PIERS PLOWMAN: THE THREE VERSIONS

General Editor

GEORGE KANE

PIERS PLOWMAN: CONCORDANCE

WILL'S VISIONS OF PIERS PLOWMAN, DO-WELL, DO-BETTER AND DO-BEST

A LEMMATIZED ANALYSIS OF THE ENGLISH VOCABULARY OF
THE A, B, AND C VERSIONS AS PRESENTED IN THE ATHLONE EDITIONS,
WITH SUPPLEMENTARY CONCORDANCES OF THE LATIN
AND FRENCH MACARONICS

BY
JOSEPH S. WITTIG

THE ATHLONE PRESS
LONDON & NEW YORK

First published in 2001 by
THE ATHLONE PRESS
A Continuum imprint
The Tower Building, 11 York Road, London SE1 7NX
370 Lexington Avenue, New York, NY 10017-6503

British Library Cataloguing in Publication Data
A catalogue record for this book is available
from the British Library

ISBN 0 485 11545 X   HB

Library of Congress Cataloging-in-Publication Data
A catalog record for this book is available from
The Library of Congress

Printed and bound in Great Britain by
St Edmundsbury Press, Bury St Edmunds

CONTENTS

PREFACE

This project was conceived at the University of North Carolina at Chapel Hill in 1986 when George Kane, intending to make a *Piers Plowman* glossary, asked me about the feasibility of my producing computer-generated concordances of the several versions of the poem. Kane already had on punch-cards an absolute alphabetical word list of B text vocabulary made for him at King's College in 1974 from corrected page proofs of the Athlone B edition. For Kane's immediate use, I had this B list printed in the University of North Carolina Computing Center. But the concordance project would require all three texts in machine-readable form on disk, so the Athlone editions of A and B were scanned and George Russell provided on disk a working copy of his edition of C, which was expected to be out "before long." As a start, I uploaded the texts to a university mainframe, ran the Oxford Concordance Program on each version to produce a concordance of spellings, redirected the output to disk, and downloaded it to microcomputer; there, the real task of making this concordance began.

It was evident from the outset that a great deal of analysis would be required before a usable, that is a lemmatized, concordance could be produced. Kane, who was in any event going to have to lemmatize for his glossary, made the primary analysis from printouts of B, and as his work on the glossary and mine on the concordance have progressed I have benefited at every stage from his observations, corrections, and advice. I completed a first version of the consolidated concordance in 1990; after publication of the Athlone C version in 1997, changes made as that edition finally evolved had to be taken into account. The concordance has since then undergone further refining and correcting.

Professor Robert Lewis of the University of Michigan generously provided *MED* head-forms, along with useful comments, for words beyond "W4," the last fascicle of that dictionary available when this book was nearing completion. I would like to thank also John Alford, Larry D. Benson, Hoyt N. Duggan, and Thorlac Turville-Petre for encouragement and valuable suggestions. And I thank my wife, Ellen W. Wittig, who has borne for so long my preoccupation with this project.

It need hardly be said that I alone am responsible for those inadequacies which remain.

J.S.W.
Chapel Hill
January 2001

INTRODUCTION

This book is a concordance to the Athlone texts of the A, B and C versions of William Langland's *Piers Plowman* edited by George Kane, George Kane and E. Talbot Donaldson, and George Russell and George Kane. Its main component is the Middle English of the poems. The French and Latin macaronics are treated in supplementary sections.

Although in this age of computers one can fairly easily produce a mechanical concordance of spellings, such an absolute alphabetical listing for the three texts would not be of much use. This concordance as it stands is a product of the analysis of these spellings with regard to orthography, dialect, in some cases morphology, and semantic value. Thus it collects, while cross-referencing them, all the forms of the M.E. verb "run" (from *arne* and *ern* to *yarn* and *yerne*) under a single headword (*rennen*); and it distinguishes homographs such as *loue* ("love" and "praise"), *moot* (noun "moat" and verb "must"), *lik* (adjectival and prepositional functions). All of the Middle English vocabulary of the three texts has been subjected to lemmatization by such analysis. In the case of the Latin and French macaronic elements this did not seem necessary.

Langland's English vocabulary, as here analysed, presents 158,809 occurrences of 14,661 different spellings (unique "tokens") gathered under 5,447 headwords ("types"). Among the latter, seventy-four combinations of two (rarely three) separate forms have been treated as one "word" (e.g., *holy_chirche*), and fourteen spellings have been analysed as two "words" (e.g., *fenel|sed*); all instances of either sort are listed in an appendix. Appendices also give ranked lists of the highest frequency English spellings and highest frequency headwords. Langland's Latin consists in 1,718 different spellings occurring a total of 6,491 times, his French of just 45 different spellings occurring a total of 104 times. The total vocabulary of these texts thus comprises 16,424 spellings which occur a total of 165,404 times.

The lemmatized Middle English entries are presented as follows. Each entry consists of three parts: headword, report of frequencies and spellings, and a list of contexts.

HEADWORDS

The concordance headwords are taken from spellings present in the Athlone editions and are almost always the dominant spelling of the grammatically prior form in these texts. One exception is *decre*, an editorial correction of a scribal spelling error. These headwords are followed by the headforms under which the word can be found in a standard dictionary (nearly always the *MED*). The headword is taken, when possible, from the B version (the one most widely read today and the last whose revision Langland completed). If the word does not occur in B, or if A or C has a grammatically prior form (e.g., a singular for a noun, an infinitive for a verb), the headform comes from A or C. If a word not in B occurs in both A and C, the headform is taken from A unless C has a grammatically prior form.

Grammatical priority has been defined as follows. For nouns a singular is prior to a plural, for adjectives and adverbs a positive degree to a comparative, a comparative to a superlative. For nouns and adjectives, the headword is a form without an inflectional ending or a final -e if such a form occurs. For verbs, the headword is an infinitive (one in -n if such a form occurs). Failing an infinitive, the order is 1st person singular present indicative, 2nd person singular present indicative, and so on, taking the persons in order, singular before plural, present before past, indicative before subjunctive before imperative, and finally participle (present before past). As in the *MED* and *OED*, gerunds are given separate entries.

Where there is a choice of spelling for the headword I have generally chosen the predominant one. Thus if the headword is from B, it is the predominant spelling of the grammatically prior form in the B version. When no spelling predominates, the first one to occur has generally been chosen.

A few exceptions to these conventions have been made in order to keep related words together or to keep the concordance aligned as much as possible with George Kane's forthcoming *Glossary*. For example, *plouȝ* has been used as headword for the noun (B usually spells it *plow*) to keep it with the verb *plouȝ*; past tense *founded* appears as headword even though the infinitive *fonden* occurs (the latter has a secondary sense, the former the primary one) because the *Glossary* will treat the primary sense first.

One of the simple part-of-speech tags listed alphabetically in the list of Abbreviations comes immediately after each headword. If two or more headwords are spelled identically or nearly so, the tags have appended numbers to distinguish them: e.g., **auowe v1** ("declare"), **auowed v2** ("made a vow").

REFERENCES TO *MED* (AND *OED*) HEADWORDS

Where possible the lexically corresponding *MED* headform immediately follows the concordance headword: thus **abate v** *abaten v.* If no dictionary is specifically named (as in the preceding example) reference is to the *MED*. The *MED* does not treat many proper nouns; when the *OED* has an appropriate sense for a proper noun not in the *MED*, a reference is given to the *OED* head. The *MED* treats many compounds under the first simplex (e.g., **handmaiden n** under *honde n.*); though I have given the *MED* head, readers should be aware that the *OED* usually has a separate entry for compounds. In a few instances when the *OED* offers supplementary information about a word significant for its form or sense in *Piers Plowman*, the *OED* headform appears after the one from the *MED*; in a few for which the *OED* seems to offer superior sense for Langland's contexts, the *OED* headform precedes one from the *MED*. A few words appear only in the *OED*. Technical legal terms are defined most fully in John Alford's *GLD* (*Piers Plowman: A Glossary of Legal Diction*), and two words (*paulynes*, *pryuees*) are best referred directly to it. Two others seem best referred directly to Latin (*decourreþ*, *pridie*; the *MED* treats the former under *deccoren*). Finally, words which I have not found in the *MED* or *OED* (nearly all of them proper nouns) are marked *n.i.d.*, "not in (these two) dictionaries."

ALPHABETICAL ORDER

To accommodate Middle English special characters and the spelling systems of the texts, the headwords and cross references in this concordance are sorted using the following adjustments to the Roman A – Z order.

I represents both the vowel I and the consonant J (as in *iuggen*, "judge"); when I stands for J it is alphabetized under J.

Y represents the palatal glide /j/ as in *yer* and the vowel /i/ as in *knyght*. Vocalic Y is alphabetized as I; the palatal consonant is alphabetized as Y in the modern Roman alphabet. *y-* prefixed words (deriving from Old English *ge-*) are alphabetized under I. Thus, for example, *ylik* is listed under I. But past participles in *y-* are listed under the finite verb if finite forms occur (thus *ymaked* is under *maken*); cross references (*ymaked > maken*) direct the reader to the headword.

Thorn (þ,Þ) is alphabetized as *t* plus *h*, and thus thorn-initial spellings will be found under T.

U and V represent the vowel U, the consonant V, and occasionally the glide W. (V generally appears initially, U internally.)   U and V are accordingly alphabetized as U when they stand for the vowel (or W) and as V when they stand for the consonant.

Yogh (ȝ,Ȝ) represents a variety of sounds, some derived from Old English G and some from that graph's falling together with the French graph z. When it represents the development of velar G (*drouȝ, heiȝe, knyȝt*) it is alphabetized between G and H.   When it represents the development of palatal G (*ȝer, ȝifte*) it is alphabetized as Y.   In these texts final yogh can also represent S (e.g., *argumentȝ, elementȝ*) and occasionally Z (*baptiȝe, chastiȝen, Ȝacheus*) and is alphabetized accordingly.

The resulting alphabetical order is the following.

A B C D E F G *Ȝ[='gh']* H IY*[=I]* I*[=J]* K L M N O P Q R
S*[and ȝ=s]* T*[including Þ as th]* UV*[=UW]* UV*[=V]* W X YȜ*[=Y]* *Ȝ[=Z]*

REPORT OF FREQUENCIES AND SPELLINGS

A summary report of a word's frequencies and various spellings follows each headword. If no spellings are listed for a version, its spelling is identical to the headword. If various spellings occur, all are listed along with their subfrequency; subforms are listed alphabetically for each version, except that past participles in y- are listed last. For example, for **after adv** one will find the summary:

A 40 after (1) aftir (39); B 99; C 87 after (2) aftir (4) aftur (81).

(B's ninety-nine instances all appear in the spelling of the headword.)

LIST OF CONTEXTS

Each occurrence is presented within its full line of context. The target word is printed in *distinctive type*. If a word occurs twice in a line the line is printed twice and first one word, then the other, distinguished. For Latin macaronics which are longer or less than one line in print, the context has sometimes been adjusted. Contexts are ordered first by version (A B C) and, within each version, by text order.

WORDS FOR WHICH CONTEXTS ARE NOT PRINTED

For the conjunction *and* (which occurs a total of 10,620 times, about once in every line and a half) I give only a brief summary report (headword and list of forms), followed by a substantial list of contexts in which the word means "if." For thirty-three other words of high frequency and little semantic complexity (listed on page xv), after the normal headword and summary of forms I report line references only instead of contexts. This compromise was necessary in order to keep the book from becoming unmanageably large.

WORDS PRESENTED ACCORDING TO SUBFORMS

For ten high-frequency words, whether they are reported with a line of context or by line reference only, it seemed useful to distinguish the occurrences by subform rather than to present one massive list arranged by version and text-order. These ten words are the verb *ben* and the personal pronouns (*he, heo, hij, I, it, þei, þow, we, ye*). For these words, after the normal headword and summary report, each form is presented separately, arranged first in absolute alphabetical order, then by version. Graphic variation between *i/y, ou/ow,* and *th/þ* have been reported but have not been made the basis for separating forms. For example, the occurrences of *he* are presented in the order *a* C, *he* A, *he* B, *he* C, *him/hym* A, *hym* B, *him/hym* C, *his* A, *his* B, *his* C, *hise* A, *hise* B, *hise* C; those for *hij* are ordered *hem* A, *hem* B, *hem* C, *her* C, *here* A, *here* B, *here* C, *hy* A, *hy* C, *hij* A, *hij* B, *hir* B, *hire* A, *hire* B.

ASSIGNMENT OF FORMS TO HEADWORDS

The concordance follows the *MED* in taking primary account of etymology. It makes exception in the case of some Old Scandinavian and Old English alternatives, where it employs the predominant form: thus *chirche*, not *kirk*, *fro*, not *from*, but *yate*, not *gate*.

Semantic decisions and consequent headword assignment are in most cases clearly indicated by the requirements of context and usage; in the latter consideration the *MED* was invaluable. In the case of homographs the policy has been to align the concordance with Kane's draft *Glossary*, and the user is alerted by cross-references (discussed below). Proper nouns are subdivided in only a few instances. Where the text suggests that the poet is punning, the assignment to headword is made by deciding the primary contextual sense.

Grammatical decisions and consequent lemmatization are a corollary of sophisticated concordancing. An undifferentiated list of several thousand *that*s would ignore the importance of the form in Middle English usage; accordingly it has been analysed as demonstrative adjective, demonstrative pronoun, relative pronoun, and conjunction. Similarly adjectives and adverbs with the same form are distinguished, as are adverbs from prepositions. The concordance follows the *MED* in separating noun from adjective. Assignments to grammatical categories follow traditional grammatical rules: e.g., an adverb is a word which modifies a verb, an adjective, or another adverb; a preposition takes an object; a conjunction links words, phrases, or clauses; a subordinating conjunction introduces a clause. Almost always the assignment is straightforward, but it is possible to disagree reasonably over such distinctions as that between predicate adjective and adverb.

CROSS-REFERENCES

This concordance offers two kinds of cross references. One pertains to meaning, the other to form.

cf. cross-references meaning. It signals words of related meaning whose entries are separated because of different etymons: e.g., **lawe n** *cf. layes*, **layes n** *cf. lawe*. It also calls attention to difficult homographs: e.g., **loue v1** *cf. v2*, **loue v2** *cf. v1* ("love" and "praise").

> ("see") and **&>** ("see also") cross-reference forms and are intended to help the reader find forms (spellings) under the headword(s) to which they have been assigned. One can look up any form from the Athlone editions of *PP* in that form's expected alphabetical position; if the form has been placed under a headword spelled differently, one will find a cross reference to the headword: e.g., *is > ben*.

> ("SEE") CROSS REFERENCES

In giving cross references for forms, I have tried to err on the side of generosity. Nearly all forms which differ significantly from the headword under which they are found have been cross-referenced, including competing spellings, "irregular" morphological forms such as the past stems of strong verbs, irregular past stems of weak verbs, and mutated stems of any part of speech. Thus one will find *dung > donge*, *drogh > drawe*, *kept > kepen*, *men > man*. And cross references always indicate when a subform appears under two or more headwords: e.g., *mouþe > mouþ, mouþen*.

Cross references are not given for forms which differ from a headword merely in a normal inflectional suffix such as *-e*, *-es*, *-is*, *-er*, *-est*, *-ed*, *-id*, *-eþ*, *-ing*. Thus *drynkes* is not cross referenced to **drynke n** nor *dryuyng* to **dryuen v**.

Cross references do not distinguish *i/y* spellings: rather than *bicam bycam* > *bicome* the reader will find simply *bicam* > *bicome*. Cross references for groups of forms which differ from one another merely in trivial spelling variants or in normal inflectional suffixes have been abbreviated. Thus separate cross references are not given for forms in *-ed/-id*, *-es/-is*, *-eþ/-iþ/-eth*. Nor have I given cross references which would appear immediately before or immediately after the entry in which a form is to be found. Thus there is no cross reference for *biknewe* (the reference would immediately precede **biknowen**) or for *bynom* (the reference would immediately follow **bynymen**). In using the concordance, then, the reader can look for any form as that form is spelled in the texts. If it does not appear as a headword, there is most likely a cross reference for it. If there is no cross reference, either the form differs from a headword in that location by just a normal inflectional suffix and can be found among the subforms of the headword; or it will be found among the subforms of the headword which immediately precedes or immediately follows.

&> ("SEE ALSO") CROSS REFERENCES

Frequently a spelling represents homographs found under more than one headword. When one sees **mete n**, **mete v1**, **mete v2** one knows that the spelling *mete* occurs under all three headwords. As mentioned above, a spelling with a routine graphemic variant will not be cross-referenced: thus *gile* and/or *gyle* may occur under both **gile n** and **gyle v** (the report of subforms for each headword indicates that *gyle* appears under both.)

If a form identical to a headword occurs also as a subform under some other headword(s), there is a "see also" cross reference following the headword: e.g., **abite v *abiten v.* &>** *habite* (signalling that *abite* is both the concordance headword for the verb and a subform of **habite n**).

If a form identical to two or more headwords also occurs as a subform under some other headword(s), a "see also" cross reference is inserted immediately after the identical headwords. For example, after **mete n**, **mete v1**, **mete v2** one finds *mete &> meten*.

All homographs are listed in an appendix.

A CONCORDANCE NOT A GLOSSARY

Unlike Tomonori Matsushita's *Glossarial Concordance to William Langland's **The Vision of Piers Plowman**: the B-Text* (2 vols. Tokyo: Yushodo P, 1998), this book consolidates the A, B and C versions of the Athlone edition in a fully lemmatized presentation. It is not designed to double as a glossary, stopping short of lexicography with attaching the corresponding *MED* (or *OED*) equivalents to its headwords. In my understanding the primary function of a concordance is to afford ready, systematically presented location of the individual words of a text in their immediate context. In the circumstances of *Piers Plowman* that function imposes two sequences of presentation subsequent to the alphabetical one: the first by version, the second by occurrence within each version. Within that treble sequence it would not be feasible to do lexicographical justice to the poet's idiosyncratic use of a fluidly polysemous medium while maintaining the usefulness of the concordance as such. Too many words in the poem have too many meanings; for these, a brief gloss would be hopelessly inadequate, often seriously misleading. It is expected that a serious user of this book will have the *MED* at hand.

MAN AND THE MACHINE

Computers are wonderfully faithful gatherers and sorters, and one could expect a computer-generated concordance to be a faultlessly consistent object. Alas, here human intervention has had to manipulate nearly every line of the computer's output, since available software does not cope very well with the vagaries of Middle English spelling and special characters (ʒ = ʒ, y, s, or z, y = i or y, þ = th, u = u or v) and no existing software can make the decisions required for lemmatizing, distinguishing homographs, analyzing grammatical usage, and labeling forms. Hours of subsequent editing by eye and hand have both refined the machine's original output and threatened to disrupt its admirable but mechanical consistency. I have used computer programs to help implement decisions and to recheck the results. But despite painstaking effort to avoid, find, and correct human errors which have crept in along the way, some, I fear, will have escaped detection.

WORDS REPORTED BY LINE REFERENCES ONLY

a indef art	I pron	þan conj
ac conj	if conj	thanne adv1
as conj	it pron	þat pron rel
but conj	ne conj	þat conj
er conj	neuere adv	þe def art
for conj	no adv	þei pron
forþi adv	noȝt adv	þis adj dem
he pron	or conj	þow pron
heo pron	quod v	þus adv
hij pron	she pron	we pron
how conj	so adv	ye pron

ABBREVIATIONS

adj	adjective
adj dem	demonstrative adjective
adv	adverb
adv correl	correlative adverb
art def	definite article
art indef	indefinite article
conj	conjunction
exclam	exclamation (interjection)
ger	gerund
GLD	John Alford, *Piers Plowman: A Glossary of Legal Diction*
letter	of the alphabet
MED	*Middle English Dictionary*
n	noun
n.i.d.	not found in dictionary (*MED* and *OED*)
n prop	proper noun (name)
num	number
OED	*Oxford English Dictionary*
prep	preposition
pron	pronoun
pron dem	demonstrative pronoun
pron indef	indefinite pronoun
prtcl	particle
ptp	past participle
prp	present participle
v	verb

MAIN CONCORDANCE: MIDDLE
ENGLISH

A

a *letter* *a n.* A 1; B 1
A. 8.120 'Abstinence þe abbesse myn *a* b c me tauȝte,
B. 7.138 'Abstynence þe Abbesse myn *a* b c me tauȝte,

a *num* *o num. cf. oon* A 10 a (9) an (1); B 18; C 12
A. 1.99 And nouȝt to fasten *a* friday in fyue score wynter,
A. 3.134 She may neiȝ as muche do in *a* moneþ ones
A. 3.237 It is a permutacioun apertly, *a* peny[worþ] for anoþer.
A. 4.142 Couþe nouȝt warpen *a* word to wiþsigge resoun,
A. 5.5 Er I hadde faren *a* furlong feyntise me h[ent]e
A. 5.6 Þat I ne miȝte ferþere *a* fote for defaute of slepyng.
A. 5.100 May no sugre ne swet þing swage it *an* vnche,
A. 6.118 Shulde I neuere ferþere *a* foote for no freris preching.'
A.10.1 'Sire dowel dwelliþ,' quaþ wyt, 'nouȝt *a* day hennes,
A.11.34 Ȝiue hem to here ȝerisȝiue þe value of *a* grote.
B.Pr.192 The maȝe among vs alle þeiȝ we mysse *a* sherewe,
B. 3.145 [She] may neiȝ as muche do in *a* Monþe one[s]
B. 3.258 It is a permutacion apertly, *a* penyworþ for anoþer.
B. 4.38 For [þei wolde do for *a* dyner or a doȝeyne capons
B. 5.5 Ac er I hadde faren *a* furlong feyntise me hente
B. 5.6 That I ne myȝte ferþer *a* foot for defaute of slepynge.
B. 5.267 Ne haue *a* peny to my pitaunce, [for pyne of my soule],
B. 5.372 That I, Gloton, girte it vp er I hadde gon *a* myle,
B. 5.417 But I kan fynden in a feld or in *a* furlang an hare
B. 5.421 Ac in Canoun nor in decretals I kan noȝt rede *a* lyne.
B. 5.633 Sholde I neuere ferþer *a* foot for no freres prechyng.'
B. 6.37 'Ye, and yet *a* point', quod Piers, 'I preye [þee] of moore:
B. 7.111 In two lynes it lay and noȝt *a* [lettre] moore,
B. 9.1 'SIre Dowel dwelleþ', quod Wit, 'noȝt *a* day hennes
B.10.48 ȝyue hem to hir yeresȝyue þe [value] of *a* grote.
B.16.86 And Piers for pure tene þat *a* pil he [l]auȝte;
B.16.222 And is noȝt but gendre of *a* generacion bifore Iesu crist in heuene:
B.18.194 If þat þei touchede *a* tree and þe [trees] fruyt eten.
C. 3.183 He may ny as muche do in *a* monthe ones
C. 4.38 For þey wolde do for *a* dyner oþer a d[o]seyne capones
C. 6.336 And deyede with *a* drop water; so doth alle synnes
C. 7.32 Ac y can fynden in a feld and in *a* forlong an hare
C. 7.286 [Sh]olde y neuere forthere [*a*] foet for no frere prechynge.'
C. 9.285 In two lynes hit lay and nat *a* lettre more
C.10.128 'Sire dowel dwelleth,' quod wit, 'nat *a* day hennes
C.10.232 Excepte onliche of vch kynde *a* payre
C.17.105 Noþer they [conn]eth ne [know]eth *a* cours by[fore] anoþer.
C.20.41 To fordoen hit on *a* day, and in thre dayes aftur
C.20.199 Yf that thei touche[d *a*] tre and of þe [trees] fruyt eten.
C.20.305 Yf they touched *a* tre or toek þerof an appul.

a *exclam* *a interj.* A 1; B 4; C 5
A. 1.41 '*A* madame mercy,' quaþ I, 'me likiþ wel ȝoure wordis.
B. 1.43 '[*A*] madame, mercy', quod I, 'me likeþ wel youre wordes.
B.13.448 To crie *a* largesse bifore oure lord, youre good loos to shewe.
B.17.127 '*A*, swete sire', I seide þo, 'wher I shal bileue,
B.18.15 Thanne was feiþ in a fenestre and cryde '*a*! fili dauid!'
C. 1.41 '*A* madame, mercy,' [quod I], 'me lyketh wel ȝoure wordes.
C. 4.164 A shyreues Clerk cryede, '*a*! capias mede
C. 7.108 To crye *a* largesse tofore oure lord ȝoure good loos to 'shewe.
C.19.96 '*A*, sire,' y saide, 'shal nat we bileue,
C.20.13 Thenne was faith in a fenestre and criede '*a*! fil[i] dauid!'

a *art indef* *a indef.art.* A 316 a (290) an (26); B 1052 a (969) an (83); C 1010 a (933) an (77)

A.Pr.1, A.Pr.2, A.Pr.2, A.Pr.3, A.Pr.5, A.Pr.6, A.Pr.8, A.Pr.8, A.Pr.10, A.Pr.11, A.Pr.12, A.Pr.14, A.Pr.14, A.Pr.15, A.Pr.15, A.Pr.17, A.Pr.50, A.Pr.62, A.Pr.65, A.Pr.65, A.Pr.66, A.Pr.82, A.Pr.84, A.Pr.89, A.1.3, A.1.36, A.1.45, A.1.61, A.1.66, A.1.85, A.1.88, A.1.130, A.1.139, A.1.154, A.1.161, A.1.163, A.1.173, A.2.8, A.2.10, A.2.21, A.2.32, A.2.40, A.2.41, A.2.85, A.2.94, A.2.95, A.2.96, A.2.96, A.2.119, A.2.128, A.2.129, A.2.143, A.2.160, A.2.176, A.2.190, A.2.192, A.3.3, A.3.23, A.3.34, A.3.34, A.3.39, A.3.44, A.3.44, A.3.47, A.3.82, A.3.99, A.3.110, A.3.118, A.3.131, A.3.149, A.3.156, A.3.159, A.3.166, A.3.178, A.3.180, A.3.192, A.3.194, A.3.196, A.3.196, A.3.199, A.3.225, A.3.227, A.3.235, A.3.237, A.3.242, A.3.256, A.3.270, A.3.276, A.4.16, A.4.29, A.4.33, A.4.34, A.4.45, A.4.54, A.4.55, A.4.67, A.4.72, A.4.82, A.4.88, A.4.104, A.4.121, A.4.130, A.4.136, A.4.136, A.5.11, A.5.23, A.5.31, A.5.31, A.5.48, A.5.60, A.5.61, A.5.62, A.5.62, A.5.62, A.5.63, A.5.64, A.5.71, A.5.73, A.5.91, A.5.98, A.5.102, A.5.110, A.5.111, A.5.112, A.5.117, A.5.125, A.5.126, A.5.127, A.5.129,

A.5.131, A.5.138, A.5.138, A.5.155, A.5.156, A.5.163, A.5.164, A.5.164, A.5.164, A.5.165, A.5.165, A.5.166, A.5.176, A.5.179, A.5.184, A.5.188, A.5.188, A.5.189, A.5.189, A.5.192, A.5.194, A.5.201, A.5.224, A.5.251, A.6.3, A.6.4, A.6.5, A.6.5, A.6.6, A.6.7, A.6.7, A.6.8, A.6.20, A.6.25, A.6.40, A.6.45, A.6.46, A.6.53, A.6.54, A.6.59, A.6.67, A.6.72, A.6.82, A.6.87, A.6.101, A.6.115, A.6.116, A.6.117, A.6.120, A.7.1, A.7.1, A.7.4, A.7.7, A.7.7, A.7.7, A.7.23, A.7.38, A.7.43, A.7.56, A.7.57, A.7.141, A.7.141, A.7.154, A.7.162, A.7.164, A.7.165, A.7.167, A.7.174, A.7.175, A.7.177, A.7.179, A.7.198, A.7.223, A.7.250, A.7.260, A.7.266, A.7.266, A.7.267, A.7.271, A.7.271, A.7.271, A.8.3, A.8.25, A.8.53, A.8.89, A.8.119, A.8.122, A.8.130, A.8.136, A.8.151, A.8.159, A.8.175, A.9.2, A.9.8, A.9.16, A.9.24, A.9.25, A.9.25, A.9.25, A.9.54, A.9.56, A.9.56, A.9.56, A.9.61, A.9.77, A.9.86, A.9.88, A.9.112, A.10.2, A.10.6, A.10.8, A.10.17, A.10.20, A.10.34, A.10.46, A.10.49, A.10.76, A.10.81, A.10.82, A.10.102, A.10.123, A.10.124, A.10.124, A.10.143, A.10.147, A.10.157, A.10.166, A.10.175, A.10.184, A.10.186, A.10.187, A.10.187, A.10.207, A.11.1, A.11.17, A.11.20, A.11.29, A.11.41, A.11.48, A.11.50, A.11.62, A.11.66, A.11.68, A.11.73, A.11.87, A.11.95, A.11.106, A.11.119, A.11.120, A.11.133, A.11.141, A.11.182, A.11.197, A.11.204, A.11.211, A.11.211, A.11.212, A.11.212, A.11.213, A.11.214, A.11.214, A.11.237, A.11.239, A.11.241, A.11.279, A.11.285, A.11.304, A.11.312, A.12.15, A.12.27, A.12.35, A.12.48, A.12.49, A.12.50, A.12.58, A.12.61, A.12.66, A.12.68, A.12.69, A.12.71, A.12.71, A.12.77, A.12.77, A.12.84, A.12.91, A.12.96, A.12.104

B.Pr.1, B.Pr.2, B.Pr.2, B.Pr.3, B.Pr.5, B.Pr.6, B.Pr.8, B.Pr.8, B.Pr.10, B.Pr.11, B.Pr.12, B.Pr.14, B.Pr.14, B.Pr.15, B.Pr.15, B.Pr.17, B.Pr.51, B.Pr.53, B.Pr.65, B.Pr.68, B.Pr.68, B.Pr.69, B.Pr.85, B.Pr.108, B.Pr.112, B.Pr.123, B.Pr.123, B.Pr.128, B.Pr.139, B.Pr.139, B.Pr.146, B.Pr.147, B.Pr.148, B.Pr.149, B.Pr.149, B.Pr.158, B.Pr.159, B.Pr.165, B.Pr.168, B.Pr.169, B.Pr.182, B.Pr.191, B.Pr.191, B.Pr.194, B.Pr.208, B.Pr.211, B.Pr.216, B.1.3, B.1.38, B.1.47, B.1.63, B.1.68, B.1.87, B.1.90, B.1.114, B.1.115, B.1.142, B.1.157, B.1.160, B.1.161, B.1.165, B.1.180, B.1.187, B.1.189, B.2.8, B.2.10, B.2.24, B.2.25, B.2.28, B.2.35, B.2.40, B.2.41, B.2.66, B.2.69, B.2.103, B.2.121, B.2.131, B.2.132, B.2.155, B.2.164, B.2.165, B.2.182, B.2.199, B.2.217, B.2.231, B.2.233, B.3.3, B.3.24, B.3.35, B.3.35, B.3.40, B.3.45, B.3.45, B.3.48, B.3.55, B.3.56, B.3.93, B.3.110, B.3.121, B.3.129, B.3.142, B.3.160, B.3.169, B.3.172, B.3.179, B.3.191, B.3.193, B.3.205, B.3.207, B.3.209, B.3.209, B.3.212, B.3.245, B.3.246, B.3.248, B.3.256, B.3.258, B.3.263, B.3.278, B.3.295, B.3.300, B.3.301, B.3.309, B.3.322, B.3.326, B.3.326, B.3.327, B.3.331, B.3.338, B.3.338, B.3.347, B.3.349, B.4.16, B.4.38, B.4.46, B.4.47, B.4.58, B.4.62, B.4.68, B.4.69, B.4.85, B.4.95, B.4.101, B.4.118, B.4.138, B.4.147, B.4.160, B.4.160, B.4.164, B.4.166, B.4.167, B.4.167, B.4.168, B.4.170, B.5.12, B.5.31, B.5.31, B.5.32, B.5.65, B.5.77, B.5.78, B.5.79, B.5.79, B.5.79, B.5.80, B.5.81, B.5.86, B.5.86, B.5.92, B.5.93, B.5.111, B.5.119, B.5.121, B.5.131, B.5.137, B.5.142, B.5.153, B.5.153, B.5.158, B.5.159, B.5.159, B.5.160, B.5.166, B.5.166, B.5.174, B.5.179, B.5.179, B.5.191, B.5.193, B.5.194, B.5.194, B.5.195, B.5.196, B.5.201, B.5.209, B.5.210, B.5.211, B.5.213, B.5.215, B.5.222, B.5.222, B.5.231, B.5.233, B.5.239, B.5.240, B.5.241, B.5.247, B.5.252, B.5.253, B.5.259, B.5.270, B.5.283, B.5.285, B.5.293, B.5.304, B.5.305, B.5.313, B.5.314, B.5.314, B.5.314, B.5.315, B.5.315, B.5.317, B.5.327, B.5.330, B.5.335, B.5.339, B.5.339, B.5.341, B.5.341, B.5.344, B.5.346, B.5.353, B.5.354, B.5.359, B.5.390, B.5.406, B.5.406, B.5.417, B.5.417, B.5.420, B.5.429, B.5.435, B.5.452, B.5.482, B.5.485, B.5.491, B.5.497, B.5.506, B.5.510, B.5.515, B.5.516, B.5.517, B.5.517, B.5.518, B.5.519, B.5.519, B.5.520, B.5.532, B.5.537, B.5.553, B.5.558, B.5.559, B.5.566, B.5.567, B.5.572, B.5.580, B.5.585, B.5.595, B.5.600, B.5.607, B.5.607, B.5.615, B.5.624, B.5.630, B.5.631, B.5.632, B.5.635, B.5.639, B.5.640, B.5.641, B.6.1, B.6.1, B.6.4, B.6.7, B.6.7, B.6.7, B.6.21, B.6.44, B.6.49, B.6.49, B.6.61, B.6.62, B.6.150, B.6.151, B.6.154, B.6.154, B.6.169, B.6.177, B.6.179, B.6.186, B.6.187, B.6.191, B.6.194, B.6.195, B.6.196, B.6.212, B.6.239, B.6.256, B.6.266, B.6.276, B.6.282, B.6.282, B.6.283, B.6.287, B.6.287, B.6.287, B.6.328, B.6.331, B.7.3, B.7.23, B.7.45, B.7.51, B.7.76, B.7.107, B.7.137, B.7.140, B.7.148, B.7.152, B.7.158, B.7.181, B.7.197, B.8.2, B.8.8, B.8.20, B.8.28, B.8.29, B.8.29, B.8.29, B.8.43, B.8.53, B.8.63, B.8.65, B.8.65, B.8.65, B.8.70, B.8.86, B.8.96, B.8.98, B.8.101, B.8.122, B.9.2, B.9.6, B.9.8, B.9.14, B.9.18, B.9.21, B.9.33, B.9.39, B.9.40, B.9.47, B.9.51, B.9.74, B.9.81, B.9.84, B.9.84, B.9.86, B.9.93, B.9.104, B.9.106, B.9.106, B.9.116, B.9.127, B.9.132, B.9.135, B.9.144, B.9.150, B.9.152, B.9.153, B.9.155, B.9.161, B.9.165, B.9.166, B.9.166, B.10.1, B.10.17, B.10.20, B.10.25, B.10.37, B.10.55, B.10.62, B.10.64, B.10.95, B.10.95, B.10.99, B.10.100, B.10.101, B.10.101, B.10.108, B.10.142, B.10.154, B.10.167, B.10.168, B.10.181, B.10.189, B.10.238, B.10.269, B.10.270, B.10.272, B.10.295, B.10.309, B.10.311, B.10.311, B.10.312, B.10.312, B.10.313, B.10.313, B.10.314, B.10.314, B.10.322, B.10.328, B.10.332, B.10.332, B.10.354, B.10.356, B.10.377, B.10.400, B.10.420, B.10.426, B.10.439, B.10.443, B.10.460, B.10.468, B.10.474, B.11.1, B.11.5, B.11.6, B.11.9, B.11.23, B.11.36, B.11.37, B.11.47, B.11.57, B.11.67, B.11.68, B.11.80, B.11.82, B.11.97, B.11.112, B.11.116, B.11.125, B.11.130, B.11.141, B.11.174, B.11.186, B.11.217, B.11.217, B.11.219, B.11.243, B.11.248, B.11.249, B.11.249, B.11.250, B.11.260, B.11.260, B.11.262, B.11.264, B.11.264, B.11.266, B.11.292, B.11.295, B.11.296, B.11.296, B.11.299, B.11.300, B.11.300, B.11.303,

B.11.303, B.11.306, B.11.307, B.11.314, B.11.324, B.11.326, B.11.350, B.11.379, B.11.379, B.11.381, B.11.390, B.11.391, B.11.396, B.11.402, B.11.425, B.11.427, B.11.427, B.11.430, B.12.19, B.12.57, B.12.59, B.12.66, B.12.68, B.12.76, B.12.99, B.12.103, B.12.105, B.12.107, B.12.132, B.12.137, B.12.138, B.12.147, B.12.150, B.12.152, B.12.161, B.12.178, B.12.179, B.12.189, B.12.201, B.12.205, B.12.206, B.12.208, B.12.208, B.12.229, B.12.242, B.12.242, B.12.255, B.12.264, B.12.283, B.12.292, B.12.292, B.12.294, B.12.296, B.13.2, B.13.3, B.13.25, B.13.30, B.13.36, B.13.44, B.13.49, B.13.54, B.13.55, B.13.57, B.13.74, B.13.88, B.13.88, B.13.93, B.13.94, B.13.95, B.13.95, B.13.100, B.13.102, B.13.112, B.13.117, B.13.120, B.13.125, B.13.129, B.13.139, B.13.151, B.13.152, B.13.153, B.13.172, B.13.172, B.13.174, B.13.185, B.13.185, B.13.192, B.13.193, B.13.194, B.13.196, B.13.221, B.13.224, B.13.226, B.13.235, B.13.246, B.13.246, B.13.247, B.13.247, B.13.248, B.13.253, B.13.261, B.13.265, B.13.267, B.13.268, B.13.269, B.13.273, B.13.275, B.13.275, B.13.284, B.13.284, B.13.287, B.13.289, B.13.301, B.13.302, B.13.327, B.13.330, B.13.335, B.13.335, B.13.335, B.13.336, B.13.337, B.13.341, B.13.344, B.13.344, B.13.361, B.13.362, B.13.363, B.13.371, B.13.371, B.13.380, B.13.390, B.13.397, B.13.409, B.13.414, B.13.415, B.13.420, B.13.443, B.13.444, B.13.447, B.13.447, B.13.447, B.13.449, B.13.453, B.13.456, B.13.458, B.13.459, B.14.3, B.14.12, B.14.18, B.14.25, B.14.34, B.14.49, B.14.85, B.14.92, B.14.93, B.14.97, B.14.126, B.14.137, B.14.142, B.14.149, B.14.151, B.14.198, B.14.213, B.14.215, B.14.235, B.14.241, B.14.242, B.14.243, B.14.249, B.14.249, B.14.252, B.14.255, B.14.264, B.14.265, B.14.267, B.14.268, B.14.271, B.14.283, B.14.297, B.14.300, B.14.302, B.14.303, B.14.304, B.14.308, B.14.308, B.14.313, B.14.319, B.14.320, B.15.3, B.15.5, B.15.10, B.15.12, B.15.16, B.15.17, B.15.21, B.15.40, B.15.43, B.15.51, B.15.58, B.15.67, B.15.89, B.15.98, B.15.111, B.15.113, B.15.122, B.15.123, B.15.124, B.15.124, B.15.125, B.15.140, B.15.142, B.15.149, B.15.150, B.15.151, B.15.151, B.15.158, B.15.162, B.15.166, B.15.166, B.15.167, B.15.167, B.15.168, B.15.178, B.15.180, B.15.187, B.15.187, B.15.204, B.15.207, B.15.214, B.15.216, B.15.230, B.15.279, B.15.284, B.15.285, B.15.316, B.15.320, B.15.333, B.15.338, B.15.338, B.15.346, B.15.347, B.15.349, B.15.349, B.15.351, B.15.375, B.15.375, B.15.376, B.15.382, B.15.397, B.15.401, B.15.409, B.15.413, B.15.415, B.15.436, B.15.441, B.15.456, B.15.462, B.15.462, B.15.467, B.15.474, B.15.483, B.15.502, B.15.507, B.15.507, B.15.509, B.15.516, B.15.519, B.15.527, B.15.527, B.15.559, B.15.562, B.15.588, B.16.3, B.16.4, B.16.13, B.16.20, B.16.27, B.16.31, B.16.44, B.16.55, B.16.68, B.16.73, B.16.77, B.16.91, B.16.91, B.16.92, B.16.101, B.16.128, B.16.139, B.16.139, B.16.147, B.16.160, B.16.163, B.16.170, B.16.171, B.16.172, B.16.173, B.16.177, B.16.178, B.16.179, B.16.185, B.16.188, B.16.191, B.16.192, B.16.204, B.16.225, B.16.248, B.16.250, B.16.254, B.16.255, B.16.260, B.16.261, B.16.269, B.17.1, B.17.1, B.17.2, B.17.11, B.17.11, B.17.11, B.17.15, B.17.33, B.17.45, B.17.51, B.17.51, B.17.53, B.17.54, B.17.56, B.17.59, B.17.74, B.17.76, B.17.96, B.17.96, B.17.105, B.17.140, B.17.141, B.17.143, B.17.151, B.17.152, B.17.154, B.17.160, B.17.168, B.17.170, B.17.172, B.17.186, B.17.198, B.17.202, B.17.202, B.17.206, B.17.206, B.17.207, B.17.208, B.17.210, B.17.210, B.17.215, B.17.223, B.17.223, B.17.227, B.17.232, B.17.235, B.17.241, B.17.243, B.17.248, B.17.266, B.17.267, B.17.270, B.17.278, B.17.282, B.17.282, B.17.283, B.17.306, B.17.321, B.17.323, B.18.2, B.18.3, B.18.5, B.18.11, B.18.13, B.18.15, B.18.16, B.18.40, B.18.46, B.18.48, B.18.51, B.18.52, B.18.58, B.18.64, B.18.69, B.18.72, B.18.73, B.18.78, B.18.78, B.18.95, B.18.97, B.18.113, B.18.115, B.18.116, B.18.119, B.18.119, B.18.124, B.18.124, B.18.128, B.18.139, B.18.142, B.18.161, B.18.213, B.18.230, B.18.231, B.18.233, B.18.235, B.18.240, B.18.252, B.18.252, B.18.260, B.18.262, B.18.263, B.18.267, B.18.272, B.18.272, B.18.288, B.18.290, B.18.299, B.18.307, B.18.335, B.18.337, B.18.337, B.18.354, B.18.356, B.18.358, B.18.359, B.18.371, B.18.379, B.18.380, B.18.382, B.18.384, B.18.398, B.18.399, B.18.408, B.18.423, B.18.428, B.19.7, B.19.28, B.19.29, B.19.42, B.19.98, B.19.99, B.19.100, B.19.106, B.19.118, B.19.128, B.19.155, B.19.160, B.19.167, B.19.202, B.19.227, B.19.237, B.19.237, B.19.250, B.19.261, B.19.262, B.19.263, B.19.263, B.19.272, B.19.273, B.19.273, B.19.279, B.19.279, B.19.280, B.19.282, B.19.305, B.19.318, B.19.324, B.19.325, B.19.327, B.19.330, B.19.336, B.19.354, B.19.357, B.19.362, B.19.363, B.19.365, B.19.365, B.19.369, B.19.369, B.19.374, B.19.388, B.19.396, B.19.409, B.19.409, B.19.410, B.19.412, B.19.416, B.19.432, B.19.435, B.19.438, B.19.439, B.19.457, B.19.458, B.19.458, B.19.459, B.19.465, B.20.16, B.20.31, B.20.36, B.20.56, B.20.57, B.20.60, B.20.64, B.20.71, B.20.87, B.20.91, B.20.104, B.20.113, B.20.117, B.20.118, B.20.129, B.20.132, B.20.134, B.20.138, B.20.145, B.20.145, B.20.146, B.20.146, B.20.148, B.20.152, B.20.157, B.20.160, B.20.161, B.20.162, B.20.163, B.20.164, B.20.172, B.20.176, B.20.176, B.20.176, B.20.179, B.20.181, B.20.181, B.20.217, B.20.218, B.20.221, B.20.223, B.20.225, B.20.255, B.20.255, B.20.258, B.20.263, B.20.265, B.20.267, B.20.267, B.20.278, B.20.292, B.20.300, B.20.302, B.20.304, B.20.312, B.20.313, B.20.317, B.20.325, B.20.325, B.20.326, B.20.336, B.20.344, B.20.363, B.20.364, B.20.367, B.20.374, B.20.380

C.Pr.1, C.Pr.2, C.Pr.2, C.Pr.3, C.Pr.6, C.Pr.8, C.Pr.15, C.Pr.16, C.Pr.17, C.Pr.19, C.Pr.29, C.Pr.51, C.Pr.63, C.Pr.66, C.Pr.66, C.Pr.67, C.Pr.83, C.Pr.134, C.Pr.135, C.Pr.139, C.Pr.146, C.Pr.161, C.Pr.166, C.Pr.167, C.Pr.168, C.Pr.169, C.Pr.170, C.Pr.170, C.Pr.178, C.Pr.182, C.Pr.185, C.Pr.186, C.Pr.199, C.Pr.207, C.1.3, C.1.36, C.1.45, C.1.59, C.1.64, C.1.83, C.1.86, C.1.108, C.1.141, C.1.153, C.1.156, C.1.157, C.1.161, C.1.176, C.1.183, C.1.185, C.1.194, C.2.9, C.2.11, C.2.24, C.2.25, C.2.28, C.2.29, C.2.30, C.2.35, C.2.37, C.2.43, C.2.68, C.2.71, C.2.86, C.2.121, C.2.147, C.2.148, C.2.171, C.2.180, C.2.195, C.2.213, C.2.227, C.2.241, C.2.243, C.3.3, C.3.25, C.3.38, C.3.38, C.3.42, C.3.47, C.3.47, C.3.51, C.3.54, C.3.60, C.3.70, C.3.104, C.3.106, C.3.106, C.3.114, C.3.114, C.3.121, C.3.131, C.3.133, C.3.135, C.3.142, C.3.142, C.3.147, C.3.158, C.3.166, C.3.180, C.3.198, C.3.215, C.3.218, C.3.225, C.3.244, C.3.245, C.3.245, C.3.250, C.3.251, C.3.255, C.3.256, C.3.262, C.3.264, C.3.265, C.3.265, C.3.268, C.3.287, C.3.292, C.3.305, C.3.305, C.3.309, C.3.314, C.3.335, C.3.335, C.3.344, C.3.345, C.3.348, C.3.354, C.3.374, C.3.375, C.3.378, C.3.381, C.3.381, C.3.382, C.3.392, C.3.404, C.3.405, C.3.409, C.3.410, C.3.434, C.3.448, C.3.453, C.3.454, C.3.462, C.3.462, C.3.462, C.3.475, C.3.479, C.3.479, C.3.480, C.3.490, C.3.490, C.3.495, C.3.497, C.4.16, C.4.26, C.4.38, C.4.44, C.4.45, C.4.61, C.4.65, C.4.81, C.4.91, C.4.113, C.4.135, C.4.144, C.4.159, C.4.162, C.4.162, C.4.164, C.5.2, C.5.2, C.5.7, C.5.12, C.5.15, C.5.16, C.5.25, C.5.27, C.5.28, C.5.28, C.5.50, C.5.84, C.5.96, C.5.97, C.5.98, C.5.100, C.5.100, C.5.112, C.5.133, C.5.134, C.5.160, C.5.160, C.5.168, C.5.177, C.5.186, C.5.190, C.6.6, C.6.22, C.6.27, C.6.45, C.6.49, C.6.75, C.6.79, C.6.79, C.6.79, C.6.80, C.6.81, C.6.85, C.6.86, C.6.104, C.6.128, C.6.128, C.6.133, C.6.134, C.6.134, C.6.135, C.6.156, C.6.161, C.6.161, C.6.178, C.6.199, C.6.201, C.6.203, C.6.204, C.6.209, C.6.217, C.6.218, C.6.219, C.6.221, C.6.223, C.6.230, C.6.230, C.6.235, C.6.237, C.6.241, C.6.242, C.6.245, C.6.245, C.6.250, C.6.251, C.6.260, C.6.261, C.6.262, C.6.268, C.6.268, C.6.284, C.6.287, C.6.289, C.6.294, C.6.305, C.6.306, C.6.308, C.6.313, C.6.341, C.6.348, C.6.352, C.6.359, C.6.360, C.6.368, C.6.368, C.6.369, C.6.371, C.6.371, C.6.371, C.6.372, C.6.372, C.6.374, C.6.385, C.6.388, C.6.393, C.6.397, C.6.397, C.6.399, C.6.399, C.6.402, C.6.403, C.6.404, C.6.411, C.6.412, C.6.417, C.6.431, C.7.6, C.7.22, C.7.22, C.7.27, C.7.31, C.7.32, C.7.32, C.7.33, C.7.42, C.7.48, C.7.54, C.7.66, C.7.80, C.7.103, C.7.104, C.7.107, C.7.107, C.7.107, C.7.109, C.7.113, C.7.116, C.7.124, C.7.127, C.7.130, C.7.131, C.7.137, C.7.151, C.7.155, C.7.160, C.7.161, C.7.162, C.7.162, C.7.163, C.7.164, C.7.164, C.7.165, C.7.177, C.7.182, C.7.197, C.7.202, C.7.204, C.7.213, C.7.214, C.7.219, C.7.227, C.7.232, C.7.243, C.7.251, C.7.257, C.7.267, C.7.283, C.7.284, C.7.285, C.7.288, C.7.296, C.7.299, C.7.300, C.7.304, C.7.307, C.8.2, C.8.5, C.8.5, C.8.5, C.8.19, C.8.35, C.8.40, C.8.46, C.8.46, C.8.46, C.8.46, C.8.60, C.8.61, C.8.111, C.8.152, C.8.166, C.8.174, C.8.176, C.8.182, C.8.183, C.8.188, C.8.222, C.8.246, C.8.251, C.8.268, C.8.280, C.8.304, C.8.304, C.8.310, C.8.310, C.8.310, C.8.348, C.8.348, C.8.352, C.9.3, C.9.27, C.9.50, C.9.92, C.9.94, C.9.95, C.9.111, C.9.116, C.9.119, C.9.148, C.9.148, C.9.150, C.9.154, C.9.157, C.9.158, C.9.212, C.9.222, C.9.248, C.9.249, C.9.249, C.9.250, C.9.259, C.9.269, C.9.275, C.9.281, C.9.282, C.9.297, C.9.301, C.9.343, C.9.346, C.9.346, C.10.2, C.10.8, C.10.20, C.10.32, C.10.33, C.10.33, C.10.33, C.10.39, C.10.62, C.10.62, C.10.64, C.10.64, C.10.68, C.10.83, C.10.100, C.10.104, C.10.118, C.10.129, C.10.133, C.10.135, C.10.141, C.10.144, C.10.147, C.10.179, C.10.179, C.10.215, C.10.216, C.10.217, C.10.223, C.10.240, C.10.240, C.10.242, C.10.260, C.10.263, C.10.263, C.10.263, C.10.267, C.10.269, C.10.271, C.10.285, C.10.285, C.10.306, C.11.1, C.11.14, C.11.17, C.11.36, C.11.46, C.11.69, C.11.76, C.11.80, C.11.114, C.11.121, C.11.129, C.11.131, C.11.165, C.11.168, C.11.182, C.11.195, C.11.224, C.11.249, C.11.252, C.11.258, C.11.265, C.11.294, C.11.303, C.12.9, C.12.47, C.12.51, C.12.60, C.12.65, C.12.76, C.12.76, C.12.78, C.12.93, C.12.132, C.12.135, C.12.135, C.12.136, C.12.145, C.12.146, C.12.146, C.12.148, C.12.159, C.12.162, C.12.197, C.12.197, C.12.199, C.12.199, C.12.200, C.12.216, C.12.217, C.13.8, C.13.20, C.13.33, C.13.33, C.13.35, C.13.39, C.13.55, C.13.55, C.13.56, C.13.73, C.13.74, C.13.88, C.13.88, C.13.92, C.13.95, C.13.97, C.13.100, C.13.106, C.13.109, C.13.110, C.13.110, C.13.113, C.13.114, C.13.114, C.13.117, C.13.117, C.13.120, C.13.121, C.13.126, C.13.129, C.13.133, C.13.161, C.13.196, C.13.198, C.13.209, C.13.210, C.13.218, C.13.233, C.13.234, C.13.234, C.13.237, C.14.15, C.14.23, C.14.26, C.14.31, C.14.33, C.14.33, C.14.34, C.14.40, C.14.43, C.14.44, C.14.48, C.14.50, C.14.52, C.14.72, C.14.76, C.14.82, C.14.83, C.14.91, C.14.94, C.14.96, C.14.105, C.14.118, C.14.119, C.14.128, C.14.140, C.14.144, C.14.145, C.14.147, C.14.147, C.14.163, C.14.174, C.14.174, C.14.185, C.14.205, C.14.211, C.14.216, C.15.2, C.15.3, C.15.29, C.15.29, C.15.29, C.15.32, C.15.33, C.15.35, C.15.35, C.15.41, C.15.49, C.15.55, C.15.58, C.15.60, C.15.85, C.15.95, C.15.95, C.15.100, C.15.101, C.15.102, C.15.102, C.15.107, C.15.109, C.15.119, C.15.125, C.15.156, C.15.161, C.15.161, C.15.170, C.15.170, C.15.172, C.15.190, C.15.193, C.15.198, C.15.223, C.15.247, C.15.300, C.16.35, C.16.39, C.16.54, C.16.73, C.16.76, C.16.81, C.16.82, C.16.83, C.16.84, C.16.84, C.16.89, C.16.89, C.16.92, C.16.95, C.16.104, C.16.105, C.16.107, C.16.111, C.16.121, C.16.133, C.16.136, C.16.139, C.16.144, C.16.147, C.16.153, C.16.154, C.16.155, C.16.158, C.16.167, C.16.168, C.16.172, C.16.177, C.16.177, C.16.178, C.16.202, C.16.205, C.16.213, C.16.227, C.16.251, C.16.265, C.16.266, C.16.268, C.16.286, C.16.296, C.16.298, C.16.299, C.16.299, C.16.300, C.16.300, C.16.301, C.16.305, C.16.319, C.16.321, C.16.352, C.16.355, C.16.370, C.16.371, C.16.373, C.16.373, C.17.9, C.17.38, C.17.54, C.17.73, C.17.74, C.17.74, C.17.112, C.17.115, C.17.127, C.17.151, C.17.158, C.17.159, C.17.165, C.17.166, C.17.166, C.17.168, C.17.171, C.17.178, C.17.179, C.17.183, C.17.222, C.17.225, C.17.239, C.17.248, C.17.253, C.17.258, C.17.258, C.17.260, C.17.267, C.17.270, C.17.277, C.17.277, C.17.287, C.17.287, C.17.290, C.17.299, C.17.308, C.17.308, C.17.309, C.17.313, C.18.4, C.18.6, C.18.12, C.18.17, C.18.31, C.18.35, C.18.44, C.18.61, C.18.83, C.18.85, C.18.91, C.18.91, C.18.91, C.18.100, C.18.109, C.18.124, C.18.124, C.18.125, C.18.139, C.18.155, C.18.158, C.18.166, C.18.166, C.18.181, C.18.182, C.18.185, C.18.193, C.18.194, C.18.200, C.18.201, C.18.221, C.18.223, C.18.224, C.18.225, C.18.227, C.18.230, C.18.240, C.18.262, C.18.264, C.18.266, C.18.270, C.18.271, C.18.276, C.18.277, C.18.285, C.19.1, C.19.1, C.19.2, C.19.12, C.19.12, C.19.12, C.19.16, C.19.34, C.19.49, C.19.49, C.19.51, C.19.54, C.19.55, C.19.58, C.19.73, C.19.86, C.19.87, C.19.114, C.19.115, C.19.115, C.19.125, C.19.129, C.19.130, C.19.130, C.19.130, C.19.131, C.19.132, C.19.136, C.19.151, C.19.164, C.19.172, C.19.172, C.19.173, C.19.174, C.19.176, C.19.176, C.19.181, C.19.189, C.19.189, C.19.193, C.19.198, C.19.201, C.19.207, C.19.209, C.19.214, C.19.232, C.19.233, C.19.241, C.19.241, C.19.251, C.19.259, C.19.262, C.19.263, C.19.264, C.19.286, C.19.301, C.19.303, C.20.2, C.20.3, C.20.9, C.20.11, C.20.13, C.20.14, C.20.39, C.20.46, C.20.48, C.20.51, C.20.52, C.20.58, C.20.66, C.20.75, C.20.80, C.20.80, C.20.98, C.20.100, C.20.116, C.20.118, C.20.119, C.20.122, C.20.122, C.20.127, C.20.127, C.20.131, C.20.142, C.20.145, C.20.164, C.20.222, C.20.239, C.20.240, C.20.242, C.20.244, C.20.249, C.20.261, C.20.261, C.20.268, C.20.270, C.20.271, C.20.275, C.20.280, C.20.280, C.20.285, C.20.305, C.20.306, C.20.307, C.20.315, C.20.315, C.20.326, C.20.327, C.20.332, C.20.348,

C.20.357,   C.20.360,   C.20.378,   C.20.383,   C.20.397,   C.20.398,   C.20.413,   C.20.421,
C.20.422,   C.20.424,   C.20.426,   C.20.441,   C.20.442,   C.20.451,   C.20.466,   C.20.471,
C.20.472,   C.21.7,   C.21.28,   C.21.29,   C.21.42,   C.21.98,   C.21.99,   C.21.100,   C.21.106,
C.21.118,   C.21.128,   C.21.155,   C.21.160,   C.21.167,   C.21.202,   C.21.227,   C.21.237,
C.21.237,   C.21.250,   C.21.261,   C.21.262,   C.21.263,   C.21.272,   C.21.273,
C.21.273,   C.21.279,   C.21.279,   C.21.280,   C.21.282,   C.21.305,   C.21.318,   C.21.324,
C.21.325,   C.21.327,   C.21.330,   C.21.336,   C.21.354,   C.21.357,   C.21.362,   C.21.363,
C.21.365,   C.21.365,   C.21.369,   C.21.369,   C.21.374,   C.21.388,   C.21.396,   C.21.409,
C.21.409,   C.21.410,   C.21.412,   C.21.416,   C.21.432,   C.21.435,   C.21.438,   C.21.439,
C.21.457,   C.21.458,   C.21.458,   C.21.459,   C.21.465,   C.22.16,   C.22.19,   C.22.31,   C.22.36,
C.22.56,   C.22.57,   C.22.60,   C.22.64,   C.22.71,   C.22.87,   C.22.91,   C.22.104,   C.22.113,
C.22.117,   C.22.118,   C.22.129,   C.22.132,   C.22.134,   C.22.138,   C.22.145,   C.22.145,
C.22.146,   C.22.146,   C.22.148,   C.22.152,   C.22.157,   C.22.160,   C.22.161,   C.22.162,
C.22.163,   C.22.164,   C.22.172,   C.22.176,   C.22.176,   C.22.176,   C.22.179,   C.22.181,
C.22.181,   C.22.217,   C.22.218,   C.22.221,   C.22.223,   C.22.225,   C.22.255,   C.22.255,
C.22.258,   C.22.263,   C.22.265,   C.22.267,   C.22.267,   C.22.278,   C.22.292,   C.22.300,
C.22.302,   C.22.304,   C.22.312,   C.22.313,   C.22.317,   C.22.325,   C.22.325,   C.22.326,
C.22.336,   C.22.344,   C.22.363,   C.22.364,   C.22.367,   C.22.374,   C.22.380.

a prep *a prep.(1) cf. on* A 12 a (7) an (5); B 19 a (9) an (10); C 39 a (23) an (16)

A.Pr.13	Ac as I beheld into þe Est *an* hei3 to þe sonne
A. 3.63	*An* aunter 3e haue 3oure hire þerof h[e]re;
A. 3.259	*An* aunter it [noi3ide me non] ende wile I make.
A. 4.32	And betwyn hymself & his sone sette hym *a* benche,
A. 5.213	Sleuþe for sorewe fil doun *a* swowe
A. 6.58	A[nd] nameliche *an* ydel þe name of god almi3t;
A. 7.41	Nyme hem nou3t, *an* aunter þou mowe hem nou3t deserue.
A. 7.292	Deyneþ nou3t to dyne *a* day ni3t olde wortis.
A. 8.115	Þe foulis in þe firmament, who fynt hem *a* wynter?
A. 9.58	Blisse of þ[e] briddis brou3te me *a* slepe;
A.10.190	In gelosie, ioyeles, & ianglyng [*a*] bedde,
A.11.279	*A* goode friday, I fynde, a feloun was sauid
B.Pr.13	[Ac] as I biheeld into þe Eest, *an* hei3 to þe sonne,
B.Pr.128	And siþen in þe Eyr *an* hei3 an Aungel of heuene
B.Pr.140	And to þe Aungel *an* hei3 answerde after:
B. 1.90	He is a god by þe gospel, *a* grounde and o lofte,
B. 3.66	*An* auenture pride be peynted þere and pomp of þe world;
B. 6.42	Nyme it no3t *an* auenture [þow] mowe it no3t deserue.
B. 6.308	Deyne[þ] no3t to dyne *a* day ny3t olde wortes.
B.11.107	'He seiþ sooþ', quod Scripture þo, and skipte *an* hei3 and preched.
B.12.202	So it fareþ by þat felon þat *a* good friday was saued;
B.12.218	And aresonedest Reson, *a* rebukynge as it were,
B.13.401	As þere no nede was goddes name *an* Idel.
B.15.559	An Aungel men herden *an* heigh at Rome crye,
B.16.172	And þanne mette I wiþ a man, *a* mydlenten sonday,
B.16.189	The light of al þat lif haþ *a* londe and a watre,
B.16.189	The light of al þat lif haþ a londe and *a* watre,
B.17.118	And Hope þe Hostile[r] shal be þer [*an* helyng þe man lith];
B.18.315	And al oure lordshipe, I leue, *a* londe and [in helle]:
B.19.191	Anoon after *an* heigh vp into heuene
B.20.383	And þat freres hadde *a* fyndyng þat for nede flateren
C. 2.58	Were beden to þe Bridale *a* bothe half þe contre,
C. 5.186	Lo! in heuene *an* heyh was an holy comune
C. 6.124	Til y, wrathe, wexe *an* hey and walke with hem bothe;
C. 7.218	And-nameliche-*an*-ydel-þe-name-of-god-almyhty.
C. 8.197	Tho was [Peres] proud and potte hem alle *a* werke
C. 8.330	Deyne[th noght] to dyne *a* day nyhte olde wortes;
C. 9.154	With a bagge at his bak *A* begyneld wyse,
C. 9.282	For y can construe vch a word and kennen hit the *an* englische.'
C.11.252	*A* gode friday, y fynde, a feloun was ysaued
C.12.41	'A saith soth,' quod scripture tho, and skypte *an* heyh and prechede.
C.14.7	Ne to spille speche, As to speke *an* ydel,
C.14.14	Is ycalde Caritas, kynde loue *an* engelysche,
C.14.131	The thef þat hadde grace of god *a* gode fryday, As thow toldest,
C.14.141	So hit f[areth] by þat *a* goed fryday was saued:
C.15.19	And how louyng he is to vch lyf *a* londe and o watere
C.16.37	Elles is al *an* ydel al oure lyuynge here,
C.16.188	Thenne ys racio my rihte name, reson *an* englische;
C.17.222	An angel men herde *an* hye at rome crye,
C.18.105	And anoon he hihte Elde *an* hy for to clymbe
C.18.181	And thenne mette y with a man *a* myddelento[n] sonenday,
C.18.212	*A* thre he is þer he is and hereof bereth wittnesse
C.18.241	Where god [ri3t me] gate cam gangynge *a* thre];
C.19.4	Lo, here the lettre,' quod he, '*a* latyn and [an] ebrew;
C.19.4	Lo, here the lettre,' quod he, 'a latyn and [*an*] ebrew;
C.19.75	And lefte hym þere *a* lechyng to lyue yf he myhte
C.19.98	In thre persones, *a* parceles departable fram oþere,
C.19.177	That serueth this swynkares to [see] by *a* nyhtes,
C.19.196	And melteth myhte into mercy, as we may se *a* wynter
C.20.29	Alle þat lyueth or loketh *a* londe or a watre.
C.20.29	Alle þat lyueth or loketh a londe or *a* watre.
C.20.61	The wal of the temple tocleyef euene [*a*] to peces;
C.20.349	We haen ylost oure lordschipe *a* londe and in helle:

C.21.191	Anoon aftur *an* heyh vp into heuene
C.21.236	And som he lered to laboure *a* londe and a watre
C.21.236	And som he lered to laboure a londe and *a* watre
C.21.328	And calde þat hous vnite, holy chirche *an* englisch
C.21.402	Of spiritus Iusticie thow spekest moche *an* ydel.'
C.22.299	Of all taletellares and titerares *an* ydel.
C.22.383	And þat freres hadde *a* fyndynge þat for nede flateren

a &> he, heo

aaron n prop *OED Aaron 1* A 1
A. 3.243	[A3ens isra[e]l and *aaron* and moyses his broþer].

abasshed ptp *abaishen v.* B 2; C 4 abasched (3) abaschet (1)
B.10.292	[Th]anne shul burel clerkes ben *abasshed* to blame yow or to greue,
B.20.48	Forþi be no3t *abasshed* to bide and to be nedy
C. 6.17	And [bold haue] y be, nat *abaschet* to agulte
C. 9.86	And ben *abasched* for to begge and wollen nat be aknowe
C.15.162	Shal neuere buyren be *abasched* þat hath this abouten hym
C.22.48	Forthy be nat *abasched* to byde and to be nedy

abate v *abaten v.* A 1; B 1
A. 7.169	To *abate* þe barly bred & þe benis ygrounde,
B.12.59	Ac grace is a gras þer[for] þo greuaunces to *abate*.

abaue v *OED abave v., MED abaven v.,* A 1; B 1; C 1
A. 7.201	And [*a*]baue hem wiþ b[e]nes for bollnyng of here wombe,
B. 6.215	[And] *aba[u]e* hem wiþ benes for bollynge of hir womb[e];
C. 8.225	And [*a*]baue hem wiþ benes for bollynge of here wombe;

abbesse n *abbesse n.* A 1; B 2; C 2
A. 8.120	'Abstinence þe *abbesse* myn a b c me tau3te,
B. 5.153	I haue an Aunte to Nonne and an *Abbesse* boþe;
B. 7.138	'Abstynence þe *Abbesse* myn a b c me tau3te,
C. 5.176	For þe abbot of engelonde and the *abbesse* his nese
C. 6.128	Y haue an Aunte to nonne and an *abbesse*;

abbot n *abbot n.* B 1; C 1
B.10.331	And þanne shal þe *Abbot* of Abyngdoun and al his issue for euere
C. 5.176	For þe *abbot* of engelonde and the abbesse his nese

abedde adv *abedde adv.* B 2; C 5
B. 5.388	Were I brou3t *abedde*, but if my tailende it made,
B. 5.410	And ligge *abedde* in lenten and my lemman in myne armes,
C. 6.44	And louelokest to loke vppon a[nd] lykyngest *abedde*
C.7.26	And ligge *abedde* in lente and my lemman in myn armus
C.10.259	And thogh he be louelich to loke[n] on and lossum *abedde*,
C.10.262	Ac lat he[r] be vnlouely and vnlofsum *abedde*,
C.10.270	In ielosye, ioyles and iangelynge *abedde*,

abeggeth adv *abeggeth adv.* C 2
C. 8.138	That no faytrye were founde in folk þat goth *abeggeth*.
C. 8.245	And go abribeth and *abeggeth* and no man beten his hungur:

abel n prop *n.i.d.* C 4
C.10.247	Aftur þat Caym þ[e] corsed hadde ykuld *abel*,
C.18.217	And *Abel* of hem bothe and alle thre o kynde;
C.18.219	And *abel* here issue, aren bote oen in manhede.
C.18.229	And as *abel* of Adam and of his wyf Eue

abide v *abiden v.* A 6 abide (4) abyde (1) abideþ (1); B 10 abide (7) abyde (1) abiden (1) abidynge (1); C 15 abyde (12) abideth (1) abidynge (1) abydyng (1)
A. 2.174	Ac marchauntis mette wiþ hym & made him *abide*;
A. 2.196	Saue mede þe maiden no mo durste *abide*.
A. 7.138	He *abideþ* wel þe betere þat bummiþ nou3t to ofte.'
A. 9.55	Blisse of þe briddis made me *abide*,
A. 9.96	But dobest bede for hem *abide* þere for euere.
A.12.45	And 3if þou desyre with him for to *abyde*
B. 2.215	Ac Marchaunt3 metten with hym and made hym *abyde*
B. 2.237	Saue Mede þe mayde na mo dorste *abide*.
B. 8.64	Blisse of þe briddes [*abide* me made],
B. 8.106	But dobest bede for hem [*abide*] þer for euere.
B.11.378	Amende þow, if þow my3t, for my tyme is to *abide*.
B.15.313	For we [by] goddes [beheestes] *abiden* alwey
B.19.294	And bold and *abidynge* bismares to suffre;
B.20.46	Ther nede haþ ynome me þat I moot nede *abide*
B.20.79	And þere *abide* and bikere ayeins Beliales children.'
B.20.131	And garte good feiþ flee and fals to *abide*,
C. 1.133	Estward til heuene, euere to *abyde*
C. 2.202	For to wisse hem þe way and with mede *abyde*
C. 2.225	A[c] marchauntes mette with hym and made hym *abyde*
C. 2.253	Saue mede þe mayde no ma durste *abyde*.
C. 4.35	For there is wrath and wranglynge then wol they *abyde*;
C. 8.287	Lat hem *abyde* til the bord be drawe; Ac bere hem none crommes
C. 9.40	And *abyde* þer in my blisse body and soule for euere.'

C.10.63   Blisse of þe briddes *abyde* me made
C.10.225   Boske ȝow to þat boet and *abideth* þerynne
C.18.135   Byg and *abydyng*, and bold in his barnhoed
C.20.344   For vs were bettere nat be then *abyde* in his sihte.
C.21.294   And bold and *abidynge* busmares to soffre
C.22.46   Ther nede hath ynome me þat y moet nede *abyde*
C.22.79   And þere *abyde* and bikere aȝeyn beliales childrene.'
C.22.131   And gert goed faith fle and fals to *abyde*

abien v *abien v.* A 4 abigge (2) abiggen (1) abiȝe (1); B 11 abye (1)
    abien (1) abyen (1) abigge (1) abiggen (1) abouȝt (1) abouȝte (4)
    abugge (1); C 9 abygge (1) abyggen (1) abouhte (3) aboute (1) abugge
    (1) abuggen (1) abuye (1)
A. 2.92   Ȝe shuln *abigge* boþe, be god þat me made.
A. 3.230   Shal *abiȝe* it bitterly or þe bok liȝeþ.
A. 7.73   And deme hem nouȝt for ȝif þou dost þou shalt it dere *abiggen*,
A. 7.151   'Or þou shalt *abigge* be þe lawe, be þe ordre þat I bere'.
B. 2.128   Ye shul *abiggen* boþe, by god þat me made!
B. 3.251   Shal *abien* it bittre or þe book lieþ.
B. 6.81   Deme-hem-noȝt-for-if-þow-doost-þow-shalt-it-deere-*abugge*-
B. 6.166   'Or þow shalt *abigge* be þe lawe, by þe ordre þat I bere!'
B. 9.91   The commune for hir vnkyndenesse, I drede me, shul *abye*;
B. 9.146   Here *abouȝte* þe barn þe belsires giltes,
B.10.286   Bittre *abouȝte* þe giltes of two badde preestes,
B.12.42   Iob þe Iew his ioye deere *abouȝte*;
B.13.375   And [what body] borwed of me *abouȝte* þe tyme
B.18.388   Be it any þyng *abouȝt*, þe boldnesse of hir synnes,
B.18.403   Thow shalt *abyen* it bittre!' and bond hym wiþ cheynes.
C. 2.144   Ȝe shal *abyggen* bothe þat amende þe sonner.
C. 6.247   So what buyrn of me borewede *abouhte* the tyme.'
C. 8.41   For thow shalt ȝelden hit, so may be, or sumdel *abuggen* hit.
C. 8.83   Deme-hem-nat-[for]-yf-thow-doest-thow-shalt-hit-dere-*abygge*.
C.10.234   Here *aboute* þe barn the belsires gultes
C.13.16   How bittere he hit *abouhte*, as þe book telleth!
C.16.221   The bittorere he shal *abugge* but yf he wel worche.
C.20.430   Be hit eny thyng *abouhte*, the boldenesse of here synne[s],
C.20.446   Thow shal[t] *abuye* bittere!' and b[o]nde hym with chaynes.

abyngdoun n prop *n.i.d.* B 1
B.10.331   And þanne shal þe Abbot of *Abyngdoun* and al his issue for euere

abite v *abiten v. &> habite* B 1; C 1 abiteth
B.16.26   And in blowyng tyme *abite* þe floures but if þise piles helpe.
C.18.32   Couetyse cometh of þat wynde and Caritas hit *abiteth*

ablende v *ablenden v.* B 2 ablende (1) ablente (1); C 2 ablende (1)
    ablente (1)
B.18.137   The while þis light and þis leme shal Lucifer *ablende*.
B.18.325   Lucifer loke ne myȝte, so light hym *ablente*.
C.20.140   The while this lihte and this l[em]e shal lucifer *ablende*.
C.20.368   Lucifer loke ne myhte, so liht hym *ablen[t]e*,

ablyndeþ v *ablinden v.* B 1 ablyndeþ
B.10.270   Siþen a beem [is] in þyn owene *ablyndeþ* þiselue–

abostede v *abosten v.* C 1
C. 8.152   A bretener cam braggyng, *abostede* [Peres] also:

abouȝt(e abouhte > abien

aboute adv *abouten adv.* A 23 aboute (21) abouten (1) abowte (1); B 30;
    C 33 aboute (32) abouten (1)
A.Pr.29   Coueite not in cuntre to cairen *aboute*
A.Pr.40   Bidderis & beggeris faste *aboute* ȝede
A. 1.90   Þe clerkis þat knowe it shulde kenne it *aboute*,
A. 1.93   And riden & rappe doun in reaumes *aboute*,
A. 2.17   And lakkide my lore to lordis *aboute*,
A. 2.39   Þat iche feld nas ful of folk al *aboute*.
A. 2.43   Of kniȝtes of cuntr[e], of comeres *aboute*,
A. 2.109   And bad gile go gyue gold al *aboute*,
A. 2.123   And let somoune alle þe segges [in shires *abouten*],
A. 2.184   And ȝaf pardoun for panis poundmel *aboute*.
A. 4.68   Ac wisdom & wyt were *aboute* faste
A. 6.6   In a [weþewindes] wyse [ywounden] *aboute*;
A. 7.286   And þo nolde wastour not werche, but wandrite *aboute*,
A. 8.30   And bynde brugges *aboute* þat tobroke were,
A. 8.127   And þoruȝ here wordis I wok & waitide *aboute*,
A. 9.1   Thus, yrobid in rosset, I rombide *aboute*
A. 9.12   Ȝif þei knewen any cuntre or costis *aboute*
A. 9.36   Þat as wyndis & watris wa[l]wen *aboute*;
A.10.105   And riȝt so be romberis þat rennen *aboute*
A.10.110   In ensaumple [þat] suche shulde not renne *aboute*,
A.10.217   And so comiþ dobest *aboute* and bringeþ doun mody,
A.11.202   And þat is riȝtful religioun, none renneris *aboute*.
A.12.61   I stode stille in a stodie and stared *abowte*.
B.Pr.29   Coueiten noȝt in contree to [cairen] *aboute*

B.Pr.40   Bidderes and beggeres faste *aboute* yede
B.Pr.151   And pleide wiþ hem perillousli and possed *aboute*.
B. 1.92   The clerkes þat knowen [it] sholde kennen it *aboute*
B. 1.95   Riden and rappen doun in Reaumes *aboute*,
B. 2.86   The Countee of Coueitise and alle þe costes *aboute*,
B. 2.145   And bad gile '[go] gyu[e] gold al *aboute*,
B. 2.159   And leten somone alle segges in shires *aboute*,
B. 2.177   To bere Bisshopes *aboute* abrood in visitynge.
B. 2.225   And [gaf] pardoun for pens poundemele *aboute*.
B. 4.81   Ac wisdom and wit were *aboute* faste
B. 5.147   That whan þei preche þe peple in many places *aboute*
B. 5.439   I [yarn] *aboute* in youþe and yaf me nauȝt to lerne,
B. 5.518   In a wiþwynde[s] wise ywounden *aboute*.
B. 6.302   And þo [n]olde Wastour noȝt werche, but wandre[d] *aboute*,
B. 7.28   And [bynde] brugges [*aboute*] þat tobroke were,
B. 7.145   And [þoruȝ hir wordes I wook] and waited *aboute*,
B. 8.1   Thus, yrobed in russet, I romed *aboute*
B. 8.12   If þei knewe any contree or costes [*aboute*]
B. 8.40   That as wyndes and [watres] walkeþ *aboute*;
B. 9.208   And so comeþ dobest [*aboute*] and bryngeþ adoun mody,
B.11.130   As a reneyed caytif recchelesly rennen *aboute*.
B.13.368   Or by nyȝte or by daye *aboute* was ich euere
B.15.329   For þat þei beggen *aboute* in buyldynge þei spende,
B.15.529   [And nauȝt to] huppe *aboute* in Engelond to halwe mennes Auteres
B.17.59   And as naked as a nedle and noon help *aboute*.
B.18.296   Thise þritty wynter, as I wene, [he wente *aboute*] and preched.
B.18.305   For þe body, while it on bones yede, *aboute* was euere
B.20.70   And pride [bar it bare] boldely *aboute*
B.20.164   And threw drede of dispair a doȝeyne myle *aboute*.
C.Pr.31   Coueyten noȝt in contre[y] to cayren *aboute*
C.Pr.41   Bidders and beggers fast *aboute* ȝede
C. 1.88   Clerkes þat knowen hit sholde kenne it *aboute*
C. 1.91   Rydon and rappe adoun in reumes *aboute*
C. 2.161   And bade gyle '[g]o gyue gold al *aboute*,
C. 2.175   And leten somne alle seggus in vche syde *aboute*,
C. 2.235   And gaf pardon for pans poundmele *aboute*.
C. 4.77   Ac wyles and wyt were *aboute* faste
C. 4.183   'Y wolde hit were,' quod the kynge, 'wel al *aboute*.
C. 5.29   Or beggest thy bylyue *aboute* at men hacches
C. 5.159   And pryked *aboute* on palfrayes fram places to maneres,
C. 7.53   And ȝede *aboute* in my ȝouthe and ȝaf me to no thedom
C. 7.163   In a wethewynde wyse ywrithe al *aboute*;
C. 8.324   And tho wolde wastor nat worche bote wandre[d] *aboute*
C. 9.107   The whiche aren lunatyk lollares and lepares *aboute*
C. 9.137   The whiche [arn] lunatyk loreles and lepares *aboute*
C. 9.153   And what freke on this folde fiscuth *aboute*
C. 9.294   And thorw here wordes [y] awoke and waytede *aboute*
C.10.1   Thus, yrobed in russet, y romede *aboute*
C.10.12   Yf they knewe eny contre oþer costes *aboute*
C.10.46   That as wyndes and wederes wal[k]eth *aboute*;
C.10.190   And ȝut were best to ben *aboute* and brynge hit to hepe
C.10.266   Ther ne is squier ne knyhte in contreye *aboute*
C.12.65   As a [reneyed] Caytyf [rechelesliche rennen *aboute*].
C.13.134   And y bowed my body, bihel[d]e al *aboute*
C.15.160   And bere hit in thy bosom *aboute* where þou wendest
C.16.338   Thogh y my byliue sholde begge *aboute* at menne hacches.
C.17.279   And nat in Ingelond to huppe *aboute* and halewe men auters
C.19.58   And as naked as an nedle and noen helpe *abouten*.
C.20.329   This thritty wynter, as y wene, and wente *aboute* and prechede.
C.20.337   For þe body, whiles hit on bones ȝede, *aboute* was hit euere
C.22.70   And pryde [baer] hit baer baldly *aboute*
C.22.164   And th[re]w drede of dispayr a doysayne myle *aboute*.

aboute prep *abouten prep.* A 5; B 21 about (1) aboute (19) abouten (1);
    C 17 aboute (16) abouten (1)
A. 1.6   How besy þei ben *aboute* þe mase?
A. 6.73   Þe mot is of mercy þe Maner al *aboute*,
A. 7.161   And buffetide þe bretoner *aboute* þe chekis
A. 8.105   Ne *aboute* my [belyue] so besy be namore:
A. 8.112   [By foules, þat are not] besy *aboute* þe bely ioye:
B.Pr.161   Beren beiȝes ful briȝte *abouten* hire nekkes.
B.Pr.178   That dorste haue bounden þe belle *aboute* þe cattes nekke;
B.Pr.179   Ne hangen it *aboute* [his] hals al Engelond to wynne;
B. 1.6   How bisie þei ben *aboute* þe maȝe?
B. 2.62   I kan noȝt rekene þe route þat ran *aboute* Mede.
B. 5.492   *Aboute* mydday, whan moost liȝt is and meel tyme of Seintes,
B. 5.586   The moot is of mercy þe Manoir *aboute*;
B. 6.176   He buffetted þe Bretoner *aboute* þe chekes
B. 7.123   Ne *aboute* my [bilyue] so bisy be na moore;
B. 7.130   By foweles [þat are] noȝt bisy *aboute* þe [bely ioye];
B.11.17   Concupiscencia carnis colled me *aboute* þe nekke
B.11.418   Ac whan he mamelede *about* mete, and entremetede to knowe
B.12.257   I leue it flawme ful foule þe fold al *aboute*
B.13.251   And buxom and busy *aboute* breed and drynke

B.13.346   *Aboute* þe mouþ, or byneþe bigynneþ to grope,
B.14.160   Ac beggeris *aboute* Midsomer bredlees þei [soupe],
B.15.283   Antony adayes *aboute* noon tyme
B.18.67   Er sonday *aboute* sonne risyng'; and sank wiþ þat til erþe.
B.18.134   Which deide and deeþ þoled þis day *aboute* mydday,
B.19.362   To deluen a dych depe *aboute* vnitee
B.20.191   He buffetted me *aboute* þe mouþ [and bette out my wangteeþ];
C.Pr.180   Bere beyus of bryghte gold *aboute* here nekkes
C.Pr.187   And hongen hit *aboute* þe cattes halse; thanne here we mowe
C.Pr.195   That derste haue ybounde þe belle *aboute* þe kattes nekke
C.Pr.196   Ne hanged it *aboute* his hals al yngelond to wynne;
C. 1.6   Hou bisy þei ben *aboute* þe mase?
C. 2.64   Y kan nouȝt rykene þe route þat ran *aboute* mede.
C. 6.180   *Aboute* þe mouthe and bynethe bygan y to grope,
C. 7.132   *Aboute* mydday, when most liht is and mel tyme of sayntes,
C. 8.173   A boffatede þe Bretoner *aboute* the chekes
C. 9.247   Ac *aboute* mydday at mele tyme y mette with hem ofte,
C.13.226   Ac when he mamelede *aboute* mete and musede to knowe
C.15.162   Shal neuere buyren be abasched þat hath this *abouten* hym
C.16.13   Ac beggares *aboute* myssomur bredles they soupe,
C.20.69   Ar soneday *aboute* sonne rysynge'; and sank with þat til erthe.
C.20.137   [Which] deyede and deth tholede this day *aboute* mydday
C.21.362   To deluen a dich depe *aboute* vnite
C.22.191   He boffeted me *aboute* þe mouthe and beet out my wangteeth

aboute &> abien

aboue adv *aboven adv.* B 3; C 3
B. 5.194   Wiþ an hood on his heed, a hat *aboue*,
B.15.441   Preestes and prechours and a pope *aboue*,
B.19.280   [That] caste for to ke[l]e a crokke to saue þe fatte *aboue*.
C.13.22   And brouhte hem all *aboue* þat in bale rotede!
C.18.86   And thenne *aboue* is bettere fruyt, ac bothe two ben gode,
C.21.280   That caste for to kele a crok [to] saue þe fatte *aboue*.

aboue prep *aboven prep.* A 1; B 10 aboue (8) abouen (2); C 7
A. 9.86   Dobest is *aboue* hem boþe & beriþ a bisshopis croce;
B. 8.96   Dobest is *aboue* boþe and bereþ a bisshopes crosse;
B. 9.14   Dobest is *aboue* boþe, a Bisshopes peere;
B.10.361   That is, loue þi lord god leuest *abouen* alle,
B.11.139   For þei beþ, as oure bokes telleþ, *aboue* goddes werkes:
B.11.219   Thanne is bileue a lele help, *aboue* logyk or lawe.
B.11.357   And brouȝten forþ hir briddes al *aboue* þe grounde.
B.14.151   ȝueþ hym a cote *aboue* his couenaunt, riȝt so crist ȝyueþ heuene
B.14.290   Ne to be Mair *aboue* men ne Mynystre vnder kynges;
B.17.133   Louye hem lik myselue, ac oure lord *abouen* alle.'
B.19.470   Ye ben but membres and I *aboue* alle.
C. 7.208   That ȝe louye hym [as] lord leely *aboue* alle.
C.10.141   Dobest is *aboue* bothe, a bishopis pere,
C.12.74   They b[e]t[h], as oure bokes telleth, [*aboue*] godes werkes:
C.13.166   And brouhte forth here briddes al *aboue* þe grounde.
C.16.34   Ho doth wel or bet or beste *aboue* alle;
C.19.102   And hym *aboue* alle and hem as mysulue;
C.21.470   ȝe ben bote membres and y *aboue* alle.

abouhte > abien; abowte > aboute

abraham n prop *n.i.d.* B 9 Abraham (8) Abrahames (1); C 13 abraham (12) Abrahammus (1)
B.16.81   Adam and *Abraham* and Ysaye þe prophete,
B.16.173   As hoor as an haweþorn and *Abraham* he highte.
B.16.177   And of *Abrahames* hous an heraud of armes,
B.17.28   *Abraham* seiþ þat he seiȝ hoolly þe Trinite,
B.17.30   And alle þre but o god; þus *Abraham* me tauȝte;
B.17.44   It is ful hard for any man on *Abraham* bileue
B.17.130   And alle þre but o god? þus *Abraham* me tauȝte;
B.17.134   'After *Abraham*', quod he, 'þat heraud of armes,
B.18.143   For Adam and Eue and *Abraham* wiþ oþere
C. 8.281   In al manere ese in *Abrahammus* lappe.
C.13.5   ȝut ret me þat *abraham* and Iob weren wonder ryche
C.13.7   *Abraham* for his [auȝte] hadde moche tene
C.13.10   And *Abraham* not hardy ones to letten hym
C.13.24   Spryngeth and spredeth, so spedde þe fader *Abraham*
C.18.112   Adam and *Abraham* and ysaye þe prophete,
C.18.182   As hoer as a hauthorn, and *abraham* he hihte.
C.19.29   *Abraham* saith þat he seyh holly þe trinitee,
C.19.31   And alle thre bote o god; thus *abraham* bereth witenesse
C.19.53   Bothe *abraham* and sp[e]s he mette at ones
C.19.99   And alle thre bote o god? thus *abraham* me tauhte.
C.19.109   And as *Abraham* þe olde of o god the tauhte
C.20.146   For Adam and Eue And *abraham* with oþere

abrede adv *abrode adv.(1), OED abreid adv.* C 1
C. 3.260   He sholde haue [ben] lord of þat lond alenghe and *abrede*

abribeth adv *abribeþ adv.* C 1
C. 8.245   And go *abribeth* and abeggeth and no man beten his hungur:

abrood adv *abrode adv.(1)* B 3; C 2 abroed (1) abrood (1)
B. 2.177   To bere Bisshopes aboute *abrood* in visitynge.
B. 5.141   And siþen þei blosmede *abrood* in boure to here shriftes.
B.14.61   For þoruȝ his breeþ beestes woxen and *abrood* yeden:
C. 9.143   Vnlouke his legges *abrood* or ligge at his ese,
C.15.260   [For] thorw his breth bestes wexe and *abroed* ȝeden:

absence n *absence n.* B 1; C 1
B.19.124   And whan he [was woxen] moore, in his moder *absence*,
C.21.124   And when he was wexen more, in his moder *absence*,

absoloun n prop *n.i.d.* C 1
C. 3.408   How he *absoloun* to hangynge brouhte;

absolucion n *absolucioun n.* A 1 absolucioun; B 1
A. 8.66   Hadde þe same *absolucioun* þat sent was to peris.
B. 7.64   Ha[dde] þe same *absolucion* þat sent was to Piers.

abstinence n *abstinence n.* A 3; B 3 Abstinence (2) Abstynence (1); C 2
A. 5.211   Er *abstinence* myn aunte haue ygyue me leue,
A. 6.106   Þat on hattiþ *abstinence*, and [humylite] anoþer,
A. 8.120   '*Abstinence* þe abbesse myn a b c me tauȝte,
B. 5.383   Til *Abstinence* myn Aunte haue ȝyue me leeue,
B. 5.620   That oon hatte *Abstinence*, and humilite anoþer;
B. 7.138   '*Abstynence* þe Abbesse myn a b c me tauȝte,
C. 6.440   Til *abstinence* myn aunte haue ȝeue me leue;
C. 7.272   That on hatte a[b]stinence and vmbletee a[n]oþer,

abugge(n abuye > abien

ac conj *ac conj.* A 91; B 294; C 269
A.Pr.13, A.Pr.35, A.Pr.78, A.Pr.87, A.1.25, A.1.42, A.1.115, A.1.119, A.1.164, A.2.106, A.2.149, A.2.174, A.2.192, A.2.197, A.3.11, A.3.53, A.3.57, A.3.76, A.3.96, A.3.97, A.3.177, A.3.238, A.3.275, A.4.24, A.4.29, A.4.68, A.4.119, A.4.134, A.4.146, A.4.153, A.5.22, A.5.84, A.5.94, A.5.142, A.5.234, A.5.245, A.6.1, A.6.47, A.6.59, A.6.95, A.6.104, A.6.110, A.7.24, A.7.25, A.7.117, A.7.126, A.7.135, A.7.188, A.7.204, A.7.243, A.7.270, A.8.25, A.8.49, A.8.52, A.8.55, A.8.82, A.8.134, A.8.155, A.8.163, A.9.18, A.9.40, A.9.49, A.9.76, A.9.102, A.9.109, A.10.10, A.10.16, A.10.32, A.10.45, A.10.64, A.10.66, A.10.71, A.10.88, A.10.95, A.10.139, A.11.38, A.11.45, A.11.54, A.11.57, A.11.72, A.11.77, A.11.96, A.11.116, A.11.137, A.11.142, A.11.149, A.11.211, A.11.230, A.11.231, A.11.241
B.Pr.5, B.Pr.13, B.Pr.35, B.Pr.81, B.Pr.107, B.Pr.176, B.Pr.180, B.Pr.214, B.1.25, B.1.44, B.1.126, B.1.130, B.1.190, B.2.63, B.2.65, B.2.142, B.2.162, B.2.169, B.2.188, B.2.215, B.2.230, B.2.234, B.2.238, B.3.11, B.3.64, B.3.87, B.3.107, B.3.186, B.3.190, B.3.259, B.3.291, B.3.299, B.3.338, B.3.347, B.4.32, B.4.36, B.4.81, B.4.136, B.4.151, B.4.167, B.4.177, B.4.190, B.5.5, B.5.22, B.5.104, B.5.114, B.5.159, B.5.169, B.5.178, B.5.226, B.5.298, B.5.349, B.5.353, B.5.396, B.5.421, B.5.463, B.5.513, B.5.560, B.5.572, B.5.576, B.5.609, B.5.617, B.5.618, B.5.625, B.6.22, B.6.23, B.6.125, B.6.134, B.6.139, B.6.145, B.6.148, B.6.202, B.6.218, B.6.259, B.6.286, B.6.319, B.6.321, B.7.19, B.7.23, B.7.45, B.7.47, B.7.50, B.7.53, B.7.76, B.7.78, B.7.100, B.7.154, B.7.157, B.7.185, B.8.22, B.8.33, B.8.44, B.8.55, B.8.58, B.8.85, B.8.112, B.8.119, B.9.10, B.9.17, B.9.31, B.9.57, B.9.58, B.9.121, B.9.150, B.9.178, B.9.193, B.9.204, B.10.32, B.10.49, B.10.52, B.10.59, B.10.68, B.10.71, B.10.124, B.10.143, B.10.164, B.10.185, B.10.190, B.10.200, B.10.212, B.10.245, B.10.266, B.10.279, B.10.311, B.10.321, B.10.322, B.10.334, B.10.335, B.10.357, B.10.395, B.10.399, B.10.402, B.10.405, B.10.437, B.11.70, B.11.79, B.11.82, B.11.103, B.11.108, B.11.129, B.11.131, B.11.160, B.11.162, B.11.192, B.11.195, B.11.198, B.11.239, B.11.254, B.11.315, B.11.320, B.11.351, B.11.369, B.11.382, B.11.409, B.11.416, B.11.418, B.11.432, B.12.25, B.12.31, B.12.59, B.12.60, B.12.68, B.12.70, B.12.77, B.12.128, B.12.133, B.12.159, B.12.196, B.12.199, B.12.214, B.12.226, B.12.235, B.12.236, B.12.272, B.12.285, B.12.287, B.13.29, B.13.40, B.13.41, B.13.43, B.13.60, B.13.68, B.13.73, B.13.74, B.13.78, B.13.131, B.13.148, B.13.179, B.13.190, B.13.227, B.13.230, B.13.255, B.13.274, B.13.409, B.13.411, B.13.431, B.14.73, B.14.75, B.14.90, B.14.95, B.14.126, B.14.145, B.14.155, B.14.160, B.14.170, B.14.174, B.14.189, B.14.192, B.14.204, B.14.207, B.14.216, B.14.218, B.14.279, B.15.1, B.15.90, B.15.101, B.15.116, B.15.125, B.15.129, B.15.135, B.15.146, B.15.156, B.15.162, B.15.199, B.15.207, B.15.227, B.15.228, B.15.231, B.15.236, B.15.247, B.15.249, B.15.266, B.15.276, B.15.295, B.15.298, B.15.305, B.15.332, B.15.342, B.15.347, B.15.350, B.15.353, B.15.387, B.15.397, B.15.414, B.15.432, B.15.486, B.15.489, B.15.574, B.15.579, B.15.596, B.15.605, B.16.3, B.16.46, B.16.48, B.16.55, B.16.113, B.16.144, B.16.161, B.16.261, B.17.60, B.17.64, B.17.66, B.17.89, B.17.99, B.17.112, B.17.133, B.17.187, B.17.194, B.17.248, B.17.285, B.17.286, B.17.305, B.17.319, B.17.347, B.18.75, B.18.78, B.18.276, B.18.375, B.18.376, B.18.377, B.18.395, B.18.396, B.19.13, B.19.30, B.19.63, B.19.69, B.19.96, B.19.157, B.19.430, B.20.35, B.20.231, B.20.245, B.20.284, B.20.288
C.Pr.6, C.Pr.62, C.Pr.78, C.Pr.101, C.Pr.134, C.Pr.193, C.Pr.197, C.1.24, C.1.42, C.1.107, C.1.116, C.1.123, C.1.125, C.1.128, C.1.186, C.2.24, C.2.65, C.2.67, C.2.158, C.2.178, C.2.201, C.2.225, C.2.240, C.2.244, C.2.248, C.2.254, C.3.12, C.3.68, C.3.115, C.3.232, C.3.234, C.3.236, C.3.258, C.3.336, C.3.374, C.3.383, C.3.394, C.3.407, C.3.444, C.3.452, C.3.478, C.3.493, C.3.500, C.4.32, C.4.36, C.4.40, C.4.55, C.4.77, C.4.133, C.4.151, C.4.171, C.5.70, C.5.90, C.5.94, C.5.124, C.5.156, C.5.167, C.5.168, C.5.178, C.6.151, C.6.160, C.6.317, C.6.411, C.7.12, C.7.32, C.7.34, C.7.69, C.7.158, C.7.205, C.7.219, C.7.223, C.7.261, C.7.269, C.7.270, C.7.307, C.8.20, C.8.51, C.8.91, C.8.131, C.8.137, C.8.141, C.8.208, C.8.228, C.8.251, C.8.265, C.8.271, C.8.287,

C.8.294, C.8.308, C.8.339, C.8.341, C.9.23, C.9.27, C.9.46, C.9.71, C.9.98, C.9.106,
C.9.113, C.9.176, C.9.189, C.9.204, C.9.247, C.9.252, C.9.303, C.9.305, C.9.331,
C.10.38, C.10.51, C.10.57, C.10.82, C.10.99, C.10.108, C.10.137, C.10.143, C.10.167,
C.10.183, C.10.188, C.10.239, C.10.242, C.10.245, C.10.256, C.10.262, C.10.272,
C.10.303, C.11.29, C.11.40, C.11.51, C.11.66, C.11.74, C.11.106, C.11.111, C.11.126,
C.11.130, C.11.222, C.11.224, C.11.230, C.11.236, C.11.299, C.12.37, C.12.42, C.12.66,
C.12.66, C.12.104, C.12.107, C.12.128, C.12.133, C.12.141, C.12.166, C.12.187,
C.12.210, C.13.1, C.13.26, C.13.31, C.13.46, C.13.61, C.13.127, C.13.179, C.13.191,
C.13.199, C.13.217, C.13.224, C.13.226, C.13.239, C.14.12, C.14.13, C.14.17, C.14.19,
C.14.23, C.14.24, C.14.26, C.14.30, C.14.77, C.14.103, C.14.135, C.14.138, C.14.153,
C.14.166, C.14.168, C.14.179, C.14.194, C.14.207, C.14.209, C.15.45, C.15.48, C.15.64,
C.15.74, C.15.78, C.15.80, C.15.84, C.15.175, C.15.204, C.15.212, C.15.225, C.15.304,
C.16.13, C.16.21, C.16.45, C.16.48, C.16.59, C.16.119, C.16.254, C.16.276, C.16.342,
C.16.352, C.16.353, C.16.356, C.16.361, C.16.367, C.16.369, C.17.29, C.17.32, C.17.79,
C.17.122, C.17.136, C.17.156, C.17.168, C.17.293, C.18.56, C.18.60, C.18.86, C.18.137,
C.18.145, C.18.147, C.18.152, C.18.162, C.18.180, C.18.199, C.18.277, C.19.44,
C.19.59, C.19.63, C.19.65, C.19.81, C.19.153, C.19.160, C.19.214, C.19.232, C.19.267,
C.19.285, C.19.299, C.19.307, C.19.327, C.20.68, C.20.77, C.20.80, C.20.281, C.20.298,
C.20.405, C.20.407, C.20.418, C.20.419, C.20.435, C.20.438, C.20.439,
C.20.445, C.21.13, C.21.30, C.21.63, C.21.69, C.21.96, C.21.157, C.21.430, C.22.35,
C.22.231, C.22.245, C.22.284, C.22.288

acale adj *acale adj.* B 1; C 1
B.18.394   For blood may suffre blood boþe hungry and *acale*
C.20.437   For bloed may s[uffr]e bloed bothe afurst and *acale*

accidie n *accidie n.* B 1; C 1
B. 5.359   And after al þis excesse he hadde an *Accidie*
C. 6.417   And aftur al this exces he hadde an *accidie*;

accord- > acorden

accuseþ v *accusen v.* A 1 acusiþ; B 1; C 3 accused (2) acuseth (1)
A. 3.161   For consience *acusiþ* þe to cunge [þe] for euere.'
B. 3.174   For Conscience *accuseþ* þee to congeien þee for euere.'
C.Pr.95   Consience cam and *[ac]cu[s]ed* hem–and þe comune herde hit–
C. 2.248   Ac Consience to þe kyng *accused* hem bothe
C. 3.220   For Consience *acuseth* the to congeye the foreuere.'

acloye v *acloien v.* C 1
C.20.294   [With] crokes and kalketrappes [a]*cloye* we hem vchone.'

acombre v *acombren v.* A 2 acumbrid; B 6 acombre (2) acombred (3) acombreþ (1); C 6 acombre (2) acombred (3) acombreth (1)
A. 1.170   ʒe ben *acumbrid* wiþ coueitise, ʒe [conne] not out crepe;
A. 1.177   To counforte þe carful *acumbrid* wiþ synne.
B. 1.32   Thoruʒ wyn and þoruʒ wommen þer was loth *acombred*,
B. 1.196   [Ye] ben *acombred* wiþ coueitise; [ye] konne noʒt [out crepe],
B. 1.203   To conforten þe carefulle *acombred* wiþ synne.
B. 2.51   And lat no conscience *acombre* þee for coueitise of Mede.'
B.12.55   [So catel and kynde wit *acombreþ* ful manye;
B.19.220   And *acombre* þee, Conscience, but if crist þee helpe.
C. 1.31   Thorw wyn and thorw wom[m]en there was loot *acombred*;
C. 1.191   And ben *acombred* with coueytise: thei can nouʒt [out crepe]
C. 1.198   That conforteth alle carefole *acombred* with synne.
C. 2.54   *Acombre* neuere thy Consience for coueityse of mede.'
C.14.17   Ac catel and kynde wit *acombreth* for monye;
C.21.220   And *acombre* þe, Consience, bote yf Crist the helpe.

acordaunce n *accordaunce n.* C 2
C. 3.337   *Acordaunce* in kynde, in case and in nombre
C. 3.395   That is vnite, *acordaun[c]e* in case, in gendre and in noumbre,

acorden v *accorden v.* A 6 accorde (1) accordiþ (1) accordyng (1) acorde (1) acorden (1) acordite (1); B 13 acorde (6) acorded (2) acordede (1) acordeden (1) acorden (1) acordeþ (2); C 19 acorde (7) acorded (1) acordede (3) acorden (2) acordeth (6)
A. 3.205   Takiþ mede of here maistris as þei mowe *accorde*;
A. 4.78   Wyt *accordiþ* þerewiþ & seide þe same:
A. 4.144   Þe king *acordite*, be crist, to resonis sawis
A. 5.177   Þei couþe [not] here consience *acorden* togidere
A.10.88   Ac ʒif clene consience *acorde* þat þiself dost wel
A.10.91   Be counseil of consience, *accordyng* holy chirche,
B. 3.218   Taken Mede of hir maistres as þei mowe *acorde*;
B. 3.319   Mercy or no mercy as Truthe [may] *acorde*.
B. 4.91   Wit *acorde*[þ] þerwiþ and [witnessede] þe same:
B. 4.158   [Kynde] wit *acorded* þerwiþ and comendede hise wordes,
B. 5.328   Thei kouþe noʒt, by hir Conscience, *acorden* [togideres]
B. 9.118   And siþenes by assent of hemself as þei two myʒte *acorde*;
B.11.43   Til Concupiscencia carnis *acorded* alle my werkes.
B.11.404   Caton *acordeþ* þerwiþ: Nemo sine crimine viuit.'
B.13.122   Til I se þo seuene and myself *acorde*
B.17.309   That þe kyng may do no mercy til boþe men *acorde*
B.18.234   That alle þe wyse of þis world in o wit *acor[de]*den
B.20.303   That wiþ Conscience *acordede* and Cardynale vertues.
B.20.353   And *acorde* wiþ Conscience and kisse hir eiþer ooþer.'

C. 3.274   Taken mede of here maistres as þei mowen *acorde*;
C. 3.356   He *acordeth* with crist in kynde, verbum caro factum est;
C. 3.362   *Acordeth* in alle kyndes with his antecedent.
C. 3.372   To *acorde* in alle kynde and in alle kyn nombre,
C. 3.377   That here loue to his lawe Thorw al þe lond *acorde*.
C. 3.393   How þat cliauntes *acorde* acounteth mede litel.
C. 3.472   Mercy or no mercy as most trewe *acorden*.
C. 4.87   Witt *acordede* therwith and witnessede þe same:
C. 5.183   And comuners [to] *acorde* in alle kyn treuthe.
C. 6.386   They couthe nat by here Consience *acorden* for treuthe
C. 8.242   And salomon þe sage with þe same *acordeth*:
C. 9.69   Catoun *acordeth* therwith: cui des videto.
C.11.310   Til Concupiscencia Carnis *acorded* til al my werkes.
C.12.161   Crist *acordeth* efte herwith; clerkes wyteth þe sothe,
C.13.212   Caton *acordeth* therwith: nemo sine crimine viuit.'
C.19.289   That may no kynge mercy graunte til bothe men *acorde*
C.20.243   That alle þe wyse of th[is] world in o wit *acordede*
C.22.303   That with Consience *acordede* and cardinal vertues.
C.22.353   And *acorde* with Consience and kusse here ayther oþer.'

acorse(- > acurseþ

acountable adj *accountable adj.* C 1
C.13.67   Aren alle *acountable* to crist and to þe kyng of heuene,

acounte n *accounte n. &> acounten* A 3 acountes (2) acountis (1); B 4 acounte (1) acountes (3); C 5 acounte (2) acountes (3)
A.Pr.91   Become clerkis of *acountis* þe king for to serue;
A. 7.81   Til I come to his *acountes* as my crede me techiþ–
A. 8.172   And come [alle] before crist *acountes* to ʒelden,
B. 5.427   Ruþe is to here rekenyng whan we shul rede *acountes*:
B. 6.89   Til I come to hise *acountes* as my [crede] me [techeþ]–
B. 7.194   And comen alle [bi]fore crist *acountes* to yelde,
B.19.462   Counseilleþ me bi hir *acounte* and my clerkes writynge.
C. 7.40   Reuthe is to here rekenynge when we shal rede *acountes*,
C. 8.98   Til y come til his *acountes* as my crede telleth,
C. 9.340   And comen alle bifore Crist *acountes* to ʒelde,
C.13.35   And rikene byfore resoun a resonable *acounte*
C.21.462   Conseileth me bi here *acounte* and my clerkes writyng.

acounten v *accounten v.* B 4 acounte (2) acountede (1) acounten (1); C 9 acounte (3) acounted (2) acounten (2) acounteth (2)
B. 4.11   And *acounte* wiþ þee, Conscience, so me crist helpe,
B.11.16   And bad me for my contenaunce *acounten* Clergie liʒte.
B.11.132   And conscience *acounte* wiþ hym] and casten hym in arerage,
B.19.412   Or þat *acountede* Conscience at a cokkes feþere.
C. 3.393   How þat cliauntes acorde *acounteth* mede litel.
C. 4.11   And *acounte* with the, Consience, so me Crist helpe,
C. 7.33   And holden a knyhtus Court and *acounte* with þe reue
C. 8.159   They *acounteth* nat of corsyng[e] ne holy kyrke dredeth–
C. 9.240   *Acounted* byfore [crist] but Consience excuse hym.
C.10.96   Lordes þat lyuen as hem lust and no lawe *acounten*,
C.11.297   As doth the reue or Conturrollor þat rykene moet and *acounten*
C.12.67   And consience *acounte* with hym and casten hym in arrerag[e]
C.21.412   Or þat *acounted* Consience [at] a cokkes fether.

acouped ptp *acoupen v.(1)* B 1
B.13.458   Til conscience *acouped* hym þerof in a curteis manere,

acquitaunce n *aquitaunce n.* B 1
B.14.190   [We] sholde take þe *Acquitaunce* as quyk and to þe queed shewen it:

acre n *aker n.(1)* A 4 akir; B 4; C 5 aker
A. 7.4   I haue an half *akir* to er[e]n be þe heiʒe weiʒe;
A. 7.5   Hadde y [erid] þat half *akir*
A. 7.98   To erien þis half *akir* helpen hym manye;
A. 7.108   And holpen [to] ere þe half *akir* wiþ 'hey trolly lolly'.
B. 6.4   I haue an half *acre* to erie by þe heiʒe weye;
B. 6.5   Hadde I eryed þis half *acre* and sowen it after
B. 6.106   To erie þis half *acre* holpen hym manye;
B. 6.116   And holpen ere þ[e] half *acre* wiþ 'how trolly lolly'.
C. 6.267   And yf y ʒede to þe taueorne or þe plough y pynched on his half *aker*
C. 8.2   Ich haue an half *aker* to erye by þe heye [way];
C. 8.3   Haued ich yered þis half *aker* and ysowed hit aftur
C. 8.113   To erien this half *ak[er]* holpen hym monye;
C. 8.123   And holpe erye this half *aker* with 'hey trollilolly'.

actif adj *actif adj.* A 2; B 8; C 7 actif (1) actyf (6)
A. 7.233   *Actif* lif oþer contemplatif; crist wolde it alse.
A.11.183   *Actif* it is hoten; [husbondis] it vsen,
B. 6.249   Contemplatif lif or *Actif* lif; crist wolde [it als].
B.13.225   Al yde[l] ich hatie for of *Actif* is my name.
B.13.238   And þat am I, *Actif*, þat ydelnesse hatie,
B.13.272   Of haukyn þe *Actif* man and how he was yclopþed.
B.13.457   Thus haukyn þe *Actif* man hadde ysoiled his cote

B.14.26   Than Haukyn þe *Actif* man, and þow do by my techyng,
B.14.323   'Allas', quod Haukyn þe *Actif* man þo, 'þat after my cristendom
B.16.2   For Haukyns loue þe *Actif* man euere I shal yow louye.
C. 7.299   Thenne was oen hihte *actif*; an hosbande he semede.
C.15.213   And for me *Actyf*, his man, þat ydelnesse ha[t]e.
C.15.232   'Pees!' quod pacience, 'y preye ȝow, sire *actyf*,
C.15.245   'Hastow,' quod *actyf*, 'ay such mete with the?'
C.15.250   'Haue, *Actyf*,' quod pacience, 'and eet this when þe hungreth
C.16.114   Quod *Actyf* tho al angryliche and Arguinge as hit were:
C.16.158   Thenne hadde *Actyf* a ledare þat hihte lib[e]rum arbitrium;

action n *accioun* n. C 2 action (1) actions (1)
C. 1.94   And halden with h[y]m and [with] here þat han trewe *action*
C. 5.196   Of alle maner *actions* and eche man loue other.

acumbrid > acombre

acurseþ v *acursen* v. A 1 acursid; B 4 acorse (1) acorsed (2) acurseþ (1);
            C 4 acorse (1) acorsed (2) acorsede (1)
A.10.155   For alle þat comen of þat caym *acursid* þei were,
B.Pr.99   Lest crist in Consistorie *acorse* ful manye.
B.15.413   Thoruȝ a cristene clerk *acorsed* in his soule–
B.18.93   Callede hem caytyues, *acorsed* for euere:
B.18.107   Which is lif þat oure lord in alle lawes *acurseþ*.
C.Pr.127   Lest crist in constorie *acorse* of [ȝow] manye.
C.18.222   That *acorsede* alle couples þat no kynde forth brouhte:
C.20.96   Calde hem Caytyues, *acorsed* for euere.
C.22.263   Pilours and pikeharneys in vch a parsch *acorsed*.

acuseth > accuseþ

aday adv *a dai,adai phrase & adv.* C 1
C. 1.27   In his dronkenesse *aday* his doughteres he dighte

adayes adv *adaies adv.* B 1 adayes
B.15.283   Antony *adayes* aboute noon tyme

adam n *Adam* n. A 4; B 26 Adam (24) Adames (2); C 27 Adam (24)
            adames (3)
A. 1.63   *Adam* & Eue he eggide to ille,
A. 6.90   Þo *Adam* & Eue eten here bane,
A.10.141   Aftir þat *adam* & [heo] eten þe appil
A.11.283   Or *adam*, or ysaye, or any of þe prophetis
B. 1.65   *Adam* and Eue he egged to ille,
B. 5.603   Tho *Adam* and Eue eten apples vnrosted
B. 9.124   [After þat *Adam* and heo eten þe appul].
B. 9.188   Noȝt as *Adam* and Eue whan Caym was engendred;
B.10.115   Why sholde we þat now ben for þe werkes of *Adam*
B.10.424   Or *Adam* or Ysaye or any of þe prophetes
B.11.206   Of *Adames* issue and Eue ay til god man deide;
B.11.417   *Adam*, whiles he spak noȝt, hadde paradis at wille,
B.12.230   Kynde] kenned *Adam* to knowe hise pryue membres,
B.12.233   Why *Adam* hiled noȝt first his mouþ þat eet þe Appul
B.15.63   [*Adam* and Eue putte out of Paradis]
B.16.81   *Adam* and Abraham and Ysaye þe prophete,
B.16.205   *Adam*, oure aller fader. Eue was of hymselue,
B.18.143   For *Adam* and Eue and Abraham wiþ oþere
B.18.153   That *Adam* and Eue haue shul bote.
B.18.178   *Adam* and Eue and oþere mo in helle.
B.18.192   That *Adam* and Eue and alle þat hem suwede
B.18.195   *Adam* afterward, ayeins his defence,
B.18.218   Forþi god, of his goednesse, þe firste gome *Adam*,
B.18.222   And after god Auntrede hymself and took *Adames* kynd[e]
B.18.281   If *Adam* ete þe Appul alle sholde deye
B.18.314   And now for þi laste lesynge] ylorn we haue *Adam*,
B.18.344   *Adam* and his issue at my wille herafter;
B.18.358   And as *Adam* and alle þoruȝ a tree deyden,
B.18.359   *Adam* and alle þoruȝ a tree shul turne to lyue,
B.19.54   For he yaf *Adam* and Eue and oþere mo blisse
C. 1.61   And Eue he eggede to ylle,
C. 7.250   That *Adam* and Eue aȝenes vs alle shette:
C.10.214   Aftur þat *Adam* and Eue hadden ysyneged;
C.10.248   S[e]th, *adames* sone, seth[en] was engendred.
C.10.289   As *Adam* dede and Eue, as y wel er tolde.
C.11.256   And ar *Adam* oþer ysaye oþer eny of þe profetes
C.12.114   Of *Adames* issue and Eue ay til god man deyede;
C.13.225   *Adam*, whiles he spak nat, hadde paradys at wille
C.14.162   And *Adam* and Eue and alle othere bestes
C.16.225   Potte out of paradys *Adam* and Eue:
C.18.68   *Adam* was as tre and we aren as his apples,
C.18.112   *Adam* and Abraham and ysaye þe prophete,
C.18.215   And o god almyhty, yf alle men ben of *Adam*.
C.18.216   Eue of *Adam* was and out of hym ydrawe
C.18.218   And thise thre þat y Carp of, *Adam* and Eue
C.18.229   And as abel of *Adam* and of his wyf Eue
C.20.146   For *Adam* and Eue And abraham with oþere

C.20.156   That *Adam* and Eue haue shullen bote.
C.20.181   *Adam* and Eue and other mo in helle.
C.20.197   That *Adam* and Eue and al his issue
C.20.200   *Adam* afturward, aȝenes his defense,
C.20.227   Forthy god, of his goednesse, þe furste [gome] *Adam*,
C.20.231   And aftur god auntred hymselue and toek *Adames* kynde
C.20.303   That *Adam* and Eue and all his issue
C.20.397   And as *Adam* and alle thorw a tre deyede,
C.20.398   *Adam* and alle thorw a tre shal turne to lyue.
C.21.54   For he ȝaf *Adam* and Eue and oþere mo blisse

addre n *naddre* n. B 2 Addere (1) Addre (1); C 3 addere (1) addre (2)
B.18.335   For in my paleis, Paradis, in persone of an *Addre*
B.18.354   Thow, lucifer, in liknesse of a luþer *Addere*
C.20.315   Not in fourme of a fende bote in fourme of an *Addre*
C.20.326   And as thowe bigyledest godes ymag[e] in goynge of an *addre*,
C.20.378   For in my palays, paradys, in persone of an *addere*

adiectyf n *adjectif adj.& n.* C 5 adiectif (1) adiectyf (4)
C. 3.336   Ac *adiectif* and sustantif vnite asken,
C. 3.343   Thenne *adiectyf* an[d] sustantyf, for englisch was it neuere.'
C. 3.361   This is relacion rect, ryht [as] *adiectyf* and sustantyf
C. 3.394   Ac *adiectyf* and sustantyf is as y [e]r tolde,
C. 3.405   As hic & hec homo askyng an *adiectyf*

ado n *ado* n. C 1
C. 5.163   Lytel hadde lordes *ado* to ȝeue lond fro [here] heyres

adoun adv *adoun adv.* A 3; B 18 adoun (14) adown (4); C 17 adoun (12)
            adoune (1) adown (3) adowne (1)
A. 4.79   'Betere is þat boote bale *adoun* bringe,
A. 5.7   I sat softely [*adoun*] & seide my beleue,
A. 9.88   A pik is in þat potent to pungen *adoun* þe wykkide,
B. 4.92   'Bettre is þat boote bale *adoun* brynge,
B. 5.7   [I] sat softely *adoun* and seide my bileue,
B. 8.98   A pik is [in] þat potente to [punge] *adown* þe wikked,
B. 9.208   And so comeþ dobest [aboute] and bryngeþ *adoun* mody,
B.10.335   [Ac] dowel shal dyngen hym *adoun* and destruye his myȝte.'
B.16.51   And palleþ *adoun* þe pouke pureliche þoruȝ grace
B.16.73   I preide Piers to pulle *adoun* an Appul and he wolde,
B.16.79   For euere as þei dropped *adoun* þe deuel was redy
B.16.128   And knokked on hem wiþ a corde, and caste *adoun* hir stalles
B.16.131   'I shal ouerturne þis temple and *adoun* þrowe,
B.17.67   He lighte *adown* of Lyard and ladde hym in his hande,
B.18.29   Deeþ seiþ he shal fordo and *adoun* brynge
B.18.35   And forbete and *adoun* brynge bale deeþ for euere:
B.18.141   And þat deeþ *adown* brouȝte, deeþ shal releue.'
B.18.253   To breke and to bete *adoun* [alle] þat ben ayeins [hym],
B.19.51   Mighte no deeþ hym fordo ne *adoun* brynge
B.20.132   And boldeliche bar *adoun* wiþ many a bright Noble
B.20.227   And hadden almoost vnitee and holynesse *adown*.
C.Pr.64   But holi chirche and charite choppe *adoun* suche shryuars
C. 1.91   Rydon and rappe *adoun* in reumes aboute
C. 3.43   And ȝut be thy bedman and brynge *adoun* Consience
C. 3.107   Ful *adoun* and forbrent forth alle þe rewe.
C. 3.238   To berne and to bruttene, to bete *adoun* strenghtes.
C. 4.88   'Betere is þat boote bale *adoun* brynge
C. 8.29   To bores and to bokkes þat breketh *adoun* myn hegges
C.10.95   And with the pyk pulte *adoun* preuaricatores legis.
C.18.50   And thenne [f]alle y *adoune* the pouke with the thridde shoriere
C.19.66   [A l]ihte a[dou]n of lyard and ladde hym in his hand[e]
C.20.28   Deth saith a wol fordo and *adown* brynge
C.20.34   And forbete [and *adown*] b[r]ynge bale deth for euere:
C.20.55   And 'yf thow be Crist and [kynges] sone come *adoun* of th[e] rode;
C.20.262   To breke and to bete *adoun* all þat ben agaynes hym
C.21.51   Myhte no deth hym fordo ne *adown* brynge
C.22.132   And baldeliche baer *adoun* with many a brihte noble
C.22.227   And hadden almost vnite and holynesse *adowne*.

adrad ptp *adreden* v. B 3; C 2
B.19.21   For alle derke deueles arn *adrad* to heren it,
B.19.305   To demen as a domesman *adrad* was he neuere,
B.20.352   And be *adrad* of deþ and wiþdrawe hym fram pryde
C.21.305   To demen as a domesman *adrad* was he neuere,
C.22.352   And be *adrad* of deth and withdrawe hym fro pruyde

adrencheth v *adrenchen* v. B 2 adreynt (1) adreynten (1); C 3 adreint (1)
            adreynt (1) adrencheth (1)
B.10.414   And men þat maden it amydde þe flood *adreynten*.
B.20.377   'He lyþ [*adreynt*] and dremeþ,' seide Pees, 'and so do manye oþere.
C.10.163   A[s] somme hangeth hemsulue and oþerwhile *adrencheth*.
C.10.245   Ac why þe world was *adreynt*, holy writ telleth,
C.22.377   'He lyeth *adreint* [and dremeth],' saide pees, 'and so doth many
            oþere.

afaite(- > affaiten; afeerd > afere

9

afeld *adv afelde adv.* A 1; B 3; C 3 afeld (2) afelde (1)
A. 4.130　Þat lawe shal ben a labourer & lede *afeld* donge,
B. 4.147　That lawe shal ben a laborer and lede *afeld* donge,
B. 6.142　Or helpe make morter or bere Muk *afeld.*
B. 6.288　To drawe *afeld* my donge while þe droȝte lasteþ.
C. 4.144　That lawe shal ben a labourer and lede *afelde* donge
C. 8.198　In daubynge and in deluynge, in donge *afeld* berynge,
C. 8.311　To drawe *afeld* my donge þe while þe drouthe lasteth.

afere *v aferen v.* A 3 aferd; B 10 afere (1) afered (8) afereþ (1); C 11 afeerd (1) aferd (3) afere (1) afered (5) afereth (1)
A. 1.10　I was *af+erd* of hire face þeiȝ heo fair were,
A. 4.49　Wrong was *aferd* þo & wisdom he souȝte
A. 7.113　Þanne were faitours *aferd* & feynide hem blynde;
B. 1.10　I was *afered* of hire face þeiȝ she fair weere
B. 4.63　Wrong was *afered* þ[o] and wisdom he souȝte
B. 6.121　Tho were faitours *afered* and feyned hem blynde;
B.10.452　Beþ noȝt [*afered* of þat folk], for I shal [ȝyue yow tonge],
B.11.63　And þo fond I þe frere *afered* and flittynge boþe
B.15.385　Wherfore I am *afered* of folk of holy kirke,
B.18.120　For þe vertue þat hire folwede *afered* was she neuere.
B.18.430　And it *afereþ* þe fend, for swich is þe myȝte
B.19.205　And was *afered* [for] þe light, for in fires [lik]nesse
B.20.166　And bad hym fonde to fighte and *afere* wanhope.
C. 1.10　Y was *afeerd* of here face thow she fayre were
C. 4.66　Tho was wrong *afered* and wisdom a souhte;
C. 8.128　Tho were faytours *aferd* and fayned hem blynde;
C. 8.179　Tho were faytours *afered* and flowen into [Peres] bernes
C.11.277　Beth nat *aferd* of þat folk for y shal ȝeue ȝow tonge,
C.15.164　Noþer fuyr ne floed ne be *aferd* of enemye:
C.19.82　Were *afered* and flowe fram þe man ywounded.
C.20.123　For þe vertue þat her folwede *afered* was she neuere.
C.20.474　And hit *afereth* th[e] fende, for such is þe myhte
C.21.205　And was *afered* for the lihte, for in fuyres liknesse
C.22.166　And baed hym fonde to fihte and *afere* wanhope.

aferes *n aferen n.(pl.)* C 1
C. 6.152　For there aren many felle frekes myn *aferes* to aspye,

affaiten *v afaiten v.* A 1; B 3 afaiteþ (1) affaiten (1) affaiteþ (1); C 2 afayte (1) affayten (1)
A. 5.49　For to *affaiten* hire flessh þat fers was to synne:
B. 5.66　To *affaiten* hire flessh þat fiers was to synne.
B.11.384　Frenche men and fre men *affaiteþ* þus hire children:
B.14.299　It *afaiteþ* þe flessh fram folies ful manye,
C. 6.7　To *affayten* here flesshe þat fers was to synne.
C. 8.30　And *afayte* thy faucones [wylde foules to culle]

affiaunce *n affiaunce n.* B 1; C 1
B.16.238　Myn *affiaunce* and my feiþ is ferme in þis bileue
C.18.254　Myen *affiaunce* and my faith is ferme in [t]his bileue

affrayned *v afrainen v.* B 1
B.16.274　I *affrayned* hym first fram whennes he come,

afyngred *ptp afingred ppl.* A 1 afyngrid; B 3; C 6 afyngered (2) afyngred (4)
A.12.59　The fyrste ferly I fond *afyngrid* me made;
B.10.60　Boþe *afyngred* and afurst, and for chele quake;
B.14.162　Afurst soore and *afyngred*, and foule yrebuked
B.19.127　Sore *afyngred* folk, mo þan fyue þousand.
C. 9.85　Bothe *afyngred* and afurste, to turne þe fayre outward
C.11.41　Bothe *afyngred* and afurst, and for defaute spille;
C.11.48　Mony tym[e] mendenauntes myhte goen *afyngred*.
C.16.15　Afurste and *afyngered* and foule rebuked
C.17.68　And fedde þat *afyn[g]red* were and in defaute lyuede.
C.21.127　Sore *afyngered* folk, mo then fyue thousend.

afore *adv afore adv.* B 1
B.14.134　Hewen þat han hir hire *afore* arn eueremoore nedy,

afore *prep afore prep.* B 6
B. 5.12　And wiþ a cros *afore* þe kyng comsede þus to techen.
B. 5.23　How pertly *afore* þe peple [preche gan Reson].
B.12.79　Giltier as *afore* god, and gretter in synne,
B.16.45　And feccheþ awey my floures som tyme *afore* boþe myne eighen.
B.17.306　Any creature [be] coupable *afore* a kynges Iustice
B.20.130　And [knokked] Conscience in Court *afore* hem alle;

afrounted *v afrounten v.* B 1; C 1
B.20.5　That *afrounted* me foule and faitour me called.
C.22.5　That *afrounted* me foule and faytour me calde.

after *adv after adv.* A 40 after (1) aftir (39); B 99; C 87 after (2) aftir (4) aftur (81)
A.Pr.49　And hadde leue to leiȝe al here lif *aftir.*
A.Pr.51　Wenten to walsyngham, & here wenchis *aftir;*

A.Pr.97　I sauȝ in þat sem[b]le as ȝe shuln here *aftir,*
A. 1.22　And rekne hem in resoun; reherse þou hem *aftir.*
A. 1.66　And siþen on an Eldir hongide him *aftir.*
A. 1.134　Loke þou suffre hym to seyn & siþþe lere it *aftir.*
A. 2.67　Þei to haue & to holde & here eires *aftir*
A. 2.98　Werchiþ be wysdom & be wyt *aftir;*
A. 2.146　And mede in þe myddis, & al þis mene *aftir.*
A. 2.153　And consience to þe king carpide it *aftir.*
A. 3.45　For to be hire bedeman & hire baude *aftir*
A. 3.241　Þat agag of amaleg & [al] his peple *aftir*
A. 3.257　Þat god hati[de him for euere] & alle hise heires *aftir.*
A. 5.2　To here matynes & masse, and to þe mete *aftir.*
A. 5.87　[For pilgrymes, for palmers, for all þe peple] *aftir,*
A. 5.92　[Þanne] I wysshe it were myn [and al þe webbe *aftir*].
A. 5.157　Þanne goþ [glotoun in], and grete oþis *aftir.*
A. 5.170　Hikke þe hostiler hitte his hood *aftir*
A. 5.183　And whoso repentiþ raþest shulde rise *aftir*
A. 5.191　[Þat] alle þat herden þat horn held here nose *aftir*
A. 6.46　For treuþe wolde loue me þe wers a long tyme *aftir.*
A. 7.162　Þat he lokide lik a lanterne al his lif *aftir;*
A. 7.195　And helpe hem of alle þing [*aftir*] þat hem nedi[þ].
A. 7.224　He hadde maugre of his maister eueremore *aftir,*
A. 7.298　And þanne curse þe king & alle þe counseil *aftir*
A. 8.4　For hym & for hise heires eueremore *aftir,*
A. 8.32　[Pore] wydewis þat wiln not be wyues *aftir,*
A. 8.77　And gon & faiten wiþ here fauntis for eueremore *aftir.*
A. 8.121　And consience com *aftir* & kennide me betere.'
A. 8.141　As daniel deui[n]ide in dede it fel *aftir:*
A. 9.45　Folewe þi flesshis wil & þe fendis *aftir,*
A.10.37　Lif þat ay shal laste, & al his lynage *aftir.*
A.10.92　Loke þou wisse þi wyt & þi werkis *aftir;*
A.10.151　Alle þat comen of þat caym crist hatid *aftir.*
A.11.67　Þat he gilide þe womman & þe wy *aftir,*
A.11.81　I wolde his eiȝen wern in his ars & his hele *aftir*
A.11.128　Logik I lerid hire, & al þe lawe *aftir,*
A.11.221　For I haue seiȝe it myself, & siþþen red it *aftir,*
A.11.245　& suche [[shewiþ] þis sermoun þat [sewiþ] *aftir*]:
A.12.79　He halsed me, and I asked him *after*
B.Pr.49　And hadden leue to lyen al hire lif *after.*
B.Pr.54　Wenten to walsyngham, and hire wenches *after;*
B.Pr.140　And to þe Aungel an heiȝ answerde *after:*
B.Pr.202　I seye for me', quod Mous, 'I se so muchel *after,*
B.Pr.218　I seiȝ in þis assemblee, as ye shul here *after.*
B. 1.22　And rekene hem by reson: reherce þow hem *after.*
B. 1.68　And siþen on an Eller hanged hym [*after*].
B. 1.146　Loke þou suffre hym to seye and siþen lere it *after.*
B. 2.102　'And þei to haue and to holde, and hire heires *after.*
B. 2.134　Wercheþ by wisdom and by wit [*after*];
B. 2.185　And Mede in þe myddes and [al þis meynee] *after.*
B. 2.192　And Conscience to þe kyng carped it *after.*
B. 3.46　For to ben hire Bedeman and hire [baude *after*].
B. 3.262　That Agag of Amalec and al his peple *after*
B. 3.279　That god hated hym for euere and alle hise heires *after.*
B. 3.314　His boost of his benefice worþ bynomen hym *after.*
B. 5.2　To here matyns and masse and to þe mete] *after.*
B. 5.107　For Pilgrymes, for Palmeres, for al þe peple *after,*
B. 5.112　[Thanne I wisshe] it were myn and al þe web *after.*
B. 5.116　Whoso vndernymeþ me herof, I hate hym dedly *after.*
B. 5.179　[I] haue a flux of a foul mouþ wel fyue dayes *after;*
B. 5.186　Esto sobrius!' he seide and assoiled me *after,*
B. 5.245　And ben hire brocour *after* and bouȝt it myselue.
B. 5.251　'Ye, I haue lent lordes loued me neuere *after,*
B. 5.306　Thanne goþ Gloton In and grete oþes *after.*
B. 5.321　Hikke þe [Hostiler] hitte his hood *after*
B. 5.334　And whoso repente[þ] raþest sholde aryse *after*
B. 5.343　That alle þat herde þat horn helde hir nos[e] *after*
B. 5.559　Truþe wolde loue me þe lasse a long tyme *after.*
B. 6.5　Hadde I eryed þis half acre and sowen it *after*
B. 6.177　That he loked lik a lanterne al his lif *after.*
B. 6.240　He hadde maugree of his maister eueremoore *after,*
B. 6.317　And þanne corseþ þe kyng and al [þe] counseil *after*
B. 7.4　For hym and for hise heires eueremoore *after.*
B. 7.95　And goon [and] faiten with [hire] fauntes for eueremoore *after.*
B. 7.139　And Conscience cam *afte[r]* and kenned me [bettre].'
B. 7.163　As Daniel diuined in dede it fel *after:*
B. 8.49　Folwe þi flesshes wille and þe fendes *after,*
B. 9.49　Lif þat ay shal laste, [and] al his lynage *after.*
B.10.109　That bi[w]iled þe womman and þe [wye] *after,*
B.10.128　I wolde his eiȝe were in his ars and his [hele] *after,*
B.10.176　Logyk I lerned hire, and [al þe lawe *after*],
B.10.222　Tel Clergie þis[e] tokene[s], and [to] Scripture *after,*
B.10.362　And *after* alle cristene creatures, in commune ech man ooþer;
B.10.385　God gaf hym grace of wit and alle goodes *after*

B.11.46 Coueitise of ei3es conforted me anoon *after*
B.11.124 By þe blood þat he bou3te vs wiþ, and þoru3 bapteme *after*:
B.11.133 And putten hym *after* in prison in purgatorie to brenne;
B.11.182 [Hir euencristene as hemself] and hir enemyes *after*.
B.11.259 [Al]þou3 it be sour to suffre, þe[r] comeþ swete [*after*].
B.11.327 I sei3 þe sonne and þe see and þe sond *after*,
B.11.338 As whan þei hadde ryde in Rotey tyme anoon [reste þei] *after*;
B.12.120 And leiden hand þeron to liften it vp loren here lif *after*.
B.12.140 And loue shal lepen out *after* into þ[is] lowe erþe,
B.13.3 In manere of a mendynaunt many yer *after*,
B.13.34 And þanne clergie and Conscience and Pacience cam *after*.
B.13.89 And þanne shullen hise guttes goþele and he shal galpen *after*.
B.13.96 And but [þe] first [leef] be lesyng leue me neuere *after*.
B.13.104 'Dowel', quod þis doctour and [drank *after*],
B.13.154 And al þe wit of þe wodnesday of þe nexte wike *after*;
B.13.169 Do kyng and quene and alle þe comune *after*
B.13.171 And as þow demest wil þei do alle hir dayes *after*:
B.13.326 And þat [by] watte [he] wiste wille wiste it *after*.
B.14.21 And siþen sende þee to Satisfaccion for to [sonnen] it *after*:
B.14.23 Shal neuere [myx] bymolen it, ne moþe *after* biten it,
B.14.115 And *after* þow sendest hem somer þat is hir souereyn ioye
B.14.154 Here for3ifnesse of hir synnes, and heuene blisse *after*.
B.14.186 And if vs fille þoru3 folie to falle in synne *after*
B.14.306 For þer þat Pouerte passeþ pees folweþ *after*,
B.15.192 And wiþ warm water at hise ei3en wasshen hem *after*.
B.15.360 That whilom warned bifore what sholde falle *after*.
B.15.581 And han clerkes to kepen vs þerInne & hem þat shul come *after*.
B.16.19 That I herde nempne his name anoon I swowned *after*,
B.16.76 And waggede widwehode and it wepte *after*;
B.16.123 For I haue saued yowself and youre sones *after*,
B.16.132 And in þre daies *after* edifie it newe,
B.16.169 Estward and westward I waited *after* faste
B.17.62 Hope cam hippynge *after* þat hadde so ybosted
B.17.83 Feiþ folwede *after* faste and fondede to mete hym,
B.17.132 O god wiþ al my good, and alle gomes *after*
B.18.1 Wolleward and weetshoed wente I forþ *after*
B.18.42 To fordoon it on o day, and in þre dayes *after*
B.18.74 And [hir] armes *after* of eiþer of þo þeues.
B.18.185 To be mannes meynpernour for eueremoore *after*.
B.18.193 Sholden deye downrighte and dwelle in pyne *after*
B.18.222 And *after* god Auntrede hymself and took Adames kynd[e]
B.19.3 To here holly þe masse and to be housled *after*.
B.19.75 Kynges come *after*, knelede and offrede [sense],
B.19.152 Christus [rex] resurgens, [and it aroos *after*],
B.19.163 Peter parceyued al þis and pursued *after*,
B.19.191 Anoon *after* an heigh vp into heuene
B.19.268 Al þat hise oxen eriede þei to harewen *after*.
B.19.327 And of al holy writ he made a roof *after*;
B.19.387 [My3t] to maken it and men to ete it *after*
B.20.97 Kynde cam *after* wiþ many kene soores
B.20.100 Deeþ cam dryuynge *after* and al to duste passhed
B.20.103 That he hitte euene, þat euere stired *after*.
B.20.136 An[d] to þe Arches in haste he yede anoon *after*
B.20.177 And þere dyed þat doctour er þre dayes *after*.
C.Pr.16 Westward y waytede in a while *aftir*
C.Pr.50 And hadde leue to lye [al here lyf *aftir*].
C.Pr.52 Wenten to Walsyngham and here wenches *aftir*;
C.Pr.210 Y seye for me,' quod þe mous, 'y se so muche *aftur*,
C.Pr.224 Al y say slepynge, as 3e shal here [a]*ftur*,
C.2.192 On secatours and such men cometh softly *aftur*.
C.2.198 And mede in þe myddes and al this me[y]n[e] *aftur*.
C.2.200 Of many maner men for mede sake seude *aftur*.
C.2.206 And consience to þe kyng carpede hit *aftur*.
C.3.103 And goode mennes for here gultes gloweth on fuyr *aftur*.
C.3.250 Wherby he may as a man for eueremore lyue *aftur*
C.3.318 And yf th[e] lele and lege be luyther men *aftur*
C.3.321 And bynyme hit hem anone and neueremore *aftur*
C.3.340 Grace of good ende and gret ioye *aftur*:
C.3.342 What is relacion rect and indirect *aftur*,
C.3.432 That god [hated hym] for euere and alle [his] eyres *aftur*.
C.3.443 Shal no mede be maistre neueremore *aftur*
C.3.494 A sholde haue yfonde [felle wordes folwynge] *aftur*:
C.4.28 Fayn were to folowe hem and faste ryden *aftur*
C.4.192 To wage thyn and helpe wynne þat thow wilnest *aftur*
C.5.174 Bred withouten beggynge to lyue by euere *aftur*
C.6.71 And þat he wiste by watte tolde hit wille *aftur*
C.6.161 Y haue a flux of a foul mouth wel fyue daies *aftur*;
C.6.168 Esto sobrius!' he saide, and assoiled hym *aftur*
C.6.192 Y lay by þe louelokest and louede here neuere *aftur*.
C.6.249 'Y haue lent lordes and ladyes þat louede me neuere *aftur*
C.6.252 That chaffared with my cheuesaunces cheued selde *aftur*.'
C.6.361 Thenne goth glotoun in and grete othes *aftur*.
C.6.378 Hicke þe hackenayman hit his hod *aftur*

C.6.392 And hoso repente[th] rathest sholde aryse *aftur*
C.6.401 That alle þat herde þ[at] hor[n] helde here nose *aftur*
C.7.204 A wolde loue me þe lasse a long tyme *aftur*.
C.8.3 Haued ich yered þis half aker and ysowed hit *aftur*
C.8.174 Þat a lokede lyke a l[a]nterne al his lyf *aftur*,
C.9.50 Shal haue grace of a good ende and greet ioye *aftur*.
C.9.171 And goen and fayten with here fauntes for eueremore *aftur*.
C.9.182 Or bylowe thorw luther men and lost here catel *aftur*
C.9.308 And sethen *aftur* his sones, and sayde hem what they thouhte;
C.10.193 For to lese þerfore her lond and her lyf *aftur*.
C.11.116 Logyk y lerned here and al þe lawe *aftur*
C.11.210 God gaf hym grace of wit and of goed *aftur*,
C.12.3 Couetyse-of-yes conforted me *aftur* and saide,
C.12.68 And potten hym *aftur* in prisoun in purgatorie to brenne
C.12.145 Althouh h[it] be sour to soffre þer cometh a swete *aftur*
C.12.203 Bitokeneth treuly in tyme comyng *aftur*
C.12.213 And asketh [hym *after*] ho shal hit haue,
C.12.243 And tho that dede þe dede ydampned þerfore *aftur*
C.13.14 And delyuerede the weye his wyf with moche welthe *aftur*.
C.13.74 That oure lord loketh *aftur* of vch a lyf þat wynneth
C.13.135 And seyhe þe sonne and þe see and þe sond *aftur*
C.13.146 As when þei hadde [ryde in] roteye[tyme] anon they reste *aftur*;
C.14.63 And all lewede þat leide hand þeron loren lyf *aftur*,
C.14.85 And loue shal lepe out *aftur* into þis lowe erthe
C.15.3 In manere of [a] mendenaunt mony 3er *aftur*.
C.15.25 And thenne cam concyence and clergie *aftur*
C.15.51 Thenne resoun radde anoon riht *aftur*
C.15.90 Bothe disches and dobelares with alle þe deyntees *aftur*
C.15.96 And thenne shal [his gottes gothelen] and [he shal] galpe [*after*].
C.15.103 And bote þe furste leef be lesyng[e] leue me neuere *aftur*.
C.15.111 'Dowel?' quod þis doctour, and he dronke *aftur*
C.15.148 And whan he hadde yworded thus wiste no man *aftur*
C.15.150 And resoun ran *aftur* and riht with hym 3ede;
C.15.167 And maistre of alle here mebles and of here moneye *aftur*,
C.15.291 [And] *aftur* thow sendest hem somer þat is here souereyne ioye
C.17.98 That whilum warnede byfore what sholde [f]alle *aftur*.
C.18.108 A waggede wedewhed and hit wepte *aftur*;
C.18.160 And ar thre dayes *aftur* edefye hit newe.'
C.19.61 Hope cam huppynge *aftur* þat hadde so ybosted
C.19.80 Bothe fayth and his felawe spes folewede faste *aftur*
C.20.1 Wollewaerd and watschoed wente y forth *aftur*
C.20.41 To fordoen hit on a day, and in thre dayes *aftur*
C.20.76 And here arme[s] *aftur* of e[ither] of tho theues.
C.20.231 And *aftur* god auntred hymsulue and toek Adames kynde
C.20.317 And byhihtest here and hym *aftur* to knowe
C.21.3 To here holly þe masse and to [be] hoseled *aftur*.
C.21.75 Kynges cam *aftur*, knelede and offrede [sense],
C.21.152 Christus [rex] resurgens, and hit aroos *aftur*,
C.21.163 Peter perseyued al this and pursuede *aftur*,
C.21.191 Anoon *aftur* an heyh vp into heuene
C.21.268 All þat his oxes erede they t[o] harwe[n] *aftur*.
C.21.327 And of all holy writ he made a roef *aftur*
C.21.387 Myhte to make hit and men to eten hit [*aftur*]
C.22.97 Kynde cam *aftur* with many k[e]ne sores,
C.22.100 Deth cam dryuyng *aftur* and al to duste paschte
C.22.103 That he hi[t]te euene, þat euere stured *aftur*.
C.22.136 And [t]o þe Arches in haste he 3ede anoen *aftur*
C.22.177 And þere deyede þat doctour ar thre dayes *aftur*.

after prep *after prep.* A 25 after (5) aftir (20); B 81; C 70 after (3) aftir (2) aftur (65)

A.1.110 And was þe louelokest [of si3t] *aftir* oure lord
A.1.118 *Aftir* here deþ day & dwelle wiþ þat shrewe.
A.1.167 Chewen here charite & chiden *aftir* more.
A.3.62 Oþer to grede *aftir* godis men whan 3e [g]iue dolis,
A.3.90 Þe king fro counseil com & callide *aftir* mede
A.5.58 Enuye wiþ heuy herte askide *aftir* shrift,
A.5.201 And *aftir* al þis surfet an axesse he hadde
A.5.225 Shal non ale *aftir* mete holde me þennis
A.6.24 Axen *aftir* hym, er now in þis place.'
A.7.157 And houpide *aftir* hungir þat herde hym at þe ferste:
A.7.251 And *aftir* many maner metis his mawe is alongid.
A.7.280 Hungir [eet] þis in haste & askide *aftir* more.
A.8.100 Þat *aftir* þi deþ day to helle shalt þou wende.'
A.8.183 Þat, *aftir* oure deþ day, dowel reherse
A.9.108 Disputyng on dowel day *aftir* oþer,
A.10.48 *Aftir* þe grace of god [þe grettest is Inwyt].
A.10.195 To folewe *aftir* þe flicche, fecche þei it neuere;
A.10.214 And *aftir* here day day shuln dwelle wiþ þe same
A.11.92 Þei3 dobest drawe on hym day *aftir* oþer.'
A.11.108 Þei two, [as] I hope, *aftir* my besekyng,
A.12.7 Þou woldest konne þat I can and carpen hit *after*;
A.12.35 Clergie into a caban crepte anon *after*,
A.12.36 And drow þe dore *after* him and bad me go do wel

A.12.39	To be hure man ȝif I most for eueremore *after*,
A.12.94	And þerfore do *after* dowel whil þi dayes duren,
B. 1.112	[And was þe louelokest of liȝt *after* oure lord
B. 1.129	*After* hir deþ day and dwelle with þat sherewe.
B. 1.193	Chewen hire charite and chiden *after* moore.
B. 2.27	And Mede is manered *after* hym [as men of] kynde [carpeþ]:
B. 3.71	Or to greden *after* goddes men whan ye [gyue] doles
B. 3.101	The kyng fro conseil cam and called *after* Mede
B. 3.318	But *after* þe dede þat is doon oon doom shal rewarde
B. 5.75	Enuye wiþ heuy herte asked *after* shrifte,
B. 5.262	Ne þyne heires *after* þee haue ioie of þat þow wynnest,
B. 5.359	And *after* al þis excesse he hadde an Accidie
B. 5.453	Shal noon ale *after* mete holde me þennes
B. 5.536	Asken *after* hym er now in þis place.
B. 6.172	And houped *after* hunger þat herde hym at þe firste,
B. 6.209	And helpen hem of alle þyng [*after* þat] hem nedeþ.
B. 6.267	And *after* many maner metes his mawe is [alonged].
B. 6.296	[Hunger eet þis] in haste and axed *after* moore.
B. 7.118	[That] *after* þi deeþ day þe deuel shal haue þi soule.'
B. 7.205	That, *after* oure deeþ day, dowel reherce
B. 8.118	Disputyng [o]n dowel day *after* ooþer,
B. 9.60	For *after* þe grace of god þe gretteste is Inwit.
B. 9.155	And haue a Sauour *after* þe sire; selde sestow ooþer.
B. 9.174	To folwen *after* þe flicche, fecche þei it neuere;
B. 9.200	And *after* hir deeþ day shul dwelle wiþ þe same
B.10.139	Theiȝ dobest drawe on hym day *after* ooþer.'
B.10.156	They two, as I hope, *after* my [bis]echyng
B.11.207	And *after* his resurexcion Redemptor was his name,
B.11.261	And *after* þat bitter bark, be þe shelle aweye,
B.11.263	So *after* pouerte or penaunce paciently ytake:
B.11.337	And *after* cours of concepcion noon took kepe of ooþer,
B.11.342	That wolde [bere] *after* bol[e], ne boor after sowe,
B.11.342	That wolde [bere] after bol[e], ne boor *after* sowe;
B.12.180	Ther þe lewed liþ stille and lokeþ *after* lente,
B.12.183	And þat is *after* person or parissh preest, [and] parauenture vnkonnynge
B.12.188	That lyuynge *after* lettrure saue[d] hym lif and soule.
B.12.217	And so I seye by þee þat sekest *after* þe whyes,
B.13.37	Conscience called *after* mete and þanne cam Scripture
B.13.184	*After* yeresȝeues or ȝiftes, or yernen to rede redels?
B.14.60	For if þow lyue *after* his loore, þe shorter lif þe bettre:
B.14.117	Thanne may beggeris, as beestes, *after* boote waiten
B.14.165	Heuene *after* hir hennes goyng þat here han swich defaute.
B.14.261	*After* hir endynge here, heueneriche blisse.
B.14.323	'Allas', quod Haukyn þe Actif man þo, 'þat *after* my cristendom
B.15.1	AC *after* my wakynge it was wonder longe
B.15.131	The whiche arn preestes inparfite and prechours *after* siluer,
B.15.159	That he ne wolde aske *after* his, and ouþerwhile coueite
B.15.254	Craueþ ne coueiteþ ne crieþ *after* moore:
B.15.279	Except þat Egidie *after* an hynde cride,
B.15.290	Poul *after* his prechyng paniers he made
B.15.405	Menynge as *after* mete; þus Makometh hire enchauntede.
B.15.416	And ben manered *after* Makometh þat no man vseþ trouþe.
B.15.459	Heþen is to mene *after* heeþ and vntiled erþe,
B.15.471	So [menen] riȝtfulle men [*after*] mercy and truþe.
B.15.475	In menyng *after* mete folweþ men þat whistlen;
B.15.479	And as þo foules to fynde fode *after* whistlyng
B.15.543	For coueitise *after* cros; þe croune stant in golde.
B.16.87	He hitte *after* hym, [happe] how it myȝte,
B.16.138	Eche day *after* ooþer hir tyme þei awaiteden
B.16.168	And *after* Piers þe Plowman pried and stared.
B.16.171	*After* Piers þe Plowman; many a place I souȝte.
B.16.178	[I] seke *after* a segge þat I seiȝ ones,
B.16.248	And conforted many a careful þat *after* his comynge waite[n],
B.17.1	'I am Spes, [a spie], quod he], 'and spire *after* a Knyght
B.17.18	'Whoso wercheþ *after* þis writ, I wol vndertaken,
B.17.134	'*After* Abraham', quod he, 'þat heraud of armes,
B.17.140	For god is *after* an hand; yheer now and knowe it.
B.18.409	'*After* sharpe shoures', quod pees, 'moost shene is þe sonne;
B.18.410	Is no weder warmer þan *after* watry cloudes;
B.18.412	Than *after* werre and wo whan loue and pees ben maistres.
B.19.123	*After* þe kynde þat he cam of; þere comsede he do wel.
B.19.257	And *after* craftes conseil cloþeþ yow and fede.
B.19.352	Wiþ þe lord þat lyueþ *after* þe lust of his body,
B.19.398	Ne *after* Conscience, by crist! while I kan selle
B.19.401	And noȝt hakke *after* holynesse; hold þi tonge, Conscience!
B.20.30	*After* þe kynges counseil and þe comune like.
B.20.71	Wiþ a lord þat lyueþ *after* likyng of body,
B.20.90	The lord þat lyued *after* lust þo aloud cryde
B.20.91	*After* Confort a knyght to come and bere his baner:
B.20.169	And lif fleiȝ for feere to phisik *after* helpe
B.20.183	And Elde *after* [hym]; and ouer myn heed yede
B.20.247	To lered ne to lewed, but lyueþ *after* youre reule.

B.20.386	And siþþe he gradde *after* Grace til I gan awake.
C.Pr.14	Estward y beheld *aftir* þe sonne
C. 1.124	Hewes in þe haliday *after* hete wayten
C. 1.131	*Aftur* here deth day and dwelle ther wrong is;
C. 1.190	[C]hewen here charite and chiden *aftur* more
C. 2.27	And mede is manered *aftur* hym as men of kynde carpeth:
C. 2.80	Mede and suche men þat *aftur* mede wayten
C. 2.109	*After* here deth dwellen day withouten ende
C. 3.128	The kyng fram conseyl come [and] calde *aftur* mede
C. 3.249	Loketh *aftur* lordschipe or oþer large mede
C. 3.471	But *aftur* þe dede þat is ydo the doom shal recorde
C. 6.63	Enuye with heuy herte asked *aftur* shrifte,
C. 6.147	[*Afturward, aftur* mete], she and she chydde
C. 6.417	And *aftur* al this exces he hadde an accidie;
C. 7.67	Shal non ale *aftur* m[e]te holde me thennes
C. 7.181	Axen *aftur* hym [er] now in þis place.'
C. 8.90	And *aftur* here warnynge and wor[d]ynge worche þou þeraftur:
C. 8.91	Ac *aftur* here doynge do thow nat, my dere sone,' quod Peres,
C. 8.168	And houped *aftur* hunger þat herde hym at þe furste.
C. 8.278	And laȝar þe lene beggare þat longede *aftur* crommes–
C. 8.283	Alle þat gr[eden at] thy gate for godes loue *aftur* fode
C. 8.318	Hunger eet al in haste and askede *aftur* more.
C. 9.76	To aglotye with here gurles þat greden *aftur* fode.
C. 9.110	And aren meuynge *aftur* þe mone; moneyeles þey walke
C. 9.229	Bothe matynes and masse; and *aftir* mete in churches
C. 9.351	That *aftur* oure deth day dowel reherce
C.10.114	Disputyng vppon dowel day *aftur* other
C.10.299	And *aftur* here deth day dwellen sollen in helle
C.11.219	And yf we sholde wurche *aftur* here werkes to wy[n]nen vs heuene
C.12.115	And *aftur* his resureccoun redemptor was his name
C.12.147	And *aftur* þat bittere barke, be þe scale aweye,
C.12.149	So *aftur* [pouerte or penaunce] pacientliche ytake
C.12.199	But as an hosebonde hopeth *aftur* an hard wynter,
C.13.145	*Aftur* cors of concepcion noon toek kepe of oþer,
C.13.150	That wolde bere *aftur* bole ne boer aftur sowe;
C.13.150	That wolde bere aftur bole ne boer *aftur* sowe;
C.14.120	There þe lewede lyth stille and loketh *aftur* lente
C.14.123	And þat is *aftur* person other parsche preest, and parauntur bothe lewede
C.14.127	That lyuynge *Aftur* lettrure saued hy[m] lyf and soule.
C.14.156	And so y sey by þe þat sekest *aftur* þe whyes,
C.15.42	Clergie cald *aftur* mete and thenne cam scripture
C.15.259	For if thow lyu[e] *aftur* his lore the shortere lyf þe betere:
C.15.293	Thenne may beggares, as bestes, *aftur* blisse aske
C.16.101	*Aftur* here endynge here heueneryche blisse.
C.16.278	As inparfite prestes and prechours *aftur* suluer,
C.16.293	That he ne askede *aftur* his and oþerewhiles coueytede
C.17.17	Paul *aftur* his prechyng paniars he made
C.17.160	And *aftur* his leryng they lyue and by lawe of kynde
C.17.176	Menyng as *aftur* mete; thus macumeth here enchauntede.
C.17.205	For couetyse *aftur* cros; the corone stand in golde.
C.18.179	And hit *aftur* þe fende, happe how hit myhte.
C.18.179	In inwit and in alle wittes *aftur* liberum Arbitrium
C.18.266	And conforted many a carfol þere þat *aftur* his comyng loke[n].
C.19.1	'I am spes, a spie,' quod he, 'and spere *aftur* a knyȝte
C.19.19	'And ho[so] worcheth *aftur* this writ, y wol vndertaken,
C.20.452	'*Aftur* sharp[e] shoures,' quod pees, 'most shene is þe sonne;
C.20.453	Is no wedore warmore then *aftur* watri cloudes;
C.20.455	Then *aftur* werre and wrake when loue and pees ben maistres.
C.21.123	*Aftur* þe kynde þat he cam of; þer comsede he do wel.
C.21.257	And *aftur* craftes consail clotheth ȝow and fedeth.
C.21.352	With the lord þat lyueth *aftur* the lust of his body,
C.21.398	Ne *aftur* Consience, bi Crist! [while] y c[an] sulle
C.21.401	And nat hacky *aftur* holinesse; hold thy tonge, consience!
C.22.30	*Aftur* þe kynges conseyl and þe comune lyke.
C.22.71	With a lord þat lyueth *aftur* likyng of body,
C.22.90	The lord þat lyuede *aftur* lust tho aloud cryede
C.22.91	*Aftur* conforte, a knyhte, [to] come and beer his baner:
C.22.169	And lyf fley for fere to fisyk *aftur* helpe
C.22.183	And Elde *aftur* hym; and ouer myn heued ȝede
C.22.247	To lered ne to lewed, but lyueth *aftur* ȝoure reule.
C.22.386	And sethe he gradde *aftur* grace tyl y gan awake.

after *conj* after *conj.* A 1 aftir; B 1; C 2 aftur

A.10.141	*Aftir* þat adam & [heo] eten þe appil
B. 9.124	[*After* þat Adam and heo eten þe appul].
C.10.214	*Aftur* þat Adam and Eue hadden ysyneged;
C.10.247	*Aftur* þat Caym þ[e] corsed hadde ykuld abel,

afterward *adv* after-ward *adv.* A 2 aftirward; B 5 afterward (4) afterwardes (1); C 6 afterward (1) afturward (5)

A.11.171	And *aftirward* his wyf I worsshipide boþe,
A.11.181	And siþen *aftirward* to se sumwhat of dobest'.
B. 4.171	The kyng callede Conscience and *afterward* Reson

B.10.228 And *afterwardes* [his] wif [I] worshiped boþe,
B.16.228 Wessh hir feet and wiped hem, and *afterward* þei eten
B.17.131 And Hope *afterward* he bad me to louye
B.18.195 Adam *afterward*, ayeins his defence,
C. 1.64 And *afterward* anhengede hym hey vppon an hellerne.
C. 6.147 [*Afturward*, aftur mete], she and she chydde
C.17.63 And *afturward* awayte ho hath moest nede
C.18.243 Wosch he[re] feet and wypede hem and *afturward* they eten.
C.19.100 And hope *afturward* of god more me toelde
C.20.200 Adam *afturward*, aȝenes his defense,

aftir(- aftur- > after-

afuyre adj *afire adv.& pred.adj.* C 2
C. 7.52 Forsleuthed in my seruice and set [hous] *afuyre*
C.16.180 Bote as wode were *afuyre* thenne worcheth bothe

afurst ptp *ofthirst ppl.* A 1 aþrest; B 2; C 4 afurst (2) afurste (2)
A.12.82 Mi name is feuere on þe ferþe day; I am *aþrest* euere.
B.10.60 Boþe afyngred and *afurst*, and for chele quake;
B.14.162 *Afurst* soore and afyngred, and foule yrebuked
C. 9.85 Bothe afyngred and *afurste*, to turne þe fayre outward
C.11.41 Bothe afyngred and *afurst*, and for defaute spille;
C.16.15 *Afurste* and afyngered and foule rebuked
C.20.437 For bloed may s[uffr]e bloed bothe *afurst* and acale

agag n prop *n.i.d.* A 2; B 2; C 2
A. 3.241 Þat *agag* of amaleg & [al] his peple aftir
A. 3.262 And riȝt as *agag* hadde happe shal somme
B. 3.262 That *Agag* of Amalec and al his peple after
B. 3.286 And riȝt as *Agag* hadde happe shul somme.
C. 3.415 That *agag* of amalek and alle his leege peple
C. 3.439 And riht as *agag* hadde happe shal somme:

agayn(- > ayein

agasteþ v *agasten v.* A 1 agast; B 4 agasteþ (1) agast (3); C 2 agast (1) agaste (1)
A. 2.173 And gile doþ him to go *agast* for to deiȝe.
B. 2.214 And Gyle dooþ hym to go *agast* for to dye.
B.13.267 And werkmen were *agast* a lite; þis wole be þouȝt longe:
B.14.281 Thanne is it good by good skile, al þat *agasteþ* pride.
B.19.299 Wiþ god, and nauȝt *agast* but of gile one.
C. 2.224 And gyle doth hym to gone *agaste* for to deye.
C.21.299 With god and nat *agast* bote of gyle one.

age n *age n.* A 1; B 4; C 5
A. 5.111 In a torn tabbard of twelue wynter *age*,
B. 5.195 In a [torn] tabard of twelf wynter *age*
B.12.7 To amende it in þi myddel *age*, lest myȝt þe faill[e]
B.20.159 Sleuþe wax wonder yerne and soone was of *age*
B.20.189 'Ye, leue, lurdeyn?' quod he, and leyde on me wiþ *Age*,
C. 6.203 In a tore tabard of twelue wynter *age*;
C.10.249 And god sente to seth so sone he was of *age*
C.18.245 He bihihte vs issue and ayr in oure olde *age*;
C.22.159 Sleuthe wax wonder ȝerne and sone was of *age*
C.22.189 'Ȝe, leue, lordeyne?' quod he, and leide on me with *age*

ageyn(- agens > ayein

aglotye v *aglotien v.* C 1
C. 9.76 To *aglotye* with here gurles that greden aftur fode.

ago ptp *agon v.* B 1 ago
B.18.274 Boþe þis lord and þis light, is longe *ago* I knew hym.

ague n *ague n.* B 2 Ague (1) Agues (1); C 2 ague (1) aguwes (1)
B.13.335 Or an *Ague* in swich an Angre and som tyme a Feuere
B.20.84 Biles and bocches and brennynge *Agues*,
C. 6.79 Or an *ague* in suche [an] angre and som tyme a feuere
C.22.84 Byles and boches and brennynge *aguwes*,

agulten v *agilten v.* B 4 agulte (3) agulten (1); C 3 agulte
B.14.8 To *agulte* god or good man by aught þat I wiste,
B.15.309 And þanne wolde lordes and ladies be looþ to *agulte*,
B.15.392 And for hir lyuynge þat lewed men be þe loþer god *agulten*.
B.17.300 And now am sory þat I so þe Seint Spirit *agulte*,
C. 6.17 And [bold haue] y be, nat abaschet to *agulte*
C.17.44 Thenne wolde lordes and ladyes be loth to *agulte*,
C.19.280 And now am sory þat y so the seynte spirit *agulte*,

aguwes > ague

ay adv *ai adv.* A 3; B 7; C 17
A. 9.44 *Ay* is þi soule sauf but þou þiself wilt
A.10.37 Lif þat *ay* shal laste, & al his lynage aftir.
A.11.24 And he þat haþ holy writ *ay* in his mouþe
B. 8.48 *Ay* is þi soule saaf but [þow þiselue wole
B. 9.49 Lif þat *ay* shal laste, [and] al his lynage after.

B.10.32 Ac he þat haþ holy writ *ay* in his mouþe
B.11.206 Of Adames issue and Eue *ay* til god man deide;
B.14.221 For þe poore is *ay* prest to plese þe riche
B.14.255 Meschief is [*ay* a mene] and makeþ hym to þynke
B.18.362 And my grace to growe *ay* gretter and widder.
C. 3.137 And *ay* the lengur y late [the] go the lasse treuthe is with the,
C. 5.95 And *ay* loste an[d] loste and at þe laste hym happed
C. 8.218 And helpe hem of alle thyng *ay* as hem nedeth.
C.10.40 That *ay* is saef and sound þat sitte withynne þe borde.
C.11.29 Ac he þat hath holy writ *ay* in his mouth
C.12.101 For god, as þe gospel saith, goth *ay* as þe pore
C.12.114 Of Adames issue and Eue *ay* til god man deyede;
C.13.4 And *ay* þe lengere they lyuede the lasse goed they hadde:
C.13.59 Ther þe messager is *ay* merye and his mouth ful of songes
C.14.133 And god is *ay* gracious to alle þat gredeth to hym
C.14.214 And hope hangeth *ay* þeron to haue þat treuthe deserueth:
C.15.245 'Hastow,' quod actyf, '*ay* such mete with the?'
C.16.62 For þe pore is *ay* prest to plese þe ryche
C.16.95 Meschief is *ay* a mene and maketh hym to thenke
C.17.146 And *ay* hopeth eft to be with here body at þe laste
C.18.232 Is and *ay* were [& worþ wiþouten ende].
C.20.400 And my grace to growe *ay* [gretter] and wyddore.

aiels n *aiel n.* B 1 Aiels
B.15.323 To ȝyue from youre heires þat youre *Aiels* yow lefte,

ayer > eyr; ayleth > eyleþ; ayr > eyr,heir; ayres > heir

aysches n *asshe n.(2)* C 1
C. 3.126 That fuyr shal falle and forbrenne al to blew *aysches*

ayþer(es > eiþer

aiþes n *eithe n.* B 1; C 1 aythes
B.19.273 Wiþ two [*aiþes*] þat þei hadde, an oold and a newe:
C.21.273 With two *aythes* þat they hadde, an oelde and a newe:

aker > acre

akeþ v *aken v.* A 1 akiþ; B 2 akeþ (1) oke (1); C 1 oke
A. 7.240 Of alle þe wyke [hy] werkiþ nouȝt, so here wombe *akiþ*.'
B. 6.256 Of al a wike werche noȝt, so oure wombe *akeþ*.'
B.17.197 Boþe meue and amende, þouȝ alle my fyngres *oke*.
C.19.163 Bothe meue and amende, thogh alle my fyngeres *oke*.

akir > acre

aknowe ptp *aknouen ppl.* C 1
C. 9.86 And ben abasched for to begge and wollen nat be *aknowe*

al adj *al lim.adj.& n. &> oueral,wiþalle* A 166 al (42) all (1) alle (123); B 567 al (190) all (1) alle (373) aller (3); C 674 al (205) alere (2) all (58) alle (409)
A.Pr.18 Of *alle* maner of men, þe mene & þe riche,
A.Pr.49 And hadde leue to leiȝe *al* here lif aftir.
A.Pr.55 I fond þere Freris, *alle* þe foure ordris,
A.Pr.67 And seide þat hymself miȝte assoile hem *alle*
A.Pr.109 *Al* þis I sauȝ slepyng & seue siþes more.
A. 1.14 For he is fadir of feiþ & fourmide ȝow *alle*
A. 1.34 *Al* is not good to þe gost þat þe gut [ask]iþ,
A. 1.52 For riȝtfulliche resoun shulde rewele ȝow *alle*,
A. 1.67 He is lettere of loue, leiȝeþ hem *alle*;
A. 1.83 'Whanne *alle* tresours arn triȝed treuþe is þe beste,
A. 1.115 A[c] lucifer lowest liþ of hem *alle*;
A. 1.117 And *alle* þat werchen with wrong wenden þei shuln
A. 1.122 Þere treuþe is in trinite & tron[iþ] h[e]m *alle*.
A. 1.124 Whanne *alle* tresours arn triȝed treuþe is þe beste.
A. 1.140 And þat falliþ to þe fadir þat fourmide vs *alle*,
A. 1.142 Mekliche for oure misdedis to amende vs *alle*.
A. 1.166 Vnkynde to here kyn & ek to *alle* cristene,
A. 1.175 Date & dabitur vobis for I dele ȝow *alle*.
A. 1.181 Whan *alle* tresouris arn triȝede treuþe is þe beste.
A. 2.11 *Alle* here fyue fyngris were frettid wiþ rynges
A. 2.24 Gile haþ begon hire so heo grauntiþ *alle* his wille;
A. 2.25 And *al* is liȝeris ledyng þat hy liȝen togideris,
A. 2.27 Þere miȝte be *alle* ȝif þou wilt whiche þei ben *alle*
A. 2.29 Knowe hem þere ȝif þou canst and kep þe from hem *alle*
A. 2.33 *Alle* þe riche retenaunce þat regniþ wiþ false
A. 2.46 *Alle* to wytnesse wel what þe writ wolde.
A. 2.61 Wiþ *alle* þe lordsshipe of leccherie in lengþe & in brede;
A. 2.63 And *al* þe Ile of vsurie, & auarice þe faste,
A. 2.65 Wiþ *alle* þe delites of lust þe deuil for to serue,
A. 2.66 In *al* þe signiure of slouþe I se[se] hem togidere;
A. 2.68 Wiþ *al* þe purtenaunce of purcatorie into þe pyne of helle;
A. 2.117 Til mede be þi weddit wyf þoruȝ wyt of vs *alle*,
A. 2.123 And let somoune *alle* þe segges [in shires abouten],
A. 2.124 And *alle* be boun, beggeris & oþere,

A. 2.137　And *alle* þe denis & southdenis, as destreris hem diȝte,
A. 2.143　And makiþ of lyere a lang carte to leden *al* þis oþere,
A. 2.146　And mede in þe myddis, & *al* þis mene aftir.
A. 2.149　Ac gile was forgoere and gyede hem *alle*.
A. 2.151　But prikede forþ on his palfray & passide hem *alle*,
A. 2.157　And do hem hange be þe hals & *alle* þat hem maynteniþ.
A. 2.159　But riȝt as þe lawe lokis let falle on hem *alle*.'
A. 2.164　And bringeþ mede to me maugre hem *alle*.
A. 2.171　And bad hym fle for fer & hise feris *alle*.
A. 2.195　*Alle* fledden for fer & flowen into hernis;
A. 3.1　　Now is mede þe maide, & no mo of hem *alle*,
A. 3.12　Þat woniþ at westmenstre worsshipeþ hire *alle*;
A. 3.18　For *al* consiences cast a[nd] craft as I trowe'.
A. 3.19　Mildeliche mede þanne merciede hem *alle*
A. 3.53　Ac god *alle* good folk such grauyng defendiþ
A. 3.77　Of *alle* suche selleris siluer to take,
A. 3.121　As comoun as þe cartewey to knaue & to [*alle*],
A. 3.140　To holde lemmanis & lotebies *alle* here lif dayes,
A. 3.154　And *alle* þat meynteniþ hire men meschaunce hem betide!
A. 3.198　To alienes, to *alle* men, to honoure hem with ȝeftis.
A. 3.200　Emperours & Erlis & *alle* maner lordis
A. 3.212　*Alle* kyn crafty men craue mede for here prentis;
A. 3.241　Þat agag of amaleg & [*al*] his peple aftir
A. 3.255　And *al* his sed for þat synne [shend]fully ende.
A. 3.257　Þat god hati[de him for euere] & *alle* hise heires aftir.
A. 3.264　And dauid shal be dyademid & daunten hem *alle*,
A. 4.101　Til lordis & ladies louen *alle* treuþe,
A. 4.111　And *alle* rome renneris, for robberis be ȝonde,
A. 4.147　And *al* my lige ledis to lede þus euene.'
A. 5.20　Þat dedly synne er domisday shal fordon hem *alle*.
A. 5.41　Sekiþ seint treuþe for he may saue ȝou *alle*
A. 5.47　And behiȝte to hym þat vs *alle* made
A. 5.53　Of *alle* þat I haue had enuye in myn herte.'
A. 5.87　[For pilgrymes, for palmers, for *all* þe peple] aftir,
A. 5.92　[Þanne] I wysshe it were myn [and *al* þe webbe aftir].
A. 5.99　[Þat] *al* my brest bolniþ for bittir of my galle.
A. 5.191　[Þat] *alle* þat herden þat horn held here nose aftir
A. 5.199　Þat wiþ *al* þe wo of þe world his wyf & his wenche
A. 5.201　And aftir *al* þis surfet an axesse he hadde
A. 5.212　And ȝet haue I hatid hire *al* my lif tyme.'
A. 5.228　*Al* þat I wykkidly wan siþen I wyt hadde,
A. 5.249　And lepe with hym ouer lond *al* his lif tyme,
A. 6.30　I haue ben his folewere *al* þis fourty wynter;
A. 6.56　And ȝe shuln lepe þe liȝtliere *al* ȝoure lif tyme;
A. 6.74　And *alle* þe wallis ben of wyt to holde wil þeroute;
A. 6.77　*Alle* þe housis ben helid, hallis & chaumbris,
A. 6.113　It is wel hard, be myn hed, any of ȝow *alle*,
A. 6.120　'Mercy [is] a maiden [þere], haþ miȝt ouer [hem] *alle*;
A. 6.121　And she is sib to *alle* synful, & hire sone alse,
A. 7.21　And *alle* maner of men þat be þe mete libbiþ,
A. 7.28　A[nd] ek laboure for þi loue *al* my lyue tyme,
A. 7.62　And *alle* kyne crafty men þat conne lyue in treuþe,
A. 7.87　And monewe me in his memorie among *alle* cristene.
A. 7.125　Ȝe eten þat [hy] shulde ete þat eren for vs *alle*;
A. 7.134　Shuln haue of myn almesse *al* þe while I libbe,
A. 7.156　'Now be þe peril of my soule!' quaþ peris, 'I shal appeire ȝow *alle*,'
A. 7.162　Þat he lokide lik a lanterne *al* his lif aftir;
A. 7.193　And it ben my blody breþeren, for god bouȝte vs *alle*.
A. 7.195　And helpe hem of *alle* þing [aftir] þat hem nedi[þ].
A. 7.208　And *alle* maner of men þat þou miȝte aspien,
A. 7.213　'I wolde not greue god,' quaþ peris, 'for *al* þe gold on ground.
A. 7.216　Go to genesis þe geaunt, engendrour of vs *alle*:
A. 7.240　Of *alle* þe wyke [hy] werkiþ nouȝt, so here wombe akiþ.'
A. 7.276　*Alle* þe pore peple pesecoddis fetten;
A. 7.298　And þanne curse þe king & *alle* þe counseil aftir
A. 8.6　And [*alle*] þat holpen to erien or to sowen,
A. 8.45　Men of lawe hadde lest for le[ttr]id þei ben *alle*;
A. 8.57　Þise þre for þrallis ben þrowe among vs *alle*
A. 8.63　*Alle* libbyng laboureris þat lyuen be here hondis,
A. 8.79　Þanne of *alle* oþer maner men þat on þis molde wandriþ.
A. 8.92　And I behynde hem boþe beheld *al* þe b[u]lle.
A. 8.117　Haue þei no garner [to go] to, but god fynt hem *alle*.'
A. 8.144　And þe enleuene sterris ha[i]lsiden hym *alle*.
A. 8.149　*Al* þis makiþ me on metelis to þinke
A. 8.152　And how þe prest inpugnid it *al* be [pu]re resoun,
A. 8.156　He passiþ *al* þe pardoun [of] seint petris chirche.
A. 8.172　And come [*alle*] before crist acountes to ȝelden,
A. 8.179　Forþi I counseil *alle* cristene [to] criȝe god mercy,
A. 9.2　　*Al* a somer sesoun for to seke dowel
A. 9.79　Þe bagges & þe [bi]gerdlis, he haþ broken hem *alle*
A. 9.91　Þei han crounide o king to kepe hem *alle*,
A. 9.99　And rewele þe reaum be red of hem *alle*.
A. 10.16　Ac þe cunstable of þe castel, þat kepiþ hem *alle*,

A. 10.21　And sire godefrey go wel, grete lordis *alle*.
A. 10.27　'Kynde,' quaþ he, 'is creatour of *alle* kenis bestis,
A. 10.28　Fadir & fourmour, þe ferste of *alle* þing.
A. 10.31　Aungelis & *alle* þing arn at his wille,
A. 10.34　And *al* at his wil was wrouȝt wiþ a speche.
A. 10.37　Lif þat ay shal laste, & *al* his lynage aftir.
A. 10.42　Inwit & *alle* wyttes enclosid ben þerinne,
A. 10.45　Ac in þe herte is hire hom heiȝest of *alle*.
A. 10.84　And *alle* kynde scoleris in scole to lerne.
A. 10.137　Kinges & kniȝtes, & *alle* kyne clerkis
A. 10.151　*Alle* þat comen of þat caym crist hatid aftir,
A. 10.155　For *alle* þat comen of þat caym acursid þei were,
A. 10.156　And *alle* þat couplide hem with þat kyn crist hatide [dedliche].
A. 10.163　And is as muche to mene, among vs *alle*,
A. 10.173　*Alle* shuln deiȝe for his dedis be dounes & hilles,
A. 10.177　Ellis shal *alle* diȝen & to helle wenden."
A. 10.178　[Þus] þoruȝ curside caym cam care vpon *alle*,
A. 10.197　Forþi I counseile *alle* cristene coueite not be weddit
A. 10.201　And [þanne] glade ȝe god þat *al* good sendiþ.
A. 11.12　Þanne *al* þe precious perrie þat in paradis wexiþ.
A. 11.16　Þanne *alle* þe soþe sawis þat salamon seide euere.
A. 11.49　Litel louiþ he þat lord þat leniþ hym *al* þat blisse.
A. 11.64　And [ek] defame þe fadir þat vs *alle* made,
A. 11.69　And *alle* here seed for here synne þe same wo suffride?"
A. 11.72　Ac austyn þe olde for *alle* suche prechide,
A. 11.80　For *alle* þat wilneþ to wyte þe [whyes] of god almiȝt,
A. 11.85　–*Al* was as he wolde; lord yworsshipid be þou,
A. 11.86　And *al* worþ as þou wilt, whatso we telle–
A. 11.89　Siþen he wilneþ to wyte which þei ben *alle*.
A. 11.128　Logik I lerid hire, & *al* þe lawe aftir,
A. 11.129　And *alle* þe musons of musik I made hire [to] knowe.
A. 11.134　[Of] *alle* kynne craftis I contreuide tolis,
A. 11.163　*Alle* þise sciences, sikir, I myself
A. 11.185　And *alle* kyne crafty men þat cunne here foode wynne,
A. 11.218　And welawey wers and I [wo]lde *al* telle.'
A. 11.220　Wern dowel, & dobet, & dobest of hem *alle*,
A. 11.224　Forþi I wende þat þo wyes wern dobest of *alle*.'
A. 11.244　Oure enemys and *alle* men þat arn nedy & pore,
A. 11.246　*Alle* kynne creatures þat to crist be[n] l[yche]
A. 11.271　And *al* holy chirche holden hem in helle.
A. 11.273　For *alle* cunnyng clerkis siþþe crist ȝede on erþe
A. 11.278　Þanne wrouȝte I vnwisly wiþ *alle* þe wyt þat I lere.
A. 11.280　Þat hadde lyued *al* his lyf wiþ lesinges & þeft[e],
A. 11.285　A robbere hadde remission raþere þanne þei *alle*,
A. 11.301　Þe help of þe holy gost to answere hem [*alle*]'.
A. 12.11　*Al* þat þou askest asoylen I wolde.'
A. 12.62　'*Al* hayl,' quod þo, and I answered, 'welcome, & with whom be ȝe?'
A. 12.110　Now *alle* kenne creatures þat cristene were euere
A. 12.114　And *alle* lordes þat louyn him lely in herte,
B.Pr.18　Of *alle* manere of men, þe meene and þe riche,
B.Pr.49　And hadden leue to lyen *al* hire lif after.
B.Pr.58　I fond þere Freres, *alle* þe foure ordres,
B.Pr.70　And seide þat hymself myȝte assoillen hem *alle*
B.Pr.103　Amonges foure vertues, [most vertuous of *alle*],
B.Pr.119　And for profit of *al* þe peple Plowmen ordeyned
B.Pr.143　Thanne [comsed] *al* þe commune crye in vers of latyn
B.Pr.153　And if we grucche of his gamen he wol greuen vs *alle*,
B.Pr.159　Seide for a souereyn [salue] to [hem *alle*]
B.Pr.175　*Al* þ[e] route of Ratons to þis reson assented.
B.Pr.177　Ther ne was Raton in þe route, for *al* þe Reaume of Fraunce,
B.Pr.179　Ne hangen it aboute [his] hals *al* Engelond to wynne;
B.Pr.181　And leten hire labour lost and *al* hire longe studie.
B.Pr.183　Strook forþ sternely and stood bifore hem *alle*
B.Pr.186　To c[r]acchen vs & *al* oure kynde þouȝ we cropen vnder benches;
B.Pr.187　Forþi I counseille *al* þe commune to late þe cat worþe,
B.Pr.223　Of *alle* kynne lybbynge laborers lopen forþ somme,
B.Pr.231　[*Al* þis I seiȝ slepyng and seuene sythes more].
B. 1.14　For he is fader of feiþ, and formed yow *alle*
B. 1.36　[*Al* is nouȝt] good to þe goost þat þe gut askeþ,
B. 1.54　For riȝtfully reson sholde rule yow *alle*,
B. 1.69　He is lettere of loue, lieþ hem *alle*;
B. 1.85　'Whan *alle* tresors arn tried treuþe is þe beste;
B. 1.110　And *alle* þat hoped it myȝte be so, noon heuene myȝte hem holde,
B. 1.126　Ac Lucifer lowest liþ of hem *alle*;
B. 1.128　And *alle* þat werchen with wrong wende þei shulle
B. 1.133　Ther Treuþe is in Trinitee and troneþ hem *alle*.
B. 1.135　Whan *alle* tresors arn tried treuþe is þe beste.
B. 1.150　And *alle* hise werkes he wrouȝte with loue as hym liste;
B. 1.166　And þat falleþ to þe fader þat formed vs *alle*,
B. 1.168　Mekely for oure mysdedes to amenden vs *alle*.
B. 1.192　Vnkynde to hire kyn and to *alle* cristene,

B. 1.201   "Date & dabitur vobis, for I deele yow *alle*."
B. 1.207   Whan *alle* tresors ben tried treuþe is þe beste.
B. 2.29   My fader þe grete god is and ground of *alle* graces,
B. 2.43   And *al* is lieres ledynge þat [lady] is þus ywedded.
B. 2.45   [There] my3tow witen if þow wilt whiche þei ben *alle*;
B. 2.47   Knowe hem þere if þow kanst and kepe [þee from hem *alle*],
B. 2.54   That *al* þe riche retenaunce þat regneþ with [fals]
B. 2.56   Of *alle* manere of men, þe meene and þe riche.
B. 2.86   The Countee of Coueitise and *alle* þe costes aboute,
B. 2.87   That is vsure and Auarice; *al* I hem graunte
B. 2.89   [Wiþ] *al* þe lordshipe of leccherie in lengþe and in brede,
B. 2.94   And *al* day to drynken at diuerse Tauernes,
B. 2.104   Wiþ *alle* þe [p]urtinaunces of Purgatorie into þe pyne of helle.
B. 2.153   Til Mede be þi wedded wif þoru3 wi[t] of vs *alle*,
B. 2.159   And leten somone *alle* segges in shires aboute,
B. 2.160   And *alle* be bown, beggers and oþere,
B. 2.174   Erchedekenes and Officials and *alle* youre Registrers,
B. 2.182   And makeþ of lyere a lang cart to leden *alle* þise oþere,
B. 2.185   And Mede in þe myddes and [*al* þis meynee] after.
B. 2.188   Ac Gyle was Forgoer and gyed hem *alle*.
B. 2.190   And priked [forþ on] his palfrey and passed hem *alle*
B. 2.196   And doon hem hange by þe hals and *alle* þat hem maynteneþ.
B. 2.198   But ri3t as þe lawe [lokeþ] lat falle on hem *alle*.'
B. 2.203   /And bryngeþ Mede to me maugree hem *alle*.
B. 2.212   And bad hym fle for fere and hise [feeres] *alle*.
B. 2.236   *Alle* fledden for fere and flowen into hernes;
B. 3.1   NOw is Mede þe mayde and na mo of hem *alle*
B. 3.12   [That] wonyeþ [at] westmynstre worshipeþ hire *alle*.
B. 3.19   For *al* Consciences cast [and] craft, as I trowe'.
B. 3.20   Mildely Mede þanne merciede hem *alle*
B. 3.39   And [þei3] Fals[hede] hadde yfolwed þee *alle* þise fift[ene] wynter,
B. 3.56   And a cours of kynde wherof we comen *alle*;
B. 3.64   Ac god *alle* good folk swich grauynge defendeþ,
B. 3.88   Of *alle* swiche Selleris siluer to take,
B. 3.132   As commune as [þe] Cartwey to [knaue and to *alle*],
B. 3.151   To [holde] lemmans and lotebies *alle* hire lifdaies,
B. 3.164   And *al* þe comune in care þat coueiten lyue in truþe.
B. 3.167   And *alle* þat maynteneþ hire men, meschaunce hem bitide!
B. 3.211   To aliens, to *alle* men, to honouren hem with 3iftes;
B. 3.213   Emperours and Erles and *alle* manere lordes
B. 3.225   *Alle* kynne craft[y] men crauen Mede for hir Prentices;
B. 3.242   And *alle* þat helpen þe Innocent and holden with þe ri3tfulle,
B. 3.262   That Agag of Amalec and *al* his peple after
B. 3.269   Moebles and vnmoebles, and *al* þow my3t fynde,
B. 3.277   And *al* his seed for þat synne shenfulliche ende.
B. 3.279   That god hated hym for euere and *alle* hise heires after.
B. 3.288   And Dauid shal be diademed and daunten hem *alle*,
B. 3.305   *Alle* þat beren baselard, brood swerd or launce,
B. 3.321   *Al* shal be but oon court, and oon [burn] be Iustice,
B. 4.39   Moore þan for] loue of oure lord or *alle* hise leeue Seintes.
B. 4.114   Til lordes and ladies louen *alle* truþe
B. 4.115   And haten *alle* harlotrie to heren or to mouþen it;
B. 4.128   And *alle* Rome renneres, for Robberes [of] biyonde,
B. 4.157   *Alle* ri3tfulle recordede þat Reson truþe tolde.
B. 4.168   And [also] a Sherreues clerk bisherewed *al* þe route:
B. 4.180   I wole haue leaute in lawe, and lete be *al* youre ianglyng;
B. 4.184   [And] *alle* youre lige beestes to lede þus euene'.
B. 5.11   And how Reson gan arayen hym *al* þe Reaume to preche
B. 5.20   That dedly synne er domesday shal fordoon hem *alle*.
B. 5.57   Sekeþ Seynt Truþe, for he may saue yow *alle*
B. 5.64   And bihi3te to hym þat vs *alle* made
B. 5.70   [Of *alle* þat] I haue [had enuye] in myn herte.'
B. 5.89   [This was *al* his curteisie where þat euere he shewed hym].
B. 5.107   For Pilgrymes, for Palmeres, for *al* þe peple after,
B. 5.112   [Thanne I wisshe] it were myn and *al* þe web after.
B. 5.120   That *al* my [brest] maketh for bitter of my galle.
B. 5.151   Or ellis *al* riche and ryden; I, wraþe, reste neuere
B. 5.161   For she hadde child in chirietyme; *al* oure Chapitre it wiste.
B. 5.180   *Al* þe wikkednesse þat I woot by any of oure breþeren,
B. 5.181   I cou[3]e it [vp] in oure Cloistre þat *al* [þe] Couent woot it.'
B. 5.237   'Vsedestow euere vsurie', quod Repentaunce, 'in *al* þi lif tyme?'
B. 5.271   Til þow make restitucion', [quod Repentaunce], 'and rekene wiþ hem *alle*;
B. 5.274   For a[l] þat ha[þ] of þi good, haue god my trouþe,
B. 5.282   And *al* þe wikkednesse in þis world þat man my3te werche or þynke
B. 5.343   That *alle* þat herde þat horn helde hir nos[e] after
B. 5.357   Wiþ *al* þe wo of þ[e] world his wif and his wenche
B. 5.359   And after *al* þis excesse he hadde an Accidie
B. 5.384   And yet haue I hated hire *al* my lif tyme.'
B. 5.408   Than *al* þat euere Marc made, Mathew, Iohan and Lucas.
B. 5.409   Vigilies and fastyng dayes, *alle* þise late I passe,
B. 5.456   *Al* þat I wikkedly wan siþen I wit hadde,

B. 5.475   And lepe wiþ hym ouer lond *al* his lif tyme,
B. 5.477   [Th]anne hadde Repentaunce ruþe and redde hem *alle* to knele.
B. 5.478   'I shal biseche for *alle* synfulle oure Saueour of grace
B. 5.479   To amenden vs of oure mysdedes: do mercy to vs *alle*,
B. 5.482   And siþen suffredest [hym] to synne, a siknesse to vs *alle*,
B. 5.495   And blewe *alle* þi blessed into þe blisse of Paradys.
B. 5.499   And *al* þat Marc haþ ymaad, Mathew, Iohan and Lucas
B. 5.508   That *alle* Seintes [for synful] songen at ones
B. 5.542   I haue ben his folwere *al* þis [fourty] wynter,
B. 5.563   That ye louen oure lord god leuest of *alle* þynges.
B. 5.569   And ye shul lepe þe li3tloker *al* youre lif tyme.
B. 5.587   And *alle* þe walles ben of wit to holden wil oute;
B. 5.590   And *alle* þe houses ben hiled, halles and chambres,
B. 5.628   It is [wel] hard, by myn heed, any of yow *alle*
B. 5.635   'Mercy is a maiden þere haþ my3t ouer [hem] *alle*;
B. 5.636   And she is sib to *alle* synfulle and hire sone also,
B. 6.19   And *alle* manere of men þat [by þe] mete libbeþ,
B. 6.26   And [ek] labour[e] for þi loue *al* my lif tyme,
B. 6.68   And *alle* kynne crafty men þat konne lyuen in truþe,
B. 6.95   And mengen [me] in his memorie amonges *alle* cristene.
B. 6.144   And *al* is þoru3 suffraunce þat vengeaunce yow ne takeþ.
B. 6.171   'Now by þe peril of my soule!' quod Piers, 'I shal apeire yow *alle*',
B. 6.177   That he loked lik a lanterne *al* his lif after.
B. 6.207   [And it] are my blody breþeren for god bou3te vs *alle*;
B. 6.209   And helpen hem of *alle* þyng [after þat] hem nedeþ.
B. 6.222   And *alle* manere of men þat þow my3t aspie
B. 6.229   'I wolde no3t greue god', quod Piers, 'for *al* þe good on grounde!
B. 6.232   Go to Genesis þe geaunt, engendrour of vs *alle*:
B. 6.256   Of *al* a wike werche no3t, so oure wombe akeþ.'
B. 6.292   *Al* þe pouere peple pescoddes fetten;
B. 6.317   And þanne corseþ þe kyng and *al* [þe] counseil after
B. 7.6   And *alle* þat holpen to erye or to sowe,
B. 7.15   And in as muche as þei mowe amenden *alle* synfulle,
B. 7.61   *Alle* libbynge laborers þat lyuen [by] hir hondes,
B. 7.76   Ac Gregory was a good man and bad vs gyuen *alle*
B. 7.77   That askeþ for his loue þat vs *al* leneþ:
B. 7.97   Than of *alle* [oþere] manere men þat on þis moolde [wandreþ]
B. 7.110   And I bihynde hem boþe biheld *al* þe bulle.
B. 7.135   Haue þei no gerner to go to but god fynt hem *alle*.'
B. 7.166   And þe elleuene sterres hailsed hym *alle*.
B. 7.173   *Al* þis makeþ me on metels to þynke
B. 7.178   [He] passeþ *al* þe pardon of Seint Petres cherche.
B. 7.194   And comen *alle* [bi]fore crist acountes to yelde,
B. 7.201   Forþi I counseille *alle* cristene to crie god mercy,
B. 8.2   *Al* a somer seson for to seke dowel.
B. 8.88   The bagges and þe bigirdles, he haþ [b]roke hem *alle*
B. 8.101   [Thei han] crowne[d a] kyng to [kepen] hem [*alle*],
B. 8.109   And rule þe Reme by [rede of hem *alle*],
B. 9.15   That he bit moot be do; he [boldeþ] hem *alle*;
B. 9.17   Ac þe Constable of [þe] Castel þat kepeþ [hem *alle*]
B. 9.22   And sire Godefray Go-wel, grete lordes [*alle*]
B. 9.26   'Kynde', quod [he], 'is creatour of *alle* kynnes [beestes],
B. 9.27   Fader and formour, [þe first of *alle* þynges];
B. 9.30   Aungeles and *alle* þyng arn at his wille
B. 9.33   [And *al* at his wil was wrou3t wiþ a speche],
B. 9.41   The lettre, for *al* his lordshipe, I leue, were neuere ymaked.
B. 9.49   Lif þat ay shal laste, [and] *al* his lynage after.
B. 9.54   Inwit and *alle* wittes [en]closed ben þerInne
B. 9.65   And *alle* þat lyuen good lif are lik to god almy3ty:
B. 9.73   *Alle* þise lakken Inwit and loore [hem] bihoueþ.
B. 9.85   For *alle* þe mebles on þis moolde and amende it my3te.
B. 9.90   [So] Iewes [shul] ben oure loresmen, shame to vs *alle*!
B. 9.107   To *alle* trewe tidy men þat trauaille desiren,
B. 9.126   And *alle* þat come of þat Caym come to yuel ende,
B. 9.142   *Alle* shul deye for hise dedes by [dounes] and hulles,
B. 9.147   And *alle* for hir [fore]fadres ferden þe werse.
B. 9.164   "I am via & veritas", seiþ crist, "I may auaunce *alle*."
B. 9.176   Forþi I counseille *alle* cristene coueite no3t be wedded
B. 9.206   To helen and to helpen, is dobest of *alle*.
B.10.12   Than *al* þe precious perree þat in paradis wexeþ.
B.10.16   Than *alle* þe sooþ sawes þat Salomon seide euere.
B.10.63   Litel loueþ he þat lord þat lent hym *al* þat blisse
B.10.77   In Religion and in *al* þe Reme amonges riche and pouere
B.10.80   That girles for [oure] giltes he forgrynt hem *alle*,
B.10.106   And leyden fautes vpon þe fader þat formede vs *alle*,
B.10.111   And *al* hir seed for hir synne þe same deeþ suffrede?
B.10.127   For *alle* þat wilneþ to wite þe [whyes] of god almy3ty,
B.10.132   *Al* was as [he] wold[e]–lord, yworshiped be þ[ow],
B.10.133   And *al* worþ as þow wolt whatso we dispute–
B.10.136   Siþþe he wilneþ to wite whiche þei ben [*alle*].
B.10.145   But *al* lau3ynge he louted and loked vpon Studie
B.10.176   Logyk I lerned hire, and [*al* þe lawe after],
B.10.177   And *alle* [þe] Musons in Musik I made hire to knowe.

B.10.182	Of *alle* kynne craftes I contreued tooles,
B.10.208	And *alle* þat lakkeþ vs or lyeþ oure lord techeþ vs to louye,
B.10.220	*Alle* þise Sciences I myself sotilede and ordeynede.
B.10.239	Wiþ *alle* þe articles of þe feiþ þat falleþ to be knowe.
B.10.246	For *al* is but oon god and ech is god hymselue:
B.10.251	Who was his Auctour? *alle* þe foure Euaungelistes.
B.10.253	*Alle* þe clerkes vnder crist ne koude þis assoille,
B.10.258	*Al* þat þe book bit bi holi cherches techyng.
B.10.268	*Alle* þat lakkeþ any lif and lakkes han hemselue:
B.10.274	*Alle* maner men to amenden bi hire myȝtes;
B.10.284	In *alle* maner þoruȝ mansede preestes.
B.10.285	The bible bereþ witnesse þat *al[le]* þe [barnes] of Israel
B.10.308	But *al* is buxomnesse þere and bokes, to rede and to lerne].
B.10.331	And þanne shal þe Abbot of Abyngdoun and *al* his issue for euere
B.10.361	That is, loue þi lord god leuest abouen *al*,
B.10.362	And after *alle* cristene creatures, in commune ech man ooþer;
B.10.385	God gaf hym grace of wit and *alle* goodes after
B.10.391	And *al* holy chirche holdeþ hem boþe [in helle]!
B.10.421	That hadde lyued *al* his lif wiþ lesynges and þefte,
B.10.426	A Robbere was yraunsoned raþer þan þei *alle*,
B.10.436	That Salomon seiþ I trowe be sooþ and certein of vs *alle*:
B.10.442	And wherby wiste men which [is] whit if *alle* þyng blak were,
B.10.446	And he þat may *al* amende haue mercy on vs alle,
B.10.446	And he þat may al amende haue mercy on vs *alle*,
B.10.453	Konnyng [and clergie] to conclude hem *alle*".
B.11.21	That leden þee wole to likynge *al* þi lif tyme'.
B.11.43	Til Concupiscencia carnis acorded *alle* my werkes.
B.11.51	Than dowel or dobet among my dedes *alle*.
B.11.61	And þanne was Fortune my foo for *al* hir faire [biheste],
B.11.101	Þyng þat *al* þe world woot, wherfore sholdestow spare
B.11.119	For crist cleped vs *alle*, come if we wolde,
B.11.123	'Thanne may *alle* cristene come', quod I, 'and cleyme þere entree
B.11.138	Mercy *al* to amende and Mekenesse hir folwe;
B.11.144	That *al* þe clergie vnder crist ne myȝte me cracche fro helle,
B.11.170	And took it moises vpon þe mount *alle* men to lere].
B.11.172	Or any Science vnder sonne, þe seuene artȝ and *alle*–
B.11.173	But þei ben lerned for oure lordes loue, lost is *al* þe tyme,
B.11.178	And þat *alle* manere men, enemyes and frendes,
B.11.197	[*Alle* myȝte god haue maad riche men if he wolde],
B.11.199	For *alle* are we cristes creatures and of his cofres riche,
B.11.211	And euery man helpe ooþer for hennes shul we *alle*:
B.11.225	I conseille *alle* cristne clyue noȝt þeron to soore,
B.11.240	And *al* was ensample, [sooþliche], to vs synfulle here
B.11.242	And [pacient as pilgrymes] for pilgrymes are we *alle*.
B.11.256	And *alle* þe wise þat euere were, by auȝt I kan aspye,
B.11.298	The same I segge for soþe by *alle* swiche preestes.
B.11.321	And slepynge I seiȝ *al* þis, and siþen cam kynde
B.11.335	Reson I seiȝ sooþly sewen *alle* beestes,
B.11.339	Males drowen hem to males [*al* mornyng] by hemselue,
B.11.343	Boþe hors and houndes and *alle* oþere beestes
B.11.370	That Reson rewarded and ruled *alle* beestes
B.11.381	He myȝte amende in a Minute while *al* þat mysstandeþ,
B.11.398	For *al* þat he [wrouȝt] was wel ydo, as holy writ witnesseþ:
B.12.30	Feiþ, hope and Charite, and *alle* ben goode,
B.12.44	Alisaundre þat *al* wan, elengliche ended.
B.12.45	Catel and kynde wit was combraunce to hem *alle*.
B.12.108	Come for *al* his kynde wit to cristendom and be saued;
B.12.121	Forþi I conseille *alle* creatures no clergie to dispise
B.12.128	Ac kynde wit comeþ of *alle* kynnes siȝtes,
B.12.135	For *alle* hir kynde knowyn[g] co[m] but of diuerse siȝtes.
B.12.155	Why I haue told [þee] *al* þis, I took ful good hede
B.12.216	*Alle* þe clerkes vnder crist ne kouþe þe skile assoille:
B.12.251	To *alle* hem þat it holdeþ til hir tail be plukked.
B.12.258	And *alle* þe oþere þer it lith enuenymeþ þoruȝ his attre.
B.12.277	'*Alle* þise clerkes', quod I, "þat [o]n crist leuen
B.13.18	[For *alle*] creatures þat crepen [or walken] of kynde ben engendred;
B.13.39	Of Austyn, of Ambrose, of [*alle*] þe foure Euangelistes:
B.13.69	That Poul in his Pistle to *al* þe peple tolde:
B.13.124	For oon Piers þe Plowman haþ impugned vs *alle*,
B.13.125	And set *alle* sciences at a sop saue loue one;
B.13.141	Thow loue leelly þi soule *al* þi lif tyme;
B.13.143	Thyn enemy in *alle* wise eueneforþ wiþ þiselue.
B.13.154	And *al* þe wit of þe wodnesday of þe nexte wike after;
B.13.167	Maister of *alle* þo men þoruȝ myȝt of þis redels,
B.13.169	Do kyng and quene and *alle* þe comune after
B.13.170	Yeue þee *al* þat þei may yeue, as þee for best yemere;
B.13.171	And as þow demest wil þei do *alle* hir dayes after:
B.13.173	*Al* þe wit of þis world and wiȝt mennes strengþe
B.13.189	For *al* þat Pacience me profreþ proud am I litel.
B.13.197	Than *alle* þo þat offrede into Gaȝophilacium?'
B.13.208	And conformen kynges to pees; and *alle* kynnes londes,
B.13.209	Sarsens and Surre, and so forþ *alle* þe Iewes,

B.13.225	*Al* yde[l] ich hatie for of Actif is my name.
B.13.239	For *alle* trewe trauaillours and tiliers of þe erþe
B.13.252	For hym and for *alle* hise, founde I þat his pardoun
B.13.263	*Al* londoun, I leue, likeþ wel my wafres,
B.13.279	Willyng þat *alle* men wende he were þat he is noȝt,
B.13.311	*Al* he wolde þat men wiste of werkes and wordes
B.13.323	*Al* þat he wiste wikked by any wight tellen it,
B.13.336	That takeþ me *al* a tweluemonþe, til þat I despise
B.13.349	And as [lef] in lente as out of lente, *alle* tymes yliche.
B.13.365	How I myȝte haue it *al* my wit I caste,
B.13.419	He hateþ to here þerof and *alle* þat it telleþ.
B.14.17	That shal clawe þi cote of *alle* kynnes filþe:
B.14.32	*All* þat lyueþ and lokeþ liflode wolde I fynde
B.14.37	Vitailles of grete vertues for *alle* manere beestes
B.14.45	In menynge þat *alle* men myȝte þe same
B.14.49	A pece of þe Paternoster [and profrede vs *alle*];
B.14.50	And þanne was it fiat voluntas tua [sholde fynde vs *alle*].
B.14.56	In [ondynge] and in handlynge and in *alle* þi fyue wittes,
B.14.116	And blisse to *alle* þat ben, boþe wilde and tame."
B.14.118	That *al* hir lif han lyued in langour and defaute.
B.14.146	And lyuen as lawe techeþ, doon leaute to hem *alle*,
B.14.148	And rewarden *alle* double richesse þat rewful hertes habbeþ.
B.14.153	And *alle* þat doon hir deuoir wel han double hire for hir trauaille,
B.14.166	For *alle* myȝtestow haue maad noon mener þan ooþer
B.14.176	Thoruȝ derþe, þoruȝ droghte, *alle* hir dayes here,
B.14.180	For how þow confortest *alle* creatures clerkes bereþ witnesse:
B.14.183	[To hores, to harlotes, to *alle* maner peple].
B.14.185	And be clene þoruȝ þat cristnyng of *alle* kynnes synne.
B.14.195	And principalliche of *al[l]*e peple but þei be poore of herte.
B.14.196	Ellis is *al* on ydel, al þat euere [we diden],
B.14.196	Ellis is al on ydel, *al* þat euere [we diden],
B.14.199	Ellis is *al* oure labour lost–lo, how men writeþ
B.14.203	The fend folweþ hem *alle* and fondeþ hem to helpe,
B.14.224	And eiþer hateþ ooþer in *alle* maner werkes.
B.14.259	And in þat secte oure saueour saued *al* mankynde.
B.14.260	Forþi [*al*] poore þat pacient is [of pure riȝt] may cleymen,
B.14.264	And for goddes loue leueþ *al* and lyueþ as a beggere.
B.14.266	Hir fader and *alle* hire frendes, and folweþ hir make–
B.14.278	'[*Al* þis] in englissh', quod Pacience, 'it is wel hard to expounen,
B.14.281	Thanne is it good by good skile, *al* þat agasteþ pride.
B.14.298	Wiþ sobretee fram *alle* synne and also ȝit moore;
B.14.302	A frend in *alle* fondynges, [of foule yueles leche],
B.14.303	And for þe [lewde] euere [yliche] a lemman of *alle* clennesse:
B.14.321	Now god þat *alle* good gyueþ graunte his soule reste
B.15.30	And þat is wit and wisdom, þe welle of *alle* craftes;
B.15.33	And whan I loue leelly oure lord and *alle* oþere
B.15.39	How þow coueitest to calle me, now þow knowest [*alle*] my names.
B.15.45	Thow woldest knowe and konne þe cause of *alle* [hire] names,
B.15.48	*Alle* þe sciences vnder sonne and alle þe sotile craftes
B.15.48	Alle þe sciences vnder sonne and *alle* þe sotile craftes
B.15.52	It were ayeins kynde', quod he, 'and *alle* kynnes reson
B.15.53	That any creature sholde konne *al* except crist oone.
B.15.68	Ayein cristes counseil and *alle* clerkes techynge,
B.15.94	Right so out of holi chirche *alle* yueles [spredeþ]
B.15.142	For a wrecchede hous [he held] *al* his lif tyme,
B.15.161	Clerkes kenne me þat crist is in *alle* places
B.15.169	He is glad wiþ *alle* glade and good til alle wikkede
B.15.169	He is glad wiþ alle glade and good til *alle* wikkede
B.15.170	And leneþ and loueþ *alle* þat oure lord made.
B.15.173	*Al* þat men seyn, he leet it sooþ and in solace takeþ,
B.15.174	And *alle* manere meschiefs in myldenesse he suffreþ.
B.15.189	Pride wiþ *al* þe appurtenaunces, and pakken hem togideres,
B.15.214	Ne at Ancres þere a box hangeþ; *alle* swiche þei faiten.
B.15.259	Ac I ne lakke no lif, but lord amende vs *alle*,
B.15.259	In *alle* manere angres, haue þis at herte
B.15.260	That þeiȝ þei suffrede *al* þis, god suffrede for vs moore
B.15.271	In hunger, in hete, in *alle* manere angres.
B.15.296	I sholde noȝt þise seuen daies siggen hem *alle*
B.15.303	[For *al* þe curteisie þat beestes konne þei kidde þat folk ofte,
B.15.344	Forþi I counseille *alle* cristene to conformen hem to charite,
B.15.372	Grammer, þe ground of *al*, bigileþ now children,
B.15.378	[And as vsher vnder hym to fourmen vs *alle*
B.15.381	That sholde konne and knowe *alle* kynnes clergie
B.15.428	*Alle* þat ben at debaat and bedemen were trewe
B.15.438	Elleuene holy men *al* þe world tornede
B.15.440	Sholde *alle* maner men; we han so manye maistres,
B.15.446	And þoruȝ miracles, as men mow rede, *al* þat marche he tornede
B.15.482	That is god of his grace, gyueþ *alle* men blisse.
B.15.484	Where þat his wille is to worshipen vs *alle*,
B.15.504	For *alle* paynymes preieþ and parfitly bileueþ
B.15.518	*Alle* þat wilned and wolde wiþ Inwit bileue it.
B.15.525	And for þe riȝt of *al* þis reume and alle reumes cristene.

B.15.525 And for þe riȝt of al þis reume and *alle* reumes cristene.
B.15.527 He is a forbisene to *alle* bisshopes and a briȝt myrour,
B.15.561 And þo þat han Petres power arn apoisoned *alle*."
B.15.602 And þat his loore be lesynges, and lakken it *alle*,
B.16.11 And to haue my fulle of þat fruyt forsake *a[l]* oþ[er] saule[e].
B.16.21 That Piers þe Plowman *al* þe place me shewed
B.16.41 Wiþ *alle* þe wiles þat he kan, and waggeþ þe roote
B.16.57 For *alle* are þei aliche longe, noon lasse þan ooþer,
B.16.70 Thanne bereþ þe crop kynde fruyt and clennest of *alle*,
B.16.80 And gadrede hem *alle* togideres, boþe grete and smale,
B.16.130 And seide it in sighte of hem *alle* so þat alle herden:
B.16.130 And seide it in sighte of hem alle so þat *alle* herden:
B.16.133 And maken it as muche ouþer moore in *alle* manere poyntes
B.16.163 Iusted in Iherusalem, a ioye to vs *alle*.
B.16.183 That oon dooþ *alle* dooþ and ech dooþ bi his one.
B.16.184 The firste haþ myȝt and maiestee, makere of *alle* þynges;
B.16.189 The light of *al* þat lif haþ a londe and a watre,
B.16.190 Confortour of creatures; of hym comeþ *alle* blisse.
B.16.205 Adam, oure *aller* fader. Eue was of hymselue,
B.16.213 Hym þat first formed al, þe fader of heuene.
B.16.224 Which is þe holy goost of *alle*, and alle is but o god.
B.16.224 Which is þe holy goost of alle, and *alle* is but o god.
B.16.236 Myself and my meynee; and *alle* þat male weere
B.16.252 Seide þat he seiȝ here þat sholde saue vs *alle*,
B.16.267 And bettre wed for us [wage] þan we ben *alle* worþi,
B.16.271 The myght of goddes mercy þat myȝte vs *alle* amende.'
B.17.3 To rule *alle* Reames wiþ; I bere þe writ [riȝt] here.'
B.17.9 [And þus my lettre meneþ; [ye] mowe knowe it *al*].'
B.17.17 [Is] here *alle* þi lordes lawes?' quod I; 'ye, leue al', he seide.
B.17.30 And *alle* þre but o god; þus Abraham me tauȝte;
B.17.38 And siþþe riȝt as myself so louye *alle* peple.
B.17.40 Than he þat gooþ wiþ two staues to sighte of vs *alle*;
B.17.100 Til he haue eten *al* þe barn and his blood ydronke.
B.17.119 And *alle* þat feble and feynte be, þat Feiþ may noȝt teche,
B.17.122 Til I haue salue for *alle* sike; and þanne shal I turne
B.17.123 And come ayein bi þis contree and conforten *alle* sike
B.17.126 *Alle* þat lyuen in Feiþ and folwen his felawes techynge.'
B.17.130 And *alle* þre but o god? þus Abraham me tauȝte;
B.17.132 O god wiþ *al* my good, and alle gomes after
B.17.132 O god wiþ al my good, and *alle* gomes after
B.17.133 Louye hem lik myselue, ac oure lord abouen *alle*.'
B.17.153 *Al* þat þe pawme parceyueþ profitable to feele.
B.17.154 Thus are þei *alle* but oon, as it an hand weere,
B.17.159 And as þe hand halt harde and *alle* þyng faste
B.17.162 [Halt] *al* þe wyde world wiþInne hem þre,
B.17.164 Heuene and helle and *al* þat is þerInne.
B.17.171 *Al* þe myȝt myd hym is in makynge of þynges.
B.17.184 And *alle* [þre] but o god as is myn hand and my fyngres.
B.17.186 *Al* is but an hand, [howso I turne it.
B.17.197 Boþe meue and amende, þouȝ *alle* my fyngres oke.
B.17.214 That *alle* kynne cristene clenseþ of synnes.
B.17.219 To *alle* vnkynde creatures þat coueite to destruye
B.17.250 *Al* þi labour is lost and al þi long trauaille;
B.17.250 Al þi labour is lost and *al* þi long trauaille;
B.17.253 To *alle* vnkynde creatures; crist hymself witnesseþ:
B.17.254 Be vnkynde to þyn euenecristene and *al* þat þow kanst bidde,
B.17.256 And purchace *al* þe pardoun of Pampilon and Rome,
B.17.301 Confesse me and crye his grace, [crist] þat *al* made,
B.17.307 Be raunsoned for his repentaunce þer *alle* reson hym dampneþ.
B.17.311 Thus it fareþ by swich folk þat [folwen] *al* hire [wille],
B.17.317 To amende *al* þat amys is, and his mercy gretter
B.17.318 Than oure wikkede werkes as holy writ telleþ–
B.17.349 For vnkyndenesse is þe contrarie of *alle* kynnes reson.
B.17.353 *Alle* manere men mercy and forȝifnesse,
B.18.3 And yede forþ lik a lorel *al* my lif tyme.
B.18.18 Thanne I frayned at Feiþ what *al* þat fare bymente,
B.18.30 *Al* þat lyueþ [or] lokeþ in londe [or] in watre.
B.18.32 That, for *al* þat deeþ kan do, wiþInne þre daies to walke
B.18.39 And *al* þe court on hym cryde 'crucifige!' sharpe.
B.18.44 And ȝit makin it as muche in *alle* manere poyntes,
B.18.61 The wal waggede and cleef and *al* þe world quaued.
B.18.83 For *alle* þei were vnhardy þat houed [þer] or stode
B.18.98 The gree ȝit haþ he geten for *al* his grete wounde,
B.18.99 For youre champion chiualer, chief knyȝt of yow *alle*,
B.18.107 Which is lif þat oure lord in *alle* lawes acurseþ.
B.18.115 Mercy highte þat mayde, a meke þyng wiþ *alle*,
B.18.154 For of *alle* venymes foulest is þe scorpion;
B.18.159 *Al* þat deeþ [d]ide first þoruȝ þe deueles entisyng,
B.18.161 So shal grace that bigan [*al*] make a good [ende
B.18.176 'My wil is to wende', quod she, 'and welcome hem *alle*
B.18.192 That Adam and Eue and *alle* þat hem suwede
B.18.212 So god þat bigan *al* of his goode wille
B.18.215 The which vnknytteþ *alle* care and comsynge is of reste.

B.18.225 To wite what *alle* wo is [þat woot of] alle ioye.
B.18.225 To wite what alle wo is [þat woot of] *alle* ioye.
B.18.234 That *alle* þe wise of þis world in o wit acor[de]den
B.18.237 And *alle* þe elementȝ', quod þe book, 'herof beren witnesse.
B.18.238 That he was god þat *al* wroȝte þe wolkne first shewed:
B.18.253 To breke and to bete adoun [*alle*] þat ben ayeins [hym],
B.18.254 [And to haue out of helle *alle* þat ben hem].
B.18.256 In *alle* myȝtes of man and his moder gladie,
B.18.257 And conforte *al* his kyn and out of care brynge,
B.18.258 And *al* þe Iewene Ioye vnioynen and vnlouken;
B.18.268 Care and [c]ombraunce is comen to vs *alle*.
B.18.272 That swich a lord and [a] light sholde lede hem *alle* hennes.'
B.18.281 If Adam ete þe Appul *alle* sholde deye
B.18.309 I rede we fle', quod [þe fend], 'faste *alle* hennes,
B.18.311 For þi lesynges, Lucifer, lost is *al* oure praye.
B.18.313 For we leued þi lesynges [we lopen out *alle*;
B.18.315 And *al* oure lordshipe, I leue, a londe and [in helle]:
B.18.318 [The] lord of myght and of ma[y]n and *alle* manere vertues,
B.18.328 For *alle* synfulle soules, to saue þo þat ben worþi.
B.18.331 That if [þei] ete þe Appul *alle* sholde deye,
B.18.334 Wiþ gile þow hem gete ageyn *alle* reson.
B.18.341 And *al* þat man haþ mysdo I man wole amende.
B.18.344 Adam and *al* his issue at my wille herafter;
B.18.350 Thow fettest myne in my place [maugree] *alle* resoun,
B.18.358 And as Adam and *alle* þoruȝ a tree deyden,
B.18.359 Adam and *alle* þoruȝ a tree shul turne to lyue,
B.18.372 And haue out of helle *alle* mennes soules.
B.18.376 For we beþ breþeren of blood, [ac] noȝt in baptisme *alle*.
B.18.377 Ac *alle* þat beþ myne hole breþeren, in blood and in baptisme,
B.18.385 Ther doom to þe deeþ dampneþ *alle* wikked,
B.18.389 I [may] do mercy þoruȝ [my] rightwisnesse and *alle* my wordes trewe,
B.18.396 Ac my rightwisnesse and right shul rulen *al* helle,
B.18.397 And mercy *al* mankynde bifore me in heuene.
B.18.404 Astroth and *al* þe route hidden hem in hernes;
B.18.405 They dorste noȝt loke on oure lord, þe [leeste] of hem *alle*,
B.18.415 And Pees þoruȝ pacience *alle* perils stoppeþ.
B.19.8 And riȝt lik in *alle* [lymes] to oure lord Ies[u].
B.19.17 That *alle* kynne creatures sholden knelen and bowen
B.19.21 For *alle* derke deueles arn adrad to heren it,
B.19.25 Than Iesu or Iesus þat *al* oure Ioye com of?'
B.19.59 To maken *alle* folk free þat folwen his lawe].
B.19.60 And siþ [*alle* hise lele liges largely he yeueþ]
B.19.81 For *alle* þe Aungeles of heuene at his burþe knelede,
B.19.82 And al þe wit of þe world was in þo þre kynges.
B.19.96 Ac for *alle* þise preciouse presentȝ oure lord [prynce] Iesus
B.19.107 Til he hadde *alle* hem þat he for bledde.
B.19.131 And *alle* he heeled and halp þat hym of grace askede;
B.19.153 Verray m[a]n bifore hem *alle* and forþ wiþ hem yede.
B.19.163 Peter parceyued *al* þis and pursued after,
B.19.166 And as *alle* þise wise wyes weren togideres
B.19.174 Deidest and deeþ þoledest and deme shalt vs *alle*,
B.19.181 And lelliche bileue al þis; I loue hem and blesse hem:
B.19.184 [Myght [men] to assoille of *alle* manere synne[s],
B.19.185 To *alle* maner men mercy and forȝifnesse]
B.19.190 And assoille men of *alle* synnes saue of dette one.
B.19.202 In liknesse of a lightnynge he lighte on hem *alle*
B.19.203 And made hem konne and knowe *alle* kynne langages.
B.19.206 Spiritus paraclitus ouerspradde hem *alle*.
B.19.216 To *alle* kynne creatures þat [k]an hi[se] fyue wittes,
B.19.219 For Antecrist and his *al* þe world shul greue
B.19.249 In pouerte and in [pacience] to preie for *alle* cristene.
B.19.250 And *alle* he lered to be lele, and ech a craft loue ooþer,
B.19.251 [Ne no boost ne] debat [be] among hem [*alle*].
B.19.253 '[That *al* craft and konnyng come] of my ȝifte.
B.19.265 And Ioyned to hem oon Iohan, moost gentil of *alle*,
B.19.266 The pris neet of Piers plow, passynge *alle* oþere.
B.19.268 *Al* þat hise oxen eriede þei to harewen after.
B.19.272 And harewede in an handwhile *al* holy Scripture
B.19.291 To suffren *al* þat god sente, siknesse and Angres.
B.19.308 He dide equyte to *alle* eueneforþ his [knowynge].
B.19.315 'Hareweþ *alle* þat konneþ kynde wit by conseil of þise docto[urs],
B.19.327 And of *al* holy writ he made a roof after;
B.19.337 Conscience and *alle* cristene and Cardinale vertues,
B.19.354 *Al* þe world in a while þoruȝ oure wit', quod Pryde.
B.19.355 Quod Conscience to *alle* cristene þo, 'my counseil is to wende
B.19.361 And cryde and comaundede *alle* cristene peple
B.19.364 Conscience comaundede þo *alle* cristene to delue,
B.19.367 Thanne *alle* kynne cristene saue comune wommen
B.19.382 The lord of lust shal be letted *al* þis lente, I hope.
B.19.384 That han laboured lelly *al* þis lenten tyme.
B.19.391 'How?' quod *al* þe comune; 'þow conseillest vs to yelde
B.19.392 *Al* þat we owen any wight er we go to housel?'

B.19.397	By Iesu! for *al* youre Ianglynge, wiþ Spiritus Iusticie,
B.19.425	And Grace þat þow gr[e]dest so of, gyour of *alle* clerkes;
B.19.427	Emperour of *al* þe world, þat alle men were cristene.
B.19.427	Emperour of al þe world, þat *alle* men were cristene.
B.19.428	Inparfit is þat pope þat *al* [peple] sholde helpe
B.19.439	As for a trewe tidy man *alle* tymes ylike,
B.19.440	And worshiped he be þat wro3te *al*, boþe good and wikke,
B.19.456	And *alle* þo faire vertues as vices þei semeþ.
B.19.461	*Al* þat myn Auditour or ellis my Styward
B.19.470	Ye ben but membres and I aboue *alle*.
B.19.471	And siþ I am youre *aller* heed I am youre aller heele
B.19.471	And siþ I am youre aller heed I am youre *aller* heele
B.19.474	Of Spiritus Iusticie for I Iugge yow *alle*.
B.20.34	[God] gouerneþ *alle* goode vertues.
B.20.40	And god as his grete Ioye goostliche he lefte
B.20.49	Siþ he þat wro3te *al* þe world was wilfulliche nedy,
B.20.53	Antecrist cam þanne, and *al* þe crop of truþe
B.20.60	And *al* þe Couent cam to welcome [a] tyraunt
B.20.61	And *alle* hise as wel as hym, saue oonly fooles;
B.20.64	And a fals fend Antecrist ouer *alle* folk regnede.
B.20.66	Defyed *alle* falsnesse and folk þat it vsede;
B.20.78	And crye we [on] *al* þe comune þat þei come to vnitee
B.20.89	Wiþ deeþ þat is dredful to vndo vs *alle*!
B.20.100	Deeþ cam dryuynge after and *al* to duste passhed
B.20.112	Amonges *alle* manere men, wedded and vnwedded,
B.20.130	And [knokked] Conscience in Court afore hem *alle*;
B.20.135	And ouertilte *al* his truþe wiþ 'tak þis vp amendement'.
B.20.151	And kille *a[l]* erþely creatur[e] saue conscience oone.
B.20.208	'Lerne to loue', quod kynde, 'and leef *alle* oþere.'
B.20.243	And curteisliche conforted hem and called in *alle* freres,
B.20.244	And seide, 'sires, sooþly welcome be ye *alle*
B.20.254	That in mesure god made *alle* manere þynges,
B.20.262	*Alle* oþere in bataille ben yholde Brybours,
B.20.264	Monkes and Moniales and *alle* men of Religion,
B.20.276	That *alle* þynges vnder heuene ou3te to ben in comune.
B.20.283	*Alle* þat ben hir parisshens penaunce enioigne,
B.20.299	Of *alle* taletelleris and titeleris in ydel.
B.20.320	Saue Piers þe Plowman þat haþ power ouer *alle*
B.20.341	'Ye? go þi gate!' quod Pees, 'by god! for *al* þi phisik,
B.20.365	[And] for [hem] þat ye ben holden to *al* my lif tyme,
B.20.372	That is þe souerayn[e] salue for *alle* [synnes of kynde].
C.Pr.10	*Al* þe welthe of the world and þe wo bothe,
C.Pr.13	*Al* y say slepynge as y shal [3ow] telle.
C.Pr.20	Of *alle* manere [of] men, þe mene and þe [riche],
C.Pr.50	And hadde leue to lye [*al* here lyf aftir].
C.Pr.56	I fonde þer Freris, *alle* þe foure ordres,
C.Pr.68	[And] sayde þat hymself myhte assoylen hem *alle*
C.Pr.100	*Al* þe world wot wel hit myghte nou3t be trewe
C.Pr.104	That *al* þe world be [þe] wors, as holy writ telleth.
C.Pr.121	God shal take vengeaunce on *alle* suche prestis
C.Pr.145	Kynde wytt and þe comune contreued *alle* craftes
C.Pr.173	'And yf we groche of his game a wol greue vs [*alle*],
C.Pr.192	*Alle* þe[e] route of ratones to þis resoun assentide;
C.Pr.194	Ther ne was [raton in] þe route, for *al* þe reame of Fraunce,
C.Pr.196	Ne hanged it aboute his hals *al* yngelond to wynne;
C.Pr.198	And leten here labour ylost and *al* here longe study.
C.Pr.200	Strok forth sturnely and stod byfore hem *alle*
C.Pr.203	To crache vs and *alle* oure kynde thogh we crope vnder benches;
C.Pr.224	*Al* y say slepynge, as 3e shal here [a]ftur,
C.Pr.235	[*Al* þis y say slepynge and seuene sythes more].
C. 1.14	For he is fader of fayth and formor of *alle*;
C. 1.17	Wherfore he hette þe elementis to helpe 3ow *alle* tymes
C. 1.34	*Al* is nat good to þe gost þat þe gott ascuth
C. 1.50	For ri3tfulliche resoun sholde reule 3ow *alle*
C. 1.60	Fader of falshede fond hit firste of *alle*.
C. 1.65	He is lettere of loue and lyeth *alle* tymes;
C. 1.75	[To] leue on me and loue me *al* thy lyf tyme.'
C. 1.81	'When *alle* tresores ben tried treuthe is þe beste;
C. 1.110	Ther he faylede and ful and his felawes *alle*;
C. 1.128	Ac lucifer lowest lith of hem *alle*;
C. 1.130	And *alle* þat worchen þat wikked is wenden thei sholle
C. 1.132	And *alle* þat han wel ywrouthe wende þey sholle
C. 1.142	For to louye thy lord leuest of *alle*,
C. 1.162	And þat falleth to þe fader þat formede vs *alle*,
C. 1.164	Mekeliche for oure mysdedes to amende vs *alle*.
C. 1.189	Vnkynde to here kyn and to *alle* cristene,
C. 1.196	"Date & dabitur vobis, y dele 3ow *alle*."
C. 1.198	That conforteth *alle* carefole acombred with synne.
C. 1.199	So loue is lecche of lyf and lysse of *alle* payne
C. 1.202	"Whenne *alle* tresores ben tried treuthe is þe beste."
C. 2.12	On *alle* here fyue fyngeres ful richeliche yrynged,
C. 2.32	That neuere lyede ne lauhede in *al* his lyf tyme;
C. 2.49	Knowe hem wel yf þou kanst and kepe the fro hem *alle*
C. 2.57	*Al* þe riche retenaunce þat ro[t]eth hem o fals lyuynge
C. 2.77	'*Al* þat loueth and byleueth vp lykyng of mede,
C. 2.96	With *al* þe lordschip of leccherye in lenghe and in Brede,
C. 2.101	*Al* day to drynke at diuerse tauernes,
C. 2.111	With *alle* þe [p]urtinaunc[e] of purgatorye and þe peyne of helle.'
C. 2.122	And ar this weddyng be wrouhte wo to *al* 3oure consayle!
C. 2.175	And leten somne *alle* seggus in vche syde aboute,
C. 2.176	And bade hem *alle* be bowen, beggares and othere,
C. 2.195	And maketh of lyare a lang cart to lede *al* this othere,
C. 2.198	And mede in þe myddes and *al* this me[y]n[e] aftur.
C. 2.201	Ac gyle was forgoere to gyen *al* th[e] peple,
C. 2.204	And prykede forth on pacience and passed hem *alle*
C. 2.209	Y wolde be awreke [o]n tho wreches and on here werkes *alle*,
C. 2.210	And do hem hange by þe halse and *alle* þat hem maynteyneth.
C. 2.212	But riht as þe lawe loketh lat falle on hem *alle*.'
C. 2.217	And bryngeth mede to me maugrey hem *alle*.
C. 2.222	And bad falsnesse to fle and his feres *alle*.
C. 2.252	*Alle* fledde for fere and flowen into hernes;
C. 3.1	Now is mede þe mayde and na mo of hem *alle*
C. 3.8	Y wol forgyue here *al* gultes, so me god helpe.'
C. 3.20	For *al* Consiences cast and craft, as y trowe.'
C. 3.21	Myldeliche mede thenne mercyede hem *alle*
C. 3.41	[And] Falshede yfonde the *al* this fourty wyntur,
C. 3.60	And [a] cours of kynde wherof we comen *alle*.
C. 3.68	Ac god to *alle* good folk suche grauynge defendeth,
C. 3.104	*Al* this haue we seyn, þat som tyme thorw a breware
C. 3.107	Ful adoun and forbrent forth *alle* þe rewe.
C. 3.116	Of *alle* suche sullers seluer to take
C. 3.126	That fuyr shal falle and forbrenne *al* to blew aysches
C. 3.144	That *alle* [women, wantowen], shal [be] war [by] þe one
C. 3.145	And bitterliche banne the and *alle* þat bereth thy name
C. 3.169	As comyn as þe cartway to knaues and to *alle*,
C. 3.189	To holde lemmanes and lotebyes *al* here lyfdayes
C. 3.202	And *al* þe comune in care and in coueytise;
C. 3.212	That *al* þe witt of the world is woxe into Gyle.
C. 3.235	Bothe here and elleswhere, in *alle* kyne londes.
C. 3.252	To helpe heyliche *alle* his oste or elles graunte
C. 3.253	*Al* þat his men may wynne, do ther[mid] here beste.
C. 3.267	To aliens, to *alle* men, to honoure hem with 3eftes;
C. 3.269	Emperours and Erles and *alle* manere lordes
C. 3.271	The pope and *alle* prelates presentes vnderfongen
C. 3.280	*Alle* kyn crafty men crauen mede for here prentises;
C. 3.339	That [is] þe gyft þat god gyueth to *alle* lele lyuynge,
C. 3.351	And take hym for his trauaile *al* þat treuthe wolde,
C. 3.354	That is god, the ground of *al*, a graciouse antecedent.
C. 3.362	Acordeth in *alle* kyndes with his antecedent.
C. 3.364	*Alle* kyn kynde to knowe and to folowe
C. 3.372	To acorde in *alle* kynde and in alle kyn nombre,
C. 3.372	To acorde in alle kynde and in *alle* kyn nombre,
C. 3.373	Withouten coest and care and *alle* kyn trauayle.
C. 3.377	That here loue to his lawe Thorw *al* þe lond acorde.
C. 3.385	Thow the kyng and þe comune *al* the coest hadde.
C. 3.386	Such inparfit peple repreueth *alle* resoun
C. 3.397	But þat *alle* maner men, wymmen and childrene
C. 3.415	That agag of amalek and *alle* his leege peple
C. 3.419	Haste the with *al* thyn oste to þe lond of Amalek
C. 3.420	And *al* þat leueth on þat lond oure [lord] wol þat thow sle hit;
C. 3.422	Mebles and vnmebles, man and *al* [thynges],
C. 3.424	For eny mede of money *al* that thow myhte [fynde],
C. 3.430	And *al* [h]is [sede] for þat synne shentfolyche ende.
C. 3.432	That god [hated hym] for euere and *alle* [his] eyres aftur.
C. 3.441	And dauid shal be ydyademed and [d]aunte *alle* oure enemyes
C. 3.458	For *alle* þat bereth baslard, br[ode] swerd oþer launce,
C. 3.465	Here sauter and here seuene p[s]almes for *alle* synful preyen;
C. 3.474	*Al* shal be but [o] couert and o [buyrne] be Iustice.
C. 4.76	Consience knoweth hit wel and *al* þe Comune trewe.'
C. 4.98	So *alle* my claymes ben quyt by so þe kyng assente.'
C. 4.109	Til lordes and ladies louen *alle* treuthe
C. 4.110	And hatien *al* harlotrie to heren oþer to mouthen hit;
C. 4.119	And til þe kynges consayl be *alle* comune profit
C. 4.121	For *alle* manere men þat me fynt neodefole;
C. 4.125	And *alle* Rome rennares for ruyflares in Fraunce
C. 4.151	Ac *al* ryhtful recordede þat resoun treuthe sayde,
C. 4.174	Y wol haue leutee for my lawe and late be *al* 3oure iangl[ing]
C. 4.178	And *alle* 3oure lege l[e]des to lede thus euene.'
C. 4.180	'But [y] reule thus *alle* reumes reuet[h] me my syhte,
C. 4.181	And brynge *alle* men to bowe withouten bittere wounde,
C. 4.182	Withouten mercement or manslauht amende *alle* reumes.'
C. 4.186	And Consience in *alle* my Courtes be a[s] kynges Iustice.'
C. 4.193	More then *alle* thy marchauntes or thy mytrede Bysshopes
C. 4.195	The kyng comaundede Consience tho to congeye *alle* his offeceres
C. 5.59	For hit ben eyres of heuene *alle* þat ben ycrouned
C. 5.88	Fiat voluntas dei fynt vs *alle* thynges.'

C. 5.101   That *alle* tymes of my tyme to profit shal turne.'
C. 5.114   Resoun reuerentliche tofore *al* þe reume prechede
C. 5.122   That dedly synne ar domesday shal fordon hem *alle*.
C. 5.125   How resoun radde *al* the reume to heuene.
C. 5.139   And so wrot the wyse to wyssen vs *alle*:
C. 5.147   The reule of *alle* religious rihtful and obedient:
C. 5.167   Ac ȝe leten ȝow *alle* as lordes, ȝoure lond lyth so brode.
C. 5.168   Ac þer shal come a kyng and confesse ȝow *alle*
C. 5.183   And comuners [to] acorde in *alle* kyn treuthe.
C. 5.185   That o wit and o wil *al* ȝoure wardes kepe.
C. 5.190   Is cause of *alle* combraunc[e] to confounde a reume.'
C. 5.193   Amonges *alle* kyne kynges ouer cristene peple.
C. 5.194   'Comaunde þat *alle* confessours þat eny kyng shryueth
C. 5.196   Of *alle* maner actions and eche man loue other.
C. 6.5   And bihyhte to hym þat vs *alle* made
C. 6.11   Of *alle* þat y haue hated in myn herte.'
C. 6.13   And shryue the sharpeliche and shak of *alle* pruyde.'
C. 6.26   In *alle* [manere] maneres my name to be knowe;
C. 6.39   In *alle* kyne couent contreuede how y myhte
C. 6.59   *Al* [y] wolde þat men wiste when it to pruyde souneth.
C. 6.64   And cryede 'mea culpa', corsynge *alle* his enemyes;
C. 6.80   That taketh me *al* [a] twelmonthe til þat y despise
C. 6.110 Inpacient in *alle* penaunc[e] and pleyned, as hit were,
C. 6.114 In *alle* manere angres þat y hadde or felede.
C. 6.115 Amonges *alle* manere men my dwellyng is som tyme,
C. 6.126 Or *alle* riche and ryde, reste shal y nat, wrathe,
C. 6.138 Til "thow lixt!" and "thow lixt!" be lady ouer hem *alle*;
C. 6.142 That *alle* ladyes me lot[h]eth þat louyet[h] eny worschipe.
C. 6.162 *Al* þat y wiste wykked by eny of oure couent
C. 6.163 Y cou[ȝ]e hit vp in oure Cloystre þat *al* þe couent woet hit.'
C. 6.183 As leef in lente as out of lente, *alle* tymes ylyche,'
C. 6.239 Vsedest [thow] euere vsurye in *al* thy lyf tyme?'
C. 6.256 For þe pope with *alle* his pentauncers power hem fayleth
C. 6.264 How y myhte haue hit *al* my wit y caste
C. 6.287 Were y a frere, in good fayth, for *al* þe gold on erthe
C. 6.295 Til thow haue ymad thy myhte to alle restitucioun.
C. 6.296 For *alle* that hauen of thy good, haue god my treuthe.
C. 6.310 *Al-þat-y-wikkedly-wan-sithen-y-witte-hadde*:
C. 6.329 [And lepe wiþ hym ouer lond *al* his lif tyme]
C. 6.334 For *al* the wrecchednesse of this world and wikkede dedes
C. 6.336 And deyede with a drop water; so doth *alle* synnes
C. 6.337 Of *alle* manere men þat [mid] goode wille
C. 6.401 That *alle* þat herde þ[at] hor[n] helde here nose aftur
C. 6.415 With *al* þe wo of th[e] world his wyf and his wenche
C. 6.417 And aftur al this exces he hadde an accidie.
C. 6.424 'Thow lord [þat] aloft art and *alle* lyues shope.
C. 6.437 Of my luyther ly[uyng] in *al* my lyf tyme.'
C. 6.441 And ȝut haue y [ha]ted here *al* my lyf tyme.'
C. 7.24   Th[en] *al* þat euere Mark made, Matheu, Iohn or lucas
C. 7.25   Vigilies and fastyngdayes y can forȝeten hem *alle*
C. 7.79   He hateth to here thereof and *alle* þat þerof carpeth.
C. 7.119 Tho was repentaunce aredy and redde hem *alle* to knele:
C. 7.120 'Y shal byseke for *alle* synnefole oure sauiour of grace
C. 7.121 To Amende vs of oure mysdedes, do mercy to vs *alle*.
C. 7.124 And sethe soffredes[t] hym to synege, a sykenesse to vs *alle*,
C. 7.139 And *al* þat mark hath ymade, Matheu, Ion and lucas
C. 7.149 Haue reuthe of *alle* these rybaudes þat repenten hem sore
C. 7.153 That *alle* seyntes for synfol songen with dauid:
C. 7.189 [I]ch haue ybe his foloware *al* this fourty wynter
C. 7.191 In *alle* kyne craftes þat he couthe deuise
C. 7.206 ȝe mote go thorw mekenesse, *alle* men and wommen,
C. 7.208 That ȝe louye hym [as] lord leely aboue *alle*.
C. 7.212 Otherwyse then ȝe wolden they wrouhte ȝow *alle* tymes.
C. 7.216 And ȝe shal lepe þe lihtloker *al* ȝoure lyf tyme:
C. 7.234 And *al* þe wallyng is aȝen þat y wil ne sholde hit wynne,
C. 7.237 And *alle* þe hous[es] been yheled, halles and chaumbres,
C. 7.250 That Adam and Eue aȝenes vs *alle* shette:
C. 7.258 In thyne hole herte to herborwe *alle* trewe
C. 7.259 And fynde *alle* manere fode to here soules
C. 7.276 Noen of hem *alle* helpe may in betere
C. 7.281 Hit is ful hard, be myn heued, eny of ȝow *alle*
C. 7.287 'ȝus!' quod [Perus] þe [plouhman], and pokede hem *alle* to gode,
C. 7.288 'Mercy is a mayden there hath myhte ouer hem *alle*
C. 7.289 And she is sib to *alle* synfole and here sone bothe
C. 8.17   And *alle* manere men þat by þe molde is susteyned
C. 8.25   And labory for tho thow louest *al* my lyf tyme,
C. 8.57   And wende with *alle* tho þat wolden lyue in treuthe.'
C. 8.58   [He] caste on his clothes of *alle* kyn craftes;
C. 8.66   And *alle* þat helpen me [to] erye or elles to wedy
C. 8.69   And *alle* kyne crafty men þat conne lyue in treuthe,
C. 8.86   Lat god yworthe with *al*, as holy wryt techeth:
C. 8.89   *Al* þat they hoten, y hote; heiliche thow soffre hem
C. 8.96   He shal haue my soule þat *alle* soules made

C. 8.104 And men[g]e me in his memorie amongus *alle* cristene.
C. 8.110 Y wol worschipe þerwith treuthe *al* my lyue
C. 8.167 'Now, by Crist!' quod [Peres] the [plouhman], 'y shal apayre ȝow *alle*,'
C. 8.174 Þat a lokede lyke a l[a]nterne *al* his lyf aftur;
C. 8.191 And freres of *alle* þe fyue ordres, alle for fere of hunger.
C. 8.197 Tho was [Peres] proud and potte hem *alle* a werke
C. 8.200 In *alle* kyne trewe craft þat man couthe deuyse.
C. 8.204 Tho hadde [Peres] pitee vppon *alle* pore peple
C. 8.215 'Ther is no fi[al] loue with this folk for *al* here fayre speche
C. 8.216 And hit are my blody bretherne for god bouhte vs *alle*.
C. 8.218 And helpe hem of *alle* thyng ay as hem nedeth.
C. 8.231 And *alle* manere [of] men þat thow myhte aspye
C. 8.235 'Y wolde nat greue [god],' quod Peres, 'for *al* þe good on erthe!
C. 8.250 And ledares for here laboryng ouer *al* þe lordes godes;
C. 8.253 Byno[m] hym *al* þat he hadde and ȝaf hit to his felawe
C. 8.259 "Yblessed be *al* tho that here bylyue biswynketh
C. 8.268 Of *al* a woke worche nat, so oure wombe greueth.'
C. 8.281 In *al* manere ese in Abrahammus lappe.
C. 8.283 *Alle* þat gr[eden at] thy gate for godes loue aftur fode
C. 8.288 Til *alle* thyne nedy neyhbores haue noen ymaked.
C. 8.315 *Alle* þe pore peple tho pesecoddes fe[tt]e;
C. 8.318 Hunger eet *al* in haste and askede aftur more.
C. 8.337 And thenne a corseth þe kyng and *alle* þe kynges Iustices
C. 9.6   And *alle* þat holpe hym to erye, to sette or to sowe
C. 9.20   To be [peres] to þe apostles *alle* peple to reule
C. 9.43   *Alle* þe peple hadde pardon ynow þat parfitliche lyuede.
C. 9.57   Thise foure sholde be fre to *alle* folk þat hit nede[th].
C. 9.58   *Alle* libbyng laborers þat lyuen with here handes
C. 9.102 For *alle* þat haen here hele and here yesyhte
C. 9.128 And *alle* manere munstrals, me woet wel þe sothe,
C. 9.131 Men suffreth *al* þat suche sayen and in solace taketh
C. 9.166 For hit blameth *all* beggarie, be ȝe ful certayn.
C. 9.179 And *alle* pore pacient apayed of goddes sonde,
C. 9.188 And *alle* holy Eremytes haue shal þe same;
C. 9.191 *Al* þat holy Ermytes hatede and despisede,
C. 9.202 *Al* they holy Ermytes were of heye kynne,
C. 9.220 For holy churche hoteth *alle* manere peple
C. 9.256 The cause of *al* this caytiftee cometh of many bischopes
C. 9.261 Thy berkeres aren a[l] blynde that bringeth forth thy lombren:
C. 9.265 Thy shep ben ner *al* shabbede; the wolf shyt wolle:
C. 9.284 And y byhynde hem bothe byheld *alle* þe bulle.
C. 9.310 And the eleuene s[t]erres haylsede hym *alle*;
C. 9.318 *Al* this maketh me on meteles to studie
C. 9.340 And comen *alle* bifore Crist acountes to ȝelde,
C. 9.344 Thow we be founden in the fraternite of *alle* fyue ordres
C. 9.347 Forthy y consayle *alle* cristene to crye god mercy
C.10.2   *Alle* a somur seson for to seke dowel
C.10.56 'Y haue no kynde kno[w]yng,' [quod y], 'to conseyue *al* this speche
C.10.67 And merueilousliche me mette amyddes *al* þat blisse.
C.10.82 Dobeth doth *al* this Ac ȝut he doth more.
C.10.84 And helpeth *alle* men of þat he may spare.
C.10.85 The bagges and þe bigerdeles, he hath [b]roken hem *alle*
C.10.104 Crounede oen to be a kyng to kepen vs *alle*
C.10.105 And reule *alle* reumes by here thre wittes
C.10.110 Of dowel and dobet and ho doth best of *alle*.'
C.10.143 Ac þe constable of þ[e] Castel þat kepeth hem *alle*
C.10.148 And sire go[dfray] go-wel, grete lordes *alle*.
C.10.152 'Kynde is creatour,' quod wit, 'of [alle] kyne thynges,
C.10.153 Fader and formour of *al* þat forth groweth
C.10.156 Angeles and *alle* thyng aren at his wille;
C.10.168 For they louyeth and bylyueth *al* here lyf tyme
C.10.169 On catel more then on kynde that *alle* kyne thynges wrouhte,
C.10.171 Inwit and *alle* wittes closed been þerynne:
C.10.180 Of þ[e] blessed baptist bifore *alle* his gestes.
C.10.188 Ac thenne dede we *alle* wel, and wel bet ȝut, to louye
C.10.191 That *alle* landes loueden and in on lawe bileuede.
C.10.220 *Alle* þat come of Caym Caytyue[s] were euere
C.10.230 *Alle* sholle deye for his dedes by dales and hulles
C.10.255 For y am via & veritas and may auauncen *alle*."
C.10.278 Forthy y conseyle *alle* cristene coueyte neuere be wedded
C.10.297 Awayten and wasten *alle* þat they cacche mowe;
C.10.305 Helen and helpen, is dobest of *alle*.
C.11.10 Then *al* þe preciouse perye þat eny prince weldeth.
C.11.13 More then holynesse or hendenesse or *al* þat seyntes techeth.
C.11.23 The sauter saith þe same of *alle* suche ryche:
C.11.45 Lytel loueth he þat lord þat lente hym *al* þat blisse
C.11.57 In religion and in *al* þe reume amongus riche and pore
C.11.92 *Alle* kynne kunnynges and comsynges of dowel,
C.11.116 Logyk y lerned here and *al* þe lawe aftur
C.11.117 And *alle* þe musons in musyk y made here to knowe.
C.11.122 Of *alle* kyne craftes y contreuede toles,
C.11.144 And *al* þat holi churche herof can þe lere

C.11.152 And *alle* thre bote o god, and herof he made
C.11.154 *Alle* þe Clerkes vnder Crist ne couthe this assoile
C.11.155 Bote thus hit bilongeth to bileue *alle* þat liketh dowel.
C.11.180 That lede þe wol to lykynge *Al* thy lyf tyme.'
C.11.199 Were hit *al* soth þat 3e seyn, thow scripture and thow clergie,
C.11.221 Thenne wrouhte [we] vnwysly for *alle* 3oure wyse techynge.
C.11.225 Thenne *al* þe kynde wyt þat 3e can bothe and kunnyng of 3oure bokes.
C.11.243 Of holy kirke þat sholde kepe *alle* cristene soules
C.11.245 Bote holy churche, herborw to *alle* þat ben yblessed.
C.11.253 That vnlawefulliche hadde ylyued *al* his lyf tyme
C.11.258 A robbare was yraunsomed rather then thei *alle*,
C.11.278 Connyng and clergie to conclude [hem] *alle*".
C.11.298 Of *al* þat they haen had of hym þat is here maistre.
C.11.305 *All* þat treuth attacheth and testifieth for gode
C.11.310 Til Concupiscencia Carnis acorded til *al* my werkes.
C.12.2   'That wit shal turne to wrechednesse for wil hath *al* his wille!'
C.12.13   And thenne was fortune my foo for *al* her fayre biheste
C.12.17   To restitute resonably for *al* vnrihtfole wynnynge.
C.12.35   Thyng þat *al* þe world woet wherfore sholdest thow spare
C.12.54   For crist clepede vs *alle*, come yf we wolde,
C.12.58   'Thenne may *alle* cristene come,' [quod y], 'and clayme þer entre
C.12.73   Mercy *al* [to] amende and mekenesse her folowe;
C.12.79   That *al* þe cristendoem vnde[r] Crist ne myhte me crache fro [helle]
C.12.91   And on Troianus treuthe to thenke *alle* tyme[s] in 3oure lyue
C.12.94   Or eny science vnder sonne, the seuene ars and *alle*–
C.12.95   Bote loue and leute hem lede ylost is *al* þe tyme
C.12.118 And euery man helpe other for hennes shal we *al*
C.12.129 And *al* was ensample, sothly, to vs synfole here
C.12.131 And pacient as pilgrimes for pilgrimes are we *alle*.
C.12.142 And *alle* þe wyse þat euere were, by auhte y can aspye,
C.12.151 The which is þe cornel of confort for *alle* cristene soules.
C.12.164 *Al* þat thow has[t] here hastly go and sulle hit;
C.12.167 Forsaek *al* and sue me and so is th[e] beste:"
C.12.168 3ut conseileth Crist in commen vs *al*:
C.12.171 And *al* þat þe world wolde and my will folowe:
C.12.177 Preueth pacient pouerte prince of *alle* vertues.
C.12.178 And by þe grayn þat groweth god vs *all* techeth
C.12.186 At the laste launceth vp whereby we lyuen *all*.
C.12.191 As lynsed, leksed and lentesedes *all*
C.12.230 So of rychesse ope rychesse ariste *alle* vices.
C.12.245 So coueytise of catel was combraunce to hem *alle*.
C.13.3   Oure prince iesu pouerte chees and his apostles *alle*
C.13.19   *Alle* his sorwe to solace thorw that song turnede
C.13.20   And Iob bykam as a iolyf man and *al* his ioye newe.
C.13.22   And brouhte hem *all* aboue þat in bale rotede!
C.13.67   Aren *alle* acountable to crist and to þe kyng of heuene,
C.13.71   *Alle* maner men [in] meschief yfalle
C.13.78   As Crist hymsulf comaundeth *alle* cristene peple:
C.13.96   As *al* þat þe ryche may rayme and rihtfuly dele
C.13.98   As þe ryche man for *al* his mone, and more as by þe gospell:
C.13.99   So pore and pacient parfitest lyf is of *alle*.
C.13.143 Resoun y sey sothly sewe *alle* bestes
C.13.147 Males drow hem to males *a[l* mour]nynge by hemsulue
C.13.180 Was þat y seyh resoun sewen *alle* bestes
C.13.198 He myhte amende in a myntewhile *al* þat [mys]standeth
C.13.199 Ac he soffreth in ensaumple þat we sholde soffren *alle*.
C.13.220 'To se moche and soffre *al*, certes, is dowel.'
C.14.11   Clerkes þat conne *al*, y hope they can do bettere;
C.14.53   Come for *al* his kynde wit thorw cristendoem to be saued,
C.14.63   And *all* lewede þat leide hand þeron loren lyf aftir.
C.14.64   Forthy y conseyle *all* creatures no cler[gie] to despice
C.14.79   For *al* here kynde knowyng cam bote of diuerse syhtes,
C.14.99   Why y haue tolde [the] *al* þis, y toek ful gode hede
C.14.109 'He þat can nat swymmen,' y sayde, 'hit semeth to *alle* wittes.'
C.14.133 And god is ay gracious to *alle* þat gredeth to hym
C.14.155 *Alle* þe Clerkes vnder Crist ne couthe [þe skyle] assoile:
C.14.162 And Adam and Eue and *alle* othere bestes
C.14.188 And to lele and lyfholy þat loueth *alle* treuthe.
C.14.199 'Alle* thise clerkes,' quod y tho, 'þat [o]n crist leuen
C.14.217 For *al* worth as god wol;' and þerwith he vanschede.
C.15.8   And vansche *alle* my vertues and my fayre lotus;
C.15.13   And how þis coueytyse ouercome *al* kyne sectes,
C.15.20   For *alle* a wisseth and 3eueth wit þat walketh oþer crepeth.
C.15.36   Concience knewe h[y]m wel and welcomede hem *all*;
C.15.44   Of Austyn, of Ambrose, of *alle* þe foure euaangeli[st]es:
C.15.59   Thenne cam contricion þat hadd coked for hem *all*
C.15.71   *Alle* þat coueyte[d] to come to eny kyne ioye,
C.15.79   For *alle* be we brethrene thogh we be diuerse yclothed.
C.15.89   Þat in þ[e] mawe of þat maystre *alle* þo metes were
C.15.90   Bothe disches and dobelares with *alle* þe deyntees aftur.
C.15.131 *Alle* kyne connynges and *alle* kyne craftes

C.15.131 *Alle* kyne connynges and *alle* kyne craftes
C.15.135 And preueth by puyre skile inparfyt *alle* thynges–
C.15.154 Y wolde, and y will hadde, wynnen *all* fraunce
C.15.166 To haue *alle* londes at thy likyng and the here lord make
C.15.167 And maistre of *alle* here mebles and of here moneye aftur,
C.15.168 The kyng and *alle* þe comune and clergie to þe loute
C.15.171 *Al* th[e] wit of this world and wyhte menne strenghe
C.15.194 Peres prentys þe plouhman, *alle* peple to conforte.'
C.15.196 'Hastow vsed or haunted *al* thy lyf tyme?"
C.15.221 In his mouthe mercy and amende vs *all*:
C.15.235 Hit am y þat fynde *alle* folke and fram hunger saue
C.15.243 In menynge þat *alle* men myhte þe same
C.15.247 A pece of þe paternoster and profred vs *all*.
C.15.249 And thenne was hit fiat voluntas tua þat sholde fynde vs *alle*.
C.15.255 In [ond]ynge and [in] handlynge [and] in *alle* thy fyue wittes,
C.15.275 And þat is charite, chaumpion chief of *all* vertues,
C.15.276 And þat is pore pacient *alle* perelles to soffre.'
C.15.292 And blisse to *all* þat been, bothe wilde and tame."
C.15.294 That *al* here lyf haen lyued in langour and defaute.
C.15.301 Many man hath his ioye here for *al* here wel dedes
C.16.18   That *al* here lyf leden in lownesse and in pouerte.
C.16.22   Riht so haue reuthe on [thy renkes] *alle*
C.16.23   And amende vs [of] thy mercy and make vs *alle* meke,
C.16.26   And confessioun to kulle *alle* kyne synnes
C.16.28   And these ben dowel and dobet and dobest of *alle*.
C.16.31   And [operis satisfaccio] for soules paieth and *alle* synnes quyteth.
C.16.32   Thise thre withoute doute tholieth *alle* pouerte
C.16.34   Ho doth wel or bet or beste aboue *alle*;
C.16.37   Elles is al an ydel *al* oure lyuynge here,
C.16.40   Elles is *alle* oure labour loest–loo how men writeth
C.16.44   The fend followeth hem *alle* and fondeth hem to helpe
C.16.99   And in þat secte oure saueour saued *al* mankynde.
C.16.100 Forthy *alle* pore þat pacient is of puyr rihte may claymen
C.16.104 And for goddes loue leueth *al* and lyueth as a beggare.
C.16.106 Here fader and *alle* here frendes and goth forth with here paramours.
C.16.117 'Y can nat construe *al* this,' quod Actiua vita.
C.16.122 *Al* þat may potte of pruyde in place þer he regneth;
C.16.134 With sobrete fro *alle* synnes and also 3ut more;
C.16.138 And frende in *alle* fondynges and of foule eueles leche:
C.16.152 And sobrete 3eueth here swete drynke and solaceth here in *all* angrys.
C.16.156 Now god þat *al* [good] gyueth graunte his soule reste
C.16.190 And þat is wit and wysdoem, the welle of *alle* craftes;
C.16.195 And when y louye lelly oure lord and *alle* oþere
C.16.201 How þou coueytest to calle me, now þou knowest *al* my namus.
C.16.207 Thow woldest knowe and conne þe cause of *all* here names
C.16.210 *Alle* þe sciences vnder sonne and alle þe sotil craftes
C.16.210 Alle þe sciences vnder sonne and *alle* þe sotil craftes
C.16.214 Hit were a3eyns kynde,' quod he, 'and *alle* kyne resoun
C.16.215 That eny creature sholde conne *al* excepte crist one.
C.16.246 Riht [so] oute of holy churche *al* euel spredeth
C.16.261 Of vsererus, of hores, of *alle* euel wynnynges,
C.16.295 For thogh me souhte *alle* þe sektes of susturne and brethurne
C.16.302 He is glad with *alle* glade as gurles þat lawhen alle
C.16.302 He is glad with alle glade as gurles þat lawhen *alle*
C.16.311 *Alle* sekness[e] and sorwes for solac[e] he hit taketh
C.16.312 And *alle* manere meschiefs as munstracie of heuene.
C.16.320 Oen aperis-tu-manum *alle* thynges hym fyndeth;
C.16.327 What sorwe he soffrede in ensaumple of vs *alle*
C.16.332 Pruyde with *alle* [þe] purtinaunces and pakketh hem togyderes
C.16.349 And cheef charite with hem and chaste *al* here lyu[e].
C.17.18   And wan with his handes *al* þat hym nedede.
C.17.33   In tokenynge þat trewe man *alle* tymes sholde
C.17.36   Toke lyflode of luyther wynnynges in *all* here lyf tyme.
C.17.50   And conforte *alle* cristene wolde holy [kirke] amende.
C.17.108 Gramer, þe grounde of *al*, bigileth nouthe childrene,
C.17.128 *Alle* kyne cristene cleuynge on o will,
C.17.134 And o god þat *al* bygan with gode herte they honoureth
C.17.141 Loue god for he is goed and grounde of *alle* treuthe;
C.17.144 For when *alle* frendes faylen and fleen away in deynge
C.17.170 Be maistre ouer *alle* tho men and on this manere a wrouhte:
C.17.224 And [tho] þat haen petres power aren apo[y]sened *alle*."
C.17.237 *Alle* londes into loue And þat in lytel tyme;
C.17.238 The pope with *alle* prestes pax vobis sholde make
C.17.240 Hadde *al* surie as hymsulue wolde and sarrasines in equitee.
C.17.242 Bote thorw pacience and priue gyle he was prince ouer hem *all*.
C.17.249 And *alle* maner men þat on this molde libbeth
C.17.255 For *alle* paynyme preyeth and parfitliche bileueth
C.17.269 *Alle* þat wilnede and wolde with inwit bileue hit.
C.17.276 And aly holy kirke honoured thorw that deyng.
C.17.277 He is a forbisene to *alle* bisshopis and a briht myrrour
C.17.310 And that his lore was lesynges and lakken hit *alle*

C.17.314 Thorw Moises and Macometh and myhte of god þat made *al*.
C.18.5 Erber of *alle* pryuatees and of holynesse.
C.18.15 And solaceth *alle* soules sorwful in purgatory.'
C.18.22 *Alle* thre yliche long and yliche large.
C.18.45 And with *alle* þe wyles þat he can waggeth þe rote
C.18.48 So this lordeynes lithereth þerto þat *alle* þe leues falleth
C.18.59 Hit is *al* of o kynde, and þat shal y preuen.
C.18.72 The whiche þe seynt spirit seweth, the sonne of *al* heuene,
C.18.101 And bryngeth forth fruyt, folk of *alle* nacion,
C.18.111 And gadered hem *alle* togyderes, bothe grete & smale,
C.18.140 Ne noon so faythfol fisciscyen, for *all* þat bysouhte hym
C.18.157 And drof hem out, *alle* þat þer bouhte and solde,
C.18.179 In inwit and in *alle* wittes aftur liberum Arbitrium
C.18.188 O speche and [o] spirit Springeth out of *alle*;
C.18.194 The thridde is þat halt *al*, a thyng by hymsulue;
C.18.195 Holy goest is his name and he is in *all*.'
C.18.199 Ac leue hit lelly *al* thy lyftyme.
C.18.215 And o god almyhty, yf *alle* men ben of Adam.
C.18.217 And Abel of hem bothe and *alle* thre o kynde;
C.18.222 That acorsede *alle* couples þat no kynde forth brouhte:
C.18.225 Ne withoute a soware be suche seed; this we seen *alle*.
C.18.236 In matrimonie aren thre and of o man cam *alle* thre
C.18.237 And to godhede goth thre and o god is *all* thre.
C.18.239 'Hastow ysey this,' y seyde, '*alle* thre and o god?'
C.18.252 Mysulue and my mayne; and *alle* þat male were
C.18.268 Saide þat a seyh here þat sholde saue vs *alle*:
C.18.283 And bettere wed for vs wagen then we ben *alle* worthy;
C.18.287 The myhte of goddes mercy that myhte vs *alle* amende.'
C.19.3 To reule *alle* reumes þerwith in riȝhte and in resoun.
C.19.18 'Is here *al* thy lordes l[aw]es?' quod y; 'ȝe, leef me,' he saide,
C.19.31 And *alle* thre bote o god; thus abraham bereth witenesse
C.19.39 The which *alle* men aren holde ouer al thyng to honoure
C.19.39 The which alle men aren holde ouer *al* thyng to honoure
C.19.41 *Alle* manere men as moche as ouresulue.
C.19.90 Til he haue eten *al* þ[e] barn and his bloed dronken
C.19.95 That his lycame shal lechen at þe laste vs *alle*.'
C.19.99 And *alle* thre bote o god? thus abraham me tauhte.
C.19.101 And lered me for his loue to louye *al* mankynde
C.19.102 And hym aboue *alle* and hem as mysulue;
C.19.105 And moest inparfyt of *alle* persones; and pacientliche soffre
C.19.106 *Alle* manere men and thogh y myhte venge
C.19.110 Loke thow louye and bileue *al* thy lyftyme.
C.19.113 For god þat *al* bygan in bigynnynge of the worlde
C.19.129 Thus are they *alle* bote oen as hit an hand were,
C.19.132 So is þe fader a fol god, the fu[r]ste of hem *alle*
C.19.134 And he fader and for[m]eour, þe furste of *alle* thynges–
C.19.135 And *al* þe myhte with hym is, was and worth euere.
C.19.146 *Alle* þat þe fyngeres and þe fust feleth and toucheth.
C.19.150 And *alle* thre is bote o god as myn hoend and my fyngeres.
C.19.152 *Al* is bote oen hoend howso y turne hit.
C.19.163 Bothe meue and amende, thogh *alle* my fyngeres oke.
C.19.180 That *alle* kyne cristene clanseth of synne[s].
C.19.185 To *alle* vnkynde creatures þat coueyten to destruye
C.19.216 *Al* thy labor is loste and al thy longe trauaile;
C.19.216 Al thy labor is loste and *al* thy longe trauaile;
C.19.219 To *alle* vnkynde creatures, as Crist hymsulue witnesseth:
C.19.220 Be vnkynde to thyn emcristene and *al* þat thow canst bidde,
C.19.222 And purchace the pardoun of pampilon and Rome
C.19.237 Bute riȝtfulliche, as men [r]at, *al* his richesse cam hym
C.19.242 For godes tretor he is [to]ld for *al* his trewe catel
C.19.246 And is in helle for *al* þat, how wol riche nouthe
C.19.281 Confesse me and crye his grace, god þat *al* made,
C.19.287 Be yraunsomed for his repentaunce þer *alle* resoun hym dampneth.
C.19.297 To amende *al* þat amys is and his mercy grettore
C.19.298 Thenne *Al* oure wikkede werkes as holy writ telleth:
C.19.329 For vnkyndenesse is þe contrarie of *alle* kyne resoun.
C.19.333 *Alle* manere men mercy and forȝeuenesse
C.20.3 And ȝede forth ylike a lorel *al* my lyf tyme
C.20.16 Thenne y [f]raynede at fayth what *al* þat fare bymente
C.20.29 *Alle* þat lyueth or loketh a londe or a watre.
C.20.31 That for *al* þat deth can do, withynne thre dayes to walke
C.20.38 And *alle* þe Court [on hym] cryede 'crucifige!' [sharpe].
C.20.43 And ȝut maken hit as moche in *alle* manere poyntes,
C.20.45 And as wyde as hit euere was; this we witnesseth *alle*.'
C.20.85 For *alle* [they were] vnhardy þat houed þer or stode
C.20.101 The gre ȝut hath he geten for *al* his grete wound[e]
C.20.102 For ȝoure chaumpioun Chiualer, chief knyht of ȝow *alle*,
C.20.107 And ȝoure childerne, cherles, cheue shal neuere
C.20.110 The which is lif þat oure lord in *all* lawes defendeth.
C.20.118 Mercy hihte þat mayde, a mylde thynge with *alle*,
C.20.157 For of *alle* venymes [fou]lest is the scorpioun;
C.20.162 *All* þat deth and þe deuel dede formost to Eue
C.20.164 So shal grace þat bigan *al* maken a goed ende

C.20.179 'My wil is to wende,' quod pees, 'and welcomen hem *alle*
C.20.188 Mercy, [my sustur], and me to maynprisen hem *alle*
C.20.197 That Adam and Eue and *al* his issue
C.20.214 Yf *all* þe world were whit or swanwhit all thynges?
C.20.214 Yf all þe world were whit or swanwhit *all* thynges?
C.20.221 So god þat bigan *al* of his gode wille
C.20.224 The which vnknytteth *alle* care and comsyng is of reste.
C.20.234 To wyte what *al* wo is þat woet of alle ioye:
C.20.234 To wyte what al wo is þat woet of *alle* ioye:
C.20.243 That *alle* þe wyse of th[is] world in o wit acordede
C.20.246 And *all* þe elementis,' quod the boek, 'hereof bereth witnesse.
C.20.247 That he was god þat *al* wrouhte the welkene furste shewede:
C.20.257 Quakid as quyk thyng and *a[l]* toquasch[ed] þe roch[e].
C.20.262 To breke and to bete adoun *all* þat ben agaynes hym
C.20.263 And to haue out [of helle] *alle* þat hym liketh.
C.20.265 And comforte *alle* his kyn and out of care brynge
C.20.266 And *alle* þe iewene ioye vnioynen and vnlouken;
C.20.273 For here cometh with croune þe kynge of *all* glorie.'
C.20.276 Care and combraunce is come to vs *all*.
C.20.280 That such a lord and a lihte sh[olde] lede hem *alle* hennes.
C.20.281 Ac [r]ise vp, Ragamoffyn, and [r]eche me *alle* þe barres
C.20.288 Coltyng and *al* his kyn, the car to saue.
C.20.303 That Adam and Eue and *all* his issue
C.20.327 So hath god bigiled vs *alle* in goynge of a weye.'
C.20.336 That if his soule hider cam hit sholde shende vs *all*.
C.20.340 Hit shal vndo vs deueles and down bryngen vs *all*.
C.20.343 Y rede we flee,' quod the fende, 'faste *all* hennes
C.20.353 And wyte[th] hem *al* þe wrechednesse þat wrouhte is on erthe.
C.20.361 'The lord of myhte and of mayne þat made *all* thynges.
C.20.371 For *alle* synfole soules, to saue oure bothe rihte.
C.20.374 That if they ete þe appul *alle* sholde deye,
C.20.377 With gyle thow hem gete agaynes *all* resoun.
C.20.389 And *al* þat m[a]n mysdede, y man to amenden hit
C.20.397 And as Adam and *alle* thorwe a tre deyede,
C.20.398 Adam and *alle* thorw a tre shal turne to lyue.
C.20.406 Bote of comune coppes, *alle* cristene soules;
C.20.414 And haue out of helle *alle* mennes soules.
C.20.418 For we beth brethrene of bloed Ac nat in baptisme *alle*.
C.20.419 Ac *alle* þat beth myn hole breth[r]ene, in bloed and in baptisme,
C.20.427 Ther þat doem to þe deth dampneth *alle* wikkede
C.20.431 [Y] may do mercy of my rihtwysnesse and *alle* myn wordes trewe
C.20.434 And so of *alle* wykkede y wol here take veniaunce.
C.20.439 Ac my rihtwysnesse and rihte shal r[ul]en [*al*] helle
C.20.440 And mercy *a[l]* mankynde bifore me in heuene.
C.20.447 Astarot and *alle* [þe route] hidden hem in hernes;
C.20.448 They dorste nat loke on oure lord, the leste of hem *alle*,
C.20.458 And pees thorw pacience *alle* perelles stop[peth].'
C.21.8 And riht lyke in *alle* lymes to oure lord iesu.
C.21.17 T[hat] *alle* kyn creatures sholde knelen and bowen
C.21.21 For *alle* derke deueles aren drad to heren hit
C.21.25 Then iesu or iesus þat *all* oure ioye cam of ?'
C.21.59 To make *alle* folk fre þat folweth his lawe.
C.21.60 And sethe [*all* his lele leges largeliche he ȝeueth]
C.21.81 For *alle* þe angelis of heuene at his burthe knelede
C.21.82 And *al* þe wit of the world was in [þo] thre kynges.
C.21.96 Ac for *all* this precious presentes oure lord prince iesu[s]
C.21.107 Til he hadde *all* hem þat he fore bledde.
C.21.131 And *all* he heled and halp þat hym of grace asked;
C.21.153 Verray man bifore [hem] *alle*, and forth with hem ȝede.
C.21.163 Peter perseyued *al* this and pursuede aftur,
C.21.166 And as *al* thise wyse weyes weren togyderes
C.21.167 In an hous *al* bishut and here dore ybarred
C.21.168 Crist cam in, and *al* closed bothe dore and ȝates,
C.21.174 Deyedest and deth tholedest and deme shalt vs *all*
C.21.181 And leelliche bileuen *al* this; y loue hem and blesse hem:
C.21.184 /Myhte men to assoyle of *alle* manere synnes,
C.21.185 To *alle* manere men mercy and forȝeuenesse\
C.21.190 And assoile men of *alle* synnes saue of dette one.
C.21.202 In liknesse of a lihtynge a lyhte on hem *alle*
C.21.203 And made hem konne & knowe *alle* kyne langages.
C.21.206 Spiritus paraclitus ouerspradde hem *alle*.
C.21.216 To *alle* kyne creatures þat can his fyue wittes,
C.21.219 For Auntecrist and hise *al* the world shal greue;
C.21.249 In pouerte and in pacience to preye for *alle* cristene;
C.21.250 And *al* he lered to be lele, and vch a craft loue oþere,
C.21.251 Ne no boest ne debaet be among hem *alle*.
C.21.253 'That *all* craft and connyng c[o]m[e] of my ȝefte.
C.21.265 And ioyned til hem oen iohann, most gentill of *all*,
C.21.266 The pris neet of [Peres plouh], passynge *alle* oþere.
C.21.268 *All* þat his oxes erede they t[o] harwe[n] aftur.
C.21.272 And harwed in an handwhile *al* holy scripture
C.21.291 To soffre *al* þat god sente, seeknesse and angeres.
C.21.295 And ple[ieþ] *al* with pacience and parce michi domine

C.21.308 He dede equite to *alle* eueneforth his knowyng.
C.21.315 'Harweth *alle* þa[t] conneth kynde wit bi consail of [this] doctours
C.21.327 And of *all* holy writ he made a roef aftur
C.21.337 Consience and *alle* cristene and cardinale vertues,
C.21.354 *Alle* the world in a while thorw oure wit,' quod pruyde.
C.21.355 Quod Consience to *alle* cristene tho, 'my consayl is [to] wende
C.21.361 And cryede and comaundede *alle* cristene peple
C.21.364 Consience comaundede t[h]o *alle* cristene to delue
C.21.367 Thenne *alle* kyne cristene saue commune wommen
C.21.382 The lord of lust shal be ylette *al* this lente, y hope.
C.21.384 That haen labored lelly *al* this lenten tyme.
C.21.391 'How?' quod *alle* þe comune; 'thow conseylest vs to ȝelde
C.21.392 *Al* þat we owen eny wyhte or we go to hosele?'
C.21.397 By iesu! for *al* ȝoure iangelyng, [with] spiritus Iusticie
C.21.425 And grace that thow gredest so of, gyour of *all* Clerkes;
C.21.427 Emperour of *al* þe world, þat all men were cristene.
C.21.427 Emperour of al þe world, þat *all* men were cristene.
C.21.428 Inparfit is þat pope þat *all* peple sholde helpe
C.21.439 As for a trewe tydy man *alle* tymes ylyke.
C.21.440 And worschiped be he þat wrouhte *all*, bothe gode and wicke.
C.21.456 And *al* tho fayre vertues as vises thei semeth.
C.21.461 *Al* þat myn Auditour or elles my styward
C.21.470 Ȝe ben bote membres and y aboue *alle*.
C.21.471 And sethe y am ȝoure *alere* heued y am ȝoure alere hele
C.21.471 And sethe y am ȝoure alere heued y am ȝoure *alere* hele
C.21.474 Of spiritus iusticie for y iuge ȝow *alle*.
C.22.34 God gouerneth *all* gode vertues.
C.22.40 And god *al* his grete ioye goestliche he lefte
C.22.49 Sethe [he] þat wrouhte *al* þe worlde was willefolliche nedy
C.22.53 Auntecrist cam thenne and *al* the crop of treuthe
C.22.60 And *al* þe couent cam to welcome a tyraunt
C.22.61 And *alle* hise as wel as hym, saue onelich foles,
C.22.64 And a fals fende auntecrist ouer *all* folke regnede.
C.22.66 Defyede *all* falsnesse and folke þat hit vsede
C.22.78 And crye we on *al* þe comune þat thei come to vnite
C.22.89 With deth þat is dredful to vndoen vs *alle*!'
C.22.100 Deth cam dryuyng aftur and *al* to duste paschte
C.22.112 Amonges *alle* manere men, wedded and vnwedded,
C.22.113 And gaderet[h] a greet oest *alle* agayn Consience.
C.22.124 His wepne was *al* wyles, to wynnen and to hyden;
C.22.130 And knokked Consience in Court bifore hem *alle*;
C.22.135 And ouertulde *al* his treuthe with 'taek this [vp] amendement.'
C.22.151 And culle *all* erthely creature saue Consience one.
C.22.208 'Lerne to loue,' quod kynde, 'and leef *all* othere.'
C.22.243 And cortey[s]liche confortede hem and calde in *all* freres
C.22.244 And saide, 'syres, soethly welcome be ȝe *alle*
C.22.254 That in mesure god made *alle* [manere] thynges
C.22.262 *Alle* oþere in bataile been yholde brybours,
C.22.264 Monkes and monyales and *alle* men of religioun,
C.22.276 That *alle* thynges vnder heuene ou[h]te to be in comune.
C.22.283 *Alle* þat been here parschienes penauns[e] enioynen
C.22.299 Of *all* taletellares and titerares an ydel.
C.22.320 Saue [Peres the Plouhman] þat haeth power ouer *alle*
C.22.341 'Ȝe? go thy gate!' quod pees, 'bi god! for *al* thi fisyk,
C.22.365 And for hem þat ȝe aren holde to *al* my lyf tyme
C.22.372 That is the souereyne salue for *alle* [synnes of kynde].

al adv *al adv.& conj.* A 13; B 38 al (37) alle (1); C 38 al (35) all (1) alle (2)

A.Pr.26 *Al* for loue of oure lord lyuede wel streite
A. 1.31 And *al* he wytide it wyn þ[at] wykkide dede.
A. 2.39 Þat iche feld nas ful of folk *al* aboute.
A. 2.89 For *al* be lesinges þou lyuest, & leccherous werkis;
A. 2.109 And bad gile go gyue gold *al* aboute,
A. 2.128 Sette mede on a shirreue shod *al* newe,
A. 4.82 And profride pees a presaunt *al* of purid gold;
A. 6.73 Þe mot is of mercy þe Maner *al* aboute,
A. 7.160 And wrong hym so be þe wombe þat *al* watride his eiȝen,
A. 7.170 Þei hadde be ded þis day & doluen *al* warm.
A. 7.183 *Al* for coueitise of his corn to [cacche] awey hungir.
A.10.179 And *al* for se[þ] & his sister children spouside eiþer oþer,
A.11.98 But *al* lauȝinge he loutide & lokide vpon studie
B.Pr.26 *Al* for loue of oure lord lyueden [wel] streyte
B.Pr.190 But fedeþ hym *al* wiþ venyson, defame we hym neuere;
B. 1.31 And *al* he witte it wyn þat wikked dede:
B. 2.125 For *al* bi lesynges þow lyuest and lecherouse werkes;
B. 2.145 And bad gile '[go] gyu[e] gold *al* aboute,
B. 2.164 Sette Mede vpon a Sherreue shoed *al* newe,
B. 4.95 And profrede Pees a present *al* of pure[d] golde.
B. 4.150 *Al* to construe þis clause for þe kynges profit,
B. 5.287 For þe good þat þow hast geten bigan *al* wiþ falshede,
B. 5.385 Thanne cam Sleuþe *al* bislabered wiþ two slymy eiȝen.
B. 5.498 And *al* to solace synfulle þow suffredest it so were:
B. 6.117 'Now by þe peril of my soule!' quod Piers *al* in pure tene,

B. 6.175 And wrong hym so by þe wombe þat [*al* watrede his eiȝen].
B. 9.157 And *al* for þei wroȝte wedlokes ayein [þe wille of god].
B.10.4 And *al* starynge dame Studie sterneliche [seide].
B.10.103 And *al* to spare to [spille þat spende] shal anoþer.
B.10.296 And *al* for youre holynesse; haue ye þis in herte.
B.11.115 *Al* for tene of hir text trembled myn herte,
B.11.357 But *al* for loue of oure lord and þe bet to loue þe peple.
B.11.357 And brouȝten forþ hir briddes *al* aboue þe grounde.
B.11.400 *Al* to murþe wiþ man þat moste wo þolie,
B.12.46 Felice hir fairnesse fel hire *al* to sclaundre,
B.12.248 And deleþ it noȝt til his deeþ day, þe tail[le is *al* of] sorwe.
B.12.257 I leue it flawme ful foule þe fold *al* aboute,
B.13.144 Cast coles on his heed of *alle* kynde speche;
B.13.402 Swoor þerby swiþe ofte and *al* biswatte his cote;
B.14.11 *Al* for coueitise of my cristendom in clennesse to kepen it.
B.15.40 'Ye ben as a bisshop', quod I, *al* bourdynge þat tyme,
B.15.443 *Al* was hethynesse som tyme Engelond and Walis
B.15.520 *Al* for to enforme þe faith; in fele contrees deyeden,
B.16.18 'Piers þe Plowman!' quod I þo, and *al* for pure Ioye
B.18.248 Quaked as quyk þyng and *al* biquasshed þe roche.
B.19.6 That Piers þe Plowman was peynted *al* blody
B.19.167 In an hous *al* bishet and hir dore ybarred
B.19.168 Crist cam In, and *al* closed boþe dore and yates,
B.19.295 And pleieþ *al* wiþ pacience and Parce michi domine;
B.20.113 And gaderede a greet hoost *al* agayn Consience.
B.20.124 His wepne was *al* wiles, to wynnen and to hiden;
C.Pr.28 *Al* for loue of oure lord lyueden [ful streyte]
C.Pr.115 And *al* was for vengeance he bet noght his children
C. 1.30 And *al* he witte [it] wyn [þat] wikkede dede:
C. 2.46 And *al* is lyares ledynge th[at] lady is thus ywedded.
C. 2.161 And bade gyle '[g]o gyue gold *al* aboute,
C. 3.203 Religioun he *al* toreueth and oute of reule to lybbe.
C. 4.91 And profrede pees a present *al* of puyre golde.
C. 4.183 'Y wolde hit were,' quod the kynge, 'wel *al* aboute.'
C. 5.162 He loketh *al* lourynge and lordeyne hym calleth.
C. 6.23 Lauhyng *al* aloude for lewede men sholde
C. 6.292 Ȝut were me leuer, by oure lord, lyue *al* by wellecresses
C. 6.342 For the good that thow hast gete bygan *al* with falshede
C. 7.1 Thenne cam sleuthe *al* byslobered with two slim[y] yes.
C. 7.138 And *a[l]* to solace synfole thow soffredest it so were:
C. 7.163 In a wethewynde wyse ywrithe *al* aboute;
C. 8.124 Quod [Peres] þe [plouhman] *al* in puyre tene:
C. 8.172 And wronge hym so by þe wombe þat *al* watrede his yes;
C. 8.187 *Al* for drede of here deth, such duntus ȝaf hunger.
C. 8.191 And freres of alle þe fyue ordres, *alle* for fere of hunger.
C.10.235 And *al* for here forfadres ferden þe worse.
C.11.4 *Al* staryng dame studie sterneliche sayde.
C.11.80 And gode men for oure gultes he *al* togrynt to deth.
C.11.83 But *al* lauhynge he louted and loked vppon stud[i]e,
C.12.50 *Al* for tene of here tyxst tremblede myn herte
C.13.134 And y bowed my body, bihel[d]e *al* aboute
C.13.166 And brouhte forth here briddes *al* aboue þe grounde.
C.13.191 They reule hem al by resoun Ac renkes ful fewe.
C.15.142 Caste coles on his heued of *alle* kyn[de] speche,
C.16.19 For *al* myhtest þou haue ymad men of grete welthe
C.16.37 Elles is *al* an ydel al oure lyuynge here,
C.16.114 Quod Actyf tho *al* angryliche and Arguinge as hit were:
C.16.202 'Ȝe beth as a bischop,' quod y, *al* bourdynge þat tyme,
C.16.267 That were bysnewed *al* with snowe and snakes withynne
C.18.39 And *al* forb[i]t Caritas rihte to þe bare stalke.
C.18.57 And askede efte tho where hit were *al* [of] o kynde.
C.20.62 The hard roch *al* toroef and riht derk nyht hit semede;
C.20.290 *Al* hoet on here hedes þat entrith ney þe walles;
C.21.6 That [Peres] þe [plouhman] was peynted *al* blody

al &> oueral, wiþalle

alay n *alai n.* B 1 alay
B.15.349 As in lussheburwes is a luþer *alay*, and yet lokeþ he lik a sterlyng;

alayed ptp *alaien v.* B 2; C 1
B.15.353 Ac þe metal, þat is mannes soule, [myd] synne is foule *alayed*.
B.15.354 Boþe lettred and lewed beþ *alayed* now wiþ synne
C.17.80 Is *alayed* with leccherye and oþer lustes of synne

alarme exclam *alarme interj.& n.* B 2; C 2
B.20.92 '*Alarme!* alarme!' quod þat lord, 'ech lif kepe his owene!'
B.20.92 'Alarme! *alarme!*' quod þat lord, 'ech lif kepe his owene!'
C.22.92 '*Alarme!* alarme!' quod þat lord, 'vch lyf kepe his owene!'
C.22.92 'Alarme! *alarme!*' quod þat lord, 'vch lyf kepe his owene!'

alas > allas

albertes n prop *n.i.d.* A 1 albertis; B 1
A.11.160 Experimentis of alkenemye of *albertis* makyng,
B.10.217 Experimentȝ of Alkenamye [of *Albertes* makynge,

alday adv *al-dai, al-daies phr.& adv.* B 1; C 1
B.15.359 Astronomiens *alday* in hir Art faillen
C.17.97 Astronomiens *alday* in here arte faylen

aldremen n *alder-man n.* C 1
C. 4.188 Audiatis alteram partem amonges *aldremen* and comeneres,

ale n *ale n. &> penyale* A 10 ale (9) nale (1); B 19 ale (18) Nale (1); C 23
A.Pr.42 Flite þanne for here foode, fouȝten at þe *ale*.
A. 5.152 'I haue good *ale*, gossib,' quaþ heo; 'glotoun, wilt þou assaie?'
A. 5.167 Ȝeue glotoun wiþ glad chiere good *ale* to hansele.
A. 5.184 And grete sire glotoun wiþ a galoun *ale*.
A. 5.225 Shal non *ale* aftir mete holde me þennis
A. 7.107 Þanne seten somme & sungen at þe *ale*,
A. 7.285 Wiþ good *ale* & glotonye h[y] gart hym to slepe.
A. 7.289 Ne non halpeny *ale* in no wyse drynke,
A.10.59 And ek in sottis þou miȝt se, þat sitten at þe *nale*.
A.10.60 Þei helde an here hed til Inwyt be drenchit,

B.Pr.42 [Flite þanne] for hire foode, fouȝten at þe *ale*.
B. 5.177 I ete þere unhende fissh and feble *ale* drynke.
B. 5.218 Peny *ale* and puddyng ale she poured togideres;
B. 5.218 Peny ale and puddyng *ale* she poured togideres;
B. 5.302 'I haue good *Ale*, gossib', quod she, 'Gloton, woltow assaye?'
B. 5.318 Geue Gloton wiþ glad chere good *ale* to hansele.
B. 5.335 And greten sire Gloton wiþ a Galon *ale*.
B. 5.403 Wiþ ydel tales at þe *ale* and ouþerwhile [in] chirche[s];
B. 5.437 Boþ[e] bred and *ale*, buttre, melk and chese
B. 5.453 Shal noon *ale* after mete holde me þennes
B. 6.115 [Th]anne seten somme and songen atte *Nale*
B. 6.301 Wiþ good *Ale* as Gloton taȝte [þei] garte [hym to] slepe.
B. 6.305 Ne noon halfpeny *ale* in none wise drynke,
B. 6.309 May no peny *ale* hem paie, ne no pece of bacoun,
B.14.232 And þouȝ his glotonye be to good *ale* he goþ to cold beddyng
B.15.126 Hadde he neuere [saued] siluer þerto [for spendyng at *ale*];
B.19.400 Thikke *ale* and þynne ale; þat is my kynde,
B.19.400 Thikke ale and þynne *ale*; þat is my kynde,
B.20.223 Than I do to drynke a drauȝte of good *ale*.'
C.Pr.43 Fayteden for here foode, foughten at þe *ale*.
C. 6.159 For y ete more fysch then flesche there and feble *ale* drynke.
C. 6.226 Peny *ale* and poddyng ale [h]e poured togederes,
C. 6.226 Peny ale and poddyng *ale* [h]e poured togederes,
C. 6.228 Þe beste *ale* lay in m[y] bour and in my bed chau[m]bre
C. 6.357 'Y haue good *ale*, gossip Glotoun, woltow assaye?'
C. 6.375 Geuen glotoun with glad chere good *ale* to hansull.
C. 6.393 And grete syre glotoun with a galoun *ale*.
C. 6.434 [On] fastyng dayes bifore noen fedde me with *ale*,
C. 7.19 With ydele tales at þe *ale* and oþerwhile in chirches;
C. 7.51 Bothe Bred and *ale*, Botere, mylke and chese
C. 7.67 Shal non *ale* aftur m[e]te holde me thennes
C. 8.122 Thenne seet somme and songen at the *ale*
C. 8.323 And thenne gloton with gode *ale* garte hunger slepe.
C. 8.327 Ne noon halpeny *ale* in none wyse drynke
C. 8.331 May no peny *ale* hem pay ne no pece of bacoun
C. 9.92 There is payne and peny *ale* as for a pytaunce ytake
C. 9.156 Thorw which craft a couthe come to bred and to *ale*
C. 9.195 For hit ben but boyes, bollares at þe *ale*,
C.16.73 And thogh his glotonye be of gode *ale* he goth to a colde beddynge
C.21.400 Thikke *ale* [&] thynne ale; þat is my kynde
C.21.400 Thikke ale [&] thynne *ale*; þat is my kynde
C.22.223 Then y do to drynke a drauht of goed *ale*.'

aleggen v *alleggen v.* A 1 alegged; B 1; C 1 allegge
A.12.107 When he saw þes sawes busyly *alegged*
B.11.89 'They wole *aleggen* also', quod I, 'and by þe gospel preuen:
C.12.30 Thei wolle *allegge* also and by þe gospel preuen:

alenghe adv *alengthe adv.* C 1
C. 3.260 He sholde haue [ben] lord of þat lond *alenghe* and abrede

alere > al; alery > aliry

aliche adv *aliche adv.* B 1 aliche
B.16.57 For alle are þei *aliche* longe, noon lasse þan ooþer,

aliens n *alien n.* A 1 alienes; B 1; C 1
A. 3.198 To *alienes*, to alle men, to honoure hem with ȝeftis.
B. 3.211 To *aliens*, to alle men, to honouren hem with ȝiftes;
C. 3.267 To *aliens*, to alle men, to honoure hem with ȝeftes;

alyhte v *alighten v.* C 1
C.11.141 And byleef lely how goddes [l]o[u]e *alyhte*

aliry adv *aliri adv.or adj.* A 1 alery; B 1; C 1 alery
A. 7.114 Somme leide here leg *alery* as suche lorellis cunne,
B. 6.122 Somme leide hir le[g] *aliry* as swiche lo[r]els konneþ
C. 8.129 [Somme] leyde here legges *alery* as suche lorelles conneth

alisaundre n1 prop *n.i.d.* B 1 alisaundre
B.12.44 *Alisaundre* þat al wan, elengliche ended.

alisaundre n2 prop *n.i.d.* A 1; B 2; C 2 alisandre (1) Alisaundre (1)
A. 6.16 In armonye, in *alisaundre*, in manye oþere places.
B. 5.528 In Armonye, in *Alisaundre*, in manye oþere places.
B.15.521 In ynde, in *alisaundre*, in ermonye and spayne,
C. 7.173 In Armonye, in *Alisaundre* [and in damaske].
C.17.272 In ynde, in *alisandre*, in Armonye [and] spayne

alyue adj *alive adv.& adj.* B 2; C 1
B. 8.116 Ellis [n]oot [no man] þat now is *alyue*.'
B.20.110 Fortune gan flatere þanne þo fewe þat were *alyue*
C.22.110 Fortune gan flateren thenne t[h]o fewe þat were *alyue*

alkenamye n *alkamie n.* A 1 alkenemye; B 1
A.11.160 Experimentis of *alkenemye* of albertis makyng,
B.10.217 Experimentȝ of *Alkenamye* [of Albertes makynge,

alle > al adj,adv, wiþalle

allas exclam *alas int.* A 1; B 12; C 8 alas (1) allas (7)
A. 5.54 Lecchour seide '*allas*!' & to oure lady criede
B. 5.71 Lechour seide '*allas*!' and [to] oure lady cryde
B. 9.66 *Allas* þat drynke shal fordo þat god deere bouȝte,
B. 9.86 *Allas* þat a cristene creature shal be vnkynde til anoþer!
B.11.44 '*Allas*, eiȝe!' quod Elde and holynesse boþe,
B.14.132 *Allas* þat richesse shal reue and robbe mannes soule
B.14.323 '*Allas*', quod Haukyn þe Actif man þo, 'þat after my cristendom
B.15.128 *Allas*, ye lewed men, muche lese ye on preestes!
B.15.322 *Allas*, lordes and ladies, lewed counseil haue ye
B.15.391 *Allas*, þanne, but oure looresmen lyue as þei leren vs,
B.15.492 *Allas*, þat men so longe [sholde bileue on Makometh]!
B.16.270 '*Allas*!' I seide, 'þat synne so longe shal lette
B.20.140 '*Allas*!' quod Conscience and cryde, 'wolde crist of his grace
C. 6.170 Thenne seyde lecherye '*alas*!' and to oure lady cryede,
C.12.1 '*Allas*, eye!' quod elde and holynesse bothe,
C.16.1 *Allas* þat rychesse shal reue and robbe mannes soule
C.16.274 *Allas*! lewed men, moche lese ȝe þat fynde
C.17.56 *Allas*, lordes and ladyes, lewede consayle haue ȝe
C.17.187 *Allas*, þat men so longe on Macometh bileueth!
C.18.286 '*Allas*!' y saide, 'þat synne so longe shal lette
C.22.140 '*Allas*!' quod Consience and cryede, 'wolde crist of his grace

allegge > aleggen; alle(r > al

allie n *allie n.* A 1
A.10.47 Inwyt is þe [*allie*] þat anima desiriþ;

allone adj *alone adv.& adj.* B 1
B.11.344 Medled noȝt wiþ hir makes, [saue man *allone*].

allouable adj *allouable adj.* C 1
C.17.130 Loue lawe withoute leutee? *allouable* was hit neuere!

allowaunce n *allouaunce n.* B 2 allowaunce (1) alowaunce (1); C 2 allouaunce
B.11.221 Is litel *allowaunce* maad, but if bileue hem helpe;
B.14.110 To haue *allowaunce* of his lord; by þe lawe he it cleymeþ.
C. 9.270 When thy lord loketh to haue *allouaunce* of his bestes
C.15.286 To haue *allouaunce* of his lord; by [þe] lawe he [hit] claymeth.

allowe v *allouen v.* B 7 allowe (1) allowed (5) alloweþ (1); C 11 alloued (2) alloueth (2) allowe (1) allowed (1) alloweth (1) aloueth (1) alowed (1) alowede (2)
B.10.439 Wher fo[r loue] a man worþ *allowed* þere and hise lele werkes,
B.10.441 And be *allowed* as he lyued so; for by luþere men knoweþ þe goode.
B.12.290 Ne wolde neuere trewe god but [trewe] truþe were *allowed*.
B.13.435 Ne no mysproud man amonges lordes ben *allowed*.
B.14.311 [For] lordes *alloweþ* hym litel or listneþ to his reson;
B.15.4 And some lakkede my lif–*allowed* it fewe–
B.16.233 He wiste my wille bi hym; he wol me it *allowe*.
C. 3.74 God in þe gospel suche grauynge nouȝt *alloueth*:
C. 3.205 Ther he is *alowed* and ylet by þat laste shal eny while
C. 7.95 Ne no mysproud man amongus lordes be [*alow*]ede.
C. 8.249 And þat best labored best was *alloued*
C.12.140 And aytheres werkes and wille] riht wel *alowede*
C.12.195 Worth *allowed* of oure lord at here laste ende
C.14.212 Ne wolde neuere trewe god bote trewe treuthe were *alloued*.
C.16.145 For lordes *alloueth* hym litel or leggeth ere to his resoun;
C.17.136 Ac oure lord *aloueth* no loue but lawe be þe cause;
C.18.82 That oure lord *alloweth*, as lered men vs techeth,
C.18.250 Where y walke in this worlde a wol hit me *allowe*.

almaries n *almerie n.* B 1; C 1
B.14.247 Ther Auarice haþ *Almaries* and yren bounden cofres.
C.16.87 There Auaryce hath *almaries* and yrebounden coffres.

almesdede n *almes-dede n.* B 2 almesdede (1) almesdedes (1); C 2 Almesdede (1) Almesdedes (1)
B. 5.594   Of *almesdedes* are þe hokes þat þe gates hangen on.
B.13.412   Dooþ noon *almes[dede]*; dred hym of no synne;
C. 7.72   Doth non *Almesdede*, drat hym nat of synne,
C. 7.242   The hokes aren *Almesdedes* þat þe ʒates hange on.

almesfull adj *almesful adj.* C 1
C. 6.48   They to wene þat y were wel holy and *almesfull*

almesse n *almesse n.* A 2; B 8 almesse (7) almesses (1); C 6 Almesse (4) Almesses (1) Almusse (1)
A. 7.119   And ʒelde ʒow of ʒour *almesse* þat ʒe ʒiuen vs here,
A. 7.134   Shuln haue of myn *almesse* al þe while I libbe,
B. 3.75   For þus [bit god in] þe gospel goode men doon hir *almesse*.
B. 6.127   And yelde yow [of] youre *Almesse* þat ye ʒyue vs here;
B. 6.146   And na moore er morwe, myn *almesse* shul þei haue,
B. 7.74   And in þe stories he techeþ to bistowe þyn *almesse*:
B.15.84   For as [me þynkeþ] ye forsakeþ no mannes *almesse*,
B.15.311   Founde þei þat freres wolde forsake hir *almesses*
B.15.420   Of tirauntʒ þat teneþ trewe men taken any *almesse*,
B.15.423   To lyue by litel and in lowe houses by *seke* mennes *almesse*.
C. 8.133   And ʒelde ʒow of ʒoure *Almesse* þat ʒe ʒeuen vs here;
C. 9.96   These are *Almusse* to helpe þat han suche charges
C. 9.141   Loken louhliche to lache men *Almesse*,
C. 9.192   As rychesses and reuerences and ryche menne *Almesse*,
C.13.79   The messager aren th[e] mendenantʒ þat lyuen by menne *almesse*,
C.17.47   Wolde religious refuse rauenours *Almesses*.

almest > almoost

almyʒty adj *al-mighti adj.* A 5 almiʒt (3) almyʒthi (1) almiʒty (1); B 15 almyghty (4) almyʒty (11); C 17 almyghty (2) almyhten (1) almyhty (14)
A. 6.58   A[nd] nameliche an ydel þe name of god *almiʒt*,
A.10.132   And lyuen as here law[e] wil[e]; it likeþ god *almiʒty*
A.11.32   More þanne musik, or makyng of god *almiʒt*,
A.11.80   For alle þat wilneþ to wyte þe [whyes] of god *almiʒt*,
A.12.26   In þe passioun, whan pilat aposed god *almyʒthi*,
B. 5.134   I wole amende þis if I may þoruʒ myʒt of god *almyʒty*.'
B. 5.571   And-nameliche-on-ydel-þe-name-of-god-*almyʒty*.
B. 7.82   For beggeres borwen eueremo and hir borgh is god *almyʒty*
B. 9.45   And in þis manere was man maad þoruʒ myʒt of god *almyʒty*,
B. 9.65   And alle þat lyuen good lif are lik to god *almyʒty*:
B. 9.95   He dooþ noʒt wel þat dooþ þus, ne drat noʒt god *almyʒty*,
B. 9.193   A[c] if þei leden þus hir lif it likeþ god *almyʒty*,
B.10.127   For alle þat wilneþ to wite þe [whyes] of god *almyʒty*,
B.10.438   In þe hondes of *almyʒty* god, and he woot þe soþe
B.11.288   That if þei trauaille truweliche, and truste in god *almyʒty*,
B.12.154   And diden [hir] homage honurably to hym þat was *almyʒty*.
B.15.295   Ac moost þoruʒ [meditacion] and mynde of god *almyghty*.
B.15.394   For þei loue and bileue in o [lord] *almyghty*
B.17.37   To bileeue and louye in o lord *almyghty*
B.18.419   For inpossible is no þyng to hym þat is *almyghty*.'
C.Pr.221   Deuyne ʒe, for y ne dar, by dere god *almyhten*.
C. 1.26   Wykked[ly] wroghte and wrathed god *almyhty*.
C. 1.111   That hadde [lu]st to be lyk his lord þat was *almyghty*:
C. 5.99   So hope y to haue of hym þat is *almyghty*
C. 6.427   Sworn godes soule and his sides and "so helpe [me] god *almyhty*"
C. 7.218   And-nameliche-an-ydel-þe-name-of-god-*almyhty*.
C.13.102   That yf th[ey] trauaile treulyche and trist in god *almyhty*
C.14.98   And deden here homage honerably to hym þat was *almyhty*.
C.15.277   'Where pouerte and pacience plese more god *almyhty*
C.17.135   And ayther loueth and byleueth in o [lord] *almyhty*.
C.17.152   Louen as by lawe of kynde oure lord god *almyhty*.
C.18.95   Shollen serue for þe lord sulue, and so fareth god *almyhty*.
C.18.210   O god *almyhty* þat man made and wrouhte
C.18.215   And o god *almyhty*, yf alle men ben of Adam.
C.19.38   To godhede but o god and on god *almyhty*
C.19.42   And for to louye and bileue in o lord *almyhty*
C.20.462   For inposible is no thynge to hym þat is *almyhty*.'

almoost adv *al-most adv.* B 2; C 2 almest (1) almost (1)
B. 4.174   And gan wexe wroþ with lawe for Mede *almoost* hadde shent it.
B.20.227   And hadden *almoost* vnitee and holynesse adown.
C. 3.209   Han *almest* mad, but marye the helpe,
C.22.227   And hadden *almost* vnite and holynesse adowne.

almusse > almesse

aloft adv *alofte adv.* B 2 aloft (1) alofte (1); C 6 aloft (2) alofte (3) aloofte (1)
B.12.220   Why some be alouʒ & some *aloft*, þi likyng it were;
B.18.145   Leue þow neuere þat yon light hem *alofte* brynge
C.Pr.177   We myhte be lordes *alofte* and lyue as vs luste.'
C. 1.113   Luppen *alofte* [in lateribus Aquilonis]

C. 6.410   For to lyfte hym *aloft* [and] leyde hym on his knees.
C. 6.424   'Thow lord [þat] *aloft* art and alle lyues shope.
C.20.44   Bothe as longe and as large *aloofte* and o grounde
C.20.148   Leue [þou] neuere þat ʒone liht hem *alofte* brynge

alogh > alouʒ

along adv *along adv.& prep.* A 1; B 1; C 1
A. 5.124   To drawe þe list *along*, þe lengere it semide;
B. 5.208   To drawe þe [list] *along*, þe lenger it semed;
C. 6.216   To drawe the lyst *along* the lengur hit semede;

alonged ptp *alonged ppl.* A 1 alongid; B 1
A. 7.251   And aftir many maner metis his mawe is *alongid*.
B. 6.267   And after many maner metes his mawe is [*alonged*].

aloofte > aloft

alose v *alosen v.* C 1
C.19.103   Noþer lacke ne *alose* ne leue þat þer were

aloud adv *aloude adv.* B 2; C 5 aloud (1) aloude (3) alowed (1)
B.19.159   And lyues and lokynge and *aloud* cride
B.20.90   The lord þat lyued after lust þo *aloud* cryde
C. 2.134   Lokede vp to oure lord and *alowed* sayde:
C. 6.23   Lauhyng al *aloude* for lewede men sholde
C.20.360   'What lord artow?' quod lucifer; a voys *aloude* saide:
C.21.159   And lyues and lokynge and *aloude* criede
C.22.90   The lord þat lyuede aftur lust tho *aloud* cryede

aloueth > allowe

alouʒ adv *aloue adv.* B 2 alogh (1) alouʒ (1)
B.12.220   Why some be *alouʒ* & some aloft, þi likyng it were;
B.12.234   Raþer þan his likame *alogh*; lewed asken þus clerkes.

alowaunce > allowaunce; alowed > allowe,aloud; alowede > allowe; als > also,as

also adv *also adv.* A 16 als (1) alse (4) also (11); B 37 als (8) also (29); C 38 alse (1) also (37)
A.Pr.96   Barouns [and] burgeis & bondage *also*
A. 2.122   Þanne was fals fayn, & fauel *als* bliþe,
A. 3.211   Asken mede & messe penis & here mete *alse*;
A. 4.53   Wysdom wan þo & so dede wyt *also*
A. 5.144   But wende to walsyngham, & my wyf *alse*,
A. 6.121   And she is sib to alle synful, & hire sone *alse*,
A. 7.141   A bretoner, a braggere, he bostide hym *also*,
A. 7.233   Actif lif oþer contemplatif; crist wolde it *alse*.
A. 8.31   Marie maidenis [and] maken hem nonnes,
A.10.200   Wydeweris & wydewis werchiþ riʒt *also*;
A.10.204   Of lif & of loue & of lawe *also*
A.10.210   And þat ben fals folk, & fals eires *also*, foundlynges & [leiʒeris],
A.11.95   [And] *also* doumb as a dore drouʒ hym asid.
A.11.199   Dobet doþ ful wel, & dewid he is *also*,
A.12.19   'Dauid godes derling defendyþ hit *also*:
A.12.102   Of peres þe plowman and mechel puple *also*.
B.Pr.96   And *also* route of Ratons rende rende mennes cloþes
B.Pr.217   Barons and Burgeises and bond[age] *als*.
B. 1.205   And *also* þe graiþe gate þat goþ into heuene.
B. 3.72   On auenture ye haue youre hire here and youre heuene *als*.
B. 3.224   Asken Mede and massepens and here mete [*als*];
B. 3.331   *Also* wroþ as þe wynd weex Mede in a while.
B. 4.18   And *also* Tomme trewe-tonge-tel-me-no-tales-
B. 4.168   And [*also*] a Sherreues clerk bisherewed al þe route:
B. 4.195   *Als* longe as [I lyue] lyue we togideres.'
B. 5.228   But wenden to walsyngham, and my wyf *als*,
B. 5.636   And she is sib to alle synfulle and hire sone *also*,
B. 6.36   *Als* longe as I lyue I shal þee mayntene.'
B. 6.154   A Bretoner, a braggere, [he b]osted Piers *als*
B. 6.249   Contemplatif lif or Actif lif; crist wolde [it *als*].
B. 9.179   [Wideweres and wodewes] wercheþ [riʒt *also*];
B. 9.191   Of lif and of [loue] and [of lawe *also*]
B.10.158   Thanne was [I] *also* fayn as fowel of fair morwe,
B.10.166   And *also* þe [longe] launde þat lecherie hatte,
B.10.342   Salomon seiþ *also* þat siluer is worst to louye:
B.10.409   And his wif wiþ hise sones and *also* hire wyues;
B.11.89   'They wole aleggen *also*', quod I, 'and by þe gospel preuen:
B.11.95   And in þe Sauter *also* seiþ dauid þe prophete
B.11.310   And *also* in þe Sauter seiþ Dauid to ouerskipperis,
B.12.117   And his sones *also* for þat synne myscheued,
B.14.3   And *also* I haue an houswif, hewen and children–
B.14.125   And hir [ladies] *also* lyueda hir lif in murþe.
B.14.298   Wiþ sobretee fram alle synne and *also* ʒit moore;
B.15.225   I haue yseyen charite *also* syngen and reden
B.15.266   Ac he suffrede in ensample þat we sholde suffren *also*,
B.15.294   And *also* Marie Maudeleyne by mores lyuede and dewes,

24

B.15.357 Wederwise shipmen and witty clerkes *also*
B.15.370 Astronomyens *also* aren at hir wittes ende;
B.15.607 And siþen þat þe Sarȝens and *also* þe Iewes
B.17.212 So dooþ þe Sire and þe sone and *also* spiritus sanctus
B.18.71 Two þeues [þat tyme] þoled deeþ [*also*]
B.18.343 And lif for lif *also*, and by þat lawe I clayme
B.19.438 And trauailleþ and tilieþ for a tretour *also* soore
C. 1.78 And *also* kenne me kyndly on crist to bileue.
C. 1.87 And *also* lyk [to] oure lord by saynt Lukes wordes. ,
C. 2.72 That Gyle hath gyue to falsnesse and grauntid *also* medę,'
C. 2.150 Forthy worcheth by wisdom and by witt *also*,
C. 3.228 And gryp[en] my gold and gyue hit where þe liked.
C. 3.261 And *also* kyng of þat kuth his kyn for to helpe,
C. 3.301 Harlotes and hoores and *also* fals leches,
C. 4.18 And *also* th[omm]e trewe-tonge-telle-me-no-tales-
C. 5.53 And *also* moreouer me [sem]eth, syre resoun,
C. 5.182 And *also*,' quod resoun, 'y rede ȝow ryche
C. 6.112 As som tyme in somur and *also* in heruest,
C. 6.187 And handlyng and halsyng and *also* thorw kyssyng,
C. 8.152 A bretener cam braggyng, abostede [Peres] *also*:
C. 8.299 For thow hast wel awroke me and *also* wel ytauhte me.'
C. 9.65 And *also* gileth hym þat gyueth and taketh agayne his wille.
C. 9.77 And hemsulue *also* soffre muche hungur
C. 9.317 And his fadur Is[rael] and *also* his dame.
C.11.95 For he is sib to þe seuene ars–and *also* my suster
C.12.30 Thei wolle allegge *also* and by þe gospel preuen:
C.12.183 [And] oþer sedes *also* in þe same wyse
C.13.123 [To] ouerskippperes *also* in þe sauter sayth dauid:
C.14.28 So grace withouten grace of god and *also* gode werkes
C.15.85 And *also* a gnedy glotoun with two grete chekes,
C.16.134 With sobrete fro alle synnes and *also* ȝut more;
C.16.181 And ayther is otheres hete and *also* of o will;
C.16.259 And þerto trewe of ȝoure tonge and of ȝoure tayl *also*
C.16.322 And *also* a can clergie, credo in deum patrem,
C.16.347 And *also* gladliche he hit gaf to gomes þat hit nedede.
C.16.350 Ich haue yseye charite *also* syngen and rede,
C.17.93 Doen her deuer day and nyhte; dede we so *alse*
C.17.106 Astron[o]myens *also* aren at here wittes ende;
C.17.270 Mony [a] seynte sethe soffrede deth *also*,
C.17.315 And sethe þat th[e] sarresynes and *also* þe iewes
C.18.65 Swettore and saueriore and *also* more grettore
C.18.152 Ac y saued ȝow sondry tymes and *also* y fe[d] ȝow
C.18.251 Y circumsised my sone *also* for his sake,
C.19.108 'A saide soeth,' quod the samaritaen, 'and so y rede the *also*.
C.21.438 And trauaileth and tulieth for a tretour *also* sore

alþouȝ *conj* al-though *conj*. B 5; C 4 althouh (3) althow (1)
B.11.259 [*Al*]*þouȝ* it be sour to suffre, þe[r] comeþ swete [after].
B.11.270 *Alþouȝ* Salomon seide, as folk seeþ in þe bible,
B.12.14 *Alþouȝ* þow strike me wiþ þi staf, wiþ stikke or wiþ yerde,
B.12.101 *Alþouȝ* men made bokes [þe maister was god]
B.18.330 [*Al*]*þouȝ* Reson recorde, and riȝt of myselue,
C. 2.124 *Althow* fals were here fader and fikel tonge her belsyre
C.12.145 *Althouh* h[it] be sour to soffre þer cometh a swete aftur.
C.14.46 [*Althouh* men maden bokes] God was here maystre
C.20.373 *Althouh* resoun record[e], and rihte of mysulue,

alwey *adv* al-wei *adv*. A 1; B 2; C 1
A. 9.20 Ergo he nis not *alwey* at hom among ȝow Freris;
B. 8.24 Ergo he nys noȝt *alwey* [at hoom] amonges yow freres;
B.15.313 For we [by] goddes [behestes] abiden *alwey*
C.10.28 Ergo he [n]is nat *alwey* at hom amonges ȝow freres;

am > ben

amaistrye *v* amaistren *v*. A 3 amaistrie (1) amaistried (1) amaistrien (1); B 3 amaistren (1) amaistrye (1) amaistried (1); C 3 amaystre (1) amaystred (1) amaystrye (1)
A. 2.112 For he may mede *amaistrien* and maken at my wille'.
A. 2.118 For we haue mede *amaistried* wiþ oure mery speche
A. 7.197 And how I miȝte *amaistrie* hem & make hem to werche.'
B. 2.148 For [he] may Mede *amaistrye* and maken at my wille'.
B. 2.154 For we haue Mede *amaistried* wiþ oure murie speche
B. 6.211 And how I myȝte *amaistren* hem and make hem to werche.'
C. 2.164 For he may mede *amaystrye* [and maken at my wille].'
C. 2.170 For we haue mede *amaystred* [with] oure mery [speche]
C. 8.220 How y myhte *amaystre* hem to louye and labory

amalec *n prop* *n.i.d.* A 1 amaleg; B 2; C 2 amalek
A. 3.241 Þat agag of *Amaleg* & [al] his peple aftir
B. 3.262 That Agag of *Amalec* and al his peple after
B. 3.266 Weend to *Amalec* with þyn oost & what þow fyndest þere sle it.
C. 3.415 That agag of *amalek* and alle his leege peple
C. 3.419 Haste the with al thyn oste to þe lond of *Amalek*

ambrose *n prop* *n.i.d.* B 2; C 2
B.13.39 Of Austyn, of *Ambrose*, of [alle] þe foure Euangelistes:
B.19.269 Oon hihte Austyn and *Ambrose* anoþer,
C.15.44 Of Austyn, of *Ambrose*, of alle þe foure euaungeli[st]es:
C.21.269 Oen hihte Austyn and *Ambros[e]* anoþer,

ameddes > amyd

amendement *n* amendement *n*. B 2; C 3
B.10.369 And siþen heþen to helpe in hope of *amendement*.
B.20.135 And ouertilte al his truþe wiþ 'tak þis vp *amendement*'.
C. 3.122 In *amendement* of mayres and oþer stywardes
C. 6.102 Graunte me, gode lord, grace of *amendement*.'
C.22.135 And ouertulde al his treuthe with 'taek this [vp] *amendement*.'

amenden *v* amenden *v*. A 13 amende; B 57 amende (42) amended (2) amenden (13); C 49 amende (44) amended (1) amenden (4)
A. 1.142 Mekliche for oure misdedis to *amende* vs alle.
A. 3.83 For to *amende* [meiris and] men þat kepiþ þe lawis,
A. 4.77 *Amende* þat mysdede, & eueremore þe betere.'
A. 4.83 'Haue þis of me, man,' quaþ heo, 'to *amende* þi skaþe,
A. 6.83 His man hattiþ *amende* ȝow, for many man he knowiþ.
A. 6.88 Biddiþ *amende* ȝow meke hym to his maister ones
A. 7.69 Þei arn askapid good auntir, now god hem *amende*.'
A. 7.257 Þere arn mo liȝeris þan lechis, lord hem *amende*.
A. 8.29 Wykkide weyes wiȝtly to *amende*,
A.10.215 But ȝif god [g]iue h[e]m grace here to *amende*.
A.11.47 Is non to nymen hym In ne his [noye] *amende*,
A.11.79 And for his muchel mercy to *amende* vs here.
A.11.251 And siþen he[þen] to helpe in hope hem to *amende*.
B. 1.168 Mekely for oure mysdedes to *amende* vs alle.
B. 2.100 And þanne wanhope to awaken h[y]m so wiþ no wil to *amende*
B. 3.57 Who may scape [þe] sclaundre, þe scaþe is soone *amended*.
B. 3.94 For to *amenden* Maires and men þat kepen [þe] lawes,
B. 4.90 *Amenden* þat [mysdede] and eueremoore þe bettre.'
B. 4.96 'Haue þis [of me, man]', quod she, 'to *amenden* þi scaþe,
B. 5.134 I wole *amende* þis if I may þoruȝ myȝt of god almyȝty.'
B. 5.187 And bad me wilne to wepe my wikkednesse to *amende*.
B. 5.266 I nolde cope vs wiþ þi catel ne oure kirk *amende*
B. 5.479 To *amenden* vs of oure mysdedes: do mercy to vs alle,
B. 5.596 His man hatte *amende*-yow, for many m[a]n h[e] knoweþ.
B. 5.601 Biddeþ *amende*-yow meke hym til his maister ones
B. 6.77 They ben ascaped good a, [now] god hem *amende*.'
B. 6.273 [Ther are mo lieres þan] leches; lord hem *amende*!
B. 7.15 And in as muche as þei mowe *amenden* alle synfulle,
B. 7.27 Wikkede weyes wightly *amende*
B. 9.78 At myseise and at myschief and mowe hem *amende*
B. 9.85 For alle þe mebles on þis moolde and he *amende* it myȝte.
B. 9.201 But god gyue hem grace here to *amende*.
B.10.61 Is noon to nyme hym [in, ne] his [n]oy *amende*,
B.10.126 And for his muche mercy to *amende* [vs] here.
B.10.274 Alle maner men to *amenden* bi hire myȝtes;
B.10.324 And *amende* Monyals, Monkes and Chanons,
B.10.446 And he þat may al *amende* haue mercy on vs alle,
B.11.104 Thouȝ þow se yuel seye it noȝt first; be sory it nere *amended*.
B.11.138 Mercy al to *amende* and Mekenesse hir folwe;
B.11.210 And of þat ech man may forbere *amende* þere it nedeþ,
B.11.378 *Amende* þow, if þow myȝt, for my tyme is to abide.
B.11.381 He myȝte *amende* in a Minute while al þat mysstandeþ,
B.11.426 As shal shame, and shenden hym, and shape hym to *amende*.
B.12.7 To *amende* it in þi myddel age, lest myȝt þe faill[e]
B.12.10 *Amende* þee while þow myȝt; þow hast ben warned ofte
B.12.15 It is but murþe as for me to *amende* my soule.
B.12.95 For boþe ben as Mirours to *amenden* [by] defautes
B.12.195 [Th]at buxomliche biddeþ it and ben in wille to *amenden* hem.
B.12.229 And if þer were he wolde *amende*, and in swich wille deieþ–
B.13.207 Ther nys wo in þis world þat we ne sholde *amende*;
B.13.257 For may no blessynge doon vs boote but if we wile *amende*,
B.13.408 Ne no mercy *amenden* þe man þat so deieþ.
B.14.20 And engreynen it wiþ good wille and goddes grace to *amende* þe,
B.14.170 Ac god, of þi goodnesse gyue hem grace to *amende*.
B.14.188 Shulde *amenden* vs as manye siþes as man wolde desire.
B.15.109 And *amende*[n] hem þat [þei] mysdoon moore for youre ensaumples
B.15.249 Ac I ne lakke no lif, but lord *amende* vs alle,
B.15.562 A medicyne moot þerto þat may *amende* prelates.
B.15.568 If preesthode were parfit þe peple sholde *amende*
B.16.271 The myght of goddes mercy þat myȝte vs alle *amende*.'
B.17.197 Boþe meue and *amende*, þouȝ alle my fyngres oke.
B.17.240 In as muche as þei mowen *amenden* and paien;
B.17.317 To *amende* al þat amys is, and his mercy gretter
B.17.338 To man þat mercy askeþ and *amende* þenkeþ".
B.17.354 And louye hem lik hymself, and his lif *amende*.
B.18.155 May no medicyne [*amende*] þe place þer he styngeþ

B.18.341   And al þat man haþ mysdo I man wole *amende*.
B.19.442   And [Piers] *amende* þe pope, þat pileþ holy kirke
B.20.109   And kynde cessede [sone] to se þe peple *amende*.
B.20.362   'That is ouerlonge', quod þis Lymytour, 'I leue. I shal *amende* it!'
C.Pr.215   Til þat meschief *amende* hem þat many man chasteth.
C. 1.77   And preyede here pitously to preye for me to *amende*
C. 1.164   Mekeliche for oure mysdedes to *amende* vs alle.
C. 2.107   And awake with wanhope and no wille to *amende*,
C. 2.144   ȝe shal abyggen bothe but ȝe *amende* þe sonner.
C. 2.249   And sayde, 'syre kyng, by crist! but clerkes *amende*,
C. 3.65   Bothe wyndowes and wowes y wol *amende* and glase
C. 3.100   Graunte gylours on erthe grace to *amende*
C. 3.136   Bothe to the and to thyne in hope thow shost *amende*;
C. 4.86   And *amende* þat is mysdo and eueremore þe betere.'
C. 4.92   'Haue this, man, of me,' quod she, 'to *amende* thy scathe
C. 4.182   Withouten mercement or manslauht *amende* alle reumes.'
C. 5.170   And *amende* ȝow monkes, moniales and chanons,
C. 6.61   'Now god for his goodnesse gyue the grace to *amende*,'
C. 6.169   And bad hym bid to god be his helpe to *amende*.
C. 7.121   To *Amende* vs of oure mysdedes, do mercy to vs alle.
C. 7.127   And bicam man of a mayde mankynde to *amende*
C. 7.244   His man hatte *amende-ȝow*, many man hym knoweth.
C. 7.248   Biddeth *amende-ȝow* [hym] to his maistre grace
C. 8.79   They ben ascaped good aunter, now god hem *amende*.'
C. 9.16   And bitynge in badde men but yf they wol *amende*,
C. 9.30   *Amende* mesondewes þerwith and myseyse men fynde
C. 9.31   And wyckede wayes with here goed *amende*
C. 9.33   *Amende* in som manere wyse and ma[y]dones helpe;
C. 9.160   Buth nat in this bulle,' quod [Peres], 'til they ben *amended*
C. 9.238   *Amend[e]* hym and mercy aske and mekeliche hym shryue,
C.10.300   Bote god ȝeue hem grace her [g]oynge here to *amende*.
C.12.73   Mercy al [to] *amende* and mekenesse her folowe;
C.13.198   He myhte *amende* in a myntewhile al þat [mys]standeth
C.14.211   And yf þer were a wolde [*amende*], and in suche a wille deyeth–
C.15.221   In his mouthe mercy and *amende* vs all:
C.15.227   For may no blessynge dawe vs bote but yf we wol *amende*
C.16.23   And *amende* vs [of] thy mercy and make vs alle meke,
C.16.263   And *amenden* [hem] of here mysdedes more for [ȝoure]
           ensaumples
C.17.50   And conforte alle cristene wolde holy [kirke] *amende*.
C.17.202   To *amende* and to make, as with men of holy churche,
C.17.225   A medecyne moste þerto þat m[ay] *amende* prelates.
C.17.250   Yf prestehode were parfyt and preyede thus the peple sholde
           amende
C.18.287   The myhte of goddes mercy that myhte vs alle *amende*.'
C.19.163   Bothe meue and *amende*, thogh alle my fyngeres oke.
C.19.206   In as moche as they mowen *amenden* and payen;
C.19.297   To *amende* al þat amys is and his mercy grettore
C.19.318   To man þat mercy asketh and *amende* thenketh."
C.19.334   And louye h[e]m yliche hymsulue [and his lyf] *amende*.
C.20.158   May no medecyne *amende* the place there he styngeth
C.20.389   And al þat m[a]n mysdede, y man to *amende* brouhte
C.21.442   And [Peres] *amende* þe pope þat pileth holi churche
C.22.109   And kynde sesede [sone] to se þe peple *amende*.
C.22.362   'That is ouerlonge,' quod this lymitour, 'y leue; y schal *amenden*
           hit!'

amendes n *amendes n.*   A 2 amendis; B 6; C 4
A. 4.75   And he *amendis* mowe make let maynprise hym haue,
A. 5.173   Whoso hadde þe hood shulde haue *amendis* of þe cloke.
B. 2.119   For Mede is muliere of *Amendes* engendred
B. 4.88   And he *amendes* mowe make lat maynprise hym haue,
B. 4.103   For Mede haþ [maad myne *amendes*]; I may na moore axe.'
B. 5.324   Whoso hadde þe hood sholde han *amendes* of þe cloke.
B.18.327   And seide to Sathan, 'lo! here my soule to *amendes*
B.18.342   Membre for membre [was *amendes* by þe olde lawe],
C. 2.123   For mede is moilere, *amendes* was here dame;
C. 2.125   *Amendes* was here moder by trewe menne lokynge,
C. 2.126   And withouten here moder *amendes* mede may [nat] be wedded.
C. 4.84   Yf he *amendes* may [make] lat maynprise hym haue

amercy v *amercen v.*   B 1
B. 6.39   And þouȝ [þow] mowe *amercy* hem lat mercy be taxour

amyd prep *amidde adv.& prep.*   A 2 amydde; B 5 amyd (1) amydde (3)
           amyddes (1); C 6 ameddes (1) amydde (4) amyddes (1)
A. 7.166   And hitte hunger þerwiþ *amydde* hise lippes,
A. 9.25   Let bringe a man in a bot amydde a brood watir;
B. 5.283   Nis na moore to þe mercy of god þan [*amyd*] þe see a gleede:
B. 8.29   Lat brynge a man in a boot *amydde* [a] bro[od] watre;
B.10.414   And men þat maden it *amydde* þe flood adreynten.
B.12.198   Riȝt as som man yeue me mete and [sette me *amydde* þe floor;
B.16.14   *Amyddes* mannes body; þe more is of þat stokke.
C. 6.335   Fareth as flo[nke] of fuyr þat ful *amydde* Temese

C. 9.122   And thauh a mete with the mayre *ameddes* þe strete
C.10.33   Lat bryng a man in a boet *amydde* a brood water;
C.10.67   And merueilousliche me mette *amyddes* al þat blisse.
C.13.43   Thogh the messager make his way *amydde* the fayre whete
C.14.137   Riht As sum man ȝeueth me mete and sette me *Amydde* þe flore;

amyddes adv *amidde adv.& prep. &> amyd* B 2 amyddes
B.13.83   Were molten leed in his mawe and Mahoun *amyddes*.
B.13.246   Saue a pardon wiþ a peis of leed and two polles *amyddes*.

amys adj *amis pred.adj.*   A 1; B 3; C 2 amis (1) amys (1)
A. 1.151   For þe same mesour ȝe mete, *amys* oþer ellis,
B. 1.177   For þe same mesur[e] þat ye mete, *amys* ouþer ellis,
B. 6.327   Whan ye se [mone] *amys* and two monkes heddes,
B.17.317   To amende al þat *amys* is, and his mercy gretter
C. 1.173   For þe same mesure þat ȝe meteth, *amis* other elles,
C.19.297   To amende þat *amys* is and his mercy grettore

among prep *amonges prep.*   A 21 among (20) amonges (1); B 70 among
           (30) amonges (40); C 60 among (19) amonge (6) amonges (24)
           amongus (11)
A. 3.41   *Among* clerkis & kniȝtes consience to felle'.
A. 3.86   *Among* þise lettride lordis þis latyn amountiþ
A. 3.156   Such a maister is mede *among* men of goode.'
A. 4.134   Ac [whanne] resoun *among* þise renkis reherside þise wordis,
A. 5.121   Ne hadde [þe] grace of gile gon *among* my ware
A. 5.123   Þanne drouȝ I me *among* drapers my donet to lere,
A. 5.125   *Among* þe riche rayes I rendrit a lessoun;
A. 7.87   And monewe me in his memorie *among* alle cristene.
A. 7.89   And dele *among* my frendis & my dere children,
A. 8.57   Þise þre for þrallis ben þrowe *among* vs alle
A. 8.78   Þere ben mo mysshapen *amonges* hem, whoso takiþ hede,
A. 8.140   Am l[ower]e lordis þat londis shuln be departid'.
A. 8.176   Þeiȝ þou be founde in þe fraternite *among* þe foure ordris,
A. 9.14   'Marie,' quaþ þe maistris, '*among* vs he dwelliþ,
A. 9.20   Ergo he nis not alwey at hom *among* ȝow Freris;
A.10.128   *Among* men of þis molde þat mek ben & kynde.
A.10.163   And is as muche to mene, *among* vs alle,
A.11.10   *Among* hogges þat hauen hawen at wille.
A.11.35   Menstralsie & merþe *among* men is nouþe
A.11.54   Ac *among* [mene] men hise mercy & his werkis,
A.11.182   'It is a wel lel[e] lif,' quaþ she, '*among* þe lewide peple;
B.Pr.103   *Amonges* foure vertues, [most vertuous of alle],
B.Pr.192   The maȝe *among* vs alle þeiȝ we mysse a sherewe,
B. 3.42   *Amonges* [clerkes and (kny3tes) Conscience to [felle]'.
B. 3.97   *Among* þise lettrede l[or]des þis latyn [amounteþ]
B. 3.169   Swich a maister is Mede *among* men of goode.'
B. 3.301   And swich pees *among* þe peple and a parfit truþe
B. 5.130   *Amonges* Burgeises haue I be, [bigg]yng at Londoun,
B. 5.169   *Among* Monkes I myȝte be ac many tyme I shonye
B. 5.205   Ne hadde þe grace of gyle ygo *amonges* my [ware]
B. 5.207   Thanne drouȝ I me *among* drapiers my donet to lerne,
B. 5.209   *Among* þe riche Rayes I rendred a lesson;
B. 5.239   I lerned *among* lumbardes [a lesson and of Iewes],
B. 5.257   'Artow manlich *among* þi neȝebores of þi mete and drynke?'
B. 5.259   *Amonges* my neȝebores namely swich a name ich haue.'
B. 6.95   And mengen [me] in his memorie *amonges* alle cristene.
B. 6.97   And dele *among* my [frendes] and my deere children.
B. 6.163   Plentee *among* þe peple þe while my plowȝ liggeþ'.
B. 6.228   And biloue þee *amonges* [lowe] men: so shaltow lacche grace.'
B. 7.96   Ther is moore mysshapen *amonges* þise beggeres
B. 7.162   *Amonges* lower lordes þi lond shal be departed'.
B. 7.198   Theiȝ [þow] be founde in þe fraternite [*among*] þe foure ordres
B. 8.18   '[Marie]', quod þe [maistres, '*amonges* vs he dwelleþ],
B. 8.24   Ergo he nys noȝt alwey [at hoom] *amonges* yow freres;
B. 8.114   How dowel, dobet and dobest doon *among* þe peple.'
B. 9.75   And fynde fele witnesses *among* þe foure doctours,
B.10.10   *Among* hogges þat han hawes at wille.
B.10.49   Ac [mynstralcie and murþe] *amonges* men is nouþe
B.10.68   Ac *amonges* meene men his mercy and hise werkes.
B.10.77   In Religion and in al þe Reme *amonges* riche and pouere
B.10.297   [*Amonges* riȝtful religious þis rule sholde be holde.
B.10.454   Dauid makeþ mencion, he spak *amonges* kynges,
B.11.51   Than dowel or dobet *among* my dedes alle.
B.11.86   'If I dorste', quod I, '*amonges* men þis metels auowe!'
B.11.204   No beggere ne boye *amonges* vs but if it synne made:
B.11.244   Many tyme god haþ ben met *among* nedy peple,
B.11.166   And how *among* þe grene gras growed so manye hewes,
B.13.229   Ouþer mantel or moneie *amonges* lordes Mynstrals.
B.13.258   Ne mannes masse make pees *among* cristene peple
B.13.277   As in apparaill and in porte proud *amonges* þe peple;
B.13.435   Ne no mysproud man *amonges* lordes ben allowed.
B.13.453   In a welhope, [for he wrouȝte so], *amonges* worþi seyntes],
B.14.27   Ne no Mynstrall be moore worþ *amonges* pouere and riche

B.14.72   *Amonges* cristene creatures, if cristes wordes ben trewe.
B.14.73   Ac vnkyndenesse caristiam makeþ *amonges* cristen peple,
B.14.74   [Oþer] plentee makeþ pryde *amonges* poore and riche.
B.14.76   For þe meschief and þe meschaunce *amonges* men of Sodome
B.14.157   For muche murþe is *amonges* riche, as in mete and cloþyng,
B.14.158   And muche murþe in May is *amonges* wilde beestes;
B.14.308   And an hardy man of herte *among* an heep of þeues.
B.15.22   'What are ye called?' quod I, 'in þat court loue *among* cristes peple?'
B.15.237   In court *amonges* [þe commune] he comeþ but selde
B.15.244   [*Amonges* erchebisshopes and bisshopes, [for beggeres sake],
B.15.258   *Amonges* cristene men þis myldenesse sholde laste
B.15.273   Woneden in wildernesse *among* wilde beestes,
B.15.335   How I myȝte mo þerInne *amonges* hem sette.
B.15.375   [Ne] nauȝt oon *among* an hundred þat an Auctour kan construwe,
B.15.403   And if he *among* þe peple preched, or in places come,
B.15.524   *Amonges* vnkynde cristene for cristes loue he deyede,
B.15.530   And crepe [in] *amonges* curatours, confessen ageyn þe lawe:
B.15.531   Many man for cristes loue was martired [*amonges*] Romayne[s]
B.15.538   And þo was plentee and pees *amonges* poore and riche,
B.16.28   Coueitise comþ of þat wynd and crepeþ *among* þe leues
B.16.256   *Amonges* patriarkes and prophetes pleyinge togideres.
B.17.213   [Fostren forþ *amonges* folk loue and bileue]
B.19.251   [Ne no boost ne] debat [be] *among* hem [alle].
B.19.311   *Among* þ[e] foure vertues and vices destruye.
B.19.420   That no Cardynal coome *among* þe comune peple,
B.19.422   At Auynoun *among* Iewes–Cum sancto sanctus eris &c–
B.19.455   For Spiritus prudencie *among* þe peple is gyle,
B.20.112   *Amonges* alle manere men, wedded and vnwedded,
C.Pr.88   That is lele loue and lyf *among* lered and lewed,
C.Pr.131   *Amonge* foure vertues, most vertuous of vertues,
C. 3.44   *Amonge* kynges and knyhtes and clerkes and the lyke.'
C. 3.49   *Among* knyhtes and clerkes consience to turne.
C. 3.98   That Innocence is herde in heuene *amonge* seyntes
C. 3.125   *Amonge* thise lettred lordes this latyn is to mene
C. 3.215   Such a maistre is mede *among* men of gode.'
C. 3.454   And such pees *among* þe peple and a parfit treuthe
C. 4.26   Whiche a maistre mede was *amonges* pore and ryche.
C. 4.188   Audiatis alteram partem *amonges* aldremen and comeneres,
C. 5.4   *Amonges* lollares of londone and lewede Ermytes,
C. 5.193   *Amonges* alle kyne kynges ouer cristene peple.
C. 6.30   Proud of aparayle in port *amongus* þe peple
C. 6.60   As to be preised *amongus* þe peple thow [y] pore seme:
C. 6.96   *Amongus* marchauntes many tymes and nameliche in londone.
C. 6.115   *Amonges* alle manere men my dwellyng is som tyme,
C. 6.143   *Amonges* wyues and wydewes [y am woned] to sitte
C. 6.151   *Amonges* monkes y myhte be Ac mony tyme y spare
C. 6.158   Y haue no luste, lef me, to longe *amonges* monkes
C. 6.213   Ne hadde þe grace of Gyle go *among* my ware
C. 6.215   Thenne drow y me *amonge* drapers my donet to lere,
C. 6.217   *Amongus* the ryche rayes y rendrede a lessoun,
C. 6.241   Y lernede *among* lumbardus a lessoun and of iewes,
C. 6.435   Out of resoun *among* rybaudes here rybaudrye to here.
C. 7.95   Ne no mysproud man *amongus* lordes be [alow]ede.
C. 7.113   In a welhope for a wrouhte so *amongus* worthy seyntes
C. 8.104   And men[g]e me in his memorie *amongus* alle cristene.
C. 8.106   And delen *amongus* my douhteres and my dere childre[n].
C. 9.18   Lechery *amonges* lordes and here luyther custumes,
C. 9.172   Ther aren mo mysshape *amonges* suche beggeres
C. 9.190   And in borwes *among* brewesteres and beggen in churches–
C.10.28   Ergo he [n]is nat alwey at hom *amonges* ȝow freres;
C.11.8   *Among* hoggus þat han hawes at wille.
C.11.32   Litel is he loued or leet [by] *among* lordes at festes.
C.11.57   In religion and in al þe reume *amongus* riche and pore
C.11.79   *Amonges* hem þat haen hawes at wille,
C.11.279   Dauid maketh mensioun he spake *among* kynges
C.12.112   No heuedere ne boy *among* vs but [yf] hit synne ma[d]e:
C.13.2   *Among* Pilours in pees yf pacience hym folowe.
C.15.203   Or mantel or mone *amonges* lordes munstrals.
C.15.228   Ne mannes prayere maky pees *amonges* cristene peple
C.15.271   *Amonges* cristene creatures, yf cristes wordes be trewe:
C.16.10   Muche murthe is in may *amonge* wilde bestes
C.16.12   And moche murthe *among* ryche men is þat han meble ynow and hele.
C.16.265   Ypocrisye is a braunche of pruyde and most *amonges* clerkes
C.16.362   *Amongus* þe comune in Court a cometh bote selde
C.17.28   And woneden in wildernesses *amonges* wilde bestes.
C.17.199   And tho was p[lente] and p[ees] *amonges* pore and ryche;
C.17.275   *Amonges* v[n]kynde cristene in holy [kirke] was slawe
C.17.280   And crepe in *amonges* curatours and confessen aȝeyn þe lawe:
C.17.281   Many man for cristes loue was martired *amonges* Romaynes
C.17.288   And *amonges* here enemyes in mortel batayles
C.17.308   That iesus was bote a iogelour, a iapare *amonges* þe comune,
C.19.179   Fostren forth *amongus* folke loue and bileue

C.21.251   Ne no boest ne debaet be *among* hem alle.
C.21.311   *Among* th[e] foure vertues and vices distruye.
C.21.420   That no cardinal come *among* þe comune peple
C.21.422   At Auenon *among* iewes–cum sancto sanctus eris &c–
C.21.455   For spiritus prudencie *among* þe peple is gyle,
C.22.112   *Amonges* alle manere men, wedded and vnwedded,

amonge adv *amonges adv. &> among* B 1
B.14.238   Wiþoute mournynge *amonge*, and meschief to bote].

amonges -us > among

amortisede v *amortisen v.* B 1; C 1 amorteysed
B.15.321   Er þei *amortisede* to monkes or [monyales] hir rente[s].
C.17.55   Ar they *amorteysed* eny more for monkes or for Chanoun[s].

amorwe adv *amorwen adv.* C 2 amorwe (1) amorwen (1)
C. 3.308   The huyre of his hewe ouer eue til *amorwe*:
C. 7.13   Y haue [made] voues fourty and forȝeten hem *amorwen*.

amounteþ v *amounten v.* A 1 amountiþ; B 1
A. 3.86   Among þise lettride lordis þis latyn *amountiþ*
B. 3.97   Among þise lettrede l[or]des þis latyn [*amounteþ*]

ampulles n *ampulle n.* A 1 ampollis; B 1; C 1 Aunpolles
A. 6.8   An hundrit of *ampollis* on his hat seten,
B. 5.520   An hundred of *Ampulles* on his hat seten,
C. 7.165   An hundret of *Aunpolles* on his hat se[t]e,

an > a,on

ancre n *ancre n.* A 3 ancris (2) ankeris (1); B 4 Ancres; C 3 ancre (1) Ankeres (1) Ankerus (1)
A.Pr.28   As *ancris* & Ermytes þat holden hem in [here] cellis,
A. 7.133   *Ankeris* & heremytes þat holde hem in here sellis,
A.10.136   Boþe maidenis & [mynchons], monkes & *ancris*,
B.Pr.28   As *Ancres* and heremites þat holden hem in hire selles,
B. 6.145   Ac *Ancres* and heremites þat eten but at Nones
B.15.214   Ne at *Ancres* þere a box hangeþ; alle swiche þei faiten.
B.15.417   *Ancres* and heremytes and Monkes and freres
C.Pr.30   As *Ankeres* and Eremites þat holdeth hem in here selles
C. 3.142   Or in a wel wors, wo[en ther as an *ancre*,
C. 8.146   *Ankerus* and Eremytes þat eten but at nones

and conj *and conj.* A 1338 and (619) & (719); B 4519 and (4484) & (35); C 4763 and (4733) & (30)
Often with sense "if," as illustrated in following instances:
A. 2.154   'Be crist,' quaþ þe king, '& I miȝte cacche
A. 4.120   For I seiȝe it be myself, & it so were
A.11.218   And welawey wers *and* I [wo]lde al telle.'
B. 2.133   [She] myȝte kisse þe kyng for cosyn *and* she wolde.
B. 2.193   'By crist!' quod þe kyng, '*and* I cacche myȝte
B. 3.130   Bitwene heuene and helle, [*and*] erþe þouȝ men souȝte.
B. 4.137   I seye it be myself *and* it so were
B. 5.90   'I wolde ben yshryue', quod þis sherewe, '*and* I for shame dorste.
B. 6.253   'Yet I preie [þee]', quod Piers, 'p[u]r charite, *and* [þow] konne
B. 9.83   Ne faille payn ne potage *and* prelates dide as þei sholden.
B. 9.85   'For alle þe mebles on þis moolde *and* he amende it myȝte.
B.10.266   Ac blame þow neuere body *and* þow be blameworþy;
B.11.100   Thouȝ þe tale [were] trewe, *and* it touche[d] synne.
B.11.138   Mercy al to amende *and* Mekenesse hir folwe;
B.11.286   *And* þei hir deuoir dide as Dauid seiþ in þe Sauter:
B.13.110   But cheeste be þer charite sholde be, *and* yonge children dorste pleyne.
B.13.114   And seide hymself, 'sire doctour, *and* it be youre wille,
B.13.163   Tene þee any tyme, *and* þow take it wiþ þe.
B.13.164   [And ek, haue god my soule, *and* þow wilt it craue
B.13.200   'Me were leuere, by oure lord, *and* I lyue sholde,
B.14.26   Than Haukyn þe Actif man, *and* þow do by my techyng,
B.15.430   The heuedes of holy chirche, *and* þei holy were,
B.16.73   I preide Piers to pulle adoun an Appul *and* he wolde.
B.17.97   *And* [he be] baþed in þat blood, baptised as it were,
B.17.245   So wole crist of his curteisie, *and* men crye hym mercy,
B.17.351   That he ne may louye, *and* hym like, and lene of his herte
B.18.414   That loue, *and* hym liste, to laughynge ne brouȝte;
B.19.26   'Thow knowest wel', quod Conscience, '*and* þow konne reson,
B.20.9   *And* þow nome na moore þan nede þee tauȝte?
B.20.210   '*And* þow loue lelly lakke shal þee neuere
C. 2.207   'Now, by crist!' quod þe kyng, '*and* y cacche myhte
C. 3.44   Amonge kynges and knyhtes and clerkes *and* the lyke.'
C. 3.140   Thow tene me and treuthe: *and* thow mowe be atake
C. 3.167   Bytwene heuene *and* helle, and erthe thogh men soughte.
C. 4.134   Y sey it [by] mysulf,' quod resoun, '*and* it so were
C. 6.91   'ȝus! redily,' quod repentaunce, '*and* thow be ryht sory
C. 6.289   Ne take a meles mete of thyn *and* myn herte hit wiste
C. 8.136   'ȝoure prayeres,' quod [Peres], '*and* ȝe p[ar]fyt weren,
C. 8.160   For ther worth no plente,' quod [Perus], '*and* þe plouh lygge.'

C. 8.232 In meschief or in malese, *and* thow mowe hem helpe,
C. 9.19 *And* suche liue as þei lereth men oure lord treuthe hem graunteth
C. 9.71 Ac þat most neden aren oure neyhebores *and* we nyme gode he[d]e
C.11.94 And ouer skripture þe skilfole *and* screueynes were trewe
C.12.32 'And wherof serueth lawe,' quod leaute, ' *and* no lyf vndertoke [hit],
C.12.73 Mercy al [to] amende *and* mekenesse her folowe;
C.15.117 *And* 3e fare thus with 3oure syke freres, ferly me thynketh
C.15.121 And saide hymsulue, 'sire doctour, [*and*] hit be 3oure wille,
C.15.159 Tene þe eny tyme *and* þou take pacience
C.15.178 Me were leuere, by oure lord, *and* y leue sholde,
C.19.211 So wol Crist of his cortesye, *and* men crien hym mercy,
C.20.457 That loue, *and* hym luste, to l[a]u[h]ynge [ne] brouhte;
C.21.26 'Thow knowest wel,' quod Concience, '*and* þou kunne resoun,
C.22.9 *And* thow nome no more then nede the tauhte?
C.22.210 'And thow loue lelly lacke shal the neuere

andrew n prop *n.i.d.* B 1; C 1 Androwe
B.15.292 Peter fisshed for his foode and his felawe *Andrew*;
C.17.19 Peter fischede for his fode And his fere *Androwe*;

angel(- > aungel

angre n *anger n.* A 1 angir; B 6 angre (2) angres (4); C 6 anger (2)
       angeres (1) angre (1) angres (1) angrys (1)
A.10.143 An aungel in *angir* hi3te h[e]m to wende
B.12.11 Wiþ poustees of pestilences, wiþ pouerte and with *angres*;
B.13.335 Or an Ague in swich an *Angre* and som tyme a Feuere
B.15.259 In alle manere *angres*, haue þis at herte
B.15.271 In hunger, in hete, in alle manere *angres*.
B.17.342 And þou3 þat men make muche doel in hir *angre*
B.19.291 To suffren al þat god sente, siknesse and *Angres*.
C. 6.79 Or an ague in suche [an] *angre* and som tyme a feuere
C. 6.114 In alle manere *angres* þat y hadde or felede.
C.12.207 Angelis in here *anger* on this wyse hem gretteth:
C.16.152 And sobrete 3eueth here swete drynke and solaceth here in all
       angrys.
C.19.322 And thogh that men make moche deul in here *anger*
C.21.291 To soffre al þat god sente, seeknesse and *angeres*.

angre v *angren v.* A 1 angriþ; B 2 angre (1) angreþ (1); C 1 Angry
A. 5.97 And whoso haþ more þanne I, þat *angriþ* myn herte.
B. 5.118 [And] whoso haþ moore þan I, þat *angreþ* [myn herte].
B.14.245 And þou3 Auarice wolde *angre* þe poore he haþ but litel my3te,
C.16.85 And thogh Auaryce wolde *Angry* [þe] pou[r]e he hath bote lytel
       myhte

angryliche adv *angrili adv.* C 1
C.16.114 Quod Actyf tho al *angryliche* and Arguinge as hit were:

angrys > angre

anhengede *anhongen v.* C 1
C. 1.64 And afterward *anhengede* hym hey vppon an hellerne.

any pron *ani lim.adj.* A 3; B 5; C 6 eny
A. 2.155 Fals oþer fauel oþer *any* of his feris,
A. 6.113 It is wel hard, be myn hed, *any* of 3ow alle,
A.11.283 Or adam, or ysaye, or *any* of þe prophetis
B. 3.324 And what smyth þat *any* smyþeþ be smyte þerwiþ to deþe;
B. 5.180 Al þe wikkednesse þat I woot by *any* of oure breþeren,
B. 5.628 It is [wel] hard, by myn heed, *any* of yow alle
B.10.367 Or delit in wyn and wildefowel and wite *any* in defaute.
B.10.424 Or Adam or Ysaye or *any* of þe prophetes
C. 3.466 Haukyng or huntyng yf *eny* of hem hit vse
C. 6.162 Al þat y wiste wykked by *eny* of oure couent
C. 7.281 Hit is ful hard, be myn heued, *eny* of 3ow alle
C.11.256 And ar Adam oþer ysaye oþer *eny* of the profetes
C.18.110 For euere as Elde hadde *eny* down, þe deuel was redy
C.20.385 The same sore shal he haue þat *eny* so smyteth:

any adj *ani lim.adj.* A 25 any (24) eny (1); B 93 any (92) anye (1); C
    106 eny
A. 2.32 And become a good man for *any* coueitise, I rede.'
A. 2.36 Þat fals & fauel be *any* fyn halden,
A. 2.100 3if *any* Leaute wile loke þei ligge togidere.
A. 2.161 To atache þis tiraunt[is] 'for *any* tresour, I hote;
A. 2.162 Feteriþ falsnesse faste for *any* skynes 3eftis,
A. 2.168 Er he be put on þe pillorie, for *any* preyour, I hote.'
A. 3.249 For *any* mylionis of mone murdre hem ichone;
A. 5.153 'Hast þou,' quaþ he, '*any* hote spices?'
A. 6.114 To gete ingang at *any* gate but grace be þe more.'
A. 7.59 And whoso helpiþ me to eren, or *any* þing swynke,
A. 7.204 Ac 3if þou fynde *any* frek þat fortune haþ apeirid
A. 7.238 *Eny* l[e]f of lechecraft lere it me, my dere,
A. 8.7 Or *any* maner mester þat mi3te peris helpen,
A. 8.60 Þat *any* mede of mene men for motyng resceyueþ.
A. 9.4 3if *any* wi3t wiste where dowel was at Inne;

A. 9.12 3if þei knewen *any* cuntre or costis aboute
A. 9.89 Þat waiten *any* wikkidnesse dowel to tenen.
A.10.57 And ek wantoun & wilde, wiþoute *any* resoun.
A.10.73 And cheuissh[en] hym for *any* charge whan he childhod passiþ,
A.10.188 Or wedde *any* wydewe for any wele of godis,
A.10.188 Or wedde any wydewe for *any* wele of godis,
A.10.211 Vngracious to gete loue or *any* good ellis,
A.11.5 'Wel art þou wys, wyt,' quaþ she, '*any* wisdomis to telle
A.11.8 Wiþ suche wise wordis to wisse *any* foolis!
A.11.186 Wiþ *any* trewe trauaille toille for here foode,
B.Pr.156 Mi3te we wiþ *any* wit his wille wiþstonde
B. 2.12 And þeron [riche] Rubies as rede as *any* gleede.
B. 2.64 Were moost pryuee with Mede of *any* men me þou3te.
B. 2.77 Than for *any* vertue or fairnesse or any free kynde.
B. 2.77 Than for any vertue or fairnesse or *any* free kynde.
B. 2.136 If *any* [lewte] wol loke þei ligge togidres,
B. 2.194 Fals or Fauel or *any* of hise feeris,
B. 2.200 To attachen þo Tyraunt3 'for *any* [tresor], I hote;
B. 2.201 Fettreþ [Falsnesse faste] for *any* kynnes 3iftes,
B. 2.207 Er he be put on þe Pillory for *any* preyere I hote.'_
B. 3.306 Ax ouþer hachet or *any* wepene ellis,
B. 3.313 Huntynge or haukynge if *any* of hem vse
B. 4.177 Ac Reson shal rekene wiþ yow if I regne *any* while,
B. 5.51 And er he gyue *any* grace gouerne first hymselue.
B. 5.154 Hir [were] leuere swowe or swelte þan suffre *any* peyne.
B. 5.172 And if I telle *any* tales þei taken hem togidres,
B. 5.303 'Hastow', quod he, '*any* hote spices?'
B. 5.400 And if I bidde *any* bedes, but if it be in wraþe,
B. 5.429 If *any* man dooþ me a bienfait or helpeþ me at nede
B. 5.629 To geten ing[o]ng at *any* gate but grace be þe moore.'
B. 6.65 And whoso helpeþ me to erie [or *any* þyng swynke]
B. 6.218 A[c] if þow fynde *any* freke þat Fortune haþ apeired
B. 6.254 *Any* leef of lechecraft lere it me, my deere;
B. 7.7 Or *any* [maner] mestier þat my3te Piers [helpe],
B. 7.59 That *any* Mede of mene men for motyng takeþ.
B. 7.79 In hym þat takeþ is þe trecherie if *any* treson walke,
B. 8.4 If *any* wi3t wiste wher dowel was at Inne;
B. 8.12 If þei knewe *any* contree or costes [aboute]
B. 8.99 That waiten *any* wikkednesse dowel to tene.
B. 9.35 And Eue of his ryb bon wiþouten *any* mene.
B. 9.100 To spille *any* speche or any space of tyme:
B. 9.100 To spille any speche or *any* space of tyme:
B. 9.154 That bryngeþ forþ *any* barn but if he be þe same
B. 9.167 Or wedden *any* wodewe for [wele] of hir goodes
B.10.5 'Wel artow wis, [wit', quod she], '*any* wisdomes to telle
B.10.8 'Wiþ swiche wise wordes to wissen *any* sottes!'
B.10.268 Alle þat lakkeþ *any* lif and lakkes han hemselue.
B.10.294 And drede to wraþe yow in *any* word youre werkmanship to lette,
B.10.305 For if heuene be on þis erþe, and ese to *any* soule,
B.11.172 Or *any* Science vnder sonne, þe seuene art3 and alle–
B.11.222 For it is ouerlonge er logyk *any* lesson assoille.
B.11.308 Or in masse or in matyns makeþ *any* defaute:
B.11.350 If *any* Mason made a molde þerto muche wonder it were.
B.12.25 Ac if þer were *any* wight þat wolde me telle
B.12.124 And medle no3t muche wiþ hem to meuen *any* wraþe
B.12.145 If *any* frere were founde þere I 3yue þee fyue shillynges!
B.12.173 If hym likeþ and lest, þan *any* lewed [sooþly].
B.13.98 Of dowel and dobet, and if do[best] be *any* penaunce.'
B.13.103 'What is dowel, sire doctour?' quod I; 'is [dobest] *any* penaunce?'
B.13.123 I am vnhardy', quod he, 'to *any* wi3t to preuen it.
B.13.163 Tene þee *any* tyme, and þow take it wiþ þe:
B.13.281 And inobedient to ben vndernome of *any* lif lyuynge;
B.13.323 Al þat he wiste,wikked by *any* wight tellen it,
B.13.331 Ther is no lif þat me loueþ lastynge *any* while.
B.13.363 And if my Neghebore hadde a[n] hyne or *any* beest ellis
B.13.389 So if I kidde *any* kyndenesse myn euencristen to helpe
B.14.19 Dobet shal beten it and bouken it as bright as *any* scarlet
B.14.156 That god rewarded double reste to *any* riche wye.
B.14.291 Selde is *any* poore yput to punysshen any peple.
B.14.291 Selde is any poore yput to punysshen *any* peple.
B.14.331 Or maistrie ouer *any* man mo þan of hymselue.
B.14.332 'I were no3t worþi, woot god', quod haukyn, 'to werien *any* cloþes,
B.15.6 Lordes or ladies or *any* lif ellis,
B.15.53 That *any* creature sholde konne al except crist oone.
B.15.176 'Haþ he *anye* rentes or richesse or any riche frendes?'
B.15.176 'Haþ he anye rentes or richesse or *any* riche frendes?'
B.15.328 If *any* peple parfourne þat text it are þise poore freres,
B.15.376 Ne rede a lettre in *any* langage but in latyn or englissh.
B.15.377 Go now to *any* degree, and but if gile be maister,
B.15.420 Of tiraunt3 þat teneþ trewe men taken *any* almesse,
B.15.532 Er cristendom [were] knowe þere, or *any* cros honoured
B.16.12 Lord!' quod I, 'if *any* wight wite whiderout it groweþ?'
B.16.65 To asken hym *any* moore þerof, and bad hym ful faire

B.16.99   For to werchen his wille wiþouten *any* synne:
B.16.107   Til he was parfit praktisour if *any* peril fille.
B.16.129   That in chirche chaffareden or chaungeden *any* moneie;
B.17.44   It is ful hard for *any* man on Abraham bileue
B.17.286   Ac þis is þe worste wise þat *any* wight myghte
B.17.288   For coueitise of *any* kynnes þyng þat crist deere bouȝte.
B.17.289   [How myȝte he aske mercy, or *any* mercy hym helpe],
B.17.298   Ne haue pite for *any* preiere þer þat he pleyneþ.'
B.17.306   *Any* creature [be] coupable afore a kynges Iustice
B.18.97   To [bete a body ybounde wiþ *any* briȝt wepene].
B.18.129   Of *any* kynnes creature, conceyued þoruȝ speche
B.18.322   For *any* wye or warde wide opned þe yates.
B.18.388   Be it *any* þyng abouȝt, þe boldnesse of hir synnes,
B.19.77   Or *any* kynnes catel; but knowelich[ede] hym souereyn
B.19.278   Er he [dide] *any* [dede] deuyse wel þe ende;
B.19.293   Maken hym, for *any* mournynge, þat he nas murie in soule
B.19.307   For present or for preiere or *any* Prynces lettres.
B.19.392   Al þat we owen *any* wight er we go to housel?'
B.20.310   If *any* surgien were [in] þe seg[e] þat softer koude plastre.
B.20.342   But þow konne [*any*] craft þow comest nouȝt herInne.
C.Pr.176   Myghte [we] with *eny* wyt his wille w[i]þsytte
C. 1.143   Dey rather þen do *eny* dedly synne:
C. 2.66   Were most pryue with mede of *eny* men [me] thoghte.
C. 2.214   [T]o atache tho tyrauntes, 'for *eny* tresor, y hote;
C. 2.215   Lat fetere falsnesse faste for *eny* skynes ȝeftes,
C. 2.219   Ar he be put on þe pylorye for *eny* preyere ich hote.'
C. 3.69   To writen [i]n wyndowes of *eny* wel dedes,
C. 3.109   For to spyre and to aspye, for *eny* speche of suluer,
C. 3.113   That vsurers oþer regraters for *eny* skynes ȝeftes
C. 3.139   Ȝut y forgyue þe þis gult; godes forb[o]de *eny* more
C. 3.191   Ther she is wel with *eny* kyng wo is þ[e] rewme
C. 3.205   Ther he is alowed and ylet by þat laste shal *eny* while
C. 3.254   Forthy y consayl no kynge *eny* conseyl aske
C. 3.295   That *eny* man Mede toke but he hi[t] myhte deserue,
C. 3.424   For *eny* mede of money al that thow myhte [fynde],
C. 3.459   Ax oþer hachet or *eny* kyne w[e]pne,
C. 3.477   And yf *eny* smyth smeth[e] hit be smyte þerwith to dethe:
C. 4.51   'Bere sikerlyche *eny* seluer to seynt Gyles doune.
C. 4.138   Ne gete my grace thorw *eny* gyfte ne glosynge spe[ch]e
C. 4.171   Ac resoun shal rykene with ȝow yf y regne *eny* while
C. 5.20   Or *eny* other kynes craft þat to þe comune nedeth,
C. 5.25   To wurche as a werkeman *eny* while to duyren.'
C. 5.152   For yf heuene be on this erthe or ese to [*eny*] soule
C. 5.194   'Comaunde þat alle confessours þat *eny* kyng shryueth
C. 6.28   To telle *eny* tale, y trowed me wysor
C. 6.29   To carpe and to consayle then *eny* Clerk or lewed;
C. 6.35   Vantyng vp my vaynglorie for *eny* vndernymynge;
C. 6.117   Harm of *eny* man, byhynde or bifore.
C. 6.119   Here were leuer swowe or swelte then soffre *eny* payne.
C. 6.142   That alle ladyes me lot[h]eth þat louyet[h] *eny* worschipe.
C. 6.154   And yf y telle *eny* tales they taken hem togyderes
C. 6.248   'Lenedest [thow] euere *eny* lord for loue of his mayntenaunce?'
C. 6.262   And yf my neyhebore hadde an hyne or *eny* beste elles
C. 6.358   'Hastow,' quod he, '*eny* hote spyces?'
C. 8.37   And when ȝe mersyen *eny* man late mercy be taxour,
C. 8.228   Ac yf thow fynde *eny* folke þat fals men han apayred
C. 8.260   Thorw *eny* lele labour as thorw lymes and handes:
C. 8.266   Yf ȝe can or knowe *eny* kyne thyng[e] of fisyk
C. 9.7   Or *eny* manere mester þat myhte [Peres] auayle
C. 9.48   That conforteth suche in *eny* caes and coueyteth nat he[re] ȝiftes
C. 9.155   And can *eny* craft in caes he wolde hit vse,
C.10.4   Yf *eny* wiht wiste where dowel was at ynne;
C.10.12   Yf they knewe *eny* contre oþer costes aboute
C.11.6   To *eny* foel or to flaterere or to frentike peple,'
C.11.10   Then al þe precious perye þat *eny* prince weldeth.
C.11.62   Ne for drede of *eny* deth withdraweth h[e]m fro pruyde
C.11.259   Withoute penaunce oþer passioun oþer *eny* other peyne
C.12.94   Or *eny* science vnder sonne, the seuene ars and alle–
C.12.121   And pore peple fayle we nat while *eny* peny vs lasteth
C.12.157   Or *eny* welthe in this world, his wyf or his childrene,
C.13.122   Or in masse or in matynes maketh *eny* defaute:
C.13.161   Yf *eny* mason made a molde þerto moche wonder me thynketh.
C.13.206   And ar thow lacke *eny* lyf loke ho is to preyse
C.14.15   And þat is dobet, yf *eny* suche be, a blessed man þat helpeth
C.14.36   Then *eny* connyng of kynde wit but clergi hit reule.
C.14.67   And medle we nat moche with hem to meuen *eny* wrathe
C.14.89   Yf *eny* frere we[re] founde þere y ȝeue the fyue shillynges!

C.14.113   Yf hym liketh and luste, then *eny* lewede sothly.
C.14.182   Then for *eny* kyn he come of or for his kynde wittes.
C.15.71   Alle þat coueyte[d] to come to *eny* kyne ioye,
C.15.78   Ac me thynketh loth, thogh y latyn knowe, to lacken *eny* secte
C.15.105   Of dowel and dobet and yf dobe[s]t [be] *eny* penaunce.'
C.15.110   'What is dowel, sire doctour?' quod y; 'is dobest *eny* penaunce?'
C.15.155   Withoute brutteny[n]ge or buyren or *eny* bloed shedynge.
C.15.159   Tene þe *eny* tyme and þou take pacience
C.15.283   Then *eny* pore pacient; and þat preue y be resoun.
C.16.126   Selde is *eny* pore ypot to p[u]nesche *eny* peple.
C.16.126   Selde is *eny* pore ypot to p[u]nesche *eny* peple.
C.16.142   And euere þe lasse þat [*eny*] lede þe lihtere his herte is there,
C.16.215   That *eny* creature sholde conne al excepte crist one.
C.16.220   The witt[i]ore þat *eny* wihte is, but yf he worche þeraftur,
C.16.307   Ne þat *eny* gome wolde gyle [ne greue oþere]
C.17.3   And ȝut oþerwhile wroeth withouten *eny* synne.'
C.17.55   Ar they amorteysed *eny* more for monkes or for Chanoun[s].
C.17.61   Or ar prestes or pardoners or *eny* peple elles.
C.17.112   Go now to *eny* degre and bote gyle be holde a maistre
C.17.282   Or cristendoem were knowe þere or *eny* croos honoured.
C.18.132   For to worchen his wille withouten *eny* synne.
C.18.185   An heraud of Armes Ar *eny* lawe were.'
C.18.211   Semblable to hymsulue ar *eny* synne were,
C.19.27   'Ȝoure wordes aren wonderfol,' quod y; 'where *eny* of [hem] be
           trewe
C.19.104   *Eny* wikkedere in þe worlde then y were mysulue
C.19.111   And yf kynde wit carpe hereaȝen or *eny* kyne thouhtes
C.19.267   Ac this is þe worste wyse þat *eny* wihte
C.19.269   For coueytise of *eny* kyne thynge þat Crist dere bouhte.
C.19.270   How myhte he aske mercy or *eny* mercy hym defende
C.19.286   *Eny* creature be coupable bifore a kynges iustice
C.20.100   To bete a body ybounde with *eny* briht wypene.
C.20.132   Of *eny* kyn[nes] creature, conceyued thorw speche
C.20.365   For *eny* wey or warde wyde open[ed] þe ȝates.
C.20.384   Or *eny* manere membre maymeth oþer herteth,
C.20.394   Here *eny* synfole soule souereynliche by maistrie,
C.20.430   Be hit *eny* thyng abouhte, the boldenesse of here synne[s],
C.21.77   Or *eny* kyne catel; bote knoweleched hym souereyn
C.21.278   Ar he dede *eny* dede deuyse wel þe ende;
C.21.293   Makyn hym, for *eny* mornynge, þat he ne was murye in soule
C.21.307   For presente or for preyere or *eny* prinses lettres.
C.21.392   Al þat we owen *eny* wyhte or we go to hosele?'
C.22.310   Yf *eny* surgien were in þe sege that softur couthe plastre.
C.22.342   Bote thow conne *eny* craft thow comest nat hereynne.

aniente *v* *anienten v.* B 1; C 2 anyente (1) anyented (1)
B.17.290   That wikkedliche and wilfulliche wolde mercy *aniente*?
C.19.271   That wikkedliche and wilfulliche wolde mercy *anyente*?
C.20.386   So lyf shal lyf le[t]e ther lyf hath lyf an[y]en[t]ed

aniȝtes *adv* *anightes adv.* B 1; C 2 anyhtes
B.17.211   [That serueþ þise swynkeres to be by *aniȝtes*],
C. 5.16   Or haue an horn and be hayward and lygge þeroute [*a*]nyhtes
C.22.196   *Anyhtes* nameliche, when we naked were,

anker- > ancre; *anoen* > anoon

anoyed *ptp* *anoien v.* A 2; B 2
A. 2.131   Þ[o] hadde notories none; *anoyed* þei were
A. 3.176   In normandie was he nouȝt *anoyed* for my sake,
B. 2.167   Tho hadde Notaries none; *anoyed* þei were
B. 5.93   I haue a neȝebore [neiȝ] me, I haue *anoyed* hym ofte,

anoon *adv* *an-on adv.* A 2 anon; B 12 anon (1) anoon (11); C 22 anoen
           (9) anon (6) anone (1) anoon (6)
A.10.165   And com to noe *anon*, and bad hym nouȝt lette
A.12.35   Clergie into a caban crepte *anon* after,
B. 9.134   And com to Noe *anon* and bad hym noȝt lette:
B.11.46   Coueitise of eiȝes conforted me *anoon* after
B.11.338   As whan þei hadde ryde in Rotey tyme *anoon* [reste þei] after;
B.11.405   Tho cauȝte I colour *anoon* and comsed to ben ashamed
B.16.19   That I herde nempne his name *anoon* I swowned after,
B.18.319   Dukes of þis dymme place, *anoon* vndo þise yates
B.19.18   *Anoon* as men nempned þe name of god Iesu;
B.19.191   *Anoon* after an heigh vp into heuene
B.20.17   Nede *anoon* righte nymeþ hym vnder maynprise.
B.20.35   Ac nede is next hym for *anoon* he mekeþ
B.20.51   Whan nede ha[dde] vndernome me þus *anoon* I fil aslepe
B.20.136   An[d] to þe Arches in haste he yede *anoon* after
C.Pr.111   *Anon* as it was tolde hym that þe children of Israel
C.Pr.113   And his sones slawe *anon* he ful for sorwe
C. 1.115   'Nere hit for northerne men *anon* y wolde ȝow telle
C. 3.321   And bynyme hit hem *anone* and neueremore aftur
C. 4.150   Reherce the[r] *anon* ryhte þat myhte resoun stoppe.
C. 6.339   Repente þe *anon*,' quod repentaunce ryhte to the vsurer,

C. 7.294	Anoþer *anoen* riht nede he sayde he hadde
C. 9.164	Hit nedeth nat nouthe *anoon* for to preche
C.13.41	His erende and his lettre sheweth and is *anoon* delyuered.
C.13.146	As when þei hadde [ryde in] roteye[tyme] *anon* they reste aftur;
C.13.213	Tho cauhte y colour *anoen* and comesede to ben aschamed
C.13.216	And saide *anoen* to mysulue, 'slepynge hadde y grace
C.13.239	Ac when nede nymeth hym vp *anoen* he is aschamed
C.15.51	Thenne resoun radde *anoon* riht aftur
C.18.105	And *anoon* he hihte Elde an hy for to clymbe
C.20.362	Dukes of this demme place, *anoen* vndoth this ȝates
C.21.18	*Anoon* as men nemned þe name of god iesu;
C.21.191	*Anoon* aftur an heyh vp into heuene
C.22.17	Nede *anoen* riht nymeth hym vnder maynprise.
C.22.35	A[c] nede is nexst hym for *anoen* he meketh
C.22.51	Whenne nede hadde vndernome [me] thus *anoen* y ful aslepe
C.22.136	And [t]o þe Arches in haste he ȝede *anoen* aftur

anoþer *pron other pron.* A 4; B 13; C 16 another (10) anoþer (6)

A. 1.104	Cherubyn & seraphyn, such seuene & *anoþer*;
A. 3.237	It is a permutacioun apertly, a peny[worþ] for *anoþer*.
A. 6.106	Þat on hattiþ abstinence, and [humylite] *anoþer*,
A. 8.111	And but ȝif luk leiȝe he leriþ vs *anoþer*,
B.Pr.185	'Thouȝ we [hadde] kille[d] þe cat ȝet sholde þer come *anoþer*
B. 1.106	Cherubyn and Seraphyn, swiche seuene & [*anoþer*];
B. 3.258	It is a permutacion apertly, a penyworþ for *anoþer*.
B. 5.620	That oon hatte Abstinence, and humilite *anoþer*;
B. 7.71	*Anoþer* that were moore nedy; so þe nedieste sholde be holpe.
B. 7.129	And but if luc lye he lereþ vs [*anoþer*]
B. 9.86	Allas þat a cristene creature shal be vnkynde til *anoþer*!
B.10.103	And al to spare to [spille þat spende] shal *anoþer*.
B.11.75	Ich haue muche merueille of yow, and so haþ many *anoþer*,
B.15.369	Neiþer þei konneþ ne knoweþ oon cours bifore *anoþer*,
B.16.272	I wepte for hise wordes; wiþ þat sauȝ I *anoþer*
B.18.47	'Tolle, tolle!' quod *anoþer*, and took of kene þornes
B.19.269	Oon highte Austyn and Ambrose *anoþer*
C.Pr.202	'Thow we hadde ykuld þe Cat ȝut shulde ther come *another*
C. 1.106	Cherubyn and Ceraphyn, suche seuene and *anoþer*,
C. 3.296	And for to vndertake [to] trauaile for *another*
C. 3.314	Hit is a permutacoun apertly, on peneworth for *another*.
C. 3.320	May desa[u]owe that thei dede and do[uwe] þerwith *another*
C. 6.24	Wene y were witty and wiser then *another*;
C. 6.38	Summe tyme in o sekte, summe tyme in *another*,
C. 7.272	That on hatte a[b]stinence and vmbletee *a[n]oþer*,
C. 7.294	*Anoþer* anoen riht nede he sayde he hadde
C. 7.302	And loure on me and lihtly chyde and sygge y louede *another*.
C. 9.123	A reuerenseth hym ryht nauht, no rather then *another*:
C.17.105	Noþer they [conn]eth ne [know]eth a cours by[fore] *anoþer*.
C.18.196	'This is myrke thyng for me,' quod y, 'and for many *anoþer*'
C.18.288	[Y] wepte for his wordes; with þat saw y *a[n]other*
C.20.47	'Tolle, tolle!' quod *another*, and toek of kene thornes
C.21.269	Oen hihte Austyn and Ambros[e] *anoþer*,

anoþer *adj other adj.* B 1 anoþer

B.16.33	That it norisseþ nyce sightes and [*anoþer*] tyme wordes

answere *n answere n.* A 1; B 1; C 1

A.12.29	God gaf him non *answere* but gan his tounge holde.
B.18.298	Wheiþer he were god or goddes sone; he [g]af me short *answere*.
C.20.331	Where he were god or godes sone; he gaf me short *answere*.

answere *v answeren v.* A 3 answere (2) answered (1); B 6 answerde (3) answere (3); C 2 answerede (1) onswerie (1)

A.11.299	For to *answere* hem haue ȝe no doute,
A.11.301	Þe help of þe holy gost to *answere* hem [alle]'.
A.12.62	'Al hayl,' quod on þo, and I *answered*, 'welcome, & with whom be ȝe?'
B.Pr.140	And to þe Aungel an heiȝ *answerde* after:
B. 5.292	For he shal *answere* for þee at þe heiȝe dome,
B.10.119	Ymaginatif herafterward shal *answere* to [youre] purpos.
B.11.252	And hastily god *answerde*, and eiþeres wille [lowed],
B.15.382	And *answere* to Argumentȝ and [assoile] a Quodlibet–
B.18.316	Eft þe light bad vnlouke and Lucifer *answerde*
C. 6.347	For he shal *onswerie* for the at the hey dome,
C.20.359	For efte þat lihte bade vnlouke [and lucifer *answerede*].

antecedent *n antecedent adj.& n.* C 3

C. 3.354	That is god, the ground of al, a graciouse *antecedent*.
C. 3.362	Acordeth in alle kyndes with his *antecedent*.
C. 3.379	Lawe, l[o]ue and lewete and hym lord *antecedent*,

antecrist *n Antecrist n.* B 7; C 7 auntecrist

B.19.219	For *Antecrist* and hise al þe world shul greue
B.19.226	And wepne to fighte wiþ whan *Antecrist* yow assailleþ.'
B.20.53	*Antecrist* cam þanne, and al þe crop of truþe
B.20.64	And a fals fend *Antecrist* ouer alle folk regnede.

B.20.69	*Antecrist* hadde þus soone hundredes at his baner,
B.20.128	To holden wiþ *Antecrist*, hir temporaltees to saue.
B.20.216	That wiþ *Antecrist* helden harde ayein Conscience.
C.21.219	For *Auntecrist* and hise al the world shal greue
C.21.226	And wepne to fihte with when *Auntecrist* ȝow assaileth.'
C.22.53	*Auntecrist* cam thenne and al the crop of treuthe
C.22.64	And a fals fende *auntecrist* ouer all folke regnede.
C.22.69	*Auntecrist* hadde thus sone hondredes at his baner
C.22.128	To holde with *auntecrist*, here temperalte[s] to saue.
C.22.216	That with *auntecrist* helden harde aȝeyn Consience.

antony *n prop n.i.d.* B 4; C 1

B.15.272	*Antony* and Egidie and oþere holy fadres
B.15.276	Ac neiþer *Antony* ne Egidie ne heremyte þat tyme
B.15.283	*Antony* adayes aboute noon tyme
B.15.421	But doon as *Antony* dide, dominyk and Fraunceys,
C.17.12	Bothe *Antony* and arseny and oþer fol monye.

apaied *ptp apaien v.* B 2 apaied (1) apayed (1); C 4 apayed

B. 6.108	Therwiþ was Perkyn *apayed* and preised hem [yerne].
B. 6.195	And ech a pouere man wel *apaied* to haue pesen for his hyre,
C. 2.47	Soffre and thow shalt see suche as ben *apayed*
C. 8.115	Therwith was [Perkyn] *apayed* and payede wel here huyre.
C. 9.179	And alle pore pacient *apayed* of goddes sonde,
C.15.63	Pacience was wel *apayed* of this propre seruice

apayre(d > apeire; aparayl(- > apparaill(-

apart *adv apart adv.* A 1 aparte; B 2; C 1

A. 5.175	And preisiden þe peneworthis [*aparte*] be hemseluen.
B. 5.326	And preised þ[e] penyworþes *apart* by hemselue.
B.13.47	Bifore Pacience breed to brynge, [bitynge *apart*],
C. 6.384	And preisede th[e] penworthis *apart* by hemsulue

apartye *adv apartie adv.* C 1

C.15.53	And bringe breed for pacience, bytyng *apartye*,

apeel *n appel n.* C 3 apeel (1) appeles (2)

C. 2.189	And on pore prouisores and *appeles* in þe Arches.
C. 2.247	And putte hem thorw *appeles* in þe popes grace.
C.19.288	The[r] þat partye pursueth the *apeel* is so huge

apeire *v aspeiren v.* A 8 apeire (4) apeirid (1) apeiride (1) apeiriþ (1) appeire (1); B 8 apeire (4) apeired (3) apeireþ (1); C 5 apayre (3) apayred (1) appeyreth (1)

A. 3.117	Apoisonide popis, *apeiride* holy chirche;
A. 5.38	'Lest þe king & his counseil ȝour comunes *apeir[e]*
A. 5.75	To *apeire* hym be my power I pursuide wel ofte,
A. 6.51	And þanne ȝoure neiȝebours next in none wise *apeir[e]*
A. 7.156	'Now be þe peril of my soule!' quaþ peris, 'I shal *appeire* ȝow alle,'
A. 7.204	Ac ȝif þou fynde any frek þat fortune haþ *apeirid*
A. 8.50	Þat is Innocent & nedy, & no man *apeiriþ*,
A.11.63	And fyndiþ forþ fantasies oure feiþ to *apeire*,
B. 3.128	[A]poisoned popes, [a]peired holy chirche.
B. 5.46	'Lest þe kyng and his conseil youre comunes *apeire*
B. 5.95	To *apeire* hym bi my power pursued wel ofte],
B. 5.564	And þanne youre neȝebores next in none wise *apeire*
B. 6.132	Whiche þei were in þis world hise werkmen *apeired*.
B. 6.171	'Now by þe peril of my soule!' quod Piers, 'I shal *apeire* yow alle',
B. 6.218	A[c] if þow fynde any freke þat Fortune haþ *apeired*
B. 7.48	That is Innocent and nedy and no man *apeireþ*,
C. 3.165	He hath apoisend popes, he *appeyreth* holy churche.
C. 5.144	'Laste þe kyng and his consayl ȝoure comunes *apayre*
C. 7.211	And thenne ȝoure neyhebores nexst in none wyse *apayre*
C. 8.167	'Now, by Crist!' quod [Peres] the [plouhman], 'y shal *apayre* ȝow alle,
C. 8.228	Ac yf thow fynde eny folke þat fals men han *apayred*

apend- > appendeþ; apere(n > appere

apereþ *v apperen v.(2)* B 1; C 1 appereth

B.14.243	And Pouerte nys but a petit þyng, *apereþ* noȝt to his nauele,
C.16.83	And pouerte is bote a pety thyng, *appereth* nat to his nauele,

apertli *adv aperteli adv.* A 3 apertly; B 2 apertli (1) apertly (1); C 1 apertly

A. 1.98	Þat is þe professioun *apertly* þat apendiþ to kniȝtes,
A. 3.237	It is a permutacioun *apertly*, a peny[worþ] for anoþer.
A. 5.15	Was *apertly* for pride & for no poynt ellis.
B. 1.100	[That] is [þe] profession *apertli* þat apendeþ to knyȝtes,
B. 3.258	It is a permutacion *apertly*, a penyworþ for anoþer.
C. 3.314	Hit is a permutacoun *apertly*, on peneworth for another.

apetit > appetit

apeward *n ape n.* A 1; B 1; C 1 hapeward

A. 6.116	'Ne I,' quaþ an *apeward*, 'be auȝt þat I knowe.'
B. 5.631	'Nor I', quod an *Apeward*, 'by auȝt þat I knowe.'

C. 7.284   'Ne y,' quod an *hapeward*, 'by auht þat y knowe.'

aples > appul

apoisoned ptp *apoisonen v.* A 1 apoisonide; B 2; C 2 apoisend (1)
apoysened (1)

A. 3.117   *Apoisonide* popis, apeiride holy chirche;
B. 3.128   *[A]poisoned* popes, [a]peired holy chirche.
B.15.561   And þo þat han Petres power arn *apoisoned* alle."
C. 3.165   He hath *apoisend* popes, he appeyreth holy churche.
C.17.224   And [tho] þat haen petres power aren *apo[y]sened* alle."

apose(d aposid(e > appose

apostata adj *apostata n.(? & adj.)* A 1; B 1; C 1 appostata
A. 1.102   And whoso passiþ þat poynt is *apostata* in his ordre.
B. 1.104   And whoso passe[þ] þat point [is] *Apostata* in [his] ordre.
C. 1.98   And hoso passeth þat poynt is *apostata* of knyghthed.

apostle n *apostle n.* A 6 apostel (2) apostil (1) apostlis (2) apostolis (1); B 15 Apostel (2) Apostle (4) Apostles (9); C 15 apostel (6) apposteles (1) apostle (1) apostles (5) apostlis (2)

A. 7.3   Quaþ perkyn þe plouʒman, 'be seint poule þe *apostel*,
A. 8.18   Han pardoun wiþ þe *apostlis* whanne þei passe hennis,
A.10.109   Poule þe *apostel* in his pistil wrot it
A.11.25   And can telle of tobie & of þe twelue *apostlis*,
A.11.289   Or poule þe *apostil* þat no pite hadde
A.12.4   He passeþ þe *apostolis* lyf, and [peryth] to aungelys.
B. 7.16   Arn peres wiþ þe *Apostles*–þ[u]s pardon Piers sheweþ–
B.10.33   And kan telle of Tobye and of [þe] twelue *Apostles*
B.10.346   And preiseden pouerte with pacience; þe *Apostles* bereþ witnesse
B.10.430   Or Poul þe *Apostle* þat no pite hadde
B.11.97   Falsnesse ne faiterie? for somwhat þe *Apostle* seide
B.13.66   Preched of penaunces þat Poul þe *Apostle* suffrede
B.15.418   Peeren to *Apostles* þoruʒ hire parfit lyuynge.
B.16.159   Suffreþ myne *Apostles* in [pays] and in [pees] gange.'
B.16.198   Patriarkes and prophetes and *Apostles* were þe children,
B.17.261   Poul þe *Apostel* preueþ wheiþer I lye:
B.17.341   As Poul þe *Apostle* to þe peple tauʒte:
B.18.243   Peter þe *Apostel* parceyued his gate,
B.19.147   And goon into Galilee and gladen hise *Apostles*
B.19.155   Telle þe comune þat þer cam a compaignie of hise *Apostles*
B.19.169   To Peter and to [h]ise *Apostles* and seide pax vobis;
C. 9.20   To be [peres] to þe *apostles* alle peple to reule
C.11.30   And can telle of treuthe and of þe twelue *aposteles*
C.11.148   Patriarkes and prophetes, *apostles* and angelis,
C.11.266   [Or] Poul þe *apostel* [þat] no pite hadde
C.12.33   Falsnesse ne fayterye? for sumwhat þe *apostel* saide:
C.13.3   Oure prince iesu pouerte chees and his *apostles* alle
C.15.72   And how þat poul þe *apostel* penaunce tholede
C.15.75   A[s] poul þe *apostle* prechede to þe peple ofte:
C.18.207   Patriarches and prophetes and *apostles* were the childrene.
C.19.227   Paul the *apostel* preueth where y lye:
C.19.321   As Paul þe *apostel* in his episteles techeth:
C.20.252   Peter þe *Apostel* perseyued his gate
C.21.147   And goen into Galilee and gladien his *apostlis*
C.21.155   Telle þe comune þat þer cam a companie of his *apostles*
C.21.169   To peter and to his *apostlis* and saide pax vobis;

apparailed > apparaille

apparaill n *appareil n.* A 1 apparail; B 5 apparaill (3) apparaille (2); C 2 aparayl (1) aparayle (1)
A. 9.111   Was no pride on his *apparail* ne no pouert noþer,
B. 8.121   Was no pride on his *apparaill* ne pouerte neiþer;
B.11.186   In a pouere mannes *apparaille* pursue[þ] vs euere,
B.11.236   For his pouere *apparaill* and pilgrymes wedes
B.11.243   And in þe *apparaill* of a pouere man and pilgrymes liknesse
B.13.277   As in *apparaill* and in porte proud amonges þe peple;
C. 6.30   Proud of *aparayle* in port amongus þe peple
C.17.72   Prestes on *aparayl* and on purnele now spene.

apparaille v *appareillen v.* A 5 aparailid (1) aparailide (2) aparaille (2); B 5 apparailed (2) apparaille (2) apparailled (1); C 4 aparayled (2) aparaylede (1) aparayle (1)
A.Pr.23   And summe putte hem to pride, *aparailide* hem þereaftir,
A. 2.135   'And let *apparaille* þise prouisours in palfreis wise;
A. 2.176   *Aparailide* hym as a prentice þe peple to serue.
A. 6.4   *Aparailid* as a paynym in pilgrim[ys] wyse.
A. 7.52   'And I shal *apparaille* me,' quaþ perkyn, 'in pilgrym[ys] wyse,
B.Pr.23   And somme putten hem to pride, *apparailed* hem þerafter,
B. 2.171   'And late *apparaille* þise prouisours in palfreyes wise;
B. 2.217   *Apparailed* hym as [a p]rentice þe peple to serue.
B. 5.516   *Apparailled* as a paynym in pilgrymes wise.
B. 6.57   'And I shal *apparaille* me', quod Perkyn, 'in pilgrymes wise
C.Pr.25   And summe putte hem to pruyde, [a]*paraylede* hem þeraftir
C. 2.227   [A]*paraylede* hym [as a] prentys the peple to serue.

C. 7.161   [A]*parayled* as a paynyem in pilgrimes wyse.
C. 8.56   'And [y] shal [ap]*parayle* me,' quod Perkyn, 'in pilgrimes wyse

appeire(th > apeire; appel > appul

appele v *appelen v.* B 1
B.11.423   Pryde now and presumpcion, parauenture, wol þee *appele*

appeles > apeel

appendeþ v *appenden v.* A 2 apendiþ; B 2 apendeþ (1) appendeþ (1); C 1 apendeth
A. 1.43   Tel me to whom þat tresour *apendiþ*.'
A. 1.98   Þat is þe professioun apertly þat *apendiþ* to kniʒtes,
B. 1.45   Tel me to whom þat tresour *appendeþ*.'
B. 1.100   [That] is [þe] profession apertli þat *apendeþ* to knyʒtes,
C. 1.97   Is þe professioun and puyr ordre that *apendeth* to knyghtes

appere v *apperen v.(1)* A 1 aperen; B 3 appere (1) appered (1) apperynge (1); C 5 apere (2) apperede (1) apperynge (1)
A. 3.103   Þanne was consience callid to comen & *aperen*
B. 3.114   [Th]anne was Consience called to come and *appere*
B.12.148   To pastours and to poetes *appered* þe Aungel
B.19.92   And presented hym wiþ pitee *apperynge* by Mirre;
C.Pr.190   And *apere* in his presence þe while hym pleye lyketh
C. 3.151   Thenne was Consience ykald to come and *apere*
C.11.149   And þe trewe trinite to Austyn *apperede*
C.14.92   To pastours and to poetes *Appered* þe Angel
C.21.92   And presented hym with pyte *apperynge* bi Mirre

appereth > apereþ

appetit n *appetit n.* A 1 apetit; B 1
A. 7.248   Aris vp er *ap[e]ti[t]* ha[ue] eten his fille;
B. 6.264   [A]rys vp er *Appetit* haue eten his fille.

appil apples > appul

appose v *apposen v.* A 6 apose (2) aposed (1) aposid (2) aposide (1); B 9 appose (4) apposed (2) apposede (1) apposeden (1) apposen (1); C 8 apose (3) aposed (1) apposede (2) apposede (2)
A. 1.45   Þo þe peple hym *aposide* with a peny in þe temple
A. 3.5   'I wile assaie hire myself, and soþly *apose*
A. 8.126   Þe prest & perkyn *aposid* eiþer oþer,
A.11.298   'Wh[anne] ʒe ben *aposid* of princes or of prestis of þe lawe
A.12.8   Presumptuowsly, parauenture, *apose* so manye
A.12.26   In þe passioun, whan pilat *aposed* god almyʒthi,
B. 1.47   Tho þe poeple hym *apposede* wiþ a peny in þe temple
B. 3.5   'I [wol] assayen hire myself and sooþliche *appose*
B. 7.144   The preest and Perkyn [a]*pposeden* eiþer ooþer,
B.12.215   Raþer þan þat ooþer þeef, þouʒ þow woldest *appose*,
B.12.232   Lewed men many tymes maistres þei *apposen*
B.13.85   [And *appose* hym] what penaunce is, of which he preched raþer.'
B.13.97   And þanne is tyme to take and to *appose* þis doctour
B.13.222   Pacience *apposed* hym and preyde he sholde telle
B.15.383   I dar noʒt siggen it for shame–if swiche were *apposed*
C. 1.45   Whenne þe peple *aposed* hym of a peny in þe temple
C. 3.5   'Y shal asaye hire mysulue and sothliche *appose*
C. 5.10   In hele and [vnnit] oen me *apposede*:
C.14.154   Rather then þat oþer [theef], thogh thow woldest *apose*,
C.15.92   And *apose* hym what penaunce is and purgatorie on erthe
C.15.104   And thenne is tyme to take and *apose* this doctour
C.15.191   Pacience *apposede* hym and preyede a sholde telle
C.16.163   And preyde pacience þat y *apose* hym moste.

appostata > apostata

approcheþ v *approchen v.* B 2 approched (1) approcheþ (1); C 3 approcheth (1) aproched (1) aprochede (1)
B.15.547   Shul [ouer]torne as templers dide; þe tyme *approcheþ* faste.
B.18.172   Whan Pees in Pacience ycloþed *approched* ner hem tweyne
C.17.209   Sholle ouerturne as templers dede; þe tyme *approcheth* faste.
C.18.138   Til plenitudo temporis [h]y tyme *aprochede*,
C.20.175   Whenne pees in pacience yclothed *aproched* her ayþer oþer

appul n *appel n.* A 2 appil (1) applis (1); B 8 apples (2) appul (6); C 9 aples (1) appel (1) apples (4) appul (3)
A. 7.277   Benes & [b]ake *applis* hy brouʒte in here lappe[s],
A.10.141   Aftir þat adam & [heo] eten þe *appil*
B. 5.603   Tho Adam and Eue eten *apples* vnrosted:
B. 6.293   Benes and baken *apples* þei broʒte in hir lappes,
B. 9.124   [After þat Adam and heo eten þe *appul*].
B. 9.152   Impe on an Ellere, and if þyn *appul* be swete
B.12.233   Why Adam hiled noʒt first his mouþ þat eet þe *Appul*
B.16.73   I preide Piers to pulle adoun an *Appul* and he wolde,
B.18.281   If Adam ete þe *Appul* alle sholde deye
B.18.331   That if [þei] ete þe *Appul* alle sholde deye,
C. 8.316   Benes and bake *aples* they brouhten in here lappe

C.10.207 For god saith hymsulue, "shal neuere goed *appel*
C.18.61   Me may se on an *appul* tree monye tyme and ofte
C.18.62   Of o kynde *apples* aren nat iliche grete
C.18.68   Adam was as tre and we aren as his *apples*,
C.18.70   Summe litel, somme large, ylik *apples* of kynde,
C.18.121 To go ransake þat ragman and reue hym of his *apples*
C.20.305 Yf they touched a tre or toek þerof an *appul*.
C.20.374 That if they ete þe *appul* alle sholde deye,

appultree n *appel-tre n.* B 1
B.18.288 And in semblaunce of a serpent sete vpon þe *Appultree*

appurtenaunces n *appurtenaunce n.* B 1
B.15.189 Pride wiþ al þe *appurtenaunces*, and pakken hem togideres,

aprill n *april n.* B 1
B.13.268 In þe date of oure driȝte, in a drye *Aprill*,

aproched(e > approcheþ; ar > ben,er; aray > array,arraye; araye(n > arraye

arate v *araten v.* B 3 arate (1) arated (2); C 3 arate (1) arated (1) aratede (1)
B.11.102 To reden it in Retorik to *arate* dedly synne?
B.11.376 And Reson *arated* me and seide, 'recche þee neuere
B.14.163 And *arated* of riche men þat ruþe is to here.
C. 5.11   Romynge in remembraunce thus resoun me *aratede*:
C.12.36   To rehercen hit by retoryk to *arate* dedly synne?
C.16.16   [And *arated* of] ryche men þat reuthe is to here.

arbitreres n *arbitratour n.* C 1
C. 6.382 And that the bettere thyng, be *arbitreres*, bote sholde þe worse.

archangel n *archangel n.(1)* A 1 archaungelis; B 2 Archangeles (1) Archaungeles (1); C 2 Archangel (1) Archangeles (1)
A. 1.106 And ouer his meyne made hem *archaungelis*,
B. 1.108 And ouer his meynee made hem *Archangeles*;
B.19.150 That Aungeles and *Archaungeles*, er þe day spronge,
C. 1.108 He was an *Archangel* of heuene, on of goddes knyghtes;
C.21.150 That Angeles and *Archangeles*, ar the day spronge,

arches n *arche n.* B 2; C 3
B. 2.61   Forgoers and vitaillers and [v]okettes of þe *Arches*;
B.20.136 An[d] to þe *Arches* in haste he yede anoon after
C. 2.63   Vorgoers and vitalers and voketes of the *Arches*;
C. 2.189 And on pore prouisores and appeles in þe *Arches*.
C.22.136 And [t]o þe *Arches* in haste he ȝede anoen aftur

archidekenes > erchdekenes; are > ben

aredy adj *aredi adj.& adv.* C 2
C. 6.97   When he solde and y nat thenne was y *aredy*
C. 7.119 Tho was repentaunce *aredy* and redde hem alle to knele:

aren > ben

arerage n *arrerage n.* B 5 arerage (3) arerages (1) Arrerage (1); C 5 arrerage
B.10.476 That seruauntȝ þat seruen lordes selde fallen in *arerage*,
B.11.129 Ac he may renne in *arerage* and rome fro home,
B.11.132 And conscience acounte wiþ hym] and casten hym in *arerage*,
B.11.134 For hise *arerages* rewarden hym þere [riȝt] to þe day of dome,
B.14.108 And þat at þe rekenyng in *Arrerage* fel raþer þan out of dette.
C. 9.273 Redde racionem villicacionis or in *arrerage* fall!
C.11.296 Selde falleth þe seruant so depe in *arrerage*
C.12.64   Ac he may renne in *arrerage* and rome fro home
C.12.67   And consience acounte with hym and casten hym in *arrerag[e]*
C.15.284 Hit are but fewe folk of this ryche that ne falleth in *arrerage*

arere adv *arrere adv* A 1; B 1; C 1
A. 5.195 Sum tyme asid, & sum tyme *arere*,
B. 5.347 Som tyme aside and som tyme *arere*,
C. 6.405 Sum tyme asyde and sum tyme *arere*,

arerid ptp *areren v.* A 1
A. 2.48   To be fastnid wiþ fals þe fyn is *arerid*.

aresonedest v *aresounen v.* B 1; C 4 aresenede (1) aresonede (2) aresounede (1)
B.12.218 And *aresonedest* Reson, a rebukynge as it were,
C.13.129 Thus rechelesnesse in a rage *aresenede* clergie
C.13.183 Thenne y [a]resonede resoun and ryht til hym y sayde,
C.13.194 And resoun *aresounede* me and sayde, 'reche þe neuere
C.13.244 Why ȝe worden to me thus was for y *aresonede* Resoun.'

areste adv *areste adv.* B 1; C 1
B. 5.232 I roos whan þei were *areste* and riflede hire males.'
C. 6.236 Y roes and ryflede here males when the[y] *areste* were.'

arewes > arwes

argue v *arguen v.* A 1 arguen; B 1; C 2 Arguen (1) Arguinge (1)
A.11.131 Aristotel & oþere mo to *arguen* I tauȝte;
B.10.179 Aristotle and oþere mo to *argue* I tauȝte;
C.11.119 Aristotel and oþere [mo] to *Arguen* y tauhte;
C.16.114 Quod Actyf tho al angryliche and *Arguinge* as hit were:

argueres n *arguer n.* B 1
B.10.120 Austyn to swiche *Argueres* [he] telleþ þis teme:

argumentȝ n *argument n.* B 2; C 1 argumentis
B.15.382 And answere to *Argumentȝ* and [assoile] a Quodlibet–
B.17.139 Or Eretikes wiþ *argumentȝ*, þyn hond þow hem shewe.
C.19.112 Or eretikes with *argumentis*, thien hoend thow hem shewe.

aryht adv *a-right adv.* C 1
C.17.157 Louyeth nat þat lord *aryht* as by þe legende sanctorum

arise v *arisen v.* A 12 aris (1) arise (7) arisen (2) ariseþ (1) arisiþ (1); B 17 arys (1) arise (8) aryse (3) ariseþ (2) aroos (2) naroos (1); C 22 arise (2) aryse (12) aryseth (2) ariste (1) aroes (1) aroos (4)
A. 3.276 And make of lawe a labourer, such loue shal *arise.*'
A. 5.178 Til robyn þe ropere was red to *arisen*,
A. 5.186 Bargoynes & beuerechis begonne for to *arise*,
A. 7.132 Til god of his grace gare h[e]m to *arise*.
A. 7.139 Þanne gan wastour *arise* & wolde haue yfouȝte;
A. 7.248 *Aris* vp er ap[e]ti[t] ha[ue] eten his fille;
A. 7.305 Or fyue ȝer be fulfild such famyn shal *arise*;
A. 8.47   Of princes & prelatis here pencioun shulde *arise*,
A. 8.171 At þe dredful dom whanne dede shal *arisen*
A. 9.30   For ȝif he ne *arise* þe raþere & [rauȝte þe stere],
A.10.119 For þoruȝ suffraunce se þou miȝt how soueraynes *ariseþ*,
A.10.121 And þus of dred & h[is] dede dobest *arisiþ*,
B. 3.300 And make of lawe a laborer; swich loue shal *arise*
B. 5.329 Til Robyn þe Ropere [arise þei bisouȝte],
B. 5.334 And whoso repente[þ] raþest sholde *aryse* after
B. 5.337 [Bargaynes and beuerages bigonne to *arise*],
B. 6.118 'But ye *arise* þe raþer and rape yow to werche
B. 6.138 Til god of his [grace gare hem to *arise*].
B. 6.264 [A]*rys* vp er Appetit haue eten his fille.
B. 6.324 Er fyue [yer] be fulfilled swich famyn shal *aryse*.
B. 8.34   For if he ne *arise* þe raþer and rauȝte þe steere
B.10.359 That whoso wolde and wilneþ wiþ crist to *arise*,
B.11.428 Lat hym ligge, loke noȝt on hym til hym list *aryse*.
B.11.440 And I *aroos* vp riȝt wiþ þat and [reuerenced] hym [faire,
B.12.171 That he þat knoweþ clergie kan sonner *arise*
B.17.139 And gyueþ youre good to þat god þat grace of *ariseþ*.
B.18.427 '[*Arise*þ] and reuerence[þ] goddes resurexion,
B.19.52   That he *naroos* and regnede and rauysshed helle.
B.19.152 Christus [rex] resurgens, [and it *aroos* after],
C. 3.358 In nombre, Rotye and *aryse* and remissioun to haue,
C. 3.453 And maky of lawe [a] laborer; suche loue shal *aryse*
C. 5.15   Repe or been a rypereue and *aryse* erly
C. 6.62   Quod repentaunce riht with þat; and thenne *aroos* enuye.
C. 6.387 Til Robyn þe Ropere *aryse* they bisouhte
C. 6.392 And hoso repente[th] rathest sholde *aryse* aftur
C. 6.395 Bargaynes and Beuereges bygan to a[*rys*]e
C. 8.125 'But ȝe *aryse* þe rather and rape ȝow to worche
C. 8.344 Ar fewe ȝeres be fulfeld famyne shal *aryse*.
C.10.52   To repenten and *arise* and rowe out of synne
C.11.231 And mercy of mercy nedes moet *aryse*
C.12.230 So of rychesse ope rychesse *ariste* alle vices.
C.13.235 Lat hym lygge, lok nat on hym til hym luste [a]*ryse*.
C.13.244 And [y] *aroes* vp riht with þat and reuerensed hym fayre
C.14.111 Þat he þat knoweth clergie conne sonnore *aryse*
C.15.27   And y *aroos* and romede forth and with resoun we mette.
C.17.139 And lele men lyue as lawe techeth and loue þerof *aryseth*
C.19.252 And gyueth ȝoure goed to þat god þat grace of *aryseth*.
C.20.264 And y, boek, wol be brente bote he *aryse* to lyue
C.20.470 '*Arise* and go reuerense godes resureccio[n]
C.21.52   That he ne *aroos* and regnede and raueschede helle.
C.21.152 Christus [rex] resurgens, and hit *aroos* aftur,

aristotle n prop *n.i.d.* A 2 Aristotel (1) Aristotle (1); B 4; C 4 Aristotel
A.11.131 *Aristotel* & oþere mo to arguen I tauȝte;
A.11.270 *Aristotle* & he, who wrouȝte betere?
B.10.179 *Aristotle* and oþere mo to argue I tauȝte;
B.10.388 *Aristotle* and he, who wissed men bettre?
B.12.43   *Aristotle* and oþere mo, ypocras and virgile,
B.12.268 [Swiche tales telleþ *Aristotle* þe grete clerk]:
C.11.119 *Aristotel* and oþere [mo] to Arguen y tauhte;
C.11.214 *Aristotel* and he, ho tauhte men bettere?
C.12.175 *Aristotel*, Ennedy, enleuene hundred,
C.14.193 Wher þey ben in hell or in heuene or *Aristotel* þe wyse.

arme n1 *arm n.* A 3 armes; B 6 arme (1) armes (5); C 3 armes (2) armus (1)

A. 7.252 And ȝif þou diȝete þe þus I dar ley myn *armes*
A.10.189 Þat neuere shal bere [barne] but it be in *armes*.
A.12.42 Þat lady þan low and lauȝthe me in here *armes*
B. 5.410 And ligge abedde in lenten and my lemman in myne *armes*
B. 6.268 And if þow diete þee þus I dar legge myne [*armes*]
B. 9.168 That neuere shal barn bere but it be in *armes*.
B.14.242 And haþ hondes and *armes* of [a long] lengþe,
B.15.122 [And beere] bedes in hir hand and a book vnder hir *arme*.
B.18.74 And [hir] *armes* after of eiþer of þo þeues.
C. 7.26 And ligge abedde in lente and my lemman in myn *armus*
C.16.82 And hath hondes and *Armes* of a longe lenthe
C.20.76 And here *arme[s]* aftur of e[ither] of tho theues.

armed v *armen v.* B 5 armed (2) armede (1) yarmed (2); C 5 armed (3) yarmed (2)

B.19.144 Kepen it fro nyghtcomeris wiþ knyghtes *yarmed*
B.19.351 Wiþ swiche colours and queyntise comeþ pride *yarmed*
B.20.116 And *armede* hym in ydelnesse and in heigh berynge.
B.20.123 And *armed* hym in Auarice and hungriliche lyuede.
B.20.144 And *armed* hym [in] haste [in] harlotes wordes,
C.21.144 Kepen hit fro nyhtecomares with knyhtes y[*ar*]*med*
C.21.351 With such colours and queyntis[e] cometh pruyde *yArmed*
C.22.116 And *armed* hym in ydelnesse and in hey berynge.
C.22.123 And *Armed* hym in Auarice and hungriliche lyuede.
C.22.144 And *Armed* hym in haste in harlotes wordes

armes n2 *armes n.(pl.)* &> *arme n1* B 9; C 7

B. 5.500 Of þyne douȝt[iest] dedes was doon in oure *armes*:
B.16.95 And þanne sholde Iesus Iuste þerfore bi Iuggement of *armes*
B.16.177 And of Abrahames hous an heraud of *armes*;
B.17.134 'After Abraham', quod he, 'þat heraud of *armes*,
B.18.16 As dooþ an heraud of *armes* whan Auentrous comeþ to Iustes.
B.18.22 'This Iesus of his gentries wol Iuste in Piers *armes*,
B.19.12 Quod Conscience and kneled þo, 'þise arn Piers *armes*,
B.19.339 And sente forþ Surquidous, his sergeaunt of *Armes*,
B.20.94 And er heraudes of *Armes* hadden discryued lordes,
C.18.128 That iesus sholde iouste þerfore by iugement of *Armes*
C.18.185 An heraud of *Armes* Ar eny lawe were.'
C.20.14 As doth an heraud of *Armes* when Auntres cometh to ioustes.
C.20.21 That this iesus of his gentrice shal iouste in Pers *Armes*,
C.21.12 Quod Conciense and knelede tho, 'this aren [Peres] *Armes*,
C.21.339 And sente forth surquido[us], his seriaunt[e] of *Armes*,
C.22.94 And ar heroudes of *Armes* hadden descreued lordes,

armonye n *armonie n.* A 1; B 2 Armonye (1) ermonye (1); C 2

A. 6.16 In *armonye*, in alisaundre, in manye oþere places.
B. 5.528 In *Armonye*, in Alisaundre, in manye oþere places.
B.15.521 In ynde, in alisaundre, in *ermonye* and spayne,
C. 7.173 In *Armonye*, in Alisaundre [and in damaske].
C.17.272 In ynde, in alisandre, in *Armonye* [and] spayne

armure n *armure n.* &> *cote_armure* B 1; C 1

B. 1.158 That myȝte noon *Armure* it lette ne none heiȝe walles.
C. 1.154 [That myȝte] non *Armure* hit lette ne none heye walles.

armus > arme; arn > ben; arne > rennen; arnede > erende; aroes aroos > arise

array n *arrai n.* B 1; C 2 aray

B. 2.17 Hire *array* me rauysshed; swich richesse sauȝ I neuere.
C. 2.16 Here *aray* with here rychesse raueschede my herte;
C. 5.157 Haen ryde out of *aray*, here reule euele yholde,

arraye v *arraien v.* A 1 araye; B 2 arayen (1) arraye (1); C 1 aray

A. 4.16 'I shal *araye* me to ryde,' quaþ resoun, 'reste þe a while,'
B. 4.16 'I shal *arraye* me to ryde,' quod Reson, 'reste þee a while',
B. 5.11 And how Reson gan *arayen* hym al þe Reaume to preche;
C. 4.16 'Y shal *aray* me to ryde,' quod resoun, 'reste the [a] while,'

arrerage > arerage; ars > art,ers

arseny n prop *n.i.d.* C 1

C.17.12 Bothe Antony and *arseny* and oþer fol monye.

arst(e > erst

art n *art n.(1)* &> *ben* A 1 ars; B 3 art (1) artȝ (2); C 4 ars (3) arte (1)

A.11.107 Is sib to þe seuene *ars* þat scripture is nempnid.
B.10.155 Is sib to [þe] seuen *artȝ*, [þat] Scripture is [nempned].
B.11.172 Or any Science vnder sonne, þe seuene *artȝ* and alle–
B.15.359 Astronomiens alday in hir *Art* faillen
C.11.95 For he is sib to þe seuene *ars*–and also my suster
C.12.94 Or eny science vnder sonne, the seuene *ars* and alle–
C.17.97 Astronomiens alday in here *arte* faylen
C.17.115 That sholde þe seuene *ars* conne and assoile a quodlibet

articles n *article n.* B 1

B.10.239 Wiþ alle þe *articles* of þe feiþ þat falleþ to be knowe.

artow > ben

arwed ptp *arghen v.* C 1

C. 3.237 Hast *arwed* many hardy man þat hadde wille to fyhte,

arwes n *arwe n.* B 3 arewes (1) arwes (2); C 3

B. 3.326 By sixe sonnes and a ship and half a shef of *Arwes*;
B.20.117 He bar a bowe in his hand and manye brode *arewes*,
B.20.226 And brode hoked *arwes*, goddes herte and hise nayles,
C. 3.479 Be sixe [s]onnes [and] a ship and half a shef of *Arwes*,
C.22.117 He baer a bowe in his hoend and many brode *arwes*,
C.22.226 And brode hokede *Arwes*, goddes herte and his nayles,

as conj *as conj.* &> *theras* A 180; B 620; C 677 als (1) as (676)

A.Pr.2, A.Pr.3, A.Pr.9, A.Pr.13, A.Pr.19, A.Pr.28, A.Pr.32, A.Pr.33, A.Pr.44, A.Pr.57, A.Pr.58, A.Pr.65, A.Pr.97, A.Pr.102, A.1.13, A.1.29, A.1.85, A.1.85, A.1.120, A.1.123, A.1.154, A.1.154, A.1.156, A.1.161, A.1.161, A.1.163, A.1.163, A.1.180, A.2.7, A.2.18, A.2.26, A.2.53, A.2.95, A.2.137, A.2.144, A.2.159, A.2.176, A.2.192, A.2.193, A.2.193, A.3.9, A.3.18, A.3.34, A.3.36, A.3.67, A.3.91, A.3.121, A.3.121, A.3.133, A.3.133, A.3.134, A.3.135, A.3.148, A.3.171, A.3.175, A.3.205, A.3.214, A.3.215, A.3.251, A.3.253, A.3.262, A.4.15, A.4.87, A.4.96, A.4.96, A.4.119, A.4.131, A.4.143, A.4.154, A.4.154, A.4.158, A.4.158, A.5.22, A.5.36, A.5.60, A.5.60, A.5.64, A.5.70, A.5.71, A.5.82, A.5.82, A.5.86, A.5.110, A.5.120, A.5.196, A.5.224, A.5.239, A.6.2, A.6.4, A.6.26, A.6.26, A.6.40, A.6.40, A.6.72, A.6.78, A.6.99, A.7.17, A.7.17, A.7.81, A.7.114, A.7.131, A.7.131, A.7.147, A.7.149, A.7.185, A.7.214, A.7.243, A.7.275, A.8.15, A.8.22, A.8.74, A.8.85, A.8.86, A.8.86, A.8.118, A.8.141, A.8.147, A.8.159, A.8.164, A.8.168, A.8.184, A.9.6, A.9.10, A.9.15, A.9.16, A.9.36, A.9.43, A.9.54, A.9.60, A.9.77, A.9.77, A.9.90, A.9.100, A.9.114, A.10.39, A.10.39, A.10.61, A.10.123, A.10.126, A.10.132, A.10.140, A.10.163, A.10.181, A.10.182, A.10.185, A.10.186, A.10.206, A.10.212, A.11.18, A.11.22, A.11.28, A.11.48, A.11.85, A.11.86, A.11.95, A.11.108, A.11.110, A.11.110, A.11.151, A.11.168, A.11.170, A.11.175, A.11.191, A.11.235, A.11.248, A.11.248, A.11.263, A.11.268, A.11.292, A.11.297, A.11.310, A.12.5, A.12.5, A.12.33, A.12.60, A.12.74, A.12.90, A.12.112

B.Pr.2, B.Pr.3, B.Pr.9, B.Pr.13, B.Pr.19, B.Pr.28, B.Pr.32, B.Pr.33, B.Pr.44, B.Pr.60, B.Pr.61, B.Pr.68, B.Pr.95, B.Pr.101, B.Pr.102, B.Pr.120, B.Pr.164, B.Pr.165, B.Pr.182, B.Pr.206, B.Pr.218, B.Pr.224, B.1.13, B.1.29, B.1.87, B.1.87, B.1.130, B.1.131, B.1.134, B.1.150, B.1.157, B.1.160, B.1.180, B.1.180, B.1.182, B.1.187, B.1.187, B.1.189, B.1.189, B.1.206, B.2.7, B.2.12, B.2.12, B.2.23, B.2.27, B.2.58, B.2.59, B.2.66, B.2.68, B.2.90, B.2.98, B.2.131, B.2.158, B.2.176, B.2.183, B.2.198, B.2.217, B.2.233, B.2.234, B.2.234, B.3.9, B.3.19, B.3.35, B.3.37, B.3.78, B.3.89, B.3.102, B.3.132, B.3.132, B.3.144, B.3.144, B.3.145, B.3.146, B.3.158, B.3.184, B.3.188, B.3.218, B.3.227, B.3.228, B.3.237, B.3.274, B.3.286, B.3.319, B.3.331, B.3.335, B.4.15, B.4.41, B.4.43, B.4.100, B.4.109, B.4.109, B.4.121, B.4.136, B.4.148, B.4.175, B.4.178, B.4.181, B.4.191, B.4.191, B.4.195, B.5.22, B.5.44, B.5.77, B.5.77, B.5.81, B.5.102, B.5.106, B.5.121, B.5.146, B.5.174, B.5.193, B.5.204, B.5.225, B.5.255, B.5.258, B.5.258, B.5.269, B.5.288, B.5.288, B.5.291, B.5.340, B.5.348, B.5.365, B.5.394, B.5.398, B.5.423, B.5.452, B.5.483, B.5.514, B.5.516, B.5.538, B.5.538, B.5.553, B.5.553, B.5.585, B.5.591, B.5.607, B.5.613, B.6.18, B.6.18, B.6.36, B.6.64, B.6.89, B.6.122, B.6.137, B.6.137, B.6.139, B.6.160, B.6.164, B.6.189, B.6.196, B.6.196, B.6.198, B.6.227, B.6.230, B.6.259, B.6.291, B.6.301, B.7.13, B.7.15, B.7.15, B.7.20, B.7.41, B.7.92, B.7.103, B.7.104, B.7.104, B.7.136, B.7.141, B.7.163, B.7.170, B.7.172, B.7.181, B.7.186, B.7.206, B.8.6, B.8.10, B.8.19, B.8.20, B.8.40, B.8.47, B.8.56, B.8.63, B.8.69, B.8.86, B.8.86, B.8.100, B.8.110, B.8.124, B.8.131, B.9.37, B.9.39, B.9.51, B.9.51, B.9.83, B.9.89, B.9.118, B.9.123, B.9.159, B.9.162, B.9.165, B.9.188, B.9.196, B.9.198, B.9.202, B.10.18, B.10.36, B.10.62, B.10.83, B.10.85, B.10.95, B.10.105, B.10.132, B.10.133, B.10.142, B.10.142, B.10.149, B.10.149, B.10.156, B.10.158, B.10.197, B.10.202, B.10.210, B.10.210, B.10.227, B.10.261, B.10.263, B.10.265, B.10.273, B.10.276, B.10.281, B.10.290, B.10.293, B.10.314, B.10.321, B.10.323, B.10.343, B.10.352, B.10.356, B.10.382, B.10.387, B.10.390, B.10.401, B.10.402, B.10.404, B.10.405, B.10.413, B.10.419, B.10.432, B.10.441, B.10.450, B.10.455, B.10.480, B.10.481, B.11.80, B.11.109, B.11.130, B.11.139, B.11.151, B.11.155, B.11.157, B.11.179, B.11.182, B.11.200, B.11.200, B.11.200, B.11.203, B.11.205, B.11.209, B.11.227, B.11.229, B.11.230, B.11.242, B.11.247, B.11.253, B.11.260, B.11.270, B.11.274, B.11.277, B.11.280, B.11.286, B.11.295, B.11.301, B.11.312, B.11.324, B.11.338, B.11.349, B.11.381, B.11.398, B.11.410, B.11.415, B.11.426, B.11.437, B.12.15, B.12.31, B.12.32, B.12.34, B.12.36, B.12.54, B.12.63, B.12.65, B.12.73, B.12.76, B.12.79, B.12.88, B.12.91, B.12.95, B.12.99, B.12.103, B.12.105, B.12.138, B.12.161, B.12.167, B.12.176, B.12.182, B.12.184, B.12.192, B.12.197, B.12.198, B.12.200, B.12.201, B.12.205, B.12.207, B.12.210, B.12.218, B.12.223, B.12.237, B.12.249, B.12.259, B.12.261, B.12.288, B.13.2, B.13.22, B.13.33, B.13.51, B.13.51, B.13.74, B.13.99, B.13.100, B.13.100, B.13.116, B.13.118, B.13.135, B.13.170, B.13.171, B.13.177, B.13.212, B.13.215, B.13.216, B.13.220, B.13.221, B.13.253, B.13.273, B.13.277, B.13.282, B.13.283, B.13.284, B.13.289, B.13.295, B.13.330, B.13.318, B.13.330, B.13.338, B.13.343, B.13.348, B.13.348, B.13.349, B.13.349, B.13.387, B.13.388, B.13.400, B.13.401, B.13.432, B.13.440, B.14.19, B.14.19, B.14.30, B.14.46, B.14.58, B.14.63, B.14.69, B.14.71, B.14.94, B.14.96, B.14.99, B.14.99, B.14.117, B.14.129, B.14.131, B.14.142, B.14.143, B.14.146, B.14.149, B.14.155, B.14.157, B.14.188, B.14.188, B.14.190, B.14.214, B.14.257, B.14.264, B.14.265, B.14.269, B.14.282, B.14.289, B.15.7, B.15.12, B.15.27, B.15.40, B.15.64, B.15.77, B.15.77, B.15.84, B.15.90, B.15.92, B.15.104, B.15.136, B.15.162, B.15.164, B.15.166, B.15.166, B.15.167, B.15.168, B.15.185, B.15.202, B.15.204, B.15.205, B.15.206, B.15.216, B.15.219, B.15.222, B.15.227, B.15.282, B.15.301, B.15.330, B.15.333,

B.15.338, B.15.341, B.15.343, B.15.349, B.15.355, B.15.363, B.15.378, B.15.386,
B.15.387, B.15.388, B.15.391, B.15.405, B.15.408, B.15.421, B.15.436, B.15.446,
B.15.450, B.15.450, B.15.458, B.15.460, B.15.467, B.15.470, B.15.474, B.15.479,
B.15.493, B.15.495, B.15.497, B.15.547, B.15.556, B.15.556, B.15.580, B.16.58,
B.16.61, B.16.69, B.16.79, B.16.133, B.16.134, B.16.134, B.16.170, B.16.173, B.16.173,
B.16.195, B.16.216, B.16.225, B.16.242, B.16.242, B.17.38, B.17.47, B.17.47, B.17.50,
B.17.59, B.17.59, B.17.65, B.17.97, B.17.104, B.17.120, B.17.128, B.17.136, B.17.141,
B.17.143, B.17.147, B.17.152, B.17.154, B.17.159, B.17.169, B.17.175, B.17.184,
B.17.200, B.17.201, B.17.202, B.17.202, B.17.203, B.17.207, B.17.209, B.17.215,
B.17.221, B.17.223, B.17.227, B.17.229, B.17.230, B.17.235, B.17.240, B.17.240,
B.17.243, B.17.274, B.17.276, B.17.293, B.17.310, B.17.318, B.17.322, B.17.341,
B.17.356, B.18.2, B.18.13, B.18.16, B.18.26, B.18.44, B.18.45, B.18.45, B.18.58,
B.18.79, B.18.106, B.18.108, B.18.113, B.18.117, B.18.160, B.18.163, B.18.196,
B.18.201, B.18.208, B.18.217, B.18.240, B.18.244, B.18.248, B.18.252, B.18.296,
B.18.358, B.18.371, B.19.18, B.19.36, B.19.36, B.19.37, B.19.50, B.19.55, B.19.57,
B.19.71, B.19.99, B.19.105, B.19.106, B.19.109, B.19.115, B.19.139, B.19.156,
B.19.166, B.19.180, B.19.194, B.19.231, B.19.233, B.19.244, B.19.254, B.19.305,
B.19.333, B.19.333, B.19.363, B.19.373, B.19.389, B.19.389, B.19.423, B.19.429,
B.19.433, B.19.434, B.19.435, B.19.436, B.19.439, B.19.446, B.19.453, B.19.456,
B.19.476, B.19.478, B.19.479, B.19.481, B.20.1, B.20.6, B.20.20, B.20.36, B.20.36,
B.20.42, B.20.57, B.20.61, B.20.61, B.20.98, B.20.129, B.20.199, B.20.237, B.20.241,
B.20.277, B.20.285, B.20.291, B.20.312, B.20.326, B.20.367, B.20.370, B.20.381,
B.20.381

C.Pr.2, C.Pr.3, C.Pr.8, C.Pr.9, C.Pr.11, C.Pr.13, C.Pr.15, C.Pr.17, C.Pr.21,
C.Pr.30, C.Pr.34, C.Pr.35, C.Pr.58, C.Pr.66, C.Pr.93, C.Pr.104, C.Pr.111, C.Pr.129,
C.Pr.130, C.Pr.177, C.Pr.182, C.Pr.199, C.Pr.223, C.Pr.224, C.Pr.227, C.Pr.228, C.1.13,
C.1.28, C.1.83, C.1.83, C.1.119, C.1.153, C.1.156, C.1.176, C.1.176, C.1.178, C.1.183,
C.1.183, C.1.185, C.1.185, C.1.201, C.2.8, C.2.23, C.2.27, C.2.28, C.2.41, C.2.47,
C.2.55, C.2.56, C.2.61, C.2.68, C.2.97, C.2.110, C.2.129, C.2.145, C.2.147, C.2.149,
C.2.196, C.2.212, C.2.227, C.2.243, C.2.244, C.2.244, C.3.9, C.3.16, C.3.20, C.3.38,
C.3.54, C.3.62, C.3.78, C.3.80, C.3.89, C.3.89, C.3.130, C.3.142, C.3.169, C.3.169,
C.3.182, C.3.182, C.3.183, C.3.184, C.3.196, C.3.230, C.3.241, C.3.250, C.3.274,
C.3.284, C.3.288, C.3.307, C.3.309, C.3.326, C.3.326, C.3.333, C.3.348, C.3.360,
C.3.361, C.3.363, C.3.375, C.3.381, C.3.384, C.3.388, C.3.394, C.3.405, C.3.413,
C.3.427, C.3.439, C.3.472, C.3.484, C.3.484, C.3.487, C.3.498, C.4.15, C.4.41, C.4.48,
C.4.96, C.4.104, C.4.104, C.4.117, C.4.118, C.4.133, C.4.145, C.4.169, C.4.172, C.4.186,
C.4.194, C.5.2, C.5.5, C.5.6, C.5.25, C.5.32, C.5.38, C.5.48, C.5.62, C.5.94, C.5.112,
C.5.124, C.5.124, C.5.142, C.5.148, C.5.160, C.5.167, C.5.169, C.5.178, C.6.12, C.6.32,
C.6.36, C.6.37, C.6.60, C.6.76, C.6.82, C.6.86, C.6.110, C.6.112, C.6.156, C.6.176,
C.6.182, C.6.183, C.6.183, C.6.199, C.6.201, C.6.212, C.6.255, C.6.276, C.6.277,
C.6.290, C.6.313, C.6.332, C.6.335, C.6.343, C.6.343, C.6.346, C.6.398, C.6.406,
C.6.422, C.6.431, C.7.10, C.7.36, C.7.66, C.7.92, C.7.100, C.7.117, C.7.125, C.7.129,
C.7.159, C.7.161, C.7.183, C.7.183, C.7.192, C.7.197, C.7.197, C.7.208, C.7.232,
C.7.232, C.7.239, C.7.253, C.7.265, C.8.16, C.8.16, C.8.22, C.8.59, C.8.63, C.8.86,
C.8.87, C.8.88, C.8.98, C.8.129, C.8.137, C.8.157, C.8.161, C.8.186, C.8.203, C.8.218,
C.8.236, C.8.239, C.8.239, C.8.260, C.8.280, C.8.297, C.8.314, C.9.13, C.9.19, C.9.24,
C.9.60, C.9.70, C.9.72, C.9.88, C.9.92, C.9.93, C.9.105, C.9.108, C.9.112, C.9.114,
C.9.115, C.9.118, C.9.118, C.9.120, C.9.127, C.9.180, C.9.181, C.9.192, C.9.194,
C.9.196, C.9.211, C.9.215, C.9.227, C.9.235, C.9.244, C.9.246, C.9.248, C.9.274,
C.9.314, C.9.327, C.9.332, C.9.352, C.10.6, C.10.10, C.10.19, C.10.20, C.10.39, C.10.46,
C.10.83, C.10.83, C.10.96, C.10.99, C.10.102, C.10.106, C.10.120, C.10.159, C.10.163,
C.10.165, C.10.178, C.10.199, C.10.199, C.10.204, C.10.216, C.10.236, C.10.289,
C.10.289, C.10.293, C.10.301, C.11.15, C.11.63, C.11.65, C.11.87, C.11.87, C.11.96,
C.11.96, C.11.100, C.11.100, C.11.135, C.11.150, C.11.196, C.11.207, C.11.218,
C.11.232, C.11.234, C.11.236, C.11.250, C.11.251, C.11.262, C.11.265, C.11.275,
C.11.280, C.11.297, C.11.301, C.12.29, C.12.43, C.12.59, C.12.65, C.12.74, C.12.80,
C.12.86, C.12.101, C.12.101, C.12.102, C.12.111, C.12.113, C.12.116, C.12.116,
C.12.117, C.12.119, C.12.119, C.12.120, C.12.131, C.12.134, C.12.146, C.12.184,
C.12.190, C.12.191, C.12.192, C.12.196, C.12.199, C.12.211, C.12.221, C.12.227,
C.12.229, C.13.8, C.13.16, C.13.20, C.13.23, C.13.28, C.13.39, C.13.50, C.13.52,
C.13.54, C.13.63, C.13.64, C.13.64, C.13.64, C.13.73, C.13.78, C.13.80, C.13.84,
C.13.87, C.13.88, C.13.91, C.13.94, C.13.95, C.13.96, C.13.97, C.13.98, C.13.98,
C.13.109, C.13.114, C.13.124, C.13.128, C.13.146, C.13.152, C.13.155, C.13.160,
C.13.184, C.13.185, C.13.185, C.13.193, C.13.197, C.13.215, C.13.223, C.13.243,
C.14.7, C.14.12, C.14.20, C.14.31, C.14.44, C.14.48, C.14.50, C.14.69, C.14.83,
C.14.105, C.14.116, C.14.122, C.14.124, C.14.131, C.14.136, C.14.137, C.14.139,
C.14.140, C.14.144, C.14.146, C.14.149, C.14.169, C.14.201, C.14.210, C.14.217,
C.15.2, C.15.14, C.15.14, C.15.14, C.15.32, C.15.33, C.15.38, C.15.39, C.15.57, C.15.57,
C.15.73, C.15.75, C.15.93, C.15.106, C.15.107, C.15.107, C.15.116, C.15.116, C.15.124,
C.15.126, C.15.169, C.15.169, C.15.174, C.15.185, C.15.189, C.15.190, C.15.198,
C.15.220, C.15.244, C.15.257, C.15.262, C.15.268, C.15.270, C.15.293, C.15.303,
C.16.21, C.16.55, C.16.97, C.16.104, C.16.105, C.16.109, C.16.114, C.16.124, C.16.143,
C.16.180, C.16.187, C.16.194, C.16.202, C.16.226, C.16.236, C.16.236, C.16.238,
C.16.241, C.16.243, C.16.271, C.16.271, C.16.278, C.16.289, C.16.291, C.16.298,
C.16.299, C.16.299, C.16.300, C.16.301, C.16.302, C.16.303, C.16.312, C.16.344,
C.16.352, C.16.371, C.17.37, C.17.59, C.17.65, C.17.85, C.17.90, C.17.118, C.17.120,
C.17.139, C.17.149, C.17.152, C.17.156, C.17.157, C.17.176, C.17.182, C.17.182,
C.17.185, C.17.188, C.17.190, C.17.193, C.17.202, C.17.209, C.17.219, C.17.219,
C.17.235, C.17.240, C.17.287, C.18.1, C.18.6, C.18.18, C.18.21, C.18.68, C.18.68,
C.18.71, C.18.74, C.18.75, C.18.78, C.18.82, C.18.87, C.18.88, C.18.98, C.18.110,
C.18.182, C.18.182, C.18.204, C.18.221, C.18.227, C.18.229, C.18.233, C.18.240,
C.18.258, C.18.259, C.19.41, C.19.41, C.19.45, C.19.45, C.19.48, C.19.55, C.19.58,
C.19.58, C.19.93, C.19.97, C.19.102, C.19.109, C.19.114, C.19.114, C.19.115, C.19.117,

C.19.121, C.19.126, C.19.127, C.19.129, C.19.131, C.19.133, C.19.150, C.19.166,
C.19.167, C.19.168, C.19.168, C.19.169, C.19.173, C.19.175, C.19.181, C.19.187,
C.19.189, C.19.193, C.19.195, C.19.196, C.19.201, C.19.206, C.19.206, C.19.209,
C.19.219, C.19.237, C.19.240, C.19.255, C.19.257, C.19.274, C.19.290, C.19.298,
C.19.300, C.19.302, C.19.321, C.19.336, C.20.2, C.20.11, C.20.14, C.20.25, C.20.43,
C.20.44, C.20.44, C.20.45, C.20.45, C.20.58, C.20.63, C.20.81, C.20.109, C.20.111,
C.20.116, C.20.116, C.20.120, C.20.163, C.20.166, C.20.201, C.20.206, C.20.215,
C.20.226, C.20.249, C.20.253, C.20.257, C.20.261, C.20.318, C.20.326, C.20.329,
C.20.358, C.20.397, C.20.404, C.20.413, C.20.433, C.21.18, C.21.36, C.21.36, C.21.37,
C.21.50, C.21.55, C.21.57, C.21.71, C.21.99, C.21.105, C.21.106, C.21.109, C.21.115,
C.21.139, C.21.156, C.21.166, C.21.180, C.21.194, C.21.231, C.21.233, C.21.244,
C.21.254, C.21.305, C.21.333, C.21.333, C.21.363, C.21.373, C.21.389, C.21.389,
C.21.423, C.21.429, C.21.433, C.21.433, C.21.435, C.21.436, C.21.439, C.21.446,
C.21.453, C.21.456, C.21.476, C.21.478, C.21.479, C.21.481, C.22.1, C.22.6, C.22.20,
C.22.36, C.22.36, C.22.42, C.22.57, C.22.61, C.22.61, C.22.98, C.22.129, C.22.199,
C.22.237, C.22.241, C.22.277, C.22.285, C.22.291, C.22.312, C.22.326, C.22.367,
C.22.370, C.22.381, C.22.381

asaye > assayen

ascapen v *escapen v.* A 2 askape (1) askapid (1); B 2 ascaped (1) ascapen
(1); C 3 ascaped (1) askape (2)

A. 2.167   And ȝif ȝe lacche leiȝere let him not *askape*
A. 7.69   Þei arn *askapid* good auntir, now god hem amende.'
B. 2.206   And if ye lacche lyere lat hym noȝt *ascapen*
B. 6.77   They ben *ascaped* good auenture, [now] god hem amende.'
C. 2.218   And yf ȝe lacchen lyare lat hym nat *askape*
C. 3.61   Ho may *askape* þe sclaundre, þe skathe myhte sone be mended;
C. 8.79   They ben *ascaped* good aunter, now god hem amende.'

aschamed > ashamed; ascuth > asken

asele v *asselen v.* A 2 asele (1) asselid (1); B 1 asseled; C 3 aseled (2)
asseled (1)

A. 2.35   Sire symonye is assent to *asele* þe chartres
A. 2.77   In þe date of þe deuil þe dede is *asselid*
B. 2.113   'In þe date of þe deuel þ[e] dede [is *asseled*]
C. 2.117   'In þe date of þe deuel th[e] dede is *aseled*
C.19.6   'Is hit *asseled*?' y saide; 'may men yse th[e] lettres?'
C.19.9   Were hit þerwith *aseled* y woet wel þe sothe

aseth > assetȝ

ashamed ptp *ashamed ppl.* A 1 asshamide; B 2; C 4 aschamed (3)
ashamed (1)

A. 5.206   Þanne was þat shrewe *asshamide* & shrapide hise eris,
B.11.405   Tho cauȝte I colour anoon and comsed to ben *ashamed*
B.20.284   And [be] *ashamed* in hir shrift; ac shame makeþ hem wende
C. 6.422   A wax *ashamed*, þat shrewe, and shrofe hym a[s] swythe
C.13.213   Tho cauhte y colour anoen and comesede to ben *aschamed*
C.13.239   Ac when nede nymeth hym vp anoen he is *aschamed*
C.22.284   And be *aschamed* in here shryft; ac shame maketh [hem] wende

aside adv *aside adv.* A 2 asid; B 5; C 4 asyde

A. 5.195   Sum tyme *asid*, & sum tyme arere,
A.11.95   [And] also doumb as a dore drouȝ hym *asid*.
B. 5.347   Som tyme *aside* and som tyme arere,
B.10.142   And as doumb as [a dore] drouȝ hym [*aside*].
B.17.60   Feiþ hadde first siȝte of hym, ac he fleiȝ *aside*
B.17.64   Ac whan he hadde sighte of þat segge *aside* he gan hym drawe
B.20.152   Lyf lepte *aside* and lauȝte hym a lemman.
C. 6.405   Sum tyme *asyde* and sum tyme arere,
C.19.59   Fayth [hadde furst siht of hym] Ac he fleyh *asyde*
C.19.63   Ac when he hadde sihte of this s[egg]e *asyde* he gan hym drawe
C.22.152   Lyf lepte *asyde* and lauhte hym a lemman.

askap- > ascapen

asken v *asken v.* A 21 aske (1) asked (2) asken (3) askest (1) askide (5)
askiþ (4) axe (1) axen (2) axide (2); B 49 aske (7) asked (9) askede
(3) asken (9) askeþ (16) askynge (1) axe (2) axed (1) yasked (1); C 59
ascuth (3) aske (15) asked (4) askede (10) asken (6) asketh (17) askyng
(1) askynge (1) axen (1) eschete (1)

A.Pr.19   Worching & wandringe as þe world *askiþ*.
A. 1.34   Al is not good to þe gost þat þe gut [*ask]iþ*,
A. 1.47   And he *askide* of hem of whom spak þe lettre,
A. 1.100   But holde wiþ hym & wiþ hire þat *aske* þe treuþe,
A. 1.136   Þat loue is þe leuest þing þat oure lord *askiþ*.
A. 1.178   Loue is þe leueste þing þat oure lord *askiþ*,
A. 3.207   Mynstralis for here merþis mede þei *asken*;
A. 3.211   *Asken* mede & messe penis & here mete alse;
A. 4.90   For mede haþ mad my mendis; I may no more *axen*.'
A. 5.58   Enuye wiþ heuy herte *askide* aftir shrift,
A. 5.149   And heo *askide* of hym whidirward he wolde.
A. 6.24   *Axen* aftir hym, er now in þis place.'
A. 7.68   For holy chirche is holden of hem no tiþes to *asken*,
A. 7.280   Hungir [eet] þis in haste & *askide* aftir more.

A. 9.5 And what man he miȝte be of many man I *askide*.
A.11.112 And *axide* hire þe heiȝe wey where clergie [dwell]ide,
A.11.114 '*Axe* þe heiȝe wey,' quaþ heo, 'from henis to suffre
A.11.178 And *axide* how wyt ferde & his wif studie,
A.12.11 Al þat þou *askest* asoylen I wolde.'
A.12.27 And *asked* Iesu on hy þat herden hit an hundred.
A.12.79 He halsed me, and I *asked* hym after
B.Pr.19 Werchynge and wandrynge as þe world *askeþ*.
B.Pr.120 To tilie and to trauaille as trewe lif *askeþ*.
B. 1.36 [Al is nouȝt] good to þe goost þat þe gut *askeþ*,
B. 1.49 And [he] *asked* of h[e]m of whom spak þe lettre,
B. 1.102 But holden wiþ hym and with here þat [*asken* þe] truþe,
B. 3.220 Mynstrales for hir myrþe Mede þei *aske*;
B. 3.224 *Asken* Mede and massepens and hire mete [als];
B. 3.236 Or resten in þyne holy hilles: þis *askeþ* Dauid.
B. 4.103 For Mede haþ [maad myne amendes] I may na moore *axe*.'
B. 5.75 Enuye wiþ heuy herte *asked* after shrifte,
B. 5.299 And [heo] *asked* [of hym] whiderward he wolde.
B. 5.423 I foryete it as yerne, and if men me it *axe*
B. 5.536 *Asken* after hym er now in þis place.'
B. 6.76 For holy chirche is [holde] of hem no tiþe to [*aske*]
B. 6.296 [Hunger eet þis] in haste and *axed* after moore.
B. 7.77 That *askeþ* for his loue þat vs al leneþ.
B. 8.5 And what man he myȝte be of many man I *asked*.
B.10.160 And *asked* hire þe heighe wey where Clergie dwelte,
B.10.162 '*Aske* þe heighe wey', quod she, 'hennes to Suffre-
B.10.206 To do good for goddes loue and gyuen men þat *asked*,
B.10.235 And *askede* how wit ferde and his wif studie].
B.12.111 Ȝyue mercy for hire mysdedes, if men it wole *aske*
B.12.194 And grace *asked* of god þat [graiþ is hem euere]
B.12.234 Raþer þan his likame alogh; lewed *asken* þus clerkes.
B.13.308 *Askeþ* at hym or at hym and he yow kan telle
B.14.111 Ioye þat neuere ioye hadde of riȝtful Iugge he *askeþ*,
B.14.229 That mete or money of oþere men moot *asken*.
B.14.262 Muche hardier may he *asken* þat here myȝte haue his wille
B.15.159 That he ne wolde *aske* after his, and ouþerwhile coueite
B.15.505 In [o] gre[et] god, and his grace *asken*,
B.15.542 And now is werre and wo, and whoso why *askeþ*:
B.16.65 To *asken* hym any moore þerof, and bad hym ful faire
B.16.242 Mercy for oure mysdedes as many tyme as we *aske*:
B.17.289 [How myȝte he *aske* mercy, or any mercy hym helpe],
B.17.294 Thus "vengeaunce, vengeaunce!" verrey charite *askeþ*.
B.17.302 And myldeliche his mercy *aske*; myghte I noȝt be saued?'
B.17.338 To man þat mercy *askeþ* and amende þenkeþ".
B.18.122 Eiþer *asked* ooþer of þis grete wonder,
B.18.297 I haue assailled hym with synne and som tyme *yasked*.
B.18.347 And þat grace gile destruye good feiþ it *askeþ*.
B.19.76 Mirre and muche gold wiþouten merc[ede] *askynge*
B.19.131 And alle he heeled and halp þat hym of grace *askede*;
B.19.230 [To wynne wiþ truþe þat] þe world *askeþ*,
B.19.476 Ne craue of my comune but as my kynde *askeþ*.'
B.19.479 [Haue] þow mayst [þyn askyng] as þi lawe *askeþ*:
B.20.188 Haddestow be hende', quod I, 'þow woldest haue *asked* leeue.'
B.20.266 Of lewed and of lered; þe lawe wole and *askeþ*
B.20.331 And in haste *askede* what his wille were.
C.Pr.21 Worchyng and wondryng as þ[e] world *ascuth*.
C. 1.34 Al is nat good to þe gost þat þe gott *ascuth*
C. 1.46 And god *askede* at hem hoes was þe koyne.
C. 3.246 May nat be sold sothliche, so many part *asketh*
C. 3.254 Forthy y consayl no kynge eny consayl *aske*
C. 3.276 Munstrals for here m[yrth]e mede thei *asken*;
C. 3.279 *Asken* mede and mas pans and here mete bothe;
C. 3.300 That pre manibus is paied or his pay *asketh*.
C. 3.302 They asken here huyre ar thei hit haue deserued
C. 3.336 Ac adiectif and sustantif vnite *asken*,
C. 3.405 As hic & hec homo *askyng* an adiectyf
C. 4.97 And mede hath made my mendes y may no more *asken*.
C. 5.62 /God and good men, as here degre *asketh*:
C. 6.14 '[I], pr[uyde], pacientlyche penaunce *aske*.
C. 6.56 *Ascuth* at hym or at h[ym] and he ȝow can telle
C. 6.63 Enuye with heuy herte *asked* aftur shrifte
C. 6.354 And whode[r]ward he wolde the breuhwyf hym *askede*.
C. 7.36 Y forȝete hit as ȝerne and yf eny man hit *aske*
C. 7.181 *Axen* aftur hym [er] now in þis place.'
C. 8.78 For holy chirche is ho[ld]e of hem no tythe to *aske*,
C. 8.318 Hunger eet al in haste and *askede* aftur more.
C. 9.238 Amend[e] hym and mercy *aske* and mekeliche hym shryue,
C.10.5 And what man a myhte be of mony m[a]n y *askede*.
C.11.102 And *askede* here þe hey way whare clergie dwelte,
C.11.104 '*Aske* þe hey wey,' [quod he], 'hennes to soffre-
C.12.166 Ac ȝef hem forth to pore folk þat for my loue hit *aske*;
C.12.213 And *asketh* [hym after] ho shal hit haue,

C.13.50 And ȝut be ylette, as y leue, for the lawe *asketh*
C.14.56 To ȝeue mercy for mysde[de]s ȝif men hit wol *aske*
C.14.132 Was for A ȝeld hym creaunt to crist and his grace *askede*.
C.15.287 Ioye þat neuere ioye hadde of rihtfull iuge he *asketh*
C.15.293 Thenne may beggares, as bestes, aftur blisse *aske*
C.16.102 Moche hardyore may he *aske* þat here myhte haue his wille
C.16.293 That he ne *askede* aftur his and oþerewhiles coueytede
C.17.70 That pore peple by puyre riht here part myhte *aske*.
C.17.204 And now is werre and wo and whoso why *asketh*:
C.17.256 In þe gre[te] god and his grace *asken*
C.18.8 Thenne gan y *aske* what hit hihte and he me sone tolde:
C.18.24 And *askede* [e]fte of hym of what wode they were.
C.18.57 And *askede* efte tho where hit were all [of] o kynde.
C.18.78 And more lykynde to oure lord then lyue as kynde *asketh*
C.18.259 As we wilnede and wolde with mou[th]e and herte *aske*.
C.19.270 How myhte he *aske* mercy or eny mercy hym defende
C.19.275 Thus "veniaunce, veniaunce!" verray charite *asketh*.
C.19.282 And myldeliche his mercy *aske*; myhte y nat be saued?'
C.19.318 To man þat mercy *asketh* and amende thenketh."
C.20.125 Ayþer *asked* oþer of this grete Wonder,
C.20.330 Y haue ass[a]yled hym with synne and som tyme ich *askede*
C.20.387 So þat lyf quyte lyf; þe olde lawe hit *asketh*.
C.20.417 Ac to be merciable to man thenne my kynde [hit] *asketh*
C.20.442 And namliche at such a nede þat nedes helpe *asketh*:
C.21.76 Mirre and moche gold withouten merc[ede] *askynge*
C.21.131 And all he heled and halp þat hym of grace *asked*;
C.21.230 To wynne with treuthe þat the world *asketh*,
C.21.476 Ne craue of my comune bote as my kynde *asketh*.'
C.21.479 [Haue þou mayst] thyn askyng as thy lawe *asketh*:
C.22.188 Haddest thow be hende,' quod y, 'thow wost haue *asked* leue.'
C.22.266 Of lewed and of lered; the lawe wol and *asketh*
C.22.331 And in haste *eschete* what his wille were.

askyng ger *askinge ger. &> asken* B 1; C 1
B.19.479 [Haue] þow mayst [þyn *askyng*] as þi lawe askeþ:
C.21.479 [Haue þou mayst] thyn *askyng* as thy lawe asketh:

aslepe adv *aslepe adv.(1)* A 1; B 6; C 4
A. 5.8 And so I babelide on my bedis þei brouȝte me *aslepe*.
B. 2.52 Thus lefte me þat lady liggynge *aslepe*,
B. 5.8 And so I bablede on my bedes þei brouȝte me *aslepe*.
B.11.5 And in a wynkynge [worþ til I weex] *aslepe*.
B.15.11 Til reson hadde ruþe on me and rokked me *aslepe*,
B.19.5 I fel eftsoones *aslepe*, and sodeynly me mette
B.20.51 Whan nede ha[dde] vndernome me þus anoon I fil *aslepe*
C. 2.55 Thus le[f]te me þat lady lyggynge as *aslepe*,
C. 5.108 Wepyng and waylyng til y was *aslepe*.
C.21.5 Y ful eftesones *aslepe* and sodeynliche me mette
C.22.51 Whenne nede hadde vndernome [me] thus anoen y ful *aslepe*

asoile(n > assoillen

asonder adv *asonder adv.& pred.adj.* A 1 assondir; B 1
A. 8.101 And piers for [pure] tene pulde it *assondir*
B. 7.119 And Piers for pure tene pulled it [*asonder*]

asondry adj *asondri adj.& adv.* B 1
B.17.167 And aren serel[e]pes by hemself; *asondry* were þei neuere;

aspare v *asparen v.* B 1
B.15.140 And [nempneþ hym] a nygard þat no good myȝte *aspare*

aspele v *cf. spelen v.* C 1
C. 6.432 And spilde þat y *aspele* myhte; y kan nat speke for shame

aspie v *aspien v.* A 5 aspie (4) aspien (1); B 8 aspide (1) aspie (5) aspye (1) aspied (1); C 14 aspyde (1) aspie (1) aspye (7) aspyed (2) aspiede (1) aspyeth (1)
A. 2.187 Spiceris speke wiþ h[i]m to *aspie* here ware,
A. 7.121 'Ȝef it be soþ,' quaþ peris, 'þat ȝe seyn, I shal it sone *aspie*.
A. 7.208 And alle maner of men þat þou miȝte *aspien*,
A.11.226 Kinghod & kniȝthod, for auȝt I can *aspien*,
A.12.103 And whan þis werk was wrouȝt, ere wille myȝte *aspie*,
B. 5.170 For þere ben manye felle frekes my feeris to *aspie*,
B. 6.129 'If it be soþ', quod Piers, 'þat ye seyn, I shal it soone *aspie*.
B. 6.222 And alle manere of men þat þow myȝt *aspie*,
B. 8.130 And wheiþer he be man or [no man] þis man wolde *aspie*,
B.11.256 And alle þe wise þat euere were, by auȝt I kan *aspye*,
B.16.170 And yede forþ as an ydiot in contree to *aspie*
B.17.35 And now com[s]eþ Spes and spekeþ, þat [haþ] *aspied* þe lawe,
B.19.335 Now is Piers to þe plow; pride it *aspide*
C. 2.48 That mede is thus ymaried; tomorwe þou shalt *aspye*.
C. 2.238 Spysours speken to hym to *aspye* he[re] ware,
C. 3.109 For to spyre and to *aspye*, for eny speche of suluer,
C. 4.53 What wey y wende wel ȝerne he *aspyeth*
C. 6.152 For there aren many felle frekes myn aferes to *aspye*,

C. 8.231   And alle manere [of] men þat thow myhte *aspye*
C. 9.147   And when he is rysen rometh out and riȝt wel *aspyeth*
C. 9.208   Long labour and litte wynnynge and at the laste they *aspyde*
C.12.142 And alle þe wyse þat euere were, by auhte y can *aspye*,
C.14.167 Was neuere man vppon molde þat myhte hit *aspie*.
C.15.151 Saue Concience and clergie y couthe no mo *aspye*.
C.19.36   And now cometh this sp[es and speketh] that hath *aspyed* þe lawe,
C.21.301 [Shal] nat be *aspyed* thorw spiritus iusticie.
C.21.335 Now is [Peres] to the [plouh]; Pryde hit *aspiede*

assay n *assai n. &>* assayen B 1
B.10.261 Swich as þow semest in siȝte be in *assay* yfounde:

assayen v *assaine v.* A 2 assaie; B 5 assaie (1) assaye (2) assaien (1)
   assayen (1); C 6 asaye (1) assay (2) assaie (1) assaye (2)
A. 3.5   'I wile *assaie* hire myself, and soþly apose
A. 5.152 'I haue good ale, gossib,' quaþ heo; 'glotoun, wilt þou *assaie*?'
B. 3.5   'I [wol] *assayen* hire myself and soopliche appose
B. 5.302 'I haue good Ale, gossib', quod she, 'Gloton, woltow *assaye*?'
B.16.74   And suffre me to *assaien* what sauour it hadde.
B.16.106 And dide hym *assaie* his surgenrie on hem þat sike were
B.18.69   And some seide he was a wicche; 'good is þat we *assaye*
C. 3.5   'Y shal *asaye* here mysulue and sothliche appose
C. 6.357 'Y haue good ale, gossip Glotoun, woltow *assaye*?'
C. 8.22   Y wolde [*assaye*] som tyme, for solace as hym wolde
C.16.164 And he soffrede me and saide, '*assay* his oþer name.'
C.18.103 *Assay* what sauour hit hadde and saide þat tyme,
C.20.71   And somme saide, 'he can of soercerie; goed is þat we *assaie*

assaille v *assaillen v.* B 7 assaille (3) assailled (1) assaillede (1) assaillen
   (1) assailleþ (1); C 7 assaile (2) assayled (1) assailede (1) assailen (2)
   assaileth (1)
B. 2.97   And þanne to sitten and soupen til sleep hem *assaille*,
B.14.202 For seuene synnes þer ben *assaillen* vs euere;
B.18.297 I haue *assailled* hym with synne and som tyme yasked
B.19.226 And wepne to fighte wiþ whan Antecrist yow *assailleþ*.'
B.20.126 Symonye hym [suede] to *assaille* Conscience,
B.20.296 The while coueitise and vnkyndenesse Conscience *assaillede*,
B.20.374 And comen wiþ a kene wille Conscience to *assaille*.
C.13.63   Wolde noon suche *assailen* hym for such as hym foloweth
C.16.43   For seuene synnes þer ben þat *ass[a]ilen* vs euere;
C.20.330 Y haue *ass[a]yled* hym with synne and som tyme ich askede
C.21.226 And wepne to fihte with when Auntecrist ȝow *assaileth*.'
C.22.126 Symonye hym suede to *assaile* Consience
C.22.296 The while Couetyse and vnkyndenesse Consience *assailede*,
C.22.374 And comen with a kene wil Consience to *assaile*.

assaut n *assaut n.* B 1
B.20.300 Ypocrisie and h[ij] an hard *assaut* þei [ȝeuen].

asse n *asse n.* B 1; C 1
B.18.11   Barefoot on an *Asse* bak bootles cam prikye
C.20.9   Barfoet on an *asse* bake boetles cam priky[e]

asseled > asele

assembled ptp *assemblen v.* B 1
B. 2.57   To marien þis mayde [was] many m[a]n *assembled*,

assemblee n *assemble n.* B 1
B.Pr.218 I seiȝ in þis *assemblee*, as ye shul here after.

assent n *assent n. &>* assenten A 1; B 3; C 1 assente
A. 4.150 Ȝif it be þat buxumnesse be at myn *assent*.'
B. 4.187 If ye bidden buxumnesse be of myn *assent*.'
B. 9.118 And siþenes by *assent* of hemself as þei two myȝte acorde;
B.14.269 As by *assent* of sondry parties and siluer to boote,
C.16.109 As by *assente* of sondry p[arti]es and suluer to bote,

assente > assent, assenten

assenten v *assenten v.* A 8 assent (2) assente (5) assentiþ (1); B 11
   assente (7) assented (2) assenten (1) assenteþ (1); C 12 assente (8)
   assented (1) assentede (1) assenteth (1) assentide (1)
A. 2.35   Sire symonye is *assent* to asele þe chartres
A. 2.106 Hereto *assentiþ* Cyuyle, ac symonye ne wolde
A. 3.107 'Wilt þou wedde þis womman ȝif I wile *assente*?
A. 4.89   So [þat] ȝe *assente* I can sey no more,
A. 4.151 'And I *assente*,' quaþ þe king, 'be seinte marie my lady,
A. 7.39   Loke þou tene no tenaunt but treuþe wile *assent*,
A. 7.50   'I *assente*, be seint Iame,' seide þe kniȝt þanne,
A. 9.100 And oþere wise & ellis nouȝt but as þei þre *assent*[e].'
B.Pr.175 Al þ[e] route of Ratons to þis reson *assented*.
B. 2.68   Thei *assented* for siluer to seye as boþe wolde.
B. 2.142 Herto *assenteþ* Cyuyle, ac Symonye ne wolde
B. 3.118 'Woltow wedde þis womman if I wole *assente*?
B. 4.102 So þat [ye] *assente* I kan seye no [moore],
B. 4.182 Quod Conscience to þe kyng, 'but þe commune wole *assente*

B. 4.188 'And I *assente*', seiþ þe kyng, 'by Seinte Marie my lady,
B. 6.38   Loke [þow] tene no tenaunt but truþe wole *assente*,
B. 6.55   'I *assente*, by Seint Iame', seide þe knyȝt þanne,
B. 8.110 And ooþer wise [and ellis noȝt] but as þei þre *assent[e]*.'
B.17.287 Synnen ayein þe Seint Spirit, *assenten* to destruye
C.Pr.192 Alle th[e] route of ratones to þis resoun *assentide*;
C. 2.70   Thei *assentede* hit were so at syluere prayere.
C. 2.158 Hereto *assenteth* syuyle, ac symonye ne wolde
C. 2.173 To be maried for mone med[e] hath *assented*.'
C. 3.155 'Woltow wedde this m[ai]de yf y wol *assente*?
C. 4.98   So alle my claymes ben quyt by so þe kyng *assente*.'
C. 4.187 'Y *assente*,' sayde resoun, 'by so ȝowsulue yhere
C. 4.190 Ne no supersedias sende but y *assente*,' quod resoun.
C. 8.36   Loke ȝe tene no tenaunt but treuthe wol *assente*
C. 8.54   'Y *assente*, by seynt Gyle,' sayde þe knyht thenne,
C.10.106 Bute oþerewise ne elles nat but as they thre *assent[e]*.'
C.19.268 Synegen aȝen þe seynte spirit, *assente* to destruye

asserue v *asserven v.* A 1; B 1
A. 7.185 And ȝaf hem mete & monie as þei miȝte *asserue*.
B. 6.198 And yaf hem mete [and money as þei] myȝte [*asserue*].

assetȝ n *asseth n.* B 1; C 1 aseth
B.17.241 And if it suffise noȝt for *assetȝ*, þat in swich a wille deyeþ,
C.19.207 And yf hit suffic[e] nat for *ase[t]h* þat in suche a will deyeth

asshamide > ashamed

asshamidest v *OED ashame v., MED ashamen v.* A 1
A. 3.177 Ac þou þiself, soþly, *asshamidest* hym ofte;

assigne v *assignen v.* A 1; B 1
A. 4.109 Til seint Iame be souȝt þere I shal *assigne*,
B. 4.126 And til Seint Iames be souȝt þere I shal *assigne*,

assoillen v *assoilen v.* A 5 asoylen (1) assoile (2) assoilid (1) assoilide (1);
   B 16 assoile (1) assoiled (3) assoileþ (1) assoille (8) assoilled (2)
   assoillen (1); C 19 asoile (1) assoile (6) assoyle (3) assoiled (6)
   assoilede (2) assoylen (1)
A.Pr.67   And seide þat hymself miȝte *assoile* hem alle
A. 3.39   I shal *assoile* þe myself for a sem of whete,
A. 3.46   Þanne he *assoilide* hire sone, & siþen he seide,
A. 3.133 Heo is *assoilid* [as] sone as hireself likiþ.
A.12.11   Al þat þou askest *asoylen* I wolde.'
B.Pr.70   And seide þat hymself myȝte *assoillen* hem alle
B. 3.40   I shal *assoille* þee myself for a seem of whete,
B. 3.47   Thanne he *assoiled* hire soone and siþen he seide,
B. 3.144 She is *assoiled* as soone as hireself likeþ.
B. 3.237 And Dauid *assoileþ* it hymself as þe Sauter telleþ:
B. 5.186 Esto sobrius!' he seide and *assoiled* me after,
B. 5.270 Thow art an vnkynde creature; I kan þee noȝt *assoille*
B. 5.273 That þow hast maad ech man good I may þee noȝt *assoille*:
B.10.253 Alle þe clerkes vnder crist ne koude þis *assoille*,
B.11.222 For it is ouerlonge er logyk any lesson *assoile*,
B.12.216 Alle þe clerkes vnder crist ne kouþe þe skile *assoille*.
B.15.382 And answere to Argumentȝ and [*assoile*] a Quodlibet–
B.17.199 That whoso synneþ in þe Seint Spirit *assoilled* worþ he neuere,
B.19.184 [Myght [men] to *assoille* of alle manere synne[s],
B.19.190 And *assoille* men of alle synnes saue of dette one.
B.19.395 And so to ben *assoilled* and siþþen ben houseled.'
C.Pr.68   [And] sayde þat hymself myhte *assoylen* hem alle
C. 3.42   Y shal *assoyle* the mysulue for a seem [of] whete
C. 3.50   And he *assoilede* here sone and sethen a sayde,
C. 3.182 He is *assoiled* [as] sone as heresulue lyketh.
C. 3.359 Of oure sory synnes to be *assoiled* and yclansed
C. 6.168 Esto sobrius!' he saide, and *assoiled* hym aftur
C. 6.257 To *assoyle* the of th[y] synne sine restitucion[e]:
C. 6.294 Thow art an vnkynde creature; y can the nat *assoile*
C. 9.4   For hym and [for] his ayres for euere to ben *assoiled*.
C.11.154 Alle þe Clerkes vnder Crist ne couthe this *assoile*
C.12.6   He shal *asoile* [the] thus sone how so euere thow wynne hit.
C.12.16   And saide he myhte [me nat] *assoile* but y suluer hadde.
C.12.139 And here aytheres wille [hasteliche god *assoilede*
C.14.155 Alle þe Clerkes vnder Crist ne couthe [þe skyle] *assoile*:
C.17.115 That sholde þe seuene ars conne and *assoile* a quodlibet
C.19.165 That hoso synegeth in þe seynt spirit *assoiled* worth he neuere,
C.21.184 /Myhte men to *assoyle* of alle manere synnes,
C.21.190 And *assoile* men of alle synnes saue of dette one.
C.21.395 And so to ben *assoiled* and sennes be hoseled.'

assondir > asonder; astarot > astroth

asterte v *asterten v.* B 1; C 1
B.11.402 For man was maad of swich a matere he may noȝt wel *asterte*
C.13.210 Man was made of such [a] matere he may nat wel *asterte*

astronomye n *astronomie n.(1)* A 1; B 2; C 1
A.11.155 *Astronomye* is hard þing & euil for to knowe;
B.10.212 Ac *Astronomye* is hard þyng and yuel for to knowe;
B.19.244 As Astronomyens þoru3 *Astronomye*, and Philosofres wise.
C.21.244 A[s] astro[nomy]ens thorw *astronomye*, & philosopheres wyse;

astronomyens n *astronomien n.* B 3 Astronomiens (1) Astronomyens (2);
    C 3 astronomiens (1) astronomyens (2)
B.15.359 *Astronomiens* alday in hir Art faillen
B.15.370 *Astronomyens* also aren at hir wittes ende;
B.19.244 As *Astronomyens* þoru3 Astronomye, and Philosofres wise.
C.17.97 *Astronomiens* alday in here arte faylen
C.17.106 *Astron[o]myens* also aren at here wittes ende;
C.21.244 A[s] *astro[nomy]ens* thorw astronomye, & philosopheres wyse;

astroth n prop *n.i.d.* B 1; C 2 Astarot
B.18.404 *Astroth* and al þe route hidden hem in hernes;
C.20.287 *Astarot*, hoet out and haue out oure knaues,
C.20.447 *Astarot* and alle [þe route] hidden hem in hernes;

aswage v *asswagen v.* B 1; C 1
B. 5.123 May no sugre ne swete þyng *aswage* my swellyng,
C. 6.88 May no sugre ne swete thyng *aswage* my swellynge

at prep *at prep.* A 92; B 236 at (232) atte (4); C 241 at (240) att (1)
A.Pr.37 And haue wyt *at* wille to wirche 3if hem list.
A.Pr.42 Flite þanne for here foode, fou3ten *at* þe ale.
A.Pr.47 For to seke seint Iame & seintes *at* rome;
A.Pr.59 Manye of þise maistris may cloþe hem *at* lyking
A.Pr.82 To haue a licence & leue *at* lundoun to dwelle,
A.Pr.85 Seriauntis it semide þat seruide *at* þe barre;
A. 1.18 Of [woll]ene, of [lyn]ene, of liflode *at* nede
A. 1.19 In mesurable maner to make 3ow *at* ese;
A. 1.24 Þat oþer is mete *at* meel for myseise of þiselue;
A. 1.54 And tutour of 3our tresour, & take it 3ow *at* nede;
A. 1.108 To be buxum *at* his bidding; he bad hem nou3t ellis.
A. 1.138 [Þer] þou art m[er]y *at* mete, 3if men bidde þe 3edde.
A. 2.40 In myddis a mounteyne *at* mydmorewe tide
A. 2.51 And he[o] be bou[n] *at* his bode his bidding to fulfille,
A. 2.52 *At* bedde & at boord buxum and hende,
A. 2.52 At bedde & *at* boord buxum and hende,
A. 2.69 3eldinge for þis þing *at* o 3eris ende
A. 2.105 It shal besette 3oure soulis wel sore *at* þe laste.'
A. 2.112 For he may mede amaistrien and maken *at* my wille'.
A. 2.138 For þei shuln bere þise bisshopis & bringe hem *at* reste.
A. 2.160 And comaundite a cunstable þat com *at* þe ferste
A. 2.169 Dreed at þe dore stood & þat doom herde,
A. 3.4 To take mede þe maide & make hire *at* ese.
A. 3.12 Þat woniþ at westmenstre worsshipeþ hire alle;
A. 3.24 Þanne lau3te hy leue, þise lordis *at* mede.
A. 3.30 And in constory *at* court callen here names.
A. 3.87 Þat fuyr shal falle & forbrenne *at* þe laste
A. 3.102 [But I be holly a3our heste honge me ellys).'
A. 3.187 Dede hym hoppe for hope to haue me *at* wille.
A. 4.114 Vpe forfaiture of þat fe, who fynt hym [*at* douere],
A. 4.123 Be vnpunisshit *at* my power for peril of my soule,
A. 4.150 3if it be þat buxumnesse be *at* myn assent.'
A. 5.14 And þe southwestryne wynd on satirday *at* eue
A. 5.27 And kep[e] it in hire coffre for catel *at* nede.
A. 5.40 And 3e þat seke seint Iame & seintes *at* rome,
A. 5.115 For sum tyme I seruide symme *at* þe nok
A. 5.169 And *at* þe newe feire nempnide it to selle.
A. 5.190 And bleu3 þe rounde ryuet *at* þe riggebones ende
A. 5.214 Til Vigilate [þe veil] fet watir [*at*] his ei3en,
A. 5.244 Dampne me nou3t *at* domisday for þat I dede so ille.'
A. 6.15 *At* bedlem, at babiloyne, I haue ben in boþe;
A. 6.15 At bedlem, *at* babiloyne, I haue ben in boþe;
A. 6.39 He [wiþ]halt non hyne his hire þat he ne haþ it *at* eue.
A. 6.67 Þanne shalt þou blenche *at* a b[erw]e, bere no fals wytnesse;
A. 6.114 To gete ingang *at* any gate but grace be þe more.'
A. 7.42 For þou shalt 3elde it a3en *at* one 3eris ende
A. 7.48 And nameliche *at* mete suche men eschew[e],
A. 7.56 And heng his hoper *at* his hals in stede of a scrippe:
A. 7.94 And ben his pilgrym *at* þe plou3 for pore menis sake.
A. 7.95 My plou3pote shal be my pyk & putte *at* þe rotis,
A. 7.104 *At* hei3 prime peris let þe plou3 stande
A. 7.107 Þanne seten somme & sungen *at* þe ale,
A. 7.111 Shal no greyn þat here growiþ glade 3ow *at* nede;
A. 7.135 Inou3 iche day *at* non, ac no more til on þe morewe
A. 7.137 Ones *at* noon is ynou3 þat no werk vsiþ;
A. 7.154 And countide peris *at* a pese & his plou3 boþe,
A. 7.157 And houpide aftir hungir þat herde hym *at* þe ferste:
A. 7.249 Let nou3t sire surfet sitten *at* þi bord;
A. 8.5 And bad hym holde hym *at* hom & erien his lai3es.
A. 8.19 *At* þe day of dom at here deis to sitten.

A. 8.19 At þe day of dom *at* here deis to sitten.
A. 8.53 Shal no deuil *at* his deþ day derie hym a myte
A. 8.91 And peris *at* his preyour þe pardoun vnfoldiþ,
A. 8.150 Manye tymes *at* mydni3t whan men shulde slepe,
A. 8.155 Dowel *at* þe day of dome is digneliche vndirfongen;
A. 8.171 *At* þe dredful dom whanne dede shal arisen
A. 8.184 Þat *at* þe day of dome we dede as he hi3te.
A. 9.4 3if any wi3t wiste where dowel was *at* Inne,
A. 9.20 Ergo he nis not alwey *at* hom among 3ow Freris;
A. 9.87 Is hokid *at* þat on ende to holde men in good lif.
A. 9.93 And were vnbuxum *at* his bidding, and bold to don ille,
A. 10.31 Aungelis & alle þing arn *at* his wille,
A. 10.34 And al his wil was wrou3t wiþ a speche,
A. 10.59 And ek in sottis þou mi3t se, þat sitten *at* þe nale.
A. 10.181 And [were] marie[d] *at* meschief as men do now here children.
A. 11.10 Among hogges þat hauen hawen *at* wille.
A. 11.15 Or ricchesse or rentis, & reste *at* here wille.
A. 11.39 *At* mete [in here] merþe, whanne mynstralis ben stille,
A. 11.43 Þus þei dryuelen *at* here deis þe deite to knowe,
A. 11.45 Ac þe carful may cri3en & carpe *at* þe 3ate,
A. 11.60 Þat defouliþ oure f[eiþ] *at* fest[is] þere þei sitten.
A. 11.152 And louen hem þat li3en on vs, & lenen hem *at* here nede,
A. 11.174 Fairere vndirfonge ne frendliere mad *at* ese
A. 11.180 To lere *at* 3ow dowel & dobet þereaftir,
A. 11.201 For mendynaunt3 *at* meschief þ[o] men were dewid,
A. 11.227 Helpiþ nou3t to heuene[ward] *at* one 3eris ende.
A. 11.267 For to reule his reaum ri3t *at* his wille.
A. 11.313 Wiþoute penaunce *at* here partyng, into [þe] hei3e blisse.
A. 12.55 Þus we lau3þe oure leue, lowtyng *at* onys,
A. 12.70 *At* my bak of broke bred þi bely for to fylle,
A. 12.71 A bagge ful of a beggere.' I bou3þe hit *at* onys.
A. 12.72 Than maunged I wit[h him] vp *at* þe fulle.
B.Pr.37 And han wit *at* wille to werken if [hem liste].
B.Pr.42 [Flite þanne] for hire foode, fou3ten *at* þe ale.
B.Pr.47 For to seken Seint Iame and Seintes *at* Rome;
B.Pr.62 Manye of þise maistre[s mowe] cloþen hem *at* likyng
B.Pr.85 To haue a licence and leue *at* London to dwelle,
B.Pr.91 Liggen *at* Londoun in Lenten and ellis.
B.Pr.98 Arn doon vndeuoutliche; drede is *at* þe laste
B.Pr.107 Ac of þe Cardinals *at* court þat kau3te of þat name,
B.Pr.146 Wiþ þat ran þer a route of Ratons *at* ones
B.Pr.150 And ouerleep hem li3tliche and lau3te hem *at* wille
B.Pr.157 We my3te be lordes o lofte and lyuen *at* oure ese.'
B.Pr.212 Sergeant3 it [s]emed þat serueden *at* þe barre,
B. 1.18 Of wollene, of lynnen, of liflode *at* nede
B. 1.19 In mesurable manere to make yow *at* ese;
B. 1.24 [That oþer is] mete *at* meel for mysese of þiselue;
B. 1.56 And tutour of youre tresor, and take it yow *at* nede;
B. 1.110 To be buxom *at* his biddyng, he bad hem nou3t ellis.
B. 2.94 And al day to drynken *at* diuerse Tauernes,
B. 2.105 Yeldynge for þis þyng *at* one [yeres ende]
B. 2.141 It shal bisitte youre soules [wel] soure *at* þe laste.'
B. 2.148 For [he] may Mede amaistrye and maken *at* my wille'.
B. 2.181 And fecchen [oure] vitailles *at* Fornicatores.
B. 2.199 And comaunded a Constable þat com *at* þe firste
B. 2.208 Drede *at* þe dore stood and þe doom herde,
B. 3.4 To take Mede þe maide and maken hire *at* ese.
B. 3.12 [That] wonyeþ [*at*] westmynstre worsshipeþ hire alle.
B. 3.18 To be wedded *at* þi wille and where þee leef likeþ
B. 3.25 Thanne lau3te þei leue, þise lordes, *at* Mede.
B. 3.31 And in Consistorie *at* court callen hire names.
B. 3.98 That fir shal falle & [forbrenne *at* þe laste]
B. 3.113 But I be holly *at* youre heste hange me [ellis].'
B. 3.196 And bere hire bras *at* þi bak to Caleis to selle,
B. 3.200 And dide hem hoppe for hope to haue me *at* wille.
B. 3.245 Of god *at* a gret nede whan þei gon hennes.
B. 3.265 Be buxom *at* his biddynge to his wille to fulfille.
B. 3.296 Ne no pelure in his [panelon] for pledynge *at* þe barre;
B. 3.340 For þat lyne was no lenger *at* þe leues ende.
B. 4.131 V[p] forfeture of þat fee, wh[o] fynt [hym] *at* Douere,
B. 4.140 Ben vnpunysshed [*at*] my power for peril of my soule,
B. 4.169 'For ofte haue I', quod he, 'holpen yow *at* þe barre
B. 5.14 And þe Southwestrene wynd on Saterday *at* euen
B. 5.27 And kepe it in hire cofre for catel *at* nede.
B. 5.49 'It is þi [tresor if treson ne were], and tryacle *at* þy nede.'
B. 5.56 And ye þat seke Seynt Iames and Seyntes [*at*] Rome,
B. 5.130 Amonges Burgeises haue I be, [bigg]yng *at* Londoun,
B. 5.163 Til "þow lixt!" and "þow lixt!" lopen out *at* ones
B. 5.178 Ac ouþer while whan wyn comeþ, [whan] I drynke *at* eue,
B. 5.199 For som tyme I serued Symme *at* [Nok]
B. 5.247 And lene folk þat lese wole a lippe *at* euery noble.
B. 5.275 [Is] holden *at* þe hei3e doom to helpe þee to restitue,
B. 5.292 For he shal answere for þee *at* þe hei3e dome,

B. 5.320	And *at* þe newe feire nempned it to selle.
B. 5.342	And blew [þe] rounde ruwet *at* [þe] ruggebones ende
B. 5.371	And ouerseyen me *at* my soper and som tyme at Nones
B. 5.371	And ouerseyen me at my soper and som tyme *at* Nones
B. 5.375	And sat som tyme so longe þere þat I sleep and eet *at* ones.
B. 5.391	Raxed and [remed] and rutte *at* þe laste.
B. 5.403	Wiþ ydel tales *at* þe Ale and ouþerwhile [in] chirche[s];
B. 5.429	If any man dooþ me a bienfait or helpeþ me *at* nede
B. 5.442	Til vigilate þe veille fette water *at* hise eiȝen
B. 5.470	Dampne me noȝt *at* domesday for þat I dide so ille.'
B. 5.488	On good fryday for mannes sake *at* ful tyme of þe daye;
B. 5.508	That alle Seintes [for synful] songen *at* ones
B. 5.527	[*At*] Bethlem, [at] Babiloyne, I haue ben in boþe,
B. 5.527	[At] Bethlem, [*at*] Babiloyne, I haue ben in boþe,
B. 5.552	He wiþhalt noon hewe his hire þat he ne haþ it *at* euen.
B. 5.580	Thanne shaltow blenche *at* a Bergh, bere-no-fals-witnesse;
B. 5.629	To geten ing[o]ng *at* any gate but grace ne moore.'
B. 6.43	For þow shalt yelde it ayein *at* one yeres [ende]
B. 6.48	For in Charnel *at* chirche cherles ben yuel to knowe,
B. 6.53	And namely *at* mete swiche men eschuwe,
B. 6.61	And [heng his] hoper *at* [his] hals in stede of a Scryppe:
B. 6.102	And ben his pilgrym *atte* plow for pouere mennes sake.
B. 6.103	My plow[pote] shal be my pi[k] and [putte *at*] þe rotes,
B. 6.112	*At* heiȝ prime Piers leet þe plow3 stonde
B. 6.115	[Th]anne seten somme and songen *atte* Nale
B. 6.119	Shal no greyn þat [here] groweþ glade yow *at* nede;
B. 6.145	Ac Ancres and heremites þat eten but *at* Nones
B. 6.169	And sette Piers *at* a pese and his plow3 boþe,
B. 6.172	And houped after hunger þat herde hym *at* þe firste.
B. 6.206	And for defaute of foode þis folk is *at* my wille.
B. 6.265	Lat noȝt sire Surfet sitten *at* þi borde;
B. 7.5	And bad hym holde hym *at* home and erien hise leyes,
B. 7.17	*At* þe day of dome at [hire] deys [to] sitte.
B. 7.17	At þe day of dome *at* [hire] deys [to] sitte.
B. 7.46	Than pro dei pietate [pleden *at* þe barre].
B. 7.51	Shal no deuel *at* his deeþ day deren hym a myte
B. 7.58	Hi[s] pardon is [wel] petit *at* hi[s] partyng hennes
B. 7.109	And Piers *at* his preiere þe pardon vnfoldeþ;
B. 7.133	The foweles in þe [firmament], who fynt hem *at* wynter?
B. 7.177	Dowel *at* þe day of dome is digneliche vnderfongen;
B. 7.193	*At* þe dredful dome, whan dede shulle rise
B. 7.200	I sette youre patentes and youre pardon *at* one pies hele.
B. 7.206	*At* þe day of dome we dide as he hiȝte.
B. 8.4	If any wiȝt wiste wher dowel was *at* Inne;
B. 8.24	Ergo he nys noȝt alwey [*at* hoom] amonges yow freres;
B. 8.97	Is hoked [*at*] þat oon ende to [holde men in good lif].
B. 8.103	[And were vnbuxum *at* his biddyng, and bold to don ille],
B. 9.30	Aungeles and alle þyng arn *at* his wille
B. 9.33	[And al his wil was wrouȝt wiþ a speche],
B. 9.59	What anima is leef or looþ; he l[e]t hire *at* his wille,
B. 9.78	*At* myseise and at myschief and mowe hem amende
B. 9.78	At myseise and *at* myschief and mowe hem amende
B. 9.82	Sholde no cristene creature cryen *at* þe yate
B.10.10	Among hogges þat han hawes *at* wille.
B.10.15	Or richesse or rentes, and reste *at* hir wille,
B.10.53	*At* mete in hir murþe whan Mynstrals beþ stille,
B.10.57	Thus þei dryuele *at* hir deys þe deitee to knowe,
B.10.59	Ac þe carefulle may crie and carpen *at* þe yate
B.10.74	And prechen *at* Seint Poules, for pure enuye of clerkes,
B.10.96	Homliche *at* oþere mennes houses and hatien hir owene.
B.10.104	I haue yherd heiȝe men etynge *at* þe table
B.10.203	And louen hem þat lyen on vs and lene hem [*at* hir nede]
B.10.231	Fairer vnderfongen ne frendlier *at* ese
B.10.295	And be prester *at* youre preiere þan for a pound of nobles,
B.10.314	An heep of houndes *at* his ers as he a lord were,
B.10.319	In many places þer þei [persons ben, be þei purely] *at* ese,
B.10.339	Helpeþ noȝt to heueneward [*at*] oone [y]eris ende,
B.10.399	[Ac] *at* hir mooste meschief [mercy were þe beste],
B.10.417	[*At* domesday þe deluuye worþ of deþ and fir at ones;
B.10.417	[At domesday þe deluuye worþ of deþ and fir *at* ones;
B.10.457	Whan man was *at* meschief wiþoute þe moore grace.
B.10.469	And passen Purgatorie penauncelees *at* hir hennes partyng
B.11.29	Thow shalt fynde Fortune þee faille *at* þi mooste nede
B.11.65	Be buried *at* hire hous but at my parisshe chirche;
B.11.65	Be buried at hire hous but *at* my parisshe chirche;
B.11.67	[*At* kirke] þere a man were cristned by kynde he sholde be buryed.
B.11.118	That vnderfonged me *atte* font for oon of goddes chosene.
B.11.121	And bad hem souke for synne [saufte] *at* his breste
B.11.131	A[c] reson shal rekene wiþ hym [and rebuken hym *at* þe laste,
B.11.141	'[I] Troianus, a trewe kny3t, [take] witnesse *at* a pope
B.11.201	For [*at*] Caluarie of cristes blood cristendom gan sprynge,
B.11.217	Crist to a commune womman seide, in [comen] *at* a feste,
B.11.300	And a title, a tale of noȝt, to his liflode *at* meschief.
B.11.333	Blisse and bale boþe I seiȝ *at* ones,
B.11.347	I hadde wonder *at* whom and wher þe pye
B.11.358	And some briddes *at* þe bile þoru3 breþyng conceyued,
B.11.417	Adam, whiles he spak noȝt, hadde paradis *at* wille,
B.12.26	What were dowel and dobet and dobest *at* þe laste,
B.12.52	And þo men þat þei moost haten mynistren it *at* þe laste;
B.12.84	And to mansede men meschief *at* hire ende.
B.12.91	Dampneþ vs *at* þe day of dome as [dide he caractes] þe Iewes.
B.12.110	To vnloken it *at* hir likyng, and to þe lewed peple
B.12.123	Take we hir wordes *at* worþ, for hir witnesse be trewe,
B.12.200	As þo þat seten *at* þe syde table or wiþ þe souereynes of þe halle,
B.13.5	First how Fortune me failed *at* my mooste nede;
B.13.8	And [peple] þat was pouere *at* litel pris þei sette,
B.13.21	I lay doun longe in þis þoȝt and *at* þe laste I slepte,
B.13.36	And seten bi oureselue *at* [a] side borde;
B.13.42	Of þat men myswonne þei made hem wel *at* ese,
B.13.68	Ac o word þei ouerhuppen *at* ech tyme þat þei preche
B.13.88	He shal haue a penaunce in his paunche and puffe *at* ech a worde,
B.13.125	And set alle sciences *at* a sop saue loue one;
B.13.136	'*A[t]* youre preiere', quod Pacience þo, 'so no man displese hym;
B.13.231	Farten ne fiþelen *at* festes ne harpen,
B.13.308	Askeþ *at* hym or at hym and he yow kan telle
B.13.308	Askeþ at hym or *at* hym and he yow kan telle
B.13.366	And hul I hadde my dong *at* þe laste I stale it,
B.13.383	[I]n haly daies *at* holy chirche whan ich herde masse
B.13.437	And for loue of [hir] lorde liþeþ hem *at* festes;
B.13.443	The pouere for a fool sage sittyng *at* þ[i] table,
B.14.59	Or þoru3 hunger or þoru3 hete, *at* his wille be it;
B.14.70	And lyueden wiþouten liflode and *at* þe laste þei woken.
B.14.108	And þat *at* þe rekenyng in Arrerage fel raþer þan out of dette.
B.14.133	Fram þe loue of oure lord *at* his laste ende!
B.14.143	As he þat noon hadde and haþ hire *at* þe laste.
B.14.147	Crist of his curteisie shal conforte yow *at* þe laste,
B.14.200	In fenestres *at* þe freres–if fals be þe foundement.
B.14.213	Ther þe poore presseþ bifore wiþ a pak *at* his rugge:
B.14.222	And buxom *at* hi[s] biddyn[g] for his broke loues,
B.14.223	And buxomnesse and boost [ben] eueremoore *at* werre,
B.15.14	And wherof I cam & of what kynde, I coniured hym *at* þe laste
B.15.20	*At* mydnyght, at mydday, my vois so is knowe
B.15.20	At mydnyght, *at* mydday, my vois so is knowe
B.15.87	Ayein youre rule and Religion; I take record *at* Iesus
B.15.126	Hadde he neuere [saued] siluer þerto [for spendyng *at* ale];
B.15.178	For a frend þat fyndeþ hym failed hym neuere *at* nede:
B.15.190	And bouken hem *at* his brest and beten hem clene,
B.15.192	And wiþ warm water *at* hise eiȝen wasshen hem after.
B.15.214	Ne *at* Ancres þere a box hangeþ; alle swiche þei faiten.
B.15.217	And þe murieste of mouþ *at* mete where he sitteþ.
B.15.259	In alle manere angres, haue þis *at* herte
B.15.341	Hem þat han as ye han; hem ye make *at* ese.
B.15.370	Astronomyens also aren *at* hir wittes ende;
B.15.428	Alle þat ben *at* debaat and bedemen were trewe:
B.15.445	Austyn [þe kyng cristnede *at* Caunterbury],
B.15.485	And feden vs and festen vs for eueremoore *at* oones].
B.15.559	An Aungel men herden an heigh *at* Rome crye,
B.16.20	And lay longe in a louedreem; and *at* þe laste me þouȝte
B.16.141	Sittynge *at* þe soper he seide þise wordes:
B.16.227	Thre men, to my si3te, I made wel *at* ese,
B.17.76	Herberwed hym *at* an hostrie and þe hostiler called:
B.17.89	'Ac þi frend and þi felawe þow fyndest me *at* nede.'
B.17.150	That touched and tastede *at* techynge of þe pawme
B.17.248	Ac hewe fir *at* a flynt foure hundred wynter;
B.17.270	Ech a riche, I rede, reward *at* hym take
B.17.296	Leue I neuere þat oure lord [*at* þe laste ende]
B.17.345	And lightliche oure lord *at* hir lyues ende;
B.18.18	Thanne I frayned *at* Feiþ what al þat fare bymente,
B.18.50	'Aue, raby', quod þat rybaud and þrew reedes *at* hym.
B.18.100	ȝilt hym recreaunt re[m]yng, riȝt *at* Iesus wille.
B.18.191	[*At*] þe bigynn[yng god] gaf þe doom hymselue
B.18.204	And wo into wele mowe wenden *at* þe laste.
B.18.291	And so þow haddest hem out and hider *at* þe laste.'
B.18.344	Adam and al his issue *at* my wille herafter;
B.18.374	And be *at* my biddyng wherso [best] me likeþ.
B.18.399	And nameliche *at* swich a nede þer nedes help bihoueþ:
B.19.61	Places in Paradis *at* hir partynge hennes
B.19.81	For alle þe Aungeles of heuene *at* his burþe knelede,
B.19.94	[Erþeliche] honeste þynges w[as] offred þus *at* ones
B.19.108	In his Iuuentee þis Iesus *at* Iewene feeste
B.19.115	So *at* þat feeste first as I bifore tolde
B.19.142	Killeden hym on cros wise *at* Caluarie on Friday,
B.19.192	He wente, and wonyeþ þere, and wol come *at* þe laste
B.19.196	And demen hem *at* domesday, boþe quyke and dede,
B.19.399	Boþe dregges and draf and drawe *at* oon hole
B.19.412	Or þat acountede Conscience *at* a cokkes feþere.

B.19.422	*At* Auynoun among Iewes–Cum sancto sanctus eris &c–
B.19.431	Qui pluit super Iustos & iniustos *at* ones
B.19.473	And what I take of yow two, I take it *at* þe techynge
B.20.3	I ne wiste wher to ete ne *at* what place,
B.20.19	That he dronke *at* ech dych er he [deye for þurst].
B.20.20	So nede *at* gret nede may nymen as for his owene
B.20.69	Antecrist hadde þus soone hundredes *at* his baner,
B.20.150	Ne careþ noȝt how Kynde slow and shal come *at* þe laste
B.20.157	And geten in hir glorie a gadelyng *at* þe laste,
B.20.162	Oon Tomme two-tonge, atteynt *at* ech [a q]ueste.
B.20.175	And Elde auntred hym on lyf, and *at* þe laste he hitte
B.20.192	And gyued me in goutes: I may noȝt goon *at* large.
B.20.197	I ne myghte in no manere maken it *at* hir wille.
B.20.255	And sette [it] *at* a certain and [at] a siker nombre.
B.20.255	And sette [it] at a certain and [*at*] a siker nombre.
B.20.301	[Ypocrisie *at* þe yate harde gan fighte]
B.20.329	And cam þere Conscience was and knokked *at* þe yate.
B.20.344	Coom in þus ycoped *at* a Court þere I dwelde,
B.20.346	And *at* þe laste þis lymytour, þo my lord was oute,
C.Pr.38	And [han] wytt *at* wille to worche yf þei wolde.
C.Pr.43	Fayteden for here fode, foughten *at* þe ale.
C.Pr.48	To seke seynt Iame and seyntes [*at*] Rome;
C.Pr.83	To haue a licence and leue [*at*] Londoun to dwelle
C.Pr.89	Leyen [*at*] Londoun in lenton and elles.
C.Pr.126	Ar don vndeuouteliche; drede is *at* þe laste
C.Pr.134	Ac of þe Cardinales *at* Court þat caught han such a name
C.Pr.162	Seriantȝ it semede that serue[d] *at* þe barre,
C.Pr.167	Than ran þer a route of ratones [*at* ones]
C.Pr.171	And ouerlep hem lightliche and laghte hem *at* wille
C.Pr.208	Wyttenesse *at* holy wryt whoso kan rede:
C.1.19	And, in mesure thow muche were, to make ȝow *at*ese
C.1.46	And god askede *at* hem hoes was þe koyne.
C.1.52	A tutor of ȝoure tresor and take it ȝow *at* nede;
C.1.204	To lere the what loue is;' and leue *at* me she lauhte.
C.2.70	Thei assentede hit were so *at* sylueres prayere.
C.2.101	Al day to drynke *at* diuerse tauernes,
C.2.157	Hit shal [bi]sitte ȝoure soules ful so[u]re *at* þe laste.'
C.2.164	For he may mede amaystrye [and maken *at* my wille].'
C.2.179	Thenne gan gyle borwen hors *at* many gret maystres
C.2.194	And fecchen oure vitailes *a[t]* fornicatores,
C.2.213	And comaundede a Constable that cam *at* þe furste
C.2.220	Drede stod *at* þe dore and [þe] d[om]e herde.
C.3.4	To take mede þe mayde and maken here *at* ese.
C.3.19	For to wedde *at* thy wille [and] where the leef li[k]eth
C.3.26	[W]henne they hadde lauhte here leue *at* this lady mede
C.3.34	And in constorie *at* court do calle ȝoure names.
C.3.150	But y be holly *at* thyn heste; lat hange me elles.'
C.3.241	And as his wyrdus were ordeyned *at* þe wille of oure lorde.
C.3.255	*A[t]* Concience þat coueiteth to conquere a reume.
C.3.303	And Gylours gyuen byfore and goode men *at* þe ende
C.3.375	As a kyng to clayme the comune *at* his wille
C.3.376	To folowe and to fynde hym and [f]eche *at* hem his consayl
C.3.418	To be buxum *at* my byddyng his [b]o[n]e to fulfille.
C.3.449	Ne no pelure in his panelon for pledyng *at* þe barre.
C.3.492	That l[yne] was no lengur and *at* þe leues ende
C.4.132	Whiles mede hath the maistrie þer motyng is *at* [þe] Barr[e].
C.4.155	That mekenesse worth maystre ouer mede *at* þe laste.'
C.5.29	Or beggest thy bylyue aboute *at* men hacches
C.5.57	Sholde nother swynke ne swete ne swerien *at* enquestes
C.5.95	And ay loste an[d] loste and *at* þe laste hym happed
C.5.97	And sette his los *at* a leef at the laste ende,
C.5.97	And sette his los at a leef *at* the laste ende,
C.5.116	And the southweste wynde on saturday *At* euene
C.5.129	And kepe hit in here cofre for catel *at* nede.
C.5.160	A[n] hep of houndes *at* h[is] ers as he a lord were
C.5.165	In many places ther thei persones ben, be hemsulue *at* ese,
C.5.197	And ȝe þat seketh seynt Iames and seyntes [*at*] Rome,
C.6.56	Ascuth *at* hym or at h[ym] and he ȝow can telle
C.6.56	Ascuth at hym or *at* h[ym] and he ȝow can telle
C.6.66	A wroth hais f[u]ste vppon wrath; hadde [he] wesches *at* wille
C.6.113	But y hadde weder *at* my wille y witte god þe cause
C.6.123	Thus Beggares and Barones *at* debat aren ofte
C.6.136	For he hadde childe in the chapun co[t]e; he worth chalenged *at* þe
C.6.145	How lytel I louye letyse *at* þe style.
C.6.160	Ac other while when wyn cometh and when y drynke late *at* euen
C.6.207	For som tyme y serued symme *at* þe style
C.6.245	Y lene folk þat lese wole a lyppe [*at*] vch a noble
C.6.265	And but y hadde of here wey *at* the laste y stale hit
C.6.272	In halydayes *at* holy churche when y herde masse
C.6.291	Y rede no faythful frere *at* thy feste to sytte
C.6.297	[Ben] haldyng *at* the heye dome to helpe the restitue.
C.6.324	Dampne me nat *at* domesday for þat y dede so ylle.'
C.6.347	For he shal onswerie for the *at* the hey dome,
C.6.400	A[nd] blew his rownd ruet *at* [þe] ry[g]bones ende
C.6.408	[A] thromblede *at* the thresfold and threw to þe erthe.
C.6.429	And ouersopped *at* my soper and som tyme at nones
C.6.429	And ouersopped at my soper and som tyme *at* nones
C.7.7	R[a]xlede and r[e]mede and rotte *at* þe laste.
C.7.19	With ydele tales *at* þe ale and oþerwhile in chirches;
C.7.27	Til matynes and masse be ydo; thenne haue y a memorie *at* þe freres.
C.7.42	Yf eny man do[th] me a beenfeet or helpeth me *at* nede
C.7.56	Til vigilate the veile fette water *at* his eyus
C.7.97	And for loue of here lord ly[th]eth hem *at* festes;
C.7.103	The pore for a f[o]l sage sittynge *at* thy table,
C.7.227	Thenne shaltow blenche *at* a berw, bere-no-fals-witnesse,
C.7.282	To geten ingang *at* eny ȝate bote grace be þe more.'
C.7.293	To loke how me liketh hit,' and toek his leue *at* Peres.
C.8.45	*At* churche in the Charnel cherles Aren euele to knowe
C.8.51	Ac [manliche] *at* mete suche men eschewe
C.8.111	And ben a pilgrym *at* þe plouh for profit to pore and ryche.'
C.8.119	*At* hey prime [Peres] leet þe plouh stande
C.8.122	Thenne seet somme and songen *at* the ale
C.8.126	Shal no grayn þat here groweth gladyen ȝow *at* nede;
C.8.146	Ankerus and Eremytes þat eten but *at* nones
C.8.166	And sette [Peres] *at* a [pes], playne hym whare he wolde.
C.8.168	And houped aftur hunger þat herde hym *at* the furste.
C.8.196	But lyflode for his la[b]our and his loue *at* nones.
C.8.274	*At* noon ne at no tyme and nameliche at sopere
C.8.274	At noon ne *at* no tyme and nameliche at sopere
C.8.274	At noon ne at no tyme and nameliche *at* sopere
C.8.275	Lat nat sire sorfeet sitt[en] *at* thy borde;
C.8.283	Alle þat gr[den *at*] thy gate for godes loue aftur fode
C.9.5	And bad hym holden hym *at* hoem and eryen his leyes.
C.9.21	And deme with hem *at* domesday bothe quyke and dede.
C.9.45	But they pre manibus were payed for pledynge *at* þe barre
C.9.53	His pardoun is ful petyt *at* his partynge hennes
C.9.87	What h[e]m nede[th] *at* here neyhebores at noon and at eue.
C.9.87	What h[e]m nede[th] at here neyhebores *at* noon and at eue.
C.9.87	What h[e]m nede[th] at here neyhebores at noon and *at* eue.
C.9.142	In hope to sitte *at* euen by þe hote coles,
C.9.143	Vnlouke his legges abrood or ligge *at* his ese,
C.9.154	With a bagge *at* his bak A begyneld wyse,
C.9.184	That lakketh this meschiefes mekeliche and myldeliche *at* herte
C.9.195	For hit ben but boyes, bollares *at* þe ale,
C.9.208	Long labour and litte wynnynge and *at* the laste they aspyde
C.9.245	Or sonendayes *at* euensong? se we wel fewe!
C.9.247	Ac aboute mydday *at* mele tyme y mette with hem ofte,
C.9.253	He sat *at* þe syde benche and at þe seconde table;
C.9.253	He sat at þe syde benche and *at* þe seconde table;
C.9.283	And [Peres] *at* his preeyre the pardon vnfoldeth
C.9.304	Caton counteth hit *at* nauht and Canonistres at lasse.
C.9.304	Caton counteth hit at nauht and Canonistres *at* lasse.
C.9.322	For hoso doth wel here *at* þe day of dome
C.9.339	*At* þe dredful dome, when dede shullen ryse
C.9.352	*At* þe day of dome we dede as he tauhte.
C.10.4	Yf eny wiht wiste where dowel was *at* ynne;
C.10.28	Ergo he [n]is nat alwey *at* hom amonges ȝow freres;
C.10.156	Angeles and alle thyng aren *at* his wille;
C.10.189	Oure enemyes enterely and helpe hem *at* here nede.
C.10.241	The eritage þat þe eyer sholde haue is *at* þe kynges wille.
C.11.8	Among hoggus þat han hawes *at* wille.
C.11.32	Litel is he loued or leet [by] among lordes *at* festes.
C.11.33	Nowe is þe manere *at* mete when munstrals ben stille
C.11.38	Thus they dreuele *a[t]* the deyes the deite to knowe
C.11.40	Ac þe carfole may crye and quake *at* þe ȝate,
C.11.54	And prech[en] *at* seynt poules, [for] puyr enuye of clerkes,
C.11.66	Ac be more a wynneth and hath þe world *at* his wille
C.11.79	Amonges hem þat haen hawes *at* wille,
C.11.188	Thow shalt fynde fortune þe fayle *At* thy moste nede
C.11.230	[Ac] *at* he[re] moste meschef mercy were þe beste
C.11.249	*At* domesday a deluuye worth of deth and fuyr at ones.
C.11.249	At domesday a deluuye worth of deth and fuyr *at* ones.
C.11.302	Lewede men in good bileue and lene hem *at* here nede.'
C.12.26	And now y am pore and penyles *at* litel pris he sette[th] me.
C.12.53	That vnderfeng me *at* þe fonte for on of godes chosene.
C.12.56	And bad hem souke for synne saue *at* his breste
C.12.66	A[c] reson shal rekene with hym and rebuken hym *at* þe laste
C.12.109	*A[t]* Caluarie of cristis bloed cristendoem gan sprynge
C.12.186	*At* the laste launceth vp whereby we lyuen all.
C.12.195	Worth allowed of oure lord *at* here laste ende
C.12.208	Ȝoure sorwe into solace shal turne *at* þe laste
C.12.228	And haen þe world *at* he[re] wille oþerwyse to leuene.
C.13.23	As grayn þat lith in greut and thorw grace *at* the laste
C.13.32	Rather then þe ryche thogh they renne *at* ones.
C.13.64	And as safly as þe messager and a[s] sone *at* his hostiele.

C.13.75 Withoute wyles or wronges or wymmen *at* þe stuyues;
C.13.141 Blisse and bale bothe y sey *at* ones
C.13.158 Y hadde wonder *at* wh[om] and where þe pye
C.13.169 'Where hadde thise wilde suche wit and *at* what scole?'
C.13.225 Adam, whiles he spak nat, hadde paradys *at* wille
C.14.55 To v[n]louken hit *at* here lykynge the lewed to helpe,
C.14.66 Take we here wordes *at* worthe, for here wittenesse[e] b[e] trewe,
C.14.139 As tho þat sitten *at* þe syde table or with þe souereyns [of þe] halle
C.14.175 And haue hem [in] haste *at* þyn owen wille
C.15.5 Furste how fortune me faylede *At* my moste nede;
C.15.10 And peple þat was pore *at* litel pris [þei] setten
C.15.41 And seten by ouresulue *at* a syde table.
C.15.47 Of þat men myswonne they made hem wel *at* ese
C.15.65 For [this] doctour *at* þe hey deys dranke wyn [so] faste–
C.15.70 *At* poules byfore þe peple what penaunce they soffrede,
C.15.95 He shal haue a penaunce in his paunche and poffe *at* vch a worde
C.15.144 Ʒef hym eft and eft, euere *at* his nede,
C.15.166 To haue alle londes *at* thy likyng and the here lord make
C.15.205 Farten ne fythelen *at* festes ne harpe,
C.15.258 Wheþer thorw hunger or [thorw] hete, *at* his wille be hit;
C.15.269 [And] lyuede withouten lyflode and [*at*] the laste awakede.
C.16.2 Fro þe loue of oure lord *at* his laste ende.
C.16.36 And bote these thre þat y spak of *at* domesday vs defende
C.16.41 In fenestres *at* þe freres–yf fals be þe fondement.
C.16.54 There þe pore preseth byfore with a pak *at* his rugge,
C.16.63 And buxum *at* his biddyng for his breed and his drynke
C.16.64 And buxumnesse and b[o]est [b]en eueremore *at* werre
C.16.160 'He þat hath lond and lordschipe,' quod he, '*at* þe laste ende
C.16.161 Shal be porest of power *at* his partynge hennes.'
C.16.171 *At* mydnyhte, at mydday, my vois is so yknowe
C.16.171 At mydnyhte, *at* mydday, my vois is so yknowe
C.16.176 Layk or leue, *at* my lykyng chese
C.16.284 That thus goth here godes *at* þe laste ende
C.16.317 [Rentes or other richesse to releue hym *at* his nede]?'
C.16.334 Bouketh hem *at* his breste and beteth h[em] ofte
C.16.338 Thogh y my byliue sholde begge aboute *at* menne hacches.
C.16.343 He is þe murieste of mouthe *at* mete þer he sitteth
C.17.106 Astron[o]myens also aren *at* here wittes ende;
C.17.137 For lechours louyen aʒen þe lawe and *at* þe laste ben dampned
C.17.138 And theues louyen and leute hatien and *at* þe laste ben hanged
C.17.146 And ay hopeth eft to be with here body *at* þe laste
C.17.222 An angel men herde an hye *at* rome crye,
C.18.153 With [two] fisches and [fyue] loues, fyue thousen[d] *at* ones,
C.18.262 *At* ones on an auter in worschipe of th[e] trinite
C.19.53 Bothe abraham and sp[e]s and he mette *at* ones
C.19.95 That his lycame shal lechen *at* þe laste vs alle.'
C.19.124 Touchede and tastede *at* techyng of the paume
C.19.214 Ac hewe fuyr *at* a flynt foure hundret wynter,
C.19.277 Leue y neuere þat oure lord *at* þe laste ende
C.19.325 And lihtliche oure lord *at* here lyues ende
C.20.16 Thenne y [f]raynede *at* fayth what al þat fare bymente
C.20.93 Bothe my lond and my licame *at* ʒoure likynge taketh hit.
C.20.103 Ʒelde hym [re]creaunt remyng, riht *at* iesu[s] wille.
C.20.196 *At* the bigynnynge god gaf the doem hymsulue
C.20.209 And wo into wele moet wende *at* þe laste.
C.20.286 That no liht lepe in *at* louer ne at loupe.
C.20.286 That no liht lepe in at louer ne *at* loupe.
C.20.293 Set Mahond *at* þe mang[n]el and mullestones throweth;
C.20.321 And so haddest hem out and hiddere *at* þe laste.'
C.20.352 Bote oure lord *at* þe laste lyares h[e] rebuke[th]
C.20.355 That ʒe belyen nat this lewed men for *at* the laste dauid
C.20.392 And gyle [be] bigyled thorw grace *at* þe laste:
C.20.416 And be *at* my biddynge, at blisse or at payne.
C.20.416 And be at my biddynge, *at* blisse or at payne.
C.20.416 And be at my biddynge, at blisse or *at* payne.
C.20.442 And namliche *at* such a nede þat nedes helpe asketh:
C.21.61 Places in paradys *at* here partyng hennes
C.21.81 For alle þe angelis of heuene *at* his burthe knelede
C.21.94 Ertheliche honeste thynges was offred thus *at* ones
C.21.108 In his iuuentee this iesus *at* iewene feste
C.21.115 So *at* þat feste furste as y before tolde
C.21.142 Culden hym on cros wyse *at* Caluarie on fryday
C.21.192 He wente and woneth there and wol come *at* þe laste
C.21.196 And demen hem *at* domesday, bothe quyke and dede,
C.21.399 Bothe dregges and draf and drawe *at* on hole
C.21.412 Or þat acounted Consience [*at*] a cokkes fether.
C.21.422 *At* Auenon among iewes–cum sancto sanctus eris &c–
C.21.431 Qui pluit super iustos & iniustos *at* ones
C.21.473 And what y take of ʒow two y take hit *at* þe techynge
C.22.3 Y ne wiste where to ete ne *at* what place
C.22.19 That he dronke *at* vch a dy[c]h ar he deye for furste.
C.22.20 So nede *at* greet nede may nyme as for his owne
C.22.69 Auntecrist hadde thus sone hondredes *at* his baner

C.22.150 Ne careth nat how kynde slowh and shal come *at* þe laste.
C.22.157 And geten in here glorie a gadlyng *at* þe laste,
C.22.162 Oen Tomme two-tonge, ateynt *at* vch [a q]ueste.
C.22.175 And Elde auntered hym on lyf and *at* þe laste he hitte
C.22.192 And gyued me in gowtes: y may nat go *at* large.
C.22.197 Y ne myhte in none manere maken hit *at* here wille
C.22.255 And sette hit *at* a serteyne and at a syker nombre
C.22.255 And sette hit at a serteyne and *at* a syker nombre
C.22.301 Ypocrisye *at* þe ʒate harde gan fyhte
C.22.329 And cam þer Consience was and knokked *at* þe ʒate.
C.22.344 Kam ynne thus ycoped *at* a Court þer y dwelte
C.22.346 And *at* þe laste this lymytour, tho my lord was oute,

atach- > attachen

atake ptp *ataken v.* C 1
C. 3.140 Thow tene me and treuthe: and thow mowe be *atake*

atamede v *attamen v.* B 1; C 1
B.17.71 [And breide to hise boteles and boþe he *atamede*];
C.19.70 And vnbokelede his boteles and bothe he *atamede*.

ateynt > atteynt

aþynkeþ v *athinken v.* B 1; C 1 athynketh
B.18.89 He sighed and seide, 'soore it me *aþynkeþ*!
C. 6.100 Now hit *athynketh* me in my thouhte þat euere y so wrouhte.

aþrest > afurst

atyer n *atir n.* C 1
C. 2.15 For to telle of here *atyer* no tyme haue y nouthe.

atymye v *atemien v.* C 2
C.19.244 Sethe he withoute wyles wan and wel myhte *atymye*
C.19.248 With wyles and with luyther whitus and ʒut wollen nat *atymye*

atired ptp *atiren v.* A 2 atirid; B 2
A. 2.15 'What is þis womman,' quaþ I, 'þus worþily *atirid*?'
A. 2.130 And fauel vpon fair speche, fe[int]liche *atirid*.
B. 2.19 'What is þis womman', quod I, 'so worþili *atired*?'
B. 2.166 And Fauel on [Fair Speche] fe[ynt]ly *atired*.

ato > atwo

atones adv *at ones phr.* B 1
B.17.55 Boþe þe heraud and hope and he mette *atones*

attachen v *attachen v.* A 2 atache (1) atachid (1); B 3 attached (2) attachen (1); C 4 atache (1) atached (1) attached (1) attacheth (1)
A. 2.161 To *atache* þis tiraunt[is] 'for any tresour, I hote,
A. 2.198 And ek wep & wrang whan heo was *atachid*.
B. 2.200 To *attachen* þo Tyrauntʒ 'for any [tresor], I hote;
B. 2.239 And ek wepte and wrong whan she was *attached*.
B.16.261 'It is a precious present', quod he, 'ac þe pouke it haþ *attached*,
C. 2.214 [T]o *atache* tho tyrauntes, 'for eny tresor, y hote;
C. 2.255 And bothe wepte and wrang when she was *attached*.
C.11.305 All þat treuth *attacheth* and testifieth for gode
C.18.277 'Hit is a precious present,' quod he, 'Ac the pouke hit hath *atached*

atte > at

atteynt ptp *atteinten v.* B 1; C 1 ateynt
B.20.162 Oon Tomme two-tonge, *atteynt* at ech [a q]ueste.
C.22.162 Oen Tomme two-tonge, *ateynt* at vch [a q]ueste.

attese > at,ese

attre n *atter n.* B 1
B.12.258 And alle þe oþere þer it lith enuenymeþ þoruʒ his *attre*.

atwene adv *atwein adv.* C 1
C.Pr.114 Fro his chayere þer he sat and brake his nekke *atwene*.

atwynne adv *atwinne adv.* C 1
C.18.189 Of o wit and o will, [they] were neuere *atwynne*

atwo adv *atwo adv.* B 1; C 3 ato
B.19.338 Blowe hem doun and breke hem and bite *atwo* þe mores.
C. 8.64 My plouhpote shal be my pykstaff and pyche *ato* þe rotes
C.20.75 A cachepol cam [forth] a[nd] craked *ato* he[re] legges
C.21.338 Blowe hem doun and B[r]eke hem and b[y]te *ato* þe mores.

auctour n *auctour n.* B 3; C 1 Autor
B.10.251 Who was his *Auctour*? alle þe foure Euaungelistes.
B.15.120 And who was myn *Auctour*, muche wonder me þinkeþ
B.15.375 [Ne] nauʒt oon among an hundred þat an *Auctour* kan construwe,
C.11.147 Ho was his *Autor* And hym of god tauhte?

audience n *audience n.* B 1; C 1 audiense
B.13.433 Sholde noon harlot haue *audience* in halle n[e] in Chambre
C. 7.93 Sholde non harlote haue *audiense* in halle ne in chaumbre

auditour n *auditour n.* B 1; C 1
B.19.461   Al þat myn *Auditour* or ellis my Styward
C.21.461   Al þat myn *Auditour* or elles my styward

auȝt pron *ought pron.* A 3 auȝt (2) ouȝt (1); B 11 aught (1) auȝt (8) ouȝt (2); C 8 auht (4) auhte (2) ouht (2)
A. 6.116   'Ne I,' quaþ an apeward, 'be *auȝt* þat I knowe.'
A. 9.78   Whiles he haþ *ouȝt* of his owene he helpiþ þere nede is;
A.11.226   Kinghod & kniȝthod, for *auȝt* I can aspie,
B. 5.422   If I bigge and borwe *auȝt*, but if it be ytailed,
B. 5.432   I am noȝt lured wiþ loue but þer ligge *auȝt* vnder þe þombe.
B. 5.481   And of nauȝt madest *auȝt* and man moost lik to þiselue,
B. 5.631   'Nor I', quod an Apeward, 'by *auȝt* þat I knowe.'
B. 8.87   [Whiles he haþ *ouȝt* of his owene he helpeþ þer nede is];
B.10.338   Kynghod [and] knyȝthod, [for *auȝt*] I kan awayte,
B.11.256   And alle þe wise þat euere were, by *auȝt* I kan aspye,
B.13.10   But quik he biqueþe [hem] *auȝt* [or sholde helpe] quyte hir dettes;
B.13.299   And if he gyueþ *ouȝt* to pouere gomes, telle what he deleþ;
B.13.415   And if he *auȝt* wole here it is an harlotes tonge.
B.14.8   To agulte god or good man by *aught* þat I wiste,
C. 6.111   On god when me greued *auht* and grochede of his sonde:
C. 7.35   Yf y b[y]gge and borwe [*ouh*]t, but yf hit be ytayled,
C. 7.45   Y am nat luyred with loue but þer lygge *ouht* vnder þe t[h]umbe.
C. 7.123   And [of nauhte madest] *auhte* and man lache thysulue
C. 7.284   'Ne y,' quod an hapeward, 'by *auht* þat y knowe.'
C. 8.234   Yf thow hast wonne *auht* wikkedliche, wiseliche despene hit:
C.12.142   And alle þe wyse þat euere were, by *auhte* y can aspye,
C.15.12   Bote quyke he byqu[e]th hem *auht* or wolde helpe quyte here dettes;

auȝt adv *ought adv.* A 1 ouȝt; B 3; C 2 auht
A. 6.20   'Knowist þou *ouȝt* a corseint,' quaþ þei, 'þat men callen treuþe?
B. 5.532   'Knowestow *auȝt* a corsaint', [quod þei], 'þat men calle truþe?
B.15.106   And hatien to here harlotrie, and [*au]ȝt* to vnderfonge
B.15.551   Right so, ye clerkes, for ȝoure coueitise er [come *auȝt*] longe
C. 7.177   'Knowest thow *auht* a corsent,' quod they, 'þat men calleth treuthe?
C.17.214   Riht so, ȝe clerkes, ȝoure coueytise ar come *auht* longe

auȝte n *aught n.* &> owe C 1
C.13.7   Abraham for his [*auȝte*] hadde moche tene

auȝtest > owe; auht(e > auȝt

aultoun n prop *n.i.d.* B 1; C 1
B.14.304   The sixte is a path of pees; ye! þoruȝ þe paas of *Aultoun*
C.16.139   The sixte is a path of pees; ȝe! thorwe þe pase of *Aultoun*

auncer n *auncel n.* A 1 aunsel; B 1; C 1
A. 5.132   Þanne [myn owne] *aunsel* dede, [whanne] I weiȝede treweþe.
B. 5.216   Than myn owene *Auncer* [whan I] weyed truþe.
C. 6.224   Then myn [owene] *auncer* when y wayed treuthe.

aungel n *aungel n.* A 6 aungel (3) aungelis (1) aungelys (2); B 18 angel (1) Aungel (6) Aungeles (11); C 17 angel (3) angeles (8) angelis (5) Angels (1)
A. 8.36   '[And] I shal sende myself seynt Michel myn *aungel*
A.10.31   *Aungelis* & alle þing arn at his wille,
A.10.143   An *aungel* in angir hiȝte h[e]m to wende
A.10.157   Forþi he sente to se[þ], & se[i]de hym be an *aungel*
A.12.4   He passeþ þe apostolis lyf, and [peryth] to *aungelys*.
A.12.95   Þat þi play be plentevous in paradys with *aungelys*.
B.Pr.128   And siþen in þe Eyr an *Aungel* of heuene
B.Pr.131   But suffren and seruen; forþi seide þe *Aungel*,
B.Pr.140   And to þe *Aungel* an heiȝ answerde after:
B. 7.34   'And I shal sende myselue Seint Michel myn [a]*ngel*
B. 9.30   *Aungeles* and alle þyng arn at his wille
B. 9.127   [For] god sente to Se[þ] and seide by an *Aungel*,
B.12.148   To pastours and to poetes appered þe *Aungel*
B.14.122   *Aungeles* þat in helle now ben hadden ioye som tyme,
B.15.559   An *Aungel* men herde an heigh at Rome crye,
B.16.71   Maidenhode, *Aungeles* peeris, and [erst] wole be ripe
B.18.371   And þanne shal I come as a kyng, crouned, wiþ *Aungeles*,
B.18.407   Manye hundred of *Aungeles* harpeden and songen,
B.19.72   And cam to take mankynde kynges and *Aungeles*
B.19.74   *Aungeles* out of heuene come knelynge and songe,
B.19.79   Into hir kyngene kiþ by counseil of *Aungeles*.
B.19.81   For alle þe *Aungeles* of heuene at his burþe knelede,
B.19.150   That *Aungeles* and Archaungeles, er þe day sprenge,
B.20.241   Lat hem be as beggeris or lyue by *Aungeles* foode.'
C. 9.37   'And y shal sende ȝow mysulue seynt Mihel myn *Angel*
C.10.156   *Angeles* and alle thyng aren at his wille,
C.11.148   Patriarkes and prophetes, apostles and *angelis*;
C.12.207   *Angelis* in here anger on this wyse hem grette:
C.14.92   To pastours and to poetes Appered þe *Angel*
C.15.298   *Angeles* þat in helle now ben hadden som tyme ioye
C.17.222   An *angel* men herde an hye at rome crye,

C.18.89   For þat is euene with *angelis* and angeles pere.
C.18.89   For þat is euene with angelis and *angeles* pere.
C.20.413   And thenne shal y come as [a] kynge, croune[d], with *angeles*
C.20.450   Many hundret of *Angels* harpeden and songen,
C.21.72   And cam to take mankynde kynges and *angeles*
C.21.74   *Angele[s]* out of heuene come knel[yng] and songe,
C.21.79   Into here kyngene kuth by consail of *Angelis*.
C.21.81   For alle þe *angelis* of heuene at his burthe knelede
C.21.150   That *Angeles* and Archangeles, ar the day spronge,
C.22.241   Lat hem be as beggares or lyue by *angeles* fode.'

aunsel > auncer

aunte n *aunte n.* A 2; B 3; C 3
A. 5.211   Er abstinence myn *aunte* haue ygyue me leue,
A. 5.250   For he hadde leiȝe be latro luciferis [*aunte*].
B. 5.153   I haue an *Aunte* to Nonne and an Abbesse boþe;
B. 5.383   Til Abstinence myn *Aunte* haue ȝyue me leeue,
B. 5.476   For he hadde leyen by Latro, luciferis *Aunte*.
C. 6.128   Y haue an *Aunte* to nonne and an abbesse;
C. 6.330   For he hadde layȝe by latro, luciferes *aunte*.
C. 6.440   Til abstinence myn *aunte* haue ȝeue me leue;

auntecrist > antecrist; aunter -ir > auenture

auntrede v *auntren v.* B 2 auntred (1) Auntrede (1); C 3 auntered (1) auntred (1) auntreth (1)
B.18.222   And after god *Auntrede* hymself and took Adames kynd[e]
B.20.175   And Elde *auntred* hym on lyf, and at þe laste he hitte
C.10.216   As an hewe þat erieth nat *aun[t]reth* hym to sowe
C.20.231   And aftur god *auntred* hymsulue and toek Adames kynde
C.22.175   And Elde *auntered* hym on lyf and at þe laste he hitte

auntres > auentrous; auntur > auenture

austyn n prop *n.i.d.* A 2; B 9 Austyn (8) Austynes (1); C 8 Austyn (7) Austynes (1)
A.11.72   Ac *austyn* þe olde for alle suche prechide,
A.11.303   Þat [was] *austyn* þe olde, & hiȝeste of þe foure,
B.10.120   *Austyn* to swiche Argueres [he] telleþ þis teme:
B.10.249   *Austyn* þe olde herof made bokes,
B.10.459   Was *Austyn* þe olde, and heiȝest of þe foure,
B.13.39   Of *Austyn*, of Ambrose, of [alle] þe foure Euangelistes:
B.14.319   Thus lered me a lettred man for oure lordes loue, Seint *Austyn*:
B.15.37   *Austyn* and Ysodorus, eiþer of hem boþe
B.15.289   Til he foundede freres of *Austynes* ordre, [or ellis freres lyen].
B.15.445   *Austyn* [þe kyng cristnede at Caunterbury],
B.19.269   Oon highte *Austyn* and Ambrose anoþer,
C.11.146   *Austyn* þe olde herof made bokes;
C.11.149   And þe trewe trinite to *Austyn* apperede
C.11.285   Was *Austyn* þe oelde þat euere man wiste,
C.15.44   Of *Austyn*, of Ambrose, of alle þe foure euaungeli[st]es:
C.16.153   Thus lered me a le[tte]red man for oure lordes loue, seynt *Austyn*:
C.16.199   *Austyn* and ysodorus, either of hem bothe
C.17.15   Foules hym fedde yf frere *Austynes* be trewe
C.21.269   Oen hihte *Austyn* and Ambros[e] anoþer,

auter n *auter n.* A 2; B 3 Auter (1) Auteres (1) Auters (1); C 3 auter (1) auters (2)
A. 3.50   'Wiste I þat,' quaþ þe womman, 'þere nis wyndowe ne *auter*
A. 5.90   [Awey] fro þe *auter* myn eiȝe I turne
B. 5.110   Awey fro þe *Auter* turne I myne eiȝen
B.10.318   To Religiouse þat han no rouþe þouȝ it reyne on hir *Auters*.
B.15.529   [And nauȝt to] huppe aboute in Engelond to halwe mennes *Auteres*
C. 5.164   To religious þat haen no reuthe thow it ryne on here *auters*.
C.17.279   And nat in Ingelond to huppe aboute and halewe men *auters*
C.18.262   At ones on an *auter* in worschipe of th[e] trinite

autor > auctour

auaille v *availen v.* B 4 auaille (3) auailled (1); C 4 availe (1) auayle (1) availe (1) availle (1)
B.10.278   [Thouȝ] it *auailled* noȝt þe commune it myȝte auaille yowselue.
B.10.278   [Thouȝ] it auailled noȝt þe commune it myȝte *auaille* yowselue.
B.17.93   'Haue hem excused', quod he; 'hir help may litel *auaille*.
B.20.179   May noȝt a myte *auaille* to med[l]e ayein Elde.'
C. 9.7   Or eny manere mester þat myhte [Peres] *auayle*
C. 9.275   Ther as mede ne mercy may nat a myte *availle*
C.19.83   'Haue hem excused,' quod [t]he samaritaen; 'here helpe may nat *availe*.
C.22.179   May nat a myte *avayle* to medlen aȝen Elde.'

auarice n *avarice n.* A 3; B 6; C 6 Auarice (1) auaryce (4) auaris (1)
A. 1.171   So [harde] haþ *auarice* haspide ȝow togideres.
A. 2.63   And al þe Ile of vsurie, & *auarice* þe faste,
A. 8.40   Vsure, & *auarice*, & oþes I defende,
B. 1.197   So harde haþ *Auarice* yhasped [yow] togideres.

B. 2.87   That is vsure and *Auarice*; al I hem graunte
B.14.245 And þouȝ *Auarice* wolde angre þe poore he haþ but litel myȝte,
B.14.247 Ther *Auarice* haþ Almaries and yren bounden cofres.
B.15.247 Ac *auarice* haþ þe keyes now and kepeþ for his kynnesmen
B.20.123 And armed hym in *Auarice* and hungriliche lyuede.
C. 1.192 So harde haþ *auaryce* yhapsed hem togederes.
C. 2.94   With vsurye and *Auaryce* and other fals sleythus
C.16.85 And thogh *Auaryce* wolde Angry [þe] pou[r]e he hath bote lytel myhte
C.16.87 There *Auaryce* hath almaries and yrebounden coffres.
C.16.367 Ac *auaris* oþerwhiles halt hym withoute þe gate.
C.22.123 And Armed hym in *Auarice* and hungriliche lyuede.

auarous adj *averous adj.* A 1 auerous; B 3 Auarous (1) auarouse (2); C 4 Auerous
A. 9.80   Þat þe Erl *auerous* hadde, or his eires,
B. 8.89   That þe Erl *Auarous* [hadde, or] hise heires,
B.15.85 Of vsurers, of hoores, of *Auarouse* chapmen,
B.15.136 Curatours of holy kirke, as clerkes þat ben *auarouse*,
C. 1.188 *Auerous* and euel willed when þei ben auaunsed,
C.10.86 Þat þe Erl *Auerous* held and his ayres
C.14.21 And holy chirche horen helpe, *Auerou[s]* and coueytous,
C.16.281 Curatours of holy [kirke] and clerkes þat ben *Auerous*,

auaunce v *avauncen v.* A 3 auauncid (2) auaunciþ (1); B 4 auaunce (1) auaunced (3); C 3 avauncen (1) avaunsed (2)
A. 1.165 Arn none hardere þan [hy] whanne [hy] ben *auauncid*,
A. 3.32   Þat he ne worþ ferst *auauncid* for I am beknowe
A. 4.116 Oþer prouisour, or prest þat þe pope *auaunciþ*.
B. 1.191 Are [none hardere] þan hij whan þei ben *auaunced*,
B. 3.33   That he ne worþ first *auaunced*, for I am biknowen
B. 9.164 "I am via & veritas", seiþ crist, "I may *auaunce* alle."
B.11.290 And þe title þat ye take ordres by telleþ ye ben *auaunced*:
C. 1.188 *Auerous* and euel willed when þei ben *avaunsed*,
C.10.255 For y am via & veritas and may *avauncen* alle."
C.13.104 The tytle [þat] ȝe take ordres by telleth ȝe ben *avaunsed*

auees > aues

auenge v *avengen v.* B 2 auenge (1) avenge (1); C 3 auenge (1) avenge (1) avenged (1)
B.13.329 *Auenge* me fele tymes, oþer frete myselue wiþInne;
B.20.384 And countrepledeþ me, Conscience; now kynde me *avenge*,
C. 3.93   The whiche crien on here knees þat crist hem *auenge*,
C. 6.139 And thenne awake y, wrathe, and wolde be *avenged*.
C.22.384 And countrepledeth me, Consience; now kynde me *avenge*

auenon > auynoun

auentrous adj *aventurous adj.* B 1; C 1 Auntres
B.18.16 As dooþ an heraud of armes whan *Auentrous* comeþ to Iustes.
C.20.14 As doth an heraud of Armes when *Auntres* cometh to ioustes.

auenture n *aventure n.* A 4 aunter (3) auntir (1); B 6; C 4 aunter (1) Auntur (3)
A. 3.63   An *aunter* ȝe haue ȝoure hire þerof h[e]re;
A. 3.259 An *aunter* it [noiȝide me non] ende wile I make.
A. 7.41   Nyme hem nouȝt, an *aunter* þou mowe hem nouȝt deserue.
A. 7.69   Þei arn askapid good *auntir*, now god hem amende.'
B. 3.66   An *auenture* pride be peynted þere and pomp of þe world;
B. 3.72   On *auenture* ye haue youre hire here and youre heuene als.
B. 3.281 On *auenture* it noyed m[e] noon ende wol I make,
B. 6.42   Nyme it noȝt an *auenture* [þow] mowe it noȝt deserue.
B. 6.77   They ben ascaped good *auenture*, [now] god hem amende.'
B.13.72 In englissh on *auenture* it sholde be rehersed to ofte,
C. 3.70   An *Auntur* pruyde be paynted there and pomp of the world,
C. 3.434 An *Auntur* hit nuyede me noen ende wol y make,
C. 8.40   Nym hit nat an *auntur* thow mowe hit nauht deserue
C. 8.79   They ben ascaped good *aunter*, now god hem amende.'

auer n *aver n.(2)* C 1
C. 6.32   Me wilnynge þat men wen[y]e y were as in *auer*

auereys n prop *n.i.d.* B 1; C 1 Aueroy
B.13.91 And preuen it by hir Pocalips and passion of Seint *Auereys*
C.15.98 And prouen hit by here pocalips and þe passioun of seynt *Aueroy*

auerous > auarous

aues n *ave n.* B 1; C 1 Auees
B.15.181 He kan portreye wel þe Paternoster and peynte it with *Aues*
C.16.323 And purtraye wel þe paternoster and peynten hit with *Auees*.

auynet n *avinete n.* B 1
B.12.259 By þe po feet is vnderstande, as I haue lerned in *Auynet*,

auynoun n prop *n.i.d.* B 1; C 1 Auenon
B.19.422 At *Auynoun* among Iewes–Cum sancto sanctus eris &c–

C.21.422 At *Auenon* among iewes–cum sancto sanctus eris &c–

auisen v *avisen v.* B 1; C 2 auyse (1) auysen (1)
B.15.320 And *auisen* hem bifore a fyue dayes or sixe
C. 4.21   And lat warrokye [hym] w[e]l with *auys[e]*-þe-byfore;
C.17.54 Yf lewede men knewe this latyn a litel they wolden *auysen* hem

auoutrye n *avoutrie n.* B 1
B.12.74 That what womman were in *auoutrye* taken, whe[r] riche or poore,

auow n *avoue n.* A 2 auowe (1) auowes (1); B 3 auow (1) auowes (2); C 1 auowe
A.Pr.68 Of falsnesse of fastyng & of *auowes* broken
A. 5.221 And made *auowe* tofore god for his foule slouþe:
B.Pr.71 Of falshede of fastynge [and] of *Auowes* ybroken.
B. 5.397 I haue maad *auowes* fourty and foryete hem on þe morwe;
B. 5.449 And made *auow* tofore god for his foule sleuþe:
C. 7.63   And made [*a]uowe* tofore god for his foule sleuthe:

auowe v1 *avouen v.(1)* A 1; B 3; C 4 avowe
A. 3.236 In marchaundie is no mede, I may it wel *auowe*;
B. 3.257 In marchaundise is no Mede, I may it wel *auowe*;
B.11.86 'If I dorste', quod I, 'amonges men þis metels *auowe*!'
B.18.216 For til modicum mete with vs, I may it wel *auowe*,
C. 3.313 In Marchandise is no mede, y may hit wel *avowe*;
C.15.113 And thenne dost thow wel and wysly, y dar hit wel *avowe*.'
C.15.139 And *avowe* byfore god and forsaken hit neuere
C.20.225 For til [modicum] mete with vs, y may hit wel *avowe*,

auowed v2 *avouen v.(2)* A 1 auowide (1); B 1
A. 5.209 And *auowide* to faste, for hungir or þrist:
B. 5.381 And *auowed* to faste for hunger or þurste:

away(e > awey

awayte v *awaiten v.* B 4 awayte (1) awaited (1) awaiteden (1) awaitestow (1); C 4 awayte (2) awayten (1) awaytest (1)
B.10.338 Kynghod [and] knyȝthod, [for auȝt] I kan *awayte*,
B.13.360 And *awaited* þoruȝ [wittes wyes] to bigile;
B.16.138 Eche day after ooþer hir tyme þei *awaiteden*
B.16.257 'What *awaitestow*?' quod he, 'and what woldestow haue?'
C. 6.279 Or in[to] pruyslond my prenties my profit to *awayte*,
C.10.297 *Awayten* and wasten alle þat they cacche mowe;
C.17.63 And afturward *awayte* ho hath moest nede
C.18.273 'What [*a]waytest* thow,' quod fayth, 'and what wost thow haue?'

awaken v *awaken v.* A 1 awake; B 14 awake (4) awaked (5) awakede (2) awaken (1) awakeþ (1) awakned (1); C 16 awake (6) awaked (1) awakede (6) awaketh (1) awakned (1) awoke (1)
A. 7.304 He shal *awake* [þoruȝ] water wastours to chaste;
B. 2.100 And þanne wanhope to *awaken* h[y]m so wiþ no wil to amende
B. 5.135 Now *awakeþ* Wraþe wiþ two white eiȝen,
B. 5.392 'What! *awake*, renk!' quod Repentaunce, 'and rape þee to shryfte!'
B. 6.323 He shal *awake* [þoruȝ] water wastours to chaste;
B.10.334 Ac er þat kyng come Caym shal *awake*,
B.11.406 And *awaked* þerwiþ; wo was me þanne
B.13.1   And I *awaked* þerwiþ, witlees nerhande,
B.14.335 And wepte and wailede, and þerwiþ I *awakede*.
B.16.167 And I *awaked* þerwiþ and wiped myne eiȝen,
B.17.356 And wente awey as wynd and þerwiþ I *awakede*.
B.19.1   Thus I *awaked* and wroot what I hadde ydremed,
B.19.481 And I *awakned* þerwiþ and wroot as me mette.
B.20.1   Thanne as I wente by þe wey, whan I was thus *awaked*,
B.20.386 And siþþe he gradde after Grace til I gan *awake*.
C.Pr.217 And [ȝ]e route of ratones of reste men *awake*
C. 2.107 And *awake* with wanhope and no wille to amende,
C. 5.1   Thus y *awakede*, woet god, whan y wonede in Cornehull,
C. 6.103 Thenne *awakede* wrathe with two w[hy]te eyes
C. 6.139 And thenne *awake* y, wrathe, and wolde be avenged.
C. 7.8   'What! *awake*, renke!' quod repentaunce, 'and rape [þe] to shryfte.'
C. 8.343 He shal *awake* thorw water wastors to chaste;
C. 9.294 And thorw here wordes [y] *awoke* and waytede aboute
C.13.214 And *awakede* þerwith; wo was me þanne
C.15.1   And y *awakede* þerwith, witteles nerhande,
C.15.269 [And] lyuede withouten lyflode and [at] the laste *awakede*.
C.15.304 Ac when deth *awaketh* hem of here we[le] þat were er so ryche
C.19.336 And wente away as wynd and þerwith y *awakede*.
C.21.481 And y [*a]wakned* þerwith and wroet as [me] mette.
C.22.1   [Thenne] as y wente by the way, when y was thus *awaked*,
C.22.386 And sethe he gradde aftur grace tyl y gan *awake*.

awey adv *awei adv.* A 11 awey (10) aweye (1); B 28 awey (26) aweye (2); C 22 away (8) awaye (1) awey (11) aweye (2)
A. 1.164 Manye chapelleins arn chast ac charite is *aweye*;
A. 2.177 Liȝtliche liȝere lep *awey* þennes,
A. 4.44   Brekiþ vp my berne doris, beriþ *awey* my whete,
A. 4.92   Wrong wendiþ not so *awey* er I wyte more.

A. 4.93   Le[pe] he so liȝtly *awey*, lauȝen he wolde,
A. 5.89   Þat bar *awey* my bolle & my broken shete.
A. 5.90   [*Awey*] fro þe auter myn eiȝe I turne
A. 7.183   Al for coueitise of his corn to [cacche] *awey* hungir.
A.10.9   And wolde wynne hire *awey* with wyles ȝif he miȝte.
A.10.170   Clene *awey* þe cursid blood þat caym haþ ymakid.
A.11.218   And wel*awey* wers and I [wo]lde al telle.'
B. 1.190   Manye Chapeleyns arn chaste ac charite is *aweye*;
B. 2.218   Liȝtliche Lyere leep *awey* þanne,
B. 3.270   Bren it; bere it noȝt *awey* be it neuer so riche;
B. 4.57   Brekeþ vp my bern[e] dore[s], bereþ *awey* my whete,
B. 4.105   Wrong wendeþ noȝt so *awey* [er] I wite moore.
B. 4.106   Lope he so liȝtly [*awey*], lauȝen he wolde,
B. 5.109   That [bar] *awey* my bolle and my broke shete.
B. 5.110   *Awey* fro þe Auter turne I myne eiȝen
B. 9.9   And wolde wynne hire *awey* wiþ wiles [if] he myȝte.
B. 9.139   Clene *awey* þe corsed blood þat Caym haþ ymaked.
B. 9.210   And dryueþ *awey* dowel þoruȝ dedliche synnes.'
B.11.261   And after þat bitter bark, be þe shelle *aweye*,
B.12.80   Than þe womman þat þere was, and wenten *awey* for shame.
B.12.177   How contricion is comended for it cacheþ *awey* synne:
B.12.265   And wel *awey* of wynge swifter þan þe Pecock,
B.14.84   Which dryueþ *awey* dedly synne and dooþ it to be venial.
B.14.209   Of wit and of wisdom, þat fer *awey* is bettre
B.16.45   And feccheþ *awey* my floures som tyme afore boþe myne eighen.
B.16.126   And lefte baskettes ful of broke mete, bere *awey* whoso wolde.'
B.17.45   And wel *awey* worse ȝit for to loue a sherewe.
B.17.54   To a Iustes in Ierusalem he [I]aced *awey* faste.
B.17.91   How þat feiþ fleiȝ *awey* and Spes his felawe boþe
B.17.313   [Drede of desperacion [þanne] dryueþ *awey* grace
B.17.356   And wente *awey* as wynd and þerwiþ I awakede.
B.19.156   And biwicched hem as þei woke and *awey* stolen it.
B.20.56   In ech a contree þer he cam he kutte *awey* truþe
B.20.168   And wayued *awey* wanhope and wiþ lif he fighteþ.
B.20.174   And dryuen *awey* deeþ wiþ Dyas and drogges.
C. 2.228   Lyhtliche lyare lep *aweye* þenne,
C. 3.423   Bern hit; bere hit nat *awey* be hit neuer so riche;
C. 4.60   And breketh vp my bern[e] dores and [b]ereth *awey* my whete
C. 4.100   Wrong goth nat so *away* ar y wete more.
C. 4.101   Lope he so lihtliche [*awey*], lawen he wolde
C. 7.222   Loke þou bere n[ouht] þere *away* but yf hit be thyn owene.
C.10.136   And wol[d]e wynne here *awaye* with wyles [ȝif] he myhte.
C.10.227   Clene *awey* þe corsed bloed þat of Caym spronge.
C.12.147   And aftur þat bittere barke, be þe scale *aweye*,
C.12.238   That fals folk fecche *aweye* felonliche his godes;
C.14.117   How contricioun is comended for hit cacheth *awey* synne:
C.17.144   For when alle frendes faylen and fleen *away* in deynge
C.18.49   And fecccheth *away* þe fruyt som tyme byfore bothe myn yes.
C.18.154   And lefte baskes ful of Broke mete, bere *awey* hoso wolde.
C.19.52   To ioust in Ierusalem he Iaced *awey* faste.
C.19.138   Sholde n[o] wri[h]t worche were they *awey*.
C.19.293   Drede of disparacion thenne dryueth [*away*] grace
C.19.336   And wente *away* as wynd and þerwith y awakede.
C.21.156   And bywiched [hem] as they woke and *away* stelen hit.
C.22.56   In vch a Contrey ther he cam [he] kutte *away* treuthe
C.22.168   And wayued *away* wanhope and with lyf he fihteth.
C.22.174   And dryue *awey* deth with dyaes and drogges.

awoke > awaken

awreke v *awreken v.* A 1; B 3 awreke (2) awroke (1); C 8 awrek (1) awreke (5) awroke (2)

A. 7.158   '*Awreke* me on wasto[urs],' quaþ peris, 'þat þis world [shend]iþ.'
B. 6.173   '*Awreke* me of wastours', quod he, 'þat þis world shendeþ.'
B. 6.201   'I am wel *awroke* of wastours þoruȝ þy myȝte.
B.20.203   *Awreke* me if youre wille be for I wolde ben hennes.'
C. 2.209   Y wolde be *awreke* [o]n tho wreches and on here werkes alle.
C. 8.158   '*Awreke* me of this wastors þat maketh this world dere–
C. 8.170   *Awreke* [me] of this wastors for þe knyhte wil nat.'
C. 8.207   'Y am wel *awroke* of wastours thorw thy myhte
C. 8.299   For thow hast wel *awroke* me and also wel ytauhte me.'
C.10.287   *Awrek* þe þerwith on wyfyng, for godes werk y holde hit:
C.17.4   'Ho is wroeth and wolde be *awreke*, holy writ preueth,' quod he,
C.22.203   *Awreke* me ȝif ȝoure wille be for y wolde be hennes.'

awurchynge adv *awirching adv.* C 1

C. 3.51   'We han a wyndowe *awurchynge* wol stande vs [wel] heye;

ax n *axe n.* B 2; C 2

B. 3.306   *Ax* ouþer hachet or any wepene ellis,
B.12.106   And haþ noon hap wiþ his *ax* his enemy to hitte,
C. 3.459   *Ax* oþer hachet or eny kyne w[e]pne,
C.14.51   And hath non hap with his *ax* his enemye to hutte,

axe(d -en > asken

axesse n *accesse n.* A 1

A. 5.201   And aftir al þis surfet an *axesse* he hadde

axide > asken

ayein adv *ayen adv.* A 5 aȝen; B 9 ageyn (1) ayein (8); C 8 agayne (2) aȝeyn (4) aȝeyne (2)

A. 4.40   He borewide of me bayard & brouȝte him neuere *aȝen*,
A. 5.227   And ȝet wile I ȝelde *aȝen*, ȝif I so muchel haue,
A. 6.103   And geten it *aȝen* þoruȝ grace & þoruȝ no gift ellis.
A. 7.42   For þou shalt ȝelde it *aȝen* at one ȝeris ende
A. 8.27   And siþen selle it *aȝen* & saue þe wynnyng,
B. 4.53   He borwed of me bayard [and] brouȝte hym [neuere *ayein*],
B. 5.455   And yet wole I yelde *ayein*, if I so muche haue,
B. 5.617   And [gete it *ayein* þoruȝ] grace [ac þoruȝ no gifte ellis].
B. 6.43   For þow shalt yelde it *ayein* at one yeres [ende]
B. 7.25   And siþenes selle it *aȝeyn* and saue þe wynnyng,
B.17.123   And come *ayein* bi þis contree and conforten alle sike
B.19.246   He wissed hem wynne it *ayein* þoruȝ wightnesse of handes
B.20.172   And þei gyuen hym *ageyn* a glaȝene howue.
B.20.225   And shotten *ayein* wiþ shot, many a shef of oþes,
C. 3.332   And efte haue hit *aȝeyne* of hem þat don ylle.
C. 6.309   Hyhte ȝeuan-ȝelde-*aȝey*-yf-y-so-moche-haue-
C. 7.269   And geten hit *agayne* thorw grace Ac thorw no gifte elles.
C. 9.29   And sethe sullen hit *aȝeyn* and saue þe wynnyng[e],
C.16.315   That neuere payed peny *aȝeyn* in places þer he prewede.'
C.21.246   He wissede [h]e[m] wynne hit *aȝeyn* thorw whitnesse of handes
C.22.172   And they gyuen hym *agayne* a glasene houe.
C.22.225   And shoten *aȝeyn*[e with] shotte many a shef of othes

ayein prep *ayen prep.* A 20 ageyns (2) agens (1) aȝeyn (1) aȝen (6) aȝens (10); B 52 agayn (2) agein (1) ageyn (5) ageynes (1) ayein (26) ayeins (17); C 53 agayn (2) agayne (2) agaynes (3) aȝeyn (10) aȝeyne (4) aȝeynes (4) aȝeyns (3) aȝen (18) aȝenes (6) aȝens (1)

A. 3.81   And suffre hem to selle sumdel *aȝens* resoun.'
A. 3.141   And bringen forþ barnes *aȝens* forboden lawis.
A. 3.146   And leiþ *aȝen* þe lawe & lettiþ þe treuþe
A. 3.243   [*Aȝens* isra[e]l and aaron and moyses his broþer.]
A. 3.268   And whoso trespassiþ [to treuþe, or] takiþ [*aȝeyn* his wille],
A. 4.35   How wrong *aȝen* his wil hadde his wyf take,
A. 7.301   Ne stryue *aȝen* þe statut, so sternely he lokide.
A. 8.24   *Aȝens* clene consience here catel to selle.
A. 8.71   And [ek] giliþ þe gyuere *ageyns* his wille.
A. 9.41   Þat is charite þe champioun, chief helpe *aȝens* synne.
A. 9.92   Þat ȝif dowel & dobet dede *aȝens* dobest
A.10.93   For ȝif þou comist *aȝen* consience þou combrist þiseluen,
A.10.142   *Aȝens* þe hest of hym þat hem of nouȝt made,
A.10.160   *Ageyns* godis hest girlis hy geten
A.10.180   *Aȝen* þe lawe of oure lord le[iȝe]n togideris,
A.10.213   *Aȝens* dowel hy don euele, & þe deuil plesen,
A.11.65   And carp[en] *aȝens* clergie crabbide wordis:
A.11.150   He kenniþ vs þe contrarie, *aȝens* catonis wordis,
A.11.153   And do good a[g]en euil; god hymself hotiþ
A.12.60   As I ȝede thurgh ȝouþe, *aȝen* prime dayes,
B. 3.92   And suffre hem to selle somdel *ayeins* reson.'
B. 3.152   And bryngeþ forþ barnes *ayein* forbode lawes.
B. 3.156   And liþ *ayein* þe lawe and letteþ hym þe gate
B. 3.293   And whoso trespaseþ [to] truþe or takeþ *ayein* his wille,
B. 4.48   How wrong *ayeins* his wille hadde his wif taken,
B. 5.430   I am vnkynde *ayeins* [his] curteisie and kan nouȝt vnderstonden it,
B. 5.608   To suffren hym and segge nouȝt *ayein* þi sires wille.
B. 6.314   *Ayeins* Catons counseil comseþ he to Iangle:
B. 6.316   He greueþ hym *ageyn* god and gruccheþ ageyn Reson,
B. 6.316   He greueþ hym *ageyn* god and gruccheþ *ageyn* Reson,
B. 6.320   Ne stryuen *ayeins* [þe] statut, so sterneliche he loked.
B. 7.22   *Ayein* clene Conscience hir catel to selle.
B. 7.69   And [ek g]ileþ þe gyuere *ageynes* his wille.
B. 8.45   [Th]at is charite þe champion, chief help *ayein* synne.
B. 8.102   That if dowel [and] dobet dide *ayein* dobest
B. 9.130   Yet [seþ], *ayein* þe sonde of oure Saueour of heuene,
B. 9.157   And al for þei wroȝte wedlokes *ayein* [þe wille of god].
B. 9.199   *Ayeins* dowel þei doon yuel and þe deuel [plese],
B.10.40   *Ayein* þe lawe of oure lord, and lyen on hemselue,
B.10.107   And carpen *ayein* cler[gie] crabbede wordes:
B.10.201   He kenneþ vs þe contrarie *ayein* Catons wordes,
B.10.204   And do good a[g]ein yuel; god hymself hoteþ:
B.11.64   *Ayeins* oure firste forward, for I seide I nolde
B.12.287   Ac truþe þat trespased neuere ne trauersed *ayeins* his lawe,
B.13.132   He wol noȝt *ayein* holy writ speken, I dar vndertake.'
B.13.413   Lyueþ *ayein* þe bileue and no lawe holdeþ.
B.15.52   It were *ayeins* kynde', quod he, 'and alle kynnes reson
B.15.54   *Ayein* swiche Salomon spekeþ and despiseþ hir wittes
B.15.68   *Ayein* cristes counseil and alle clerkes techynge,
B.15.87   *Ayein* youre rule and Religion; I take record at Iesus

B.15.530   And crepe [in] amonges curatours, confessen *ageyn* þe lawe:
B.16.165   *Ayeins* deeþ and þe deuel: destruyed hir boþeres myȝtes,
B.17.287   Synnen *ayein* þe Seint Spirit, assenten to destruye
B.18.38   The Iewes and þe Iustice *ayeins* Iesu þei weere,
B.18.88   '*Ayein* my wille it was, lord, to wownde yow so soore.'
B.18.195   Adam afterward, *ayeins* his defence,
B.18.199   *Ayeins* Reson. [I], rightwisnesse, recorde þus wiþ truþe
B.18.253   To breke and to bete adoun [alle] þat ben *ayeins* [hym],
B.18.267   'Swich a light, *ayeins* oure leue laȝar [i]t fette.
B.18.334   Wiþ gile þow hem gete *ageyn* alle reson.
B.18.348   So leue [it] noȝt, lucifer, *ayein* þe lawe I fecche hem,
B.18.357   Graciousliche þi gile haue quyt: go gile *ayein* gile!
B.18.361   Now bigynneþ þi gile *ageyn* þee to turne
B.19.317   '*Ayeins* þi greynes', quod Grace, 'bigynneþ for to ripe,
B.19.359   To goon *agayn* Pride but Grace weere wiþ vs.'
B.19.446   *Ayein* þe olde lawe and newe lawe, as Luc [bereþ] witness[e]:
B.20.72   That kam *ayein* conscience þat kepere was and gyour
B.20.79   And þere abide and bikere *ayeins* Beliales children.'
B.20.113   And gaderede a greet hoost al *agayn* Conscience.
B.20.179   May noȝt a myte auaille to med[l]e *ayein* Elde.'
B.20.216   That wiþ Antecrist helden harde *ayein* Conscience.
B.20.220   Coomen *ayein* Conscience; wiþ Coueitise þei helden.
C. 3.120   'And soffre hem som tyme to selle *aȝeyne* þe lawe.'
C. 3.190   And bringeth forth bar[n]es *aȝenes* forbodene lawes:
C. 3.194   He lyth *aȝeyn* þe lawe and le[tte]th hym þe gate
C. 3.410   *Agaynes* godes comandement, god tok such a vengeaunce
C. 3.446   And hoso taketh *aȝeyn* treuthe or transuerseth aȝeyns resoun
C. 3.446   And hoso taketh aȝeyn treuthe or transuerseth *aȝeyns* resoun
C. 5.74   For the ryhte of this reume ryden *aȝeyn* oure enemyes
C. 6.76   *Aȝeyn* þe consayl of Crist, as clerkes fyndeth in bokes:
C. 7.43   Y am vnkynde *aȝen* his cortesie [and] can nat vnderstande hit
C. 7.73   Lyueth *aȝen* þe bileue and no lawe kepeth
C. 7.150   That euere they gulte *aȝeyn* þe, god, in gost or in dede.'
C. 7.250   That Adam and Eue *aȝenes* vs alle shette:
C. 8.336   *Aȝenes* Catones consayle comseth he to gruche:
C. 8.340   Ne stryue *aȝeynes* [þe] statuyt, [so sturnliche a lokede].
C. 9.26   *Aȝen* clene Consience for couetyse of wynnynge.
C. 9.65   And also gileth hym þat gyueth and taketh *agayne* his wille.
C. 9.104   Lyuen *aȝen* goddes lawe and þe lore of holi churche.
C. 9.213   *Aȝen* þe lawe he lyueth yf latyn be trewe:
C. 9.219   Lollen *aȝen* þe byleue and lawe of holy churche.
C.10.217   On a leye land *aȝeynes* his lordes wille,
C.10.219   Þat lycame haen *aȝen* þe lawe þat oure lord ordeynede.
C.10.298   *Aȝen* dowel they do yuele and þe deuel serue
C.11.34   The lewed *aȝen* þe lered þe holy lore to disp[u]te
C.14.209   Ac treuth þat trespassed neuere ne trauersede *aȝens* his lawe
C.16.214   Hit were *aȝeyns* kynde,' quod he, 'and alle kyne resoun
C.16.216   *Aȝenes* suche salamon speketh and despiseth here wittes
C.16.241   *Aȝen* þe consayl of crist, as holy clergie witnesseth:
C.16.285   That lyuen *aȝen* holy lore and þe loue of charite.'
C.17.137   For lechours louyen *aȝen* þe lawe and at þe laste ben dampned
C.17.235   *Aȝen* þe lore of oure lord as seynt luk witnesseth–
C.17.280   And crepe in amonges curatours and confessen *aȝeyn* þe lawe:
C.19.170   So hoso synegeth *aȝeyn* þe seynt spirit hit semeth þat he greueth
C.19.268   Synegen *aȝen* þe seynte spirit, assente to destruye
C.20.37   The iewes and þe iustic[e] *aȝeyns* iesus þey were,
C.20.90   '*Aȝeyn* my will hit was,' quod he, 'þat y ȝow wounde made.'
C.20.200   Adam afturward, *aȝenes* his defense,
C.20.204   *Aȝeynes* resoun; y, rihtwysnesse, recorde [þus] with treuthe
C.20.262   To breke and to bete adoun all þat ben *agaynes* hym
C.20.275   'Such a lyht *aȝenes* oure leue laȝar hit fette;
C.20.314   *Aȝeyne* his loue and his leue on his londe ȝedest,
C.20.377   With gyle thow hem gete *agaynes* all resoun.
C.20.381   *Aȝeyne* my loue and my leue: þe olde lawe techeth
C.20.393   So leue hit nat, lucifer, *aȝeyne* þe lawe y feche
C.20.399   And now bygynneth thy gyle *agayne* the to turne
C.21.317   '*Aȝeynes* thy graynes,' quod grace, 'bigynneth for to rype,
C.21.359   To goen *agayn* pruyde bute grace were with vs.'
C.21.446   *Aȝen* þe olde lawe and newe lawe, as Luk bereth witnesse:
C.22.72   That cam *aȝen* Consience þat kepar was and gyour
C.22.79   And þere abyde and bikere *aȝeyn* beliales childrene.'
C.22.113   And gaderet[h] a greet oest alle *agayn* Consience.
C.22.179   May nat a myte avayle to medlen *aȝen* Elde.'
C.22.216   That with auntecrist helden harde *aȝeyn* Consience.
C.22.220   Comen *aȝen* Consience; with couetyse they helden.

aȝeynward adv *ayen-ward adv.* C 1
C.19.77   'And þat more goth for his medicyne y make the good *aȝeynward*

B

b letter *b n.* A 1; B 1
A. 8.120 'Abstinence þe abbesse myn a *b* c me tauȝte,
B. 7.138 'Abstynence þe Abbesse myn a *b* c me tauȝte,

baar > beren; babelide > bablede

baberlipped adj *baberlipped adj.* A 1 babirlippid; B 1; C 1 baburlippid
A. 5.109 He was [betil]browid & *babirlippid* wiþ two bleride eiȝen,
B. 5.190 He was bitelbrowed and *baberlipped* wiþ two blered eiȝen;
C. 6.198 He was bitelbrowed and *baburlippid* with two blered eyes

baby n *babe n.* B 1; C 1
B.17.98 And þanne plastred wiþ penaunce and passion of þat *baby*,
C.19.94 And ȝut bote they l[e]ue lelly vpon þat litel *baby*,

babiloyne n *Babiloine n.* A 1; B 2 Babiloigne (1) Babiloyne (1); C 1
A. 6.15 At bedlem, at *babiloyne*, I haue ben in boþe;
B. 5.527 [At] Bethlem, [at] *Babiloyne*, I haue ben in boþe,
B.15.510 That bere bisshopes names of Bethleem and *Babiloigne*.
C. 7.172 In bedlem and in *babiloyne* y haue be in bothe,

bablede v *babelen v.* A 1 babelide; B 1
A. 5.8 And so I *babelide* on my bedis þei brouȝte me aslepe.
B. 5.8 And so I *bablede* on my bedes þei brouȝte me aslepe.

baburlippid > baberlipped; bacbite > bakbite

bacheler n *bacheler n.* A 1 bacheleris; B 3 bacheler (2) Bachelers (1); C 3 bacheler (2) bachelers (1)
A.Pr.90 I sauȝ bisshopis bolde & *bacheleris* of deuyn
B.Pr.87 Bisshopes and *Bachelers*, boþe maistres and doctours,
B.16.179 A ful bold *bacheler*; I knew hym by his blasen.'
B.18.85 But þis blynde *bacheler* baar hym þoruȝ þe herte.
C.Pr.85 Bischopes and *bachelers*, bothe maystres and doctours,
C. 9.249 A *bacheler* [o]r a be[au]pere beste hym bysemede
C.20.87 Bote this blynde *bacheler* that bar hym thorw the herte.

baches n *bach n.(1)* A 1; B 1; C 1
A. 6.2 But blustrid forþ as bestis ouer [*baches*] & hilles
B. 5.514 But blustreden forþ as beestes ouer [*baches*] and hilles
C. 7.159 But blostrede forth as bestes ouer *baches* and hulles

bacon n *bacoun n.* A 3 bacoun; B 5 bacon (4) bacoun (1); C 7 bacon (3) bacoun (4)
A. 7.268 And I seiȝe, be my soule, I haue no salt *bacoun*,
A. 7.293 May no penyale hem paye, ne no pece of *bacoun*,
A.10.196 But ȝif þei boþe be forsworn þat *bacoun* þei tyne.
B. 5.193 And as a bondeman[nes] *bacon* his berd was [yshaue].
B. 6.284 And yet I seye, by my soule! I haue no salt *bacon*
B. 6.309 May no peny ale hem paie, ne no pece of *bacoun*,
B. 9.175 But þei boþe be forswore þat *bacon* þei tyne.
B.13.92 That neiþer *bacon* ne braun, blancmanger ne mortrews
C. 6.201 And as a bondemannes *bacoun* his berd was yshaue,
C. 8.306 And ȝut y say[e], be my soule! y haue no sal[t] *bacoun*
C. 8.331 May no peny ale hem pay ne no pece of *bacoun*
C. 9.148 Where he may rathest haue a repaest or a ronde of *bacoun*,
C.10.277 Bote they bothe be forswore þat *bacon* þei tyne.
C.15.67 Brawen and bloed of gees, *bacon* and colhoppes.
C.15.99 That noþer *bacon* ne brawn, blaunmanger ne mortrewes

bad > bidden

badde adj *badde adj.* B 1; C 2
B.10.286 Bittre abouȝte þe giltes of two *badde* preestes,
C. 9.16 And bitynge in *badde* men but yf they wol amende,
C.17.74 And to a *badde* peny with a gode printe:

baddely adv *baddeliche adv.* B 1; C 2 baddeliche (1) baddelyche (1)
B.15.536 *Baddely* ybedded, no book but conscience,
C. 4.55 ȝut is he bold for to borw Ac *baddelyche* he payeth:
C.17.197 *Baddeliche* ybedded, no boek but Consience

baddenesse n *badnesse n.* B 1
B.12.48 The beaute of hir body; in *baddenesse* she despended.

bade baed > bidden; baer > bare,beren; bagbitares > bakbiteris

bagge n *bagge n.(1)* A 4 bagge (3) bagges (1); B 5 bagge (4) bagges (1); C 10 bagge (7) bagges (3)
A.Pr.41 Til here bely & here *bagge* were bratful ycrammid;
A. 6.7 A *bagge* & a bolle he bar be his side;
A. 9.79 Þe *bagges* & þe [bi]gerdlis, he haþ broken hem alle
A.12.71 A *bagge* ful of a beggere.' I bouȝþe hit at onys.
B.Pr.41 [Til] hire bel[y] and hire *bagg[e* were bret]ful ycrammed,
B. 5.519 A bolle and a *bagge* he bar by his syde.
B. 8.88 The *bagges* and þe bigirdles, he haþ [b]roke hem alle
B.14.249 A beggeris *bagge* þan an yren bounde cofre.
B.20.142 And boold and bidynge while his *bagge* lasteþ.'
C.Pr.42 Til here [bely] and here [*bagge*] w[ere] bretful ycrammed,
C. 5.52 Withoute *bagge* or botel but my wombe one.
C. 7.164 A bolle and a *bagge* a bar by his syde;
C. 9.98 Ac beggares with *bagges* þe whiche brewhous[es] ben here churches,
C. 9.120 Withoute *bagge* and bred as þe book telleth:
C. 9.139 For they bereth none *bagges* ne boteles vnder clokes
C. 9.154 With a *bagge* at his bak A begyneld wyse,
C.10.85 The *bagges* and þe bigerdeles, he hath [b]roken hem alle
C.16.89 A beggares *bagge* then an yrebounden coffre.
C.22.142 And bolde and [b]ydynge while his *bagge* lasteth.'

bayard n *baiard n.(1)* A 1; B 3 bayard (2) Bayardes (1); C 4
A. 4.40 He borewide of me *bayard* & brouȝte him neuere aȝen,
B. 4.53 He borwed of me *bayard* [and] brouȝte hym [neuere ayein],
B. 4.124 Til Bisshopes *Bayardes* ben beggeris Chaumbres,
B. 6.193 For þat was bake for *bayard* was boote for many hungry;
C. 4.56 He borwed of me *bayard* a[nd] brouhte hym hom neuere
C. 8.178 And þat was bake for *bayard* may be here bote.'
C. 8.192 For þat was bake for *bayard* was bote for many hungry,
C.19.72 Enbaumed hym and boend his heued and on *bayard* hym sette

baillifs n *baillif n.* A 1; B 2 baillies (1) baillifs (1); C 2 bailifs (1) Baylifs (1)
A. 3.2 Wiþ bedelis & *baillifs* ybrouȝt to þe king.
B. 2.60 Bedelles and *baillifs* and Brocours of chaffare,
B. 3.2 Wiþ Bedeles and *baillies* brouȝt [to] þe kyng.
C. 2.62 Bydels and *bailifs* and brokeres of chaffar[e],
C. 3.2 [With] Bedeles and *Baylifs* ybrouhte byfor þe kyng.

bak n *bak n.* A 7 bak (6) bakkis (1); B 8 bak (7) bakkes (1); C 4 bak (3) bake (1)
A. 2.136 Sire symonye hymself shal sitte on here *bakkis*;
A. 3.183 And bar here bras on þi *bak* to caleis to selle,
A. 3.186 And bateride hym on þe *bak*, boldite his herte.
A. 5.74 And blamide hym behynde his *bak* to bringe hym in fame;
A. 8.15 And bere hem boþe on here *bak* as here baner shewiþ,
A. 8.76 Or his *bak* or his bon þei breken in his ȝouþe,
A.12.70 At my *bak* of broke bred þi bely for to fylle,
B. 2.172 Sire Symonye hymself shal sitte vpon hir *bakkes*.
B. 3.196 And bere hire bras at þi *bak* to Caleis to selle,
B. 3.199 I batred hem on þe *bak* and boldede hire hertes.
B. 5.94 [And blamed hym bihynde his *bak* to brynge hym in fame;
B. 7.94 Or [his] *bak* or [his] boon [þei] brekeþ in his youþe,
B.13.316 What on *bak*, and what on body half, and by þe two sides
B.13.324 And blame men bihynde hir *bak* and bidden hem meschaunce.
B.18.11 Barefoot on an Asse *bak* bootles cam prikye
C. 6.69 And blame men byhynde here *bak* and bidde hem meschaunce;
C. 9.154 With a bagge at his *bak* A begyneld wyse,
C. 9.170 Or þe *bak* or som bon þey breke of he[re] children
C.20.9 Barfoet on an asse *bake* boetles cam priky[e]

bakbite v *bakbiten v.* B 1; C 1 bacbite
B. 2.81 To *bakbite* and to bosten and bere fals witnesse,
C. 2.88 To *bacbite* and to boste and bere fals witnesse,

bakbiteris n *bakbitere n.* B 1; C 1 bagbitares
B.16.43 *Bakbiteris* [brewe]cheste, brawleris and chideris,
C.18.46 Thorw *bagbitares* and braule[r]s and thorw bolde chidares

bakbityng ger *bakbiting ger.* B 3 bakbityng (1) bakbitynge (2); C 2 bacbitynge (1) bakbytynge (1)
B. 5.88 Wiþ *bakbitynge* and bismere and berynge of fals witnesse;

B. 5.131   And gart *bakbityng* be a brocour to blame mennes ware.
B.15.238 For braulynge and *bakbitynge* and berynge of fals witnesse.
C. 6.95   ʒut am y brokour of *bakbytynge* to blame menne w[a]re
C.16.363 For braulyng and *bacbitynge* and berynge of fals witnesse.

bake ptp *baken v. &> bak* A 2 bake (1) ybake (1); B 7 bake (2) baken
    (1) ybake (3) ybaken (1); C 5 bake (4) ybake (1)
A. 7.267   A lof of benis & bren *ybake* for my children;
A. 7.277   Benes & [b]ake applis hy brouȝte in here lappe[s],
B. 6.182   Or ellis benes [and] bren *ybaken* togideres.'
B. 6.193   For þat was *bake* for bayard was boote for many hungry;
B. 6.283   [A lof] of benes and bran *ybake* for my fauntes.
B. 6.293   Benes and *baken* apples þei broȝte in hir lappes,
B.13.266 Wiþ [bake] breed fro Stratford; þo gonnen beggeris wepe
B.15.433 It is vnsauory, forsoþe, ysoden or *ybake*;
B.15.463 He fedde hem wiþ no venyson ne fesauntȝ *ybake*
C. 8.178   And þat was *bake* for bayard may be here bote.'
C. 8.192   For þat was *bake* for bayard was bote for many hungry,
C. 8.316   Benes and *bake* aples they brouhten in here lappe
C. 8.332   But hit be [fresh] flesch or fisch yfried or *ybake*
C. 9.93   And colde flesche and fische as venisoun were *bake*;

bakers n *bakere n.* A 1 bakeris; B 1; C 3 bakeres
A. 3.68   Breweris & *bakeris*, bocheris & cokes,
B. 3.79   Brew[e]rs and *Bak[e]rs*, Bochiers and Cokes;
C.Pr.225 Bothe *Bakeres* and Breweres, Bochers and other,
C. 3.80   As *Bakeres* a[nd] Breweres, Bocheres and cokes;
C. 4.120 And til byschopes ben *bakeres*, Breweres and taylours

bakken v *bakken v.* A 1
A.11.188 To breke beggeris bred & *bakken* hem with cloþis,

bakkes n *cf. bak n.3. &> bak* B 1; C 1
B.10.366 And oure *bakkes* þat moþeeten be and seen beggeris go naked,
C.13.72   Fynde beggares bred, *bakkes* for þe colde,

bakkis > bak

baksteres n *baxter n.* A 1 baxteris; B 1
A.Pr.98   *Baxteris* & bocheris & breusteris manye,
B.Pr.219 *Baksteres* and Brewesteres and Bochiers manye,

balayshed > baleied; bald- > bold(-

bale n *bale n.(1)* A 4; B 6; C 7
A. 4.76   And be borugh for his *bale* & b[ig]gen hym bote,
A. 4.79   'Betere is þat boote *bale* adoun bringe,
A. 4.80   Þanne *bale* be bet & bote neuere þe betere.'
A.10.147 And brouȝt forþ a barn þat muche *bale* wrouȝte;
B. 4.89   And be borȝ for his *bale* and buggen hym boote,
B. 4.92   'Bettre is þat boote *bale* adoun brynge,
B. 4.93   Than *bale* be ybet and boote neuer þe bettre.'
B.11.122 And drynke boote for *bale*, brouke it whoso myȝte.
B.11.333 Blisse and *bale* boþe I seiȝ at ones,
B.18.202 For it is botelees *bale*, þe byte þat þei eten.'
C. 4.85   And be borw for his *bale* and buggen hym bote
C. 4.88   'Betere is þat bote *bale* adoun brynge
C. 4.89   Then *bale* be ybete and bote neuer þe betere.'
C.12.57   And drynke bote for *bale*, brouke hit hoso myhte.\
C.13.22   And brouhte hem all aboue þat in *bale* rotede!
C.13.141 Blisse and *bale* bothe y sey at ones
C.20.207 For hit is boteles *bale*, the bite that they eten.'

bale adj *bale adj.* B 1; C 1
B.18.35   And forbete and adoun brynge *bale* deeþ for euere;
C.20.34   And forbete [and adown] b[r]ynge *bale* deth for euere:

baleys n *baleis n.(2)* A 1 baleis; B 2 baleys (1) baleises (1); C 1 baleyse
A.11.133 And bet hem wiþ a *baleis* but ȝif þei wolde lerne.
B.10.181 And bette hem wiþ a *baleys* but if þei wolde lerne.
B.12.12   And wiþ þise bittre *baleises* god beteþ his deere children:
C.11.121 And be[t] hem with a *baleyse* bute yf þei wolde lerne.

baleised ptp *baleisen v.* B 1; C 1 balayshed
B. 5.175   And *baleised* on þe bare ers and no brech bitwene.
C. 6.157   And *balayshed* on þe bare ers and no brech bytwene.

balkes n *balke n.* A 1 balkis; B 1; C 1
A. 7.99   Dikeris & delueres dy[gg]eþ vp þe *balkis*.
B. 6.107   Dikeres and Delueres digged vp þe *balkes*;
C. 8.114   Dikares and deluares digged vp þe *balkes*

balled adj *balled adj.* A 1 ballid; B 2; C 2
A.11.41   And bringe forþ a *ballid* resoun, t[a]k[e] bernard to witnesse,
B.10.55   And bryngen forþ a *balled* reson, taken Bernard to witnesse,
B.20.184 And made me *balled* bifore and bare on þe croune;
C.11.36   And brynge forth [a] *balle[d]* reso[n], taken bernard to witnesse
C.22.184 And made me *balled* bifore and baer on þe crowne;

ballokknyf n *ballok n.* B 1
B.15.124 A baselard or a *ballokknyf* wiþ botons ouergilte,

bande v *OED band v.1* C 1
C. 6.218   To brochen hem with a batnelde and *bande* hem togyderes,

bane n *bane n.* A 1; C 1
A. 6.90   Þo Adam & Eue eten here *bane*,
C. 8.349   Shal brynge *bane* and batayle on bothe half þe mone;

baner n *banere n.* A 1; B 3; C 3
A. 8.15   And bere hem boþe on here bak as here *baner* shewiþ,
B.20.69   Antecrist hadde þus soone hundredes at his *baner*,
B.20.91   After Confort a knyght to come and bere his *baner*:
B.20.96   And bar þe *baner* bifore deeþ; bi riȝt he it cleymede.
C.22.69   Auntecrist hadde thus sone hondredes at his *baner*
C.22.91   Aftur conforte, a knyhte, [to] come and beer his *baner*:
C.22.96   And baer þe *baner* bifore deth; bi riht he hit claymede.

banyer n *banerer n.* B 1
B.15.436 And be gide and go bifore as a good *Banyer*,

banisshit ptp *banishen v.* A 1
A. 3.274   Vnkyndenesse is comaundour, & kyndenesse is *banisshit*.

bank n *banke n.(1)* A 1; B 2
A.Pr.8   Vndir a brood *bank* be a bourn[e] side,
B.Pr.8   Vnder a brood *bank* by a bourn[e] syde,
B.17.105 For [an] Outlaw[e is] in þe wode and vnder *bank* lotieþ,

banne v *bannen v.* A 3 banne (2) bannide (1); B 6 banne (3) banned (1)
    banneþ (2); C 5 banne (4) banneth (1)
A. 1.60   May *banne* þat he born was to body or to soule.
A.10.171 "Bestis þat now ben shuln *banne* þe tyme
A.11.7   And blamide hym [and *bannide* hym] & bad hym be stille–
B. 1.62   May *banne* þat he born was to bodi or to soule.
B. 7.89   The book *banneþ* beggerie and blameþ hem in þis manere:
B. 9.140   Beestes þat now ben shul *banne* þe tyme
B.10.7   And blamed hym and *banned* hym and bad hym be stille–
B.11.31   Bittrely shaltow *banne* þanne, boþe dayes and nyȝtes,
B.15.252 Neiþer he blameþ ne *banneþ*, bosteþ ne preiseþ,
C. 1.58   May *banne* þat he born was [to] body [or to] soule.
C. 3.145   And bitterliche *banne* the and alle þat bereth thy name
C. 9.162   The boek *banneth* beggarie and blameth hit in this manere:
C.10.228 Bestes þat now beth shal *banne* þe tyme
C.11.190 Bitterliche shaltow *banne* thenne, bothe dayes and nyhtes,

bannebury n prop *OED Banbury* C 1
C. 2.114   Butte þe Bedel of *Bannebury* sokene,

bapteme n *bapteme n.* B 6 bapteme (3) baptisme (3); C 5 bapteme (3) baptisme (2)
B.11.82   Ac [a] barn wiþouten *bapteme* may noȝt be saued:
B.11.124 By þe blood þat he bouȝte vs wiþ, and þoruȝ *bapteme* after:
B.14.184 Thou tauȝtest hem in þe Trinite to taken *bapteme*
B.18.376 For we beþ breþeren of blood, [ac] noȝt in *baptisme* alle.
B.18.377 Ac alle þat beþ myne hole breþeren, in blood and in *baptisme*,
B.19.323 And of his *baptisme* and blood þat he bledde on roode
C.12.59   By þ[e] bloed [that] he bouhte vs with and *bapteme*, as he tauhte;
C.14.201 Withoute *bapteme*, as by here bokes, beth nat ysaued.'
C.20.418 For we beth brethrene of bloed Ac nat in *baptisme* alle.
C.20.419 Ac alle þat beth myn hole breth[r]ene, in bloed and in *baptisme*,
C.21.323 And of his *bapteme* and bloed þat he bledde on rode

baptised > baptiȝe

baptist n *baptist n.(1)* A 1; B 4 Baptist (3) baptiste (1); C 5 baptist (2) baptiste (3)
A.11.282 Sonnere hadde he saluacioun þanne seint Ion þe *baptist*,
B.10.423 He was sonner ysaued þan seint Iohan þe *Baptist*
B.16.82   Sampson and Samuel and Seint Iohan þe *Baptist*,
B.16.250 Of a [buyrn] þat baptised hym–Iohan *Baptist* was his name–
B.19.38   And þo þat bicome cristene bi counseil of þe *baptis[t]e*
C.10.180 Of þ[e] blessed *baptist* bifore alle his gestes.
C.11.255 He was sunnere ysaued then seynt Iohn þe *baptiste*
C.18.118 Sampson and samuel and seynt Iohann þe *Baptiste*,
C.18.267 Forthy y seke hym,' he saide, 'for seynt Iohann þe *Baptiste*
C.21.38   And tho þat bycome cristene bi consail of þe *baptist*

baptiȝe v *baptisen v.* B 7 baptised (3) baptiȝe (2) baptiȝed (2); C 2 baptised (1) ybaptised (1)
B.10.351 That is *baptiȝed* beþ saaf, be he riche or pouere.'
B.11.77   Raþer þan to *baptiȝe* barnes þat ben Catecumelynges.
B.11.79   Ac muche moore meritorie, me þynkeþ, is to *baptiȝe*,
B.11.80   For a *baptiȝed* man may, as maistres telleþ,
B.15.517 And *baptised* and bishined wiþ þe blode of his herte
B.16.250 Of a [buyrn] þat *baptised* hym–Iohan Baptist was his name–
B.17.97   And [he be] baþed in þat blood, *baptised* as it were,

C.17.268 And *baptised* and bis[hin]ede with þe bloed of his herte
C.19.88 And with þe bloed of þat barn enbaumed and *ybaptised*.

baptiȝynge ger *baptising ger.* B 1
B.11.78 *Baptiȝynge* and buryinge boþe beþ ful nedefulle;

bar > bare,beren

barayne adj *baraine adj.* B 1; C 1 bareyne
B.18.106 But [as] *barayne* be and [by] vsurie [libben],
C.20.109 [But] as *bareyne* be and by vsure libbe,

bare adj *bar adj.* B 4; C 5 baer (2) bar (1) bare (2)
B. 5.175 And baleised on þe *bare* ers and no brech bitwene.
B.16.35 And forbiteþ þe blosmes riȝt to þe *bare* leues.
B.20.70 And pride [bar it *bare*] boldely aboute
B.20.184 And made me balled bifore and *bare* on þe croune;
C. 6.150 Til bothe here hedes were *bar* and blody here chekes.
C. 6.157 And balayshed on þe *bare* ers and no brech bytwene.
C.18.39 And al forb[i]t Caritas rihte to þe *bare* stalke.
C.22.70 And pryde [baer] hit *baer* baldly aboute
C.22.184 And made me balled bifore and *baer* on þe crowne;

barefoot adj *barfot adj.& adv.* B 1; C 2 barfoet (1) barfoot (1)
B.18.11 *Barefoot* on an Asse bak bootles cam prikye
C. 9.121 *Barfoot* and bredles, beggeth they of no man
C.20.9 *Barfoet* on an asse bake boetles cam priky[e]

bareyne > barayne; baren > beren; barfoet -foot > barefoot

bargayn n *bargaine n.* A 1 bargoynes; B 2 bargaynes; C 3 bargayn (1) bargaynes (2)
A. 5.186 *Bargoynes* & beuerechis begonne for to arise,
B. 2.88 In *bargaynes* and brocages wiþ þe Burgh of þefte,
B. 5.337 [*Bargaynes* and beuerages bigonne to arise],
C. 2.95 In *bargaynes* and Brocages with the borw of thefte,
C. 5.96 A boute suche a *bargayn* he was þe bet euere
C. 6.395 *Bargaynes* and Beuereges bygan to a[rys]e

bark n *bark n.* B 2 bark (1) barke (1); C 2 barke
B.11.260 As on a walnote wiþoute is a bitter *barke*,
B.11.261 And after þat bitter *bark*, be þe shelle aweye;
C.12.146 As on a walnote withoute is a bittere *barke*
C.12.147 And aftur þat bittere *barke*, be þe scale aweye,

barly n *barli n.* A 3; B 2; C 2
A. 5.133 I bouȝte hire *barly*; heo breuȝ it to selle.
A. 7.129 Or ȝe shuln ete *barly* bred & of þe bro[k] drynke;
A. 7.169 To abate þe *barly* bred & þe benis ygrounde,
A. 5.217 I bouȝte hire *barly*; she brew it to selle.
B. 6.135 Or ye shul eten *barly* breed and of þe broke drynke;
C. 6.225 Y bouhte here *barly*; [a] brew hit to sulle.
C. 8.142 Or ȝe shal ete *barly* breed and of þe broke drynke.

barm n *barm n.* B 1 barm
B.17.73 Enbawmed hym and bond his heed and in his [barm] hym leide,

barn n *barn n.* A 7 barn (3) barne (1) barnes (3); B 20 barn (15) barnes (5); C 15 barn (9) barne (1) barnes (4) bernes (1)
A. 2.3 Þat bar þe blisside *barn* þat bouȝte vs on þe rode,
A. 3.141 And bringen forþ *barnes* aȝens forboden lawis.
A. 3.250 *Barnes* and bestis brenne hem to deþe."
A. 8.75 And bringen forþ *barnes* þat bois ben holden.
A.10.147 And brouȝt forþ a *barn* þat muche bale wrouȝte;
A.10.189 Þat neuere shal bere [*barne*] but it be in armes.
A.12.117 Þat *barn* bryng vs to blys þat bled vpon þe rode amen.
B. 2.3 That bar þ[e] blis[sed] *barn* þat bouȝte vs on þe Rode,
B. 3.152 And bryngeþ forþ *barnes* ayein forbode lawes.
B. 7.93 And bryngen forþ *barnes* þat bastardes men calleþ.
B. 9.80 For moore bilongeþ to þe litel *barn* er he þe lawe knowe
B. 9.146 Here abouȝte þe *barn* þe belsires giltes,
B. 9.154 That bryngeþ forþ any *barn* but if he be þe same
B. 9.168 That neuere shal *barn* bere but it be in armes.
B.10.285 The bible bereþ witnesse þat al[le] þe [*barnes*] of Israel
B.10.327 [Bynymen] that hir *barnes* claymen, and blame yow foule:
B.11.77 Raþer þan to baptiȝe *barnes* þat ben Catecumelynges.
B.11.82 Ac [a] *barn* wiþouten bapteme may noȝt be saued:
B.12.146 Ne in none [beggers] cote [n]as þat *barn* born,
B.12.187 Wel may þe *barn* blesse þat hym to book sette,
B.15.456 [And] so it fareþ by a *barn* þat born is of wombe,
B.17.96 Wiþouten þe blood of a *barn* born of a mayde.
B.17.100 Til he haue eten al þe *barn* and his blood ydronke.
B.18.133 Siþ þis *barn* was ybore ben xxxti wynter passed
B.18.233 That þo þis *barn* was ybore, as blased a sterre
B.18.235 That swich a *barn* was ybore in Bethleem þe Citee
C. 2.3 That bar þ[e] blessid *bar[n]* þat bouhte [vs] on þe rode,
C. 3.190 And bringeth forth *bar[n]es* aȝenes forbodene lawes:

C. 5.70 Ac sythe bondemen *barnes* haen be mad bisshopes
C. 5.172 And Barones and here *barnes* blame ȝow and repreue:
C. 8.305 And bred for my *barnes* of benes and of peses.
C.10.234 Here aboute þe *barn* the belsires gultes
C.14.126 Wel may þe *barne* blesse þat hym to boek sette,
C.17.58 With þat ȝoure *bernes* and ȝoure bloed by goed lawe may clayme!
C.19.86 Withoute þe bloed of a *barn* he beth nat ysaued
C.19.87 The whiche *barn* mote nedes be born of a mayde,
C.19.88 And with þe bloed of þat *barn* enbaumed and ybaptised.
C.19.90 Til he haue eten al þ[e] *barn* and his bloed dronken
C.20.136 Sethe this *barn* was ybore ben thritty wynter ypassed,
C.20.242 [That tho] this *barn* was ybore þ[er] blased a sterre
C.20.244 That such a *barn* was ybore in Bethleem þe Citee

barnhoed n *barnhede n* C 1
C.18.135 Byg and abydyng, and bold in his *barnhoed*

baroun n *baroun n.* A 4 barouns; B 6 Barones (1) Barons (3) baroun (2); C 6 barones (5) Baroun (1)
A.Pr.96 *Barouns* [and] burgeis & bondage also
A. 3.144 *Barouns* & burgeis she bringeþ in sorewe;
A. 3.192 Þe leste brol of his blood a *barouns* pere.
B.Pr.217 *Barons* and Burgeises and bond[age] als
B. 3.163 *Barons* and Burgeises she bryngeþ in sorwe,
B. 3.205 The leeste brol of his blood a *Barones* piere.
B.10.326 And *Barons* wiþ Erles beten hem þoruȝ Beatus virres techyng;
B.13.165 There nys neiþer emperour ne emperesse, erl ne *baroun*,
B.20.129 And cam to þe kynges counseille as a kene *baroun*
C.Pr.223 As *Barones* and Burgeys and bondemen of thorpus.
C. 3.262 The leeste brolle of his blod a *Barones* pere.
C. 5.71 And bar[o]nes *bastardus* haen be Erchedekenes
C. 5.172 And *Barones* and here barnes blame ȝow and repreue:
C. 6.123 Thus Beggares and *Barones* at debat aren ofte
C.22.129 And cam to þe kynges consail as a kene *Baroun*

barre n *barre n.* A 1; B 5 barre (4) barres (1); C 7 barre (4) barres (3)
A.Pr.85 Seriauntis it semide þat seruide at þe *barre*;
B.Pr.212 Sergeantȝ it [s]emed þat serueden at þe *barre*,
B. 3.296 Ne no pelure in his [panelon] for pledynge at þe *barre*;
B. 4.169 'For ofte haue I', quod he, 'holpen yow at þe *barre*,
B. 7.46 Than pro dei pietate [pleden at þe *barre*].
B.18.321 And wiþ þat breeþ helle brak with Belialles *barres*;
C.Pr.162 Seriantȝ it semede þat serue[d] at þe *barre*,
C. 3.449 Ne no pelure in his panelon for pledyng at þe *barre*.
C. 4.132 Whiles mede hath the maistrie þer motyng is at [þe] *Barr[e]*.
C. 7.239 The *barres* aren of buxumnesse as bretherne of o wombe;
C. 9.45 But they pre manibus were payed for pledynge at þe *barre*;
C.20.281 Ac [r]ise vp, Ragamoffyn, and [r]eche me alle þe *barres*
C.20.364 And with þat breth helle braek with belialles *barres*;

barre v *barren v.* C 1
C.20.284 Ar we thorw brihtnesse be b[l]ente go *barre* þe ȝates;

barst > brast

baselard n *baselard n.(1)* A 1; B 3 baselard (2) baselardes (1); C 1 baslard
A.11.214 A bidowe or a *baselard* he beriþ be his side;
B. 3.305 Alle þat beren *baselard*, brood swerd or launce,
B.15.121 But if many preest [forbeere] hir *baselardes* and hir broches
B.15.124 A *baselard* or a ballokknyf wiþ botons ouergilte,
C. 3.458 For alle þat bereth *baslard*, br[ode] swerd oþer launce,

baskettes n *basket n.* B 1; C 1 basketes
B.16.126 And lefte *baskettes* ful of broke mete, bere awey whoso wolde.'
C.18.154 And lefte *basketes* ful of Broke mete, bere awey hoso wolde.

baslard > baselard

bastard n *bastard n.* A 1; B 5 bastard (4) bastardes (1); C 7 bastard (4) bastardus (3)
A. 2.95 [And] as a *bastard* yborn of belsab[ubb]is kynde;
B. 2.24 But sooþnesse wolde noȝt so for she is a *Bastard*.
B. 2.131 And [as] a *Bastard* ybore of Belsabubbes kynne.
B. 5.158 And maad hem Ioutes of Ianglyng þat dame Iohane was a *bastard*,
B. 7.93 And bryngen forþ barnes þat *bastardes* men calleþ.
B.16.69 Thanne Continence is neer þe crop as kaylewey *bastard*.
C. 2.24 Ac sothnesse wolde nat so for she is a *bastard*.
C. 2.147 And as a *bastard* ybore byȝete was he neuere.
C. 5.68 Bondemen and *bastardus* and beggares children,
C. 5.71 And bar[o]nes *bastardus* haen be Erchedekenes
C. 6.133 And made hem ioutes of iangelynge: "dame Ione was a *bastard*
C. 9.169 Bringeth forth *bastardus*, beggares of kynde,
C.10.263 A *bastard*, a bond oen, a begeneldes douhter

bat > batte

bataille n *bataille n.* B 5 bataille (4) batailles (1); C 9 bataile (3) batayle (3) bataies (1) batayles (2)

B. 3.323   *Batailles* shul none be, ne no man bere wepene,
B.12.105 And as a blynd man in *bataille* bereþ wepne to fiȝte
B.16.164 On cros vpon Caluarie crist took þe *bataille*
B.18.64   'For a bitter *bataille*', þe dede body seide;
B.20.262 Alle oþere in *bataille* ben yholde Brybours,
C.Pr.108 Thei were discomfited in *batayle* and losten Archa domini
C.Pr.112 Were disconfit in *batayle* and Archa domini lorn
C. 3.476 *Bataile*s sholle neuere eft be ne man bere eg toel
C. 8.49   Bute they be of bounte, of *batayles* or of treuthe.
C. 8.349 Shal brynge bane and *batayle* on bothe half þe mone;
C.14.50 And as a blynde man in *bataile* bereth wepene to fyhte
C.17.288 And amonges here enemyes in mortel *batayles*
C.20.66 'For a dede body saide,'
C.22.262 Alle oþere in *bataile* been yholde brybours,

batauntliche adv *batauntliche adv.* B 1; C 1

B.14.214 *Batauntliche* as beggeris doon, and boldeliche he craueþ
C.16.55 *Batauntliche* as beggares doon, and baldeliche he craueth

bateride > batred

baþed ptp *bathen v.* B 1

B.17.97 And [he be] *baþed* in þat blood, baptised as it were,

batnelde n *batnedle n.* C 1

C. 6.218 To brochen hem with a *batnelde* and bande hem togyderes,

batred v *bateren v.* A 1 bateride; B 1

A. 3.186 And *bateride* hym on þe bak, boldite his herte,
B. 3.199 I *batred* hem on þe bak and boldede hire hertes

batte n *bat n* A 1; C 1 bat

A. 7.165 And wiþ a bene *batte* he[ȝe]de [hem] betwene,
C.18.91 And bad hit be, of a *bat* of erthe, a man and a maide,

baude n *baude n.* A 2; B 3; C 3 baud (1) baude (1) baudes (1)

A. 3.45   For to be hire bedeman & hire *baude* aftir.
A. 3.118 I[s] not a betere *baude*, be hym þat me made,
B. 3.46   For to ben hire Bedeman and hire [*baude* after].
B. 3.129 Is noȝt a bettre *baude*, by hym þat me made,
B. 6.71   And danyel þe dees pleyere and Denote þe *baude*
C. 3.166 Is nat a bettere *baud*, by hym þat me made,
C. 6.189 Sotiled songes and sente out olde *baudes*
C. 8.72   And danyel þe dees playere and denote þe *baude*

baudekyn n *baudekin n.(2)* A 1; B 1

A. 3.40   And ek be þi *baudekyn*, & bere wel þin arnede
B. 3.41   And [ek] be þi [*baudekyn*] and bere wel þ[yn erende]

baw exclam *bau interj.* B 2; C 2 bawe

B.11.140 'Ye? *baw* for bokes!' quod oon was broken out of helle.
B.19.396 'Ye? *baw*!' quod a Brewere, 'I wol noȝt be ruled,
C.12.75 'ȝe? *bawe* for bokes!' quod oen was broken out of helle.
C.21.396 'ȝe? *bawe*!' quod a breware, 'y wol nat be yruled,

baxteris > baksteres; be > ben,by

beaupeere n *beau adj.* B 1; C 2 beaupere

B.18.231 Book highte þat *beaupeere*, a bold man of speche.
C. 9.249 A bacheler [o]r a *be[au]pere* beste hym bysemede
C.20.240 Boek hihte þat *beaupere*, a bolde man of speche.

beaute n *beaute n.* B 1; C 2

B.12.48 The *beaute* of hir body; in baddenesse she despended.
C.13.11 Ne for brihtnesse of here *beaute* here wolde to be byknowe.
C.17.163 *Beaute* sanȝ bounte blessed was [hit] neuere

becauȝte v *bicacchen v.* C 1

C.14.62 And his sones for his synnes sorwe hem [*becauȝte*]

beches n *beche n.* A 1 bechis; B 1; C 1

A. 5.18 *Bechis* & broode okis wern blowen to [þe] grounde,
B. 5.18 *Beches* and brode okes were blowen to þe grounde
C. 5.120 *Beches* and brode okes were blowe to þe grounde

becom(- > bicome

bed n *bed n.(1) &> bedchambre,bidden* A 6 bed (1) bedde (5); B 6 bed (1) bedde (5); C 7 bed (3) bedde (4)

A.Pr.43 In glotonye, god wot, go þei to *bedde*,
A. 2.52 At *bedde* & at boord buxum and hende,
A. 5.200 Bere hym to his *bed* & brouȝte hym þerinne.
A. 7.91 I bar hom þat I borewide er I to *bedde* ȝede.
A.10.190 In gelosie, ioyeles, and ianglyng [a] *bedde*,
A.11.52 [Mendynauntȝ] meteles miȝte go to *bedde*.
B.Pr.43 In glotonye, god woot, go þei to *bedde*,
B. 5.358 Baren hym to his *bed* and brouȝte hym þerInne,

B. 6.99 I bar hom þat I borwed er I to *bedde* yede.
B. 9.169 [In Ielousie, ioyelees, and ianglynge on *bedde*,
B.10.66 Mendinauntȝ metelees myȝte go to *bedde*.
B.17.325 And if his hous be vnhiled and reyne on his *bedde*
C.Pr.44 In glotonye þ[o] gomus goth þei to *bedde*
C. 6.416 Beren hym to his *bed* and brouhten hym þerynne
C. 7.4   Were y brouhte [o]n *bed*, but yf my taylende hit made,
C. 8.108 I bar hoem þat y borwed ar y to *bedde* ȝede.
C. 9.145 Drynke druie and depe and drawe hym thenne to *bedde*;
C. 9.255 Ne no blanke[t] on his *bed* ne whyte bred byfore hym.
C.19.305 And if his hous be vnheled and reyne on his *bedde*

bedbourde n *bed n.(1) + bourde n.* A 1 bedbourd; B 1; C 1

A.10.203 Shulde no *bedbourd* be; but þei were boþe clene
B. 9.190 Sholde no [*bedbourde*] be; but þei boþe were clene
C.10.290 For sholde no *bedbourde* be bote yf they bothe were

bedchambre n *bed n.(1)* A 1 bedchaumbre; B 1; C 1 bed_chaumbre

A. 5.136 Þe beste in my *bedchaumbre* lay be þe wouȝ.
B. 5.220 The beste [in my *bedchambre*] lay [by þe walle],
C. 6.228 Þe beste ale lay in m[y] bour and in my *bed chau[m]bre*

bedde > bed

bedden v *bedden v.* B 2 bedden (1) ybedded (1); C 1 ybedded

B. 2.98   And breden as Burgh swyn, and *bedden* hem esily
B.15.536 Baddely *ybedded*, no boek but conscience,
C.17.197 Baddeliche *ybedded*, no boek but Consience

beddyng ger *bedding ger.* B 1; C 1 beddynge

B.14.232 And þouȝ his glotonye be to good ale he goþ to cold *beddyng*
C.16.73 And thogh his glotonye be of gode ale he goth to a colde *beddynge*

beddrede > bedrede

bede n *bede n. &> bidden* A 1 bedis; B 6 bede (1) bedes (5); C 3 bede (1) bedes (2)

A. 5.8   And so I babelide on my *bedis* þei brouȝte me aslepe.
B. 5.8   And so I bablede on my *bedes* þei brouȝte me aslepe.
B. 5.400 And if I bidde any *bedes*, but if it be in wraþe,
B.11.150 Wiþouten *bede* biddyng his boone was vnderfongen
B.12.28 And þere bidde my *bedes* but whan ich ete or slepe.
B.15.122 [And beere] *bedes* in hir hand and a book vnder hir arme.
B.19.375 Some þoruȝ *bedes* biddynge and some [by] pilgrymag[e]
C. 7.16   And yf y bidde eny *bedes*, but yf hit be in wrath,
C.12.85 Withouten *bed[e]* biddyng his bone was vnderfonge
C.21.375 Somme thorw *bedes* biddynge and [somme] bi pilgrimag[e]

bedel n *bidel n.* A 2 bedel (1) bedelis (1); B 3 Bedel (1) bedeles (1) bedelles (1); C 3 Bedel (1) Bedeles (1) bydels (1)

A. 2.74   Bette þe *bedel* of bukyngham shire,
A. 3.2   Wiþ *bedelis* & baillifs ybrouȝt to þe king.
B. 2.60   *Bedelles* and baillifs and Brocours of chaffare,
B. 2.110 Bette þe *Bedel* of Bokynghamshire,
B. 3.2   Wiþ *Bedeles* and baillies brouȝt [to] þe kyng.
C. 2.62   *Bydels* and bailifs and brokeres of chaffar[e],
C. 2.114 Butte þe *Bedel* of Bannebury sokene,
C. 3.2   [With] *Bedeles* and Baylifs ybrouhte byfor þe kyng.

bedeman n *bedeman n.* A 1; B 3 Bedeman (1) bedemen (2); C 3 bedemen (1) bedman (2)

A. 3.45   For to be hire *bedeman* & hire baude aftir.
B. 3.46   For to ben hire *Bedeman* and hire [baude after].
B.15.205 For þer are beggeris and bidderis, *bedemen* as it were,
B.15.428 Alle þat ben at debaat and *bedemen* were trewe:
C. 3.43   And ȝut be thy *bedman* and brynge adoun Consience
C. 3.48   For to ben here *bedman* and bere wel here ernde
C. 3.275 Bothe Beg[g]eres and *bedemen* crauen mede for here preyeres;

beden v *beden v. &> bidden* C 1

C.10.267 That he ne wol bowe to þat bonde to *beden* here an hosebonde

bedl(e)hem > bethleem; bedman > bedeman

bedrede adj *bedreden adj.* A 3 beddrede (1) bedrede (2); B 4 bedrede (1) bedreden (2) bedredene (1); C 4 bedreden (1) bedredene (2) bedredne (1)

A. 7.130 But he be blynd, or brokesshankid, or *beddrede* ligge:
A. 7.177 Blynde & *bedrede* were botind a þousand
A. 8.84   Blynde & *bedrede*, & broken here membris,
B. 6.191 Blynde and *bedreden* were bootned a þousand;
B. 7.30   Pouere peple [*bedredene*] and prisons [in stokkes]
B. 7.102 Blynde and *bedreden* and broken here membres
B.13.447 And a blynd man for a bourdeour, or a *bedrede* womman
C. 5.21   [Hem þat *bedreden* be] byleue t[o] fynden?'
C. 7.107 And a blynd man for a bordor or a *bedredene* womman
C. 9.34   Pore peple *bedredene* and prisones in stokkes
C. 9.178 Blynde and *bedredne* and broken here membres,

beelsyre > belsires

beem n *bem n.* B 2
B.10.270 Siþen a *beem* [is] in þyn owene ablyndeþ þiselue–
B.10.282 Lewed men may likne yow þus, þat þe *beem* liþ in youre eiзen,

been > ben; beenfeet -fete > bienfait; beer(e > beren

beest n *beste n. &> ben* A 16 beste (1) bestis (15); B 44 beest (6) beestes
(35) bestes (3); C 34 beste (3) bestes (29) bestis (2)
A. 3.250 Barnes and *bestis* brenne hem to deþe."
A. 3.252 Coueitide here catel, kilde nouзt hire *bestis,*
A. 3.253 But brouзte wiþ hym þe *bestis* as þe bible [telliþ],
A. 4.143 But stari[den for] stodyenge [and] stoden as *bestis.*
A. 6.2 But blustrid forþ as *bestis* ouer [baches] & hilles
A. 6.31 Boþe sowen his seed, & sewide hise *bestis,*
A. 7.128 [Cacche cowes] from his corn, [and] kepen hise *bestis,*
A. 7.181 And become knaues to kepe peris *bestis,*
A. 8.74 But as wilde *bestis* wiþ wehe, & worþ vp togideris
A.10.27 'Kynde,' quaþ he, 'is creatour of alle kenis *bestis,*
A.10.33 For þoruз þe woord þat he warp wexe forþ *bestis,*
A.10.61 And ben braynwood as *bestis,* so here blood wexiþ.
A.10.171 "*Bestis* þat now ben shuln banne þe tyme
A.10.174 Boþe fisshis & foulis, forþ mi[d] oþere *bestis,*
A.10.175 Outtake þe eiзte soulis, aftur of iche *beste* a couple
A.11.310 Þanne pore peple, as plouзmen, and pastours of *bestis,*
B. 3.267 Burnes and *beestes,* bren hem to deþe;
B. 3.274 Forbar hym and his *beestes* boþe as þe bible witnesseþ
B. 5.514 But blustreden forþ as *beestes* ouer [baches] and hilles
B. 5.543 Boþe ysowen his seed and suwed hise *beestes,*
B. 6.140 To kepe kyen in þe feld, þe corn fro þe *beestes,*
B. 7.92 But as wilde *bestes* with wehee worþen vppe and werchen,
B. 8.54 To fleynge foweles, to fisshes and to *beestes.*
B. 9.26 'Kynde', quod [he], 'is creatour of alle kynnes [*beestes*],
B. 9.32 For þoruз þe word þat he [warp] woxen forþ *beestes,*
B. 9.140 *Beestes* þat now ben shul banne þe tyme
B. 9.143 And þe foweles þat fleen forþ wiþ oþere *beestes,*
B.10.248 Makere of man [and his make] and of *beestes* boþe.
B.10.408 But briddes and *beestes* and þe blissed Noe
B.10.413 And shilden vs from shame þerinne, as Noes ship dide *beestes;*
B.10.416 That ben Carpenters holy kirk to make for cristes owene *beestes:*
B.11.328 And where þat briddes and *beestes* by hir mak[e þei] yeden,
B.11.335 Reson I seiз sooþly sewen alle *beestes,*
B.11.343 Boþe hors and houndes and alle oþere *beestes*
B.11.355 For fere of oþere foweles and for wilde *beestes.*
B.11.362 Ther neiþer burn ne *beest* may hir briddes rechen.
B.11.370 That Reson rewarded and ruled alle *beestes*
B.12.129 Of briddes and of *beestes,* [by] tastes of truþe.
B.12.219 /And willest of briddes & *beestes* and of hir bredyng knowe,
B.12.224 How euere *beest* oþer brid haþ so breme wittes.
B.12.236 Ac of briddes and of *beestes* men by olde tyme
B.13.15 Of kynde and of his konnynge, and how curteis he is to *bestes,*
B.13.363 And if my Neghebore hadde a[n] hyne or any *beest* ellis
B.14.37 Vitailles of grete vertues for alle manere *beestes*
B.14.44 And *bestes* by gras and by greyn and by grene rootes,
B.14.61 For þoruз his breeþ *beestes* woxen and abrood yeden:
B.14.62 Ergo þoruз his breeþ [boþe] men and *beestes* lyuen,
B.14.65 And out of þe flynt sprong þe flood þat folk and *beestes* dronken.
B.14.112 And seiþ, "lo! briddes and *beestes* þat no blisse ne knoweþ
B.14.117 Thanne may beggeris, as *beestes,* after boote waiten
B.14.158 And muche murþe in May is amonges wilde *beestes;*
B.15.273 Woneden in wildernesse amonge wilde *beestes,*
B.15.280 And þoruз þe mylk of þat mylde *beest* þe man was sustened;
B.15.299 Neiþer bere ne boor ne ooþer *beest* wilde,
B.15.303 [For al þe curteisie þat *beestes* konne þei kidde þat folk ofte,
B.15.305 Ac god sente hem foode by foweles and by no fierse *beestes*
B.15.460 As in wildernisse wexeþ wilde *beestes*
B.16.124 Youre bodies, youre *beestes,* and blynde men holpen,
B.19.263 That oon was Luk, a large *beest* and a lowe chered,
B.19.264 And Mark, and Mathew þe þridde, myghty *beestes* boþe;
C. 3.421 Man, womman and wyf, childe, wedewe and *bestes,*
C. 3.427 Forbar hym and his *beste bestes,* as þe byble wittenesseth,
C. 6.262 And yf my neyhebore hadde an hyne or eny *beste* elles
C. 7.159 But blostrede forth as *bestes* ouer baches and hulles
C. 7.187 And to sowen his seed [and] suewen his *bestes,*
C. 8.189 And lame men he lechede with longes of *bestes.*
C. 9.225 In frithes and in forestes for fox and other *beste*
C. 9.270 When thy lord loketh to haue allouaunce of his *bestes*
C.10.228 *Bestes* þat now beth shal banne þe tyme
C.10.231 And þe foules þat fl[e]eth forth with oþer *bestes,*
C.11.239 Bote briddes and *bestis* and þe blessed Noe
C.11.248 For lewed folk, goddes foles and his fre *bestes:*
C.13.136 And where þat briddes and *bestis* by here make þei зeden,
C.13.143 Resoun y sey sothly sewe alle *bestes*

C.13.180 Was þat y seyh resoun sewen alle *bestes*
C.13.186 That thow ne reul[e]st rather renkes then other *bestes.*
C.13.190 They ouerdoen hit day and nyhte and so doth nat oþer *bestes;*
C.14.80 Of briddes and of *bestes,* of blisse and of sorwe.
C.14.88 Bote of clennesse of clerkes and kepares of *bestes:*
C.14.162 And Adam and Eue and alle othere *bestes*
C.14.169 To briddes and to *bestes,* As here bokes telleth
C.15.18 Of kynde and [of] his connynge and what connynge he зaf *bestes*
C.15.242 *Bestes* by gra[s] and by grayn and by grene rotes,
C.15.260 [For] thorw his breth *bestes* wexe and abroed зeden:
C.15.261 Ergo thorw his breth *bestes* lyueth, bothe men and fisches.
C.15.264 And oute of þe flynt sprange þe flood þat folk and *bestes* dronke.
C.15.288 And saith, "loo! briddes and *bestes* þat no blisse ne knoweth
C.15.293 Thenne may beggares, as *bestes,* aftur blisse aske
C.16.10 Muche murthe is in may amonge wilde *bestes*
C.17.28 And woneden in wildernesses amonges wilde *bestes.*
C.17.29 Ac durste no *beste* byte hem by day ne by nyhte
C.17.32 Ac *bestes* brouhte hem no mete bute onliche þe foules
C.21.263 That oen was luc, a large *beste* and a lou chered,
C.21.264 And Marc and Mathewe the thridde, myhty *bestes* bothe;

beet > beten; beeþ > ben; befall- befel > bifalle

beflobered v *befloberen v.* B 1
B.13.400 And foule *beflobered* it, as wiþ fals speche,

befor- > bifore; begeneldes > begyneld; beggar- > begger-

begge v *beggen v. &> buggen* A 3 begge (2) beggiþ (1); B 8 begge (5)
beggen (1) beggeþ (2); C 17 begge (10) beggen (1) beggest (1)
beggeth (5)
A. 7.221 He shal go [*begge* & bidde] & no man bete his hungir;
A. 8.68 But зif þe suggestioun be soþ þat [shapiþ hem to] *begge.*
A. 8.69 For he þat *beggiþ* or bit, but he haue nede,
B. 6.192 That seten to *begge* siluer soone were þei heeled,
B. 6.237 He shal [go] *begge* and bidde and no man bete his hunger.
B. 7.66 But if þe suggestion be sooþ þat shapeþ hem to *begge,*
B. 7.67 For he þat *beggeþ* or bit, but he haue nede,
B.11.278 To beggeris þat *begge* and bidden for goddes loue.
B.15.256 Neiþer he biddeþ ne *beggeþ* ne borweþ to зelde.
B.15.329 For þat þei *beggen* aboute in buyldynge þei spende,
B.20.238 For lomere he lyeþ þat liflode moot *begge*
C. 5.29 Or *beggest* thy bylyue aboute at men hacches.
C. 5.51 Now with hym, now with here: on this wyse y *begge*
C. 5.90 Ac it semeth no sad parfitnesse in Citees to *b[e]gge*
C. 6.313 For me is leuere in this lyue as a lorel *begge*
C. 9.62 Bote the sugestioun be soth þat shapeth h[e]m to *begge*
C. 9.63 For he þat *beg[g]eth* or biddeth, but y[f he] haue nede,
C. 9.86 And ben abasched for to *begge* and wollen nat be aknowe
C. 9.121 Barfoot and bredles, *beggeth* they of no man
C. 9.161 Ne no beggare[s] þat *beggeth* but yf they haue nede.'
C. 9.190 And in borwes among brewesteres and *beggen* in churches–
C.10.185 And holy churche helpe to, so sholde no man *begge*
C.16.70 That mete or moneye of straunge men moet *begge.*
C.16.338 Thogh y my byliue sholde *begge* aboute at menne hacches.
C.16.372 For noþer he *beggeth* ne biddeth ne borweth to зelde
C.16.374 To *begge* or to borwe but of god one:
C.17.2 Or *beggeth* or biddeth, be he ryche or pore,
C.22.238 For lomere he lyeth þat lyflode moet *begge*

beggere n *beggere n. &> buggere* A 10 beggere (3) beggeris (7); B 39
beggere (8) beggeres (11) beggeris (17) beggers (3); C 37 beggare (11)
beggares (24) Beggeres (1) beggers (1)
A.Pr.40 Bidderis & *beggeris* faste aboute зede
A. 2.124 And alle be boun, *beggeris* & oþere,
A. 3.206 *Beggeris* for here bidding biddiþ of men mede;
A. 7.189 Of *beggeris* & bidderis what best is to done.
A. 7.199 Bolde *beggeris* & bigge, þat mowe here breed beswynken,
A. 7.287 Ne no *beggere* ete bred þat benis in come,
A. 8.67 *Beggeris* & bidderis ben not in þe bulle
A.10.115 To be blissid for þi beryng, [з]e, *b[e]ggere* þeiз þou were.
A.11.188 To breke *beggeris* bred & bakken hem with cloþis,
A.12.71 A bagge ful of a *beggere.*' I bouзte hit at onys.
B.Pr.40 Bidderes and *beggeres* faste aboute yede
B. 2.160 And alle be bown, *beggers* and oþere,
B. 3.219 *Beggeres* for hir biddynge bidden [of] men Mede;
B. 4.124 Til Bisshopes Bayardes ben *beggeris* Chaumbres,
B. 5.150 Til þei be boþe *beggers* and by my spiritualte libben,
B. 5.440 And euere siþþe be *beggere* [by cause of my] sleuþe:
B. 6.194 And many a *beggere* for benes buxom was to swynke,
B. 6.203 'Of *beggeris* and bidderis what best be to doone.
B. 6.213 Bolde *beggeris* and bigge þat mowe hir breed biswynke,
B. 6.303 Ne no *beggere* ete breed þat benes Inne [come],
B. 7.65 *Beggeres* [and] bidderes beþ noзt in þe bulle
B. 7.82 For *beggeres* borwen eueremo and hir borgh is god almyзty

B. 7.84   Forþi biddeþ noȝt, ye *beggeres*, but if ye haue nede;
B. 7.96   Ther is moore mysshapen amonges þise *beggeres*
B. 9.92   Bisshopes shul be blamed for *beggeres* sake.
B. 9.94   And biddeþ þe *beggere* go for his broke cloþes:
B.10.85   And brekeþ noȝt to þe *beggere* as þe book techeþ:
B.10.366   And oure bakkes þat moþeeten be and seen *beggeris* go naked,
B.11.198   [Ac] for þe beste ben som riche and some *beggeres* and pouere.
B.11.200   And breþeren as of oo blood, as wel *beggeres* as Erles.
B.11.204   No *beggere* ne boye amonges vs but if it synne made:
B.11.278   To *beggeris* þat begge and bidden for goddes loue.
B.12.146   Ne in none [*beggers*] cote [n]as þat barn born,
B.12.201   But as a *beggere* bordlees by myself on þe grounde.
B.13.241   *Beggeris* and bidderis of my breed crauen,
B.13.266   Wiþ [bake] breed fro Stratford; þo gonnen *beggeris* wepe
B.13.302   Boldest of *beggeris*; a bostere þat noȝt haþ,
B.13.439   Haue *beggeres* bifore hem þe whiche ben goddes minstrales
B.14.117   Thanne may *beggeris*, as beestes, after boote waiten
B.14.160   Ac *beggeris* aboute Midsomer bredlees þei [soupe],
B.14.214   Batauntliche as *beggeris* doon, and boldeliche he craueþ
B.14.249   A *beggeris* bagge þan an yren bounde cofre.
B.14.264   And for goddes loue leueþ al and lyueþ as a *beggere*.
B.15.205   For þer are *beggeris* and bidderis, bedemen as it were,
B.15.227   Ac biddynge as *beggeris* biheld I hym neuere:
B.15.244   [Amonges erchebisshopes and bisshopes, [for *beggeres* sake],
B.15.342   Ac Religiouse þat riche ben sholde raþer feeste *beggeris*
B.20.239   Than he þat laboureþ for liflode and leneþ it *beggeris*.
B.20.241   Lat hem be as *beggeris* or lyue by Aungeles foode.'
C.Pr.41   Bidders and *beggers* fast aboute ȝede
C. 2.176   And bade hem alle be bowen, *beggares* and othere,
C. 3.275   Bothe *Beg[g]eres* and bedemen crauen mede for here preyeres;
C. 5.68   Bondemen and bastardus and *beggares* children,
C. 6.49   And non so bolde a *beggare* to bidde and to craue,
C. 6.123   Thus *Beggares* and Barones at debat aren ofte
C. 6.125   Or til they bothe be *beggares* and by [my] spiritual[t]e libbe
C. 7.54   And sethe a *beggare* haue y be for my foule sleuthe:
C. 7.99   Haue *beggares* byfore hem þe whiche ben goddes mu[n]strals
C. 8.193   Drosenes and dregges drynke for many *beggares*.
C. 8.201   Was no *beggare* so bold, but yf a blynd were,
C. 8.209   Of *beggares* and biddares what beste be to done.
C. 8.223   Bolde *beggares* and bygge þat mowe here breed byswynke,
C. 8.264   To *beggares* and to boys þat loth ben to worche.
C. 8.278   And laȝar þe lene *beggare* þat longede aftur crommes–
C. 8.325   Ne no *beggare* eten bred þat benes ynne were
C. 9.61   *Beggares* and Biddares beth nat in þ[e] bulle
C. 9.98   Ac *beggares* with bagges þe whiche brewhous[es] ben here
           churches.
C. 9.105   A[nd] ȝut ar ther oþere *beggares*, in hele as hit semeth
C. 9.161   Ne no *beggare[s]* þat beggeth but yf they haue nede.'
C. 9.169   Bringeth forth bastardus, *beggares* of kynde,
C. 9.172   Ther aren mo mysshape amonges suche *beggares*
C.12.112   No *beggare* ne boy among vs but [yf] hit synne ma[d]e:
C.12.116   And we his blody bretherne, as wel *beggares* as lordes.
C.13.72   Fynde *beggares* bred, bakkes for þe colde,
C.13.95   For þe wil is as moche worthe of a wrecche *beggare*
C.14.140   Bote as a *beggare* bordles be mysulue on þe grounde.
C.15.293   Thenne may *beggares*, as bestes, aftur blisse aske
C.15.300   And now he buyth hit bittere; he is a *beggare* of helle.
C.16.13   Ac *beggares* aboute myssomur bredles they soupe
C.16.55   Batauntliche as *beggares* doen, and baldeliche he craueth
C.16.89   A *beggares* bagge then an yrebounden coffre.
C.16.104   And for goddes loue leueth al and lyueth as a *beggare*.
C.16.352   Ac biddyng als a *beggare* byhelde y hym neuere.
C.16.366   With bisshopes a wolde be for *beggares* sake
C.22.239   Then he þat laboreth for lyflode and leneth hit *beggares*.
C.22.241   Lat hem be as *beggares* or lyue by angeles fode.'

beggerie n *beggerie n.* B 1; C 2 beggarie

B. 7.89   The book banneþ *beggerie* and blameþ hem in þis manere:
C. 9.162   The boek banneth *beggarie* and blameth hit in this manere:
C. 9.166   For hit blameth all *beggarie*, be ȝe ful certayn.

beggeris > beggere,buggere

beggynge ger *begging ger.* C 3

C. 5.174   Bred withouten *beggynge* to lyue by euere aftur
C.17.8   Withoute borwynge or *beggynge* bote of god one,
C.17.27   Withoute borwynge or *beggynge*, or þe boek lyeth,

begyneld n *beggild n.* C 2 begeneldes (1) begyneld (1)

C. 9.154   With a bagge at his bak A *begyneld* wyse,
C.10.263   A bastard, a bond oen, a *begeneldes* douhter

begynne > bigynnen

begynnere n *biginner n.* A 1

A.10.53   Of good speche & [going] he is þe *begynnere*;

begynneþ > bigynnen; begynnung > bigynnyng

begon ptp *biginen v.* A 1

A. 2.24   Gile haþ *begon* hire so heo grauntiþ alle his wille;

begonne > bigynnen; begrucchiþ > bigruccheþ; beheld > biholde; behest(es > biheste; behiȝte behyhte > bihote; behynde > bihynde; behold- > biholde; behote > bihote; behouiþ > bihoueþ

beiȝe n *bei n.* B 3 beiȝe (2) beiȝes (1); C 3 beygh (2) beyus (1)

B.Pr.161   Beren *beiȝes* ful briȝte abouten hire nekkes,
B.Pr.165   Were þer a belle on hire *beiȝe*, by Iesu, as me þynkeþ,
B.Pr.176   Ac þo þe belle was ybrouȝt and on þe *beiȝe* hanged
C.Pr.180   Bere *beyus* of bryghte gold aboute here nekkes
C.Pr.182   Wer ther a belle on here *beygh*, by iesu, as me thynketh,
C.Pr.193   Ac tho þe belle was ybroughte and on þe *beygh* hangid

beyre num *bo num.* C 1

C.20.36   To se how douhtyliche deth sholde do and demen [h]er *beyre* rihte.

beyus > beiȝe

bekene n *beken n.* B 1; C 1 bekne

B.17.266   Ye brenne but ye blase noȝt; þat is a blynd *bekene*:
C.19.232   Ȝe brenneth ac ȝe blaseth nat; and þat is a blynde *bekne*:

bekenne > bikenne; beknew beknowe > biknowe; beleue > bileue,bileuen

bele adj *bel adj.* B 1; C 1

B.15.115   Ye aren enblaunched wiþ *bele* paroles and wiþ [*bele* cloþes]
C.16.270   That ben enblaunched with *bele* paroles and with *bele* clothes

bely n *beli n.* A 4 bely (3) belly (1); B 2; C 1

A.Pr.41   Til here *bely* & here bagge were bratful ycrammid;
A. 8.112   [By foules, þat are not] besy aboute þe *bely* ioye:
A.12.70   At my bak of broke bred þi *bely* for to fylle,
A.12.74   [But ete as hunger me mete til my *belly* swellyd.
B.Pr.41   [Til] hire *bel[y]* and hire bagg[e were bret]ful ycrammed;
B. 7.130   By foweles [þat are] noȝt bisy aboute þe [*bely* ioye],
C.Pr.42   Til here [*bely*] and here [bagge] w[ere] bretful ycrammed,

belialles n *Belial n.* B 2 Beliales (1) Belialles (1); C 3 Belial (1) beliales (1) belialles (1)

B.18.321   And wiþ þat breeþ helle brak with *Belialles* barres;
B.20.79   And þere abide and bikere ayeins *Beliales* children.'
C.20.282   That *Belial*, thy beelsyre, beet with thy dame
C.20.364   And with þat breth helle braek with *belialles* barres;
C.22.79   And þere abyde and bikere aȝeyn *beliales* childrene.'

belyen > bilye; belyue > bilyue

belle n *belle n.* B 6 belle (5) belles (1); C 6 belle (5) belles (1)

B.Pr.165   Were þer a *belle* on hire beiȝe, by Iesu, as me þynkeþ,
B.Pr.168   To bugge a *belle* of bras or of briȝt siluer
B.Pr.176   Ac þo þe *belle* was ybrouȝt and on þe beiȝe hanged
B.Pr.178   That dorste haue bounden þe *belle* aboute þe cattes nekke,
B.Pr.188   And be we neuere [so] bolde þe *belle* hym to shewe.
B.20.59   And Religiouse reuerenced hym and rongen hir *belles*,
C.Pr.182   Wer ther a *belle* on here beygh, by iesu, as me thynketh,
C.Pr.185   A *belle* to byggen of bras oþer of] bryghte syluer
C.Pr.193   Ac tho þe *belle* was ybroughte and on þe beygh hangid
C.Pr.195   That derste haue ybounde þe *belle* aboute þe kattes nekke
C.Pr.205   And be [we] neuere so bold the *belle* hym [to] shewe.
C.22.59   And religious reuerensed hym and rongen here *belles*

belly > bely

belouȝ v *bilaughen v.* A 1

A. 8.107   And beloure þat I [be]louȝ er þeiȝ liflode me faile.

beloure v *bilouren v.* A 1

A. 8.107   And *beloure* þat I [be]louȝ er þeiȝ liflode me faile.

belowen > bilye

belsabubbes n *Belzabub n.* A 1 belsabubbis; B 1

A. 2.95   [And] as a bastard yborn of *belsab[ubb]is* kynde;
B. 2.131   And [as] a Bastard ybore of *Belsabubbes* kynne.

belsires n *bel adj.* B 1; C 3 beelsyre (1) belsyre (1) belsires (1)

B. 9.146   Here abouȝte þe barn þe *belsires* giltes,
C. 2.124   Althow fals were here fader and fikel tonge her *belsyre*
C.10.234   Here aboute þe barn the *belsires* gultes
C.20.282   That Belial, thy *beelsyre*, beet with thy dame

bemen- > bymeene

ben v *ben v.* A 648 am (18) are (1) arn (27) art (8) be (130) ben (74) best (1) beþ (5) is (222) nas (3) nere (3) nis (4) was (80) were (63) wern (9); B 1990 am (55) ar (2) are (32) aren (6) arn (31) art (17) artow (7) be (389) beest (1) beeþ (1) ben (176) beþ (23) is (687) nas (3) nere (3) nis (1) nys (6) was (332) weere (15) were (199) weren (3) ybe (1); C 1981 am (46) ar (13) are (6) aren (52) arn (1) art (19) artow (5) be (436) been (12) beeþ (1) ben (132) best (2) beth (34) buth (1) is (661) ys (6) nas (1) nere (3) nis (2) was (310) wer (1) were (227) weren (9) ybe (1)

am A 18

A. 1.73 'Holy chirche I *am*,' quaþ heo, 'þou auȝtest me to knowe;
A. 3.32 Þat he ne worþ ferst auauncid for I *am* beknowe
A. 3.52 Þat iche segge shal se I *am* sistir of ȝour hous.'
A. 4.13 'I *am* fayn of þat foreward,' seiþ þe frek þanne,
A. 4.47 I *am* not hardy [for hym vnneþe] to loke.'
A. 4.155 'I *am* redy,' quaþ resoun, 'to reste wiþ ȝow euere;
A. 5.105 'I *am* sory,' quaþ enuye, 'I am but selde oþere,
A. 5.105 'I am sory,' quaþ enuye, 'I *am* but selde oþere,
A. 5.217 "I *am* sory for my synne," sey to þiseluen,
A. 6.86 And *am* sory for my synnes & so shal I euere
A. 7.75 'For [now] I *am* old & hor & haue of myn owene
A. 7.123 And I *am* his [h]olde hyne & auȝte hym to warne.
A.11.258 –ȝet *am* I neuere þe ner for nouȝt I haue walkid
A.12.23 "I *am* not hardy," quod he, "þat I herde wiþ erys,
A.12.33 But as he seyþ, such I *am*, when he with me carpeþ.'
A.12.63 'I *am* dwellyng with deth, and hunger I hatte.
A.12.82 Mi name is feuere on þe ferþe day; I *am* aþrest euere.
A.12.83 I *am* masager of deþ; men haue I tweyne:

am B 55

B. 1.75 'Holi chirche I *am*', quod she; 'þow ouȝtest me to knowe.
B. 3.33 That he ne worþ first auaunced, for I *am* biknowen
B. 3.63 That [ech] segge shal [see] I *am* suster of youre house.'
B. 4.13 'I *am* fayn of þat foreward,' seide þe freke þanne,
B. 4.60 I am noȝt hardy for hym vnneþe to loke.'
B. 4.155 And seide, 'madame, I *am* youre man what so my mouþ Iangle.
B. 4.192 'I *am* redy', quod Reson, 'to reste wiþ yow euere;
B. 5.128 'I *am* sory', quod [enuye], 'I am but selde ooþer,
B. 5.128 'I am sory', quod [enuye], 'I *am* but selde ooþer,
B. 5.137 'I *am* wraþe', quod he, 'I was som tyme a frere,
B. 5.174 And *am* chalanged in þe Chapitrehous as I a child were
B. 5.258 'I *am* holden', quod he, 'as hende as hound is in kichene;
B. 5.402 I *am* occupied eche day, halyday and ooþer,
B. 5.413 I [a]m noȝt shryuen som tyme but if siknesse it make
B. 5.430 I *am* vnkynde ayeins [his] curteisie and kan nouȝt vnderstonden it,
B. 5.432 I *am* noȝt lured wiþ loue but þer ligge auȝt vnder þe þombe.
B. 5.445 "I *am* sory for my synn[e]", seye to þiselue.
B. 5.599 And *am* sory for my synnes and so [shal I] euere
B. 5.642 Thow shalt seye I *am* þi Suster.' I ne woot where þei bicome.
B. 6.83 'For now I *am* old and hoor and haue of myn owene
B. 6.131 And I *am* his [h]olde hyne and [auȝte] hym to warne.
B. 6.201 'I *am* wel awroke of wastours þoruȝ þy myȝte.
B. 9.164 "I *am* via & veritas", seiþ crist, "I may auaunce alle."
B.10.377 'This is a long lesson', quod I, 'and litel *am* I þe wiser;
B.12.1 'I *am* ymaginatif', quod he; 'ydel was I neuere
B.13.111 I wolde permute my penaunce with youre, for I *am* in point to dowel.'
B.13.123 'I *am* vnhardy', quod he, 'to any wiȝt to preuen it.
B.13.156 And herwith *am* I welcome þer I haue it wiþ me.
B.13.189 For al þat Pacience me profreþ proud *am* I litel.
B.13.224 'I *am* a Mynstrall', quod þat man, 'my name is Actiua vita.
B.13.238 And þat *am* I, Actif, þat ydelnesse hatie,
B.14.1 'I haue but oon hool hater', quod haukyn, 'I *am* þe lasse to blame
B.15.16 'I *am* cristes creature', quod he, 'and [of his kyn a party],
B.15.23 'The whiles I quykne þe cors', quod he, 'called *am* I anima;
B.15.25 And for þat I kan [and] knowe called *am* I mens;
B.15.32 Thanne *am* I Conscience ycalled, goddes clerk and his Notarie;
B.15.36 Thanne *am* I spirit spechelees; Spiritus þanne ich hatte.
B.15.385 Wherfore I *am* afered of folk of holy kirke.
B.16.3 Ac ȝit I *am* in a weer what charite is to mene.'
B.16.142 'I *am* sold þoruȝ [som] of yow; he shal þe tyme rewe
B.16.176 'I *am* feiþ', quod þat freke, 'it falleþ noȝt to lye,
B.16.234 I *am* ful siker in soule þerof, and my sone boþe.
B.17.1 'I *am* Spes, [a spie', quod he], 'and spire after a Knyght
B.17.109 For he seigh me þat *am* Samaritan suwen Feiþ & his felawe
B.17.300 And now *am* sory þat I so þe Seint Spirit agulte,
B.18.126 'And *am* wendynge to wite what þis wonder meneþ.'
B.18.356 And I in liknesse of a leode, þat lord *am* of heuene,
B.18.365 For I þat *am* lord of lif, loue is my drynke,
B.18.384 And I þat *am* kyng of kynges shal come swich a tyme
B.19.410 'I *am* a Curatour of holy kirke, and cam neuere in my tyme
B.19.466 'I *am* kyng wiþ croune þe comune to rule,
B.19.469 Ther I may hastilokest it haue, for I *am* heed of lawe;
B.19.471 And siþ I *am* youre aller heed I am youre aller heele

B.19.471 And siþ I am youre aller heed I *am* youre aller heele
B.20.336 'I *am* a Surgien', seide þe [frere], 'and salues kan make.

am C 46

C. 1.72 'Holy churche y *am*,' quod she; 'þou oughtest me to knowe.
C. 2.33 And y *am* his dere doughter, ducchesse of heuene.
C. 3.36 That he ne worth furste vaunsed, for y *am* byknowe
C. 3.67 That euery seg shal se y *am* sustre of ȝoure ordre.'
C. 4.13 'Y *am* fayn of that foreward, in fayth,' tho quod Consience,
C. 4.63 Y *am* nat hardy for hym vnnethe to loke.'
C. 5.23 Y *am* to wayke to wurcche with sykel or with sythe
C. 6.93 'I *am* sory,'sayde enuye, 'y am [but] selde othur;
C. 6.93 'I am sory,'sayde enuye, 'y *am* [but] selde othur;
C. 6.95 ȝut *am* y brokour of bakbytynge to blame menne w[a]re
C. 6.105 'I *am* wr[a]the,' quod þat weye, 'wol gladliche smyte
C. 6.143 Amonges wyues and wydewes [y *am* woned] to sitte
C. 6.156 ȝut *am* y chalenged in oure chapitrehous as y a childe were
C. 7.18 Y *am* occupied vch day, haliday and oþere,
C. 7.28 Y *am* nat shryue som tyme but yf seknesse hit make
C. 7.43 Y *am* vnkynde aȝen his cortesie [and] can nat vnderstande hit
C. 7.45 Y *am* nat luyred with loue but þer lygge ouht vnder þe t[h]umbe.
C. 7.59 "Y *am* sory for my synnes", sey to thysuluen
C. 7.246 Y *am* sory [for] my synnes, and so [shal y] euere;
C. 8.92 'For now y *am* olde and hoer and haue of myn owene
C. 8.207 'Y *am* wel awroke of wastours thorw thy myhte
C.10.255 For y *am* via & veritas and may avauncen alle."
C.12.26 And now y *am* pore and penyles at litel pris he sette[th] me.
C.14.1 'I *am* ymagenatyf,' quod he; 'ydel was y neuere
C.15.193 'Ich *am* a mynstral,' quod this man, 'my name is actiua vita,
C.15.211 Y *am* sory þat y sowe or sette but for mysulue.
C.15.235 Hit *am* y þat fynde alle folke and fram hunger saue
C.16.167 'Y *am* cristes creature,' quod he, 'and cristene in mony a place
C.16.183 And whiles y quyke þe cors ycald *am* y Anima;
C.16.185 And [for] þat y can and knowe ycald *am* y [mens];
C.16.192 Thenne *am* y Concience ycald, goddes Clerk and his notarie;
C.16.194 Thenne *am* y liberum Arbitrium, as le[tt]red men telleth;
C.16.198 Thenne *am* y [y] spirit spechelees; spiritus then y hote.
C.18.175 Sethe y be tresoun *am* take and to ȝoure will, iewes,
C.18.184 'I *am* with fayth,' quod þat freke, 'hit falleth nat me to lye,
C.19.1 'I *am* spes, a spie,' quod he, 'and spere aftur a knyȝte
C.19.280 And now *am* sory þat y so the seynte spirit agulte,
C.20.129 'And *am* wendynge to wyte what þis wonder meneth.'
C.20.403 For y þat *am* lord of lyf, loue is my drynke,
C.20.426 And y þat *am* kynge o[f] kynges shal come such a tyme
C.21.410 'Ich *am* a Curatour of holi [kirke] and cam neuer in my tyme
C.21.466 'Y *am* kyng with croune the comune to reule
C.21.469 Ther y may hastilokest hit haue, for y *am* heed of lawe;
C.21.471 And sethe y *am* ȝoure alere heued y am ȝoure alere hele
C.21.471 And sethe y am ȝoure alere heued y *am* ȝoure alere hele
C.22.336 'Y *am* a surgien,' saide the frere, 'and salues can make.

ar B 2

B.10.216 Yet *ar* þer fibicches in [forelles] of fele mennes [wittes],
B.13.183 'What!' quod Clergie to Conscience, '*ar* ye coueitous nouþe

ar C 13

C.Pr.126 *Ar* don vndeuouteliche; drede is at þe laste
C. 8.294 Ther *ar* many luther leches Ac lele leches fewe;
C. 9.105 A[nd] ȝut *ar* ther oþere beggares, in hele as hit semeth
C. 9.236 Vnder this obedience *ar* we vchone
C. 9.260 For many wakere wolues *ar* wr[iþ]en into thy foldes;
C.10.14 For ȝe *ar* men of this molde þat moste wyde walken
C.10.45 The godes of this grounde *ar* like þe grete wawes
C.11.18 That coueite can and caste thus *ar* cleped into consayle:
C.11.234 Seldom *ar* they seyen so lyue as they lere;
C.16.165 'Leue liberum arbitrium,' quod y, 'of what lond *ar* ȝe?
C.17.83 Thus *ar* ȝe luyþer ylikned to lossheborw[e] sterlynges
C.18.60 Ac somme *ar* swettore then somme and so[nner]e wollen rotye.
C.22.334 'He is syke,' saide Pees, 'and so *ar* many other.

are A 1

A. 8.112 [By foules, þat *are* not] besy aboute þe bely ioye:

are B 32

B. 1.21 *Are* none nedfulle but þo; and nempne hem I þynke
B. 1.70 That trusten on his tresour bitraye[d *are*] sonnest.'
B. 1.140 'Thow doted daffe!' quod she, 'dulle *are* þi wittes.
B. 1.191 *Are* [none hardere] þan hij whan þei ben auaunced,
B. 3.80 For þise *are* men on þis molde þat moost harm wercheþ
B. 3.231 'Ther *are* two manere of Medes, my lord, [bi] youre leue.
B. 4.34 'Ther *are* wiles in hire wordes, and with Mede þei dwelleþ;
B. 5.594 Of almesdedes ben *are* þe hokes þat þe gates hangen on.
B. 5.618 A[c] þer *are* seuen sustren þat seruen truþe euere
B. 6.98 For þouȝ I deye today my dettes *are* quyte.
B. 6.207 [And it] *are* my blody breþeren for god bouȝte vs alle;
B. 6.273 [Ther *are* mo lieres þan] leches; lord hem amende!
B. 7.130 By foweles [þat *are*] noȝt bisy aboute þe [bely ioye];

51

B. 9.65 And alle þat lyuen good lif *are* lik to god almyȝty:
B.10.21 [That] swiche craftes k[onne] to counseil [*are*] cleped;
B.10.437 Ther *are* witty and wel libbynge ac hire werkes ben yhudde
B.10.464 Than *are* þise [kete] clerkes þat konne manye bokes,
B.11.199 For alle *are* we cristes creatures and of his cofres riche,
B.11.242 And [pacient as pilgrymes] for pilgrymes *are* we alle.
B.12.5 And how fele fernyeres *are* faren and so fewe to come;
B.12.17 And bidde for hem þat ȝyueþ þee breed, for þer *are* bokes y[n]owe
B.15.22 'What *are* ye called', quod I, 'in þat court among cristes peple?'
B.15.201 For þer *are* [pure] proude herted men, pacient of tonge
B.15.205 For þer *are* beggeris and bidderis, bedemen as it were,
B.15.328 If any peple parfourne þat text it *are* þise poore freres,
B.16.44 And leiþ a laddre þerto, of lesynges *are* þe ronges,
B.16.57 For alle *are* þei aliche longe, noon lasse þan ooþer,
B.16.121 'Thanne *are* ye cherles', [chidde Iesus], 'and youre children boþe,
B.17.154 Thus *are* þei alle but oon, as it an hand weere.
B.19.35 Boþe his loore and his lawe; now *are* þei lowe cherles.
B.20.234 'And for þei *are* pouere, parauenture, for patrymoyne [hem] faille[þ],
B.20.334 'He is sik', seide Pees, 'and so *are* manye oþere.

are C 6

C. 8.216 And hit *are* my blody bretherne for god bouhte vs alle.
C. 9.96 These *are* Almusse to helpe þat han suche charges
C.12.131 And pacient as pilgrimes for pilgrimes *are* we alle.
C.15.284 Hit *are* but fewe folk of this ryche that ne falleth in arrerage
C.19.129 Thus *are* they alle bote oen as hit an hand were,
C.21.35 Bothe his lore and his lawe; now *are* they lowe cherles.

aren B 6

B.15.115 Ye *aren* enblaunched wiþ bele paroles and wiþ [bele cloþes]
B.15.116 Ac youre werkes and wordes þervnder *aren* ful [wol]ueliche.
B.15.370 Astronomyens also *aren* at hir wittes ende;
B.17.167 And *aren* serel[e]pes by hemself; asondry were þei neuere;
B.19.22 And synfulle *aren* solaced and saued by þat name,
B.19.39 *Aren* frankeleyns, free men þoruȝ fullynge þat þei toke

aren C 52

C.Pr.93 And summe *aren* as seneschalles and seruen oþer lordes
C. 1.21 *Aren* non [ni]defole but tho and nemne hem y thenke
C. 1.139 'Thow dotede daffe!' quod she, 'dulle *aren* thy wittes.
C. 1.186 Mony chapeleynes *aren* chaste ac charite hem fayleth;
C. 1.187 *Aren* none hardore ne hungriore then men of holy chirche,
C. 1.195 For this *aren* wordes ywryten in þe ewangelie:
C. 6.123 Thus Beggares and Barones at debat *aren* ofte
C. 6.152 For there *aren* many felle frekes myn aferes to aspye,
C. 7.89 Ryht so flateres and fooles *aren* þe fendes procuratours
C. 7.239 The barres aren of buxumnesse as bretherne of o wombe;
C. 7.242 The hokes *aren* Almesdedes þat þe ȝates hange on.
C. 7.271 And *aren* porteres ouer þe posternes þat to þ[e] place bilongen.
C. 8.45 At churche in the Charnel cherles *Aren* euele to knowe
C. 8.261 This *aren* euidences,' quod hunger, 'for hem þat wolle nat swynke
C. 9.71 Ac þat most neden *aren* oure neyhebores and we nyme gode he[d]e,
C. 9.107 The whiche *aren* lunatyk lollares and lepares aboute
C. 9.110 And *aren* meuynge aftur þe mone; moneyeles þey walke
C. 9.118 Hit *aren* as his postles, suche peple, or as his priue disciples
C. 9.126 For hit *aren* murye mouthed men, munstrals of heuene
C. 9.172 Ther *aren* mo mysshape amonges suche beggares
C. 9.261 Thy berkeres *aren* a[l] blynde that bringeth forth thy lombren:
C.10.77 *Aren* thre fayre vertues and ben nat fer to fynde.
C.10.156 Angeles and alle thyng *aren* at his wille,
C.10.273 The fruyt þat they brynge forth *aren* many foule wordes;
C.11.26 Harlotes for here harlotrye *aren* holpe ar nedy pore;
C.11.289 *Aren* noen rather yraueschid fro þe rihte bileue
C.12.188 *Aren* tidiore and touore to mannes byhofte
C.12.192 *Aren* not so worthy as whete ne so wel mowe
C.13.67 *Aren* alle acountable to crist and to þe kyng of heuene,
C.13.79 The messager *aren* th[e] mendenantȝ þat lyuen by menne almesse,
C.13.174 Mony selcouthes y seyh *aren* nat to segge nouthe
C.15.305 Then *aren* hit puyre pore thynges in purgatorie or in hell.
C.16.3 Hewen þat haen here huyre byfore *aren* eueremore pore
C.16.21 Ac for þe beste, as y hope, *aren* som pore and ryche.
C.17.106 Astron[o]myens also *aren* at here wittes ende;
C.17.224 And [tho] þat haen petres power *aren* apo[y]sened alle."
C.18.62 Of o kynde apples *aren* nat iliche grete
C.18.64 Tho that sitten in þe sonne syde sannore *aren* rype,
C.18.68 Adam was as tre and of his apples,
C.18.81 'Ȝe, sire, y sayde, 'and sethen þer *aren* but tweyne lyues
C.18.206 The whiche *aren* childrene of charite and holy church [the] moder.
C.18.219 And abel here issue, *aren* bote oen in manhede.
C.18.236 In matrimonie *aren* thre and of o man cam alle thre
C.19.27 'Ȝoure wordes *aren* wonderfol,' quod y; 'where eny of [hem] be trewe
C.19.33 He can no certeyn somme telle and somme *aren* in his lappe.
C.19.39 The which alle men *aren* holde ouer al thyng to honoure
C.19.85 Noþer faith ne fyn hope, so festred *aren* his woundes.
C.21.12 Quod Conciense and knelede tho, 'this *aren* [Peres] Armes,

---

C.21.21 For alle derke deueles *aren* drad to heren hit
C.21.39 *Aren* frankeleynes, fre men Thorw follyng þat they toke
C.22.234 'And for thei *aren* pore, parauntur, for patrimonye hem faileth,
C.22.365 And for hem þat ȝe *aren* holde to al my lyf tyme

arn A 27

A. 1.21 *Arn* none nedful but þo & nempne hem I þenke,
A. 1.68 Þat tresten on his tresour betraid *arn* sonnest.'
A. 1.83 'Whanne alle tresours *arn* triȝed treuþe is þe beste.
A. 1.124 Whanne alle tresours *arn* triȝed treuþe is þe beste.
A. 1.129 'Þou dotide daffe,' quaþ heo, 'dulle *arn* þine wittes.
A. 1.164 Manye chapelleins *arn* chast ac charite is aweye;
A. 1.165 *Arn* none hardere þan [hy] whanne [hy] ben auauncid,
A. 1.174 For þise *arn* þe wordis writen in þe Euaungelie:
A. 1.181 Whan alle tresouris *arn* triȝede treuþe is þe beste.
A. 3.69 For þise *arn* men of þise molde þat most harm werchiþ
A. 3.218 'Þere *arn* to maner of medis, my lord, be ȝour leue.
A. 6.104 Ac þere *arn* seuene sistris þat [seruen] treuþe euere,
A. 7.49 For it *arn* þe deuelis disours I do þe to vndirstonde.
A. 7.69 Þei *arn* askapid good auntir, now god hem amende.'
A. 7.257 Þere *arn* mo liȝeris þan lechis, lord hem amende.
A. 7.259 'Be seint pernel,' quaþ peris, 'þise *arn* profitable wordis.
A. 9.70 *Arn* þre faire vertues, & ben not f[e]r to fynde.
A.10.31 Aungelis & alle þing *arn* at his wille,
A.10.192 Þe fruyt þat þei bringe forþ *arn* manye foule wordis.
A.11.37 Glotonye & grete oþis, þise *arn* games nowadayes.
A.11.159 Ȝet *arn* þere febicchis of Forellis of many manis wittes,
A.11.216 *Arn* more in his mynde þan þe memorie of his foundours.
A.11.237 Þat *arn* vncristene in þat caas may cristene an heþene,
A.11.244 Oure enemys and alle men þat *arn* nedy & pore,
A.11.291 And *arn* no[ne], forsoþe, souereynes in heuene
A.11.307 *Arn* none raþere yrauisshid fro þe riȝte beleue
A.11.308 Þanne *arn* þise [k]ete clerkis þat conne many bokis,

arn B 31

B.Pr.98 *Arn* doon vndeuoutliche; drede is at þe laste
B.Pr.164 And ouþer while þei *arn* elliswhere, as I here telle.
B. 1.85 'Whan alle tresors *arn* tried treuþe is þe beste;
B. 1.135 Whan alle tresors *arn* tried truþe is þe beste.
B. 1.190 Manye Chapeleyns *arn* chaste ac charite is aweye;
B. 5.619 And *arn* porters of þe Posternes þat to þe place longeþ.
B. 6.275 'By Seint [Pernele]', quod Piers, 'þise *arn* profitable wordes!
B. 7.16 *Arn* peres wiþ þe Apostles–þ[u]s pardon Piers sheweþ–
B. 8.39 The goodes of þis grounde *arn* like þe grete wawes,
B. 9.30 Aungeles and alle þyng *arn* at his wille
B. 9.171 The fruyt þat [þei] brynge forþ *arn* [manye] foule wordes;]
B. 9.195 [That] oþergenes ben geten for gedelynges *arn* holden,
B.10.51 Glotonye and grete oþes, þis[e *arn* games nowadaies].
B.10.354 That [*arn*] vncristene in þat caas may cristen an heþen,
B.10.463 *Arn* none raþer yrauysshed fro þe riȝte bileue
B.11.176 For Seint Iohan seide it, and soþe *arn* his wordes:
B.13.128 And [demeþ] þat dowel and dobet *arn* two Infinites,
B.13.429 Riȝt so flatereris and fooles *arn* þe fendes disciples
B.14.134 Hewen þat han hir hire afore *arn* eueremoore nedy,
B.15.131 The whiche *arn* preestes inparfite and prechours after siluer,
B.15.134 So harlotes and hores *arn* holpe wiþ swiche goodes.
B.15.486 Ac who beþ þat excuseþ hem þat [*arn*] persons and preestes,
B.15.561 And þo þat han Petres power *arn* apoisoned alle."
B.15.580 *Arn* ferme as in þe feiþ, goddes forbode ellis,
B.15.606 *Arn* folk of oon feiþ; þe fader god þei honouren.
B.17.26 'Youre wordes *arn* wonderfulle', quod I, 'which of yow is trewest
B.17.32 He kan noȝt siggen þe somme, and some *arn* in his lappe.
B.18.150 Now youre goode dayes *arn* doon as daniel prophecied;
B.19.12 Quod Conscience and kneled þo, 'þise *arn* Piers armes,
B.19.21 For alle derke deueles *arn* adrad to heren it,

arn C 1

C. 9.137 The whiche [*arn*] lunatyk loreles and lepares aboute

art A 8

A. 1.82 How I may sauen my soule, þat seint *art* yho[ld]en.'
A. 1.138 [Þer] þou *art* m[er]y at erthe, ȝif men bidde þe ȝedde.
A. 7.211 [Or with werk or with word þe while þou *art* here].
A. 9.63 'What *art* þou,' quaþ I þo, 'þat my name knowist?'
A. 9.65 'Wot ich?' quaþ I; 'who *art* þou?' 'þouȝt,' seide he þanne.
A. 9.67 'Art þou þouȝt, þo?' quod I; 'þou couþest me telle
A.11.5 'Wel *art* þou wys, wyt,' quaþ she, 'any wisdomis to telle

art B 17

B. 1.84 How I may saue my soule þat Seint *art* yholden.'
B. 3.338 Ac þow *art* lik a lady þat radde a lesson ones
B. 5.270 Thow *art* an vnkynde creature; I kan þee noȝt assoille
B. 5.503 That *art* oure fader and oure broþer, be merciable to vs,
B. 7.137 Thow *art* lettred a litel; who lerned þeȝ on boke?'
B. 8.72 'What *art* [þ]ow', quod I þo, 'þat my name knowest?'

B. 8.74 'Woot I?' [quod I; 'who *art* þow]?' 'þou3t', seide he þanne.
B. 9.185 Whiles þow *art* yong [and yeep] and þi wepene [yet] kene
B.11.18 And seide, 'þow *art* yong and yeep and hast yeres ynowe
B.11.374 'I haue wonder [in my wit], þat witty *art* holden,
B.13.204 Whan þow *art* wery [for]walked; wille me to counseille'.
B.18.188 'What, rauestow?' quod Rightwisnesse, 'or þow *art* right dronke?
B.18.364 That *art* doctour of deeþ drynk þat þow madest.
B.19.173 Thow *art* my lord, I bileue, god lord Iesu;
B.19.175 And now *art* lyuynge and lokynge and laste shalt euere."
B.19.408 Leue it wel [þow *art*] lost, boþe lif and soule.'
B.20.356 'Thow *art* welcome', quod Conscience; 'kanstow heele sike?

art C 19

C. 1.80 How y may saue my soule, þat saynt *art* yholde.'
C. 3.490 Thow *art* lyk a lady þat a lessoun radde
C. 5.33 Or thow *art* broke, so may be, in body or in membre
C. 6.294 Thow *art* an vnkynde creature; y can the nat assoile
C. 6.424 'Thow lord [þat] aloft *art* and alle lyues shope.
C. 7.143 That *art* furste oure fadur and of flesch oure broþer
C.10.70 'What *art* thow', quod y [þo], 'þat my name knowest?'
C.10.72 'Woet y?' quod y; 'who *art* thow?' 'thouhte,' sayde he thenne.
C.10.74 '*Art* thow thouht?' quod y tho; 'thow couthest me wisse
C.10.286 And whil þou *art* 3ong an[d] 3ep and thy wepene kene
C.11.177 And saide, 'þou *art* 3ong and 3ep and hast 3eres ynowe
C.12.215 "And *art* so loth to leue that lete shal thow nedes:
C.13.184 'Y haue wonder in my wit, so wys as thow *art* holden,
C.20.193 'Rauest thow?' quod rihtwisnesse, 'or thow *art* riht dronke!
C.20.402 That *art* doctour of deth drynke þat thow madest.
C.21.173 Thow *art* my lord, y bileue, god lord iesu;
C.21.175 And now *art* lyuynge and lokynge and laste shalt euere."
C.21.404 Vnblessed *art* thow, breware, but yf the god helpe.
C.22.356 'Thow *art* welcome,' quod Consience; 'can[st] thow hele syke?

artow B 7

B. 5.257 '*Artow* manlich among þi ne3ebores of þi mete and drynke?'
B. 8.76 '*Artow* þou3t?' quod I þoo; 'þow koudest me [telle]
B.10.5   'Wel *artow* wis, [wit, quod she], 'any wisdomes to telle
B.11.416 Ac for þyn entremetynge here *artow* forsake:
B.15.50 'Thanne *artow* inparfit', quod he, 'and oon of prides kny3tes.
B.18.317 What lord *artow*?' quod Lucifer; þe light soone seide
B.19.404 Vnblessed *artow*, Brewere, but if þee god helpe.

artow C 5

C.11.5   'Wel *artow* wyse,' quod she to wyt, 'suche wysdomes to shewe
C.13.224 Ac for thyn entremetynge her *artow* forsake:
C.16.212 'Thenne *artow* inparfit', quod he, 'and oen of pruydes knyhtes.
C.18.183 'Of whennes *artow*?' quod y, and hendeliche hym grette.
C.20.360 'What lord *artow*?' quod lucifer; a voys aloude saide:

be A 130

A.Pr.53 Cloþide hem in copis to *be* knowen from oþere;
A.Pr.76 His sel shulde not *be* sent to disseyue þe peple.
A.Pr.89 Þanne gete a mom of here mouþ til mony *be* shewid.
A. 1.40 And for þou shuldist *be* war I wisse þe þe beste.'
A. 1.53 And kynde wyt *be* wardeyn 3oure welþe to kepe,
A. 1.108 To *be* buxum at his bidding; he bad hem nou3t ellis.
A. 1.121 Mowe *be* sikur þat here soule shal wende into heuene,
A. 1.133 Þis I trowe *be* treuþe; who can teche þe betere,
A. 1.152 3e shuln *be* wei3e þerwiþ whanne 3e wende hennes.
A. 1.153 For þ[ei3 3e] *be* trewe of 3oure tunge & treweliche wynne,
A. 2.19 And so shulde [heo] not *be* for wrong was hire sire;
A. 2.48 To *be* fastnid wiþ fals þe fyn is arerid.
A. 2.51 And he[o] *be* bou[n] at his bidding his bidding to fulfille,
A. 2.59 To *be* present in pride for pouere [or for] riche,
A. 2.82 [And] er þis weddyng *be* wrou3t wo þe betide!
A. 2.101 And 3if þe iustice iugge hire to *be* ioyned with fals,
A. 2.102 3et *be* war of þe weddyng for witty is treuþe.
A. 2.117 Til mede *be* þi weddit wyf þoru3 wyt of vs alle,
A. 2.124 And alle *be* boun, beggeris & oþere,
A. 2.134 Þat somenours shulde *be* sadelit & serue hem ichone,
A. 2.156 I wolde *be* wroken of þise wrecchis þat werchen so ille,
A. 2.168 Er he *be* put on þe pillorie, for any preyour, I hote.
A. 3.26 And bidden hire *be* blyþe, 'for we ben þin owene
A. 3.40 And ek *be* þi baudekyn, & bere wel þin arnede
A. 3.45 For to *be* hire bedeman & hire baude aftir.
A. 3.49 Sikir shulde þi soule *be* heuene to haue'.
A. 3.56 *Be* war what þi ri3t hond werchiþ or deliþ,
A. 3.57 A[c] so preuyliche parte it þat pride *be* not sei3e,
A. 3.75 Ne bou3te none burgages, *be* 3e wel certayn.
A. 3.102 [But I *be* holly at 3our heste honge me ellysi].'
A. 3.108 For heo is fayn of þi Felasshipe, for to *be* þi make.'
A. 3.131 To *be* cursid in constorie heo countiþ not a risshe;
A. 3.138 She blissiþ þise bisshopis 3if þei *be* lewid;
A. 3.180 And dreddist to *be* ded for a dym cloud,
A. 3.188 Hadde I *be* march[al] of his men, *be* marie of heuene,
A. 3.190 He shulde haue *be* lord of þat lond in lengþe & in brede,
A. 3.199 Mede makiþ hym *be* louid & for a man holde.

A. 3.245 To *be* buxum & boun his bidding to fulfille.
A. 3.263 Samuel shal slen hym, & saul shal *be* blamid,
A. 3.264 And dauid shal *be* dyademid & daunten hem alle,
A. 3.266 Shal no more mede *be* maister on erþe,
A. 4.26 In cheker & in chauncerie, to *be* dischargid of þinges,
A. 4.76 And *be* borugh for his bale & b[ig]gen hym bote;
A. 4.80 Þanne bale *be* bet & bote neuere þe betere.'
A. 4.94 And ofte þe boldere *be* to bete myn hynen.
A. 4.99 Þat mede muste *be* meynpernour resoun þei besou3te.
A. 4.102 And pernelis purfile *be* put in hire hucche;
A. 4.103 Til childris cherisshing *be* chastisid with 3erdis,
A. 4.104 And harlotis holynesse *be* holde for an [heþyng];
A. 4.105 Til clerkis & kni3tes *be* curteis of here mouþes,
A. 4.109 Til seint Iame *be* sou3t þere I shal assigne,
A. 4.115 But if he *be* marchaunt, oþer his man, oþer messang[er] with lettres,
A. 4.123 *Be* vnpunisshit at my power for peril of my soule,
A. 4.127 And bad Nullum [bonum *be*] irremuneratum.
A. 4.140 But he *be* cokewald ycald, kitte of my nose.'
A. 4.150 3if it *be* þat buxumnesse be at myn assent.'
A. 4.150 3if it *be* þat buxumnesse be at myn assent.'
A. 4.152 *Be* my counseil ycome of clerkes and Erlis.
A. 4.156 So consience *be* of 3our counseil, kepe I no betere.'
A. 5.39 And *be* steward of 3oure stede til 3e be stewid betere.
A. 5.39 And *be* steward of 3oure stede til 3e be stewid betere.
A. 5.51 And suffre to *be* misseid, & so dide I neuere.
A. 5.122 It hadde *be* vnsold þis seue 3er, so me god helpe.
A. 5.151 And siþen I wile *be* shriuen & synne no more.'
A. 5.171 And bed bette *be* bocher þe on his side.
A. 5.192 And wisshide it hadde *be* wexid wiþ a wysp of firsen.
A. 5.222 'Shal no sonneday *be* þis seue 3er, but seknesse it make,
A. 6.53 And so bo[wiþ] forþ *be* a [brok], *be* buxum of speche,
A. 6.57 So shalt þou se swere nou3t but it *be* for nede,
A. 6.62 Loke þou breke no bowis þere but it *be* þin owene
A. 6.70 And þanne shalt þou [se] sey soþ, so it *be* to done;
A. 6.95 Ac *be* war þanne of wraþþe, þat wykkide shrewe,
A. 6.112 But 3if 3e *be* sibbe to summe of þis seuene
A. 6.114 To gete ingang at any gate but grace *be* more.'
A. 7.12 But 3if it *be* holy day oþer holy euen;
A. 7.45 And þat þou *be* trewe of [þi] tunge, & talis þou hate,
A. 7.46 But it *be* of wysdom or of wyt þi werkmen to chaste,
A. 7.95 My plou3pote shal *be* my pyk & putte at þe rotis,
A. 7.116 'We haue none [lymes] to laboure wiþ, lord, ygracid *be* 3e;
A. 7.121 '3ef it *be* soþ,' quaþ peris, 'þat 3e seyn, I shal it sone aspie.
A. 7.130 But he *be* blynd, or brokesshankid, or beddrede ligge:
A. 7.170 Þei hadde *be* ded þis day & doluen al warm.
A. 7.190 For I wot wel, *be* þou ywent, hy wile werche ille;
A. 7.230 And þat he weniþ wel to haue I wile it *be* hym bereuid".
A. 7.255 And *be* fayn be my feiþ his fesik to leten,
A. 7.261 Wende now whanne þi wille is, þat wel *be* þou euere.'
A. 7.294 But 3if it *be* fressh flessh oþer fissh yfried,
A. 7.296 But he *be* hei3liche hirid ellis wile he chide,
A. 7.305 Or fyue 3er *be* fulfild such famyn shal arise;
A. 8.32 [Pore] wydewis þat wiln not *be* wyues aftir,
A. 8.68 But 3if þe suggestioun *be* soþ þat [shapiþ hem to] begge.
A. 8.105 Ne aboute my [belyue] so besy *be* namore.
A. 8.123 Quoniam literaturam non cognoui, þat mi3te *be* þi teme.'
A. 8.133 For þat I sai3 slepyng 3if it so *be* mi3te.
A. 8.140 Among l[ower]e lordis þi londis shuln *be* departid'.
A. 8.167 *Be* þou neuere þe baldere to breke þe ten hestis;
A. 8.176 Þei3 þou *be* founde in þe fraternite among þe foure ordris,
A. 8.180 And marie his moder *be* mene betwene,
A. 9.5   And what man he mi3te *be* of many man I askide.
A. 9.35 Þe goodis of þis ground *be* lik þe grete wawes,
A. 9.98 Corounid on to *be* kyng & *be* h[ere] counseil werchen,
A. 9.114 But as I bad þou3t bo þe mene betwene,
A.10.60 Þei helde ale in here hed til Inwyt *be* drenchit,
A.10.66 Ac þe fadir & þe Frendis for fauntis shuln *be* blamid
A.10.100 And *be* glad of þe grace þat god haþ Isent þe.
A.10.113 3if þou *be* man maried, monk, oþer chanoun,
A.10.115 To *be* blissid for þi beryng, [3]e, b[e]ggere þei3 þou were.
A.10.117 *Be* paied wiþ þe porcioun, pore oþer riche,
A.10.134 Þei *be* þe riccheste of reaumes & þe rote of dowel.
A.10.169 Til fourty dayes *be* fulfild, þat flood haue ywasshe
A.10.183 For coueitise of catel vnkyndely *be* maried.
A.10.189 Þat neuere shal bere [barne] but it *be* in armes.
A.10.196 But 3if þei boþe *be* forsworn þat bacoun þei tyne.
A.10.197 Forþi I counseile alle cristene coueite not *be* weddit
A.10.203 Shulde no bedbourd *be*; but þei were boþe clene
A.11.7   And blamide hym [and bannide hym] & bad hym *be* stille–
A.11.18 But it *be* cardit wiþ coueitise as cloþeris don here wolle,
A.11.61 For now is iche boy bold, & he *be* riche,
A.11.62 To tellen of þe trinite to *be* holden a sire,
A.11.85 –Al was as he wolde; lord yworsshipid *be* þou,

A.11.91 I dar *be* his bolde boruȝ do bet wile he neuere,
A.11.123 Þat iche wiȝt *be* in wille his wyt þe to shewen;
A.11.236 Mowe *be* sauid so, & so is oure beleue.
A.11.247 We *be* holde heiȝly to herie & honoure,
A.11.250 Þat is, iche cristene [creature] *be* kynde to oþer,
A.12.39 To *be* hure man ȝif I most for eueremore after,
A.12.62 'Al hayl,' quod on þo, and I answered, 'welcome, & with whom *be* ȝe?'
A.12.95 Þat þi play *be* plentevous in paradys with aungelys.
A.12.96 Þou shalt *be* lauȝth into lyȝth with loking of an eye
A.12.98 And *be* prest to preyeres and profitable werkes.'

be B 389

B.Pr.79 His seel sholde noȝt *be* sent to deceyue þe peple.
B.Pr.127 And for þi riȝtful rulyng *be* rewarded in heuene'.
B.Pr.157 We myȝte *be* lordes o lofte and lyuen at oure ese.'
B.Pr.174 And if hym wraþeþ *be* war and his wey shonye.'
B.Pr.188 And *be* we neuere [so] bolde þe belle hym to shewe.
B.Pr.203 Shal neuere þe cat ne þe kiton by my counseil *be* greued,
B.Pr.216 Than gete a mom of hire mouþ til moneie *be* shewed.
B.1.55 And kynde wit *be* wardeyn youre welþe to kepe
B.1.110 To *be* buxom at his biddyng, he bad hem nouȝt ellis.
B.1.120 And alle þat hoped it myȝte so, noon heuene myȝte hem holde,
B.1.132 Mowe *be* siker þat hire soul[e] sh[a]l wende to heuene
B.1.145 This I trowe *be* truþe; who kan teche þee bettre,
B.1.149 May no synne *be* on hym seene þat vseþ þat spice,
B.1.176 Thouȝ ye *be* myȝt[y] to mote beeþ meke [of] youre werkes,
B.1.179 For þouȝ ye *be* trewe of youre tonge and treweliche wynne,
B.2.32 And what man *be* merciful and leelly me loue
B.2.33 Shal al my lord and I his leef in þe heiȝe heuene.
B.2.48 And lakke hem noȝt but lat hem worþe til leaute *be* Iustice
B.2.66 And as a Brocour brouȝte hire to *be* wiþ fals enioyned.
B.2.80 To *be* Princes in pride and pouerte to despise,
B.2.101 For he leueþ *be* lost, þis is [his] laste ende.
B.2.103 A dwellynge wiþ þe deuel and dampned *be* for euere
B.2.118 And er þis weddynge *be* wroȝt wo þee bitide!
B.2.137 And [if þe] Iustic[e] Iugg[e] hire to *be* Ioyned [wiþ] Fals
B.2.138 Yet *be* war of [þe] weddynge; for witty is truþe,
B.2.153 Til Mede *be* þi wedded wif þoruȝ wi[t] of vs alle,
B.2.160 And alle *be* bown, beggers and oþere,
B.2.170 That Somonours sholde *be* Sadeled and serven hem echone,
B.2.195 I wolde *be* wroken of þo wrecches þat wercheþ so ille,
B.2.207 Er he *be* put on þe Pillory for any preyere I hote.'_
B.3.18 To *be* wedded at þi wille and wher þee leef likeþ
B.3.27 And beden hire *be* bliþe: 'for we beþ þyne owene
B.3.41 And [ek] *be* þi [baudekyn] and bere wel þ[yn erende]
B.3.50 Syker sholde þi soule *be* heuene to haue'.
B.3.52 For to *be* youre frend, frere, and faile yow neuere.
B.3.66 An auenture pride *be* peynted þere and pomp of þe world;
B.3.86 Ne bouȝte none burgages, *be* ye [wel] certeyne.
B.3.113 But I *be* holly at youre heste hange me [ellis].'
B.3.119 For she is fayn of þi felaweshipe, for to *be* þi make.'
B.3.142 To *be* corsed in Consistorie she counteþ noȝt a [risshe];
B.3.149 She blesseþ þise Bisshopes [if] þei *be* lewed;
B.3.193 And dreddest to *be* ded for a dym cloude,
B.3.203 He sholde haue *be* lord of þat lond in lengþe and in brede,
B.3.265 *Be* buxom at his biddynge his wil to fulfille.
B.3.270 Bren it; bere it noȝt awey *be* it neuer so riche;
B.3.287 Samuel shal sleen hym and Saul shal *be* blamed
B.3.288 And Dauid shal *be* diademed and daunten hem alle,
B.3.290 Shal na moore Mede *be* maister [on erþe],
B.3.303 That Moyses or Messie *be* come into [myddel]erþe,
B.3.307 Shal *be* demed to þe deeþ but if he do it smyþye
B.3.321 Al shal *be* but oon court, and oon [burn] *be* Iustice,
B.3.321 Al shal be but oon court, and oon [burn] *be* Iustice,
B.3.323 Batailles shul none *be*, ne no man bere wepene,
B.3.324 And what smyth þat any smyþeþ *be* smyte þerwiþ to deþe;
B.3.337 'I leue wel, lady', quod Conscience, 'þat þi latyn *be* trewe.
B.4.23 For he wol make wehee twies er [we] *be* þere.'
B.4.89 And *be* borȝ for his bale and buggen hym boote,
B.4.93 Than bale *be* ybet and boote neuer þe bettre.'
B.4.107 And [ofte] þe boldere *be* to bete myne hewen.
B.4.112 That Mede moste *be* maynpernour Reson þei bisouȝte.
B.4.116 Til pernelles purfill *be* put in hire hucche,
B.4.117 And childrene cherissynge *be* chast[ised] wiþ yerdes,
B.4.118 And harlottes holynesse *be* holden for an [heþyng];
B.4.119 Til clerkene coueitise *be* to cloþe þe pouere and fede,
B.4.122 And til prechours prechynge *be* preued on hemselue;
B.4.123 Til þe kynges counseil *be* þe commune profit;
B.4.126 And til Seint Iames *be* souȝt þere I shal assigne,
B.4.132 But it *be* Marchaunt or his man or Messager wiþ lettres,
B.4.144 And bad Nullum bonum *be* irremuneratum.
B.4.164 But he *be* knowe for a Cokewold kut of my nose.'
B.4.180 I wole haue leaute in lawe, and lete *be* al youre ianglyng;

B.4.181 And as moost folk witnesseþ wel wrong shal *be* demed.'
B.4.187 If ye bidden buxomnesse *be* of myn assent.'
B.4.189 [*Be*] my counseil co[men] of clerkes and of Erles.
B.4.193 So Conscience *be* of [y]oure counseil [kepe I] no bettre.'
B.5.35 'Late no wynnyng [forwanye hem] while þei *be* yonge,
B.5.47 And *be* Stywar[d] of youre sted[e] til ye *be* [stewed] bettre'.
B.5.47 And *be* Stywar[d] of youre sted[e] til ye *be* [stewed] bettre'.
B.5.52 'And ye þat han lawes to [loke], lat truþe *be* youre coueitise
B.5.68 And suffre to *be* mysseyd, and so dide I neuere.
B.5.91 I wolde *be* gladder, by god! þat Gybbe hadde meschaunce
B.5.97 And [doon] his frendes *be* his foon þoruȝ my false tonge.
B.5.130 Amonges Burgeises haue I *be*, [bigg]yng at Londoun,
B.5.131 And gart bakbityng *be* a brocour to blame mennes ware.
B.5.150 Til þei *be* boþe beggers and by my spiritualte libben,
B.5.155 I haue *be* cook in hir kichene and þe Couent serued
B.5.169 Among Monkes I myȝte *be* ac many tyme I shonye
B.5.234 Thow haddest *be* bettre worþi ben hanged þerfore.'
B.5.264 And þat was wonne wiþ wrong wiþ wikked men *be* despended.
B.5.291 Bisette it hymself as best [*be*] for þi soule.
B.5.301 And siþen I wole *be* shryuen and synne na moore.'
B.5.366 Shryue þee and *be* shamed þerof and shewe it with þi mouþe.'
B.5.373 And yspilt þat myȝte *be* spared and spended on som hungry;
B.5.378 'This shewynge shrift', quod Repentaunce, 'shal *be* meryt to þe.'
B.5.386 'I moste sitte [to *be* shryuen] or ellis sholde I nappe;
B.5.400 And if I bidde any bedes, but if it *be* in wraþe,
B.5.411 Til matyns and masse *be* do, and þanne [moste] to þe freres;
B.5.415 I haue *be* preest and person passynge þritty wynter,
B.5.422 If I bigge and borwe auȝt, but if it *be* ytailed,
B.5.440 And euere siþþe *be* beggere [by cause of] my sleuþe:
B.5.450 'Shal no Sonday *be* þis seuen yer, but siknesse it [make],
B.5.502 Bidde and biseche, if it *be* þi wille,
B.5.503 That art oure fader and oure broþer, *be* merciable to vs,
B.5.570 So shaltow se swere-noȝt-but-it-*be*-for-nede-
B.5.575 Loke [þow] breke no bowes þere but if it *be* [þyn] owene.
B.5.583 Thanne [shalt þow] see seye-sooþ-so-it-*be*-to-doone-
B.5.609 A[c] *be* war þanne of Wraþe, þat wikked sherewe,
B.5.627 But if ye *be* sibbe to some of þise seuene
B.5.629 To geten ing[o]ng at any gate but grace *be* þe moore.'
B.5.639 'Bi seint Poul!' quod a pardoner, 'paraventure I *be* noȝt knowe þere;
B.6.39 And þouȝ [þow] mowe amercy hem lat mercy *be* taxour
B.6.46 Thouȝ he *be* þyn vnderlyng here wel may happe in heuene
B.6.50 And þat þow *be* trewe of þi tonge and tales þow hatie
B.6.51 But if [it *be*] of wisdom or of wit þi werkmen to chaste;
B.6.103 My plow[pote] shal *be* my pi[k] and [putte at] þe rotes,
B.6.114 Sholde *be* hired þerafter whan heruest tyme come.
B.6.124 'We haue no lymes to laboure with; lord, ygraced *be* [y]e!
B.6.129 'If it *be* sooþ', quod Piers, 'þat ye seyn, I shal it soone aspie.
B.6.136 But if he *be* blynd or brokelegged or bolted wiþ Irens,
B.6.180 They hadde *be* [dede and] doluen, ne deme þow noon ooþer.
B.6.203 'Of beggeris and bidderis what best *be* to doone.
B.6.204 For I woot wel, *be* þow went þei wol werche ille;
B.6.205 Meschief it makeþ þei *be* so meke nouþe,
B.6.227 And if þow wilt *be* gracious to god do as þe gospel techeþ
B.6.271 And *be* fayn, by my feiþ, his Phisik to lete,
B.6.277 Wend now whan [þi wil is], þat wel *be* þow euere.'\
B.6.310 But if it *be* fressh flessh ouþer fissh [y]fryed,
B.6.312 But he *be* heiȝliche hyred ellis wole he chide,
B.6.324 Er fyue [yer] *be* fulfilled swich famyn shal aryse.
B.6.329 Thanne shal deeþ wiþdrawe and derþe *be* Iustice,
B.7.12 Wiþ Patriarkes and prophetes in paradis to *be* felawe.
B.7.66 But if þe suggestion *be* sooþ þat shapeþ hem to begge,
B.7.71 Anoþer that were moore nedy; so þe nedieste sholde *be* holpe.
B.7.88 Lat vsage *be* youre solas of seintes lyues redyng;
B.7.123 Ne aboute my [bilyue] so bisy *be* na moore;
B.7.150 Of þat I seiȝ slepynge, if it so *be* myȝte,
B.7.162 Amonges lower lordes þi lond shal *be* departed.'
B.7.189 *Be* [þow] neuer þe bolder to breke þe x hestes,
B.7.198 Theiȝ [þow] *be* founde in þe fraternite [among] þe foure ordres
B.7.202 And Marie his moder *be* meene bitwene,
B.8.5 And what man he myȝte *be* of many man I asked.
B.8.14 For [ye] *be* men of þis moolde þat moost wide walken,
B.8.108 Crouned oon to *be* kyng, [and by hir counseil werchen],
B.8.124 But as I bad þoȝt þoo *be* mene bitwene,
B.8.130 And wheiþer he *be* man or [no man] þis man wolde aspie,
B.9.15 That he bit moot *be* do; he [boldeþ] hem alle;
B.9.86 Allas þat a cristene creature shal *be* vnkynde til anoþer!
B.9.89 Whi [ne wol] we cristene of cristes good *be* as kynde?
B.9.92 Bisshopes shul be blamed for beggeres sake.
B.9.128 "Thyn issue in þyn issue, I wol þat þei *be* wedded,
B.9.138 Til fourty daies *be* fulfild, þat flood haue ywasshen
B.9.150 Ac I fynde, if þe fader *be* fals and a sherewe,
B.9.152 Impe on an Ellere, and if þyn appul *be* swete
B.9.154 That bryngeþ forþ any barn but if he *be* þe same

B. 9.168 That neuere shal barn bere but it *be* in armes.
B. 9.175 But þei boþe *be* forswore þat bacon þei tyne.
B. 9.176 Forþi I counseille alle cristene coueite noȝt *be* wedded
B. 9.180 For no londes, but for loue, leue ye *be* wedded
B. 9.190 Sholde no [bedbourde] *be*; but þei boþe were clene
B.10.7   And blamed hym and banned hym and bad hym *be* stille–
B.10.18 But it *be* carded wiþ coueitise as cloþeres [don] hir wolle.
B.10.132 Al was as [he] wold[e]–lord, yworshiped *be* þ[ow],
B.10.171 That ech wight *be* in wille his wit þee to shewe.
B.10.202 [And] biddeþ vs *be* as breþeren and [blissen] oure enemys
B.10.239 Wiþ alle þe articles of þe feiþ þat falleþ to *be* knowe.
B.10.261 Swich as þow semest in siȝte *be* in assay yfounde:
B.10.262 And lat no body *be* by þi beryng bigiled
B.10.263 But *be* swich in þi soule as þow semest wiþoute:
B.10.264 Thanne is dobest to *be* boold to blame þe gilty,
B.10.266 Ac blame þow neuere body and þow *be* blameworþy:
B.10.277 For goddes word wolde noȝt *be* lost, for þat wercheþ euere;
B.10.295 And *be* prester at youre preiere þan for a pound of nobles,
B.10.297 [Amonges riȝtful religious þis rule sholde *be* holde.
B.10.305 For if heuene *be* on þis erþe, and ese to any soule,
B.10.319 In many places þer þei [persons ben, þe þei purely] at ese,
B.10.351 That is baptiȝed beþ saaf, *be* he riche or pouere.'
B.10.353 Mowen *be* saued so, and [so] is oure bileue;
B.10.363 And þus bilongeþ to louye þat leueþ [to] *be* saued.
B.10.366 And oure bakkes þat moþeeten *be* and seen beggeris go naked,
B.10.368 For euery cristene creature sholde *be* kynde til ooþer,
B.10.396 Thouȝ hir goost *be* vngracious god for to plese.
B.10.436 That Salomon seiþ I trowe *be* sooþ and certein of vs alle:
B.10.441 And allowed as he lyued so; for by luþere men knoweþ þe goode.
B.11.23 Til þow *be* a lord and haue lond leten þee I nelle
B.11.39 If truþe wol witnesse it *be* wel do Fortune to folwe
B.11.58 And preien for þee pol by pol if þow *be* pecuniosus.'
B.11.65 *Be* buried at hire hous but at my parisshe chirche;
B.11.67 [At kirke] þere a man were cristned by kynde he sholde *be* buryed.
B.11.82 Ac [a] barn wiþouten bapteme may noȝt *be* saued:
B.11.103 Ac *be* [þow] neueremoore þe firste [þe] defaute to blame;
B.11.104 Thouȝ þow se yuel seye it noȝt first; *be* sory it nere amended.
B.11.164 Yblissed be truþe þat so brak helle yates
B.11.174 For no cause to cacche siluer þerby, ne to *be* called a maister,
B.11.212 And *be* we noȝt vnkynde of oure catel, ne of oure konnyng neiþer,
B.11.241 That we sholde *be* lowe and loueliche, [and lele ech man to oþer],
B.11.259 [Al]þouȝ it *be* sour to suffre, þe[r] comeþ swete [after].
B.11.261 And after þat bitter bark, *be* þe shelle aweye,
B.11.276 Whoso wole *be* pure parfit moot possession forsake
B.11.304 If fals latyn *be* in þat lettre þe lawe it impugneþ,
B.11.312 The bisshop shal *be* blamed bifore god, as I leue,
B.11.388 And er þow lakke my lif loke [þyn] *be* to preise.
B.11.391 Ech a lif wolde *be* laklees, leue þow noon oþer.
B.11.396 For *be* a man fair or foul it falleþ noȝt to lakke
B.12.33 That is, if þow *be* man maryed þi make þow louye
B.12.35 Riȝt so if þow *be* Religious ren þow neuere ferþer
B.12.38 And if þow *be* maiden to marye and myȝt wel continue,
B.12.58 And Richesse riȝt so but if þe roote *be* trewe.
B.12.90 Riȝt so goddes body, breþeren, but it *be* worþili taken,
B.12.108 Come for al his kynde wit to cristendom and *be* saued;
B.12.123 Take we hir wordes at worþ, for hir witnesse *be* trewe,
B.12.172 Out of synne and *be* saaf, þouȝ he synne ofte,
B.12.174 For if þe clerk ne konnynge he knoweþ what is synne,
B.12.191 Ther lewed þeues ben lolled vp; loke how þei *be* saued!
B.12.212 For he is in þe loweste of heuene, if oure bileue *be* trewe,
B.12.220 Why some *be* alouȝ & some aloft, þi likyng it were;
B.12.251 To alle hem þat it holdeþ til hir tail *be* chastised.
B.12.255 His ledene is in oure lordes ere lik a pies chiteryng:
B.12.256 And whan his caroyne shal come in caue to *be* buryed
B.12.270 And wheiþer he *be* saaf or noȝt saaf, þe soþe woot no clergie,
B.12.273 To wissen vs [wyes] þerwiþ þat wiss[h]en to *be* saued–
B.12.288 But lyueþ as his lawe techeþ and leueþ þer *be* no bettre,
B.13.35 Pacience and I [prestly] were put to *be* [mettes],
B.13.71 Holi writ bit men *be* war–I wol noȝt write it here
B.13.72 In englissh on auenture it sholde *be* reherced to ofte,
B.13.86 Pacience parceyued what I þouȝte and [preynte] on me to *be* stille
B.13.96 And but [þe] first [leef] *be* lesyng leue me neuere after.
B.13.98 Of dowel and dobet, and if do[best] *be* any penaunce.'
B.13.106 'By þis day, sire doctour', quod I, 'þanne [in dowel *be* ye noȝt]!
B.13.110 But cheeste þer charite sholde be, and yonge children dorste pleyne,
B.13.110 But cheeste *be* þer charite sholde be, and yonge children dorste pleyne,
B.13.113 And preynte vpon pacience to preie me *be* stille,
B.13.114 And seide hymself, 'sire doctour, and it *be* youre wille,
B.13.134 Pacience haþ *be* in many place, and paraunter [knoweþ]
B.13.157 Vndo it; lat þis doctour deme if dowel *be* þerInne.
B.13.182 And *be* Pilgrym wiþ pacience til I haue preued moore.'

B.13.206 If Pacience *be* oure partyng felawe and pryue with vs boþe
B.13.250 And þanne wolde I *be* prest to þe peple paast for to make,
B.13.259 Til pride *be* pureliche fordo, and [þat] þoruȝ payn defaute.
B.13.262 So er my wafres *be* ywroȝt muche wo I þolye.
B.13.267 And werkmen were agast a lite; þis wole *be* þouȝt longe:
B.13.289 As best for his body *be* to haue a [bold] name;
B.13.406 That into wanhope he [worþ] and wende nauȝt to *be* saued.
B.13.452 Thise solaceþ *be* soule til hymself *be* falle
B.14.2   Thouȝ he *be* soiled and selde clene: I slepe þerInne o nyȝtes;
B.14.5   It haþ *be* laued in lente and out of lente boþe
B.14.27 Ne no Mynstrall *be* moore worþ amonges pouere and riche
B.14.30 And flour to fede folk wiþ as best *be* for þe soule;
B.14.35 'Whoso leueþ yow, by oure lord! I leue noȝt he *be* blessed.'
B.14.38 And seide, 'lo! here liflode ynogh, if oure bileue *be* trewe.
B.14.55 By so þat þow *be* sobre of siȝte and of tonge,
B.14.59 Or þoruȝ hunger or þoruȝ hete, at his wille *be* it;
B.14.71 And if men lyuede as mesure wolde sholde neuere moore *be* defaute
B.14.75 [Ac] mesure is [so] muche worþ it may noȝt *be* to deere.
B.14.84 Which dryueþ awey dedly synne and dooþ it to *be* venial.
B.14.90 Ac shrift of mouþ moore worþi is if man *be* y[n]liche contrit,
B.14.91 For shrift of mouþe sleeþ synne *be* it neuer so dedly-
B.14.102 'Wheiþer paciente pouerte', quod Haukyn, '*be* moore plesaunt to oure d[riȝte]
B.14.144 It may noȝt *be*, ye riche men, or Mathew on god lyeþ:
B.14.185 And *be* clene þoruȝ þat cristnyng of alle kynnes synne.
B.14.192 Ac þe parchemyn of þis patente of pouerte *be* moste,
B.14.195 And principalliche of al[l]e peple but þei *be* poore of herte.
B.14.200 In fenestres at þe freres–if fals *be* þe foundement.
B.14.201 Forþi cristene sholde *be* in commune riche, noon coueitous for hymselue.
B.14.232 And þouȝ his glotonye *be* to good ale he goþ to cold beddyng
B.14.248 And wheiþer *be* liȝter to breke? lasse boost [it] makeþ
B.14.258 And wheiþer he *be* or *be* noȝt, he bereþ þe signe of pouerte
B.14.258 And wheiþer he be or *be* noȝt, he bereþ þe signe of pouerte
B.14.272 And put hym to *be* pacient and pouerte weddeþ,
B.14.290 Ne to *be* Mair aboue men ne Mynystre vnder kynges;
B.14.324 I ne hadde *be* deed and doluen for dowelis sake!
B.15.102 Shal neuere flour ne fruyt [wexe] ne fair leef *be* grene.
B.15.104 And *be* kynde as bifel for clerkes and curteise of cristes goodes,
B.15.125 Ac a Porthors þat sholde *be* his Plow, Placebo to sigge–
B.15.145 Thus goon hire goodes, *be* þe goost faren.
B.15.236 Ac if coueitise *be* of þe counseil he wol noȝt come þerInne.
B.15.309 And þanne wolde lordes and ladies *be* looþ to agulte,
B.15.377 Go now to any degree, and but if gile *be* maister,
B.15.390 And so may Sarȝens *be* saued, Scribes and [Grekes].
B.15.392 And for hir lyuynge þat lewed men *be* þe loþer god agulten.
B.15.424 Grace sholde growe and *be* grene þoruȝ hir goode lyuynge,
B.15.436 And *be* gide and go bifore as a good Banyer,
B.15.442 That goddes salt sholde *be* to saue mannes soule.
B.15.453 Til it *be* fulled vnder foot or in fullyng stokkes,
B.15.457 Til it *be* cristned in cristes name and confermed of þe bisshop
B.15.489 They wol *be* wrooþ for I write þus, ac to witnesse I take
B.15.496 To *be* pastours and preche þe passion of Iesus,
B.15.514 Men myȝte noȝt *be* saued but þoruȝ mercy and grace,
B.15.565 If possession *be* poison and inparfite hem make
B.15.575 That no man sholde *be* bisshop but if he hadde boþe
B.15.602 And þat his loore *be* lesynges, and lakken it alle,
B.15.603 And hopen þat he *be* to come þat shal hem releue;
B.16.71 Maidenhode, Aungeles peeris, and [erst] wole *be* ripe
B.16.94 That Piers fruyt floured and felle to *be* rype.
B.16.152 And kiste hym to *be* caught þerby and kulled of þe Iewes.
B.16.156 Thow shalt *be* myrour to many men to deceyue,
B.16.158 Thouȝ I bi treson *be* take [to] youre [iewene] wille
B.16.202 And þat it may *be* so and sooþ [sheweþ it manhode]:
B.16.217 Na moore myȝte god *be* man but if he moder hadde.
B.16.263 No no buyrn *be* oure borgh, ne brynge vs fram his daunger–
B.17.95 Neiþer Feiþ ne fyn hope, so festred *be* hise woundes,
B.17.97 And [he *be*] baþed in þat blood, baptised as it were,
B.17.115 And þanne shal Feiþ *be* forster here and in þis Fryth walke,
B.17.118 And Hope þe Hostile[r] shal *be* þer [an helyng þe man lith];
B.17.119 And alle þat feble and feynte *be*, þat Feiþ may noȝt teche,
B.17.236 Wol brennen and blasen, *be* þei togideres,
B.17.254 *Be* vnkynde to þyn euenecristene and al þat þow kanst bidde,
B.17.257 And Indulgences ynowe, and *be* ingratus to þi kynde,
B.17.281 For euery manere good [man may] *be* likned
B.17.292 "Vengeaunce, vengeaunce! forȝyue *be* it neuere
B.17.302 And myldeliche his mercy aske; myghte I noȝt *be* saued?'
B.17.306 Any creature [*be*] coupable afore a kynges Iustice
B.17.307 *Be* raunsoned for his repentaunce þer alle reson hym dampneþ.
B.17.323 That oon is a wikkede wif þat wol noȝt *be* chastised;
B.17.325 And if his hous *be* vnhiled and reyne on his bedde
B.17.330 Til he *be* blereighed or blynd and [þe borre] in þe þrote,
B.17.334 The wif is oure wikked flessh þat wol noȝt *be* chastised

B.18.13 As is þe kynde of a knyght þat comeþ to be dubbed,
B.18.24 That crist be noȝt [y]knowe here for consummatus deus
B.18.54 And [seide], 'if þat þow sotil be [biselue] now [þow help].
B.18.55 If þow be crist and kynges sone com down of þe roode:
B.18.70 Wher he be deed or noȝt deed doun er he be taken.'
B.18.70 Wher he be deed or noȝt deed doun er he be taken.'
B.18.101 For be þis derknesse ydo deeþ worþ [yvenquisshed];
B.18.106 But [as] barayne be and [by] vsurie [libben],
B.18.132 And þat my tale be trewe I take god to witnesse.
B.18.136 In menynge þat man shal fro merknesse be drawe
B.18.151 'Thoruȝ experience', quod [heo], 'I hope þei shul be saued;
B.18.156 Til he be deed and do þerto; þe yuel he destruyeþ,
B.18.185 To be mannes meynpernour for eueremoore after.
B.18.200 That hir peyne be perpetuel and no preiere hem helpe.
B.18.214 And suffrede to be sold to se þe sorwe of deying,
B.18.255 And I, book, wole be brent but Iesus rise to lyue
B.18.260 And bileue on a newe lawe be lost, lif and soule.'
B.18.293 For god wol noȝt be bigiled', quod Gobelyn, 'ne byiaped.
B.18.310 For vs were bettre noȝt be þan biden his sighte.
B.18.339 That gilours be bigiled and þat is good reson:
B.18.374 And be at my biddyng wherso [best] me likeþ.
B.18.375 A[c] to be merciable to man þanne my kynde [it] askeþ
B.18.378 Shul noȝt be dampned to þe deeþ þat [dureþ] wiþouten ende:
B.18.388 Be it any þyng abouȝt, þe boldnesse of hir synnes,
B.18.390 And þouȝ holy writ wole þat I be wroke of hem þat diden ille–
B.18.391 They shul be clensed clerliche and [keuered] of hir synnes
B.18.393 And my mercy shal be shewed to manye of my [halue]breþeren,
B.19.3   To here holly þe masse and to be housled after.
B.19.27 That knyght, kyng, conquerour may be o persone.
B.19.28 To be called a knyght is fair for men shul knele to hym.
B.19.29 To be called a kyng is fairer for he may knyghtes make.
B.19.30 Ac to be conquerour called, þat comeþ of special grace,
B.19.62 He may [be wel] called conquerour, and þat is crist to mene.
B.19.138 To be kaiser or kyng of þe kyngdom of Iuda.
B.19.162 For þat womm[a]n witeþ may noȝt wel be counseille.
B.19.178 Blessed mote þow be, and be shalt for euere.
B.19.178 Blessed mote þow be, and be shalt for euere.
B.19.179 And blessed mote þei be, in body and in soule,
B.19.188 Thus haþ Piers power, b[e] his pardon paied,
B.19.222 Shullen come and be curatours ouer kynges and Erles;
B.19.223 And Pride shal be Pope, Prynce of holy chirche,
B.19.243 Boþe of wele and of wo [and be ware bifore],
B.19.250 And alle he lered to be lele, and ech a craft loue ooþer,
B.19.251 [Ne no boost ne] debat [be] among hem [alle].
B.19.252 'Thouȝ some be clenner þan some, ye se wel', quod Grace,
B.19.255 And who þat moost maistries kan be myldest of berynge.
B.19.298 And he þat ete of þat seed sholde be [euene] trewe
B.19.347 Shal be coloured so queyntely and couered vnder [oure] Sophistrie
B.19.382 The lord of lust shal be letted at þis lente, I hope.
B.19.396 'Ye? baw!' quod a Brewere, 'I wol noȝt be ruled,
B.19.407 But Conscience [be þi] comune[s] and Cardinale vertues
B.19.437 [So blessed be Piers þe Plowman þat peyneþ hym to tilye],
B.19.440 And worshiped be he wroȝte al, boþe good and wikke,
B.19.441 And suffreþ þat synfulle be [til som tyme þat þei repente].
B.19.443 And cleymeþ bifore þe kyng to be kepere ouer cristene,
B.19.475 So I may boldely be housled for I borwe neuere,
B.20.38 [Philosophres] forsoke wele for þei wolde be nedy
B.20.39 And woneden [wel elengely] and wolde noȝt be riche.
B.20.48 Forþi be noȝt abasshed to bide and to be nedy
B.20.48 Forþi be noȝt abasshed to bide and to be nedy
B.20.108 Leue pride pryuely and be parfite cristene.
B.20.185 So harde he yede ouer myn heed it wole be sene euere.
B.20.188 Haddestow be hende', quod I, 'þow woldest haue asked leeue.'
B.20.203 Awreke me if youre wille be for I wolde ben hennes.'
B.20.204 'If þow wolt be wroken wend into vnitee
B.20.241 Lat hem be as beggeris or lyue by Aungeles foode.'
B.20.244 And seide, 'sires, sooþly welcome be ye alle
B.20.248 And I wol be youre boruȝ: ye shal haue breed and cloþes
B.20.252 Frere Fraunceys and Domynyk, for loue to be holye.
B.20.284 And [be] ashamed in hir shrift; ac shame makeþ hem wende
B.20.288 Ac while he is in westmynstre he wol be bifore
B.20.323 That frere flaterere be fet and phisike yow sike.'
B.20.352 And be adrad of deeþ and wiþdrawe hym fram pryde
         be C 437
C.Pr.54 Clothed hem in copis to be knowe fram othere
C.Pr.62 Ac sith charite hath be Chapman and [c]hief to shryue lordes
C.Pr.77 His seel sholde nouȝt be ysent in deseyte of þe peple.
C.Pr.100 Al þe world wot wel hit myghte nouȝt be trewe
C.Pr.104 That al þe world be [þe] wors, as holy writ telleth.
C.Pr.120 And ȝe shulde be here fadres and techen hem betre
C.Pr.151 And for thy rightful ruylynge be rewardid in heuene.'
C.Pr.166 Than gete a Mum of here mouth [til] moneye [be] shewed.
C.Pr.177 We myhte be lordes alofte and lyue as vs luste.'

C.Pr.205 And be [we] neuere so bold the belle hym [to] shewe.
C.Pr.211 Shal neuer þe Cat ne [þe] kytoun be my conseil be greued
C. 1.15 To be fayful to hym [he] ȝaf ȝow fyue wittes
C. 1.51 And kynde witte be wardeyn ȝoure welthe to kepe
C. 1.111 That hadde [lu]st to be lyk his lord þat was almyghty:
C. 1.125 Ac thei caren nat thow hit be cold, knaues, when þe[i] worche.
C. 1.144 And this y trowe be treuth; [ho] kan tecche þe bettre
C. 1.172 Thow ȝe be myhty to mote beth meke in ȝoure werkes,
C. 1.174 ȝe shal be weye þerwith whenne ȝe wende hennes.
C. 2.51 Lacke hem nat but lat hem worthe til leutee be Iustice
C. 2.68 And [as] a brokor brouhte here to be [with fals enioyned].
C. 2.108 For a leueth be lost when he his lyf leteth,\
C. 2.122 And ar this weddyng be wrouhte wo to al ȝoure consayle!
C. 2.126 And withouten here moder amendes mede may [nat] be wedded.
C. 2.139 That mede may be wedded to no man bot treuthe,
C. 2.152 Where matrymonye may be of mede and of falshede.
C. 2.169 Til mede be thy wedded wyf wolle we nat stunte,
C. 2.173 To be maried for mone med[e] hath assented.'
C. 2.176 And bade hem alle be bowen, beggares and othere,
C. 2.209 Y wolde be awreke [o]n tho wreches and on here werkes alle,
C. 2.219 Ar he be put on þe pylorye for eny preyere ich hote.'
C. 3.28 And beden here be blythe: 'for we beth thyn owene
C. 3.43 And ȝut be thy bedman and brynge adoun Consience
C. 3.56 'Y shal be ȝoure frende, frere, and fayle ȝow neuere
C. 3.61 Ho may askape þe sclaundre, þe skathe myhte sone be mended;
C. 3.70 An Auntur pruyde be paynted there and pomp of the world,
C. 3.85 Ne bouhte none burgages, be ȝe ful certayn.
C. 3.114 Be yfranchised for a fre man and haue a fals name.
C. 3.132 And wilned to be buxsled withouten his leue,
C. 3.140 Thow tene me and treuthe: and thow mowe be atake
C. 3.144 That alle [women, wantowen], shal [be] war [by] þe one
C. 3.150 But y be holly at thyn heste; lat hange me elles.'
C. 3.156 For she is fayn of thy felawschipe, for to be thy make.'
C. 3.180 To be cursed in constorie a counteth nat a rusche;
C. 3.246 May nat be sold sothliche, so many part asketh
C. 3.248 The leste ladde þat longeth with hym, be þe londe ywonne,
C. 3.256 For sholde neuere Consience be my constable were y a kyng,' quod mede,
C. 3.257 'Ne be Marschal ouer my men there y moste fyhte.
C. 3.306 And but hit prestly be ypayed þe payere is to blame,
C. 3.310 That bothe the lord and the laborer be leely yserued.
C. 3.318 And yf th[e] lele and lege be luyther men aftur
C. 3.328 And [soffrede] hym lyu[e] in mysbileue; y leue he be in helle.
C. 3.355 And man is relatif rect yf he be rihte trewe:
C. 3.359 Of oure sory synnes to be assoiled and yclansed
C. 3.390 Be the peccunie ypaied, thow parties chyde,
C. 3.402 And coueytede oure kynde and be kald in oure name–
C. 3.418 To be buxam at my byddyng his [b]o[n]e to fulfille.
C. 3.423 Bern hit; bere hit nat awey be hit neuer so riche;
C. 3.440 Samuel shal sle hym and sauel shal be yblamed
C. 3.441 And dauid shal be ydyademed and [d]aunte alle oure enemyes
C. 3.443 Shal no mede be maistre neueremore aftur
C. 3.445 Tho shal be maistres on molde trewe men to helpe.
C. 3.456 That here kyng be ycome fro þe Court of heuene,
C. 3.460 Shal be demed to þe deth but yf he do hit smythye
C. 3.474 Al shal be but [o] couert and o [buyrne] be Iustice;
C. 3.474 Al shal be but [o] couert and o [buyrne] be Iustice;
C. 3.476 Batailes sholle neuere eft be ne man bere eg toel
C. 3.477 And yf eny smyth smeth[e] hit be smyte þerwith to dethe:
C. 4.85 And be borw for his bale and buggen hym bote
C. 4.89 Then bale be ybete and bote neuer þe betere.'
C. 4.102 And efte the baldore be to bete myn hewes.
C. 4.107 That mede myhte be maynpernour [resoun] thei bysouhte.
C. 4.111 Tyl purnele porfiel be putte in here whicche
C. 4.112 And [chyldren] chersyng be chasted with ȝerdes
C. 4.113 And harlotes holynesse be an heye ferie;
C. 4.114 Til Clerkene Coueytise be cloth for þe pore
C. 4.116 And religious outryderes be reclused in here Cloistres
C. 4.117 And be as Benet hem bad, dominik and frounceys;
C. 4.119 And til þe kynges consayl be alle comune profit
C. 4.122 And til saynt Iames be souhte there pore sykke lyggen,
C. 4.123 In prisones and in pore cotes be pilgrimages to Rome
C. 4.129 But [it] be marchaunt or his man or messager [with] lettres,
C. 4.137 Be vnpunisched in my power for perel of [my] soule
C. 4.141 And bad nullum bonum be irremuneratum.
C. 4.159 But he be knowe for a cokewold kut of my nose.'
C. 4.174 Y wol haue leutee for my lawe and late be al ȝoure iangl[ing]
C. 4.175 And by lele and lyfholy my lawe shal be demed.'
C. 4.185 But be my cheef Chaunceller in Cheker and in parlement
C. 4.186 And Consience in alle my Courtes be a[s] kynges Iustice.'
C. 5.16 Or haue an horn and be hayward and lygge þeroute [a]nyhtes
C. 5.21 [Hem þat bedreden be] byleue t[o] fynden?'
C. 5.33 Or thow art broke, so may be, in body or in membre

C. 5.34 Or ymaymed thorw som myshap whereby thow myhte *be* excused?'
C. 5.50 To *be* welcome when y come oþerwhile in a monthe,
C. 5.66 For sholde no clerke *be* crouned but yf he come were
C. 5.70 Ac sythe bondemen barnes haen *be* mad bisshopes
C. 5.71 And bar[o]nes bastardus haen *be* Erchedekenes
C. 5.72 And so[p]ares and here sones for suluer han *be* knyhtes,
C. 5.80 Lyfholynesse and loue hath *be* longe hennes
C. 5.81 And wol til hit *be* wered out [or] oþerwyse ychaunged.
C. 5.91 But he *be* obediencer to prior or to mynistre.'
C. 5.145 And be stewar[d] of ȝoure stedes til ȝe be stewed bettere.'
C. 5.145 And be stewar[d] of ȝoure stedes til ȝe *be* stewed bettere.'
C. 5.152 For yf heuene *be* on this erthe or ese to [eny] soule
C. 5.165 In many places ther thei persones ben, *be* hemsulue at ese,
C. 5.175 And constantyn shal *be* here cook and coueerour of here churches,
C. 5.179 Clerkes and holy [kyrke] shal *be* clothed newe.'
C. 6.9 And soffre to *be* mysseyde, and so dyde y neuere.
C. 6.16 Haue *be* vnbuxum, y byseche god of mercy;
C. 6.17 And [bold haue] y *be*, nat abaschet to agulte
C. 6.26 In alle [manere] maneres my name to *be* knowe;
C. 6.40 *Be* holden for holy and honoured by þat enchesoun;
C. 6.60 As to be preised amongus þe peple thow [y] pore seme:
C. 6.91 'ȝus! redily,' quod repentaunce, 'and thow *be* ryht sory
C. 6.125 Or til they bothe *be* beggares and by [my] spiritual[t]e libbe
C. 6.130 Y haue *be* coek in here kychene and the couent serued
C. 6.138 Til "thow lixt!" and "thow lixt!" *be* lady ouer hem alle;
C. 6.139 And thenne awake y, wrathe, and wolde *be* avenged.
C. 6.151 Amonges monkes y myhte *be* Ac mony tyme y spare
C. 6.169 And bad hym bid to god *be* his helpe to amende.
C. 6.206 'Y haue *be* coueytous, þis kaytif, 'y biknowe hit here.
C. 6.214 Hit hadde *be* vnsold this seuene ȝer, so me god helpe.
C. 6.238 Thow wolt *be* hanged heye þerfore, here oþer in helle.
C. 6.332 By so hit *be* in thyn herte as y here thy tonge.
C. 6.333 [T]rist and mychel mercy and ȝut þou myhte *be* saued.
C. 6.346 To bysetten hit hymsulue as beste *be* for thy soule.
C. 6.356 And sennes sitte and *be* shryue and synege no more.'
C. 6.402 And wesched hit hadde [*be* wexed] with a weps of breres.
C. 7.2 'Y moste sitte to *be* shryue or elles sholde y nappe;
C. 7.16 And yf y bidde eny bedes, but yf hit *be* in wrath,
C. 7.27 Til matynes and masse *be* ydo; thenne haue y a memorie at þe freres.
C. 7.30 I haue *be* prest and persoun passynge thritty wyntur
C. 7.35 Yf y b[y]gge and borwe [ouh]t, but yf hit *be* ytayled,
C. 7.54 And sethe a beggare haue y *be* for my foule sleuthe.
C. 7.64 'Shal no sonday *be* this seuene ȝere, but seknesse hit make,
C. 7.95 Ne no mysproud man amongus lordes *be* [alow]ede.
C. 7.112 Thise solaseth þe soule til hymsulue *be* yfalle
C. 7.142 Bidde and biseche the, yf hit *be* thy wille,
C. 7.145 That what tyme we synnefole men wolden *be* sory
C. 7.172 In bedlem and in babiloyne y haue *be* in bothe,
C. 7.217 [So] shalt thow se swere-nat-but-it-*be*-for-nede—
C. 7.222 Loke þou bere n[ouht] away but yf hit *be* thyn owene.
C. 7.230 Thenne shaltow se say-soth-so-hit-*be*-to-done—
C. 7.260 ȝef loue and leute and oure lawe [*be*] trewe:
C. 7.261 Ac *be* war thenne of wrath, þat wikkede shrewe,
C. 7.282 To geten ingang at ȝate bote grace *be* þe more.'
C. 7.298 Treuth telleth [this to hym], þat y *be* excused.'
C. 8.37 And when ȝe mersyen eny man late mercy *be* taxour,
C. 8.41 For thow shalt ȝelden hit, so may *be*, or sumdel abuggen hit.
C. 8.43 Thogh he *be* here thyn vnderlynge in heuene parauntur
C. 8.47 Hit bicometh to the, knyhte, to *be* corteys and hende,
C. 8.49 Bute they *be* of bounte, of batayles or of treuthe.
C. 8.64 My plouhpote shal *be* my pykstaff and pyche ato þe rotes
C. 8.121 He sholde *be* huyred þeraftur when heruost tyme come.
C. 8.143 But yf he *be* blynde or brokelegged or bolted with yren,
C. 8.178 And þat was bake for bayard may *be* here bote.'
C. 8.195 To *be* his holde hewe thow he hadde no more
C. 8.209 Of beggares and biddares what beste *be* to done.
C. 8.210 For y woet wel, *be* [thow] went, worche þei wol ful ille;
C. 8.259 "Yblessed *be* al tho that here bylyue biswynketh
C. 8.262 That here lyflode *be* lene and lyte worth here clothes.'
C. 8.270 ȝe han manged ouer moche; þat maketh ȝow so syke.
C. 8.287 Lat hem abyde til the bord drawe; Ac bere hem none crommes
C. 8.292 And *be* fayn, be my fayth, his fysik to leete
C. 8.298 Wende nouthe when thow wol[t] and wel [*be*] thow euere.
C. 8.332 But hit *be* [fresh] flesch or fisch yfried or ybake
C. 8.334 But he heyliche yhuyred elles wol he chy[d]e;
C. 8.344 Ar fewe ȝeres *be* fulfeld famyne shal aryse.
C. 8.350 And thenne shal deth withdrawe and derthe *be* Iustice
C. 9.20 To *be* [peres] to þe apostles alle peple to reule
C. 9.57 Thise foure sholde *be* to alle folk þat hit nede[th].
C. 9.62 Bote the sugestioun *be* soth þat shapeth h[e]m to begge
C. 9.86 And ben abasched for to begge and wollen nat *be* aknowe
C. 9.99 But they *be* blynde or tobroke or elles be syke,
C. 9.99 But they be blynde or tobroke or elles *be* syke,

C. 9.166 For hit blameth all beggarie, *be* ȝe ful certayn.
C. 9.213 Aȝen þe lawe he lyueth yf latyn *be* trewe:
C. 9.221 Vnder obedience *be* and buxum to þe lawe:
C. 9.223 And vnder obedience *be* by dayes and by nyhtes;
C. 9.237 And hoso breketh this, *be* wel waer, but yf he repente,
C. 9.299 Of that y seyh slepynge, if hit so *be* myhte,
C. 9.335 *Be* ȝe neuere þe baldere to breke þe ten hestes
C. 9.344 Thow we *be* founden in the fraternite of alle fyue ordres
C. 9.348 And marie his moder *be* oure mene to hym
C.10.5 And what man a myhte *be* of mony m[a]n y askede.
C.10.98 Sholde no bisshop *be* here biddynges to withsite.
C.10.101 And crounede oen to *be* kyng to kull withoute synne
C.10.104 Crounede oen to *be* a kyng to kepen vs alle
C.10.120 Bote as y bad thouht tho *be* mene betwene
C.10.226 Til fourty [dayes] be fulfild and floed haue ywasche
C.10.233 That in thi [s]hingled ship shal *be* with þe ysaued."
C.10.238 That þe sire by hymsulue doth þe sone sholde *be* þe worse.
C.10.240 For thogh þe fader *be* a frankeleyn and for a felon be hanged
C.10.240 For thogh þe fader be a frankeleyn and for a felon *be* hanged
C.10.259 And thogh he *be* louelich to loke[n] on and lossum abedde,
C.10.262 Ac lat he[r] *be* vnlouely and vnlofsum abedde,
C.10.264 That no cortesye can, bute [knowe late here *be*]
C.10.265 For riche or yrented wel, thouh he *be* reueled for elde
C.10.277 Bote they bothe *be* forsore þat bacon þei tyne.
C.10.278 Forthy y conseyle alle cristene coueyte neuere *be* wedded
C.10.282 And loke þat loue *be* more þe cause then lond oþer nobles.
C.11.15 Bote wit þe cardet with coueytise as clotheres kemben here wolle.
C.11.71 *Be* large þerof whil hit lasteth to ledes þat ben nedy
C.11.78 Forthy, wit,' quod she, '*be* waer holy writ to shewe
C.11.107 For yf thow coueytest to *be* ryche to clergie comest thow neuere.
C.11.157 Ne man mouhte haue mery[t]e [thereof] mouhte hit *be* ypreued:
C.11.182 Til thow *be* a lord and haue lond leten y þe nelle
C.11.227 Thogh here gost *be* vngracious god for to plese.
C.11.251 Laste ȝe *be* loste as þe laboreres were þat lab[o]red vnder Noe.
C.11.264 Mouhte sleylokeste *be* slawe and sente hym to w[e]rre,
C.12.10 And preeye for the pol by pol yf thow *be* peccuniosus.'
C.12.14 And pouerte pursuede me and potte me to *be* lowe.
C.12.37 Ac *be* [thow] neueremore þe furste the defaute to blame;
C.12.39 Thyng þat wolde *be* pryue publische thow hit neuere;
C.12.96 Of hym þat trauaileth [t]heron bote treuthe *be* his lyuynge.
C.12.122 For in here likenesse oure lord lome hath *be* yknowe.
C.12.130 That we sholde *be* low and louelich and lele vch man til oþer
C.12.145 Althouh h[it] *be* sour to soffre þer cometh a swete aftur.
C.12.147 And aftur þat bittere barke, *be* þe scale aweye,
C.12.158 For þe loue of oure lord lo[w]eth hym to *be* pore,
C.12.196 And for here pacience *be* ypresed as for puyr martir
C.12.235 For, how [euere hit] *be* ywonne, but hit [be] wel despene[d]
C.12.235 For, how [euere hit] be ywonne, but hit [*be*] wel despene[d]
C.12.237 For if he *be* fer þerfro fol ofte hath he drede
C.13.11 Ne for brihtnesse of here beaute here spouse to *be* byknowe.
C.13.29 Bothe t[w]o ben gode, *be* ȝe ful certeyn,
C.13.37 The marchaunt mote nede *be* ylet lenger then the messager
C.13.44 Wol no wys man *be* wroth ne his wed take—
C.13.50 And ȝut *be* ylette, as y leue, for the lawe asketh
C.13.57 And dredeth to *be* ded þerfore and he in derke mette
C.13.83 That þe lawe ȝeueth leue such low folk to *be* excused,
C.13.118 Yf fals latyn *be* in þat lettre þe lawe hit enpugneth,
C.13.124 The bishop shal *be* blamed before god, as y leue,
C.13.201 So is soffrance souereynliche, so hit *be* for godes loue.
C.13.209 Vch a lede wolde *be* lacles, leef thow non other.
C.13.233 For shal neuere, ar shame come, a shrewe wel [*be*] chaste[d].
C.14.12 Ac hit soffiseth to *be* saued [to] be such as y tauhte.
C.14.12 Ac hit soffiseth to be saued [to] *be* such as y tauhte.
C.14.15 And þat is dobet, yf eny suche *be*, a blessed man þat helpeth
C.14.16 That pees *be* and pacience and pore withoute defaute:
C.14.20 As loreles to *be* lordes and lewede men techares,
C.14.29 May nat *be*, [be] þ[ow] syker, thogh we bidde euere.
C.14.29 May nat be, [*be*] þ[ow] syker, thogh we bidde euere.
C.14.31 As to *be* bore or bygete in such a constillacioun;
C.14.53 Come for al his kynde wit thorw cristendoem to *be* saued,
C.14.66 Take we here wordes at worthe, for here witteness[e] b[*e*] trewe,
C.14.112 Out of synne and saef, thogh he synege ofte,
C.14.114 For yf þe clerke *be* connynge [he] knoweth what is synne
C.14.134 And wol no wikkede man [*be*] lost bote if he wol hymsulue:
C.14.151 For he is in þe loweste of heuene, yf oure byleue *be* trewe,
C.14.165 Sey hit and soffred hit And saide hit *be* sholde:
C.14.191 And wher he *be* saef or nat saef þe sothe woet no clergie
C.14.195 To wissen vs weyes þerwith þat wenen to *be* saued—
C.14.210 Bote lyue[th] as his lawe t[echeth] and leueth þer *be* no bettere,
C.14.215 And þat is loue and large huyre, yf þe lord *be* trewe,
C.15.40 Pacience and y [prestly weren] pot to *be* mettes
C.15.76 Holy writ byt men *be* waer and wysly hem kepe

C.15.79 For alle be we brethrene thogh we be diuerse yclothed.
C.15.79 For alle be we brethrene thogh we be diuerse yclothed.
C.15.93 And why a lyueth nat as a lereth.' 'lat be,' quod pacience,
C.15.103 And bote þe furste leef be lesyng[e] leue me neuere aftur.
C.15.105 Of dowel and dobet and yf dobe[s]t [be] eny penaunce.'
C.15.120 And preynte vppon pacience to preie me be stille
C.15.121 And saide hymsulue, 'sire doctour, [and] hit be 3oure wille,
C.15.129 Shal no such motyef be meued for me bote [þ]ere
C.15.136 Bote lele loue and treuthe that loth is to be founde.'
C.15.162 Shal neuere buyren be abasched þat hath this abouten hym
C.15.164 Noþer fuyr ne floed ne be aferd of enemye:
C.15.222 And thenne wolde y be bysy and buxum to helpe
C.15.229 Til pruyde be puyreliche fordo and þat thorw payn defaute:
C.15.237 And saide, 'lo! here lyflode ynow yf oure beleue be trewe
C.15.254 By so þat þou be sobre of syhte and of tonge,
C.15.258 Wheþer thorw hunger or [thorw] hete, at his wille be hit;
C.15.270 And yf men lyuede as mesure wolde sholde neuere[more] be defaute
C.15.271 Amonges cristene creatures, yf cristes wordes be trewe:
C.16.41 In fenestres at þe freres–yf fals be þe fondement.
C.16.42 Forthy cristene sholde be in comune ryche, noon coueytous for
hymsulue.
C.16.73 And thogh his glotonye be of gode ale he goth to a colde beddynge
C.16.88 And where be [lyh]tere to breke? lasse boest hit maketh
C.16.98 And where he be or be nat, a bereth þe signe of pouerte
C.16.98 And where he be or be nat, a bereth þe signe of pouerte
C.16.112 And potte hym to be pacient and pouerte weddeth,
C.16.125 Ne to be mair ouer men ne mynistre vnder kynges;
C.16.161 Shal be porest of power at his partynge hennes.
C.16.166 And yf thow be cristes creature, for cristes loue telle me.'
C.16.178 And may nat be withoute a body to bere me where hym liketh.'
C.16.228 And doth hym to be deynous and deme þat beth nat lered.
C.16.255 Shal neuere flour ne fruyt wexe ne fayre leue be grene.
C.16.257 And be corteys and kynde of holy kyrke godes,
C.16.275 Vnk[ynd]e curatours to be kepares of 3oure soules.
C.16.280 And þat with gyle was gete vngraciousliche be yspened.
C.16.287 That maistres commenden moche. Where may hit be yfounde?
C.16.357 In [þat] sekte sethe to selde hath he be [knowen].
C.16.360 In kynges Court a cometh yf his consaile be trewe
C.16.361 Ac yf couetyse be of his consaile a wol nat come þerynne.
C.16.366 With bisshopes a wolde be for beggares sake
C.17.2 Or beggeth or biddeth, be he ryche or pore,
C.17.4 'Ho is wroeth and wolde be awreke, holy writ preueth,' quod he,
C.17.5 'A passeth cheef charite yf holy churche be trewe:
C.17.10 To his selide cam and soffred be mylked.
C.17.15 Foules hym fedde yf frere Austynes be trewe
C.17.39 "Wyf! be ywar," quod he; "what haue we herynne?
C.17.40 Lord leue," quod þat lede, " no stole thynge be herynne!"
C.17.44 Thenne wolde lordes and ladyes be loth to agulte
C.17.46 And marchaunt3 merciable wolde be and men of lawe bothe
C.17.94 Ther sholde be plente and pees perpetuel euere.
C.17.112 Go now to eny degre and bote gyle be holde a maistre
C.17.123 For sarrasynes may be saued as yf they so byleued
C.17.136 Ac oure lord aloueth no loue but lawe be þe cause:
C.17.146 And ay hopeth eft to be with here body at þe laste
C.17.148 And þat is charite, leue chield, to be cher ouer thy soule;
C.17.151 'Hit may be so þat sarresynes haen such a manere charite,
C.17.167 And pursuede to haue be pope, prince of holy chirche,
C.17.170 Be maistre ouer alle tho men and on this manere a wrouhte:
C.17.192 To be p[astor]s and preche the passioun of iesus
C.17.229 For if possession be poysen and inparfit hem make,
C.17.265 That men myhte nat be saued but thorw mercy and grace
C.17.287 For as þe kynde is of a knyhte or [of] a kynge to be take
C.17.289 To be culd and ouercome the comune to defende,
C.17.296 Moises to be maister þerof til messie come
C.17.311 And hopen þat he be to come þat shal hem releue
C.17.313 And haen a suspectioun to be saef, bothe sarresynes & iewes,
C.18.55 And þe fruyt was fayre, non fayrere be myhte,
C.18.91 And bad hit be, of a bat of erthe, a man and a maide,
C.18.127 That elde felde efte þe fruyt, or full to be fayre,
C.18.169 And kuste iesus to be knowe þerby and cauht of þe iewes.
C.18.173 Thow shalt be myrrour to monye men to disceue.
C.18.175 Sethe y be tresoun am take and to 3oure will, iewes,
C.18.225 Ne withoute a soware be suche seed; this we seyn alle.
C.19.27 '3oure wordes aren wonderfol,' quod y; 'where eny of [hem] be trewe
C.19.35 Sethe the furste sufficede to bileue and be saued?
C.19.87 The whiche barn mote nedes be born of a mayde,
C.19.91 And 3ut [b]e plasterud with pacience when fondynges [priketh
hym]–
C.19.139 Riht so failed þe sone, the syre be ne myhte
C.19.147 Bote [be he] greued with here grype the holy goost lat falle.
C.19.182 The blase be yblowen out, 3ut brenneth þe weke–
C.19.202 Wol brennen and blasen, be they togyderes,
C.19.220 Be vnkynde to thyn emcristene and al þat thow canst bidde,

C.19.223 And indulgences ynowe and be ingrat[u]s to thy kynde,
C.19.224 The holy goest hereth the nat ne helpeth the, be thow certeyne.
C.19.245 Lordliche for to lyue and lykyngliche be clothed
C.19.262 For euery manere goed man may be likned to a torche
C.19.273 "Veniaunce, veniaunce! for3eue be hit neuere
C.19.282 And myldeliche his mercy aske; myhte y nat be saued?'
C.19.286 Eny creature be coupable bifore a kynges iustice
C.19.287 Be yraunsomed for his repentaunce þer alle resoun hym dampneth.
C.19.303 That [oon] is a wikkede wyf þat wol nat be chasted;
C.19.305 And if his hous be vnheled and reyne on his bedde
C.19.310 Til he be blereyede or blynde and þe borre in [the] throte,
C.19.314 The wyf is oure wikkede flesche [þat] wol nat be chasted
C.19.323 And be inpacient in here penaunc[e], puyr resoun knoweth
C.20.11 As is þe kynde of a knyhte þat cometh to be dobbet,
C.20.23 That Crist be nat yknowe for consumm[a]tus deus
C.20.54 And saiden, 'yf he sotil be hymsulue now he wol helpe;'
C.20.55 And 'yf thow be Crist and [kynges] sone come adoun of th[e] rode;
C.20.72 Wher he be ded or nat ded down or he be taken.'
C.20.72 Wher he be ded or nat ded down or he be taken.'
C.20.104 For be this derkenesse ydo deth worth yvenkused;
C.20.109 [But] as bareyne be and by vsure libbe,
C.20.135 And þat my tale [be] trewe y take god to witnesse.
C.20.139 In menynge þat man shal fro me[r]kenesse be ydrawe
C.20.159 Til he [be] ded [and] ydo þerto; [þe yuel] he destruyeth,
C.20.205 That her peyne [be] perpetuel [and] no preyer hem helpe.
C.20.223 And soffred to be sold to se þe sorwe of deynge,
C.20.264 And y, boek, wol be brente bote he aryse to lyue
C.20.268 And bile[u]e on a newe lawe be ylost, lyf and soule.'
C.20.284 Ar we thorw brihtnesse be b[l]ente go barre þe 3ates;
C.20.323 [For] god wol nat be [bi]gyled,' quod gobelyne, 'n[e] byiaped.
C.20.338 To lere men to [be] lele and vch man to louye oþer;
C.20.339 The which lyf and lawe, be hit longe yvysed,
C.20.344 For vs were bettere nat be then abyde in his sihte.
C.20.372 Myne they [be] and of me; y may þe bet hem clayme.
C.20.392 And gyle [be] bigyled thorw grace at þe laste:
C.20.416 And be at my biddynge, at blisse or at payne.
C.20.417 Ac to be merciable to man thenne my kynde [hit] asketh
C.20.420 Shal neuere in helle eft come be he ones oute:
C.20.430 Be hit eny thyng abouhte, the boldenesse of here synne[s],
C.20.432 For holy writ wol þat y be wreke of here harm þat wrouhte ille–
C.20.436 To be merciable to monye of my haluebretherne.
C.21.3 To here holly þe masse and to [be] hoseled aftur.
C.21.27 That knyht, kyng, conquerour may be o persone.
C.21.28 To be cald a knyht is fayr for men shal knele to hym;
C.21.29 To be cald a kyng is fairor for he may knyhtes make;
C.21.30 Ac to be conquerour cald, þat cometh of special grace
C.21.62 He may be wel called conquerour and that is Crist to mene.
C.21.100 And many wyles and wyt þat wol be a ledare.
C.21.138 To be Cayser or kyng of the kyngdoem of Iuda
C.21.162 For þat womman witeth [may] nat [wel be] conseyl.
C.21.178 Yblessed mote thow be and be shalt for euere.
C.21.178 Yblessed mote thow be and be shalt for euere.
C.21.179 And yblessed mote they be, in body and in soule,
C.21.188 Thus hath Peres power, be his pardoun payed,
C.21.222 Shal come and be curatours ouer kynges and Erles;
C.21.223 And [pryde shal] be pope, prince of holy chirche,
C.21.243 Bothe of wele and of wo and be ywaer bifore,
C.21.248 And somme he [l]ered to lyue in longyng to be hennes,
C.21.250 And al he lered to be lele, and vch a craft loue oþere,
C.21.251 Ne no boest ne debaet be among hem alle.
C.21.252 'Thouh somme be clenner then somme, 3e sen wel,' quod grace,
C.21.255 And [ho] þat moest maistries can be myldest of berynge
C.21.298 And he þat ete of þat seed sholde be euene trewe
C.21.301 [Shal] nat be aspyed thorw spiritus iusticie.
C.21.347 Shal be coloured so queyntly and keuered vnder [o]ure sophistrie
C.21.358 For witterly, y woet wel, we be nat of strenghe
C.21.365 And make a moche moet þat myhte be a strenghe
C.21.382 The lord of lust shal be ylette al this lente, y hope.
C.21.395 And so to ben assoiled and sennes be hoseled.'
C.21.396 '3e? bawe!' quod a breware, 'y wol nat be yruled,
C.21.407 Bote Consience [be] thy comune[s] and cardinale vertues
C.21.437 So yblessed be [Peres] the [plouhman] þat peyneth hym to tulie
C.21.440 And worschipede de he þat wrouhte all, bothe gode and wicke,
C.21.441 And soffreth þat synnefole be til som tyme þat þei repente.
C.21.443 And claymeth bifore þe kynge to be kepare ouer cristene
C.21.444 And counteth nat thow cristene be culde and yrobbed
C.21.475 So y may boldely be hoseled for y borwe neuere
C.22.13 Ne wyht no[n] wol be his borwe ne wed hath [non] to legge;
C.22.38 Philosopheres forsoke wel[e] for they wolde be nedy
C.22.39 And woneden wel elyngly and wolden nat be riche.
C.22.48 Forthy be nat abasched to byde and to be nedy
C.22.48 Forthy be nat abasched to byde and to be nedy
C.22.108 Leue pruyde priueyliche and be parfyt cristene.

C.22.185 So harde he ȝede ouer myn heued hit wol *be* sene euere.
C.22.188 Haddest thow *be* hende,' quod y, 'thow wost haue asked leue.'
C.22.203 Awreke me ȝif ȝoure wille *be* for y wolde be hennes.'
C.22.203 Awreke me ȝif ȝoure wille be for y wolde *be* hennes.'
C.22.204 'Yf thow wol[t] *be* wreke wende into vnite
C.22.207 'Consaileth me, kynde,' quod y, 'what craft *be* beste to lere?'
C.22.241 Lat hem *be* as beggares or lyue by angeles fode.'
C.22.244 And saide, 'syres, soethly welcome *be* ȝe alle
C.22.248 [And] y wol *be* ȝoure borwh: ȝe shal haue breed and clothes
C.22.252 Frere fraunceys and domynyk, for loue to *be* holy.
C.22.276 That alle thynges vnder-heuene ou[h]te to *be* in comune.
C.22.284 And *be* aschamed in here shryft; ac shame maketh [hem] wende
C.22.288 Ac while he is in Westmynstre he wol *be* bifore
C.22.323 That frere flaterare *be* fet and fisyk ȝow seke.'
C.22.352 And *be* adrad of deth and withdrawe hym fro pruyde

beon C 12

C. 5.15 Repe or *been* a rypereue and aryse erly
C. 7.69 Ac wheche *been* þe braunches þat bryngeth men to sleuthe?
C. 7.237 And alle þe hous[es] *been* yheled, halles and chaumbres,
C. 8.139 ȝe *been* wastours, y woet wel, and waste and deuouren
C. 9.226 That in wilde wodes *been* or in waste places,
C.10.166 Such lyther lyuyng men lome *been* ryche
C.10.171 Inwit and alle wittes closed *been* þerynne:
C.15.292 And blisse to all þat *been*, bothe wilde and tame."
C.19.320 *Been* seeknes[e] and oþere sorwes þat we soffren ouhte,
C.22.261 Bote hy ben nempned in þe nombre of þat *been* ywaged.
C.22.262 Alle oþere in bataile *been* yholde brybours,
C.22.283 Alle þat *been* here parschienes penauns[e] enioynen

beest B 1

B. 5.589 Botrased wiþ bileef-so-or-þow-*beest*-noȝt-saued;

beeþ B 1

B. 1.176 Thouȝ ye be myȝt[y] to mote *beeþ* meke [of] youre werkes,

beeþ C 1

C. 8.52 For hit *beeþ* þe deueles dysors to drawe men to synne;

ben A 74

A.Pr.61 Siþen charite haþ *ben* chapman & chief to shryue lordis
A.Pr.94 *Ben* ylope to lundoun be leue of hire bisshop.
A.Pr.95 And *ben* clerkis of þe kinges bench þe cuntre to shende.
A. 1.6   How besy þei *ben* aboute þe mase?
A. 1.16 For to worsshipe hym þerewiþ whiles ȝe *ben* here.
A. 1.150 Þeiȝ ȝe m1ȝty to mote beþ mek of ȝour werkis,
A. 1.165 Arn none hardere þan [hy] whanne [hy] *ben* auauncid,
A. 1.170 Ȝe *ben* acumbrid wiþ coueitise, ȝe [conne] not out crepe;
A. 2.21 I auȝte *ben* hiȝere þanne heo for I com of a betere.
A. 2.27 Þere miȝte þou wyte ȝif þou wilt whiche þei *ben* alle
A. 3.26 And bidden hire be blyþe, 'for we *ben* þin owene
A. 3.65 Meiris & ma[ce]ris, hij þat *ben* mene
A. 3.220 To hem þat werchen wel whiles þei *ben* here.
A. 3.222 Tak no mede, my lord, of [men] þat *ben* trewe
A. 4.130 Þat lawe shal *ben* a labourer & lede afeld donge,
A. 5.33 'Let no wynnyng forwanye hem whiles þei *ben* ȝonge'.
A. 5.77 And don hise frendis *ben* hise fon þoruȝ my false tunge.
A. 5.114 'I haue [*ben*] coueit[ous],' quaþ [þat caitif], 'I [bi]knowe [hit] h[e]re,
A. 6.15 At bedlem, at babiloyne, I haue *ben* in boþe;
A. 6.30 I haue *ben* his folewere al þis fourty wynter;
A. 6.74 And alle þe wallis *ben* of wyt to holde wil þeroute;
A. 6.75 Þe kirnelis *ben* of cristendom þat kynde to saue,
A. 6.77 Alle þe housis *ben* helid, hallis & chaumbris,
A. 6.105 And *ben* porteris þe posternis þat to þe place longiþ:
A. 7.90 For þeiȝ I deiȝe today my dettis *ben* quyt;
A. 7.94 And *ben* his pilgrym at þe plouȝ for pore menis sake.
A. 7.116 Shulde þou hirid þereaftir whan heruist ȝeme come.
A. 7.122 Ȝe *ben* wastours, I wot wel, & treuþe wot þe soþe,
A. 7.191 Meschief it makiþ h[y] *ben* so mek nouþe,
A. 7.193 And it *ben* my blody breþeren, for god bouȝte vs alle.
A. 7.209 Þat nedy *ben* or nakid, and nouȝt han to spende,
A. 7.239 For summe of my seruauntis *ben* seke oþer while,
A. 8.45 Men of lawe hadde lest for le[ttr]id þei *ben* alle;
A. 8.57 Þise þre for þrallis *ben* þrowe among vs alle
A. 8.67 Beggeris & bidderis *ben* not in þe bulle,
A. 8.75 And bringen forþ barnes þat bois *ben* holden.
A. 8.78 Þere *ben* mo mysshapen amonges hem, whoso takiþ hede,
A. 8.82 Ac olde men & hore þat helpeles *ben* of strengþe,
A. 8.106 Of preyours & of penaunce my plouȝ *ben* hereaftir,
A. 8.165 Forþi I rede ȝow renkes þat riche *ben* on erþe
A. 8.169 Þat han þe [welþe of þis] world, & wise men *ben* holden.
A. 8.182 Suche werkis to werche, whiles we *ben* here,
A. 9.70 Arn þre faire vertues, & *ben* not f[e]r to fynde.
A.10.22 Þise sixe yset to saue þe castel:
A.10.23 To kepe þise womman þise wise men *ben* chargid,
A.10.42 Inwit & alle wyttes enclosid *ben* þerinne,
A.10.61 And *ben* braynwood as bestis, so here blood wexiþ.

A.10.67 But þei witen hem fro wauntounesse whiles þei *ben* ȝon[g]e.
A.10.68 And ȝif þei *ben* pore & cateles, to kepe hem fro ille,
A.10.70 Fro folies, & fynde hem til þei *ben* wise.
A.10.85 Þanne is dobet to *ben* ywar for betyng of þe ȝarde,
A.10.106 Fro religioun to religioun, reccheles *ben* þei euere;
A.10.128 Among men of þis molde þat mek *ben* & kynde.
A.10.131 Formest & ferst to folk þat *ben* weddit
A.10.135 For of here kynde þei comen þat confessours *ben* nempnid,
A.10.140 *Ben* conseyuid in cursid tyme as kaym was on Eue:
A.10.171 "Bestis þat now *ben* shuln banne þe tyme
A.10.176 Þat in þe [shynglid] ship shal *ben* ysauid;
A.10.209 Þat oþere gatis *ben* geten for gadelynges ben holden;
A.10.209 Þat oþere gatis ben geten for gadelynges *ben* holden;
A.10.210 And þat *ben* fals folk, & fals eires also, foundlynges & [leiȝeris],
A.11.6   To flatereris or to folis þat frentyk *ben* of wittis,'
A.11.21 Þat suche craftis conne [to counseil *ben* yclepid],
A.11.22 And *ben* seruid as sires þat serue þe deuil.
A.11.39 At mete [in here] merþe, whanne mynstralis *ben* stille,
A.11.89 Siþen he wilneþ to wyte which þei *ben* alle.
A.11.145 For dobet & dobest *ben* drawen of louis [co]le.
A.11.151 And [biddiþ] vs *ben* as breþeren, & blissen oure enemys,
A.11.189 Counforte þe carful þat in castel *ben* fetterid,
A.11.195 Sire dobest haþ *ben* [in office], so is he best worþi
A.11.246 Alle kynne creatures þat to crist be[n] l[yche]
A.11.297 And is as muche to mene, to men þat *ben* lewid,
A.11.298 'Wh[anne] ȝe *ben* aposid of princes or of prestis of þe lawe
A.12.21 Til þo wrecches *ben* in wil here synne to lete."

ben B 176

B.Pr.56 Cloþed hem in copes to *ben* knowen from oþere;
B.Pr.64 Siþ charite haþ *ben* chapman and chief to shryue lordes
B.Pr.104 That Cardinals *ben* called and closynge yates
B.Pr.209 What þis metels bymeneþ, ye men þat *ben* murye,
B. 1.6   How bisie þei *ben* aboute þe maȝe?
B. 1.16 For to worshipe hym þerwiþ while ye *ben* here.
B. 1.42 And for þow sholdest *ben* ywar I wisse þee þe beste.'
B. 1.178 Ye shulle *ben* weyen þerwiþ whan ye wenden hennes:
B. 1.191 Are [none hardere] þan hij whan þei *ben* auaunced,
B. 1.196 [Ye] *ben* acombred wiþ coueitise; [ye] konne noȝt [out crepe],
B. 1.200 Fo[r] þise [*ben* wordes] writen in þe [euaungelie]:
B. 1.207 Whan alle tresors *ben* tried treuþe is þe beste.
B. 2.28 I ouȝte *ben* hyere þan she; I kam of a betere.
B. 2.45 [There] myȝtow witen if þow wilt whiche þei *ben* alle
B. 3.46 For to *ben* hire Bedeman and hire [baude after].
B. 3.76 Maires and Maceres þat menes *ben* bitwene
B. 3.201 Hadde I *ben* Marchal of his men, by Marie of heuene!
B. 3.233 To [hem] þat [werchen wel] while þei *ben* here.
B. 3.292 Thise shul *ben* Maistres on moolde [trewe men] to saue.
B. 4.29 In [c]heker and in Chauncerye, to *ben* descharged of þynges.
B. 4.124 Til Bisshopes Bayardes *ben* beggeris Chaumbres,
B. 4.140 *Ben* vnpunysshed [at] my power for peril of my soule,
B. 4.147 That lawe shal *ben* a laborer and lede afeld donge,
B. 5.90 'I wolde *ben* yshryue', quod þis sherewe, 'and I for shame dorste.
B. 5.168 They hadde þanne ben Infamis, þei kan so yuele hele co[unseil].
B. 5.170 For þere ben manye felle frekes my feeris to aspie,
B. 5.198 'I haue *ben* coueitous', quod þis caytif, 'I biknowe it here.
B. 5.206 It hadde *ben* vnsold þis seuen yer, so me god helpe.
B. 5.234 Thow haddest be bettre worþi *ben* hanged þerfore.'
B. 5.245 And *ben* hire brocour after and bouȝt it myselue.
B. 5.322 And bad Bette þe Bocher *ben* on his syde.
B. 5.344 And wisshed it hadde *ben* wexed wiþ a wispe of firses.
B. 5.527 [At] Bethlem, [at] Babiloyne, I haue *ben* in boþe,
B. 5.542 I haue *ben* his folwere al þis [fourty] wynter,
B. 5.587 And alle þe walles *ben* of wit to holden wil oute;
B. 5.588 [The] kernele[s *ben* of] cristendom [þat] kynde to saue,
B. 5.590 And alle þe houses *ben* hiled, halles and chambres,
B. 5.621 Charite and Chastite *ben* hi[r]e chief maydenes;
B. 6.48 For in Charnel at chirche cherles *ben* yuel to knowe,
B. 6.54 For it *ben* þe deueles disours, I do þe to vnderstonde.'
B. 6.77 They *ben* ascaped good auenture, [now] god hem amende.'
B. 6.102 And *ben* his pilgrym atte plow for pouere mennes sake.
B. 6.130 Ye *ben* wastours, I woot wel, and truþe woot þe soþe,
B. 6.223 That nedy *ben* [or naked, and nouȝt han to spende,
B. 7.13 Bysshopes yblessed, if þei *ben* as þei sholde
B. 7.55 Thise *ben* tresores trewe folk to helpe,
B. 7.100 Ac olde men and hore þat helplees *ben* of strengþe,
B. 7.124 Of preieres and of penaunce my plouȝ shal *ben* herafter,
B. 7.187 Forþi I rede yow renkes þat riche *ben* on erþe
B. 7.191 That haue þe welþe of þis world and wise men *ben* holden
B. 7.204 Swiche werkes to werche, while we *ben* here,
B. 8.79 Arn þre faire vertues, and *ben* noȝt fer to fynde.
B. 8.128 'Wher dowel [and] dobet and dobest *ben* in londe
B. 9.23 Thise [sixe] *ben* set to [saue] þis lady anima
B. 9.54 Inwit and alle wittes [en]closed *ben* þerInne,

B. 9.62 And þat *ben* glotons, glubberes; hir god is hire wombe:
B. 9.90 [So] Iewes [shul] *ben* oure loresmen, shame to vs alle!
B. 9.102 Is moost yhated vpon erþe of hem þat *ben* in heuene:
B. 9.112 For of hir kynde þei come þat Confessours *ben* nempned,
B. 9.123 Conceyued *ben* in [cursed] tyme as Caym was on Eue
B. 9.140 Beestes þat now *ben* shul banne þe tyme
B. 9.145 That in [þe] shyngled ship shul *ben* ysaued."
B. 9.160 For coueitise of catel vnkyndely *ben* [maried].
B. 9.186 Wreke þee wiþ wyuyng if þow wolt *ben* excused:
B. 9.195 [That] oþergates *ben* geten for gedelynges arn holden,
B.10.6 To flatereres or to fooles þat frenetike *ben* of wittes',
B.10.25 And þat þei *ben* lordes of ech a lond þat out of lawe libbeþ,
B.10.115 Why sholde we þat now *ben* for þe werkes of Adam
B.10.136 Siþþe he wilneþ to wite whiche þei *ben* [alle].
B.10.138 I dar *ben* his bolde borgh þat dobet wole he neuere,
B.10.193 For dobet and dobest *ben* [drawen] of loues [scole].
B.10.256 Ne man hadde no merite my3te it *ben* ypreued:
B.10.275 This text was told yow to *ben* ywar er ye tau3te
B.10.292 [Th]anne shul burel clerkes *ben* abasshed to blame yow or to greue,
B.10.319 In many places þer þei [persons *ben*, be þei purely] at ese,
B.10.416 That *ben* Carpenters holy kirk to make for cristes owene beestes:
B.10.432 And now *ben* [swiche] as Souereyns wiþ Seintes in heuene,
B.10.437 Ther are witty and wel libbynge ac hire werkes *ben* yhudde
B.10.444 Forþi lyue we forþ wiþ [liþere] men; I leue fewe *ben* goode,
B.11.77 Raþer þan to bapti3e barnes þat *ben* Catecumelynges,
B.11.173 But þei *ben* lerned for oure lordes loue, lost is al þe tyme,
B.11.198 [Ac] for þe beste þer som riche and some beggeres and pouere.
B.11.213 For woot no man how nei3 it is to *ben* ynome fro boþe.
B.11.233 For in hir liknesse oure lord [lome] haþ ben yknowe.
B.11.244 Many tyme god haþ *ben* met among nedy peple,
B.11.268 And lasse he dredeþ deeþ and in derke to *ben* yrobbed
B.11.280 As Dauid seiþ in þe Sauter: to swiche þat *ben* in wille
B.11.290 And þe title þat ye take ordres by telleþ ye *ben* auaunced:
B.11.364 Manye selkouþes I sei3 *ben* no3t to seye nouþe.
B.11.405 Tho cau3te I colour anoon and comsed to *ben* ashamed
B.12.10 Amende þee while þow my3t; þow hast *ben* warned ofte
B.12.24 [In manye places pleyden þe parfiter to *ben*].
B.12.30 Feiþ, hope and Charite, and alle *ben* goode,
B.12.85 For goddes body my3te no3t *ben* of breed wiþouten clergie,
B.12.95 For boþe *ben* as Mirours with mesure [by] defautes
B.12.191 Ther lewed þeues *ben* lolled vp; loke how þei be saued!
B.12.195 [Th]at buxomliche biddeþ it and *ben* in wille to amenden hem.
B.12.274 And þe bettre for hir bokes to bidden we *ben* holden–
B.13.12 And how þat lewed men *ben* lad, but oure lord hem helpe,
B.13.18 [For alle] creatures þat crepen [or walken] of kynde *ben* engendred;
B.13.73 And greue þerwiþ [þat goode *ben*]–ac gramariens shul re[d]e:
B.13.255 Ac if my3t of myracle hym faille it is for men *ben* no3t worþi.
B.13.281 And inobedient to *ben* vndernome of any lif lyuynge;
B.13.314 Haþ manye moles and spottes; it moste *ben* ywasshe.'
B.13.409 [Ac] whiche *ben* þe braunches þat bryngen a man to sleuþe?
B.13.420 Thise *ben* þe braunches, beþ war, þat bryngen a man to wanhope.
B.13.435 Ne no mysproud man amonges lordes *ben* allowed.
B.13.439 Haue beggeres bifore hem þe whiche *ben* goddes minstrales
B.14.72 Amonges cristene creatures, if cristes wordes *ben* trewe.
B.14.116 And blisse to alle þat *ben*, boþe wilde and tame."
B.14.122 Aungeles þat in helle now ben hadden ioye som tyme,
B.14.131 And whan he dyeþ *ben* disalowed, as Dauid seiþ in þe Sauter:
B.14.169 Of þe good þat þow hem gyuest ingrati *ben* manye,
B.14.202 For seuene synnes þer *ben* assaillen vs euere;
B.14.223 And buxomnesse and boost [*ben*] eueremoore at werre,
B.15.40 'Ye *ben* as a bisshop', quod I, al bourdynge þat tyme,
B.15.97 Ther some bowes *ben* leued and some bereþ none
B.15.136 Curatours of holy kirke, as clerkes þat *ben* auarouse,
B.15.155 And wollen lene þer þei leue lelly to *ben* paied.
B.15.232 In þat secte siþþe to selde haþ he *ben* [knowe].
B.15.324 And [bisette] to bidde for yow to swiche þat *ben* riche,
B.15.325 And *ben* founded and feffed ek to bidde for oþere.
B.15.330 And on hemself som, and swiche as *ben* hir laborers;
B.15.332 Ac clerkes and kny3tes and communers þat *ben* riche,
B.15.336 Right so ye riche, ye robeþ þat *ben* riche
B.15.342 Ac Religiouse þat riche *ben* sholde raþer feeste beggeris
B.15.343 Than burgeises þat riche *ben* as þe book techeþ,
B.15.399 This Makometh was cristene [man], and for he moste no3t *ben* pope
B.15.416 And *ben* manered after Makometh þat no man vseþ trouþe.
B.15.425 And folkes sholden [fynde], þat *ben* in diuerse siknesse,
B.15.428 Alle þat *ben* at debaat and bedemen were trewe:
B.15.437 And hardie hem þat bihoueth *ben*, and 3yue hem good euidence.
B.15.473 That loþ *ben* to louye wiþouten lernyng of ensaumples.
B.15.487 That heuedes of holy chirche *ben*, þat han hir wil here,
B.15.577 O3ias seiþ for swiche þat sike *ben* and feble,
B.16.6 The leues lele wordes, þe lawe of holy chirche;
B.16.247 Thus haue I *ben* his heraud here and in helle
B.16.267 And bettre wed for us [wage] þan we *ben* alle worþi,

B.17.25 Ye! and sixti þousand biside forþ þat *ben* no3t seyen here.'
B.17.88 And graunted hym to *ben* his [gome]; 'graunt mercy', he seide;
B.17.107 Who is bihynde and who bifore and who *ben* on horse;
B.17.148 The fyngres þat fre *ben* to folde and to serue
B.17.263 That riche *ben* and reson knoweþ ruleþ wel youre soule;
B.17.272 For þat *ben* vnkynde to hise, hope I noon ooþer
B.17.321 Thre þynges þer *ben* þat doon a man by strengþe
B.17.333 Thise þre þat I telle of *ben* þus to vnderstonde:
B.17.340 *Ben* siknesse and sorwes þat we suffren o[u3]te,
B.17.343 And *ben* inpacient in hir penaunce, pure reson knoweþ
B.18.133 Siþ þis barn was ybore *ben* xxxti wynter passed
B.18.253 To breke and to bete adoun [alle] þat *ben* ayeins [hym],
B.18.278 For by right and by reson þe renkes þat *ben* here
B.18.328 For alle synfulle soules, to saue þo þat *ben* worþi.
B.18.329 Myne þei *ben* and of me; I may þe bet hem cleyme.
B.18.412 Than after werre and wo whan loue and pees *ben* maistres.
B.19.64 Is to wissen vs þerwiþ, þat whan we *ben* tempted,
B.19.100 And manye wiles and wit þat wole *ben* a ledere.
B.19.248 And some he lered to lyue in longynge to *ben* hennes,
B.19.260 My prowor and my Plowman Piers shal *ben* on erþe,
B.19.301 [Shal] nou3t *ben* espied [þoru3] Spiritus Iusticie.
B.19.344 'And Piers bern worþ ybroke; and þei þat *ben* in vnitee
B.19.365 And make a muche moot þat myghte *ben* a strengþe
B.19.395 And so to *ben* assoilled and siþþen ben houseled.
B.19.395 And so to ben assoilled and siþþen *ben* houseled.'
B.19.444 And counteþ no3t þou3 cristene *ben* killed and robbed,
B.19.470 Ye *ben* but membres and I aboue alle.
B.20.13 No wight noon wol *ben* his boru3, ne wed haþ noon to legge;
B.20.203 Awreke me if youre wille be for I wolde *ben* hennes.'
B.20.235 They wol flatere [to] fare wel folk þat *ben* riche.
B.20.261 [But þei *ben* nempned in þe noumbre of hem þat ben ywaged].
B.20.261 [But þei ben nempned in þe noumbre of hem þat *ben* ywaged].
B.20.262 Alle oþere in bataille *ben* yholde Brybours,
B.20.276 That alle þynges vnder heuene ou3te to *ben* in comune.
B.20.282 *Ben* Curatours called to knowe and to hele,
B.20.283 Alle þat *ben* hir parisshens penaunce enioigne,
B.20.305 'Go salue þo þat sike *ben* and þoru3 synne ywounded.'
B.20.365 [And] for [hem] þat ye *ben* holden to al my lif tyme,

ben C 132

C.Pr.87 *Ben* charged with holy chirche charite to tylie,
C.Pr.94 And *ben* in stede of stewardus and sitten and demen.
C.Pr.97 And boxes *ben* yset forth ybounde with yren
C.Pr.132 That Cardinales *ben* cald and closyng 3ates
C.Pr.191 And yf hym wratheth *ben* war and his way [shonye].'
C.Pr.220 What þis meteles bymeneth, 3e men þat *ben* merye,
C. 1.6 Hou bisy þei *ben* aboute þe mase?
C. 1.40 And wysseth þe to *ben* ywar what wolde þe desseyue.'
C. 1.81 'When alle tresores *ben* tried treuthe is þe beste;
C. 1.175 For thow 3e *ben* trewe of 3oure tong[e] and treweliche wynne
C. 1.176 And *ben* as chast as a child þat chyht noþer ne fyhteth,
C. 1.188 Auerous and euel willed when þei *ben* avaunsed,
C. 1.191 And *ben* acombred with coueytise: thei can nou3t [out crepe]
C. 1.202 "Whenne alle tresores *ben* tried treuthe is þe bettre."
C. 2.30 Y ouhte *ben* herrore then he; y com of a bettere.
C. 2.47 Soffre and thow shalt see suche as *ben* apayed
C. 2.87 To *ben* pr[inces] in pruyde and pouert to dispice,
C. 2.106 And sue forth suche felawschipe til they *ben* falle in Slewthe
C. 3.48 For to *ben* here bedman and bere wel here ernde
C. 3.187 He blesseth this bischopes thow thei *ben* lewede;
C. 3.258 Ac hadde y, mede, *ben* marchel o[f] his men in Fraunce
C. 3.260 He sholde haue [*ben*] lord of þat lond alenghe and abrede
C. 3.366 In whiche *ben* gode and euel, and graunte here n[eyther] will.
C. 3.457 Moises or messie, þat men *ben* so trewe.
C. 4.98 So alle my claymes *ben* quyt by so þe kyng assente.'
C. 4.120 And til byschopes *ben* bakeres, Breweres and taylours
C. 4.144 That lawe shal *ben* a laborer and lede afelde donge
C. 5.59 For hit *ben* eyres of heuene alle þat ben ycrouned
C. 5.59 For hit ben eyres of heuene alle þat *ben* ycrouned
C. 5.137 'Late no wynnynge forwanyen hem while thei *ben* 3onge
C. 5.165 In many places ther thei persones *ben*, he hemsulue at ese,
C. 6.116 With lewed and lered þat leef *ben* to here
C. 6.297 [*Ben*] haldyng at the heye dome to helpe the restitue.
C. 6.379 And bade b[et]te þe bochere *ben* on his syde.
C. 7.99 Haue beggeres byfore hem þe whiche *ben* goddes mu[n]strals
C. 7.146 For dedes that we han don ylle dampned sholde we *ben* neuere
C. 7.235 The carneles *ben* of cristendom þat kynde to saue,
C. 7.270 Ac ther *ben* seuene susteres þat seruen treuthe euere
C. 7.273 Charite and chastite *ben* his chief maydenes,
C. 8.79 They *ben* ascaped good aunter, now god hem amende.'
C. 8.107 For thouh y dey today my dette[s *ben*] yquited;
C. 8.111 And *ben* a pilgrym at þe plouh for profit to pore and ryche.'
C. 8.211 Meschef hit maketh they *ben* so meke nouthe
C. 8.264 To beggares and to boys þat loth *ben* to worche.

C. 9.4   For hym and [for] his ayres for euere to *ben* assoiled.
C. 9.13 Bishopis yblessed, yf they *ben* as they sholde,
C. 9.86 And *ben* abasched for to begge and wollen nat be aknowe
C. 9.98 Ac beggares with bagges þe whiche brewhous[es] *ben* here churches,
C. 9.138 For vnder godes secret seal here synnes *ben* keuered.
C. 9.160 Buth nat in this bulle,' quod [Peres], 'til they *ben* amended
C. 9.176 Ac olde [men] and hore þat helples *ben* and nedy
C. 9.195 For hit *ben* but boyes, bollares at þe ale,
C. 9.214 Kyndeliche, by Crist, *ben* suche ycald lollares.
C. 9.265 Thy shep *ben* ner al shabbede; the wolf shyt wolle:
C. 9.333 Forthy y rede ȝow renkes þat riche *ben* on this erthe
C. 9.337 That haen þe welthe of this world and wise men *ben* holde
C. 9.350 Suche werkes to worche the while we *ben* here
C.10.77 Aren thre fayre vertues and *ben* nat fer to fynde.
C.10.124 'Whare dowel and dobet And dobest *ben* in londe
C.10.149 Thise fyue *ben* sette for to saue Anima
C.10.190 And ȝut were best to *ben* aboute and brynge hit to hepe
C.10.192 Bishope[s] sholde *ben* hereaboute and bryng this to hepe
C.10.209 And is no more to mene but men þat *ben* bygeten
C.10.218 So was Caym conseyued and so *ben* corsed wreches
C.10.288 ȝe þat han wyues *ben* war and wo[r]cheth nat out of tyme
C.10.294 That oþergatus *ben* gete for gadelynges ben holden
C.10.294 That oþergatus ben gete for gadelynges *ben* holden
C.11.33 Nowe is þe manere at mete when munstrals *ben* stille
C.11.71 Be large þerof whil this lasteth to ledes þat *ben* nedy
C.11.125 Thus thorw my lore *ben* men ylered thogh y loke demme.
C.11.245 Bote holy churche, herborw to alle þat *ben* yblessed.
C.11.247 That [*ben*] carpentars vnder Crist holy kirke to make
C.12.28 The sauter sayth hit is no synne for suche men þat *ben* trewe
C.12.97 So loue and leute *ben* oure lordes bokes
C.12.153 And lasse drat [dethe] or in derke to *ben* yrobbed
C.12.184 That *ben* layd in louhe erthe, ylore as hit were,
C.12.187 A[c] sedes þat ben sowen and mowen soffre wyntres
C.12.189 Then sedes þat [in somer] sowe *ben* and mowen nat with forstes
C.12.225 Riht so, sothly, suche þat *ben* bischopes,
C.13.29 Bothe t[w]o *ben* gode, be ȝe ful certeyn,
C.13.66 The marchaunt is no more to mene but men þat *ben* ryche
C.13.104 The tytle [þat] ȝe take ordres by telleth ȝe *ben* avaunsed
C.13.213 Tho cauhte y colour anoen and comesede to *ben* aschamed
C.14.130 There lewede theues *ben* lolled vp; loke how þei be saued!
C.14.130 There lewede theues ben lolled vp; loke how þei *ben* saued!
C.14.193 Wher þey *ben* in hell or in heuene or Aristotel þe wyse.
C.14.196 And þe bettere for here bokes to bidden we *ben* yholde–
C.15.15 And how þat lewede men *ben* lad, but oure lord hem helpe,
C.15.298 Angeles þat in helle now *ben* hadden som tyme ioye
C.15.302 And lordes and ladyes *ben* cald for ledes þat they haue
C.16.28 And these *ben* dowel and dobet and dobest of alle.
C.16.43 For seuene synnes þer *ben* þat ass[a]ilen vs euere;
C.16.64 And buxumnesse and b[o]est [b]en eueremore at werre
C.16.270 That *ben* enblaunched with bele paroles and with bele clothes
C.16.281 Curatours of holy [kirke] and clerkes þat *ben* Auerous,
C.16.325 There pore men and prisones *ben* and paye for here fode,
C.17.52 To make men louye mesure þat monkes *ben* and freres:
C.17.57 To feffe suche and fede þat founded *ben* to þe fulle
C.17.137 For lechours louyen aȝen þe lawe and at þe laste *ben* dampned
C.17.138 And theues louyen ȝe leute hatien and at þe laste *ben* hanged
C.17.156 Ac many manere men þer *ben*, as sarresynes and iewes,
C.17.230 The heuedes of holy churche and tho þat *ben* vnder hem,
C.18.44 And leyth a laddere þerto, of lesynges *ben* þe ronges,
C.18.86 And thenne aboue is bettere fruyt, ac bothe two *ben* gode,
C.18.191 'Su[t]he they *ben* suyrelepus,' quod y, 'they haen sondry names?'
C.18.215 And o god almyhty, yf alle men *ben* of Adam.
C.18.265 Thus haue y *ben* his heraud here and in helle
C.18.279 Ne noen bern *ben* oure borw ne bryngen vs [fro his] daunger–
C.18.283 And bettere wed for vs wagen then we *ben* alle worthy;
C.19.122 The fyngres þat fre ben to folde and to cluche
C.19.229 That riche *ben* and resoun knoweth; reule wel ȝoure soul[e];
C.19.247 Excuse hem þat *ben* vnkynde and ȝut here [catel] ywonne
C.19.253 For þat *ben* vn[k]ynde to hise, hope ȝe noen oþer
C.19.301 Thre thynges ther *ben* þat doth a man to sterte
C.19.313 Thise thre that y telle of thus *ben* [to] vnderstande:
C.20.111 Now *ben* ȝoure gode dayes ydoen, as daniel of ȝow telleth;
C.20.136 Sethe this barn was ybore *ben* thritty wynter ypassed,
C.20.154 'Thorw experiense,' quod he, 'y hope they shal *ben* saued;
C.20.262 To breke and to bete adoun all þat ben agaynes hym
C.20.300 For bi riht and by resoun þ[e] renkes þat *ben* here
C.20.309 And sethen we haen *ben* sesed seuene thousand wynter
C.20.455 Then aftur werre and wrake when loue and pees *ben* maistres.
C.21.22 And synfole *ben* solaced and saued by þat name.
C.21.64 Is to wissen vs þerwith, þat when we *ben* ytempted
C.21.260 My prowour and my [plouhman Peres] shal *ben* on erthe
C.21.344 'And Peres berne worth broke and þei þat *ben* in vnite
C.21.395 And so to *ben* assoiled and sennes be hoseled.'

C.21.470 ȝe *ben* bote membres and y aboue alle.
C.22.235 Thei wol flatere to fare wel folk þat *ben* riche.
C.22.261 Bote hy *ben* nempned in þe nombre of hem þat been ywaged.
C.22.282 *Ben* curatours cald to knowe and to hele,
C.22.305 'Go salue tho þat syke [*ben*] and thorw synne ywounded.'

best A 1

A. 6.76 And boterasid wiþ beleue [so] oþer þou [*be*]st not sauid;

best C 2

C. 7.236 Ibotrased with bileue-so-or-t[hou]-*best*-not-ysaued;
C.21.408 Leue hit [wel thou] *be*[*st*] lost, bothe lyf and soule.'

beþ A 5

A. 1.150 Þeiȝ ȝe ben miȝty to mote *beþ* mek of ȝour werkis;
A. 6.107 Charite & chastite *beþ* hire chief maidenes,
A. 9.117 'Where þat dowel, & dobet, & dobest *beþ* in londe,
A.10.15 *Beþ* maistris of þis maner þis maide to kepe.
A.11.192 Þ[i]s *be*[*þ*] dobet; so beriþ witnesse þe sauter:

beþ B 23

B. 3.27 And beden hire be bliþe: 'for we *beþ* þyne owene
B. 3.304 And haue wonder in hire hertes þat men *beþ* so trewe.
B. 5.566 And so boweþ forþ by a brook, *beþ*-buxom-of-speche,
B. 7.65 Beggeres [and] bidderes *beþ* noȝt in þe bulle
B. 9.187 Whan ye han wyued *beþ* war and wercheþ in tyme,
B.10.27 "Lo!" seiþ holy lettrure, "whiche [lordes] *beþ* þise sherewes";
B.10.53 At mete in hir murþe whan Mynstrals *beþ* stille,
B.10.83 Ne *beþ* plenteuouse to þe pouere as pure charite wolde,
B.10.351 Saaf, þat is baptiȝed *beþ*, be he riche or pouere.'
B.10.452 *Beþ* noȝt [afered of þat folk], for I shal [ȝyue yow tonge],
B.11.78 Baptiȝynge and buryinge boþe *beþ* ful nedefulle;
B.11.139 For þei *beþ*, as oure bokes telleþ, aboue goddes werkes:
B.13.420 Thise ben þe braunches, *beþ* war, þat bryngen a man to wanhope.
B.15.154 Men *beþ* merciable to mendinauntȝ and to poore,
B.15.354 Boþe lettred and lewed *beþ* alayed now wiþ synne
B.15.486 Ac who *beþ* þat excuseþ hem þat [arn] persons and preestes,
B.16.7 The blosmes *beþ* buxom speche and benigne lokynge.
B.17.262 Forþi *beþ* war, ye wise men þat wiþ þe world deleþ;
B.17.264 *Beþ* noȝt vnkynde, I conseille yow, to youre euenecristene.
B.18.279 Body and soule *beþ* myne, boþe goode and ille.
B.18.376 For we *beþ* breþeren of blood, [ac] noȝt in baptisme alle.
B.18.377 Ac alle þat *beþ* myne hole breþeren, in blood and in baptisme,
B.19.358 For witterly, I woot wel, we *beþ* noȝt of strengþe

beth C 34

C. 1.172 Thow ȝe be myhty to mote *beth* meke in ȝoure werkes,
C. 2.154 ȝut *beth* ywar of þe weddynge; for witty is treuthe
C. 3.28 And beden here be blythe: 'for we *beth* thyn owene
C. 7.80 This *beth* þe branches, beth ywar, þat bryngeth a man to wanhope.
C. 7.80 This beth þe branches, *beth* ywar, þat bryngeth a man to wanhope.
C. 7.213 And so [boweth] forth by [a] brok, [*beth*-buxum-of-speche],
C. 9.51 *Beth* ywar, ȝe wis men and witty of þe lawe,
C. 9.61 Beggares and Biddares *beth* nat in þ[e] bulle
C. 9.242 Breke þis obedience þat *beth* so fer fram chirche.
C.10.228 Bestes þat now *beth* shal banne þe tyme
C.11.24 "Lo!" saith holy letrure, "whiche lordes *beth* this schrewes";
C.11.153 [Bisily] bokes; ho *beth* his witnesses?
C.11.268 And now *beth* this seyntes, by that men saith, and souereynes in heuene,
C.11.277 *Beth* nat aferd of þat folk for y shal ȝeue ȝow tonge,
C.11.288 And is to mene no more to men þat *beth* lewed:
C.12.74 They *be*[*t*]*h*, as oure bokes telleth, [aboue] godes werkes:
C.13.80 *Beth* nat ybounde, as beth [þ]e ryche, to [bothe two] lawes,
C.13.80 Beth nat ybounde, as *beth* [þ]e ryche, to [bothe two] lawes,
C.13.112 The same y segge for sothe by suche þat *beth* prestes
C.13.115 Euele *beth* thei ysoffred, suche þat [shenden] þe masse
C.14.177 For here fetheres þat fayre *beth* to fle fer hem letteth.
C.14.201 Withoute bapteme, as by here bokes, *beth* nat ysaued.'
C.15.225 Ac yf myhte of myracle hym fayle hit is for men *beth* nat worthy
C.16.202 'ȝe *beth* as a bischop,' quod y, al bourdynge þat tyme,
C.16.228 And doth hym to be deynous and deme þat *beth* nat lered.
C.16.250 Tho bowes þat bereth nat and *beth* nat grene yleued,
C.19.86 Withoute þe bloed of a barn he *beth* nat ysaued;
C.19.228 Forthy *beth* ywar, ȝe wyse men þat with the world deleth,
C.19.230 *Beth* nat vnkynde, y conseyle ȝow, to ȝoure emcristene.
C.20.301 Body and soule *beth* myne, bothe gode and ille.
C.20.354 *Beth* ywaer, ȝe wyse clerkes and ȝe witty of lawe,
C.20.382 That gylours [*beth*] bigiled and [in] here gyle falle
C.20.418 For we *beth* brethrene of bloed Ac nat in baptisme alle.
C.20.419 Ac alle þat *beth* myn hole breth[r]ene, in bloed and in baptisme,

buth C 1

C. 9.160 *Buth* nat in this bulle,' quod [Peres], 'til they ben amended

ybe B 1

B.14.96 And as it neuere [n]adde *ybe* to noȝte bryngeþ dedly synne

ybe C 1

C. 7.189 [I]ch haue *ybe* his foloware al this fourty wynter

is A 222

A.Pr.39 Qui loquitur turpiloquium [*is*] luciferis hyne.
A.Pr.64 Þe moste meschief on molde *is* mountyng vp faste.
A.Pr.77 It *is* not be þe bisshop þat þe boy prechiþ,
A.Pr.83 To synge for symonye for siluer *is* swete.
A. 1.11 And seide 'mercy madame, what *is* þis to mene?'
A. 1.12 'Þe tour [on] þe toft,' quaþ heo, 'treuþe *is* þereinne,
A. 1.14 For he *is* fadir of feiþ & fourmide ʒow alle
A. 1.23 Þat on *is* vesture fro chele þe to saue;
A. 1.24 Þat oþer *is* mete at meel for myseise of þiselue;
A. 1.33 Mesure *is* medicine þeiʒ þou muche ʒerne.
A. 1.34 Al *is* not good to þe gost þat þe gut [ask]iþ,
A. 1.35 Ne liflode to þe lykam þat lef *is* to þe soule.
A. 1.37 Þat *is* þe wrecchide world [wolde] þe betraye.
A. 1.57 'Þe dungeon in þe dale þat dredful *is* of siʒt:
A. 1.59 'Þ[at] *is* þe castel of care; who[so] comiþ þereinne
A. 1.61 Þereinne woniþ a wy þat wrong *is* yhoten;
A. 1.67 He *is* lettere of loue, leiʒeþ hem alle;
A. 1.83 'Whanne alle tresours arn triʒed treuþe *is* þe beste;
A. 1.85 It *is* as derworþi a dreury as dere god hymseluen.
A. 1.86 For whoso *is* trewe of his tunge, telliþ non oþer,
A. 1.88 He *is* a god be þe gospel on ground & on lofte,
A. 1.98 Þat *is* þe professioun apertly þat apendiþ to kniʒtes,
A. 1.102 And whoso passiþ þat poynt *is* apostata in his ordre.
A. 1.122 Þere treuþe *is* in trinite & tron[iþ] h[e]m alle.
A. 1.124 Whanne alle tresours arn triʒed treuþe *is* þe beste.
A. 1.126 Þat treuþe *is* þe tresour triʒest on erþe.'
A. 1.130 It *is* a kynde knowyng þat kenneþ in þin herte
A. 1.136 Þat loue *is* þe leuest þing þat oure lord askiþ,
A. 1.160 Þat feiþ wiþoute fait *is* feblere þan nouʒt,
A. 1.163 It *is* as lewid as a laumpe þat no liʒt is inne.
A. 1.163 It *is* as lewid as a laumpe þat no liʒt *is* inne.
A. 1.164 Manye chapelleins arn chast ac charite *is* aweye;
A. 1.172 Þ[at] *is* no treuþe of trinite but treccherie of helle,
A. 1.176 Þat *is* þe lok of loue þat letiþ out my grace
A. 1.178 Loue *is* þe leueste þing þat oure lord askiþ,
A. 1.181 Whan alle tresouris arn triʒede treuþe *is* þe beste.
A. 1.182 Now haue I told þe what treuþe *is*, þat no tresor is betere,
A. 1.182 Now haue I told þe what treuþe is, þat no tresor *is* betere,
A. 2.14 Þere nis no quen queyntere þat quyk *is* o lyue.
A. 2.15 'What *is* þis womman,' quaþ I, 'þus worþily atirid?'
A. 2.16 'Þat *is* mede þe maide, haþ noiʒede me ful ofte.
A. 2.18 In þe popis paleis heo *is* preuy as myselue;
A. 2.25 And al *is* liʒeris ledyng þat hy liʒen togideris.
A. 2.35 Sire symonye *is* assent to asele þe chartres
A. 2.48 To be fastnid wiþ fals þe fyn *is* arerid.
A. 2.71 Þere to wone wiþ wrong while god *is* in heuene.'
A. 2.77 In þe date of þe deuil þe dede *is* asselid
A. 2.83 For mede *is* molere of [m]endis engendrit
A. 2.87 Worþi *is* þe werkman his mede to haue.
A. 2.94 Þat fals *is* a faitour [and] feyntles of werkis,
A. 2.96 And mede *is* a mulere, [a maiden of gode];
A. 2.99 Lediþ hire to lundoun þere lawe is yhandlit
A. 2.102 Ʒet be war of þe weddyng for witty *is* treuþe.
A. 2.103 For consience *is* of his counseil & knowiþ ʒow ichone,
A. 2.194 And *is* welcome whanne he wile & woniþ wiþ hem ofte.
A. 3.1 Now *is* mede þe maide, & no mo of hem alle,
A. 3.59 Who *is* curteis or kynde or coueitous, or ellis,
A. 3.108 For heo *is* fayn of þi Felasshipe, for to be þi make.'
A. 3.111 She *is* freel of hire feiþ, fikel of hire speche;
A. 3.118 I[s] not a betere baude, be hym þat me made,
A. 3.120 She *is* tykil of hire tail, talewys of hire tunge,
A. 3.133 Heo *is* assoilid [as] sone as hireself likiþ.
A. 3.136 She *is* preuy wiþ þe pope, prouisours it knowiþ;
A. 3.142 Þere she *is* wel wiþ þe king wo is þe reaume,
A. 3.142 Þere she is wel wiþ þe king wo *is* þe reaume,
A. 3.143 For she *is* fauourable to fals & fouliþ treuþe ofte;
A. 3.150 Lawe *is* so lordlich & loþ to make ende,
A. 3.153 Þis *is* þe lif of þat lady, now lord ʒif hire sorewe!
A. 3.156 Such a maister *is* mede among men of goode.'
A. 3.164 Þere þat meschief *is* gret mede may helpe,
A. 3.195 Þat *is* þe riccheste reaume þat re[yn] ouer[houiþ].
A. 3.216 Mede *is* worþi þe maistrie to haue'.
A. 3.225 Þere *is* a mede mesurles þat maistris desiriþ;
A. 3.235 *Is* no maner of mede but a mesurable hire;
A. 3.236 In marchaundie *is* no mede, I may it wel auowe;
A. 3.237 It *is* a permutacioun apertly, a peny[worþ] for anoþer.
A. 3.273 Þat lawe is lord waxen & leute is pore,
A. 3.273 Þat lawe is lord waxen & leute *is* pore,
A. 3.274 Vnkyndenesse *is* comaundour, & kyndenesse is banisshit.
A. 3.274 Vnkyndenesse is comaundour, & kyndenesse *is* banisshit.
A. 4.58 But ʒif mede it make [þi] meschief *is* vppe,
A. 4.79 'Betere *is* þat boote bale adoun bringe,

A. 4.146 'Ac it *is* wel hard, be myn hed, herto to bringe it.
A. 5.83 He *is* douʒtiere þanne I–I dar non harm don hym,
A. 5.204 Þe ferste woord þat he spak was 'where *is* þe bolle?'
A. 5.219 For *is* no gilt here so gret þat his goodnesse nis more'.
A. 6.35 Þere *is* no labourer in his lordsshipe þat he louiþ beter
A. 6.38 He *is* þe presteste payere þat pore men knowen;
A. 6.40 He *is* as louʒ as a lomb & loueliche of speche.
A. 6.47 Ac ʒe þat wilneþ to wende, þis *is* þe weye þider.
A. 6.68 He *is* fre[þ]id in wiþ Floreynes & oþere [fees] manye.
A. 6.73 Þe mot *is* of mercy þe Maner al aboute,
A. 6.79 Þe tour þere treuþe *is* hymself is vp to þe sonne;
A. 6.79 Þe tour þere treuþe is hymself *is* vp to þe sonne;
A. 6.110 Ac whoso *is* sib to þis sistris, so me god helpe,
A. 6.111 He *is* wondirliche welcome & faire vndirfonge.
A. 6.113 It *is* wel hard, be myn hed, any of ʒow alle,
A. 6.120 'Mercy [*is*] a maiden [þere], haþ miʒt ouer [hem] alle;
A. 6.121 And she *is* sib to alle synful, & hire sone alse,
A. 7.19 Þat han silk & sendel, sewiþ it whanne tyme *is*,
A. 7.68 For holy chirche *is* holden of hem no tiþes to asken,
A. 7.70 Dame merciþ wharne whanne tyme *is* piers wyf hatte;
A. 7.86 He *is* holden, I hope, to haue me in mynde,
A. 7.97 Now *is* peris & þe pilgrimes to þe plouʒ faren;
A. 7.137 Ones at noon *is* ynouʒ þat no werk vsiþ;
A. 7.189 Of beggeris & bidderis what best *is* to done.
A. 7.228 "He þat haþ shal haue to helpe þere nede *is*,
A. 7.250 L[o]ue hym nouʒt, for he *is* a lecchour & likerous of tunge,
A. 7.251 And aftir many maner metis his mawe *is* alongid.
A. 7.260 Þis *is* a louely lessoun, lord it þe forʒelde.
A. 7.261 Wende now whanne þi wille *is*, þat wel be þou euere.'
A. 8.50 Þat *is* Innocent & nedy, & no man apeiriþ,
A. 8.55 Ac to bigge watir ne wynd, ne wyt *is* þe þridde,
A. 8.59 His pardoun in purcatorie wel [petit] *is*, I trowe,
A. 8.62 Siþen ʒe sen it *is* þus sewiþ ʒow bope:
A. 8.70 He *is* fals wiþ þe fend & [defraudiþ] þe nedy,
A. 8.110 Þat louiþ god lelly, his liflode *is* þe more:
A. 8.138 Daniel seide, 'sire king, þi sweuene *is* to mene
A. 8.155 Dowel at þe day of dome *is* digneliche vndirfongen;
A. 8.159 Þis *is* [a] l[e]f of oure beleue, as lettrid men vs [tech]iþ:
A. 8.164 It *is* not so sikir for þe soule, certis, as is do wel.
A. 8.164 It is not so sikir for þe soule, certis, as *is* do wel.
A. 9.21 He *is* oþerwhile elliswhere to wisse þe peple.'
A. 9.29 And ʒet *is* he sauf & sound, & so hym behouiþ.
A. 9.34 Þe watir *is* liknid to þe world þat waniþ & waxiþ;
A. 9.37 Þe boot *is* lik[nid] to þe body þat britel is of kynde,
A. 9.37 Þe boot is lik[nid] to þe body þat britel *is* of kynde,
A. 9.41 Þat *is* charite þe champioun, chief helpe aʒens synne.
A. 9.44 Ay *is* þi soule sauf but þou þiself wilt
A. 9.71 Whoso *is* mek of his mouþ, mylde of his speche,
A. 9.75 And [*is*] nouʒt drunkelewe ne deynous, dowel hym folewiþ.
A. 9.77 He *is* as louʒ as a lomb, louelich of speche,
A. 9.78 Whiles he haþ ouʒt of his owene he helpiþ þere nede *is*;
A. 9.82 And *is* ronne to religioun, & haþ rendrit þe bible,
A. 9.86 Dobest *is* aboue hem boþe & beriþ a bisshopis croce.
A. 9.87 *Is* hokid at þat on ende to holde men in good lif.
A. 9.88 A pik *is* in þat potent to pungen adoun þe wykkide,
A. 9.106 Ellis wot no man þat now *is* o lyue.'
A. 9.118 Here is wil wolde wyte ʒif wit couþe hym teche.'
A.10.3 Of erþe & eir it *is* mad, medlit togideris,
A.10.12 Dobet *is* hire damysele, sire dowelis [douʒter],
A.10.17 *Is* a wys kniʒt withalle, sire [inwit] he hatte,
A.10.26 [And what [kenis] þing *is* kynde, conne ʒe me telle]?'
A.10.27 'Kynde,' quaþ he, '*is* creatour of alle kenis bestis,
A.10.29 And þat *is* þe grete god þat gynnyng had neuere,
A.10.32 Ac man *is* hym most lik of mark & of shap.
A.10.38 Þat *is* þe castel þat kynde made, caro it hatte,
A.10.43 For loue of þat lady þat lif *is* ynempnid.
A.10.44 Þat *is* Anima, þat oueral in þe body wandriþ,
A.10.45 Ac in þe herte *is* hire hom heiʒest of alle.
A.10.46 Heo *is* lyf & ledere, a lemman of heuene.
A.10.47 Inwyt *is* þe [allie] þat anima desiriþ;
A.10.48 Aftir þe grace of god [þe grettest *is* Inwyt].
A.10.49 Inwyt in þe heuid *is*, & an help to þe soule,
A.10.50 For þoruʒ his connyng *is* kept caro & anima
A.10.53 Of good speche & [going] he *is* þe begynnere,
A.10.54 In manis brayn *is* he most & miʒtiest to knowe.
A.10.55 Þere *is* his bour bremest but ʒif blod it make;
A.10.56 For whan blood *is* bremere þanne brayn, þan is Inwit bounde,
A.10.56 For whan blood is bremere þanne brayn, þan *is* Inwit bounde,
A.10.69 Þanne *is* holichirche owyng to helpe hem & saue
A.10.72 *Is* chief souereyn ouer hymself his soule to ʒeme,
A.10.75 For werche he wel oþer wrong, þe wyt *is* his owene.
A.10.76 Þanne *is* dowel a duc þat destroyeþ vices,
A.10.79 And þat *is* dred of god, dowel it makiþ.

A.10.80 It *is* begynnyng of goodnesse god for to douten.
A.10.82 For doute men doþ þe bet; dred *is* such a maister
A.10.85 Þanne *is* dobet to ben ywar for betyng of þe ȝarde,
A.10.108 Thrift oþer þedom with þo *is* selde yseiȝe:
A.10.111 And for wisdom *is* writen & witnessid in chirches:
A.10.122 Which *is* þe flour & þe fruyt fostrid of boþe.
A.10.123 Riȝt as a rose, [þat red *is* and] swet,
A.10.130 Such wer[kis] to werche [þat] he *is* wiþ paied.
A.10.163 And *is* as muche to mene, among vs alle,
A.10.186 It *is* an vncomely copil, be crist, as [me þinkeþ],
A.10.216 Þanne *is* dowel to dreden, & dobet to suffre,
A.10.218 And þat *is* wykkide wil þat many werk shendiþ.'
A.11.17 Wisdom and wyt now *is* not worþ a risshe
A.11.29 Litel *is* he louid or lete by þat suche a lessoun techiþ,
A.11.35 Menstralsie & merþe among men is nouþe
A.11.47 *Is* non to nymen hym In ne his [noye] amende,
A.11.53 God *is* muche in þe [gorge] of þis grete maistris,
A.11.61 For now *is* iche boy bold, & he be riche,
A.11.88 What *is* dowel fro dobet; now def mote he worþe,
A.11.103 [To] kenne me kyndely to knowe what *is* dowel'.
A.11.105 I shal kenne þe to my cosyn þat clergie *is* hoten.
A.11.107 *Is* sib to þe seuene ars þat scripture is nempnid.
A.11.107 Is sib to þe seuene ars þat scripture is nempnid.
A.11.113 'And tel me sum tokne to hym, for tyme *is* þat I wende'.
A.11.140 It *is* no science forsoþe for to sotile þereinne.
A.11.143 For þere þat loue *is* lord lakkiþ neuere grace.
A.11.155 Astronomye is hard þing & euil for to knowe;
A.11.156 Geometrie & geomesie *is* gynful of speche:
A.11.158 For sorcerie *is* þe souerayn bok þat to þat science longiþ.
A.11.182 'It *is* a wel lel[e] lif,' quaþ she, 'among þe lewide peple;
A.11.183 Actif it *is* hoten; [husbondis] it vsen,
A.11.194 [Dredles] þis *is* dobet; [dobest wot þe soþe].
A.11.195 Sire dobest haþ ben [in office], so *is* he best worþi
A.11.197 Forþi *is* dobest [a] bisshopis pere,
A.11.199 Dobet doþ ful wel, & dowel *is* also,
A.11.202 And þat *is* riȝtful religioun, none renneris aboute,
A.11.211 Ac now *is* religioun a ridere & a rennere [be stretis],
A.11.217 Þis *is* þe lif of þis lordis þat lyuen shulde wiþ dobet,
A.11.229 Poul prouiþ it *is* vnpossible, riche men in heuene.
A.11.233 And prouen it be þe pistil þat petir *is* nempnid:
A.11.235 'Þat *is* in extremis,' quaþ scripture, 'as sarisines & Iewis
A.11.236 Mowe be sauid so, & so *is* oure beleue.
A.11.241 For cristene han a degre & *is* þe comun speche:
A.11.250 Þat *is*, iche cristene [creature] be kynde to oþer,
A.11.254 Ne mecaberis, ne sle nouȝt, *is* þe kynde englissh;
A.11.259 To wyte what *is* dowel witterly in herte,
A.11.297 And *is* as muche to mene, to men þat ben lewid,
A.11.306 And *is* to mene in oure mouþ, more ne lesse,
A.12.43 And sayde, 'my cosyn kynde wit knowen *is* wel wide,
A.12.44 And his loggyng *is* with lyf þat lord is of erþe,
A.12.44 And his loggyng is with lyf þat lord *is* of erþe,
A.12.82 Mi name *is* feuere on þe ferþe day; I am aþrest euere.
A.12.84 Þat on *is* called cotidian, a courrour of oure hous;
A.12.87 Fro deþ þat *is* oure duk swyche dedis we brynge.'
A.12.90 But lyue as þis lyf *is* ordeyned for the.
A.12.101 And wrouȝthe þat here *is* wryten and oþer werkes boþe
A.12.105 And *is* closed vnder clom, crist haue his soule.
B.Pr.39 Qui loquitur turpiloquium *is* luciferes hyne.
B.Pr.67 The mooste meschief on Molde *is* mountynge [vp] faste.
B.Pr.80 It *is* noȝt by þe bisshop þat þe boy precheþ;
B.Pr.86 [To] syngen for symonie for siluer *is* swete.
B.Pr.98 Arn doon vndeuoutliche; drede *is* at þe laste
B.Pr.105 There [crist *is* in] kyngdom, to close and to shette,
B.Pr.191 For bettre *is* a litel los þan a long sorwe.
B.Pr.194 Ther þe cat *is* a kitoun þe court is ful elenge;
B.Pr.194 Ther þe cat is a kitoun þe court *is* ful elenge;
B.1.12 'The tour on þe toft', quod she, 'truþe *is* þerInne,
B.1.14 For he *is* fader of feiþ, and formed yow alle
B.1.23 That oon [*is*] vesture from [chele] þee to saue;
B.1.24 [That oþer *is*] mete at meel for mysese of þiselue,
B.1.35 Mesure *is* medicine þouȝ þow muchel yerne.
B.1.36 [Al *is* nouȝt] good to þe goost þat þe gut askeþ,
B.1.37 Ne liflode to þ[e] likame [þat leef is to þ[e] soule.
B.1.39 That *is* þe wrecched world wolde þee bitraye.
B.1.59 'Th[e] dongeon in þe dale þat dredful *is* of siȝte–
B.1.61 'That *is* þe castel of care; whoso comþ þerInne
B.1.63 TherInne wonyeþ a [wye] þat wrong *is* yhote;
B.1.69 He *is* lettere of loue, lieþ hem alle;
B.1.85 'Whan alle tresors arn tried treuþe *is* þe beste;
B.1.87 It *is* as dereworþe a drury as deere god hymseluen.
B.1.88 [For] who *is* trewe of his tonge, telleþ noon ooþer,
B.1.90 He *is* a god by þe gospel, a grounde and o lofte,
B.1.100 [That] *is* [þe] profession apertli þat apendeþ to knyȝtes,

B.1.104 And whoso passe[þ] þat point [*is*] Apostata in [his] ordre.
B.1.131 And enden, as I er seide, in truþe þat *is* þe beste.
B.1.133 Ther Treuþe *is* in Trinitee and troneþ hem alle.
B.1.135 Whan alle tresors arn tried truþe *is* þe beste.
B.1.137 That Treuþe *is* tresor þe trieste on erþe.'
B.1.142 It *is* a kynde knowyng þat kenneþ in þyn herte
B.1.148 For truþe telleþ þat loue *is* triacle of heuene:
B.1.159 Forþi *is* loue ledere of þe lordes folk of heuene
B.1.160 And a meene, as þe Mair *is*, bitwene þe [commune] & þe [kyng];
B.1.161 Right so *is* loue a ledere and þe lawe shapeþ;
B.1.164 And in þe herte þere *is* þe heed and þe heiȝe welle.
B.1.186 That Feiþ withouten feet *is* [feblere þan nouȝt],
B.1.189 It *is* as lewed as a lampe þat no liȝt is Inne.
B.1.189 It is as lewed as a lampe þat no liȝt *is* Inne.
B.1.190 Manye Chapeleyns arn chaste ac charite *is* aweye;
B.1.198 [Th]at *is* no truþe of þe Trinite but tricherie of helle,
B.1.202 [Th]at *is* þe lok of loue [þat] leteþ out my grace
B.1.204 Loue *is* leche of lif and next oure lord selue,
B.1.207 Whan alle tresors ben tried treuþe *is* þe beste.
B.1.208 Now haue I told þee what truþe *is*, þat no tresor is bettre,
B.1.208 Now haue I told þee what truþe is, þat no tresor *is* bettre,
B.2.19 'What *is* þis womman', quod I, 'so worþili atired?'
B.2.20 'That *is* Mede þe mayde, haþ noyed me ful ofte,
B.2.21 And ylakked my lemman þat leautee *is* hoten.
B.2.23 In þe popes Paleis she *is* pryuee as myselue,
B.2.24 But sooþnesse wolde noȝt so for she *is* a Bastard.
B.2.27 And Mede *is* manered after hym [as men of] kynde [carpeþ]:
B.2.29 My fader þe grete god *is* and ground of alle graces,
B.2.43 And al *is* lieres ledynge þat [lady] is þus ywedded.
B.2.43 And al is lieres ledynge þat [lady] *is* þus ywedded.
B.2.76 That Mede *is* ymaried moore for hire goodes
B.2.78 Falsnesse *is* fayn of hire for he woot hire riche;
B.2.87 That *is* vsure and Auarice; al I hem graunte
B.2.101 For he leueþ be lost, þis *is* [his] laste ende.
B.2.107 And with hym to wonye [in] wo while god *is* in heuene.'
B.2.113 'In þe date of þe deuel þ[e] dede [*is* asseled]
B.2.119 For Mede *is* muliere of Amendes engendred
B.2.130 That Fals *is* fe[ynt]lees and fikel in hise werkes,
B.2.132 And Mede *is* muliere, a maiden of goode;
B.2.135 Ledeþ hire to Londoun þere [lawe] [*is* yhandled],
B.2.138 Yet be war of [þe] weddynge; for witty *is* truþe,
B.2.139 [For] Conscience *is* of his counseil and knoweþ yow echone;
B.2.179 Shul seruen myself þat Cyuyle *is* nempned.
B.2.235 And *is* welcome whan he wile and woneþ with hem ofte.
B.3.1 NOw *is* Mede þe mayde and na mo of hem alle
B.3.55 It *is* a freletee of flessh–ye fynden it in bokes–
B.3.57 Who may scape [þe] sclaundre, þe scaþe *is* soone amended;
B.3.58 It *is* synne of þe seuene sonnest relessed.
B.3.119 For she *is* fayn of þi felaweshipe, for to be þi make.'
B.3.122 She *is* frele of hire feiþ, fikel of hire speche;
B.3.129 *Is* noȝt a bettre baude, by hym þat me made,
B.3.131 She *is* tikel of hire tail, talewis of tonge,
B.3.144 She *is* assoiled as soone as hireself likeþ.
B.3.147 She *is* pryuee wiþ þe pope, prouisours it knoweþ;
B.3.153 Ther she *is* wel wiþ þe kyng wo is þe Reaume,
B.3.153 Ther she is wel wiþ þe kyng wo *is* þe Reaume,
B.3.154 For she *is* fauourable to fals and [f]ouleþ truþe ofte.
B.3.161 Lawe *is* so lordlich and looþ to maken ende.
B.3.166 This *is* þe lif of þat lady, now lord ȝyue hire sorwe,
B.3.169 Swich a maister *is* Mede among men of goode.'
B.3.177 Ther þat meschief *is* [most] Mede may helpe.
B.3.208 That *is* þe richeste Reaume þat reyn ouerhoueþ.
B.3.229 Mede *is* worþi, [me þynkeþ], þe maistrie to haue'.
B.3.246 Ther *is* [a] Mede mesurelees þat maistres desireþ;
B.3.256 It *is* no manere Mede but a mesurable hire.
B.3.257 In marchaundise *is* no Mede, I may it wel auowe;
B.3.258 It *is* a permutacion apertly, a penyworþ for anoþer.
B.3.282 For so *is* þis world went wiþ hem þat han power
B.3.283 That whoso seiþ hem soþe[s] *is* sonnest yblamed.
B.3.318 But after þe dede þat *is* doon oon doom shal rewarde
B.3.351 And þat *is* þe tail of þe text of þat [teme ye] shewed,
B.3.353 The soule þat þe soude takeþ by so muche *is* bounde.'
B.4.35 Theras wraþe and wranglynge *is* þer wynne þei siluer,
B.4.36 Ac [þ]ere *is* loue and leautee [hem likeþ] noȝt come þere:
B.4.72 But if Mede it make þi meschief *is* vppe,
B.4.92 'Bettre *is* þat boote bale adoun brynge
B.4.183 It *is* [wel] hard, by myn heed, hert[o] to brynge it,
B.5.49 'It *is* þi [tresor if treson ne were], and tryacle at þy nede.'
B.5.100 That boþe lif and lyme *is* lost þoruȝ my speche.
B.5.103 He *is* douȝtier þan I; I dar [noon harm doon hym],
B.5.122 For enuye and yuel wil *is* yuel to defie.
B.5.127 'Sorwe [for] synn[e] *is* sauacion of soules.'
B.5.142 And now *is* fallen þerof a fruyt þat folk han wel leuere

B. 5.152 [That] I ne moste folwe this folk, for swich *is* my grace.
B. 5.258 'I am holden', quod he, 'as hende as hound *is* in kichene;
B. 5.265 For were I frere of þat hous þer good feiþ and charite *is*
B. 5.275 [Is] holden at þe heiȝe doom to helpe þee to restitue,
B. 5.355 *Is* noon so hungry hound in hertford shire
B. 5.362 The firste word þat he [spak] was 'where *is* þe bolle?'
B. 5.401 That I telle wiþ my tonge *is* two myle fro myn herte.
B. 5.426 And my seruauntȝ som tyme: hir salarie *is* bihynde;
B. 5.427 Ruþe *is* to here rekenyng whan we shul rede acountes:
B. 5.447 For *is* no gilt here so gret þat his goodnesse [i]s moore.'
B. 5.447 For *is* no gilt here so gret þat his goodnesse [i]s moore.'
B. 5.492 Aboute mydday, whan moost liȝt *is* and meel tyme of Seintes,
B. 5.551 He *is* þe presteste paiere þat pouere men knoweþ;
B. 5.553 He *is* as lowe as a lamb and louelich of speche;
B. 5.560 Ac [ye þat] wilneþ to wende, þis *is* þe wey þider.
B. 5.581 He *is* fryþed In wiþ floryns and oþere fees manye;
B. 5.586 The moot *is* of mercy þe Manoir aboute;
B. 5.592 The brugg[e] *is* of bidde-wel-þe-bet-may-þow-spede;
B. 5.593 Ech piler *is* of penaunce, of preieres-to-Seyntes,
B. 5.625 A[c] who *is* sib to þise [sustren], so me god helpe,
B. 5.626 He *is* wonderly welcome and faire vnderfongen.
B. 5.628 It *is* [wel] hard, by myn heed, any of yow alle
B. 5.635 'Mercy *is* a maiden þere haþ myȝt ouer [hem] alle;
B. 5.636 And she *is* sib to alle synfulle and hire sone also,
B. 6.11 That ye haue silk and Sandel to sowe whan tyme *is*
B. 6.76 For holy chirche *is* [holde] of hem no tiþe to [aske],
B. 6.78 Dame werch-whan-tyme-*is* Piers wif hiȝte;
B. 6.94 [He *is*] holden, I hope, to haue me in [mynde]
B. 6.105 Now *is* Perkyn and [þe] pilgrimes to þe plow faren.
B. 6.144 And al *is* þoruȝ suffrance þat vengeaunce yow ne takeþ;
B. 6.151 For it *is* an vnresonable Religion þat haþ riȝt noȝt of certein.'
B. 6.206 And for defaute of foode þis folk *is* at my wille.
B. 6.244 "He þat haþ shal haue and helpe þere [nede *is*]
B. 6.252 He *is* blessed by þe book in body and in soule:
B. 6.266 L[o]ue hym noȝt for he [a] lech[our] and likerous of tunge,
B. 6.267 And after many maner metes his mawe *is* [alonged].
B. 6.276 /[Th]is *is* a louely lesson; lord it þee foryelde.
B. 6.277 Wend now whan [þi wil *is*], þat wel be þow euere.'\
B. 7.48 That is Innocent and nedy and no man apeireþ,
B. 7.58 Hi[s] pardon *is* [wel] petit at hi[s] partyng hennes
B. 7.68 He *is* fals wiþ þe feend and defraudeþ þe nedy,
B. 7.73 Cui des videto *is* Catons techyng,
B. 7.78 For wite ye neuere who *is* worþi, ac god woot who haþ nede.
B. 7.79 In hym þat takeþ *is* þe trecherie if any treson walke.
B. 7.82 For beggeres borwen eueremo and hir borgh *is* god almyȝty
B. 7.96 Ther *is* moore mysshapen amonges þise beggeres
B. 7.128 That loueþ god lelly his liflode *is* ful esy:
B. 7.160 Daniel seide, 'sire kyng, þi [sweuene *is* to mene]
B. 7.177 Dowel at þe day of dome *is* digneliche vnderfongen;
B. 7.181 This *is* [a leef of] oure bileue, as lettred men vs techeþ:
B. 7.186 [It] *is* noȝt so siker for þe soule, certes, as is dowel.
B. 7.186 [It] *is* noȝt so siker for þe soule, certes, as *is* dowel.
B. 8.25 He *is* ouþerwhile elliswhere to wisse þe peple.'
B. 8.33 Ac yet *is* he saaf and sound, and so hym bihoueþ,
B. 8.38 The water *is* likned to þe world þat wanyeþ and wexeþ;
B. 8.41 The boot *is* likned to [þe] body þat brotel of kynde,
B. 8.41 The boot is likned to [þe] body þat brotel *is* of kynde,
B. 8.45 [Th]at *is* charite þe champion, chief help ayein synne.
B. 8.48 Ay *is* þi soule saaf but [þow þiselue wole
B. 8.55 Ac man maad moost þerof and moost *is* to blame
B. 8.80 Whoso *is* [meke of his mouþ, milde of his speche],
B. 8.84 And *is* noȝt dronkelewe ne [d]eynous, dowel hym folweþ.
B. 8.86 He *is* as lowe as a lamb, louelich of speche;
B. 8.87 [Whiles he haþ ouȝt of his owene he helpeþ þer nede *is*];
B. 8.91 And *is* ronne to Religion, and haþ rendred þe bible,
B. 8.96 Dobest *is* aboue boþe and bereþ a bisshopes crosse;
B. 8.97 *Is* hoked [at] þat oon ende to [holde men in good lif].
B. 8.98 A pik *is* [in] þat potente to [punge] adown þe wikked
B. 8.116 Ellis [n]oot [no man] þat now is alyue;
B. 8.129 Here *is* wil wolde wite if wit koude [hym teche];
B. 8.131 And werchen as þei þre wolde; th[i]s *is* his entente.'
B. 9.3 Of erþe and Eyr [it *is*] maad, medled togideres,
B. 9.12 Dobet *is* hire damyselle, sire doweles douȝter,
B. 9.14 Dobest *is* aboue boþe, a Bisshopes peere;
B. 9.16 [By his leryng *is* lad þat lady Anima].
B. 9.18 *Is* a wis knyȝt wiþalle, sire Inwit he hatte,
B. 9.25 'What kynnes þyng *is* kynde?' quod I; 'kanstow me telle?'
B. 9.26 'Kynde', quod [he], '*is* creatour of alle kynnes [beestes],
B. 9.28 And þat *is* þe grete god þat gynnyng hadde neuere,
B. 9.31 Ac man *is* hym moost lik of marc and of [shape].
B. 9.50 [Th]at *is* þe Castel þat kynde made; caro it hatte,
B. 9.55 For loue of þe lady anima þat lif *is* ynempned.
B. 9.57 A[c] in þe herte *is* hir hoom and hir mooste reste.

B. 9.58 Ac Inwit *is* in þe heed and to þe herte he lokeþ
B. 9.59 What anima *is* leef or looþ; he l[e]t hire at his wille.
B. 9.60 For after þe grace of god þe gretteste *is* Inwit.
B. 9.62 And þat ben glotons, glubberes; hir god *is* hire wombe:
B. 9.64 That lyuen synful lif here hir soule *is* lich þe deuel.
B. 9.69 [Holy chirche is owynge to helpe hem and saue.
B. 9.93 He *is* [Iugged wiþ] Iudas þat ȝyueþ a Iaper siluer
B. 9.102 *Is* moost yhated vpon erþe of hem þat ben in heuene;
B. 9.103 And siþþe to spille speche þat [spire] *is* of grace
B. 9.110 [Dowel in þis world *is* trewe wedded libbynge folk],
B. 9.120 In erþe [þe] heuene [*is*]; hymself [was þe] witnesse.
B. 9.148 The gospel *is* hera[g]ein in o degre, I fynde.
B. 9.165 It *is* an vncomly couple, by crist! as me þynkeþ,
B. 9.184 Fo[r] lecherie in likynge *is* lymeyerd of helle.
B. 9.202 Dowel, my [deere], *is* to doon as lawe techeþ;
B. 9.204 Ac to loue and to lene], leue me, þat *is* dobet;
B. 9.206 To helen and to helpen, *is* dobest of alle.
B. 9.207 [Thanne *is* dowel] to drede, and dobet to suffre,
B. 9.209 And þat *is* wikked wille þat many werk shendeþ,
B.10.17 Wisdom and wit now *is* noȝt worþ a [risshe]
B.10.37 Litel *is* he loued [or lete by] þat swich a lesson [techeþ],
B.10.49 Ac [mynstralcie and murþe] amonges men *is* nouþe,
B.10.61 *Is* noon to nyme hym [in, ne] his [n]oy amende.
B.10.67 God *is* muche in þe gorge of þise grete maistres,
B.10.75 That folk *is* noȝt fermed in þe feiþ ne free of hire goodes
B.10.76 Ne sory for hire synnes; so *is* pride woxen
B.10.79 [For god *is* def nowadayes and deyneþ [noȝt vs to here],
B.10.81 And yet þe wrecches of þis world *is* noon ywar by ooþer,
B.10.97 Elenge *is* þe halle, ech day in þe wike,
B.10.135 What *is* dowel fro dobet, [now] deef mote he worþe,
B.10.151 [To] kenne me kyndely to knowe what *is* dowel.'
B.10.153 I shal kenne þee to my Cosyn þat Clergie *is* hoten.
B.10.155 *Is* sib to [þe] seuen artȝ, [þat] Scripture is [nempned].
B.10.155 Is sib to [þe] seuen artȝ, [þat] Scripture *is* [nempned].
B.10.161 'And tel me som tokene [to hym], for tyme *is* þat I wende'.
B.10.188 It *is* no Science forsoþe for to sotile Inne:
B.10.191 For þere þat loue *is* ledere lakke[þ] neuere grace.
B.10.199 This *is* Catons kennyng to clerkes þat he lereþ.
B.10.211 For *is* no science vnder sonne so souereyn for þe soule.
B.10.212 Ac Astronomye *is* hard þyng and yuel for to knowe;
B.10.213 Geometrie and Geomesie [*is*] gynful of speche;
B.10.215 For sorcerie *is* þe Souereyn book þat to [þat] Scienc[e] [l]ongeþ.
B.10.223 To counseille þee kyndely to knowe what *is* dowel.'
B.10.238 'It *is* a commune lyf', quod Clergie, 'on holy chirche to bileue
B.10.240 And þat *is* to bileue lelly, boþe lered and lewed,
B.10.244 Thoruȝ þe help of þe holy goost þe which *is* of boþe;
B.10.246 For al *is* but oon god and ech is god hymselue:
B.10.246 For al is but oon god and ech *is* god hymselue:
B.10.257 [So] *is* dobet to suffre for þ[i] soules helþe
B.10.259 And þat *is*, man, bi þy myȝt, for mercies sake,
B.10.264 Thanne *is* dobest to be boold to blame þe gilty,
B.10.270 Siþen a beem [*is*] in þyn owene ablyndeþ þiselue–
B.10.283 And þe festu *is* fallen for youre defaute
B.10.306 It *is* in cloistre or in scole, by manye skiles I fynde.
B.10.308 But al *is* buxomnesse þere and bokes, to rede and to lerne].
B.10.309 In scole þere *is* scorn but if a clerk wol lerne,
B.10.311 Ac now *is* Religion a rydere, a [rennere by stretes],
B.10.320 Of þe pouere haue þei no pite, and þat *is* hir [pure chartre];
B.10.329 Of Costantyns cofres [þer þe catel *is* Inne]
B.10.336 'Thanne is dowel and dobet', quod I, 'dominus and knyȝthode?'
B.10.342 Salomon seiþ also þat siluer *is* worst to louye'.
B.10.350 And preuen it by [þe pistel þat Peter *is* nempned]:
B.10.351 That *is* baptiȝed beþ saaf, be he riche or pouere.'
B.10.352 'That *is* in extremis', quod Scripture, '[as] Sarȝens & Iewes
B.10.353 Mowen be saued so, and [so] *is* oure bileue.
B.10.361 That *is*, loue þi lord god leuest abouen alle,
B.10.371 And seiþ "slee noȝt þat semblable *is* to myn owene liknesse
B.10.373 *Is* slee noȝt but suffre and [so] for þe beste,
B.10.377 'This *is* a long lesson', quod I, 'and litel am I þe wiser.
B.10.378 Where dowel *is* or dobet derkliche ye shewen.
B.10.412 Of holi chirche þat herberwe *is*, and goddes hous to saue
B.10.415 The culorum of þis clause curatours *is* to mene,
B.10.442 And wherby wiste men which [*is*] whit if alle þyng blak were,
B.10.462 And *is* to mene to [Englissh] men, moore ne lesse,
B.10.481 The which *is* mannes soule to saue, as god seiþ in þe gospel:
B.11.55 For whiles Fortune *is* þi frend freres wol þee louye,
B.11.79 Ac muche moore meritorie, me þynkeþ, *is* to baptiȝe,
B.11.96 It *is* licitum for lewed men to [legge] þe soþe
B.11.105 [Th]yng þat *is* pryue, publice þow it neuere;
B.11.137 'That *is* sooþ', seide Scripture; 'may no synne lette
B.11.160 [This matere *is* merk for many, ac men of holy chirche,
B.11.167 Loue and lewtee *is* a leel science,
B.11.168 For þat *is* þe book blissed of blisse and of ioye;

B.11.173 But þei ben lerned for oure lordes loue, lost *is* al þe tyme,
B.11.183 For hem þat haten vs *is* oure merite to louye,
B.11.213 For woot no man how neiȝ it *is* to ben ynome fro boþe.
B.11.215 Ne vndernyme noȝt foule, for *is* noon wiþoute defaute.
B.11.219 Thanne *is* bileue a lele help, aboue logyk or lawe.
B.11.221 *Is* litel alowaunce maad, but if bileue hem helpe;
B.11.222 For it *is* ouerlonge er logyk any lesson assoille,
B.11.223 And lawe *is* looþ to louye but if he lacche siluer.
B.11.232 Why I meue þis matere *is* moost for þe pouere;
B.11.260 As a walnote wiþoute is a bitter barke,
B.11.262 *Is* a kernel of confort kynde to restore.
B.11.266 Of which crist *is* a kernell to conforte þe soule.
B.11.267 And wel sikerer he slepeþ, þe [segge] þat *is* pouere,
B.11.269 Than he þat *is* riȝt riche; Reson bereþ witnesse.
B.11.275 And *is* to mene to men þat on þis moolde lyuen;
B.11.296 It *is* a careful knyȝt, and of a caytif kynges makyng,
B.11.303 A chartre *is* chalangeable bifore a chief Iustice;
B.11.306 The gome þat gloseþ so chartres for a goky is holden.
B.11.307 So *is* it a goky, by god! þat in his gospel failleþ,
B.11.315 A[c] neuer neiþer *is* blamelees, þe bisshop ne þe Chapeleyn;
B.11.316 For hir eiþer *is* endited, and that [of] 'Ignorancia
B.11.319 The which I preise, þer pacience *is*, moore parfit þan richesse.
B.11.378 Amende þow, if þow myȝt, for my tyme is to abide.
B.11.379 Suffraunce *is* a souerayn vertue, and a swift vengeaunce.
B.11.382 Ac he suffreþ for som mannes goode, and so *is* oure bettre.
B.11.389 For *is* no creature vnder crist can formen hymseluen,
B.11.409 [To wite] what dowel *is*, [ac wakyng neuere]'.
B.11.411 '[What *is* dowel?' quod þat wiȝt]; 'ywis, sire', I seide,
B.11.412 'To se muche and suffre moore, certes, *is* dowel.'
B.11.434 Thanne woot þe dronken [wye] wherfore he *is* to blame.'
B.11.439 'Certes', quod he, 'þat *is* sooþ'; and shoop hym for to walken,
B.12.15 It *is* but murþe as for me to amende my soule.
B.12.18 To telle men what dowel *is*, dobet and dobest boþe,
B.12.19 And prechours to preuen what it *is* of many a peire freres.'
B.12.29 'Poul in his pistle', quod he, 'preueþ what *is* dowel:
B.12.33 That *is*, if þow be man maryed þi make þow louye
B.12.37 And hold þee vnder obedience þat heigh wey *is* to heuene.
B.12.56 Wo *is* hym þat hem weldeþ but he hem [wel] despende:
B.12.59 Ac grace *is* a gras þer[for] þo greuaunces to abate.
B.12.61 Pacience and pouerte þe place [*is*] þer it groweþ,
B.12.68 Ac grace *is* a gifte of god and of greet loue spryngeþ,
B.12.70 Ac yet *is* Clergie to comende and kynde wit boþe,
B.12.71 And namely Clergie for cristes loue, þat of Clergie *is* roote.
B.12.83 So clergie *is* confort to creatures þat repenten,
B.12.86 The which body *is* boþe boote to þe riȝtfulle
B.12.93 For kynde wit *is* of his kyn and neiȝe Cosynes boþe
B.12.109 Which *is* þe cofre of cristes tresor, and clerkes kepe þe keyes
B.12.126 For Clergie *is* kepere vnder crist of heuene;
B.12.163 That ooþer *is* lewed of þat labour, lerned neuere swymme.
B.12.164 Which trowestow of þo two [in Themese] *is* in moost drede,
B.12.166 Or þe swymmere þat *is* saaf by so hymself like,
B.12.168 And *is* in drede to drenche, þat neuere dide swymme?'
B.12.174 For if þe clerk be konnynge he knoweþ what *is* synne,
B.12.177 How contricion *is* comended for it cacheþ awey synne:
B.12.183 And þat *is* after person or parissh preest, [and] parauenture vnkonnynge
B.12.189 Dominus pars hereditatis mee *is* a murye verset
B.12.194 And grace asked of god þat [graiþ *is* hem euere]
B.12.206 For he þat *is* ones a þef is eueremoore in daunger,
B.12.206 For he þat *is* ones a þef is eueremoore in daunger,
B.12.212 For he *is* in þe loweste of heuene, if oure bileue be trewe,
B.12.227 He *is* þe pies patron and putteþ it in hir ere
B.12.228 [That þ]ere þe þorn *is* þikkest to buylden and brede;
B.12.239 And feblest fowel of fliȝt *is* þat fleeþ or swymmeþ.
B.12.240 And þat [*is*] þe pecok & þe Pehen [wiþ hir proude feþeres
B.12.244 For þe trailynge of his tail ouertaken *is* he soone.
B.12.245 And his flessh *is* foul flessh and his feet boþe,
B.12.248 And deleþ it noȝt til his deeþ day, þe tail[*is* al of] sorwe.
B.12.250 So *is* possession peyne of pens and of nobles
B.12.259 By þe po feet *is* vnderstande, as I haue lerned in Auynet,
B.12.263 So *is* þe riche [reuerenced] by reson of hise goodes.
B.12.264 The larke þat *is* a lasse fowel is moore louelich of ledene,
B.12.264 The larke þat *is* a lasse fowel is moore louelich of ledene,
B.12.267 To lowe libbynge men þe larke *is* resembled.
B.12.272 Ac god *is* so good, I hope þat siþþe he gaf hem wittes
B.12.284 And he *is* saaf, seiþ þe book, and his soule in heuene.
B.12.285 [Ac] þer *is* fullynge of Font and fullynge in blood shedyng
B.12.286 And þoruȝ fir *is* fullyng, and þat is ferme bileue:
B.12.286 And þoruȝ fir *is* fullyng, and þat is ferme bileue:
B.12.291 And wheiþer it worþ [of truþe] or noȝt, [þe] worþ [of] bileue *is* gret,
B.13.15 Of kynde and of his konnynge, and how curteis he is to bestes.
B.13.16 And how louynge he *is* to [ech lif] on londe and on watre–
B.13.52 'Here *is* propre seruice', quod Pacience, 'þer fareþ no Prince bettre.'

B.13.65 'It *is* noȝt foure dayes þat þis freke, bifore þe deen of Poules,
B.13.76 They prechen þat penaunce *is* profitable to þe soule.
B.13.85 [And appose hym] what penaunce *is*, of which he preched raþer.'
B.13.93 *Is* neiþer fissh n[e] flessh, but fode for a penaunt.
B.13.97 And þanne *is* tyme to take and to appose þis doctour
B.13.103 'What *is* dowel, sire doctour?' quod I; 'is [dobest] any penaunce?'
B.13.103 'What is dowel, sire doctour?' quod I; '*is* [dobest] any penaunce?'
B.13.115 What *is* dowel and dobet? ye dyuynours knoweþ.'
B.13.119 'Now þow, Clergie', quod Conscience, 'carp[e] what *is* dowel.'
B.13.121 Ther þe lord of lif wonyeþ, to leren [hem] what *is* dowel.
B.13.155 The myddel of þe Moone [*i*]s þe [m]yght of boþe.
B.13.172 'It *is* but a dido', quod þis doctour, 'a disours tale.
B.13.193 For þer [*is*] no tresour [þerto] to a trewe wille.
B.13.205 'That *is* sooþ', [seide] Conscience, 'so me god helpe.
B.13.211 'That *is* sooþ', [seide] Clergie, 'I se what þow menest.
B.13.219 There vnkyndenesse and coueitise *is*, hungry contrees boþe.
B.13.224 'I am a Mynstrall', quod þat man, 'my name *is* Actiua vita.
B.13.225 Al yde[l] ich hatie for Actif *is* my name.
B.13.255 Ac if myȝt of myracle hym faille it *is* for men ben noȝt worþi
B.13.264 And louren whan þei lakken hem; it *is* noȝt longe ypassed
B.13.279 Willyng þat alle men wende he were þat he *is* noȝt,
B.13.331 Ther *is* no lif þat me loueþ lastynge any while.
B.13.407 The whiche *is* sleuþe so slow þat may no sleiȝtes helpe it,
B.13.410 [*Is* whan men] moorneþ noȝt for hise mysdedes, ne makeþ no sorwe;
B.13.414 Ech day *is* halyday with hym or an heiȝ ferye,
B.13.415 And if he auȝt wole here it *is* an harlotes tonge.
B.14.28 Than Hauky[n] wi[l] he wafrer, [which *is*] Actiua vita.'
B.14.64 It *is* founden þat fourty wynter folk lyuede withouten tulyyng,
B.14.75 [Ac] mesure *is* [so] muche worþ it may noȝt be to deere.
B.14.88 Ergo contricion, feiþ and conscience *is* kyndeliche dowel,
B.14.90 Ac shrift of mouþ moore worþi *is* if man be y[n]liche contrit,
B.14.97 That it neuere eft *is* sene ne soor, but semeþ a wounde yheeled.'
B.14.100 'Ther parfit truþe and poore herte *is*, and pacience of tonge,
B.14.101 There *is* Charite þe chief, chaumbrere for god hymselue.'
B.14.115 And after þow sendest hem somer þat *is* hir souereyn ioye
B.14.126 Ac god *is* of [a] wonder wille, by þat kynde wit sheweþ,
B.14.155 Ac it *is* but selde yseien, as by holy seintes bokes,
B.14.157 For muche murþe *is* amonges riche, as in mete and cloþyng,
B.14.158 And muche murþe in May *is* amonges wilde beestes,
B.14.161 And yet *is* wynter for hem worse, for weetshoed þei [gange],
B.14.163 And arated of riche men þat ruþe *is* to here.
B.14.196 Ellis *is* al on ydel, al þat euere [we diden],
B.14.199 Ellis *is* al oure labour lost–lo, how men writeþ
B.14.206 And þat *is* plesaunt to pride in poore and in riche.
B.14.207 [Ac] þe riche *is* reuerenced by reson of his richesse.
B.14.208 Ther þe poore *is* put bihynde, and parauenture kan moore
B.14.209 Of wit and of wisdom, þat fer awey *is* bettre
B.14.218 Ac in pouerte þer pacience *is* pride haþ no myȝte,
B.14.221 For þe poore *is* ay prest to plese þe riche
B.14.226 [For] if þei pleyne [þe feblere *is* þe poore];
B.14.228 [For lowliche he lokeþ, and louelich *is* his speche
B.14.234 For whan he streyneþ hym to strecche þe strawe *is* his shetes.
B.14.236 That *is* welawo whan he wakeþ and wepeþ for colde,
B.14.237 And som tyme for his synnes; so he *is* neuere murie
B.14.241 For men knowen wel þat Coueitise *is* of [a] kene wille
B.14.255 Meschief *is* [ay a mene] and makeþ hem to þynke
B.14.256 That god *is* his grettest help and no gome ellis,
B.14.260 Forþi [al] poore þat pacient *is* [of pure riȝt] may cleymen,
B.14.267 Muche *is* [þat maide] to loue of [a man] þat swich oon takeþ,
B.14.268 [Moore] þan [a maiden *is*] þat is maried þoruȝ brocage
B.14.268 [Moore] þan [a maiden is] þat *is* maried þoruȝ brocage
B.14.273 The which *is* sib to god hymself, [so neiȝ is pouerte].'
B.14.273 The which is sib to god hymself, [so neiȝ *is* pouerte].'
B.14.275 What *is* Pouerte, pacience', quod he, 'properly to mene?'
B.14.278 '[Al þis] in englissh', quod Pacience, 'it *is* wel hard to expounen,
B.14.280 Pouerte *is* þe firste point þat pride moost hateþ;
B.14.281 Thanne *is* it good by good skile, al þat agasteþ pride.
B.14.282 Riȝt as contricion *is* confortable þyng, conscience woot wel,
B.14.284 So pouerte propreliche penaunce [*is* to þe body,
B.14.289 [O]r as Iustice to Iugge men enioyned *is* no poore,
B.14.291 Selde *is* any poore yput to punysshen any peple.
B.14.294 Selde *is* poore [riȝt] riche but of riȝtful heritage.
B.14.297 The ferþe *is* a fortune þat florissheþ þe soule
B.14.301 The fifte *is* moder of [myȝt and of mannes] helþe,
B.14.304 The sixte *is* a path of pees; ye! þoruȝ þe paas of Aultoun
B.14.307 And euer þe lasse þat he [lede], þe [liȝter] *is* of herte:
B.14.310 The seuenþe *is* welle of wisedom and fewe wordes sheweþ,
B.14.313 The eighteþe *is* a lele labour and looþ to take moore,
B.14.316 The nynþe *is* swete to þe soule, no sugre swetter,
B.14.317 For pacience *is* payn for pouerte hymselue,
B.14.325 So hard it *is*', quod haukyn, 'to lyue and to do synne.
B.15.18 *Is* neiþer Peter þe Porter ne Poul wiþ [þe] fauchon
B.15.20 At mydnyght, at mydday, my vois so *is* knowe

B.15.26 And whan I make mone to god memoria *is* my name;
B.15.28 Thanne *is* Racio my riȝte name, reson on englissh;
B.15.29 And whan I feele þat folk telleþ my firste name *is* sensus,
B.15.30 And þat *is* wit and wisdom, þe welle of alle craftes;
B.15.34 Thanne *is* lele loue my name, and in latyn Amor;
B.15.44 'That *is* sooþ', seide he; 'now I se þi wille.
B.15.56 To englisshe men þis *is* to mene, þat mowen speke and here,
B.15.64 And riȝt as hony *is* yuel to defie and engleymeþ þe mawe,
B.15.69 That *is* Non plus sapere quam oportet sapere.
B.15.95 There inparfit preesthode *is*, prechours and techeris.
B.15.98 Ther *is* a meschief in þe more of swiche manere [stokkes].
B.15.100 [*Is* þe] roote of þe right feiþ to rule þe peple;
B.15.101 A[c] þer þe roote *is* roten, reson woot be soþe,
B.15.111 [For ypocrisie] in latyn *is* likned to a [loþly] dongehill
B.15.129 Ac þing þat wikkedly *is* wonne, and wiþ false sleightes,
B.15.133 [This] þat wiþ gile was geten vngraciousliche *is* [s]pended.
B.15.144 By lered, by lewed, þat looþ *is* to [s]pende
B.15.149 'What *is* charite?' quod I þo; 'a childissh þyng', he seide:
B.15.152 I haue lyued in londe', quod [I], 'my name *is* longe wille,
B.15.161 Clerkes kenne me þat crist *is* in alle places
B.15.164 Charite] *is* noȝt chaumpions fight ne chaffare as I trowe.'
B.15.167 And *is* as glad of a gowne of a gray russet
B.15.169 He *is* glad wiþ alle glade and good til alle wikkede
B.15.182 And ouþerwhile he *is* woned to wenden on pilgrymages
B.15.186 And whan he *is* wery of þat werk þan wole he som tyme
B.15.200 What *is* þe wille and wherfore þat many wight suffreþ:
B.15.207 Ac it *is* moore to haue hir mete [on] swich an esy manere
B.15.216 For charite *is* goddes champion, and as a good child hende,
B.15.219 And *is* compaignable and confortatif as crist bit hymselue:
B.15.231 Ac it *is* fern [and fele yeer in] Fraunceis tyme;
B.15.235 In kynges court he comeþ ofte þer þe counseil *is* trewe,
B.15.255 The mooste liflode he lyueþ by *is* loue in goddes passion;
B.15.262 Of oure foes þat dooþ vs falsnesse; þat *is* oure fadres wille.
B.15.337 And helpeþ hem þat helpeþ yow and ȝyueþ þer no nede *is*,
B.15.347 Ac þer *is* a defaute in þe folk þat þe feiþ kepeþ.
B.15.348 Wherfore folk *is* þe febler and noȝt ferm of bileue.
B.15.349 As in lussheburwes *is* a luþer alay, and yet lokeþ he lik a sterlyng;
B.15.350 The merk of þat monee *is* good ac þe metal is feble;
B.15.350 The merk of þat monee is good ac þe metal *is* feble;
B.15.353 Ac þe metal, þat *is* mannes soule, [myd] synne is foule alayed.
B.15.353 Ac þe metal, þat is mannes soule, [myd] synne *is* foule alayed.
B.15.373 For *is* noon of þise newe clerkes, whoso nymeþ hede,
B.15.433 It *is* vnsauory, forsoþe, ysoden or ybake;
B.15.434 So *is* mannes soule, sooþly, þat seeþ no goo[d] ensampl[e]
B.15.452 Clooþ þat comeþ fro þe weuyng *is* noȝt comly to were
B.15.456 [And] so it fareþ by a barn þat born *is* of wombe;
B.15.458 It *is* heþene as to heueneward and helplees to þe soule.
B.15.459 Heþen *is* to mene after heeþ and vntiled erþe.
B.15.472 [And by þe hond fedde foules [*i*]*s* folk vnderstonde
B.15.482 That *is* god of his grace, gyueþ alle men blisse.
B.15.484 Where þat his wille *is* to worshipen vs alle,
B.15.508 And þat *is* rouþe for riȝtful men þat in þe Reawme wonyen,
B.15.526 Holy chirche *is* honoured heiȝliche þoruȝ his deying;
B.15.527 He *is* a forbisene to alle bisshopes and a briȝt myrour,
B.15.533 It *is* ruþe to rede how riȝtwise men lyuede,
B.15.539 And now *is* rouþe to rede how þe rede noble
B.15.540 *Is* reuerenced er þe Roode, receyued for [þe] worþier
B.15.542 And now *is* werre and wo, and whoso why askeþ:
B.15.545 That in grotes *is* ygraue and in gold nobles.
B.15.570 Euery bisshop þat bereþ cros, by þat he *is* holden
B.15.584 Dilige deum & proximum *is* parfit Iewen lawe;
B.16.3 Ac ȝit I am in a weer what charite *is* to mene.'
B.16.4 'It *is* a ful trie tree', quod he, 'trewely to telle.
B.16.5 Mercy *is* þe more þerof; þe myddul stok is ruþe;
B.16.5 Mercy is þe more þerof; þe myddul stok *is* ruþe;
B.16.14 Amyddes mannes body; þe more *is* of þat stokke.
B.16.27 The world *is* a wikked wynd to hem þat willen truþe.
B.16.31 The flessh *is* a fel wynd, and in flouryng tyme,
B.16.37 That *is* þe passion and þe power of oure prince Iesu.
B.16.47 That *is* lieutenaunt to loken it wel bi leue of myselue:
B.16.60 'That *is* sooþ', [seide] Piers, 'so it may bifalle.
B.16.69 Thanne Continence *is* neer þe crop as kaylewey bastard.
B.16.85 There *is* derknesse and drede and þe deuel maister.
B.16.148 And which tokne to þis day to muche *is* yvsed,
B.16.149 That *is* kissynge and fair contenaunce and vnkynde wille.
B.16.155 And gile in þi glad chere and galle *is* in þi laughyng.
B.16.185 Pater *is* his propre name, a persone by hymselue.
B.16.186 The secounde of þa[t] sire *is* Sothfastnesse filius,
B.16.197 That *is* children of charite, and holi chirche þe moder.
B.16.207 And eiþer *is* oþeres ioye in þre sondry persones.
B.16.209 And þus *is* mankynde and manhede of matrimoyne yspronge
B.16.211 Migh[t] *is* [in] matrimoyne þat multiplieþ þe erþe
B.16.215 That *is*, creatour weex creature to knowe what was boþe.

B.16.219 Ne matrimoyne withouten Mul[eri]e *is* noȝt muche to preise:
B.16.220 Thus in þre persones *is* parfitliche [pure] manhede,
B.16.221 That *is* man and his make and mulliere children;
B.16.222 And *is* noȝt but gendre of a generacion bifore Iesu crist in heuene:
B.16.223 So *is* þe fader forþ with þe sone and fre wille of boþe,
B.16.224 Which is þe holy goost of alle, and alle is but o god.
B.16.224 Which is þe holy goost of alle, and alle *is* but o god.
B.16.230 Ful trewe toknes bitwene vs *is* to telle whan me likeþ.
B.16.238 Myn affiaunce and my feiþ *is* ferme in þis bileue.'
B.16.258 'I wolde wite', quod I þo, 'what is in youre lappe.'
B.16.260 'This *is* a present of muche pris; what prynce shal it haue?'
B.16.261 'It *is* a precious present', quod he, 'ac þe pouke it haþ attached,
B.16.265 Til he come þat I carpe of; crist *is* his name
B.16.268 That *is* lif for lif; or ligge þus euere
B.17.4 '*Is* it enseled?' I seide; 'may men see þ[e] lettres?'
B.17.6 And þat *is* cros and cristendom and crist þeron to honge;
B.17.7 And whan it *is* enseled [þerwiþ] I woot wel þe soþe
B.17.17 [*Is*] here alle þi lordes lawes?' quod I; 'ye, leue me', he seide.
B.17.26 'Youre wordes arn wonderfulle', quod I, 'which of yow *is* trewest
B.17.42 It *is* lighter to lewed men o lesson to knowe
B.17.44 It *is* ful hard for any man on Abraham bileue
B.17.46 It *is* lighter to leeue in þre louely persones
B.17.105 For [an] Outlaw[e *is*] in þe wode and vnder bank lotieþ,
B.17.107 Who *is* bihynde and who bifore and who ben on horse;
B.17.108 For he halt hym hardier on horse þan he þat *is* [on] foote.
B.17.117 Which *is* þe wey þat I wente and wher forþ to Ierusalem;
B.17.140 For god *is* after an hand; yheer now and knowe it.
B.17.144 The pawme *is* [þe piþ of] þe hand, and profreþ forþ þe fyngres
B.17.147 The holy goost of heuene: he *is* as þe pawme.
B.17.152 The fader *is* [þanne] as a fust wiþ fynger to touche–
B.17.158 How he þat *is* holy goost sire and sone preueþ.
B.17.164 Heuene and helle and al þat *is* þerInne
B.17.165 Thus it *is*–nedeþ no man trowe noon ooþer–
B.17.169 And as my fust *is* ful hand y[f]olden togideres
B.17.170 So *is* þe fader a ful god, formour and shappere:
B.17.171 Al þe myȝt myd hym *is* in makynge of þynges.
B.17.173 Keruynge and compasynge [*i*]*s* craft of þe fyngres.
B.17.174 Right so *is* þe sone þe Science of þe fader
B.17.175 And ful god as *is* þe fader, no febler ne no bettre.
B.17.176 The pawme *is* pureliche þe hand, haþ power by hymselue
B.17.182 So *is* þe holy goost god, neiþer gretter ne lasse
B.17.183 Than *is* þe sire [or] þe sone and in þe same myghte,
B.17.184 And alle [þre] but o god as *is* myn hand and my fyngres.
B.17.186 Al *is* but an hand, [howso I turne it.
B.17.187 Ac who *is* hurte in þe hand], euene in þe myddes,
B.17.202 For god þe fader *is* as a fust; þe sone is as a fynger;
B.17.202 For god þe fader is as a fust; þe sone *is* as a fynger;
B.17.203 The holy goost of heuene [he] *is* as þe pawme.
B.17.206 [For] to a torche or a tapur þe Trinite *is* likned,
B.17.218 So is [þe] holy goost god and grace wiþoute mercy
B.17.250 Al þi labour *is* lost and al þi long trauaille;
B.17.252 So *is* þe holi goost god and grace wiþouten mercy
B.17.266 Ye brenne but ye blase noȝt; þat *is* a blynd bekene:
B.17.273 But þei dwelle þer Diues *is* dayes wiþouten ende.
B.17.274 Thus *is* vnkyndenesse þe contrarie þat quencheþ, as it were,
B.17.280 The which *is* lif and loue, þe leye of mannes body.
B.17.286 Ac þis *is* þe worste wise þat any wight myghte
B.17.291 Innocence *is* next god and nyght and day it crieþ
B.17.305 Ac it *is* but selden yseiȝe, þer sooþnesse bereþ witnesse,
B.17.308 For þer þat partie pursueþ þe [peel] *is* lo[þ]
B.17.316 Noght of þe nounpower of god, þat he ne *is* myghtful
B.17.317 To amende al þat amys *is*, and his mercy gretter
B.17.320 His sorwe *is* satisfaccion for [swich] þat may noȝt paie.
B.17.323 That oon *is* a wikkede wif þat wol noȝt be chastised;
B.17.334 The wif *is* oure wikked flessh þat wol noȝt be chastised
B.17.337 And "þat *is* lightly forȝyuen and forȝeten boþe
B.17.348 That *is* coueitise and vnkyndenesse þat quencheþ goddes mercy;
B.17.349 For vnkyndenesse *is* þe contrarie of alle kynnes reson.
B.18.13 As *is* þe kynde of a knyght þat comeþ to be dubbed,
B.18.21 '*Is* Piers in þis place?' quod I, and he preynte on me.
B.18.69 And some seide he was a wicche; 'good *is* þat we assaye
B.18.103 And youre fraunchise þat fre was fallen *is* in þraldom;
B.18.107 Which *is* lif þat oure lord in alle lawes acurseþ.
B.18.135 And þat *is* cause of þis clips þat closeþ now þe sonne,
B.18.142 'That þow tellest', quod Truþe, '*is* but a tale of waltrot!
B.18.147 It *is* trufle þat þow tellest; I, truþe, woot þe soþe,
B.18.148 For þat *is* ones in helle out comeþ [it] neuere.
B.18.154 For of alle venymes foulest *is* þe scorpion;
B.18.162 And bigile þe gilour, and þat *is* good] sleighte:
B.18.167 'That *is* sooþ', seide Mercy, 'and I se here by Sowþe
B.18.176 'My wil *is* to wende', quod she, 'and welcome hem alle
B.18.182 Loue þat *is* my lemman swiche lettres me sente
B.18.202 For it *is* botelees bale, þe byte þat þei eten.'

B.18.206 For no wight woot what wele *is* þat neuere wo suffrede,
B.18.207 Ne what *is* hoot hunger þat hadde neuere defaute.
B.18.209 Sholde wite witterly what day *is* to meene.
B.18.211 Wite what wo *is*, ne were þe deeþ of kynde.
B.18.215 The which vnknytteþ alle care and comsynge *is* of reste.
B.18.217 Woot no wight, as I wene, what [*is* ynogh] to mene.
B.18.225 To wite what alle wo *is* [þat woot of] alle ioye.
B.18.227 Shal lere hem what langour *is* and lisse wiþouten ende.
B.18.228 Woot no wight what werre *is* þer þat pees regneþ,
B.18.229 Ne what *is* witterly wele til weylawey hym teche.'
B.18.265 For here comeþ wiþ crowne þat kyng *is* of glorie." '
B.18.268 Care and [c]ombraunce *is* comen to vs alle.
B.18.270 And lede it þer [laʒar *is*] and lightliche me bynde.
B.18.274 Boþe þis lord and þis light, *is* longe ago I knew hym.
B.18.276 And where he wole *is* his wey; ac ware hym of þe perils:
B.18.280 For hymself seide, þat Sire *is* of heuene,
B.18.283 And [siþen] he þat Sooþnesse *is* seide þise wordes,
B.18.286 'That *is* sooþ', seide Sathan, 'but I me soore drede,
B.18.292 'It *is* noʒt graiþly geten þer gile is þe roote,
B.18.292 'It is noʒt graiþly geten þer gile *is* þe roote,
B.18.308 Wiþ glorie and with gret light; god it is, I woot wel.
B.18.311 For þi lesynges, Lucifer, lost *is* al oure praye.
B.18.339 That gilours be bigiled and þat *is* good reson:
B.18.353 So þat þoruʒ gile þow gete þoruʒ grace it *is* ywonne.
B.18.360 And gile *is* bigiled and in his gile fallen:
B.18.365 For I þat am lord of lif, loue *is* my drynke,
B.18.379 It *is* noʒt vsed in erþe to hangen a feloun
B.18.409 'After sharpe shoures', quod pees, 'moost shene *is* þe sonne;
B.18.410 *Is* no weder warmer þan after watry cloudes;
B.18.419 For inpossible *is* no þyng to hym þat is almyghty.'
B.18.419 For inpossible is no þyng to hym þat *is* almyghty.'
B.18.430 And it afereþ þe fend, for swich *is* þe myʒte
B.19.10 '*Is* þis Iesus þe Iustere', quod I, 'þat Iewes dide to deþe?
B.19.11 Or it *is* Piers þe Plowman? who peynted hym so rede?'
B.19.14 *Is* crist wiþ his cros, conquerour of cristene.'
B.19.19 Ergo *is* no name to þe name of Iesus,
B.19.24 *Is* crist moore of myʒt and moore worþi name
B.19.28 To be called a knyght *is* fair for men shul knele to hym.
B.19.29 To be called a kyng *is* fairer for he may knyghtes make.
B.19.36 As wide as þe world *is* [wonyeþ þer noon]
B.19.57 And bond [hym] as [he *is* bounde] wiþ bondes of yrene.
B.19.62 He may [be wel] called conquerour, and þat *is* crist to mene.
B.19.64 *Is* to wissen vs þerwiþ, þat whan we ben tempted,
B.19.89 Gold *is* likned to leautee þat laste shal euere
B.19.93 For Mirre *is* mercy to mene and mylde speche of tonge.
B.19.106 As kynde *is* of a Conquerour, so comsede Iesu
B.19.111 For wyn *is* likned to lawe and lifholynesse,
B.19.207 Quod Conscience and knelede, 'þis *is* cristes messager
B.19.208 And comeþ fro þe grete god; grace *is* his name.
B.19.333 As wide as þe world *is* wiþ Piers to tilie truþe.
B.19.335 Now *is* Piers to þe plow; pride it aspide
B.19.348 That Conscience shal noʒt knowe who *is* cristene or heþene,
B.19.355 Quod Conscience to alle cristene þo, 'my counseil *is* to wende
B.19.385 Here *is* breed yblessed, and goddes body þervnder.
B.19.393 'That *is* my conseil', quod Conscience, 'and Cardinale vertues;
B.19.400 Thikke ale and þynne ale; þat *is* my kynde,
B.19.409 'Thanne *is* many a [lif] lost', quod a lewed vicory.
B.19.417 "The contree *is* þe corseder þat Cardinals come Inne,
B.19.428 Inparfit *is* þat pope þat al [peple] sholde helpe
B.19.436 As for hymself and hise seruauntʒ, saue he *is* first yserued.
B.19.455 For Spiritus prudencie among þe peple *is* gyle,
B.20.12 That *is* mete whan men hym werneþ and he no moneye weldeþ.
B.20.23 For *is* no vertue bi fer to Spiritus temperancie,
B.20.33 Wenynge *is* no wysdom, ne wys ymaginacion:
B.20.35 Ac nede *is* next hym for anoon he mekeþ
B.20.89 Wiþ deeþ þat *is* dredful to vndo vs alle!'
B.20.141 That Coueitise were cristene þat is so kene [to fighte],
B.20.207 'Counseille me, kynde', quod I, 'what craft *is* best to lerne?'
B.20.269 It *is* wikked to wage yow; ye wexen out of noumbre.
B.20.270 Heuene haþ euene noumbre and helle *is* wiþoute noumbre.
B.20.280 And yuele *is* þis yholde in parishes of Engelonde,
B.20.288 Ac while he *is* in westmynstre he wol be bifore
B.20.313 'Ther *is* a Surgien in þ[e] sege þat softe kan handle,
B.20.315 Oon frere Flaterere *is* phisicien and surgien.'
B.20.317 For here *is* many a man hurt þoruʒ ypocrisye.'
B.20.334 'He *is* sik', seide Pees, 'and so are manye oþere.
B.20.335 Ypocrisie haþ hurt hem; ful hard *is* if þei keuere.'
B.20.357 Here *is* Contricion', quod Conscience, 'my cosyn, ywounded.
B.20.360 [And] lat hem ligge ouerlonge and looþ *is* to chaunge;
B.20.362 'That *is* ouerlonge', quod þis Lymytour, 'I leue. I shal amende it!'
B.20.372 That *is* þe souerayn[e] salue for alle [synnes of kynde].

is C 667 **is** (661) **ys** (6)
C.Pr.40 Qui turpiloquium loquitur [*is*] luciferes knaue.

C.Pr.78 Ac it *is* nouʒt by þe bischop þat þe boy precheþ,
C.Pr.84 And synge þer for symonye [for] seluer *is* swete.
C.Pr.88 That *is* lele loue and lyf among lered and lewed,
C.Pr.126 Ar don vndeuouteliche; drede *is* at þe laste
C.Pr.133 Thare Crist *is* in kynedom to close with heuene.
C.Pr.207 Ther þe Cat [*is*] a kytoun þe Court is ful elynge.
C.Pr.207 Ther þe Cat [is] a kytoun þe Court *is* ful elynge.
C.Pr.214 But soffre and sey nouʒt; and [so] *is* þe beste
C. 1.12 'The tour vppon þe tofte,' quod she, 'treuthe *is* þerynne
C. 1.14 For he *is* fader of fayth and formor of alle;
C. 1.23 The firste *is* fode and vesture þe seconde
C. 1.33 Mesure *is* medecyne thogh þow muche ʒerne.
C. 1.34 Al *is* nat good to þe gost þat þe gott ascuth
C. 1.35 Ne liflode to þe lycame þat lef *is* [to] þe soule.
C. 1.37 [That] *is* þe wrecchede world wolde þe bigyle.
C. 1.57 'That *is* þe Castel of care; whoso cometh þerynne
C. 1.59 Therynne wonyeth a wyghte þat wrong *is* [ihote];
C. 1.65 He *is* lettere of loue and lyeth alle tymes;
C. 1.67 To combre men with coueytise, þat *is* his kynde and his lore.'
C. 1.81 'When alle tresores is tried treuthe *is* þe beste;
C. 1.83 Hit *is* a[s] derworthe a druerie as dere god hymseluen.
C. 1.84 For who *is* trewe of his tonge and of his two handes
C. 1.86 He *is* a god by þe gospel and graunte may hele
C. 1.97 *Is* þe professioun and puyr ordre that apendeth to knyghtes
C. 1.98 And hoso passeth þat poynt *is* appostata of knyghthed.
C. 1.117 'Hit *is* sikerore bi southe þer þe sonne regneth
C. 1.121 And helle *is* þer he is and [he] þere ybounde.
C. 1.121 And helle is þer he *is* and [he] þere ybounde.
C. 1.130 And alle þat worchen þat wikked *is* wenden thei sholle
C. 1.131 Aftur here deth day and dwelle ther wrong *is*;
C. 1.134 There treuthe *is*, þe tour that trinite ynne sitteth.
C. 1.136 Tha[n] treuthe and trewe loue *is* no tresor bettre.'
C. 1.141 Hit *is* a kynde knowynge that kenet in thyn herte
C. 1.146 For treuthe telleth þat loue *ys* triacle [for] synne
C. 1.148 Loue *is* [þe] plonte of pees, most precious of vertues,
C. 1.155 Forthi *is* loue ledare of [þe] lordes folk of heuene
C. 1.156 And a mene, as þe Mayre *is*, bitwene þe kyng and þe comune;
C. 1.157 Ryht so *is* loue [a] ledare and þe lawe shapeth;
C. 1.160 And in þe herte þer *is* þe hed and þe heye welle.
C. 1.182 That fayth withouten feet *is* feblore then nauth
C. 1.185 Hit *is* as lewed as a laumpe þat no liht is ynne.
C. 1.185 Hit is as lewed as a laumpe þat no liht *is* ynne.
C. 1.193 And þat *is* no treuthe of þe trinite but triccherye [and] synne
C. 1.197 Þat *is* þe lok of loue [þat] vnloseth grace
C. 1.199 So loue *is* lecche of lyf and lysse of alle payne
C. 1.202 "Whenne alle tresores ben tried treuthe *is* þe beste."
C. 1.204 To lere the what loue *is*;' and leue at me she lauhte.
C. 2.19 'That *is* mede þe mayde, hath niyed me ful ofte
C. 2.20 And [lakked] my lemman þat leute *is* hoten
C. 2.23 In þe popes palays he *is* pryue as mysulue.
C. 2.24 Ac sothnesse wolde nat so for she *is* a bastard.
C. 2.27 And mede *is* manered aftur hym as men of kynde carpeth:
C. 2.46 And al *is* lyares ledynge th[at] lady is thus ywedded.
C. 2.46 And al is lyares ledynge th[at] lady *is* thus ywedded.
C. 2.48 That mede *is* thus ymaried; tomorwe þou shalt aspye.
C. 2.83 That mede *is* maried more for here richesse
C. 2.85 Falsnesse *is* fayn of here for he wot here ryche;
C. 2.117 'In þe date of the deuel th[e] dede *is* aseled
C. 2.123 For mede *is* moilere, amendes was here dame;
C. 2.146 That fals *is* faythles, the fende his syre
C. 2.146 That fals is faythles, the fende *is* his syre
C. 2.148 And mede *is* moylore, [a] mayden of gode;
C. 2.154 ʒut beth ywar of þe weddynge; for witty *is* treuthe
C. 2.155 And Consience *is* of his consayl and knoweth ʒow [echone];
C. 2.245 And *is* welcome when he cometh and woneth with hem ofte.
C. 3.1 Now *is* mede þe mayde and na mo of hem alle
C. 3.59 Hit *is* but frelete of fleysche–ʒe fyndeth [hit in] bokes–
C. 3.62 Hit *is* synne as of seuene noon sannour relesed.
C. 3.88 And [t]how thei fillen nat ful þat for lawe *is* seled
C. 3.98 That Innocence *is* herde in heuene amonge seyntes
C. 3.112 Hit *is* nat seemely, forsothe, in Citee [ne] in borw toun
C. 3.125 Amonge thise lettred lordes this latyn *is* to mene
C. 3.137 And ay the lengur y late [the] go the lasse treuthe *is* with the,
C. 3.156 For she *is* fayn of thy felawschipe, for to be thy make.'
C. 3.159 For she [*is*] frele of here fayth, fikel of here speche
C. 3.166 *Is* nat a bettere baud, by hym þat me made,
C. 3.168 For she *is* tikel of here tayl, talewys of tonge,
C. 3.182 He *is* assoiled [as] sone as heresulue lyketh.
C. 3.185 He *is* priue with þe pope, prouysours it knoweth,
C. 3.191 Ther she *is* wel with eny kyng wo is þ[e] rewme
C. 3.191 Ther she is wel with eny kyng wo *is* þ[e] rewme
C. 3.192 For she *is* fauerable to fals the whiche defouleth treuthe.
C. 3.197 Thorw which loueday *is* loste þat leute myhte wynne;

C. 3.199 Lawe *is* so lordliche and loth to make ende;
C. 3.204 Ther ne *is* Cite vnder sonne ne noon so ryche reume
C. 3.205 Ther he *is* alowed and ylet by þat laste shal eny while
C. 3.212 That al þe witt of the world *is* woxe into Gyle.
C. 3.215 Such a maistre *is* mede among men of gode.'
C. 3.223 Ther þat meschief *is* greet mede may helpe;
C. 3.244 Vnconnynge *is* þat Consience a kyndom to sulle
C. 3.245 For þat [*is*] conquere[d] thorw a comune helpe, a kyndom or
              ducherie,
C. 3.251 And þat *is* þe kynde of a kyng þat conquereth on his enemys,
C. 3.282 *Is* no lede þat leueth þat he ne loueth mede
C. 3.285 Mede *is* worthy, me thynketh, þe maistrye to haue.'
C. 3.287 That mede [*is*] euermore a mayntenour of Gyle,
C. 3.291 Ac ther *is* mede and mercede and bothe men demen
C. 3.294 And þat *is* nother resoun ne ryhte ne [i]n no rewme lawe
C. 3.300 That pre manibus *is* paied or his pay asketh.
C. 3.304 When þe dede *is* ydo and þe day endit.
C. 3.305 And þat *is* no mede but a mercede, a manere dewe dette,
C. 3.306 And but hit prestly be ypayed þe payere *is* to blame,
C. 3.309 And ther *is* resoun as a reue rewardynge treuthe
C. 3.313 In Marchandise *is* no mede, y may hit wel avowe;
C. 3.314 Hit *is* a permutacoun apertly, on peneworth for another.
C. 3.317 To here [lele] and lege, loue [*is*] the cause;
C. 3.329 So god gyueth no [grace] þat "si" [ne] *is* the glose
C. 3.333 Thus *is* mede and mercede as two maner relacions,
C. 3.338 And ayther *is* otheres helpe; of hem cometh retribucoun
C. 3.339 That [*is*] þe gyft þat god gyueth to alle lele lyuynge,
C. 3.342 What *is* relacion rect and indirect aftur,
C. 3.344 'Relacioun rect,' quod Consience, '*is* a record of treuthe–
C. 3.354 That *is* god, the ground of al, a graciouse antecedent.
C. 3.355 And man *is* relatif rect yf he be rihte trewe:
C. 3.361 This *is* relacion rect, ryht [as] adiectyf and sustantyf
C. 3.363 Indirect thyng *is* as hoso coueytede
C. 3.367 Þat *is* nat resonable ne rect to refuse my syre name,
C. 3.371 So indirect *is* inlyche to coueyte
C. 3.374 A[c] relacoun rect *is* a ryhtful custume,
C. 3.394 Ac adiectyf and sustantyf *is* as y [e]r tolde,
C. 3.395 That *is* vnite, acordaun[c]e in case, in gendre and in noumbre,
C. 3.396 And *is* to [mene] in oure mouth more n[e] mynne
C. 3.404 Thus *is* man and mankynde in maner of [a] sustantyf,
C. 3.435 For so is the world went with hem þat han powere
C. 3.436 That he þat sayth men sothe[s] *is* sonnest yblamed.
C. 3.450 Muchel [euel] *is* thorw mede mony tymes ysoffred
C. 3.471 But aftur þe dede þat *is* ydo the doom shal recorde
C. 3.489 'I leue the,' quod Consience, 'for þat latyn *is* trewe.
C. 3.500 Ac he þat resceyueth or rec[ett]eth here *is* rescetour of Gyle.'
C. 4.22 For hit *is* þe wone of wil to wynse and to kyke
C. 4.35 For there *is* wrath and wranglynge there wol they abyde;
C. 4.36 Ac there *is* loue and leutee hit lyketh nat here hertes:
C. 4.55 Зut *is* he bold for to borw Ac baddelyche he payeth:
C. 4.86 And amende þat *is* mysdo and eueremore þe betere.'
C. 4.88 'Betere *is* þat bote bale adoun brynge
C. 4.132 Whiles mede mathe the maistrie þer motyng *is* at [þe] Barr[e].
C. 4.177 Hit *is* ful hard, by myn heued, herto to brynghen hit
C. 5.31 The whiche *is* lollarne lyf þat lytel is preysed
C. 5.31 The whiche is lollarne lyf þat lytel *is* preysed
C. 5.38 And what *is* beste for the body, as the boek telleth,
C. 5.46 *Is* paternoster and my primer, placebo and dirige,
C. 5.85 *Is* the leuest labour þat oure lord pleseth.
C. 5.92 'That *is* soth,' y saide, 'and so y beknowe
C. 5.99 So hope y to haue of hym þat *is* almyghty
C. 5.103 The l[y]f þat *is* louable and leele to thy soule.'
C. 5.153 Hit *is* in C[l]oystre or in scole, by many skilles y fynde.
C. 5.155 In scole *is* loue and louhnesse and lykyng to lerne.
C. 5.166 Of þe pore haueth thei no pite and þat *is* here puyre chartre.
C. 5.181 'For þe comune *is* the kynges tresor, Consience woet wel.
C. 5.190 *Is* cause of alle combraunc[e] to confounde a reume.
C. 6.83 To the soutere of southewerk, suche *is* his grace.
C. 6.87 For enuye and euyl wil *is* euel to defye.
C. 6.115 Amonges alle manere men my dwellyng *is* som tyme,
C. 6.127 That y ne mot folowe this folk: my fortune *is* non oþer.
C. 6.153 That *is* Priour and supriour and oure pater Abbas.
C. 6.303 There shal he wite witturly what vsure *is* to mene
C. 6.304 And [what] penaunce the prest shal haue þat p[r]oud *is* of his tithes.
C. 6.313 For me *is* leuere in this lyue as a lorel begge
C. 6.413 *Ys* non so hungry hound in hertford shyre
C. 7.17 That y telle with my tonge *is* t[wo] myle fro myn herte.
C. 7.20 Goddes payne and his passioun *is* puyre selde in my thouhte.
C. 7.39 And my seruauntes som tyme here salerie *is* bihynde;
C. 7.40 Reuthe *is* to here rekenynge when we shal rede acountes,
C. 7.61 For *is* no gult [here] so greet þat his goodnesse is more.'
C. 7.61 For is no gult [here] so greet þat his goodnesse *is* more.'
C. 7.70 *Is* when men mourneth not for his mysdedes,

C. 7.132 Aboute mydday, when most liht *is* and mel tyme of sayntes,
C. 7.195 He *is* þe presteste payere þat eny pore man knoweth;
C. 7.197 He *is* as louh as a lombe by leel of his tonge.
C. 7.205 Ac hoso wol wende þer treuthe *is*, this is þe way thede[r]:
C. 7.205 Ac hoso wol wende þer treuthe is, this *is* þe way thede[r]:
C. 7.209 That *is* to sey sothly зe sholde rather deye
C. 7.228 *Is* frithed in with floreynes and othere fees monye;
C. 7.233 The mote *is* of mercy, the manere in þe myddes
C. 7.234 And al þe wallyng *is* of wyt for wil ne sholde hit wynne;
C. 7.241 Vche piler *is* of penaunc[e] and preyeres to seyntes;
C. 7.278 And ho *is* sib to þis seuene, so me god helpe,
C. 7.279 *Is* wonderliche welcome and fayre vnderfonge;
C. 7.280 Ho *is* nat syb to this seuene, sothly to telle,
C. 7.281 Hit *is* ful hard, be myn heued, eny of зow alle
C. 7.288 'Mercy *is* a mayden there hath myhte ouer hem alle
C. 7.289 And she *is* sib to alle synfole and here sone bothe
C. 7.307 Ac þe way *is* ful wikked but hoso hadde a gyde
C. 8.10 That зe [han] selk and sendel to sowe whan tyme *is*
C. 8.17 And alle manere men þat by þe molde *is* susteyned
C. 8.78 For holy chirche *is* ho[ld]e of hem no tythe to aske,
C. 8.80 Dame worch-when-tyme-*is* [Peres] wyf hehte;
C. 8.97 And defenden hit fro þe fende, and so *is* my beleue,
C. 8.103 He *is* holdyng, y hope, to haue me in his masse
C. 8.112 Now is perkyn and þ[e] pilgrimes to þe plouh faren.
C. 8.213 Hit *is* nat for loue, leue hit, thei labore thus faste
C. 8.215 'Ther *is* no fi[al] loue with this folk for al here fayre speche
C. 9.47 That innocent and nedy *is* and no man harm wolde,
C. 9.53 His pardoun *is* ful petyt at his partynge hennes
C. 9.55 For hit *is* symonye to sulle þat sent is of grace,
C. 9.55 For hit is symonye to sulle þat sent *is* of grace,
C. 9.56 Þat *is* wit and watur and wynde and fuyre the ferthe;
C. 9.64 He *is* fals and faytour and defraudeth the nedy
C. 9.70 Woet no man, as y wene, who *is* worthy to haue
C. 9.82 That reuthe *is* to rede or in ryme shewe
C. 9.92 There *is* payne and peny ale as for a pytaunce ytake
C. 9.140 The whiche *is* lollarne lyf and lewede Ermytes;
C. 9.146 And whenne hym lyketh and luste, his leue is to ryse
C. 9.147 And when he *is* rysen rometh out and riзt wel aspyeth
C. 9.216 He þat lolleth *is* lame or his leg out of ioynte
C. 9.250 And fo[r] þe cloth þat keuereth hym ykald he *is* a frere,
C. 9.263 The tarre *is* vntydy þat to þe [tripe] bylongeth;
C. 9.264 Here salue *is* of supersedeas in sumnoures boxes;
C. 9.266 How, herde! where *is* thyn ho[u]nd[e] and thyn hardy herte
C. 9.269 And many a fayre flees falsliche *is* ywasche!
C. 9.272 And þe wolle worth weye, wo *is* the thenne!
C. 9.332 Hit *is* nat so syker for þe soule, certes, as [is] dowel.
C. 9.332 Hit is nat so syker for þe soule, certes, as [*is*] dowel.
C.10.29 He *is* otherwhile elleswher to wisse the peple.'
C.10.37 [A] bendeth and boweth, the body *is* so vnstable,
C.10.38 A[c] зut *is* he saef and sound; and so hit fareth by þe rihtfole.
C.10.40 That ay *is* saef and sound þat sitte withynne þe borde.
C.10.44 The water *is* likned to þe wor[l]d þat wanyeth and waxeth;
C.10.47 The boet *is* liknet to oure body þat bretil is of kynde,
C.10.47 The boet is liknet to oure body þat bretil *is* of kynde,
C.10.78 Ho[so] *is* trewe of his tonge and of his two handes
C.10.81 And *is* nat dronklewe ne dedeynus, dowel h[y]m foleweth.
C.10.83 He *is* [as] logh as a lomb and loueliche of speche
C.10.88 And *is* ronne [t]o religioun and hath rendred þe bible
C.10.92 Lene hem and loue hem", this latyn *is* to mene.
C.10.125 Here *is* oen wolde ywyte yf wit couthe teche;
C.10.130 Of erthe and ayer [hit *is*] maed, ymedled togyderes,
C.10.139 Dobet *is* here damysele, sire dowelus douhtur,
C.10.141 Dobest *is* aboue bothe, a bishopis pere,
C.10.142 And by his leryng *is* lad þat lady Anima.
C.10.144 *Is* a wise knyhte withalle, sire inwit he hatte,
C.10.151 'What kynne thyng *is* kynde?' quod y; 'canst thow me telle?'
C.10.152 'Kynde *is* creatour,' quod wit, 'of [alle] kyne thynges,
C.10.154 The which *is* god grettest [þat gynnynge hadde] neuere,
C.10.157 Man *is* hym most lyk of membres and of face
C.10.170 The which *is* loue and lyf þat last withouten ende.
C.10.174 Inwit *is* in the heued and anima in herte
C.10.176 For þat *is* goddes oune goed, his grace and his tresour,
C.10.209 And *is* no more to mene but men þat ben bygeten
C.10.212 And þat my sawe *is* soth þe sauter bereth witnesse.
C.10.236 The gospel *is* hereagayn, as gomus may rede:
C.10.241 The eritage þat þe eyer sholde haue *is* at þe kynges wille.
C.10.242 Ac þe gospel *is* a glose ther and huydeth þe grayth treuthe;
C.10.266 Ther ne *is* squier ne knyhte in contreye aboute
C.10.285 That lecherye *is* a lykyng thynge, a lymзerd of helle.
C.10.301 And thus *is* dowel, my frende, to do as lawe techeth:
C.10.303 Ac to louye and to l[e]ne, leef me, þat *is* dobet;
C.10.305 Helen and helpen, *is* dobest of alle.
C.10.307 The more he *is* worthy and worth, of wyse and goed ypresed.'

C.11.14 Wysdom and wit now *is* nat worth a carse
C.11.19 He *is* reuerensed and yrobed þat can robbe þe peple
C.11.27 And þat *is* no riht ne resoun for rather me sholde
C.11.32 Litel *is* he loued or leet [by] among lordes at festes.
C.11.33 Nowe *is* þe manere at mete when munstrals ben stille
C.11.42 *Is* non so hende to haue hym [in] but hote hym go þer god is.
C.11.42 Is non so hende to haue hym [in] but hote hym go þer god *is*.
C.11.44 God *is* nat in þat hoem ne his helpe nother.
C.11.55 That folk *is* nat ferme[d] in þe faith ne fre of here godes
C.11.56 Ne sory for here synnes; so [*is*] pruyde enhanced
C.11.59 For god *is* deef nowadayes and deyneth [nat vs] to here
C.11.61 And ʒut th[e] wrechus of this world *is* noen ywar by oþer
C.11.70 And *is* to mene no more bote "who[so] muche goed weldeth
C.11.77 For *is* no wit worth now but hit of wynnynge soune.
C.11.80 The which *is* a lykyng and luste, þe loue of þe world.'
C.11.89 With þat ʒe kenne me kyndeliche to knowe what *is* dowel.'
C.11.93 Of dobet [and] of dobest–for doctour he *is* knowe
C.11.95 For he *is* sib to þe seuene ars–and also my suster
C.11.103 'And telle me som tokene,' quod y, 'for tyme *is* þat y wende.'
C.11.110 To clergie shaltow neuere come ne knowe what *is* dowel.
C.11.129 Hit *is* no science sothly bote a sothfaste bileue.
C.11.131 For loue *is* a lykyng thyng and loth for to greue.
C.11.133 For of dobet and dobest here doctour *is* dere loue.'
C.11.158 Thus bileue and le[ute], and loue is the thridde
C.11.244 For Archa Noe, nymeth hede, *ys* no more to mene
C.11.246 The culorum of this clause curatores *is* to mene
C.11.271 Ho *is* worthy for wele or for wykkede [pyne]:
C.11.288 And *is* to mene no more ho best *beth* lewed:
C.11.298 Of al þat they haen had of hym þat *is* here maistre
C.12.7 For while fortune *is* thy frende freres wol the louye
C.12.28 The sauter sayth hit *is* no synne for suche men þat ben trewe
C.12.38 Thouh tho[w] se, say nat sum tyme þat *is* treuthe.
C.12.72 'That *is* soth,' saide scripture; ' may no synne lette
C.12.95 Bote loue and leute hem lede ylost *is* al þe tyme
C.12.146 As on a walnote withoute *is* a bittere barke
C.12.148 *Is* a cornel of comfort kynde to restore,
C.12.151 The which *is* þe cornel of comfort for alle cristene soules.
C.12.152 And wel sikorere he slepeth, þe segg þat *is* pore,
C.12.154 Then he þat *is* rihte ryche; reson bereth witnesse:
C.12.163 "Yf thow likest to lyue," quod god, "þe lyf þat *is* parfit,
C.12.167 Forsaek al and sue me and al *is* th[e] beste:"
C.12.180 Bote if þe seed þat sowen *is* in the sloo sterue
C.12.220 Hit lasteth nat longe þat *is* lycour-swete,
C.12.236 Worldly wele *y[s]* wykked thyng to hem þat hit kepeth.
C.12.242 And ʒut as many man ymorthred for his moneye and his godes
C.12.247 That rote *is* of robbares, the rychess[e] withynne!
C.13.41 His erende and his lettre sheweth and *is* anoon delyuered.
C.13.45 Ne non haiward *is* hote his wed for to taken.
C.13.59 Ther þe messager is ay merye and his mouth ful of songes
C.13.65 Ʒe wyte, ʒe wyse men, what this *is* to mene:
C.13.66 The marchaunt *is* no more to mene but men þat ben ryche
C.13.91 Ther *is* no lawe, as y leue, wol lette hym þe gate
C.13.92 Ther god *is* gateward hymsulf and vch a gome knoweth.
C.13.95 For þe wil *is* as moche worthe of a wrecche beggare
C.13.99 So pore and pacient parfitest lyf *is* of alle.
C.13.110 For hit *is* a carfol knyhte and of a Caytif kynges makynge
C.13.117 A Chartre *is* chaleniable byfore a chief Iustice,
C.13.120 The gome þat gloseth so Chartres for a goky *is* halden.
C.13.121 So [*is* hit] a goky, by god! þat in [his] gospel fayleth
C.13.127 Ac neuer noþer *is* blameles, the bischop ne þe chapeleyn,
C.13.160 Ther *is* no wriht, as y wene, sholde worch here neste to paye;
C.13.192 And perfore merueileth me, for man *is* moste yliche the,
C.13.200 *Is* no vertue so fair ne of valewe ne profit
C.13.201 So *is* soffrance souereynliche, so hit be for godes loue.
C.13.206 And ar thow lacke eny lyf loke ho *is* to preyse
C.13.207 For *is* no creature vnder Crist þat can hymsulue make
C.13.217 To wyte what dowel *is* Ac wakynge neuere.'
C.13.219 'What *is* dowel?' quod þat wyhte; 'ywis, sire,' y saide,
C.13.220 'To se moche and soffre al, certes, *is* dowel.'
C.13.239 Ac when nede nymeth hym vp anoen he *is* aschamed
C.13.240 And thenne woet he wherfore and why he *is* to blame.'
C.13.245 'Ʒe, certes,' quod he, 'þat *is* soth', and shop hym to walke;
C.14.2 Thogh y sete by mysulue, suche *is* my grace.
C.14.6 Noþer to lye ne to lacke ne lere þat *is* defended
C.14.14 *Is* ycalde Caritas, kynde loue an engelysche,
C.14.15 And þat *is* dobet, yf eny suche be, a blessed man þat helpeth
C.14.18 Wo *is* hym þat hem weldeth but he hem wel despene:
C.14.23 Ac grace *is* a graes þerfore to don hem [growe efte];
C.14.33 So grace *is* a gifte of god and kynde wit a chaunce
C.14.35 And ʒut *is* clergie to comende for cristes loue more
C.14.54 Whiche [*is* the] coffre of cristis tresor, and clerkes kepeth þe keyes
C.14.70 For clergy *is* cristes vycary to conforte and to cure;
C.14.101 That *is*, how lewede men and luythere lyhtloker were ysaued

C.14.107 That oþer *is* lewed of þat labour, lerned neuere swymme.
C.14.108 Which trowest [þou] of tho two in temese [*is*] in moste drede?'
C.14.114 For yf þe clerke be connynge [he] knoweth what *is* synne
C.14.117 How contricioun *is* comended for hit cacheth awey synne:
C.14.123 And þat *is* aftur person other parsche preest, and parauntur bothe
lewede
C.14.128 Dominus pars hereditatis [mee] *is* A merye verset;
C.14.133 And god *is* ay gracious to alle þat gredeth to hym
C.14.145 For he þat *is* ones a thef is eueremore in daunger
C.14.145 For he þat is ones a thef *is* eueremore in daunger
C.14.151 For he *is* in þe loweste of heuene, yf oure byleue be trewe,
C.14.171 And feblest foul of flyh[t *is*] þat fleeth oþer swym[m]eth:
C.14.172 That *is*, þe pocok and þe popeiay with here proude fetheres
C.14.178 His le[d]ene *is* vnloueliche and lothliche his careyne
C.14.179 Ac for his peynted pennes þe pecok *is* honoured
C.14.185 The larke þat is a lasse foul *is* louoloke[re] of ledene
C.14.185 The larke þat is a lasse foul *is* louoloke[re] of ledene
C.14.187 To lowe lyuynge men þe larke *is* resembled
C.14.194 Ac god *is* so gode, y hope þat seth he gaf hem wittes
C.14.206 And he *is* saef, saith the boek, and his soule in heuene.
C.14.207 Ac þer *is* follyng of fonte and follyng in bloed [s]hedyng
C.14.208 And thorw fuyr *is* fullyng; and [þat] *is* ferme bileue
C.14.208 And thorw fuyr is fullyng; and [þat] *is* ferme bileue:
C.14.213 And wher hit worth or worth nat, the bileue *is* gret of treuthe
C.14.215 And þat *is* loue and large huyre, yf þe lord be trewe,
C.15.19 And how louyng he *is* to vch lyf a londe and o watere
C.15.58 'This *is* a semely seruyce,' saide pacience.
C.15.69 'Hit *is* nat thre daies doen this doctour þat he prechede
C.15.80 Ac y wiste neuere freke þat frere *is* ycald of þe fyue mendynantʒ
C.15.82 They preche þat penaunce *is* profitable to þe soule
C.15.92 And apose hym what penaunce *is* and purgatorie on erthe
C.15.100 *Is* noþer fische ne flesche but fode for [a] penant[e].
C.15.104 And thenne *is* tyme to take and to apose this doctour
C.15.110 'What *is* dowel, sire doctour?' quod y; 'is dobest eny penaunce?'
C.15.110 'What is dowel, sire doctour?' quod y; '*is* dobest eny penaunce?'
C.15.122 What *is* dowel and dobet? ʒe deuynours knoweth.'
C.15.127 'Now þou, Clergie,' quod Consience, 'carpe what *is* dowel.'
C.15.136 Bote lele loue and treuthe that loth *is* to be founde.'
C.15.170 'This *is* a dido,' quod this doctour, 'a dysores tale!
C.15.181 That they knoweth nat,' quod Concience, 'what *is* kynde pacience.
C.15.188 There vnkyndenesse and coueytise [*is*], hungry contreys bothe.
C.15.193 'Ich am a mynstral,' quod this man, 'my name *is* actiua vita,
C.15.225 Ac yf myhte of myracle hym fayle hit *is* for men beth nat worthy
C.15.263 Hit *is* founde þat fourty wynter folke lyuede and tylde nat
C.15.272 'What *is* [properly] parfit pacience?' quod Actiua vita.
C.15.275 And þat *is* charite, chaumpion chief of all vertues,
C.15.276 And þat *is* pore pacient alle perelles to soffre.'
C.15.291 [And] aftur thow sendest hem somer þat *is* here souereyne ioye
C.15.300 And now he buyth hit bittere; he *is* a beggare of helle.
C.16.5 When his d[eu]er *is* doen and his dayes iourne
C.16.6 Thenne may men wyte what he *is* worth and what he hath deserued
C.16.10 Muche murthe *is* in may amonge wilde bestes
C.16.12 And moche murthe among ryche men *is* þat han meble ynow and
hele.
C.16.14 And ʒut *is* wynter for hem worse for weetshoed þey g[ang]e,
C.16.16 [And arated of] ryche men þat reuthe *is* to here.
C.16.37 Elles *is* al an ydel al oure lyuynge here,
C.16.40 Elles *is* alle oure labour loest–loo how men writeth
C.16.47 And þat *is* plesant to pruyde in pore and in ryche.
C.16.48 A[c] þe ryche *is* reuerenced by resoun of his rychesse
C.16.49 There þe pore *is* potte behynde and parauntur can more
C.16.50 Of wit and of wisdoem þat fer way *is* bettere
C.16.59 Ac in pouerte þer pacience *is* pruyde hath no myhte
C.16.62 For þe pore *is* ay prest to plese þe ryche
C.16.67 For yf they bothe pleyne the pore *is* bote feble;
C.16.69 For lo[w]lyche he loketh and lo[uelych]e is his speche
C.16.75 For when he streyneth hym to strecche the strawe *is* his shetes.
C.16.77 Þat *is* welowo when he [w]aketh and wepeth for colde;
C.16.78 So he *is* neuere[more ful] merye, so meschief hym folleweth.
C.16.81 For men knowen wel þat coueytise *is* of a kene will
C.16.83 And pouerte *is* bote a pety thyng, appereth nat to his nauele.
C.16.95 Meschief *is* ay a mene and maketh hym to thenke
C.16.96 That god *is* his gretteste helpe and no gome elles
C.16.100 Forthy alle pore þat pacient *is* of puyr rihte may claymen
C.16.107 Moche *is* [þat] mayde to louye of a man þat such oen taketh,
C.16.108 More then þat mayde *is* þat is maried by brocage,
C.16.108 More then þat mayde is þat *is* maried by brocage,
C.16.113 The whiche *is* syb to crist [hym]sulue and semblable bothe.'
C.16.115 'What *is* pouerte, pacience?' quod he; 'y preye þat thow telle hit.'
C.16.119 In engelysch *is* ful hard Ac sumdel y shal telle the.
C.16.120 Pouerte *is* the furste poynte þat pruyde moest hateth;
C.16.121 Thenne *is* [hit] goed by goed skill, thouh hit greue a litel,
C.16.126 Selde *is* eny pore ypot to p[u]nesche eny peple.

C.16.129 Selde *is* pore rihte ryche but of rihtfole eritage.
C.16.133 The furthe *is* a fortune þat florischeth þe soule
C.16.137 [The fifte *is*] moder of myhte and of mannes helthe
C.16.139 The sixte *is* a path of pees; ʒe! thorwe þe pase of Aultoun
C.16.142 And euere þe lasse þat [eny] lede þe lihtere his herte *is* there,
C.16.144 The seuethe *is* a welle of wysdoem and fewe wordes sheweth
C.16.147 The eyʒte *is* a lel labour and loeth to take more
C.16.150 The nythe *is* swete to [þe] soul[e], no sucre swettore,
C.16.151 For pacience *is* his paniter and pouerte payn here fyndeth
C.16.169 *Is* noþer Peter the porter ne poul with the fauchen
C.16.171 At mydnyhte, at mydday, my vois *is* so yknowe
C.16.179 'Thenne *is* þat body bettere þen þou?' quod y. 'Nay,' quod he, 'no bettere,
C.16.181 And ayther *is* otheres hete and also of o will;
C.16.182 And so *is* man þat hath his mynde myd liberum Arbitrium.
C.16.188 Thenne *ys* racio my rihte name, reson an englische;
C.16.189 And when y fele þat folke telleth my furste name *is* sensus
C.16.190 And þat *is* wit and wysdoem, the welle of alle craftes;
C.16.196 Thenne *is* lele loue my name and in latyn Amor;
C.16.206 'That *is* soth,' he sayde; 'now y se thy wille.
C.16.218 To engelische men this *is* to mene, þat mowen speke and here,
C.16.220 The witt[i]ore þat eny wihte *is*, but yf he worche þeraftur,
C.16.226 And riht as hony *is* euel to defie,
C.16.247 There inparfit preesthoode *is*, prechares and techares.
C.16.251 There *is* a meschief in þe more of suche manere stokkes.
C.16.253 *Is* þe rote of [the] rihte fayth to reule þe peple;
C.16.254 Ac þer þe rote *is* roton, resoun woet þe sothe,
C.16.265 Ypocrisye *is* a braunche of pruyde and most amonges clerkes
C.16.266 And *is* ylikned in latyn to a lothly donghep
C.16.276 Ac thyng þat wykkedliche *is* wonne and with fals sleythes
C.16.286 'Charite,' quod y tho, 'þat *is* a thyng forsothe
C.16.298 'Charite *is* a childische thyng, as holy churche witnesseth:
C.16.302 He *is* glad with alle glade as gurles þat lawhen alle
C.16.308 For drede of god þat so goed *is* and thusgates vs techeth:
C.16.324 And oþerwhile his wone *is* to w[e]nde [o]n pilgrimages
C.16.343 He *is* þe murieste of mouthe at mete þer he sitteth
C.16.356 Ac hit *is* fer and fele ʒer in franceys tyme;
C.16.365 For ouerlong *is* here lawe but yf þay lacche suluer.
C.16.369 Ac thorw Coueytyse and his consaile ycongeyed *is* he ofte.
C.17.1 'There *is* no such,' y sayde, 'þat som tyme ne borweth
C.17.4 'Ho is wroeth and wolde be awreke, holy writ preueth,' quod he,
C.17.41 This *is* no more to mene bote men of holy churche
C.17.49 And charite þat chield *is* now sholde chaufen of hymsulue
C.17.75 Of moche [m]one þe metal *is* nauhte
C.17.76 And ʒut *is* þe printe puyr trewe and parfitliche ygraue.
C.17.77 And so hit fareth by false cristene: here follynge *is* trewe,
C.17.79 Ac þe metal þat *is* mannes soule of [many of] this techares
C.17.80 *Is* alayed with leccherye and oþer lustes of synne
C.17.90 As they ywoned were; in wham *is* defaute?
C.17.91 Nat in god þat he ne *is* goed and þe grounde bothe;
C.17.109 For *is* [now] noon, hoso nymeth hede,
C.17.125 'What *is* holy churche, chere frende?' quod y; 'Charite,' he saide;
C.17.140 The whiche *is* þe heued of charite and hele of mannes soule:
C.17.141 Loue god for he *is* goed and grounde of alle treuthe;
C.17.143 Loue thy frende þat folleweth thy wille, that *is* thy fayre soule.
C.17.148 And þat *is* charite, leue chield, to be cher ouer thy soule;
C.17.150 'Where sarresynes,' y saide, 'yse nat what *is* charite?'
C.17.153 Hit *is* kyndly thyng creature his creatour to honoure,
C.17.154 For þer *is* no man þat mynde hath þat ne meketh [hym] and bysecheth
C.17.162 Thenne *is* lawe ylefte and leute vnknowe.
C.17.164 Ne kynde sanʒ cortesie in no contreye *is* preysed.
C.17.194 Hit *is* reuthe to rede how riht holy men lyuede,
C.17.200 And now *is* reuthe to rede how þe rede noble
C.17.201 *Is* reuerenced byfore the rode and resceyued for the worthiore
C.17.204 And now *is* werre and wo and whoso why asketh:
C.17.207 That in grotes *is* graue and in golde nobles.
C.17.233 For were presthode more parfyte, that *is*, þe pope formost
C.17.247 The whiche *is* þe hy holy gost þat out of heuene descendet[h]
C.17.259 And þat *is* reuthe for rihtfole men þat in þ[e] reume wonyeth
C.17.277 He *is* a forbisene to alle bisshopis and a briht myrrour
C.17.287 For as þe kynde *is* of a knyhte or [of] a kynge to be take
C.17.290 So *is* þe kynde of a curatour for criste[s] loue to preche
C.18.14 The whiche *is* Caritas ykald, Cristes oune foode,
C.18.31 The world *is* a wikkede wynd to hem þat wo[l] treuthe;
C.18.35 Thenne *is* þe flesch a fel wynde and in flouryng tyme
C.18.41 The which *is* þe passioun & þe penaunce & þe parfitnesse of iesus
C.18.51 The whiche *is* spiritus sanctus and sothfaste bileue
C.18.52 And that *is* grace of þe holy gost; and thus gete y the maystrye.'
C.18.59 Hit *is* al of o kynde, and þat shal y preuen,
C.18.77 And chaste leden here lyf, *is* lyf of contemplacioun,
C.18.86 And thenne aboue *is* bettere fruyt, ac bothe two ben gode,
C.18.88 Thenne *is* virginite, more vertuous and fayrest, as in heuene,

C.18.89 For þat *is* euene with angelis and angeles pere.
C.18.97 And in heuene *is* priueoste and next hym by resoun
C.18.100 'This *is* a propre plonte,' quod y–'and priueliche hit bloweth
C.18.116 There *is* derkenesse and drede and þe deuel maister.
C.18.151 'Thenne *is* saton ʒoure saueour,' quod iesus, '& hath ysaued ʒow ofte.
C.18.158 And saide, 'this *is* an hous of orysones and of holynesse
C.18.159 And when þat my will *is* y wol hit ouerthrowe
C.18.186 'What *is* his [conn]esaunc[e],' quod y, 'in his cote Armure?'
C.18.192 'That *is* soth,' saide he thenne, 'the syre hatte pater
C.18.193 And þe seconde *is* a sone of þe sire, filius;
C.18.194 The thridde *is* þat halt al, a thyng by hymsulue;
C.18.195 Holy goest *is* his name and he is in all.'
C.18.195 Holy goest is his name and he *is* in all.'
C.18.196 'This *is* myrke thyng for me,' quod y, 'and for many anoþer,
C.18.212 A thre he *is* þer he is and hereof bereth wittnesse
C.18.212 A thre he is þer he *is* and hereof bereth wittnesse
C.18.214 That he *is* thre persones departable y preue hit by mankynde,
C.18.220 Matrimonye withoute moylere *is* nauht moche to preyse
C.18.232 *Is* and ay were [& worþ wiþouten ende].
C.18.233 And as thre persones palpable is puy[r]lich bote o mankynde,
C.18.234 The which *is* man and his make and moilere here issue,
C.18.235 So i[n] god [and] godes sone i/s] thre persones, the trinite.
C.18.237 And to godhede goth thre and o god *is* all thre.
C.18.246 Fol trewe tokenes bitwene vs *is* wh[at] tyme þat y met[t]e hym,
C.18.254 Myen affiaunce and my faith *is* ferme in [t]his bileue
C.18.274 'I wolde ywyte,' quod y tho, 'what *is* in thy lappe.'
C.18.276 'This *is* a present of moche pris; what prince shal hit haue?'
C.18.277 'Hit *is* a preciouse present,' quod he, 'Ac the pouke hit hath attached
C.18.281 Til he come þat y carpe of; Crist *is* his name
C.18.284 And þat *is* lyf for lyf or ligge thus euere
C.19.5 That that y sey *is* soeth se hoso liketh.'
C.19.6 '*Is* hit asseled?' y saide; 'may men yse th[e] lettres?'
C.19.8 The which *is* Cr[oes] and cristendoem and cr[ist] þer[o]n [to] hang[e];
C.19.18 '*Is* here al thy lordes l[aw]es?' quod y; 'ʒe, leef me,' he saide.
C.19.43 Hit *is* liht for lewed and for lered bothe.
C.19.74 *Is* syxe myle or seuene bisyde þe newe marcat,
C.19.114 Ferde furste as a f[u]ste, and ʒut *is*, as y leue,
C.19.118 The paume *is* the pethe of the hand and profereth [forth] the fyngeres
C.19.121 The holy goest of heuene: he *is* as þe paume.
C.19.126 The fader *is* thenne as þe fuste with fynger and with paume
C.19.131 And as þe fuste *is* a ful hand yfolde togyderes,
C.19.132 So *is* þe fader a fol god, the fu[r]ste of hem alle
C.19.133 As my fuste *is* furste ar y my fyngours shewe,
C.19.135 And al þe myhte with hym *is*, was and worth euere.
C.19.136 The fyngeres *is* a fol hand for failed they or thombe
C.19.141 The paume *is* puyrliche the hand and hath power by hymsulue
C.19.148 Thus *is* the holy goste god, noyther grettore ne lassore
C.19.149 Then *is* the syre or þe sone and of þe same myhte
C.19.150 And alle thre *is* bote o god as myn hoend and my fyngeres.
C.19.152 Al *is* bote oen hoend howso y turne hit.
C.19.153 Ac ho *is* herte in the hand euene in þe myddes
C.19.168 For [g]o[d] the fader *is* as þe fust; þe sone is as þe fynger.
C.19.168 For [g]o[d] the fader is as þe fust; þe sone *is* as þe fynger;
C.19.169 The holy gost of heuene he *is* as þe paume.
C.19.172 For to a torche or a taper þe trinite *is* likned,
C.19.184 So *is* þe holi gost god and grace withouten mercy
C.19.216 Al thy labor *is* loste and al thy longe trauaile,
C.19.218 So *is* þe holy gost god and grace withouten mercy
C.19.232 ʒe brenneth ac ʒe blaseth nat; and þat *is* a blynde bekne:
C.19.242 For godes tretor he *is* [to]ld for al his trewe catel
C.19.246 And *is* in helle for al þat, how wol riche nouthe
C.19.250 [That that wickedliche *is* wonne to wasten hit and make frendes?]
C.19.254 Bote they dwelle there diues *is* dayes withouten ende.
C.19.255 Thus *is* vnkyndenesse [the contrarie that] quencheth, as hit were,
C.19.261 The which *is* lyf and loue, the leye of mannes body.
C.19.267 Ac this *is* the worste wyse þat eny wiht myhte
C.19.272 Innocence *is* next god and nyht and day hit crieth
C.19.276 And sethe Charite þat holy churche *is* chargeth this so sore
C.19.285 Ac hit *is* bote selde yseyen, there sothnesse bereth witnesse,
C.19.288 The[r] þat partye pursueth the apeel *is* so huge
C.19.296 And nat of þe nownpower of god, þat he ne *is* ful of myhte
C.19.297 To amende al þat amys *is* and his mercy grettore
C.19.300 As sorwe of herte *is* satisfaccioun for suche þat may nat paye
C.19.303 That [oon] *is* a wikkede wyf þat wol nat be chasted;
C.19.314 The wyf *is* oure wikkede flesche [þat] wol nat be chasted
C.19.317 And "þat *is* lihtliche forʒeue and forʒete bothe
C.19.328 That *is* coueytise and vnkyndenesse whiche quencheth godes mercy
C.19.329 For vnkyndenesse *is* þe contrarie of alle kyne resoun.
C.19.330 For þer ne *is* sike ne sory ne non so moche wrecche
C.20.11 As *is* þe kynde of a knyhte þat cometh to be dobbet,
C.20.19 '*Is* Peres in this place?' quod y, and he printe on me.

C.20.71 And somme saide, 'he can of soercerie; goed *is* þat we assaie
C.20.106 And ȝoure franchise þat fre was yfallen *is* i[n] thraldoem;
C.20.110 The which *is* lif þat oure lord in all lawes defendeth.
C.20.138 And þat *is* cause of this clips þat [c]loseth now þe sonne.
C.20.145 'That thow tellest,' quod treuthe, '*is* bote a tale of walterot!
C.20.150 Hit *is* truyfle þat thow tellest; y, treuthe, woet þe sothe,
C.20.151 [For] þat ones *is* in helle out cometh hit neuere.
C.20.157 For of alle venymes [fou]lest *is* þe scorpioun;
C.20.165 And bigile þe gilour, and þat *is* goed sleythe:
C.20.170 'That *is* soth,' saide mercy, 'and y se here bi southe
C.20.179 'My wil *is* to wende,' quod pees, 'and welcomen hem alle
C.20.185 Loue þat *is* my lemman such lettres me sente
C.20.207 For hit *is* boteles bale, the bite that they eten.'
C.20.211 For no wiht woet what wele *is* þat neuere wo soffrede
C.20.212 Ne what *is* hoet hunger þat hadde neuere defaute.
C.20.216 Sholde ywyte witterly what day *is* to mene.
C.20.220 Ywyte what wo *is* ne were þe deth of kynde.
C.20.224 The which vnknytteth alle care and comsyng *is* of reste.
C.20.226 Ne woet no wyht, as y wene, what *is* ynow to mene.
C.20.234 To wyte what al wo *is* þat woet of alle ioye:
C.20.236 Shal lere hem what l[angour] *is* and lisse withouten ende.
C.20.237 For woet no wiht what werre *is* þer [þat] pees regneth
C.20.238 Ne what *is* witterliche wele til welaway hym teche.'
C.20.276 Care and combraunce *is* come to vs all.
C.20.278 And lede hit þer laȝar *is* and lihtliche me bynde.
C.20.296 Bothe this lord and this lihte, *ys* longe ygo y knewe hym.
C.20.298 And where he wol *is* his way, ac waer hym of þe perelles:
C.20.302 For hymsulue said, þat sire *is* of heuene.
C.20.307 And sethe he *is* a lele lord y leue þat he wol nat
C.20.311 Thenne were he vnwrast of his word þat witnesse *is* of treuthe.'
C.20.312 'That *is* soeth,' saide satoun, 'bote y me sore doute
C.20.322 'Hit *is* nat graythly ygete ther gyle is þe rote
C.20.322 'Hit *is* nat graythly ygete ther gyle is þe rote
C.20.342 With glorie and with [grete] lihte; god hit *is* ich woet wel.
C.20.353 And wyte[th] hem al þe wrechednesse þat wrouhte *is* on erthe.
C.20.356 Witnesseth in his writyng[e] what *is* lyares mede:
C.20.396 So þat [thorw] gyle was gete thorw grace *is* now ywonne
C.20.403 For y þat am lord of lyf, loue *is* my drynke,
C.20.421 Hit *is* nat vsed [i]n erthe to hangen [a] felo[n]
C.20.452 'Aftur sharp[e] shoures,' quod pees, 'most shene *is* þe sonne;
C.20.453 *Is* no wedore warmore then aftur watri cloudes;
C.20.462 For inposible *is* no thynge to hym þat is almyhty.'
C.20.462 For inposible is no thynge to hym þat *is* almyhty.'
C.20.474 And hit afereth th[e] fende, for such *is* þe myhte
C.21.10 '*Is* this iesus the ioustare,' quod y, 'þat iewes dede to dethe?
C.21.11 Or hit *is* [Peres þe Plouhman? who] paynted hym so rede?'
C.21.14 *Is* Crist with his croes, conquerour of Cristene.'
C.21.19 Ergo *is* no name to þe name of iesus
C.21.24 *Is* Crist more of myhte and more worth[y] name
C.21.28 To be cald a knyht *is* fayr for men shal knele to hym;
C.21.29 To be cald a kyng *is* fairor for he may knyhtes make;
C.21.36 As wyd[e] as þe worlde *is* wonyeth þer none
C.21.57 And bonde [hym] as he *is* bounde with bondes of yre.
C.21.62 He may be wel called conquerour and that *is* Crist to mene.
C.21.64 *Is* to wissen vs þerwith, þat when we ben ytempted
C.21.89 Gold *is* likened to lewetee that laste shal euere
C.21.93 For Mirre *is* mercy to mene and mylde speche of tonge.
C.21.106 As kynde *is* of a conquerour, so comesede iesu
C.21.111 For wyn *is* likned to lawe and lyfholinesse
C.21.207 Quod Consience and knelede, 'this *is* Cristes messager
C.21.208 And cometh fro the grete god; grace *is* his name.
C.21.333 As wyde as the world *is* with Peres to tulye treuthe
C.21.335 Now *is* [Peres] to the [plouh]; Pryde hit aspiede
C.21.348 That Consience shal nat knowe [ho *is* cristene or hethene]
C.21.355 Quod Consience to alle cristene tho, 'my consayl *is* [to] wende
C.21.385 Here *is* bred yblessed and godes body peru'nder.
C.21.393 'That *is* my conseil,' quod Consience, 'and cardinale vertues,
C.21.400 Thikke ale [&] thynne ale; þat *is* my kynde
C.21.409 'Thenne *is* many [a lyf] ylost,' quod a lewed vicory.
C.21.417 "The contreye *is* þe corsedore þat cardinals cometh ynne
C.21.428 Inparfit *is* þat pope þat all peple sholde helpe
C.21.436 As for hymsulue and his seruauntes, saue he *is* furste yserued.
C.21.455 For spiritus prudencie among þe peple *is* gyle
C.22.12 That *is* mete when men hym werneth [and] he no money weldeth
C.22.23 [For *is* no vertue by fer to spiritus temperancie],
C.22.33 Wenyng *is* no wisdoem ne wyse ymaginacioun:
C.22.35 A[c] nede *is* nexst hym for anoen he meketh
C.22.89 With deth þat *is* dredful to vndoen vs alle!
C.22.141 That couetyse were cristene þat *is* so kene to fihte
C.22.269 Hit *is* wikked to wage ȝow; ȝe wexeth out of nombre.
C.22.270 [Heuene haeth euene nombre and helle *is* withoute nombre].
C.22.280 And euele *is* this yholde in parsches of yngelond
C.22.288 Ac while he *is* in Westmynstre he wol be bifore

C.22.313 'Ther *is* a surgien in the sege that softe can handele
C.22.315 Oen frere flaterrere *is* fiscicien and surgien.'
C.22.317 For here *is* many [a] man hert thorw ypocrisye.'
C.22.334 'He *is* syke,' saide Pees, 'and so ar many other.
C.22.335 Ypocrysye haeth her[t]e hem; ful hard *is* yf thei keuere.'
C.22.357 Here *is* contricioun,' quod Consience, 'my cosyn, ywounded.
C.22.360 And lat hem lygge ouerlonge and loeth *is* to chaungen;
C.22.362 'That *is* ouerlonge,' quod this lymitour, 'y leue; y schal amenden hit!'
C.22.372 That *is* the souereyne salue for alle [synnes of kynde].

nas A 3

A. 2.38 Þer *nas* halle ne hous to herberwe þe peple,
A. 2.39 Þat iche feld *nas* ful of folk al aboute.
A. 4.135 Þere *nas* man in þe mothalle, more ne lesse,

nas B 3

B.12.146 Ne in none [beggers] cote [*n*]*as* þat barn born,
B.19.293 Maken hym, for any mournynge, þat he *nas* murie in soule,
B.19.372 Ther *nas* no cristene creature þat kynde wit hadde

nas C 1

C.20.310 And neuere [*n*]*as* þeraȝeyne and now wolde bigynne,

nere A 3

A. 5.179 And nempnide hym for a noumpere þat no debate *nere*.
A. 5.240 To haue helle for euere ȝif þat hope *nere*.
A.11.51 *Nere* mercy in mene men more þan in riche

nere B 3

B.Pr.200 *Nere* þe cat of þ[e] court þat kan yow ouerlepe;
B. 5.330 And nempned hym for a nounpere þat no debat *nere*.
B.11.104 Thouȝ þow se yuel seye it noȝt first; be sory it *nere* amended.

nere C 3

C. 1.115 '*Nere* hit for northerne men anon y wolde ȝow telle
C. 3.173 Shyreues of shyres were shent yf he *nere*,
C.15.210 *Nere* hit þat þe parsche [prest] preyeth for me on sonendayes,

nis A 4

A. 2.14 Þere *nis* no quen queyntere þat quyk is o lyue.
A. 3.50 'Wiste I þat,' quaþ þe womman, 'þere *nis* wyndowe ne auter
A. 5.219 For is no gilt here so gret þat his goodnesse *nis* more'.
A. 9.20 Ergo he *nis* not alwey at hom among ȝow Freris;

nys B 7 nis (1) nys (6)

B. 5.283 *Nis* na moore to þe mercy of god þan [amyd] þe see a gleede:
B. 8.24 Ergo he *nys* noȝt alwey [at hoom] amonges yow freres;
B.11.349 Ther *nys* wriȝte, as I wene, sholde werche hir nes[t] to paye;
B.13.165 There *nys* neiþer emperour ne emperesse, erl ne baroun,
B.13.207 Ther *nys* wo in þis world þat we ne sholde amende.
B.14.243 And Pouerte *nys* but a petit þyng, apereþ noȝt to his nauele,
B.17.350 For þer *nys* sik ne sory, ne noon so muche wrecche

nis C 2

C.10.28 Ergo he [*n*]*is* nat alwey at hom amonges ȝow freres;
C.15.165 Þer [*n*]*is* wyht in this world þat wolde the lette

was A 80

A.Pr.1 IN a somer sesoun whanne softe *was* the sonne
A.Pr.7 I *was* wery [for]wandrit & wente me to reste
A.Pr.12 Þat I *was* in a wildernesse, wiste I neuere where;
A. 1.10 I *was* aferd of hire face þeiȝ heo fair were,
A. 1.60 May banne þat he born *was* to body or to soule.
A. 1.110 And *was* þe louelokest [of siȝt] aftir oure lord
A. 1.147 Þat he *was* miȝtful & mek & mercy gan graunte
A. 2.8 And *was* war of a womman wondirliche cloþide,
A. 2.19 And so shulde [heo] not be for wrong *was* hire sire;
A. 2.41 *Was* piȝt vp a pauyloun proud for þe nones,
A. 2.47 In what maner þat mede in mariage *was* feffid;
A. 2.72 In witnesse of whiche þing wrong *was* þe furste,
A. 2.113 Þo þis gold *was* gyue gret was þe þonking
A. 2.113 Þo þis gold was gyue gret *was* þe þonking
A. 2.122 Þanne *was* fals fayn, & fauel als bliþe,
A. 2.149 Ac gile *was* forgoere and gyede hem alle.
A. 2.179 He *was* nowhere welcome for his many talis,
A. 2.198 And ek wep & wrang whan heo *was* atachid.
A. 3.11 Ac þere *was* merþe & mynstralcie mede to plese;
A. 3.103 Þanne *was* consience callid to comen & aperen
A. 3.176 In normandie *was* he nouȝt anoyed for my sake,
A. 4.49 Wrong *was* aferd þo & wisdom he souȝte.
A. 4.67 And wisten wel þat wrong *was* a shrewe euere.
A. 5.3 Þanne wakide I of my wynkyng, & wo *was* wiþalle
A. 5.15 *Was* apertly for pride & for no poynt ellis.
A. 5.30 He warnide watte his wyf *was* to blame
A. 5.31 Þat hire hed *was* worþ a mark & his hod not worþ a grote.
A. 5.49 For to affaiten hire flessh þat fers *was* to synne:
A. 5.60 He *was* as pale as a p[e]let, [in] þe palesie he semide;
A. 5.61 He *was* cloþid in a caurymaury, I [couþe] it nouȝt descryue;
A. 5.66 His body *was* bolnid for wr[aþþe] þat he bot his lippe[s],
A. 5.80 Boþe his lyme & his lif *was* lost þoruȝ my tunge.
A. 5.109 He *was* [betil]browid & babirlippid wiþ two bleride eiȝen,
A. 5.113 He shulde wandre on þat walsshe, so *was* it þredbare.

A. 5.116 And *was* his prentis ypliȝt his profit to loke.
A. 5.118 Wykkidly to weiȝe *was* my ferste lessoun.
A. 5.129 My wyf *was* a wynstere & wollene cloþ made,
A. 5.140 Rose þe regratour *was* hire riȝte name;
A. 5.178 Til robyn þe ropere *was* red to arisen,
A. 5.185 Þere *was* lauȝing & louryng & 'lete go þe cuppe!'
A. 5.204 Þe ferste woord þat he spak *was* 'where is þe bolle?'
A. 5.206 Þanne *was* þat shrewe asshamide & shrapide hise eris,
A. 5.234 Ac for þere *was* nouȝt wherewith he wepte swiþe sore.
A. 7.24 Ac on þe tem trewely tauȝt *was* I neuere.
A. 7.100 Þerewiþ *was* perkyn payed, and preisid hem ȝerne.
A. 7.147 To kepen hym as couenaunt *was* fro curside shrewis,
A. 7.152 'I *was* not wonid to werche,' quaþ wastour, 'now wile I not begynne,'
A. 7.173 Þat hunger *was* not hardy on hem for to loke.
A. 7.184 And pieris *was* proud þerof, & putte hem in office,
A. 7.284 Þanne *was* folk fayn, & fedde hunger with þe beste;
A. 7.297 Þat he *was* werkman ywrouȝt warie þe tyme,
A. 7.300 Ac while hunger *was* here maister wolde þere non chide,
A. 8.66 Hadde þe same absolucioun þat sent *was* to peris.
A. 8.81 Þat euere he *was* man wrouȝt whanne he shal henne fare.
A. 8.94 And *was* writen riȝt þus in witnesse of treuþe:
A. 8.148 Þat Iosep *was* Iustice Egipt to kepe–
A. 9.4 Ȝif any wiȝt wiste where dowel *was* at Inne;
A. 9.6 *Was* neuere wiȝt as I wen[t]e þat me wisse couþe
A. 9.110 He *was* long & lene, lyk to non oþer,
A. 9.111 *Was* no pride on his apparail ne no pouert noþer,
A.10.34 And al at his wil *was* wrouȝt wiþ a speche,
A.10.41 Þoruȝ miȝt of þe maieste man *was* ymakid.
A.10.140 Ben conseyuid in cursid tyme as kaym *was* on Eue:
A.10.161 Þat god *was* wroþ wiþ here werkis & [suche wordis seide]:
A.11.2 Þat lene *was* of lich & of lo[uȝ] chere.
A.11.3 She *was* wondirliche wroþ þat wyt so tauȝte,
A.11.85 –Al was as he wolde; lord yworsshipid be þou,
A.11.93 And whanne þat wyt *was* war how his wif tolde
A.11.100 And whanne I *was* war of his wil to his wif gan I knele,
A.11.173 *Was* neuere [gome] vpon þis ground, siþþe god makid heuene,
A.11.176 Þat I *was* of wyttis hous & wiþ his wyf dame stodie.
A.11.261 I *was* markid wiþoute mercy, & myn name entrid
A.11.272 And *was* þere neuere in þis world to wysere of werkis,
A.11.279 A goode friday, I fynde, a feloun was sauid
A.11.294 Þat clergie of cristis mouþ comendite [*was* hit] neuere,
A.11.303 Þat [*was*] austyn þe olde, & hiȝeste of þe foure,
A.12.41 Kynde [wit] hure confessour, hure cosyn *was* Inne.
A.12.100 Þat þis speche *was* spedelich, and sped him wel faste,
A.12.103 And whan þis werk *was* wrouȝt, ere wille myȝte aspie,
      was B 332
B.Pr.1 IN a somer seson whan softe *was* þe sonne
B.Pr.7 I *was* wery forwandred and wente me to reste
B.Pr.12 That I *was* in a wildernesse, wiste I neuere where.
B.Pr.51 To ech a tale þat þei tolde hire tonge *was* tempred to lye
B.Pr.176 Ac þo þe belle *was* ybrouȝt and on þe beiȝe hanged
B.Pr.177 Ther ne *was* Raton in þe route, for al þe Reaume of Fraunce,
B. 1.10 I was afered of hire face þeiȝ she fair weere
B. 1.32 Thoruȝ wyn and þoruȝ wommen þer *was* loth acombred,
B. 1.62 May banne þat he born *was* to bodi or to soule.
B. 1.112 [And *was*] þe louelokest of liȝt after oure lord
B. 1.156 *Was* neuere leef vpon lynde lighter þerafter,
B. 1.173 That he *was* myȝtful and meke and mercy gan graunte
B. 2.8 And *was* war of a womman [wonder]liche ycloþed,
B. 2.15 Hire Robe *was* ful riche, of reed scarlet engreyned,
B. 2.18 I hadde wonder what she *was* and whos wif she were.
B. 2.25 For Fals *was* hire fader þat haþ a fikel tonge
B. 2.53 And how Mede *was* ymaried in Metels me þouȝte;
B. 2.57 To marien þis mayde [*was*] many m[a]n assembled,
B. 2.108 In witnesse of which þyng wrong *was* þe firste,
B. 2.149 Tho þis gold *was* ygyue gret was þe þonkyng
B. 2.149 Tho þis gold was ygyue gret *was* þe þonkyng
B. 2.158 Thanne *was* Fal[s] fayn and Fauel as bliþe,
B. 2.188 Ac Gyle *was* Forgoer and gyed hem alle.
B. 2.220 He *was* nowher welcome for his manye tales,
B. 2.239 And ek wepte and wrong whan she *was* attached.
B. 3.11 A[c] þer *was* murþe & Mynstralcie Mede to plese;
B. 3.114 [Th]anne *was* Conscience called to come and appere
B. 3.189 In Normandie *was* he noȝt noyed for my sake,
B. 3.275 Ooþerwise þan he *was* warned of þe prophete,
B. 3.339 *Was* omnia probate, and þat plesed hire herte
B. 3.340 For þat lyne *was* no lenger at þe leues ende.
B. 4.62 That wrong *was* a wikked luft and wroȝte muche sorwe.
B. 4.63 Wrong *was* afered þ[o] and wisdom he souȝte
B. 5.3 Thanne waked I of my wynkyng and wo *was* withalle
B. 5.15 *Was* pertliche for pride and for no point ellis.

B. 5.30 He warnede watte his wif *was* to blame
B. 5.31 [That] hire heed *was* worþ [a] marc & his hood noȝt a grote.
B. 5.66 To affaiten hire flessh þat fiers *was* to synne.
B. 5.77 He *was* as pale as a pelet, in þe palsy he semed.
B. 5.78 [He *was*] cloþed in a kaurymaury–I couþe it nouȝt discryue–
B. 5.83 His body *was* [b]ollen for wraþe þat he boot hise lippes,
B. 5.86 Ech a word þat he warp *was* of a Neddres tonge;
B. 5.87 Of chidynge and chalangynge *was* his chief liflode,
B. 5.89 [This *was*] al his curteisie where þat euere he shewed hym].
B. 5.132 Whan he solde and I nouȝt þanne *was* I redy
B. 5.137 'I am wraþe', quod he, 'I *was* som tyme a frere,
B. 5.157 I *was* þe Prioresse potager and oþere pouere ladies,
B. 5.158 And maad hem Ioutes of Ianglyng þat dame Iohane *was* a bastard,
B. 5.159 And dame Clarice a knyȝtes douȝter ac a cokewold *was* hir sire,
B. 5.166 Seint Gregory *was* a good pope and hadde a good forwit:
B. 5.190 He *was* bitelbrowed and baberlipped wiþ two blered eiȝen;
B. 5.193 And as a bondeman[nes] bacon his berd *was* [yshaue]
B. 5.197 She sholde noȝt [wandre] on þat wel[ch]e, so *was* it þredbare.
B. 5.200 And *was* his prentice ypliȝt his profit to [loke].
B. 5.202 Wikkedly to weye *was* my firste lesson.
B. 5.213 My wif *was* a [wynnestere] and wollen cloþ made,
B. 5.224 Rose þe Regrater *was* hir riȝte name;
B. 5.231 'ȝis, ones I *was* yherberwed', quod he, 'wiþ an heep of chapmen;
B. 5.233 'That was no restitucion', quod Repentaunce, 'but a robberis þefte;
B. 5.264 And þat *was* wonne wiþ wrong wiþ wikked men be despended.
B. 5.336 There *was* lauȝynge and lourynge and 'lat go þe cuppe!'
B. 5.353 Ac Gloton *was* a gret cherl and grym in þe liftyng;
B. 5.362 The firste word þat he [spak] *was* 'where is þe bolle?'
B. 5.370 There no nede *was* nyne hundred tymes;
B. 5.396 Ac neiþer of oure lord ne of oure lady þe leeste þat euere *was* maked.
B. 5.399 Ne riȝt sory for my synnes yet, [so þee I], *was* I neuere.
B. 5.462 And for þer *was* noȝt wher[wiþ] he wepte swiþe soore.
B. 5.484 For þoruȝ þat synne þi sone sent *was* to erþe
B. 5.490 But in oure secte *was* þe sorwe and þi sone it ladde:
B. 5.500 Of þyne douȝt[iest] dedes *was* doon in oure armes:
B. 5.513 Ac þere *was* [wye] noon so wys þe wey þider kouþe,
B. 6.22 Ac on þe teme trewely tauȝt *was* I neuere.
B. 6.108 Therwiþ *was* Perkyn apayed and preised hem [yerne].
B. 6.160 To kepen hym as couenaunt *was* fro cursede sherewes,
B. 6.167 'I *was* noȝt wont to werche', quod Wastour, 'now wol I noȝt bigynne!'
B. 6.185 That hunger *was* noȝt hardy on hem for to loke.
B. 6.193 For þat *was* bake for bayard was boote for many hungry;
B. 6.193 For þat was bake for bayard *was* boote for many hungry;
B. 6.194 And many a beggere for benes buxum *was* to swynke,
B. 6.197 And [Piers *was*] proud þerof] and putte hem [in office]
B. 6.300 Thanne *was* folk fayn and fedde hunger wiþ þe beste;
B. 6.313 [That] he *was* werkman wroȝt [warie] þe tyme.
B. 6.319 Ac whiles hunger *was* hir maister þer wolde noon chide
B. 7.64 Ha[dde] þe same absolucion þat sent *was* to Piers.
B. 7.76 Ac Gregory *was* a good man and bad vs gyuen alle
B. 7.99 That euere [he *was* man] wroȝt whan [he] shal hennes fare.
B. 7.112 And *was* writen riȝt þus in witnesse of truþe:
B. 7.171 That Ioseph *was* Iustice Egipte to loke;
B. 8.4 If any wiȝt wiste wher dowel *was* at Inne;
B. 8.6 *Was* neuere wiȝt as I wente þat me wisse kouþe
B. 8.120 He *was* long and lene, lik to noon ooþer;
B. 8.121 *Was* no pride on his apparaill ne pouerte neiþer;
B. 8.126 What *was* Dowel fro dobet and dobest from hem boþe.
B. 9.33 [And al at his wil *was* wrouȝt wiþ a speche],
B. 9.36 For he *was* synguler hymself and seide faciamus,
B. 9.45 And in þis manere *was* man maad þoruȝ myȝt of god almyȝty,
B. 9.53 Thorgh myȝt of þe mageste man *was* ymaked.
B. 9.115 The wif *was* maad þe w[y]e for to helpe werche,
B. 9.116 And þus *was* wedlok ywroȝt wiþ a mene persone,
B. 9.119 And þus *was* wedlok ywroȝt and god hymself it made.
B. 9.120 In erþe [be] heuene [is]; hymself [*was*] þe] witnesse.
B. 9.123 Conceyued ben in [cursed] tyme as Caym *was* on Eue
B. 9.188 Noȝt as Adam and Eue whan Caym *was* engendred;
B.10.1 Thanne hadde wit a wif *was* hote dame Studie,
B.10.2 That lene *was* of [liche] and of [lowe chere].
B.10.3 She *was* wonderly wroþ þat wit [so] tauȝte,
B.10.102 That *was* maad for meles men to eten Inne,
B.10.132 Al *was* as [he] wold[e]–lord, yworshiped be þ[ow],
B.10.140 And whan þat wit *was* ywar [how his wif] tolde
B.10.147 And whan I *was* war of his wille to his wif gan I [knele]
B.10.158 Thanne *was* [I] also fayn as fowel of fair morwe,
B.10.230 *Was* neuere gome vpon þis ground, siþ god made [heuene],
B.10.233 That I *was* of wittes hous and wiþ his wif dame Studie.
B.10.236 I seide to h[y]m sooþly þat sent *was* I þider
B.10.251 Who *was* his Auctour? alle þe foure Euaungelistes.
B.10.275 This text *was* told yow to ben ywar er ye tauȝte
B.10.380 And þat I man maad *was*, and my name yentred
B.10.402 Ac hir werkes, as holy writ seiþ, [*was*] euere þe contrarie.

B.10.405 Ac I wene it worþ of manye as *was* in Noes tyme
B.10.407 *Was* neuere wrighte saued þat wroȝte þeron, ne ooþer werkman ellis,
B.10.410 Of w[r]ightes þat it wroȝte *was* noon of hem ysaued.
B.10.420 On good Friday, I fynde, a felon *was* ysaued
B.10.423 He *was* sonner ysaued þan seint Iohan þe Baptist
B.10.426 A Robbere *was* yraunsoned raþer þan þei alle,
B.10.447 For soþest word þat euer god seide *was* þo he seide Nemo bonus.
B.10.449 That] Clergie of cristes mouþ comended *was* it [neuere],
B.10.457 Whan man *was* at meschief wiþoute þe moore grace.
B.10.459 *Was* Austyn þe olde, and heiȝest of þe foure,
B.11.7 [For] I *was* rauysshed riȝt þere; Fortune me fette
B.11.14 And Coueitise of eiȝes [þat ooþer man]
B.11.27 Thanne *was* þer oon þat hiȝte Elde, þat heuy *was* of chere;
B.11.27 Thanne *was* þer oon þat hiȝte Elde, þat heuy *was* of chere;
B.11.61 And þanne *was* Fortune my foo for al hir faire [biheste],
B.11.111 This *was* hir teme and hir text–I took ful good hede–
B.11.113 And whan þe peple *was* plener comen þe porter vnpynned þe yate
B.11.140 'Ye? baw for bokes!' quod oon *was* broken out of helle.
B.11.142 How [I] *was* ded and dampned to dwellen in pyne
B.11.150 Wiþouten bede biddyng his boone *was* vnderfongen
B.11.155 That *was* an vncristene creature, as clerkes fyndeþ in bokes:
B.11.157 *Was* þat Sarsen saued, as Seint Gregorie bereþ witnesse.
B.11.207 And after his resurexcion Redemptor *was* his name,
B.11.238 So bi hise werkes þei wisten þer he *was* Iesus.
B.11.240 And al *was* ensample, [sooþliche], to vs synfulle here
B.11.249 *Was* a pure pouere maide and to a pouere man ywedded.
B.11.272 Wiser þan Salomon *was* bereþ witnesse and tauȝte
B.11.273 That parfit pouerte *was* no possession to haue,
B.11.325 I *was* fet forþ by [forbisenes] to knowe
B.11.341 Ther ne *was* cow ne cowkynde þat conceyued hadde
B.11.398 For al þat he [wrouȝt] *was* wel ydo, as holy writ witnesseþ:
B.11.402 For man *was* maad of swich a matere he may noȝt wel asterte
B.11.406 And awaked þerwiþ; wo was me þanne
B.11.419 The wisedom and þe wit of god, he *was* put fram blisse.
B.11.438 Why ye wisse me þus', quod I, '*was* for I rebuked Reson.'
B.12.1 'I am ymaginatif', quod he; 'ydel *was* I neuere
B.12.45 Catel and kynde wit *was* combraunce to hem alle.
B.12.73 In þe olde lawe as þe lettre telleþ, þat *was* þe lawe of Iewes,
B.12.76 A womman, as [we] fynde[n], *was* gilty of þat dede,
B.12.80 Than þe womman þat þere *was*, and wenten awey for shame.
B.12.101 Alþouȝ men made bokes [þe maister *was* god]
B.12.127 *Was* þer neuere [kyng ne] knyȝt but clergie hem made.
B.12.133 Ac þoruȝ hir science sooþly *was* neuere soule ysaued
B.12.137 And seiden hir wordes [ne] hir wisdomes [w]as but a folye;
B.12.154 And doute [hir] homage honurably to hym þat *was* almyȝty.
B.12.186 Wo *was* hym marked þat wade moot wiþ he lewed!
B.12.193 *Was* for he yald hym creaunt to crist & knewliched hym gilty,
B.12.202 So it fareþ by þat felon þat a good friday *was* saued;
B.12.261 That *was* writen, and þei witnesse to werche as it wolde.
B.12.283 "Troianus *was* a trewe knyght and took neuere cristendom
B.12.295 And wit and wisdom', quod þat wye, '*was* som tyme tresor
B.12.296 To kepe wiþ a commune; no catel *was* holde bettre,
B.13.7 And how þat freres folwede folk þat was riche
B.13.8 And [peple] þat *was* pouere at litel pris þei sette,
B.13.9 And no corps in hir kirkȝerd n[e] in hir kirk *was* buryed
B.13.25 And þere I [mette] a maister, what man he *was* I nyste,
B.13.33 This maister *was* maad sitte as for þe mooste worþi,
B.13.43 Ac hir sauce *was* ouer sour and vnsauourly grounde
B.13.48 And me þat *was* his [mette oþer mete boþe],
B.13.59 Pacience *was* proud of þat propre seruice
B.13.139 [Th]us [lerede] me ones a lemman, loue *was* hir name.
B.13.192 The goode wil of a wight *was* neuere bouȝt to þe fulle,
B.13.265 There *was* a careful commune whan no cart com to towne
B.13.270 My wafres were gesene whan Chichestre *was* Maire.'
B.13.272 Of haukyn þe Actif man and how he *was* ycloþed.
B.13.274 Ac it *was* moled in many places wiþ manye sondry plottes,
B.13.283 *Was* noon swich as hymself], ne [noon] so po[pe] holy;
B.13.319 It *was* fouler bi fele fold þan it first semed.
B.13.320 It *was* bidropped wiþ wraþe and wikkede wille,
B.13.342 I waitede wisloker and þanne *was* it soilled
B.13.355 [*Was*] colomy þoruȝ coueitise and vnkynde desiryng.
B.13.362 'The worste withInne *was*; a greet wit I let it.
B.13.368 Or by nyȝte or by daye aboute *was* ich euere
B.13.381 Moore þan it *was* worþ, and yet wolde I swere
B.13.397 That my mynde ne *was* moore on my good in a doute
B.13.401 As þere no nede *was* goddes name an Idel:
B.14.39 For lent neuere *was* lif but liflode were shapen,
B.14.47 But I [listnede and] lokede what liflode it *was*
B.14.50 And þanne *was* it fiat voluntas tua [sholde fynde vs alle].
B.14.66 And in Elyes tyme heuene *was* yclosed
B.14.106 I wiste neuere renk þat riche *was*, þat whan he rekene sholde,
B.14.121 For to wroþerhele *was* he wroȝt þat neuere was Ioye shapen.
B.14.121 For to wroþerhele was he wroȝt þat neuere *was* Ioye shapen.

B.14.244 And louely layk *was* it neuere bitwene þe longe and þe shorte.
B.14.322 That þ[u]s first wroot to wissen men what Pouerte *was* to mene.'
B.15.1 AC after my wakynge it *was* wonder longe
B.15.2 Er I koude kyndely knowe what *was* dowel,
B.15.120 And who *was* myn Auctour, muche wonder me þinkeþ
B.15.133 [This] þat wiþ gile *was* geten vngraciousliche is [s]pended.
B.15.230 And in a freres frokke he *was* yfounden ones,
B.15.245 For to wonye wiþ hem his wone *was* som tyme,
B.15.280 And þoruȝ þe mylk of þat mylde beest þe man *was* sustened;
B.15.298 Ac þer ne *was* leoun ne leopard þat on laundes wenten,
B.15.312 And bidden hem bere it þere it [yborwed *was*].
B.15.366 And what to leue and to lyue by; þe lond *was* so trewe.
B.15.371 Of þat *was* calculed of þe element þe contrarie þei fynde.
B.15.399 This Makometh *was* cristene [man], and for he moste noȝt ben pope
B.15.443 Al *was* hethynesse som tyme Engelond and Walis
B.15.451 [Enformed] hem what fullynge and feiþ *was* to mene.
B.15.523 In sauacion of [mannes soule] seint [Thomas] *was* ymartired;
B.15.531 Many man for cristes loue *was* martired [amonges] Romayne[s]
B.15.538 And þo *was* plentee and pees amonges poore and riche,
B.15.583 In stoon for it stedefast *was* and stonde sholde euere.
B.15.593 And whan he lifte vp Laȝar þat leid *was* in graue
B.16.23 Wiþ þre piles *was* it vnderpight; I parceyued it soone.
B.16.79 For euere as þei dropped adoun þe deuel *was* redy
B.16.100 And in þe wombe of þat wenche *was* he fourty woukes
B.16.107 Til he *was* parfit praktisour if any peril fille.
B.16.118 That he *was* leche of lif and lord of heigh heuene.
B.16.134 As euere it *was* and as wid; wherfore I hote yow
B.16.145 It *was* hymself sooþly and seide 'tu dicis'.
B.16.150 And [þus] *was* wiþ Iudas þo þat Iesus bitrayed:
B.16.160 On a þursday in þesternesse þus *was* he taken;
B.16.161 Thoruȝ Iudas and Iewes Iesus *was* [ynome]
B.16.187 Wardeyn of þat wit haþ; *was* euere wiþouten gynnyng.
B.16.204 In tokenynge of þe Trinite, *was* [taken out of a man],
B.16.205 Adam, oure aller fader. Eue *was* of hymselue,
B.16.206 And þe issue þat þei hadde it *was* of hem boþe,
B.16.215 That is, creatour weex creature to knowe what *was* boþe.
B.16.216 As widewe wiþouten wedlok *was* neuere ȝit yseyȝe,
B.16.250 Of a [buyrn] þat baptised hym–Iohan Baptist *was* his name–
B.17.12 Wheron [*was*] writen two wordes on þis wise yglosed.
B.17.14 This *was* the tixte, trewely; I took ful good yeme.
B.17.15 The glose *was* gloriously writen wiþ a gilt penne:
B.17.56 Where a man *was* wounded and wiþ þeues taken.
B.17.69 And parceyued bi his pous he *was* in peril to dye
B.17.87 And suwed þat Samaritan þat *was* so ful of pite,
B.17.92 For sighte of þ[e] sorweful [segge] þat robbed *was* with þeues.
B.17.102 That he ne *was* robbed or rifled, rood he þere or yede,
B.17.111 He *was* vnhardy, þat harlot, and hidde hym in Inferno.
B.17.125 For þe barn *was* born in Bethleem þat with his blood shal saue
B.17.141 The fader *was* first as a fust wiþ o fynger foldynge
B.17.149 Bitoknen sooþly þe sone þat sent *was* til erþe,
B.18.15 Thanne *was* feiþ in a fenestre and cryde 'a! fili dauid!'
B.18.68 Some seide þat he *was* goddes sone þat so faire deide:
B.18.69 And some seide he *was* a wicche; 'good is þat we assaye
B.18.72 Vpon a croos bisides crist; so *was* þe comune lawe.
B.18.75 Ac *was* no bo[y] so boold goddes body to touche;
B.18.76 For he *was* knyȝt and kynges sone kynde foryaf þat [þrowe]
B.18.81 Maugree his manye teeþ he *was* maad þat tyme
B.18.88 'Ayein my wille it *was*, lord, to wownde yow so soore.'
B.18.95 To do þe blynde bete [þe dede], it *was* a boyes counseille.
B.18.96 Cursede cayt[yues]! knyghthood *was* it neuere
B.18.103 And youre fraunchise þat fre *was* fallen is in þraldom;
B.18.120 For þe vertue þat hire folwede afered *was* she neuere.
B.18.133 Siþ þis barn *was* ybore ben xxxti wynter passed
B.18.140 And þat *was* tynt þoruȝ tree, tree shal it wynne.
B.18.166 For he[o] woot moore þan we; he[o] *was* er we boþe.'
B.18.221 To wite what wele was, kyndeliche [to] knowe it.
B.18.230 Thanne *was* þer a wight wiþ two brode eiȝen,
B.18.233 That þo þis barn *was* ybore þer blased a sterre
B.18.235 That swich a barn *was* ybore in Bethleem þe Citee
B.18.238 That he *was* god þat al wroȝte þe wolkne first shewed.
B.18.242 The water witnesse[þ] þat he *was* god for he wente on it;
B.18.284 And siþen I [*was*] seised seuene [þousand] wynter
B.18.300 And whan I seiȝ it was so, [s]lepynge I wente
B.18.301 To warne Pilates wif what done man *was* Iesus,
B.18.305 For þe body, while it on bones yede, aboute *was* euere
B.18.342 Membre for membre [*was* amendes by þe olde lawe],
B.18.346 And boþe quykne and quyte þat queynt *was* þoruȝ synne;
B.18.413 *Was* neuere werre in þis world ne wikkednesse so kene
B.19.6 That Piers þe Plowman *was* peynted al blody
B.19.40 And gentil men wiþ Iesu, for Iesu[s] *was* yfulled
B.19.47 And from fendes þat in hem [*was*] and false bileue.
B.19.48 Tho *was* he Iesus of Iewes called, gentile prophete,
B.19.53 And þo *was* he conquerour called of quyke and of dede,

B.19.56 [And took [Lucifer þe loþely] þat lord *was* of helle
B.19.58 Who *was* hardiere þan he? his herte blood he shadde
B.19.70 Faithly for to speke, his firste name *was* Iesus.
B.19.71 Tho he *was* born in Bethleem, as þe book telleþ,
B.19.80 And þere *was* þat word fulfilled þe which þow of speke,
B.19.82 And al þe wit of þe world *was* in þo þre kynges.
B.19.94 [Erþeliche] honeste þynges w[as] offred þus at ones
B.19.97 *Was* neiþer kyng ne conquerour til he [comsed] wexe
B.19.117 And þanne *was* he [cleped and] called noȝt [oonly] crist but Iesu,
B.19.121 That he þoruȝ grace *was* gete and of no gome ellis.
B.19.124 And whan he [*was* woxen] moore, in his moder absence,
B.19.129 The which *was* dobet, where þat he wente.
B.19.132 And þo *was* he called in contre þe comune peple,
B.19.134 For dauid *was* doghtiest of dedes in his tyme;
B.19.139 Ne ouer Iewes Iustice, as Iesus *was*, hem þouȝte.
B.19.182 And whan þis dede *was* doon do best he [þouȝte],
B.19.204 I wondred what þat *was* and waggede Conscience,
B.19.205 And *was* afered [for] þe light, for in fires [lik]nesse
B.19.245 And some to ryde and to recouere þat [vnriȝt]fully *was* wonne:
B.19.263 That oon *was* Luk, a large beest and a lowe chered,
B.19.289 The þridde seed þat Piers sew *was* Spiritus fortitudinis,
B.19.290 And who[so] ete [of] þat seed hardy *was* euere
B.19.297 The ferþe seed þat Piers sew *was* Spiritus Iusticie,
B.19.305 To demen as a domesman adrad *was* he neuere
B.19.329 And whan þis dede *was* doon Grace deuysede
B.20.1 Thanne as I wente by þe wey, whan I *was* thus awaked,
B.20.8 [*Was*] by techynge and by tellynge of Spiritus temperancie,
B.20.42 So [he *was* nedy], as seiþ þe book in manye sondry places,
B.20.49 Siþ he þat wroȝte wil þe world was wilfulliche nedy,
B.20.63 [Th]an to lyue lenger siþ [Leute] *was* so rebuked
B.20.72 That kam ayein conscience þat kepere *was* and gyour
B.20.88 There *was* 'harrow!' and 'help! here comeþ kynde
B.20.95 Elde þe hoore; [he] *was* in þe vauntwarde
B.20.124 His wepne *was* al wiles, to wynnen and to hiden;
B.20.158 Oon þat muche wo wroȝte, Sleuþe *was* his name.
B.20.159 Sleuþe wax wonder yerne and soone *was* of age
B.20.161 Hir sire *was* a Sysour þat neuere swoor truþe,
B.20.187 Siþ whanne *was* þe wey ouer mennes heddes?
B.20.193 And of þe wo þat I *was* Inne my wif hadde ruþe
B.20.195 For þe lyme þat she loued me fore and leef *was* to feele
B.20.214 And þere *was* Conscience Conestable, cristene to saue,
B.20.221 'By [þe] Marie!' quod a mansed preest, [*was*] of þe March of
          [Irlonde],
B.20.329 And cam þere Conscience *was* and knokked at þe yate.
B.20.330 Pees vnpynned it, *was* Porter of vnitee,
B.20.345 And *was* my lordes leche and my ladies boþe.
B.20.346 And at þe laste þis lymytour, þo my lord *was* oute,
B.20.370 And wake for hise wikked werkes as he *was* wont to doone.

was C 310

C.Pr.1 In a somur sesoun whan softe *was* þe sonne
C.Pr.15 And say a tour; as [y] trow[e], treuthe *was* thereynne.
C.Pr.111 Anon as it *was* tolde hym that þe children of Irael
C.Pr.115 And al *was* for vengeance he bet noght his children
C.Pr.117 God *was* wel þe wrother and took þe raþer vengeance.
C.Pr.193 Ac tho þe belle *was* ybroughte and on þe beygh hangid
C.Pr.194 Ther ne *was* [raton in] þe route, for al þe reame of Fraunce,
C.1.10 Y *was* afeerd of here face thow she fayre were
C.1.31 Thorw wyn and thorw wom[e]n there *was* loot acombred;
C.1.46 And god askede at hem hoes *was* þe koyne.
C.1.58 May banne þat he born *was* [to] body [or to] soule.
C.1.108 He *was* an Archangel of heuene, on of goddes knyghtes;
C.1.111 That hadde [lu]st to be lyk his lord þat *was* almyghty:
C.1.152 *Was* neuer lef vppon lynde lyhtere theraftur\
C.1.169 That he *was* myhtfull and meke and mercy gan graunte
C.2.9 And [*was* war of] a womman wonderly yclothed.
C.2.10 She *was* purfiled [with] pelure, non puyrere on erthe,
C.2.14 Here robynge *was* rychere þen y rede couthe;
C.2.17 [Wh]os wyf a were and what *was* here name,
C.2.25 Oon fauel *was* he[re] fader þat hath a fykel tonge
C.2.56 And y say how mede *was* maried, metyng as it were.
C.2.67 Ac Fauel *was* þe furste þat fette here out of chambre
C.2.112 In wittenesse of [which] thyng wrong *was* þe furste,
C.2.123 For mede is moilere, amendes *was* here dame;
C.2.125 Amendes *was* here moder by trewe menne lokynge,
C.2.147 And as a bastard ybore byȝete *was* he neuere.
C.2.165 Tho this gold *was* ygyue grete was the thonkynge
C.2.165 Tho this gold was ygyue grete *was* the thonkynge
C.2.174 Thenne *was* [falsnesse] fayn and [fauel] blythe,
C.2.201 Ac gyle *was* forgoere to gyuen al th[e] peple,
C.2.221 What *was* þe kynges wille and wyghtliche wente
C.2.230 He *was* nawher welcome for his many tales,
C.2.255 And bothe wepte and wrang when she *was* attached.
C.3.12 Ac there *was* myrthe and mynstracie mede to plese;

C.3.151 Thenne *was* Consience ykald to come and apere
C.3.343 Thenne adiectyf an[d] sustantyf, for englisch *was* it neuere.'
C.3.431 Thus *was* kyng sauel ouercome thorw coueytise of mede,
C.3.491 *Was* omnia probate; þat plesede here herte.
C.3.492 That l[yne] *was* no lengur and at þe leues ende
C.4.26 Whiche a maistre mede *was* amonges pore and ryche.
C.4.65 How wrong *was* a wykked man and muche wo wrouhte.
C.4.66 Tho *was* wrong afered and wisdom a souhte;
C.4.71 Thorw wrong and his werkes there *was* mede yknowe
C.5.35 'When y [ȝut] ȝong *was*, many ȝer hennes,
C.5.96 A boute suche a bargayn he *was* þe bet euere
C.5.108 Wepyng and waylyng til y *was* aslepe.
C.5.115 And preuede þat this pestelences *was* for puyre synne
C.5.117 *Was* pertliche for pruyde and for no poynt elles.
C.5.132 He warnede watte his wyf *was* to blame
C.5.133 [That] here hed *was* worth half marc and his hoed nat a grote.
C.5.186 Lo! in heuene an heyh *was* an holy comune
C.5.188 Were wittiore and worthiore then he þat *was* his maister.
C.6.7 To affayten here flesshe þat fers *was* to synne.
C.6.18 God and goode men so gret *was* myn herte.
C.6.37 *Was* non such as [my]sulue ne non so popholy;
C.6.51 Thyng þat neuere *was* thouthe and ȝut [y] swor [y] seyh hit
C.6.68 Chidynge and chalengynge *was* his cheef lyflode
C.6.97 When he solde and y nat thenne *was* y aredy
C.6.132 I *was* the Prioresse potager and oþer pore ladies
C.6.133 And made hem ioutes of iangelynge: "dame Ione *was* a bastard
C.6.134 And dame clarice a knyhtes douhter, a cokewolde *was* here syre,
C.6.148 And y, wrath, *was* war and w[o]rthe on hem bothe
C.6.181 Til bothe oure wil *was* oen and to þe werk we ȝeden,
C.6.193 When y *was* olde and hoor and hadde ylore þat kynde
C.6.198 He *was* bitelbrowed and baburlippid with two blered eyes
C.6.201 And as a bondemannes bacoun his berd *was* yshaue,
C.6.205 He sholde [nat] wandre [o]n þat walch, so *was* hit thredbare.
C.6.208 And was his prentis yplyht his profit to wayte
C.6.210 Wykkedliche to waye *was* my furste lessoun.
C.6.221 My wyf *was* a webbe and wollone cloth made
C.6.232 Rose þe regrater was here ryhte name;
C.6.235 'Ȝus! ones y *was* herberwed,' quod he, 'with an heep of chapmen;
C.6.237 'That *was* a rufol restitucioun,' quod repentaunce, 'for sothe;
C.6.284 That my muynde ne *was* more [o]n my godes in a doute
C.6.308 Thenne *was* there a walschman was wonderly sory,
C.6.308 Thenne was there a walschman *was* wonderly sory,
C.6.316 And for þer *was* nat wherwith a wep swythe sore.
C.6.394 There *was* leyhing and louryng and 'lat go the coppe!'
C.6.411 Ac gloton *was* a greet cherl and gr[ym] in þe luftynge
C.6.420 The furste [word] þat he spake *was* '[wh]o halt þe bolle?'
C.6.428 There no nede ne *was*, many sythe falsly;
C.7.12 Ac of oure lord ne of oure lady þe leste þat euere *was* maked.
C.7.119 Tho *was* repentaunce aredy and redde hem alle to knele:
C.7.126 For thorw þat synne thy sone ysent *was* til erthe
C.7.140 Of thy douhtiokest dedes *was* don in oure sekte:
C.7.158 Ac þer *was* wye non so wys þat the way thider couthe
C.7.160 Til late *was* and longe þat thei a lede mette
C.7.299 Thenne *was* here actif; an hosbande he semede.
C.8.20 Ac [on þe] t[ee]me treuely ytauhte *was* y neuere.
C.8.61 A buschel of breedcorn brouht *was* þerynne.
C.8.115 Therwith *was* [Perkyn] apayed and payede wel here huyre.
C.8.157 To kepe hym and his catel as couenant *was* bitwene hem:
C.8.164 'I *was* nat woned to worche,' quod wastour, 'now wol y nat bygynne!'
C.8.178 And þat *was* bake for bayard may be here bote.'
C.8.181 That hunger *was* nat hardy on hem for to loke.
C.8.192 For þat was bake for bayard *was* bote for many hungry,
C.8.192 For þat *was* bake for bayard was bote for many hungry,
C.8.194 There *was* no ladde þat lyuede þat ne lowede hym to Peres
C.8.197 Tho *was* [Peres] proud and potte hem alle a werke
C.8.201 *Was* no beggare so bold, but yf a blynd were,
C.8.249 And þat best labored best *was* alloued
C.8.251 Ac he þat *was* a wreche and wolde nat trauaile
C.8.322 Thenne [*was*] folke fayn and fedde hunger dentie[f]liche
C.8.335 Þat he *was* werkeman ywrouhte warien þe tyme.
C.8.339 Ac whiles hungur *was* here maistre ther wolde non chyde
C.9.286 And *was* ywryte ryhte thus in witnesse of treuthe
C.9.315 That Ioseph *was* Iustice Egipte to saue;
C.10.4 Yf eny wiht wiste where dowel *was* at ynne;
C.10.6 *Was* neuere wihte [as y wente] þat me wisse couthe
C.10.116 He *was* long and lene, ylyk to noon other;
C.10.117 *Was* no pruyde on his parail ne pouerte noythere;
C.10.122 What *was* dowel fro dobet and dobest fro hem bothe.
C.10.195 The[r]of *was* he robbed and ruyfled or he on rode deyede
C.10.213 Caym þe corsede creature conseyued *was* in synne
C.10.218 So *was* Caym conseyued and so ben corsed wreches
C.10.245 Ac why þe world *was* adreynt, holy writ telleth,
C.10.246 *Was* for mariages ma[ugre kynd]e þat men made þat tyme.

C.10.248 S[e]th, adames sone, seth[en] *was* engendred.
C.10.249 And god sente to seth so sone he *was* of age
C.11.1 Thenne hadde wit a wyf *was* hote dame studie
C.11.3 She *was* wonderly wroth þat wit me so tauhte;
C.11.81 And when wit *was* ywar what studie menede
C.11.85 And when y *was* war of his wille to þat womman gan y louten
C.11.100 Thenne *was* y as fayn as foul of faire morwen,
C.11.147 Ho *was* his Autor And hym of god tauhte?
C.11.166 For y *was* rauysched rihte there; fortune me fette
C.11.173 And coueytise-of-yes ycalde *was* þat oþer.
C.11.186 Thenne *was* [there] oen þat hihte Elde þat heuy was of chere;
C.11.186 Thenne was [there] oen þat hihte Elde þat heuy *was* of chere;
C.11.196 Sir wanhope *was* sib to hym, as som men me tolde,
C.11.203 That y man ymaed *was* and my name yentred
C.11.235 Wittnesseth godes word þat *was* neuere vntrewe:
C.11.236 Ac y wene hit worth of monye as *was* in noes tyme
C.11.238 *Was* neuere wrihte þat þeron wrouhte ne werkman ysaued
C.11.241 Of wryhtes þat hit wrouhte *was* noen of hem ysaued.
C.11.252 A gode friday, y fynde, a feloun *was* ysaued
C.11.255 He *was* sunnere ysaued then seynt Iohn þe baptiste
C.11.258 A robbare *was* yraunsomed rather then thei alle,
C.11.274 That clergie of cristes mouthe com[e]nded *was* euere.
C.11.285 *Was* Austyn þe oelde þat euere man wiste,
C.12.13 And thenne *was* fortune my foo for al her fayre biheste
C.12.48 And whan þe peple *was* plenere ycome þe porter vnpynnede þe gate
C.12.75 'Ʒe? bawe for bokes!' quod oen *was* broken out of helle.
C.12.77 How y *was* ded and dampned to dwellen in [pyne]
C.12.85 Withouten bed[e] biddyng his bone *was* vnderfonge
C.12.115 And aftur his resureccoun redemptor *was* his name
C.12.127 So by [h]is werkes thei wisten þat he *was* iesu
C.12.129 And al *was* ensample, sothly, to vs synfole here
C.12.135 *Was* a puyre pore mayde and to a pore man ywedded.
C.12.217 That many mothe *was* maistre ynne in A myntewhyle;
C.12.245 So coueytise of catel *was* combraunce to hem alle.
C.13.8 For in greet pouerte he *was* put: a prince, as hit were,
C.13.149 Ther ne [was] cow ne cowkynde þat conseyued hadde
C.13.151 Ther ne was no kyne kynde þat conseyued hadde
C.13.180 *Was* þat y seyh resoun sewen alle bestes
C.13.210 Man *was* made of such [a] matere he may nat wel asterte
C.13.214 And awakede þerwith; wo *was* me thenne
C.13.218 And thenne *was* ther a wyhte, what he was y neste.
C.13.218 And thenne was ther a wyhte, what he *was* y neste.
C.13.227 The wisdom and the wit of god he *was* pot out of blisse.
C.13.244 Why ʒe worden to me thus *was* for y aresonede Resoun.'
C.14.1 'I am ymagenatyf,' quod he; 'ydel *was* y neuere
C.14.4 And wissed the [wel] ofte what dowel *was* to mene
C.14.46 [Althouh men maden bokes] God *was* here maystre
C.14.77 Ac thorw here science sothly *was* neuere soule ysaued
C.14.82 And saide here wordes ne here wysdomes *was* but a folye;
C.14.90 Ne in no cote ne Caytyfs hous [crist *was* ybore
C.14.98 And deden here homage honerably to hym þat *was* almyhty.
C.14.125 Muchel wo *was* hym marked þat wade shal with þe lewede!
C.14.132 *Was* for A ʒeld hym creaunt to crist and his grace askede.
C.14.141 So hit f[areth] by þe feloun þat a goed fryday *was* saued:
C.14.159 *Was* neuere creature vnder crist þat knewe wel þe bygynnyng
C.14.164 Of goed and of wykke kynde *was* þe furste;
C.14.167 *Was* neuere man vppon molde þat myhte hit aspie.
C.14.205 'Troianes *was* a trewe knyhte and toek neuere cristendoem
C.14.216 And a cortesye more þen couenant *was*, what so clerkes carpe,
C.15.9 And how þat freres folewede folk þat *was* ryche
C.15.10 And peple þat *was* pore at litel pris [þei] setten
C.15.38 The maistre *was* maed sitte As for þe moste worthy;
C.15.48 Ac here sauce *was* ouersour and vnsauerly ygrounde
C.15.54 And to me þat *was* his mette tho, and oþer mete bothe.
C.15.60 And brouhte forth a pytaunce, *was* pro h[a]c orabit [ad te] omnis
C.15.63 Pacience *was* wel apayed of this propre seruice
C.15.152 [And] pacience properliche spak, tho Peres *was* thus ypassed,
C.15.238 For lente neuere *was* lyf but lyflode were shape,
C.15.249 And thenne *was* hit fiat voluntas tua þat sholde fynde vs alle.
C.15.265 And in Elies tyme heuene *was* yclosed
C.15.281 [Y wiste neuere renke þat ryche *was* þat whan he rekene sholde]
C.15.297 For to wroþerhele *was* he wrouht þat neuere was ioye yschape.
C.15.297 For to wroþerhele was he wrouht þat neuere *was* ioye yschape.
C.16.84 And louely layk *was* hit neuere bytwene a longe and a short
C.16.154 That puyre pouerte and pacience *was* a louh lyuynge on erthe,
C.16.157 That wroet thus to wisse men what pouerte *was* to mene.'
C.16.162 Thenne hadde y wonder what he *was*, þat l[i]berum Arbitrium,
C.16.280 And þat with gyle *was* gete vngraciousliche be yspened.
C.16.355 And in a frere f[r]oude he *was* founde ones
C.17.24 Bote thre little loues and loue *was* here soule.
C.17.38 To his wyf; when he *was* blynde he herde a la[m]be blete:
C.17.103 And what lyue by and leue, the londe *was* so trewe.
C.17.107 Of þat *was* kalculed of þe clymat the contrarie þey fynde,

C.17.130 Loue lawe withoute leutee? allouable *was* hit neuere!
C.17.163 Beaute sanʒ bounte blessed *was* [hit] neuere
C.17.165 Me fynde[th] þat Macometh *was* a man ycristened
C.17.168 Ac for he *was* lyk a lossheborw y leue oure lord hym lette.
C.17.178 For Macometh to men swaer hit *was* a messager of heuene
C.17.199 And tho *was* p[lente] and p[ees] amonges pore and ryche;
C.17.242 Bote thorw pacience and priue gyle *was* porter ouer hem all.
C.17.275 Amonges v[n]kynde cristene in holy [kirke] *was* slawe
C.17.281 Many man for cristes loue *was* martired amonges Romaynes
C.17.302 Tho he luft vp lasar þat layde *was* in graue;
C.17.308 That iesus *was* bote a iogelour, a iapare amonges þe comune,
C.17.310 And that his lore *was* lesynges and lakken hit alle
C.18.55 And þe fruyt *was* fayre, non fayrere be myhte;
C.18.68 Adam *was* as tre and we aren as his apples,
C.18.90 Hit *was* þe furste fruyte þat þe fader of heuene blessed,
C.18.110 For euere as Elde hadde eny down, þe deuel *was* redy
C.18.133 And in þe wombe of þat wenche *was* he fourty wokes
C.18.139 That suche a surgien sethen ysaye *was* þer neuere
C.18.148 That he *was* god or godes sone for þat grete wonder;
C.18.216 Eue of Adam *was* and out of hym ydrawe
C.18.227 *Was* þe sone in hymsulue, in a simile as Eue was,
C.18.227 Was þe sone in hymsulue, in a simile as Eue *was*,
C.19.13 Whereon *was* writen two wordes on this wyse yglosed:
C.19.15 This *was* the tyxt trewly; y toek ful good gome.
C.19.16 The glose *was* gloriously writen with a gult penne:
C.19.68 And parseued by his poues he *was* in perel to deye
C.19.92 For wente neuere man this way þat he ne *was* here yruyfled
C.19.123 Bitokneth soethly þe sone þat sente *was* til erthe,
C.19.135 And al þe myhte with hym is, *was* and worth euere.
C.19.241 And for he *was* a nygard and a nythynge to the nedfol pore,
C.20.13 Thenne *was* faith in a fenestre and criede 'a! fil[i] dauid!'
C.20.45 And as wyde as hit euere *was*; this we witnesseth alle.'
C.20.70 Somme saide he *was* godes sone þat so fayre deyede:
C.20.74 Vppon cros bisyde Crist; so *was* þe comune lawe.
C.20.77 Ac *was* no boie so bold godes body to touche;
C.20.78 For he *was* knyht and kynges sone kynde forʒaf þat [þrowe]
C.20.83 Maugre his mony teth he *was* mad þat tyme
C.20.90 'Aʒeyn my will hit *was*,' quod he, 'þat y ʒow wounde made.'
C.20.98 [To do] þe blynde bete the dede, [hit] *was* a boyes [conseille].
C.20.99 Corsede Caytifues! knyhthoed *was* hit neuere
C.20.106 And ʒoure franchise fre *was* yfallen is i[n] thraldoem;
C.20.123 For þe vertue þat her folewede afered *was* she neuere.
C.20.136 Sethe this barn *was* ybore ben thritty wynter ypassed,
C.20.143 And] that *was* tynt thorw tre, tre shal hit wynne.
C.20.169 For he woet more then we; he *was* ar we bothe.'
C.20.230 To wyte what wele [*was*], kyndeliche to knowe [hit].
C.20.239 Thenne wa[s] ther a wihte with two brode yes;
C.20.242 [That tho] this barn *was* ybore þ[er] blased a sterre
C.20.244 That such a barn *was* ybore in Bethleem þe Citee
C.20.247 That he *was* god þat al wrouhte the welkene furste shewede:
C.20.251 The water witnesseth þat he *was* god for a wente on h[it];
C.20.333 And when y seyh hit *was* so, y sotiled how y myhte
C.20.337 For þe body, whiles hit on bones ʒede, aboute *was* hit euere
C.20.391 And bothe quykie and quyte that queynte *was* thorw synne
C.20.396 So þat [thorw] gyle *was* gete thorw grace is now ywonne
C.20.456 *Was* neuere werre in this world ne wikkedere enuye
C.21.6 That [Peres] þe [plouhman] *was* peynted al blody
C.21.40 And Ientel men with iesu for iesu[s] *was* yfolled
C.21.47 And fro fendes þat in hem *was* and false bileue.
C.21.48 Tho *was* he iesu[s] of iewes [cald], gentel profete,
C.21.53 And tho *was* he conquerour cald of quyke and of dede
C.21.56 And toek lucifer the loethliche þat lord *was* of helle
C.21.58 Ho *was* hardior then he? his herte bloed he she[d]de
C.21.70 Faythly for to speke his furste name *was* iesus.
C.21.71 Tho he *was* bore in Bedlehem, as þe boek telleth,
C.21.80 And þer *was* þat word fulfuld þe which þou of speke,
C.21.82 And al þe wit of the world *was* in [þo] thre kynges.
C.21.94 Ertheliche honeste thynges *was* offred thus at ones
C.21.97 *Was* noþer kyng ne conquerour til he comsed wexe
C.21.117 And tho *was* he cleped and calde not [onl]y Crist but iesu,
C.21.121 That he thorw grace *was* gete and of no gome elles.
C.21.124 And when he *was* wexen more, in his moder absence,
C.21.129 The which *was* dobet, where þat he wente.
C.21.132 And tho *was* he cald in contreye of þe comune peple,
C.21.134 For dauid *was* douhtiest of dedes in his tyme
C.21.139 Ne ouer Iewes Iustice as iesus *was*, hem thouhte.
C.21.182 And when this dede *was* doen do best he thouhte,
C.21.204 Y wondred what þat *was* and wagged Consience
C.21.205 And *was* afered for the lihte, for in fuyres liknesse
C.21.245 And somme to ryde & to rekeuere that vnrihtfulliche *was* wonne:
C.21.263 That oen *was* luc, a large beste and a lou chered,
C.21.289 The thridde seed that [Peres] sewe *was* spiritus fortitudinis
C.21.290 And hoso ete of þa[t] seed hardy *was* euere

C.21.293 Makyn hym, for eny mornynge, þat he ne *was* murye in soule
C.21.297 The ferthe seed that [Peres] sewe *was* spiritus Iusticie
C.21.305 To demen as a domesman adrad *was* he neuere
C.21.329 And when this dede *was* doen grace deuysed
C.21.372 Ther ne *was* cristene creature that kynde wit hadde
C.22.1 [Thenne] as y wente by the way, when y *was* thus awaked,
C.22.8 *Was* bi techyng and by tellyng of spiritus temperancie
C.22.42 So he *was* nedy, as saith the boek in mony sondry places,
C.22.49 Sethe [he] þat wrouhte al þe worlde *was* willefolliche nedy
C.22.63 Then to lyue lengere sethe leautee *was* so rebuked
C.22.72 That cam aȝen Consience þat kepar *was* and gyour
C.22.88 There was 'harow!' and 'helpe! here cometh kynde
C.22.95 Elde þe hore; he *was* in þe Vawwarde
C.22.124 His wepne *was* al wyles, to wynnen and to hyden;
C.22.158 Oen þat moche wo wrouhte, sleuthe *was* his name.
C.22.159 Sleuthe wax wonder ȝerne and sone *was* of age
C.22.161 Here syre *was* a sysour þat neuere swoer treuthe
C.22.187 Sennes whanne *was* þe way ouer menne heuedes?
C.22.193 And of þe wo þat y *was* ynne my wyf hadde reuthe
C.22.195 For þe lyme þat she loued me fore and leef *was* to fele
C.22.214 And there *was* Consience Constable, cristene to saue,
C.22.221 'By þe Marie!' quod a mansed prest, *was* of þe march of Ireland,
C.22.329 And cam þer Consience *was* and knokked at þe ȝate.
C.22.330 Pees vnpynned hyt, *was* porter of vnite,
C.22.345 And was my lordes leche and my ladyes bothe,
C.22.346 And at þe laste this lymytour, tho my lord *was* oute,
C.22.370 And wake for his wikkede werkes as he *was* woned [to do].

weere B 15

B.Pr.2 I shoop me into [a] shrou[d] as I a sheep *weere*;
B. 1.10 I was afered of hire face þeiȝ she fair *weere*
B. 1.71 Thanne hadde I wonder in my wit what womman it *weere*
B.15.3 And so my wit weex and wanyed til I a fool *weere*.
B.16.236 Myself and my meynee; and alle þat male *weere*
B.17.154 Thus are þei alle but oon, as it an hand *weere*,
B.18.38 The Iewes and þe Iustice ayeins Iesu þei *weere*,
B.18.196 Freet of þat fruyt and forsook, as it *weere*,
B.18.208 If no nyȝt ne *weere*, no man as I leeue
B.19.357 Praye we þat a pees *weere* in Piers berne þe Plowman.
B.19.359 To goon agayn Pride but Grace *weere* wiþ vs.'
B.19.363 That holy chirche stode in [holynesse] as it a Pyl *weere*.
B.20.32 Of þat he weneþ wolde falle if his wit ne *weere*;
B.20.57 And gerte gile growe as he a god *weere*.
B.20.196 On nyghtes namely, whan we naked *weere*,

wer C 1

C.Pr.182 *Wer* ther a belle on here beygh, by iesu, as me thynketh,

were A 63

A.Pr.2 I shop me into a shroud as I a shep *were*;
A.Pr.41 Til here bely & here bagge *were* bratful ycrammid;
A.Pr.52 Grete lobies & longe þat loþ *were* to swynke
A.Pr.65 Þere prechide a pardoner as he a prest *were*;
A.Pr.75 *Were* þe bisshop yblissid & worþ boþe hise eris
A.Pr.79 Þat þe pore peple of þe parissh shulde haue ȝif þei ne *were*.
A.Pr.81 Þat here parissh w[ere] pore siþþe þe pestilence tyme,
A. 1.10 I was aferd of hire face þeiȝ heo fair *were*,
A. 1.69 Þanne hadde I wondir in my wyt what womman it *were*
A. 1.72 What he[o] *were* witterly þat wisside me so faire.
A. 2.11 Alle here fyue fyngris *were* frettid wiþ rynges
A. 2.34 *Were* beden to þe b[ri]dale on boþe two sides.
A. 2.131 Þ[o] hadde notories none; anoyed þei *were*
A. 3.6 What man of þis world þat hire *were* leuist;
A. 3.36 And seide [wel] softely, in shrifte as it *were*,
A. 3.106 What þat his wille *were* & what he do shulde.
A. 3.124 Shirreues of shires *were* shent ȝif heo ne *were*.
A. 3.124 Shirreues of shires were shent ȝif heo ne *were*.
A. 4.68 Ac wisdom & wyt *were* aboute faste
A. 4.74 'God wot,' quaþ wysdom, 'þat *were* not þe beste.
A. 4.120 For I seiȝe it be myself, & it so *were*
A. 4.121 Þat I *were* king wiþ croune to kepe a reaume,
A. 5.63 Of a Freris frokke *were* þe foresleuys.
A. 5.82 I hailside hym as hendely as I his frend *were*:
A. 5.92 [Þanne] I wysshe it *were* myn [and al þe webbe aftir].
A. 5.96 I wolde þat iche wiȝt *were* my knaue.
A. 5.172 Þere *were* chapmen chosen þat chaffare to preise:
A. 5.176 Þere *were* oþes an hep, [whoso it herde];
A. 5.224 And here masse & matynes as I a monk *were*]
A. 6.1 Ac þere w[ere] fewe men so wys þat [þe [wey] þider couþe,
A. 6.87 Whanne I þenke þereon, þeiȝ I *were* a pope.'
A. 7.1 'Þis *were* a wikkide weye, but whoso hadde a gide
A. 7.2 Þat miȝte folewe vs iche fote [forto] we *were* þere.'
A. 7.6 I wolde wende wiþ ȝow til ȝe *were* þere'.
A. 7.7 'Þis *were* a long lettyng,' quaþ a lady in a scleire.
A. 7.101 Oþere werkmen þere *were* [þat] wrouȝte ful faste,
A. 7.113 Þanne *were* faitours aferd & feynide hem blynde;

A. 7.177 Blynde & bedrede *were* botind a þousand
A. 7.196 [Now wolde I] wite, ȝif þou wistest, what *were* þe beste,
A. 8.30 And bynde brugges aboute þat tobroke *were*,
A. 8.42 Þanne wepe þe marchauntis merye; many wepe for ioye,
A. 8.122 '*Were* þou a prest, piers,' quaþ he, 'þou miȝtest preche wh[an] þe liki[de];
A. 9.32 Þere *were* þe manis lif lost for lacchesse of hymselue.
A. 9.93 And were vnbuxum at his bidding, and bold to don ille.
A. 9.109 Ac er we ywar *were* wiþ wyt gonne we mete.
A.10.115 To be blissid for þi beryng, [ȝ]e, b[e]ggere þeiȝ þou *were*.
A.10.155 For alle þat comen of þat caym acursid þei *were*,
A.10.181 And [were] marie[d] at meschief as men do now here children.
A.10.203 Shulde no bedbourd be; but þei *were* boþe clene.
A.11.11 Þei do but drauele þeron; draf *were* hem leuere
A.11.14 Þat hem *were* leuere lond, & lordsshipe on erþe,
A.11.141 Ne *were* þe loue þat liþ þerein a wel lewid þing it were.
A.11.141 Ne were þe loue þat liþ þerein a wel lewid þing it *were*.
A.11.172 And tolde hire þe toknes þat me ytauȝt *were*.
A.11.201 For mendynauntȝ at meschief þ[o] men *were* dewid,
A.11.262 In þe legende of lif longe er I *were*,
A.11.292 As þise þat wrouȝte wykkidly in world whanne þei *were*
A.12.6 Þe *were* lef to lerne but loþ for to stodie.
A.12.14 That he shewe me hit ne sholde but ȝif [I schriuen] *were*
A.12.17 Þat hit *were* boþe skaþe and sklaundre to holy cherche
A.12.40 With þat she wolde me wisse wher þe toun *were*
A.12.80 Of when þat he *were*, and wheder þat he wolde.
A.12.110 Now alle kenne creatures þat cristene *were* euere

were B 199

B.Pr.41 [Til] hire bel[y] and hire bagg[e *were* bret]ful ycrammed;
B.Pr.55 Grete lobies and longe þat loþe *were* to swynke
B.Pr.68 Ther preched a pardoner as he a preest *were*;
B.Pr.78 *Were* þe Bisshop yblessed and worþ boþe hise eris
B.Pr.82 That þe [pouere peple] of þe parisshe sholde haue if þei ne *were*.
B.Pr.84 That hire parissh[e] wer[e] pouere siþ þe pestilence tyme,
B.Pr.165 *Were* þer a belle on hire beiȝe, by Iesu, as me þynkeþ,
B. 1.33 And þere gat in glotonie gerles þat *were* cherles.
B. 1.74 What she *were* witterly þat wissed me so faire.
B. 2.11 Fetisliche hire fyngres *were* fretted with gold wyr
B. 2.18 I hadde wonder what she was and whos wif she *were*.
B. 2.55 *Were* boden to þe bridale on boþe two sides,
B. 2.64 *Were* moost pryuee with Mede of any men me þouȝte.
B. 2.96 And in fastynge dayes to frete er ful tyme *were*.
B. 2.167 Tho hadde Notaries none; anoyed þei *were*
B. 3.6 What man of þis [world] þat hire *were* leuest.
B. 3.37 And seide [wel] softely, in shrift as it *were*,
B. 3.117 What his wille *were* and what he do [sholde].
B. 3.135 Sherreues of Shires *were* shent if she ne *were*.
B. 3.135 Sherreues of Shires were shent if she ne *were*.
B. 3.346 This text þat ye han told *were* [trewe] for lordes,
B. 4.81 Ac wisdom and wit *were* aboute faste
B. 4.87 'God woot', quod wisdom, 'þat *were* noȝt þe beste.
B. 4.137 I seye it by myself and it so *were*
B. 4.138 That I *were* kyng with coroune to kepen a Reaume,
B. 4.149 Clerkes þat *were* Confessours coupled hem togideres
B. 5.13 He preued þat þise pestilences *were* for pure synne,
B. 5.16 Pyries and Plumtrees *were* puffed to þe erþe
B. 5.18 Beches and brode okes *were* blowen to þe grounde
B. 5.49 'It is þi [tresor if treson ne *were*], and tryacle at þy nede.'
B. 5.80 Of a Freres frokke *were* þe foresleues.
B. 5.102 I hailse[d] hym hendely as I his frend *were*:
B. 5.112 [Thanne I wisshe] it *were* myn and al þe web after.
B. 5.117 I wolde þat ech wight *were* my knaue.
B. 5.154 Hir [*were*] leuere swowe or swelte þan suffre any peyne.
B. 5.167 That no Prioresse *were* preest, for þat he [purueiede];
B. 5.174 And am chalanged in þe Chapitrehous as I a child *were*
B. 5.232 I roos whan þei *were* areste and riflede hire males.'
B. 5.235 'I wende riflynge *were* restitucion for I lerned neuere rede on boke,
B. 5.265 For þe beste book in oure hous, þeiȝ brent gold *were* þe leues,
B. 5.268 For þe beste book in oure hous, þeiȝ brent gold *were* þe leues,
B. 5.269 And I wiste witterly þow *were* swich as þow tellest.
B. 5.286 But if it *were* wiþ þi tonge or ellis wiþ þi hondes.
B. 5.323 Þere *were* chapmen ychose þis chaffare to preise:
B. 5.327 [There *were* oþes an heep, whoso it herde];
B. 5.377 Fedde me bifore] noon whan fastyng dayes *were*.'
B. 5.388 *Were* I brouȝt abedde, but if my tailende it made,
B. 5.389 Sholde no ryngynge do me ryse er I *were* ripe to dyne.'
B. 5.452 And here matyns and masse as I a monk *were*]
B. 5.498 And al to solace synfulle þow suffredest it so *were*:
B. 5.600 Whan I þynke þeron, þeiȝ I *were* a Pope."
B. 6.1 'This *were* a wikkede wey but whoso hadde a gyde
B. 6.7 'This *were* a long lettyng', quod a lady in a Scleyre.
B. 6.109 Oþere werkmen þer *were* þat wroȝten ful [faste],

B. 6.121 Tho *were* faitours afered and feyned hem blynde;
B. 6.132 Whiche þei *were* in þis world hise werkmen apeired.
B. 6.191 Blynde and bedreden *were* bootned a þousand;
B. 6.192 That seten to begge siluer soone *were* þei heeled,
B. 6.210 Now wolde I wite, [if þow wistest], what *were* þe beste,
B. 7.28 And [bynde] brugges [aboute] þat tobroke *were*,
B. 7.38 Thanne *were* Marchauntȝ murie; many wepten for ioye
B. 7.70 For if he wiste he *were* noȝt nedy he wolde [it ȝyue]
B. 7.71 Anoþer that *were* moore nedy; so þe nedieste sholde be holpe.
B. 7.140 '*Were* þow a preest, [Piers]', quod he, 'þow myȝtest preche [whan þee liked]
B. 8.36 [There] *were* [þe mannes] lif lost [for] lachesse of hymselue.
B. 8.103 [And *were* vnbuxum at his biddyng, and bold to don ille],
B. 8.119 A[c] er we [war *were*] wiþ wit gonne we mete.
B. 9.41 The lettre, for al þe lordshipe, I leue, *were* neuere ymaked.
B. 9.72 Madde men and maydenes þat helplese *were*;
B. 9.105 Wolde neuere þe feiþful fader [h]is fiþele *were* vntempred
B. 9.190 Sholde no [bedbourde] be; but þei boþe *were* clene
B.10.11 Thei doon but dr[a]uele þeron; draf *were* hem leuere
B.10.14 That hem *were* leuere lond and lordshipe on erþe,
B.10.65 Ne *were* mercy in meene men moore þan in riche
B.10.105 Carpen as þei clerkes *were* of crist and of hise myȝtes,
B.10.128 I wolde his eiȝe *were* in his ers and his [hele] after,
B.10.189 [Ne *were* þe loue þat liþ þerinne a wel lewed þyng it were].
B.10.189 [Ne were þe loue þat liþ þerinne a wel lewed þyng it *were*].
B.10.229 And tolde [hire] þe tokenes þat me tauȝt *were*.
B.10.276 That ye *were* swiche as ye sey[d]e to salue wiþ oþere.
B.10.314 An heep of houndes at his ers as he a lord *were*,
B.10.381 In þe legende of lif longe er I *were*,
B.10.399 [Ac] at hir mooste meschief [mercy *were* þe beste],
B.10.433 Tho þat wrouȝte wikkedlokest in world þo þei *were*;
B.10.442 And wherby wiste men which [is] whit if alle þyng blak *were*,
B.10.443 And who *were* a good man but if þer were som sherewe?
B.10.443 And who were a good man but if þer *were* som sherewe?
B.11.59 By wissynge of þis wenche I [dide], hir wordes *were* so swete,
B.11.67 [At kirke] þere a man *were* cristned by kynde he sholde be buryed.
B.11.74 Where my body *were* buryed by so ye hadde my siluer.
B.11.100 Thouȝ þe tale [*were*] trewe, and it touche[d] synne.
B.11.112 'Multi to a mangerie and to þe mete *were* sompned,
B.11.117 Wheiþer I *were* chosen or noȝt chosen; on holi chirche I þouȝte
B.11.148 And [for] he wepte and wilned [þat I] *were* [saued]
B.11.226 For some wordes I fynde writen, *were* of Feiþes techyng,
B.11.235 Cleophas ne knew hym noȝt þat he crist *were*
B.11.246 Seint Iohan and oþere seintes *were* seyen in poore cloþyng,
B.11.248 Iesu crist on a Iewes doȝter liȝte, gentil womman þouȝ she *were*
B.11.256 And alle þe wise þat euere *were*, by auȝt I kan aspye,
B.11.350 If any Mason made a molde þerto muche wonder it *were*.
B.11.368 Of hir kynde and hir colour to carpe it *were* to longe.
B.11.413 'Haddestow suffred', he seide, 'slepynge þo þow *were*,
B.11.431 [To blame or] to bete hym þanne] it *were* but pure synne.
B.11.441 And if his wille *were* he wolde his name telle].
B.12.6 And of þi wilde wantownesse [whiles] þow yong *were*
B.12.21 Seide, 'Caton conforted his sone þat, clerk þouȝ he *were*,
B.12.25 Ac if þer *were* any wight þat wolde me telle
B.12.26 What *were* dowel and dobet and dobest at þe laste,
B.12.74 That what womman *were* in auoutrye taken, whe[r] riche or poore,
B.12.115 But he *were* preest or preestes sone, Patriark or prophete.
B.12.118 And manye mo oþer men, þat *were* no leuites.
B.12.144 Ne of lordes þat *were* lewed men, but of þe hyeste lettred oute:
B.12.145 If any frere *were* founde þere I ȝyue þee fyue shillynges!
B.12.151 [Riche men rutte þo and in hir reste *were*
B.12.157 How þat lewed men liȝtloker þan lettrede *were* saued,
B.12.209 It *were* neiþer reson ne riȝt to rewarde boþe yliche.
B.12.218 And aresonedest Reson, a rebukynge as it *were*,
B.12.220 Why some ben alouȝ & some aloft, þi likyng it *were*;
B.12.276 For lettred men *were* lewed yet ne were loore of hir bokes.'
B.12.276 For lettred men were lewed yet ne *were* loore of hir bokes.'
B.12.289 And if þer *were* he wolde amende, and in swich wille deieþ–
B.12.290 Ne wolde neuere trewe god but [trewe] truþe wern allowed.
B.13.2 And as a freke þat [fey] *were* forþ gan I walke
B.13.35 Pacience and I [prestly] *were* put to be [mettes],
B.13.83 *Were* molten leed in his mawe and Mahoun amyddes.
B.13.148 Ac for to fare þus wiþ þi frend, folie it *were*;
B.13.177 And took Clergie and Conscience to conseil as it *were*
B.13.200 'Me *were* leuere, by oure lord, and I lyue sholde,
B.13.215 Conscience þo wiþ Pacience passed, pilgrymes as it *were*.
B.13.267 And werkmen *were* agast a lite; þis wolde be þouȝt longe:
B.13.270 My wafres *were* gesene whan Chichestre was Maire.'
B.13.279 Willyng þat alle men wende he *were* þat he is noȝt,
B.13.291 Willynge þat men wende his wit *were* þe beste,
B.13.350 Swiche werkes with hem *were* neuere out of seson
B.13.388 As whan I lened and leued it lost or longe er it *were* paied.
B.13.434 Ther wise men *were*, witnesseþ goddes wordes,

B.14.7 And [laþered] wiþ þe losse of catel [forto me] looþ [*were*]
B.14.39 For lent neuere was lif but liflode *were* shapen,
B.14.124 Right so reson sheweþ þat [þo renkes] þat *were* [lordes]
B.14.129 For þei han hir hire heer and heuene as it *were*,
B.14.138 What he *were* worþi for his werk and what he haþ deserued,
B.14.332 'I *were* noȝt worþi, woot god', quod haukyn, 'to werien any cloþes,
B.15.12 Til I seiȝ, as it sorcerie *were*, a sotil þyng wiþ alle.
B.15.15 If he *were* cristes creature [for cristes loue] me to tellen.
B.15.47 'Ye, sire!' I seide, 'by so no man *were* greued
B.15.52 It *were* ayeins kynde', quod he, 'and alle kynnes reson
B.15.73 Bettre it *were* [by] manye doctours to [bi]leuen swich techyng
B.15.108 Loþe *were* lewed men but þei youre loore folwede
B.15.112 That *were* bisnewed wiþ snow and snakes wiþInne,
B.15.113 Or to a wal þat *were* whitlymed and were foul wiþInne;
B.15.113 Or to a wal þat were whitlymed and *were* foul wiþInne;
B.15.205 For þer are beggeris and bidderis, bedemen as it *were*,
B.15.223 Edmond and Edward, [eiþer] *were* kynges
B.15.334 That *were* ful of faire trees, and I fondede and caste
B.15.383 I dar noȝt siggen it for shame–if swiche *were* apposed
B.15.428 Alle þat ben at debaat and bedemen *were* trewe:
B.15.430 The heuedes of holy chirche, and þei holy *were*,
B.15.532 Er cristendom [*were*] knowe þere, or any cros honoured.
B.15.566 [Charite] *were* to deschargen hem for holy chirches sake,
B.15.568 If preesthode *were* parfit þe peple sholde amende
B.15.601 And [ȝit] wenen þo wrecches þat he *were* pseudopropheta
B.16.93 Til plenitudo temporis [tyme] comen *were*
B.16.105 That, þouȝ he *were* wounded with his enemy, to warisshen hymselue]
B.16.106 And dide hym assaie his surgenrie on hem þat sike *were*.
B.16.175 And of whennes he *were* and whider þat he [þ]ouȝte.
B.16.196 To ocupie hym here til issue *were* spronge,
B.16.198 Patriarkes and prophetes and Apostles *were* þe children,
B.17.97 And [he be] baþed in þat blood, baptised as it *were*,
B.17.129 In þre persones departable þat perpetuele *were* euere,
B.17.167 And aren serel[e]pes by hemself; asondry *were* þei neuere;
B.17.192 *Were* þe myddel of myn hand ymaymed or yperissed
B.17.194 Ac þouȝ my þombe and my fyngres boþe *were* toshullen,
B.17.207 As wex and a weke *were* twyned togideres,
B.17.274 Thus is vnkyndenesse þe contrarie þat quencheþ, as it *were*,
B.18.7 That noon harlot *were* so hardy to leyen hond vpon hym.
B.18.83 For alle þei *were* vnhardy þat houed [þer] or stode
B.18.211 Wite what wo is, ne *were* þe deeþ of kynde.
B.18.290 And toldest hire a tale, of treson *were* þe wordes;
B.18.294 We haue no trewe title to hem, for þoruȝ treson *were* þei dampned.'
B.18.298 Wheiþer I *were* god or goddes sone; he [g]af me short answere;
B.18.310 For vs *were* bettre noȝt be þan biden his sighte.
B.18.380 Ofter þan ones þouȝ he *were* a tretour.
B.18.398 For I *were* an vnkynde kyng but I my kynde helpe,
B.19.34 The Iewes þat *were* gentil men, Ies[u] þei despised,
B.19.369 And [a sisour and a somonour] þat *were* forsworen ofte;
B.19.371 And for siluer *were* forswore–sooþly þei wiste it.
B.19.427 Emperour of al þe world, þat alle men *were* cristene.
B.20.62 Whiche foolis *were* wel [gladdere] to deye
B.20.65 [And] þat *were* mylde men and holye þat no meschief dradden;
B.20.68 They cursed and hir conseil, *were* it clerk or lewed.
B.20.110 Fortune gan flatere þanne þo fewe þat *were* alyue
B.20.141 That Coueitise *were* cristene þat is so kene [to fighte],
B.20.194 And wisshed ful witterly þat I *were* in heuene.
B.20.271 Forþi I wolde witterly þat ye *were* in þe Registre
B.20.308 And þat Piers [pardon] *were* ypayed, redde quod debes.
B.20.310 If any surgien *were* [in] þe seg[e] þat softer koude plastre.
B.20.331 And in haste askede what his wille *were*.
B.20.347 He saluede so oure wommen til some *were* wiþ childe.'

were **C 227**

C.Pr.2 Y shope me into [a] shroud[e] as y a shep *were*;
C.Pr.11 Wynkyng as hit *were*, witterliche y sigh hit;
C.Pr.42 Til here [bely] and here [bagge] w[*ere*] bretful ycrammed,
C.Pr.53 Grete lobies and longe þat loth *were* to swynke
C.Pr.66 Ther precede a Pardoner as he a prest *were*,
C.Pr.76 *Were* þe bischop yblessed and worth bothe his eres
C.Pr.80 That þe [pore] peple [of þe] parsch[e] sholde haue yf þei ne *were*.
C.Pr.82 That here parsch[e] *were* pore sithe þ[e] pestelence tyme,
C.Pr.106 Ful on hem þat fre *were* thorwe two fals prestis!
C.Pr.108 Thei *were* discomfited in batayle and losten Archa domini
C.Pr.112 *Were* disconfit in batayle and Archa domini lorn
C.Pr.116 And for þei *were* prestis and men of holy chirche
C.Pr.218 Ne *were* þe Cat of þe Court and ȝonge kitones toward;
C. 1.10 Y was aferd of here face thow she fayre *were*
C. 1.19 And, in mesure thow muche *were*, to make ȝow attese
C. 1.29 In his glotonye bygat gurles þat *were* cherles
C. 1.68 Thenne hadde y wonder in my wit what woman he *were*
C. 1.71 What she *were* wytterly þat wissede me so [faire].
C. 2.17 [Wh]os wyf a *were* and what was here name,

C. 2.56 And y say how mede was maried, metyng as it *were*.
C. 2.58 *Were* beden to þe Bridale a bothe half þe contre,
C. 2.59 Of many manere men þat of mede[s] kynne *were*,
C. 2.66 *Were* most pryue with mede of eny men [me] thoghte.
C. 2.70 Thei assentede hit *were* so at syluere prayere.
C. 2.124 Althow fals *were* hir fader and fikel tonge her belsyre
C. 2.128 And god graunte[de] hit *were* so so no gyle were,
C. 2.128 And god graunte[de] hit were so so no gyle *were*,
C. 2.131 That god wolde *were* ydo withoute som deseyte.
C. 3.6 What man of this world þat here [*were* leuest].
C. 3.111 Ar he *were* vnderfonge fre and felawe in ʒoure rolles.
C. 3.154 What his wille *were* and what he do sholde.
C. 3.173 Shyreues of shyres *were* shent yf he nere,
C. 3.241 And as his wyrdus *were* ordeyned at þe wille of oure lorde.
C. 3.256 For sholde neuere Consience be my constable *were* y a kyng,' quod mede.
C. 3.384 For they wilnen and wolden as beste *were* for hemsulue
C. 4.28 Fayn *were* to folowe hem and faste ryden aftur
C. 4.77 Ac wyles and wyt *were* aboute faste
C. 4.83 'God woot,' quod [wysdom], 'þat *were* nat the beste.
C. 4.134 Y sey it [by] mysulf,' quod resoun, 'and it so *were*
C. 4.135 That y *were* kyng with c[r]oune to kepe [a] reume,
C. 4.146 Clerkes [þat were confessours] co[u]plede hem togederes
C. 4.183 'Y wolde hit *were*,' quod the kynge, 'wel al aboute.
C. 5.66 For sholde no clerke be crouned but yf he come *were*
C. 5.118 P[iri]es and plumtrees *were* po[ff]ed to þe erthe.
C. 5.120 Beches and brode okes *were* blowe to þe grounde
C. 5.124 Ac y shal sey as y sayh, slepynge as hit *were*,
C. 5.160 A[n] hep of houndes at h[is] ers as he a lord *were*
C. 5.188 *Were* wittiore and worthiore then he þat was his maister.
C. 5.192 And no grace [to] graunte til good loue *were*
C. 6.24 Wene y *were* witty and wiser then another;
C. 6.32 Me wilnynge þat men wen[t]e y *were* as in auer,
C. 6.48 They to wene þat y *were* wel holy and almesfull
C. 6.65 His clothes *were* of corsemen[t] and of kene wordes.
C. 6.110 Inpacient in alle penaunc[e] and pleyned, as hit *were*,
C. 6.129 Here *were* leuer swowe or swelte then soffre eny payne.
C. 6.150 Til bothe here hedes *were* bar and blody here chekes.
C. 6.156 ʒut am y chalenged in oure chapitrehous as y a childe *were*
C. 6.184 Such werkes with vs *were* neuere out of sesoun
C. 6.277 As whenne y lenede and leuede hit lost or longe or hit *were* payed.
C. 6.287 *Were* y a frere, in good fayth, for al þe gold on erthe
C. 6.290 Thow *were* such as thow sayst; y sholde rather s[t]erue:
C. 6.292 ʒut *were* me leuer, by oure lord, lyue al by wellecresses
C. 6.300 Yf he wiste thow *were* such when he resseyued thyn offrynge.
C. 6.380 There *were* chapmen ychose this chaffare to preyse;
C. 6.385 And there othes an heep for on sholde haue þe worse.
C. 6.388 And nempned hym for a noumper þat no debat *were*.
C. 7.4 *Were* y brouhte [o]n bed, but yf my taylende hit made,
C. 7.5 Sholde no ryngyng do me ryse til y *were* rype to dyne.'
C. 7.66 And here mateynes and masse as y a monke *were*,
C. 7.94 There wyse men *were*, wittnesseth goddes wordes,
C. 7.138 And a[l] to solace synfole thow soffredest it so *were*:
C. 7.203 *Were* hit itolde treuthe þat y toke mede
C. 7.301 *Were* y seuen nyhte fro here syhte s[ynnen] he wolde
C. 8.5 'Th[is] *were* a long lettyng,' quod [a] lady in a slayre;
C. 8.22 Y wolde [assaye] som tyme, for solace as hit *were*.'
C. 8.116 Oþer werkemen þer *were* þat wrouhten fol ʒerne,
C. 8.128 Tho *were* faytours aferd and fayned hem blynde;
C. 8.138 That no faytrye *were* founde in folk þat goth abeggeth.
C. 8.179 Tho *were* faytours afered and flowen into [Peres] bernes
C. 8.201 Was no beggare so bold, but yf a blynd *were*,
C. 8.219 Now nedde y wyte, ar thow wendest, what *were* þe beste;
C. 8.280 And sethen y say hym sitte as he a syre *were*
C. 8.325 Ne no beggare eten bred þat benes ynne *were*
C. 9.41 Tho *were* Marchauntes mury; many wopen for ioye
C. 9.44 Men of lawe hadde lest þat loth *were* to plede
C. 9.45 But they pre manibus *were* payed for pledynge at þe barre;
C. 9.67 Bote ther he wiste *were* wel grete nede.
C. 9.93 And colde flesche and fische as venisoun *were* bake;
C. 9.95 *Were* a feste with suche folk or so fele cockes.
C. 9.114 To profecye of þe peple, pleinge as hit *were*
C. 9.202 Al they holy Ermytes *were* of heye kynne,
C. 9.205 Whilen *were* werkmen, webbes and taylours
C. 9.211 And clothed hem in copes, clerkes as hit *were*
C. 9.248 [C]o[m]e in his cope as he a Clerk *were*;
C. 9.259 Vigilare *were* fayrere for thow haste a greet charge.
C. 10.115 And ar we ywar *were* with wit gan we mete.
C. 10.190 And ʒut *were* best to ben aboute and brynge hit to hepe
C. 10.194 The catel that Crist hadde, then clothes hit *were*;
C. 10.199 To wende as wyde as þe worlde *were*
C. 10.220 Alle þat come of Caym Caytyue[s] *were* euere

C. 10.269 That his wyf *were* wexe or a walet ful of nobles.
C. 10.290 For sholde no bedbourde be bote yf they bothe *were*
C. 11.9 They do bote dr[a]uele þeron; draf *were* hem leuere
C. 11.47 Ne *were* mercy in m[e]ne men more then in riht riche
C. 11.94 And ouer skripture þe skilfole and screueynes *were* trewe
C. 11.199 *Were* hit al soth þat ʒe seyn, thow scripture and thow clergie,
C. 11.204 In þe legende of lyf longe ar y *were*.
C. 11.217 *Were* wonder goed and wisest in here tyme
C. 11.224 A[c] me *were* leuere, by oure lord, a lyppe of goddes grace
C. 11.230 [Ac] at he[re] moste meschef mercy *were* þe beste
C. 11.251 Laste ʒe be loste as þe laboreres *were* þat lab[o]red vnder Noe.
C. 11.269 Tho that worste wrouhten while thei here *were*.
C. 12.4 'Rechelesnesse reche the neuere; By so thow riche *were*
C. 12.11 By wissyng of this wenche y dede, here wordes *were* so swete,
C. 12.22 Wher my body *were* yber[i]ed by so ʒe hadde my [suluer].'
C. 12.27 Y wolde it *were* no synne,' y saide, 'to seien þat were treuthe.
C. 12.27 Y wolde it were no synne,' y saide, 'to seien þat *were* treuthe.
C. 12.47 'Multi to a mangerye and to þe mete *were* sompned
C. 12.52 Where y *were* chose [or nat chose]; on holy churche y thouhte
C. 12.83 And for a wilnede wepynge þat y *were* ysaued
C. 12.124 Cleophas ne knewe hym nat þat he Crist *were*
C. 12.142 And alle þe wyse þat euere *were*, by auhte y can aspye,
C. 12.184 That ben layd in louhe erthe, ylore as hit *were*.
C. 13.8 For in greet pouerte he was put: a prince, as hit *were*,
C. 13.114 And a title, a tale of nauht, to his lyflode as hit *were*.
C. 13.152 That ne lees the lykynge of lost of flesch, as hit *were*,
C. 13.178 Of here kynde and here colour to carpe hit *were* to longe.
C. 13.221 'Haddestow soffred,' he sayde, 'slepyng tho thow *were*,
C. 13.247 And yf his wille *were* A wolde his name telle.
C. 14.38 Lawe of loue oure lord wrouht] long ar crist *were*.
C. 14.60 Bote hit *were* pres[t] or prestis sone, patriarke or p[ro]phete.
C. 14.71 Bothe lewede and lerede *were* lost yf clergie ne were.
C. 14.71 Bothe lewede and lerede were lost yf clergie ne *were*.
C. 14.89 Yf eny frere we[re] founde þere y ʒeue the fyue shillynges!
C. 14.95 Ryche men rotte tho and in here reste *were*
C. 14.101 That is, how lewede men and luythere lyhtloker *were* ysaued
C. 14.148 Hit *were* no resoun ne riht to rewarde bothe ylyche.
C. 14.166 Ac why a wolde þat wykke *were*, y wene and y leue
C. 14.198 For letrede men *were* lewede ʒut ne were lore of [here bokes].'
C. 14.198 For letrede men were lewede ʒut ne *were* lore of [here bokes].'
C. 14.211 And yf þer *were* a wolde [amende], and in suche a wille deyeth—
C. 14.212 Ne wolde neuere trewe god bote trewe treuthe *were* alloued.
C. 15.2 And as a freke þ[at] fay *were* forth can y walken
C. 15.33 Ilyk[e peres] the [ploghman], as he a palmere *were*,
C. 15.89 Þat in þ[e] mawe of þat maystre alle þo metes *were*,
C. 15.174 And toek Clergie and Consience to conseyle as hit *were*.
C. 15.178 Me *were* leuere, by oure lord, and y leue sholde,
C. 15.233 For þoʒ nere payn [of] plouh ne potage *were*
C. 15.238 For lente neuere was lyf but lyflode *were* shape,
C. 15.248 And y lystnede and lokede what lyflode hit *were*
C. 15.296 Other here or elliswher, elles hit *were* reuthe;
C. 15.304 Ac when deth awaketh hem of here we[le] þat *were* er so ryche
C. 16.114 Quod Actyf tho al angryliche and Arguinge as hit *were*:
C. 16.180 Bote as wode *were* afuyre thenne worcheth bothe
C. 16.209 'ʒe, sire!' y sayde, 'by so no man *were* ygreued,
C. 16.214 Hit *were* aʒeyns kynde,' quod he, 'and alle kyne resoun
C. 16.234 To teche þe ten comaundementʒ ten sythe *were* bettere
C. 16.262 Loeth *were* lewed [men] bote they ʒoure lore folwede[n]
C. 16.267 That *were* bysnewed al with snowe and snakes withynne
C. 16.268 Or to a wal ywhitlymed and *were* blak withynne;
C. 16.337 'Were y with hym by Cr[i]st,' quod y, 'y wolde neuere fro hym
C. 16.348 Edmond and Edward, ayþer *were* seyntes,
C. 17.6 Holy writ witnesseth þer *were* suche eremytes,
C. 17.68 And fedde þat afyn[g]red *were* and in defaute lyuede.
C. 17.90 As they ywoned *were*; in wham is defaute?
C. 17.231 Hit *were* charite to deschargen hem for holy churche sake,
C. 17.233 For *were* presthode more parfyte, that is, þe pope formost
C. 17.250 Yf presthode *were* parfyt and preyede thus the peple sholde amende
C. 17.282 Or cristendoem *were* knowe þere or eny croos honoured.
C. 18.6 Euene in þe myddes an ympe, as hit *were*,
C. 18.24 And askede [e]fte of hym of what wode they *were*.
C. 18.27 Thre persones indepartable, perpetuel *were* euere,
C. 18.47 And shaketh hit; ne *were* hit vndershored hit sholde nat stande.
C. 18.54 Where þe fruyt *were* fayre or foul for to loke on.
C. 18.57 And askede efte tho where hit *were* all [of] o kynde.
C. 18.126 Til plenitudo temporis tyme ycome *were*
C. 18.185 An heraud of Armes Ar eny lawe *were*.'
C. 18.189 Of o wit and o will, [they] *were* neuere atwynne
C. 18.205 To ocupien hym here til issue *were* spronge
C. 18.207 Patriarches and prophetes and apostles *were* the childrene.
C. 18.211 Semblable to hymsulue ar eny synne *were*,
C. 18.232 Is and ay *were* [& worþ wiþouten ende].

C.18.252 Mysulue and my mayne; and alle þat male *were*
C.19.9   *Were* hit þerwith aseled y woet wel þe sothe
C.19.82   *Were* afered and flowe fram þe man ywounded.
C.19.103 Noþer lacke ne alose ne leue þat þer *were*
C.19.104 Eny wikkedere in þe worlde then y *were* mysulue
C.19.129 Thus are they alle bote oen as hit an hand *were*,
C.19.138 Sholde n[o] wri[h]t worche *were* they awey.
C.19.158 *Were* þe myddel of myn hand [ymaymed or ypersed
C.19.160 Ac thouh my thombe and my fyngeres bothe *were* toshullen
C.19.173 As wexe and a weke *were* twyned togyderes
C.19.255 Thus is vnkyndenesse [the contrarie that] quencheth, as hit *were*,
C.20.37   The iewes and þe iustic[e] aʒeyns iesus þey *were*
C.20.63   The erthe toquasch[t]e and quoek as hit quyk *were*
C.20.85   For alle [they *were*] vnhardy þat houed þer or stode
C.20.116 Out of þe west as hit *were* a wenche, as me thouhte,
C.20.201 Freet of th[at] fruyt and forsoke, as hit *were*,
C.20.214 Yf all þe world *were* whit or swanwhit all thynges?
C.20.215 Yf no nyht ne *were* no man, [as] y leue,
C.20.218 He hadde nat wist witterly where deth *were* sour or swete.
C.20.220 Ywyte what wo is ne *were* þe deth of kynde.
C.20.311 Thenne *were* the vnwrast of hys word þat witnesse is of treuthe.'
C.20.331 Where he *were* god or godes sone; he gaf me short answere.
C.20.344 For vs *were* bettere nat be then abyde in his sihte.
C.20.422 Oftur then ones thogh [he] *were* [a] tretou[r].
C.20.441 For y *were* an vnkynde kyng bote y my kyn helpe
C.21.34   The iewes and þat *were* gentel men iesu thei despisede,
C.21.357 Preye we þat a pees *were* in [Peres] berne [þe Plouhman]
C.21.359 To goen agayn pruyde bute grace *were* with vs.'
C.21.363 That holi churche stoede in holinesse as hit [a pyle *were*].
C.21.427 Emperour of al þe world, þat all men *were* cristene.
C.22.32   Of þat he weneth wolde falle yf his wit ne *were*,
C.22.57   And garte gyle [growe] þere as he a god *were*.
C.22.62   [Whiche foles] *were* wel gladere to deye
C.22.65   And þat *were* mylde men and holy þat no meschief dradden,
C.22.68   Thei corsede and here consail, *were* hit Clerk or lewed.
C.22.110 Fortune gan flateren thenne t[h]o fewe þat *were* alyue
C.22.141 That couetyse *were* cristene þat is so kene to fihte
C.22.194 And wesched wel witterly þat y *were* in heuene.
C.22.196 Anyhtes nameliche, when we naked *were*,
C.22.271 Forthy y wolde witterly þat ʒe *were* in [þe] registre
C.22.308 And þat Peres pardon *were* ypayd, redde quod debes.
C.22.310 Yf eny surgien *were* in þe sege that softur couthe plastre.
C.22.331 And in haste eschete what his wille *were*.
C.22.347 He salued so oure wymmen til some *were* with childe.'

weren B 3
B.11.283 If preestes *weren* [wise] þei wolde no siluer take
B.19.166 And as alle þise wise wyes *weren* togideres
B.20.118 *Weren* feþered wiþ fair biheste and many a fals truþe.

weren C 9
C. 6.41   Wilnynge þat men wen[d]e myne werkes *weren* þe beste
C. 8.136 'ʒoure prayeres,' quod [Peres], 'and ʒe p[ar]fyt *weren*,
C.13.5   ʒut ret me þat abraham and Iob *weren* wonder ryche
C.15.40   Pacience and y [prestly *weren*] pot to be mettes
C.20.248 Tho þat *weren* in heuene token stella comata
C.21.166 And as al thise wyse weyes *weren* togyderes
C.21.369 And a sisour and [clause] sompnour þat *weren* forsworen ofte;
C.21.371 And for suluer *weren* forswore–soth[ly] thei wisten hit.
C.22.118 *Weren* fythered with fayre biheste and many a fals treuthe.

wern A 9
A. 4.132 Clerkis þat *wern* confessours couplide hem togideris,
A. 5.13   And prouide þat þise pestilences *wern* for pur synne,
A. 5.16   Piries & pl[umtr]es *wern* pu[ffid] to þe erþe
A. 5.18   Bechis & broode okis *wern* blowen to [þe] grounde,
A. 7.180 And lame menis lymes *wern* li[þ]id þat tyme,
A.10.159 And siþen se[þ] & his suster [sed] *wern* spousid to kaymes;
A.11.81   I wolde his eiʒen *wern* in his ars & his hele aftir
A.11.220 *Wern* dowel, & dobet, & dobest of hem alle,
A.11.224 Forþi I wende þat þo wyes *wern* dobest of alle.'

benche n *benche n.* A 3 bench (2) benche (1); B 3 benche (2) benches (1); C 3 benche (2) benches (1)
A.Pr.95   And ben clerkis of þe kinges *bench* þe cuntre to shende.
A. 4.32   And betwyn hymself & his sone sette hym a *benche*,
A. 5.158 Cisse þe so[wes]tere sat on þe *bench*,
B.Pr.186 To c[r]acchen vs & al oure kynde þouʒ we cropen vnder *benches*;
B. 4.45   And bitwene hymself and his sone sette hym on *benche*,
B. 5.307 Cesse þe [sowestere] sat on þe *benche*,
C.Pr.203 To crache vs and alle oure kynde thogh we crope vnder *benches*;
C. 6.362 Sesse þe [sywestere] saet on þe *benche*,
C. 9.253 He sat at þe syde *benche* and at þe seconde table;

bendeth v *benden v.(1)* C 1
C.10.37   [A] *bendeth* and boweth, the body is so vnstable,

bene n *bene n.* A 6 bene (1) benes (2) benis (3); B 7 bene (1) benes (6); C 6 bene (1) benes (5)
A. 7.165 And wiþ a *bene* batte he[ʒe]de [hem] betwene,
A. 7.169 To abate þe barly bred & þe *benis* ygrounde,
A. 7.201 And [a]baue hem wiþ b[e]nes for bollnyng of here wombe,
A. 7.267 A lof of *benis* & bren ybake for my children;
A. 7.277 *Benes* & [b]lake applis hy brouʒte in here lappe[s],
A. 7.287 Ne no beggere ete bred þat *benis* in come,
B. 6.182 Or ellis *benes* [and] bren ybaken togideres.'
B. 6.194 And many a beggere for *benes* buxum was to swynke,
B. 6.215 [And] aba[u]e hem wiþ *benes* for bollynge of hir womb[e];
B. 6.283 [A lof] of *benes* and bran ybake for my fauntes.
B. 6.293 *Benes* and baken apples þei broʒte in here lappes,
B. 6.303 Ne no beggere ete breed þat *benes* Inne [come],
B.11.171 'Lawe wiþouten loue', quod Troianus, 'ley þer a *bene*!'
C. 8.177 'Haue mercy on hem, hunger,' quod [Peres], 'and lat me ʒeue hem *benes*
C. 8.225 And [a]baue hem with *benes* for bollyng of here wombe;
C. 8.305 And bred for my barnes of *benes* and of peses.
C. 8.316 *Benes* and bake aples they brouhten in here lappe
C. 8.325 Ne no beggare eten bred þat *benes* ynne were
C.12.93   For lawe withouten leute, ley þer a *bene*!

benefice n *benefice n.* B 1; C 1 benefices
B. 3.314 His boost of his *benefice* worþ bynomen hym after.
C. 3.33   And bygge ʒow *benefices*, [here bonchef] to haue,

beneyt n prop *n.i.d.* B 2 Beneit (1) Beneyt (1); C 1 Benet
B. 4.121 As Seynt *Beneit* hem bad, Bernard and Fraunceis;
B.15.422 [Boþe] *Beneit* and Bernard, þe whiche hem first tauʒte
C. 4.117 And be as *Benet* hem bad, dominik and fraunceys;

beneþ(e > byneþe

benigne adj *benigne adj.* B 2; C 2 benigne (1) benyngne (1)
B.16.7   The blosmes beþ buxom speche and *benigne* lokynge.
B.18.116 A ful *benigne* burde and Buxom of speche.
C.18.11   The whiche blosmes buirnes *benigne* speche hit calleth,
C.20.119 A fol *benyngne* buyrde and buxum of speche.

benigneliche adv *benigneli adv.* B 1; C 1 benyngnelyche
B.12.112 Buxomliche and *benigneliche* and bidden it of grace.
C.14.57   Buxumliche and *benyngnelyche* and bidden hit of grace.

benyngn- > benigne(-

benyson n *benisoun n.* B 1
B.13.235 For no breed þat I brynge forþ, saue a *benyson* on þe sonday

benom > bynymen; ; bequest > biqueste; ber > beren

berd n *berd n.(1)* B 1; C 1
B. 5.193 And as a bondeman[nes] bacon his *berd* was [yshaue].
C. 6.201 And as a bondemannes bacoun his *berd* was yshaue,

bere n *bere n.* B 1; C 1 beres
B.15.299 Neiþer *bere* ne boor ne ooþer beest wilde,
C. 9.197 That wonede whilom in wodes with *beres* and lyons.

bere v1 *beren v.(2)* B 1; C 1
B.11.342 That wolde [*bere*] after bol[e], ne boor after sowe.
C.13.150 That *bere* aftur bole ne boer aftur sowe;

bere &> beren

beren v2 *beren v.(1)* A 21 bar (6) bere (8) beriþ (5) born (1) yborn (1); B 88 baar (1) bar (13) baren (1) beere (2) ber (1) bere (21) beren (3) bereþ (35) berþ (1) born (6) ybore (4); C 74 baer (8) bar (5) beer (1) bere (19) beren (1) bereth (31) bore (2) born (2) ybore (5)
A. 1.60   May banne þat he *born* was to body or to soule.
A. 2.3   Þat *bar* þe blisside barn þat bouʒte vs on þe rode,
A. 2.95   [And] as a bastard *yborn* of belsab[ubb]is kynde;
A. 2.138 For þei shuln *bere* þise bisshopis & bringe hem at reste.
A. 3.40   And ek be þi baudekyn, & *bere* wel þin arnede
A. 3.183 And *bar* here bras on þi bak to caleis to selle,
A. 4.44   Brekiþ vp my berne doris, *beriþ* awey my whete,
A. 4.112 *Bere* no siluer ouer se þat signe of king shewi[þ],
A. 5.89   Þat *bar* awey my bolle & my broken shete.
A. 5.200 *Bere* hym to his bed & brouʒte hem slepe:
A. 6.5   He *bar* a burdoun ybounde wiþ a brood list,
A. 6.7   A bagge & a bolle he *bar* be his side;
A. 6.67   Þanne shalt þou blenche at a b[erw]e, *bere* no fals wytnesse;
A. 7.91   I *bar* hom þat I borewide er I to bedde ʒede.
A. 7.151 'Or þou shalt abigge be þe lawe, be þe ordre þat I *bere*'.
A. 8.15   And *bere* hem boþe on here bak as here baner shewiþ,
A. 8.135 Ac for þe bible *beriþ* wytnesse
A. 9.86   Dobest is aboue hem boþe & *beriþ* a bisshopis croce;
A.10.189 Þat neuere shal *bere* [barne] but it be in armes.

A.11.192 Þ[i]s be[þ] dobet; so *beriþ* witnesse þe sauter:
A.11.214 A bidowe or a baselard he *beriþ* be his side;
B.Pr.161 *Beren* bei3es ful bri3te abouten hire nekkes,
B. 1.62 May banne þat he *born* was to bodi or to soule.
B. 2.3 That *bar* þ[e] blis[sed] barn þat bou3te vs on þe Rode,
B. 2.38 And how ye shul saue yourself? þe Sauter *bereþ* witnesse:
B. 2.81 To bakbite and to bosten and *bere* fals witnesse,
B. 2.131 And [as] a Bastard *ybore* of Belsabubbes kynne.
B. 2.177 To *bere* Bisshopes aboute abrood in visitynge.
B. 3.41 And [ek] be þi [baudekyn] and *bere* wel þ[yn erende]
B. 3.196 And *bere* hire bras at þi bak to Caleis to selle,
B. 3.270 Bren it; *bere* it no3t awey be it neuer so riche,
B. 3.305 Alle þat *beren* baselard, brood swerd or launce,
B. 3.323 Batailles shul none be, ne no man *bere* wepene,
B. 4.57 Brekeþ vp my bern[e] dore[s], *bereþ* awey my whete,
B. 4.129 *Bere* no siluer ouer see þat signe of kyng sheweþ,
B. 5.109 That [*bar*] awey my bolle and my broke shete.
B. 5.140 Til þei *beere* leues of lowe speche lordes to plese,
B. 5.146 And freres fyndeþ hem in defaute, as folk *bereþ* witnesse,
B. 5.290 *Ber* it to þe Bisshop, and bid hym of his grace
B. 5.358 *Baren* hym to his bed and brou3te hym þerInne,
B. 5.517 He *bar* a burdoun ybounde wiþ a brood liste,
B. 5.519 A bolle and a bagge he *bar* by his syde.
B. 5.580 Thanne shaltow blenche at a Bergh, *bere*-no-fals-witnesse;
B. 6.99 I *bar* hom þat I borwed er I to bedde yede.
B. 6.142 Or helpe make morter or *bere* Muk afeld.
B. 6.166 'Or þow shalt abigge by þe lawe, by þe ordre þat I *bere*!'
B. 7.52 That he ne worþ saaf [sikerly]; þe Sauter *bereþ* witnesse:
B. 7.85 For whoso haþ to buggen hym breed, þe book *bereþ* witnesse,
B. 7.157 Ac for þe book bible *bereþ* witnesse
B. 8.96 Dobest is aboue boþe and *bereþ* a bisshopes crosse;
B. 9.76 And þat I lye no3t of þat I lere þee, luc *bereþ* witnesse.
B. 9.168 That neuere shal barn *bere* but it be in armes.
B.10.89 How þe book bible of hym *bereþ* witnesse.
B.10.252 And Crist cleped hymself so, þe [scripture] *bereþ* witnesse:
B.10.285 The bible *bereþ* witnesse þat al[le] þe [barnes] of Israel
B.10.346 And preiseden pouerte with pacience; þe Apostles *bereþ* witnesse
B.11.157 Was þat Sarsen saued, as Seint Gregorie *bereþ* witnesse.
B.11.227 That saued synful men as Seint Iohan *bereþ* witnesse:
B.11.253 Boþe Marthaes and Maries, as Mathew *bereþ* witnesse.
B.11.269 Than he þat is ri3t riche; Reson *bereþ* witnesse:
B.11.272 Wiser þan Salomon was *bereþ* witnesse and tau3te
B.11.274 And lif moost likynge to god as luc *bereþ* witnesse:
B.12.65 As þe book *bereþ* witnesse to burnes þat kan rede:
B.12.105 And as a blynd man in bataille *bereþ* wepne to fi3te
B.12.146 Ne in none [beggers] cote [n]as þat barn *born*,
B.12.184 To lere lewed men as luc *bereþ* witnesse:
B.13.135 That no clerk ne kan, as crist *bereþ* witnesse:
B.13.152 I *bere* þer, [in a bouste] faste ybounde, dowel,
B.13.440 As he seiþ hymself; seynt Iohan *bereþ* witnesse.
B.14.86 And brynge his soule to blisse, so þat feiþ *bere* witnesse
B.14.180 For how þow confortest alle creatures clerkes *bereþ* witnesse:
B.14.258 And wheiþer he be or be no3t, he *bereþ* þe signe of pouerte
B.15.41 'For bisshopes yblessed *bereþ* manye names,
B.15.90 Ac of curatours of cristen peple, as clerkes *bereþ* witnesse.
B.15.97 Ther some bowes ben leued and some *bereþ* none
B.15.122 [And *beere*] bedes in hir hand and a book vnder hir arme.
B.15.171 Corseþ he no creature ne he kan *bere* no wraþe,
B.15.184 Thou3 he *bere* hem no breed he *bereþ* hem swetter liflode,
B.15.184 Thou3 he *bere* hem no breed he *bereþ* hem swetter liflode;
B.15.312 And bidden hem *bere* it þere it [yborwed was].
B.15.456 [And] so it fareþ by a barn þat *born* is of wombe,
B.15.510 That *bere* bisshopes names of Bethleem and Babiloigne.
B.15.528 And souereynliche to swiche þat of surrye *bereþ* þe name],
B.15.570 Euery bisshop þat *bereþ* cros, by þat he is holden
B.16.70 Thanne *bereþ* þe crop kynde fruyt and clennest of alle,
B.16.83 *Bar* hem forþ bo[lde]ly–no body hym letted–
B.16.126 And lefte baskettes ful of broke mete, *bere* awey whoso wolde.'
B.16.180 'What *berþ* þat buyrn', quod I þo, 'so blisse þee bitide?'
B.16.254 For in his bosom bar a þyng þat he blissed euere.
B.17.3 To rule alle Reames wiþ; I *bere* þe writ [ri3t] here.'
B.17.96 Wiþouten þe blood of a barn *born* of a mayde,
B.17.125 For þe barn was *born* in Bethleem þat with his blood shal saue
B.17.305 Ac it is but selden ysei3e, þer sooþnesse *bereþ* witnesse,
B.18.85 But þis blynde bacheler þanne *bar* hym þoru3 þe herte.
B.18.133 Siþ þis barn was *ybore* ben xxxti wynter passed
B.18.232 'By goddes body', quod þis book, 'I wol *bere* witnesse
B.18.233 That þo þis barn was *ybore* þer blased a sterre
B.18.235 That swich a barn was *ybore* in Bethleem þe Citee
B.18.237 And alle þe element3', quod þe book, 'herof *beren* witnesse.
B.18.429 For goddes blissede body it *bar* for oure boote;
B.19.49 And kyng of hir kyngdom and croune *bar* of þornes.
B.19.71 Tho he was *born* in Bethleem, as þe book telleþ,

B.19.446 Ayein þe olde lawe and newe lawe, as Luc [*bereþ*] witness[e]:
B.20.70 And pride [*bar* it bare] boldely aboute
B.20.91 After Confort a knyght to come and *bere* his baner:
B.20.96 And *bar* þe baner bifore deeþ; bi ri3t he it cleymede.
B.20.117 He *bar* a bowe in his hand and manye brode arewes
B.20.132 And boldeliche *bar* adoun wiþ many a bright Noble
B.20.286 That borweþ and *bereþ* it þider and þanne biddeþ frendes
C.Pr.180 *Bere* beyus of bryghte gold aboute here nekkes
C. 1.58 May banne þat he *born* was [to] body [or to] soule.
C. 2.3 That *bar* þ[e] blissid bar[n] þat bouhte [vs] on þe rode,
C. 2.28 For shal neuer breere *bere* berye as a vine,
C. 2.88 To bacbite and to boste and *bere* fals witnesse.
C. 2.147 And as a bastard *ybore* by3ete was he neuere.
C. 2.180 And shop þat a shereue sholde *bere* mede
C. 3.48 For to ben here bedman and *bere* wel here ernde
C. 3.145 And bitterliche banne the and alle þat *bereth* thy name
C. 3.423 Bern hit; *bere* hit nat awey be hit neuer so riche;
C. 3.458 For alle þat *bereth* baslard, br[ode] swerd oþer launce,
C. 3.476 Bataines sholle neuere eft be ne man *bere* eg toel
C. 4.51 'Bere sikerlyche eny seluer to seynt Gyles doune.
C. 4.60 And breketh vp my bern[e] dores and [b]ereth awey my whete
C. 4.126 *Bere* no seluer ouer see þat sygne of kyng sheweth,
C. 6.345 *Bere* hit to th[e] bischop and bide hym of his grace
C. 6.416 *Beren* hym to his bed and brouhten hym þerynne
C. 7.100 As he sayth hymsulf; seynt Ion *bereth* witnesse:
C. 7.162 He *bar* a bordoun ybounde with a brood liste,
C. 7.164 A bolle and a bagge a *bar* by his syde;
C. 7.222 Loke þou *bere* n[ouht] þere away but yf hit be thyn owene.
C. 7.227 Thenne shaltow blenche at a berw, *bere*-no-fals-witnesse,
C. 8.108 I *bar* hoem þat y borwed ar y to bedde 3ede.
C. 8.287 Lat hem abyde til þe bord be drawe; Ac *bere* hem none crommes
C. 9.139 For they *bereth* none bagges ne boteles vnder clokes
C. 9.305 Ac for þe boek bible *bereth* witnesse
C.10.93 Dobest *bere* sholde þe bisshopes [c]rose
C.10.212 And þat my sawe is soth þe sauter *bereth* witnesse:
C.11.213 And demede wel and wysly; wymmen *bereth* wittenesse:
C.12.134 And seynt marie his moder, as Mathew *bereth* witnesse,
C.12.154 Then he þat is rihte ryche; reson *bereth* witnesse:
C.13.55 For þat on *bereth* but a box, a breuet þerynne,
C.14.31 As to be *bore* or bygete in such a constillacioun;
C.14.50 And as a blynde man in bataile *bereth* wepene to fyhte
C.14.90 Ne in no cote ne Caytyfs hous [crist was *ybore*
C.14.124 To lere lewede men As luk *bereth* witnesse:
C.15.160 And *bere* hit in thy bosom aboute where þou wendest
C.15.220 As þe boek *bereth* witnesse þat he bere myhte
C.15.220 As þe boek *bereth* witnesse þat he bere myhte
C.16.98 And where he be or be nat, a *bereth* þe signe of pouerte
C.16.178 And may nat be withoute a body to *bere* me where hym liketh.'
C.16.203 'For bisshopes yblessed *bereth* many names,
C.16.249 Þere som bowes *bereth* leues and som bereth none:
C.16.249 Þere som bowes bereth leues and som *bereth* none:
C.16.250 Tho bowes þat *bereth* nat and beth nat grene yleued,
C.16.291 As poul in his pistul of hym *bereth* wittenesse.
C.17.261 That *bereth* name of Neptalym, of Niniue [and] of damaske.
C.17.278 And souereynliche [to] suche þat of surie *bereth* þe name
C.18.25 'Thise thre shorriares,' quod he,' that *bereth* vp this plonte
C.18.114 *Baer* hem forth baldly–no body hym lette–
C.18.154 And lefte basketes ful of Broke mete, *bere* awey hoso wolde.
C.18.212 A thre he is þer he is and hereof *bereth* wittnesse
C.18.221 As þe bible *bereth* witnesse, A boek of þe olde lawe,
C.18.270 For in his bosome a *baer* [a] thyng þat [a] blessede [euere].
C.19.31 And alle thre bote o god; thus abraham *bereth* witenesse
C.19.87 The whiche barn mote nedes be *born* of a mayde,
C.19.240 Clothes of moest cost, as clerkes *bereth* witnesse:
C.19.285 Ac hit is bote selde yseyen, there sothnesse *bereth* witnesse,
C.20.87 Bote this blynde bacheler that *bar* hym thorw the herte.
C.20.136 Sethe this barn was *ybore* ben thritty wynter ypassed,
C.20.241 'By godes body,' quod this boek, 'y wol [b]ere witnesse
C.20.242 [That tho] this barn was *ybore* þ[er] blased a sterre
C.20.244 That such a barn was *ybore* in Bethleem þe Citee
C.20.244 And all þe elementis,' quod the boek, 'hereof *bereth* witnesse.
C.20.473 For godes blessed body hit *baer* for oure bote.
C.21.49 And kyng of here kyngdoem and croune *baer* of thornes.
C.21.71 Tho he was *bore* in Bedlehem, as þe boek telleth,
C.21.446 A3en þe olde lawe and newe lawe, as Luk *bereth* witnesse.
C.22.70 And pryde [*baer*] hit baer baldly aboute
C.22.91 Aftur conforte, a knyhte, [to] come and *beer* his baner:
C.22.96 And *baer* þe baner bifore deth; bi riht he hit claymede.
C.22.117 He *baer* a bowe in his hoend and many brode arewes,
C.22.132 And baldeliche *baer* adoun with many a brihte noble
C.22.286 That borweth and *bereth* hit theddere and thenne biddeth frendes

bereuid > bireue

bergh n *bergh n.* A 1 berwe; B 1; C 1 berw
A. 6.67   Þanne shalt þou blenche at a *b[erw]e*, bere no fals wytnesse;
B. 5.580   Thanne shaltow blenche at a *Bergh*, bere-no-fals-witnesse;
C. 7.227   Thenne shaltow blenche at a *berw*, bere-no-fals-witnesse,

berye n *berie n.* C 1
C. 2.28   For shal neuer breere bere *berye* as a vine,

beryng ger *bering ger.* A 1; B 8 beryng (1) berynge (7); C 4 berynge
A.10.115   To be blissid for þi *beryng*, [ȝ]e, b[e]ggere þeiȝ þou were.
B. 5.88   Wiþ bakbitynge and bismere and *berynge* of fals witnesse;
B.10.262   And lat no body be by þi *beryng* bigiled
B.11.302   [Moore þan cure] for konnyng or 'knowen for clene [of] *berynge*'.
B.13.276   Of scornyng and of scoffyng and of vnskilful *berynge*;
B.15.202   And buxome as of *berynge* to burgeises and to lordes,
B.15.238   For braulynge and bakbitynge and *berynge* of fals witnesse.
B.19.255   And who þat moost maistries kan be myldest of *berynge*.
B.20.116   And armede hym in ydelnesse and in heigh *berynge*.
C. 8.198   In daubynge and in deluynge, in donge afeld *berynge*,
C.16.363   For braulyng and bacbityng and *berynge* of fals witnesse.
C.21.255   And [ho] þat moest maistries can be myldest of *berynge*.
C.22.116   And armed hym in ydelnesse and in hey *berynge*.

berke v *berken v.* C 1
C. 9.262   Dispergentur oues, þe dogge dar nat *berke*.

berkeres n *berker n.* C 1
C. 9.261   Thy *berkeres* aren a[l] blynde that bringeth forth thy lombren:

bern n *bern n.(2)* &> *brennen,burn* A 2 berne (1) bernis (1); B 4 bern (1) berne (2) Bernes (1); C 5 berne (3) bernes (1) bernis (1)
A. 4.44   Brekiþ vp my *berne* doris, beriþ awey my whete,
A. 7.171   Faitours for fer flowen into *bernis*
B. 4.57   Brekeþ vp my *bern[e]* dore[s], bereþ awey my whete,
B. 6.183   Faitours for fere flowen into *Bernes*
B.19.344   'And Piers *bern* worþ ybroke; and þei þat ben in vnitee
B.19.357   Praye we þat a pees weere in Piers *berne* þe Plowman.
C. 4.60   And breketh vp my *bern[e]* dores and [b]ereth awey my whete
C. 8.179   Tho were faytours afered and flowen into [Peres] *bernes*
C.12.214   Þe catel þat he kepeth so in coffres and in *bernis*,
C.21.344   'And Peres *berne* worth broke and þei þat ben in vnite
C.21.357   Preye we þat a pees were in [Peres] *berne* [þe Plouhman]

bernard n prop *n.i.d.* A 1; B 4; C 2
A.11.41   And bringe forþ a ballid resoun, t[a]k[e] *bernard* to witnesse,
B. 4.121   As Seynt Beneyt hem bad, *Bernard* and Fraunceis;
B.10.55   And bryngen forþ a balled reson, taken *Bernard* to witnesse,
B.15.60   "Beatus est", seiþ Seint *Bernard*, "qui scripturas legit
B.15.422   [Boþe] Beneit and *Bernard*, þe whiche hem first tauȝte
C.11.36   And brynge forth [a] balle[d] reso[n], taken *bernard* to witnesse
C.16.222   "Beatus," saith seynt *Bernard*, "qui scripturas legit

berne > bern,brennen; bernes > barn,bern; berthe > burþe; berw(e > bergh; beseche besek- > bisech-; besette > bisitten; besy > bisy; beside > biside; besouȝte > bisechen; besshette > bishetten

best adj *best adj.* A 16 best (1) beste (15); B 33 best (8) beste (25); C 28 best (1) beste (27)
A. 1.40   And for þou shuldist be war I wisse þe þe *beste*.'
A. 1.83   'Whanne alle tresours arn triȝed treuþe is þe *beste*;
A. 1.124   Whanne alle tresours arn triȝed treuþe is þe *beste*.
A. 1.181   Whan alle tresouris arn triȝede treuþe is þe *beste*.
A. 2.127   Þanne fette fauel folis of þe *beste*,
A. 4.9   For he shal rewele my reaume & rede me þe *beste*
A. 4.27   And riden faste for resoun shulde rede hem þe *beste*
A. 4.74   'God wot,' quaþ wysdom, 'þat were not þe *beste*.
A. 5.136   Þe *beste* in my bedchaumbre lay be þe wouȝ.
A. 7.23   'Be crist,' quaþ a kniȝt þo, 'þou [kenn]ist vs þe *beste*;
A. 7.189   Of beggeris & biddaris what *best* is to done.
A. 7.196   [Now wolde I] wite, ȝif þou wistest, what were þe *beste*,
A. 7.284   Þanne was folk fayn, & fedde hunger with þe *beste*;
A. 7.290   But of þe *beste* & þe brunneste þat breusteris sellen.
A. 8.62   Siþen ȝe sen it is þus sewiþ to þe *beste*.
A.11.154   And seide it hymself in ensaumple for þe *beste*:
B. 1.42   And for þow sholdest ben ywar I wisse þee þe *beste*.'
B. 1.85   'Whan alle tresors arn tried treuþe is þe *beste*;
B. 1.131   And enden, as I er seide, in truþe þat is þe *beste*,
B. 1.135   Whan alle tresors arn tried truþe is þe *beste*.
B. 1.207   Whan alle tresors ben tried treuþe is þe *beste*.
B. 2.163   [Thanne fette Fauel] foles [of þe *beste*],
B. 4.9   For he shal rule my Reaume and rede me þe *beste*
B. 4.30   And riden faste for Reson sholde rede hem þe *beste*
B. 4.87   'God woot', quod wisdom, 'þat were noȝt þe *beste*.
B. 5.220   The *beste* [in my bedchambre] lay [by þe walle],
B. 5.268   For þe *beste* book in oure hous, þeiȝ brent gold were þe leues,
B. 5.291   Bisette it hymself as *best* [be] for þi soule.

B. 5.483   And for þe *beste* as I bileue whateuere þe book telleþ:
B. 6.21   'By crist!' quod a knyȝt þoo, '[þow] kenne[st] vs þe *beste*,
B. 6.203   'Of beggeris and bidderis what *best* be to doone.
B. 6.210   Now wolde I wite, [if þow wistest], what were þe *beste*,
B. 6.300   Thanne was folk fayn and fedde hunger wiþ þe *beste*;
B. 6.306   But of þe *beste* and þe brunneste þat [brewesteres] selle.
B.10.373   Is slee noȝt but suffre and [so] for þe *beste*,
B.10.399   [Ac] at hir mooste meschief [mercy were þe *beste*],
B.11.198   [Ac] for þe *beste* ben som riche and some beggeres and pouere
B.11.257   Preise[n] pouerte for *best* lif if Pacience it folw[e],
B.12.147   But in a Burgeises place, of Bethlem þe *beste*:
B.13.170   Yeue þee al þat þei may yeue, as þee for *beste* yemere;
B.13.289   As *best* for his body be to haue a [bold] name;
B.13.291   Willynge þat men wende his wit were þe *beste*,
B.13.313   'By crist!' quod Conscience þo, 'þi *beste* cote, Haukyn,
B.14.30   And flour to fede folk wiþ as *best* be for þe soule.
B.15.586   And on þat lawe þei l[e]ue and leten it þe *beste*.
B.19.182   And whan þis dede was doon do *best* he [þouȝte],
B.19.433   As brighte as to þe *beste* man or to þe beste womman.
B.19.433   As brighte as to þe beste man or to þe *beste* womman.
B.20.207   'Counseille me, kynde', quod I, 'what craft is *best* to lerne?'
C.Pr.214   But soffre and sey nouȝt; and [so] is þe *beste*
C. 1.81   'When alle tresores ben tried treuthe is þe *beste*;
C. 1.202   "Whenne alle tresores ben tried treuthe is þe *beste*."
C. 3.253   Al þat his men may wynne, do ther[mid] here *beste*.
C. 3.384   For they wilnen and wolden as *beste* were for hemsulue
C. 3.427   Forbar hym and his *beste* bestes, as þe byble wittenesseth,
C. 4.9   For he shal reulen my rewme and rede me the *beste*
C. 4.83   'God woot', quod [wysdom], 'þat were nat the *beste*.
C. 5.38   And what is *beste* for the body, as the boek telleth,
C. 6.41   Wilnynge þat men wen[d]e myne werkes weren þe *beste*
C. 6.228   Þe *beste* ale lay in m[y] bour and in my bed chau[m]bre
C. 6.346   To bysetten hit hymsulue as *beste* be for thy soule.
C. 7.125   And for [þe] *beste*, as y beleue, what[euere] þe boek telle:
C. 8.19   'By Crist' quod a knyhte tho, 'a kenneth vs þe *beste*
C. 8.209   Of beggares and biddares what *beste* be to done.
C. 8.219   Now wolde y wyte, ar thow wendest, what were þe *beste*,
C. 8.328   Bote of the *beste* and þe brouneste þat brewestares sullen.
C.10.190   And ȝut were *best* to ben aboute and brynge hit to hepe
C.11.230   [Ac] at he[re] moste meschef mercy were þe *beste*
C.12.143   Preise[n] pouerte for *best* [lif] if pacience hit folowe
C.12.167   Forsaek al and sue me and so is th[e] *beste*:"
C.14.91   Bote in a burgeises hous], the *beste* of þe toune.
C.15.126   And he þat doth as he techeth y halde hit for þe *beste*:
C.16.21   Ac for þe *beste*, as y hope, aren som pore and ryche.
C.17.297   And on þat lawe they leue and leten hit for þe *beste*.
C.21.433   As brihte as to þe *beste* man or to þe beste womman.
C.21.433   As brihte as to þe beste man or to þe *beste* womman.
C.22.207   'Consaileth me, kynde,' quod y, 'what craft be *beste* to lere?'

best &> ben; beste > beest,best; bestes -is > beest; beswynken > biswynke

best adv *best adv.* A 7 best (6) beste (1); B 8; C 10 best (5) beste (5)
A. 5.24   He bad wastour go werche what he *best* couþe
A. 7.79   He shal haue my soule þat *best* haþ deserued,
A. 7.105   To ouersen hem hymself; whoso *best* wrouȝte
A. 8.26   And bad h[e]m begge boldely what [hem *best*] likeþ,
A.10.95   Ac ȝif þou werchist be godis word I warne þe þe *beste*,
A.11.142   Ac for it lat *best* be loue I loue it þe *beste*
A.11.195   Sire dobest haþ ben [in office], so is he *best* worþi
B. 5.24   He bad wastour go werche what he *best* kouþe
B. 6.87   He shal haue my soule þat *best* haþ deserued,
B. 6.113   To ouersen hem hymself; whoso *best* wrouȝte
B. 7.24   [And bad hem] buggen boldely [what] hem *best* liked
B. 9.99   He dooþ *best* þat wiþdraweþ hym by daye and by nyȝte
B.10.190   Ac for it leteþ *best* bi loue I loue it þe bettre,
B.15.156   Ac charite þat Poul preiseþ *best*, and moost plesaunt to oure [Saueour]–
C. 5.43   That laboure þat y lerned *beste* þerwith lyuen y sholde:
C. 8.120   [To] ouersey hem hymsulue; hoso *beste* wrouhte
C. 8.249   And þat *best* labored best was alloued
C. 8.249   And þat best labored *best* was alloued
C. 9.28   [And] bad hem bugge boldly what hem *best* likede
C. 9.249   A bacheler [o]r a be[au]pere *beste* hym bysemede
C.10.110   Of dowel and dobet and ho doth *best* of alle.'
C.12.105   For vch frende fedeth other and fondeth hou *beste* to quite
C.16.34   Ho doth wel or bet or *beste* aboue alle;
C.21.182   And when this dede was doen do *best* he thouhte

bet &> ben; beste > beest,best; bestes -is > beest; beswynken > biswynke

bet adv *bet adv.& adj.* &> *beten, cf. bettre* A 5; B 3; C 7 bet (6) bette (1)
A.Pr.63   But holy chirche & [hy] holden *bet* togidere
A. 1.127   'Ȝet haue I no kynde knowyng,' quaþ I, '[ȝe mote kenne me *bet*]
A. 7.44   And mysbede nouȝt þi bondemen, þe *bet* shalt þou spede;

A.10.82   For doute men doþ þe *bet*; dred is such a maister
A.11.91   I dar be his bolde boruȝ do *bet* wile he neuere,
B. 5.592   The brugg[e] is of bidde-wel-þe-*bet*-may-þow-spede;
B.11.175   But al for loue of oure lord and þe *bet* to loue þe peple.
B.18.329   Myne þei ben and of me; I may þe *bet* hem cleyme.
C. 5.96   A boute suche a bargayn he was þe *bet* euere
C. 7.240   The Brygge hatte b[id]-wel-the-*bet*-may-th[ow]-spede;
C. 8.42   Misbede nat thy bondeman, the *bette* may th[ow] spede;
C.10.188   Ac thenne dede we alle wel, and wel *bet* ȝut, to louye
C.14.10   And thenne dost thow wel, withoute drede; ho can do *bet* no force.
C.16.34   Ho doth wel or *bet* or beste aboue alle;
C.20.372   Myne they [be] and of me; y may þe *bet* hem clayme.

bete v1 *beten v.(2)* &> *beten* A 1; B 1; C 1 beten
A. 7.221   He shal go [begge & bidde] & no man *bete* his hungir;
B. 6.237   He shal [go] begge and bidde and no man *bete* his hunger.
C. 8.245   And go abribeth and abeggeth and no man *beten* his hungur:

beten v2 *beten v.(1)* &> *bete* A 7 beet (2) bet (2) bete (2) betiþ (1); B 20
    beet (1) bete (10) beten (3) beteþ (2) bette (3) ybet (1); C 20 beet (3)
    bet (2) bete (13) beteth (1) ybete (1)
A. 4.46   And ȝet he betiþ me þerto & liþ be my maiden.
A. 4.80   Þanne bale be *bet* & bote neuere þe betere.'
A. 4.94   And ofte þe boldere be to *bete* myn hynen.
A. 5.218   And *beet* þiself on þe brest & bidde hym of grace,
A. 7.71   His douȝter hattiþ do riȝt [so] or þi damme shal þe *bete*;
A. 7.163   He *beet* hem so boþe he brast ner here mawis.
A.11.133   And *bet* hem wiþ a baleis but ȝif þei wolde lerne.
B. 4.59   And yet he *beteþ* me þerto and lyþ by my mayde.
B. 4.93   Than bale be *ybet* and boote neuer þe betere.'
B. 4.107   And [ofte] þe boldere be to *bete* myne hewen.
B. 5.33   And *bete* Beton þerwith but if she wolde werche.
B. 5.446   And *beet* þiself on þe brest and bidde hym of grace,
B. 6.79   His douȝter hiȝte do-riȝt-so-or-þi-dame-shal-þee-*bete*;
B. 6.178   He *bette* hem so boþe he brast ner hire [mawes].
B.10.181   And *bette* hem wiþ a baleys but if þei wolde lerne.
B.10.323   And *bete* yow, as þe bible telleþ, for brekynge of youre rule,
B.10.326   And Barons wiþ Erles *beten* hem þoruȝ Beatus virres techyng;
B.11.431   [To blame or] to *bete* hym þanne] it were but pure synne.
B.12.12   And wiþ þise bittre baleises god *beteþ* his deere children:
B.14.19   Dobet shal *beten* it and bouken it as bright as any scarlet
B.15.190   And bouken hem at his brest and *beten* hem clene,
B.16.127   And mysseide þe Iewes manliche and manaced hem to *bete*
B.18.95   To do þe blynde *bete* [þe dede], it was a boyes counseille.
B.18.97   To [*bete* a body ybounde wiþ any briȝt wepene].
B.18.253   To breke and to *bete* adoun [alle] þat ben ayeins [hym],
B.20.27   And *bete* men ouer bittre, and so[m body] to litel,
B.20.191   He buffetted me aboute þe mouþ [and *bette* out my wangteeþ]
C.Pr.115   And al was for vengeance he *bet* noght his children
C. 3.238   To berne and to bruttene, to *bete* adoun strenghtes.
C. 4.89   Then bale be *ybete* and boote neuer þe betere.'
C. 4.102   And efte the baldore be to *bete* myn hewes.
C. 5.135   And *bete* Betene þerwith but yf a wolde worche.
C. 5.169   And *bete* ȝow, as þe bible telleth, for brekynge of ȝoure reule
C. 6.141   Byte and *bete* and brynge forth suche thewes
C. 7.60   And *bete* thysulue [o]n þe breste and bidde hym of grace
C. 8.81   His douhter hihte do-rihte-so-or-thy-dame-shal-þe-*bete*;
C. 8.163   'Or y shal *bete* the by the lawe and brynge þe in stokkes.'
C. 8.175   [He] *beet* hem so bothe he barste ner her gottes
C.11.121   And *be[t]* hem with a baleyse bute yf þei wolde lerne.
C.13.238   To blame hym or to *bete* hym thenne y halde hit but synne.
C.16.334   Bouketh hem at his breste and *beteth* h[em] ofte
C.20.98   [To do] þe blynde bete the dede, [hit] was a boyes [conseille].
C.20.100   To beke a body ybounde with eny briht wypene.
C.20.262   To breke and to *bete* adoun all þat ben agaynes hym
C.20.282   That Belial, thy beelsyre, *beet* with thy dame
C.22.27   And *bete* men ouer bitere and som body to litel,
C.22.191   He boffeted me aboute þe mouthe and *beet* out my wangteeth

betene > beton; beter(- > bettre; beth > ben

bethleem n prop *n.i.d.* A 1 bedlem; B 7 Bethleem (4) Bethlem (3); C 4
    Bedlehem (1) bedlem (2) Bethleem (1)
A. 6.15   At *bedlem*, at babiloyne, I haue ben in boþe;
B. 5.527   [At] *Bethlem*, [at] Babiloyne, I haue ben in boþe,
B.12.147   But in a Burgeises place, of *Bethlem* þe beste:
B.12.149   And bad hem go to *Bethlem* goddes burþe to honoure
B.15.510   That bere bisshopes names of *Bethleem* and Babiloigne.
B.17.125   For þe barn was born in *Bethleem* þat with his blood shal saue
B.18.235   That swich a barn was ybore in *Bethleem* þe Citee
B.19.71   Tho he was born in *Bethleem*, as þe book telleþ,
C. 7.172   In *bedlem* and in babiloyne y haue ben in bothe,
C.14.93   And bad hem go to *Bedlem* goddes berthe to honoure
C.20.244   That such a barn was ybore in *Bethleem* þe Citee
C.21.71   Tho he was bore in *Bedlehem*, as þe boek telleth,

betide > bitide; betilbrowid > bitelbrowed

betyng ger *beting ger.* A 1; B 1; C 1 betynge
A.10.85   Þanne is dobet to ben ywar for *betyng* of þe ȝarde,
B.13.147   And but he bowe for þis *betyng* blynd mote he worþe!"
C.15.147   And bote he bowe for this *betynge* blynde mote he worthen.'

beton n prop *cf. OED Betty* A 1 Betoun; B 2; C 2 betene
A. 5.148   And *Betoun* þe breustere bad h[ym] good morewe,
B. 5.33   And bete *Beton* þerwith but if she wolde werche.
B. 5.298   [Ac] *Beton* þe Brewestere bad hym good morwe
C. 5.135   And bete *Betene* þerwith but yf a wolde worche.
C. 6.353   By *betene* hous the brewestere þat bad hym good morwen

betray- > bitraye; betrauaile > bytrauayle; betre > bettre

bette n prop *cf. OED Bartholomew* &> *bet,beten* A 2; B 3; C 3 bette (2)
    butte (1)
A. 2.74   *Bette* þe bedel of bukyngham shire,
A. 5.171   And bed *bette* þe bocher be on his side.
B. 2.110   *Bette* þe Bedel of Bokynghamshire,
B. 5.32   [He] bad *Bette* kutte a bouȝ ouþer tweye
B. 5.322   And bad *Bette* þe Bocher ben on his syde.
C. 2.114   *Butte* þe Bedel of Bannebury sokene.
C. 5.134   He bad *b[e]tte* kutte a bo[u]he or twene
C. 6.379   And bade *b[et]te* þe bochere ben on his side.

bettre adj *bettre adj. cf. bet* A 13 betere; B 27; C 26 betere (6) bettere
    (18) bettre (2)
A. 1.8   Haue þei worsshipe in þis world þei kepe no *betere*:
A. 1.182   Now haue I told þe what treuþe is, þat no tresour is *betere*,
A. 2.10   Icorounid in a coroune, þe king haþ non *betere*,
A. 2.21   I auȝte ben hiȝere þanne heo for I com of a *betere*.
A. 3.118   I[s] not a *betere* baude, be hym þat me made,
A. 4.77   Amende þat mysdede, & eueremore þe *betere*.'
A. 4.79   'Betere is þat boote bale adoun bringe,
A. 4.80   Þanne bale be *bet* & bote neuere þe *betere*.'
A. 4.156   So consience be of ȝour counseil, kepe I no *betere*.'
A. 7.150   Warnide wastour & wisside hym *betere*,
A. 8.121   And consience com aftir & kennide me *betere*.'
A.11.264   And I leue on oure lord & on no lettrure *betere*.
A.12.31   Of þat he wolde wite wis him no *betere*;
B.Pr.191   For *bettre* is a litel los þan a long sorwe.
B. 1.8   Haue þei worship in þis world þei [kepe] no *bettre*;
B. 1.208   Now haue I told þee what truþe is, þat no tresor is *bettre*,
B. 2.10   Ycorouned [in] a coroune, þe kyng haþ noon *bettre*.
B. 2.28   I ouȝte ben hyere þan she; I kam of a *bettre*.
B. 3.129   Is noȝt a *bettre* baude, by hym þat me made,
B. 4.90   Amenden þat [mysdede] and eueremoore þe *bettre*.'
B. 4.92   'Bettre is þat boote bale adoun brynge
B. 4.93   Than bale be *ybet* and boote neuer þe *bettre*.'
B. 4.193   So Conscience be of [y]oure counseil [kepe I] no *bettre*.'
B. 6.165   Warnede wastour and wissed hym *bettre*
B. 7.139   And Conscience cam afte[r] and kenned me [*bettre*].'
B.11.258   And boþe *bettre* and blesseder by many fold þan Richesse.
B.11.382   Ac he suffreþ for som mannes goode, and so is oure *bettre*.
B.12.197   As Seint Iohan and oþer Seintes þat deserued hadde *bettre*.
B.12.274   And þe *bettre* for hir bokes to bidden we ben holden–
B.12.288   But lyueþ as his lawe techeþ and leueþ þer be no *bettre*,
B.12.296   To kepe wiþ a commune; no catel was holde *bettre*,
B.14.60   For if þow lyue after his loore, þe shorter lif þe *bettre*:
B.14.209   Of wit and of wisdom, þat fer awey is *bettre*
B.15.73   *Bettre* it were [by] manye doctours to [bi]leuen swich techyng
B.16.267   And *bettre* wed for us [wage] þan we ben alle worþi,
B.17.175   And ful god as is þe fader, no febler ne no *bettre*.
B.17.332   That sholde brynge in *bettre* wode or blowe it til it brende.
B.18.310   For vs were *bettre* noȝt be þan biden his sighte.
B.20.16   And þouȝ he come so to a clooþ and kan no *bettre* cheuyssaunce
B.20.318   'We han no nede', quod Conscience; 'I woot no *bettre* leche
C. 1.8   Ha[u]e thei worship in this world thei wilneth no *bettere*;
C. 1.136   Tha[n] treuthe and trewe loue is no tresor *bettre*.'
C. 2.11   And crouned [in] a croune, þe kyng haþ non *bettre*;
C. 2.30   Y ouhte ben herrore then he; y com of a *bettre*.
C. 3.166   Is nat a *bettere* baud, by hym þat me made,
C. 4.86   And amende þat is mysdo and eueremore þe *betere*.'
C. 4.88   'Betere is þat bote bale adoun brynge
C. 4.89   Then bale be *ybete* and boote neuer þe *betere*.'
C. 6.243   And len[e] for loue of þe wed the whych y lette *bettere*
C. 6.382   And that the *bettere* thyng, be arbitreres, bote sholde þe worse.
C. 8.162   Warnede wastour and wissede hym *betere*:
C.12.141   Ac pouerte god potte byfore and preuede for þe *betere*:
C.12.144   And bothe *bettere* and blessedere by many fold then richesse.
C.14.136   A[s] seynt Ioh[a]n and oþer seyntes þat haen [de]serued *bettere*.
C.14.210   Bote lyue[th] as his lawe t[echeth] and leueth þer be no *bettere*,
C.15.259   For if thow lyu[e] aftur his lore the shortere lyf þe *betere*:

C.16.50   Of wit and of wisdoem þat fer way is *bettere*
C.16.179 'Thenne is þat body *bettere* þen þou?' quod y. 'Nay,' quod he, 'no bettere,
C.16.179 'Thenne is þat body bettere þen þou?' quod y. 'Nay,' quod he, 'no *bettere*,
C.16.234 To teche þe ten comaundementȝ ten sythe were *bettere*
C.18.86   And thenne aboue is *bettere* fruyt, ac bothe two ben gode,
C.18.283 And *bettere* wed for vs wagen then we ben alle worthy;
C.19.312 That sholde brynge in *bettere* wode or blowen hit til hit brente.
C.20.344 For vs were *bettere* nat be then abyde in his sihte.
C.22.16   And thow he come so to a cloth and can no *bettere* cheuesaunce
C.22.318 'We haen no nede,' quod Consience; 'y woet no *bettere* leche

bettre adv *bettre adv.* A 21 beter (1) betere (20); B 27; C 21 betre (2) betere (2) bettere (13) bettre (4)

A.Pr.31   And somme chosen [hem] to chaffare, þei cheuide þe *betere*
A.Pr.88   Tho[u] miȝtest *betere* mete myst on maluerne hilles
A. 1.32   Dred delitable drynk & þou shalt do þe *betere*
A. 1.133 Þis I trowe be treuþe; who can teche þe *betere*,
A. 5.17   In ensaumple, se[gges], þat ȝe shulde do þe *betere*;
A. 5.36   'And libbe as ȝe lere vs, we wile leue ȝow þe *betere*'.
A. 5.39   And be steward of ȝoure stede til ȝe be stewid *betere*
A. 6.35   Þere is no labourer in his lordsshipe þat he louiþ *beter*
A. 7.138 He abideþ wel þe *betere* þat bummiþ nouȝt to ofte.'
A. 7.210 Wiþ mete or [wiþ] mone let make hem [fare þe *betere*],
A. 8.35   Releue religioun & renten hem *betere*
A. 9.49   Ac ȝif I may lyuen & loken I shal go lerne *betere*.
A. 9.64   'Þat þou wost wel,' quaþ he, '& no wiȝt *betere*.'
A.10.10   Ac kynde knowiþ [þis] wel and kepiþ hire þe *betere*,
A.10.89   Wilne þou neuere in þis world, [wy], for to do *betere*,
A.11.31   For ȝif harlotrie ne halp[e] hem [maken], haue god my trouþe,
A.11.142 Ac for it lat best be loue I loue it þe *betere*,
A.11.165 I bekenne þe crist,' quaþ she, 'I can teche þe no *betere*.'
A.11.206 And seide it in ensaumple þat þei shulde do þe *betere*:
A.11.270 Aristotle & he, who wrouȝte *betere*?
A.12.3   And whoso coueyteþ don *betere* þan þe boke telleþ,
B.Pr.31   And somme chosen [hem to] chaffare; þei cheueden þe *bettre*,
B.Pr.66   But holy chirche and hij holde *bettre* togidres
B.Pr.215 Thow myȝtest *bettre* meete myst on Maluerne hilles
B. 1.34   Forþi dred delitable drynke and þow shalt do þe *bettre*;
B. 1.138 'Yet haue I no kynde knowyng', quod I, 'ye mote kenne me *bettre*
B. 1.145 This I trowe be truþe; who kan teche þee *bettre*,
B. 3.272 Spille it and spare it noȝt, þow shalt spede þe *bettre*."
B. 5.17   In ensample, [segges, þat ye] sholden do þe *bettre*;
B. 5.44   [Lyue] as ye leren vs; we shul leue yow þe *bettre*.'
B. 5.47   And be Stywar[d] of youre sted[e] til ye be [stewed] *bettre*'.
B. 5.234 Thow haddest be *bettre* worþi ben hanged þerfore.'
B. 5.418 *Bettre* þan in Beatus vir or in Beati omnes
B. 6.45   And mysbede noȝt þi bondem[a]n, þe *bettre* [shalt] þow spede;
B. 6.224 Wiþ mete or wiþ mone lat make hem fare þe *bettre*].
B. 7.33   Releue Religion and renten hem *bettre*
B. 8.58   Ac if I may lyue and loke I shal go lerne *bettre*.'
B. 8.73   'That þow woost wel', quod he, 'and no wiȝt *bettre*.'
B. 9.10   Ac kynde knoweþ þis wel and kepeþ hire þe *bettre*,
B. 9.98   And [dredeþ hym] noȝt for drede of vengeaunce dooþ þerfore þe *bettre*;
B.10.190 Ac for it leteþ best bi loue I loue it þe *bettre*,
B.10.383 I leue it wel by oure lord and on no lettrure *bettre*.
B.10.388 Aristotle and he, who wissed men *bettre*?
B.11.254 Ac pouerte god putte bifore and preised þe *bettre*:
B.11.387 Forþi I rede', quod reson, '[þow] rule þi tonge *bettre*,
B.13.52   'Here is propre seruice', quod Pacience, 'þer fareþ no Prince *bettre*.'
B.15.426 The *bettre* for hir biddynges in body and in soule.
B.16.231 First he fonded me if I, [feiþ], louede *bettre*
C.Pr.33   And summe chesen chaffare; þei cheue[den] þe *bettre*
C.Pr.120 And ȝe shulde be here fadres and techen hem *betre*
C.Pr.165 Thow myghtest *betre* meten myst on maluerne hulles
C. 1.137 'I haue no kynde knowyng,' quod y, '[ȝe mot] kenne me *bettere*
C. 1.144 And this y trowe be treuth; [ho] kan tecche þe *bettere*
C. 3.425 Spille hit, spare hit nat and thow shalt spede th[e] *bettere*."
C. 5.119 In ensau[m]ple, seggus, þat we sholde do þe *bettere*;
C. 5.142 Lyue as ȝe lereth vs; we shall leue ȝow þe *bettere*.'
C. 5.145 And be stewar[d] of ȝoure stedes til ȝe be stewed *bettere*.'
C. 7.276 Noen of hem alle helpe may in *betere*
C. 9.36   Releue Religion and renten hem *bettere*.
C.10.57   Ac yf y may lyue and loke y shal go lerne *bettere*.'
C.10.71   'That þou [wost] w[el],' quod he, 'and no wyht *bettere*.'
C.10.137 A[c] kynde knoweth this wel and kepeth here þe *betere*
C.11.130 Ac for hit lereth men to louie y beleue þeron þ[e] *bettere*
C.11.208 Y leue hit wel by oure lord and on no lettrure *bettere*.
C.11.214 Aristotel and he, ho tauhte men *bettere*?
C.14.11   Clerkes þat conne al, y hope they can do *bettere*;
C.14.196 And þe *bettere* for here bokes to bidden we ben yholde–
C.15.123 'Y haue yseide,' quod þat segg, 'y can sey no *bettere*.'

C.17.122 Ac ȝif prestes doen here deuer wel we shal do þe *bettre*

betwene betwyn > bitwene; beþ > ben

beuerages n *beverage n.* A 1 beuerechis; B 1; C 1 Beuereges
A. 5.186 Bargoynes & *beuerechis* begonne for to arise,
B. 5.337 [Bargaynes and *beuerages* bigonne to arise],
C. 6.395 Bargaynes and *Beuereges* bygan to a[rys]e

beȝende beȝonde > biyonde

by prep *by prep.* &> by_so A 133 be (121) by (12); B 368 bi (44) by (324); C 352 be (27) bi (32) by (293)
A.Pr.8   Vndir a brood bank *be* a bourn[e] side,
A.Pr.77   It is not *be* þe bisshop þat þe boy prechiþ,
A.Pr.94   Ben ylope to lundoun *be* loue of hire bisshop,
A. 1.28   Dede he his douȝter[n] þat þe deuil lykide,
A. 1.30   And leccherie h[i]m lauȝte & lay *be* hem boþe;
A. 1.88   He is a god *be* þe gospel on ground & on lofte,
A. 1.89   And ek lyk to oure lord *be* seint lukis wordis.
A. 1.92   Kinges & kniȝtes shulde kepe it *be* resoun,
A. 1.123 Forþi I seye as I seide er, *be* siȝte of þise textis:
A. 1.128 *Be* what craft in my cors it compsiþ, & where.'
A. 1.180 Forþi I seiȝe as I seide er, *be* siȝte of þise tixtes:
A. 2.4   Kenne me *be* sum craft to k[now]e þe false'.
A. 2.36   Þat fals & fauel *be* any fyn halden,
A. 2.78   *Be* siȝte of sire symonye & signes of notories.
A. 2.89   For al *be* lesinges þou lyuest, & leccherous werkis;
A. 2.92   Ȝe shuln abigge boþe, *be* god þat me made.
A. 2.98   Werchiþ *be* wysdom & *be* wyt aftir;
A. 2.98   Werchiþ *be* wysdom & *be* wyt aftir;
A. 2.133 Þanne swor cyuyle & seide *be* þe rode
A. 2.154 '*Be* crist,' quaþ þe king, '& I miȝte cacche
A. 2.157 And do hem hange *be* þe hals & alle þat hem maynteniþ,
A. 3.7   And ȝif heo werche *be* wyt & my wil folewe
A. 3.10   Tok mede *be* þe myddel & brouȝte hire to chaumbre.
A. 3.15   Counforti[de] hire kyndely *be* clergie[s] leue,
A. 3.37   'Þeiȝ lerid & lewide hadde leiȝe *be* ichone,
A. 3.118 I[s] not a betere baude, *be* hym þat me made,
A. 3.129 He[o] takiþ þe trewe *be* þe top, teiȝeþ hym faste,
A. 3.145 *Be* Iesu, wiþ hire Iuelx ȝoure Iustice she shendiþ,
A. 3.188 Hadde I be march[al] of his men, *be* marie of heuene,
A. 3.215 Quaþ þe king to consience, '*be* crist, as me þinkiþ,
A. 3.218 'Þere arn a maner of medis, my lord, *be* ȝour leue.
A. 3.240 God sente hym to segge *be* samuels mouþ
A. 4.4   'Nay *be* [Crist],' quaþ consience, 'cunge me raþere!
A. 4.29   Ac consience com arst to court *be* a myle wey
A. 4.46   And ȝet he betiþ me þerto & liþ *be* my maiden.
A. 4.56   'Whoso werchiþ *be* wil wraþþe makiþ ofte.
A. 4.57   I sey it *be* myself, þou shalt it sone fynde,
A. 4.70   Þe king swor *be* crist & *be* his croune boþe
A. 4.70   Þe king swor be crist & *be* his croune boþe
A. 4.117 And ȝet,' quaþ resoun, '*be* þe rode, I shal no reuþe haue
A. 4.120 For I seiȝe it *be* myself, & it so were
A. 4.144 Þe king acordite, *be* crist, to resonis sawis
A. 4.146 'Ac it is wel hard, *be* myn hed, herto to bringe it.
A. 4.148 '*Be* hym þat [rauȝte] on þe rode,' quaþ resoun to þe king,
A. 4.151 'And I assente,' quaþ þe king, '*be* seinte marie my lady,
A. 5.62   A kertil & a courtepy, a knyf *be* his side,
A. 5.75   To apeire hym *be* my power I pursuide wel ofte,
A. 5.131 Þe pound þat heo [payede] *by* peisid a quarter more
A. 5.135 For laboureris & louȝ folk þat lay *be* h[y]mselue;
A. 5.136 Þe beste in my bedchaumbre lay *be* þe wouȝ.
A. 5.166 Of vpholderis an hep, erliche *be* þe morewe,
A. 5.175 And preisiden þe penewortis [aparte] *be* hemseluen.
A. 5.177 Þei couþe [not] *be* here consience acorden togidere
A. 5.231 And wiþ þe residue & þe remenaunt, *be* þe roode of chestre,
A. 5.250 For he hadde leiȝe *be* latro luciferis [aunte].
A. 6.7   A bagge & a bolle he bar *be* his side,
A. 6.12   And sen *be* his signes whom he souȝt hadde.
A. 6.17   Ȝe mowe se *be* my signes þat sitten on myn hat
A. 6.44   'Nay, *be* þe peril of my soule!' quaþ piers & gan to swere:
A. 6.53   And so bo[wiþ] forþ *be* a [brok], be buxum of speche,
A. 6.59   Þanne shalt þou come *be* a croft, ac come þou nouȝt þereinne,
A. 6.64   Þei hote stele nouȝt, ne sle nouȝt; strik forþ *be* boþe.
A. 6.102 Þus miȝt þou lese his loue, to lete wel *be* þiselue,
A. 6.113 It is wel hard, *be* myn hed, any of ȝow alle,
A. 6.115 '*Be* crist,' quaþ a cuttepurs, 'I haue no kyn þere.'
A. 6.116 'Ne I,' quaþ an apeward, '*be* auȝt þat I knowe.'
A. 6.123 Þou miȝt gete grace [here] so þou go *be* tyme.'
A. 7.3   Quaþ perkyn þe plouȝman, '*be* seint poule þe apostel,
A. 7.4   I haue an half akir to er[e]n *be* þe heiȝe weiȝe,
A. 7.21   And alle maner of men þat *be* þe mete libbiþ,
A. 7.23   '*Be* crist,' quaþ a kniȝt þo, 'þou [kenn]ist vs þe beste;

A. 7.26	'Be seint poule,' quaþ perkyn, 'for þou profrist þe so lowe
A. 7.36	'Be my power, piers, I pliȝte þe my treuþe
A. 7.50	'I assente, be seint Iame,' seide þe kniȝt þanne,
A. 7.51	'For to werche be þi woord while my lif duriþ.'
A. 7.60	Shal haue be oure lord þe more here in heruist,
A. 7.92	And wiþ þe residue & þe remenaunt, be þe rode of chestre,
A. 7.109	'Be þe prince of paradis!' quaþ piers þo in wraþþe,
A. 7.151	'Or þou shalt abigge be þe lawe, be þe ordre þat I bere'.
A. 7.151	'Or þou shalt abigge be þe lawe, be þe ordre þat I bere'.
A. 7.156	'Now be þe peril of my soule!' quaþ peris, 'I shal appeire ȝow alle,'
A. 7.159	Hungir in haste þanne hente wastour be þe mawe,
A. 7.160	And wrong hym so be þe wombe þat al watride his eiȝen,
A. 7.170	Þei hadde be ded be þis day & doluen al warm.
A. 7.178	[Þat leyȝe [blereyed] and brokelegged by þe hye waye];
A. 7.255	And be fayn be my feiþ his fesik to leten,
A. 7.259	'Be seint pernel,' quaþ peris, 'þise arn profitable wordis.
A. 7.263	Er I haue dyned be þis day & ydronke boþe.'
A. 7.268	And I seiȝe, be my soule, I haue no salt bacoun,
A. 7.269	Ne no cokenay, be crist, colopis to maken.
A. 7.273	Be þis liflode I mote lyue til lammasse tyme;
A. 7.274	Be þat I hope to haue heruest in my croft,
A. 7.283	Be þat it neiȝide ner heruest [þat] newe corn com to chepyng.
A. 8.23	And for þei swere be here soule, & so god muste hem helpe,
A. 8.63	Alle libbyng laboureris þat lyuen be here hondis,
A. 8.109	Be þat þe sauter vs seiþ, & so dede manye oþere.
A. 8.112	[By foules, þat are not] besy aboute þe bely ioye:
A. 8.114	And shewiþ it vs be ensaumple oureselue to wisse.
A. 8.152	And how þe prest inpugnid it al be [pu]re resoun,
A. 8.174	What þou dedist day [by day] þe dom wile reherce.
A. 9.24	Be a forebisene,' quaþ þe Frere, 'I shal þe faire shewen:
A. 9.33	Riȝt þus [it] fariþ,' quaþ þe Frere, 'be folk here on erþe.
A. 9.54	[And] as I wente be a wode, walkyng myn one,
A. 9.62	Com & callide me be my kynde name.
A. 9.98	Corounid on to be kyng & be h[ere] counseil werchen,
A. 9.99	And rewele þe reaum be red of hem alle,
A.10.18	And haþ fyue faire sones be his furste wyf:
A.10.91	Be counseil of consience, accordyng holy chirche,
A.10.95	Ac ȝif þou werchist be godis word I warne þe þe beste,
A.10.105	And riȝt so be romberis þat rennen aboute
A.10.157	Forþi he sente to se[þ], & se[i]de hym be an aungel
A.10.173	Alle shuln deiȝe for his dedis be dounes & hilles,
A.10.186	It is an vncomely copil, be crist, as [me þinkeþ],
A.11.13	I say be þo,' quaþ she, 'þat shewen be here werkis
A.11.13	I say be þo,' quaþ she, 'þat shewen be here werkis
A.11.29	Litel is he louid or lete by þat suche a lessoun techiþ,
A.11.116	And rid forþ be ricchesse, ac reste þou not þereinne,
A.11.142	Ac for it lat best be loue I loue it þe betere,
A.11.196	Be þat god in þe gospel grauntiþ & techiþ;
A.11.209	Riȝt so be religioun, it roileþ & steruiþ
A.11.211	Ac now is religioun a ridere & a rennere [be stretis],
A.11.214	A bidowe or a baselard he beriþ be his side,
A.11.232	'Contra,' quaþ I, 'be crist! þat can I be wi[þsigg]e,
A.11.233	And prouen it be þe pistil þat petir is nempnid:
A.11.275	And be here werkis & here wordis wissen vs to dowel,
A.11.276	And ȝif I shal werke be here werkis to wynne me heuene,
A.12.32	For he cam nouȝt by cause to lerne to dowel
A.12.108	By Iames and by Ierom, by Iop and by oþere,
A.12.108	By Iames and by Ierom, by Iop and by oþere,
A.12.108	By Iames and by Ierom, by Iop and by oþere,
A.12.108	By Iames and by Ierom, by Iop and by oþere,
A.12.115	God saue hem sound by se and by land.
A.12.115	God saue hem sound by se and by land.
B.Pr.8	Vnder a brood bank by a bourn[e] syde,
B.Pr.52	Moore to seye sooþ, it semed bi hire speche.
B.Pr.80	It is noȝt by þe bisshop þat þe boy precheþ;
B.Pr.165	Were þer a belle on hire beiȝe, by Iesu, as me þynkeþ,
B.Pr.197	For may no renk þer reste haue for Ratons by nyȝte,]
B.Pr.203	Shal neuere þe cat ne no kiton by my counseil be greued,
B.Pr.210	Deuyne ye, for I ne dar, by deere god in heuene.
B. 1.22	And rekene hem by reson: reherce þow hem after.
B. 1.28	Dide by hise douȝtres þat þe deuel liked;
B. 1.30	And Leccherie hym lauȝte, and lay by hem boþe;
B. 1.90	He is a god by þe gospel, a grounde and o lofte,
B. 1.91	And [ek] ylik to oure lord by Seint Lukes wordes.
B. 1.94	Kynges and knyȝtes sholde kepen it by reson,
B. 1.134	Forþi I seye, as I seyde er, by siȝte of þise textes:
B. 1.139	By what craft in my cors it comseþ, and where.'
B. 1.163	And for to knowen it kyndely, it comseþ by myght,
B. 1.206	Forþi I seye as I seide er by [siȝte of þise] textes:
B. 2.4	Kenne me by som craft to knowe þe false.'
B. 2.79	And Fauel wiþ his fikel speche feffeþ by þis chartre
B. 2.114	By siȝte of sire Symonie and Cyuyles leeue.'
B. 2.125	For al bi lesynges þow lyuest and lecherouse werkes;

B. 2.128	Ye shul abiggen boþe, by god þat me made!
B. 2.134	Wercheþ by wisdom and by wit [after];
B. 2.134	Wercheþ by wisdom and by wit [after];
B. 2.193	'By crist!' quod þe kyng, 'and I cacche myȝte
B. 2.196	And doon hem hange by þe hals and alle þat hem maynteneþ.
B. 3.7	And if she werche bi wit and my wil folwe
B. 3.10	Took Mede bi þe myddel and broȝte hire into chambre.
B. 3.15	Conforte[d] hire kyndely by clergies leue,
B. 3.38	'Theiȝ [lered and lewed] hadde leyen by þee [echone],
B. 3.100	Yiftes or yeresyeues bycause of hire Offices.
B. 3.129	Is noȝt a bettre baude, by hym þat me made,
B. 3.140	[She] takeþ þe trewe bi þe top, tieþ h[y]m faste,
B. 3.155	By Iesus! wiþ hire Ieweles youre Iustices she shendeþ
B. 3.201	Hadde I ben Marchal of his men, by Marie of heuene!
B. 3.228	Quod þe kyng to Conscience, 'by crist, as me þynkeþ,
B. 3.231	'Ther are two manere of Medes, my lord, [bi] youre leue.
B. 3.261	God sente to Saul by Samuel þe prophete
B. 3.326	By sixe sonnes and a ship and half a shef of Arwes;
B. 3.353	The soule þat þe soude takeþ by so muche is bounde.'
B. 4.4	'Nay, by crist!' quod Conscience; 'congeye me [raþer]!
B. 4.40	Forþi, Reson, lat hem ride þo riche by hemselue,
B. 4.59	And yet he beteþ me þerto and lyþ by my mayde.
B. 4.70	'Whoso wercheþ by wille wraþe makeþ ofte.
B. 4.71	I seye it by myself, þow shalt it wel fynde,
B. 4.83	The kyng swor by crist and by his crowne boþe
B. 4.83	The kyng swor by crist and by his crowne boþe
B. 4.134	And yet', quod Reson, 'by þe Rode! I shal no ruþe haue
B. 4.137	I seye it by myself and it so were
B. 4.178	And deme yow, bi þis day, as ye han deserued.
B. 4.179	Mede shal noȝt maynprise yow, by þe marie of heuene!
B. 4.183	It is [wel] hard, by myn heed, hert[o] to brynge it,
B. 4.185	'By hym þat rauȝte on þe Rode!' quod Reson to þe kynge,
B. 4.188	'And I assente', seiþ þe kyng, 'by Seinte Marie my lady,
B. 5.79	[A] kirtel and [a] Courtepy, a knyf by his syde,
B. 5.91	I wolde be gladder, by god! þat Gybbe hadde meschaunce
B. 5.95	To apeire hym bi my power pursued wel ofte,
B. 5.150	Til þei be boþe beggers and by my spiritualte libben,
B. 5.165	Hadde þei had knyues, by crist! eiþer hadde kild ooþer.
B. 5.180	Al þe wikkednesse þat I woot by any of oure breþeren,
B. 5.183	Counseil þat þow knowest by contenaunce ne by [speche];
B. 5.183	Counseil þat þow knowest by contenaunce ne by [speche];
B. 5.215	[Th]e pound þat she paied by peised a quartron moore
B. 5.219	For laborers and lowe folk þat lay by hymselue.
B. 5.220	The beste [in my bedchambre] lay [by þe walle],
B. 5.249	And took it by tale here and tolde hem þere lasse.'
B. 5.317	[Of] vpholderes an heep, erly by þe morwe,
B. 5.326	And preised þ[e] penyworþes apart by hemselue.
B. 5.328	Thei couþe noȝt, by hir Conscience, acorden [togideres]
B. 5.351	Clement þe Cobelere kauȝte hym by þe myddel
B. 5.393	'If I sholde deye bi þis day [I drede me sore].
B. 5.440	And euere siþþe be beggere [by cause of my] sleuþe:
B. 5.459	And wiþ þe residue and þe remenaunt, by þe Rode of Chestre,
B. 5.476	For he hadde leyen by Latro, luciferis Aunte.
B. 5.501	And by so muche [it] semeþ þe sikerer we mowe
B. 5.519	A bolle and a bagge he bar by his syde.
B. 5.524	And se bi hise signes whom he souȝt hadde.
B. 5.529	Ye may se by my signes þat sitten on myn hatte
B. 5.557	'Nay, by [þe peril of] my soul[e]!' quod Piers and gan to swere:
B. 5.566	And so boweþ forþ by a brook, beþ-buxom-of-speche.
B. 5.572	Thanne shaltow come by a croft, [ac] come þow noȝt þerInne;
B. 5.577	Thei hiȝte Stele-noȝt-[ne]-Sle-noȝt; strik forþ by boþe.
B. 5.616	Thus myȝtestow lesen his loue, to lete wel by þiselue,
B. 5.628	It is [wel] hard, by myn heed, any of yow alle
B. 5.630	'By Crist!' quod a kuttepurs, 'I haue no kyn þere.'
B. 5.631	'Nor I', quod an Apeward, 'by auȝt þat I knowe.'
B. 5.639	'Bi seint Poul!' quod a pardoner, 'parauenture I be noȝt knowe þere;
B. 5.641	'By crist!' quod a comune womman, 'þi compaignie wol I folwe.
B. 6.3	Quod Perkyn þe Plowman, 'by Seint Peter of Rome!
B. 6.4	I haue an half acre to erie by þe heiȝe weye;
B. 6.19	And alle manere of men þat [by þe] mete libbeþ,
B. 6.21	'By crist!' quod a knyȝt þoo, '[þow] kenne[st] vs þe beste,
B. 6.24	'By Seint Poul!' quod Perkyn, '[for þow profrest þee so lowe]
B. 6.34	'By my power, Piers, I pliȝte þee my trouþe
B. 6.55	'I assente, by Seint Iame', seide þe knyȝt þanne,
B. 6.56	'For to werche by þi wor[d] while my lif dureþ.
B. 6.66	Shal haue leue, by oure lord, to lese here in heruest
B. 6.100	And wiþ þe residue and þe remenaunt, by þe Rode of Lukes!
B. 6.101	I wol worshipe þerwiþ truþe by my lyue,
B. 6.117	'Now by þe peril of my soule!' quod Piers al in pure tene,
B. 6.166	'Or þow shalt abigge by þe lawe, by þe ordre þat I bere!'
B. 6.166	'Or þow shalt abigge by þe lawe, by þe ordre þat I bere!'
B. 6.171	'Now by þe peril of my soule!' quod Piers, 'I shal apeire yow alle',
B. 6.174	Hunger in haste þoo hente wastour by þe [mawe]

B. 6.175 And wrong hym so *by* þe wombe þat [al watrede his eiȝen].
B. 6.252 He is blessed *by* þe book in body and in soule:
B. 6.271 And be fayn, *by* my feiþ, his Phisik to lete,
B. 6.275 'By Seint [Pernele]', quod Piers, 'þise arn profitable wordes!
B. 6.279 [Er] I haue dyned *bi* þis day and ydronke boþe.'
B. 6.284 And yet I seye, *by* my soule! I haue no salt bacon
B. 6.285 Ne no cokeney, *by* crist! coloppes to maken.
B. 6.289 *By* þis liflode [I moot] lyue til lammesse tyme,
B. 6.290 *By* þat I hope to haue heruest in my crofte;
B. 6.299 *By* þat it neȝed neer heruest newe corn cam to chepyng.
B. 6.328 And a mayde haue þe maistrie, and multiplie *by* eiȝte,
B. 7.21 And for þei swere *by* hir soule and so god moste hem helpe
B. 7.61 Alle libbynge laborers þat lyuen [*by*] hir hondes,
B. 7.127 *By* þat þe Sauter [vs] seith, [and] so dide othere manye.
B. 7.130 *By* foweles [þat are] noȝt bisy aboute þe [bely ioye];
B. 7.132 And sheweþ vs *by* ensampl[e] vs selue to wisse.
B. 7.196 [What] þow didest day *by* day þe doom wole reherce.
B. 8.28 *By* a forbisne', quod þe frere, 'I shal þee faire shewe.
B. 8.37 [Riȝt] þus it [fareþ]', quod þe frere, '*by* folk here on erþe.
B. 8.63 And as I wente *by* a wode, walkyng myn one],
B. 8.71 Cam and called me *by* my kynde name.
B. 8.108 Crouned oon to be kyng, [and *by* hir counseil werchen],
B. 8.109 And rule þe Reme *by* [rede of hem alle],
B. 9.16 [*By* his leryng is lad þat lady Anima].
B. 9.19 And haþ fyue faire sones *bi* his firste wyue:
B. 9.42 And so it semeþ *by* hym [þere he seide in þe bible
B. 9.99 He dooþ best þat wiþdraweþ hym *by* daye and by nyȝte
B. 9.99 He dooþ best þat wiþdraweþ hym *by* daye and *by* nyȝte
B. 9.117 First *by* þe fadres wille and þe frendes conseille,
B. 9.118 And siþenes *by* assent of hemself as þei two myȝte acorde;
B. 9.127 [For] god sente to Se[þ] and seide *by* an Aungel,
B. 9.142 Alle shul deye for hise dedes *by* [dounes] and hulles,
B. 9.165 It is an vncomly couple, *by* crist! as me þynkeþ,
B. 10.13 I seye *by* [þo]', quod she, 'þat sheweþ by hir werkes
B. 10.13 I seye by [þo]', quod she, 'þat sheweþ *by* hir werkes
B. 10.26 The Sauter seiþ þe same *by* swiche þat doon ille:
B. 10.37 Litel is he loued [or lete *by*] þat swich a lesson [techeþ],
B. 10.81 And yet þe wrecches of þis world is noon ywar *by* ooþer,
B. 10.99 Now haþ ech riche a rule to eten *by* hymselue
B. 10.113 "Of þat [ye] clerkes vs kenneþ of crist *by* þe gospel:
B. 10.164 And ryd forþ *by* richesse, ac rest þow noȝt þerInne,
B. 10.190 Ac for it leteþ best *bi* loue I loue it þe bettre,
B. 10.258 Al þat þe book bit *bi* holi cherches techyng;
B. 10.259 And þat is, man, *bi* þy myȝt, for mercies sake,
B. 10.262 And lat no body be *by* þi beryng bigiled
B. 10.274 Alle maner men to amenden *bi* hire myȝtes;
B. 10.303 Riȝt so [*by*] religion, [it] ro[i]leþ [and] stereþ
B. 10.306 It is in cloistre or in scole, *by* manye skiles I fynde.
B. 10.311 Ac now is Religion a rydere, a [rennere *by* stretes],
B. 10.347 That þei han Eritage in heuene, and *by* trewe riȝte,
B. 10.349 'Contra!' quod I, '*by* crist! þat kan I [wiþseye],
B. 10.350 And preuen it *by* [þe pistel þat Peter is nempned]:
B. 10.383 I leue it wel *by* oure lord and on no lettrure bettre.
B. 10.392 And if I sh[al] werche *by* hir werkes to wynne me heuene,
B. 10.411 God lene it fare noȝt so *bi* folk þat þe feiþ techeþ
B. 10.441 And be allowed as he lyued so; for *by* luþere men knoweþ þe
                goode.
B. 10.455 And myȝte no kyng ouercomen hym as *by* konnynge of speche.
B. 11.2 And lakked me in latyn and liȝt *by* me sette,
B. 11.28 'Man', quod he, 'if I mete wiþ þe, *by* Marie of heuene!
B. 11.58 And preien for þee pol *by* pol if þow be pecuniosus.'
B. 11.59 *By* wissynge of þis wenche I [dide], hir wordes were so swete,
B. 11.67 [At kirke] þere a man were cristned *by* kynde he sholde be buryed.
B. 11.71 '*By* my feiþ! frere', quod I, 'ye faren lik þise woweris
B. 11.73 Riȝt so, *by* þe roode! rouȝte ye neuere
B. 11.87 'ȝis, by Peter and *by* Poul!' quod he and took hem boþe to witnesse:
B. 11.87 'ȝis, by Peter and *by* Poul!' quod he and took hem boþe to witnesse:
B. 11.89 'They wole aleggen also', quod I, 'and *by* þe gospel preuen:
B. 11.124 *By* þe blood þat he bouȝte vs wiþ, and þoruȝ bapteme after:
B. 11.135 But if Contricion wol come and crye *by* his lyue
B. 11.152 *By* loue and by lernyng of my lyuynge in truþe,
B. 11.152 By loue and *by* lernyng of my lyuynge in truþe;
B. 11.154 Lo! ye lordes, what leautee dide *by* an Emperour of Rome
B. 11.188 To knowen vs *by* oure kynde herte and castynge of oure eiȝen,
B. 11.190 And exciteþ vs *by* þe Euuangelie þat, whan we maken festes,
B. 11.238 So *bi* hise werkes þei wisten þat he was Iesus,
B. 11.239 Ac *by* cloþyng þei knewe hym noȝt, [so caitifliche he yede].
B. 11.256 And alle þe wise þat euere were, *by* auȝt I kan aspye,
B. 11.258 And boþe bettre and blesseder *by* many fold þan Richesse.
B. 11.290 And þe title þat ye take ordres *by* telleþ ye ben auaunced:
B. 11.298 The same I segge for soþe *by* alle swiche preestes
B. 11.307 So is it a goky, *by* god! þat in his gospel failleþ,
B. 11.322 And nempned me *by* my name and bad me nymen hede,

B. 11.325 I was fet forþ *by* [forbisenes] to knowe
B. 11.328 And where þat briddes and beestes *by* hir mak[e þei] yeden,
B. 11.339 Males drowen hem to males [al mornyng] *by* hemselue,
B. 11.420 And riȝt so ferde Reson *bi* þee; þow wiþ rude speche
B. 12.2 Thouȝ I sitte *by* myself in siknesse n[e] in helþe.
B. 12.95 For boþe ben as Mirours to amenden [*by*] defautes
B. 12.122 Ne sette short *bi* hir science, whatso þei don hemselue.
B. 12.129 Of briddes and of beestes, [*by*] tastes of truþe.
B. 12.134 Ne broȝt *by* hir bokes to blisse ne to ioye,
B. 12.201 But as a beggere bordlees *by* myself on þe grounde.
B. 12.202 So it fareþ *by* þat felon þat a good friday was saued;
B. 12.205 But *by* mannysh as a soleyn and serued on [þe] erþe.
B. 12.211 That oure lord ne hadde hym liȝtly out, so leue I [*by*] þe þef in
                heuene.
B. 12.213 And wel lose[l]y he lolleþ þere *by* þe lawe of holy chirche:
B. 12.217 And so I seye *by* þee sekest after þe whyes
B. 12.236 Ac of briddes and of beestes men *by* olde tyme
B. 12.259 *By* þe po feet is vnderstande, as I haue lerned in Auynet,
B. 12.263 So is þe riche [reuerenced] *by* reson of hise goodes.
B. 12.266 And of flessh *by* fele fold fatter and swettter;
B. 13.36 And seten *bi* oureselue at [a] side borde.
B. 13.91 And preuen it *by* hir Pocalips and passion of Seint Auereys
B. 13.105 'Do noon yuel to þyn euencristen, nouȝt *by* þi power.'
B. 13.116 '*By* þis day, sire doctour', quod I, 'þanne [in dowel be ye noȝt]!
B. 13.158 For, *by* hym þat me made, myȝte neuere pouerte,
B. 13.188 'Nay, *by* crist!' quod Conscience to Clergie, 'god þee foryelde;
B. 13.200 'Me were leuere, *by* oure lord, and I lyue sholde,
B. 13.220 And as þe[i] wente *by* þe weye–of dowel þei carped–
B. 13.271 I took [greet] kepe, *by* crist! and Conscience boþe,
B. 13.282 And so singuler *by* hymself [as to siȝte of þe peple
B. 13.284 Yhabited as an heremyte, an ordre *by* hymselue,
B. 13.313 '*By* crist!' quod Conscience þo, 'þi beste cote, Haukyn,
B. 13.316 What on bak, and what on body half, and *by* þe two sides
B. 13.319 It was fouler *bi* fele fold þan it first semed.
B. 13.323 Al þat he wiste wikked *by* any wight tellen it,
B. 13.325 And he wiste *by* wille [to watte tellen it],
B. 13.326 And þat [*by*] watte [he] wiste wille wiste it after,
B. 13.343 Wiþ likynge of lecherie as *by* lokynge of his eiȝe.
B. 13.366 And but I hadde *by* ooþer wey at þe laste I stale it,
B. 13.368 Or *by* nyȝte or by daye aboute was ich euere
B. 13.368 Or by nyȝte or *by* daye aboute was ich euere
B. 13.451 That *bi* his lyue liþed hem and loued hem to here.
B. 14.8 To agulte god or good man *by* aught þat I wiste,
B. 14.12 And kouþe I neuere, *by* crist! kepen it clene an houre
B. 14.26 Than Haukyn þe Actif man, and þow do *by* my techyng,
B. 14.35 'Whoso leueþ yow, *by* oure lord! I leue noȝt he be blessed.'
B. 14.43 The Corlew *by* kynde of þe Eyr, moost clennest flessh of briddes,
B. 14.44 And bestes *by* gras and by greyn and by grene rootes,
B. 14.44 And bestes by gras and *by* greyn and by grene rootes,
B. 14.44 And bestes by gras and by greyn and *by* grene rootes,
B. 14.109 Ther þe poore dar plede and preue *by* pure reson
B. 14.110 To haue allowaunce of his lord; *by* þe lawe he it cleymeþ.
B. 14.126 Ac god is of [a] wonder wille, *by* þat kynde wit sheweþ,
B. 14.128 Riȝt so fareþ god *by* som riche; ruþe me it þynkeþ,
B. 14.140 So I seye *by* yow riche, it semeþ noȝt þat ye shulle
B. 14.155 Ac it is but selde yseien, as *by* holy seintes bokes,
B. 14.207 [Ac] þe riche is reuerenced *by* reson of his richesse
B. 14.240 And *by* þe nekke namely hir noon may hente ooþer;
B. 14.269 As *by* assent of sondry parties and siluer to boote,
B. 14.271 So it [preueþ] *by* ech a persone þat possession forsakeþ
B. 14.281 Thanne is it good *by* good skile, al þat agasteþ pride.
B. 15.46 And of [myne] if þow myȝtest, me þynkeþ *by* it speche.'
B. 15.73 Bettre it were [*by*] manye doctours to [bi]leuen swich techyng
B. 15.96 [And] se it *by* ensaumple in somer tyme on trowes:
B. 15.144 *By* lered, by lewed, þat loob is to [s]pende
B. 15.144 By lered, *by* lewed, þat loob is to [s]pende
B. 15.163 And so I trowe trewely, *by* þat men telleþ of [it,
B. 15.195 '*By* crist! I wolde I knewe hym', quod I, 'no creature leuere.'
B. 15.198 'Clerkes haue no knowyng', quod he, 'but *by* werkes and wordes.
B. 15.209 Therfore *by* colour ne by clergie knowe shaltow [hym] neuere,
B. 15.209 Therfore by colour ne *by* clergie knowe shaltow [hym] neuere,
B. 15.255 The mooste liflode he lyueþ *by* is loue in goddes passion;
B. 15.274 Monkes and mendinauntȝ, men *by* hemselue
B. 15.281 And day *bi* day hadde he hire noȝt his hunger for to slake,
B. 15.284 Hadde a brid þat brouȝte hym breed þat he *by* lyuede,
B. 15.294 And also Marie Maudeleyne *by* mores lyuede and dewes,
B. 15.301 And if þei kouþe han ycarped, *by* crist! as I trowe,
B. 15.305 Ac god sente hem foode *by* foweles and by no fierse beestes
B. 15.305 Ac god sente hem foode by foweles and *by* no fierse beestes
B. 15.313 For we [*by*] goddes [behestes] abiden alwey
B. 15.351 And so it fareþ *by* som folk now; þei han a fair speche,
B. 15.362 Wisten *by* þe walkne what sholde bitide;
B. 15.365 *By* þe seed þat þei sewe what þei sel[l]e myȝte,

B.15.366	And what to leue and to lyue *by*; þe lond was so trewe.
B.15.423	To lyue *by* litel and in lowe houses by lele mennes almesse.
B.15.423	To lyue by litel and in lowe houses *by* lele mennes almesse.
B.15.456	[And] so it fareþ *by* a barn þat born is of wombe;
B.15.472	[And *by*] þe hond fedde foules [i]s folk vnderstonde
B.15.477	Louen and bileuen *by* lettred mennes doynges,
B.15.478	And *by* hire wordes and werkes wenen and trowen;
B.15.481	And *by* þe man þat made þe feste þe mageste bymeneþ
B.15.513	In ensaumple þat men sholde se *by* sadde reson
B.15.564	Takeþ hire landes, ye lordes, and leteþ hem lyue *by* dymes.
B.15.570	Euery bisshop þat bereþ cros, *by* þat he is holden
B.15.592	And *by* þat mangerie [þei] myȝte wel se þat Messie he semede;
B.16.47	That is lieutenaunt to loken it wel *bi* leue of myselue:
B.16.88	Filius *by* þe fader wille and frenesse of spiritus sancti
B.16.95	And þanne sholde Iesus Iuste þerfore *bi* Iuggement of armes
B.16.158	Thouȝ I *bi* treson be take [to] youre [iewene] wille
B.16.179	A ful bold bacheler; I knew hym *by* his blasen.'
B.16.183	That oon dooþ alle dooþ and ech dooþ *bi* his one.
B.16.185	Pater is his propre name, a persone *by* hymselue.
B.16.188	The þridde highte þe holi goost, a persone *by* hymselue,
B.16.233	He wiste my wille *bi* hym; he wol me it allowe.
B.17.41	And riȝt so, *bi* þe roode, Reson me sheweþ
B.17.61	And nolde noȝt neghen hym *by* nyne londes lengþe.
B.17.65	Dredfully, *bi* þis day! as doke dooþ fram þe faucon.
B.17.69	And parceyued *bi* his pous he was in peril to dye
B.17.123	And come ayein *bi* þis contree and conforten alle sike
B.17.167	And aren serel[e]pes *by* hemself; asondry were þei neuere;
B.17.176	The pawme is pureliche þe hand, haþ power *by* hymselue
B.17.198	*By* þis skile', [he seide], 'I se an euidence
B.17.211	[That serueþ þise swynkeres to se *by* aniȝtes],
B.17.258	The holy goost hereþ þee noȝt ne helpe may þee *by* reson.
B.17.265	For manye of yow riche men, *by* my soule, men telleþ,
B.17.283	And who[so] morþereþ a good man, me þynkeþ, *by* myn Inwit,
B.17.311	Thus it fareþ *by* swich folk þat [folwen] al hire [wille],
B.17.321	Thre þynges þer ben þat doon a man *by* strengþe
B.17.344	That þei han cause to contrarie *by* kynde of hir siknesse;
B.18.8	And how Osanna *by* Organye olde folk songen,
B.18.45	Boþe as long and as large *bi* lofte and by grounde.'
B.18.45	Boþe as long and as large bi lofte and *by* grounde.'
B.18.86	The blood sprong doun *by* þe spere and vnspered [his] eiȝen.
B.18.106	But [as] barayne be and [*by*] vsurie [libben],
B.18.167	'That is sooþ', seide Mercy, 'and I se here *by* Sowþe
B.18.173	Rightwisnesse hire reuerenced *by* hir riche cloþyng
B.18.232	'*By* goddes body', quod þis book, 'I wol bere witnesse
B.18.277	If he reu[e] me my riȝt he robbeþ me *by* maistrie.
B.18.278	For *by* right and by reson þe renkes þat ben here
B.18.278	For by right and *by* reson þe renkes þat ben here
B.18.289	And eggedest hem to ete, Eue *by* hirselue,
B.18.342	Membre for membre [was amendes *by* þe olde lawe],
B.18.343	And lif for lif also, and *by* þat lawe I clayme
B.18.349	But *by* right and by reson raunsone here my liges:
B.18.349	But by right and *by* reson raunsone here my liges:
B.18.352	To recouere hem þoruȝ raunsoun and *by* no reson ellis.
B.18.355	Getest *bi* gile þo þat god louede;
B.18.400	Thus *by* lawe', quod oure lord, 'lede I wole fro hennes
B.18.416	'Trewes', quod Truþe, 'þow tellest vs sooþ, *by* Iesus!
B.19.20	Ne noon so nedeful to nempne *by* nyȝte ne by daye.
B.19.20	Ne noon so nedeful to nempne by nyȝte ne *by* daye.
B.19.22	And synfulle aren solaced and saued *by* þat name,
B.19.38	And þo pat bicome cristene *bi* counseil of þe baptis[t]e
B.19.66	And se *bi* his sorwe þat whoso loueþ ioye
B.19.79	Into hir kyngene kiþ *by* counseil of Aungeles.
B.19.92	And presented hym wiþ pitee apperynge *by* Mirre;
B.19.98	In þe manere of a man and þat *by* muchel sleighte,
B.19.122	He wroȝte þat *by* no wit but þoruȝ word one,
B.19.157	Ac Marie Maudeleyne mette hym *by* þe weye
B.19.170	And took Thomas *by* þe hand and tauȝte hym to grope
B.19.217	Tresour to lyue *by* to hir lyues ende,
B.19.232	They lelly to lyue *by* labour of grace.
B.19.233	And *by* wit to wissen oþere as grace hem wolde teche.
B.19.235	[*By*] sellynge and buggynge hir bilyue to wynne.
B.19.237	And lyue, *by* þat labour], a lele lif and a trewe.
B.19.239	To wynne wiþ hir liflode of loore of his techynge;
B.19.315	'Hareweþ alle þat konneþ kynde wit *by* conseil of þise docto[urs],
B.19.319	'*By* god! Grace', quod Piers, 'ye moten gyue tymber,
B.19.375	Some þoruȝ bedes biddynge and some [*by*] pilgrymag[e]
B.19.397	*By* Iesu! for al youre langlynge, wiþ Spiritus Iusticie,
B.19.405	But þow lyue *by* loore of Spiritus Iusticie,
B.19.419	Forþi', quod þis vicory, '*by* verray god I wolde
B.19.453	But [it soune], as *by* sighte, somwhat to wynnyng.
B.19.459	Thanne louȝ þer a lord and, '*by* þis light!' seide,

B.19.462	Counseilleþ me *bi* hir acounte and my clerkes writynge.
B.19.465	And þanne cam þer a kyng and *by* his croune seide,
B.19.468	And if me lakkeþ to lyue *by* þe lawe wole I take it
B.20.1	Thanne as I wente *by* þe wey, whan I was thus awaked,
B.20.8	[Was] *by* techynge and by tellynge of Spiritus temperancie,
B.20.8	[Was] by techynge and *by* tellynge of Spiritus temperancie,
B.20.14	And he [cacche] in þat caas and come þerto *by* sleighte
B.20.23	For is no vertue *bi* fer to Spiritus temperancie.
B.20.96	And bar þe baner bifore deeþ; *bi* riȝt he it cleymede.
B.20.212	And [I] *by* conseil of kynde comsed to rome
B.20.221	'*By* [þe] Marie!' quod a mansed preest, [was] of þe March of [Irlonde],
B.20.241	Lat hem be as beggeris or lyue *by* Aungeles foode.'
B.20.268	Forþi', quod Conscience, '*by* crist! kynde wit me telleþ
B.20.275	And preche men of Plato, and preue it *by* Seneca
B.20.314	And moore of phisik *bi* fer, and fairer he plastreþ;
B.20.341	'Ye? go þi gate!' quod Pees, '*by* god! for al þi phisik,
B.20.380	'*By* crist!' quod Conscience þo, 'I wole bicome a pilgrym,
C.Pr.78	Ac it is nouȝt *by* þe bischop þat þe boy precheþ,
C.Pr.103	I leue, *by* oure lord, for loue of ȝoure coueytise
C.Pr.182	Wer ther a belle on here beygh, *by* iesu, as me thynketh,
C.Pr.211	Shal neuer þe Cat ne [þe] kytoun *be* my conseil be greued
C.Pr.221	Deuyne ȝe, for y ne dar, *by* dere god almyhten.
C.1.4	Cam doun fro þe castel and calde me *by* name
C.1.22	And rekene hem *by* rewe: reherse hem wher þe liketh.
C.1.28	And lay *by* hem bothe as þe boke telleth;
C.1.86	He is a god *by* þe gospel and graunte may hele
C.1.87	And also lyk [to] oure lord *by* saynt Lukes wordes.
C.1.90	Kynges and knyghtes sholde kepen hit *by* resoun,
C.1.117	'Hit is sikerore *bi* southe þer þe sonne regneth
C.1.118	Then in þe north *by* many notes, no man leue other.
C.1.138	*By* what wey it wexeth and wheder out of my menynges.'
C.1.159	And for to knowe hit kyndly, hit comeseth *by* myhte
C.1.201	Forthi y may seye, as y saide eer, *by* s[ih]t of this tex[t]es:
C.2.4	Kenne me *by* sum craft to knowe þe false.'
C.2.86	And fauel þat hath a fals speche Feffeth hem *by* þis lettre
C.2.118	*By* syhte of sire Simonye and syuyles leue.'
C.2.125	Amendes was here moder *by* trewe menne lokynge,
C.2.141	For *by* lesynges ȝe lacchen largeliche mede.
C.2.150	Forthy worcheth *by* wisdom and by witt also,
C.2.150	Forthy worcheth by wisdom and *by* witt also,
C.2.183	And ryde on hem and on reue[s] righte faste *by* mede.
C.2.207	'Now, *by* crist!' quod þe kyng, 'and y cacche myhte
C.2.210	And do hem hange *by* þe halse and alle þat hem maynteyneth.
C.2.249	And sayde, 'syre kyng, *by* crist! but clerkes amende,
C.3.7	And yf she worche wysely and *by* wys men consayl
C.3.10	Took mede *by* þe myddel and myldeliche here brouhte
C.3.11	Into Boure with blisse and *by* here gan sitte.
C.3.16	Confortede here as they couthe *by* the clerkes leue
C.3.40	'Thow le[r]ed men and le[w]ed haued layn *by* the bothe
C.3.143	[And marre þe with myschef], *be* seynte mary my lady,
C.3.144	That alle [women, wantowen], shal [be] war [*by*] þe one
C.3.166	Is nat a bettere baud, *by* hym þat me made,
C.3.171	Lyggeth *by* here, when hem lust, lered and lewed.
C.3.178	And taketh [þe] tre[we] *by* the top and te[i]eth hym f[aste]
C.3.193	*By* iesu! with here ieweles the Iustices she shendeth;
C.3.205	Ther he is alowed and ylet *by* þat laste shal eny while
C.3.284	Quod þe kyng to Consience, '*by* crist, as me thynketh,
C.3.288	As þe sauhter sayth *by* such þat ȝeueth mede:
C.3.307	As *by* the book þat byt nobody withholde
C.3.414	How god sente to sauel *by* samuel þe prophete
C.3.428	Otherwyse then god wolde and warnede hym *by* þe prophete,
C.3.479	*Be* sixe [s]onnes [and] a ship and half a shef of Arwes;
C.4.4	'Nay, *by* Crist!' quod Consience, 'congeie me [rather]!
C.4.47	And how he raueschede Rose the ryche wydewe *by* nyhte
C.4.62	And ȝut he manes[c]heth me and myne and lyth *be* my mayde.
C.4.79	The kyng [s]wor *by* Crist and by his croune bothe
C.4.79	The kyng [s]wor by Crist and *by* his croune bothe
C.4.99	'Nay, *by* crist!' quod þe kyng, 'for Consiences sake
C.4.131	And [ȝut],' quod resoun, '*by* þe rode! y shal no reuthe haue
C.4.134	Y sey it [*by*] mysulf,' quod resoun, 'and it so were
C.4.139	Ne thorw mede mercy, *by* marie of heuene!
C.4.154	And sayden, 'we seyn wel, syre resoun, *be* thi wordes
C.4.172	And deme ȝow, *by* þis day, as ȝe haen deserued.
C.4.173	Mede shal nat maynprise [ȝow], *by* marye of heuene!
C.4.175	And *by* lele and lyfholy my lawe shal be demed.'
C.4.177	Hit is ful hard, *by* myn heued, herto to bryngen it
C.4.179	'*By* hym þat rauhte [on] þe rode,' quod resoun to the kyng,
C.4.194	Or lumbardus of lukes þat leuen *by* lone as iewes.'
C.5.3	And lytel ylet *by*, leueth me for sothe,
C.5.6	For as y cam *by* Consience with resoun y mette
C.5.26	'Thenne hastow londes to lyue *by*,' quod resoun, 'or lynage ryche
C.5.42	Yf y *be* labour sholde lyuen and lyflode deseruen,

C. 5.55 For *by* þe lawe of leuyticy þat oure lord ordeynede,
C. 5.89 Quod Consience, '*by* Crist, y can nat se this lyeth;
C. 5.153 Hit is in C[l]oystre or in scole, *by* many skilles y fynde.
C. 5.174 Bred withouten beggynge to lyue *by* euere aftur
C. 6.36 And ȝut so synguler *be* mysulue as to syhte of [þe] peple
C. 6.40 Be holden for holy and honoured *by* þat enchesoun;
C. 6.70 And þat a wiste *by* wille to watekyn he tolde hit
C. 6.71 And þat he wiste *by* watte tolde hit wille aftur
C. 6.125 Or til they bothe be beggares and *by* [my] spiritual[t]e libbe
C. 6.162 Al þat y wiste wykked *by* eny of oure couent
C. 6.165 Consayl þat thow knowest *by* continaunce ne by speche.
C. 6.165 Consayl þat thow knowest by continaunce ne *by* speche.
C. 6.191 *By* sorserie sum tyme and sum tyme by maistrie.
C. 6.191 By sorserie sum tyme and sum tyme *by* maistrie.
C. 6.192 Y lay *by* þe louelokest and louede here neuere aftur.
C. 6.223 The pound th[at] he payede *by* peysed a quarter more
C. 6.227 For laboreres and louh folk þat lay *by* hymsulue
C. 6.253 'Now redily,' quod repentaunce, 'and *by* þe rode, y leue,
C. 6.265 And but y hadde *by* other wey at the laste y stale hit
C. 6.292 ȝut were me leuer, *by* oure lord, lyue al by wellecresses
C. 6.292 ȝut were me leuer, by oure lord, lyue al *by* wellecresses
C. 6.295 Til thow haue ymad *by* thy myhte to alle men restitucioun.
C. 6.307 And arste shal come to heuene, [*by* hym þat me made]!'
C. 6.330 For he hadde layȝe *by* latro, luciferes aunte.
C. 6.331 'Be þe rode,' quod repentaunce, 'thow romest toward heuene
C. 6.341 For thow hast no good, *by* good fayth, to gete the with a wastel.
C. 6.353 *By* betene hous the brewestere þat bad hym good morwen
C. 6.374 And of vphalderes an heep, [e]rly *by* þe morwe,
C. 6.382 And that the bettere thyng, *be* arbitreres, bote sholde þe worse.
C. 6.384 And preisede th[e] penworthis apart *by* hemsulue
C. 6.386 They couthe nat *by* here Consience acorden for treuthe
C. 6.409 Clement þe coblere cauhte hym *by* þe myddel
C. 7.9 'Yf y sholde deye *be* þis day y drede me sore.
C. 7.111 That *by* his lyue l[yth]ed hem and louede hem to here.
C. 7.141 And *by* so muche hit semeth the sykerloker we mowe
C. 7.164 A bolle and a bagge a bar *by* his syde;
C. 7.169 And se *by* [his] signes wham a souht hadde.
C. 7.174 ȝe may se *be* [my] signes þat sitten on my cappe
C. 7.201 'Nay, *bi* þe perel of my soule!' Peres gan to swerie,
C. 7.213 And so [boweth] forth *by* [a] brok, [beth-buxum-of-speche],
C. 7.219 Thenne shalt thow come *by* a croft Ac come thow [nat] þerynne;
C. 7.224 Thei hatte stele-nat and sle-nat; stryk forth *by* bothe
C. 7.268 Thus myhte thow lesen his loue, to lete wel *by* thysulue,
C. 7.281 Hit is ful hard, *be* myn heued, eny of ȝow alle
C. 7.283 '*By* Crist!' quod a cottepors, 'y haue no kyn there.'
C. 7.284 'Ne y,' quod an hapeward, '*by* auht þat y knowe.'
C. 7.305 [Quod contemplacion, '*by* Crist, thow y care soffre],
C. 8.1 Qvod [perkyn] þe [plouhman], '*be* seynt petur of Rome!
C. 8.2 Ich haue an half aker to erye *by* þe heye [way];
C. 8.17 And alle manere men þat *by* þe molde is susteyned
C. 8.19 '*By* Crist!' quod a knyhte tho, 'a kenneth vs þe beste
C. 8.21 Y wolde y couthe,' quod the knyhte, '*by* Crist and his moder!
C. 8.33 '*By* my power, [Peres], y plyhte the my treuthe
C. 8.54 'Y assente, *by* seynt Gyle,' sayde the knyht thenne,
C. 8.55 'For to worche *by* thy wit and my wyf bothe.'
C. 8.67 Shal haue leue, *by* oure lord, to [lese here in heruest]
C. 8.88 What þei comaunde as *by* þe kyng countreplede hit neuere;
C. 8.109 And with þe res[i]due and þe remenant, *by* the rode of lukes!
C. 8.163 'Or y shal bete the *by* the lawe and brynge þe in stokkes.'
C. 8.167 'Now, *by* Crist!' quod [Peres] the [plouhman], 'y shal apayre ȝow alle,'
C. 8.171 Hunger in haste tho hente wastour *by* þe mawe
C. 8.172 And wronge hym so *by* þe wombe þat al watrede his yes;
C. 8.233 Loke *by* thy lyue lat hem nat forfare.
C. 8.263 '*By* Crist!' quod [Peres] þe [plouhman] tho, 'this prouerbis [wol y] shewe
C. 8.282 And ȝif thow [the pore *be* thy] pouer, [Peres], y þe rede;
C. 8.292 And be fayn, *be* my fayth, his fysik to leete
C. 8.296 '*By* seynte Poul!' quod Peres, 'thow poyntest neyh þe treuthe
C. 8.301 Ar y haue ydyned *be* þis day and ydronke bothe.'
C. 8.306 And ȝut y say[e], *be* my soule! y haue no sal[t] bacoun
C. 8.307 Ne no cokeney, *be* Crist! colloppes to make.
C. 8.312 *By* this lyflode we mote lyue til l[a]masse tyme
C. 8.313 And *by* [t]hat y hope to haue heruost in my croft[e];
C. 8.321 *By* that hit nyhed neyh heruost and newe corn cam to chepyng.
C. 9.17 Drede nat for no deth to distruye *by* here power
C. 9.25 And for they sw[e]re *by* here soule and [so] god mote hem helpe
C. 9.32 And brugges tobrokene *by* þe heye wayes
C. 9.142 In hope to sitte at euen *by* þe hote coles,
C. 9.152 In idelnesse and in ese and *by* otheres trauayle.
C. 9.189 Ac Ermytes þat inhabiten *by* the heye weye
C. 9.199 And summe lyuede *by* here letterure and labour of here handes
C. 9.201 And briddes brouhte somme bred þat they *by* lyuede.

C. 9.204 Ac thise Ermytes þat edifien thus *by* the heye weye
C. 9.214 Kyndeliche, *by* Crist, ben suche ycald lollares.
C. 9.215 As *by* þe engelisch of oure eldres of olde mennes techynge
C. 9.223 And vnder obedience be *by* dayes and by nyhtes;
C. 9.223 And vnder obedience be by dayes and *by* nyhtes;
C. 9.244 As matynes *by* þe morwe til masse bygynne,
C. 9.303 Ac men setteth nat *by* sowngewarie for me seth hit often fayle;
C. 9.342 And how we dede day *be* day the doem wol reherce.
C. 9.346 Y sette nat *by* pardon a pese ne nat a pye hele.
C.10.23 Seuene sithe, sayth þe boek, synegeth day *by* day
C.10.32 *By* a forbisene,' quod þe frere, 'y shal the fayre shewe:
C.10.38 A[c] ȝut is he saef and sound; and so hit fareth *by* þe rihtfole.
C.10.41 So hit fareth,' quod þe frere, '*by* þe ryhtful mannus fallynge.
C.10.62 *By* a wi[d]e wildernesse and by a wode syde.
C.10.62 By a wi[d]e wildernesse and *by* a wode syde.
C.10.69 Cam and calde me *be* my kynde name.
C.10.105 And reule alle reumes *by* here thre wittes
C.10.142 And *by* his leryng is lad þat lady Anima.
C.10.145 And hath fyue fayre sones *by* his furste wyue:
C.10.165 As þe sauter sayth *by* synnefole shrewes:
C.10.172 *By* loue and by leute, þerby lyueth anima
C.10.172 By loue and *by* leute, þerby lyueth anima
C.10.173 And lyf lyueth *by* inwit and leryng of kynde.
C.10.211 That lele legityme *by* þe lawe may claymen.
C.10.230 Alle sholle deye for his dedes *by* dales and hulles
C.10.238 That þe sire *by* hymsulue doth þe sone sholde be þe worse.
C.11.11 Y syg hit *by* suche,' quod [she], 'þat sheweth by here werkes
C.11.11 Y syg hit by suche,' quod [she], 'þat sheweth *by* here werkes
C.11.32 Litel is he loued or leet [*by*] among lordes at festes.
C.11.61 And ȝut th[e] wrechus of this world is noen ywar *by* oþer
C.11.72 And yf thow haue litel, leue sone, loke *by* þy lyue
C.11.106 And ryde forth *by* rychesse [ac] reste nat þerynne,
C.11.124 And caste [mette] *by* squire bothe lyne and leuele.
C.11.139 '*By* Crist,' quod Clergie, 'yf thow coueyte dowel
C.11.162 And lakkede [me in] latyn and lyhte *by* me sette
C.11.187 'Man,' quod [he], 'yf y me[t]e with the, *by* marie of heuene,
C.11.208 Y leue hit wel *by* oure lord and on no lettrure bettere.
C.11.223 That hoso doth *by* ȝoure doctrine doth wel, y leue,
C.11.242 A[c] me were leuere, *by* oure lord, a lyppe of goddes grace
C.11.242 God lene hit fare nat so *by* folk þat þe faith techen
C.11.265 Lelly as *by* his lokes, with a le[tt]re of gyle?
C.11.268 And now beth this seyntes, *by* that men saith, and souereynes in heuene.
C.11.270 *By* that þat salamon saith hit semeth þat no wyht woet
C.11.281 Sothly,' saide rechelesnesse, 'ȝe se *by* many euydences
C.12.10 And preeye for the pol *by* pol yf thow be peccuniosus.'
C.12.11 *By* wissyng of this wenche y dede, here wordes were so swete,
C.12.19 '*By* my faith! frere,' quod y, 'ȝe fare lyke þe woware
C.12.21 Riht so, *by* þe rode, rouhte ȝe neuere
C.12.30 Thei wolle allegge also and *by* þe gospel preuen
C.12.36 To rehercen hit *by* retoryk to arate dedly synne?
C.12.59 *By* þ[e] bloed [that] he bouhte vs with and bapteme, as he tauhte:
C.12.70 Bote yf contricioun and confessioun crye *by* his lyue
C.12.127 So *by* [h]is werkes thei wisten þat he was iesu
C.12.128 As *by* clothyng they knewe hym nat, so caytifliche he ȝede.
C.12.142 And alle þe wyse þat euere were, *by* auhte y can aspye,
C.12.144 And bothe bettere and blessedere *by* many fold then richesse.
C.12.178 And *by* þe grayn þat groweth god vs all techeth.
C.13.27 Thogh y preyse pouerte thus and preue hit *by* ensau[m]ples,
C.13.28 Worthiore as *by* holy writ and wyse fylosofres.
C.13.42 And thogh they wen[de] *by* the wey, tho two togederes,
C.13.70 And haue reuthe and releue with his rychesse *by* his power
C.13.79 The messager aren th[e] mendenantȝ þat lyuen *by* menne almesse,
C.13.89 And sheweth be seel and seth by lettre with what lord he dwelleth,
C.13.89 And sheweth be seel and seth *by* lettre with what lord he dwelleth,
C.13.98 As þe ryche man for al his mone, and more as *by* þe gospell:
C.13.104 The tytle [þat] ȝe take ordres *by* telleth ȝe ben avaunsed
C.13.112 The same y segge for sothe *by* suche þat beth prestes
C.13.121 So [is hit] a goky, *by* god! þat in [his] gospel fayleth
C.13.133 To knowe *by* vch a creature kynde to louye.
C.13.136 And where þat briddes and bestis *by* here make þei ȝeden,
C.13.147 Males drow hem to males a[l mour]nynge *by* hemsulue
C.13.191 They reule hem a[l] by resoun Ac renkes ful fewe.
C.13.228 Rihte so ferde Resoun *by* the; for thy rude speche
C.13.241 'ȝe seggeth soth, *be* my soule,' quod y, 'I haue sey hit ofte.
C.14.2 Thogh y sete *by* mysulue, suche is my grace.
C.14.65 Ne sette shorte *by* here science, whatso þei doen hemsulue.
C.14.72 Kynde wittede men [c]an a clergie *by* hemsulue,
C.14.78 Ne brouhte *by* here bokes to blisse ne to ioye,
C.14.140 Bote as a beggare bordles *be* mysulue on þe grounde.
C.4.144 Bote as a soleyn *by* hymsulue [and] yserued [o]n þe [erthe].

C.14.150 That oure [lord] ne hauede [hym] lihtliche out, so leue y [*by*] þ[e]
               thef in heuene.
C.14.152 And wel lo[s]liche he lolleth þere *by* þe lawe of holy churche:
C.14.156 And so y sey *by* þe þat sekest aftur þe whyes,
C.14.201 Withoute bapteme, as *by* here bokes, beth nat ysaued.'
C.15.41 And seten *by* ouresulue at a syde table.
C.15.98 And prouen hit *by* here pocalips and þe passioun of seynt Aueroy
C.15.128 'Haue me excused,' quod Clergie, '*be* crist, but in scole.
C.15.135 And preueth *by* puyre skile inparfyt alle thynges–
C.15.157 For, *by* hym þat me made, myhte neuere pouerte
C.15.177 '*By* Crist!' quod Consience, 'clergie, y wol nat lye;
C.15.178 Me were leuere, *by* oure lord, and y leue sholde,
C.15.189 And as they wente *by* þe way–of dowel can they carpe–
C.15.241 The Cryket *by* kynde of þe fuyr and corleu by þe wynde,
C.15.241 The Cryket by kynde of þe fuyr and corleu *by* þe wynde,
C.15.242 Bestes *by* gra[s] and by grayn and by grene rotes,
C.15.242 Bestes by gra[s] and *by* grayn and by grene rotes,
C.15.242 Bestes by gra[s] and by grayn and *by* grene rotes,
C.15.283 Then eny pore pacient; and þat preue y *be* resoun.
C.15.285 There þe pore dar plede and preue *by* puyr resoun
C.15.286 To haue allouaunce of his lord; *by* [þe] lawe he [hit] claymeth.
C.16.8 So y sey *by* 3ow ryche, hit semeth nat þat 3e sholle
C.16.48 A[c] þe ryche is reuerenced *by* resoun of his rychesse
C.16.80 And *by* þe nekke namelyche here noen may henten other;
C.16.108 More then pat mayde is þat is maried *by* brocage,
C.16.109 As *by* assente of sondry p[arti]es and suluer to bote,
C.16.111 So hit fareth *by* vch a persone þat possession forsaket
C.16.121 Thenne is [hit] goed *by* goed skill, thouh hit greue a litel,
C.16.208 And of myn yf thow myhtes[t], me thynketh *by* thy speche.'
C.16.248 And s[e] hit *by* ensample In somur tyme on trees
C.16.292 I knewe neuere, *by* Crist, clerk noþer lewed
C.16.297 And so y trowe truely, *by* þat me telleth of charite.'
C.16.337 'Were y with hym *by* Cr[i]st,' quod y, 'y wolde neuere fro hym
C.16.341 *By* clothyng ne by carpynge knowe shaltow hym neuere
C.16.341 By clothyng ne *by* carpynge knowe shaltow hym neuere
C.17.7 Solitarie *by* hemsulue in here selles lyuede
C.17.21 Marie Maudeleyne *by* mores lyuede and dewes;
C.17.29 Ac durste no beste byte hem *by* day ne by nyhte;
C.17.29 Ac durste no beste byte hem by day ne *by* nyhte;
C.17.58 With þat 3oure bernes and 3oure bloed *by* goed lawe may clayme!
C.17.70 That pore peple *by* puyre riht here part myhte aske.
C.17.77 And so hit fareth *by* false cristene: here follynge is trewe,
C.17.99 Shipmen and sheepherdes *by* þe seuene sterres
C.17.102 *By* the seed þat they sewe what þey sulle myhte
C.17.103 And what lyue *by* and leue, the londe was so trewe.
C.17.152 Louen as *by* lawe of kynde oure lord god almyhty.
C.17.157 Louyeth nat þat lord aryht as *by* þe legende sanctorum
C.17.160 And aftur his leryng they lyue and *by* lawe of kynde
C.17.227 Taketh here londe[s], 3e lordes, and lat hem lyue *by* dymes
C.17.264 In ensaumple þat men sholde se *by* sad resoen
C.17.283 Euery bisshope *bi* þe lawe sholde buxumliche walke
C.17.301 *By* þe myracles þat he made messie he semede
C.18.67 And so hit fareth sothly, sone, *by* oure kynde.
C.18.97 And in heuene is priueoste and next hym *by* resoun
C.18.120 Filius *by* þe fadres wille fley with spiritus sanctus
C.18.128 That iesus sholde iouste þerfore *by* iugement of Armes
C.18.194 The thridde is þat halt al, a thyng *by* hymsulue;
C.18.214 That he is thre persones departable y preue hit *by* mankynde,
C.18.241 Where god [ri3t *be* my gate cam gangynge a thre];
C.19.60 And [n]olde nat neyhele hym *by* nyne londes lenghe.
C.19.68 And parseued *by* his poues he was in perel to deye
C.19.141 The paume is puyrliche the hand and hath power *by* hymsulue
C.19.164 *Bi* this simile,' he saide, 'y se an euydence
C.19.177 That serueth this swynkares to [see] *by* a nyhtes,
C.19.231 For mony of 3ow riche men, *by* my soule y lye nat,
C.19.264 And hoso morthereth a goed man, me thynketh *bi* myn inwit,
C.19.291 Thus hit fareth *bi* such folk þat folewen here owene will,
C.19.324 That they haen cause to contrarien *bi* kynde of here seknes[e];
C.20.7 And how osanna *by* orgene oelde folke songe.
C.20.88 The bloed sprang down *by* the spere and vnspered [his] yes.
C.20.109 [But] as bareyne be and *by* vsure libbe,
C.20.170 'That is soth,' saide mercy, 'and y se here *bi* southe
C.20.235 So hit shal fare *bi* this folk: here folye and here synne
C.20.241 '*By* godes body,' quod this book, 'y wol [b]ere witnesse
C.20.299 Yf he reue me my rihte A robbeth me [*by*] maistrie
C.20.300 For *bi* riht and by resoun þ[e] renkes þat ben here
C.20.300 For bi riht and *by* resoun þ[e] renkes þat ben here
C.20.316 And entisedest Eue to eten *bi* here one–
C.20.394 Here eny synfole soule souereynliche *by* maistrie
C.20.395 Bote [*by*] riht and [by] resoun raunsome here my lege[s]:
C.20.395 Bote [by] riht and [*by*] resoun raunsome here my lege[s]:
C.20.443 Thus *by* lawe,' quod oure lord, 'lede y wol fro hennes
C.20.459 'Trewes,' quod treuthe; 'thow tellest vs soeth, *by* iesus!

C.21.20 Ne noen so niedfol to nemnie *by* nyhte ne by day
C.21.20 Ne noen so niedfol to nemnie by nyhte ne *by* day
C.21.22 And synfole ben solaced and saued *by* þat name.
C.21.38 And tho þat bycome cristene *bi* consail of þe baptist
C.21.66 And se *bi* his sorwe þat hoso loueth ioye
C.21.79 Into here kyngene kuth *by* consail of Angelis.
C.21.92 And presented hym with pyte apperynge *bi* Mirre
C.21.98 In þe manere of a man and þat *by* moche sleythe,
C.21.122 He wrouhte þat *by* no wyt bote thorw word one,
C.21.157 Ac Marie Maudeleyne mette hym *by* þe weye
C.21.170 And toek Thomas *by* the hoende and tauhte hym to grope
C.21.217 Tresor to lyue *by* to here lyues ende
C.21.232 They leely to lyue *bi* labour of tonge
C.21.233 And *bi* wit to wissen oþere as grace hem wolde teche.
C.21.235 [*By*] sullyng and buggynge here bileue to wynne.
C.21.237 And lyue *by* þat laboure a leele lyf and a trewe.
C.21.239 To wynne with here lyflode *bi* lore of his techynge];
C.21.315 'Harweth alle þa[t] conneth kynde wit *bi* consail of [this] doctours
C.21.319 '*By* god! grace,' quod [Peres], '3e moet gyue tymber
C.21.375 Somme thorw bedes biddynge and [somme] *bi* pilgrimag[e]
C.21.397 *By* iesu! for al 3oure iangelyng, [with] spiritus Iustice
C.21.398 Ne aftur Consience, *bi* Crist! [while] y c[an] sulle
C.21.405 Bote thow lyue *bi* lore of spiritus Iusticie,
C.21.419 Forthy,' quod this vicory, '*bi* verray god y wolde
C.21.453 Bote hit sowne, as *bi* sihte, somwhat to wynnynge.
C.21.459 Thenne lowh ther a lord and '*bi* this lihte!' saide,
C.21.462 Conseileth me *bi* here acounte and my clerkes wrytyng.
C.21.465 And thenne cam þer a kyng and *bi* his corone saide,
C.21.468 And yf me lakketh to lyue *by* þe lawe wol y take hit
C.22.1 [Thenne] as y wente *by* the way, when y was thus awaked,
C.22.8 Was *bi* techyng and by tellyng of spiritus temperancie
C.22.8 Was bi techyng and *by* tellyng of spiritus temperancie
C.22.14 And he cacche in þat caes and come therto *by* sleithe
C.22.23 [For is no vertue *by* fer to spiritus temperancie],
C.22.96 And baer þe baner bifore deth; *bi* riht he hit claymede,
C.22.212 And y *bi* conseil of kynde comsed to Rome
C.22.221 '*By* þe Marie!' quod a mansed prest, was of þe march of Ireland,
C.22.241 Lat hem be as beggares or lyue *by* angeles fode.'
C.22.268 For[thy],' quod Consience, '*bi* Crist! kynde wit me telleth
C.22.275 And preche men of plato and preuen hit *by* seneca
C.22.314 And more of fysyk *bi* fer, and fayror he plastereth;
C.22.341 '3e? go thy gate!' quod pees, '*bi* god! for al thi fisyk,
C.22.380 '*By* Crist!' quod Consience tho, 'y wol bicome a pilgrime

by_so conj *bi conj.2* B 7 by_so (6) bi_so (1); C 11 by_so (9) bi_so (2)
B.11.74 Where my body were buryed *by so* ye hadde my siluer.
B.12.166 Or þe swymmere þat is saaf *by so* hymself like,
B.14.55 *By so* þat þow be sobre of si3te and of tonge,
B.14.279 Ac somdeel I shal seyen it, *by so* þow vnderstonde.
B.15.47 'Ye, sire!' I seide, '*by so* no man were greued'
B.19.447 It semeþ *bi so* hymself hadde his wille
B.20.222 'I counte na moore Conscience *by so* I cacche siluer
C. 4.98 So alle my claymes ben quyt *by so* þe kyng assente.'
C. 4.187 'Y assente,' sayde resoun, '*by so* 3owsulue yhere
C. 5.39 And sykerost for þe soule, *by so* y wol contenue.
C. 6.332 *By so* hit be in thyn herte as y here thy tonge.
C.10.306 For þe more a man may do, *by so* þat a do hit,
C.12.4 'Rechelesnesse reche the neuere; *By so* thow riche were
C.12.22 Wher my body were yber[i]ed *by so* 3e hadde my [suluer].'
C.15.254 *By so* þat þou be sobre of syhte and of tonge,
C.16.209 '3e, sire!' y sayde, '*by so* no man were ygreued,
C.21.447 Hit semeth *bi so* hymsulue hadde his wille
C.22.222 'Y counte no more Consience *bi so* y cache suluer

bible n *bible n.* A 7; B 16; C 8 bible (7) byble (1)
A. 3.253 But brou3te wiþ hym þe bestis as þe *bible* [telliþ],
A. 7.215 '3e, I hote þe,' quaþ hungir, 'oþer ellis þe *bible* lei3eþ.
A. 7.219 And sapience seiþ þe same, I sai3 it in þe *bible*:
A. 8.124 'Lewide lorel,' quaþ peris, 'litel lokest þou on þe *bible*;
A. 8.135 Ac for þe *bible* beriþ wytnesse
A. 9.82 And is ronne to religioun, & haþ rendrit þe *bible*,
A.11.126 And þat [I] grete wel his wyf for I wrot hire þe *bible*,
B. 3.274 Forbar hym and his beestes boþe as þe *bible* witnesseþ,
B. 6.231 'Ye I [h]ote þee', quod hunger, 'or ellis þe *bible* lieþ.
B. 6.235 And Sapience seiþ þe same–I sei3 it in þe *bible*:
B. 7.142 'Lewed lorel!' quod Piers, 'litel lokestow on þe *bible*;
B. 7.157 Ac for þe book *bible* bereþ witnesse
B. 8.91 And is ronne to Religion, and haþ rendred þe *bible*,
B. 9.42 And so it semeþ by hym [þere he seide in þe *bible*
B.10.89 How þe book *bible* of hym bereþ witnesse:
B.10.174 And þat I grete wel his wif, for I wroot hire [þe *bible*],
B.10.285 The *bible* bereþ witnesse þat al[le] þe [barnes] of Israel
B.10.323 And bete yow, as þe *bible* telleþ, for brekynge of youre rule,
B.10.333 That þis worþ sooþ, seke ye þat ofte ouerse þe *bible*:

B.11.270 Alþouȝ Salomon seide, as folk seeþ in þe *bible*,
B.11.394 The wise and þe witty wroot þus in þe *bible*:
B.13.185 I shal brynge yow a *bible*, a book of þe olde lawe,
B.15.89 Of þis matere I myȝte make a long *bible*,
C. 3.427 Forbar hym and his beste bestes, as þe *byble* wittenesseth,
C. 3.485 'Loo what salamon sayth,' quod she, 'in sapiense in þe *bible*!
C. 5.169 And bete ȝow, as þe *bible* telleth, for brekynge of ȝoure reule
C. 8.237 'ȝe, y bihote the,' quod hunger, 'or elles þe *bible* lyeth.
C. 9.305 Ac for þe boek *bible* bereth witnesse
C.10.88 And is ronne [t]o religioun and hath rendred þe *bible*
C.11.114 And sey y gre[t]e wel his wyf, for y wrot here a *bible*
C.18.221 As þe *bible* bereth witnesse, A boek of þe olde lawe,

bicam > bicome; bycause > by,cause

bicche n *bicche n.* A 1; B 1; C 1 byche
A. 5.194 And þanne gan he to go [lik a glemans *bicche*],
B. 5.346 And þanne gan he to go lik a glemannes *bicche*
C. 6.404 And thenne gan he go lyke a glemans *byche*

bicome v *bicomen v.* A 6 becom (1) become (3) becomiþ (1) bicome (1);
    B 13 bicam (5) bicom (1) bicome (4) bicomeþ (3); C 17 bicam (4)
    bycam (4) bicome (1) bycome (2) bicometh (3) bycometh (2) bykam
    (1)
A.Pr.91 *Become* clerkis of acountis þe king for to serue;
A. 1.112 Þanne fil he wiþ [his] felawis & fendis *bicome*;
A. 2.32 And *become* a good man for any coueitise, I rede.'
A. 3.196 It *becom[iþ]* a king þat kepiþ a reaume
A. 7.181 And *become* knaues to kepe peris bestis,
A.11.94 He *beco[m]* so confus he couþe nouȝt mele,
B. 3.209 It *bicomeþ* a kyng þat kepeþ a Reaume
B. 5.485 And *bicam* man of a maide mankynde to saue,
B. 5.642 Thow shalt seye I am þi Suster.' I ne woot where þei *bicome*.
B.10.141 He *bicom* so confus he couþe noȝt [mele],
B.11.202 And blody breþeren we *bicome* þere of o body ywonne,
B.15.516 And *bicam* man of a maide and metropolitanus,
B.18.60 The day for drede wiþdrouȝ and derk *bicam* þe sonne;
B.18.213 *Bicam* man of a mayde mankynde to saue
B.19.38 And þo þat *bicome* cristene bi counseil of þe baptis[t]e
B.19.42 It *bicomeþ* to a kyng to kepe and to defende,
B.19.99 As it *bicomeþ* a conquerour to konne manye sleightes,
B.20.41 And cam and took mankynde and *bicam* nedy.
B.20.380 'By crist!' quod Conscience þo, 'I wole *bicome* a pilgrym,
C. 3.265 Hit *bycometh* for a kyng þat shal kepe a reume
C. 5.61 Hit *bycometh* for clerkes Crist for to serue,
C. 7.127 And *bicam* man of a mayde mankynde to amende.
C. 8.47 Hit *bicometh* to the, knyhte, to be corteys and hende,
C.11.143 And *bycam* man of þat maide withoute mankynde;
C.12.110 And blody bretherne we *bycome* þere of o body ywonne,
C.13.20 And Iob *bykam* as a iolyf man and al his ioye newe.
C.15.149 Where Peres the plogman *bycam*, so priueyliche he wente.
C.17.267 And *bicam* man of a mayde and metropol[it]anus
C.18.134 And *bycam* man of þat maide mankynde to saue,
C.20.60 The daye for drede withdrouh and derke *bicam* þe sonne;
C.20.222 *Bycam* man of a mayde mankynde to saue
C.21.38 And tho þat *bycome* cristene bi consail of þe baptist
C.21.42 Hit *bicometh* [to] a kyng to kepe and to defende
C.21.99 As hit *bicometh* a conquerour to conne mony sleythes,
C.22.41 And cam and toek mankynde and *bicam* nedy.
C.22.380 'By Crist!' quod Consience tho, 'y wol *bicome* a pilgrime

bid > bidden; biddares > bidderis

bidden v *bidden v.* A 29 bad (16) bed (1) bede (1) beden (1) bidde (5)
    bidden (1) biddiþ (3) bit (1); B 78 bad (31) bede (1) beden (3) bid (1)
    bidde (16) bidden (7) biddeþ (10) biddynge (1) bit (7) boden (1); C 56
    bad (17) bade (6) baed (2) bede (5) bid (3) byd (1) bidde (9) bidden
    (2) biddeth (6) biddyng (1) bide (1) bit (1) byt (2)
A. 1.108 To be buxum at his bidding; he *bad* hem nouȝt ellis.
A. 1.138 [Þer] þou art m[er]y at mete, ȝif men *bidde* þe ȝedde.
A. 2.34 Were *beden* to þe b[ri]dale on boþe two sides.
A. 2.109 And *bad* gile go gyue gold al aboute,
A. 2.171 And *bad* hym fle for fer & hise feris alle.
A. 3.26 And *bidden* hire be blyþe, 'for we ben þin owene
A. 3.206 Beggeris for here bidding *biddiþ* of men mede;
A. 4.127 And *bad* Nullum [bonum be] irremuneratum.
A. 5.24 He *bad* wastour go werche what he best couþe
A. 5.145 And *bidde* þe rode of bromholm bringe me out of dette.'
A. 5.148 And Betoun þe breustere *bad* h[ym] good morewe,
A. 5.171 And *bed* bette þe bocher on his side.
A. 5.218 And beet þiself on þe brest & *bidde* hym of grace,
A. 6.88 *Biddiþ* amende ȝow meke hym to his maister ones
A. 7.66 Treuþe tolde me ones & *bad* me telle it forþ.
A. 7.142 And *bad* hym go pisse wiþ his plou[ȝ]: 'pilide shrewe!
A. 7.202 And ȝif þe [g]omes grucche *bidde* hem gon & sywnke,

A. 7.221 He shal go [begge & *bidde*] & no man bete his hungir;
A. 8.5 And *bad* hym holde hym at hom & erien his laiȝes.
A. 8.26 And *bad* h[e]m begge boldely what [hem best] likeþ,
A. 8.69 For he þat beggiþ or *bit*, but he haue nede,
A. 9.96 But dobest *bede* for hem abide þere for euere.
A. 9.114 But as I *bad* þouȝt þo be mene betwene,
A.10.165 And com to noe anon, and *bad* hym nouȝt lette
A.11.7 And blamide hym [and bannide hym] & *bad* hym be stille–
A.11.151 And [*biddiþ*] vs ben as breþeren, & blissen oure enemys,
A.12.36 And drow þe dore after him and *bad* me go do wel
A.12.75 Þer *bad* me hunger haue gode day but I helde me stille;
A.12.106 And so *bad* Iohan but busily wel ofte
B. 1.110 To be buxom at his biddyng, he *bad* hem nouȝt ellis.
B. 2.55 Were *boden* to þe bridale on boþe two sides,
B. 2.145 And *bad* gile '[go] gyu[e] gold al aboute,
B. 2.212 And *bad* hym fle for fere and hise [feeres] alle.
B. 3.27 And *beden* hire be bliþe: 'for we beþ þyne owene
B. 3.75 For þus [*bit* god in] þe gospel goode men doon hir almesse.
B. 3.219 Beggeres for hir biddynge *bidden* [of] men Mede.
B. 4.33 And *bad* Reson ryde faste and recche of hir neiþer.
B. 4.121 As Seynt Beneyt hem *bad*, Bernard and Frauuceis;
B. 4.144 And *bad* Nullum bonum be irremuneratum.
B. 4.187 If ye *bidden* buxomnesse be of myn assent.'
B. 5.24 He *bad* wastour go werche what he best kouþe
B. 5.32 [He] *bad* Bette kutte a bouȝ ouþer tweye
B. 5.187 And *bad* me wilne to wepe my wikkednesse to amende.
B. 5.229 And *bidde* þe Roode of Bromholm brynge me out of dette.'
B. 5.290 Ber it to þe Bisshop, and *bid* hym my grace,
B. 5.298 [Ac] Beton þe Brewestere *bad* hym good morwe
B. 5.322 And *bad* Bette þe Bocher ben on his syde.
B. 5.400 And if I *bidde* any bedes, but if it be in wraþe,
B. 5.446 And beet þiself on þe brest and *bidde* hym of grace,
B. 5.502 *Bidde* and biseche, if it be þi wille,
B. 5.592 The brugg[e] is of *bidde*-wel-þe-bet-may-þow-spede;
B. 5.601 *Biddeþ* amende-yow meke hym til his maister ones
B. 6.74 Treuþe tolde me ones and *bad* me telle it [forþ]:
B. 6.155 And *bad* hym go pissen with his plowȝ: '[pyuysshe] sherewe!
B. 6.216 And if þe gomes grucche *bidde* hem go [and] swynke,
B. 6.237 He shal [go] begge and *bidde* and no man bete his hunger.
B. 7.5 And *bad* hym holde hym at home and erien hise leyes,
B. 7.24 [And *bad* hem] buggen boldely [what] hem best liked
B. 7.67 For he þat beggeþ or *bit*, but he haue nede,
B. 7.76 Ac Gregory was a good man and *bad* vs gyuen alle
B. 7.81 And he þat *biddeþ* borweþ and bryngeþ hymself in dette.
B. 7.84 Forþi *biddeþ* noȝt, ye beggeres, but if ye haue nede,
B. 8.106 But dobest *bede* for hem [abide] þer for euere.
B. 8.124 But as I *bad* þoȝt þoo be mene bitwene,
B. 9.15 That he mot *bit* bcode do; he [boldeþ] hem alle:
B. 9.94 And *biddeþ* þe beggere go for his broke cloþes:
B. 9.134 And com to Noe anon and *bad* hym noȝt lette:
B.10.7 And blamed hym and banned hym and *bad* hym be stille–
B.10.202 [And] *biddeþ* vs be as breþeren and [blissen] oure enemys
B.10.258 Al þat þe book *bit* bi holi cherches techyng;
B.11.16 And *bad* me for my contenaunce acounten Clergie liȝte.
B.11.121 And *bad* hem souke for synne [saufte] at his breste
B.11.265 To wepe and to wel *bidde*, wherof wexeþ Mercy
B.11.278 To beggeris þat begge and *bidden* for goddes loue.
B.11.322 And nempned me by my name and *bad* me nymen hede,
B.11.399 Euery creature in his kynde encreesse [he *bad*]
B.12.9 Pouerte or penaunce, or preyeres *bidde*:
B.12.17 And *bidde* for hem þat ȝyue[þ] þee breed, for þer are bokes y[n]owe
B.12.28 And þere *bidde* my bedes but whan ich ete or slepe.
B.12.54 And loue hem noȝt as oure lord *bit*, lesen hir soules:
B.12.112 Buxomliche and benigneliche and *bidden* it of grace.
B.12.149 And *bad* hem go to Bethlem goddes burþe to honoure
B.12.195 [Th]at buxomliche *biddeþ* it and ben in wille to amenden hem.
B.12.274 And þe bettre for hir bokes to *bidden* we ben holden–
B.13.23 And *bad* me come to his court, wiþ clergie sholde I dyne.
B.13.71 Holi writ *bit* men be war–I wol noȝt write it here–
B.13.236 Whan þe preest preieþ þe peple hir Paternoster to *bidde*
B.13.324 And blame men bihynde hir bak and *bidden* hem meschaunce;
B.15.185 Loueþ hem as oure lord *biddeþ* and lokeþ how þei fare.
B.15.219 And is compaignable and confortatif and crist *bit* hymselue:
B.15.227 Ac *biddynge* as beggeris biheld I hym neuere.
B.15.256 Neiþer he *biddeþ* ne beggeþ ne borweþ to yelde.
B.15.312 And *bidden* hem bere it þere it [yborwed was].
B.15.324 And [bisette] to *bidde* for yow to swiche þat ben riche,
B.15.325 And ben founded and feffed ek to *bidde* for oþere.
B.16.22 And *bad* me toten on þe tree, on top and on roote.
B.16.65 To asken hym any moore þerof, and *bad* hym ful faire
B.17.131 And Hope afterward he *bad* me to louye
B.17.246 Boþe forȝyue and foryete, and ȝit *bidde* for vs
B.17.254 Be vnkynde to þyn euenecristene and al þat þow kanst *bidde*,

B.18.53   And *beden* hym drynken his deeþ [to lette and] hise daies [lengþe],
B.18.262 A spirit spekeþ to helle and *biddeþ* vnspere þe yates:
B.18.316 Eft þe light *bad* vnlouke and Lucifer answerde
B.19.143 And siþen buriede his body, and *beden* þat men sholde
B.20.166 And *bad* hym fonde to fighte and afere wanhope.
B.20.286 That borweþ and bereþ it þider and þanne *biddeþ* frendes
B.20.376 And [*bad*] Contricion [come] to kepe þe yate.
C. 2.58   Were *beden* to þe Bridale a bothe half þe contre,
C. 2.161 And *bade* gyle '[g]o gyue gold al aboute,
C. 2.176 And *bade* hem alle be bowen, beggares and othere,
C. 2.222 And *bad* falsnesse to fle and his feres alle.
C. 3.28   And *beden* here be blythe: 'for we beth thyn owene
C. 3.307 As by the book þat *byt* nobody withholde
C. 4.117 And be as Benet hem *bad*, dominik and frounceys;
C. 4.141 And *bad* nullum bonum be irremuneratum.
C. 5.126 He *bad* wastoures [g]o wurche and wynne here sustinaunce
C. 5.134 He *bad* b[e]tte kutte a bo[u]he or twene
C. 6.49   And non so bolde a beggare to *bidde* and to craue,
C. 6.69   And blame men byhynde here bak and *bidde* hem meschaunce;
C. 6.169 And *bad* hym bid to god be his helpe to amende.
C. 6.169 And bad hym *bid* to god be his helpe to amende.
C. 6.345 Bere hit to th[e] bischop and *bide* hym of his grace
C. 6.353 By betene hous the brewestere þat *bad* hym good morwen
C. 6.379 And *bade* b[et]te þe bochere ben on his syde.
C. 7.16   And yf y *bidde* eny bedes, but yf hit be in wrath,
C. 7.60   And bete thysulue [o]n þe breste and *bidde* hym of grace
C. 7.142 *Bidde* and biseche the, yf hit be thy wille,
C. 7.240 The Brygge hatte *b[id]*-wel-the-bet-may-th[ow]-spede;
C. 7.248 *Biddeth* amende-ȝow meke [hym] to his maistre grace
C. 8.76   Treuthe t[o]lde me ones and *bad* me telle hit fort[h]:
C. 8.151 And *bad* hym go pisse with his plogh, pyuische shrewe.
C. 8.205 And *bade* hunger in haste hye hym out of contraye
C. 8.226 And yf þe [g]lomes gruche *bid[d]e* hem go and swynke
C. 9.5   And *bad* hym holden hym at hoem and eryen his leyes
C. 9.28   [And] *bad* hem bugge boldly what hem best likede
C. 9.63   For he þat beg[g]eth or *biddeth*, but y[f he] haue nede,
C.10.120 Bote as y *bad* thouht tho be mene betwene
C.10.223 And *bad* go shapen a ship of shides and bordes.
C.11.43   Thenne semeth hit to my sihte to suche þat so *biddeth*
C.11.175 And *bade* me for my contin[au]nce counte cler[gie] lihte.
C.12.56   And *bad* hem souke for synne saue at his breste
C.14.29   May nat be, [be] þ[ow] syker, thogh we *bidde* euere.
C.14.57   Buxumliche and benyngnelyche and *bidden* hit of grace.
C.14.93   And *bad* men go to Bedlem goddes berthe to honoure
C.14.196 And þe bettere for here bokes to *bidden* we ben yholde–
C.15.26   And *beden* me ryse and rome; with reson sholde y dyne.
C.15.76   Holy writ *byt* men be waer and wysly hem kepe
C.16.352 Ac *biddyng* als a beggare byhelde y hym neuere.
C.16.372 For noþer he beggeth ne *biddeth* ne borweth to ȝelde.
C.17.2   Or beggeth or *biddeth*, be he ryche or pore,
C.17.59   For god *bad* his blessed as þe boek techeth–
C.17.62   Helpe thy kyn, Crist *bid*, for þer [coms]eth charite
C.17.190 That they ne wente [þe wey] as holy writ *byd*:
C.18.91   And *bad* hit be, of a bat of erthe, a man and a maide,
C.19.212 Bothe forȝeue and forȝete and ȝut *bidde* for vs
C.19.220 Be vnkynde to thyn emcristene and al þat thow canst *bidde*,
C.20.53   And *beden* hym drynke his deth to lette and his dayes lenghe
C.20.270 A spirit speketh to helle and *bit* vnspere þe ȝates:
C.20.359 For efte þat lihte *bade* vnlouke [and lucifer answerede].
C.21.143 And sethen bur[ie]den his body and *beden* þat men sholde
C.22.166 And *baed* hym fonde to fihte and afere wanhope.
C.22.286 That borweth and bereth hit theddere and thenne *biddeth* frendes
C.22.376 And *baed* contricioun come to kepe þe ȝate.

bidderis n *bidder n.* A 3; B 5 bidderes (2) bidderis (3); C 3 biddares (2) bidders (1)
A.Pr.40   *Bidderis* & beggeris faste aboute ȝede
A. 7.189 Of beggeris & *bidderis* what best is to done.
A. 8.67   Beggeris & *bidderis* ben not in þe bulle
B.Pr.40   *Bidderes* and beggeres faste aboute yede
B. 6.203 'Of beggeris and *bidderes* what best be to doone.
B. 7.65   Beggeres [and] *bidderes* beþ noȝt in þe bulle
B.13.241 Beggeris and *bidderis* of my breed crauen,
B.15.205 For þer are beggeris and *bidderis*, bedemen as it were,
C.Pr.41   *Bidders* and beggers fast aboute ȝede.
C. 8.209 Of beggares and *biddares* what beste be to done.
C. 9.61   Beggares and *Biddares* beth nat in þ[e] bulle

biddyng ger *biddynge ger. &>* bidden A 7 bidding (5) biddyng (2); B 12 biddyng (8) biddynge (3) biddynges (1); C 7 biddyng (3) byddyng (1) biddynge (2) biddynges (1)
A. 1.75   Þou brouȝtest me borewis my *biddyng* to werche,
A. 1.108 To be buxum at his *bidding*; he bad hem nouȝt ellis.
A. 2.51   And he[o] be bou[n] at his bode his *bidding* to fulfille,

A. 3.206 Beggeris for here *bidding* biddiþ of men mede;
A. 3.245 To be buxom & boun his *bidding* to fulfille.
A. 6.71   [And] loke þat þou leiȝe nouȝt for no manis *biddyng*.
A. 9.93   And were vnbuxum at his *bidding*, and bold to don ille,
B. 1.77   [Thow] brouȝtest me borwes my *biddyng* to [werche],
B. 1.110 To be buxom at his *biddyng*, he bad hem nouȝt ellis.
B. 3.219 Beggeres for hir *biddynge* bidden [of] men Mede;
B. 3.265 Be buxom at his *biddynge* his wil to fulfille.
B. 5.584 In-[no]-manere-ellis-noȝt-for-no-mannes-*biddyng*.
B. 8.103 [And were vnbuxum at his *biddyng*, and bold to don ille],
B.11.150 Wiþouten bede *biddyng* his boone was vnderfongen
B.11.153 Brouȝte me fro bitter peyne þer no *biddyng* myȝte.'
B.14.222 And buxom at hi[s] *biddyn[g]* for his broke loues,
B.15.426 The bettre for hir *biddynges* in body and in soule.
B.18.374 And be at my *biddyng* wherso [best] me likeþ.
B.19.375 Some þoruȝ bedes *biddynge* and some [by] pilgrymag[e]
C. 1.74   Thow broughtest me borewes my *biddyng* to fulfille,
C. 3.418 To be buxum at my *byddyng* his [b]o[n]e to fulfille.
C.10.98   Sholde no bisshop be here *biddynges* to withsite.
C.12.85   Withouten bed[e] *biddyng* his bone was vnderfonge
C.16.63   And buxum at his *biddyng* for his breed and his drynke
C.20.416 And be at my *biddynge*, at blisse or at payne.
C.21.375 Somme thorw bedes *biddynge* and [somme] bi pilgrimag[e]

bide > bidden,biden; bydels > bedel

biden v *biden v.* A 1; B 4 bide (1) biden (1) bideþ (1) bidynge (1); C 2 byde (1) bydynge (1)
A.10.168 Busk[en hem] to þat boot & *biden* þereInne
B. 9.137 Buskeþ yow to þat boot and *bideþ* þerInne
B.18.310 For vs were bettre noȝt þe þan *biden* his sighte.
B.20.48   Forþi be noȝt abasshed to *bide* and to be nedy
B.20.142 And boold and *bidynge* while his bagge lasteþ.'
C.22.48   Forthy be nat abasched to *byde* and to be nedy
C.22.142 And bolde and [*b*]*ydynge* while his bagge lasteth.'

bidowe n *bideu n.* A 1
A.11.214 A *bidowe* or a baselard he beriþ be his side;

bidropped ptp *bidroppen v.* B 1 bidropped
B.13.320 It was *bidropped* wiþ wraþe and wikkede wille,

bienalis > biennals

bienfait n *benefete n.* A 1; B 2 bienfait (1) bienfeet (1); C 2 beenfeet (1) beenfete (1)
A. 6.98   Þe boldnesse of þi *bienfait* makiþ þe blynd þanne,
B. 5.429 If any man dooþ me a *bienfait* or helpeþ me at nede
B. 5.612 The boldnesse of þi *bienfe[et]* makeþ þee blynd þanne,
C. 7.42   Yf eny man do[th] me a *beenfeet* or helpeth me at nede
C. 7.264 The boldenesse of thy *beenfet[e]* maketh the blynd thenne;

biennals n *biennal n.* A 1 bienalis; B 1; C 1 bionales
A. 8.154 *Bienalis* & trienalis & bisshopis lettres.
B. 7.176 *Biennals* and triennals and Bisshopes lettres.
C. 9.321 *Bionales* and trionales and bisshopes lettres.

bifalle v *bifallen v.* A 7 befalle (1) befalliþ (1) befel (4) byfel (1); B 14 bifalle (4) bifalleþ (1) bifel (9); C 13 bifalle (2) byfalle (1) byfalleth (2) biful (5) byful (2) byfull (1)
A.Pr.6   Me *befel* a ferly, of fairie me þouȝte:
A. 1.50   "Reddite cesari," quaþ god, "þat cesari *befall[iþ]*,
A. 5.42   Qui cum patre & filio; Faire mote ȝow *befalle*.'
A. 5.245 Ac what *befel* of þis feloun I can not faire shewe;
A. 8.147 It *befel* as his fadir seide in faraos tyme
A. 9.8   Til it *befel* on a Friday two Freris I mette,
A.12.58   Many ferlys me *byfel* in a fewe ȝeris.
B.Pr.6   Me *bifel* a ferly, of Fairye me þoȝte.
B. 1.52   "Reddite Cesari," quod god, "þat Cesari *bifalleþ*,
B. 5.58   Qui cum patre & filio; þat faire hem *bifalle*
B. 5.471 What *bifel* of þis feloun I kan noȝt faire shewe.
B. 7.170 It *bifel* as his fader seide in Pharaoes tyme
B. 7.172 It *bifel* as his fader tolde, hise frendes þere hym souȝte.
B. 8.8   Til it *bifel* on a Friday two freres I mette,
B. 9.162 As *bifel* of þe folk þat I bifore [shewed],
B.11.295 As *bifel* for a knyȝt, or foond hym for his strengþe.
B.15.104 And be kynde as *bifel* for clerkes and curteise of cristes goodes,
B.16.60   'That is sooþ,' [seide] Piers, 'so it may *bifalle*.
B.16.139 Til it *bifel* on a friday, a litel bifore Pasqe.
B.19.242 And some to se and to seye what sholde *bifalle*,
B.20.350 He may se and here [here, so] may *bifalle*.
C.Pr.7   Me *biful* for to slepe, for werynesse ofwalked,
C. 1.48   "Reddite cesari," sayde god, "þat cesar[i] *byfalleth*,
C. 5.199 Qui cum patre & filio; þat fayre hem *byfalle*
C. 6.27   Semyng a souerayn oen whereso me *byfull*
C. 6.325 What *byful* of this feloun y can nat fayre shewe;

C. 9.129   To vnderfongen hem fayre *byfalleth* for þe ryche
C. 9.314   Hit *biful* as his fadur saide in farao his tyme
C.10.8   Til hit *biful* [o]n [a] fryday two freres y mette,
C.13.109   As *byful* for a knyht or fond hym for his strenthe.
C.18.166   This *biful* on a fryday, a litel bifore Pasche,
C.20.379   Falsliche [thow] fettest there þat me *biful* to loke,
C.21.242   And somme to se and to saye what sholde *bifalle*
C.22.350   He may se and here here, so may *bifalle*,

bifore adv *biforen adv.* A 5 before (4) beforn (1); B 23 before (2) bifore
(21); C 17 before (1) bifore (8) byfore (8)
A. 5.9   Þanne sauȝ I meke[l] more þan I *before* tolde,
A. 5.10   [For I [sauȝ] þe feld ful of folk þat I *before* tolde],
A. 6.11   And þe vernicle *beforn* for men shulde knowe
A. 7.226   And ȝaf [it] hym in haste þat hadde ten *before*,
A.10.185   As fel of þe folk [þat I] *before* shewide.
B. 5.9   [Th]anne [mette me] muche moore þan I *bifore* tolde,
B. 5.10   For I seiȝ þe feld ful of folk þat I *before* [tolde],
B. 5.523   And þe vernycle *bifore*, for men sholde knowe
B. 6.242   And yaf [it hym in haste þat hadde ten *bifore*];
B. 9.162   As bifel of þe folk þat I *bifore* [shewed].
B.11.254   Ac pouerte god putte *bifore* and preised þe bettre:
B.13.315   'Ye, whoso toke hede', quod haukyn, 'bihynde and *bifore*,
B.14.139   And noȝt to fonge *bifore* for drede of disalowyng.
B.14.142   Riȝt as a seruaunt takeþ his salarie *bifore*, & siþþe wolde clayme
            moore
B.14.213   Ther þe poore preesseþ *bifore* wiþ a pak at his rugge;
B.15.153   And fond I neuere ful charite, *before* ne bihynde.
B.15.320   And auisen hem *bifore* a fyue dayes or sixe
B.15.360   That whilom warned *bifore* what sholde falle after.
B.15.436   And be gide and go *bifore* as a good Banyer,
B.16.140   The þursday *bifore*, þere he made his [cene],
B.17.107   Who is bihynde and who *bifore* and who ben on horse;
B.19.16   Patriarkes and prophetes prophecied *bifore*
B.19.55   That longe hadde yleyen *bifore* as Luciferis cherles,
B.19.115   So at þat feeste first as I *bifore* tolde
B.19.148   And his moder Marie; þus men *bifore* de[uyn]ede.
B.19.243   Boþe of wele and of wo [and be ware *bifore*],
B.20.184   And made me balled *bifore* and bare on þe croune;
B.20.288   Ac while he is in westmynstre he wol be *bifore*
C. 3.303   And Gylours gyuen *byfore* and goode men at þe ende
C. 4.21   And lat warrokye [hym] w[e]l with auyseth-þe-*byfore*;
C. 5.109   Thenne mette me muche more then y *byfore* tolde
C. 6.117   Harm of eny man, byhynde or *bifore*.
C. 7.168   And þe vernicle *bifore* for men sholde yknowe
C.12.141   Ac pouerte god potte *byfore* and preuede for þe betere:
C.16.3   Hewen þat haen here huyre *byfore* aren eueremore pore
C.16.7   A[nd] nat to fonge *byfore* for drede [of] dessallouwynge.
C.16.54   There þe pore preseth *byfore* with a pak at his rugge,
C.17.98   That whilum warnede *byfore* what sholde [f]alle aftur.
C.21.16   Patriarkes & prophetes profecied *bifore*
C.21.55   That longe hadden leye *bifore* as luciferes cherles
C.21.115   So at þat feste furste as y *before* tolde
C.21.148   And his moder marie; thus men *bifore* deuynen.
C.21.243   Bothe of wele and of wo and be ywaer *bifore*,
C.22.184   And made me balled *bifore* and baer on þe crowne;
C.22.288   Ac while he is in Westmynstre he wol be *bifore*

bifore prep *biforen prep.* A 4 before; B 32; C 47 before (1) bifore (19)
byfor (1) byfore (26)
A. 3.104   *Before* þe kyng & his counseil, clerkis & oþere.
A. 3.173   And þou hast famid me foule *before* þe king here.
A. 8.39   And *before* þe face of my fadir fourme ȝoure setis.
A. 8.172   And come [alle] *before* crist acountes to ȝelden,
B.Pr.183   Strook forþ sternely and stood *bifore* hem alle
B. 3.115   *Bifore* þe kyng and his conseil, clerkes and oþere.
B. 3.186   Ac þow hast famed me foule *bifore* þe kyng here.
B. 5.377   Fedde me *biforee* noon whan fastyng dayes were.'
B. 7.194   And comen alle [bi]fore crist acountes to yelde,
B.10.451   Thouȝ ye come *bifore* kynges and clerkes of þe lawe
B.11.189   Wheiþer we loue þe lordes here *bifore* þe lord of blisse;
B.11.303   A chartre is chalangeable *bifore* a chief Iustice.
B.11.312   The bisshop shal be blamed *bifore* god, as I leue,
B.11.393   Of hire defautes foule *bifore* hem reherced].
B.13.47   *Bifore* Pacience breed to brynge, [bitynge apart],
B.13.65   'It is noȝt foure dayes þis freke, *bifore* þe deen of Poules,
B.13.74   Ac I wiste neuere freke þat as a frere yede *bifore* men on englissh
B.13.82   That disshes and doublers [þis doctour *bifore*]
B.13.439   Haue beggeres *bifore* hem þe whiche ben goddes minstrales
B.13.440   To crie a largesse *bifore* oure lord, youre good loos to shewe.
B.15.239   In þe Consistorie *bifore* þe Commissarie he comeþ noȝt ful ofte
B.15.302   Thei wolde haue yfed þat folk *bifore* wilde foweles;
B.15.369   Neiþer þei konneþ ne knoweþ oon cours *bifore* anoþer.
B.15.595   Dide hym rise and rome riȝt *bifore* þe Iewes.

B.16.139   Til it bifel on a friday, a litel *bifore* Pasqe.
B.16.222   And is noȝt but gendre of a generacion *bifore* Iesu crist in heuene:
B.18.40   Tho putte forþ a p[e]lour *bifore* Pilat and seide,
B.18.80   *Bifore* Pilat and ooþer peple in þe place he houed.
B.18.124   And which a light and a leme lay *bifore* helle.
B.18.373   Fendes and f[e]ndekynes *bifore* me shul stande
B.18.397   And mercy al mankynde *bifore* me in heuene.
B.19.7   And com in wiþ a cros *bifore* þe comune peple,
B.19.119   For *bifore* his moder Marie made he þat wonder
B.19.153   Verray m[a]n *bifore* hem alle and forþ wiþ hem yede.
B.19.443   And cleymeþ *bifore* þe kyng to be kepere ouer cristene,
B.20.96   And bar þe baner *bifore* deeþ; bi riȝt he it cleymede.
C.Pr.200   Strok forth sturnely and stod *byfore* hem alle
C. 2.103   And fastyng dayes to frete *byfore* noone and drynke
C. 3.2   [With] Bedeles and Baylifs ybrouhte *byfor* þe kyng.
C. 3.152   *Byfore* þe kyng and his consayl, clerkes and oþere.
C. 3.232   Ac thow hast famed me foule *byfore* þe kyng here
C. 3.293   Mede many tymes men ȝeueth *byfore* þe doynge
C. 4.30   *Byfore* þe kyng an[d] Consience yf þe comune playne
C. 5.106   *Byfore* þe cross on my knees knokked y my brest,
C. 5.113   And Consience his crocer *byfore* þe kyng stande.
C. 6.434   [On] fastyng dayes *bifore* noen fedde me with ale,
C. 7.99   Haue beggares *byfore* hem þe whiche ben goddes mu[n]strals
C. 9.240   Acounted *byfore* [crist] but Consience excuse hym.
C. 9.255   Ne no blanke[t] on his bed ne whyte bred *byfore* hym.
C. 9.323   Worth fayre vnderfonge *byfore* god þat tyme
C. 9.340   And comen alle *bifore* Crist acountes to ȝelde,
C.10.180   Of þ[e] blessed baptist *bifore* alle his gestes.
C.11.276   Thogh ȝe come *bifore* kynges and clerkes of þe law[e]
C.12.160   And lyf lastyng for euere *byfore* oure lord in heuene:
C.13.35   And rikene *byfore* resoun a resonable acounte
C.13.117   A Chartre is chaleniable *byfore* a chief Iustice.
C.13.124   The bishop shal be blamed *before* god, as y leue,
C.15.22   That iustus *bifore* iesu in die iudicij non saluabitur bote vix helpe;
C.15.70   At poules *byfore* þe peple what penaunce they soffrede,
C.15.138   *Byfore* perpetuel pees y shal proue þat y saide
C.15.139   And avowe *byfore* god and forsaken hit neuere
C.15.209   For no breed þat y betrauaile to [brynge] *byfore* lordes.
C.16.364   In constorie *bifore* [þe] commissarie a cometh nat ful ofte
C.17.31   And faire *byfore* tho men fauneden with þe tayles.
C.17.60   To helpe thy fader formost *byfore* freres or monkes
C.17.84   That fayre *byfore* folk prechen and techen
C.17.105   Noþer they [conn]eth ne [know]eth a cours *by[fore]* anoþer.
C.18.49   And feccheth away þe fruyt som tyme *byfore* bothe myn yes.
C.18.98   And for þe fayrest fruyte *byfore* hym, as of erthe,
C.18.166   This biful on a fryday, a litel *bifore* Pasche,
C.19.286   Eny creature be coupable *bifore* a kynges iustice
C.20.39   Thenne potte hym forth a pelour *byfore* pilatus and saide,
C.20.82   *Byfore* pilatus and oþere peple in þe place he houed.
C.20.127   And which a lihte and a leem lay *bifore* helle.
C.20.415   Fendes and fendekynes *byfore* me shal stande
C.20.440   And mercy a[l] mankynde *byfore* me in heuene.
C.21.7   And cam in with a cros *bifore* þe comune peple
C.21.119   For *bifore* his moder Marie made he þat wonder
C.21.153   Verray man *bifore* [hem] alle, and forth with hem ȝede.
C.21.443   And claymeth *bifore* þe kynge to be kepare ouer cristene
C.22.96   And baer þe baner *bifore* deth; bi riht he hit claymede.
C.22.130   And knokked Consience in Court *bifore* hem alle;

biful- > bifalle; byg > bigge; bigan > bigynnen

bygat v *biyeten v.* C 4 bygat (1) bygete (1) bygeten (1) byȝete (1)
C. 1.29   In his glotonye *bygat* gurles þat were cherles
C. 2.147   And as a bastard ybore *byȝete* was he neuere.
C.10.209   And is no more to mene but men þat ben *bygeten*
C.14.31   As to be bore or *bygete* in such a constillacioun;

bigerdeles -dlis > bigirdles; bygete(n > begat

bigge adj *big adj. &> buggen* A 1; B 1; C 2 byg (1) bygge (1)
A. 7.199   Bolde beggeris & *bigge*, þat mowe here breed beswynken,
B. 6.213   Bolde beggeris and *bigge* þat mowe hir breed biswynke,
C. 8.223   Bolde beggares and *bygge* þat mowe here breed byswynke,
C.18.135   *Byg* and abydyng, and bold in his barnhoed

biggen > buggen; biggere > buggere

biggyng prp *biggen v.* B 1
B. 5.130   Amonges Burgeises haue I be, [bigg]yng at Londoun,

bigile v *bigilen v.* A 2; B 14 bigile (6) bigiled (6) bigileþ (2); C 17 bigile
(2) bigyle (2) bygile (1) bygyle (1) bigiled (3) bigyled (2) bigiledest
(1) bigyledest (1) bigileth (3) bygyleth (1)
A.11.76   Suffre sathan his sed to *bigile*,
A.11.83   Suffren sathan his sed to *bigile*,

B.10.123 Suffre Sathan his seed to *bigile*,
B.10.130 Suffre Sathan his seed to *bigile*,
B.10.198 And so shaltow fals folk and feiþlees *bigile*:
B.10.262 And lat no body be by þi beryng *bigiled*
B.11.41   Ne shal noȝt greue þee [graiþly], ne *bigile* [þee], but þow wolt.'
B.13.360 And awaited þoruȝ [wittes wyes] to *bigile*;
B.14.204 Ac wiþ richesse þ[o] Ribaud[es] raþest men *bigileþ*.
B.15.372 Grammer, þe ground of al, *bigile*þ now children,
B.15.412 And siþþe oure Saueour suffred þe Sarȝens so *bigiled*
B.18.160 And riȝt as [þe gilour] þoruȝ gile [*bigiled* man formest]
B.18.162 And *bigile* þe gilour, and þat is good] sleighte:
B.18.293 For god wol noȝt be *bigiled*', quod Gobelyn, 'ne byiaped.
B.18.339 That gilours be *bigiled* and þat is good reson:
B.18.360 And gile is *bigiled* and in his gile fallen:
C. 1.37   [That] is þe wrecchede world wolde þe *bigyle*
C. 3.92   That *bygyleth* goode men and greueth men wrongly,
C. 3.95   That so *bigileth* hem of here goed, þat god on hem sende
C.11.17   And lette with a loueday [lewed] treuthe and *bigile*
C.11.308 Ne shal nat greue þe gr[ayth]ly ne *bigyle* the, but thow wolle.'
C.14.5   And conseyled the for cristes sake no creature is *bygile*,
C.15.77   That no fals frere thorw flaterynge hem *bygyle*;
C.16.45   Ac with rychesse tho rybaudes rathest men *bigileth*.
C.17.108 Gramer, þe grounde of al, *bigileth* nouthe childrene,
C.20.163 And riht as the gylour thorw gyle *bigile[d]* man formost
C.20.165 And *bigile* þe gilour, and þat is goed sleythe:
C.20.323 [For] god wol nat be [*bi*]*gyled*,' quod gobelyne, 'n[e] byiaped.
C.20.326 And as thowe *bigyledest* godes ymag[e] in goynge of an addre,
C.20.327 So hath god *bigiled* vs alle in goynge of a weye.'
C.20.380 *Byglosedest* hem and *bigiledest* hem and my gardyne breke
C.20.382 That gylours [beth] *bigiled* and [in] here gyle falle
C.20.392 And gyle [be] *bigyled* thorw grace at þe laste:

bigynnen *v biginnen v.* A 4 begynne (2) begynneþ (1) begonne (1); B 19
    bigan (9) bigynne (1) bigynnen (1) bigynneþ (5) bigonne (3); C 23
    bigan (9) bygan (5) bigynne (3) bygynne (2) bigynneth (2) bygynneth
    (2)
A. 2.56   Þus *begynne* þe gomes & gredde wel heiȝe:
A. 5.146 Now *begynneþ* glotoun for to [go to] shrift,
A. 5.186 Bargoynes & beuerechis *begonne* for to arise,
A. 7.152 'I was not wonid to werche', quaþ wastour, 'now wile I not
            begynne,'
B. 2.74   [Th]us *bigynnen* þ[e] gomes [and] greden [wel] heiȝe:
B. 5.287 For þe good þat þow hast geten *bigan* al wiþ falshede,
B. 5.296 Now *bigynneþ* Gloton for to go to shrifte
B. 5.337 [Bargaynes and beuerages *bigonne* to arise],
B. 5.340 Hise guttes *bigonne* to goþelen as two gredy sowes;
B. 5.390 He *bigan* Benedicite with a bolk and his brest knokked,
B. 6.167 'I was noȝt wont to werche', quod Wastour, 'now wol I noȝt
            bigynne!'
B.13.346 Aboute þe mouþ, or byneþe *bigynneþ* to grope,
B.14.149 And as an hyne þat hadde his hire er he *bigonne*,
B.18.48   And *bigan* of [grene] þorn a garland to make,
B.18.161 So shal grace that *bigan* [al] make a good [ende
B.18.181 For Iesus Iustede wel Ioye *bigynneþ* dawe:
B.18.212 So god þat *bigan* al of his goode wille
B.18.361 Now *bigynneþ* þi gile ageyn þee to turne
B.19.110 And þere *bigan* god of his grace to do wel:
B.19.116 *Bigan* god of his grace and goodnesse to dowel,
B.19.213 [Th]anne *bigan* grace to go wiþ Piers Plowman
B.19.317 'Ayeins þi greynes', quod Grace, '*bigynneþ* for to ripe,
B.19.325 And þerwiþ Grace *bigan* to make a good foundement,
C. 1.104 And god whan he *bigan* heuene in þat grete blisse
C. 5.100 A gobet of his grace and *bigynne* a tyme
C. 5.102 'Y rede the,' quod resoun tho, 'rape the to *bigynne*
C. 6.180 Aboute þe mouthe and bynethe *bygan* y to grope
C. 6.342 For the good that thow hast gete *bygan* al with falshede
C. 6.350 Now *bygynneth* glotoun for to go to shryfte
C. 6.395 Bargaynes and Beuereges *bygan* to a[rys]e
C. 7.6   A *bigan* benedicite with a bolk and his breste knokkede,
C. 8.164 'I was nat woned to worche,' quod wastour, 'now wol y nat
            bygynne!'
C. 9.244 As matynes by þe morwe til masse *bygynne*,
C.17.134 And o god þat al *bygan* with gode herte they honoureth
C.19.113 For god þat al *bygan* in bigynnynge of the worlde
C.20.48   And *bigan* of grene thorn a garlond to make,
C.20.164 So shal grace þat *bigan* al maken a goed ende
C.20.184 For iesus ioustede wel ioy *bigynneth* dawe:
C.20.221 So god þat *bigan* al of his gode wille
C.20.310 And neuere [n]as þeraȝeyne and now wolde *bigynne*,
C.20.399 And now *bygynneth* thy gyle agayne the to turne
C.21.110 And þer *bigan* god of his grace to do wel:
C.21.116 *Bigan* god of his grace and goodnesse to do wel
C.21.213 Thenne *bigan* grace to go with [Peres Plouhman]
C.21.317 'Aȝeynes thy graynes,' quod grace, '*bigynneth* for to rype,

C.21.325 And þerwith grace *bigan* to make a goode fo[un]dement

bigynnyng ger *biginninge ger.* A 1 begynnyng; B 1; C 5 bigynnyng (1)
    bygynnyng (1) bygynnynge (2) bygynnynge (1)
A.10.80   It is *begynnyng* of goodnesse god for to douten.
B.18.191 [At] þe *bigynn[yng]* god] gaf þe doom hymselue
C. 8.238 Go to oure *bygynnynge* tho god the world made,
C.14.159 Was neuere creature vnder crist þat knewe wel þe *bygynnyng*
C.18.203 God [that] *bigynnyng* hadde neuere bote tho hym goed thouhte
C.19.113 For god þat al *bygan* in *bigynnynge* of the worlde
C.20.196 At the *bigynnynge* god gaf the doem hymsulue

bigirdles n *bigirdel n.* A 1 bigerdlis; B 1; C 1 bigerdeles
A. 9.79   Þe bagges & þe [*bi*]*gerdlis*, he haþ broken hem alle
B. 8.88   The bagges and þe *bigirdles*, he haþ [b]roke hem alle
C.10.85   The bagges and þe *bigerdeles*, he hath [b]roken hem alle

byglosedest v *biglossen v.* C 1
C.20.380 *Byglosedest* hem and bigiledest hem and my gardyne breke

bigonne > bigynnen

bigruccheþ v *bigrucchen v.* A 1 begrucchiþ; B 1; C 2 begrucheth (1)
    bigruchen (1)
A. 7.61   And make hym mery wiþ þe corn whoso it *begrucchiþ*.
B. 6.67   And make h[y]m murie þermyd, maugree whoso *bigruccheþ* it.
C. 8.68   And m[a]ken hym merye þermy[d], maugrey ho[so] *bigruchen* hit;
C. 8.155 And maken vs murye þer[with] maugreye h[o] *begrucheth*.'

biheeld biheld(e > biholde

biheste n *biheste n.* A 1 behest; B 4 behestes (1) biheste (3); C 5 biheste
    (3) byheste (1) bihestes (1)
A. 3.116 Ȝoure fadir he[o] fellide þoruȝ false *behest*,
B. 3.127 Youre fader she felled þoruȝ false *biheste*,
B.11.61   And þanne was Fortune my foo for al hir faire [*biheste*],
B.15.313 For we [by] goddes [*behestes*] abiden alwey
B.20.118 Weren feþered wiþ fair *biheste* and many a fals truþe.
C.10.250 That for no kyne catel ne no kyne *byheste*
C.12.13   And thenne was fortune my foo for al her fayre *biheste*
C.18.122 That thorw fals *biheste* and fruyt furste man disseyued.
C.20.320 And dust hem breke here buxumnesse thorw fals *bihestes*
C.22.118 Weren fythered with fayre *biheste* and many a fals treuthe.

bihighte -hiȝte -hihte(- > bihote

bihynde adv *bihinden adv.& pred.adj.* A 1 behynde; B 8; C 6 bihynde (2)
    byhynde (3) behynde (1)
A. 3.33   Þere cunnyng clerkis shuln clokke *behynde*.'
B. 3.34   Ther konnynge clerkes shul clokke *bihynde*.'
B. 5.426 And my seruauntȝ som tyme: hir salarie is *bihynde*;
B.13.315 'Ye, whoso toke hede', quod haukyn, '*bihynde* and bifore,
B.14.208 Ther þe poore is put *bihynde*, and parauenture kan moore
B.15.153 And fond I neuere ful charite, before ne *bihynde*.
B.15.437 And hardie hem þat *bihynde* ben, and ȝyue hem good euidence.
B.17.107 Who is *bihynde* and who bifore and who ben on horse;
B.19.340 And his Spye Spille-loue, oon Spek-yuel-*bihynde*.
C. 3.37   There connynge clerkes shal clokke *bihynde*.'
C. 6.117 Harm of eny man, *byhynde* or bifore.
C. 7.39   And my seruauntes som tyme here salerie is *bihynde*;
C.15.7   That y lyuede longe, leue me *byhynde*
C.16.49   There þe pore is potte *behynde* and parauntur can more
C.21.340 And his spye spille-loue, oen speke-euele-*bihynde*.

bihynde prep *behinde prep.* A 2 behynde; B 4; C 2 byhynde
A. 5.74   And blamide hym *behynde* his bak to bringe hym in fame;
A. 8.92   And I *behynde* hem boþe beheld al þe b[u]lle.
B. 5.94   [And blamed hym *bihynde* his bak to brynge hym in fame;
B. 7.110 And I *bihynde* hem boþe biheld al þe bulle.
B.13.324 And blame men *bihynde* oure bak and bidden hem meschaunce;
B.16.49   Manacen *bihynde* me, my fruyt for to fecche.
C. 6.69   And blame men *byhynde* here bak and bidde hem meschaunce.
C. 9.284 And y *byhynde* hem bothe byheld alle þe bulle.

byhofte n *bihofþe n.* C 1
C.12.188 Aren tidiore and touore to mannes *byhofte*

biholde v *biholden v.* A 4 beheld (2) beholde (1) beholdis (1); B 8 biheeld
    (1) biheld (3) biholde (3) biholdest (1); C 6 beheld (2) byheld (1)
    bihelde (1) byhelde (1) byholde (1)
A.Pr.13   Ac as I *beheld* into þe Est an heiȝ to þe sonne
A. 5.91   & *beholde* how heyne haþ a newe cote;
A. 8.92   And I behynde hem boþe *beheld* al þe b[u]lle.
A. 8.125 On salamonis sawis [seldom] þou *beholdis*:
B.Pr.13   [Ac] as I *biheeld* into þe Eest, an heiȝ to þe sonne,
B. 5.111 And *biholde* [how H]eyne haþ a newe cote;
B. 7.110 And I bihynde hem boþe *biheld* al þe bulle.
B. 7.143 On Salomons sawes selden þow *biholdest*:

B.11.9   And in a Mirour þat hiȝte middelerþe she made me *biholde*,
B.11.345   Briddes I *biheld* þat in buskes made nestes;
B.15.227   Ac biddynge as beggeris *biheld* I hym neuere.
B.17.68   And to þe wye he wente hise woundes to *biholde*,
C.Pr.14   Estward y *beheld* aftir þe sonne
C. 9.284   And y byhynde hem bothe *byheld* alle þe bulle.
C.13.134   And y bowed my body, *bihel[d]e* al aboute
C.13.156   Briddes y *beheld* [þat] in bosches made nestes;
C.16.352   Ac biddyng als a beggare *byhelde* y hym neuere.
C.19.67   And to th[e] wey a wente his woundes to *byholde*

bihote v *bihoten* v. A 4 behiȝte (2) behote (2); B 7 bihighte (1) bihiȝte (4) bihote (2); C 10 behyhte (1) behote (1) bihihte (4) bihyhte (1) byhihtest (1) bihote (2)
A. 3.28   Hendely þanne heo *behiȝte* hem þe same,
A. 5.47   And *behiȝte* to hym þat vs alle made
A. 5.226   Til I haue euesong herd, I *behote* [to] þe rode.
A. 7.262   'I *behote* god,' quaþ hunger, 'henis nile I wende
B. 3.29   Hendiliche heo þanne *bihiȝte* hem þe same,
B. 5.64   And *bihiȝte* to hym þat vs alle made
B. 5.454   Til I haue euensong herd: I *bihote* to þe Roode.
B. 6.278   '[I] *bihote* god', quod hunger, 'hennes [nil] I wende
B.16.239   For hymself *bihiȝte* to me and to myn issue boþe
B.18.332   I *bihiȝte* hem noȝt here helle for euere.
B.20.111   And *bihighte* hem long lif, and lecherie he sente
C. 3.30   And Mede hendeliche *behyhte* hem þe same,
C. 6.5   And *bihyhte* to hym þat vs alle made
C. 7.68   Til y haue euensong yherd: y *bihote* to þe rode.'
C. 8.237   'Ȝe, y *bihote* the,' quod hunger, 'or elles þe bible lyeth.
C. 8.300   'Y *behote* the,' quod hunger, 'þat hennes ne wol y wende
C.18.245   He *bihihte* vs issue and ayr in oure olde age;
C.18.257   To me and [to] myn issue more he me *bihihte*,
C.20.317   And *byhihtest* here and hym aftur to knowe
C.20.375   Y *bihihte* hem nat here helle for euere.
C.22.111   And *bihihte* hem long lyf and lecherye he sente

bihoueþ v *bihoven* v. A 3 behouiþ; B 6; C 2 bihoueth (1) byhoueth (1)
A. 8.116   Whan þe frost fresiþ foode hem *behouiþ*;
A. 9.29   And ȝet is he sauf & sound, & so hym *behouiþ*.
A.10.74   Saue hymself fro synne, for so hym *behouiþ*,
B. 5.38   "[Lo], þe leuere child þe moore loore *bihoueþ*";
B. 7.134   [Whan þe frost freseþ fode hem *bihoueþ*];
B. 8.33   Ac yet is he saaf and sound, and so hym *bihoueþ*,
B. 9.73   Alle þise lakken Inwit and loore [hem] *bihoueþ*.
B.17.319   Ac er his rightwisnesse to ruþe torne som restitucion *bihoueþ*,
B.18.399   And nameliche at swich a nede þer nedes help *bihoueþ*:
C. 7.295   To falewe with fiue ȝo[k]es; 'forthy me *bihoueth*
C. 9.89   What other *byhoueth* þat hath many childrene

byiaped v *bijapen* v. B 1; C 2 byiaped (1) byiapede (1)
B.18.293   For god wol noȝt be bigiled', quod Gobelyn, 'ne *byiaped*.
C. 1.63   Iudas he *byiapede* thorw iewene suluer
C.20.323   [For] god wol nat be [bi]gyled,' quod gobelyne, 'n[e] *byiaped*.

bykam > bicome

bikenne n *bikennen* v. A 3 bekenne; B 2; C 2 bykenne
A. 2.31   I may no lengere lette, lord I þe *bekenne*,
A. 9.50   I *bekenne* [ȝow] crist þat on þe crois deiȝede.'
A.11.165   I *bekenne* þe crist,' quaþ she, 'I can teche þe no betere.'
B. 2.50   Now I *bikenne* þee crist', quod she, 'and his clene moder,
B. 8.59   'I *bikenne* þee crist', quod he, 'þat on [þe] cros deyde.'
C. 2.53   For y *bykenne* the crist,' quod she, 'and his clene moder,
C.10.58   'Y *bykenne* the Crist,' quod he, 'þat on þe cross deyede.'

bikere v *bikeren* v. B 1; C 1
B.20.79   And þere abide and *bikere* ayeins Beliales children.'
C.22.79   And þere abyde and *bikere* aȝeyn beliales childrene.'

biknowen v *biknouen* v. A 2 beknowe (1) biknowe (1); B 5 beknew (1) biknewe (1) biknowe (1) biknowen (2); C 7 beknowe (1) biknewe (1) biknewen (1) biknowe (1) byknowe (2) byknowen (1)
A. 3.32   Þat he ne worþ ferst auauncid for I am *beknowe*
A. 5.114   'I haue [ben] coueit[ous],' quaþ [þat caitif], 'I [bi]knowe [hit] h[e]re,
B.Pr.205   And þouȝ it costned me catel *biknowen* it I nolde
B. 3.33   That he ne worþ first auaunced, for I am *biknowen*
B. 5.198   'I haue ben coueitous', quod þis caytif, 'I *biknowe* it here.
B.10.422   And for he *bekne[w* on] þe cros and to crist shrof hym
B.19.149   The knyghtes þat kepten it *biknewe* hemseluen
C.Pr.213   And thow hit costed m[e] catel *byknowen* [hit] y ne wolde
C. 3.36   That he ne worth furste vaunsed, for y am *byknowe*
C. 5.92   'That is soth,' y saide, 'and so y *beknowe*
C. 6.206   'Y haue be coueitous,' quod this kaytif, 'y *biknowe* hit here.
C.11.254   And for he *biknewe* on þe croes and to crist shrof hym
C.13.11   Ne for brihtnesse of here beaute here spouse to be *byknowe*,

C.21.149   The knyhtes þat kepten hit *biknewen* hemsuluen

bile n *bil n.(1)* B 1
B.11.358   And some briddes at þe *bile* þoruȝ breþyng conceyued,

bileef > bileuen; bileeue > bileue,bileuen

biles n *bile n.(2)* B 1; C 1 byles
B.20.84   *Biles* and bocches and brennynge Agues,
C.22.84   *Byles* and boches and brennynge aguwes,

bileue n *bileve n. &> bileuen,bilyue* A 6 beleue; B 37 bileeue (1) bileue (36); C 38 beleue (3) bileue (25) byleue (10)
A. 5.7   I sat softely [adoun] & seide my *beleue*,
A. 8.159   Þis is [a] l[e]f of oure *beleue*, as lettrid men vs [tech]iþ:
A.11.236   Mowe be sauid so, & so is oure *beleue*.
A.11.238   And for his lele *beleue*, whanne he his lif tyneþ,
A.11.249   And souereynliche to suche þat sewen oure *beleue*:
A.11.307   Arn none raþere yrauisshid fro þe riȝte *beleue*
B. 5.7   [I] sat softely adoun and seide my *bileue*,
B. 7.181   This is [a leef of] oure *bileue*, as lettred men vs techeþ:
B.10.207   And [souereynly] to swiche [þat] suwen oure *bileue*;
B.10.250   And hymself ordeyned to sadde vs in *bileue*.
B.10.353   Mowen be saued so, and [so] is oure *bileue*.
B.10.355   And for his lele *bileue*, whan he þe lif tyneþ,
B.10.463   Arn none raþer yrauysshed fro þe riȝte *bileue*
B.10.465   Ne none sonner saued, ne sadder of *bileue*,
B.10.470   Into þe [parfit] blisse of Paradis for hir pure *bileue*,
B.11.110   [The *bileue* [of oure] lord þat lettred men techeþ].
B.11.219   Thanne is *bileue* a lele help, aboue logyk or lawe.
B.11.221   Is litel alowaunce maad, but if *bileue* hem helpe;
B.12.212   For he is in þe loweste of heuene, if oure *bileue* be trewe,
B.12.286   And þoruȝ fir is fullyng, and þat is ferme *bileue*:
B.12.291   And wheiþer it worþ [of truþe] or noȝt, [þe] worþ [of] *bileue* is gret,
B.13.210   Turne into þe trewe feiþ and intil oon *bileue*.'
B.13.217   Sobretee and symple speche and sooþfast *bileue*,
B.13.413   Lyueþ ayein þe *bileue* and no lawe holdeþ.
B.14.38   And seide, 'lo! here liflode ynogh, if oure *bileue* be trewe.
B.14.46   Lyue þoruȝ leel *bileue*, [as oure lord] witnesseþ:
B.14.193   And of pure pacience and parfit *bileue*.
B.15.72   That [lome] þe lewed peple of hir *bileue* doute.
B.15.348   Wherfore folk is þe febler and noȝt ferm of *bileue*.
B.15.358   Han no *bileue* to þe lifte ne to þe [lodesterre].
B.15.387   [Ac] if þei ouerhuppe, as I hope noȝt, oure *bileue* suffiseþ,
B.15.393   For Sarȝens han somwhat semynge to oure *bileue*,
B.15.439   Into lele *bileue*; þe lightloker me þinkeþ
B.15.502   Han a lippe of oure *bileue*, þe lightlier me þynkeþ
B.15.515   And þoruȝ penaunce and passion and parfit bile[ue]
B.15.608   Konne þe firste clause of oure *bileue*, Credo in deum patrem omnipotentem,
B.16.210   And bitokneþ þe Trinite and trewe *bileue*.
B.16.238   Myn affiaunce and my feiþ is ferme in þis *bileue*
B.17.121   And hostele hem and heele þoruȝ holy chirche *bileue*
B.17.213   [Fostren forþ amonges folk loue and *bileue*]
B.19.47   And from fendes þat in hem [was] and false *bileue*.
B.19.334   [And þe [lond] of *bileue*, þe lawe of holy chirche]
B.19.346   Confession and Contricion, and youre carte þe *bileeue*
C. 7.73   Lyueth aȝen þe *bileue* and no lawe kepeth
C. 8.97   And defenden hit fro þe fende, and so is my *beleue*,
C. 9.219   Lollen aȝen þe *byleue* and lawe of holy churche.
C.11.129   Hit is no science sothly bote a sothfaste *bileue*,
C.11.158   Thus *bileue* and le[ute], and loue is the thridde
C.11.289   Aren noen rather yraueschid fro þe rihte *bileue*
C.11.291   Ne none sanere ysa[u]ed ne saddere in *bileue*,
C.11.295   And passen purgatorie penaunceles for here parfit *bileue*:
C.11.302   Lewede men in good *bileue* and lene hem at here nede.'
C.12.44   The *bileue* of oure lord þat lettred men techeth.
C.12.87   Loue withoute lele *bileue* a[nd] my lawe riht[ful]
C.13.90   Knowelecheth hym cristene and of holy kirke *byleue*,
C.14.151   For he is in þe loweste of heuene, yf oure *byleue* be trewe,
C.14.208   And thorw fuyr is fullyng; and [þat] is ferme *bileue*:
C.14.213   And wher hit worth or worth nat, the *bileue* is gret of treuthe
C.15.186   Sobrete [and] symple speche and sothfaste *bileue*
C.15.237   And saide, 'lo! here lyflode ynow yf oure *beleue* be trewe
C.15.244   Leue thorw lele *bileue*, As oure lord wittenesseth:
C.16.233   That bothe le[r]ed and le[w]ed of here *beleue* douten.
C.17.22   Loue and lele *byleue* held lyf and soule togyderes,
C.17.88   Lewed men han no *byleue*, [so] lettred men erren;
C.17.96   Haen no *byleue* to þe lyft ne to þe lodesterr[e].
C.17.119   Thogh hit suffice for oure sauacioun soethfaste *byleue*,
C.17.126   [Lif in] loue and leutee in o *byleue* a[nd] lawe,
C.17.127   A loueknotte of leutee and of lele *byleue*,
C.17.158   And lyuen oute of lele *byleue* for they l[e]ue on a mene.
C.17.253   Haen a lyppe of oure *bileue*, the lihtlokour me thynketh

C.17.266 And thorw penaunce and passioun and parfyt *bileue*;
C.17.294 Bischope[s] and bokes the *bileue* to teche.
C.17.316 Conne þe furste clause of oure *bileue*, credo in deum patrem,
C.18.51   The whiche is spiritus sanctus and sothfaste *bileue*
C.18.209 Bitokeneth þe trinite and trewe *bileue*.
C.18.254 Myen affiaunce and my faith is ferme in [t]his *bileue*
C.19.179 Fostren forth amongus folke loue and *bileue*
C.19.194 Til þat loue and *bileue* leliche to hym blowe.
C.21.47   And fro fendes þat in hem was and false *bileue*.
C.21.334 And þe londe of *bileue*, the lawe of holi churche.
C.21.346 Confessioun and contricioun, and ȝoure Carte, the *bileue*,

bileue &> bileuen, bilyue

bileuen v1 *bileven v.(1)* A 1 beleue; B 2 bileue (1) bileuen (1); C 3
    bileue (2) byleueth (1)
A. 7.164 N[e] hadde peris [wiþ] a pese lof preyede hym *beleue*,
B. 6.179 Ne hadde Piers wiþ a pese loof preyed [hym *bileue*]
B.15.73 Bettre it were [by] manye doctours to [bi]leuen swich techyng
C. 3.348 As a leel laborer *byleueth* [with] his maister
C. 8.176 Ne hadde [Peres] with a pese loof preyede hym *b[ile]ue*.
C.12.212 And þat his gost shal go and [his] goed *bileue*

bileuen v2 *bileven v.(2)* &> bileue A 4 beleue; B 32 bileef (1) bileeue (1)
    bileue (19) bileued (1) bileuede (1) bileuen (2) bileuest (1) bileueþ (6);
    C 36 beleue (2) byleef (1) bileue (18) byleue (2) bileued (1) byleued
    (1) bileuede (1) bileuen (1) byleuen (1) bileuest (1) bileueth (2)
    byleueth (4) bylyueth (1)
A. 1.79   And ek kenne me kyndely on crist to *beleue*,
A. 6.76   And boterasid wiþ *beleue* [so] oþer þou [be]st not sauid;
A. 7.80   And defende it fro þe fend, for so I *beleue*,
A.11.77 Ac *beleue* lelly o[n þe] lore of holy chirche,
B. 1.81   And [ek] kenne me kyndely on crist to *bileue*,
B. 5.483 And for þe beste as I *bileue* whateuere þe book telleþ:
B. 5.589 Botrased wiþ *bileef*-so-or-þow-beest-noȝt-saued;
B. 6.88   And [defende it fro þe fend], for so I *bileue*,
B.10.118 And maken men in mys *bileue* þat muse on hire wordes.
B.10.124 Ac *bileueþ* lelly in þe loore of holy chirche,
B.10.238 'It is a commune lyf', quod Clergie, 'on holy chirche to *bileue*
B.10.240 And þat is to *bileue* lelly, boþe lered and lewed,
B.10.254 But þus it bilongeþ to lewed þat willen dowel.
B.12.182 But as his loresman lereþ hym *bileueþ* and troweþ,
B.13.273 He hadde a cote of cristendom as holy kirke *bileueþ*.
B.14.87 That whiles he lyuede he *bileuede* in þe loore of holy chirche.
B.15.394 For þei loue and *bileue* in o [lord] almyghty
B.15.395 And we lered and lewed [*bileueþ* in oon god;
B.15.396 Cristene and vncristene on oon god *bileueþ*].
B.15.477 Louen and *bileuen* by lettred mennes doynges,
B.15.492 Allas, þat men so longe [sholde *bileue* on Makometh]!
B.15.504 For alle paynymes preieþ and parfitly *bileueþ*
B.15.518 Alle þat wilned and wolde wiþ Inwit *bileue* it.
B.15.572 Tellen hem and techen hem on þe Trinite to *bileue*,
B.15.579 Ac we cristene creatures þat on þe cros *bileuen*
B.16.200 In menynge þat man moste on o god *bileue*,
B.17.31   And haþ saued þat *bileued* so and sory for hir synnes,
B.17.37   To *bileeue* and louye in o lord almyghty
B.17.44   It is ful hard for any man on Abraham *bileue*
B.17.127 'A, swete sire', I seide þo, 'wher I shal *bileue*,
B.17.135 Sette [faste] þi feiþ and ferme *bileue*;
B.18.260 And *bileue* on a newe lawe be lost, lif and soule.'
B.19.120 That she first and formest ferme sholde *bileue*
B.19.173 Thow art my lord, I *bileue*, god lord Iesu,
B.19.177 "Thomas, for þow trowest þis and treweliche *bileuest* it
B.19.181 And lelliche *bileue* al þis; I loue hem and blesse hem:
C. 1.78   And also kenne me kyndly on crist to *bileue*.
C. 2.77   'Al þat loueth and *byleueth* vp lykyng of mede,
C. 3.357 In case, credere in ecclesia, in holy kyrke to *bileue*;
C. 3.398 Sholde confourme hem to o kynde on holy kyrke to *bileue*
C. 7.125 And for [þe] beste, as y *beleue*, what[euere] þe boek telle:
C. 7.236 Ibotrased with *bileue*-so-or-t[hou]-best-noȝt-ysaued;
C.10.168 For they louyeth and *bylyueth* al here lyf tyme
C.10.191 That alle landes loueden and in on lawe *bileuede*.
C.11.130 Ac for hit lereth men to louie y *beleue* þeron þ[e] bettere
C.11.141 And *byleef* lelly how goddes [l]o[u]e alyhte
C.11.150 And he vs saide as he sey, and so y *bileue*,
C.11.155 Bote thus hit bilongeth to *bileue* alle þat liketh dowel.
C.13.87   For if he loueth and *byleueth* as the lawe techeth–
C.14.13   Ac to louye and lene and lyue wel and *byleue*
C.14.122 But as his loresman [lereth hym] *byleueth* and troweth,
C.16.359 Of tho that lelelyche lyuen and louen and *byleuen*:
C.17.123 For sarrasynes may be saued so yf they so *byleued*
C.17.133 That lelyche they *byleue*, and ȝut here lawe diuerseth,
C.17.135 And ayther loueth and *byleueth* in o [lord] almyhty.
C.17.187 Allas, þat men so longe on Macometh *bileueth*!

C.17.255 For alle paynyme preyeth and parfitliche *bileueth*
C.17.269 Alle þat wilnede and wolde with inwit *bileue* hit.
C.17.286 And enchaunten hem to charite on holy churche to *bileue*.
C.18.249 I withsaet nat his heste; y hope and *bileue*
C.19.28   And lele to *bileue* on for [lif and] for soule?
C.19.32   And hath ysaued þat *bileued* so and sory for here synnes;
C.19.35   Sethe the furste sufficede to *bileue* and be saued?
C.19.42   And for to louye and *bileue* in o lord almyhty
C.19.44   Ac for to *bileue* in o lord þat lyueth in thre persones
C.19.96   'A, sire', y saide, 'shal nat we *bileue*,
C.19.110 Loke thow louye and *bileue* al thy lyftyme.
C.20.268 And *bile[u]e* on a newe lawe be ylost, lyf and soule.'
C.21.120 That [sh]e furste and formoste [ferme sholde] *bileue*
C.21.173 Thow art my lord, y *bileue*, god lord iesu,
C.21.177 "Thomas, for thow trowest this and treweliche *bileuest* hit
C.21.181 And leelliche *bileuen* al this; y loue hem and blesse hem:

bilye v *bilien v.(2)* A 1 belowen; B 4 bilieþ (1) bilye (1) bilowen (2); C 2
    belyen (1) bylowe (1)
A. 5.76   And *belowen* hym to lordis to don hym lese siluer,
B. 2.22   And *bilowen* h[ym] to lordes þat lawes han to kepe.
B. 5.96   And [*bilowen*] hym to lordis to doon hym lese siluer,
B. 5.407 Or lesynge[s] to lauȝen [of] and *bilye* my neȝebores,
B.10.22 Thei lede lordes wiþ lesynges and *bilieþ* truþe.
C. 9.182 Or *bylowe* thorw luther men and lost here catel aftur
C.20.355 That ȝe *belyen* nat this lewed men for at the laste dauid

bilyue n *bilive n.* A 1 belyue; B 4 bileue (1) bilyue (3); C 7 bileue (1)
    byleue (1) bilyue (1) byliue (1) bylyue (3)
A. 8.105 Ne aboute my [*belyue*] so besy be namore;
B. 7.123 Ne aboute my [*bilyue*] so bisy be na moore;
B.11.301 He [ouȝte no] *bileue*, as I leue, to lacche þoruȝ his croune
B.19.235 [By] sellynge and buggynge hir *bilyue* to wynne.
B.20.7   That þow toke to þi *bilyue*, to cloþes and to sustenaunce,
C. 1.18   And brynge forth ȝoure *bilyue*, bothe lynnen and wollene,
C. 5.21   [Hem þat bedreden be] *byleue* t[o] fynden?'
C. 5.29   Or beggest thy *bylyue* aboute at men hacches
C. 8.259 "Yblessed be al tho that here *bylyue* biswynketh
C.16.338 Thogh y my *byliue* sholde begge aboute at menne hacches.
C.21.235 [By] sullyng and buggynge here *bileue* to wynne.
C.22.7   That thow toke to [thy *bylyue*], to clothes and to sustinaunce

bylyueth > bileuen

bille n *bille n.* A 1; B 2; C 1
A. 4.34   Þanne com pes into þe parlement & putte vp a *bille*
B. 4.47   [Th]anne com pees into [þe] parlement and putte [vp] a *bille*
B.13.247 Hadde ich a clerc þat couþe write I wolde caste hym a *bille*
C. 4.45   Thenne cam p[ees] into [þe] parlement and putte vp a *bille*

bilongeþ v *bilongen v.* B 7; C 8 bilongen (1) bilongeth (3) bylongeth (4)
B.Pr.110 For in loue and lettrure þe eleccion *bilongeþ*;
B. 9.80   For moore *bilongeþ* to þe litel barn er he þe lawe knowe
B.10.254 But þus it *bilongeþ* to bileue to lewed þat willen dowel.
B.10.363 And þus *bilongeþ* to louye þat leueþ [to] be saued.
B.16.191 So þre *bilongeþ* for a lord þat lordshipe cleymeþ:
B.17.166 That þre þynges *bilongeþ* in oure [fader] of heuene
B.17.179 And to vnfolde þe fust, [for hym it *bilongeþ*,
C. 1.43   Telleth me to wham þat tresour *bylongeth*.'
C. 5.69   Thyse *bylongeth* to labory and lordes kyn to serue.
C. 7.271 And aren porteres ouer þe posternes þat to þ[e] place *bilongen*
C. 9.231 Thus hit *bylongeth* for lord[e], for lered and for lewed
C. 9.263 The tarre is vntydy þat to þe [tripe] *bylongeth*;
C.11.155 Bote thus hit *bilongeth* to bileue alle þat liketh dowel.
C.18.200 Thre *bilongeth* to a lord þat leiaunce claymeth,
C.19.144 And to vnfolde þe fust, for hym hit *bilongeth*,

biloue v *biloven v.* B 2 biloue (1) biloued (1); C 1 byloued
B. 3.212 Mede makeþ hym *biloued* and for a man holden.
B. 6.228 And *biloue* þee amonges [lowe] men: so shaltow lacche grace.'
C. 3.268 Mede maketh hym *byloued* and for a man yholde.

bilowe(n > bilye

bymeene v1 *bimenen v.(2)* A 2 bemene (1) bemeniþ (1); B 7 bymeene (2)
    bymeneþ (4) bymente (1); C 6 bemene (1) bymene (1) bymeneth (3)
    bymente (1)
A. 1.1   What þe mounteyne [be]meniþ, & ek þe [m]erke dale,
A. 1.58   What may it [be]mene, madame I þe biseche?'
B.Pr.209 What þis metels *bymeneþ*, ye men þat ben murye,
B. 1.1   What þ[e] Mountaigne *bymeneþ* and þe merke dale
B. 1.11   And seide, 'mercy, madame, what [may] þis [by]meene?'
B. 1.60   What may it [by]mene, madame, I [þee] biseche?'
B.15.481 And by þe man þat made þe feste þe mageste *bymeneþ*
B.18.18 Thanne I frayned at Feiþ what al þat fare *bymente*,
B.18.170 But [loue] sente hire som lettre what þis light *bymeneþ*

C.Pr.220 What þis meteles *bymeneth*, ȝe men þat ben merye,
C. 1.1 What the montaigne *bymeneth* and þe merke dale
C. 1.11 And sayde, 'mercy, madame, what may this [be]mene?'
C. 1.56 What may hit *bymene*, madame, y [þe] byseche?'
C.20.16 Thenne y [f]raynede at fayth what al þat fare *bymente*
C.20.173 Bote loue haue ysente her som lettre what this liht *bymeneth*

bymeneþ v2 *bimenen v.(1) &> bymeene* B 1
B.15.147 And *bymeneþ* goode meteȝyueres and in mynde haueþ

bymente > bymeene

bymolen v *bimolen v.* B 2
B.14.4 That wollen *bymolen* it many tyme maugree my chekes.
B.14.23 Shal neuere [myx] *bymolen* it, ne moþe after biten it,

bynam > bynymen

bynden v *binden v.* A 3 bynde (1) bounde (1) ybounde (1); B 17 bynde (4) bynden (2) bond (3) bounde (3) bounden (2) ybounde (3); C 16 bynde (4) boend (1) bond (1) bonde (2) bounde (1) ybounde (7)
A. 6.5 He bar a burdoun *ybounde* wiþ a brood list,
A. 8.30 And *bynde* brugges aboute þat tobroke were,
A.10.56 For whan blood is bremere þanne brayn, þan is Inwit *bounde*,
B.Pr.101 To *bynden* and vnbynden as þe book telleþ,
B.Pr.178 That dorste haue *bounden* þe belle aboute þe cattes nekke,
B. 2.210 Falsnesse and his felawship to fettren and to *bynden*.
B. 3.353 The soule þat þe soude takeþ by so muche is *bounde*.'
B. 5.517 He bar a burdoun *ybounde* wiþ a brood liste,
B. 7.28 And [*bynde*] brugges [aboute] þat tobroke were,
B.13.152 I bere þer, [in a bouste] faste *ybounde*, dowel.
B.14.247 Ther Auarice haþ Almaries and yren *bounden* cofres.
B.14.249 A beggeris bagge þan an yren *bounde* cofre.
B.17.73 Enbawmed hym and *bond* his heed and in his [barm] hym leide,
B.18.34 And legge it þer hym likeþ, and Lucifer *bynde*,
B.18.97 To [bete a body *ybounde*] wiþ any briȝt wepene].
B.18.270 And lede it þer [laȝar is] and lightliche me *bynde*.
B.18.403 Thow shalt abyen it bittre!' and *bond* hym wiþ cheynes.
B.19.57 And *bond* [hym] as [he is bounde] wiþ bondes of yrene.
B.19.57 And bond [hym] as [he is *bounde*] wiþ bondes of yrene.
B.19.189 To *bynde* and vnbynde boþe here and elli[s],
C.Pr.97 And boxes ben yset forth *ybounde* with yren
C.Pr.129 To *bynde* and vnbynde as þe boke telleth,
C.Pr.195 That derste haue *ybounde* þe belle aboute þe kattes nekke.
C. 1.121 And helle is þer he is and [he] þere *ybounde*.
C. 7.162 He bar a burdoun *ybounde* with a brood liste,
C.10.263 A bastard, a *bond* oen, a begeneldes douhter
C.13.80 Beth nat *ybounde*, as beth [þ]e ryche, to [bothe two] lawes,
C.19.54 In a wi[d]e wildernesse where theues hadde *ybounde*
C.19.72 Enbaumed hym and *boend* his heued and on bayard hym sette
C.20.33 And legge hit þere hym liketh and lucifer *bynde*
C.20.100 To bete a body *ybounde* with eny briht wypene.
C.20.278 And lede hit þer laȝar is and lihtliche me *bynde*.
C.20.446 Thow shal[t] abuye bittere!' and *b[o]nde* hym with chaynes.
C.21.57 And *bonde* [hym] as he is bounde with bondes of yre.
C.21.57 And bonde [hym] as he is *bounde* with bondes of yre.
C.21.189 To *bynde* and vnbynde bothe here and elles

byneþe adv *binethen adv.* A 1 beneþe; B 3; C 2 beneth (1) bynethe (1)
A.Pr.15 A dep dale *beneþe*, a dungeoun þereinne
B.Pr.15 A deep dale *byneþe*, a dongeon þerInne
B.13.346 Aboute þe mouþ, or *byneþe* bigynneþ to grope,
B.16.67 'Heer now *byneþe*', quod he þo, 'if I nede hadde,
C. 6.180 Aboute þe mouthe and *bynethe* bygan y to grope,
C.18.84 'Here *beneth* y may nyme, yf y nede hadde,

bynymen v *binimen v.* A 1 benom; B 3 bynam (1) bynymen (1) bynomen (1); C 3 bynyme (1) bynoem (1) bynom (1)
A. 7.225 And *benom* hym his nam for he nolde werche,
B. 3.314 His boost of his benefice worþ *bynomen* hym after.
B. 6.241 And *bynam* hym his Mnam for he [n]olde werche,
B.10.327 [*Bynymen*] that hir barnes claymen, and blame yow foule:
C. 3.321 And *bynyme* hit hem anone and neueremore aftur
C. 8.253 *Byno[m]* hym al þat he hadde and ȝaf hit to his felawe
C.13.9 *Bynoem* [hym] his hosewyf [and helde here hymsulue]

bionales > biennals

biquasshed v *biquasshen v.* B 1
B.18.248 Quaked as quyk þyng and al *biquasshed* þe roche.

biqueste n *biqueste n.* A 1 bequest; B 1; C 1
A. 7.77 Forþi I wile er I wende do w[r]yte my *bequest*.
B. 6.85 Forþi I wole er I wende do write my *biqueste*.
C. 8.94 Forthy y wol ar y wende do wryte my *biqueste*.

biqueþe v *biquethen v.* B 1; C 1 byqueth
B.13.10 But quik he *biqueþe* [hem] auȝt [or sholde helpe] quyte hir dettes;

C.15.12 Bote quyke he *byqu[e]th* hem auht or wolde helpe quyte here dettes;

bireue v *bireuen v.* A 1 bereuid; B 1; C 1
A. 7.230 And þat he weniþ wel to haue I wile it be hym *bereuid*'.
B. 6.246 And þat he weneþ wel to haue I wole it hym *bireue*"
C. 8.257 And þat he weneth wel to haue y wol hit hym *bireue*".

birewe v *bireuen v.* B 1
B.12.252 And þouȝ þe riche repente þanne and *birewe* þe tyme

byschytten > bischetten; bischop(- > bisshop

bisechen v *bisechen v.* A 10 beseche (1) beseke (2) besouȝte (5) biseche (1) byseke (1); B 17 biseche (7) bisechen (1) biseke (1) bisouȝte (8); C 22 biseche (3) bysuche (5) bysechen (1) bysecheth (1) biseke (1) byseke (1) bysoughte (1) bisouhte (5) bysouhte (3) bisowte (1)
A. 1.58 What may it [be]mene, madame I þe *biseche*?'
A. 1.144 But mekly wiþ mouþe mercy he *besouȝte*
A. 3.76 Ac mede þe maide þe mair heo *besouȝte*
A. 4.81 Þanne gan mede to meke hire, & mercy *besouȝte*,
A. 4.99 Þat mede muste be meynpernour resoun þei *besouȝte*.
A. 5.52 But now wile I meke me & mercy *beseke*
A. 5.237 Þo dismas my broþer *besouȝte* þe of grace,
A. 5.243 But for þi muchel mercy mytygacioun I *beseche*;
A.11.99 In signe þat I shulde *beseke* hire of grace.
A.12.116 Marie moder and may, for man þou *byseke*
B. 1.60 What may it [by]meene, madame, I [þee] *biseche*?'
B. 1.170 But mekely wiþ mouþe mercy [he] *bisouȝte*
B. 3.87 Ac Mede þe mayde þe Mair [she] *bisouȝt[e]*
B. 4.94 [Th]anne gan Mede to me[k]en hire, and mercy *bisouȝte*,
B. 4.112 That Mede moste be maynpernour Reson þei *bisouȝte*.
B. 5.69 But now [wole I] meke me and mercy *biseche*
B. 5.281 'Haue mercy in þi mynde, and wiþ þi mouþ *biseche* it–
B. 5.329 Til Robyn þe Ropere [arise þei *bisouȝte*],
B. 5.465 Tho Dysmas my broþer *bisouȝte* [þee] of grace
B. 5.469 But for þi muchel mercy mitigacion I *biseche*:
B. 5.478 'I shal *biseche* for alle synfulle oure Saueour of grace
B. 5.502 Bidde and *biseche*, if it be þi wille,
B.10.146 In signe þat I sholde *bisechen* hire of grace.
B.11.56 And [festne] þee [in] hir Fraternitee and for þe *biseke*
B.13.384 Hadde I neuere wille, woot god, witterly to *biseche*
B.20.106 Conscience of his curteisie [þo] kynde he *bisouȝte*
B.20.170 And *bisouȝte* hym of socour and of his salue hadde;
C. 1.56 What may hit bymene, madame, y [þe] *byseche*?'
C. 1.166 Bote mekeliche with mouth mercy he *bysoughte*
C. 3.77 ȝut mede the Mayr myldeliche he *bysouhte*,
C. 3.115 Ac Mede þe mayde þe mayr heo *bisowte*
C. 4.90 Then gan mede to m[e]ken here and mercy *bisouhte*
C. 4.107 That mede myhte be maynpernour [resoun] thei *bysouhte*.
C. 6.10 But now wol y meke me and mercy *byseche*
C. 6.16 Haue be vnbuxum, þy *bysuche* god of mercy;
C. 6.92 For thy synnes souereynly and *biseke* god of mercy.'
C. 6.273 Hadde y neuere will, [woot god], witterly to *bysuche*
C. 6.319 Tho dysmas my brother *bisouhte* [þe] of grace
C. 6.323 For thy mochel mercy mitigacioun y *biseche*:
C. 6.387 Til Robyn þe Ropere aryse they *bisouhte*
C. 7.120 'Y shal *byseke* for alle synnefole oure sauiour of grace
C. 7.142 Bidde and *biseche* the, yf hit be thy wille,
C.11.84 Semyng þat y sholde *bysechen* here of grace.
C.12.8 And festene the in ther f[r]aternite and for the *bysuche*
C.17.154 For þer is no man þat mynde hath þat ne meketh [hym] and *bysecheth*
C.17.244 Prelates and prestis preeye and *biseche*
C.18.140 Ne noon so faythfol fisciscyen, for all þat *bysouhte* hym
C.22.106 Concience of his cortesye tho kynde he *bisouhte*
C.22.170 And *bisouhte* hym of socour and of h[is] salue hadde

bisechyng ger *bisechinge ger.* A 1 besekyng; B 1
A.11.108 Þei two, [as] I hope, aftir my *besekyng*,
B.10.156 They two, as I hope, after my [*bis*]echyng

bisegede v *bisegen v.* B 1; C 1 biseged
B.20.215 And *bisegede* [sikerly] wiþ seuene grete geauntȝ
C.22.215 And *biseged* s[iker]ly with seuene grete geauntes

biseye v *bisen v.* B 1; C 1 byseye
B.20.202 Lo! Elde þe hoore haþ me *biseye*.
C.22.202 Lo! Elde þe hore hath me *byseye*;

biseke > bisechen

bysemede v *bisemen v.* C 1
C. 9.249 A bacheler [o]r a be[au]pere beste hym *bysemede*

bisette v *bisetten v.* B 5; C 2 bysette (1) bysetten (1)
B. 5.261 'God lene þee neuere grace] þi good wel to *bisette*,

B. 5.263   Ne þyne executours wel *bisette* þe siluer þat þow hem leuest;
B. 5.291   *Bisette* it hymself as best [be] for þi soule.
B.12.47   And Rosamounde riȝt so reufulliche [*bisette*]
B.15.324 And [*bisette*] to bidde for yow to swiche þat ben riche,
C. 6.254   Shal neuere seketoure[s] wel *bysette* the syluer þat thow hem leuest
C. 6.346   To *bysetten* hit hymsulue as beste be for thy soule.

bisherewed v *bishreuen* v. B 1
B. 4.168   And [also] a Sherreues clerk *bisherewed* al þe route:

bishetten v *bishetten* v. A 1 besshette; B 2 bishet (1) bishetten (1); C 2 byschytten (1) bishut (1)
A. 2.175   *Besshette* hym in here shoppis to shewen here ware;
B. 2.216   And *bishetten* hym in hire shoppes to shewen hire ware;
B.19.167 In an hous al *bishet* and hir dore ybarred
C. 2.226   And *byschytten* hym in here shoppe[s] to shewen hire ware;
C.21.167 In an hous al *bishut* and here dore ybarred

bishined v *bishinen* v. B 1; C 1 bishinede
B.15.517 And baptised and *bishined* wiþ þe blode of his herte
C.17.268 And baptised and *bis[hin]ede* with þe bloed of his herte

bishop(- > bisshop; bishut > bishetten

bisy adj *bisi* adj. A 3 besy; B 4 bisy (2) bisie (1) busy (1); C 2 bisy (1) bysy (1)
A. 1.6   How *besy* þei ben aboute þe mase?
A. 8.105   Ne aboute my [belyue] so *besy* be namore;
A. 8.112   [By foules, þat are not] *besy* aboute þe bely ioye:
B. 1.6   How *bisie* þei ben aboute þe maȝe?
B. 7.123   Ne aboute my [bilyue] so *bisy* be na moore;
B. 7.130   By foweles [þat are] noȝt *bisy* aboute þe [bely ioye];
B.13.251 And buxom and *busy* aboute breed and drynke
C. 1.6   Hou *bisy* þei ben aboute þe mase?
C.15.222 And thenne wolde y be *bysy* and buxum to helpe

biside adv *bisides* adv. A 1 beside; B 2
A. 2.42   And ten þousand of tentis teldit *beside*
B. 6.150   Thei shul haue payn and potage and [a pitaunce *biside*],
B.17.25   Ye! and sixti þousand *biside* forþ þat ben noȝt seyen here.'

biside prep *bisides* prep. B 2 biside (1) bisides (1); C 3 bisyde (2) byside (1)
B.17.75   Wel sixe Mile or seuene *biside* þe newe Market;
B.18.72   Vpon a croos *bisides* crist; so was þe comune lawe.
C. 6.54   And sygge to suche þat sytte me *byside*:
C.19.74   Is syxe myle or seuene *bisyde* þe newe marcat,
C.20.74   Vppon cros *bisyde* Crist; so was þe comune lawe.

bisily > busily

bisynesse n *bisinesse* n. B 1; C 1 bisinesse
B.14.320 A blessed lif wiþouten *bisynesse* for body and soule:
C.16.155 A blessed lyf withoute *bisinesse* bote onelyche for þe soule:

bisitten v *bisitten* v. A 1 besette; B 2 bisitte (1) bisitten (1); C 1 bisitte
A. 2.105   It shal *besette* ȝoure soulis wel sore at þe laste.'
B. 2.141   It shal *bisitte* youre soules [wel] soure at þe laste.'
B.10.365 It shal *bisitten* vs ful soure þe siluer þat we kepen,
C. 2.157   Hit shal [*bi*]*sitte* ȝoure soules ful so[u]re at þe laste.'

bislabered ptp *bislobben* v. B 1; C 1 byslobered
B. 5.385   Thanne cam Sleuþe al *bislabered* & worþ two slymy eiȝen;
C. 7.1   Thenne cam sleuthe al *byslobered* with two slim[y] yes.

bismere n *bismare* n. B 2 bismares (1) bismere (1); C 1 busmares
B. 5.88   Wiþ bakbitynge and *bismere* and berynge of fals witnesse;
B.19.294 And bold and abidynge *bismares* to suffre;
C.21.294 And bold and abidynge *busmares* to soffre

bisnewed ptp *bisneued* ppl. B 1; C 1 bysnewed
B.15.112 That were *bisnewed* wiþ snow and snakes wiþInne,
C.16.267 That were *bysnewed* al with snowe and snakes withynne

bysoughte -souȝte -souhte -sowte > bisechen

bisperede v *bisperren* v. B 1
B.15.143 And þat he spared and *bisperede* [s]pende we in murþe."

bisshop n *bishop* n. A 12 bisshop (4) bisshopis (8); B 31 bisshop (15) bisshopes (15) bysshopes (1); C 30 bischop (7) bischope (1) bischopes (5) byschopes (1) bischopis (1) bishop (1) bishope (1) bishopes (1) bishopis (2) bisshop (1) bisshope (1) bisshopes (6) bysshopes (1) bisshopis (1)
A.Pr.66   Brouȝte forþ a bulle wiþ *bisshopis* selis
A.Pr.75   Were þe *bisshop* yblissid & worþ boþe hise eris
A.Pr.77   It is not be þe *bisshop* þat þe boy prechiþ,
A.Pr.80   Personis & parissh prestis pleynide hem to here *bisshop*
A.Pr.90   I sauȝ *bisshopis* bolde & bacheleris of deuyn
A.Pr.94   Ben ylope to lundoun be leue of hire *bisshop*,

A. 2.138   For þei shuln bere þise *bisshopis* & bringe hem at reste.
A. 3.138   She blissiþ þise *bisshopis* ȝif þei be lewid;
A. 8.13   *Bisshopis* þat blissen, & boþe lawes lettren.
A. 8.154   Bienalis & trienalis & *bisshopis* lettres.
A. 9.86   Dobest is aboue hem boþe & beriþ a *bisshopis* croce;
A.11.197 Forþi is dobest [a] *bisshopis* pere,
B.Pr.69   Brouȝte forþ a bulle wiþ *Bisshopes* seles,
B.Pr.78   Were þe *Bisshop* yblessed and worþ boþe hise eris
B.Pr.80   It is noȝt by þe *bisshop* þat þe boy precheþ,
B.Pr.83   Persons and parisshe preestes pleyned hem to þe *Bisshop*
B.Pr.87   *Bisshopes* and Bachelers, boþe maistres and doctours,
B. 2.177   To bere *Bisshopes* aboute abrood in visitynge.
B. 3.149   She blesseþ þise *Bisshopes* [if] þei be lewed;
B. 4.124   Til *Bisshopes* Bayardes ben beggeris Chaumbres,
B. 5.290   Ber it to þe *Bisshop*, and bid hym of his grace
B. 5.640   I wol go fecche my box wiþ my breuettes & a bulle with *bisshopes* lettres
B. 6.149   Ne Postles, but þei preche konne and haue power of þe *bisshop*:
B. 7.13   *Bysshopes* yblessed, if þei ben as þei sholde
B. 7.176   Biennals and triennals and *Bisshopes* lettres.
B. 8.96   Dobest is aboue boþe and bereþ a *bisshopes* crosse;
B. 9.14   Dobest is aboue boþe, a *Bisshopes* peere;
B. 9.92   *Bisshopes* shul be blamed for beggeres sake.
B.11.293 Or þe *bisshop* þat blessed yow [and embaumed youre fyngres].
B.11.312 The *bisshop* shal be blamed bifore god, as I leue,
B.11.315 A[c] neuer neiþer is blamelees, þe *bisshop* ne þe Chapeleyn;
B.15.40   'Ye ben as a *bisshop*', quod I, al bourdynge þat tyme,
B.15.41   'For *bisshopes* yblessed bereþ manye names,
B.15.138 Or [endeþ] intestate and þanne [entreþ þe *bisshop*]
B.15.244 [Amonges erchebisshopes and *bisshopes*, [for beggeres sake],
B.15.457 Til it be cristned in cristes name and confermed of þe *bisshop*
B.15.510 That bere *bisshopes* names of Bethleem and Babiloigne.
B.15.527 He is a forbisene to alle *bisshopes* and a briȝt myrour:
B.15.554 Togideres loue leelly, leueþ it wel, ye *bisshopes*,
B.15.570 Euery *bisshop* þat bereþ cros, by þat he is holden
B.15.575 That no man sholde be *bisshop* but if he hadde boþe
B.20.319 Than person or parisshe preest, penitauncer or *bisshop*,
B.20.327 Boldely to þe *bisshop* and his brief hadde
C.Pr.67   Brouth forth a bulle with *bischopis* selys
C.Pr.76   Were þe *bischop* yblessed and worth bothe his eres
C.Pr.78   Ac it is nouȝt by þe *bischop* þat þe boy precheþ,
C.Pr.81   Persones and parsche prestis pleyned [hem] to þe *bischop*
C.Pr.85   *Bischopes* and bachelers, bothe maystres and doctours,
C. 3.187   He blesseth this *bischopes* thow thei ben lewede:
C. 4.120   And til *byschopes* ben bakeres, Breweres and taylours
C. 4.193   More then alle thy marchauntes or thy mytrede *Bysshopes*
C. 5.70   Ac sythe bondemen barnes haen be mad *bisshopes*
C. 6.345   Bere hit to th[e] *bischop* and bide hym of his grace
C. 9.13   *Bishopis* yblessed, yf they ben as they sholde,
C. 9.256   The cause of al this caytiftee cometh of many *bischopes*
C. 9.321   Bionales and trionales and *bisshopes* lettres.
C.10.93   Dobest bere sholde þe *bisshopes* [c]rose
C.10.98   Sholde no *bisshop* be here biddynges to withsite.
C.10.141 Dobest is aboue bothe, a *bishopis* pere,
C.10.192 *Bishope*[s] sholde ben hereaboute and bryng this to hepe
C.12.225 Riht so, sothly, suche þat ben *bischopes*,
C.13.107 Or þe *bischop* þat blessed ȝow and enbaumed ȝoure fyngeres:
C.13.124 The *bishop* shal be blamed before god, as y leue,
C.13.127 Ac neuer noþer is blameles, the *bischop* ne þe chapeleyn,
C.16.202 'Ȝe beth as a *bischop*,' quod y, al bourdynge þat tyme,
C.16.203 'For *bisshopes* yblessed bereth many names,
C.16.366 With *bisshopes* a wolde be for beggares sake
C.17.217 Togederes louyen lelelyche, l[e]ueth hit [wel], *bisshopes*,
C.17.277 He is a forbisene to alle *bisshopis* and a briht myrrour
C.17.283 Euery *bisshope* bi þe lawe sholde buxumliche walke
C.17.294 *Bischope*[s] and bokes the bileue to teche.
C.22.319 Then person oþer parsche prest, penytauncer or *bischope*
C.22.327 Baldly to þe *bishope* and his breef hadde

bistowe v *bistouen* v. B 1
B. 7.74   And in þe stories he techeþ to *bistowe* þyn almesse:

bistrideþ v *bistriden* v. B 1; C 1 bystrideth
B.17.81   For I may noȝt lette', quod þat Leode and lyard he *bistrideþ*
C.19.78   For y may nat lette,' quod that lede; and lyard he *bystrideth*

biswatte ptp *bisweten* v. B 1
B.13.402 Swoor þerby swiþe ofte and al *biswatte* his cote;

biswynke v *biswinken* v. A 1 beswynken; B 2 biswynke (1) biswynken (1); C 3 byswynke (1) byswynken (1) biswynketh (1)
A. 7.199   Bolde beggeris & bigge, þat mowe here breed *beswynken*,
B. 6.213   Bolde beggeris and bigge þat mowe hir breed *biswynke*,
B.15.488 Wiþouten trauaille þe tiþe deel þat trewe men *biswynken*?
C. 8.140   That lele land tilynge men leely *byswynken*.

C. 8.223   Bolde beggares and bygge þat mowe here breed *byswynke*,
C. 8.259   "Yblessed be al tho that here bylyue *biswynketh*

bit > bidden

byte n *bite n. &> biten* B 1; C 1 bite
B.18.202   For it is botelees bale, þe *byte* þat þei eten.'
C.20.207   For hit is boteles bale, the *bite* that they eten.'

byteche v *bitechen v.* C 1
C.15.182   Forthy,' quod Concience, 'crist y the *byteche*;

bitelbrowed adj *bitelbrouwed adj.* A 1 betilbrowid; B 1; C 1
A. 5.109   He was [*betil*]*browid* & babirlippid wiþ two bleride eiȝen,
B. 5.190   He was *bitelbrowed* and baberlipped wiþ two blered eiȝen;
C. 6.198   He was *bitelbrowed* and baburlippid with two blered eyes

biten v *biten v.(1)* A 1 bot; B 6 bite (2) biten (2) bitynge (1) boot (1); C
    7 byte (4) biten (1) bytyng (1) bitynge (1)
A. 5.66   His body was bolnid for wr[aþþe] þat he *bot* his lippe[s],
B. 5.83   His body was [b]ollen for wraþe þat he *boot* hise lippes,
B.13.47   Bifore Pacience breed to brynge, [*bitynge* apart],
B.14.23   Shal neuere [myx] bymolen it, ne moþe after *biten* it,
B.19.338   Blowe hem doun and breke hem and *bite* atwo þe mores.
B.20.359   The plastres of þe person and poudres *biten* to soore;
B.20.361   Fro lenten to lenten he lat hise plastres *bite*.'
C. 6.141   *Byte* and bete and brynge forth suche thewes
C. 9.16   And *bitynge* in badde men but yf they wol amende,
C.15.53   And bringe breed for pacience, *bytyng* apartye,
C.17.29   Ac durste no beste *byte* hem by day ne by nyhte
C.21.338   Blowe hem doun and B[r]eke hem and *b[y]te* ato þe mores.
C.22.359   The plasteres of the persoun and poudres *b[it]en* to sore;
C.22.361   Fro lente to lente he lat his plastres *byte*.'

bitere > bittre

bythenke v *bithinken v.* C 1
C. 6.107   To sle hym sleyliche sleythes y *bythenke*.

bitide v *bitiden v.* A 3 betide; B 7 bitidde (1) bitide (5) bitit (1); C 3
    bytydde (1) bytyde (1) bitit (1)
A. 2.82   [And] er þis weddyng be wrouȝt wo þe *betide*!
A. 3.110   Er I wedde such a wif wo me *betide*!
A. 3.154   And alle þat meynteniþ hire men meschaunce hem *betide*!
B. 2.118   And er þis weddynge be wroȝt wo þee *bitide*!
B. 3.121   Er I wedde swich a wif wo me *bitide*!
B. 3.167   And alle þat maynteneþ hire men, meschaunce hem *bitide*!
B.11.403   That som tyme hym *bitit* to folwen his kynde;
B.12.116   [Saul for he sacrificed sorwe hym *bitidde*,
B.15.362   Wisten by þe walkne what sholde *bitide*;
B.16.180   'What berþ þat buyrn', quod I þo, 'so blisse þee *bitide*?'
C. 3.158   Ar y wedde suche a wyf wo me *bytyde*!
C.13.211   That some tyme hym *bitit* to folewen his kynde;
C.14.61   Saul for he sacreficede sorwe hym *bytydde*

bityme adv *bitime adv.* B 1; C 1 bytymes
B. 5.638   Thow myȝt gete grace þere so þow go *bityme*.'
C. 7.291   Thow myhte gete grace there so thow go *bytymes*.'

bitit > bitide

bitokneþ v *bitoknen v.* B 7 bitoknen (1) bitokneþ (6); C 9 bitokened (1)
    bytokenen (1) bitokeneth (3) bitokneth (3)
B.12.241   *Bitokneþ* riȝt riche men þat reigne here on erþe.
B.15.466   The calf *bitokneþ* clennesse in hem þat kepeþ lawes,
B.16.210   And *bitokneþ* þe Trinite and trewe bileue,
B.16.212   And *bitokneþ* trewely, telle if I dorste,
B.17.146   And *bitokneþ* trewely, telle whoso liketh,
B.17.149   *Bitoknen* sooþly þe sone þat sent was til erþe,
B.18.127   'Haue no merueille', quod mercy; 'murþe it *bitokneþ*.
C.12.203   *Bitokeneth* treuly in tyme comyng aftur
C.14.173   *Bytokenen* riht ryche men þat reygne here on erthe.
C.18.26   *Bytokeneth* trewely the trinite of heuene,
C.18.162   Ac þe ouerturnynge of the temple *bitokened* his resureccioun.
C.18.209   *Bitokeneth* þe trinite and trewe bileue.
C.18.263   And ma[k]e sacrefice so: somwhat hit *bitokneth*;
C.19.120   And *bitokeneth* trewly, telle hoso liketh,
C.19.123   *Bitokneth* soethly the sone þat sente was til erthe,
C.20.130   'Haue no merueyle,' quod Mercy; 'merthe hit *bitokneth*.

bitraye v *bitraien v.* A 4 betraid (1) betraye (2) betrayen (1); B 5 bitraye
    (3) bitrayed (2); C 2 bytraye (1) bytrayeth (1)
A. 1.37   Þat is þe wrecchide world [wolde] þe *betraye*.
A. 1.68   Þat tresten on his tresour *betraid* arn sonnest.'
A. 5.216   And seide, 'war þe for wanhope wile þe *betraye*;
A.11.84   [O]r Iudas þe Iew Iesu *betraye*[n].
B. 1.39   That is þe wrecched world wolde þee *bitraye*.
B. 1.70   That trusten on his tresour *bitraye*[d are] sonnest.'

B. 5.444   And seide, 'ware þee, for wanhope wo[l] þee *bitraye*.
B.10.131   Or Iudas [þe Iew] Iesu *bitraye*.
B.16.150   And [þus] was wiþ Iudas þo þat Iesus *bitrayed*:
C. 1.66   That tristeth in tresor of erthe he *bytrayeth* sonest.
C. 7.58   And sayde, 'war the for wanhope wo[l the] *bytraye*.

bytrauayle v *bitravaillen v.* C 2 betrauaile (1) bytrauayle (1)
C. 8.241   Bytu[lye] and *bytrauayle* trewely [ȝ]oure lyflode:
C.15.209   For no breed þat y *betrauaile* to [brynge] byfore lordes.

bitter n *bitter adj.as n.* A 1 bittir; B 1
A. 5.99   [Þat] al my brest bolniþ for *bittir* of my galle.
B. 5.120   That al my [brest] bolneþ for *bitter* of my galle.

bitter adj *bitter adj.* B 6 bitter (5) bittre (1); C 5 bittere (4) bittur (1)
B.11.153   Brouȝte me fro *bitter* peyne þer no biddyng myȝte.'
B.11.260   As on a walnote wiþoute is a *bitter* barke,
B.11.261   And after þat *bitter* bark, be þe shelle aweye,
B.12.12   And wiþ þise *bittre* baleises god beteþ his deere children:
B.13.44   In a morter, Post mortem, of many *bitter* peyne
B.18.64   'For a *bitter* bataille', þe dede body seide;
C. 4.181   And brynge alle men to bowe withouten *bittere* wounde,
C.12.146   As on a walnote withoute is a *bittere* barke
C.12.147   And aftur þat *bittere* barke, be þe scale aweye,
C.15.49   In a morter, post mortem, of many *bittere* peynes
C.20.66   'For a *bittur* bataile,' þe ded body saide;

bittere > bittre; bitterly -liche > bittrely

bitternesse n *bitternesse n.* B 1; C 1
B.18.363   [þe *bitternesse* þat þow hast browe, now brouke it þiselue];
C.20.401   The *bitternesse* þat thow hast browe, now brouk hit thysulue;

bittre adv *bittere adv. &> bitter* B 4; C 5 bitere (1) bittere (3) bittorere
    (1)
B. 3.251   Shal abien it *bittre* or þe book lieþ.
B.10.286   *Bittre* abouȝte þe giltes of two badde preestes,
B.18.403   Thow shalt abyen it *bittre*!' and bond hym wiþ cheynes.
B.20.27   And bete men ouer *bittre*, and so[m body] to litel,
C.13.16   How *bittere* he hit abouhte, as þe book telleth!
C.15.300   Now he buyth hit *bittere*; he is a beggare of helle.
C.16.221   The *bittorere* he shal abugge but yf he wel worche.
C.20.446   Thow shal[t] abuye *bittere*!' and b[o]nde hym with chaynes.
C.22.27   And bete men ouer *bitere* and som body to litel

bittrely adv *bitterli adv.* A 1 bitterly; B 1; C 2 bitterliche
A. 3.230   Shal abiȝe it *bitterly* or þe bok liȝeþ.
B.11.31   *Bittrely* shaltow banne þanne, boþe dayes and nyȝtes,
C. 3.145   And *bitterliche* banne the and alle þat bereth thy name
C.11.190   *Bitterliche* shaltow banne thenne, bothe dayes and nyhtes,

bittur > bitter

bytulye v *bitilien v.* C 1
C. 8.241   *Bytu[lye]* and bytrauayle trewely [ȝ]oure lyflode:

bitwene adv *bitwene adv.* A 4 betwene; B 5; C 3 betwene (1) bytwene
    (2)
A.Pr.17   A fair feld ful of folk fand I þere *betwene*
A. 8.180   And marie his modir to be mene *betwene*,
A. 9.114   But as I bad þouȝt þo be mene *betwene*,
A.10.193   Haue þei no children but ch[este], & choppis [*betwene*].
B.Pr.17   A fair feeld ful of folk fond I þer *bitwene*
B. 5.175   And baleised on þe bare ers and no brech *bitwene*.
B. 7.202   And Marie his moder be mene *bitwene*,
B. 8.124   But as I bad þoȝt þoo be mene *bitwene*,
B. 9.172   Haue þei no children but cheeste and [*choppes*] *bitwene*.
C.Pr.19   A fair feld ful of folk fond y þer *bytwene*
C. 6.157   And balayshed on þe bare ers and no brech *bytwene*.
C.10.120   Bote as y bad thouht tho be mene *betwene*

bitwene prep *bitwene prep.* A 8 betwene (1) betwyn (7); B 11; C 10
    bitwene (6) bytwene (4)
A. 3.66   *Betwyn* þe king & þe comunes, to kepe þe lawis,
A. 3.119   *Betwyn* heuene & helle, & erþe þeiȝ men souȝte.
A. 4.32   And *betwyn* hymself & his sone sette hym a benche,
A. 5.55   To make mercy for his mysdede *betwyn* god & hym
A. 5.79   *Betwyn* hym & his meyne I haue mad wraþþe;
A. 7.165   And wiþ a bene batte he[ȝe]de [hem] *betwene*,
A.10.202   For in [vn]tyme, treweliche, *betwyn* m[a]n & womm[a]n,
A.10.206   As *betwyn* sengle & sengle, siþþe lawe haþ ygrauntid
B. 1.160   And a meene, as þe Mair is, *bitwene* þe [commune] & þe [kyng],
B. 3.76   Maires and Maceres þat menes ben *bitwene*
B. 3.130   *Bitwene* heuene and helle, [and] erþe þouȝ men souȝte.
B. 4.45   And *bitwene* hymself and his sone sette hym on benche,
B. 5.72   To maken mercy for hi[s] mysded[e] *bitwene* god and [hym]
B. 5.99   *Bitwene* [meyne and meyne] I make debate ofte
B. 9.189   For in vntyme, trewely, *bitwene* man and womman

B.13.174　Kan noȝt [parfournen] a pees *bitwene* [þe pope] and hise enemys,
B.13.175　Ne *bitwene* two cristene kynges kan no wiȝt pees make
B.14.244　And louely layk was it neuere *bitwene* þe longe and þe shorte.
B.16.230　Ful trewe toknes *bitwene* vs is to telle whan me likeþ.
C. 1.156　And a mene, as þe Mayre is, *bitwene* þe kyng and þe comune;
C. 3.167　*Bytwene* heuene and helle, and erthe thogh men soughte.
C. 3.382　*Bytwene* two lo[n]des for a trewe marke.
C. 4.43　And *bytwene* hymsulue and his sone sette tho sire resoun
C. 8.157　To kepe hym and his catel as couenant was *bitwene* hem:
C.10.274　Haen þei no childerne bute cheste and [c]hoppes hem *bitwene*.
C.12.126　Til he blessed here bred and brake hit hem *bitwene*.
C.16.84　And louely layk was hit neuere *bytwene* a longe and a short.
C.17.248　To make a perpetuel pees *bitwene* þe prince of heuene
C.18.246　Fol trewe tokenes *bitwene* vs is wh[at] tyme þat y met[t]e hym,

biwicched v *biwicchen v.* B 1; C 1 bywiched
B.19.156　And *biwicched* hem as þei woke and awey stolen it.
C.21.156　And *bywiched* [hem] as they woke and away stelen hit.

biwiled v *biwilen v.* B 1
B.10.109　That *bi[w]iled* þe womman and þe [wye] after,

biyete n *biyete n.* B 1
B. 2.41　To oon fals fikel-tonge, a fendes *biyete*.

byȝete > bygat

biyonde adv *biyonde adv.* A 2 beȝonde; B 2; C 1 beȝende
A. 3.99　I haue a kniȝt, consience, com late fro *beȝonde*,
A. 4.111　And alle rome renneris, for robberis of *beȝonde*,
B. 3.110　I haue a knyȝt, Conscience, cam late fro *biyonde*;
B. 4.128　And alle Rome renneres, for Robberes [of] *biyonde*,
C. 3.147　Y haue a knyght, Consience, cam late fro *beȝende*;

blak adj *blak adj.* B 1; C 1
B.10.442　And wherby wiste men which [is] whit if alle þyng *blak* were,
C.16.268　Or to a wal ywhitlymed and were *blak* withynne;

blame v *blamen v.* A 5 blame (1) blamid (2) blamide (2); B 20 blame (12) blamed (5) blameþ (2) yblamed (1); C 13 blame (8) blamed (1) blameth (2) yblamed (2)
A. 3.263　Samuel shal slen hym, & saul shal be *blamid*,
A. 5.30　He warnide watte his wyf was to *blame*
A. 5.74　And *blamide* hym behynde his bak to bringe hym in fame;
A.10.66　Ac þe fadir & þe Frendis for fauntis shuln be *blamid*
A.11.7　And *blamide* hym [and bannide hym] & bad hym be stille–
B. 3.283　That whoso seiþ hem soþe[s] is sonnest *yblamed*.
B. 3.287　Samuel shal sleen hym and Saul shal be *blamed*
B. 5.30　He warnede watte his wif was to *blame*
B. 5.94　[And *blamed* hym bihynde his bak to brynge hym in fame;
B. 5.131　And gart bakbityng be a brocour to *blame* mennes ware.
B. 7.89　The book banneþ beggerie and *blameþ* hem in þis manere:
B. 8.55　Ac man haþ moost þerof and moost is to *blame*
B. 9.92　Bisshopes shul be *blamed* for beggeres sake.
B.10.7　And *blamed* hym and banned hym and bad hym be stille–
B.10.264　Thanne is dobest to be boold to *blame* þe gilty,
B.10.266　Ac *blame* þow neuere body and þow be blameworþy:
B.10.292　[Th]anne shul burel clerkes ben abasshed to *blame* yow or to greue,
B.10.327　[Bynymen] that hir barnes claymen, and *blame* yow foule:
B.11.103　Ac be [þow] neueremoore þe firste [þe] defaute to *blame*;
B.11.312　The bisshop shal be *blamed* bifore god, as I leue,
B.11.431　[To *blame* or] to bete hym þanne it were but pure synne.
B.11.434　Thanne woot þe dronken [wye] wherfore he is to *blame*.'
B.13.324　And *blame* men bihynde hir bak and bidden hem meschaunce;
B.14.1　'I haue but oon hool hater', quod haukyn, 'I am þe lasse to *blame*
B.15.252　Neiþer he *blameþ* ne banneþ, bosteþ ne preiseþ,
C. 3.306　And but hit prestly be ypayed þe payere is to *blame*,
C. 3.436　That he þat sayth men sothe[s] is sonnest *yblamed*.
C. 3.440　Samuel shal sle hym and sauel shal be *yblamed*
C. 5.132　He warnede watte his wyf was to *blame*
C. 5.172　And Barones and here barnes *blame* ȝow and repreue:
C. 6.69　And *blame* men byhynde here bak and bidde hem meschaunce;
C. 6.95　ȝut am y brokour of bakbytynge to *blame* menne w[a]re
C. 9.162　The boek banneth beggarie and *blameth* hit in this manere:
C. 9.166　For hit *blameth* all beggarie, be ȝe ful certayn.
C.12.37　Ac be [thow] neueremore þe furste the defaute to *blame*;
C.13.124　The bishop shal be *blamed* before god, as y leue,
C.13.238　To *blame* hym or to bete hym thenne y halde hit but synne.
C.13.240　And thenne woet he wherfore and why he is to *blame*.'

blamelees adj *blameles adj.* B 1; C 1 blameles
B.11.315　A[c] neuer neiþer is *blamelees*, þe bisshop ne þe Chapeleyn;
C.13.127　Ac neuer noþer is *blameles*, the bischop ne þe chapeleyn,

blameworþy adj *blameworthi adj.* B 1
B.10.266　Ac blame þow neuere body and þow be *blameworþy*:

blancmanger n *blankmanger n.* B 1; C 1 blaunmanger
B.13.92　That neiþer bacon ne braun, *blancmanger* ne mortrews,
C.15.99　That noþer bacon ne brawn, *blaunmanger* ne mortrewes

blanket n *blanket n.* C 1
C. 9.255　Ne no *blanke[t]* on his bed ne whyte bred byfore hym.

blase n *blase n. &> blasen vb* B 1; C 1
B.17.216　The *blase* þerof yblowe out, yet brenneþ þe weke–
C.19.182　The *blase* be yblowen out, ȝut brenneth þe weke–

blasen n *blasoun n.* B 1
B.16.179　A ful bold bacheler; I knew hym by his *blasen*.'

blasen v *blasen v.(1)* B 6 blase (3) blased (1) blasen (1) blaseþ (1); C 6 blase (2) blased (1) blasen (1) blaseth (2)
B.17.223　As dooþ a kex or a candle þat caught haþ fir and *blaseþ*,
B.17.226　Til þe holy goost gynne to glowe and to *blase*,
B.17.236　Wol brennen and *blasen*, be þei togideres,
B.17.260　Ne brenne ne *blase* clere, fo[r] blowynge of vnkyndenesse.
B.17.266　Ye brenne but ye *blase* noȝt; þat is a blynd bekene:
B.18.233　That þo þis barn was ybore þer *blased* a sterre
C.19.189　A[s] doth a kix [o]r a candle þat cauht hath fuyr and *blaseth*,
C.19.192　Til the holy goest gynne to glowe and [to] *blase*,
C.19.202　Wol brennen and *blasen*, be they togyderes,
C.19.226　Ne brenne ne *blase* clere for blowynge of vnkyndenesse.
C.19.232　ȝe brenneth ac ȝe *blaseth* nat; and þat is a blynde bekne:
C.20.242　[That tho] this barn was ybore þ[er] *blased* a sterre

blaunmanger > blancmanger

blede v *bleden v.* A 2 bled (1) bledde (1); B 4 bledde (2) bledden (1) blede (1); C 4 bledde (2) bledden (1) blede (1)
A. 7.167　And *bledde* into þe bodyward a bolle ful of growel,
A.12.117　Þat barn bryng vs to blys þat *bled* vpon þe rode amen.
B.16.237　*Bledden* blood for þat lordes loue and hope to blisse þe tyme.
B.18.395　Ac blood may noȝt se blood *blede* but hym rewe:
B.19.107　Til he hadde alle hem þat he for *bledde*.
B.19.323　And of his baptisme and blood þat he *bledde* on roode
C.18.253　*Bledden* bloed for þat lordes loue [and] hope to blisse þ[e] tyme.
C.20.438　Ac bloed may nat se blood *blede* bote hym rewe:
C.21.107　Til he hadde all hem þat he fore *bledde*.
C.21.323　And of his bapteme and bloed þat he *bledde* on rode

blenche v *blenchen v.* A 1; B 1; C 1
A. 6.67　Þanne shalt þou *blenche* at a b[erw]e, bere no fals wytnesse;
B. 5.580　Thanne shaltow *blenche* at a Bergh, bere-no-fals-witnesse;
C. 7.227　Thenne shaltow *blenche* at a berw, bere-no-fals-witnesse,

blende v *blenden v.(1)* B 2 blende (1) blente (1); C 3 blende (1) blente (2)
B. 5.494　[Th]at liȝt þat lepe out of þee, Lucifer [it] *blent[e]*
B.10.134　And þo þat vseþ þise hauylons [for] to *blende* mennes wittes,
C. 7.134　The lihte þat lup oute of the, lucifer hit *blente*
C.20.284　Ar we thorw brihtnesse be *b[l]ente* go barre þe ȝates;
C.20.292　And sheteth out shot ynow his sheltrom to *blende*;

blered v *bleren v.(1)* A 2 bleride; B 2; C 2
A.Pr.71　He bunchi[de] hem wiþ his breuet & *bleri[de]* here eiȝe[n]
A. 5.109　He was [betil]browid & babirlippid wiþ two *bleride* eiȝen,
B.Pr.74　He bonched hem with his breuet and *blered* hire eiȝen
B. 5.190　He was bitelbrowed and baberlipped wiþ two *blered* eiȝen,
C.Pr.72　A bounchede hem with his b[reuet] and *blered* here yes
C. 6.198　He was bitelbrowed and baburlippid with two *blered* eyes

blereighed adj *blere-eied adj.* A 1 blereyed; B 1; C 1 blereyede
A. 7.178　[Þat leyȝe [*blereyed*] and brokelegged by þe hye waye];
B.17.330　Til he be *blereighed* or blynd and [þe borre] in þe þrote;
C.19.310　Til he be *blereyede* or blynde and þe borre in [the] throte,

bleride > blered

blesse v *blessen v.* A 5 blissen (1) blissid (1) blisside (1) blissiþ (1) yblissid (1); B 24 blesse (2) blessed (8) blessede (1) blesseder (1) blesseþ (1) blissed (4) blissede (2) yblessed (4) yblissed (1); C 27 blesse (2) blessed (11) blessede (1) blessedere (1) blesseth (1) blessid (1) yblessed (10)
A.Pr.75　Were þe bisshop *yblissid* & worþ boþe hise eris
A. 2.3　Þat bar þe *blisside* barn þat bouȝte vs on þe rode,
A. 3.138　She *blissiþ* þise bisshopis ȝif þei be lewid;
A. 8.13　Bisshopis þat *blissen*, & boþe lawes kenne,
A.10.115　To be *blissid* for þi beryng, [ȝ]e, b[e]ggere þeiȝ þou were.
B.Pr.78　Were þe Bisshop *yblessed* and worþ boþe hise eris
B. 2.3　That bar þ[e] *blis[sed]* barn þat bouȝte vs on þe Rode,
B. 3.138　She *blesseþ* þise Bisshopes [if] þei be lewed;
B. 5.495　And blewe alle þi *blessed* into þe blisse of Paradys.
B. 6.252　He is *blessed* by þe book in body and in soule;
B. 7.13　Bysshopes *yblessed*, if þei ben as þei sholde
B.10.408　But briddes and beestes and þe *blissed* Noe

B.11.164   *Yblissed* be truþe þat so brak helle yates
B.11.168   For þat is þe book *blissed* of blisse and of ioye;
B.11.237   Til he *blessede* and brak þe breed þat þei eten.
B.11.258   And boþe bettre and *blesseder* by many fold þan Richesse.
B.11.293   Or þe bisshop þat *blessed* yow [and embaumed youre fyngres].
B.12.187   Wel may þe barn *blesse* þat hym to book sette,
B.14.35   'Whoso leueþ yow, by oure lord! I leue noȝt he be *blessed.*'
B.14.320   A *blessed* lif wiþouten bisynesse for body and soule:
B.15.41   'For bisshopes *yblessed* bereþ manye names,
B.16.254   For in his bosom he bar a þyng þat he *blissed* euere.
B.18.429   For goddes *blissede* body it bar for oure boote;
B.19.146   That þat *blissede* body of burieles [sholde risen]
B.19.178   *Blessed* mote þow be, and be shalt for euere.
B.19.179   And *blessed* mote þei be, in body and in soule,
B.19.181   And lelliche bileue al þis; I loue hem and *blesse* hem:
B.19.385   Here is breed *yblessed*, and goddes body þervnder.
B.19.437   [So *blessed* be Piers þe Plowman þat peyneþ hym to tilye],
C.Pr.76   Were þe bischop *yblessed* and worth bothe his eres
C. 2.3   That bar þ[e] *blessid* bar[n] þat bouhte [vs] on þe rode,
C. 3.187   He *blesseth* this bischopes thow thei ben lewede;
C. 7.135   And brouhte thyne *yblessed* fro thennes into þe blisse of heuene.
C. 8.259   "*Yblessed* be al tho that here bylyue biswynketh"
C. 9.13   Bishopis *yblessed*, yf they ben as they sholde,
C.10.180   Of þ[e] *blessed* baptist bifore alle his gestes.
C.11.239   Bote briddes and bestis and þe *blessed* Noe
C.11.245   Bote holy churche, herborw to alle þat ben *yblessed*.
C.12.126   Til he *blessed* here bred and brake hit hem bitwene.
C.12.144   And bothe bettere and *blessedere* by many fold then richesse.
C.13.107   Or þe bischop þat *blessed* ȝow and enbaumed ȝoure fyngeres.
C.14.15   And þat is dobet, yf eny suche be, a *blessed* man þat helpeth
C.14.126   Wel may þe barne *blesse* þat hym to boek sette,
C.16.155   A *blessed* lyf withoute bisinesse bote onelyche for þe soule:
C.16.203   'For bisshopes *yblessed* bereth many names,–
C.17.59   For god bad his *blessed* as þe boek techeth–
C.17.163   Beaute sanȝ bounte *blessed* was [hit] neuere
C.18.90   Hit was þe furste fruyte þat þe fader of heuene *blessed*,
C.18.270   For in his bosome a baer [a] thyng þat [a] *blessede* [euere].
C.20.473   For goddes *blessed* body hit baer for oure bote
C.21.146   That þat *blessed* body of buyrielles sholde ryse
C.21.178   *Yblessed* mote thow be and be shalt for euere.
C.21.179   And *yblessed* mote they be, in body and in soule,
C.21.181   And leelliche bileuen al this; y loue hem and *blesse* hem:
C.21.385   Here is bred *yblessed* and godes body þervnder.
C.21.437   So *yblessed* be [Peres] the [plouhman] þat peyneth hym to tulie

blessynge ger *blessinge ger.* A 1 blissing; B 2; C 2
A. 7.236   God ȝiueþ [hem] his *blissing* þat here liflode so wynneþ.'
B.13.249   And þat his *blessynge* and hise bulles bocches myȝte destruye:
B.13.257   For may no *blessynge* doon vs boote but if we wile amende.
C.15.218   For founde y þat his *blessynge* and his bulle [bocches] myhte [destruye],
C.15.227   For may no *blessynge* doen vs bote but yf we wol amende

blete v *bleten v.* C 1
C.17.38   To his wyf; when he was blynde he herde a la[m]be *blete:*

bleuȝ > blowe

blew adj *bleu adj. &> blowe* C 1
C. 3.126   That fuyr shal falle and forbrenne al to *blew* aysches

blewe > blowe

blynd adj *blind adj.* A 5 blynd (2) blynde (3); B 17 blynd (8) blynde (9); C 20 blynd (3) blynde (17)
A. 6.98   Þe boldnesse of þi bienfait makiþ þe *blynd* þanne,
A. 7.113   Þanne were faitours aferd & feynide hem *blynde;*
A. 7.130   But he be *blynd*, or brokesshankid, or beddrede ligge:
A. 7.177   *Blynde* & bedrede were botind a þousand
A. 8.84   *Blynde* & bedrede, & broken here membris,
B. 5.612   The boldnesse of þi bienfe[et] makeþ þee *blynd* þanne,
B. 6.121   Tho were faitours afered and feyned hem *blynde;*
B. 6.136   But if he be *blynd* or brokelegged or bolted wiþ Irens,
B. 6.191   *Blynde* and bedreden were bootned a þousand;
B. 7.102   *Blynde* and bedreden and broken hire membres,
B.10.272   I rede ech a *blynd* bosard do boote to hymselue,
B.12.105   And as a *blynd* man in bataille bereþ wepne to fiȝte
B.13.147   And but he bowe for þis betyng *blynd* mote he worþe!"
B.13.447   And a *blynd* man for a bourdeour, or a bedrede womman
B.16.108   And souȝte out þe sike and [saluede *blynde* and crokede,
B.16.124   Youre bodies, youre beestes, and *blynde* men holpen.
B.17.266   Ye brenne but ye blase noȝt; þat is a *blynd* bekene:
B.17.330   Til he be blereighed or *blynd* and [þe borre] in þe þrote;
B.18.82   To [Iusten wiþ Iesus, þis *blynde* Iew Longeus].
B.18.85   But þis *blynde* bacheler baar hym þoruȝ þe herte.
B.18.95   To do þe *blynde* bete [þe dede], it was a boyes counseille.

B.19.125   He made lame to lepe and yaf light to *blynde*
C. 7.107   And a *blynd* man for a bordor or a bedredene womman
C. 7.264   The boldenesse of thy beenfet[e] maketh the *blynd* thenne;
C. 8.128   Tho were faytours aferd and fayned hem *blynde;*
C. 8.143   But yf he be *blynde* or brokelegged or bolted with yren,
C. 8.188   *Blynde* and Brokelegged he botened a thousand
C. 8.201   Was no beggare so bold, but yf a *blynd* were,
C. 9.97   And to conforte suche coterelles and crokede men and *blynde.*
C. 9.99   But they be *blynde* or tobroke or elles be syke,
C. 9.178   *Blynde* and bedredne and broken here membres,
C. 9.261   Thy berkeres aren a[l] *blynde* that bringeth forth thy lombren:
C.14.50   And as a *blynde* man in bataile bereth wepene to fyhte
C.15.147   And bote he bowe for this betynge *blynde* mote he worthen.'
C.17.38   To his wyf; when he was *blynde* he herde a la[m]be blete:
C.18.141   A lechede hem of here langour, bothe lasares and *blynde,*
C.19.232   Ȝe brenneth ac ȝe blaseth nat; and þat is a *blynde* bekne:
C.19.310   Til he be blereyede or *blynde* and be borre in [the] throte,
C.20.84   [To] iouste with iesus, this *blynde* iewe longies
C.20.87   Bote this *blynde* bacheler that bar hym thorw the herte.
C.20.98   [To do] þe *blynde* bete the dede, [hit] was a boyes [conseille].
C.21.125   He made lame to lepe and ȝaf liht to *blynde*

blisse n *blisse n. &> blissen* A 12 blys (1) blisse (11); B 33; C 24
A.Pr.27   In hope [for] to haue heueneriche *blisse,*
A. 2.30   Ȝif þou wilnest to wone wiþ treuþe in his *blisse.*
A. 3.92   And brouȝte hire to bo[ure] wiþ *blisse* & wiþ ioye.
A. 3.219   Þat on god of his grace gyueþ in his *blisse*
A. 4.91   'Nay,' quaþ þe king, 'so god ȝiue me *blisse,*
A. 9.55   *Blisse* of þe briddis made me abide,
A. 9.58   *Blisse* of þ[e] briddis brouȝte me a slepe;
A.10.36   Ȝaf hym gost of his godhed & grauntide hym *blisse,*
A.11.49   Litel louiþ he þat lond leniþ hym al þat *blisse,*
A.11.66   "Why wolde oure sauiour suffre such a worm in his *blisse*
A.11.313   Wiþoute penaunce at here partyng, into [þe] heiȝe *blisse.*
A.12.117   Þat barn bryng vs to *blys* þat bled vpon þe rode amen.
B.Pr.27   In hope [for] to haue heueneriche *blisse.*
B.Pr.106   And to opene it to hem and heuene *blisse* shewe.
B. 1.113   Til he brak buxomnesse; his *blisse* gan he tyne
B. 3.103   And brouȝte hire to boure wiþ *blisse* and wiþ ioye.
B. 3.232   That oon god of his grace [gyueþ] in his *blisse*
B. 5.495   And blewe alle þi blessed into þe *blisse* of Paradys.
B. 6.47   That he worþ worþier set and wiþ moore *blisse:*
B. 8.64   *Blisse* of þe briddes [abide me made],
B. 9.48   And of his grete grace graunted hym *blisse,*
B.10.63   Litel loueþ he þat lord þat lent hym al þat *blisse*
B.10.108   "Why wolde oure Saueour suffre swich a worm in his *blisse*
B.10.427   Wiþouten penaunce of purgatorie, to perpetuel *blisse.*
B.10.470   Into þe [parfit] *blisse* of Paradis for hir pure bileue,
B.11.26   'The freke þat folwede my wille failled neuere *blisse.*'
B.11.168   For þat is þe book blissed of *blisse* and of ioye;
B.11.189   Wheiþer we loue þe lordes here bifore þe lord of *blisse;*
B.11.333   *Blisse* and bale boþe I seiȝ at ones,
B.11.419   The wisedom and wit of god, he was put fram *blisse.*
B.12.134   Ne broȝt by hir bokes to *blisse* ne to ioye,
B.12.152   Tho it shon to shepherdes, a shewer of *blisse].*
B.12.196   Ac þouȝ þat þeef hadde heuene he hadde noon heiȝ *blisse,*
B.14.86   And brynge his soule to *blisse,* so feiþ beriþ witnesse
B.14.112   And seiþ, "lo! briddes and beestes þat no *blisse* ne knoweþ
B.14.116   And *blisse* to alle þat ben, boþe wilde and tame."
B.14.154   Here forȝifnesse of hir synnes, and heuene *blisse* after.
B.14.215   For his pouerte and pacience a perpetuel *blisse:*
B.14.261   After hir endynge here, heueneriche *blisse.*
B.15.175   Coueiteþ he noon erþely good, but heueneriche *blisse.*'
B.15.482   That is god of his grace, gyueþ alle men *blisse.*
B.16.108   'What berþ þat buyrn', quod I þo, 'so *blisse* þee bitide?'
B.16.190   Confortour of creatures; of hym comeþ alle *blisse.*
B.17.34   Siþ þe firste suffiseþ to sauacion and to *blisse?*
B.19.54   For he yaf Adam and Eue and oþere mo *blisse*
C.Pr.29   In hope to haue a good ende and heuenriche *blisse,*
C. 1.104   And god whan he bigan heuene in þat grete *blisse*
C. 3.11   Into Boure with *blisse* and by here gan sitte.
C. 7.135   And brouhte thyne yblessed fro thennes into þe *blisse* of heuene.
C. 9.40   And abyde þer in my *blisse* body and soule for euere.'
C.10.63   *Blisse* of þe briddes abyde me made
C.10.67   And merueilousliche me mette amyddes al þat *blisse.*
C.11.45   Lytel loueth he þat lord þat lente hym al þat *blisse*
C.11.201   Sholde sitte in goddis sihte ne se god in his *blisse:*
C.11.260   Passe[d] forth paciently to perpetuel *blisse.*
C.12.159   He shal haue an hundredfold of heueneryche *blisse*
C.13.141   *Blisse* and bale bothe y sey at ones,
C.13.227   The wisdom and the wit of god he was pot out of *blisse.*
C.14.78   Ne brouhte by here bokes to *blisse* ne to ioye,
C.14.80   Of briddes and of bestes, of *blisse* and of sorwe.
C.14.96   Tho hit shoen to shepherdes, a shewere of *blisse.*

C.14.135   Ac thogh th[at] theef hadde heuene he hadde noen hey *blisse*
C.15.288   And saith, "loo! briddes and bestes þat no *blisse* ne knoweth
C.15.292   And *blisse* to all þat been, bothe wilde and tame."
C.15.293   Thenne may beggares, as bestes, aftur *blisse* aske
C.16.101   Aftur here endynge here heueneryche *blisse*.
C.20.347   For we leued on thy lesynges [there losten we *blisse*;
C.20.416   And be at my biddynge, at *blisse* or at payne.
C.21.54   For he 3af Adam and Eue and oþere mo *blisse*

blissed(e > blesse

blissen v *blissen v. &> blesse* A 1; B 2 blisse (1) blissen (1); C 1 blisse
A.11.151   And [biddiþ] vs ben as breþeren, & *blissen* oure enemys,
B.10.202   [And] biddeþ vs be as breþeren and [*blissen*] oure enemys,
B.16.237   Bledden blood for þat lordes loue and hope to *blisse* þe tyme.
C.18.253   Bledden bloed for þat lordes loue [and] hope to *blisse* þ[e] tyme.

blissid(e > blesse; blissing > blessynge; blissiþ > blesse

bliþe adj *blithe adj.* A 2 bliþe (1) blyþe (1); B 2; C 2 blythe
A. 2.122   Þanne was fals fayn, & fauel als *bliþe*,
A. 3.26   And bidden hire be *blyþe*, 'for we ben þin owene
B. 2.158   Thanne was Fal[s] fayn and Fauel as *bliþe*,
B. 3.27   And beden hire be *blyþe*: 'for we beþ þyne owene
C. 2.174   Thenne was [falsnesse] fayn and [fauel] *blythe*,
C. 3.28   And beden here be *blythe*: 'for we beth thyn owene

blod(e > blood

blody adj *blodi adj.* A 2; B 6; C 7
A. 4.64   Pees putte forþ his heued & his panne *blody*:
A. 7.193   And it ben my *blody* breþeren, for god bou3te vs alle.
A. 8.78   Pees putte forþ his heed, and his panne *blody*:
B. 6.207   [And it] are my *blody* breþeren for god bou3te vs alle;
B.11.202   And *blody* breþeren we bicome þere of o body ywonne,
B.16.111   Boþe meseles and mute and in þe menyson *blody*,
B.19.6   That Piers þe Plowman was peynted al *blody*
B.19.13   Hise colours and his cote Armure; ac he þat comeþ so *blody*
C. 4.74   3ut pees put forth his heued and his panne *blody*:
C. 6.150   Til bothe here hedes were bar and *blody* here chekes.
C. 8.216   And hit are my *blody* bretherne for god bouhte vs alle.
C.12.110   And *blody* bretherne we bycome þere of o body ywonne,
C.12.116   And we his *blody* bretherne, as wel beggares as lordes.
C.21.6   That [Peres] þe [plouhman] was peynted al *blody*
C.21.13   His colours and his cote armure; ac he þat cometh so *blody*

blood n *blod n.* A 5 blod (1) blood (4); B 25 blode (1) blood (24); C 27 bloed (23) blod (1) blode (1) blood (2)
A. 3.192   Þe leste brol of his *blood* a barouns pere.
A.10.55   Þere is his bour bremest but 3if *blod* it make;
A.10.56   For whan *blood* is bremere þanne brayn, þan is Inwit bounde,
A.10.61   And ben braynwood as bestis, so here *blood* wexiþ.
A.10.170   Clene awey þe cursid *blood* þat caym haþ ymakid.
B. 1.155   And whan it hadde of þis fold flessh and *blood* taken
B. 3.205   The leeste brol of his *blood* a Barones piere.
B. 5.493   Feddest wiþ þi fresshe *blood* oure forefadres in derknesse:
B. 9.139   Clene awey þe corsed *blood* þat Caym haþ ymaked.
B.11.124   By þe *blood* þat he bou3te vs wiþ, and þoru3 bapteme after:
B.11.200   And breþeren as of oo *blood*, as wel beggeres as Erles.
B.11.201   For [at] Caluarie of cristes *blood* cristendom gan sprynge,
B.12.285   [Ac] þer is fullynge of Font and fullynge in *blood* shedyng
B.15.517   And baptised and bishined wiþ þe *blode* of his herte
B.16.237   Bledden *blood* for þat lordes loue and hope to blisse þe tyme.
B.17.96   Wiþouten þe *blood* of a barn born of a mayde.
B.17.97   And [he] be] baþed in þat *blood*, baptised as it were,
B.17.100   Til he haue eten al þe barn and his *blood* ydronke
B.17.125   For þe barn was born in Bethleem þat with his *blood* shal saue
B.17.293   That shente vs and shedde oure *blood*, forshapte vs as it [semed]:
B.18.86   The *blood* sprong doun by þe spere and vnspered [his] ei3en.
B.18.376   For we beþ breþeren of *blood*, [ac] no3t in baptisme alle.
B.18.377   Ac alle þat beþ myne hole breþeren, in *blood* and in baptisme,
B.18.394   For *blood* may suffre blood boþe hungry and acale
B.18.394   For blood may suffre *blood* boþe hungry and acale
B.18.395   Ac *blood* may no3t se blood blede but hym rewe:
B.18.395   Ac blood may no3t se *blood* blede but hym rewe:
B.19.58   Who was hardiere þan he? his herte *blood* he shadde
B.19.323   And of his baptisme and *blood* þat he bledde on roode
B.19.445   And fynt folk to fi3te and cristen *blood* to spille
C. 1.151   /A[nd] when hit hadde of þe folde flesch and *blode* taken
C. 3.262   The leeste brolle of his *blod* a Barones pere.
C. 5.78   Popes and patrones pore gentel *blood* refused
C. 7.133   Feddest tho with thy [fresshe] *blood* oure forfadres in helle:
C.10.227   Clene awey þe corsed *bloed* þat of Caym spronge.
C.12.59   By þ[e] *bloed* [that] he bouhte vs with and bapteme, as he tauhte:
C.12.109   A[t] Caluarie of cristis *bloed* cristendoem gan sprynge
C.14.207   Ac þer is follyng of fonte and follyng in *bloed* [s]hedyng

C.15.67   Brawen and *bloed* of gees, bacon and colhoppes.
C.15.155   Withoute brutteny[n]ge of buyren or eny *bloed* shedynge.
C.17.58   With þat 3oure bernes and 3oure *bloed* by goed lawe may clayme!
C.17.268   And baptised and bis[hin]ede with þe *bloed* of his herte
C.18.253   Bledden *bloed* for þat lordes loue [and] hope to blisse þ[e] tyme.
C.19.86   Withoute þe *bloed* of a barn he beth nat ysaued.
C.19.88   And with þe *bloed* of þat barn enbaumed and ybaptised.
C.19.90   Til he haue eten al þ[e] barn and his *bloed* dronken
C.19.274   That shent vs and shedde oure *bloed*, forschupte vs as hit semede:
C.20.88   The *bloed* sprang down by þe spere and vnspered [his] yes.
C.20.418   For we beth brethrene of *bloed* Ac nat in baptisme alle.
C.20.419   Ac alle þat beth myn hole breth[r]ene, in *bloed* and in baptisme,
C.20.437   For *bloed* may s[uffr]e bloed bothe afurst and acale
C.20.437   For bloed may s[uffr]e *bloed* bothe afurst and acale
C.20.438   Ac *bloed* may nat se bloed blede bote hym rewe:
C.20.438   Ac bloed may nat se *bloed* blede bote hym rewe:
C.21.58   Ho was hardior then he? his herte *bloed* he she[d]de
C.21.323   And of his bapteme and *bloed* þat he bledde on rode
C.21.445   And fynde[th] folke to fihte and cristene *bloed* to spille

blosmede v *blosmen v.* B 1
B. 5.141   And siþen þei *blosmede* abrood in boure to here shriftes.

blosmes n *blosme n.* B 2; C 2
B.16.7   The *blosmes* beþ buxom speche and benigne lokynge.
B.16.35   And forbiteþ þe *blosmes* ri3t to þe bare leues.
C.18.10   Thorw louely lokyng[e] hit lyueth and launseth vp *blosmes*,
C.18.11   The whiche *blosmes* buirnes benigne speche hit calleth.

blostrede > blustreden

blowe v1 *blouen v.(1)* A 2 bleu3 (1) blowen (1); B 9 blew (2) blewe (1) blowe (4) blowen (1) yblowe (1); C 8 blew (1) blewe (1) blowe (4) blowen (1) yblowen (1)
A. 5.18   Bechis & broode okis wern *blowen* to [þe] grounde,
A. 5.190   And *bleu3* þe rounde ryuet at þe riggebones ende
B. 5.18   Beches and brode okes were *blowen* to þe grounde
B. 5.342   And *blew* [þe] rounde ruwet at [þe] ruggebones ende
B. 5.495   And *blewe* alle þi blessed into þe blisse of Paradys.
B. 5.507   And *blew* it wiþ Beati quorum remisse sunt iniquitates,
B.16.32   Thoru3 likynge and lustes so loude he gynneþ *blowe*
B.17.216   The blase þerof *yblowe* out, yet brenneþ þe weke–
B.17.228   Til þat lele loue ligge on hym and *blowe*.
B.19.338   *Blowe* hem doun and breke hem and bite atwo þe mores.
C. 5.120   Beches and brode okes were *blowe* to þe grounde
C. 6.400   A[nd] *blew* his rownd ruet at [þe] ry[g]bones ende
C. 7.152   And *Blewe* hit with beati quorum remisse sunt iniquitates &
C.18.36   Thorw lecherie and lustes so loude he gynneth *blowe*
C.19.182   The blase is *yblowen* out, 3ut brenneth þe weke–
C.19.194   Til þat loue and bileue leliche to hym *blowe*.
C.19.312   That sholde brynge in bettere wode or *blowen* hit til hit brente.
C.21.338   *Blowe* hem doun and B[r]eke hem and b[y]te ato þe mores.

bloweth v2 *blouen v.(2)* C 1
C.18.100   'This is a propre plonte,' quod y–'and priueliche hit *bloweth*

blowyng ger *blouing ger.(2)* B 1
B.16.26   And in *blowyng* tyme abite þe floures but if þise piles helpe.

blowynge ger *blouing ger.(1)* B 1; C 1
B.17.260   Ne brenne ne blase clere, fo[r] *blowynge* of vnkyndenesse.
C.19.226   Ne brenne ne blase clere for *blowynge* of vnkyndenesse.

blustreden v *blusteren v.* A 1 blustrid; B 1; C 1 blostrede
A. 6.2   But *blustrid* forþ as bestis ouer [baches] & hilles
B. 5.514   But *blustreden* forþ as beestes ouer [baches] and hilles
C. 7.159   But *blostrede* forth as bestes ouer baches and hulles

bocches n *bocche n.* B 2; C 2 bocches (1) boches (1)
B.13.249   And þat his blessynge and hise bulles *bocches* my3te destruye:
B.20.84   Biles and *bocches* and brennynge Agues,
C.15.218   For founde y þat his blessynge and his bulle [*bocches*] myhte [destruye],
C.22.84   Byles and *boches* and brennynge aguwes,

bocher n *bocher n.* A 3 bocher (1) bocheris (2); B 3 Bocher (1) Bochiers (2); C 3 bochere (1) Bocheres (1) Bochers (1)
A.Pr.98   Baxteris & *bocheris* & breusteris manye,
A. 3.68   Breweris & bakeris, *bocheris* & cokes,
A. 5.171   And bed bette þe *bocher* be on his side.
B.Pr.219   Baksteres and Brewesteres and *Bochiers* manye,
B. 3.79   Brew[e]rs and Bak[e]rs, *Bochiers* and Cokes;
B. 5.322   And bad Bette þe *Bocher* be on his syde.
C.Pr.225   Bothe Bakeres and Breweres, *Bochers* and other,
C. 3.80   As Bakeres a[nd] Breweres, *Bocheres* and cokes;
C. 6.379   And bade b[et]te þe *bochere* ben on his syde.

boches > bocches; bochiers > bocher

bode n *bod n.(2)* A 2
A. 2.51   And he[o] be bou[n] at his *bode* his bidding to fulfille,
A. 3.251   And for he kilde not þe king as crist [him] *bode* sente,

boden > bidden

body n *bodi n.* A 6; B 41 bodi (1) body (37) bodie (1) bodye (1) bodies (1); C 37 body (36) bodies (1)
A. 1.60   May banne þat he born was to *body* or to soule.
A. 1.169   Ʒe curatours þat kepe ʒow clene of ʒour *body*,
A. 5.66   His *body* was bolnid for wr[aþþe] þat he bot his lippe[s],
A. 9.37   Þe boot is lik[nid] to þe *body* þat britel is of kynde,
A. 9.43   Þat, þeiʒ þi *body* bowe as bot doþ in þe watir,
A.10.44   Þat is Anima, þat oueral in þe *body* wandriþ,
B. 1.62   May banne þat he born was to *bodi* or to soule.
B. 1.195   [Ye] curatours [þat] kepen [yow] clene of [youre] *bod[y]*,
B. 5.83   His *body* was [b]ollen for wraþe þat he boot hise lippes,
B. 6.252   He is blessed by þe book in *body* and in soule:
B. 8.41   The boot is liknyd to [þe] *body* þat brotel is of kynde,
B. 8.47   [That], þouʒ þ[i] *body* bowe as boot dooþ in þe watre,
B. 9.56   Ouer al in mannes *body* he[o] walkeþ and wandreþ,
B.10.262   And lat no *body* be by þi beryng bigiled
B.10.266   Ac blame þow neuere *body* and þow be blameworþy:
B.11.74   Where my *body* were buryed by so ye hadde my siluer.
B.11.202   And blody breþeren we bicome þere of o *body* ywonne,
B.12.48   The beaute of hir *body*; in baddenesse she despended.
B.12.85   For goddes *body* myʒte noʒt ben of breed wiþouten clergie,
B.12.86   The which *body* is boþe boote to þe riʒtfulle
B.12.90   Riʒt so goddes *body*, breþeren, but it be worþili taken,
B.13.289   As best for his *body* be to haue a [bold] name;
B.13.316   What on bak, and what on *body* half, and by þe two sides
B.13.375   And [what *body*] borwed of me abouʒte þe tyme
B.14.130   And greet likynge to lyue wiþouten labour of *bodye*,
B.14.263   In lond and in lordshipe and likynge of *bodie*
B.14.284   So pouerte propreliche penaunce [is to þe *body*,
B.14.320   A blessed lif wiþouten bisynesse for *body* and soule:
B.15.426   The bettre for hir biddynges in *body* and in soule.
B.16.14   Amyddes mannes *body*; þe more is of þat stokke.
B.16.83   Bar hem forþ bo[lde]ly–no *body* hym letted–
B.16.124   Youre *bodies*, youre beestes, and blynde men holpen,
B.17.280   The which is lif and loue, þe leye of mannes *body*.
B.18.64   'For a bitter bataille', þe dede *body* seide;
B.18.75   Ac was no bo[y] so boold goddes *body* to touche;
B.18.97   To [bete a *body* ybounde wiþ any briʒt wepene].
B.18.232   'By goddes *body*', quod þis book, 'I wol bere witnesse
B.18.279   *Body* and soule beþ myne, boþe goode and ille.
B.18.305   For þe *body*, while it on bones yede, aboute was euere
B.18.429   For goddes blissede *body* it bar for oure boote:
B.19.143   And siþen buriede his *body*, and beden þat men sholde
B.19.146   That þat blissede *body* of burieles [sholde risen]
B.19.179   And blessed mote þei be, in *body* and in soule,
B.19.352   Wiþ þe lord þat lyueþ after þe lust of his *body*,
B.19.385   Here is breed yblessed, and goddes *body* þervnder.
B.20.27   And bete men ouer bittre, and so[m *body*] to litel,
B.20.71   Wiþ a lord þat lyueþ after likyng of *body*,
C. 1.58   May banne þe born was [to] *body* [or to] soule.
C. 1.147   And most souerayne salue for soule and for *body*.
C. 3.105   Many burgages ybrent and *bodies* þerynne
C. 3.307   As by the book þat byt no*body* withholde
C. 5.33   Or thow art broke, so may be, in *body* or in membre
C. 5.38   And what is beste for the *body*, as the boek telleth.
C. 7.128   And madest thysulue with thy sone oure soule & *body* ilych:
C. 9.40   And abyde þer in my blisse *body* and soule for euere.'
C. 9.203   Forsoken lond and lordschipe and lykyng[e] of *body*.
C.10.37   [A] bendeth and boweth, the *body* is so vnstable,
C.10.47   The boet is liknet to oure *body* þat bretil is of kynde,
C.11.12   Þat [they] louyen lond and lordschipe and lykynge of *body*
C.12.22   Wher my *body* were yber[i]ed by so ʒe hadde my [suluer].'
C.12.88   Saued me, sarrasyn, soule and *body* bothe.'
C.12.110   And blody bretherne we bycome there of o *body* ywonne,
C.12.206   Pouerte and penaunce and persecucoun of *body*.
C.13.134   And y bowed my *body*, bihel[d]e al aboute
C.16.103   In lond and in lordschipe [and] lykynge of *body*
C.16.178   And may nat be withoute a *body* to bere me where hym liketh.'
C.16.179   'Thenne is þat *body* bettere þen þou?' quod y. 'Nay,' quod he, 'no bettere,
C.17.146   And ay hopeth eft to be with here *body* at þe laste
C.18.114   Baer hem forth baldly–no *body* hym lette–
C.19.261   The which is lyf and loue, the leye of mannes *body*.
C.20.66   'For a bittur bataile,' þe ded *body* saide;
C.20.77   Ac was no boie so bold godes *body* to touche;
C.20.100   To bete a *body* ybounde with eny briht wypene.

C.20.241   'By godes *body*,' quod this boek, 'y wol [b]ere witnesse
C.20.301   *Body* and soule beth myne, bothe gode and ille.
C.20.337   For þe *body*, whiles hit on bones ʒede, aboute was hit euere
C.20.473   For godes blessed *body* hit baer for oure bote.
C.21.143   And sethen bur[ie]den his *body* and beden þat men sholde
C.21.146   That þat blessed *body* of buyrielles sholde ryse
C.21.179   And yblessed mote they be, in *body* and in soule,
C.21.352   With the lord þat lyueth aftur the lust of his *body*,
C.21.385   Here is bred yblessed and godes *body* þervnder.
C.22.27   And bete men ouer bitere and som *body* to litel,
C.22.71   With a lord þat lyueth aftur likyng of *body*

bodily adj *bodiliche adj.* B 1
B.15.576   *Bodily* foode and goostly foode to] gyue þere it nedeþ:

bodyward adv *bodi n.* A 1
A. 7.167   And bledde into þe *bodyward* a bolle ful of growel,

boek > book; boend > bynden; boende > bonde; boer > boor; boerd > borde; boest > boost; boet > boot; boetles > bootles; boffatede -eted > buffetted

boy n *boie n.(1)* A 3 boy (2) bois (1); B 4 boy (2) boye (1) boyes (1); C 8 boy (2) boie (2) boyes (2) boys (2)
A.Pr.77   It is not be þe bisshop þat þe *boy* prechiþ,
A. 8.75   And bringen forþ barnes þat *bois* ben holden.
A.11.61   For now is iche *boy* bold, & he be riche,
B.Pr.80   It is noʒt by þe bisshop þat þe *boy* precheþ;
B.11.204   No beggere ne *boye* amonges vs but if it synne made:
B.18.75   Ac was no bo[y] so boold goddes body to touche;
B.18.95   To do þe blynde bete [þe dede], it was a *boyes* counseille.
C.Pr.78   Ac it is nouʒt by þe bischop þat þe *boy* precheþ,
C. 8.264   To beggares and to *boys* þat loth ben to worche.
C. 9.127   And godes *boys*, bourdyors as the book telleth:
C. 9.195   For hit ben but *boyes*, bollares at þe ale,
C.12.112   No beggare ne *boy* among vs but [yf] hit synne ma[d]e:
C.20.77   Ac was no *boie* so bold godes body to touche;
C.20.79   That hadde no *boie* hardynesse hym to touche in deynge.
C.20.98   [To do] þe blynde bete the dede, [hit] was a *boyes* [conseille].

boylaunt prp *boillen v.* C 1
C.20.289   Brumstoen *boylaunt*, brennyng out cast hit,

boyste > bouste; bok(e -es > book

bokelees adj *OED bookless a.* B 1
B.15.127   [He syngeþ seruice *bokelees*], seiþ it with ydel wille.

bokynghamshire n prop *n.i.d.* A 1 bukyngham; B 1
A. 2.74   Bette þe bedel of *bukyngham* shire,
B. 2.110   Bette þe Bedel of *Bokynghamshire*,

bokkes > bukkes

bold adj *bold adj.* A 7 baldere (1) bold (2) bolde (3) boldere (1); B 16 bold (5) bolde (5) bolder (1) boldere (1) boldest (1) boold (3); C 16 baldere (1) baldore (1) bald (1) bold (8) bolde (6)
A.Pr.90   I sauʒ bisshopis *bolde* & bacheleris of deuyn
A. 4.94   And ofte þe *boldere* be to bete myn hynen.
A. 7.199   *Bolde* beggeris & bigge, þat mowe here breed beswynken,
A. 8.167   Be þou neuere þe *baldere* to breke þe ten hestis;
A. 9.93   And were vnbuxum at his bidding, and *bold* to don ille,
A.11.61   For now is iche boy *bold*, & he be riche,
A.11.91   I dar be his *bolde* boruʒ do bet wile he neuere,
B.Pr.188   And be we neuere [so] *bolde* þe belle hym to shewe.
B. 2.83   Vnbuxome and *bolde* to breke þe ten hestes;
B. 4.107   And [ofte] þe *boldere* be to bete myne hewen.
B. 6.213   *Bolde* beggeris and bigge þat mowe hir breed biswynke,
B. 7.189   Be [þow] neuer þe *bolder* to breke þe x hestes,
B. 8.103   [And were vnbuxum at his biddyng, and *bold* to don ille],
B.10.138   I dar ben his *bolde* borgh þat dobet wole he neuere,
B.10.264   Thanne is dobest to be *boold* to blame þe gilty,
B.13.280   Forwhy he bosteþ and braggeþ wiþ manye *bolde* oþes;
B.13.289   As best for his body be to haue a [*bold*] name;
B.13.302   *Boldest* of beggeris; a bostere þat noʒt haþ,
B.16.179   A ful *bold* bacheler; I knew hym by his blasen.'
B.18.75   Ac was no bo[y] so *boold* goddes body to touche;
B.18.231   Book highte þat beaupeere, a *bold* man of speche.
B.19.294   And *bold* and abidynge bismares to suffre;
B.20.142   And *boold* and bidynge while his bagge lasteþ.'
C.Pr.205   And be [we] neuere so *bold* the belle hym [to] shewe.
C. 2.90   Vnbuxum and *bold* to breke þe ten hestes;
C. 4.55   Ʒut is he *bold* to borw Ac baddelyche he payeth:
C. 4.102   And efte the *baldore* be to bete myn hewes.
C. 6.17   And [*bold* haue] y be, nat abaschet to agulte
C. 6.34   Bostyng and braggynge with many *bolde* othes,
C. 6.49   And non so *bolde* a beggare to bidde and to craue,
C. 8.201   Was no beggare so *bold*, but yf a blynd were,

C. 8.223 *Bolde* beggares and bygge þat mowe here breed byswynke,
C. 9.335 Be ȝe neuere þe *baldere* to breke þe ten hestes
C.18.46 Thorw bagbitares and braule[r]s and thorw *bolde* chidares
C.18.135 Byg and abydyng, and *bold* in his barnhoed
C.20.77 Ac was no boie so *bold* godes body to touche;
C.20.240 Boek hihte þat beaupere, a *bolde* man of speche.
C.21.294 And *bold* and abidynge busmares to soffre
C.22.142 And *bolde* and [b]ydynge while his bagge lasteth.'

boldede > boldeþ

boldely adv *boldeli(che adv.* A 1; B 7 boldely (5) boldeliche (2); C 7
    baldeliche (2) baldly (3) boldely (1) boldly (1)
A. 8.26 And bad h[e]m begge *boldely* what [hem best] likeþ,
B. 7.24 [And bad hem] buggen *boldely* [what] hem best liked
B.14.214 Batauntliche as beggeris doon, and *boldeliche* he craueþ
B.16.83 Bar hem forþ *bo[lde]ly*–no body hym letted–
B.19.475 So I may *boldely* be housled for I borwe neuere
B.20.70 And pride [bar it bare] *boldely* aboute
B.20.132 And *boldeliche* bar adoun wiþ many a bright Noble
B.20.327 *Boldely* to þe bisshop and his brief hadde
C. 9.28 [And] bad hem bugge *boldly* what hem best likede
C.16.55 Batauntliche as beggares doen, and *baldeliche* he craueth
C.18.114 Baer hem forth *baldly*–no body hym lette–
C.21.475 So y may *boldely* be hoseled for y borwe neuere
C.22.70 And pryde [baer] hit baer *baldly* aboute
C.22.132 And *baldeliche* baer adoun with many a brihte noble
C.22.327 *Baldly* to þe bishope and his breef hadde

boldenesse > boldnesse

boldeþ v *bolden v.* A 1 boldite; B 2 boldede (1) boldeþ (1)
A. 3.186 And bateride hym on þe bak, *boldite* his herte,
B. 3.199 I batred hem on þe bak and *boldede* hire hertes
B. 9.15 That he bit moot be do; he [*boldeþ*] hem alle;

boldite > boldeþ; boldly > boldely

boldnesse n *boldnesse n.* A 1; B 2; C 2 boldenesse
A. 6.98 Þe *boldnesse* of þi bienfait makiþ þe blynd þanne
B. 5.612 The *boldnesse* of þi bienfe[et] makeþ þee blynd þanne
B.18.388 Be it any þyng abouȝt, þe *boldnesse* of hir synnes,
C. 7.264 The *boldenesse* of thy beenfet[e] maketh the blynd thenne;
C.20.430 Be hit eny thyng abouhte, the *boldenesse* of here synne[s],

bole n *bole n.(1)* B 1; C 1
B.11.342 That wolde [bere] after *bol[e]*, ne boor after sowe;
C.13.150 That wolde bere aftur *bole* ne boer aftur sowe;

bolk n *bolk n.* B 1; C 1
B. 5.390 He bigan Benedicite with a *bolk* and his brest knokked,
C. 7.6 A bigan benedicite with a *bolk* and his breste knokkede,

bollares n *bollere n.* C 1
C. 9.195 For hit ben but boyes, *bollares* at þe ale,

bolle n *bolle n.* A 4; B 3; C 3
A. 5.89 Þat bar awey my *bolle* & my broken shete.
A. 5.204 Þe ferste woord þat he spak was 'where is þe *bolle*?'
A. 6.7 A bagge & a *bolle* he bar be his side;
A. 7.167 And bledde into þe bodyward a *bolle* ful of growel,
B. 5.109 That [bar] awey my *bolle* and my broke shete.
B. 5.362 The firste word þat he [spak] was 'where is þe *bolle*?'
B. 5.519 A *bolle* and a bagge he bar by his syde,
C. 6.420 The furste [word] þat he spak was '[wh]o halt þe *bolle*?'
C. 7.164 A *bolle* and a bagge a bar by his syde,
C.20.407 Ac thy drynke worth deth and depe helle thy *bolle*.

bollen ptp *bollen v.* B 1
B. 5.83 His body was [b]ollen for wraþe þat he boot hise lippes,

bollynge ger *bollinge ger.* B 1; C 1 bollyng
B. 6.215 [And] aba[u]e hem wiþ benes for *bollynge* of hir womb[e];
C. 8.225 And [a]baue hem with benes for *bollyng* of here wombe;

bollnyng ger *bolning ger.* A 1
A. 7.201 And [a]baue hem wiþ b[e]nes for *bollnyng* of here wombe,

bolneþ v *bolnen v.* A 2 bolnid (1) bolniþ (1); B 1
A. 5.66 His body was *bolnid* for wr[aþþe] þat he bot his lippe[s],
A. 5.99 [Þat] al my brest *bolniþ* for bittir of my galle.
B. 5.120 That al my [brest] *bolneþ* for bitter of my galle.

bolted ptp *bolten v.* B 1; C 1
B. 6.136 But if he be blynd or brokelegged or *bolted* wiþ Irens,
C. 8.143 But yf he be blynde or brokelegged or *bolted* with yren,

bon n *bon n.* A 2 bon (1) bones (1); B 4 boon (1) bon (1) bones (2); C 4
    bon (1) bones (2) bonis (1)
A. 7.83 Þe [k]ir[k]e shal haue my caroyn & kepe my *bones*,

A. 8.76 Or his bak or his *bon* þei breken in his ȝouþe,
B. 6.91 The kirke shal haue my caroyne and kepe my *bones*
B. 7.94 Or [his] bak or [his] *boon* [þei] brekeþ in his youþe
B. 9.35 And Eue of his ryb *bon* wiþouten any mene.
B.18.305 For þe body, while it on *bones* yede, aboute was euere
C. 8.100 The kyrke shal haue my caroyne and kepe my *bones*
C. 9.157 And ouermore to [a]n [ha]tur to hele with his *bonis*
C. 9.170 Or þe bak or som *bon* þey breke of he[re] children
C.20.337 For þe body, whiles hit on *bones* ȝede, aboute was hit euere

bonched v *bonchen v.* A 1 bunchide; B 1; C 1 bounchede
A.Pr.71 He *bunchi[de]* hem wiþ his breuet & bleri[de] here eiȝe[n]
B.Pr.74 He *bonched* hem with his breuet and blered hire eiȝen
C.Pr.72 A *bounchede* hem with his b[reuet] and blered here yes

bonchef n *bonchef n.* C 1
C. 3.33 And bygge ȝow benefices, [here *bonchef*] to haue,

bond n *bond n. &> bynden* B 1 bondes; C 2 bond (1) bondes (1)
B.19.57 And bond [hym] as [he is bounde] wiþ *bondes* of yrene.
C. 5.14 Mowen or mywen or make *bond* to sheues,
C.21.57 And *bonde* [hym] as he is bounde with *bondes* of yre.

bondage n *bondage n.* A 1; B 1
A.Pr.96 Barouns [and] burgeis & *bondage* also
B.Pr.217 Barons and Burgeises and *bond[age]* als

bonde n *bonde n.(1) &> bynden* C 3 boende (1) bonde (2)
C. 3.201 Trewe Burgeys and *bonde* he bryngeth to nauhte ofte
C.10.267 That he ne wol bowe to þat *bonde* to beden here an hosebonde
C.15.14 As wel lered as lewede and lorde as þe [*b*]oende,

bondeman n *bonde-man n.* A 2 bondemen; B 2 bondeman (1)
    bondemannes (1); C 5 bondeman (1) bondemannes (1) bondemen (3)
A. 7.44 And mysbede nouȝt þi *bondemen*, þe bet shalt þou spede;
A.10.138 Barouns & burgeis, & *bondemen* of tounes.
B. 5.193 And as a *bondeman[nes]* bacon his berd was [yshaue].
B. 6.45 And mysbede noȝt þi *bondem[a]n*, þe bettre [shalt] þow spede;
C.Pr.223 As Barones and Burgeys and *bondemen* of thorpus.
C. 5.68 *Bondemen* and bastardus and beggares children,
C. 5.70 Ac sythe *bondemen* barnes haen be mad bisshopes
C. 6.201 And as a *bondemannes* bacoun his berd was yshaue,
C. 8.42 Misbede nat thy *bondeman*, the bette may th[ow] spede;

bone > boone; bones -is > bon

book n *bok n.(1)* A 10 bok (3) boke (3) bokes (1) bokis (3); B 58 bok (1)
    boke (3) bokes (23) book (31); C 53 boek (20) boke (4) bokes (25)
    book (4)
A. 1.159 For Iames þe ientil ioynide in his *bokis*
A. 2.80 And seide to cyuyle, 'now sorewe on þi *bokes*,
A. 3.230 Shal abiȝe it bitterly or þe *bok* liȝeþ.
A. 6.26 'I knowe hym as kyndely as clerk doþ his *bokis*.
A. 8.119 Þou art le[ttr]id a litel; who lernide þe on *boke*?'
A. 9.17 Seue siþes, seiþ þe *bok*, [synneþ] þe riȝtful;
A.11.130 Plato þe poete, I putte hym ferst to *boke*;
A.11.158 For sorcerie is þe *bok* þat to þat science longiþ.
A.11.308 Þanne arn þise [k]ete clerkis þat conne many *bokis*,
A.12.3 And whoso coueyteþ don betere þan þe *boke* telleþ,
B.Pr.101 To bynden and vnbynden as þe *book* telleþ,
B. 1.185 For Iames þe gentile [loyned] in hise *bokes*
B. 2.116 And seide [to] Cyuyle, 'now sorwe [on þi *bokes*]
B. 3.55 It is a freletee of flessh–ye fynden it in *bokes*–
B. 3.251 Shal abien it bittre or þe *book* lieþ.
B. 3.333 Se what Salomon seiþ in Sapience *bokes*!
B. 5.148 I, wraþe, walke wiþ hem and wisse hem of my *bokes*.
B. 5.235 'I wende riflynge were restitucion for I lerned neuere rede on *boke*,
B. 5.268 For þe beste *book* in oure hous, þeiȝ brent gold were þe leues,
B. 5.483 And for þe beste as I bileue whateuere þe *book* telleþ:
B. 5.558 'I knowe hym as kyndely as clerc doþ hise *bokes*.
B. 6.252 He is blessed by þe *book* in body and in soule:
B. 7.85 For whoso haþ to buggen hym breed, þe *book* bereþ witnesse,
B. 7.89 The *book* banneþ beggerie and blameþ hem in þis manere:
B. 7.137 Thow art lettred a litel; who lerned þee on *boke*?'
B. 7.157 Ac for þe *book* bible bereþ witnesse
B. 8.21 Seuene siþes, seiþ þe *book*, synneþ þe rightfulle;
B.10.85 And brekeþ noȝt to þe beggere as þe *book* techeþ:
B.10.89 How þe *book* bible of hym bereþ witnesse,
B.10.178 Plato þe poete, I putte [hym] first to *boke*;
B.10.215 For sorcerie is þe Souereyn *book* þat to [þat] Scienc[e] [l]ongeþ.
B.10.249 Austyn þe olde herof made *bokes*,
B.10.258 Al þat þe *book* bit bi holi cherches techyng;
B.10.308 But al is buxomnesse þere and *bokes*, to rede and to lerne].
B.10.434 And þo þat wisely wordeden and writen manye *bokes*
B.10.464 Than are þise [kete] clerkes þat konne manye *bokes*,

B.10.473   That euere þe[i] kouþe [konne on *book*] moore þan Credo in deum
           patrem,
B.11.139   For þei beþ, as oure *bokes* telleþ, aboue goddes werkes:
B.11.140   'Ye? baw for *bokes*!' quod oon was broken out of helle.
B.11.155   That was an vncristene creature, as clerkes fyndeþ in *bokes*:
B.11.168   For þat is þe *book* blissed of blisse and of ioye;
B.11.277   Or selle it, as seiþ þe *book*, and þe siluer dele
B.12.17   And bidde for hem þat ȝyueþ þee breed, for þer are *bokes* y[n]owe
B.12.57   Sapience, seiþ þe *bok*, swelleþ a mannes soule:
B.12.65   As þe *book* bereþ witnesse to burnes þat kan rede:
B.12.100   Na moore kan no Clerk but if he cauȝte it first þoruȝ *bokes*.
B.12.101   Alþouȝ men made *bokes* [þe maister was god]
B.12.134   Ne broȝt by hir *bokes* to blisse ne to ioye,
B.12.187   Wel may þe barn blesse þat hym to *book* sette,
B.12.274   And þe bettre for hir *bokes* to bidden we ben holden–
B.12.276   For lettred men were lewed yet ne were loore of hir *bokes*.'
B.12.284   And he is saaf, seiþ þe *book*, and his soule in heuene.
B.13.185   I shal brynge yow a bible, a *book* of þe olde lawe,
B.13.201   Haue pacience parfitliche þan half þi pak of *bokes*.'
B.14.67   That no reyn ne roon; þus rede men in *bokes*,
B.14.69   Seuene slepe, as seiþ þe *book*, seuene hundred wynter
B.14.155   Ac it is but selde yseien, as by holy seintes *bokes*,
B.15.122   [And beere] bedes in hir hand and a *book* vnder hir arme.
B.15.278   But of foweles þat fleeþ; þus fyndeþ men in *bokes*.
B.15.282   But selden and sondry tymes, as seiþ þe *book* and techeþ,
B.15.343   Than burgeises þat riche ben as þe *book* techeþ,
B.15.536   Baddely ybedded, no *book* but conscience,
B.18.231   *Book* highte þat beaupeere, a bold man of speche.
B.18.232   'By goddes body', quod þis *book*, 'I wol bere witnesse
B.18.237   And alle þe elementȝ, quod þe *book*, 'herof beren witnesse.
B.18.255   And I, *book*, wole be brent but Iesus rise to lyue
B.19.71   Tho he was born in Bethleem, as þe *book* telleþ,
B.20.42   So [he was nedy], as seiþ þe *book* in manye sondry places,
C.Pr.129   To bynde and vnbynde as þe *boke* telleth,
C. 1.28   And lay by hem bothe as þe *boke* telleth;
C. 1.181   For Iames þe gentele iuge[d] in his *bokes*
C. 3.59   Hit is but frelete of fleysche–ȝe fyndeth [hit in] *bokes*–
C. 3.307   As by the *book* þat byt nobody withholde
C. 5.38   And what is beste for the body, as the *boek* telleth,
C. 5.146   Gregory þe grete Clerk gart wryte in *bokes*
C. 6.76   Aȝeyn þe consayl of Crist, as clerkes fyndeth in *bokes*:
C. 7.125   And for [þe] beste, as y beleue, what[euere] þe *boek* telle:
C. 7.183   'I knowe hym as kyndely as Clerk doth his *bokes*.'
C. 9.120   Withoute bagge and bred as þe *book* telleth;
C. 9.127   And godes boys, bourdyors as the *book* telleth:
C. 9.162   The *boek* banneth beggarie and blameth hit in this manere:
C. 9.305   Ac for þe *boek* bible bereth witnesse
C.10.23   Seuene sithe, sayth þe *boek*, synegeth day by day
C.11.65   And breketh nat here bred to þe pore as þe *boke* hoteth:
C.11.113   Sey [to] hym thysulue ouerse m[y] *bokes*
C.11.118   Plato þe poete y putte hym furste to *boke*;
C.11.146   Austyn þe olde herof made *bokes*;
C.11.153   [Bisily] *bokes*; ho beth his witnesses?
C.11.225   Thenne al þe kynde wyt þat ȝe can bothe and kunnyng of ȝoure
           bokes.
C.11.272   Thus y, rechelesnesse, haue yrad registres and *bokes*
C.12.74   They b[e]t[h], as oure *bokes* telleth, [aboue] goddes werkes:
C.12.75   'ȝe? bawe for *bokes*!' quod oen was broken out of helle.
C.12.97   So loue and leute ben oure lordes *bokes*
C.13.16   How bittere he hit abouhte, as þe *book* telleth!
C.13.128   For ignorancia non excusat as ych haue herd in *bokes*.'
C.14.45   No more can no clerk but if hit come of *bokes*.
C.14.46   [Althouh men maden *bokes*] God was here maystre
C.14.78   Ne brouhte by here *bokes* to blisse ne to ioye,
C.14.126   Wel may þe barne blesse þat hym to *boek* sette,
C.14.157   How creatures han kynde wit and how clerkes come to *bokes*
C.14.169   To briddes and to bestes, As here *bokes* telleth
C.14.196   And þe bettere for here *bokes* to bidden we ben yholde–
C.14.198   For letrede men were lewede ȝut ne were lore of [here *bokes*].'
C.14.201   Withoute bapteme, as by here *bokes*, beth nat ysaued.'
C.14.206   And he is saef, saith the *boek*, and his soule in heuene.
C.15.179   Haue pacience parfitlyche then half thy pak of *bokes*.
C.15.220   As þe *boek* bereth witnesse þat he bere myhte
C.15.266   That no reyn ne roen; thus z[r]at men [i]n *bokes*,
C.15.268   Seuene slepen, as saith þe *boek*, more then syxty wynter
C.17.27   Withoute borwynge or beggynge, or þe *boek* lyeth,
C.17.59   For god bad his blessed as þe *boek* techeth–
C.17.197   Baddeliche ybedded, no *boek* but Consience
C.17.294   Bischope[s] and *bokes* the bileue to teche.
C.18.221   As þe bible bereth witnesse, A *boek* of þe olde lawe,
C.19.238   And hymsulue, sayth þe *boek*, sotiled how he myhte
C.20.240   *Boek* hihte þat beaupere, a bolde man of speche.
C.20.241   'By godes body,' quod this *boek*, 'y wol [b]ere witnesse

C.20.246   And all þe elementis,' quod the *boek*, 'hereof bereth witnesse.
C.20.264   And y, *boek*, wol be brente bote he aryse to lyue
C.21.71   Tho he was bore in Bedlehem, as þe *boek* telleth,
C.22.42   So he was nedy, as saith the *boek* in mony sondry places,

boold > *bold*; *boon* > *bon*

boone n *bon n.(2)* B 1; C 2 bone
B.11.150   Wiþouten bede biddyng his *boone* was vnderfongen
C. 3.418   To be buxum at my byddyng his [b]o[n]e to fulfille.
C.12.85   Withouten bed[e] biddyng his *bone* was vnderfonge

boor n *bor n.* A 1 boris; B 3 boor (2) bores (1); C 2 boer (1) bores (1)
A. 7.32   And [to] *boris* & [to] bukkes þat breken myn heggis,
B. 6.30   To *bores* and to [bukkes] þat breken myne hegges,
B.11.342   That wolde [bere] after bol[e], ne *boor* after sowe;
B.15.299   Neiþer bere ne *boor* ne ooþer beest wilde,
C. 8.29   To *bores* and to bokkes þat breketh adoun myn hegges
C.13.150   That wolde bere aftur bole ne *boer* aftur sowe;

boord > *borde*

boost n *bost n.* A 1 bost; B 4; C 3 boest
A. 1.111   Til he brak buxumnesse þoruȝ *bost* of hymseluen.
B. 3.314   His *boost* of his benefice worþ bynomen hym after.
B.14.223   And buxomnesse and *boost* [ben] eueremoore at werre,
B.14.248   And wheiþer be liȝter to breke? lasse *boost* [it] makeþ
B.19.251   [Ne no *boost* ne] debat [be] among hem [alle].
C.16.64   And buxomnesse and *b[o]est* [b]en eueremore at werre
C.16.88   And where be [lyh]tere to breke? lasse *boest* hit maketh
C.21.251   Ne no *boest* ne debaet be among hem alle.

boot n *bot n.(1)* &> *biten* A 6 boot (4) bot (2); B 6; C 6 boet (4) bote
(2)
A. 9.25   Let bringe a man in a *bot* amydde a brood watir;
A. 9.26   Þe wynd, & þe watir, & þe waggyng of þe *boot*
A. 9.31   Þe wynd wolde wiþ þe watir þe *boot* ouerþrowe.
A. 9.37   Þe *boot* is lik[nid] to þe body þat britel is of kynde,
A. 9.43   Þat, þeiȝ þi body bowe as *bot* doþ in þe watir,
A.10.168   Busk[en hem] to þat *boot* & biden þerelnne
B. 8.29   Lat brynge a man in a *boot* amydde [a] bro[od] watre,
B. 8.30   The wynd and þe water and þe [waggyng of þe *boot*]
B. 8.35   The wynd wolde wiþ þe water þe *boot* ouerþrowe.
B. 8.41   The *boot* is likned to [þe] body þat brotel is of kynde,
B. 8.47   [That], þouȝ þ[i] body bowe as *boot* dooþ in þe watre,
B. 9.137   Buskeþ yow to þat *boot* and bideþ þerInne
C.10.33   Lat bryng a man in a *boet* amydde a brood water;
C.10.34   The wynde and þe water and [þe] wag[g]yng of the *bote*
C.10.36   For stonde he neuere so stifliche, thorw steryng of þe *bote*
C.10.39   Thow he falle he falleth nat but [as] hoso ful in a *boet*
C.10.47   The *boet* is liknet to oure body þat bretil is of kynde,
C.10.225   Boske ȝow to þat *boet* and abideth þerynne

boote n *bote n.(1)* A 3 boote (1) bote (2); B 14 boote (12) bote (2); C 10
bote
A. 4.76   And be borugh for his bale & b[ig]gen hym *bote*;
A. 4.79   'Betere is þat *boote* bale adoun bringe,
A. 4.80   Þanne bale be bet & *bote* neuere þe betere.'
B. 4.89   And be borȝ for his bale and buggen hym *boote*,
B. 4.92   'Bettre is þat *boote* bale adoun brynge
B. 4.93   Than bale be ybet and *boote* neuer þe bettre.'
B. 6.193   For þat was bake for bayard was *boote* for many hungry;
B.10.272   I rede ech a blynd bosard do *boote* to hymselue,
B.11.122   And drynke none *boote* for bale, brouke a whoso myȝte.
B.12.86   The which body is boþe *boote* to þe riȝtfulle
B.13.257   For may no blessynge doon vs *boote* but if we wile amende,
B.13.340   [For] Goddes word [ne grace] gaf me neuere *boote*,
B.14.117   Thanne may beggeris, as beestes, after *boote* waiten
B.14.238   Wiþoute mournynge amonge, and meschief to *bote*].
B.14.269   As by assent of sondry parties and siluer to *boote*,
B.18.153   That Adam and Eue haue shul *bote*].
B.18.429   For goddes blissede body it bar for oure *boote*;
C. 4.85   And be borw for his bale and buggen hym *bote*
C. 4.88   'Betere is þat *bote* bale adoun brynge
C. 4.89   Then bale be ybete and *bote* neuer þe betere.'
C. 8.178   And þat was bake for bayard may be here *bote*.'
C. 8.192   For þat was bake for bayard was *bote* for many hungry,
C.12.57   And drynke *bote* for bale, brouke hit hoso myhte.\
C.15.227   For may no blessynge doen vs *bote* but yf we wol amende
C.16.109   As by assente of sondry p[arti]es and suluer to *bote*,
C.20.156   That Adam and Eue haue shullen *bote*
C.20.473   For godes blessed body hit baer for oure *bote*

bootles adj *boteles adj.* B 1; C 1 boetles
B.18.11   Barefoot on an Asse bak *bootles* cam prikye
C.20.9   Barfoet on an asse bake *boetles* cam priky[e]

bootned v *botnen v.(1) cf. bote v.* A 1 botind; B 1; C 1 botened
A. 7.177   Blynde & bedrede were *botind* a þousand
B. 6.191   Blynde and bedreden were *botned* a þousand;
C. 8.188   Blynde and Brokelegged he *botened* a thousand

borde n *bord n.* A 3 boord (1) bord (1) bordis (1); B 4 borde (2) bordes
    (2); C 6 boerd (1) bord (1) borde (2) bordes (2)
A. 2.52   At bedde & at *boord* buxum and hende,
A. 7.249   Let nouȝt sire surfet sitten at þi *bord*;
A.10.166   Swiþe to shapen a sship of shidis & *bordis*;
B. 6.265   Lat noȝt sire Surfet sitten at þi *borde*;
B. 9.135   "Swiþe go shape a ship of shides and of *bordes*;
B.10.406   Tho he shoop þat ship of shides and *bordes*:
B.13.36   And seten bi oureselue at [a] side *borde*.
C. 8.275   Lat nat sire sorfeet sitt[en] at thy *borde*;
C. 8.287   Lat hem abyde til the *bord* be drawe; Ac bere hem none crommes
C.10.40   That ay is saef and sound þat sitte withynne þe *borde*.
C.10.223   And bad go shapen a ship of shides and *bordes*.
C.11.237   Tho he shoop þe ship of shides and *bordes*:
C.15.173   Profitable for bothe parties;' and potte þe *boerd* fro hym

bordiours > bourdeour

bordlees adj *bord-les adj.* B 1; C 1 bordles
B.12.201   But as a beggere *bordlees* by myself on þe grounde.
C.14.140   Bote as a beggare *bordles* be mysulue on þe grounde.

bordor > bourdeour; bordoun > burdoun; bore > beren; bores > boor;
borewede -eþ -ide > borwe; borewes -is > borgh;

borgh n *borgh n.* A 3 borewis (1) borugh (1) boruȝ (1); B 8 borgh (3)
    borȝ (1) boruȝ (2) borwe (1) borwes (1); C 5 borw (2) borwe (1)
    borewes (1) borwh (1)
A. 1.75   Þou brouȝtest me *borewis* my biddyng to werche,
A. 4.76   And be *borugh* for his bale & b[ig]gen hym bote;
A.11.91   I dar be his bolde *boruȝ* do bet wile he neuere,
B. 1.77   [Thow] brouȝtest me *borwes* my biddyng to [werche],
B. 4.89   And be *borȝ* for his bale and buggen hym boote;
B. 7.82   For beggeres borwen eueremo and hir *borgh* is god almyȝty
B.10.138   I dar ben his bolde *borgh* þat dobet wole he neuere,
B.14.191   And putten of so þe pouke, and preuen vs vnder *borwe*.
B.16.263   Ne no buyrn be oure *borgh*, ne brynge vs fram his daunger–
B.20.13   Ne wight noon wol ben his *boruȝ*, ne wed haþ noon to legge;
B.20.248   And I wol be youre *boruȝ*: ye shal haue breed and cloþes
C. 1.74   Thow broughtest me *borewes* my biddyng to fulfille,
C. 4.85   And be *borw* for his bale and buggen hym bote
C.18.279   Ne noen bern ben oure *borw* ne bryngen vs [fro his] daunger–
C.22.13   Ne wyht no[n] wol be his *borwe* ne wed hath [non] to legge;
C.22.248   [And] y wol be ȝoure *borwh*: ȝe shal haue breed and clothes

boris > boor; born > beren

borre n *burre n.(1)* B 1; C 1
B.17.330   Til he be blereighed or blynd and [þe *borre*] in þe þrote;
C.19.310   Til he be blereyede or blynde and þe *borre* in [the] throte,

borugh boruȝ > borgh; borw > borgh,borwe,burgh

borwe v *borwen v. &> borgh* A 2 borewide; B 14 borwe (4) borwed (3)
    borwen (1) borwest (1) borweþ (4) yborwed (1); C 14 borewede (1)
    boreweth (1) borw (1) borwe (3) borwed (2) borwede (1) borwen (1)
    borwest (1) borweth (3)
A. 4.40   He *borewide* of me bayard & brouȝte him neuere aȝen,
A. 7.91   I bar hom þat I *borewide* er I to bedde ȝede.
B. 4.53   He *borwed* of me bayard [and] brouȝte hym [neuere ayein],
B. 4.109   As longe as [I lyue], but lowenesse hym *borwe*.'
B. 5.254   'Hastow pite on pouere men þat [for pure nede] *borwe*?'
B. 5.288   And as longe as þow lyuest þerwith þow yeldest noȝt but *borwest*;
B. 5.422   If I bigge and *borwe* auȝt, but if it be ytailed,
B. 6.99   I bar hom þat I *borwed* er I to bedde yede.
B. 7.81   And he þat biddeþ *borweþ* and bryngeþ hymself in dette.
B. 7.82   For beggeres *borwen* eueremo and hir borgh is god almyȝty
B.13.375   And [what body] *borwed* of me abouȝte þe tyme
B.14.296   Ne *borweþ* of hise neighebores but þat he may wel paie:
B.15.256   Neiþer he biddeþ ne beggeþ ne *borweþ* to yelde.
B.15.312   And bidden hem bere it þere it [*yborwed* was].
B.19.475   So I may boldely be housled for I *borwe* neuere,
B.20.286   That *borweþ* and bereþ it þider and þanne biddeþ frendes
C. 2.179   Thenne gan gyle *borwen* hors at many gret maystres
C. 4.55   Ȝut is he bold for to *borw* Ac baddelyche he payeth:
C. 4.56   He *borwed* of me bayard a[nd] brouhte hym hom neuere
C. 6.247   So what buyrn of me *borewede* abouhte the tyme;
C. 6.343   And as longe as thow lyuest therwith þou ȝeldest nat bote *borwest*;
C. 7.35   Yf y b[y]gge and *borwe* [ouh]t, but yf hit be ytayled,
C. 8.108   I bar hoem þat y *borwed* ar y to bedde ȝede.
C.16.131   Ne *boreweth* of his neyhebore but þat he may wel paye
C.16.315   That neuere payed peny aȝeyn in places þer he *borwede*.'

C.16.372   For noþer he beggeth ne biddeth ne *borweth* to ȝelde.
C.16.374   To begge or to *borwe* but of god one:
C.17.1   'There is no such,' y sayde, 'þat som tyme ne *borweth*
C.21.475   So y may boldely be hoseled for y *borwe* neuere
C.22.286   That *borweth* and bereth hit theddere and thenne biddeth frendes

borwes > borgh,burgh; borwh > borgh

borwynge C 2
C.17.8   Withoute *borwynge* or beggynge bote of god one,
C.17.27   Withoute *borwynge* or beggynge, or þe boek lyeth,

bosard n *busard n.* B 1
B.10.272   I rede ech a blynd *bosard* do boote to hymselue,

bosches > buskes; boske(de > buskeþ

bosom n *bosom n.* B 1; C 2 bosom (1) bosome (1)
B.16.254   For in his *bosom* he bar a þyng þat he blissed euere.
C.15.160   And bere hit in thy *bosom* aboute where þou wendest
C.18.270   For in his *bosome* a baer [a] thyng þat [a] blessede [euere].

bost > boost

bosten v *bosten v.* A 1 bostide; B 6 bosted (1) bosten (2) bosteþ (2)
    ybosted (1); C 3 boste (1) bostyng (1) ybosted (1)
A. 7.141   A bretoner, a braggere, he *bostide* hym also,
B. 2.81   To bakbite and to *bosten* and bere fals witnesse,
B. 6.154   A Bretoner, a braggere, [he *b]osted* Piers als
B.13.280   Forwhy he *bosteþ* and braggeþ wiþ manye bolde oþes;
B.13.305   Of dedes þat he neuere dide demen and *bosten*,
B.15.252   Neiþer he blameþ ne banneþ, *bosteþ* ne preiseþ,
B.17.62   Hope cam hippynge after þat hadde so *ybosted*
C. 2.88   To bacbite and to *boste* and bere fals witnesse,
C. 6.34   *Bostyng* and braggynge with many bolde othes,
C.19.61   Hope cam huppynge aftur þat hadde so *ybosted*

bostere n *boster n.* B 1
B.13.302   Boldest of beggeris; a *bostere* þat noȝt haþ,

bot > biten,boot,but

bote v *boten v.(1) &> boot,boote,but; cf. bootned v.* C 1
C. 6.382   And that the bettere thyng, be arbitreres, *bote* sholde þe worse.

botel n *botel n.(1)* B 1 boteles; C 3 botel (1) boteles (2)
B.17.71   [And breide to hise *boteles* and boþe he atamede];
C. 5.52   Withoute bagge or *botel* but my wombe one.
C. 9.139   For they bereth none bagges ne *boteles* vnder clokes
C.19.70   And vnbokelede his *boteles* and bothe he atamede.

botelees adj *boteles adj.(1)* B 1; C 1 boteles
B.18.202   For it is *botelees* bale, þe byte þat þei eten.'
C.20.207   For hit is *boteles* bale, the bite that they eten.'

boteles > botel,botelees; botened > bootned; boterasid > botrased; botere >
buttre

boþe num *bothe num.* A 49; B 176 boþe (173) boþer (1) boþeres (2); C
    189 both (2) bothe (186) boþe (1)
A.Pr.75   Were þe bisshop yblissid & worþ *boþe* hise eris
A.Pr.100   Taillours, t[okk]eris & to[ll]eris *boþe*,
A. 1.15   *Boþe* wiþ fel & wiþ face, & ȝaf ȝow fyue wyttes
A. 1.30   And leccherie h[i]m lauȝte & lay be hem *boþe*;
A. 2.6   *Boþe* fals & fauel & hise feris manye.'
A. 2.34   Were beden to þe b[ri]dale on *boþe* two sides.
A. 2.54   Symonye & cyuyle stondiþ forþ *boþe*
A. 2.92   Ȝe shuln abigge boþe, be god þat me made.
A. 3.125   She doþ men lese here land & here lif *boþe*;
A. 4.2   Ȝe shuln sauȝte, forsoþe, & serue me *boþe*.
A. 4.38   '*Boþe* my gees & my gris hise gadelynges fecchen;
A. 4.59   For *boþe* þi lyf & þi lond liþ in his grace.'
A. 4.70   Þe king swor be crist & be his croune *boþe*
A. 4.98   And to counseile þe king & consience *boþe*;
A. 5.80   *Boþe* his lyme & his lif was lost þoruȝ my tunge.
A. 5.119   Watte þe waffrer & his wyf *boþe*,
A. 6.15   At bedlem, at babiloyne, I haue ben in *boþe*;
A. 6.29   *Boþe* sowe [and sette] while I swynke miȝte.
A. 6.31   *Boþe* sowen his seed, & sewide hise bestis,
A. 6.48   Ȝe mote go þoruȝ meknesse, *boþe* men & wyues,
A. 6.64   Þei hote stele nouȝt, ne sle nouȝt; strik forþ be *boþe*.
A. 7.27   I shal swynken & sweten & sowe for vs *boþe*,
A. 7.117   Ac we preye for ȝow, peris, & for ȝoure plouȝ *boþe*,
A. 7.127   *Boþe* to setten & to sowen, & sauen his telþe,
A. 7.154   And countide peris at a pese & his plouȝ *boþe*,
A. 7.163   He beet hem so *boþe* he brast ner here mawis.
A. 7.263   Er I haue dyned be þis day & ydronke *boþe*.'
A. 8.13   Bisshopis þat blissen, & *boþe* lawes kenne,
A. 8.15   And bere hem *boþe* on here bak as here baner shewiþ,

A. 8.46   For so seiþ þe sauter & sapience *boþe*:
A. 8.92   And I behynde hem *boþe* beheld al þe b[u]lle.
A. 8.134   Ac catoun construiþ it [nay] & canonistris *boþe*:
A. 9.86   Dobest is aboue hem *boþe* & beriþ a bisshopis croce;
A.10.13   And seruiþ þis lady lelly *boþe* late & raþe.
A.10.40   Þat he wrouȝte wiþ werkis & with wordis *boþe*.
A.10.94   [And so witnesseþ goddis worde and holiwrit *boþe*]:
A.10.122   Which is þe flour & þe fruyt fostrid of *boþe*.
A.10.136   *Boþe* maidenis & [mynchons], monkes & ancris,
A.10.174   *Boþe* fisshis & foulis, forþ mi[d] oþere bestis,
A.10.196   But ȝif þei *boþe* be forsworn þat bacoun þei tyne.
A.10.203   Shulde no bedbourd be; but þei were *boþe* clene
A.11.46   *Boþe* for hungir & for þrest, & for chele quak[e];
A.11.115   *Boþe* wele & wo ȝif þat þou wile lerne,
A.11.171   And aftirward his wyf I worsshipide *boþe*,
A.11.269   *Boþe* in werk & in woord, in world in his tyme?
A.12.9   That myȝthe turne m[e] to tene & theologie *boþe*.
A.12.17   Þat hit were *boþe* skaþe and sklaundre to holy cherche
A.12.85   Tercian þat oþer; trewe drinkeres *boþe*.
A.12.101   And wrouȝthe þat here is wryten and oþer werkes *boþe*
B.Pr.78   Were þe Bisshop yblessed and worþ *boþe* hise eris
B.Pr.87   Bisshopes and Bachelers, *boþe* maistres and doctours,
B.Pr.116   The kyng and knyȝthod and clergie *boþe*
B.Pr.163   *Boþe* in wareyne and in waast where hem [leue] like[þ];
B. 1.15   *Boþe* with fel and with face, and yaf yow fyue wittes
B. 1.30   And Leccherie hym lauȝte, and lay by hem *boþe*;
B. 2.6   *Boþe* Fals and Fauel and hi[s]e feeres manye.'
B. 2.55   Were boden to þe bridale on *boþe* two sides,
B. 2.67   Whan Symonye and Cyuylle seighe hir *boþer* wille
B. 2.68   Thei assented for siluer to seye as *boþe* wolde.
B. 2.72   Symonye and Cyuylle stonden forþ *boþe*
B. 2.128   Ye shul abiggen *boþe*, by god þat me made!
B. 2.169   Ac þanne swoor Symonye and Cyuylle
B. 3.136   She dooþ men lese hire lond and hire lif *boþe*;
B. 3.274   Forbar hym and his beestes *boþe* as þe bible witnesseþ
B. 4.2   Ye shul sauȝtne, forsoþe, and serue me *boþe*.
B. 4.51   '*Boþe* my gees and my grys hise gadelynges feccheþ.
B. 4.73   For hope þi lif and þi lond lyþ in his grace.'
B. 4.83   The kyng swor by crist and by his crowne *boþe*
B. 4.111   And to counseille þe kyng and Conscience [*boþe*]
B. 5.100   That *boþe* lif and lyme is lost þoruȝ my speche.
B. 5.150   Til he be *boþe* beggers and by my spirituelte libben,
B. 5.153   I haue an Aunte to Nonne and an Abbesse *boþe*;
B. 5.156   Manye Monþes wiþ hem, and wiþ Monkes *boþe*.
B. 5.171   *Boþe* Priour and Suppriour and oure Pater Abbas;
B. 5.252   And haue ymaad many a knyȝt *boþe* Mercer and draper
B. 5.308   Watte þe warner and his wif *boþe*,
B. 5.374   Ouer delicatly on [feeste] dayes dronken and eten *boþe*,
B. 5.436   *Boþe* flessh and fissh and manye oþere vitailles;
B. 5.437   *Boþ[e]* bred and ale, buttre, melk and chese
B. 5.527   [At] Bethlem, [at] Babiloyne, I haue ben in *boþe*,
B. 5.541   *Boþe* sowe and sette while I swynke myȝte.
B. 5.543   *Boþe* ysowen his seed and suwed hise beestes,
B. 5.561   Ye moten go þoruȝ mekenesse, *boþe* men and wyues,
B. 5.577   Thei hiȝte Stele-noȝt-[ne]-Sle-noȝt; strik forþ by *boþe*;
B. 6.25   I shal swynke and swete and sowe for vs *boþe*,
B. 6.125   Ac we preie for yow, Piers, and for youre plowȝ *boþe*,
B. 6.169   And sette Piers at a pese and his plowȝ *boþe*,
B. 6.178   He bette hem so *boþe* he brast ner hire [mawes].
B. 6.255   For some of my seruauntȝ and myself *boþe*
B. 6.279   [Er] I haue dyned bi þis day and ydronke *boþe*.'
B. 7.14   Legistres of *boþe* lawes þe lewed þerwiþ to preche,
B. 7.110   And I bihynde hem *boþe* biheld al þe bulle.
B. 8.16   *Boþe* princes paleises and pouere mennes cotes,
B. 8.17   And dowel and do yuele, wher þei dwelle *boþe*.'
B. 8.96   Dobest is aboue *boþe* and bereþ a bisshopes crosse;
B. 8.126   What was Dowel fro dobet and dobest from hem *boþe*.
B. 9.13   To seruen þis lady leelly, *boþe* late and raþe.
B. 9.14   Dobest is aboue *boþe*, a Bisshopes peere;
B. 9.52   [Th]at he wroȝte wiþ werk and wiþ word *boþe*;
B. 9.175   But þei *boþe* be forsworn þat bacon þei tyne.
B. 9.190   Sholde no [bedbourde] be; but þei *boþe* were clene
B. 9.205   To ȝyuen and to yemen *boþe* yonge and olde,
B.10.60   *Boþe* afyngred and afurst, and for chele quake;
B.10.149   As longe as I lyue, *boþe* late and raþe,
B.10.163   *Boþe*-wele-and-wo if þat þow wolt lerne,
B.10.228   And afterwardes [his] wif [I] worshiped *boþe*,
B.10.240   And þat is to bileue lelly, *boþe* lered and lewed,
B.10.244   Thoruȝ þe help of þe holy goost þe which is of *boþe*,
B.10.247   God þe fader, god þe sone, god holy goost of *boþe*,
B.10.248   Makere of man [and his make] and of beestes *boþe*.
B.10.344   And patriarkes and prophetes and poetes *boþe*
B.10.391   And al holy chirche holdeþ hem *boþe* [in helle]!

B.11.15   Pride of parfit lyuynge pursued hem *boþe*
B.11.31   Bittrely shaltow banne þanne, *boþe* dayes and nyȝtes,
B.11.44   'Allas, eiȝe!' quod Elde and holynesse *boþe*,
B.11.63   And þo fond I þe frere afered and flittynge *boþe*
B.11.78   Baptiȝynge and buryinge *boþe* beþ ful nedefulle;
B.11.87   'ȝis, by Peter and by Poul!' quod he and took hem *boþe* to witnesse:
B.11.208   And we hise breþeren þoruȝ hym ybouȝt, *boþe* riche and pouere.
B.11.213   For woot no man hou neiȝ it is to ben ynome fro *boþe*.
B.11.224   *Boþe* logyk and lawe, þat loueþ noȝt to lye,
B.11.253   *Boþe* Marthaes and Maries, as Mathew bereþ witnesse.
B.11.258   And *boþe* bettre and blesseder by many fold þan Richesse.
B.11.331   Man and his make I myȝte [se] *boþe*
B.11.332   Pouerte and plentee, *boþe* pees and werre,
B.11.333   Blisse and bale *boþe* I seiȝ at ones,
B.11.343   *Boþe* hors and houndes and alle oþere beestes
B.11.401   In fondynge of þe flessh and of þe fend *boþe*,
B.12.18   To telle men what dowel is, dobet and dobest *boþe*,
B.12.34   And lyue forþ as lawe wole while ye lyuen *boþe*.
B.12.70   Ac yet is Clergie to comende and kynde wit *boþe*,
B.12.86   The which body is *boþe* boote to þe riȝtfulle
B.12.88   As cristes caracte[s] conforrede, and *boþe* coupable shewed
B.12.93   For kynde wit is of his kyn and neiȝe Cosynes *boþe*
B.12.95   For *boþe* ben as Mirours to amenden [by] defautes
B.12.96   And lederes for lewed men and for lettred *boþe*.
B.12.161   And *boþe* naked as a nedle, hir noon [sadder] þan ooþer.
B.12.209   It were neiþer reson ne riȝt to rewarde *boþe* yliche.
B.12.245   And his flessh is foul flessh and his feet *boþe*,
B.13.48   And me þat was his [mette oþer mete *boþe*].
B.13.145   *Boþe* wiþ wer[k] and with wor[d] fonde hise loue to wynne;
B.13.155   The myddel of þe Moone [i]s þe [m]yght of *boþe*.
B.13.206   If Pacience be oure partyng felawe and pryue with vs *boþe*
B.13.219   There vnkyndenesse and coueitise is, hungry contrees *boþe*.
B.13.271   I took [greet] kepe, by crist! and Conscience *boþe*,
B.13.286   Lakkynge lettrede men and lewed men *boþe*;
B.13.378   And *boþe* to kiþ and to kyn vnkynde of þat ich hadde;
B.14.5   It haþ be laued in lente and out of lente *boþe*
B.14.62   Ergo þoruȝ his breeþ [*boþe*] men and beestes lyuen,
B.14.95   Ac satisfaccion sekeþ out þe roote, and *boþe* sleeþ and voideþ,
B.14.116   And blisse to alle þat ben, *boþe* wilde and tame."
B.14.152   *Boþe* to riche and to noȝt riche þat rewfulliche libbeþ;
B.14.257   And he his seruaunt, as he seiþ, and his sute *boþe*.
B.14.270   Moore for coueitise of [catel] þan kynde loue of *boþe*–
B.15.37   Austyn and Ysodorus, eiþer of hem *boþe*
B.15.105   Trewe of youre tonge and of youre tail *boþe*,
B.15.139   And makeþ murþe þer[wiþ] and hise me[yne] *boþe*;
B.15.221   *Boþe* in grey and in grys and in gilt harneis,
B.15.285   And þouȝ þe gome hadde a gest god fond hem *boþe*.
B.15.293   Som þei solde and som þei soden, and so þei lyued *boþe*.
B.15.354   *Boþe* lettred and lewed beþ alayed now wiþ synne
B.15.367   Now faileþ þe folk of þe flood and of þe lond *boþe*,
B.15.384   Thei sholde faillen of hir Philosophie and in Phisik *boþe*.
B.15.422   [*Boþe*] Beneit and Bernard, þe whiche hem first tauȝte
B.15.490   *Boþe* Mathew and Marc and Memento domine dauid:
B.15.544   *Boþe* riche and Religious, þat roode þei honoure
B.15.574   Ac ysaie of yow spekeþ and oȝias *boþe*,
B.15.575   That no man sholde be bisshop but if he hadde *boþe*
B.15.590   *Boþe* of miracles and merueilles, and how he men festede,
B.16.45   And feccheþ awey my floures som tyme afore *boþe* myne eighen.
B.16.80   And gadrede hem alle togideres, *boþe* grete and smale,
B.16.110   And sike and synfulle *boþe* so] to goode turnede:
B.16.111   *Boþe* meseles and mute and in þe menyson blody,
B.16.121   'Thanne are ye cherles', [chidde Iesus], 'and youre children *boþe*,
B.16.165   Ayeins deeþ and þe deuel: destruyed hir *boþer*es myȝtes,
B.16.193   Of hym[self] and of his seruaunt, and what [suffreþ hem] *boþe*.
B.16.206   And þe issue þat þei hadde it was of hem *boþe*,
B.16.215   That is, creatour weex creature to knowe what was *boþe*.
B.16.223   So is þe fader forþ with þe sone and fre wille of *boþe*,
B.16.234   I am ful siker in soule þerof, and my sone *boþe*.
B.16.239   For hymself bihiȝte to me and to myn issue *boþe*
B.16.244   And doon hym worship with breed and with wyn *boþe*,
B.17.55   *Boþe* þe heraud and hope and he mette atones
B.17.71   [And breide to hise boteles and *boþe* he atamede];
B.17.91   How þat feiþ fleiȝ awey and Spes his felawe *boþe*
B.17.128   As Feiþ and his felawe enformed me *boþe*,
B.17.156   The paume for [he] putteþ forþ fyngres and þe fust *boþe*
B.17.163   *Boþe* wolkne and þe wynd, water and erþe,
B.17.180   And receyue þat þe fyngres recheþ and refuse *boþe*
B.17.194   Ac þouȝ my þombe and my fyngres *boþe* were toshullen
B.17.197   *Boþe* meue and amende, þouȝ alle my fyngres oke.
B.17.208   And þanne a fir flawmynge forþ out of *boþe*,
B.17.246   *Boþe* forȝyue and foryete, and ȝit bidde for vs
B.17.309   That þe kyng may do no mercy til *boþe* men acorde
B.17.337   And "þat is lightly forȝyuen and forȝeten *boþe*

B.17.352	Good wille, good word [*boþe*], wisshen and willen
B.18.37	To se how doghtiliche deeþ sholde do and deme hir *boþeres* right.
B.18.45	*Boþe* as long and as large bi lofte and by grounde.'
B.18.73	A Cachepol cam forþ and craked *boþe* hir legges
B.18.166	For he[o] woot moore þan we; he[o] was er we *boþe*.'
B.18.197	The loue of oure lord and his loore *boþe*,
B.18.224	*Boþe* in heuene and in erþe, and now til helle he þenkeþ
B.18.261	'Suffre we', seide truþe; 'I here and see *boþe*
B.18.274	*Boþe* þis lord and þis light, is longe ago I knew hym.
B.18.279	Body and soule beþ myne, *boþe* goode and ille.
B.18.346	And *boþe* quykne and quyte þat queynt was þoruȝ synne;
B.18.394	For blood may suffre blood *boþe* hungry and acale
B.19.35	*Boþe* his loore and his lawe; now are þei lowe cherles.
B.19.78	*Boþe* of [s]ond, sonne and see, and siþenes þei wente
B.19.104	And som tyme he gaf good and grauntede heele *boþe*.
B.19.113	And crist counseileþ þus and comaundeþ *boþe*,
B.19.114	[*Boþe*] to lered and to lewede, to louyen oure enemys.
B.19.164	*Boþe* Iames and Iohan, Iesu to seke,
B.19.168	Crist cam In, and al closed *boþe* dore and yates,
B.19.189	To bynde and vnbynde *boþe* here and elli[s],
B.19.196	And demen hem at domesday, *boþe* quyke and dede,
B.19.243	*Boþe* of wele and of wo [and be ware bifore],
B.19.264	And Mark, and Mathew þe þridde, myghty beestes *boþe*;
B.19.399	*Boþe* dregges and draf and drawe at oon hole.'
B.19.408	Leue it wel [þow art] lost, *boþe* lif and soule.
B.19.440	And worshiped be he þat wroȝte al, *boþe* good and wikke,
B.20.44	"*Boþe* fox and fowel may fle to hole and crepe
B.20.251	For loue lafte þei lordshipe, *boþe* lond and scole,
B.20.337	Conscience knoweþ me wel and what I kan *boþe*.'
B.20.345	And was my lordes leche and my ladies *boþe*.
C.Pr.10	Al þe welthe of the world and þe wo *bothe*,
C.Pr.76	Were þe bischop yblessed and worth *bothe* his eres
C.Pr.85	Bischopes and bachelers, *bothe* maystres and doctours,
C.Pr.181	And colers of crafty werk, *bothe* knyghte[s] and squieres.
C.Pr.225	*Bothe* Bakeres and Breweres, Bochers and other,
C. 1.18	And brynge forth ȝoure bilyue, *bothe* lynnen and wollene,
C. 1.28	And lay by hem *bothe* as þe boke telleth;
C. 1.32	Forthy drede delitable drynke *bothe* day and nyghtes.
C. 2.6	[*Boþe*] fals and fauel and fikel tonge lyare
C. 2.58	Were beden to þe Bridale a *bothe* half þe contre,
C. 2.69	When simonye and syuile ysey[e] þer *bothe* wille
C. 2.74	Thenne simonye and syuyle standeth forth *bothe*
C. 2.93	Th[e] count[e] of coueytise [he] consenteth to hem *bothe*,
C. 2.144	Ȝe shal abyggen *bothe* but ȝe amende þe sonner.
C. 2.248	Ac Consience to þe kyng accused hem *bothe*
C. 2.255	And *bothe* wepte and wrang when she was attached.
C. 3.40	'Thow le[r]ed men and le[w]ed haued layn by the *bothe*
C. 3.65	*Bothe* wyndowes and wowes y wol amende and glase
C. 3.78	*Bothe* Schyreues and seriauntes and suche as kepeth lawes,
C. 3.91	*Bothe* thorw fuyr and flood a[nd] thorw fals peple
C. 3.99	That louten for hem to oure lord and to oure lady *bothe*
C. 3.136	*Bothe* to the and to thyne in hope thow shost amende;
C. 3.174	For he doth men lesen here lond and here lyf *bothe*;
C. 3.235	*Bothe* here and elleswhere, in alle kyne londes.
C. 3.275	*Bothe* Beg[g]eres and bedemen crauen mede for here preyeres;
C. 3.279	Asken mede and mas pans and here mete *bothe*;
C. 3.291	Ac ther is mede and mercede and *bothe* men demen
C. 3.310	That *bothe* the lord and the laborer be leely yserued.
C. 3.319	*Bothe* kyng and Cayser and þe crouned pope
C. 3.331	*Bothe* gyue and graunte there his grace lyketh
C. 3.334	Rect and indirect, reninde *bothe*
C. 3.365	And withoute ca[s]e to cache [to] and come to *bothe* nombres,
C. 3.380	*Bothe* heued and here kyng, haldyng with no parteyȝe
C. 4.2	Ȝe shal sauhtene, forsothe, and serue me *bothe*.
C. 4.49	'*Bothe* my gees and my grys and my g[r]as he taketh.
C. 4.79	The kyng [s]wor by Crist and by his croune *bothe*
C. 4.143	And yf ȝe wor[c]he it in werke y wedde *bothe* myn handes
C. 5.44	And so y leue in london and [vp] lond[on] *bothe*.
C. 5.156	Ac mony day, men telleth, *bothe* monkes and chanons
C. 6.52	And lyed o my lycame and on my lyf *bothe*;
C. 6.106	*Bothe* with stoon and with staf and stele vppon myn enemye;
C. 6.124	Til y, wrathe, wexe an hey and walke with hem *bothe*;
C. 6.125	Or til they *bothe* be beggares and by [my] spiritual[t]e libbe
C. 6.131	Mony monthes with hem and with monkes *bothe*.
C. 6.148	And y, wrath, was war and w[o]rthe on hem *bothe*
C. 6.150	Til *bothe* here hedes were bar and blody here chekes.
C. 6.181	Til *bothe* oure wil was oen and to þe werk we ȝeden,
C. 6.202	With his hood on his heued and his hat *bothe*,
C. 6.250	And haue ymad many a knyht *bothe* mercer and draper
C. 7.49	*Bothe* flesch and fysch and vitailes kepte so longe
C. 7.51	*Bothe* Bred and ale, Botere, mylke and chese
C. 7.172	In bedlem and in babiloyne y haue be in *bothe*,
C. 7.186	*Bothe* to sowe and to sette þe while y swynke myhte
C. 7.224	Thei hatte stele-nat and sle-nat; stryk forth by *bothe*
C. 7.289	And she is sib to alle synfole and here sone *bothe*
C. 8.24	'Y shal swynke and swete and sowe for vs *bothe*
C. 8.55	'For to worche by thy wit and my wyf *bothe*.'
C. 8.131	'A[c] we praye for ȝow, [peres] and for ȝoure plouh *bothe*
C. 8.145	*Bothe* of my corn and of my cloth to kepe hem fram defaute.
C. 8.175	[He] beet hem so *bothe* he barste ner her gottes
C. 8.267	For somme of my seruauntes and mysulf *bothe*
C. 8.301	Ar y haue ydyned þis day and ydronke *bothe*.'
C. 8.349	Shal brynge bane and batayle on *bothe* half þe mone;
C. 9.21	And deme with hem at domesday *bothe* quyke and dede.
C. 9.75	*Bothe* in mylke and in mele to make with papelotes
C. 9.80	*Bothe* to carde and to kembe, to cloute and to wasche,
C. 9.85	*Bothe* afyngred and afurste, to turne þe fayre outward
C. 9.106	Ac hem wanteth wyt, men and women *bothe*,
C. 9.149	Suluer or sode mete and sum tyme *bothe*,
C. 9.229	*Bothe* matynes and masse; and aftir mete in churches
C. 9.284	And y byhynde hem *bothe* byheld alle þe bulle.
C.10.16	*Bothe* princes paleis and pore menne cotes
C.10.17	And dowel and do euele, where þei dwellen *bothe*.'
C.10.122	What was dowel fro dobet and dobest fro hem *bothe*.
C.10.140	To serue þat lady leely *bot[h]* late and rathe.
C.10.141	Dobest is aboue *bothe*, a bishopis pere,
C.10.181	Euery man þat hath inwit and his hele *bothe*
C.10.205	For of here kynde þey come, *bothe* confessours and martres,
C.10.277	Bote they *bothe* be forswore þat bacon þei tyne.
C.10.290	For sholde no bedbourde be bote yf they *bothe* were
C.10.304	To ȝeue and to ȝeme *bothe* ȝonge and olde,
C.11.41	*Bothe* afyngred and afurst, and for defaute spille;
C.11.87	As longe as y lyue, *bothe* late and rathe,
C.11.105	*Bothe*-wele-and-wo yf þou wilt lerne;
C.11.108	*Bothe* wymmen and wyn, wr[a]the, [enuy] and slewthe
C.11.124	And caste [mette] by squire *bothe* lyne and leuele.
C.11.190	Bitterliche shaltow banne thenne, *bothe* dayes and nyhtes,
C.11.216	Wittenesseth þat here wordes and here werkes *bothe*
C.11.218	And holi churche, as y here, haldeth *bothe* in helle!
C.11.225	Thenne al þe kynde wyt þat ȝe can *bothe* and kunnyng of ȝoure bokes.
C.12.1	'Allas, eye!' quod elde and holynesse *bothe*,
C.12.88	Saued me, sarrasyn, soule and body *bothe*.'
C.12.144	And *bothe* bettere and blessedere by many fold then richesse.
C.13.29	*Bothe* t[w]o ben gode, be ȝe ful certeyn,
C.13.34	And sholden wende o wey where *bothe* mosten reste
C.13.36	What oen hath, what [o]þer hath and what they hadde *bothe*,
C.13.69	*Bothe* louye and lene le[l]e and vnlele
C.13.80	Beth nat ybounde, as beth [þ]e ryche, to [*bothe* two] lawes,
C.13.139	Man and his make y myhte seen *bothe*
C.13.140	Pouerte and plente, *bothe* pees and werre,
C.13.141	Blisse and bale *bothe* y sey at ones
C.13.155	As in derne dedes, *bothe* drynkyng and elles.
C.13.189	In wommen, in wedes and in wordes *bothe*
C.14.32	That wit wexeth therof and oþer w[y]rdes *bothe*:
C.14.71	*Bothe* lewede and lerede were lost yf clergie ne were.
C.14.105	And *bothe* naked as a nedle, here noen heuegore then othere.
C.14.123	And þat is aftur person other parsche preest, and parauntur *bothe* lewede
C.14.148	Hit were no resoun ne riht to rewarde *bothe* ylyche.
C.15.54	And to me þat was his mette tho, and oþer mete *bothe*.
C.15.61	Consience confortede vs, *bothe* clergie and scripture,
C.15.90	*Bothe* disches and dobelares with alle þe deyntees aftur.
C.15.173	Profitable for *bothe* parties;' and potte þe boerd fro hym
C.15.188	There vnkyndenesse and coueytise [is], hungry contreys *bothe*.
C.15.261	Ergo thorw his breth bestes lyueth, *bothe* men and fisches,
C.15.292	And blisse to all þat been, *bothe* wilde and tame."
C.16.67	For yf they *bothe* pleyne the pore is bote feble;
C.16.97	And he [h]is seruant, a[s] he saith, and of his se[u]te *bothe*.
C.16.113	The whiche is syb to crist [hym]sulue and semblable *bothe*.'
C.16.159	A knewe Consience ful wel and clergie *bothe*.
C.16.175	And som tyme to soffre *bothe* [sorwe] and [tene],
C.16.180	Bote as wode were afuyre thenne worcheth *bothe*
C.16.199	Austyn and ysodorus, either of hem *bothe*
C.16.233	That *bothe* le[r]ed and le[w]ed of here beleue douten
C.16.283	Leueth hit wel, lordes, *both* lewed and lered,
C.16.346	*Bothe* in gray and in grys and in gult harneys,
C.17.12	*Bothe* Antony and arseny and oþer fol monye.
C.17.20	Som they so[l]de and som they s[o]de and so they lyuede *bothe*.
C.17.46	And marchauntȝ merciable wolde be and men of lawe *bothe*
C.17.91	Nat in god þat he ne is goed and þe grounde *bothe*;
C.17.104	Now failleth this folk, *bothe* follwares and shipmen,
C.17.206	*Bothe* riche and religiou[s] þat rode they honouren
C.17.313	And haen a suspectioun to be saef, *bothe* sarresynes & iewes,
C.18.49	And feccheth away þe fruyt som tyme byfore *bothe* myn yes.
C.18.86	And thenne aboue is bettere fruyt, ac *bothe* two ben gode,

C.18.102 *Bothe* parfit and inparfit.' Puyr fayn y wolde
C.18.111 And gadered hem alle togyderes, *bothe* grete & smale,
C.18.141 A lechede hem of here langour, *bothe* lasares and blynde,
C.18.202 Of hymsulue and his seruant, and what soffreth hem *bothe*.
C.18.213 The werkes þat hymsulue wr[o]uhte and this world *bothe*:
C.18.217 And Abel of hem *bothe* and alle thre o kynde;
C.18.231 So oute of þe syre and of þe sone þe seynt spirit of hem *bothe*
C.18.255 For hymsulue saide y sholde [haue], y and myn issue *bothe*,
C.18.261 Worschipe hym with wyn and with breed *bothe*
C.19.25 *Bothe* Iosue and Ieudith and Iudas Macabeus,
C.19.43 Hit is liht for lewed and for lered *bothe*.
C.19.53 *Bothe* abraham and sp[e]s and he mette at ones
C.19.70 And vnbokelede his boteles and *bothe* he atamede.
C.19.80 *Bothe* fayth and his felawe spes folewede faste aftur
C.19.81 Ac y sewede the samaritaen and saide how they *bothe*
C.19.97 As faith and his felawe spes enfourmede me *bothe*,
C.19.160 Ac thouh my thombe and my fyngeres *bothe* were toshullen
C.19.163 *Bothe* meue and amende, thogh alle my fyngeres oke.
C.19.174 And thenne [a fuyr flaumynge] forth of hem *bothe*.
C.19.212 *Bothe* forȝeue and forȝete and ȝut bidde for vs
C.19.289 That may no kynge mercy graunte til *bothe* men acorde
C.19.317 And "þat is lihtliche forȝeue and forȝete *bothe*
C.19.332 Goed wil, goed word *bothe*, wischen and wilnen
C.20.44 *Bothe* as longe and as large aloofte and o grounde
C.20.93 *Bothe* my lond and my licame at ȝoure likynge taketh hit.
C.20.169 For he woet more then we; he was ar we *bothe*.'
C.20.202 The loue of oure lord and his lore *bothe*
C.20.233 *Bothe* in heuene and in erthe, and now to helle he thenketh
C.20.269 'Soffre we,' sayde treuthe; 'y here and se lihte'
C.20.296 *Bothe* this lord and this lihte, ys longe ygo y knewe hym.
C.20.301 Body and soule beth myne, *bothe* gode and ille.
C.20.318 As two godes, with god, *bothe* goed and ille.
C.20.319 Thus with treson and tricherie thow troyledest hem *bothe*
C.20.370 'Lo! me here, ' quod oure lord, 'lyf and soule *bothe*,
C.20.371 For alle synfole soules, to saue oure *bothe* rihte.
C.20.391 And *bothe* quykie and quyte that queynte was thorw synne
C.20.437 For bloed may s[uffr]e bloed *bothe* afurst and acale
C.21.35 *Bothe* his lore and his lawe; now are they lowe cherles.
C.21.78 *Bothe* of sand, sonne and see and sennes þei wente
C.21.104 And som tyme he gaf goed and graunted hele *bothe*;
C.21.113 And Crist consayleth [þu]s and comaundeth *bothe*,
C.21.114 *Bothe* to lered and to lewed, to louye oure enemyes.
C.21.164 *Bothe* Iames and Iohann, iesu to seke,
C.21.168 Crist cam in, and al closed *bothe* dore and ȝates,
C.21.189 To bynde and vnbynde *bothe* here and elles
C.21.196 And demen hem at domesday, *bothe* quyke and dede,
C.21.243 *Bothe* of wele and of wo and be ywaer bifore,
C.21.264 And Marc and Mathewe the thridde, myhty bestes *bothe*;
C.21.399 *Bothe* dregges and draf and drawe at on hole
C.21.408 Leue hit [wel thou] be[st] lost, *bothe* lyf and soule.'
C.21.440 And worschiped be he þat wrouhte all, *bothe* gode and wicke,
C.22.44 "*Bothe* fox and foule may fle to hole and crepe
C.22.251 For loue lefte they lordschipe, *bothe* lond and scole,
C.22.337 Consience knoweth me wel and what y can *bothe*.'
C.22.345 And was my lordes leche and my ladyes *bothe*.

botind > bootned

botons n *botoun n.* B 1
B.15.124 A baselard or a ballokknyf wiþ *botons* ouergilte,

botrased ptp *boterassen v.* A 1 boterasid; B 1; C 1 Ibotrased
A. 6.76 And *boterasid* wiþ beleue [so] oþer þou [be]st not sauid;
B. 5.589 *Botrased* wiþ bileef-so-or-þow-beest-noȝt-saued;
C. 7.236 *Ibotrased* with bileue-so-or-t[hou]-best-not-ysaued;

bouȝ n *bough n.* A 1 bowis; B 3 bouȝ (1) bowes (2); C 3 bouhe (1) bowes (2)
A. 6.62 Loke þou breke no *bowis* þere but it be þin owene.
B. 5.32 [He] bad Bette kutte a *bouȝ* ouþer tweye
B. 5.575 Loke [þow] breke no *bowes* þere but if it be [þyn] owene.
B.15.97 Ther some *bowes* ben leued and some bereþ none
C. 5.134 He bad b[e]tte kutte a *bo[u]he* or twene
C.16.216 Þere som *bowes* bereth leues and som bereth none:
C.16.250 Tho *bowes* þat bereth nat and beth nat grene yleued,

bouȝt(e bouȝþe > buggen; bouhe > bouȝ; bouhte > buggen

bouken v *bouken v.* B 2; C 1 bouketh
B.14.19 Dobet shal beten it and *bouken* it as bright as any scarlet
B.15.190 And *bouken* hem at his brest and beten hem clene,
C.16.334 *Bouketh* hem at his breste and beteth h[em] ofte

boumode > bummiþ; boun > bown; bounched > bonched; bounde(n > bynden,yrebounden

bountee n *bounte n.* B 1; C 2 bounte
B.14.150 And whan he haþ doon his deuoir wel men dooþ hym ooþer bountee
C. 8.49 Bute they be of *bounte*, of batayles or of treuthe.
C.17.163 Beaute sanȝ *bounte* blessed was [hit] neuere

bour n *bour n.* A 3 bour (2) boure (1); B 4 bour (1) boure (3); C 3 bour (2) Boure (1)
A. 3.14 Buski[de] hem to þe *bour* þere þe burde dwelliþ,
A. 3.92 And brouȝte hire to *bo[ure]* wiþ blisse and wiþ ioye.
A.10.55 Þere is his *bour* bremest but ȝif blod it make;
B. 2.65 Ac Fauel was þe firste þat fette hire out of *boure*
B. 3.14 Busked hem to þe *bour* þer þe burde dwelle[þ],
B. 3.103 And brouȝte hire to *boure* wiþ blisse and wiþ ioye.
B. 5.141 And siþen þei blosmede abrood in *boure* to here shriftes.
C. 3.11 Into *Boure* with blisse and by here gan sitte.
C. 3.15 Boskede hem to þe *bour* ther th[e] buyrde dwel[leth],
C. 6.228 Þe beste ale lay in m[y] *bour* and in my bed chau[m]bre

bourdeour n *bourdour n.* B 1; C 3 bordiours (1) bordor (1) bourdyors (1)
B.13.447 And a blynd man for a *bourdeour*, or a bedrede womman
C. 7.107 And a blynd man for a *bordor* or a bedredene womman
C. 9.127 And godes boys, *bourdyors* as the book telleth:
C. 9.136 Godes munstrals and his mesagers and his mury *bordiours*

bourdynge prp *bourden v.(1)* B 1; C 1
B.15.40 'Ye ben as a bisshop', quod I, al *bourdynge* þat tyme,
C.16.202 'Ȝe beth as a bischop,' quod y, al *bourdynge* þat tyme,

bourdyors > bourdeour

bourne n *bourne n.* A 1; B 1
A.Pr.8 Vndir a brood bank be a *bourn[e]* side,
B.Pr.8 Vnder a brood bank by a *bourn[e]* syde,

bouste n *boiste n.* A 1 boyste; B 1
A.12.69 'Go we forþ,' quod þe gom, 'I haue a gret *boyste*
B.13.152 I bere þer, [in a *bouste*] faste ybounde, dowel

bowe n *boue n.(1) &> bowen* B 1; C 2 bowe (1) bowes (1)
B.20.117 He bar a *bowe* in his hand and manye brode arewes,
C.20.291 Setteth *bo[w]es* of brake and brasene gonnes
C.22.117 He baer a *bowe* in his hoend and many brode arwes,

bowen v *bouen v.(1) &> bown* A 2 bowe (1) bowiþ (1); B 4 bowe (2) bowen (1) boweþ (1); C 7 bowe (3) bowed (1) bowen (1) boweth (2)
A. 6.53 And so bo[wiþ] forþ be a [brok], be buxum of speche,
A. 9.43 Þat, þeiȝ þi body bowe as bot doþ in þe watir,
B. 5.566 And so *boweþ* forþ by a brook, beþ-buxom-of-speche,
B. 8.47 [That], þouȝ þ[i] body *bowe* as boot dooþ in þe watre,
B.13.147 And but he *bowe* for þis betyng blynd mote he worþe!"
B.19.17 That alle kynne creatures sholden knelen and *bowen*
C. 4.181 And brynge alle men to *bowe* withouten bittere wounde,
C. 7.213 And so [*boweth*] forth by [a] brok, [beth-buxum-of-speche],
C.10.37 [A] bendeth and *boweth*, the body is so vnstable,
C.10.267 That he ne wol *bowe* to þat bonde to beden here an hosebonde
C.13.134 And y *bowed* my body, bihel[d]e al aboute
C.15.147 And bote he *bowe* for this betynge blynde mote he worthen.'
C.21.17 T[hat] alle kyn creatures sholde knelen and *bowen*

bowes > bouȝ,bowe; bowis > bouȝ

bown adj *boun adj.* A 3 boun; B 1; C 1 bowen
A. 2.51 And he[o] be *bou[n]* at his bode his bidding to fulfille,
A. 2.124 And alle be *boun*, beggeris & oþere,
A. 3.245 To be buxum & *boun* his bidding to fulfille.
B. 2.160 And alle be *bown*, beggers and oþere,
C. 2.176 And bade hem alle be *bowen*, beggares and othere,

box n *box n.(2)* B 3; C 3 box (1) boxes (2)
B. 5.640 I wol go fecche my *box* wiþ my breuettes & a bulle with bisshopes lettres
B.13.194 Hadde noȝt [Marie] Maudeleyne moore for a *box* of salue
B.15.214 Ne at Ancres þere a *box* hangeþ; alle swiche þei faiten.
C.Pr.97 And *boxes* ben yset forth ybounde with yren
C. 9.264 Here salue is of supersedeas in sumnoures *boxes*;
C.13.55 For þat on bereth but a *box*, a breuet þerynne,

braek > breke

braggere n *braggere n.* A 1; B 1
A. 7.141 A bretoner, a *braggere*, he bostide hym also,
B. 6.154 A Bretoner, a *braggere*, [he b]osted Piers als

braggeþ v *braggen v.* B 1; C 2 braggyng (1) braggynge (1)
B.13.280 Forwhy he bosteþ and *braggeþ* wiþ manye bolde oþes;
C. 6.34 Bostyng and *braggynge* with many bolde othes,
C. 8.152 A bretener cam *braggyng*, abostede [Peres] also:

brayn n *brain* n. A 2
A.10.54   In manis *brayn* is he most & miჳtiest to knowe.
A.10.56   For whan blood is bremere þanne *brayn*, þan is Inwit bounde,

braynwood adj *brain* n. A 1
A.10.61   And ben *braynwood* as bestis, so here blood wexiþ.

brak > breke

brake n *brake* n.(2) C 1
C.20.291   Setteth bo[w]es of *brake* and brasene gonnes

brake v *braken* v. &> *breke* C 1
C. 6.431   And as an hound þat eet gras so gan y to *brake*

bran > bren; branches > braunche

bras n *bras* n. A 1; B 2; C 1
A. 3.183   And bar here *bras* on þi bak to caleis to selle,
B.Pr.168   To bugge a belle of *bras* or of briჳt siluer
B. 3.196   And bere hire *bras* at þi bak to Caleis to selle,
C.Pr.185   A belle to byggen of *bras* oþer of] bryghte syluer

brasene adj *brasen* adj. C 1
C.20.291   Setteth bo[w]es of brake and *brasene* gonnes

brast v *bresten* v. A 1; B 1; C 1 barste
A. 7.163   He beet hem so boþe he *brast* ner here mawis.
B. 6.178   He bette hem so boþe he *brast* ner hire [mawes].
C. 8.175   [He] beet hem so bothe he *barste* ner her gottes

bratful > bretful; braulers > brawleris

braulynge ger *brauling* ger. B 1; C 1 braulyng
B.15.238   For *braulynge* and bakbitynge and berynge of fals witnesse.
C.16.363   For *braulyng* and bacbitynge and berynge of fals witnesse.

braun > brawen

braunche n *braunch* n. B 3 braunches; C 3 branches (1) braunche (1) braunches (1)
B.13.409   [Ac] whiche ben þe *braunches* þat bryngen a man to sleuþe?
B.13.420   Thise ben þe *braunches*, beþ war, þat bryngen a man to wanhope.
B.15.75   And of þe *braunches* þat burioneþ of hem and bryngen men to helle.
C. 7.69   Ac wheche been þe *braunches* þat bryngeth men to sleuthe?
C. 7.80   This beth þe *branches*, beth ywar, þat bryngeth a man to wanhope.
C.16.265   Ypocrisye is a *braunche* of pruyde and most amonges clerkes

brawen n *barun* n. B 2 braun (1) brawen (1); C 2 brawen (1) brawn (1)
B.13.63   Wombe cloutes and wilde *brawen* and egges yfryed wiþ grece.
B.13.92   That neiþer bacon ne *braun*, blancmanger ne mortrews,
C.15.67   *Brawen* and bloed of gees, bacon and colhoppes.
C.15.99   That noþer bacon ne *brawn*, blaunmanger ne mortrewes

brawleris n *braulere* n. B 1; C 1 braulers
B.16.43   Bakbiteris [brewe]cheste, *brawleris* and chideris,
C.18.46   Thorw bagbitares and *braule[r]s* and thorw bolde chidares

brawn > brawen

brech n *brech* n. B 1; C 1
B. 5.175   And baleised on þe bare ers and no *brech* bitwene.
C. 6.157   And balayshed on þe bare ers and no *brech* bytwene.

bred > breed

bredcorn n *bred* n.(1) A 1 breed_corn; B 1; C 1 breedcorn
A. 7.57   'A busshel of *breed* corn br[yng m]e þereinne,
B. 6.62   'A busshel of *bredcorn* brynge me þerInne,
C. 8.61   A buschel of *breedcorn* brouht was þerynne.

bredde(n > brede v1

brede n *brede* n.(2) A 2; B 2; C 1
A. 2.61   Wiþ alle þe lordsshipe of leccherie in lengþe & in *brede*;
A. 3.190   He shulde haue be lord of þat lond in lengþe & in *brede*,
B. 2.89   [Wiþ] al þe lordshipe of leccherie in lengþe and in *brede*,
B. 3.203   He sholde haue be lord of þat lond in lengþe and in *brede*,
C. 2.96   With al þe lordschip of leccherye in lenghe and in *Brede*,

brede v1 *breden* v.(3) B 4 bredden (2) brede (1) bredeþ (1); C 1 bredde
B.11.348   Lerned to legge þe stikkes in whiche she leyeþ and *bredeþ*.
B.11.356   And some troden, [I took kepe], and on trees *bredden*,
B.11.359   And some caukede; I took kepe how pecokkes *bredden*.
B.12.228   [That þ]ere þe þorn is þikkest to buylden and *brede*;
C.13.165   And som treden, y toke kepe, and on trees *bredde*

breden v2 *broden* v.(1) B 1
B. 2.98   And *breden* as Burgh swyn, and bedden hem esily

bredyng ger *bredinge* ger.(2) B 1
B.12.219   /And willest of briddes & beestes and of hir *bredyng* knowe,

bredlees adj *bredles* adj. B 1; C 2 bredles
B.14.160   Ac beggeris aboute Midsomer *bredlees* þei [soupe],
C. 9.121   Barfoot and *bredles*, beggeth they of no man
C.16.13   Ac beggares aboute myssomur *bredles* they soupe

breed n *bred* n.(1) &> *bredcorn* A 8 bred (7) breed (1); B 24 bred (1) breed (23); C 23 bred (15) breed (8)
A. 7.129   Or ჳe shuln ete barly *bred* & of þe bro[k] drynke;
A. 7.169   To abate þe barly *bred* & þe benis ygrounde,
A. 7.199   Bolde beggeris & bigge, þat mowe here *breed* beswynken,
A. 7.200   Wiþ houndis *bred* & hors bred holde vp here hertis,
A. 7.200   Wiþ houndis bred & hors *bred* holde vp here hertis,
A. 7.287   Ne no beggere ete *bred* þat benis in come,
A.11.188   To breke beggeris *bred* & bakken hem with cloþis,
A.12.70   At my bak of broke *bred* þi bely for to fylle,
B. 5.173   And doon me faste frydayes to [þerf] *breed* and to watre;
B. 5.437   Boþ[e] *bred* and ale, buttre, melk and chese
B. 6.135   Or ye shul eten barly *breed* and of þe broke drynke;
B. 6.213   Bolde beggeris and bigge þat mowe hir *breed* biswynke,
B. 6.214   Wiþ houndes *breed* and horse breed hoold vp hir hertes,
B. 6.214   Wiþ houndes breed and horse *breed* hoold vp hir hertes,
B. 6.303   Ne no beggere ete *breed* þat benes Inne [come],
B. 7.85   For whoso haþ to buggen hym *breed*, þe book bereþ witnesse,
B. 7.86   He haþ ynouჳ þat haþ *breed* ynouჳ, þouჳ he haue noჳt ellis:
B. 7.125   And wepen whan I sholde [werche] þouჳ whete *breed* me faille.
B.11.237   Til he blessede and brak þe *breed* þat þei eten.
B.12.17   And bidde for hem þat ჳyueþ þee *breed*, for þer are bokes y[n]owe
B.12.85   For goddes body myჳte noჳt ben of *breed* wiþouten clergie,
B.13.47   Bifore Pacience *breed* to brynge, [bitynge apart],
B.13.235   For no *breed* þat I brynge forþ, saue a benyson on þe sonday
B.13.241   Beggeris and bidderis of my *breed* crauen,
B.13.251   And buxom and busy aboute *breed* and drynke
B.13.260   For er I haue *breed* of mele ofte moot I swete,
B.13.266   Wiþ [bake] *breed* fro Stratford; þo gonnen beggeris wepe
B.15.184   Thouჳ he bere hem no *breed* he bereþ hem swetter liflode;
B.15.284   Hadde a brid þat brouჳte hym *breed* þat he by lyuede,
B.16.244   And doon hym worship with *breed* and wiþ wyn boþe,
B.19.385   Here is *breed* yblessed, and goddes body þervnder.
B.20.248   And I wol be youre boruჳ: ye shal haue *breed* and cloþes
C. 5.174   *Bred* withouten beggynge to lyue by euere aftur
C. 6.146   For she had haly *bred* ar y my herte gan change.
C. 6.155   And doen me faste fridayes to *bred* and to water;
C. 7.51   Bothe *Bred* and ale, Botere, mylke and chese
C. 8.142   Or ჳe shal ete barly *breed* and of þe broke drynke.
C. 8.223   Bolde beggares and bygge þat mowe here *breed* byswynke,
C. 8.224   With houndes *bred* and hors breed hele hem when þei hungren
C. 8.224   With houndes bred and hors *breed* hele hem when þei hungren
C. 8.305   And *bred* for my barnes of benes and of peses.
C. 8.325   Ne no beggare eten *bred* þat benes ynne were
C. 9.120   Withoute bagge and *bred* as þe book telleth:
C. 9.156   Thorw which craft a couthe come to *bred* and to ale
C. 9.201   And briddes brouhte somme *bred* þat they by lyuede.
C. 9.255   Ne no blanke[t] on his bed ne whyte *bred* byfore hym.
C.11.65   And breketh nat here *bred* to þe pore as þe boke hoteth:
C.12.126   Til he blessed here *bred* and brake hit hem bitwene.
C.13.72   Fynde beggares *bred*, bakkes for þe colde,
C.15.53   And bringe *breed* for pacience, bytyng apartye,
C.15.209   For no *breed* þat y betrauaile to [brynge] byfore lordes.
C.16.63   And buxum at his biddyng for his *breed* and his drynke
C.18.261   Worschipe hym with wyn and with *breed* bothe
C.21.385   Here is *bred* yblessed and godes body þervnder.
C.22.248   [And] y wol be ჳoure borwh: ჳe shal haue *breed* and clothes

breedcorn > bredcorn; breef > brief; breere > brere

breeþ n *breth* n.(1) B 3; C 3 breth
B.14.61   For þoruჳ his *breeþ* beestes woxen and abrood yeden:
B.14.62   Ergo þoruჳ his *breeþ* [boþe] men and beestes lyuen,
B.18.321   And wiþ þat *breeþ* helle brak with Belialles barres.
C.15.260   [For] thorw his *breth* bestes wexe and abrood ჳeden:
C.15.261   Ergo thorw his *breth* bestes lyueth, bothe men and fisches,
C.20.364   And with þat *breth* helle braek with belialles barres;

breide v *breiden* v.(1) B 1
B.17.71   [And *breide* to hise boteles and boþe he atamede];

breke v *breken* v. A 12 brak (1) breke (3) breken (2) brekiþ (1) broke (1) broken (4); B 26 brak (5) breke (8) breken (1) brekeþ (3) broke (5) broken (2) ybroke (1) ybroken (1); C 25 braek (1) brake (2) breke (10) breketh (4) broke (4) broken (3) ybrokene (1)
A.Pr.68   Of falsnesse of fastyng & of auowes *broken*.
A.1.111   Til he *brak* buxumnesse þoruჳ bost of hymseluen.
A. 4.44   *Brekiþ* vp my berne doris, beriþ awey my whete,
A. 5.89   Þat bar awey my bolle & my *broken* shete.
A. 6.62   Loke þou *breke* no bowis þere but it be þin owene.

A. 7.32   And [to] boris & [to] bukkes þat *breken* myn heggis,
A. 8.76   Or his bak or his bon þei *breken* in his ʒouþe,
A. 8.84   Blynde & bedrede, & *broken* here membris,
A. 8.167   Be þou neuere þe baldere to *breke* þe ten hestis;
A. 9.79   Þe bagges & þe [bi]gerdlis, he haþ *broken* hem alle
A.11.188   To *breke* beggeris bred & bakken hem wiþ cloþis,
A.12.70   At my bak of *broke* bred þi bely for to fylle,
B.Pr.71   Of falshede of fastynge [and] of Auowes *ybroken*.
B. 1.113   Til] he *brak* buxomnesse; his blisse gan he tyne
B. 2.83   Vnbuxome and bolde to *breke* þe ten hestes;
B. 4.57   *Brekeþ* vp my bern[e] dore[s], bereþ awey my whete,
B. 5.109   That [bar] awey my bolle and my *broke* shete.
B. 5.242   Swiche dedes I dide write if he his day *breke*;
B. 5.575   Loke [þow] *breke* no bowes þere but if it be [þyn] owene.
B. 6.30   To bores and to [bukkes] þat *breken* myne hegges,
B. 7.94   Or [his] bak or [his] boon [þei] *brekeþ* in his youþe
B. 7.102   Blynde and bedreden and *broken* hire membres
B. 7.189   Be [þow] neuer þe boldere to *breke* þe ten hestes;
B. 8.88   The bagges and þe bigirdles, he haþ [b]*roke* hem alle
B. 9.94   And biddeþ þe beggere go for his *broke* cloþes:
B.10.85   And *brekeþ* noʒt to þe beggere as þe book techeþ:
B.10.288   Archa dei myshapped and Ely *brak* his nekke.
B.11.140   'Ye? baw for bokes!' quod oon was *broken* out of helle.
B.11.164   Yblissed be truþe þat so *brak* helle yates
B.11.237   Til he blessede and *brak* þe breed þat þei eten.
B.14.222   And buxom at hi[s] biddyn[g] for his *broke* loues,
B.14.248   And wheiþer he liʒter to *breke*? lasse boost [it] makeþ
B.16.126   And lefte baskettes ful of *broke* mete, bere awey whoso wolde.'
B.18.253   To *breke* and to bete adoun [alle] þat ben ayeins [hym],
B.18.287   For þow gete hem wiþ gile and his Gardyn *breke*,
B.18.321   And wiþ þat breeþ helle *brak* with Belialles barres;
B.19.338   Blowe hem doun and *breke* hem and bite atwo þe mores.
B.19.344   'And Piers bern worþ *ybroke*; and þei þat ben in vnitee
C.Pr.69   Of falsnss[e of] fastyng[e and] of vowes *ybrokene*.
C.Pr.114   Fro his chayere [for he sat and *brake* his nekke atwene.
C. 2.90   Vnbuxum and bold to *breke* þe ten hestes;
C. 4.60   And *breketh* vp my bern[e] dores and [b]ereth awey my whete
C. 5.33   Or thow art *broke*, so may be, in body or in membre
C. 8.29   To bores and to bokkes þat *breketh* adoun myn hegges
C. 9.170   Or þe bak or som bon þey *breke* of he[re] children
C. 9.178   Blynde and bedredne and *broken* here membris,
C. 9.237   And hoso *breketh* this, be wel waer, but yf he repente,
C. 9.242   *Breke* þis obedience þat beth so fer fram chirche
C. 9.277   Mercy for mede and my lawe *breke*.'
C. 9.335   Be ʒe neuere þe baldere to *breke* þe ten hestes
C.10.85   The bagges and þe bigerdeles, he hath [b]*roken* hem alle
C.11.65   And *breketh* nat here bred to þe pore as þe boke hoteth:
C.12.75   'ʒe? bawe for bokes!' quod oen was *broken* out of helle.
C.12.126   Til he blessed here bred and *brake* hit hem bitwene.
C.16.88   And where be [lyh]tere to *breke*? lasse boest hit maketh
C.18.154   And lefte basketes ful of *Broke* mete, bere awey hoso wolde.
C.20.262   To *breke* and to bete adoun all þat ben agaynes hym
C.20.313   For thow gete hem with gyle and his gardyn *broke*,
C.20.320   And dust hem *breke* here buxumnesse thorw fals bihestes
C.20.364   And with þat breth helle *braek* with belialles barres,
C.20.380   Byglosedest hem and bigiledest hem and my gardyne *breke*
C.21.338   Blowe hem doun and *B[r]eke* hem and b[y]te ato þe mores.
C.21.344   'And Peres berne worth *broke* and þei þat ben in vnite

brekynge ger *brekinge ger.* B 1; C 1
B.10.323   And bete yow, as þe bible telleþ, for *brekynge* of youre rule,
C. 5.169   And bete ʒow, as þe bible telleth, for *brekynge* of ʒoure reule

breme adj *breme adj.* A 2 bremere (1) bremest (1); B 1
A.10.55   Þere is his bour *bremest* but ʒif blod it make;
A.10.56   For whan blood is *bremere* þanne brayn, þan is Inwit bounde,
B.12.224   How euere beest ouþer brid haþ so *breme* wittes.

bren n *bran n.* &> brennen A 1; B 2 bran (1) bren (1)
A. 7.267   A lof of benis & *bren* ybake for my children;
B. 6.182   Or ellis benes [and] *bren* ybaken togideres.'
B. 6.283   [A lof] of benes and *bran* ybake for my fauntes.

brennen v *brennen v.* A 1 brenne; B 10 bren (2) brende (1) brenne (3) brennen (1) brenneþ (1) brennynge (1) brent (1); C 12 bern (1) berne (1) brenne (2) brennen (1) brenneth (2) brennyng (1) brennynge (1) brente (2) ybrent (1)
A. 3.250   Barnes and bestis *brenne* hem to deþe."
B. 3.267   Burnes and beestes, *bren* hem to deþe;
B. 3.270   *Bren* it; bere it noʒt awey be it neuer so riche;
B.11.133   And putten hym after in prison in purgatorie to *brenne*.
B.17.216   The blase þerof yblowe out, yet *brenneþ* þe weke–
B.17.236   Wol *brennen* and blasen, be þei togideres,
B.17.260   Ne *brenne* ne blase clere, fo[r] blowynge of vnkyndenesse.
B.17.266   Ye *brenne* but ye blase noʒt; þat is a blynd bekene:

B.17.332   That sholde brynge in bettre wode or blowe it til it *brende*.
B.18.255   And I, book, wole be *brent* but Iesus rise to lyue
B.20.84   Biles and bocches and *brennynge* Agues,
C. 3.105   Many burgages *ybrent* and bodies þerynne
C. 3.238   To *berne* and to bruttene, to bete adoun strenghtes
C. 3.423   *Bern* hit; bere hit nat awey be hit neuer so riche;
C.12.68   And potten hym aftur in prisoun in purgatorie to *brenne*
C.19.182   The blase be yblowen out, ʒut *brenneth* þe weke–
C.19.202   Wol *brennen* and blasen, be they togyderes,
C.19.226   Ne *brenne* ne blase clere for blowynge of vnkyndenesse.
C.19.232   ʒe *brenneth* ac ʒe blaseth nat; and þat is a blynde bekne:
C.19.312   That sholde brynge in bettere wode or blowen hit til hit *brente*.
C.20.264   And y, book, wol be *brente* bote he aryse to lyue
C.20.289   Brumstoen boylaunt, *brennyng* out cast hit,
C.22.84   Byles and boches and *brennynge* aguwes,

brennyng ger *brenninge ger.* &> brennen B 1
B.15.83   If I lye on yow to my lewed wit, ledeþ me to *brennyng*!

brent ptp *burnen v.* &> brennen B 1
B. 5.268   For þe beste book in oure hous, þeiʒ *brent* gold were þe leues,

brente > brennen

brere n *brer n.* A 1; C 2 breere (1) breres (1)
A.10.124   Out of a raggit rote and a rouʒ *brere*
C. 2.28   For shal neuer *breere* bere berye as a vine,
C. 6.402   And wesched hit hadde [be wexed] with a weps of *breres*.

brest n *brest n.* A 2; B 5 brest (4) breste (1); C 5 brest (1) breste (4)
A. 5.99   [Þat] al my *brest* bolniþ for bittir of my galle.
A. 5.218   And beet þiself on þe *brest* & bidde hym of grace,
B. 5.120   That al my [*brest*] bolneþ for bitter of my galle.
B. 5.390   He bigan Benedicite with a bolk and his *brest* knokked,
B. 5.446   And beet þiself on þe *brest* and bidde hym of grace,
B.11.121   And bad hem souke for synne [saufte] at his *breste*
B.15.190   And bouken hem at his *brest* and beten hem clene,
C. 5.106   Byfore þe cross on my knees knokked y my *brest*,
C. 7.6   A bigan benedicite with a bolk and his *breste* knokkede,
C. 7.60   And bete thysulue [o]n þe *breste* and bydde hym of grace
C.12.56   And bad hem souke for synne saue at his *breste*
C.16.334   Bouketh hem at his *breste* and beteth h[em] ofte

bretener > bretoner

bretful adj *bredful adj.* A 1 bratful; B 1; C 1
A.Pr.41   Til here bely & here bagge were *bratful* ycrammid;
B.Pr.41   [Til] hire bel[y] and hire bagg[e were *bret*]ful ycrammed;
C.Pr.42   Til here [bely] and here [bagge] w[ere] *bretful* ycrammed,

breth > breeþ; bretherne -rene -urne > broþer

breþyng ger *brethinge ger.* B 1
B.11.358   And some briddes at þe bile þoruʒ *breþyng* conceyued,

bretil > brotel

bretoner n *Britoner n.* A 2; B 2; C 2 bretener (1) Bretoner (1)
A. 7.141   A *bretoner*, a braggere, he bostide hym also,
A. 7.161   And buffetide þe *bretoner* aboute þe chekis
B. 6.154   A *Bretoner*, a braggere, [he b]osted Piers als
B. 6.176   He buffetted þe *Bretoner* aboute þe chekes
B. 8.152   A *bretener* cam braggyng, abostede [Peres] also:
C. 8.173   A boffatede þe *Bretoner* aboute the chekes

breuʒ > brew

breuhwyf n *breuwif n.* C 1
C. 6.354   And whode[r]ward he wolde the *breuhwyf* hym askede.

breuster- > brewester-

breuet n *brevet n.* A 1; B 2 breuet (1) breuettes (1); C 2
A.Pr.71   He bunchi[de] hem wiþ his *breuet* & bleri[de] here eiʒe[n]
B.Pr.74   He bonched hem with his *breuet* and blered hire eiʒen
B. 5.640   I wol go fecche my box wiþ my *breuettes* & a bulle with bisshopes lettres
C.Pr.72   A bounchede hem with his *b[reuet]* and blered here yes
C.13.55   For þat on bereth but a box, a *breuet* þerynne,

brew v *breuen v.* A 1 breuʒ; B 2 brew (1) browe (1); C 2 brew (1) browe (1)
A. 5.133   I bouʒte hire barly; heo *breuʒ* it to selle.
B. 5.217   I bouʒte hire barly; she *brew* it to selle.
B.18.363   [Þe bitternesse þat þow hast *browe*, now brouke it þiselue];
C. 6.225   Y bouhte here barly; [a] *brew* hit to sulle.
C.20.401   The bitternesse þat thow hast *browe*, now brouk hit thysulue;

breware > brewere

brewecheste adj *breuecheste n.* B 1
B.16.43   Bakbiteris [*brewe*]*cheste*, brawleris and chideris,

brewere n *breuere n.* A 1 breweris; B 3 Brewere (2) Brewers (1); C 6 breware (3) Breweres (3)
A. 3.68   *Breweris* & bakeris, bocheris & cokes,
B. 3.79   *Brew[e]rs* and Bak[e]rs, Bochiers and Cokes;
B.19.396   'Ye? baw!' quod a *Brewere*, 'I wol noȝt be ruled,
B.19.404   Vnblessed artow, *Brewere*, but if þee god helpe.
C.Pr.225   Bothe Bakeres and *Breweres*, Bochers and other,
C. 3.80   As Bakeres a[nd] *Breweres*, Bocheres and cokes;
C. 3.104   Al this haue we seyn, þat som tyme thorw a *breware*
C. 4.120   And til byschopes ben bakeres, *Breweres* and tayllours
C.21.396   'ȝe? bawe!' quod a *breware*, 'y wol nat be yruled,
C.21.404   Vnblessed art thow, *breware*, but yf the god helpe.

brewestere n *breuster n.* A 3 breustere (1) breusteris (2); B 3 Brewestere (1) brewesteres (2); C 3 brewestares (1) brewestere (1) brewesteres (1)
A.Pr.98   Baxteris & bocheris & *breusteris* manye,
A. 5.148   And Betoun þe *breustere* bad h[ym] good morewe,
A. 7.290   But of þe beste & þe brunneste þat *breusteris* sellen.
B.Pr.219   Baksteres and *Brewesteres* and Bochiers manye,
B. 5.298   [Ac] Beton þe *Brewestere* bad hym good morwe
B. 6.306   But of þe beste and þe brunneste þat [*brewesteres*] selle.
C. 6.353   By betene hous the *brewestere* þat bad hym good morwen
C. 8.328   Bote of the beste and þe brouneste þat *brewestares* sullen.
C. 9.190   And in borwes among *brewesteres* and beggen in churches–

brewhouses n *beruhous n.* C 1
C. 9.98   Ac beggares with bagges þe whiche *brewhous[es]* ben here churches,

brybours n *bribour n.* B 1; C 1
B.20.262   Alle oþere in bataille ben yholde *Brybours*,
C.22.262   Alle oþere in bataile been yholde *brybours*,

brid n *brid n.* A 2 briddis; B 16 brid (2) briddes (14); C 10 briddes
A. 9.55   Blisse of þe *briddis* made me abide,
A. 9.58   Blisse of þ[e] *briddis* brouȝte me a slepe;
B. 8.64   Blisse of þe *briddes* [abide me made],
B.10.408   But *briddes* and beestes and þe blissed Noe
B.11.328   And where þat *briddes* and beestes by hir mak[e þei] yeden,
B.11.345   *Briddes* I biheld þat in buskes made nestes;
B.11.351   Ac yet me merueilled moore how many oþere *briddes*
B.11.357   And brouȝten forþ hir *briddes* al aboue þe grounde.
B.11.358   And some *briddes* at þe bile þoruȝ breþyng conceyued,
B.11.362   Ther neiþer burn ne beest may hir *briddes* rechen.
B.12.129   Of *briddes* and of beestes, [by] tastes of truþe.
B.12.219   /And willest of *briddes* & beestes and of hir bredyng knowe,
B.12.224   How euere beest ouþer *brid* haþ so breme wittes.
B.12.236   Ac of *briddes* and of beestes men by olde tyme
B.14.43   The Corlew by kynde of þe Eyr, moost clennest flessh of *briddes*,
B.14.112   And seiþ, "lo! *briddes* and beestes þat no blisse ne knoweþ
B.15.284   Hadde a *brid* þat brouȝte hym breed þat he by lyuede,
B.15.314   Til *briddes* brynge vs [wherby] we sholde lyue.
C. 9.201   And *briddes* brouhte somme bred þat they by lyuede,
C.10.63   Blisse of þe *briddes* abyde me made
C.11.239   Bote *briddes* and bestis and þe blessed Noe
C.13.136   And where þat *briddes* and bestis by here make þei ȝeden,
C.13.156   *Briddes* y beheld [þat] in bosches made nestes;
C.13.162   And ȝut me merueylede more [how] mony [other] *briddes*
C.13.166   And brouhte forth here *briddes* al aboue þe grounde.
C.14.80   Of *briddes* and of bestes, of blisse and of sorwe.
C.14.169   To *briddes* and to bestes, As here bokes telleth
C.15.288   And saith, "loo! *briddes* and bestes þat no blisse ne knoweth

bridale n *bridale n.* A 1; B 2; C 1
A. 2.34   Were beden to þe *b[ri]dale* on boþe two sides.
B. 2.44   Tomorwe worþ ymaked þe maydenes *bridale*;
B. 2.55   Were boden to þe *bridale* on boþe two sides,
C. 2.58   Were beden to þe *Bridale* a bothe half þe contre,

briddes > brid

brydel n *bridel n.* A 1 bridel; B 1
A. 4.20   Hange on hym þe heuy *bridel* to holde his hed lowe,
B. 4.22   Hange on hym þe heuy *brydel* to holde his heed lowe,

brief n *bref n.* B 1; C 1 breef
B.20.327   Boldely to þe bisshop and his *brief* hadde
C.22.327   Baldly to þe bishope and his *breef* hadde

brygge > brugge: bright > briȝt

brighte adv *brighte adv. &> briȝt* B 1; C 1 brihte
B.19.433   As *brighte* as to þe beste man or to þe beste womman.
C.21.433   As *brihte* as to þe beste man or to þe beste womman.

briȝt adj *bright adj.* B 7 bright (2) briȝt (3) briȝte (2); C 5 bryghte (2) briht (2) brihte (1)
B.Pr.161   Beren beiȝes ful *briȝte* abouten hire nekkes,
B.Pr.168   To bugge a belle of bras or of *briȝt* siluer
B.12.222   Wherof þei cacche hir colours so clere and so *briȝte*,
B.14.19   Dobet shal beten it and bouken it as *bright* as any scarlet
B.15.527   He is a forbisene to alle bisshopes and a *briȝt* myrrour,
B.18.97   To [bete a body ybounde wiþ any *briȝt* wepene].
B.20.132   And boldeliche bar adoun wiþ many a *bright* Noble
C.Pr.180   Bere beyus of *bryghte* aboute here nekkes
C.Pr.185   A belle to byggen of bras oþer of] *bryghte* syluer
C.17.277   He is a forbisene to alle bisshopis and a *briht* myrrour
C.20.100   To bete a body ybounde with eny *briht* wypene.
C.22.132   And baldeliche baer adoun with many a *brihte* noble

brihtnesse n *brightnesse n.* C 2
C.13.11   Ne for *brihtnesse* of here beaute here spouse to be byknowe.
C.20.284   Ar we thorw *brihtnesse* be b[l]ente go barre þe ȝates;

brynge v *bringen v.* A 28 bryng (2) bringe (8) bringe (1) bringen (2) bringeþ (3) brouȝt (1) brouȝte (9) brouȝtest (1) ybrouȝt (1); B 65 bringe (1) bryng (1) brynge (27) bryngen (5) bryngeþ (7) broȝt (1) broȝte (3) brouȝt (2) brouȝte (15) brouȝten (1) brouȝtest (1) ybrouȝt (1); C 68 bryng (2) bringe (1) brynge (26) bryngen (3) bringeth (3) bryngeth (5) broughtest (1) brouht (1) brouhte (21) brouhten (2) brouth (1) ybroughte (1) ybrouhte (1)
A.Pr.66   *Brouȝte* forþ a bulle wiþ bisshopis selis
A. 1.75   Þou *brouȝtest* me borewis my biddyng to werche,
A. 2.138   For þei shuln bere þise bisshopis & *bringe* hem at reste.
A. 2.164   And *bringeþ* mede to me maugre hem alle.
A. 3.2   Wiþ bedelis & baillifs *ybrouȝt* to þe king.
A. 3.10   Tok mede be þe myddel & *brouȝte* hire to chaumbre.
A. 3.92   And *brouȝte* hire to bo[ure] wiþ blisse & wiþ ioye.
A. 3.141   And *bringen* forþ barnes aȝens forboden lawis.
A. 3.144   Barouns & burgeis she *bringeþ* in sorewe;
A. 3.253   But *brouȝte* wiþ hym þe bestis as þe bible [telliþ],
A. 4.40   He borewide of me bayard & *brouȝte* him neuere aȝen,
A. 4.79   'Betere is þat boote bale adoun *bringe*,
A. 4.146   'Ac it is wel hard, be myn hed, herto to *bringe* it.
A. 5.8   And so I babelide on my bedis þei *brouȝte* me aslepe.
A. 5.74   And blamide hym behynde his bak to *bringe* hym in fame;
A. 5.145   And bidde þe rode of bromholm *bringe* me out of dette.'
A. 5.200   Bere hym to his bed & *brouȝte* hym þerinne.
A. 7.57   'A busshel of breed corn *br[yng m]e* þereinne,
A. 7.277   Benes & [b]ake applis hy *brouȝte* in here lappe[s],
A. 8.75   And *bringen* forþ barnes þat bois ben holden.
A. 9.25   Let *bringe* a man in a bot amydde a brood watir;
A. 9.58   Blisse of þ[e] briddis *brouȝte* me a slepe;
A.10.147   And *brouȝt* forþ a barn þat muche bale wrouȝte;
A.10.192   Þe fruyt þat þei *bringe* forþ arn manye foule wordis.
A.10.217   And so comiþ dobest aboute, and *bringeþ* doun mody,
A.11.41   And *bringe* forþ a ballid resoun, t[a]k[e] bernard to witnesse,
A.12.87   Fro deþ þat is oure duk swyche dedis we *brynge*.'
A.12.117   Þat barn *bryng* vs to blys þat bled vpon þe rode amen.
B.Pr.69   *Brouȝte* forþ a bulle wiþ Bisshopes seles,
B.Pr.176   Ac þo þe belle was *ybrouȝt* and on þe beiȝe hanged
B. 1.77   [Thow] *brouȝtest* me borwes my biddyng to [werche],
B. 2.66   And as a Brocour *brouȝte* hire to be wiþ fals enioyned.
B. 2.203   /And *bryngeþ* Mede to me maugree hem alle.
B. 3.2   Wiþ Bedeles and baillies *brouȝt* [to] þe kyng.
B. 3.10   Took Mede bi þe myddel and *broȝte* hire into chambre.
B. 3.103   And *brouȝte* hire to boure wiþ blisse and wiþ ioye.
B. 3.152   And *bryngeþ* forþ barnes ayein forbode lawes.
B. 3.163   Barons and Burgeises she *bryngeþ* in sorwe,
B. 4.53   He borwed of me bayard [and] *brouȝte* hym [neuere ayein],
B. 4.92   'Bettre is þat boote bale adoun *brynge*
B. 4.183   It is [wel] hard, by myn heed, hert[o] to *brynge* it,
B. 5.8   And so I bablede on my bedes þei *brouȝte* me aslepe.
B. 5.94   [And blamed hym bihynde his bak to *brynge* hym in fame;
B. 5.229   And bidde þe Roode of Bromholm *brynge* me out of dette.'
B. 5.358   Baren hym to his bed and *brouȝte* hym þerInne,
B. 5.388   Were I *brouȝt* abedde, but if my tailende it made,
B. 6.62   'A busshel of bredcorn *brynge* me þerInne,
B. 6.293   Benes and baken apples þei *broȝte* in hir lappes,
B. 7.81   And he þat biddeþ borweþ and *bryngeþ* hymself in dette.
B. 7.93   And *bryngen* forþ barnes þat bastardes men calleþ.
B. 8.29   Lat *brynge* a man in a boot amydde [a] bro[od] watre;
B. 9.154   That *bryngeþ* forþ any barn but if he be þe same
B. 9.171   The fruyt þat [þei] *brynge* forþ arn [manye] foule wordes;]
B. 9.208   And so comeþ dobest [aboute] and *bryngeþ* adoun mody,
B.10.55   And *bryngen* forþ a balled reson, taken Bernard to witnesse,
B.10.315   And but if his knaue knele þat shal his coppe *brynge*
B.11.8   And into þe lond of longynge [and] loue she me *brouȝte*
B.11.33   And pride of parfit lyuynge to muche peril þee *brynge*.'

B.11.153 *Brouʒte* me fro bitter peyne þer no biddyng myʒte.'
B.11.357 And *brouʒten* forþ hir briddes al aboue þe grounde.
B.12.134 Ne *broʒt* by hir bokes to blisse ne to ioye,
B.13.47 Bifore Pacience breed to *brynge*, [bitynge apart],
B.13.53 /And he *brouʒte* vs of Beati quorum of Beatus virres makyng,
B.13.56 'Bryng pacience som pitaunce pryuelyche', quod Conscience,
B.13.185 I shal *brynge* yow a bible, a book of þe olde lawe,
B.13.235 For no breed þat I *brynge* forþ, saue a benyson on þe sonday
B.13.409 [Ac] whiche ben þe braunches þat *bryngen* a man to sleuþe?
B.13.420 Thise ben þe braunches, beþ war, þat *bryngen* a man to wanhope.
B.13.426 Lest þo þre maner men to muche sorwe yow *brynge*:
B.14.86 And *brynge* his soule to blisse, so þat feiþ bere witnesse
B.14.96 And as it neuere [n]adde ybe to noʒte *bryngeþ* dedly synne
B.15.75 And of þe braunches þat burioneþ of hem and *bryngen* men to helle,
B.15.284 Hadde a brid þat *brouʒte* hym breed þat he by lyuede,
B.15.308 And lawefulle men to lifholy men liflode *brynge*;
B.15.314 Til briddes *brynge* vs [wherby] we sholde lyue.
B.15.398 *Brouʒte* Sarʒens of Surree, and see in what manere.
B.15.410 Makometh in mysbileue men and wommen *brouʒte*,
B.15.427 Hir preieres and hir penaunces to pees sholde *brynge*
B.15.598 And þoruʒ his pacience hir power to pure noʒt he *brouʒte*:
B.16.263 Ne no buyrn be oure borgh, ne *brynge* vs fram his daunger–
B.17.33 What neded it [now] a newe lawe to [*brynge*]
B.17.94 May no medicyne [vnder mone] þe man to heele *bringe*,
B.17.332 That sholde *brynge* in bettre wode or blowe it til it brende.
B.18.29 Deeþ seiþ he shal fordo and adoun *brynge*
B.18.35 And forbete and adoun *brynge* bale deeþ for euere:
B.18.131 Wiþouten [wommene] wem into þis world *broʒte* hym.
B.18.141 And þat deeþ adown *brouʒte*, deeþ shal releue.'
B.18.145 Leue þow neuere þat yon light hem alofte *brynge*
B.18.257 And conforte al his kyn and out of care *brynge*
B.18.414 That loue, and hym liste, to laughynge ne *brouʒte*;
B.19.51 Mighte no deeþ hym fordo ne adoun *brynge*
B.19.284 Ne [sholde] no scornere out of skile hym *brynge*;
B.20.201 And cryede to kynde: 'out of care me *brynge*!
C.Pr.67 *Brouth* forth a bulle with bischopis selys
C.Pr.193 Ac tho þe belle was *ybroughte* and on þe beygh hangid
C.1.18 And *brynge* forth ʒoure bilyue, bothe lynnen and wollene,
C.1.74 Thow *broughtest* me borewes my biddyng to fulfille,
C.2.31 The fader þat me forth *brouhte* filius dei he hoteth,
C.2.68 And [as] a brokor *brouhte* here to be [with fals enioyned].
C.2.142 That ʒe nymeth [and] notaries to nauhte gynneth *brynge*
C.2.217 And *bryngeth* mede to me maugrey hem alle.
C.3.2 [With] Bedeles and Baylifs *ybrouhte* byfor þe kyng.
C.3.10 Took mede by þe myddel and myldeliche here *brouhte*
C.3.43 And ʒut be thy bedman and *brynge* adoun Consience
C.3.190 And *bringeth* forth bar[n]es aʒenes forbodene lawes:
C.3.201 Trewe Burgeys and bonde he *bryngeth* to nauhte ofte
C.3.408 How he absoloun to hangynge *brouhte*;
C.4.56 He borwed of me bayard a[nd] *brouhte* hym hom neuere
C.4.88 'Betere is þat bote bale adoun *brynge*
C.4.177 Hit is ful hard, by myn heued, herto to *bryngen* hit
C.4.181 And *brynge* alle men to bowe withouten bittere wounde,
C.6.141 Byte and bete and *brynge* forth suche thewes
C.6.416 Beren hym to his bed and *brouhten* hym þerynne
C.7.4 Were y *brouhte* [o]n bed, but yf my taylende hit made,
C.7.69 Ac wheche been þe braunches þat *bryngeth* men to sleuthe?
C.7.80 This beth þe branches, beth ywar, þat *bryngeth* a man to wanhope.
C.7.86 Laste tho manere men to muche sorwe ʒow *brynge*:
C.7.135 And *brouhte* thyne yblessed fro thennes into þe blisse of heuene.
C.8.61 A buschel of breedcorn *brouht* was þerynne.
C.8.163 'Or y shal bete the by the lawe and *brynge* þe in stokkes.'
C.8.316 Benes and bake aples they *brouhten* in here lappe
C.8.349 Shal *brynge* bane and batayle on bothe half þe mone;
C.9.169 *Bringeth* forth bastardus, beggares of kynde,
C.9.201 And briddes *brouhte* somme bred þat they by lyuede.
C.9.261 Thy berkeres aren a[l] blynde that *bringeth* forth thy lombren:
C.10.33 Lat *bryng* a man in a boet amydde a brood water;
C.10.190 And ʒut were best to ben aboute and *brynge* hit to hepe
C.10.192 Bishope[s] sholde ben hereaboute and *bryng* this to hepe
C.10.273 The fruyt þat they *brynge* forth aren many foule wordes;
C.11.36 And *brynge* forth [a] balle[d] reso[n], taken bernard to witnesse
C.11.167 And into þe lond of longyng [and loue] she me *brouhte*
C.11.192 And pruyde-of-parfit-lyuynge to moche perel the *brynge*.'
C.13.22 And *brouhte* hem all aboue þat in bale rotede!
C.13.166 And *brouhte* forth here briddes al aboue þe grounde.
C.14.78 Ne *brouhte* by here bokes to blisse ne þe ioye,
C.15.53 And *bringe* breed for pacience, bytyng apartye,
C.15.60 And *brouhte* forth a pytaunce, was pro h[a]c orabit [ad te] omnis
C.15.209 For no breed þat y betrauaile to [*brynge*] byfore lordes,
C.17.32 Ac bestes *brouhte* hem no mete bute onliche þe foules
C.17.181 Thus macumeth in misbileue man & womman *brouhte*

C.17.236 His preyeres with his pacience to pees sholde *brynge*
C.17.306 And her power thorw his pacience to puyr nauht *brouhte*.
C.18.79 And folewe þat the flesche wole and fruyt forth *brynge*.
C.18.101 And *bryngeth* forth fruyt, folk of alle nacion,
C.18.222 That acorsede alle couples þat no kynde forth *brouhte*:
C.18.279 Ne noen bern ben oure borw ne *bryngen* vs [fro his] daunger–
C.19.34 What nedede hit thanne a newe lawe to *brynge*
C.19.55 A man, as me tho thouhte, to moche care they *brouhte*
C.19.84 Ne no medicyne vnder molde the man to hele *brynge*,
C.19.312 That sholde *brynge* in bettere wode or blowen hit til hit brente.
C.20.28 Deth saith a wol fordo and adown *brynge*
C.20.34 And forbete [and adown] b[r]ynge bale deth for euere:
C.20.134 Withouten wommane wem into this world *brouhte* hym.
C.20.144 And þat deth down *brouhte*, deth shal releue.'
C.20.148 Leue [þou] neuere þat ʒone liht hem alofte *brynge*
C.20.265 And comforte alle his kyn and out of care *brynge*
C.20.340 Hit shal vndo vs deueles and down *bryngen* vs all.
C.20.457 That loue, and hym luste, to l[a]u[h]ynge [ne] *brouhte*;
C.21.51 Myhte no deth hym fordo ne adown *brynge*
C.21.284 Ne sholde no scornare out of skille hym *brynge*
C.22.201 And cryede to kynde: 'out of care me *brynge*!

britel > brotel

brocage n *brokage* n. B 2 brocage (1) brocages (1); C 2 brocage (1) Brocages (1)
B.2.88 In bargaynes and *brocages* wiþ þe Burgh of þefte,
B.14.268 [Moore] þan [a maiden is] þat is maried þoruʒ *brocage*
C.2.95 In bargaynes and *Brocages* with the borw of thefte,
C.16.108 More then þat mayde is þat is maried by *brocage*,

brochen n *brochen* v. A 1 brochide; C 1 brochen
A.5.126 *Brochide* hem wiþ a pakke nedle, & pleit hem togidere;
C.6.218 To *brochen* hem with a batnelde and bande hem togyderes,

broches n *broche* n.(1) A 1 brochis; B 3; C 2
A.Pr.72 And rauʒte wiþ his rageman ryngis & *brochis*.
B.Pr.75 And rauʒte wiþ his Rageman rynges and *broches*.
B.15.121 But if many preest [forbeere] hir baselardes and hir *broches*
B.17.249 But þow haue tow to take it wiþ, tonder or *broches*,
C.Pr.73 And raughte with his Rageman Rynges and *Broches*.
C.19.215 Bote thow haue tasch to take hit with, tender [or] *broches*,

brocour n *brokour* n. B 4 Brocour (3) Brocours (1); C 3 brokeres (1) brokor (1) brokour (1)
B.2.60 Bedelles and baillifs and *Brocours* of chaffare,
B.2.66 And as a *Brocour* brouʒte hire to be wiþ fals enioyned.
B.5.131 And gart bakbityng be a *brocour* to blame mennes ware.
B.5.245 And ben hire *brocour* after and bouʒt hymselue.
C.2.62 Bydels and bailifs and *brokeres* of chaffar[e],
C.2.68 And [as] a *brokor* brouhte here to be [with fals enioyned].
C.6.95 ʒut am y *brokour* of bakbytynge to blame menne w[a]re

brode adj *brod* adj. A 4 brood (3) broode (1); B 10 brode (6) brood (4); C 8 brode (6) brood (2)
A.Pr.8 Vndir a *brood* bank be a bourn[e] side,
A.5.18 Bechis & *broode* okis wern blowen to [þe] grounde.
A.6.5 He bar a burdoun ybounde wiþ a *brood* list,
A.9.25 Let bringe a man in a bot amydde a *brood* watir;
B.Pr.8 Vnder a *brood* bank by a bourn[e] syde,
B.3.305 Alle þat beren baselard, *brood* swerd or launce,
B.5.18 Beches and *brode* okes were blowen to þe grounde
B.5.517 He bar a burdoun ybounde wiþ a *brood* liste,
B.8.29 Lat brynge a man in a bot amydde [a] bro[od] watre;
B.10.321 Ac þei leten hem as lordes, hire lon[d þ]is so *brode*.
B.13.242 Faitours and freres and folk wiþ *brode* crounes.
B.18.230 Thanne was þer a wight wiþ two *brode* eiʒen;
B.20.117 He bar a bowe in his hand and manye *brode* arewes,
B.20.226 And *brode* hoked arwes, goddes herte and hise nayles,
C.3.458 For alle þat bereth baslard, br[ode] swerd oþer launce,
C.5.120 Beches and *brode* okes were blowe to þe grounde
C.5.167 Ac ʒe leten ʒow alle as lordes, ʒoure lond lyth so *brode*.
C.7.162 He bar a bordoun ybounde with a *brood* liste,
C.10.33 Lat bryng a man in a boet amydde a *brood* water;
C.20.239 Thenne wa[s] ther a wihte with two *brode* yes;
C.22.117 He baer a bowe in his hoend and many *brode* arwes,
C.22.226 And *brode* hokede Arwes, goddes herte and his nayles,

broʒt(e > brynge; brok > brook; broke > breke,brook

brokelegged adj *breken* v. A 1; B 1; C 2
A.7.178 [þat leyʒe [blereyed] and *brokelegged* by þe hye waye];
B.6.136 But if he be blynd or *brokelegged* or bolted wiþ Irens,
C.8.143 But yf he be blynde or *brokelegged* or bolted with yren,
C.8.188 Blynde and *Brokelegged* he botened a thousand

broken > breke; brokeres > brocour

brokesshankid adj *breken v.* A 1
A. 7.130   But he be blynd, or *brokesshankid*, or beddrede ligge:

brokor -our > brocour

brol n *brol n.* A 1; B 1; C 1 brolle
A. 3.192   Þe leste *brol* of his blood a barouns pere.
B. 3.205   The leeste *brol* of his blood a Barones piere.
C. 3.262   The leeste *brolle* of his blod a Barones pere.

bromholm n prop *n.i.d.* A 1; B 1
A. 5.145   And bidde þe rode of *bromholm* bringe me out of dette.'
B. 5.229   And bidde þe Roode of *Bromholm* brynge me out of dette.'

brood(e > brode

brook n *brok n.(3)* A 2 brok; B 2 broke (1) brook (1); C 2 brok (1) broke (1)
A. 6.53   And so bo[wiþ] forþ be a [*brok*], be buxum of speche,
A. 7.129   Or ʒe shuln ete barly bred & of þe *bro[k]* drynke;
B. 5.566   And so boweþ forþ by a *brook*, beþ-buxom-of-speche,
B. 6.135   Or ye shul eten barly breed and of þe *broke* drynke;
C. 7.213   And so [boweth] forth by [a] *brok*, [beth-buxum-of-speche],
C. 8.142   Or ʒe shal ete barly breed and of þe *broke* drynke.

brotel adj *brotel adj.* A 1 britel; B 1; C 1 bretil
A. 9.37   Þe boot is lik[nid] to þe body þat *britel* is of kynde,
B. 8.41   The boot is likned to [þe] body þat *brotel* is of kynde,
C.10.47   The boet is liknet to oure body þat *bretil* is of kynde,

broþer n *brother n.* A 7 breþeren (4) broþer (3); B 15 breþeren (11) broþer (3) broþeres (1); C 16 bretherne (6) brethrene (3) brethurne (1) brother (4) broþer (2)
A. 1.64   Counseilid kaym to kiln his *broþer*,
A. 3.243   [Aʒens isra[e]l and aaron and moyses his *broþer*].
A. 5.237   Þo dismas my *broþer* besouʒte þe of grace,
A. 6.78   Wiþ no led but [wiþ] loue & louʒnesse, as *breþeren* of o wombe.
A. 7.193   And it ben my blody *breþeren*, for god bouʒte vs alle.
A.11.151   And [biddiþ] vs ben as *breþeren*, & blissen oure enemys,
A.11.191   Obedient as *breþeren* & sustren to oþere,
B. 1.66   Counseilled Kaym to killen his *broþer*,
B. 5.180   Al þe wikkednesse þat I woot by any of oure *breþeren*,
B. 5.465   Tho Dysmas my *broþer* bisouʒte [þee] of grace
B. 5.503   That art oure fader and oure *broþer*, be merciable to vs,
B. 5.591   Wiþ no leed but wiþ loue and lowe[nesse] as *breþeren* [of o wombe].
B. 6.207   [And it] are my blody *breþeren* for god bouʒte vs alle;
B.10.202   [And] biddeþ vs be as *breþeren* and [blissen] oure enemys
B.10.269   Why meuestow þi mood for a mote in þi *broþeres* eiʒe,
B.11.200   And *breþeren* as of oo blood, as wel beggeres as Erles.
B.11.202   And blody *breþeren* we bicome þere of o body ywonne,
B.11.208   And we hise *breþeren* þoruʒ hym ybouʒt, boþe riche and pouere.
B.12.90   Riʒt so goddes body, *breþeren*, but it be worþili taken,
B.18.376   For we beþ *breþeren* of blood, [ac] noʒt in baptisme alle.
B.18.377   Ac alle þat beþ myne hole *breþeren*, in blood and in baptisme,
B.19.254   Lokeþ þat no[on] lakke oþer, but loueþ as *breþeren*;
C.Pr.107   For Offines s[yn]ne and fines his *brother*
C. 1.62   Conseylede Caym to cullen his *brother*,
C. 6.319   Tho dysmas my *brother* bisouhte [þe] of grace
C. 7.143   That art furste oure fadur and of flesch oure *broþer*
C. 7.239   The barres aren of buxumnesse as *bretherne* of o wombe;
C. 8.216   And hit are my blody *bretherne* for god bouhte vs alle.
C. 9.316   His eleuene *bretherne* hym for nede souhte
C.10.251   Soffre his seed seden with Caymus seed his *brother*.
C.12.110   And blody *bretherne* we bycome þere of o body ywonne,
C.12.116   And we his blody *bretherne*, as wel beggeres as lordes.
C.12.170   He moet forsaken hymsulue his suster and his *broþer*
C.15.79   For alle be we *brethrene* thogh we be diuerse yclothed.
C.16.295   For thogh me souhte alle þe sektes of susturne and *brethurne*
C.20.418   For we beth *brethrene* of bloed Ac nat in baptisme alle.
C.20.419   Ac alle þat beth myn hole *breth[r]ene*, in bloed and in baptisme,
C.21.254   Loke þat noen lacke oþere bute loueth as *bretherne*

broughtest brouʒt- brouht(- > brynge

brouke v *brouken v.* B 2; C 2 brouk (1) brouke (1)
B.11.122   And drynke boote for bale, *brouke* it whoso myʒte.
B.18.363   [Þe bitternesse þat þow hast browe, now *brouke* it þiselue];
C.12.57   And drynke bote for bale, *brouke* hit hoso myhte.\
C.20.401   The bitternesse þat thow hast browe, now *brouk* hit thysulue;

brouneste > brunneste; brouth > brynge; browe > brew

browes n *broue n.* A 1
A.12.12   Skornfully þ[o] scripture she[t] vp h[ere] *browes*,

bruges > brugges

brugge n *brigge n.* A 1 brugges; B 2 brugge (1) brugges (1); C 2 Brygge (1) brugges (1)
A. 8.30   And bynde *brugges* aboute þat tobroke were,
B. 5.592   The *brugg[e]* is of bidde-wel-þe-bet-may-þow-spede;
B. 7.28   And [bynde] *brugges* [aboute] þat tobroke were,
C. 7.240   The *Brygge* hatte b[id]-wel-the-bet-may-th[ow]-spede;
C. 9.32   And *brugges* tobrokene by the heye wayes

brugges n prop *n.i.d. &>* brugge B 1; C 1 Bruges
B.13.391   And if I sente ouer see my seruaunt3 to *Brugges*,
C. 6.278   And yf y sente ouer see my seruauntes to *Bruges*

brumstoen n *brimston n.* C 1
C.20.289   *Brumstoen* boylaunt, brennyng out cast hit,

brunneste adj *broun adj.* A 1; B 1; C 1 brouneste
A. 7.290   But of þe beste & þe *brunneste* þat breusteris sellen.
B. 6.306   But of þe beste and þe *brunneste* þat [brewesteres] selle.
C. 8.328   Bote of the beste and þe *brouneste* þat brewestares sullen.

brusshe n *brushe n.* B 1
B.13.459   Why he ne hadde [w]asshen it or wiped it wiþ a *brusshe*.

bruttene v *britnen v.* C 1
C. 3.238   To berne and to *bruttene*, to bete adoun strenghtes.

bruttenynge ger *britning ger.* C 1
C.15.155   Withoute *brutteny[n]ge* of buyren or eny bloed shedynge.

buffetted v *buffeten v.* A 1 buffetide; B 2; C 2 boffatede (1) boffeted (1)
A. 7.161   And *buffetide* þe bretoner aboute þe chekis
B. 6.176   He *buffetted* þe Bretoner aboute þe chekes
B.20.191   He *buffetted* me aboute þe mouþ and bette out my wangteeþ;
C. 8.173   A *boffatede* þe Bretoner aboute the chekes
C.22.191   He *boffeted* me aboute þe mouthe and beet out my wangteeth

buggen v *bien v.* A 12 begge (1) bigge (1) biggen (4) bouʒte (5) bouʒþe (1); B 22 bigge (2) biggen (1) bouʒt (2) bouʒte (8) bugge (4) buggen (4) ybouʒt (1); C 21 begge (2) beggeth (1) bygge (2) byggen (1) bouhte (9) boute (1) bugge (3) buggen (1) buyth (1)
A. 2.3   Þat bar þe blisside barn þat *bouʒte* vs on þe rode,
A. 3.70   To þe pore peple þat parcelmel *biggen*,
A. 3.72   And ri[chen] þoruʒ regrat[r]ie & rentis hem *biggen*
A. 3.75   Ne *bouʒte* none burgages, be ʒe wel certayn.
A. 4.76   And be borugh for his bale & *b[ig]gen* hym bote;
A. 5.133   I *bouʒte* hire barly; heo breuʒ it to selle.
A. 5.137   And whoso bummide þerof, *bouʒte* it þereaftir,
A. 7.193   And it ben my blody *breþeren*, for god *bouʒte* vs alle.
A. 7.264   'I haue no peny,' quaþ piers, 'pulettis to *biggen*,
A. 8.26   And bad h[e]m *begge* boldely what [hem best] likeþ,
A. 8.55   Ac to *bigge* watir ne wynd, ne wyt is þe þridde,
A.12.71   A bagge ful of a beggere.' I *bouʒþe* hit at onys.
B.Pr.168   To *bugge* a belle of bras or of briʒt siluer
B. 2.3   That bar þ[e] blis[sed] barn þat *bouʒte* vs on þe Rode,
B. 3.81   To þe pouere peple þat parcelmele *buggen*.
B. 3.83   Thei richen þoruʒ regratrie and rentes hem *biggen*
B. 3.86   Ne *bouʒte* none burgages, be ye [wel] certeyne.
B. 4.89   And be borʒ for his bale and *buggen* hym boote,
B. 5.217   I *bouʒte* hire barly; she brew it to selle.
B. 5.221   And whoso bummed þerof *bouʒte* it þerafter,
B. 5.245   And ben hire brocour after and *bouʒt* it myselue.
B. 5.422   If I *bigge* and borwe auʒt, but if it be ytailed,
B. 6.207   [And it] are my blody *breþeren* for god *bouʒte* vs alle;
B. 6.280   'I haue no peny', quod Piers, 'pulettes to *bugge*,
B. 7.24   [And bad hem] *buggen* boldely [what] hem best liked
B. 7.53   Ac to *bugge* water ne wynd ne wit ne fir þe ferþe,
B. 7.85   For whoso haþ to *buggen* hym breed, þe book bereþ witnesse,
B. 9.66   Allas þat drynke shal fordo þat god deere *bouʒte*,
B.11.124   By þe blood þat he *bouʒte* vs wiþ, and þoruʒ bapteme after:
B.11.208   And we hise *breþeren* þoruʒ hym *ybouʒt*, boþe riche and pouere.
B.13.192   The goode wil of a wight was neuere *bouʒt* to þe fulle,
B.14.231   For his rentes ne wol nauʒt reche no riche metes to *bigge*;
B.17.288   For coueitise of any kynnes þyng þat crist deere *bouʒte*.
B.19.279   And lerned men a ladel *bugge* wiþ a long stele
C.Pr.185   A belle to *byggen* of bras oþer of[bryghte syluer
C. 2.3   That bar þ[e] blessid bar[n] þat *bouhte* [vs] on þe rode,
C. 3.33   And *bygge* ʒow benefices, [here bonchef] to haue,
C. 3.82   Rychen thorw regraterye and rentes hem *beggeth*
C. 3.85   Ne *bouhte* none burgages, be ʒe ful certayn.
C. 3.86   Thei han no pite on the peple þat parselmele mot *begge*;
C. 4.85   And be borw for his bale and *buggen* hym bote
C. 5.96   A *boute* suche a bargayn he was þe bet euere
C. 6.225   Y *bouhte* here barly; [a] brew hit to sulle.
C. 6.229   And hoso boumode therof *bouhte* hit þeraftur,
C. 7.35   Yf y b[y]gge and borwe [ouh]t, but yf hit be ytayled,
C. 8.216   And hit are my blody bretherne for god *bouhte* vs alle.

C. 8.302 'Y haue no peny,' quod [Peres], 'polettes for to *begge*,
C. 9.28 [And] bad hem *bugge* boldly what hem best likede
C.12.59 By þ[e] bloed [that] he *bouhte* vs with and bapteme, as he tauhte:
C.15.300 And now he *buyth* hit bittere; he is a beggare of helle.
C.16.72 For his rentes wol nat reche ryche metes to *bugge*;
C.18.157 And drof hem out, alle þat þer *bouhte* and solde,
C.18.164 And pursuede hym priueliche and for pans hym *bouhte*–
C.19.269 For coueytise of eny kyne thynge þat Crist dere *bouhte*.
C.21.279 And lered men a ladel *bugge* with a longe stale

buggere n *biere n.* A 2 beggeris (1) biggere (1); B 1
A. 2.44 For sisours, for somenours, for selleris, for *beggeris*,
A.11.212 A ledere of l[oue]d[a]ies & a lond *biggere*;
B.10.312 A ledere of louedayes and a lond *buggere*,

buggynge ger *biinge ger.* B 1; C 1
B.19.235 [By] sellynge and *buggynge* hir bilyue to wynne.
C.21.235 [By] sullyng and *buggynge* here bileue to wynne.

buylden v *bilden v.* B 1
B.12.228 [That þ]ere þe þorn is þikkest to *buylden* and brede;

buyldynge ger *bildinge ger.* B 1
B.15.329 For þat þei beggen aboute in *buyldynge* þei spende,

buyr- > bur-; buyth > buggen; bukyngham > bokynghamshire

bukkes n *bukke n.* A 1; B 1; C 1 bokkes
A. 7.32 And [to] boris & [to] *bukkes* þat breken myn heggis,
B. 6.30 To bores and to [*bukkes*] þat breken myne hegges,
C. 8.29 To bores and to *bokkes* þat breketh adoun myn hegges

bulle n *bulle n.* A 6 bulle (4) bulles (1) bullis (1); B 9 bulle (6) bulles (3); C 9 bulle (7) bulles (2)
A.Pr.66 Brouȝte forþ a *bulle* wiþ bisshopis selis
A.Pr.70 Comen vp knelynge to kissen his *bulle*.
A. 3.137 Sire symonye & hireself seliþ þe *bullis*;
A. 8.67 Beggeris & bidderis ben not in þe *bulle*
A. 8.92 And I behynde hem boþe beheld al þe *b[u]lle*.
A. 8.170 [To purchace pardoun and þe popes *bulles*],
B.Pr.69 Brouȝte forþ a *bulle* wiþ Bisshopes seles,
B.Pr.73 Comen vp knelynge to kissen hi[s] *bull[e]*.
B. 3.148 Sire Symonie and hirselue seleþ [þe] *bulles*.
B. 5.640 I wol go fecche my box wiþ my breuettes & a *bulle* with bisshopes lettres
B. 7.39 And preiseden Piers þe Plowman þat purchaced þis *bulle*.
B. 7.65 Beggeres [and] bidderes beþ noȝt in þe *bulle*
B. 7.110 And I bihynde hem boþe biheld al þe *bulle*.
B. 7.192 To purchace pardon and þe popes *bulles*.
B.13.249 And þat his blessynge and hise *bulles* bocches myȝte destruye:
C.Pr.67 Brouth forth a *bulle* with bischopis selys
C.Pr.71 Comen [vp] knel[yng] to kyssen his *bull[e]*.
C. 3.186 For symonye and hereselue seleth [þe] *bulles*.
C. 9.42 And prey[se]de [Peres] the [plouhman] þat purchased þis *bull[e]*.
C. 9.61 Beggares and Biddares beth nat in þ[e] *bulle*
C. 9.160 Buth nat in this *bulle*,' quod [Peres], 'til they ben amended
C. 9.284 And y byhynde hem bothe byheld alle þe *bulle*.
C. 9.338 To pur[c]hace ȝow pardoun and the popes *bulles*.
C.15.218 For founde y þat his blessynge and his *bulle* [bocches] myhte [destruye],

bummiþ v *bomben v.* A 2 bummide (1) bummiþ (1); B 1 bummed; C 1 boumode
A. 5.137 And whoso *bummide* þerof, bouȝte it þereaftir,
A. 7.138 He abideþ wel þe betere þat *bummiþ* nouȝt to ofte.'
B. 5.221 And whoso *bummed* þerof bouȝte it þerafter,
C. 6.229 And hoso *boumode* therof bouhte hit þeraftur,

bunchide > bonched

burde n *birde n.(1)* A 1; B 3 burde (2) burdes (1); C 3 buyrde (2) buyrdes (1)
A. 3.14 Buski[de] hem to þe bour þere þe *burde* dwelliþ,
B. 3.14 Busked hem to þe bour þer þe *burde* dwelle[þ],
B.18.116 A ful benigne *burde* and Buxom of speche
B.19.135 The *burdes* þo songe, Saul interfecit mille et dauid decem milia.
C. 3.15 Boskede hem to þe bour ther th[e] *buyrde* dwel[leth],
C.20.119 A fol benyngne *buyrde* and buxum of speche.
C.21.135 The *buyrdes* tho songe, Saul interfecit mille & dauid decem milia.

burdoun n *burdoun n.* A 1; B 1; C 1 bordoun
A. 6.5 He bar a *burdoun* ybounde wiþ a brood list,
B. 5.517 He bar a *burdoun* ybounde wiþ a brood liste,
C. 7.162 He bar a *bordoun* ybounde with a brood liste,

burel adj *burel n.(1)* B 1
B.10.292 [Th]anne shul *burel* clerkes ben abasshed to blame yow or to greue,

burgages n *burgage n.* A 1; B 1; C 2
A. 3.75 Ne bouȝte none *burgages*, be ȝe wel certayn.
B. 3.86 Ne bouȝte none *burgages*, be ye [wel] certeyne.
C. 3.85 Ne bouhte none *burgages*, be ȝe ful certayn.
C. 3.105 Many *burgages* ybrent and bodies þerynne

burgeises n *burgeis n.* A 3 burgeis; B 6; C 3 burgeises (1) Burgeys (2)
A.Pr.96 Barouns [and] *burgeis* & bondage also
A. 3.144 Barouns & *burgeis* she bringeþ in sorewe;
A.10.138 Barouns & *burgeis*, & bondemen of tounes.
B.Pr.217 Barons and *Burgeises* and bond[age] als
B. 3.163 Barons and *Burgeises* she bryngeþ in sorwe,
B. 5.130 Amonges *Burgeises* haue I be, [bigg]yng at Londoun,
B.12.147 But in a *Burgeises* place, of Bethlem þe beste:
B.15.202 And buxome as of berynge to *burgeises* and to lordes,
B.15.343 Than *burgeises* þat riche ben as þe book techeþ,
C.Pr.223 As Barones and *Burgeys* and bondemen of thorpus.
C. 3.201 Trewe *Burgeys* and bonde he bryngeth to nauhte ofte
C.14.91 Bote in a *burgeises* hous], the beste of þe toune.

burgh n *burgh n.(1)* A 1; B 2; C 3 borw (2) borwes (1)
A.12.52 Til ȝe come to þe *burg[h]* quod bonum est tenete.
B. 2.88 In bargaynes and brocages wiþ þe *Burgh* of þefte,
B. 2.98 And breden as *Burgh* swyn, and bedden hem esily
C. 2.95 In bargaynes and Brocages with the *borw* of thefte,
C. 3.112 Hit is nat seemely, forsothe, in Citee [ne] in *borw* toun
C. 9.190 And in *borwes* among brewesteres and beggen in churches–

burye v *birien v.* B 7 burye (1) buried (1) buryed (4) buriede (1); C 2 burieden (1) yberied (1)
B.11.65 Be *buried* at hire hous but at my parisshe chirche;
B.11.67 [At kirke] þere a man were cristned by kynde he sholde be *buryed*.
B.11.74 Where my body were *buryed* by so ye hadde my siluer.
B.11.76 Whi youre Couent coueiteþ to confesse and to *burye*
B.12.256 And whan his caroyne shal come in caue to be *buryed*
B.13.9 And no corps in hir kirkȝerd n[e] in hir kirk was *buryed*
B.19.143 And siþen *buriede* his body, and beden þat men sholde
C.12.22 Wher my body were *yber[i]ed* by so ȝe hadde my [suluer].'
C.21.146 And sethen *bur[ie]den* his body and beden þat men sholde

burieles n *biriels n.* B 1; C 1 buyrielles
B.19.146 That þat blissede body of *burieles* [sholde risen]
C.21.146 That þat blessed body of *buyrielles* sholde ryse

buryinge ger *biriinge ger.* B 1
B.11.78 Baptiȝynge and *buryinge* boþe beþ ful nedefulle;

burioneþ v *bourjounen v.* B 1
B.15.75 And of þe braunches þat *burioneþ* of hem and bryngen men to helle,

burn n *bern n.(1)* B 7 buyrn (3) burn (2) burnes (2); C 6 bern (1) buyren (2) buyrn (1) buyrne (1) buirnes (1)
B. 3.267 *Burnes* and beestes, bren hem to deþe;
B. 3.321 Al shal be but oon court, and oon [*burn*] be Iustice;
B.11.362 Ther neiþer *burn* ne beest may hir briddes rechen.
B.12.65 As þe book bereþ witnesse to *burnes* þat kan rede:
B.16.180 'What berþ þat *buyrn*', quod I þo, 'so blisse þee bitide?'
B.16.250 Of a [*buyrn*] þat baptised hym–Iohan Baptist was his name–
B.16.263 Ne no *buyrn* be oure borgh, ne brynge vs fram his daunger–
C. 3.474 Al shal be but [o] couert and o [*buyrne*] be Iustice;
C. 6.247 So what *buyrn* of me borewede abouhte the tyme.'
C.15.155 Withoute brutteny[n]ge of *buyren* or eny bloed shedynge.
C.15.162 Shal neuere *buyren* be abasched þat hath this abouten hym
C.18.11 The whiche blosmes *buirnes* benigne speche hit calleth.
C.18.279 Ne noen *bern* ben oure borw ne bryngen vs [fro his] daunger–

burþe n *birthe n.* B 3; C 3 berthe (1) burthe (2)
B.12.149 And bad hem go to Bethlem goddes *burþe* to honoure
B.18.240 And tendeden [hire] as a torche to reuerensen his *burþe*;
B.19.81 For alle þe Aungeles of heuene at his *burþe* knelede,
C.14.93 And bad hem go to Bedlem goddes *berthe* to honoure
C.20.249 And tenden h[ere] as a torche to reuerensen his *burthe*;
C.21.81 For alle þe angelis of heuene at his *burthe* knelede

buschel > busshel; busy > bisy

busily adv *bisili adv.* A 2 busily (1) busyly (1); C 1 bisily
A.12.106 And so bad Iohan but *busily* wel ofte
A.12.107 When he saw þes sawes *busyly* alegged
C.11.153 [*Bisily*] bokes; ho beth his witnesses?

busken v *busken v.* A 2 busken (1) buskide (1); B 2 busked (1) buskeþ (1); C 2 boske (1) boskede (1)
A. 3.14 *Buski[de]* hem to þe bour þere þe burde dwelliþ,
A.10.168 *Busk[en* hem] to þat boot & biden þereInne
B. 3.14 *Busked* hem to þe bour þer þe burde dwelle[þ],

B. 9.137 *Buskeþ* yow to þat boot and bideþ þerInne
C. 3.15 *Boskede* hem to þe bour ther th[e] buyrde dwel[leth],
C.10.225 *Boske* ʒow to þat boet and abideth þerynne

buskes n *bush n.(1)* B 1; C 1 bosches
B.11.345 Briddes I biheld þat in *buskes* made nestes;
C.13.156 Briddes y beheld [þat] in *bosches* made nestes;

busmares > bismere

busshel n *busshel n.(1)* A 1; B 1; C 1 buschel
A. 7.57 'A *busshel* of breed corn br[yng m]e þereinne,
B. 6.62 'A *busshel* of bredcorn brynge me þerInne,
C. 8.61 A *buschel* of breedcorn brouht was þerynne.

but prep *but conj.* A 4; B 9; C 19 bot (1) bote (7) but (10) bute (1)
A. 1.21 Arn none nedful *but* þo & nempne hem I þenke,
A. 7.291 Laboureris þat haue no land [to] lyue on [*but*] here handis
A. 8.98 *But* do wel & haue wel, & god shal haue þi soule
A.10.193 Haue þei no children *but* ch[este], & choppis [betwene].
B. 1.21 Are none nedfulle *but* þo; and nempne hem I þynke
B. 6.307 Laborers þat haue no land to lyue on *but* hire handes
B. 7.116 *But* do wel and haue wel, and god shal haue þi soule,
B. 9.172 Haue þei no children *but* cheeste and [choppes] bitwene.
B.13.127 *But* Dilige deum and Domine quis habitabit;
B.13.150 Kynde loue coueiteþ noʒt no catel *but* speche.
B.14.296 Ne borweþ of hise neighebores *but* þat he may wel paie:
B.15.536 Baddely ybedded, no book *but* conscience,
B.15.537 Ne no richesse *but* þe roode to reioisse hem Inne:
C. 1.21 Aren non [ni]defole *but* tho and nemne hem y thenke
C. 2.139 That mede may be wedded to no man *bot* treuthe,
C. 2.178 Ac hakeneys hadde thei none *bote* hakeneys to huyre;
C. 5.41 Lyf þat me [l]ykede *but* in this longe clothes.
C. 5.52 Withoute bagge or botel *but* my wombe one.
C. 7.77 A wexeth wroth and wol not here *but* wordes of murthe;
C. 8.329 Laborers þat han no lond to lyue on *but* here handes
C. 9.90 And hath no catel *but* his craft to clothe h[e]m and to fede
C. 9.290 *Bote* do wel and haue wel, and [god] shal haue thy soule
C.10.209 And is no more to mene *but* men þat ben bygeten
C.10.274 Haen þei no childerne *bute* cheste and [c]hoppes hem bitwene.
C.10.293 *Bote* wyues and wedded men, as holy writ techeth:
C.15.134 *Bote* dilige deum & p[roximu]m [and] domine quis habitabit
C.15.136 *Bote* lele loue and treuthe that loth is to be founde.'
C.16.131 Ne boreweth of his neyhebore *but* þat he may wel paye
C.17.116 *Bo[t]e* they fayle in philosophie and philosoferes lyuede:
C.17.197 Baddeliche ybedded, no boek *but* Consience
C.17.198 Ne no rychesse *but* þe rode to reioysen hem ynne:
C.20.87 *Bote* this blynde bacheler that bar hym thorw the herte.

but conj *but conj.* A 99; B 266; C 268 bote (122) but (135) bute (11)
    A.Pr.5, A.Pr.63, A.1.81, A.1.100, A.1.144, A.1.155, A.1.161, A.1.172, A.2.93, A.2.150, A.2.151, A.2.159, A.3.102, A.3.167, A.3.235, A.3.253, A.3.267, A.4.5, A.4.45, A.4.58, A.4.95, A.4.96, A.4.110, A.4.115, A.4.125, A.4.140, A.4.143, A.4.149, A.5.50, A.5.52, A.5.57, A.5.57, A.5.105, A.5.112, A.5.144, A.5.222, A.5.243, A.6.2, A.6.57, A.6.62, A.6.63, A.6.78, A.6.112, A.6.114, A.7.1, A.7.12, A.7.16, A.7.39, A.7.46, A.7.110, A.7.130, A.7.265, A.7.286, A.7.288, A.7.290, A.7.294, A.7.296, A.8.21, A.8.41, A.8.68, A.8.69, A.8.74, A.8.111, A.8.117, A.8.177, A.9.44, A.9.74, A.9.96, A.9.100, A.9.105, A.9.114, A.10.51, A.10.55, A.10.67, A.10.99, A.10.189, A.10.194, A.10.196, A.10.199, A.10.203, A.10.212, A.10.215, A.11.11, A.11.18, A.11.48, A.11.90, A.11.98, A.11.133, A.11.225, A.11.257, A.12.6, A.12.14, A.12.29, A.12.33, A.12.67, A.12.74, A.12.75, A.12.90

    B.Pr.66, B.Pr.131, B.Pr.190, B.Pr.206, B.1.83, B.1.102, B.1.121, B.1.170, B.1.181, B.1.187, B.1.198, B.2.24, B.2.48, B.2.129, B.2.189, B.2.198, B.3.108, B.3.113, B.3.180, B.3.256, B.3.307, B.3.318, B.3.321, B.4.5, B.4.58, B.4.72, B.4.108, B.4.109, B.4.127, B.4.132, B.4.142, B.4.164, B.4.182, B.4.186, B.5.33, B.5.67, B.5.69, B.5.74, B.5.74, B.5.125, B.5.128, B.5.196, B.5.228, B.5.233, B.5.236, B.5.260, B.5.286, B.5.288, B.5.388, B.5.395, B.5.400, B.5.413, B.5.417, B.5.422, B.5.432, B.5.450, B.5.469, B.5.490, B.5.514, B.5.570, B.5.575, B.5.591, B.5.627, B.5.629, B.6.1, B.6.17, B.6.18, B.6.51, B.6.118, B.6.136, B.6.145, B.6.149, B.6.281, B.6.302, B.6.304, B.6.306, B.6.310, B.6.312, B.6.331, B.7.66, B.7.67, B.7.84, B.7.92, B.7.129, B.7.135, B.7.199, B.8.48, B.8.56, B.8.83, B.8.106, B.8.110, B.8.115, B.8.124, B.9.79, B.9.154, B.9.168, B.9.173, B.9.175, B.9.180, B.9.190, B.9.201, B.10.11, B.10.18, B.10.39, B.10.62, B.10.84, B.10.137, B.10.145, B.10.181, B.10.246, B.10.254, B.10.263, B.10.281, B.10.308, B.10.309, B.10.315, B.10.337, B.10.343, B.10.348, B.10.364, B.10.372, B.10.373, B.10.376, B.10.408, B.10.443, B.10.456, B.10.477, B.11.41, B.11.65, B.11.72, B.11.135, B.11.145, B.11.156, B.11.173, B.11.175, B.11.204, B.11.221, B.11.223, B.11.294, B.11.299, B.11.392, B.11.431, B.12.15, B.12.27, B.12.28, B.12.36, B.12.56, B.12.58, B.12.90, B.12.100, B.12.107, B.12.115, B.12.127, B.12.135, B.12.137, B.12.138, B.12.144, B.12.147, B.12.182, B.12.201, B.12.205, B.12.288, B.12.290, B.13.10, B.13.12, B.13.45, B.13.93, B.13.96, B.13.110, B.13.147, B.13.168, B.13.172, B.13.203, B.13.257, B.13.341, B.13.366, B.13.380, B.13.417, B.14.1, B.14.39, B.14.47, B.14.58, B.14.93, B.14.97, B.14.119, B.14.155, B.14.195, B.14.198, B.14.243, B.14.245, B.14.246, B.14.250, B.14.253, B.14.294, B.15.59, B.15.108, B.15.121, B.15.130, B.15.162, B.15.175, B.15.180, B.15.198, B.15.210, B.15.212, B.15.237, B.15.240, B.15.249, B.15.278, B.15.282, B.15.376, B.15.377, B.15.391, B.15.421, B.15.464,

B.15.464, B.15.514, B.15.575, B.16.26, B.16.194, B.16.217, B.16.222, B.16.224, B.17.30, B.17.70, B.17.86, B.17.130, B.17.154, B.17.184, B.17.186, B.17.227, B.17.249, B.17.266, B.17.273, B.17.305, B.18.28, B.18.85, B.18.16, B.18.142, B.18.170, B.18.249, B.18.255, B.18.259, B.18.286, B.18.349, B.18.395, B.18.398, B.18.406, B.19.37, B.19.77, B.19.117, B.19.122, B.19.220, B.19.254, B.19.299, B.19.359, B.19.404, B.19.405, B.19.407, B.19.421, B.19.453, B.19.470, B.19.476, B.20.247, B.20.261, B.20.321, B.20.342

    C.Pr.36, C.Pr.64, C.Pr.214, C.1.79, C.1.100, C.1.166, C.1.177, C.1.183, C.1.193, C.2.26, C.2.51, C.2.144, C.2.203, C.2.212, C.2.249, C.3.59, C.3.150, C.3.209, C.3.226, C.3.295, C.3.305, C.3.306, C.3.381, C.3.397, C.3.460, C.3.471, C.3.474, C.4.5, C.4.41, C.4.61, C.4.103, C.4.124, C.4.129, C.4.159, C.4.180, C.4.185, C.4.190, C.5.9, C.5.66, C.5.91, C.5.135, C.5.161, C.6.8, C.6.10, C.6.85, C.6.90, C.6.93, C.6.113, C.6.174, C.6.174, C.6.204, C.6.265, C.6.343, C.7.4, C.7.16, C.7.28, C.7.35, C.7.45, C.7.64, C.7.75, C.7.159, C.7.217, C.7.222, C.7.238, C.7.282, C.7.307, C.8.15, C.8.36, C.8.49, C.8.125, C.8.143, C.8.146, C.8.196, C.8.201, C.8.214, C.8.303, C.8.324, C.8.326, C.8.328, C.8.332, C.8.334, C.8.352, C.9.16, C.9.45, C.9.62, C.9.63, C.9.67, C.9.99, C.9.161, C.9.195, C.9.234, C.9.237, C.9.240, C.9.276, C.9.292, C.9.345, C.10.39, C.10.80, C.10.99, C.10.106, C.10.106, C.10.111, C.10.120, C.10.158, C.10.164, C.10.258, C.10.261, C.10.264, C.10.275, C.10.277, C.10.280, C.10.290, C.10.300, C.11.9, C.11.15, C.11.42, C.11.64, C.11.70, C.11.75, C.11.77, C.11.83, C.11.121, C.11.129, C.11.152, C.11.155, C.11.239, C.11.245, C.11.308, C.12.16, C.12.20, C.12.70, C.12.80, C.12.95, C.12.96, C.12.112, C.12.180, C.12.182, C.12.199, C.12.227, C.12.235, C.13.40, C.13.55, C.13.66, C.13.108, C.13.113, C.13.164, C.13.238, C.14.18, C.14.30, C.14.36, C.14.45, C.14.52, C.14.60, C.14.79, C.14.82, C.14.83, C.14.88, C.14.91, C.14.122, C.14.134, C.14.140, C.14.144, C.14.160, C.14.210, C.14.212, C.15.12, C.15.15, C.15.22, C.15.50, C.15.100, C.15.103, C.15.118, C.15.124, C.15.128, C.15.129, C.15.147, C.15.153, C.15.197, C.15.211, C.15.227, C.15.238, C.15.257, C.15.284, C.15.295, C.16.36, C.16.39, C.16.67, C.16.83, C.16.85, C.16.86, C.16.90, C.16.93, C.16.129, C.16.155, C.16.180, C.16.220, C.16.221, C.16.262, C.16.277, C.16.296, C.16.362, C.16.365, C.16.374, C.17.8, C.17.24, C.17.30, C.17.32, C.17.41, C.17.42, C.17.112, C.17.136, C.17.242, C.17.265, C.17.308, C.18.19, C.18.81, C.18.203, C.18.219, C.18.233, C.19.31, C.19.38, C.19.69, C.19.94, C.19.99, C.19.128, C.19.129, C.19.147, C.19.150, C.19.152, C.19.193, C.19.215, C.19.237, C.19.254, C.19.285, C.20.27, C.20.109, C.20.145, C.20.173, C.20.258, C.20.264, C.20.267, C.20.312, C.20.315, C.20.352, C.20.395, C.20.406, C.20.438, C.20.441, C.20.449, C.21.37, C.21.77, C.21.117, C.21.122, C.21.220, C.21.254, C.21.299, C.21.359, C.21.404, C.21.405, C.21.407, C.21.421, C.21.453, C.21.470, C.21.476, C.22.247, C.22.261, C.22.321, C.22.342

but &> iohan_but; bute > but; buth > ben; butte > bette

buttre n *butere n.* B 1; C 1 Botere
B. 5.437 Boþ[e] bred and ale, *buttre*, melk and chese
C. 7.51 Bothe Bred and ale, *Botere*, mylke and chese

buxom adj *buxom adj.* A 4 buxum; B 9 buxom (7) buxome (1) buxum (1); C 6 buxum
A. 1.108 To be *buxum* at his bidding; he bad hem nouʒt ellis.
A. 2.52 At bedde & at boord *buxum* and hende,
A. 3.245 To be *buxum* & boun his bidding to fulfille.
A. 6.53 And so bo[wiþ] forþ be a [brok], be *buxum* of speche.
B. 1.110 To be *buxom* at his biddyng, he bad hem nouʒt ellis.
B. 3.265 Be *buxom* at his biddynge his wil to fulfille.
B. 5.566 And so boweþ forþ by a brook, beþ-*buxom*-of-speche.
B. 6.194 And many a beggere for benes *buxom* was to swynke,
B.13.251 And *buxom* and busy aboute breed and drynke
B.14.222 And *buxom* at hi[s] biddyn[g] for his broke loues,
B.15.202 And *buxome* as of berynge to burgeises and to lordes,
B.16.7 The blosmes beþ *buxom* speche and benigne lokynge.
B.18.116 A ful benigne burde and *Buxom* of speche.
C. 3.418 To be *buxum* at my byddyng his [b]o[n]e to fulfille.
C. 7.213 And so [boweth] forth by [a] brok, [beth-*buxum*-of-speche],
C. 9.221 Vnder obedience to be and *buxum* to þe lawe:
C.15.222 And thenne wolde y be bysy and *buxum* to helpe
C.16.63 And *buxum* at his biddyng for his breed and his drynke
C.20.119 A fol benyngne buyrde and *buxum* of speche.

buxomliche adv *buxonli adv.* B 2; C 2 buximliche
B.12.112 *Buxomliche* and benigneliche and bidden it of grace.
B.12.195 [Th]at *buxomliche* biddeþ it and ben in wille to amenden hem.
C.14.57 *Buxumliche* and benyngnelyche and bidden hit of grace.
C.17.283 Euery bisshope bi þe lawe sholde *buxumliche* walke

buxomnesse n *buxomnesse n.* A 2 buxumnesse; B 4; C 3 buxumnesse
A. 1.111 Til he brak *buxumnesse* þoruʒ bost of hymseluen.
A. 4.150 ʒif it be þat *buxumnesse* be at myn assent.'
B. 1.113 Til] he brak *buxomnesse*; his blisse gan he tyne
B. 4.187 If ye bidden *buxomnesse* be of myn assent.'
B.10.308 But al is *buxomnesse* þere and bokes, to rede and to lerne].
B.14.223 And *buxomnesse* and boost [ben] eueremoore at werre,
C. 7.239 The barres aren of *buxumnesse* as bretherne of o wombe;
C.16.64 And *buxumnesse* and b[o]est [b]en eueremore at werre
C.20.320 And dust hem breke here *buxumnesse* thorw fals bihestes

buxum(- > buxom(-

C

c letter *c n.* A 1; B 1

A. 8.120   'Abstinence þe abbesse myn a b *c* me tauʒte,
B. 7.138   'Abstynence þe Abbesse myn a b *c* me tauʒte,

caas n *cas n.* A 3 cas; B 4 caas (3) cas (1); C 12 caes (3) case (8) kaes (1)

A. 3.258   Þe culorum of þis [*cas*] kepe I not to shewe;
A. 8.51   Counfortiþ hym in þat *cas*, coueitiþ nouʒt his goodis,
A.11.237   Þat arn vncristene in þat *cas* may cristene an heþene,
B. 3.280   The culorum of þis *cas* kepe I noʒt to [shewe];
B. 7.49   Conforteþ hym in þat *caas*, [coueiteþ noʒt hise] ʒiftes,
B.10.354   That [arn] vncristene in þat *caas* may cristen an heþen,
B.20.14   And he [cacche] in þat *caas* and come þerto by sleighte
C. 3.337   Acordaunce in kynde, in *case* and in nombre
C. 3.347   In kynde and in *case* and in cours of nombre.
C. 3.357   In *case*, credere in ecclesia, in holy kyrke to bileue;
C. 3.365   And withoute *ca[s]e* to cache [to] and come to bothe nombres,
C. 3.387   And halt hem vnstedefast for hem lakkeþ *case*.
C. 3.389   Of the cours of *case* so thei cache suluer.
C. 3.395   That is vnite, acordaun[c]e in *case*, in gendre and in noumbre,
C. 3.399   And coueyte þe *case*, when thei couthe vnderstande,
C. 3.433   The culorum of this *kaes* kepe y nat to shewe;
C. 9.48   That conforteth suche in eny *caes* and coueyteth nat he[re] ʒiftes
C. 9.155   And can eny craft in *caes* he wolde hit vse,
C.22.14   And he cacche in þat *caes* and come therto by sleithe

cabane n *caban n.* A 2 caban; B 1

A. 3.178   Crope into a *caban* for cold of þi nailes;
A.12.35   Clergie into a *caban* crepte anon after,
B. 3.191   Crope into a *Cabane* for cold of þi nayles;

cacchen v *cacchen v.* A 4 cacche; B 23 cacche (11) cacchen (1) caccheþ (2) cacheþ (1) caught (2) caughte (1) cauʒte (2) kauʒte (3); C 17 cacche (5) cach (1) cache (4) cacheth (1) caught (1) cauht (2) cauhte (3)

A. 2.154   'Be crist,' quaþ þe king, '& I miʒte *cacche*
A. 7.128   [*Cacche* cowes] from his corn, [and] kepen hise bestis,
A. 7.183   Al for coueitise of his corn to [*cacche*] awey hungir.
A.11.87   And now comiþ a conyon & wolde *cacche* of my wittes
B.Pr.107   Ac of þe Cardinals at court þat *kauʒte* þat name,
B.Pr.189   [The while he *caccheþ* conynges he coueiteþ noʒt [o]ure caroyne
B.Pr.207   Coupled and vncoupled to *cacche* what þei mowe.
B. 2.36   How construeþ David þe kyng of men þat [*caccheþ*] Mede,
B. 2.193   'By crist!' quod þe kyng, 'and I *cacche* myʒte
B. 5.256   That wolde kille hem if he *cacche* hem myʒte for coueitise of hir skynnes
B. 5.351   Clement þe Cobelere *kauʒte* hym by þe myddel
B.11.174   For no cause to *cacche* siluer þerby, ne to be called a maister,
B.11.405   Tho *cauʒte* I colour anoon and comsed to ben ashamed
B.12.100   Na moore kan no Clerk but if he *cauʒte* it first þoruʒ bokes.
B.12.141   And clennesse shal *cacchen* it and clerkes shullen it fynde:
B.12.177   How contricion is comended for it *cacheþ* awey synne:
B.12.222   Wherof þei *cacche* hir colours so clere and so briʒte,
B.12.242   For pursue a pecok or a pehen to *cacche*,
B.13.298   And large to lene, [loos] þerby to *cacche*].
B.13.334   That I *cacche* þe crampe, þe Cardiacle som tyme,
B.13.404   'And *kauʒte* siknesse somtyme for my [surfetes] ofte
B.14.239   And if Coueitise *cacche* þe poore þei may noʒt come togideres,
B.16.152   And kiste hym to be *caught* þerby and kulled of þe Iewes.
B.17.223   As dooþ a kex or a candle þat *caught* haþ fir and blaseþ,
B.19.128   Thus he confortede carefulle and *caughte* a gretter name
B.20.14   And he [*cacche*] in þat caas and come þerto by sleighte
B.20.222   'I counte na moore Conscience by so I *cacche* siluer
C.Pr.134   Ac of þe Cardinales at Court þat *caught* han such a name
C. 2.207   'Now, by crist!' quod þe kyng, 'and y *cacche* myhte
C. 3.365   And withoute ca[s]e to *cache* [to] and come to bothe nombres,
C. 3.389   Of the cours of case so thei *cache* suluer.
C. 6.78   That y *cache* þe crompe, the cardiacle sume tyme
C. 6.40   Clement þe coblere *cauhte* hym by þe myddel
C.10.297   Awayten and wasten alle þat they *cacche* mowe;
C.13.213   Tho *cauhte* y colour anoen and comesede to ben aschamed
C.14.86   And clennesse shal *cach* hit and clerkes shollen hit fynde:
C.14.117   How contricioun is comended for hit *cacheth* awey synne:

C.14.174   For pursue a pocok or a pohen to *cacche*
C.16.79   And thogh coueytyse [*cacche*] þe pore they may nat come togyderes
C.18.169   And kuste iesus to be knowe þerby and *cauht* of þe iewes.
C.19.189   A[s] doth a kix [o]r a candle þat *cauht* hath fuyr and blaseth,
C.21.128   Thus he comfortede carefole and *cauhte* a grettere name,
C.22.14   And he *cacche* in þat caes and come therto by sleithe
C.22.222   'Y counte no more Consience bi so y *cache* suluer

cachepol n *cacche-pol n.* B 2; C 2

B.18.46   'Crucifige!' quod a *Cachepol*, '[he kan of wicchecraft]!'
B.18.73   A *Cachepol* cam forþ and craked boþe hir legges
C.20.46   'Crucifige!' q[uo]d a *cachepol*, 'he can of wycchecrafte!'
C.20.75   A *cachepol* cam [forth] a[nd] craked ato he[re] legges

cacheþ > cacchen; caes > caas

caym n prop *Caim n.* A 11 caym (6) caymes (1) kaym (2) kaymes (2); B 10 Caym (7) Caymes (2) Kaym (1); C 9 Caym (7) Caymes (1) Caymus (1)

A. 1.64   Counseilid *kaym* to kiln his broþer,
A.10.140   Ben conseyuid in cursid tyme as *kaym* was on Eue:
A.10.148   *Caym* þei hym callide, in cursid tyme engendrit.
A.10.151   Alle þat comen of þat *caym* crist hatid aftir,
A.10.154   For þei mariede men wiþ curside men of *caymes* kyn.
A.10.155   For alle þat comen of þat *caym* acursid þei were,
A.10.158   To kepe his kynrede fro *kaymes*, þei couplide nouʒt togideris,
A.10.159   And siþen se[þ] & his suster [sed] wern spousid to *kaymes*;
A.10.170   Clene awey þe cursid blood þat *caym* haþ ymakid.
A.10.172   Þat euere curside *caym* com on þis erþe;
A.10.178   [Þus] þoruʒ curside *caym* cam care vpon alle,
B. 1.66   Counseilled *Kaym* to killen his broþer,
B. 9.123   Conceyued ben in [cursed] tyme as *Caym* was on Eue
B. 9.126   And alle þat come of þat *Caym* come to yuel ende,
B. 9.129   And noʒt þi kynde wiþ *Caymes* ycoupled n[e] yspoused".
B. 9.131   *Caymes* kynde and his kynde coupled togideres,
B. 9.139   Clene awey þe corsed blood þat *Caym* haþ ymaked.
B. 9.141   That euere cursed *Caym* coom on þis erþe:
B. 9.156   And þus þoruʒ cursed *Caym* cam care vpon erþe,
B. 9.188   Noʒt as Adam and Eue whan *Caym* was engendred;
B.10.334   Ac er þat kyng come *Caym* shal awake,
C. 1.62   Conseylede *Caym* to cullen his brother,
C.10.213   *Caym* þe corsede creature conseyued was in synne
C.10.218   So was *Caym* conseyued and so ben corsed wreches
C.10.220   Alle þat come of *Caym* Caytyue[s] were euere
C.10.221   And for þe synne of *Caymes* seed sayede god to Noe:
C.10.227   Clene awey þe corsed bloed þat of *Caym* spronge,
C.10.229   That euere corsed *Caym* cam on þis erthe;
C.10.247   Aftur þat *Caym* þ[e] corsed hadde ykuld abel,
C.10.251   Soffre his seed seden with *Caymus* seed his brother.

cayphas n prop *n.i.d.* B 1; C 1

B.19.140   [Her]of *Cayphas* hadde enuye and oþere Iewes,
C.21.140   Hereof hadde *Cayphas* enuye and oþer iewes

caiser- > kaiser

cairen v *cairen v.* A 3 cairen (1) cairiþ (2); B 3 cairen (1) caireþ (1) kaireþ (1); C 2 cayren (1) kayres (1)

A.Pr.29   Coueite not in cuntre to *cairen* aboute,
A. 4.22   Þanne consience on his capil *cairiþ* forþ faste,
A. 5.147   And *ca[iriþ]* hym to [k]ir[k]eward hise [coupe] to shewe.
B.Pr.29   Coueiten noʒt in contree to [*cairen*]
B. 4.24   Thanne Conscience [o]n his capul [*caireþ*] forþ faste,
B. 5.297   And [*kaireþ*] hym to kirkeward his coupe to shewe.
C.Pr.31   Coueyten noʒt in contre[y] to *cayren* aboute
C. 6.351   And *kayres* hym to kyrkeward his coup[e] to shewe.

caytif n *caitif n.* A 1 caitif; B 5 caytif (3) caytyues (2); C 8 Caytif (1) Caytyf (2) Caytyfs (1) Caitifues (1) Caytyues (2) kaytif (1)

A. 5.114   'I haue [ben] coueit[ous],' quaþ [þat *caitif*], 'I [bi]knowe [hit] h[e]re,
B. 5.198   'I haue ben coueitous', quod þis *caytif*, 'I biknowe it here.
B.11.130   As a reneyed *caytif* recchelesly rennen aboute.
B.18.93   Callede hem *caytyues*, acorsed for euere,

B.18.96   Cursede *cayt[yues]*! knyghthood was it neuere
B.19.403   '*Caytif*!' quod Conscience, 'cursede wrecche!
C. 6.206   'Y haue be couetous,' quod this *kaytif*, 'y biknowe hit here.
C. 8.243   "The slowe *Caytif* for colde wolde no corn tylye;
C.10.220   Alle þat come of Caym *Caytyue[s]* were euere
C.12.65   As a [reneyed] *Caytyf* [rechelesliche rennen aboute].
C.14.90   Ne in no cote ne *Caytyfs* hous [crist was ybore
C.20.96   Calde hem *Caytyues*, acorsed for euere.
C.20.99   Corsede *Caytifues*! knyhthoed was hit neuere
C.21.403   '*Caytyf*!' quod Consience, 'corsede wreche!

caytif adj *caitif adj.* B 1; C 1
B.11.296   It is a careful kny3t, and of a *caytif* kynges makyng,
C.13.110   For hit is a carfol knyhte and of a *Caytif* kynges makynge

caitifliche adv *caitifli adv.* B 1; C 2 caytifliche
B.11.239   Ac by cloþyng þei knewe hym no3t, [so *caitifliche* he yede].
C. 3.242   *Caytifliche* thow, Consience, conseiledest þe kyng leten
C.12.128   Ac by clothyng they knewe hym nat, so *caytifliche* he 3ede.

caytiftee > cheitiftee; caytyues > caytif

cake n *cake n.* A 2; B 1; C 1
A. 7.179   Hungir hem helide wiþ an hot[e] *cake*.
A. 7.266   A fewe cruddis & crem, & [a]n [hauer] *cake*,
B. 6.282   A fewe cruddes and creme and [a *cake* of otes],
C. 8.304   A fewe croddes and craym and a *cake* of otes

cakebreed n *cake n.* B 1 Cakebreed
B.16.229   Calues flessh and *Cakebreed*; and knewe what I þou3te.

calabre n *Calabre n.* A 1; B 1; C 1 callabre
A. 7.254   And ek his cloke [of] *calabre* & þe knoppis of gold,
B. 6.270   And his cloke of *Calabre* [and] þe knappes of golde,
C. 8.291   And his cloke of *callabre* for his comune[s] legge

calculed ptp *calculen v.* B 1; C 1 kalculed
B.15.371   Of þat was *calculed* of þe element þe contrarie þei fynde.
C.17.107   Of þat was *kalculed* of þe clymat the contrarie þey fynde.

cald(e > callen

caleis n prop *n.i.d.* A 1; B 1
A. 3.183   And bar here bras on þi bak to *caleis* to selle,
B. 3.196   And bere hire bras at þi bak to *Caleis* to selle,

calf n *calf n.(1)* A 1; B 6 calf (4) calues (2); C 1
A. 7.271   And ek a cow & a *calf*, & a carte mare
B. 6.287   And ek a cow and a *calf*, and a cart mare
B.15.465   And wiþ *calues* flessh he fedde þe folk þat he louede.
B.15.466   The *calf* bitokneþ clennesse in hem þat kepeþ lawes,
B.15.467   For as þe Cow þoru3 kynde mylk þe *calf* norisseþ til an Oxe,
B.15.470   Right as þe cow *calf* coueiteþ [swete melk]
B.16.229   *Calues* flessh and Cakebreed; and knewe what I þou3te.
C. 8.310   And a cow with a *calf* and a cart m[a]re

callabre > calabre

callen v *callen v.* A 13 calde (1) calle (1) called (2) callen (2) callid (1)
    callide (4) calliþ (1) ycald (1); B 52 calle (4) called (35) callede (5)
    callen (3) calleþ (3) ycalled (2); C 52 cald (10) calde (16) calle (3)
    called (1) callede (2) callen (1) calleth (6) callide (1) kald (1) kalde (1)
    ycald (5) ycalde (2) ykald (3)
A. 1.4   Com doun fro þat [clyf] & *callide* me faire,
A. 3.3   Þe king *calliþ* a clerk–I can not his name–
A. 3.30   And in constory at court *callen* here names.
A. 3.90   Þe king fro counseil com & *callide* aftir mede
A. 3.103   Þanne was consience *callid* to comen & aperen
A. 4.17   And *calde* catoun his knaue, curteis of speche:
A. 4.140   But he be cokewald, *callid*, kitte of my nose.'
A. 6.20   'Knowist þou ou3t a corseint,' quaþ þei, 'þat men *callen* treuþe?
A. 9.62   Com & *callide* me be my kynde name.
A.10.25   'What *calle* 3e þat castel,' quaþ I, 'þat kynde haþ ymakid?
A.10.148   Caym þei hym *callide*, in cursid tyme engendrit.
A.12.49   She *called* me a clerioun þat
A.12.84   Þat on is *called* cotidian, a courrour of oure hous;
B.Pr.104   That Cardinals ben *called* and closynge yates
B. 1.4   Cam doun from [þe] Castel and *called* me faire,
B. 3.3   The kyng *called* a clerk–[I kan] no3t his name–
B. 3.31   And in Consistorie at court *callen* hire names.
B. 3.101   The kyng fro conseil cam and *called* after Mede
B. 3.114   [Th]anne was Conscience *called* to come and appere
B. 4.17   And *called* Caton his knaue, curteis of speche,
B. 4.166   For þe mooste commune of þat court *called* hire an hore.
B. 4.171   The kyng *callede* Conscience and afterward Reson
B. 5.532   'Knowestow au3t a corsaint', [quod þei], 'þat men *calle* truþe?
B. 7.93   And bryngen forþ barnes þat bastardes men *calleþ*.
B. 8.71   Cam and *called* me by my kynde name.

B.10.293   And carpen no3t as þei carpe now, [and] *calle* yow doumbe
             houndes:
B.11.13   Concupiscencia carnis men *called* þe elder mayde
B.11.14   And Coueitise of ei3es [þat ooþer was *ycalled*].
B.11.174   For no cause to cacche siluer þerby, ne to be *called* a maister,
B.11.192   'Ac *calleþ* hem carefulle þerto, þe croked and þe pouere;
B.11.205   In þe olde lawe, as [þe] lettre telleþ, mennes sones men *calle[d]* vs
B.13.31   Conscience *called* hym In and curteisliche seide
B.13.37   Conscience *called* after mete and þanne cam Scripture
B.15.22   'What are ye *called*', quod I, 'in þat court among cristes peple?'
B.15.23   'The whiles I quykne þe cors', quod he, '*called* am I anima';
B.15.25   And for þat I kan [and] knowe *called* am I mens;
B.15.32   Thanne am I Conscience *ycalled*, goddes clerk and his Notarie;
B.15.39   How þow coueitest to *calle* me, now þow knowest [alle] my
             names.
B.15.431   Crist *calleþ* hem salt for cristene soules,
B.15.594   And vnder stoon deed and stank; wiþ stif vois hym *callede*:
B.16.135   Of preieres and of parfitnesse þis place þat ye *callen*:
B.16.245   And *called* me foot of his feiþ, his folk for to saue
B.17.53   Comynge from a contree þat men *called* Ierico;
B.17.76   Herberwed hym at an hostrie and þe hostiler *called*:
B.18.93   *Callede* hem caytyues, acorsed for euere.
B.18.426   And *callede* kytte my wif and Calote my doghter:
B.19.9   And þanne *called* I Conscience to kenne me þe soþe:
B.19.15   'Why *calle* [ye] hym crist, siþen Iewes *calle[d]* hym Iesus?
B.19.15   'Why *calle* [ye] hym crist, siþen Iewes *calle[d]* hym Iesus?
B.19.23   And ye *callen* hym crist; for what cause, telleþ me.
B.19.28   To be *called* a knyght is fair for men shul knele to hym.
B.19.29   To be *called* a kyng is fairer for he may knyghtes make.
B.19.30   Ac to be conquerour *called*, þat comeþ of special grace,
B.19.48   Tho was he Iesus of Iewes *called*, gentile prophete,
B.19.53   And þo was he conquerour *called* of quyke and of dede,
B.19.62   He may [be wel] *called* conquerour, and þat is crist to mene.
B.19.85   Maistres and lettred men, Magi hem *callede*.
B.19.117   And þanne was he [cleped and] *called* no3t [oonly] crist but Iesu,
B.19.132   And þo was he *called* in contre of þe comune peple,
B.19.136   Forþi þe contree þer Iesu cam *called* hym fili dauid.
B.19.328   And *called* þat hous vnitee, holy chirche on englissh.
B.20.5   That afrounted me foule and faitour me *called*.
B.20.243   And curteisliche conforted hem and *called* in alle freres,
B.20.282   Ben Curatours *called* to knowe and to hele,
B.20.304   Conscience *called* a leche þat koude wel shryue:
C.Pr.132   That Cardinales ben *cald* and closyng 3ates
C. 1.4   Cam doun fro þe castel and *calde* me by name
C. 3.3   The kyng *callede* a clerke–y can nat his name–
C. 3.34   And in constorie at court do *calle* 3oure names.
C. 3.128   The kyng fram conseyl come [and] *calde* aftur mede
C. 3.151   Thenne was Consience *ykald* to come and apere
C. 3.402   And coueytede oure kynde and be *kald* in oure name–
C. 4.17   And *kalde* Catoun his knaue, Corteys of speche,
C. 4.161   For þe comune *calde* here queynte comune hore.
C. 5.162   He loketh al lourynge and lordeyne hym *calleth*.
C. 7.177   'Knowest thow auht a corsent,' quod they, 'þat men *calleth* treuthe?
C. 9.214   Kyndeliche, by Crist, ben suche *ycald* lollares.
C. 9.250   And fo[r] þe cloth þat keuereth hym *ykald* is a frere,
C.10.69   Cam and *calde* me be my kynde name.
C.11.172   Concupiscencia carnis men *calde* þ[e] eldre maide
C.11.173   And coueyitise-of-yes *ycalde* was þat oþer.
C.12.104   "Ac *calleth* the carefole þerto, the crokede and the pore;
C.12.113   In þe olde lawe, as þe lettre telleth, mennes sones me *calde* vs
C.14.14   Is *ycalde* Caritas, kynde loue an engelysche,
C.15.42   Clergie *cald* aftur mete and thenne cam scripture
C.15.80   Ac y wiste neuere freke þat frere is *ycald* of þe fyue mendynant3
C.15.302   And lordes and ladyes ben *cald* for ledes þat they haue
C.16.183   And whiles y quyke þe cors *ycald* am y Anima;
C.16.185   And [for] þat y can and knowe *ycald* am y [mens];
C.16.192   Thenne am y Concience *ycald*, goddes Clerk and his notarie;
C.16.201   How þou coueytest to *calle* me, now þou knowest al my namus.
C.18.11   The whiche blosmes buirnes benigne speche hit *calleth*.
C.18.12   And þerof cometh a goed fruyt þe wiche men *calleth* werkes
C.18.14   The whiche is Caritas *ykald*, Cristes oune fode,
C.18.80   That [lyf Actiua] lettred men in here langage *calleth*.'
C.19.51   Comynge fram a contraye þat men *calde* Ierico;
C.20.96   *Calde* hem Caytyues, acorsed for euere.
C.20.469   And *calde* kitte my wyf and Calote my douhter:
C.21.9   And thenne *calde* y Consience to kenne me þe sothe:
C.21.15   'Whi *calle* 3e hym Crist sennes iewes callede hym iesus?
C.21.15   'Whi *calle* 3e hym Crist sennes iewes *callede* hym iesus?
C.21.23   And 3e *callen* hym Crist; for what cause, telleth me.
C.21.28   To be *cald* a knyht is fayr for men shal knele to hym;
C.21.29   To be *cald* a kyng is fairor for he may knyhtes make;
C.21.30   Ac to be conquerour *cald*, þat cometh of special grace
C.21.48   Tho was he iesu[s] of iewes [*cald*], gentel profete,

C.21.53   And tho was he conquerour *cald* of quyke and of dede
C.21.62   He may be wel *called* conquerour and that is Crist to mene.
C.21.85   Maistres & lettred men, Magi hem *calde*.
C.21.117   And tho was he cleped and *calde* not [onl]y Crist but iesu,
C.21.132   And tho was he *cald* in contreye of þe comune peple,
C.21.136   Forthy þe contre þer iesu cam *calde* hym fili dauid
C.21.328   And *calde* þat hous vnite, holy chirche an englisch.
C.22.5   That afrounted me foule and faytour me *calde*.
C.22.243   And cortey[s]liche confortede hem and *calde* in all freres
C.22.282   Ben curatours *cald* to knowe and to hele,
C.22.304   Consience *calde* a leche þat couthe wel shryue:

calote n prop *n.i.d.* B 1; C 1
B.18.426   And callede kytte my wif and *Calote* my doghter:
C.20.469   And calde kitte my wyf and *Calote* my douhter:

caluarie n prop *Calvarie n.* A 2; B 7 Caluarie (6) caluarye (1); C 5
            Caluary (1) Caluarie (4)
A. 5.236   'Crist, þat on *caluarie* vpon þe [cros] diȝedist,
A.11.28   On crois vpon *caluarie*, as clerkis vs techiþ,
B. 5.464   'Crist, þat on *Caluarie* vpon þe cros deidest,
B.10.36   [On cros vpon *caluarye* as clerkes vs techeþ],
B.11.201   For [at] *Caluarie* of cristes blood cristendom gan sprynge,
B.16.164   On cros vpon *Caluarie* crist took þe bataille
B.19.41   And vpon *Caluarie* on cros ycrouned kyng of Iewes.
B.19.142   Killeden hym on cros wise at *Caluarie* on Friday,
B.19.322   That crist vpon *Caluarie* for mankynde on pyned.
C. 6.318   'Crist, þat on *Caluarie* on þe crosse deyedest,
C.12.109   A[t] *Caluarie* of cristis bloed cristendoem gan sprynge
C.21.41   And vpon *Caluarie* on cros ycrouned kyng of iewes.
C.21.142   Culden hym on cros wyse at *Caluarie* on fryday
C.21.322   That Crist vpon *Caluary* for mankynde on peyned.

calues > *calf; cam* > *comen*

cammaca n *camaca n.* C 1
C.16.301   As of a cote of *ca[mm]aca* or of clene scarlet.

cammokes n *cammok n.* B 1; C 1
B.19.312   'For comunliche in contrees *cammokes* and wedes
C.21.312   'For cominliche in Contrayes *cammokes* and wedes

can > *ginneþ,konne*

candle n *candel n.* B 1; C 2
B.17.223   As dooþ a kex or a *candle* þat caught haþ fir and blaseþ,
C. 3.106   And thorw a *candle* clemynge in [a] cursed place
C.19.189   A[s] doth a kix [o]r a *candle* þat cauht hath fuyr and blaseth,

canoen > *canoun*

canon n *canoun n.(2)* A 2 canoun (1) chanoun (1); B 2 canon (1)
            Chanons (1); C 3 chanons (2) Chanouns (1)
A.10.113   ȝif þou be man maried, monk, oþer *chanoun*,
A.11.33   Wolde neuere king, ne kniȝt, ne *canoun* of seint poulis
B.10.47   [W]olde neuere kyng ne knyȝt ne [c]*anon* of Seint Poules
B.10.324   And amende Monyals, Monkes and *Chanons*,
C. 5.156   Ac mony day, men telleth, bothe monkes and *chanons*,
C. 5.170   And amende ȝow monkes, moniales and *chanons*,
C.17.55   Ar they amorteysed eny more for monkes or for *Chanoun[s]*.

canonistres n *canonistre n.* A 1 canonistris; B 1; C 1
A. 8.134   Ac catoun construiþ it [nay] & *canonistris* boþe:
B. 7.155   Caton and *Canonistres* counseillen vs to leue
C. 9.304   Caton counteth hit at nauht and *Canonistres* at lasse.

canoun n *canoun n.(1)* &> *canon* B 1; C 1 Canoen
B. 5.421   Ac in *Canoun* nor in decretals I kan noȝt rede a lyne.
C.15.84   'A[c] this doctour and dyuynour,' quod y, 'and decretistre of
            Canoen,

canst > *konne*

cantel n *cantel n.* C 1
C.14.163   A *cantel* of kynde wyt here kynde to saue.

canterbury > *caunterbury*

capede v *capen v.* C 1
C.15.108   Cowhede and *capede*, and consience hym herde

capel -il caples > *capul; capon(e)s* > *chapun*

cappe n *cappe n.* C 1
C. 7.174   ȝe may se be [my] signes þat sitten on my *cappe*

capul n *capel n.* A 2 capelis (1) capil (1); B 5 caples (3) capul (2); C 3
            capel (1) caples (2)
A. 2.126   Þanne car[i]de hy fo[r] *capelis* to carien hem þider;
A. 4.22   Þanne consience on his *capil* cairiþ forþ faste,
B. 2.162   Ac þanne cared þei for *caples* to carien hem þider;

B. 4.24   Thanne Conscience [o]n his *capul* [caireþ] forþ faste,
B.17.110   On my *Capul* þat highte caro–of mankynde I took it–
B.19.331   And gaf hym *caples* to his carte, contricion and confession;
B.19.345   Shulle come out, Conscience; and youre [*caples* two],
C. 4.24   Thenne Consience on his *capel* comesed to pryke
C.21.331   And gaf hym *caples* to his Carte, Contrissioun & confessioun;
C.21.345   Shal come oute, Consience; and ȝoure [*caples* two],

car n *carre n.* C 1
C.20.288   Coltyng and al his kyn, the *car* to saue.

caractes n *carecte n.* B 3
B.12.78   [For] þoruȝ *caractes* þat crist wroot þe Iewes knewe hemselue
B.12.88   As cristes *caracte[s]* confortede, and boþe coupable shewed
B.12.91   Dampneþ vs at þe day of dome as [dide þe *caractes*] þe Iewes.

carde v *carden v.* A 1 cardit; B 1 carded; C 2 carde (1) cardet (1)
A.11.18   But it be *cardit* wiþ coueitise as cloþeris don here wolle;
B.10.18   But it be *carded* wiþ coueitise as cloþeres [don] hir wolle.
C. 9.80   Bothe to *carde* and to kembe, to cloute and to wasche,
C.11.15   Bote hit be *cardet* with coueytise as clotheres kemben here wolle.

cardiacle n *cardiacle n.* B 2 Cardiacle (1) Cardiacles (1); C 2 cardiacle
            (1) cardiacles (1)
B.13.334   That I cacche þe crampe, þe *Cardiacle* som tyme,
B.20.82   Coughes and *Cardiacles*, Crampes and tooþaches,
C. 6.78   That y cache þe crompe, the *cardiacle* sume tyme
C.22.82   Cowhes and *cardiacles*, crampes and toethaches,

cardynal n *cardinal n.* A 1 cardinal; B 6 Cardynal (2) Cardinals (4); C 8
            cardinal (2) cardinale (1) Cardinales (1) Cardynales (1) cardinals (2)
            Cardynals (1)
A.12.15   Of þe kynde *cardinal* wit, and cristned in a font,
B.Pr.107   Ac of þe *Cardinals* at court þat kauȝte of þat name,
B.19.224   Coueitise and vnkyndenesse *Cardinals* hym to lede.
B.19.413   I knew neuere *Cardynal* þat he ne cam fro þe pope.
B.19.417   "The contree is þe corseder þat *Cardinals* come Inne,
B.19.420   That no *Cardynal* coome among þe comune peple,
B.19.449   And crist of his curteisie þe *Cardinals* saue
C.Pr.134   Ac of þe *Cardinales* at Court þat caught han such a name
C.16.368   Kynge[s] and *Cardynals* kn[o]wen hym sum tyme
C.17.166   And a *cardinal* of Court, a gret clerk withalle,
C.21.224   Coueytise and vnkyndenesse *Cardynales* hym [to] lede.
C.21.413   Y knewe neuere *cardinale* þat he ne cam fro þe pope
C.21.417   "The contreye is þe corsedore þat *Cardinals* cometh ynne,
C.21.420   That no *cardinal* come among þe comune peple
C.21.449   And Crist of his cortesye þe *cardinals* saue

cardinale adj *cardinal adj.* B 13 Cardinale (6) Cardynale (5) Cardinals (1)
            Cardynales (1); C 13 cardinal (3) cardinale (8) Cardinales (2)
B.Pr.104   That *Cardinals* ben called and closynge yates
B.19.274   And Grace gaf [Piers] greynes, *Cardynal[es]* vertues,
B.19.316   And tilieþ [to] hir techynge þe *Cardynale* vertues.'
B.19.337   Conscience and alle cristene and *Cardinale* vertues,
B.19.343   [Th]e sedes [þat sire] Piers [sew], þe *Cardynale* vertues.
B.19.393   'That is my conseil', quod Conscience, 'and *Cardynale* vertues;
B.19.407   But Conscience [be þi] comune[s] and *Cardinale* vertues
B.19.411   Man to me þat me kouþe telle of *Cardinale* vertues,
B.19.452   The counseil of Conscience or *Cardinale* vertues,
B.20.21   Wiþouten conseil of Conscience or *Cardynale* vertues,
B.20.73   Ouer kynde cristene and *Cardynale* vertues.
B.20.122   Ouercome Conscience and *Cardinale* vertues;
B.20.303   That wiþ Conscience acordede and *Cardynale* vertues.
C.Pr.132   That *Cardinales* ben cald and closyng ȝates
C.21.274   And grace gaf Peres graynes, *cardinales* vertues,
C.21.316   And tulieth [to] here techynge the *cardinal* vertues.'
C.21.337   Consience and alle cristene and *cardinale* vertues,
C.21.343   þe sedes that sire [Peres] sewe, þe *cardinale* vertues.
C.21.393   'That is my conseil,' quod Consience, 'and *cardinale* vertues,
C.21.407   Bote Consience [be] thy comune[s] and *cardinale* vertues
C.21.411   Man to me þat me couthe telle of *cardinal[e]* vertues
C.21.452   The conseyl of Consience or *cardinal[e]* vertues
C.22.21   Withouten consail of Consience or *cardinale* vertues
C.22.73   Ouer kynde cristene and *cardinale* vertues.
C.22.122   Ouercome Consience and *cardinal* vertues
C.22.303   That with Consience acordede and *cardinal* vertues.

cardit > *carde*

care n *care n.(1)* A 3; B 11; C 11
A. 1.59   'Þ[at] is þe castel of *care*; who[so] comiþ þereinne
A. 2.115   And comen to counforte fro *care* þe false,
A.10.178   [Þus] þoruȝ curside caym cam *care* vpon alle,
B. 1.61   'That is þe castel of *care*; whoso comþ þerInne
B. 2.151   And comen to conforten from *care* þe false
B. 3.164   And al þe comune in *care* þat coueiten lyue in truþe,

B. 9.156 And þus þoru3 cursed Caym cam *care* vpon erþe,
B.13.160 Coold ne *care* ne compaignye of þeues,
B.14.175 Conforte þo creatures þat muche *care* suffren
B.18.215 The which vnknytteþ alle *care* and comsynge is of reste.
B.18.257 And conforte al his kyn and out of *care* brynge,
B.18.268 *Care* and [c]ombraunce is comen to vs alle.
B.20.165 For *care* Conscience þo cryde vpon Elde
B.20.201 And cryde to kynde: 'out of *care* me brynge!
C. 1.57 'That is þe Castel of *care*; whoso cometh þerynne
C. 3.202 And al þe comune in *care* and in coueytise;
C. 3.373 Withouten coest and *care* and alle kyn trauayle.
C. 7.305 [Quod contemplacion, 'by Crist, thow y *care* soffre],
C.18.172 And kene *care* in thy kissyng and combraunce to thysulue.
C.19.55 A man, as me tho thouhte, to moche *care* they brouhte
C.20.224 The which vnknytteth alle *care* and comsyng is of reste.
C.20.265 And comforte alle his kyn and out of *care* brynge
C.20.276 *Care* and combraunce is come to vs all.
C.22.165 For *care* Consience tho cryede vpon elde
C.22.201 And cryede to kynde: 'out of *care* me brynge!

care v *caren v.* A 1 caride; B 4 care (2) cared (1) careþ (1); C 5 care (2) caren (1) careth (2)
A. 2.126 Þanne car[i]de hy fo[r] capelis to carien hem þider,
B. 2.162 Ac þanne *cared* þei for caples to carien hem þider;
B.14.57 Darstow neuere *care* for corn ne cloþ ne for drynke,
B.19.381 'I *care* no3t', quod Conscience, 'þou3 pride come nouþe.
B.20.150 Ne *careþ* no3t how Kynde slow and shal come at þe laste
C. 1.125 Ac thei *caren* nat thow hit be cold, knaues, when þe[i] worche.
C. 9.109 *Careth* they for no colde ne counteth of non hete
C.15.256 Dar þe nat *care* for no corn ne for cloth ne for drynke
C.21.381 'Y *care* nat,' quod Consience, 'thow pryde come nouthe;
C.22.150 Ne *careth* nat how kynde slowh and shal come at þe laste

careful adj *careful adj.* A 4 carful; B 9 careful (4) carefulle (5); C 7 carefole (4) carfol (2) carfole (1)
A. 1.177 To counforte þe *carful* acumbrid wiþ synne.
A.10.184 A *carful* concepcioun comiþ of such weddyng
A.11.45 Ac þe *carful* may cri3en & carpe at þe 3ate,
A.11.189 Counforte þe *carful* þat in castel ben fetterid,
B. 1.203 To conforten þe *carefulle* acombred wiþ synne.
B. 9.161 [A] *careful* concepcion comeþ of [swich weddynge]
B.10.59 Ac þe *carefulle* may crie and carpen at þe yate
B.11.192 'Ac calleþ þe *carefulle* þerto, þe croked and þe pouere;
B.11.296 It is a *careful* kny3t, and of a caytif kynges makyng,
B.13.265 There was a *careful* commune whan no cart com to towne
B.14.179 Conforte þi *carefulle*, crist, in þi rich[e],
B.16.264 And conforted many a *careful* þat after his comynge waite[n],
B.19.128 Thus he confortede *carefulle* and caughte a gretter name,
C. 1.198 That conforteth alle *carefole* acombred with synne.
C.11.40 Ac þe *carfole* may crye and quake at þe 3ate,
C.12.104 "Ac calleth þe *carefole* þerto, the crokede and the pore;
C.13.110 For hit is a *carfol* knyhte and of a Caytif kynges makynge
C.18.266 And conforted many a *carfol* þere þat aftur his comyng loke[n].
C.19.65 Ac so sone so the samaritaen hadde sihte of this *carefole*
C.21.128 Thus he comfortede *carefole* and cauhte a grettere name,

carefully adv *carefulli adv.* A 1 carfulliche; B 1
A. 5.59 And *carfulliche* his cope [comsiþ] he to shewe.
B. 5.76 And *carefully* [his coupe] he comse[þ] to shewe.

careyne n *careine n.* A 1 caroyn; B 5 careyne (2) caroyne (3); C 3 careyne (1) caroyne (2)
A. 7.83 Þe [k]ir[k]e shal haue my *caroyn* & kepe my bones,
B.Pr.189 [The while he caccheþ conynges he coueiteþ no3t [o]ure *caroyne*
B. 6.91 The kirke shal haue my *caroyne* and kepe my bones,
B.12.256 And whan his *caroyne* shal come in caue to be buryed
B.14.334 To couere my *careyne*', quod he, and cride mercy faste
B.15.35 And whan I flee fro þe flessh and forsake þe *careyne*
C. 8.100 The kyrke shal haue my *caroyne* and kepe my bones
C.14.178 His le[d]ene is vnloueliche and lothliche his *careyne*
C.16.197 And when y fle fro þe [flessh] and feye leue þe *caroyne*

carfol(e carful(- > careful(-; caride > care

carien v *carien v.* A 2 cariede (1) carien (1); B 2 carie (1) carien (1); C 2 carie (1) caryeth (1)
A. 2.126 Þanne car[i]de hy fo[r] capelis to *carien* hem þider;
A. 6.32 And kepide his corn, & *cariede* it to house,
B. 2.162 Ac þanne cared þei for caples to *carien* hem þider;
B.19.330 A cart highte cristendom to *carie* [home] Piers sheues,
C. 9.151 And *ca[ry]eth* hit hoem to his cote and cast hym to lyuene
C.21.330 A Cart hihte Cristendoem to *carie* hoem Peres sheues

carneles > kerneles; caroyn(e > careyne

carolden v *carolen v.* B 1; C 1 caroled
B.18.424 Til þe day dawed þise damyseles [*carolden*]
C.20.467 Til þe day dawed thes damoyseles *caroled*

carpen v *carpen v.* A 7 carpe (1) carpen (4) carpeþ (1) carpide (1); B 26 carpe (9) carped (5) carpede (2) carpen (7) carpeþ (2) ycarped (1); C 20 Carp (1) carpe (9) carped (1) carpede (3) carpen (1) carpeth (4) karpe (1)
A. 2.153 And consience to þe king *carpide* it aftir.
A.11.38 Ac 3if þei *carpen* of crist, þise clerkis & þise lewid,
A.11.45 Ac þe carful may cri3en & *carpe* at þe 3ate,
A.11.56 Clerkis and k[ete] men *carpen* of god faste,
A.11.65 And *carp[en]* a3ens clergie crabbide wordis:
A.12.7 Þou woldest konne þat I can and *carpen* hit after;
A.12.33 But as he seyþ, such I am, when he with me *carpeþ*.'
B. 2.27 And Mede is manered after hym [as men of] kynde [*carpeþ*]:
B. 2.192 And Conscience to þe kyng *carped* it after.
B.10.52 Ac if þei *carpen* of crist, þise clerkes and þise lewed,
B.10.59 Ac þe carefulle may crie and *carpen* at þe yate
B.10.70 Clerkes and [kete] men *carpen* of god faste
B.10.105 *Carpen* as þei clerkes were of crist and of hise my3tes,
B.10.107 And *carpen* ayein cler[gie] crabbede wordes:
B.10.293 And *carpen* no3t as þei carpe now, [and] calle yow doumbe houndes:
B.10.293 And carpen no3t as þei *carpe* now, [and] calle yow doumbe houndes:
B.10.307 For in cloistre comeþ [no] man to [*carpe*] ne to fi3te
B.11.216 For whateuere clerkes *carpe* of cristendom or ellis,
B.11.368 Of hir kynde and hir colour to *carpe* it were to longe.
B.13.58 And Conscience conforted vs and *carped* vs murye tales:
B.13.101 Coughed and *carped*, and Conscience hym herde
B.13.113 'Now þow, Clergie', quod Conscience, '*carp[e]* what is dowel.'
B.13.179 Ac Conscience *carped* loude and curteisliche seide,
B.13.220 And as þe[i] wente by þe weye–of dowel þei *carped*–
B.13.416 Whan men *carpen* of crist or clennesse of soul[e]
B.15.117 Iohannes Crisostomus of clerkes [*carpeþ*] and preestes:
B.15.301 And if þei kouþe han *ycarped*, by crist! as I trowe,
B.16.265 Til he come þat I *carpe* of; crist is his name
B.17.138 And if Conscience *carpe* þerayein, or kynde wit eyþer,
B.19.69 Ac to *carpe* moore of crist and how he com to þat name,
B.19.176 Crist *carpede* þanne and curteisliche seide,
B.19.199 Thus Conscience of crist and of þe cros *carpede*
B.20.333 *Carpe* I wolde wiþ contricion, and þerfore cam I hider.'
C. 2.27 And mede is manered aftur hym as men of kynde *carpeth*:
C. 2.206 And consience to þe kyng *carpede* hit aftur.
C. 4.32 Ac Consience knewe hem wel and *carped* to resoun:
C. 6.29 To *carpe* and to consayle then eny Clerk or lewed;
C. 7.76 When me *carpeth* of Crist or clannesse of soule
C. 7.79 He hateth to here thereof and alle þat þerof *carpeth*.
C.11.50 Clerkes and knyhtes *carpen* of god ofte
C.13.178 Of here kynde and here colour to *carpe* hit were to longe.
C.15.127 'Now þou, Clergie', quod Consience, '*carpe* what is dowel.'
C.15.189 And as they wente by þe way–of dowel can they *carpe*–
C.16.272 Iohannes Crisostomus *carpeth* thus of clerkes [and prestes]:
C.17.69 Y dar nat *carpe* of clerkes now þat cristes [tresor] kepe
C.18.218 And thise thre þat y *Carp* of, Adam and Eue
C.18.281 Til he come þat y *carpe* of; Crist is his name
C.19.111 And yf kynde wit *carpe* herea3en or eny kyne thouhtes
C.21.69 Ac to *carpe* more of Crist and how he cam to þat name;
C.21.176 Crist *Carpede* thenne and cortey[s]liche seide,
C.21.199 Thus Consience of Crist and of þe cros *carpede*
C.22.333 *Karpe* y wolde with Contricioun and þerfore [cam y] heddere.'

carpenters n *carpenter n.* A 1 carpenteris; B 2; C 2 carpentares (1) carpenters (1)
A.11.135 Of *carpenteris* & kerueris; [I] kende ferst masons,
B.10.183 Of *Carpent[ers* and] kerueres; [I kenned first] Masons
B.10.416 That ben *Carpenters* holy kirk to make for cristes owene beestes.
C.11.123 Of *carpent[ers* and] keruers, and contreuede þe compas
C.11.247 That [ben] *carpentares* vnder Crist holy kirke to make

carpyng ger *carping ger.* A 1 carping; B 2 carpyng (1) carpynge (1); C 2 carpynge
A.11.96 Ac for no *carping* I couþe, ne knelyng to þe ground,
B.Pr.204 [Ne] *carpynge* of þis coler þat costed me neuere;
B.10.143 A[c] for no *carpyng* I kouþe, ne knelyng to þe grounde,
C.Pr.212 Ne *carp[ynge]* of [þis] cole[r] þat costede me neuere.
C.16.341 By clothyng ne by *carpynge* knowe shaltow hym neuere

carse n *cresse n.* C 2 carse (1) cresses (1)
C. 8.320 With craym and with croddes, with *cresses* and oþere erbes.
C.11.14 Wysdom and wit now is nat worth a *carse*

cart n *cart n.* A 3 carte; B 7 cart (5) carte (2); C 7 cart (5) carte (2)
A. 2.141 And let cartesadil þe Comissare, oure *carte* shal he drawe,
A. 2.143 And makiþ of lyere a lang *carte* to leden al þis oþere,
A. 7.271 And ek a cow & a calf, & a *carte* mare
B. 2.180 And [lat] Cartsadle þe Commissarie; oure *cart* shal he [drawe]
B. 2.182 And makeþ of lyere a lang *cart* to leden alle þise oþere,
B. 6.287 And ek a cow and a calf, and a *cart* mare
B.13.265 There was a careful commune when no *cart* com to towne
B.19.330 A *cart* highte cristendom to carie [home] Piers sheues,
B.19.331 And gaf hym caples to his *carte*, contricion and confession;
B.19.346 Confession and Contricion, and youre *carte* þe bileeue
C. 2.193 And lat cop[l]e þe commissare; oure *cart* shal he drawe
C. 2.195 And maketh of lyare a lang *cart* to lede al this othere,
C. 5.13 Or koke for my cokeres or to þe *Cart* piche,
C. 8.310 And a cow with a calf and a *cart* m[a]re
C.21.330 A *Cart* hihte Cristendoem to carie hoem Peres sheues,
C.21.331 And gaf hym caples to his *Carte*, Contrissioun & confessioun;
C.21.346 Confessioun and contricioun, and ȝoure *Carte*, the bileue,

carte v *carten v.* C 1
C. 5.65 And knaue[s] vncrounede to *carte* and to worche.

carteres n *carter n.* C 1
C. 9.206 And *carteres* knaues and Clerkes withouten grace,

cartewey > cartwey

cartsadle v *cart-sadelen v.* A 1 cartesadil; B 1
A. 2.141 And let *cartesadil* þe Comissare, oure carte shal he drawe.
B. 2.180 And [lat] *Cartsadle* þe Commissarie; oure cart shal he [drawe]

cartwey n *cart n.* A 1 cartewey; B 1; C 1 cartway
A. 3.121 As comoun as þe *cartewey* to knaue & to [alle],
B. 3.132 As commune as [þe] *Cartwey* to [knaue and to alle],
C. 3.169 As comyn as þe *cartway* to knaues and to alle,

cartwhel n *cart n.* C 1
C.15.161 In þe corner of a *car[t]whel* with a crow croune.

cas(e > caas

cast s *cast n. &> casten* A 1; B 1; C 1
A. 3.18 For al consiences *cast* a[nd] craft as I trowe'.
B. 3.19 For al Consciences *cast* [and] craft, as I trowe'.
C. 3.20 For al Consiences *cast* and craft, as y trowe.'

castel n *castel n.* A 7; B 6; C 6 castel (5) chastel (1)
A. 1.59 'Þ[at] is þe *castel* of care; who[so] comiþ þereinne
A.10.2 In a *castel* þat kynde made of foure skenis þinges.
A.10.16 Ac þe cunstable of þe *castel*, þat kepiþ hem alle,
A.10.22 Þise sixe ben yset to saue þe *castel*;
A.10.25 'What calle ȝe þat *castel*,' quaþ I, 'þat kynde haþ ymakid?
A.10.38 Þat is þe *castel* þat kynde made, caro it hatte,
A.11.189 Counforte þe carful þat in *castel* ben fetterid,
B. 1.4 Cam doun from [þe] *Castel* and called me faire,
B. 1.61 'That is þe *castel* of care; whoso comþ þerInne
B. 9.2 In a *Castel* þat kynde made of foure kynnes þynges.
B. 9.17 Ac þe Constable of [þe] *Castel* þat kepeþ [hem alle]
B. 9.50 [Th]at is þe *Castel* þat kynde made; caro it hatte,
B.13.120 'I haue seuene sones', he seide, seruen in a *Castel*
C. 1.4 Cam doun fro þe *castel* and calde me by name
C. 1.57 'That is þe *Castel* of care; whoso cometh þerynne
C. 2.92 With [þe] *chastel* of cheste and chaterynge out of resoun;
C. 3.141 In the *Castel* of Corf y shal do close the,
C.10.129 In a *Castel* þat kynde made of foure kyne thynges.
C.10.143 Ac þe constable of þ[e] *Castel* þat kepeth hem alle

casten v *casten v.* A 5 cast (1) caste (3) casten (1); B 22 cast (2) caste (12) casten (6) casteþ (2); C 16 cast (4) caste (10) casten (2)
A. 4.72 & comaundid a cunstable to *caste* hym in yrens]:
A. 5.168 Clement þe cobeler *cast* of his cloke
A. 7.15 *Caste* hem cloþis for cold for so wile treuþe.
A. 7.54 He *caste* on his cloþis, ycloutid & hole,
A. 9.94 Þanne shulde þe kyng come & *casten* hem in presoun,
B.Pr.117 *Casten* þat þe commune sholde [hire communes] fynde.
B. 4.85 And comaundede a Constable to *casten* hym in Irens:
B. 5.319 Clement þe Cobelere *caste* of his cloke
B. 6.16 *Casteþ* hem cloþes [for cold] for so [wol] truþe.
B. 6.59 [He] *caste* on [hise] cloþes, ycloutid and hole,
B. 8.104 Thanne [sholde] þe kyng come and *casten* hem in [prison,
B.11.132 And conscience acounte wiþ hym and *casten* hym in arerage,
B.11.410 And as I *caste* vp myne eiȝen oon loked on me.
B.12.160 Tak two stronge men and in Themese *cast* hem,
B.13.144 *Cast* coles on his heed of alle kynde speche;
B.13.247 Hadde ich a clerc þat couþe write I wolde *caste* hym a bille
B.13.356 Moore to good þan to god þe gome his loue *caste*,
B.13.365 How I myȝte haue it al my wit I *caste*,

B.15.334 That were ful of faire trees, and I fondede and *caste*
B.15.402 The corn þat she croppede he *caste* it in his ere,
B.16.42 And *casteþ* vp to þe crop vnkynde Neighebores,
B.16.75 And Piers *caste* to þe crop and þanne comsed it to crye;
B.16.128 And knokked on hem wiþ a corde, and *caste* adoun hir stalles
B.16.137 Thei *casten* and contreueden to kulle hym whan þei myȝte;
B.19.141 And for to doon hym to deþe day and nyȝt þei *casten*.
B.19.280 [That] *caste* for to ke[l]e a crokke to saue þe fatte aboue.
B.20.121 Thanne cam Coueitise and *caste* how he myȝte
C.Pr.144 *Caste* þat þe comun[e] sholde here comunes fynde.
C. 4.81 And comaundede a Constable to *caste* [hym] in yrones
C. 6.264 How y myhte haue hit al my wit y *caste*
C. 6.376 Clement þe Coblere *cast* of his cloke
C. 8.58 [He] *caste* on his clothes of alle kyn craftes,
C. 9.151 And ca[ry]eth hit hoem to his cote and *cast* hym to lyuene
C.11.16 Ho can *caste* and contreue to disseyue þe ri[gh]tfole,
C.11.18 That coueite can and *caste* thus ar cleped into consayle:
C.11.124 And *caste* [mette] by squire bothe lyne and leuele,
C.12.67 And consience acounte with hym and *casten* hym in arerag[e]
C.14.104 Take two stronge men and in temese *cast* hem,
C.15.142 *Caste* coles on his heued of alle kyn[de] speche,
C.20.289 Brumstoen boylaunt, brennyng out *cast* hit,
C.21.141 And for to do hym to dethe day and nyhte they *casten*,
C.21.280 That *caste* for to kele a crok [to] saue þe fatte aboue.
C.22.121 Thenne cam couetyse and *caste* how he myhte

castynge ger *casting ger.* B 1 castynge
B.11.188 To knowen vs by oure kynde herte and *castynge* of oure eiȝen,

cat n *cat n.* B 9 cat (6) cattes (3); C 8 Cat (6) cattes (1) kattes (1)
B.Pr.149 For a *cat* of a [court] cam whan hym liked
B.Pr.170 [And hangen it vpon þe *cattes* hals; þanne here we mowen]
B.Pr.178 That dorste haue bounden þe belle aboute þe *cattes* nekke,
B.Pr.185 'Thouȝ we [hadde] kille[d] þe *cat* yet sholde þer come anoþer
B.Pr.187 Forþi I counseille al þe commune to late þe *cat* worþe,
B.Pr.194 Ther þe *cat* is a kitoun þe court is ful elenge.
B.Pr.200 Nere þe *cat* of þ[e] court þat kan yow ouerlepe;
B.Pr.203 Shal neuere þe *cat* ne þe kiton by my counseil be greued,
B. 5.255 'I haue as muche pite of pouere men as pedlere haþ of *cattes*,
C.Pr.170 For a *Cat* of a Court cam whan hym likede
C.Pr.187 And hongen hit aboute þe *cattes* halse; thanne here we mowe
C.Pr.195 That derste haue ybounde þe belle aboute þe *kattes* nekke
C.Pr.202 'Thow we hadde ykuld þe *Cat* ȝut shulde ther come anoþer
C.Pr.204 Forthy y conseile for oure comune profit lat þe *Cat* yworthe
C.Pr.207 Ther þe *Cat* [is] a kytoun þe Court is ful elynge.
C.Pr.211 Shal neuer þe *Cat* ne [þe] kytoun be my conseil greued
C.Pr.218 Ne were þe *Cat* of þe Court and ȝonge kitones toward;

catecumelynges n *cathecumine n.* B 1
B.11.77 Raþer þan to baptiȝe barnes þat ben *Catecumelynges*.

catel n *catel n.* A 9; B 28; C 31
A. 3.252 Coueitide here *catel*, kilde nouȝt hire bestis,
A. 4.69 To ouercome þe king wiþ *catel* ȝif þei miȝte.
A. 5.27 And kep[e] it in hire coffre for *catel* at nede.
A. 6.60 Þ[e] croft hattiþ coueite nouȝt menis *catel* ne here wyues,
A. 7.84 For of my corn & my *catel* [he] crauide þe tiþ[e];
A. 7.206 Counforte hem wiþ þi *catel* for cristis loue of heuene;
A. 8.24 Aȝens clene consience here *catel* to selle.
A.10.183 For coueitise of *catel* vnkyndely be maried.
A.10.199 For coueitise of *catel* or of kynrede riche.
B.Pr.205 And þouȝ it costned me *catel* biknowen it I nolde
B. 3.68 And þi cost and þi coueitise and who þe *catel* ouȝte.
B. 3.273 And for he coueited hir *catel* and þe kyng spared,
B. 4.82 To ouercomen þe kyng wiþ *catel* if þei myȝte.
B. 5.27 And kepe it in hire coffre for *catel* at nede.
B. 5.266 I nolde cope vs wiþ þi *catel* ne oure kirk amende
B. 5.573 Th[e] croft hatte Coueite-noȝt-mennes-*catel*-ne-hire-wyues-
B. 6.92 For of my corn and [my] *catel* [h]e craued þe tiþe;
B. 6.147 And *catel* to [cope] hem wiþ þat han Cloistres and chirches.
B. 6.220 Conforte h[e]m wiþ þi *catel* for cristes loue of heuene.
B. 7.22 Ayein clene Conscience hir *catel* to selle.
B. 9.160 For coueitise of *catel* vnkyndely ben [maried].
B. 9.177 For coueitise of *catel* ne of kynrede riche.
B.10.29 And moost vnkynde to þe commune þat moost *catel* weldeþ:
B.10.329 Of Costantyns cofres [þer þe *catel* is Inne]
B.10.477 But þo þat kepen þe lordes *catel*, clerkes and Reues.
B.11.212 And be we noȝt vnkynde of oure *catel* ne of oure konnyng neiþer,
B.11.294 For made neuere kyng no knyȝt but he hadde *catel* to spende
B.12.45 *Catel* and kynde wit was combraunce to hem alle,
B.12.55 [So *catel* and kynde wit acombreþ ful manye;
B.12.292 To kepe wiþ a commune; no *catel* was holde bettre,
B.13.150 Kynde loue coueiteþ noȝt no *catel* but speche.
B.14.7 And [laþered] wiþ þe losse of *catel* [forto me] looþ [were]
B.14.270 Moore for coueitise of [*catel*] þan kynde loue of boþe–

B.15.429   "Salt saueþ *catel*", siggen þise wyues:
B.19.77   Or any kynnes *catel*; but knowelich[ede] hym souereyn
B.19.292   Mighte no [lyere wiþ lesynges] ne los of worldly *catel*
B.20.209   'How shal I come to *catel* so to cloþe me and to feede?'
C.Pr.213   And thow hit costed m[e] *catel* byknowen [hit] y ne wolde
C. 3.72   Thi cost and here couetyse and ho þe *catel* ouhte.
C. 3.323   That kyng oþer kayser hem gaf, *Catel* oþer rente.
C. 3.426   And for a coueytede here *catel* and the kyng sparede,
C. 4.78   To ouercome þe kyng [with] *catel* y[f] they myhte.
C. 5.129   And kepe hit in here cofre for *catel* at nede.
C. 6.288   Y ne wolde cope me with thy *catel* ne oure kyrke mende
C. 7.220   The croft hatte coueyte-nat-menne-*catel*-ne-here-wyues-
C. 8.101   For of my corn and my *catel* he craued [þe] tythe.
C. 8.157   To kepe hym and his *catel* as couenant was bitwene hem:
C. 8.229   Conforte hem with thy *catel*, for so comaundeth treuthe;
C. 9.90   And hath no *catel* but his craft to clothe h[e]m and to fede
C. 9.182   Or bylowe thorw luther men and lost here *catel* aftur
C.10.169   On *catel* more then on kynde that alle kyne thynges wrouhte,
C.10.194   The *catel* that Crist hadde, thre clothes hit were;
C.10.250   That for no kyne *catel* ne no kyne byheste
C.10.257   For coueytise of *catel* and connynge chapmen;
C.10.279   For coueytise of *catel* in none kyne wyse;
C.12.214   Þe *catel* þat he kepeth so in coffres and in bernis,
C.12.241   For coueytyse of *catel* to culle hym þat hit kepeth.
C.12.245   So coueytise of *catel* was combraunce to hem alle.
C.13.108   For made neuere kyng no knyhte but he hadde *catel* to spene
C.14.17   Ac *catel* and kynde wit acombreth fol monye;
C.15.145   Conforte hym with thy *catel* and with thy kynde speche;
C.16.110   More for coueytise of *catel* then kynde loue of þe mariage.
C.17.212   How tho corsede cristene *catel* and richesse worschipede;
C.19.242   For godes tretor he is [to]ld for al his trewe *catel*
C.19.247   Excuse hem þat ben vnkynde and ʒut here [*catel*] ywonne
C.21.77   Or eny kyne *catel*; boþe knoweleched hym souereyn
C.21.292   Myhte no lyare with lesynge[s] ne losse of worldly *catel*
C.22.209   'How shal y come to *catel* so to clothe me and to fede?'

cateles adj *catelles adj.* A 1
A.10.68   And ʒif þei ben pore & *cateles*, to kepe hem fro ille,

caton n prop *Caton n.* A 5 catonis (1) catoun (4); B 12 Caton (7) Catons
   (4) Catoun (1); C 7 Caton (3) Catones (1) Catoun (3)
A. 4.17   And calde *catoun* his knaue, curteis of speche:
A. 8.134   Ac *catoun* construiþ it [nay] & canonistris boþe:
A.10.97   *Catoun* counseilliþ–tak kep of his teching–
A.11.146   In oþer science it seiþ, I saiʒ it in *catoun*,
A.11.150   He kenniþ vs þe contrarie, aʒens *catonis* wordis,
B. 4.17   And called *Caton* his knaue, curteis of speche,
B. 6.314   Ayeins *Catons* counseil comseþ he to Iangle:
B. 7.72   *Caton* kenneþ me þus and þe clerc of stories.
B. 7.73   Cui des videto is *Catons* techyng,
B. 7.155   *Caton* and Canonistres counseillen vs to leue
B.10.194   In ooþer Science it seiþ, I seiʒ it in *Catoun*,
B.10.199   This is *Catons* kennyng to clerkes þat he lereþ.
B.10.201   He kenneþ vs þe contrarie ayein *Catons* wordes,
B.10.343   And *Caton* kenneþ vs to coueiten it nauʒt but as nede techeþ:
B.11.404   *Caton* acordeþ þerwiþ: Nemo sine crimine viuit.'
B.12.21   Seide, '*Caton* conforted his sone þat, clerk þouʒ he were,
B.19.296   And couered hym vnder conseille of *Caton* þe wise:
C. 4.17   And kalde *Catoun* his knaue, Corteys of speche,
C. 7.34   Ac y can nat construe *catoun* ne clergialiche reden.
C. 8.336   Aʒenes *Catones* consayle comseth he to gruche:
C. 9.69   *Catoun* acordeth therwith: cui des videto.
C. 9.304   *Caton* counteth hit at nauht and Canonistres at lasse.
C.13.212   *Caton* acordeth therwith: nemo sine crimine viuit.'
C.21.296   And keuered hym vnder consayl of *Caton* the wyse:

cattes > cat; caudel > cawdel; caught(e cauʒte cauht(-> cacchen

cauken v *cauken v.* B 2 caukede (1) cauken (1); C 2 cauke (1) caukede
   (1)
B.11.359   And some *caukede*; I took kepe how pecokkes bredden.
B.12.229   And kynde kenned þe pecok to *cauken* in swich a [wise.
C.13.170   And how þe pocok *caukede* [y toke kepe þerof],
C.14.161   He tauhte þe tortle to tre[d]e, the pocok to *cauke*

caunterbury n prop *OED Canterbury* B 1; C 1 Canterbury
B.15.445   Austyn [þe kyng cristnede at *Caunterbury*],
C.17.274   In sauacioun of mannes soule seynte Thomas of *Canterbury*

caurymaury > kaurymaury

cause n *cause n.* A 1; B 11; C 12
A.12.32   For he cam not by *cause* to lerne to dowel
B. 3.100   Yiftes or yeresyeues by*cause* of hire Offices.
B. 5.440   And euere siþþe be beggere [by *cause* of my] sleuþe:
B.11.174   For no *cause* to cacche siluer þerby, ne to be called a maister,

B.12.225   Clergie ne kynde wit ne knew neuere þe *cause*,
B.12.226   Ac kynde knoweþ þe *cause* hymself, no creature ellis.
B.13.126   And no text ne takeþ to mayntene his *cause*
B.15.45   Thow woldest knowe and konne þe *cause* of alle [hire] names,
B.17.344   That þei han *cause* to contrarie by kynde of hir siknesse;
B.18.135   And þat is *cause* of þis clips þat closeþ now þe sonne,
B.19.23   And ye callen hym crist; for what *cause*, telleþ me.
B.19.63   Ac þe *cause* þat he comeþ þus wiþ cros of his passion
C. 3.317   To here [lele] and lege, loue [is] the *cause*;
C. 5.190   Is *cause* of alle combraunc[e] to confounde a reume.'
C. 6.113   But y hadde weder at my wille y witte god þe *cause*
C. 9.256   The *cause* of al this caytiftee cometh of many bischopes
C.10.282   And loke þat loue be more þe *cause* then lond oþer nobles.
C.16.207   Thow woldest knowe and conne þe *cause* of all here names,
C.17.131   God lereth no lyf to l[eu]e withouten lele *cause*.
C.17.136   Ac oure lord aloueth no loue but lawe be þe *cause*:
C.19.324   That they haen *cause* to contrarien bi kynde of here sekness[e];
C.20.138   And þat is *cause* of this clips that [c]loseth now þe sonne,
C.21.23   And ʒe callen hym Crist; for what *cause*, telleth me.
C.21.63   Ac the *cause* that he cometh thus with cros [of] his passioun

caue n *cave n.(1)* B 1
B.12.256   And whan his caroyne shal come in *caue* to be buryed

cawdel n *caudel n.* B 1; C 1 caudel
B. 5.354   And kouʒed vp a *cawdel* in Clementes lappe.
C. 6.412   And cowed vp a *caudel* in Clementis lappe.

cellis > selle

cene n *cene n.* B 1 cene
B.16.140   The þursday bifore, þere he made his [*cene*],

ceraphyn > seraphyn

certein n *certain n.* B 6 certain (1) certein (4) certeyn (1); C 4 certeyne
   (3) serteyne (1)
B. 6.151   For it is an vnresonable Religion þat haþ riʒt noʒt of *certein*.'
B.13.376   Wiþ presentes pryuely, or paide som *certeyn*;
B.20.255   And sette [it] at a *certain* and [at] a siker nombre.
B.20.258   Han Officers vnder hem, and ech of hem a *certein*.
B.20.267   A *certein* for a certein, saue oonliche of freres.
B.20.267   A certein for a *certein*, saue oonliche of freres.
C.22.255   And sette hit at a *serteyne* and at a syker nombre
C.22.258   Haen officerys vnder hem and vch of hem a *certeyne*.
C.22.267   A *certeyne* for a certeyne saue oenliche of freres.
C.22.267   A certeyne for a *certeyne* saue oenliche of freres.

certein adj *certain adj.* A 1 certayn; B 3 certein (2) certeyne (1); C 6
   certayn (2) certeyn (2) certeyne (2)
A. 3.75   Ne bouʒte none burgages, be ʒe wel *certayn*.
B. 3.86   Ne bouʒte none burgages, be ye [wel] *certeyne*.
B.10.436   That Salomon seiþ I trowe be sooþ and *certein* of vs alle:
B.20.265   Hir ordre and hir reule wole to han a *certein* noumbre
C. 3.85   Ne bouhte none burgages, be ʒe ful *certayn*.
C. 9.166   For hit blameth all beggarie, be ʒe ful *certayn*.
C.13.29   Bothe t[w]o ben gode, be ʒe ful *certeyn*,
C.19.33   He can no *certeyn* somme telle and somme aren in his lappe.
C.19.224   The holy goest hereth the nat ne helpeth the, be thow *certeyne*.
C.22.265   Here ordre and here reule wol to haue a *certeyne* nombre

certes adv *certes adv.* A 3 certis (2) sertis (1); B 7; C 11 certes (8) sertes
   (3)
A. 2.116   And seide, '*certis* cesse shuln we neuere
A. 8.164   It is not so sikir for þe soule, *certis*, as is do wel.
A. 9.18   Ac whoso synneþ, I seiʒe, *sertis*, me þinkiþ
B. 2.152   And seiden, '*certes*, cessen shul we neuere
B. 7.186   [It] is noʒt so siker for þe soule, *certes*, as is dowel.
B. 8.22   A[c] whoso synneþ, I sei[e, *certes*], me þynkeþ
B.11.412   'To se muche and suffre moore, *certes*, is dowel.'
B.11.439   '*Certes*', quod he, 'þat is sooþ'; and shoop hym for to walken,
B.18.295   '*Certes* I drede me', quod þe deuel, 'lest truþe [do] hem fecche.
B.20.340   '*Certes*', seide his felawe, 'sire Penetrans domos.'
C. 5.22   '*Sertes*,' y sayde, 'and so me god helpe,
C. 9.258   *Certes*, hoso durste sygge hit, Simon quasi dormit;
C. 9.332   Hit is nat so syker for þe soule, *certes*, as [is] dowel.
C.10.25   And hoso synegeth,' y sayde, '*certes* he doth nat wel;
C.13.195   Why y soffre or nat soffre; *certes*,' he sayde,
C.13.220   'To se moche and soffre al, *certes*, is dowel.'
C.13.245   'ʒe, *certes*,' quod he, 'þat is soth', and shop hym to walke,
C.15.114   '*Sertes*, sire,' thenne saide y, 'hit semeth nou[th]e here,
C.18.16   'Now, *certes*,' y sayde, and siʒte for ioye,
C.18.58   'ʒe, *sertes*,' he sayde, 'and sothliche leue hit.
C.22.340   '*Certes*,' saide his felawe, 'sire penetrans domos.'

cesar n prop *cesar n.* A 2; B 1; C 1 Sesares
A. 1.46   ʒif þei [shulde] worsshipe þerwiþ *cesar* þe king.

A. 1.49   *"Cesar,"* þ[ei] seide, "we se wel ichone."
B. 1.48   [If] þei sholde [worshipe þerwiþ *Cesar* þe kyng].
C. 1.47   *"Sesares,"* thei sayde, "sothliche we knoweth."

cese > cessen

cesse n prop *n.i.d.* A 1 Cisse; B 1; C 1 Sesse
A. 5.158   *Cisse* þe so[wes]tere sat on þe bench,
B. 5.307   *Cesse* þe [sowestere] sat on þe benche,
C. 6.362   *Sesse* þe [sywestere] saet on þe benche,

cessen v *cesen v.* A 3 cesse (2) sessiþ (1); B 5 cesse (1) cessede (1)
   cessen (2) cesseþ (1); C 6 cese (1) cesseth (1) sese (3) sesede (1)
A. 2.116   And seide, 'certis *cesse* shuln we neuere
A. 4.1   *'Sessiþ,'* seide þe king, 'I suffre ȝow no lengere.
A. 8.104   I shal *cesse* of my sowyng,' quaþ peris, '& swynke not so harde,
B. 2.152   And seiden, 'certes, *cessen* shul we neuere
B. 4.1   *'CEsseþ,'* sei[de] þe kyng, 'I suffre yow no lenger.
B. 7.122   I shal *cessen* of my sowyng', quod Piers, '& swynke noȝt so harde,
B.20.107   To *cesse* and suffre, and see wher þei wolde
B.20.109   And kynde *cessede* [sone] to se þe peple amende.
C. 2.168   And sayde softly, *'sese* shal we neuere;
C. 4.1   *'[Cesseth],'* saide þe kynge, 'y soffre ȝow no lengore.
C. 9.228   And vppon sonendayes to *cese* goddes seruice to here,
C.14.41   "That seth hymsulue synnelees *sese* nat, y hote,
C.22.107   To *sese* and soffre and se wher they wolde
C.22.109   And kynde *sesede* [sone] to se þe peple amende.

chafe v *chaufen v.* B 1; C 2 chaufe (1) chaufen (1)
B.12.125   Lest cheste *cha[fe]* vs to choppe ech man oþer:
C.14.68   Laste cheste *chauf[e]* vs to [c]hoppe vch man oþer.
C.17.49   And charite þat chield is now sholde *chaufen* of hymsulue

chaffare n *chaffare n.* A 3; B 9; C 3
A.Pr.31   And somme chosen [hem] to *chaffare,* þei cheuide þe betere
A. 5.143   Ne neuere wykkidly weiȝe ne wykkide *chaffare* make,
A. 5.172   Þere were chapmen chosen þat *chaffare* to preise;
B.Pr.31   And somme chosen [hem to] *chaffare;* þei cheueden þe bettre,
B. 2.60   Bedelles and baillifs and Brocours of *chaffare,*
B. 5.133   To lye and to loure on my neȝebore and to lakke his *chaffare.*
B. 5.227   And neuere wikkedly weye ne wikke *chaffare* vse,
B. 5.244   I haue lent lordes and ladies my *chaffare*
B. 5.246   Eschaunges and cheuysaunces, wiþ swich *chaffare* I dele,
B. 5.323   Ther were chapmen ychose þis *chaffare* to preise:
B.13.379   And whoso cheped my *chaffare,* chiden I wolde
B.15.164   Charite] is noȝt chaumpions fight ne *chaffare* as I trowe.'
C.Pr.33   And somme chesen *chaffare;* þei cheue[den] þe bettre
C. 2.62   Bydels and bailifs and brokeres of *chaffar[e],*
C. 6.380   There were chapmen ychose this *chaffare* to preyse;

chaffare v *chaffaren v.* B 4 chaffared (1) chaffareden (1) chaffareþ (2); C
   5 chaffare (2) chaffared (1) chaffaren (1) ychaffared (1)
B.14.315   And [þou3] he *chaffareþ* he chargeþ no losse, mowe he charite
   wynne:
B.15.107   Tiþes [of vn]trewe þyng ytilied or *chaffared,*
B.15.165   'Charite', quod he, 'ne *chaffareþ* noȝt, ne chalangeþ, ne craueþ.'
B.16.129   That in chirche *chaffareden* or chaungeden any moneie:
C. 5.94   Ac ȝut y hope, as he þat ofte hath *ychaffared*
C. 6.252   That *chaffared* with my cheuesaunces cheued selde aftur.'
C. 8.248   *Chaffare* and cheue þerwith in chele and in hete.
C.12.227   That *chaff[ar]en* as chapmen and chide bote they wynne
C.16.149   And thogh he *chaffare* he chargeth no loes may he charite wynne:

chayere n *chaiere n.* C 1
C.Pr.114   Fro his *chayere* þer he sat and brake his nekke atwene.

chaynes > cheyne

chalange v *chalengen v.* B 5 chalange (2) chalanged (1) chalangen (1)
   chalangeþ (1); C 5 chalenge (2) chalenged (2) chalengen (1)
B.Pr.93   In Cheker and in Chauncelrie *chalangen* hise dettes
B. 5.174   And am *chalanged* in þe Chapitrehous as I a child were
B.15.31   And whan I *chalange* or chalange noȝt, chepe or refuse,
B.15.31   And whan I chalange or *chalange* noȝt, chepe or refuse,
B.15.165   'Charite', quod he, 'ne chaffareþ noȝt, ne *chalangeþ,* ne craueþ.'
C.Pr.91   In Cheker and in Chancerye *chalengen* his dettes
C. 6.136   For he hadde childe in the chapun co[t]e; he worth *chalenged* at þe
   eleccioun."
C. 6.156   Ȝut am y *chalenged* in oure chapitrehous as y a childe were
C.16.191   And when y *chalenge* [or chalenge] nat, chepe or refuse
C.16.191   And when y chalenge [or *chalenge*] nat, chepe or refuse

chalangeable adj *chalengeable adj.* B 1; C 1 chaleniable
B.11.303   A chartre is *chalangeable* bifore a chief Iustice;
C.13.117   A Chartre is *chaleniable* byfore a chief Iustice;

chalangynge ger *chalenginge ger.* B 3; C 1 chalengynge
B. 5.87   Of chidynge and *chalangynge* was his chief liflode,

B.11.425   Shal neuere *chalangynge* ne chidynge chaste a man so soone
B.15.345   For charite wiþouten *chalangynge* vnchargeþ þe soule,
C. 6.68   Chidynge and *chalengynge* was his cheef lyflode

chaleng- > chalange; chaleniable > chalangeable

chambre n *chaumbre n.* &> bedchambre A 2 chaumbre (1) chaumbris (1);
   B 6 chambre (4) chambres (1) Chaumbres (1); C 4 chambre (1)
   chaumbre (2) chaumbres (1)
A. 3.10   Tok mede be þe myddel & brouȝte hire to *chaumbre.*
A. 6.77   Alle þe housis ben helid, hallis & *chaumbris,*
B. 3.10   Took Mede bi þe myddel and broȝte hire into *chambre.*
B. 4.124   Til Bisshopes Bayardes ben beggeris *Chaumbres,*
B. 5.590   And alle þe houses ben hiled, halles and *chambres,*
B.10.101   Or in a *chambre* wiþ a chymenee, and leue þe chief halle
B.13.433   Sholde noon harlot haue audience in halle n[e] in *Chambre*
B.16.92   That oon Iesus a Iustices sone moste Iouke in hir *chambre*
C. 2.67   Ac Fauel was þe furste þat fette here out of *chambre*
C. 7.93   Sholde non harlote haue audiense in halle ne in *chaumbre*
C. 7.237   And alle þe hous[es] been yheled, halles and *chaumbres,*
C.18.125   That oen Iesus, a Iustices sone, most iouken in here *chaumbre*

champion n *champioun n.* A 1 champioun; B 3 champion (2) chaumpions
   (1); C 1 chaumpion
A. 9.41   Þat is charite þe *champioun,* chief helpe aȝens synne.
B. 8.45   [Th]at is charite þe *champion,* chief help ayein synne.
B.15.164   Charite] is noȝt *chaumpions* fight ne chaffare as I trowe.'
B.15.216   For charite is goddes *champion,* and as a good child hende.
C.15.275   And þat is charite, *chaumpion* chief of all vertues,

champion adj *cf. champioun n.* B 1; C 1 chaumpioun
B.18.99   For youre *champion* chiualer, chief knyȝt of yow alle,
C.20.102   For ȝoure *chaumpioun* Chiualer, chief knyht of ȝow alle,

chancerye > chauncelrie; change > chaunge; chanons -oun(s > canon

chapeleyn n *chapelein n.* A 1 chapelleins; B 3 Chapeleyn (1) Chapeleyns
   (2); C 3 chapeleyn (1) chapeleynes (2)
A. 1.164   Manye *chapelleins* arn chast ac charite is aweye;
B. 1.190   Manye *Chapeleyns* arn chaste ac charite is aweye;
B. 6.12   Chesibles for *Chapeleyns* chirches to honoure.
B.11.315   A[c] neuer neiþer is blamelees, þe bisshop ne þe *Chapeleyn;*
C. 1.186   Mony *chapeleynes* aren chaste ac charite hem fayleth;
C. 8.11   Chesibles for *chapeleynes* churches to honoure.
C.13.127   Ac neuer noþer is blameles, the bischop ne þe *chapeleyn,*

chapellis n *chapele n.* A 1
A. 7.20   Chesiblis for *chapellis* chirches to honoure.

chapitre n *chapitre n.* B 2 Chapitle (1) Chapitre (1); C 1
B. 3.320   Kynges Court and commune Court, Consistorie and *Chapitle,*
B. 5.161   For she hadde child in chirietyme; al oure *Chapitre* it wiste.
C. 3.473   Kyngus Court and comune Court, constorie and [c]hap[itre],

chapitrehous n *chapitre n.* B 1; C 1
B. 5.174   And am chalanged in þe *Chapitrehous* as I a child were
C. 6.156   Ȝut am y chalenged in oure *chapitrehous* as y a childe were

chapman n *chap-man n.* A 3 chapman (1) chapmen (2); B 5 chapman (1)
   chapmen (4); C 6 Chapman (1) chapmen (5)
A.Pr.61   Siþen charite haþ ben *chapman* & chief to shryue lordis
A. 5.32   He chargide *chapmen* to chastice here children:
A. 5.172   Þere were *chapmen* chosen þat chaffare to preise;
B.Pr.64   Siþ charite haþ ben *chapman* and chief to shryue lordes
B. 5.34   He chargede *Chapmen* to chasti3en hir children:
B. 5.231   '3is, ones I was yherberwed', quod he, 'wiþ an heep of *chapmen;*
B. 5.323   Ther were *chapmen* ychose þis chaffare to preise:
B.15.85   Of vsurers, of hoores, of Auarouse *chapmen;*
C.Pr.62   Ac sith charite hath be *Chapman* and [c]hief to shryue lordes
C. 5.136   He chargede *Chapmen* to chasten here children:
C. 6.235   '3us! ones y was herberwed,' quod he, 'with an heep of *chapmen;*
C. 6.380   There were *chapmen* ychose this chaffare to preyse;
C.10.257   For coueytise of catel and connynge *chapmen,*
C.12.227   That chaff[ar]en as *chapmen* and chide bote they wynne

chapun n *capoun n.* B 2 capons; C 2 capones (1) chapun (1)
B. 4.38   For [þei wolde do for a dyner or a do3eyne *capons*
B.15.474   Ri3t as *capons* in a court comeþ to mennes whistlyng,
C. 4.38   For þey wolde do for a dyner oþer a d[o]seyne *capones*
C. 6.136   For he hadde childe in the *chapun* co[t]e; he worth chalenged at þe
   eleccioun."

charge n *charge n.* A 1; C 2 charge (1) charges (1)
A.10.73   And cheuissh[en] hym for any *charge* whan he childhod passiþ,
C. 9.96   These are Almusse to helpe þat han suche *charges*
C. 9.259   Vigilare were fayrere for thow haste a greet *charge.*

charge v *chargen v.* A 2 chargid (1) chargide (1); B 4 charge (1) chargede (1) chargeþ (2); C 8 charge (2) charged (2) chargede (1) chargeth (3)
A. 5.32   He *chargide* chapmen to chastice here children:
A.10.23   To kepe þise womman þise wise men ben *chargid*,
B. 5.34   He *chargede* Chapmen to chastiȝen hir children:
B.14.315   And [þouȝ] he chaffareþ he *chargeþ* no losse, mowe he charite wynne
B.17.295   And siþ holy chirche and charite *chargeþ* þis so soore
B.20.237   Lat hem chewe as þei chose and *charge* hem with no cure
C.Pr.87   Ben *charged* with holy chirche charite to tylie,
C. 5.136   He *chargede* Chapmen to chasten here children:
C. 7.257   And *charge* charite a churche to make
C. 9.73   *Charged* with childrene and chief lordes rente.
C.16.149   And thogh he chaffare he *chargeth* no loes may he charite wynne:
C.16.290   Charite þat *chargeth* nauht ne chyt thow me greue hym,
C.19.276   And sethe Charite þat holy churche is *chargeth* this so sore
C.22.237   Late hem chewe as thei chose and *charge* hem with no cure.

charite n *charite n.* A 7; B 36; C 38
A.Pr.61   Siþen *charite* haþ ben chapman & chief to shryue lordis
A. 1.162   Chastite wiþoute *charite* worþ cheynide in helle;
A. 1.164   Manye chapelleins arn chast ac *charite* is aweye;
A. 1.167   Chewen here *charite* & chiden aftir more.
A. 1.168   Such chastite wiþoute *charite* worþ cheynid in helle.
A. 6.107   *Charite* & chastite beþ hire chief maidenes,
A. 9.41   Þat is *charite* þe champioun, chief helpe aȝens synne.
B.Pr.64   Siþ *charite* haþ ben chapman and chief to shryue lordes
B. 1.188   Chastite wiþouten *charite* worþ cheyned in helle;
B. 1.190   Manye Chapeleyns arn chaste ac *charite* is aweye;
B. 1.193   Chewen hire *charite* and chiden after moore.
B. 1.194   Swich chastite wiþouten *charite* worþ cheyned in helle.
B. 5.265   For were I frere of þat hous þer good feiþ and *charite* is
B. 5.607   In a cheyne of *charite* as þow a child were,
B. 5.621   *Charite* and Chastite ben hi[r]e chief maydenes;
B. 8.45   [Th]at is *charite* þe champion, chief help ayein synne.
B.10.83   Ne beþ plenteuouse to þe pouere as pure *charite* wolde,
B.12.30   Feiþ, hope and *Charite*, and alle ben goode,
B.12.31   And sauen men sondry tymes, ac noon so soone as *Charite*.
B.13.110   But cheeste be þer *charite* sholde be, and yonge children dorste pleyne.
B.14.98   'Where wonyeþ *Charite*?' quod Haukyn; 'I wiste neuere in my lyue
B.14.101   There is *Charite* þe chief, chaumbrere for god hymselue.'
B.14.315   And [þouȝ] he chaffareþ he *chargeþ* no losse, mowe he charite wynne
B.15.79   Moore for pompe þan for pure *charite*; þe peple woot þe soþe.
B.15.148   In preieres and in penaunces, and in parfit *charite*.'
B.15.149   'What is *charite*?' quod I þo; 'a childissh þyng', he seide:
B.15.153   And fond I neuere ful *charite*, before ne bihynde.
B.15.156   Ac *charite* þat Poul preiseþ best, and moost plesaunt to oure [Saueour]–
B.15.164   *Charite*] is noȝt chaumpions fight ne chaffare as I trowe.'
B.15.165   '*Charite*', quod he, 'ne chaffareþ noȝt, ne chalangeþ, ne craueþ.'
B.15.216   For *charite* is goddes champion, and as a good child hende,
B.15.224   And seintes yset; [stille] *charite* hem folwede.
B.15.225   I haue yseyen *charite* also syngen and reden
B.15.250   And gyue vs grace, goode god, *charite* to folwe.
B.15.344   Forþi I counseille alle cristene to conformen hem to *charite*,
B.15.345   For *charite* wiþouten chalangynge vnchargeþ þe soule,
B.15.566   [*Charite*] were to deschargen hem for holy chirches sake,
B.16.3   Ac ȝit I am in a weer what *charite* is to mene.'
B.16.9   And so þoruȝ god and goode men groweþ þe fruyt *Charite*.'
B.16.197   That is children of *charite*, and holi chirche þe moder.
B.17.294   Thus "vengeaunce, vengeaunce!" verrey *charite* askeþ.
B.17.295   And siþ holy chirche and *charite* chargeþ þis so soore
B.17.297   Wol loue [þat lif] þat [lakkeþ *charite*],
C.Pr.62   Ac sith *charite* hath be Chapman and [c]hief to shryue lordes
C.Pr.64   But holi chirche and *charite* choppe adoun suche shryuars
C.Pr.87   Ben charged with holy chirche *charite* to tylie,
C. 1.184   Chastite withouten *charite* worth c[h]eyned in helle;
C. 1.186   Mony chapeleynes aren chaste ac *charite* hem fayleth;
C. 1.190   [C]hewen here *charite* and chiden aftur more
C. 2.37   He shal lese for here loue [a] lippe of trewe *charite*;
C. 2.143   Holy churche, and *charite* ȝe cheweth and deuoureth.
C. 7.257   And charge *charite* a churche to make
C. 7.273   *Charite* and chastite ben his chief maydenes,
C.10.42   Thow he thorw fondynges falle he falleth nat out of *charite*;
C.11.63   Ne parteth with þe pore as puyr *charite* wolde,
C.15.275   And þat is *charite*, chaumpion chief of all vertues,
C.16.35   And holy churche and *charite* herof a chartre made.
C.16.149   And thogh he chaffare he chargeth no loes may he *charite* wynne:
C.16.285   That lyuen aȝen holy lore and þe loue of *charite*.'
C.16.286   '*Charite*,' quod y tho, 'þat is a thyng forsothe
C.16.290   *Charite* þat chargeth nauht ne chyt thow me greue hym,

C.16.297   And so y trowe treuly, by þat me telleth of *charite*.'
C.16.298   '*Charite* is a childische thyng, as holy churche witnesseth:
C.16.349   And cheef *charite* with hem and chaste all here lyu[e].
C.16.350   Ich haue yseye *charite* also syngen and rede,
C.17.5   'A passeth cheef *charite* yf holy churche be trewe:
C.17.49   And *charite* þat chield is now sholde chaufen of hymsulue
C.17.62   Helpe thy kyn, Crist bid, for þer [coms]eth *charite*
C.17.64   And þer helpe yf thow has[t]; and þat halde y *charite*.
C.17.125   'What is holy churche, chere frende?' quod y; '*Charite*,' he saide:
C.17.140   The whiche is þe heued of *charite* and hele of mannes soule:
C.17.148   And þat is *charite*, leue chield, to be cher ouer thy soule;
C.17.150   'Where sarresynes,' y saide, 'yse nat what is *charite*?'
C.17.151   'Hit may be so þat sarresynes haen such a manere *charite*,
C.17.231   Hit were *charite* to deschargen hem for holy churche sake,
C.17.286   And enchaunten hem to *charite* on holy churche to bileue.
C.18.2   Thow couthest telle me and teche me [in] *charite* [to] leue.
C.18.206   The whiche aren childrene of *charite* and holy church [the] moder.
C.19.275   Thus "veniaunce, veniaunce!" verray *charite* asketh.
C.19.276   And sethe *Charite* þat holy churche is chargeth this so sore
C.19.278   Wol louye þat lyf þat loue and *Charite* destruyeth.'

charme n *charme n.* B 3; C 2
B.13.341   But þoruȝ a *charme* hadde I chaunce and my chief heele.'
B.17.20   For, þouȝ I seye it myself, I haue saued with þis *charme*
B.17.23   Lo! here in my lappe þat leeued on þat *charme*,
C. 6.85   But thorw a *charme* hadde y chaunce and my chef hele.
C.19.21   For, thogh y sey hit mysulue, y haue saued with this *charme*

charnel n *charnel n.(1)* B 1; C 1
B. 6.48   For in *Charnel* at chirche cherles ben yuel to knowe,
C. 8.45   At churche in the *Charnel* cherles Aren euele to knowe

chartre n *chartre n.(1)* A 1 chartres; B 6 chartre (5) chartres (1); C 6 chartre (5) Chartres (1)
A. 2.35   Sire symonye is assent to asele þe *chartres*
B. 2.69   Thanne leep liere forþ and seide, 'lo! here a *chartre*
B. 2.79   And Fauel wiþ his fikel speche feffeþ by þis *chartre*
B.10.320   Of þe pouere haue þei no pite, and þat is hir [pure *chartre*];
B.11.127   For may no cherl *chartre* make ne his c[h]atel selle
B.11.303   A *chartre* is chalangeable bifore a chief Iustice;
B.11.306   The gome þat gloseþ so *chartres* for a goky is holden.
C. 2.71   Thenne lup lyare forth and saide, 'loo! here a *Chartre*
C. 5.166   Of þe pore haueth thei no pite and þat is here puyre *chartre*.
C.12.62   For may no cherl *chartre* make ne his chatel sulle
C.13.117   A *Chartre* is chaleniable byfore a chief Iustice;
C.13.120   The gome þat gloseth so *Chartres* for a goky is halden.
C.16.35   And holy churche and charite herof a *chartre* made.

chaste adj *chaste adj.* A 2 chast; B 2; C 3 chast (1) chaste (2)
A. 1.154   And ek as *chast* as a child þat in chirche wepiþ,
A. 1.164   Manye chapelleins arn *chast* ac charite is aweye;
B. 1.180   And as *chaste* as a child þat in chirche wepeþ,
B. 1.190   Manye Chapeleyns arn *chaste* ac charite is aweye;
C. 1.176   And ben as *chast* as a child þat chyht noþer ne fyhteth,
C. 1.186   Mony chapeleynes aren *chaste* ac charite hem fayleth;
C.16.349   And cheef charite with hem and *chaste* all here lyu[e].

chaste adv *chaste adv.* C 1
C.18.77   And *chaste* leden here lyf, is lyf of contemplacioun,

chaste v *chasten v.* A 4; B 4; C 7 chaste (1) chasted (4) chasten (1) chasteth (1)
A. 7.46   But it be of wysdom or of wyt þi werkmen to *chaste*;
A. 7.299   Suche lawis to loke laboureris to *chast[e]*.
A. 7.304   He shal awake [þoruȝ] water wastours to *chaste*;
A.11.198   Prince ouer godis peple to prechen or to *chaste*.
B. 6.51   But if [it be] of wisdom or of wit þi werkmen to *chaste*;
B. 6.318   Swiche lawes to loke laborers to [*chaste*].
B. 6.323   He shal awake [þoruȝ] water wastours to *chaste*;
B.11.425   Shal neuere chalangynge ne chidynge *chaste* a man so soone
C.Pr.215   Til þat meschief amende hem þat many man *chasteth*.
C. 4.112   And [chyldren] chersyng be *chasted* with ȝerdes
C. 5.136   He chargede Chapmen to *chasten* here children:
C. 8.343   He shal awake thorw water wastors to *chaste*;
C.13.233   For shal neuere, ar shame come, a shrewe wel [be] *chaste[*d].
C.19.303   That [oon] is a wikkede wyf þat wol nat be *chasted*;
C.19.314   The wyf is oure wikkede flesche [þat] wol nat be *chasted*

chastel > castel; chastice > chastiȝen

chastilet n *castelet n.* B 1
B. 2.85   Wiþ þe *Chastilet* of cheste and chaterynge out of reson,

chastised > chastiȝen

chastite n *chastite n.* A 3; B 3; C 2
A. 1.162   *Chastite* wiþoute charite worþ cheynide in helle;

A. 1.168   Such *chastite* wiþoute charite worþ cheynid in helle.
A. 6.107   Charite & *chastite* beþ hire chief maidenes,
B. 1.188   *Chastite* wiþouten charite worþ cheyned in helle;
B. 1.194   Swich *chastite* wiþouten charite worþ cheyned in helle.
B. 5.621   Charite and *Chastite* ben hi[r]e chief maydenes;
C. 1.184   *Chastite* withouten charite worth c[h]eyned in helle;
C. 7.273   Charite and *chastite* ben his chief maydenes,

chastiȝen v *chastisen v.* A 2 chastice (1) chastisid (1); B 4 chastised (3)
    chastiȝen (1); C 1 chastisid
A. 4.103   Til childris cherisshing be *chastisid* with ȝerdis;
A. 5.32   He chargide chapmen to *chastice* here children:
B. 4.117   And childrene cherissynge be *chast[ised]* wiþ yerdes,
B. 5.34   He chargede Chapmen to *chastiȝen* hir children:
B.17.323   That oon is a wikkede wif þat wol noȝt be *chastised*;
B.17.334   The wif is oure wikked flessh þat wol noȝt be *chastised*
C.Pr.110   And *chastisid* hem noght þerof and nolde noght rebuken hem

chatel n *chatel n.* B 1; C 1
B.11.127   For may no cherl chartre make ne his *c[h]atel* selle
C.12.62   For may no cherl chartre make ne his *chatel* sulle

chaterynge ger *chateringe ger.* B 1; C 1
B. 2.85   Wiþ þe Chastilet of cheste and *chaterynge* out of reson,
C. 2.92   With [þe] chastel of cheste and *chaterynge* out of resoun;

chatre v *chateren v.* B 1; C 1 chattere
B.14.227   And if he chide or *chatre* hym cheueþ þe worse,
C.16.68   And yf he chyde or *chattere* hym cheueth þe worse

chaufe(n > chafe; chaumbre > chambre,bedchambre

chaumbrere n *chaumberere n.* B 1
B.14.101   There is Charite þe chief, *chaumbrere* for god hymselue.'

chaumbres > chambre; ; chaump- > champion

chaunce n *chaunce n.* B 1; C 2
B.13.341   But þoruȝ a charme hadde I *chaunce* and my chief heele.'
C. 6.85   But thorw a charme hadde y *chaunce* and my chef hele.
C.14.33   So grace is a gifte of god and kynde wit a *chaunce*

chaunceller n *chaunceler n.* C 1
C. 4.185   But be my cheef *Chaunceller* in Cheker and in parlement

chauncelrie n *chauncerie n.* A 1 chauncerie; B 2 Chauncelrie (1)
    Chauncerye (1); C 1 Chancerye
A. 4.26   In cheker & in *chauncerie*, to be dischargid of þinges,
B.Pr.93   In Cheker and in *Chauncelrie* chalangen hise dettes
B. 4.29   In [c]heker and in *Chauncerye*, to ben descharged of þynges.
C.Pr.91   In Cheker and in *Chancerye* chalengen his dettes

chaunge v *chaungen v.* B 3 chaunge (1) chaunged (1) chaungeden (1); C
    5 change (1) chaunge (1) chaungede (1) chaungen (1) ychaunged (1)
B.11.369   Ac þat moost meued me and my mood *chaunged*,
B.16.129   That in chirche chaffareden or *chaungeden* any moneie;
B.20.360   [And] lat hem ligge ouerlonge and looþ is to *chaunge*;
C. 5.81   And wol til hit be wered out [or] oþerwyse *ychaunged*.
C. 6.146   For she had haly bred ar y my herte gan *change*.
C.12.209   And out of wo into wele ȝoure wirdes shal *chaunge*."
C.13.179   Ac þat most meuede me and my mood *chaungede*
C.22.360   And lat hem lygge ouerlonge and loeth is to *chaungen*;

cheef > chief; cheere > chere; chees > chese; cheest > cheste; chef > chief

cheyne n *chaine n.* B 3 cheyne (1) cheynes (2); C 1 chaynes
B. 5.607   In a *cheyne* of charite as þow a child were,
B.17.113   That he worþ fettred, þat feloun, faste wiþ *Cheynes*,
B.18.403   Thow shalt abyen it bittre!' and bond hym wiþ *cheynes*.
C.20.446   Thow shal[t] abuye bittere!' and b[o]nde hym with *chaynes*.

cheyne v *chainen v.* A 2 cheynid (1) cheynide (1); B 2 cheyned; C 2
    cheyne (1) cheyned (1)
A. 1.162   Chastite wiþoute charite worþ *cheynide* in helle;
A. 1.168   Such chastite wiþoute charite worþ *cheynid* in helle.
B. 1.188   Chastite wiþouten charite worþ *cheyned* in helle;
B. 1.194   Swich chastite wiþouten charite worþ *cheyned* in helle.
C. 1.184   Chastite withouten charite worth *c[h]eyned* in helle;
C.20.285   Cheke and *cheyne* we and vch a [c]hine stoppe

cheitiftee n *caitifte n.* B 1; C 2 caytiftee (1) Cheytyftee (1)
B.20.236   And siþen þei chosen chele and *cheitiftee*
C. 9.256   The cause of al this *caytiftee* cometh of many bischopes
C.22.236   And sethen thei chosen chele and *Cheytyftee*

cheke n *cheke n.* A 5 chekis; B 10 cheke (1) chekes (9); C 7 chekes
A. 4.37   And margerete of hire maydenhed maugre hire *chekis*.
A. 5.65   So lokide he wiþ lene *chekis*, lourande foule.
A. 5.110   [And] as a l[e]erene purs lollide his *chekis*.
A. 7.145   And make vs merye þerwiþ maugre þi *chekis*'.

A. 7.161   And buffetide þe bretoner aboute þe *chekis*
B. 4.50   And Margrete of hir maydenhede maugree hire *chekes*.
B. 5.82   So loked he wiþ lene *chekes*, lourynge foule.
B. 5.164   And eiþer hit[t]e ooþer vnder þe *cheke*.
B. 5.191   And [lik] a leþeren purs lolled hise *chekes*
B. 6.40   And mekenesse þi maister maugree Medes *chekes*;
B. 6.158   And maken vs murye þer[wiþ] maugree þi *chekes*.'
B. 6.176   He buffetted þe Bretoner aboute þe *chekes*
B.13.78   'Ac þis goddes gloton', quod I, 'wiþ hise grete *chekes*
B.13.100   As rody as a Rose [ruddede] hise *chekes*,
B.14.4   That wollen bymolen it many tyme maugree my *chekes*,
C. 6.150   Til bothe here hedes were bar and blody here *chekes*.
C. 6.199   And as a letherne pors lollede his *chekes*
C. 8.38   And Mekenesse thy maystre maugre mede *chekes*
C. 8.173   A boffatede þe Bretoner aboute þe *chekes*
C. 9.209   That faytede in frere clothinge hadde fatte *chekes*.
C.15.85   And also a gnedy glotoun with two grete *chekes*,
C.15.107   As rody as a rose rodded his *chekes*,

cheke v *chekken v.(1)* C 1
C.20.285   *Cheke* and cheyne we and vch a [c]hine stoppe

cheker n *cheker n.(2)* A 1; B 2; C 2
A. 4.26   In *cheker* & in chauncerie, to be dischargid of þinges,
B.Pr.93   In *Cheker* and in Chauncelrie chalangen hise dettes
B. 4.29   In [c]*heker* and in Chauncerye, to ben descharged of þynges.
C.Pr.91   In *Cheker* and in Chancerye chalengen his dettes
C. 4.185   But be my cheef Chaunceller in *Cheker* and in parlement

chele n *chele n.* A 2; B 3; C 2
A. 1.23   Þat on is vesture fro *chele* þe to saue;
A.11.46   Boþe for hungir & for þrest, & for *chele* quak[e];
B. 1.23   That oon [is] vesture from [*chele*] þee to saue;
B.10.60   Boþe afyngred and afurst, and for *chele* quake;
B.20.236   And siþen þei chosen *chele* and cheitiftee
C. 8.248   Chaffare and cheue þerwith in *chele* and in hete.
C.22.236   And sethen thei chosen *chele* and Cheytyftee

chepe n prop *chep n.* A 1; B 1
A. 5.164   A ribibour, a ratoner, & a rakiere of *chepe*,
B. 5.314   A Ribibour, a Ratoner, a Rakiere of *Chepe*,

chepe v *chepen v.* B 2 Chepe (1) cheped (1); C 1
B.13.379   And whoso *cheped* my chaffare, chiden I wolde
B.15.31   And whan I chalange or chalange noȝt, *chepe* or refuse,
C.16.191   And when y chalenge [or chalenge] nat, *chepe* or refuse

chepyng ger *chepinge ger.* A 2; B 2; C 2 chepyng (1) chepynge (1)
A. 4.43   Forstalliþ my feiris, fiȝteþ in my *chepyng*,
A. 7.283   Be þat it neiȝide ner heruest [þat] newe corn com to *chepyng*.
B. 4.56   Forstalleþ my feires, fiȝteþ in my *Chepyng*,
B. 6.299   By þat it neȝed neer heruest newe corn cam to *chepyng*.
C. 4.59   Forstalleth my fayres and fyhteth in my *chepyng[e]*
C. 8.321   By that hit nyhed neyh heruost and newe corn cam to *chepyng*.

cher adj *OED chary a., cf. MED cher adj.* C 2 cher (1) chere (1)
C.17.125   'What is holy churche, *chere* frende?' quod y; 'Charite,' he saide;
C.17.148   And þat is charite, leue chield, to be *cher* ouer thy soule.

cherche > chirche,holy_chirche

chere n *chere n.(1)* A 2 chere (1) chiere (1); B 8 cheere (1) chere (6)
    chiere (1); C 6 chere (5) chiere (1)
A. 5.167   Ȝeue glotoun wiþ glad *chiere* good ale to hansele.
A.11.2   Þat lene was of lich & of lo[uȝ] *chere*.
B. 4.165   Mede mornede þo and made heuy *chere*
B. 5.318   Geue Gloton wiþ glad *chere* good ale to hansele.
B.10.2   That lene was of [liche] and of [lowe *chere*].
B.11.27   Thanne was þer oon þat hiȝte Elde, þat heuy was of *chere*;
B.11.187   And lokeþ on vs in hir liknesse and þat wiþ louely *chere*
B.16.155   And gile is in þi glad *chere* and galle is in þi laughyng.
B.20.114   This lecherie leide on wiþ [laughynge] *chiere*
B.20.349   Lat in þe frere and his felawe, and make hem fair *cheere*.
C. 4.160   Mede mornede tho and made heuy *chere*
C. 6.375   Geuen glotoun with glad *chere* good ale to hansull.
C.11.186   Thenne was [there] oen þat hihte Elde þat heuy was of *chere*;
C.17.30   Bote myldelyche when þey metten maden lowe [*c*]*here*
C.22.114   This lecherye leyde [o]n with lauhyng *chere*
C.22.349   Lat in þe frere and his felawe and make hem fayere *chiere*.

chered ptp *chered pp.* B 2
B.19.263   That oon was Luk, a large beest and a lowe *chered*,
B.20.2   Heuy *chered* I yede and elenge in herte.
C.21.263   That oen was luc, a large beste and a lou *chered*,
C.22.2   Heuy *chered* y ȝede and [e]lyng in herte.

cheries > chiries

cherissynge ger *cherishinge ger.* A 1 cherisshing; B 1; C 1 chersyng
A. 4.103   Til childris *cherisshing* be chastisid with ȝerdis;
B. 4.117   And childrene *cherissynge* be chast[ised] wiþ yerdes,
C. 4.112   And [chyldren] *chersyng* be chasted with ȝerdes

cherl n *cherl n.* A 1 cherlis; B 10 cherl (3) cherles (7); C 9 cherl (3) cherles (6)
A. 3.247   Children & *cherlis*, choppe hem to deþe.
B. 1.33   And þere gat in glotonye gerles þat were *cherles*.
B. 5.353   Ac Gloton was a gret *cherl* and grym in þe liftyng;
B. 6.48   For in Charnel at chirche *cherles* ben yuel to knowe,
B.11.127   For may no *cherl* chartre make ne his c[h]atel selle
B.16.121   'Thanne are ye *cherles*', [chidde Iesus], 'and youre children boþe,
B.18.104   And ye, *cherles*, and youre children cheue shulle [ye] neuere,
B.19.35   Boþe his loore and his lawe; now are þei lowe *cherles*.
B.19.37   But vnder tribut and taillage as tikes and *cherles*.
B.19.55   That longe hadde yleyen bifore as Luciferis *cherles*,
B.20.146   And leet leautee a *cherl* and lyere a fre man.
C. 1.29   In his glotonye bygat gurles þat were *cherles*
C. 6.411   Ac gloton was a greet *cherl* and gr[ym] in þe luftynge
C. 8.45   At churche in the Charnel *cherles* Aren euele to knowe
C.12.62   For may no *cherl* chartre make ne his chatel sulle
C.20.107   And alle ȝoure childerne, *cherles*, cheue shal neuere
C.21.35   Bothe his lore and his lawe; now are þei lowe *cherles*.
C.21.37   Bote vnder tribuyt and talage as tykes and *cherles*.
C.21.55   That longe hadden leye bifore as luciferes *cherles*
C.22.146   And leet leautee a *cherl* and lyare a fre man.

chersyng > cherissynge

cherubyn n *cherubin n.* A 1; B 1; C 1
A. 1.104   *Cherubyn* & seraphyn, such seuene & anoþer;
B. 1.106   *Cherubyn* and Seraphyn, swiche seuene & [anoþer],
C. 1.106   *Cherubyn* and Ceraphyn, suche seuene and anoþer,

cheruelles n *chervel n.* A 1 chiriuellis; B 1; C 1 chiruulles
A. 7.278   Chibollis, & *chiriuellis*, & ri[p]e chiries manye,
B. 6.294   Chibolles and *Cheruelles* and ripe chiries manye;
C. 8.309   Chibolles and *chiruulles* and cheries samrede

chese n *chese n.* A 1 chesis; B 3 chese (2) cheses (1); C 3 chese (2) cheses (1)
A. 7.265   Noþer gees ne gris, but two grene *chesis*,
B. 5.92   Than þouȝ I hadde þis wouke ywonne a weye of Essex *chese*.
B. 5.437   Boþ[e] bred and ale, buttre, melk and *chese*
B. 6.281   Neiþer gees ne grys, but two grene *cheses*,
C. 7.51   Bothe Bred and ale, Botere, mylke and *chese*
C. 8.303   Noþer goos ne gries but two grene *cheses*,
C. 9.150   Loef oþer half loef other a lompe of *chese*

chese v *chesen v.* A 2 chosen; B 9 chese (1) chose (1) chosen (5) chosene (1) ychose (1); C 11 chees (1) chese (2) chesen (1) chose (4) chosen (1) chosene (1) ychose (1)
A.Pr.31   And somme *chosen* [hem] to chaffare, þei cheuide þe betere
A. 5.172   Þere were chapmen *chosen* þat chaffare to preise;
B.Pr.31   And somme *chosen* [hem to] chaffare; þei cheueden þe bettre,
B. 5.323   Ther were chapmen *ychose* þis chaffare to preise:
B.11.117   Wheiþer I were *chosen* or noȝt chosen; on holi chirche I þouȝte
B.11.117   Wheiþer I were chosen or noȝt *chosen*; on holi chirche I þouȝte
B.11.118   That vnderfonged me atte font for oon of goddes *chosene*.
B.15.38   Nempnede me þus to name; now þow myȝt *chese*
B.18.201   Forþi lat hem chewe as þei *chosen* and chide we noȝt, sustres,
B.20.236   And siþen þei *chosen* chele and cheitiftee
B.20.237   Lat hem chewe as þei *chose* and charge hem with no cure
C.Pr.33   And summe *chesen* chaffare; þei cheue[den] þe bettre
C. 6.380   There were chapmen *ychose* this chaffare to preyse;
C.12.52   Where y were *chose* [or nat chose]; on holy churche y thouhte
C.12.52   Where y were chose [or nat *chose*]; on holy churche y thouhte
C.12.53   That vnderfeng me at þe fonte for on of godes *chosene*.
C.13.3   Oure prince iesu pouerte *chees* and his apostles alle
C.16.176   Layk or leue, at my lykyng *chese*
C.16.200   Nempned me thus to name; now þou myhte *chese*
C.20.206   Forthy [let] hem che[w]e as they *chose* and chyde we nat, sustres,
C.22.236   And sethen thei *chosen* chele and Cheytyftee
C.22.237   Late hem chewe as thei *chose* and charge hem with no cure.

chesibles n *chesible n.* A 1 chesiblis; B 1; C 1
A. 7.20   *Chesiblis* for chapellis chirches to honoure.
B. 6.12   *Chesibles* for Chapeleyns chirches to honoure.
C. 8.11   *Chesibles* for chapeleynes churches to honoure.

cheste n1 *cheste n.* B 1; C 1
B.12.114   Hadde neuere lewed man leue to leggen hond on þat *cheste*
C.14.59   Hadde neuere lewede [man] leue to legge hand on þat *cheste*

cheste n2 *chest n.* A 1; B 4 cheeste (2) cheste (2); C 4
A.10.193   Haue þei no children but ch[este], & choppis [betwene].

B. 2.85   Wiþ þe Chastilet of *cheste* and chaterynge out of reson,
B. 9.172   Haue þei no children but *cheeste* and [choppes] bitwene.
B.12.125   Lest *cheste* cha[fe] vs to choppe ech man oþer:
B.13.110   But *cheeste* be þer charite sholde be, and yonge children dorste pleyne,
C.Pr.105   What *cheste* and meschaunce to þe children of Irael
C. 2.92   With [þe] chastel of *cheste* and chaterynge out of resoun;
C.10.274   Haen þei no childerne bute *cheste* and [c]hoppes hem bitwene.
C.14.68   Laste *cheste* chauf[e] vs to [c]hoppe vch man oþer.

chestre n prop *n.i.d.* A 2; B 2; C 1
A. 5.231   And wiþ þe residue & þe remenaunt, be þe roode of *chestre*,
A. 7.92   And wiþ þe residue & þe remenaunt, be þe rode of *chestre*,
B. 5.395   But I kan rymes of Robyn hood and Randolf Erl of *Chestre*,
B. 5.459   And wiþ þe residue and þe remenaunt, bi þe Rode of *Chestre*,
C. 7.11   Y can rymes of robyn hode and of randolf Erle of *Chestre*

chetes n *chete n.(2)* C 1
C. 4.169   'Thorw ȝoure lawe, as y leue, y lese many *chetes*;

cheue v *cheven v.* A 1 cheuide; B 3 cheue (1) cheueden (1) cheueþ (1); C 5 cheue (2) cheued (1) cheueden (1) cheueth (1)
A.Pr.31   And somme chosen [hem] to chaffare, þei *cheuide* þe betere
B.Pr.31   And somme chosen [hem to] chaffare; þei *cheueden* þe bettre,
B.14.227   And if he chide or chatre hym *cheueþ* þe worse,
B.18.104   And ye, cherles, and youre children *cheue* shulle [ye] neuere,
C.Pr.33   And summe chesen chaffare; þei *cheue*[den] þe bettre
C. 6.252   That chaffared with my cheuesaunces *cheued* selde aftur.'
C. 8.248   Chaffare and *cheue* þerwith in chele and in hete.
C.16.68   And yf he chyde or chattere hym *cheueth* þe worse
C.20.107   And alle ȝoure childerne, cherles, *cheue* shal neuere

cheuenteyn > chieftayn

cheuyssaunce n *chevisaunce n.* B 2 cheuysaunces (1) cheuyssaunce (1); C 2 cheuesaunce (1) cheuesaunces (1)
B. 5.246   Eschaunges and *cheuysaunces*, wiþ swich chaffare I dele,
B.20.16   And þouȝ he come so to a clooþ and kan no bettre *cheuyssaunce*
C. 6.252   That chaffared with my *cheuesaunces* cheued selde aftur.'
C.22.16   And thow he come so to a cloth and can no bettre *cheuesaunce*

cheuisshen v *chevishen v.* A 1
A.10.73   And *cheuissh*[en] hym for any charge whan he childhod passiþ,

chewe v *cheuen v.* A 1 chewen; B 3 chewe (2) chewen (1); C 6 chewe (4) chewen (1) cheweth (1)
A. 1.167   *Chewen* here charite & chiden aftir more.
B. 1.193   *Chewen* hire charite and chiden after moore.
B.18.201   Forþi lat hem *chewe* as þei chosen and chide we noȝt, sustres,
B.20.237   Lat hem *chewe* as þei chose and charge hem with no cure
C. 1.190   [C]hewen here charite and chiden aftur more
C. 2.143   Holy churche, and charite ȝe *cheweth* and deuoureth.
C. 8.285   Lene hem som of thy loef thouh thow þe lasse *chewe*.
C.15.45   Ac of this mete þat maystre myhte nat we[l c]hewe;
C.20.206   Forthy [let] hem *che[w]e* as they chose and chyde we nat, sustres,
C.22.237   Late hem *chewe* as thei chose and charge hem with no cure.

chibolles n *chibolle n.* A 1 chibollis; B 1; C 1 chibolles
A. 7.278   *Chibollis*, & chiriuellis, & ri[p]e chiries manye,
B. 6.294   *Chibolles* and Cheruelles and ripe chiries manye;
C. 8.309   *Chibolles* and chiruulles and cheries samrede

chichestre n prop *n.i.d.* B 1
B.13.270   My wafres were gesene whan *Chichestre* was Maire.'

chidares > chideres

chiden v *chiden v.* A 5 chide (4) chiden (1); B 11 chidde (2) chide (7) chiden (2); C 14 chydde (2) chide (1) chyde (8) chiden (1) chyht (1) chyt (1)
A. 1.167   Chewen here charite & *chiden* aftir more.
A. 3.165   And þou knowist, consience, I ca[m] nouȝt to *chide*,
A. 4.39   I dar not for fer of hym fiȝte ne *chide*.
A. 7.296   But he be heiȝliche hirid ellis wile he *chide*,
A. 7.300   Ac while hunger was here maister wolde þere non *chide*,
B. 1.193   Chewen hire charite and *chiden* after moore.
B. 3.178   And þow knowest, Conscience, I kam noȝt to *chide*,
B. 4.52   I dar noȝt for fere of h[y]m fiȝte ne *chide*.
B. 6.312   But he be heiȝliche hyred ellis wole he *chide*;
B. 6.319   Ac whiles hunger was hir maister þer wolde noon *chide*
B.13.322   Lyinge and la[kk]ynge and leue tonge to *chide*,
B.13.379   And whoso cheped my chaffare, *chiden* I wolde
B.14.227   And if he *chide* or chatre hym cheueþ þe worse,
B.16.121   'Thanne are ye cherles', [*chidde* Iesus], 'and youre children boþe,
B.18.201   Forþi lat hem chewe as þei chosen and *chide* we noȝt, sustres,
B.18.418   And leteþ no peple', quod pees, 'parceyue þat we *chidde*;
C. 1.176   And ben as chast as a child þat *chyht* noþer ne fyhteth,
C. 1.190   [C]hewen here charite and *chiden* aftur more

C. 3.224   And þ[ou] knowe[st], Consience, y cam nat to *chyde*
C. 3.390   Be the peccunie ypaied, thow parties *chyde*,
C. 5.154   For in C[l]oystre cometh no man to *chyde* ne to fyhte;
C. 6.147   [Afturward, aftur mete], she and she *chydde*
C. 7.302   And loure on me and lihtly *chyde* and sygge y louede another.
C. 8.334   But he be heyliche yhuyred elles wol he *chy[d]e*;
C. 8.339   Ac whiles hungur was here maistre ther wolde non *chyde*
C.12.227   That chaff[ar]en as chapmen and *chide* bote they wynne
C.16.68   And yf he *chyde* or chattere hym cheueth þe worse
C.16.290   Charite þat chargeth nauht ne *chyt* thow me greue hym,
C.20.206   Forthy [let] hem che[w]e as they chose and *chyde* we nat, sustres,
C.20.461   'And lat no peple,' quod pees, 'perseyue þat we *chydde*;

chideris n *chidere n.* B 1; C 1 chidares
B.16.43   Bakbiteris [brewe]cheste, brawleris and *chideris*,
C.18.46   Thorw bagbitares and braule[r]s and thorw bolde *chidares*

chidynge ger *chidinge ger.* B 2; C 1 chidynge
B. 5.87   Of *chidynge* and chalangynge was his chief liflode,
B.11.425   Shal neuere chalangynge ne *chidynge* chaste a man so soone
C. 6.68   *Chidynge* and chalengynge was his cheef lyflode

chief n *cher n.* B 1
B.14.101   There is Charite þe *chief*, chaumbrere for god hymselue.'

chief adj *chef adj.* A 4; B 10; C 13 cheef (6) chef (1) chief (6)
A.Pr.61   Siþen charite haþ ben chapman & *chief* to shryue lordis
A. 6.107   Charite & chastite beþ hire *chief* maidenes,
A. 9.41   Þat is charite þe champioun, *chief* helpe aȝens synne.
A.10.72   Is *chief* souereyn ouer hymself his soule is ȝeme,
B.Pr.64   Siþ charite haþ ben chapman and *chief* to shryue lordes
B. 5.87   Of chidynge and chalangynge was his *chief* liflode,
B. 5.621   Charite and Chastite ben hi[r]e *chief* maydenes;
B. 8.45   [Th]at is charite þe champion, *chief* help ayein synne.
B.10.101   Or in a chambre wiþ a chymenee, and leue þe *chief* halle
B.11.303   A chartre is chalangeable bifore a *chief* Iustice;
B.13.341   But þoruȝ a charme hadde I chaunce and my *chief* heele.'
B.18.99   For youre champion chiualer, *chief* knyȝt of yow alle,
B.19.406   The *chief* seed þat Piers sew, ysaued worstow neuere.
B.19.472   And holy chirches *chief* help and Chieftayn of þe comune,
C.Pr.62   Ac sith charite hath be Chapman and [c]*hief* to shryue lordes
C. 4.185   But be my *cheef* Chaunceller in Cheker and in parlement
C. 6.68   Chidynge and chalengynge was his *cheef* lyflode
C. 6.85   But thorw a charme hadde y chaunce and my *chef* hele.
C. 7.273   Charite and chastite ben his *chief* maydenes,
C. 9.73   Charged with childrene and *chief* lordes rente.
C.13.117   A Chartre is chaleniable byfore a *chief* Iustice;
C.15.275   And þat is charite, chaumpion *chief* of all vertues,
C.16.349   And *cheef* charite with hem and chaste all here lyu[e].
C.17.5   'A passeth *cheef* charite yf holy churche be trewe:
C.20.102   For ȝoure chaumpioun Chiualer, *chief* knyht of ȝow alle,
C.21.406   The *cheef* seed þat [Peres] sewe, ysaued wo[r]st þou neuere.
C.21.472   And holy churche *cheef* helpe and cheuenteyn of þe comu[n]e

chieftayn n *chevetaine n.* B 1; C 1 cheuenteyn
B.19.472   And holy chirches chief help and *Chieftayn* of þe comune,
C.21.472   And holy churche cheef helpe and *cheuenteyn* of þe comu[n]e

chield ptp *chillen v. &> child* C 1
C.17.49   And charite þat *chield* is now sholde chaufen of hymsulue

chiere > chere; chyht > chiden

child n *child n.* A 13 child (1) childe (1) children (10) childris (1); B 32
child (6) childe (3) children (22) childrene (1); C 32 chield (1) child (1)
(1) childe (6) childerne (4) children (8) chyldren (1) childrene (10)
childurne (1)
A.Pr.35   Ac Iaperis & iangleris, Iudas *children*,
A. 1.154   And ek as chast as a *child* þat in chirche wepiþ,
A. 3.239   Why þe vengeaunce fel on saul & on his *children*?
A. 3.247   *Children* & cherlis, choppe hem to deþe.
A. 4.103   Til *childris* cherisshing be chastisid with ȝerdis;
A. 5.32   He chargede chapmen to chastice here *children*:
A. 7.89   And dele among my frendis & my dere *children*,
A. 7.267   A lof of benis & bren ybake for my *children*;
A. 8.83   And wommen wiþ *childe* þat werche ne mowe,
A.10.103   I haue [lernid] how lewid men han [lerid] here *children*
A.10.179   And al for se[þ] & his sister *children* spouside eiþer oþer,
A.10.181   And [were] marie[d] at meschief as men do now here *children*.
A.10.193   Haue þei no *children* but ch[este], & choppis [betwene].
B.Pr.35   Ac Iaperes and Iangeleres, Iudas *children*,
B. 1.180   And as chaste as a *child* þat in chirche wepeþ,
B. 3.260   Whi þ[at] vengeaunce fel on Saul and on his *children*?
B. 3.268   Widwes and wyues, wommen and *children*,
B. 4.117   And *childrene* cherissynge be chast[ised] wiþ yerdes,
B. 5.34   He chargede Chapmen to chastiȝen hir *children*:

B. 5.38   "[Lo], þe leuere *child* þe moore loore bihoueþ";
B. 5.40   Whoso spareþ þe spryng spilleþ hise *children*.'
B. 5.161   For she hadde *child* in chirietyme; al oure Chapitre it wiste.
B. 5.174   And am chalanged in þe Chapitrehous as I a *child* were
B. 5.607   In a cheyne of charite as þow a *child* were,
B. 6.97   And dele among my [frendes] and my deere *children*.
B. 7.101   And wommen wiþ *childe* þat werche ne mowe,
B. 9.70   And] fynden hem þat hem fauted, and faderlese *children*,
B. 9.158   Forþi haue þei maugre of hir mariages þat marie so hir *children*,
B. 9.172   Haue þei no *children* but cheeste and [choppes] bitwene.
B.11.209   Forþi loue we as leue [*children* shal], and ech man laughe of ooþer,
B.11.384   Frenche men and fre men affaiteþ þus hire *children*:
B.12.12   And wiþ þise bittre baleises god beteþ his deere *children*:
B.13.110   But cheeste be þer charite sholde be, and yonge *children* dorste
            pleyne.
B.14.3   And also I haue an houswif, hewen and *children*–
B.15.216   For charite is goddes champion, and as a good *child* hende,
B.15.248   And for his seketoures & his seruauntȝ, & som for hir *children*].
B.15.372   Grammer, þe ground of al, bigileþ now *children*,
B.16.121   'Thanne are ye cherles', [chidde Iesus], 'and youre *children* boþe,
B.16.197   That is *children* of charite, and holi chirche þe moder.
B.16.198   Patriarkes and prophetes and Apostles were þe *children*,
B.16.221   That is man and his make and mulliere *children*;
B.18.104   And ye, cherles, and youre *children* cheue shulle [ye] neuere,
B.18.130   And grace of þe holy goost; weex greet wiþ *childe*;
B.20.79   And þere abide and bikere ayeins Beliales *children*.'
B.20.347   He salude so oure wommen til some were wiþ *childe*.'
C.Pr.105   What cheste and meschaunce to þe *children* of Irael
C.Pr.111   Anon as it was tolde hym þat þe *children* of Irael
C.Pr.115   And al was for vengeance he bet noght his *children*
C. 1.176   And ben as chast as a *child* þat chyht noþer ne fyhteth,
C. 3.397   But þat alle maner men, wymmen and *childrene*
C. 3.421   Man, womman and wyf, *childe*, wedewe and bestes,
C. 4.112   And [*chyldren*] chersyng be chasted with ȝerdes,
C. 5.68   Bondemen and bastardus and beggares *children*,
C. 5.136   He chargede Chapmen to chasten here *children*:
C. 5.138   For hoso spareth þe spry[n]g spilleth h[is] *children*;
C. 6.136   For he hadde *childe* in the chapun co[t]e; he worth chalenged at þe
            eleccioun."
C. 6.156   Ȝut am y chalenged in oure chapitrehous as y a *childe* were,
C. 8.106   And delen amongus my douhteres and my dere *childre[n]*,
C. 9.73   Charged with *childrene* and chief lordes rente.
C. 9.89   What other byhoueth þat hath many *childrene*
C. 9.170   Or þe bak or som bon þey breke of he[re] *children*
C. 9.177   And wymmen with *childe* þat worche ne mowe,
C. 9.227   As wolues þat wuryeth men, wymmen and *childrene*
C.10.256   Ac fewe folke now folweth this for thei ȝeue her *childurne*
C.10.274   Haen þei no *childerne* bute cheste and [c]hoppes hem bitwene.
C.12.117   Forthy loue we as leue *childerne*, lene hem þat nedeth
C.12.157   Or eny welthe in this world, his wyf or his *childrene*,
C.16.303   And sory when he seth men sory, as thow seest *childerne*
C.17.108   Gramer, þe grounde of al, bigileth nouthe *childerne*,
C.17.148   And þat is charite, leue *chield*, to be cher ouer thy soule;
C.17.291   And deye for his dere *childrene* to de[struy]e dedly synne,
C.18.206   The whiche aren *childerne* of charite and holy church [the] moder,
C.18.207   Patriarches and prophetes and apostles were the *childerne*.
C.20.107   And alle ȝoure *childerne*, cherles, cheue shal neuere
C.20.133   And grace of the holy goost; wax grete with *childe*,
C.22.79   And þere abyde and bikere aȝeyn beliales *childrene*.'
C.22.347   He salued so oure wymmen til some were with *childe*.'

childhod n *childhod n.* A 1
A.10.73   And cheuissh[en] hym for any charge whan he *childhod* passiþ,

childissh adj *childish adj.* B 1; C 1 childische
B.15.149   'What is charite?' quod I þo; 'a *childissh* þyng', he seide:
C.16.298   'Charite is a *childische* thyng, as holy churche witnesseth:

children(- -dris -durne > child

chillynge ger *chilling ger.* A 1 chillyng; B 1; C 1 chillyng
A. 7.295   And chaud, & pluys chaud, for *chillyng* of h[ere] mawe.
B. 6.311   And þat chaud and plus chaud for *chillynge* of hir mawe.
C. 8.333   And þat chaut and pluchaut for *chillyng* of h[ere] mawe.

chymenee n *chimene n.* B 1
B.10.101   Or in a chambre wiþ a *chymenee*, and leue þe chief halle

chyn n *chin n.* B 1; C 1
B. 5.192   Wel sidder þan his *chyn*; þei chyueled for elde;
C. 6.200   Wel syddore then his *chyn*, ycheueled for elde,

chine n *chine n.* C 1
C.20.285   Cheke and cheyne we and vch a [c]*hine* stoppe

chirche n *chirche n.* &> *holy_chirche* A 10 chirche (5) chirches (2) kirke (3); B 19 cherche (1) chirche (8) chirches (3) kirk (4) kirke (3); C 21 chirche (2) *chirches* (1) churche (5) churches (6) kyrke (6) kyrkes (1)

A. 1.154   And ek as chast as a child þat in *chirche* wepiþ,
A. 2.183   And senten hym on sundais wiþ selis to *chirche*,
A. 5.1   Þe king & [his] kniȝtes to þe *[k]ir[k]e* wente
A. 5.85   Whanne I come to þe *[k]ir[k]e* & knel[e] to þe rode,
A. 5.162   Claris of cokkislane & þe clerk of þe *chirche*,
A. 5.223   Þat I ne shal do me er day to þe dere *chirche*
A. 7.20   Chesiblis for chapellis *chirches* to honoure.
A. 7.83   Þe *[k]ir[k]e* shal haue my caroyn & kepe my bones,
A. 8.156   He passiþ al þe pardoun [of] seint petris *chirche*.
A.10.111   And for wisdom is writen & witnessid in *chirches*:
B. 1.180   And as chaste as a child þat in *chirche* wepeþ,
B. 2.224   And senten hym [on Sondayes wiþ seles] to *chirch[e]*,
B. 3.60   And I shal couere youre *kirk*, youre cloistre do maken,
B. 5.1   The kyng and hise knyȝtes to þe *kirke* wente
B. 5.105   Whan I come to þe *kirk* and knele to þe Roode
B. 5.266   I nolde cope vs wiþ þi catel ne oure *kirk* amende
B. 5.311   Clarice of Cokkeslane and þe Clerk of þe *chirche*,
B. 5.403   Wiþ ydel tales at þe Ale and ouþerwhile [in] *chirche[s]*;
B. 5.451   That I ne shal do me er day to þe deere *chirche*
B. 6.12   Chesibles for Chapeleyns *chirches* to honoure.
B. 6.48   For in Charnel at *chirche* cherles ben yuel to knowe,
B. 6.91   The *kirke* shal haue my caroyne and kepe my bones
B. 6.147   And catel to [cope] hem wiþ þat han Cloistres and *chirches*.
B. 7.178   [He] passeþ al þe pardon of Seint Petres *cherche*.
B.11.65   Be buried at hire hous but at my parisshe *chirche*;
B.11.67   [At *kirke*] þere a man were cristned by kynde he sholde be buried.
B.13.9   And no corps in hir kirkȝerd n[e] in hir *kirk* was buryed
B.16.129   That in *chirche* chaffareden or chaungeden any moneie;
B.19.2   And dighte me derely and dide me to *chirche*
C. 2.234   And senten hym on sonendayes with seeles to *churche*,
C. 3.64   And y shal cuuere ȝoure *kyrke* and ȝoure clo[i]stre make;
C. 5.12   'Can thow seruen,' he sayde, 'or syngen in a *churche*
C. 5.30   Or faytest vppon frydayes or festeday[es] in *churches*,
C. 5.60   And in quoer and in *kyrkes* Cristes mynistres:
C. 5.104   'Ȝe! and contynue,' quod Consience, 'and to þe *kyrke* wen[d]e.'
C. 5.105   And to þe *kyrke* y gan go god to honoure;
C. 5.175   And constantyn shal be here cook and couerour of here *churches*,
C. 6.288   Y ne wolde cope me with thy catel ne oure *kyrke* mende
C. 6.366   Claryce of cockes lane and the clerc of þe *churche*,
C. 7.19   With ydele tales at þe ale and oþerwhile in *chirches*;
C. 7.65   That y ne shal do me ar day to þe dere *chirche*
C. 7.257   And charge charite a *churche* to make
C. 8.11   Chesibles for chapeleynes *churches* to honoure.
C. 8.45   At *churche* in the Charnel cherles Aren euele to knowe
C. 8.100   The *kyrke* shal haue my caroyne and kepe my bones
C. 9.98   Ac beggares with bagges þe whiche brewhous[es] ben here *churches*,
C. 9.190   And in borwes among brewesteres and beggen in *churches*–
C. 9.229   Bothe matynes and masse; and aftir mete in *churches*
C. 9.242   Breke þis obedience þat beth so fer fram *chirche*.
C.21.2   And dihte me derely and dede me to *kyrke*

chiries n *cheri n.* A 1; B 1; C 2 cheries
A. 7.278   Chibollis, & chiriuellis, & ri[p]e *chiries* manye,
B. 6.294   Chibolles and Cheruelles and ripe *chiries* manye;
C. 8.309   Chibolles and chiruulles and *cheries* samrede
C.12.221   As pesecoddes, pere ionettes, plommes and *cheries*;

chirietyme n *cheri n.* B 1
B. 5.161   For she hadde child in *chirietyme*; al oure Chapitre it wiste.

chiriuelles chiruulles > cheruelles; chyt > chiden

chiteryng ger *chiteringe ger.* B 1
B.12.255   His ledene be in oure lordes ere lik a pies *chiteryng*;

chiualer n *chevaler n.* B 1; C 1
B.18.99   For youre champion *chiualer*, chief knyȝt of yow alle,
C.20.102   For ȝoure chaumpioun *Chiualer*, chief knyht of ȝow alle,

chyueled v *chiveren v.* B 1; C 1 ycheueled
B. 5.192   Wel sidder þan his chyn; þei *chyueled* for elde,
C. 6.200   Wel syddore then his chyn, *ycheueled* for elde,

choppe v *choppen v.* A 1; B 1; C 2
A. 3.247   Children & cherlis, *choppe* hem to deþe.
B.12.125   Lest cheste cha[fe] vs to *choppe* ech man oþer:
C.Pr.64   But holi chirche and charite *choppe* adoun suche shryuars
C.14.68   Laste cheste chauf[e] vs to *[c]hoppe* vch man oþer.

choppes n *chop n.(1)* A 1 choppis; B 1; C 1
A.10.193   Haue þei no children but ch[este], & *choppis* [betwene].
B. 9.172   Haue þei no children but cheeste and [*choppes*] bitwene.

C.10.274   Haen þei no childerne bute cheste and [*c*]*hoppes* hem bitwene.

chose(- > chese; church(- > chirche, holi_chirche

circumscised v *circumcisen v.* B 1; C 1 circumsised
B.16.235   I *circumscised* my sone siþen for his sake,
C.18.251   Y *circumsised* my sone also for his sake,

cisse > cesse

cite n *cite n.* B 3 Cite (1) Citee (1) Citees (1); C 6 Cite (1) Citee (2) Citees (2) Cytees (1)
B.Pr.160   'I haue yseyen segges', quod he, 'in þe *Cite* of Londoun
B.14.81   [So] thei sonken into helle, þe *Citees* echone.
B.18.235   That swich a barn was ybore in Bethleem þe *Citee*
C.Pr.179   Sayde, 'y haue seyen grete syres in *Cytees* and in townes
C. 3.90   Many sondry sorwes in *Citees* falleth ofte
C. 3.112   Hit is nat seemely, forsothe, in *Citee* [ne] in borw toun
C. 3.204   Ther ne is *Cite* vnder sonne ne noon so ryche reume
C. 5.90   Ac it semeth no sad parfitnesse in *Citees* to b[e]gge
C.20.244   That such a barn was ybore in Bethleem þe *Citee*

cyuylle n *civile adj.as n.* A 7 cyuyle; B 12 Cyuyle (5) Cyuyles (1) Cyuylle (6); C 12 syuile (4) syuyle (7) syuyles (1)
A. 2.54   Symonye & *cyuyle* stondiþ forþ boþe
A. 2.80   And seide to *cyuyle*, 'now sorewe on þi bokes,
A. 2.106   Hereto assentiþ *Cyuyle*, ac symonye ne wolde
A. 2.132   Þat symonye & *cyuyle* shulde on here fet gange.
A. 2.133   Þanne swor *cyuyle* & seide be þe rode
A. 2.140   Shuln serue myself þat *cyuyle* hatte;
A. 2.165   Symonye & *cyuyle*, I sen[d]e hem to warne
B. 2.63   Ac Symonie and *Cyuylle* and Sisours of courtes
B. 2.67   Whan Symonye and *Cyuylle* seighe hir boþer wille
B. 2.71   And preide *Cyuylle* to see and Symonye to rede it.
B. 2.72   Symonye and *Cyuylle* stonden forþ boþe
B. 2.114   By siȝt of sire Symonie and *Cyuyles* leeue.'
B. 2.116   And seide [to] *Cyuyle*, 'now sorwe [on] þi bokes]
B. 2.142   Herto assenteþ *Cyuyle*, ac Symonye ne wolde
B. 2.168   For Symonye and *Cyuylle* sholde on hire feet gange.
B. 2.169   Ac þanne swoor Symonye and *Cyuylle* boþe
B. 2.179   Shul seruen myself þat *Cyuyle* is nempned.
B. 2.204   [Symonye and *Cyuyle*, I sende hem to warne
B.20.137   And tornede *Cyuyle* into Symonye, and siþþe he took þe Official.
C. 2.65   Ac simonye and *syuile* and sysores of contrees
C. 2.69   When simonye and *syuile* ysey[e] þer bothe wille
C. 2.73   And preyeth *syuile* to se and s[y]monye to rede hit.
C. 2.74   Thenne simonye and *syuyle* standeth forth bothe
C. 2.76   Thenne saide symonye þat *syuyle* it herde:
C. 2.118   By syhte of sire Simonye and *syuyles* leue.'
C. 2.130   For *syuile* and thisylue selde fulfulleth
C. 2.158   Hereto assenteth *syuyle*, ac symonye ne wolde
C. 2.184   Symonye and *syuyle* seyden and sworen
C. 2.186   'And y mysulue, *syuyle*, and symonye my felawe
C. 2.246   Symonye and *syuile* senten to Rome,
C.22.137   And turnede *syuyle* into symonye and sethe he toek þe official.

clayme(de -en > cleymen

claymes n *claim n.* C 1
C. 4.98   So alle my *claymes* ben quyt by so þe kyng assente.'

claymeþ > cleymen; clannesse > clennesse

clanse v *clensen v.* B 3 clensed (2) clenseþ (1); C 4 clanse (1) clansed (1) clanseth (1) yclansed (1)
B.16.109   And commune wommen conuertede and *clensed* of synne,
B.17.214   That alle kynne cristene *clenseþ* of synnes.
B.18.391   They shul be *clensed* clerliche and [keuered] of hir synnes
C. 3.359   Of oure sory synnes to be assoiled and *yclansed*
C.16.25   And sende vs contricion [cleriche] to *clanse* with oure soules
C.18.142   And comen wommen conuertede and *clansed* hem of synne
C.19.180   That alle kynne cristene *clanseth* of synne[s].

clarice n prop *n.i.d.* A 1 Claris; B 2; C 2 clarice (1) Claryce (1)
A. 5.162   *Claris* of cokkislane & þe clerk of þe chirche,
B. 5.159   And dame *Clarice* a knyȝtes douȝter ac a cokewold was hir sire,
B. 5.311   *Clarice* of Cokkeslane and þe Clerk of þe chirche,
C. 6.134   And dame *clarice* a knyhtes douhter, a cokewolde was here syre,
C. 6.366   *Claryce* of cockes lane and the clerc of þe churche,

clause n *clause n.* A 3; B 4; C 3
A. 4.133   For to construe þis *clause* declynede faste,
A. 8.44   For he co[pie]de þus here *clause* þei [couden] hym gret mede.
A. 8.90   For I shal construe iche *clause* & kenne it þe on englissh.'
B. 4.150   Al to construe þis *clause* for þe kynges profit,
B. 7.108   For I [shal] construe ech *clause* and kenne it þee on englissh.'
B.10.415   The culorum of þis *clause* curatours is to mene,

B.15.608   Konne þe firste *clause* of oure bileue, Credo in deum patrem
                  omnipotentem,
C. 4.147   To construe this *c[l]ause*, kyndeliche what it meneth.
C.11.246   The culorum of this *clause* curatores is to mene
C.17.316   Conne þe furste *clause* of oure bileue, credo in deum patrem,

clausemele adv *clause-mel adv.*   B 1
B. 5.419   Construe *clause[m]el[e]* and kenne it to my parisshens.

clawen v *clauen v.*   B 4 clawe (2) clawen (1) claweþ (1);   C 2 clawe
B.Pr.154   Cracchen vs or *clawen* vs, and in hise clouches holde
B.10.289   Forþi, ye Correctours, *claweþ* heron and correcteþ first yowselue,
B.14.17   That shal *clawe* þi cote of alle kynnes filþe:
B.17.191   To clucche or to *clawe*, to clippe or to holde.
C.Pr.174   To his clees *clawe* vs and [in] his cloches halde
C.19.157   To cluche or to *clawe*, to clippe or to holde.

cleef v *cleven v.(2)*   B 1
B.18.61   The wal waggede and *cleef* and al þe world quaued.

cleer > cler

clees n *claue n.(1)*   C 1
C.Pr.174   To his *clees* clawe vs and [in] his cloches halde

cleymen v *claimen v.*   A 2 cleyme (1) cleymeþ (1);   B 14 clayme (2)
   claymen (1) claymeþ (1) cleyme (4) cleymede (1) cleymen (1) cleymeþ
   (4);   C 15 clayme (4) claymede (1) claymen (3) claymeth (7)
A. 1.91   For cristene & vncristene *cleymeþ* it ichone.
A. 8.139   Þat [vncouþe] kni3t[is] shal come þi kingdom to *cleyme*;
B. 1.93   For cristen and vncristen *cleymeþ* it echone.
B. 7.161   That vnkouþe kny3tes shul come þi kyngdom to *cleyme*;
B.10.327   [Bynymen] that hir barnes *claymen*, and blame yow foule:
B.10.348   Ther riche men no ri3t may *cleyme* but of ruþe and grace.'
B.11.123   'Thanne may alle cristene come', quod I, 'and *cleyme* þere entree
B.14.110   To haue allowaunce of his lord; by þe lawe he it *cleymeþ*.
B.14.142   Ri3t as a seruaunt takeþ his salarie bifore, & siþþe wolde *clayme*
                  moore
B.14.260   Forþi [al] poore þat pacient is [of pure ri3t] may *cleymen*,
B.16.191   So þre bilongeþ for a lord þat lordshipe *cleymeþ*:
B.18.20   'And fecche þat þe fend *claymeþ*, Piers fruyt þe Plowman.'
B.18.329   Myne þei ben and of me; I may þe bet hem *cleyme*.
B.18.343   And lif for lif also, and by þat lawe I *clayme*
B.19.443   And *cleymeþ* bifore þe kyng to be kepere ouer cristene,
B.20.96   And bar þe baner bifore deeþ; bi ri3t he it *cleymede*.
C. 1.89   For cristene and vncristene *claymeth* it echone.
C. 3.322   Noyther [thei ne] here ayres hardy to *claymen*
C. 3.375   As a kyng to *clayme* the comune at his wille
C. 3.378   So comune *claymeth* of a kyng thre kyne thynges,
C.10.211   That lele legityme be þe lawe may *claymen*.
C.12.58   'Thenne may alle cristene come,' [quod y], 'and *clayme* þer entre
C.15.286   To haue allouaunce of his lord; by [þe] lawe he [hit] *claymeth*.
C.16.100   Forthy alle pore þat pacient is of puyr rihte may *claymen*
C.17.58   With þat 3oure bernes and 3oure blood by goed lawe may *clayme*!
C.17.71   Of þat þat holy churche of þe olde lawe *claymeth*
C.18.200   Thre bilongeth to a lord þat leiaunce *claymeth*,
C.20.18   'And feche þat þe fende *claymeth*, pers fruyt þe plouhman.'
C.20.372   Myne they [be] and of me; y may þe bet hem *clayme*.
C.21.443   And *claymeth* bifore þe kynge to be kepare ouer cristene
C.22.96   And baer þe baner bifore deth; bi riht he hit *claymede*.

clement n prop *n.i.d.*   A 2;   B 4 Clement (3) Clementes (1);   C 4 Clement
   (3) Clementis (1)
A. 5.168   *Clement* þe cobeler cast of his cloke
A. 5.181   In couenaunt þat *clement* [shulde þe cuppe felle],
A. 5.319   *Clement* þe Cobelere caste of his cloke
B. 5.332   In couenaunt þat *Clement* sholde þe cuppe fille,
B. 5.351   *Clement* þe Cobelere kau3te hym by þe myddel
B. 5.354   And kou3ed vp a cawdel in *Clementes* lappe.
C. 6.376   *Clement* þe Coblere cast of his cloke
C. 6.390   In couenaunt þat *clement* sholde the coppe fulle
C. 6.409   *Clement* þe coblere cauhte hym by þe myddel
C. 6.412   And cowed vp a caudel in *Clementis* lappe.

clemynge prp *clemen v.*   C 1
C. 3.106   And thorw a candle *clemynge* in [a] cursed place

clemp > clymbe

clene adj *clene adj.*   A 8;   B 22 clene (18) clenner (1) clennere (1) clennest
   (2);   C 13 clene (10) clenner (1) clennest (1) clenneste (1)
A. 1.169   3e curatours þat kepe 3ow *clene* of 3our body,
A. 3.21   Coupis of *clene* gold [and] pecis of siluer,
A. 5.253   Criede vpward to crist & to his [*clene*] modir
A. 6.27   *Clene* consience & wyt kende me to his place,
A. 7.288   But coket, or clermatyn, or of *clene* whete,
A. 8.24   A3ens *clene* consience here catel to selle.

A.10.88   Ac 3if *clene* consience acorde þat þiself dost wel
A.10.203   Shulde no bedbourd be; but þei were boþe *clene*
B. 1.195   [Ye] curatours [þat] kepen [yow] *clene* of [youre] bod[y],
B. 2.50   Now I bikenne þee crist', quod she, 'and his *clene* moder,
B. 3.22   Coupes of *clene* gold and coppes of siluer,
B. 5.511   Cride vpward to Crist and to his *clene* moder
B. 6.304   But Coket [or] clermatyn or of *clene* whete,
B. 7.22   Ayein *clene* Conscience hir catel to selle.
B. 9.190   Sholde no [bedbourde] be; but þei boþe were *clene*
B.10.265   Syþenes þow seest þiself as in soule *clene*;
B.11.81   Thoru3 contricion [*clene*] come to þe hei3e heuene–
B.11.302   [Moore þan cure] for konnyng or 'knowen for *clene* [of] berynge'.
B.13.295   And noon so holy as he ne of lif *clennere*,
B.14.2   Thou3 it be soiled and selde *clene*: I slepe þerInne o ny3tes;
B.14.12   And kouþe I neuere, by crist! kepen it *clene* an houre
B.14.22   Dobest [shal kepe it *clene* from vnkynde werkes].
B.14.43   The Corlew by kynde of þe Eyr, moost *clennest* flessh of briddes,
B.14.185   And be *clene* þoru3 þat cristnyng of alle kynnes synne.
B.15.190   And bouken hem at his brest and beten hem *clene*,
B.16.70   Thanne bereþ þe crop kynde fruyt and *clennest* of alle,
B.18.119   A comely creature [and a *clene*]; truþe she highte.
B.19.252   'Thou3 some be *clenner* þan some, ye se wel', quod Grace,
B.19.379   *Clennesse* [of þe] comune and clerkes *clene* lyuynge
B.19.458   And coloureþ it for a konnynge and a *clene* lyuynge.'
C. 2.53   For y bykenne the crist,' quod she, 'and his *clene* moder,
C. 3.23   Coupes of *clene* gold [and] coppes of syluer,
C. 7.156   Criede vpward to Crist and to his *clene* moder
C. 8.326   Bote clermatyn and coket and of *clene* whete,
C. 9.26   A3en *clene* Consience for couetyse of wynnynge.
C.10.291   *Clene* of lyf and in loue of soule and in lele wedlok.
C.16.301   As of a cote of ca[mm]aca or of *clene* scarlet.
C.18.93   And þe *clennest* creature furste creat[our] knowe.
C.18.94   In kynges Court and in knyhtes, the *clenneste* men and fayreste
C.20.122   A comely creature and a *clene*; Treuthe she hihte.
C.21.252   'Thouh somme be *clenner* then somme, 3e sen wel,' quod grace,
C.21.379   *Clannesse* of þe comune and clerkes *clene* lyuynge
C.21.458   And coloureth hit for a connyng and a *clene* lyuynge.'

clene adv *clene adv.*   A 1;   B 3;   C 3
A.10.170   *Clene* awey þe cursid blood þat caym haþ ymakid.
B. 9.139   *Clene* awey þe corsed blood þat Caym haþ ymaked.
B.11.30   And Concupiscencia carnis *clene* þee forsake–
B.20.369   Til Contricion hadde *clene* foryeten to crye and to wepe
C.10.227   *Clene* awey þe corsed blood of Caym spronge.
C.11.189   And Concupiscencia Carnis *clene* the forsake–
C.22.369   Til Contricioun hadde *clene* for3ete to crye and to wepe

clennesse n *clennesse n.*   B 6;   C 4 clannesse (2) clennesse (2)
B.12.141   And *clennesse* shal cacchen it and clerkes shullen it fynde:
B.13.416   Whan men carpen of crist or *clennesse* of soul[e]
B.14.11   Al for coueitise of my cristendom in *clennesse* to kepen it.
B.14.303   And for þe [lewde] euere [yliche] a lemman of alle *clennesse*,
B.15.466   The calf bitokneþ *clennesse* in hem þat kepeþ lawes,
B.19.379   *Clennesse* [of þe] comune and clerkes clene lyuynge
C. 7.76   When me carpeth of Crist or *clennesse* of soule
C.14.86   And *clennesse* shal cach hit and clerkes shollen hit fynde:
C.14.88   Bote of *clennesse* of clerkes and kepares of bestes:
C.21.379   *Clannesse* of þe comune and clerkes clene lyuynge

clennest(e > clene; clensed -eþ > clanse

cleophas n prop *n.i.d.*   B 1;   C 1
B.11.235   *Cleophas* ne knew hym no3t þat he crist were
C.12.124   *Cleophas* ne knewe hym nat þat he Crist were

clepe v *clepen v.*   A 1 yclepid;   B 6 clepe (1) cleped (5);   C 6 cleped (2)
   clepede (3) clepie (1)
A.11.21   Þat suche craftis conne [to counseil ben *yclepid*],
B.10.21   [That] swiche craftes k[onne] to counseil [are] *cleped*;
B.10.252   And Crist *cleped* hymself so, þe [scripture] bereþ witnesse:
B.11.119   For crist *cleped* vs alle, come if we wolde,
B.11.191   We sholde no3t *clepe* oure kyn þerto ne none kynnes riche:
B.19.117   And þanne was he [*cleped* and] called no3t [oonly] crist but Iesu,
B.20.182   The compaignye of confort men *cleped* it som tyme.
C. 6.149   Tyl ayþer *clepede* oþer "hore!" and o[f] with the clothes
C.11.18   That coueite can and caste thus ar *cleped* into consayle:
C.12.54   For crist *clepede* vs alle, come yf we wolde,
C.12.103   We sholde nat *clepie* knyhtes þerto ne none kyne ryche:
C.21.117   And tho was he *cleped* and calde not [onl]y Crist but iesu,
C.22.182   The company of comfort men *clepede* hit som tyme.

cler adj *cler adj.*   A 1;   B 2 cler (1) clere (1);   C 1 cleer
A. 6.72   Þanne shalt þou come to a court, *cler* as þe sonne.
B. 5.585   Thanne shaltow come to a court, *cler* as þe sonne.
B.12.222   Wherof þei cacche hir colours so *clere* and so bri3te,
C. 7.232   And so shaltow come to a Court as *cleer* as þe sonne.

clerc > clerk

clere adv *cler adv.* B 1; C 1
B.17.260 Ne brenne ne blase *clere*, fo[r] blowynge of vnkyndenesse.
C.19.226 Ne brenne ne blase *clere* for blowynge of vnkyndenesse.

clereliche > clerliche; clerge -y > clergie

clergially adv *clergialli adv.* B 1; C 1 clergialiche
B.Pr.124 And knelynge to þe kyng *clergially* he seide,
C. 7.34 Ac y can nat construe catoun ne *clergialiche* reden.

clergie n *clergie n.* A 14 clergie (13) clergies (1); B 56 clergie (54)
clergies (2); C 55 clerge (1) clergi (1) clergy (1) clergie (51) clergies
(1)
A. 3.15 Counforti[de] hire kyndely be *clergie[s]* leue,
A. 3.152 *Clergie* and coueitise he[o] coupliþ togidere.
A.10.107 Ne men þat conne manye craftis, *clergie* [it telliþ],
A.11.65 And carp[en] a3ens *clergie* crabbide wordis,
A.11.105 I shal kenne þe to my cosyn þat *clergie* is hoten.
A.11.112 And axide hire þe hei3e wey where *clergie* [dwell]ide,
A.11.117 For 3if þou coupl[e] þe wiþ hym to *clergie* comist þou neuere;
A.11.124 So shalt þou come to *clergie* þat can many wyttes.
A.11.169 And er I com to *clergie* coude I neuere stynte.
A.11.177 Curteisliche *clergi[e]* c[o]llide me & kiste,
A.11.294 Þat *clergie* of cristis mouþ comendite [was hit] neuere,
A.12.1 'Crist wot,' quod *clergie*, 'knowe hit 3if þe lyke,
A.12.13 And on *clergie* crieþ on cristes holy name
A.12.35 *Clergie* into a caban crepte anon after,
B.Pr.116 The kyng and kny3thod and *clergie* boþe
B. 3.15 Conforte[d] hire kyndely by *clergies* leue,
B. 3.165 *Clergie* and coueitise she coupleþ togidres.
B.10.107 And carpen ayein *cler[gie]* crabbede wordes:
B.10.153 I shal kenne þee to my Cosyn þat *Clergie* is hoten.
B.10.160 And asked hire þe heighe wey where *Clergie* dwelte,
B.10.165 For if þow coupl[e] þee [wiþ hym] to *clergie* comest [þow] neuere;
B.10.172 [So] shaltow come to *Clergie* þat kan manye [wittes].
B.10.222 Tel *Clergie* þis[e] tokene[s], and [to] Scripture after,
B.10.226 And [er] I com to *clergie* [koude I] neuere stynte.
B.10.234 [Curteisly *clergie* collede me and kiste,
B.10.238 'It is a commune lyf', quod *Clergie*, 'on holy chirche to bileue
B.10.449 That] *Clergie* of cristes mouþ comended was it [neuere],
B.10.453 Konnyng [and *clergie*] to conclude hem alle]
B.11.16 And bad me for my contenaunce acounten *Clergie* li3te.
B.11.144 That al þe *clergie* vnder crist ne my3te me cracche fro helle,
B.11.166 Ther no *clergie* ne kouþe, ne konnyng of lawes.
B.11.414 Thow sholdest haue knowen þat *clergie* kan & [conceyued] moore
           þoru3 Res[on],
B.11.415 For Reson wolde haue reherced þee ri3t as *Clergie* seid;
B.11.424 That *Clergie* þi compaignye kepeþ no3t to suwe.
B.11.430 Of *clergie* ne of his counseil ne counte[þ] no3t a risshe.
B.12.64 *Clergie* and kynde wit comeþ of si3te and techyng
B.12.66 Of quod scimus comeþ *Clergie*, [a] konnynge of heuene,
B.12.70 Ac yet is *Clergie* to comende and kynde wit boþe,
B.12.71 And namely *Clergie* for cristes loue, þat of Clergie is roote.
B.12.71 And namely Clergie for cristes loue, þat of *Clergie* is roote.
B.12.77 Ac crist of his curteisie þoru3 *clergie* hir saued.
B.12.81 [Thus *Clergie* þere] conforted þe womman.
B.12.83 So *clergie* is confort to creatures þat repenten.
B.12.85 For goddes body my3te no3t ben of breed wiþouten *clergie*,
B.12.92 Forþi I counseille þee for cristes sake *clergie* þat þow louye;
B.12.121 Forþi I conseille alle creatures no *clergie* to dispise
B.12.126 For *Clergie* is kepere vnder crist of heuene;
B.12.127 Was þer neuere [kyng ne] kny3t þat *clergie* hem made.
B.12.138 A[s] to þe *clergie* of crist counted it but a trufle:
B.12.156 How þow contrariedest *clergie* wiþ crabbede wordes,
B.12.171 That he þat knoweþ *clergie* kan sonner arise
B.12.225 *Clergie* ne kynde wit ne knew neuere þe cause,
B.12.270 And wheiþer he be saaf or no3t saaf, þe soþe woot no *clergie*.
B.13.23 And bad me come to his court, wiþ *clergie* sholde I dyne.
B.13.24 And for Conscience of *Clergie* spak I com wel þe raþer.
B.13.34 And þanne *clergie* and Conscience and Pacience cam after.
B.13.119 'Now þow, *Clergie*', quod Conscience, 'carp[e] what is dowel.'
B.13.177 And took *Clergie* and Conscience to conseil as it were
B.13.180 'Frendes, fareþ wel', and faire spak to *clergie*,
B.13.183 'What!' quod *Clergie* to Conscience, 'ar ye coueitous nouþe
B.13.188 'Nay, by crist!' quod Conscience to *Clergie*, 'god þee foryelde;
B.13.199 And siþen softeliche he seide in *clergies* ere,
B.13.202 *Clergie* of Conscience no congie wolde take,
B.13.211 'That is sooþ', [seide] *Clergie*, 'I se what þow menest.
B.15.78 In housynge, in haterynge, [in] heigh *clergie* shewynge
B.15.209 Therfore by colour ne by *clergie* knowe shaltow [hym] neuere,
B.15.381 That sholde konne and knowe alle kynnes *clergie*
B.19.467 And holy kirke and *clergie* fro cursed men to [de]fende.
B.20.228 Conscience cryede, 'help, *Clergie* or I falle

B.20.375 Conscience cryed eft [*Clergie* to helpe],
C.Pr.152 Consience to *Clergie* and to þe kynge sayde:
C.11.91 Y shal kenne þe to *clergie*, my cosyn, þat knoweth
C.11.96 And *clergi[es]* wedded wyf, as wyse as hymsulue
C.11.98 So with þat *clergie* can and consail of scripture
C.11.102 And askede here þe hey way whare *clergie* dwelte;
C.11.107 For yf thow coueytest to be ryche to *clergie* comest thow neuere.
C.11.110 To *clergie* shaltow neuere come ne knowe what is dowel.
C.11.111 A[c] if þow happe,' quod he, 'þat þou hitte on *clergie*
C.11.135 And to *clergie* y cam as clerkes me saide.
C.11.139 'By Crist,' quod *Clergie*, 'yf thow coueyte dowel
C.11.161 And continaunce made on *clergie*, to congeie me hit semede,
C.11.175 And bade me for my contin[au]nce counte *cler[gie]* lihte.
C.11.199 Were hit al soth þat 3e seyn, thow scripture and thow *clergie*,
C.11.202 For *clergie* saith þat he seyh in þe seynt euaungelie
C.11.222 Ac y countresegge the nat, *clergie*, ne thy connyng, scripture;
C.11.274 That *clergie* of cristes mouthe com[e]nded was it euere.
C.11.278 Connyng and *clergie* to conclude [hem] alle".
C.11.312 *Clergie* [and] his conseile y counted ful litel.
C.12.98 And cristis oune *clergie*; he cam fro heuene to teche hit
C.13.129 Thus rechelesnesse in a rage aresenede *clergie*
C.13.131 Til þat kynde cam *clergie* to helpe
C.13.222 Thow sholdest haue yknowe þat *clergie* ca[n] & conseyued mor[e]
           [thorw] resoun
C.13.223 For resoun wolde haue rehersed þe riht as *clergie* seide;
C.13.232 Ne *clergie* of his connynge kepeth [t]he nat shewe.
C.13.237 Of *clergie* ne of kynde wyt counteth he nat a rusche.
C.14.30 Ac *clergie* cometh bote of syhte and kynde wit of sterres.
C.14.34 And *clergie* a connynge of kynde wittes techyng.
C.14.35 And 3ut is *clergie* to comende for cristes loue more
C.14.36 Then eny connyng of kynde wit but *clergi* hit reule.
C.14.43 Forthy y conseile vch a creature *clergie* to honoure
C.14.64 Forthy y conseyle all creatures no *cler[gie]* to despice
C.14.70 For *clergy* is cristes vycary to conforte and to cure;
C.14.71 Bothe lewede and lerede were lost yf *clergie* ne were.
C.14.72 Kynde wittede men [c]an a *clergie* by hemsulue;
C.14.83 As to þe *clergie* of crist thei counted hit but a tryfle:
C.14.100 How þou contra[r]idest *clergie* with crabbed wordes,
C.14.111 Þat he þat knoweth *clergie* conne sonnore aryse
C.14.191 And wher he be saef or nat saef þe sothe woet no *clergie*
C.15.25 And thenne cam concyence and *clergie* aftur
C.15.42 *Clergie* cald aftur mete and thenne cam scripture
C.15.61 Consience confortede vs, bothe *clergie* and scripture,
C.15.127 'Now þou, *Clergie*,' quod Consience, 'carpe what is dowel.'
C.15.128 'Haue me excused,' quod *Clergie*, 'be crist, but in scole.
C.15.151 Saue Conscience and *clergie* y couthe no mo aspye.
C.15.168 The kyng and alle þe comune and *clergie* to þe loute
C.15.174 And toek *Clergie* and Conscience to conseyle as hit were.
C.15.176 And sethe a saide to *clergie* so þat y hit herde:
C.15.177 'By Crist!' quod Consience, '*clergie*, y wol nat lye;
C.16.159 A knewe Consience ful wel and *clergie* bothe.
C.16.237 In housynge, in helynge, in h[eyh] *clergie* schewynge
C.16.241 A3en þe consayl of crist, as holy *clergie* witnesseth:
C.16.322 And also a can *clergie*, credo in deum patrem,
C.21.467 And holy kyrke and *clerge* fro cursed men to defende.
C.22.228 Consience cryede, 'helpe, *Clergie*, or y falle
C.22.375 Consience cryede efte *clergie* [to] helpe

clergyse n *clergise n.* C 1
C.20.405 Ac y wol drynke of no dische ne of deep *clergyse*

clerioun n *clergeoun n.* A 1
A.12.49 She called me a *clerioun* þat

clerk n *clerk n.* A 25 clerk (6) clerkes (1) clerkis (18); B 98 clerc (5)
clerk (20) clerkene (1) clerkes (72); C 84 clerc (1) clerk (16) clerke (3)
clerkene (1) clerkes (62) clerkus (1)
A.Pr.91 Become *clerkis* of acountis þe king for to serue;
A.Pr.95 And ben *clerkis* of þe kinges bench þe cuntre to shende.
A. 1.90 Þe *clerkis* þat knowe it shulde kenne it aboute,
A. 3.3 Þe king calliþ a *clerk*–I can not his name–
A. 3.9 Curteisliche þe *clerk* þanne, as þe king hi3te,
A. 3.25 Wiþ þat come *clerkis* to conforten hire þe same,
A. 3.33 Þere cunnyng *clerkis* shuln clokke behynde.'
A. 3.41 Among *clerkis* & kni3tes consience to felle'.
A. 3.104 Before þe kyng & his counseil, *clerkis* & oþere.
A. 3.132 For heo copiþ þe Comissarie and c[ot]iþ hise *clerkis*
A. 3.209 Men þat [kenne] *clerkis* crauen of h[e]m mede;
A. 4.105 Til *clerkis* & kni3tes be curteis of here mouþes,
A. 4.132 *Clerkis* þat wern confessours couplide hem togideris,
A. 4.152 Be my counseil ycome of *clerkes* and Erlis.
A. 5.162 Claris of cokkislane & þe *clerk* of þe chirche,
A. 6.26 'I knowe hym as kyndely as *clerk* doþ his bokis.
A. 8.137 Þat nabugodonosor nempne þise *clerkis*–

A.9.16	'Contra,' quaþ I as a *clerk* & comside to dispute:
A.10.137	Kinges & kni3tes, & alle kyne *clerkis*,
A.11.28	On crois vpon caluarie, as *clerkis* vs techiþ,
A.11.38	Ac 3if þei carpen of crist, þise *clerkis* & þise lewid,
A.11.56	*Clerkis* and k[ete] men carpen of god faste,
A.11.204	Gregory þe grete *clerk*, a good pope in his tyme,
A.11.273	For alle cunnyng *clerkis* siþþe crist 3ede on erþe
A.11.308	Þanne arn þise [k]ete *clerkis* þat conne many bokis,
B.Pr.114	And þanne cam kynde wit and *clerkes* he made
B.1.92	The *clerkes* þat knowen [it] sholde kennen it aboute
B.2.58	As of kny3tes and of *clerkes* and ooþer commune peple,
B.2.59	As Sisours and Somonours, Sherreues and hire *clerkes*,
B.3.3	The kyng called a *clerk*–[I kan] no3t his name–
B.3.9	Curteisly þe *clerk* þanne, as þe kyng hi3te,
B.3.26	Wiþ þat comen *clerkes* to conforten hire þe same
B.3.34	Ther konnynge *clerkes* shul clokke bihynde.'
B.3.42	Amonges [*clerkes*] and [kny3tes] Conscience to [felle]'.
B.3.115	Bifore þe kyng and his conseil, *clerkes* and oþere.
B.3.143	For she copeþ þe Commissarie and coteþ hise *clerkes*
B.3.222	Men þat [kenne *clerkes*] crauen [of hem] Mede;
B.3.332	'I kan no latyn?' quod she, '*clerkes* wite þe soþe!
B.3.347	Ac yow failed a konnynge *clerk* þat kouþe þe leef han torned.
B.4.119	Til *clerkene* coueitise be cloþe þe pouere and fede,
B.4.149	*Clerkes* þat were Confessours coupled hem togideres
B.4.168	And [also] a Sherreues *clerk* bisherewed al þe route:
B.4.189	[Be] my counseil co[men] of *clerkes* and of Erles.
B.5.31	Clarice of Cokkeslane and þe *Clerk* of þe chirche,
B.5.538	'I knowe hym as kyndely as *clerc* doþ hise bokes.
B.7.72	Caton kenneþ me þus and þe *clerc* of stories.
B.7.159	That Nabugodonosor nempne[þ þise] *clerkes*–
B.8.20	'Contra!' quod I as a *clerc* and comsed to disputen:
B.9.113	Kynges and kny3tes, kaysers and [*clerkes*];
B.10.36	[On cros vpon caluarye as *clerkes* vs techeþ],
B.10.52	Ac if þei carpen of crist, þise *clerkes* and þise lewed,
B.10.70	*Clerkes* and [kete] men carpen of god faste
B.10.74	And prechen at Seint Poules, for pure enuye of *clerkes*,
B.10.105	Carpen as þei *clerkes* were of crist and of hise my3tes,
B.10.113	"Of þat [ye] *clerkes* vs kenneþ of crist by þe gospel:
B.10.199	This is Catons kennyng to *clerkes* þat he lereþ.
B.10.253	Alle þe *clerkes* vnder crist ne koude þis assoille,
B.10.292	[Th]anne shul burel *clerkes* ben abasshed to blame yow or to greue,
B.10.298	Gregorie þe grete *clerk* and þe goode pope
B.10.309	In scole þere is scorn but if a *clerk* wol lerne,
B.10.403	Forþi wise witted men and wel ylettrede *clerkes*
B.10.418	Forþi I counseille yow *clerkes*, of holy [kirke] þe wri3tes,
B.10.451	Thou3 ye come bifore kynges and *clerkes* of þe lawe
B.10.464	Than are þise [kete] *clerkes* þat konne manye bokes,
B.10.472	Ye, men knowe *clerkes* þat han corsed þe tyme
B.10.477	But þo þat kepen þe lordes catel, *clerkes* and Reues.
B.10.480	As *clerkes* of holy [k]ir[k]e þat kepen cristes tresor,
B.11.204	For an vncristene creature; *clerkes* wite þe soþe
B.11.155	That was an vncristene creature, as *clerkes* fyndeþ in bokes:
B.11.216	For whateuere *clerkes* carpe of cristendom or ellis,
B.12.21	Seide, 'Caton conforted his sone þat, *clerk* þou3 he were,
B.12.69	Knew neuere *clerk* how it comeþ forþ, ne kynde wit þe weyes:
B.12.98	Ne countreplede *clerkes*, I counseille þee for euere.
B.12.100	Na moore kan no *Clerk* but if he cau3te it first þoru3 bokes.
B.12.107	Na moore kan a kynde witted man, but *clerkes* hym teche,
B.12.109	Which is þe cofre of cristes tresor, and *clerkes* kepe þe keyes
B.12.141	And clennesse shal cacchen it and *clerkes* shullen it fynde:
B.12.153	*Clerkes* knewen it wel and comen wiþ hir present3
B.12.158	Than *clerkes* or kynde witted men of cristene peple.
B.12.174	For if þe *clerk* be konnynge he knoweþ what is synne,
B.12.178	And þis conforteþ ech a *clerk* and coureþ fro wanhope.
B.12.216	Alle þe *clerkes* vnder crist ne kouþe þe skile assoille:
B.12.234	Raþer þan his likame alogh; lewed asken þus *clerkes*.
B.12.235	Kynde knoweþ whi he dide so, ac no *clerk* ellis.
B.12.268	[Swiche tales telleþ Aristotle þe grete *clerk*]:
B.12.277	'Alle þise *clerkes*', quod I þo, "þat [o]n crist leuen
B.13.11	And how þis Coueitise ouercom *clerkes* and preestes;
B.13.116	'Dowel', quod þis doctour, 'do as *clerkes* techeþ.
B.13.135	That no *clerk* ne kan, ne crist as I leue,
B.13.247	Hadde ich a *clerc* þat couþe write I wolde caste hym a bille
B.13.292	[Or for his crafty konnynge or of *clerkes* þe wisest,
B.13.338	And seye þat no *clerc* ne kan, ne crist as I leue,
B.13.431	Ac *clerkes* þat knowen holy writ sholde kenne lordes
B.13.436	[*Clerkes* and kni3tes welcomeþ kynges minstrales,
B.14.180	For how þow confortest alle creatures *clerkes* bereþ witnesse:
B.15.32	Thanne am I Conscience ycalled, goddes *clerk* and his Notarie;
B.15.68	Ayein cristes counseil and alle *clerkes* techynge,
B.15.82	Gooþ to þe glose of þ[e] vers, ye grete *clerkes*;
B.15.90	Ac of curatours of cristen peple, as *clerkes* bereþ witnesse,
B.15.104	And be kynde as bifel for *clerkes* and curteise of cristes goodes,
B.15.117	Iohannes Crisostomus of *clerkes* [carpeþ] and preestes:
B.15.136	Curatours of holy kirke, as *clerkes* þat ben auarouse,
B.15.161	*Clerkes* kenne me þat crist is in alle places
B.15.197	'Wheiþer *clerkes* knowen hym', quod I, 'þat kepen holi kirke?'
B.15.198	'*Clerkes* haue no knowyng', quod he, 'but by werkes and wordes.
B.15.211	And þat knoweþ no *clerk* ne creature on erþe
B.15.332	Ac *clerkes* and kny3tes and communers þat ben riche,
B.15.357	Wederwise shipmen and witty *clerkes* also
B.15.373	For is noon of þise newe *clerkes*, whoso nymeþ hede,
B.15.388	As *clerkes* in Corpus Christi feeste syngen and reden
B.15.404	Thanne wolde þe coluere come to þe *clerkes* ere
B.15.413	Thoru3 a cristene *clerk* acorsed in his soule·
B.15.415	How englisshe coluere fede þat coueitise hi3te,
B.15.444	Til Gregory garte *clerkes* to go here and preche.
B.15.546	For coueitise of þat cros [*clerkes*] of holy kirke
B.15.551	Right so, ye *clerkes*, for youre coueitise er [come au3t] longe
B.15.581	And han *clerkes* to kepen vs þerInne & hem þat shul come after.
B.19.270	Gregori þe grete *clerk* and [þe goode Ierom];
B.19.379	Clennesse [of þe] comune and *clerkes* clene lyuynge
B.19.414	And we *clerkes*, whan þei come, for hir comunes paieþ,
B.19.425	And Grace þat þow gr[e]dest so of, gyour of alle *clerkes*;
B.19.462	Counseilleþ me bi hir acounte and my *clerkes* writynge.
B.20.68	They cursed and hir conseil, were it *clerk* or lewed.
C.Pr.141	And þenne cam kynde wytt [& *clerkus* he made
C.1.88	*Clerkes* þat knowen hit sholde kenne hit aboute
C.1.122	Euene þe contrarie sitteth Crist, *Clerkes* wyteth þe sothe:
C.2.60	Of knyghtes, of *clerkes* [and] other comune peple,
C.2.61	As sysores [and] sompnores, shyryues and here *clerkes*,
C.2.249	And sayde, 'syre kyng, by crist! but *clerkes* amende,
C.3.3	The kyng callede a *clerc*–y can nat his name–
C.3.9	Cortesliche þe *Clerk* thenne, as þe kyng hyhte,
C.3.16	Confortede here as they couthe by the *clerkes* leue
C.3.27	Thenne come *clerkes* to conforte here the same
C.3.37	There connynge *clerkes* shal clokke byhynde.'
C.3.44	Amonge kynges and knyhtes and *clerkes* and þe lyke.'
C.3.49	Among knyhtes and *clerkes* consience to turne.
C.3.152	Byfore þe kyng and his consayl, *clerkes* and oþere.
C.3.181	For a copeth þe commissarie and coteth his *clerkes*
C.3.211	For *clerkes* and coueitise mede hath knet togederes
C.3.277	Maistres þat kenneth *clerkes* craueth therfore mede;
C.3.286	'Nay,' quod Consience to þe kyng, '*clerkes* witeth þe sothe,
C.4.114	Til *Clerkene* Coueytise be cloth for þe pore
C.4.146	*Clerkes* [þat were confessours] co[u]plede hem togederes
C.4.164	A shyreues *Clerk* cryede, 'a! capias mede
C.5.54	Me sholde constrayne no *Cler[k]* to no knaues werkes,
C.5.56	*Clerkes* ycrouned, of kynde vnderstondynge,
C.5.61	Hit bycometh for *clerkes* Crist for to serue,
C.5.66	For sholde no *clerke* be crouned but yf he come were
C.5.146	Gregory þe grete *Clerk* gart wryte in bokes
C.5.179	*Clerkes* and holy [kyrke] shal be clothed newe.'
C.6.29	To carpe and to consayle then eny *Clerk* or lewed;
C.6.76	A3eyn þe consayl of Crist, as *clerkes* fyndeth in bokes:
C.6.82	And segge þat no *clerk* ne can, ne Crist as y leue,
C.6.366	Claryce of cockes lane and þe *clerc* of þe churche,
C.7.91	*Clerkes* þat knoweth this sholde kenne lordes
C.7.96	*Clerkes* and knyhtes welcometh kynges munstrals
C.7.183	'I knowe hym as kyndely as *Clerk* doth his bokes.
C.9.206	And carteres knaues and *Clerkes* withouten grace,
C.9.211	And clothed hem in copes, *clerkes* as hit were
C.9.248	[C]o[m]e in his cope as he a *Clerk* were;
C.10.20	'Contra!' quod y as a *Clerk* and comsed to despute
C.11.50	*Clerkes* and knyhtes carpen of god ofte
C.11.54	And prech[en] at seynt poules, [for] puyr enuye of *clerkes*,
C.11.135	And to clergie y cam as *clerkes* me saide.
C.11.154	Alle þe *Clerkes* vnder Crist ne couthe this assoile
C.11.233	Wel ywitted men and wel ylettred *clerkes*,
C.11.276	Thogh 3e come bifore kynges and *clerkes* of þe law[e]
C.11.286	Saide thus in his sarmon for ensau[m]ple of grete *clerkes*,
C.11.290	Comuneliche then *clerkes* most knowyng in konnyng
C.11.301	As *clerkes* of holy [k]ir[k]e þat [kepe] sholde and saue
C.12.78	For an vncristene creature; [*clerkes*] woet þe sothe
C.12.161	Crist acordeth efte herwith; *clerkes* wyteth þe sothe,
C.12.226	Erles and Erchedekenes and oþere riche *clerkes*
C.14.11	*Clerkes* þat conne al, y hope they can do bettere;
C.14.45	No more can no *clerk* but if hit come of bokes.
C.14.52	No more can a kynde witted man, but *clerkes* hym teche,
C.14.54	Whiche [is the] coffre of cristis tresor, and *clerkes* kepeth þe keyes
C.14.86	And clennesse shal cach hit and *clerkes* shollen hit fynde:
C.14.88	Bote of clennesse of angeles and of bestes:
C.14.97	*Clerkes* kn[e]we [þe] comet and comen with here presentes
C.14.102	The[n] connynge *clerkes* of kynde vnderstondynge.
C.14.114	For yf þe *clerke* be connynge [he] knoweth what is synne

C.14.118   And þat conforteth vch a *clerk* and keuereth fro wanhope,
C.14.155   Alle þe *Clerkes* vnder Crist ne couthe [þe skyle] assoile:
C.14.157   How creatures han kynde wit and how *clerkes* come to bokes
C.14.199   'Alle this *clerkes*,' quod y tho, 'þat [o]n crist leuen
C.14.216   And a cortesye more þen couenant was, what so *clerkes* carpe,
C.16.192   Thenne am y Concience ycald, goddes *Clerk* and his notarie;
C.16.265   Ypocrisye is a braunche of pruyde and most amonges *clerkes*
C.16.272   Iohannes Crisostomus carpeth thus of *clerkes* [and prestes]:
C.16.281   Curatours of holy [kirke] and *clerkes* þat ben Auerous,
C.16.292   I knewe neuere, by Crist, *clerk* noþer lewed
C.16.339   Where *clerkes* knowe hym nat,' quod y, 'þat kepen holy churche?'
C.17.69   Y dar nat carpe of *clerkes* now þat cristes [tresor] kepe
C.17.120   As *Clerkes* in corpus cristi feste syngen and reden
C.17.166   And a cardinal of Court, a gret *clerk* withalle,
C.17.175   Thenne sholde þe coluere come to þe *clerkes* ere,
C.17.208   For couetyse of th[at] croes *clerkes* of holi churche
C.17.214   Riht so, ʒe *clerkes*, ʒoure coueytise ar come auht longe
C.19.240   Clothes of moest cost, as *clerkes* bereth witnesse:
C.20.354   Beth ywaer, ʒe wyse *clerkes* and ʒe witty of lawe,
C.21.270   Gregory the grete *Clerk* and [þe gode Ieroem];
C.21.379   Clannesse of þe comune and *clerkes* clene lyuynge
C.21.414   And we *Clerkes*, when they come, for here comunes paieth,
C.21.425   And grace that thow gredest so of, gyour of all *Clerkes*;
C.21.462   Conseileth me bi here acounte and my *clerkes* writyng.
C.22.68   Thei corsede and here consail, were hit *Clerk* or lewed.

clerkysh adj *OED clerkish a.* C 1
C. 6.42   And connyngest of my craft, *Clerkysh* oþer other,

clerliche adv *clerkli adv.* B 1; C 1 clereliche
B.18.391   They shul be clensed *clerliche* and [keuered] of hir synnes
C.16.25   And sende vs contricion [*clereliche*] to clanse with oure soules

clermatyn n *cler-matin n.* A 1; B 1; C 1
A. 7.288   But coket, or *clermatyn*, or of clene whete,
B. 6.304   But Coket [or] *clermatyn* or of clene whete,
C. 8.326   Bote *clermatyn* and coket and of clene whete

cleueth -ynge > *clyueþ*

cliauntes n *client n.* C 1
C. 3.393   How þat *cliauntes* acorde acounteth mede litel.

clycat > *cliket*

clyf n *clif n.* A 1
A. 1.4   Com doun fro þat [*clyf*] & callide me faire,

cliket n *cliket n.* A 1; B 1; C 1 clycat
A. 6.91   For he haþ þe keiʒes & þe *cliket* þeiʒ þe king slepe
B. 5.604   For he haþ þe keye and þe *cliket* þouʒ þe kyng slepe.
C. 7.252   And he hath þe keye and þe *clycat* thow þe kyng slepe

cliketted ptp *cliketed ppl.* A 1 ycliket; B 1; C 1 yclyketed
A. 6.100   Ikeiʒid & *ycliket* to kepe þe þeroute
B. 5.614   Keyed and *cliketted* to kepe þee wiþouten,
C. 7.266   Ykeyed and *yclyketed* to [kepe] the withouten,

clymat n *climat n.* C 1
C.17.107   Of þat was kalculed of þe *clymat* the contrarie þey fynde.

clymbe v *climben v.* A 1; C 2 clemp (1) clymbe (1)
A.10.101   For ʒif þou comsist to *clymbe*, & coueitest herre,
C.18.105   And anoon he hihte Elde an hy for to *clymbe*
C.18.107   And Elde *clemp* to þe c[r]opward; thenne comsed hit to crye.

clyngest v *clingen v.* B 1; C 1 clingest
B.14.52   Or whan þow clomsest for cold or *clyngest* for drye.
C.15.251   Or when thow cl[o]msest fo[r] colde or *clingest* for drouthe.

clippe v *clippen v.(1)* B 2; C 2 clippe (1) cluppe (1)
B.17.191   To clucche or to clawe, to *clippe* or to holde.
B.18.417   *Clippe* we in couenaunt, and ech of vs [kisse] ooþer,
C.19.157   To cluche or to clawe, to *clippe* or to holde.
C.20.460   *Cluppe* we in couenaunt and vch of vs kusse oþere.'

clips n *eclipse n.* B 1; C 1
B.18.135   And þat is cause of þis *clips* þat closeþ now þe sonne,
C.20.138   And þat is cause of this *clips* þat [c]loseth now þe sonne,

clyueþ v *cleven v.(1)* B 2 clyue (1) clyueþ (1); C 3 cleueth (2) cleuynge (1)
B.11.225   I conseille alle cristne *clyue* noʒt þeron to soore,
B.17.335   For kynde *clyueþ* on hym euere to contrarie þe soule;
C. 7.304   I may nat come for a kitte, so a *cleueth* on me:
C.17.128   Alle kyne cristene *cleuynge* on o will,
C.19.315   For kynde *cleueth* on hym euere to contrarie þe soule;

cloches > *clouches*

cloistre n *cloistre n.* A 1; B 7 cloistre (5) cloistres (2); C 6 cloistre (1) Cloystre (4) Cloistres (1)
A.11.210   Þat out of couent & *cloistre* coueiten to libben".
B. 3.60   And I shal couere youre kirk, youre *cloistre* do maken,
B. 4.120   And Religiouse Romeris Recordare in hir *cloistres*
B. 5.181   I cou[ʒ]e it [vp] in oure *Cloistre* þat al [þe] Couent woot it.'
B. 6.147   And catel to [cope] hem wiþ þat han *Cloistres* and chirches.
B.10.304   That out of couent and *cloistre* coueiten to libbe.
B.10.306   It is in *cloistre* or in scole, by manye skiles I fynde.
B.10.307   For in *cloistre* comeþ [no] man to [carpe] ne to fiʒte
C. 3.64   And y shal cuuere ʒoure kyrke and ʒoure clo[i]stre make;
C. 4.116   And religious outryderes be reclused in here *Cloistres*
C. 5.151   That out of couent and *Cloystre* coueyteth to dwelle.
C. 5.153   Hit is in C[l]oystre or in scole, by many skilles y fynde.
C. 5.154   For in C[l]oystre cometh no man to chyde ne to fyhte;
C. 6.163   Y cou[ʒ]e hit vp in oure *Cloystre* þat al þe couent woet hit.'

cloke n *cloke n.(1)* A 5; B 5; C 6 cloke (5) clokes (1)
A. 5.168   Clement þe cobeler cast of his *cloke*
A. 5.173   Whoso hadde þe hood shulde haue amendis of þe *cloke*.
A. 5.180   Hikke þe hostiller þanne hadde þe *cloke*
A. 6.10   And many crouch [o]n his *cloke*, & keiʒes of rome,
A. 7.254   And ek his *cloke* [of] calabre & þe knoppis of gold,
B. 5.319   Clement þe Cobelere caste of his *cloke*
B. 5.324   Whoso hadde þe hood sholde han amendes of þe *cloke*.
B. 5.331   Hikke þe hostiler [þanne] hadde þe *cloke*
B. 5.522   And many crouch on his *cloke* and keyes of Rome,
B. 6.270   And his *cloke* of Calabre [and] þe knappes of golde,
C. 6.376   Clement þe Coblere cast of his *cloke*
C. 6.381   That hoso hadde the hood sholde nat haue þe *cloke*
C. 6.389   Hicke þe hostiler hadde þe *cloke*
C. 7.167   And many crouch on his *cloke* [and] kayes of Rome
C. 8.291   And his *cloke* of callabre for his comune[s] legge
C. 9.139   For they bereth none bagges ne boteles vnder *clokes*,

clokke v *clokken v.(2)* A 1; B 1; C 1
A. 3.33   Þere cunnyng clerkis shuln *clokke* behynde.'
B. 3.34   Ther konnynge clerkes shul *clokke* bihynde.'
C. 3.37   There connynge clerkes shal *clokke* byhynde.'

clom n *clom n.(2)* A 1
A.12.105   And is closed vnder *clom*, crist haue his soule.

clomsest v *clomsen v.* B 1; C 1
B.14.52   Or whan þow *clomsest* for cold or clyngest for drye.
C.15.251   Or when thow *cl[o]msest* fo[r] colde or clingest for drouthe.

clooþ > *cloþ*

close v *closen v.* A 4 close (1) closed (1) closid (2); B 8 close (2) closed (3) closeþ (1) closynge (1) yclosed (1); C 10 close (3) closed (3) closeth (1) closyng (1) yclosed (2)
A. 6.99   And so worst þou dryuen out as dew & þe dore *closid*,
A. 7.96   And helpe my cultir to kerue & *close* þe forewis.'
A.10.5   Kynde haþ *closid* þereinne, craftili wiþalle,
A.12.105   And is *closed* vnder clom, crist haue his soule.
B.Pr.104   That Cardinals ben called and *closynge* yates
B.Pr.105   There [crist is in] kyngdom, to *close* and to shette,
B. 5.613   And [so] worstow dryuen out as dew and þe dore *closed*,
B. 6.104   And helpe my cultour to kerue and [*close*] þe furwes.'
B. 9.5   Kynde haþ *closed* þerInne, craftily wiþalle,
B.14.66   And in Elyes tyme heuene was *yclosed*
B.18.135   And þat is cause of þis clips þat *closeþ* now þe sonne,
B.19.168   Crist cam In, and al *closed* boþe dore and yates,
C.Pr.132   That Cardinales ben cald and *closyng* ʒates
C.Pr.133   Thare Crist is in kynedom to *close* with heuene.
C. 3.141   In the Castel of Corf y shal do *close* the,
C. 7.265   So worth thow dryuen out as de[w] and þe dore *yclosed*,
C. 8.65   And helpe my Coltur to kerue and cl[o]se þe forwes;
C.10.132   Kynde hath *closed* therynne, craftily withalle,
C.10.171   Inwit and alle wittes *closed* been þerynne.
C.15.265   And in Elies tyme heuene was *yclosed*
C.20.138   And þat is cause of this clips þat [c]loseth now þe sonne,
C.21.168   Crist cam in, and al *closed* bothe dore and ʒates,

cloþ n *cloth n.* A 6 cloþ (1) cloþis (5); B 20 clooþ (3) cloþ (3) cloþes (14); C 25 cloth (9) clothes (16)
A. 2.182   Wysshen hym & wypide him & wounde hym in *cloþis*,
A. 5.129   My wyf was a wynstere & wollene *cloþ* made,
A. 7.15   Caste hem *cloþis* for cold for so wile treuþe.
A. 7.54   He caste on his *cloþis*, ycloutid & hole,
A. 8.43   And ʒaf wille for his writyng wollene *cloþis*;
A.11.188   To breke beggeris bred & bakken hem with *cloþis*,
B.Pr.199   And also ye route of Ratons rende mennes *cloþes*
B. 5.213   My wif was a [wynnestere] and wollen *cloþ* made,
B. 6.14   Makeþ *cloþ*, I counseille yow, and kenneþ so youre douʒtres.

B. 6.16   Casteþ hem *clopes* [for cold] for so [wol] truþe.
B. 6.59   [He] caste on [hise] *clopes*, yclouted and hole,
B. 9.94   And biddeþ þe beggere go for his broke *clopes*:
B.11.34   'Ye? recche þee neuere', quod Rechelesnesse, stood forþ in raggede
           clopes;
B.11.433   And shame shrapeþ hise *clopes* and hise shynes wassheþ,
B.13.29   A[c] Pacience in þe Paleis stood in pilgrymes *clopes*
B.14.57   Darstow neuere care for corn ne for *clop* ne for drynke,
B.14.177   Wo in wynter tymes for wantynge of *clopes*,
B.14.332   'I were noȝt worþi, woot god', quod haukyn, 'to werien any *clopes*,
B.15.115   Ye aren enblaunched wiþ bele paroles and wiþ [bele *clopes*]
B.15.452   *Cloop* þat comeþ fro þe weuyng is noȝt comly to were
B.16.253   I hadde wonder of hise wordes and of hise wide *clopes*
B.19.287   Sholde no curious *cloop* comen on his rugge,
B.20.7   That þow toke to þi bilyue, to *clopes* and to sustenaunce,
B.20.16   And þouȝ he come so to a *cloop* and kan no bettre cheuyssaunce
B.20.143   And þanne lough lyf and leet daggen hise *clopes*,
B.20.248   And I wol be youre boruȝ: ye shal haue breed and *clopes*
C. 4.114   Til Clerkene Coueitise be *cloth* for þe pore
C. 5.18   Or shap shon or *cloth* or shep and kyne kepe,
C. 5.41   Lyf þat me [l]ykede but in this longe *clothes*.
C. 6.65   His *clothes* were of corsemen[t] of and of kene wordes,
C. 6.149   Tyl ayþer clepede oþer "hore!" and o[f] with the *clothes*
C. 6.221   My wyf was a webbe and wollone *cloth* made
C. 8.13   Consience conseyleth ȝow *cloth* for to make
C. 8.58   [He] caste on his *clothes* of alle kyn craftes,
C. 8.145   Bothe of my corn and of my *cloth* to kepe hem fram defaute.
C. 8.262   That here lyflode be lene and lyte worth here *clothes*.'
C. 9.250   And fo[r] þe *cloth* þat keuereth hym ykald he is a frere,
C.10.194   The catel that Crist hadde, thre *clothes* hit were;
C.10.202   In meschief for defaute of mete ne for myssyng of *clothes*:
C.11.193   'ȝe? reche þe neuere,' quod rechelesnesse, stod forth in ragged
           clothes;
C.12.125   For his pore parail and pilgrimes *clothes*
C.15.256   Dar þe nat care for no corn ne for *cloth* ne for drynke,
C.16.270   That ben enblaunched with bele paroles and with bele *clothes*
C.16.351   Ryden and rennen in raggede *clothes*
C.18.269   Thenne hadde y wonder of his wordes and of [his] wyde *clothes*
C.19.240   *Clothes* of moest cost, as clerkes bereth witnesse:
C.21.287   Sholde no curious *cloth* comen on his rugge
C.22.7   That thow toke to [thy bylyue], to *clothes* and to sustinaunce
C.22.16   And thow he come so to a *cloth* and can no bettere cheuesaunce
C.22.143   And thenne lowh lyf and lette dagge his *clothes*
C.22.248   [And] y wol be ȝoure borwh: ȝe shal haue breed and *clothes*

cloþen v*clothen v.* A 5 cloþe (1) cloþid (1) cloþide (2) ycloþid (1); B 12
    cloþe (2) cloþed (2) cloþen (1) cloþeþ (1) ycloþed (6); C 16 clothe (3)
    clothed (4) clotheth (2) yclothed (7)
A.Pr.53   *Clopide* hem in copis to be knowen from oþere:
A.Pr.59   Manye of þise maistris may *clope* hem at lyking
A. 1.3   A louely lady of lire in lynene *yclopid*
A. 2.8   And was war of a womman wondirliche *clopide*,
A. 5.61   He was *clopid* in a caurymaury, I [coupe] it nouȝt descryue;
B.Pr.56   *Cloped* hem in copes to ben knowen from oþere:
B.Pr.62   Manye of þise maistre[s mowe] *clopen* hem at likyng
B. 1.3   A louely lady of leere in lynnen *ycloped*
B. 2.8   And was war of a womman [wonder]liche *ycloped*,
B. 4.119   Til clerkene coueitise be to *clope* þe pouere and fede,
B. 5.78   [He was] *cloped* in a kaurymaury–I koupe it nouȝt discryue–
B.13.272   Of haukyn þe Actif man and how he was *ycloped*.
B.15.535   Fer fro kyth and fro kyn yuele *ycloped* yeden,
B.18.168   Where pees comeþ pleyinge in pacience *ycloped*.
B.18.172   Whan Pees in Pacience *ycloped* approched ner hem tweyne
B.19.257   And after craftes conseil *clopeþ* yow and fede.
B.20.209   'How shal I come to catel so to *clope* me and to feede?'
C.Pr.54   *Clothed* hem in copis to be knowe fram othere
C. 1.3   A louely lady of [lere] in lynnene [y]*clothed*
C. 2.9   And [was war of] a womman wonderly *yclothed*.
C. 5.2   [K]ytte and y in a cote, *yclothed* as a lollare
C. 5.179   Clerkes and holy [kyrke] shal be *clothed* newe.'
C. 9.90   And hath no catel but his craft to *clothe* h[e]m and to fede
C. 9.211   And *clothed* hem in copes, clerkes as hit were
C.13.84   As none tythes to tythe ne to *clothe* the nakede
C.15.79   For alle be we brethrene thogh we be diuerse *yclothed*.
C.16.326   *Clotheth* hem and conforteth hem and of Crist precheth hem,
C.17.196   Fer fro [k]uthe and fro kyn euele *yclothed* ȝeden,
C.19.245   Lordliche for to lyue and lykyngliche be *clothed*
C.20.171   Where cometh pees pleyinge in pacience *yclothed*.
C.20.175   Whenne pees in pacience *yclothed* aproched her ayþer oþer
C.21.257   And aftur craftes consail *clotheth* ȝow and fedeth.
C.22.209   'How shal y come to catel so to *clothe* me and to fede?'

cloþeres n*clother n.* A 1 cloþeris; B 1; C 1 clotheres
A.11.18   But it be cardit wiþ coueitise as *cloþeris* don here wolle;

B.10.18   But it be carded wiþ coueitise as *cloperes* [don] hir wolle.
C.11.15   Bote hit be cardet with coueytise as *clotheres* kemben here wolle.

cloþyng ger*clothing ger.* A 1 cloþing; B 6 cloþyng (5) cloþynge (1); C 6
    clothinge (1) clothyng (5)
A.Pr.24   In cuntenaunce of *clobing* comen disgisid.
B.Pr.24   In contenaunce of *clopynge* comen d[is]gised.
B.11.239   Ac by *clopyng* þei knewe hym noȝt, [so caitifliche he yede].
B.11.246   Seint Iohan and oþere seintes were seyen in poore *clopyng*,
B.14.157   For muche murþe is amonges riche, as in mete and *clopyng*,
B.15.103   Forþi wolde ye lettrede leue þe lecherie of *clopyng*,
B.18.173   Rightwisnesse hire reuerenced by hir riche *clopyng*
C.Pr.26   In continance [of] *clothyng* in many kyne gyse.
C. 9.209   That faytede in frere *clothinge* hadde fatte chekes.
C.12.128   Ac by *clothyng* þei knewe hym nat, so caytifliche he ȝede.
C.16.256   For wolde ȝe lettered leue þ[e] lecherye of *clothyng*
C.16.341   By *clothyng* ne by carpynge knowe shaltow hym neuere.
C.20.176   Rihtwisnesse reuerenced pees in here rich *clothyng*

clouches n *cloke n.(2)* B 1; C 1 cloches
B.Pr.154   Cracchen vs or clawen vs, and in hise *clouches* holde
C.Pr.174   To his clees clawe vs and [in] his *cloches* halde

cloude n *cloud n.* A 1 cloud; B 2 cloude (1) cloudes (1); C 3 cloudes
A. 3.180   And dreddist to be ded for a dym *cloud*,
B. 3.193   And dreddest to be ded for a dym *cloude*,
B.18.410   Is no weder warmer þan after watry *cloudes*;
C.10.159   And as thow seest the sonne sum tyme for *cloudes*,
C.14.73   Of *cloudes* and of costumes they contreuede mony thynges
C.20.453   Is no wedore warmore then aftur watri *cloudes*;

cloute v *clouten v.(1)* A 1 ycloutid; B 1 yclouted; C 1
A. 7.54   He caste on his *clopis*, ycloutid & hole,
B. 6.59   [He] caste on [hise] *clopes*, yclouted and hole,
C. 9.80   Bothe to carde and to kembe, to *cloute* and to wasche,

cloutes n *clout n.(1)* B 2; C 1
B. 2.223   Wesshen hym & wiped hym & wounden hym in *cloutes*,
B.13.63   Wombe *cloutes* and wilde brawen and egges yfryed wiþ grece.
C. 2.233   Thei woschen hym and wypeden hym and wonden hym in *cloutes*,

clucche v *clicchen v.* B 1; C 2 cluche
B.17.191   To *clucche* or to clawe, to clippe or to holde.
C.19.122   The fyngres þat fre ben to folde and to *cluche*
C.19.157   To *cluche* or to clawe, to clippe or to holde.

cluppe > clippe

cobelere n *cobelere n.* A 1 cobeler; B 2; C 2 coblere
A. 5.168   Clement þe *cobeler* cast of his cloke
B. 5.319   Clement þe *Cobelere* caste of his cloke
B. 5.351   Clement þe *Cobelere* kauȝte hym by þe myddel
C. 6.376   Clement þe *Coblere* cast of his cloke
C. 6.409   Clement þe *coblere* cauhte hym by þe myddel

cockes n *cokel n. &> cokkeslane* C 1
C. 9.95   Were a feste with suche folk or so fele *cockes*.

coek > cook; coeld > cold; coest > cost

coffes n *cuffe n.* A 1 cuffis; B 1; C 1
A. 7.55   Hise cokeris & his *cuffis* for cold of his nailes,
B. 6.60   [Hise] cokeres and [hise] *coffes* for cold of [hise] nailes,
C. 8.59   His cokeres and his *coffes*, as kynde wit hym tauhte,

cofre n *cofre n.* A 1 coffre; B 7 cofre (4) cofres (3); C 5 coffre (2)
    coffres (2) cofre (1)
A. 5.27   And kep[e] it in hire *coffre* for catel at nede.
B. 5.27   And kepe it in hire *cofre* for catel at nede.
B.10.329   Of Costantyns *cofres* [þer þe catel is Inne]
B.11.199   For alle are we cristes creatures and of his *cofres* riche,
B.12.109   Which is þe *cofre* of cristes tresor, and clerkes kepe þe keyes
B.13.300   Pouere of possession in purs and in *cofre*;
B.14.247   Ther Auarice haþ Almaries and yren bounden *cofres*.
B.14.249   A beggeris bagge þan an yren bounde *cofre*.
C. 5.129   And kepe hit in here *cofre* for catel at nede.
C.12.214   Þe catel þat he kepeth so in *coffres* and in bernis,
C.14.54   Whiche [is the] *coffre* of cristis tresor, and clerkes kepeth þe keyes
C.16.87   There Auaryce hath almaries and yrebounden *coffres*.
C.16.89   A beggares bagge then an yrebounden *coffre*.

cogheþ v*coughen v.* B 4 cogheþ (1) coughed (1) couȝe (1) kouȝed (1); C
    4 coueth (1) couȝe (1) cowed (1) cowhede (1)
B. 5.181   I cou[ȝ]e it [vp] in oure Cloistre þat al [þe] Couent woot it.'
B. 5.354   And kouȝed vp a cawdel in Clementes lappe.
B.13.101   *Coughed* and carped, and Conscience hym herde
B.17.331   *Cogheþ* and curseþ þat crist gyue h[y]m sorwe
C. 6.163   Y cou[ȝ]e hit vp in oure Cloystre þat al þe couent woet it.'

C. 6.412　And *cowed* vp a caudel in Clementis lappe.
C.15.108　*Cowhede* and capede, and consience hym herde
C.19.311　*Coueth* and corseth þat Crist ȝeue hym sorwe

coyn n *coin n.(1)* A 1; B 1; C 3 coyne (2) koyne (1)
A. 4.113　Neiþer grotis ne gold ygraue wiþ kynges *coyn*,
B. 4.130　Neiþer [grotes ne gold ygraue wiþ kynges *coyn*]
C. 1.46　And god askede at hem hoes was þe *koyne*.
C.17.81　That god coueyteth nat þe *coyne* þat crist hymsulue printede
C.17.82　And for þe synne of þe soule forsaketh his oune *coyne*.

cok n *cok n.(1)* B 1 cokkes; C 2 cok (1) cokkes (1)
B.19.412　Or þat acountede Conscience at a *cokkes* feþere.
C.13.171　How vncortey[s]liche þat *cok* his kynde for[th] strenede
C.21.412　Or þat acounted Consience [at] a *cokkes* fether.

coke v *cokken v.(2)* B 1; C 2 coke (1) koke (1)
B.19.238　And some he tauȝte to tilie, to [*coke*] and to thecche,
C. 5.13　Or *koke* for my cokeres or to þe Cart piche,
C.21.238　And somme he tauhte to tulye, to [*coke*] and to [thecche,

coked ptp *coken v.* C 1
C.15.59　Thenne cam contricion þat hadd *coked* for hem all

cokeney n *coken-ei n.(1)* A 1 cokenay; B 1; C 1
A. 7.269　Ne no *cokenay*, be crist, colopis to maken.
B. 6.285　Ne no *cokeney*, by crist! coloppes to maken.
C. 8.307　Ne no *cokeney*, be Crist! colloppes to make.

cokeres n1 *coker n.* A 1 cokeris; B 1; C 1
A. 7.55　Hise *cokeris* & his cuffis for cold of his nailes,
B. 6.60　[Hise] *cokeres* and [hise] coffes for cold of [hise] nailes,
C. 8.59　His *cokeres* and his coffes, as kynde wit hym tauhte,

cokeres n2 *cokker n.(3)* C 1
C. 5.13　Or koke for my *cokeres* or to þe Cart piche,

cokes > cook

coket n *coket n.(2)* A 1; B 1; C 1
A. 7.288　But *coket*, or clermatyn, or of clene whete,
B. 6.304　But *Coket* [or] clermatyn or of clene whete,
C. 8.326　Bote clermatyn and *coket* and of clene whete

cokewold n *cokewold n.* A 1 cokewald; B 2; C 2 cokewold (1) cokewolde (1)
A. 4.140　But he be *cokewald* ycald, kitte of my nose.'
B. 4.164　But he be knowe for a *Cokewold* kut of my nose.'
B. 5.159　And dame Clarice a knyȝtes douȝter ac a *cokewold* was hir sire,
C. 4.159　But he be knowe for a *cokewold* kut of my nose.'
C. 6.134　And dame clarice a knyhtes douhter, a *cokewolde* was here syre,

cokkes > cok

cokkeslane n *cok n.(1)* A 1 cokkislane; B 1; C 1 cockes_lane
A. 5.162　Claris of *cokkislane* & þe clerk of þe chirche,
B. 5.311　Clarice of *Cokkeslane* and þe Clerk of þe chirche,
C. 6.366　Claryce of *cockes lane* and the clerc of þe churche,

cold n *cold n.* A 3; B 7 cold (5) colde (1) coold (1); C 5 colde
A. 3.178　Crope into a caban for *cold* of þi nailes;
A. 7.15　Caste hem cloþis for *cold* for so wile treuþe.
A. 7.55　Hise cokeris & his cuffis for *cold* of his nailes,
B. 3.191　Crope into a Cabane for *cold* of þi nayles;
B. 6.16　Casteþ hem cloþes [for *cold*] for so [wol] truþe.
B. 6.60　[Hise] cokeres and [hise] coffes for *cold* of [hise] nailes,
B.11.285　Ne neiþer kirtel ne cote, þeiȝ þei for *cold* sholde deye,
B.13.160　*Coold* ne care ne compaignye of þeues,
B.14.52　Or whan þow clomsest for *cold* or clyngest for drye.
B.14.236　That is welawo whan he wakeþ and wepeþ for *colde*,
C. 8.243　"The slowe Caytif for *colde* wolde no corn tylye;
C. 9.109　Careth they for no colde ne counteth of non hete
C.13.72　Fynde beggares bred, bakkes for þe *colde*,
C.15.251　Or when thow cl[o]msest fo[r] *colde* or clingest for drouthe.
C.16.77　Þat is welowo when he [w]aketh and wepeth for *colde*;

cold adj *cold adj.* B 2; C 5 coeld (2) cold (1) colde (2)
B.13.261　And er þe commune haue corn ynouȝ many a *cold* morwenyng;
B.14.232　And þouȝ his glotonye be to good ale he goþ to *cold* beddyng
C. 1.125　Ac thei caren nat thow hit be *cold*, knaues, when þe[i] worche.
C. 9.93　And *colde* flesche and fische as venisoun were bake;
C.16.73　And thogh his glotonye be of gode ale he goth to a *colde* beddynge
C.17.303　Quadriduanus *coeld* quyk dede hym walke.
C.18.144　Quadriduanus *coeld*, quyk dede hym rome.

cole n1 *col n.(1)* A 1; B 1 coles
A. 7.270　Ac I haue persile & poret, & many *cole* plantis,
B. 6.286　Ac I haue percile and pore[t] and manye [plaunte *coles*],

coler n *coler n.* B 3 coler (2) colers (1); C 3 coler (2) colers (1)
B.Pr.162　And somme *colers* of crafty werk; vncoupled þei wen[d]en
B.Pr.169　And knytten it on a *coler* for oure commune profit
B.Pr.204　[Ne] carpynge of þis *coler* þat costed me neuere;
C.Pr.181　And *colers* of crafty werk, bothe knyghte[s] and squieres.
C.Pr.186　And knytten hit on a *coler* for oure comune profyt
C.Pr.212　Ne carp[ynge] of [þis] cole[r] þat costede me neuere.

coles n2 *col n.(2)* &> *cole* B 1; C 2
B.13.144　Cast *coles* on his heed of alle kynde speche;
C. 9.142　In hope to sitte at euen by þe hote *coles*,
C.15.142　Caste *coles* on his heued of alle kyn[de] speche,

colhoppes > coloppes

collateral adj *collateral adj.* B 1; C 1
B.14.300　A *collateral* confort, cristes owene ȝifte:
C.16.136　A *collateral* confort, cristes oune sonde:

colled ptp *collen v.* A 1 collide; B 2 colled (1) collede (1)
A.11.177　Curteisliche clergi[e] c[o]llide me & kiste,
B.10.234　[Curteisly clergie *collede* me and kiste,
B.11.17　Concupiscencia carnis *colled* me aboute þe nekke

colloppes > coloppes

colomy adj *colmi adj.* B 1 colomy
B.13.355　[Was] *colomy* þoruȝ coueitise and vnkynde desiryng.

coloppes n *colloppe n.* A 1 colopis; B 1; C 2 colhoppes (1) colloppes (1)
A. 7.269　Ne no cokenay, be crist, *colopis* to maken.
B. 6.285　Ne no cokeney, by crist! *coloppes* to maken.
C. 8.307　Ne no cokeney, be Crist! *colloppes* to make.
C.15.67　Brawen and bloed of gees, bacon and *colhoppes*.

colour n *colour n.* B 10 colour (4) colours (6); C 9 colour (4) coloures (2) colours (3)
B. 3.238　Tho þat entren of o *colour* and of one wille
B.11.330　Wiþ fleckede feþeres and of fele *colours*.
B.11.365　I seiȝ floures in þe fryth and hir faire *colours*
B.11.368　Of hir kynde and hir *colour* to carpe it were to longe.
B.11.405　Tho cauȝte I *colour* anoon and comsed to ben ashamed
B.12.222　Wherof þei cacche hir *colours* so clere and so briȝte,
B.15.209　Therfore by *colour* ne by clergie knowe shaltow [hym] neuere,
B.19.13　Hise *colours* and his cote Armure; ac he þat comeþ so blody
B.19.241　And some to [kerue and compace], and *colours* to make;
B.19.351　Wiþ swiche *colours* and queyntise comeþ pride yarmed
C.13.138　With flekede fetheres and of fele *colours*.
C.13.175　Ne what o[f] floures on felde and of here fayre *coloures*
C.13.178　Of here kynde and here *colour* to carpe hit were to longe.
C.13.213　Tho cauhte y *colour* anoen and comesede to ben aschamed
C.18.21　And of o kyne *colour* & kynde, as me thoghte,
C.20.213　Ho couthe kyndeliche whit *colour* descreue
C.21.13　His *colours* and his cote armure; ac he þat cometh so blody
C.21.241　[And somme to kerue a]nd compace and *coloures* to make;
C.21.351　With such *colours* and queyntis[e] cometh pruyde yArmed

coloureþ v *colouren v.* B 2 coloured (1) coloureþ (1); C 2 coloured (1) coloureth (1)
B.19.347　Shal be *coloured* so queyntely and couered vnder [oure] Sophistrie
B.19.458　And *coloureþ* it for a konnynge and a clene lyuynge.'
C.21.347　Shal be *coloured* so queyntly and keuered vnder [o]ure sophistrie
C.21.458　And *coloureth* hit for a connyng and a clene lyuynge.'

coltyng n prop *n.i.d.* C 1
C.20.288　*Coltyng* and al his kyn, the car to saue.

coltur > cultour

coluere n *culver n.* B 3; C 5 coluer (2) coluere (3)
B.15.404　Thanne wolde þe *coluere* come to þe clerkes ere
B.15.407　That þe *coluere* þat com so com from god of heuene
B.15.415　How englisshe clerkes a *coluere* fede þat coueitise hiȝte,
C.17.173　Corn [þat þe] *coluere* eet when he come in places,
C.17.175　Thenne sholde þe *coluere* come to þe clerkes ere,
C.17.177　And when þe *coluer* ca[m] th[us] then knelede þe peple
C.17.179　And sothliche þat god sulue in suche a *coluere* lyknesse
C.17.246　And crie to Crist a wolde his *coluer* sende

com > comen; comandement > comaundement

comaunde v *commaunden v.* A 5 comaunde (2) comaundid (1) comaundite (2); B 11 comaunde (2) comaunded (3) comaundede (3) comaundeþ (2) commaunded (1); C 14 comaunde (5) comaundede (6) comaundeth (3)
A. 1.20　And *comaundite* of his curteisie in comoun þre þinges;
A. 2.160　And *comaundite* a cunstable þat com at þe ferste
A. 4.6　'And I *comaunde* þe,' quaþ þe king to consience þanne,
A. 4.8　*Comaunde* hym þat he come my counseil to here,

A. 4.72 & *comaundid* a cunstable to caste hym in yrens]:
B. 1.20 And *comaunded* of his curteisie in commune þree þynges;
B. 2.199 And *comaundede* a Constable þat com at þe firste
B. 2.209 And how þe kyng *comaunded* Constables and sergeaunt3
B. 4.6 'And I *comaunde* þee', quod þe kyng to Conscience þanne,
B. 4.8 *Comaunde* hym þat he come my counseil to here,
B. 4.85 And *comaundede* a Constable to casten hym in Irens:
B.11.181 [And] *comaundeþ* ech creature to conformen hym to louye
B.13.46 Conscience curteisly þo *commaunded* Scripture
B.19.113 And crist counseileþ þus and *comaundeþ* boþe,
B.19.361 And cryde and *comaundede* alle cristene peple
B.19.364 Conscience *comaundede* þo alle cristene to delue,
C. 1.20 And *comaundede* of his cortesye in comune thre thynges;
C. 2.213 And *comaundede* a Constable that cam at þe furste
C. 4.6 'And y *comaunde* [the],' quod the kyng to Consience thenne,
C. 4.8 *Comaunde* hym þat he come my consayle to here
C. 4.81 And *comaunde* a Constable to caste [hym] in yrones
C. 4.195 The kyng *comaundede* Consience tho to congeye alle his offeceres
C. 5.194 '*Comaunde* þat alle confessours þat eny kyng shryueth
C. 8.88 What þei *comaunde* as by þe kyng countreplede hit neuere:
C. 8.229 Conforte hem with thy catel, for so *comaundeth* treuthe;
C.13.78 As Crist hymsulf *comaundeth* alle cristene peple:
C.15.52 That Consience *comaunde* sholde to do come scripture
C.21.113 And Crist consayleth [þu]s and *comaundeth* bothe,
C.21.361 And cryede and *comaundede* alle cristene peple
C.21.364 Consience *comaundede* t[h]o alle cristene to delue

comaundement n *commaundement n.* B 2 comaundement (1)
comaundement3 (1); C 4 comandement (2) comaundement3 (1)
comaundementis (1)

B.14.292 /Ergo pouerte and poore men parfournen þe *comaundement*
B.15.74 And tellen men of þe ten *comaundement3*, and touchen þe seuene synnes
C. 3.410 Agaynes godes *comandement*, god tok such a vengeaunce
C.11.140 Kepe þe ten *comaundementis* and kepe þe fro synne
C.16.127 Ergo pouerte and pore men parforme þe *comandement*
C.16.234 To teche þe ten *comaundement3* ten sythe were bettere

comaundour n *commaundour n.* A 1

A. 3.274 Vnkyndenesse is *comaundour*, & kyndenesse is banisshit.

combraunce n *combraunce n.* B 2; C 4

B.12.45 Catel and kynde wit was *combraunce* to hem alle.
B.18.268 Care and [c]*ombraunce* is comen to vs alle.
C. 5.190 Is cause of alle *combraunc[e]* to confounde a reume.'
C.12.245 So coueytise of catel was *combraunce* to hem alle.
C.18.172 And kene care in thy kissyng and *combraunce* to thysulue.
C.20.276 Care and *combraunce* is come to vs all.

combre v *combren v.* A 1 combrist; C 1

A.10.93 For 3if þou comist a3en consience þou *combrist* þiseluen,
C. 1.67 To *combre* men with coueytise, þat is his kynde and his lore.'

comely > **comly**

comen v *comen v.* &> *commune* A 61 cam (5) com (18) come (22) comen
(7) comist (2) comiþ (6) ycome (1); B 226 cam (52) com (19) come
(86) comen (16) comest (2) comeþ (33) comynge (1) coom (2) coom
(2) coome (6) coomen (1) kam (6); C 228 kam (32) cam (82) com (1)
come (87) comen (11) comest (2) cometh (37) comyng (1) comynge
(1) ycome (3)

A.Pr.24 In cuntenaunce of cloþing *comen* disgisid.
A.Pr.70 *Comen* vp knelynge to kissen his bulle.
A. 1.4 *Com* doun fro þat [clyf] & callide me faire,
A. 1.59 'Þ[at] is þe castel of care; who[so] *comiþ* þereinne
A. 2.21 I au3te ben hi3ere þanne heo for I *com* of a betere.
A. 2.115 And *comen* to counforte fro care þe false,
A. 2.152 And *come* to þe kinges court & consience tolde,
A. 2.160 And comaundite a cunstable þat *com* at þe ferste
A. 3.25 Wiþ þat *come* clerkis to conforten hire þe same,
A. 3.34 Þanne þere a confessour ycopid as a frere;
A. 3.90 Þe king fro counseil *com* & callide aftir mede
A. 3.99 I haue a kni3t, consience, *com* late fro be3onde;
A. 3.103 Þanne was consience callid to *comen* & aperen
A. 3.165 And þou knowist, consience, I *ca[m]* nou3t to chide,
A. 3.275 Ac kynde wyt shal *come* 3et, & consience togidere,
A. 4.8 Comaunde hym þat he *come* my counseil to here,
A. 4.21 And 3et wile [h]e make many wehe er we *come* þere.'
A. 4.29 Ac consience *com* arst to court be a myle wey
A. 4.31 Curteisliche þe king þanne *com* in to resoun,
A. 4.34 Þanne *com* pes into þe parlement & putte vp a bille
A. 4.152 Be my counseil *ycome* of clerkes and Erlis.
A. 5.11 And consience wiþ a cros *com* for to preche,
A. 5.85 Whanne I *come* to þe [k]ir[k]e & knel[e] to þe rode,
A. 5.107 Þanne *com* coueitise; I can hym nou3t descryue,
A. 5.139 Whanne it *com* in cuppemel; þat craft my wyf vside.

A. 6.13 Þis folk fraynide hym faire [fro] whenis þat he *come*.
A. 6.49 Til 3e *come* into consience þat crist wyte þe soþe,
A. 6.59 Þanne shalt þou come be a croft, ac *come* þou nou3t þereinne;
A. 6.59 Þanne shalt þou *come* be a croft, ac come þou nou3t þereinne;
A. 6.72 Þanne shalt þou *come* to a court, cler as þe sonne.
A. 7.34 For þise *comiþ* to my croft & croppiþ my whete.'
A. 7.81 Til I *come* to his acountes as my crede me techiþ–
A. 7.106 Shulde ben hirid þereaftir whan heruist tyme *come*.
A. 7.283 Be þat it nei3ide ner heruest [þat] newe corn *com* to chepyng.
A. 7.287 Ne no beggere ete bred þat benis in *come*,
A. 8.121 And consience *com* aftir & kennide me betere.'
A. 8.139 Þat [vncouþe] kni3t[is] shal *come* þi kingdom to cleyme;
A. 8.172 And *come* [alle] before crist acountes to 3elden,
A. 9.62 *Com* & callide me be my kynde name.
A. 9.94 Þanne shulde þe kyng *come* & casten hem in presoun,
A.10.24 Til kynde *come* oþer sende [and] kepe hire hymselue.'
A.10.93 For 3if þou *comist* a3en consience þou combrist þiseluen,
A.10.135 For of here kynde þei *comen* þat confessours ben nempnid,
A.10.151 Alle þat *comen* of þat caym crist hatid aftir,
A.10.153 [Þat] of seth & his sistir siþþe forþ *come*
A.10.155 For alle þat *comen* of þat caym acursid þei were,
A.10.165 And *com* to noe anon, and bad hym nou3t lette
A.10.172 Þat euere curside caym *com* on þis erþe;
A.10.178 [Þus] þoru3 curside caym *cam* care vpon alle,
A.10.184 A carful concepcioun *comiþ* of such weddyng
A.10.217 And so *comiþ* dobest aboute, and bringeþ doun mody,
A.11.87 And now *comiþ* a conyon & wolde cacche of my wittes
A.11.117 For 3if þou coupl[e] be with hym to clergie *comist* þou neuere;
A.11.120 Til þou *come* to a court, kepe wel þi tunge
A.11.124 So shalt þou *come* to clergie þat can many wyttes.
A.11.169 And er I *com* to clergie coude I neuere stynte.
A.11.240 Ac cristene men, god wot, *comiþ* not so to heuene,
A.12.32 For he *cam* not by cause to lerne to dowel
A.12.52 Til 3e *come* to þe burg[h] quod bonum est tenete.
A.12.57 And ere I *cam* to þe court quod bonum est tenete
A.12.77 With þat *cam* a knaue with a confessoures face,
B.Pr.24 In contenaunce of cloþynge *comen* d[is]gised.
B.Pr.73 *Comen* vp knelynge to kissen hi[s] bull[e].
B.Pr.112 Thanne *kam* þer a kyng; kny3thod hym ladde;
B.Pr.114 And þanne *cam* kynde wit and clerkes he made
B.Pr.148 *Comen* to a counseil for þe commune profit.
B.Pr.149 For a cat of a [court] *cam* whan hym liked
B.Pr.185 'Thou3 we [hadde] kille[d] þe cat yet sholde þer *come* anoþer
B. 1.4 *Cam* doun from [þe] Castel and called me faire,
B. 1.61 'That is þe castel of care; whoso *comþ* þerInne
B. 2.26 And neuere sooþ seide siþen he *com* to erþe,
B. 2.28 I ou3te ben hyere þan she; I *kam* of a bettre.
B. 2.151 And *comen* to conforten from care þe false
B. 2.191 And to þe kynges court and Conscience tolde,
B. 2.199 And comaunded a Constable þat *com* at þe firste
B. 3.26 Wiþ þat *comen* clerkes to conforten hire þe same
B. 3.35 Thanne *cam* þer a Confessour coped as a frere;
B. 3.56 And a cours of kynde wherof we *comen* alle;
B. 3.101 The kyng fro conseil *cam* and called after Mede
B. 3.110 I haue a kny3t, Conscience, *cam* late fro biyonde;
B. 3.114 [Th]anne was Conscience called to *come* and appere
B. 3.178 And þow knowest, Conscience, I *kam* no3t to chide,
B. 3.299 Ac kynde loue shal *come* 3it and Conscience togideres
B. 3.303 That Moyses or Messie be *come* into [myddel]erþe,
B. 4.8 Comaunde hym þat he *come* my counseil to here,
B. 4.36 Ac [þ]ere is loue and leautee [hem like]þ no3t *come* þere:
B. 4.43 As Conscience hym kenned til þei *come* to þe kynge
B. 4.44 Curteisly þe kyng þanne *com* [in to] Reson,
B. 4.47 [Th]anne *com* pees into [þe] parlement and putte [vp] a bille
B. 4.189 [Be] my counseil *co[men]* of clerkes and Erles.
B. 5.105 Whan I *come* to þe kirk and knele to þe Roode
B. 5.178 Ac ouþer while whan wyn *comeþ*, [whan] I drynke at eue,
B. 5.188 [Th]anne *cam* Coueitise; [I kan] hym na3t discryue,
B. 5.223 [Whan] it *cam* In cuppemele, þis craft my wif vsed.
B. 5.385 Thanne *cam* Sleuþe al bislabered wiþ two slymy ei3en.
B. 5.412 *Come* I to Ite missa est I holde me yserued.
B. 5.525 This folk frayned hym [faire] fro whennes he *come*.
B. 5.562 Til ye *come* into Conscience þat crist wite þe soþe,
B. 5.572 Thanne shaltow come by a croft, [ac] *come* þow no3t þerInne;
B. 5.572 Thanne shaltow *come* by a croft, [ac] come þow no3t þerInne;
B. 5.585 Thanne shaltow *come* to a court, cler as þe sonne.
B. 6.32 For [þise] *comeþ* to my croft and croppeþ my whete.'
B. 6.89 Til I *come* to hise acountes as my [crede] me [techeþ]–
B. 6.114 Sholde be hired þerafter whan heruest tyme *come*.
B. 6.299 By þat it ne3ed neer heruest newe corn *cam* to chepyng.
B. 6.303 Ne no beggere ete breed þat benes Inne [*come*],
B. 7.139 And Conscience *cam* afte[r] and kenned me [bettre].'
B. 7.161 That vnkouþe kny3tes shul *come* þi kyngdom to cleyme;

B. 7.194	And *comen* alle [bi]fore crist acountes to yelde,		B.18.11	Barefoot on an Asse bak bootles *cam* prikye
B. 8.71	*Cam* and called me by my kynde name.		B.18.13	As is þe kynde of a knyght þat *comeþ* to be dubbed,
B. 8.104	Thanne [sholde] þe kyng *come* and casten hem in [prison,		B.18.16	As dooþ an heraud of armes whan Auentrous *comeþ* to Iustes.
B. 9.24	Til kynde *come* or sende [and kepe] hire [hymselue].'		B.18.36	Thanne *cam* Pilatus with muche peple, sedens pro tribunali,
B. 9.112	For of hir kynde þei *come* þat Confessours ben nempned,		B.18.55	If þow be crist and kynges sone *com* down of þe roode;
B. 9.114	Maidenes and martires out of o man *come.*		B.18.62	Dede men for þat dene *come* out of depe graues
B. 9.126	And alle þat *come* of þat Caym come to yuel ende,		B.18.73	A Cachepol *cam* forþ and craked boþe hir legges
B. 9.126	And alle þat come of þat Caym *come* to yuel ende,		B.18.78	Ac þer *cam* forþ a kny3t wiþ a kene spere ygrounde,
B. 9.134	And *com* to Noe anon and bad hym no3t lette:		B.18.109	Whan crist *cam* hir kyngdom þe crowne sholde [lese]:
B. 9.141	That euere cursed Caym *coom* on þis erþe;		B.18.114	*Cam* walkynge in þe wey; to helleward she loked.
B. 9.156	And þus þoru3 cursed Caym *cam* care vpon erþe,		B.18.117	Hir suster, as it semed, *cam* so[fte]ly walkynge
B. 9.161	[A] careful concepcion *comeþ* of [swich weddynge]		B.18.148	For þat is ones in helle out *comeþ* [it] neuere.
B. 9.208	And so *comeþ* dobest [aboute] and bryngeþ adoun mody,		B.18.165	Rightwisnesse *come* rennynge; reste we þe while,
B.10.165	For if þow coupl[e] þee [wiþ hym] to clergie *comest* [þow] neuere;		B.18.168	Where pees *comeþ* pleyinge in pacience ycloþed.
B.10.168	Til þow come to a court, kepe-wel-þi-tunge–		B.18.252	For [Iesus as a] geaunt wiþ a gyn [*comeþ*] yonde]
B.10.172	[So] shaltow *come* to Clergie þat kan manye [wittes].		B.18.265	For here *comeþ* wiþ crowne þat kyng is of glorie." '
B.10.226	And [er] I *com* to clergie [koude I] neuere stynte.		B.18.268	Care and [c]ombraunce is *comen* to vs alle.
B.10.307	For in cloistre *comeþ* [no] man to [carpe] ne to fi3te		B.18.269	If þis kyng *come* In mankynde wole he fecche
B.10.322	Ac þer shal *come* a kyng and confesse yow Religiouses,		B.18.307	And now I se wher a soule *comeþ* [silynge hiderward]
B.10.334	Ac er þat kyng *come* Caym shal awake,		B.18.320	That crist may *come* In, þe kynges sone of heuene!'
B.10.357	Ac cristene men wiþoute moore maye no3t *come* to heuene,		B.18.371	And þanne shal I *come* as a kyng, crouned, wiþ Aungeles,
B.10.451	Thou3 ye *come* bifore kynges and clerkes of þe lawe		B.18.381	And if þe kyng of þat kyngdom *come* in þat tyme
B.11.11	And knowe þat þow coueitest and *come* þerto paraunter'.		B.18.384	And I þat am kyng of kynges shal *come* swich a tyme
B.11.50	Coueitise of ei3es *com* ofter in mynde		B.19.7	And *com* in wiþ a cros bifore þe comune peple,
B.11.53	'Haue no conscience', [quod she],'how þow *come* to goode;		B.19.13	Hise colours and his cote Armure; ac he þat *comeþ* so blody
B.11.81	Thoru3 contricion [clene] *come* to þe hei3e heuene–		B.19.25	Than Iesu or Iesus þat al oure Ioye *com* of?'
B.11.113	And whan þe peple was plener *comen* þe porter vnpynned þe yate		B.19.30	Ac to be conquerour called, þat *comeþ* of special grace,
B.11.119	For crist cleped vs alle, *come* if we wolde,		B.19.63	Ac þe cause þat he *comeþ* þus wiþ cros of his passion
B.11.123	'Thanne may alle cristene *come*', quod I, 'and cleyme þere entree		B.19.72	And *cam* to take mankynde kynges and Aungeles
B.11.135	But if Contricion wol *come* and crye by his lyue		B.19.74	Aungeles out of heuene *come* knelynge and songe,
B.11.217	Crist to a commune womman seide, in [*comen*] at a feste,		B.19.75	Kynges *come* after, knelede and offrede [sense],
B.11.259	[Al]þou3 it be sour to suffre, þe[r] *comeþ* swete [after].		B.19.86	That o kyng *cam* wiþ Reson couered vnder sense.
B.11.321	And slepynge I sei3 al þis, and siþen *cam* kynde		B.19.91	The þridde kyng þo *kam* knelynge to Iesu
B.12.5	And how fele fernyeres are faren and so fewe to *come*;		B.19.123	After þe kynde þat he *cam* of; þere comsede he do wel.
B.12.64	Clergie and kynde wit *comeþ* of si3te and techyng		B.19.136	Forþi þe contree þer Iesu *cam* called hym fili dauid,
B.12.66	Of quod scimus *comeþ* Clergie, [a] konnynge of heuene,		B.19.151	*Come* knelynge to þe corps and songen
B.12.67	And of quod vidimus *comeþ* kynde wit, of si3te of diuerse peple.		B.19.155	Telle þe comune þat þer *cam* a compaignie of hise Apostles.
B.12.69	Knew neuere clerk how it *comeþ* forþ, ne kynde wit þe weyes:		B.19.160	In ech a compaignie þer she *cam*, Christus resurgens.
B.12.108	*Come* for al his kynde wit to cristendom and be saued;		B.19.161	Thus *cam* it out þat crist ouercoom, recouerede and lyuede:
B.12.128	Ac kynde wit *comeþ* of alle kynnes si3tes,		B.19.168	Crist *cam* In, and al closed boþe dore and yates,
B.12.135	For alle hir kynde knowyn[g] *co[m]* but of diuerse si3tes.		B.19.186	In couenaunt þat þei *come* and knewelich[e] to paie
B.12.153	Clerkes knewen it wel and *comen* wiþ hir present3		B.19.192	He wente, and wonyeþ þere, and wol *come* at þe laste
B.12.181	And haþ no contricion er he *come* to shrifte; & þanne kan he litel telle		B.19.200	And counseiled me to knele þerto; and þanne *cam*, me þou3te,
B.12.256	And whan his caroyne shal *come* in caue to be buryed		B.19.208	And *comeþ* fro þe greet god; grace is his name.
B.13.22	And as crist wolde þer *com* Conscience to conforte me þat tyme		B.19.222	Shullen *come* and be curatours ouer kynges and Erles;
B.13.23	And bad me *come* to his court, wiþ clergie sholde I dyne.		B.19.253	'[That al craft and konnyng *come*] of my 3ifte.
B.13.24	And for Conscience of Clergie spak I *com* wel þe raþer.		B.19.287	Sholde no curious clooþ *comen* on his rugge,
B.13.34	And þanne clergie and Conscience and Pacience *come* after.		B.19.341	Thise two *coome* to Conscience and to cristen peple
B.13.37	Conscience called after mete and þanne *cam* Scripture		B.19.345	Shulle *come* out, Conscience; and youre [caples two],
B.13.133	'Thanne passe we ouer til Piers *come* and preue þis in dede.		B.19.351	Wiþ swiche colours and queyntise *comeþ* pride yarmed
B.13.218	To conforte hym and Conscience if þei *come* in place		B.19.360	And þanne *kam* Kynde wit Conscience to teche,
B.13.265	There was a careful commune whan no cart *com* to towne		B.19.381	'I care no3t', quod Conscience, 'þou3 pride come nouþe.
B.13.310	And what I kouþe and knew and what kyn I *com* of.		B.19.383	'*Comeþ*', quod Conscience, 'ye cristene, and dyneþ,
B.14.83	And þoru3 feiþ *comeþ* contricion, conscience woot wel,		B.19.410	'I am a Curatour of holy kirke, and *cam* neuere in my tyme
B.14.239	And if Coueitise cacche þe poore þei may no3t *come* togideres,		B.19.413	I knew neuere Cardynal þat he ne *cam* fro þe pope.
B.15.14	And wherof I *cam* & of what kynde. I coniured hym at þe laste		B.19.414	And we clerkes, whan þei *come*, for hir comunes paieþ,
B.15.235	In kynges court he *comeþ* ofte þer þe counseil is trewe,		B.19.417	"The contree is þe corseder þat Cardinals *come* Inne,
B.15.236	Ac if coueitise be of þe counseil he wol no3t *come* þerInne.		B.19.420	That no Cardynal *coome* among þe comune peple,
B.15.237	In court amonges [þe commune] he *comeþ* but selde		B.19.424	And þow Conscience in kynges court, and sholdest neuere *come* þennes;
B.15.239	In þe Consistorie bifore þe Commissarie he *comeþ* no3t ful ofte		B.19.465	And þanne *cam* þer a kyng and by his croune seide,
B.15.403	And if he among þe peple preched, or in places *come*,		B.20.14	And he [cacche] in þat caas and *come* þerto by sleighte
B.15.404	Thanne wolde þe coluere *come* to þe clerkes ere		B.20.16	And þou3 he *come* so to a clooþ and kan no bettre cheuyssaunce
B.15.407	That þe coluere þat *com* so com from god of heuene		B.20.41	And *cam* and took mankynde and bicam nedy.
B.15.407	That þe coluere þat com so *com* from god of heuene		B.20.53	Antecrist *cam* þanne, and al þe crop of truþe
B.15.452	Clooþ þat *comeþ* fro þe weuyng is no3t comly to were		B.20.56	In ech a contree þer he *cam* he kutte awey truþe
B.15.474	Ri3t as capons in a court *comeþ* to mennes whistlyng,		B.20.60	And al þe Couent *cam* to welcome [a] tyraunt
B.15.551	Right so, ye clerkes, for youre coueitise er [*come* au3t] longe		B.20.72	That *kam* ayein conscience þat kepere was and gyour
B.15.581	And han clerkes to kepen vs þerInne & hem þat shul *come* after.		B.20.74	'I conseille', quod Conscience þo, '*comeþ* wiþ me, ye fooles,
B.15.585	And took it Moyses to teche men til Messie *coome*,		B.20.76	And crye we to kynde þat he *come* and defende vs
B.15.603	And hopen þat he be to *come* þat shal hem releue;		B.20.78	And crye we [on] al þe comune þat þei *come* to vnitee
B.16.28	Coueitise *comþ* of þat wynd and crepeþ among þe leues		B.20.80	Kynde Conscience þo herde and *cam* out of þe planetes
B.16.93	Til plenitudo temporis [tyme] *comen* tyme		B.20.88	There was 'harrow!' and 'help! here *comeþ* kynde
B.16.102	To haue yfou3te wiþ þe fend er ful tyme *come*.		B.20.91	After Confort a knyght to *come* and bere his baner:
B.16.174	I frayned hym first fram whennes he *come*		B.20.97	Kynde *cam* after wiþ many kene soores
B.16.190	Confortour of creatures; of hym *comeþ* alle blisse.		B.20.100	Deeþ *cam* dryuynge after and al to duste passhed
B.16.265	Til he *come* þat I carpe of; crist is his name		B.20.121	Thanne *cam* Coueitise and caste how he my3te
B.16.274	I affrayned hym first fram whennes he *come*,		B.20.129	And *cam* to þe kynges counseille as a kene baroun
B.17.53	*Comynge* from a contree þat men called Ierico;		B.20.139	Departen er deeþ *cam* and deuors shapte.
B.17.62	Hope *cam* hippynge after þat hadde so ybosted		B.20.150	Ne careþ no3t how Kynde slow and shal *come* at þe laste
B.17.77	'Haue, kepe þis man', [quod he], 'til I *come* fro þe Iustes.		B.20.206	And loke þow konne som craft er þow *come* þennes.'
B.17.85	To ouertaken hym and talke to hym er þei to towne *coome*.		B.20.209	'How shal I *come* to catel so to cloþe me and to feede?'
B.17.123	And *come* ayein bi þis contree and conforten alle sike			

B.20.213 Thoruȝ Contricion and Confession til I *cam* to vnitee.
B.20.218 Proude preestes *coome* with hym; [passynge an hundred]
B.20.220 *Coomen* ayein Conscience; wiþ Coueitise þei helden.
B.20.230 Freres herden hym crye and *comen* hym to helpe,
B.20.233 That þei *come* for coueitise, to haue cure of soules.
B.20.316 Quod Contricion to Conscience, 'do hym *come* to vnitee,
B.20.326 To curen as a Curatour; and *cam* with hi[s] lettr[e]
B.20.328 In contrees þer he *coome* confessions to here;
B.20.329 And *cam* þere Conscience was and knokked at þe yate.
B.20.333 Carpe I wolde wiþ contricion, and þerfore *cam* I hider.'
B.20.342 But þow konne [any] craft þow *comest* nouȝt herInne.
B.20.344 *Coom* in þus ycoped at a Court þere I dwelde,
B.20.355 And *cam* to Conscience and curteisly hym grette.
B.20.374 And *comen* wiþ a kene wille Conscience to assaille.
B.20.376 And [bad] Contricion [*come*] to kepe þe yate.
C.Pr.71 *Comen* [vp] knel[yng] to kyssen his bull[e].
C.Pr.95 Consience *cam* and [ac]cu[s]ed hem–and þe comune herde hit–
C.Pr.139 Thenne *cam* the[r] a kyng; knygh[t]hede hym la[dd]e;
C.Pr.141 And thenne *cam* kynde wytt [& clerkus he made
C.Pr.169 *Comen* til a conseyl for [þe] comune profyt.
C.Pr.170 For a Cat of a Court *cam* whan hym likede
C.Pr.202 'Thow we hadde ykuld þe Cat ȝut shulde ther *come* another
C.1.4 *Cam* doun fro þe castel and calde me by name
C.1.57 'That is þe Castel of care; whoso *cometh* þerynne
C.2.30 Y ouhte ben herrore then he; y *com* of a bettere.
C.2.167 And *comen* ful courteysly to conforte the false
C.2.192 On secatours and such men *cometh* softly aftur.
C.2.205 And *kam* to þe kynges Court and Consience tolde,
C.2.213 And comaundede a Constable that *cam* at þe furste
C.2.245 And is welcome when he *cometh* and woneth with hem ofte.
C.3.27 Thenne *come* clerkes to conforte here the same
C.3.38 Thenne *come* þer a confessour ycoped as a frere;
C.3.60 And [a] cours of kynde wherof we *comen* alle.
C.3.128 The kyng fram conseyl *come* [and] calde aftur mede
C.3.147 Y haue a knyght, Consience, *cam* late fro beȝende;
C.3.151 Thenne was Consience ykald to *come* and apere
C.3.224 And þ[ou] knowe[st], Consience, y *cam* nat to chyde
C.3.239 In contrees there the kyng *cam*, consience hym lette
C.3.338 And ayther is otheres helpe; of hem *cometh* retribucoun
C.3.352 So of ho[l] herte *cometh* hope and hardy relacoun
C.3.365 And withoute ca[s]e to cache [to] and *come* to bothe nombres,
C.3.452 A[c] kynde loue shal *come* ȝut and Consience togyderes
C.3.456 That here kyng be *ycome* fro þe Court of heuene,
C.4.8 Comaunde hym þat he *come* my consayle to here
C.4.33 'Here *cometh*,' quod Consience, 'þat Coueytise seruen.
C.4.42 Corteyslyche þe kyng thenne *cam* and grette resoun
C.4.45 Thenne *cam* p[ees] into [þe] parlement and putte vp a bille
C.5.6 For as y *cam* by Consience with resoun y mette
C.5.50 To be welcome when y *come* oþerwhile in a monthe,
C.5.66 For sholde no clerke be crouned but yf he *come* were
C.5.154 For in C[l]oystre *cometh* no man to chyde ne to fyhte;
C.5.168 Ac þer shal *come* a kyng and confesse ȝow alle
C.5.178 Ac ar þat kyng *come*, as cronicles me tolde,
C.6.58 And what y couthe and knewe and what kyn y *cam* of.'
C.6.160 Ac other while when wyn *cometh* and when y drynke late at euen
C.6.196 Thenne *cam* coueytse; y can hym nat descreue,
C.6.231 When hit *cam* in coppemele; this crafte my wyf vsede.
C.6.307 And arste shal *come* to heuene, [by hym þat me made]!'
C.6.338 Confessen hem and cryen hym mercy; shal neuere *come* in helle.
C.7.1 Thenne *cam* sleuthe al byslobered with two slim[y] yes.
C.7.170 This folk frayned hym furste fro whennes he *come*.
C.7.207 Til ȝe *come* into Consience, yknowe of god sulue,
C.7.219 Thenne shalt thow *come* by a croft Ac come thow [nat] þerynne;
C.7.219 Thenne shalt thow come by a croft Ac *come* thow [nat] þerynne;
C.7.232 And so shaltow *come* to a Court as cleer as þe sonne.
C.7.304 I may nat *come* for a kitte, so a cleueth on me:
C.8.31 For þey *cometh* to my croft my corn to diffoule.'
C.8.98 Til y *come* til his acountes as my crede telleth,
C.8.121 He sholde be huyred þeraftur when heruost tyme *come*.
C.8.152 A bretener *cam* braggyng, abostede [Peres] also:
C.8.321 By that hit nyhed neyh heruost and newe corn *cam* to chepyng.
C.9.125 We sholde [haue] hem to house and helpe hem when they *come*:
C.9.156 Thorw which craft a couthe *come* to bred and to ale
C.9.248 [C]o[m]e in his cope as he a Clerk were;
C.9.254 *Cam* no wyn in his wombe thorw þe woke longe
C.9.256 The cause of al this caytiftee *cometh* of many bischopes
C.9.340 And *comen* alle bifore Crist acountes to ȝelde,
C.10.53 To contricion, to confessioun, til he *come* til his ende.
C.10.69 *Cam* and calde me be my kynde name.
C.10.150 Til kynde *come* o[r] sende and kepe here hymsulue.'
C.10.205 For of here kynde þey *come*, bothe confessours and martres,
C.10.220 Alle þat *come* of Caym Caytyue[s] were euere
C.10.229 That euere corsed Caym *cam* on þis erthe;

C.11.107 For yf thow coueytest to be ryche to clergie *comest* thow neuere.
C.11.110 To clergie shaltow neuere *come* ne knowe what is dowel.
C.11.135 And to clergie y *cam* as clerkes me saide.
C.11.170 And knowe þat þou coueytest and *come* þerto parauntur.'
C.11.276 Thogh ȝe *come* bifore kynges and clerkes of þe law[e]
C.12.5 [Haue no consience how þou *come* to good]; confesse the to som frere.
C.12.48 And whan þe peple was plenere *ycome* þe porter vnpynnede þe gate
C.12.54 For crist clepede vs alle, *come* yf we wolde,
C.12.58 'Thenne may alle cristene *come*,' [quod y], 'and clayme þer entre
C.12.98 And cristis oune clergie; he *cam* fro heuene to teche hit
C.12.145 Althouh h[it] be sour to soffre þer *cometh* a swete aftur.
C.12.169 "Hoso coueiteth to *come* to my kyneriche
C.12.203 Bitokeneth treuly in tyme *comyng* aftur
C.13.85 Ne in none enquestes to *come* ne cont[u]max thogh he worche
C.13.131 Til þat kynde *cam* clergie to helpe
C.13.233 For shal neuere, ar shame *come*, a shrewe wel [be] chaste[d].
C.14.30 Ac clergie *cometh* bote of syhte and kynde wit of sterres,
C.14.39 And crist *cam* and confermede and holy kyrke made
C.14.45 No more can no clerk but if hit *come* of bokes.
C.14.53 *Come* for al his kynde wit thorw cristendoem to be saued,
C.14.79 For al here kynde knowyng *cam* bote of diuerse syhtes,
C.14.97 Clerkes kn[e]we [þe] comet and *comen* with here presentes
C.14.121 And hath no contricion ar he *come* to shrifte; and thenne can he lytel telle,
C.14.157 How creatures han kynde wit and how clerkes *come* to bokes
C.14.158 And how þe floures in þe fryth *cometh* to fayre hewes:
C.14.182 Then for eny kyn he *come* of or for his kynde wittes.
C.15.25 And thenne *cam* concyence and clergie aftur
C.15.32 [Pacience as a pore thyng *cam*] and preeyede mete pur charite;
C.15.42 Clergie cald aftur mete and thenne *cam* scripture
C.15.52 That Consience comaunde sholde to do *come* scripture
C.15.59 Thenne *cam* contricion þat hadd coked for hem all
C.15.71 Alle þat coueyte[d] to *come* to eny kyne ioye,
C.15.187 To conforte hym and Consience yf they *come* in place
C.16.29 Cordis contricio *cometh* of sor[w]e of herte
C.16.30 And oris confessio *cometh* of [knowlechyng and] shrifte of mouthe
C.16.79 And thogh coueytyse [cacche] þe pore they may nat *come* togyderes
C.16.360 In kynges Court a *cometh* yf his consaile be trewe
C.16.361 Ac yf couetyse be of his consaile a wol nat *come* þerynne
C.16.362 Amongus þe comune in Court a *cometh* bote selde
C.16.364 In constorie bifore [þe] commissarie a *cometh* nat ful ofte
C.17.10 To his selle selde *cam* and soffred be mylked.
C.17.149 Contrarie her nat as in Consience yf thow wol[t] *come* to heuene.'
C.17.173 Corn [þat þe] coluere eet when he *come* in places
C.17.175 Thenne sholde þe coluere *come* to þe clerkes ere,
C.17.177 And when þe coluer *ca[m]* th[us] then knelede þe peple
C.17.214 Riht so, ȝe clerkes, ȝoure coueytise ar *come* auht longe
C.17.296 Moises to be maister þerof til messie *come*
C.17.311 And hopen þat he be to *come* þat shal hem releue;
C.18.4 Til we *cam* into a contre, cor hominis hit heihte,
C.18.12 And þerof *cometh* a goed fruyt þe wiche men calleth werkes
C.18.32 Couetyse *cometh* of þat wynde and Caritas hit abiteth
C.18.126 Til plenitudo temporis tyme *ycome* were
C.18.136 To haue yfouhte with þe fende Ar fol tyme *come*.
C.18.236 In matrimonie aren thre and of o man *cam* alle thre
C.18.241 Where god [riȝt be my gate *cam* gangynge a thre];
C.18.281 Til he *come* þat y carpe of; Crist is his name
C.18.290 And y fraynede hym furst fro whennes he *come*,
C.19.36 And now *cometh* this sp[es and speketh] that hath aspyed þe lawe,
C.19.49 Thenne sey we a samaritaen *cam* sittynge on a muyle;
C.19.51 *Comynge* fram a contraye þat men callide Ierico;
C.19.61 Hope cam huppynge aftur þat hadde so ybosted
C.19.237 Bute riȝtfulliche, as men [r]at, al his richesse *cam* hym
C.20.9 Barfoet on an asse bake boetles *cam* priky[e]
C.20.11 As is þe kynde of a knyhte þat *cometh* to be dobbet,
C.20.14 As doth an heraud of Armes when Auntres *cometh* to ioustes.
C.20.35 Thenne *cam* Pilatus with moche peple, sedens pro tribunali,
C.20.55 And 'yf thow be Crist and [kynges] sone *come* adoun of th[e] rode;
C.20.64 And dede men for þat dene *cam* oute of depe graues
C.20.75 A cachepol *cam* [forth] a[nd] craked ato he[re] legges
C.20.80 Ac þer forth a knyhte with a kene spere ygrounde,
C.20.117 *Cam* walkynge in þe way; to hellward she lokede
C.20.120 Here suster, as hit semede, *cam* softly walkynge
C.20.151 [For] þat ones is in helle out *cometh* hit neuere.'
C.20.168 Rihtwisnesse *come* rennynge; reste we the while
C.20.171 Where *cometh* pees pleiynge in pacience yclothed.
C.20.261 For iesus as a geaunt with a gyn *cometh* ȝende
C.20.273 For here *cometh* with croune þe kynge of all glorie.'
C.20.276 Care and combraunce is *come* to vs all.
C.20.277 Yf this kyng *come* in mankynde wol he fecche

C.20.336   That if his soule hider *cam* hit sholde shende vs all.
C.20.341   And now y se where his soule *cometh* sylinge hid[er]ward
C.20.363   That Crist may *come* in, the kynges sone of h[e]uene!'
C.20.413   And thenne shal y *come* as [a] kynge, croune[d], with angeles
C.20.420   Shal neuere in helle eft *come* be he ones oute:
C.20.423   And yf þe kynge of þe kyngdoem *come* in þe tyme
C.20.426   And y þat am kynge o[f] kynges shal *come* such a tyme
C.21.7   And *cam* in with a cros bifore þe comune peple
C.21.13   His colours and his cote armure; ac he þat *cometh* so blody
C.21.25   Then iesu or iesus þat all oure ioye *cam* of ?'
C.21.30   Ac to be conquerour cald, þat *cometh* of special grace
C.21.63   Ac the cause that he *cometh* thus with cros [of] his passioun
C.21.69   Ac to carpe more of Crist and how he *cam* to þat name;
C.21.72   And *cam* to take mankynde kynges and angeles
C.21.74   Angele[s] out of heuene *come* knel[yng] and songe,
C.21.75   Kynges *cam* aftur, knelede and offrede [sense].
C.21.86   That [o] kyng *cam* with reson ykyuered vnder ensense.
C.21.91   The thridde kyng *cam* [þo] knel[ynge] to iesu
C.21.123   Aftur þe kynde þat he *come* of; þer comsede he do wel.
C.21.136   Forthy þe contre þer iesu *cam* calde hym fili dauid
C.21.151   *Comen* knelyng to þ[e] Cors and songen
C.21.155   Telle þe comune þat þer *cam* a companie of his apostles
C.21.160   In vch a companye þer he *cam*, christus resurgens.
C.21.161   Thus *cam* hit out þat Crist ouerkam, rekeuerede and lyuede:
C.21.168   Crist *cam* in, and al closed bothe dore and ʒates,
C.21.186   In couenaunt þat they *come* and knolech[e] to pay
C.21.192   He wente and woneth there and wol *come* at þe laste
C.21.200   And conseyled me to knele þerto; and thenne *cam*, me thouhte,
C.21.208   And *cometh* fro the grete god; grace is his name.
C.21.222   Shal *come* and be curatours ouer kynges and Erles;
C.21.253   'That all craft and connyng *c[o]m[e]* of my ʒefte.
C.21.287   Sholde no curious cloth *comen* on his rugge
C.21.341   Thise two *cam* to Consience and to cristene peple
C.21.345   Shal *come* oute, Consience; and ʒoure [caples two],
C.21.351   With such colours and queyntis[e] *cometh* pruyde yArmed
C.21.360   And thenne *cam* kynde wit Consience to teche
C.21.381   'Y care nat,' quod Consience, 'thow pryde *come* nouthe;
C.21.383   *Cometh*,' quod Consience, 'ʒe cristene, and dyneth
C.21.410   'Ich am a Curatour of holi [kirke] and *cam* neuer in my tyme
C.21.413   Y knewe neuere cardinale þat he ne *cam* fro þe pope
C.21.414   And we Clerkes, when they *come*, for here comunes paieth,
C.21.417   "The contreye is þe corsedore þat cardinals *cometh* ynne
C.21.420   That no cardinal *come* among þe comune peple
C.21.424   And thow, Consience, in kynges Court and sholdest neuer *come* thennes;
C.21.465   And thenne *cam* þer a kyng and bi his corone saide,
C.22.14   And he cacche in þat caes and *come* therto by sleithe
C.22.16   And thow me *come* so to a cloth and can no bettere cheuesaunce
C.22.41   And *cam* and toek mankynde and bicam nedy.
C.22.53   Auntecrist *cam* thenne and al the crop of treuthe
C.22.56   In vch a Contrey ther he *cam* [he] kutte awey treuthe
C.22.60   And al þe couent *cam* to welcome a tyraunt
C.22.72   That *cam* aʒen Consience þat kepar was and gyour
C.22.74   'Y consail,' quod Consi[e]nce tho, '*cometh* with me, ʒe foles,
C.22.76   And crye we to kynde þat he *come* and defende vs
C.22.78   And crye we on al þe comune þat thei *come* to vnite
C.22.80   Kynde Consience tho herde and *cam* oute of þe planetes
C.22.88   There was 'harow!' and 'helpe! here *cometh* kynde
C.22.91   Aftur conforte, a knyhte, [to] *come* and beer his baner:
C.22.97   Kynde *cam* aftur with many k[e]ne sores,
C.22.100   Deth *cam* dryuyng aftur and al to duste paschte
C.22.121   Thenne *cam* couetyse and caste how he myhte
C.22.129   And *cam* to þe kynges consail as a kene Baroun
C.22.139   Departen ar dethe *come* and deuors shupte.
C.22.150   Ne careth nat how kynde slowh and shal *come* at þe laste
C.22.206   And loke thow conne som craft ar thow *come* thennes.'
C.22.209   'How shal y *come* to catel so to clothe me and to fede?'
C.22.213   Thorw contricion and confessioun til y *cam* to vnite.
C.22.218   Proute prestes *cam* with hym; passyng an hundred
C.22.220   *Comen* aʒen Consience; with couetyse they helden.
C.22.230   Freres herde hym crye and *comen* hym to helpe
C.22.233   That they *cam* for Couetyse, to haue cure of soules.
C.22.316   Quod contricion to Consience, 'do hym *come* to vnite
C.22.326   To curen as a curatour; and *kam* with his lettre
C.22.328   In contreys þer he *cam* confessiones to here;
C.22.329   And *cam* þer Consience was and knokked at þe ʒate.
C.22.333   Karpe y wolde with Contricioun and þerfore [*cam* y] heddere.'
C.22.342   Bote thow conne eny craft thow *comest* nat hereynne.
C.22.344   *Kam* ynne thus ycoped at a Court þer y dwelte
C.22.355   And *cam* to Consience and cortey[s]liche hym grette.
C.22.374   And *comen* with a kene wil Consience to assaile.
C.22.376   And baed contricioun *come* to kepe þe ʒate.

comende v *commenden v.* A 1 comendite; B 4 comende (1) comended (2) comendede (1); C 4 comende (1) comended (2) commenden (1)

A.11.294   Þat clergie of cristis mouþ *comendite* [was hit] neuere,
B. 4.158   [Kynde] wit acorded þerwiþ and *comendede* hise wordes,
B.10.449   That] Clergie of cristes mouþ *comended* was it [neuere],
B.12.70   Ac yet is Clergie to *comende* and kynde wit boþe,
B.12.177   How contricion is *comended* for it cacheþ awey synne:
C.11.224   That clergie of cristes mouthe *com[e]nded* was euere.
C.14.35   And ʒut is clergie to *comende* for cristes loue more
C.14.117   How contricioun is *comended* for hit cacheth awey synne:
C.16.287   That maistres *commenden* moche. Where may hit be yfounde?

comeneres > communers

comeres n *comer n.* A 2 comeres (1) comeris (1); B 1; C 1
A. 2.43   Of kniʒtes of cuntr[e], of *comeres* aboute,
A. 2.192   F[or] knowing of *comeris* copide hym as a Frere.
B. 2.233   For knowynge of *comeres* coped hym as a Frere.
C. 2.243   For knowyng of *co[mere]s* copeden hym as a frere.

comesed -eth > comseþ

comet n *comete n.* C 1
C.14.97   Clerkes kn[e]we [þe] *comet* and comen with here presentes

comfort(- > confort(-; comin(e > commune

comynge ger *cominge ger.* &> comen B 2; C 2 comyng (1) comynge (1)
B.16.248   And conforted many a careful þat after his *comynge* waite[n],
B.18.401   Tho [ledes] þat [I] lou[e], and leued in my *comynge*;
C.18.266   And conforted many a carfol þere þat aftur his *comyng* loke[n].
C.20.444   Tho [ledes] þat y louye and leued in my *comynge*;

cominliche > communliche; comisare -rie > commissarie

comly adj *comli adj.& n.* B 2 comely (1) comly (1); C 1 comely
B.15.452   Clooþ þat comeþ fro þe weuyng is noʒt *comly* to were
B.18.119   A *comely* creature [and a clene]; truþe she highte.
C.20.122   A *comely* creature and a clene; Treuthe she hihte.

commaunded > comaunde; commen > commune; commenden > comende

commissarie n *commissarie n.* A 2 Comissare (1) Comissarie (1); B 3; C 3
A. 2.141   And let cartesadil þe *Comissare*, oure carte shal he drawe,
A. 3.132   For heo copiþ þe *Comissarie* and c[ot]iþ hise clerkis
B. 2.180   And [lat] Cartsadle þe *Commissarie*; oure cart shal he [drawe]
B. 3.143   For she copeþ þe *Commissarie* and coteþ hise clerkes
B.15.239   In þe Consistorie bifore þe *Commissarie* he comeþ noʒt ful ofte
C. 2.193   And lat cop[l]e þe *commissarie*; oure cart shal he drawe
C. 3.181   For a copeth þe *commissarie* and coteth his clerkes
C.16.364   In constorie bifore [þe] *commissarie* a cometh nat ful ofte

commune n *commune n.* A 3 comune (1) comunes (2); B 39 commune (20) communes (2) comune (14) comunes (3); C 45 comine (2) commune (1) comune (37) comunes (5)
A. 3.66   Betwyn þe king & þe *comunes*, to kepe þe lawis,
A. 5.38   'Lest þe king & his counseil ʒour *comunes* apeir[e]
A.11.222   How crist counseiliþ þe *comune* & kenneþ hem þis tale:
B.Pr.113   Might of þe *communes* made hym to regne.
B.Pr.115   For to counseillen þe kyng and þe *commune* saue.
B.Pr.117   Casten þat þe *commune* sholde [hire communes] fynde.
B.Pr.117   Casten þat þe commune sholde [hire *communes*] fynde.
B.Pr.118   The *commune* contreued of kynde wit craftes,
B.Pr.121   The kyng and þe *commune* and kynde wit þe þridde
B.Pr.143   Thanne [comsed] al þe *commune* crye in vers of latyn
B.Pr.187   Forþi I counseille al þe *commune* to late þe cat worþe,
B. 1.160   And a meene, as þe Mair is, bitwene þe [*commune*] & þe [kyng];
B. 3.77   The kyng and þe *comune* to kepe þe lawes,
B. 3.164   And al þe *comune* in care þat coueiten lyue in truþe.
B. 3.316   Ouer[carke] þe *commune* ne to þe Court sompne,
B. 4.80   Conscience and þe *commune* kn[e]wen [wel] þe soþe,
B. 4.151   Ac noʒt for confort of þe *commune* ne for þe kynges soule.
B. 4.182   Quod Conscience to þe kyng, 'but þe *commune* wole assente
B. 5.46   'Lest þe kyng and his conseil youre *comunes* apeire
B. 5.48   And siþen he counseiled þe kyng his *comune* to louye:
B. 9.91   The *commune* for hir vnkyndenesse, I drede me, shul abye;
B.10.29   And moost vnkynde to þe *commune* þat moost catel weldeþ:
B.10.278   [Thouʒ] it auailled noʒt þe *commune* it myʒte auaille yowselue.
B.12.296   To kepe wiþ a *commune*; no catel was holde bettre,
B.13.169   Do kyng and quene and alle þe *comune* after
B.13.261   And er þe *commune* haue corn ynouʒ many a cold morwenyng;
B.13.265   There was a careful *commune* whan no cart com to towne
B.15.237   In court amonges [þe *commune*] he comeþ but selde
B.15.553   If knyghthod and kynde wit and þe *commune* [and] conscience
B.19.155   Telle þe *comune* þat þer cam a compaignie of hise Apostles
B.19.214   And counseillede hym and Conscience þe *comune* to sompne:
B.19.379   Clennesse [of þe] *comune* and clerkes clene lyuynge

B.19.391   'How?' quod al þe *comune*; 'þow conseillest vs to yelde
B.19.407   But Conscience [be þi] *comune[s]* and Cardinale vertues
B.19.414   And we clerkes, whan þei come, for hir *comunes* paieþ,
B.19.416   The *comune* clamat cotidie, ech a man til ooþer,
B.19.451   For þe *comune*', quod þis Curatour, 'counten ful litel
B.19.466   'I am kyng wiþ croune þe *comune* to rule,
B.19.472   And holy chirches chief help and Chieftayn of þe *comune*,
B.19.476   Ne craue of my *comune* but as my kynde askeþ.'
B.19.477   'In condicion', quod Conscience, 'þat þow [þe *comune*] defende
B.20.78   And crye we [on] al þe *comune* þat þei come to vnitee.
C.Pr.95   Consience cam and [ac]cu[s]ed hem–and þe *comune* herde hit–
C.Pr.142   For to conseillen þe kyng and þe *comune* saue.
C.Pr.144   Caste þat þe *comun[e]* sholde here comunes fynde.
C.Pr.144   Caste þat þe *comun[e]* sholde here *comunes* fynde.
C.Pr.145   Kynde wytt and þe *comune* contreued alle craftes
C.Pr.148   Thenne kynde witt to þe kynge and to þe *comune* saide:
C. 1.156   And a mene, as þe Mayre is, bitwene þe kyng and þe *comune*;
C. 3.202   And al *comune* in care and in coueytise;
C. 3.207   And custumes of coueytise þe *comune* to destruye.
C. 3.375   As a kyng to clayme the *comune* at his wille
C. 3.378   So *comune* claymeth of a kyng thre kyne thynges,
C. 3.385   Thow the kyng and þe *comune* al the coest hadde.
C. 3.469   Ouerkarke þe *comune* ne to þe Court sompne
C. 4.30   Byfore þe kyng an[d] Consience yf þe *comune* playne
C. 4.76   Consience knoweth hit wel and al þe *Comune* trewe.'
C. 4.161   For þe *comune* calde here queynte comune hore.
C. 4.176   Quod Consience to þe kyng, 'withoute þe *comune* helpe
C. 5.20   Or eny other kynes craft þat to þe *comune* nedeth,
C. 5.75   In confort of the *comune* and the kynges worschipe,
C. 5.144   'Laste þe kyng and his consayl ȝoure *comunes* apayre
C. 5.180   And sethe a consailede þe kyng his *comine* to louie:
C. 5.181   'For þe *comune* is the kynges tresor, Consience woet wel.
C. 5.186   Lo! in heuene an heyh was an holy *comune*
C. 8.84   'Consayle nat þe *comune* þe kyng to desplese
C. 8.291   And his cloke of callabre for his *comune[s]* legge
C. 9.10   And ryhtfulliche in reumes ruylen þe *comune*
C.15.11   Ne no cors of pore *comine* in here kyrkeȝerde most lygge
C.15.168   The kyng and alle þe *comune* and clergie to þe loute
C.16.362   Amongus þe *comune* in Court a cometh bote selde
C.17.216   Ȝif knyhthoed and kynde wit and þe *comune* and consience
C.17.289   To be culd and ouercome the *comune* to defende,
C.17.308   That iesus was bote a iogelour, a iapare amonges þe *comune*,
C.21.155   Telle þe *comune* þat þer cam a companie of his apostles
C.21.214   And conseilede hym and Consience the *comune* to sompne:
C.21.379   Clannesse of þe *comune* and clerkes clene lyuynge
C.21.391   'How?' quod alle þe *comune*; 'thow conseylest vs to ȝelde
C.21.407   Bote Consience [be] thy *comune[s]* and cardinale vertues
C.21.414   And we Clerkes, when they come, for here *comunes* paieth,
C.21.416   The *comu[n]e* clamat cotidie, vch a man to oþer,
C.21.451   [For] þe *comune*,' quod this curatour, 'counteth ful litel
C.21.466   'Y am kyng with croune þe *comune* to reule
C.21.472   And holy churche cheef helpe and cheuenteyn of þe *comu[n]e*
C.21.476   Ne craue of my *comune* bote as my kynde asketh.'
C.21.477   'In condicioun,' quod Consience, 'þat þou [þe] *comune* defende
C.22.78   And crye we on al þe *comune* þat thei come to vnite

commune *adj comune adj.* A 3 comoun (2) comun (1); B 23 commune
   (15) comune (8); C 23 comen (1) comyn (1) commen (1) commune
   (1) comune (19)

A. 1.20   And comaundite of his curteisie in *comoun* þre þinges;
A. 3.121   As *comoun* as þe cartewey to knaue & to [alle],
A.11.241   For cristene han a degre & is þe *comun* speche:
B.Pr.148   Comen to a counseil for þe *commune* profit.
B.Pr.169   And knytten it on a coler for oure *commune* profit
B. 1.20   And comaunded of his curteisie in *commune* þree þynges,
B. 2.58   As of knyȝtes and of clerkes and ooþer *commune* peple,
B. 3.132   As *commune* as [þe] Cartwey to [knaue and to alle],
B. 3.320   Kynges Court and *commune* Court, Consistorie and Chapitle,
B. 4.123   Til þe kynges counseil be þe *commune* profit;
B. 4.166   For þe mooste *commune* of þat court called hire an hore.
B. 5.641   'By crist!' quod a *commune* womman, 'þi compaignie wol I folwe.
B. 7.54   Thise foure þe fader of heuene made to þis foold in *commune*;
B.10.238   'It is a *commune* lyf', quod Clergie, 'on holy chirche to bileue
B.10.362   And after alle cristene creatures, in *commune* ech man ooþer;
B.10.466   Than Plowmen and pastours and [pouere] *commune* laborers,
B.11.217   Crist to a *commune* womman seide, in [comen] at a feste,
B.14.201   Forþi cristene sholde be in *commune* riche, noon coueitous for
           hymselue.
B.16.109   And *commune* wommen conuertede and clensed of synne,
B.18.72   Vpon a croos bisides crist; so was þe *comune* lawe.
B.19.7   And com in wiþ a cros bifore þe *comune* peple,
B.19.132   And þo was he called in contre of þe *comune* peple,
B.19.367   Thanne alle kynne cristene saue *comune* wommen
B.19.420   That no Cardynal coome among þe *comune* peple,

B.20.30   After þe kynges counseil and þe *comune* like.
B.20.276   That alle þynges vnder heuene ouȝte to ben in *comune*.
C.Pr.169   Comen til a conseyl for [þe] *comune* pryfyt.
C.Pr.186   And knytten hit on a coler for oure *comune* profyt
C.Pr.204   Forthy y conseile for oure *comune* profit lat þe Cat yworthe
C. 1.20   And comaundede of his cortesye in *comune* thre thynges.
C. 2.22   In kynges court, in *comune* court contra[r]ieth my techynge.
C. 2.60   Of knyghtes, of clerkes [and] other *comune* peple,
C. 3.169   As *comyn* as þe cartway to knaues and to alle,
C. 3.245   For þat [is] conquere[d] thorw a *comune* helpe, a kyndom or
           ducherie,
C. 3.473   Kyngus Court and *comune* Court, constorie and [c]hap[itre],
C. 4.119   And til kynges consayl be alle *comune* profit
C. 4.161   For þe comune calde here queynte *comune* hore.
C.11.292   Then ploughmen an[d] pastours and pore *comune* peple.
C.12.168   Ȝut conseileth Crist in *commen* vs all:
C.16.42   Forthy cristene sholde be in *comune* ryche, noon coueytous for
           hymsulue.
C.18.142   And *comen* wommen conuertede and clansed hem of synne
C.20.74   Vppon cros bisyde Crist; so was þe *comune* lawe.
C.20.406   Bote of *comune* coppes, alle cristene soules;
C.21.7   And cam in with a cros bifore þe *comune* peple
C.21.132   And tho was he cald in contreye of þe *comune* peple,
C.21.367   Thenne alle kyne cristene saue *commune* wommen
C.21.420   That no cardinal come among þe *comune* peple
C.22.30   Aftur þe kynges conseyl and þe *comune* lyke.
C.22.276   That alle thynges vnder heuene ou[h]te to be in *comune*.

communers *n communer n.* B 1; C 2 comeneres (1) comuners (1)
B.15.332   Ac clerkes and knyȝtes and *communers* þat ben riche,
C. 4.188   Audiatis alteram partem amonges aldremen and *comeneres*,
C. 5.183   And *comuners* [to] acorde in alle kyn treuthe.

comoun > **commune**

compace *v compassen v.* B 1; C 1
B.19.241   And some to [kerue and *compace*], and colours to make;
C.21.241   [And somme to kerue a]nd *compace* and coloures to make;

compacience *n compacience n.* B 1; C 1
B.13.80   That he precheþ [and] preueþ noȝt [*com]pacience*', I tolde.
C.15.87   That a precheth and preueth nat *compacience*,' ich tolde,

compaignable *adj compaignable adj.* B 1; C 1 compenable
B.15.219   And is *compaignable* and confortatif as crist bit hymselue:
C.16.344   And *compenable* in companye a[s] Crist hymsulue techeth:

compaignye *n compaignie n.* B 7 compaignie (3) compaignye (4); C 6
   companie (1) companye (4) compeny (1)
B. 5.641   'By crist!' quod a comune womman, 'þi *compaignie* wol I folwe.
B.11.424   That Clergie þi *compaignye* kepeþ noȝt to suwe.
B.13.160   Coold ne care ne *compaignye* of þeues,
B.19.155   Telle þe comune þat þer cam a *compaignie* of hise Apostles
B.19.160   In ech a *compaignie* þer she cam, Christus resurgens.
B.20.120   Conscience and his *compaignye*, of holy [kirke] þe techeris.
B.20.182   The *compaignye* of confort men cleped it som tyme
C.13.243   As shame: ther he sheweth hym vch man shoneth his *companye*.
C.16.344   And compenable in *companye* a[s] Crist hymsulue techeth:
C.21.155   Telle þe comune þat þer cam a *companie* of his apostles
C.21.160   In vch a *companye* þer he cam, christus resurgens.
C.22.120   Consience and his *companye*, of holy [kirke] þe techares.
C.22.182   The *compeny* of comfort men clepede hit som tyme.

compas *n compas n.* C 1
C.11.123   Of carpent[ers and] keruers, and contreuede þe *compas*

compasynge *ger compassinge ger.* B 1
B.17.173   Keruynge and *compasynge* [i]s craft of þe fyngres.

compenable > **compaignable**; *compeny* > **compaignye**

comseþ *v comsen v.* A 7 compsiþ (2) comside (1) comsist (1) comsiþ (2)
   cumside (1); B 19 comsed (7) comsede (5) comseþ (7); C 15 comesed
   (3) comesede (2) comeseth (1) comsed (5) comsede (1) comseth (3)

A. 1.128   Be what craft in my cors it *compsiþ*, & where.'
A. 1.139   For in kynde knowyng in herte þer *comsiþ* a miȝt,
A. 3.93   [Curteisly] þe king *compsiþ* to telle.
A. 5.23   How consience wiþ a cros *cumside* to preche.
A. 5.59   And carfulliche his cope [*comsiþ*] he to shewe.
A. 9.16   'Contra,' quaþ I as a clerk & *comside* to dispute:
A.10.101   For ȝif þou *comsist* to clymbe, & coueitest herre,
B.Pr.143   Thanne [*comsed*] al þe commune crye in vers of latyn
B. 1.139   By what craft in my cors it *comseþ*, and where.'
B. 1.163   And for to knowen it kyndely, it *comseþ* by myght,
B. 1.165   For in kynde knowynge in herte þer [*comseþ* a myȝt],
B. 3.104   Curteisly þe kyng *comse[þ]* to telle.
B. 5.12   And wiþ a cros afore þe kyng *comsede* þus to techen.

B. 5.76   And carefully [his coupe] he *comse[þ]* to shewe.
B. 6.314   Ayeins Catons counseil *comseþ* he to Iangle:
B. 8.20   'Contra!' quod I as a clerc and *comsed* to disputen:
B.11.405   Tho cauȝte I colour anoon and *comsed* to ben ashamed
B.12.280   'Contra!' quod Ymaginatif þoo and *comsed* to loure,
B.16.75   And Piers caste to þe crop and þanne *comsed* it to crye;
B.17.35   And now *com[s]eþ* Spes and spekeþ, þat [haþ] aspied þe lawe,
B.18.57   'Consummatum est', quod crist and *comsede* for to swoune.
B.19.97   Was neiþer kyng ne conquerour til he [*comsed*] wexe
B.19.106   As kynde is of a Conquerour, so *comsede* Iesu
B.19.123   After þe kynde þat he cam of; þere *comsede* he do wel.
B.20.212   And [I] by conseil of kynde *comsed* to rome
B.20.242   Conscience of þis counseil þo *comsede* for to laughe,
C. 1.159   And for to knowe hit kyndly, hit *comeseth* by myhte
C. 1.161   For [in] kynde knowynge [in] herte ther *comseth* a myhte
C. 4.24   Thenne Consience on his capel *comesed* to pryke
C. 8.336   Aȝenes Catones consayle *comseth* he to gruche:
C.10.20   'Contra!' quod y as a Clerk and *comsed* to despute
C.13.213   Tho cauhte y colour anoen and *comesede* to ben aschamed
C.14.202   'Contra!' quod ymagynatif tho and *comesed* to loure
C.17.62   Helpe thy kyn, Crist bid, for þer [*coms*]*eth* charite
C.18.107   And Elde clemp to þe c[r]opward; thenne *comsed* hit to crye.
C.20.57   'Consummatum est,' quod Crist and *comsed* for to swoene.
C.21.97   Was noþer kyng ne conquerour til he *comsed* wexe
C.21.106   As kynde is of a conquerour, so *comesede* iesu
C.21.123   Aftur þe kynde þat he cam of; þer *comsede* he do wel.
C.22.212   And y bi conseil of kynde *comsed* to Rome
C.22.242   Con[s]ience of this con[s]ail tho *comesed* for to lawhe

comsynge ger *comsing ger.* B 1; C 2 comsyng (1) comsynges (1)
B.18.215   The which vnknytteþ alle care and *comsynge* is of reste.
C.11.92   Alle kynne kunnynges and *comsynges* of dowel.
C.20.224   The which vnknytteth alle care and *comsyng* is of reste.

comþ > comen; comun(e > commune; comunely -liche > comunliche; comuners > communers; comunes > commune

comunliche adv *communeli adv.* B 1; C 4 cominliche (1) comuneliche (1) comunely (1) comunlyche (1)
B.19.312   'For *comunliche* in contrees cammokes and wedes
C.11.290   *Comuneliche* then clerkes most knowyng in konnyng
C.14.19   Ac *comunlyche* connynge and vnkynde ryche[sse]
C.16.141   For þer as pouerte passeth þes followeth *comunely*
C.21.312   'For *cominliche* in Contrayes cammokes and wedes

conceiledest > counseillen

conceyuen v *conceiven v.* A 3 conseyue (1) conseyuede (1) conseyuid (1); B 7 conceyued (5) conceyuen (1) conseyued (1); C 8 conceyued (1) conseyue (1) conseyued (6)
A. 7.35   Curteisliche þ[e] kniȝt [*conseyuede*] þise wordis;
A. 9.48   'I haue no kynde knowyng,' quaþ I, 'to *conseyue* þi wordis,
A.10.140   Ben *conseyuid* in cursid tyme as kaym was on Eue:
B. 6.33   Curteisly þe knyȝt [*conseyued*] þise wordes:
B. 8.57   'I haue no kynde knowyng', quod I, 'to *conceyuen* [þi] wordes
B. 9.123   *Conceyued* ben in [cursed] tyme as Caym was on Eue
B.11.341   Ther ne was cow ne cowkynde þat *conceyued* hadde
B.11.358   And some bridded at þe bile þoruȝ breþyng *conceyued*,
B.11.414   Thow sholdest haue knowen þat clergie kan & [*conceyued*] moore
                þoruȝ Res[on],
B.18.129   Of any kynnes creature, *conceyued* þoruȝ speche
C. 8.32   Courteisliche the knyhte thenne [*co[nseyu]ed*] thise wordes:
C.10.56   'Y haue no kynde kno[w]yng,' [quod y], 'to *conseyue* al this speche
C.10.213   Caym þe corsede creature *conseyued* was in synne
C.10.218   So was Caym *conseyued* and so ben corsed wreches
C.13.149   Ther ne [was] cow ne cowkynde þat *conseyued* hadde
C.13.151   Ther ne was no kyne kynde þat *conseyued* hadde
C.13.222   Thow sholdest haue yknowe þat clergie ca[n] & *conseyued* mor[e]
                [thorw] resoun
C.20.132   Of eny kyn[nes] creature, *conceyued* thorw speche

concepcion n *concepcioun n.* A 1 concepcioun; B 2; C 1
A.10.184   A carful *concepcioun* comiþ of such weddyng
B. 9.161   [A] careful *concepcion* comeþ of [swich weddynge]
B.11.337   And after cours of *concepcion* noon took kepe of ooþer,
C.13.145   Aftur cors of *concepcion* noon toek kepe of oþer,

concience -nse > conscience

conclude v *concluden v.* B 1; C 1
B.10.453   Konnyng [and clergie] to *conclude* hem alle”.
C.11.278   Connyng and clergie to *conclude* [hem] alle”.

condicion n *condicioun n.* B 1; C 1 condicioun
B.19.477   'In *condicion*', quod Conscience, 'þat þow [þe comune] defende
C.21.477   'In *condicioun*,' quod Consience, 'þat þou [þe] comune defende

conestable > constable

confermen v *confermen v.* B 3 confermed (2) confermen (1); C 1 confermede
B.10.358   For þat crist for cristene men deide, and *confermed* þe lawe
B.13.213   And *confermen* fauntekyns ooþer folk ylered
B.15.457   Til it be cristned in cristes name and *confermed* of þe bisshop
C.14.39   And crist cam and *confermede* and holy kyrke made

confessen v *confessen v.* B 5 confesse (4) confessen (1); C 6 confesse (3) confessede (1) confessen (2)
B.10.322   Ac þer shal come a kyng and *confesse* yow Religiouses,
B.11.54   Go *confesse* þee to som frere and shewe hym þi synnes.
B.11.76   Whi youre Couent coueiteþ to *confesse* and to burye
B.15.530   And crepe [in] amonges curatours, *confessen* ageyn þe lawe:
B.17.301   *Confesse* me and crye his grace, [crist] þat al made,
C. 5.168   Ac þer shal come a kyng and *confesse* ȝow alle
C. 6.338   *Confessen* hem and cryen hym mercy; shal neuere come in helle:
C.12.5   [Haue no consience how þou come to good]; *confesse* the to som
                frere.
C.12.15   And flittyng fond y the frere þat me *confessede*
C.17.280   And crepe in amonges curatours and *confessen* aȝeyn þe lawe:
C.19.281   *Confesse* me and crye his grace, god þat al made,

confession n *confessioun n.* B 6 confession (5) confessions (1); C 8 confessiones (1) confessioun (7)
B.12.175   And how contricion wiþoute *confession* conforteþ þe soule,
B.14.187   *Confession* and knowlichynge [and] crauynge þi mercy
B.19.331   And gaf hym caples to his carte, contricion and *confession*;
B.19.346   *Confession* and Contricion, and youre carte þe bileeue
B.20.213   Thoruȝ Contricion and *Confession* til I cam to vnitee.
B.20.328   In contrees þer he coome *confessions* to here;
C.10.53   To contricion, to *confessioun*, til he come til his ende.
C.12.70   Bote yf contricioun and *confessioun* crye by his loue
C.14.115   And how contricion withoute *confessioun* conforteth þe soule,
C.16.26   And *confessioun* to kulle alle kyne synnes
C.21.331   And gaf hym caples to his Carte, Contrissioun & *confessioun*;
C.21.346   *Confessioun* and contricioun, and ȝoure Carte, the bileue,
C.22.213   Thorw contricion and *confessioun* til y cam to vnite.
C.22.328   In contreys þer he cam *confessiones* to here;

confessour n *confessour n.* A 6 confessour (3) confessoures (1) confessours (2); B 7 confessour (5) Confessours (2); C 7 confessour (4) confessours (3)
A. 3.34   Þanne com þere a *confessour* ycoped as a frere;
A. 4.128   Let þi *confessour*, sire king, construe it þe on englissh,
A. 4.132   Clerkis þat wern *confessours* couplide hem togideris,
A.10.135   For of here kynde þei comen þat *confessours* ben nempnid,
A.12.41   Kynde [wit] hure *confessour*, hure cosyn was Inne.
A.12.77   With þat cam a knaue with a *confessoures* face,
B. 3.35   Thanne cam þer a *Confessour* coped as a frere;
B. 4.145   Late [þi] *Confessour*, sire kyng, construe [it þee on englissh],
B. 4.149   Clerkes þat were *Confessours* coupled hem togidere
B. 9.112   For of hir kynde þei come þat *Confessours* ben nempned,
B.11.70   Ac yet I cryde on my *Confessour* þat [so konnyng heeld hym]:
B.14.18   Dowel shal wasshen it and wryngen it þoruȝ a wis *confessour*:
B.20.371   For confort of his *confessour* Contricion he lafte,
C. 3.38   Thenne come þer a *confessour* ycoped as a frere;
C. 4.142   Lat thy *Confessour*, syre kyng, construe this in englische
C. 4.146   Clerkes [þat were *confessours*] co[u]plede hem togederes
C. 5.194   'Comaunde þat alle *confessours* þat eny kyng shryueth
C.10.205   For of here kynde þey come, þe *confessours* and martres,
C.12.197   Or for a *confessour* ykud þat counteth nat a ruche
C.22.371   For confort of his *confessour* Contricioun he lefte

conformen v *conformen v.* B 3; C 1 confourme
B.11.181   [And] comaundeþ ech creature to *conformen* hym to louye
B.13.208   And *conformen* kynges to pees; and alle kynnes londes,
B.15.344   Forþi I counseille alle cristene to *conformen* hem to charite,
C. 3.398   Sholde *confourme* hem to o kynde on holy kyrke to bileue

confort n *comfort n.* B 9; C 8 comfort (1) confort (6) conforte (1)
B. 4.151   Ac noȝt for *confort* of þe commune ne for þe kynges soule.
B.11.262   Is a kernel of *confort* kynde to restore.
B.12.83   So clergie is *confort* to creatures þat repenten,
B.13.450   And in his deeþ deyinge þei don hym gret *confort*
B.14.286   /And Contricion *confort* and cura animarum.
B.14.300   A collateral *confort*, cristes owene ȝifte:
B.20.91   After *Confort* a knyght to come and bere his baner:
B.20.182   The compaignye of *confort* men cleped it som tyme
B.20.371   For *confort* of his confessour Contricion he lafte,
C. 5.75   In *confort* of the comune and the kynges worschipe,
C. 7.110   And in his deth deynge they don hym greet *confort*
C.12.148   Is a cornel of *confort* kynde to restore,
C.12.151   The which is þe cornel of *confort* for alle cristene soules.

C.16.136 A collateral *confort*, cristes oune sonde:
C.22.91 Aftur *conforte*, a knyhte, [to] come and beer his baner:
C.22.182 The compeny of *comfort* men clepede hit som tyme.
C.22.371 For *confort* of his confessour Contricioun he lefte

confortable adj *comfortable adj.* B 1
B.14.282 Riȝt as contricion is *confortable* þyng, conscience woot wel,

confortatif adj *comfortatif adj.& n.* B 1
B.15.219 And is compaignable and *confortatif* as crist bit hymselue:

conforte > *confort,conforten*

conforten v *comforten v.* A 7 conforten (1) counforte (4) counfortide (1)
  counfortiþ (1); B 30 conforte (11) conforted (9) confortede (2)
  conforten (4) confortest (1) conforteþ (3); C 26 comforte (2)
  comfortede (1) conforte (10) conforted (2) confortede (5) conforteth (6)
A. 1.177 To *counforte* þe carful acumbrid wiþ synne.
A. 2.115 And comen to *counforte* fro care þe false,
A. 3.15 *Counforti[de]* hire kyndely be clergie[s] leue,
A. 3.25 Wiþ þat come clerkis to *conforten* hire þe same,
A. 7.206 *Counforte* hem wiþ þi catel for cristis loue of heuene;
A. 8.51 *Counfortiþ* hym in þat cas, coueitiþ nouȝt his goodis,
A.11.189 *Counforte* þe carful þat in castel ben fetterid,
B. 1.203 To *conforten* þe carefulle acombred wiþ synne.
B. 2.151 And comen to *conforten* from care þe false
B. 3.15 *Conforte[d]* hire kyndely by clergies leue,
B. 3.26 Wiþ þat comen clerkes to *conforten* hire þe same
B. 6.220 *Conforte* h[e]m wiþ þi catel for cristes loue of heuene;
B. 7.49 *Conforteþ* hym in þat caas, [coueiteþ noȝt hise] ȝiftes,
B. 7.152 And which a pardon Piers hadde þe peple to *conforte*,
B.11.46 Coueitise of eiȝes *conforted* me anoon after
B.11.52 Coueitise of eiȝes [ofte me *conforted*];
B.11.266 Of which crist is a kernell to *conforte* þe soule.
B.12.21 Seide, 'Caton *conforted* his sone þat, clerk þouȝ he were,
B.12.81 [Thus Clergie þere] *conforted* þe womman.
B.12.88 As cristes caracte[s] *confortede*, and boþe coupable shewed
B.12.175 And how contricion wiþoute confession *conforteþ* þe soule,
B.12.178 And þis *conforteþ* ech a clerk and coureþ fro wanhope,
B.13.22 And as crist wolde þer com Conscience to *conforte* me þat tyme
B.13.58 And Conscience *conforted* vs and carped vs murye tales:
B.13.218 To *conforte* hym and Conscience if þei come in place
B.13.394 Miȝte neuere me *conforte* in þe mene [tyme]
B.14.147 Crist of his curteisie shal *conforte* yow at þe laste,
B.14.175 *Conforte* þo creatures þat muche care suffren
B.14.179 *Conforte* þi carefulle, crist, in þi rich[e],
B.14.180 For how þow *confortest* alle creatures clerkes bereþ witnesse:
B.16.248 And *conforted* many a careful þat after his comynge waite[n],
B.17.123 And come ayein bi þis contree and *conforten* alle sike
B.18.257 And *conforte* al his kyn and out of care brynge,
B.19.128 Thus he *confortede* carefulle and cauȝte a gretter name
B.20.67 And what kyng þat hem *conforted*, knowynge [hir gile],
B.20.243 And curteisliche *conforted* hem and called in alle freres,
B.20.358 *Conforte* hym', quod Conscience, 'and tak kepe to hise soores.
C. 1.198 That *conforteth* alle carefole acombred with synne.
C. 2.167 And comen ful courteysly to *conforte* the false
C. 3.16 *Confortede* here as they couthe by the clerkes leue
C. 3.27 Thenne come clerkes to *conforte* here the same
C. 6.281 Myhte neuere me *comforte* in the mene tyme
C. 8.229 *Conforte* hem with thy catel, for so comaundeth treuthe;
C. 9.48 That *conforteth* suche in eny caes and coueyteth nat he[re] ȝiftes
C. 9.97 And to *conforte* suche coterelles and crokede men and blynde.
C.11.176 Concupiscencia Carnis *confortede* me o[n] this manere
C.12.3 Coueityse-of-yes *conforted* me aftur and saide,
C.14.70 For clergy is cristes vycary to *conforte* and to cure;
C.14.115 And how contricion withoute confessioun *conforteth* þe soule,
C.14.118 And þat *conforteth* vch a clerk and keuereth fro wanhope,
C.15.61 Consience *confortede* vs, bothe clergie and scripture,
C.15.145 *Conforte* hym with thy catel and with thy kynde speche;
C.15.187 To *conforte* hym and Consience yf they come in place
C.15.194 Peres prentys þe plouhman, alle peple to *conforte*.'
C.16.326 Clotheth hem and *conforteth* hem as Crist precheth hem,
C.17.50 And *conforte* alle cristene wolde holy [kirke] amende.
C.18.73 And *conforteth* hem in here continence þat lyuen in
      contemplacioun,
C.18.266 And *conforted* many a carfol þere þat aftur his comyng loke[n].
C.20.265 And *comforte* alle his kyn and out of care brynge
C.21.128 Thus he *comfortede* carefole and cauhte a grettere name,
C.22.67 And what kyng þat hem *confortede*, knowynge here gyle,
C.22.243 And cortey[s]liche *confortede* hem and calde in all freres,
C.22.358 *Conforte* hym,' quod Consience, 'and taek kepe to his sores.

confortour n *comfortour n.* B 1
B.16.190 *Confortour* of creatures; of hym comeþ alle blisse.

confounde v *confounden v.* C 1
C. 5.190 Is cause of alle combraunc[e] to *confounde* a reume.'

confourme > *conformen*

confus adj *confused pp.* A 1; B 1
A.11.94 He beco[m] so *confus* he couþe nouȝt mele,
B.10.141 He bicom so *confus* he couþe noȝt [mele],

congeien v *congeien v.* A 2 cunge; B 3 congeye (1) congeyed (1)
  congeien (1); C 6 congeie (2) congeye (2) conieyed (1) ycongeyed (1)
A. 3.161 For consience acusiþ þe to *cunge* [þe] for euere.'
A. 4.4 'Nay be [Crist],' quaþ consience, '*cunge* me raþere!
B. 3.174 For Conscience accuseþ þee to *congeien* þee for euere.'
B. 4.4 'Nay, by crist!' quod Conscience; '*congeye* me [raþer]!'
B.13.198 Thus curteisliche Conscience *congeyed* first þe frere,
C. 3.220 For Consience acuseth the to *congeye* the foreuere.'
C. 4.4 'Nay, by Crist!' quod Consience, '*congeie* me [rather]!'
C. 4.195 The kyng comaundede Consience tho to *congeye* alle his offeceres
C.11.161 And continaunce made on clergie, to *congeie* me hit semede,
C.15.175 Ac Concience, y toek kepe, *coniey[e]d* sone this doctour
C.16.369 Ac thorw Coueytyse and his consaile *ycongeyed* is he ofte.

congie n *conge n.* B 1
B.13.202 Clergie of Conscience no *congie* wolde take,

conynges n *coning n.* B 1
B.Pr.189 [The while he caccheþ *conynges* he coueiteþ noȝt [o]ure caroyne

conyon n *conjoun n.* A 1
A.11.87 And now comiþ a *conyon* & wolde cacche of my wittes

conieyed > *congeien*

coniured v *conjuren v.* B 1
B.15.14 And wherof I cam & of what kynde. I *coniured* hym at þe laste

conne > *konne*

connesaunce n *conissaunce n.* C 1
C.18.186 'What is his [*conn]esaunc[e]*,' quod y, 'in his cote Armure?'

conneth > *konne*; *connyng(-* > *konnyng*

conquere v *conqueren v.* B 1 conquered; C 4 conquere (1) conquered (1)
  conquerede (1) conquereth (1)
B.19.50 And þo *conquered* he on cros as conquerour noble;
C. 3.245 For þat [is] *conquere[d]* thorw a comune helpe, a kyndom or
      ducherie,
C. 3.251 And þat is þe kynde of a kyng þat *conquereth* on his enemys,
C. 3.255 A[t] Concience þat coueiteth to *conquere* a reume.
C.21.50 And tho *conquerede* he on cros as conquerour noble;

conquerour n *conquerour n.* B 10; C 10
B.19.14 Is crist wiþ his cros, *conquerour* of cristene.'
B.19.27 That knyght, kyng, *conquerour* may be o persone.
B.19.30 Ac to be *conquerour* called, þat comeþ of special grace,
B.19.43 And *conquerour* of [his] conquest hise lawes and his large.
B.19.50 And þo conquered he on cros as *conquerour* noble;
B.19.53 And þo was he *conquerour* called of quyke and of dede,
B.19.62 He may [be wel] called *conquerour*, and þat is crist to mene.
B.19.97 Was neiþer kyng ne *conquerour* til he [comsed] wexe
B.19.99 As it bicomeþ a *conquerour* to konne manye sleightes,
B.19.106 As kynde is of a *Conquerour*, so comsede Iesu
C.21.14 Is Crist with his croes, *conqueror* of Cristene.'
C.21.27 That knyht, kyng, *conquerour* may be o persone.
C.21.30 Ac to be *conquerour* cald, þat cometh of special grace,
C.21.43 And *conquerour* of his conqueste his layes and his large.
C.21.50 And tho conquerede he on cros as *conquerour* noble;
C.21.53 And tho was he *conquerour* cald of quyke and of dede
C.21.62 He may be wel called *conquerour* and that is Crist to mene.
C.21.97 Was noþer kyng ne *conquerour* til he comsed wexe
C.21.99 As hit bicometh a *conquerour* to conne mony sleythes
C.21.106 As kynde is of a *conquerour*, so comesede iesu

conquest n *conqueste n.* B 1; C 1 conqueste
B.19.43 And conquerour of [his] *conquest* hise lawes and his large.
C.21.43 And conquerour of his *conqueste* his layes and his large.

consail(- > *counseil,counseillen*

conscience n *conscience n.* A 38 consience (37) consiences (1); B 150
  conscience (149) Consciences (1); C 160 Concience (11) concyence (1)
  Conciense (1) Conscience (2) Consience (143) Consiences (2)
A. 2.103 For *consience* is of his counseil & knowiþ ȝow ichone,
A. 2.152 And come to þe kinges court & *consience* tolde,
A. 2.153 And *consience* to þe king carpide it aftir.
A. 3.18 For al *consiences* cast a[nd] craft as I trowe'.
A. 3.41 Among clerkis & kniȝtes *consience* to felle'.
A. 3.99 I haue a kniȝt, *consience*, com late fro beȝonde;

A.3.103	Þanne was *consience* callid to comen & aperen	

A.3.103　Þanne was *consience* callid to comen & aperen
A.3.105　Knelynge, *consience* to þe kyng loutide,
A.3.109　Quaþ *consience* to þe kyng, 'crist it [me] forbede!
A.3.161　For *consience* acusiþ þe te cunge [þe] for euere.'
A.3.165　And þou knowist, *consience*, I ca[m] nouʒt to chide,
A.3.167　Wel þou wost, *consience*, but ʒif þou wilt leiʒe,
A.3.193　[Cowardly þou *consience* conceiledest him þennes]
A.3.215　Quaþ þe king to *consience*, 'be crist, as me þinkiþ,
A.3.217　'Nay,' quaþ *consience* to þe king & knelide to þe erþe,
A.3.260　[I] *consience* knowe þis, for kynde [w]it me tauʒte,
A.3.275　Ac kynde wyt shal come ʒet, & *consience* togidere,
A.4.3　　Kisse hire,' quaþ þe king, '*consience*, I hote!'
A.4.4　　'Nay be [Crist],' quaþ *consience*, 'cunge me raþere!
A.4.6　　'And I comaunde þe,' quaþ þe king to *consience* þanne,
A.4.11　　And counte wiþ [þe] *consience*, so me crist helpe,
A.4.22　　Þanne *consience* on his capil cairiþ forþ faste,
A.4.29　　Ac *consience* com arst to court be a myle wey
A.4.48　　[Þe king kneuʒ] he seide soþ for *consience* hym tolde.
A.4.66　　*Consience* & þe king kneuʒ wel þe soþe,
A.4.98　　And to counseile þe king & *consience* boþe;
A.4.156　So *consience* be of ʒour counsail, kepe I no betere.'
A.5.11　　And *consience* wiþ a cros com for to preche,
A.5.23　　How *consience* wiþ a cros cumside to preche
A.5.177　Þei couþe [not] be here *consience* acorden togidere
A.6.27　　Clene *consience* & wyt kende me to his place,
A.6.49　　Til ʒe come into *consience* þat crist wyte þe soþe,
A.8.24　　Aʒens clene *consience* here catel to selle.
A.8.121　And *consience* com aftir & kennide me betere.'
A.10.88　Ac ʒif clene *consience* acorde þat þiself dost wel
A.10.91　Be counseil of *consience*, accordyng holy chirche,
A.10.93　For ʒif þou comist aʒen *consience* þou combrist þiseluen,
A.11.309　Ne none sonnere ysauid, ne saddere of *consience*,
B.2.51　　And lat no *conscience* acombre þee for coueitise of Mede.'
B.2.139　[For] *Conscience* is of his counseil and knoweþ yow echone;
B.2.191　And com to þe kynges court and *Conscience* tolde,
B.2.192　And *Conscience* to þe kyng carped it after.
B.3.19　　For al *Consciences* cast [and] craft, as I trowe'.
B.3.42　　Amonges [clerkes] and [knyʒtes] *Conscience* to [felle]'.
B.3.67　　For [god] knoweþ þi *conscience* and þi kynde wille
B.3.110　I haue a knyʒt, *Conscience*, cam late fro biyonde;
B.3.114　[Th]anne was *Conscience* called to come and appere
B.3.116　Knelynge, *Conscience* to þe kyng louted,
B.3.120　Quod *Conscience* to þe kyng, 'crist it me forbede!
B.3.174　For *Conscience* accuseþ þe to congeien þee for euere.'
B.3.178　And þow knowest, *Conscience*, I kam noʒt to chide,
B.3.180　Wel þow woost, [*Conscience*], but if þow wolt [lie],
B.3.206　Cowardly þow, *Conscience*, conseiledest hym þennes
B.3.228　Quod þe kyng to *Conscience*, 'by crist, as me þynkeþ,
B.3.230　'Nay', quod *Conscience* to þe kyng and kneled to þe erþe,
B.3.284　I, *Conscience*, knowe þis for kynde wit me tauʒte
B.3.299　Ac kynde loue shal come ʒit and *Conscience* togideres
B.3.337　'I leue wel, lady', quod *Conscience*, 'þat þi latyn be trewe.
B.4.3　　Kis hire', quod þe kyng, '*Conscience*, I hote!'
B.4.4　　'Nay, by crist!' quod *Conscience*; 'congeye me [raþer]!
B.4.6　　'And I comaunde þee', quod þe kyng to *Conscience* þanne,
B.4.11　　And acounte wiþ þee, *Conscience*, so me crist helpe,
B.4.24　　Þanne *Conscience* [o]n his capul [caireþ] forþ faste,
B.4.32　　A[c] *Conscience* knew hem wel, þei loued coueitise.
B.4.41　　For *Conscience* know[e þei] noʒt, ne crist, as I trowe.'
B.4.43　　As *Conscience* hym kenned til þei come to þe kynge.
B.4.61　　The kyng knew he seide sooþ, for *Conscience* hym tolde
B.4.80　　*Conscience* and þe commune kn[e]wen [wel] þe soþe,
B.4.111　And to counseille þe kyng and *Conscience* [boþe]
B.4.171　The kyng callede *Conscience* and afterward Reson
B.4.182　Quod *Conscience* to þe kyng, 'but þe commune wole assente
B.4.193　So *Conscience* be of [y]oure counsail [kepe I] no bettre.'
B.5.328　Thei couþe noʒt, by hir *Conscience*, acorden [togideres]
B.5.539　*Conscience* and kynde wit kenned me to his place
B.5.562　Til ye come into *Conscience* þat crist wite þe soþe,
B.7.22　　Ayein clene *Conscience* hir catel to selle.
B.7.139　And *Conscience* cam afte[r] and kenned me [bettre].'
B.11.53　'Haue no *conscience*', [quod she],'how þow come to goode;
B.11.66　For I herde ones how *Conscience* it tolde,
B.11.132　And *conscience* acounte wiþ hym] and casten hym in arerage,
B.13.22　And as crist wolde þer com *Conscience* to conforte me þat tyme
B.13.24　And for *Conscience* of Clergie spak I com wel þe raþer.
B.13.27　*Conscience* knew hym wel and welcomed hym faire.
B.13.31　*Conscience* called hym In and curteisliche seide
B.13.34　And þanne clergie and *Conscience* and Pacience cam after.
B.13.37　*Conscience* called after mete and þanne cam Scripture
B.13.46　*Conscience* curteisly þo commaunded Scripture
B.13.56　'Bryng pacience som pitaunce pryuelliche', quod *Conscience*,
B.13.58　And *Conscience* conforted vs and carped vs murye tales:

B.13.101　Coughed and carped, and *Conscience* hym herde
B.13.112　Than *Conscience* curteisly a contenaunce made,
B.13.119　'Now þow, Clergie', quod *Conscience*, 'carp[e] what is dowel.'
B.13.131　'I kan noʒt heron', quod *Conscience*, 'ac I knowe Piers.
B.13.177　And took Clergie and *Conscience* to conseil as it were
B.13.179　Ac *Conscience* carped loude and curteisliche seide,
B.13.183　'What!' quod Clergie to *Conscience*, 'ar ye coueitous noube
B.13.188　'Nay, by crist!' quod *Conscience* to Clergie, 'god þee foryelde;
B.13.198　Thus curteisliche *Conscience* congeyed first þe frere,
B.13.202　Clergie of *Conscience* no congie wolde take,
B.13.205　'That is sooþ', [seide] *Conscience*, 'so me god helpe.
B.13.215　*Conscience* þo wiþ Pacience passed, pilgrymes as it were.
B.13.218　To conforte hym and *Conscience* if þei come in place
B.13.223　To *Conscience* what craft he kouþe, and to what contree he wolde.
B.13.271　I took [greet] kepe, by crist! and *Conscience* boþe,
B.13.313　'By crist!' quod *Conscience* þo, 'þi beste cote, Haukyn,
B.13.390　Vpon a cruwel coueitise m[y *conscience*] gan hange.
B.13.458　Til *conscience* acouped hym þerof in a curteis manere,
B.14.16　'And I shal kenne þee', quod *Conscience*, 'of Contricion to make
B.14.83　And þoruʒ feiþ comeþ contricion, *conscience* woot wel,
B.14.88　Ergo contricion, feiþ and *conscience* is kyndeliche dowel,
B.14.189　A[c] if þe [pouke] wolde plede herayein, and punysshe vs in *conscience*,
B.14.282　Riʒt as contricion is confortable þyng, *conscience* woot wel,
B.15.32　Thanne am I *Conscience* ycalled, goddes clerk and his Notarie;
B.15.242　And þat *Conscience* and crist haþ yknyt faste
B.15.536　Baddely ybedded, no book but *conscience*,
B.15.553　If knyghthod and kynde wit and þe commune [and] *conscience*
B.17.138　And if *Conscience* carpe þerayein, or kynde wit eyþer,
B.19.9　　And þanne called I *Conscience* to kenne me þe soþe:
B.19.12　Quod *Conscience* and kneled þo, 'þise arn Piers armes,
B.19.26　'Thow knowest wel', quod *Conscience*, 'and þow konne reson,
B.19.199　Thus *Conscience* of crist and of þe cros carpede
B.19.204　I wondred what þat was and waggede *Conscience*,
B.19.207　Quod *Conscience* and knelede, 'þis is cristes messager
B.19.209　Knele now', quod *Conscience*, 'and if þow kanst synge
B.19.212　And cride wiþ *Conscience*, 'help vs, [crist], of grace!'
B.19.214　And counseillede hym and *Conscience* þe comune to sompne:
B.19.220　And acombre þee, *Conscience*, but if crist þee helpe.
B.19.256　And crouneþ *Conscience* kyng and makeþ craft youre Stiward,
B.19.337　*Conscience* and alle cristene and Cardinale vertues,
B.19.341　Thise two coome to *Conscience* and to cristen peple
B.19.345　Shulle come out, *Conscience*; and youre [caples two],
B.19.348　That *Conscience* shal noʒt knowe who is cristene or heþene,
B.19.355　Quod *Conscience* to alle cristene þo, 'my counseil is to wende
B.19.360　And þanne kam Kynde wit *Conscience* to teche,
B.19.364　*Conscience* comaundede þo alle cristene to delue,
B.19.381　'I care noʒt', quod *Conscience*, 'þouʒ pride come nouþe.
B.19.383　'Comeþ', quod *Conscience*, 'ye cristene, and dyneþ,
B.19.393　'That is my conseil', quod *Conscience*, 'and Cardinale vertues;
B.19.398　Ne after *Conscience*, by crist! while I kan selle
B.19.401　And noʒt hakke after holynesse; hold þi tonge, *Conscience*!
B.19.403　'Caytif!' quod *Conscience*, 'cursede wrecche!
B.19.407　But *Conscience* [be þi] comune[s] and Cardinale vertues
B.19.412　Or þat acountede *Conscience* at a cokkes feþere.
B.19.424　And þow *Conscience* in kynges court, and sholdest neuere come þennes;
B.19.452　The counseil of *Conscience* or Cardinale vertues
B.19.477　'In condicion', quod *Conscience*, 'þat þow [þe comune] defende
B.20.21　Wiþouten conseil of *Conscience* or Cardynale vertues,
B.20.72　That kam ayein *conscience* þat kepere was and gyour
B.20.74　'I conseille', quod *Conscience* þo, 'comeþ wiþ me, ye fooles,
B.20.80　Kynde *Conscience* þo herde and cam out of þe planetes
B.20.106　*Conscience* of his curteisie [þo] kynde he bisouʒte
B.20.113　And gaderede a greet hoost al agayn *Conscience*.
B.20.120　*Conscience* and his compaignye, of holy [kirke] þe techeris.
B.20.122　Ouercome *Conscience* and Cardinale vertues;
B.20.126　Symonye hym [suede] to assaille *Conscience*;
B.20.130　And [knokked] *Conscience* in Court afore hem alle;
B.20.140　'Allas!' quod *Conscience* and cryde, 'wolde crist of his grace
B.20.147　*Conscience* and counseil, he counted [it] f[o]llye.
B.20.151　And kille a[l] erþely creatur[e] saue *conscience* oone.
B.20.165　For care *Conscience* þo cryde vpon Elde
B.20.214　And þere was *Conscience* Conestable, cristene to saue
B.20.216　That wiþ Antecrist helden harde ayein *Conscience*.
B.20.220　Coomen ayein *Conscience*; wiþ Coueitise þei helden.
B.20.222　'I counte na moore *Conscience* by so I cacche siluer
B.20.228　*Conscience* cryede, 'help, Clergie or I falle
B.20.231　Ac for þei kouþe noʒt wel hir craft *Conscience* forsook hem.
B.20.232　Nede neghede þo neer and *Conscience* he tolde
B.20.242　*Conscience* of þis counseil þo comsede for to laughe,
B.20.268　Forþi', quod *Conscience*, 'by crist! kynde wit me telleþ
B.20.294　Enuye herfore hatede *Conscience*,

B.20.296 The while coueitise and vnkyndenesse *Conscience* assaillede.
B.20.297 In vnitee holy chirche *Conscience* held hym
B.20.303 That wiþ *Conscience* acordede and Cardynale vertues.
B.20.304 *Conscience* called a leche þat koude wel shryue:
B.20.316 Quod Contricion to *Conscience*, 'do hym come to vnitee,
B.20.318 'We han no nede', quod *Conscience*; 'I woot no bettre leche
B.20.322 I may wel suffre', seide *Conscience*, 'syn ye desiren,
B.20.329 And cam þere *Conscience* was and knokked at þe yate.
B.20.337 *Conscience* knoweþ me wel and what I kan boþe.'
B.20.353 And acorde wiþ *Conscience* and kisse hir eiþer ooþer.'
B.20.355 And cam to *Conscience* and curteisly hym grette.
B.20.356 'Thow art welcome', quod *Conscience*; 'kanstow heele sike?
B.20.357 Here is Contricion', quod *Conscience*, 'my cosyn, ywounded.
B.20.358 Conforte hym', quod *Conscience*, 'and tak kepe to hise soores.
B.20.374 And comen wiþ a kene wille *Conscience* to assaille.
B.20.375 *Conscience* cryed eft [Clergie to helpe],
B.20.380 'By crist!' quod *Conscience* þo, 'I wole bicome a pilgrym,
B.20.384 And countredeþ me, *Conscience*; now kynde me avenge,
C.Pr.95 *Consience* cam and [ac]cu[s]ed hem–and þe comune herde hit–
C.Pr.138 Contreplede hit noght', quod *Conscience*, 'for holi [k]ir[k]e sake.'
C.Pr.143 *Conscience* & kynde wit] and knyghthed togedres
C.Pr.152 *Consience* to Clergie and to þe kynge sayde:
C.Pr.160 *Consience* and þe kynge into Court wente
C. 2.54 Acombre neuere thy *Consience* for coueityse of mede.'
C. 2.155 And *Consience* is of his consayl and knoweth зow [echone];
C. 2.205 And kam to þe kynges Court and *Consience* tolde,
C. 2.206 And *consience* to þe kyng carpede hit aftur.
C. 2.248 Ac *Consience* to þe kyng accused hem bothe
C. 3.20 For al *Consiences* cast and craft, as y trowe.'
C. 3.43 And зut be thy bedman and brynge adoun *Consience*
C. 3.49 Among knyhtes and clerkes *consience* to turne.
C. 3.71 For god knoweth thi *consience* [and þy kynde wille,
C. 3.147 Y haue a knyght, *Consience*, cam late fro beзende;
C. 3.151 Thenne was *Consience* ykald to come and apere
C. 3.153 Knelyng, *consience* to þe kyng loutede;
C. 3.157 Quod *Consience* to the kyng, 'Crist hit me forbede!
C. 3.220 For *Consience* acuseth the to congeye the foreuere.'
C. 3.224 And þ[ou] knowe[st], *Consience*, y cam nat to chyde
C. 3.239 In contrees there the kyng cam, *consience* hym lette
C. 3.242 Caytifliche thow, *Consience*, conseiledest þe kyng leten
C. 3.244 Vnconnynge is þat *Consience* a kyndom to sulle
C. 3.255 A[t] *Concience* þat coueiteth to conquere a reume.
C. 3.256 For sholde neuere *Consience* be my constable were y a kyng,' quod mede,
C. 3.263 Vnconnyngliche [þow], *Consience*, conseiledest hym thenne
C. 3.284 Quod þe kyng to *Consience*, 'by crist, as me thynketh,
C. 3.286 'Nay,' quod *Consience* to þe kyng, 'clerkes witeth þe sothe,
C. 3.341 Quod the kyng to *Consience*, 'knowen y wolde
C. 3.344 'Relacioun rect,' quod *Consience*, 'is a record of treuthe–
C. 3.437 [I], *Consience*,knowe this for kynde wit me tauhte
C. 3.452 A[c] kynde loue shal come зut and *Consience* togyderes
C. 3.489 'I leue the, lady,' quod *Consience*, 'for þat latyn is trewe.
C. 4.3 Kusse here,' quod the kyng, '*Consience*, y hote!'
C. 4.4 'Nay, by Crist!' quod *Consience*, 'congeie me [rather]!
C. 4.6 'And y comaunde [the],' quod the kyng to *Consience* thenne,
C. 4.11 And acounte with the, *Consience*, so me Crist helpe,
C. 4.13 'Y am fayn of that foroward, in fayth,' tho quod *Consience*,
C. 4.24 Thenne *Consience* on his capel comesed to pryke
C. 4.30 Byfore þe kyng an[d] *Consience* yf þe comune playne
C. 4.32 Ac *Consience* knewe hem wel and carped to resoun:
C. 4.33 'Here cometh,' quod *Consience*, 'þat Coueytise seruen.
C. 4.41 Bute dede as *Consience* hym kennede til he þe kyng mette.
C. 4.64 [The kyng knew he sayde soth for *Consience* hym tolde]
C. 4.76 *Consience* knoweth hit wel and al þe Comune trewe.'
C. 4.99 'Nay, by crist!' quod þe kyng, 'for *Consiences* sake
C. 4.106 And for to consayle þe kynge on *Consience* thei lokede;
C. 4.152 And kynde [wit] and *Consience* corteysliche thonkede
C. 4.157 And cryede to *Consience*, the kyng myhte hit here:
C. 4.166 The kyng to consayl tho toek *Consience* and resoun
C. 4.176 Quod *Consience* to þe kyng, 'withoute þe comune helpe
C. 4.186 And *Consience* in alle my Courtes be a[s] kynges Iustice.'
C. 4.195 The kyng comaundede *Consience* tho to congeye alle his offeceres
C. 5.6 For as y cam by *Consience* with resoun y mette
C. 5.83 For in my *Consience* y knowe what Crist w[o]lde y wrouhte.
C. 5.89 Quod *Consience*, 'by Crist, y can nat se this lyeth;
C. 5.104 'зe! and contynue,' quod *Consience*, 'and to þe kyrke ywen[d]e.'
C. 5.113 And *Consience* his crocer byfore þe kyng stande.
C. 5.181 'For þe comune is the kynges tresor, *Consience* woet wel.
C. 6.386 They couthe nat by here *Consience* acorden for treuthe
C. 7.184 *Consience* and kynde wyt kenned me to his place
C. 7.207 Til зe come into *Consience*, yknowe of god sulue,
C. 8.13 *Consience* conseyleth зow cloth for to make
C. 8.53 Ne countreplede nat *Consience* ne holy kyrke ryhtes.'

C. 9.26 Aзen clene *Consience* for coueytse of wynnynge.
C. 9.240 Acounted byfore [crist] but *Consience* excuse hym.
C.12.5 [Haue no *consience* how þou come to good]; confesse the to som frere.
C.12.67 And *consience* acounte with hym and casten hym in arrerag[e]
C.15.25 And thenne cam *concyence* and clergie aftur
C.15.30 *Concience* knewe hym [wel] welcomede hym fayre.
C.15.36 *Concience* knewe h[y]m wel and welcomede hem all;
C.15.52 That *Consience* comaunde sholde to do come scripture
C.15.61 *Consience* confortede vs, bothe clergie and scripture,
C.15.108 Cowhede and capede, and *consience* hym herde
C.15.119 Thenne *consience* corteyslyche a continaunce made
C.15.127 'Now þou, Clergie,' quod *Consience*, 'carpe what is dowel.'
C.15.151 Saue *Concience* and clergie y couthe no mo aspye.
C.15.174 And toek Clergie and *Consience* to conseyle as hit were.
C.15.175 Ac *Concience*, y toek kepe, coniey[e]d sone this doctour
C.15.177 'By Crist!' quod *Consience*, 'clergie, y wol nat lye;
C.15.181 That they knoweth nat,' quod *Consience*, 'what is kynde pacience.
C.15.182 Forthy,' quod *Concience*, 'crist y the byteche;
C.15.187 To conforte hym and *Consience* yf they come in place
C.15.195 'What manere munstracye, my dere frende,' quod *Concience*,
C.16.159 A knewe *Consience* ful wel and clergie bothe.
C.16.192 Thenne am y *Concience* ycald, goddes Clerk and his notarie;
C.17.149 Contrarie her nat as in *Consience* yf thow wol[t] come to heuene.'
C.17.197 Baddeliche ybedded, no boek but *Consience*
C.17.216 зif knyhthoed and kynde wit þe comune and *consience*
C.21.9 And thenne calde y *Consience* to kenne me þe sothe:
C.21.12 Quod *Conciense* and knelede tho, 'this aren [Peres] Armes,
C.21.26 'Thow knowest wel,' quod *Concience*, 'and þou kunne resoun,
C.21.199 Thus *Consience* of Crist and of þe cros carpede
C.21.204 Y wondred what þat was and wagged *Consience*
C.21.207 Quod *Consience* and knelede, 'this is Cristes messager
C.21.209 Knele now,' quod *Consience*, 'and yf thow canst synge,
C.21.212 And criden with *Consience*, 'helpe vs, [Crist], of grace!'
C.21.214 And conseilede hym and *Consience* the comune to sompne:
C.21.220 And acombre þe, *Consience*, bote yf Crist the helpe.
C.21.256 And crouneth *Consience* kyng and maketh craft зoure styward
C.21.337 *Consience* and alle cristene and cardinale vertues,
C.21.341 Thise two cam to *Consience* and to cristene peple
C.21.345 Shal come oute, *Consience*; and зoure [caples two],
C.21.348 That *Consience* shal nat knowe [ho is cristene or hethene]
C.21.355 Quod *Consience* to alle cristene tho, 'my consayl is [to] wende
C.21.360 And thenne cam kynde wit *Consience* to teche
C.21.364 *Consience* comaundede t[h]o alle cristene to delue
C.21.381 'Y care nat,' quod *Consience*, 'thow pryde come nouthe;
C.21.383 Cometh,' quod *Consience*, 'зe cristene, and dyneth
C.21.393 'That is my conseil,' quod *Consience*, 'and cardinale vertues,
C.21.398 Ne aftur *Consience*, bi Crist! [while] y c[an] sulle
C.21.401 And nat hacky aftur holinesse; hold thy tonge, *consience*!
C.21.403 'Caytyf!' quod *Consience*, 'corsede wreche!
C.21.407 Bote *Consience* [be] thy comune[s] and cardinale vertues
C.21.412 Or þat acounted *Consience* [at] a cokkes fether.
C.21.424 And thow, *Consience*, in kynges Court and sholdest neuer come thennes;
C.21.452 The conseyl of *Consience* or cardinal[e] vertues
C.21.477 'In condicioun,' quod *Consience*, 'þat þou [þe] comune defende
C.22.21 Withouten consail of *Consience* or cardinale vertues
C.22.72 That cam aзen *Consience* þat kepar was and gyour
C.22.74 'Y consail,' quod *Consi[e]nce* tho, 'cometh with me, зe foles,
C.22.80 Kynde *Consience* tho herde and cam oute of the planetes
C.22.106 *Concience* of his cortesye tho kynde he bisouhte
C.22.113 And gaderet[h] a greet oest alle agayn *Consience*.
C.22.120 *Consience* and his companye, of holy [kirke] þe techares.
C.22.122 Ouercome *Consience* and cardinal vertues
C.22.126 Symonye hym suede to assaile *Consience*
C.22.130 And knokked *Consience* in Court bifore hem alle;
C.22.140 'Allas!' quod *Consience* and cryede, 'wolde crist of his grace
C.22.147 *Consience* and conseil, he counted hit folye.
C.22.151 And culle all erthely creature saue *Consience* one.
C.22.165 For care *Consience* tho cryede vpon elde
C.22.214 And there was *Consience* Constable, cristene to saue,
C.22.216 That with auntecrist helden harde aзeyn *Consience*.
C.22.220 Comen aзen *Consience*; with couetyse they helden.
C.22.222 'Y counte no more *Consience* bi so y cache suluer
C.22.228 *Consience* cryede, 'helpe, Clergie, or y falle
C.22.231 A[c] for they couthe nat wel here crafte *Consience* forsoek hem.
C.22.232 Nede neyhede tho ner and *Consience* he toelde
C.22.242 Con[s]ience of this con[s]ail tho comesed to lawhe
C.22.268 For[thy],' quod *Consience*, 'bi Crist! kynde wit me telleth
C.22.294 Enuye herfore hatede *Consience*
C.22.296 The while Couetyse and vnkyndenesse *Consience* assailede.
C.22.297 In vnite holi church *Consience* heeld hym
C.22.303 That with *Consience* acordede and cardinal vertues.

C.22.304 *Consience* calde a leche þat couthe wel shryue:
C.22.316 Quod contricion to *Consience*, 'do hym come to vnite
C.22.318 'We haen no nede,' quod *Consience*; 'y woet no bettere leche
C.22.322 Y may wel soffre,' sayde *Consience*, 'sennes ȝe desiren,
C.22.329 And cam þer *Consience* was and knokked at þe ȝate.
C.22.337 *Consience* knoweth me wel and what y can bothe.'
C.22.353 And acorde with *Consience* and kusse here ayther oþer.'
C.22.355 And cam to *Consience* and cortey[s]liche hym grette.
C.22.356 'Thow art welcome,' quod *Consience*; 'can[st] thow hele syke?
C.22.357 Here is contricioun,' quod *Consience*, 'my cosyn, ywounded.
C.22.358 Conforte hym,' quod *Consience*, 'and taek kepe to his sores.
C.22.374 And comen with a kene wil *Consience* to assaile.
C.22.375 *Consience* cryede efte clergie [to] helpe
C.22.380 'By Crist!' quod *Consience* tho, 'y wol bicome a pilgrime
C.22.384 And countrepledeth me, *Consience*; now kynde me avenge

conseil(- > counseil(-; conseyu(- > conceyuen

consenteth v *consenten v.* C 1
C. 2.93Th[e]   count[e] of coueytise [he] *consenteth* to hem bothe,

consience(- > conscience

consistorie n *consistorie n.* A 3 constorie (2) constory (1); B 6; C 5
          constorie
A. 2.139 Paulynes peple, for pleyntes in *constorie*,
A. 3.30   And in *constory* at court callen here names.
A. 3.131 To be cursid in *constorie* heo countiþ not a risshe;
B.Pr.99   Lest crist in *Consistorie* acorse ful manye.
B. 2.178 Paulynes pryuees for pleintes in *Consistorie*
B. 3.31   And in *Consistorie* at court callen hire names.
B. 3.142 To be corsed in *Consistorie* she counteþ noȝt a [risshe];
B. 3.320 Kynges Court and commune Court, *Consistorie* and Chapitle,
B.15.239 In þe *Consistorie* bifore þe Commissarie he comeþ noȝt ful ofte
C.Pr.127 Lest crist in *constorie* acorse of [ȝow] manye.
C. 3.34   And in *constorie* at court do calle ȝoure names.
C. 3.180 To be cursed in *constorie* a counteth nat a rusche;
C. 3.473 Kyngus Court and comune Court, *constorie* and [c]hap[itre],
C.16.364 In *constorie* bifore [þe] commissarie a cometh nat ful ofte

conspire v *conspiren v.* A 1; B 2 conspire (1) conspired (1)
A.11.19   Þat can construe deseites, & *conspire* wrongis,
B.10.19   [That] kan con[strue] deceites and *conspire* wronges
B.10.429 Or who [dide] worse þan Dauid þat vries deeþ *conspired*,

constable n *constable n.* A 3 cunstable; B 6 Conestable (1) Constable (4)
          Constables (1); C 6
A. 2.160 And comaundite a *cunstable* þat com at þe ferste
A. 4.72   & comaundid a *cunstable* to caste hym in yrens]:
A.10.16   Ac þe *cunstable* of þe castel, þat kepiþ hem alle,
B. 2.199 And comaunded a *Constable* þat com at þe firste
B. 2.209 And how þe kyng comaunded *Constables* and sergeauntȝ
B. 3.315 Shal neiþer kyng ne knyght, *Constable* ne Meire
B. 4.85   And comaundede a *Constable* to casten hym in Irens:
B. 9.17   Ac þe *Constable* of [þe] Castel þat kepeþ [hem alle]
B.20.214 And þere was Conscience *Conestable*, cristene to saue,
C. 2.213 And comaunded a *Constable* that cam at þe furste
C. 3.256 For sholde neuere Consience be my *constable* were y a kyng,' quod
          mede,
C. 3.468 Shal nother kyng ne knyght, *Constable* ne Mayre
C. 4.81   And comaundede a *Constable* to caste [hym] in yrones
C.10.143 Ac þe *constable* of þ[e] Castel þat kepeth hem alle
C.22.214 And there was Consience *Constable*, cristene to saue,

constantyne > costantyn

constellacioun n *constellacioun n.* A 1; C 1 constillacioun
A.10.146 In þat curside *constellacioun* þei knewe togideris,
C.14.31   As to be bore or bygete in such a *constillacioun*;

constory(- > consistorie

constrayne v *constreinen v.* C 2
C. 5.54   Me sholde *constrayne* no Cler[k] to no knaues werkes,
C.20.435 A[c] ȝut my kynde [in] my kene ire shal *constrayne* my will–

construe v *construen v.* A 6 construe (4) construide (1) construiþ (1); B 11
          construe (7) construeþ (1) construwe (1) construed (1); C 6
A.Pr.58   For coueitise of copis *construide* it as þei wolde.
A. 4.128 Let þi confessour, sire king, *construe* it þe on englissh,
A. 4.133 For to *construe* þis clause declynede faste,
A. 8.90   For I shal *construe* iche clause & kenne it þe on englissh.'
A. 8.134 Ac catoun *construiþ* it [nay] & canonistris boþe,
A.11.19   Þat can *construe* deseites, & conspire wrongis,
B.Pr.61   For coueitise of copes *construwed* it as þei wolde.
B.Pr.144 To þe kynges counseil, *construe* whoso wolde,
B. 2.36   How *construeþ* David þe kyng of men þat [caccheþ] Mede,
B. 4.145 Late [þi] Confessour, sire kyng, *construe* [it þee on englissh],

B. 4.150 Al to *construe* þis clause for þe kynges profit,
B. 5.278 Cum sancto sanctus eris: *construwe* me þis on englissh.'
B. 5.419 *Construe* clause[m]el[e] and kenne it to my parisshens.
B. 7.108 For I [shal] *construe* ech clause and kenne it þee on englissh.'
B.10.19   [That] kan con[strue] deceites and conspire wronges
B.14.277 'I kan noȝt *construe*,' quod haukyn; 'ye moste kenne me þis on
          englissh.'
B.15.375 [Ne] nauȝt oon among an hundred þat an Auctour kan *construwe*,
C. 4.142 Lat thy Confessour, syre kyng, *construe* this in englische
C. 4.147 To *construe* this c[l]ause, kyndeliche what it meneth.
C. 7.34   Ac y can nat *construe* catoun ne clergialiche reden.
C. 9.282 For y can *construe* vch a word and kennen hit the an englische.'
C.16.117 'Y can nat *construe* al this,' quod Actiua vita.
C.17.111 Ne [can] *construe* kyndelyche þat poetes made.

contemplacion n *contemplacioun n.* B 1; C 4 contemplacion (1)
          contemplacioun (3)
B.20.274 And lerne logyk and lawe and ek *contemplacion*,
C. 7.305 [Quod *contemplacion*, 'by Crist, thow y care soffre],
C.18.73   And conforteth hem in here continence þat lyuen in
                          contemplacioun,
C.18.77   And chaste leden here lyf, is lyf of *contemplacioun*,
C.22.274 And lerne logyk and lawe and eke *contemplacioun*

contemplatif adj *contemplatif adj.& n.* A 1; B 1
A. 7.233 Actif lif oþer *contemplatif*; crist wolde it alse.
B. 6.249 *Contemplatif* lif or Actif lif; crist wolde [it als].

contenaunce n *contenaunce n.* A 1 cuntenaunce; B 5; C 5 continance (1)
          continaunce (4)
A.Pr.24   In *cuntenaunce* of cloþing comen disgisid.
B.Pr.24   In *contenaunce* of cloþynge comen d[is]gised.
B. 5.183 Counseil þat þow knowest by *contenaunce* ne by [speche];
B.11.16   And bad me for my *contenaunce* acounten Clergie liȝte.
B.13.112 Than Conscience curteisly a *contenaunce* made,
B.16.149 That is kissynge and fair *contenaunce* and vnkynde wille.
C.Pr.26   In *continance* [of] clothyng in many kyne gyse.
C. 6.165 Consayl þat thow knowest by *continaunce* ne by speche.
C.11.161 And *continaunce* made on clergie, to congeie me hit semede,
C.11.175 And bade me for my *contin[au]nce* counte cler[gie] lihte.
C.15.119 Thenne consience corteyslyche a *continaunce* made

contenue > continue; continance -aunce > contenaunce

continence n *continence n.* B 1; C 1
B.16.69   Thanne *Continence* is neer þe crop as kaylewey bastard.
C.18.73   And conforteth hem in here *continence* þat lyuen in
                          contemplacioun,

continue v *continuen v.* B 2; C 3 contenue (1) contynue (2)
B. 9.182 And euery maner seculer [man] þat may noȝt *continue*
B.12.38   And if þow be maiden to marye and myȝt wel *continue*,
C. 5.39   And sykerost for þe soule, by so y wol *continue*.
C. 5.104 'Ȝe! and *contynue*,' quod Consience, 'and to þe kyrke ywen[d]e.'
C.10.283 And euery maner seculer man þat may nat *contynue*

contraye(s > contree

contrarie n *contrarie n.* A 1; B 6; C 7 contrarie (5) contrarye (2)
A.11.150 He kenniþ vs þe *contrarie*, aȝens catonis wordis,
B.10.201 He kenneþ vs þe *contrarie* ayein Catons wordes,
B.10.402 Ac hir werkes, as holy writ seiþ, [was] euere þe *contrarie*.
B.12.50   That wise wordes wolde shewe and werche þe *contrarie*:
B.15.371 Of þat was calculed of þe element þe *contrarie* þei fynde.
B.17.274 Thus is vnkyndenesse þe *contrarie* þat quencheþ, as it were,
B.17.349 For vnkyndenesse is þe *contrarie* of alle kynnes reson.
C. 1.122 Euene þe *contrarie* sitteth Crist, Clerkes wyteth þe sothe:
C. 9.194 Coueyten þe *contrarye* for as coterelles they libbeth.
C.10.239 Ac Westm[in]stre lawe, y woet wel, worcheth þe *contra[r]ye*;
C.17.107 Of þat was kalculed of þe clymat the *contrarie* þey fynde.
C.17.161 And when kynde hath his cours and no *contrarie* fyndeth
C.19.255 Thus is vnkyndenesse [the *contrarie* that] quencheth, as hit were,
C.19.329 For vnkyndenesse is þe *contrarie* of alle kyne resoun.

contrarie v *contrarien v.* B 5 contrarie (2) contrariedest (1) contrarien (1)
          contrarieþ (1); C 8 contraridest (1) contrarie (2) contraryed (1)
          contrarien (1) contraryen (1) contrarieth (2)
B. 5.54   For whoso *contrarieþ* truþe, he telleþ in þe gospel,
B.12.156 How þow *contrariedest* clergie wiþ crabbede wordes,
B.15.569 That *contrarien* cristes lawe and cristendom dispise.
B.17.335 For kynde clyueþ on hym euere to *contrarie* þe soule;
B.17.344 That þei han cause to *contrarie* by kynde of hir siknesse,
C.Pr.59   For coueytise of copis *contraryed* somme doctours.
C. 2.22   In kynges court, in comune court *contra[r]ieth* my techynge.
C.10.244 That kynde folweth kynde and *contrarieth* neuere:
C.14.100 How þou *contra[r]idest* clergie with crabbed wordes,
C.17.149 *Contrarie* her nat as in Consience yf thow wol[t] come to heuene.'

C.17.251 That *contra[r]yen* now cristes law[e] and cristendoem dispisen.
C.19.315 For kynde cleueth on hym euere to *contrarie* þe soule;
C.19.324 That they haen cause to *contrarien* bi kynde of here sekness[e];

contree n *contree n.* A 4 cuntre; B 17 contre (1) contree (11) contrees (5);
    C 20 contraye (2) Contrayes (1) contre (4) contrees (3) contrey (2)
    contreye (5) contreyes (1) contreys (2)
A.Pr.29 Coueite not in *cuntre* to cairen aboute
A.Pr.95 And ben clerkis of þe kinges bench þe *cuntre* to shende.
A. 2.43 Of kniȝtes of *cuntr[e]*, of comeres aboute,
A. 9.12 ȝif þei knewen any *cuntre* or costis aboute
B.Pr.29 Coueiten noȝt in *contree* to [cairen] aboute
B. 8.12 If þei knewe any *contree* or costes [aboute]
B. 8.15 And knowen *contrees* and courtes and many kynnes places,
B.13.219 There vnkyndenesse and coueitise is, hungry *contrees* boþe.
B.13.223 To Conscience what craft he kouþe, and to what *contree* he wolde.
B.15.520 Al for to enforme þe faith; in fele *contrees* deyeden,
B.16.170 And yede forþ as an ydiot in *contree* to aspie
B.17.53 Comynge from a *contree* þat men called Ierico;
B.17.116 And kennen outcom[en] men þat knowen noȝt þe *contree*
B.17.123 And come ayein bi þis *contree* and conforten alle sike
B.19.132 And þo was he called in *contre* of þe comune peple,
B.19.136 Forþi þe *contree* þer Iesu cam called hym fili dauid,
B.19.312 'For comunliche in *contrees* cammokes and wedes
B.19.417 "The *contree* is þe corseder þat Cardinals come Inne,
B.20.56 In ech a *contree* þer he cam he kutte away truþe
B.20.224 And so seiden sixty of þe same *contree*,
B.20.328 In *contrees* þer he coome confessions to here;
C.Pr.31 Coueyten noȝt in *contre[y]* to cayren aboute
C. 2.58 Were beden to þe Bridale a bothe half þe *contre*,
C. 2.65 Ac simonye and syuile and sysores of *contrees*
C. 3.239 In *contrees* there the kyng cam, consience hym lette
C. 8.205 And bade hunger in haste hye hym out of *contraye*
C. 9.111 With a good will, witteles, mony wyde *contreyes*
C.10.12 Yf they knewe eny *contre* oþer costes aboute
C.10.15 And knowen *contrees* and Courtes and many kynne plases,
C.10.266 Ther ne is squier ne knyhte in *contreye* aboute
C.15.188 There vnkyndenesse and coueytise [is], hungry *contreys* bothe.
C.17.164 Ne kynde sanȝ cortesie in no *contreye* is preysed.
C.18.4 Til we cam into a *contre*, cor hominis hit heihte,
C.19.51 Comynge fram a *contraye* þat men callide Ierico;
C.21.132 And tho was he cald in *contreye* of þe comune peple,
C.21.136 Forthy þe *contre* þer iesu cam calde hym fili dauid,
C.21.312 'For cominliche in *Contrayes* cammokes and wedes
C.21.417 "The *contreye* is þe corsedore þat cardinals cometh ynne,
C.22.56 In vch a *Contrey* ther he cam [he] kutte awey treuthe
C.22.224 And so sayde syxty of þe same *contreye*
C.22.328 In *contreys* þer he cam confessiones to here;

contreplede > countrepledeþ

contreue v *contreven v.* A 1 contreuide; B 3 contreued (2) contreueden
    (1); C 7 contreue (1) contreued (1) contreuede (5)
A.11.134 [Of] alle kynne craftis I *contreuide* tolis,
B.Pr.118 The commune *contreued* of kynde wit craftes,
B.10.182 Of alle kynne craftes I *contreued* tooles,
B.16.137 Thei casten and *contreueden* to kulle hym whan þei myȝte;
C.Pr.145 Kynde wytt and þe comune *contreued* alle craftes
C. 6.39 In alle kyne couent *contreuede* how y myhte
C.11.16 Ho can caste and *contreue* to disseyue þe ri[gh]tfole,
C.11.122 Of alle kyne craftes y *contreuede* toles,
C.11.123 Of carpent[ers and] keruers, and *contreuede* þe compas
C.14.73 Of cloudes and of costumes they *contreuede* mony thynges
C.14.160 Bote kynde þat *contreuede* hit furst of his corteyse wille.

contricion n *contricioun n.* B 22; C 17 contricion (8) contricioun (8)
    Contrissioun (1)
B.11.81 Thoruȝ *contricion* [clene] come to þe heiȝe heuene–
B.11.135 But if *Contricion* wol come and crye by his lyue
B.12.175 And how *contricion* wiþoute confession conforteþ þe soule,
B.12.177 How *contricion* is comended for it cacheþ away synne:
B.12.181 And haþ no *contricion* er he come to shrifte; & þanne kan he litel
    telle
B.14.16 'And I shal kenne þee', quod Conscience, 'of *Contricion* to make
B.14.83 And þoruȝ feiþ comeþ *contricion*, conscience woot wel,
B.14.85 And þouȝ a man myȝte noȝt speke *contricion* myȝte hym saue
B.14.88 Ergo *contricion*, feiþ and conscience is kyndeliche dowel,
B.14.93 Ther *contricion* dooþ but dryueþ it doun into a venial synne,
B.14.282 Riȝt as *contricion* is confortable þyng, conscience woot wel,
B.14.286 /And *Contricion* confort and cura animarum;
B.19.331 And gaf hym caples to his carte, *contricion* and confession;
B.19.346 Confession and *Contricion*, and youre carte þe bileeue,
B.20.213 Thoruȝ *Contricion* and Confession til I cam to vnitee.
B.20.316 Quod *Contricion* to Conscience, 'do hym come to vnitee,
B.20.333 Carpe I wolde wiþ *contricion*, and þerfore cam I hider.'

B.20.357 Here is *Contricion'*, quod Conscience, 'my cosyn, ywounded.
B.20.363 And gooþ gropeþ *Contricion* and gaf hym a plastre
B.20.369 Til *Contricion* hadde clene foryeten to crye and to wepe
B.20.371 For confort of his confessour *Contricion* he lafte,
B.20.376 And [bad] *Contricion* [come] to kepe þe yate.
C.10.53 To *contricion*, to confessioun, til he come til his ende.
C.12.70 Bote yf *contricioun* and confessioun crye by his lyue
C.14.115 And how *contricion* withoute confessioun conforteth þe soule,
C.14.117 How *contricioun* is comended for hit cacheth awey synne:
C.14.121 And hath no *contricion* ar he come to shrifte; and thenne can he
    lytel telle,
C.15.59 Thenne cam *contricion* þat hadd coked for hem all
C.16.25 And sende vs *contricion* [clereliche] to clanse with oure soules
C.21.331 And gaf hym caples to his Carte, *Contrissioun* & confessioun;
C.21.346 Confession and *contricioun*, and ȝoure Carte, þe bileue,
C.22.213 Thorw *contricion* and confessioun til y cam to vnite.
C.22.316 Quod *contricion* to Consience, 'do hym come to vnite
C.22.333 Karpe y wolde with *Contricioun* and þerfore [cam y] heddere.'
C.22.357 Here is *contricioun'*, quod Consience, 'my cosyn, ywounded.
C.22.363 And goeth gropeth *contricion* and gaf hym a plastre
C.22.369 Til *Contricioun* hadde clene forȝete to crye and to wepe
C.22.371 For confort of his confessour *Contricioun* he lefte
C.22.376 And baed *contricioun* come to kepe þe ȝate.

contrit adj *contrit adj.* B 1
B.14.90 Ac shrift of mouþ moore worþi is if man be y[n]liche *contrit*,

contumax adj *contumax adj.* C 1
C.13.85 Ne in none enquestes to come ne *cont[u]max* thogh he worche

conturrollor n *countrollour n.* C 1
C.11.297 As doth the reue or *Conturrollor* þat rykene moet and acounten

conuerte v *converten v.* B 1 conuertede; C 3 conuerte (1) conuerted (1)
    conuertede (1)
B.16.109 And commune wommen *conuertede* and clensed of synne,
C.17.186 Sholden *conuerte* hem to Crist and cristendoem to take.
C.18.142 And comen wommen *conuertede* and clansed hem of synne,
C.20.189 And þat Crist hath *conuerted* the kynde of rihtwisnesse

cook n *cok n.(6)* A 2 cokes (1) cookis (1); B 3 cook (1) cokes (2); C 4
    coek (1) cokes (2) cook (1)
A.Pr.104 *Cookis* & here knaues crieþ 'hote pyes, hote!
A. 3.68 Breweris & bakeris, bocheris & *cokes*,
B.Pr.226 *Cokes* and hire knaues cryden, 'hote pies, hote!
B. 3.79 Brew[e]rs and Bak[e]rs, Bochiers and *cokes*,
B. 5.155 I haue be *cook* in hir kichene and þe Couent serued
C.Pr.230 *Cokes* and here knaues cryede, 'hote pyes, hote!
C. 3.80 As Bakeres a[nd] Breweres, Bocheres and *cokes*;
C. 5.175 And constantyn shal be here *cook* and couerour of here churches,
C. 6.130 Y haue be *coek* in here kychene and the couent serued

coold > cold; coom(- > comen

cope n *cope n.* A 2 copis; B 4 copes; C 6 cope (1) copes (3) copis (2)
A.Pr.53 Cloþide hem in *copis* to be knowen from oþere;
A.Pr.58 For coueitise of *copis* construide it as þei wolde.
B.Pr.56 Cloþed hem in *copes* to ben knowen from oþere;
B.Pr.61 For coueitise of *copes* construwed it as þei wolde.
B. 6.188 And kitten hir *copes* and courtepies hem maked
B.20.58 Freres folwede þat fend for he gaf hem *copes*,
C.Pr.54 Clothed hem in *copis* to be knowe fram othere;
C.Pr.59 For coueytise of *copis* contraryed somme doctours.
C. 8.185 They curuen here *copes* and courtepies hem made
C. 9.211 And clothed hem in *copes*, clerkes as hit were
C. 9.248 [C]o[m]e in his *cope* as he a Clerk were;
C.22.58 Freres folewed þat fende for he ȝaf hem *copes*

cope v *copen v.* A 3 copide (1) copiþ (1) ycopid (1); B 6 cope (2) coped
    (2) copeþ (1) ycoped (1); C 5 cope (1) copeden (1) copeth (1) ycoped
    (2)
A. 2.192 F[or] knowing of comeris *copide* hym as a Frere.
A. 3.34 Þanne com þere a confessour *ycopid* as a frere;
A. 3.132 For heo *copiþ* þe Comissarie and c[ot]iþ hise clerkis
B. 2.233 For knowynge of comeres *coped* hym as a Frere.
B. 3.35 Thanne cam þer a Confessour *coped* as a frere;
B. 3.143 For she *copeþ* þe Commissarie and coteþ hise clerkes
B. 5.266 I nolde *cope* vs wiþ þi catel ne oure kirk amende
B. 6.147 And catel to [*cope*] hem wiþ þat han Cloistres and chirches,
B.20.344 Coom in þus *ycoped* at a Court þer I dwelde.
C. 2.243 For knowyng of co[mere]s *copeden* hym as a frere.
C. 3.38 Thenne come þer a confessour *ycoped* as a frere;
C. 3.181 For a *copeth* þe commissarie and coteth his clerkes
C. 6.288 Y ne wolde *cope* me with thy catel ne oure kyrke mende
C.22.344 Kam ynne thus *ycoped* at a Court þer y dwelte

cope &> coupe

copiede v *copien v.* A 1
A. 8.44   For he *co[pie]de* þus here clause þei [couden] hym gret mede.

copil cople > couple

coppe n *cuppe n.* A 3 coupis (1) cuppe (2); B 5 coppe (1) coppes (1)
   coupes (1) cuppe (2); C 6 coppe (3) coppes (2) coupes (1)
A. 3.21   *Coupis* of clene gold [and] pecis of siluer,
A. 5.181   In couenaunt þat clement [shulde þe *cuppe* felle],
A. 5.185   Þere was lauȝing & louryng & 'lete go þe *cuppe!*'
B. 3.22   *Coupes* of clene gold and coppes of siluer,
B. 3.22   Coupes of clene gold and *coppes* of siluer,
B. 5.332   In couenaunt þat Clement sholde þe *cuppe* fille,
B. 5.336   There was lauȝynge and lourynge and 'lat go þe *cuppe*!'
B.10.315   And but if his knaue knele þat shal his *coppe* brynge
C. 3.23   *Coupes* of clene gold [and] coppes of syluer,
C. 3.23   Coupes of clene gold [and] *coppes* of syluer,
C. 5.161   And but if his knaue knele þat shal his *coppe* holde
C. 6.390   In couenaunt þat clement sholde the *coppe* fulle
C. 6.394   There was leyhing and louryng and 'lat go the *coppe*!'
C.20.406   Bote of comune *coppes*, alle cristene soules;

coppemele > cuppemele

corde n *corde n.* B 1 corde
B.16.128   And knokked on hem wiþ a *corde*, and caste adoun hir stalles

corecte > correcte

corf n prop *n.i.d.* C 1
C. 3.141   In the Castel of *Corf* y shal do close the,

corlew n *curleu n.* B 1; C 1 corleu
B.14.43   The *Corlew* by kynde of þe Eyr, moost clennest flessh of briddes,
C.15.241   The Cryket by kynde of þe fuyr and *corleu* by þe wynde,

corn n *corn n.* &> *bredcorn* A 6; B 7 corn (6) cornes (1); C 10 corn (8)
   corne (1) cornes (1)
A. 6.32   And kepide his *corn*, & cariede it to house,
A. 7.61   And make hym mery wiþ þe *corn* whoso it begrucchiþ.
A. 7.84   For of my *corn* & my catel [he] crauide þe tiþ[e];
A. 7.128   [Cacche cowes] from his *corn*, [and] kepen hise bestis,
A. 7.183   Al for coueitise of his *corn* to [cacche] awey hungir.
A. 7.283   Be þat it neiȝide ner heruest [þat] newe *corn* com to chepyng.
B. 6.92   For of my *corn* and [my] catel [h]e craued þe tiþe;
B. 6.140   To kepe kyen in þe feld, þe *corn* fro þe beestes,
B. 6.299   By þat it neȝed neer heruest newe *corn* cam to chepyng.
B.13.261   And er þe commune haue *corn* ynouȝ many a cold morwenyng;
B.14.57   Darstow neuere care for *corn* ne cloþ ne for drynke,
B.15.402   The *corn* þat she croppede he caste it in his ere,
B.19.318   Ordeigne þee an hous, Piers, to herberwe Inne þi *cornes*.'
C. 5.17   And kepe my *corn* in my croft f[or] pykares and theues
C. 8.31   For þey cometh to my croft my *corn* to diffoule.'
C. 8.101   For of my *corn* and my catel he craued [þe] tythe.
C. 8.145   Bothe of my *corn* and of my cloth to kepe hem fram defaute.
C. 8.243   "The slowe Caytif for colde wolde no *corn* tylye;
C. 8.321   By that hit nyhed neyh heruost and newe *corn* cam to chepyng.
C.13.46   Ac if þe marchaunt make his way ouer menne *corne*
C.15.256   Dar þe nat care for no *corn* ne for cloth ne for drynke
C.17.173   *Corn* [þat þe] coluere eet when he come in places
C.21.318   Ordeyne the an hous, [Peres], to herborwe in thy *cornes*.'

cornehull n prop *corn. n.* C 1
C. 5.1   Thus y awakede, woet god, whan y wonede in *Cornehull*,

cornel > kernel

corner n *conren n.(1)* C 1
C.15.161   In þe *corner* of a car[t]whel with a crow croune.

corone coroune > crowne; corounid > croune; corps > cors

correcte v *correcten v.* B 2 correcte (1) correcteþ (1); C 1 corecte
B.10.289   Forþi, ye Correctours, claweþ heron and *correcteþ* first yowselue,
B.19.303   And to *correcte* [þ]e kyng if [þe kyng] falle in gilt.
C.21.303   And to *corecte* the kyng and the kyng falle in [g]ulte.

correctours n *correctour n.* B 1
B.10.289   Forþi, ye *Correctours*, claweþ heron and correcteþ first yowselue,

corrupcions n *corrupcioun n.* B 1; C 1 corupcions
B.20.99   So kynde þoruȝ *corrupcions* kilde ful manye.
C.22.99   So kynde thorw *corupcions* kulde fol mony.

cors n *cors n.* &> *cours* A 1; B 4 corps (2) cors (2); C 3
A. 1.128   Be what craft in my *cors* it compsiþ, & where.'
B. 1.139   By what craft in my *cors* it comseþ, and where.'
B.13.9   And no *corps* in hir kirkȝerd n[e] in hir kirk was buryed
B.15.23   'The whiles I quykne þe *cors*', quod he, 'called am I anima;
B.19.151   Come knelynge to þe *corps* and songen

C.15.11   Ne no *cors* of pore comine in here kyrkeȝerde most lygge
C.16.183   And whiles y quyke þe *cors* ycald am y Anima;
C.21.151   Comen knelyng to þ[e] *Cors* and songen

corsaint n *cor-seint n.* A 1 corseint; B 1; C 1 corsent
A. 6.20   'Knowist þou ouȝt a *corseint*,' quaþ þei, 'þat men callen treuþe?
B. 5.532   'Knowestow auȝt a *corsaint*,' [quod þei], 'þat men calle truþe?
C. 7.177   'Knowest thow auht a *corsent*,' quod they, 'þat men calleth treuthe?

corsed(- > curseþ

corsement n *cursement n.* C 1
C. 6.65   His clothes were of *corsemen[t]* and of kene wordes.

corsent > corsaint; corseth > curseþ

corsynge ger *cursing ger.* &> *curseþ* C 1
C. 8.159   They acounteth nat of *corsyng[e]* ne holy kyrke dredeth–

corteys(- cortes- > curteis(-; corupcions > corrupcions

cosyn n *cosine n.* A 5 cosenes (1) cosyn (4); B 4 cosyn (3) Cosynes (1);
   C 2
A. 2.97   She miȝte kisse þe king for *cosyn* ȝif he[o] wolde.
A.11.105   I shal kenne þe to my *cosyn* þat clergie is hoten.
A.12.41   Kynde [wit] hure confessour, hure *cosyn* was Inne.
A.12.43   And sayde, 'my *cosyn* kynde wit knowen is wel wide,
A.12.53   Ken him to my *cosenes* hous þat kinde wit hyȝth.
B. 2.133   [She] myȝte kisse þe kyng for *cosyn* and she wolde.
B.10.153   I shal kenne þee to my *Cosyn* þat Clergie is hoten.
B.12.93   For kynde wit is of his kyn and neiȝe *Cosynes* boþe
B.20.357   Here is Contricion', quod Conscience, 'my *cosyn*, ywounded.
C.11.91   Y shal kenne þe to clergie, my *cosyn*, þat knoweth
C.22.357   Here is contricioun,' quod Consience, 'my *cosyn*, ywounded.

cost n1 *cost n.(1)* B 1; C 1
B. 3.68   And þi *cost* and þi coueitise and who þe catel ouȝte.
C. 3.72   Thi *cost* and here couetyse and ho þe catel ouhte.

cost n2 *cost n.(2)* B 1; C 4 coest (2) cost (2)
B.13.41   Ac [he eet] mete of moore *cost*, mortrews and potages.
C. 3.373   Withouten *coest* and care and alle kyn trauayle.
C. 3.385   Thow the kyng and þe comune al the *coest* hadde.
C.15.46   Forthy eet he mete of more *cost*, mortrewes and potages.
C.19.240   Clothes of moest *cost*, as clerkes bereth witnesse:

costantyn n prop *n.i.d.* B 2 Costantyn (1) Costantyns (1); C 2 Constantyn
B.10.329   Of *Costantyns* cofres [þer þe catel is Inne]
B.15.557   Whan *Costantyn* of curteisie holy kirke dowed
C. 5.175   And *constantyn* shal be here cook and couerour of here churches.
C.17.220   Whan *Constantyn* of cortesye holy kirke dowede

coste n *coste n.* &> *costed* A 1 costis; B 3 coste (1) costes (2); C 1
   costes
A. 9.12   Ȝif þei knewen any cuntre or *costis* aboute
B. 2.86   The Countee of Coueitise and alle þe *costes* aboute,
B. 8.12   If þei knewe any contree or *costes* [aboute]
B.18.113   [Where] out of þe west *coste* a wenche as me þouȝte
C.10.12   Yf they knewe eny contre oþer *costes* aboute

costed v *costen v.* B 2 coste (1) costed (1); C 2 costed (1) costede (1)
B.Pr.204   [Ne] carpynge of þis coler þat *costed* me neuere;
B.13.382   That it *coste* me muche moore; swoor manye oþes.
C.Pr.212   Ne carp[ynge] of [þis] cole[r] þat *costede* me neuere.
C.Pr.213   And thow hit *costed* m[e] catel byknowen [hit] y ne wolde

costned v *costnen v.* B 1
B.Pr.205   And þouȝ it *costned* me catel biknowen it I nolde

costumes > custume

cote n1 *cote n.(1)* B 2 cote (1) cotes (1); C 8 cote (4) cotes (4)
B. 8.16   Boþe princes paleises and pouere mennes *cotes*,
B.12.146   Ne in none [beggers] *cote* [n]as þat barn born,
C. 4.123   In prisones and in pore *cotes* be pilgrimages to Rome
C. 5.2   [K]ytte and y in a *cote*, yclothed as a lollare
C. 6.136   For he hadde childe in the chapun *co[t]e*; he worth chalenged at þe
            eleccioun."
C. 9.72   As prisones in puttes and pore folk in *cotes*,
C. 9.83   The wo of this wommen þat wonyeth in *cotes*
C. 9.151   And ca[ry]eth hit hoem to his *cote* and cast hym to lyuene
C.10.16   Bothe princes paleis and pore menne *cotes*
C.14.90   Ne in no *cote* ne Caytyfs hous [crist was ybore

cote n2 *cote n.(2)* A 1; B 9; C 1
A. 5.91   & beholde how heyne haþ a newe *cote*,
B. 5.111   And biholde [how H]eyne haþ a newe *cote*;
B.11.285   Ne neiþer kirtel ne *cote*, þeiȝ þei for cold sholde deye,
B.13.273   He hadde a *cote* of cristendom as holy kirke bileueþ.
B.13.313   'By crist!' quod Conscience þo, 'þi beste *cote*, Haukyn,

B.13.354 Thanne Pacience parceyued of pointes [his] *cote*
B.13.402 Swoor þerby swiþe ofte and al biswatte his *cote*;
B.13.457 Thus haukyn þe Actif man hadde ysoiled his *cote*
B.14.17 That shal clawe þi *cote* of alle kynnes filþe:
B.14.151 ȝyueþ hym a *cote* aboue his couenaunt, riȝt so crist ȝyueþ heuene
C.16.301 As of a *cote* of ca[mm]aca or of clene scarlet.

cote_armure n *cote-armure n.* B 1; C 2
B.19.13 Hise colours and his *cote Armure*; ac he þat comeþ so blody
C.18.186 'What is his [conn]esaunc[e],' quod y, 'in his *cote Armure*?'
C.21.13 His colours and his *cote armure*; ac he þat cometh so blody

coterelles n *coterel n.(1)* C 2
C.9.97 And to conforte suche *coterelles* and crokede men and blynde.
C.9.194 Coueyten þe contrarye for as *coterelles* they libbeth.

coteþv *coten v.(1)* A 1 cotiþ; B 1; C 1 coteth
A.3.132 For heo copiþ þe Comissarie and *c[ot]iþ* hise clerkis
B.3.143 For she copeþ þe Commissarie and *coteþ* hise clerkes
C.3.181 For a copeth þe commissarie and *coteth* his clerkes

cotidian n *cotidian adj.& n.* A 1
A.12.84 Þat on is called *cotidian*, a courrour of oure hous;

cottepors > kuttepurs; coude(stow > konne; couden > kidde,konne; couert >
court; coughed > cogheþ

coughes n *cough n.* B 1; C 1 cowhes
B.20.82 *Coughes* and Cardiacles, Crampes and tooþaches,
C.22.82 *Cowhes* and cardiacles, crampes and toethaches,

couȝe > cogheþ; counfort- > conforten

counseil n *counseil n. &> counseillen* A 11; B 43 conseil (10) conseille
(2) counseil (27) counseille (4); C 45 consail (10) consayl (13)
consaile (3) consayle (5) conseil (5) conseyl (6) conseile (1) conseyle
(1) conseille (1)
A.2.103 For consience is of his *counseil* & knowiþ ȝow ichone,
A.3.90 Þe king fro *counseil* com & callide aftir mede
A.3.104 Before þe kyng & his *counseil*, clerkis & oþere.
A.4.8 Comaunde hym þat he come my *counseil* to here,
A.4.152 Be my *counseil* ycome of clerkes and Erlis.
A.4.156 So consience be of ȝour *counseil*, kepe I no betere.'
A.5.38 'Lest þe king & his *counseil* ȝour comunes apeir[e]
A.7.298 And þanne curse þe king & alle þe *counseil* aftir
A.9.98 Corounid on to be kyng & þe h[ere] *counseil* werchen,
A.10.91 Be *counseil* of consience, accordyng holy chirche,
A.11.21 Þat suche craftis conne [to *counseil* ben yclepid],
B.Pr.144 To þe kynges *counseil*, construe whoso wolde.
B.Pr.148 Comen to a *counseil* for þe commune profit.
B.Pr.180 [Ac] helden hem vnhardy and hir *counseil* feble,
B.Pr.203 Shal neuere þe cat ne þe kiton by my *counseil* be greued,
B.2.139 [For] Conscience is of his *counseil* and knoweþ yow echone;
B.3.101 The kyng fro *conseil* cam and called after Mede
B.3.115 Bifore þe kyng and his *conseil*, clerkes and oþere.
B.4.8 Comaunde hym þat he come my *counseil* to here,
B.4.123 Til þe kynges *counseil* be þe commune profit;
B.4.189 [Be] my *counseil* co[men] of clerkes and of Erles.
B.4.193 So Conscience be of [y]oure *counseil* [kepe I] no bettre.'
B.5.46 'Lest þe kyng and his *conseil* youre comunes apeire
B.5.168 They hadde þanne ben Infamis, þei kan so yuele hele *co[unseil]*.
B.5.183 *Counseil* þat þow knowest by contenaunce ne by [speche];
B.6.314 Ayeins Catons *counseil* comseþ he to Iangle:
B.6.317 And þanne corseþ þe kyng and al [þe] *counseil* after
B.8.108 Crouned oon to be kyng, [and by hir *counseil* werchen],
B.9.117 First by þe fadres wille and þe frendes *conseille*,
B.10.21 [That] swiche craftes k[onne] to *counsel* [are] cleped;
B.11.430 Of clergie ne of his *counseil* he counteþ noȝt a risshe.
B.13.177 And took Clergie and Conscience to *conseil* as it were
B.13.204 Whan þow art wery [for]walked; wille me to *counseille*'.
B.15.68 Ayein cristes *counseil* and alle clerkes techynge,
B.15.235 In kynges court he comeþ ofte þer þe *counseil* is trewe,
B.15.236 Ac if coueitise be of þe *counseil* he wol noȝt come þerInne.
B.15.322 Allas, lordes and ladies, lewed *counseil* haue ye
B.18.95 To do þe blynde bete [þe dede], it was a boyes *counseille*.
B.19.38 And þo þat bicome cristene bi *counseil* of þe baptis[t]e
B.19.79 Into hir kyngene kiþ by *counseil* of Aungeles.
B.19.162 For þat womm[a]n witeþ may noȝt wel be *counseille*.
B.19.257 And after craftes *conseil* cloþeþ yow and fede.
B.19.296 And couered hym vnder *conseille* of Caton þe wise:
B.19.315 'Hareweþ alle þat konneþ kynde wit by *conseil* of þise docto[urs],
B.19.355 Quod Conscience to alle cristene þo, 'my *counseil* is to wende
B.19.393 'That is my *conseil*', quod Conscience, 'and Cardinale vertues;
B.19.452 The *counseil* of Conscience or Cardinale vertues,
B.20.21 Wiþouten *conseil* of Conscience or Cardynale vertues,
B.20.30 After þe kynges *counseil* and þe comune like.

B.20.68 They cursed and hir *conseil*, were it clerk or lewed.
B.20.129 And cam to þe kynges *counseille* as a kene baroun
B.20.147 Conscience and *counseil*, he counted [it] f[o]lye.
B.20.212 And [I] by *conseil* of kynde comsed to rome
B.20.242 Conscience of þis *counseil* þo comsede for to laughe,
C.Pr.169 Comen til a *conseyl* for [þe] comune profyt.
C.Pr.197 [Ac helden hem vnhardy and here *conseil* feble]
C.Pr.211 Shal neuer þe Cat ne [þe] kytoun be my *conseil* be greued
C.2.122 And ar this weddyng be wrouthe wo to al ȝoure *consayle*!
C.2.155 And Consience is of his *consayl* and knoweth ȝow [echone];
C.3.7 And yf she worche wysely and by wys men *consayl*
C.3.128 The kyng fram *conseyl* come [and] calde aftur mede
C.3.146 And teche the to louye treuthe and take *consail* of resoun
C.3.152 Byfore þe kyng and his *consayl*, clerkes and oþere.
C.3.254 Forthy y consayl no kynge eny *conseyl* aske
C.3.376 To folowe and to fynde hym and [f]eche at hem his *consayl*
C.4.8 Comaunde hym þat he come my *consayle* to here,
C.4.119 And til þe kynges *consayl* be alle comune profit
C.4.166 The kyng to *consayl* tho toek Consience and resoun
C.5.144 'Laste þe kyng and his *consayl* ȝoure comunes apayre
C.5.184 Lat no kyne *consayl* ne couetyse ȝow parte,
C.6.76 Aȝeyn þe *consayl* of Crist, as clerkes fyndeth in bokes:
C.6.165 *Consayl* þat thow knowest by continaunce ne by speche.
C.8.336 Aȝenes Catones *consayle* comseth he to gruche:
C.11.18 That coueite can and caste thus ar cleped into *consayle*;
C.11.98 So with þat clergie can and *consail* of scripture
C.11.312 Clergie [and] his *conseile* y counted ful litel.
C.15.174 And toek Clergie and Consience to *conseyle* as hit were.
C.16.241 Aȝen þe *consayl* of crist, as holy clergie witnesseth.
C.16.360 In kynges Court a cometh yf his *consaile* be trewe
C.16.361 Ac yf couetyse be of his *consaile* a wol nat come þerynne.
C.16.369 Ac thorw Coueytyse and his *consaile* ycongeyed is he ofte.
C.17.56 Allas, lordes and ladyes, lewede *consayle* haue ȝe
C.20.98 [To do] þe blynde bete the dede, [hit] was a boyes [*conseille*].
C.21.38 And tho þat bycome cristene bi *consail* of þe baptist
C.21.79 Into here kyngene kuth by *consail* of Angelis.
C.21.162 For þat womman witeth [may] nat [wel be] *conseyl*.
C.21.257 And aftur craftes *consail* clotheth ȝow and fedeth.
C.21.296 And keuered hym vnder *consayl* of Caton the wyse:
C.21.315 'Harweth alle þa[t] conneth kynde wit bi *consail* of [this] doctours
C.21.355 Quod Consience to alle cristene tho, 'my *consail* is [to] wende
C.21.393 'That is my *conseil*,' quod Consience, 'and cardinale vertues,
C.21.452 The *conseyl* of Consience or cardinal[e] vertues
C.22.21 Withouten *consail* of Consience or cardinale vertues,
C.22.30 Aftur þe kynges *conseyl* and þe comune lyke.
C.22.68 Thei corsede and here *consail*, were hit Clerk or lewed.
C.22.129 And cam to þe kynges *consail* as a kene Baroun
C.22.147 Consience and *conseil*, he counted hit folye.
C.22.212 And y bi *conseil* of kynde comsed to Rome
C.22.242 Con[s]ience of this *con[s]ail* tho comesed for to lawhe

counseille > counseil,counseillen

counseillen v *counseilen v.* A 8 conceiledest (1) counseil (1) counseile (2)
counseillid (1) counseilide (1) counseilliþ (2); B 26 conseiledest (1)
conseille (4) conseillest (1) counseiled (3) counseileþ (1) counseille (11)
counseilled (1) counseillede (1) counseillen (2) counseilleþ (1); C 26
consail (1) consayl (1) consayle (4) consailede (1) consaileth (1)
consayleth (1) conseile (3) conseyle (3) conseyled (2) conseilede (2)
conseyede (1) conseiledest (2) conseylest (1) conseileth (2) conseyleth
(1) conseillen (1)
A.1.64 *Counseilid* kaym to kiln his broþer,
A.3.174 For kilde I neuere no king ne *counseilide* þeraftir,
A.3.193 [Cowardly þou consience *conceiledest* him þennes]
A.4.98 And to *counseile* þe king & consience boþe;
A.8.179 Forþi I *counseil* alle cristene [to] criȝe god mercy,
A.10.97 Catoun *counseilliþ*–tak kep of his teching–
A.10.197 Forþi I *counseile* alle cristene coueite not be weddit
A.11.222 How crist *counseilliþ* þe comune & kenneþ hem þis tale:
B.Pr.115 For to *counseillen* þe kyng and þe commune saue.
B.Pr.187 Forþi I *counseille* al þe commune to late þe cat worþe,
B.1.66 *Counseilled* Kaym to killen his broþer,
B.3.187 For killed I neuere no kyng, ne *counseiled* þerafter,
B.3.206 Cowardly þow, Conscience, *conseiledest* hym þennes
B.4.111 And to *counseille* þe kyng and Conscience [boþe]
B.5.48 And siþen he *counseiled* þe kyng his commune to louye:
B.6.14 Makeþ cloþ, I *counseille* yow, and kenneþ so youre douȝtres.
B.7.155 Caton and Canonistres *counseillen* vs to leue
B.7.201 Forþi I *counseille* alle cristene to crie god mercy,
B.9.176 Forþi I *counseille* alle cristene coueite noȝt be wedded
B.10.223 To *counseille* þee kyndely to knowe what is dowel.'
B.10.418 Forþi I *counseille* yow clerkes, of holy [kirke] þe wriȝtes,
B.11.225 I *conseille* alle cristne clyue noȝt þeron to soore,
B.12.92 Forþi I *counseille* þee for cristes sake clergie þat þow louye;

145

B.12.98   Ne countreplede clerkes, I *counseille* þee for euere.
B.12.121   Forþi I *conseille* alle creatures no clergie to dispise
B.15.344   Forþi I *counseille* alle cristene to conformen hem to charite,
B.17.264   Beþ noȝt vnkynde, I *conseille* yow, to youre euenecristene.
B.19.113   And crist *counseileþ* þus and comaundeþ boþe,
B.19.200   And *counseiled* me to knele þerto; and þanne cam, me þouȝte,
B.19.214   And *counseillede* hym and Conscience þe comune to sompne:
B.19.391   'How?' quod al þe comune; 'þow *conseillest* vs to yelde
B.19.462   *Counseilleþ* me bi hir acounte and my clerkes writynge.
B.20.74   'I *conseille*', quod Conscience þo, 'comeþ wiþ me, ye fooles,
B.20.207   'Counseille me, kynde', quod I, 'what craft is best to lerne?'
C.Pr.142   For to *conseillen* þe kyng and þe commune saue.
C.Pr.204   Forthy y *conseile* for oure comune profit lat þe Cat yworthe
C. 1.62   *Conseylede* Caym to cullen his brother,
C. 3.233   For kulde y neuere no kyng ne *conseilede* so to done;
C. 3.242   Caytifliche thow, Consience, *conseiledest* þe kyng leten
C. 3.254   Forthy y *consayl* no kynge eny conseyl aske
C. 3.263   Vnconnyngliche [þow], Consience, *conseiledest* hym thenne
C. 4.106   And for to *consayle* þe kynge on Consience thei lokede;
C. 5.180   And sethe a *consailede* þe kyng his comine to louie:
C. 6.29   To carpe and to *consayle* then eny Clerk or lewed;
C. 8.13   Consience *conseyleth* ȝow cloth for to make
C. 8.84   'Consayle nat þe comune þe kyng to desplese
C. 9.347   Forthy y *consayle* alle cristene to crye god mercy
C.10.278   Forthy y *conseyle* alle cristene coueyte neuere be wedded
C.12.168   ȝut *conseileth* Crist in commen vs all:
C.14.5   And *conseyled* the for cristes sake no creature to bygile,
C.14.43   Forthy y *conseile* vch a creature clergie to honoure
C.14.64   Forthy y *conseyle* all creatures no cler[gie] to despice
C.19.230   Beth nat vnkynde, y *conseyle* ȝow, to ȝoure emcristene.
C.21.113   And Crist *consayleth* [þu]s and comaundeth bothe,
C.21.200   And *conseyled* me to knele þerto; and thenne cam, me thouhte,
C.21.214   And *conseilede* hym and Consience þe comune to sompne:
C.21.391   'How?' quod alle þe comune; 'thow *conseylest* vs to ȝelde
C.21.462   *Conseileth* me bi here acounte and my clerkes writyng.
C.22.74   'Y *consail*,' quod Consi[e]nce tho, 'comeþ with me, ȝe foles,
C.22.207   'Consaileth me, kynde,' quod y, 'what craft be beste to lere?'

counte v *counten v. &> countee* A 3 counte (1) countide (1) countiþ (1);
   B 8 counte (1) counted (2) counten (1) counteþ (4); C 14 counte (2)
   counted (3) counteth (9)
A. 3.131   To be cursid in constorie heo *countiþ* not a risshe;
A. 4.11   And *counte* wiþ [þe] consience, so me crist helpe,
A. 7.154   And *countide* peris at a pese & his plouȝ boþe,
B. 3.142   To be corsed in Consistorie she *counteþ* noȝt a [risshe];
B.11.430   Of clergie ne of his counseil he *counteþ* noȝt a risshe.
B.12.138   A[s] to þe clergie of crist *counted* it but a trufle:
B.19.304   For *counteþ* he no kynges wraþe when he in Court sitteþ;
B.19.444   And *counteþ* noȝt þouȝ cristene ben killed and robbed,
B.19.451   For þe comune', quod þis Curatour, '*counten* ful litel
B.20.147   Conscience and counseil, he *counted* [it] f[o]lye.
B.20.222   'I *counte* na moore Conscience by so I cacche siluer
C. 3.180   To be cursed in constorie a *counteth* nat a rusche.
C. 9.109   Careth they for no colde ne *counteth* of non hete
C. 9.304   Caton *counteth* hit at nauht and Canonistres at lasse.
C.10.258   Of kyn ne of kynrede *counteth* men bote litel.
C.11.175   And bade me for my contin[au]nce *counte* cler[gie] lihte.
C.11.312   Clergie [and] his conseile y *counted* ful litel.
C.12.197   Or for a confessour ykud þat *counteth* nat a ruche
C.13.237   Of clergie ne of kynde wyt *counteth* he nat a rusche.
C.14.83   As to þe clergie of crist thei *counted* hit but a tryfle:
C.21.304   For *counteth* he no kynges wreth when he in Court sitteth;
C.21.444   And *counteth* nat thow cristene be culde and yrobbed,
C.21.451   [For] the comune,' quod this curatour, '*counteth* ful litel
C.22.147   Consience and conseil, he *counted* hit folye.
C.22.222   'Y *counte* no more Consience bi so y cache suluer

countee n *counte n.(3)* B 1; C 1 counte
B. 2.86   The *Countee* of Coueitise and alle þe costes aboute,
C. 2.93   Th[e] *count[e]* of coueytise [he] consenteth to hem bothe,

countrepledeþ v *countre- pref. 2.* B 2 countreplede (1) countrepledeþ (1);
   C 4 contreplede (1) countreplede (2) countrepledeth (1)
B.12.98   Ne *countreplede* clerkes, I counseille þee for euere.
B.20.384   And *countrepledeþ* me, Conscience; now kynde me avenge
C.Pr.138   *Contreplede* hit noght,' quod Conscience, 'for holi [k]ir[k]e sake.'
C. 8.53   Ne *countreplede* nat Consience ne holy kyrke ryhtes.'
C. 8.88   What þei comaunde as by þe kyng *countreplede* hit neuere;
C.22.384   *Countrepledeth* me, Consience; now kynde me avenge

countresegge v *countre- pref. 2.* C 1
C.11.222   Ac y *countresegge* the nat, clergie, ne thy connyng, scripture.

coupable adj *coupable adj.& n.* B 2; C 1
B.12.88   As cristes caracte[s] confortede, and boþe *coupable* shewed

B.17.306   Any creature [be] *coupable* afore a kynges Iustice
C.19.286   Eny creature be *coupable* bifore a kynges iustice

coupe n *coupe n.(2)* A 3 cope (1) coupe (2); B 3; C 2 coupe
A. 5.59   And carfulliche his *cope* [comsiþ] he to shewe.
A. 5.147   And ca[iriþ] hym to [k]ir[k]eward hise [*coupe*] to shewe.
A. 5.247   And knowelechide his [*coupe*] to crist ȝet eftsones,
B. 5.76   And carefully [his *coupe*] he comse[þ] to shewe.
B. 5.297   And [kaireþ] hym to kirkeward his *coupe* to shewe.
B. 5.473   And knoweliched his [*coupe*] to crist yet eftsoones,
C. 6.327   And knolechede [his *coupe* to Crist] ȝut eftsones,
C. 6.351   And kayres hym to kyrkeward his *coup[e]* to shewe.

coupes -is > coppe

couple n *couple n. &> coupleþ* A 2 copil (1) couple (1); B 2; C 1
   couples
A.10.175   Outtake þe eiȝte soulis, & of iche beste a *couple*
A.10.186   It is an vncomely *copil*, be crist, as [me þinkeþ],
B. 9.144   Excepte oonliche of ech kynde a *couple*
B. 9.165   It is an vncomly *couple*, by crist! as me þynkeþ,
C.18.222   That acorsede alle *couples* þat no kynde forth brouhte:

coupleþ v *couplen v.* A 5 couple (1) couplide (3) coupliþ (1); B 6 couple
   (1) coupled (3) coupleþ (1) ycoupled (1); C 2 cople (1) couplede (1)
A. 3.152   Clergie and coueitise he[o] *coupliþ* togidere.
A. 4.132   Clerkis þat wern confessours *couplide* hem togideris,
A.10.156   And alle þat *couplide* hem with þat kyn crist hatide [dedliche].
A.10.158   To kepe his kynrede fro kaymes, þei *couplide* nouȝt togideris;
A.11.117   For ȝif þou *coupl[e]* þe with hym to clergie comist þou neuere;
B.Pr.207   *Coupled* and vncoupled to cacche what þei mowe.
B. 3.165   Clergie and coueitise she *coupleþ* togidres.
B. 4.149   Clerkes þat were Confessours *coupled* hem togideres
B. 9.129   And noȝt þi kynde wiþ Caymes *ycoupled* n[e] yspoused".
B. 9.131   Caymes kynde and his kynde *coupled* togideres,
B.10.165   For if þow *coupl[e]* þe [wiþ hym] to clergie comest [þow] neuere;
C. 2.193   And lat *cop[l]e* þe commissarie; oure cart shal he drawe
C. 4.146   Clerkes [þat were confessours] *co[u]plede* hem togederes

courrour n *coror n.* A 1
A.12.84   Þat on is called cotidian, a *courrour* of oure hous;

cours n *cours n.* B 3; C 6 cors (1) cours (5)
B. 3.56   And a *cours* of kynde wherof we comen alle;
B.11.337   And after *cours* of concepcion noon took kepe of ooþer,
B.15.369   Neiþer þei konneþ ne knoweþ oon *cours* bifore anoþer.
C. 3.60   And [a] *cours* of kynde wherof we comen alle.
C. 3.347   In kynde and in case and in *cours* of nombre.
C. 3.389   Of the *cours* of case so thei cache suluer.
C.13.145   Aftur *cors* of concepcion noon toek kepe of oþer,
C.17.105   Noþer they [conn]eth ne [know]eth a *cours* by[fore] anoþer.
C.17.161   And when kynde hath his *cours* and no contrarie fyndeth

court n *court n.(1)* A 6; B 28 court (26) courtes (2); C 29 couert (2)
   Court (25) courtes (2)
A. 2.152   And come to þe kinges *court* & consience tolde,
A. 3.30   And in constory at *court* callen here names.
A. 4.29   Ac consience com arst to *court* be a myle wey
A. 6.72   Þanne shalt þou come to a *court*, cler as þe sonne.
A.11.120   Til þou come to a *court*, kepe wel þi tunge
A.12.57   And ere I cam to þe *court* quod bonum est tenete
B.Pr.107   Ac of þe Cardinals at *court* þat kauȝte of þat name,
B.Pr.111   Forþi I kan & kan nauȝt of *court* speke moore.
B.Pr.149   For a cat of a [*court*] cam whan hym liked
B.Pr.194   Ther þe cat is a kitoun þe *court* is ful elenge;
B.Pr.200   Nere þe cat of þ[e] *court* þat kan yow ouerlepe;
B. 2.63   Ac Symonie and Cyuylle and Sisours of *courtes*
B. 2.191   And com to þe kynges *court* and Conscience tolde,
B. 3.31   And in Consistorie at *court* callen hire names.
B. 3.316   Ouer[carke] þe commune ne to þe *Court* sompne,
B. 3.320   Kynges *Court* and commune Court, Consistorie and Chapitle,
B. 3.320   Kynges Court and commune *Court*, Consistorie and Chapitle,
B. 3.321   Al shal be but oon *court*, and oon [burn] be Iustice.
B. 4.166   For þe mooste comune of þat *court* called hire an hore.
B. 5.585   Thanne shaltow come to a *court*, cler as þe sonne.
B. 8.15   And knowen contrees and *courtes* and many kynnes places,
B.10.168   Til þow come to a *court*, kepe-wel-þi-tunge-
B.13.23   And bad me come to his *court*, wiþ clergie sholde I dyne.
B.15.17   In cristes *court* yknowe wel and of [cristene in many a place].
B.15.21   That ech a creature of his *court* welcomeþ me faire.'
B.15.22   'What are ye called', quod I, 'in þat *court* among cristes peple?'
B.15.235   In kynges *court* he comeþ ofte þer þe counseil is trewe,
B.15.237   In *court* amonges [þe commune] he comeþ but selde
B.15.474   Riȝt as capons in a *court* comeþ to mennes whistlyng,
B.18.39   And al þe *court* on hym cryde 'crucifie!' sharpe.
B.19.304   For *counteþ* he no kynges wraþe when he in *Court* sitteþ;

B.19.424 And þow Conscience in kynges *court*, and sholdest neuere come
　　　　　þennes;
B.20.130 And [knokked] Conscience in *Court* afore hem alle;
B.20.344 Coom in þus ycoped at a *Court* þere I dwelde,
C.Pr.134 Ac of þe Cardinales at *Court* þat caught han such a name
C.Pr.160 Consience and þe kynge into *Court* wente
C.Pr.170 For a Cat of a *Court* cam whan hym likede
C.Pr.207 Ther þe Cat [is] a kytoun þe *Court* is ful elynge.
C.Pr.218 Ne were þe Cat of þe *Court* and 3onge kitones toward;
C. 1.105 Made knyghtes in his *Couert* creatures tene,
C. 2.22   In kynges *court*, in comune court contra[r]ieth my techynge.
C. 2.22   In kynges court, in comune *court* contra[r]ieth my techynge.
C. 2.205 And kam to þe kynges *Court* and Consience tolde,
C. 3.34   And in constorie at *court* do calle 3oure names.
C. 3.456 That here kyng ycome fro þe *Court* of heuene,
C. 3.469 Ouerkarke þe comune ne to þe *Court* sompne
C. 3.473 Kyngus *Court* and comune Court, constorie and [c]hap[itre],
C. 3.473 Kyngus Court and comune *Court*, constorie and [c]hap[itre],
C. 3.474 Al shal be but [o] *couert* and o [buyrne] be Iustice;
C. 4.186 And Consience in alle my *Courtes* be a[s] kynges Iustice.'
C. 7.33   And holden a knyhtus *Court* and acounte with þe reue
C. 7.232 And so shaltow come to a *Court* as cleer as þe sonne.
C.10.15   And knowen contrees and *Courtes* and many kynne plases,
C.16.168 And in cristes *court* yknowe wel and of his kynne a party.
C.16.360 In kynges *Court* a cometh yf his consaile be trewe
C.16.362 Amongus þe comune in *Court* a cometh bote selde
C.17.166 And a cardinal of *Court*, a gret clerk withalle,
C.18.94   In kynges *Court* and in knyhtes, the clenneste men and fayreste
C.20.38   And alle þe *Court* [on hym] cryede 'crucifige!' [sharpe].
C.21.304 For counteth he no kynges wreth when he in *Court* sitteth;
C.21.424 And thow, Consience, in kynges *Court* and sholdest neuer come
　　　　　thennes;
C.22.130 And knokked Consience in *Court* bifore hem alle;
C.22.344 Kam ynne thus ycoped at a *Court* þer y dwelte

courteis- > *curteis-*

courtepy n *courte-pi* n. A 1; B 2 Courtepy (1) courtepies (1); C 1
　　courtepies
A. 5.62   A kertil & a *courtepy*, a knyf be his side,
B. 5.79   [A] kirtel and [a] *Courtepy*, a knyf by his syde,
B. 6.188 And kitten hir copes and *courtepies* hem maked
C. 8.185 They curuen here copes and *courtepies* hem made

couth(- > *konne; coupe* > *kidde,konne; coupest* > *konne*

coueiten v *coveiten* v. A 10 coueite (4) coueyte (1) coueiten (1) coueitest
　　(1) coueyteþ (1) coueitide (1) coueitiþ (1); B 25 coueite (6) coueited
　　(3) coueiten (4) coueitest (2) coueiteþ (10); C 30 coueite (1) coueyte
　　(7) coueyted (2) coueitede (1) coueyteth (3) coueyten (3) coueytest (3)
　　coueiteth (3) coueyteth (6)
A.Pr.29   *Coueite* not in cuntre to cairen aboute
A. 3.248 Loke þou kille þe king; *coueite* nou3t hise godis;
A. 3.252 *Coueitide* here catel, kilde nou3t hire bestis,
A. 6.60   Þ[e] croft hattiþ *coueite* nou3t menis catel ne here wyues,
A. 8.51   Coumfortiþ hym in þat cas, *coueitiþ* nou3t his goodis,
A. 9.103 More kynde knowyng I *coueyte* to lere,
A.10.101 For 3if þou comsist to clymbe, & *coueitest* herre,
A.10.197 Forþi I counseile alle cristene *coueite* not be weddit
A.11.210 Þat out of couent & cloistre *coueiten* to libben".
A.12.3   And whoso *coueyteþ* don betere þan þe boke telleþ,
B.Pr.29   *Coueiten* no3t in contree to [cairen] aboute
B.Pr.189 [The while he cacche þ conynges he *coueite þ* no3t [o]ure caroyne
B. 3.164 And al þe comune in care þat *coueiten* lyue in truþe.
B. 3.273 And for he *coueited* hir catel and þe kyng spared,
B. 5.573 Th[e] croft hatte *Coueite*-no3t-mennes-catel-ne-hire-wyues-
B. 7.49   Conforteþ hym in þat caas, [*coueiteþ* no3t hise] 3iftes,
B. 8.113 More kynde knowynge I *coueite* to lerne,
B. 9.176 Forþi I counseille alle cristene *coueite* no3t be wedded
B.10.304 That out of couent and cloistre *coueiten* to libbe.
B.10.343 And Caton kenneþ vs to *coueiten* it nau3t but as nede techeþ:
B.11.11   And knowe þat þow *coueitest* and come þerto parauntur'.
B.11.76   Whi youre Couent *coueiteþ* to confesse and to burye
B.11.125 For þou3 a cristen man *coueited* his cristendom to reneye,
B.13.149 For he þat loueþ þee leelly litel of þyne *coueiteþ*.
B.13.150 Kynde loue *coueiteþ* no3t no catel but speche.
B.14.312 He tempreþ þe tonge to truþeward [þat] no tresor *coueiteþ*,
B.15.39   How þow *coueitest* to calle me, now þow knowest [alle] my
　　　　　names.
B.15.159 That he ne wolde aske after his, and ouþerwhile *coueite*
B.15.175 *Coueiteþ* he noon erþely good, but heueneriche blisse.'
B.15.254 Craueþ ne *coueiteþ* ne crieþ after moore:
B.15.470 Right as þe cow calf *coueiteþ* [swete melk];
B.17.124 That craueþ it [or] *coueiteþ* it [and] crieþ þerafter.
B.17.219 To alle vnkynde creatures þat *coueite* to destruye

B.18.169 Loue haþ *coueited* hire longe; leue I noon ooþer
B.20.253 And if ye *coueite* cure, kynde wol yow [telle]
C.Pr.31   *Coueyten* no3t in contre[y] to cayren aboute
C. 3.255 A[t] Concience þat *coueiteth* to conquere a reume.
C. 3.363 Indirect thyng is as hoso *coueytede*
C. 3.371 So indirect is inlyche to *coueyte*
C. 3.399 And *coueyte* þe case, when thei couthe vnderstande,
C. 3.402 And *coueytede* oure kynde and be kald in oure name–
C. 3.426 And for a *coueytede* here catel and the kyng sparede,
C. 5.151 That out of couent and Cloystre *coueyteth* to dwelle.
C. 7.220 The croft hatte *coueyte*-nat-menne-catel-ne-here-wyues-
C. 9.48   That conforteth suche in eny caes and *coueyteth* nat he[re] 3iftes
C. 9.194 *Coueyten* þe contrarye for as coterelles they libbeth.
C.10.109 More kynd[e] knowynge *coueyte* y to here
C.10.278 Forthy y conseyle alle cristene *coueyte* neuere be wedded
C.11.18   That *coueite* can and caste thus ar cleped into consayle:
C.11.107 For yf thow *coueytest* to be ryche to clergie comest thow neuere.
C.11.139 'By Crist,' quod Clergie, 'yf thow *coueyte* dowel
C.11.170 And knowe þat þou *coueytest* and come þerto parauntur.'
C.12.60   For thogh a cristene man *coueitede* his cristendom to renoye
C.12.169 "Hoso *coueiteth* to come to my kyneriche
C.15.71   Alle þat *coueyte*[d] to come to eny kyne ioye,
C.15.153 'That loueth lely,' quod he, 'bote litel thyng *coueyteth*.
C.16.146 A trempeth þe tonge to treuthward þat no tresor *coueyteth*:
C.16.201 How þou *coueytest* to calle me, now þou knowest al my namus.
C.16.293 That he ne askede aftur his and oþerwhiles *coueytede*
C.16.370 And hoso *coueyteth* to knowe [hym] such a kynde hym foloweth
C.17.81   That god *coueyteth* nat þe coyne þat crist hymsulue printede
C.17.228 Yf þe kynges *coueyte* in cristes pees to lyuene.
C.19.185 To alle vnkynde creatures þat *coueyten* to destruye
C.20.172 Loue hath *coueyted* here longe; leue y non oþere
C.22.253 And yf 3e *coueiteth* cure kynde wol 3ow telle

coueitise n *coveitise* n. A 10; B 47; C 48 coueitise (1) coueityse (1)
　　coueytise (25) coueytyse (5) coueytise (16)
A.Pr.58   For *coueitise* of copis construide it as þei wolde.
A. 1.170 3e ben acumbrid wiþ *coueitise*, 3e [conne] not out crepe;
A. 2.32   And become a good man for any *coueitise*, I rede.'
A. 2.62   Wiþ þe kingdom of *coueitise* I croune hem togidere;
A. 3.152 Clergie and *coueitise* he[o] coupliþ togidere,
A. 5.107 Þanne com *coueitise*; I can hym nou3t descryue,
A. 7.183 Al for *coueitise* of his corn to [cacche] awey hungir.
A.10.183 For *coueitise* of catel vnkyndely be maried.
A.10.198 For *coueitise* of catel or of kynrede riche,
A.11.18   But it be cardit wiþ *coueitise* as cloþeris don here wolle;
B.Pr.61   For *coueitise* of copes construwed it as þei wolde.
B. 1.196 [Ye] ben acombred wiþ *coueitise* ye konne no3t [out crepe],
B. 2.51   And lat no conscience acombre þee for *coueitise* of Mede.'
B. 2.86   The Countee of *Coueitise* and alle þe costes aboute,
B. 3.68   And þi cost and þi *coueitise* and who þe catel ou3te.
B. 3.165 Clergie and *coueitise* she coupleþ togidres,
B. 4.32   A[c] Conscience knew hem wel, þei loued *coueitise*,
B. 4.119 Til clerkene *coueitise* be to cloþe þe pouere and fede,
B. 5.52   'And ye þat han lawes to [loke], lat truþe be youre *coueitise*,
B. 5.188 [Th]anne cam *Coueitise*; [I kan] hym na3t discryue,
B. 5.256 That wolde kille hem if he cacche hem my3te for *coueitise* of hir
　　　　　skynnes
B. 9.160 For *coueitise* of catel vnkyndely ben [maried].
B. 9.177 For *coueitise* of catel ne of kynrede riche;
B.10.18   But it be carded wiþ *coueitise* as cloþeres [don] hir wolle.
B.10.287 Offyn and Fynes; for hir *coueitise*
B.11.14   And *Coueitise* of ei3es [þat ooþer was ycalled].
B.11.32   *Coueitise* of ei3e, þat euere þow hir knewe–
B.11.40   Concupiscencia carnis ne *Coueitise* of ei3es
B.11.46   *Coueitise* of ei3es conforted me anoon after
B.11.50   *Coueitise* of ei3es com ofter in mynde
B.11.52   *Coueitise* of ei3es [ofte me conforted];
B.13.11   And how þis *Coueitise* ouercom clerkes and preestes,
B.13.219 There vnkyndenesse and *coueitise* is, hungry contrees boþe.
B.13.355 [Was] colomy þoru3 *coueitise* and vnkynde desiryng.
B.13.390 Vpon a cruwel *coueitise* m[y conscience] gan hange.
B.14.11   Al for *coueitise* of my cristendom in clennesse to kepen it.
B.14.239 And if *Coueitise* cacche þe poore þei may no3t come togideres,
B.14.241 For men knowen wel þat *Coueitise* is of [a] kene wille
B.14.270 Moore for *coueitise* of [catel] þan kynde loue of boþe–
B.15.62   *Coueitise* to konne and to knowe scienc[e]
B.15.67   For in þe likynge liþ a pride and licames *coueitise*
B.15.236 Ac if *coueitise* be of þe counseil he wol no3t come þerInne.
B.15.415 How englisshe clerkes a coluere fede þat *coueitise* hi3te,
B.15.543 For *coueitise* after cros; þe croune stant in golde.
B.15.546 For *coueitise* of þat cros [clerkes] of holy kirke
B.15.551 Right so, ye clerkes, for youre *coueitise* er [come au3t] longe
B.16.28   *Coueitise* comþ of þat wynd and crepeþ among þe leues
B.17.277 Vnkynde cristene men, for *coueitise* and enuye

B.17.288   For *coueitise* of any kynnes þyng þat crist deere bou3te.
B.17.348   That is *coueitise* and vnkyndenesse þat quencheþ goddes mercy;
B.19.224   *Coueitise* and vnkyndenesse Cardinals hym to lede.
B.20.121   Thanne cam *Coueitise* and caste how he my3te
B.20.141   That *Coueitise* were cristene þat is so kene [to fighte],
B.20.220   Coomen ayein Conscience; wiþ *Coueitise* þei helden.
B.20.233   That þei come for *coueitise*, to haue cure of soules.
B.20.296   The while *coueitise* and vnkyndenesse Conscience assaillede.
B.20.351   That lif þoru3 his loore shal leue *coueitise*
C.Pr.59   For *coueytise* of copis contraryed somme doctours.
C.Pr.103   I leue, by oure lord, for loue of 3oure *coueytise*
C. 1.67   To combre men with *coueytise*, þat is his kynde and his lore.'
C. 1.191   And ben acombred with *coueytise*: thei can nou3t [out crepe]
C. 2.54   Acombre neuere thy Consience for *coueytise* of mede.'
C. 2.93   Th[e] count[e] of *coueytise* [he] consenteth to hem bothe,
C. 2.250   Thy kynedom thorw *Coueytise* wol out of kynde wende,
C. 3.72   Thi cost and here *coueytise* and ho þe catel ouhte.
C. 3.202   And al þe comune in care and in *coueytise*;
C. 3.207   And custumes of *coueytise* þe comune to destruye.
C. 3.211   For clerkes and *coueitise* mede hath knet togederes
C. 3.431   Thus was kyng sauel ouercome thorw *coueytise* of mede,
C. 4.33   'Here cometh,' quod Consience, 'þat *Coueytise* seruen.
C. 4.114   Til Clerkene *Coueytise* be cloth for þe pore
C. 5.184   Lat no kyne consayl ne *coueytise* 3ow parte,
C. 6.196   Thenne cam *coueytise*; y can hym nat descreue,
C. 9.26   A3en clene Consience for *coueytise* of wynnynge.
C.10.257   For *coueytise* of catel and connynge chapmen;
C.10.279   For *coueytise* of catel in none kyne wyse;
C.11.15   Bote hit be cardet with *coueytise* as clotheres kemben here wolle.
C.11.173   And *coueytise*-of-yes ycalde was þat oþer.
C.11.191   *Coueytise*-of-yes þat euere thow here knewe–
C.11.307   Concupiscencia carnis [ne *coueytise*-of-yes]
C.12.3   *Coueytise*-of-yes conforted me aftur and saide,
C.12.241   For *coueytyse* of catel to culle hym þat hit kepeth.
C.12.245   So *coueytise* of catel was combraunce to hem alle.
C.15.13   And how þis *coueytise* ouercome al kyne sectes,
C.15.188   There vnkyndenesse and *coueytise* [is], hungry contreys bothe.
C.16.79   And thogh *coueytyse* [cacche] þe pore they may nat come
            togyderes
C.16.81   For men knowen wel þat *coueytise* is of a kene will
C.16.110   More for *coueytise* of catel then kynde loue of þe mariage.
C.16.224   *Coueytyse* to conne and to knowe scienc[e]
C.16.361   Ac yf *coueytise* be of his consaile a wol nat come þerynne.
C.16.369   Ac thorw *Coueytyse* and his consaile ycongeyed is he ofte.
C.17.205   For *coueytise* aftur cros; the corone stand in golde.
C.17.208   For *coueytise* of th[at] croes clerkes of holi churche
C.17.214   Riht so, 3e clerkes, 3oure *coueytise* ar come auht longe
C.18.32   *Coueytise* cometh of þat wynde and Caritas hit abiteth
C.19.258   Vnkynde cristene men, for *coueytise* and enuye
C.19.269   For *coueytise* of eny kyne thynge þat Crist dere bouhte.
C.19.328   That is *coueytise* and vnkyndenesse whiche quencheth godes
            mercy
C.21.224   *Coueytise* and vnkyndenesse Cardynales hym [to] lede.
C.22.121   Thenne cam *coueytise* and caste how he myhte
C.22.141   That *coueytise* were cristene þat is so kene to fihte,
C.22.220   Comen a3en Consience; with *coueytise* they helden.
C.22.233   That they cam for *Coueytise*, to haue cure of soules.
C.22.296   The while *Coueytise* and vnkyndenesse Consience assailede.
C.22.351   That lyf thorw his lore shal leue *Coueytyse*

coueitous adj *coveitous adj.* A 2; B 3; C 3 coueytous (2) couetous (1)
A. 3.59   Who is curteis or kynde or *coueitous*, or ellis.
A. 5.114   'I haue [ben] coueit[ous],' quaþ [þat caitif], 'I [bi]knowe [hit]
            h[e]re,
B. 5.198   'I haue ben *coueitous*', quod þis caytif, 'I biknowe it here.
B.13.183   'What!' quod Clergie to Conscience, 'ar ye *coueitous* nouþe
B.14.201   Forþi cristene sholde be in commune riche, noon *coueitous* for
            hymselue.
C. 6.206   'Y haue be *couetous*,' quod this kaytif, 'y biknowe hit here.
C.14.21   And holy chirche horen helpe, Auerou[s] and *coueytous*,
C.16.42   Forthy cristene sholde be in comune ryche, noon *coueytous* for
            hymsulue.

couenaunt n *covenant n.* A 3; B 6; C 6 couenant (3) couenaunt (3)
A. 5.181   In *couenaunt* þat clement [shulde þe cuppe felle],
A. 7.29   In *couenaunt* þat þou kepe holy[k]ir[k]e and myself
A. 7.147   To kepen hym as *couenaunt* was fro curside shrewis,
B. 5.332   In *couenaunt* þat Clement sholde þe cuppe fille,
B. 6.27   In *couenaunt* þow kepe holy kirke and myselue
B. 6.160   To kepen hym as *couenaunt* was fro cursede sherewes,
B.14.151   3yueþ hym a cote aboue his *couenaunt*, ri3t so crist 3yueþ heuene
B.18.417   Clippe we in *couenaunt*, and ech of vs [kisse] ooþer,
B.19.186   In *couenaunt* þat þei come and knewelich[e] to paie
C. 6.390   In *couenaunt* þat clement sholde the coppe fulle

C. 8.26   In *couenant* þat thow kepe holy kerke and mysulue
C. 8.157   To kepe hym and his catel as *couenant* was bitwene hem:
C.14.216   And a cortesye more þen *couenant* was, what so clerkes carpe,
C.20.460   Cluppe we in *coueenaunt* and vch of vs kusse oþere.'
C.21.186   In *coueenaunt* þat they come and knolech[e] to pay

couent n *couvent n.* A 1; B 6 couent (5) Couentes (1); C 6
A.11.210   þat out of *couent* & cloistre coueiten to libben".
B. 5.138   And þe *Couentes* Gardyner for to graffen Impes.
B. 5.155   I haue be cook in hir kichene and þe *Couent* serued
B. 5.181   I cou[3]e it [vp] in oure Cloistre þat al [þe] *Couent* woot it.'
B.10.304   That out of *couent* and cloistre coueiten to libbe.
B.11.76   Whi youre *Couent* coueiteþ to confesse and to burye
B.20.60   And al þe *Couent* cam to welcome [a] tyraunt
C. 5.151   That out of *couent* and Cloystre coueyteth to dwelle.
C. 6.39   In alle kyne *couent* contreuede how y myhte
C. 6.130   Y haue be coek in here kychene and the *couent* serued
C. 6.162   Al þat y wiste wykked by eny of oure *couent*
C. 6.163   Y cou[3]e hit vp in oure Cloystre þat al þe *couent* woet hit.'
C.22.60   And al þe *couent* cam to welcome a tyraunt

couere v *coveren v.(1)* B 6 couere (2) couered (3) couereþ (1); C 7 cuuere
            (1) keuered (3) keuereth (2) ykuuered (1)
B. 3.60   And I shal *couere* youre kirk, youre cloistre do maken,
B.12.178   And þis conforteþ ech a clerk and *couereþ* fro wanhope,
B.14.334   To *couere* my careyne', quod he, and cride mercy faste.
B.19.86   That o kyng cam wiþ Reson *couered* vnder sense.
B.19.296   And *couered* hym vnder conseille of Caton þe wise:
B.19.347   Shal be coloured so queyntely and *couered* vnder [oure] Sophistrie
C. 3.64   And y shal *cuuere* 3oure kyrke and 3oure clo[i]stre make;
C. 9.138   For vnder godes secret seal here synnes ben *keuered*.
C. 9.250   And fo[r] þe cloth þat *keuereth* hym ykald he is a frere,
C.14.118   And þat conforteth vch a clerk and *keuereth* fro wanhope,
C.21.86   That [o] kyng cam with reson *ykuuered* vnder ensense.
C.21.296   And *keuered* hym vnder consayl of Caton the wyse:
C.21.347   Shal be coloured so queyntly and *keuered* vnder [o]ure sophistrie

coueerour n *coverour n.* C 1
C. 5.175   And constantyn shal be here cook and *couerour* of here churches,

coueth > cogheþ; couet- > coueit-

cow n *cou n.* A 1; B 5 cow (4) kyen (1); C 3 cow (2) kyne (1)
A. 7.271   And ek a *cow* & a calf, & a carte mare
B. 6.140   To kepe *kyen* in þe feld, þe corn fro þe beestes,
B. 6.287   And ek a *cow* and a calf, and a cart mare
B.11.341   Ther ne was *cow* ne cowkynde þat conceyued hadde
B.15.467   For as þe *Cow* þoru3 kynde mylk þe calf norisseþ til an Oxe,
B.15.470   Right as þe *cow* calf coueiteþ [swete melk];
C. 5.18   Or shap shon or cloth or shep and *kyne* kepe,
C. 8.310   And a *cow* with a calf and a cart m[a]re
C.13.149   Ther ne [was] *cow* ne cowkynde þat conseyued hadde

cowardly adv *couardli adv.* A 1; B 1
A. 3.193   [Cowardly] þou consience conceiledest him þennes]
B. 3.206   *Cowardly* þow, Conscience, conseiledest hym þennes

cowed > cogheþ

cowes n *choughe n.* A 1
A. 7.128   [Cacche cowes] from his corn, [and] kepen hise bestis,

cowhede > cogheþ; cowhes > coughes

cowkynde n *cou n.* B 1; C 1
B.11.341   Ther ne was cow ne *cowkynde* þat conceyued hadde
C.13.149   Ther ne [was] cow ne *cowkynde* þat conseyued hadde

crabbede ptp *crabbed ppl.* A 1 crabbide; B 2; C 1 crabbed
A.11.65   And carp[en] a3ens clergie *crabbide* wordis:
B.10.107   And carpen ayein cler[gie] *crabbede* wordes:
B.12.156   How þow contrariedest clergie wiþ *crabbede* wordes,
C.14.100   How þou contra[r]idest clergie with *crabbed* wordes,

cracchen v *cracchen v.* B 4 cracche (1) cracched (1) cracchen (2); C 3
            crache
B.Pr.154   *Cracchen* vs or clawen vs, and in hise clouches holde
B.Pr.186   To c[r]acchen vs & al oure kynde þou3 we cropen vnder benches;
B.11.144   That al þe clergie vnder crist ne my3te me *cracche* fro helle.
B.15.454   Wasshen wel wiþ water and wiþ taseles *cracched*,
C.Pr.203   To *crache* vs and alle oure kynde thogh we crope vnder benches;
C. 6.140   And thenne y crye and *crache* with my kene nayles,
C.12.79   That al þe cristendoem vnde[r] Crist ne myhte me *crache* fro
            [helle]

cradel n *cradel n.* C 1
C. 9.79   To rise to þe reule to rokke þe *cradel*,

craft n *craft n.(1)* A 12 craft (7) craftis (5); B 27 craft (18) crafte (1) craftes (8); C 29 craft (19) crafte (2) craftes (8)

A.Pr.101 Masonis, mynours, & manye oþere *craftis*,
A. 1.128 Be what *craft* in my cors it compsiþ, & where.'
A. 2.4 Kenne me be sum *craft* to k[now]e þe false'.
A. 2.188 For he coude on here *craft* & kneuȝ manye gommes.
A. 3.18 For al consiences cast a[nd] *craft* as I trowe'.
A. 5.25 And wynne þat he wastide wiþ sum maner *craft*,
A. 5.139 Whanne it com in cuppemel; þat *craft* my wyf vside.
A. 5.242 Ne neuere wen[e] to wynne wiþ *craft* þat [I owe],
A. 8.34 Sette scoleris to scole or [to] summe skynes *craftis*,
A.10.107 Ne men þat conne manye *craftis*, clergie [it telliþ],
A.11.21 Þat suche *craftis* conne [to counseil ben yclepid],
A.11.134 [Of] alle kynne *craftis* I contreuide tolis,
B.Pr.118 The commune contreued of kynde wit *craftes*,
B.Pr.222 Masons, Mynours and many oþere *craftes*;
B. 1.139 By what *craft* in my cors it comseþ, and where.'
B. 2.4 Kenne me by som *craft* to knowe þe false'.
B. 2.229 For he kouþe [on] hir *craft* and knew manye gommes.
B. 3.19 For al Consciences cast [and] *craft*, as I trowe'.
B. 5.25 And wynnen his wastyng wiþ som maner *crafte*.
B. 5.223 [Whan] it cam In cuppemele, þis *craft* my wif vsed.
B. 5.468 Ne neuere wene to wynne wiþ *craft* þat I owe],
B. 5.547 In taillours *craft* and tynkeris craft, what truþe kan deuyse,
B. 5.547 In taillours *craft* and tynkeris craft, what truþe kan deuyse,
B. 7.32 Sette Scolers to scole or to som [kynnes] *craftes*,
B.10.21 [That] swiche *craftes* k[onne] to counseil [are] cleped;
B.10.182 Of alle kynne *craftes* I contreued tooles,
B.13.223 To Conscience what *craft* he kouþe, and to what contree he wolde.
B.15.30 And þat is wit and wisdom, þe welle of alle *craftes*;
B.15.48 Alle þe sciences vnder sonne and alle þe sotile *craftes*
B.17.173 Keruynge and compasynge [i]s *craft* of þe fyngres.
B.19.234 And some he kennede *craft* and konnynge of sighte,
B.19.250 And alle he lered to be lele, and ech a *craft* loue ooþer,
B.19.253 '[That al *craft* and konnyng come] of my ȝifte.
B.19.256 And crouneþ Conscience kyng and makeþ *craft* youre Stiward,
B.19.257 And after *craftes* conseil cloþeþ yow and fede.
B.20.206 And loke þow konne som *craft* er þow come þennes.'
B.20.207 'Counseille me, kynde', quod I, 'what *craft* is best to lerne?'
B.20.231 Ac for þei kouþe noȝt wel hir *craft* Conscience forsook hem.
B.20.342 But þow konne [any] *craft* þow comest noȝt herInne.
C.Pr.145 Kynde wytt and þe comune contreued alle *craftes*
C. 2.4 Kenne me by sum *craft* to knowe þe false.'
C. 2.239 For a can on here *craft* and knoweth manye gommes.
C. 3.20 For al Consiences cast and *craft*, as y trowe'.
C. 4.170 Mede and men of ȝoure *craft* muche treuthe letteth.
C. 5.20 Or eny other kynes *craft* þat to þe comune nedeth,
C. 6.42 And connyngest of my *craft*, Clerkysh oþer other,
C. 6.231 When hit cam in coppemele; this *crafte* my wyf vsede.
C. 6.322 Ne neuere wene to wynne with *craft* þat y knowe;
C.11.122 Of alle kyne *craftes* y contreuede toles,
C.15.131 Alle kyne connynges and alle kyne *craftes*
C.15.192 What *craft* þat he couthe and cortey[s]liche he saide:
C.16.190 And þat is wit and wysdoem, þe welle of alle *craftes*;
C.16.210 Alle þe sciences vnder sonne and alle þe sotil *craftes*
C.21.234 And somme he kende *craft* and konnynge of syhte,
C.21.250 And al he lered to be lele, and vch a *craft* loue oþere,
C.21.253 'That all *craft* and connyng c[o]m[e] of my ȝefte.
C.21.256 And crouneth Consience kyng and maketh *craft* ȝoure styward,
C.21.257 And aftur *craftes* consail clotheth ȝow and fedeth.
C.22.206 And loke thow conne som *craft* ar thow come thennes.'
C.22.207 'Consaileth me, kynde,' quod y, 'what *craft* be beste to lere?'
C.22.231 A[c] for they couthe nat wel here *crafte* Consience forsoek hem.
C.22.342 Bote thow conne eny *craft* thow comest nat hereynne.

crafty adj *crafti adj.* A 3; B 4; C 3

A. 3.212 Alle kyn *crafty* men craue mede for here prentis;
A. 7.62 And alle kyne *crafty* men þat conne lyue in treuþe,
A.11.185 And alle kyne *crafty* men þat cunne here foode wynne,
B.Pr.162 And somme colers of *crafty* werk; vncoupled þei wen[d]en
B. 3.225 Alle kynne *craft[y]* men crauen Mede for hir Prentices;
B. 6.68 And alle kynne *crafty* men þat konne lyuen in truþe,
B.13.292 [Or for his *crafty* konnynge or of clerkes þe wisest,
C.Pr.181 And colers of *crafty* werk, bothe knyghte[s] and squieres.
C. 3.280 Alle kyn *crafty* men crauen mede for here prentises;
C. 8.69 And alle kyne *crafty* men þat conne lyue in treuthe,

craftily adv *craftili adv.* A 1; B 1; C 1

A.10.5 Kynde haþ closid þereinne, *craftily* wiþalle,
B. 9.5 Kynde haþ closed þerInne, *craftily* wiþalle,
C.10.132 Kynde hath closed therynne, *craftily* withalle,

craym > creme

craked v *craken v.* B 1; C 1

B.18.73 A Cachepol cam forþ and *craked* boþe hir legges
C.20.75 A cachepol cam [forth] a[nd] *craked* ato he[re] legges

crampe n *crampe n.(1)* B 2 crampe (1) Crampes (1); C 2 crampes (1) crompe (1)

B.13.334 That I cacche þe *crampe*, þe Cardiacle som tyme,
B.20.82 Coughes and Cardiacles, *Crampes* and tooþaches,
C. 6.78 That y cache þe *crompe*, the cardiacle sume tyme
C.22.82 Cowhes and cardiacles, *crampes* and toethaches,

craue v *craven v.* A 3 craue (1) crauen (1) crauide (1); B 10 craue (2) craued (1) crauen (3) craueþ (4); C 9 craue (3) craued (1) crauede (1) crauen (2) craueth (2)

A. 3.209 Men þat [kenne] clerkis *crauen* of h[e]m mede;
A. 3.212 Alle kyn crafty men *craue* mede for here prentis;
A. 7.84 For of my corn & my catel [he] *crauide* þe tiþ[e];
B. 3.222 Men þat [kenne clerkes] *crauen* [of hem] Mede;
B. 3.225 Alle kynne craft[y] men *crauen* Mede for hir Prentices;
B. 6.92 For of my corn and [my] catel [h]e *craued* þe tiþe;
B.13.164 [And ek, haue god my soule, and þow wilt it *craue*
B.13.241 Beggeris and bidderis of my breed *crauen*,
B.14.214 Batauntliche as beggeris doon, and boldeliche he *craueþ*
B.15.165 'Charite', quod he, 'ne chaffareþ noȝt, ne chalangeþ, ne *craueþ*.
B.15.254 *Craueþ* ne coueiteþ ne crieþ after moore:
B.17.124 That *craueþ* it [or] coueiteþ it [and] crieþ þerafter.
B.19.476 Ne *craue* of my comune but as my kynde askeþ.'
C. 3.275 Bothe Beg[g]eres and bedemen *crauen* mede for here preyeres;
C. 3.277 Maistres þat kenneth clerkes *craueth* therfore mede;
C. 3.280 Alle kyn crafty men *crauen* mede for here prentises;
C. 6.49 And non so bolde a beggare to bidde and to *craue*,
C. 8.101 For of my corn and my catel he *craued* [þe] tythe.
C.12.150 Maketh man to haue mynde in god and his mercy to *craue*,
C.15.34 *Crauede* and cryede for cristes loue of heuene
C.16.55 Batauntliche as beggares doen, and baldeliche he *craueth*
C.21.476 Ne *craue* of my comune bote as my kynde asketh.'

crauynge ger *craving ger.* B 1

B.14.187 Confession and knowlichynge [and] *crauynge* þi mercy

creatour n *creatour n.* A 1; B 3; C 3

A.10.27 'Kynde,' quaþ he, 'is *creatour* of alle kenis bestis,
B. 9.26 'Kynde,' quod [he], 'is *creatour* of alle kynnes [beestes],
B.11.326 Thorugh ech a creature kynde my *creatour* to louye.
C.10.152 'Kynde is *creatour*,' quod wit, 'of [alle] kyne thynges,
C.17.153 Hit is kyndly thyng creature his *creatour* to honoure,
C.18.93 And þe clennest creature furste *creat[our]* knowe.

creature n *creature n.* A 3 creature (1) creatures (2); B 39 creature (25) creatures (14); C 29 creature (20) creatures (9)

A.11.246 Alle kynne *creatures* þat to crist be[n] l[yche]
A.11.250 Þat is, iche cristene [*creature*] be kynde to oþer,
A.12.110 Now alle kenne *creatures* þat cristene were euere
B. 5.270 Thow art an vnkynde *creature*; I kan þee noȝt assoille
B. 9.82 Sholde no cristene *creature* cryen at þe yate
B. 9.86 Allas þat a cristene *creature* shal be vnkynde til anoþer!
B.10.362 And after alle cristene *creatures*, in commune ech man ooþer;
B.10.368 For euery cristene *creature* sholde be kynde til oþer,
B.11.143 For an vncristene *creature*; clerkes wite þe soþe
B.11.155 That was an vncristene *creature*, as clerkes fyndeþ in bokes:
B.11.181 [And] comaundeþ ech *creature* to conformen hym to louye
B.11.199 For alle are we *creatures* and of his cofres riche,
B.11.326 Thorugh ech a *creature* kynde my creatour to louye.
B.11.389 For is no *creature* vnder crist can formen hymseluen,
B.11.399 Euery *creature* in his kynde encreesse [he bad]
B.12.83 So clergie is confort to *creatures* þat repenten,
B.12.121 Forþi I conseille alle *creatures* no clergie to dispise
B.12.226 Ac kynde knoweþ þe cause hymself, no *creature* ellis. ·
B.12.279 Ne no *creature* of cristes liknesse withouten cristendom worþ saued.'
B.13.18 [For alle] *creatures* þat crepen [or walken] of kynde ben engendred;
B.14.72 Amonges cristene *creatures*, if cristes wordes ben trewe.
B.14.175 Conforte þo *creatures* þat muche care suffren
B.14.180 For how þow confortest alle *creatures* clerkes bereþ witnesse:
B.15.15 If he were cristes *creature* [for cristes loue] me to tellen.
B.15.16 'I am cristes *creature*', quod he, 'and [of his kyn a party],
B.15.21 That ech a *creature* of his court welcomeþ me faire.'

B.15.53   That any *creature* sholde konne al except crist oone.
B.15.171 Corseþ he no *creature* ne he kan bere no wraþe,
B.15.195 'By crist! I wolde I knewe hym', quod I, 'no *creature* leuere.'
B.15.211 And þat knoweþ no clerk ne *creature* on erþe
B.15.579 Ac we cristene *creatures* þat on þe cros bileuen
B.16.190 Confortour of *creatures*; of hym comeþ alle blisse.
B.16.215 That is, creatour weex *creature* to knowe what was boþe.
B.17.219 To alle vnkynde *creatures* þat coueite to destruye
B.17.253 To alle vnkynde *creatures*; crist hymself witnesseþ:
B.17.306 Any *creature* [be] coupable afore a kynges Iustice
B.18.119 A comely *creature* [and a clene]; truþe she highte.
B.18.129 Of any kynnes *creature*, conceyued þoruȝ speche
B.19.17   That alle kynne *creatures* sholden knelen and bowen
B.19.216 To alle kynne *creatures* þat [k]an hi[se] fyue wittes,
B.19.372 Ther nas no cristene *creature* þat kynde wit hadde
B.20.151 And kille a[l] erþely *creatur[e]* saue conscience oone.
C. 1.105 Made knyghtes in his Couert *creatures* tene,
C. 6.294 Thow art an vnkynde *creature*; y can the nat assoile
C.10.213 Caym þe corsede *creature* conseyued was in synne
C.12.78 For an vncristene *creature*; [clerkes] woet þe sothe
C.13.133 To knowe by vch a *creature* kynde to louye.
C.13.207 For is no *creature* vnder Crist þat can hymsulue make
C.13.208 And if *creatures* cristene couth make hemsulue
C.14.5   And conseyled the for cristes sake no *creature* to bygile,
C.14.43 Forthy y conseile vch a *creature* clergie to honoure
C.14.64 Forthy y conseyle all *creatures* no cler[gie] to despice
C.14.157 How *creatures* han kynde wit and how clerkes come to bokes
C.14.159 Was neuere *creature* vnder crist þat knewe wel þe bygynnyng
C.15.223 Vch a kyne *creature* þat on crist leueth.
C.15.271 Amonges cristene *creatures*, yf cristes wordes be trewe:
C.16.166 And yf thow be cristes *creature*, for cristes loue telle me.'
C.16.167 'Y am cristes *creature*,' quod he, 'and cristene in mony a place
C.16.172 That vch a *creature* þat loueth crist welcometh me faire.'
C.16.215 That eny *creature* sholde conne al excepte crist one.
C.17.153 Hit is kyndly thyng *creature* his creatour to honoure,
C.18.93 And þe clennest *creature* furste creat[our] knowe.
C.19.185 To alle vnkynde *creatures* þat coueyten to destruye
C.19.219 To alle vnkynde *creatures*, as Crist hymsulue witnesseth:
C.19.286 Eny *creature* be coupable bifore a kynges iustice
C.20.122 A comely *creature* and a clene; Treuthe she highte.
C.20.132 Of eny kyn[nes] *creature*, conceyued thorw speche
C.21.17   T[hat] alle kyn *creatures* sholde knelen and bowen
C.21.216 To alle kyne *creatures* þat can his fyue wittes,
C.21.372 Ther ne was cristene *creature* that kynde wit hadde
C.22.151 And culle all erthely *creature* saue Consience one.

creaunt adj *creaunt adj.* B 2; C 2 creaunt (1) cryant (1)

B.12.193 Was for he yald hym *creaunt* to crist & knewliched hym gilty,
B.12.214 A[c] why þat oon þeef on þe cros *creaunt* hym yald
C.14.132 Was for A ȝeld hym *creaunt* to crist and his grace askede.
C.14.153 Ac why þat [on] theef vppon þe cros *cryant* hym ȝelde

crede n *crede n.(2)* A 1; B 1; C 3

A. 7.81   Til I come to his acountes as my *crede* techiþ–
B. 6.89   Til I come to hise acountes as my [*crede*] me [techeþ]–
C. 3.360 And lyue as oure *crede* vs kenneth with crist withouten ende.
C. 8.98   Til y come til his acountes as my *crede* telleth,
C.17.293 Ac we cristene conneth þe [*crede*] and haen of oure tonge

creme n *creme n.(2)* A 1 crem; B 1; C 2 craym

A. 7.266 A fewe cruddis & *crem*, & [a]n [hauer] cake,
B. 6.282 A fewe cruddes and *creme* and [a cake of otes],
C. 8.304 A fewe croddes and *craym* and a cake of otes
C. 8.320 With *craym* and with croddes, with cresses and oþere erbes.

crepe v *crepen v.* A 3 crepe (1) crepte (1) crope (1); B 8 crepe (3) crepen (1) crepeþ (2) crope (1) cropen (1); C 6 crepe (4) crepeth (1) crope (1)

A. 1.170 Ȝe ben acumbrid wiþ coueitise, ȝe [conne] not out *crepe*;
A. 3.178 *Crope* into a caban for cold of þi nailes;
A.12.35 Clergie into a caban *crepte* anon after,
B.Pr.186 To c[r]acchen vs & al oure kynde þouȝ we *cropen* vnder benches;
B. 1.196 [Ye] ben acombred wiþ coueitise, [ye] konne noȝt [out *crepe*],
B. 3.191 *Crope* into a Cabane for cold of þi nayles;
B.13.18 [For alle] creatures þat *crepen* [or walken] of kynde ben engendred;
B.15.530 And *crepe* [in] amonges curatours, confessen ageyn þe lawe:
B.16.28 Coueitise comþ of þat wynd and *crepeþ* among þe leues
B.18.428 And *crepe[þ]* to þe cros on knees and kisse[þ] it for a Iuwel
B.20.44   "Boþe fox and fowel may fle to hole and *crepe*
C.Pr.203 To cracche vs and alle oure kynde thogh we *crope* vnder benches;
C. 1.191 And ben acombred with coueytise: thei can nouȝt [out *crepe*]
C.15.20 For alle a wisseth and ȝeueth wit þat walketh oþer *crepeth*.
C.17.280 And *crepe* in amonges curatours and confessen aȝeyn þe lawe:
C.20.471 And *crepe* to þe croes on knees and kusse hit for a iewel

---

C.22.44   "Bothe fox and foule may fle to hole and *crepe*

cresses > carse; *cryant* > creaunt

cryen v *crien v.* A 11 criede (4) crieþ (2) criȝe (2) criȝede (1) criȝen (1) criȝide (1); B 42 cride (5) cryden (1) crie (12) cried (2) cryed (1) cryede (1) cryen (1) crieþ (4); C 42 cryde (1) criden (1) crie (1) crye (12) cried (1) criede (6) cryede (16) crien (2) cryen (1) crieth (1)

A.Pr.104 Cookis & here knaues *crieþ* 'hote pyes, hote!
A. 1.77   Þanne I knelide on my knes & *criȝide* hire of grace;
A. 2.1   Ȝet knelide I on my knes & *criȝede* hire of grace,
A. 5.46   And lay longe er heo lokide, & 'lord mercy' *criede*,
A. 5.54   Lecchour seide 'allas!' & to oure lady *criede*
A. 5.88   Þanne I *criȝe* on my knes þat crist gyue hym sorewe
A. 5.215 And flattide it on his face & faste on him *criede*
A. 5.253 *Criede* vpward to crist & to his [clene] modir
A. 8.179 Forþi I counseil alle cristene [to] *criȝe* god mercy,
A.11.45 Ac þe carful may *criȝen* & carpe at þe ȝate,
A.12.13 And on clergie *crieþ* on cristes holy name
B.Pr.143 Thanne [comsed] al þe commune *crye* in vers of latyn
B.Pr.226 Cokes and hire knaues *cryden*, 'hote pies, hote!
B. 1.79   Thanne I [kneled] on my knees and *cried* hire of grace;
B. 2.1   YEt [kneled I] on my knees and *cried* hire of grace,
B. 5.63   And lay longe er she loked, and 'lord, mercy!' *cryde*,
B. 5.71   Lechour seide 'allas!' and [to] oure lady *cryde*
B. 5.108 Thanne I *crye* on my knees þat crist ȝyue h[y]m sorwe
B. 5.443 And flatte it on his face and faste on hym *crye*
B. 5.511 *Cride* vpward to Crist and to his clene moder
B. 7.201 Forþi I counseille alle cristene to *crie* god mercy,
B. 9.82   Sholde no cristene creature *cryen* at þe yate
B.10.59 Ac þe carefulle may *crie* and carpen at þe yate
B.11.70 Ac yet I *cryde* on my Confessour þat [so konnyng heeld hym]:
B.11.135 But if Contricion wol come and *crye* by his lyue
B.12.254 Thouȝ he *crye* to crist þanne wiþ kene wil, I leue
B.13.448 To *crie* a largesse bifore oure lord, youre good loos to shewe.
B.14.334 To couere my careyne', quod he, and *cride* mercy faste
B.15.254 Craueþ ne coueiteþ ne *crieþ* after moore:
B.15.279 Except þat Egidie after an hynde *cride*,
B.15.559 An Aungel men herden an heigh at Rome *crye*,
B.16.75 And Piers caste to þe crop and þanne comsed it to *crye*;
B.17.124 That craueþ it [or] coueiteþ it [and] *crieþ* þerafter.
B.17.245 So wole crist of his curteisie, and men *crye* hym mercy,
B.17.291 Innocence is next god and nyght and day it *crieþ*
B.17.301 Confesse me and *crye* his grace, [crist] þat al made,
B.18.15 Thanne was feiþ in a fenestre and *cryde* 'a! fili dauid!'
B.18.39 And al þe court on hym *cryde* 'crucifige!' sharpe.
B.18.87 Thanne fil þe knyȝt vpon knees and *cryde* [Iesu] mercy:
B.18.263 A vois loude in þat light to lucifer *crieþ*,
B.19.159 And lyues and lokynge and aloud *cride*
B.19.212 And *cride* wiþ Conscience, 'help vs, [crist], of grace!'
B.19.361 And *cryde* and comaundede alle cristene peple
B.20.76 And *crye* we to kynde þat he come and defende vs
B.20.78 And *crye* we [on] al þe comune þat þei come to vnitee
B.20.90 The lord þat lyued after lust þo aloud *cryde*
B.20.140 'Allas!' quod Conscience and *cryde*, 'wolde crist of his grace
B.20.165 For care Conscience þo *cryde* vpon Elde
B.20.201 And *cryde* to kynde: 'out of care me brynge!
B.20.228 Conscience *cryede*, 'help, Clergie or I falle
B.20.230 Freres herden hym *crye* and comen hym to helpe,
B.20.369 Til Contricion hadde clene foryeten to *crye* and to wepe
B.20.375 Conscience *cryed* eft [Clergie to helpe],
C.Pr.230 Cokes and here knaues *cryede*, 'hote pyes, hote!
C. 1.76   Thenne y knelede on my knees and *criede* here of grace
C. 2.1   And thenne y kneled [o]n my knees and *cried* here of grace,
C. 3.93   The whiche *crien* on here knees þat crist hem auenge
C. 4.157 And *cryede* to Consience, the kyng myhte hit here:
C. 4.164 A shyreues Clerk *cryede*, 'a! capias mede
C. 6.4   And [lay] long ar he lokede and 'lord, mercy!' *cryede*
C. 6.64   And *cryede* 'mea culpa', corsynge alle his enemyes;
C. 6.140 And thenne y *crye* and crache with my kene nayles,
C. 6.170 Thenne seyde lecherye 'alas!' and to oure lady *cryede*,
C. 6.338 Confessen hem and *crye* hym mercy; shal neuere come in helle:
C. 7.57   And flatte hit on his face and faste on hym *cryede*
C. 7.108 To *crye* a largesse tofore oure lord ȝoure good loos to shewe.
C. 7.147 Yf we knowlechede and *cryde* Crist þerfore mercy:
C. 7.156 *Criede* vpward to Crist and to his clene moder
C. 9.347 Forthy y consayle alle cristene to *crye* god mercy
C.11.40 Ac þe carfole may *crye* and quake at þe ȝate,
C.12.70 Bote yf contricioun and confessioun *crye* by his lyue
C.13.13 That þe kynde [kyng] *criede* hym mercy
C.15.34 Craude and *cryede* for cristes loue of heuene
C.17.222 An angel men herde an hye at rome *crye*,
C.17.246 And *crie* to Crist a wolde his coluer sende

C.18.107 And Elde clemp to þe c[r]opward; thenne comsed hit to *crye*.
C.19.211 So wol Crist of his cortesye, and men *crien* hym mercy,
C.19.272 Innocence is next god and nyht and day hit *crieth*
C.19.281 Confesse me and *crye* his grace, god þat al made,
C.20.13   Thenne was faith in a fenestre and *criede* 'a! fil[i] dauid!'
C.20.38   And alle þe Court [on hym] *cryede* 'crucifige!' [sharpe].
C.20.89   Tho ful the knyhte vppon knees and *criede* iesu mercy:
C.21.159 And lyues and lokynge and aloude *criede*
C.21.212 And *criden* with Consience, 'helpe vs, [Crist], of grace!'
C.21.361 And *cryede* and comaundede alle cristene peple
C.22.76   And *crye* we to kynde þat he come and defende vs
C.22.78   And *crye* we on al þe comune þat thei come to vnite
C.22.90   The lord þat lyuede aftur lust tho aloud *cryede*
C.22.140 'Allas!' quod Consience and *cryede*, 'wolde crist of his grace
C.22.165 For care Consience tho *cryede* vpon elde
C.22.201 And *cryede* to kynde: 'out of care me brynge!
C.22.228 Consience *cryede*, 'helpe, Clergie, or y falle
C.22.230 Freres herde hym *crye* and comen hym to helpe
C.22.369 Til Contricioun hadde clene forʒete to *crye* and to wepe
C.22.375 Consience *cryede* efte clergie [to] helpe

criket n *criket n.* B 1; C 1 Cryket
B.14.42   Fissh to lyue in þe flood and in þe fir þe *Criket*,
C.15.241 The *Cryket* by kynde of þe fuyr and corleu by þe wynde,

crisostomus > iohannes_crisostomus

crist n prop *Crist n.* A 36 crist (33) cristes (1) cristis (2); B 146 crist (116) cristes (30); C 140 crist (117) cristes (20) cristis (3)
A. 1.79   And ek kenne me kyndely on *crist* to beleue,
A. 1.103 And *crist*, king[ene] kin[g], kniʒtide tene,
A. 2.154 'Be *crist*,' quaþ þe king, '& I miʒte cacche
A. 3.109 Quaþ consience to þe kyng, '*crist* it [me] forbede!
A. 3.215 Quaþ þe kyng to consience, 'be *crist*, as me þinkiþ,
A. 3.251 And for he kilde not þe king as *crist* [him] bode sente,
A. 4.4   'Nay be [*Crist*],' quaþ consience, 'cunge me raþere!
A. 4.11   And counte wiþ [þe] consience, so me *crist* helpe,
A. 4.70   Þe king swor be *crist* & be his croune boþe
A. 4.144 Þe king acordite, be *crist*, to resonis sawis
A. 5.88   Þanne I criʒe on my knes þat *crist* gyue hym sorewe
A. 5.236 '*Crist*, þat on caluarie vpon þe [cros] diʒedist,
A. 5.247 And knowelechide his [coupe] to *crist* ʒet eftsones,
A. 5.253 Criede vpward to *crist* & to his [clene] modir
A. 6.49   Til ʒe come into consience þat *crist* wyte þe soþe,
A. 6.115 'Be *crist*,' quaþ a cuttepurs, 'I haue no kyn þere.'
A. 7.23   'Be *crist*,' quaþ a kniʒt þo, 'þou [kenn]ist vs þe beste;
A. 7.206 Counforte hem wiþ þi catel for *cristis* loue of heuene;
A. 7.233 Actif lif oþer contemplatif; *crist* wolde it alse.
A. 7.269 Ne no cokenay, be *crist*, colopis to maken.
A. 8.172 And come [alle] before *crist* acountes to ʒelden,
A. 9.50   I bekenne [ʒow] *crist* þat on þe crois deiʒede.'
A.10.151 Alle þat comen of þat caym *crist* hatid aftir,
A.10.156 And alle þat couplide hem with þat kyn *crist* hatide [dedliche].
A.10.186 It is an vncomely copil, be *crist*, as [me þinkeþ],
A.11.38   Ac ʒif þei carpen of *crist*, þise clerkis & þise lewid,
A.11.165 I bekenne þe *crist*,' quaþ she, 'I can teche þe no betere.'
A.11.222 How *crist* counseilliþ þe comune & kenneþ hem þis tale:
A.11.232 'Contra,' quaþ I, 'be *crist*! þat kan I þe wi[þsigg]e,
A.11.246 Alle kynne creatures þat to *crist* be[n] l[yche]
A.11.273 For alle cunnyng clerkis siþþe *crist* ʒede on erþe
A.11.281 And for he kneuʒ on þe crois & to *crist* shr[o]f hym,
A.11.294 Þat clergie of *cristis* mouþ comendite [was hit] neuere,
A.12.1   '*Crist* wot,' quod clergie, 'knowe hit ʒif þe lyke,
A.12.13   And on clergie crieþ on *cristes* holy name
A.12.105 And is closed vnder clom, *crist* haue his soule.
B.Pr.88   That han cure vnder *crist*, and crownynge in tokene
B.Pr.99   Lest *crist* in Consistorie acorse ful manye.
B.Pr.105 There [*crist* is in] kyngdom, to close and to shette,
B.Pr.125 '*Crist* kepe þee, sire kyng, and þi kyngryche,
B. 1.81   And [ek] kenne me kyndely on *crist* to bileue,
B. 1.105 [And] *crist*, kyngene kyng, knyʒted ten,
B. 2.50   Now I bikenne þee *crist*', quod she, 'and his clene moder,
B. 2.193 'By *crist*!' quod þe kyng, 'and I cacche myʒte
B. 3.120 Quod Conscience to þe kyng, '*crist* it me forbede!
B. 3.228 Quod þe kyng to Conscience, 'by *crist*, as me þynkeþ,
B. 4.4   'Nay, by *crist*!' quod Conscience; 'congeye me [raþer]!
B. 4.11   And acounte wiþ þee, Conscience, so me *crist* helpe,
B. 4.41   For Conscience know[e þei] noʒt, ne *crist*, as I trowe.'
B. 4.83   The kyng swor by *crist* and by his crowne boþe
B. 4.104 'Nay,' quod þe kyng, 'so me *crist* helpe,
B. 5.108 Thanne I crye on my knees þat *crist* ʒyue h[y]m sorwe
B. 5.165 Hadde þei had knyues, by *crist*! eiþer hadde kild ooþer.
B. 5.464 '*Crist*, þat on Caluarie vpon þe cros deidest,
B. 5.473 And knoweliched his [coupe] to *crist* yet eftsoones,

B. 5.511 Cride vpward to *Crist* and to his clene moder
B. 5.562 Til ye come into Conscience þat *crist* wite þe soþe,
B. 5.630 'By *Crist*!' quod a kuttepurs, 'I haue no kyn þere.'
B. 5.641 'By *crist*!' quod a comune womman, 'þi compaignie wol I folwe.
B. 6.21   'By *crist*!' quod a knyʒt þoo, '[þow] kenne[st] vs þe beste,
B. 6.220 Conforte h[e]m wiþ þi catel for *cristes* loue of heuene;
B. 6.249 Contemplatif lif or Actif lif; *crist* wolde [it als].
B. 6.285 Ne no cokeney, by *crist*! coloppes to maken.
B. 7.194 And comen alle [bi]fore *crist* acountes to yelde,
B. 8.59   'I bikenne þee *crist*', quod he, 'þat on [þe] cros deyde.'
B. 9.89   Whi [ne wol] we cristene of *cristes* good be as kynde?
B. 9.164 "I am via & veritas", seiþ *crist*, "I may auaunce alle."
B. 9.165 It is an vncomly couple, by *crist*! as me þynkeþ.
B.10.52   Ac if þei carpen of *crist*, þise clerkes and þise lewed,
B.10.105 Carpen as þei clerkes were of *crist* and of hise myʒtes,
B.10.113 "Of þat [ye] clerkes vs kenneþ of *crist* by þe gospel:
B.10.252 And *Crist* cleped hymself so, þe [scripture] bereþ witnesse:
B.10.253 Alle þe clerkes vnder *crist* ne koude þis assoille
B.10.349 'Contra!' quod I, 'by *crist*! þat kan I [wiþseye],
B.10.358 For þat *crist* for cristene men deide, and conformed þe lawe
B.10.359 That whoso wolde and wilneþ wiþ *crist* to arise,
B.10.416 That ben Carpenters holy kirk to make for *cristes* owene beestes:
B.10.422 And for he bekne[w on] þe cros and to *crist* shrof hym,
B.10.449 That] Clergie of *cristes* mouþ comended was it [neuere],
B.10.480 As clerkes of holy [k]ir[k]e þat kepen *cristes* tresor,
B.11.119 For *crist* cleped vs alle, come if we wolde,
B.11.144 That al þe clergie vnder *crist* ne myʒte me cracche fro helle,
B.11.185 [For] oure Ioye and oure [Iuel], Iesu *crist* of heuene,
B.11.199 For alle are we *cristes* creatures and of his cofres riche,
B.11.201 For [at] Caluarie of *cristes* blood cristendom gan sprynge,
B.11.217 *Crist* to a commune womman seide, in [comen] at a feste,
B.11.235 Cleophas ne knew hym noʒt þat he *crist* were,
B.11.248 Iesu *crist* on a Iewes doʒter liʒte, gentil womman þouʒ she were,
B.11.266 Of which *crist* is a kernell to conforte þe soule.
B.11.389 For is no creature vnder *crist* can formen hymseluen,
B.12.71   And namely Clergie for *cristes* loue, þat of Clergie is roote.
B.12.77   Ac ʒif of his curteisie þoruʒ clergie hir saued.
B.12.78   [For] þoruʒ caractes þat *crist* wroot þe Iewes knewe hemselue
B.12.82   Holy kirke knoweþ þis þat *cristes* writyng saued;
B.12.88   As *cristes* caracte[s] confortede, and boþe coupable shewed
B.12.92   Forþi I counseille þee for *cristes* sake clergie þat þow louye,
B.12.109 Which is þe cofre of *cristes* tresor, and clerkes kepe þe keyes
B.12.126 For Clergie is kepere vnder *crist* of heuene,
B.12.138 A[s] to þe clergie of *crist* counted it but a trufle:
B.12.193 Was for he yald hym creaunt to *crist* & knewliched hym gilty,
B.12.216 Alle þe clerkes vnder *crist* ne kouþe þe skile assoille:
B.12.254 Thouʒ he crye to *crist* þanne wiþ kene wil, I leue
B.12.277 'Alle þise clerkes', quod I þo, "þat [o]n *crist* leuen
B.12.279 Ne no creature of *cristes* liknesse withouten cristendom worþ
          saued.'
B.13.22   And as *crist* wolde þer com Conscience to conforte me þat tyme
B.13.77   And what meschief and maleese *crist* for man þolede,
B.13.135 That no clerk ne kan, as *crist* bereþ witnesse:
B.13.188 'Nay, by *crist*!' quod Conscience to Clergie, 'god þee foryelde';
B.13.271 I took [greet] kepe, by *crist*! and Conscience boþe,
B.13.313 'By *Crist*!' quod Conscience þo, 'þi beste cote, Haukyn,
B.13.338 And seye þat no clerc ne kan, ne *crist* as I leue,
B.13.416 Whan men carpen of *crist* or clennesse of soul[e]
B.14.12   And kouþe I neuere, by *crist*! kepen it clene an houre
B.14.72   Amonges cristene creatures, if *cristes* wordes ben trewe.
B.14.147 *Crist* of his curteisie shal conforte yow at þe laste,
B.14.151 ʒyueþ mede aboue his couenaunt, riʒt so *crist* ʒyueþ heuene
B.14.179 Conforte þi carefulle, *crist*, in þi rich[e],
B.14.181 Thus in genere of gentries Iesu *crist* seide,
B.14.300 A collateral confort, *cristes* owene ʒifte:
B.15.15   If he were *cristes* creature [for *cristes* loue] me to tellen.
B.15.15   If he were *cristes* creature [for *cristes* loue] me to tellen.
B.15.16   'I am *cristes* creature', quod he, 'and [of his kyn a party],
B.15.17   In *cristes* court yknowe wel and of [cristene in many a place].
B.15.22   'What are ye called', quod I, 'in þat court among *cristes* peple?'
B.15.53   That any creature sholde konne al except *crist* oone.
B.15.68   Ayein *cristes* counseil and alle clerkes techynge,
B.15.104 And be kynde as bifel for clerkes and curteise of *cristes* goodes,
B.15.161 Clerkes kenne me þat *crist* is in alle places
B.15.195 'By *crist*! I wolde I knewe hym', quod I, 'no creature leuere.'
B.15.219 And is compaignable and confortatif as *crist* bit hymselue:
B.15.242 And þat Conscience and *crist* haþ yknyt faste,
B.15.246 And *cristes* patrymonye to þe poore parcelmele dele;
B.15.301 And if þei kouþe han ycarped, by *crist*! as I trowe,
B.15.431 *Crist* calleþ hem salt for cristene soules,
B.15.447 To *crist* and to cristendom and cros to honoure,
B.15.457 Til it be cristned in *cristes* name and confermed of þe bisshop
B.15.491 What pope or prelat now parfourneþ þat *crist* highte,

B.15.495 That þei ne wente as *crist* wisseþ, siþen þei wille haue name,
B.15.499 For cristene and vncristene *crist* seide to prechours
B.15.524 Amonges vnkynde cristene for *cristes* loue he deyede,
B.15.531 Many man for *cristes* loue was martired [amonges] Romayne[s]
B.15.541 Than *cristes* cros þat ouercam deeþ and dedly synne.
B.15.569 That contrarien *cristes* lawe and cristendom dispise.
B.15.587 And ȝit knewe þei *crist* þat cristendom tauȝte,
B.16.164 On cros vpon Caluarie *crist* tooke þe bataille
B.16.199 And *Crist* and cristendom and cristene holy chirche.
B.16.222 And is noȝt but gendre of a generacion bifore Iesu *crist* in heuene:
B.16.265 Til he come þat I carpe of; *crist* is his name
B.17.6 And þat is cros and cristendom and *crist* þeron to honge;
B.17.245 So wole *crist* of his curteisie, and men crye hym mercy,
B.17.253 To alle vnkynde creatures; *crist* hymself witnesseþ:
B.17.288 For coueitise of any kynnes þyng þat *crist* deere bouȝte.
B.17.301 Confesse me and crye hym grace, [*crist*] þat al made,
B.17.331 Cogheþ and curseþ þat *crist* gyue h[y]m sorwe
B.18.9 And of *cristes* passion and penaunce, þe peple þat ofrauȝte.
B.18.24 That *crist* be noȝt [y]knowe here for consummatus deus
B.18.55 If þow be *crist* and kynges sone com down of þe roode:
B.18.57 'Consummatum est', quod *crist* and comsede for to swoune.
B.18.72 Vpon a croos bisides *crist*; so was þe comune lawe.
B.18.109 Whan *crist* cam hir kyngdom þe crowne sholde [lese]:
B.18.320 That *crist* may come In, þe kynges sone of heuene!'
B.19.14 Is *crist* wiþ his cros, conquerour of cristene.'
B.19.15 'Why calle [ye] hym *crist*, siþen Iewes calle[d] hym Iesus?
B.19.23 And ye callen hym *crist*; for what cause, telleþ me.
B.19.24 Is *crist* moore of myȝt and moore worþi name
B.19.62 He may [be wel] called conquerour, and þat is *crist* to mene:
B.19.69 Ac to carpe moore of *crist* and how he com to þat name,
B.19.113 And *crist* counseileþ þus and comaundeþ boþe,
B.19.117 And þanne was he [cleped and] called noȝt [oonly] *crist* but Iesu,
B.19.161 Thus cam it out þat *crist* ouercoom, recouerede and lyuede:
B.19.168 *Crist* cam In, and al closed boþe dore and yates,
B.19.176 *Crist* carpede þanne and curteisliche seide,
B.19.199 Thus Conscience of *crist* and of þe cros carpede
B.19.207 Quod Conscience and knelede, 'þis is *cristes* messager
B.19.212 And cride wiþ Conscience, 'help vs, [*crist*], of grace!'
B.19.220 And acombre þee, Conscience, but if *crist* þee helpe.
B.19.322 That *crist* vpon Caluarie for mankynde on pyned.
B.19.398 Ne after Conscience, by *crist*! while I kan selle
B.19.449 And *crist* of his curteisie þe Cardinals saue
B.20.140 'Allas!' quod Conscience and cryde, 'wolde *crist* of his grace
B.20.268 Forþi', quod Conscience, 'by *crist*! kynde wit me telleþ
B.20.380 'By *crist*!' quod Conscience þo, 'I wole bicome a pilgrym,
C.Pr.86 That han cure vnder *crist* and crownyng in tokene
C.Pr.127 Lest *crist* in constorie acorse of [ȝow] manye.
C.Pr.133 Thare *Crist* is in kynedom to close with heuene.
C.Pr.149 '*Crist* kepe þe, [sire] kynge, and thy kyneriche
C.1.78 And also kenne me kyndly on *crist* to bileue.
C.1.122 Euene þe contrarie sitteth *Crist*, Clerkes wyteth þe sothe:
C.2.53 For y bykenne the *crist*,' quod she, 'and his clene moder,
C.2.207 'Now, by *crist*!' quod þe kyng, 'and y cacche myhte
C.2.249 And sayde, 'syre kyng, by *crist*! but clerkes amende,
C.3.93 The whiche crien on here knees þat *crist* hem auenge,
C.3.157 Quod Consience to the kyng, '*Crist* hit me forbede!
C.3.284 Quod þe kyng to Consience, 'by *crist*, as me thynketh,
C.3.356 He acordeth with *crist* in kynde, verbum caro factum est;
C.3.360 And lyue as oure crede vs kenneth with *crist* withouten ende.
C.4.4 'Nay, by *Crist*!' quod Consience, 'congeie me [rather]!
C.4.11 And acounte with the, Consience, so me *Crist* helpe,
C.4.79 The kyng [s]wor by *Crist* and by his croune borde
C.4.99 'Nay, by *crist*!' quod þe kyng, 'for Consiences sake
C.5.60 And in quoer and in kyrkes *Cristes* mynistres:
C.5.61 Hit bycometh for clerkes *Crist* for to serue,
C.5.83 For in my Consience y knowe what *Crist* w[o]lde y wrouhte.
C.5.89 Quod Consience, 'by *Crist*, y can nat se this lyeth;
C.6.76 Aȝeyn þe consayl of *Crist*, as clerkes fyndeth in bokes:
C.6.82 And segge þat no clerk ne can, ne *Crist* as y leue,
C.6.318 '*Crist*, þat on Caluarie on þe crosse deyedest
C.6.327 And knolechede [his coupe to *Crist*] ȝut eftsones.
C.7.76 When me carpeth of *Crist* or clannesse of soule
C.7.147 Yf we knowlechede and cryde *Crist* þerfore mercy:
C.7.156 Criede vpward to *Crist* and to his clene moder
C.7.283 'By *Crist*!' quod a cottepors, 'y haue no kyn there.'
C.7.305 [Quod contemplacion, 'by *Crist*, thow y care soffre],
C.8.19 'By *Crist*!' quod a knyhte tho, 'a kenneth vs þe beste
C.8.21 Y wolde y couthe,' quod the knyhte, 'by *Crist* and his moder!
C.8.167 'Now, by *Crist*!' quod [Peres] the [plouhman], 'y shal apayre ȝow alle,'
C.8.263 'By *Crist*!' quod [Peres] þe [plouhman] tho, 'this prouerbis [wol y] shewe
C.8.307 Ne no cokeney, be *Crist*! colloppes to make.

C.9.214 Kyndeliche, by *Crist*, ben suche ycald lollares.
C.9.240 Acounted byfore [*crist*] but Consience excuse hym.
C.9.340 And comen alle bifore *Crist* acountes to ȝelde,
C.10.58 'Y bykenne the *Crist*,' quod he, 'þat on þe cross deyede.'
C.10.108 'Ac ȝut sauereth [me nat] thy sawes, so me *Crist* spede!
C.10.194 The catel that *Crist* hadde, thre clothes hit were;
C.11.31 Or of þe passioun of *Crist* or of purgatorie þe peynes,
C.11.139 'By *Crist*,' quod Clergie, 'yf thow coueyte dowel
C.11.154 Alle þe Clerkes vnder *Crist* ne couthe this assoile
C.11.247 That [ben] carpentares vnder *Crist* holy kirke to make
C.11.254 And for he biknewe on þe croes and to *crist* shrof hym
C.11.274 For clergie of *cristes* mouthe com[e]nded was euere.
C.11.275 For *Crist* saide to sayntes and to suche as he louede,
C.12.54 For *crist* clepede vs alle, come yf we wolde,
C.12.79 That al þe cristendoem vnde[r] *Crist* ne myhte me crache fro [helle]
C.12.98 And *cristis* oune clergie; he cam fro heuene to teche hit
C.12.109 A[t] Caluarie of *cristis* bloed cristendoem gan sprynge
C.12.124 Cleophas ne knewe hym nat þat he *Crist* were
C.12.161 *Crist* acordeth efte herwith; clerkes wyteth þe sothe,
C.12.168 ȝut conseileth *Crist* in commen vs al:
C.12.205 For *crist* saide [so] to seyntes þat for his sake tholeden
C.13.67 Aren alle acountable to *crist* and to þe kyng of heuene,
C.13.78 As *Crist* hymsulf comaundeth alle cristene peple:
C.13.207 For is no creature vnder *Crist* þat can hymsulue make
C.14.5 And conseyled the for *cristes* sake no creature to bygile,
C.14.35 And ȝut is clergie to comende for *cristes* loue more
C.14.38 Lawe of loue oure lord wrouht] long ar *crist* were.
C.14.39 And *crist* cam and confermede and holy kyrke made
C.14.54 Whiche [is the] coffre of *cristis* tresor, and clerkes kepeth þe keyes
C.14.70 For clergy is *cristes* vycary to conforte and to cure;
C.14.83 As to þe clergie of *crist* thei counted hit but a tryfle:
C.14.90 Ne in no cote he Caytyfs hous [*crist* was ybore
C.14.132 Was for *a* ȝeld hym creaunt to *crist* and his grace askede:
C.14.155 Alle þe Clerkes vnder *Crist* ne couthe [þe skyle] assoile.
C.14.159 Was neuere creature vnder *crist* þat knewe wel þe bygynnyng
C.14.199 'Alle thise clerkes,' quod y tho, 'þat [o]n *crist* leuen
C.15.34 Crauede and cryede for *cristes* loue of heuene
C.15.83 And what meschief and maleese *crist* for man tholede.
C.15.128 'Haue me excused,' quod Clergie, 'be *crist*, but in scole.
C.15.177 'By *Crist*!' quod Consience, 'clergie, y wol nat lye;
C.15.182 Forthy,' quod Concience, 'crist y þe byteche;
C.15.223 Vch a kyne creature þat on *crist* leueth.
C.15.271 Amonges cristene creatures, yf *cristes* wordes be trewe:
C.16.113 The whiche is syb to *crist* [hym]sulue and semblable bothe.'
C.16.136 A collateral confort, *cristes* oune sonde:
C.16.166 And yf thow be *cristes* creature, for cristes loue telle me.'
C.16.166 And yf thow be *cristes* creature, for *cristes* loue telle me.'
C.16.167 'Y am *cristes* creature,' quod he, 'and cristene in mony a place
C.16.168 And in *cristes* court yknowe wel and of his kynne a party.
C.16.172 That vch a creature þat loueth *crist* welcometh me faire.'
C.16.215 That eny creature sholde conne al excepte *crist* one.
C.16.241 Aȝen þe consayl of *crist*, as holy clergie witnesseth:
C.16.292 I knewe neuere, by *Crist*, clerk noþer lewed
C.16.326 Clotheth hem and conforteth hem and of *Crist* precheth hem,
C.16.337 'Were y with hym by *Cr[i]st*,' quod y, 'y wolde neuere fro hym
C.17.62 Helpe thy kyn, *Crist* bid, for þer [coms]eth charite
C.17.69 Y dar nat carpe of clerkes now þat *cristes* [tresor] kepe
C.17.81 That god coueyteth nat þe coyne þat *crist* hymsulue printede
C.17.186 Sholden conuerte hem to *Crist* and cristendoem to take.
C.17.203 Thenne *cristes* cros þat ouercome deth and dedly synne.
C.17.228 Yf the kynges coueyte in *cristes* pees to lyuene
C.17.246 And crie to *Crist* a wolde his coluer sende
C.17.251 That contra[r]ryen now *cristes* law[e] and cristendoem dispisen.
C.17.281 Many man for *cristes* loue was martired amonges Romaynes
C.17.290 So is þe kynde of a curatour for *criste[s]* loue to preche
C.17.298 And ȝut knewe they *crist* þat cristendoem tauhte
C.18.14 The whiche is Caritas ykald, *Cristes* oune fode,
C.18.155 'Vnkynde and vnkunnynge!' quod *Crist*, and with a roep smeot hem
C.18.208 And *Crist* and cristendoem and cristene holy churche.
C.18.281 Til he come þat y carpe of; *Crist* is his name
C.19.8 The which is Cr[oes] and cristendoem and *cr[ist]* þer[o]n [to] hang[e];
C.19.211 So wol *Crist* of his cortesye, and men crien hym mercy,
C.19.219 To alle vnkynde creatures, as *Crist* hymsulue witnesseth:
C.19.269 For coueytise of eny kyne thynge þat *Crist* dere bouhte.
C.19.311 Coueth and corseth þat *Crist* ȝeue hym sorwe
C.20.23 That *Crist* be nat yknowe for consumm[a]tus deus
C.20.55 And 'yf thow be *Crist* and [kynges] sone come adoun of th[e] rode,
C.20.57 'Consummatum est,' quod *Crist* and comsed for to swoene.
C.20.74 Vppon cros bisyde *Crist*; so was þe comune lawe.

C.20.112 When *Crist* thorw croos ouercam зoure kyndoem sholde tocleue:
C.20.189 And þat *Crist* hath conuerted the kynde of rihtwisnesse
C.20.363 That *Crist* may come in, the kynges sone of h[e]uene!'
C.21.14 Is *Crist* with his croes, conquerour of Cristene.'
C.21.15 'Whi calle зe hym *Crist* sennes iewes callede hym iesus?
C.21.23 And зe callen hym *Crist*; for what cause, telleth me.
C.21.24 Is *Crist* more of myhte and more worth[y] name
C.21.62 He may be wel called conquerour and þat is *Crist* to mene.
C.21.69 Ac to carpe more of *Crist* and how he cam to þat name;
C.21.113 And *Crist* consayleth [þu]s and comaundeth bothe,
C.21.117 And tho was he cleped and calde not [onl]y *Crist* but iesu,
C.21.161 Thus cam hit out þat *Crist* ouerkam, rekeuerede and lyuede:
C.21.168 *Crist* cam in, and al closed bothe dore and зates,
C.21.176 *Crist* Carpede thenne and cortey[s]liche saide,
C.21.199 Thus Consience of *Crist* and of þe cros carpede
C.21.207 Quod Consience and knelede, 'this is *Cristes* messager
C.21.212 And criden with Consience, 'helpe vs, [*Crist*], of grace!'
C.21.220 And acombre þe, Consience, bote yf *Crist* the helpe.
C.21.322 That *Crist* vpon Caluary for mankynde on peyned.
C.21.398 Ne aftur Consience, bi *Crist*! [while] y c[an] sulle
C.21.449 And *Crist* of his cortesye þe cardinals saue
C.22.140 'Allas!' quod Consience and cryede, 'wolde *crist* of his grace
C.22.268 For[thy],' quod Consience, 'bi *Crist*! kynde wit me telleth
C.22.380 'By *Crist*!' quod Consience tho, 'y wol bicome a pilgrime

cristen adj *Cristen adj.& n.* A 12 cristene; B 60 cristen (6) cristene (53)
cristne (1); C 51 cristene
A. 1.91 For *cristene* & vncristene cleymeþ it ichone.
A. 1.166 Vnkynde to here kyn & ek to alle *cristene*,
A. 3.265 And o *cristene* king kepe vs ichone.
A. 7.87 And monewe me in his memorie among alle *cristene*.
A. 8.179 Forþi I counseil alle *cristene* [to] criзe god mercy,
A.10.197 Forþi I counseile alle *cristene* coueite not be weddit
A.11.239 Haue eritage in heuene as an heiз *cristene*.
A.11.240 Ac *cristene* men, god wot, comiþ not so to heuene,
A.11.241 For *cristene* han a degre & is þe comun speche:
A.11.250 þat is, iche *cristene* [creature] be kynde to oþer,
A.11.290 *Cristene* kynde to kille to deþe?
A.12.110 Now alle kenne creatures þat *cristene* were euere
B. 1.93 For *cristen* and vncristen cleymeþ it echone.
B. 1.192 Vnkynde to hire kyn and to alle *cristene*,
B. 3.289 And oon *cristene* kyng kepen [vs echone].
B. 6.95 And mengen [me] in his memorie amonges alle *cristene*.
B. 7.201 Forþi I counseille alle *cristene* to crie god mercy,
B. 9.82 Sholde no *cristene* creature cryen at þe yate
B. 9.86 Allas þat a *cristene* creature shal be vnkynde til anoþer!
B. 9.89 Whi [ne wol] we *cristene* of cristes good be as kynde?
B. 9.176 Forþi I counseille alle *cristene* coueite noзt be wedded
B.10.356 Haue heritage [in] heuene as [an heiз] *cristene*.
B.10.357 Ac *cristene* men wiþoute moore maye noзt come to heuene,
B.10.358 For þat crist for *cristene* men deide, and confermed þe lawe
B.10.362 And after alle *cristene* creatures, in commune ech man ooþer;
B.10.368 For euery *cristene* creature sholde be kynde til ooþer,
B.10.431 *Cristene* kynde to kille to deþe?
B.11.123 'Thanne may alle *cristene* come', quod I, 'and cleyme þere entree
B.11.125 For þouз a *cristen* man coueited his cristendom to reneye,
B.11.225 I conseille alle *cristne* clyue noзt þeron to soore,
B.12.158 Than clerkes or kynde witted men of *cristene* peple.
B.13.175 Ne bitwene two *cristene* kynges kan no wiзt pees make
B.13.258 Ne mannes masse make pees among *cristene* peple.
B.14.72 Amonges *cristene* creatures, if cristes wordes ben trewe.
B.14.73 Ac vnkyndenesse caristiam makeþ amonges *cristen* peple,
B.14.201 Forþi *cristene* sholde be in commune riche, noon coueitous for
hymselue.
B.15.17 In cristes court yknowe wel and of [*cristene* in many a place].
B.15.90 Ac of curatours of *cristen* peple, as clerkes bereþ witnesse,
B.15.258 Amonges *cristene* men þis myldenesse sholde laste
B.15.344 Forþi I counseille alle *cristene* to conformen hem to charite,
B.15.396 *Cristene* and vncristene on oon god bileueþ].
B.15.399 This Makometh was *cristene* [man], and for he moste noзt ben
pope
B.15.413 Thoruз a *cristene* clerk acorsed in his soule–
B.15.431 Crist calleþ hem salt for *cristene* soules,
B.15.499 For *cristene* and vncristene crist seide to prechours
B.15.524 Amonges vnkynde *cristene* for cristes loue he deyede,
B.15.525 And for þe riзt of al þis reume and alle reumes *cristene*.
B.15.579 Ac we *cristene* creatures þat on þe cros bileuen
B.15.609 Prelates of *cristene* prouinces sholde preue if þei myзte
B.16.199 And Crist and cristendom and *cristene* holy chirche
B.17.214 That alle kynne *cristene* clenseþ of synnes.
B.17.277 Vnkynde *cristene* men, for coueitise and enuye
B.19.14 Is crist wiþ his cros, conquerour of *cristene*.'
B.19.38 And þo þat bicome *cristene* bi counseil of þe baptis[t]e
B.19.249 In pouerte and in [pacience] to preie alle *cristene*

B.19.337 Conscience and alle *cristene* and Cardinale vertues,
B.19.341 Thise two coome to Conscience and to *cristen* peple
B.19.348 That Conscience shal noзt knowe who is *cristene* or heþene,
B.19.355 Quod Conscience to alle *cristene* þo, 'my counseil is to wende
B.19.361 And cryde and comaundede alle *cristene* peple
B.19.364 Conscience comaundede þo alle *cristene* to delue,
B.19.367 Thanne alle kynne *cristene* saue comune wommen
B.19.372 Ther nas no *cristene* creature þat kynde wit hadde
B.19.383 'Comeþ', quod Conscience, 'ye *cristene*, and dyneþ,
B.19.427 Emperour of al þe world, þat alle men were *cristene*.
B.19.443 And cleymeþ bifore þe kyng to be kepere ouer *cristene*,
B.19.444 And counteþ noзt þouз *cristene* ben killed and robbed,
B.19.445 And fynt folk to fiзte and *cristen* blood to spille
B.20.73 Ouer kynde *cristene* and Cardynale vertues.
B.20.108 Leue pride pryuely and be parfite *cristene*.
B.20.141 That Coueitise were *cristene* þat is so kene [to fiзte],
B.20.214 And þere was Conscience Conestable, *cristene* to saue,
C. 1.89 For *cristene* and vncristene claymeth it echone.
C. 1.189 Vnkynde to here kyn and to alle *cristene*,
C. 3.442 And o *cristene* kyng kepe vs echone.
C. 5.193 Amonges alle kyne kynges ouer *cristene* peple.
C. 8.104 And men[g]e me in his memorie amongus alle *cristene*.
C. 9.347 Forthy y consayle alle *cristene* to crye god mercy,
C.10.278 Forthy y conseyle alle *cristene* coueyte neuere be wedded
C.11.243 Of holy kirke þat sholde kepe alle *cristene* soules
C.11.267 *Cristene* [kynde] to culle to dethe?
C.12.58 'Thenne may alle *cristene* come,' [quod y], 'and clayme þer entre
C.12.60 For thogh a *cristene* man coueitede his cristendom to renoye
C.12.151 The which is þe cornel of confort for alle *cristene* soules.
C.13.78 As Crist hymsulf comaundeth alle *cristene* peple:
C.13.90 Knowelecheth hym *cristene* and of holy kirke byleue,
C.13.208 And if creatures *cristene* couth make hemsulue
C.15.228 Ne mannes prayere maky pees amonges *cristene* peple
C.15.271 Amonges *cristene* creatures, yf cristes wordes be trewe:
C.16.42 Forthy *cristene* sholde be in comune ryche, noon coueytous for
hymsulue.
C.16.167 'Y am cristes creature,' quod he, 'and *cristene* in mony a place
C.17.50 And conforte alle *cristene* wolde holy [kirke] amende.
C.17.77 And so hit fareth by false *cristene*: here follynge is trewe,
C.17.128 Alle kyne *cristene* cleuynge on o will,
C.17.183 And seth oure saueour soffrede such a fals *cristene*
C.17.212 How tho corsede *cristene* catel and richesse worschipede;
C.17.234 That with moneye maynteyneth men [t]o werre vppon *cristene*
C.17.275 Amonges v[n]kynde *cristene* in holy [kirke] was slawe
C.17.293 Ac we *cristene* conneth þe [crede] and haen of oure tonge
C.18.208 And Crist and cristendom and *cristene* holy churche
C.19.180 That alle kyne *cristene* clanseth of synne[s].
C.19.258 Vnkynde *cristene* men, for coueytise and enuye
C.20.406 Bote of comune coppes, alle *cristene* soules;
C.21.14 Is Crist with his croes, conquerour of *Cristene*.'
C.21.38 And tho þat bycome *cristene* bi consail of þe baptist
C.21.249 In pouerte and in pacience to preye for alle *cristene*;
C.21.337 Consience and alle *cristene* and cardinale vertues,
C.21.341 Thise two cam to Consience and to *cristene* peple
C.21.348 That Consience shal nat knowe [ho is *cristene* or hethene]
C.21.355 Quod Consience to alle *cristene* tho, 'my consayl is [to] wende
C.21.361 And cryede and comaundede alle *cristene* peple
C.21.364 Consience comaundede t[h]o alle *cristene* to delue
C.21.367 Thenne alle kyne *cristene* saue commune wommen
C.21.372 Ther ne was *cristene* creature that kynde wit hadde
C.21.383 Cometh,' quod Consience, 'зe *cristene*, and dyneth
C.21.427 Emperour of al þe world, þat alle men were *cristene*
C.21.443 And claymeth bifore þe kynge to be kepare ouer *cristene*
C.21.444 And counteth nat thow *cristene* be culde and yrobbed
C.22.73 Ouer kynde *cristene* and cardinale vertues.
C.22.108 Leue pruyde priueyliche and be parfyt *cristene*.
C.22.141 That couetyse were *cristene* þat is so kene to fihte
C.22.214 And there was Consience Constable, *cristene* to saue,

cristen v *cristnen v.* A 2 cristene (1) cristned (1); B 4 cristen (1) cristned
(2) cristnede (1); C 1 ycristened
A.11.237 þat arn vncristene in þat cas may *cristene* an heþene,
A.12.15 Of þe kynde cardinal wit, and *cristned* in a font,
B.10.354 That [arn] vncristene in þat caas may *cristen* an heþen,
B.11.67 [At kirke] þere a man were *cristned* by kynde he sholde be buryed.
B.15.445 Austyn [þe kyng *cristnede* at Caunterbury],
B.15.457 Til it be *cristned* in cristes name and confermed of þe bisshop
C.17.165 Me fynde[th] þat Macometh was a man *ycristened*

cristendom n *Cristendom n.* A 1; B 18; C 14 cristendoem (12) cristendom
(2)
A. 6.75 þe kirnelis ben of *cristendom* þat kynde to saue,
B. 5.588 [The] kernele[s ben of *cristendom* [þat] kynde to saue,

B.11.125 For þou3 a cristen man coueited his *cristendom* to reneye,
B.11.201 For [at] Caluarie of cristes blood *cristendom* gan sprynge,
B.11.216 For whateuere clerkes carpe of *cristendom* or ellis,
B.12.108 Come for al his kynde wit to *cristendom* and be saued;
B.12.279 Ne no creature of cristes liknesse withouten *cristendom* worþ
         saued.'
B.12.283 "Troianus was a trewe knyght and took neuere *cristendom*
B.13.273 He hadde a cote of *cristendom* as holy kirke bileueþ.
B.14.11 Al for coueitise of my *cristendom* in clennesse to kepen it.
B.14.323 'Allas', quod Haukyn þe Actif man þo, 'þat after my *cristendom*
B.15.352 Crowne and *cristendom*, þe kynges mark of heuene,
B.15.447 To crist and to *cristendom* and cros to honoure,
B.15.532 Er *cristendom* [were] knowe þere, or any cros honoured.
B.15.569 That contrarien cristes lawe and *cristendom* dispise.
B.15.587 And 3it knewe þei crist þat *cristendom* tau3te,
B.16.199 And Crist and *cristendom* and cristene holy chirche.
B.17.6 And þat is cros and *cristendom* and crist þeron to honge;
C. 7.235 The carneles ben of *cristendom* þat kynde to saue,
C.12.60 For thogh a cristene man coueitede his *cristendom* to renoye,
C.12.79 That al þe *cristendoem* vnde[r] Crist ne myhte me crache fro
         [helle]
C.12.109 A[t] Caluarie of cristis bloed *cristendoem* gan sprynge
C.14.53 Come for al his kynde wit thorw *cristendoem* to be saued,
C.14.205 'Troianes was a trewe knyhte and toek neuere *cristendoem*
C.17.78 *Cristendoem* of holy kyrke, the kynges marke of heuene,
C.17.186 Sholden conuerte hem to Crist and *cristendoem* to take.
C.17.251 That contra[r]ryen now cristes law[e] and *cristendoem* dispisen.
C.17.282 Or *cristendoem* were knowe þere or eny croos honoured.
C.17.298 And 3ut knewe they crist þat *cristendoem* tauhte,
C.18.208 And Crist and *cristendoem* and cristene holy churche.
C.19.8 The which is Cr[oes] and *cristendoem* and cr[ist] þer[o]n [to]
         hang[e];
C.21.330 A Cart hihte *Cristendoem* to carie hoem Peres sheues

cristene cristne(e > cristen

cristnyng gen *cristning ger.* B 1
B.14.185 And be clene þoru3 þat *cristnyng* of alle kynnes synne.

cri3- > cryen

croce n *croce n.* A 1; C 1 crose
A. 9.86 Dobest is aboue hem boþe & beriþ a bisshopis *croce*;
C.10.93 Dobest bere sholde þe bisshopes [c]*rose*

crocer n *crocer n.* C 1
C. 5.113 And Consience his *crocer* byfore þe kyng stande.

croddes > cruddes; croes > cros

croft n *croft n.* A 4; B 4 croft (3) crofte (1); C 5 croft (4) crofte (1)
A. 6.59 Þanne shalt þou come be a *croft*, ac come þou nou3t þereinne;
A. 6.60 Þ[e] *croft* hattiþ coueite nou3t menis catel ne here wyues,
A. 7.34 For þise comiþ to my *croft* & croppiþ my whete.'
A. 7.274 Be þat I hope to haue heruest in my *croft*,
B. 5.572 Thanne shaltow come by a *croft*, [ac] come þow no3t þerInne;
B. 5.573 Th[e] *croft* hatte Coueite-no3t-mennes-catel-ne-hire-wyues-
B. 6.32 For [þise] comeþ to my *croft* and croppeþ my whete.'
B. 6.290 By þat I hope to haue heruest in my *crofte*,
C. 5.17 And kepe my corn in my *croft* f[or] pykares and theues
C. 7.219 Thenne shalt thow come by a *croft* Ac come thow [nat] þerynne;
C. 7.220 The *croft* hatte coueyte-nat-menne-catel-ne-here-wyues-
C. 8.31 For þey cometh to my *croft* my corn to diffoule.'
C. 8.313 And by [t]hat y hope to haue heruost in my *croft*[e];

crois > cros; crok > crokke

croked adj *croked ppl.* B 2 croked (1) crokede (1); C 3 croked (1)
    crokede (2)
B.11.192 'Ac calleþ þe carefulle þerto, þe *croked* and þe pouere,
B.16.108 And sou3te out þe sike and [saluede blynde and *crokede*,
C. 2.29 Ne on a *croked* kene thorn kynde fyge wexe:
C. 9.97 And to conforte suche coterelles and *crokede* men and blynde.
C.12.104 "Ac calleth the carefole þerto, the *crokede* and the pore;

crokes n *crok n.* C 1
C.20.294 [With] *crokes* and kalketrappes [a]cloye we hem vchone.'

crokke n *crokke n.* B 1; C 1 crok
B.19.280 [That] caste for to ke[l]e a *crokke* to saue þe fatte aboue.
C.21.280 That caste for to kele a *crok* [to] saue þe fatte aboue.

crommes n *crome n.* C 2
C. 8.278 And la3ar þe lene beggare þat longede aftur *crommes*–
C. 8.287 Lat hem abyde til the bord be drawe; Ac bere hem none *crommes*

crompe > crampe

cronicles n *cronicle n.* C 1
C. 5.178 Ac ar þat kyng come, as *cronicles* me tolde,

croos > cros

crop n *crop n.* B 5; C 2
B.16.42 And casteþ vp to þe *crop* vnkynde Neighebores,
B.16.69 Thanne Continence is neer þe *crop* as kaylewey bastard.
B.16.70 Thanne bereþ þe *crop* kynde fruyt and clennest of alle,
B.16.75 And Piers caste to þe *crop* and þanne comsed it to crye;
B.20.53 Antecrist cam þanne, and al þe *crop* of truþe
C.18.75 These haen þe [hete] of þe holi goest as þe *crop* of tre [the] sonne.
C.22.53 Auntecrist cam thenne and al the *crop* of treuthe

crope(n > crepe

croppeþv *croppen v.* A 1 croppiþ; B 2 croppede (1) croppeþ (1)
A. 7.34 For þise comiþ to my croft & *croppiþ* my whete.'
B. 6.32 For [þise] comeþ to my croft and *croppeþ* my whete.'
B.15.402 The corn þat she *croppede* he caste it in his ere,

cropward n *crop n.* C 1
C.18.107 And Elde clemp to þe c[r]*opward*; thenne comsed hit to crye.

cros n *cros n.* A 6 crois (3) cros (3); B 27 croos (1) cros (25) crosse (1);
    C 21 croes (5) croos (2) cros (11) cross (2) crosse (1)
A. 5.11 And consience wiþ a *cros* com for to preche,
A. 5.23 How consience wiþ a *cros* cumside to preche.
A. 5.236 'Crist, þat on caluarie vpon þe [*cros*] di3edist,
A. 9.50 I bekenne [3ow] crist þat on þe *crois* dei3ede.'
A.11.28 On *crois* vpon caluarie, as clerkis vs techiþ,
A.11.281 And for he kneu3 on þe *crois* & to crist shr[o]f hym,
B. 5.12 And wiþ a *cros* afore þe kyng comsede þus to techen.
B. 5.241 And lene it for loue of þe *cros*, to legge a wed and lese it.
B. 5.464 'Crist, þat on Caluarie vpon þe *cros* deidest,
B. 8.59 'I bikenne þee crist', quod he, 'þat on [þe] *cros* deyde.'
B. 8.96 Dobest is aboue boþe and bereþ a bisshopes *crosse*;
B.10.36 [On *cros* vpon caluarye as clerkes vs techeþ],
B.10.422 And for he bekne[w on] þe *cros* and to crist shrof hym
B.12.214 A[c] why þat oon þeef on þe *cros* creaunt hym yald
B.15.447 To crist and to cristendom and *cros* to honoure,
B.15.532 Er cristendom [were] knowe þere, or any *cros* honoured.
B.15.541 Than cristes *cros* þat ouercam deeþ and dedly synne.
B.15.543 For coueitise after *cros*; þe croune stant in golde.
B.15.546 For coueitise of þat *cros* [clerkes] of holy kirke
B.15.570 Euery bisshop þat bereþ *cros*, by þat he is holden
B.15.579 Ac we cristene creatures þat on þe *cros* bileuen
B.16.164 On *cros* vpon Caluarie crist took þe bataille
B.17.6 And þat is *cros* and cristendom and crist þeron to honge;
B.18.72 Vpon a croos bisides crist; so was þe comune lawe.
B.18.428 And crepe[þ] to þe *cros* on knees and kisse[þ] it for a Iuwel
B.19.7 And com in wiþ a *cros* bifore þe comune peple,
B.19.14 Is crist wiþ his *cros*, conquerour of cristene.'
B.19.41 And vpon Caluarie on *cros* ycrouned kyng of Iewes.
B.19.50 And þo conquered he on *cros* as conquerour noble,
B.19.63 Ac þe cause þat he comeþ þus wiþ *cros* of his passion
B.19.142 Killeden hym on *cros* wise at Caluarie on Friday,
B.19.199 Thus Conscience of crist and of þe *cros* carpede
B.19.321 And Grace gaf hym þe *cros*, wiþ þe [garland] of þornes,
C. 5.106 Byfore þe *cross* on my knees knokked y my brest,
C. 6.318 'Crist, þat on Caluarie on þe *crosse* deyedest
C.10.58 'Y bykenne the Crist,' quod he, 'þat on þe *cross* deyede.'
C.11.254 And for he biknewe on þe *croes* and to crist shrof hym
C.14.153 Ac why þat [on] theef vppon þe *cros* cryant hym 3elde
C.17.203 Thenne cristes *cros* þat ouercome deth and dedly synne.
C.17.205 For couetyse aftur *cros*; the corone stand in golde.
C.17.208 For couetyse of th[at] *croes* clerkes of holi churche
C.17.282 Or cristendoem were knowe þere or eny *croos* honoured.
C.19.8 The which is Cr[oes] and cristendoem and cr[ist] þer[o]n [to]
         hang[e];
C.20.74 Vppon *cros* bisyde Crist; so was þe comune lawe.
C.20.112 When Crist thorw *croos* ouercam 3oure kyndoem sholde tocleue;
C.20.471 And crepe to þe *croes* on knees and kusse hit for a iewel
C.21.7 And cam in with a *cros* bifore þe comune peple
C.21.14 Is Crist with his *croes*, conquerour of Cristene.'
C.21.41 And vpon Caluarie on *cros* ycrouned kyng of iewes.
C.21.50 And tho conquerede he on *cros* as conquerour noble;
C.21.63 Ac the cause that he cometh thus with *cros* [of] his passioun
C.21.142 Culden hym on *cros* wyse at Caluarie on fryday
C.21.199 Thus Consience of Crist and of þe *cros* carpede
C.21.321 And grace gaf hym þe *cros* with [the garlond] of thornes

crose > croce; cross(e > cros

crouch n *crouche n.* A 1; B 1; C 1
A. 6.10 And many *crouch* [o]n his cloke, & kei3es of rome,

B. 5.522   And many *crouch* on his cloke and keyes of Rome,
C. 7.167   And many *crouch* on his cloke [and] kayes of Rome

croune v *corounen v.(1)* &> *crowne* A 4 corounid (1) croune (1) crounide
   (1) icorounid (1); B 7 crouned (2) crouneþ (2) crowned (1) Ycorouned
   (1) ycrouned (1); C 11 crouned (4) crounede (2) crouneth (2)
   ycrouned (3)
A. 2.10   *Icorounid* in a coroune, þe king haþ non betere;
A. 2.62   Wiþ þe kingdom of coueitise I *croune* hem togidere;
A. 9.91   Þei han *crounide* o king to kepe hem alle,
A. 9.98   *Corounid* on to be kyng & be h[ere] counseil werchen,
B. 2.10   *Ycorouned* [in] a coroune, þe kyng haþ noon bettre.
B. 8.101   [Thei han] *crowne[d* a] kyng to [kepen] hem [alle],
B. 8.108   *Crouned* oon to be kyng, [and by hir counseil werchen],
B.11.313   That *crouneþ* swiche goddes knyȝtes, þat konneþ noȝt sapienter
B.18.371   And þanne shal I come as a kyng, *crouned*, wiþ Aungeles,
B.19.41   And vpon Caluarie on cros *ycrouned* kyng of lewes.
B.19.256   And *crouneþ* Conscience kyng and makeþ craft youre Stiward,
C. 2.11   And *crouned* [in] a croune, þe kyng haþ non bettre;
C. 3.319   Bothe kyng and Cayser and þe *crouned* pope
C. 5.56   Clerkes *ycrouned*, of kynde vnderstondynge,
C. 5.59   For hit ben eyres of heuene alle þat ben *ycrouned*
C. 5.66   For sholde no clerke but yf he come were
C.10.101   And *crounede* oen to be kyng to kull withoute synne
C.10.104   *Crounede* oen to be a kyng to kepen vs alle
C.13.125   That *crouneth* suche goddes knyhtes that conne [nat] sapienter
C.20.413   And thenne shal y come as [a] kynge, *croune[d*, with angeles
C.21.41   And vpon Caluarie on cros *ycrouned* kyng of iewes.
C.21.256   And *crouneth* Consience kyng and maketh craft ȝoure styward

crounes > crowne

crow n *croue n.* C 1
C.15.161   In þe corner of a car[t]whel with a *crow* croune.

crowne n *coroune n.* A 3 coroune (1) croune (2); B 16 coroune (2) croune
   (6) crounes (1) crowne (7); C 14 corone (2) croune (10) crounes (1)
   crowne (1)
A. 2.10   *Icorounid* in a *coroune*, þe king haþ non betere;
A. 4.70   Þe king swor be crist & be his *croune* boþe
A. 4.121   Þat I were king wiþ *croune* to kepe a reaume,
B. 2.10   *Ycorouned* [in] a *coroune*, þe kyng haþ noon bettre.
B. 4.83   The kyng swor by crist and by his *crowne* boþe
B. 4.138   That I were kyng with *coroune* to kepen a Reaume,
B.11.36   A man may stoupe tyme ynoȝ whan he shal tyne þe *crowne*.'
B.11.299   That han neiþer konnynge ne kyn, but a *crowne* one
B.11.301   He [ouȝte no] bileue, as I leue, to lacche þoruȝ his *croune*
B.13.242   Faitours and freres and folk wiþ brode *crounes*.
B.15.229   Ycalled and ycrymyled and his *crowne* yshaue.
B.15.352   *Crowne* and cristendom, þe kynges mark of heuene,
B.15.543   For coueitise after cros; þe *croune* stant in golde.
B.18.109   Whan crist cam hir kyngdom þe *crowne* sholde [lese]:
B.18.265   For here cometh wiþ *crowne* þat kyng is of glorie."'
B.19.49   And kyng of hir kyngdom and *croune* bar of þornes.
B.19.465   And þanne cam þer a kyng and by his *croune* seide,
B.19.466   'I am kyng wiþ *croune* þe comune to rule,
B.20.184   And made me balled bifore and bare on þe *croune*;
C. 2.11   And crouned [in] a *croune*, þe kyng haþ non bettre;
C. 4.79   The kyng [s]wor by Crist and by his *croune* bothe
C. 4.135   That y were kyng with *c[r]oune* to kepe [a] reume,
C. 5.177   Shal haue a knok vppon here *crounes* and incurable þe wounde:
C.11.195   A man may stoupe tyme ynowe when he shal tyne þe *croune*.'
C.13.113   That [hath] noþer connyng ne kyn bote a *croune* one
C.15.161   In þe corner of a car[t]whel with a crow *croune*.
C.16.354   Ycalled and ycrimyled and his *croune* yshaue.
C.17.205   For couetyse aftur cros; the *corone* stand in golde.
C.20.273   For here cometh with *croune* þe kynge of all glorie.'
C.21.49   And kyng of here kyngdoem and *croune* baer of thornes.
C.21.465   And thenne cam þer a kyng and bi his *corone* saide,
C.21.466   'Y am kyng with *croune* the comune to reule
C.22.184   And made me balled bifore and baer on þe *crowne*;

crowned > croune

crownynge ger *corouning ger.* B 1; C 1 crownyng
B.Pr.88   That han cure vnder crist, and *crownynge* in tokene
C.Pr.86   That han cure vnder crist and *crownyng* in tokene

cruddes n *crud n.* A 1 cruddis; B 1; C 2 croddes
A. 7.266   A fewe *cruddis* & crem, & [a]n [hauer] cake,
B. 6.282   A fewe *cruddes* and creme and [a cake of otes],
C. 8.304   A fewe *croddes* and craym and a cake of otes
C. 8.320   With craym and with *croddes*, with cresses and oþere erbes.

cruwel adj *cruel adj.* B 1
B.13.390   Vpon a *cruwel* coueitise m[y] conscience] gan hange.

cuffis > coffes; culd(- culle(- > killen

culorum n *culorum n.* A 1; B 2; C 2
A. 3.258   Þe *culorum* of þis [cas] kepe I not to shewe;
B. 3.280   The *culorum* of þis cas kepe I noȝt to [shewe];
B.10.415   The culorum of þis clause *curatours* is to mene,
C. 3.433   The *culorum* of this kaes kepe y nat to shewe;
C.11.246   The *culorum* of this clause curatores is to mene

cultour n *culter n.* A 1 cultir; B 2 cultour (1) kultour (1); C 2 coltur
A. 7.96   And helpe my *cultir* to kerue & close þe forewis.'
B. 3.308   Into sikel or to siþe, to Shaar or to *kultour*:
B. 6.104   And helpe my *cultour* to kerue and [close] þe furwes.'
C. 3.461   Into sykel or [t]o sythe, to shar oþer to *coltur*:
C. 8.65   And helpe my *Coltur* to kerue and cl[o]se þe forwes;

*cumside > comseþ; cunge > congeien; cunne > konne; cunnyng > konnyng;
cunstable > constable; cuntenaunce > contenaunce; cuntre > contree; cuppe
> coppe*

cuppemele adv *cuppe n.* A 1 cuppemel; B 1; C 1 coppemele
A. 5.139   Whanne it com in *cuppemel*; þat craft my wyf vside.
B. 5.223   [Whan] it cam In *cuppemele*, þis craft my wif vsed.
C. 6.231   When hit cam in *coppemele*; this crafte my wyf vsede.

curatour n *curatour n.* A 1 curatours; B 11 Curatour (3) curatours (8); C
   11 curatores (1) curatour (4) curatours (6)
A. 1.169   Ȝe *curatours* þat kepe ȝow clene of ȝour body,
B. 1.195   [Ye] *curatours* [þat] kepen [yow] clene of [youre] bod[y],
B.10.415   The culorum of þis clause *curatours* is to mene,
B.13.13   Thoruȝ vnkonnynge *curatours* to incurable peynes;
B.15.90   Ac of *curatours* of cristen peple, as clerkes bereþ witnesse,
B.15.136   *Curatours* of holy kirke, as clerkes þat ben auarouse,
B.15.530   And crepe [in] amonges *curatours*, confessen ageyn þe lawe:
B.19.222   Shullen come and be *curatours* ouer kynges and Erles;
B.19.410   'I am a *Curatour* of holy kirke, and cam neuere in my tyme
B.19.451   For þe comune', quod þis *Curatour*, 'counten ful litel
B.20.282   Ben *Curatours* called to knowe and to hele,
B.20.326   To curen as a *Curatour*; and cam with hi[s] lettr[e]
C.11.246   The culorum of this clause *curatores* is to mene
C.15.16   Thorw vnkunynge *curatours* to incurable peynes;
C.16.275   Vnk[ynd]e *curatours* to be kepares of ȝoure soules.
C.16.281   *Curatours* of holy [kirke] and clerkes þat ben Auerous,
C.17.280   And crepe in amonges *curatours* and confessen aȝeyn þe lawe:
C.17.290   So is þe kynde of a *curatour* for criste[s] loue to preche
C.21.222   Shal come and be *curatours* ouer kynges and Erles;
C.21.410   'Ich am a *Curatour* of holi [kirke] and cam neuer in my tyme
C.21.451   [For] the comune,' quod this *curatour*, 'counteth ful litel
C.22.282   Ben *curatours* cald to knowe and to hele,
C.22.326   To curen as a *curatour*; and kam with his lettre

cure n *cure n.(1)* &> *curen* B 5; C 4
B.Pr.88   That han *cure* vnder crist, and crownynge in tokene
B.11.302   [Moore þan *cure*] for konnyng or 'knowen for clene [of] berynge'.
B.20.233   That þei come for coueitise, to haue *cure* of soules.
B.20.237   Lat hem chewe as þei chose and charge hem with no *cure*
B.20.253   And if ye coueite *cure*, kynde wol yow [telle]
C.Pr.86   That han *cure* vnder crist and crownyng in tokene
C.22.233   That they cam for Couetyse, to haue *cure* of soules.
C.22.237   Late hem chewe as thei chose and charge hem with no *cure*.
C.22.253   And yf ȝe coueiteth *cure* kynde wol ȝow telle

curen v *curen v.(2)* B 1; C 2 cure (1) curen (1)
B.20.326   To *curen* as a Curatour; and cam with hi[s] lettr[e]
C.14.70   For clergy is cristes vycary to conforte and to *cure*;
C.22.326   To *curen* as a curatour; and kam with his lettre

curious adj *curious adj.* B 1; C 1
B.19.287   Sholde no *curious* clooþ comen on his rugge,
C.21.287   Sholde no *curious* cloth comen on his rugge

curseþ v *cursen v.* A 10 curse (1) cursid (4) curside (5); B 18 corsed (3)
   corsede (1) corseder (1) corseþ (2) cursed (6) cursede (3) curseþ (1)
   ycursed (1); C 18 corsed (5) corsede (6) corsedore (1) corseth (2)
   corsynge (1) cursed (3)
A. 3.131   To be *cursid* in constorie heo countiþ not a risshe;
A. 7.147   To kepen hym as couenaunt was fro *curside* shrewis,
A. 7.298   And þanne *curse* þe king & alle þe counseil aftir
A.10.140   Ben conseyuid in *cursid* tyme as kaym was on Eue:
A.10.146   In þat *curside* constellacioun þei knewe togiderus,
A.10.148   Caym þei hym callide, in *cursid* tyme engendrit.
A.10.154   For þei mariede hem wiþ *curside* men of caymes kyn.
A.10.170   Clene awey þe *cursid* blood þat caym haþ ymakid.
A.10.177   Þat euere *curside* caym com on þis erþe,
A.10.178   [Þus] þoruȝ *curside* caym cam care vpon alle,
B. 3.142   To be *corsed* in Consistorie she counteþ noȝt a [risshe];
B. 6.160   To kepen hym as coueenaunt was fro *cursede* sherewes,

B. 6.317   And þanne *corseþ* þe kyng and al [þe] counseil after
B. 9.123   Conceyued ben in [*cursed*] tyme as Caym was on Eue
B. 9.139   Clene awey þe *corsed* blood þat Caym haþ ymaked.
B. 9.141   That euere *cursed* Caym coom on þis erþe
B. 9.156   And þus þoruȝ *cursed* Caym cam care vpon erþe,
B.10.472   Ye, men knowe clerkes þat han *corsed* þe tyme
B.15.171   *Corseþ* he no creature ne he kan bere no wraþe,
B.17.276   For þat kynde dooþ vnknyþe fordooþ, as þise *corsede* þeues,
B.17.331   Cogheþ and *curseþ* þat crist gyue h[y]m sorwe
B.18.96   *Cursede* cayt[yues]! knyghthood was it neuere
B.19.403   'Caytif!' quod Conscience, '*cursede* wrecche!
B.19.417   "The contree is þe *corseder* þat Cardinals come Inne,
B.19.432   And sent þe sonne to saue a *cursed* mannes tilþe
B.19.467   And holy kirke and clergie fro *cursed* men to [de]fende.
B.20.68   They *cursed* and hir conseil, were it clerk or lewed.
B.20.263   Pylours and Pykeharneys, in ech a [parisshe] *ycursed*._
C. 3.106   And thorw a candle clemynge in [a] *cursed* place
C. 3.180   To be *cursed* in constorie a counteth nat a rusche;
C. 6.64   And cryede 'mea culpa', *corsynge* alle his enemyes;
C. 8.337   And thenne a *corseth* þe kyng and alle þe kynges Iustices
C.10.213   Caym þe *corsede* creature conseyued was in synne
C.10.218   So was Caym conseyued and so ben *corsed* wreches
C.10.227   Clene awey þe *corsed* bloed þat of Caym spronge.
C.10.229   That euere *corsed* Caym cam on þis erthe;
C.10.247   Aftur þat Caym þ[e] *corsed* hadde ykuld abel,
C.17.212   How tho *corsede* cristene catel and richesse worschipede;
C.19.257   For þat kynde doth vnkynde fordoth, as this *corsede* theues,
C.19.311   Coueth and *corseth* þat Crist ȝeue hym sorwe
C.20.99   *Corsede* Caytifues! knyhthood was hit neuere
C.21.403   'Caytyf!' quod Consience, '*corsede* wreche!
C.21.417   "The contreye is þe *corsedore* þat cardinals cometh ynne
C.21.432   And sente þe so[nn]e to saue a *corsed* mannes tulthe
C.21.467   And holy kyrke and clerge fro *corsed* men to defende.
C.22.68   Thei *corsede* and here consail, were hit Clerk or lewed.

curteis adj *courteis adj.& n.*   A 3; B 4 curteis (3) curteise (1); C 4 corteys
   (3) corteyse (1)
A. 3.59   Who is *curteis* or kynde or coueitous, or ellis.
A. 4.17   And calde catoun his knaue, *curteis* of speche:
A. 4.105   Til clerkis & kniȝtes be *curteis* of here mouþes,
B. 4.17   And called Caton his knaue, *curteis* of speche,
B.13.15   Of kynde and of his konnynge, and how *curteis* he is to bestes,
B.13.458   Til conscience acouped hym þerof in a *curteis* manere,
B.15.104   And be kynde as bifel for clerkes and *curteise* of cristes goodes,
C. 4.17   And kalde Catoun his knaue, *Corteys* of speche,
C. 8.47   Hit bicometh to the, knyhte, to be *corteys* and hende,
C.14.160   Bote kynde þat contreuede hit furst of his *corteyse* wille.
C.16.257   And be *corteys* and kynde of holy kyrke godes,

curteisie n *courteisie n.*   A 1; B 11; C 10 cortesie (2) cortesye (8)
A. 1.20   And comaundite of his *curteisie* in comoun þre þinges,
B. 1.20   And comaunded of his *curteisie* in commune þree þynges;
B. 5.89   [This was al his *curteisie* where þat euere he shewed hym].
B. 5.430   I am vnkynde ayeins [his] *curteisie* and kan nouȝt vnderstonden it,
B.10.316   He loureþ on hym and [lakkeþ] hym: who [lered] hym *curteisie*?
B.12.77   Ac crist of his *curteisie* þoruȝ clergie hir saued.
B.14.147   Crist of his *curteisie* shal conforte yow at þe laste,
B.15.303   [For al þe *curteisie* þat beestes konne þei kidde þat folk ofte,
B.15.557   Whan Costantyn of *curteisie* holy kirke dowed
B.17.245   So wole crist of his *curteisie*, and men crye hym mercy,
B.19.449   And crist of his *curteisie* þe Cardinals saue
B.20.106   Conscience of his *curteisie* [þo] kynde he bisouȝte
C. 1.20   And comaundede of his *cortesye* in comune thre thynges.
C. 3.315   And thow the kyng of his *cortesye*, Cayser or pope,
C. 7.43   Y am vnkynde aȝen his *cortesie* [and] can nat vnderstande hit
C.10.264   That no *cortesye* can, bute [knowe late here be]
C.14.216   And a *cortesye* more þen couenant was, what so clerkes carpe,
C.17.164   Ne kynde sanȝ *cortesie* in no contreye is preysed
C.17.220   Whan Constantyn of *cortesye* holy kirke dowede
C.19.211   So wol Crist of his *cortesye*, and men crien hym mercy,
C.21.449   And Crist of his *cortesye* þe cardinals saue
C.22.106   Concience of his *cortesye* tho kynde he bisouhte

curteisly adv *courteisliche adv.*   A 6 curteisliche (5) curteisly (1); B 14
   curteisly (9) curteisliche (5); C 12 corteisliche (1) corteysliche (5)
   corteyslyche (2) cortesliche (1) courteysly (1) courteisliche (2)
A. 3.9   *Curteisliche* þe clerk þanne, as þe king hiȝte,
A. 3.93   [*Curteisly*] þe king compsiþ to telle;
A. 4.31   *Curteisliche* þe king þanne com in to resoun,
A. 7.35   *Curteisliche* þ[e] kniȝt [conseyuede] þise wordis;
A. 7.149   *Curteisliche* þe kniȝt þanne as his kynde wolde
A.11.177   *Curteisliche* clergi[e] c[o]llide me & kiste,
B. 3.9   *Curteisly* þe clerk þanne, as þe kyng hiȝte,
B. 3.104   *Curteisly* þe kyng comse[þ] to telle;

B. 4.44   *Curteisly* þe kyng þanne com [in to] Reson,
B. 6.33   *Curteisly* þe knyȝt [conseyued] þise wordes:
B. 6.164   *Curteisly* þe knyȝt þanne, as his kynde wolde,
B.10.234   [*Curteisly*] clergie collede me and kiste,
B.13.31   Conscience called hym In and *curteisliche* seide
B.13.46   Conscience *curteisly* þo commaunded Scripture
B.13.112   Than Conscience *curteisly* a contenaunce made,
B.13.179   Ac Conscience carped loude and *curteisliche* seide,
B.13.198   Thus *curteisliche* Conscience congeyed first þe frere,
B.19.176   Crist carpede þanne and *curteisliche* seide,
B.20.243   And *curteisliche* conforted hem and called in alle freres,
B.20.355   And cam to Conscience and *curteisly* hym grette.
C. 2.167   And comen ful *courteysly* to conforte the false
C. 3.9   *Cortesliche* þe Clerk thenne, as þe kyng hyhte,
C. 3.130   *Cortesliche* þe kynge, as his kynde wolde,
C. 4.42   *Corteyslyche* þe kyng thenne cam and grette resoun
C. 4.152   And kynde [wit] and Consience *corteysliche* thonkede
C. 8.32   *Courteisliche* the knyhte thenne co[nseyu]ed thise wordes:
C. 8.161   *Courteisliche* the knyhte thenne, as his kynde wolde,
C.15.119   Thenne consience *corteyslyche* a continaunce made
C.15.192   What craft þat he couthe and *cortey[s]liche* he saide:
C.21.176   Crist Carpede thenne and *cortey[s]liche* saide,
C.22.243   And *cortey[s]liche* confortede hem and calde in all freres,
C.22.355   And cam to Consience and *cortey[s]liche* hym grette.

curuen > kerue; custe > kissen

custume n *custume n.*   B 1 custumes; C 4 costumes (1) custume (1)
   custumes (2)
B.12.97   Forþi lakke þow neuere logik, lawe ne hise *custumes*,
C. 3.207   And *custumes* of coueytise þe comune to destruye.
C. 3.374   A[c] relacoun rect is a ryhtful *custume*,
C. 9.18   Lechery amonges lordes and here luyther *custumes*,
C.14.73   Of cloudes and of *costumes* they contreuede mony thynges

cuttepurs > kuttepurs; cuuere > couere

D

daffe n *daffe n.* A 1; B 2; C 3
A. 1.129 'Þou dotide *daffe*,' quaþ heo, 'dulle arn þine wittes.
B. 1.140 'Thow doted *daffe*!' quod she, 'dulle are þi wittes.
B.11.427 For lat a dronken *daffe* in a dyk falle,
C. 1.139 'Thow dotede *daffe*!' quod she, 'dulle aren thy wittes.
C.10.178 As lo[t] dede and Noe, and herodes þe *daffe*
C.13.234 For lat a dronkene *daffe* in a dykke falle,

daggen v *daggen v.(1)* B 1; C 1 dagge
B.20.143 And þanne lough lyf and leet *daggen* hise cloþes,
C.22.143 And thenne lowh lyf and lette *dagge* his clothes

day n *dai n. &> holy_day* A 41 day (28) dayes (13); B 93 day (59) daye
(4) daies (8) dayes (22); C 75 day (47) daye (3) daies (3) dayes (20)
days (2)
A.Pr.103 And driueþ forþ þe longe *day* wiþ dieu saue dame emme;
A. 1.27 For loth, in his lyf *dayes*, for lykyng of drink
A. 1.96 For dauid, in hise *dayes*, dubbide kniȝtes,
A. 1.118 Aftir here deþ *day* & dwelle wiþ þat shrewe.
A. 2.190 And wiþheld him half [a] ȝer & elleuene *dayes*.
A. 3.98 Henis to þi deþ *day* do þou so no more.
A. 3.135 As ȝoure secre sel in seue score *dayes*.
A. 3.140 To holde lemmanis & lotebies alle here lif *dayes*,
A. 5.71 I miȝte not many *day* do as a man [au]ȝte,
A. 5.156 And a [ferþingworþ] of [fenelsed] for fastyng *dayes*.'
A. 6.80 He may do wiþ þe *day* sterre what hym dere likiþ;
A. 7.12 But ȝif it be holy *day* oþer holy euen;
A. 7.135 Inouȝ iche *day* at non, ac no more til on þe morewe
A. 7.170 Þei hadde be ded þis *day* & doluen al warm.
A. 7.244 Þat þou drynke no *day* er þou dyne somwhat,
A. 7.263 Er I haue dyned þis *day* & ydronke boþe.'
A. 7.292 Deyneþ nouȝt to dyne a *day* niȝt olde wortis.
A. 8.19 At þe *day* of dom at here deis to sitten.
A. 8.22 For þei h[o]lde nouȝt here haly *dayes* as holy chirche techiþ,
A. 8.53 Shal no deuil at his deþ *day* derie hym a myte
A. 8.100 Þat aftir þi deþ *day* to helle shalt þou wende.'
A. 8.155 Dowel at þe *day* of dome is digneliche vndirfongen;
A. 8.174 What þou dedist *day* [by day] þe dom wile reherce.
A. 8.174 What þou dedist day [by *day*] þe dom wile reherce.
A. 8.183 Þat, aftir oure deþ *day*, dowel reherse
A. 8.184 Þat at þe *day* of dome we dede as he hiȝte.
A. 9.23 'How seue siþes þe sadde man synneþ on þe *day*;
A. 9.39 Synnes þe sad man seuene [siþes] in þe *day*.
A. 9.107 Þouȝt & I þus þre *dayes* we ȝeden,
A. 9.108 Disputyng on dowel *day* aftir oþer,
A.10.1 'Sire dowel dwelliþ,' quaþ wyt, 'nouȝt a *day* hennes,
A.10.169 Til fourty *dayes* be fulfild, þat flood haue ywasshe
A.10.214 And aftir here deþ *day* shuln dwelle with þe same
A.11.92 Þeiȝ dobest drawe on hym *day* aftir oþer.'
A.12.60 As I ȝede thurgh ȝouþe, aȝen prime *dayes*,
A.12.66 I shal felle þat freke in a fewe *dayes*.'
A.12.75 Þer bad me hunger haue gode *day* but I helde me stille;
A.12.81 'With deþ I duelle,' quod he, '*dayes* and nyȝtes.'
A.12.82 Mi name is feuere on þe ferþe *day*; I am aþrest euere.
A.12.94 And þerfore do after dowel whil *day* is on erthe.'
B.Pr.225 And dryueþ forþ þe longe *day* with 'Dieu saue dame Emme'.
B. 1.98 /For Dauid in hise *dayes* dubbed knyȝtes,
B. 1.121 But fellen out in fendes liknesse [ful] nyne *dayes* togideres
B. 1.129 After hir deþ *day* and dwelle with þat sherewe.
B. 2.94 And al *day* to drynken at diuerse Tauernes,
B. 2.96 And in fastynge *dayes* to frete er ful tyme were.
B. 2.231 And [wiþ]helden hym an half yeer and elleuene *dayes*.
B. 3.109 Hennes to þi deeþ *day* do [þow] so na moore.
B. 3.146 As youre secret seel in sixe score *dayes*.
B. 3.312 And dyngen vpon Dauid eche *day* til eue;
B. 4.178 And deme yow, bi þis *day*, as ye han deserued.
B. 5.179 [I] haue a flux of a foul mouþ wel fyue *dayes* after;
B. 5.242 Swiche dedes I dide write if he his *day* breke;
B. 5.305 A ferþyngworþ of fenel seed for fastynge *dayes*.'
B. 5.374 Ouer delicatly on [feeste] *dayes* dronken and eten boþe,
B. 5.377 Fedde me bifore] noon whan fastyng *dayes* were.'

B. 5.393 'If I sholde deye bi þis *day* [I drede me sore].
B. 5.402 I am occupied eche *day*, halyday and ooþer,
B. 5.409 Vigilies and fastyng *dayes*, alle þise late I passe,
B. 5.451 That I ne shal do me er *day* to þe deere chirche
B. 5.488 On good fryday for mannes sake at ful tyme of þe *daye*;
B. 5.496 The þridde *day* [þer]after þow yedest in oure sute;
B. 6.260 That þow drynke no *day* er þow dyne somwhat.
B. 6.279 [Er] I haue dyned bi þis *day* and ydronke boþe.'
B. 6.308 Deyne[þ] noȝt to dyne a *day* nyȝt olde wortes.
B. 7.17 At þe *day* of dome at [hire] deys [to] sitte.
B. 7.51 Shal no deuel at his deeþ *day* deren hym a myte
B. 7.118 [That] after þi deeþ *day* þe deuel shal haue þi soule.'
B. 7.177 Dowel at þe *day* of dome is digneliche vnderfongen;
B. 7.196 [What] þow didest *day* by day þe doom wole reherce.
B. 7.196 [What] þow didest day by day þe doom wole reherce.
B. 7.205 That, after oure deeþ *day*, dowel reherce
B. 7.206 At þe *day* of dome we dide as he hiȝte.
B. 8.27 'How seuen siþes þe sadde man [synneþ on þe *day*].
B. 8.43 Synneþ þe sadde man [seuen siþes a *day*].
B. 8.117 Thoȝt and I þus þre *daies* we yeden,
B. 8.118 Disputyng [o]n dowel *day* after ooþer,
B. 9.1 'SIre Dowel dwelleþ', quod Wit, 'noȝt a *day* hennes
B. 9.99 He dooþ best þat wiþdraweþ hym by *daye* and by nyȝte
B. 9.138 Til fourty *daies* be fulfild, þat flood haue ywasshen
B. 9.200 And after hir deeþ *day* shul dwelle wiþ þe same
B.10.97 Elenge is þe halle, ech *day* in þe wike,
B.10.139 Theiȝ dobest drawe on hym *day* after ooþer.'
B.10.364 And but we do þus in dede, [er] þe *day* of dome,
B.11.31 Bittrely shaltow banne þanne, boþe *dayes* and nyȝtes,
B.11.134 For hise arerages rewarden hym þere [riȝt] to þe *day* of dome,
B.11.314 Synge ne psalmes rede ne seye a masse of þe *day*.
B.12.91 Dampneþ vs at þe *day* of dome as [dide þe caractes] þe Iewes.
B.12.248 And deleþ it noȝt til his deeþ *day*, þe tail[le is al of] sorwe.
B.13.65 'It is noȝt foure *dayes* þat þis freke, bifore þe deen of Poules,
B.13.106 'By þis *day*, sire doctour', quod I, '[þanne [in dowel ne ye noȝt]!
B.13.171 And as þow demest wil þei do alle hir *dayes* after:
B.13.348 As wel fastyng *dayes* [as] Fridaies [and] forboden nyȝtes,
B.13.368 Or by nyȝte or by *daye* aboute was ich euere
B.13.383 [I]n haly chirche whan ich herde masse
B.13.414 Ech *day* is halyday with hym or an heiȝ ferye.
B.14.107 Whan he drogh to his deeþ *day* þat he ne dredde hym soore,
B.14.136 And til he haue doon his deuoir and his *dayes* iournee.
B.14.176 Thoruȝ derþe, þoruȝ droghte, alle hir *dayes* here,
B.15.281 And *day* bi day hadde he hire noȝt his hunger for to slake,
B.15.281 And day bi *day* hadde he hire noȝt his hunger for to slake,
B.15.296 I sholde noȝt þise seuen *daies* siggen hem alle
B.15.320 And auisen hem bifore a fyue *dayes* or sixe
B.15.401 Daunted a dowue and *day* and nyȝt hire fedde.
B.15.560 "Dos ecclesie þis *day* haþ ydronke venym
B.16.132 And in þre *daies* after edifie it newe,
B.16.138 Eche *day* after ooþer hir tyme þei awaiteden
B.16.148 And which tokne to þis *day* to muche is yvsed,
B.16.166 Deide and dee[þ] fordide, and *day* of nyȝt made.
B.16.266 That shal deliuere vs som *day* out of þe deueles power
B.17.65 Dredfully, bi þis *day*! as doke dooþ fram þe faucon.
B.17.112 Ac er þis day þre *dai* vndertaken
B.17.112 Ac er þis *day* þre *daies* I dar vndertaken
B.17.255 Delen and do penaunce *day* and nyght euere,
B.17.273 But þei dwelle þer Diues is *dayes* wiþouten ende.
B.17.291 Innocence is next god and nyght and *day* it crieþ
B.18.32 That, for al þat deeþ kan do, wiþInne þre *daies* to walke
B.18.42 To fordoon it on o *day*, and in þre dayes after
B.18.42 To fordoon it on o day, and in þre *dayes* after
B.18.53 And beden hym drynken his deeþ [to ketle and] hise *daies* [lengþe],
B.18.60 The *day* for drede wiþdrouȝ and derk bicam þe sonne;
B.18.108 Now youre goode *dayes* arn doon as daniel prophecied;
B.18.123 Of þe dyn and þe derknesse and how þe *day* rowed,
B.18.134 Which deide and þoled þis *day* aboute mydday,
B.18.177 That many *day* myȝte I noȝt se for merknesse of synne,
B.18.209 Sholde wite witterly what *day* is to meene.
B.18.424 Til þe *day* dawed þise damyseles [carolden]
B.19.20 Ne noon so nedeful to nempne by nyȝte ne by *daye*.

157

B.19.101   And so dide Iesu in hise *dayes*, whoso [dorste] telle it.
B.19.141   And for to doon hym to deþe *day* and nyȝt þei casten.
B.19.150   That Aungeles and Archaungeles, er þe *day* spronge,
B.20.177   And þere dyed þat doctour er þre *dayes* after.
B.20.293   And suffre þe dede in dette to þe *day* of doome.
C.Pr.229   And dryueth forth [þe longe] *da[y]* with 'd[ieu] saue dame Emme.'
C. 1.32   Forthy drede delitable drynke bothe *day* and nyghtes.
C. 1.102   Dauid in his *daies* dobbed knyghtes,
C. 1.114   Thenne sitten in þe sonne syde þere þe *day* roweth?'
C. 1.131   Aftur here deth *day* and dwelle ther wrong is;
C. 2.101   Al *day* to drynke at diuerse tauernes,
C. 2.103   And fastyng *dayes* to frete byfore noone and drynke
C. 2.109   After here deth dwellen *day* withouten ende
C. 2.241   And [wiþ]helden hym [a] half ȝere and eleue *dayes*.
C. 3.184   As ȝoure secrete seel in sixe score *dayes*.
C. 3.304   When þe dede is ydo and þe *day* endit.
C. 4.172   And deme ȝow, by this *day*, as ȝe haen deserued.
C. 5.156   Ac mony *day*, men telleth, bothe monkes and chanons
C. 6.161   Y haue a flux of a foul mouth wel fyue *daies* aftur;
C. 6.182   As wel fastyng *dayes* and frydayes and heye fest[e] euenes.
C. 6.360   A ferthyngworth [of] fenkel sed[e] for fastyng *dayes*.'
C. 6.434   [On] fastyng *dayes* bifore noen fedde me with ale,
C. 7.9   'Yf y sholde deye be þis *day* y drede me sore.
C. 7.18   Y am occupied vch *day*, haliday and oþere,
C. 7.25   Vigilies and fastyng*dayes* y can forȝeten hem alle
C. 7.65   That y ne shal do me ar *day* to þe dere chirche
C. 7.136   The thridde *day* þeraftur thow ȝedest i[n] oure sekte;
C. 8.276   And loke þou drynke no *day* ar thow dyne sumwhat.
C. 8.301   Ar y haue ydyned be þis *day* and ydronke bothe.'
C. 8.330   Deyne[th noght] to dyne a *day* nyhte olde wortes;
C. 9.94   Fridays and fastyng*days* a ferthingworth of moskeles
C. 9.223   And vnder obedience be by *dayes* and by nyhtes;
C. 9.233   Vigilies and fastyng*days* forthermore to knowe
C. 9.322   For hoso doth wel here at þe *day* of dome
C. 9.342   And how we dede *day* be day the doem wol reherce.
C. 9.342   And how we dede day be *day* the doem wol reherce.
C. 9.351   That aftur oure deth *day* dowel reherce
C. 9.352   At þe *day* of dome we dede as he tauhte.
C.10.23   Seuene sithe, sayth þe boek, synegeth *day* by day
C.10.23   Seuene sithe, sayth þe boek, synegeth day by *day*
C.10.31   'How seuene sithes þe sad man synegeth on þe *day*.
C.10.113   Thouht and y thus thre *dayes* we ȝeden
C.10.114   Disputyng vppon dowel *day* aftur other
C.10.128   'Sire dowel dwelleth,' quod wit, 'nat a *day* hennes
C.10.226   Til fourty [*dayes*] be fulfild and floed haue ywasche
C.10.299   And after her deth *day* dwellen shollen in helle
C.11.190   Bitterliche shaltow banne thenne, bothe *dayes* and nyhtes,
C.12.69   And for his rechelesnes rewarde hym þere riht to þe *day* of dome
C.13.126   Syng ne [psalmes] rede [ne sey a masse of the *daye*].
C.13.190   They ouerdoen hit *day* and nyhte and so doth nat oþer bestes;
C.15.69   'Hit is nat thre *daies* doen this doctour þat he prechede
C.16.5   When his d[eu]er is doen and his *dayes* iourne
C.16.321   Fiat-voluntas-tua festeth hym vch a *daye*.
C.17.29   Ac durste no beste byte hem by *day* ne by nyhte
C.17.93   Doen her deuer *day* and nyhte; dede we so alse
C.17.171   He endaunted a douue and *day* and nyhte here fedde;
C.17.223   "Dos ecclesie this *day* hath ydronke venym
C.17.245   Deuouteliche *day* and nyhte, withdrawe hem fro synne
C.18.160   And ar thre *dayes* aftur edefye hit newe.'
C.18.282   That shal delyuere vs som *day* out of þe deueles power
C.19.221   Dele and do penaunce *day* and nyht euere
C.19.254   Bote they dwelle there diues is *dayes* withouten ende.
C.19.272   Innocence is next god and nyht and *day* hit crieth
C.20.31   That for al þat deth can do, withynne thre *dayes* to walke
C.20.41   To fordoen hit on a *day*, and in thre dayes aftur
C.20.41   To fordoen hit on a day, and in thre *dayes* aftur
C.20.53   And beden hym drynke his deth to lette and his *dayes* lenghe
C.20.60   The *daye* for drede withdrouh and derke bicam þe sonne;
C.20.111   Now ben ȝoure gode *dayes* ydoen, as daniel of ȝow telleth;
C.20.126   Of the dene and the derkenesse and how þe *day* roued
C.20.137   [Which] deyede and deth tholede this *day* aboute mydday
C.20.180   That many *day* myhte y nat se for merkenesse of synne,
C.20.216   Sholde ywyte witterly what *day* is to mene.
C.20.467   Til þe *day* dawed thes damoyseles caroled
C.21.20   Ne noen so niedfol to nemnie by nyhte ne by *day*
C.21.101   And so dede iesu in his *dayes*, whoso durste tellen hit.
C.21.141   And for to do hym to dethe *day* and nyhte they casten,
C.21.150   That Angeles and Archangeles, ar the *day* spronge,
C.22.177   And þere deyede þat doctour ar thre *dayes* aftur.
C.22.293   And soffren þe dede in dette to þe *day* of dome.

dayes > *day, halyday*

---

dale n *dale n.*   A 3; B 3; C 4 dale (3) dales (1)
A.Pr.15   A dep *dale* beneþe, a dungeoun þereinne
A. 1.1   What þe mounteyne [be]meniþ, & ek þe [m]erke *dale*,
A. 1.57   'Þe dungeon in þe *dale* þat dredful is of siȝt:
B.Pr.15   A deep *dale* byneþe, a dongeon þerInne
B. 1.1   What þ[e] Mountaigne bymeneþ and þe merke *dale*
B. 1.59   'Th[e] dongeon in þe *dale* þat dredful is of siȝte–
C.Pr.17   And seigh a depe *dale*; deth, as y leue,
C. 1.1   What the montaigne bymeneth and þe merke *dale*
C. 1.55   'The dep *dale* and þe derk, so vnsemely to se to,
C.10.230   Alle sholle deye for his dedes by *dales* and hulles

damaske n prop *damask n.*   B 1; C 3
B.15.494   Of Naȝareth, of Nynyue, of Neptalym and *Damaske*,
C. 7.173   In Armonye, in Alisaundre [and in *damaske*].
C.17.189   Of nasareth, of [n]yneue, of neptalym [and] *damaske*,
C.17.261   That bereth name of Neptalym, of Niniue [and] of *damaske*.

dame n *dame n.*   A 5 dame (4) damme (1); B 11; C 11
A. 7.70   *Dame* werche whanne tyme is piers wyf hatte;
A. 7.71   His douȝter hattiþ do riȝt [so] or þi *damme* shal þe bete;
A.11.1   Þanne hadde wyt a wyf þat hatte *dame* studie,
A.11.14   And sterneliche staringe *dame* studie seide:
A.11.176   Þat I was of wyttis hous & wiþ his wyf *dame* stodie.
B. 5.37   My sire seide to me, and so dide my *dame*,
B. 5.158   And maad hem Ioutes of Ianglyng þat *dame* Iohane was a bastard,
B. 5.159   And *dame* Clarice a knyȝtes douȝter ac a cokewold was hir sire,
B. 5.160   And *dame* Pernele a preestes fyle; Prioresse worþ she neuere
B. 5.497   A synful Marie þe seiȝ er seynte Marie þi *dame*,
B. 6.78   *Dame* werch-whan-tyme-is Piers wif hiȝte;
B. 6.79   His douȝter hiȝte do-riȝt-so-or-þi-*dame*-shal-þee-bete;
B.10.1   Thanne hadde wit a wif was hote *dame* Studie,
B.10.4   And al starynge *dame* Studie sterneliche [seide].
B.10.233   That I was of wittes hous and wiþ his wif *dame* Studie.
B.13.339   To þe Soutere of Southwerk or of Shordych *dame* Emme;
C. 2.123   For mede is moilere, amendes was here *dame*;
C. 6.133   And made hem ioutes of iangelynge: "*dame* Ione was a bastard,
C. 6.134   And *dame* clarice a knyhtes douhter, a cokewolde was here syre,
C. 6.135   And *dame* purnele a prestis fyle; Prioresse worth he neuere
C. 7.137   A synful marie þe sey ar seynte marye þy *dame*
C. 8.80   *Dame* worch-when-tyme-is [Peres] wyf hehte;
C. 8.81   His douhter hihte do-rihte-so-or-thy-*dame*-shal-þe-bete;
C. 9.317   And his fadur Is[rael] and also his *dame*.
C.11.1   Thenne hadde wit a wyf was hote *dame* studie
C.11.4   Al staryng *dame* studie sterneliche sayde.
C.20.282   That Belial, thy beelsyre, beet with thy *dame*

damyselle n *damisele n.*   A 1 damysele; B 3 damyseles (2) damyselle (1);   C 2 damysele (1) damoyseles (1)
A.10.12   Dobet is hire *damysele*, sire dowelis [douȝter],
B. 9.12   Dobet is hire *damyselle*, sire doweles douȝter,
B.11.12   Thanne hadde Fortune folwynge hire two fair *damyseles*:
B.18.424   Til þe day dawed þise *damyseles* [carolden]
C.10.139   Dobet is here *damysele*, sire dowelus douhtur,
C.20.467   Til þe day dawed thes *damoyseles* caroled

damme > *dame*

dampnacion n *dampnacioun n.*   B 1
B.12.87   And deeþ and *dampnacion* to hem þat deyeþ yuele,

dampneþ v *dampnen v.*   A 1 dampne; B 11 dampne (1) dampned (6) dampnede (1) dampneþ (3); C 13 dampne (2) dampned (5) dampnede (2) dampneth (3) ydampned (1)
A. 5.244   *Dampne* me nouȝt at domisday for þat I dede so ille.'
B. 2.103   A dwellynge wiþ þe deuel and *dampned* be for euere
B. 5.470   *Dampne* me noȝt at domesday for þat I dide so ille.'
B.10.435   Of wit and of wisedom wiþ *dampned* soules wonye.
B.11.142   How [I] was ded and *dampned* to dwellen in pyne
B.12.91   *Dampneþ* vs at þe day of dome as [dide þe caractes] þe Iewes.
B.15.550   Reson and rightful doom þ[o] Religiouse d[ampn]ede.
B.17.268   That] Diues deyde, *dampned* for his vnkyndenesse
B.17.307   Be raunsoned for his repentaunce þer alle reson hym *dampneþ*.
B.18.294   We haue no trewe title to hem, for þoruȝ treson were þei *dampned*.'
B.18.378   Shul noȝt be *dampned* to þe deeþ þat [dureþ] wiþouten ende:
B.18.385   Ther doom to þe deeþ *dampneþ* alle wikked,
C. 6.324   *Dampne* me nat at domesday for þat y dede so ylle.'
C. 7.146   For dedes that we han don ylle *dampned* sholde we ben neuere
C. 9.158   And lyueth lyke a lollare, goddes lawe hym *dampneth*.
C.12.77   How y was ded and *dampned* to dwellen in [pyne]
C.12.243   And tho that dede þe dede *ydampned* þerfore aftur
C.17.137   For lechours louyen aȝen þe lawe and at þe laste ben *dampned*
C.17.213   Resoun and rihtful doem tho religious *dampnede*.
C.17.215   Shal *dampne* dos ecclesie and depose ȝow for ȝoure pruyde:

C.19.234 That diues deyede, *dampned* for his vnkyndenesse
C.19.243 And *dampned* a dwelleth with þe deuel in helle.
C.19.287 Be yraunsomed for his repentaunce þer alle resoun hym *dampneth*.
C.20.308 Reuen vs of oure riht sethe resoun hem *dampnede*.
C.20.427 Ther þat doem to þe deth *dampneth* alle wikkede

dandy > handy_dandy

daniel n prop *n.i.d.* A 3; B 6 Daniel (5) danyel (1); C 3 daniel (1) danyel (2)

A. 8.136 How *Dani[el]* deui[n]ide þe drem[is] of a king
A. 8.138 *Daniel* seide, 'sire king, þi sweuene is to mene
A. 8.141 As *daniel* deui[n]ide in dede it fel aftir:
B. 6.71 And *danyel* þe dees pleyere and Denote þe baude
B. 7.158 How *Daniel* diuined þe dre[mes] of a kyng
B. 7.160 *Daniel* seide, 'sire kyng, þi [sweuene is to mene]
B. 7.163 As *Daniel* diuined in dede it fel after:
B.15.599 *Daniel* of hire vndoynge deuyned and seide
B.18.108 Now youre goode dayes arn doon as *daniel* prophecied;
C. 8.72 And *danyel* þe dees playere and denote þe baude
C. 9.306 How *danyel* deuynede and vndede þe dremes of kynges,
C.20.111 Now ben ȝoure gode dayes ydoen, as *daniel* of ȝow telleth;

dar v1 *durren v. &> darstow* A 11 dar (7) durst (1) durste (3); B 28 dar (16) dorste (12); C 24 dar (12) derste (1) dorste (1) durste (10)

A.Pr.38 Þat poule prechiþ of hem I *dar* not proue it here:
A. 2.196 Saue mede þe maiden no mo *durste* abide.
A. 3.189 I *durste* han leid my lif & no lesse wed
A. 4.39 I *dar* not for fer of hym fiȝte ne chide.
A. 5.83 He is douȝtiere þanne I–I *dar* non harm don hym,
A. 6.81 Deþ *dar* not do þing þat he defendiþ.
A. 7.252 And ȝif þou diȝete þe þus I *dar* ley myn armes
A. 9.113 I *durste* meue no mater to make hym to iangle,
A.11.91 I *dar* be his bolde boruȝ do bet wile he neuere,
A.11.109 Shuln wisse þe to dowel, I *dar* wel vndirtake.'
A.12.76 For gronyng of my guttys I *durst* gon no ferther].
B.Pr.38 That Poul precheþ of hem I [*dar*] nat preue it here;
B.Pr.152 'For doute of diuerse d[e]uele þat are noȝt wel loke,
B.Pr.178 That *dorste* haue bounden þe belle aboute þe cattes nekke,
B.Pr.210 Deuyne ye, for I ne *dar*, by deere god in heuene.
B. 2.34 And what man takeþ Mede, myn heed *dar* I legge,
B. 2.237 Saue Mede þe mayde na mo *dorste* abide.
B. 3.202 I *dorste* haue leyd my lif and no lasse wedde
B. 4.52 I *dar* noȝt for fere of h[y]m fiȝte ne chide.
B. 5.90 'I wolde ben yshryue', quod þis sherewe, 'and I for shame *dorste*.
B. 5.103 He is douȝtier þan I; I *dar* [noon harm don hym].
B. 5.356 *Dorste* lape of þat leuynges, so vnlouely [it] smauȝte.
B. 6.268 And if þow diete þee þus I *dar* legge myne [armes]
B. 8.123 I *dorste* meue no matere to maken hym to Iangle,
B.10.138 I *dar* ben his bolde borgh þat dobet wole he neuere,
B.10.157 Shullen wissen þee to dowel, I *dar* [wel] vndertake.'
B.11.86 'If I *dorste*', quod I, 'amonges men þis metels auowe!'
B.13.110 But cheeste be þer charite sholde be, and yonge children *dorste* pleyne
B.13.132 He wol noȝt ayein holy writ speken, I *dar* vndertake.'
B.14.109 Ther þe poore *dar* plede and preue by pure reson
B.15.383 I *dar* noȝt siggen it for shame–if swiche were apposed
B.15.414 [Ac] for drede of þe deeþ I *dar* noȝt telle truþe,
B.15.549 Moore tresor þan trouþe? I *dar* telle þe soþe;
B.16.212 And bitokneþ trewely, telle if I *dorste*,
B.16.214 The sone, if I *dorste* seye, resembleþ wel þe widewe:
B.17.112 Ac er þis day þre daies I *dar* vndertaken
B.18.158 So shal þis deeþ fordo, I *dar* my lif legge,
B.18.405 They *dorste* noȝt loke on oure lord, þe [leeste] of hem alle,
B.19.101 And so dide Iesu in hise dayes, whoso [*dorste*] telle it.
C.Pr.195 That *derste* haue ybounde þe belle aboute þe kattes nekke
C.Pr.221 Deuyne ȝe, for y ne *dar*, by dere god almyhten.
C. 2.36 And what [man] mede loueth, my lyf [*dar* y] wedde,
C. 2.253 Saue mede þe mayde no ma *durste* abyde.
C. 3.214 For pore men *dar* nat pleyne ne no pleynt shewe,
C. 3.236 Ac thow thysulue onliche, ho[so] hit segge *durste*,
C. 3.259 Y *durste* haue yleyd my lyf and no lasse wedde
C. 4.50 I *dar* nat for his felawschipe, in fayth,' pees sayde,
C. 4.191 'And y *dar* lege my lyf þat loue wol lene þe seluer
C. 6.414 *Durste* lape of þat lyuynge, so vnlouely hit smauhte.
C. 8.202 Þat *durste* withsitte þat [Peres] sayde for fere of syre hunger
C. 8.289 And yf thow dyete the thus y *dar* legge myn eres
C. 9.258 Certes, hoso *durste* sygge hit, Simon quasi dormit;
C. 9.262 Dispergentur oues, þe dogge *dar* nat berke.
C.10.119 Y *durste* meue no matere to maken hym to iangle,
C.15.113 And thenne dost thow wel and wysly, y *dar* hit wel avowe.'
C.15.285 There þe pore *dar* plede and preue by puyr resoun
C.17.29 Ac *durste* no beste byte hem by day ne by nyhte
C.17.69 Y *dar* nat carpe of clerkes now þat cristes [tresor] kepe

C.17.211 More tresor then treuthe? Y *dar* nat telle þe sothe
C.19.64 And dredfully withdrow hym and *durste* go no nerre.
C.20.161 And so shal this deth fordo, y *dar* my lyf legge,
C.20.448 They *dorste* nat loke on oure lord, the leste of hem alle,
C.21.101 And so dede iesu in his dayes, whoso *durste* tellen hit.

darstow v2 *thurven v.* B 1; C 1 dar
B.14.57 *Darstow* neuere care for corn ne cloþ ne for drynke,
C.15.256 *Dar* þe nat care for no corn ne for cloth ne for drynke

date n *date n.(2)* A 1; B 2; C 1
A. 2.77 In þe *date* of þe deuil þe dede is asselid
B. 2.113 'In þe *date* of þe deuel þ[e] dede [is asseled]
B.13.268 In þe *date* of oure driȝte, in a drye Aprill,
C. 2.117 'In þe *date* of the deuel th[e] dede is aseled

daubynge ger *daubing ger.* C 1
C. 8.198 In *daubynge* and in deluynge, in donge afeld berynge,

daunce v *dauncen v.* B 1; C 1 daunse
B.18.180 [Thanne] I shal *daunce* þerto; do þow so suster.
C.20.183 And y shal *daunse* þerto; do thow so sustur .

dauncelid ptp *daunselen v.* A 1
A.11.30 Or *daun[cel]id* or drawe forþ; þise disours wyte þe soþe.

daunger n *daunger n.* B 2; C 2
B.12.206 For he þat is ones a þef is eueremoore in *daunger*,
B.16.263 Ne no buyrn be oure borgh, ne brynge vs fram his *daunger*–
C.14.145 For he þat is ones a thef is eueremore in *daunger*
C.18.279 Ne noen bern ben oure borw ne bryngen vs [fro his] *daunger*–

daunse > daunce

daunsynge ger *dauncinge ger.* C 1
C.10.179 Ȝaf his douhter for a *daunsynge* in a disch þe heued

daunten v *daunten v.* A 1; B 3 daunted (2) daunten (1); C 1 daunte
A. 3.264 And dauid shal be dyademid & *daunten* hem alle,
B. 3.288 And Dauid shal be diademed and *daunten* hem alle,
B.10.38 Or *daunted* or drawe forþ; I do it on god hymselue.
B.15.401 *Daunted* a dowue and day and nyȝt hire fedde.
C. 3.441 And dauid shal be ydyademed and [*d*]*aunte* alle oure enemyes

dauid n prop *cf. David n.* A 4; B 23 Dauid (22) David (1); C 17 Dauid (16) dauyd (1)

A. 1.96 For *dauid*, in hise dayes, dubbide kniȝtes,
A. 3.264 And *dauid* shal be dyademid & daunten hem alle,
A.11.288 Or who dede wers þanne *dauid* þat vrie destroyede,
A.12.19 '*Dauid* godes derling defendyþ hit also:
B. 1.98 /For *Dauid* in hise dayes dubbed knyȝtes,
B. 2.36 How construeþ *David* þe kyng of men þat [caccheþ] Mede,
B. 3.236 Or resten in þyne holy hilles: þis askeþ *Dauid*.
B. 3.237 And *Dauid* assoileþ it hymself as þe Sauter telleþ:
B. 3.288 And *Dauid* shal be diademed and daunten hem alle,
B. 3.312 And dyngen vpon *Dauid* eche day til eue;
B.10.290 And þanne mowe ye [manly] seye, as *Dauid* made þe Sauter,
B.10.429 Or who [dide] worse þan *Dauid* þat vries deeþ conspired,
B.10.454 *Dauid* makeþ mencion, he spak amonges kynges,
B.11.94 And in þe Sauter also seiþ *dauid* þe prophete
B.11.280 As *Dauid* seiþ in þe Sauter: to swiche þat ben in wille
B.11.286 þei hir deuoir dide as *Dauid* seiþ in þe Sauter:
B.11.310 And also in þe Sauter seiþ *Dauid* to ouerskipperis,
B.12.13 And *Dauid* in þe Sauter seiþ, of swiche þat loueþ Iesus,
B.13.432 What *Dauid* seiþ of swiche men as þe Sauter telleþ:
B.14.94 As *Dauid* seiþ in þe Sauter: et quorum tecta sunt peccata.
B.14.131 And whan he dyeþ ben disalowed, as *Dauid* seiþ in þe Sauter:
B.15.490 Boþe Mathew and Marc and Memento domine *dauid*:
B.18.15 Thanne was feiþ in a fenestre and cryde 'a! fili *dauid*!'
B.19.133 For þe dedes þat he dide, Fili *dauid*, Iesus.
B.19.134 For *dauid* was doghtiest of dedes in his tyme;
B.19.135 The burdes þo songe, Saul interfecit mille et *dauid* decem milia.
B.19.136 Forþi þe contree þer Iesu cam called hym fili *dauid*,
C. 1.102 *Dauid* in his daies dobbed knyghtes,
C. 2.39 Y do hit vppon *dauyd*; the doumbe wil noȝt lyen:
C. 2.41 And *dauid* vndoth hymself as þe doumbe sheweth:
C. 3.441 And *dauid* shal be ydyademed and [*d*]aunte alle oure enemyes
C. 7.92 Wh[at] *dauid* sayth of such men as þe sauter telleth:
C. 7.153 That alle seyntes for synfol songen with *dauid*:
C.11.263 Or *dauid* þe douhty þat de[uyn]ed how vrye
C.11.279 *Dauid* maketh mensioun he spake among kynges
C.13.123 [To] ouerskipperes also in þe sauter sayth *dauid*:
C.14.69 And do we as *dauid* techeth for doute of godes veniance:
C.15.306 *Dauid* in þe sauter of suche maketh mynde and sayth: dormierunt
C.20.13 Thenne was faith in a fenestre and criede 'a! fil[i] *dauid*!'
C.20.355 That ȝe belyen nat this lewed men for at the laste *dauid*
C.21.133 For þe dedes þat he dede, fili *dauid*, iesus.

C.21.134   For *dauid* was douhtiest of dedes in his tyme
C.21.135   The buyrdes tho songe, Saul interfecit mille & *dauid* decem milia.
C.21.136   Forthy þe contre þer iesu cam calde hym fili *dauid*

dawe n prop *n.i.d.* A 1; B 2; C 2
A. 5.163   *Dawe* þe dykere & a dusȝeyn oþere,
B. 5.313   *Dawe* þe dykere and a doȝeyne oþere,]
B. 6.330   And *Dawe* þe dykere deye for hunger
C. 6.369   *Dawe* þe dikere with a dosoyne harlotes
C. 8.351   And *dawe* þe deluare dey for defaute

dawe v *dauen* v.   B 2 dawe (1) dawed (1); C 2 dawe (1) dawed (1)
B.18.181   For Iesus Iustede wel Ioye bigynneþ *dawe*:
B.18.424   Til þe day *dawed* þise damyseles [carolden]
C.20.184   For iesus ioustede wel ioy bigynneth *dawe*:
C.20.467   Til þe day *dawed* thes damoyseles caroled

debat n *debat* n.   A 1 debate; B 4 debaat (1) debat (2) debate (1); C 3 debaet (1) debat (2)
A. 5.179   And nempnide hym for a noumpere þat no *debate* nere.
B. 5.99   Bitwene [meyne and meyne] I make *debate* ofte
B. 5.330   And nempned hym for a nounpere þat no *debat* nere.
B.15.428   Alle þat ben at *debaat* and bedemen were trewe:
B.19.251   [Ne no boost ne] *debat* [be] among hem [alle]
C. 6.123   Thus Beggares and Barones at *debat* aren ofte
C. 6.388   And nempned hym for a noumper þat no *debat* were.
C.21.251   Ne no boest ne *debaet* be among hem alle.

deceite n *deceite* n.   A 1 deseites; B 2 deceite (1) deceites (1); C 3 deseite (1) deseyte (2)
A.11.19   Þat can construe *deseites*, & conspire wrongis,
B.10.19   [That] kan con[strue] *deceites* and conspire wronges
B.18.333   For þe dede þat þei dide, þi *deceite* it made;
C.Pr.77   His seel sholde nouȝt be ysent in *deseyte* of þe peple.
C. 2.131   That god wolde were ydo withoute som *deseyte*.
C.20.376   For the [dede] that they dede, thi *deseite* hit made;

deceyue v *deceiven* v.   A 2 desceyue (1) disseyue (1); B 3 deceyue; C 5 desseyue (1) disceue (2) disseyue (1) disseyued (1)
A.Pr.76   His sel shulde not be sent to *disseyue* þe peple.
A.11.164   Foundit hem formest folk to *desceyue*.
B.Pr.79   His seel sholde noȝt be sent to *deceyue* þe peple.
B.10.221   Founded hem formest folk to *deceyue*.
B.16.156   Thow shalt be myrour to many men to *deceyue*,
C. 1.40   And wysseth þe to ben ywar what wolde þe *desseyue*.'
C.11.16   Ho can caste and contreue to *disseyue* þe ri[gh]tfole,
C.17.184   *Disceue* so the sarrasyns, sothlyche me thynketh
C.18.122   That thorw fals biheste and fruyt furste man *disseyued*,
C.18.173   Thow shalt be myrrour to monye men to *disceue*.

declare v *declaren* v.   B 1; C 3 declare (2) declareth (1)
B.14.288   Selde sit pouerte þe soþe to *declare*,
C. 2.151   And ledeth here to londone there lawe may *declare*
C. 9.49   And for þe loue of oure lord lawe for hem *declareth*
C.16.123   Selde syt pouerte þe soth to *declare*

declynede v *declinen* v.   A 1
A. 4.133   For to construe þis clause *declynede* faste,

decourreþ v *cf. Latin decorio*   B 1
B.14.194   Of pompe and of pride þe parchemyn *decourreþ*,

[decre] n *decre* n.   A 1 degre; B 1 decrees; C 1 decres
A.11.241   For cristene han a *degre* & is þe comun speche:
B.15.380   Doctours of *decrees* and of diuinite maistres,
C.17.114   Doctours of *decre[s]* and of diuinite maistres

decretals n *decretal* n.   B 1
B. 5.421   Ac in Canoun nor in *decretals* I kan noȝt rede a lyne.

decretistre n *decretiste* n.   C 1
C.15.84   'A[c] this doctour and dyuynour,' quod y, 'and *decretistre* of Canoen,

ded adj *ded* adj., *ded* adj.as n. *cf. ded* ptp   A 3 ded (2) dede (1); B 15 ded (1) dede (8) deed (6); C 15 ded (7) dede (8)
A. 1.161   And as *ded* as a dorenail but ȝif þe dede folewe.
A. 7.170   Þei hadde be *ded* be þis day & doluen al warm.
A. 8.171   At þe dredful dom whanne *dede* shal arisen
B. 1.187   And as *deed* as a dore[nail] but if þe ded[e] folwe:
B. 6.180   They hadde be [*dede* and] doluen, ne deme þow noon ooþer.
B. 7.193   At þe dredful dome, whan *dede* shulle rise
B.11.142   How [I] was *ded* and dampned to dwellen in pyne
B.14.324   I ne hadde be *deed* and doluen for dowelis sake!
B.15.594   And vnder stoon *deed* and stank; wiþ stif vois hym callede:
B.18.62   *Dede* men for þat dene come out of depe graues
B.18.64   'For a bitter bataille', þe *dede* body seide;
B.18.70   Wher he be *deed* or noȝt deed doun er he be taken.'

B.18.70   Wher he be *deed* or noȝt *deed* doun er he be taken.'
B.18.95   To do þe blynde bete [þe *dede*], it was a boyes counseille.
B.18.156   Til he be *deed* and do þerto; þe yuel he destruyeþ,
B.19.53   And þo was he conquerour called of quyke and of *dede*,
B.19.196   And demen hem at domesday, boþe quyke and *dede*,
B.20.293   And suffre þe *dede* in dette to þe day of doome.
C. 1.183   And as *ded* as [a] dore nayl but yf þe ded[e] folowe:
C. 9.21   And deme with hem at domesday bothe quyke and *dede*.
C. 9.339   At þe dredful dome, when *dede* shullen ryse
C.12.77   How y was *ded* and dampned to dwellen in [pyne]
C.12.185   And thorw þe grace of god and grayn *dede* [i]n erthe
C.13.57   And dredeth to be *ded* þerfore and he in derke mette
C.20.64   And *dede* men for þat dene cam oute of depe graues
C.20.66   'For a bittur bataile,' þe *ded* body saide;
C.20.72   Wher he be *ded* or nat ded down or he be taken.'
C.20.72   Wher he be *ded* or nat *ded* down or he be taken.'
C.20.98   [To do] þe blynde bete the *dede*, [hit] was a boyes [conseille].
C.20.159   Til he [be] *ded* [and] ydo þerto; [þe yuel] he destruyeth,
C.21.53   And tho was he conquerour cald of quyke and of *dede*
C.21.196   And demen hem at domesday, bothe quyke and *dede*,
C.22.293   And soffren þe *dede* in dette to þe day of dome.

ded ptp *deden* v.   A 1; B 1
A. 3.180   And dreddist to be *ded* for a dym cloud,
B. 3.193   And dreddest to be *ded* for a dym cloude,

ded &> doon; deddly > dedly

dede n *dede* n. *&> ded,doon* A 15 dede (11) dedis (4); B 32 dede (21) dedes (11) dedis (11); C 27 dede (15) dedes (11) dedis (1)
A.Pr.102   As dikeris & delueris þat doþ here *dede* ille
A. 1.31   And al he wytide it wyn þ[at] wykkide *dede*.
A. 1.161   And as ded as a dorenail but ȝif þe *dede* folewe.
A. 2.77   In þe date of þe deuil þe *dede* is asselid
A. 2.125   To wende wiþ hem to westmynstre to wytnesse þ[is] *dede*.
A. 3.61   To writen in wyndowis of ȝoure wel *dedis*,
A. 3.242   Shulde diȝe for a *dede* þat don hadde here eldren
A. 4.54   For þat wrong hadde wrouȝt so wykkide a *dede*,
A. 4.108   And do it in *dede* to drawe vs to goode;
A. 5.252   Wepynge & weylyng for here wykkide *dedis*;
A. 8.141   As daniel deui[n]ide in *dede* it fel aftir:
A.10.121   And þus of dred & h[is] *dede* dobest arisiþ.
A.10.173   Alle shuln deiȝe for his *dedis* be dounes & hilles,
A.10.205   Þat *dede* derne do no man ne shulde.
A.12.87   Fro deþ þat is oure duk swyche *dedis* we brynge.'
B.Pr.152   'For doute of diuerse d[e]des we dar noȝt wel loke,
B.Pr.224   As dykeres and delueres þat doon hire *ded[e]* ille
B. 1.31   And al he witte it wyn þat wikked *dede*:
B. 1.187   And as deed as a dore[nail] but if þe *ded[e]* folwe:
B. 2.113   'In þe date of þe deuel þ[e] *dede* [is asseled]
B. 2.161   To wenden wiþ hem to westmynstre to witnesse þis *dede*.
B. 3.65   To writen in wyndowes of hir wel *dedes*,
B. 3.70   To writen in wyndowes of youre wel *dedes*
B. 3.263   Sholden deye for a *dede* þat doon hadde hire eldres.
B. 3.318   But after þe *dede* þat is doon oon doom shal rewarde
B. 4.68   For þat wrong hadde ywroȝt so wikked a *dede*,
B. 5.43   And dooþ it in *dede*, it shal drawe yow to goode.
B. 5.242   Swiche *dedes* I dide write if he his day breke;
B. 5.500   Of þyne douȝt[iest] *dedes* was doon in oure armes:
B. 5.505   That euere þei wraþed þee in þis world in word, þouȝt or *dedes*.'
B. 7.163   As Daniel diuined in *dede* it fel after:
B. 9.142   Alle shul deye for hise *dedes* by [dounes] and hulles,
B. 9.192   That [*dede* derne] do no man ne sholde.
B.10.364   And but we do þus in *dede*, [er] þe day of dome,
B.11.51   Than dowel or dobet among my *dedes* alle.
B.12.76   A womman, as [we] fynde[n], was gilty of þat *dede*,
B.13.133   'Thanne passe we ouer til Piers come and preue þis in *dede*.
B.13.305   Of *dedes* þat he neuere dide demen and bosten:
B.14.328   That [euere he] dide *dede* þat deere god displesed;
B.18.90   For þe *dede* þat I haue doon I do me in youre grace.
B.18.187   And þat þis *dede* shal dure dormiam & requiescam.'
B.18.333   For þe *dede* þat þei dide, þi deceite it made;
B.19.133   For þe *dedes* þat he dide, Fili dauid, Iesus.
B.19.134   For dauid was doghtiest of *dedes* in his tyme;
B.19.182   And whan þis *dede* was doon do best he [þouȝte],
B.19.278   Er he [dide] any [*dede*] deuyse wel þe ende;
B.19.329   And whan þis *dede* was doon Grace deuysede
C.Pr.228   As dykers and deluers þat doth here *dedis* ylle
C. 1.30   And al he witte [it] wyn [þat] wikkede *dede*:
C. 1.183   And as ded as [a] dore nayl but yf þe *ded[e]* folowe:
C. 2.117   'In þe date of the deuel th[e] *dede* is aseled
C. 3.69   To writen [i]n wyndowes of eny wel *dedes*,
C. 3.304   When þe *dede* is ydo and þe day endit.
C. 3.416   Sholde deye der[f]ly for *dedes* of here eldres.

C. 3.471 But aftur þe *dede* þat is ydo the doom shal recorde
C. 5.9 And no *dede* to do but drynke and slepe.
C. 6.334 For al the wrecchednesse of this world and wikkede *dedes*
C. 7.140 Of thy douhtiokest *dedes* was don in oure sekte:
C. 7.146 For *dedes* that we han don ylle dampned sholde we ben neuere
C. 7.150 That euere they gulte aȝeyn þe, god, in gost or in *dede*.'
C.10.230 Alle sholle deye for his *dedes* by dales and hulles
C.10.237 Holy writ witnesseth þat for no wikkede *dede*
C.10.292 For þat *dede* derne do no man sholde
C.12.243 And tho that dede þe *dede* ydampned þerfore aftur
C.13.155 As in derne *dedes*, bothe drynkyng and elles.
C.15.301 Many man hath his ioye here for al here wel *dedes*
C.16.193 And when y wol do or [nat do] gode *dedes* or ille
C.20.92 Of þe *dede* þat y haue do y do me in ȝoure grace;
C.20.192 And that this *dede* shal duyre, dormiam & requiescam.'
C.20.376 For the [*dede*] that they dede, thi deseite hit made;
C.21.133 For þe *dedes* þat he dede, fili dauid, iesus.
C.21.134 For dauid was douhtiest of *dedes* in his tyme
C.21.182 And when this *dede* was doen do best he thouhte
C.21.278 Ar he dede eny *dede* deuyse wel þe ende;

deden > doon

dedeynus adj *disdeinous adj.* C 1
C.10.81 And is nat dronklewe ne *dedeynus*, dowel h[y]m foleweth.

dedist > doon

dedly adj *dedli adj.* A 4; B 15 dedly (12) dedlich (1) dedliche (1) deedly (1); C 9 deddly (1) dedly (8)
A. 1.132 No *dedly* synne to do, diȝe þeiȝ þou shuldist.
A. 5.20 Þat *dedly* synne er domisday shal fordon hem alle.
A. 9.40 Ac *dedly* synne doþ he nouȝt, for dowel hym helpiþ,
A. 9.46 And don *dedly* synne & drenche þiselue.
B. 1.144 No *dedly* synne to do, deye þeiȝ þow sholdest,
B. 5.20 That *dedly* synne er domesday shal fordoon hem alle.
B. 8.44 Ac *dedly* synne doþ he noȝt for dowel hym [helpeþ],
B. 8.50 And] do *deedly* synne and drenche þi[selue].
B. 9.210 And dryueþ awey dowel þoruȝ *dedliche* synnes.'
B.10.243 Fro þe *dedly* deeþ and [þe] deueles power
B.11.102 To reden it in Retorik to arate *dedly* synne?
B.13.387 As if I hadde *dedly* synne doon I dredde noȝt þat so soore
B.13.405 And þanne I dradde to deye in *dedlich* synne',
B.14.79 Diden *dedly* synne þat þe deuel liked,
B.14.84 Which dryueþ awey *dedly* synne and dooþ it to be venial.
B.14.89 And surgiens for *dedly* synnes whan shrift of mouþe failleþ.
B.14.91 For shrift of mouþe sleeþ synne be it neuer so *dedly*–
B.14.96 And as it neuere [n]adde ybe to noȝte bryngeþ *dedly* synne
B.15.541 Than cristes cros þat ouercam deeþ and *dedly* synne.
C. 1.143 Dey rather þen do eny *dedly* synne:
C. 5.122 That *dedly* synne ar domesday shal fordon hem alle.
C. 6.276 As thow y *deddly* synne dede y dradde [hit] nat so sore
C. 7.210 Thenne eny *dedly* synne do for drede or for preeyere.
C. 9.239 Y drede me, and he dey, hit worth for *dedly* synne
C.10.43 So *dedly* synne doth he nat for dowel hym helpeth.
C.12.36 To rehercen hit by retoryk to arate *dedly* synne?
C.17.203 Thenne cristes cros þat ouercome deth and *dedly* synne.
C.17.291 And deye for his dere childrene to de[struy]e *dedly* synne,

dedly adv *dedli adv.* A 2 dedly (1) *dedliche* (1); B 2; C 1
A. 8.162 Soulis þat han ysynned seue siþes *dedly*.
A.10.156 And alle þat couplide hem with þat kyn crist hatide [*dedliche*].
B. 5.116 Whoso vndernymeþ me herof, I hate hym *dedly* after.
B. 7.184 Soules þat haue synned seuen siþes *dedly*.
C. 9.330 Soules þat haue syneged seuene sythes *dedly*.

deed(ly > ded(ly; deef > def

deel n *del n.(2) &> dele* B 1
B.15.488 Wiþouten trauaille þe tiþe *deel* þat trewe men biswynken?

deele > dele

deen n *den n.(2)* A 2 denis; B 2 deen (1) denes (1)
A.Pr.92 Archidekns & *denis* þat dignites hauen
A. 2.137 And alle þe *denis* & southdenis, as destreris hem diȝte,
B. 2.173 *Denes* and Southdenes, drawe yow togideres;
B.13.65 'It is noȝt foure dayes þat þis freke, bifore þe *deen* of Poules,

deep adj *dep adj.* A 2 dep (1) depe (1); B 4 deep (2) depe (2); C 5 deep (1) dep (1) depe (3)
A.Pr.15 A *dep* dale beneþe, a dungeoun þereinne
A.Pr.16 Wiþ *depe* dikes & derke & dredful of siȝt.
B.Pr.15 A *deep* dale byneþe, a dongeon þerInne
B.Pr.16 Wiþ *depe* diches and derke and dredfulle of siȝte.
B. 1.115 Into a *deep* derk helle to dwelle þere for euere;
B.18.62 Dede men for þat dene come out of *depe* graues

C.Pr.17 And seigh a *depe* dale; deth, as y leue,
C. 1.55 'The *dep* dale and þe derk, so vnsemely to se to,
C.20.64 And dede men for þat dene cam oute of *depe* graues
C.20.405 Ac y wol drynke of no dische ne of *deep* clergyse
C.20.407 Ac thy drynke worth deth and *depe* helle thy bolle.

deere adj *dere adj.(1)* A 4 dere; B 11 deere (10) derrest (1); C 15 dere
A. 1.85 It is as derworþi a dreury as *dere* god hymseluen.
A. 5.223 Þat I ne shal do me er day to þe *dere* chirche
A. 7.89 And dele among my frendis & my *dere* children,
A. 7.238 Eny l[e]f of lechecraft lere it me, my *dere*,
B.Pr.210 Deuyne ye, for I ne dar, by *deere* god in heuene.
B. 1.87 It is as dereworþe a drury as *dere* god hymseluen.
B. 2.13 And Diamaundes of *derrest* pris and double manere Saphires,
B. 5.451 That I ne shal do me er day to þe *deere* chirche
B. 6.97 And dele among my [frendes] and my *deere* children.
B. 6.161 'And fro þise wastours wolueskynnes þat makeþ þe world *deere*,
B. 6.254 Any leef of lechecraft lere it me, my *deere*;
B. 9.202 Dowel, my [*deere*], is to doon as lawe techeþ:
B.12.12 And wiþ þise bittre baleises god beteþ his *deere* children:
B.14.75 [Ac] mesure is [so] muche worþ it may noȝt be to *deere*.
B.14.328 That [euere he] dide dede þat *deere* god displesed;
C.Pr.221 Deuyne ȝe, for y ne dar, by *dere* god almyhten.
C. 1.83 Hit is a[s] derworthe a druerie as *dere* god hymseluen.
C. 2.33 And y am his *dere* doughter, ducchesse of heuene.
C. 7.65 That y ne shal do me er day to þe *dere* chirche
C. 8.91 Ac aftur here doynge do thow nat, my *dere* sone,' quod Peres,
C. 8.106 And delen amongus my douhteres and my *dere* childre[n].
C. 8.158 'Awreke me of this wastors þat maketh this world *dere*–
C.10.13 Wher þat dowel dwelleth; '*dere* frendes, telleth me,
C.10.127 And what þey drede and doute, *dere* sire, telleth.'
C.10.198 Sholde doute no deth ne no *dere* ȝeres
C.11.133 For of dobet and dobest here doctour is *dere* loue.'
C.13.18 Derworthe and *dere* god, do we so mala",
C.13.168 Dompynges dyuede; '*dere* God,' y sayde,
C.15.195 'What manere munstracye, my *dere* frende,' quod Concience,
C.17.291 And deye for his *dere* childrene to de[struy]e dedly synne,

deere adv *dere adv.* A 3 dere; B 5; C 3 dere
A. 6.80 He may do wiþ þe day sterre what hym *dere* likiþ;
A. 7.73 And deme hem nouȝt for ȝif þou dost þou shalt it *dere* abiggen,
A. 7.275 Þanne may I diȝte þi dyner as þe *dere* likeþ;
B. 6.81 Deme-hem-noȝt-for-if-þow-doost-þow-shalt-it-*deere*-abugge-
B. 6.291 [Th]anne may I diȝte þi dyner as [þee] *deere* likeþ.'
B. 9.66 Allas þat drynke shal fordo þat god *deere* bouȝte,
B.12.42 Iob þe Iew his ioye *deere* abouȝte;
B.17.288 For coueitise of any kynnes þyng þat crist *deere* bouȝte.
C. 8.83 Deme-hem-nat-[for]-yf-thow-doest-thow-shalt-hit-*dere*-abygge-
C. 8.314 Thenne may y dyhte [þ]y dyner as me *dere* lyketh.'
C.19.269 For coueytise of eny kyne thynge þat Crist *dere* bouhte.

deere &> deren

dees n *de n. &> deys* B 1; C 1
B. 6.71 And danyel þe *dees* pleyere and Denote þe baude
C. 8.72 And danyel þe *dees* playere and denote þe baude

deeþ n *deth n.* A 16 deth (1) deþ (11) deþe (4); B 70 deeþ (57) deþ (4) deþe (8) deþes (1); C 64 deth (55) dethe (8) dethus (1)
A. 1.118 Aftir here *deþ* day & dwelle wiþ þat shrewe.
A. 1.145 To haue pite on þat peple þat pynede hym to *deþe*.
A. 3.98 Henis to þe *deþe* do þou so no more.
A. 3.247 Children & cherlis, choppe hem to *deþe*.
A. 3.250 Barnes and bestis brenne hem to *deþe*."
A. 6.81 *Deþ* dar not do þing þat he defendiþ.
A. 8.53 Shal no deuil at his *deþ* day derie hym a myte
A. 8.100 Þat aftir þi *deþ* day to helle shalt þou wende.'
A. 8.183 Þat, aftir oure *deþ* day, dowel reherse
A.10.214 And aftir here *deþ* day shuln dwelle with þe same
A.11.290 Cristene kynde to kille to *deþe*?
A.12.63 'I am dwellyng with *deth*, and hunger I hatte.
A.12.81 'With *deþ* I duelle,' quod he, 'dayes and nyȝtes.
A.12.83 I am masager of *deþ*; men haue I tweyne:
A.12.87 Fro *deþ* þat is oure duk swyche dedis we brynge.'
A.12.104 *Deþ* delt him a dent and drof him to þe erþe
B. 1.129 After hir *deþ* day and dwelle with þat sherewe.
B. 1.171 To haue pite [on] þat peple þat peyned hym to *deþe*.
B. 3.109 Hennes to þi *deeþ* day do [þow] so na moore.
B. 3.267 Burnes and beestes, bren hem to *deþe*.
B. 3.307 Shal be demed to þe *deeþ* but if he do it smyþye
B. 3.324 And what smyth þat any smyþeþ be smyte þerwiþ to *deþe*:
B. 5.489 Ther þiself ne þi sone no sorwe in *deeþ* feledest,
B. 6.329 Thanne shal *deeþ* wiþdrawe and derþe be Iustice
B. 7.51 Shal no deuel at his *deeþ* day deren hym a myte
B. 7.57 Whan þei drawen on to [þe *deþ*] and Indulgences wolde haue,

161

B. 7.118 [That] after þi *deeþ* day þe deuel shal haue þi soule.'
B. 7.205 That, after oure *deeþ* day, dowel reherce
B. 9.200 And after hir *deeþ* day shul dwelle wiþ þe same
B.10.82 Ne for drede of þe *deeþ* wiþdrawe noȝt hir pride,
B.10.111 And al hir seed for hir synne þe same *deeþ* suffrede?
B.10.243 Fro þe dedly *deeþ* and [þe] deueles power
B.10.417 [At domesday þe deluuye worþ of *deþ* and fir at ones;
B.10.429 Or who [dide] worse þan Dauid þat vries *deeþ* conspired,
B.10.431 Cristene kynde to kille to *deþe*?
B.11.177 Whoso loueþ noȝt, leue me, he lyueþ in *deeþ* deyinge.
B.11.268 And lasse he dredeþ *deeþ* and in derke to ben yrobbed
B.12.75 Wiþ stones men sholde hir strike and stone hire to *deþe*.
B.12.87 And *deeþ* and dampnacion to hem þat deyeþ yuele,
B.12.248 And deleþ it noȝt til his *deeþ* day, þe tail[le is al of] sorwe.
B.13.425 In youre *deeþ* deyinge I drede me soore
B.13.450 And in his *deeþ* deyinge þei don hym gret confort
B.14.58 Ne *deeþ* drede [ne deuel], but deye as god likeþ
B.14.107 Whan he drogh to his *deeþ* day þat he ne dredde hym soore,
B.15.414 [Ac] for drede of þe *deeþ* I dar noȝt telle truþe,
B.15.522 In dolful *deþ* deyeden for hir faith.
B.15.541 Than cristes cros þat ouercam *deeþ* and dedly synne.
B.16.165 Ayeins *deeþ* and þe deuel: destruyed hir boþeres myȝtes,
B.16.166 Deide and *dee[þ]* fordide, and day of nyȝt made.
B.17.19 Shal neuere deuel hym dere ne *deeþ* in soule greue;
B.18.29 *Deeþ* seiþ he shal fordo and adoun brynge
B.18.32 That, for al þat *deeþ* kan do, wiþInne þre daies to walke
B.18.35 And forbete adoun brynge bale *deeþ* for euere:
B.18.37 To se how doghtiliche *deeþ* sholde do and deme hir boþeres right.
B.18.53 And beden hym drynken his *deeþ* [to lette and] hise daies [lengþe],
B.18.65 'Lif and *deeþ*, in þis derknesse hir oon fordooþ hir ooþer.
B.18.71 Two þeues [þat tyme] þoled *deeþ* [also]
B.18.101 For be þis derkenesse ydo *deeþ* worþ [yvenquisshed];
B.18.134 Which deide and *deeþ* þoled þis day aboute mydday,
B.18.141 And þat *deeþ* adown brouȝte, deeþ shal releue.'
B.18.141 And þat deeþ adown brouȝte, *deeþ* shal releue.'
B.18.158 So shal þis *deeþ* fordo, I dar my lif legge,
B.18.159 Al þat *deeþ* [d]ide first þoruȝ þe deueles entisyng,
B.18.211 Wite what wo is, ne were þe *deeþ* of kynde.
B.18.275 May no *deeþ* [þis lord] dere, ne no deueles queyntise,
B.18.302 For Iewes hateden hym and han doon hym to *deþe*.
B.18.345 And þat *deeþ* in hem fordide my deeþ shal releue
B.18.345 And þat deeþ in hem fordide my *deeþ* shal releue
B.18.364 That art doctour of *deeþ* drynk þat þow madest.
B.18.378 Shul noȝt be dampned to þe *deeþ* þat [dureþ] wiþouten ende:
B.18.382 There [a] feloun þole sholde *deeþ* ooþer Iuwise
B.18.385 Ther doom to þe *deeþ* dampneþ alle wikked,
B.19.10 'Is þis Iesus þe Iustere', quod I, 'þat Iewes dide to *deþe*?
B.19.51 Mighte no *deeþ* hym fordo ne adoun brynge
B.19.141 And for to doon hym to *deþe* day and nyȝt þei casten,
B.19.174 Deidest and *deeþ* þoledest and deme shalt vs alle,
B.19.306 Neiþer of duc ne of *deeþ* þat he ne dide lawe
B.20.89 Wiþ *deeþ* þat is dredful to vndo vs alle!'
B.20.96 And bar þe baner bifore *deeþ*; bi riȝt he it cleymede.
B.20.100 *Deeþ* cam dryuynge after and al to duste passhed
B.20.105 Swowned and swelted for sorwe of [*deþes*] dyntes.
B.20.139 Departen er *deeþ* cam and deuors shapte.
B.20.154 Shal do þee noȝt drede, neiþer *deeþ* ne elde,
B.20.174 And dryuen awey *deeþ* wiþ Dyas and drogges.
B.20.200 And *deeþ* drogh neiȝ me; for drede gan I quake,
B.20.352 And be adrad of *deeþ* and wiþdrawe hym fram pryde
C.Pr.17 And seigh a depe dale; *deth*, as y leue,
C. 1.131 Aftur here *deth* day and dwelle ther wrong is;
C. 1.167 To haue pitee on þat peple þat paynede hym to *dethe*.
C. 2.109 After here *deth* dwellen day withouten ende
C. 3.460 Shal be demed to þe *deth* but yf he do hit smythye
C. 3.477 And yf eny smyth smeth[e] hit be smyte þerwith to *dethe*:
C. 7.85 In ȝoure *deth* deynge y drede me sore
C. 7.710 And in his *deth* deynge they don hym greet confort
C. 8.187 Al for drede of here *deth*, such duntus ȝaf hunger.
C. 8.350 And thenne shal *deth* withdrawe and derthe be Iustice
C. 9.17 Drede nat for no *deth* to distruye by here power
C. 9.52 For whenne ȝe drawe to þe *deth* and indulgences wolde haue
C. 9.351 That aftur oure *deth* day dowel reherce
C.10.198 Sholde doute no *deth* ne no dere ȝeres
C.10.299 And after her *deth* day dwellen shollen in helle
C.11.60 And gode men for oure gultes he al togrynt to *deth*.
C.11.62 Ne for drede of eny *deth* withdraweth h[e]m fro pruyde
C.11.249 At domesday a deluuye worth of *deth* and fuyr at ones.
C.11.267 Cristene [kynde] to culle to *dethe*?
C.12.153 And lasse drat [*dethe*] or in derke to ben yrobbed
C.14.42 To strike with stoen or with staf this strompet to *dethe*."
C.15.257 Ne d[e]*th* drede ne deuel, [but] deye as god liketh
C.15.282 When he drow to þe *deth* that he ne dradd hym sarrore

C.15.304 Ac when *deth* awaketh hem of here we[le] þat were er so ryche
C.16.313 Of *deth* ne of derthe drad he neuere
C.17.203 Thenne cristes cros þat ouercome *deth* and dedly synne.
C.17.270 Mony [a] seynte sethe soffrede *deth* also,
C.19.20 Shal neuere deuel hym dere ne *deth* in soule greue;
C.20.28 *Deth* saith a wol fordo and adown brynge
C.20.31 That for al þat *deth* can do, withynne thre dayes to walke
C.20.34 And forbete [and adown] b[r]ynge bale *deth* for euere:
C.20.36 To se how douhtyliche *deth* sholde do and demen [h]er beyre rihte.
C.20.53 And beden hym drynke his *deth* to lette and his dayes lenghe
C.20.67 'Lyf & *deth*, in this derkenesse here oen fordoth her oþer.
C.20.73 T[w]o theues tho tholed *deth* þat tyme
C.20.104 For be this derkenesse ydo *deth* worth yvenkused;
C.20.137 [Which] deyede and *deth* tholede this day aboute mydday,
C.20.144 And þat *deth* down brouhte, deth shal releue.'
C.20.144 And þat deth down brouhte, *deth* shal releue.'
C.20.161 And so shal this *deth* fordo, y dar my lyf legge,
C.20.162 All þat *deth* and þe deuel dede formost to Eue
C.20.218 He hadde nat wist witterly where *deth* were sour or swete.
C.20.220 Ywyte what wo is ne were þe *deth* of kynde.
C.20.297 May no *deth* this lord dere ne [n]o deueles quentyse
C.20.390 And þat *deth* fordede my deth to releue
C.20.390 And þat deth fordede my *deth* to releue
C.20.402 That art doctour of *deth* drynke þat thow madest.
C.20.407 Ac thy drynke worth *deth* and depe helle thy bolle.
C.20.424 Ther a thief tholie sholde *deth* oþer iewyse
C.20.427 Ther þat doem to þe *deth* dampneth alle wikkede
C.21.10 'Is this iesus þe ioustare,' quod y, 'þat iewes dede to *dethe*?
C.21.51 Myhte no *deth* hym fordo ne adown brynge
C.21.141 And for to do hym to *dethe* day and nyhte they casten,
C.21.174 Deyedest and *deth* tholedest and deme shalt vs all
C.21.306 Noþer of deuk ne of *deth* þat he ne dede lawe
C.22.89 With *deth* þat is dredful to vndoen vs alle!'
C.22.96 And baer þe baner bifore *deth*; bi riht he hit claymede.
C.22.100 *Deth* cam dryuyng aftur and al to duste paschte
C.22.105 Swowened and swel[t]e for sorwe of *dethus* duntes.
C.22.139 Departen ar *dethe* come and deuors shupte.
C.22.154 Shal do the nat drede, noþer *deth* ne elde,
C.22.174 And dryue awey *deth* with dyaes and drogges.
C.22.200 And *deth* drow ney me; for drede gan y quaken
C.22.352 And be adrad of *deth* and withdrawe hym fro pruyde

def adj *def adj.* A 1; B 3 deef (1) def (1) deue (1); C 2 deef (1) deue (1)
A.11.88 What is dowel fro dobet; now *def* mote he worþe,
B.10.79 [For god is *def* nowadayes and deyneþ [noȝt vs to here],
B.10.135 What is dowel fro dobet, [now] *deef* mote he worþe,
B.19.130 For *deue* þoruȝ hise doynges and dombe speke [and herde],
C.11.59 For god is *deef* nowadayes and deyneth [nat vs] to here
C.21.130 For *deue* thorw his doynges and dombe speke [&] herde

defame v *defamen v.* A 1; B 1
A.11.64 And [ek] *defame* þe fadir þat vs alle made,
B.Pr.190 But fedeþ hym al wiþ venyson, *defame* we hym neuere;

defaute n *defaute n.* A 4; B 21 defaute (19) defautes (2); C 21
A. 2.104 And ȝif he fynde ȝow in *defaute*, & wiþ fals holden,
A. 5.6 Þat I ne miȝte ferþere a fote for *defaute* of slepyng.
A. 7.192 And for *defaute* of foode þus faste hy werchiþ.
A. 8.145 'Beau fitȝ,' quaþ his fadir, 'for *defaute* we shuln,
B. 2.140 And if he fynde yow in *defaute*, and with [fals] holde,
B. 5.6 That I ne myȝte ferþer a foot for *defaute* of slepynge.
B. 5.146 And freres fyndeþ hem in *defaute*, as folk bereþ witnesse,
B. 6.206 And for *defaute* of foode þis folk is at my wille.
B. 7.168 'Beau fitȝ', quod his fader, 'for *defaute* we shullen,
B. 9.84 A Iew wolde noȝt se a Iew go Ianglyng for *defaute*
B.10.283 And þe festu is fallen for youre *defaute*
B.10.367 Or delit in wyn and wildefowel and wite any in *defaute*.
B.11.103 Ac be [þow] neueremoore þe firste [þe] *defaute* to blame;
B.11.215 Ne vndernyme noȝt foule, for is noon wiþoute *defaute*.
B.11.308 Or in masse or in matyns makeþ any *defaute*:
B.11.393 Of hire *defautes* foule bifore hem reherced]
B.12.95 For boþe ben as Mirours to amenden [by] *defautes*
B.13.259 Til pride be pureliche fordo, and [þat] þoruȝ payn *defaute*.
B.14.71 And if men lyuede as mesure wolde sholde neuere moore be *defaute*
B.14.114 And makest hem wel neiȝ meke and mylde for *defaute*,
B.14.118 That al hir lif han lyued in langour and *defaute*.
B.14.165 Heuene after hir hennes goyng þat here han swich *defaute*.
B.15.135 A[c] goddes folk for *defaute* þerof forfaren and spillen
B.15.347 Ac þer is a *defaute* in þe folk þat þe feiþ kepeþ,
B.18.207 Ne what is hoot hunger þat hadde neuere *defaute*.
C. 2.156 And yf he fynde ȝow in *defaute* and with the fals holde,
C. 7.306 Famyne and *defaute*, folwen y wol Peres;
C. 8.145 Bothe of my corn and of my cloth to kepe hem fram *defaute*.

C. 8.212   And for *defaute* this folk folweth myn hestes.
C. 8.244   In somur for his sleuthe he shal haue *defaute*
C. 8.351   And dawe þe deluare dey for *defaute*
C. 9.100   Thouh he falle for *defaute* þat fayteth for his lyflode
C. 9.207   H[e]lden ful hungry hous and hadde muche *defaute*,
C. 9.312   'Beau fitȝ,' quod the fadur, 'for *defaute* we shal,
C.10.202   In meschief for *defaute* of mete ne for myssyng of clothes:
C.11.41   Bothe afyngred and afurst, and for *defaute*
C.12.37   Ac be [thow] neueremore þe furste the *defaute* to blame;
C.13.122   Or in masse or in matynes maketh eny *defaute*:
C.14.16   That pees be and pacience and pore withoute *defaute*:
C.15.229   Til pruyde be puyreliche fordo and þat thorw payn *defaute*:
C.15.270   And yf men lyuede as mesure wolde sholde neuere[more] be
                defaute
C.15.290   And makest hem wel neyh meke and mylde for *defaute*
C.15.294   That al here lyf haen lyued in langour and *defaute*.
C.17.68   And fedde þat afyn[g]red were and in *defaute* lyuede.
C.17.90   As they ywoned were; in wham is *defaute*?
C.20.212   Ne what is hoet hunger þat hadde neuere *defaute*.

defence n *defense n.* B 1; C 1 defense
B.18.195   Adam afterward, ayeins his *defence*,
C.20.200   Adam afturward, aȝenes his *defense*,

defende v *defenden v.* A 7 defende (2) defendeþ (1) defendite (1) defendiþ
    (2) defendyþ (1); B 10 defende (7) defended (1) defenden (1)
    defendeþ (1); C 16 defende (9) defended (1) defenden (3) defendeth
    (3)
A. 3.53   Ac god alle good folk such grauyng *defendiþ*
A. 6.81   Deþ dar not do þing þat he *defendiþ*.
A. 7.80   And *defende* it fro þe fend, for so I beleue,
A. 7.168   Ne hadde þ[e] fisician ferst *defendite* him watir
A. 8.40   Vsure, & auarice, & oþes I *defende*,
A.12.18   Sitthe theologie þe trewe to tellen hit *defendeþ*;
A.12.19   'Dauid godes derling *defendyþ* hit also:
B. 3.64   Ac god alle good folk swich grauynge *defendeþ*,
B. 6.88   And [*defende* it fro þe fend], for so I bileue,
B.15.19   That wole *defende* me þe dore, dynge I neuer so late.
B.16.246   And *defende* hem fro þe fend, folk þat on me leneden.
B.19.42   It bicomeþ to a kyng to kepe and to *defende*,
B.19.46   And *defended* from foule yueles, feueres and Fluxes,
B.19.467   And holy kirke and clergie fro cursed men to [de]fende.
B.19.477   'In condicion', quod Conscience, 'þat þow [þe comune] *defende*
B.20.76   And crye we to kynde þat he come and *defende* vs
B.20.257   Kynges and knyghtes þat kepen and *defenden*
C. 3.68   Ac god to alle good folk suche grauynge *defendeth*,
C. 8.34   To *defende* þe in fayth, fyhte thow y sholde.'
C. 8.97   And *defenden* hit fro þe fende, and so is my beleue,
C. 9.9   Kyngus and knyhtus þat holy kyrke *defenden*
C.14.6   Noþer to lye ne to lacke ne lere þat is *defended*
C.16.36   And bote these thre þat y spak of at domesday vs *defende*
C.16.135   Hit *defendeth* þe flesche fram folies ful monye,
C.16.170   That wol *defende* me [þe] dore, dynge y neuere so late.
C.17.289   To be culd and ouercome the comune to *defende*,
C.19.270   How myhte he aske mercy or eny mercy hym *defende*
C.20.110   The which is lif þat oure lord in all lawes *defendeth*.
C.21.42   Hit bicometh [to] a kyng to kepe and to *defende*
C.21.467   And holy kyrke and clerge fro cursed men to *defende*.
C.21.477   'In condicioun,' quod Consience, 'þat þou [þe] comune *defende*
C.22.76   And crye we to kynde þat he come and *defende* vs
C.22.257   Kynges and knyhtes þat ke[p]en and *defenden*

defense > defence; deffye > defyen; deffouled > deroulen

defyed v1 *defien v.(1)* B 1; C 1 defyede
B.20.66   *Defyed* alle falsnesse and folk þat it vsede;
C.22.66   *Defyede* all falsnesse and folke þat hit vsede

defyen v2 *defien v.(2)* A 2 defie; B 5 defie (4) defyen (1); C 5 deffye (1)
    defie (1) defye (2) defyen (1)
A.Pr.108   Of þe ryn & of þe rochel, þe rost to *defie*!
A. 5.210   'Shal neuere fissh on þe Friday *defie* in my wombe
B.Pr.230   Of þe Ryn and of þe Rochel þe roost to *defie*!'
B. 5.122   For enuye and yuel wil is yuel to *defie*.
B. 5.382   'Shal neuere fyssh on [þe] Fryday *defyen* in my wombe
B.13.403   And moore mete eet and dronk þan kynde myȝte *defie*,
B.15.64   And riȝt as hony is yuel to *defie* and engleymeþ þe mawe,
C.Pr.234   Of þe r[yn]e and of þe rochele the roost [to] *defie*!'
C. 6.87   For enuye and euyl wil is euel to *defye*.
C. 6.430   More then my kynde myhte *deffye*
C. 6.439   Shal neuere fysch [o]n þe fryday *defyen* in my wombe
C.16.226   And riht as hony is euel to *defie*,

defoulen v *defoulen v.* A 1 defoulíþ; B 2 defouled (1) defoulen (1); C 3
    deffouled (1) defouleth (1) diffoule (1)
A.11.60   Þat *defouliþ* oure f[eiþ] at fest[is] þere þei sitten.

B.14.24   Ne fend ne fals man *defoulen* it in þi lyue.
B.15.534   How þei *defouled* hir flessh, forsoke hir owene wille,
C. 3.192   For she is fauerable to fals the whiche *defouleth* treuthe.
C. 8.31   For þey cometh to my croft my corn to *diffoule*.'
C.17.195   How they *deffoule[d]* here flesche, forsoke here owne wille,

defraudeþ v *defrauden v.* A 1 defraudiþ; B 1; C 1 defraudeth
A. 8.70   He is fals wiþ þe fend & [*defraudiþ*] þe nedy,
B. 7.68   He is fals wiþ þe feend and *defraudeþ* þe nedy,
C. 9.64   He is fals and faytour and *defraudeth* the nedy

degre n *degre n. &> decre* A 1; B 3 degre (2) degree (1); C 4 degre (2)
    degrees (1) degres (1)
A.11.90   But he lyue in þe leste *degre* þat longiþ to dowel
B. 9.148   The gospel is hera[g]ein in o *degre*, I fynde:
B.10.137   But he lyue in þe [leeste *degre*] þat longeþ to dowel
B.15.377   Go now to any *degree*, and but if gile be maister,
C. 5.62   /God and good men, as here *degre* asketh:
C.17.112   Go now to eny *degre* and bote gyle be holde a maistre
C.18.56   A[c] in thre *degrees* hit grewe; grete ferly me thouhte,
C.18.83   Why groweth this fruyt in thre *degres*?' 'A goed skil,' he saide.

deye v *dien v.* A 17 deiȝe (8) deiȝede (1) diȝe (6) diȝedist (1) diȝen (1); B
    56 deide (8) deyde (2) deyden (1) deidest (3) deye (26) deyede (1)
    deyeden (2) deyen (1) deieþ (3) deyeþ (3) dye (4) dyed (1) dyeþ (1); C
    57 dey (6) deye (24) deyede (17) deyedest (3) deyeth (4) dye (1) dyen
    (2)
A. 1.132   No dedly synne to do, diȝe þeiȝ þou shuldist.
A. 1.141   Lokide on vs wiþ loue, & let his sone *deiȝe*
A. 2.173   And gile doþ him to go agast for to *deiȝe*.
A. 3.242   Shulde *diȝe* for a dede þat don hadde here eldren
A. 3.254   God seide to samuel þat saul shulde *deiȝe*,
A. 4.5   But resoun rede me þerto [raþer] wole I *deiȝe*.'
A. 5.236   'Crist, þat on caluarie vpon þe [cros] *diȝedist*,
A. 7.90   For þeiȝ I *deiȝe* today my dettis ben quyt;
A. 7.112   And þeiȝ ȝe *deiȝe* for doel þe deuil haue þat recche!'
A. 7.258   Þei do men *diȝe* þoruȝ here drynkes er destenye it wolde.'
A. 8.37   Þat no deuil shal ȝow dere, *diȝe* whan ȝe diȝe,
A. 8.37   Þat no deuil shal ȝow dere, diȝe whan ȝe *diȝe*,
A. 9.47   God wile suffre þe to *deiȝe* so for þiself hast þe maistrie.'
A. 9.50   I bekenne [ȝow] crist þat on þe crois *deiȝede*.'
A.10.173   Alle shuln *deiȝe* for his dedis be dounes & hilles,
A.10.177   Ellis shal alle *diȝen* & to helle wenden."
A.11.208   Þei *diȝe* for þe drouȝte, whanne þei dreiȝe lengen;
B. 1.144   No dedly synne to do, *deye* þeiȝ þow sholdest,
B. 1.167   Loked on vs wiþ loue and leet his sone *dye*
B. 2.214   And Gyle dooþ hym to go agast for to *dye*.
B. 3.263   Sholden *deye* for a dede þat doon hadde hire eldres.
B. 3.276   God seide to Samuel þat Saul sholde *deye*
B. 4.5   But Reson rede me þerto raþer wol I *deye*.'
B. 5.393   'If I sholde *deye* bi þis day [I drede me sore].
B. 5.464   'Crist, þat on Caluarie vpon þe cros *deidest*,
B. 5.487   And siþþe wiþ þi selue sone in oure s[u]te *deidest*
B. 6.98   For þouȝ I *deye* today my dettes are quyte;
B. 6.120   And þouȝ ye *deye* for doel þe deuel haue þat recch[e]!'
B. 6.274   They do men *deye* þoruȝ hir drynkes er destynee it wolde.'
B. 6.330   And Dawe þe dykere *deye* for hunger
B. 8.59   'I bikenne þee crist', quod he, 'þat on [þe] cros *deyde*.'
B. 9.142   Alle shul *deye* for hise dedes by [dounes] and hulles,
B.10.302   Thei *deyen* for drouȝte, whan þei drie [lenge]
B.10.358   For þat crist for cristene men *deide*, and conferred þe lawe
B.11.206   Of Adames issue and Eue ay til god man *deide*;
B.11.285   Ne neiþer kirtel ne cote, þeiȝ þei for cold sholde *deye*,
B.12.87   And deeþ and dampnacion to hem þat *deyeþ* yuele,
B.12.207   And as lawe likeþ to lyue or to *deye*:
B.12.289   And if þer were he wolde amende, and in swich wille *deieþ*–
B.13.405   And þanne I dradde to *deye* in dedlich synne',
B.13.408   Ne no mercy amenden me man þat so *deyeþ*].
B.14.58   Ne deeþ drede [ne deuel], but *deye* as god likeþ
B.14.131   And whan he *dyeþ* ben disalowed, as Dauid seiþ in þe Sauter:
B.14.135   And selden *deyeþ* he out of dette þat dyneþ er he deserue it,
B.15.497   And as hymself seide [so] to lyue and *dye*:
B.15.519   Many a seint syþen haþ suffred to *deye*
B.15.520   Al for to enforme þe faith; in fele contrees *deyeden*,
B.15.522   In dolful deþ *deyeden* for hir faith.
B.15.524   Amonges vnkynde cristene for cristes loue he *deyede*,
B.16.166   *Deide* and dee[þ] fordide, and day of nyȝt made.
B.17.69   And parceyued bi his pous he was in peril to *dye*
B.17.241   And if it suffise noȝt for asset[ȝ], þat in swich a wille *deyeþ*,
B.17.268   That] Diues *deyde*, dampned for his vnkyndenesse
B.17.299   'I pose I hadde synned so and sholde [nouþe] *deye*,
B.18.28   'Nay', quod [feiþ, 'but] þe fend and fals doom [to *deye*].
B.18.56   Thanne shul we leue þat lif þee loueþ and wol noȝt lete þee *deye*.'
B.18.58   Pitousliche and pale, as a prison þat *deieþ*,

B.18.68   Some seide þat he was goddes sone þat so faire *deide*:
B.18.134 Which *deide* and deeþ þoled þis day aboute mydday,
B.18.193 Sholden *deye* downrighte and dwelle in pyne after
B.18.281 If Adam ete þe Appul alle sholde *deye*
B.18.303 I wolde haue lengþed his lif for I leued if he *deide*
B.18.331 That if [þei] ete þe Appul alle sholde *deye*,
B.18.358 And as Adam and alle þoruȝ a tree *deide*
B.18.366 And for þat drynke today I *deide* vpon erþe.
B.18.387 Wheiþer þei *deye* or deye noȝt for þat þei diden ille.
B.18.387 Wheiþer þei deye or *deye* noȝt for þat þei diden ille.
B.19.174 *Deidest* and deeþ þoledest and deme shalt vs alle,
B.20.19   That he dronke at ech dych er he [*deye* for þurst].
B.20.50   Ne neuere noon so nedy ne pouerer *deide*.
B.20.62   Whiche foolis were wel [gladdere] to *deye*
B.20.177 And þere *dyed* þat doctour er þre dayes after.
B.20.312 For fastynge of a fryday he ferde as he wolde *deye*.
C.Pr.102 That lewed men in mysbileue lyuen and *dyen*.
C. 1.143 *Dey* rather þen do eny dedly synne:
C. 1.163 Lokede on vs with loue [and] let his sone *deye*
C. 2.224 And gyle doth hym to gone agaste for to *deye*.
C. 3.401 For þat lordes loue that for oure loue *deyede*
C. 3.411 That saul for þat synne and his sone *deyede*
C. 3.416 Sholde *deye* der[f]ly for dedes of here eldres.
C. 3.429 God sayde to samuel þat sauel sholde *deye*
C. 4.5   But resoun rede me þertyl rather wo[l] y *dey*.'
C. 5.40   And foen[d y] nere, in fayth, seth my frendes *deyede*
C. 5.149 *Dyen* for drouthe whenne they drye lygge,
C. 6.318 'Crist, þat on Caluarie on þe crosse *deyedest*
C. 6.336 And *deyede* with a drop water; so doth alle synnes
C. 7.9   'Yf y sholde *deye* be þis day y drede me sore.
C. 7.129 And sethe in oure secte, as hit semed, *deyedest*,
C. 7.209 That is to sey sothly ȝe sholde rather *deye*
C. 8.107 For thouh y *dey* today my dette[s ben] yquited;
C. 8.127 And thow ȝe *deye* for deul þe deuel haue þat reche!'
C. 8.295 They don men *deye* thorw here drynkes Ar destyne hit wolde.'
C. 8.351 And dawe þe deluare *dey* for defaute
C. 9.239 Y drede me, and he *dey*, hit worth for dedly synne
C.10.58   'Y bykenne the Crist,' quod he, 'þat on þe cross *deyede*.'
C.10.60   And gyue me grace on þis grounde with good ende to *deye*.'
C.10.195 The[r]of was he robbed and ruyfled or he on rode *deyede*
C.10.230 Alle sholle *deye* for his dedes by dales and hulles
C.12.114 Of Adames issue and Eue ay til god man *deyede*;
C.12.182 Sholde neuere whete wexe but whete furste *deyede*;
C.14.146 And as þe lawe lyketh to lyue oþer to *dye*
C.14.211 And yf þer were a wolde [amende], and in suche a wille *deyeth*–
C.15.257 Ne d[e]th drede ne deuel, [but] *deye* as god liketh
C.16.4   And selde *deyeth* [he] oute of dette [þat] dyne[th] ar he deserue hit.
C.17.193 And as hymsulue saide so to lyue and *deye*:
C.17.271 For to enf[ou]rme þe fayth ful wydewhare *deyede*,
C.17.291 And *deye* for his dere childrene to de[struy]e dedly synne,
C.19.68   And parseued by his poues he was in perel to *deye*
C.19.207 And yf hit suffic[e] nat for ase[t]h þat in suche a will *deyeth*
C.19.234 That diues *deyede*, dampned for his vnkyndenesse
C.19.279 'Y pose y hadde syneged so and sholde nouthe *deye*
C.20.27 'Nay,' quod faith, 'bote the fende and fals doem to *deye*.
C.20.56 Thenne shal we leue that lyf þe loueth and wol nat late the *deye*.'
C.20.58 Pitousliche and pale, as [a] prisoun þat *deyede*
C.20.70 Somme saide he was godes sone þat so fayre *deyede*:
C.20.137 [Which] *deyede* and deth tholede this day aboute mydday
C.20.198 Sholde *deye* downriht and d[welle] in payne euere
C.20.304 [Sh]olde *deye* with doel and here dwelle euere
C.20.335 Y wolde haue lenghed his lyf for y leued, yf he *deyede*,
C.20.374 That if they ete þe appul alle sholde *deye*,
C.20.397 And as Adam and alle thorwe a tre *deyede*,
C.20.404 And for þat drynke today y *deyede* as hit semede.
C.20.429 Where they *deye* or dey nat, dede they neuere so ille.
C.20.429 Where they deye or *dey* nat, dede they neuere so ille.
C.21.174 *Deyedest* and deth tholedest and deme shalt vs all
C.22.19 That he dronke at vch a dy[c]h ar he *deye* for furste.
C.22.50 Ne neuere noen so nedy ne porore *deyede*.'
C.22.62 [Whiche foles] were wel gladere to *deye*
C.22.177 And þere *deyede* þat doctour ar thre dayes aftur.
C.22.312 For fastyng of a fryday a feerde as he wolde *deye*.

deyes > deys; deiȝe(de > deye

deying ger *diinge ger.* B 6 deying (3) deyinge (3); C 7 deyng (1) deynge (6)

B. 7.35   That no deuel shal yow dere ne [in youre *deying* fere yow],
B.11.177 Whoso loueþ noȝt, leue me, he lyueþ in deeþ *deyinge*.
B.13.425 In youre deeþ *deyinge* I drede me soore
B.13.450 And in his deeþ *deyinge* þei don hym gret confort
B.15.526 Holy chirche is honoured heiȝliche þoruȝ his *deying*;
B.18.214 And suffrede to be sold to se þe sorwe of *deying*,

C. 7.85   In ȝoure deth *deynge* y drede me sore
C. 7.110 And in his deth *deynge* they don hym greet confort
C. 9.38   That no deuel shal ȝow dere ne despeyre in ȝoure d[e]ynge
C.17.144 For when alle frendes faylen and fleen away in *deynge*
C.17.276 And alle holy kirke honoured thorw that *deyng*.
C.20.79 That hadde no boie hardynesse hym to touche in *deynge*.
C.20.223 And soffred to be sold to se þe sorwe of *deynge*,

deile > dele

deyneþ v *deinen v.(1)* A 1; B 2; C 2 deyneth

A. 7.292 *Deyneþ* nouȝt to dyne a day niȝt olde wortis.
B. 6.308 *Deyne[þ]* noȝt to dyne a day nyȝt olde wortes.
B.10.79 [For god is def nowadayes and *deyneþ* [noȝt vs to here],
C. 8.330 *Deyne[th* noght] to dyne a day nyhte olde wortes;
C.11.59 For god is deef nowadayes and *deyneth* [nat vs] to here

deyng(e > deying

deynous adj *deinous adj.* A 1; B 1; C 1

A. 9.75   And [is] nouȝt drunkelewe ne *deynous*, dowel hym folewiþ.
B. 8.84   And is noȝt dronkelewe ne [d]eynous, dowel hym folweþ.
C.16.228 And doth hym to be *deynous* and deme þat beth nat lered.

deyntee n *deinte n.* B 2 deyntee (1) deyntees (1); C 3 deynte (1) deyntees (2)

B.11.48   That of dowel ne dobet no *deyntee* me þouȝte;
B.14.123 And diues in *deyntees* lyuede and in douce vie;
C.11.311 Of dowel ne of dobet no *deynte* me thouhte;
C.15.90 Bothe disches and dobelares with alle þe *deyntees* aftur.
C.15.299 And dyues in *deyntees* lyuede and [in] douce vie

deys n *deis n.* A 2 deis; B 3 dees (1) deys (2); C 2 deyes (1) deys (1)

A. 8.19   At þe day of dom at here *deis* to sitten.
A.11.43 Þus þei dryuelen at here *deis* þe deite to knowe,
B. 7.17   At þe day of dome at [hire] *deys* [to] sitte.
B.10.57 Thus þei dryuele at hir *deys* þe deitee to knowe,
B.13.61 For þis poctour on þe heiȝe *dees* drank wyn so faste:
B.11.38 Thus they dreuele a[t] the *deyes* the deite to knowe
C.15.65 For [this] doctour at þe hey *deys* dranke wyn [so] faste–

deitee n *deite n.* A 1 deite; B 1; C 1 deite

A.11.43 Þus þei dryuelen at here deis þe *deite* to knowe,
B.10.57 Thus þei dryuele at hir deys þe *deitee* to knowe,
C.11.38 Thus they dreuele a[t] the deyes the *deite* to knowe

dele v *delen v.* A 9 deile (1) dele (5) delen (1) deliþ (1) delt (1); B 17 deel (1) deele (3) dele (6) delen (1) deleþ (6); C 12 dele (6) delen (1) delest (1) deleth (4)

A. 1.173 And a lering to lewide men þe lattere to *dele*.
A. 1.175 Date & dabitur vobis for I *dele* ȝow alle.
A. 3.56   Be war what þi riȝt hond werchiþ or *deliþ*,
A. 7.67   Deleantur de libro; I shulde not *dele* wiþ hem,
A. 7.89   And *dele* among my frendis & my dere children.
A. 8.73   Þei wedde no womman þat hy wiþ *delen*
A.11.162 Ȝif þou þenke do wel *deile* þerewith neuere.
A.11.243 Godis word witnessiþ we shuln ȝiue & *dele*
A.12.104 Deþ *delt* him a dent and drof him to þe erþe
B. 1.199 And lernynge to lewed men þe latter to *deele*.
B. 1.201 "Date & dabitur vobis, for I *deele* yow alle."
B. 5.246 Eschaunges and cheuysaunces, wiþ swich chaffare I *dele*,
B. 6.75   Deleantur de libro viuencium; I sholde noȝt *dele* wiþ hem,
B. 6.97   And *dele* among my [frendes] and my deere children.
B. 7.91   [Thei] wedde [no] womman þat [þei] wiþ *deele*
B.10.28   Thilke þat god [moost gyueþ] leest good þei *deleþ*,
B.10.87   And lordeþ in [ledes] þe lasse good he *deleþ*.
B.10.219 If þow þynke to dowel *deel* þerwiþ neuere.
B.11.277 Or selle it, as seiþ þe book, and þe siluer *dele*
B.12.248 And *deleþ* it noȝt til his deeþ day, þe tail[le is al of] sorwe.
B.13.299 And if he gyueþ ouȝt to pouere gomes, þenke what he *deleþ*,
B.15.246 And cristes patrymonye to þe poore parcelmele *dele*;
B.17.255 *Delen* and do penaunce day and nyght euere,
B.17.262 Forþi beþ war, ye wise men þat wiþ þe world *deleþ*;
B.19.325 'For I wole *dele* today and [dyuyde] grace
B.19.349 Ne no manere marchaunt þat wiþ moneye *deleþ*.
C. 1.196 "Date & dabitur vobis, for y *dele* ȝow alle."
C. 3.76   Ywyte what thow *delest* with thi ryhte syde.
C. 8.77   Del[e]antur de libro viuencium; y sholde nat *dele* with hem
C. 8.106 And *delen* amongus my douhteres and my dere childre[n].
C. 9.168 Ne weddeth none wymmen þat they with *deleth*,
C.11.67 And lordeth in ledes the lasse goed he *deleth*.
C.11.69 How he tolde in a tyme and tauhte his sone *dele*:
C.13.96 As al þat þe ryche may rayme and rihtfuly *dele*
C.19.221 *Dele* and do penaunce day and nyht euere,
C.19.228 Forthy beth ywar, ȝe wyse men þat with the world *deleth*,
C.21.215 'For y wol *dele* today and deuyde grace

C.21.349   Ne no manere Marchaunt þat with moneye *deleth*

delicat *adj* *delicat adj.* C 1
C. 8.277   Thenk þat [diues] for his *delicat* lyf to þe deuel wente

delicatly *adv* *delicatli adv.* B 3; C 2 delicatlyche (1) delycatly (1)
B. 5.184   And drynk nat ouer *delicatly*, ne to depe neiþer,
B. 5.374   Ouer *delicatly* on [feeste] dayes dronken and eten boþe,
B.14.251   Ne dooþ hym noȝt dyne *delicatly* ne drynke wyn ofte.
C. 6.166   And drynke nat ouer *delycatly* n[e] to depe neyther
C.16.91   Ne doth men dyne *delicatlyche* ne drynke wyne ofte.

delynge *ger* *deling ger.* B 1; C 1 delyng
B.19.376   And oþ[er] pryue penaunc[e], and somme þoruȝ penyes *delynge*.
C.21.376   Or oþer priue penauns[e] and somme thorw pans *delyng*.

delit *v* *deliten v.* A 1 delyted; B 2 delit (1) delited (1)
A. 1.29   [*Delyted* hym in drynke as the deuyl wolde],
B. 1.29   *Delited* hym in drynke as þe deuel wolde,
B.10.367   Or *delit* in wyn and wildefowel and wite any in defaute.

delitable *adj* *delitable adj.* A 1; B 1; C 1
A. 1.32   Dred *delitable* drynk & þou shalt do þe betere;
B. 1.34   Forþi dred *delitable* drynke and þow shalt do þe bettre;
C. 1.32   Forthy drede *delitable* drynke bothe day and nyghtes.

delites *n* *delit n.(1)* A 1
A. 2.65   Wiþ alle þe *delites* of lust þe deuil for to serue,

deliuere *v* *deliveren v.* B 2 deliuere (1) deliuereþ (1); C 3 delyuere (1) delyuered (1) delyuerede (1)
B.15.346   And many a prison fram purgatorie þoruȝ hise preieres *deliuereþ*.
B.16.266   That shal *deliuere* vs som day out of þe deueles power
C.13.14   And *delyuerede* the weye his wyf with moche welthe aftur.
C.13.41   His erende and his lettre sheweth and is anoon *delyuered*.
C.18.282   That shal *delyuere* vs som day out of þe deueles power

delt > dele

deluuye *n* *diluvie n.* B 1; C 1
B.10.417   [At domesday þe *deluuye* worþ of deþ and fir at ones;
C.11.249   At domesday a *deluuye* worth of deth and fuyr at ones.

deluare(s > delueres

deluen *v* *delven v.* A 4 deluen (1) doluen (3); B 7 delue (1) deluen (2) doluen (3) idolue (1); C 2 delue (1) deluen (1)
A. 6.33   Dyke[d] & d[o]luen & do what he hiȝte,
A. 7.170   Þei hadde be ded be þis day & *doluen* al warm.
A. 7.176   And *doluen* drit & dung to ditte out hunger.
A.11.187   Diken or *deluen*, dowel it hatte.
B. 5.545   Idyke[d] and Id[o]lue, Ido þat [he] hoteþ.
B. 6.141   Diken or *deluen* or dyngen vpon sheues
B. 6.180   They hadde be [dede and] *doluen*, ne deme þow noon ooþer.
B. 6.190   And *doluen* [drit] and [dung] to [ditte out] hunger.
B.14.324   I ne hadde be deed and *doluen* for dowelis sake!
B.19.362   To *deluen* a dych depe aboute vnitee
B.19.364   Conscience comaundede þo alle cristene to *delue*,
C.21.362   To *deluen* a dich depe aboute vnite
C.21.364   Consience comaundede t[h]o alle cristene to *delue*

delueres *n* *delver* A 2 delueres (1) delueris (1); B 2; C 3 deluare (1) deluares (1) deluers (1)
A.Pr.102   As dikeris & *delueris* þat doþ here dede ille
A. 7.99   Dikeris & *delueres* dy[gg]eþ vp þe balkis.
B.Pr.224   As dykeres and *delueres* þat doon hire ded[e] ille
B. 6.107   Dikeres and *Delueres* digged vp þe balkes;
C.Pr.228   As dykers and *deluers* þat doth here dedis ylle
C. 8.114   Dikares and *deluares* digged vp þe balkes;
C. 8.351   And dawe þe *deluare* dey for defaute

deluynge *ger* *delving ger.* C 1
C. 8.198   In daubynge and in *deluynge*, in donge afeld berynge,

demen *v* *demen v.* A 6 demde (1) deme (3) demide (1) demist (1); B 21 deme (9) demed (4) demen (5) demest (2) demeþ (1); C 18 deme (7) demed (3) demede (3) demen (5)
A. 1.84   I do it on Deus caritas to *deme* þe soþe.
A. 3.175   Ne dide as þou *demist*; I do it on þe king.
A. 5.95   I *deme* men þere [hy] don ille, & ȝet I do wers;
A. 7.73   And *deme* hem nouȝt for ȝif þou dost þou shalt it dere abiggen,
A. 8.153   And [dem]ide þat dowel indulgence passiþ,
A.11.268   De[m]de he not wel & wisly, as holy [writ] techiþ,
B.Pr.96   And in stede of Stywardes sitten and *demen*.
B. 1.86   I do it on Deus caritas to *deme* þe soþe.
B. 3.188   Ne dide as þow *demest*; I do it on þe kynge.
B. 3.307   Shal be *demed* to þe deeþ but if he do it smyþye
B. 4.178   And *deme* yow, bi þis day, as ye han deserued.
B. 4.181   And as moost folk witnesseþ wel wrong shal be *demed*.'

B. 5.115   [I] *deme* [men þere hij] doon ille, [and yet] I do werse;
B. 6.81   *Deme*-hem-noȝt-for-if-þow-doost-þow-shalt-it-deere-abugge-
B. 6.180   They hadde be [dede and] doluen, ne *deme* þow noon ooþer.
B. 7.175   And *demed* þat dowel Indulgences passe[þ],
B.10.387   He *demed* wel and wisely as holy writ telleþ;
B.13.128   And [*demeþ*] þat dowel and dobet arn two Infinites,
B.13.157   Vndo it; lat þis doctour *deme* if dowel be þerInne.
B.13.171   And as þow *demest* wil þei do alle hir dayes after:
B.13.305   Of dedes þat he neuere dide *demen* and bosten;
B.15.27   And whan I *deme* domes and do as truþe techeþ
B.15.552   Shal þei *demen* dos ecclesie, and [depose yow for youre pride]:
B.18.37   To se how doghtiliche deeþ sholde do and *deme* hir boþeres right.
B.19.174   Deidest and deeþ þoledest and *deme* shalt vs alle,
B.19.196   And *demen* hem at domesday, boþe quyke and dede,
B.19.305   To *demen* as a domesman adrad was he neuere
C.Pr.94   And ben in stede of stewardus and sitten and *demen*.
C. 1.82   I do it [o]n deus caritas to *deme* þe sothe.
C. 3.291   Ac ther is mede and mercede and bothe men *demen*
C. 3.460   Shal be *demed* to þe deth but yf he do hit smythye
C. 4.172   And *deme* ȝow, by this day, as ȝe haen deserued.
C. 4.175   And by lele and lyfholy my lawe shal be *demed*.'
C. 6.20   *Demed* for here vuel vices and exitede oþere
C. 8.83   *Deme*-hem-nat-[for]-yf-thow-doest-thow-shalt-hit-dere-abygge.
C. 9.21   And *deme* with hem at domesday bothe quyke and dede.
C. 9.320   And *demede* þat dowel indulgences passeth,
C.10.102   That wolde nat do as dobest *de[m]ede* and tauhte.
C.11.213   And *demede* wel and wysly; wymmen bereth wittenesse:
C.16.187   And when y *deme* domus and do as treuthe techeth
C.16.228   And doth hym to be deynous and *deme* þat beth nat lered.
C.20.36   To se how douhtyliche deth sholde do and *demen* [h]er beyre rihte.
C.21.174   Deyedest and deth tholedest and *deme* shalt vs all
C.21.196   And *demen* hem at domesday, bothe quyke and dede,
C.21.305   To *demen* as a domesman adrad was he neuere

demynge *ger* *deming ger.* C 1
C.12.80   Bote onlyche loue and leaute as in my lawes *demynge*.

demme > dym,dymme

dene *n* *dine n.(1)* B 2 dene (1) dyn (1); C 2
B.18.62   Dede men for þat *dene* come out of depe graues
B.18.123   Of þe *dyn* and þe derknesse and how þe day rowed,
C.20.64   And dede men for þat *dene* cam oute of depe graues
C.20.126   Of the *dene* and the derkenesse and how þe day roued

denes -is > deen

denyede *v* *denien v.* C 1
C.11.262   As in likyng of lecherye no lyf *denyede*!

denote *n prop* *n.i.d.* B 1; C 1
B. 6.71   And danyel þe dees pleyere and *Denote* þe baude
C. 8.72   And danyel þe dees playere and *denote* þe baude

dent > dynt

dentiefliche *adv* *deintifliche adv.* C 1
C. 8.322   Thenne [was] folke fayn and fedde hunger *dentie[f]liche*

dep > deep

departable *adj* *departable adj.* B 2; C 4
B.17.29   Thre persones in parcelles *departable* fro ooþer
B.17.129   In þre persones *departable* þat perpetuele were euere,
C.18.187   'Thre persones in o pensel,' quod he, '*departable* fram oþere.
C.18.214   That he is thre persones *departable* y preue hit by mankynde,
C.19.30   Thre persones parselmele *depar[t]able* fram oþere
C.19.98   In thre persones, a parceles *departable* fram oþere,

departen *v* *departen v.* A 1 departid; B 2 departed (1) departen (1); C 2 departe (1) departen (1)
A. 8.140   Among l[ower]e lordis þi londis shuln be *departid'.*
B. 7.162   Amonges lower lordes þi lond shal be *departed*.'
B.20.139   *Departen* er deeþ cam and deuors shapte.
C.17.147   In murthe or in mournynge and neuere[more] to *departe*.
C.22.139   *Departen* ar dethe come and deuors shupte.

depe *adv* *depe adv. &> deep* A 2 depe (1) deppere (1); B 8 depe (6) depper (2); C 9 depe (8) deppore (1)
A. 1.114   Summe in eir, summe in erþe, summe in helle *depe*.
A.11.139   And þe *deppere* I deuynide þe derkere me þouȝte;
B. 1.125   Somme in Eyr, somme in erþe, somme in helle *depe*.
B. 5.184   And drynk nat ouer delicatly, ne to *depe* neiþer,
B.10.187   And þe *depper* I deuyne[d] þe derker me [þouȝte].
B.12.210   And riȝt as Troianus þe trewe knyȝt [tilde] noȝt *depe* in helle
B.13.90   For now he haþ dronken so *depe* he wole deuyne soone
B.14.6   Wiþ þe sope of siknesse þat sekeþ wonder *depe*,
B.15.199   Ac Piers þe Plowman parceyueþ moore *depper*

B.19.362   To deluen a dych *depe* aboute vnitee
C. 1.127   Summe in erthe, summe in ayr, summe in helle *depe*.
C. 6.166   And drynke nat ouer delycatly n[e] to *depe* neyther
C. 9.145   Drynke druie and *depe* and drawe hym thenne to bedde;
C.11.128   And þe *deppore* y deuine the derkore me thynketh hit.
C.11.296   Selde falleth þe seruant so *depe* in arrerage
C.11.300   Selde falleth so foule and so *depe* in synne
C.14.149   And riht as troianes þe trewe knyhte [telde] nat *depe* in helle
C.15.97   [For] now he hath dronke so *depe* a wol deuyne sone
C.21.362   To deluen a dich *depe* aboute vnite

depose v *deposen v.* B 1; C 1
B.15.552   Shal þei demen dos ecclesie, and [*depose* yow for youre pride]:
C.17.215   Shal dampne dos ecclesie and *depose* 3ow for 3oure pruyde:

depper(e -ore > depe

depraue v *depraven v.* A 1; B 2; C 1
A. 3.166   Ne to *depraue* þi persone wiþ a proud herte.
B. 3.179   Ne [to] *depraue* þi persone wiþ a proud herte.
B. 5.145   Thise possessioners preche and *depraue* freres;
C. 3.225   Ne to *depraue* thy persone with a pro[u]d herte.

dere > deere,deren

derely adv *dereli adv.(1)* B 1; C 1
B.19.2   And dighte me *derely* and dide me to chirche
C.21.2   And dihte me *derely* and dede me to kyrke

deren v *deren v.* A 2 dere (1) derie (1); B 6 deere (1) dere (4) deren (1); C 4 dere
A. 8.37   Þat no deuil shal 3ow *dere*, di3e whan 3e di3e,
A. 8.53   Shal no deuil at his deþ day *derie* hym a myte
B. 7.35   That no deuel shal yow *dere* ne [in youre deying fere yow],
B. 7.51   Shal no deuel at his deeþ day *deren* hym a myte
B.14.171   For may no derþe hem *deere*, droghte ne weet,
B.17.19   Shal neuere deuel hym *dere* ne deeþ in soule greue;
B.18.26   For no dynt shal hym *dere* as in deitate patris.'
B.18.275   May no deeþ [þis lord] *dere*, ne no deueles queyntise,
C. 9.38   That no deuel shal 3ow *dere* ne despeyre in 3oure d[e]ynge
C.19.20   Shal neuere deuel hym *dere* ne deth in soule greue;
C.20.25   For no d[yn]t shal hym *dere* as in deitate patris.'
C.20.297   May no deth this lord *dere* ne [n]o deueles quentyse

dereworþe adj *dereworthe adj.* A 1 derworþi; B 1; C 3 derworth (1) derworthe (2)
A. 1.85   It is as *derworþi* a dreury as dere god hymseluen.
B. 1.87   It is as *dereworþe* a drury as dere god hymseluen.
C. 1.83   Hit is a[s] *derworthe* a druerie as dere god hymseluen.
C. 6.89   Ne *derworth* drynke dryue hit fro myn herte.
C.13.18   *Derworthe* and dere god, do we so mala",

derfly adv *derfli adv.* C 1
C. 3.416   Sholde deye *der[f]ly* for dedes of here eldres.

derie > deren

derk adj *derk adj.* A 2 derke (1) derkere (1); B 5 derk (2) derke (2) derker (1); C 5 derk (2) derke (2) derkore (1)
A.Pr.16   Wiþ depe dikes & *derke* & dredful of si3t.
A.11.139   And þe deppere I deuynide þe *derkere* me þou3te;
B.Pr.16   Wiþ depe diches and *derke* and dredfulle of si3te.
B. 1.115   Into a deep *derk* helle to dwelle þere for euere;
B.10.187   And þe depper I deuyne[d] þe *derker* me [þou3te].
B.18.60   The day for drede wiþdrou3 and *derk* bicam þe sonne;
B.19.21   For alle *derke* deueles arn adrad to heren it,
C. 1.55   'The dep dale and þe *derk*, so vnsemely to se to,
C.11.128   And þe deppore y deuine the *derkore* me thynketh hit.
C.20.60   The daye for drede withdrouh and *derk* bicam þe sonne;
C.20.62   The hard roch al toroef and riht *derk* nyht hit semede;
C.21.21   For alle *derke* deueles aren drad to heren hit

derke n *derk n.* &> derk B 1; C 2
B.11.268   And lasse he dredeþ deeþ and in *derke* to ben yrobbed
C.12.153   And lasse drat [dethe] or in *derke* to ben yrobbed
C.13.57   And dredeth to be ded þerfore and he in *derke* mette

derkenesse > dernkesse

derkliche adv *deckliche adv.* B 1
B.10.378   Where dowel is or dobet *derkliche* ye shewen.

derknesse n *derknesse n.* B 8; C 6 derkenesse
B. 5.493   Feddest wiþ þi fresshe blood oure forefadres in *derknesse*:
B.16.85   There is *derknesse* and drede and þe deuel maister.
B.16.251   That to patriarkes & prophetes and ooþer peple in *derknesse*
B.17.237   And solacen hem þat mowe [no3t] se, þat sitten in *derknesse*,
B.18.65   'Lif and deeþ, in þis *derknesse* hir oon fordooþ hir ooþer.
B.18.101   For be þis *derknesse* ydo deeþ worþ [yvenquisshed];

B.18.111   I drow me in þat *derknesse* to descendit ad inferna
B.18.123   Of þe dyn and þe *derknesse* and how þe day rowed,
B.18.116   There is *derknesse* and drede and þe deuel maister.
C.19.203   And solacen [hem] þat mowen nat se, sittynge in *derkeness[e]*,
C.20.67   'Lyf & deth, in this *derkenesse* here oen fordoth her oþer.
C.20.104   For be this *derkenesse* ydo deth worth yvenkused;
C.20.114   Y [d]row [me] in þat *derkenesse* to descendit ad inferna
C.20.126   Of the dene and the *derkenesse* and how þe day roued

derkore > derk

derling n *dereling n.* A 1
A.12.19   'Dauid godes *derling* defendyþ hit also:

derne adj *derne adj.* A 1; B 3; C 3
A.10.205   Þat dede *derne* do no man ne shulde.
B. 2.176   As [de]uoutrye and diuorses and *derne* vsurie,
B. 9.192   That [dede *derne*] do no man ne sholde.
B.13.55   In a dissh of *derne* shrifte, Dixi & confitebor tibi.
C. 3.292   A desert for som doynge, *derne* oþer elles.
C.10.292   For þat dede *derne* do no man sholde.
C.13.155   As in *derne* dedes, bothe drynkyng and elles.

derne adv *derne adv.* B 1
B.11.352   Hidden and hileden hir egges ful *derne*

dernely adv *dernliche adv.* C 1
C.13.163   Hudden and helede here egges *dernely*

derrest > deere; derste > dar

derþe n *derthe n.* B 3; C 2 derthe
B. 6.329   Thanne shal deeþ wiþdrawe and *derþe* be Iustice,
B.14.171   For may no *derþe* hem deere, droghte ne weet,
B.14.176   Thoru3 *derþe*, þoru3 droghte, alle hir dayes here,
C. 8.350   And thenne shal deth withdrawe and *derthe* be Iustice
C.16.313   Of deth ne of *derthe* drad he neuere

derworth- > dereworþe

desauowe v *disavouen v.* C 1
C. 3.320   May *desa[u]owe* that thei dede and do[uwe] þerwith another

desceyue > deceyue

descendeth v *descenden v.* C 1
C.17.247   The whiche is þe hy holy gost þat out of heuene *descendet[h]*

deschargen v *dischargen v.* A 1 dischargid; B 2 descharged (1) deschargen (1); C 1
A. 4.26   In cheker & in chauncerie, to be *dischargid* of þinges
B. 4.29   In [c]heker and in Chauncerye, to ben *descharged* of þynges.
B.15.566   [Charite] were to *deschargen* hem for holy chirches sake,
C.17.231   Hit were charite to *deschargen* hem for holy churche sake,

descreue(d descryue > discryue; deseit- > deceite

desert n *esert n.(1)* C 1
C. 3.292   A *desert* for som doynge, derne oþer elles.

deserue v *deserven v.* A 5 deserue (1) deseruid (3) deseruyþ (1); B 9 deserue (3) deserued (6); C 18 deserue (7) deserued (5) deseruen (1) deserueth (2) discerue (1) diserue (1) diserued (1)
A. 5.239   Þi wil w[orþ]e vpon me, as I haue wel *deseruid*
A. 7.41   Nyme hem nou3t, an aunter þou mowe hem nou3t *deserue*.
A. 7.79   He shal haue my soule þat best haþ *deseruid*,
A. 7.203   And he shal soupe swettere whanne he it haþ *deseruid*.
A.12.92   And mannes merþe w[or]þ no mor þan he *deseruyþ* here
B. 4.178   And deme yow, bi þis day, as ye han *deserued*
B. 6.42   Nyme it no3t an aunture [þow] mowe it no3t *deserue*.
B. 6.87   He shal haue my soule þat best haþ *deserued*,
B. 6.217   And he shal soupe swetter whan he it haþ *deserued*.
B.12.197   As Seint Iohan and oþere Seintes þat *deserued* hadde bettre.
B.14.127   To 3yue many m[e]n his [mercymonye] er he it haue *deserued*.
B.14.135   And selden deyeþ he out of dette þat dyneþ er he *deserue* it,
B.14.138   What he were worþi for his werk and what he haþ *deserued*,
B.14.314   Than he may [soþly] *deserue*, in somer or in wynter;
C. 2.136   For y, man, of thy mercy mede haue *diserued*."
C. 2.137   And se[t]he man may [o]n heye mede of god *diserue*
C. 3.295   That eny man Mede toke but he hi[t] myhte *deserue*,
C. 3.298   Ne haue hap to his hele mede to *deserue*.
C. 3.302   They asken here huyre ar thei hit haue *deserued*
C. 4.172   And deme 3ow, by this day, as 3e haen *deserued*.
C. 5.32   There ryhtfulnesse rewardeth ryht as men *deserueth*–
C. 5.42   Yf y be labour sholde lyuen and lyflode *deseruen*,
C. 5.45   The lomes þat y labore with and lyflode *deserue*
C. 8.40   Nym hit nat an auntur thow mowe hit nauht *deserue*
C. 8.203   And 3af hem mete and money as þei myhte *deserue*.
C. 8.227   And h[e] shal soupe swetture when [he] hit hath *deserued*.

C.13.86 Halyday or holy euene his mete to *discerue*.
C.14.136 A[s] seynt Ioh[a]n and oþer seyntes þat haen [*de]serued* bettere.
C.14.214 And hope hangeth ay þeron to haue þat treuthe *deserueth*:
C.16.4 And selde deyeth [he] oute of dette [þat] dyne[th] ar he *deserue* hit.
C.16.6 Thenne may men wyte what he is worth and what he hath *deserued*
C.16.148 Then he may sothly *deserue* in Somur or in wynter;

desire v *desiren v.* A 7 desyre (1) desiren (1) desiriþ (5); B 8 desire (1) desiren (3) desireþ (4); C 2 desiren (1) desireth (1)
A. 1.158 Þanne malkyn of hire maidenhed þat no man *desiriþ*.
A. 3.88 Þe hous and þe hom[e] of hem þat *desiren*
A. 3.225 Þere is a mede mesurles þat maistris *desiriþ*;
A. 3.231 Prestis & personis þat plesing *desiriþ*,
A.10.47 Inwyt is þe [allie] þat anima *desiriþ*.
A.10.125 Springeþ & sprediþ, þat spiceris *desiriþ*,
A.12.45 And 3if þou *desyre* with him for to abyde
B. 1.184 Than Malkyn of hire maydenhede þat no man *desireþ*.
B. 3.99 The hou[s] and [þe] ho[m] of hem þat *desireþ*
B. 3.246 Ther is [a] Mede mesurelees þat maistres *desireþ*;
B. 3.252 Preestes and persons þat plesynge *desireþ*,
B. 9.107 To alle trewe tidy men þat trauaille *desiren*,
B.14.188 Shulde amenden vs as manye siþes as man wolde *desire*.
B.15.469 And maidenes and mylde men mercy wolde *desire*.
B.20.322 I may wel suffre', seide Conscience, 'syn ye *desiren*,
C. 1.180 Then malkyn of here maydenheed [þat] no man [*desir]eth*.
C.22.322 Y may wel soffre,' sayde Consience, 'sennes 3e *desiren*,

desiryng ger *desiringe ger.* B 1
B.13.355 [Was] colomy þoru3 coueitise and vnkynde *desiryng*.

despeyre v *despeiren v.* C 1
C. 9.38 That no deuel shal 3ow dere ne *despeyre* in 3oure d[e]ynge

despende v *dispenden v.* B 5 despende (1) despended (4); C 3 despene (2) despened (1)
B. 5.264 And þat was wonne wiþ wrong wiþ wikked men be *despended*.
B.10.330 That Gregories godchildren [vngodly] *despended*.
B.12.48 The beaute of hir body; in baddenesse she *despended*.
B.12.56 Wo is hym þat hem weldeþ but he hem [wel] *despende*:
B.14.103 Than richesse ri3tfulliche wonne and resonably *despended*?'
C. 8.234 Yf thow hast wonne auht wikkedliche, wiseliche *despene* hit:
C.12.235 For, how [euere hit] be ywonne, but hit [be] wel *despene[*d]
C.14.18 Wo is hym þat hem weldeth but he hem wel *despene*:

desperacion n *desperacioun n.* B 1; C 1 disparacion
B.17.313 [Drede of *desperacion* [þanne] dryueþ awey grace
C.19.293 Drede of *disparacion* thenne dryueth [away] grace

despise v *despisen v.* B 9 despise (3) despised (2) despiseþ (2) dispise (2); C 11 despice (1) despise (1) despised (1) despisede (1) despiseth (2) dispice (2) dispisede (1) dispisen (1) dispiseth (1)
B. 2.80 To be Princes in pride and pouerte to *despise*,
B. 5.149 Thus þei speken of spiritualte þat eiþer *despiseþ* ooþer
B.12.121 Forþi I conseille alle creatures no clergie to *dispise*
B.13.336 That takeþ me al a tweluemonþe, til þat I *despise*
B.15.54 Ayein swiche Salomon spekeþ and *despiseþ* hir wittes
B.15.569 That contrarien cristes lawe and cristendom *dispise*
B.18.41 'This Iesus of oure Iewes temple Iaped and *despised*,
B.18.92 Thanne gan Feiþ felly þe false Iewes *despise*;
B.19.34 The Iewes þat were gentil men, Ies[u] þei *despised*,
C. 2.87 To ben pr[inces] in pruyde and pouert to *dispise*,
C. 6.80 That taketh me al [a] twelmonthe til þat y *dispise*
C. 6.122 Thus thei speke and dispute þat vchon *dispiseth* oþer.
C. 7.118 For a lythed and louede þat godes lawe *despiseth*:
C. 9.191 Al þat holy Ermytes hatede and *dispisede*,
C.14.64 Forthy y conseyle all creatures no cler[gie] to *despice*
C.16.216 A3enes suche salamon speketh and *despiseth* here wittes
C.17.251 That contra[r]yen now cristes law[e] and cristendoem *dispisen*.
C.20.40 'This iesus of oure iewene temple iaped and *despised*,
C.20.95 Thenne gan faith f[el]ly þe false iewes *dispice*,
C.21.34 The iewes þat were gentel men iesu thei *dispisede*,

desplese > displese

despoilen v *despoilen v.* C 1
C.13.58 With robbares and reuares þat ryche men *despoilen*

dispute > disputen; dessallouwynge > disalowyng; desseyue > deceyue

destynee n *destine n.* A 1 destenye; B 1; C 1 destyne
A. 7.258 Þei do men di3e þoru3 here drynkes er *destenye* it wolde.'
B. 6.294 They do men deye þoru3 hir drynkes er *destynee* it wolde.'
C. 8.295 They don men deye thorw here drynkes Ar *destyne* hit wolde.'

destreris n *destrer n.* A 1
A. 2.137 And alle þe denis & southdenis, as *destreris* hem di3te,

destruye v *destroien v.* A 5 destroye (1) destroyede (1) destroyeþ (1) destroi3eþ (1) distroyeþ (1); B 17 destroye (2) destruye (11) destruyed (1) destruye3þ (3); C 18 destrueth (1) destruye (8) destruyeth (2) distrueth (1) distruye (4) distruyeth (2)
A.Pr.22 [Wonne] þat þise wastours wiþ glotonye *destroi3eþ*.
A. 7.30 Fro wastours [and wikkide men] þat wolde me *destroye*,
A. 7.124 Suche wastours in þis world his werkmen *distroyeþ*;
A.10.76 Þanne is dowel a duc þat *destroyeþ* vices,
A.11.288 Or who dede wers þanne dauid þat vrie *destroyede*,
B.Pr.22 Wonnen þat [þise] wastours with glotonye *destruyeþ*.
B.Pr.198 [And] many m[a]nnes malt we mees wolde *destruye*,
B. 2.14 Orientals and Ewages enuenymes to *destroye*.
B. 3.271 For Mede ne for monee loke þow *destruye* it.
B. 6.28 Fro wastours and wikked men þat [wolde me *destruye*],
B.10.335 [Ac] dowel shal dyngen hym adoun and *destruye* his my3te.'
B.13.249 And þat his blessynge and hise bulles bocches my3te *destruye*:
B.16.40 And þanne fondeþ þe fend my fruyt to *destruye*
B.16.165 Ayeins deeþ and þe deuel: *destruyed* hir boþeres my3tes,
B.17.219 To alle vnkynde creatures þat coueite to *destruye*
B.17.279 For þat þe holy goost haþ to kepe þ[o] harlotes *destruyeþ*,
B.17.287 Synnen ayein þe Seint Spirit, assenten to *destruye*
B.18.156 Til he be deed and do þerto; þe yuel he *destruyeþ*,
B.18.236 That mannes soule sholde saue and synne *destroye*.
B.18.347 And þat grace gile good feiþ it askeþ.
B.19.311 Among þ[e] foure vertues and vices *destruye*.
B.20.382 To seken Piers þe Plowman, þat pryde [my3te] *destruye*,
C.Pr.24 And wonne þat þis wastors with glotony *destrueth*.
C.Pr.216 For many mannys malt we muys wolde *distruye*
C. 3.207 And custumes of coueytise þe comune to *destruye*.
C. 9.17 Drede nat for no deth to *distruye* by here power
C.12.234 Ouerplente pruyde norischeth þer pouerte hit *distrueth*.
C.14.22 Druy[e]th vp dowel and *distruyeth* dobest.
C.15.218 For founde y þat his blessynge and his bulle [bocches] myhte [*destruye*],
C.16.174 'Of [fele] tyme to fihte,' quod he, 'falsnesse to *destruye*
C.17.217 And deye for his dere childrene to *de[struy]e* dedly synne,
C.18.43 And thenne fondeth þe fende my fruyte to *destruye*
C.19.185 To alle vnkynde creatures þat coueyten to *destruye*
C.19.260 For that the holy goest hath to kepe tho harlotes *distruyeth*,
C.19.268 Synegen a3en þe seynte spirit, assente to *destruye*
C.19.278 Wol louye þat lyf þat loue and Charite *destruyeth*.'
C.20.159 Til he [be] ded [and] ydo þerto; [þe yuel] he *destruyeth*,
C.20.245 That mannes soule sholde saue and synne *distruye*.
C.21.311 Among th[e] foure vertues and vices *distruye*.
C.22.382 To seke [Peres the Plouhman], þat pruyde myhte *destruye*,

deth- > deeþ

dette n *dette n.* A 2 dette (1) dettis (1); B 11 dette (8) dettes (3); C 13 dette (8) dettes (5)
A. 5.145 And bidde þe rode of bromholm bringe me out of *dette*.'
A. 7.90 For þei3 I dei3e today my *dettis* ben quyt;
B.Pr.93 In Cheker and in Chauncelrie chalangen hise *dettes*
B. 5.229 And bidde þe Roode of Bromholm brynge me out of *dette*.'
B. 6.98 For þou3 I deye today my *dettes* are quyte;
B. 7.81 And he þat biddeþ borweþ and bryngeþ hymself in *dette*.
B.13.10 But quik he biqueþe [hem] au3t [or sholde helpe] quyte hir *dettes*;
B.14.108 And þat at þe rekenyng in Arrerage fel raþer þan out of *dette*.
B.14.135 And selden deyeþ he out of *dette* þat dyneþ er he deserue it,
B.19.190 And assoille men of alle synnes saue of *dette* one.
B.20.10 And nede haþ no lawe ne neuere shal falle in *dette*
B.20.293 And suffre þe dede in *dette* to þe day of doome.
B.20.321 And Indulgence may do but if *dette* lette it.
C.Pr.91 In Cheker and in Chancerye chalengen his *dettes*
C. 3.305 And þat is no mede but a mercede, a manere dewe *dette*,
C. 6.299 Shal parte with the in purgatorye and helpe paye thy *dette*
C. 8.101 For thouh y dey today my *dette[*s ben] yquited;
C. 9.274 Thyn huyre, herde, as y hope, hath nat to quyte thy *dette*
C.13.38 For þe parcel[s] of his pauper and oþer pruye *dettes*
C.13.76 And 3ut more, to maken pees and quyten menne *dettes*
C.15.12 Bote quyke he byqu[e]th hem auht or wolde helpe quyte here *dettes*;
C.16.4 And selde deyeth [he] oute of *dette* [þat] dyne[th] ar he deserue hit.
C.21.190 And assoile men of alle synnes saue of *dette* one.
C.22.10 And nede hath no lawe ne neuere shal falle in *dette*
C.22.293 And soffren þe dede in *dette* to þe day of dome.
C.22.321 And indulgence may do but yf *dette* lette hit.

deuk > duc; deul > doel; deux > mesondieux; deue > def

deuel n *devel n.* A 11 deuelis (1) deuil (9) deuyl (1); B 27 deuel (18) deueles (9); C 18 deuel (13) deueles (5)
A. 1.28 Dede be his dou3ter[n] þat þe *deuil* lykide,
A. 1.29 [Delyted hym in drynke as the *deuyl* wolde],
A. 2.65 Wiþ alle þe delites of lust þe *deuil* for to serue,

A. 2.77   In þe date of þe *deuil* þe dede is asselid
A. 7.49   For it arn þe *deuelis* disours I do þe to vndirstonde.
A. 7.112   And þei3 3e dei3e for doel þe *deuil* haue þat recche!'
A. 8.37   Þat no *deuil* shal 3ow dere, di3e whan 3e di3e,
A. 8.53   Shal no *deuil* at his deþ day derie hym a myte
A.10.194   Þei3 þei don hem to dunmowe, but 3if þe *deuil* helpe
A.10.213   A3ens dowel hy don euele, & þe *deuil* plesen,
A.11.22   And ben seruid as sires þat serue þe *deuil*.
B. 1.28   Dide by hise dou3tres þat þe *deuel* liked;
B. 1.29   Delited hym in drynke as þe *deuel* wolde,
B. 2.103   A dwellynge wiþ þe *deuel* and dampned be for euere
B. 2.113   'In þe date of þe *deuel* þ[e] dede [is asseled]
B. 5.624   Heo haþ holpe a þousand out of þe *deueles* punfolde.
B. 6.54   For it ben þe *deueles* disours, I do þe to vnderstonde.'
B. 6.120   And þou3 ye deye for doel þe *deuel* haue þat recch[e]!'
B. 7.35   That no *deuel* shal yow dere ne [in youre deying fere yow],
B. 7.51   Shal no *deuel* at his deeþ day deren hym a myte
B. 7.118   [That] after þi deeþ day þe *deuel* shal haue þi soule.'
B. 9.64   That lyuen synful lif here hir soule is lich þe *deuel*.
B. 9.173   [Th]ou3 þei do hem to Dunmowe, but if þe *deuel* helpe
B. 9.199   Ayeins dowel þei doon yuel and þe *deuel* [plese],
B.10.243   Fro þe dedly deeþ and [þe] *deueles* power
B.14.58   Ne deeþ drede [ne *deuel*], but deye as god likeþ
B.14.79   Diden dedly synne þat þe *deuel* liked,
B.16.79   For euere as þei dropped adoun þe *deuel* was redy
B.16.85   There is derknesse and drede and þe *deuel* maister.
B.16.120   And seide he wro3te þoru3 wichecraft & wiþ þe *deueles* my3te:
B.16.165   Ayeins deeþ and þe *deuel*: destruyed hir boþeres my3tes,
B.16.266   That shal deliuere vs som day out of þe *deueles* power
B.17.19   Shal neuere *deuel* hym dere ne deeþ in soule greue;
B.18.159   Al þat deeþ [d]ide first þoru3 þe *deueles* entisyng,
B.18.275   May no deeþ [þis lord] dere, ne no *deueles* queyntise,
B.18.282   And dwelle wiþ vs *deueles*; þis þretynge [dri3ten] made.
B.18.295   'Certes I drede me', quod þe *deuel*, 'lest truþe [do] hem fecche.
B.19.21   For alle derke *deueles* arn adrad to heren it,
C. 2.117   'In þe date of the *deuel* th[e] dede is aseled
C. 8.52   For hit beeþ þe *deueles* dysors to drawe men to synne;
C. 8.127   And thow 3e deye for deul þe *deuel* haue þat reche!'
C. 8.277   Thenk þat [diues] for his delicat lyf to þe *deuel* wente
C. 9.38   That no *deuel* shal 3ow dere ne despeyre in 3oure d[e]ynge
C.10.275   Thogh they [do] hem to donemowe, bote þe *deuel* helpe
C.10.298   A3en dowel they do yuele and þe *deuel* serue
C.15.257   Ne d[e]þ drede ne *deuel*, [but] deye as god liketh
C.18.110   For euere as Elde hadde eny down, þe *deuel* was redy
C.18.116   There is derkenesse and drede and þe *deuel* maister.
C.18.282   That shal delyuere vs som day out of þe *deueles* power
C.19.20   Shal neuere *deuel* hym dere ne deth in soule greue;
C.19.243   And dampned a dwelleth with þe *deuel* in helle.
C.20.162   All þat deth and þe *deuel* dede formost to Eue
C.20.297   May no deth this lord dere ne [n]o *deueles* quentyse
C.20.325   'Forthy y drede me,' quod þe *deuel*, 'laste treuthe wol hem fecche.
C.20.340   Hit shal vndo vs *deueles* and down bryngen vs all.
C.21.21   For alle derke *deueles* aren drad to heren hit

deuer > deuoir; deuyde > dyuyde; deuil > deuel

deuyn n *divine n.* A 1
A.Pr.90   I sau3 bisshopis bolde & bacheleris of *deuyn*

deuyne v *divinen v.* A 3 deuinide (2) deuynide (1); B 9 deuyne (3)
deuyned (2) deuynede (1) deuyneþ (1) diuined (2); C 9 deuine (1)
deuinede (1) deuyne (3) deuyned (2) deuynede (1) deuyneth (1)
A. 8.136   How Dani[el] *deui[n]ide* þe drem[is] of a king
A. 8.141   As daniel *deui[n]ide* in dede it fel aftir:
A.11.139   And þe deppere I *deuynide* þe derkere me þou3te;
B.Pr.210   *Deuyne* ye, for I ne dar, by deere god in heuene.
B. 7.158   How Daniel *diuined* þe dre[mes] of a kyng
B. 7.163   As Daniel *diuined* in dede it fel after:
B.10.187   And þe depper I *deuyne[d]* þe derker me [þou3te].
B.13.90   For now he haþ dronken so depe he wole *deuyne* soone
B.15.599   Daniel of hire vndoynge *deuyned* and seide
B.15.604   Moyses eft or Messie hir maistres *deuyneþ*
B.19.148   And his moder Marie; þus men bifore *de[uyn]ede*,
B.19.240   And some to *deuyne* and diuide, [figures] to kenne:
C.Pr.221   *Deuyne* 3e, for y ne dar, by dere god almyhten.
C. 9.306   How danyel *deuynede* and vndede þe dremes of kynges,
C.10.100   Thus dowel and dobet *de[uin]ede* and a dobest
C.11.128   And þe deppore y *deuine* þe derkore me thynketh hit.
C.11.263   Or dauid þe douhty þat *de[uyn]ed* how vrye
C.15.97   [For] now he hath dronke so depe a wol *deuyne* sone
C.17.312   Moises oþer Macometh here maystres *deuyneth*
C.21.148   And his moder marie; thus men bifore *deuyned*.
C.21.240   And somme to *deuyne* and deuyde, [figu]res to kenne;

deuinour(s > diuinour

---

deuyse v *devisen v.* B 4 deuyse (2) deuysede (1) dyuyse (1); C 4 deuise
(1) deuyse (2) deuysed (1)
B. 5.547   In taillours craft and tynkeris craft, what truþe kan *deuyse*,
B.16.66   'To [*dyuyse*] þe fruyt þat so faire hangeþ'.
B.19.278   Er he [dide] any [dede] *deuyse* wel þe ende;
B.19.329   And whan þis dede was doon Grace *deuysede*
C. 7.191   In alle kyne craftes þat he couthe *deuise*
C. 8.200   In alle kyne trewe craft þat man couthe *deuyse*.
C.21.278   Ar he dede eny dede *deuyse* wel þe ende;
C.21.329   And when this dede was doen grace *deuysed*

deuoir n *dever n.* A 1 deuer; B 5; C 3 deuer
A.12.2   I haue do my *deuer* þe dowel to teche,
B.11.286   And þei hir *deuoir* dide as Dauid seiþ in þe Sauter:
B.13.212   I shal dwelle as I do my *deuoir* to shewe,
B.14.136   And til he haue doon his *deuoir* and his dayes iournee.
B.14.150   And whan he haþ doon his *deuoir* wel men dooþ hym ooþer
                bountee,
B.14.153   And alle þat doon hir *deuoir* wel han double hire for hir trauaille,
C.16.5   When his *d[eu]er* is doen and his dayes iourne
C.17.93   Doen her *deuer* day and nyhte; dede we so alse
C.17.122   Ac 3if prestes doen here *deuer* wel we shal do þe bettre

deuors n *divorce n.* B 2 deuors (1) diuorses (1); C 1
B. 2.176   As [de]uoutrye and *diuorses* and derne vsurie,
B.20.139   Departen er deeþ cam and *deuors* shapte.
C.22.139   Departen ar dethe come and *deuors* shupte.

deuouren v *devouren v.* C 3 deuouren (1) deuoureth (2)
C. 2.143   Holy churche, and charite 3e cheweth and *deuoureth*.
C. 8.139   3e been wastours, y woet wel, and waste and *deuouren*
C.16.282   Lihtliche þat they leue loseles hit *deuoureth*.

deuouteliche adv *devoutli adv.* C 1
C.17.245   *Deuouteliche* day and nyhte, withdrawe hem fro synne

deuoutours n *devoutour n.* C 1
C. 2.187   Wol Ryde vppon Rectores and ryche men *deuoutours*,

deuoutrye n *devoutrie n.* B 1
B. 2.176   As [de]*uoutrye* and diuorses and derne vsurie,

dew adj *due adj.* A 1; B 1; C 2 dew (1) dewe (1)
A. 6.99   And so worst þou dryuen out as *dew* & þe dore closid,
B. 5.613   And [so] worstow dryuen out as *dew* and þe dore closid,
C. 3.305   And þat is no mede but a mercede, a manere *dewe* dette,
C. 7.265   So worth thow dryuen out as *de[w]* and þe dore yclosed,

dewes n *deu n.* B 1; C 1
B.15.294   And also Marie Maudeleyne by mores lyuede and *dewes*,
C.17.21   Marie Maudeleyne by mores lyuede and *dewes*;

dewid > douwe

diademed ptp *diademen v.* A 1 dyademid; B 1; C 1 ydyademed
A. 3.264   And dauid shal be *dyademid* & daunten hem alle,
B. 3.288   And Dauid shal be *diademed* and daunten hem alle,
C. 3.441   And dauid shal be *ydyademed* and [d]aunte alle oure enemyes

dyaes > dyas

diamaundes n *diamaunt n.* B 1
B. 2.13   And *Diamaundes* of derrest pris and double manere Saphires,

diapenidion n *dia- pref.* A 1 dyapendyon; B 1
A. 5.101   Ne no *dyapendyon* dryue it fro myn herte.
B. 5.124   Ne no *Diapenidion* dryue it fro myn herte.

dyas n *dia n.* B 1; C 1 dyaes
B.20.174   And dryuen awey deeþ wiþ *Dyas* and drogges.
C.22.174   And dryue away deth with *dyaes* and drogges.

dych n *diche n.* A 1 dikes; B 4 dych (2) diches (1) dyk (1); C 3 dich (1)
dych (1) dykke (1)
A.Pr.16   Wiþ depe *dikes* & derke & dredful of si3t.
B.Pr.16   Wiþ depe *diches* and derke and dredfulle of si3te.
B.11.427   For lat a dronken daffe in a *dyk* falle,
B.19.362   To deluen a *dych* depe aboute vnitee
B.20.19   That he dronke at ech *dych* er he [deye for þurst].
C.13.234   For lat a dronkene daffe in a *dykke* falle,
C.21.362   To deluen a *dich* depe aboute vnite
C.22.19   That he dronke at vch a *dy[c]h* ar he deye for furste.

dide(- > doon

dido n *dido n.* B 1; C 1
B.13.172   'It is but a *dido*', quod þis doctour, 'a disours tale.
C.15.170   'This is a *dido*,' quod this doctour, 'a dysores tale!

dye(d -n > deye

diete n *diete n.* A 1 diȝete; B 1; C 1 dyete
A. 7.252 And ȝif þou *diȝete* þe þus I dar ley myn armes
B. 6.268 And if þow *diete* þee þus I dar legge myne [armes]
C. 8.289 And yf thow *dyete* the thus y dar legge myn eres

dyeþ > deye; diffoule > defoulen

dyggeþ v *diggen v.* A 1; B 1 digged; C 1 digged
A. 7.99 Dikeris & delueres *dy[gg]eþ* vp þe balkis.
B. 6.107 Dikeres and Delueres *digged* vp þe balkes;
C. 8.114 Dikares and deluares *digged* vp þe balkes;

dighte > diȝte

digneliche adv *digneli adv.* A 1; B 1
A. 8.155 Dowel at þe day of dome is *digneliche* vndirfongen;
B. 7.177 Dowel at þe day of dome is *digneliche* vnderfongen;

dignites n *dignite n.* A 1
A.Pr.92 Archideknes & denis þat *dignites* hauen

diȝe -dist -n > deye; diȝete > diete

diȝte v *dighten v.* A 2; B 2 dighte (1) diȝte (1); C 3 dighte (1) dihte (1) dyhte (1)
A. 2.137 And alle þe denis & southdenis, as destreris hem *diȝte*,
A. 7.275 Þanne may I *diȝte* þi dyner as þe dere likeþ.'
B. 6.291 [Th]anne may I *diȝte* þi dyner as [þee] deere likeþ.'
B.19.2 And *dighte* me derely and dide me to chirche
C. 1.27 In his dronkenesse aday his doughteres he *dighte*
C. 8.314 Thenne may y *dyhte* [þ]y dyner as me dere lyketh.'
C.21.2 And *dihte* me derely and dede me to kyrke

dyk > dych; dykares > dikere

diken v *dichen v.* A 2 dyked (1) diken (1); B 2 diken (1) idyked (1)
A. 6.33 *Dyke[d]* & d[o]luen & do what he hiȝte,
A.11.187 *Diken* or deluen, dowel it hatte.
B. 5.545 *Idyke[d]* and Id[o]lue, Ido þat [he] hoteþ.
B. 6.141 *Diken* or deluen or dyngen vpon sheues

dykere n *dicher n.* A 3 dykere (1) dikeris (2); B 4 dykere (2) dikeres (1) dykeres (1); C 3 dikares (1) dikere (1) dykers (1)
A.Pr.102 As *dikeris* & delueris þat doþ here dede ille
A. 5.163 Dawe þe *dykere* & a dusȝeyn oþere,
A. 7.99 *Dikeris* & delueres dy[gg]eþ vp þe balkis.
B.Pr.224 As *dykeres* and delueres þat doon hire ded[e] ille
B. 5.313 Dawe þe *dykere* and a doȝeyne oþere,]
B. 6.107 *Dikeres* and Delueres digged vp þe balkes;
B. 6.330 And Dawe þe *dykere* deye for hunger.
C.Pr.228 As *dykers* and deluers þat doth here dedis ylle
C. 6.369 Dawe þe *dikere* with a dosoyne harlotes
C. 8.114 *Dikares* and deluares digged vp þe balkes;

dikes dykke > dych

dym adj *dim adj* A 1 dym; B 2 dym (1) dymme (1); C 1 demme
A. 3.180 And dreddist to be ded for a *dym* cloud,
B. 3.193 And dreddest to be ded for a *dym* cloude,
B.18.319 Dukes of þis *dymme* place, anoon vndo þise yates
C.20.362 Dukes of this *demme* place, anoen vndoth this ȝates

dymes n *dime n.* B 1; C 1
B.15.564 Takeþ hire landes, ye lordes, and leteþ hem lyue by *dymes*.
C.17.227 Taketh here londe[s], ȝe lordes, and lat hem lyue by *dymes*

dymme adv *dimme adv.* &> dym A 1; B 1; C 1 demme
A.11.136 And lernide h[e]m lyuel & lyne þeiȝ I loke *dymme*.
B.10.184 And lerned hem leuel and lyne þouȝ I loke *dymme*.
C.11.125 Thus thorw my lore ben men ylered thogh y loke *demme*.

dymmed ptp *dimmen v.* A 1 dymmede; B 1; C 1 dymmede
A. 5.197 Whanne he drouȝ to þe dore þanne *dymmede* hise eiȝen;
B. 5.349 A[c] whan he drouȝ to þe dore þanne *dymmed* hise eiȝen;
C. 6.407 And when he drow to the dore thenne *dymmede* his yes;

dyn > dene

dyne v *dinen v.(2)* A 6 dyne (5) dyned (1); B 10 dyne (7) dyned (1) dyneþ (2); C 10 dyne (7) dyneth (2) ydyned (1)
A.Pr.105 Goode gees & gris; go we *dyne*, go we!'
A. 5.57 Drinke but wiþ þe doke & *dyne* but ones.
A. 5.72 Such wynd in my wombe wexiþ er I *dyne*.
A. 7.244 Þat þou drynke no day er þou *dyne* sumwhat,
A. 7.263 Er I haue *dyned* be þis day & ydronke boþe.'
A. 7.292 Deyneþ nouȝt to *dyne* a day niȝt olde wortis.
B.Pr.227 Goode gees and grys! go we *dyne*, go we!'
B. 5.74 Drynke but [wiþ] þe doke and *dyne* but ones.
B. 5.389 Sholde no ryngynge do me ryse er I were ripe to *dyne*.'
B. 6.260 That þow drynke no day er þow *dyne* somwhat.

B. 6.279 [Er] I haue *dyned* bi þis day and ydronke boþe.'
B. 6.308 Deyne[þ] noȝt to *dyne* a day nyȝt olde wortes.
B.13.23 And bad me come to his court, wiþ clergie sholde I *dyne*.
B.14.135 And selden deyeþ he out of dette þat *dyneþ* er he deserue it,
B.14.251 Ne dooþ hym noȝt *dyne* delicatly ne drynke wyn ofte.
B.19.383 'Comeþ', quod Conscience, 'ye cristene, and *dyneþ*,
C.Pr.231 Goode gees and grys! ga we *dyne*, ga we!'
C. 6.174 Drynke but with þe doke and *dyne* but ones.
C. 7.5 Sholde no ryngyng do me ryse til y were rype to *dyne*.'
C. 8.276 And loke þou drynke no day ar thow *dyne* sumwhat.
C. 8.301 Ar y haue *ydyned* be þis day and ydronke boþe.'
C. 8.330 Deyne[th noght] to *dyne* a day nyhte olde wortes;
C.15.26 And beden me ryse and rome; with reson sholde y *dyne*.
C.16.4 And selde deyeth [he] oute of dette [þat] *dyne[th]* ar he deserue hit.
C.16.91 Ne doth men *dyne* delicatlyche ne drynke wyne ofte.
C.21.383 Cometh,' quod Consience, 'ȝe cristene, and *dyneth*

dyner n *diner n.* A 1; B 3; C 3
A. 7.275 Þanne may I diȝte þi *dyner* as þe dere likeþ.'
B. 4.38 For [þei wolde do for a *dyner* or a doȝeyne capons
B. 6.291 [Th]anne may I diȝte þi *dyner* as [þee] deere likeþ.'
B.13.28 Thei wesshen and wipeden and wenten to þe *dyner*.
C. 4.38 For þey wolde do for a *dyner* oþer a d[o]seyne capones
C. 8.314 Thenne may y dyhte [þ]y *dyner* as me dere lyketh.'
C.15.31 They woschen and wypeden and wenten to þe *dyner*.

dyngen v *dingen v.* B 4 dynge (1) dyngen (3); C 1 dynge
B. 3.312 And *dyngen* vpon Dauid eche day til eue;
B. 6.141 Diken or deluen or *dyngen* vpon sheues
B.10.335 [Ac] dowel shal *dyngen* hym adoun and destruye his myȝte.'
B.15.19 That wole defende me þe dore, *dynge* I neuer so late.
C.16.170 That wol defende me [þe] dore, *dynge* y neuere so late.

dynt n *dint n.* A 1 dent; B 2 dynt (1) dyntes (1); C 3 dynt (1) duntes (1) duntus (1)
A.12.104 Deþ delt him a *dent* and drof him to þe erþe
B.18.26 For no *dynt* shal hym dere as in deitate patris.'
B.20.105 Swowned and swelted for sorwe of [deþes] *dyntes*.
C. 8.187 Al for drede of here deth, such *duntus* ȝaf hunger.
C.20.25 For no *d[yn]t* shal hym dere as in deitate patris.'
C.22.105 Swowened and swel[t]e for sorwe of dethus *duntes*.

dirige n *dirige n.* C 2
C. 3.464 Prestes and persones placebo and *dirige*,
C. 5.46 Is paternoster and my primer, placebo and *dirige*,

disalowed ptp *disallouen v.* B 1
B.14.131 And whan he dyeþ ben *disalowed*, as Dauid seiþ in þe Sauter:

disalowyng ger *disalouing ger.* B 1; C 1 dessallouwynge
B.14.139 And noȝt to fonge bifore for drede of *disalowyng*.
C.16.7 A[nd] nat to fonge byfore for drede [of] *dessallouwynge*.

discerue > deserue; disceue > deceyue; disch(e > dissh; dischargid > deschargen

disciple n *disciple n.* A 1 disciplis; B 2 disciples; C 2 disciple (1) disciples (1)
A.11.295 For he seide it hymself to summe of his *disciplis*:
B.13.429 Riȝt so flatereris and fooles arn þe fendes *disciples*
B.15.88 That seide to hise *disciples*, "Ne sitis personarum acceptores".
C. 9.118 Hit aren as his postles, suche peple, or as his priue *disciples*
C.18.165 Of Ieudas þe iew, iesus oune *disciple*.

discomfited ptp *discomfiten v.* C 2 discomfited (1) disconfit (1)
C.Pr.108 Thei were *discomfited* in batayle and losten Archa domini
C.Pr.112 Were *disconfit* in batayle and Archa domini lorn

discrete adj *discrete aƒ.* C 1
C. 5.84 Preeyeres of a parfit man and penaunce *d[iscret]e*

discryue v1 *descriven v.* A 2 descryue; B 3 discryue (2) discryuen (1); C 2 descreue
A. 5.61 He was cloþid in a caurymaury, I [couþe] it nouȝt *descryue*;
A. 5.107 Þanne com coueitise; I can hym nouȝt *descryue*,
B. 5.78 [He was] cloþed in a kaurymaury–I kouþe it nouȝt *discryue*–
B. 5.188 [Th]anne cam Coueitise; [I kan] hym naȝt *discryue*,
B.16.53 'Now faire falle yow, Piers', quod I, 'so faire ye *discryuen*'
C. 6.196 Thenne cam couetyse; y can hym nat *descreue*,
C.20.213 Ho couthe kyndeliche whit colour *descreue*

discryued v2 *descrien v.* B 1 discryued; C 1 descreued
B.20.94 And er heraudes of Armes hadden *discryued* lordes,
C.22.94 And ar heroudes of Armes hadden *descreued* lordes,

diserue(d > deserue

disgised ptp *disgisen v.* A 1 disgisid; B 1
A.Pr.24 In cuntenaunce of cloþing comen *disgisid*.

B.Pr.24   In contenaunce of cloþynge comen d[is]gised.

dysmas n prop *n.i.d.* A 1 dismas; B 1; C 1
A. 5.237   Þo *dismas* my broþer besouȝte þe of grace,
B. 5.465   Tho *Dysmas* my broþer bisouȝt [þee] of grace
C. 6.319   Tho *dysmas* my brother bisouhte [þe] of grace

disours n *disour n.* A 2; B 2; C 2 dysores (1) dysors (1)
A. 7.49   For it arn þe deuelis *disours* I do þe to vndirstonde.
A.11.30   Or daun[cel]id or drawe forþ; þise *disours* wyte þe soþe.
B. 6.54   For it ben þe deueles *disours*, I do þe to vnderstonde.'
B.13.172   'It is but a dido', quod þis doctour, 'a *disours* tale.
C. 8.52   For hit beeþ þe deueles *dysors* to drawe men to synne;
C.15.170   'This is a dido,' quod this doctour, 'a *dysores* tale!

dispair n *despeir n.* B 1; C 1 dispayr
B.20.164   And threw drede of *dispair* a doȝeyne myle aboute.
C.22.164   And th[re]w drede of *dispayr* a doysayne myle aboute.

disparacion > desperacion; dispice dispise(- > despise

dispit n *despit n.* C 1
C. 8.184   Sp[it]teden and spradden donge in *dispit* of hunger.

displese v *displesen v.* B 2 displese (1) displesed (1); C 1 desplese
B.13.136   'A[t] youre preiere', quod Pacience þo, 'so no man *displese* hym:
B.14.328   That [euere he] dide dede þat deere god *displesed*;
C. 8.84   'Consayle nat þe comune þe kyng to *desplese*

disputen v *disputen v.* A 2 dispute (1) disputyng (1); B 7 dispute (5) disputen (1) disputyng (1); C 7 despute (2) dispute (3) disputen (1) disputyng (1)
A. 9.16   'Contra,' quaþ I as a clerk & comside to *dispute*:
A. 9.108   *Disputyng* on dowel day aftir oþer,
B. 8.20   'Contra!' quod I as a clerc and comsed to *disputen*:
B. 8.118   *Disputyng* [o]n dowel day after oþer,
B.10.112   Here lyeþ youre lore", þise lordes gynneþ *dispute*,
B.10.133   And al worþ as þow wolt whatso we *dispute*–
B.10.255   For hadde neuere freke fyn wit þe feiþ to *dispute*,
B.11.116   And in a weer gan I wexe, and wiþ myself to *dispute*
B.11.320   Ac muche moore in metynge þus wiþ me gan oon *dispute*,
C. 6.122   Thus thei speke and *dispute* þat vchon dispiseth oþer.
C. 6.137   Thus sytte they, sustres, sum tyme and *disputen*
C.10.20   'Contra!' quod y as a Clerk and comsed to *despute*
C.10.114   *Disputyng* vppon dowel day aftur other
C.11.34   The lewed aȝen þe lered þe holy lore to *disp[u]te*
C.11.156   For hadde neuere frek fyn wi[t] the faith to *dispute*
C.12.51   And in a wer gan y wex and with mysulue to *despute*

disseyue(d > deceyue

dissh n *dish n.* B 2 dissh (1) disshes (1); C 3 disch (1) dische (1) disches (1)
B.13.55   In a *dissh* of derne shrifte, Dixi & confitebor tibi.
B.13.82   That *disshes* and doublers [þis doctour bifore]
C.10.179   Ȝaf his douhter for a daunsynge in a *disch* þe heued
C.15.90   Bothe *disches* and dobelares with alle þe deyntees aftur.
C.20.405   Ac y wol drynke of no *dische* ne of deep clergyse

dysshere n *dishere n.* A 1 disshere; B 1; C 1 disshere
A. 5.165   A ropere, a redyngking, & rose þe *disshere*;
B. 5.315   A Ropere, a Redyngkyng and Rose þe *dyssher[e]*,
C. 6.372   A ropere, a redyngkynge and Rose þe *disshere*,

distroyeþ distrueth distruy- > destruye

ditte v *ditten v.* A 1; B 1
A. 7.176   And doluen drit & dung to *ditte* out hunger.
B. 6.190   And doluen [drit] and [dung] to [*ditte* out] hunger.

dyuen v *diven v.* B 2 dyued (1) dyuen (1); C 2 dyuede (1) dyuen (1)
B.12.162   That oon [kan] konnynge and kan swymmen and *dyuen*;
B.12.165   He þat neuere ne *dyued* ne noȝt kan of swymmyng,
C.13.168   Dompynges *dyuede*; 'dere God', y sayde,
C.14.106   That oen hath connyng and can swymmen and *dyuen*;

diuerse adj *diverse adj.* B 5; C 2
B.Pr.152   'For doute of *diuerse* d[e]des we dar noȝt wel loke,
B. 2.94   And al day to drynken at *diuerse* Tauernes,
B.12.67   And of quod vidimus comeþ kynde wit, of siȝte of *diuerse* peple.
B.12.135   For alle hir kynde knowyn[g] co[m] out of *diuerse* siȝtes.
B.15.425   And folkes sholden [fynde], þat ben in *diuerse* siknesse,
C. 2.101   Al day to drynke at *diuerse* tauernes,
C.14.79   For al here kynde knowyng cam bote of *diuerse* syhtes,

diuerse adv *diverse adv.* C 1
C.15.79   For alle be we brethrene thogh we be *diuerse* yclothed.

diuerseth v *diversen v.* C 1
C.17.133   That lelyche they byleue, and ȝut here lawe *diuerseth*,

diues n prop *dives n.* B 3; C 4 diues (3) dyues (1)
B.14.123   And *diues* in deyntees lyuede and in douce vie;
B.17.268   That] *Diues* deyde, dampned for his vnkyndenesse
B.17.273   But þei dwelle þer *Diues* is dayes wiþouten ende.
C. 8.277   Thenk þat [*diues*] for his delicat lyf to þe deuel wente
C.15.299   And *dyues* in deyntees lyuede and [in] douce vie
C.19.234   That *diues* deyede, dampned for his vnkyndenesse
C.19.254   Bote they dwelle there *diues* is dayes withouten ende.

dyuyde v *dividen v.* B 2 diuide (1) dyuyde (1); C 2 deuyde
B.19.215   'For I wole dele today and [*dyuyde*] grace
B.19.240   And some to deuyne and *diuide*, [figures] to kenne;
C.21.215   'For y wol dele today and *deuyde* grace
C.21.240   And somme to deuyne and *deuyde*, [figu]res to kenne;

diuined > deuyne; dyuyneris > diuinour

diuinite n *divinite n.* B 2; C 1
B. 7.141   As diuinour in *diuinite*, wiþ Dixit inspiens to þi teme.'
B.15.380   Doctours of decrees and of *diuinite* maistres,
C.17.114   Doctours of decre[s] and of *diuinite* maistres

diuinour n *divinour n.* A 1 dyuynour; B 4 deuinour (1) dyuyneris (1) diuinour (1) dyuynours (1); C 2 deuynours (1) dyuynour (1)
A.11.302   Þe douȝtiest doctour or *dyuynour* of þe trinite.
B. 7.141   As *diuinour* in diuinite, wiþ Dixit inspiens to þi teme.'
B.10.458   The douȝtieste doctour and *deuinour* of þe trinitee
B.12.130   [*Dyuyneris*] toforn vs [viseden and markeden]
B.13.115   What is dowel and dobet? ye *dyuynours* knoweþ.'
C.15.84   'A[c] this doctour and *dyuynour*,' quod y, 'and decretistre of Canoen,
C.15.122   What is dowel and dobet? ȝe *deuynours* knoweth.'

dyuyse > deuyse; diuorses > deuors; do > doon,dowel; dobbed -et > dubbed; dobelares > doublers

dobest n *don v.* A 19; B 23; C 17
A. 9.69   'Dowel,' quaþ he, '& dobet, & *dobest* þe þridde
A. 9.86   *Dobest* is aboue hem boþe & beriþ a bisshopis croce;
A. 9.92   Þat ȝif dowel & dobet dede aȝens *dobest*
A. 9.96   But *dobest* bede for hem abide þere for euere.
A. 9.97   Þus dowel, & dobet, & *dobest* þe þridde,
A. 9.104   How dowel, dobet & *dobest* don on þis erþe.'
A. 9.117   'Where þat dowel, & dobet, & *dobest* beþ in londe,
A.10.14   Þus dowel, & dobet, & *dobest* þe þridde,
A.10.121   And þus of dred & h[is] dede *dobest* arisiþ,
A.10.127   So *dobest* out of dobet & dowel gynneþ springe
A.10.217   And so comiþ *dobest* aboute, and bringeþ doun mody,
A.11.92   Þeiȝ *dobest* drawe on hym day aftir oþer.'
A.11.145   For dobet & *dobest* ben drawen of louis s[co]le.
A.11.181   And siþen aftirward to se sumwhat of *dobest*.'
A.11.194   [Dredles] þis is dobet; [*dobest* wot þe soþe].
A.11.195   Sire *dobest* haþ ben [in office], so is he best worþi
A.11.197   Forþi is *dobest* [a] bisshopis pere,
A.11.220   Wern dowel, & dobet, & *dobest* of hem alle,
A.11.224   Forþi I wende þat þo wyes wern *dobest* of alle.'
B. 8.78   'Dowel', [quod he], 'and dobet and *dobest* þe þridde
B. 8.96   *Dobest* is aboue boþe and bereþ a bisshopes crosse;
B. 8.102   That if dowel [and] dobet dide ayein *dobest*
B. 8.106   But *dobest* bede for hem [abide] þer for euere.
B. 8.107   Thus dowel and dobet and *dobest* þe þridde
B. 8.114   How dowel, dobet and *dobest* doon among þe peple.'
B. 8.126   What was Dowel fro dobet and *dobest* from hem boþe.
B. 8.128   'Wher dowel [and] dobet and *dobest* ben in londe
B. 9.14   *Dobest* is aboue boþe, a Bisshopes peere;
B. 9.206   To helen and to helpen, is *dobest* of alle.
B. 9.208   And so comeþ *dobest* [aboute] and bryngeþ adoun mody,
B.10.139   Theiȝ *dobest* drawe on hym day after oþer.'
B.10.193   For dobet and *dobest* ben [drawen] of loues [scole].
B.10.237   Dowel and dobet and *dobest* to lerne.
B.10.264   Thanne is *dobest* to be boold to blame þe gilty,
B.12.18   To telle men what dowel is, dobet and *dobest* boþe,
B.12.26   What were dowel and dobet and *dobest* at þe laste,
B.13.98   Of dowel and dobet, and if *do[best]* be any penaunce.'
B.13.103   'What is dowel, sire doctour?' quod I; 'is [*dobest*] any penaunce?'
B.13.118   And *dobest* doþ hymself so as he seiþ and precheþ;
B.13.129   Whiche Infinites wiþ a feiþ fynden out *dobest*,
B.13.138   Disce and dowel, doce and dobet, dilige and *dobest*:
B.14.22   *Dobest* [shal kepe it clene from vnkynde werkes].
C.10.76   'Dowel and dobet,' quod he, ' and *dobest* the thridde
C.10.93   *Dobest* bere sholde þe bisshopes [c]rose
C.10.99   Ac *dobest* sholde drede hem nat but do as god hihte:
C.10.100   Thus dowel and dobet de[uin]ede a *dobest*
C.10.102   That wolde nat do as *dobest* de[m]ede and tauhte.
C.10.103   Thus dowel and dobet and *dobest* the thridde
C.10.122   What was dowel fro dobet and *dobest* fro hem bothe.

C.10.124 'Whare dowel and dobet And *dobest* ben in londe
C.10.141 *Dobest* is aboue bothe, a bishopis pere,
C.10.305 Helen and helpen, is *dobest* of alle.
C.11.93 Of dobet [and] of *dobest*–for doctour he is knowe
C.11.133 For of dobet and *dobest* here doctour is dere loue.'
C.11.159 That [doth] men dowel, dobet and *dobest*.'
C.14.22 Druy[e]th vp dowel and distruyeth *dobest*.
C.15.105 Of dowel and dobet and yf dobe[s]t [be] eny penaunce.'
C.15.110 'What is dowel, sire doctour?' quod y; 'is *dobest* eny penaunce?'
C.16.28 And these ben dowel and dobet and *dobest* of alle.

dobet n *don v.* A 21; B 29; C 19

A. 9.69 'Dowel,' quaþ he, '& *dobet*, & dobest þe þridde,
A. 9.76 *Dobet* þus doþ, ac he doþ muche more.
A. 9.90 And as dowel & *dobet* dede hem to vndirstonde,
A. 9.92 Þat ȝif dowel & *dobet* dede aȝens dobest
A. 9.97 Þus dowel, & *dobet*, & dobest þe þridde,
A. 9.104 How dowel, *dobet* & dobest don on þis erþe.'
A. 9.117 'Where þat dowel, & *dobet*, & dobest beþ in londe,
A.10.12 *Dobet* is hire damysele, sire dowelis [douȝter],
A.10.14 Þus dowel, & *dobet*, & dobest þe þridde,
A.10.85 Þanne is *dobet* to ben ywar for betyng of þe ȝarde,
A.10.118 Þus in dred liþ dowel, [and] *dobet* to suffre,
A.10.127 So dobest out of *dobet* & dowel gynneþ springe
A.10.216 Þanne is dowel to dreden, [and] *dobet* to suffre,
A.11.88 What is dowel fro *dobet*; now def mote he worþe,
A.11.145 For *dobet* & dobest ben drawen of louis s[co]le.
A.11.180 To lere at ȝow dowel & *dobet* þereaftir,
A.11.192 Þ[i]s be[þ] *dobet*; so beriþ witnesse þe sauter:
A.11.194 [Dredles] þis is *dobet*; [dobest wot þe soþe].
A.11.199 *Dobet* doþ ful wel, & dewid he is also,
A.11.217 Þis is þe lif of þis lordis þat lyuen shulde wiþ *dobet*,
A.11.220 Wern dowel, & *dobet*, & dobest of hem alle,
B. 8.78 'Dowel', [quod he], 'and *dobet* and dobest þe þridde
B. 8.85 *Dobet* [þus dooþ], ac he dooþ muche moore.
B. 8.100 And [as] dowel and *dobet* [dide] hem [to vnderstonde],
B. 8.102 That if dowel [and] *dobet* dide ayein dobest
B. 8.107 Thus dowel and *dobet* and dobest þe þridde
B. 8.114 How dowel, *dobet* and dobest doon among þe peple.'
B. 8.126 What was Dowel fro *dobet* and dobest from hem boþe.
B. 8.128 'Wher dowel [and] *dobet* and dobest ben in londe
B. 9.12 *Dobet* is hire damyselle, sire doweles douȝter,
B. 9.204 Ac to loue and to lene], leue me, þat is *dobet*;
B. 9.207 [Thanne is dowel] to drede, and *dobet* to suffre,
B.10.135 What is dowel fro *dobet*, [now] deef mote he worþe,
B.10.138 I dar ben his bolde borgh þat *dobet* wole he neuere,
B.10.193 For *dobet* and dobest ben [drawen] of loues [scole].
B.10.237 Dowel and *dobet* and dobest to lerne.
B.10.257 [So] is *dobet* to suffre for þ[i] soules helþe
B.10.336 'Thanne is dowel and *dobet*', quod I, 'dominus and knyȝthode?'
B.10.378 Where dowel is or *dobet* derkliche ye shewen.
B.11.48 That of dowel ne *dobet* no deyntee me þouȝte;
B.11.51 Than dowel or *dobet* among my dedes alle.
B.12.18 To telle men what dowel is, *dobet* and dobest boþe,
B.12.26 What were dowel and *dobet* and dobest at þe laste,
B.13.98 Of dowel and *dobet*, and if do[best] be any penaunce.'
B.13.115 What is dowel and *dobet*? ye dyuynours knoweþ.'
B.13.117 [That trauailleþ to teche oþere I holde it for a *dobet*].
B.13.128 And [demeþ] þat dowel and *dobet* arn two Infinites,
B.13.138 Disce and dowel, doce and *dobet*, dilige and dobest
B.14.19 *Dobet* shal beten it and bouken it as bright as any scarlet
B.19.129 The which was *dobet*, where þat he wente.
C.10.76 'Dowel and *dobet*,' quod he, ' and dobest the thridde
C.10.82 Dobeth doth al this Ac ȝut he doth more.
C.10.100 Thus dowel and *dobet* de[uin]ede a dobest
C.10.103 Thus dowel and *dobet* and dobest the thridde
C.10.110 Of dowel and *dobet* and ho doth best of alle.'
C.10.122 What was dowel fro *dobet* and dobest fro hem bothe.
C.10.124 'Whare dowel and *dobet* And dobest ben in londe
C.10.139 *Dobet* is here damysele, sire dowelus douhtur,
C.10.303 Ac to louye and to l[e]ne, leef me, þat is *dobet*;
C.11.93 Of *dobet* [and] of dobest–for doctour he is knowe
C.11.133 For of *dobet* and dobest here doctour is dere loue.'
C.11.159 That [doth] men dowel, *dobet* and dobest.'
C.11.311 Of dowel ne of *dobet* no deynte me thouhte;
C.14.15 And þat is *dobet*, yf eny suche be, a blessed man þat helpeth
C.15.105 Of dowel and *dobet* and yf dobe[s]t [be] eny penaunce.'
C.15.122 What is dowel and *dobet*? ȝe deuynours knoweth.'
C.15.125 That trauayleth to teche oþere y halde hit for a *dobet*;
C.16.28 And these ben dowel and *dobet* and dobest of alle.
C.21.129 The which was *dobet*, where þat he wente.

doctour n *doctour n.* A 2 doctor (1) doctour (1); B 20 doctour (14) doctours (6); C 19 doctour (14) doctours (5)

A. 2.73 And piers þe pardoner, poulynes *doctor*,
A.11.302 Þe douȝtiest *doctour* or dyuynour of þe trinite,
B.Pr.87 Bisshopes and Bachelers, boþe maistres and *doctours*,
B. 9.75 And fynde fele witnesses among þe foure *doctours*,
B.10.458 The douȝtieste *doctour* and deuinour of þe trinitee
B.13.61 For þis *doctour* on þe heiȝe dees drank wyn so faste:
B.13.82 That disshes and doublers [þis *doctour* bifore]
B.13.97 And þanne is tyme to take and to appose þis *doctour*
B.13.99 And I sat stille as Pacience seide, and þus soone þis *doctour*,
B.13.103 'What is dowel, sire *doctour*?' quod I; 'is [dobest] any penaunce?'
B.13.104 'Dowel', quod þis *doctour* and [drank after],
B.13.106 'By þis day, sire *doctour*', quod I, 'þanne [in dowel be ye noȝt]!'
B.13.114 And seide hymself, 'sire *doctour*, and it be youre wille,
B.13.116 'Dowel', quod þis *doctour*, 'do as clerkes techeþ,
B.13.157 Vndo it; lat þis *doctour* deme if dowel be þerInne.
B.13.172 'It is but a dido', quod þis *doctour*, 'a disours tale.
B.15.73 Bettre it were [by] manye *doctours* to [bi]leuen swich techyng
B.15.243 Thei vndoon it vn[digne]ly, þo *doctours* of lawe.
B.15.380 *Doctours* of decrees and of diuinite maistres,
B.18.364 That art *doctour* of deeþ drynk þat þow madest.
B.19.315 'Hareweþ alle þat konneþ kynde wit by conseil of þise docto[urs]',
B.20.177 And þere dyed þat *doctour* er þre dayes after.
C.Pr.59 For coueytise of copis contraryed somme *doctours*.
C.Pr.85 Bischopes and bachelers, bothe maystres and *doctours*,
C.11.93 Of dobet [and] of dobest–for *doctour* he is knowe
C.11.133 For of dobet and dobest here *doctour* is dere loue.'
C.15.65 For [this] *doctour* at þe hey deys dranke wyn [so] faste–
C.15.69 'Hit is nat thre daies doen this *doctour* þat he prechede
C.15.84 'A[c] this *doctour* and dyuynour,' quod y, 'and decretistre of Canoen,
C.15.104 And thenne is tyme to take and to appose this *doctour*
C.15.106 Y sae[t] stille as pacience wolde and thus sone this *doctour*,
C.15.110 'What is dowel, sire *doctour*?' quod y; 'is dobest eny penaunce?'
C.15.111 'Dowel!' quod this *doctour*, and he dronke aftur;
C.15.121 And saide hymsulue, 'sire *doctour*, [and] hit be ȝoure wille,
C.15.124 Bote do as *doctours* techeth, for dowel y hit holde;
C.15.170 'This is a dido,' quod this *doctour*, 'a dysores tale!
C.15.175 Ac Concience, y toek kepe, coniey[e]d sone this *doctour*
C.17.114 *Doctours* of decre[s] and of diuinite maistres
C.20.402 That art *doctour* of deth drynke þat thow madest.
C.21.315 'Harweth alle þa[t] conneth kynde wit bi consail of [this] *doctours*
C.22.177 And þere deyede þat *doctour* ar thre dayes aftur.

doctrine n *doctrine n.* B 1; C 1

B. 2.109 And Piers þe Pardoner of Paulynes *doctrine*,
C.11.223 That hoso doth by ȝoure *doctrine* doth wel, y leue,

doel n *dol n.(2)* A 2; B 4; C 3 deul (2) doel (1)

A. 5.207 And gan grete grymly & gret *doel* ma[k]e
A. 7.112 And þeiȝ ȝe deiȝe for *doel* þe deuil haue þat recche!'
B. 5.379 And þanne gan Gloton greete and gret *doel* to make
B. 6.120 And þouȝ ye deye for *doel* þe deuel haue þat recch[e]!'
B.15.146 Ac for goode men, god woot, greet *doel* men maken,
B.17.342 And þouȝ þat men make muche *doel* in hir angre
C. 8.127 And thow ȝe deye for *deul* þe deuel haue þat reche!'
C.19.322 And thogh that men make moche *deul* in here anger
C.20.304 [Sh]olde deye with *doel* and here dwelle euere

doem > doom; doen -est > doon

dogge n *dogge n.* A 1; B 1; C 1

A. 5.98 Þus I lyue loueles, [lyk] a lyþer *dogge*,
B. 5.119 [Th]us I lyue louelees lik a luþer *dogge*
C. 9.262 Dispergentur oues, þe *dogge* dar nat berke.

doghter > douȝter; doghty(- > douhty(-; doȝter > douȝter

doynge ger *doinge ger.* B 3 doynge (1) doynges (2); C 5 doynge (4) doynges (1)

B.15.477 Louen and bileuen by lettred mennes *doynges*,
B.19.130 For deue þoruȝ hise *doynges* and dombe speke [and herde],
B.19.430 A[c] wel worþe Piers þe plowman þat pursueþ god in *doynge*,
C. 3.292 A desert for som *doynge*, derne oþer elles.
C. 3.293 Mede many tymes men ȝeueth bifore þe *doynge*
C. 8.91 Ac aftur here *doynge* do thow nat, my dere sone,' quod Peres.
C.21.130 For deue thorw his *doynges* and dombe speke [&] herde
C.21.430 Ac wel worth Peres the plouhman þat pursueth god in *doyng[e]*,

doysayne > doȝeyne

doke n *doke n.* A 1; B 2; C 1

A. 5.57 Drinke but wiþ þe *doke* & dyne but ones.
B. 5.74 Drynke but [wiþ] þe *doke* and dyne but ones.
B.17.65 Dredfully, bi þis day! as *doke* dooþ fram þe faucon.

C. 6.174   Drynke but with þe *doke* and dyne but ones.

doles n *dol n.(1)* A 1 dolis; B 1
A. 3.62   Oþer to grede aftir godis men whan ȝe [g]iue *dolis*,
B. 3.71   Or to greden after goddes men whan ye [gyue] *doles*

dolful adj *dolful adj.* B 1 dolful
B.15.522   In *dolful* deþ deyeden for hir faith.

doluen > deluen; dombe > doumbe

dome n *dom n.* A 6 dom (3) dome (2) doom (1); B 19 dome (8) domes (2) doom (8) doome (1); C 17 doem (5) dome (9) doom (2) domus (1)
A. 2.169   Dreed at þe dore stood & þat *doom* herde,
A. 8.19   At þe day of *dom* at here deis to sitten.
A. 8.155   Dowel at þe day of *dome* is digneliche vndirfongen;
A. 8.171   At þe dredful *dom* whanne dede shal arisen
A. 8.174   What þou dedist day [by day] þe *dom* wile reherce.
A. 8.184   Þat at þe day of *dome* we dede as he hiȝte.
B. 2.208   Drede at þe dore stood and þe *doom* herde,
B. 3.318   But after þe dede þat is doon oon *doom* shal rewarde
B. 5.275   [Is] holden at þe heiȝe *doom* to helpe þee to restitue,
B. 5.292   For he shal answere for þee at þe heiȝe *dome*,
B. 7.17   At þe day of *dome* at [hire] deys [to] sitte.
B. 7.177   Dowel at þe day of *dome* is digneliche vnderfongen;
B. 7.193   At þe dredful *dome*, whan dede shulle rise
B. 7.196   [What] þow didest day by day þe *doom* wole reherce.
B. 7.206   At þe day of *dome* we dide as he hiȝte.
B.10.364   And but we do þus in dede, [er] þe day of *dome*,
B.11.134   For hise arerages rewarden hym þere [riȝt] to þe day of *dome*,
B.11.145   But oonliche loue and leautee and my laweful *domes*.
B.12.91   Dampneþ vs at þe day of *dome* as [dide þe caractes] þe Iewes.
B.15.27   And whan I deme *domes* and do as truþe techeþ
B.15.550   Reson and rightful *doom* þ[o] Religiouse d[ampn]ede.
B.18.28   'Nay', quod feiþ, 'but] þe fend and fals *doom* [to deye].
B.18.191   [At] þe bigynn[yng god] gaf þe *doom* hymselue
B.18.385   Ther *doom* to þe deeþ dampneþ alle wikked,
B.20.293   And suffre þe dede in dette to þe day of *doome*.
C. 2.132   Y, Theo[lo]gie, þe tixt knowe yf trewe *doom* wittenesseth,
C. 2.220   Drede stod at þe dore and [þe] d[om]e herde,
C. 3.471   But aftur þe dede þat is ydo the *doom* shal recorde
C. 6.297   [Ben] haldyng at the heye *dome* to helpe the restitue.
C. 6.347   For he shal onswerie for the at the hey *dome*,
C. 9.322   For hoso doth wel here at þe day of *dome*
C. 9.339   At þe dredful *dome*, when dede shullen ryse
C. 9.342   And how we dede day be day þe *doem* wol reherce.
C. 9.352   At þe day of *dome* we dede as he tauhte.
C.12.69   And for his rechelesnes rewarde hym þere riht to þe day of *dome*
C.12.89   'Lo! lordes, what leute dede and leele *dome* yvsed.
C.16.187   And when y deme *domus* and do as treuthe techeth
C.17.213   Resoun and rihtfol *doem* tho religious dampnede.
C.20.27   'Nay,' quod faith, 'bote the fende and fals *doem* to deye.
C.20.196   At the bigynnyge god gaf the *doem* hymsulue
C.20.427   Ther *doem* to þe deth dampneth alle wikkede
C.22.293   And soffren þe dede in dette to þe day of *dome*.

domesday n *domesdai n.* A 2 domisday; B 4; C 6
A. 5.20   Þat dedly synne er *domisday* shal fordon hem alle.
A. 5.244   Dampne me nouȝt at *domisday* for þat I dede so ille.'
B. 5.20   That dedly synne er *domesday* shal fordoon hem alle.
B. 5.470   Dampne me noȝt at *domesday* for þat I dede so ille.'
B.10.417   [At *domesday* þe deluuye worþ of deþ and fir at ones;
B.19.196   And demen hem at *domesday*, boþe quyke and dede,
C. 5.122   That dedly synne ar *domesday* shal fordon hem alle.
C. 6.324   Dampne me nat at *domesday* for þat y dede so ylle.'
C. 9.21   And deme with hem at *domesday* bothe quyke and dede.
C.11.249   At *domesday* a deluuye worth of deth and fuyr at ones.
C.16.36   And bote these thre þat y spak of at *domesday* vs defende
C.21.196   And demen hem at *domesday*, bothe quyke and dede,

domesman n *domesman n.* B 1; C 1
B.19.305   To demen as a *domesman* adrad was he neuere
C.21.305   To demen as a *domesman* adrad was he neuere

dominyk n prop *n.i.d.* B 2 dominyk (1) Domynyk (1); C 2 dominik (1) domynyk (1)
B.15.421   But doon as Antony dide, *dominyk* and Fraunceys,
B.20.252   Frere Fraunceys and *Domynyk*, for loue to be holye.
C. 4.117   And be as Benet hem bad, *dominik* and fraunceys;
C.22.252   Frere fraunceys and *domynyk*, for loue to be holy.

dompynges n *domping n.* C 1
C.13.168   *Dompynges* dyuede; 'dere God,' y sayde,

domus > doom; don > doon

done n *OED done ppl. a. (n.)* &> *doon* B 1
B.18.301   To warne Pilates wif what *done* man was Iesus,

donemowe > dunmowe

donet n *donet n.* A 1; B 1; C 1
A. 5.123   Þanne drouȝ I me among drapers my *donet* to lere,
B. 5.207   Thanne drouȝ I me among drapiers my *donet* to lerne,
C. 6.215   Thenne drow y me amonge drapers my *donet* to lere,

donge n *dong n.* A 3 dong (1) donge (1) dung (1); B 4 donge (3) dung (1); C 7
A. 4.130   Þat lawe shal ben a labourer & lede afeld *donge*,
A. 7.176   And doluen drit & *dung* to ditte out hunger.
A. 7.272   To drawe on feld my *dong* while þe drouȝt lastiþ.
B. 3.310   Spynne or sprede *donge* or spille hymself with sleuþe.
B. 4.147   That lawe shal ben a laborer and lede afeld *donge*,
B. 6.190   And doluen [drit] and [*dung*] to [ditte out] hunger.
B. 6.288   To drawe afeld my *donge* while þe droȝte lasteþ.
C. 4.144   That lawe shal ben a laborer and lede afelde *donge*,
C. 8.184   Sp[it]teden and spradden *donge* in dispit of hunger.
C. 8.198   In daubynge and in deluynge, in *donge* afeld berynge,
C. 8.311   To drawe afeld my *donge* þe while þe drouthe lasteth.
C.12.224   On fat lond ful of *donge* foulest wedes groweth.
C.12.229   Riht as wedes waxeth in wose and in *donge*
C.12.231   Lo! lond ouerleyd with marl and with *donge*,

dongehill n *donghep n.* B 1
B.15.111   [For ypocrisie] in latyn is likned to a [loþly] *dongehill*

dongeon n *dongoun n.* A 2 dungeon (1) dungeoun (1); B 2
A.Pr.15   A dep dale beneþe, a *dungeoun* þereinne
A. 1.57   'Þe *dungeon* in þe dale þat dredful is of siȝt:
B.Pr.15   A deep dale byneþe, a *dongeon* þerInne
B. 1.59   Th[e] *dongeon* in þe dale þat dredful is of siȝte–

donghep n *donghep n.* C 1
C.16.266   And is ylikned in latyn to a lothly *donghep*

doom > dome

doon v *don v. cf. dowel* A 92 dede (11) dedist (1) dide (3) do (44) don (15) done (4) dost (2) doþ (12); B 248 dide (46) diden (6) didest (1) do (89) don (6) doon (46) doone (8) doost (1) dooþ (35) doþ (7) ido (1) ydo (2); C 199 ded (1) dede (36) deden (1) dyde (1) do (83) doen (12) doest (1) don (10) done (4) dost (2) doth (40) dust (1) ydo (6) ydoen (1)
A.Pr.102   As dikeris & delueris þat *doþ* here dede ille
A. 1.25   And drink whanne þe driȝep, ac *do* it nouȝt out of resoun
A. 1.28   *Dede* be his douȝter[n] þat þe deuil lykide,
A. 1.32   Dred delitable drynk & þou shalt *do* þe betere;
A. 1.51   Et que sunt dei deo oþer ellis ȝe *don* ille.''
A. 1.84   I *do* it on Deus caritas to deme þe soþe.
A. 1.87   *Doþ* þe werkis þerwiþ & wilneþ no man ille,
A. 1.97   [Di]de hem swere on h[ere] swerd to serue treuþe euere.
A. 1.132   No dedly synne to *do*, diȝe þeiȝ þou shuldist.
A. 2.157   And *do* hem hange be þe hals & alle þat hem maynteniþ.
A. 2.173   And gile *doþ* him to go agast for to deiȝe.
A. 3.98   Henis to þi deþ day *do* þou so no more.
A. 3.106   What þat his wille were & what he *do* shulde.
A. 3.125   She *doþ* men lese here land & here lif boþe;
A. 3.134   She may neiȝ as muche *do* in a moneþ ones
A. 3.175   Ne *dide* as þou demist; I *do* it on þe king.
A. 3.175   Ne dide as þou demist; I *do* it on þe king.
A. 3.187   *Dede* hym hoppe for hope to haue me at wille.
A. 3.242   Shulde diȝe for a dede þat *don* hadde here eldren
A. 3.269   Leaute shal *do* hym lawe [and no] lif ellis.
A. 4.25   Folewide hem faste for hy hadden to *done*
A. 4.53   Wysdom wan þo & so *dede* wyt also
A. 4.84   For I wile wage for wrong, he [wile] *do* so no more.'
A. 4.108   And *do* it in dede to drawe vs to goode;
A. 5.17   In ensaumple, se[gges], þat ȝe shulde *do* þe betere;
A. 5.51   And suffre to be misseid, & so *dide* I neuere.
A. 5.71   I miȝte not many day *do* as a man [au]ȝte,
A. 5.76   And belowen hym to lordis to *don* hym lese siluer,
A. 5.77   And don hise frendis hen hise fon þoruȝ my false tunge.
A. 5.83   He is douȝtiere þanne I–I dar non harm *don* hym,
A. 5.95   I deme men þere [hy] *don* ille, & ȝet I do wers;
A. 5.95   I deme men þere [hy] don ille, & ȝet I *do* wers;
A. 5.132   Þanne [myn owne] aunsel *dede*, [whanne] I weiȝede treweþe.
A. 5.223   Þat I ne shal *do* me er day to þe dere chirche
A. 5.244   Dampne me nouȝt at domisday for þat I *dede* so ille.'
A. 6.26   'I knowe hym as kyndely as clerk *doþ* his bokis.
A. 6.28   And *dede* me sure hym [siþþe] to serue hym for euere;
A. 6.33   Dyke[d] & d[o]luen & *do* what he hiȝte,
A. 6.70   And þanne shalt þou [se] sey soþ, so it be to *done*;

A. 6.80	He may *do* wiþ þe day sterre what hym dere likiþ;
A. 6.81	Deþ dar not *do* þing þat he defendiþ.
A. 7.49	For it arn þe deuelis disours I *do* þe to vndirstonde.
A. 7.71	His douȝter hattiþ *do* riȝt [so] or þi damme shal þe bete;
A. 7.73	And deme hem nouȝt for ȝif þou *dost* þou shalt it dere abiggen,
A. 7.77	Forþi I wile er I wende *do* w[r]yte my bequest.
A. 7.102	Eche man on his maner made hymself to *done*,
A. 7.189	Of beggeris & bidderis what best is to *done*.
A. 7.214	Miȝte I synneles *do* as þou seist?' seide peris þanne.
A. 7.258	Þei *do* men diȝe þoruȝ here drynkes er destenye it wolde.'
A. 8.98	But *do* wel & haue wel, & god shal haue þi soule,
A. 8.99	And *do* euele & haue euele, & hope þou non oþer
A. 8.109	Be þat þe sauter vs seiþ, & so *dede* manye oþere.
A. 8.161	Þat pardoun, & penaunce, & preyours *do* salue
A. 8.164	It is not so sikir for þe soule, certis, as is *do* wel.
A. 8.174	What þou *dedist* day [by day] þe dom wile reherce.
A. 8.184	Þat at þe day of dome we *dede* as he hiȝte.
A. 9.13	'Where þat dowel dwelli[þ], *do* me to wisse'.
A. 9.19	[Þat] dowel & *do* euele mowe not dwelle togidere.
A. 9.40	Ac dedly synne *doþ* he nouȝt, for dowel hym helpiþ;
A. 9.43	Þat, þeiȝ þi body bowe as bot *doþ* in þe watir,
A. 9.46	And *don* dedly synne & drenche þiseluen.
A. 9.68	Where dowel dwelliþ, & *do* me to wisse.'
A. 9.76	Dobet þus *doþ*, ac he doþ muche more.
A. 9.76	Dobet þus doþ, ac he *doþ* muche more.
A. 9.85	And wiþ glad wil *doþ* hem good for so god [hiȝte].
A. 9.90	And as dowel *dede* hem to vndirstonde,
A. 9.92	Þat ȝif dowel & dobet *dede* aȝens dobest
A. 9.93	And were vnbuxum at his bidding, and bold to *don* ille,
A. 9.104	How dowel, dobet & dobest *don* on þis erþe.'
A.10.11	And haþ *don* hire to sire dowel, duk of þise marchis.
A.10.82	For doute men *dop* þe bet; dred is such a maister
A.10.88	Ac ȝif clene consience acorde þat þiself *dost* wel
A.10.89	Wilne þou neuere in þis world, [wy], for to *do* betere,
A.10.181	And [were] marie[d] at meschief as men *do* now here children.
A.10.194	Þeiȝ þei *don* hem to dunmowe, but ȝif þe deuil helpe
A.10.205	Þat dede derne *do* no man ne shulde.
A.10.213	Aȝens dowel hy *don* euele, & þe deuil plesen,
A.11.11	Þei *do* but drauele þeron; draf were hem leuere
A.11.18	But it be cardit wiþ coueitise as cloþeris *don* here wolle;
A.11.91	I dar be his bolde boruȝ *do* bet wile he neuere.
A.11.144	Leue lelly þeron ȝif þou þenke *do* wel,
A.11.153	And *do* good a[g]ens euil; god hymself hotiþ
A.11.162	Ȝif þou þenke *do* wel deile þerewith neuere.
A.11.199	Dobet *doþ* ful wel, & dewid he is also,
A.11.206	And seide it in ensaumple þat þei shulde *do* þe betere:
A.11.287	Þanne marie þe maudeleyn who miȝte *do* wers?
A.11.288	Or who *dede* wers dauid þat vrie destroyede,
A.12.2	I haue *do* my deuer þe dowel to teche,
A.12.3	And whoso coueyteþ *don* betere þan þe boke telleþ,
A.12.10	Ȝif I wiste witterly þou woldest *don* þerafter,
A.12.36	And drow þe dore after him and bad me go *do* wel
A.12.94	And þerfore *do* after dowel whil þi dayes duren,
B.Pr.98	Arn *doon* vndeuoutliche; drede is at þe laste
B.Pr.224	As dykeres and delueres þat *doon* hire ded[e] ille
B. 1.25	And drynke whan þ[ee] drie[þ], ac *do* [it] noȝt out of reson
B. 1.28	*Dide* by hise douȝtres þat þe deuel liked;
B. 1.34	Forþi dred delitable drynke and þow shalt *do* þe bettre;
B. 1.53	Et que sunt dei deo or ellis ye *don* ille."
B. 1.86	I *do* it on Deus caritas to deme þe soþe.
B. 1.89	*Doþ* þe werkes þerwiþ and wilneþ no man ille,
B. 1.99	*Dide* hem sweren on hir swerd to seruen truþe euere.
B. 1.144	No dedly synne to *do*, deye þeiȝ þow sholdest,
B. 2.196	And *doon* hem hange by þe hals and alle þat hem maynteneþ.
B. 2.214	And Gyle *doþ* hym to go agast for to dye.
B. 3.60	And I shal couere youre kirk, youre cloistre *do* maken,
B. 3.61	Wowes *do* whiten and wyndowes glaȝen,
B. 3.62	*Do* peynten and portraye [who] paie[d] for þe makynge
B. 3.75	For þus [bit god in] þe gospel goode men *doon* hir almesse.
B. 3.109	Hennes to þi deeþ day *do* [þow] so na moore.
B. 3.117	What his wille were and what he *do* [sholde].
B. 3.136	She *doþ* men lese hire lond and hire lif boþe;
B. 3.145	[She] may neiȝ as muche *do* in a Monþe one[s]
B. 3.159	And *doþ* men lese þoruȝ hire loue þat lawe myȝte wynne;
B. 3.188	Ne *dide* as þow demest; I do it on þe kynge.
B. 3.188	Ne dide as þow demest; I *do* it on þe kynge.
B. 3.200	And *dide* hem hoppe for hope to haue me at wille.
B. 3.243	Wiþouten Mede *doþ* hem good and þe truþe helpeþ
B. 3.263	Sholden deye for a dede þat *doon* hadde hire eldres.
B. 3.294	Leaute shal *don* hym lawe and no lif ellis.
B. 3.307	Shal be demed to þe deeþ but if he *do* it smyþye
B. 3.317	Ne putte hem in panel to *doon* hem pliȝte hir truþe;
B. 3.318	But after þe dede þat is *doon* oon doom shal rewarde

B. 4.28	Folwed h[e]m faste for þei hadde to *doone*
B. 4.38	For [þei] wolde *do* for a dyner or a doȝeyne capons
B. 4.97	For I wol wage for wrong, he wol *do* so na moore.'
B. 5.17	In ensample, [segges, þat ye] sholden *do* þe bettre;
B. 5.37	My sire seide to me, and so *dide* my dame,
B. 5.43	And *doþ* it in dede, it shal drawe yow to goode.
B. 5.68	And suffre to be mysseyd, and so *dide* I neuere.
B. 5.96	And [bilowen] hym to lordes to *doon* hym lese siluer,
B. 5.97	And [*doon*] his frendes be his foon þoruȝ my false tonge.
B. 5.103	He is douȝtier þan I; I dar [noon harm *doon* hym],
B. 5.115	[I] deme [men þere hij] *doon* ille, [and yet] I do werse;
B. 5.115	[I] deme [men þere hij] doon ille, [and yet] I *do* werse;
B. 5.173	And *doon* me faste frydayes to [þerf] breed and to watre;
B. 5.242	Swiche dedes I *dide* write if he his day breke;
B. 5.389	Sholde no ryngynge *do* me ryse er I were ripe to dyne.'
B. 5.411	Til matyns and masse be *do*, and þanne [moste] to þe freres;
B. 5.429	If any man *doþ* me a bienfait or helpeþ me at nede
B. 5.451	That I ne shal *do* me er day to þe deere chirche
B. 5.470	Dampne me noȝt at domesday for þat I *dide* so ille.'
B. 5.479	To amenden vs of oure mysdedes: *do* mercy to vs alle,
B. 5.500	Of þyne douȝt[iest] dedes was *doon* in oure armes:
B. 5.538	'I knowe hym as kyndely as clerc *doþ* hise bokes.
B. 5.540	And *diden* me suren hym [siþþen] to seruen hym for euere,
B. 5.545	Idyke[d] and Id[o]lue, I*do* þat [he] hoteþ.
B. 5.548	I weue and I wynde and *do* what truþe hoteþ.
B. 5.583	Thanne [shalt þow] see seye-sooþ-so-it-be-to-*doone*–
B. 6.54	For it ben þe deueles disours, I *do* þe to vnderstonde.'
B. 6.64	To pilgrymage as palmeres *doon* pardon to haue.
B. 6.79	His douȝter hiȝte *do*-riȝt-so-or-þi-dame-shal-þee-bete;
B. 6.81	Deme-hem-noȝt-for-if-þow-*doost*-þow-shalt-it-deere-abugge–
B. 6.85	Forþi I wole er I wende *do* write my biqueste.
B. 6.110	Ech man in his manere made hymself to *doone*,
B. 6.196	And what Piers preide hem to *do* as prest as a Sperhauk.
B. 6.203	'Of beggeris and bidderis what best be to *doone*.
B. 6.226	Theiȝ þei *doon* yuele lat [þow] god yworþe:
B. 6.227	And if þow wilt be gracious to god *do* as þe gospel techeþ
B. 6.230	Miȝte I synnelees *do* as þow seist?' seide Piers þanne.
B. 6.274	They *do* men deye þoruȝ hir drynkes er destynee it wolde.'
B. 7.45	Ac many a Iustice and Iurour wolde for Iohan *do* moore
B. 7.116	But *do* wel and haue wel, and god shal haue þi soule,
B. 7.117	And *do* yuel and haue yuel, [and] hope þow noon ooþer
B. 7.127	By þat þe Sauter [vs] seith, [and] so *dide* othere manye.
B. 7.183	That pardon and penaunce and preieres *doon* saue
B. 7.196	[What] þow *didest* day by day þe doom wole reherce.
B. 7.206	At þe day of dome we *dide* as he hiȝte.
B. 8.13	'Where þat dowel dwelleþ, *doþ* me to witene.'
B. 8.17	And dowel and *do* yuele, wher þei dwelle togideres.
B. 8.23	[That] dowel and *do* yuele mowe noȝt dwelle togideres.
B. 8.44	Ac dedly synne *doþ* he noȝt for dowel hym [helpeþ],
B. 8.47	[That], þouȝ þ[i] body bowe as boot *doþ* in þe watre,
B. 8.50	And] *do* deedly synne and drenche þi[selue]
B. 8.77	Where dowel dwelleþ, and *do* me [to wisse].'
B. 8.85	Dobet [þus *doþ*], ac he doþ muche moore.
B. 8.85	Dobet [þus doþ], ac he *doþ* muche moore.
B. 8.95	And wiþ glad wille *doþ* hem good for so god hoteþ.
B. 8.100	And [as] dowel and dobet [*dide*] hem [to vnderstonde],
B. 8.102	That if dowel [and] dobet *dide* ayein dobest
B. 8.103	[And were vnbuxum at his biddyng, and bold to *don* ille],
B. 8.114	How dowel, dobet and dobest *doon* among þe peple.'
B. 9.11	And [haþ] *doo[n]* hire wiþ sire dowel, duc of þise Marches.
B. 9.15	That he bit moot be *do*; he [boldeþ] hem alle;
B. 9.67	And *doþ* god forsaken hem þat he shoop to his liknesse:
B. 9.83	Ne faille payn ne potage and prelates *dide* as þei sholden.
B. 9.95	He *doþ* noȝt wel þat doþ þus, ne drat noȝt god almyȝty,
B. 9.95	He doþ noȝt wel þat *doþ* þus, ne drat noȝt god almyȝty,
B. 9.97	That dredeþ god, he *doþ* wel; þat dredeþ hym for loue
B. 9.98	And [dredeþ hym] noȝt for drede of vengeaunce *doþ* þerfore þe bettre;
B. 9.99	He *doþ* best þat wiþdraweþ hym by daye and by nyȝte
B. 9.173	[Th]ouȝ þei *do* hem to Dunmowe, but if þe deuel helpe
B. 9.192	That [dede derne] *do* no man ne sholde.
B. 9.199	Ayeins dowel þei *do* yuel and þe deuel [plese]
B. 9.202	Dowel, my [deere], is to *doon* as lawe techeþ:
B.10.11	Thei *doon* but dr[a]uele þeron; draf were hem leuere
B.10.18	But it be carded wiþ coueitise as cloþeres [*don*] hir wolle.
B.10.26	The Sauter seiþ þe same by swiche þat *doon*.
B.10.38	Or daunted or drawe forþ; I *do* it on god hymselue.
B.10.42	Drynken and dreuelen and *do* men for to gape,
B.10.197	Whoso gloseþ as gylours *doon*, go me to þe same,
B.10.204	And *do* good a[g]ein yuel; god hymself hoteþ
B.10.206	To *do* good for goddes loue and gyuen men þat asked,
B.10.219	If þow þynke to *dowel* deel þerwiþ neuere.
B.10.272	I rede ech a blynd bosard *do* boote to hymselue,

B.10.300	And seiþ it in ensample [þat] þei sholde *do* þerafter:
B.10.317	Litel hadde lordes to *doon* to зyue lond from hire heires
B.10.364	And but we *do* þus in dede, [er] þe day of dome,
B.10.401	As Salomon *dide* and swiche oþere, þat shewed grete wittes
B.10.404	As þei seyen hemself selde *doon* þerafter:
B.10.413	And shilden vs from shame þerinne, as Noes ship *dide* beestes;
B.10.428	Than Marie Maudeleyne [who myзte *do*] werse?
B.10.429	Or who [*dide*] worse þan Dauid þat vries deeþ conspired,
B.11.38	'And Deus disponit', quod he; 'lat god *doon* his wille.
B.11.39	If truþe wol witnesse it be wel *do* Fortune to folwe
B.11.59	By wissynge of þis wenche I [*dide*], hir wordes were so swete,
B.11.120	Sarзens and scismatikes and so he *dide* þe Iewes:
B.11.154	Lo! ye lordes, what leautee *dide* by an Emperour of Rome
B.11.159	And on Troianus truþe to þenke, and *do* truþe to þe peple.
B.11.286	And þei hir deuoir *dide* as Dauid seiþ in þe Sauter.
B.11.318	This lokynge on lewed preestes haþ *doon* me lepe from pouerte
B.11.377	Why I suffre or noзt suffre; þiself hast noзt to *doone*.
B.11.398	For al þat he [wrouзt] was wel *ydo*, as holy writ witnesseþ:
B.11.421	Lakkedest and losedest þyng þat longed noзt to *doone*.
B.12.22	To solacen hym som tyme; [so] I *do* whan I make:
B.12.27	Wolde I neuere *do* werk, but wende to holi chirche
B.12.32	For he *dooþ* wel, wiþouten doute, þat dooþ as lewte techeþ
B.12.32	For he *dooþ* wel, wiþouten doute, þat *dooþ* as lewte techeþ
B.12.91	Dampneþ vs at þe day of dome as [*dide* þe caractes] þe Iewes.
B.12.122	Ne sette short bi hir science, whatso þei *don* hemselue.
B.12.154	And *diden* [hir] homage honurably to hym þat was almyзty.
B.12.168	And is in drede to drenche, þat neuere *dide* swymme?'
B.12.235	Kynde knoweþ whi he *dide* so, ac no clerk ellis.
B.13.105	'*Do* noon yuel to þyn euencristen, nouзt by þi power.'
B.13.111	I wolde permute my penaunce with youre, for I am in point to *dowel*.'
B.13.116	'Dowel', quod þis doctour, '*do* as clerkes techeþ.
B.13.118	And dobest *doþ* hymself so as he seiþ and precheþ:
B.13.169	*Do* kyng and quene and alle þe comune after
B.13.171	And as þow demest wil þei *do* alle hir dayes after:
B.13.212	I shal dwelle as I *do* my deuoir to shewe,
B.13.228	Couþe I lye [and] *do* men lauзe, þanne lacchen I sholde
B.13.257	For may no blessynge *doon* vs boote but if we wile amende,
B.13.290	And entremetten hym ouer al þer he haþ noзt to *doone*;
B.13.305	Of dedes þat he neuere *dide* demen and bosten;
B.13.306	And of werkes þat he wel *dide* witnesse and siggen,
B.13.359	Lened for loue of þe wed and looþ to *do* truþe;
B.13.387	As if I hadde dedly synne *doon* I dredde noзt þat so soore
B.13.412	*Dooþ* noon almes[dede]; dred hym of no synne;
B.13.423	And han likynge to liþen hem [in hope] to *do* yow lauзe–
B.13.450	And in his deeþ deyinge þei *don* hym gret confort
B.14.26	Than Haukyn þe Actif man, and þow *do* by my techyng,
B.14.79	*Diden* dedly synne þat þe deuel liked,
B.14.84	Which dryueþ awey dedly synne and *dooþ* it to be venial.
B.14.93	Ther contricion *dooþ* but dryueþ it doun into a venial synne
B.14.136	And til he haue *doon* his deuoir and his dayes iournee.
B.14.146	And lyuen as lawe techeþ, *doon* leaute to hem alle,
B.14.150	And whan he haþ *doon* his deuoir wel men dooþ hym ooþer bountee,
B.14.150	And whan he haþ doon his deuoir wel men *dooþ* hym ooþer bountee,
B.14.153	And alle þat *doon* hir deuoir wel han double hire for hir trauaille.
B.14.196	Ellis is al on ydel, al þat euere [we *diden*],
B.14.214	Batauntliche as beggeris *doon*, and boldeliche he craueþ
B.14.251	Ne *dooþ* hym noзt dyne delicatly ne drynke wyn ofte.
B.14.325	So hard it is', quod haukyn, 'to lyue and to *do* synne.
B.14.328	That [euere he] *dide* dede þat deere god displesed;
B.15.27	And whan I deme domes and *do* as truþe techeþ
B.15.59	But he *do* þerafter, it dooþ hym double scaþe.
B.15.59	But he do þerafter, it *dooþ* hym double scaþe.
B.15.193	[Th]anne he syngeþ whan he *doþ* so, and som tyme wepynge,
B.15.261	In ensample we sholde *do* so, and take no vengeaunce
B.15.262	Of oure foes þat *dooþ* vs falsnesse; þat is oure fadres wille.
B.15.264	Sholde neuere Iudas ne Iew haue Iesu *doon* on roode,
B.15.368	Shepherdes and shipmen, and so *do* þise tilieris.
B.15.386	Lest þei ouerhuppen as ooþere *doon* in office and in houres.
B.15.406	And *dide* folk þanne falle on knees; for he swoor in his prechyng
B.15.421	But *doon* as Antony dide, dominyk and Fraunceys,
B.15.421	But doon as Antony *dide*, dominyk and Fraunceys,
B.15.547	Shul [ouer]torne as templers *dide*; þe tyme approcheþ faste.
B.15.595	*Dide* hym rise and rome riзt bifore þe Iewes.
B.16.106	And *dide* hym assaie his surgenrie on hem þat sike were
B.16.114	Quatriduanus quelt quyk *dide* hym walke.
B.16.183	That oon *dooþ* alle dooþ and ech dooþ bi his one.
B.16.183	That oon dooþ alle *dooþ* and ech dooþ bi his one.
B.16.183	That oon dooþ alle dooþ and ech *dooþ* bi his one.
B.16.243	And siþþe he sente me to seye I sholde *do* sacrifise
B.16.244	And *doon* hym worship with breed and wiþ wyn boþe,

B.17.65	Dredfully, bi þis day! as doke *dooþ* fram þe faucon.
B.17.212	So *dooþ* þe Sire and þe sone and also spiritus sanctus
B.17.223	As *dooþ* a kex or a candle þat caught haþ fir and blaseþ,
B.17.224	Na moore *dooþ* sire ne sone ne seint spirit togidres
B.17.255	Delen and *do* penaunce day and nyght euere,
B.17.276	For þat kynde *dooþ* vnkynde fordooþ, as þise corsede þeues,
B.17.309	That þe kyng may *do* no mercy til boþe men acorde
B.17.321	Thre þynges þer ben þat *doon* a man by strengþe
B.17.328	It *dooþ* hym worse þan his wif or wete to slepe;
B.18.16	As *dooþ* an heraud of armes whan Auentrous comeþ to Iustes.
B.18.32	That, for al þat deeþ kan *do*, wiþInne þre daies to walke
B.18.37	To se how doghtiliche deeþ sholde *do* and deme hir boþeres right.
B.18.90	For þe dede þat I haue *doon* I do me in youre grace.
B.18.90	For þe dede þat I haue doon I *do* me in youre grace.
B.18.95	To *do* þe blynde bete [þe dede], it was a boyes counseille.
B.18.101	For be þis derknesse *ydo* deeþ worþ [yvenquisshed];
B.18.108	Now youre goode dayes arn *doon* as daniel prophecied;
B.18.156	Til he be deed and *do* þerto; þe yuel he destruyeþ,
B.18.159	Al þat deeþ [*d]ide* first þoruз þe deueles entisyng,
B.18.180	[Thanne] I shal daunce þerto; *do* þow so suster.
B.18.295	'Certes I drede me', quod þe deuel, 'lest truþe [*do*] hem fecche.
B.18.301	To warne Pilates wif what done man was Iesus,
B.18.302	For Iewes hateden hym and han *doon* hym to deþe.
B.18.333	For þe dede þat þei *dide*, þi deceite it made;
B.18.387	Wheiþer þei deye or deye noзt for þat þei *diden* ille.
B.18.389	I [may] *do* mercy þoruз [my] rightwisnesse and alle my wordes trewe;
B.18.390	And þouз holy writ wole þat I be wroke of hem þat *diden* ille–
B.19.2	And dighte me derely and *dide* me to chirche
B.19.10	'Is þis Iesus þe Iustere', quod I, 'þat Iewes *dide* to deþe?
B.19.44	And so *dide* Iesus þe Iewes; he Iustified and tauзte hem
B.19.101	And so *dide* Iesu in hise dayes, whoso [dorste] telle it.
B.19.110	And þere bigan god of his grace to *do* wel
B.19.116	Bigan god of his grace and goodnesse to *dowel*,
B.19.123	After þe kynde þat he cam of; þere comsede he *do* wel.
B.19.133	For þe dedes þat he *dide*, Fili dauid, Iesus.
B.19.141	And for to *doon* hym to deþe day and nyзt þei casten.
B.19.182	And whan þis dede was *doon* do best he [þouзte],
B.19.182	And whan þis dede was doon *do* best he [þouзte],
B.19.211	Thanne song I þat song; so *dide* manye hundred,
B.19.278	Er he [*dide*] any [dede] deuyse wel he ende;
B.19.306	Neiþer of duc ne of deeþ, þat he ne *dide* lawe
B.19.308	He *dide* equyte to alle eueneforþ his [knowynge].
B.19.309	Thise foure sedes Piers sew, and siþþe he *dide* hem harewe
B.19.314	And so *doon* vices vertues; [f]orþi', quod Piers,
B.19.329	And whan þis dede was *doon* Grace deuysede
B.20.6	'[Coudes]tow noзt excuse þee as *dide* þe kyng and oþere:
B.20.26	He shal *do* moore þan mesure many tyme and ofte,
B.20.154	Shal *do* þee noзt drede, neiþer deeþ ne elde,
B.20.223	Than I *do* to drynke a drauзte of good ale.'
B.20.306	Shrift shoop sharp salue and made men *do* penaunce
B.20.316	Quod Contricion to Conscience, '*do* hym come to vnitee,
B.20.321	And Indulgence may *do* but if dette lette it.
B.20.370	And wake for hise wikked werkes as he was wont to *doone*.
B.20.373	Sleuþe seigh þat and so *dide* pryde,
B.20.377	'He lyþ [adreynt] and dremeþ', seide Pees, 'and so *do* manye oþere.
B.20.379	And [*doþ*] men drynke dwale]; þei drede no synne.'
C.Pr.109	And for here syre sey hem synne and suffred hem *do* ille
C.Pr.119	That soffreth men *do* sacrefyce and worschipe maumettes
C.Pr.123	Than euere he *dede* on Offi[n] and Fines [or on her] fader.
C.Pr.126	Ar *don* vndeuouteliche; drede is at þe laste
C.Pr.228	As dykers and deluers þat *doth* here dedis ylle
C.1.24	And drynke þat *doth* the good–a[c] drynke nat out of tyme.
C.1.49	Et que sunt dei deo or [elles] зe *don* ylle."
C.1.82	I *do* it [o]n deus caritas to deme þe soothe.
C.1.85	And *doth* þe werkes þerwith and wilneth no man ylle.
C.1.103	*Dede* hem swere on here swerd to serue treuthe euere.
C.1.143	Dey rather þen *do* eny dedly synne:
C.2.39	Y *do* hit vppon dauyd; the doumbe wil noзt lyen.
C.2.131	That god wolde were *ydo* withoute som deseyte.
C.2.210	And *do* hem hange by þe halse and alle þat hem maynteyneth.
C.2.224	And gyle *doth* hym to gone agaste for to deye.
C.3.34	And in constorie at court *do* calle зoure names.
C.3.66	And [*do*] peynten and purtrayen who payede for þe makyng
C.3.81	For thyse men *don* most harm to þe mene peple,
C.3.141	In the Castel of Corf y shal *do* close the,
C.3.154	What his wille were and what he *do* sholde.
C.3.174	For he *doth* men lesen here lond and here lyf bothe;
C.3.183	He may ny as muche *do* in a monthe ones
C.3.233	For kulde y neuere no kyng ne conseilede so to *done*;
C.3.253	Al þat his men may wynne, *do* ther[mid] here beste.
C.3.304	When þe dede is *ydo* and þe day endit.
C.3.320	May desa[u]owe that thei *dede* and do[uwe] þerwith another

C. 3.332	And efte haue hit aзeyne of hem þat *don* ylle.
C. 3.447	Lewete shal *do* hym lawe and no lyf elles.
C. 3.460	Shal be demed to þe deth but yf he *do* hit smythye
C. 3.470	Ne potte [hem] in panele [to] *do* [hem] plihte here treuthe;
C. 3.471	But aftur þe dede þat is *ydo* the doom shal recorde
C. 4.38	For þey wolde *do* for a dyner oþer a d[o]seyne capones
C. 4.41	Bute *dede* as Consience hym kennede til he þe kyng mette.
C. 4.93	For y wol wage for wrong; he wol *do* so no mare.'
C. 5.9	And no dede to *do* but drynke and slepe.
C. 5.119	In ensau[m]ple, seggus, þat we sholde *do* þe bettere;
C. 6.9	And soffre to be mysseyde, and so *dyde* y neuere.
C. 6.53	Of werkes þat y wel *dede* witnesses take
C. 6.109	The harm þat y haue *do* with hand and with tonge.
C. 6.155	And *doen* me faste fridayes to bred and to water;
C. 6.276	As thow y deddly synne *dede* y dradde [hit] nat so sore
C. 6.324	Dampne me nat at domesday for þat y *dede* so ylle.'
C. 6.336	And deyede with a drop water; so *doth* alle synnes
C. 7.5	Sholde no ryngyng *do* me ryse til y were rype to dyne.'
C. 7.27	Til matynes and masse be *ydo*; thenne haue y a memorie at þe freres.
C. 7.42	Yf eny man *do[th]* me a beenfeet or helpeth me at nede
C. 7.65	That y ne shal *do* me ar day to þe dere chirche
C. 7.72	*Doth* non Almesdede, drat hym nat of synne,
C. 7.83	And han lykyng to lythen hem in hope to *do* зow lawhe–
C. 7.110	And in his deth deynge they *don* hym greet confort
C. 7.121	To Amende vs of oure mysdedes, *do* mercy to vs alle.
C. 7.140	Of thy douhtiokest dedes was *don* in oure sekte:
C. 7.146	For dedes that we han *don* ylle dampned sholde we ben neuere
C. 7.183	'I knowe hym as kyndely as Clerk *doth* his bokes.
C. 7.210	Thenne eny dedly synne *do* for drede or for preeyere.
C. 7.230	Thenne shaltow se say-soth-so-hit-be-to-*done*-
C. 8.63	To pilgrimag[e] as palmeres *doen* to wynne.
C. 8.81	His douhter hihte *do*-rihte-so-or-thy-dame-shal-þe-bete;
C. 8.83	Deme-hem-nat-[for]-yf-thow-*doest*-thow-shalt-hit-dere-abygge.'
C. 8.91	Ac aftur here doynge *do* thow nat, my dere sone,' quod Peres,
C. 8.94	Forthy y wol ar y wende *do* wryte my biqueste.
C. 8.117	Vch man in his manere made hymsulue to *done*
C. 8.209	Of beggares and biddares what beste be to *done*.
C. 8.236	Myhte y synneles *do* as thow sayst?' sayde Peres þe plouhman.
C. 8.295	They *don* men deye thorw here drynkes Ar destyne hit wolde.'
C. 9.112	Riht as Peter *dede* and poul saue þat þey preche nat
C. 9.132	And зut more to suche men me *doth* ar they passe;
C. 9.290	Bote *do* wel and haue wel, and [god] shal haue thy soule
C. 9.291	And *do* yuele and haue euele and hope thow non oþere
C. 9.322	For hoso *doth* wel here at þe day of dome
C. 9.329	That pardoun and penaunc[e] and preyere[s] *don* saue
C. 9.342	And how we *dede* day be day the doem wol reherce.
C. 9.352	At þe day of dome we *dede* as he tauhte.
C.10.17	And dowel and *do* euele, where þei dwellen bothe.'
C.10.25	And hoso synegeth,' y sayde, 'certes he *doth* nat wel;
C.10.26	For hoso synegeth sicurly *doth* euele
C.10.27	And dowel and *do* euele may nat dwelle togyderes.
C.10.43	So dedly synne *doth* he nat for dowel hym helpeth.
C.10.75	Where þat dowel dwelleth And *do* me to knowe.'
C.10.82	Dobet *doth* al this Ac зut he doth more.
C.10.82	Dobet doth al this Ac зut he *doth* more.
C.10.99	Ac dobest sholde drede hem nat but *do* as god hihte:
C.10.102	That wolde nat *do* as dobest de[m]ede and tauhte.
C.10.110	Of dowel and dobet and ho *doth* best of alle.'
C.10.138	And hath *do* here with sire dowel, duk of this marches.
C.10.178	As lo[t] *dede* and Noe, and herodes þe daffe
C.10.188	Ac thenne *dede* we alle wel, and wel bet зut, to louye
C.10.203	Hoso lyueth in lawe and in loue *doth* wel
C.10.238	That þe sire by hymsulue *doth* þe sone sholde be þe worse.
C.10.275	Thogh they [*do*] hem to donemowe, bote þe deuel helpe
C.10.289	As Adam *dede* and Eue, as y whil er tolde.
C.10.292	For þat dede derne *do* no man sholde
C.10.298	Aзen dowel they *do* yuele and þe deuel serue
C.10.301	And thus is dowel, my frende, to *do* as lawe techeth:
C.10.306	For þe more a man may *do*, by so þat a do hit,
C.10.306	For þe more a man may do, by so þat a *do* hit,
C.11.9	They *do* bote dr[a]uele þeron; draf were hem leuere
C.11.159	Leue hit lelly and loke þou *do* þeraftur
C.11.159	That [*doth*] men dowel, dobet and dobest.'
C.11.223	That hoso *doth* by зoure doctrine doth wel, y leue,
C.11.223	That hoso doth by зoure doctrine *doth* wel, y leue,
C.11.261	Then marie maudelene who myhte *do* worse?
C.11.297	As *doth* the reue or Conturrollor þat rykene moet and acounten
C.11.304	'Et deus disponit,' quod he; 'la[t] god *do* his wille.
C.12.11	By wissyng of this wenche y *dede*, here wordes were so swete,
C.12.55	Sarrasynes and sismatikes and so a *ded* þe iewes.
C.12.89	'Lo! lordes, what leute *dede* and leele dome yvsed.
C.12.92	And louye for oure lordes loue and *do* leute euermore.

C.12.243	And tho that *dede* þe dede ydampned þerfore aftur
C.13.18	Derworthe and dere god, *do* we so mala",
C.13.40	Ther þe messager *doth* no more but with his mouth telleth
C.13.190	They ouerdoen hit day and nyhte and so *doth* nat oþer bestes;
C.14.10	And thenne *dost* thow wel, withoute drede; ho can do bet no force.
C.14.10	And thenne dost thow wel, withoute drede; ho can *do* bet no force.
C.14.11	Clerkes þat conne al, y hope they can *do* bettre;
C.14.23	Ac grace is a graes þerfore to *don* hem [growe efte];
C.14.27	And sent forth the seynt espirit to *do* loue sprynge:
C.14.65	Ne sette shorte by here science, whatso þei *doen* hemsulue.
C.14.69	And *do* we as dauid techeth for doute of godes veniance:
C.14.98	And *deden* here homage honerably to hym þat was almyhty.
C.15.52	That Consience comaunde sholde to *do* come scripture
C.15.69	'Hit is nat thre daies *doen* this doctour þat he prechede
C.15.112	'*Do* thy neyhebore non harm ne thysulue nother
C.15.113	And thenne *dost* thow wel and wysly, y dar hit wel avowe.'
C.15.124	Bote *do* as doctours techeth, for dowel y hit holde;
C.15.126	And he þat *doth* as he techeth y halde hit for þe beste:
C.15.202	[Cou]de y lye and *do* men lawhe thenne lacchen y scholde
C.15.227	For may no blessynge *doen* vs bote yf we wol amende
C.16.5	When his d[eu]er is *doen* and his dayes iourne
C.16.34	Ho *doth* wel or bet or beste aboue alle;
C.16.55	Batauntliche as beggares *doen*, and baldeliche he craueth
C.16.91	Ne *doth* men dyne delicatlyche ne drynke wyne ofte.
C.16.177	To *do* wel or wykke, a will with a resoun,
C.16.187	And when y deme domus and *do* as treuthe techeth
C.16.193	And when y wol *do* or [nat do] gode dedes or ille
C.16.193	And when y wol do or [nat *do*] gode dedes or ille
C.16.228	And *doth* hym to be deynous and deme þat beth nat lered.
C.16.336	Thenne syngeth he when he *doth* so and som tyme w[e]pynge:
C.17.93	*Doen* her deuer day and nyhte; dede we so alse
C.17.93	Doen her deuer day and nyhte; *dede* we so alse
C.17.118	That they ouerhippe nat for hastite, as y hope they *do* nat,
C.17.122	Ac зif prestes *doen* here deuer wel we shal do þe bettre
C.17.122	Ac зif prestes doen here deuer wel we shal *do* þe bettre
C.17.209	Sholle ouerturne as templers *dede*; þe tyme approcheth faste.
C.17.303	Quadriduanus coeld quyk *dede* hym walke.
C.17.307	And зut they seyen sothly, and so *doen* þe sarrasynes,
C.18.144	Quadriduanus coeld, quyk *dede* hym rome.
C.19.178	So *doth* þe sire and þe sone and seynt spirit togyderes
C.19.189	A[s] *doth* a kix [o]r a candle þat cauht hath fuyr and blaseth,
C.19.190	No more *doth* sire ne sone ne seynt spirit togyderes
C.19.221	Dele and *do* penaunce day and nyht euere
C.19.257	For þat kynde *doth* vnkynde fordoth, as this corsede theues,
C.19.301	Thre thynges ther ben þat *doth* a man to sterte
C.19.308	Hit *doth* hym worse then his wyf or wete to slepe;
C.20.14	As *doth* an heraud of Armes when Auntres cometh to ioustes.
C.20.31	That for al þat deth can *do*, withynne thre dayes to walke
C.20.36	To se how douhtyliche deth sholde *do* and demen [h]er beyre rihte.
C.20.92	Of þe dede þat y haue *do* y do me in зoure grace;
C.20.92	Of þe dede þat y haue do y *do* me in зoure grace;
C.20.98	[To *do*] þe blynde bete the dede, [hit] was a boyes [conseille].
C.20.104	For be this derkenesse *ydo* deth worth yvenkused;
C.20.111	Now ben зoure gode dayes *ydoen*, as daniel of зow telleth;
C.20.159	Til he [be] ded [and] *ydo* þerto; [þe yuel] he destruyeth,
C.20.162	All þat deth and þe deuel *dede* formost to Eue
C.20.183	And y shal daunse þerto; *do* thow so sustur
C.20.320	And *dust* hem breke here buxumnesse thorw fals bihestes
C.20.376	For the [dede] that they *dede*, thi deseite hit made;
C.20.429	Where they deye or dey nat, *dede* they neuere so ille.
C.20.431	[Y] may *do* mercy of my rihtwysnesse and alle myn wordes trewe
C.21.2	And dihte me derely and *dede* me to kyrke
C.21.10	'Is this iesus the ioustare,' quod y, 'þat iewes *dede* to dethe?
C.21.44	And so *dede* iesus þe iewes; he iustified and tauhte hem
C.21.101	And so *dede* iesu in his dayes, whoso durste tellen hit.
C.21.110	And þer bigan god of his grace to *do* wel:
C.21.116	Bigan god of his grace and goodnesse to *do* wel
C.21.123	Aftur þe kynde he cam of; þer comsede he *do* wel.
C.21.133	For þe dedes þat he *dede*, fili dauid, iesus.
C.21.141	And for to *do* hym to dethe day and nyhte they casten,
C.21.182	And when this dede was *doen* do best he thouhte
C.21.182	And when this dede was doen *do* best he thouhte
C.21.211	[Thanne] sang [y] þat song; so *dede* many hundret
C.21.278	Ar he *dede* eny dede deuyse wel þe ende;
C.21.306	Noþer of deuk ne of deth þat he ne *dede* lawe
C.21.308	He *dede* equite to alle eueneforth his knowyng.
C.21.309	Thise foure sedes [Peres] sewe and sennes he *dede* hem harewe
C.21.314	And so *doth* vices vertues; forthy,' quod [Peres],
C.21.329	And when this dede was *doen* grace deuysed
C.21.329	And when this dede was doen grace deuysed
C.22.6	'Couthest thow nat excuse the as *dede* the kyng and oþere;
C.22.26	He shal *do* more þe[n] mesure mony tymes and often
C.22.154	Shal *do* the nat drede, noþer deth ne elde,

C.22.223   Then y *do* to drynke a drauht of goed ale.'
C.22.306   Shrift schupte scharp salue and made men *do* penauns[e]
C.22.316   Quod contricion to Consience, '*do* hym come to vnite
C.22.321   And indulgence may *do* but yf dette lette hit.
C.22.370   And wake for his wikkede werkes as he was woned [to *do*].
C.22.373   Sle[u]th seyh þat and so *dede* pruyde
C.22.377   'He lyeth adreint [and dremeth],' saide pees, 'and so *doth* mony
                  oþere.
C.22.379   And *doth* men drynke dwale; [they] drat no synne.'

dore n *dore n.(1) &> dorenayl* A 6 dore (5) doris (1); B 8 dore (7) dores
           (1); C 8 dore (7) dores (1)
A. 2.169   Dreed at þe *dore* stood & þat doom herde,
A. 4.44   Brekiþ vp my berne *doris*, beriþ awey my whete,
A. 5.197   Whanne he drouȝ to þe *dore* þanne dymmede hise eiȝen;
A. 6.99   And so worst þou dryuen out as dew & þe *dore* closid,
A.11.95   [And] also doumb as a *dore* drouȝ hym asid.
A.12.36   And drow þe *dore* after him and bad me go do wel
B. 2.208   Drede at þe *dore* stood and þe doom herde,
B. 4.57   Brekeþ vp my bern[e] *dore[s]*, bereþ awey my whete,
B. 5.349   A[c] whan he drouȝ to þe *dore* þanne dymmed hise eiȝen;
B. 5.613   And [so] worstow dryuen out as dew and þe *dore* closed,
B.10.142   And as doumb as [a *dore*] drouȝ hym [aside].
B.15.19   That wole defende me þe *dore*, dynge I neuer so late.
B.19.167   In an hous al bishet and hir *dore* ybarred
B.19.168   Crist cam In, and al closed boþe *dore* and yates,
C. 1.183   And as ded as [a] *dore* nayl but yf þe ded[e] folowe:
C. 2.220   Drede stod at þe *dore* and [þe] d[om]e herde,
C. 4.60   And breketh vp my bern[e] *dores* and [b]ereth awey my whete
C. 6.407   And when he drow to þe *dore* thenne dymmede his yes;
C. 7.265   So worth thow dryuen out as de[w] and þe *dore* yclosed,
C.16.170   That wol defende me [þe] *dore*, dynge y neuere so late.
C.21.167   In an hous al bishut and here *dore* ybarred
C.21.168   Crist cam in, and al closed bothe þe *dore* and ȝates,

dorenail n *dore n.(1)* A 1 ; B 1 ; C 1 dore_nayl
A. 1.161   And as ded as a *dorenail* but ȝif þe dede folewe.
B. 1.187   And as deed as a *dore[nail]* but if þe ded[e] folwe:
C. 1.183   And as ded as [a] *dore nayl* but yf þe ded[e] folowe:

dorste > dar; doseyne dosoyne > doȝeyne; dost > doon

doted ptp *doten v.* A 1 dotide; B 1 ; C 1 dotede
A. 1.129   'Þou *dotide* daffe,' quaþ heo, 'dulle arn þine wittes.
B. 1.140   'Thow *doted* daffe!' quod she, 'dulle are þi wittes.
C. 1.139   'Thow *dotede* daffe!' quod she, 'dulle aren thy wittes.

doþ > doon

double adj *double adj.* B 5
B. 2.13   And Diamaundes of derrest pris and *double* manere Saphires,
B.14.148   And rewarden alle *double* richesse þat rewful hertes habbeþ.
B.14.153   And alle þat doon hir deuoir wel han *double* hire for hir trauaille,
B.14.156   That god rewarded *double* reste to any riche wye.
B.15.59   But he do þerafter, it dooþ hym *double* scaþe.

doublefold adj *doublefold adj.& adv.* A 1 ; B 1 ; C 1
A. 8.177   And haue indulgence *doublefold*, but dowel þe helpe
B. 7.199   And haue Indulgences *doublefold*, but dowel [þee] helpe
C. 9.345   And haue indulgences *doublefold*, but dowel vs helpe

doublers n *doubler n.* B 1 ; C 1 dobelares
B.13.82   That disshes and *doublers* [þis doctour bifore]
C.15.90   Bothe disches and *dobelares* with alle þe deyntees aftur.

douȝter n *doughter n.* A 3 douȝter (2) douȝtern (1); B 8 doghter (1)
           doȝter (1) douȝter (4) douȝtres (2); C 11 doughter (1) doughteres (1)
           douhter (6) douhteres (2) douhtur (1)
A. 1.28   Dede be his *douȝter[n]* þat þe deuil lykide,
A. 7.71   His *douȝter* hattiþ do riȝt [so] or þi damme shal þe bete;
A.10.12   Dobet is hire damysele, sire dowelis [*douȝter*],
B. 1.28   Dide by hise *douȝtres* þat þe deuel liked;
B. 2.30   Oo god wiþouten gynnyng, and I his goode *douȝter*;
B. 5.159   And dame Clarice a knyȝtes *douȝter* ac a cokewold was hir sire,
B. 6.14   Makeþ cloþ, I counseille yow, and kenneþ so youre *douȝtres*.
B. 6.79   His *douȝter* hiȝte do-riȝt-so-or-þi-dame-shal-þee-bete;
B. 9.12   Dobet is hire damysele, sire doweles *douȝter*,
B.11.248   Iesu crist on a Iewes *doȝter* liȝte, gentil womman þouȝ she were,
B.18.426   And callede kytte my wif and Calote my *doghter*:
C. 1.27   In his dronkenesse aday his *doughteres* he dighte
C. 2.33   And y am his dere *doughter*, ducchesse of heuene.
C. 2.127   For treuthe plyhte þe trewthe to wedde on of here *douhteres*,
C. 3.369   For hoso wolde to wyue haue my worliche *douhter*
C. 6.134   And dame clarice a knyhtes *douhter*, a cokewolde was here syre,
C. 8.81   His *douhter* hihte do-rihte-so-or-thy-dame-shal-þe-bete;
C. 8.106   And delen amongus my *douhteres* and my dere childre[n].
C.10.139   Dobet is here damysele, sire dowelus *douhtur*,

C.10.179   Ȝaf his *douhter* for a daunsynge in a disch þe heued
C.10.263   A bastard, a bond oen, a begeneldes *douhter*
C.20.469   And calde kitte my wyf and Calote my *douhter*:

douhty adj *doughti adj.& n.* A 2 douȝtiere (1) douȝtiest (1); B 4 doghtiest
           (1) douȝtier (1) douȝtiest (1) douȝtieste (1); C 3 douhty (1) douhtiest
           (1) douhtiokest (1)
A. 5.83   He is *douȝtiere* þanne I–I dar non harm don hym,
A.11.302   Þe *douȝtiest* doctour or dyuynour of þe trinite,
B. 5.103   He is *douȝtier* þan I; I dar [noon harm doon hym],
B. 5.500   Of þyne *douȝt[iest]* dedes was doon in oure armes:
B.10.458   The *douȝtieste* doctour and deuinour of þe trinitee
B.19.134   For dauid was *doghtiest* of dedes in his tyme;
C.11.263   Or dauid þe *douhty* þat de[uyn]ed how vrye
C.21.134   For dauid was *douhtiest* of dedes in his tyme

douhtyliche adv *doughtiliche adv.* B 1 doghtiliche; C 1
B.18.37   To se how *doghtiliche* deeþ sholde do and deme hir boþeres right.
C.20.36   To se how *douhtyliche* deth sholde do and demen [h]er beyre rihte.

douhtur > douȝter

doumb adj *domb adj.* A 1 ; B 3 dombe (1) doumb (1) doumbe (1); C 3
           dombe (1) doumbe (2)
A.11.95   [And] also *doumb* as a dore drouȝ hym asid.
B.10.142   And as *doumb* as [a dore] drouȝ hym [aside].
B.10.293   And carpen noȝt as þei carpe now, [and] calle yow *doumbe*
                  houndes:
B.19.130   For deue þoruȝ hise doynges and *dombe* speke [and herde],
C. 2.39   Y do hit vppon dauyd; þe *doumbe* wil noȝt lyen:
C. 2.41   And dauid vndoth hymself as þe *doumbe* sheweth:
C.21.130   For deue thorw his doynges and *dombe* speke [&] herde

doun adv *doun adv. &> vp_so_doun* A 4; B 11 doun (10) down (1); C
           10 doun (2) down (8)
A. 1.4   Com *doun* fro þat [clyf] & callide me faire,
A. 1.93   And riden & rappe *doun* in reaumes aboute,
A. 5.213   Sleuþe for sorewe fil *doun* a swowe
A.10.217   And ȝo comiþ dobest aboute, and bringeþ *doun* mody,
B. 1.4   Cam *doun* from [þe] Castel and called me faire,
B. 1.95   Riden and rappen *doun* in Reaumes aboute,
B.13.21   I lay *doun* longe in þis þoȝt and at þe laste I slepte,
B.14.93   Ther contricion dooþ but dryueþ it *doun* into a venial synne
B.16.30   Thanne with þe firste pil I palle hym *doun*, potencia de[i patris].
B.18.55   If þow be crist and kynges sone com *down* of þe roode;
B.18.70   Wher he be deed or noȝt deed *doun* er he be taken.'
B.18.84   To touchen hym or to tasten hym or taken *doun* of roode,
B.18.86   The blood sprong *doun* by þe spere and vnspered [his] eiȝen.
B.19.338   Blowe hem *doun* and breke hem and bite atwo þe mores.
B.20.54   Torned it [tid] vp so doun and ouertilte þe roote,
C. 1.4   Cam *doun* fro þe castel and calde me by name
C.18.34   And with þe furste planke y palle hym *down*, potencia dei patris.
C.18.110   For euere as Elde hadde eny *down*, þe deuel was redy
C.20.72   Wher he be deed or nat ded *down* or he be taken.'
C.20.86   To touchen hym or to t[ast]en hym or taken *down* [of rode]
C.20.88   The bloed sprang *down* by the spere and vnspered [his] yes.
C.20.144   And þat deth *down* brouhte, deth shal releue.'
C.20.340   Hit shal vndo vs deueles and *down* bryngen vs all.
C.21.338   Blowe hem *doun* and B[r]eke hem and b[y]te ato þe mores.
C.22.54   Turned hit tyd vp so *down* and ouertulde þe rote

dounes n *doune n.* A 1 ; B 1 ; C 1 doune
A.10.173   Alle shuln deiȝe for his dedis be *dounes* & hilles,
B. 9.142   Alle shul deye for hise dedes by [*dounes*] and hulles,
C. 4.51   'Bere sikerlyche eny seluer to seynt Gyles *doune*.

doute n *doute n. &> douten* A 3 ; B 4; C 3
A. 9.60   Þat euere dremide driȝt in *doute*, as I wene.
A.10.82   For *doute* men doþ þe bet; dred is such a maister
A.11.299   For to answere men ne no *doute*,
B.Pr.152   'For *doute* of diuerse d[e]des we dar noȝt wel loke,
B. 8.69   That euer dremed [driȝt] in [*doute*], as I wene.
B.12.32   For he dooþ wel, wiþouten *doute*, þat dooþ as lewte techeþ.
B.13.397   That my mynde ne was moore on my good in a *doute*
C. 6.284   That my muynde ne was more [o]n my godes in a *doute*
C.14.69   And do we as dauid techeth for *doute* of godes veniance:
C.16.32   Thise thre withoute *doute* tholieth alle pouerte

douten v *douten v.* A 1 ; B 1 doute; C 4 doute (3) douten (1)
A.10.80   It is begynnyng of goodnesse god for to *douten*.
B.15.72   That [lome] þe lewed peple of hir bileue *doute*;
C.10.127   And what þey drede and *doute*, dere sire, telleth.'
C.10.198   Sholde *doute* no deth ne no dere ȝeres.
C.16.233   That bothe le[r]ed and le[w]ed of here beleue *douten*.
C.20.312   'That is soeth,' saide satoun, 'bote y me sore *doute*

douue > dowue

douwe v *douen v.(2)* A 2 dewid; B 1 dowed; C 2 douwe (1) dowede (1)
A.11.199 Dobet doþ ful wel, & *dewid* he is also,
A.11.201 For mendynaunt3 at meschief þ[o] men were *dewid*,
B.15.557 Whan Costantyn of curteisie holy kirke *dowed*
C. 3.320 May desa[u]owe that thei dede and *do[uwe]* þerwith another
C.17.220 Whan Constantyn of cortesye holy kirke *dowede*

douere n prop *n.i.d.* A 1; B 1
A. 4.114 Vpe forfaiture of þat fe, who fynt hym [at *douere*],
B. 4.131 V[p] forfeture of þat fee, wh[o] fynt [hym] at *Douere*,

dowed(e > douwe

dowel n *don v. &> doon (B.10.219, 13.111, 19.116)* A 44 dowel (43)
  dowelis (1); B 69 dowel (67) doweles (1) dowelis (1); C 52 dowel
  (50) do_wel (1) dowelus (1)
A. 8.153 And [dem]ide þat *dowel* indulgence passiþ,
A. 8.155 *Dowel* at þe day of dome is digneliche vndirfongen;
A. 8.177 And haue indulgence doublefold, but *dowel* þe helpe
A. 8.183 Þat, aftir oure deþ day, *dowel* reherse
A. 9.2 Al a somer sesoun for to seke *dowel*,
A. 9.4 3if any wi3t wiste where *dowel* was at Inne'.
A. 9.13 'Where þat *dowel* dwelli[þ], do me to wisse'.
A. 9.19 [Þat] *dowel* & do euele mowe not dwelle togidere.
A. 9.40 Ac dedly synne doþ he nou3t, for *dowel* hym helpiþ,
A. 9.53 Þus I wente wydewhere *dowel* to seken,
A. 9.68 Where *dowel* dwelliþ, & do me to wisse.'
A. 9.69 '*Dowel*,' quaþ he, '& dobet, & dobest þe þridde,
A. 9.75 And [is] nou3t drunkelewe ne deynous, *dowel* hym folewiþ.
A. 9.89 Þat waiten any wikkidnesse *dowel* to tenen.
A. 9.90 And as *dowel* & dobet dede hem to vndirstonde,
A. 9.92 Þat 3if *dowel* & dobet dede a3ens dobest
A. 9.97 Þus *dowel*, & dobet, & dobest þe þridde,
A. 9.104 How *dowel*, dobet & dobest don on þis erþe.'
A. 9.108 Disputyng on *dowel* day aftir oþer,
A. 9.117 'Where þat *dowel*, & dobet, & dobest beþ in londe,
A.10.1 'Sire *dowel* dwelliþ,' quaþ wyt, 'nou3t a day hennes,
A.10.11 And haþ don hire to sire *dowel*, duk of þise marchis.
A.10.12 Dobet is hire damysele, sire *dowelis* [dou3ter],
A.10.14 Þus *dowel*, & dobet, & dobest þe þridde,
A.10.76 Þanne is *dowel* a duc þat destroyeþ vices,
A.10.79 And þat is dred of god, *dowel* it makiþ.
A.10.118 Þus in dred liþ *dowel*, [and] dobet to suffre,
A.10.127 So dobest out of dobet & *dowel* gynneþ springe
A.10.134 Þei be þe riccheste of reaumes & þe rote of *dowel*.
A.10.213 A3ens *dowel* hy don euele, & þe deuil plesen,
A.10.216 Þanne is *dowel* to dreden, & dobet to suffre,
A.11.88 What is *dowel* fro dobet; now def mote he worþe,
A.11.90 But he lyue in þe leste degre þat longiþ to *dowel*
A.11.103 [To] kenne me kyndely to knowe what is *dowel*'.
A.11.109 Shuln wisse þe to *dowel*, I dar wel vndirtake.'
A.11.180 To lere at 3ow *dowel* & dobet þereaftir,
A.11.187 Diken or deluen, *dowel* it hatte.
A.11.220 Wern *dowel*, & dobet, & dobest of hem alle,
A.11.259 To wyte what is *dowel* witterly in herte,
A.11.275 And be here werkis & here wordis wissen vs to *dowel*,
A.12.2 I haue do my deuer þe *dowel* to teche,
A.12.32 For he cam not by cause to lerne to *dowel*
A.12.54 Sey I sente him þis segge, and þat he shewe hym *dowel*.'
A.12.94 And þerfore do after *dowel* whil þi dayes duren,
B. 7.174 And how þe preest preued no pardon to *dowel*
B. 7.175 And demed þat *dowel* Indulgences passe[þ],
B. 7.177 *Dowel* at þe day of dome is digneliche vnderfongen;
B. 7.186 [It] is no3t so siker for þe soule, certes, as is *dowel*.
B. 7.199 And haue Indulgences doublefold, but *dowel* [þee] helpe
B. 7.205 That, after oure deeþ day, *dowel* reherce
B. 8.2 Al a somer seson for to seke *dowel*,
B. 8.4 If any wi3t wiste wher *dowel* was at Inne.
B. 8.13 'Where þat *dowel* dwelleþ, dooþ me to witene.'
B. 8.17 And *dowel* and do yuele, wher þei dwelle boþe.'
B. 8.23 [That] *dowel* and do yuele mowe no3t dwelle togideres.
B. 8.44 Ac dedly synne doþ he no3t for *dowel* hym [helpeþ],
B. 8.56 But if he werche wel þerwiþ as *dowel* hym techeþ.'
B. 8.62 [Th]us I wente widewher [*dowel* to seke,
B. 8.77 Where *dowel* dwelleþ, and do me [to wisse].'
B. 8.78 '*Dowel*', [quod he], 'and dobet and dobest þe þridde
B. 8.84 And is no3t dronkelewe ne [d]eynous, *dowel* hym folweþ.
B. 8.99 That waiten any wikkednesse *dowel* to tene.
B. 8.100 And [as] *dowel* and dobet [dide] hem [to vnderstonde],
B. 8.102 That if *dowel* [and] dobet dide ayein dobest
B. 8.107 Thus *dowel* and dobet and dobest þe þridde
B. 8.114 How *dowel*, dobet and dobest doon among þe peple.'
B. 8.118 Disputyng [o]n *dowel* day after ooþer,

B. 8.126 What was *Dowel* fro dobet and dobest from hem boþe.
B. 8.128 'Wher *dowel* [and] dobet and dobest ben in londe,
B. 9.1 'SIre *Dowel* dwelleþ', quod Wit, 'no3t a day hennes,
B. 9.11 And [haþ] doo[n] hire wiþ sire *dowel*, duc of þise Marches.
B. 9.12 Dobet is hire damyselle, sire *doweles* dou3ter,
B. 9.110 [*Dowel* in þis world is trewe wedded libbynge folk],
B. 9.199 Ayeins *dowel* þei doon yuel and þe deuel [plese],
B. 9.202 *Dowel*, my [deere], is to doon as lawe techeþ:
B. 9.207 [Thanne is *dowel*] to drede, and dobet to suffre,
B. 9.210 And dryueþ awey *dowel* þoru3 dedliche synnes.'
B.10.135 What is *dowel* fro dobet, [now] deef mote he worþe,
B.10.137 But he lyue in þe [leeste degre] þat longeþ to *dowel*
B.10.151 [To] kenne me kyndely to knowe what is *dowel*.'
B.10.157 Shullen wissen þee to *dowel*, I dar [wel] vndertake.'
B.10.192 Loke þow loue lelly if þee likeþ *dowel*,
B.10.223 To counseille þee kyndely to knowe what is *dowel*.'
B.10.237 *Dowel* and dobet and dobest to lerne.
B.10.254 But þus it bilongeþ to bileue to lewed þat willen *dowel*.
B.10.335 [Ac] *dowel* shal dyngen hym adoun and destruye his my3te.'
B.10.336 'Thanne is *dowel* and dobet', quod I, 'dominus and kny3thode?'
B.10.378 Where *dowel* is or dobet derkliche ye shewen.
B.11.48 That of *dowel* ne dobet no deyntee me þou3te;
B.11.51 Than *dowel* or dobet among my dedes alle.
B.11.409 [To wite] what *dowel* is, [ac wakyng neuere].'
B.11.411 '[What is *dowel*?' quod þat wi3t]; 'ywis, sire', I seide,
B.11.412 'To se muche and suffre moore, certes, is *dowel*.'
B.12.18 To telle men what *dowel* is, dobet and dobest boþe,
B.12.26 What were *dowel* and dobet and dobest at þe laste,
B.12.29 'Poul in his pistle', quod he, 'preueþ what is *dowel*.'
B.13.98 Of *dowel* and dobet, and if do[best] be any penaunce.'
B.13.103 'What is *dowel*, sire doctour?' quod I; 'is [dobest] any penaunce?'
B.13.104 '*Dowel*', quod þis doctour and [drank after],
B.13.106 'By þis day, sire doctour', quod I, 'þanne [in *dowel* be ye no3t]!
B.13.115 What is *dowel* and dobet? ye dyuynours knoweþ.
B.13.116 '*Dowel*', quod þis doctour, 'do as clerkes techeþ.
B.13.119 'Now þow, Clergie', quod Conscience, 'carp[e] what is *dowel*.'
B.13.121 Ther þe lord of lif wonyeþ, to leren [hem] what is *dowel*.
B.13.128 And [demeþ] þat *dowel* and dobet arn two Infinites,
B.13.138 Disce and *dowel*, doce and dobet, dilige and dobest:
B.13.152 I bere þer, [in a bouste] faste ybounde, *dowel*,
B.13.157 Vndo it; lat þis doctour deme if *dowel* be þerInne.
B.13.220 And as þe[i] wente by þe weye–of *dowel* þei carped–
B.14.18 *Dowel* shal wasshen it and wryngen it þoru3 a wis confessour:
B.14.88 Ergo contricion, feiþ and conscience is kyndeliche *dowel*,
B.14.324 I ne hadde be deed and doluen for *dowelis* sake!
B.15.2 Er I koude kyndely knowe what was *dowel*
C. 9.319 And how þe prest preuede no pardon to *do wel*
C. 9.320 And demede þat *dowel* indulgences passeth,
C. 9.324 So *dowel* passeth pardoun and pilgrimages to Rome.
C. 9.332 Hit is nat so syker for þe soule, certes, as [is] *dowel*
C. 9.345 And haue indulgences doublefold, but *dowel* vs helpe
C. 9.351 That aftur oure deth day *dowel* reherce
C.10.2 Alle a somur seson for to seke *dowel*
C.10.4 Yf eny wiht wiste wher *dowel* was at ynne;
C.10.13 Wher þat *dowel* dwelleth; 'dere frendes, telleth me,
C.10.17 And *dowel* and do euele, where þei dwellen bothe.'
C.10.27 And *dowel* and do euele may nat dwelle togyderes.
C.10.43 So dedly synne doth he nat for *dowel* hym helpeth.
C.10.75 Where þat *dowel* dwelleth And do me to knowe.'
C.10.76 '*Dowel* and dobet,' quod he, ' and dobest the thridde
C.10.81 And is nat dronklewe ne dedeynus, *dowel* h[y]m foleweth.
C.10.100 Thus *dowel* and dobet de[uin]ede a dobest
C.10.103 Thus *dowel* and dobet and dobest the thridde
C.10.110 Of *dowel* and dobet and ho doth best of alle.'
C.10.114 Disputyng vppon *dowel* day aftur other
C.10.122 What was *dowel* fro dobet and dobest fro hem bothe.
C.10.124 'Whare *dowel* and dobet And dobest ben in londe
C.10.128 'Sire *dowel* dwelleth,' quod wit, 'nat a day hennes
C.10.138 And hath do here with sire *dowel*, duk of this marches.
C.10.139 Dobet is here dameysele, sire *dowelus* douhtur,
C.10.298 A3en *dowel* they do yuele and þe deuel serue
C.10.301 And thus is *dowel*, my frende, to do as lawe techeth.
C.11.76 And þat loueth lordes now and leten hit a *dowel*
C.11.89 With þat 3e kenne me kyndeliche to knowe what is *dowel*.'
C.11.92 Alle kynne kunnynges and comsynges of *dowel*,
C.11.99 Thow shalt kunne and knowe kyndeliche *dowel*.'
C.11.110 To clergie shaltow neuere come ne knowe what is *dowel*.
C.11.132 Lerne for to louie yf þe lik[e] *dowel*
C.11.138 To kenne and to knowe kyndeliche *dowel*.
C.11.139 'By Crist,' quod Clergie, 'yf thow coueyte *dowel*
C.11.155 Bote thus hit bilongeth to bileue alle þat liketh *dowel*.
C.11.159 That [doth] men *dowel*, dobet and dobest.'
C.11.311 Of *dowel* ne of dobet no deynte me thouhte;

C.13.217 To wyte what *dowel* is Ac wakynge neuere.'
C.13.219 'What is *dowel*?' quod þat wyhte; 'ywis, sire,' y saide,
C.13.220 'To se moche and soffre al, certes, is *dowel*.'
C.14.4   And wissed the [wel] ofte what *dowel* was to mene
C.14.22   Druy[e]th vp *dowel* and distruyeth dobest.
C.15.105 Of *dowel* and dobet and yf dobe[s]t [be] eny penaunce.'
C.15.110 'What is *dowel*, sire doctour?' quod y; 'is dobest eny penaunce?'
C.15.111 '*Dowel*?' quod this doctour, and he dronke aftur;
C.15.115 In þat ȝe parteth nat with vs pore, þat ȝe passeth *dowel*
C.15.118 [Bu]t *dowel* endite ȝow in die iudicij.'
C.15.122 What is *dowel* and dobet? ȝe deuynours knoweth.'
C.15.124 Bote do as doctours techeth, for *dowel* y hit holde;
C.15.127 'Now þou, Clergie,' quod Consience, 'carpe what is *dowel*.'
C.15.189 And as they wente by the way–of *dowel* can they carpe–
C.16.28   And these ben *dowel* and dobet and dobest of alle.

down > doun, vp_so_doun

downrighte adv *dounright adv.* B 1; C 1 downriht
B.18.193 Sholden deye *downrighte* and dwelle in pyne after
C.20.198 Sholde deye *downriht* and d[welle] in payne euere

dowue n *douve n.* B 2; C 2 douue (1) dowue (1)
B.15.401 Daunted a *dowue* and day and nyȝt hire fedde;
B.15.409 And þus þoruȝ wiles of his wit and a whit *Dowue*
C.17.171 He endaunted a *douue* and day and nyhte here fedde;
C.17.239 And take hede [how] Macometh thorw a mylde *dowue*

doȝeyne num *doseine num.* A 1 dusȝeyn; B 3; C 3 doysayne (1) doseyne
  (1) dosoyne (1)
A. 5.163 Dawe þe dykere & a *dusȝeyn* oþere,
B. 4.38   For [þei wolde do for a dyner or a *doȝeyne* capons
B. 5.313 Dawe þe dykere and a *doȝeyne* oþere,]
B.20.164 And threw drede of dispair a *doȝeyne* myle aboute.
C. 4.38   For þey wolde do for a dyner oþer a *d[o]seyne* capones
C. 6.369 Dawe þe dikere with a *dosoyne* harlotes
C.22.164 And th[re]w drede of dispayr a *doysayne* myle aboute.

drad(- > drede

draf n *draf n.* A 1; B 2; C 2
A.11.11 Þei do but drauele þeron; *draf* were hem leuere
B.10.11 Thei doon but dr[a]uele þeron; *draf* were hem leuere
B.19.399 Boþe dregges and *draf* and drawe at oon hole
C.11.9   They do bote dr[a]uele þeron; *draf* were hem leuere
C.21.399 Bothe dregges and *draf* and drawe at on hole

drank(e > drynken

draper n *draper n.* A 1 drapers; B 2 draper (1) drapiers (1); C 2 draper
  (1) drapers (1)
A. 5.123 Þanne drouȝ I me among *drapers* my donet to lere,
B. 5.207 Thanne drouȝ I me among *drapiers* my donet to lerne,
B. 5.252 And haue ymaad many a knyȝt boþe Mercer and *draper*
C. 6.215 Thenne drow y me amonge *drapers* my donet to lere,
C. 6.250 And haue ymad many a knyht bothe mercer and *draper*

drat > drede

drauȝte n *draught n.* B 1; C 1 drauht
B.20.223 Than I do to drynke a *drauȝte* of good ale.'
C.22.223 Then y do to drynke a *drauht* of goed ale.'

drauele > dreuelen

drawe v *drauen v.* A 11 drawe (6) drawen (1) drouȝ (3) drow (1); B 22
  drawe (11) drawen (2) drogh (2) drouȝ (4) drow (1) drowe (1) drowen
  (1); C 23 drawe (12) drow (7) drowe (2) ydrawe (2)
A. 2.141 And let cartesadil þe Comissare, oure carte shal he *drawe*,
A. 4.108 And do it in dede to *drawe* vs to goode;
A. 5.123 Þanne *drouȝ* I me among drapers my donet to lere,
A. 5.124 To *drawe* þe list along, þe lengere it semide;
A. 5.197 Whanne he *drouȝ* to þe dore þanne dymmede hise eiȝen;
A. 7.272 To *drawe* on feld my dong while þe drouȝt lastiþ.
A.11.30 Or daun[cel]id or *drawe* forþ; þise disours wyte þe soþe.
A.11.92 Þeiȝ dobest *drawe* on hym day aftir oþer.'
A.11.95 [And] also doumb as a dore *drouȝ* hym asid.
A.11.145 For dobet & dobest ben *drawen* of louis s[co]le.
A.12.36 And *drow* þe dore after him and bad me go do wel
B. 2.173 Denes and Southdenes, *drawe* yow togideres;
B. 2.180 And [lat] Cartsadle þe Commissarie; oure cart shal he [*drawe*]
B. 5.43   And dooþ it in dede, it shal *drawe* yow to goode.
B. 5.207 Thanne *drouȝ* I me among drapiers my donet to lerne,
B. 5.208 To *drawe* þe [list] along, þe lenger it semed;
B. 5.349 A[c] whan he *drouȝ* to þe dore þanne dymmed hise eiȝen;
B. 6.288 To *drawe* afeld my donge while þe droȝte lasteþ.

B. 7.57   Whan þei *drawen* on to [þe deþ] and Indulgences wolde haue,
B.10.38 Or daunted or *drawe* forþ; I do it on god hymselue.
B.10.139 Theiȝ dobest *drawe* on hym day after ooþer.'
B.10.142 And as doumb as [a dore] *drouȝ* hym [aside].
B.10.193 For dobet and dobest ben [*drawen*] of loues [scole].
B.11.42 'Ye! farewel, Phippe', quod Faunteltee, and forþ gan me *drawe*
B.11.339 Males *drowen* hem to males [al mornyng] by hemselue,
B.11.340 And [femeles to femeles ferded and *drowe*].
B.13.50 And siþþe he [*drouȝ*] vs drynke, Di[u] perseuerans,
B.14.107 Whan he *drogh* to his deeþ day þat he ne dredde hym soore,
B.17.64 Ac whan he hadde sighte of þat segge aside he gan hym *drawe*
B.18.111 I *drow* me in þat derknesse to descendit ad inferna
B.18.136 In menynge þat man shal fro merknesse be *drawe*
B.19.399 Boþe dregges and draf and *drawe* at oon hole
B.20.200 And deeþ *drogh* neiȝ me; for drede gan I quake,
C. 2.193 And lat cop[l]e þe commissarie; oure cart shal he *drawe*
C. 6.215 Thenne *drow* y me amonge drapers my donet to lere,
C. 6.216 To *drawe* the lyst along the lengur hit semede;
C. 6.407 And when he *drow* to the dore thenne dymmede his yes;
C. 8.52   For hit beeþ þe deueles dysors to *drawe* men to synne;
C. 8.190 Prestes and oþer peple towarde [Peres] they *drowe*
C. 8.287 Lat hem abyde til the bord be *drawe*; Ac bere hem none crommes
C. 8.311 To *drawe* afeld my donge þe while þe drouthe lasteth.
C. 9.52   For whenne ȝe *drawe* to þe deth and indulgences wolde haue
C. 9.145 Drynke druie and depe and *drawe* hym thenne to bedde;
C.11.309 'Ȝe! farewel, fyppe,' quod fauntelete and forth gan me *drawe*
C.13.100 Vch a parfi[t] prest to pouerte sholde *drawe*
C.13.147 Males *drow* hem to males a[l mour]nynge by hemsulue,
C.13.148 And femeles to femeles ferddede and *drowe*.
C.15.56 And sethe he *drow* vs drynke, di[u] p[er]seuerans,
C.15.282 When he *drow* to þe deth that he ne dradd hym sarrore,
C.18.216 Eue of Adam was and out of hym *ydrawe*
C.18.228 Wh[om] god wolde oute of þe wey [*d]rawe*.
C.19.63 Ac when he hadde sihte of this s[egg]e asyde he gan hym *drawe*
C.20.114 Y [*d]row* [me] in þat derkenesse to descendit ad inferna
C.20.139 In menynge þat man shal fro me[r]kenesse be *ydrawe*
C.21.399 Bothe dregges and draf and *drawe* at on hole
C.22.200 And deth *drow* ney me; for drede gan y quaken

drede n *drede n.* A 6 dred (4) drede (1) dreed (1); B 15 drede; C 18
  drede
A. 2.169 *Dreed* at þe dore stood & þat doom herde,
A. 5.19   And turnide vpward here tail in toknyng of *drede*
A.10.79 And þat is *dred* of god, dowel it makiþ.
A.10.82 For doute men doþ þe bet; *dred* is such a maister
A.10.118 Þus in *dred* liþ dowel, [and] dobet to suffre,
A.10.121 And þus of *dred* & h[is] dede dobest arisiþ,
B.Pr.98 Arn doon vndeuoutliche; *drede* is at þe laste
B. 2.208 *Drede* at þe dore stood and þe doom herde,
B. 2.211 Thanne *Drede* wente wyȝtliche and warned þe False
B. 5.19   [And] turned vpward hire tai[l] in tokenynge of *drede*
B. 9.98 And [dredeþ hym] noȝt for *drede* of vengeaunce dooþ þerfore þe
     bettre;
B.10.82 Ne for *drede* of þe deeþ wiþdrawe noȝt hir pride,
B.12.164 Which trowestow of þo two [in Themese] is in moost *drede*,
B.12.168 And is in *drede* to drenche, þat neuere dide swymme?'
B.14.139 And noȝt to fonge bifore for *drede* of disalowyng.
B.15.414 [Ac] for *drede* of þe deeþ I dar noȝt telle truþe,
B.16.85 There is derknesse and *drede* and þe deuel maister.
B.17.313 [*Drede* of desperacion [þanne] dryueþ awey grace
B.18.60 The day for *drede* wiþdrouȝ and derk bicam þe sonne;
B.20.164 And threw *drede* of dispair a doȝeyne myle aboute.
B.20.200 And deeþ drogh neiȝ me; for *drede* gan I quake,
C.Pr.126 Ar don vndeuouteliche; *drede* is at þe laste
C. 2.220 *Drede* stod at þe dore and [þe] d[om]e herde,
C. 5.121 And turned vpward here tayl in tokenynge of *drede*
C. 7.210 Thenne eny dedly synne do for *drede* or for preeyere.
C. 7.308 That myhte folowe vs vch fote for *drede* of mysturnynge.'
C. 8.187 Al for *drede* of here deth, such duntus ȝaf hunger.
C.11.62 Ne for *drede* of eny deth withdraweth h[e]m fro pruyde
C.12.237 For if he be fer þerfro fol ofte hath he *drede*
C.12.246 Lo, how pans purchaseth fayre places and d[r]ede,
C.14.10 And thenne dost thow wel, withoute *drede*; ho can do bet no force.
C.14.108 Which trowest [þou] of tho two in temese [is] in moste *drede*?'
C.16.7   A[nd] nat to fonge byfore for *drede* [of] dessallouwynge.
C.16.308 For *drede* of god þat so goed is and thusgates vs techeth:
C.18.116 There is derkenesse and *drede* and þe deuel maister.
C.19.293 *Drede* of disparacion thenne dryueth [away] grace
C.20.60 The daye for *drede* withdrouh and derke bicam þe sonne;
C.22.164 And th[re]w *drede* of dispayr a doysayne myle aboute.
C.22.200 And deth drow ney me; for *drede* gan y quaken

drede v *dreden v.* A 3 dred (1) dreddist (1) dreden (1); B 22 dradde (1) dradden (1) drat (1) dred (2) dredde (2) dreddest (1) drede (10) dredeþ (4); C 21 drad (2) dradd (1) dradde (1) dradden (1) drat (3) drede (11) dredeth (2)

A. 1.32   *Dred* delitable drynk & þou shalt do þe betere;
A. 3.180   And dreddist to be ded for a *dym* cloud,
A.10.216   Þanne is dowel to *dreden*, & dobet to suffre,
B. 1.34   Forþi *dred* delitable drynke and þow shalt do þe bettre;
B. 3.193   And dreddest to be ded for a *dym* cloude,
B. 5.393   'If I sholde deye bi þis day [I *drede* me sore].
B. 9.91   The commune for hir vnkyndenesse, I *drede* me, shul abye;
B. 9.95   He dooþ noȝt wel þat dooþ þus, ne *drat* noȝt god almyȝty,
B. 9.97   That *dredeþ* god, he dooþ wel; þat dredeþ hym for loue
B. 9.97   That *dredeþ* god, he dooþ wel; þat *dredeþ* hym for loue
B. 9.98   And [*dredeþ* hym] noȝt for drede of vengeaunce dooþ þerfore þe bettre;
B. 9.207   [Thanne is dowel] to *drede*, and dobet to suffre,
B.10.294   And *drede* to wraþe yow in any word youre werkmanship to lette,
B.11.268   And lasse he *dredeþ* deeþ and in derke to ben yrobbed
B.13.387   As if I hadde dedly synne doon I *dredde* noȝt þat so soore
B.13.405   And þanne I *dradde* to deye in dedlich synne',
B.13.412   Dooþ noon almes[dede]; *dred* hym of no synne;
B.13.425   In youre deeþ deyinge I *drede* me soore
B.14.58   Ne deeþ *drede* [ne deuel], but deye as god likeþ
B.14.107   Whan he drogh to his deeþ day þat he ne *dredde* hym soore,
B.18.286   'That is sooþ', seide Sathan, 'but I me soore *drede*,
B.18.295   'Certes I *drede* me', quod þe deuel, 'lest truþe [do] hem fecche.
B.20.65   [And] þat were myȝtilche men and holye þat no meschief *dradden*;
B.20.154   Shal do þee noȝt *drede*, neiþer deeþ ne elde,
B.20.379   And [doþ men drynke dwale]; þei *drede* no synne.'
C. 1.32   Forthy *drede* delitable drynke bothe day and nyghtes.
C. 6.276   As thow y deddly synne dede y *dradde* [hit] nat so sore
C. 7.9   'Yf y sholde deye be þis day y *drede* me sore.
C. 7.72   Doth non Almesdede, *drat* hym nat of synne,
C. 7.85   In ȝoure deth deynge y *drede* me sore
C. 8.159   They acounteth nat of corsyng[e] ne holy kyrke *dredeth*–
C. 9.14   Lele and fol of loue and no lord *drede*,
C. 9.17   *Drede* nat for no deth to distruye by here power
C. 9.239   Y *drede* me, and he dey, hit worth for dedly synne
C.10.99   Ac dobest sholde *drede* hem nat but do as god hihte:
C.10.127   And what þey *drede* and doute, dere sire, telleth.'
C.12.153   And lasse *drat* [dethe] or in derke to ben yrobbed
C.13.57   And *dredeth* to be ded þerfore and he in derke mette
C.15.257   Ne d[e]th *drede* ne deuel, [but] deye as god liketh
C.15.282   When he drow to þe deth that he ne *dradd* hym sarrore
C.16.313   Of deth ne of derthe *drad* he neuere
C.20.325   'Forthy y *drede* me,' quod þe deuel, 'laste treuthe wol hem fecche.
C.21.21   For alle derke deueles aren *drad* to heren hit
C.22.65   And þat were mylde men and holy þat no meschief *dradden*,
C.22.154   Shal do the nat *drede*, noþer deth ne elde,
C.22.379   And doth men drynke dwale; [they] *drat* no synne.'

dredful adj *dredeful adj.* A 3; B 4 dredful (3) dredfulle (1); C 2

A.Pr.16   Wiþ depe dikes & derke & *dredful* of siȝt.
A. 1.57   'Þe dungeon in þe dale þat *dredful* is of siȝt:
A. 8.171 At þe *dredful* dom whanne dede shal arisen
B.Pr.16   Wiþ depe diches and derke and *dredfulle* of siȝte.
B. 1.59   'Th[e] dongeon in þe dale þat *dredful* is of siȝte–
B. 7.193 At þe *dredful* dome, whan dede shulle rise
B.20.89   Wiþ deeþ þat is *dredful* to vndo vs alle!'
C. 9.339 At þe *dredful* dome, when dede shullen ryse
C.22.89   With deth þat is *dredful* to vndoen vs alle!'

dredfully adv *dredefulli adv.* B 1; C 1

B.17.65   *Dredfully*, bi þis day! as doke dooþ fram þe faucon.
C.19.64   And *dredfully* withdrow hym and durste go no nerre.

dredles adv *dredeles adv.* A 1

A.11.194 [*Dredles*] þis is dobet; [dobest wot þe soþe].

dreed > drede

dregges **n** *dregges n.* B 1; C 2

B.19.399 Boþe *dregges* and draf and drawe at oon hole
C. 8.193 Drosenes and *dregges* drynke for many beggares.
C.21.399 Bothe *dregges* and draf and drawe at on hole

dreiȝe > drye; dremed > dremeþ

dremels n *dremels n.* B 1; C 1 dremeles

B.13.14   And how þat Ymaginatif in *dremels* me tolde
C.15.17   And how þat ymaginatyf in *dremeles* me tolde

dremes n *drem n.(2)* A 1 dremis; B 1; C 1

A. 8.136 How Dani[el] deui[n]ide þe *drem[is]* of a king
B. 7.158 How Daniel diuined þe *dre[mes]* of a kyng

C. 9.306   How danyel deuynede and vndede þe *dremes* of kynges,

dremeþ v *dremen v.* A 1 dremide; B 4 dremed (2) dremeþ (1) ydremed (1); C 3 dremede (1) dremeth (1) ydremed (1)

A. 9.60   Þat euere *dremide* driȝt in doute, as I wene.
B. 8.69   That euer *dremed* [driȝt] in [doute], as I wene.
B.18.7   Of gerlis and of Gloria laus gretly me *dremed*,
B.19.1   Thus I awaked and wroot what I hadde *ydremed*,
B.20.377   'He lyþ [adreynt] and *dremeþ*', seide Pees, 'and so do manye oþere.
B.20.6   Of gurles and of gloria laus greetliche me *dremede*
C.21.1   Thus y wakede and wrot what y hadde *ydremed*
C.22.377   'He lyeth adreint [and *dremeth*],' saide pees, 'and so doth mony oþere.

drenche v *drenchen v.* A 2 drenche (1) drenchit (1); B 2

A. 9.46   And don dedly synne & *drenche* þiseluen.
A.10.60   Þei helde ale in here hed til Inwyt be *drenchit*,
B. 8.50   And] do deedly synne and *drenche* þi[selue].
B.12.168   And is in drede to *drenche*, þat neuere dide swymme?'

dreury > drury

dreuelen v *drevelen v.* A 2 drauele (1) dryuelen (1); B 3 drauele (1) dreuelen (1) dryuele (1); C 2 drauele (1) dreuele (1)

A.11.11   Þei do but *drauele* þeron; draf were hem leuere
A.11.43   Þus þei *dryuelen* at here deis þe deite to knowe
B.10.11   Thei doon but *dr[a]uele* þeron; draf were hem leuere
B.10.42   Drynken and *dreuelen* and do men for to gape,
B.10.57   Thus þei *dryuele* at hir deys þe deitee to knowe,
C.11.9   They do bote *dr[a]uele* þeron; draf were hem leuere
C.11.38   Thus they *dreuele* a[t] the deyes the deite to knowe

drye n *drie n.(1)* A 1 driȝe; B 2; C 1

A. 6.18   Þat I haue walkid wel wide in wet & in *driȝe*,
B. 5.530   That I haue walked [wel] wide in weet and in *drye*
B.14.52   Or whan þow clomsest for cold or clyngest for *drye*.
C. 7.175   /[Y haue] ywalked ful wyde in wete and in *drye*

drye adj *drie adj.(1)* A 1 dreiȝe; B 3 drie (1) drye (2); C 2 drye (1) druye (1)

A.11.208   Þei diȝe for þe drouȝte, whanne þei *dreiȝe* lengen;
B.10.302   Thei deyen for drouȝte, whan þei *drie* [lenge];
B.13.268   In þe date of oure driȝte, in a *drye* Aprill,
B.17.326   He sekeþ and sekeþ til he slepe *drye*.
C. 5.149   Dyen for drouthe whenne they *drye* lygge,
C.19.306   A seketh and seketh til he slepe *druye*.

drieþ v *drien v.(1)* A 1 driȝeþ; B 1; C 1 druyeth

A. 1.25   And drink whanne þe *driȝeþ*, ac do it nouȝt out of resoun
B. 1.25   And drynke whan þ[ee] *drie[þ]*, ac do [it] noȝt out of reson
C.14.22   *Druy[e]th* vp dowel and distruyeth dobest.

driȝe > drye; driȝeþ > drieþ

driȝt n *driht n.* A 1; B 1

A. 9.60   Þat euere dremide *driȝt* in doute, as I wene.
B. 8.69   That euer dremed [*driȝt*] in [doute], as I wene.

driȝte n *Drihten n.* B 3 driȝte (2) driȝten (1)

B.13.268   In þe date of oure *driȝte*, in a drye Aprill,
B.14.102   'Wheiþer paciente pouerte', quod Haukyn, 'be moore plesaunt to oure d[*riȝte*]
B.18.282   And dwelle wiþ vs deueles; þis þretynge [*driȝten*] made.

drynke n *drinke n. &> drynken* A 6 drink (2) drynk (1) drynke (1) drinkes (1) drynkes (1); B 16 drynke (14) drynkes (2); C 18 drynke (16) drynkes (2)

A. 1.25   And *drink* whanne þe driȝeþ, ac do it nouȝt out of resoun
A. 1.27   For loth, in his lyf dayes, for lykyng of *drink*
A. 1.29   [Delyted hym in *drynke* as the deuyl wolde],
A. 1.32   Dred delitable *drynk* & þou shalt do þe betere;
A. 7.258   Þei do men diȝe þoruȝ here *drynkes* er destenye it wolde.'
A.11.121   F[ro] lesinges & li[þer] speche & likerous *drinkes*.
B. 1.25   And *drynke* whan þ[ee] drie[þ], ac do [it] noȝt out of reson
B. 1.27   For Lot, in hise lifdayes, for likynge of *drynke*,
B. 1.29   Delited hym in *drynke* as þe deuel wolde,
B. 1.34   Forþi dred delitable *drynke* and þow shalt do þe bettre;
B. 5.257   'Artow manlich among þi neȝebores of þi mete and *drynke*?'
B. 6.274   They do men deye þoruȝ hir *drynkes* er destynee it wolde.'
B. 9.66   Allas þat *drynke* shal fordo þat god deere bouȝte,
B.10.169   Fro-lesynges-and-liþer-speche-and-likerouse-*drynkes*.
B.13.50   And siþþe he [drouȝ] vs *drynke*, Di[u] perseuerans,
B.13.251   And buxom and busy aboute breed and *drynke*
B.14.57   Darstow neuere care for corn ne cloþ ne for *drynke*,
B.14.78   For [men] mesured noȝt hemself of [mete] and dr[y]nke,
B.14.318   And sobretee swete *drynke* and good leche in siknesse.
B.18.365   For I þat am lord of lif, loue is my *drynke*,
B.18.366   And for þat *drynke* today I deide vpon erþe.

B.18.368 May no *drynke* me moiste, ne my þurst slake,
C. 1.24 And *drynke* þat doth the good–a[c] drynke nat out of tyme.
C. 1.25 Loot in his lyue thorw likerous *drynke*
C. 1.32 Forthy drede delitable *drynke* bothe day and nyghtes.
C. 6.89 Ne derworth *drynke* dryue hit fro myn herte
C. 8.193 Drosenes and dregges *drynke* for many beggares.
C. 8.295 They don men deye thorw here *drynkes* Ar destyne hit wolde.'
C.10.177 That many lede leseth thorw lykerous *drynke*,
C.10.187 Meble ne vnmeble, mete noþer *drynke*.
C.13.188 In mete out of mesure and mony tymes in *drynke*,
C.15.56 And sethe he drow vs *drynke*, di[u] p[er]seuerans,
C.15.215 Fro Mihelmasse to Mihelmasse y fynde mete and *drynke*.
C.15.256 Dar þe nat care for no corn ne for cloth ne for *drynke*
C.16.63 And buxum at his biddyng for his breed and his *drynke*
C.16.152 And sobrete 3eueth here swete *drynke* and solaceth here in all angrys.
C.20.403 For y þat am lord of lyf, loue is my *drynke*,
C.20.404 And for þat *drynke* today y deyede as hit semede.
C.20.407 Ac thy *drynke* worth deth and depe helle thy bolle.
C.20.409 May no pyement ne pomade ne preciouse *drynkes*

drynken v *drinken v.* A 5 drinke (1) drynke (3) ydronke (1); B 31 drank
(2) drynk (2) drynke (13) drynken (3) dronk (1) dronke (2) dronken (5)
ydronke (3); C 32 dranke (1) drynke (20) dronke (6) dronken (1)
dronkene (1) ydronke (3)

A. 5.57 *Drinke* but wiþ þe doke & dyne but ones.
A. 7.129 Or 3e shuln ete barly bred & of þe bro[k] *drynke*;
A. 7.244 Þat þou *drynke* no day er þou dyne sumwhat,
A. 7.263 Er I haue dyned be þis day & *ydronke* boþe.'
A. 7.289 Ne non halpeny ale in no wyse *drynke*,
B. 2.94 And al day to *drynken* at diuerse Tauernes,
B. 5.74 *Drynke* but [wiþ] þe doke and dyne but ones.
B. 5.177 I ete þere unþende fissh and feble ale *drynke*.
B. 5.178 Ac ouþer while whan wyn comeþ, [whan] I *drynke* at eue,
B. 5.184 And *drynk* nat ouer delicatly, ne to depe neiþer,
B. 5.374 Ouer delicatly on [feeste] dayes *dronken* and eten boþe,
B. 5.376 For loue of tales in Tauernes [to] *drynke* þe moore I [hyed;
B. 6.135 Or ye shul eten barly breed and of þe broke *drynke*;
B. 6.260 That þow *drynke* no day er þow dyne somwhat.
B. 6.279 [Er] I haue dyned bi þis day and *ydronke* boþe.'
B. 6.305 Ne noon halfpeny ale in none wise *drynke*,
B.10.42 *Drynken* and dreuelen and do men for to gape,
B.11.122 And *drynke* boote for bale, brouke it whoso my3te.
B.11.427 For lat a *dronken* daffe in a dyk falle,
B.11.434 Thanne woot þe *dronken* [wye] wherfore he is to blame.'
B.13.61 For þis doctour on þe hei3e dees *drank* wyn so faste:
B.13.90 For now he haþ *dronken* so depe he wole deuyne soone
B.13.104 'Dowel', quod þis doctour and [*drank* after],
B.13.403 And moore mete eet and *dronk* þan kynde my3te defie,
B.14.65 And out of þe flynt sprong þe flood þat folk and beestes *dronken*.
B.14.251 Ne dooþ hym no3t dyne delicatly ne *drynke* wyn ofte.
B.15.315 For hadde ye potage and payn ynogh and penyale to *drynke*,
B.15.560 "Dos ecclesie þis day haþ *ydronke* venym
B.17.100 Til he haue eten al þe barn and his blood *ydronke*.
B.18.53 And beden hym *drynken* his deeþ [to lette and] hise daies [lengþe],
B.18.188 'What, rauestow?' quod Rightwisnesse, 'or þow art right *dronke*?
B.18.364 That art doctour of deeþ *drynk* þat þow madest.
B.18.370 That I *drynke* ri3t ripe Must, Resureccio mortuorum.
B.20.19 That he *dronke* at ech dych er he [deye for þurst].
B.20.223 Than I do to *drynke* a drau3te of good ale.'
B.20.379 And [doþ men *drynke* dwale]; þei drede no synne.'
C. 1.24 And drynke þat doth the good–a[c] *drynke* nat out of tyme.
C. 2.101 Al day to *drynke* at diuerse tauernes,
C. 2.103 And fastyng dayes to frete byfore noone and *drynke*
C. 5.9   And no dede to do but *drynke* and slepe.
C. 6.159 For y ete more fysch then flesche there and feble ale *drynke*.
C. 6.160 Ac other while when wyn cometh and when y *drynke* late at euen
C. 6.166 And *drynke* nat ouer delycatly n[e] to depe neyther
C. 6.174 *Drynke* but with þe doke and dyne but ones.
C. 6.363 Watte þe w[a]rnare and his wyf *dronke*,
C. 6.419 Then [wakede he] wel wanne and wolde haue *ydronke*;
C. 8.142 Or 3e shal ete barly breed and of þe broke *drynke*.
C. 8.276 And loke þou *drynke* no day ar thow dyne sumwhat.
C. 8.301 Ar y haue ydyned be þis day and *ydronke* bothe.'
C. 8.327 Ne noon halpeny ale in none wyse *drynke*
C. 9.145 *Drynke* druie and depe and drawe hym thenne to bedde;
C.12.57 And *drynke* bote for bale, brouke hit hoso myhte.\
C.13.234 For lat a *dronkene* daffe in a dykke falle,
C.15.65 For [this] doctour at þe hey deys *dranke* wyn [so] faste–
C.15.97 [For] now he hath *dronke* so depe a wol deuyne sone
C.15.111 'Dowel?' quod this doctour, and he *dronke* aftur;
C.15.264 And oute of þe flynt spronge þe floed þat folk and bestes *dronke*.
C.16.91 Ne doth men dyne delicatlyche ne *drynke* wyne ofte.
C.17.223 "Dos ecclesie this day hath *ydronke* venym

C.19.90 Til he haue eten al þ[e] barn and his bloed *dronken*
C.20.53 And beden hym *drynke* his deth to lette and his dayes lenghe
C.20.193 'Rauest thow?' quod rihtwisnesse, 'or thow art riht *dronke*!
C.20.402 That art doctour of deth *drynke* þat thow madest.
C.20.405 Ac y wol *drynke* of no dische ne of deep clergyse
C.20.412 And [y] *drynke* riht rype m[o]st, resureccio mortuorum.
C.22.19 That he *dronke* at vch a dy[c]h ar he deye for furste.
C.22.223 Then y do to *drynke* a drauht of goed ale.'
C.22.379 And doth men *drynke* dwale; [they] drat no synne.'

drinkeres n *drinkere n.* A 1
A.12.85 Tercian þat oþer; trewe *drinkeres* boþe.

drynkynge ger *drinkinge ger.* B 1; C 2 drynkyng
B.11.336 In etynge, in *drynkynge* and in engendrynge of kynde.
C.13.144 In etynge, [in] *drynkyng* [and] in engend[eryng] of kynde.
C.13.155 As in derne dedes, bothe *drynkyng* and elles.

drit n *drit n.* A 1; B 1
A. 7.176 And doluen *drit* & dung to ditte out hunger.
B. 6.190 And doluen [*drit*] and [dung] to [ditte out] hunger.

dryuele(n > dreuelen

dryuen v *driven v.* A 5 dryue (2) dryuen (1) driueþ (1) drof (1); B 10
dryue (2) dryuen (2) dryueþ (5) dryuynge (1); C 10 dryue (5) dryuen
(1) dryueth (2) dryuyng (1) drof (1)
A.Pr.103 And *driueþ* forþ þe longe day wiþ dieu saue dame emme;
A. 5.101 Ne no dyapendyon *dryue* it fro myn herte.
A. 6.99 And so worst þou *dryuen* out as dew & þe dore closid,
A. 7.126 Ac treuþe shal teche 3ow his tem for to *dryue*,
A.12.104 Deþ delt him a dent and *drof* him to þe erþe.
B.Pr.225 And *dryueþ* forþ þe longe day with 'Dieu saue dame Emme'.
B. 5.124 Ne no Diapenidion *dryue* it fro myn herte,
B. 5.613 And [so] worstow *dryuen* out as dew and þe dore closed,
B. 6.134 Ac truþe shal teche yow his teme to *dryue*,
B. 9.210 And *dryueþ* awey dowel þoru3 dedliche synnes.'
B.14.84 Which *dryueþ* awey dedly synne and dooþ it to be venial.
B.14.93 Ther contricion dooþ but *dryueþ* it doun into a venial synne
B.17.313 [Drede of desperacion [þanne] *dryueþ* awey grace
B.20.100 Deeþ cam *dryuynge* after and al to duste passhed
B.20.174 And *dryuen* awey deeþ wiþ Dyas and drogges.
C.Pr.229 And *dryueth* forth [þe longe] da[y] with 'd[ieu] saue dame Emme.'
C. 5.19 Heggen or harwen or swyn or gees *dryue*
C. 6.89 Ne derworth drynke *dryue* hit fro myn herte
C. 7.265 So worth thow *dryuen* out as de[w] and þe dore yclosed,
C. 7.296 To goo with a good wil and graytheliche hem *dryue*.
C. 8.141 Ac treuthe shal teche 3ow his teme to *dryue*
C.18.157 And *drof* hem out, alle þat þer bouhte and solde,
C.19.293 Drede of disparacion thenne *dryueth* [away] grace
C.22.100 Deth cam *dryuyng* aftur and al to duste paschte
C.22.174 And *dryue* awey deth with dyaes and drogges.

drogges n *drogge n.* B 1; C 1
B.20.174 And dryuen awey deeþ wiþ Dyas and *drogges*.
C.22.174 And dryue awey deth with dyaes and *drogges*.

drogh > drawe

dro3te n *droughte n.* A 2 drou3t (1) drou3te (1); B 4 droghte (2) dro3te (1)
drou3te (1); C 3 drouthe
A. 7.272 To drawe on feld my dong while þe *drou3t* lastiþ.
A.11.208 Þei di3e for þe *drou3te*, whanne þei drei3e lengen;
B. 6.288 To drawe afeld my donge while þe *dro3te* lasteþ.
B.10.302 Thei deyen for *drou3te*, whan þei drie [lenge];
B.14.171 For may no derþe hem deere, *droghte* ne weet,
B.14.176 Thoru3 derþe, þoru3 *droghte*, alle hir dayes here,
C. 5.149 Dyen for *drouthe* whenne they drye lygge,
C. 8.311 To drawe afeld my donge þe while þe *drouthe* lasteth.
C.15.251 Or when thow cl[o]msest fo[r] colde or clingest for *drouthe*.

dronk(e > drynken

dronkelewe adj *dronkeleue adj.* A 1 drunkelewe; B 1; C 1 dronklewe
A. 9.75 And [is] nou3t *drunkelewe* ne deynous, dowel hym folewiþ.
B. 8.84 And is no3t *dronkelewe* ne [d]eynous, dowel hym foleweþ.
C.10.81 And is nat *dronkelewe* ne dedeynus, dowel h[y]m foleweth.

dronken(e > drynken

dronkenesse n *dronkenesse n.* C 1
C. 1.27 In his *dronkenesse* aday his doughteres he dighte

dronklewe > dronkelewe

drop n *drope n.(1)* C 1
C. 6.336 And deyede with a *drop* water; so doth alle synnes

dropped v *droppen v.* B 1
B.16.79   For euere as þei *dropped* adoun þe deuel was redy

drosenes n *drosen n.* C 1
C. 8.193   *Drosenes* and dregges drynke for many beggares.

drouȝ > drawe; drouȝt(e drouthe > droȝte; drow(- > drawe; druerie > drury

druie adv *drie adv.* C 1
C. 9.145   Drynke *druie* and depe and drawe hym thenne to bedde;

druye > drie; druyeth > drieþ; drunkelewe > dronkelewe

drury n *druerie n.* A 1 dreury; B 1; C 1 druerie
A. 1.85   It is as derworþi a *dreury* as dere god hymseluen.
B. 1.87   It is as dereworþe a *drury* as deere god hymseluen.
C. 1.83   Hit is a[s] derworthe a *druerie* as dere god hymseluen.

dubbed v *dubben v.* A 1 dubbide; B 2; C 2 dobbed (1) dobbet (1)
A. 1.96   For dauid, in hise dayes, *dubbide* kniȝtes,
B. 1.98   /For Dauid in hise dayes *dubbed* knyȝtes,
B.18.13   As þe kynde of a knyght þat comeþ to be *dubbed*,
C. 1.102   Dauid in his daies *dobbed* knyghtes,
C.20.11   As is þe kynde of a knyhte þat cometh to be *dobbet*,

duc n *duk n.* A 3 duc (1) duk (2); B 3 duc (2) dukes (1); C 3 deuk (1)
    duk (1) dukes (1)
A.10.11   And haþ don hire to sire dowel, *duk* of þise marchis.
A.10.76   Þanne is dowel a *duc* þat destroyeþ vices,
A.12.87   Fro deþ þat is oure *duk* swyche dedis we brynge.'
B. 9.11   And [haþ] doo[n] hire wiþ sire dowel, *duc* of þise Marches.
B.18.319   *Dukes* of þis dymme place, anoon vndo þise yates
B.19.306   Neiþer of *duc* ne of deeþ, þat he ne dide lawe
C.10.138   And hath do here with sire dowel, *duk* of this marches.
C.20.362   *Dukes* of this demme place, anoen vndoth this ȝates
C.21.306   Noþer of *deuk* ne of deth þat he ne dede lawe

ducchesse n *ducchesse n.* C 1
C. 2.33   And y am his dere doughter, *ducchesse* of heuene.

ducherie n *ducherie n.* C 1
C. 3.245   For þat [is] conquere[d] thorw a comune helpe, a kyndom or
            ducherie,

duelle > dwellen; duyre(- > dure; duk(es > duc

dulle adj *dul adj.* A 1; B 1; C 1
A. 1.129   'Þou dotide daffe,' quaþ heo, '*dulle* arn þine wittes.
B. 1.140   'Thow doted daffe!' quod she, '*dulle* are þi wittes.
C. 1.139   'Thow dotede daffe!' quod she, '*dulle* aren thy wittes.

dung > donge; dungeon -oun > dongeon

dunmowe n prop *n.i.d.* A 1; B 1; C 1 donemowe
A.10.194   Þeiȝ þei don hem to *dunmowe*, but ȝif þe deuil helpe
B. 9.173   [Th]ouȝ þei do hem to *Dunmowe*, but if þe deuel helpe
C.10.275   Thogh they [do] hem to *donemowe*, bote þe deuel helpe

duntes -us > dynt

dure v *duren v.* A 4 duren (1) duriþ (3); B 11 dure (3) durede (1) durest
    (1) dureþ (6); C 9 duyre (2) duyred (1) duyren (1) duyreth (2) dure
    (1) dureth (1)
A. 1.76   To loue me lelly whiles þi lif *duriþ*.'
A. 7.51   'For to werche be þi woord while my lif *duriþ*.'
A.11.102   For to werche ȝour wil [while] my lif *duriþ*,
A.12.94   And þerfore do after dowel whil þi dayes *duren*,
B. 1.78   To louen me leelly while þi lif *dureþ*.'
B. 6.56   'For to werche by þi wor[d] while my lif *dureþ*.'
B.10.92   For we haue no lettre of oure lif how longe it shal *dure*.
B.10.150   For to worche oure wille while my lif *dureþ*,
B.10.210   Forþi loke þow louye as longe as þow *durest*,
B.13.51   'As longe', quod [he], 'as [lif] and lycame may *dure*'.
B.14.159   And so forþ while somer lasteþ hir solace *dureþ*.
B.15.240   For hir lawe *dureþ* ouerlonge but if þei lacchen siluer,
B.18.63   And tolde why þat tempeste so longe tyme *durede*:
B.18.187   And þat þis dede shal *dure* dormiam & requiescam.'
B.18.378   Shul noȝt be dampned to þe deeþ þat [dureþ] wiþouten ende:
C. 1.107   Lucifer, louelokest tho, ac litel while it *duyred*.
C. 3.29   For to worche thy wille the while þou myhte dure.'
C. 5.25   To wurche as a werkeman eny while to *duyren*.'
C.11.88   For to worche ȝoure wille while my lyf *duyreth*
C.12.222   That lihtlich launseth vp litel while *dureth*
C.15.57   'As longe,' quod he, ' as lyf and lycame may *duyre*.'
C.16.11   And so forth whiles somur laste[th] here solace *duyreth*
C.20.65   And tolde why þ[at] tempest so longe tyme *durede*:
C.20.192   And that this dede shal *duyre*, dormiam & requiescam.'

durst(e > dar; dusȝeyn > doȝeyne; dust > doon

duste n *dust n.* B 1; C 1
B.20.100   Deeþ cam dryuynge after and al to *duste* passhed
C.22.100   Deth cam dryuyng aftur and al to *duste* paschte

dwale n *dwale n.* B 1; C 1
B.20.379   And [doþ men drynke *dwale*]; þei drede no synne.'
C.22.379   And doth men drynke *dwale*; [they] drat no synne.'

dwellen v *dwellen v.* A 17 duelle (1) dwelle (5) dwellen (1) dwelleþ (1)
    dwellide (1) dwellyng (1) dwelliþ (7); B 22 dwelde (1) dwelle (11)
    dwellen (1) dwelleþ (8) dwelte (1); C 21 dwelle (8) dwellen (4)
    dwelleth (7) dwelte (2)
A.Pr.82   To haue a licence & leue at lundoun to *dwelle*,
A. 1.118   Aftir here deþ day & *dwelle* wiþ þat shrewe.
A. 3.14   Buski[de] hem to þe bour þere þe burde *dwelliþ*,
A. 6.21   Canst þou wisse vs þe wey where þat wy *dwelliþ*?'
A. 6.41   And ȝif ȝe wilneþ wyte where þat wy *dwelliþ*
A. 7.182   And preiȝede pur charite wiþ peris for to *dwelle*,
A. 9.13   'Where þat dowel *dwelli[þ]*, do me to wisse'.
A. 9.14   'Marie,' quaþ þe maistris, 'among vs he *dwelliþ*,
A. 9.19   [Þat] dowel & do euele mowe not *dwelle* togidere.
A. 9.68   Where dowel *dwelliþ*, & do me to wisse.'
A. 9.105   'But wyt can wisse þe,' quaþ þouȝt, 'where þo þre *dwellen*,
A.10.1   'Sire dowel *dwelliþ*,' quaþ wyt, 'nouȝt a day hennes,
A.10.214   And aftir here deþ day shuln *dwelle* with þe same
A.11.112   And axide hire þe heiȝe wey where clergie [*dwell*]ide,
A.12.46   I shal þe wisse [wynlyche] where þat he [*dwelle*'.
A.12.63   'I am *dwellyng* with deth, and hunger I hatte.
A.12.81   'With deþ I *duelle*,' quod he, 'dayes and nyȝtes.
B.Pr.85   To haue a licence and leue at London to *dwelle*,
B. 1.115   Into a deep derk helle to *dwelle* þere for euere;
B. 1.129   After hir deþ day and *dwelle* with þat sherewe.
B. 3.14   Busked hem to þe bour þer þe burde *dwelle[þ]*,
B. 4.34   'Ther are wiles in hire wordes, and with Mede þei *dwelleþ*;
B. 5.533   [Kanstow] wissen vs þe wey wher þat wye *dwelleþ*?'
B. 5.554   And if ye wilneþ wite where þat [wye] *dwelleþ*
B. 8.13   'Where þat dowel *dwelleþ*, dooþ me to witene.'
B. 8.17   And dowel and do yuele, wher þei *dwelle* boþe.'
B. 8.18   '[Marie]', quod þe [maistres, 'amonges vs he *dwelleþ*],
B. 8.23   [That] dowel and do yuele mowe noȝt *dwelle* togideres.
B. 8.77   Where dowel *dwelleþ*, and do me [to wisse].'
B. 8.115   'But wit konne wisse þee', quod þoȝt, 'where þo þre *dwelle*
B. 9.1   'SIre Dowel *dwelleþ*', quod Wit, 'noȝt a day hennes
B. 9.200   And after hir deeþ day shul *dwelle* wiþ þe same
B.10.160   And asked hire þe heighe wey where Clergie *dwelte*,
B.11.142   How [I] was ded and dampned to *dwellen* in pyne
B.13.212   I shal *dwelle* as I do my deuoir to shewe,
B.17.273   But þei *dwelle* þer Diues is dayes wiþouten ende.
B.18.193   Sholden deye downrighte and *dwelle* in pyne after
B.18.282   And *dwelle* wiþ vs deueles; þis pretynge [driȝten] made.
B.20.344   Coom in þus ycoped at a Court þere I *dwelde*,
C.Pr.83   To haue a licence and leue [at] Londoun to *dwelle*
C. 1.131   Aftur here deth day and *dwelle* ther wrong is;
C. 2.109   After here deth *dwellen* day withouten ende
C. 3.15   Boskede hem to þe bour ther th[e] buyrde *dwel[leth]*,
C. 5.151   That out of couent and Cloystre coueyteth to *dwelle*.
C. 9.39   And sende ȝoure soules þer y mysulue *dwelle*
C.10.13   Wher þat dowel *dwelleth*; 'dere frendes, telleth me,
C.10.17   And dowel and do euele, where þei *dwellen* bothe.'
C.10.27   And dowel and do euele may nat *dwelle* togyderes.
C.10.75   Where þat dowel *dwelleth* And do me to knowe.'
C.10.111   'Bote wit wol the wisse,' quod thouhte, 'where tho thre *dwelleth*,
C.10.128   'Sire dowel *dwelleth*,' quod wit, 'nat a day hennes
C.10.299   And after her deth day *dwellen* shollen in helle
C.11.102   And askede here þe hey way whare clergie *dwelte*;
C.12.77   How y was ded and dampned to *dwellen* in [pyne]
C.13.89   And sheweth be seel and seth by lettre with what lord he *dwelleth*,
C.19.243   And dampned a *dwelleth* with þe deuel in helle.
C.19.254   Bote they *dwelle* there diues is dayes withouten ende.
C.20.198   Sholde deye downriht and d[welle] in payne euere
C.20.304   [Sh]olde deye with doel and here *dwelle* euere
C.22.344   Kam ynne thus ycoped at a Court þer y *dwelte*

dwellynge ger *dwellinge ger.* B 1; C 1 dwellyng
B. 2.103   A *dwellynge* wiþ þe deuel and dampned be for euere
C. 6.115   Amonges alle manere men my *dwellyng* is som tyme,

dwelte > dwellen

E

ebrew n *Ebreu n.* C 1

C.19.4 Lo, here the lettre,' quod he, 'a latyn and [an] *ebrew*;

ech adj *ech pron. &> echone* A 16 eche (2) iche (14); B 61 ech (58) eche (3); C 51 eche (4) vcche (1) vch (43) vche (3)

A. 2.39 Þat *iche* feld nas ful of folk al aboute.
A. 3.52 Þat *iche* segge shal se I am sistir of зour hous.'
A. 5.96 I wolde þat *iche* wiзt were my knaue;
A. 5.230 Þat *iche* man shal haue his er I hennis wende,
A. 7.2 Þat miзte folewe vs *iche* fote [forto] we were þere.'
A. 7.102 *Eche* man on his maner made hymself to done,
A. 7.135 Inouз *iche* day at non, ac no more til on þe morewe
A. 7.231 Kynde wyt wolde þat *iche* wiзt wrouзte
A. 8.90 For I shal construe *iche* clause & kenne it þe on englissh.'
A.10.71 A[c] *iche* wiзt in þis world þat haþ wys vndirstonding
A.10.175 Outtake þe eiзte soulis, & of *iche* beste a couple
A.10.207 Þat *iche* man haue a make in [mariage] of wedlak
A.11.61 For now is *iche* boy bold, & he be riche,
A.11.123 *iche* wiзt be in wille his wyt þe to shewen;
A.11.250 Þat is, *iche* cristene [creature] be kynde to oþer,
A.11.257 *Eche* man for his misdede but mercy it make.'
B.Pr.51 To *ech* a tale þat þei tolde hire tonge was tempred to lye
B.Pr.122 Shopen lawe and leaute, *ech* [lif] to knowe his owene.
B.Pr.208 Forþi *ech* a wis wiзt I warne, wite wel his owene.'
B. 3.63 That [*ech*] segge shal [see] I am suster of youre house.'
B. 3.309 *Ech* man to pleye with a plow, Pykoise or spade,
B. 3.312 And dyngen vpon Dauid eche day til eue;
B. 5.86 *Ech* a word þat he warp was of a Neddres tonge;
B. 5.117 I wolde þat *ech* wight were my knaue.
B. 5.273 That þow hast maad *ech* man good I may þee noзt assoille:
B. 5.402 I am ocupied *eche* day, halyday and ooþer,
B. 5.458 That *ech* man shal haue his er I hennes wende;
B. 5.593 *Ech* piler is of penaunce, of preieres-to-Seyntes;
B. 6.2 That [myзte] folwen vs *ech* foot': þus þis folk hem mened.
B. 6.110 *Ech* man in his manere made hymself to doone,
B. 6.195 And *ech* a pouere man wel apaied to haue pesen for his hyre,
B. 6.247 Kynde wit wolde þat *ech* wiзt wroзte,
B. 7.108 For I [shal] construe *ech* clause and kenne it þee on englissh.'
B. 9.144 Excepte oonliche of *ech* kynde a couple
B.10.25 And þat þei ben lordes of *ech* a lond þat out of lawe libbeþ:
B.10.97 Elenge is þe halle, *ech* day in þe wike,
B.10.99 Now haþ *ech* riche a rule to eten by hymselue
B.10.171 That *ech* wight be in wille his wit þee to shewe.
B.10.246 For al is but oon god and *ech* is god hymselue:
B.10.272 I rede *ech* a blynd bosard do boote to hymselue,
B.10.310 And gret loue and likyng for *ech* [loweþ hym to] ooþer.
B.10.362 And after alle cristene creatures, in commune *ech* man ooþer;
B.10.376 *Ech* man for hi[s] mysded[e] but mercy it [make]."'
B.11.97 If hem likeþ and lest; *ech* a lawe it graunteþ,
B.11.181 [And] comaundeþ *ech* creature to conformen hym to louye
B.11.194 Youre festynge and youre faire зifte; *ech* frend quyteþ so ooþer.
B.11.209 Forþi loue we as leue [children shal], and *ech* man laughe of ooþer,
B.11.210 And of þat *ech* man may forbere amende þere it nedeþ,
B.11.241 That we sholde be lowe and loueliche, [and lele *ech* man to oþer],
B.11.326 Thorugh *ech* a creature kynde my creatour to louye.
B.11.391 *Ech* a lif wolde be laklees, leue þow noon oþer.
B.12.125 Lest cheste cha[fe] vs to choppe *ech* man oþer:
B.12.178 And þis conforteþ *ech* a clerk and coucreþ fro wanhope,
B.13.16 And how louynge he is to [*ech* lif] on londe and on watre–
B.13.68 Ac o word þei ouerhuppen at *ech* tyme þat þei preche
B.13.88 He shal haue a penaunce in his paunche and puffe at *ech* a worde,
B.13.344 For *ech* a maide þat he mette he made hire a signe
B.13.414 *Ech* day is halyday with hym or an heiз ferye,
B.14.271 So it [preueþ] by *ech* a persone þat possession forsakeþ
B.15.21 That *ech* a creature of his court welcomeþ me faire.'
B.16.138 *Eche* day after ooþer hir tyme þei awaiteden
B.16.183 That oon dooþ alle dooþ and *ech* dooþ bi his one.
B.17.106 And [may] *ech* man see and good mark take
B.17.270 *Ech* a riche, I rede, reward at hym take
B.18.417 Clippe we in couenaunt, and *ech* of vs [kisse] ooþer,
B.19.160 In *ech* a compaignie þer she cam, Christus resurgens.
B.19.227 And gaf *ech* man a grace to gide wiþ hymseluen

B.19.250 And alle he lered to be lele, and *ech* a craft loue ooþer,
B.19.394 [Or] *ech* man forзyue ooþer, and þat wole þe Paternoster:
B.19.416 The comune clamat cotidie, *ech* a man til ooþer,
B.19.457 *Ech* man subtileþ a sleiзte synne to hide
B.20.19 That he dronke at *ech* dych er he [deye for þurst].
B.20.56 In *ech* a contree þer he cam he kutte awey truþe
B.20.92 'Alarme! alarme!' quod þat lord, '*ech* lif kepe his owene!'
B.20.162 Oon Tomme two-tonge, atteynt at *ech* [a q]ueste.
B.20.258 Han Officers vnder hem, and *ech* of hem a certein.
B.20.263 Pylours and Pykeharneys, in *ech* a [parisshe] ycursed.
C. 2.175 And leten somne alle seggus in *vche* syde aboute,
C. 3.462 *Vche* man to pley with a plogh, a pikois oþer a spade,
C. 5.196 Of alle maner actions and *eche* man loue other.
C. 6.178 For *eche* mayde þer y mette y kutte awey a signe
C. 6.245 Y lene folk þat lese wole a lyppe [at] *vch* a noble
C. 6.312 That *eche* man shal haue his ar y hennes wende
C. 7.18 Y am occupied *vch* day, haliday and oþere,
C. 7.50 Til *eche* lyf hit lothed to loke þeron or smylle hit;
C. 7.241 *Vche* piler is of penaunc[e] and preyeres to seyntes;
C. 7.308 That myhte folowe vs *vch* fote for drede of mysturnynge.'
C. 8.117 *Vch* man in his manere made hymsulue to done
C. 9.116 To зeue *vch* a wyht wyt, welthe and his hele
C. 9.232 *Vcche* halyday to here holly þe seruise,
C. 9.282 For y can construe *vch* a word and kennen hit the an englische.'
C.10.232 Excepte onliche of *vch* kynde a payre
C.12.105 For *vch* frende fedeth other and fondeth hou beste to quite
C.12.106 Meles and manschipes, *vch* man oþere.
C.12.130 That we sholde be low and louelich and lele *vch* man til oþer
C.13.74 That oure lord loketh aftur of *vch* a lyf þat wynneth
C.13.92 Ther god is gateward hymsulf and *vch* a gome knoweth.
C.13.94 In þat a wilneth and wolde *vch* wyht as hymsulue.
C.13.100 *Vch* a parfi[t] prest to pouerte sholde drawe
C.13.133 To knowe by *vch* a creature kynde to louye.
C.13.196 '*Vch* a segge for hymsulue, salamon vs techeth:
C.13.209 In *vch* a lede wolde be lacles, leef thow non other.
C.13.243 As shame: ther he sheweth hym *vch* man shoneth his companye.
C.14.43 Forthy y conseile *vch* a creature clergie to honoure
C.14.68 Laste cheste chauf[e] vs to [c]hoppe *vch* man oþer.
C.14.118 And þat conforteth *vch* a clerk and keuereth fro wanhope,
C.15.19 And how louyng he is to *vch* lyf a londe and o watere
C.15.95 He shal haue a penaunce in his paunche and poffe at *vch* a worde
C.15.223 *Vch* a kyne creature þat on crist leueth.
C.16.111 So hit fareth by *vch* a persone þat possession forsaket
C.16.172 That *vch* a creature þat loueth crist welcometh me faire.'
C.16.321 Fiat-voluntas-tua festeth hym *vch* a daye.
C.19.251 *Vch* a riche y rede reward herof take
C.20.285 Cheke and cheyne we and *vch* a [c]hine stoppe
C.20.338 To lere men to [be] lele and *vch* man to louye oþer;
C.20.460 Cluppe we in couenaunt and *vch* of vs kusse oþere.'
C.21.160 In *vch* a companye þer he cam, christus resurgens.
C.21.227 And gaf *vch* man a grace to gye with hymsuluen
C.21.250 And al he lered to be lele, and *vch* a craft loue oþere,
C.21.394 Or *vch* man forзeue oþer, and þat wol þe paternost[er]:
C.21.416 The comu[n]e clamat cotidie, *vch* a man to oþer,
C.21.457 *Vch* man sotileth a sleythe synne to huyde
C.22.19 That he dronke at *vch* a dy[c]h ar he deye for furste.
C.22.56 In *vch* a Contrey ther he cam [he] kutte awey treuthe
C.22.92 'Alarme! alarme!' quod þat lord, '*vch* lyf kepe his owene!'
C.22.162 Oen Tomme two-tonge, ateynt at *vch* [a q]ueste.
C.22.258 Haen officerys vnder hem and *vch* of hem a certeyne.
C.22.263 Pilours and pikeharneys in *vch* a parsch acorsed.

echone pron *ech on pron.phrase* A 11 ichone; B 12 echone (11) ech_one (1); C 9 echone (3) vchon (1) vchone (5)

A. 1.17 And þerfore he hiзte þe erþe to helpe зow *ichone*
A. 1.49 "Cesar," þ[ei] seide, "we se wel *ichone*."
A. 1.91 For cristene & vncristene cleymeþ it *ichone*.
A. 2.103 For consience is of his counseil & knowiþ зow *ichone*,
A. 2.134 Þat somenours shulde be sadelit & serue hem *ichone*,
A. 3.20 Of here grete goodnesse, & [g]af hem *ichone*
A. 3.37 'Þeiз lerid & lewide hadde leiзe be þe *ichone*,
A. 3.80 'For my loue,' quaþ þat lady, 'loue hem *ichone*,

A. 3.249 For any mylionis of mone murdre hem *ichone*;
A. 3.265 And o cristene king kepe vs *ichone*.
A. 7.194 Treuþe tauȝte me ones to loue hem *ichone*
B. 1.17   And þerfore he hiȝte þe erþe to helpe yow *echone*
B. 1.51   "Cesar[i]s", þei seiden, "we seen wel *echone*."
B. 1.93   For cristen and vncristen cleymeþ it *echone*.
B. 2.139 [For] Conscience is of his counseil and knoweþ yow *echone*;
B. 2.170 That Somonours sholde be Sadeled and seruen hem *echone*,
B. 3.21   Of hire grete goodnesse, and gaf hem *echone*
B. 3.38   'Theiȝ [lered and lewed] hadde leyen by þee [*echone*],
B. 3.91   'For my loue', quod þat lady, 'loue hem *echone*,
B. 3.289 And oon cristene kyng kepen [vs *echone*].
B. 6.208 Treuþe tauȝte me ones to louen hem *ech one*,
B.11.63   As quasi modo geniti gentil men *echone*
B.14.81   [So] thei sonken into helle, þe Citees *echone*.
C. 1.89   For cristene and vncristene claymeth it *echone*.
C. 2.155 And Consience is of his consayl and knoweth ȝow *echone*];
C. 3.22   Of here grete goodnesse and gaf hem *vchone*
C. 3.442 And o cristene kyng kepe vs *echone*.
C. 6.122 Thus thei speke and dispute þat *vchon* dispiseth oþer.
C. 8.217 Treuthe tauhte me ones to louye hem *vchone*
C. 9.236 Vnder this obedience ar we *vchone*,
C.12.111 As quasi modo geniti gentel men *vchone*,
C.20.294 [With] crokes and kalketrappes [a]cloye we hem *vchone*.'

edifie v *edifien v.* B 2; C 3 edefien (1) edefye (1) edifien (1)
B.16.132 And in þre daies after *edifie* it newe,
B.18.43   *Edifie* it eft newe–here he stant þat seide it–
C. 9.204 Ac thise Ermytes þat *edifien* thus by the heye weye
C.18.160 And ar thre dayes aftur *edefye* hit newe.'
C.20.42   *Edefien* hit eft newe–here he stant þat saide hit–

edmond n prop *n.i.d.* B 1; C 1
B.15.223 *Edmond* and Edward, [eiþer] were kynges
C.16.348 *Edmond* and Edward, ayþer were seyntes,

edward n prop *n.i.d.* B 1; C 1
B.15.223 Edmond and *Edward*, [eiþer] were kynges
C.16.348 Edmond and *Edward*, ayþer were seyntes,

edwyted v *edwiten v.* B 1; C 1 Edwitede
B. 5.363 His wif [*edwyted*] hym þo [of wikkednesse and synne],
C. 6.421 His wyf and his inwit *Edwitede* hym of his synne;

eefte > eft; eer > er; eere > ere

eest n *est n.* A 1 Est; B 2 Eest (1) est (1); C 1 eest
A.Pr.13   Ac as I beheld into þe *Est* an heiȝ to þe sonne
B.Pr.13   [Ac] as I biheeld into þe *Eest*, an heiȝ to þe sonne,
B.18.118 Euene out of þe *Est* and westward she lokede,
C.20.121 Euene oute of þe *eest* and westward she thouhte,

eft adv *eft adv.* A 2; B 10; C 18 eefte (1) eft (7) efte (10)
A. 6.101 Happily an hundrit wynter er þou *eft* entre.
A.11.82   Þat euere *eft* wilneþ to wyte why [þat] god wolde
B. 3.348 And if ye seche Sapience *eft* fynde shul ye þat folweþ,
B. 5.615 Happily an hundred wynter er þow *eft* entre.
B.10.129 That euere [*eft*] wilneþ to wite why þat god wolde
B.14.97   That it neuere *eft* is sene ne soor, but semeþ a wounde yheeled.'
B.15.604 Moyses *eft* or Messie hir maistres deuyneþ.
B.17.114 And neuere *eft* greue gome þat gooþ þis ilke gate:
B.18.4   Til I weex wery of þe world and wilned *eft* to slepe
B.18.43   Edifie it *eft* newe–here he stant þat seide it–
B.18.316 *Eft* þe light bad vnlouke and Lucifer answerde
B.20.375 Conscience cryed *eft* [Clergie to helpe],
C. 3.332 And *efte* haue hit aȝeyne of hem þat don ylle.
C. 3.476 Batailes sholle neuere *eft* be ne man bere eg toel
C. 4.102 And *efte* the baldore be to bete myn hewes.
C. 7.267 Haplice an hundred wynter ar thow *eft* entre.
C.12.161 Crist acordeth *efte* herwith; clerkes wyteth þe sothe,
C.13.132 And in þe myrour of mydelerthe made him *efte* to loke,
C.14.23   Ac grace is a graes þerfore to don hem [growe *efte*];
C.15.144 Ȝef hym *eft* and eft, euere at his nede,
C.15.144 Ȝef hym eft and *eft*, euere at his nede,
C.17.146 And ay hopeth *eft* to be with here body at þe laste
C.18.24   And askede [e]*fte* of hym of what wode they were.
C.18.57   And askede *efte* tho where hit were all [of] o kynde.
C.18.127 That elde felde *efte* þe fruyt, or full to be rype.
C.20.4   Til y waxe wery of the world and wilnede *eefte* to slepe
C.20.42   Edefien hit *eft* newe–here he stant þat saide hit–
C.20.359 For *efte* þat lihte bade vnlouke [and lucifer answerede].
C.20.420 Shal neuere in helle *eft* come be he ones oute:
C.22.375 Consience cryede *efte* clergie [to] helpe

eftsoones adv *eftsones adv.* A 1 eftsones; B 3 eftsoone (1) eftsoones (2); C 2 eftsones (1) eftsones (1)
A. 5.247 And knowelechide his [coupe] to crist ȝet *eftsones*,
B. 5.473 And knoweliched his [coupe] to crist yet *eftsones*,
B. 6.170 And manaced [hym] and his men if þei mette *eftsoone*.
B.19.5   I fel *eftsoones* aslepe, and sodeynly me mette
C. 6.327 And knolechede [his coupe to Crist] ȝut *eftsones*,
C.21.5   Y ful *eftesones* aslepe and sodeynliche me mette

eg n *egge n.(2), egge tol n.* C 1
C. 3.476 Batailes sholle neuere eft be ne man bere *eg* toel

eggedest v *eggen v.(1)* A 2 eggide (1) eggiþ (1); B 2 egged (1) eggedest (1); C 1 eggede
A. 1.63   Adam & Eue he *eggide* to ille,
A.10.52   He *eggiþ* eiȝe siȝt & heryng to gode;
B. 1.65   Adam and Eue he *egged* to ille,
B.18.289 And *eggedest* hem to ete, Eue by hirselue,
C. 1.61   Adam and Eue he *eggede* to ylle,

egges n *egge n.(1)* B 3; C 1
B.11.352 Hidden and hileden hir *egges* ful derne
B.11.354 In Mareys and moores [manye] hidden hir *egges*]
B.13.63   Wombe cloutes and wilde brawen and *egges* yfryed wiþ grece.
C.13.163 Hudden and helede here *egges* dernely

eggi- > eggedest

egidie n prop *n.i.d.* B 3; C 1 Egide
B.15.272 Antony and *Egidie* and oþere holy fadres
B.15.276 Ac neiþer Antony ne *Egidie* ne heremyte þat tyme
B.15.279 Except þat *Egidie* after an hynde cride,
C.17.9   Excepte þat *Egide* a hynde oþerwhile

egipte n prop *Egipte n.* A 1 Egipt; B 1; C 1
A. 8.148 Þat Iosep was Iustice *Egipt* to kepe–
B. 7.171 That Ioseph was Iustice *Egipte* to loke;
C. 9.315 That Ioseph was Iustice *Egipte* to saue;

egre adj *egre adj.* B 1; C 1
B.13.81   And wisshed witterly, wiþ wille ful *egre*,
C.15.88   And wished witterly with will ful *egre*

egreliche adv *egreli adv.* B 2; C 1 egrelich
B.16.64   And *egreliche* he loked on me and þerfore I spared
B.19.378 *Egreliche* ernynge out of mennes eighen.
C.21.378 *Egrelich* ernynge oute [of] menne yes.

eye > eiȝe; eyer > heir; eighen > eiȝe; eighte > eiȝte

eighteþe num *eightethe ord. num.* B 1; C 1 eyȝte
B.14.313 The *eighteþe* is a lele labour and looþ to take moore
C.16.147 The *eyȝte* is a lel labour and loeth to take more

eiȝte num *eighte card. num.* A 1 eiȝte; B 2 eighte (1) eiȝte (1); C 1 eyhte
A.10.175 Outtake þe *eiȝte* soulis, & of iche beste a couple
B. 6.328 And a mayde haue þe maistrie, and multiplie by *eiȝte*,
B.20.343 I knew swich oon ones, noȝt *eighte* wynter [passed],
C.22.343 Y knewe such oen ones, nat *eyhte* wynter passed,

eyhte > eighteþe

eyleþ v *eilen v.* A 2 eileþ; B 3 eileþ (1) eyleþ (2); C 2 ayleth
A. 7.120 For we mowe no[þer] swynke ne swete, such seknesse vs *eileþ*'.
A. 7.241 'I wot wel,' quaþ hunger, 'what seknesse hem *eileþ*.
B. 6.128 For we may [neiþer] swynke ne swete, swich siknesse vs *eyleþ*.'
B. 6.657 'I woot wel', quod hunger, 'what siknesse yow *eyleþ*.
B.15.251 For whoso myȝte meete [wiþ] hym swiche maneres hym *eileþ*:
C. 8.134 We may nother swynke ne swete, suche sekenes vs *ayleth*;
C. 8.269 'Y wot wel,' quod hungur, 'what sekenesse ȝow *ayleth*.

eyr n *air n.(1)* A 2 eir; B 4; C 3 ayer (1) ayr (1) eir (1)
A. 1.114 Summe in *eir*, summe in erþe, summe in helle depe.
A.10.3   Of erþe & *eir* it is mad, medlit togideris;
B.Pr.128 And siþen in þe *Eyr* an heiȝ an Aungel of heuene
B. 1.125 Somme in *Eyr*, somme in erþe, somme in helle depe.
B. 9.3   Of erþe and *Eyr* [it is] maad, medled togideres,
B.14.43   The Corlew by kynde of þe *Eyr*, moost clennest flessh of briddes,
C. 1.127 Summe in erthe, summe in *ayr*, summe in helle depe.
C.10.130 Of erthe and *ayer* [hit is] maed, ymedled togyderes,
C.15.219 Lette this luythere [*eir*] and leche þe sike–

eires > heir

eiþer pron *either pron.* A 2 eiþer; B 19 eiþer (13) eyþer (4) eiþeres (2); C 17 ayther (5) aytheres (2) ayþer (6) either (3) eyþer (1)
A. 8.126 Þe prest & perkyn aposid *eiþer* oþer,
A.10.179 And al for se[þ] & his sister children spouside *eiþer* oþer,
B. 5.149 Thus þei speken of spiritualte þat *eiþer* despiseþ ooþer
B. 5.164 And *eiþer* hit[t]e ooþer vnder þe cheke.

B. 5.165	Hadde þei had knyues, by crist! *eiþer* hadde kild ooþer.
B. 7.144	The preest and Perkyn [a]pposeden *eiþer* ooþer,
B. 9.88	*Eyþer* of hem helpeþ ooþer of þat þat h[y]m nedeþ,
B.11.179	Loue hir *eyþer* ooþer, and lene hem as hemselue.
B.11.252	And hastily god answerde, and *eiþeres* wille [lowed],
B.11.316	For hir *eiþer* is endited, and that [of] 'Ignorancia
B.13.176	Profitable to *eiþer* peple;' and putte þe table fro hym,
B.13.347	Til *eiþeres* wille wexeþ kene and to þe werke yeden,
B.14.224	And *eiþer* hateþ ooþer in alle maner werkes.
B.15.37	Austyn and Ysodorus, *eiþer* of hem boþe
B.15.223	Edmond and Edward, [*eiþer*] were kynges
B.16.207	And *eiþer* is oþeres ioye in þre sondry persones,
B.17.138	And if Conscience carpe þerayein, or kynde wit *eyþer*,
B.17.310	And *eyþer* haue equyte, as holy writ telleþ:
B.18.74	And [hir] armes after of *eiþer* of þo þeues.
B.18.122	*Eiþer* asked ooþer of þis grete wonder,
B.20.353	And acorde wiþ Conscience and kisse hir *eiþer* ooþer.'
C. 3.338	And *ayther* is otheres helpe; of hem cometh retribucoun
C. 6.149	Tyl *ayþer* clepede oþer "hore!" and o[f] with the clothes
C. 6.188	Exited *either* oþer til oure olde synne;
C.10.281	And [wedewares and wedewes] weddeth *ayþer* oþer;
C.12.139	And here *aytheres* wille [hasteliche god assoilede
C.12.140	And *aytheres* werkes and wille] riht wel alowede
C.16.65	And *ayther* hateth oþer and may nat wone togyderes.
C.16.181	And *ayther* is otheres hete and also of o will;
C.16.199	Austyn and ysodorus, *either* of hem bothe
C.16.348	Edmond and Edward, *ayþer* were seyntes,
C.17.135	And *ayther* loueth and byleueth in o [lord] almyhty.
C.17.172	In *ayþer* of his eres prieueliche he hadde
C.19.290	That *eyþer* haue equitee, as holy writ witnesseth:
C.20.76	And here arme[s] aftur of *e[ither]* of tho theues.
C.20.125	*Ayþer* asked oþer of this grete Wonder,
C.20.175	Whenne pees in pacience yclothed aproched her *ayþer* oþer
C.22.353	And acorde with Consience and kusse here *ayther* oþer.'

eiȝe n1 *eie n.(1)* A 12 eiȝe (2) eiȝen (9) eye (1); B 36 eighen (6) eiȝe (4)
     eiȝen (20) eiȝes (6); C 27 eye (1) eyes (5) eyus (1) yes (20)

A.Pr.71	He bunchi[de] hem wiþ his breuet & bleri[de] here *eiȝe[*n]
A. 5.44	And made wil to wepe watir wiþ his *eiȝen*.
A. 5.90	[Awey] fro þe auter myn *eiȝe* I turne
A. 5.109	He was [betil]browid & babirlippid wiþ two bleride *eiȝen*.
A. 5.197	Whanne he drouȝ to þe dore þanne dymmede hise *eiȝen*;
A. 5.203	Þanne wakide he of his wynkyng & wypide his *eiȝen*;
A. 5.214	Til Vigilate [þe veil] fet watir [at] his *eiȝen*,
A. 5.246	Wel I woot he wep faste watir wiþ his *eiȝen*,
A. 7.160	And wrong hym so be þe wombe þat al watride his *eiȝen*,
A.10.52	He eggiþ *eiȝe* siȝt & heryng to gode;
A.11.81	I wolde his *eiȝen* wern in his ars & his hele aftir
A.12.96	Þou shalt be lauȝth into lyȝth with loking of an *eye*
B.Pr.74	He bonched hem with his breuet and blered hire *eiȝen*
B. 2.90	As in werkes and in wordes and waityn[g] with *eiȝes*
B. 5.61	And [made] wille to wepe water wiþ hise *eiȝen*.
B. 5.110	Awey fro þe Auter turne I myne *eiȝen*
B. 5.135	Now awakeþ Wraþe wiþ two white *eiȝen*,
B. 5.190	He was bitelbrowed and baberlipped wiþ two blered *eiȝen*;
B. 5.349	A[c] whan he drouȝ to þe dore þanne dymmed hise *eiȝen*;
B. 5.361	Thanne waked he of his wynkyng and wiped hise *eiȝen*;
B. 5.385	Thanne cam Sleuþe al bislabered wiþ two slymy *eiȝen*.
B. 5.442	Til vigilate þe veille fette water at hise *eiȝen*
B. 5.472	Wel I woot he wepte faste water wiþ hise *eiȝen*,
B. 6.175	And wrong hym so be þe wombe þat [al watrede his *eiȝen*].
B.10.128	I wolde his *eiȝe* were in his ers and his [hele] after,
B.10.269	Why meuestow þi mood for a mote in þi broþeres *eiȝe*,
B.10.282	Lewed men may likne yow þus, þat þe beem liþ in youre *eiȝen*,
B.11.14	And Coueitise of *eiȝes* [þat ooþer was ycalled].
B.11.32	Coueitise of *eiȝe*, þat euere þow hir knewe–
B.11.40	Concupiscencia carnis ne Coueitise of *eiȝes*
B.11.46	Coueitise of *eiȝes* conforted me anoon after
B.11.50	Coueitise of *eiȝes* com ofter in mynde
B.11.52	Coueitise of *eiȝes* [ofte me conforted];
B.11.188	To knowen vs by oure kynde herte and castynge of oure *eiȝen*,
B.11.410	And as I caste vp myne *eiȝen* oon loked on me.
B.12.99	For as a man may noȝt see þat mysseþ hise *eiȝen*,
B.13.343	Wiþ likynge of lecherie as by lokynge of his *eiȝe*.
B.14.327	And wepte water wiþ hise *eighen* and weyled þe tyme
B.15.192	And wiþ warm water at hise *eiȝen* wasshen hem after.
B.16.45	And feccheþ awey my floures som tyme afore boþe myne *eighen*,
B.16.116	And wepte water wiþ hise *eiȝen*; þer sei3en it manye.
B.16.167	And I awaked þerwiþ and wiped myne *eiȝen*
B.17.329	For smoke and smolder [smerteþ] hise *eighen*
B.17.347	Ac þe smoke and þe smolder þat smyt in oure *eighen*,
B.18.59	The lord of lif and of liȝt þo leide hise togideres.
B.18.86	The blood sprong doun by þe spere and vnspered [his] *eiȝen*.
B.18.230	Thanne was þer a wiȝt wiþ two brode *eiȝen*;

B.19.378	Egreliche ernynge out of mennes *eighen*.
C.Pr.72	A bounchede hem with his b[reuet] and blered here *yes*
C. 2.97	As in werkes and in wordes and waytyng[e] of *yes*,
C. 6.2	And made will to wepe water with his *eyes*
C. 6.103	Thenne awakede wrathe with two w[hy]te *eyes*
C. 6.177	In word, in wedes, in waytynge of *eyes*.
C. 6.198	He was bitelbrowed and baburlippid with two blered *eyes*
C. 6.326	Wel y woet a wepte faste water with his *yes*
C. 6.407	And when he drow to the dore thenne dymmede his *yes*;
C. 7.1	Thenne cam sleuthe al byslobered with two slim[y] *yes*.
C. 7.56	Til vigilate the veile fette water at his *eyus*
C. 8.172	And wronge hym so by þe wombe þat al watrede his *yes*;
C.11.173	And coueytise-of-*yes* ycalde was þat oþer.
C.11.191	Coueytse-of-*yes* þat euere thow here knewe–
C.11.307	Concupiscencia carnis [ne coueytise-of-*yes*]
C.12.3	Coueytse-of-*yes* conforted me [anon] aftur and saide,
C.14.44	For as a man may nat se þat misseth his *yes*,
C.16.335	And with warm water of his *yes* woketh h[em] til [t]he[y] white:
C.18.49	And feccheth away þe fruyt som tyme byfore bothe myn *yes*.
C.18.146	And wepte watur with [his] *yes*; the why weten fewe.
C.19.309	For smoke & smolder] smerteth his [*yes*]
C.19.327	Ac þe smoke and þe smolder þat smyt in oure *yes*,
C.20.50	'Aue, raby,' quod þat ribaud, and redes shotte vp to his *yes*.
C.20.59	The lord of lyf and of liht tho leyde his *eyes* togederes.
C.20.88	The bloed sprang down by the spere and vnspered [his] *yes*.
C.20.233	Thenne wa[s] ther a wihte with two brode *yes*
C.20.383	And hoso hit out a mannes *eye* or elles his foreteth
C.21.378	Egrelich ernynge oute [of] menne *yes*.

eiȝe n2 *eie n(2)* B 1; C 1 eye

B.11.44	'Allas, *eiȝe*!' quod Elde and holynesse boþe,
C.12.1	'Allas, *eye*!' quod elde and holynesse bothe,

ek adv&conj *ek adv. and conj.* A 20; B 15; C 1 eke

A. 1.1	What þe mounteyne [be]meniþ, & *ek* þe [m]erke dale,
A. 1.2	And *ek* þe feld ful of folk I shal ȝow faire shewe.
A. 1.79	And *ek* kenne me kyndely on crist to beleue,
A. 1.89	And *ek* lyk to oure lord be seint lukis wordis.
A. 1.137	And *ek* þe plante of pes; preche it in þin harpe
A. 1.154	And *ek* as chast as a child þat in chirche wepiþ,
A. 1.166	Vnkynde to here kyn & *ek* to alle cristene,
A. 1.179	And *ek* þe graiþ gate þat goþ into heuene.
A. 2.198	And *ek* wep & wrang whan heo was atachid.
A. 3.40	And *ek* be þi baudekyn, & bere wel þin arnede
A. 3.169	And *ek* grepe my gold & gyue it where þe likiþ.
A. 3.191	And *ek* king of þat kiþ his kyn for to helpe,
A. 7.28	A[nd] *ek* laboure for þi loue al my lif tyme,
A. 7.254	And *ek* his cloke [of] calabre & þe knoppis of gold,
A. 7.271	And *ek* a cow & a calf, & a carte mare
A. 8.71	And [*ek*] giliþ þe gyuere ageyns his wille.
A.10.57	And *ek* wantoun & wilde, wiþoute any resoun.
A.10.59	And *ek* in sottis þou miȝt se, þat sitten at þe nale.
A.11.64	And [*ek*] defame þe fadir þat vs alle made,
A.11.118	And *ek* þe longe launde þat leccherie hatte,
B. 1.81	And [*ek*] kenne me kyndely on crist to bileue,
B. 1.91	And [*ek*] ylik to oure lord by Seint Lukes wordes.
B. 1.152	And [*ek*] þe pl[ante] of pees, moost precious of vertues.
B. 2.93	Glotonye he [gyueþ] hem *ek* and grete oþes togidere,
B. 2.239	And *ek* wepte and wrong whan she was attached.
B. 3.41	And [*ek*] be þi [baudekyn] and bere wel þ[yn erende]
B. 3.182	And [*ek*] griped my gold [and] gyue it where þee liked.
B. 3.204	And [*ek*] kyng of þat kiþ his kyn for to helpe,
B. 6.26	And [*ek*] labour[e] for þi loue al my lyf tyme,
B. 6.287	And *ek* a cow and a calf, and a cart mare
B. 7.69	And [*ek* g]ileþ þe gyuere ageynes his wille.
B.10.471	That inparfitly here knewe and *ek* lyuede.
B.13.164	[And *ek*, haue god my soule, and þow wilt it craue
B.15.325	And ben founded and feffed *ek* to bidde for oþere.
B.20.274	And lerne logyk and lawe and *ek* contemplacion,
C.22.274	And lerne logyk and lawe and *eke* contemplacioun

elde n *elde n.* A 1; B 19; C 22

A. 3.89	To haue ȝeftis [or ȝerisȝiuys] in ȝouþe or in *elde*.
B. 5.192	Wel sidder þan his chyn; þei chyueled for *elde*;
B.11.27	Thanne was þer oon þat hiȝte *Elde*, þat heuy was of chere;
B.11.35	'Folwe forþ þat Fortune wole; þow hast wel fer til *Elde*.
B.11.44	'Allas, eiȝe!' quod *Elde* and holynesse boþe,
B.11.60	Til I for[yede] youþe and yarn into *Elde*.
B.12.8	In þyn olde *elde*, þat yuele kan suffre
B.13.6	And how þat *Elde* manaced me, myȝte we euere mete;
B.13.353	And of hir harlotrye and horedom in hir *elde* tellen.
B.20.95	*Elde* þe hoore; [he] was in þe vauntwarde
B.20.154	Shal do þee noȝt drede, neiþer deeþ ne *elde*,
B.20.165	For care Conscience þo cryde vpon *Elde*

B.20.167 And *Elde* hente good hope and hastiliche he shifte hym
B.20.173 Lyf leeued þat lechecraft lette sholde *Elde*
B.20.175 And *Elde* auntred hym on lyf, and at þe laste he hitte
B.20.179 May noȝt a myte auaille to med[l]e ayein *Elde*.'
B.20.183 And *Elde* after [hym]; and ouer myn heed yede
B.20.186 'Sire yuele ytauȝt *Elde*!' quod I, 'vnhende go wiþ þe!
B.20.198 So *Elde* and [heo] hadden it forbeten.
B.20.202 Lo! *Elde* þe hoore haþ me biseye.
C. 6.200 Wel syddore then his chyn, ycheueled for *elde*,
C.10.265 For riche or yrented wel, thouh he be reueled for *elde*
C.11.186 Thenne was [there] oen þat hihte *Elde* þat heuy was of chere;
C.11.194 'Folowe forth þat fortune wole; þou hast [wel] fer to *elde*.
C.12.1 'Allas, eye!' quod *elde* and holynesse bothe,
C.12.12 Til y forȝet ȝouthe and ȝorn into *elde*.
C.15.6 And how *elde* man[a]ced me, so myhte happe
C.18.105 And anoon he hihte *Elde* an hy for to clymbe
C.18.107 And *Elde* clemp to þe c[r]opward; thenne comsed hit to crye.
C.18.110 For euere as *Elde* hadde eny down, þe deuel was redy
C.18.127 That *elde* felde efte þe fruyt, or full to be rype.
C.22.95 *Elde* þe hore; he was in þe Vawwarde
C.22.154 Shal do the nat drede, noþer deth ne *elde*,
C.22.165 For care Consience tho cryede vpon *elde*
C.22.167 And *elde* hente gode hope and hastiliche [he] sh[ifte] hym
C.22.173 Lyf leuede þat lechecraft lette sholde *Elde*
C.22.175 And *Elde* auntered hym on lyf and at þe laste he hitte
C.22.179 May nat a myte avayle to medlen aȝen *Elde*.'
C.22.183 And *Elde* aftur hym; and ouer myn heued ȝede
C.22.186 'Syre euele yt[a]uȝte *Elde*,' quod y, 'vnhende go with the!
C.22.198 So *Elde* and hee hit hadde forbete.
C.22.202 Lo! *Elde* þe hore hath me byseye;

elder *adj old adj.* B 1; C 1 eldre
B.11.13 Concupiscencia carnis men called þe *elder* mayde
C.11.172 Concupiscencia carnis men calde þ[e] *eldre* maide

eldir > eller

eldres *n eldre n.* A 1 eldren; B 1; C 2
A. 3.242 Shulde diȝe for a dede þat don hadde here *eldren*
B. 3.263 Sholden deye for a dede þat doon hadde hire *eldres*.
C. 3.416 Sholde deye der[f]ly for dedes of here *eldres*.
C. 9.215 As by þe engelisch of oure *eldres* of olde mennes techynge

eleccion *n eleccioun n.* B 1; C 2 eleccioun (1) eleccoun (1)
B.Pr.110 For in loue and lettrure þe *eleccion* bilongeþ;
C.Pr.137 For in loue and lettrure lith þe grete *eleccoun*.
C. 6.136 For he hadde childe in the chapun co[t]e; he worth chalenged at þe *eleccioun*."

element *n element n.* B 2 element (1) elementȝ (1); C 2 elementis
B.15.371 Of þat was calculed of þe *element* þe contrarie þei fynde.
B.18.237 And alle þe *elementȝ*', quod þe book, 'herof beren witnesse.
C. 1.17 Wherfore he hette þe *elementis* to helpe ȝow alle tymes
C.20.246 And all þe *elementis*,' quod þe boek, 'hereof bereth witnesse.

elenge *adj elenge adj.* B 3; C 2 elyng (1) elynge (1)
B.Pr.194 Ther þe cat is a kitoun þe court is ful *elenge*;
B.10.97 *Elenge* is þe halle, ech day in þe wike,
B.20.2 Heuy chered I yede and *elenge* in herte.
C.Pr.207 Ther þe Cat [is] a kytoun þe Court is ful *elynge*.
C.22.2 Heuy chered y ȝede and [*e*]*lyng* in herte.

elengliche *adv elengli adv.* B 2 elengely (1) elengliche (1); C 1 elyngly
B.12.44 Alisaundre þat al wan, *elengliche* ended.
B.20.39 And woneden [wel *elengely*] and wolde noȝt be riche.
C.22.39 And woneden wel *elyngly* and wolden nat be riche.

eleue(- > elleuene

ely *n prop n.i.d.* B 1
B.10.288 Archa dei myshapped and *Ely* brak his nekke.

elyes *n prop n.i.d.* B 1; C 1 Elies
B.14.66 And in *Elyes* tyme heuene was yclosed
C.15.265 And in *Elies* tyme heuene was yclosed

elyng(e > elenge; elyngly > elengliche

eller *n eller n* A 1 Eldir; B 2 Eller (1) Ellere (1); C 1 hellerne
A. 1.66 And siþen on an *Eldir* hongide him aftir.
B. 1.68 And siþen on an *Eller* hanged hym [after].
B. 9.152 Impe on an *Ellere*, and if þyn appul be swete
C. 1.64 And afterward anhengede hym hey vppon an *hellerne*.

elles(- > ellis(-

elleuene *num elleven card. num.* A 4 elleuene (2) enleuene (2); B 5; C 6 eleue (1) eleuene (3) enleuene (2)
A. 2.190 And wiþheld him half [a] ȝer & *elleuene* dayes.

A. 3.168 Þou hast hongid on myn half *enleuene* tymes,
A. 5.141 Sheo haþ yholde huxterie *elleuene* wynter.
A. 8.144 And þe *enleuene* sterris ha[i]lsiden hym alle.
B. 2.231 And [wiþ]helden hym an half yeer and *elleuene* dayes.
B. 3.181 Thow hast hanged on myn half *elleuene* tymes,
B. 5.225 She haþ holden hukkerye [*elleuene* wynter].
B. 7.166 And þe *elleuene* sterres hailsed hym alle.
B.15.438 *Elleuene* holy men al þe world tornede
C. 2.241 And [wiþ]helden hym [a] half ȝere and *eleue* dayes.
C. 3.227 Thow hast hanged on my half *enleuene* tymes,
C. 6.233 [He] ha[th] holde hokkerye this *eleuene* wynter.'
C. 9.310 And the *eleuene* s[t]erres haylsede hym alle;
C. 9.316 His *eleuene* bretherne hym for nede souhte
C.12.175 Aristotel, Ennedy, *enleuene* hundred,

ellis *adj elles adj.* A 11; B 20; C 12 elles
A. 1.108 To be buxum at his bidding; he bad hem nouȝt *ellis*.
A. 1.151 For þe same mesour ȝe mete, amys oþer *ellis*,
A. 3.59 Who is curteis or kynde or coueitous, or *ellis*.
A. 3.101 'ȝa lord,' quaþ þat lady, 'lord forbede *ellis*;
A. 3.269 Leaute shal do hym lawe [and no] lif *ellis*.
A. 5.15 Was apertly for pride & for no poynt *ellis*.
A. 6.103 And geten it aȝen þoruȝ grace & þoruȝ no gift *ellis*.
A. 8.160 And so I leue lelly, lord forbede *ellis*,
A.10.65 For no werk þat þei werche, wykkide oþer *ellis*.
A.10.208 And [werche] on his wyf & on no womman *ellis*.
A.10.211 Vngracious to gete loue or any good *ellis*.
B. 1.110 To be buxum at his biddyng, he bad hem nouȝt *ellis*.
B. 1.177 For þe same mesur[e] þat ye mete, amys ouþer *ellis*,
B. 3.112 'Ye, lord', quod þat lady, 'lord forbede *ellis*!
B. 3.294 Leaute shal don hym lawe and no lif *ellis*.
B. 5.15 Was pertliche for pride and for no point *ellis*.
B. 5.584 In-[no]-manere-*ellis*-noȝt-for-no-mannes-biddyng.
B. 5.617 And [gete it ayein þoruȝ] grace [ac þoruȝ no gifte *ellis*].
B. 7.86 He haþ ynouȝ þat haþ breed ynouȝ, þouȝ he haue noȝt *ellis*:
B. 7.182 And so I leue leelly, lor[d] forb[e]de *ellis*,
B.10.407 Was neuere wrighte saued þat wroȝte þeron, ne ooþer werkman *ellis*,
B.11.216 For whateuere clerkes carpe of cristendom or *ellis*,
B.12.226 Ac kynde knoweþ þe cause hymself, no creature *ellis*.
B.12.235 Kynde knoweþ whi he dide so, ac no clerk *ellis*.
B.13.363 And if my Neghebore hadde a[n] hyne or any beest *ellis*
B.14.256 That god is his grettest help and no gome *ellis*,
B.15.6 Lordes or ladies or any lif *ellis*,
B.15.580 Arn ferme as in þe feiþ, goddes forbode *ellis*,
B.16.143 That euere he his Saueour solde for siluer or *ellis*.'
B.18.352 To recouere hem þoruȝ raunsoun and by no reson *ellis*,
C. 1.173 For þe same mesure þat ȝe meteth, amis other *elles*,
C. 3.292 A desert for som doynge, derne oþer *elles*.
C. 3.447 Lewete shal do hym lawe and no lyf *elles*.
C. 5.117 Was pertliche for pruyde and for no poynt *elles*.
C. 6.262 And yf my neyhebore hadde an hyne or eny beste *elles*
C. 7.231 In-none-manere-*elles*-nat-for-no-mannes-preeyre.
C. 7.269 And geten hit agayne thorw grace Ac thorw no gifte *elles*.
C. 9.198 Summe hadde lyflode of h[ere] lynage and of no lyf *elles*
C. 9.328 And so y leue lely–lord forbede *elles*–
C.13.155 As in derne dedes, bothe drynkyng and *elles*.
C.16.96 That god is his gretteste helpe and no gome *elles*
C.17.61 Or ar prestes or pardoners or eny peple *elles*

ellis *adv elles adv.* A 9 ellis (8) ellys (1); B 19; C 27 elles
A. 1.51 Et que sunt dei deo oþer *ellis* ȝe don ille."
A. 3.102 [But I be holly at ȝour heste honge me *ellys*].'
A. 7.215 'ȝe, I hote þe,' quaþ hungir, 'oþer *ellis* þe bible leiȝeþ.
A. 7.296 But he be heiȝliche hirid *ellis* wile he chide,
A. 9.100 And oþere wise & *ellis* nouȝt but as þei þre assent[e].'
A. 9.106 *Ellis* wot no man þat now is o lyue.'
A.10.177 *Ellis* shal alle diȝen & to helle wenden."
A.11.260 For howso I werche in þis world, [wrong] oþer *ellis*,
A.11.263 Or *ellis* [vn]writen as witnessiþ þe gospel:
B.Pr.91 Liggen at Londoun in Lenten and *ellis*.
B. 1.53 Et que sunt dei deo or *ellis* ye don ille."
B. 3.113 But I be holly at youre heste hange me [*ellis*].'
B. 5.151 Or *ellis* al riche and ryden; I, wraþe, reste neuere
B. 5.286 But if it were wiþ þi tonge or *ellis* wiþ þi hondes.
B. 5.386 'I moste sitte [to be shryuen] or *ellis* sholde I nappe;
B. 6.182 Or *ellis* benes [and] bren ybaken togideres.'
B. 6.231 'Ye I [h]ote þee', quod hunger, 'or *ellis* þe bible lieþ.
B. 6.312 But he be heiȝliche hyred *ellis* wole he chide,
B. 8.110 And ooþer wise [and *ellis* noȝt] but as þei þre assent[e].'
B. 8.116 *Ellis* [n]oot [no man] þat now is alyue.'
B.10.382 Or *ellis* vnwriten for wikkednesse as holy writ witnesseþ:
B.10.440 Or *ellis* for his yuel wille and enuye of herte,

B.14.196 *Ellis* is al on ydel, al þat euere [we diden],
B.14.199 *Ellis* is al oure labour lost–lo, how men writeþ
B.15.289 Til he foundede freres of Austynes ordre, [or *ellis* freres lyen].
B.19.121 That he þoruȝ grace was gete and of no gome *ellis*.
B.19.189 To bynde and vnbynde boþe here and *elli[s]*,
B.19.461 Al þat myn Auditour or *ellis* my Styward
C.Pr.89 Leyen [at] Londoun in lenton and *elles*.
C. 1.49 Et que sunt dei deo or [*elles*] ȝe don ylle."
C. 3.94 Here on this erthe or *elles* in helle,
C. 3.150 But y be holly at thyn heste; lat hange me *elles*.'
C. 3.252 To helpe heyliche alle his oste or *elles* graunte
C. 3.299 Y halde hym ouer hardy or *elles* nat trewe
C. 7.2 'Y moste sitte to be shryue or *elles* sholde y nappe;
C. 7.75 But harlotrie and horedom or *elles* of som wynnynge;
C. 8.66 And alle þat helpen me [to] erye or *elles* to wedy
C. 8.237 'ȝe, y bihote the,' quod hunger, 'or *elles* þe bible lyeth.'
C. 8.334 But he be heyliche yhuyred *elles* wol he chy[d]e;
C. 9.99 But they be blynde or tobroke or *elles* be syke,
C. 9.212 Or oen of som ordre or *elles* a profete.
C.10.106 Bute oþerwise ne *elles* nat but as they thre assent[e].'
C.10.112 *Elles* knowe y noen þat can in none kynneryche.'
C.13.48 Oþer his hatt or his hoed or *elles* his gloues
C.15.296 Other here or elliswher, *elles* hit were reuthe;
C.16.37 *Elles* is al an ydel al oure lyuynge here,
C.16.40 *Elles* is alle oure labour loest–loo how men writeth
C.17.11 *Elles* foules fedde hem in frythes þer they wonede,
C.17.16 For he ordeyned þat ordre or *elles* þey gabben.
C.19.151 Vnfolden or folden, a fuste wyse or *elles*,
C.19.263 Or *elles* [to] a taper to reuerense with the trinite
C.20.383 And hoso hit out a mannes eye or *elles* his foreteth
C.21.121 That he thorw grace was gete and of no gome *elles*.
C.21.189 To bynde and vnbynde bothe here and *elles*,
C.21.461 Al þat myn Auditour or *elles* my styward

elliswhere adv *elleswher adv.* A 1; B 4; C 4 elleswher (1) ellesswhere (2)
    elliswher (1)
A. 9.21 He is oþerwhile *elliswhere* to wisse þe peple.'
B.Pr.164 And ouþer while þei arn *elliswhere*, as I here telle.
B. 8.25 He is ouþerwhile *elliswhere* to wisse þe peple.'
B.14.120 Ouþer here or *elliswhere*, kynde wolde it neuere:
B.17.200 Neiþer here ne *elliswhere*, as I herde telle:
C. 3.235 Bothe here and *elleswhere*, in alle kyne londes.
C.10.29 He is otherwhile *elleswher* to wisse þe peple.'
C.15.296 Other here or *elliswher*, elles hit were reuthe;
C.19.166 Noþer here ne *elleswhere*, as y herde telle:

emaus n prop *n.i.d.* B 1; C 1 Emaux
B.11.234 Witnesse in þe Pask wyke, whan he yede to *Emaus*;
C.12.123 Witnesse in þe paske woke when he ȝede to *Emaux*:

embaumed v *embaumem v.* B 2 embaumed (1) enbawmed (1); C 3
    enbaumed
B.11.293 Or þe bisshop þat blessed yow [and *embaumed* youre fyngres].
B.17.73 *Enbawmed* hym and bond his heed and in his [barm] hym leide,
C.13.107 Or þe bischop þat blessed ȝow and *enbaumed* ȝoure fyngeres.
C.19.72 *Enbaumed* hym and boend his heued and on bayard hym sette
C.19.88 And with þe bloed of þat barn *enbaumed* and ybaptised.

emcristen(e > euencristen; emforth > euenforþ

emme n prop *n.i.d. &> French* B 1
B.13.339 To þe Soutere of Southwerk or of Shordych dame *Emme*;

emperesse n *emperesse n.* B 1
B.13.165 There nys neiþer emperour ne *emperesse*, erl ne baroun,

emperour n *emperour n.* A 1 Emperours; B 4 emperour (3) emperours
    (1); C 2 Emperour (1) Emperours (1)
A. 3.200 *Emperours* & Erlis & alle maner lordis
B. 3.213 *Emperours* and Erles and alle manere lordes
B.11.154 Lo! ye lordes, what leautee dide by an *Emperour* of Rome
B.13.165 There nys neiþer *emperour* ne emperesse, erl ne baroun,
B.19.427 *Emperour* of al þe world, þat alle men were cristene.
C. 3.269 *Emperours* and Erles and alle manere lordes
C.21.427 *Emperour* of al þe world, þat all men were cristene.

enba- > embaumed

enblaunched ptp *emblaunchen v.* B 1; C 1
B.15.115 Ye aren *enblaunched* wiþ bele paroles and wiþ [bele cloþes]
C.16.270 That ben *enblaunched* with bele paroles and with bele clothes

enchaunten v *enchaunten v.* B 3 enchaunted (2) enchauntede (1); C 4
    enchaunted (2) enchauntede (1) enchaunten (1)
B. 2.42 Fauel þoruȝ his faire speche haþ þis folk *enchaunted*,
B.15.405 Menynge as after mete; þus Makometh hire *enchauntede*,
B.20.378 The frere wiþ his phisyk þis folk haþ *enchaunted*,

C. 2.45 Fauel thorw his flaterynge speche hath mede foule *enchaunted*,
C.17.176 Menyng as aftur mete; thus macumeth here *enchauntede*,
C.17.286 And *enchaunten* hem to charite on holy churche to bileue.
C.22.378 The frere with his fisyk this folk hath *enchaunted*

enchesoun n *enchesoun n.* C 1
C. 6.40 Be holden for holy and honoured by þat *enchesoun*;

enclosed ptp *enclosen v.* A 1 enclosid; B 1
A.10.42 Inwit & alle wyttes *enclosid* ben þerinne,
B. 9.54 Inwit and alle wittes [*en*]closed ben þerInne,

encombre v *encombren v.* B 1; C 1
B.19.228 That ydelnesse *encombre* hym noȝt, enuye ne pride:
C.21.228 That ydelnesse *encombre* h[y]m nat, enuye ne pryde:

encountre prep *encountre prep.* C 1
C.18.238 Lo! treys *encountre* treys,' quod he, 'in godhede and in manhede.'

encreesse v *encresen v.* B 1
B.11.399 Euery creature in his kynde *encreesse* [he bad]

endaunted v *endaunten v.* C 1
C.17.171 He *endaunted* a douue and day and nyhte here fedde;

ende n *ende n.(1)* A 12; B 32; C 39
A. 1.95 Til treuþe hadde termined here trespas to þe *ende*.
A. 1.116 For pride þat he put out his peyne haþ non *ende*.
A. 2.69 ȝeldinge for þis þing at o ȝeris *ende*
A. 3.150 Lawe is so lordlich & loþ to make *ende*,
A. 3.227 And þerof sei[þ] þe sauter in a salmis *ende*
A. 3.259 An aunter it [noiȝide me non] *ende* wile I make.
A. 5.190 And bleuȝ þe rounde ryuet at þe riggebones *ende*
A. 7.42 For þou shalt ȝelde it aȝen at one ȝeris *ende*
A. 9.87 Is hokid at þat on *ende* to holde men in good lif.
A.10.145 In tene & trauaille to here lyues *ende*.
A.11.227 Helpiþ nouȝt to heuene[ward] at one ȝeris *ende*,
A.12.109 And for he medleþ of makyng he made þis *ende*.
B. 1.97 Til treuþe hadde ytermyned hire trespas to þe *ende*.
B. 1.127 For pride þat he putte out his peyne haþ noon *ende*.
B. 2.101 For he leueþ be lost, þis is [his] laste *ende*.
B. 2.105 Yeldynge for þis þyng at one [yeres *ende*]
B. 3.161 Lawe is so lordlich and looþ to maken *ende*;
B. 3.248 And þerof seiþ þe Sauter in a Salmes *ende*
B. 3.281 On auenture it noyed m[e] noon *ende* wol I make,
B. 3.340 For þat lyne was no lenger at þe leues *ende*.
B. 5.236 And I kan no frenssh in feiþ but of þe ferþest *ende* of Northfolk.'
B. 5.342 And blew [þe] rounde ruwet at [þe] ruggebones *ende*
B. 6.43 For þow shalt yelde it ayein at one yeres [*ende*]
B. 8.97 Is hoked [at] þat oon *ende* to [holde men in good lif].
B. 9.126 And alle þat come of þat Caym come to yuel *ende*,
B.10.339 Helpeþ noȝt to heueneward [at] oone [y]eris *ende*,
B.12.4 And manye tymes haue meued þee to [mynne] on þyn *ende*,
B.12.84 And to mansede men meschief at hire *ende*.
B.14.105 Thouȝ men rede of richesse riȝt to þe worldes *ende*,
B.14.133 Fram þe loue of oure lord at his laste *ende*!
B.14.225 If wraþe wrastle wiþ þe poore he haþ þe worse *ende*
B.15.370 Astronomyens also aren at hir wittes *ende*;
B.16.157 Ac [to] þe [worldes *ende*] þi wikkednesse shal worþe vpon þiselue:
B.16.240 Lond and lordshipe and lif wiþouten *ende*.
B.17.273 But þei dwelle þer Diues is dayes wiþouten *ende*.
B.17.296 Leue I neuere þat oure lord [at þe laste *ende*]
B.17.345 And lightliche oure lord at hir lyues *ende*
B.18.161 So shal grace that bigan [al] make a good [*ende*
B.18.203 'And I shal preue', quod Pees, 'hir peyne moot haue *ende*,
B.18.227 Shal lere hem what langour is and lisse wiþouten *ende*.
B.18.378 Shul noȝt be dampned to þe deeþ þat [dureþ] wiþouten *ende*:
B.19.198 And wikkede to wonye in wo wiþouten *ende*.'
B.19.217 Tresour to lyue by riȝt to hir lyues *ende*,
B.19.278 Er he [dide] any [dede] deuyse wel þe *ende*;
C.Pr.29 In hope to haue a good *ende* and heuenriche blisse,
C. 1.93 Til treuthe hadde termyned here trespas to þe *ende*
C. 1.129 For pruyde th[at] hym pokede his payne hath non *ende*.
C. 2.35 Shal haue grace to good ynow and a good *ende*,
C. 2.109 After here deth dwellen day withouten *ende*
C. 3.199 Lawe is so lordliche and loth to make *ende*;
C. 3.303 And Gylours gyuen byfore and goode men at þe *ende*
C. 3.340 Grace of good *ende* and gret ioye aftur.
C. 3.360 And lyue as oure crede vs kenneth with crist withouten *ende*.
C. 3.434 An Auntur hit nuyede me noen *ende* wol y make,
C. 3.492 That l[yne] was no lengur and at þe leues *ende*
C. 5.97 And sette his los at a leef at the laste *ende*,
C. 5.111 Y saw þe felde ful of folk fram *ende* til oþer
C. 6.400 A[nd] blew his rownd ruet at [þe] ry[g]bones *ende*
C. 9.50 Shal haue grace of a good *ende* and greet ioye aftur.
C.10.53 To contricion, to confessioun, til he come til his *ende*.

C.10.60   And gyue me grace on þis grounde with good *ende* to deye.'
C.10.94   And halie with þe hoked *ende* [i]lle men to gode
C.10.170   The which is loue and lyf þat last withouten *ende*.
C.12.195   Worth allowed of oure lord at here laste *ende*
C.13.25   And þe gentel Iob; here ioye hath non *ende*.
C.15.280   Thogh men rede of rychesse rihte to þe worldes *ende*
C.16.2   Fro þe loue of oure lord at his laste *ende*.
C.16.66   Yf wrathe wrastle with þe pore he hath þe worse *ende*
C.16.160   'He þat hath lond and lordschipe,' quod he, 'at þe laste *ende*
C.16.284   That thus goth here godes at þe laste *ende*
C.17.106   Astron[o]myens also aren at here wittes *ende*;
C.18.174   Wo to tho þat thy wyles vysen to þe wo[r]ldes *ende*:
C.18.232   Is and ay were [& worþ wiþouten *ende*].
C.18.256   Lond and lordschip ynow and lyf withouten *ende*.
C.19.254   Bote they dwelle there diues is dayes withouten *ende*.
C.19.277   Leue y neuere þat oure lord at þe laste *ende*
C.19.325   And lihtliche oure lord at here lyues *ende*
C.20.164   So shal grace þat bigan al maken a goed *ende*
C.20.208   'And y shal pre[u]e,' quod pees, 'here payne moet haue *ende*
C.20.236   Shal lere hem what l[angour] is and lisse withouten *ende*.
C.21.198   And wikked to wonye in wo withouten *ende*.'
C.21.217   Tresor to lyue by to here lyues *ende*
C.21.278   Ar he dede eny dede deuyse wel þe *ende*;

ende v *enden v.* A 3 ende (2) enden (1); B 4 ende (1) ended (1) enden (1)
  endeþ (1); C 3 ende (2) endit (1)
A. 1.120   And *enden* as I er seide, in perfite werkis,
A. 3.255   And al his sed for þat synne [shend]fully *ende*.
A. 9.52   And [g]iue þe grace on þis erþe in good lif to *ende*'.
B. 1.131   And *enden*, as I er seide, in truþe þat is þe beste,
B. 3.277   And al his seed for þat synne shenfulliche *ende*.
B.12.44   Alisaundre þat al wan, elengliche *ended*.
B.15.138   Or [endeþ] intestate and þanne [entreþ] þe bisshop]
C. 3.304   When þe dede is ydo and þe day *endit*.
C. 3.430   And al [h]is [sede] for þat synne shentfolyche *ende*.
C. 9.292   Bote he þat euele lyueth euele shal *ende*.'

endynge ger *endinge ger.* B 1; C 1
B.14.261   After hir *endynge* here, heueneriche blisse.
C.16.101   Aftur here *endynge* here heueneryche blisse.

endit > ende

enditen v *enditen v.* B 2 endited (1) enditen (1); C 2 endite
B.11.316   For hir eiþer is *endited*, and that [of] 'Ignorancia
B.15.374   [That kan versifie faire ne formaliche *enditen*],
C.15.118   [Bu]t dowel *endite* 3ow in die iudicij.'
C.17.110   þat can versifye vayre or formallych *endite*

enemy n *enemi n.* A 2 enemys; B 11 enemy (5) enemyes (2) enemys (4);
  C 16 enemy (1) enemye (5) enemyes (9) enemys (1)
A.11.151   And [biddiþ] vs ben as breþeren, & blissen oure *enemys*,
A.11.244   Oure *enemys* and alle men þat arn nedy & pore,
B.10.202   [And] biddeþ vs be as breþeren and [blissen] oure *enemys*
B.11.178   And þat alle manere men, *enemyes* and frendes,
B.11.182   [Hir euencristene as hemself] and hir *enemyes* after.
B.12.106   And haþ noon nap wiþ his ax his *enemy* to hitte,
B.13.143   Thyn *enemy* in alle wise eueneforþ wiþ þiselue.
B.13.162   Ne [neiþer] fuyr ne flood ne feere of þyn *enemy*
B.13.174   Kan no3t [parfournen] a pees bitwene [þe pope] and hise *enemys*,
B.13.445   For to saue þi soule from sathan þyn *enemy*.
B.16.105   That, þou3 he were wounded with his *enemy*, to warisshen
             hymselue;
B.19.112   And lawe lakkede þo for men louede no3t hir *enemys*,
B.19.114   [Boþe] to lered and to lewede, to louyen oure *enemys*.
C. 3.243   In his *enemyes* handes his heritage of Fraunce.
C. 3.251   And þat is þe kynde of a kyng þat conquereth on his *enemys*,
C. 3.441   And dauid shal be ydyademed and [d]aunte alle oure *enemyes*
C. 5.74   For the ryhte of this reume ryden a3eyn oure *enemyes*
C. 6.64   And cryede 'mea culpa', corsynge alle his *enemyes*;
C. 6.106   Bothe with stoon and with staf and stele vppon myn *enemye*;
C. 7.105   For to saue thy soule fram satan thyn *enemye*
C.10.189   Oure *enemyes* enterely and helpe hem at here nede.
C.14.51   And hath non hap with his ax his *enemye* to hutte,
C.15.140   That disce, doce, dilige deum and thyn *enemy*,
C.15.164   Noþer fuyr ne floed ne be aferd of *enemye*:
C.17.142   Loue thyn *enemye* entierely goddes heste to fulfille;
C.17.288   And amonges here *enemyes* in mortel batayles
C.21.112   And lawe lakked tho for men loued nat her *enemyes*
C.21.114   Bothe to lered and to lewed, to louye oure *enemyes*.

enforme v *enfourmen v.* B 4 enforme (1) enformed (2) enformeþ (1); C 2
  enfourme (1) enfourmede (1)
B. 3.241   And *enformeþ* pouere [peple] and pursueþ truþe:
B.15.451   [*Enformed*] hem what fullynge and feiþ was to mene.

B.15.520   Al for to *enforme* þe faith; in fele contrees deyeden,
B.17.128   As Feiþ and his felawe *enformed* me boþe,
C.17.271   For to *enf[ou]rme* þe fayth ful wydewhare deyede,
C.19.97   As faith and his felawe spes *enfourmede* me bothe,

engelisch(e > englissh

engelond n prop *Engelond n.* B 4 Engelond (3) Engelonde (1); C 4
  engelonde (1) Ingelond (1) yngelond (2)
B.Pr.179   Ne hangen it aboute [his] hals al *Engelond* to wynne;
B.15.443   Al was hethynesse som tyme *Engelond* and Walis
B.15.529   [And nau3t to] huppe aboute in *Engelond* to halwe mennes Auteres
B.20.280   And yuele is þis yholde in parisshes of *Engelonde*,
C.Pr.196   Ne hanged it aboute his hals al *yngelond* to wynne;
C. 5.176   For þe abbot of *engelonde* and the abbesse his nese
C.17.279   And nat in *Ingelond* to huppe aboute and halewe men auters
C.22.280   And euele is this yholde in parsches of *yngelond*

engenderyng > engendrynge

engendreþ v *engendren v.* A 2 engendrit; B 4 engendred (3) engendreþ
  (1); C 3 engendred (1) engendrede (1) engendreth (1)
A. 2.83   For mede is molere of [m]endis *engendrit*
A.10.148   Caym þei hym callide, in cursid tyme *engendrit*.
B. 2.119   For Mede is muliere of Amendes *engendred*
B. 9.188   No3t as Adam and Eue whan Caym was *engendred*;
B.12.238   And þat þe faireste fowel foulest *engendreþ*,
B.13.18   [For alle] creatures þat crepen [or walke̦n] of kynde ben
             engendred;
C.10.215   Withouten repentaunce of here rechelesnesse a rybaud þei
             engendrede.
C.10.248   S[e]th, adames sone, seth[en] was *engendred*.
C.14.170   Þat þe fayrest foul foulest *engendreth*

engendrynge ger *engendring ger.* B 1; C 1 engenderyng
B.11.336   In etynge, in drynkynge and in *engendrynge* of kynde.
C.13.144   In etynge, [in] drynkyng [and] in *engend[eryng]* of kynde.

engendrit > engendreþ

engendrour n *engendrour n.* A 1; B 1
A. 7.216   Go to genesis þe geaunt, *engendrour* of vs alle:
B. 6.232   Go to Genesis þe geaunt, *engendrour* of vs alle:

engleymeþ v *engleimen v.* B 2; C 1 engleymeth
B.15.57   The man þat muche hony eteþ his mawe it *engleymeþ*,
B.15.64   And ri3t as hony is yuel to defie and *engleymeþ* þe mawe,
C.16.219   The man þat moche hony eet his mawe hit *engleymeth*;

englissh n *English n.* A 3; B 10; C 7 engelisch (1) engelysch (1)
  engelysche (1) englisch (1) englische (3)
A. 4.128   Let þi confessour, sire king, construe it þe on *englissh*,
A. 8.90   For I shal construe iche clause & kenne it þe on *englissh*.'
A.11.254   Ne mecaberis, ne sle nou3t, is þe kynde *englissh*;
B. 4.145   Late [þi] Confessour, sire kyng, construe [it þee on *englissh*],
B. 5.278   Cum sancto sanctus eris: construwe me þis on *englissh*.'
B. 7.108   For I [shal] construe ech clause and kenne it þee on *englissh*.'
B.13.72   In *englissh* on auenture it sholde be rehersed to ofte,
B.13.74   Ac I wiste neuere freke þat as a frere yede bifore men on *englissh*
B.14.277   'I kan no3t construe', quod haukyn; 'ye moste kenne me þis on
             englissh.'
B.14.278   '[Al þis] in *englissh*', quod Pacience, 'it is wel hard to expounen,
B.15.28   Thanne is Racio my ri3te name, reson on *englissh*;
B.15.376   Ne rede a lettre in any langage but in latyn or *englissh*.
B.19.328   And called þat hous vnitee, holy chirche on *englissh*.
C. 4.142   Lat thy Confessour, syre kyng, construe this in *englische*
C. 9.215   As by þe *engelisch* of oure eldres of olde mennes techynge
C. 9.282   For y can construe vch a word and kennen hit the an *englische*.'
C.14.14   Is ycalde Caritas, kynde loue an *engelysche*,
C.16.119   In *engelysch* is ful hard Ac sumdel y shal telle the.
C.16.218   Thenne ys racio my rihte name, reson an *englische*;
C.21.328   And calde þat hous vnite, holy chirche an *englisch*.

englissh adj *English adj.* B 3 englissh (1) englisshe (2); C 2 engelische
  (1) englisch (1)
B.10.462   And is to mene to [*Englissh*] men, moore ne lesse,
B.15.56   To *englisshe* men þis is to mene, þat mowen speke and here,
B.15.415   How *englisshe* clerkes a coluere fede þat coueitise hi3te,
C. 3.343   Thenne adiectyf an[d] sustantyf, for *englisch* was it neuere.'
C.16.218   To *engelische* men this is to mene, þat mowen speke and here,

engreynen v *engreinen v.* B 2 engreyned (1) engreynen (1)
B. 2.15   Hire Robe was ful riche, of reed scarlet *engreyned*,
B.14.20   And *engreynen* it wiþ good wille and goddes grace to amende þe,

enhanced ptp *enhauncen v.* C 1
C.11.56   Ne sory for here synnes; so [is] pruyde *enhanced*

eny > any

enioigne v *enjoinen v.* A 2 enioynede (1) enioynide (1); B 6 enioigne (1) enioyned (4) enioyneþ (1); C 7 enioyne (1) enioyned (2) enioynen (2) enioyneth (2)

A. 6.85   I perfourmde þe penaunce þe prest me *enioynide*,
A.10.4   Wiþ wynd & wiþ watir wi[tti]liche *enioynede*.
B. 2.66   And as a Brocour brou3te hire to be wiþ fals *enioyned*.
B. 5.598   I parfourned þe penaunce þe preest me *enioyned*
B. 9.4   Wiþ wynd and wiþ water witt[i]ly *enioyned*.
B.13.411   [Ac] penaunce þat þe preest *enioyneþ* parfourneþ yuele;
B.14.289   [O]r as Iustice to Iugge men *enioyned* is no poore,
B.20.283   Alle þat ben hir parisshens penaunce *enioigne*,
C. 2.68   And [as] a brokor brouhte here to be [with fals *enioyned*].
C. 2.153   And thow Iustices enioyne hem thorw I[u]roures othes
C. 5.195   *Enioyne* hem pees for here penaunce and perpetuel for3e[ue]nesse
C. 7.71   The penauns[e] þat þe prest *enioyneth* parformeth euele,
C.10.131   With wynd and with water wittyly *enioyned*.
C.16.124   Or a[s] iustice to iuge men, me *enioyneth* þerto no pore,
C.22.283   Alle þat been here parschienes penauns[e] *enioynen*

enleuene > elleuene

ennedy n prop *n.i.d.* C 1

C.12.175   Aristotel, *Ennedy*, enleuene hundred,

enpugneth > impugnen

enquestes n *enqueste n.* C 2

C. 5.57   Sholde nother swynke ne swete ne swerien at *enquestes*
C.13.85   Ne in none *enquestes* to come ne cont[u]max thogh he worche

ensample n *ensaumple n.* A 8 ensaumple (6) ensaumplis (2); B 16 ensample (7) ensamples (5) ensaumple (2) ensaumples (2); C 13 ensample (2) ensaumple (7) ensaumples (4)

A. 1.146   Here mi3t þou sen *ensaumplis* in hymself one
A. 4.119   Ac I may shewe *ensaumplis* as I se [oþer],
A. 5.17   In *ensaumple*, se[gges], þat 3e shulde do þe betere;
A. 8.114   And shewiþ it vs be *ensaumple* oureselue to wisse.
A.10.110   In *ensaumple* [þat] suche shulde not renne aboute,
A.11.154   And seide it hymself in *ensaumple* for þe beste:
A.11.206   And seide it in *ensaumple* þat þei shulde do þe betere:
A.11.274   Taken *ensaumpl[e]* of here sawis in sarmonis þat þei maken,
B. 1.172   Here my3tow sen *ensample[s]* in hymself oone
B. 4.136   Ac I may shewe *ensamples* as I se ouþ[er].
B. 5.17   In *ensample*, [segges, þat ye] sholden do þe bettre;
B. 7.132   And sheweþ vs by *ensampl[e]* vs selue to wisse.
B.10.300   And seiþ it in *ensample* [þat] þei sholde do þerafter:
B.10.475   I se *ensamples* myself and so may manye oþer,
B.11.240   And al was *ensample*, [sooþliche], to vs synfulle here
B.12.237   *Ensamples* token and termes, as telleþ þ[ise] poetes,
B.15.96   [And] se it by *ensaumple* in somer tyme on trowes:
B.15.109   And amende[n] hem þat [þei] mysdoon moore for youre *ensaumples*
B.15.261   In *ensample* we sholde do so, and take no vengeaunce
B.15.266   Ac he suffrede in *ensample* þat we sholde suffren also,
B.15.268   Pacientes Vincunt verbi gracia, and [verred] *ensamples* manye.
B.15.434   So is mannes soule, sooþly, þat seeþ no goo[d] *ensampl[e]*
B.15.473   That loþ ben to louye wiþouten lernyng of *ensaumples*.
B.15.513   In *ensaumple* þat men sholde se by sadde reson
C. 1.168   Here myhtow se *ensaumples* in hymself one
C. 1.194   And a luther *ensau[m]ple*, leef me, [to] þe lewed peple.
C. 4.133   Ac y may s[hew]en *ensaumples* as y see othere.
C. 5.119   In *ensau[m]ple*, seggus, þat we sholde do þe bettere;
C.10.243   For god seid *ensaumple* of suche manere issue
C.11.286   Saide thus in his sarmon for *ensau[m]ple* of grete clerkes,
C.12.129   And al was *ensample*, sothly, to vs synfole here
C.13.27   Thogh y preyse pouerte thus and preue hit by *ensau[m]ples*
C.13.199   Ac he soffreth in *ensaumple* þat we sholde soffren alle.
C.16.248   And s[e] hit by *ensample* In somur tyme on trees
C.16.263   And amenden [hem] of here mysdedes more for [3oure] *ensaumples*
C.16.327   What sorwe he soffrede in *ensaumple* of vs alle
C.17.264   In *ensaumple* þat men sholde se by sad resoen

enseled ptp *enselen v.* B 2

B.17.4   'Is it *enseled*?' I seide; 'may men see þ[e] lettres?'
B.17.7   And whan it is *enseled* [þerwiþ] I woot wel þe soþe

ensense n *encens n.* C 1

C.21.86   That [o] kyng cam with reson ykyuered vnder *ensense*.

enspireth v *enspiren v.(2)* C 1

C.16.244   Spryngeth and spredeth and *enspireth* þe peple

entente n *entente n.* B 1

B. 8.131   And werchen as þei þre wolde; th[i]s is his *entente*.'

enterely adv *enterli adv.* C 2 enterely (1) entierely (1)

C.10.189   Oure enemyes *enterely* and helpe hem at here nede.
C.17.142   Loue thyn enemye *entierely* goddes heste to fulfille;

entermetynge > entremetynge

entice v *enticen v.* B 2 entice (1) entisynge (1); C 2 entise (1) entisedest (1)

B.13.321   Wiþ enuye and yuel speche *entisynge* to fighte,
B.13.430   To *entice* men þoru3 hir tales to synne and harlotrie.
C. 7.90   To *entise* men thorw here tales to synne and harlotrie.
C.20.316   And *entisedest* Eue to eten bi here one–

entierely > enterely; entise(dest > entice

entisyng ger *enticing ger.* &> entice B 1

B.18.159   Al þat deeþ [d]ide first þoru3 þe deueles *entisyng*,

entre > entree,entreþ; entred > entreþ

entree n *entre n.* B 1; C 1 entre

B.11.123   'Thanne may alle cristene come', quod I, 'and cleyme þere *entree*
C.12.58   'Thenne may alle cristene come,' [quod y], 'and clayme þer *entre*

entremetede > entremetten

entremetynge ger *entermeting ger.* B 1; C 1 entermetynge

B.11.416   Ac for þyn *entremetynge* here artow forsake:
C.13.224   Ac for thyn entermetynge her artow forsake:

entremetten v *entermeten v.* B 2 entremetede (1) entremetten (1)

B.11.418   Ac whan he mamelede about mete, and *entremetede* to knowe
B.13.290   And *entremetten* hym ouer al þer he haþ no3t to doone;

entreþ v *entren v.* A 2 entre (1) entrid (1); B 5 entre (1) entred (1) entren (1) entreþ (1) yentred (1); C 4 entre (1) entred (1) entrith (1) yentred (1)

A. 6.101   Happily an hundrit wynter er þou eft *entre*.
A.11.261   I was markid wiþoute mercy, & myn name *entrid*
B. 3.238   Tho þat *entren* of o colour and of one wille
B. 5.615   Happily an hundred wynter er þow eft *entre*.
B.10.380   And þat I man maad was, and my name *yentred*
B.15.138   Or [endeþ] intestate and þanne [*entreþ* þe bisshop]
B.20.354   Thus þoru3 hende speche [þe frere *entred*]
C. 7.267   Hapliche an hundred wynter ar thow eft *entre*.
C.11.203   That y man ymaed was and my name *yentred*
C.20.290   Al hoet on here hedes þat *entrith* ney þe walles;
C.22.354   Thus thorw hende speche [the frere *entred*]

enuenymes n *envenim n.* B 1

B. 2.14   Orientals and Ewages *enuenymes* to destroye.

enuenymeþ v *envenimen* B 1

B.12.258   And alle þe oþere þer it lith *enuenymeþ* þoru3 his attre.

enuye n *envie n.* A 6; B 19; C 19 enuy (1) enuye (18)

A. 2.60   Wiþ þe Erldom of *enuye* for euere to laste,
A. 5.53   Of alle þat I haue had *enuye* in myn herte.'
A. 5.58   *Enuye* wiþ heuy herte askide aftir shrift,
A. 5.105   'I am sory,' quaþ *enuye*, 'I am but selde oþere,
A. 6.96   For he haþ *enuye* to hym þat in þin herte sitteþ
A.10.7   Anima he[o] ha[tte]; to hire [haþ] *enuye*
B. 2.84   And þe Erldom of *Enuye* and [Ire] togideres,
B. 5.70   [Of alle þat] I haue [had *enuye*] in myn herte.'
B. 5.75   *Enuye* wiþ heuy herte asked after shrifte,
B. 5.122   For *enuye* and yuel wil is yuel to defie.
B. 5.128   'I am sory,' quod [*enuye*], 'I am but selde ooþer,
B. 5.610   [For] he haþ *enuye* to hym þat in þyn herte sitteþ
B. 9.7   Anima she hatte; [to hir haþ *enuye*]
B.10.74   And prechen at Seint Poules, for pure *enuye* of clerkes,
B.10.440   Or ellis for his yuel wille and *enuye* of herte,
B.11.106   Neiþer for loue [looue] it no3t ne lakke it for *enuye*:
B.13.321   Wiþ *enuye* and yuel speche entisynge to fighte,
B.16.136   *Enuye* and yuel wil [arne] in þe Iewes.
B.17.277   Vnkynde cristene men, for coueitise and *enuye*
B.18.49   And sette it sore on his heed and seide in *enuye*;
B.19.140   [Her]of Cayphas hadde *enuye* and oþere Iewes,
B.19.228   That ydelnesse encombre hym no3t, *enuye* ne pride:
B.20.246   Holdeþ yow in vnitee, and haueþ noon *enuye*
B.20.273   *Enuye* herde þis and heet freres go to scole
B.20.294   *Enuye* herfore hatede Conscience,
C. 2.91   The Erldom of *enuye* and yre he hem graunteth,
C. 6.62   Quod repentaunce riht with þat; and thenne aroos *enuye*.
C. 6.63   *Enuye* with heuy herte asked aftur shrifte
C. 6.87   For *enuye* and euyl wil is euel to defye.
C. 6.93   'I am sory,'sayde *enuye*, 'y am [but] selde othur;
C. 7.262   For he hath *enuye* to hym þat in thyn herte setteth
C.10.134   Anima she hatte; to here hath *enuye*

C.11.54 And prech[en] at seynt poules, [for] puyr *enuye* of clerkes,
C.11.108 Bothe wymmen and wyn, wr[a]the, [*enuy*] and slewthe
C.12.40 Nother for loue [loue] it [nat] ne lacke hit for *enuye*:
C.18.163 *Enuye* and euel wil ern in þe iewes
C.19.258 Vnkynde cristene men, for coueytise and *enuye*
C.20.49 And sette hit sore on his heued and saide in *Enuye*.
C.20.456 Was neuere werre in this world ne wikkedere *enuye*
C.21.140 Hereof hadde Cayphas *enuye* and oþer iewes
C.21.228 That ydelnesse encombre h[y]m nat, *enuye* ne pryde:
C.22.246 Holdeth ȝow in vnite and haueth noen *enuye*
C.22.273 *Enuye* herde this and heete freres go to scole
C.22.294 *Enuye* herfore hatede Consience,

episteles n *epistel n.* C 1
C.19.321 As Paul þe apostel in his *episteles* techeth:

equyte n *equite n.* B 2; C 3 equite (1) equitee (2)
B.17.310 And eyþer haue *equyte*, as holy writ telleþ:
B.19.308 He dide *equyte* to alle eueneforþ his [knowynge].
C.17.240 Hadde al surie as hymsulue wolde and sarrasines in *equitee.*
C.19.290 That eyþer haue *equitee*, as holy writ witnesseth:
C.21.308 He dede *equite* to alle eueneforth his knowyng.

er adv *er adv.* A 4; B 3; C 5 eer (1) er (4)
A. 1.120 And enden as I *er* seide, in perfite werkis,
A. 1.123 Forþi I seye as I seide *er*, be siȝte of þise textis:
A. 1.180 Forþi I seiȝe as I seide *er* be siȝte of þise tixtes:
A. 8.107 And beloure þat I [be]louȝ *er* þeiȝ liflode me faile.
B. 1.131 And enden, as I *er* seide, in truþe þat is þe beste,
B. 1.134 Forþi I seye, as I seyde *er*, by siȝte of þise textes:
B. 1.206 Forþi I seye as I seide *er* by [siȝte of þise] textes:
C. 1.201 Forthi y may seye, as y saide *eer*, by s[ih]t of this tex[t]es:
C. 3.394 Ac adiectyf and sustantyf is as y [*e*]r tolde,
C. 7.181 Axen aftur hym [*er*] now in þis place.'
C.10.289 As Adam dede and Eue, as y whil *er* tolde.
C.15.304 Ac when deth awaketh hem of here we[le] þat were *er* so ryche

er prep *er prep.* A 3; B 11; C 10 ar
A. 5.20 Þat dedly synne *er* domisday shal fordon hem alle.
A. 5.223 Þat I ne shal do me *er* day to þe dere chirche
A. 6.24 Axen aftir hym, *er* now in þis place.'
B. 5.20 That dedly synne *er* domesday shal fordoon hem alle.
B. 5.451 That I ne shal do me *er* day to þe deere chirche
B. 5.497 A synful Marie þe seiȝ *er* seynte Marie þi dame,
B. 5.536 Asken after hym *er* now in þis place.'
B. 6.146 And na moore *er* morwe, myn almesse shul þei haue,
B.10.364 And but we do þus in dede, [*er*] þe day of dome,
B.15.540 Is reuerenced *er* þe Roode, receyued for [þe] worþier
B.17.112 Ac *er* þis day þre daies I dar vndertaken
B.18.67 *Er* sonday aboute sonne risyng'; and sank wiþ þat til erþe.
B.18.166 For he[o] woot moore þan we; he[o] was *er* we boþe.'
B.20.177 And þere dyed þat doctour *er* þre dayes after.
C. 5.122 That dedly synne *ar* domesday shal fordon hem alle.
C. 6.146 For she had haly bred *ar* y my herte gan change.
C. 7.65 That y ne shal do me *ar* day to þe dere chirche
C. 7.137 A synful marie þe sey *ar* seynte marye þy dame,
C.11.26 Harlotes for here harlotrye aren holpe *ar* nedy pore;
C.17.61 Or *ar* prestes or pardoners or eny peple elles.
C.18.160 And *ar* thre dayes aftur edefye hit newe.'
C.20.69 *Ar* soneday aboute sonne rysynge'; and sank with þat til erthe.
C.20.169 For he woet more then we; he was *ar* we bothe.'
C.22.177 And þere deyede þat doctour *ar* thre dayes aftur.

er conj *er conj.(1)* A 30 er (27) ere (2) or (1); B 66; C 60 ar (54) or (6)
   A.1.71, A.2.82, A.2.168, A.3.110, A.4.21, A.4.92, A.5.5, A.5.46, A.5.72,
A.5.193, A.5.211, A.5.230, A.5.232, A.6.101, A.7.77, A.7.91, A.7.188, A.7.244, A.7.245,
A.7.248, A.7.258, A.7.263, A.7.305, A.8.181, A.9.11, A.9.109, A.11.169, A.11.262,
A.12.57, A.12.103
   B.Pr.155, B.1.73, B.2.96, B.2.118, B.2.207, B.3.121, B.3.325, B.4.23, B.4.105,
B.5.5, B.5.51, B.5.63, B.5.345, B.5.372, B.5.389, B.5.458, B.5.460, B.5.615, B.6.85,
B.6.99, B.6.202, B.6.260, B.6.261, B.6.264, B.6.274, B.6.279, B.7.203, B.7.203, B.8.11,
B.8.119, B.9.80, B.10.226, B.10.275, B.10.334, B.10.381, B.11.222, B.11.388, B.12.181,
B.13.260, B.13.261, B.13.262, B.13.388, B.14.127, B.14.135, B.14.149, B.15.2,
B.15.321, B.15.532, B.15.551, B.15.567, B.16.102, B.16.115, B.17.85, B.17.319,
B.18.70, B.19.150, B.19.225, B.19.278, B.19.320, B.19.392, B.20.19, B.20.93, B.20.94,
B.20.139, B.20.206, B.20.338
   C.Pr.175, C.1.70, C.2.122, C.2.219, C.3.111, C.3.158, C.3.302, C.3.478, C.4.100,
C.5.178, C.6.4, C.6.101, C.6.277, C.6.312, C.7.267, C.8.94, C.8.108, C.8.208, C.8.219,
C.8.271, C.8.276, C.8.301, C.8.344, C.9.132, C.9.349, C.10.11, C.10.115,
C.11.204, C.11.256, C.12.232, C.13.206, C.13.233, C.14.26, C.14.38, C.14.121, C.16.4,
C.17.55, C.17.214, C.17.232, C.17.282, C.18.136, C.18.145, C.18.185, C.18.211,
C.19.133, C.19.299, C.20.72, C.20.284, C.21.150, C.21.225, C.21.278, C.21.320,
C.21.392, C.22.19, C.22.93, C.22.94, C.22.139, C.22.206, C.22.338

erber > herber

erbes n *herbe n.* C 1
C. 8.320 With craym and with croddes, with cresses and oþere *erbes*.

erchebisshopes n *archebishop n.* B 1
B.15.244 [Amonges *erchebisshopes* and bisshopes, [for beggeres sake],

erchedekenes n *archedeken.* A 1 archideknes; B 1; C 2
A.Pr.92 *Archidekns* & denis þat dignites hauen
B. 2.174 *Erchedekenes* and Officials and alle youre Registrers,
C. 5.71 And bar[o]nes bastardus haen be *Erchedekenes*
C.12.226 Erles and *Erchedekenes* and oþere riche clerkes

erd n *erd n.(1)* A 1 erde; B 1; C 1
A. 7.187 Hom into his owene *er[d]e* & holde him þere euere.
B. 6.200 Hoom [in]to his owene [*e*]rd and holden hym þere [euere].
C. 8.206 Hoem [in]to his owene [*e*]rd and halde hym þere euere.

ere n *ere n.(1)* &> *er,erien* A 5 ere (1) eris (3) erys (1); B 10 eere (1) ere
  (7) eris (2); C 8 ere (5) eres (3)
A.Pr.75 Were þe bisshop yblissid & worþ boþe hise *eris*
A. 4.14 And riȝt renneþ to resoun & rouniþ in his *ere*;
A. 4.129 And ȝif þou werche [it in] werk I wedde myne *eris*
A. 5.206 Þanne was þat shrewe asshamide & shrapide hise *eris*,
A.12.23 "I am not hardy," quod he, "þat I herde with *erys*,"
B.Pr.78 Were þe Bisshop yblessed and worþ boþe hise *eris*
B. 4.14 And [riȝt renneþ] to Reson and rouneþ in his *ere*;
B. 4.146 And if [þow] werch[e] it in werk I wedde myne *eris*
B.12.227 He is þe pies patron and putteþ it in hir *ere*
B.12.255 His ledene be in oure lordes *ere* lik a pies chiteryng;
B.13.199 And siþen softeliche he seide in clergies *ere*;
B.15.402 The corn þat she croppede he caste it in his *ere*,
B.15.404 Thanne wolde þe coluere come to þe clerkes *eere*
B.20.134 He Iogged to a Iustice and Iusted in his *eere*
B.20.190 And hitte me vnder þe *ere*; vnneþe [may] ich here.
C.Pr.76 Were þe bischop yblessed and worth bothe his *eres*
C. 4.14 And rood forth to resoun and rouned in his *ere*
C. 8.289 And yf thow dyete the thus y dar legge myn *eres*
C.16.145 For lordes alloueth hym litel or leggeth *ere* to his resoun;
C.17.172 In ayþer of his *eres* priueliche he hadde
C.17.175 Thenne sholde þe coluere come to þe clerkes *ere*,
C.22.134 He iogged til a iustice and iustede in his *ere*
C.22.190 And hitte me vnder þe *ere*; vnnethe may ich here.

erede > erien; eremites > heremyte; eren > erien

erende n *erende n.* A 1 arnede; B 1; C 2 erende (1) ernde (1)
A. 3.40 And ek to þi baudekyn, & bere wel þin *arnede*
B. 3.41 And [ek] to þi [baudekyn] and bere wel þ[yn *erende*]
C. 3.48 For to ben here bedman and bere wel here *ernde*
C.13.41 His *erende* and his lettre sheweth and is anoon delyuered.

eretikes n *heretike n. &.adj.* B 1; C 1
B.17.139 Or *Eretikes* wiþ argumentȝ, þyn hond þow hem shewe.
C.19.112 Or *eretikes* with argumentis, thien hoend thow hem shewe.

erien v *eren v.(1)* A 9 ere (1) eren (4) erid (1) erien (3); B 10 ere (1) erie
  (4) erye (2) eryed (1) eriede (1) erien (1); C 10 erede (1) erye (5)
  erien (1) eryen (1) erieth (1) yered (1)
A. 7.4 I haue an half akir to *er[e]n* be þe heiȝe weiȝe;
A. 7.5 Hadde y [*erid*] þat half akir
A. 7.25 Ac kenne me,' quaþ þe kniȝt, '& I wile [conne] *eren*.'
A. 7.59 And whoso helpiþ me to *eren*, or any þing swynke,
A. 7.98 To *erien* þis half akir helpen hym manye;
A. 7.108 And holpen [to] *ere* þe half akir wiþ 'hey trolly lolly'.
A. 7.125 Ȝe eten þat [hy] shulde ete þat *eren* for vs alle.
A. 8.5 And bad hym holde hym at hom & *eren* his laiȝes.
A. 8.6 And [alle] þat holpen to *erien* or to sowen,
B. 6.4 I haue an half acre to *erie* by þe heiȝe weye;
B. 6.5 Hadde I *eryed* þis half acre and sowen it after
B. 6.23 [Ac] kenne me', quod þe knyȝt, 'and [I wole konne *erie*].'
B. 6.65 And whoso helpeþ me to *erie* [or any þyng swynke]
B. 6.106 To *erie* þis half acre holpen hym manye;
B. 6.116 And holpen *ere* þ[e] half acre wiþ 'how trolly lolly'.
B. 7.5 And bad hym holde hym at home and *erien* hise leyes,
B. 7.6 And alle þat holpen to *erye* or to sowe,
B.14.29 'And I shal purueie þee paast', quod Pacience, 'þouȝ no plouȝ *erye*,
B.19.268 Al þat hise oxen *eriede* þei to harewen after.
C. 8.2 Ich haue an half aker to *erye* by þe heye [way];
C. 8.3 Haued ich *yered* þis half aker and ysowed hit aftur
C. 8.66 And alle þat helpen me [to] *erye* or elles to wedy
C. 8.113 To *erien* this half ak[er] holpen hym monye;
C. 8.123 And holpe *erye* this half aker with 'hey trollilolly.'
C. 9.5 And bad hym holden hym at hoem and *eryen* his leyes
C. 9.6 And alle þat holpe hym to *erye*, to sette or to sowe
C.10.216 As an hewe þat *erieth* nat aun[t]reth hym to sowe
C.15.234 Pruyde wolde potte hymsulf forth thogh no plough *erye*.

C.21.268 All þat his oxes *erede* they t[o] harwe[n] aftur.

eris > ere; eritage > heritage

erl n *erl n.* A 4 Erl (1) Erlis (3); B 8 Erl (3) Erles (5); C 5 Erl (1) Erle (1) Erles (3)

A. 3.200 Emperours & *Erlis* & alle maner lordis
A. 4.152 Be my counseil ycome of clerkes and *Erlis*.
A. 9.80 Þat þe *Erl* auerous hadde, or his eires,
A.11.219 'I wende þat kinghed, & kniȝthed, & caiseris wiþ *Erlis*
B. 3.213 Emperours and *Erles* and alle manere lordes
B. 4.189 [Be] my counseil co[men] of clerkes and of *Erles*.
B. 5.395 But I kan rymes of Robyn hood and Randolf *Erl* of Chestre,
B. 8.89 That þe *Erl* Auarous [hadde, or] hise heires,
B.10.326 And Barons wiþ *Erles* beten hem þoruȝ Beatus virres techyng;
B.11.200 And breþeren as of oo blood, as wel beggeres as *Erles*.
B.13.165 There nys neiþer emperour ne emperesse, *erl* ne baroun,
B.19.222 Shullen come and be curatours ouer kynges and *Erles*;
C. 3.269 Emperours and *Erles* and alle manere lordes
C. 7.11 Y can rymes of robyn hode and of randolf *Erle* of Chestre,
C.10.86 Þat þe *Erl* Auerous held and his ayres
C.12.226 *Erles* and Erchedekenes and oþere riche clerkes
C.21.222 Shal come and be curatours ouer kynges and *Erles*;

erldom n *erldom n.* A 1; B 1; C 1

A. 2.60 Wiþ þe *Erldom* of enuye for euere to laste,
B. 2.84 And þe *Erldom* of Enuye and [Ire] togideres,
C. 2.91 The *Erldom* of enuye and yre he hem graunteth,

erly adv *erli adv.* A 1 erliche; B 1; C 2

A. 5.166 Of vpholderis an hep, *erliche* be þe morewe,
B. 5.317 [Of] vpholderes an heep, *erly* by þe morwe,
C. 5.15 Repe or been a rypereue and aryse *erly*
C. 6.374 And of vphalderes an heep, [e]*rly* by þe morwe,

ermyte(s > heremyte; ermonye > armonye n; ern > rennen; ernde > erende; ernynge > rennen

errant adj *erraunt adj.* C 1

C. 6.306 Then an *errant* vsurer, haue god my treuthe,

erren v *erren v.* C 1

C.17.88 Lewed men han no byleue, [so] lettred men *erren*;

ers n *ars n.* A 1 ars; B 3; C 3

A.11.81 I wolde his eiȝen wern in his *ars* & his hele aftir
B. 5.175 And baleised on þe bare *ers* and no brech bitwene.
B.10.128 I wolde his eiȝe were in his *ers* and his [hele] after,
B.10.314 An heep of houndes at his *ers* as he a lord were,
C. 5.160 A[n] hep of houndes at h[is] *ers* as he a lord were
C. 6.157 And balayshed on þe bare *ers* and no brech bytwene.
C. 6.305 For an hore of here *ers* wynnynge may hardiloker tythe

erst adv *erest adv.* A 1 arst; B 1; C 1 arste

A. 4.29 Ac consience com *arst* to court be a myle wey
B.16.71 Maidenhode, Aungeles peeris, and [*erst*] wole be ripe
C. 6.307 And *arste* shal come to heuene, [by hym þat me made]!'

erþe n *erthe n.(1)* A 26; B 49; C 57 erthe

A. 1.7 Þe moste partie of þis peple þat passiþ on þis *erþe*,
A. 1.17 And þerfore he hiȝte þe *erþe* to helpe ȝow ichone
A. 1.114 Summe in eir, summe in *erþe*, summe in helle depe.
A. 1.126 Þat treuþe is þe tresour triȝest on *erþe*.'
A. 2.9 Ipurfilid wiþ pelure, þe pureste [o]n *erþe*,
A. 2.57 'Wyten & wytnessen þat wonen vpon *erþe*,
A. 3.119 Betwyn heuene & helle, & *erþe* þeiȝ men souȝte.
A. 3.217 'Nay,' quaþ consience to þe king & knelide to þe *erþe*,
A. 3.266 Shal no more mede be maister on *erþe*,
A. 5.16 Piries & pl[umtr]es wern pu[ffid] to þe *erþe*
A. 5.45 Pernel proud herte plat hire to þe *erþe*
A. 5.198 He [þr]umblide on þe presshewold & [þrew] to þe *erþe*
A. 8.2 To take his tem & [tilien þe *erþe*],
A. 8.88 Here penaunce & here purcatorie vpon þis pur *erþe*.
A. 8.165 Forþi I rede ȝow renkes þat riche ben on *erþe*
A. 9.33 Riȝt þus [it] fariþ,' quaþ he Frere, 'be folk here on *erþe*.
A. 9.52 And [g]iue þe grace on þis *erþe* in good lif to ende'.
A. 9.104 How dowel, dobet & dobest don on þis *erþe*.'
A.10.3 Of *erþe* & eir it is mad, medlit togideris;
A.10.126 Or as whete out of weed waxiþ, out of þe *erþe*,
A.10.172 Þat euere curside caym com on þis *erþe*;
A.11.14 Þat hem were leuere lond, & lordsshipe on *erþe*,
A.11.184 Trewe tilieris on *erþe*, taillours & souteris
A.11.273 For alle cunnyng clerkis siþþe crist ȝede on *erþe*
A.12.44 And his loggyng is with lyf þat lord is of *erþe*,
A.12.104 Deþ delt him a dent and drof him to þe *erþe*
B. 1.7 The mooste partie of þis peple þat passeþ on þis *erþe*,
B. 1.17 And þerfore he hiȝte þe *erþe* to helpe yow echone

B. 1.125 Somme in Eyr, somme in *erþe*, somme in helle depe.
B. 1.137 That Treuþe is tresor þe trieste on *erþe*.'
B. 1.154 Til it hadde of þe *erþe* [y]eten [hitselue].
B. 2.9 Purfiled wiþ Pelure, þe [pureste on] *erþe*,
B. 2.26 And neuere sooþ seide siþen he com to *erþe*,
B. 2.75 Witeþ and witnesseþ þat wonieþ vpon *erþe*
B. 3.130 Bitwene heuene and helle, [and] *erþe* þouȝ men souȝte.
B. 3.230 'Nay', quod Conscience to þe kyng and kneled to þe *erþe*.
B. 3.290 Shal na moore Mede be maister [on *erþe*],
B. 4.26 Whiche maistries Mede makeþ on þis *erþe*.
B. 5.16 Pyries and Plumtrees were puffed to þe *erþe*
B. 5.62 Pernele proud-herte platte hire to þe *erþe*
B. 5.350 He [þr]umbled on þe presshfold and þrew to þe *erþe*.
B. 5.484 For þoruȝ þat synne þi sone sent was to *erþe*
B. 7.2 To [t]aken his teme and tilien þe *erþe*,
B. 7.106 Hir penaunce and hir Purgatorie [vp]on þis [pure] *erþe*,
B. 7.187 Forþi I rede yow renkes þat riche ben on *erþe*
B. 8.37 [Riȝt] þus it [fareþ]', quod þe frere, 'by folk here on *erþe*.
B. 9.3 Of *erþe* and Eyr [it is] maad, medled togideres,
B. 9.102 Is moost yhated vpon *erþe* of hem þat ben in heuene;
B. 9.120 In *erþe* [þe] heuene [is]; hymself [was þe] witnesse.
B. 9.141 That euere cursed Caym coom on þis *erþe*.
B. 9.156 And þus þoruȝ cursed Caym cam care vpon *erþe*,
B.10.14 That hem were leuere lond and lordshipe on *erþe*,
B.10.305 For if heuene be on þis *erþe*, and ese to any soule,
B.12.140 And loue shal lepen out after into þ[is] *erþe*,
B.12.205 But by hymself as a soleyn and serued on [þe] *erþe*.
B.12.241 Bitokneþ riȝt riche men þat reigne here on *erþe*.
B.13.239 For alle trewe trauaillours and tiliers of þe *erþe*
B.13.372 Of my nexte Neghebore, nymen of his *erþe*:
B.14.41 First þe wilde worm vnder weet *erþe*,
B.15.211 And þat knoweþ no clerk ne creature on *erþe*
B.15.364 Tilieris þat tiled þe *erþe* tolden hir maistres
B.15.459 Heþen is to mene after heeþ and vntiled *erþe*,
B.15.511 [Whan þe hye kyng of heuene sente his sone to *erþe*
B.16.211 Migh[t] is [in] matrimoyne þat multiplieþ þe *erþe*
B.17.149 Bitoknen soofly þe sone þat sent was til *erþe*,
B.17.163 Boþe wolkne and þe wynd, water and *erþe*,
B.18.67 Er sonday aboute sonne risyng'; and sank wiþ þat til *erþe*.
B.18.224 Boþe in heuene and in *erþe*, and now til helle he þenkeþ
B.18.241 The light folwede þe lord into þe lowe *erþe*.
B.18.247 The *Erþe* for heuynesse þat he wolde suffre
B.18.366 And for þat drynke today I deide vpon *erþe*.
B.18.379 It is noȝt vsed in *erþe* to hangen a feloun
B.19.73 Reuerenced hym [riȝt] faire wiþ richesses of *erþe*.
B.19.260 My prowor and my Plowman Piers shal ben on *erþe*,
B.20.240 And siþen freres forsoke þe felicite of *erþe*
C.Pr.227 As taylers and tanners and tulyers [of] þe *erthe*,
C. 1.7 The moste party of this peple þat passeth on þis *erthe*,
C. 1.66 That tristeth in tresor of *erthe* he bytrayeth sonest.
C. 1.127 Summe in *erthe*, summe in ayr, summe in helle depe.
C. 1.150 Til hit hadde of *erthe* yȝoten hitsilue.
C. 2.10 She was purfiled [with] pelure, non puyrere on *erthe*,
C. 2.82 Wyten and witnessen þat wonyen on *erthe*
C. 2.138 Hit semeth sothly riȝt so on *erthe*
C. 3.94 Here on this *erthe* or elles in helle,
C. 3.100 Graunte gylours on *erthe* grace to amende
C. 3.101 And haue here penaunce on puyre *erthe* and nat þe peyne of helle.
C. 3.167 Bytwene heuene and helle, and *erthe* thogh men soughte.
C. 3.324 For god gaf salomon grace vpon *erthe*,
C. 5.118 P[iri]es and plumtrees were po[ff]ed to þe *erthe*
C. 5.152 For yf heuene be on this *erthe* or ese to [eny] soule
C. 6.3 P[ur]nele proude herte platte here to þe *erthe*
C. 6.269 Of my neyhebore nexst, nymen of his *erthe*;
C. 6.287 Were y a frere, in good fayth, for al þe gold on *erthe*
C. 6.408 [A] thromblede at the thresfold and threw to þe *erthe*.
C. 7.126 For thorw þat synne thy sone ysent was til *erthe*
C. 8.235 'Y wolde nat greue [god],' quod Peres, 'for al þe good on *erthe*!
C. 9.2 To taken his teme and tilion þe *erthe*
C. 9.186 Here penaunce and here purgatorie vppon this puyre *erthe*
C. 9.333 Forthy y rede ȝow renkes þat riche ben on this *erthe*
C.10.24 The rihtfulluste ren[k] þat regneth [o]n *erthe*.
C.10.49 Synegeth seue sithe þe saddest man on *erthe*
C.10.130 Of *erthe* and ayer [hit is] maed, ymedled togyderes,
C.10.160 May nat shyne ne shewe on schalkes on *erthe*,
C.10.200 To tulie þe *erthe* with tonge and teche men to louye.
C.10.229 That euere corsed Caym cam on þis *erthe*;
C.11.200 Y leue neuere þat lord ne lady þat lyueth her [o]n *erthe*
C.12.184 That ben layd in louhe *erthe*, ylore as hit were,
C.12.185 And thorw þe grace of god and grayn dede [i]n *erthe*
C.13.15 Iob þe gentele, what ioye hadde he on *erthe*?
C.14.85 And loue shal lepe out aftur into this lowe *erthe*
C.14.144 Bote as a soleyn by hymsulue [and] yserued [o]n þe [*erthe*].

C.14.173 Bytokenen riht ryche men þat reygne here on *erthe*.
C.15.92 And apose hym what penaunce is and purgatorie on *erthe*
C.15.240 Þe worm and wonte vnder *erthe* and in water fisches,
C.16.154 That puyre pouerte and pacience was a louh lyuynge on *erthe*,
C.17.101 Tilyares þat tilede þe *erthe* tolden here maystres
C.17.262 For when þe hye kyng of heuene sente his so[n]e til *erthe*
C.18.91 And bad hit be, of a bat of *erthe*, a man and a maide,
C.18.96 Maydones and martres ministrede [hym] here on *erthe*
C.18.98 And for þe fayrest fruyte byfore hym, as of *erthe*,
C.19.123 Bitokneth soethly the sone þat sente was til *erthe*,
C.20.63 The *erthe* toquasch[t]e and quoek as hit quyk were
C.20.69 Ar soneday aboute sonne rysynge'; and sank with þat til *erthe*.
C.20.233 Bothe in heuene and in *erthe*, and now to helle he thenketh
C.20.250 The lihte folewede þe lord into þe lowe *erthe*.
C.20.256 Þe *erthe* for heuynesse þat he wolde soffre
C.20.353 And wyte[th] hem al þe wrechednesse þat wrouhte is on *erthe*.
C.20.421 Hit is nat vsed [i]n *erthe* to hangen [a] felo[n]
C.20.472 And rihtfollokest A relyk, noon richore on *erthe*.
C.21.73 Reuerensed hym riht fayre with richesses of *erthe*.
C.21.260 My prowour and my [plouhman Peres] shal ben on *erthe*
C.22.240 And senne freres forsoke the felic[it]e of *erthe*

erþely adj *ertheli adj.* B 3 erþeliche (1) erþely (2); C 2 ertheliche (1) erthely (1)
B.15.175 Coueiteþ he noon *erþely* good, but heueneriche blisse.'
B.19.94 [*Erþeliche*] honeste þynges w[as] offred þus at ones
B.20.151 And kille a[l] *erþely* creatur[e] saue conscience oone.
C.21.94 *Ertheliche* honeste thynges was offred thus at ones
C.22.151 And culle all *erthely* creature saue Consience one.

eschaunges n *eschaunge n.* B 2; C 1
B.5.246 *Eschaunges* and cheuysaunces, wiþ swich chaffare I dele,
B.13.393 To marchaunden wiþ [my] moneie and maken [here] *eschaunges*,
C.6.280 To marchaunde with my moneye and maken here *eschaunges*,

eschete > asken

eschetes n *eschete n.* B 1
B.4.175 And seide, 'þoru3 [youre] lawe, as I leue, I lese manye *eschetes*;

eschuwe v *escheuen v.* A 1 eschewe; B 1; C 1 eschewe
A.7.48 And nameliche at mete suche men *eschew[e]*,
B.6.53 And namely at mete swiche men *eschuwe*,
C.8.51 Ac [manliche] at mete suche men *eschewe*

ese n *ese n.* A 4; B 11; C 10
A.Pr.54 Shopen hem Ermytes here *ese* to haue.
A.1.19 In mesurable maner to make 3ow at *ese*;
A.3.4 To take mede þe maide & make hire at *ese*.
A.11.174 Fairere vndirfonge ne frendliere mad at *ese*
B.Pr.57 Shopen hem heremytes hire *ese* to haue.
B.Pr.157 We my3te be lordes o lofte and lyuen at oure *ese*.'
B.1.19 In mesurable manere to make yow at *ese*;
B.3.4 To take Mede þe maide and maken hire at *ese*.
B.10.231 Fairer vnderfongen ne frendlier at *ese*
B.10.305 For if heuene be on þis erþe, and *ese* to any soule,
B.10.319 In many places þer þei [persons ben, be þei purely] at *ese*,
B.13.42 Of þat men myswonne þei made hem wel at *ese*,
B.15.341 Hem þat han as ye han; hem ye make at *ese*.
B.16.227 Thre men, to my si3te, I made wel at *ese*,
B.18.210 Sholde neuere ri3t riche man þat lyueþ in reste and *ese*
C.Pr.55 And [shopen] he[m] heremites here *ese* to haue.
C.1.19 And, in mesure thow muche were, to make 3ow at*ese*
C.3.4 To take mede þe mayde and maken here at *ese*.
C.5.152 For yf heuene be on this erthe or *ese* to [eny] soule
C.5.165 In many places ther thei persones ben, be hemsulue at *ese*,
C.8.281 In al manere *ese* in Abrahammus lappe.
C.9.143 Vnlouke his legges abrood or ligge at his *ese*,
C.9.152 In idelnesse and in *ese* and by otheres trauayle.
C.13.54 As þe messager may ne with so moche *ese*.
C.15.47 Of þat men myswonne they made hem wel at *ese*

esy adj *esi adj.* B 2
B.7.128 That loueþ god lelly his liflode is ful *esy*:
B.15.207 Ac it is moore to haue hir mete [on] swich an *esy* manere

esily adv *esili adv.* B 1
B.2.98 And breden as Burgh swyn, and bedden hem *esily*

espied ptp *aspien v.* B 1
B.19.301 [Shal] nou3t ben *espied* [þoru3] Spiritus Iusticie.

espirit n *espirit n.* C 1
C.14.27 And sent forth the seynt *espirit* to do loue sprynge:

essex n prop *OED Essex* B 1
B.5.92 Than þou3 I hadde þis wouke ywonne a weye of *Essex* chese.

est > eest

estward adv *estward adv.* B 1; C 2
B.16.169 *Estward* and westward I waited after faste
C.Pr.14 *Estward* y beheld aftir þe sonne
C.1.133 *Estward* til heuene, euere to abyde

eten v *eten v.* A 12 eet (2) ete (6) eten (4); B 42 eet (8) et (1) ete (16) eten (14) eteþ (2) etynge (1); C 26 eet (8) ete (10) eten (8)
A.6.90 Þo Adam & Eue *eten* here bane,
A.7.125 3e *eten* þat [hy] shulde ete þat eren for vs alle.
A.7.125 3e eten þat [hy] shulde *ete* þat eren for vs alle.
A.7.129 Or 3e shuln *ete* barly bred & of þe bro[k] drynke;
A.7.131 Þei shuln *ete* as good as I, so me god helpe,
A.7.245 And *ete* nou3t, I hote þe, er hunger þe take
A.7.248 Aris vp er ap[e]ti[t] ha[ue] *eten* his fille;
A.7.280 Hungir [*eet*] þis in haste & askide aftir more.
A.7.287 Ne no beggere *ete* bred þat benis in come,
A.8.108 Þe prophet his p[a]yn *e[et]* in penaunce & in wepyng
A.10.141 Aftir þat adam & [heo] *eten* þe appil
A.12.74 [But *ete* as hunger me hete til my belly swellyd.
B.5.121 I my3te no3t *ete* many yeres as a man ou3te
B.5.177 I *ete* þere vnþende fissh and feble ale drynke.
B.5.374 Ouer delicatly on [feeste] dayes dronken and *eten* boþe,
B.5.375 And sat som tyme so longe þere þat I sleep and *eet* at ones.
B.5.603 Tho Adam and Eue apples vnrosted:
B.6.135 Or ye shul *eten* barly breed and of þe broke drynke;
B.6.137 [Thei] shal *ete* [as good as I, so me god helpe],
B.6.145 Ac Ancres and heremites þat *eten* but at Nones
B.6.181 '[Lat] hem lyue', he seide, 'and lat hem *ete* wiþ hogges,
B.6.261 *Ete* no3t, I hote þee, er hunger þee take
B.6.264 [A]rys vp er Appetit haue *eten* his fille.
B.6.296 [Hunger *eet* þis] in haste and axed after moore.
B.6.303 Ne no beggere *ete* bred þat benes Inne [come],
B.7.126 The prophete his payn *eet* in penaunce and in sorwe
B.9.124 [After þat Adam and heo *eten* þe appul].
B.10.99 Now haþ ech riche a rule to *eten* by hymselue
B.10.102 That was maad for meles men to *eten* Inne,
B.10.104 I haue yherd hei3e men *etynge* at þe table
B.11.237 Til he blessede and brak þe breed þat þei *eten*.
B.12.28 And þere bidde my bedes but whan ich *ete* or slepe.
B.12.123 Why Adam hiled no3t first his mouþ *eet* þe Appul
B.13.40 Ac þis maister [of þise men] no maner flessh [*eet*],
B.13.41 Ac [he *eet*] mete of moore cost, mortrews and potages.
B.13.62 He *eet* manye sondry metes, mortrews and puddynges,
B.13.107 For ye han harmed vs two in þat ye *eten* þe puddyng,
B.13.403 And moore mete *eet* and dronk þan kynde my3te defie,
B.14.51 'Haue, haukyn', quod Pacience, 'and *et* þis whan þe hungreþ
B.15.57 The man þat muche hony *eteþ* his mawe it engleymeþ,
B.15.180 And if he soupeþ *eteþ* but a sop of Spera in deo.
B.16.228 Wessh hir feet and wiped hem, and afterward þei *eten*
B.17.100 Til he haue *eten* al þe barn and his blood ydronke.
B.18.194 If þat þei touchede a tree and þe [trees] fruyt *eten*.
B.18.202 For it is botelees bale, þe byte þat þei *eten*.'
B.18.281 If Adam *ete* þe Appul alle sholde deye
B.18.289 And eggedest hem to *ete*, Eue by hirselue,
B.18.331 That if [þei] *ete* þe Appul alle sholde deye,
B.19.277 And whoso *ete* þat ymagynen he sholde,
B.19.282 He þat *ete* of þat seed hadde swich a kynde:
B.19.290 And who[so] *ete* [of] þat seed hardy was euere
B.19.298 And he þat *ete* of þat seed sholde be [euene] trewe
B.19.387 [My3t] to maken it and men to *ete* it after
B.20.3 I ne wiste wher to *ete* ne at what place,
C.6.86 Y myhte nat *ete* many 3er as a man ouhte
C.6.159 For y *ete* more fysch then flesche there and feble ale drynke.
C.6.431 And as an hound þat *eet* gras so gan y to brake
C.8.142 Or 3e shal *ete* barly breed and of þe broke drynke.
C.8.146 Ankerus and Eremytes þat *eten* but at nones
C.8.271 Ac *ete* nat, y hote, Ar hungur the take
C.8.318 Hunger *eet* al in haste and askede aftur more.
C.8.325 Ne no beggare *eten* bred þat benes ynne were
C.15.46 Forthy eet he mete of more cost, mortrewes and potages.
C.15.66 And *ete* manye sondry metes, mortrewes and poddynges,
C.15.250 'Haue, Actyf,' quod pacience, 'and *eet* this when þe hungreth
C.16.219 The man þat moche hony *eet* his mawe hit engleymeth;
C.17.23 Marie Egipciaca *eet* in thritty wynter
C.17.173 Corn [þat þe] coluere *eet* when he come in places
C.18.243 Wosch he[re] feet and wypede hem and afturward they *eten*.
C.19.90 Til he haue *eten* al þ[e] barn and his bloed dronken
C.20.199 Yf that thei touche[d a] tre and of þe [trees] fruyt *eten*.
C.20.207 For hit is boteles bale, the bite that they *eten*.'

C.20.316 And entisedest Eue to *eten* bi here one–
C.20.374 That if they *ete* þe appul alle sholde deye,
C.21.277 [And] hoso *ete* þat ymageny he sholde,
C.21.282 He þat *eet* of that seed hadde such a kynde:
C.21.290 And hoso *ete* of þa[t] seed hardy was euere
C.21.298 And he þat *ete* of þat seed sholde be euene trewe
C.21.387 Myhte to make hit and men to *eten* hit [aftur]
C.22.3 Y ne wiste where to *ete* ne at what place

etynge ger *etinge ger. &> eten* B 1; C 1
B.11.336 In *etynge*, in drynkynge and in engendrynge of kynde.
C.13.144 In *etynge*, [in] drynkyng [and] in engend[eryng] of kynde.

euangelistes > euaungelistes

euaungelie n *evangelie n.* A 1; B 2; C 3 euaungelie (2) ewangelie (1)
A. 1.174 For þise arn þe wordis writen in þe *Euaungelie*:
B. 1.200 Fo[r] þise [ben wordes] writen in þe [*euaungelie*]:
B.11.190 And exciteþ vs by þe *Euaungelie* þat, whan we maken festes,
C. 1.195 For this aren wordes ywryten in þe *ewangelie*:
C.11.202 For clergie saith þat he seyh in þe seynt *euaungelie*
C.12.102 And, as þe *euaungelie* witnesseth, when we maken festes

euaungelistes n *evangelist n.* B 2 Euaungelistes (1) euaungelistes (1); C 1
B.10.251 Who was his Auctour? alle þe foure *Euaungelistes*.
B.13.39 Of Austyn, of Ambrose, of [alle] þe foure *Euaungelistes*:
C.15.44 Of Austyn, of Ambrose, of alle þe foure *euaungeli[st]es*:

eue n prop *n.i.d. &> euen* A 3; B 16; C 21
A. 1.63 Adam & *Eue* he eggide to ille,
A. 6.90 Þo Adam & *Eue* eten here bane,
A.10.140 Ben conseyuid in cursid tyme as kaym was on *Eue*:
B. 1.65 Adam and *Eue* he egged to ille,
B. 5.603 Tho Adam and *Eue* eten apples vnrosted:
B. 9.35 And *Eue* of his ryb bon wiþouten any mene.
B. 9.123 Conceyued ben in [cursed] tyme as Caym was on *Eue*
B. 9.188 Noȝt alle may þat han with Caym was engendred;
B.11.206 Of Adames issue and *Eue* ay til god man deide;
B.12.231 And tauȝte hym and *Eue* to helien hem wiþ leues.
B.15.63 [Adam and *Eue* putte out of Paradis]:
B.16.205 Adam, oure aller fader. *Eue* was of hymselue,
B.18.143 For Adam and *Eue* and Abraham wiþ oþere
B.18.153 That Adam and *Eue* haue shul bote].
B.18.178 Adam and *Eue* and oþere mo in helle.
B.18.192 That Adam and *Eue* and alle þat hem suwede
B.18.289 And eggedest hem to ete, *Eue* by hirselue,
B.18.402 And for þi lesynge, lucifer, þat þow leighe til *Eue*
B.19.54 For he yaf Adam and *Eue* and oþere mo blisse
C. 1.61 Adam and *Eue* he eggede to ylle,
C. 7.250 That Adam and *Eue* and aȝenes vs alle shette:
C.10.214 Aftur þat Adam and *Eue* hadden ysyneged;
C.10.289 As Adam dede and *Eue*, as y whil er tolde.
C.12.114 Of Adames issue and *Eue* ay til god man deyede;
C.14.162 And Adam and *Eue* and alle othere bestes
C.16.225 Potte out of paradys Adam and *Eue*:
C.18.216 *Eue* of Adam was and out of hym ydrawe
C.18.218 And thise thre þat y Carp of, Adam and *Eue*
C.18.227 Was þe sone in hymsulue, in a simile as *Eue* was,
C.18.229 And as abel of Adam and of his wyf *Eue*
C.20.146 For Adam and *Eue* And abraham with oþere
C.20.156 That Adam and *Eue* haue shullen bote.
C.20.162 All þat deth and þe deuel dede formost to *Eue*
C.20.181 Adam and *Eue* and other mo in helle.
C.20.197 That Adam and *Eue* and al his issue
C.20.303 That Adam and *Eue* and all his issue
C.20.316 And entisedest *Eue* to eten bi here one–
C.20.348 And now for a later lesynge þat thow lowe til *Eue*
C.20.445 Ac for þe lesynge þat thow low, lucifer, til *eue*
C.21.54 For he ȝaf Adam and *Eue* and oþere mo blisse

euel(e > yuel,yuele; eueles > yuel n

euen n *even n.* A 5 eue (3) euen (2); B 7 eue (2) euen (5); C 10 eue (2)
euen (5) euene (2) euenes (1)
A. 5.14 And þe southwestryne wynd on satirday at *eue*
A. 6.39 He [wiþ]halt non hyne his hire þat he ne haþ it at *eue*.
A. 6.66 And hold wel þin haliday heiȝ til *euen*.
A. 7.12 But ȝif it be holy day oþer holy *euen*;
A. 7.172 And fla[ppid]e on wiþ flailes fro morewe til *eue*,
B. 3.312 And dyngen vpon Dauid eche day til *eue*;
B. 5.14 And þe Southwestrene wynd on Saterday at *euen*
B. 5.178 Ac ouþer while whan wyn comeþ, [whan] I drynke at *eue*,
B. 5.552 He wiþhalt noon hewe his hire þat he ne haþ it at *euen*.
B. 5.579 And hold wel þyn haliday heighe til *euen*,
B. 6.184 And flapten on wiþ flailes fro morwe til *euen*
B.14.15 That I ne flobre it foule fro morwe til *euen*.'

C. 3.308 The huyre of his hewe ouer *eue* til amorwe:
C. 5.116 And the southweste wynde on saturday At *euene*
C. 6.160 Ac other while when wyn cometh and when y drynke late at *euen*
C. 6.182 As wel fastyng dayes and frydayes and heye fest[e] *euenes*.
C. 7.196 He withhalt non hewe his huyre ouer *euen*;
C. 7.226 And hold wel þ[in] haliday heye til *euen*.
C. 8.180 And flapton on with f[lay]les fro morwen til *euen*
C. 9.87 What h[e]m nede[th] at here neyhebores at noon and at *eue*.
C. 9.142 In hope to sitte at *euen* by þe hote coles,
C.13.86 Halyday or holy *euene* his mete to discerue.

euencristen n *even adj.* B 9 euencristen (4) euencristene (2) euenecristene
(3); C 6 emcristen (1) emcristene (4) euencristene (1)
B. 2.95 And þere to Iangle and Iape and Iugge hir *euencristen*,
B. 5.433 The kyndenesse þat myn *euencristene* kidde me fernyere,
B.11.182 [Hir *euencristene* as hemself] and hir enemyes after.
B.13.105 'Do noon yuel to þyn *euencristen*, nouȝt by þi power.'
B.13.330 As a shepsteres shere ysherewed [myn *euencristen*]:
B.13.389 So if I kidde any kyndenesse myn *euencristen* to helpe
B.17.137 Thyn *euenecristene* eueremoore eueneforþ with þiselue.
B.17.254 Be vnkynde to þyn *euenecristene* and al þat þow kanst bidde,
B.17.264 Beþ noȝt vnkynde, I conseille yow, to youre *euenecristene*.
C. 2.102 And there to iangele and iape and iuge here *Emcristene*,
C. 6.75 Lyke a schupestares sharre and shrewed myn *euencristene*
C. 7.46 The kyndenesse þat myn *emcristen* kud me ferneȝer,
C.10.79 And thorw lele labour lyueth and loueth his *emcristene*
C.19.220 Be vnkynde to thyn *emcristene* and al þat thow canst bidde,
C.19.230 Beth nat vnkynde, y conseyle ȝow, to ȝoure *emcristene*.

euene adj *even adj.* B 1; C 2
B.20.270 Heuene haþ *euene* noumbre and helle is wiþoute noumbre.
C.18.89 For þat is *euene* with angelis and angeles pere.
C.22.270 [Heuene haeth *euene* nombre and helle is withoute nombre].

euene adv *even adv.* A 2; B 6; C 10
A. 4.147 And all my lige ledis to lede þus *euene*.'
A. 8.128 And sauȝ þe sonne *euene* souþ sitte þat tyme,
B. 4.184 [And] alle youre lige leodes to lede þus *euene*'.
B. 7.146 And seiȝ þe sonne [*euene*] South sitte þat tyme,
B.17.187 Ac who is hurte in þe hand], *euene* in þe myddes,
B.18.118 *Euene* out of þe Est and westward she lokede,
B.19.298 And he þat ete of þat seed sholde be [*euene*] trewe
B.20.103 That he hitte *euene*, þat euere stired after.
C. 1.122 *Euene* þe contrarie sitteth Crist, Clerkes wyteth þe sothe:
C. 4.178 And alle ȝoure lege l[e]des to lede thus *euene*.'
C.13.68 That holde mote þe hey way, *euene* the ten hestes,
C.16.53 The hey way to heueneward he halt hit nat fol *euene*
C.18.6 *Euene* in þe myddes an ympe, as hit were,
C.19.153 Ac ho is herte in the hand *euene* in þe myddes
C.20.61 The wal of the temple tocleyef *euene* [a] to peces;
C.20.121 *Euene* oute of þe eest and westward she thouhte,
C.21.298 And he þat ete of þat seed sholde be *euene* trewe
C.22.103 That he hi[t]te *euene*, þat euere stured aftur.

euene &> euen; euenecristene > euencristen

eueneforþ adv *evenforth adv.* B 2
B.13.143 Thyn enemy in alle wise *eueneforþ* wiþ þiselue.
B.17.137 Thyn euenecristene eueremoore *eueneforþ* with þiselue.

eueneforþ prep *evenforth prep.* B 1; C 3 emforth (2) eueneforth (1)
B.19.308 He dide equyte to alle *eueneforþ* his [knowynge].
C.15.141 [Hertely þou hym] helpe *emforth* thy myhte,
C.16.223 Et verba vertit in opera *emforth* his power."
C.21.308 He dede equite to alle *eueneforth* his knowyng.

euensong n *evensong n.* A 2 euesong; B 2; C 4
A. 5.187 And seten so til *euesong* & songe [vmbe]while
A. 5.226 Til I haue *euesong* herd, I behote [to] be rode.
B. 5.338 And seten so til *euensong* and songen vmwhile
B. 5.454 Til I haue *euensong* herd: I bihote to þe Roode.
C. 6.396 And seten so til *euenson[g]* and songen vmbywhile
C. 7.68 Til y haue *euensong* yherd: y bihote to þe rode.'
C. 9.230 To heren here *euensong* euery man ouhte.
C. 9.245 Or sonendayes at *euensong*? se we wel fewe!

euere adv *ever adv.* A 35; B 81 euer (3) euere (78); C 69 euer (2) euere
(67)
A.Pr.45 Slep & sleuþe sewiþ hem *euere*.
A. 1.97 [Di]de hem swere on h[ere] swerd to serue treuþe *euere*.
A. 2.12 Of þe pureste perreiȝe þat prince werde *euere*.
A. 2.37 And feffe mede þer[myd] in mariage for *euere*.
A. 2.50 In foreward þat falshed shal fynde hire for *euere*,
A. 2.60 Wiþ þe Erldom of enuye for *euere* to laste,
A. 2.121 Iuggen ȝow ioyntly in ioye for *euere*'.
A. 2.166 Þat holy chirche for hem worþ harmid for *euere*;

A. 3.149 Þe mase for a mene man þei3 he mote *euere*.
A. 3.161 For consience acusiþ þe to cunge [þe] for *euere*.'
A. 3.179 Wendist þat wynter wolde han last *euere*;
A. 3.257 Þat god hati[de him for *euere* & alle hise heires aftir.
A. 4.52 Þei3 pees & his power pleynide hem *euere*'.
A. 4.67 And wisten wel þat wrong was a shrewe *euere*.
A. 4.110 Þat no man go to galis but 3if he go for *euere*.
A. 4.155 'I am redy,' quaþ resoun, 'to reste wiþ 3ow *euere*;
A. 5.84 Ac hadde I maistrie & mi3t I wolde murdre hym for *euere*.
A. 5.240 To haue helle for *euere* 3if þat hope nere.
A. 6.28 And dede me sure hym [siþþe] to serue hym for *euere*;
A. 6.86 And am sory for my synnes & so shal I *euere*
A. 6.104 Ac þere arn seuene sistris þat [seruen] treuþe *euere*,
A. 7.187 Hom into his owene er[d]e & holde him þere *euere*.
A. 7.261 Wende now whanne þi wille is, þat wel be þou *euere*.'
A. 8.81 Þat *euere* he was man wrou3t whanne he shal henne fare.
A. 9.15 And *euere* haþ [as] I hope, & euere shal hereaftir.'
A. 9.15 And euere haþ [as] I hope, & *euere* shal hereaftir.'
A. 9.60 Þat *euere* dremide dri3t in doute, as I wene.
A. 9.96 But dobest bede for hem abide þere for *euere*.
A.10.106 Fro religioun to religioun, reccheles ben þei *euere*;
A.10.172 Þat *euere* curside caym com on þis erþe;
A.11.16 Þanne alle þe soþe sawis þat salamon seide *euere*.
A.11.82 Þat *euere* eft wilneþ to wyte why [þat] god wolde
A.11.286 Wiþoute penaunce of purcatorie to haue paradis for *euere*.
A.12.82 Mi name is feuere on þe ferþe day; I am aþrest *euere*.
A.12.110 Now alle kenne creatures þat cristene were *euere*
B.Pr.45 Slep and slewþe seweþ hem *euere*.
B. 1.99 Dide hem sweren on hir swerd to seruen truþe *euere*.
B. 1.115 Into a deep derk helle to dwelle þere for *euere*;
B. 2.103 A dwellynge wiþ þe deuel and dampned be for *euere*
B. 2.157 Iuggen yow ioyntly in ioie for *euere*.
B. 2.205 That holy chirche for hem worþ harmed for *euere*.]
B. 3.160 The ma3e for a mene man þou3 he mote *euere*!
B. 3.174 For Conscience accuseþ þee to congeien þee for *euere*.'
B. 3.192 Wendest þat wynter wolde han ylasted *euere*;
B. 3.279 That god hated hym for *euere* and alle hise heires after.
B. 4.66 Thei3 pees and his power pleyned h[e]m *euere*'.
B. 4.127 That no man go to Galis but if he go for *euere*.
B. 4.192 'I am redy,' quod Reson, 'to reste wiþ yow *euere*;
B. 5.89 [This was al his curteisie where þat *euere* he shewed hym].
B. 5.104 Ac hadde I maistrie and my3t [I wolde murþere hym for *euere*].
B. 5.230 'Repentedestow *euere*', quod Repentaunce, 'or restitucion madest?'
B. 5.237 'Vsedestow *euere* vsurie', quod Repentaunce, 'in al þi lif tyme?'
B. 5.250 'Lentestow *euere* lordes for loue of hire mayntenaunce?'
B. 5.396 Ac neiþer of oure lord ne of oure lady þe leeste þat *euere* was
          maked.
B. 5.408 Than al þat *euere* Marc made, Mathew, Iohan and Lucas.
B. 5.440 And *euere* siþþe be beggere [by cause of my] sleuþe:
B. 5.505 That *euere* þei wraþed þee in þis world in word, þou3t or dedes.'
B. 5.540 And diden me suren hym [siþþen] to seruen hym for *euere*,
B. 5.599 And am sory for my synnes and so [shal I] *euere*
B. 5.618 A[c] þer are seuen sustren þat seruen truþe *euere*
B. 6.200 Hoom [in]to his owene [e]rd and holden hym þere [*euere*].
B. 6.277 Wend now whan [þi wil is], þat wel be þow *euere*.'\
B. 7.99 That *euere* [he was man] wro3t whan [he] shal hennes fare.
B. 8.19 And *euere* haþ as I hope, and euere shal herafter.
B. 8.19 And euere haþ as I hope, and *euere* shal herafter.'
B. 8.69 That *euer* dremed [dri3t] in [doute], as I wene.
B. 8.106 But dobest bede for hem [abide] þer for *euere*.
B. 9.141 That *euere* cursed Caym coom on þis erþe:
B.10.16 Than alle þe sooþ sawes þat Salomon seide *euere*.
B.10.129 That *euere* [eft] wilneþ to wite why þat god wolde
B.10.277 For goddes word wolde no3t be lost, for þat wercheþ *euere*;
B.10.331 And þanne shal þe Abbot of Abyngdoun and al his issue for *euere*
B.10.402 Ac hir werkes, as holy writ seiþ, [was] *euere* þe contrarie.
B.10.447 For soþest word þat *euer* god seide was þo he seide Nemo bonus.
B.10.473 That *euere* þe[i] kouþe [konne on book] moore þan Credo in deum
          patrem,
B.11.32 Coueitise of ei3e, þat *euere* þow hir knewe—
B.11.186 In a pouere mannes apparaille pursue[þ] vs *euere*,
B.11.256 And alle þe wise þat *euere* were, by au3t I kan aspye,
B.12.98 Ne countreplede clerkes, I counseille þee for *euere*.
B.12.194 And grace asked of god þat [grai3 is hem *euere*]
B.12.224 How *euere* beest ouþer brid haþ so breme wittes.
B.12.253 That *euere* he gadered so grete and gaf þerof so litel,
B.13.6 And how þat Elde manaced me, my3te we *euere* mete;
B.13.60 And made hym murþe wiþ his mete, ac I mornede *euere*
B.13.368 Or by ny3te or by daye aboute was ich *euere*
B.14.196 Ellis is al on ydel, al þat *euere* [we diden],
B.14.202 For seuene synnes þer ben assaillen [vs *euere*];
B.14.303 And for þe [lewde] *euere* [yliche] a lemman of alle clennesse.
B.14.307 And *euer* þe lasse þat he [lede], þe [li3ter] he is of herte:

B.14.326 Synne seweþ vs *euere*', quod he and sory gan wexe,
B.14.328 That [*euere* he] dide dede þat deere god displesed;
B.14.330 That *euere* he hadde lond ouþer lordshipe lasse oþer moore,
B.15.555 The lordshipe of londes [lese ye shul for *euere*],
B.15.583 In stoon for it stedefast was and stonde sholde *euere*.
B.16.2 For Haukyns loue þe Actif man *euere* I shal yow louye.
B.16.79 For *euere* as þei dropped adoun þe deuel was redy
B.16.134 As *euere* it was and as wid; wherfore I hote yow
B.16.143 That *euere* he his Saueour solde for siluer or ellis.'
B.16.187 Wardeyn of þat wit haþ; was *euere* wiþouten gynnyng.
B.16.254 For in his bosom he bar a þyng þat he blissed *euere*.
B.16.268 That is lif for lif; or ligge þus *euere*
B.17.129 In þre persones departable þat perpetuele were *euere*,
B.17.255 Delen and do penaunce day and nyght *euere*,
B.17.335 For kynde clyueþ on hym *euere* to contrarie þe soule:
B.18.35 And forbete and adoun brynge bale deeþ for *euere*:
B.18.93 Callede hem caytyues, acorsed for *euere*.
B.18.305 For þe body, while it on bones yede, aboute was *euere*
B.18.332 I bihi3te hem no3t here helle for *euere*.
B.19.45 The lawe of lif þat laste shal *euere*,
B.19.89 Gold is likned to leautee þat laste shal *euere*
B.19.175 And now art lyuynge and lokynge and laste shalt *euere*."
B.19.178 Blessed mote þow be, and be shalt for *euere*.
B.19.290 And who[so] ete [of] þat seed hardy was *euere*
B.20.103 That he hitte euene, þat *euere* stired after.
B.20.185 So harde he yede ouer myn heed it wole be sene *euere*.
B.20.205 And hold þee þere *euere* til I sende for þee.
C.Pr.46 Slep and slewthe sueth [hem] *euer*.
C.Pr.123 Than *euere* he dede on Offi[n] and Fines [or on her] fader.
C. 1.103 Dede hem swere on here swerd to serue treuthe *euere*.
C. 1.133 Estward til heuene, *euere* to abyde
C. 2.251 And holy churche thorw hem worth harmed for *euere*.'
C. 3.198 The mase for a mene man thow he mote *euere*!
C. 3.220 For Consience acuseth the to congeye the for *euere*.'
C. 3.432 That god [hated hym] for *euere* and alle [his] eyres aftur.
C. 4.70 Of pees and his power thow he pleyne *euere*.'
C. 4.124 So þat noon go to galys but yf he go for *euere*;
C. 5.96 A boute suche a bargayn he was þe bet *euere*
C. 5.174 Bred withouten beggynge to lyue by *euere* aftur
C. 6.100 Now hit athynketh me in my thouhte þat *euere* y so wrouhte.
C. 6.234 'Repentedest [thow e]*uere*,' quod repentaunce, '[or] Restitucioun
          madest?'
C. 6.239 Vsedest [thow] *euere* vsurye in al thy lyf tyme?'
C. 6.248 'Lenedest [thow] *euere* eny lord for loue of his mayntenaunce?'
C. 7.12 Ac of oure lord ne of oure lady þe leste þat *euere* was maked.
C. 7.24 Th[en] al þat *euere* Mark made, Matheu, Iohn or lucas.
C. 7.150 That *euere* they gulte a3eyn þe, god, in gost or in dede.'
C. 7.185 And maden me sykere[n] sethen to seruen hym for *euere*,
C. 7.246 Y am sory [for] my synnes, and so [shal y] *euere*,
C. 7.270 Ac ther ben seuene susteres þat seruen treuthe *euere*
C. 8.206 Hoem [in]to his owene [e]rd and halde hym þere *euere*.
C. 8.298 Wende nouthe when thow wol[t] and wel [be thow] *euere*
C. 9.4 For hym and [for] his ayres for *euere* to ben assoiled.
C. 9.40 And abyde þer in my blisse body and soule for *euere*.'
C.10.19 And *euere* hath, as y hope, and euere wol hereaftur.'
C.10.19 And euere hath, as y hope, and *euere* wol hereaftur.'
C.10.51 Ac fre wil and fre wit foleweth man *euere*
C.10.220 Alle þat come of Caym Caytyue[s] were *euere*
C.10.229 That *euere* corsed Caym cam on þis erthe;
C.11.191 Couetyse-of-yes þat thow here knewe—
C.11.274 That clergie of cristes mouthe com[e]nded was *euere*—
C.11.285 Was Austyn þe oelde þat *euere* man wiste,
C.12.6 He shal asoile [the] thus sone how so *euere* thow wynne hit.
C.12.142 And alle þe wyse þat *euere* were, by auhte y can aspye,
C.12.160 And lyf lastyng for *euere* byfore oure lord in heuene:
C.12.235 For, how [*euere* hit] be ywonne, but hit [be] wel despene[d]
C.13.205 Forthy,' quod Resoun, 'y rede thow reule thy tonge *euere*
C.14.29 May nat be, [þe] þ[ow] syker, thogh we bidde *euere*.
C.15.64 And made [hym] mer[þe] with [h]is mete Ac y mournede *euere*
C.15.144 3ef hym eft and eft, *euere* at his nede,
C.15.303 And slepeth, as hit semeth, and somur *euere* hem foleweth.
C.16.43 For seuene synnes þer ben þat ass[a]ilen vs *euere*;
C.16.142 And þe lasse þat [eny] lede þe lihtere his herte is there,
C.17.94 Ther sholde be plente and pees perpetuel *euere*.
C.17.218 The lordschipe of londes lese 3e shal for *euer*
C.18.27 Thre persones indepartable, perpetuel were *euere*,
C.18.110 For *euere* as Elde hadde eny down, þe deuel was redy
C.18.270 For in his bosome a baer [a] thyng þat [a] blessede [*euere*].
C.18.284 And þat is lyf for lyf or ligge thus *euere*
C.19.135 And al þe myhte with hym is, was and worth *euere*.
C.19.221 Dele and do penaunce day and nyht *euere*
C.19.315 For kynde cleueth on hym *euere* to contrarie þe soule:
C.20.34 And forbete [and adown] b[r]ynge bale deth for *euere*:

C.20.45   And as wyde as hit *euere* was; this we witnesseth alle.'
C.20.96   Calde hem Caytyues, acorsed for *euere*.
C.20.198   Sholde deye downriht and d[welle] in payne *euere*
C.20.304   [Sh]olde deye with doel and here dwelle *euere*
C.20.337   For þe body, whiles hit on bones 3ede, aboute was hit *euere*
C.20.375   Y bihihte hem nat here helle for *euere*.
C.21.45   The lawe of lyf that laste shal *euere*
C.21.89   Gold is likened to lewetee that laste shal *euere*
C.21.175   And now art lyuynge and lokynge and laste shalt *euere*."
C.21.178   Yblessed mote thow be and be shalt for *euere*.
C.21.290   And hoso ete of þa[t] seed hardy was *euere*
C.22.103   That he hi[t]te euene, þat *euere* stured aftur.
C.22.185   So harde he 3ede ouer myn heued hit wol be sene *euere*.
C.22.205   And halde the there *euere* til y sende for the.

eueremoore adv *evermor adv.* A 5 eueremore; B 12 eueremo (1)
eueremoore (11); C 10 eueremore (8) euermore (2)
A. 4.77   Amende þat mysdede, & *eueremore* þe betere.'
A. 7.224   He hadde maugre of his maister *eueremore* aftir,
A. 8.4   For hym & for hise heires *eueremore* aftir,
A. 8.77   And gon & faiten wiþ here fauntis for *eueremore* aftir.
A.12.39   To be hure man 3if I most for *eueremore* aftir,
B. 4.90   Amenden þat [mysdede] and *eueremoore* þe bettre.'
B. 6.240   He hadde maugree of his maister *eueremoore* after,
B. 7.4   For hym and for hise heires *eueremoore* after.
B. 7.82   For beggeres borwen *eueremo* and hir borgh is god almy3ty
B. 7.95   And goon [and] faiten with [hire] fauntes for *eueremoore* after.
B.12.206   For he þat is ones a þef is *eueremoore* in daunger,
B.14.134   Hewen þat han hir hire afore arn *eueremoore* nedy,
B.14.223   And buxomnesse and boost [ben] *eueremoore* at werre,
B.15.179   Fiat voluntas tua fynt hym *eueremoore*,
B.15.485   And feden vs and festen vs for *eueremoore* at oones].
B.17.137   Thyn euenecristene *eueremoore* eueneforþ with þiselue,
B.18.185   To be mannes meynpernour for *eueremoore* after.
C. 3.250   Wherby he may as a man for *eueremore* lyue aftur.
C. 3.287   That mede [is] *euermore* a mayntenour of Gyle,
C. 3.403   And nyme hym into oure noumbre, now and *eueremore*:
C. 4.86   And amende þat is mysdo and *eueremore* þe betere.'
C. 9.171   And goen and fayten with here fauntes for *eueremore* aftur.
C.12.92   And louye for oure lordes loue and do leute *euermore*.
C.14.145   For he þat is ones a thef is *eueremore* in daunger
C.16.3   Hewen þat haen here huyre byfore aren *eueremore* pore
C.16.64   And buxumnesse and b[o]est [b]en *eueremore* at werre
C.17.66   That his mede and his manhede for *eueremore* shal laste:

euery adj *everi pron.* B 10; C 7
B. 5.247   And lene folk þat lese wole a lippe at *euery* noble.
B. 8.53   Wit and free wil, to *euery* wi3t a porcion,
B. 9.182   And *euery* maner seculer [man] þat may no3t continue
B.10.368   For *euery* cristene creature sholde be kynde til ooþer,
B.11.211   And *euery* man helpe ooþer for hennes shul we alle:
B.11.399   *Euery* creature in his kynde encreesse [he bad]
B.11.437   As shame: þere he sheweþ hym, [hym shonyeþ *euery* man].
B.15.263   For wel may *euery* man wite, if god hadde wold hymselue,
B.15.570   *Euery* bisshop þat bereþ cros, by þat he is holden
B.17.281   For *euery* manere good [man may] be likned
C. 3.67   That *euery* seg shal se y am sustre of 3oure ordre.'
C. 9.230   To heren here euensong *euery* man ouhte.
C.10.181   *Euery* man þat hath inwit and his hele bothe
C.10.283   And *euery* maner seculer man þat may nat contynue
C.12.118   And *euery* man helpe other for hennes shal we alle
C.17.283   *Euery* bisshope bi þe lawe sholde buxumliche walke
C.19.262   For *euery* manere goed man may be likned to a torche

euermore > eueremoore

euesynges n *evesing n.* B 1; C 1
B.17.231   Ysekeles in *euesynges* þoru3 hete of þe sonne
C.19.197   Isekeles in *euesynges* thorwe hete of the sonne

euesong > euensong

euidence n *evidence n.* B 3 euidence (2) euydence (1); C 4 euydence (2)
euidences (1) euydences (1)
B.15.437   And hardie hem þat bihynde ben, and 3yue hem good *euidence*.
B.17.198   By þis skile', [he seide], 'I se an *euidence*
B.18.152   For venym fordooþ venym, [þer fecche I *euydence*
C. 8.261   This aren *euidences*,' quod hunger, 'for hem þat wolle nat swynke
C.11.281   Sothly,' saide rechelesnesse, '3e se by many *euydences*
C.19.164   Bi this simile,' he seide, 'y se an *euydence*
C.20.155   For venym fordoth venym, þer feche y *euydence*

euil > yuel

ewages n *ewage adj.* B 1
B. 2.14   Orientals and *Ewages* enuenymes to destroye.

ewangelie > euaungelie

except prep *excep ppl. (& conj.)* B 4 except (2) excepte (2); C 3 excepte
B. 9.144   *Excepte* oonliche of ech kynde a couple
B.11.98   *Excepte* persons and preestes and prelates of holy chirche.
B.15.53   That any creature sholde konne al *except* crist oone.
B.15.279   *Except* þat Egidie after an hynde cride,
C.10.232   *Excepte* onliche of vch kynde a payre
C.16.215   That eny creature sholde conne al *excepte* crist one.
C.17.9   *Excepte* þat Egide a hynde oþerwhile

excesse n *excess n.* B 1; C 1 exces
B. 5.359   And after al þis *excesse* he hadde an Accidie
C. 6.417   And aftur al this *exces* he hadde an accidie;

exciteþ v *exciten* B 1; C 2 exited (1) exitede (1)
B.11.190   And *exciteþ* vs by þe Euaungelie þat, whan we maken festes,
C. 6.20   Demed for here vuel vices and *exitede* oþere
C. 6.188   *Exited* either oþer til oure olde synne;

excuse v *excusen v.* A 1 excuse; B 6 excuse (3) excused (2) excuseþ (1);
C 9 excuce (1) excuse (3) excused (5)
A. 3.160   'Excuse þe 3if þou canst; I can no more sei3e,
B. 3.173   'Excuse þee if þow kanst; I kan na moore seggen,
B. 9.186   Wreke þee wiþ wyuyng if þow wolt ben *excused*:
B.12.20   I sei3 wel he seide me sooþ, and somwhat me to *excuse*
B.15.486   Ac who beþ þat *excuseþ* hem þat [arn] persons and preestes,
B.17.93   'Haue hem *excused*', quod he; 'hir help may litel auaille.
B.20.6   '[Coudes]tow no3t *excuse* þee as dide þe kyng and oþere:
C. 3.219   'Excuce the yf thow kanst; y can no more segge
C. 5.34   Or ymaymed thorw som myshap whereby thow myhte be
excused?'
C. 7.298   Treuth telleth [this to hym], þat y be *excused*.'
C. 9.240   Acounted byfore [crist] but Consience *excuse* hym.
C.13.83   That þe lawe 3eueth leue such low folk to be *excused*,
C.15.128   'Haue me *excused*,' quod Clergie, 'be crist, but in scole.
C.19.83   'Haue hem *excused*,' quod [t]he samaritaen; 'here helpe may nat
availe.
C.19.247   *Excuse* hem þat ben vnkynde and 3ut here [catel] ywonne
C.22.6   'Couthest thow nat *excuse* the as dede the kyng and oþere:

executours n *executour n. cf. seketoures* B 4
B. 5.263   Ne þyne *executours* wel bisette þe siluer þat þow hem leuest;
B.12.260   *Executours*, false frendes, þat fulfille no3t his wille
B.15.132   *Executours* and Sodenes, Somonours and hir lemmannes.
B.20.291   As sisours and *executours*; þei [shul] 3yue þe freres

exited(e > exciteþ

experience n *experience n.* B 1; C 1 experiense
B.18.151   'Thoru3 *experience*', quod [heo], 'I hope þei shul be saued;
C.20.154   'Thorw *experiense*,' quod he, 'y hope they shal ben saued;

experiment3 n *experiment n.* A 1 experimentis; B 1
A.11.160   *Experimentis* of alkenemye of albertis makyng,
B.10.217   *Experiment3* of Alkenamye [of Albertes makynge,

expounen v *expounen v.* B 1
B.14.278   '[Al þis] in englissh', quod Pacience, 'it is wel hard to *expounen*,

eye(s > ei3e

F

face n *face n.* A 6; B 4; C 4

A.1.10	I was aferd of hire *face* þei3 heo fair were,
A.1.15	Boþe wiþ fel & wiþ *face*, & 3af 3ow fyue wyttes
A.5.215	And flattide it on his *face* & faste on him criede
A.7.222	Matheu wiþ þe manis *face* [mouþ]iþ þise wordis:
A.8.39	And before þe *face* of my fadir fourme 3oure setis.
A.12.77	With þat cam a knaue with a confessoures *face*,
B.1.10	I was afered of hire *face* þei3 she fair weere
B.1.15	Boþe with fel and with *face*, and yaf yow fyue wittes
B.5.443	And flatte it on his *face* and faste on hym cryde
B.6.238	Mathew wiþ mannes *face* mouþe[þ] þise wordes:
C.1.10	Y was aferd of here *face* thow she fayre were
C.7.57	And flatte hit on his *face* and faste on hym cryede
C.8.240	þat sayth, "with swynke and with [swetande] *face*
C.10.157	Man is hym most lyk of membres and of *face*

fader n *fader n.* A 11 fadir (10) fadris (1); B 38 fader (34) fadres (4); C 34 fader (26) faderes (1) faders (1) fadres (2) fadur (4)

A.1.14	For he is *fadir* of feiþ & fourmide 3ow alle
A.1.62	*Fadir* of falshed, he foundi[de] it hymselue.
A.1.140	And þat falliþ to þe *fadir* þat fourmide vs alle,
A.3.116	3oure *fadir* he[o] fellide þoru3 false behest,
A.6.54	Forto 3e fynden a foorþe, 3oure *fadris* honouriþ;
A.8.39	And before þe face of my *fadir* fourme 3oure setis.
A.8.145	'Beau fit3,' quaþ his *fadir*, 'for defaute we shuln,
A.8.147	It befel as his *fadir* seide in faraos tyme
A.10.28	*Fadir* & fourmour, þe ferste of alle þing.
A.10.66	Ac þe *fadir* & þe Frendis for fauntis shuln be blamid
A.11.64	And [ek] defame þe *fadir* þat vs alle mаde,
B.1.14	For he is *fader* of feiþ, and formed yow alle
B.1.64	*Fader* of falshede, [he] founded it hymselue.
B.1.166	And þat falleþ to þe *fader* þat formed vs alle,
B.2.25	For Fals was hire *fader* þat haþ a fikel tonge
B.2.29	My *fader* þe grete god is and ground of alle graces,
B.3.127	Youre *fader* she felled þoru3 false biheste,
B.5.503	That art oure *fader* and oure broþer, be merciable to vs,
B.5.567	[Forto] ye fynden a ford, oure-*fadres*-honoureþ;
B.7.54	Thise foure þe *fader* of heuene made to þis foold in commune;
B.7.168	'Beau fit3', quod his *fader*, 'for defaute we shullen,
B.7.170	It bifel as his *fader* seide in Pharaoes tyme
B.7.172	It bifel as his *fader* tolde, hise frendes þere hym sou3te.
B.9.27	*Fader* and formour, [þe first of alle þynges,
B.9.105	Wolde neuere þe feiþful *fader* [h]is fiþele were vntempred
B.9.117	First by þe *fadres* wille and þe frendes conseille,
B.9.150	Ac I fynde, if þe *fader* be fals and a sherewe,
B.10.106	And leyden fautes vpon þe *fader* þat formede vs alle,
B.10.247	God þe *fader*, god þe sone, god holy goost of boþe,
B.14.266	Hir *fader* and alle hire frendes, and folweþ hir make–
B.15.262	Of oure foes þat dooþ vs falsnesse; þat is oure *fadres* wille.
B.15.272	Antony and Egidie and oþere holy *fadres*
B.15.419	Wolde neuere þe feiþful *fader* þat [þ]ise Ministres sholde
B.15.606	Arn folk of oon feiþ; þe *fader* god þei honouren.
B.16.88	Filius by þe *fader* wille and frenesse of spiritus sancti
B.16.205	Adam, oure aller *fader*, Eue was of hymselue,
B.16.213	Hym þat first formed al, þe *fader* of heuene
B.16.223	So is þe *fader* forþ with þe sone and fre wille of boþe,
B.17.141	The *fader* was first as a fust wiþ o fynger foldynge
B.17.152	The *fader* is [þanne] as a fust wiþ fynger to touche–
B.17.161	Right so þe *fader* and þe sone and Seint Spirit þe þridde
B.17.166	That þre þynges bilongeþ in oure [*fader*] of heuene
B.17.170	So is þe *fader* a ful god, formour and shappere:
B.17.174	Right so þe sone þe Science of þe *fader*
B.17.175	And ful god as is þe *fader*, no febler ne no bettre.
B.17.202	For god þe *fader* is as a fust; þe sone is as a fynger;
B.17.229	And þanne flawmeþ he as fir on *fader* and on filius
B.17.238	So wol þe *fader* for3yue folk of mylde hertes
B.17.247	[Fro] þe *fader* of heuene for3ifnesse to haue.
C.Pr.120	And 3e shulde be here *fadres* and techen hem betre
C.Pr.122	Wel hardere and grettere on suche shrewed *faderes*
C.Pr.123	Than euere he dede on Offi[n] and Fines [or on her] *fader*.
C.1.14	For he is *fader* of fayth and formor of alle;
C.1.60	*Fader* of falshede fond hit firste of alle.

C.1.162	And þat falleth to þe *fader* þat formede vs alle,
C.2.25	Oon fauel was he[re] *fader* þat hath a fykel tonge
C.2.31	The *fader* þat me forth brouhte filius dei he hoteth,
C.2.124	Althow fals were here *fader* and fikel tonge her belsyre
C.3.164	3oure *fader* she [f]elde, fals and she togederes;
C.5.36	My *fader* and my frendes foende me to scole
C.6.15	For y, formost and furste, to *fader* and moder
C.7.143	That art furste oure *fadur* and of flesch oure broþer,
C.7.214	Forto 3e fynde a ford, 3oure-*fader*[s]-honoureth;
C.9.312	'Beau fit3,' quod þe *fadur*, 'for defaute we shal,
C.9.314	Hit biful as his *fadur* saide in farao his tyme
C.9.317	And his *fadur* Is[rael] and also his dame.
C.10.153	*Fader* and formour of al þat forth groweth
C.10.240	For thogh þe *fader* be a frankeleyn and for a felon be hanged
C.12.156	His *fader* or his frendes, fre[m]de oþer sybbe,
C.13.24	Spryngeth and spredeth, so spedde þe *fader* Abraham
C.16.27	And satisfaccioun þe whiche folfilleth þe *fader* will of heuene;
C.16.106	Here *fader* and alle here frendes and goth forth with here paramours;
C.17.60	To helpe thy *fader* formost byfore freres or monkes
C.18.90	Hit was þe furste fruyte þat þe *fader* of heuene blessed,
C.18.120	Filius by þe *fadres* wille fley with spiritus sanctus
C.18.226	Now go we to godhede: in god, *fader* of heuene,
C.19.126	The *fader* is thenne as þe fuste with fynger and with paume
C.19.132	So is þe *fader* a fol god, the fu[r]ste of hem alle
C.19.134	And he *fader* and for[m]eour, þe furste of alle thynges–
C.19.168	For [g]o[d] þe *fader* is as þe fust; þe sone is as þe fynger;
C.19.195	And thenne flaumeth he as fuyr on *fader* and on filius
C.19.204	So wol þe *fader* for3eue folke of mylde hertes
C.19.213	To þe *fader* of heuene for3e[ue]nesse to haue.

faderlese adj *faderles adj.* B 1
B.9.70	And] fynden hem þat hem fauted, and *faderlese* children,

fadir fadres fadur > fader; fay > fey; fayere > fair; fayful(- > feiþful(-

faillen v *failen v.* A 9 faile (6) failiþ (1) faille (2); B 34 faile (3) failed (4) faileþ (1) fayleþ (1) faille (15) failled (1) faillen (3) failleþ (6); C 32 faile (2) fayle (11) failed (2) faylede (3) faylen (2) faileth (4) fayleth (6) faylle (1) failleth (1)

A.2.93	Wel 3e wyte, wernardis, but 3if 3oure wyt *faile*,
A.2.110	'And nameliche to þe notories, þat hem non *fail*[e];
A.4.157	'I graunte,' quaþ þe king, 'godis forbode he *faille*!
A.7.16	For I shal lene hem lyflode, but 3if þe lond *faile*,
A.7.256	And lerne to laboure wiþ lond lest liflode hym *faile*.
A.7.306	Þoru3 flood [and] foule wederis fruytes shuln *fa[i]lle*,
A.8.107	And beloure þat I [be]lou3 er þei3 liflode me *faile*.
A.10.58	In 3onge fauntes & folis, wiþ hem *failiþ* Inwyt,
A.11.207	"Whanne fisshes *faile* þe flood or þe fresshe watir
B.2.92	There as wil wolde and werkmanshipe *fayleþ*.'
B.2.129	Wel ye witen, wernardes, but if youre wit *faille*,
B.2.146	And namely to þe Notaries þat hem noon *faille*.
B.3.52	For to be youre frend, frere, and *faile* yow neuere
B.3.347	Ac yow *failed* a konnynge clerk þat kouþe þe leef han torned.
B.4.156	I falle in floryns', quod þat freke, 'and *faile* speche ofte.'
B.4.194	'I graunte [gladly]', quod þe kyng, 'goddes forbode [he *faile*]!
B.6.17	For I shal lenen hem liflode but if þe lond *faille*
B.6.272	And lerne to laboure wiþ lond [lest] liflode [hym *faille*].
B.6.325	Thoru3 flo[od] and foule wedres fruytes shul *faille*.
B.7.125	And wepen whan I sholde [werche] þou3 whete breed me *faille*.
B.7.154	Ac I haue no sauour in songewarie for I se it ofte *faille*.
B.9.83	Ne *faille* payn ne potage and prelates dide as þei sholden.
B.10.301	Whan fisshes *faillen* þe flood or þe fresshe water
B.10.398	In good þan in god; forþi hem grace *failleþ*.
B.11.26	'The freke þat folwede my wille *failled* neuere blisse.'
B.11.29	Thow shalt fynde Fortune þee *faille* at þi mooste nede
B.11.279	For *failed* neuere man mete þat my3tful god serueþ;
B.11.307	So is it a goky, by god! þat in his gospel *failleþ*,
B.12.7	To amende it in þi myddel age, lest my3t þe *faill*[e]
B.13.5	First how Fortune me *failed* at my mooste nede;
B.13.255	Ac if my3t of myracle hym *faille* it is for men ben no3t worþi
B.14.33	And þat ynogh; shal noon *faille* of þyng þat hem nedeþ:
B.14.89	And surgiens for dedly synnes whan shrift of mouþe *failleþ*.

B.15.178   For a frend þat fyndeþ hym *failed* hym neuere at nede:
B.15.359   Astronomiens alday in hir Art *faillen*
B.15.367   Now *failleþ* þe folk of þe flood and of þe lond boþe,
B.15.384   Thei sholde *faillen* of hir Philosophie and in Phisik boþe.
B.15.432   [Ac] fressh flessh ouþer fissh, whan it salt *failleþ*,
B.17.190   For peyne of þe pawme power hem *failleþ*
B.17.251   For may no fir flaumbe make, *faille* it [h]is kynde.
B.19.218   And wepne to fighte wiþ þat wole neuere *faille*.
B.20.31   And Spiritus prudencie in many a point shal *faille*
B.20.234   'And for þei are pouere, parauenture, for patrymoyne [hem]
             faille[þ]
C. 1.120   Ther he *faylede* and ful and his felawes alle;
C. 1.186   Mony chapeleynes aren chaste ac charite hem *fayleth*;
C. 2.99   There þat wille wolde and wer[k]manschip *faileth*.
C. 2.162   And [name]liche [to] the notaries þat [hem noon] *fayle*.
C. 3.56   'Y shal be ȝoure frende, frere, and *fayle* ȝow neuere
C. 3.350   To pay hym yf he parforme and haue pite yf he *faileth*
C. 5.148   Ryht as fysches in floed whan hem *fayleth* water
C. 6.256   For þe pope with alle his pentauncers power hem *fayleth*
C. 8.15   For y shal lene hem lyflode but [yf] þe lond *faylle*
C. 8.293   And lerne to labory with lond lest lyflode h[y]m *fayle*.
C. 8.346   Thorw flodes and foule wederes fruyttes shollen *fayle*;
C. 9.303   Ac men setteth nat by sowngewarie for me seth hit often *fayle*;
C.10.167   Of gold and of oþer goed ac goddes grace hem *fayleth*.
C.11.188   Thow shalt fortune þe *fayle* if thy moste nede
C.11.229   In goed then in god; forthy hem grace *faileth*.
C.12.121   And pore peple *fayle* we nat while eny peny vs lasteth
C.13.121   So [is hit] a goky, by god! þat in [his] gospel *fayleth*
C.15.5   Furste how fortune me *faylede* At my moste nede;
C.15.225   Ac yf myhte of myracle hym *fayle* hit is for men beth nat worthy
C.16.319   A frende he hath þat fyn[t] hym þat *faylede* hym neuere.
C.17.97   Astronomiens alday in here arte *faylen*
C.17.104   Now *failleth* this folk, bothe follwares and shipmen;
C.17.116   Bo[t]e they *fayle* in philosophie and philosoferes lyuede.
C.17.144   For when alle frendes *faylen* and fleen away in deynge
C.18.30   [And fro fallynge the stok; hit *fayle* nat of his myhte].
C.19.136   The fyngeres is a fol hand for *failed* they or thombe
C.19.139   Riht so *failed* þe sone, the syre be ne myhte
C.19.156   For peyne of þe paume power hem *fayleth*
C.19.217   For may no fuyr flaume make, *faile* hit his kynde.
C.21.218   And wepne to fihte with þat wol neuere *fayle*.
C.22.31   And spiritus Prudencie in many a poynt shal *faile*
C.22.234   'And for thei aren pore, parauntur, for patrimonye hem *faileth*,

fayn adj *fain adj. &> fayne* A 6; B 7; C 8
A. 2.122   Þanne was fals *fayn*, & fauel als bliþe,
A. 3.108   For heo is *fayn* of þi Felasshipe, for to be þi make.'
A. 4.13   'I am *fayn* of þat foreward,' seiþ þe frek þanne,
A. 7.255   And be *fayn* be my feiþ his fesik to leten,
A. 7.284   Þanne was folk *fayn*, & fedde hunger with þe beste,
A.11.110   Þanne was I [as] *fayn* as foul of fair morewen,
B. 2.78   Falsnesse is *fayn* of hire for he woot hire riche;
B. 2.158   Thanne was Fal[s] *fayn* and Fauel as bliþe,
B. 3.119   For she is *fayn* of þi felaweshipe, for to be þi make.'
B. 4.13   'I am *fayn* of þat foreward', seide þe freke þanne,
B. 6.271   And be *fayn*, by my feiþ, his Phisik to lete,
B. 6.300   Thanne was folk *fayn* and fedde hunger wiþ þe beste,
B.10.158   Thanne was [I] also *fayn* as fowel of fair morwe,
C. 2.85   Falsnesse is *fayn* of here for he wot here ryche;
C. 2.174   Thenne was [falsnesse] *fayn* and [fauel] blythe,
C. 3.156   For she is *fayn* of thy felawschipe, for to be thy make.'
C. 4.13   'Y am *fayn* of that foreward, in fayth,' tho quod Consience,
C. 4.28   *Fayn* were to folowe hem and faste ryden aftur
C. 8.292   And be *fayn*, be my fayth, his fysik to leete
C. 8.322   Thenne [was] folke *fayn* and fedde hunger dentie[f]liche
C.11.100   Thenne was y as *fayn* as foul of faire morwen,

fayne adv *fain adv.* A 1 fayn; B 1; C 1 fayn
A.12.67   'I wolde folwe þe *fayn*, but fentesye me hendeþ;
B.11.392   Ne þow shalt fynde but fewe *fayne* [wolde] heere
C.18.102   Bothe parfit and inparfit.' Puyr *fayn* y wolde

fayned > feynen

fair adj *fair adj. &> faire* A 9 fair (6) faire (3); B 31 fair (14) faire (13)
     fairer (2) faireste (1) feirest (1); C 42 fayere (1) fair (2) fayr (1) faire
     (1) fayre (28) fayrere (2) fayrest (4) fayreste (1) faior (1) feyr (1)
A.Pr.17   A *fair* feld ful of folk fand I þere betwene
A. 1.10   I was aferd of hire face þeiȝ heo *fair* were,
A. 2.23   Fauel wiþ *fair* speche haþ forgid hem togidere;
A. 2.114   To false & to fauel for here *faire* ȝeftis,
A. 2.130   And fauel vpon *fair* speche, fe[int]liche atirid.
A. 2.191   Freris wiþ *fair* speche fetten hym þennes;
A. 9.70   Arn þre *faire* vertues, & ben not f[e]re to fynde.
A.10.18   And haþ fyue *faire* sones be his furste wyf:

A.11.110   Þanne was I [as] *fayn* as foul of *fair* morewen,
B.Pr.17   A *fair* feeld ful of folk fond I þer bitwene
B. 1.10   I was afered of hire face þeiȝ she *fair* weere
B. 2.42   Fauel þoruȝ his *faire* speche haþ þis folk enchaunted,
B. 2.150   To Fals and to Fauel for hire *faire* ȝiftes,
B. 2.166   And Fauel on [*Fair* Speche] fe[ynt]ly atired.
B. 2.232   Freres wiþ *fair* speche fetten hym þennes;
B. 8.79   Arn þre *faire* vertues, and ben noȝt fer to fynde.
B. 9.19   And haþ fyue *faire* sones bi his firste wyue:
B.10.158   Thanne was [I] also *fayn* as fowel of *fair* morwe,
B.11.12   Thanne hadde Fortune folwynge hire two *fair* damyseles:
B.11.61   And þanne was Fortune my foo for al hir *faire* [biheste],
B.11.194   Youre festynge and youre *faire* ȝifte; ech frend quyteþ so ooþer.
B.11.365   I seiȝ floures in þe fryth and hir *faire* colours
B.11.396   For be a man *fair* or foul it falleþ noȝt to lakke
B.12.221   And of þe floures in þe Fryth and of hire *faire* hewes,
B.12.238   And þat þe *faireste* fowel foulest engendreþ,
B.13.296   Or *feirest* of feitures of forme and of shafte,
B.14.25   Shal noon heraud ne harpour haue a *fairer* garnement
B.15.102   Shal neuere flour ne fruyt [wexe] ne *fair* leef be grene.
B.15.334   That were ful of *faire* trees, and I fondede and caste
B.15.351   And so it fareþ by som folk now; þei han a *fair* speche,
B.16.1   'NOw *faire* falle yow', quod I þo, 'for youre *faire* shewyng!
B.16.29   And forfreteþ neiȝ þe fruyt þoruȝ manye *faire* sightes.
B.16.149   That is kissynge and *fair* contenaunce and vnkynde wille.
B.16.154   'Falsnesse I fynde in þi *faire* speche
B.17.210   Fostren forþ a flawmbe and a *fair* leye
B.19.28   To be called a knyght is *fair* for men shul knele to hym.
B.19.29   To be called a kyng is *fairer* for he may knyghtes make.
B.19.456   And alle þo *faire* vertues as vices þei semeþ.
B.20.118   Weren feþered wiþ *fair* biheste and many a fals truþe.
B.20.349   Lat in þe frere and his felawe, and make hem *fair* cheere.
C.Pr.19   A *fair* feld ful of folk fond y þer bytwene
C. 1.10   Y was afeerd of hire face thow she *fayre* were
C. 2.166   That [fals] and [fauel] hadde for he[re] *fayre* ȝeftes,
C. 2.242   Freres [with] *fayre* speche fetten hym thennes;
C. 6.46   Prout of my *fayre* fetures and for y song shille;
C. 8.215   'Ther is no fi[al] loue with this folk for al here *fayre* speche
C. 9.85   Bothe afyngred and afurste, to turne þe *fayre* outward
C. 9.259   Vigilare were *fayrere* for thow haste a greet charge.
C. 9.269   And many a *fayre* flees falsliche is ywasche!
C.10.77   Aren thre *fayre* vertues and ben nat fer to fynde.
C.10.145   And hath fyue *fayre* sones by his furste wyue:
C.11.100   Thenne was y as *fayn* as foul of *faire* morwen,
C.11.171   Thenne hadde fortune folwyng here two *fayre* maydenes:
C.12.13   And thenne was fortune my foo for al her *fayre* biheste
C.12.246   Lo, how pans purchaseth *fayre* places and d[r]ede,
C.13.43   Thogh the messager make his way amydde the *fayre* whete
C.13.175   Ne what o[f] floures on felde and of here *fayre* coloures
C.13.200   Is no vertue so *fair* ne of valewe ne profit
C.14.158   And how þe floures in þe fryth cometh to *fayre* hewes:
C.14.170   Þat þe *fayrest* foul foulest engendreth
C.14.177   For here fetheres þat *fayre* beth to fle fer hem letteth.
C.14.180   More þan for his *fayre* flesch or for his merye note.
C.15.8   And vansche alle my vertues and my *fayre* lotus.
C.16.255   Shal neuere flour ne fruyt wexe ne *fayre* leue be grene.
C.17.143   Loue thy frende þat followeth thy wille, that is thy *fayre* soule.
C.18.29   The fruyt of this *fayre* tre fro thre wikkede wyndes
C.18.33   And forfret þat fruyt thorw many *fayre* s[ih]tus.
C.18.54   Where þe fruyt were *fayre* or foul for to loke on.
C.18.55   And þe fruyt was *fayre*, non fayrere be myhte,
C.18.55   And þe fruyt was fayre, non *fayrere* be myhte,
C.18.88   Thenne is virginite, more vertuous and *fayrest*, as in heuene,
C.18.92   In menynge þat the *fayrest* thyng the furste thynge sholde honoure
C.18.94   In kynges Court and in knyhtes, the clenneste men and *fayreste*
C.18.98   And for þe *fayrest* fruyte byfore hym, as of erthe,
C.18.171   'Falsnesse y fynde in thy *fayre* speche
C.18.247   How he fondede me furste; my *fayre* sone ysaak
C.19.176   Fostren forth a flaume and a *feyr* lye
C.21.28   To be cald a knyht is *fayr* for men shal knele to hym;
C.21.29   To be cald a kyng is *faior* for he may knyhtes make;
C.21.456   And al tho *fayre* vertues as vises thei semeth.
C.22.118   Weren fythered with *fayre* biheste and many a fals treuthe.
C.22.349   Lat in þe frere and his felawe and make hem *fayere* chiere.

fayre n *fair n.* C 1
C. 3.370   I wolde feffe hym with here *fayre* and [with] here foule taylende.

faire adv *faire adv. &> fair* A 10 faire (9) fairere (1); B 26 faire (24)
     fairer (2); C 20 fair (1) fayr (1) faire (3) fayre (13) fayror (1) vayre
     (1)
A. 1.2   And ek þe feld ful of folk I shal ȝow *faire* shewe.
A. 1.4   Com doun fro þat [clyf] & callide me *faire*,
A. 1.56   Þanne I fraynide hire *faire* for him þat hire made,

A. 1.72   What he[o] were witterly þat wisside me so *faire*.
A. 5.42   Qui cum patre & filio; *Faire* mote ȝow befalle.'
A. 5.245   Ac what befel of þis feloun I can not *faire* shewe;
A. 6.13   Þis folk fraynide hym *faire* [fro] whenis þat he come.
A. 6.111   He is wondirliche welcome & *faire* vndirfonge.
A. 9.24   Be a forebisene,' quaþ þe Frere, 'I shal þe *faire* shewen:
A.11.174   *Fairere* vndirfonge ne frendliere mad at ese
B. 1.2   And þe feld ful of folk I shal yow *faire* shewe.
B. 1.4   Cam doun from [þe] Castel and called me *faire*,
B. 1.58   Thanne I frayned hire *faire* for hym þat [hire] made,
B. 1.74   What she were witterly þat wissed me so *faire*.
B. 5.58   Qui cum patre & filio; þat *faire* hem bifalle
B. 5.471   What bifel of þis feloun I kan noȝt *faire* shewe
B. 5.525   This folk frayned hym [*faire*] fro whennes he come.
B. 5.626   He is wonderly welcome and *faire* vnderfongen.
B. 8.28   By a forbisne,' quod þe frere, 'I shal þe *faire* shewe.
B.10.231   *Fairer* vnderfongen ne frendlier at ese
B.11.440   And I aroos vp riȝt wiþ þat and [reuerenced] hym [*faire*,
B.13.27   Conscience knew hym wel and welcomed hym *faire*.
B.13.180   'Frendes, fareþ wel', and *faire* spak to clergie,
B.15.9   'God loke yow, lordes', ne loutede *faire*,
B.15.21   That ech a creature of his court welcomeþ me *faire*.'
B.15.374   [That kan versifie *faire* ne formaliche enditen],
B.16.1   'NOw *faire* falle yow', quod I þo, 'for youre faire shewyng!
B.16.53   'Now *faire* falle yow, Piers', quod I, 'so faire ye discryuen
B.16.53   'Now faire falle yow, Piers', quod I, 'so *faire* ye discryuen
B.16.65   To asken hym any moore þerof, and bad hym ful *faire*
B.16.66   'To [dyuyse] þe fruyt þat so *faire* hangeþ'.
B.16.226   I roos vp and reuerenced hym and riȝt *faire* hym grette.
B.18.68   Some seide þat he was goddes sone þat so *faire* deide:
B.19.73   Reuerenced hym [riȝt] *faire* wiþ richesses of erþe.
B.19.480   The viker hadde fer hoom and *faire* took his leeue
B.20.314   And moore of phisik bi fer, and *fairer* he plastreþ;
C. 1.2   And þe feld ful of folk y shal ȝou *fair* shewe.
C. 1.54   [Thanne] y fraynede her *fayr* for hym þat here made,
C. 1.71   What she were wytterly þat wissede me so [*faire*].
C. 5.199   Qui cum patre & filio; þat *fayre* hem byfalle
C. 6.325   What byful of this feloun y can nat *fayre* shewe;
C. 7.279   Is wonderliche welcome and *fayre* vnderfonge;
C. 9.129   To vnderfongen hem *fayre* byfalleth for þe ryche
C. 9.323   Worth *fayre* vnderfonge byfore god þat tyme
C.10.32   By a forbisene,' quod þe frere, 'y shal þe *fayre* shewe.
C.13.246   And [y] aroes vp riht with þat and reuerensed hym *fayre*
C.15.30   Concience knewe hym [wel and] welcomede hym *fayre*.
C.16.172   That vch a creature þat loueth crist welcometh me *faire*.'
C.17.31   And *faire* byfore tho men faunede with þe tayles.
C.17.84   That *fayre* byfore folk prechen and techen
C.17.110   Þat can versifye *vayre* or formallych endite
C.18.242   Y roos vp and reuerensed god and riȝt *fayre* hym grette,
C.20.70   Somme saide he was godes sone þat so *fayre* deyede:
C.21.73   Reuerensed hym riht *fayre* with richesses of erthe.
C.21.480   The vicory hadde fer hoem and [*fayre*] toek his leue
C.22.314   And more of fysyk bi fer, and *fayror* he plastereth;

fayre(s &> feire; fayrenesse > fairnesse

fairye n *fairie n.* A 1 fairie; B 1
A.Pr.6   Me befel a ferly, of *fairie* me þouȝte:
B.Pr.6   Me bifel a ferly, of *Fairye* me þoȝte.

fairnesse n *fairnesse n.* B 2; C 1 fayrenesse
B. 2.77   Than for any vertue or *fairnesse* or any free kynde.
B.12.46   Felice hir *fairnesse* fel hire al to sclaundre,
C.13.172   And ferlyede of his *fayrenesse* and of his foul le[den]e.

fait > feet; faiten > faytest

faiterie n *faiterie n.* B 1; C 2 fayterye (1) faytrye (1)
B.11.92   Falsnesse ne *faiterie*? for somwhat þe Apostle seide
C. 8.138   That no *faytrye* were founde in folk þat goth abeggeth.
C.12.33   Falsnesse ne *fayterye*? for sumwhat þe apostel saide:

faytest v *faiten v.(1)* A 1 faiten; B 2 faiten; C 5 faytede (1) fayteden (1) fayten (1) faytest (1) fayteth (1)
A. 8.77   And goon & *faiten* wiþ here fauntis for eueremore aftir.
B. 7.95   And goon [and] *faiten* with [hire] fauntes for eueremoore after.
B.15.214   Ne at Ancres þere a box hangeþ; alle swiche þei *faiten*.
C.Pr.43   *Fayteden* for here fode, foughten at þe ale.
C. 5.30   Or *faytest* vppon frydayes or festeday[es] in churches.
C. 9.100   Thouh he falle for defaute þat *fayteth* for his lyflode
C. 9.171   And goen and *fayten* with here fauntes for eueremore aftur.
C. 9.209   That *faytede* in frere clothinge hadde fatte chekes.

faith(ful -les > feiþ(-

faithly adv *feithli adv.* B 1; C 1 faythly
B.19.70   *Faithly* for to speke, his firste name was Iesus.

C.21.70   *Faythly* for to speke his furste name was iesus.

faityng ger *faiting ger.* B 1 faityng
B.10.39   But þoo þat feynen hem foolis, and wiþ *faityng* libbeþ

faitour n *faitour n.* A 5 faitour (1) faitours (4); B 9 faitour (2) faitours (7); C 8 faytors (1) faytour (3) faytours (4)
A. 2.94   Þat fals is a *faitour* [and] feyntles of werkis,
A. 2.144   As fo[bb]is & *faitours* þat on here feet iotten.'
A. 7.113   Þanne were *faitours* aferd & feynide hem blynde;
A. 7.171   *Faitours* for fer flowen into bernis
A.11.58   Freris and *faitours* han founden vp suche questiouns
B. 2.183   As [fobbes] and *Faitours* þat on hire feet [iotten].'
B. 6.72   And frere *faitour* and folk of hi[s] ordre,
B. 6.121   Tho were *faitours* afered and feyned hem blynde;
B. 6.183   *Faitours* for fere flowen into Bernes
B. 9.196   As fals folk, fondlynges, *faitours* and lieres,
B.10.72   Freres and *faitours* han founde [vp] swiche questions
B.13.242   *Faitours* and freres and folk wiþ brode crounes.
B.15.215   Fy on *faitours* and in fautores suos!
B.20.5   That afrounted me foule and *faitour* me called.
C. 2.196   As fobbes and *faytours* þat on here feet rennen.'
C. 8.73   And frere *faytour* and folk of þat ordre,
C. 8.128   Tho were *faytours* aferd and fayned hem blynde;
C. 8.179   Tho were *faytours* afered and flowen into [Peres] bernes
C. 9.64   He is fals and *faytour* and defraudeth the nedy
C.10.295   And fals folk and fondlynges, *faytors* and lyares,
C.11.52   Freres and *faytours* haen founde vp suche questions
C.22.5   That afrounted me foule and *faytour* me calde.

faytrye > faiterie

falaes adj *fallace adj.* C 1
C.16.232   Mouen motyues, mony tymes insolibles and *falaes*,

falewe v *falwen v.(1)* C 1
C. 7.295   To *falewe* with fiue ȝo[k]es; 'forthy me bihoueth

fall > falle

fallas n *fallace n.* C 1
C.11.20   Thorw *fallas* and fals questes and thorw fikel speche.

falle v *fallen v.* A 10 falle (3) fallen (1) falliþ (1) fel (3) fil (2); B 51 falle (22) fallen (6) falleþ (5) fel (8) felle (1) fellen (3) fil (4) fille (2); C 55 fall (1) falle (23) falleth (11) fallyng (1) ful (11) full (1) fullen (1) valle (1) yfalle (4) yfallen (1)
A.Pr.62   Manye ferlis han *fallen* in a fewe ȝeris.
A. 1.112   Þanne *fil* he wiþ [his] felawis & fendis bicome;
A. 1.140   And þat *falliþ* to be fadir þat fourmide vs alle.
A. 2.159   But riȝt as þe lawe lokis let *falle* on hem alle.'
A. 3.87   Þat fuyr shal *falle* & forbrenne at þe laste
A. 3.239   Why þe vengeaunce *fel* on saul & on his children?
A. 5.213   Sleuþe for sorewe *fil* doun a swowe
A. 8.141   As daniel deui[n]ide in dede it *fel* aftir:
A. 9.27   Makeþ þe man many tymes to *falle* & to stande.
A.10.185   As *fel* of þe folk [þat I] before shewide.
B.Pr.65   Manye ferlies han *fallen* in a fewe yeres.
B. 1.114   And *fel* fro þat felawshipe in a fendes liknesse
B. 1.121   But *fellen* out in fendes liknesse [ful] nyne dayes togideres
B. 1.124   Whan þise wikkede wenten out wonderwise þei *fellen*,
B. 1.166   And þat *falleþ* to þe fader þat formed vs alle,
B. 2.198   But riȝt as þe lawe [lokeþ] lat *falle* on hem alle.'
B. 3.98   That fir shal *falle* & [forbrenne at þe laste]
B. 3.260   Whi þ[at] vengeaunce *fel* on Saul and on his children?
B. 3.325   And er þis fortune *falle* fynde men shul þe worste
B. 4.156   I *falle* in floryns', quod þat freke, 'and faile speche ofte.'
B. 5.142   And now is *fallen* þerof a fruyt þat folk han wel leuere
B. 7.163   As Daniel diuined in dede it *fel* after:
B. 8.31   Makeþ þe man many tyme to *falle* and to stonde.
B.10.239   Wiþ alle þe articles of þe feiþ þat *falleþ* to be knowe.
B.10.283   And þe festu is *fallen* for youre defaute
B.10.476   That seruauntȝ þat seruen lordes selde *fallen* in arerage,
B.10.479   Selden *falle* so foule and so fer in synne
B.11.99   It *falleþ* noȝt for þat folk no tales to telle
B.11.396   For be a man fair or foul it *falleþ* noȝt to lakke
B.11.427   For lat a dronken daffe in a dyk *falle*,
B.12.46   Felice hir fairnesse *fel* hire al to sclaundre,
B.13.452   Thise solaceþ þe soule til hymself be *falle*
B.14.80   Vengeaunce *fil* vpon hem for hir vile synnes;
B.14.108   And þat at þe rekenyng in Arrerage *fel* raþer þan out of dette.
B.14.186   And if vs *fille* þoruȝ folie to falle in synne after
B.14.186   And if vs fille þoruȝ folie to *falle* in synne after
B.15.51   For swich a lust and likyng Lucifer *fel* from heuene:
B.15.300   That ne *fil* to hir feet and fawned wiþ þe tailles;
B.15.360   That whilom warned bifore what sholde *falle* after.

B.15.406 And dide folk þanne *falle* on knees; for he swoor in his prechyng
B.15.567 And purgen hem of poison er moore peril *falle*.
B.16.1   'NOw faire *falle* yow', quod I þo, 'for youre faire shewyng!
B.16.53   'Now faire *falle* yow, Piers', quod I, 'so faire ye discryuen
B.16.94   That Piers fruyt floured and *felle* to be rype.
B.16.107 Til he was parfit praktisour if any peril *fille*.
B.16.176 'I am feiþ', quod þat freke, 'it *falleþ* noȝt to lye;
B.17.314 That mercy in hir mynde may noȝt *fallen*;
B.17.336 And þouȝ it *falle* it fynt skiles þat "frelete it made",
B.18.87   Thanne *fil* þe knyȝt vpon knees and cryde [Iesu] mercy:
B.18.94   'For þis foule vileynye vengeaunce to yow *falle*!
B.18.103 And youre fraunchise þat fre was *fallen* is in þraldom;
B.18.312 First þoruȝ þe we *fellen* fro heuene so heiȝe:
B.18.360 And gile is bigiled and in his gile *fallen*:
B.18.369 Til þe vendage *falle* in þe vale of Iosaphat,
B.19.5   I *fel* eftsoones aslepe and sodeynly me mette
B.19.303 And to correcte [þ]e kyng if [þe kyng] *falle* in gilt.
B.20.10   And nede haþ no lawe ne neuere shal *falle* in dette
B.20.32   Of þat he weneþ wolde *falle* if his wit ne weere;
B.20.51   Whan nede ha[dde] vndernome me þus anoon I *fil* aslepe
B.20.176 A Phisicien wiþ a furred hood þat he *fel* in a palsie,
B.20.228 Conscience cryede, 'help, Clergie or I *falle*
C.Pr.63   Mony ferlyes han *falle* in a fewe ȝeres.
C.Pr.106 *Ful* on hem þat fre were thorwe two fals prestis!
C.Pr.113 And his sones slawe anon he *ful* for sorwe
C. 1.120 Ther he faylede and *ful* and his felawes alle;
C. 1.126 Wonderwyse, holy wryt telleth, how þei *fullen*,
C. 1.162 And þat *falleth* to þe fader þat formede vs alle,
C. 2.106 And sue forth suche felawschipe til they ben *falle* in Slewthe
C. 2.212 But riht as þe lawe loketh lat *falle* on hem alle.'
C. 3.90   Many sondry sorwes in Citees *falleth* ofte
C. 3.97   Morreyne or other meschaunc[e]: and mony tymes hit *falleth*
C. 3.102 And thenne *falleth* ther fuyr on fals men houses
C. 3.107 *Ful* adoun and forbrent forth alle þe rewe.
C. 3.126 That fuyr shal *falle* and forbrenne al to blew aysches
C. 3.478 Ac ar this fortune *falle* fynde ne shal the worste
C. 6.335 Fareth as flo[nke] of fuyr þat *ful* amydde Temese
C. 7.112 Thise solaseth þe soule til hymsulue be *yfalle*
C. 9.100 Thouh he *falle* for defaute þat fayteth for his lyflode
C. 9.180 As mesels and mendenantes, men *yfalle* in meschief
C. 9.183 Or thorw fuyr or thorw floed *yfalle* into pouerte,
C. 9.273 Redde racionem villicacionis or in arrerage *fall*!
C.10.22   *Fallyng* fro ioye, iesu woet þe sothe!
C.10.39   Thow he *falle* he falleth nat but [as] hoso ful in a boet
C.10.39   Thow he *falleth* he falleth nat but [as] hoso ful in a boet
C.10.39   Thow he falle he falleth nat but [as] hoso *ful* in a boet
C.10.42   Thow he thorw fondynges *falle* he falleth nat out of charite;
C.10.42   Thow he thorw fondynges falle he *falleth* nat out of charite;
C.11.296 Selde *falleth* þe seruant so depe in arrerage
C.11.300 Selde *falleth* so foule and so depe in synne
C.13.71   Alle maner men [in] meschief *yfalle*,
C.13.234 For lat a dronkene daffe in a dykke *falle*,
C.15.284 Hit are but fewe folk of this ryche that ne *falleth* in arrerage
C.16.213 For such a lust and lykynge lucifer *ful* fram heuene:
C.17.98   That whilum warnede byfore what sholde [f]*alle* aftur.
C.17.232 And purge hem of þe olde poysen Ar more perel *falle*.
C.18.48   So this lordeynes lithereth þerto þat alle þe leues *falleth*
C.18.50   And thenne [f]*alle* y adoune the pouke with the thridde shoriere
C.18.106 And shaken hit sharpeliche; the rype sholden *falle*.
C.18.127 That elde felde efte þe fruyt, or *full* to be rype.
C.18.184 'I am with fayth,' quod þat freke, 'hit *falleth* nat me to lye,
C.19.147 Bote [be he] greued with here grype the holy goost lat *falle*.
C.19.294 That mercy in here mynde may nat thenne *falle*;
C.19.316 And thogh he *falle* he fynte skiles þat "freelete hit made"
C.20.89   Tho *ful* the knyhte vppon knees and criede iesu mercy:
C.20.97   'For þis [fou]l vilanye vengeaunce [to] ȝow [f]*all[e]*!
C.20.106 And ȝoure franchise þat fre was *yfallen* is i[n] thraldoem;
C.20.346 And out of heuene hidore thy pryde made vs *falle*.
C.20.382 That gylours [beth] bigiled and [in] here gyle *falle*
C.20.411 Til þe ventage *valle* in þe vale of Iosophat
C.21.5   Y *ful* eftesones aslepe and sodeynliche me mette
C.21.303 And to corecte the kyng and the kyng *falle* in [g]ulte.
C.22.10   And nede hath no lawe ne neuere shal *falle* in dette
C.22.32   Of þat he weneth wolde *falle* yf his wit ne were;
C.22.51   Whenne nede hadde vndernome [me] thus anoen y *ful* aslepe
C.22.176 A fisician with a forred hoed that he *ful* in a palesye
C.22.228 Consience cryede, 'helpe, Clergie, or y *falle*

fallyng ger *fallinge ger. &> falle* B 2 fallyng (1) fallynge (1); C 3 fallyng
      (1) fallynge (2)
B.16.25   'For wyndes, wiltow wite', quod he, 'to witen it fro *fallyng*:
B.19.65   Therwith to fiȝte and [f]enden vs fro *fallynge* in[to] synne,
C.10.41   So hit fareth,' quod þe frere, 'by þe ryhtful mannus *fallynge*.
C.18.30   [And fro *fallynge* the stok; hit fayle nat of his myhte].

C.21.65   Therwith to fihte and fende vs fro *fallyng* into synne

fals n *fals n.* A 18 fals (16) false (2); B 19; C 16
A. 2.6   Boþe *fals* & fauel & hise feris manye.'
A. 2.22   Tomorewe worþ þe mariage mad of mede & of *fals*;
A. 2.33   Alle þe riche retenaunce þat regniþ wiþ *false*
A. 2.36   Þat *fals* & fauel be any fyn halden;
A. 2.48   To be fastnid wiþ *fals* þe fyn is arerid.
A. 2.49   Þanne fauel fettiþ hire forþ & to *fals* takiþ
A. 2.55   And vnfolde þe feffement þat *fals* haþ ymakid;
A. 2.88   And þou hast fastnid hire wiþ *fals*, fy on þi law[e]!
A. 2.94   Þat *fals* is a faitour [and] feyntles of werkis,
A. 2.101 And ȝif þe iustice iugge hire to be ioyned with *fals*,
A. 2.104 And ȝif he fynde ȝow in defaute, & wiþ *fals* holden,
A. 2.114 To *false* & to fauel for here faire ȝeftis,
A. 2.122 Þanne was *fals* fayn, & fauel als bliþe,
A. 2.129 And *fals* sat on a sisour þat softeliche trottide,
A. 2.145 *Fals* & fauel fariþ forþ togidere,
A. 2.155 *Fals* oþer fauel oþer any of his feris,
A. 3.96   Ac wers wrouȝtest þou neuere þan þo þou *fals* toke.
A. 3.143 For she is fauourable to *fals* & fouliþ treuþe ofte;
B. 2.6   Boþe *Fals* and Fauel and hi[s]e feeres manye.'
B. 2.25   For *Fals* was hire fader þat haþ a fikel tonge
B. 2.41   To oon *fals* fikel-tonge, a fendes biyete.
B. 2.54   That al þe riche retenaunce þat regneþ with [*fals*]
B. 2.66   And as a Brocour brouȝte hire to be wiþ *fals* enioyned.
B. 2.73   And vnfoldeþ þe feffement that *Fals* hath ymaked.
B. 2.124 And þow hast fest hire [wiþ] *Fals*; fy on þi lawe!
B. 2.130 That *Fals* is fe[ynt]lees and fikel in hise werkes,
B. 2.137 And [if þe] Iustic[e] Iugg[e] hire to be Ioyned [wiþ] *Fals*
B. 2.140 And if he fynde yow in defaute, and with [*fals*] holde,
B. 2.150 To *Fals* and to Fauel for hire faire ȝiftes,
B. 2.158 Thanne was *Fal[s]* fayn and Fauel as bliþe,
B. 2.165 And *Fals* sat on a Sisour þat softeli trotted,
B. 2.184 *Fals* and Fauel fareþ forþ togideres
B. 2.194 *Fals* or Fauel or any of hise feeris
B. 3.107 Ac worse wroȝtest [þ]ow neuere þan þo þow *Fals* toke.
B. 3.154 For she is fauourable to *fals* and [f]ouleþ truþe ofte.
B.20.55   And [made] *fals* sprynge and sprede and spede mennes nedes.
B.20.131 And garte good feiþ flee and *fals* to abide,
C. 2.6   [Boþe] *fals* and fauel and fikel tonge lyare
C. 2.44   To oon *fals* faythlesse of þe fendes kynne
C. 2.68   And [as] a brokor brouhte here to be [with *fals* enioyned].
C. 2.75   And vnfoldeth the feffament þat *fals* hath ymaked.
C. 2.124 Althow *fals* were here fader and fikel tonge her belsyre
C. 2.140 And thow hast feffed here with *fals*; fy on suche lawe.
C. 2.146 That *fals* is faythles, the fende is his syre
C. 2.166 That [*fals*] and [fauel] hadde for he[re] fayre ȝeftes,
C. 2.182 And *fals* and fauel fecche forth sysores
C. 2.197 Thenne *fals* and fauel ryde forth togederes
C. 2.208 *Fals* or fauel or here felawe lyare
C. 3.138 For wors wrouhtest [thow] neuere then tho thow *fals* toke.
C. 3.164 ȝoure fader she [f]elde, *fals* and she togederes;
C. 3.192 For she is fauerable to *fals* the whiche defouleth treuthe.
C.22.55   And made *fals* sprynge and sprede and spe[d]e menne nedes.
C.22.131 And gert goed faith fle and *fals* to abyde

fals adj *fals adj., adj. as n.* A 14 fals (6) false (8); B 39 fals (22) false
      (17); C 45 fals (34) false (11)
A. 2.4   Kenne me be sum craft to k[now]e þe *false*'.
A. 2.111 And feffe *false* wytnesse wiþ floreynes ynowe,
A. 2.115 And comen to counforte fro care þe *false*,
A. 2.170 And wiȝtliche wente to warne þe *false*,
A. 3.116 ȝoure fadir he[o] fellide þoruȝ *false* behest,
A. 3.118 To vnfetere þe *fals*, fle where hym lykiþ.
A. 5.77   And don hise frendis ben hise fon þoruȝ my *false* tunge.
A. 6.67   Þanne shalt þou blenche at a b[erw]e, bere no *fals* wytnesse;
A. 7.205 Wiþ fuyr or wiþ *false* men, fond suche [to] knowen;
A. 8.70   He is *fals* wiþ þe fend & [defraudiþ] þe nedy,
A. 9.38   Þat þoruȝ þe fend, & þe flessh, & þe *false* world,
A.10.139 Ac *fals* folk & feiþles, þeuis & leiȝeris,
A.10.210 And þat ben *fals* folk, & fals eires also, foundlynges & [leiȝeris],
A.10.210 And þat ben fals folk, & *fals* eires also, foundlynges & [leiȝeris],
B. 2.4   Kenne me by som craft to knowe þe *false*'.
B. 2.81   To bakbite and to bosten and bere *fals* witnesse,
B. 2.147 And feffe *fal[s]* witness[e] wiþ floryns ynowe,
B. 2.151 And comen to conforten from care þe *false*
B. 2.211 Thanne Drede wente wyȝtliche and warned þe *False*
B. 3.127 Youre fader she felled þoruȝ *false* biheste,
B. 3.139 To vnfetter þe *fals*, fle where hym likeþ.
B. 5.88   Wiþ bakbitynge and bismere and berynge of *fals* witnesse;
B. 5.97   And [doon] his frendes be his foon þoruȝ my *false* tonge.
B. 5.580 Thanne shaltow blenche at a Bergh, bere-no-*fals*-witnesse;
B. 6.219 [Wiþ fir or wiþ] *false* men, fonde swiche to knowe.

B. 7.68	He is *fals* wiþ þe feend and defraudeþ þe nedy,
B. 8.42	That þoru3 þe fend and þe flessh and þe [*false*] worlde
B. 9.121	Ac *fals* folk, feiþlees, þeues and lyeres,
B. 9.150	Ac I fynde, if þe fader be *fals* and a sherewe,
B. 9.196	As *fals* folk, fondlynges, faitours and lieres,
B.10.198	And so shaltow *fals* folk and feiþlees bigile:
B.11.304	If *fals* latyn be in þat lettre þe lawe it impugneþ,
B.12.260	Executours, *false* frendes, þat fulfille no3t his wille
B.13.327	And made of frendes foes þoru3 a *fals* tonge.
B.13.358	[Thoru3] *false* mesures and met, and wiþ fals witnesse;
B.13.358	[Thoru3] false mesures and met, and wiþ *fals* witnesse;
B.13.400	And foule beflobered it, as wiþ *fals* speche.
B.14.24	Ne fend ne *fals* man defoulen it in þi lyue.
B.14.200	In fenestres at þe freres–if *fals* be þe foundement.
B.14.295	Wynneþ he no3t wiþ wi3tes *false* ne wiþ vnseled mesures
B.15.129	Ac þing þat wikkedly is wonne, and wiþ *false* sleightes,
B.15.238	For braulynge and bakbitynge and berynge of *fals* witnesse.
B.15.507	Thus in a feiþ leue þat folk, and in a *fals* mene,
B.18.28	'Nay', quod [feiþ, 'but] þe fend and *fals* doom [to deye].
B.18.92	Thanne gan Feiþ felly þe *false* Iewes despise;
B.18.110	What for feere of þis ferly and of þe *false* Iewes
B.19.47	And from fendes þat in hem [was] and *false* bileue.
B.19.221	And *false* prophetes fele, flatereris and gloseris,
B.19.247	And fecchen it fro *false* men wiþ Foluyles lawes.
B.19.370	Witynge and wilfully wiþ þe *false* helden.
B.20.64	And a *fals* fend Antecrist ouer alle folk regnede.
B.20.118	Weren feþered wiþ fair biheste and many a *fals* truþe.
B.20.285	And fleen to þe freres, as *fals* folk to westmynstre
C.Pr.106	Ful on hem þat fre were þorwe two *fals* prestis!
C. 2.4	Kenne me by sum craft to knowe þe *false*.'
C. 2.57	Al þe riche retenaunce þat ro[t]eth hem o *fals* lyuynge
C. 2.86	And fauel þat hath a *fals* speche Feffeth hem by þis lettre
C. 2.88	To bacbite and to boste and bere *fals* witnesse,
C. 2.94	With vsurye and Auaryce and other *fals* sleythus
C. 2.156	And yf he fynde 3ow in defaute and with the *fals* holde,
C. 2.163	And feffe *fals* witnesse with floreynes ynowe,
C. 2.167	And comen ful courteysly to conforte the *false*
C. 3.91	Bothe thorw fuyr and flood a[nd] thorw *fals* peple
C. 3.102	And thenne falleth ther fuyr on *fals* men houses
C. 3.114	Be yfranchised for a fre man and haue a *fals* name.
C. 3.177	To vnfetere the *fals*, fle wher hym liketh,
C. 3.301	Harlotes and hoores and also *fals* leches,
C. 6.72	And made of frendes foes thorw fikel and *fals* tonge.
C. 6.258	'With *false* wordes and w[ittes] haue y ywonne my godes
C. 6.293	Then haue my fode and my fyndynge of *fals* mene wynnyngus.
C. 7.227	Thenne shaltow blenche at a berw, bere-no-*fals*-witnesse,
C. 8.228	Ac yf thow fynde eny folke þat *fals* men han apayred
C. 9.64	He is *fals* and faytour and defraudeth the nedy
C.10.295	And *fals* folk and fondlynges, faytors and lyares,
C.11.20	Thorw fallas and *fals* questes and thorw fikel speche.
C.12.198	Fere ne famyne ne *fals* mennes tonges.
C.12.238	That *fals* folk fecche aweye felonliche his godes;
C.13.118	Yf *fals* latyn be in þat lettre þe lawe hit enpugneth,
C.15.77	That no *fals* frere thorw flaterynge hem bygyle;
C.16.41	In fenestres at þe freres–yf *fals* be þe fondement.
C.16.130	Wynneth he nat with w[ih]tus *false* ne with vnselede mesures
C.16.276	Ac thyng þat wykkedliche is wonne and with *fals* sleithes
C.16.363	For braulyng and bacbitynge and berynge of *fals* witnesse.
C.17.77	And so hit fareth by *false* cristene: here follynge is trewe,
C.17.183	And seth oure saueour soffrede such a *fals* cristene
C.17.258	Thus in a fayth l[e]ueth þat folk and in a *fals* mene,
C.18.122	That thorw *fals* biheste and fruyt furste man disseyued.
C.20.27	'Nay,' quod faith, 'bote the fende and *fals* doem to deye.
C.20.95	Thenne gan faith f[el]ly þe *false* iewes dispice,
C.20.113	What for fere of this ferly and of þe *false* iewes
C.20.320	And dust hem breke here buxumnesse thorw *fals* bihestes
C.21.47	And fro fendes þat in hem was and *false* bileue.
C.21.221	And *false* profetes fele, flateres and glosares,
C.21.247	And fechen hit fro *false* men with foleuiles lawes.
C.21.370	Wytyng and wilfully with the *false* helden
C.22.64	And a *fals* fende auntecrist ouer all folke regnede.
C.22.118	Weren fythered with fayre biheste and many a *fals* treuthe.
C.22.285	And fle to þe freres, as *fals* folk to Westmynstre

falshede n *falshede n.* A 3 falshed; B 4; C 4

A. 1.62	Fadir of *falshed*, he foundi[de] it hymselue.
A. 2.50	In foreward þat *falshed* shal fynde hire for euere,
A. 3.38	And þei3 *falshed* hadde folewid þe þis fiftene wynter,
B.Pr.71	Of *falshede* of fastynge [and] of Auowes ybroken.
B. 1.64	Fader of *falshede*, [he] founded it hymselue.
B. 3.39	And [þei3] *Fals[hede]* hadde yfolwed þee alle þise fift[ene] wynter,
B. 5.287	For þe good þat þow hast geten bigan al wiþ *falshede*,
C. 1.60	Fader of *falshede* fond hit firste of alle.

C. 2.152	Where matrymonye may be of mede and of *falshede*.
C. 3.41	[And] *Falshede* yfonde the al this fourty wyntur,
C. 6.342	For the good that thow hast gete bygan al with *falshede*

falsliche adv *falsli adv.* B 2; C 3 falsly (1) falsliche (2)

B.18.336	*Falsliche* þow fettest þyng þat I louede.
B.18.351	*Falsliche* and felonliche; good feiþ me it tau3te
C. 6.428	There no nede ne was, many sythe *falsly*;
C. 9.269	And many a fayre flees *falsliche* is ywasche!
C.20.379	*Falsliche* [thow] fettest there þat me biful to loke,

falsnesse n *falsnesse n.* A 4; B 8; C 13

A.Pr.68	Of *falsnesse* of fastyng & of auowes broken.
A. 2.58	Þat I, fauel, feffe *falsnesse* to mede,
A. 2.162	Feteriþ *falsnesse* faste for any skynes 3eftis,
A. 2.172	Þanne *fal[s]nesse* for feer flei3 to þe Freris;
B. 2.78	*Falsnesse* is fayn of hire for he woot hire riche;
B. 2.201	Fettreþ [*Falsnesse* faste] for any kynnes 3iftes,
B. 2.210	*Falsnesse* and his felawship to fettren and to bynden.
B. 2.213	[Thanne] *Falsnesse* for fere flei3 to þe Freres;
B.11.92	*Falsnesse* ne faiterie? for somwhat þe Apostle seide
B.15.262	Of oure foes þat dooþ vs *falsnesse*; þat is oure fadres wille.
B.16.154	'*Falsnesse* I fynde in þi faire speche
B.20.66	Defyed alle *falsnesse* and folk þat it vsede;
C.Pr.69	Of *falsness[e of]* fastyng[e and] of vowes ybrokene.
C. 2.72	That Gyle hath gyue to *falsnesse* and grauntid also mede,'
C. 2.79	That foleweth *falsnesse*, Fauel and lyare,
C. 2.85	*Falsnesse* is fayn of here for he wot here ryche;
C. 2.105	/This lyf to folowe *falsnesse* and folk þat on hym leueth,
C. 2.174	Thenne was [*falsnesse*] fayn and [fauel] blythe,
C. 2.215	Lat fetere *falsnesse* faste for eny skynes 3eftes,
C. 2.222	And bad *falsnesse* to fle and his feres alle.
C. 2.223	*Falsnesse* for fere tho fleyh to þe freres;
C.12.33	*Falsnesse* ne fayterye? for sumwhat þe apostel saide:
C.16.174	'Of [fele] tyme to fihte,' quod he, '*falsnesse* to destruye
C.18.171	'*Falsnesse* y fynde in thy fayre speche
C.22.66	Defyede all *falsnesse* and folke þat hit vsede

fame n *fame n.(1)* A 1; B 1

A. 5.74	And blamide hym behynde his bak to bringe hym in *fame*;
B. 5.94	[And blamed hym bihynde his bak to brynge hym in *fame*;

famed ptp *famen v.(1)* A 1 famid; B 1; C 1

A. 3.173	And þou hast *famid* me foule before þe king here.
B. 3.186	Ac þow hast *famed* me foule bifore þe kyng here.
C. 3.232	Ac thow hast *famed* me foule byfore þe kyng here

famyn n *famine n.* A 1; B 1; C 4 famyn (1) famyne (3)

A. 7.305	Or fyue 3er be fulfild such *famyn* shal arise;
B. 6.324	Er fyue [yer] be fulfilled swich *famyn* shal aryse.
C. 7.306	*Famyne* and defaute, folwen y wol Peres;
C. 8.214	But for fere of *famyen*, in fayth,' sayde [Peres].
C. 8.344	Ar fewe 3eres be fulfeld *famyne* shal aryse.
C.12.198	Fere ne *famyne* ne fals mennes tonges.

fand > fynden; fange > fonge

fantasies n *fantasie n.* A 2; B 1; C 1 fantasyes

A.Pr.36	Fonden hem *fantasies* & foolis hem make,
A.11.63	And fyndiþ forþ *fantasies* oure feiþ to apeire,
B.Pr.36	[Fonden] hem *fantasies* and fooles hem makeþ,
C.Pr.37	Fyndeth out foule *fantasyes* and foles hem maketh

farao(s > pharoes

fare n *fare n.(1)* B 2; C 2

B.18.18	Thanne I frayned at Feiþ what al þat *fare* bymente,
B.18.125	'Ich haue ferly of þis *fare*, in feiþ', seide truþe,
C.20.16	Thenne y [f]raynede at fayth what al þat *fare* bymente
C.20.128	'Y haue ferly of this *fare*, in faith,' seide Treuthe,

fare v *faren v.* A 7 fare (2) faren (2) fariþ (2) ferde (1); B 30 fare (10) faren (5) fareþ (11) ferde (3) ferden (1); C 23 fare (8) faren (1) fareth (10) feerde (1) ferde (2) ferden (1)

A. 2.145	Fals & fauel *fariþ* forþ togidere,
A. 5.5	Er I hadde *faren* a furlong feyntise me h[ent]e
A. 7.97	Now is peris & þe pilgrimes to þe plou3 *faren*;
A. 7.210	Wiþ mete or [wiþ] mone let make hem [*fare* þe betere],
A. 8.81	Þat euere he was man wrou3t whanne he shal henne *fare*.
A. 9.33	Ri3t þus [it] *fariþ*,' quaþ þe Frere, 'be folk here on erþe.
A.11.178	And axide how wyt *ferde* & his wif studie,
B. 2.184	Fals and Fauel *fareþ* forþ togideres
B. 5.5	Ac er I hadde *faren* a furlong feyntise me hente
B. 6.105	Now is Perkyn and [þe] pilgrimes to þe plow *faren*.
B. 6.224	Wiþ mete or wiþ mone lat make hem *fare* þe bettre].
B. 7.99	That euere [he was man] wro3t whan [he] shal hennes *fare*.
B. 8.37	[Ri3t] þus it [*fareþ*]', quod þe frere, 'by folk here on erþe.

B. 9.147   And alle for hir [fore]fadres *ferden* þe werse.
B.10.95   Nouȝt to *fare* as a fiþelere or a frere to seke festes,
B.10.235   And askede how wit *ferde* and his wif studie].
B.10.411   God lene it *fare* noȝt so bi folk þat þe feiþ techeþ
B.11.42   'Ye! *farewel*, Phippe', quod Faunteltee, and forþ gan me drawe
B.11.71   'By my feiþ! frere', quod I, 'ye *faren* lik þise woweris
B.11.420   And riȝt so *ferde* Reson bi þee; þow wiþ rude speche
B.12.5   And how fele fernyeres are *faren* and so fewe to come;
B.12.202   So it *fareþ* by þat felon þat a good friday was saued;
B.13.52   'Here is propre seruice', quod Pacience, 'þer *fareþ* no Prince bettre.'
B.13.109   And if ye *fare* so in youre Fermerye, ferly me þynkeþ
B.13.148   Ac for to *fare* þus wiþ þi frend, folie it were;
B.13.180   'Frendes, *fareþ* wel', and faire spak to clergie,
B.14.128   Riȝt so *fareþ* god by som riche; ruþe me it þynkeþ,
B.15.145   Thus goon hire goodes, be þe goost *faren*.
B.15.185   Loueþ hem as oure lord biddeþ and lokeþ how þei *fare*.
B.15.333   Fele of yow *fareþ* as if I a forest hadde
B.15.351   And so it *fareþ* by som folk now; þei han a fair speche,
B.15.456   [And] so it *fareþ* by a barn þat born is of wombe;
B.17.311   Thus it *fareþ* by swich folk þat [folwen] al hire [wille],
B.18.226   So it shal *fare* by þis folk: hir folie and hir synne
B.20.235   They wol flatere [to] *fare* wel folk þat ben riche.
B.20.290   And so it *fareþ* with muche folk þat to freres shryueþ,
B.20.312   For fastynge of a fryday he *ferde* as he wolde deye.
C. 5.8   And lymes to labory with and louede wel *fare*
C. 6.335   *Fareth* as flo[nke] of fuyr þat ful amydde Temese
C. 8.112   Now is perkyn and þ[e] pilgrimes to þe plouh *faren*.
C.10.38   A[c] ȝut is he saef and sound; and so hit *fareth* by þe rihtfole.
C.10.41   So hit *fareth*,' quod þe frere, 'by þe ryhtful mannus fallynge.
C.10.235   And al for here forfadres *ferden* þe worse.
C.11.73   Get þe loue þerwith thogh thow worse *fare*".
C.11.242   God lene hit *fare* nat so by folk þat þe faith techen
C.11.309   'Ȝe! *farewel*, fyppe,' quod fauntelete and forth gan me drawe
C.12.19   'By my faith! frere,' quod y, 'ȝe *fare* lyke þe woware
C.13.228   Rihte þe Resoun by þe; for thy *ferde* Resoun þe
C.14.141   So hit f[areth] by þe feloun þat a goed fryday was saued:
C.15.117   And ȝe *fare* thus with ȝoure syke freres, ferly me thynketh
C.16.111   So hit *fareth* by vch a persone þat possession forsaket
C.17.77   And so hit *fareth* by false cristene: here follynge is trewe,
C.18.67   And so hit *fareth* sothly, sone, by oure kynde.
C.18.95   Shollen serue for þe lord sulue, and so *fareth* god almyhty.
C.19.114   *Ferde* furste as a f[u]ste, and ȝut is, as y leue,
C.19.291   Thus hit *fareth* bi such folke þat folewen here owene will,
C.20.235   So hit shal *fare* bi this folk: here folye and here synne
C.22.235   Thei wol flatere to *fare* wel folk þat ben riche.
C.22.290   And so hit *fareth* with moche folke þat to freres shryuen,
C.22.312   For fastyng of a fryday a *feerde* as he wolde deye.

farten v *ferten v.* B 1; C 1

B.13.231   *Farten* ne fiþelen at festes ne harpen,
C.15.205   *Farten* ne fythelen at festes ne harpe,

faste adj *fast adj.* A 1

A. 2.63   And al þe Ile of vsurie, & auarice þe *faste*,

faste adv *faste adv.* A 22; B 36; C 21 fast (1) faste (20)

A.Pr.40   Bidderis & beggeris *faste* aboute ȝede
A.Pr.64   Þe moste meschief on molde is mountyng vp *faste*.
A. 1.42   Ac þe mone on þis molde þat men so *faste* holdiþ,
A. 1.94   And taken trespassours & teiȝen hem *faste*
A. 1.113   Out of heuene into helle hobelide þei *faste*,
A. 2.162   Feteriþ falsnesse *faste* for any skynes ȝeftis,
A. 3.129   He[o] takiþ þe trewe be þe top, teiȝeþ hym *faste*,
A. 4.22   Þanne consience on his capil cairiþ forþ *faste*,
A. 4.25   Folewide hem *faste* for hy hadden to done
A. 4.27   And riden *faste* for resoun shulde rede hem þe beste
A. 4.68   Ac wisdom & wyt were aboute *faste*
A. 4.133   For to construe þis clause declynede *faste*,
A. 5.215   And flattide it on his face & *faste* on him criede
A. 5.220   Þanne sat sleuþe vp & seynide hym *faste*,
A. 5.246   Wel I woot he wep *faste* watir wiþ his eiȝen,
A. 7.10   And wyues þat han woll[e] werchiþ it *faste*,
A. 7.13   Lokiþ forþ ȝoure lynen & laboureþ þeron *faste*,
A. 7.101   Oþere werkmen þere were [þat] wrouȝte ful *faste*,
A. 7.192   And for defaute of foode þus *faste* hy werchiþ.
A. 7.303   For hungir hiderward hastiþ hym *faste*.
A.11.56   Clerkis and k[ete] men carpen of god *faste*,
A.12.100   Þat þis speche was spedelich, and sped him wel *faste*,
B.Pr.40   Bidderes and beggeres *faste* aboute yede
B.Pr.67   The mooste meschief on Molde is mountynge [vp] *faste*.
B. 1.44   Ac þe moneie [on] þis molde þat men so *faste* holdeþ,
B. 1.96   And taken transgressores and tyen hem *faste*
B. 2.201   Fettreþ [Falsnesse *faste*] for any kynnes ȝiftes,
B. 3.140   [She] takeþ þe trewe bi þe top, tieþ h[y]m *faste*,

B. 4.24   Thanne Conscience [o]n his capul [caireþ] forþ *faste*,
B. 4.28   Folwed h[e]m *faste* for þei hadde to doone
B. 4.30   And riden *faste* for Reson sholde rede hem þe beste
B. 4.33   And bad Reson ryde *faste* and recche of hir neiþer.
B. 4.42   And þanne Reson rood *faste* þe riȝte heiȝe gate
B. 4.81   Ac wisdom and wit were aboute *faste*
B. 4.167   Ac a Sisour and a Somonour sued hire *faste*,
B. 5.443   And flatte it on his face and *faste* on hym cryde
B. 5.448   Thanne sat Sleuþe vp and seyned hym [*faste*]
B. 5.472   Wel I woot he wepte *faste* water wiþ hise eiȝen,
B. 6.109   Oþere werkmen þer were þat wroȝten ful [*faste*],
B. 6.322   For hunger hiderward hasteþ hym *faste*.
B.10.70   Clerkes and [kete] men carpen of god *faste*
B.13.61   For þis doctour on þe heiȝe dees drank wyn so *faste*:
B.13.152   I bere þer, [in a bouste] *faste* ybounde, dowel,
B.14.274   'Haue god my trouþe', quod Haukyn '[I wene yow] preise *faste*
                    pouerte.
B.14.334   To couere my careyne', quod he, and cride mercy *faste*
B.15.242   And þat Conscience and crist haþ yknyt *faste*
B.15.448   And follede folk *faste*, and þe feiþ tauȝte
B.15.547   Shul [ouer]torne as templers dide; þe tyme approcheþ *faste*.
B.16.169   Estward and westward I waited after *faste*
B.17.54   To a Iustes in Ierusalem he [I]aced awey *faste*.
B.17.83   Feiþ folwede after *faste* and fondede to mete hym,
B.17.113   That he worþ fettred, þat feloun, *faste* wiþ Cheynes,
B.17.135   Sette [*faste*] þi feiþ and ferme bileue;
B.17.159   And as þe hand halt harde and alle þyng *faste*
B.18.6   Reste me þere and rutte *faste* til Ramis palmarum.
B.18.309   I rede we fle', quod [þe fend], '*faste* alle hennes,
B.19.103   And som tyme he fauȝt *faste* and fleiȝ ouþer while,
B.20.324   The frere herof herde and hiede *faste*
C.Pr.41   Bidders and beggers *faste* aboute ȝede
C.Pr.65   The moste meschief on molde mounteth vp *faste*.
C. 1.42   Ac þe moneye of þis molde þat men so *faste* kepen,
C. 1.92   And take transgressores and teyen hem *faste*
C. 2.183   And ryde on hem and on reue[s] righte *faste* by mede.
C. 2.215   Lat fetere falsnesse *faste* for eny skynes ȝeftes,
C. 3.178   And taketh [þe] tre[we] by the top and te[i]eth hym f[*aste*]
C. 4.28   Fayn were to folowe hem and *faste* ryden aftur
C. 4.77   Ac wyles and wyt were aboute *faste*
C. 6.326   Wel y woet a wepte *faste* water with his yes
C. 7.57   And flatte hit on his face and *faste* on hym cryede
C. 8.213   Hit is nat for loue, leue hit, thei labore thus *faste*
C. 8.342   For hungur hiderwardes hasteth hym *faste*.
C.11.174   And pruyde-of-parfit-lyuynge pursuede me *faste*
C.15.65   For [this] doctour at þe hey deys dranke wyn [so] *faste*–
C.17.209   Sholle ouerturne as templers dede; þe tyme approcheth *faste*.
C.19.52   To ioust in Ierusalem he Iaced awey *faste*.
C.19.80   Bothe fayth and his felawe spes folewede *faste* aftur
C.20.343   Y rede we flee,' quod the fende, '*faste* all hennes
C.21.103   And som tyme he fauht *faste* and fley oþerwhile
C.22.324   The frere herof herde and hyede *faste*

faste &> fasten

fasten v *faster v.(2)* A 2 faste (1) fasten (1); B 3 faste (2) fasten (1); C 4
faste (3) fastyng (1)

A. 1.99   And nouȝt to *fasten* a friday in fyue score wynter,
A. 5.209   And auowide to *faste*, for hungir or þrist:
B. 1.101   And nauȝt to *fasten* o friday in fyue score wynter,
B. 5.173   And doon me *faste* frydayes to [þerf] breed and to watre;
B. 5.381   And auowed to *faste* for hunger or þurste:
C. 1.99   For thei sholde nother *faste* ne forbere the serk
C. 6.155   And doen me *faste* fridayes to bred and to water;
C. 6.352   *Fastyng* on a friday forth gan he wende
C.13.81   To lene ne to lerne ne lentones to *faste*

fastyng ger *fasting ger.(2) &> fasten* A 2; B 7 fastyng (3) fastynge (4); C
10 fastyng (8) fastynge (2)

A.Pr.68   Of falsnesse of *fastyng* & of auowes broken.
A. 5.156   And a [ferþingworþ] of [fenelsed] for *fastyng* dayes.'
B.Pr.71   Of falshede of *fastynge* [and] of Auowes ybroken.
B. 2.96   And in *fastynge* dayes to frete er ful tyme were.
B. 5.305   A ferþyngworþ of fenel seed for *fastyng* dayes.'
B. 5.377   Fedde me bifore] noon whan *fastyng* dayes were.'
B. 5.409   Vigilies and *fastyng* dayes, alle þise late I passe,
B.13.348   As wel *fastyng* dayes [as] Fridaies [and] forboden nyȝtes,
B.20.312   For *fastynge* of a fryday he ferde as he wolde deye.
C.Pr.69   Of falsness[e of] *fastyng*[e and] of vowes ybrokene.
C. 2.103   And *fastyng* dayes to frete byfore noone and drynke
C. 6.182   As wel *fastyng* dayes and frydayes and heye fest[e] euenes,
C. 6.360   A ferthyngworth [of] fenkel sed[e] for *fastyng* dayes.'
C. 6.434   [On] *fastyng* dayes bifore noen fedde me with ale,
C. 7.25   Vigilies and *fastyng*dayes y can forȝeten hem alle

C. 9.94   Fridays and *fastyng*days a ferthingworth of moskeles
C. 9.233   Vigilies and *fastyng*days forthermore to knowe
C. 9.234   And fulfille th[e] *fastyng[e]* but infirmite hit made,
C.22.312   For *fastyng* of a fryday a feerde as he wolde deye.

fastnid > festne

fat adj *fat adj.* B 1 fatter; C 2 fat (1) fatte (1)
B.12.266   And of flessh by fele fold *fatter* and swetter;
C. 9.209   That faytede in frere clothinge hadde *fatte* chekes.
C.12.224   On *fat* lond ful of donge foulest wedes groweth.

fatte n *fatte n. &> fat* B 1; C 1
B.19.280   [That] caste for to ke[l]e a crokke to saue þe *fatte* aboue.
C.21.280   That caste for to kele a crok [to] saue þe *fatte* aboue.

fauchon n *fauchoun n.* B 1; C 1 fauchen
B.15.18   Is neiþer Peter þe Porter ne Poul wiþ [þe] *fauchon*
C.16.169   Is noþer Peter the porter ne poul with the *fauchen*

faucon n *faucoun n.* A 1 fauconis; B 2 faucon (1) faucons (1); C 1 faucones
A. 7.33   And fecche þe hom *fauconis* þe foulis to kille,
B. 6.31   And [fette þee hoom] *faucons* foweles to kille,
B.17.65   Dredfully, bi þis day! as doke dooþ fram þe *faucon*.
C. 8.30   And afayte thy *faucones* [wylde foules to culle]

fauȝt fauht > fiȝte; faumewarde > vauntwarde; faunede > fawned

faunt n *faunt n.* A 4 fauntes (1) fauntis (3); B 4 faunt (1) fauntes (3); C 1 fauntes
A. 8.77   And gon & faiten wiþ here *fauntis* for eueremore aftir.
A.10.58   In ȝonge *fauntes* & folis, wiþ hem failiþ Inwyt,
A.10.64   Ac in *fauntis* ne in folis þe [fend] haþ no miȝt
A.10.66   Ac þe fadir & þe Frendis for *fauntis* shuln be blamid
B. 6.283   [A lof] of benes and bran ybake for my *fauntes*.
B. 7.95   And goon [and] faiten with [hire] *fauntes* for eueremoore after.
B. 9.68   [*Fauntes* and] fooles þat fauten Inwit,
B.16.101   Til he weex a *faunt* þoruȝ hir flessh and of fightyng kouþe
C. 9.171   And goen and fayten with here *fauntes* for eueremore aftur.

fauntekyn n *fauntekin n.* B 2 fauntekyn (1) fauntekyns (1); C 3 fauntekyn (1) fauntkynes (1) fauntokynes (1)
B.13.213   And confermen *fauntekyns* ooþer folk ylered
B.19.118   A *faunt[ek]yn* ful of wit, filius Marie.
C. 9.35   Fynde hem for godes loue and *fauntkynes* to scole,
C.10.183   Ac *fauntokynes* and foles þat fauten inwit
C.21.118   A *fauntekyn* ful of wyt, filius Marie.

faunteltee n *fauntelte n.* B 2 fauntelte (1) Faunteltee (1); C 1 fauntelete
B.11.42   'Ye! farewel, Phippe,' quod *Faunteltee*, and forþ gan me drawe
B.15.150   Wiþouten *fauntelte* or folie a fre liberal wille.'
C.11.309   'ȝe! farewel, fyppe,' quod *fauntelete* and forth gan me drawe

fauntkynes fauntokynes > fauntekyn

fauten v *fauten v.* B 2 fauted (1) fauten (1); C 1
B. 9.68   [Fauntes and] fooles þat *fauten* Inwit,
B. 9.70   And] fynden hem þat hem *fauted*, and faderlese children,
C.10.183   Ac fauntokynes and foles þat *fauten* inwit

fautes n *faute n.* B 1
B.10.106   And leyden *fautes* vpon þe fader þat formede vs alle,

fauel n *favel n.* A 12; B 11; C 12
A. 2.6   Boþe fals & *fauel* & hise feris manye.'
A. 2.23   *Fauel* wiþ fair speche haþ forgid hem togidere;
A. 2.36   Þat fals & *fauel* be any fyn halden,
A. 2.49   Þanne *fauel* fettiþ hire forþ & to fals takiþ
A. 2.58   Þat I, *fauel*, feffe falsnesse to mede,
A. 2.108   Þanne fette *fauel* forþ floreynes ynowe,
A. 2.114   To false & to *fauel* for here faire ȝeftis,
A. 2.122   Þanne was fals fayn, & *fauel* als bliþe,
A. 2.127   Þanne fette *fauel* folis of þe beste,
A. 2.130   And *fauel* vpon fair speche, fe[int]liche atirid.
A. 2.145   Fals & *fauel* fariþ forþ togidere,
A. 2.155   Fals oþer *fauel* oþer any of his feris,
B. 2.6   Boþe Fals and *Fauel* and hi[s]e feeres manye.'
B. 2.42   *Fauel* þoruȝ his faire speche haþ þis folk enchaunted,
B. 2.65   Ac *Fauel* was þe firste þat fette hire out of boure
B. 2.79   And *Fauel* wiþ his fikel speche feffeþ by þis chartre
B. 2.144   Thanne fette *Fauel* forþ floryns ynowe
B. 2.150   To Fals and to *Fauel* for hire faire ȝiftes,
B. 2.158   Thanne was Fal[s] fayn and *Fauel* as bliþe,
B. 2.163   [Thanne fette *Fauel*] foles [of þe beste],
B. 2.166   And *Fauel* on [Fair Speche] fe[ynt]ly atired.
B. 2.184   Fals and *Fauel* fareþ forþ togideres
B. 2.194   Fals or *Fauel* or any of hise feeris

C. 2.6   [Boþe] fals and *fauel* and fikel tonge lyare
C. 2.25   Oon *fauel* was he[re] fader þat hath a fykel tonge
C. 2.45   *Fauel* thorw his flaterynge speche hath mede foule enchaunted,
C. 2.67   Ac *Fauel* was þe furste þat fette here out of chambre
C. 2.79   That foleweth falsnesse, *Fauel* and lyare,
C. 2.86   And *fauel* þat hath a fals speche Feffeth hem by þis lettre
C. 2.160   T[h]o fette *fauel* forth floreynes ynowe
C. 2.166   That [fals] and [*fauel*] hadde for he[re] fayre ȝeftes,
C. 2.174   Thenne was [falsnesse] fayn and [*fauel*] blythe,
C. 2.182   And fals and *fauel* fecche forth sysores
C. 2.197   Thenne fals and *fauel* ryde forth togederes
C. 2.208   Fals or *fauel* or here felawe lyare

fauourable adj *favourable adj.* A 1; B 1; C 1 fauerable
A. 3.143   For she is *fauourable* to fals & fouliþ treuþe ofte;
B. 3.154   For she is *fauourable* to fals and [f]ouleþ truþe ofte.
C. 3.192   For she is *fauerable* to fals the whiche defouleth treuthe.

fawned v *faunen v.(1)* B 1; C 1 faunede
B.15.300   That ne fil to hir feet and *fawned* wiþ þe tailles;
C.17.31   And faire byfore tho men *faunede* with þe tayles.

fe > fee; febicchis > fibicches

feble adj *feble adj.* A 2 feble (1) feblere (1); B 12 feble (7) febler (2) feblere (2) feblest (1); C 6 feble (4) feblest (1) feblore (1)
A. 1.160   Þat feiþ wiþoute fait is *feblere* þan nouȝt,
A.10.187   To ȝiuen a ȝong wenche to an old *feble*,
B.Pr.180   [Ac] helden hem vnhardy and hir counseil *feble*,
B. 1.186   That Feiþ withouten feet is [*feblere* þan nouȝt],
B. 5.177   I ete þere unþende fissh and *feble* ale drynke.
B. 5.405   I visited neuere *feble* men ne fettred [men] in puttes.
B. 9.166   To yeuen a yong wenche to [a yolde] *feble*,
B.12.239   And *feblest* fowel of fliȝt is þat fleeþ or swymmeþ.
B.14.226   [For] if þei pleyne [þe *feblere* is þe poore];
B.15.348   Wherfore folk is þe *febler* and noȝt ferm of bileue.
B.15.350   The merk of þat monee is good ac þe metal is *feble*;
B.15.577   Oȝias seiþ for swiche þat sike ben and *feble*,
B.17.119   And alle þat *feble* and feynte be, þat Feiþ may noȝt teche,
B.17.175   And ful god as is þe fader, no *febler* ne no bettre.
C.Pr.197   [Ac helden hem vnhardy and here conseil *feble*]
C. 1.182   That fayth withouten feet is *feblore* then nauth
C. 6.159   For y ete more fysch then flesche there and *feble* ale drynke.
C. 7.21   Y visitede neuere *feble* man ne fetered man in prisone.
C.14.171   And *feblest* foul of flyh[t is] þat fleeth oþer swym[m]eth:
C.16.67   For yf they bothe pleyne þe pore is bote *feble*;

fecchen v *fecchen v.* A 6 fecche (5) fecchen (1); B 21 fecche (16) fecchen (3) feccheþ (2); C 22 fecche (8) fecchen (2) feccheth (2) feche (9) fechen (1)
A. 4.7   'Rape þe to riden, & resoun þat þou *fecche*.
A. 4.38   'Boþe my gees & my gris hise gadelynges *fecchen*;
A. 5.29   And *fecche* [hom] felis fro wyuene pyne.
A. 7.33   And *fecche* þe hom fauconis þe foulis to kille,
A. 7.144   Of þ[i] flour, and þi flessh *fecche* whanne vs likeþ,
A.10.195   To folewe aftir þe flicche, *fecche* þei it neuere;
B. 2.181   And *fecchen* [oure] vitailles at Fornicatores.
B. 4.7   'Rape þee to ryde and Reson [þat] þow *fecche*.
B. 4.51   'Boþe my gees and my grys hise gadelynges *feccheþ*.
B. 5.29   And *fecche* Felice hom fro wyuen pyne.
B. 5.640   I wol go *fecche* my box wiþ my breuettes & a bulle with bisshopes lettres
B. 6.157   Of þi flour and þi flessh, *fecche* whanne vs likeþ,
B. 9.174   To folwen aftir þe flicche, *fecche* þei it neuere;
B.13.371   That a foot lond or a forow *fecchen* I wolde.
B.16.45   And *feccheþ* awey my floures som tyme afore boþe myne eighen.
B.16.49   Manacen bihynde me, my fruyt for to *fecche*,
B.16.264   Out of þe poukes pondfold no maynprise may vs *fecche*–
B.16.269   Lollynge in my lappe til swich a lord vs *fecche*.'
B.18.20   'And *fecche* þat þe fend claymeþ, Piers fruyt þe Plowman.'
B.18.33   And *fecche* fro þe fend Piers fruyt þe Plowman
B.18.152   For venym fordooþ venym, [þer *fecche* I euydence
B.18.269   If þis kyng come In mankynde wole he *fecche*
B.18.295   'Certes I drede me', quod þe deuel, 'lest truþe [do] hem *fecche*.
B.18.348   So leue [it] noȝt, lucifer, ayein þe lawe I *fecche* hem,
B.19.145   For no fren[d] sholde [it] *fecche*; for prophetes hem tolde
B.19.247   And *fecchen* it fro false men wiþ Foluyles lawes.
B.19.464   And wiþ Spiritus fortitudinis *fecche* it, [wole he, nel he].'
C. 2.182   And fals and fauel *fecche* forth sysores
C. 2.194   And *fecchen* oure vitailes a[t] fornicatores,
C. 3.376   To folewe and to fynde hym and [f]*feche* at hem his consayl
C. 4.7   'Rape the to ryde and resoun þat thow [f]*fec[c]he*.
C. 6.268   That a foet lond or a forw *fecchen* y wolde.
C. 8.154   [Of] thy flour and thy flesch, *feche* whenne vs liketh,
C. 8.347   Pruyde and pestilences shal moche peple *feche*;

C.10.276   To folwe for þe flicche, *feccheth* they hit neuere;
C.12.238   That fals folk *fecche* aweye felonliche his godes;
C.18.49   And *feccheth* away þe fruyt som tyme byfore bothe myn yes.
C.18.129   Who sholde *fecche* this fruyt, the fende or iesus suluen.
C.18.280   Fro þe poukes pondefold no maynprise may vs *feche*–
C.18.285   Lollyng in my lappe til suche a lord vs *feche*.'
C.20.18   'And *feche* þat þe fende claymeth, pers fruyt þe plouhman.'
C.20.32   And *feche* fro þe fende [Peres] fruyt þe [plouhman]
C.20.155   For venym fordoth venym, þer *feche* y euydence
C.20.277   Yf this kyng come in mankynde wol he *fecche*
C.20.325   'Forthy y drede me,' quod þe deuel, 'laste treuthe wol hem *fecche*.
C.20.393   So leue hit nat, lucifer, aзeyne þe lawe y *feche*
C.21.145   For no frende sholde hit *fecche*; for profetes hem tolde
C.21.247   And *fechen* hit fro false men with foleuiles lawes;
C.21.464   And with spiritus fortitudinis *fecche* hit, wolle he, null he.'

feden v *feden v.* A 2 fedde (1) fede (1); B 27 fed (1) fedde (8) fedden (1)
    feddest (1) fede (7) feden (3) fedeþ (4) feede (1) yfed (1); C 17 fed
    (1) fedde (8) feddest (1) fede (3) feden (2) fedeth (2)
A.Pr.93   To preche þe peple & pore men to *fede*
A. 7.284   Þanne was folk fayn, & *fedde* hunger with þe beste;
B.Pr.90   Prechen and praye for hem, and þe pouere *fede*,
B.Pr.190   But *fedeþ* hym al wiþ venyson, defame we hym neuere;
B. 4.119   Til clerkene coueitise be to cloþe þe pouere and *fede*,
B. 5.377   *Fedde* me bifore] noon whan fastyng dayes were.'
B. 5.493   *Feddest* wiþ þi fresshe blood oure forefadres in derknesse:
B. 6.251   The freke þat *fedeþ* hymself wiþ his feiþful labour
B. 6.297   Thanne pouere folk for fere *fedden* hunger yerne
B. 6.300   Thanne was folk fayn and *fedde* hunger wiþ þe beste;
B.11.193   For youre frendes wol *feden* yow, and fonde yow to quyte
B.13.422   That *fedeþ* fooles sages, flatereris and lieris,
B.14.10   To penaunce pacience and pouere men to *fede*,
B.14.30   And flour to *fede* folk wiþ as best be for þe soule;
B.15.288   Foweles hym *fedde*, fele wyntres wiþ alle,
B.15.302   Thei wolde haue *yfed* þat folk bifore wilde foweles;
B.15.306   In menynge þat meke þyng mylde þyng sholde *fede*.
B.15.340   Right so ye riche, ye robeþ and *fedeþ*
B.15.401   Daunted a dowue and day and nyзt hire *fedde*.
B.15.415   How englisshe clerkes a coluere *fede* þat coueitise hiзte,
B.15.463   He *fedde* men wiþ no venyson ne fesauntз ybake
B.15.465   And wiþ calues flessh he *fedde* þe folk þat he louede.
B.15.472   [And by þe hond *fedde* foules [i]s folk vnderstonde
B.15.485   And *feden* vs and festen vs for eueremoore at oones].
B.15.573   And *feden* hem wiþ goostly foode and [nedy folk to fynden.
B.16.125   And *fed* yow wiþ two fisshes and wiþ fyue loues,
B.19.126   And *fedde* wiþ two fisshes and with fyue loues
B.19.257   And after craftes conseil cloþeþ yow and *fede*.
B.20.209   'How shal I come to catel so to cloþe me and to *feede*?'
C. 6.434   [On] fastyng dayes bifore noen *fedde* me with ale,
C. 7.82   That *feden* foel sages, flateres and lyares
C. 7.133   *Feddest* tho with thy [fresshe] blood oure forfadres in helle:
C. 8.319   Pore folk for fere tho *fedde* honger зerne
C. 8.322   Thenne [was] folke fayn and *fedde* hunger dentie[f]liche
C. 9.90   And hath no catel but his craft to clothe h[e]m and to *fede*
C.12.105   For vch frende *fedeth* other and fondeth hou beste to quite
C.17.11   Elles foules *fedde* hem in frythes þer they wonede,
C.17.15   Foules hym *fedde* yf frere Austynes be trewe
C.17.57   To feffe suche and *fede* þat founded ben to þe fulle
C.17.68   And *fedde* þat afyn[g]red were and in defaute lyuede.
C.17.171   He endaunted a douue and day and nyhte here *fedde*;
C.17.285   *Feden* hem and follen hem and fere hem fro synne–
C.18.152   Ac y saued зow sondry tymes and also y *fe[d]* зow
C.21.126   And *fedde* with two fisches and with fyue loues
C.21.257   And aftur craftes consail clotheth зow and *fedeth*.
C.22.209   'How shal y come to catel so to clothe me and to *fede*?'

fee n *fe n.(2)* A 2 fe (1) fees (1); B 2 fee (1) fees (1); C 3 fee (1) fees (2)
A.4.114   Vpe forfaiture of þat fe, who fynt hym [at douere],
A. 6.68   He is fre[þ]id in wiþ Floreynes & oþere [*fees*] manye.
B. 4.131   V[p] forfeture of þat *fee*, wh[o] fynt [hym] at Douere,
B. 5.581   He is fryþed In wiþ floryns and oþere *fees* manye;
C. 4.128   Vp forfeture of þat *fee*, ho fyndeth h[y]m ouerward,
C. 5.77   Imade here kyn knyhtes and knyhtes *fees* ypurchased,
C. 7.228   Is frithed in with floreynes and othere *fees* monye;

feede > feden; feeld > feld

feele v *felen v.(1)* B 8 feele (5) fele (1) feledest (1) feleþ (1); C 8 fele (5)
    felede (1) feledest (1) feleth (1)
B. 5.489   Ther þiself ne þi sone no sorwe in deeþ *feledest*,
B.15.29   And whan I *feele* þat folk telleþ my firste name is sensus,
B.17.153   Al þat þe pawme parceyueþ profitable to *feele*.
B.17.181   Whan he *feleþ* þe fust and] þe fyngres wille;
B.18.220   And siþþe he suffred hym synne sorwe to *feele*,
B.19.171   And *feele* wiþ hise fyngres his flesshliche herte.

B.20.37   [For nede makeþ nede *fele* nedes lowe herted].
B.20.195   For þe lyme þat she loued me fore and leef was to *feele*
C. 6.114   In alle manere angres þat y hadde or *felede*.
C. 7.130   On a friday in fourme of man *feledest* oure sorwe:
C.16.189   And when y *fele* þat folke telleth my furste name is sensus
C.19.146   Alle þat þe fyngeres and þe fust *feleth* and toucheth.
C.20.229   And sethe he soffrede hym synne sorwe to *fele*
C.21.171   And *fele* with his fyngeres his flescheliche herte.
C.22.37   For nede maketh neede *fele* nedes louh herted.
C.22.195   For þe lyme þat she loued me fore and leef was to *fele*

feend > fend; feer > fere; feerde > fare

feere n *fere n.(1)* &> *fere* A 5 fere (2) feris (3); B 5 feere (2) feeres (2)
    feeris (1); C 4 fere (3) feres (1)
A. 2.6   Boþe fals & fauel & hise *feris* manye.'
A. 2.155   Fals oþer fauel oþer any of his *feris*,
A. 2.171   And bad hym fle for fer & hise *feris* alle.
A. 4.24   Ac [o]n wary[n] wisdom, and witty his *fere*
A. 4.141   War[yn] wisdom þo, ne [witty] his *fere*,
B. 2.6   Boþe Fals and Fauel and hi[s]e *feeres* manye.'
B. 2.194   Fals or Fauel or any of hise *feeris*
B. 2.212   And bad hym fle for fere and hise [*feeres*] alle.
B. 4.27   Oon waryn wisdom and witty his *feere*
B.17.324   Hir *feere* fleeþ hire for feere of hir tonge.
C. 2.222   And bad falsnesse to fle and his *feres* alle.
C.13.164   For no foul sholde hit fynde but his *fere* and hymsulue.
C.17.19   Peter fischede for his fode And his *fere* Androwe;
C.19.304   Here f[e]re fleeth here for fere of here tonge.

feeris n *faire n.* &> *feere* B 1
B. 5.170   For þere ben manye felle frekes my *feeris* to aspie,

feeste > feste,festen

feet n *fet n.* &> *foot* A 1 fait; B 1; C 1
A. 1.160   Þat feiþ wiþoute *fait* is feblere þan nouзt,
B. 1.186   That Feiþ withouten *feet* is [feblere þan nouзt],
C. 1.182   That fayth withouten *feet* is feblore then nauth

feffement n *feffement n.* A 1; B 1; C 1 feffament
A. 2.55   And vnfolde þe *feffement* þat fals haþ ymakid;
B. 2.73   And vnfoldeþ þe *feffement* that Fals hath ymaked.
C. 2.75   And vnfoldeth the *feffament* þat fals hath ymaked.

feffeþ v *feffen v.* A 4 feffe (3) feffid (1); B 3 feffe (1) feffed (1) feffeþ
    (1); C 5 feffe (3) feffed (1) feffeth (1)
A. 2.37   And *feffe* mede þer[myd] in mariage for euere.
A. 2.47   In what maner þat mede was *feffid*;
A. 2.58   Þat I, fauel, *feffe* falsnesse to mede,
A. 2.111   And *feffe* false wytnesse wiþ floreynes ynowe,
B. 2.79   And Fauel wiþ his fikel speche *feffeþ* by þis chartre
B. 2.147   And *feffe* fal[s] witnesse[s] wiþ floryns ynowe,
B.15.325   And ben founded and *feffed* ek to bidde for oþere.
C. 2.86   And fauel þat hath a fals speche *Feffeth* hem by þis lettre
C. 2.140   And thow hast *feffed* here with fals; fy on suche lawe.
C. 2.163   And *feffe* fals witnesse with floreynes ynowe,
C. 3.370   I wolde *feffe* hym with here fayre and [with] here foule taylende.
C.17.57   To *feffe* suche and fede þat founded ben to þe fulle

fey adj *feie adj.* B 1; C 2 fay (1) feye (1)
B.13.2   And as a freke þat [*fey*] were forþ gan I walke
C.15.2   And as a freke þ[at] *fay* were forth can y walken
C.16.197   And when y fle fro þe [flessh] and *feye* leue þe caroyne

feynen v *feinen v.* A 1 feynide; B 2 feyned (1) feynen (1); C 1 fayned
A. 7.113   Þanne were faitours aferd & *feynide* hem blynde;
B. 6.121   Tho were faitours aferd and *feyned* hem blynde,
B.10.39   But þoo þat *feynen* hem foolis, and wiþ faityng libbeþ
C. 8.128   Tho were faytours aferd and *fayned* hem blynde;

feynte adj *feint adj.* B 1 feynte
B.17.119   And alle þat feble and *feynte* be, þat Feiþ may noзt teche,

feyntise n *feintise n.* A 3 feyntise (1) fentesye (1) fentyse (1); B 1
A. 5.5   Er I hadde faren a furlong *feyntise* me h[ent]e
A.12.67   'I wolde folwe þe fayn, but *fentesye* me hendeþ;
A.12.68   Me folweþ such a *fentyse*, I may no ferþer walke.'
B. 5.5   Ac er I hadde faren a furlong *feyntise* me hente

feyntlees adj *feintles adj.* A 1 feyntles; B 1
A. 2.94   Þat fals is a faitour [and] *feyntles* of werkis,
B. 2.130   That Fals is *fe[ynt]lees* and fikel in hise werkes,

feyntly adv *feintli adv.* A 1 feintliche; B 1
A. 2.130   And fauel vpon fair speche, *fe[int]liche* atirid.
B. 2.166   And Fauel on [Fair Speche] *fe[ynt]ly* atired.

feyr > fair

feire n *feire n.* A 3 feire (2) feiris (1); B 3 feire (1) Feyre (1) feires (1); C 4 fayre (3) fayres (1)

A. 4.43 Forstalliþ my *feiris*, fiȝteþ in my chepyng,
A. 5.119 To wynchestre & to wy I [wente] to þe *feire*
A. 5.169 And at þe newe *feire* nempnide it to selle.
B. 4.56 Forstalleþ my *feires*, fiȝteþ in my Chepyng,
B. 5.203 To Wy and to Wynchestre I wente to þe *Feyre*
B. 5.320 And at þe newe *feire* nempned it to selle.
C. 4.59 Forstalleth my *fayres* and fyhteth in my chepyng[e]
C. 6.211 To wy and to wynchestre y wente to þe *fayre*
C. 6.377 And to þe newe *fayre* nempnede [hit] to sull;
C.13.52 And ȝut thow they wende o way as to wynchestre *fayre*

feirest > fair

feiþ n *feith n.* A 8; B 60 faith (2) faiþ (1) feiþ (56) Feiþes (1); C 44 faith (17) fayth (27)

A. 1.14 For he is fadir of *feiþ* & fourmide ȝow alle
A. 1.74 I vndirfang þe ferst and þi *feiþ* [þe] tauȝte.
A. 1.160 Þat *feiþ* wiþoute fait is feblere þan nouȝt,
A. 3.111 She is freel of hire *feiþ*, fikel of hire speche;
A. 3.147 Þat *feiþ* may not haue his forþ, hire floreynes go so þikke.
A. 7.255 And be fayn be my *feiþ* his fesik to leten,
A.11.60 Þat defouliþ oure f[eiþ] at fest[is] þere þei sitten.
A.11.63 And fyndiþ forþ fantasies oure *feiþ* to apeire,
B. 1.14 For he is fader of *feiþ*, and formed yow alle
B. 1.76 I vnderfeng þee first and þ[i] *feiþ* [þee] tauȝte.
B. 1.186 That *Feiþ* withouten feet is [feblere þan nouȝt],
B. 3.122 She is frele of hire *feiþ*, fikel of hire speche;
B. 3.157 That *feiþ* may noȝt haue his forþ, hire floryns go so þikke.
B. 4.37 Thei ne [gy]ueþ noȝt of [good *feiþ*, woot god þe sooþe]:
B. 5.236 And I kan no frenssh in *feiþ* but of þe ferþest ende of Northfolk.'
B. 5.265 For were I frere of þat hous þer good *feiþ* and charite is
B. 6.271 And be fayn, by my *feiþ*, his Phisik to gete
B.10.75 That folk is noȝt fermed in þe *feiþ* ne free of hire goodes
B.10.239 Wiþ alle þe articles of þe *feiþ* þat falleþ to be knowe.
B.10.255 For hadde neuere freke fyn wit þe *feiþ* to dispute,
B.10.395 Ac of fele witty in *feiþ* litel ferly I haue
B.10.411 God lene it fare noȝt so bi folk þat þe *feiþ* techeþ
B.11.71 'By my *feiþ*! frere', quod I, 'ye faren lik þise woweris
B.11.226 For some wordes I fynde writen, were of *Feiþes* techyng,
B.12.3 I haue folwed þee, in *feiþ*, þise fyue and fourty wynter,
B.12.30 *Feiþ*, hope and Charite, and alle ben goode,
B.13.129 Whiche Infinites wiþ a *feiþ* fynden out dobest,
B.13.210 Turne into þe trewe *feiþ* and intil oon bileue.'
B.14.82 Forþi mesure we vs wel and make [we] *feiþ* oure sheltrom;
B.14.83 And þoruȝ *feiþ* comeþ contricion, conscience woot wel,
B.14.86 And brynge his soule to blisse, so þat *feiþ* bere witnesse
B.14.88 Ergo contricion, *feiþ* and conscience is kyndeliche dowel,
B.15.100 [Is þe] roote of þe right *feiþ* to rule þe peple;
B.15.347 Ac þer is a defaute in þe folk þat þe *feiþ* kepeþ,
B.15.448 And follede folk faste, and þe *feiþ* tauȝte
B.15.451 [Enformed] hem what fullynge and *feiþ* was to mene.
B.15.507 Thus in a *feiþ* leue þat folk, and in a fals mene,
B.15.520 Al for to enforme þe *faith*; in fele contrees deyeden,
B.15.522 In dolful deþ deyeden for hir *faith*.
B.15.580 Arn ferme as in þe *feiþ*, goddes forbode ellis,
B.15.606 Arn folk of oon *feiþ*; þe fader god þei honouren.
B.16.176 'I am *feiþ*,' quod þat freke, 'it falleþ noȝt to lye,
B.16.231 First he fonded me if I, [*feiþ*], louede bettre
B.16.238 Myn affiaunce and my *feiþ* is ferme in þis bileue
B.16.245 And called me foot of his *feiþ*, his folk for to saue
B.17.60 *Feiþ* hadde first siȝte of hym, ac he fleiȝ aside
B.17.83 *Feiþ* folwede after faste and fondede to mete hym,
B.17.91 How þat *feiþ* fleiȝ awey and Spes his felawe boþe
B.17.95 Neiþer *Feiþ* ne fyn hope, so festred be hise woundes,
B.17.103 Saue *feiþ* and [myselue and] Spes [his felawe],
B.17.109 For he seigh me þat am Samaritan suwen *Feiþ* & his felawe
B.17.115 And þanne shal *Feiþ* be forster here and in þis Fryth walke,
B.17.119 And alle þat feble and feynte be, þat *Feiþ* may noȝt teche,
B.17.126 Alle þat lyuen in *Feiþ* and folwen his felawes techynge.'
B.17.128 As *Feiþ* and his felawe enformed me boþe,
B.17.135 Sette [faste] þi *feiþ* and ferme bileue;
B.18.15 Thanne was *feiþ* in a fenestre and cryde 'a! fili dauid!'
B.18.18 Thanne I frayned at *feiþ* what al þat fare bymente,
B.18.28 'Nay', quod [*feiþ*, 'but] þe fend and fals doom [to deye].
B.18.92 Thanne gan *Feiþ* felly þe false Iewes despise;
B.18.125 'Ich haue ferly of þis fare, in *feiþ*', seide truþe,
B.18.347 And þat grace gile destruye good *feiþ* it askeþ.
B.18.351 Falsliche and felonliche; good *feiþ* me it tauȝte
B.19.271 Thise foure, þe *feiþ* to teche, folwe[de] Piers teme
B.19.300 For gile goþ so pryuely þat good *feiþ* ouþer while
B.20.28 And greue men grettore þan good *feiþ* it wolde.
B.20.131 And garte good *feiþ* flee and fals to abide,

B.20.332 'In *faiþ*', quod þis frere, 'for profit and for helþe
C. 1.14 For he is fader of *fayth* and formor of alle;
C. 1.182 That *fayth* withouten feet is feblore then nauth
C. 3.159 For she [is] frele of here *fayth*, fikel of here speche
C. 3.195 That *fayth* may nat haue his forth, here floreynes goth so thykke,
C. 4.13 'Y am fayn of that foreward, in *fayth*,' tho quod Consience,
C. 4.37 They gyue n[ouh]t of good *fayth*, woe[t] god the sothe,
C. 4.50 Y dar nat for his felawschipe, in *fayth*,' pees sayde
C. 5.40 And foen[d y] nere, in *fayth*, seth my frendes deyede
C. 6.287 Were y a frere, in good *fayth*, for al þe gold on erthe
C. 6.341 For thow hast no good, by good *fayth*, to gete the with a wastel.
C. 8.34 To defende þe in *fayth*, fyhte thow y sholde.'
C. 8.214 But for fere of famyen, in *fayth*,' sayde [Peres].
C. 8.292 And be fayn, be my *fayth*, his fysik to leete
C.11.55 That folk is nat ferme[d] in þe *faith* ne fre of here godes
C.11.156 For hadde neuere frek fyn wi[t] the *faith* to dispute
C.11.226 For of fele witty in *faith* litel ferly y haue
C.11.242 God lene hit fare nat so by folk þat þe *faith* techen
C.11.273 And fonde y neuere in *faith*, for to telle treuthe,
C.12.19 'By my *faith*! frere,' quod y, 'ȝe fare lyke þe woware
C.14.3 Y haue folewed the, in *fayth*, mo then fourty wynter
C.16.253 Is þe rote of [the] rihte *fayth* to reule þe peple;
C.16.289 And fonde y neuere in *faith*, as freres hit precheth,
C.17.258 Thus in a *fayth* l[e]ueth þat folk and in a fals mene,
C.17.271 For to enf[ou]rme þe *fayth* ful wydewhare deyede,
C.18.184 'I am with *fayth*,' quod þat freke, 'hit falleth nat me to lye,
C.18.198 'Muse nat to moche þeron,' quod *fayth*, 'til thow more knowe
C.18.254 Myen affiaunce and my *faith* is ferme in [t]his bileue
C.18.273 'What [a]waytest thow,' quod *fayth*, 'and what wost thow haue?'
C.19.23 'He seyth soth,' saide *fayth*; 'y haue yfounde hit trewe.
C.19.26 And six thousand mo,' quod *fayth*; 'y [can] nat seyn here names.'
C.19.59 *Fayth* [hadde furst siht of hym] Ac he fleyh asyde
C.19.80 Bothe *fayth* and his felawe spes folewede faste aftur
C.19.85 No[þer] *faith* ne fyn hope, so festred aren his woundes.
C.19.97 As *faith* and his felawe spes enfourmede me bothe,
C.20.13 Thenne was *faith* in a fenestre and criede 'a! fil[i] dauid!'
C.20.16 Thenne y [f]raynede at *fayth* what al þat fare bymente,
C.20.27 'Nay,' quod *faith*, 'bote the fende and fals doem to deye.
C.20.95 Thenne gan *faith* f[el]ly þe false iewes dispice,
C.20.128 'Y haue ferly of this fare, in *faith*,' seide truþe,
C.21.271 Thise foure, the *fayth* to teche, folewe[de Peres] teme
C.21.300 For gyle goth so priuely þat goed *fayth* oþer while
C.22.28 And greue men grettore then goed *faith* hit w[o]lde.
C.22.131 And gert goed *faith* fle and fals to abyde
C.22.332 'In *fayth*,' quod this frere, 'for profyt and for helthe

feiþful adj *feithful adj.* B 3; C 4 fayful (1) faythfol (1) faythful (1) faythfull (1)

B. 6.251 The freke þat fedeþ hymself wiþ his *feiþful* labour
B. 9.105 Wolde neuere þe *feiþful* fader [h]is fiþele were vntempred
B.15.419 Wolde neuere *feiþful* fader þat [þ]ise Ministres sholde
C. 1.15 To be *fayful* to hym [he] ȝaf ȝow fyue wittes
C. 6.291 Y rede no *faythful* frere at thy feste to sytte.
C.17.35 For wolde neuere *faythfull* god þat freres and monkes
C.18.140 Ne noon so *faythfol* fisciscyen, for all þat bysouhte hym

feiþfulliche adv *feithfulli adv.* A 1; B 1; C 2 fayfulleche (1) feithfullich (1)

A. 7.63 I shal fynde hem foode þat *feiþfulliche* libbeþ,
B. 6.69 I shal fynden hem fode þat *feiþfulliche* libbeþ,
C. 1.100 But [*feithfullich*] fyghte and fende treuthe
C. 8.70 Y shal fynde hem fode þat *fayfulleche* libbeth,

feiþlees adj *feithles adj.* A 1 feiþlees; B 2; C 2 faythles (1) faythlesse (1)

A.10.139 Ac fals folk & *feiþles*, þeuis & leiȝeris,
B. 9.121 Ac fals folk, *feiþlees*, þeues and lyeres,
B.10.198 And so shaltow fals folk and *feiþlees* bigile:
C. 2.44 To oon fals *faythlesse* of þe fendes kynne.
C. 2.146 That fals is *faythles*, the fende is his syre

feitures n *feture n.(1)* B 1; C 1 fetures
B.13.296 Or feirest of *feitures* of forme and of shafte,
C. 6.46 Prout of my fayre *fetures* and for y song shille;

fel n *fel n.(1)* A 1; B 1
A. 1.15 Boþe wiþ *fel* & wiþ face, & ȝaf ȝow fyue wyttes
B. 1.15 Boþe with *fel* and with face, and yaf yow fyue wittes

fel adj *fel adj.* B 3 fel (1) felle (2); C 3 fel (1) felle (2)
B. 3.342 She sholde haue founden fel[l]e wordes folwynge þerafter:
B. 5.170 For þere ben manye *felle* frekes my feeris to aspie,
B.16.31 The flessh is a *fel* wynd, and in flouryng tyme,
C. 3.494 A sholde haue yfonde [*felle* wordes folwynge] aftur:
C. 6.152 For there aren many *felle* frekes myn aferes to aspye,
C.18.35 Thenne is þe flesch a *fel* wynde and in flouryng tyme

fel &> falle; felasshipe > felawship

felawe n *felaue n.* A 1 felawis; B 17 felawe (14) felawes (3); C 13 felawe (10) felawes (2) felowe (1)

A. 1.112   Þanne fil he wiþ [his] *felawis* & fendis bicome;
B. 7.12   Wiþ Patriarkes and prophetes in paradis to be *felawe.*
B. 9.87   Syn Iewes, þat we Iugge Iudas *felawes,*
B.12.167   Ther his *felawe* fleteþ forþ as þe flood likeþ
B.13.94   And þanne shal he testifie of [a] Trinite, and take his *felawe* to witnesse
B.13.206   If Pacience be oure partyng *felawe* and pryue with vs boþe
B.15.292   Peter fisshed for his foode and his *felawe* Andrew;
B.15.379   Flaterere his *felawe,* ferly me þynkeþ].
B.17.89   'Ac þi frend and þi *felawe* þow fyndest me at nede.'
B.17.91   How þat feiþ fleiȝ awey and Spes his *felawe* boþe
B.17.103   Saue feiþ and [myselue and] Spes [his *felawe*],
B.17.109   For he seigh me þat am Samaritan suwen Feiþ & his *felawe*
B.17.126   Alle þat lyuen in Feiþ and folwen his *felawes* techynge.'
B.17.128   As Feiþ and his *felawe* enformed me boþe,
B.19.88   Rightwisnesse vnder reed gold, Resones *felawe;*
B.19.201   Oon Spiritus paraclitus to Piers and to hise *felawes.*
B.20.340   'Certes', seide his *felawe,* 'sire Penetrans domos.'
B.20.349   Lat in þe frere and his *felawe,* and make hem fair cheere.
C. 1.120   Ther he faylede and ful and his *felawes* alle;
C. 2.186   'And y mysulue, syuyle, and symonye my *felawe*
C. 2.208   Fals or fauel or here *felawe* lyare
C. 3.111   Ar he were vnderfonge fre and *felawe* in ȝoure rolles.
C. 4.27   Ooen wareyn wisman and wilyman his *felawe*
C. 8.253   Byno[m] hym al þat he hadde and ȝaf hit to his *felawe*
C.15.101   And [thenne shal he testifie of] a trinite and take his *felowe* [t]o witnesse
C.19.80   Bothe fayth and his *felawe* spes folewede faste aftur
C.19.97   As faith and his *felawe* spes enfourmede me bothe,
C.21.88   Rihtwisnesse vnder reed gold, resones *felawe;*
C.21.201   Oen spiritus paraclitus to Peres and to his *felawes.*
C.22.340   'Certes,' saide his *felawe,* 'sire penetrans domos.'
C.22.349   Lat in þe frere and his *felawe* and make hem fayere chiere.

felawship n *felaushipe n.* A 1 Felasshipe; B 4 felaweshipe (1) felawship (2) felawshipe (1); C 4 felawschipe (3) felowschipe (1)

A. 3.108   For heo is fayn of þi *Felasshipe,* for to be þi make.'
B. 1.114   And fel fro þat *felawshipe* in a fendes liknesse
B. 2.210   Falsnesse and his *felawship* to fettren and to bynden.
B. 3.119   For she is fayn of þi *felaweshipe,* for to be þi make.'
B.11.24   That I ne shal folwe þi *felawship,* if Fortune it like.'
C. 2.106   And sue forth suche *felawschipe* til they ben falle in Slewthe
C. 3.156   For she is fayn of thy *felawschipe,* for to be thy make.'
C. 4.50   Y dar nat for his *felawschipe,* in fayth,' pees sayde,
C.11.183   That y ne shal folowe thy *felowschipe* yf fortune [hit] lyke.'

feld n *feld n.* A 6; B 7 feeld (2) feld (5); C 7 feld (5) felde (2)

A.Pr.17   A fair *feld* ful of folk fand I þere betwene
A. 1.2   And ek þe *feld* ful of folk I shal ȝow faire shewe.
A. 2.39   Þat iche *feld* nas ful of folk al aboute.
A. 5.10   [For I [sauȝ] þe *feld* ful of folk þat I before tolde],
A. 7.220   Piger propter frigus no *feld* wolde tilie;
A. 7.272   To drawe on *feld* my dong while þe drouȝt lastiþ.
B.Pr.17   A fair *feeld* ful of folk fond I þer bitwene
B. 1.2   And þe *feld* ful of folk I shal yow faire shewe.
B. 5.10   For I seiȝ þe *feld* ful of folk þat I before [tolde],
B. 5.417   But I kan fynden in a *feld* or in a furlang an hare
B. 6.140   To kepe kyen in þe *feld,* þe corn fro þe beestes.
B. 6.236   Piger [propter frigus] no *feeld* [w]olde tilie;
B.19.313   Foulen þe fruyt in þe *feld* þer þei growen togideres,
C.Pr.19   A fair *feld* ful of folk fond y þer bytwene
C. 1.2   And þe *feld* ful of folk y shal ȝou fair shewe.
C. 5.111   Y saw þe *felde* ful of folk fram ende til oþer
C. 7.32   Ac y can fynden in a *feld* and in a forlong an hare
C.12.193   In þe *feld* with þe forst and hit frese longe.
C.13.175   Ne what o[f] floures on *felde* and of here fayre coloures
C.21.313   Fouleth the fruyt in the *feld* ther thei growe togyderes

felde > feld,felle

fele adj *fele indef. num. &> feele* B 14; C 10 fele (9) vele (1)

B. 9.75   And fynde *fele* witnesses among þe foure doctours,
B.10.216   Yet ar þer fibicches in [forelles] of *fele* mennes [wittes],
B.10.395   Ac of *fele* witty in feiþ litel ferly I haue
B.11.330   Wiþ fleckede feþeres and of *fele* colours.
B.12.5   And how *fele* fernyeres are faren and so fewe to come;
B.12.266   And of flessh by *fele* fold fatter and swetter;
B.13.319   It was fouler bi *fele* fold þan it first semed.
B.13.329   Auenge me *fele* tymes, oþer frete myselue wiþInne;
B.15.70   Freres and *fele* oþere maistres þat to [þe] lewed [folk] prechen,
B.15.231   Ac it is fern [and *fele* yeer in] Fraunceis tyme;

B.15.288   Foweles hym fedde, *fele* wyntres wiþ alle,
B.15.333   *Fele* of yow fareþ as if I a forest hadde
B.15.520   Al for to enforme þe faith; in *fele* contrees deyeden,
B.19.221   And false prophetes *fele,* flatereris and gloseris,
C. 6.74   Venged me *vele* tymes other vrete myself withynne
C. 6.118   Freres folewen my [f]ore *fele* tyme and ofte
C. 9.91   And *fele* to fonge þerto and fewe panes taketh.
C. 9.95   Were a feste with suche folk or so *fele* cockes.
C.11.226   For of *fele* witty in faith litel ferly y haue
C.13.138   With flekede fetheres and of *fele* colours.
C.16.174   'Of [*fele*] tyme to fihte,' quod he, 'falsnesse to destruye
C.16.231   Freres *fele* tymes to þe folk þer they prechen
C.16.356   Ac hit is fer and *fele* ȝer in franceys tyme;
C.21.221   And false profetes *fele,* flateres and glosares,

felede(st -eþ > feele

felice n prop *n.i.d.* A 1 felis; B 2; C 1 felyce

A. 5.29   And fecche [hom] *felis* fro wyuene pyne.
B. 5.29   And fecche *Felice* hom fro wyuene pyne.
B.12.46   *Felice* hir fairnesse fel hire al to sclaundre,
C. 5.131   And fette *felyce* hoem fram wyuene pyne.

felicite n *felicite n.* B 1; C 1

B.20.240   And siþen freres forsoke þe *felicite* of erþe
C.22.240   And senne freres forsoke the *felic[it]e* of erthe

felyng ger *felinge ger.(1)* B 1; C 1 velynge

B.18.128   A maiden þat highte Marie, and moder wiþouten *felyng*
C.20.131   A mayde þat hoteth Marie, a[nd] moder withouten *velynge*

felis > felice

felle v *fellen v. &> falle,fel,fille* A 3 felle (2) fellide (1); B 2 felle (1) felled (1); C 3 felde

A. 3.41   Among clerkis & kniȝtes consience to *felle'.*
A. 3.116   ȝoure fadir he[o] *fellide* þoruȝ false behest,
A.12.66   I shal *felle* þat freke in a fewe dayes.'
B. 3.42   Amonges [clerkes] and [knyȝtes] Conscience to [*felle*]'.
B. 3.127   Youre fader she *felled* þoruȝ false beheste,
C. 3.164   ȝoure fader she [f]*elde,* fals and she togederes;
C. 3.240   That he ne *felde* nat his foes tho fortune hit wolde
C.18.127   That elde *felde* efte þe fruyt, or full to be rype.

fellen > falle

felly adv *felliche adv.* B 1; C 1

B.18.92   Thanne gan Feiþ *felly* þe false Iewes despise;
C.20.95   Thenne gan faith *f[el]ly* þe false iewes dispice,

felon > feloun

felonliche adv *felounliche adv.* B 1; C 1

B.18.351   Falsliche and *felonliche;* good feiþ me it tauȝte
C.12.238   That fals folk fecche aweye *felonliche* his godes;

feloun n *feloun n.(1)* A 2; B 6 felon (2) feloun (4); C 5 felon (2) feloun (3)

A. 5.245   Ac what befel of þis *feloun* I can not faire shewe;
A.11.279   A goode friday, I fynde, a *feloun* was sauid
B. 5.471   What bifel of þis *feloun* I kan noȝt faire shewe.
B.10.420   On good Friday, I fynde, a *felon* was ysaued
B.12.202   So it fareþ by þat *felon* þat a good friday was saued;
B.17.113   That he worþ fettred, þat *feloun,* faste wiþ Cheynes,
B.18.379   It is noȝt vsed in erþe to hangen a *feloun*
B.18.382   There [a] *feloun* þole sholde deeþ ooþer Iuwise
C. 6.325   What byful of this *feloun* y can nat fayre shewe;
C.10.240   For thogh þe fader be a frankeleyn and for a *felon* be hanged
C.11.252   A gode friday, y fynde, a *feloun* was ysaued
C.14.141   So hit f[areth] by þe *feloun* þat a goed fryday was saued:
C.20.421   Hit is nat vsed [i]n erthe to hangen [a] *felo[n]*

felow- > felaw-

femelles n *femele adj. & n.* B 2; C 2 femeles

B.11.340   And [*femelles* to femelles ferded and drowe].
B.11.340   And [femelles to *femelles* ferded and drowe].
C.13.148   And *femeles* to femeles ferddede and drowe.
C.13.148   And femeles to *femeles* ferddede and drowe.

fend n *fend n.* A 8 fend (6) fendis (2); B 30 feend (1) fend (21) fendes (8); C 25 fend (4) fende (16) fendes (5)

A. 1.38   For þe *fend* & þi flessh folewiþ togidere,
A. 1.112   Þanne fil he wiþ [his] felawis & *fendis* bicome;
A. 7.80   And defende it fro þe *fend,* for so I beleue,
A. 7.136   Lest his flessh & þe *fend* foulide his soule.
A. 8.70   He is fals wiþ þe *fend* & [defraudiþ] þe nedy,
A. 9.38   Þat þoruȝ þe *fend,* & þe flessh, & þe false world,
A. 9.45   Folewe þi flesshis wil & þe *fendis* aftir,

204

A.10.64   Ac in fauntis ne in folis þe [*fend*] haþ no miȝt
B. 1.40   For þe *fend* and þi flessh folwen togidere,
B. 1.114 And fel fro þat felawshipe in a *fendes* liknesse
B. 1.121 But fellen out in *fendes* liknesse [ful] nyne dayes togideres
B. 2.41   To oon fals fikel-tonge, a *fendes* biyete,
B. 6.88   And [defende it fro þe *fend*], for so I bileue,
B. 7.68   He is fals wiþ þe *feend* and defraudeþ þe nedy,
B. 8.42   That þoruȝ þe *fend* and þe flessh and þe [false] worlde
B. 8.49   Folwe þi flesshes wille and þe *fendes* after,
B.11.401 In fondynge of þe flessh and of þe *fend* boþe,
B.12.179 In which flood þe *fend* fondeþ a man hardest.
B.13.429 Riȝt so flatereris and fooles arn þe *fendes* disciples
B.14.24   Ne *fend* ne fals man defoulen it in þi lyue.
B.14.203 The *fend* folweþ hem alle and fondeþ hem to helpe,
B.15.141 To frend ne to fremmed: "þe *fend* haue his soule!
B.16.40   And þanne fondeþ þe *fend* my fruyt to destruye
B.16.48   Ac whan þe *fend* and þe flessh forþ wiþ þe world
B.16.96   Wheiþer sholde fonge þe fruyt, þe *fend* or hymselue.
B.16.102 To haue yfouȝte wiþ þe *fend* er ful tyme come.
B.16.246 And defende hem fro þe *fend*, folk þat on me leneden.
B.18.20   'And fecche þat þe *fend* claymeþ, Piers fruyt þe Plowman.'
B.18.28   'Nay', quod [feiþ, 'but] þe *fend* and fals doom [to deye].
B.18.33   And fecche fro þe *fend* Piers fruyt þe Plowman
B.18.198 And folwede þat þe *fend* tauȝte and his [flesshes] wille
B.18.309 I rede we fle', quod [þe *fend*], 'faste alle hennes,
B.18.373 *Fendes* and f[e]ndekynes bifore me shul stande
B.18.430 And it afereþ þe *fend*, for swich is þe myȝte
B.19.47   And from *fendes* þat in hem [was] and false bileue.
B.20.58   Freres folwede þat *fend* for he gaf hem copes,
B.20.64   And a fals *fend* Antecrist ouer alle folk regnede.
B.20.77   Fooles fro þise *fendes* lymes, for Piers loue þe Plowman.
C. 1.38   For the *fend* and thy flesch folewen togederes
C. 1.119 For theder as þe *fende* fly his fote for to sette,
C. 2.44   To oon fals faythlesse of þe *fendes* kynne.
C. 2.146 That fals is faythles, the *fende* is his syre
C. 7.89   Ryht so flateres and fooles aren þe *fendes* procuratours
C. 8.97   And defenden hit fro þe *fende*, and so is my beleue,
C.10.48   That thorw the *fend* and [the] flesch and th[e] freel worlde
C.14.110 In whiche floed þe *fende* fondeth [a] man hardest.
C.16.44 The *fend* folleweth hem alle and fondeth hem to helpe
C.18.43 And thenne fondeth the *fende* my fruyte to destruye
C.18.119 And hit aftur þe *fende*, happe how hit myhte.
C.18.129 Who sholde fecche this fruyt, the *fende* or iesus suluen.
C.18.136 To haue yfouthte with þe *fende* Ar fol tyme come.
C.20.18 'And feche þat þe *fende* claymeth, pers fruyt þe plouhman.'
C.20.27 'Nay,' quod faith, 'bote the *fende* and fals doem to deye.
C.20.32 And feche fro þe *fende* [Peres] fruyt þe [plouhman]
C.20.203 And folewede þat þe *fende* tauhte and his flesch[es] will
C.20.315 Not in fourme of a *fende* bote in fourme of an Addre
C.20.343 Y rede we flee,' quod the *fende*, 'faste all hennes,
C.20.415 *Fendes* and fendekynes byfore me shal stande
C.20.474 And hit afereth th[e] *fende*, for such is þe myhte
C.21.47 And fro *fendes* þat in hem was and false bileue.
C.22.58 Freres folewed þat *fende* for he ȝaf hem copes,
C.22.64 And a fals *fende* auntecrist ouer all folke regnede.
C.22.77 Foles fro this *fendes* lymes for [Peres] loue the [plouhman].

fende > fend,fenden

fendekynes n *fendekin* n. B 1; C 1
B.18.373 Fendes and *f[e]ndekynes* bifore me shul stande
C.20.415 Fendes and *fendekynes* byfore me shal stande

fenden v *fenden* v. B 1; C 3 fende (2) fended (1)
B.19.65 Therwith to fiȝte and [f]enden vs fro fallynge in[to] synne,
C. 1.100 But [feithfullich] fyghte and *fende* treuthe
C.21.46 And *fended* fro foule eueles, feueres and fluxes
C.21.65 Therwith to fihte and *fende* vs fro fallyng into synne

fenel n *fenel* n. cf. *fenkel* A 1; B 1
A. 5.156 And a [ferþingworþ] of [*fenel*sed] for fastyng dayes.'
B. 5.305 A ferþyngworþ of *fenel* seed for fastynge dayes.'

fenestre n *fenestre* n. B 2 fenestre (1) fenestres (1); C 2 fenestre (1) fenestres (1)
B.14.200 In *fenestres* at þe freres–if fals be þe foundement.
B.18.15 Thanne was feiþ in a *fenestre* and cryde 'a! fili dauid!'
C.16.41 In *fenestres* at þe freres–yf fals be þe fondement.
C.20.13 Thenne was faith in a *fenestre* and criede 'a! fil[i] dauid!'

fenkel n *fenkel* n. cf. *fenel* C 1
C. 6.360 A ferthyngworth [of] *fenkel* sed[e] for fastyng dayes.'

fent- > feyntise

fer adj *fer* adj.(1) A 1; B 3 fer (2) ferþest (1); C 5
A. 9.70 Arn þre faire vertues, & ben not *f[e]r* to fynde.
B. 5.236 And I kan no frenssh in feiþ but of þe *ferþest* ende of Northfolk.'
B. 8.79 Arn þre faire vertues, and ben noȝt *fer* to fynde.
B.15.535 *Fer* fro kyth and fro kyn yuele yclothed yeden,
C. 9.242 Breke þis obedience þat beth so *fer* fram chirche
C.10.77 Aren thre fayre vertues and ben nat *fer* to fynde.
C.12.237 For if he be *fer* þerfro fol ofte hath he drede
C.16.356 Ac hit is *fer* and fele ȝer in franceys tyme.
C.17.196 *Fer* fro [k]uthe and fro kyn euele yclothed ȝeden,

fer adv. *fer* adv. A 11 ferther (2) ferþer (3) ferþere (6); B 16 fer (8) ferþer (8); C 11 fer (8) forthere (2) forþere (1)
A. 2.163 And ge[rd]iþ of giles hed; let hym go no *ferþere*;
A. 5.6   Þat I ne miȝte *ferþere* a fote for defaute of slepyng.
A. 6.118 Shulde I neuere *ferþere* a foote for no freris preching.'
A. 7.188 'Ac ȝet I preye þe,' quaþ peris, 'er þou passe *ferþere*:
A. 9.11 And preiȝede hem, pur charite, er þei passide *ferþere*,
A.10.99 But suffre & sit stille & sek þou no *ferþere*,
A.11.293 And ȝet [haue] I forget[e *ferþer*] of fyue wyttis teching
A.12.30 Riȝt so I rede,' quod she, 'red þou no *ferþer*;
A.12.68 Me folweþ such a fentyse, I may no *ferþer* walke.'
A.12.76 For gronyng of my guttys I durst gon no *ferther*].
A.12.89 'Nay, wil,' quod þat wyȝth, 'wend þou no *ferther*,
B. 2.202 And girdeþ of Gyles heed; lat hym go no *ferþer*;
B. 5.6   That I ne myȝte *ferþer* a foot for defaute of slepynge.
B. 5.633 Sholde I neuere *ferþer* a foot for no freres prechyng.'
B. 8.11 And preide hem, p[u]r charite, er þei passed *ferþer*
B.10.448 [And yet haue I forgete *ferþer* of fyue wittes techyng
B.10.479 Selden falle so foule and so *fer* in synne
B.11.35 'Folwe forþ þat Fortune wole; þow hast wel *fer* til Elde.
B.12.35 Riȝt so if þow be Religious ren þow neuere *ferþer*
B.12.39 Seke þow neuere Seint *ferþer* for no soule helþe.
B.12.243 They may noȝt flee *fer* ne ful heiȝe neiþer;
B.14.209 Of wit and of wisdom, þat *fer* awey is bettre
B.18.164 Out of þe nyppe of þe North noȝt ful *fer* hennes
B.19.480 The viker hadde *fer* hoom and faire took his leeue
B.20.23 For is no vertue bi *fer* to Spiritus temperancie,
B.20.314 And moore of phisik bi *fer*, and fairer he plastreþ;
B.20.338 'I praye þee', quod Pees þo, 'er þow passe *ferþer*,
C. 7.286 [Sh]olde y neuere *forthere* [a] foet for no frere prechynge.'
C.10.11 And preyde hem, pur charite, ar they passede *forthere*
C.11.194 'Folowe forth þat fortune wole; þou hast [wel] *fer* to elde.
C.14.176 For þey may nat fle *fer* ne ful hey neyther
C.14.177 For here fetheres þat fayre beth to fle *fer* hem letteth.
C.16.50 Of wit and of wisdoem þat *fer* way is bettere
C.20.167 Out of þe nype of þe north nat ful *fer* hennes
C.21.480 The vicory hadde *fer* hoem and [fayre] toek his leue
C.22.23 [For is no vertue by *fer* to spiritus temperancie],
C.22.314 And more of fysyk bi *fer*, and fayror he plastereth;
C.22.338 'Y preye the,' quod Pees tho, 'ar thow passe *forþere*,

fer &> fere; ferddede > ferded; ferde > fare

ferded v *feren* v.(3) B 1; C 1 ferddede
B.11.340 And [femelles to femelles *ferded* and drowe].
C.13.148 And femeles to femeles *ferddede* and drowe.

ferden > fare

fere n *fer* n.(1) &> *feere* A 7 feer (1) fer (5) fere (1); B 12 feere (4) fere (8); C 11
A. 2.171 And bad hym fle for *fer* & hise feris alle.
A. 2.172 Þanne fal[s]nesse for *feer* fleiȝ to þe Freris;
A. 2.195 Alle fledden for *fer* & flowen into hernis;
A. 2.197 Ac trewely to telle heo tremblide for *fere*,
A. 4.39 I dar not for *fer* of hym fiȝte ne chide.
A. 7.171 Faitours for *fer* flowen into bernis
A. 7.281 Þanne þise folk for *fer* fetten hym manye
B. 2.212 And bad hym fle for *fere* and hise [feeres] alle.
B. 2.213 [Thanne] Falsnesse for *fere* fleiȝ to þe Freres;
B. 2.236 Alle fledden for *fere* and flowen into hernes;
B. 2.238 Ac trewely to telle she trembled for [*fere*],
B. 4.52 I dar noȝt for *fere* of h[y]m fiȝte ne chide.
B. 6.183 Faitours for *fere* flowen into Bernes
B. 6.297 Thanne pouere folk for *fere* fedden hunger yerne
B.11.355 For *fere* of oþere foweles and for wilde beestes.
B.13.162 Ne [neiþer] fuyr ne flood ne *feere* of þyn enemy
B.17.324 Hir feere fleeþ hire for *feere* of hir tonge.
B.18.110 What for *feere* of þis ferly and of þe false Iewes
B.20.169 And lif fleiȝ for *feere* to phisik after helpe
C. 2.223 Falsnesse for *fere* tho fleyh to þe freres;
C. 2.252 Alle fledde for *fere* and flowen into hernes;
C. 2.254 Ac treuliche to telle a tremblede for *fere*
C. 8.191 And freres of alle þe fyue ordres, alle for *fere* of hunger.

C. 8.202　Þat durste withsitte þat [Peres] sayde for *fere* of syre hunger
C. 8.214　But for *fere* of famyen, in fayth,' sayde [Peres].
C. 8.319　Pore folk for *fere* tho fedde honger ȝerne
C.12.198　*Fere* ne famyne ne fals mennes tonges.
C.19.304　Here f[e]re fleeth here for *fere* of here tonge.
C.20.113　What for *fere* of this ferly and of þe false iewes
C.22.169　And lyf fley for *fere* to fisyk aftur helpe

fere v *feren v.(1)*　B 1;　C 1
B. 7.35　That no deuel shal yow dere ne [in youre deying *fere* yow],
C.17.285　Feden hem and follen hem and *fere* hem fro synne–

feres > feere

ferye n *ferie n.(1)*　B 1;　C 1 ferie
B.13.414　Ech day is halyday with hym or an heiȝ *ferye*,
C. 4.113　And harlotes holynesse be an eye *ferie*;

feris > feere

ferly n *ferli n.*　A 4 ferly (2) ferlis (1) ferlys (1);　B 7 ferly (6) ferlies (1);
　C 8 ferly (7) ferlyes (1)
A.Pr.6　Me befel a *ferly*, of fairie me þouȝte:
A.Pr.62　Manye *ferlis* han fallen in a fewe ȝeris.
A.12.58　Many *ferlys* me byfel in a fewe ȝeris.
A.12.59　The fyrste *ferly* I fond afyngrid me made;
B.Pr.6　Me bifel a *ferly*, of Fairye me þoȝte.
B.Pr.65　Manye *ferlies* han fallen in a fewe yeres.
B.10.395　Ac of fele witty in feiþ litel *ferly* I haue
B.13.109　And if ye fare so in youre Fermerye, *ferly* me þynkeþ
B.15.379　Flaterere his felawe, *ferly* me þynkeþ).
B.18.110　What for feere of þis *ferly* and of þe false Iewes
B.18.125　'Ich haue *ferly* of þis fare, in feiþ', seide truþe,
C.Pr.63　Mony *ferlyes* han falle in a fewe ȝeres.
C.11.226　For of fele witty in faith litel *ferly* y haue
C.15.117　And ȝe fare thus with ȝoure syke freres, *ferly* me thynketh
C.16.296　And fynde hym, but f[i]guratyfly, a *ferly* me thynketh:
C.17.113　And flaterrere for his vscher, *ferly* me thynketh.
C.18.56　A[c] in thre degrees hit grewe; grete *ferly* me thouhte,
C.20.113　What for feere of this *ferly* and of þe false iewes
C.20.128　'Y haue *ferly* of this fare, in faith,' seide Treuthe,

ferlyede v *ferlien v.*　C 1
C.13.172　And *ferlyede* of his fayrenesse and of his foul le[den]e.

ferm adj *ferm adj.*　B 4 ferm (1) ferme (3);　C 2 ferme
B.12.286　And þoruȝ fir is fullyng, and þat is *ferme* bileue:
B.15.348　Wherfore folk is þe febler and noȝt *ferm* of bileue.
B.15.580　Arn *ferme* as in þe feiþ, goddes forbode ellis,
B.16.238　Myn affiaunce and my feiþ is *ferme* in þis bileue
C.14.208　And thorw fuyr is fullyng; and [þat] is *ferme* bileue:
C.18.254　Myen affiaunce and my faith is *ferme* in [t]his bileue

ferme n *ferme n.(2)*　B 1
B.16.16　And liberum arbitrium haþ þe lond [to] *ferme*,

ferme adv *ferme adv.*　B 2;　C 1
B.17.135　Sette [faste] þi feiþ and *ferme* bileue;
B.19.120　That she first and formest *ferme* sholde bileue
C.21.120　That [sh]e furste and formoste [*ferme* sholde] bileue

ferme &> ferm

fermed ptp *fermen v.(3)*　B 1;　C 1
B.10.75　That folk is noȝt *fermed* in þe feiþ ne free of hire goodes
C.11.55　That folk is nat *ferme[d]* in þe faith ne fre of here godes

fermerye n *fermerie n.*　B 1
B.13.109　And if ye fare so in youre Fermerye, ferly me þynkeþ

fern adj *fern adj.*　B 1
B.15.231　Ac it is *fern* [and fele yeer in] Fraunceis tyme;

fernyere adv *fern- adv.*　B 1;　C 1 ferneȝer
B. 5.433　The kyndenesse þat myn euencristene kidde me *fernyere*,
C. 7.46　The kyndenesse þat myn emcristen kud me *ferneȝer*,

fernyeres n *fern- adv.*　B 1
B.12.5　And how fele *fernyeres* are faren and so fewe to come;

fers > fiers; ferst(e > first

ferþe num *ferthe num.*　A 1;　B 3;　C 3 ferthe (2) furthe (1)
A.12.82　Mi name is feuere on þe *ferþe* day; I am aþrest euere.
B. 7.53　Ac to bugge water ne wynd ne wit ne fir þe *ferþe*,
B.14.297　The *ferþe* is a fortune þat florissheþ þe soule
B.19.297　The *ferþe* seed þat Piers sew was Spiritus Iusticie,
C. 9.56　Þat is wit and watur and wynde and fuyre þe *ferthe*;
C.16.133　The *furthe* is a fortune þat florischeth þe soule
C.21.297　The *ferthe* seed that [Peres] sewe was spiritus Iusticie

ferþer(e -est > fer

ferþyng n *ferthing n.*　A 2 ferþing;　B 2;　C 2 ferthyng (1) ferthynge (1)
A. 4.41　Ne no *ferþing* þerfore for nouȝt I couþe plete.
A. 6.45　'I nolde fonge a *ferþing* for seint Thomas shryne,
B. 4.54　Ne no *ferþyng* þerfore for [n]ouȝt I koude plede.
B. 5.558　'I nolde fange a *ferþyng* for Seint Thomas Shryne;
C. 4.57　Ne [no] *ferthyng* therfore, for nouhte y couthe plede.
C. 7.202　'Y [nolde] fonge a *ferthynge* for seynt Thomas shryne;

ferþyngworþ n *ferthing n.*　A 1 ferþingworþ;　B 1;　C 2 ferthingworth (1)
　ferthyngworth (1)
A. 5.156　And a [*ferþingworþ*] of [fenelsed] for fastyng dayes.'
B. 5.305　A *ferþyngworþ* of fenel seed for fastynge dayes.'
C. 6.360　A *ferthyngworth* [of] fenkel sed[e] for fastyng dayes.'
C. 9.94　Fridays and fastyngdays a *ferthingworth* of moskeles

fesauntȝ n *fesaunt n.*　B 1
B.15.463　He fedde hem wiþ no venyson ne *fesauntȝ* ybake

fesik > phisik; fest > festne,fust

feste n *feste n.*　A 1 festis;　B 12 feeste (4) feste (4) festes (4);　C 11 feste
　(7) festes (4)
A.11.60　Þat defouliþ oure f[eiþ] at *fest[is]* þere þei sitten.
B. 5.374　Ouer delicatly on [*feeste*] dayes dronken and eten boþe,
B.10.95　Nouȝt to fare as a fiþelere or a frere to seke *festes*,
B.11.190　And exciteþ vs by þe Euaungelie þat, whan we maken *festes*,
B.11.217　Crist to a commune womman seide, in [comen] at a *feste*,
B.13.231　Farten ne fiþelen at *festes* ne harpen,
B.13.437　And for loue of [hir] lorde liþeþ hem at *festes*;
B.13.455　Leden þo þat [liþed] hem to Luciferis *feste*
B.15.388　As clerkes in Corpus Christi *feeste* syngen and reden
B.15.462　Ye mynnen wel how Mathew seiþ, how a man made a *feste*.
B.15.481　And by þe man þat made þe *feste* þe mageste bymeneþ
B.19.108　In his Iuuentee þis Iesus at Iewene *feeste*
B.19.115　So at þat *feeste* first as I bifore tolde
C. 6.182　As wel fastyng dayes and frydayes and heye *fest[e]* euenes.
C. 6.291　Y rede no faythful frere at thy *feste* to sytte.
C. 7.97　And for loue of here lord ly[th]eth hem at *festes*;
C. 7.115　Leden tho that lythed hem to luciferes *feste*
C. 9.95　Were a *feste* with suche folk or so fele cockes.
C.11.32　Litel is he loued or leet [by] among lordes at *festes*.
C.12.102　And, as þe euaungelie witnesseth, when we maken *festes*,
C.15.205　Farten ne fythelen at *festes* ne harpe,
C.17.120　As Clerkes in corpus cristi *feste* syngen and reden
C.21.108　In his iuuente this iesus at iewene *feste*
C.21.115　So at þat *feste* furste as y before tolde

festedayes n *feste n.*　C 1
C. 5.30　Or faytest vppon frydayes or *festeday[es]* in churches,

festen v *festen v.*　B 3 feeste (1) festede (1) festen (1);　C 1 festeth
B.15.342　Ac Religiouse þat riche ben sholde raþer *feeste* beggeris
B.15.485　And feden vs and *festen* vs for eueremoore at oones].
B.15.590　Boþe of miracles and merueilles, and how he men *festede*,
C.16.321　Fiat-voluntas-tua *festeth* hym vch a daye.

festene > festne

festynge ger *festinge ger.*　B 1 festynge
B.11.194　Youre *festynge* and youre faire ȝifte; ech frend quyteþ so ooþer.

festne v *fastnen v.*　A 2 fastnid;　B 2 fest (1) festne (1);　C 1 festene
A. 2.48　To be *fastnid* wiþ fals þe fyn is arerid.
A. 2.88　And þou hast *fastnid* hire wiþ fals, fy on þi law[e]!
B. 2.124　And þow hast *fest* hire [wiþ] Fals; fy on þi lawe!
B.11.56　And [*festne*] þee [in] hir Fraternitee and for þe biseke
C.12.8　And *festene* the in ther f[r]aternite and for the byseche

festred ptp *festren v.*　B 1;　C 1
B.17.95　Neiþer Feiþ ne fyn hope, so *festred* be hise woundes,
C.19.85　Noþer faith ne fyn hope, so *festred* aren his woundes.

festu n *festu n.*　B 1
B.10.283　And þe *festu* is fallen for youre defaute

fet > fette,foot; fete > foot; feter- > fettren

feþere n *fether n.*　B 4 feþere (1) feþeres (3);　C 5 fether (1) fetheres (4)
B.11.330　Wiþ fleckede *feþeres* and of fele colours.
B.12.240　And þat [is] þe pecok & þe Pehen [wiþ hir proude *feþeres*
B.12.262　Thus þe Poete preueþ þe pecok for hise *feþeres*;
B.19.412　Or þat acounteed Conscience at a cokkes *feþere*.
C.13.138　With flekede *fetheres* and of fele colours.
C.14.172　That is, þe pocok and þe popeiay with here proude *fetheres*
C.14.177　For here *fetheres* þat fayre beth to fle fer hem letteth.
C.14.183　Thus þe poete praiseth þe pecok for his *fetheres*
C.21.412　Or þat acounted Consience [at] a cokkes *fether*.

feþered v *fetheren v.(1)* B 1; C 1 fythered
B.20.118 Weren *feþered* wiþ fair biheste and many a fals truþe.
C.22.118 Weren *fythered* with fayre biheste and many a fals treuthe.

fetisliche adv *fetisli adv.* B 1
B. 2.11 *Fetisliche* hire fyngres were fretted with gold wyr

fette v *fetten v.* A 9 fet (1) fette (3) fetten (4) fettiþ (1); B 14 fet (2) fette (8) fetten (2) fettest (2); C 10 fet (1) fette (7) fetten (1) fettest (1)
A. 2.49 Þanne fauel *fettiþ* hire forþ & to fals takiþ
A. 2.108 Þanne *fette* fauel forþ floreynes ynowe
A. 2.127 Þanne *fette* fauel folis of þe beste,
A. 2.142 And *fetten* oure vitailes [of] fornicatouris;
A. 2.191 Freris wiþ fair speche *fetten* hym þennes;
A. 3.91 And ofsente hire as swiþe; seriauntis hire *fe[tt]e*
A. 5.214 Til Vigilate [þe veil] *fet* watir [at] his eiȝen.
A. 7.276 Alle þe pore peple pesecoddis *fetten*;
A. 7.281 Þanne þou list for fer *fetten* hym manye
B. 2.65 Ac Fauel was þe firste þat *fette* hire out of boure
B. 2.144 Thanne *fette* Fauel forþ floryns ynowe
B. 2.163 [Thanne *fette* Fauel] foles [of þe beste],
B. 2.232 Freres wiþ fair speche *fetten* hym þennes;
B. 3.102 And ofsente hire as swiþe; [sergeauntȝ hire *fette*]
B. 5.442 Til vigilate þe veille *fette* water at hise eiȝen.
B. 6.31 And [*fette* þee hoom] faucons foweles to kille
B. 6.292 Al þe pouere peple pescoddes *fetten*;
B.11.7 [For] I was rauysshed riȝt here; Fortune me *fette*
B.11.325 I was *fet* forþ by [forbisenes] to knowe
B.18.267 'Swich a light, ayeins oure leue laȝar [i]t *fette*.
B.18.336 Falsliche þow *fettest* þyng þat I louede.
B.18.350 Thow *fettest* myne in my place [maugree] alle resoun,
B.20.323 That frere flaterere be *fet* and phisike yow sike.'
C. 2.67 Ac Fauel was þe furste þat *fette* here out of chambre
C. 2.160 T[h]o *fette* fauel forth floreynes ynowe
C. 2.242 Freres [with] fayre speche *fetten* hym thennes,
C. 5.131 And *fette* felyce hoem fram wyuene pyne.
C. 7.56 Til vigilate the veile *fette* water at his eyus
C. 8.315 Alle þe pore peple tho pesecoddes *fe[tt]e*;
C.11.166 For y was rauysched rihte there; fortune me *fette*
C.20.275 'Such a lyht aȝenes oure leue laȝar hit *fette*;
C.20.379 Falsliche [thow] *fettest* there þat me biful to loke,
C.22.323 That frere flaterare be *fet* and fisyk ȝow seke.'

fettren v *feteren v.* A 2 feteriþ (1) fetterid (1); B 4 fettred (2) fettren (1) fettreþ (1); C 3 fetere (1) fetered (1) fetured (1)
A. 2.162 *Feteriþ* falsnesse faste for any skynes ȝeftis,
A.11.189 Counforte þe carful þat in castel ben *fetterid*,
B. 2.201 *Fettreþ* [Falsnesse faste] for any kynnes ȝiftes,
B. 2.210 Falsnesse and his felawship to *fettren* and to bynden.
B. 5.405 I visited neuere feble men ne *fettred* [men] in puttes.
B.17.113 That he worþ *fettred*, þat feloun, faste wiþ Cheynes.
C. 2.215 Lat *fetere* falsnesse faste for eny skynes ȝeftis,
C. 7.21 Y visitede neuere feble man ne *fetered* man in prisone.
C.16.330 And when he hath visited thus *fetured* folk and oþer folke pore,

fetures > feitures

feuere n *fever n.* A 1; B 3 feuere (1) feueres (2); C 4 feuer (1) feuere (1) feueres (2)
A.12.82 Mi name is *feuere* on þe ferþe day; I am aþrest euere.
B.13.335 Or an Ague in swich an Angre and som tyme a *Feuere*
B.19.46 And defended from foule yueles, *feueres* and Fluxes,
B.20.81 And sente forþ his forreyours, *Feueres* and Fluxes,
C. 3.96 *Feuer* or foul[e] euel other fuyr on here houses,
C. 6.79 Or an ague in suche [an] angre and som tyme a *feuere*
C.21.46 And fended fro foule eueles, *feueres* and fluxes
C.22.81 And sente forth his forreours, *feueres* and fluxes,

fewe adj *feue indef. pron.* A 6; B 10; C 15
A.Pr.62 Manye ferlis han fallen in a *fewe* ȝeris.
A. 3.151 Wiþoute presentis or panis he plesiþ [wel] *fewe*.
A. 6.1 Ac þere w[ere] *fewe* men so wys þat þe [wey] þider couþe,
A. 7.266 A *fewe* cruddis & crem, & [a]n [hauer] cake,
A.12.58 Many ferlys me byfel in a *fewe* ȝeris.
A.12.66 I shal felle þat freke in a *fewe* dayes.'
B.Pr.65 Manye ferlies han fallen in a *fewe* yeres.
B. 3.162 Wiþouten presentȝ or pens [he] pleseþ wel *fewe*.
B. 6.282 A *fewe* cruddes and creme and [a cake of otes],
B.10.444 Forþi lyue we forþ wiþ [liþere] men; I leue *fewe* ben goode,
B.11.392 Ne þow shalt fynde but *fewe* fayne [wolde] heere
B.12.5 And how fele fernyeres are faren and so *fewe* to come;
B.13.227 [Ac] *fewe* robes I fonge or furrede gownes.
B.14.310 The seuenþe is welle of wisedom and *fewe* wordes sheweþ
B.15.4 And some lakkede my lif—allowed it *fewe*—
B.20.110 Fortune gan flatere þanne þo *fewe* þat were alyue

C.Pr.63 Mony ferlyes han falle in a *fewe* ȝeres.
C. 3.200 Withoute presentes oþer pans he pleseth [wel] *fewe*.
C. 8.294 Ther ar many luther leches Ac lele leches *fewe*;
C. 8.304 A *fewe* croddes and craym and a cake of otes
C. 8.344 Ar *fewe* ȝeres be fulfeld famyne shal aryse.
C. 9.91 And fele to fonge þerto and *fewe* panes taketh.
C. 9.245 Or sonendayes at euensong? se we wel *fewe*!
C.10.256 Ac *fewe* folke now folweth this for thei ȝeue her childurne
C.13.191 They reule hem al by resoun Ac renkes ful *fewe*.
C.15.201 And *fewe* robes y fonge or forrede gounes.
C.15.284 Hit ar but *fewe* folk of this ryche that ne falleth in arrerage
C.16.132 And me leneth lyhtly *fewe* men and me wene hem pore:
C.16.144 The seuethe is a welle of wysdoem and *fewe* wordes sheweth
C.18.146 And wepte watur with [his] yes; the why weten *fewe*.
C.22.110 Fortune gan flateren thenne t[h]o *fewe* þat were alyue

fy exclam *fi int.* A 1; B 2; C 1
A. 2.88 And þou hast fastnid hire wiþ fals, *fy* on þi law[e]!
B. 2.124 And þow hast fest hire [wiþ] Fals; *fy* on þi lawe!
B.15.215 *Fy* on faitours and in fautores suos!
C. 2.140 And thow hast feffed here with fals; *fy* on suche lawe.

fial adj *OED feal a.* C 1
C. 8.215 'Ther is no *fi[al]* loue with this folk for al here fayre speche

fibicches n *febicches n.(pl.)* A 1 febicchis; B 1
A.11.159 Ȝet arn þere *febicchis* of Forellis of many manis wittes,
B.10.216 Yet ar þer *fibicches* in [forelles] of fele mennes [wittes],

fiers adj *fers adj.* A 1 fers; B 2 fiers (1) fierse (1); C 1 fers
A. 5.49 For to affaiten hire flessh þat *fers* was to synne:
B. 5.66 To affaiten hire flessh þat *fiers* was to synne.
B.15.305 Ac god sente hem foode by foweles and by no *fierse* beestes
C. 6.7 To affayten here flesshe þat *fers* was to synne.

fifte num *fifte ord. num.* B 2; C 1
B.11.47 And folwed me fourty wynter and a *fifte* moore,
B.14.301 The *fifte* is moder of [myȝt and of mannes] helþe,
C.16.137 [The *fifte* is] moder of myhte and of mannes helthe

fiftene num *fiftene card. num.* A 1; B 1
A. 3.38 And þeiȝ falshed hadde folewid þe þis *fiftene* wynter,
B. 3.39 And [þeiȝ] Fals[hede] hadde yfolwed þee alle þise *fift[ene]* wynter,

fyge n *fige n.* C 1
C. 2.29 Ne on a croked kene thorn kynde *fyge* wexe:

fight n *fight n.* B 1
B.15.164 Charite] is noȝt chaumpions *fight* ne chaffare as I trowe.'

fighte(þ > fiȝte

fightyng ger *fightinge ger.* B 1
B.16.101 Til he weex a faunt þoruȝ hir flessh and of *fightyng* kouþe.

figuratyfly adv *figuratifliche adv.* C 1
C.16.296 And fynde hym, but *f[i]guratyfly*, a ferly me thynketh:

figures n *figure n.* B 1; C 1
B.19.240 And some to deuyne and diuide, [*figures*] to kenne;
C.21.240 And somme to deuyne and deuyde, [*figu]res* to kenne;

fiȝte v *fighten v.* A 4 fiȝte (1) fiȝteþ (1) fouȝten (1) yfouȝten (1); B 19 fauȝt (2) fighte (6) fighteþ (1) fiȝte (6) fiȝteþ (1) fouȝten (1) yfouȝte (2); C 26 fauht (3) fyghte (2) fihte (7) fyhte (8) fihteth (1) fyhteth (2) foughten (1) yfouhte (1) yfouthte (1)
A.Pr.42 Flite þanne for here foode, *fouȝten* at þe ale.
A. 4.39 I dar not for fer of hym *fiȝte* ne chide.
A. 4.43 Forstalliþ my feiris, *fiȝteþ* in my chepyng,
A. 7.139 Þanne gan wastour arise & wolde haue *yfouȝte*;
B.Pr.42 [Flite þanne] for hire foode, *fouȝten* at þe ale.
B. 4.52 I dar noȝt for fere of h[y]m *fiȝte* ne chide.
B. 4.56 Forstalleþ my feires, *fiȝteþ* in my Chepyng,
B. 6.35 To fulfille þis forward þouȝ I *fiȝte* sholde.
B. 6.152 [Th]anne gan wastour to wraþen hym and wolde haue *yfouȝte*;
B.10.307 For in cloistre comeþ [no] man to [carpe] ne to *fiȝte*
B.12.105 And as a blynd man in bataille bereþ wepne to *fiȝte*
B.13.337 Wiþ enuye and yuel speche entisynge to *fiȝte*,
B.16.102 To haue *yfouȝte* wiþ þe fend er ful tyme come.
B.18.367 I *fauȝt* so me þursteþ ȝit for mannes soule sake;
B.19.65 Therwith to *fiȝte* and [f]enden vs fro fallynge in[to] synne,
B.19.103 And som tyme he *fauȝt* faste and flei[ȝ] oþer while,
B.19.218 And wepne to *fighte* wiþ þat wole neuere faille.
B.19.226 And wepne to *fighte* wiþ whan Antecrist yow assailleþ.'
B.19.445 And fynt folk to *fiȝte* and cristen blood to spille
B.20.141 That Coueitise were cristene þat is so kene [to *fiȝte*],
B.20.166 And bad hym fonde to *fighte* and afere wanhope.
B.20.168 And wayued awey wanhope and wiþ lif he *fighteþ*.

B.20.301   [Ypocrisie at þe yate harde gan *fighte*]
C.Pr.43   Fayteden for here fode, *foughten* at þe ale.
C. 1.96   Treweliche to take and treweliche to *fyghte*
C. 1.100   But [feithfullich] *fyghte* and fende treuthe
C. 1.176   And ben as chast as a child þat chyht noþer ne *fyhteth*,
C. 3.237   Hast arwed many hardy man þat hadde wille to *fyhte*,
C. 3.247   Of folk þat *fauht* þerfore and folwede þe kynges wille.
C. 3.257   'Ne be Marschal ouer my men there y moste *fyhte*.
C. 4.59   Forstalleth my fayres and *fyhteth* in my chepyng[e]
C. 5.58   Ne *fyhte* in no faumewarde ne his foe greue:
C. 5.154   For in C[l]oystre cometh no man to chyde ne to *fyhte*;
C. 8.34   To defende þe in fayth, *fyhte* thow y sholde.'
C. 8.149   Thenne gan wastor to wrath hym and wolde haue *yfouhte*
C. 8.150   And to [Peres] þe [plouhman] profrede to *fyhte*
C.14.50   And as a blynde man in bataile bereth wepene to *fyhte*
C.16.174   'Of [fele] tyme to *fihte*,' quod he, 'falsnesse to destruye
C.18.136   To haue *yfouhte* with þe fende Ar fol tyme come.
C.20.408   Y *fauht* so me fursteth ȝut for mannes soule sake:
C.21.65   Therwith to *fihte* and fende vs fro fallyng into synne
C.21.103   And som tyme he *fauht* faste and fley oþerwhile
C.21.218   And wepne to *fihte* with þat wol neuere fayle
C.21.226   And wepne to *fihte* with when Auntecrist ȝow assaileth.'
C.21.445   And *fynde*[th] folke to *fihte* and cristene bloed to spille
C.22.141   That couetyse were cristene þat is so kene to *fihte*
C.22.166   And baed hym *fonde* to *fihte* and afere wanhope.
C.22.168   And wayued away wanhope and with lyf he *fihteth*.

fikel adj *fikel adj.* A 1; B 5; C 6 fikel (5) fykel (1)
A. 3.111   She is freel of hire feiþ, *fikel* of hire speche;
B. 2.25   For Fals was hire fader þat haþ a *fikel* tonge
B. 2.41   To oon fals *fikel*-tonge, a fendes biyete.
B. 2.79   And Fauel wiþ his *fikel* speche feffeþ by þis chartre
B. 2.130   That Fals is fe[ynt]lees and *fikel* in hise werkes,
B. 3.122   She is frele of hire feiþ, *fikel* of hire speche;
C. 2.6   [Boþe] fals and fauel and *fikel* tonge lyare
C. 2.25   Oon fauel was he[re] fader þat hath a *fykel* tonge
C. 2.124   Althow fals were here fader and *fikel* tonge her belsyre
C. 3.159   For she [is] frele of here fayth, *fikel* of here speche
C. 6.72   And made of frendes foes thorw *fikel* and fals tonge.
C.11.20   Thorw fallas and fals questes and thorw *fikel* speche.

fil > falle

fyle n *file n.(2)* B 1; C 1
B. 5.160   And dame Pernele a preestes *fyle*; Prioresse worþ she neuere
C. 6.135   And dame purnele a prestis *fyle*; Prioresse worth he neuere

fille n *fille n.(1)* A 1; B 1
A. 7.248   Aris vp er ap[e]ti[t] ha[ue] eten his *fille*;
B. 6.264   [A]rys vp er Appetit haue eten his *fille*.

fille v *fillen v.* A 2 felle (1) fylle (1); B 2 fille (1) filled (1); C 2 fillen (1)
fulle (1)
A. 5.181   In couenaunt þat clement [shulde þe cuppe *felle*],
A.12.70   At my bak of broke bred þi bely for to *fylle*,
B. 5.332   In couenaunt þat Clement sholde þe cuppe *fille*,
B.15.338   As whoso *filled* a tonne [ful] of a fressh ryuer
C. 3.88   And [t]how thei *fillen* nat ful þat for lawe is seled
C. 6.390   In couenaunt þat clement sholde the coppe *fulle*

fille &> falle; fylosopfres > philosofres; filosophye > philosophie

filþe n *filth n.* B 1
B.14.17   That shal clawe þi cote of alle kynnes *filþe*:

fyn n1 *fin n.(1)* B 1; C 1
B.20.45   And þe fissh haþ *fyn* to flete wiþ to reste;
C.22.45   And þe fisch hath *fyn* to flete with to reste;

fyn n2 *fin n.(2)* A 2
A. 2.36   Þat fals & fauel be any *fyn* halden,
A. 2.48   To be fastnid wiþ fals þe *fyn* is arerid.

fyn adj *fin adj.* B 2; C 2
B.10.255   For hadde neuere freke *fyn* wit þe feiþ to dispute,
B.17.95   Neiþer Feiþ ne *fyn* hope, so festred be hise woundes,
C.11.156   For hadde neuere frek *fyn* wi[t] the faith to dispute,
C.19.85   Noþer faith ne *fyn* hope, so festred aren his woundes.

fynden v *finden v.* A 22 fand (1) fynde (11) fynden (1) fyndiþ (1) fynt (3)
fond (3) founde (1) founden (1); B 73 fynde (34) fynden (10) fyndest
(2) fyndeþ (4) fynt (6) fond (7) foond (1) founde (5) founden (2)
yfounde (1) yfounden (1); C 81 fynde (37) fynden (4) fyndeth (11)
fynt (4) fynte (1) foend (2) foende (1) fond (5) fonde (3) founde (8)
founden (1) yfonde (2) yfounde (2)
A.Pr.17   A fair feld ful of folk *fand* I þere betwene
A.Pr.55   I *fond* þere Freris, alle þe foure ordris,

A. 2.50   In foreward þat falshed shal *fynde* hire for euere,
A. 2.104   And ȝif he *fynde* ȝow in defaute, & wiþ fals holden,
A. 4.57   I sey it be myself, þou shalt it sone *fynde*,
A. 4.114   Vpe forfaiture of þat fe, who *fynt* hym [at douere],
A. 6.54   Forto ȝe *fynden* a foorþe, ȝoure fadris honouriþ,
A. 7.53   And wende wiþ ȝow þe wey til we *fynde* treuþe.'
A. 7.63   I shal *fynde* hem foode þat feiþfulliche libbeþ,
A. 7.204   Ac ȝif þou *fynde* any frek þat fortune haþ apeirid
A. 8.33   *Fynde* suche here foode for oure lordis loue of heuene,
A. 8.97   'Petir,' quaþ þe prest þo, 'I can no pardoun *fynde*
A. 8.115   Þe foulis in þe firmament, who *fynt* hem a wynter?
A. 8.117   Haue þei no garner [to go] to, but god *fynt* hem alle.'
A. 8.176   Þeiȝ þou be *founde* in þe fraternite among þe foure ordris,
A. 9.70   Arn þre faire vertues, & ben not f[e]r to *fynde*.
A.10.70   Fro folies, & *fynde* hem til þei ben wise.
A.11.58   Freris and faitours han *founden* vp suche questiouns
A.11.63   And *fyndiþ* forþ fantasies oure feiþ to apeire,
A.11.168   And *fond* as she foretolde & forþ gan I wende,
A.11.279   A goode friday, I *fynde*, a feloun was sauid
A.12.59   The fyrste ferly I *fond* afyngrid me made;
B.Pr.17   A fair feeld ful of folk *fond* I þer bitwene
B.Pr.58   I *fond* þere Freres, alle þe foure ordres,
B.Pr.117   Casten þat þe commune sholde [hire communes] *fynde*.
B. 2.40   And if he *fynde* yow in defaute, and with [fals] holde,
B. 3.55   It is a freletee of flessh–ye *fynden* it in bokes–
B. 3.266   Weend to Amalec with þyn oost & what þow *fyndest* þere sle it.
B. 3.269   Moebles and vnmoebles, and al þow myȝt *fynde*,
B. 3.325   And er þis fortune falle *fynde* men shul be worste
B. 3.342   She sholde haue *founden* fel[l]e wordes folwynge þerafter.
B. 3.344   And so [mys]ferde ye, madame; ye kouþe na moore *fynde*
B. 3.348   And if ye seche Sapience eft *fynde* shul ye þat folweþ,
B. 4.71   I seye it by myself, þow shalt it wel *fynde*,
B. 4.131   V[p] forfeture of þat fee, wh[o] *fynt* [hym] at Douere,
B. 5.146   And freres *fyndeþ* hem in defaute, as folk bereþ witnesse,
B. 5.417   But I kan *fynden* in a feld or in a furlang an hare
B. 5.567   [Forto] ye *fynden* a ford, youre-fadres-honoureþ:
B. 6.58   And wende wiþ yow [þe wey] til we *fynde* truþe.'
B. 6.69   I shal *fynden* hem fode þat feiþfulliche libbeþ,
B. 6.218   A[c] if þow *fynde* any freke þat Fortune haþ apeired
B. 7.31   *Fynden* [swiche] hir foode [for oure lordes loue of heuene],
B. 7.115   'Peter!' quod þe preest þoo, 'I kan no pardon *fynde*
B. 7.133   The foweles in þe [firmament], who *fynt* hem at wynter?
B. 7.135   Haue þei no gerner to go to but god *fynt* hem alle.'
B. 7.198   Theiȝ [þow] be *founde* in þe fraternite [among] þe foure ordres
B. 8.79   Arn þre faire vertues, and ben noȝt fer to *fynde*.
B. 9.70   And] *fynden* hem þat hem fauted, and faderlese children,
B. 9.75   And *fynde* fele witnesses among þe foure doctours,
B. 9.148   The gospel is hera[g]ein in o degre, I *fynde*:
B. 9.150   Ac I *fynde*, if þe fader be fals and a sherewe,
B.10.72   Freres and faitours han *founde* [vp] swiche questions
B.10.94   And how he myȝte moost meynee manliche *fynde*.
B.10.261   Swich as þow semest in siȝte be in assay *yfounde*:
B.10.306   It is in cloistre or in scole, by manye skiles I *fynde*.
B.10.328   And þanne Freres in hir fraytour shul *fynde* a keye
B.10.420   On good Friday, I *fynde*, a felon was ysaued
B.11.25   'He shal *fynde* me his frend', quod Fortune þerafter;
B.11.29   Thow shalt *fynde* Fortune þee faille at þi mooste nede,
B.11.63   And þo *fond* I þe were afered and flittynge boþe
B.11.155   That was an vncristene creature, as clerkes *fyndeþ* in bokes.
B.11.226   For some wordes I *fynde* writen, were of Feiþes techyng,
B.11.295   As bifel for a knyȝt, or *foond* hym for his strengþe.
B.11.353   [For men sholde hem noȝt *fynde* whan þei þerfro wente;
B.11.392   Ne þow shalt *fynde* but fewe fayne [wolde] heere
B.12.76   A womman, as [we] *fynde*[n], was gilty of þat dede,
B.12.141   And clennesse shal cacchen it and clerkes shullen it *fynde*:
B.12.145   If any frere were *founde* þere I ȝyue þee fyue shillynges!
B.13.95   What he *fond* in a [forel of] a freres lyuyng,
B.13.129   Whiche Infinites wiþ a feiþ *fynden* out dobest,
B.13.240   Fro Mighelmesse to Mighelmesse I *fynde* hem wiþ wafres.
B.13.243   I *fynde* payn for þe pope and prouendre for his palfrey,
B.13.252   For hym and for alle hise, *founde* I þat his pardoun
B.13.317   Men sholde *fynde* manye frounces and manye foule plottes.'
B.14.32   All þat lyueþ and lokeþ liflode wolde I *fynde*
B.14.50   And þanne was it fiat voluntas tua [sholde *fynde* vs alle].
B.14.64   It is *founden* þat fourty wynter folk lyuede withouten tulying,
B.15.151   'Where sholde men *fynde* swich a frend wiþ so fre an herte?
B.15.153   And *fond* I neuere ful charite, before ne bihynde,
B.15.178   For a frend þat *fyndeþ* hym failed hym neuere at nede:
B.15.179   Fiat voluntas tua *fynt* hym eueremoore,
B.15.230   And in a freres frokke he was *yfounden* ones,
B.15.278   But of foweles þat fleeþ þus *fyndeþ* men in bokes.
B.15.285   And þouȝ þe gome hadde a gest god *fond* hem boþe.
B.15.307   [Riȝt so] Religiouses rightfulle men sholde [*fynde*],

B.15.311   *Founde* þei þat freres wolde forsake hir almesses
B.15.371   Of þat was calculed of þe element þe contrarie þei *fynde.*
B.15.425   And folkes sholden [*fynde*], þat ben in diuerse siknesse,
B.15.479   And as þo foules to *fynde* fode after whistlyng
B.15.573   And feden hem wiþ goostly foode and [nedy folk to *fynden.*
B.16.154   'Falsnesse I *fynde* in þi faire speche
B.17.89   'Ac þi frend and þi felawe þow *fyndest* me at nede.'
B.17.336   And þou3 it falle it *fynt* skiles þat "frelete it made",
B.19.445   And *fynt* folk to fi3te and cristen blood to spille
B.20.295   And freres to philosophie he *fond* [hem] to scole,
C.Pr.19   A fair feld ful of folk *fond* y þer bytwene
C.Pr.37   *Fyndeth* out foule fantasyes and foles hem maketh
C.Pr.56   I *fonde* þer Freris, alle þe foure ordres,
C.Pr.144   Caste þat þe comun[e] sholde here comunes *fynde.*
C. 2.156   And yf he *fynde* 3ow in defaute and with the fals holde,
C. 3.41   [And] Falshede *yfonde* the al this fourty wyntur,
C. 3.59   Hit is but frelete of fleysche–3e *fyndeth* [hit in] bokes–
C. 3.376   To folowe and to *fynde* hym and [f]eche at hem his consayl
C. 3.424   For eny mede of money al that thow myhte [*fynde*],
C. 3.478   Ac ar this fortune falle *fynde* me shal the worste
C. 3.494   A sholde haue *yfonde* [felle wordes folwynge] aftur:
C. 3.496   So hoso [s]echeth sapience *fynde* he shal [that] foloweth
C. 4.121   For alle manere men þat me *fynt* neodefole;
C. 4.128   Vp forfeiture of þat fee, ho *fyndeth* h[y]m ouerward,
C. 5.21   [Hem þat bedreden be] byleue t[o] *fynden*?'
C. 5.27   That *fynde*[th] the thy fode–for an ydel man þow semest,
C. 5.36   My fader and my frendes *foende* me to scole
C. 5.40   And *foen[d* y] nere, in fayth, seth my frendes deyede
C. 5.49   And þo þa[t] *fynden* me my fode fouchensaf, y trowe,
C. 5.76   And monkes and moniales þat mendenant[es] sholde *fynde*
C. 5.88   Fiat voluntas dei *fynt* vs alle thynges.'
C. 5.153   Hit is in C[l]oystre or in scole, by many skilles y *fynde.*
C. 5.173   Freres in here fraytour shal *fynde* þat tyme
C. 6.22   And scornede hem and oþere yf y a skil *founde,*
C. 6.76   A3eyn þe consayl of Crist, as clerkes *fyndeth* in bokes:
C. 7.32   Ac y can *fynden* in a feld and in a forlong an hare
C. 7.214   Forto 3e *fynde* a ford, 3oure-fader[s]-honoureth;
C. 7.259   And *fynde* alle manere folk fode to here soules
C. 8.70   Y shal *fynde* hem fode þat fayfulleche libbeth,
C. 8.138   That no faytrye were *founde* in folk þat goth abeggeth.
C. 8.148   What! y and myn wolle *fynde* hem what hem nedeth.'
C. 8.228   Ac yf thow *fynde* eny folke þat fals men han apayred
C. 9.30   Amende mesondewes þerwith and myseyse men *fynde*
C. 9.35   *Fynde* hem for godes loue and fauntkynes to scole,
C. 9.289   'Peter!' quod the prest tho, 'y kan no pardoun *fynde*
C. 9.344   Thow ne be *founden* in the fraternite of alle fyue ordres
C.10.77   Aren thre fayre vertues and ben nat fer to *fynde.*
C.10.182   Hath tresor ynow of treuthe to *fynden* hymsulue.
C.10.184   Frendes shal *fynde* hem and fram folye kepe
C.11.52   Freres and faytours haen *fornen* vp suche questions
C.11.184   'A shal *fynde* me his frende,' quod fortune þeraftur;
C.11.188   Thow shalt *fynde* fortune þe fayle At thy moste nede
C.11.252   A gode friday, y *fynde*, a feloun was ysaued
C.11.273   And *fonde* y neuere in faith, for to telle treuthe,
C.12.15   And flittyng *fond* y the frere þat me confessede
C.12.25   'For this frere flaterede me while he *fond* me ryche
C.12.210   Ac hoso rat of th[e] ryche the reuers may *fynde,*
C.13.72   *Fynde* beggares bred, bakkes for þe colde,
C.13.109   As byful for a knyht or *fond* hym for his strenthe.
C.13.164   For no foul sholde hit *fynde* but his fere and hymsulue.
C.14.86   And clennesse shal cach hit and clerkes shollen hit *fynde*:
C.14.89   Yf eny frere we[re] *founde* þere y 3eue the fyue shillynges!
C.15.102   What a *fond* in a forel of a frere[s] lyuynge,
C.15.136   Bote lele loue and treuthe that loth is to be *founde.*'
C.15.183   With pacience wol y passe parfitnesse to *fynde.*'
C.15.200   The pore and the ryche y pleide and payn *fynde*
C.15.215   Fro Mihelmasse to Mihelmasse y *fynde* mete and drynke.
C.15.216   Y *fynde* payn for þe po[p]le and pre[y]en hym ych wolde
C.15.218   For *founde* y þat his blessynge and his bulle [bocches] myhte
        [destruye],
C.15.235   Hit am y þat *fynde* alle folke and fram hunger saue
C.15.249   And thenne was hit fiat voluntas tua þat sholde *fynde* vs alle.
C.15.263   Hit is *founde* þat fourty wynter folke lyuede and tylde nat
C.16.151   For pacience is his paniter and pouerte payn here *fyndeth*
C.16.274   Allas! lewed men, moche lese 3e þat *fynde*
C.16.287   That maistres commenden moche. Where may hit be *yfounde*?
C.16.289   And *fonde* y neuere in faith, as freres hit precheth,
C.16.296   And *fynde* hym, but f[i]guratyfly, a ferly me thynketh:
C.16.316   'H[o] *fynt* hym his fode,' quod y, 'or what frendes hath he,
C.16.319   A frende he hath þat *fyn[t]* hym þat faylede hym neuere.
C.16.320   Oen aperis-tu-manum alle thynges hym *fyndeth*;
C.16.355   And in a frere f[r]okke he was *founde* ones
C.17.34   *Fynde* honest men and holy men and oþer rihtfole peple.

C.17.85   And worcheth nat as 3e *fyndeth* ywryte and wisseth þe peple.
C.17.107   Of þat was kalculed of þe clymat the contrarie þey *fynde.*
C.17.161   And when kynde hath his cours and no contrarie *fyndeth*
C.17.165   Me *fynde*[th] þat Macometh was a man ycristened
C.18.171   'Falsnesse y *fynde* in thy fayre speche
C.19.23   'He seyth soth,' saide fayth; 'y haue *yfounde* hit trewe.
C.19.316   And thogh he falle he *fynte* skiles þat "freelete hit made"
C.21.445   And *fynde*[th] folke to fihte and cristene blood to spille
C.22.295   And freres to filosophye he *foend* hem to scole

fyndyng ger *finding ger.* &> *fynden* B 1; C 3 fyndynge
B.20.383   And þat freres hadde a *fyndyng* þat for nede flateren
C. 3.345   Folowynge and *fyndynge* out þe fundement of a strenghe,
C. 6.293   Then haue my fode and my *fyndynge* of fals menne wynnyngus.
C.22.383   And þat freres hadde a *fyndynge* þat for nede flateren

fynes n prop *n.i.d.* B 1; C 2 fines
B.10.287   Offyn and *Fynes*; for hir coueitise
C.Pr.107   For Offines s[yn]ne and *fines* his brother
C.Pr.123   Than euere he dede on Offi[n] and *Fines* [or on her] fader.

fynger n *finger n.* A 3 fyngris; B 23 fynger (5) fyngres (18); C 22 fynger (7) fyngeres (11) fyngours (1) fyngres (3)
A. 2.11   Alle here fyue *fyngris* were frettid wiþ rynges
A. 7.11   Spynneþ it spedily, spariþ not 3oure *fyngris*
A. 7.18   And 3e loueliche ladies wiþ 3our [longe] *fyngris,*
B. 2.11   Fetisliche hire *fyngres* were fretted with gold wyr
B. 6.10   And ye louely ladies wiþ youre longe *fyngres,*
B.11.169   God wrou3te it and wroot it wiþ his [owene] *fynger,*
B.11.293   Or þe bisshop þat blessed yow [and embaumed youre *fyngres*].
B.17.141   The fader was first as a fust wiþ o *fynger* foldynge
B.17.142   Til hym [likede] and liste to vnlosen his *fynger,*
B.17.144   The pawme is [þe piþ of] þe hand, and profreþ forþ þe *fyngres*
B.17.148   The *fyngres* þat fre ben to folde and to serue
B.17.152   The fader is [þanne] as a fust wiþ *fynger* to touche–
B.17.156   The paume for [he] putteþ forþ *fyngres* and þe fust boþe.
B.17.160   Thoru3 foure *fyngres* and a thombe forþ with þe pawme,
B.17.168   Na moore [may an hand] meue wiþoute *fyngres.*
B.17.172   The *fyngres* formen a ful hand to portreye or peynten;
B.17.173   Keruynge and compasynge [i]s craft of þe *fyngres.*
B.17.177   Oþerwise þan þe wriþen fust or werkmanshipe of *fyngres.*
B.17.180   And receyue þat þe *fyngres* recheþ and refuse boþe
B.17.181   Whan he feleþ þe fust and] þe *fyngres* wille;
B.17.184   And alle [þre] but o god as is myn hand and my *fyngres.*
B.17.194   Ac þou3 my þombe and my *fyngres* boþe were toshullen
B.17.197   Boþe meue and amende, þou3 alle my *fyngres* oke.
B.17.202   For god þe fader is as a fust; þe sone is as a *fynger*;
B.19.171   And feele wiþ hise *fyngres* his flesshliche herte.
C. 2.12   On alle here fyue *fyngeres* ful richeliche yrynged,
C. 8.9   And 3e worthily wymmen with 3oure longe *fyngres,*
C.13.107   Or þe bischop þat blessed 3ow and enbaumed 3oure *fyngeres.*
C.14.37   For moyses witnesseth þat god wroet [in stoen with his *fynger*;
C.19.115   As a fuste wit[h] a *fynger* yfolde togyderes
C.19.116   Til hym likede and luste to vnlose that *fynger*
C.19.118   The paume is the pethe of the hand and profereth [forth] the *fyngeres*
C.19.122   The *fyngres* þat fre ben to folde and to cluche
C.19.126   The fader is thenne as þe fuste with *fynger* and with paume
C.19.128   And þat the *fynger* gropeth he grypeth bote yf hit greue þe paume.
C.19.130   A fuste with a *fynger* and a fol paume.
C.19.133   As my fuste is furste ar y my *fyngours* shewe,
C.19.136   The *fyngres* is a fol hand for failed they or thombe
C.19.142   Oþerwyse then þe writhen f[u]ste or werkmanschupe of *fyngres.*
C.19.145   And receue þat the *fyngeres* recheth and refuse, yf h[y]m liketh,
C.19.146   Alle þat þe *fyngeres* and þe fust feleth and toucheth.
C.19.150   And alle thre is bote o god as myn hoend and my *fyngeres,*
C.19.155   For þe *fyngeres* þat folde sholde and þe fust make
C.19.160   Ac thouh my thombe and my *fyngeres* bothe were toshullen
C.19.163   Bothe meue and amende, thogh alle my *fyngeres* oke.
C.19.168   For [g]o[d] the fader is as þe fust; þe sone is as þe *fynger*;
C.21.171   And fele with his *fyngeres* his flescheliche herte.

fynt(e > fynden; fippe > phippe

fir n *fir n.* A 2 fuyr; B 16 fir (14) fires (1) fuyr (1); C 21 fuyr (19) fuyre (1) fuyres (1)
A. 3.87   þat *fuyr* shal falle & forbrenne at þe laste
A. 7.205   Wiþ *fuyr* or wiþ false men, fond suche [to] knowen;
B. 3.98   That *fir* shal falle & [forbrenne at þe laste]
B. 6.219   [Wiþ *fuyr* or wiþ] false men, fonde swiche to knowe.
B. 7.53   Ac to bugge water ne wynd ne wit ne *fir* þe ferþe,
B.10.417   [At domesday þe deluuye worþ of deþ and *fir* at ones;
B.12.286   And þoru3 *fir* is fullyng, and þat is ferme bileue:
B.13.162   Ne [neiþer] *fuyr* ne flood ne feere of þyn enemy

B.14.42	Fissh to lyue in þe flood and in þe *fir* þe Criket,
B.17.208	And þanne a *fir* flawmynge forþ out of boþe.
B.17.209	And as wex and weke and [warm] *fir* togideres
B.17.217	Wiþouten leye or light [liþ *fir* in þe macche]–
B.17.223	As dooþ a kex or a candle þat caught haþ *fir* and blaseþ,
B.17.229	And þanne flawmeþ he as *fir* on fader and on filius
B.17.243	And as þe weke and *fir* wol maken a warm flaumbe
B.17.248	Ac hewe *fir* at a flynt foure hundred wynter;
B.17.251	For may no *fir* flaumbe make, faille it [h]is kynde.
B.19.205	And was afered [for] þe light, for in *fires* [lik]nesse
C. 3.91	Bothe thorw *fuyr* and flood a[nd] thorw fals peple
C. 3.96	Feuer or foul[e] euel other *fuyr* on here houses,
C. 3.102	And thenne falleth ther *fuyr* on fals men houses
C. 3.103	And goode mennes for here gultes gloweth on *fuyr* aftur.
C. 3.126	That *fuyr* shal falle and forbrenne al to blew aysches
C. 6.335	Fareth as flo[nke] of *fuyr* þat ful amydde Temese
C. 9.56	Þat is wit and watur and wynde and *fuyre* the ferthe;
C. 9.183	Or thorw *fuyr* or thorw floed yfalle into pouerte,
C.11.249	At domesday a deluuye worth of deth and *fuyr* at ones.
C.14.208	And thorw *fuyr* is fullyng; and [þat] is ferme bileue:
C.15.164	Noþer *fuyr* ne loue ne be aferd of enemye:
C.15.241	The Cryket by kynde of þe *fuyr* and corleu by þe wynde,
C.19.174	And thenne [a *fuyr* flaumynge] forth of hem bothe.
C.19.175	And as wex and weke and warm *fuyr* togyderes
C.19.183	Withouten leye [or] lihte lith *fuyr* in þe mache–
C.19.189	A[s] doth a kix [o]r a candle þat cauht hath *fuyr* and blaseth,
C.19.195	And thenne flaumeth he as *fuyr* on fader and on filius
C.19.209	And as þe wyke and [*fuyr* wol make a warm] flaume
C.19.214	Ac hewe *fuyr* at a flynt foure hundret wynter,
C.19.217	For may no *fuyr* flaume make, faile hit hit kynde.
C.21.205	And was afered for the lihte, for in *fuyres* liknesse

firmament n *firmament n.* A 1; B 1

A. 8.115	Þe foulis in þe *firmament*, who fynt hem a wynter?
B. 7.133	The foweles in þe [*firmament*], who fynt hem at wynter?

firses n *firse n.* A 1 firsen; B 1

A. 5.192	And wisshide it hadde be wexid wiþ a wysp of *firsen*.
B. 5.344	And wisshed it hadde ben wexed wiþ a wispe of *firses*.

first adj *first ord. num.* A 8 ferste (5) fyrste (1) furste (2); B 24 first (5) firste (19); C 27 ferste (1) firste (1) furst (1) furste (24)

A. 2.72	In witnesse of whiche þing wrong was þe *furste*,
A. 2.160	And comaundite a cunstable þat com at þe *ferste*
A. 5.118	Wykkidly to weiʒe was my *ferste* lessoun.
A. 5.204	Þe *ferste* woord þat he spak was 'where is þe bolle?'
A. 7.157	And houpide aftir hungir þat herde hym at þe *ferste*:
A.10.18	And haþ fyue faire sones be his *furste* wyf:
A.10.28	Fadir & fourmour, þe *ferste* of alle þing.
A.12.59	The *fyrste* ferly I fond afyngrid me made;
B. 2.65	Ac Fauel was þe *firste* þat fette hire out of boure
B. 2.108	In witnesse of which þyng wrong was þe *firste*,
B. 2.199	And comaunded a Constable þat com at þe *firste*
B. 3.244	Swiche manere men, my lord, shul haue þis *firste* Mede
B. 5.202	Wikkedly to weye was my *firste* lesson.
B. 5.362	The *firste* word þat he [spak] was 'where is þe bolle?'
B. 6.172	And houped after hunger þat herde hym at þe *firste*.
B. 9.19	And haþ fyue faire sones bi his *firste* wyue:
B. 9.27	Fader and formour, [þe *first* of alle þynges].
B.11.64	Ayeins oure *firste* forward, for I seide I nolde
B.11.103	Ac be [þow] neueremoore þe *firste* [þe] defaute to blame;
B.13.96	And but [þe] *first* [leef] be lesyng leue me neuere after.
B.14.280	Pouerte is þe *firste* point þat pride moost hateþ;
B.15.29	And whan I feele þat folk telleþ my *firste* name is sensus,
B.15.608	Konne þe *firste* clause of oure bileue, Credo in deum patrem omnipotentem,
B.16.30	Thanne with þe *firste* pil I palle hym doun, potencia de[i patris].
B.16.184	The *firste* haþ myʒt and maiestee, makere of alle þynges;
B.17.34	Siþ þe *firste* suffiseþ to sauacion and to blisse?
B.17.60	Feiþ hadde *first* siʒte of hym, ac he fleiʒ aside
B.17.141	The fader was *first* as a fust wiþ o fynger foldynge
B.18.157	The *first* venymouste, þoru3 [vertu] of hymselue.
B.18.218	Forþi god, of his goodnesse, þe *firste* gome Adam,
B.19.70	Faithly to speke, his *firste* name was Iesus.
B.19.276	Spiritus prudencie þe *firste* seed highte,
C. 1.23	The *firste* is fode and vesture þe seconde
C. 2.67	Ac Fauel was þe *furste* þat fette here out of chambre
C. 2.112	In wittenesse of [which] thyng wrong was the *furste*,
C. 2.213	And comaundede a Constable that cam at þe *furste*
C. 6.210	Wykkedliche to waye was my *furste* lessoun.
C. 6.420	The *furste* [word] þat he spake was '[wh]o halt þe bolle?'
C. 8.168	And houped aftur hunger þat herde hym at the *furste*.
C. 9.251	Wascheth and wypeth and with þe *furste* sitteth.
C.10.145	And hath fyue fayre sones by his *furste* wyue:

C.12.37	Ac be [thow] neueremore þe *furste* the defaute to blame;
C.14.164	Of goed and of wykke kynde was þe *furste*;
C.15.103	And bote þe *furste* leef be lesyng[e] leue me neuere aftur.
C.16.120	Pouerte is þe *furste* poynte þat pruyde moest hateth;
C.16.189	And when y fele þat folke telleth my *furste* name is sensus
C.17.316	Conne þe *furste* clause of oure bileue, credo in deum patrem,
C.18.34	And with þe *furste* planke y palle hym down, potencia dei patris.
C.18.90	Hit was þe *furste* fruyte þat þe fader of heuene blessed,
C.18.92	In menynge þat the fayrest thyng the *furste* thynge sholde honoure
C.19.35	Sethe the *furste* sufficede to bileue and be saued?
C.19.59	Fayth [hadde *furst* siht of hym] Ac he fleyh asyde
C.19.132	So is þe fader a fol god, the *fu[r]ste* of hem alle
C.19.133	As my fuste is *furste* ar y my fyngours shewe,
C.19.134	And he fader and for[m]eour, þe *furste* of alle thynges–
C.20.160	The [f]erste venemouste, thorw vertu of hymsulue.
C.20.227	Forthy god, of his goednesse, þe *furste* [gome] Adam,
C.21.70	Faythly for to speke his *furste* name was iesus.
C.21.276	Spiritus prudencie the *furste* seed hihte

first adv *first adv.* A 9 ferst (8) furst (1); B 30; C 23 firste (1) furst (3) furste (19)

A. 1.74	I vndirfang þe *ferst* and þi feiþ [þe] tauʒte.
A. 3.32	Þat he ne worþ *ferst* auauncid for I am beknowe
A. 5.117	*Ferst* I lernide to leiʒe a lef oþer tweiʒe;
A. 7.168	Ne hadde þ[e] fisician *ferst* defendite him watir
A.10.131	Formest & *ferst* to folk þat ben weddit
A.11.130	Plato þe poete, I putte hym *ferst* to boke;
A.11.132	Gramer for girles I garte *ferst* write,
A.11.135	Of carpenteris & kerueris; [I] kende *ferst* masons,
A.12.113	*Furst* to rekne Richard, kyng of þis rewme,
B. 1.76	I vnderfeng þee *first* and þ[i] feiþ [þee] tauʒte.
B. 3.33	That he ne worþ *first* auaunced, for I am biknowen
B. 5.51	And er he gyue any grace gouerne *first* hymselue.
B. 5.201	*First* I lerned to lye a leef ouþer tweyne;
B. 9.117	*First* by þe fadres wille and þe frendes conseille,
B. 9.194	For he made wedlok *first* and [þus] hymself seide:
B.10.178	Plato þe poete, I putte [hym] *first* to boke;
B.10.180	Grammer for girles I garte *first* write,
B.10.183	Of Carpent[ers and] kerueres; [I kenned *first*] Masons
B.10.289	Forþi, ye Correctours, claweþ heron and correcteþ *first* yowselue,
B.11.104	Thouʒ þow se yuel seye it noʒt *first*; be sory it nere amended.
B.12.100	Na moore kan no Clerk but if he cauʒte it *first* þoruʒ bokes.
B.12.233	Why Adam hiled noʒt *first* his mouþ þat eet þe Appul
B.13.5	*First* how Fortune me failed at my mooste neode.
B.13.153	In a signe of þe Saterday þat sette *first* þe kalender,
B.13.198	Thus curteisliche Conscience congeyed *first* þe frere,
B.13.319	It was fouler bi fele fold þan it *first* semed.
B.14.41	*First* þe wilde worm vnder weet erþe,
B.14.322	That þ[u]s *first* wroot to wissen men what Pouerte was to mene.'
B.15.422	[Boþe] Beneit and Bernard, þe whiche hem *first* tauʒte
B.16.174	I frayned hym *first* fram whennes he come
B.16.213	Hym þat *first* formed al, þe fader of heuene.
B.16.231	Þer he fonded me if I, [feiþ], louede bettre
B.16.274	I affrayned hym *first* fram whennes he come,
B.18.159	Al þat deeþ [d]ide *first* þoruʒ þe deueles entisyng,
B.18.238	That he was god þat al wroʒte þe wolkne *first* shewed:
B.18.312	*First* þoruʒ þe we fellen fro heuene so heiʒe:
B.19.115	So at þat feeste *first* as I bifore tolde
B.19.120	That she *first* and formest ferme sholde bileue
B.19.436	As for hymself and hise seruauntʒ, saue he is *first* yserued.
C. 1.60	Fader of falshede fond hit *firste* of alle.
C. 3.36	That he ne worth *furste* vaunsed, for y am byknowe
C. 5.110	Of þe matere þat me mette *furste* on Maluerne hulles
C. 6.15	For y, formost and *furste*, to fader and moder
C. 6.209	*Furste* y lerned to lye a leef oþer tweye;
C. 7.143	That art *furste* oure fadur and of flesch oure broþer
C. 7.170	This folk frayned hym *furste* fro whennes he come.
C. 9.222	*Furste*, Religious of religioun a reule to holde
C.11.118	Plato þe poete y putte hym *furste* to boke;
C.11.120	Gramer for gurles y gart *furste* write
C.12.182	Sholde neuere whete wexe but whete *furste* deyede;
C.14.160	Bote kynde þat contreuede hit *furst* of his corteyse wille.
C.15.5	*Furste* how fortune me faylede At my moste neode;
C.18.93	And þe clennest creature *furste* creat[our] knowe.
C.18.122	That thorw fals biheste and fruyt *furste* man disseyued.
C.18.247	How he fondede me *furste*; my fayre sone ysaak
C.18.290	And y fraynede hym *furst* fro whennes he come,
C.19.114	Ferde *furste* as a f[u]ste, and ʒut is, as y leue,
C.20.247	That he was god þat al wrouhte the welkene *furste* shewede:
C.20.345	For thy lesinges, lucifer, we losten *furst* oure ioye
C.21.115	So at þat feste *furste* as y before tolde
C.21.120	That [sh]e *furste* and formoste [ferme sholde] bileue
C.21.436	As for hymsulue and his seruauntes, saue he is *furste* yserued.

fisch(- > fissh(-; fiscicien fisciscyen > phisicien

fiscuth v *fisken v.* C 1

C. 9.153   And what freke on this folde *fiscuth* aboute

fisician > phisicien; fisik > phisik; fysyke > phisik n

fissh n *fish n.* A 4 fissh (2) fisshes (1) fisshis (1); B 13 fissh (7) fyssh (1) fisshes (5); C 12 fisch (2) fische (2) fysch (3) fisches (4) fysches (1)

A. 5.210   'Shal neuere *fissh* on þe Friday defie in my wombe
A. 7.294   But ȝif it be fressh flessh oþer *fissh* yfried,
A.10.174   Boþe *fisshis* & foulis, forþ mi[d] oþere bestis,
A.11.207   "Whanne *fisshes* faile þe flood or þe fresshe watir
B. 5.177   I ete þere unþende *fissh* and feble ale drynke.
B. 5.382   'Shal neuere *fyssh* on [þe] Fryday defyen in my wombe
B. 5.436   Boþe flessh and *fissh* and manye oþere vitailles;
B. 6.310   But if it be fressh flessh ouþer *fissh* [y]fryed,
B. 8.54   To fleynge foweles, to *fisshes* and to beestes.
B.10.301   Whan *fisshes* faillen þe flood or þe fresshe water
B.13.93   Is neiþer *fissh* n[e] flessh, but fode for a penaunt.
B.14.42   *Fissh* to lyue in þe flood and in þe fir þe Criket,
B.15.432   [Ac] fressh flessh ouþer *fissh*, whan it salt failleþ,
B.15.591   Wiþ two *fisshes* and fyue loues fyue þousand peple,
B.16.125   And fed yow wiþ two *fisshes* and wiþ fyue loues,
B.19.126   And fedde wiþ two *fisshes* and with fyue loues
B.20.45   And þe *fissh* haþ fyn to flete wiþ to reste;
C. 5.148   Ryht as *fysches* in floed whan hem fayleth water
C. 6.159   For y ete more *fysch* then flesche there and feble ale drynke.
C. 6.439   Shal neuere *fysch* [o]n þe fryday defyen in my wombe
C. 7.49   Bothe flesch and *fysch* and vitailes kepte so longe
C. 8.332   But hit be [fresh] flesch or *fisch* yfried or ybake
C. 9.93   And colde flesche and *fische* as venisoun were bake;
C.15.100   Is noþer *fische* ne flesche but fode for [a] penaunt.
C.15.240   Þe worm and wonte vnder erthe and in water *fisches*,
C.15.261   Ergo thorw his breth bestes lyueth, bothe men and *fisches*,
C.18.153   With [two] *fisches* and [fyue] loues, fyue thousen[d] at ones,
C.21.126   And fedde with two *fisches* and with fyue loues
C.22.45   And þe *fisch* hath fyn to flete with to reste;

fisshed v *fishen v.* B 1; C 1 fischede

B.15.292   Peter *fisshed* for his foode and his felawe Andrew;
C.17.19   Peter *fischede* for his fode And his fere Androwe;

fithele(n > fiþele(n; fythered > feþered

fiþele n *fithele n.* &> *fiþelen* B 2; C 1 fythele

B. 9.105   Wolde neuere þe feiþful fader [h]is *fiþele* were vntempred
B.13.456   Wiþ turpiloquio, a l[a]y of sorwe, and luciferis *fiþele*.
C. 7.116   With turpiloquio, a lay of sorwe and luciferes *fythele*,

fiþelen v *fithelen v.* B 2 fiþele (1) fiþelen (1); C 2 fithele (1) fythelen (1)

B.13.231   Farten ne *fiþelen* at festes ne harpen,
B.13.446   And *fiþele* þee wiþoute flaterynge of good friday þe [geste],
C. 7.106   And *fithele* the withoute flaterynge of god friday þe [g]este,
C.15.205   Farten ne *fythelen* at festes ne harpe,

fiþelere n *fithelere n.* B 1

B.10.95   Nouȝt to fare as a *fiþelere* or a frere to seke festes,

fyue num *five card.num.* A 7; B 17; C 17 fiue (1) fyue (16)

A. 1.15   Boþe wiþ fel & wiþ face, & ȝaf ȝow *fyue* wyttes
A. 1.99   And nouȝt to fasten a friday in *fyue* score wynter,
A. 2.11   Alle here *fyue* fyngris were frettid wiþ rynges
A. 7.305   Or *fyue* ȝer be fulfild such famyn shal arise;
A.10.18   And haþ *fyue* faire sones be his furste wyf:
A.11.215   Godis flessh, & his fet, & hise *fyue* woundis
A.11.293   And ȝet [haue] I forget[e þere] of *fyue* wyttis teching
B. 1.15   Boþe with fel and with face, and yaf yow *fyue* wittes
B. 1.101   And nauȝt to fasten o friday in *fyue* score wynter,
B. 5.179   [I] haue a flux of a foul mouþ wel *fyue* dayes after;
B. 6.324   Er *fyue* [yer] be fulfilled swich famyn shal aryse.
B. 9.19   And haþ *fyue* faire sones bi his firste wyue:
B.10.448   [And yet haue I forgete ferþer of *fyue* wittes techyng
B.12.3   I haue folwed þee, in feiþ, þise *fyue* and fourty wynter,
B.12.145   If any frere were founde þere I ȝyue þee *fyue* shillynges!
B.14.56   In [ondynge] and in handlynge and in alle þi *fyue* wittes,
B.15.76   And how þat folk in folies [hir *fyue* wittes mysspenden],
B.15.320   And auisen hem bifore a *fyue* dayes or sixe
B.15.591   Wiþ two fisshes and fyue loues fyue þousand peple,
B.15.591   Wiþ two fisshes and *fyue* loues fyue þousand peple,
B.16.125   And fed yow wiþ two fisshes and wiþ *fyue* loues,
B.19.126   And fedde wiþ two fisshes and with *fyue* loues
B.19.127   Sore afyngred folk, mo þan *fyue* þousand.
B.19.216   To alle kynne creatures þat [k]an hi[se] *fyue* wittes,
C. 1.15   To be fayful to hym [he] ȝaf ȝow *fyue* wittes
C. 2.12   On alle here *fyue* fyngeres ful richeliche yrynged,
C. 6.161   Y haue a flux of a foul mouth wel *fyue* daies aftur;

C. 7.295   To falewe with *fiue* ȝo[k]es; 'forthy me bihoueth
C. 8.191   And freres of alle þe *fyue* ordres, alle for fere of hunger.
C. 9.344   Thow we be founden in the fraternite of alle *fyue* ordres
C.10.145   And hath *fyue* fayre sones by his furste wyue:
C.10.149   Thise *fyue* ben sette for to saue Anima
C.14.89   Yf eny frere we[re] founde þere y ȝeue the *fyue* shillynges!
C.15.80   Ac y wiste neuere freke þat frere is ycald of þe *fyue* mendynantȝ
C.15.255   In [ond]ynge and [in] handlynge [and] in alle thy *fyue* wittes,
C.16.235   And [ho]w that folk [in folies] here *fyue* wittes myspen[en],
C.18.153   With [two] fisches and [*fyue*] loues, fyue thousen[d] at ones,
C.18.153   With [two] fisches and [fyue] loues, *fyue* thousen[d] at ones,
C.21.126   And fedde with two fisches and with *fyue* loues
C.21.127   Sore afyngered folk, mo then *fyue* thousend.
C.21.216   To alle kyne creatures þat can his *fyue* wittes,

flailes n *fleil n.* A 1; B 1; C 1 flayles

A. 7.172   And fla[ppid]e on wiþ *flailes* fro morewe til eue,
B. 6.184   And flapten on wiþ *flailes* fro morwe til euen
C. 8.180   And flapton on with *f[lay]les* fro morwen til euen

flappes n *flappe n.* B 1

B.13.67   In fame & frigore and *flappes* of scourges:

flapten v *flappen v.* A 1 flappide; B 1; C 1 flapton

A. 7.172   And *fla[ppid]e* on wiþ flailes fro morewe til eue,
B. 6.184   And *flapten* on wiþ flailes fro morwe til euen
C. 8.180   And *flapton* on with f[lay]les fro morwen til euen

flaterare > flaterere

flatere v *flateren v.(1)* B 3 flatere (2) flateren (1); C 6 flatere (1) flaterede (1) flateren (3) flaterynge (1)

B.20.110   Fortune gan *flatere* þanne þo fewe þat were alyue
B.20.235   They wol *flatere* [to] fare wel folk þat ben riche.
B.20.383   And þat freres hadde a fyndyng þat for nede *flateren*
C. 2.45   Fauel thorw his *flaterynge* speche hath mede foule enchaunted,
C. 8.147   And freres þat *flateren* nat and pore folke syke,
C.12.25   'For this frere *flaterede* me while he fond me ryche
C.22.110   Fortune gan *flateren* thenne t[h]o fewe þat were alyue
C.22.235   Thei wol *flatere* to fare wel folk þat ben riche.
C.22.383   And þat freres hadde a fyndynge þat for nede *flateren*

flaterere n *flaterer n.* A 1 flatereris; B 8 flaterere (3) flatereres (1) flatereris (3) flateres (1); C 8 flaterare (1) flaterere (1) flaterers (1) flateres (3) flaterrere (2)

A.11.6   To *flatereris* or to folis þat frentyk ben of wittis,'
B.10.6   To *flatereres* or to fooles þat frenetike ben of wittes',
B.13.422   That fedeþ fooles sages, *flatereris* and lieris,
B.13.429   Riȝt so *flatereris* and fooles arn þe fendes disciples
B.13.454   [There] *flateres* and fooles þoruȝ hir foule wordes
B.15.379   *Flaterere* his felawe, ferly me þynkeþ].
B.19.221   And false prophetes fele, *flatereris* and gloseris,
B.20.315   Oon frere *Flaterere* is phisicien and surgien.'
B.20.323   That frere *flaterere* be fet and phisike yow sike.'
C. 7.82   That feden foel sages, *flateres* and lyares,
C. 7.89   Ryht so *flateres* and fooles aren þe fendes procuratours
C. 7.114   There *flaterers* and foles with here foule wordes
C.11.6   To eny foel or to *flaterere* or to frentike peple,'
C.17.113   And *flaterrere* for his vscher, ferly me thynketh.
C.21.221   And false profetes fele, *flateres* and glosares,
C.22.315   Oen frere *flaterrere* is fiscicien and surgien.'
C.22.323   That frere *flaterare* be fet and fisyk ȝow seke.'

flaterynge ger *flatering ger.* &> *flatere* B 1; C 2

B.13.446   And fiþele þee wiþoute *flaterynge* of good friday þe [geste],
C. 7.106   And fithele the withoute *flaterynge* of god friday þe [g]este
C.15.77   That no fals frere thorw *flaterynge* hem bygyle;

flaterrere > flaterere

flatte v *flatten v.* A 1 flattide; B 1; C 1

A. 5.215   And *flattide* it on his face & faste on him criede
B. 5.443   And *flatte* it on his face and faste on hym cryde
C. 7.57   And *flatte* hit on his face and faste on hym cryede

flatterrere > flaterere

flaumbe n *flaume n.* B 3 flaumbe (2) flawmbe (1); C 3 flaumé

B.17.210   Fostren forþ a *flawmbe* and a fair leye
B.17.243   And as þe weke and fir wol maken a warm *flaumbe*
B.17.251   For may no fir *flaumbe* make, faille it [h]is kynde.
C.19.176   Fostren forth a *flaume* and a feyr lye
C.19.209   And as þe wyke and [fuyr wol make a warm] *flaume*
C.19.217   For may no fuyr *flaume* make, faile hit his kynde.

flaumeth flaumynge > flawme

flaundres n prop *OED Flanders* B 1; C 1

B. 5.312   [Sire Piers of Pridie and Pernele of *Flaundres*,

C. 6.367   Syre [Peres] of prydie and purnele of *Flaundres*,

flawmbe > flaumbe

flawme v *flaumen v.* B 3 flawme (1) flawmeþ (1) flawmynge (1); C 2
    flaumeth (1) flaumynge (1)
B.12.257 I leue it *flawme* ful foule þe fold al aboute,
B.17.208 And þanne a fir *flawmynge* forþ out of boþe.
B.17.229 And þanne *flawmeþ* he as fir on fader and on filius
C.19.174 And thenne [a fuyr *flaumynge*] forth of hem bothe.
C.19.195 And thenne *flaumeth* he as fuyr on fader and on filius

fle > flee,fleen

fleckede ptp *flekked ppl.* B 1; C 1 flekede
B.11.330 Wiþ *fleckede* feþeres and of fele colours.
C.13.138 With *flekede* fetheres and of fele colours.

fledde(n > fleen

flee v1 *flien v. &>* *fleen* A 2 flowen; B 8 fle (1) flee (1) fleen (1) fleeþ
    (2) fleynge (1) flowen (2); C 9 fle (3) fleeth (2) fley (1) flowen (3)
A. 2.195 Alle fledden for fer & *flowen* into hernis;
A. 7.171 Faitours for fer *flowen* into bernis
B. 2.236 Alle fledden for fere and *flowen* into hernes;
B. 6.183 Faitours for fere *flowen* into Bernes
B. 8.54 To *fleynge* foweles, to fisshes and to beestes.
B. 9.143 And þe foweles þat *fleen* forþ wiþ oþere beestes,
B.12.239 And feblest fowel of fliȝt is þat *fleeþ* or swymmeþ.
B.12.243 They may noȝt *flee* fer ne ful heiȝe neiþer];
B.15.278 But of foweles þat *fleeþ*; þus fyndeþ men in bokes.
B.20.44 "Boþe fox and fowel may *fle* to hole and crepe
C. 2.252 Alle fledde for fere and *flowen* into hernes;
C. 8.179 Tho were faytours afered and *flowen* into [Peres] bernes
C.10.231 And þe foules þat *fl[e]eth* forth with oþer bestes,
C.14.171 And feblest foul of flyh[t is] þat *fleeth* oþer swym[m]eth:
C.14.176 For þey may nat *fle* fer ne ful hey neyther
C.14.177 For here fetheres þat fayre beth to *fle* fer hem letteth.
C.18.120 Filius by þe fadres wille *fley* with spiritus sanctus
C.20.369 And tho that oure lord louede forth with þat liht *flowen*.
C.22.44 "Bothe fox and foule may *fle* to hole and crepe

fleen v2 *flen v.(1) &> flee* A 4 fle (2) fledden (1) fleiȝ (1); B 14 fle (3)
    fledden (1) flee (2) fleen (2) fleeþ (1) fleiȝ (5); C 15 fle (5) fledde (1)
    flee (1) fleen (1) fleeth (1) fley (2) fleyh (2) fly (1) flowe (1)
A. 2.171 And bad hym *fle* for fer & hise feris alle.
A. 2.172 Þanne fal[s]nesse for feer *fleiȝ* to þe Freris;
A. 2.195 Alle *fledden* for fer & flowen into hernis;
A. 3.128 To vnfetere þe fals, *fle* where hym lykiþ.
B. 2.212 And bad hym *fle* for fere and hise [feeres] alle.
B. 2.213 [Thanne] Falsnesse for fere *fleiȝ* to þe Freres;
B. 2.236 Alle *fledden* for fere and flowen into hernes;
B. 3.139 To vnfettre þe fals, *fle* where hym likeþ.
B.15.35 And whan I *flee* fro þe flessh and forsake þe careyne
B.17.60 Feiþ hadde first siȝte of hym, ac he *fleiȝ* aside
B.17.91 How þat feiþ *fleiȝ* awey and Spes his felawe boþe
B.17.322 For to *fleen* his owene [hous] as holy writ sheweþ.
B.17.324 Hir feere *fleeþ* hire for feere of hir tonge.
B.18.309 I rede we *fle*', quod [þe fend], 'faste alle hennes,
B.19.103 And som tyme he fauȝt faste and *fleiȝ* ouþer while,
B.20.131 And garte good feiþ *flee* and fals to abide.
B.20.169 And lif *fleiȝ* for feere to phisik after helpe
B.20.285 And *fleen* to þe freres, as fals folk to westmynstre
C. 1.119 For theder as þe fende *fly* his fote for to sette,
C. 2.222 And bad falsnesse to *fle* and his feres alle.
C. 2.223 Falsnesse for fere tho *fleyh* to þe freres;
C. 2.252 Alle *fledde* for fere and flowen into hernes;
C. 3.177 To vnfetere the fals, *fle* wher hym liketh,
C.16.197 And when y *fle* fro þe [flessh] and feye leue þe careyne
C.17.144 For when alle frendes faylen and *fleen* away in deynge
C.19.59 Fayth [hadde furst siht of hym] Ac he *fleyh* asyde
C.19.82 Were afered and *flowe* fram þe man ywounded.
C.19.304 Here f[e]re *fleeth* here for fere of here tonge.
C.20.343 Y rede we *flee*,' quod the fende, 'faste all hennes,
C.21.103 And som tyme he fauht faste and *fley* oþerwhile,
C.22.131 And gert goed faith *fle* and fals to abyde
C.22.169 And lyf *fley* for fere to fisyk aftur helpe
C.22.285 And *fle* to þe freres, as fals folk to Westmynstre

flees n *fles n.* C 1
C. 9.269 And many a fayre *flees* falsliche is ywasche!

fleeth fley > flee,fleen; flei(ȝ -h > fleen; fleynge : flee; fleysche > flessh;
flekede > fleckede

flesch(- > flessh(-

flessh n *flesh n.* A 8 flessh (7) flesshis (1); B 27 flessh (25) flesshes (2);
    C 21 fleysche (1) flesch (10) flesche (7) flesches (1) flessh (1) flesshe
    (1)
A. 1.38 For þe fend & þi *flessh* folewiþ togidere,
A. 5.49 For to affaiten hire *flessh* þat fers was to synne:
A. 7.136 Lest his *flessh* & þe fend foulide his soule.
A. 7.144 Of þ[i] flour, and þi *flessh* fecche whanne vs likeþ,
A. 7.294 But ȝif it be fressh *flessh* oþer fissh yfried,
A. 9.38 Þat þoruȝ þe fend, & þe *flessh*, & þe false world,
A. 9.45 Folewe þi *flesshis* wil & þe fendis aftir,
A.11.215 Godis *flessh*, & his fet, & hise fyue woundis
B. 1.40 For þe fend and þi *flessh* folwen togidere,
B. 1.155 And whan it hadde of þis fold *flessh* and blood taken
B. 3.55 It is a freletee of *flessh*–ye fynden it in bokes–
B. 5.66 To affaiten hire *flessh* þat fiers was to synne.
B. 5.436 Boþe *flessh* and fissh and manye oþere vitailles;
B. 6.157 Of þi flour and þi *flessh*, fecche whanne vs likeþ,
B. 6.310 But if it be fressh *flessh* ouþer fissh [y]fryed,
B. 8.42 That þoruȝ þe fend and þe *flessh* and þe [false] worlde
B. 8.49 Folwe þi *flesshes* wille and þe fendes after,
B.11.401 In fondynge of þe *flessh* and of þe fend boþe,
B.12.245 And his *flessh* is foul flessh and his feet boþe,
B.12.245 And his flessh is foul *flessh* and his feet boþe,
B.12.266 And of *flessh* by fele fold fatter and swetter;
B.13.40 Ac þis maister [of þise men] no maner *flessh* [eet],
B.13.93 Is neiþer fissh n[e] *flessh*, but fode for a penaunt.
B.14.43 The Corlew by kynde of þe Eyr, moost clennest *flessh* of briddes,
B.14.299 It afaiteþ þe *flessh* fram folies ful manye,
B.15.35 And whan I flee fro þe *flessh* and forsake þe careyne
B.15.432 [Ac] fressh *flessh* ouþer fissh, whan it salt failleþ,
B.15.465 And wiþ calues *flessh* he fedde þe folk þat he louede.
B.15.534 How þei defouled hir *flessh*, forsoke hir owene wille,
B.16.31 The *flessh* is a fel wynd, and in flouryng tyme,
B.16.48 Ac whan þe fend and þe *flessh* forþ wiþ þe world
B.16.101 Til he weex a faunt þoruȝ hir *flessh* and of fightyng kouþe
B.16.229 Calues *flessh* and Cakebreed; and knewe what I þouȝte.
B.17.334 The wif is oure wikked *flessh* þat wol noȝt be chastised
B.18.198 And folwede þat þe fend tauȝte and his [*flesshes*] wille
C. 1.38 For the fend and thy *flesch* folewen togederes,
C. 1.151 /A[nd] when hit hadde of þe folde *flesch* and blode taken
C. 3.59 Hit is but frelete of *fleysche*–ȝe fyndeth [hit in] bokes–
C. 6.7 To affayten here *flesshe* þat fers was to synne.
C. 6.159 For y ete more fysch then *flesche* there and feble ale drynke.
C. 7.49 Bothe *flesch* and fysch and vitailes kepte so longe
C. 7.143 That art furste oure fadur and of *flesch* oure broþer
C. 8.154 [Of] thy flour and thy *flesch*, feche whenne vs liketh
C. 8.332 But hit be [fresh] *flesch* or fisch yfried or ybake
C. 9.93 And colde *flesche* and fische as venisoun were bake;
C.10.48 That thorw the fend and [the] *flesch* and th[e] freel worlde
C.13.152 That ne lees the lykynge of lost of *flesch*, as hit were,
C.14.180 More þan for his fayre *flesch* or for his merye note.
C.15.100 Is noþer fische ne *flesche* but fode for [a] penant[e].
C.16.135 Hit defendeth þe *flesche* fram folies ful monye,
C.16.197 And when y fle fro þe [*flessh*] and feye leue þe careyne
C.17.195 How they deffoule[d] here *flesche*, forsoke here owne wille,
C.18.35 Thenne is þe *flesch* a fel wynde and in flouryng tyme
C.18.79 And folewe þat the *flesche* wole and fruyt forth brynge.
C.19.314 The wyf is oure wikkede *flesche* [þat] wol nat be chasted
C.20.203 And folewede þat þe fend tauhte and his *flesch[es]* will

flesshliche adj *fleshlich adj.* B 1; C 1 flescheliche
B.19.171 And feele wiþ hise fyngres his *flesshliche* herte.
C.21.171 And fele with his fyngeres his *flescheliche* herte.

flete v *fleten v.(1)* B 2 flete (1) fleteþ (1); C 1
B.12.167 Ther his felawe *fleteþ* forþ as þe flood likeþ
B.20.45 And þe fissh haþ fyn to *flete* wiþ to reste;
C.22.45 And þe fisch hath fyn to *flete* with to reste;

flex n *flex n.* B 1; C 1
B. 6.13 Wyues and widewes wolle and *flex* spynneþ;
C. 8.12 Wyue[s] and wyddewes wolle an[d] *flex* spynneth;

fly > fleen

flicche n *flicche n.* A 1; B 1; C 1
A.10.195 To folewe aftir þe *flicche*, fecche þei it neuere;
B. 9.174 To folwen after þe *flicche*, fecche þei it neuere;
C.10.276 To folwe for þe *flicche*, feccheth they hit neuere;

fliȝt n *flight n.(2)* B 2; C 1 flyht
B.12.239 And feblest fowel of *fliȝt* is þat fleeþ or swymmeþ.
B.12.249 Riȝt as þe pennes of þe pecok peyneþ hym in his *fliȝt*,
C.14.171 And feblest foul of *flyh[t* is] þat fleeth oþer swym[m]eth:

flynt n *flint n.* B 2; C 2
B.14.65   And out of þe *flynt* sprong þe flood þat folk and beestes dronken.
B.17.248   Ac hewe fir at a *flynt* foure hundred wynter;
C.15.264   And oute of þe *flynt* sprong þe floed þat folk and bestes dronke.
C.19.214   Ac hewe fuyr at a *flynt* foure hundret wynter,

flite v *fliten v.* A 1; B 1
A.Pr.42   *Flite* þanne for here foode, fouȝten at þe ale.
B.Pr.42   [*Flite* þanne] for hire foode, fouȝten at þe ale.

flittynge prp *flitten v.* B 1; C 1 flittyng
B.11.63   And þo fond I þe frere afered and *flittynge* boþe
C.12.15   And *flittyng* fond y the frere þat me confessede

flobre v *floberen v.* B 1
B.14.15   That I ne *flobre* it foule fro morwe til euen.'

flodes floed > flood

flonke n *flaunk n.* C 1
C. 6.335   Fareth as *flo[nke]* of fuyr þat ful amydde Temese

flood n *flod n.* A 3; B 10; C 8 flodes (1) floed (6) flood (1)
A. 7.306   Þoruȝ *flood* [and] foule wederis fruytes shuln fa[i]lle,
A.10.169   Til fourty dayes be fulfild, þat *flood* haue ywasshe
A.11.207   "Whanne fisshes faile þe *flood* or þe fresshe watir
B. 6.325   Thoruȝ *flo[od]* and foule wedres fruytes shul faille,
B. 9.138   Til fourty daies be fulfild, þat *flood* haue ywasshen
B.10.301   Whan fisshes faillen þe *flood* or þe fresshe water
B.10.414   And men þat maden it amydde þe *flood* adreynten.
B.12.167   Ther his felawe fleteþ forþ as þe *flood* likeþ.
B.12.179   In which *flood* þe fend fondeþ a man hardest.
B.13.162   Ne [nei]þer fuyr ne *flood* ne feere of þyn enemy
B.14.42   Fissh to lyue in þe *flood* and in þe fir þe Criket,
B.14.65   And out of þe flynt sprong þe *flood* þat folk and beestes dronken.
B.15.367   Now faileþ þe folk of þe *flood* and of þe lond boþe,
C. 3.91   Bothe thorw fuyr and *flood* a[nd] thorw fals peple
C. 5.148   Ryht as fysches in *floed* whan hem fayleth water
C. 8.346   Thorw *flodes* and foule wederes fruyttes shollen fayle;
C. 9.183   Or thorw fuyr or thorw *floed* yfalle into pouerte,
C.10.226   Til fourty [dayes] be fulfild and *floed* haue ywasche
C.14.119   In whiche *floed* þe fende fondeth [a] man hardest.
C.15.164   Noþer fuyr ne *floed* ne be aferd of enemye:
C.15.264   And oute of þe flynt spronge þe *floed* þat folk and bestes dronken.

floor n *flor n.* B 1; C 1 flore
B.12.198   Riȝt as som man yeue me mete and [sette me amydde þe *floor*];
C.14.137   Riht As sum man ȝeueth me mete and sette me Amydde þe *flore*;

floryns n *floren n.* A 4 floreynes; B 5; C 4 floreynes
A. 2.108   Þanne fette fauel forþ *floreynes* ynowe,
A. 2.111   And feffe false wytnesse wiþ *floreynes* ynowe,
A. 3.147   Þat feiþ may not haue his forþ, hire *floreynes* go so þikke.
A. 6.68   He is fre[þ]id in wiþ *Floreynes* & oþere [fees] manye.
B. 2.144   Thanne fette Fauel forþ *floryns* ynowe
B. 2.147   And feffe fal[s] witness[e] wiþ *floryns* ynowe,
B. 3.157   That feiþ may noȝt hauh forþ, hire *floryns* go so þikke.
B. 4.156   I falle in *floryns*', quod þat freke, 'and faile speche ofte.'
B. 5.581   He is fryþed In wiþ *floryns* and oþere fees manye;
C. 2.160   T[h]o fette fauel forth *floreynes* ynowe
C. 2.163   And feffe fals witnesse with *floreynes* ynowe,
C. 3.195   That fayth may nat haue his forth, here *floreynes* goth so thykke,
C. 7.228   Is frithed in with *floreynes* and othere fees monye;

florissheþ v *florishen v.* B 1; C 1 florischeth
B.14.297   The ferþe is a fortune þat *florissheþ* þe soule
C.16.133   The furthe is a fortune þat *florischeth* þe soule

flour n1 *flour n.(1)* A 1; B 5 flour (1) floures (4); C 3 flour (1) floures (2)
A.10.122   Which is þe *flour* & þe fruyt fostrid of boþe.
B.11.365   I seiȝ *floures* in þe fryth and hir faire colours
B.12.221   And of þe *floures* in þe Fryth and of hire faire hewes,
B.15.102   Shal neuere *flour* ne fruyt [wexe] ne fair leef be grene.
B.16.26   And in blowyng tyme abite þe *floures* but if þise piles helpe.
B.16.45   And feccheþ awey my *floures* som tyme afore boþe myne eighen.
C.13.175   Ne what o[f] *floures* on felde and of here fayre coloures
C.14.158   And how þe *floures* in þe fryth cometh to fayre hewes:
C.16.255   Shal neuere *flour* ne fruyt wexe ne fayre leue be grene.

flour n2 *flour n.(2)* A 1; B 2; C 1
A. 7.144   Of þ[i] *flour*, and þi flessh fecche whanne vs likeþ,
B. 6.157   Of þi *flour* and þi flessh, fecche whanne vs likeþ,
B.14.30   And *flour* to fede folk wiþ as best be for þe soule;
C. 8.154   [Of] thy *flour* and thy flesche, feche whenne vs liketh

floured v *flouren v.(1)* B 1
B.16.94   That Piers fruyt *floured* and felle to be rype.

flouryng ger *flouring ger.* B 1; C 1
B.16.31   The flessh is a fel wynd, and in *flouryng* tyme,
C.18.35   Thenne is þe flesch a fel wynde and in *flouryng* tyme

flowe > fleen; flowen > flee

flux n *flux n.* B 3 flux (1) Fluxes (2); C 3 flux (1) fluxes (2)
B. 5.179   [I] haue a *flux* of a foul mouþ wel fyue dayes after;
B.19.46   And defended from foule yueles, feueres and *Fluxes*,
B.20.81   And sente forþ his forreyours, Feueres and *Fluxes*,
C. 6.161   Y haue a *flux* of a foul mouth wel fyue daies aftur;
C.21.46   And fended fro foule eueles, feueres and *fluxes*
C.22.81   And sente forth his forreours, feueres and *fluxes*,

fobbes n *fob n.(2)* A 1 fobbis; B 1; C 1
A. 2.144   As *fo[bb]is* & faitours þat on here feet iotten.'
B. 2.183   As [*fobbes*] and Faitours þat on hire feet [iotten].'
C. 2.196   As *fobbes* and faytours þat on here feet rennen.'

fode > foode; foe(s > foo; foel > fool; foend(e > fynden; foet > foot; fol > fool,ful

fold n1 *folde n.(2), -fold suff.* B 3; C 1
B.11.258   And boþe bettre and blesseder by many *fold* þan Richesse.
B.12.266   And of flessh by fele *fold* fatter and swetter;
B.13.319   It was fouler bi fele *fold* þan it first semed.
C.12.144   And bothe bettere and blessedere by many *fold* then richesse.

fold n2 *folde n.(3)* B 3 fold (2) foold (1); C 2 folde
B. 1.155   And whan it hadde of þis *fold* flessh and blood taken
B. 7.54   Thise foure þe fader of heuene made to þis *foold* in commune;
B.12.257   I leue it flawme ful foule þe *fold* al aboute,
C. 1.151   /A[nd] when hit hadde of þe *folde* flesch and blode taken
C. 9.153   And what freke on this *folde* fiscuth aboute

folde v *folden v.(2) &> fold* B 5 folde (2) folden (1) yfolden (1) foldynge (1); C 5 folde (2) folden (1) yfolde (2)
B.17.141   The fader was first as a fust wiþ o fynger *foldynge*
B.17.148   The fyngres þat fre ben to *folde* and to serue
B.17.169   And as my fust is ful hand y[ff]olden togideres
B.17.185   Vnfolden or *folden*, my fust and my pawme
B.17.189   For þe fyngres þat *folde* sholde and þe fust make
C.19.115   As a fuste wit[h] a fynger *yfolde* togyderes
C.19.122   The fyngres þat fre ben to *folde* and to cluche
C.19.131   And as þe fuste is a ful hand *yfolde* togyderes,
C.19.151   Vnfolden or *folden*, a fuste wyse or elles,
C.19.155   For þe fyngeres þat *folde* sholde and þe fust make

foldes n *fold n.(1)* C 1
C. 9.260   For many wakere wolues ar wr[iþ]en into thy *foldes*;

foles n *fole n. &> fool* A 1 folis; B 1
A. 2.127   Þanne fette fauel *folis* of þe beste,
B. 2.163   [Thanne fette Fauel] *foles* [of þe beste],

foleuiles > foluyles; folew- > folw-; folfilleth > fulfille

folie n *folie n.* A 1 folies; B 9 folie (5) folye (2) folies (2); C 7 folye (5) folies (2)
A.10.70   Fro *folies*, & fynde hem til þei ben wise.
B.12.137   And seiden hir wordes [ne] hir wisdomes [w]as but a *folye*;
B.13.148   Ac for to fare þus wiþ þi frend, *folie* it were.
B.14.186   And if vs fille þoruȝ *folie* to falle in synne after
B.14.299   It afaiteþ þe flessh fram *folies* ful manye,
B.15.10   That folk helden me a fool; and in þat *folie* I raued
B.15.76   And how þat folk in *folies* [hir fyue wittes mysspenden],
B.15.150   Wiþouten fauntelte or *folie* a fre liberal wille.'
B.18.226   So it shal fare by þis folk: hir *folie* and hir synne
B.20.147   Conscience and counseil, he counted [it] *f[o]lye.*
C.10.184   Frendes shal fynde hem and fram *folye* kepe
C.11.306   Thow thei folowe þat fortune wole [no] *folye* ich it holde.
C.14.82   And saide here wordes ne here wysdomes was but a *folye*;
C.16.135   Hit defendeth þe flesche fram *folies* ful monye,
C.16.235   And [ho]w that folk [in *folies*] here fyue wittes myspen[en],
C.20.235   So hit shal fare bi this folk: here *folye* and here synne
C.22.147   Consience and conseil, he counted hit *folye.*

foliliche adv *folili adv.* B 1; C 1
B.15.77   As wel freres as ooþer folk, *foliliche* spenden
C.16.236   As wel freres as oþere folk, *foliliche* spenden

folis > foles,fool

folk n *folk n.* A 17; B 78 folk (76) folkes (2); C 63 folk (46) folke (17)
A.Pr.17   A fair feld ful of *folk* fand I þere betwene
A. 1.2   And ek þe feld ful of *folk* I shal ȝow faire shewe.
A. 2.39   Þat iche feld nas ful of *folk* al aboute.
A. 3.53   Ac god alle good *folk* such grauyng defendiþ
A. 3.234   Þat laboureris & louȝ *folk* taken of here maistris

A. 5.10   [For I [sauȝ] þe feld ful of *folk* þat I before tolde],
A. 5.135 For laboureris & louȝ *folk* þat lay be h[y]mselue;
A. 6.13   Þis *folk* fraynide hym faire [fro] whenis þat he come.
A. 7.281 Þanne þise *folk* for fer fetten hym manye
A. 7.284 Þanne was *folk* fayn, & fedde hunger with þe beste;
A. 9.3   And fraynide ful ofte of *folk* þat I mette
A. 9.33   Riȝt þus [it] fariþ,' quaþ þe Frere, 'be *folk* here on erþe.
A.10.131 Formest & ferst to *folk* þat ben weddit
A.10.139 Ac fals *folk* & feiþles, þeuis & leiȝeris,
A.10.185 As fel of þe *folk* [þat I] before shewide.
A.10.210 And þat ben fals *folk*, & fals eires also, foundlynges & [leiȝeris],
A.11.164 Foundit hem formest *folk* to desceyue.
B.Pr.17 A fair feeld ful of *folk* fond I þer bitwene
B. 1.2   And þe feld ful of *folk* I shal yow faire shewe.
B. 1.159 Forþi is loue ledere of þe lordes *folk* of heuene
B. 2.42 Fauel þoruȝ his faire speche haþ þis *folk* enchaunted,
B. 3.64 Ac god alle good *folk* swich grauynge defendeþ,
B. 3.255 That laborers and lowe [lewede] *folk* taken of hire maistres
B. 4.181 And as moost *folk* witnesseþ wel wrong shal be demed.'
B. 5.10 For I seiȝ þe feld ful of *folk* þat I before [tolde],
B. 5.142 And now is fallen þerof a fruyt þat *folk* han wel leuere
B. 5.146 And freres fyndeþ hem in defaute, as *folk* bereþ witnesse,
B. 5.152 [That] I ne moste folwe this *folk*, for swich is my grace.
B. 5.219 For laborers and lowe *folk* þat lay by hymselue.
B. 5.247 And lene *folk* þat lese wole a lippe at euery noble.
B. 5.525 This *folk* frayned hym [faire] fro whennes he come.
B. 6.2   That [myȝte] folwen vs ech foot': þus þis *folk* hem mened.
B. 6.72 And frere faitour and *folk* of hi[s] ordre,
B. 6.206 And for defaute of foode þis *folk* is at my wille.
B. 6.297 Thanne pouere *folk* for fere fedden hunger yerne
B. 6.300 Thanne was *folk* fayn and fedde hunger wiþ þe beste;
B. 7.55 Thise ben truþes tresores trewe *folk* to helpe,
B. 8.3   And frayned ful ofte of *folk* þat I mette
B. 8.37 [Riȝt] þus it [fareþ]', quod þe frere, 'by *folk* here on erþe.
B. 9.110 [Dowel in þis world is trewe wedded libbynge *folk*],
B. 9.121 Ac fals *folk*, feiþlees, þeues and lyeres,
B. 9.162 As bifel of þe *folk* þat I bifore [shewed].
B. 9.196 As fals *folk*, fondlynges, faitours and lieres,
B.10.75 That *folk* is noȝt fermed in þe feiþ ne free of hire goodes
B.10.198 And so shaltow fals *folk* and feiþlees bigile:
B.10.221 Founded hem formest *folk* to deceyue.
B.10.411 God lene it fare noȝt so bi *folk* þat þe feiþ techeþ
B.10.452 Beþ noȝt [afered of þat *folk*], for I shal [ȝyue yow tonge],
B.11.99 It falleþ noȝt for þat *folk* no tales to telle
B.11.270 Alþouȝ Salomon seide, as *folk* seeþ in þe bible,
B.12.53 And for þei suffren and see so manye nedy *folkes*
B.13.7   And how þat freres folwede *folk* þat was riche
B.13.190 Ac þe wil of þe wye and þe wil of *folk* here
B.13.213 And confermen fauntekyns ooþer *folk* ylered
B.13.242 Faitours and freres and *folk* wiþ brode crounes.
B.14.30 And flour to fede *folk* wiþ as best be for þe soule;
B.14.64 It is founden þat fourty wynter *folk* lyuede withouten tulying,
B.14.65 And out of þe flynt sprong þe flood þat *folk* and beestes dronken.
B.15.10 That *folk* helden me a fool; and in þat folie I raued
B.15.29 And whan I feele þat *folk* telleþ my firste name is sensus,
B.15.70 Freres and fele oþere maistres þat to [þe] lewed [*folk*] prechen,
B.15.76 And how þat *folk* in folies [hir fyue wittes mysspenden],
B.15.77 As wel freres as ooþer *folk*, foliliche spenden
B.15.135 A[c] goddes *folk* for defaute þerof forfaren and spillen
B.15.302 Thei wolde haue yfed þat *folk* bifore wilde foweles;
B.15.303 [For al þe curteisie þat beestes konne þei kidde þat *folk* ofte,
B.15.347 Ac þer is a defaute in þe *folk* þat þe feiþ kepeþ,
B.15.348 Wherfore *folk* is þe febler and noȝt ferm of bileue.
B.15.351 And so it fareþ by som *folk* now; þei han a fair speche,
B.15.367 Now faileþ þe *folk* of þe flood and of þe lond boþe,
B.15.385 Wherfore I am afered of *folk* of holy kirke,
B.15.406 And dide *folk* þanne falle on knees; for he swoor in his prechyng
B.15.425 And *folkes* sholden [fynde], þat ben in diuerse siknesse,
B.15.448 And follede *folk* faste, and þe feiþ tauȝte
B.15.465 And wiþ calues flessh he fedde þe *folk* þat he louede.
B.15.472 [And by þe hond fedde foules [i]s *folk* vnderstonde
B.15.507 Thus in a feiþ leue þat *folk*, and in a fals mene,
B.15.573 And feden hem wiþ goostly foode and [nedy *folk* to fynden.
B.15.606 Arn *folk* of oon feiþ; þe fader god þei honouren.
B.16.245 And called me foot of his feiþ, his *folk* for to saue
B.16.246 And defende hem fro þe fend, *folk* þat on me leneden.
B.17.213 [Fostren forþ amonges *folk* loue and bileue]
B.17.238 So wol þe fader forȝyue *folk* of mylde hertes
B.17.311 Thus it fareþ by swich *folk* þat [folwen] al hire [wille].
B.18.8   And how Osanna by Organye olde *folk* songen,
B.18.226 So it shal fare by þis *folk*: hir folie and hir synne
B.19.59 To maken alle *folk* free þat folwen his lawe].
B.19.127 Sore afyngred *folk*, mo þan fyue þousand.

B.19.445 And fynt *folk* to fiȝte and cristen blood to spille
B.20.64 And a fals fend Antecrist ouer alle *folk* regnede.
B.20.66 Defyed alle falsnesse and *folk* þat it vsede;
B.20.235 They wol flatere [to] fare wel *folk* þat ben riche.
B.20.285 And fleen to þe freres, as fals *folk* to westmynstre
B.20.290 And so it fareþ with muche *folk* þat to freres shryueþ,
B.20.378 The frere wiþ his phisyk þis *folk* haþ enchaunted,
C.Pr.19 A fair feld ful of *folk* fond y þer bytwene
C. 1.2   And þe feld ful of *folk* y shal ȝou fair shewe.
C. 1.155 Forthi is loue ledare of [þe] lordes *folk* of heuene
C. 2.105 /This lyf to folowe falsnesse and *folk* þat on hym leueth,
C. 3.68 Ac god to alle good *folk* suche grauynge defendeth,
C. 3.247 Of *folk* þat fauht þerfore and folwede þe kynges wille.
C. 5.67 Of frankeleynes and fremen and of *folke* ywedded.
C. 5.111 Y saw þe felde ful of *folk* fram ende til oþer
C. 6.127 That y ne mot folowe this *folk*: my fortune is non oþer.
C. 6.227 For laboreres and louh *folk* þat lay by hymsulue.
C. 6.245 Y lene *folk* þat lese wole a lyppe [at] vch a noble
C. 7.170 This *folk* frayned hym furste fro whennes he come.
C. 7.259 And fynde alle manere *folk* fode to here soules
C. 8.73 And frere faytour and *folk* of þat ordre,
C. 8.138 That no faytrye were founde in *folk* þat goth abeggeth,
C. 8.147 And freres þat flateren nat and pore *folke* syke,
C. 8.212 And for defaute this *folk* folweth myn hestes.
C. 8.215 'Ther is no fi[al] loue with this *folk* for al here fayre speche
C. 8.228 Ac yf thow fynde eny *folke* þat fals men han apayred
C. 8.319 Pore *folk* for fere tho fedde honger ȝerne
C. 8.322 Thenne [was] *folke* fayn and fedde hunger dentie[f]liche
C. 9.57 Thise foure sholde be fre to alle *folk* þat hit nede[th].
C. 9.72 As prisones in puttes and pore *folk* in cotes,
C. 9.95 Were a feste with suche *folk* or so fele cockes.
C.10.3   And fraynede ful ofte of *folke* þat y mette
C.10.256 Ac fewe *folke* now folweth this for thei ȝeue her childurne
C.10.295 And fals *folk* and fondlynges, faytors and lyares,
C.11.55 That *folk* is nat ferme[d] in þe faith ne fre of here godes
C.11.242 God lene hit fare nat so by *folk* þat þe faith techen
C.11.248 For lewed *folk*, goddes foles and his fre bestes:
C.11.277 Beth nat aferd of þat *folk* for y shal ȝeue ȝow tonge,
C.12.166 Ac ȝef hem forth to pore *folk* þat for my loue hit aske;
C.12.238 That fals *folk* fecche aweye felonliche his godes;
C.13.83 That þe lawe ȝeueth leue such low *folk* to be excused,
C.15.9   And how þat freres folwede *folk* þat was ryche
C.15.235 Hit am y þat fynde alle *folke* and fram hunger saue
C.15.263 Hit is founde þat fourty wynter *folke* lyuede and tylde nat
C.15.264 And oute of þe flynt spronge þe floed þat *folk* and bestes dronke.
C.15.284 Hit are but fewe *folk* of this ryche that ne falleth in arrerage
C.16.189 And when y fele þat *folke* telleth my furste name is sensus
C.16.231 Freres fele tymes to þe *folk* þer they prechen
C.16.235 And [ho]w that *folk* [in folies] here fyue wittes myspen[en],
C.16.236 As wel freres as oþere *folk*, foliliche spenden
C.16.330 And when he hath visited thus fetured *folk* and oþer folke pore,
C.16.330 And when he hath visited thus fetured folk and oþer *folke* pore,
C.17.84 That fayre byfore *folk* prechen and techen
C.17.104 Now failleth this *folk*, bothe follwares and shipmen;
C.17.258 Thus in a fayth l[e]ueth þat *folk* and in a fals mene,
C.18.101 And bryngeth forth fruyt, *folk* of alle nacion,
C.19.179 Fostren forth amongus *folke* loue and bileue
C.19.204 So wol þe fader forȝeue *folke* of mylde hertes
C.19.291 Thus hit fareth by such *folk* þat folewen here owene will,
C.20.7   And how osanna by orgene oelde *folke* songe.
C.20.235 So hit shal fare bi this *folk*: here folye and here synne
C.21.59 To make alle *folk* fre þat folweth his lawe.
C.21.127 Sore afyngered *folk*, mo then fyue thousend.
C.21.445 And fynde[th] *folke* to fihte and cristene bloed to spille
C.22.64 And a fals fende auntecrist ouer all *folke* regnede.
C.22.66 Defyede all falsnesse and *folke* þat hit vsede;
C.22.235 Thei wol flatere to fare wel *folk* þat ben riche.
C.22.285 And fle to þe freres, as fals *folk* to Westmynstre
C.22.290 And so hit fareth with moche *folke* þat to freres shryuen,
C.22.378 The frere with his fisyk this *folk* hath enchaunted

follen v *fulwen* v. B 2 follede (1) yfulled (1); C 2 follen (1) yfolled (1)
B.15.448 And *follede* folk faste, and þe feiþ tauȝte
B.19.40 And gentil men wiþ Iesu, for Iesu[s] was *yfulled*
C.17.285 Feden hem and *follen* hem and fere hem fro synne–
C.21.40 And Ientel men with iesu for iesu[s] was *yfolled*

folleweth > folwen; follyng(e > fullyng; follwares > folwere; folow- > folwen

folowynge ger *folwing ger.* C 1
C. 3.345 *Folowynge* and fyndynge out þe fundement of a strenghe,

foluyles n prop *cf. foleviles laues phr.* B 1; C 1 foleuiles
B.19.247 And fecchen it fro false men wiþ *Foluyles* lawes.
C.21.247 And fechen hit fro false men with *foleuiles* lawes;

folwen v *folwen v.* A 13 folewe (5) folewid (1) folewide (1) folewiþ (3)
folwe (2) folweþ (1); B 48 folwe (13) folwed (3) folwede (11) folwen
(8) folweþ (9) folwynge (3) yfolwed (1); C 56 folleweth (7) folowe
(14) folowede (1) foloweth (3) folwe (1) folwede (1) folweden (1)
folwen (1) folweth (5) folwyng (5) folwynge (2) folewe (2) folewed (2)
folewede (6) folewen (4) foleweth (5)

A. 1.38   For þe fend & þi flessh *folewiþ* togidere,
A. 1.161   And as ded as a dorenail but ȝif þe dede *folewe*.
A. 2.147   I haue no tom to telle þat hem *folewiþ*
A. 3.7   And ȝif heo werche be wyt & my wil *folewe*
A. 3.38   And þeiȝ falshed hadde *folewid* þe þis fiftene wynter,
A. 4.25   *Folewide* hem faste for hy hadden to done
A. 7.2   Þat miȝte *folewe* vs iche fote [forto] we were þere.'
A. 9.45   *Folewe* þi flesshis wil & þe fendis aftir,
A. 9.75   And [is] nouȝt drunkelewe ne deynous, dowel hym *folewiþ*.
A.10.195   To *folewe* aftir þe flicche, fecche þei it neuere;
A.12.67   'I wolde *folwe* þe fayn, but fentesye me hendeþ;
A.12.68   Me *folweþ* such a fentyse, I may no ferþer walke.'
A.12.91   Þ[ou] tomblest wiþ a trepget ȝif þou my tras *folwe*,
B. 1.40   For þe fend and þi flessh *folwen* togidere,
B. 1.187   And as deed as a dore[nail] but if þe ded[e] *folwe*:
B. 2.186   I haue no tome to telle þe tail þat [hem] *folwe[þ]*
B. 3.7   And if she werche bi wit and my wil *folwe*
B. 3.39   And [þeiȝ] Fals[hede] hadde *yfolwed* þee alle þise fift[ene] wynter,
B. 3.342   She sholde haue founden fel[l]e wordes *folwynge* þerafter:
B. 3.348   And if ye seche Sapience eft fynde shul ye þat *folweþ*,
B. 4.28   *Folwed* h[e]m faste for þei hadde to doone
B. 5.152   [That] I ne moste *folwe* this folk, for swich is my grace.
B. 5.641   'By crist!' quod a comune womman, 'þi compaignie wol I *folwe*.
B. 6.2   That [myȝte] *folwen* vs ech foot': þus þis folk hem mened.
B. 8.49   *Folwe* þi flesshes wille and þe fendes after,
B. 8.84   And is noȝt dronkelewe ne [d]eynous, dowel hym *folweþ*.
B. 9.174   To *folwen* after þe flicche, fecche þei it neuere;
B.11.12   Thanne hadde Fortune *folwynge* hire two fair damyseles:
B.11.24   That I ne shal *folwe* þi felawship, if Fortune it like.'
B.11.26   'The freke þat *folwede* my wille failled neuere blisse.'
B.11.35   'Folwe forþ þat Fortune wole; þow hast wel fer til Elde.
B.11.39   If truþe wol witnesse it be wel do Fortune to *folwe*
B.11.47   And *folwed* me fourty wynter and a fifte moore,
B.11.138   Mercy al to amende and Mekenesse hir *folwe*;
B.11.257   Preise[n] pouerte for best lif if Pacience it *folw[e]*,
B.11.375   Why þow ne sewest man and his make þat no mysfeet hem *folwe*.'
B.11.403   That som tyme hym bitit to *folwen* his kynde.
B.12.3   I haue *folwed* þee, in feiþ, þise fyue and fourty wynter,
B.13.7   And how þat freres *folwede* folk þat was riche
B.14.203   The fend *folweþ* hem alle and fondeþ hem to helpe,
B.14.205   For þer þat richesse regneþ reuerence[s] *folweþ*,
B.14.220   Ne haue power in pouerte, if pacience [it] *folwe*.
B.14.266   Hir fader and alle hire frendes, and *folweþ* hir make–
B.14.306   For þer þat Pouerte passeþ pees *folweþ* after,
B.15.108   Loþe were lewed men but þei youre loore *folwede*
B.15.224   And seintes yset; [stille] charite hem *folwede*.
B.15.250   And gyue vs grace, goode god, charite to *folwe*.
B.15.464   But wiþ foweles þat fram hym nolde but *folwede* his whistlyng:
B.15.475   In menyng after mete *folwed* men þat whistlen;
B.16.162   That on þe friday *folwynge* for mankyndes sake
B.17.83   Feiþ *folwede* after faste and fondede to mete hym,
B.17.126   Alle þat lyuen in Feiþ and *folwen* his felawes techynge.'
B.17.311   Thus it fareþ by swich folk þat [folwen] al hire [wille],
B.18.120   For þe vertue þat hire *folwede* afered was she neuere.
B.18.198   And *folwede* þat þe fend tauȝte and his [flesshes] wille
B.18.241   The light *folwede* þe lord into þe lowe erþe.
B.19.33   And fre men foule þralles þat *folwen* noȝt hise lawes.
B.19.59   To maken alle folk free þat *folwen* his lawe].
B.19.271   Thise foure, þe feiþ to teche, *folwe[de]* Piers teme
B.19.415   For hir pelure and palfreyes mete and pilours þat hem *folweþ*.
B.20.58   Freres *folwede* þat fend for he gaf hem copes,
C. 1.38   For the fend and thy flesch *folewen* togedere,
C. 1.183   And as ded as [a] dore nayl but yf þe ded[e] *folowe*:
C. 2.34   [W]hat man [that] me louyeth and my wille *foleweth*
C. 2.79   That *foleweth* falsnesse, Fauel and lyare,
C. 2.105   /This lyf to *folowe* falsnesse and folk þat on hym leueth,
C. 2.199   Y haue no tome to telle the tayl þat hem *folewe[th]*
C. 3.247   Of folk þat fauht þerfore and *folwede* þe kynges wille.
C. 3.364   Alle kyn kynde to knowe and to *folowe*
C. 3.376   To *folowe* and to fynde hym and [f]eche at hem his consayl
C. 3.494   A sholde haue yfonde [felle wordes *folwynge*] aftur:
C. 3.496   So hoso [s]echeth sapience fynde he shal [that] *foloweth*
C. 4.28   Fayn were to *folowe* hem and faste ryden aftur
C. 6.118   Freres *folewen* my [f]lore fele tyme and ofte
C. 6.127   That y ne mot *folowe* this folk: my fortune is non oþer.
C. 7.306   Famyne and defaute, *folwen* y wol Peres;
C. 7.308   That myhte *folowe* vs vch fote for drede of mysturnynge.'

C. 8.212   And for defaute this folk *folweth* myn hestes.
C. 8.348   Thre shypes and a schaef with [a vii] *folwynge*
C.10.51   Ac fre wil and fre wit *foleweth* man euere
C.10.81   And is nat dronklewe ne dedeynus, dowel h[y]m *foleweth*.
C.10.244   That kynde *folweth* kynde and contrarieth neuere:
C.10.256   Ac fewe folke now *folweth* this for thei ȝeue her childurne
C.10.276   To *folwe* for þe flicche, feccheth they hit neuere;
C.11.171   Thenne hadde fortune *folwyng* here two fayre maydenes:
C.11.183   That y ne shal *folowe* thy felowschipe yf fortune [hit] lyke.'
C.11.194   'Folowe forth þat fortune wole; þou hast [wel] fer to elde.
C.11.306   Thow thei *folowe* þat fortune wole [no] folye ich it holde.
C.12.73   Mercy al [to] amende and mekenesse her *folowe*;
C.12.143   Preise[n] pouerte for beste [lif] if pacience hit *folowe*
C.12.171   And al þat þe world wolde and my will *folowe*:
C.13.2   Among Pilours in pees yf pacience hym *folowe*.
C.13.63   Wolde noon suche assailen hym for such as hym *foloweth*
C.13.211   That some tyme hym bitit to *folewen* his kynde.
C.14.3   Y haue *folewed* the, in fayth, mo then fourty wynter
C.15.9   And how þat freres *folewede* folk þat was ryche
C.15.184   And wenten forth here way; with grete wille y *folowede*.
C.15.303   And slepeth, as hit semeth, and somur euere hem *folleweth*.
C.16.44   The fend *folleweth* hem alle and fondeth hem to helpe
C.16.46   For [þer] þat rychess[e] regneth reuerences *folleweth*
C.16.61   Ne haue power in pouerte yf pacience h[it] *folewe*.
C.16.78   So he is neuere[more ful] merye, so meschief hym *followe*,
C.16.141   For þer as pouerte passeth pes *folleweth* comunely
C.16.262   Loeth were lewed [men] bote they ȝoure lore *folwede[n]*
C.16.370   And hoso coueyteth to knowe [hym] such a kynde hym *foloweth*
C.17.143   Loue thy frende þat *folleweth* thy wille, that is thy fayre soule.
C.18.79   And *folewe* þat the flesche wole and fruyt forth brynge.
C.19.80   Bothe fayth and his felawe spes *folewede* faste aftur
C.19.291   Thus hit fareth bi such folk þat *folewen* here owene will,
C.20.123   For þe vertue þat *folewede* afered was she neuere.
C.20.203   And *folewede* þat þe fend tauhte and his flesch[es] will
C.20.250   The lihte *folewede* þe lord into þe lowe erthe.
C.21.33   And fre men foule thralles þat *folleweth* nat his lawes.
C.21.59   To make alle folk fre þat *folleweth* his lawe.
C.21.271   Thise foure, the fayth to teche, *folewe[de* Peres] teme
C.21.415   For here pelurre and palfrayes mete and pelours þat hem *folweth*.
C.22.58   Freres *folewed* þat fende for he ȝaf hem copes

folwere n *folwer n.* A 1 folewere; B 1; C 2 follwares (1) foloware (1)

A. 6.30   I haue ben his *folewere* al þis fourty wynter;
B. 5.542   I haue ben his *folwere* al þis [fourty] wynter,
C. 7.189   [I]ch haue ybe his *foloware* al this fourty wynter
C.17.104   Now failleth this folk, bothe *follwares* and shipmen;

fon > foo; fond > fynden,fonde,founded

fonde v *fonden v. &> fynden* A 1 fond; B 11 fonde (4) fonded (1)
fondede (2) fondeþ (3) founded (1); C 7 fond (1) fonde (1) fondede
(1) fondeth (4)

A. 7.205   Wiþ fuyr or wiþ false men, *fond* suche [to] knowen;
B. 6.219   [Wiþ fir or wiþ] false men, *fonde* swiche to knowe.
B.11.193   For youre frendes wol feden yow, and *fonde* yow to quyte
B.12.179   In which flood þe fend *fondeþ* a man hardest.
B.13.145   Boþe wiþ wer[k] and with wor[d] *fonde* his loue to wynne;
B.14.203   The fend *folweþ* hem alle and *fondeþ* hem to helpe,
B.15.334   That were ful of faire trees, and I *fondede* and caste
B.16.40   And þanne *fondeþ* þe fend my fruyt to destruye
B.16.231   First he *fonded* me if I, [feiþ], louede bettre
B.17.22   '[He seiþ] sooþ', seide þis heraud; 'I haue [*founded*] it ofte.
B.17.83   Feiþ folwede after faste and *fondede* to mete hym,
B.20.166   And bad hym *fonde* to fighte and afere wanhope.
C.12.105   For vch frende fedeth other and *fondeth* hou beste to quite
C.14.119   In whiche floed þe fende *fondeth* [a] man hardest.
C.15.143   *Fond* [with] wit & word his loue to wynne,
C.16.44   The fend folleweth hem alle and *fondeth* hem to helpe
C.18.43   And thenne *fondeth* the fende my fruyte to destruye
C.18.247   How he *fondede* me furste; my fayre sone ysaak.
C.22.166   And baed hym *fonde* to fihte and afere wanhope.

fondement > foundement; fonden > founded

fondynge ger *fondinge ger.* B 2 fondynge (1) fondynges (1); C 3
fondynges

B.11.401   In *fondynge* of þe flessh and of þe fend boþe,
B.14.302   A frend in alle *fondynges*, [of foule yueles leche],
C.10.42   Thow he thorw *fondynges* falle he falleth nat out of charite;
C.16.138   And frende in alle *fondynges* and of foule eueles leche:
C.19.91   And ȝut [b]e plasterud with pacience when *fondynges* [priketh
           hym]–

fondlynges n *flondling n.* A 1 foundlynges; B 1; C 1
A.10.210   And þat ben fals folk, & fals eires also, *foundlynges* & [leiȝeris],
B. 9.196   As fals folk, *fondlynges*, faitours and lieres,

C.10.295   And fals folk and *fondlynges*, faytors and lyares,

fonge v *fongen v.* A 1; B 4 fange (1) fonge (3); C 4
A. 6.45   'I nolde *fonge* a ferþing for seint Thomas shryne,
B. 5.558   'I nolde *fange* a ferþyng for Seint Thomas Shryne;
B.13.227   [Ac] fewe robes I *fonge* or furrede gownes.
B.14.139   And noȝt to *fonge* bifore for drede of disalowyng.
B.16.96   Wheiþer sholde *fonge* þe fruyt, þe fend or hymselue.
C. 7.202   'Y [nolde] *fonge* a ferthynge for seynt Thomas shryne;
C. 9.91   And fele to *fonge* þerto and fewe panes taketh.
C.15.201   And fewe robes y *fonge* or forrede gounes.
C.16.7   A[nd] nat to *fonge* byfore for drede [of] dessallouwynge.

font n *font n.* A 1; B 2; C 2 fonte
A.12.15   Of þe kynde cardinal wit, and cristned in a *font*,
B.11.118   That vnderfonged me atte *font* for oon of goddes chosene.
B.12.285   [Ac] þer is fullynge of *Font* and fullynge in blood shedyng
C.12.53   That vnderfeng me at þe *fonte* for on of godes chosene.
C.14.207   Ac þer is follyng of *fonte* and follyng in bloed [s]hedyng

foo n *fo n.* A 1 fon; B 4 foes (2) foo (1) foon (1); C 4 foe (1) foes (2) foo (1)
A. 5.77   And don hise frendis ben hise *fon* þoruȝ my false tunge.
B. 5.97   And [doon] his frendes be his *foon* þoruȝ my false tonge.
B.11.61   And þanne was Fortune my *foo* for al hir faire [biheste],
B.13.327   And made of frendes *foes* þoruȝ a fals tonge.
B.15.262   Of oure *foes* þat dooþ vs falsnesse; þat is oure fadres wille.
C. 3.240   That he ne felde nat his *foes* tho fortune hit wolde
C. 5.58   Ne fyhte in no faumewarde ne his *foe* greue:
C. 6.72   And made of frendes *foes* thorw fikel and fals tonge.
C.12.13   And thenne was fortune my *foo* for al her fayre biheste

foode n *fode n.* A 10 fode (1) foode (9); B 17 fode (5) foode (12); C 19 fode
A.Pr.42   Flite þanne for here *foode*, fouȝten at þe ale.
A. 7.22   Helpiþ hem werche wiȝtly þat wynne ȝoure *foode*.'
A. 7.63   I shal fynde hem *foode* þat feiþfulliche libbeþ,
A. 7.192   And for defaute of *foode* þus faste hy werchiþ.
A. 7.235   He þat get his *fode* here wiþ trauaile of his hondis,
A. 7.253   Þat fisik shal his furrid hood for his *foode* selle,
A. 8.33   Fynde suche here *foode* for oure lordis loue of heuene,
A. 8.116   Whan þe frost fresiþ *foode* hem behouiþ,
A.11.185   And alle kyne crafty men þat cunne here *foode* wynne,
A.11.186   Wiþ any trewe trauaille toille for here *foode*,
B.Pr.42   [Flite þanne] for hire *foode*, fouȝten at þe ale.
B. 6.20   Helpeþ hym werche wiȝtliche þat wynneþ youre *foode*.'
B. 6.69   I shal fynden hem *fode* þat feiþfulliche libbeþ,
B. 6.206   And for defaute of *foode* þis folk is at my wille.
B. 6.269   That Phisik shal hi[s] furred ho[od] for his *fode* selle,
B. 7.31   Fynden [swiche] hir *foode* [for oure lordes loue of heuene],
B. 7.134   [Whan þe frost freseþ *fode* hem bihoueþ];
B. 9.71   And widewes þat han noȝt wherwith to wynnen hem hir *foode*,
B.13.93   Is neiþer fissh n[e] flessh, but *fode* for a penaunt.
B.15.292   Peter fisshed for his *foode* and his felawe Andrew;
B.15.305   Ac god sente hem *foode* by foweles and by no fierse beestes
B.15.479   And as þo foules to fynde *fode* after whistlyng
B.15.573   And feden hem wiþ goostly *foode* and [nedy folk to fynden.
B.15.576   Bodily *foode* and goostly foode to] gyue þere it nedeþ.
B.15.576   Bodily foode and goostly *foode* to] gyue þere it nedeþ:
B.20.15   He synneþ noȝt, so:þliche, þat so wynneþ his *foode*.
B.20.241   Lat hem be as beggeris or lyue by Aungeles *foode*.'
C.Pr.43   Fayteden for here *fode*, foughten at þe ale.
C. 1.23   The firste is *fode* and vesture þe seconde
C. 5.27   That fynde[th] the thy *fode*–for an ydel man þow semest,
C. 5.49   And tho þa[t] fynden me my *fode* fouchensaf, y trowe,
C. 6.293   Then haue my *fode* and my fyndynge of fals menne wynnyngus.
C. 7.259   And fynde alle manere folk *fode* to here soules
C. 8.18   Helpeth hym worche wi[ȝt]liche þat wynneth ȝoure *fode*.'
C. 8.70   Y shal fynde hem *fode* þat fayfulleche libbeth,
C. 8.283   Alle þat gr[eden at] thy gate for godes loue aftur *fode*
C. 8.290   That fysik shal his forred hod[e] for his *fode* sulle
C. 9.76   To aglotye with here gurles that greden aftur *fode*.
C. 9.200   And somme hadde foreynes to frendes þat hem *fode* sente
C.15.100   Is noþer fische ne flesche but *fode* for [a] penant[e].
C.16.316   'H[o] fynt hym his *fode*', quod y, 'or what frendes hath he,
C.16.325   There pore men and prisones ben and paye for here *fode*,
C.17.19   Peter fischede for his *fode* And his fere Androwe;
C.18.14   The whiche is Caritas ykald, Cristes oune *fode*,
C.22.15   He synegeth nat sothlich þat so wynneth his *fode*.
C.22.241   Lat hem be as beggares or lyue by angeles *fode*.'

fool n *fol n.* A 5 folis (3) foolis (2); B 15 fool (4) fooles (9) foolis (2); C 13 foel (3) fol (1) foles (8) fooles (1)
A.Pr.36   Fonden hem fantasies & *foolis* make,
A.10.58   In ȝonge fauntes & *folis*, wiþ hem failiþ Inwyt,

A.10.64   Ac in fauntis ne in *folis* þe [fend] haþ no miȝt
A.11.6   To flatereris or to *folis* þat frentyk ben of wittis,'
A.11.8   Wiþ suche wise wordis to wisse any *foolis*!
B.Pr.36   [Fonden] hem fantasies and *fooles* hem makeþ,
B. 9.68   [Fauntes and] *fooles* þat fauten Inwit,
B.10.6   To flatereres or to *fooles* þat frenetike ben of wittes',
B.10.39   But þoo þat feynen hem *foolis*, and wiþ faityng libbeþ
B.11.68   And for I seide þus to freres a *fool* þei me helden,
B.13.422   That fedeþ *fooles* sages, flatereris and lieris,
B.13.429   Riȝt so flatereris and *fooles* arn þe fendes disciples
B.13.443   The pouere for a *fool* sage sittyng at þ[i] table,
B.13.454   [There] flateres and *fooles* þoruȝ hir foule wordes
B.15.3   And so my wit weex and wanyed til I a *fool* weere.
B.15.10   That folk helden me a *fool*; and in þat folie I raued
B.20.61   And alle hise as wel as hym, saue oonly *fooles*;
B.20.62   Whiche *foolis* were wel [gladdere] to deye
B.20.74   'I conseille', quod Conscience þo, 'cometh wiþ me, ye *fooles*,
B.20.77   *Fooles* fro þise fendes lymes, for Piers loue þe Plowman.'
C.Pr.37   Fyndeth out foule fantasyes and *foles* hem maketh
C. 7.82   That feden *foel* sages, flateres and lyares
C. 7.89   Ryht so flateres and *fooles* aren þe fendes procuratours
C. 7.103   The pore for a *f[o]l* sage sittynge at thy table,
C. 7.114   There flaterers and *foles* with here foule wordes
C.10.183   Ac fauntokynes and *foles* þat fauten inwit
C.11.6   To eny *foel* or to flaterere or to frentike peple,'
C.11.248   For lewed folk, goddes *foles* and his fre bestes:
C.12.211   How god, as þe gospelle telleth, gyueth [hym] *foel* to name,
C.22.61   And alle hise as wel as hym, saue onelich *foles*;
C.22.62   [Whiche *foles*] were wel gladere to deye
C.22.74   'Y consail', quod Consi[e]nce tho, 'cometh with me, ȝe *foles*,
C.22.77   *Foles* fro this fendes lymes for [Peres] loue the [plouhman].'

foold > fold; foon > foo; foond > fynden; foorþe > ford

foot n *fot n.* A 8 feet (2) fet (2) fete (1) foote (1) fote (2); B 15 feet (7) foot (7) foote (1); C 8 feet (3) foet (3) fote (2)
A. 2.132   Þat symonye & cyuyle shulde on here *fet* gange.
A. 2.144   As fo[bb]is & faitours þat on here *feet* iotten.'
A. 4.73   'He sh[al] not þis seue ȝer se hise *feet* ones!'
A. 5.6   Þat I ne miȝte ferþere a *fote* for defaute of slepyng.
A. 6.118   Shulde I neuere ferþere a *foote* for no freris preching.'
A. 7.2   Þat miȝte folewe vs iche *fote* [forto] we were þere.'
A.11.215   Godis flessh, & his *fet*, & hise fyue woundis
A.12.47   And þanne I kneled on my knes and kyste her [*fete*] sone,
B. 2.168   For Symonye and Cyuylle sholde on hire *feet* gange.
B. 2.183   As [fobbes] and Faitours þat on hire *feet* [iotten].'
B. 4.86   '[He shal] noȝt þise seuen yer seen his *feet* ones!'
B. 5.6   That I ne myȝte ferþer a *foot* for defaute of slepynge.
B. 5.633   Sholde I neuere ferþere a *foot* for no freres prechyng.'
B. 6.2   That [myȝte] folwen vs ech *foot*': þus þis folk hem mened.
B.12.245   And his flessh is foul flessh and his *feet* boþe,
B.12.259   By þe po *feet* is vnderstande, as I haue lerned in Auynet,
B.13.371   That a *foot* lond or a forow fecchen I wolde
B.15.300   That ne fil to hir *feet* and fawned wiþ þe tailles;
B.15.453   Til it be fulled vnder *foot* or in fullyng stokkes,
B.16.228   Wessh hir *feet* and wiped hem, and afterward þei eten
B.16.245   And called me *foot* of his feiþ, his folk for to saue
B.17.57   He myȝte neiþer steppe ne stande ne stere *foot* ne handes
B.17.108   For he halt hym hardier on horse þan he þat is [on] *foote*.
C. 1.119   For theder as þe fende fly his *fote* for to sette,
C. 2.196   As fobbes and faytours þat on here *feet* rennen.'
C. 4.82   Ther he sholde nat in seuene ȝer see his *feet* [ones].
C. 6.268   That a *foet* lond or a forw fecchen y wolde
C. 7.286   [Sh]olde y neuere forthere [a] *foet* for no frere prechynge.'
C. 7.308   That myhte folowe vs vch *fote* for drede of mysturnynge.'
C.18.243   Wosch he[re] *feet* and wypede hem and afturward they eten.
C.19.56   For he ne myhte stepe ne stande ne stere *foet* ne handes

for prep *for prep.* A 222; B 571 for (570) fore (1); C 608 for (605) fore (3)
A.Pr.26   Al *for* loue of oure lord lyuede wel streite
A.Pr.30   *For* no likerous liflode wile here likam to plese.
A.Pr.42   Flite þanne *for* here foode, fouȝten at þe ale.
A.Pr.56   Prechinge þe peple *for* profit of þe wombe;
A.Pr.58   *For* coueitise of copis construide it as þei wolde.
A.Pr.83   To synge *for* symonye for siluer is swete.
A.Pr.86   Pleten *for* penis & [poundide] þe lawe,
A.Pr.87   A[c] nouȝt *for* loue of oure lord vnlose here lippes ones.
A. 1.24   Þat oþer is mete at meel *for* myseise of þiselue;
A. 1.27   For loth, in his lyf dayes, *for* lykyng of drink
A. 1.56   Þanne I fraynide hire faire *for* him faire made,
A. 1.78   Preiȝede hire pitously [to] preiȝe *for* my sennes,
A. 1.101   And neuere leue h[e]m *for* !oue ne lacching of ȝeftis;
A. 1.116   *For* pride þat he put out his peyne haþ non ende.

A. 1.142	Mekliche *for* oure misdedis to amende vs alle.
A. 2.2	And seide, 'mercy madame, *for* marie loue of heuene
A. 2.32	And become a good man *for* any coueitise, I rede.'
A. 2.37	And feffe mede þer[myd] in mariage *for* euere.
A. 2.41	Was piȝt vp a pauyloun proud *for* þe nones,
A. 2.44	*For* sisours, for somenours, for selleris, *for* beggeris,
A. 2.44	For sisours, *for* somenours, for selleris, *for* beggeris,
A. 2.44	For sisours, for somenours, *for* selleris, *for* beggeris,
A. 2.44	For sisours, for somenours, for selleris, *for* beggeris,
A. 2.45	*For* lerid, for lewid, for laboureris of þropis,
A. 2.45	For lerid, *for* lewid, for laboureris of þropis,
A. 2.45	For lerid, for lewid, *for* laboureris of þropis,
A. 2.50	In foreward þat falshed shal fynde hire *for* euere,
A. 2.59	To be present in pride *for* pouere [or for] riche,
A. 2.59	To be present in pride for pouere [or *for*] riche,
A. 2.60	Wiþ þe Erldom of enuye *for* euere to laste,
A. 2.69	Ȝeldinge *for* þis þing at o ȝeris ende
A. 2.97	She miȝte kisse þe king *for* cosyn ȝif he[o] wolde.
A. 2.107	Til he hadde siluer *for* his selis & signes.
A. 2.114	To false & to fauel *for* here faire ȝeftis,
A. 2.121	Iuggen ȝow ioyntly in ioye *for* euere'.
A. 2.126	Þanne car[i]de hy *fo[r]* capelis to carien hem þider;
A. 2.139	Paulynes peple, *for* pleyntes in constorie,
A. 2.161	To atache þis tiraunt[is] *'for* any tresour, I hote;
A. 2.162	Feteriþ falsnesse faste *for* any skynes ȝeftis,
A. 2.166	Þat holy chirche *for* hem worþ harmid for euere;
A. 2.166	Þat holy chirche for hem worþ harmid *for* euere;
A. 2.168	Er he be put on þe pillorie, *for* any preyour, I hote.'
A. 2.171	And bad hym fle *for* fer & hise feris alle.
A. 2.172	Þanne fal[s]nesse *for* feer fleiȝ to þe Freris;
A. 2.179	He was nowhere welcome *for* his many talis,
A. 2.184	And ȝaf pardoun *for* panis poundmel aboute.
A. 2.192	F[or] knowing of comeris copide hym as a Frere.
A. 2.195	Alle fledden *for* fer & flowen into hernis;
A. 2.197	Ac trewely to telle heo tremblide *for* fere,
A. 3.18	*For* al consiences cast a[nd] craft as I trowe'.
A. 3.39	I shal assoile þe myabulf *for* a sem of whete.
A. 3.42	Þanne mede *for* hire mysdedis to þat man knelide,
A. 3.80	'For my loue,' quaþ þat lady, 'loue hem ichone,
A. 3.126	And letiþ passe prisoners & paieþ *for* hem ofte,
A. 3.130	And hangiþ hym *for* hattrede þat harmide neuere.
A. 3.149	Þe mase *for* a mene man þeiȝ he mote euere.
A. 3.161	For consience acusiþ þe to cunge [þe] *for* euere.'
A. 3.176	In normandie was he nouȝt anoyed *for* my sake,
A. 3.178	Crope into a caban *for* cold of þi nailes.
A. 3.180	And dreddist to be ded *for* a dym cloud,
A. 3.181	And hastide[st] þe homward *for* hunger of þi wombe.
A. 3.187	Dede hym hoppe *for* hope to haue me at wille.
A. 3.194	To leuen his lordsshipe *for* a litel siluer,
A. 3.199	Mede makiþ hym be louid & *for* a man holde.
A. 3.204	Seruauntis *for* here seruyse, we se wel þe soþe,
A. 3.206	Beggeris *for* here bidding biddiþ of men mede;
A. 3.207	Mynstralis *for* here merþis mede þei asken;
A. 3.212	Alle kyn crafty men craue mede *for* here prentis;
A. 3.223	Loue hem & le[n]e hem *for* oure lordis loue of heuene;
A. 3.232	Þat take mede & money *for* massis þat þei synge,
A. 3.237	It is a permutacioun apertly, a peny[worþ] *for* anoþer.
A. 3.242	Shulde diȝe *for* a dede þat don hadde here eldren
A. 3.249	*For* any mylionis of mone murdre hem ichone,
A. 3.255	And al his sed *for* þat synne [shend]fully ende.
A. 3.257	Þat god hati[de him *for* euere] & alle hise heires aftir.
A. 3.270	Shal no seriaunt *for* þat seruyse were a silk houue,
A. 4.39	I dar not *for* fer of hym fiȝte ne chide.
A. 4.41	Ne no ferþing þerfore *for* nouȝt I couþe plete.
A. 4.45	And takiþ me but a taile *for* ten quarteris otis,
A. 4.47	I am not hardy [*for* hym vnneþe] to loke.'
A. 4.71	[Þat wrong *for* his werkis shulde woo þole,
A. 4.76	And be borugh *for* his bale & b[ig]gen hym bote;
A. 4.84	For I wile wage *for* wrong, he [wile] do so no more.'
A. 4.104	And harlotis holynesse be holde *for* an [heþyng];
A. 4.110	Þat no man go to galis but ȝif he go *for* euere,
A. 4.111	And alle rome renneris, *for* robberis of beȝonde,
A. 4.123	Be vnpunisshit at my power *for* peril of my soule,
A. 4.125	Ne *for* no mede haue mercy but meknesse it made,
A. 4.139	'Whoso wilneþ hire to wyue *for* welþe of hire godis,
A. 4.143	But stari[den *for*] stodyenge [and] stoden as bestis.
A. 5.6	Þat I ne miȝte ferþere a fote *for* defaute of slepyng.
A. 5.13	And prouide þat þise pestilences wern *for* pur synne,
A. 5.15	Was apertly *for* pride & for no poynt ellis.
A. 5.15	Was apertly for pride & *for* no poynt ellis.
A. 5.27	And kep[e] it in hire coffre *for* catel at nede.
A. 5.55	To make mercy *for* his mysdede betwyn god & hym
A. 5.66	His body was bolnid *for* wr[aþþe] þat he bot his lippe[s],
A. 5.84	Ac hadde I maistrie & miȝt I wolde murdre hym *for* euere.
A. 5.86	To preye *for* þe peple as þe prest techiþ,
A. 5.87	[*For* pilgrymes, for palmers, for all þe peple] aftir,
A. 5.87	[For pilgrymes, *for* palmers, for all þe peple] aftir,
A. 5.87	[For pilgrymes, for palmers, *for* all þe peple] aftir,
A. 5.99	[Þat] al my brest bolniþ *for* bittir of my galle.
A. 5.104	'Sorewe *for* synne sauiþ wel manye.'
A. 5.115	*For* sum tyme I seruide symme at þe nok
A. 5.135	*For* laboureris & louȝ folk þat lay be h[y]mselue;
A. 5.138	A galoun *for* a grote, god wot no lasse,
A. 5.156	And a [ferþingworþ] of [fenelsed] *for* fastyng dayes.'
A. 5.179	And nempniþ hym *for* a noumpere þat no debate nere.
A. 5.208	*For* his liþer lif þat he lyued hadde,
A. 5.209	And auowide to faste, *for* hungir or þrist:
A. 5.213	Sleuþe *for* sorewe fil doun a swowe
A. 5.217	"I am sory *for* my synne," sey to þiseluen,
A. 5.221	And made auowe tofore god *for* his foule slouþe;
A. 5.238	And þou haddist mercy on þat man *for* memento sake,
A. 5.240	To haue helle *for* euere ȝif þat hope nere.
A. 5.243	But *for* þi muchel mercy mytygacioun I beseche;
A. 5.252	Wepynge & weylyng *for* here wykkide dedis;
A. 6.19	And souȝt goode seintes *for* my soule hele.'
A. 6.28	And dede me sure hym [siþþe] to serue hym *for* euere;
A. 6.45	'I nolde fonge a ferþing *for* seint Thomas shryne,
A. 6.57	So shalt þou se swere nouȝt but it be *for* nede,
A. 6.69	Loke þou plukke no plant[e] þere *for* peril of þi soule.
A. 6.71	[And] loke þat þou leiȝe nouȝt *for* no manis biddyng.
A. 6.86	And am sory *for* my synnes & so shal I euere
A. 6.118	Shulde I neuere ferþere a foote *for* no freris preching.'
A. 7.9	'Summe shal sewe þe sak *for* shedyng of þe whete;
A. 7.15	Caste hem cloþis *for* cold for so wile treuþe.
A. 7.17	As longe as I lyue *for* þe lordis loue of heuene.
A. 7.20	Chesiblis *for* chapellis chirches to honoure.
A. 7.27	I shal swynken & sweten & sowe *for* vs boþe,
A. 7.28	A[nd] ek laboure *for* þi loue al my lif tyme,
A. 7.55	Hise cokeris & his cuffis *for* cold of his nailes,
A. 7.65	And robyn þe ribaudour *for* hise rusty woordis.
A. 7.85	[I] payede hym prestly *for* peril of my soule.
A. 7.94	And ben his pilgrym at þe plouȝ *for* pore menis sake.
A. 7.112	And þeiȝ ȝe deiȝe *for* doel þe deuil haue þat recche!'
A. 7.117	Ac we preye *for* ȝow, peris, & for ȝoure plouȝ boþe,
A. 7.117	Ac we preye for ȝow, peris, & *for* ȝoure plouȝ boþe,
A. 7.125	Ȝe eten þat [hy] shulde ete þat eren *for* vs alle.
A. 7.171	Faitours *for* fer flowen into bernis
A. 7.174	For a potel of pe[s]is þat peris hadde mad
A. 7.183	Al *for* coueitise of his corn to [cacche] awey hungir.
A. 7.192	And *for* defaute of foode þus faste hy werchiþ.
A. 7.198	'Here now,' quaþ hungir, '& holde it *for* a wisdom:
A. 7.201	And [a]baue hem wiþ b[e]nes *for* bollnyng of here wombe,
A. 7.206	Counforte hem wiþ þi catel *for* cristis loue of heuene.
A. 7.213	'I wolde not greue god,' quaþ peris, '*for* al þe gold on ground.
A. 7.218	& labouren *for* þi liflode, & so oure lord hiȝte;
A. 7.253	Þat fisik shal his furrid hood *for* his foode selle,
A. 7.267	A lof of benis & bren ybake *for* my children,
A. 7.281	Þanne þise folk *for* fer fetten hym manye
A. 7.295	And chaud, & pluys chaud, *for* chillyng of h[ere] mawe.
A. 8.4	*For* hym & for hise heires eueremore aftir,
A. 8.4	For hym & *for* hise heires eueremore aftir,
A. 8.33	Fynde suche here foode *for* oure lordis loue of heuene,
A. 8.42	Þanne were marchauntis merye; many wepe *for* ioye,
A. 8.43	And ȝaf wille *for* his writyng wollene cloþis;
A. 8.49	Ac he þat spendiþ his speche & spekiþ *for* þe pore
A. 8.52	Ac *for* oure lordis loue lawe for hym shewiþ,
A. 8.52	Ac for oure lordis loue lawe *for* hym shewiþ,
A. 8.57	Þise þre *for* þrallis ben þrowe among vs alle
A. 8.60	Þat any mede of mene men *for* motyng resceyueþ.
A. 8.65	And lyuen in loue & [in] lawe, *for* here louȝ herte
A. 8.77	And gon & faiten wiþ here fauntis *for* eueremore aftir.
A. 8.87	*For* loue of here louȝ herte oure lord haþ hem grauntid
A. 8.101	And piers *for* [pure] tene pulde it assondir
A. 8.132	And *for* peris loue þe plouȝman wel pensif in herte,
A. 8.133	*For* þat I saiȝ slepyng ȝif it so be miȝte.
A. 8.145	'Beau fitȝ,' quaþ his fadir, '*for* defaute we shuln,
A. 8.146	I myself & my sones, seke þe *for* nede.
A. 8.164	It is not so sikir *for* þe soule, certis, as is do wel.
A. 8.178	I ne wolde ȝiue *for* þi patent on pye hele.
A. 9.32	Þere were þe manis lif lost *for* lacchesse of hymselue.
A. 9.96	But dobest bede *for* hem abide þere for euere.
A. 9.96	But dobest bede for hem abide þere *for* euere.
A.10.43	*For* loue of þat lady þat lif is ynempnid.
A.10.65	*For* no werk þat þei werche, wykkide oþer ellis.
A.10.66	Ac þe fadir & þe Frendis *for* fauntis shuln be blamid
A.10.73	And cheuissh[en] hym *for* any charge whan he childhod passiþ,

A.10.81	Salamon it seide *for* a soþ tale:
A.10.82	*For* doute men doþ þe bet; dred is such a maister
A.10.85	Þanne is dobet to ben ywar *for* betyng of þe ȝarde,
A.10.102	Þou miȝtest lese þi louȝnesse *for* a litel pride.
A.10.111	And *for* wisdom is writen & witnessid in chirches:
A.10.115	To be blissid *for* þi beryng, [ȝ]e, b[e]ggere þeiȝ þou were.
A.10.173	*For* loue of here louȝnesse oure lord ȝiueþ hem grace
A.10.173	Alle shuln deiȝe *for* his dedis be dounes & hilles,
A.10.183	*For* coueitise of catel vnkyndely be maried.
A.10.188	Or wedde any wydewe *for* any wele of godis,
A.10.209	*For* coueitise of catel or of kynrede riche,
A.10.209	Þat oþere gatis ben geten *for* gadelynges ben holden;
A.11.46	Boþe *for* hungir & for þrest, & for chele quak[e];
A.11.46	Boþe for hungir & *for* þrest, & for chele quak[e];
A.11.46	Boþe for hungir & for þrest, & *for* chele quak[e];
A.11.69	And alle here seed *for* here synne þe same wo suffride?"
A.11.72	Ac austyn þe olde *for* alle suche prechide;
A.11.73	And *for* suche tale telleris suche a teme shewide:
A.11.79	And *for* his muchel mercy to amende vs here.
A.11.96	Ac *for* no carping I couþe, ne knelyng to þe ground,
A.11.104	'For þi meknesse, man,' quaþ she, 'and for þi mylde speche,
A.11.104	'For þi meknesse, man,' quaþ she, 'and *for* þi mylde speche,
A.11.132	Gramer *for* girles I garte ferst write,
A.11.154	And seide it hymself in ensaumple *for* þe beste:
A.11.186	Wiþ any trewe trauaille toille *for* here foode,
A.11.200	And haþ possessions & pluralites *for* pore menis sake;
A.11.208	Þei diȝe *for* þe drouȝte, whanne þei dreiȝe lengen;
A.11.226	Kinghod & kniȝthod, *for* auȝt I can aspie,
A.11.238	And *for* his lele beleue, whanne he his lif tyneþ,
A.11.257	Eche man *for* his misdede but mercy it make.'
A.11.258	–Ȝet am I neuere þe ner *for* nouȝt I haue walkid
A.11.263	Or ellis [vn]writen *for* wykkid as witnessiþ þe gospel:
A.11.273	*For* alle cunnyng clerkis siþþe crist ȝede on erþe
A.11.277	And *for* here werkis & here wyt wende to pyne,
A.11.286	Wiþoute penaunce of purcatorie to haue paradis *for* euere.
A.11.304	Seide þis *for* a sarmoun, so me god helpe:
A.12.39	To be hure man ȝif I most *for* eueremore after,
A.12.73	*For* þe myssyng of mete no mesour I coude,
A.12.76	*For* gronyng of my guttys I durst gon no ferther].
A.12.90	But lyue as þis lyf is ordeyned *for* the.
A.12.111	God *for* his goudnesse gif hem swyche happes
A.12.116	Marie moder and may, *for* man þou byseke
B.Pr.26	Al *for* loue of oure lord lyueden [wel] streyte
B.Pr.30	*For* no likerous liflode hire likame to plese.
B.Pr.42	[Flite þanne] *for* hire foode, fouȝten at þe ale.
B.Pr.59	Prechynge þe peple *for* profit of [þe wombe];
B.Pr.61	*For* coueitise of copes construwed it as þei wolde.
B.Pr.86	[To] syngen *for* symonie for siluer is swete.
B.Pr.90	Prechen and praye *for* hem, and þe pouere fede,
B.Pr.119	And *for* profit of al þe peple Plowmen ordeyned
B.Pr.127	And *for* þi riȝtful rulyng be rewarded in heuene'.
B.Pr.148	Comen to a counseil *for* þe commune profit.
B.Pr.152	'For doute of diuerse d[e]des we dar noȝt wel loke,
B.Pr.159	Seide *for* a souereyn [salue] to [hem alle].
B.Pr.169	And knytten it on a coler *for* oure commune profit
B.Pr.177	Ther ne was Raton in þe route, *for* al þe Reaume of Fraunce,
B.Pr.197	For may no renk þer reste haue *for* Ratons by nyȝte,]
B.Pr.202	I seye *for* me', quod þe Mous, 'I se so muchel after,
B.Pr.213	Pleteden *for* penyes and pounde[d] þe lawe
B.Pr.214	[Ac] noȝt *for* loue of oure lord vnlose hire lippes ones.
B. 1.24	[That oþer is] mete at meel *for* mysese of þiselue;
B. 1.27	For Lot, in hise lifdayes, *for* likynge of drynke,
B. 1.58	Thanne I frayned hire faire *for* hym þat [hire] made,
B. 1.80	Preide hire pitously [to] preye *for* my synnes;
B. 1.103	And neuere leue hem *for* loue ne lacchynge of [yiftes];_
B. 1.115	Into a deep derk helle to dwelle þere *for* euere;
B. 1.127	*For* pride þat he putte out his peyne haþ noon ende.
B. 1.151	And lered it Moyses *for* þe leueste þyng and moost lik to heuene,
B. 1.162	Vpon man *for* hise mysdedes þe mercyment he taxeþ.
B. 1.168	Mekely *for* oure mysdedes to amenden vs alle.
B. 2.2	And seide 'mercy, madame, *for* Marie loue of heuene
B. 2.35	That he shal lese *for* hire loue a l[i]ppe of Caritatis.
B. 2.51	And lat no conscience acombre þee *for* coueitise of Mede.'
B. 2.68	Thei assented *for* siluer to seye as boþe wolde.
B. 2.76	That Mede is ymaried moore *for* hire goodes
B. 2.77	Than *for* any vertue or fairnesse or any free kynde.
B. 2.103	A dwellynge wiþ þe deuel and dampned be *for* euere.
B. 2.105	Yeldynge *for* þis þyng at one [yeres ende]
B. 2.133	[She] myȝte kisse þe kyng *for* cosyn and she wolde.
B. 2.143	Til he hadde siluer *for* his [seles] and [signes of] Notaries.
B. 2.150	To Fals and to Fauel *for* hire faire ȝiftes,
B. 2.157	Iuggen yow ioyntly in ioie *for* euere'.
B. 2.162	Ac þanne cared þei *for* caples to carien hem þider;

B. 2.178	Paulynes pryuees *for* pleintes in Consistorie
B. 2.200	To attachen þo Tyrauntȝ '*for* any [tresor], I hote;
B. 2.201	Fettreþ [Falsnesse faste] *for* any kynnes ȝiftes,
B. 2.205	That holy chirche *for* hem worþ harmed for euere.]
B. 2.205	That holy chirche for hem worþ harmed *for* euere.]
B. 2.207	Er he be put on þe Pillory *for* any preyere I hote.'_
B. 2.212	And bad hym fle *for* fere and hise [feeres] alle.
B. 2.213	[Thanne] Falsnesse *for* fere fleiȝ to þe Freres;
B. 2.220	He was nowher welcome *for* his manye tales,
B. 2.225	And [gaf] pardoun *for* pens poundemele aboute.
B. 2.233	*For* knowynge of comeres coped hym as a Frere.
B. 2.236	Alle fledden *for* fere and flowen into hernes.
B. 2.238	Ac trewely to telle she trembled *for* [fere],
B. 3.19	*For* al Consciences cast [and] craft, as I trowe'.
B. 3.40	I shal assoille þee myself *for* a seem of whete,
B. 3.43	Thanne Mede *for* hire mysdedes to þat man kneled
B. 3.62	Do peynten and portraye [who] paie[d] *for* þe makynge
B. 3.91	'For my loue', quod þat lady, 'loue hem echone,
B. 3.137	[And] leteþ passe prisoners and paieþ *for* hem ofte,
B. 3.141	And hangeþ h[y]m *for* hatrede þat harm[e]de neuere.
B. 3.160	The maȝe *for* a mene man þouȝ he mote euere!
B. 3.174	For Conscience accuseþ þee to congeien þee *for* euere.'
B. 3.189	In Normandie was he noȝt noyed *for* my sake,
B. 3.191	Crope into a Cabane *for* cold of þi nayles;
B. 3.193	And dreddest to be ded *for* a dym cloude,
B. 3.194	And [hastedest þee] homward *for* hunger of þi wombe.
B. 3.200	And dide hem hoppe *for* hope to haue me at wille.
B. 3.207	To leuen his lordshipe *for* a litel siluer,
B. 3.212	Mede makeþ hym biloued and *for* a man holden.
B. 3.217	Ser[u]auntȝ *for* hire seruyce, we seeþ wel þe soþe,
B. 3.219	Beggeres *for* hir biddynge bidden [of] men Mede;
B. 3.220	Mynstrales *for* hir myrþe Mede þei aske;
B. 3.225	Alle kynne craft[y] men crauen Mede *for* hir Prentices;
B. 3.253	That taken Mede and moneie *for* masses þat þei syngeþ,
B. 3.258	It is a permutacion apertly, a penyworþ *for* anoþer.
B. 3.263	Sholden deye *for* a dede þat doon hadde hire eldres.
B. 3.271	*For* Mede he for monee loke þow destruye it.
B. 3.271	For Mede ne *for* monee loke þow destruye it.
B. 3.277	And al his seed *for* þat synne shenfulliche ende.
B. 3.279	That god hated hym *for* euere and alle hise heires after.
B. 3.295	Shal no sergeant *for* [þat] seruice were a silk howue,
B. 3.296	Ne no pelure in his [panelon] *for* pledynge at þe barre;
B. 3.328	And Sarȝynes *for* þat siȝte shul synge Gloria in excelsis &c,
B. 3.346	This text þat ye han told were [trewe] *for* lordes,
B. 4.38	For [þei wolde do *for* a dyner or a doȝeyne capons
B. 4.39	Moore þan *for* loue of oure lord or alle hise leeue Seintes.
B. 4.52	I dar noȝt *for* fere of h[y]m fiȝte ne chide.
B. 4.54	Ne no ferþyng þerfore *for* [n]ouȝt I koude plede.
B. 4.58	And takeþ me but a taille *for* ten quarters Otes;
B. 4.60	I am noȝt hardy *for* hym vnneþe to loke.'
B. 4.84	That wrong *for* hise werkes sholde wo þolie,
B. 4.89	And be borȝ *for* his bale and buggen hym boote,
B. 4.97	For I wol wage *for* wrong, he wol do so na moore.'
B. 4.118	And harlottes holynesse be holden *for* an [heþyng];
B. 4.127	That no man go to Galis but if he go *for* euere.
B. 4.128	And alle Rome renneres, *for* Robberes [of] biyonde,
B. 4.133	Prouysour or preest or penaunt *for* hise synnes.
B. 4.140	Ben vnpunysshed [at] my power *for* peril of my soule,
B. 4.142	Ne *for* no Mede haue mercy but mekenesse it ma[de],
B. 4.150	Al to construe þis clause *for* þe kynges profit,
B. 4.151	Ac noȝt *for* confort of þe commune ne for þe kynges soule.
B. 4.151	Ac noȝt for confort of þe commune ne *for* þe kynges soule.
B. 4.163	'Whoso wilneþ hire to wif *for* welþe of hire goodes,
B. 4.164	But he be knowe *for* a Cokewold kut of my nose.'
B. 5.6	That I ne myȝte ferþer a foot *for* defaute of slepynge,
B. 5.13	He preued þat þise pestilences were *for* pure synne,
B. 5.15	Was pertliche *for* pride and for no point ellis.
B. 5.15	Was pertliche for pride and *for* no point ellis.
B. 5.27	And kepe it in hire cofre *for* catel at nede.
B. 5.36	Ne *for* no poustee of pestilence plese hem noȝt out of reson.
B. 5.72	To maken mercy *for* hi[s] mysded[e] bitwene god and [hym]
B. 5.83	His body was [b]ollen *for* wraþe þat he boot hise lippes,
B. 5.90	'I wolde ben yshryue', quod þis sherewe, 'and I *for* shame dorste.
B. 5.104	Ac hadde I maistrie and myȝt [I wolde murþere hym *for* euere].
B. 5.106	[To] preye þe peple as þe preest techeþ,
B. 5.107	*For* Pilgrymes, for Palmeres, for al þe peple after,
B. 5.107	For Pilgrymes, *for* Palmeres, for al þe peple after,
B. 5.107	For Pilgrymes, for Palmeres, *for* al þe peple after,
B. 5.120	That al my [brest] bolneþ *for* bitter of my galle.
B. 5.127	'Sorwe [*for*] synn[e] is sauacion of soules.'
B. 5.167	That no Prioresse were preest, *for* þat he [purueiede];
B. 5.192	Wel sidder þan his chyn; þei chyueled *for* elde;
B. 5.199	*For* som tyme I serued Symme atte [Nok]

B. 5.219   *For* laborers and lowe folk þat lay by hymselue.
B. 5.222   A galon *for* a grote, god woot no lesse,
B. 5.241   And lene it *for* loue of þe cros, to legge a wed and lese it.
B. 5.250   'Lentestow euere lordes *for* loue of hire mayntenaunce?'
B. 5.253   That payed neuere *for* his prentishode noȝt a peire gloues.'
B. 5.254   'Hastow pite on pouere men þat [*for* pure nede] borwe?"
B. 5.256   That wolde kille hem if he cacche hem myȝte *for* coueitise of hir
         skynnes
B. 5.267   Ne haue a peny to my pitaunce, [*for* pyne of my soule],
B. 5.268   *For* þe beste book in oure hous, þeiȝ brent gold were þe leues,
B. 5.291   Bisette it hymself as best [be] *for* þi soule.
B. 5.292   For he shal answere *for* þe at þe heiȝe dome,
B. 5.293   *For* þee and for many mo þat man shal yeue a rekenyng:
B. 5.293   For þee and *for* many mo þat man shal yeue a rekenyng:
B. 5.305   A ferþyngworþ of fenel seed *for* fastynge dayes.'
B. 5.330   And nempned hym *for* a nounpere þat no debat nere.
B. 5.376   *For* loue of tales in Tauernes [to] drynke þe moore I [hyed;
B. 5.380   *For* his luþer lif þat he lyued hadde,
B. 5.381   And auowed to faste *for* hunger or þurste:
B. 5.399   Ne riȝt sory *for* my synnes yet, [so þee I], was I neuere.
B. 5.445   "I am sory *for* my synn[e]", seye to þiselue,
B. 5.449   And made auow tofore god *for* his foule sleuþe:
B. 5.466   And haddest mercy on þat man *for* Memento sake,
B. 5.469   But *for* þi muchel mercy mitigacion I biseche:
B. 5.478   'I shal biseche *for* alle synfulle oure Saueour of grace
B. 5.483   And *for* þe beste as I bileue whateuere þe book telleþ:
B. 5.488   On good fryday *for* mannes sake at ful tyme of þe daye;
B. 5.491   The sonne *for* sorwe þerof lees [s]iȝt [for] a tyme.
B. 5.491   The sonne for sorwe þerof lees [s]iȝt [*for*] a tyme.
B. 5.508   That alle Seintes [*for* synful] songen at ones
B. 5.531   And souȝt goode Seintes *for* me soul[e] hel[e].'
B. 5.540   And diden me suren hym [siþþen] to seruen hym *for* euere,
B. 5.558   'I nolde fange a ferþyng *for* Seint Thomas Shryne;
B. 5.570   So shaltow se swere-noȝt-but-it-be-*for*-nede.'
B. 5.582   Loke þow plukke no plaunte þere *for* peril of þi soule.
B. 5.584   In-[no]-manere-ellis-noȝt-*for*-no-mannes-biddyng.
B. 5.595   Grace hatte þe gateward, a good man *for* sobe.
B. 5.599   And am sory *for* my synnes and so [shal I] euere
B. 5.632   'Wite god', quod a waf[ferer], 'wiste I þis *for* soþe
B. 5.633   Sholde I neuere ferþer a foot *for* no freres prechyng.'
B. 6.9   'Somme shul sowe þe sak *for* shedyng of þe Whete.
B. 6.12   Chesibles *for* Chapeleyns chirches to honoure.
B. 6.16   Casteþ hem cloþes [*for* cold] for so [wol] truþe.
B. 6.18   As longe as I lyue, *for* þe lordes loue of heuene.
B. 6.25   I shal swynke and swete and sowe *for* vs boþe,
B. 6.26   And [ek] labour[e] *for* þi loue al my lif tyme,
B. 6.60   [Hise] cokeres and [hise] coffes *for* cold of [hise] nailes,
B. 6.73   And Robyn þe Ribaudour *for* hise rusty wordes.
B. 6.93   I paide [hym] prestly *for* peril of my soule;
B. 6.102   And ben his pilgrym atte plow *for* pouere mennes sake.
B. 6.120   And þouȝ ye deye *for* doel þe deuel haue þat recch[e]!'
B. 6.125   Ac we preie *for* yow, Piers, and for youre plowȝ boþe,
B. 6.125   Ac we preie for yow, Piers, and *for* youre plowȝ boþe,
B. 6.183   Faitours *for* fere flowen into Bernes
B. 6.186   *For* a pot[el] of peses þat Piers hadde ymaked
B. 6.193   For þat was bake *for* bayard was boote for many hungry;
B. 6.193   For þat was bake for bayard was boote *for* many hungry;
B. 6.194   And many a beggere *for* benes buxum was to swynke,
B. 6.195   And ech a pouere man wel apaied to haue pesen *for* his hyre,
B. 6.206   And *for* defaute of foode þis folk is at my wille.
B. 6.212   'Here now', quod hunger, 'and hoold it *for* a wisdom:
B. 6.215   [And] aba[u]e hem wiþ hunger *for* bollynge of hir womb[e];
B. 6.220   Conforte h[e]m wiþ þi catel *for* cristes loue of heuene;
B. 6.229   'I wolde noȝt greue god', quod Piers, '*for* al þe good on grounde!
B. 6.234   And laboure *for* þi liflode, and so oure lord hiȝte.
B. 6.269   That Phisik shal hi[s] furred ho[od] *for* his fode selle,
B. 6.283   [A lof] of benes and bran ybake *for* my fauntes.
B. 6.297   Thanne pouere folk *for* fere fedden hunger yerne
B. 6.311   And þat chaud and plus chaud *for* chillynge of hir mawe.
B. 6.330   And Dawe þe dykere deye *for* hunger
B. 7.4   *For* hym and for hise heires eueremoore after.
B. 7.4   For hym and *for* hise heires eueremoore after.
B. 7.31   Fynden [swiche] hir foode [*for* oure lordes loue of heuene],
B. 7.38   Thanne were Marchauntȝ murie; manye wepten *for* ioye
B. 7.43   Pledours sholde peynen hem to plede *for* swiche and helpe;
B. 7.44   Princes and prelates sholde paie *for* hire trauaille:
B. 7.45   Ac many a Iustice and Iurour wolde *for* Iohan do moore
B. 7.47   Ac he þat spendeþ his speche and spekeþ *for* þe pouere
B. 7.50   [Ac] *for* oure lordes loue [lawe for hym sheweþ],
B. 7.50   [Ac] for oure lordes loue [lawe *for* hym sheweþ],
B. 7.59   That any Mede of mene men *for* motyng takeþ.
B. 7.63   And lyuen in loue and in lawe, *for* hir lowe hert[e]
B. 7.77   That askeþ *for* his loue þat vs al leneþ:

B. 7.95   And goon [and] faiten with [hire] fauntes *for* eueremoore after.
B. 7.105   *For* loue of hir lowe hert[e] oure lord haþ hem graunted
B. 7.119   And Piers *for* pure tene pulled it [asonder]
B. 7.151   And *for* Piers [loue] þe Plowman [wel] pencif in herte,
B. 7.168   'Beau fitȝ', quod his fader, '*for* defaute we shullen,
B. 7.169   I myself and my sones, seche þee *for* nede.'
B. 7.186   [It] is noȝt so siker *for* þe soule, certes, as is dowel.
B. 8.36   [There] were [þe mannes] lif lost [*for*] lachesse of hymselue.
B. 8.106   But dobest bede *for* hem [abide] þer for euere.
B. 8.106   But dobest bede for hem [abide] þer *for* euere.
B. 9.41   The lettre, *for* al þe lordshipe, I leue, were neuere ymaked.
B. 9.55   *For* loue of þe lady anima þat lif is ynempned.
B. 9.84   A Iew wolde noȝt se a Iew go Ianglyng *for* defaute
B. 9.85   *For* alle þe mebles on þis moolde and he amende it myȝte.
B. 9.91   The commune *for* hir vnkyndenesse, I drede me, shul abye;
B. 9.92   Bisshopes shul be blamed *for* beggeres sake.
B. 9.94   And biddeþ þe beggere go *for* his broke cloþes:
B. 9.97   That dredeþ god, he dooþ wel; þat dredeþ hym *for* loue
B. 9.98   And [dredeþ hym] noȝt *for* drede of vengeaunce dooþ þerfore þe
         bettre;
B. 9.142   Alle shul deye *for* hise dedes by [dounes] and hulles,
B. 9.147   And alle *for* hir [fore]fadres ferden þe werse.
B. 9.160   *For* coueitise of catel vnkyndely ben [maried].
B. 9.167   Or wedden any wodewe *for* [wele] of hir goodes
B. 9.177   *For* coueitise of catel ne of kynrede riche;
B. 9.180   *For* no londes, but for loue, loke ye be wedded
B. 9.180   For no londes, but *for* loue, loke ye be wedded
B. 9.195   [That] oþergates ben geten *for* gedelynges arn holden,
B. 9.10   Harlotes *for* hir harlotrie may haue of hir goodes,
B. 10.30   Boþe afyngred and afurst, and *for* chele quake;
B. 10.60   And prechen at Seint Poules, *for* pure enuye of clerkes,
B. 10.74   Ne sory *for* hire synnes; so is pride woxen
B. 10.76   That girles *for* [oure] giltes he forgrynt hem alle;
B. 10.80   Ne *for* drede of þe deeþ wiþdrawe noȝt hir pride,
B. 10.82   In a pryuee parlour *for* pouere mennes sake,
B. 10.100   That was maad *for* meles men to eten Inne,
B. 10.102   And al hir seed *for* hir synne þe same deeþ suffrede?
B. 10.111   Why sholde we þat now ben *for* þe werkes of Adam
B. 10.115   And *for* his muche mercy to amende [vs] here.
B. 10.126   A[c] *for* no carpyng I kouþe, ne knelyng to þe grounde,
B. 10.143   '*For* þi mekenesse, man', quod she, 'and for þi mylde speche
B. 10.152   'For þi mekenesse, man', quod she, 'and *for* þi mylde speche
B. 10.152   Grammer *for* girles I garte first write,
B. 10.180   To do good *for* goddes loue and gyuen men þat asked,
B. 10.206   For is no science vnder sonne so souereyn *for* þe soule.
B. 10.211   [So] is dobet to suffre *for* þ[i] soules helþe
B. 10.257   And þat is, man, bi þy myȝt, *for* mercies sake,
B. 10.259   Why meuestow þi mood *for* a mote in þi broþeres eiȝe,
B. 10.269   And þe festu is fallen *for* youre defaute
B. 10.283   Offyn and Fynes; *for* hir coueitise
B. 10.287   And be prester at youre preiere þan *for* a pound of nobles,
B. 10.295   And al *for* youre holynesse; haue ye þis in herte.
B. 10.296   Thei deyen *for* drouȝte, whan þei drie [lenge];
B. 10.302   And bete yow, as þe bible telleþ, *for* brekynge of youre rule.
B. 10.323   And þanne shal þe Abbot of Abyngdoun and al his issue *for* euere
B. 10.331   Kynghod [and] knyȝthod, [*for* auȝt] I kan awayte,
B. 10.338   And *for* his lele bileue, whan he þe lif tyneþ,
B. 10.355   For þat crist *for* cristene men deide, and conformed þe lawe
B. 10.358   Is slee noȝt but suffre and [so] *for* þe beste,
B. 10.373   Ech man *for* hi[s] mysded[e] but mercy it [make]." '
B. 10.376   Or ellis vnwriten *for* wikkednesse as holy writ witnesseþ:
B. 10.382   Of hir wordes þei wissen vs *for* wisest as in hir tyme,
B. 10.390   That *for* hir werkes and wit now wonyeþ in pyne,
B. 10.393   That ben Carpenters holy kirk to make *for* cristes owene beestes:
B. 10.416   Wher fo[r loue] a man worþ allowed þere and hise lele werkes,
B. 10.439   Or ellis for his yuel wille and enuye of herte,
B. 10.440   *For* soþest word þat euer god seide was þo he seide Nemo bonus.
B. 10.447   Into þe [parfit] blisse of Paradis *for* hir pure bileue,
B. 10.470   Tho wepte I *for* wo and wraþe of hir speche
B. 11.4   And bad me *for* my contenaunce acounten Clergie liȝte.
B. 11.16   And [festne] þee [in] hir Fraternitee and *for* þe biseke
B. 11.56   And preien *for* þee pol by pol if þow be pecuniosus.'
B. 11.58   And þanne was Fortune my foo *for* al hir faire [biheste],
B. 11.61   And loued me þe lasse *for* my lele speche.
B. 11.69   Falsnesse ne faiterie? *for* somwhat þe Apostle seide
B. 11.92   It is licitum *for* lewed men to [legge] þe soþe
B. 11.96   It falleþ noȝt *for* þat folk no tales to telle
B. 11.99   Neiþer *for* loue [looue] it noȝt ne lakke it for enuye:
B. 11.106   Neiþer for loue [looue] it noȝt ne lakke it *for* enuye:
B. 11.106   Al *for* tene of hir text trembled myn herte,
B. 11.115   That vnderfonged me atte font *for* oon of goddes chosene.
B. 11.118   And bad hem souke *for* synne [saufte] at his breste
B. 11.121   And drynke boote *for* bale, brouke it whoso myȝte.
B. 11.122

B.11.134	*For* hise arerages rewarden hym þere [riȝt] to þe day of dome,
B.11.136	Mercy *for* hise mysdedes wiþ mouþe [or] wiþ herte.'
B.11.140	'Ye? baw *for* bokes!' quod oon was broken out of helle.
B.11.143	*For* an vncristene creature; clerkes wite þe soþe
B.11.147	Sauacion *for* sooþnesse þat he seiȝ in my werkes;
B.11.156	Nouȝt þoruȝ preiere of a pope but *for* his pure truþe
B.11.160	[This matere is merk *for* many, ac men of holy chirche,
B.11.173	But þei ben lerned *for* oure lordes loue, clerkes wite þe soþe
B.11.174	*For* no cause to cacche siluer þerby, ne to be called a maister,
B.11.175	But al *for* loue of oure lord and þe bet to loue þe peple.
B.11.195	Ac *for* þe pouere I shal paie, and pure wel quyte hir trauaille
B.11.196	That ȝyueþ hem mete or moneie [and] loueþ hem *for* my sake.'
B.11.198	[Ac] *for* þe beste ben som riche and some beggeres and pouere.
B.11.230	And as Seint Gregorie seide, *for* mannes soule helþe
B.11.232	Why I meue þis matere is moost *for* þe pouere;
B.11.236	*For* his pouere apparaill and pilgrymes wedes
B.11.257	Preise[n] pouerte *for* best lif if Pacience it folw[e],
B.11.278	To beggeris þat begge and bidden *for* goddes loue.
B.11.284	*For* masses ne for matyns, noȝt hir mete of vsureres,
B.11.284	For masses ne *for* matyns, noȝt hir mete of vsureres,
B.11.285	Ne neiþer kirtel ne cote, þeiȝ þei *for* cold sholde deye,
B.11.291	Thanne nedeþ yow noȝt to [nyme] siluer *for* masses þat ye syngen,
B.11.295	As bifel *for* a knyȝt, or foond hym for his strengþe.
B.11.295	As bifel for a knyȝt, or foond hym *for* his strengþe.
B.11.298	The same I segge *for* soþe by alle swiche preestes
B.11.302	[Moore þan cure] *for* konnyng or 'knowen for clene [of] berynge'.
B.11.302	[Moore þan cure] for konnyng or 'knowen *for* clene [of] berynge'.
B.11.306	The gome þat gloseþ so chartres *for* a goky is holden.
B.11.355	*For* fere of oþere foweles and for wilde beestes.
B.11.355	For fere of oþere foweles and *for* wilde beestes.
B.11.382	Ac he suffreþ *for* som mannes goode, and so is oure bettre.
B.11.416	Ac *for* þyn entremetynge here artow forsake:
B.11.432	Ac whan nede nymeþ hym vp *for* [nede] lest he sterue,
B.12.15	It is but murþe as *for* me to amende my soule.
B.12.17	And bidde *for* hem þat ȝyueþ þee breed, for þer are bokes y[n]owe
B.12.39	Seke þow neuere Seint ferþer *for* no soule helþe.
B.12.71	And namely Clergie *for* cristes loue, þat of Clergie is roote.
B.12.80	Than þe womman þat þere was, and wenten awey *for* shame.
B.12.92	Forþi I counseille þee *for* cristes sake clergie þat þow louye;
B.12.96	And lederes *for* lewed men and for lettred boþe.
B.12.96	And lederes for lewed men and *for* lettred boþe.
B.12.98	Ne countreplede clerkes, I counseille þee *for* euere.
B.12.108	Come *for* al his kynde wit to cristendom and be saued;
B.12.111	Ȝyue mercy *for* hire mysdedes, if men it wole aske
B.12.117	And his sones also *for* þat synne myscheued,
B.12.244	*For* þe trailynge of his tail ouertaken is he soone.
B.12.262	Thus þe Poete preueþ þe pecok *for* hise feþeres;
B.12.274	And þe bettre *for* hir bokes to bidden we ben holden–
B.12.275	That god *for* his grace gyue hir soules reste,
B.12.292	And an hope hangynge þerInne to haue a mede *for* his truþe.
B.13.30	And preyde mete 'p[u]r charite, *for* a pouere heremyte'.
B.13.33	This maister was maad sitte as *for* þe mooste worþi,
B.13.45	But if þei synge *for* þo soules and wepe salte teris:
B.13.75	Taken it *for* his teme and telle it wiþouten glosyng.
B.13.77	And what meschief and maleese crist *for* man þolede,
B.13.93	Is neiþer fissh n[e] flessh, but fode *for* a penaunt.
B.13.117	[That trauailleþ to teche oþere I holde it *for* a dobet].
B.13.142	And so þow lere þe to louye, *for* [þe] lordes loue of heuene,
B.13.147	And but he bowe *for* þis betyng blynd mote he worþe!"
B.13.170	Yeue þee al þat þei may yeue, as þee *for* best yemere;
B.13.189	*For* al þat Pacience me profreþ proud am I litel.
B.13.191	Haþ meued my mood to moorne *for* my synnes.
B.13.194	Hadde noȝt [Marie] Maudeleyne moore *for* a box of salue
B.13.196	And þe poore widewe [purely] *for* a peire of mytes
B.13.235	*For* no breed þat I brynge forþ, saue a benyson on þe sonday
B.13.237	*For* Piers þe Plowman and þat hym profit waiten.
B.13.243	I fynde payn *for* þe pope and prouendre for his palfrey,
B.13.243	I fynde payn for þe pope and prouendre *for* his palfrey,
B.13.248	That he sente me vnder his seel a salue *for* þe pestilence,
B.13.252	*For* hym and for alle hise, founde I þat his pardoun
B.13.252	For hym and *for* alle hise, founde I þat his pardoun
B.13.289	As best *for* his body be to haue a [bold] name;
B.13.292	[Or *for* his crafty konnynge or of clerkes þe wisest,
B.13.304	And segge þyng þat he neuere seiȝ for soþe sweren it;
B.13.332	*For* tales þat I telle no man trusteþ to me.
B.13.359	Lened *for* loue of þe wed and looþ to do truþe,
B.13.385	Mercy *for* my mysdedes, þat I ne moorned moore
B.13.386	*For* losse of good, leue me, þan for likames giltes;
B.13.386	For losse of good, leue me, þan *for* likames giltes;
B.13.404	'And kauȝte siknesse somtyme *for* my [surfetes] ofte
B.13.410	[Is whan men] moorneþ noȝt *for* hise mysdedes, ne makeþ no sorwe;
B.13.437	And *for* loue of [hir] lorde liþeþ hem at festes;
B.13.443	The pouere *for* a fool sage sittyng at þ[i] table,
B.13.447	And a blynd man *for* a bourdeour, or a bedrede womman
B.14.9	And [siþþe] shryuen of þe preest, þat [*for* my synnes gaf me]
B.14.11	Al *for* coueitise of my cristendom in clennesse to kepen it.
B.14.30	And flour to fede folk wiþ as best be *for* þe soule;
B.14.37	Vitailles of grete vertues *for* alle manere beestes
B.14.52	Or whan þow clomsest *for* cold or clyngest for drye.
B.14.52	Or whan þow clomsest for cold or clyngest *for* drye.
B.14.57	Darstow neuere care *for* corn ne cloþ ne for drynke,
B.14.57	Darstow neuere care for corn ne cloþ ne *for* drynke,
B.14.80	Vengeaunce fil vpon hem *for* hir vile synnes;
B.14.89	And surgiens *for* dedly synnes whan shrift of mouþe failleþ.
B.14.101	There is Charite þe chief, chaumbrere *for* god hymselue.'
B.14.114	And makest hem wel neiȝ meke and mylde *for* defaute,
B.14.138	What he were worþi *for* his werk and what he haþ deserued,
B.14.139	And noȝt to fonge bifore *for* drede of disalowyng.
B.14.153	And alle þat doon hir deuoir wel han double hire *for* hir trauaille,
B.14.161	And yet is wynter *for* hem worse, for weetshoed þei [gange],
B.14.177	Wo in wynter tymes *for* wantynge of cloþes,
B.14.201	Forþi cristene sholde be in commune riche, noon coueitous *for* hymselue.
B.14.215	*For* his pouerte and pacience a perpetuel blisse:
B.14.222	And buxom at hi[s] biddyn[g] *for* his broke loues,
B.14.235	So *for* his glotonie and his greete sleuþe he haþ a greuous penaunce,
B.14.236	That is welawo whan he wakeþ and wepeþ *for* colde,
B.14.237	And som tyme *for* his synnes; so he is neuere murie
B.14.252	A straw *for* þe stuwes! [it] stoode noȝt, I trowe,
B.14.264	And *for* goddes loue leueþ al and lyueþ as a beggere.
B.14.265	And as a mayde *for* mannes loue hire moder forsakeþ,
B.14.270	Moore *for* coueitise of [catel] þan kynde loue of boþe–
B.14.303	And *for* þe [lewde] euere [yliche] a lemman of alle clennesse:
B.14.317	For pacience is payn *for* pouerte hymselue,
B.14.319	Thus lered me a lettred man *for* oure lordes loue, Seint Austyn.
B.14.320	A blessed lif wiþouten bisynesse *for* body and soule:
B.14.324	I ne hadde be deed and doluen *for* dowelis sake!
B.14.333	Ne neiþer sherte ne shoon, saue *for* shame one
B.15.5	And lete me *for* a lorel and looþ to reuerencen
B.15.15	If he were cristes creature [*for* cristes loue] me to tellen.
B.15.51	*For* swich a lust and likyng Lucifer fel from heuene:
B.15.79	Moore *for* pompe þan for pure charite; þe peple woot þe soþe.
B.15.79	Moore for pompe þan *for* pure charite; þe peple woot þe soþe.
B.15.81	And reuerencen þe riche þe raþer *for* hir siluer:
B.15.91	I shal tellen it *for* truþes sake; take hede whoso likeþ.
B.15.104	And be kynde as bifel *for* clerkes and curteise of cristes goodes,
B.15.109	And amende[n] hem þat [þei] mysdoon moore *for* youre ensaumples
B.15.126	Hadde he neuere [saued] siluer þerto [*for* spendyng at ale];
B.15.135	A[c] goddes folk *for* defaute þerof forfaren and spillen.
B.15.146	Ac *for* goode men, god woot, greet doel men maken,
B.15.208	Than *for* penaunce and parfitnesse þe pouerte þat swiche takeþ.
B.15.238	*For* braulynge and bakbitynge and berynge of fals witnesse.
B.15.241	And matrimoyne *for* moneie maken and vnmaken,
B.15.244	[Amonges erchebisshopes and bisshopes, [*for* beggeres sake],
B.15.247	Ac auarice haþ þe keyes now and kepeþ *for* his kynnesmen
B.15.248	And *for* his seketoures & his seruauntȝ, & som for hir children].
B.15.248	And for his seketoures & his seruauntȝ, & som *for* hir children].
B.15.260	That þeiȝ men suffrede al þis, god suffrede *for* vs moore
B.15.287	That no man myȝte hym se *for* mosse and for leues.
B.15.287	That no man myȝte hym se for mosse and *for* leues.
B.15.292	Peter fisshed *for* his foode and his felawe Andrew;
B.15.297	That lyueden þus *for* oure lordes loue many longe yeres.
B.15.324	And [bisette] to bidde *for* yow to swiche þat ben riche,
B.15.325	And ben founded and feffed ek to bidde *for* oþere.
B.15.383	I dar noȝt siggen it *for* shame–if swiche were apposed
B.15.392	Ac hir lyuynge þat lewed men be loþer god agulten.
B.15.414	[Ac] *for* drede of þe deeþ I dar noȝt telle truþe.
B.15.426	The bettre *for* hir biddynges in body and in soule.
B.15.431	Crist calleþ hem salt *for* cristene soules,
B.15.485	And feden vs and festen vs *for* eueremoore at oones].
B.15.499	*For* cristene and vncristene crist seide to prechours
B.15.508	And þat is rouþe *for* riȝtful men þat in þe Reawme wonyen,
B.15.522	In dolful deþ deyeden *for* hir faith.
B.15.524	Amonges vnkynde cristene *for* cristes loue he deyede,
B.15.525	And *for* þe riȝt of al þis reume and alle reumes cristene.
B.15.531	Many man *for* cristes loue was martired [amonges] Romayne[s]
B.15.540	Is reuerenced er þe Roode, receyued *for* [þe] worþier
B.15.543	*For* coueitise after cros; þe croune stant in golde.
B.15.546	*For* coueitise of þat cros [clerkes] of holy kirke
B.15.551	Right so, ye clerkes, *for* youre coueitise er [come auȝt] longe
B.15.552	Shal þei demen dos ecclesie, and [depose yow *for* youre pride]:
B.15.555	The lordshipe of londes [lese ye shul *for* euere],
B.15.563	That sholden preie *for* þe pees, possession hem letteþ;

B.15.566	[Charite] were to deschargen hem *for* holy chirches sake,
B.15.577	Oȝias seiþ *for* swiche þat sike ben and feble,
B.15.588	[And] *for* a parfit prophete þat muche peple sauede
B.16.1	'NOw faire falle yow', quod I þo, *'for* youre faire shewyng!
B.16.2	*For* Haukyns loue þe Actif man euere I shal yow louye.
B.16.18	'Piers þe Plowman!' quod I þo, and al *for* pure Ioye
B.16.25	'For wyndes, wiltow wite', quod he, 'to witen it fro fallyng:
B.16.86	And Piers *for* pure tene þat a pil he [l]auȝte;
B.16.112	Ofte [he] heeled swiche; he held it *for* no maistrie
B.16.143	That euere he his Saueour solde *for* siluer or ellis.'
B.16.162	That on þe friday folwynge *for* mankyndes sake
B.16.191	So þre bilongeþ *for* a lord þat lordshipe cleymeþ:
B.16.195	Sente forþ his sone as *for* seruaunt þat tyme
B.16.235	I circumscised my sone siþen *for* his sake,
B.16.237	Bledden blood *for* þat lordes loue and hope to blisse þe tyme.
B.16.242	Mercy *for* oure mysdedes as many tyme as we asken:
B.16.267	And bettre wed *for* us [wage] þan we ben alle worþi,
B.16.268	That is lif *for* lif; or ligge þus euere
B.16.272	I wepte *for* hise wordes; wiþ þat sauȝ I anoþer
B.17.27	And lelest to leue [on] *for* lif and for soule?
B.17.27	And lelest to leue [on] for lif and *for* soule?
B.17.31	And haþ saued þat bileued so and sory *for* hir synnes,
B.17.44	It is ful hard *for* any man on Abraham bileue
B.17.78	And lo, here siluer', he seide, *'for* salue to hise woundes.'
B.17.80	'What he spendeþ moore [*for* medicyne] I make þee good herafter,
B.17.92	*For* sighte of þ[e] sorweful [segge] þat robbed was with þeues.
B.17.122	Til I haue salue *for* alle sike; and þanne shal I turne
B.17.190	*For* peyne of þe pawme power hem failleþ
B.17.241	And if it suffise noȝt *for* assetȝ, þat in swich a wille deyeþ,
B.17.242	Mercy *for* his mekenesse wol maken good þe remenaunt.
B.17.246	Boþe forȝyue and foryete, and ȝit bidde *for* vs
B.17.260	Ne brenne ne blase clere, *fo[r]* blowynge of vnkyndenesse.
B.17.268	That] Diues deyde, dampned *for* his vnkyndenesse
B.17.277	Vnkynde cristene men, *for* coueitise and enuye
B.17.278	Sleeþ a man *for* hise moebles wiþ mouþ or with handes.
B.17.288	*For* coueitise of any kynnes þyng þat crist deere bouȝte.
B.17.298	Ne haue pite *for* any preiere þer þat he pleyneþ.'
B.17.307	Be raunsoned *for* his repentaunce þer alle reson hym dampneþ.
B.17.320	His sorwe is satisfaccion *for* [swich] þat may noȝt paie.
B.17.324	Hir feere fleeþ hire *for* feere of hir tonge.
B.18.17	Olde Iewes of Ierusalem *for* ioye þei songen,
B.18.24	That crist be noȝt [y]knowe here *for* consummatus deus
B.18.32	That, *for* al þat deeþ kan do, wiþInne þre daies to walke
B.18.35	And forbete and adoun brynge bale deeþ *for* euere:
B.18.60	The day *for* drede wiþdrouȝ and derk bicam þe sonne;
B.18.62	Dede men *for* þat dene come out of depe graues
B.18.64	*'For* a bitter bataille', þe dede body seide;
B.18.90	*For* þe dede þat I haue doon I do me in youre grace.
B.18.93	Callede hem caytyues, acorsed *for* euere.
B.18.94	'For þis foule vileynye vengeaunce to yow falle!
B.18.98	The gree ȝit haþ he geten *for* al his grete wounde.
B.18.110	What *for* feere of þis ferly and of þe false Iewes
B.18.120	*For* þe vertue þat hire folwede afered was she neuere.
B.18.177	That many day myȝte I noȝt se *for* merknesse of synne.
B.18.185	To be mannes meynpernour *for* eueremoore after.
B.18.247	The Erþe *for* heuynesse þat he wolde suffre
B.18.311	*For* þi lesynges, Lucifer, lost is al oure praye.
B.18.314	And now *for* þi laste lesynge] ylorn we haue Adam,
B.18.322	*For* any wye or warde wide opned þe yates.
B.18.328	*For* alle synfulle soules, to saue þo þat ben worþi.
B.18.332	I bihiȝte hem noȝt here helle *for* euere.
B.18.342	Membre *for* membre [was amendes by þe olde lawe],
B.18.343	And lif *for* lif also, and by þat lawe I clayme
B.18.366	And *for* þat drynke today I deide vpon erþe.
B.18.367	I fauȝt so me þursteþ ȝit *for* mannes soule sake;
B.18.402	And *for* þi lesynge, lucifer, þat þow leighe til Eue
B.18.428	And crepe[þ] to þe cros on knees and kisse[þ] it *for* a Iuwel
B.18.429	For goddes blissede body it bar *for* oure boote.
B.19.23	And ye callen hym crist; *for* what cause, telleþ me.
B.19.96	Ac *for* alle þise preciouse presentȝ oure lord [prynce] Iesus
B.19.107	Til he hadde alle hem þat he *for* bledde.
B.19.133	*For* þe dedes þat he dide, Fili dauid, Iesus.
B.19.178	Blessed mote þow be, and be shalt *for* euere.
B.19.205	And was afered [*for*] þe light, for in fires [lik]nesse
B.19.249	In pouerte and in [pacience] to preie *for* alle cristene.
B.19.293	Maken hym, *for* any mournynge, þat he nas murie in soule,
B.19.307	*For* present or for preiere or any Prynces lettres.
B.19.307	For present or *for* preiere or any Prynces lettres.
B.19.322	That crist vpon Caluarie *for* mankynde on pyned.
B.19.371	For siluer were forswore–sooþly þei wiste it.
B.19.377	And þanne wellede water *for* wikkede werkes
B.19.397	By Iesu! *for* al youre Ianglynge, wiþ Spiritus Iusticie,
B.19.414	And we clerkes, whan þei come, *for* hir comunes paieþ,
B.19.415	*For* hir pelure and palfreyes mete and pilours þat hem folweþ.
B.19.435	As wel *for* a wastour and wenches of þe stewes
B.19.436	As *for* hymself and hise seruauntȝ, saue he is first yserued.
B.19.438	And trauailleþ and tilieþ *for* a tretour also soore
B.19.439	As *for* a trewe tidy man alle tymes ylike.
B.19.458	And coloureþ it *for* a konnynge and a clene lyuynge.'
B.20.19	That he dronke at ech dych er he [deye *for* þurst].
B.20.20	So nede at gret nede may nymen as *for* his owene
B.20.36	And as lowe as a lomb *for* lakkyng þat hym nedeþ;
B.20.77	Fooles fro þise fendes lymes, *for* Piers loue þe Plowman.
B.20.105	Swowned and swelted *for* sorwe of [deþes] dyntes.
B.20.138	*For* a [Meneuer Mantel he] made lele matrymoyne
B.20.148	Thus relyede lif *for* a litel fortune
B.20.165	*For* care Conscience þo cryde vpon Elde
B.20.169	And lif fleiȝ *for* feere to phisik after helpe
B.20.195	For þe lyme þat she loued me *fore* and leef was to feele
B.20.200	And deeþ drogh neiȝ me; *for* drede gan I quake,
B.20.205	And hold þee þere euere til I sende *for* þee.
B.20.233	That þei come *for* coueitise, to haue cure of soules.
B.20.239	Than he þat laboureþ *for* liflode and leneþ it beggeris.
B.20.251	*For* loue lafte þei lordshipe, boþe lond and scole,
B.20.252	Frere Fraunceys and Domynyk, *for* loue to be holye.
B.20.267	A certein *for* a certein, saue oonliche of freres.
B.20.292	A parcel to preye *for* hem and [pleye] wiþ þe remenaunt,
B.20.307	*For* hir mys[fetes] þat þei wroȝt hadde,
B.20.312	*For* fastynge of a fryday he ferde as he wolde deye.
B.20.325	To a lord *for* a lettre leue to haue
B.20.332	'In faiþ', quod þis frere, *'for* profit and for helþe
B.20.332	'In faiþ', quod þis frere, 'for profit and *for* helþe
B.20.341	'Ye? go þi gate!' quod Pees, 'by god! *for* al þi phisik,
B.20.364	Of 'a pryuee paiement and I shal praye *for* yow
B.20.365	[And] *for* [hem] þat ye ben holden to al my lif tyme,
B.20.367	As frere[s] of oure Fraternytee, *for* a litel siluer.'
B.20.370	And wake *for* hise wikked werkes as he was wont to doone.
B.20.371	For confort of his confessour Contricion he lafte,
B.20.372	That is þe souerayn[e] salue *for* alle [synnes of kynde].
B.20.383	And þat freres hadde a fyndyng þat *for* nede flateren
C.Pr.7	Me biful for to slepe, *for* werynesse ofwalked,
C.Pr.28	Al *for* loue of oure lord lyueden [ful streyte]
C.Pr.32	*For* no likerous liflode here lycame to plese.
C.Pr.43	Fayteden *for* here fode, foughten at þe ale;
C.Pr.57	Prechyng þe peple *for* profyt of þe wombe;
C.Pr.59	*For* coueytise of copis contraryed somme doctours.
C.Pr.84	And synge þer *for* symonye [for] seluer is swete.
C.Pr.103	I leue, by oure lord, *for* loue of ȝoure coueytise
C.Pr.107	*For* Offines s[yn]ne and fines his brother
C.Pr.113	And his sones slawe anon he ful *for* sorwe
C.Pr.115	And al was *for* vengeance he bet noght his children
C.Pr.124	*For* ȝoure shrewed soffraunce and ȝoure oune synne.
C.Pr.138	'Contreplede hit noght,' quod Consience, *'for* holi [k]ir[k]e sake.'
C.Pr.146	And *for* most profi[t to þe peple] a plogh gonne þei make,
C.Pr.151	And *for* thy rightful ruylynge be rewardid in heuene.'
C.Pr.163	Plededen *for* penyes and pounde[d] þe lawe
C.Pr.164	And nat *for* loue of oure lord vnlose here lyppes ones.
C.Pr.169	Comen til a conseyl for [þe] comune profyt.
C.Pr.186	And knytten hit on a coler *for* oure comune profyt
C.Pr.194	Ther ne was [raton in] þe route, *for* al þe reame of Fraunce,
C.Pr.204	Forthy y conseile *for* oure comune profit lat þe Cat yworthe
C.Pr.210	Y seye *for* me,' quod þe mous, 'y se so muche aftur,
C.1.54	[Thanne] y fraynede her fayr *for* hym þat here made,
C.1.77	And preyede here pitously to preye *for* me to amende
C.1.95	And *for* no lordene loue leue þe trewe partie.
C.1.101	And neuer leue *for* loue in hope to lacche syluer.
C.1.110	Lepen out in lothly forme *for* his [luþer] wille
C.1.115	'Nere hit *for* northerne men anon y wolde ȝow telle
C.1.129	*For* pruyde th[at] hym pokede his payne hath non ende.
C.1.146	For treuthe telleth þat loue ys triacle *for* synne
C.1.147	And most souerayne salue *for* soule and for body.
C.1.147	And most souerayne salue for soule and *for* body.
C.1.158	Vp man *for* his mysdedes the mercement he taxeth.
C.1.164	Mekeliche *for* oure mysdedes to amende vs alle.
C.2.2	And sayde 'mercy, madame, *for* mary loue of heuene
C.2.37	He shal lese *for* here loue [a] lippe of trewe charite;
C.2.54	Acombre neuere thy Consience *for* coueityse of mede.'
C.2.83	That mede is maried more *for* here richesse
C.2.84	Then *for* holynesse oþer hendenesse oþer for hey kynde.
C.2.84	Then for holynesse oþer hendenesse oþer *for* hey kynde.
C.2.149	A myhte kusse the kyng as *for* his kyn[nes] womman.
C.2.159	Til he hadde seluer *for* the seel and signes of notaries.
C.2.166	That [fals] and [fauel] hadde *for* he[re] fayre ȝeftes.
C.2.173	To be maried *for* mone med[e] hath assented.'
C.2.200	Of many maner men *for* mede sake seude aftur.
C.2.214	[T]o atache tho tyrauntes, *'for* eny tresor, y hote;

C. 2.215	Lat fetere falsnesse faste *for* eny skynes ȝeftes,
C. 2.219	Ar he be put on þe pylorye *for* eny preyere ich hote.'
C. 2.223	Falsnesse *for* fere tho fleyh to þe freres;
C. 2.230	He was nawher welcome *for* his many tales,
C. 2.235	And gaf pardon *for* pans poundmele aboute.
C. 2.243	*For* knowyng of co[mere]s copeden hym as a frere.
C. 2.251	And holy churche thorw hem worth harmed *for* euere.'
C. 2.252	Alle fledde *for* fere and flowen into hernes;
C. 2.254	Ac treuliche to telle a tremblede *for* fere
C. 3.20	*For* al Consiences cast and craft, as y trowe.'
C. 3.42	Y shal assoyle the mysulue *for* a seem [of] whete
C. 3.45	Thenne mede *for* here mysdedes to th[at] man knelede
C. 3.53	In masse and in matynes *for* mede we shal synge
C. 3.54	Solempneliche and softlyche as *for* a suster of oure ordre.'
C. 3.66	And [do] peynten and purtrayen ho payede *for* þe makyng
C. 3.88	And [t]how thei fillen nat ful þat *for* lawe is seled
C. 3.89	A grypeth þerfore a[s] gret as *for* þe grayeth treuthe.
C. 3.99	That louten *for* hem to oure lord and to oure lady bothe
C. 3.103	And goode mennes *for* here gultes gloweth on fuyr aftur.
C. 3.109	For to spyre and to aspye, *for* eny speche of suluer,
C. 3.113	That vsurers oþer regrateres *for* eny skynes ȝeftes
C. 3.114	Be yfranchised *for* a fre man and haue a fals name.
C. 3.119	Loue hem *for* my loue,' quod this lady mede,
C. 3.175	He lat passe prisones [and] paieth *for* hem ofte
C. 3.179	And hangeth hym *for* ha[t]rede þat harmede nere.
C. 3.198	The mase *for* a mene man thow he mote euere!
C. 3.220	For Consience acuseth the to congeye the *foreuere*.'
C. 3.250	Wherby he may as a man *for* eueremore lyue aftur.
C. 3.264	To lete so his lordschipe *for* a litel mone.
C. 3.265	Hit bycometh *for* a kyng þat shal kepe a reume
C. 3.268	Mede maketh hym byloued and *for* a man yholde.
C. 3.273	Seruantes *for* here seruyse, [we see wel þe sothe],
C. 3.275	Bothe Beg[g]eres and bedemen crauen mede *for* here preyeres;
C. 3.276	Munstrals *for* here m[yrth]e mede thei asken;
C. 3.280	Alle kyn crafty men crauen mede *for* here prentises;
C. 3.292	A desert *for* som doynge, derne oþer elles.
C. 3.296	And for to vndertake [to] trauaile *for* another
C. 3.311	The mede þat many prest[es] taken *for* masses þat thei syngen,
C. 3.314	Hit is a permutacoun apertly, on peneworth *for* another.
C. 3.351	And take hym *for* his trauaile al þat treuthe wolde,
C. 3.368	Sethe y, his sone and his seruant, sewe *for* his ryhte.
C. 3.382	Bytwene two lo[n]des *for* a trewe marke.
C. 3.384	For they wilnen and wolden as beste were *for* hemsulue.
C. 3.400	To syke *for* here synnes and soffre harde penaunc[e]
C. 3.401	*For* þat lordes loue that for oure loue deyede
C. 3.401	For þat lordes loue that *for* oure loue deyede
C. 3.409	And se[t]he, for sauel saued a kyng *fo[r]* mede
C. 3.411	That saul *for* þat synne and his sone deyede
C. 3.416	Sholde deye der[f]ly *for* dedes of here eldres.
C. 3.424	*For* eny mede of money al that thow myhte [fynde],
C. 3.430	And al [h]is [sede] *for* þat synne shentfolyche ende.
C. 3.432	That god [hated hym] *for* euere and alle [his] eyres aftur.
C. 3.448	Shal no ser[i]aunt *for* [þat] seruic[e] werie a selk houe
C. 3.449	Ne no pelure in his panelon *for* pledyng at þe barre.
C. 3.465	Here sauter and here seuene p[s]almes *for* alle synful preyen;
C. 3.481	And saresines *for* þat syhte shal syng Credo in spiritum sanctum
C. 4.38	For þey wolde do *for* a dyner oþer a d[o]seyne capones
C. 4.39	More then *for* oure lordes loue oþer oure lady, goddes moder.'
C. 4.50	Y dar nat *for* his felawschipe, in fayth,' pees sayde,
C. 4.57	Ne [no] ferthyng therfore, *for* nouhte y couthe plede.
C. 4.61	And taketh me but a tayle *for* ten quarteres otes;
C. 4.63	Y am nat hardy *for* hym vnnethe to loke;
C. 4.80	That wrong *for* his werkes sholde w[oo] tholye
C. 4.85	And be borw *for* his bale and buggen hym bote
C. 4.93	For y wol wage *for* wrong; he wol do so no mare.'
C. 4.99	'Nay, by crist!' quod þe kyng, '*for* Consiences sake
C. 4.104	As longe as y lyue *for* his luther werkes.'
C. 4.114	Til Clerkene Coueytise be cloth *for* þe pore
C. 4.121	*For* alle manere men þat me fynt neodefole;
C. 4.124	So þat noon go to galys but yf he go *for* euere,
C. 4.125	And alle Rome rennares *for* ruyflares in Fraunce
C. 4.130	Prouisour or preest oþer penaunt *for* his synnes.
C. 4.137	Be vnpunisched in my power *for* perel of [my] soule
C. 4.153	Resoun *for* his ryhtful speche; ryche and pore hym louede
C. 4.158	'Hoso wilneth here to wy[u]le *for* welthe of here goodes
C. 4.159	But he be knowe *for* a cokewold kut of my nose.'
C. 4.174	Y wol haue leutee *for* my lawe and late be al ȝoure iangl[ing]
C. 5.3	And lytel ylet by, leueth me *for* sothe,
C. 5.13	Or koke *for* my cokeres or to þe Cart piche,
C. 5.17	And kepe my corn in my croft *f[or]* pykares and theues
C. 5.38	And what is beste *for* the body, as the boek telleth,
C. 5.39	And sykerost *for* þe soule, by so y wol contenue.
C. 5.48	Th[u]s y s[yn]ge *for* here soules of suche as me helpeth

C. 5.61	Hit bycometh *for* clerkes Crist for to serue,
C. 5.72	And so[p]ares and here sones *for* suluer han be knyhtes,
C. 5.74	*For* the ryhte of this reume ryden aȝeyn oure enemyes
C. 5.86	Non de solo,' y sayde, '*for* sothe viuit homo,
C. 5.107	S[yh]ing *for* my synnes, seggyng my paternoster,
C. 5.115	And preuede þat this pestelences was *for* puyre synne
C. 5.117	Was pertliche *for* pruyde and for no poynt elles.
C. 5.117	Was pertliche for pruyde and *for* no poynt elles.
C. 5.129	And kepe hit in here cofre *for* catel at nede.
C. 5.149	Dyen *for* drouthe whenne they drye lygge,
C. 5.169	And bete ȝow, as þe bible telleth, *for* brekynge of ȝoure reule
C. 5.195	Enioyne hem pees *for* here penaunce and perpetuel forȝe[ue]nesse
C. 6.20	Demed *for* here vuel vices and exitede oþere
C. 6.35	Vantyng vp my vaynglorie *for* eny vndernymynge;
C. 6.40	Be holden *for* holy and honoured by þat enchesoun;
C. 6.47	And what y gaf *for* godes loue to gossipus y tolde,
C. 6.61	'Now god *for* his goodnesse gyue the grace to amende,'
C. 6.92	*For* thy synnes souereynly and biseke god of mercy.'
C. 6.101	Lord, ar y lyf lete, *for* loue of thysulue
C. 6.171	'Lady, to thy leue sone loute *for* me nouthe
C. 6.173	With þat y shal,' quod þat shrewe, 'saturdayes *for* thy loue
C. 6.195	Now, lord, *for* thy lewete on lechours haue mercy.'
C. 6.200	Wel syddore then his chyn, ycheueled *for* elde,
C. 6.227	*For* laboreres and louh folk þat lay by hymsulue.
C. 6.230	A galon *for* a grote, and ȝut no grayth mesure
C. 6.237	'That was a ruful restitucioun,' quod repentaunce, '*for* sothe;
C. 6.243	And len[e] *for* loue of þe wed the whych y lette bettere
C. 6.248	'Lenedest [thow] euere eny lord *for* loue of his mayntenaunce?'
C. 6.251	Payed neuere *for* his prentished nat a payre gloues.
C. 6.274	Mercy *for* my mysdedes þat y ne mourned [o]ftur
C. 6.275	*For* lo[s] of good, leef me, then for lycames gultes.
C. 6.275	For lo[s] of good, leef me, then *for* lycames gultes.
C. 6.287	Were y a frere, in good fayth, *for* al þe gold on erthe
C. 6.320	And haddest mercy vppon þat man *for* memento sake,
C. 6.323	*For* thy mochel mercy mitigacioun y biseche.
C. 6.346	To bysetten hit hymsulue as beste be *for* thy soule.
C. 6.347	For he shal onswerie *for* the at the hey dome,
C. 6.348	*For* the and for many mo þat man shal ȝeue a rykenynge
C. 6.348	For the and *for* many mo þat man shal ȝeue a rykenynge
C. 6.360	A ferthyngworth [of] fenkel sed[e] *for* fastyng dayes.'
C. 6.386	They couthe nat by here Consience acorden *for* treuthe
C. 6.388	And nempned hym *for* a noumper þat no debat were.
C. 6.432	And spilde þat y aspele myhte; y kan nat speke *for* shame
C. 6.438	For y vowe to verray god, *for* hungur or furste,
C. 7.15	Ne ryht sory *for* my synnes—y seyh neuere þe tyme—
C. 7.54	And sethe a beggare haue y be *for* my foule sleuthe:
C. 7.59	"Y am sory *for* my synnes", sey to thysuluen
C. 7.63	And made [a]uowe tofore god *for* his foule sleuthe:
C. 7.70	Is when men mourneth not *for* his mysdedes,
C. 7.97	And *for* loue of here lord ly[th]eth hem at festes,
C. 7.103	The pore *for* a f[o]ol sage sittynge at thy table,
C. 7.107	And a blynd man *for* a bordor or a bedredene womman
C. 7.120	'Y shal byseke *for* alle synnefole oure sauiour of grace
C. 7.125	And *for* [þe] beste, as y beleue, what[euere] þe boek telle:
C. 7.131	The sonne *for* sorwe þerof lees [s]iht for a tyme.
C. 7.131	The sonne for sorwe þerof lees [s]iht *for* a tyme.
C. 7.146	*For* dedes that we han don ylle dampned sholde we ben neuere
C. 7.148	And *for* [that] muchel mercy and marie loue thi moder
C. 7.153	That alle seyntes *for* synful songen with dauid:
C. 7.176	[And] souht gode seyntes *for* my soule helthe.'\
C. 7.185	And maden me sykere[n hym] sethen to seruen hym *for* euere,
C. 7.192	Profitable as *for* þe plouh a potte me to lerne
C. 7.202	'Y [nolde] fonge a ferthynge *for* seynt Thomas shryne;
C. 7.210	Thenne eny dedly synne do *for* drede or for preeyere.
C. 7.210	Thenne eny dedly synne do for drede or *for* preeyere.
C. 7.217	[So] shalt thow se swere-nat-but-it-be-*for*-nede-
C. 7.229	Loke thow plokke no plonte þere *for* perel of thy soule.
C. 7.231	In-none-manere-elles-nat-*for*-no-mannes-preeyre.
C. 7.243	Grace hatte þe gateward, a goed man *for* sothe;
C. 7.246	Y am sory [*for*] my synnes, and so [shal y] euere,
C. 7.277	For he payeth *for* prisones in places and in peynes.
C. 7.285	'Wyte god,' quod a wafre[re], 'wiste y this *for* sothe
C. 7.286	[Sh]olde y neuere forthere [a] foet *for* no frere prechynge.'
C. 7.304	I may nat come *for* a kitte, so a cleueth on me:
C. 7.308	That myhte folowe vs vch fote *for* drede of mysturnynge.'
C. 8.7	'Y preye ȝow *for* ȝoure profit,' quod Peres to þe ladyes,
C. 8.8	'That somme sowe þe sak *for* shedynge of the whete,
C. 8.11	Chesibles *for* chapeleynes churches to honoure.
C. 8.14	*For* profit of the pore and plesaunce of ȝowsuluen.
C. 8.16	As longe as y leue, *for* [þe] lordes loue of heuene.
C. 8.22	Y wolde [assaye] som tyme, *for* solace as hit were.'
C. 8.24	'Y shal swynke and swete and sowe *for* vs bothe,
C. 8.25	And labory *for* tho thow louest al my lyf tyme,

C. 8.75   And Robyn þe rybauder *for* his rousty wordes.
C. 8.102 Y payede hit prestly *for* perel of my soule;
C. 8.111 And ben a pilgrym at þe plouh *for* profit to pore and ryche.'
C. 8.127 And thow ȝe deye *for* deul þe deuel haue þat reche!'
C. 8.131 'A[c] we praye *for* ȝow, [peres] and for ȝoure plouh bothe
C. 8.131 'A[c] we praye for ȝow, [peres] and *for* ȝoure plouh bothe
C. 8.178 And þat was bake *for* bayard may be here bote.'
C. 8.182 *For* a potte ful of potage þat [Peres] wyf made
C. 8.187 Al *for* drede of here deth, such duntus ȝaf hunger.
C. 8.191 And freres of alle þe fyue ordres, alle *for* fere of hunger.
C. 8.192 For þat was bake *for* bayard was bote for many hungry,
C. 8.192 For þat was bake for bayard was bote *for* many hungry,
C. 8.193 Drosenes and dregges drynke *for* many beggares.
C. 8.196 But lyflode *for* his la[b]our and his loue at nones.
C. 8.202 Þat durste withsitte þat [Peres] sayde *for* fere of syre hunger
C. 8.212 And *for* defaute this folk folweth myn hestes.
C. 8.213 Hit is nat *for* loue, leue hit, thei labore thus faste
C. 8.214 But *for* fere of famyen, in fayth,' sayde [Peres].
C. 8.215 'Ther is no fi[al] loue with this folk *for* al here fayre speche
C. 8.221 *For* here lyflode, lere me now, sire hunger.'
C. 8.222 'Now herkene,' quod hunger, 'and holde hit *for* a wysdom:
C. 8.225 And [a]baue hem with benes *for* bollyng of here wombe;
C. 8.235 'Y wolde nat greue [god],' quod Peres, '*for* al þe good on erthe!
C. 8.243 "The slowe Caytif *for* colde wolde no corn tylye;
C. 8.244 In somur *for* his sleuthe he shal haue defaute
C. 8.250 And ledares *for* here laboryng ouer al þe lordes godes;
C. 8.252 The lord *for* his lachesse and his luther sleuthe
C. 8.261 This aren euidences,' quod hunger, '*for* hem þat wolle nat swynke
C. 8.277 Thenk þat [diues] *for* his delical lyf to þe deuel wente
C. 8.283 Alle þat gr[eden at] thy gate *for* godes loue aftur fode
C. 8.290 That fysik shal his forred hod[e] *for* his fode sulle
C. 8.291 And his cloke of callabre *for* his comune[s] legge
C. 8.305 And bred *for* my barnes of benes and of peses.
C. 8.319 Pore folk *for* fere tho fedde honger ȝerne
C. 8.333 And þat chaut and pluchaut *for* chillyng of h[ere] mawe.
C. 8.351 And dawe þe deluare dey *for* defaute
C. 9.4   *For* hym and [for] his ayres for euere to ben assoiled.
C. 9.4   For hym and [*for*] his ayres for euere to ben assoiled.
C. 9.4   For hym and [for] his ayres *for* euere to ben assoiled.
C. 9.17 Drede nat *for* no deth to distruye by here power
C. 9.26 Aȝen clene Consience *for* coueytyse of wynnynge.
C. 9.35 Fynde hem *for* godes loue and fauntkynes to scole,
C. 9.40 And abyde þer in my blisse body and soule *for* euere.
C. 9.41 Tho were Marchauntes mury; many wopen *for* ioye
C. 9.45 But they pre manibus were payed *for* pledynge at þe barre;
C. 9.46 Ac he [that] speneth his speche and speketh *for* þe pore
C. 9.49 And *for* þe loue of oure lord lawe for hem declareth
C. 9.49 And for þe loue of oure lord lawe *for* hem declareth
C. 9.54 That mede of mene men *for* here motynge taken.
C. 9.66 For he þat gyueth *for* goddes loue wolde nat gyue, his thankes,
C. 9.68 And moste merytorie to men þat he ȝeueth *fore*.
C. 9.92 There is payne and peny ale as *for* a pytaunce ytake
C. 9.100 Thouh he falle *for* defaute þat fayteth for his lyflode
C. 9.100 Thouh he falle for defaute þat fayteth *for* his lyflode
C. 9.109 Careth they *for* no colde ne counteth of non hete
C. 9.129 To vnderfongen hem fayre byfalleth *for* þe ryche
C. 9.130 *For* þe lordes loue or þe ladyes þat they with longen.
C. 9.133 Me [g]yueth hem giftes and gold *for* grete lordes sake.
C. 9.171 And goen and fayten with here fauntes *for* eueremore aftur.
C. 9.185 *For* loue of here lowe hertes oure lord hath hem ygraunted
C. 9.225 In frithes and in forestes *for* fox and other bestes
C. 9.231 Thus hit bylongeth *for* lord[e], for lered and for lewed
C. 9.231 Thus hit bylongeth for lord[e], *for* lered and for lewed
C. 9.231 Thus hit bylongeth for lord[e], for lered and *for* lewed
C. 9.239 Y drede me, and he dey, hit worth *for* dedly synne
C. 9.246 Or labory *for* here lyflode as þe lawe wolde?
C. 9.250 And fo[r] þe cloth þat keuereth hym ykald he is a frere,
C. 9.268 Y leue, *for* thy lacchesse, thow lesest many wetheres
C. 9.276 But 'haue this *for* þat tho þat thow toke
C. 9.277 Mercy *for* mede and my lawe breke.'
C. 9.278 Loke now, *for* thy lacchesse, what lawe wol the graunte
C. 9.279 Purgatorie *for* thy paie O[r] perpetuel helle
C. 9.280 For shal no pardon preye *for* ȝow there ne no princes lettres.
C. 9.312 'Beau fitȝ,' quod the fadur, '*for* defaute we shal,
C. 9.313 Y mysulue and my sones, seche the *for* nede.'
C. 9.316 His eleuene bretherne hym *for* nede souhte
C. 9.332 Hit is nat so syker *for* þe soule, certes, as [is] dowel.
C. 10.55 Oure lyf to oure lord god *for* oure lycames gultes.'
C. 10.97 *For* here mok and here mebles suche men thenketh
C. 10.159 And as thow seest the sonne sum tyme *for* cloudes
C. 10.179 Ȝaf his douhter *for* a daunsynge in a disch þe heued
C. 10.196 And seth [he les] his lyf *for* lawe sholde loue wexe.
C. 10.202 In meschief *for* defaute of mete ne for myssyng of clothes:

C. 10.202 In meschief for defaute of mete ne *for* myssyng of clothes:
C. 10.221 And *for* þe synne of Caymes seed sayede god to Noe:
C. 10.230 Alle sholle deye *for* his dedes by dales and hulles
C. 10.235 And al *for* here forfadres ferden þe worse.
C. 10.237 Holy writ witnesseth þat *for* no wikkede dede
C. 10.240 For thogh þe fader be a frankeleyn and *for* a felon be hanged
C. 10.246 Was *for* mariages ma[ugre kynd]e þat men made þat tyme.
C. 10.250 That *for* no kyne catel ne no kyne byheste
C. 10.257 *For* coueytise of catel and connynge chapmen;
C. 10.265 *For* riche or yrented wel, thouh he be reueled for elde
C. 10.265 For riche or yrented wel, thouh he be reueled *for* elde
C. 10.268 And wedden here *for* here welthe and weschen on þe morwe
C. 10.276 To folwe þe flicche, feccheth they hit neuere;
C. 10.279 *For* coueytise of catel in none kyne wyse;
C. 10.294 That obergatus ben gete *for* gadelynges ben holden
C. 11.26 Harlotes *for* here harlotrye aren holpe ar nedy pore;
C. 11.41 Bothe afyngred and afurst, and *for* defaute spille;
C. 11.54 And prech[en] at seynt poules, [*for*] puyr enuye of clerkes,
C. 11.56 Ne sory *for* here synnes; so [is] pruyde enhanced
C. 11.60 And gode men *for* oure gultes he al togrynt to deth.
C. 11.62 Ne *for* drede of eny deth withdraweth h[e]m fro pruyde
C. 11.90 '*For* thy mekenesse, [man],' quod she, 'and for thy mylde speche
C. 11.90 'For thy mekenesse, [man],' quod she, 'and *for* thy mylde speche
C. 11.93 Of dobet [and] of dobest–*for* doctour he is knowe
C. 11.120 Gramer *for* gurles y gart furste write
C. 11.142 On þe maide Marie *for* mankynde sake
C. 11.164 Tho wepte y *for* wo and wrathe of here wordes
C. 11.175 And bade me *for* my contin[au]nce counte cler[gie] lihte.
C. 11.207 Vnwriten *for* som wikkednesse, as holy writ sheweth:
C. 11.220 That *for* here werkes and wyt wonyeth now in payne,
C. 11.221 Thenne wrouhte [we] vnwysly *for* alle ȝoure wyse techynge.
C. 11.248 *For* lewed folk, goddes foles and his fre bestes:
C. 11.271 Ho is worthy *for* wele or for wykkede [pyne]:
C. 11.271 Ho is worthy for wele or *for* wykkede [pyne]:
C. 11.286 Saide thus in his sarmon *for* ensau[m]ple of grete clerkes,
C. 11.295 And passen purgatorie penaunceles *for* here parfit bileue:
C. 11.305 All þat treuth attacheth and testifieth *for* gode
C. 12.8 And festene the in ther f[r]aternite and *for* þe byseche
C. 12.10 And preeye *for* the pol by pol yf thow be peccuniosus.'
C. 12.13 And thenne was fortune my foo *for* al her fayre biheste
C. 12.17 To restitute resonably *for* al vnrihtfole anynynge.
C. 12.28 The sauter sayth hit is no synne *for* suche men þat ben trewe
C. 12.33 Falsnesse ne fayterye? *for* sumwhat þe apostel saide:
C. 12.40 Nother *for* loue [loue] it [nat] ne lacke hit for enuye:
C. 12.40 Nother for loue [loue] it [nat] ne lacke hit *for* enuye:
C. 12.50 Al *for* tene of here tyxst tremblede myn herte
C. 12.53 That vnderfeng me at þe fonte *for* on of godes chosene.
C. 12.56 And bad hem souke *for* synne saue at his breste
C. 12.57 And drynke bote *for* bale, brouke hit hoso myhte.\
C. 12.69 And *for* his rechelesnes rewarde hym þere riht to þe day of dome
C. 12.71 Mercy *for* his mysdedes with mouthe and with herte.'
C. 12.75 'Ȝe? bawe *for* bokes!' quod oen was broken out of helle.
C. 12.78 *For* an vncristene creature; [clerkes] woet þe sothe
C. 12.82 Sauacion *for* soethnesse [þat] a sey in my werkes.
C. 12.92 And louye *for* oure lordes loue and do leute euermore.
C. 12.93 *For* lawe withouten leutee, ley þer a bene!
C. 12.125 *For* his pore parail and pilgrimes clothes
C. 12.141 Ac pouerte god potte byfore and preude *for* þe betere:
C. 12.143 Preise[n] pouerte *for* beste [lif] if pacience hit folowe
C. 12.151 The which is þe cornel of confort *for* alle cristene soules.
C. 12.158 *For* þe loue of oure lord lo[w]eth hym to be pore,
C. 12.160 And lyf lastyng *for* euere byfore oure lord in heuene:
C. 12.166 Ac ȝef hem forth to pore folk þat *for* my loue hit aske;
C. 12.173 To testifie *for* treuthe þe tale þat y shewe
C. 12.196 And *for* here pacience be ypresed as for puyr martir
C. 12.196 And for here pacience be ypresed as *for* puyr martir
C. 12.197 Or *for* a confessour ykud þat counteth nat a ruche
C. 12.204 Murthe *for* his mornyng, and þat muche plentee.
C. 12.205 For crist saide [so] to seyntes þat *for* his sake tholeden
C. 12.241 *For* coueytyse of catel to culle hym þat hit kepeth.
C. 12.242 And so is many man ymorthred *for* his moneye and his godes
C. 12.244 And he *for* his hard holdyng in helle parauntur:
C. 13.7 Abraham *for* his [auȝte] hadde moche tene
C. 13.11 Ne *for* brihtnesse of here beaute here spouse to be byknowe.
C. 13.17 And *for* a song in his sorwe, "si bona accepimus a domino &c,
C. 13.51 Marchauntȝ *for* here marchaundyse in many place to tolle.
C. 13.60 And leueth *for* his lettres þat no [lede] wole hym greue.
C. 13.63 Fynde beggares bred, bakkes *for* þe colde,
C. 13.72 Wolde noon suche assailen hym *for* such as hym foloweth
C. 13.97 And as moche mede *for* a myte þer he offreth
C. 13.98 As þe ryche man *for* al his mone, and more by þe gospell:
C. 13.105 And nedeth [ȝow] nat to nyme siluer *for* masses þat ȝe synge
C. 13.109 As byful *for* a knyht or fond hym for his strenthe.

C.13.109   As byful for a knyht or fond hym *for* his strenthe.
C.13.112   The same y segge *for* sothe by suche þat beth prestes
C.13.120   The gome þat gloseth so Chartres *for* a goky is halden.
C.13.196   'Vch a segge *for* hymsulue, salamon vs techeth:
C.13.201   So is soffrance souereynliche, so hit be *for* godes loue.
C.13.224   Ac *for* thyn entermetynge her artow forsake:
C.13.228   Rihte so ferde Resoun by; *for* thy rude speche
C.13.230   [*For*] pruyde or presumpcioun of thy parfit lyuynge,
C.14.5   And conseyled the *for* cristes sake no creature to bygile,
C.14.35   And ȝut is clergie to comende *for* cristes loue more
C.14.53   Come *for* al his kynde wit thorw cristendoem to be saued,
C.14.56   To ȝeue mercy for mysde[de]s ȝif men hit wol aske
C.14.62   And his sones *for* his synnes sorwe hem [becauȝte]
C.14.69   And do we as dauid techeth *for* doute of godes veniance:
C.14.177   *For* here fetheres þat fayre beth to fle fer hem letteth.
C.14.179   Ac *for* his peynted pennes þe pecok is honoured
C.14.180   More þan *for* his fayre flesch or for his merye note.
C.14.180   More þan for his fayre flesch or *for* his merye note.
C.14.181   Riht so men reuerence[th] more þe ryche *for* h[is] mebles
C.14.182   Then *for* eny kyn he come of or for his kynde wittes.
C.14.182   Then for eny kyn he come of or *for* his kynde wittes.
C.14.183   Thus þe poete praiseth þe pecok *for* his fetheres
C.14.184   And þe ryche *for* his rentes or for rychesse in his shopp[e].
C.14.184   And þe ryche for his rentes or *for* rychesse in his shopp[e].
C.14.196   And þe bettere *for* here bokes to bidden we ben yholde–
C.14.197   That god *for* his grace gyue here soules reste
C.15.34   Crauede and cryede *for* cristes loue of heuene
C.15.35   A meles mete *for* a pore man or moneye yf they hadde.
C.15.38   The maistre was maed sitte As *for* þe moste worthy;
C.15.39   Resoun stoed and s[t]yhlede as *for* styward of halle.
C.15.50   Bote yf they synge *for* tho soules and wepe salte teres:
C.15.53   And bringe breed *for* pacience, bytyng apartye,
C.15.59   Thenne cam contricion þat hadd coked *for* hem all
C.15.73   *For* oure lordes loue, as holy lettre telleth:
C.15.81   Þat toek this *for* his teme and tolde hit withoute glose.
C.15.83   And what meschief and maleese crist *for* man tholede.
C.15.100   Is noþer fische ne flesche but fode *for* [a] penant[e].
C.15.125   That trauayleth to teche oþere y halde hit *for* a dobet;
C.15.126   And he þat doth as he techeth y halde hit *for* þe beste:
C.15.129   Shal no such motyef be meued *for* me late [þ]ere
C.15.130   *For* Peres loue þe palmare ȝent, þat inpugnede ones
C.15.133   And no tixst ne taketh to preue this *for* trewe
C.15.147   And bote he bowe *for* this betynge blynde mote he worthen.'
C.15.169   As *for* here lord and here ledare and l[y]ue as thow techest.'
C.15.173   Profitable for bothe parties;' and potte þe boerd fro hym
C.15.209   *For* no breed þat y betrauaile to [brynge] byfore lordes
C.15.210   Nere hit þat þe parsche [prest] preyeth *for* me on sonendayes,
C.15.211   Y am sory þat y sowe or sette but *for* mysulue.
C.15.212   Ac þe prest and [þe] peple preyeth *for* Peres þe Plouheman
C.15.213   And *for* me Actyf, his man, þat ydelnesse ha[t]e.
C.15.214   [*For*] lordes and lorelles, luther and gode,
C.15.216   Y fynde payn *for* þe po[p]le and pre[y]en hym ych wolde
C.15.251   Or when thow cl[o]msest fo[r] colde or clingest for drouthe.
C.15.251   Or when thow cl[o]msest fo[r] colde or clingest *for* drouthe.
C.15.256   Dar þe nat care *for* no corn ne for cloth ne for drynke
C.15.256   Dar þe nat care for no corn ne *for* cloth ne for drynke
C.15.256   Dar þe nat care for no corn ne for cloth ne *for* drynke
C.15.290   And makest hem wel neyh meke and mylde *for* defaute
C.15.301   Many man hath his ioye here *for* al here wel dedes
C.15.302   And lordes and ladyes ben cald *for* ledes þat they haue
C.16.7   A[nd] nat to fonge byfore *for* drede [of] dessallouwynge.
C.16.9   Haue two heuenes *for* ȝoure her[berw]ynge.
C.16.14   And ȝut is wynter *for* hem worse for weetshoed þey g[ang]e,
C.16.21   Ac *for* þe beste, as y hope, aren som pore and ryche.
C.16.31   And [operis satisfaccio] *for* soules paieth and alle synnes quyteth:
C.16.42   Forthy cristene sholde be in comune ryche, noon coueytous *for* hymsulue.
C.16.56   *For* his pouerte and pacience perpetuel ioye.
C.16.63   And buxum at his biddyng *for* his breed and his drynke
C.16.76   So *for* his glotonye and his grete synne he hath a greuous penaunce
C.16.77   Þat is welowo when he [w]aketh and wepeth *for* colde;
C.16.92   A straw *for* the stuyues! hit stoed nat, [y trowe],
C.16.104   And *for* goddes loue leueth al and lyueth as a beggare.
C.16.105   As a mayde *for* mannes loue here moder fors[a]ke[th],
C.16.110   More *for* coueytise of catel then kynde loue of þe mariage.
C.16.153   Thus lered me a le[tte]red man *for* oure lordes loue, seynt Austyn.
C.16.155   A blessed lyf withoute bisinesse bote onelyche *for* þe soule:
C.16.166   And yf thow be cristes creature, *for* cristes loue telle me.'
C.16.213   *For* such a lust and lykynge lucifer ful fram heuene.
C.16.238   More *for* pompe and pruyde, as þe peple woet wel
C.16.240   And reuerence þe ryche þe rather *for* here suluer
C.16.263   And amenden [hem] of here mysdedes more *for* [ȝoure] ensaumples

C.16.305   And when a man swereth "forsoth" *for* sooth he hit troweth;
C.16.308   *For* drede of god þat so goed is and thusgates vs techeth:
C.16.311   Alle sekness[e] and sorwes *for* solac[e] he hit taketh
C.16.325   There pore and prisones ben and paye *for* here fode,
C.16.363   *For* braulyng and bacbitynge and berynge of fals witnesse.
C.16.366   With bisshopes a wolde be *for* beggares sake
C.16.373   He halt hit *for* a vyce and a foule shame
C.17.14   That no man myhte se hym *for* moes and for leues.
C.17.14   That no man myhte se hym for moes and *for* leues.
C.17.19   Peter fischede *for* his fode And his fere Androwe;
C.17.26   That lyueden thus *for* oure lordes loue monye longe ȝeres
C.17.55   Ar they amorteysed eny more *for* monkes or for Chanoun[s].
C.17.55   Ar they amorteysed eny more for monkes or *for* Chanoun[s].
C.17.65   Lo laurence *for* his largenesse, as holy lore telleth
C.17.66   That his mede and his manhede *for* eueremore shal laste:
C.17.82   And *for* þe synne of þe soule forsaketh his oune coyne.
C.17.113   And flaterrere *for* his vscher, ferly me thynketh.
C.17.118   That they ouerhippe nat *for* hastite, as y hope they do nat,
C.17.119   Thogh hit suffice *for* oure sauacioun soethfaste byleue,
C.17.159   A man þat hihte Makameth *for* messie they hym holdeth
C.17.201   Is reuerenced byfore the rode and resceyued *for* the worthiore
C.17.205   *For* couetyse aftur cros; the corone stand in golde.
C.17.208   *For* couetyse of th[at] croes clerkes of holi churche
C.17.215   Shal dampne dos ecclesie and depose ȝow *for* ȝoure pruyde:
C.17.218   The lordschipe of londes lese ȝe shal *for* euer
C.17.226   That sholde preye *for* þe pees possession hem letteth;
C.17.231   Hit were charite to deschargen hem *for* holy churche sake,
C.17.259   And þat is reuthe *for* rihtfole men þat in þ[e] reume wonyeth
C.17.260   And a perel *for* prelates þat þe pope maketh
C.17.281   Many man *for* cristes loue was martired amonges Romaynes
C.17.290   So is þe kynde of a curatour *for* criste[s] loue to preche
C.17.291   And deye *for* his dere childrene to de[struy]e dedly synne,
C.17.297   And on þat lawe they leue and leten hit *for* þe beste.
C.17.299   And *for* a parfit profete that moche peple sauede
C.18.16   'Now, certes,' y sayde, and siȝte *for* ioye,
C.18.95   Shollen serue *for* þe lord sulue, and so fareth god almyhty.
C.18.98   And *for* þe fayrest fruyte byfore hym, as of erthe,
C.18.110   *For* euere as Elde hadde eny down, þe deuel was redy
C.18.148   That he was god or godes sone *for* þat grete wonder;
C.18.164   And pursuede hym prieueliche and *for* pans hym bouhte–
C.18.196   'This is myrke thyng *for* me,' quod y, and for many anoþer,
C.18.196   'This is myrke thyng for me,' quod y, and *for* many anoþer,
C.18.204   Sente forth his sone As *for* seruant þat tyme
C.18.251   Y circumsised my sone also *for* his sake,
C.18.253   Bledden bloed *for* þat lordes loue [and] hope to blisse þ[e] tyme.
C.18.258   Mercy *for* oure mysdedes as many tymes
C.18.283   And bettere wed *for* vs wagen then we ben alle worthy;
C.18.284   And þat is lyf *for* lyf or ligge thus euere
C.18.288   [Y] wepte *for* his wordes; with þat saw y [a]nother
C.19.28   And lele to bileue on *for* [lif and] for soule?
C.19.28   And lele to bileue on for [lif and] *for* soule?
C.19.32   And hath ysaued þat bileued so and sory *for* here synnes;
C.19.40   And seth to louye and to lene *for* þat lordes sake
C.19.43   Hit is liht *for* lewed and for lered bothe.
C.19.43   Hit is liht for lewed and *for* lered bothe.
C.19.77   'And þat more goth *for* his medicyne y make the good aȝeynward
C.19.101   And lered me *for* his loue to louye al mankynde
C.19.156   *For* peyne of þe paume power hem fayleth
C.19.207   And yf hit suffic[e] nat *for* ase[t]h þat in suche a will deyeth
C.19.208   Mercy *for* his mekenesse wol maky good þe remenaunt.
C.19.212   Bothe forȝeue and forȝete and ȝut bidde *for* vs
C.19.226   Ne brenne ne blase clere *for* blowynge of vnkyndenesse.
C.19.234   That diues deyede, dampned *for* his vnkyndenesse
C.19.242   For godes tretor he is [to]ld *for* al his trewe catel
C.19.246   And is in helle *for* al þat, how wol riche nouthe
C.19.258   Vnkynde cristene men, *for* coueytise and enuye
C.19.259   Sleth a man *for* his mebles with mouthe or with handes.
C.19.269   *For* coueytise of eny kyne thynge þat Crist dere bouhte.
C.19.287   Be yraunsomed *for* his repentaunce þer alle resoun hym dampneth.
C.19.300   As sorwe of herte is satisfaccioun *for* suche þat may nat paye.
C.19.304   Here f[e]re fleeth here *for* fere of here tonge.
C.20.15   Olde iewes of Ierusalem *for* ioye they songen,
C.20.20   'Liberum dei Arbitrium *for* loue hath vndertake
C.20.23   That Crist be nat yknowe *for* consumm[a]tus deus
C.20.31   That *for* al þat deth can do, withynne thre dayes to walke
C.20.34   And forbete [and adown] b[r]ynge bale deth *for* euere:
C.20.60   The daye *for* drede withdrouh and derke bicam þe sonne;
C.20.64   And dede men *for* þat dene cam oute of depe graues
C.20.66   'For a bittur bataile,' þe ded body saide;
C.20.96   Calde hem Caytyues, acorsed *for* euere.
C.20.97   'For þis [fou]l vilanye vengeaunce [to] ȝow [f]all[e]!
C.20.101   The gre ȝut hath he geten *for* al his grete wound[e]
C.20.113   What *for* fere of this ferly and of þe false iewes

C.20.123 *For* þe vertue þat her folewede afered was she neuere.
C.20.180 That many day myhte y nat se *for* merkenesse of synne,
C.20.256 Þe erthe *for* heuynesse þat he wolde soffre
C.20.345 *For* thy lesinges, lucifer, we losten furst oure ioye
C.20.348 And now *for* a later lesynge] þat thow lowe til Eue
C.20.351 Lucifer *for* his lesynges, leue y noen oþer
C.20.357 (A litel y ouerleep *for* lesynges sake,
C.20.365 *For* eny wey or warde wyde open[ed] þe ȝates.
C.20.371 *For* alle synfole soules, to saue oure bothe rihte.
C.20.375 Y bihihte hem nat here helle *for* euere.
C.20.404 And *for* þat drynke today y deyede as hit semede.
C.20.408 Y fauht so me fursteth ȝut *for* mannes soule sake:
C.20.445 Ac *for* þe lesynge þat thow low, lucifer, til eue
C.20.471 And crepe to þe croes on knees and kusse hit *for* a iewel
C.20.473 For godes blessed body hit baer *for* oure bote
C.21.23 And ȝe callen hym Crist; *for* what cause, telleth me.
C.21.96 Ac *for* all this preciouse presentes oure lord prince iesu[s]
C.21.107 Til he hadde all hem þat he *fore* bledde.
C.21.133 *For* þe dedes þat he dede, fili dauid, iesus.
C.21.178 Yblessed mote thow be and be shalt *for* euere.
C.21.205 And was afered *for* the lihte, for in fuyres liknesse
C.21.249 In pouerte and in pacience to preye *for* alle cristene;
C.21.293 Makyn hym, *for* eny mornynge, þat he ne was murye in soule
C.21.307 *For* presente or for preyere or eny prinses lettres.
C.21.307 For presente or *for* preyere or eny prinses lettres.
C.21.322 That Crist vpon Caluary *for* mankynde on peyned.
C.21.371 And *for* suluer weren forswore–soth[ly] thei wisten hit.
C.21.377 And thenne walled watur *for* wikked werkes
C.21.397 By iesu! *for* al ȝoure iangelyng, [with] spiritus Iusticie
C.21.414 And we Clerkes, when they come, *for* here comunes paieth,
C.21.415 *For* here pelurre and palfrayes mete and pelours þat hem folweth.
C.21.435 As wel *for* a wastour [and] wenche[s] of the stuyves
C.21.436 As *for* hymsulue and his seruauntes, saue he is furste yserued.
C.21.438 And trauaileth and tulieth *for* a tretour also sore
C.21.439 As *for* a trewe tydy man alle tymes ylyke.
C.21.458 And coloureth hit *for* a connyng and a clene lyuynge.'
C.22.19 That he dronke at vch a dy[c]h ar he deye *for* furste.
C.22.20 So nede at greet nede may nyme as *for* his owne
C.22.36 And as louh as a lamb *for* lakkyng þat hym nedeth;
C.22.77 Foles fro this fendes lymes *for* [Peres] loue the [plouhman].
C.22.105 Swowened and swel[t]e *for* sorwe of dethus duntes.
C.22.138 *For* a meneuer man[t]el he made leele matrimonye
C.22.148 Thus relyed lyf *for* a litel fo[rtune]
C.22.165 *For* care Consience tho cryede vpon elde
C.22.169 And lyf fley *for* fere to fisyk aftur helpe
C.22.195 For þe lyme þat she loued me *fore* and leef was to fele
C.22.200 And deth drow ney me; *for* drede gan y quaken
C.22.205 And halde the there euere til y sende *for* the.
C.22.233 That they cam *for* Couetyse, to haue cure of soules.
C.22.239 Then he þat laboreth *for* lyflode and leneth hit beggares.
C.22.251 *For* loue lefte they lordschipe, bothe lond and scole,
C.22.252 Frere fraunceys and domynyk, *for* loue to be holy.
C.22.267 A certeyne *for* a certeyne saue oenliche of freres.
C.22.292 A parcel to preye *for* hem and [pleye] with þe remenaunt
C.22.307 *For* here mys[fetes] that thei wrouht hadde
C.22.312 *For* fastyng of a fryday a feerde as he wolde deye.
C.22.325 To a lord *for* a lettre leue to haue
C.22.332 'In fayth,' quod this frere, '*for* profyt and for helthe
C.22.332 'In fayth,' quod this frere, 'for profyt and *for* helthe
C.22.341 'Ȝe? go thy gate!' quod pees, 'bi god! *for* al thi fisyk,
C.22.364 Of 'a pryue payement and y shal preye *for* ȝow
C.22.365 And *for* hem þat ȝe aren holde to al my lyf tyme
C.22.367 [As] freres of oure fraternite *for* a litel suluer'.
C.22.370 And wake *for* his wikkede werkes as he was woned [to do].
C.22.371 *For* confort of his confessour Contricioun he lefte
C.22.372 That is the souereyne salue *for* alle [synnes of kynde].
C.22.383 And þat freres hadde a fyndynge þat *for* nede flateren

for conj *for conj. &> forto, for_to* A 148; B 466; C 463

A.Pr.60, A.Pr.83, A.1.14, A.1.27, A.1.36, A.1.38, A.1.40, A.1.52, A.1.55, A.1.86, A.1.91, A.1.96, A.1.125, A.1.135, A.1.139, A.1.151, A.1.153, A.1.159, A.1.174, A.1.175, A.2.19, A.2.21, A.2.83, A.2.89, A.2.102, A.2.103, A.2.112, A.2.118, A.2.138, A.2.188, A.3.17, A.3.26, A.3.32, A.3.58, A.3.64, A.3.69, A.3.71, A.3.74, A.3.108, A.3.132, A.3.143, A.3.155, A.3.161, A.3.174, A.3.251, A.3.260, A.4.9, A.4.25, A.4.27, A.4.48, A.4.54, A.4.59, A.4.61, A.4.84, A.4.87, A.4.90, A.4.120, A.4.126, A.4.154, A.5.10, A.5.41, A.5.106, A.5.216, A.5.219, A.5.234, A.5.244, A.5.250, A.6.11, A.6.36, A.6.46, A.6.83, A.6.91, A.6.96, A.7.15, A.7.16, A.7.26, A.7.34, A.7.42, A.7.49, A.7.58, A.7.68, A.7.73, A.7.74, A.7.75, A.7.80, A.7.84, A.7.90, A.7.120, A.7.190, A.7.193, A.7.212, A.7.223, A.7.225, A.7.239, A.7.250, A.7.303, A.8.22, A.8.23, A.8.44, A.8.45, A.8.46, A.8.69, A.8.90, A.8.135, A.9.28, A.9.30, A.9.40, A.9.42, A.9.47, A.9.85, A.10.33, A.10.50, A.10.56, A.10.74, A.10.75, A.10.90, A.10.93, A.10.101, A.10.119, A.10.135, A.10.154, A.10.155, A.10.179, A.10.182, A.10.202, A.11.31, A.11.61, A.11.80, A.11.113, A.11.117, A.11.126, A.11.138, A.11.142, A.11.143, A.11.145, A.11.158, A.11.201, A.11.221, A.11.241, A.11.253, A.11.255, A.11.260, A.11.265, A.11.281, A.11.295, A.11.300, A.12.32, A.12.109

B.Pr.63, B.Pr.86, B.Pr.110, B.Pr.129, B.Pr.149, B.Pr.191, B.Pr.193, B.Pr.197, B.Pr.201, B.Pr.210, B.1.14, B.1.27, B.1.38, B.1.40, B.1.42, B.1.54, B.1.57, B.1.88, B.1.93, B.1.98, B.1.118, B.1.136, B.1.147, B.1.148, B.1.153, B.1.165, B.1.177, B.1.179, B.1.185, B.1.200, B.1.201, B.2.24, B.2.25, B.2.78, B.2.101, B.2.119, B.2.123, B.2.125, B.2.138, B.2.139, B.2.148, B.2.154, B.2.168, B.2.229, B.3.17, B.3.27, B.3.33, B.3.67, B.3.75, B.3.80, B.3.82, B.3.85, B.3.119, B.3.143, B.3.154, B.3.168, B.3.174, B.3.187, B.3.273, B.3.282, B.3.284, B.3.329, B.3.330, B.3.340, B.4.9, B.4.19, B.4.23, B.4.28, B.4.30, B.4.38, B.4.41, B.4.61, B.4.68, B.4.73, B.4.97, B.4.100, B.4.103, B.4.143, B.4.152, B.4.166, B.4.169, B.4.174, B.4.191, B.5.10, B.5.54, B.5.57, B.5.122, B.5.129, B.5.152, B.5.161, B.5.170, B.5.235, B.5.265, B.5.274, B.5.285, B.5.287, B.5.292, B.5.431, B.5.444, B.5.447, B.5.462, B.5.470, B.5.476, B.5.484, B.5.523, B.5.549, B.5.596, B.5.604, B.5.610, B.6.16, B.6.17, B.6.24, B.6.32, B.6.43, B.6.48, B.6.54, B.6.63, B.6.76, B.6.81, B.6.82, B.6.83, B.6.88, B.6.92, B.6.98, B.6.128, B.6.151, B.6.162, B.6.193, B.6.204, B.6.207, B.6.239, B.6.241, B.6.255, B.6.266, B.6.322, B.7.20, B.7.21, B.7.41, B.7.67, B.7.70, B.7.78, B.7.80, B.7.82, B.7.85, B.7.90, B.7.108, B.7.154, B.7.156, B.7.157, B.8.14, B.8.32, B.8.34, B.8.44, B.8.46, B.8.52, B.8.95, B.9.32, B.9.36, B.9.60, B.9.63, B.9.80, B.9.111, B.9.112, B.9.127, B.9.157, B.9.159, B.9.163, B.9.184, B.9.189, B.9.194, B.10.79, B.10.92, B.10.127, B.10.161, B.10.165, B.10.174, B.10.190, B.10.191, B.10.193, B.10.211, B.10.215, B.10.246, B.10.255, B.10.277, B.10.277, B.10.305, B.10.307, B.10.310, B.10.358, B.10.368, B.10.374, B.10.384, B.10.397, B.10.422, B.10.441, B.10.445, B.10.450, B.10.452, B.11.7, B.11.45, B.11.55, B.11.64, B.11.66, B.11.68, B.11.80, B.11.84, B.11.119, B.11.125, B.11.127, B.11.139, B.11.148, B.11.168, B.11.176, B.11.183, B.11.185, B.11.193, B.11.199, B.11.201, B.11.211, B.11.213, B.11.215, B.11.216, B.11.222, B.11.226, B.11.233, B.11.242, B.11.279, B.11.292, B.11.294, B.11.316, B.11.353, B.11.378, B.11.389, B.11.396, B.11.398, B.11.402, B.11.415, B.11.427, B.11.429, B.11.438, B.12.17, B.12.32, B.12.53, B.12.72, B.12.78, B.12.85, B.12.93, B.12.95, B.12.99, B.12.116, B.12.123, B.12.126, B.12.135, B.12.139, B.12.174, B.12.177, B.12.193, B.12.206, B.12.212, B.12.242, B.12.276, B.12.293, B.13.18, B.13.24, B.13.61, B.13.90, B.13.107, B.13.111, B.13.124, B.13.149, B.13.158, B.13.178, B.13.181, B.13.193, B.13.195, B.13.225, B.13.230, B.13.239, B.13.254, B.13.255, B.13.257, B.13.260, B.13.340, B.13.344, B.13.453, B.14.39, B.14.54, B.14.60, B.14.61, B.14.76, B.14.78, B.14.91, B.14.121, B.14.129, B.14.137, B.14.157, B.14.161, B.14.166, B.14.171, B.14.180, B.14.202, B.14.205, B.14.211, B.14.221, B.14.226, B.14.228, B.14.231, B.14.234, B.14.241, B.14.246, B.14.250, B.14.306, B.14.311, B.14.317, B.15.25, B.15.41, B.15.67, B.15.80, B.15.84, B.15.111, B.15.142, B.15.178, B.15.201, B.15.205, B.15.213, B.15.216, B.15.220, B.15.240, B.15.251, B.15.263, B.15.303, B.15.313, B.15.315, B.15.329, B.15.345, B.15.356, B.15.373, B.15.393, B.15.394, B.15.399, B.15.406, B.15.467, B.15.489, B.15.504, B.15.583, B.16.57, B.16.79, B.16.123, B.16.239, B.16.249, B.16.254, B.17.20, B.17.58, B.17.81, B.17.101, B.17.105, B.17.108, B.17.109, B.17.125, B.17.140, B.17.156, B.17.178, B.17.179, B.17.189, B.17.201, B.17.202, B.17.206, B.17.251, B.17.259, B.17.265, B.17.272, B.17.276, B.17.279, B.17.281, B.17.308, B.17.329, B.17.335, B.17.349, B.17.350, B.18.26, B.18.76, B.18.83, B.18.99, B.18.101, B.18.102, B.18.138, B.18.143, B.18.148, B.18.152, B.18.154, B.18.166, B.18.181, B.18.202, B.18.205, B.18.206, B.18.216, B.18.242, B.18.252, B.18.265, B.18.273, B.18.278, B.18.280, B.18.287, B.18.293, B.18.294, B.18.302, B.18.303, B.18.305, B.18.310, B.18.313, B.18.333, B.18.335, B.18.365, B.18.376, B.18.387, B.18.394, B.18.398, B.18.419, B.18.429, B.18.430, B.19.21, B.19.28, B.19.29, B.19.40, B.19.54, B.19.81, B.19.90, B.19.93, B.19.111, B.19.112, B.19.119, B.19.130, B.19.134, B.19.145, B.19.145, B.19.162, B.19.177, B.19.205, B.19.215, B.19.219, B.19.258, B.19.300, B.19.304, B.19.312, B.19.358, B.19.451, B.19.455, B.19.469, B.19.474, B.19.475, B.20.11, B.20.23, B.20.25, B.20.35, B.20.37, B.20.38, B.20.58, B.20.195, B.20.203, B.20.231, B.20.234, B.20.234, B.20.238, B.20.278, B.20.281, B.20.317

C.Pr.79, C.Pr.84, C.Pr.101, C.Pr.109, C.Pr.116, C.Pr.137, C.Pr.170, C.Pr.206, C.Pr.216, C.Pr.219, C.Pr.221, C.1.14, C.1.36, C.1.38, C.1.50, C.1.53, C.1.84, C.1.89, C.1.99, C.1.119, C.1.135, C.1.146, C.1.149, C.1.161, C.1.173, C.1.175, C.1.181, C.1.195, C.1.196, C.2.24, C.2.28, C.2.53, C.2.85, C.2.108, C.2.123, C.2.127, C.2.130, C.2.136, C.2.141, C.2.145, C.2.154, C.2.164, C.2.170, C.2.239, C.3.18, C.3.28, C.3.36, C.3.71, C.3.81, C.3.84, C.3.131, C.3.138, C.3.156, C.3.159, C.3.168, C.3.174, C.3.181, C.3.186, C.3.192, C.3.211, C.3.214, C.3.220, C.3.233, C.3.245, C.3.256, C.3.324, C.3.343, C.3.369, C.3.384, C.3.387, C.3.409, C.3.426, C.3.435, C.3.437, C.3.458, C.3.482, C.3.483, C.3.489, C.4.9, C.4.19, C.4.22, C.4.35, C.4.38, C.4.64, C.4.72, C.4.93, C.4.96, C.4.140, C.4.161, C.5.5, C.5.6, C.5.27, C.5.55, C.5.59, C.5.66, C.5.83, C.5.138, C.5.152, C.5.154, C.5.176, C.5.181, C.6.15, C.6.23, C.6.46, C.6.84, C.6.87, C.6.94, C.6.120, C.6.136, C.6.146, C.6.152, C.6.159, C.6.178, C.6.207, C.6.256, C.6.296, C.6.305, C.6.313, C.6.316, C.6.324, C.6.330, C.6.334, C.6.341, C.6.342, C.6.347, C.6.385, C.6.438, C.7.44, C.7.58, C.7.61, C.7.113, C.7.118, C.7.126, C.7.168, C.7.234, C.7.262, C.7.277, C.8.15, C.8.31, C.8.41, C.8.52, C.8.62, C.8.78, C.8.83, C.8.92, C.8.101, C.8.107, C.8.160, C.8.170, C.8.192, C.8.210, C.8.216, C.8.229, C.8.267, C.8.279, C.8.299, C.8.342, C.9.24, C.9.25, C.9.52, C.9.55, C.9.63, C.9.66, C.9.102, C.9.119, C.9.126, C.9.138, C.9.139, C.9.166, C.9.167, C.9.194, C.9.195, C.9.217, C.9.220, C.9.259, C.9.260, C.9.280, C.9.282, C.9.303, C.9.305, C.9.322, C.10.14, C.10.26, C.10.36, C.10.43, C.10.54, C.10.168, C.10.176, C.10.201, C.10.205, C.10.207, C.10.240, C.10.243, C.10.252, C.10.254, C.10.255, C.10.256, C.10.287, C.10.290, C.10.292, C.10.306, C.11.27, C.11.59, C.11.77, C.11.95, C.11.103, C.11.107, C.11.114, C.11.130, C.11.131, C.11.133, C.11.156, C.11.166, C.11.197, C.11.202, C.11.209, C.11.226, C.11.228, C.11.244, C.11.254, C.11.275, C.11.277, C.11.284, C.12.2, C.12.7, C.12.23, C.12.25, C.12.54, C.12.60, C.12.62, C.12.83, C.12.101, C.12.105, C.12.107, C.12.118, C.12.122, C.12.131, C.12.205, C.12.235, C.12.237, C.13.1, C.13.8, C.13.12, C.13.33, C.13.38, C.13.50, C.13.55, C.13.87, C.13.95, C.13.101, C.13.106, C.13.108, C.13.110, C.13.128, C.13.154, C.13.164, C.13.192, C.13.207, C.13.223, C.13.229, C.13.233,

C.13.234, C.13.236, C.13.244, C.14.37, C.14.44, C.14.61, C.14.66, C.14.70, C.14.79,
C.14.84, C.14.114, C.14.117, C.14.132, C.14.145, C.14.151, C.14.174, C.14.176,
C.14.198, C.14.217, C.15.20, C.15.65, C.15.79, C.15.97, C.15.124, C.15.157, C.15.204,
C.15.218, C.15.224, C.15.225, C.15.227, C.15.233, C.15.238, C.15.253, C.15.259,
C.15.260, C.15.297, C.16.14, C.16.19, C.16.43, C.16.46, C.16.52, C.16.62, C.16.67,
C.16.69, C.16.72, C.16.75, C.16.81, C.16.86, C.16.90, C.16.141, C.16.145, C.16.151,
C.16.185, C.16.203, C.16.239, C.16.256, C.16.295, C.16.365, C.16.372, C.17.16,
C.17.35, C.17.59, C.17.62, C.17.86, C.17.109, C.17.123, C.17.137, C.17.141, C.17.144,
C.17.154, C.17.158, C.17.168, C.17.178, C.17.229, C.17.233, C.17.252, C.17.255,
C.17.262, C.17.287, C.18.89, C.18.140, C.18.255, C.18.267, C.18.270, C.19.21, C.19.56,
C.19.57, C.19.78, C.19.92, C.19.113, C.19.136, C.19.143, C.19.144, C.19.155, C.19.167,
C.19.168, C.19.172, C.19.217, C.19.225, C.19.231, C.19.241, C.19.244, C.19.253,
C.19.257, C.19.260, C.19.262, C.19.295, C.19.309, C.19.315, C.19.329, C.19.330,
C.20.25, C.20.78, C.20.85, C.20.102, C.20.104, C.20.105, C.20.141, C.20.146, C.20.151,
C.20.155, C.20.157, C.20.169, C.20.184, C.20.207, C.20.210, C.20.211, C.20.219,
C.20.225, C.20.237, C.20.251, C.20.261, C.20.273, C.20.295, C.20.300, C.20.302,
C.20.313, C.20.323, C.20.324, C.20.328, C.20.335, C.20.337, C.20.344, C.20.347,
C.20.355, C.20.359, C.20.376, C.20.378, C.20.403, C.20.418, C.20.432, C.20.437,
C.20.441, C.20.462, C.20.473, C.20.474, C.21.21, C.21.28, C.21.29, C.21.40, C.21.54,
C.21.81, C.21.90, C.21.93, C.21.111, C.21.112, C.21.119, C.21.130, C.21.134, C.21.145,
C.21.145, C.21.162, C.21.177, C.21.205, C.21.215, C.21.219, C.21.258, C.21.300,
C.21.304, C.21.312, C.21.358, C.21.451, C.21.455, C.21.469, C.21.474, C.21.475,
C.22.11, C.22.23, C.22.25, C.22.35, C.22.37, C.22.38, C.22.58, C.22.195, C.22.203,
C.22.231, C.22.234, C.22.234, C.22.238, C.22.278, C.22.281, C.22.317

for_to adv&prtcl *forto adv. & particle cf forto* A 38; B 72; C 68

A.Pr.27	In hope [*for*] *to* haue heueneriche blisse,
A.Pr.47	*For to* seke seint Iame & seintes at rome;
A.Pr.91	Become clerkis of acountis þe king *for to* serue;
A.1.16	*For to* worsshipe hym þerewiþ whiles ȝe ben here.
A.1.131	*For to* loue þi lord leuere þanne þiselue;
A.2.65	Wiþ alle þe delites of lust þe deuil *for to* serue,
A.2.173	And gile doþ him to go agast *for to* deiȝe.
A.2.186	*For to* wone wiþ hem, watris to loke.
A.3.27	*For to* werche þi wil while þi lif lastiþ.'
A.3.45	*For to* be hire bedeman & hire baude aftir.
A.3.83	*For to* amende [meiris and] men þat kepiþ þe lawis,
A.3.108	For heo is fayn of þi Felasshipe, *for to* be þi make.'
A.3.184	Þere I lefte wiþ my lord his lif *for to* saue,
A.3.191	And ek king of þat kiþ his kyn *for to* helpe,
A.4.28	*For to* saue hemself from shame & from harm.
A.4.133	*For to* construe þis clause declynede faste,
A.5.11	And consience wiþ a cros com *for to* preche,
A.5.49	*For to* affaiten hire flessh þat fers was to synne:
A.5.146	Now begynneþ glotoun *for to* [go to] shrift,
A.5.150	'To holy chirche', quaþ he, '*for to* here masse,
A.5.186	Bargoynes & beuerechis begonne *for to* arise,
A.6.94	And lere þe *for to* loue & hise lawes holden.
A.7.51	'*For to* werche be þi woord while my lif duriþ.'
A.7.126	Ac treuþe shal teche ȝow his tem *for to* dryue,
A.7.173	Þat hunger was not hardy on hem *for to* loke.
A.7.182	And preiȝede pur charite wiþ peris *for to* dwelle,
A.9.2	Al a somer sesoun *for to* seke dowel,
A.10.80	It is begynnyng of goodnesse god *for to* douten.
A.10.89	Wilne þou neuere in þis world, [wy], *for to* do betere,
A.10.182	For summe, as I se now, soþ *for to* telle,
A.11.102	*For to* werche ȝour wil [while] my lif duriþ,
A.11.140	It is no science forsoþe *for to* sotile þereinne.
A.11.155	Astronomye is hard þing & euil *for to* knowe;
A.11.267	*For to* reule his reaum riȝt at his wille;
A.11.299	*For to* answere hem haue ȝe no doute,
A.12.6	Þe were lef to lerne but loþ *for to* stodie;
A.12.45	And ȝif þou desyre with him *for to* abyde
A.12.70	At my bak of broke bred þi bely *for to* fylle,
B.Pr.27	In hope [*for*] *to* haue heueneriche blisse,
B.Pr.47	*For to* seken Seint Iame and Seintes at Rome;
B.Pr.115	*For to* counseillen þe kyng and þe commune saue.
B.Pr.172	And if hym list *for to* laike þanne loke we mowen
B.1.16	*For to* worshipe hym þerwiþ while ye ben here.
B.1.143	*For to* louen þi lord leuere þan þiselue.
B.1.163	And *for to* knowen it kyndely, it comseþ by myght,
B.2.214	And Gyle doþ hym to go agast *for to* dye.
B.2.227	[*For to*] wonye with hem watres to loke.
B.3.28	*For to* werche þi wille [while þi lif lasteþ].'
B.3.46	*For to* ben hire Bedeman and hire [baude after].
B.3.52	*For to* be youre frend, frere, and faile yow neuere
B.3.94	*For to* amenden Maires and men þat kepen [þe] lawes,
B.3.119	For she is fayn of þi felaweshipe, *for to* be þi make.'
B.3.197	Ther I lafte wiþ my lord his lif *for to* saue.
B.3.204	And [ek] kyng of þat kiþ his kyn *for to* helpe,
B.4.31	*For to* saue hem[seluen] from shame and from harmes.
B.5.138	And þe Couentes Gardyner *for to* graffen Impes.
B.5.296	Now bigynneþ Gloton *for to* go to shrifte

B.5.300	'To holy chirche', quod he, '*for to* here masse,
B.5.352	*For to* liften hym o lofte and leyde hym on his knowes.
B.6.56	'*For to* werche by þi wor[d] while my lif dureþ.'
B.6.185	That hunger was noȝt hardy on hem *for to* loke.
B.8.2	Al a somer seson *for to* seke dowel,
B.9.115	The wif was maad þe w[y]e *for to* helpe werche,
B.9.159	For some, as I se now, sooþ *for to* telle,
B.10.42	Drynken and dreuelen and do men *for to* gape,
B.10.134	And þo þat vseþ þise hauylons [*for*] *to* blende mennes wittes,
B.10.150	*For to* werche youre wille while my lif dureþ,
B.10.188	It is no Science forsoþe *for to* sotile Inne;
B.10.212	Ac Astronomye is hard þyng and yuel *for to* knowe;
B.10.396	Thouȝ hir goost be vngracious god *for to* plese.
B.11.19	*For to* lyue longe and ladies to louye,
B.11.57	To hir Priour prouincial a pardon *for to* haue,
B.11.72	That wedde none widwes but *for to* welden hir goodes.
B.11.323	And þoruȝ þe wondres of þis world wit *for to* take.
B.11.422	Tho hadde he [litel] likyng *for to* lere þe moore.
B.11.439	'Certes', quod he, 'þat is sooþ'; and shoop hym *for to* walken,
B.12.72	For Moyses witnesseþ þat god wroot *for to* wisse þe peple
B.12.131	[The] selkouþes þat þei seiȝen, hir sones *for to* teche.
B.12.208	And *for to* seruen a Seint and swich a þef togideres,
B.12.246	And vnlouelich of ledene and looþ *for to* here.
B.13.148	Ac *for to* fare þus wiþ þi frend, folie it were;
B.13.250	And þanne wolde I þe prest to þe peple paast *for to* make,
B.13.442	*For to* solace youre soules swiche minstrales to haue:
B.13.445	*For to* saue þi soule from sathan þyn enemy.
B.14.21	And siþen sende þee to Satisfaccion *for to* [sonnen] it after:
B.15.110	Than *for to* prechen and preuen it noȝt–ypocrisie it semeþ.
B.15.245	*For to* wonye wiþ hem his wone was som tyme,
B.15.281	And day bi day hadde he hire noȝt his hunger *for to* slake,
B.15.408	As messager to Makometh, men *for to* teche.
B.15.512	Many myracles he wrouȝte m[e]n *for to* turne,
B.15.520	Al *for to* enforme þe faith; in fele contrees deyeden
B.16.49	Manacen bihynde me, my fruyt *for to* fecche,
B.16.99	*For to* werchen his wille wiþouten any synne:
B.16.104	And lered hym lechecraft his lif *for to* saue
B.16.245	And called me foot of his feiþ, his folk *for to* saue
B.17.43	Than *for to* techen hem two, and to hard to lerne þe leeste!
B.17.45	And wel awey worse ȝit *for to* loue a sherewe.
B.17.47	Than *for to* louye and lene as wel lorels as lele.
B.17.244	*For to* murþen men [wiþ] þat in [m]erke sitten.
B.17.322	*For to* fleen his owene [hous] as holy writ sheweþ.
B.18.57	'Consummatum est', quod crist and comsede *for to* swoune.
B.19.70	Faithly *for to* speke, his firste name was Iesus.
B.19.141	And *for to* doon hym to deþe day and nyȝt þei casten.
B.19.261	And *for to* tilie truþe a teeme shal he haue.'
B.19.280	[That] caste *for to* ke[l]e a crokke to saue þe fatte aboue.
B.19.317	'Ayeins þi greynes', quod Grace, 'bigynneþ *for to* ripe,
B.20.11	For þre þynges he takeþ his lif *for to* saue.
B.20.18	And if hym list *for to* lape þe lawe of kynde wolde
B.20.242	Conscience of þis counseil þo comsede *for to* laughe,
B.20.250	Wiþ þat ye leue logik and lerneþ *for to* louye.
C.Pr.7	Me biful for werynesse of–walked,
C.Pr.142	*For to* conseillen þe kyng and þe commune saue.
C.Pr.189	And yf [hym] lust *for to* layke than loke we mowe
C.1.16	*For to* worschipe hym þerwith þe whiles ȝe lyuen here.
C.1.119	For theder as þe fende fly his fote *for to* sette,
C.1.142	*For to* louye thy lord leuest of alle,
C.1.159	And *for to* knowe hit kyndly, hit comeseth by myhte
C.2.15	*For to* telle of here atyer no tyme haue y nouthe.
C.2.202	*For to* wisse hem þe way and with mede abyde.
C.2.224	And gyle doth hym to gone agaste *for to* deye.
C.3.19	*For to* wedde at thy wille '[and] where the leef li[k]eth
C.3.29	*For to* worche thy wille the while þou myhte dure.'
C.3.48	*For to* ben here bedman and bere wel here ernde
C.3.109	*For to* spyre and to aspye, for eny speche of suluer,
C.3.156	For she is fayn of thy felawschipe, *for to* be thy make.'
C.3.261	And also kyng of þat kuth his kyn *for to* helpe,
C.3.283	And glad *for to* grype here, gret lord oþer pore.'
C.3.296	And *for to* vndertake [to] trauaile for another
C.4.55	Ȝut is he bold *for to* borw Ac baddelyche he payeth:
C.4.68	And *for to* haue here helpe handy dandy payde.
C.4.106	And *for to* consayle þe kynge on Consience thei lokede;
C.5.61	Hit bycometh for clerkes Crist *for to* serue,
C.6.350	Now bygynneth glotoun *for to* go to shryfte
C.6.355	'To holy churche,' quod he, '*for to* here masse
C.6.406	As hoso layth lynes *for to* lacche foules.
C.6.410	*For to* lyfte hym aloft [and] leyde hym on his knees.
C.7.102	*For to* solace ȝoure soules suche munstrals to haue:
C.7.105	*For to* saue thy soule fram satan thyn enemye.
C.8.13	Consience conseyleth ȝow cloth *for to* make
C.8.55	'*For to* worche by thy wit and my wyf bothe.'

C. 8.181   That hunger was nat hardy on hem *for to* loke.
C. 8.302   'Y haue no peny,' quod [Peres], 'polettes *for to* begge,
C. 9.86   And ben abasched *for to* begge and wollen nat be aknowe
C. 9.164   Hit nedeth nat nouthe anoon *for to* preche
C. 9.267   *For to* go wurye þe wolf that the wolle fou[l]eth?
C.10.2   Alle a somur seson *for to* seke dowel
C.10.149   Thise fyue ben sette *for to* saue Anima
C.11.88   *For to* worche ȝoure wille while my lyf duyreth
C.11.131   For loue is a lykyng thyng and loth *for to* greue.
C.11.132   Lerne *for to* louie yf þe lik[e] dowel
C.11.178   *For to* lyue longe and ladyes to louye
C.11.227   Thogh here gost be vngracious god *for to* plese.
C.11.273   And fonde y neuere in faith, *for to* telle treuthe,
C.12.20   That wilneth nat þe wedewe bote *for to* welde here godes.
C.12.233   Riht so, sothly, *for to* segge treuthe,
C.13.45   Ne non haiward is hote his wed *for to* taken.
C.13.47   And þe hayward happe with hym *for to* mete,
C.14.147   And *for to* seruen a seynt and suche a thef togyderes,
C.16.264   Then *for to* prechen and preue hit nat–ypocrisye hit semeth.
C.17.263   Mony myracles a wrouhte men *for to* torne,
C.17.271   *For to* enf[ou]rme þe fayth ful wydewhare deyede,
C.18.54   Where þe fruyt were fayre or foul *for to* loke on.
C.18.105   And anoon he hihte Elde an hy *for to* clymbe
C.18.132   *For to* worchen his wille withouten eny synne:
C.19.42   And *for to* louye and bileue in o lord almyhty
C.19.44   Ac *for to* bileue in o lord þat lyueth in thre persones
C.19.210   *For to* murthe men with þat in merke sitten,
C.19.245   Lordliche *for to* lyue and lykyngliche be clothed
C.20.57   'Consummatum est,' quod Crist and comsed *for to* swoene.
C.21.70   Faythly *for to* speke his furste name was iesus.
C.21.141   And *for to* do hym to dethe day and nyhte they casten,
C.21.261   And *for to* tulye treuthe a teme shal he haue.'
C.21.317   'Aȝeynes thy graynes,' quod grace, 'bigynneth *for to* rype,
C.22.11   For thre thynges he taketh [h]is lyf *for to* saue.
C.22.18   And yf [hym] lust *for to* lape the lawe of kynde wolde
C.22.242   Con[s]ience of this con[s]ail tho comesed *for to* lawhe
C.22.250   With þat ȝe l[e]ue logyk and lerneth *for to* louye.

forageres n *forager n.* B 1; C 1
B.20.85   Frenesies and foule yueles; *forageres* of kynde
C.22.85   Freneseyes and foule eueles; *forageres* of kynde

forbar > forbere

forbedeþ v *forbeden v.* A 4 forbede (3) forboden (1); B 6 forbede (3) forbedeþ (1) forbode (1) forboden (1); C 4 forbede (3) forbodene (1)
A. 3.101   'ȝa lord,' quaþ þat lady, 'lord *forbede* ellis;
A. 3.109   Quaþ consience to þe kyng, 'crist it [me] *forbede*!
A. 3.141   And bringen forþ barnes aȝens *forboden* lawis.
A. 8.160   And so I leue lelly, lord *forbede* ellis,
B. 3.112   'Ye, lord', quod þat lady, 'lord *forbede* ellis!
B. 3.120   Quod Conscience to þe kyng, 'crist it me *forbede*!
B. 3.152   And bryngeþ forþ barnes ayein *forbode* lawes.
B. 7.182   And so I leue leelly, lor[d] *forb[e]de* ellis,
B.10.209   And noȝt to greuen hem þat greueþ vs; god [þat *forbedeþ*]:
B.13.348   As wel fastyng dayes [as] Fridaies [and] *forboden* nyȝtes,
C. 3.149   'ȝe, lord,' quod that lady, 'lord hit me *forbede*
C. 3.157   Quod Consience to the kyng, 'Crist hit me *forbede*!
C. 3.190   And bringeth forth bar[n]es aȝenes *forbodene* lawes:
C. 9.328   And so y leue lely–lord *forbede* elles–

forbere v *forberen v.* B 3 forbar (1) forbeere (1) forbere (1); C 2 forbar (1) forbere (1)
B. 3.274   *Forbar* hym and his beestes boþe as þe bible witnesseþ
B.11.210   And of þat ech man may *forbere* amende þere it nedeþ,
B.15.121   But if many preest [*forbeere*] hir baselardes and hir broches
C. 1.99   For thei sholde nother faste ne *forbere* the serk
C. 3.427   *Forbar* hym and his beste bestes, as þe bible wittenesseth,

forbete v *forbeten v.* B 2 forbete (1) forbeten (1); C 2
B.18.35   And *forbete* and adoun brynge bale deeþ for euere:
B.20.198   So Elde and [heo] hadden it *forbeten*.
C.20.34   And *forbete* [and adown] b[r]ynge bale deth for euere:
C.22.198   So Elde and hee hit hadde *forbete*.

forbisene n *forebisne n.* A 1 forebisene; B 3 forbisene (1) forbisenes (1) forbisne (1); C 2
A. 9.24   Be a *forebisene*,' quaþ þe Frere, 'I shal þe faire shewen:
B. 8.28   By a *forbisne*', quod þe frere, 'I shal þee faire shewe.
B.11.325   I was fet forþ by [*forbisenes*] to knowe
B.15.527   He is a *forbisene* to alle bisshopes and a briȝt myrrour
C.10.32   By a *forbisene*,' quod þe frere, 'y shal the fayre shewe:
C.17.277   He is a *forbisene* to alle bisshopis and a briht myrrour

forbiteþ v *forbiten v.* B 1 forbiteþ; C 1 forbit
B.16.35   And *forbiteþ* þe blosmes riȝt to þe bare leues.
C.18.39   And al *forb[i]t* Caritas rihte to þe bare stalke.

forbode n *forbod n. &> forbedeþ* A 1; B 2; C 1
A. 4.157   'I graunte,' quaþ þe king, 'godis *forbode* he faille!
B. 4.194   'I graunte [gladly]', quod þe kyng, 'goddes *forbode* [he faile]!
B.15.580   Arn ferme as in þe feiþ, goddes *forbode* ellis,
C. 3.139   ȝut y forgyue þe þis gult; godes *forb[o]de* eny more

forboden(e > forbedeþ

forbrenne v *forbrennan v.* A 1; B 1; C 2 forbrenne (1) forbrent (1)
A. 3.87   Þat fuyr shal falle & *forbrenne* at þe laste.
B. 3.98   That fir shal falle & [*forbrenne* at þe laste]
C. 3.107   Ful adoun and *forbrent* forth alle þe rewe.
C. 3.126   That fuyr shal falle and *forbrenne* al to blew aysches

force n *force n.* C 1
C.14.10   And thenne dost thow wel, withoute drede; ho can do bet no *force*.

ford n *ford n.* A 1 foorþe; B 1; C 1
A. 6.54   Forto ȝe fynden a *foorþe*, ȝoure fadris honouriþ;
B. 5.567   [Forto] ye fynden a *ford*, youre-fadres-honoureþ:
C. 7.214   Forto ȝe fynde a *ford*, ȝoure-fader[s]-honoureth;

fordoon v *fordon v.* A 1 fordon; B 13 fordide (2) fordo (5) fordoon (2) fordooþ (4); C 11 fordede (1) fordo (4) fordoen (1) fordon (1) fordoth (4)
A. 5.20   Þat dedly synne er domisday shal *fordon* hem alle.
B. 5.20   That dedly synne er domesday shal *fordoon* hem alle.
B. 9.66   Allas þat drynke shal *fordo* þat god deere bouȝte,
B.13.259   Til pride be pureliche *fordo*, and [þat] þoruȝ payn defaute.
B.16.166   Deide and dee[þ] *fordide*, and day of nyȝt made.
B.17.276   For þat kynde dooþ vnkynde *fordoop*, as þise corsede þeues,
B.17.284   He *fordooþ* þe leuest light þat oure lord louyeþ.
B.18.29   Deeþ seiþ he shal *fordo* and adoun brynge
B.18.42   To *fordoon* it on o day, and in þre dayes after
B.18.65   'Lif and deeþ, in þis derknesse hir oon *fordooþ* hir ooþer.
B.18.152   For venym *fordooþ* venym, [þer fecche I euydence]
B.18.158   So shal þis deeþ *fordo*, I dar my lif legge,
B.18.345   And þat deeþ in hem *fordide* my deeþ shal releue
B.19.51   Mighte no deeþ hym *fordo* ne adoun brynge
C. 5.122   That dedly synne ar domesday shal *fordon* hem alle.
C.15.229   Til pruyde be puyreliche *fordo* and þat thorw payn defaute:
C.19.257   For þat kynde doth vnkynde *fordoth*, as this corsede theues,
C.19.265   A *fordoth* the lihte þat oure lord loketh to haue worschipe of.
C.20.28   Deth saith a wol *fordo* and adown brynge
C.20.41   To *fordoen* hit on a day, and in thre dayes aftur
C.20.67   'Lyf & deth, in this derkenesse here oen *fordoth* her oþer.
C.20.155   For venym *fordoth* venym, þer feche y euydence
C.20.161   And so shal this deth *fordo*, y dar my lyf legge,
C.20.390   And þat deth *fordede* my deth to releue
C.21.51   Myhte no deth hym *fordo* ne adown brynge

fore n *fore n. &> for prep* C 1
C. 6.118   Freres folewen my [f]ore fele tyme and ofte

forebisene > forbisene

forefadres n *forefader n.* B 2; C 2 forfadres
B. 5.493   Feddest wiþ þi fresshe blood oure *forefadres* in derknesse:
B. 9.147   And alle for hir [*fore]fadres* ferden þe werse.
C. 7.133   Feddest tho with thy [fresshe] blood oure *forfadres* in helle:
C.10.235   And al for here *forfadres* ferden þe worse.

foreynes n *forein n.* C 1
C. 9.200   And somme hadde *foreynes* to frendes þat hem fode sente

forel n *forel n.* A 1 Forellis; B 2 forel (1) forelles (1); C 1
A.11.159   ȝet arn þere febicchis of *Forellis* of many manis wittes.
B.10.216   Yet ar þer fibicches in [*forelles*] of fele mennes [wittes],
B.13.95   What he fond in a [*forel* of] a freres lyuyng,
C.15.102   What a fond in a *forel* of a frere[s] lyuynge,

foresleues n *foresleve n.* A 1 foresleuys; B 1
A. 5.63   Of a Freris frokke were þe *foresleuys*.
B. 5.80   Of a Freres frokke were þe *foresleues*.

forest n *forest n.* B 1; C 1 forestes
B.15.333   Fele of yow fareþ as if I a *forest* hadde
C. 9.225   In frithes and in *forestes* for fox and other bestes

foreteth n *foreteth n. pl.* C 1
C.20.383   And hoso hit out a mannes eye or elles his *foreteth*

foretolde v *foretellen v.* A 1
A.11.168   And fond as she *foretolde* & forþ gan I wende,

foreward > forward; forewis > forow; forfadres > forefadres; forfaiture > forfeture

forfaren v *forfaren v.(1)* B 1; C 1 forfare
B.15.135 A[c] goddes folk for defaute þerof *forfaren* and spillen.
C. 8.233 Loke by thy lyue lat hem nat *forfare*.

forfeten v *forfetern v.* B 1 forfeteþ; C 2 forfeten (1) forfeteth (1)
B.20.25 For Spiritus fortitudinis *forfeteþ* [wel] ofte;
C.13.187 Y se non so ofte *forfeten* sothly so mankynde;
C.22.25 For spiritus fortitudinis *forfeteth* wel ofte;

forfeture n *forfeture n.* A 1 forfaiture; B 1; C 1
A. 4.114 Vpe *forfaiture* of þat fe, who fynt hym [at douere],
B. 4.131 V[p] *forfeture* of þat fee, wh[o] fynt [hym] at Douere,
C. 4.128 Vp *forfeture* of þat fee, ho fyndeth h[y]m ouerward,

forfreteþ v *forfreten v.* B 1; C 1 forfret
B.16.29 And *forfreteþ* nei3 þe fruyt þoru3 manye faire sightes.
C.18.33 And *forfret* þat fruyt thorw many fayre s[ih]tus.

forgete > foryete; forgeuenesse > for3ifnesse

forgid ptp *forgen v.* A 1
A. 2.23 Fauel wiþ fair speche haþ *forgid* hem togidere;

forgifnesse > for3ifnesse; forguue(n > for3yue

forglutten v *forglotten v.* B 1; C 1 forglotten
B.10.84 But in gaynesse and glotonye *forglutten* hir good
C.11.64 Bote in gaynesse and glotonye *forglotten* here godes

forgo v *foregon v.* C 1
C.13.49 The marchaunt mote *forgo* or moneye of his porse

forgoer n *foregoer n.* A 1 forgoere; B 2 Forgoer (1) Forgoers (1); C 2 forgoere (1) vorgoers (1)
A. 2.149 Ac gile was *forgoere* and gyede hem alle.
B. 2.61 *Forgoers* and vitaillers and [v]okettes of þe Arches;
B. 2.188 Ac Gyle was *Forgoer* and gyed hem alle.
C. 2.63 *Vorgoers* and vitalers and voketes of the Arches;
C. 2.201 Ac gyle was *forgoere* to gyen al th[e] peple,

forgrynt v *cf. for-, grindan v.* B 1
B.10.80 That girles for [oure] giltes he *forgrynt* hem alle].

for3af > for3yue; for3eld(e > foryelde; for3et(- > foryete; for3eue > for3yue

forleyn ptp *forlien v.* C 1
C. 4.46 How wrong wilfully hadde his wyf *forleyn*

forlong > furlong

formaliche adv *formalli adv.* B 1; C 1 formallych
B.15.374 [That kan versifie faire ne *formaliche* enditen],
C.17.110 Þat can versifye vayre or *formallych* endite

forme n *forme n.* B 3; C 5 forme (1) fourme (4)
B. 1.117 Lopen out wiþ Lucifer in loþliche *forme*
B.13.296 Or feirest of feitures of *forme* and of shafte,
B.20.52 And mette ful merueillously þat in mannes *forme*
C. 1.110 Lepen out in lothly *forme* for his [luþer] wille
C. 7.130 On a friday in *fourme* of man feledest oure sorwe:
C.20.315 Not in *fourme* of a fende bote in fourme of an Addre
C.20.315 Not in fourme of a fende bote in *fourme* of an Addre
C.22.52 And mette ful merueylousely þat in mannes *fourme*

formen v *formen v.* A 3 fourme (1) fourmide (2); B 7 formed (3) formede (1) formen (2) fourmen (1); C 1 formede
A. 1.14 For he is fadir of feiþ & *fourmide* 3ow alle
A. 1.140 And þat falliþ to þe fadir þat *fourmide* vs alle,
A. 8.39 And before þe face of my fadir *fourme* 3oure setis.
B. 1.14 For he is fader of feiþ, and *formed* yow alle
B. 1.166 And falleþ to þe fader þat *formed* vs alle,
B.10.106 And leyden fautes vpon þe fader þat *formede* vs alle,
B.11.389 For is no creature vnder crist can *formen* hymseluen,
B.15.378 [And as vsher vnder hym to *fourmen* vs alle
B.16.213 Hym þat first *formed* al, þe fader of heuene.
B.17.172 The fyngres *formen* a ful hand to portreye or peynten;
C. 1.162 And þat falleth to þe fader þat *formede* vs alle,

formeour > formour

formest adv *formest adv.* A 2; B 3; C 7 formeste (1) formost (5) formoste (1)
A.10.131 *Formest* & ferst to folk þat ben weddit
A.11.164 Foundit hem *formest* folk to desceyue.
B.10.221 Founded hem *formest* folk to deceyue.
B.18.160 And ri3t as [þe gilour] þoru3 gile [bigiled man *formest*]
B.19.120 That she first and *formest* ferme sholde bileue
C. 1.73 Y vndirfenge þe *formeste* and fre man the made.

C. 6.15 For y, *formost* and furste, to fader and moder
C.17.60 To helpe thy fader *formost* byfore freres or monkes
C.17.233 For were presthode more parfyte, that is, þe pope *formost*
C.20.162 All þat deth and þe deuel dede *formost* to Eue
C.20.163 And riht as þe gylour thorw gyle bigiled man *formost*
C.21.120 That [sh]e furste and *formoste* [ferme sholde] bileue

formor > formour; formost(e > formest

formour n *formere n.* A 1 fourmour; B 2; C 3 formeour (1) formor (1) formour (1)
A.10.28 Fadir & *fourmour*, þe ferste of alle þing.
B. 9.27 Fader and *formour*, [þe first of alle þynges].
B.17.170 So is þe fader a ful god, *formour* and shappere:
C. 1.14 For he is fader of fayth and *formor* of alle;
C.10.153 Fader and *formour* of al þat forth groweth
C.19.134 And he fader and *for[m]eour*, þe furste of alle thynges–

fornicatouris n *fornicatour n.* A 1
A. 2.142 And fetten oure vitailes [of] *fornicatouris*;

forow n *forwe n.* A 1 forewis; B 2 forow (1) furwes (1); C 2 forw (1) forwes (1)
A. 7.96 And helpe my cultir to kerue & close þe *forewis*.'
B. 6.104 And helpe my cultour to kerue and [close] þe *furwes*.'
B.13.371 That a foot lond or a *forow* fecchen I wolde
C. 6.268 That a foet lond or a *forw* fecchen y wolde
C. 8.65 And helpe my Coltur to kerue and cl[o]se þe *forwes*;

foroward > forward; forred(e > furred

forreyours n *forreour n.* B 1; C 1 forreours
B.20.81 And sente forþ his *forreyours*, Feueres and Fluxes,
C.22.81 And sente forth his *forreours*, feueres and fluxes,

forsaken v *forsaken v.* B 18 forsaken (8) forsaken (1) forsakeþ (3) forsoke (4) forsook (2); C 19 forsaek (1) forsake (4) forsaken (3) forsaketh (4) forsoek (1) forsoke (5) forsoken (1)
B. 5.424 Sixe siþes or seuene I *forsake* it wiþ oþes.
B. 9.67 And dooþ god *forsaken* hem þat he shoop to his liknesse:
B.11.30 And Concupiscencia carnis clene þee *forsake*–
B.11.276 Whoso wole be pure parfit moot possession *forsake*
B.11.416 Ac for þyn entremetynge here artow *forsake*:
B.14.265 And as a mayde for mannes loue hire moder *forsakeþ*,
B.14.271 So it [preueþ] by ech a persone þat possession *forsakeþ*
B.15.35 And whan I flee fro þe flessh and *forsake* þe careyne
B.15.84 For as [me þynkeþ] ye *forsakeþ* no mannes almesse,
B.15.311 Founde þei þat freres wolde *forsake* hir almesses
B.15.534 How þei defouled hir flessh, *forsoke* hir owene wille,
B.16.11 And to haue my fulle of þat fruyt *forsake* a[l] oþ[er] saule[e].
B.17.312 Yuele lyuen and leten no3t til lif hem *forsake*.
B.18.196 Freet of þat fruyt and *forsook*, as it weere,
B.19.368 Repenteden and [*forsoke*] synne, saue þei one,
B.20.38 [Philosophres] *forsoke* wele for þei wolde be nedy
B.20.231 Ac for þei kouþe no3t wel hir craft Conscience *forsook* hem.
B.20.240 And siþen freres *forsoke* þe felicite of erþe
C. 7.37 Sixe sithe oþer seuene y *forsake* hit with othes
C. 9.203 *Forsoken* lond and lordschipe and lykyng[e] of body.
C.11.189 And Concupiscencia Carnis clene the *forsake*–
C.12.155 Holy [writ] witnesseth hoso *forsaketh*
C.12.167 *Forsaek* al and sue me and so is th[e] beste:"
C.12.170 He moet *forsaken* hymsulue his suster and his broþer
C.13.224 Ac for thyn entermetynge her artow *forsake*:
C.15.139 And avowe byfore god and *forsaken* hit neuere
C.16.105 As a mayde for mannes loue here moder *fors[a]ke[*th],
C.16.111 So hit fareth by vch a persone þat possession *forsaketh*
C.17.82 And for þe synne of þe soule *forsaketh* his oune coyne
C.17.195 How they deffoule[d] here flesche, *forsoke* here owne wille,
C.18.76 Wedewes and wedewares þat here own[e] wil *forsaken*
C.19.292 That euele lyuen and leten nat t[il lif] hem *forsake*.
C.20.201 Freet of th[at] fruyt and *forsoke*, as hit were,
C.21.368 Repenteden and [*forsoke*] synne, saue thei one
C.22.38 Philosoferes *forsoke* wel[e] for they wolde be nedy
C.22.231 A[c] for they couthe nat wel here crafte Consience *forsoek* hem.
C.22.240 And senne freres *forsoke* the felic[it]e of erthe

forshapte v *forshapen v.* B 1; C 1 forschupte
B.17.293 That shente vs and shedde oure blood, *forshapte* vs as it [semed]:
C.19.274 That shent vs and shedde oure bloed, *forschupte* vs as hit semede:

forsleuþe v *forsleuthen v.* B 1; C 1 forsleuthed
B. 5.438 *Forsleuþed* in my seruice til it my3te serue no man.
C. 7.52 *Forsleuthed* in my seruice and set [hous] afuyre

forsoek forsoke(n forsook > forsaken

forsoþe adv *forsoth adv.* A 5; B 3; C 4 forsoth (1) forsothe (3)
A. 4.2 3e shuln sau3te, *forsoþe*, & serue me boþe.

A. 6.82   Grace hattiþ þe [gateward], a good man *forsoþe*,
A. 6.117   'Wyte god,' quaþ a waffrer, 'wiste I þat *forsoþe*,
A.11.140   It is no science *forsoþe* for to sotile þereinne.
A.11.291   And arn no[ne], *forsoþe*, souereynes in heuene
B. 4.2   Ye shul sauȝtne, *forsoþe*, and serue me boþe,
B.10.188   It is no Science *forsoþe* for to sotile Inne;
B.15.433   It is vnsauory, *forsoþe*, ysoden or ybake;
C. 3.112   Hit is nat seemely, *forsothe*, in Citee [ne] in borw toun
C. 4.2   Ȝe shal sauhtene, *forsothe*, and serue me bothe.
C.16.286   'Charite,' quod y tho, 'þat is a thyng *forsothe*
C.16.305   And when a man swereth "*forsoth*" for sooth he hit troweth;

forst(es > frost

forstalleþ v *forestallen v.* A 1 forstalliþ; B 1; C 1 forstalleth
A. 4.43   *Forstalliþ* my feiris, fiȝteþ in my chepyng,
B. 4.56   *Forstalleþ* my feires, fiȝteþ in my Chepyng,
C. 4.59   *Forstalleth* my fayres and fyhteth in my chepyng[e]

forster n *forster n.* B 1
B.17.115   And þanne shal Feiþ be *forster* here and in þis Fryth walke,

forswore ptp *forsweren v.* A 1 forsworn; B 3 forswore (2) forsworen (1); C 3 forswore (2) forsworen (1)
A.10.196   But ȝif þei boþe be *forsworn* þat bacoun þei tyne.
B. 9.175   But þei boþe be *forswore* þat bacon þei tyne.
B.19.369   And [a sisour and a somonour] þat were *forsworen* ofte;
B.19.371   And for siluer were–sooþly þei wiste it.
C.10.277   Bote they bothe be *forswore* þat bacon þei tyne.
C.21.369   And a sisour and [a] sompnour þat weren *forsworen* ofte;
C.21.371   And for suluer weren *forswore*–soth[ly] thei wisten hit.

forþ n *ford n.* A 1; B 1; C 1 forth
A. 3.147   Þat feiþ may not haue his *forþ*, hire floreynes go so þikke.
B. 3.157   That feiþ may noȝt haue his *forþ*, hire floryns go so þikke.]
C. 3.195   That fayth may nat haue his *forþ*, here floreynes goth so thykke,

forþ adv *forth adv.* A 35; B 77; C 88 forth
A.Pr.48   Wenten *forþ* in here wey wiþ many wise talis,
A.Pr.66   Brouȝte *forþ* a bulle wiþ bisshopis selis
A.Pr.103   And driueþ *forþ* þe longe day wiþ dieu saue dame emme;
A. 2.49   Þanne fauel fettiþ hire *forþ* & to fals takiþ
A. 2.54   Symonye & cyuyle stondiþ *forþ* boþe
A. 2.108   Þanne fette fauel *forþ* floreynes ynowe,
A. 2.145   Fals & fauel fariþ *forþ* togidere,
A. 2.151   But prikede *forþ* on his palfray & passide hem alle,
A. 3.141   And bringen *forþ* barnes aȝens forboden lawis.
A. 4.22   Þanne consience on his capil cairiþ *forþ* faste,
A. 4.30   And rombide *forþ* wiþ resoun riȝt to þe king.
A. 4.64   Pees putte *forþ* his heued & his panne blody:
A. 6.2   But blustrid *forþ* as bestis ouer [baches] and hilles
A. 6.25   'Petir,' quaþ a plouȝman and putte *forþ* his hed,
A. 6.53   And so bo[wiþ] *forþ* be a [brok], be buxum of speche,
A. 6.64   Þei hote stele nouȝt, ne sle nouȝt; strik *forþ* be boþe.
A. 6.97   And pokiþ [*forþ*] pride to preise þiselue.
A. 7.13   Lokiþ *forþ* ȝoure lynen & laboureþ þeron faste.
A. 7.66   Treuþe tolde me ones & bad me telle it *forþ*:
A. 8.75   And bringen *forþ* barnes þat bois ben holden.
A. 9.115   To putte *forþ* sum purpos [to] prouen hise wittes.
A.10.33   For þoruȝ þe woord þat he warp wexe *forþ* bestis,
A.10.147   And brouȝt *forþ* a barn þat muche bale wrouȝte;
A.10.153   [Þat] of seth & his sistir siþþe *forþ* come
A.10.174   Boþe fisshis & foulis, *forþ* mi[d] oþere bestis,
A.10.192   Þe fruyt þat þei bringe *forþ* arn manye foule wordis.
A.11.20   And lede *forþ* a loueday to lette þe treuþe,
A.11.30   Or daun[cel]id or drawe *forþ*; þise disours wyte þe soþe.
A.11.41   And bringe *forþ* a ballid resoun, t[a]k[e] bernard to witnesse,
A.11.42   And putte *forþ* presumpcioun to proue þe soþe.
A.11.63   And fyndiþ *forþ* fantasies oure feiþ to apeire,
A.11.116   And rid *forþ* be ricchesse, ac reste þou not þereinne,
A.11.168   And fond as she foretolde & *forþ* gan I wende,
A.12.56   And wente *forþ* on my way with omnia probate,
A.12.69   'Go we *forþ*,' quod þe gom, 'I haue a gret boyste
B.Pr.48   Wenten *forþ* in hire wey wiþ many wise tales,
B.Pr.69   Brouȝte *forþ* a bulle wiþ Bisshopes seles,
B.Pr.183   Strook *forþ* sternely and stood bifore hem alle
B.Pr.223   Of alle kynne lybbynge laborers lopen *forþ* somme,
B.Pr.225   And dryueþ *forþ* þe longe day with 'Dieu saue dame Emme'.
B. 2.49   And haue power to punysshe hem; þanne put *forþ* þi reson.
B. 2.69   Thanne leep liere *forþ* and seide, 'lo! here a chartre
B. 2.72   Symonye and Cyuylle stonden *forþ* boþe
B. 2.144   Thanne fette Fauel *forþ* floryns ynowe
B. 2.184   Fals and Fauel fareþ *forþ* togideres
B. 2.190   And priked [*forþ* on] his palfrey and passed hem alle
B. 3.152   And bryngeþ *forþ* barnes ayein forbode lawes.
B. 4.24   Thanne Conscience [o]n his capul [caireþ] *forþ* faste,

B. 4.78   Pees putte *forþ* his heed, and his panne blody:
B. 5.514   But blustreden *forþ* as beestes ouer [baches] and hilles
B. 5.537   'Peter!' quod a Plowman, and putte *forþ* his hed:
B. 5.566   And so boweþ *forþ* by a brook, beþ-buxom-of-speche,
B. 5.577   Thei hiȝte Stele-noȝt-[ne]-Sle-noȝt; strik *forþ* by boþe;
B. 5.611   And pokeþ *forþ* pride to preise þiselue;
B. 6.74   Truþe tolde me ones and bad me telle it [*forþ*]:
B. 7.93   And bryngen *forþ* barnes þat bastardes men calleþ.
B. 8.125   [To] pute *forþ* som purpos to preuen hise wittes.
B. 9.32   For þoruȝ þe word þat he [warp] woxen *forþ* beestes,
B. 9.38   My myȝt moot helpe *forþ* wiþ my speche".
B. 9.143   And þe foweles þat fleen *forþ* wiþ oþere beestes,
B. 9.154   That bryngeþ *forþ* any barn but if he be þe same
B. 9.171   The fruyt þat [þei] brynge *forþ* arn [manye] foule wordes;]
B.10.20   And lede *forþ* a loueday to lette [þe] truþe,
B.10.38   Or daunted or drawe *forþ*; I do it on god hymselue.
B.10.55   And bryngen *forþ* a balled reson, taken Bernard to witnesse,
B.10.56   And puten *forþ* presumpcion to preue þe soþe.
B.10.164   And ryd *forþ* by richesse, ac rest þow noȝt þerInne,
B.10.444   Forþi lyue we *forþ* wiþ [liþere] men; I leue fewe ben goode,
B.11.34   'Ye? recche þee neuere', quod Rechelesnesse, stood *forþ* in raggede cloþes;
B.11.35   'Folwe *forþ* þat Fortune wole; þow hast wel fer til Elde.
B.11.42   'Ye! farewel, Phippe', quod Faunteltee, and *forþ* gan me drawe
B.11.325   I was fet *forþ* by [forbisenes] to knowe
B.11.357   And brouȝten *forþ* hir briddes al aboue þe grounde.
B.11.363   And siþen I loked on þe see and so *forþ* on þe sterres;
B.12.34   And lyue *forþ* as lawe wole while ye lyuen boþe,
B.12.69   Knew neuere clerk how it comeþ *forþ*, ne kynde wit þe weyes:
B.12.167   Ther his felawe fleteþ *forþ* as þe flood likeþ
B.13.2   And as a freke þat [fey] were *forþ* gan I walke
B.13.209   Sarsens and Surre, and so *forþ* alle þe Iewes,
B.13.235   For no breed þat I brynge *forþ*, saue a benyson on þe sonday
B.14.159   And so *forþ* while somer lasteþ hir solace dureþ.
B.15.339   And wente *forþ* wiþ þat water to woke wiþ Temese.
B.16.48   Ac whan þe fend and þe flessh *forþ* wiþ þe world
B.16.83   Bar hem *forþ* bo[lde]ly–no body hym letted–
B.16.146   Thanne wente *forþ* þat wikked man and wiþ þe Iewes mette
B.16.170   And yede *forþ* as an ydiot in contree to aspie
B.16.195   Sente *forþ* his sone as for seruaunt þat tyme
B.16.223   So is þe fader *forþ* with þe sone and fre wille of boþe,
B.16.273   Rapeliche renne *forþ* þe riȝte wey [we] wente.
B.17.11   [He plukkede] *forþ* a patente, a pece of an hard roche
B.17.25   Ye! and sixti þousand biside *forþ* þat ben noȝt seyen here.'
B.17.74   And ladde hym so *forþ* on Lyard to lex Christi, a graunge
B.17.117   Which is þe wey þat I wente and wher *forþ* to Ierusalem;
B.17.120   Hope shal lede hem *forþ* with loue as his lettre telleþ.
B.17.143   And profre[d] it *forþ* as with a pawme to what place it sholde.
B.17.144   The pawme is [þe piþ of] þe hand, and profreþ *forþ* þe fyngres
B.17.156   The paume for [he] putteþ *forþ* fyngres and þe fust boþe.
B.17.160   Thoruȝ foure fyngres and a thombe *forþ* with þe pawme,
B.17.208   And þanne a fir flawmynge *forþ* out of boþe.
B.17.210   Fostren *forþ* a flawmbe and a fair leye
B.17.213   [Fostren *forþ* amonges folk loue and bileue]
B.18.1   Wolleward and weetshoed wente I *forþ* after
B.18.3   And yede *forþ* lik a lorel al my lif tyme
B.18.40   Tho putte hym *forþ* a p[e]lour bifore Pilat and seide,
B.18.73   A Cachepol cam *forþ* and craked boþe hir legges
B.18.78   Ac þer cam *forþ* a knyȝt wiþ a kene spere ygrounde,
B.18.299   And þus haþ he trolled *forþ* [lik a tidy man] þise two and þritty wynter.
B.18.406   But leten hym lede *forþ* [what] hym liked and lete [what] hym liste.
B.19.153   Verray m[a]n bifore hem alle and *forþ* wiþ hem yede.
B.19.339   And sente *forþ* Surquidous, his sergeaunt of Armes,
B.20.81   And sente *forþ* his forreyours, Feueres and Fluxes,
B.20.149   And prike[d] *forþ* pride; preiseþ he no vertue,
C.Pr.4   Wente *forth* in þe world wondres to here
C.Pr.49   Wenten *forth* [i]n here way with many wyse tales
C.Pr.67   Brouth *forth* a bulle with bischopis selys
C.Pr.97   And boxes ben yset *forth* ybounde with yren
C.Pr.200   Strok *forth* sturnely and stod byfore hem alle
C.Pr.229   And dryueth *forth* [þe longe] da[y] with 'd[ieu] saue dame Emme.'
C. 1.18   And brynge *forth* þoure bilyue, bothe lynnen and wollene,
C. 2.31   The fader þat me *forth* brouhte filius dei he hoteth,
C. 2.52   And haue power to p[uny]schen hem; thenne put *forth* thy resoun.
C. 2.71   Thenne lup lyare *forth* and saide, 'loo! here a Chartre
C. 2.74   Thenne simonye and syuyle standeth *forth* bothe
C. 2.106   And sue *forth* suche felawschipe til they ben falle in Slewthe
C. 2.160   T[h]o fette fauel *forth* floreynes ynowe
C. 2.182   And fals and fauel fecche *forth* sysores
C. 2.197   Thenne fals and fauel ryde *forth* togederes
C. 2.204   And prykede *forth* on pacience and passed hem alle

C. 3.107   Ful adoun and forbrent *forth* alle þe rewe.
C. 3.190   And bringeth *forth* bar[n]es aȝenes forbodene lawes:
C. 3.346   And styfliche stande *forth* to strenghe þe fundement,
C. 4.14   And rood *forth* to resoun and rouned in his ere
C. 4.34   Ryde *forth*, syre resoun, and rech nat of here tales
C. 4.40   Thenne resoun rood *forth* Ac took reward of no man
C. 4.74   ȝut pees put *forth* his heued and his panne blody:
C. 4.162   A sysour and a somnour tho softliche *forth* ȝede
C. 6.141   Byte and bete and brynge *forth* suche thewes
C. 6.352   Fastyng on a friday *forth* gan he wende
C. 7.159   But blostrede *forth* as bestes ouer baches and hulles
C. 7.182   '[Peter]! quod a [plouhman], and potte *forth* his heued,
C. 7.213   And so [boweth] *forth* by [a] brok, [beth-buxum-of-speche],
C. 7.224   Thei hatte stele-nat and sle-nat; stryk *forth* by bothe
C. 7.263   And poketh *forth* pruyde to preyse thysuluen.
C. 8.76   Treuthe t[o]lde me ones and bad me telle hit *fort[h]*:
C. 9.119   For a sent hem *forth* seluerles in a somur garnement
C. 9.169   Bringeth *forth* bastardus, beggares of kynde,
C. 9.261   Thy berkeres aren a[l] blynde that bringeth *forth* thy lombren:
C.10.61   I wente *forth* wydewhare walkynge myn one
C.10.121   And potte *forth* som purpos to prouen his wittes,
C.10.153   Fader and formour of al þat *forth* groweth
C.10.231   And þe foules þat fl[e]eth *forth* with oþer bestes,
C.10.273   The fruyt þat they brynge *forth* aren many foule wordes;
C.11.36   And brynge *forth* [a] balle[d] reso[n], taken bernard to witnesse
C.11.37   And putten *forth* presumpcioun to preue þe sothe.
C.11.106   And ryde *forth* by rychesse [ac] reste nat þerynne,
C.11.193   'ȝe? reche þe neuere,' quod rechelesnesse, stod *forth* in ragged
           clothes;
C.11.194   'Folowe *forth* þat fortune wole; þou hast [wel] fer to elde.
C.11.260   Passe[d] *forth* paciently to perpetuel blisse.
C.11.309   'ȝe! farewel, fyppe,' quod fauntelete and *forth* gan me drawe
C.12.166   Ac ȝef hem *forth* to pore folk þat for my loue hit aske;
C.13.166   And brouhte *forth* here briddes al aboue þe grounde.
C.13.171   How vncortey[s]liche þat cok his kynde *for[th]* strenede
C.13.173   And sethe y lokede on þe see and so *forth* on [þe] sterres;
C.14.9   Lowe the and l[y]ue *forth* in þe lawe of holy chirche;
C.14.27   And sent *forth* the seynt espirit to do loue sprynge:
C.15.2   And as a freke þ[at] fay were *forth* can y walken
C.15.27   And y aroos and romede *forth* and with resoun we mette.
C.15.28   We reuerensede resoun and romede *forth* softly
C.15.60   And brouhte *forth* a pytaunce, was pro h[a]c orabit [ad te] omnis
C.15.184   And wenten *forth* here way; with grete wille y folowede.
C.15.234   Pruyde wolde potte hymsulf *forth* thogh no plough erye.
C.16.11   And so *forth* whiles somur laste[th] here solace duyreth
C.16.106   Here fader and alle here frendes and goth *forth* with here
           paramours.
C.16.342   Ac thorw werkes thow myhte wyte wher *forth* he walketh:
C.18.3   Thenne louh liberum Arbitrium and ladde me *forth* with tales
C.18.79   And folewe þat the flesche wole and fruyt *forth* brynge.
C.18.101   And bryngeth *forth* fruyt, folk of alle nacion,
C.18.114   Baer hem *forth* baldly–no body hym lette–
C.18.204   Sente *forth* his sone As for seruant þat tyme
C.18.222   That acorsede alle couples þat no kynde *forth* brouhte:
C.18.230   Sprang *forth* and spak, a spyer of hem tweyne,
C.19.12   A pluhte *forth* a patente, a pece of an hard roche
C.19.73   And ladde hym *forth* to lauacrum lex dei, a grang[e]
C.19.117   And profered hit *forth* as with the paume to what place hit sholde.
C.19.118   The paume is the pethe of the hand and profereth [*forth*] the
           fyngeres
C.19.174   And thenne [a fuyr flaumynge] *forth* of hem bothe.
C.19.176   Fostren *forth* a flaume and a feyr lye
C.19.179   Fostren *forth* amongus folke loue and bileue
C.20.1   Wollewaerd and watschoed wente y *forth* aftur
C.20.3   And ȝede *forth* ylike a lorel al my lyf tyme
C.20.39   Thenne potte hym *forth* a pelour bifore pilatus and saide,
C.20.75   A cachepol cam [*forth*] a[nd] craked ato he[re] legges
C.20.80   Ac þer cam *forth* a knyhte with a kene spere ygrounde,
C.20.332   Thus hath he trolled *forth* lyke a tydy man this two & thritty
           wynter.
C.20.369   And tho that oure lord louede *forth* with þat liht flowen.
C.20.449   Bote leten hym lede *forth* which hym luste and leue which hym
           likede.
C.21.153   Verray man bifore [hem] alle, and *forth* with hem ȝede
C.21.339   And sente *forth* surquido[us], his seriaunt[e] of Armes,
C.22.81   And sente *forth* his forreours, feueres and fluxes
C.22.149   And prike[d] *forth* with pruyde; preyseth he no vertue

forthenken > forþynkeþ; forther(e > fer

forthermore adv *furthermore phrase & adv.* C 1
C. 9.233   Vigilies and fastyngdays *forthermore* to knowe

forþi adv *forthi pronomial adv. & conj.* A 11; B 51; C 46 forthi (2) forthy (44)

           A.1.123, A.1.149, A.1.180, A.3.60, A.7.77, A.8.165, A.8.179, A.10.157,
A.10.197, A.11.197, A.11.224

           B.Pr.111, B.Pr.131, B.Pr.187, B.Pr.208, B.1.34, B.1.134, B.1.159, B.1.175,
B.1.206, B.3.69, B.3.264, B.4.40, B.5.176, B.5.284, B.6.85, B.7.84, B.7.187, B.7.201,
B.9.158, B.9.176, B.10.210, B.10.289, B.10.398, B.10.403, B.10.418, B.10.444,
B.11.209, B.11.214, B.11.387, B.12.92, B.12.94, B.12.97, B.12.121, B.13.441,
B.14.82, B.14.201, B.14.260, B.14.309, B.15.103, B.15.344, B.17.262, B.18.201,
B.18.218, B.19.136, B.19.225, B.19.314, B.19.419, B.20.48, B.20.268, B.20.271

           C.Pr.118, C.Pr.204, C.1.32, C.1.155, C.1.171, C.1.201, C.2.150, C.3.73, C.3.108,
C.3.254, C.4.184, C.5.82, C.7.101, C.7.295, C.7.297, C.7.303, C.8.94, C.9.159, C.9.210,
C.9.333, C.9.347, C.10.278, C.11.78, C.11.229, C.12.117, C.12.120, C.13.205, C.14.43,
C.14.64, C.15.46, C.15.182, C.16.42, C.16.100, C.17.169, C.18.267, C.19.228, C.20.206,
C.20.227, C.20.325, C.21.136, C.21.225, C.21.314, C.21.419, C.22.48, C.22.268,
C.22.271

forþynkeþ v *forthinken v.* A 1 forþinkeþ; B 1; C 2 forthenketh (1) forthynketh (1)
A.10.164   "Þat I man makide now it me *forþinkeþ*".
B. 9.133   "That I [man makede now] it me *forþynkeþ*":
C.10.252   And seth for he soffred hit god sayde, "me *forthynketh*
C.20.91   [He] syhed and saide, 'sore hit me *forthenketh*!

forto conj *forto conj. cf for_to* A 2; B 2; C 2
A. 6.54   *Forto* ȝe fynden a foorþe, ȝoure fadris honouriþ;
A. 7.2   Þat miȝte folewe vs iche fote [*forto*] we were þere.'
B. 5.567   [*Forto*] ye fynden a ford, youre-fadres-honoureþ;
B.14.7   And [laþered] wiþ þe losse of catel [*forto* me] looþ [were]
C. 7.214   *Forto* ȝe fynde a ford, ȝoure-fader[s]-honoureth;
C.10.193   *For to* lese þerfore her lond and her lyf aftur.

fortune n *fortune n.* A 1; B 16; C 18
A. 7.204   Ac ȝif þou fynde any frek þat *fortune* haþ apeirid
B. 3.325   And er þis *fortune* falle fynde men shul þe worste
B. 6.218   A[c] if þow fynde any freke þat *Fortune* haþ apeired
B.11.7   [For] I was rauysshed riȝt þere; *Fortune* me fette
B.11.12   Thanne hadde *Fortune* folwynge hire two fair damyseles:
B.11.24   That I ne shal folwe þi felawship, if *Fortune* it like.'
B.11.25   'He shal fynde me his frend', quod *Fortune* þerafter;
B.11.29   Thow shalt fynde *Fortune* þee faille at þi mooste nede
B.11.35   'Folwe forþ þat *Fortune* wole; þow hast wel fer til Elde.
B.11.39   If truþe wol witnesse it be wel do *Fortune* to folwe
B.11.55   For whiles *Fortune* is þi frend freres wol þee louye,
B.11.61   And þanne was *Fortune* my foo for al hir faire [biheste],
B.13.5   First how *Fortune* me failed at my mooste nede;
B.14.297   The ferþe is a *fortune* þat florissheþ þe soule
B.20.110   *Fortune* gan flatere þanne þo fewe þat were alyue
B.20.148   Thus relyede lif for a litel *fortune*
B.20.156   This likede lif and his lemman *fortune*
C. 3.240   That he ne felde nat his foes tho *fortune* hit wolde
C. 3.478   Ac ar this *fortune* falle fynde me shal the worste
C. 6.127   That y ne mot folowe this folk: my *fortune* is non oþer.
C.11.166   For y was rauysched rihte there; *fortune* me fette
C.11.171   Thenne hadde *fortune* folwyng two fayre maydenes:
C.11.183   That y ne shal folowe thy felowschipe yf *fortune* [hit] lyke.'
C.11.184   'A shal fynde me his frende,' quod *fortune* þeraftur;
C.11.188   Thow shalt fynde *fortune* þe fayle At thy moste nede
C.11.194   'Folowe forth þat *fortune* wole; þou hast [wel] fer to elde.
C.11.283   Withoute þe gifte of god w[it]h grace of *fortune*.
C.11.306   Thow thei folowe þat *fortune* wole [no] folye ich it holde.
C.12.7   For while *fortune* is thy frende freres wol the louye
C.12.13   And thenne was *fortune* my foo for al her fayre bihese
C.15.5   Furste how *fortune* me faylede At my moste nede;
C.16.133   The furthe is a *fortune* þat florischeth þe soule;
C.22.110   *Fortune* gan flateren thenne t[h]o fewe þat were alyue
C.22.148   Thus relyed lyf for a litel *fo[rtune]*
C.22.156   This likede lyf and his lemman *fortune*

forw(es > forow

forwalked ptp *forwalked ppl.* B 1
B.13.204   Whan þow art wery [*for*]walked; wille me to counseille'.

forwandred ptp *forwandren v.* A 1 forwandrit; B 1
A.Pr.7   I was wery [*for*]wandrit & wente me to reste
B.Pr.7   I was wery *forwandred* and wente me to reste

forwanye v *forwanien v.* A 1; B 1; C 1 forwanyen
A. 5.33   'Let no wynnyng *forwanye* hem whiles þei ben ȝonge'.
B. 5.35   'Late no wynnyng [*forwanye* hem] while þei be yonge,
C. 5.137   'Late no wynnynge *forwanyen* hem while thei ben ȝonge

forward n *foreward n.* A 3 foreward; B 3 foreward (1) forward (2); C 1 foreward
A. 2.50   In *foreward* þat falshed shal fynde hire for euere,

A. 4.13   'I am fayn of þat *foreward*,' seiþ þe frek þanne,
A. 7.37   To fulfille þe *foreward* whiles I may stande'.
B. 4.13   'I am fayn of þat *foreward*', seide þe freke þanne,
B. 6.35   To fulfille þis *forward* þouȝ I fiȝte sholde.
B.11.64 Ayeins oure firste *forward*, for I seide I nolde
C. 4.13   'Y am fayn of that *foreward*, in fayth,' tho quod Consience,

forwhy conj *forwhi pronominal adv. & conj.* B 1
B.13.280 *Forwhy* he bosteþ and braggeþ wiþ manye bolde oþes;

forwit n *forewit n.* B 1
B. 5.166 Seint Gregory was a good pope and hadde a good *forwit*:

foryaf > forȝyue

foryede v *forgon v.* B 1; C 1 forȝet
B.11.60 Til I *for[yede]* youþe and yarn into Elde.
C.12.12 Til y *forȝet* ȝouthe and ȝorn into elde.

foryelde v *foryelden v.* A 1 forȝelde; B 2; C 1 forȝeld
A. 7.260 Þis is a louely lessoun, lord it þe *forȝelde*.
B. 6.276 /[Th]is is a louely lesson; lord it þee *foryelde*.
B.13.188 'Nay, by crist!' quod Conscience to Clergie, 'god þee *foryelde*;
C. 8.297 And leelyche sayst, as y leue; lord hit þe *forȝeld*!

forȝet > foryede

foryete v *foryeten v.* A 1 forgete; B 8 forgete (1) forȝeten (1) forȝyte (1) foryete (4) foryeten (1); C 8 forȝete (5) forȝeten (3)
A.11.293 And ȝet [haue] I *forget[e* ferþer] of fyue wyttis teching
B. 5.397 I haue maad auowes fourty and *foryete* hem on þe morwe;
B. 5.423 I *foryete* it as yerne, and if men me it axe
B. 5.434 Sixty siþes I, Sleuþe, haue *foryete* it siþþe
B.10.448 [And yet haue I *forgete* ferþer of fyue wittes techyng
B.17.246 Boþe forȝyue and *foryete*, and ȝit bidde for vs
B.17.337 And "þat is lightly forȝyuen and *forȝeten* boþe
B.20.155 And [so] *forȝyte* sorwe and [of synne ȝue noȝt].'
B.20.369 Til Contricion hadde clene *foryeten* to crye and to wepe
C. 7.13 Y haue [made] voues fourty and *forȝeten* hem amorwen.
C. 7.25 Vigilies and fastyngdayes y can *forȝeten* hem alle
C. 7.36 Y *forȝete* hit as ȝerne and yf eny man hit aske
C. 7.47 Sixty sythes y, sleuthe, haue *forȝeten* hit sethe
C.19.212 Bothe forȝeue and *forȝete* and ȝut bidde for vs
C.19.317 And "þat is lihtliche forȝeue and *forȝete* bothe
C.22.155 And [s]o *forȝete* [sorwe] and [of synne ȝeue nouht].'
C.22.369 Til Contricioun hadde clene *forȝete* to crye and to wepe

forȝeue > foryeue

forȝifnesse n *foryevenesse n.* B 6 forgifnesse (1) forȝifnesse (5); C 7 forgeuenesse (1) forȝeuenesse (6)
B.14.154 Here *forȝifnesse* of hir synnes, and heuene blisse after.
B.17.225 Graunte no grace ne *for[g]ifnesse* of synnes
B.17.247 [Fro] þe fader of heuene *forȝifnesse* to haue.
B.17.353 Alle manere men mercy and *forȝifnesse*;
B.19.185 To alle maner men mercy and *forȝifnesse*]
B.20.287 Yerne of *forȝifnesse* or lenger yeres loone.
C. 5.195 Enioyne hem pees for here penaunce and perpetuel *forȝe[ue]nesse*
C. 6.436 Herof, gode god, graunte me *forȝeuenesse*,
C.19.191 Graunten [no] grace ne *forgeuenesse* of synnes
C.19.213 To þe fader of heuene *forȝe[ue]nesse* to haue.
C.19.333 Alle manere men mercy and *forȝeuenesse*
C.21.185 To alle manere men mercy and *forȝeuenesse*\
C.22.287 Ȝerne of *forȝeuenesse* or lengore ȝeres l[on]e.

forȝyte > foryete

forȝyue v *foryeven v.* A 3 forgyue; B 10 forgyue (2) forgyuen (2) forȝyue (4) forȝyuen (1) foryaf (1); C 10 forgyue (4) forȝaf (1) forȝeue (5)
A. 3.8   I wile *forgyue* hire þe gilt, so me god helpe.'
A. 3.97 Ac I *forgyue* þe þe gilt & graunte þe [my] grace;
A. 4.88 I *forgyue* hym þ[at] gilt wiþ a good wille.
B. 3.8   I wol *forgyuen* hire þ[e] gilt, so me god helpe.'
B. 3.108 But I *forgyue* þee þ[e] gilt and graunte þee my grace,
B. 4.101 I *forgyue* hym þat gilt wiþ a good wille
B.17.238 So wol þe fader *forȝyue* folk of mylde hertes
B.17.246 Boþe *forȝyue* and foryete, and ȝit bidde for vs
B.17.292 "Vengeaunce, vengeaunce! *forȝyue* be it neuere
B.17.337 And "þat is lightly *forȝyuen* and forȝeten boþe
B.18.76 For he was knyȝt and kynges sone kynde *foryaf* þat [þrowe]
B.18.184 And þat god haþ *forgyuen* and graunted me, pees, & mercy
B.19.394 [Or] ech man *forȝyue* ooþer, and þat wole þe Paternoster:
C. 3.8   Y wol *forgyue* here alle gultes, so me god helpe.'
C. 3.135 And monye a gulte y haue the *forgyue* & my grace graunted
C. 3.139 Ȝut y *forgyue* þis gult; godes forb[o]de eny more
C.19.204 So wol þe fader *forȝeue* folke of mylde hertes
C.19.212 Bothe *forȝeue* and forȝete and ȝut bidde for vs
C.19.273 "Veniaunce, veniaunce! *forȝeue* be hit neuere

C.19.317 And "þat is lihtliche *forȝeue* and forȝete bothe
C.20.78 For he was knyht and kynges sone kynde *forȝaf* þat [þrowe]
C.20.187 And þat god hath *forgyue* and graunted to mankynde
C.21.394 Or vch man *forȝeue* oþer, and þat wol þe paternost[er]:

fostren v *fostren v.* A 1 fostrid; B 2; C 2
A.10.122 Which is þe flour & þe fruyt *fostrid* of boþe.
B.17.210 *Fostren* forþ a flawmbe and a fair leye
B.17.213 [*Fostren* forþ amonges folk loue and bileue]
C.19.176 *Fostren* forth a flaume and a feyr lye
C.19.179 *Fostren* forth amongus folke loue and bileue

fote > foot

fouchensaf v *vouchen sauf v. phr.* C 2 fouchensaf (1) fouchen_saef (1)
C. 5.49 And tho þa[t] fynden me my fode *fouchensaf*, y trowe,
C.18.18 And sethen þat ȝe *fouchen saef* to sey me as hit hoteth.'

foughten fouȝten > fiȝte

foul adj *foul adj. &> fowel* A 3 foule; B 18 foul (5) foule (11) fouler (1) foulest (1); C 23 foul (4) foule (17) foulest (2)
A. 5.221 And made auowe tofore god for his *foule* slouþe:
A. 7.306 Þoruȝ flood [and] *foule* wederis fruytes shuln fa[i]lle,
A.10.192 Þe fruyt þat þei bringe forþ arn manye *foule* wordis.
B. 5.179 [I] haue a flux of a *foul* mouþ wel fyue dayes after;
B. 5.449 And made auow tofore god for his *foule* sleuþe:
B. 6.325 Thoruȝ flo[od] and *foule* wedres fruytes shul faille,
B. 9.171 The fruyt þat [þei] brynge forþ arn [manye] *foule* wordes;]
B.10.41 Spitten and spuen and speke *foule* wordes,
B.11.396 For be a man fair or *foul* it falleþ noȝt to lakke
B.12.245 And his flessh is *foul* flessh and his feet boþe,
B.13.317 Men sholde fynde manye frounces and manye *foule* plottes.'
B.13.319 It was *fouler* bi fele fold þan it first semed.
B.13.454 [There] flateres and fooles þoruȝ hir *foule* wordes
B.14.302 A frend in alle fondynges, [of *foule* yueles leche],
B.15.113 Or to a wal þat were whitlymed and were *foul* wiþInne;
B.16.77 And whan [he] meued matrimoyne it made a *foul* noise.
B.18.94 'For þis *foule* vileynye vengeaunce to yow falle!
B.18.154 For of alle venymes *foulest* is þe scorpion;
B.19.33 And fre men *foule* þralles þat folwen noȝt hise lawes.
B.19.46 And defended from *foule* yueles, feueres and Fluxes,
B.20.85 Frenesies and *foule* yueles; forageres of kynde
C.Pr.37 Fyndeth out *foule* fantasyes and foles hem maketh
C. 3.96 Feuer or *foul[e]* euel other fuyr on here houses,
C. 3.370 I wolde feffe hym with here fayre and [with] here *foule* taylende.
C. 6.161 Y haue a flux of a *foul* mouth wel fyue daies aftur;
C. 6.433 The vilony of my *foule* mouthe and of my foule mawe:
C. 6.433 The vilony of my *foule* mouthe and of my foule mawe:
C. 7.54 And sethe a beggare haue y be for my *foule* sleuthe:
C. 7.63 And made [a]uowe tofore god for his *foule* sleuthe:
C. 7.114 There flaterers and foles with here *foule* wordes
C. 8.346 Thorw flodes and *foule* wederes fruyttes shollen fayle;
C.10.273 The fruyt þat they brynge forth aren many *foule* wordes;
C.12.224 On fat lond ful of donge *foulest* wedes groweth.
C.13.172 And ferlyede of his fayrenesse and of his *foul* le[den]e.
C.13.242 Ther smyt no thyng so smerte ne smelleth so *foule*
C.16.138 And frende in alle fondynges and of *foule* eueles leche:
C.16.373 He halt hit for a vyce and a *foule* shame
C.18.54 Where þe fruyt were fayre or *foul* for to loke on.
C.18.109 A meued matrimonye; hit made a *fo[u]le* noyse.
C.20.97 'For þis *[fou]l* vilanye vengeaunce [to] ȝow [f]all[e]!
C.20.157 For of alle venymes *[fou]lest* is þe scorpioun;
C.21.33 And fre men *foule* thralles þat folleweth nat his lawes.
C.21.46 And fended fro *foule* eueles, feueres and fluxes
C.22.85 Freneseyes and *foule* eueles; forageres of kynde

foule adv *foule adv. &> foul,fowel* A 2; B 14 foule (13) foulest (1); C 7 foule (6) foulest (1)
A. 3.173 And þou hast famid me *foule* before þe king here.
A. 5.65 So lokide he wiþ lene chekis, lourande *foule*.
B. 3.186 Ac þow hast famed me *foule* bifore þe kyng here.
B. 5.82 So loked he wiþ lene chekes, lourynge *foule*.
B.10.327 [Bynymen] that hir barnes claymen, and blame yow *foule*:
B.10.479 Selden falle so *foule* and so fer in synne
B.11.215 Ne vndernyme noȝt *foule*, for is noon wiþoute defaute.
B.11.393 Of hire defautes *foule* bifore hem reherced].
B.11.436 Ther smyt no þyng so smerte, ne smelleþ so [*foule*]
B.12.238 And þat þe faireste fowel *foulest* engendreþ,
B.12.257 I leue it flawme ful *foule* þe fold al aboute,
B.13.400 And *foule* beflobered it, as wiþ fals speche,
B.14.15 That I ne flobre it *foule* fro morwe til euen.'
B.14.162 Afurst soore and afyngred, and *foule* yrebuked
B.15.353 Ac þe metal, þat is mannes soule, [myd] synne is *foule* alayed.
B.20.5 That afrounted me *foule* and faitour me called.
C. 2.45 Fauel thorw his flaterynge speche hath mede *foule* enchaunted,

C. 3.232   Ac thow hast famed me *foule* byfore þe kyng here
C.11.300   Selde falleth so *foule* and so depe in synne
C.14.170   Þat þe fayrest foul *foulest* engendreth
C.16.15   Afurste and afyngered and *foule* rebuked
C.20.350   Sethe þat satan myssaide thus *foule*
C.22.5   That afrounted me *foule* and faytour me calde.

foules > fowel; foulest > foul,foule

fouleþ v *foulen v.(1)* A 2 foulide (1) fouliþ (1); B 2 foulen (1) fouleþ (1);
    C 2 fouleth
A. 3.143   For she is fauourable to fals & *fouliþ* treuþe ofte;
A. 7.136   Lest his flessh & þe fend *foulide* his soule.
B. 3.154   For she is fauourable to fals and [f]*ouleþ* truþe ofte.
B.19.313   *Foulen* þe fruyt in þe feld þer þei growen togideres,
C. 9.267   For to go wurye þe wolf that the wolle *fou[l]eth*?
C.21.313   *Fouleth* the fruyt in the feld ther thei growe togyderes

foulis > fowel; founde(n > fynden

founded v *founden v.(2)* &> *fonde* v A 3 fonden (1) foundide (1) foundit
    (1); B 5 fonden (1) founded (3) foundede (1); C 2 fond (1) founded
    (1)
A.Pr.36   *Fonden* hem fantasies & foolis hem make,
A. 1.62   Fadir of falshed, he *foundi[de]* it hymselue.
A.11.164   *Foundit* hem formest folk to desceyue.
B.Pr.36   [*Fonden*] hem fantasies and fooles hem makeþ,
B. 1.64   Fader of falshede, [he] *founded* it hymselue.
B.10.221   *Founded* hem formest folk to deceyue.
B.15.289   Til he *foundede* freres of Austynes ordre, [or ellis freres lyen].
B.15.325   And ben *founded* and feffed ek to bidde for oþere.
C. 1.60   Fader of falshede *fond* hit firste of alle.
C.17.57   To feffe suche and fede þat *founded* ben to þe fulle

foundement n *foundement n.* B 2; C 4 fondement (1) foundement (1)
    fundement (2)
B.14.200   In fenestres at þe freres–if fals be þe *foundement*.
B.19.325   And þerwiþ Grace bigan to make a good *foundement*,
C. 3.345   Folowynge and fyndynge out þe *fundement* of a strenghe,
C. 3.346   And styfliche stande forth to strenghe þe *fundement*,
C.16.41   In fenestres at þe freres–yf fals be þe *fondement*.
C.21.325   And þerwith grace bigan to make a goode *fo[un]dement*

foundlynges > fondlynges

foundours n *foundour n.* A 1
A.11.216   Arn more in his mynde þan þe memorie of his *foundours*.

foure num *four num.* A 4; B 17; C 11
A.Pr.55   I fond þere Freris, alle þe *foure* ordris,
A. 8.176   Þei3 þou be founde in þe fraternite among þe *foure* ordris,
A.10.2   In a castel þat kynde made of *foure* skenis þinges.
A.11.303   Þat [was] austyn þe olde, & hi3este of þe *foure*,
B.Pr.58   I fond þere Freres, alle þe *foure* ordres,
B.Pr.103   Amonges *foure* vertues, [most vertuous of alle],
B. 7.54   Thise *foure* þe fader of heuene made to þis foold in commune;
B. 7.198   Thei3 [þow] be founde in þe fraternite [among] þe *foure* ordres
B. 9.2   In a Castel þat kynde made of *foure* kynnes þynges.
B. 9.75   And fynde fele witnesses among þe *foure* doctours,
B.10.251   Who was his Auctour? alle þe *foure* Euangelistes.
B.10.459   Was Austyn þe olde, and hei3est of þe *foure*,
B.13.39   Of Austyn, of Ambrose, of [alle] þe *foure* Euangelistes:
B.13.65   'It is no3t *foure* dayes þat þis freke, bifore þe deen of Poules,
B.17.160   Thoru3 *foure* fyngres and a thombe forþ with þe pawme,
B.17.248   Ac hewe fir at a flynt *foure* hundred wynter;
B.19.262   Grace gaf Piers a teeme, *foure* grete Oxen.
B.19.267   And Grace gaf Piers of his goodnesse *foure* stottes,
B.19.271   Thise *foure*, þe feiþ to teche, folwe[de] Piers teme
B.19.309   Thise *foure* sedes Piers sew, and siþþe he dide hem harewe
B.19.311   Among þ[e] *foure* vertues and vices destruye.
C.Pr.56   I fonde þer Freris, alle þe *foure* ordres,
C.Pr.131   Amonge *foure* vertues, most vertuous of vertues,
C. 9.57   Thise *foure* sholde be fre to alle folk þat hit nede[th].
C.10.129   In a Castel þat kynde made of *foure* kyne thynges.
C.15.44   Of Austyn, of Ambrose, of alle þe *foure* euaungeli[st]es:
C.19.214   Ac hewe fuyr at a flynt *foure* hundret wynter,
C.21.262   Grace gaf [Peres] a teme, *foure* grete oxen.
C.21.267   And grace [gaef Peres of his goednesse] *foure* stottes,
C.21.271   Thise *foure*, the fayth to teche, folewe[de Peres] teme
C.21.309   Thise *foure* sedes [Peres] sewe and sennes he dede hem harewe
C.21.311   Among th[e] *foure* vertues and vices distruye.

fourm- > form-

fourty num *forti num.* A 2; B 7; C 7
A. 6.30   I haue ben his folewere al þis *fourty* wynter;
A.10.169   Til *fourty* dayes be fulfild, þat flood haue ywasshe

B. 5.397   I haue maad auowes *fourty* and foryete hem on þe morwe;
B. 5.542   I haue ben his folwere al þis [*fourty*] wynter,
B. 9.138   Til *fourty* daies be fulfild, þat flood haue ywasshen
B.11.47   And folwed me *fourty* wynter and a fifte moore,
B.12.3   I haue folwed þee, in feiþ, þise fyue and *fourty* wynter,
B.14.64   It is founden þat *fourty* wynter folk lyuede withouten tulying,
B.16.100   And in þe wombe of þat wenche was he *fourty* woukes
C. 3.41   [And] Falshede yfonde the al this *fourty* wyntur,
C. 7.13   Y haue [made] voues *fourty* and for3eten hem amorwen.
C. 7.189   [I]ch haue ybe his foloware al this *fourty* wynter
C.10.226   Til *fourty* [dayes] be fulfild and floed haue ywasche
C.14.3   Y haue folewed þe, in fayth, mo then *fourty* wyntur
C.15.263   Hit is founde þat *fourty* wynter folke lyuede and tylde nat
C.18.133   And in þe wombe of þat wenche was he *fourty* wokes

fowel n *foul n.* A 7 foul (1) foules (2) foulis (4); B 22 foules (2) fowel (6)
    foweles (14); C 14 foul (6) foule (1) foules (7)
A. 5.196   As whoso leide lynes to lacche wiþ [*foules*].
A. 7.33   And fecche þe hom fauconis þe *foulis* to kille,
A. 8.112   [By *foules*, þat are not] besy aboute þe bely ioye:
A. 8.115   Þe *foulis* in þe firmament, who fynt hem a wynter?
A. 9.57   To lerne þe laies þat louely [*foulis*] maden.
A.10.174   Boþe fisshis & *foulis*, forþ mi[d] oþere bestis,
A.11.174   Þanne was I [as] fayn as *foul* of fair morewen,
B. 5.348   As whoso leiþ lynes to lacche [wiþ] *foweles*.
B. 6.31   And [fette þee hoom] faucons *foweles* to kille,
B. 7.130   By *foweles* [þat are] no3t bisy aboute þe [bely ioye];
B. 7.133   The *foweles* in þe [firmament], who fynt hem at wynter?
B. 8.54   To fleynge *foweles*, to fisshes and to beestes.
B. 8.66   To [lerne] þe layes [þat] louely *foweles* made.
B. 9.143   And þe *foweles* þat fleen forþ wiþ oþere beestes,
B.10.158   Thanne was [I] also fayn as *fowel* of fair morewen,
B.11.329   Wilde wormes in wodes, and wonderful *foweles*
B.11.355   For fere of oþere *foweles* and for wilde beestes.
B.12.238   And þat þe faireste *fowel* foulest engendreþ,
B.12.239   And feblest *fowel* of fli3t is þat fleeþ or swymmeþ.
B.12.264   The larke þat is a lasse *fowel* is moore louelich of ledene,
B.12.269   Thus he likneþ in his logik þe leeste *fowel* oute.
B.15.278   But of *foweles* þat fleeþ; þus fyndeþ men in bokes.
B.15.288   *Foweles* hym fedde, fele wyntres wiþ alle,
B.15.302   Thei wolde haue yfed þat folk bifore wilde *foweles*;
B.15.305   Ac god sente hem foode by *foweles* and by no fierse beestes
B.15.464   But wiþ *foweles* þat fram hym nolde but folwede his whistlyng:
B.15.472   [And by þe hond fedde *foules* [i]s folk vnderstonde
B.15.479   And as þo *foules* to fynde fode after whistlyng
B.20.44   “Boþe fox and *fowel* may fle to hole and crepe
C. 6.406   As hoso layth lynes for to lacche *foules*.
C. 8.30   And afayte thy faucones [wylde *foules* to culle]
C.10.231   And þe *foules* þat fl[e]eth forth with oþer bestes,
C.11.100   Thenne was y as fayn as *foul* of faire morwen,
C.13.137   Wilde wormes in wodes and wondurfol *foules*
C.13.164   For no *foul* sholde hit fynde but his fere and hymsulue.
C.14.170   Þat þe fayrest foul *foulest* engendreth
C.14.171   And feblest *foul* of flyh[t is] þat fleeth oþer swym[m]eth:
C.14.185   The larke þat is a lasse *foul* is loueloke[re] of ledene,
C.14.190   Likneth in here logik þe leste *foul* out[e].
C.17.11   Elles *foules* fedde hem in frythes þer they wonede,
C.17.15   *Foules* hym fedde yf frere Austynes be trewe
C.17.32   Ac bestes brouhte hem no mete bute onliche þe *foules*
C.22.44   “Bothe fox and *foule* may fle to hole and crepe

fox n *fox n.* A 1 foxis; B 2 fox (1) foxes (1); C 3 fox (2) foxes (1)
A. 7.31   And go hunte hardily [to] har[is] & [to] *fox[is]*,
B. 6.29   And go hunte hardiliche to hares and to *foxes*,
B.20.44   “Boþe *fox* and fowel may fle to hole and crepe
C. 8.28   And go hunte hardelyche to hares and to *foxes*,
C. 9.225   In frithes and in forestes for *fox* and other bestes
C.22.44   “Bothe *fox* and foule may fle to hole and crepe

frayned v *frainen v.* A 3 fraynide; B 5; C 5 frayned (1) fraynede (4)
A. 1.56   Þanne I *fraynide* hire faire for him þat hire made,
A. 6.13   Þis folk *fraynide* hym faire [fro] whenis þat he come.
A. 9.3   And *fraynide* ful ofte of folk þat I mette
B. 1.58   Thanne I *frayned* hire faire for hym þat [hire] made,
B. 5.525   This folk *frayned* hym [faire] fro whennes he come.
B. 8.3   And *frayned* ful ofte of folk þat I mette
B.16.174   I *frayned* hym first fram whennes he come
B.18.18   Thanne I *frayned* at Feiþ what al þat fare bymente,
C. 1.54   [Thanne] y *fraynede* her fayr for hym þat here made,
C. 7.170   This folk *frayned* hym furste fro whennes he come.
C.10.3   And *fraynede* ful ofte of folke þat y mette
C.18.290   And y *fraynede* hym furst fro whennes he come,
C.20.16   Thenne y [f]*raynede* at fayth what al þat fare bymente

fraytour n *freitour n.* B 1; C 1 fraytour
B.10.328   And þanne Freres in hir *fraytour* shul fynden a keye
C. 5.173   Freres in here *fraytour* shal fynde þat tyme

fram > fro; franceys > fraunceis; franchise > fraunchise

frankeleyn n *frankelein n.* B 1 frankeleyns; C 3 frankeleyn (1)
    frankeleynes (2)
B.19.39   Aren *frankeleyns*, free men þoruȝ fullynge þat þei toke
C. 5.67   Of *frankeleynes* and fremen and of folke ywedded.
C.10.240   For thogh þe fader be a *frankeleyn* and for a felon be hanged
C.21.39   Aren *frankeleynes*, fre men Thorw follyng þat they toke

fraternitee n *fraternite n.* A 1 fraternite; B 3 fraternite (1) Fraternitee (1)
    Fraternytee (1); C 3 fraternite
A. 8.176   Þeiȝ þou be founde in þe *fraternite* among þe foure ordris,
B. 7.198   Theiȝ [þow] be founde in þe *fraternite* [among] þe foure ordres
B.11.56   And [festne] þee [in] hir *Fraternitee* and for þe biseke
B.20.367   As frere[s] of oure *Fraternytee*, for a litel siluer'.
C. 9.344   Thow we be founden in the *fraternite* of alle fyue ordres
C.12.8   And festene the in ther *f[r]aternite* and for the byseche
C.22.367   [As] freres of oure *fraternite* for a litel suluer'.

fraunce n prop *Fraunce n.* A 1; B 2; C 6
A.10.8   A proud prikere of *Fraunce*, Princeps huius mundi,
B.Pr.177   Ther ne was Raton in þe route, for al þe Reaume of *Fraunce*,
B. 9.8   A proud prikere of *Fraunce*, Princeps huius mundi,
C.Pr.194   Ther ne was [raton in] þe route, for al þe reame of *Fraunce*,
C. 3.243   In his enemyes handes his heritage of *Fraunce*.
C. 3.258   Ac hadde y, mede, ben marchel o[f] his men in *Fraunce*
C. 4.125   And alle Rome rennares for ruyflares in *Fraunce*
C.10.135   A proued prikeare of *fraunce*, princeps huius mundi,
C.15.154   Y wolde, and y will hadde, wynnen all *fraunce*

fraunceis n prop *n.i.d.* B 4 Fraunceis (2) Fraunceys (2); C 3 franceys (1)
    fraunceys (2)
B. 4.121   As Seynt Beneyt hem bad, Bernard and *Fraunceis*;
B.15.231   Ac it is fern [and fele yeer in] *Fraunceis* tyme;
B.15.421   But doon as Antony dide, dominyk and *Fraunceys*,
B.20.252   Frere *Fraunceys* and Domynyk, for loue to be holye.
C. 4.117   And be as Benet hem bad, dominik and *fraunceys*;
C.16.356   Ac hit is fer and fele ȝer in *franceys* tyme;
C.22.252   Frere *fraunceys* and domynyk, for loue to be holy.

fraunchise n *fraunchise n.* B 1; C 1 franchise
B.18.103   And youre *fraunchise* þat fre was fallen is in þraldom;
C.20.106   And ȝoure *franchise* þat fre was yfallen is i[n] thraldoem;

fre adj *fre adj.* B 13 fre (8) free (5); C 17
B. 2.77   Than for any vertue or fairnesse or any *free* kynde.
B. 8.53   Wit and *free* wil, to euery wiȝt a porcion,
B.10.75   That folk is noȝt fermed in þe feiþ ne *free* of hire goodes
B.11.384   Frenche men and *fre* men affaiteþ þus hire children:
B.15.150   Wiþouten fauntelte or folie a *fre* liberal wille.
B.15.151   'Where sholde men fynde swich a frend wiþ so *fre* an herte?
B.16.223   So is þe fader forþ with þe sone and *fre* wille of boþe,
B.17.148   The fyngres þat *fre* ben to folde and to serue
B.18.103   And youre fraunchise þat *fre* was fallen is in þraldom;
B.19.33   And *fre* men foule þralles þat folwen noȝt hise lawes.
B.19.39   Aren frankeleyns, *free* men þoruȝ fullynge þat þei toke
B.19.59   To maken alle folk *free* þat folwen his lawe].
B.20.146   And leet leautee a cherl and lyere a *fre* man.
C.Pr.106   Ful on hem þat *fre* were thorwe two fals prestis!
C. 1.73   Y vndirfenge þe formeste and *fre* man the made.
C. 3.108   Forthy mayres þat maketh *fre* men, me thynketh þat ȝe ouhten
C. 3.111   Ar he were vnderfonge *fre* and felawe in ȝoure rolles.
C. 3.114   Be yfranchised for a *fre* man and haue a fals name.
C. 5.67   Of frankeleynes and *fremen* and of folke ywedded.
C. 9.57   Thise foure sholde be *fre* to alle folk þat hit nede[th].
C.10.51   Ac *fre* wil and fre wit foleweth man euere
C.10.51   Ac fre wil and *fre* wit foleweth man euere
C.11.55   That folk is nat ferme[d] in þe faith ne *fre* of here godes
C.11.248   For lewed folk, goddes foles and his *fre* bestes:
C.19.122   The fyngres þat *fre* ben to folde and to cluche
C.20.106   And ȝoure franchise þat fre was yfallen is i[n] thraldoem;
C.21.33   And *fre* men foule thralles þat folleweth nat his lawes.
C.21.39   Aren frankeleynes, *fre* men Thorw follyng þat they toke
C.21.59   To make alle folk *fre* þat folweth his lawe.
C.22.146   And leet leautee a cherl and lyare a *fre* man.

freel > frele; freelete > freletee; freet > frete

freke n *freke n.* A 3 frek (2) freke (1); B 11 freke (10) frekes (1); C 6
    frek (1) freke (4) frekes (1)
A. 4.13   'I am fayn of þat foreward,' seiþ þe *frek* þanne,
A. 7.204   Ac ȝif þou fynde any *frek* þat fortune haþ apeirid
A.12.66   I shal felle þat *freke* in a fewe dayes.'

B. 4.156   I falle in floryns', quod þat *freke*, 'and faile speche ofte.'
B. 5.170   For þere ben manye felle *frekes* my feeris to aspie,
B. 6.218   A[c] if þow fynde any *freke* þat Fortune haþ apeired
B. 6.251   The *freke* þat fedeþ hymself wiþ his feiþful labour
B.10.255   For hadde neuere *freke* fyn wit þe feiþ to dispute,
B.11.26   'The *freke* þat folwede my wille failled neuere blisse.'
B.13.2   And as a *freke* þat [fey] were forþ gan I walke
B.13.65   'It is noȝt foure dayes þat þis *freke*, bifore þe deen of Poules,
B.13.74   Ac I wiste neuere *freke* þat as a frere yede bifore men on englissh
B.16.176   'I am feiþ', quod þat *freke*, 'it falleþ noȝt to lye,
C. 6.152   For there aren many felle *frekes* myn aferes to aspye,
C. 9.153   And what *freke* on this folde fiscuth aboute
C.11.156   For hadde neuere *frek* fyn wi[t] the faith to dispute,
C.15.2   And as a *freke* þ[at] fay were forth can y walken
C.15.80   Ac y wiste neuere *freke* þat frere is ycald of þe fyue mendynantȝ
C.18.184   'I am with fayth,' quod þat *freke*, 'hit falleth nat me to lye,

frele adj *frele adj.* A 1 freel; B 1; C 2 freel (1) frele (1)
A. 3.111   She is *freel* of hire feiþ, fikel of hire speche;
B. 3.122   She is *frele* of hire feiþ, fikel of hire speche;
C. 3.159   For she [is] *frele* of here fayth, fikel of here speche
C.10.48   That thorw the fend and [the] flesch and th[e] *freel* worlde

freletee n *frelete n.* B 2 frelete (1) freletee (1); C 2 freelete (1) frelete (1)
B. 3.55   It is a *freletee* of flessh-ye fynden it in bokes-
B.17.336   And þouȝ it falle it fynt skiles þat "*frelete* it made",
C. 3.59   Hit is but *frelete* of fleysche-ȝe fyndeth [hit in] bokes-
C.19.316   And thogh he falle he fynte skiles þat "*freelete* hit made"

fremmed adj *fremed adj.* B 1; C 1 fremde
B.15.141   To frend ne to *fremmed*: "þe fend haue his soule!
C.12.156   His fader or his frendes, *fre[m]de* oþer sybbe,

frenche adj *Frensh adj. &> frenssh* B 1
B.11.384   *Frenche* men and fre men affaiteþ þus hire children:

frend n *frend n.* A 6 frend (1) frendis (5); B 26 frend (12) frendes (14); C
    25 frende (11) frendes (14)
A. 5.77   And don hise *frendis* ben hise fon þoruȝ my false tunge.
A. 5.82   I hailside hym as hendely as I his *frend* were:
A. 7.89   And dele among my *frendis* & my dere children,
A. 7.212   Make þe *Frendis* þermi[d] for so matheu vs techiþ:
A. 9.81   And wiþ mammones money he haþ mad hym *frendis*,
A.10.66   Ac þe fadir & þe *Frendis* for fauntis shuln be blamid
B. 3.52   For to be youre *frend*, frere, and faile yow neuere
B. 5.97   And [doon] his *frendes* be his foon þoruȝ my false tonge.
B. 5.102   I hailse[d] hym hendely as I his *frend* were:
B. 6.97   And dele among my [*frendes*] and my deere children.
B. 7.172   It bifel as his fader tolde, hise *frendes* þere hym souȝte.
B. 8.90   And wiþ Mammonaes moneie he haþ maad hym *frendes*;
B. 9.117   First by þe fadres wille and þe *frendes* conseille,
B.11.25   'He shal fynde me his *frend*', quod Fortune þerafter;
B.11.55   For whiles Fortune is þi *frend* freres wol þee louye,
B.11.178   And þat alle manere men, enemyes and *frendes*,
B.11.193   For youre *frendes* wol feden yow, and fonde yow to quyte
B.11.194   Youre festynge and youre faire ȝifte; ech *frend* quyteþ so ooþer.
B.12.260   Executours, false *frendes*, þat fulfille noȝt his wille
B.13.148   Ac for to fare þus wiþ þi *frend*, folie it were;
B.13.180   'Frendes, fareþ wel', and faire spak to clergie,
B.13.327   And made of *frendes* foes þoruȝ a fals tonge.
B.14.266   Hir fader and alle hire *frendes*, and folweþ hir make-
B.14.302   A *frend* in alle fondynges, [of foule yueles leche],
B.15.141   To *frend* ne to fremmed: "þe fend haue his soule!
B.15.151   'Where sholde men fynde swich a *frend* wiþ so fre an herte?
B.15.176   'Haþ he anye rentes or richesse or any riche *frendes*?'
B.15.178   For a *frend* þat fyndeþ hym failed hym neuere at nede:
B.17.89   'Ac þi *frend* and þi felawe þow fyndest me at nede.'
B.18.411   Ne no loue leuere, ne leuer *frendes*,
B.19.145   For no *fren[d]* sholde [it] fecche; for prophetes hem tolde
B.20.286   That borweþ and bereþ it þider and þanne biddeþ *frendes*
C. 3.56   'Y shal be ȝoure *frende*, frere, and fayle ȝow neuere
C. 5.36   My fader and my *frendes* foende me to scole
C. 5.40   And foen[d y] nere, in fayth, seth my *frendes* deyede
C. 6.72   And made of *frendes* foes thorw fikel and fals tonge.
C. 9.200   And somme hadde foreynes to *frendes* þat hem fode sente
C.10.13   Wher þat dowel dwelleth; 'dere *frendes*, telleth me,
C.10.87   And of mammonaus mone ymaked hym many *frendes*
C.10.184   *Frendes* shal fynde hem and fram folye kepe
C.10.301   And thus is dowel, my *frende*, to do as lawe techeth:
C.11.184   'A shal fynde me his *frende*,' quod fortune þerafur;
C.12.7   For while fortune is thy *frende* freres wol þe louye
C.12.105   For vch *frende* fedeth other and fondeth hou beste to quite
C.12.156   His fader or his *frendes*, fre[m]de oþer sybbe,
C.15.195   'What manere munstracye, my dere *frende*,' quod Concience,

C.16.106   Here fader and alle here *frendes* and goth forth with here
          paramours:
C.16.138   And *frende* in alle fondynges and of foule eueles leche:
C.16.316   'H[o] fynt hym his fode,' quod y, 'or what *frendes* hath he,
C.16.319   A *frende* he hath þat fyn[t] hym þat faylede hym neuere.
C.17.125   'What is holy churche, chere *frende*?' quod y; 'Charite,' he saide;
C.17.143   Loue thy *frende* þat followeth thy wille, that is thy fayre soule.
C.17.144   For when alle *frendes* faylen and fleen away in deynge
C.19.250   [That that wickedliche is wonne to wasten hit and make *frendes*?]
C.20.454   Ne no loue leuore ne leuore *frendes*
C.21.145   For no *frende* sholde hit fecche; for profetes hem tolde
C.22.286   That borweth and bereth hit theddere and thenne biddeth *frendes*

frendlier adj *frendli adj*.   A 1 frendliere; B 1
A.11.174   Fairere vndirfonge ne *frendliere* mad at ese
B.10.231   Fairer vnderfongen ne *frendlier* at ese

frenesies n *frenesie n*.   B 1; C 1 freneseyes
B.20.85   *Frenesies* and foule yueles; forageres of kynde
C.22.85   *Freneseyes* and foule eueles; forageres of kynde

frenesse n *frenesse n*.   B 1 frenesse
B.16.88   Filius by þe fader wille and *frenesse* of spiritus sancti

frenetike adj *frenetik adj*.   A 1 frentyk; B 1; C 2 frentike (1) frentyk (1)
A.11.6   To flatereris or to folis þat *frentyk* ben of wittis,'
B.10.6   To flatereres or to fooles þat *frenetike* ben of wittes',
C.11.6   To eny foel or to flaterere or to *frentike* peple,'
C.18.178   With moche noyse þat nyhte nere *frentyk* y wakede;

frenssh n *Frensh adj*.   B 1; C 1 frenche
B.5.236   And I kan no *frenssh* in feiþ but of þe ferþest ende of Northfolk.'
C.13.202   And so witnesseth wyse and wisseth þe *frenche*:

frentyk(e > frenetike

frere n *frere n*.   A 13 frere (5) freris (8); B 66 frere (26) freres (40); C 69
     frere (33) freres (35) Freris (1)
A.Pr.55   I fond þere *Freris*, alle þe foure ordris,
A.2.172   Þanne fal[s]nesse for feer fleiȝ to þe *Freris*;
A.2.191   *Freris* wiþ fair speche fetten hym þennes;
A.2.192   F[or] knowing of comeris copide hym as a *Frere*.
A.3.34   Þanne com þere a confessour ycopid as a *frere*;
A.5.63   Of a *Freris* frokke were þe foresleuys.
A.6.118   Shulde I neuere ferþere a foote for no *freris* preching.'
A.9.8   Til it befel on a Friday two *Freris* I mette,
A.9.20   Ergo he nis not alwey at hom among ȝow *Freris*;
A.9.22   'I shal seiȝe þe, my sone,' seide þe *Frere* þanne,
A.9.24   Be a forebisene,' quaþ þe *Frere*, 'I shal þe faire shewen:
A.9.33   Riȝt þus [it] fariþ,' quaþ þe *Frere*, 'be folk here on erþe
A.11.58   *Freris* and faitours han founden vp suche questiouns
B.Pr.58   I fond þere *Freres*, alle þe foure ordres,
B.2.213   [Thanne] Falsnesse for fere fleiȝ to þe *Freres*;
B.2.232   *Freres* wiþ fair speche fetten hym þennes;
B.2.233   For knowynge of comeres coped hym as a *Frere*.
B.3.35   Thanne cam þere a Confessour coped as a *frere*;
B.3.52   For to be youre frend, *frere*, and faile yow neuere
B.5.80   Of a *Freres* frokke were þe foresleues.
B.5.137   'I am wraþe', quod he, 'I was som tyme a *frere*,
B.5.144   And now persons han parceyued þat *freres* parte wiþ hem
B.5.145   Thise possessioners preche and depraue *freres*;
B.5.146   And *freres* fyndeþ hem in defaute, as folk bereþ witnesse,
B.5.265   For were I *frere* of þat hous þer good feiþ and charite is
B.5.411   Til matyns and masse be do, and þanne [moste] to þe *freres*;
B.5.633   Sholde I neuere ferþere a foot for no *freres* prechyng.'
B.6.72   And *frere* faitour and folk of hi[s] ordre,
B.8.8   Til it bifel on a Friday two *freres* I mette,
B.8.24   Ergo he nys noȝt alwey [at hoom] amonges yow *freres*;
B.8.26   'I shal seye þee, my sone', seide þe *frere* þanne,
B.8.28   By a forbisne', quod þe *frere*, 'I shal þee faire shewe.
B.8.37   [Riȝt] þus it [fareþ]', quod þe *frere*, 'by folk here on erþe.
B.10.72   *Freres* and faitours han founde [vp] swiche questions
B.10.95   Nouȝt to fare as a fiþelere or a *frere* to seke festes,
B.10.328   And þanne *Freres* in hir fraytour shul fynden a keye
B.11.54   Go confesse þee to som *frere* and shewe hym þi synnes.
B.11.55   For whiles Fortune is þi frend *freres* wol þee louye,
B.11.63   And þo fond I þe *frere* afered and flittynge boþe
B.11.68   And for I seide þus to þrere a fool þei me helden,
B.11.71   'By my feiþ! *frere*', quod I, 'ye faren lik þise woweris
B.11.84   And lewte [louȝ] on me [for] I loured [on þe *frere*];
B.12.19   And prechours to preuen what it is of many a peire *freres*.'
B.12.145   If any *frere* were founde þere I ȝyue þee fyue shillynges!
B.13.7   And how þat *freres* folwede folk þat was riche
B.13.74   Ac I wiste neuere freke þat as a *frere* yede bifore men on englissh
B.13.95   What he fond in a [forel of] a *freres* lyuyng,
B.13.198   Thus curteisliche Conscience congeyed first þe *frere*,

B.13.242   Faitours and *freres* and folk wiþ brode crounes.
B.14.200   In fenestres at þe *freres*–if fals be þe foundement.
B.15.70   *Freres* and fele oþere maistres þat to [þe] lewed [folk] prechen,
B.15.77   As wel *freres* as ooþer folk, foliliche spenden
B.15.230   And in a *freres* frokke he was yfounden ones,
B.15.289   Til he foundede *freres* of Austynes ordre, [or ellis freres lyen].
B.15.289   Til he foundede freres of Austynes ordre, [or ellis *freres* lyen].
B.15.311   Founde þei þat *freres* wolde forsake hir almesses
B.15.328   If any peple parfourne þat text it are þise poore *freres*,
B.15.417   Ancres and heremytes and Monkes and *freres*
B.20.58   *Freres* folwede þat fend for he gaf hem copes,
B.20.230   *Freres* herden hym crye and comen hym to helpe,
B.20.240   And siþen *freres* forsoke þe felicite of erþe
B.20.243   And curteisliche conforted hem and called in alle *freres*,
B.20.252   *Frere* Fraunceys and Domynyk, for loue to be holye.
B.20.267   A certein for a certein, saue oonliche of *freres*.
B.20.273   Enuye herde þis and heet *freres* go to scole
B.20.285   And fleen to þe *freres*, as fals folk to westmynstre
B.20.290   And so it fareþ with muche folk þat to *freres* shryueþ,
B.20.291   As sisours and executours; þei [shul] ȝyue þe *freres*
B.20.295   And *freres* to philosophie he fond [hem] to scole,
B.20.315   Oon *frere* Flaterere is phisicien and surgien.'
B.20.323   That *frere* flaterere be fet and phisike yow sike.'
B.20.324   The *frere* herof herde and hiede faste
B.20.332   'In faiþ', quod þis *frere*, 'for profit and for helþe
B.20.336   'I am a Surgien', seide þe [*frere*], 'and salues kan make.
B.20.349   Lat in þe *frere* and his felawe, and make hem fair cheere.
B.20.354   Thus þoruȝ hende speche [þe *frere* entred]
B.20.367   As *frere*[s] of oure Fraternytee, for a litel siluer'.
B.20.378   The *frere* wiþ his phisyk þis folk haþ enchaunted,
B.20.383   And þat *freres* hadde a fyndyng þat for nede flateren
C.Pr.56   I fonde þer *Freris*, alle þe foure ordres,
C.Pr.60   Mony of þise maistres of mendenant *freres*
C.2.223   Falsnesse for fere tho fleyh to þe *freres*;
C.2.242   *Freres* [with] fayre speche fetten hym thennes,
C.2.243   For knowyng of co[mere]s copeden hym as a *frere*.
C.3.38   Thenne come þer a confessour ycoped as a *frere*;
C.3.56   'Y shal be ȝoure frende, *frere*, and fayle ȝow neuere
C.5.173   *Freres* in here fraytour shal fynde þat tyme
C.6.118   *Freres* folewen my [f]ore fele tyme and ofte
C.6.287   Were y a *frere*, in good fayth, for al þe gold on erthe
C.6.291   Y rede no faythful *frere* at thy feste to sytte.
C.7.27   Til matynes and masse be ydo; thenne haue y a memorie at þe
          freres.
C.7.286   [Sh]olde y neuere forthere [a] foet for no *frere* prechynge.'
C.8.73   And *frere* faytour and folk of þat ordre,
C.8.147   And *freres* þat flateren nat and pore folke syke,
C.8.191   And *freres* of alle þe fyue ordres, alle for fere of hunger.
C.9.209   That faytede in *frere* clothinge hadde fatte chekes.
C.9.250   And fo[r] þe cloth þat keuereth hym ykald he is a *frere*,
C.10.8   Til hit biful [o]n [a] fryday two *freres* y mette,
C.10.18   'Sothly,' saide þe *frere*, 'a soiourneth with vs freres
C.10.18   'Sothly,' saide þe frere, 'a soiourneth with vs *freres*
C.10.28   Ergo he [n]is nat alwey at hom amonges ȝow *freres*;
C.10.30   'Y shal sey þe, my sone,' sayde þe *frere* thenne,
C.10.32   By a forbisene,' quod þe *frere*, 'y shal the fayre shewe:
C.10.41   So hit fareth,' quod þe *frere*, 'by þe ryhtful mannus fallynge.
C.11.52   *Freres* and faytours haen founde vp suche questions
C.12.5   [Haue no consience how þou come to good]; confesse the to som
          frere.
C.12.7   For while fortune is thy frende *freres* wol the louye
C.12.15   And flittyng fond y the *frere* þat me confessede
C.12.19   'By my faith! *frere*', quod y, 'ȝe fare lyke þe woware
C.12.23   And thenne louhe leaute for y loured on þe *frere*:
C.12.25   'For this *frere* flaterede me while he fond me ryche
C.14.89   Yf eny *frere* we[re] founde þere y ȝeue the fyue shillynges!
C.15.9   And how þat *freres* folewede folk þat was ryche
C.15.29   And metten with a maystre, a man lyk a *frere*.
C.15.77   That no fals *frere* thorw flaterynge hem bygyle;
C.15.80   Ac y wiste neuere freke þat *frere* is ycald of þe fyue mendynantȝ
C.15.102   What a fond in a forel of a *frere*[s] lyuynge,
C.15.117   And ȝe fare thus with ȝoure syke *freres*, ferly me thynketh
C.16.41   In fenestres at þe *freres*–yf fals be þe fondement.
C.16.231   *Freres* fele tymes to þe folk þer they prechen
C.16.236   As wel *freres* as oþere folk, foliliche spenden
C.16.289   And fonde y neuere in faith, as *freres* hit precheth,
C.16.355   And in a *frere* f[r]okke he was founde ones,
C.17.15   Foules hym fedde yf *frere* Austynes be trewe
C.17.35   For wolde neuere faythfull god þat *freres* and monkes
C.17.52   To make men louye mesure þat monkes ben and *freres*:
C.17.60   To helpe thy fader formost byfore *freres* or monkes
C.22.58   *Freres* folewed þat fende for he ȝaf hem copes
C.22.230   *Freres* herde hym crye and comen hym to helpe

C.22.240   And senne *freres* forsoke the felic[it]e of erthe
C.22.243   And cortey[s]liche confortede hem and calde in all *freres*
C.22.252   *Frere* frronceys and domynyk, for loue to be holy.
C.22.267   A certeyne for a certeyne saue oenliche of *freres*.
C.22.273   Enuye herde this and heete *freres* go to scole
C.22.285   And fle to þe *freres*, as fals folk to Westmynstre
C.22.290   And so hit fareth with moche folke þat to *freres* shryuen,
C.22.291   As sisours and secutours; they shal ȝeue þe *freres*
C.22.295   And *freres* to filosophye he foend hem to scole
C.22.315   Oen *frere* flaterrere is fiscicien and surgien.'
C.22.323   That *frere* flaterare be fet and fysyk ȝow seke.'
C.22.324   The *frere* herof herde and hyede faste
C.22.332   'In fayth,' quod this *frere*, 'for profyt and for helthe
C.22.336   'Y am a surgien,' saide the *frere*, 'and salues can make.
C.22.349   Lat in þe *frere* and his felawe and make hem fayere chiere.
C.22.354   Thus thorw hende speche [the *frere* entred]
C.22.367   [As] *frere* of oure fraternite for a litel suluer'.
C.22.378   The *frere* with his fisyk this folk hath enchaunted
C.22.383   And þat *freres* hadde a fyndynge þat for nede flateren

freseþ v *fresen v.* A 1 fresiþ; B 1; C 1 frese
A. 8.116   Whan þe frost *fresiþ* foode hem behouiþ;
B. 7.134   [Whan þe frost *freseþ* fode hem bihoueþ];
C.12.193   In þe feld with þe forst and hit *frese* longe.

fressh adj *fresh adj.* A 2 fressh (1) fresshe (1); B 5 fressh (3) fresshe (2); C 2 fresh (1) fresshe (1)
A. 7.294   But ȝif it be *fressh* flessh oþer fissh yfried,
A.11.207   "Whanne fisshes faile þe flood or þe *fresshe* watir
B. 5.493   Feddest wiþ þi *fresshe* blood oure forefadres in derknesse:
B. 6.310   But if it be *fressh* flessh ouþer fissh [y]fryed,
B.10.301   Whan fisshes faillen þe flood or þe *fresshe* water
B.15.338   As whoso filled a tonne [ful] of a *fressh* ryuer
B.15.432   [Ac] *fressh* flessh ouþer fissh, whan it salt failleþ,
C. 7.133   Feddest wiþ thy [*fresshe*] blood oure forfadres in helle:
C. 8.332   But hit be [*fresh*] flesch or fisch yfried or ybake

frete v *freten v.(1)* B 3 freet (1) frete (2); C 3 freet (1) frete (1) vrete (1)
B. 2.96   And in fastynge dayes to *frete* er ful tyme were.
B.13.329   Auenge me fele tymes, oþer *frete* myselue wiþInne;
B.18.196   *Freet* of þat fruyt and forsook, as it weere,
C. 2.103   And fastyng dayes to *frete* byfore noone and drynke
C. 6.74   Venged me vele tymes other *vrete* myself withynne
C.20.201   *Freet* of th[at] fruyt and forsoke, as it was,

freþid > fryþed

fretted ptp *freten v.(2)* A 1 frettid; B 1
A. 2.11   Alle here fyue fyngris were *frettid* wiþ rynges
B. 2.11   Fetisliche hire fyngres were *fretted* with gold wyr

friday n *fridai n.* A 4; B 14 friday (8) fryday (4) Fridaies (1) frydayes (1); C 15 friday (4) fridayes (1) fridays (1) fryday (7) frydayes (2)
A. 1.99   And nouȝt to fasten a *friday* in fyue score wynter,
A. 5.210   'Shal neuere fissh on þe *Friday* defie in my wombe
A. 9.8   Til it befel on a *Friday* two Freris I mette,
A.11.279   A goode *friday*, I fynde, a feloun was sauid
B. 1.101   And nauȝt to fasten o *friday* in fyue score wynter,
B. 5.173   And doon me faste *frydayes* to [perf] breed and to watre;
B. 5.382   'Shal neuere fyssh on [þe] *Fryday* defyen in my wombe
B. 5.488   On good *fryday* for mannes sake at ful tyme of þe daye;
B. 8.8   Til it bifel on a *Friday* two freres I mette,
B.10.420   On good *Friday*, I fynde, a felon was ysaued
B.12.192   The þef þat hadde grace of god on good *fryday*, as þow spek[e],
B.12.202   So it fareþ by þat felon þat a good *friday* was saued;
B.13.348   As wel fastyng dayes [as] *Fridaies* [and] forboden nyȝtes,
B.13.446   And fiþele þee wiþoute flaterynge of good *friday* þe [geste]
B.16.139   Til it bifel on a *friday*, a litel bifore Pasqe.
B.16.162   That on þe *friday* folwynge for mankyndes sake
B.19.142   Killeden hym on cros wise at Caluarie on *Friday*,
B.20.312   For fastynge of a *fryday* he ferde as he wolde deye.
C. 5.30   Or faytest vppon *frydayes* or festeday[es] in churches,
C. 6.155   And doen me faste *fridayes* to bred and to water;
C. 6.182   As wel fastyng dayes and *frydayes* and heye fest[e] euenes.
C. 6.352   Fastyng on a *friday* forth gan he wende
C. 6.439   Shal neuere fysch [o]n þe *fryday* defyen in my wombe
C. 7.106   And fithele the withoute flaterynge of god *friday* þe [g]este
C. 7.130   On a *friday* in fourme of man feledest oure sorwe:
C. 9.94   *Fridays* and fastyngdays a ferthingworth of moskeles
C.10.8   Til hit biful [o]n [a] *fryday* two freres y mette,
C.11.252   A gode *friday*, y fynde, a feloun was ysaued
C.14.131   The thef þat hadde grace of god a gode *fryday*, As thow toldest,
C.14.141   So hit f[areth] by þe feloun þat a goed *fryday* was saued:
C.18.166   This biful on a *friday*, a litel bifore Pasche.
C.21.142   Culden hym on cros wyse at Caluarie on *fryday*
C.22.312   For fastyng of a *fryday* a feerde as he wolde deye.

fryth n *frith n.(2)* B 3; C 3 frithes (1) fryth (1) frythes (1)
B.11.365   I seiȝ floures in þe *fryth* and hir faire colours
B.12.221   And of þe floures in þe *Fryth* and of hire faire hewes,
B.17.115   And þanne shal Feiþ be forster here and in þis *Fryth* walke,
C. 9.225   In *frithes* and in forestes for fox and other bestes
C.14.158   And how þe floures in þe *fryth* cometh to fayre hewes:
C.17.11   Elles foules fedde hem in *frythes* þer they wonede,

fryþed ptp *frithen v.* A 1 freþid; B 1; C 1 frithed
A. 6.68   He is *fre[þ]id* in wiþ Floreynes & oþere [fees] manye.
B. 5.581   He is *fryþed* In wiþ floryns and oþere fees manye;
C. 7.228   Is *frithed* in with floreynes and othere fees monye;

fro prep *from prep.* A 34 fro (28) from (6); B 92 fram (13) fro (57) from (22); C 83 fram (24) fro (59)
A.Pr.53   Cloþide hem in copis to be knowen *from* oþere;
A. 1.4   Com doun *fro* þat [clyf] & callide me faire,
A. 1.23   Þat on is vesture *fro* chele þe to saue;
A. 2.29   Knowe hem þere ȝif þou canst and kep þe *from* hem alle
A. 2.115   And comen to counforte *fro* care þe false,
A. 3.90   Þe king *fro* counseil com & callide aftir mede
A. 3.99   I haue a kniȝt, consience, com late *fro* beȝonde;
A. 4.28   For to saue hemself *from* shame & from harm.
A. 4.28   For to saue hemself from shame & *from* harm.
A. 5.29   And fecche [hom] felis *fro* wyuene pyne
A. 5.90   [Awey] *fro* þe auter myn eiȝe I turne
A. 5.101   Ne no dyapendyon dryue it *fro* myn herte.
A. 6.13   Þis folk fraynide hym faire [*fro*] whenis þat he come.
A. 6.14   '*Fro* synay,' he seide, '& fro þe sepulcre.
A. 6.14   'Fro synay,' he seide, '& *fro* þe sepulcre.
A. 7.30   *Fro* wastours [and wikkide men] þat wolde me destroye,
A. 7.80   And defende it *fro* the fend, for so I beleue.
A. 7.128   [Cacche cowes] *from* his corn, [and] kepen hise bestis,
A. 7.147   To kepen hym as coueaunt was *fro* curside shrewis,
A. 7.148   *Fro* wastours þat waite wynneres to shende.
A. 7.172   And fla[ppid]e on wiþ flailes *fro* morewe til eue,
A. 9.51   And þei seide, 'þe same saue þe *fro* myschaunce,
A.10.67   But þei witen hem *fro* wauntounesse whiles þei ben ȝon[g]e.
A.10.68   And ȝif þei ben pore & cateles, to kepe hem *fro* ille,
A.10.70   *Fro* folies, & fynde hem til þei ben wise.
A.10.74   Saue hymself *fro* synne, for so hym behouiþ;
A.10.106   *Fro* religioun to religioun, reccheles ben þei euere;
A.10.158   To kepe his kynrede *fro* kaymes, þei couplide nouȝt togideris;
A.11.88   What is dowel *fro* dobet; now def mote he worþe,
A.11.114   'Axe þe heiȝe wey,' quaþ heo, '*from* henis to suffre
A.11.121   F[*ro*] lesinges & li[þer] speche & likerous drinkes.
A.11.213   Poperiþ on a palfrey [*fro*] toune to toune;
A.11.307   Arn none raþere yrauisshid *fro* þe riȝte beleue
A.12.87   *Fro* deþ þat is oure duk swyche dedis we brynge.'
B.Pr.56   Cloþed hem in copes to ben knowen *from* oþere;
B. 1.4   Cam doun *fro* [þe] Castel and called me faire,
B. 1.23   That oon [is] vesture *from* [chele] þee to saue;
B. 1.114   And fel *fro* þat felawshipe in a fendes liknesse
B. 2.47   Knowe hem þere if þow kanst and kepe [þee *from*] hem alle],
B. 2.151   And comen to conforten *from* care þe false
B. 3.101   The kyng *fro* conseil cam and called after Mede
B. 3.110   I haue a knyȝt, Conscience, cam late *fro* biyonde;
B. 4.31   For to saue hem[seluen] *from* shame and from harmes.
B. 4.31   For to saue hem[seluen] from shame and *from* harmes.
B. 5.29   And fecche Felice hom *fro* wyuen pyne.
B. 5.110   Awey *fro* þe Auter turne I myne eiȝen
B. 5.124   Ne no Diapenidion dryue it *fro* myn herte,
B. 5.295   And what he lente yow of oure lordes good to lette yow *fro* synne.'
B. 5.401   That I telle wiþ my tonge is two myle *fro* myn herte.
B. 5.525   This folk frayned hym [faire] *fro* whennes he come.
B. 5.526   '*Fram* Synay', he seide, 'and fram [þe Sepulcre].
B. 5.526   'Fram Synay', he seide, 'and *fram* [þe Sepulcre].
B. 6.28   *Fro* wastours and wikked men þat [wolde me destruye],
B. 6.49   Or a knyȝt *from* a knaue; knowe þis in þyn herte.
B. 6.88   And [defende it *fro* þe fend], for so I bileue,
B. 6.140   To kepe kyen in þe feld, þe corn *fro* þe beestes,
B. 6.160   To kepen hym as coueaunt was *fro* cursede sherewes,
B. 6.161   'And *fro* þise wastours wolueskynnes þat makeþ þe world deere,
B. 6.184   And flapten on wiþ flailes *fro* morwe til euen
B. 7.36   And witen yow *fro* wanhope, if ye wol þus werche,
B. 8.60   And I seide 'þe same saue yow *fro* myschaunce,
B. 8.126   What was Dowel *fro* dobet and dobest from hem boþe.
B. 8.126   What was Dowel fro dobet and dobest *from* hem boþe.
B. 9.183   Wisely go wedde and ware [þee] *fro* synne,
B.10.135   What is dowel fro dobet, [now] deef mote he worþe,
B.10.169   *Fro*-lesynges-and-liþer-speche-and-likerouse-drynkes.
B.10.243   *Fro* þe dedly deeþ and [þe] deueles power
B.10.313   A prikere on a palfrey *fro* [place] to Manere,
B.10.317   Litel hadde lordes to doon to ȝyue lond *from* hire heires

B.10.413   And shilden vs *from* shame þerinne, as Noes ship dide beestes;
B.10.463   Arn none raþer yrauysshed *fro* þe riȝte bileue
B.11.129   Ac he may renne in arerage and rome *fro* home,
B.11.144   That al þe clergie vnder crist ne myȝte me cracche *fro* helle;
B.11.153   Brouȝte me *fro* bitter peyne þer no biddyng myȝte.'
B.11.213   For woot no man how neiȝ it is to ben ynome *fro* boþe.
B.11.318   This lokynge on lewed preestes haþ doon me lepe *from* pouerte
B.11.419   The wisedom and þe wit of god, he was put *fram* blisse.
B.12.178   And þis conforteþ ech a clerk and co,uereþ *fro* wanhope,
B.12.190   That haþ take *fro* Tybourne twenty stronge þeues,
B.13.176   Profitable to eiþer peple;' and putte þe table *fro* hym,
B.13.240   *Fro* Mighelmesse to Mighelmesse I fynde hem wiþ wafres.
B.13.266   Wiþ [bake] breed *fro* Stratford; þo gonnen beggeris wepe
B.13.428   Sauen þoruȝ hir sermo[n] mannes soule *fro* helle;
B.13.445   For to saue þi soule *from* sathan þyn enemy.
B.14.15   That I ne flobre it foule *fro* morwe til euen.'
B.14.22   Dobest [shal kepe it clene *from* vnkynde werkes].
B.14.133   *Fram* þe loue of oure lord at his laste ende!
B.14.298   Wiþ sobretee *fram* alle synne and also ȝit moore;
B.14.299   It afaiteþ þe flessh *fram* folies ful manye,
B.15.35   And whan I flee *fro* þe flessh and forsake þe careyne
B.15.51   For swich a lust and likyng Lucifer fel *from* heuene:
B.15.323   To ȝyue *from* youre heires þat youre Aiels yow lefte,
B.15.346   And many a prison *fram* purgatorie þoruȝ hise preieres deliuereþ.
B.15.407   That þe coluere þat com so com *from* god of heuene
B.15.452   Clooþ þat cometh *fro* þe weuyng is noȝt comly to were
B.15.464   But wiþ foweles þat *fram* hym nolde but folwede his whistlyng:
B.15.535   Fer *fro* kyth and fro kyn yuele ycloþed yeden,
B.15.535   Fer fro kyth and *fro* kyn yuele ycloþed yeden,
B.16.25   'For wyndes, wiltow wite', quod he, 'to witen it *fro* fallyng:
B.16.89   To go robbe þat Rageman and reue þe fruyt *fro* hym.
B.16.174   I frayned hym first *fram* whennes he come
B.16.246   And defende hem *fro* þe fend, folk þat on me leneden.
B.16.263   Ne no buyrn be oure borgh, ne brynge vs *fram* his daunger–
B.16.274   I affrayned hym first *fram* whennes he come,
B.17.29   Thre persones in parcelles departable *fro* ooþer
B.17.53   Comynge *from* a contree þat men called Ierico;
B.17.65   Dredfully, bi þis day! as doke dooþ *fram* þe faucon.
B.17.77   'Haue, kepe þis man', [quod he], 'til I come *fro* þe Iustes.
B.17.247   [*Fro*] þe fader of heuene forȝifnesse to haue.
B.18.33   And fecche *fro* þe fend Piers fruyt þe Plowman
B.18.136   In menynge þat man shal *fro* merknesse be drawe
B.18.306   To saue men *from* synne if hemself wolde.
B.18.312   First þoruȝ þe we fellen *fro* heuene so heiȝe:
B.18.400   Thus by lawe', quod oure lord, 'lede I wole *fro* hennes
B.19.46   And defended *from* foule yueles, feueres and Fluxes,
B.19.47   And *from* fendes þat in hem [was] and false bileue.
B.19.65   Therwith to fiȝte and [f]enden vs *fro* fallynge in[to] synne,
B.19.144   Kepen it *fro* nyghtcomeris wiþ knyghtes yarmed
B.19.208   And cometh *fro* þe grete god; grace is his name.
B.19.247   And fecchen it *fro* false men wiþ Foluyles lawes.
B.19.413   I knew neuere Cardynal þat he ne cam *fro* þe pope.
B.19.467   And holy kirke and clergie *fro* cursed men to [de]fende.
B.20.77   Fooles *fro* þise fendes lymes, for Piers loue þe Plowman.
B.20.352   And be adrad of deeþ and wiþdrawe hym *fram* pryde
B.20.361   *Fro* lenten to lenten he lat hise plastres bite.'
C.Pr.54   Clothed hem in copis to be knowe *fram* othere
C.Pr.114   *Fro* his chayere þer he sat and brake his nekke atwene.
C.1.4   Cam doun *fro* þe castel and calde me by name
C.2.49   Knowe hem wel yf þou kanst and kepe the *fro* hem alle
C.2.181   Softliche in s[am]b[u]re *fram* syse [to] syse,
C.3.128   The kyng *fram* conseyl come [and] calde aftur mede
C.3.133   Til treuthe hadde ytolde here a tokene *fram* hymsulue.
C.3.147   Y haue a knyght, Consience, cam late *fro* beȝende;
C.3.456   That here kyng he ycome *fro* þe Court of heuene.
C.5.111   Y saw þe felde ful of folk *fram* ende til oþer
C.5.131   And fette felyce hoem *fram* wyuene pyne.
C.5.159   And pryked aboute on palfrayes *fram* places to maneres,
C.5.163   Lytel hadde lordes ado to ȝeue lond *fro* [here] heyres
C.6.89   Ne derworth drynke dryue hit *fro* myn herte
C.6.349   What a lered ȝow to lyue with and to lette ȝow *fram* thefte.'
C.7.17   That y telle with my tonge is t[wo] myle *fro* myn herte.
C.7.88   Sauen thorw here sarmon mannes soule *fram* helle;
C.7.105   For to saue thy soule *fram* satan thyn enemye
C.7.135   And brouhte thyne yblessed *fro* thennes into þe blisse of heuene.
C.7.170   This folk frayned hym furste *fro* whennes he come.
C.7.171   '*Fro* synoye,' he sayde, 'and fro þe sepulcre.
C.7.171   'Fro synoye,' he sayde, 'and *fro* þe sepulcre.
C.7.256   And solace thy soule and saue the *fram* payne
C.7.301   Were y seuen nyhte *fro* here syhte s[ynnen] he wolde
C.8.27   *Fro* wastores and wikked men þat þis world struyen
C.8.46   Or a knyhte [*fram*] a knaue or a quene fram a queene.

C.8.46   Or a knyhte [fram] a knaue or a quene *fram* a queene.
C.8.97   And defenden hit *fro* þe fende, and so is my beleue,
C.8.145   Bothe of my corn and of my cloth to kepe hem *fram* defaute.
C.8.180   And flapton on with f[lay]les *fro* morwen til euen
C.9.242   Breke þis obedience þat beth so fer *fram* chirche.
C.10.22   Fallyng *fro* ioye, iesu woet þe sothe!
C.10.59   And y sayde, 'þe same saue ȝow *fro* meschaunce
C.10.122   What was dowel *fro* dobet and dobest fro hem bothe.
C.10.122   What was dowel fro dobet and dobest *fro* hem bothe.
C.10.184   Frendes shal fynde hem and *fram* folye kepe
C.10.284   Wisely go wedde and war þe *fro* synne;
C.11.62   Ne for drede of eny deth withdraweth h[e]m *fro* pruyde
C.11.140   Kepe þe ten comaundementis and kepe þe *fro* synne
C.11.289   Aren noen rather yraueschid *fro* þe rihte bileue
C.12.64   Ac he may renne in arerage and rome *fro* home,
C.12.79   That al þe cristendoem vnde[r] Crist ne myhte me crache *fro* [helle]
C.12.98   And cristis oune clergie; he cam *fro* heuene to teche hit
C.14.118   And þat conforteth vch a clerk and keuereth *fro* wanhope,
C.14.129   Hit hath take *fro* tybourne twenty stronge theues
C.15.173   Profitable for bothe parties;' and potte þe boerd *fro* hym
C.15.215   *Fro* Mihelmasse to Mihelmasse y fynde mete and drynke.
C.15.235   Hit am y þat fynde alle folke and *fram* hunger saue
C.16.2   *Fram* þe loue of oure lord at his laste ende.
C.16.134   With sobrete *fro* alle synnes and also ȝut more;
C.16.135   Hit defendeth þe flesche *fram* folies ful monye,
C.16.197   And when y fle *fro* þe [flessh] and feye leue þe caroyne
C.16.213   For such a lust and lykynge lucifer ful *fram* heuene:
C.16.337   'Were y with hym by Cr[i]st,' quod y, 'y wolde neuere *fro* hym
C.17.196   Fer *fro* [k]uthe and fro kyn euele yclothed ȝeden,
C.17.196   Fer fro [k]uthe and *fro* kyn euele yclothed ȝeden,
C.17.245   Deuouteliche day and nyhte, withdrawe hem *fro* synne
C.17.273   And *fro* mysbileue mony men turnede.
C.17.285   Feden hem and follen hem and fere hem *fro* synne–
C.18.29   The fruyt of this fayre tre *fro* thre wikkede wyndes
C.18.30   [And *fro* fallynge the stok; hit fayle nat of his myhte].
C.18.187   'Thre persones in o pensel,' quod y, 'departable *fram* oþere.
C.18.279   Ne noen bern ben oure borw ne bryngen vs [*fro* his] daunger–
C.18.280   *Fro* þe poukes pondefold no maynprise may vs feche–
C.18.290   And y fraynede hym furst *fro* whennes he come,
C.19.30   Thre persones parselmele depar[t]able *fro* oþere
C.19.51   Comynge *fram* a contraye þat men callide Ierico;
C.19.82   Were afered and flowe *fram* þe man ywounded.
C.19.98   In thre persones, a parceles departable *fram* oþere,
C.20.32   And feche *fro* þe fende [Peres] fruyt þe [plouhman]
C.20.139   In menynge þat man shal *fro* me[r]kenesse be ydrawe
C.20.443   Thus by lawe,' quod oure lord, 'lede y wol *fro* hennes
C.21.46   And fended *fro* foule eueles, feueres and fluxes
C.21.47   And *fro* fendes þat in hem was and false bileue.
C.21.65   Therwith to fihte and fende vs *fro* fallyng into synne
C.21.144   Kepen hit *fro* nyhtecomares with knyhtes y[ar]med
C.21.208   And cometh *fro* the grete god; grace is his name.
C.21.247   And fechen hit *fro* false men with foleuiles lawes;
C.21.413   Y knewe neuere cardinale þat he ne cam *fro* þe pope
C.21.467   And holy kyrke and clerge *fro* cursed men to defende.
C.22.77   Foles *fro* this fendes lymes for [Peres] loue the [plouhman].
C.22.352   And be adrad of deth and withdrawe hym *fro* pruyde
C.22.361   *Fro* lente to lente he lat his plastres byte.'

frokke n *frok n.* A 1; B 2; C 1
A.5.63   Of a Freris *frokke* were þe foresleuys.
B.5.80   Of a Freres *frokke* were þe foresleues.
B.15.230   And in a freres *frokke* he was yfounden ones,
C.16.355   And in a frere f[r]okke he was founde ones

from > fro

frost n *frost n.* A 1; B 1; C 2 forst (1) forstes (1)
A.8.116   Whan þe *frost* fresiþ foode hem behouiþ;
B.7.134   [Whan þe *frost* freseþ fode hem bihoueþ];
C.12.189   Then sedes þat [in somer] sowe ben and mowen nat with *forstes*
C.12.193   In þe feld with þe *forst* and hit frese longe.

frounces n *frounce n.(1)* B 1
B.13.317   Men sholde fynde manye *frounces* and manye foule plottes.'

fruyt n *fruit n.* A 3 fruyt (2) fruytes (1); B 20 fruyt (19) fruytes (1); C 25 fruyt (21) fruyte (3) fruyttes (1)
A.7.306   Þoruȝ flood [and] foule wederis *fruytes* shuln fa[i]lle,
A.10.122   Which is þe flour & þe *fruyt* fostrid of boþe.
A.10.192   Þe *fruyt* þat þei bringe forþ arn manye foule wordis.
B.5.142   And now is fallen þerof a *fruyt* þat folk han wel leuere
B.6.325   Thoruȝ flo[od] and foule wedres *fruytes* shul faille,
B.9.171   The *fruyt* þat [þei] brynge forþ arn [manye] foule wordes;]
B.15.102   Shal neuere flour ne *fruyt* [wexe] ne fair leef be grene.

B.16.9 And so þoruȝ god and goode men groweþ þe *fruyt* Charite.'
B.16.11 And to haue my fulle of þat *fruyt* forsake a[l] oþ[er] saule[e].
B.16.29 And forfreteþ neiȝ þe *fruyt* þoruȝ manye faire sightes.
B.16.40 And þanne fondeþ þe fend my *fruyt* to destruye
B.16.49 Manacen bihynde me, my *fruyt* for to fecche,
B.16.66 'To [dyuyse] þe *fruyt* þat so faire hangeþ'.
B.16.68 Matrimoyne I may nyme, a moiste *fruyt* wiþalle.
B.16.70 Thanne bereþ þe crop kynde *fruyt* and clennest of alle,
B.16.89 To go robbe þat Rageman and reue þe *fruyt* fro hym.
B.16.94 That Piers *fruyt* floured and felle to be rype.
B.16.96 Wheiþer sholde fonge *fruyt*, þe fend or hymselue.
B.18.20 'And fecche þat þe fend claymeþ, Piers *fruyt* þe Plowman.'
B.18.33 And fecche fro þe fend Piers *fruyt* þe Plowman
B.18.194 If þat þei touchede a tree and þe [trees] *fruyt* eten.
B.18.196 Freet of þat *fruyt* and forsook, as it weere,
B.19.313 Foulen *fruyt* in þe feld þer þei growen togideres,
C. 8.346 Thorw flodes and foule wederes *fruyttes* shollen fayle;
C.10.273 The *fruyt* þat they brynge forth aren many foule wordes;
C.16.255 Shal neuere flour ne *fruyt* wexe ne fayre leue be grene.
C.18.12 And þerof cometh a goed *fruyt* þe wiche men calleth werkes
C.18.29 The *fruyt* of this fayre tre fro thre wikkede wyndes
C.18.33 And forfret þat *fruyt* thorw many fayre s[ih]tus.
C.18.43 And thenne fondeth the fende my *fruyte* to destruye
C.18.49 And feccheth away þe *fruyt* som tyme byfore bothe myn yes.
C.18.54 Where þe *fruyt* were fayre or foul for to loke on.
C.18.55 And þe *fruyt* was fayre, non fayrere be myhte,
C.18.79 And folewe þat the flesche wole and *fruyt* forth brynge.
C.18.83 Why groweth this *fruyt* in thre degres?' 'A goed skil,' he saide.
C.18.85 Matrimonye, a moist *fruyt* þat multiplieth þe peple;
C.18.86 And thenne aboue is bettere *fruyt*, ac bothe two ben gode,
C.18.90 Hit was þe furste *fruyte* þat þe fader of heuene blessed,
C.18.98 And for þe fayrest *fruyte* byfore hym, as of erthe,
C.18.101 And bryngeth forth *fruyt*, folk of alle nacion.
C.18.122 That thorw fals biheste and *fruyt* furste man disseyued.
C.18.127 That elde felde efte þe *fruyt*, or full to be rype.
C.18.129 Who sholde fecche this *fruyt*, the fende or iesus suluen.
C.20.18 'And feche þat þe fende claymeth, pers *fruyt* þe plouhman.'
C.20.32 And feche fro þe fende [Peres] *fruyt* þe [plouhman]
C.20.199 Yf that thei touche[d a] tre and of þe [trees] *fruyt* eten.
C.20.201 Freet of th[at] *fruyt* and forsoke, as hit were,
C.21.313 Fouleth the *fruyt* in the feld ther thei growe togyderes

fuyr(- > fir

ful adj *ful adj. &> potte_ful* A 6; B 16; C 17 fol (5) ful (12)
A.Pr.17 A fair feld *ful* of folk fand I þere betwene
A. 1.2 And ek þe feld *ful* of folk I shal ȝow faire shewe.
A. 2.39 Þat iche feld nas *ful* of folk al aboute.
A. 5.10 [For I sauȝ] þe feld *ful* of folk þat I before tolde],
A. 7.167 And bledde into þe bodyward a bolle *ful* of growel,
A.12.71 A bagge *ful* of a beggere.' I bouȝþe hit at onys.
B.Pr.17 A fair feeld *ful* of folk fond I þer bitwene
B. 1.2 And þe feld *ful* of folk I shal yow faire shewe.
B. 2.96 And in fastynge dayes to frete *ful* tyme were.
B. 5.10 For I seiȝ þe feld *ful* of folk þat I before [tolde],
B. 5.488 On good fryday for mannes sake at *ful* tyme of þe daye;
B.15.153 And fond I neuere *ful* charite, before ne bihynde.
B.15.334 That were *ful* of faire trees, and I fondede and caste
B.15.338 As whoso filled a tonne [*ful*] of a fressh ryuer.
B.16.102 To haue yfouȝte wiþ þe fend er *ful* tyme come.
B.16.126 And lefte baskettes *ful* of broke mete, bere awey whoso wolde.'
B.17.87 And suwed þat Samaritan þat was so *ful* of pite,
B.17.169 And as my fust is *ful* hand y[f]olden togideres
B.17.170 So is þe fader a *ful* god, formour and shappere:
B.17.172 The fyngres formen a *ful* hand to portreye or peynten;
B.17.175 And *ful* god as is þe fader, no febler ne no bettre.
B.19.118 A faunt[ek]yn *ful* of wit, filius Marie.
C.Pr.19 A fair feld *ful* of folk fond y þer bytwene
C. 1.2 And þe feld *ful* of folk y shal ȝou fair shewe.
C. 3.88 And [t]how thei fillen nat *ful* þat for lawe is seled
C. 5.111 Y saw þe felde *ful* of folk fram ende til oþer
C. 9.14 Lele and *fol* of loue and no lord drede;
C. 9.343 A pouhe *ful* of pardon there ne prouinciales lettres,
C.10.269 That his wyf were wexe or a walet *ful* of nobles.
C.12.224 On fat lond *ful* of donge foulest wedes groweth.
C.13.59 Ther þe messager is ay merye and his mouth *ful* of songes
C.18.136 To haue yfouhte with þe fende Ar *fol* tyme come.
C.18.154 And lefte basketes *ful* of Broke mete, bere awey hoso wolde.
C.19.130 A fuste with a fynger and a *fol* paume.
C.19.131 And as þe fuste is a *ful* hand yfolde togyderes,
C.19.132 So is þe fader a *fol* god, the fu[r]ste of hem alle
C.19.136 The fyngeres is a *fol* hand for failed they or thombe
C.19.296 And nat of þe nownpower of god, þat he ne is *ful* of myhte.
C.21.118 A fauntekyn *ful* of wyt, filius Marie.

ful adv *ful adv.* A 7; B 47; C 59 fol (14) ful (45)
A.Pr.20 Summe putte hem to plouȝ, pleiȝede *ful* selde,
A.Pr.21 In settyng & sowyng swonke *ful* harde;
A. 2.16 'Þat is mede þe maide, haþ noiȝede me *ful* ofte,
A. 7.101 Oþere werkmen þere were [þat] wrouȝte *ful* faste,
A. 9.3 And fraynide *ful* ofte of folk þat I mette
A.11.199 Dobet doþ *ful* wel, & dewid he is also,
A.12.78 [Lene & rewlyche, with leggys *ful* smale].
B.Pr.20 Some putten hem to plouȝ, pleiden *ful* selde,
B.Pr.21 In settynge and sowynge swonken *ful* harde;
B.Pr.29 Lest crist in Consistorie acorse *ful* manye.
B.Pr.161 Beren beiȝes *ful* briȝte abouten hire nekkes,
B.Pr.194 Ther þe cat is a kitoun þe court is *ful* elenge;
B. 1.121 But fellen out in fendes liknesse [*ful*] nyne dayes togidere
B. 2.15 Hire Robe was *ful* riche, of reed scarlet engreyned,
B. 2.20 'That is Mede þe mayde, haþ noyed me *ful* ofte,
B. 3.349 A *ful* teneful text to hem þat takeþ Mede:
B. 4.74 Thanne wowede wrong wisdom *ful* yerne
B. 6.109 Oþere werkmen þer were þat wroȝten *ful* [faste],
B. 7.11 Han pardon þoruȝ purgatorie to passen *ful* liȝtly,
B. 7.128 That loueþ god lelly his liflode is *ful* esy:
B. 8.3 And frayned *ful* ofte of folk þat I mette
B.10.365 It shal bisitten vs *ful* siluer þat we kepen,
B.11.20 And in þis Mirour þow myȝt se [myrþes] *ful* manye
B.11.78 Baptiȝynge and buryinge boþe beþ *ful* nedefulle;
B.11.111 This was hir teme and hir text–I took *ful* good hede–
B.11.352 Hidden and hileden hir egges *ful* derne
B.12.55 [So catel and kynde wit acombreþ *ful* manye;
B.12.155 Why I haue told [þee] al þis, I took *ful* good hede
B.12.243 They may noȝt flee fer ne *ful* heiȝe neiþer];
B.12.257 I leue it flawme *ful* foule þe fold al aboute.
B.13.81 And wisshed witterly, wiþ wille *ful* egre,
B.13.203 But seide *ful* sobreliche, 'þow shalt se þe tyme
B.14.299 It afaiteþ þe flessh fram folies *ful* manye,
B.14.329 Swouned and sobbed and siked *ful* ofte
B.15.116 Ac youre werkes and wordes þervnder aren *ful* [wol]ueliche.
B.15.239 In þe Consistorie bifore þe Commissarie he comeþ noȝt *ful* ofte
B.16.4 'It is a *ful* trie tree', quod he, 'trewely to telle.
B.16.65 To asken hym any moore þerof, and bad hym *ful* faire
B.16.179 A *ful* bold bacheler; I knew hym by his blasen.'
B.16.230 *Ful* trewe toknes bitwene vs is to telle whan me likeþ.
B.16.234 I am *ful* siker in soule þerof, and my sone boþe.
B.17.14 This was the tixte, trewely; I took *ful* good yeme.
B.17.44 It is *ful* hard for any man on Abraham bileue
B.17.52 Ridynge *ful* rapely þe righte wey we yeden,
B.18.116 A *ful* benigne burde and Buxom of speche.
B.18.150 Thanne Mercy *ful* myldely mouþed þise wordes,
B.18.164 Out of þe nyppe of þe North noȝt *ful* longe,
B.19.451 For þe comune', quod þis Curatour, 'counten *ful* litel
B.20.47 And suffre sorwes *ful* soure, þat shal to Ioye torne.''
B.20.52 And mette *ful* merueillously þat in mannes forme
B.20.99 So kynde þoruȝ corrupcions kilde *ful* manye.
B.20.119 Wiþ vntidy tales he tened *ful* ofte
B.20.194 And wisshed *ful* witterly þat I were in heuene.
B.20.335 Ypocrisie haþ hurt hem; *ful* hard is if þei keuere.'
C.Pr.22 Somme potte hem to plogh, playde *ful* selde,
C.Pr.23 In settynge and sowynge swonken *ful* harde
C.Pr.28 Al for loue of oure lord lyueden [*ful* streyte]
C.Pr.207 Ther þe Cat [is] a kytoun þe Court is *ful* elynge;
C. 2.12 On alle here fyue fyngeres *ful* richeliche yrynged,
C. 2.19 'That is mede þe mayde, hath niyed me *fol* ofte
C. 2.157 Hit shal [bi]sitte ȝoure soules *ful* so[u]re at þe laste.'
C. 2.167 And comen *ful* courteysly to conforte the false
C. 3.85 Ne bouhte none burgages, be ȝe *ful* certayn.
C. 3.161 In trist of here tresor he teneth *fol* monye,
C. 3.497 A *ful* teneful tyxst to hem þat taketh mede,
C. 4.52 [A w]ayteth *ful* wel when y seluer take,
C. 4.177 Hit is *ful* hard, by myn heued, herto to bryngen hit
C. 7.175 /[Y haue] ywalked *ful* wyde in wete and in drye
C. 7.251 A *ful* leel lady vnlek hit of grace
C. 7.275 Largenesse þ[e] lady lat in *ful* monye,
C. 7.281 Hit is *ful* hard, be myn heued, eny of ȝow alle
C. 7.307 Ac þe way is *ful* wikked but hoso hadde a gyde
C. 8.116 Oþer werkemen þer were þat wrouhten *fol* ȝerne,
C. 8.210 For y woet wel, be [thow] went, worche þei wol *ful* ille;
C. 9.11 Haen pardon thorw purgatorye to passe *ful* lyhtly,
C. 9.53 His pardoun is *ful* petyt at his partynge hennes
C. 9.166 For hit blameth all beggarie, be ȝe *ful* certayn.
C. 9.207 H[e]lden *ful* hungry hous and hadde muche defaute,
C. 9.300 And of [Peres] the [plouhman] *fol* pencyf in herte
C.10.3 And frayned *ful* ofte of folke þat y mette
C.11.2 That *ful* lene lokede and lyfholy semede.
C.11.179 And in þis myrrour thow myhte se murthes *fol* monye

C.11.312   Clergie [and] his conseile y counted *ful* litel.
C.12.45   Of here teme and here tales y took *ful* good hede;
C.12.237   For if he be fer þerfro *fol* ofte hath he drede
C.13.29   Bothe t[w]o ben gode, be ȝe *ful* certeyn,
C.13.191   They reule hem al by resoun Ac renkes *ful* fewe.
C.14.17   Ac catel and kynde wit acombreth *fol* monye;
C.14.99   Why y haue tolde [the] al þis, y toek *ful* gode hede
C.14.176   For þey may nat fle fer ne *ful* hey neyther
C.15.88   And wisched witterly with will *ful* egre
C.15.180   Lettrure and longe studie letteth *fol* monye
C.16.53   The hey way to heueneward he halt hit nat *fol* euene
C.16.78   So he is neuere[more *ful*] merye, so meschief hym folleweth.
C.16.119   In engelysch is *ful* hard Ac sumdel y shal telle the.
C.16.135   Hit defendeth þe flesche fram folies *ful* monye,
C.16.159   A knewe Consience *ful* wel and clergie bothe.
C.16.364   In constorie bifore [þe] commissarie a cometh nat *ful* ofte
C.17.12   Bothe Antony and arseny and oþer *fol* monye.
C.17.271   For to enf[ou]rme þe fayth *ful* wydewhare deyede,
C.17.300   And of selcouthe sores saued men *fol* ofte.
C.18.246   *Fol* trewe tokenes bitwene vs is wh[at] tyme þat y met[t]e hym,
C.19.15   This was the tyxt trewly; y toek *ful* good gome.
C.19.50   Rydynge *ful* raply þe rihte way we ȝeden,
C.20.119   A *fol* benyngne buyrde and buxum of speche.
C.20.153   Thenne mercy *fol* myldely mouthed this wordes,
C.20.167   Out of þe nype of þe north nat *ful* fer hennes.
C.21.451   [For] þe comune,' quod this curatour, 'counteth *ful* litel.
C.22.47   And soffre sorwes *ful* soure þat shal to ioye torne."
C.22.52   And mette *ful* merueylously þat in mannes fourme
C.22.99   So kynde thorw corupcions kulde *fol* mony.
C.22.112   With vntidy tales he tened *ful* ofte
C.22.335   Ypocrysye haeth her[t]e hem; *ful* hard is yf thei keuere.'

ful &> falle

fulfille v *fulfillen v.* A 5 fulfild (2) fulfille (3); B 7 fulfild (1) fulfille (4) fulfilled (2); C 9 folfilleth (1) fulfeld (1) fulfild (1) fulfille (4) fulfuld (1) fulfulleth (1)

A. 2.51   And he[o] be bou[n] at his bode his bidding to *fulfille*,
A. 3.245   To be buxum & boun his bidding to *fulfille*.
A. 7.37   To *fulfille* þe foreward whiles I may stande'.
A. 7.305   Or fyue ȝer be *fulfild* such famyn shal arise;
A.10.169   Til fourty dayes be *fulfild*, þat flood haue ywasshe
B. 3.265   Be buxom at his biddynge his wil to *fulfille*.
B. 6.35   To *fulfille* þis forward þou3 I fi3te sholde.
B. 6.324   Er fyue [yer] be *fulfilled* swich famyn shal aryse.
B. 9.138   Til fourty daies be *fulfild*, þat flood haue ywasshen
B.10.360   He sholde louye and lene and þe lawe *fulfille*.
B.12.260   Executours, false frendes, þat *fulfille* no3t his wille
B.19.80   And þere was þat word *fulfilled* þe which þow of speke,
C. 1.74   Thow broughtest me borewes my biddyng to *fulfille*,
C. 2.130   For syuyle and thisylue selde *fulfulleth*
C. 3.418   To be buxum at my byddyng his [b]o[n]e to *fulfille*.
C. 8.344   Ar fewe ȝeres be *fulfeld* famyne shal aryse.
C. 9.234   And *fulfille* th[e] fastyng[e] but infirmite hit made,
C.10.226   Til fourty [dayes] be *fulfild* and floed haue ywasche
C.16.27   And satisfaccioun þe whiche *folfilleth* þe fader will of heuene;
C.17.142   Loue thyn enemye entierely goddes heste to *fulfille*;
C.21.80   And þer was þat word *fulfuld* þe which þou of speke,

full > falle

fulle n *fulle n.(1) &> fille* A 1; B 3; C 2
A.12.72   Than maunged I wit[h him] vp at þe *fulle*;
B.13.192   The goode wil of a wight was neuere bou3t to þe *fulle*,
B.14.178   And in somer tyme selde soupen to þe *fulle*.
B.16.11   And to haue my *fulle* of þat fruyt forsake a[l] oþ[er] saule[e].
C.17.57   To feffe suche and fede þat founded ben to þe *fulle*
C.20.410   Moiste me to þe *fulle* ne my furste slokke

fulled ptp *fullen v.(2)* B 1
B.15.453   Til it be *fulled* vnder foot or in fullyng stokkes,

fullen v *fullen v.(1) &> falle* A 1; B 1; C 1
A.11.44   And gnawen god in [þe gorge] whanne here guttis *fullen*.
B.10.58   And gnawen god [in] þe gorge whanne hir guttes *fullen*.
C.11.39   And gnawen god with gorge when here gottes *f[u]llen*.

fulliche adv *fulli adv.* B 1
B.15.61   Et verba vertit in opera *fulliche* to his power."

fullyng ger1 *fulwing ger.* B 5 fullyng (1) fullynge (4); C 5 follyng (3) follynge (1) fullyng (1)
B.12.285   [Ac] þer is *fullynge* of Font and fullynge in blood shedyng
B.12.285   [Ac] þer is fullynge of Font and *fullynge* in blood shedyng
B.12.286   And þoru3 fir is *fullyng*, and þat is ferme bileue:
B.15.451   [Enformed] hem what *fullynge* and feiþ was to mene.

B.19.39   Aren frankeleyns, free men þoru3 *fullynge* þat þei toke
C.14.207   Ac þer is *follyng* of fonte and follyng in bloed [s]hedyng
C.14.207   Ac þer is follyng of fonte and *follyng* in bloed [s]hedyng
C.14.208   And thorw fuyr is *fullyng*; and [þat] is ferme bileue:
C.17.77   And so hit fareth by false cristene: here *follynge* is trewe,
C.21.39   Aren frankeleynes, fre men Thorw *follyng* þat they toke

fullyng ger2 *fullinge ger.(2)* B 1
B.15.453   Til it be fulled vnder foot or in *fullyng* stokkes,

fundement > foundement

furlong n *furlong n.* A 1; B 2 furlang (1) furlong (1); C 1 forlong
A. 5.5   Er I hadde faren a *furlong* feyntise me h[ent]e
B. 5.5   Ac er I hadde faren a *furlong* feyntise me hente
B. 5.417   But I kan fynden in a feld or in a *furlang* an hare
C. 7.32   Ac y can fynden in a feld and in a *forlong* an hare

furred ptp *furren v.* A 1 furrid; B 3 furred (2) furrede (1); C 3 forred (2) forrede (1)
A. 7.253   þat fisik shal his *furrid* hood for his foode selle,
B. 6.269   That Phisik shal hi[s] *furred* ho[od] for his fode selle,
B.13.227   [Ac] fewe robes I fonge or *furrede* gownes.
B.20.176   A Phisicien wiþ a *furred* hood þat he fel in a palsie,
C. 8.290   That fysik shal his *forred* hod[e] for his fode sulle
C.15.201   And fewe robes y fonge or *forrede* gounes.
C.22.176   A fisician with a *forred* hoed that he ful in a palesye

furst(e > first,þurst; fursteth > þursteþ; furthe > ferþe; furwes > forow

fust n *fist n.(1)* A 1 fest; B 11; C 13 fust (4) fuste (9)
A. 5.67   And wroþliche he wroþ his *fest*, to wreke hym he þou3te,
B. 5.84   And [wroþliche he wroþ his] *fust*, to wreke hym he þou3te
B.17.141   The fader was first as a *fust* wiþ o fynger foldynge
B.17.152   The fader is [þanne] as a *fust* wiþ fynger to touche–
B.17.156   The paume for [he] putteþ forþ fyngres and þe *fust* boþe.
B.17.169   And as my *fust* is ful hand y[f]olden togideres
B.17.177   Oþerwise þan þe wriþen *fust* or werkmanshipe of fyngres.
B.17.179   And to vnfolde þe *fust*, [for hym it bilongeþ,
B.17.181   Whan he feleþ þe [*fust* and] þe fyngres wille;
B.17.185   Vnfolden or folden, my *fust* and my pawme
B.17.189   For þe fyngres þat folde sholde and þe *fust* make,
B.17.202   For god þe fader is as a *fust*; þe sone is as a fynger;
C. 6.66   A wroth f[u]ste vppon wrath; hadde [he] wesches at wille
C.19.114   Ferde furste as a f[u]ste, and 3ut is, as y leue,
C.19.115   As a *fuste* wit[h] a fynger yfolde togyderes
C.19.126   The fader is thenne as þe *fuste* with fynger and with paume
C.19.130   A *fuste* with a fynger and a fol paume.
C.19.131   And as þe *fuste* is a ful hand yfolde togyderes,
C.19.133   As my *fuste* is furste ar y my fyngours shewe,
C.19.142   Oþerwyse then þe writhen f[u]ste or werkmanschupe of fyngres.
C.19.144   And to vnfolde þe *fust*, for hym hit bilongeth,
C.19.146   Alle þat þe fyngeres and þe *fust* feleth and toucheth.
C.19.151   Vnfolden or folden, a *fuste* wyse or elles,
C.19.155   For þe fyngeres þat folde sholde and þe *fust* make
C.19.168   For [g]o[d] the fader is as þe *fust*; þe sone is as þe fynger;

G

ga > goon

gabbe v *gabben v.* C 2 gabbe (1) gabben (1)
C. 3.226   Wel thow wost, weye, but yf thow wille *gabbe*,
C.17.16   For he ordeyned þat ordre or elles þey *gabben*.

gabbyng ger *gabbinge ger.* B 2 gabbyng (1) gabbynges (1); C 3 gabbyng
   (1) gabbynge (1) gabbynges (1)
B.19.454   Of gile ne of *gabbyng* gyue þei neuere tale,
B.20.125   Wiþ glosynges and *gabbynges* he giled þe peple.
C.17.129   Withoute gyle and *gabbyng* gyue and sulle and lene.
C.21.454   Of gyle ne of *gabbyng[e]* gyueth they neuer tale
C.22.125   With glosynges and *gabbynges* he gyled þe peple.

gable n *gable n.* A 1; B 1; C 1
A. 3.48   Woldist þou glase þe *gable*, & graue þere þin name,
B. 3.49   Woldestow glaȝe þ[e] *gable* & graue [þere] þy name
C. 3.52   Wolde ȝe glase þ[e] *gable* and graue ther ȝoure name

gabrielis n prop *OED Gabriel* B 1; C 1 gabrieles
B.16.90   And þanne spak spiritus sanctus in *Gabrielis* mouþe
C.18.123   And thenne spak spiritus sanctus in *gabrieles* mouthe

gadelyng n *gadeling n.* A 2 gadelynges; B 4 gadelyng (1) gadelynges (1)
   gedelyng (1) gedelynges (1); C 2 gadelynges (1) gadlyng (1)
A. 4.38   'Boþe my gees & my gris hise *gadelynges* fecchen,
A.10.209   Þat oþere gatis ben geten for *gadelynges* ben holden;
B. 4.51   'Boþe my gees and my grys hise *gadelynges* feccheþ.
B. 9.106   Ne his gleman a *gedelyng*, a goere to tauernes.
B. 9.195   [That] oþergates ben geten for *gedelynges* arn holden,
B.20.157   And geten in hir glorie a *gadelyng* at þe laste,
C.10.294   That oþergatus ben gete for *gadelynges* ben holden
C.22.157   And geten in here glorie a *gadlyng* at þe laste,

gaderen v *gaderen v.* B 8 gadered (2) gaderede (1) gaderen (2) gadereþ (2)
   gadrede (1); C 6 gadered (2) gadereth (2) gedereth (1) ygadered (1)
B.12.51   And riche renkes riȝt so *gaderen* and sparen
B.12.253   That euere he *gadered* so grete and gaf þerof so litel,
B.13.369   Thoruȝ gile to *gaderen* þe good þat ich haue.
B.14.230   And if glotonie greue pouerte he *gadereþ* þe lasse
B.16.80   And *gadrede* hem alle togideres, boþe grete and smale,
B.19.336   And *gadered* hym a greet Oost; greuen he þynkeþ
B.20.113   And *gaderede* a greet hoost al agayn Conscience.
B.20.368   Thus he gooþ and *gadereþ* and gloseþ þere he shryueþ
C. 6.259   And with Gyle and glosynge *ygadered* þat y haue.
C.16.71   And yf glotonye greue pouerte h[e] *gadereth* þe lasse
C.18.111   And *gadered* hem alle togyderes, bothe grete & smale,
C.21.336   And *gadered* hym a grete oeste; greue he thenketh
C.22.113   And *gaderet[h]* a greet oest alle agayn Consience.
C.22.368   Thus he goeth and *gedereth* and gloseth þer he shryueth

gadlyng > gadelyng; gadrede > gaderen; gaef gaf > gyuen

gaye adj *gai adj.* B 1; C 1 gay
B.18.175   And in hire *gaye* garnementȝ whom she grete þouȝte.
C.20.178   And [in] here *gay* garnementes wham she gladie thouhte.

gailers n *gaioler n.* A 1 gaileris; B 1; C 1 gaylers
A. 3.127   And [g]iueþ þe *gaileris* gold & grotis togidere
B. 3.138   And gyueþ þe *Gailers* gold and grotes togidres
C. 3.176   And gyueth the *gaylers* gold and grotes togederes

gaynesse n *gainesse n.* B 1; C 1
B.10.84   But in *gaynesse* and glotonye forglutten hir good
C.11.64   Bote in *gaynesse* and glotonye forglotten here godes

galice > galis

galilee n prop *n.i.d.* B 2; C 2
B.19.147   And goon into *Galilee* and gladen hise Apostles
B.19.158   Goynge toward *Galilee* in godhede and manhede
C.21.147   And goen into *Galilee* and gladien his apostlis
C.21.158   Goynge toward *galilee* in godhede and manhede

galis n prop *n.i.d.* A 2; B 2 Galice (1) Galis (1); C 2 galys
A. 4.110   Þat no man go to *galis* but ȝif he go for euere;
A. 6.9   Signes of synay, & shilles of *galis*,
B. 4.127   That no man go to *Galis* but if he go for euere.
B. 5.521   Signes of Synay and shelles of *Galice*,
C. 4.124   So þat noon go to *galys* but yf he go for euere;
C. 7.166   Signes of syse and shelles of *galys*

galle n *galle n.* A 1; B 2
A. 5.99   [Þat] al my brest bolniþ for bittir of my *galle*.
B. 5.120   That al my [brest] bolneþ for bitter of my *galle*.
B.16.155   And gile in þi glad chere and *galle* is in þi laughyng.

galoches n *galoche n.* B 1; C 1
B.18.14   To geten hym gilte spores [and] *galoches* ycouped.
C.20.12   To geten h[ym] gult spores and *galoches* ycouped.

galon n *galoun n.* A 3 galoun; B 3; C 3 galon (1) galoun (2)
A. 5.138   A *galoun* for a grote, god wot no lasse,
A. 5.184   And grete sire glotoun wiþ a *galoun* ale.
A. 5.188   Til glotoun hadde ygulpid a *galoun* & a gille.
B. 5.222   A *galon* for a grote, god woot no lesse,
B. 5.335   And greten sire Gloton wiþ a *Galon* ale.
B. 5.339   Til Gloton hadde yglubbed a *galon* and a gille.
C. 6.230   A *galon* for a grote, and ȝut no grayth mesure
C. 6.393   And grete syre glotoun with a *galoun* ale.
C. 6.397   Til glotoun hadde yglobbed a *galoun* and a gylle.

galpen v *galpen v.* B 1; C 1 galpe
B.13.89   And þanne shullen hise guttes goþele and he shal *galpen* after.
C.15.96   And thenne shal [his gottes gothelen] and [he shal] *galpe* [after].

game n *game n.* A 1 games; B 4 game (2) gamen (1) games (1); C 1
A.11.37   Glotonye & grete oþis, þise arn *games* nowadayes.
B.Pr.153   And if we grucche of his *gamen* he wol greuen vs alle,
B. 5.406   I haue leuere here an harlotrye or a Somer *game* of Souters,
B. 9.104   And goddes gleman and a *game* of heuene.
B.10.51   Glotonye and grete oþes, þis[e arn *games* nowadaies].
C.Pr.173   'And yf we groche of his *game* a wol greue vs [alle],

gan > gynneþ

gange v *gangen v.* A 1; B 3; C 3 gange (2) gangynge (1)
A. 2.132   Þat symonye & cyuyle shulde on here fet *gange*.
B. 2.168   For Symonye and Cyuylle sholde on hire feet *gange*.
B.14.161   And yet is wynter for hem worse, for weetshoed þei [*gange*],
B.16.159   Suffreþ myne Apostles in [pays] and in [pees] *gange*.'
C.16.14   And ȝut is wynter for hem worse for weetshoed þey g[*ang*]e,
C.18.176   Soffreth my postles in pays and in pees *gange*.'
C.18.241   Where god [riȝt be my gate cam *gangynge* a thre];

gape v *gapen v.* B 1
B.10.42   Drynken and dreuelen and do men for to *gape*,

gardyn n *gardin n.* B 2; C 2 gardyn (1) gardyne (1)
B.16.13   'It groweþ in a *gardyn*', quod he, 'þat god made hymselue
B.18.287   For þow gete hem wiþ gile and his *Gardyn* breke,
C.20.313   For thow gete hem with gyle and his *gardyn* broke,
C.20.380   Byglosedest hem and bigiledest hem and my *gardyne* breke

gardyner n *gardiner n.* B 1
B. 5.138   And þe Couentes *Gardyner* for to graffen Impes.

gare v *geren v.* A 3 gare (1) gart (1) garte (1); B 8 gare (1) gart (1) garte
   (5) gerte (1); C 5 gart (2) garte (2) gert (1)
A. 7.132   Til god of his grace *gare* h[e]m to arise.
A. 7.285   Wiþ good ale & glotonye h[y] *gart* hym to slepe.
A.11.132   Gramer for girles I *garte* ferst write,
B. 1.122   Til god of his goodnesse [*garte* þe heuene to stekie]
B. 5.131   And *gart* bakbityng be a brocour to blame mennes ware.
B. 6.138   Til god of his [grace *gare* hem to arise.
B. 6.301   Wiþ good Ale as Gloton taȝte [þei] *garte* [hym to] slepe.
B.10.180   Grammer for girles I *garte* first write,
B.15.444   Til Gregory *garte* clerkes to go here and preche.
B.20.57   And *gerte* gile growe þere as he a god weere.
B.20.131   And *garte* good feiþ flee and fals to abide.
C. 5.146   Gregory þe grete Clerk *gart* wryte in bokes
C. 8.323   And thenne gloton with gode ale *garte* hunger slepe.
C.11.120   Gramer for gurles y *gart* furste write

C.22.57   And *garte* gyle [growe] þere as he a god were.
C.22.131 And *gert* goed faith fle and fals to abyde

garland n *gerland n.* B 2; C 2 garlond
B.18.48   And bigan of [grene] þorn a *garland* to make,
B.19.321 And Grace gaf hym þe cros, wiþ þe [*garland*] of þornes,
C.20.48   And bigan of grene thorn a *garlond* to make
C.21.321 And grace gaf hym þe cros with [the *garlond*] of thornes

garleek n *garlek n.* A 1 garlek; B 1; C 1 garlek
A. 5.155 I haue pepir, & p[ye]nye, & a pound of *garlek*,
B. 5.304 'I haue pepir and pion[e] and a pound of *garleek*,
C. 6.359 'Y haue pepur and pyonie and a pound of *garlek*,

garlekhiþe n prop *garlek n.* B 1
B. 5.316 Godefray of *Garlekhiþe* and Griffyn þe walshe;

garlekmonger n *garlek n.* C 1
C. 6.373 Godefray þe *garlekmonger* and Gryffyth þe walshe

garlond > garland

garnement n *garnement n.* B 3 garnement (2) garnementȝ (1); C 2 garnement (1) garnementes (1) ·
B.13.399 [Yet glotoun wiþ grete oþes his [*garnement*] hadde soiled
B.14.25   Shal noon heraud ne harpour haue a fairer *garnement*
B.18.175 And in hire gaye *garnementȝ* whom she grete þouȝte.
C. 9.119 For a sent hem forth seluerles in a somur *garnement*
C.20.178 And [in] here gay *garnementes* wham she gladie thouhte.

garner > gerner; gart(e > gare

gascoigne n prop *gascoine n. & adj.* A 1 gascoyne; B 1; C 1 gascoyne
A.Pr.107 'W[hit] wyn of osay, & wyn of *gascoyne*,
B.Pr.229 'Whit wyn of Oseye and wyn of *Gascoigne*,
C.Pr.233 'Whit wyn of Oseye and wyn of *gascoyne*,

gat > geten

gate n *gate n.(2) &> yate, cf. oþergates* A 2 gate (1) gates (1); B 7; C 5
A. 1.179 And ek þe graiþ *gate* þat goþ into heuene.
A.12.88   'Myȝt I so, god wot, ȝoure *gates* wolde I holden.'
B. 1.205 And also þe graiþe *gate* þat goþ into heuene.
B. 3.156 And liþ ayein þe lawe and letteþ hym þe *gate*
B. 4.42   And þanne Reson rood faste þe riȝte heiȝe *gate*
B.17.48   Go þi *gate*!' quod I to Spes, 'so me god helpe,
B.17.114 And neuere eft greue gome þat gooþ þis ilke *gate*:
B.18.243 Peter þe Apostel parceyued his *gate*,
B.20.341 'Ye? go þi *gate*!' quod Pees, 'by god! for al þi phisik,
C. 3.194 He lyth aȝeyn þe lawe and le[tte]th hym þe *gate*
C.13.91   Ther is no lawe, as y leue, wol lette hym þe *gate*
C.19.46   Go thy *gate*!' quod y to spes; 'so me god helpe,
C.20.252 Peter þe Apostel perseyued his *gate*
C.22.341 'Ȝe? go thy *gate*!' quod pees, 'bi god! for al thi fisyk,

gates > gate,yate; gatis > oþergates

gateward n *gate n.(1)* A 1; B 1; C 2
A. 6.82   Grace hattiþ þe [*gateward*], a good man forsoþe,
B. 5.595 Grace hatte þe *gateward*, a good man for soþe;
C. 7.243 Grace hatte þe *gateward*, a good man for sothe;
C.13.92   Ther god is *gateward* hymsulf and vch a gome knoweth.

gaȝophilacium n *gazofilacium n.* B 1
B.13.197 Than alle þo þat offrede into *Gaȝophilacium*?'

geaunt n *geaunt n. & adj.* A 1; B 3 geaunt (2) geauntȝ (1); C 2 geaunt (1) geauntes (1)
A. 7.216 Go to genesis þe *geaunt*, engendrour of vs alle:
B. 6.232 Go to Genesis þe *geaunt*, engendrour of vs alle:
B.18.252 For [Iesus as a] *geaunt* wiþ a gyn [comeþ yonde]
B.20.215 And bisegede [sikerly] wiþ seuene grete *geauntȝ*
C.20.261 For iesus as a *geaunt* with a gyn cometh ȝende
C.22.215 And biseged s[iker]ly with seuene grete *geauntes*

gedelyng(es > gadelyng; gedereth > gaderen; gees > goos

geffrey n prop *n.i.d.* B 1 Geffrey
B.15.123 Sir Iohan and sire *Geffrey* haþ [of siluer a girdel],

gelosie > ielousie

gendre n *gendre n.* B 1; C 1
B.16.222 And is noȝt but *gendre* of a generacion bifore Iesu crist in heuene:
C. 3.395 That is vnite, acordaun[c]e in case, in *gendre* and in noumbre,

generacion n *generacioun n.* B 1 generacion
B.16.222 And is noȝt but gendre of a *generacion* bifore Iesu crist in heuene:

genesis n *Genesis n.* A 1; B 1; C 1
A. 7.216 Go to *genesis* þe geaunt, engendrour of vs alle:

B. 6.232 Go to *Genesis* þe geaunt, engendrour of vs alle:
C. 8.239 As wyse men haen wryten and as witnesseth *Genesis*

gentel(- > gentil(-

gentil adj *gentil adj. &> gentile* B 6 gentil (5) gentile (1); C 8 gentel (6) gentill (1) Ientel (1)
B.11.203 As quasi modo geniti *gentil* men echone,
B.11.248 Iesu crist on a Iewes doȝter liȝte, *gentil* womman þouȝ she were,
B.19.34   The Iewes þat were *gentil* men, Ies[u] þei despised,
B.19.40   And *gentil* men wiþ Iesu, for Iesu[s] was yfulled
B.19.48   Tho was he Iesus of Iewes called, *gentile* prophete,
B.19.265 And Ioyned to hem oon Iohan, moost *gentil* of alle,
C. 5.78   Popes and patrones pore *gentel* blood refused
C.12.111 As quasi modo geniti *gentel* men vchone,
C.13.25   And þe *gentel* Iob; here ioye hath non ende.
C.17.132 Iewes and *gentel* sarresines iugen hemsulue
C.21.34   The iewes þat were *gentel* men iesu thei dispisede,
C.21.40   And *Ientel* men with iesu for iesu[s] was yfolled
C.21.48   Tho was he iesu[s] of iewes [cald], *gentel* profete,
C.21.265 And ioyned til hem oen iohann, most *gentill* of all,

gentile n *gentil n. &> gentil* A 3 gentil (1) ientil (1) ientile (1); B 3; C 3 gentele
A. 1.159 For Iames þe *ientil* ioynide in his bokis
A.11.23   Iob þe *ientile* in his gestis seide it:
A.11.27   To iesu þe *gentil* þat Iewis todrowe
B. 1.185 For Iames þe *gentile* [Ioyned] in hise bokes
B.10.23   Iob þe *gentile* in hise gestes witnesseþ
B.10.35   To Iesu þe *gentile* þat Iewes todrowe
C. 1.181 For Iames þe *gentele* iuge[d] in his bokes
C.11.21   Iob þe *gentele* in his g[e]stes witnesseth
C.13.15   Iob þe *gentele*, what ioye hadde he on erthe?

gentilliche adv *gentilli adv.* A 1 ientily; B 2; C 2 genteliche
A. 3.13   *Ientily* wiþ ioye þe Iustices so[mm]e
B. 3.13   *Gentilliche* wiþ ioye þe Iustices somme
B.13.232 Iape ne Iogele ne *gentilliche* pipe,
C. 3.14   *Genteliche* with ioye the Iustices somme
C.15.206 Iape ne i[o]gele ne *genteliche* pipe,

gentries n *gentrie n.* B 2; C 1 gentrice
B.14.181 Thus in genere of *gentries* Iesu crist seide
B.18.22   'This Iesus of his *gentries* wol Iuste in Piers armes,
C.20.21   That this iesus of his *gentrice* shal iouste in Pers Armes,

geomesie n *geomancie n.* A 1; B 1
A.11.156 Geometrie & *geomesie* is gynful of speche;
B.10.213 Geometrie and *Geomesie* [is] gynful of speche;

geometrie n *gemetrie n.* A 1; B 1
A.11.156 *Geometrie* & geomesie is gynful of speche;
B.10.213 *Geometrie* and Geomesie [is] gynful of speche;

gerdiþ > girdeþ; gerl- > girles

gerner n *gerner n.* A 1 garner; B 1
A. 8.117 Haue þei no *garner* [to go] to, but god fynt hem alle.'
B. 7.135 Haue þei no *gerner* to go to but god fynt hem alle.'

gert(e > gare

gerþes n *gerth n.* A 1 gerþis; B 1
A. 4.19   And let warroke hym wel wiþ [wy]tful *gerþis*,
B. 4.21   And lat warroke hym wel wiþ wit[ful] *gerþes*.

gesene adj *gesoun adj. & n.* B 1
B.13.270 My wafres were *gesene* whan Chichestre was Maire.'

gesse v *gessen v.* B 1
B. 5.414 Nouȝt twyes in two yer, and þanne [telle I vp *gesse*].

gest n *gest n.* B 1; C 3 geste (1) gestes (2)
B.15.285 And þouȝ þe gome hadde a *gest* god fond hem boþe.
C. 7.106 And fithele the withoute flaterynge of god friday þe [*g*]*este*
C.11.21   Iob þe gentele in his g[e]*stes* witnesseth
C.15.204 [Ac for] y can nat tabre ne trompy ne telle [no] *gestes*,

geste n *geste n.(1) &> gest* A 1 gestis; B 4 geste (1) gestes (3); C 2 gestes
A.11.23   Iob þe ientile in his *gestis* seide it:
B.10.23   Iob þe gentile in hise *gestes* witnesseþ
B.10.31   And Iaperis and Iogelours and Iangleris of *gestes*,
B.13.230 Ac for I kan neiþer taboure ne trompe ne telle no *gestes*,
B.13.446 And fiþele þee wiþoute flaterynge of good friday þe [*geste*],
C.10.180 Of þ[e] blessed baptist bifore alle his *gestes*.
C.15.198 As a waf[e]rer with wafres, a[nd] welcome godes *gestes*.

gestes > gest,geste

geten v *geten v.(1)* A 12 gat (1) get (1) gete (7) geten (3); B 24 gat (2) gete (12) geten (9) getest (1); C 22 gat (1) get (1) gete (14) geten (5) ygete (1)

A.Pr.34   And *gete* gold wiþ here gle giltles, I trowe.
A.Pr.89   Þanne *gete* a mom of here mouþ til mony be shewid.
A. 4.65   'Wiþoute gilt, god wot, *gat* I þis skaþe.'
A. 4.124   Ne *gete* my grace þoruȝ giftes, so me god helpe!
A. 6.103   And *geten* it aȝen þoruȝ grace & þoruȝ no gift ellis.
A. 6.114   To *gete* ingang at any gate but grace be þe more.'
A. 6.123   Þou miȝt *gete* grace [þere] so þou go be tyme.'
A. 7.235   He þat *get* his fode here wiþ trauaile of his hondis,
A.10.160   Ageyns godis hest girlis hy *geten*
A.10.209   Þat oþere gatis ben *geten* for gadelynges ben holden;
A.10.211   Vngracious to *gete* loue or any good ellis,
A.11.97   I miȝte *gete* no g[r]ayn of hise grete wyttes,
B.Pr.34   And *geten* gold with hire glee [gilt]lees, I leeue.
B.Pr.216   Than *gete* a mom of here mouþ til moneie be shewed.
B. 1.33   And þere *gat* in glotonie gerles þat were cherles.
B. 4.79   'Wiþouten gilt, god woot, *gat* I þis scaþe.'
B. 4.141   Ne *gete* my grace [þoruȝ] giftes, so me god [helpe]!
B. 5.285   For þow hast no good ground to *gete* þee wiþ a wastel
B. 5.287   For þe good þat þow hast *geten* bigan al wiþ falshede,
B. 5.617   And [*gete* it ayein þoruȝ] grace [ac þoruȝ no gifte ellis].
B. 5.629   To *geten* ing[o]ng at any gate but grace be þe moore.'
B. 5.638   Thow myȝt *gete* grace þere so þow go bityme.'
B. 9.191   And þanne *gete* ye grace of god and good ynouȝ to lyue wiþ,
B. 9.195   [That] oþergates ben *geten* for gedelynges arn holden,
B. 9.197   Vngracious to *gete* good or loue of þe peple;
B.10.144   I myȝte *gete* no greyn of his grete wittes,
B.15.133   [This] þat wiþ gile was *geten* vngraciousliche is [s]pended.
B.18.14   In *geten* hym gilte spores [and] galoches ycouped.
B.18.98   The gree ȝit haþ he *geten* for al his grete wounde,
B.18.287   For þow *gete* hem wiþ gile and his Gardyn breke,
B.18.292   'It is noȝt graiþly *geten* þer gile is þe roote,
B.18.334   Wiþ gile how hem *gete* ageyn alle reson.
B.18.353   So þat þoruȝ gile þow *gete* þoruȝ grace it is ywonne.
B.18.355   *Getest* bi gile þo þat god louede;
B.19.121   That he þoruȝ grace was *gete* and of no gome ellis.
B.20.157   And *geten* in hir glorie a gadelyng at þe laste,
C.Pr.166   Than *gete* a Mum of here mouth [til] moneye [be] shewed.
C. 4.75   'Withouten gult, god wot, [*gat* y] this s[c]athe;
C. 4.138   Ne *gete* my grace thorw eny gyfte ne glosynge spe[ch]e
C. 6.341   For thow hast no good, by good fayth, to *gete* the with a wastel.
C. 6.342   For the good that thow hast *gete* bygan al with falshede
C. 7.269   And *geten* hit agayne thorw grace Ac thorw no gifte elles.
C. 7.282   To *geten* ingang at eny ȝate bote grace be þe more.'
C. 7.291   Thow myhte *gete* grace there so thow go bytymes.'
C.10.294   That oþergatus ben *gete* for gadelynges ben holden
C.10.296   Vngracious to *gete* goed or loue of [þe] peple,
C.11.73   *Get* þe loue þerwith thogh thow worse fare".
C.11.82   I myhte *gete* no grayn of [his] grete wittes
C.16.280   And þat with gyle was *gete* vngraciousliche be yspened.
C.18.52   And that is grace of þe holy gost; and thus *gete* y the maystrye.'
C.20.12   To *geten* h[ym] gult spores and galoches ycouped.
C.20.101   The gre ȝut hath he *geten* for al his grete wound[e]
C.20.313   For thow *gete* hem with gyle and his gardyn broke,
C.20.322   'Hit is nat graythly *ygete* ther gyle is þe rote
C.20.377   With gyle thow hem *gete* agaynes all resoun.
C.20.396   So þat [thorw] gyle was *gete* thorw grace is now ywonne
C.21.121   That he thorw grace was *gete* and of no gome elles.
C.22.157   And *geten* in here glorie a gadlyng at þe laste,

geterne > gyterne; geue(n > gyuen

gybbe n prop *Gibbe n.(1)* B 1
B. 5.91   I wolde be gladder, by god! þat *Gybbe* hadde meschaunce

gide n *gide n.* A 1; B 2 gide (1) gyde (1); C 1 gyde
A. 7.1   'Þis were a wikkide weye, but whoso hadde a *gide*
B. 6.1   'This were a wikkede wey but whoso hadde a *gyde*
B.15.436   And be *gide* and go bifore as a good Banyer,
C. 7.307   Ac þe way is ful wikked but hoso hadde a *gyde*

gide v *giden v.* B 1
B.19.227   And gaf ech man a grace to *gide* wiþ hymseluen

gyen v *gien v.* A 1 gyede; B 1 gyed; C 2 gye (1) gyen (1)
A. 2.149   Ac gile was forgoere and *gyede* hem alle.
B. 2.188   Ac Gyle was Forgoer and *gyed* hem alle.
C. 2.201   Ac gyle was forgoere to *gyen* al th[e] peple,
C.21.227   And gaf vch man a grace to *gye* with hymsuluen

gif > gyuen

gifte n *yifte n.* A 13 gift (1) giftes (2) ȝeftis (9) ȝifte (1); B 26 gifte (3) giftes (4) ȝifte (5) ȝiftes (12) yiftes (2); C 25 gifte (3) giftes (2) gyft (1) gyfte (1) ȝefte (2) ȝeftes (14) ȝiftes (1) ȝyftes (1)

A. 1.101   And neuere leue h[e]m for loue ne lacching of *ȝeftis*;
A. 2.114   To false & to fauel for here faire *ȝeftis*,
A. 2.162   Feteriþ falsnesse faste for any skynes *ȝeftis*,
A. 3.89   To haue *ȝeftis* [or ȝerisȝiuys] in ȝouþe or in elde.
A. 3.115   Leri[þ] hem leccherie þat loui[þ] hire *ȝeftis*.
A. 3.171   Ȝet I may, as I miȝte, [menske] þe wiþ *ȝeftis*,
A. 3.198   To alienes, to alle men, to honoure hem with *ȝeftis*.
A. 3.201   Þoruȝ *ȝeftis* han ȝonge men to [ȝerne] & to ride.
A. 3.229   And he þat gripiþ here *giftes*, so me god helpe,
A. 4.124   Ne *gete* my grace þoruȝ *giftes*, so me god helpe!
A. 6.103   And geten it aȝen þoruȝ grace & þoruȝ no *gift* ellis.
A. 7.40   And þei pore men profre þe presauntis or *ȝeftis*
A.11.111   Gladdere þanne þe gleman þat gold haþ to *ȝifte*,
B. 1.103   And neuere leue hem for loue ne lacchynge of [*yiftes*];_
B. 2.150   To Fals and to Fauel for hire faire *ȝiftes*,
B. 2.201   Fettreþ [Falsnesse faste] for any kynnes *ȝiftes*,
B. 3.100   *Yiftes* or yeresyeues bycause of hire Offices.
B. 3.126   Lereþ hem lecherie þat loueþ hire *ȝiftes*.
B. 3.184   Yet I may, as I myȝte, menske þee wiþ *ȝiftes*,
B. 3.211   To aliens, to alle men, to honouren hem with *ȝiftes*;
B. 3.214   [Thoruȝ] *ȝiftes* han yonge men to [yerne] and to ryde.
B. 3.250   And he þat gripeþ hir [*giftes*], so me god helpe,
B. 3.334   That ȝyuen *ȝiftes*, [takeþ yeme], þe victorie wynneþ
B. 4.141   Ne *gete* my grace [þoruȝ] *giftes*, so me god [helpe]!
B. 5.53   Moore þan gold ouþer *giftes* if ye wol god plese;
B. 5.617   And [*gete* it ayein þoruȝ] grace [ac þoruȝ no *gifte* ellis].
B. 6.41   And þouȝ pouere men profre [þee] presentes and *ȝiftes*
B. 7.41   For þe Sauter saueþ hem noȝt, swiche as take *ȝiftes*,
B. 7.49   Conforteþ hym in þat caas, [coueiteþ noȝt hise] *ȝiftes*,
B.10.43   Likne men and lye on hem þat leneþ hem no *ȝiftes*,
B.10.159   Gladder þan þe gleman þat gold haþ to *ȝifte*,
B.11.194   Youre festynge and youre faire *ȝifte*; ech frend quyteþ so ooþer.
B.12.63   And þoruȝ þe *gifte* of þe holy goost as þe gospel telleþ:
B.12.68   Ac grace is a *gifte* of god and of greet loue spryngeþ,
B.13.184   After yeresȝeues or *ȝiftes*, or yernen to rede redels?
B.13.234   I haue no goode *giftes* of þise grete lordes
B.13.245   Neiþer prouendre ne personage yet of [þe] popes *ȝifte*,
B.14.300   A collateral confort, cristes owene *ȝifte*:
B.19.253   '[That al craft and konnyng come] of my *ȝifte*.
C. 2.166   That [fals] and [fauel] hadde for he[re] fayre *ȝeftes*,
C. 2.215   Lat fetere falsnesse faste for eny skynes *ȝeftes*,
C. 3.24   Rynges with rubees and othere riche *ȝeftes*,
C. 3.113   That vsurers oþer regraters for eny skynes *ȝeftes*
C. 3.117   Or presentes without pans and oþer priue *ȝeftes*.
C. 3.127   The houses and þe homes of hem þat taketh *ȝeftes*.
C. 3.163   And lereth hem lecherye þat louyeth here *ȝeftes*.
C. 3.230   Ȝut y may, as y myhte, menske þe with *ȝeftes*
C. 3.267   To aliens, to alle men, to honoure hem with *ȝeftes*.
C. 3.270   Thorw *ȝeftes* haen ȝemen to ȝerne and to ryde;
C. 3.316   Ȝeue lond or lordschipe [or] oþer large *ȝeftes*
C. 3.339   That [is] þe *gyft* þat god gyueth to alle lele lyuynge,
C. 3.451   And letteth the lawe thorw here large *ȝeftes*.
C. 3.486   That ȝeueth *ȝeftes*, taketh ȝeme, the victorie a wynneth
C. 4.138   Ne *gete* my grace thorw eny *gyfte* ne glosynge spe[ch]e
C. 7.269   And geten hit agayne thorw grace Ac thorw no *gifte* elles.
C. 8.39   And thogh pore men profre ȝow presentes and *ȝyftes*
C. 9.48   That conforteth suche in eny caes and coueyteth nat he[re] *ȝiftes*
C. 9.133   Me [g]yueth hem *giftes* and gold for grete lordes sake.
C.11.101   Gladdere then [þe] gleman þat gold hath to *ȝefte*
C.11.283   Withoute þe *gifte* of god w[it]h grace of fortune.
C.13.61   Ac ȝut myhte þe marchaunt thorw moneye and other *ȝeftes*
C.14.33   So grace is a *gifte* of god and kynde wit a chaunce
C.15.208   Y haue no gode *giftes* of thise grete lordes
C.21.253   'That all craft and connyng c[o]m[e] of my *ȝefte*.

gile n *gile n.(3)* A 7 gile (6) giles (1); B 29 gile (24) gyle (4) Gyles (1); C 37 gyle (36) gyles (1)

A. 2.24   *Gile* haþ begon hire so heo grauntiþ alle his wille;
A. 2.109   And bad *gile* go gyue gold al aboute,
A. 2.149   Ac *gile* was forgoere and gyede hem alle.
A. 2.163   And ge[rd]iþ of *giles* hed; let hym go no ferþere;
A. 2.173   And *gile* doþ him to go agast for to deiȝe.
A. 5.121   Ne hadde [þe] grace of *gile* gon among my ware
A. 8.41   Þat no *gile* go wiþ ȝow but þe graiþ treuþe.'
B. 2.70   That *Gile* wiþ hise grete oþes gaf hem togidere',
B. 2.145   And bad *gile* '[go] gyu[e] gold al aboute,
B. 2.188   Ac *Gyle* was Forgoer and gyed hem alle.
B. 2.202   And girdeþ of *Gyles* heed; lat hym go no ferþer;
B. 2.214   And *Gyle* dooþ hym to go agast for to dye.
B. 5.205   Ne hadde þe grace of *gyle* ygo amonges my [ware]

B.13.369 Thoruȝ *gile* to gaderen þe good þat ich haue.
B.15.133 [This] þat wiþ *gile* was geten vngraciousliche is [s]pended.
B.15.377 Go now to any degree, and but if *gile* be maister,
B.16.155 And gile in þi glad chere and galle is in þi laughyng.
B.18.160 And riȝt as [þe gilour] þoruȝ *gile* [bigiled man formest]
B.18.287 For þow gete hem wiþ *gile* and his Gardyn breke,
B.18.292 'It is noȝt graiþly geten þer *gile* is þe roote,
B.18.334 Wiþ *gile* þow hem gete ageyn alle reson.
B.18.347 And þat grace *gile* destruye good feiþ it askeþ.
B.18.353 So þat þoruȝ *gile* þow gete þoruȝ grace it is ywonne.
B.18.355 Getest bi *gile* þo þat god louede;
B.18.357 Graciousliche þi *gile* haue quyt: go gile ayein gile!
B.18.357 Graciousliche þi gile haue quyt: go *gile* ayein gile!
B.18.357 Graciousliche þi gile haue quyt: go gile ayein *gile*!
B.18.360 And *gile* is bigiled and in his gile fallen:
B.18.360 And gile is bigiled and in his *gile* fallen:
B.18.361 Now bigynneþ þi *gile* ageyn þee to turne
B.19.299 Wiþ god, and nauȝt agast but of *gile* one.
B.19.300 For *gile* gooþ so pryuely þat good feiþ ouþer while
B.19.454 Of *gile* ne of gabbyng gyue þei neuere tale
B.19.455 For Spiritus prudencie among þe peple is *gyle*,
B.20.57 And gerte *gile* growe þere as he a god weere.
B.20.67 And what kyng þat hem conforted, knowynge [hir *gile*],
C.Pr.12 Of treuthe and tricherye, tresoun and *gyle*
C. 2.26 And selde soth sayth bote yf he souche *gyle*,
C. 2.72 That *Gyle* hath gyue to falsnesse and grauntid also mede,'
C. 2.128 And god graunte[de] hit were so so no *gyle* were,
C. 2.129 And thow has[t] gyue here as *gyle* tauhte, now god ȝeue þe sorwe!
C. 2.161 And bade *gyle* '[g]o gyue gold al aboute,
C. 2.179 Thenne gan *gyle* borwen hors at many gret maystres
C. 2.201 Ac *gyle* was forgoere to gyen al th[e] peple,
C. 2.216 And gurdeth of *gyles* heed; lat hym goo no wyddore
C. 2.224 And *gyle* doth hym to gone agaste for to deye.
C. 3.131 Lacked here a litel w[iht] for þat she louede *gyle*
C. 3.212 That al þe witt of the world is woxe into *Gyle*.
C. 3.287 That mede [is] euermore a mayntenour of *Gyle*,
C. 3.500 Ac he þat resceyueth or rec[ett]eth here is rescetour of *Gyle*.'
C. 6.190 To wynne to my wille wymmen with *gyle*,
C. 6.213 Ne hadde þe grace of *Gyle* go among my ware
C. 6.259 And with *Gyle* and glosynge ygadered þat y haue,
C.11.265 Lelly as by his lokes, with a le[tt]re of *gyle*?
C.12.240 To synege and to souche sotiltees of *Gyle*,
C.16.280 And þat with *gyle* was gete vngraciousliche be yspened.
C.17.112 Go now to eny degre and bote *gyle* be holde a maistre
C.17.129 Withoute *gyle* and gabbyng gyue and sulle and lene.
C.17.242 Bote thorw pacience and priue *gyle* he was prince ouer hem all.
C.20.163 And riht as the gylour thorw *gyle* bigiled man formost
C.20.313 For thow gete hem with *gyle* and his gardyn broke,
C.20.322 'Hit is nat graythly ygete ther *gyle* is þe rote
C.20.377 With *gyle* thow hem gete agaynes all resoun.
C.20.382 That gylours [beth] bigiled and [in] here *gyle* falle
C.20.392 And *gyle* [be] bigyled thorw grace at þe laste:
C.20.396 So þat [thorw] *gyle* was gete thorw grace is now ywonne
C.20.399 And now bygynneth thy *gyle* agayne the to turne
C.21.299 With god and nat agast bote of *gyle* one.
C.21.300 For *gyle* goth so priueyly þat goed fayth oþer while
C.21.454 Of *gyle* ne of gabbyng[e] gyueth they neuer tale
C.21.455 For spiritus prudencie among þe peple is *gyle*
C.22.57 And garte *gyle* [growe] þere as he a god were.
C.22.67 And what kyng þat hem confortede, knowynge here *gyle*,

gyle v *gilen v.(1)* A 2 gilide (1) giliþ (1); B 2 giled (1) gileþ (1); C 3 gyle (1) gileth (1) gyled (1)
A. 8.71 And [ek] *giliþ* þe gyuere ageyns his wille.
A.11.67 Þat he *gilide* þe womman & by wy aftir,
B. 7.69 And [ek *g*]*ileþ* þe gyuere ageynes his wille.
B.20.125 Wiþ glosynges and gabbynges he *giled* þe peple.
C. 9.65 And also *gileth* hym þat gyueth and taketh agayne his wille.
C.16.307 Ne þat eny gome wolde *gyle* [ne greue oþere]
C.22.125 With glosynges and gabbynges he *gyled* þe peple.

gyles n prop *n.i.d.* C 2 Gyle (1) Gyles (1)
C. 4.51 'Bere sikerlyche eny seluer to seynt *Gyles* doune.
C. 8.54 'Y assente, by seynt *Gyle*,' sayde the knyht thenne,

gille n *gille n.* A 1; B 1; C 1 gylle
A. 5.188 Til glotoun hadde ygulpid a galoun & a *gille*.
B. 5.339 Til Gloton hadde yglubbed a galon and a *gille*.
C. 6.397 Til glotoun hadde yglobbed a galoun and a *gylle*.

gilour n *gilour n.* A 1; B 5 gilour (3) gilours (1) gylours (1); C 5 gilour (1) gylour (1) gylours (3)
A. 2.85 And þou hast gyuen hire to a *gilour*, now god ȝiue þe sorewe!
B. 2.121 And þow hast gyuen hire to a *gilour*, now god gyue þee sorwe!
B.10.197 Whoso gloseþ as *gylours* doon, go me to þe same,

B.18.160 And riȝt as [þe *gilour*] þoruȝ gile [bigiled man formest]
B.18.162 And bigile þe *gilour*, and þat is good] sleighte:
B.18.339 That *gilours* be bigiled and þat is good reson:
C. 3.100 Graunte *gylours* on erthe grace to amende
C. 3.303 And *Gylours* gyuen byfore and goode men at þe ende
C.20.163 And riht as the *gylour* thorw gyle bigiled man formost
C.20.165 And bigile þe *gilour*, and þat is goed sleythe:
C.20.382 That *gylours* [beth] bigiled and [in] here gyle falle

gilt n *gilt n.(1)* A 5; B 11 gilt (7) giltes (4); C 14 gult (3) gulte (4) gultes (7)
A. 3.8 I wile forgyue hire þe *gilt*, so me god helpe.'
A. 3.97 Ac I forgyue þe þe *gilt* & graunte þe [my] grace;
A. 4.65 'Wiþoute *gilt*, god wot, gat I þis skaþe.'
A. 4.88 I forgyue hym þ[at] *gilt* wiþ a good wille.'
A. 5.219 For is no *gilt* here so gret þat his goodnesse nis more.'
B. 3.8 I wol forgyuen hire þ[e] *gilt*, so me god helpe.'
B. 3.108 But I forgyue þee þ[e] *gilt* and graunte þee my grace;
B. 4.79 'Wiþouten *gilt*, god woot, gat I þis scaþe.'
B. 4.101 I forgyue hym þat *gilt* wiþ a good wille
B. 5.447 For is no *gilt* here so gret þat his goodnesse [i]s moore.'
B. 9.146 Here abouȝte þe barn þe belsires *giltes*,
B.10.80 That girles for [oure] *giltes* he forgrynt hem alle.
B.10.286 Bittre abouȝte þe *giltes* of two badde preestes,
B.13.256 To haue þe grace of god, and no *gilt* of [þe] pope.
B.13.386 For losse of good, leue me, þan for likames *giltes*;
B.19.303 And to correcte [þ]e kyng if [þe kyng] falle in *gilt*.
C. 3.8 Y wol forgyue here alle *gultes*, so me god helpe.'
C. 3.103 And goode mennes for here *gultes* gloweth on fuyr aftur.
C. 3.135 And monye a *gulte* y haue the forgyue & my grace graunted
C. 3.139 ȝut y forgyue the þis *gult*; godes forb[o]de eny more
C. 4.75 'Withouten *gult*, god wot, [gat y] this s[c]athe;'
C. 6.176 As in likynge of lecherye my lycames *gultes*
C. 6.275 For lo[s] of good, leef me, then for lycames *gultes*.
C. 7.61 For is no *gult* [here] so greet þat his goodnesse is more.'
C. 7.150 That euere they *gulte* aȝeyn þe, god, in gost or in dede,'
C.10.55 Oure lyf to oure lord god for oure lycames *gultes*.'
C.10.234 Here aboute þe barn the belsires *gultes*
C.11.60 And gode men for oure *gultes* he al togrynt to deth.
C.15.226 To haue þe grace of god and no *gulte* of þe pope.
C.21.303 And to corecte the kyng and the kyng falle in [g]*ulte*.

gilt ptp *gilden v.* B 3 gilt (2) gilte (1); C 3 gult
B.15.221 Boþe in grey and in grys and in *gilt* harneis,
B.17.15 The glose was gloriously writen wiþ a *gilt* penne:
B.18.14 To geten hym *gilte* spores [and] galoches ycouped.
C.16.346 Bothe in gray and in grys and in *gult* harneys,
C.19.16 The glose was gloriously writen with a *gult* penne:
C.20.12 To geten h[ym] *gult* spores and galoches ycouped.

gilty adj *gilti adj.* B 6 gilty (5) giltier (1); C 3 gulty
B. 5.367 'I, Gloton', quod þe [gome], '*gilty* me yelde
B.10.264 Thanne is dobest to be boold to blame þe *gilty*,
B.12.76 A womman, as [we] fynde[n], was *gilty* of þat dede,
B.12.79 *Giltier* as afore goed, and gretter in synne,
B.12.193 Was for he yald hym creaunt to crist & knewliched hym *gilty*,
B.19.302 Spiritus Iusticie spareþ noȝt to spille [þe] *gilty*,
C. 6.175 Y, *gulty* in gost, to god y me shryue
C. 6.425 To the, god, y glotoun, *gulty* me ȝelde
C.21.302 Spiritus iusticie spareth nat to spille [the] *gulty*

giltlees adj *giltles adj.* A 1 giltles; B 1
A.Pr.34 And gete gold wiþ here gle *giltles*, I trowe.
B.Pr.34 And geten gold with hire glee [*gilt]lees*, I leeue.

gyn n *ginne n.* B 1; C 1
B.18.252 For [Iesus as a] geaunt wiþ a *gyn* [comeþ yonde]
C.20.261 For iesus as a geaunt with a *gyn* cometh ȝende

gynful adj *ginful adj.* A 1; B 1
A.11.156 Geometrie & geomesie is *gynful* of speche;
B.10.213 Geometrie and Geomesie [is] *gynful* of speche;

gynneþ v *ginnen v.* A 12 gan (10) gynneþ (1) gonne (1); B 34 gan (28) gynne (1) gynneþ (2) gonne (2) gonnen (1); C 35 can (2) gan (28) gynne (1) gynneth (2) gonne (2)
A.Pr.11 Þanne *gan* I mete a merueillous sweuene,
A. 1.147 Þat he was miȝtful & mek & mercy *gan* graunte
A. 4.81 Þanne *gan* mede to meke hire, & mercy besouȝte,
A. 5.194 And þanne *gan* he to go [lik a glemans bicche],
A. 5.207 And *gan* grete grymly & gret doel ma[k]e
A. 6.44 'Nay, be þe peril of my soule!' quaþ piers & *gan* to swere:
A. 7.139 Þanne *gan* wastour arise & wolde haue yfouȝte;
A. 9.109 Ac er we ywar were wiþ wyt *gonne* we mete.
A.10.127 So dobest out of dobet & dowel *gynneþ* springe
A.11.100 And whanne I was war of his wil to his wif *gan* I knele,

A.11.168 And fond as she foretolde & forþ *gan* I wende,
A.12.29 God gaf him non answere but *gan* his tounge holde.
B.Pr.11 Thanne *gan* I meten a merueillous sweuene,
B. 1.113 Til he brak buxomnesse; his blisse *gan* he tyne
B. 1.173 That he was my3tful and meke and mercy *gan* graunte
B. 4.94 [Th]anne *gan* Mede to me[k]en hire, and mercy bisou3te,
B. 4.174 And *gan* wexe wroþ with lawe for Mede almoost hadde shent it,
B. 5.11 And how Reson *gan* arayen hym al þe Reaume to preche
B. 5.23 How pertly afore þe peple [preche *gan* Reson].
B. 5.346 And þanne *gan* he to go lik a glemannes bicche
B. 5.379 And þanne *gan* Gloton greete and gret doel to make
B. 5.480 God, þat of þi goodnesse [*g*]*onne* þe world make,
B. 5.557 'Nay, by [þe peril of] my soul[e]!' quod Piers and *gan* to swere:
B. 6.152 [Th]anne *gan* wastour to wraþen hym and wolde haue yfou3te;
B. 8.119 A[c] er we [war were] wiþ wit *gonne* we mete.
B.10.112 Here lyeþ youre lore", þise lordes *gynneþ* dispute,
B.10.147 And whan I was war of his wille to his wif *gan* I [knele]
B.11.42 'Ye! farewel, Phippe', quod Faunteltee, and forþ *gan* me drawe
B.11.116 And in a weer *gan* I wexe, and wiþ myself to dispute
B.11.201 For [at] Caluarie of cristes blood cristendom *gan* sprynge,
B.11.320 Ac muche moore in metynge þus wiþ me *gan* oon dispute,
B.13.2 And as a freke þat [fey] were forþ *gan* I walke
B.13.266 Wiþ [bake] breed fro Stratford; þo *gonnen* beggeris wepe
B.13.345 Semynge to synneward, and som he *gan* taste
B.13.390 Vpon a cruwel coueitise m[y conscience] *gan* hange.
B.14.34 Thanne laughed haukyn a litel and lightly *gan* swerye;
B.14.326 Synne seweþ vs euere', quod he and sory *gan* wexe,
B.16.32 Thoru3 likynge and lustes so loude he *gynneþ* blowe
B.17.64 Ac whan he hadde sighte of þat segge aside he *gan* hym drawe
B.17.226 Til þe holy goost *gynne* to glowe and to blase,
B.18.92 Thanne *gan* Feiþ felly þe false Iewes despise;
B.18.245 And lo! how þe sonne *gan* louke hire light in hirselue
B.20.110 Fortune *gan* flatere þanne þo fewe þat were alyue
B.20.200 And deeþ drogh nei3 me; for drede *gan* I quake,
B.20.301 [Ypocrisie at þe yate harde *gan* fighte]
B.20.386 And siþþe he gradde after Grace til I *gan* awake.
C.Pr.146 And for most profi[t to þe peple] a plogh *gonne* þei make,
C. 1.169 That he was myhtfull and meke and mercy *gan* graunte
C. 2.142 That 3e nymeth [and] notaries to nauhte *gynneth* brynge
C. 2.179 Thenne *gan* gyle borwen hors at many gret maystres
C. 3.11 Into Boure with blisse and by here *gan* sitte.
C. 4.90 Then *gan* mede to m[e]eken here and mercy bisouhte
C. 4.148 Mede in the mothalle tho on men of lawe *gan* wynke
C. 5.105 And to þe kyrke y *gan* go god to honoure;
C. 6.146 For she had haly bred ar y my herte *gan* change.
C. 6.179 Semyng to synneward and summe y *gan* taste
C. 6.352 Fastyng on a friday forth *gan* he wende
C. 6.398 His gottes *gan* to gothly as t[w]o g[re]dy sowes,
C. 6.404 And thenne *gan* he go lyke a glemans byche
C. 6.431 And as an hound þat eet gras so *gan* y to brake
C. 7.122 God þat of thi goodnesse *gonne* þe world make
C. 7.201 'Nay, bi þe perel of my soule!' Peres *gan* to swerie,
C. 8.149 Thenne *gan* wastor to wrath hym and wolde haue yfouhte
C.10.115 And ar we ywar were with wit *gan* we mete.
C.11.85 And when y was war of his wille to þat womman *gan* y louten
C.11.309 '3e! farewel, fyppe,' quod fauntele and forth *gan* me drawe
C.12.51 And in a wer *gan* y wex and with mysulue to despute
C.12.109 A[t] Caluarie of cristis bloed cristendoem *gan* sprynge
C.15.2 And as a freke þ[at] fay were forth *can* y walken
C.15.189 And as they wente by the way–of dowel *can* they carpe–
C.18.8 Thenne *gan* y aske what hit hihte and he me tho tolde:
C.18.36 Thorw lecherie and lustes so loude he *gynneth* blowe
C.19.63 Ac when he hadde sihte of this s[egg]e asyde he *gan* hym drawe
C.19.71 With wyn and with oyle his woundes he *gan* li[th]e,
C.19.192 Til the holy goest *gynne* to glowe and [to] blase,
C.20.95 Thenne *gan* faith f[el]ly þe false iewes dispice,
C.20.254 And lo! how þe sonne *gan* louke here lihte in hereselue
C.22.110 Fortune *gan* flateren thenne t[h]o fewe þat were alyue
C.22.200 And deth drow ney me; for drede *gan* y quaken
C.22.301 Ypocrisye at þe 3ate harde *gan* fyhte
C.22.386 And sethe he gradde aftur grace tyl y *gan* awake.

gynnyng *ger* ginninge ger. A 1; B 5; C 1 gynnynge
A.10.29 And þat is þe grete god þat *gynnyng* had neuere,
B. 2.30 Oo god wiþouten *gynnyng*, and I his goode dou3ter;
B. 9.28 And þat is þe grete god þat *gynnyng* hadde neuere,
B.10.241 On þe grete god þat *gynnyng* hadde neuere,
B.16.187 Wardeyn of þat wit haþ; was euere wiþouten *gynnyng*.
B.16.194 So god, þat *gynnyng* hadde neuere but þo hym good þou3te,
C.10.154 The which is god grettest [þat *gynnynge* hadde] neuere,

gyour *n* giour n. B 2; C 2
B.19.425 And Grace þat þow gr[e]dest so of, *gyour* of alle clerkes;
B.20.72 That kam ayein conscience þat kepere was and *gyour*

C.21.425 And grace that thow gredest so of, *gyour* of all Clerkes;
C.22.72 That cam a3en Consience þat kepar was and *gyour*

girdel *n* girdel n. B 2; C 1 gyrdel
B.13.293 Or strengest on stede, or styuest vnder *girdel*,
B.15.123 Sir Iohan and sire Geffrey haþ [of siluer a *girdel*],
C. 6.43 And strengest vppon stede and styuest vnder *gyrdel*

girdeþ *v* girden v.(2) A 1 gerdiþ; B 2 girdeþ (1) girte (1); C 1 gurdeth
A. 2.163 And *ge[rd]iþ* of giles hed; let hym go no ferþere;
B. 2.202 And *girdeþ* of Gyles heed; lat hym go no ferþer;
B. 5.372 That I, Gloton, *girte* it vp er I hadde gon a myle,
C. 2.216 And *gurdeth* of gyles heed; lat hym goo no wyddore

girles *n* girle n. A 2 girles (1) girlis (1); B 4 gerles (1) gerlis (1) girles (2); C 5 gurles
A.10.160 Ageyns godis hest *girlis* hy geten
A.11.132 Gramer for *girles* I garte ferst write,
B. 1.33 And þere gat in glotonie *gerles* þat were cherles.
B.10.80 That *girles* for [oure] giltes he forgrynt hem alle].
B.10.180 Grammer for *girles* I garte first write,
B.18.7 Of *gerlis* and of Gloria laus gretly me dremed,
C. 1.29 In his glotonye bygat *gurles* þat were cherles
C. 9.76 To aglotye with here *gurles* that greden aftur fode.
C.11.120 Gramer for *gurles* y gart furste write
C.16.302 He is glad with alle glade as *gurles* þat lawhen alle
C.20.6 Of *gurles* and of gloria laus greetliche me dremede

girte > girdeþ

gyse *n* gise n. C 1
C.Pr.26 In continance [of] clothyng in many kyne *gyse*.

gyterne *n* giterne n. B 1; C 1 geterne
B.13.233 Ne neiþer saille ne [sautrie] ne synge wiþ þe *gyterne*,
C.15.207 Ne noþer sayle ne sautrien ne syngen with þe *geterne*,

gyued *v* given v. B 1; C 1
B.20.192 And *gyued* me in goutes: I may no3t goon at large.
C.22.192 And *gyued* me in gowtes: y may nat go at large.

gyuen *v* yeven v. A 40 gaf (2) gif (1) giue (3) gyue (7) gyuen (2) giueþ (1) gyueþ (1) 3af (8) 3eue (1) 3if (1) 3iue (6) 3iuen (4) 3iueþ (2) ygyue (1); B 110 gaf (23) geue (1) giue (16) gyuen (5) gyuest (1) gyueþ (9) 3euen (1) 3yue (16) 3yuen (2) 3yueþ (9) yaf (11) yeue (10) yeuen (2) yeueþ (3) ygyue (1); C 106 gaef (2) gaf (19) geuen (1) gyue (16) gyuen (2) gyueth (12) 3af (14) 3ef (3) 3eue (20) 3euen (3) 3eueth (11) 3if (1) 3oue (1) ygyue (1)
A.Pr.73 Þus [3e *gyuen* 3oure] gold glotonis to helpe
A. 1.15 Boþe wiþ fel & wiþ face, & *3af* 3ow fyue wyttes
A. 1.105 *3af* hem mi3t in his mageste, þe meryere hem þou3te,
A. 2.64 Glotonye & grete oþes I *gyue* hem togidere,
A. 2.84 God grauntide to *gyue* mede to treuþe.
A. 2.85 And þou hast *gyuen* hire to a gilour, now god 3iue þe sorewe!
A. 2.85 And þou hast *gyuen* hire to a gilour, now god 3iue þe sorewe!
A. 2.109 And bad gile go *gyue* gold al aboute,
A. 2.113 Þo þis gold was *gyue* gret was þe þonking
A. 2.184 And *3af* pardoun for panis poundmel aboute.
A. 3.20 Of here grete goodnesse, & [*g*]*af* hem ichone
A. 3.62 Oþer to grede aftir godis men whan 3e [*g*]*iue* dolis,
A. 3.127 And [*g*]*iueþ* þe gaileris gold & grotis togidere
A. 3.153 Þis is þe lif of þat lady, now lord *3if* hire sorewe!
A. 3.169 And ek grepe my gold & *gyue* it where þe likiþ.
A. 3.197 To *3iuen* hise men mede þat mekly hym seruen,
A. 3.219 Þat on god of his grace *3yue* þe blisse
A. 4.91 'Nay,' quaþ þe king, 'so god *3iue* me blisse
A. 5.88 Þanne I cri3e on my knes þat crist *gyue* hym sorewe
A. 5.167 *3eue* glotoun wiþ glad chiere good ale to hansele.
A. 5.211 Er abstinence myn aunte haue *ygyue* me leue,
A. 7.119 And 3elde 3ow of 3our almesse þat 3e *3iuen* vs here,
A. 7.185 And *3af* hem mete & monie as þei mi3te asserue.
A. 7.226 And *3af* [it] hym in haste þat hadde ten before,
A. 7.236 God *3iueþ* [hem] his blissing þat here liflode so wynneþ.'
A. 8.43 And *3af* wille for his writyng wollene cloþis;
A. 8.178 I ne wolde *3iue* for þi patent on pye hele.
A. 8.181 Þat god *3iue* vs grace er we go hennis
A. 9.52 And [*g*]*iue* þe grace on þis erþe in good lif to ende'.
A.10.36 *3af* hym gost of his godhed & grauntide hym blisse,
A.10.116 Loke þou grucche nou3t on god þei3 he *gyue* þe litel;
A.10.129 For loue of here lou3nesse oure lord *3iueþ* hem grace
A.10.187 To *3iuen* a 3ong wenche to an old feble,
A.10.215 But 3if god [*g*]*iue* h[e]m grace here to amende.
A.11.34 *3iue* hem to here 3eris*3iue* þe value of a grote.
A.11.243 Godis word witnessiþ we shuln *3iue* & dele
A.11.248 And *3iuen* hem of oure good as good as oureseluen,
A.11.266 God *3af* h[i]m grace & ricchesse togidere

A.12.29	God *gaf* him non answere but gan his tounge holde.
A.12.111	God for his goudnesse *gif* hem swyche happes
B.Pr.76	Thus [ye] *gyuen* [youre] gold glotons to [helpe]
B. 1.15	Boþe with fel and with face, and *yaf* yow fyue wittes
B. 1.107	*Yaf* hem myȝt in his maiestee, þe murier hem þouȝte,
B. 2.31	And haþ *yeuen* me mercy to marie wiþ myselue,
B. 2.70	That Gile wiþ hise grete oþes *gyueþ* hem togidere,
B. 2.93	Glotonye he [*gyueþ*] hem ek and grete oþes togidere,
B. 2.120	God graunte[d] to *gyue* Mede to truþe,
B. 2.121	And þow hast *gyuen* hire to a gilour, now god *gyue* þee sorwe!
B. 2.121	And þow hast *gyuen* hire to a gilour, now god *gyue* þee sorwe!
B. 2.145	And bad gile '[go] *gyu[e]* gold al aboute,
B. 2.149	Tho þis gold was *ygyue* gret was þe þonkyng
B. 2.225	And [*gaf*] pardoun for pens poundemele aboute.
B. 3.21	Of hire grete goodnesse, and *gaf* hem echone
B. 3.71	Or to greden after goddes men whan ye [*gyue*] doles
B. 3.138	And *gyueþ* þe Gailers gold and grotes togidres
B. 3.166	This is þe lif of þat lady, now lord *ȝyue* hire sorwe,
B. 3.182	And [ek] griped my gold [and] *gyue* it where þee liked.
B. 3.210	To *yeue* [hise men mede] þat mekely hym serueþ,
B. 3.232	That oon god of his grace [*gyueþ*] in his blisse
B. 3.334	That *ȝyuen* ȝiftes, [takeþ yeme], þe victorie wynneþ
B. 4.37	Thei ne [*gy]ueþ* noȝt of [good feiþ, woot god þe sooþe]:
B. 4.170	And yet *yeue* ye me neuere þe worþ of a risshe.'
B. 5.51	And er he *gyue* any grace gouerne first hymselue.
B. 5.108	Thanne I crye on my knees þat crist *ȝyue* h[y]m sorwe
B. 5.293	For þee and for many mo þat man shal *yeue* a rekenyng:
B. 5.318	*Geue* Gloton wiþ glad chere good ale to hanselle.
B. 5.383	Til Abstinence myn Aunte haue *ȝyue* me leeue,
B. 5.439	I [ȝarn] aboute in youþe and *yaf* me nauȝt to lerne,
B. 6.127	And yelde yow [of] youre Almesse þat ye *ȝyue* vs here;
B. 6.198	And *yaf* hem mete [and money as þei] myȝte [asserue]
B. 6.242	And *yaf* [it hym in haste þat hadde ten bifore];
B. 7.70	For if he wiste he were noȝt nedy he wolde [it *ȝyue*]
B. 7.76	Ac Gregory was a good man and bad vs *gyuen* alle
B. 7.80	For he þat *yeueþ* yeldeþ and yarkeþ hym to reste,
B. 7.83	To yelden hem þat *yeueþ* hem and yet vsure moore:
B. 7.203	That god *gyue* vs grace er we go hennes
B. 8.52	For he *yaf* þee [to] yeresȝyue to yeme wel þiselue.
B. 8.61	And *ȝyue* yow grace on þis grounde goode men to worþe'.
B. 9.47	And þus god *gaf* hym a goost [of] þe godhede of heuene
B. 9.93	He is [lugged wiþ] Iudas þat *ȝyueþ* a Iaper siluer
B. 9.166	To *yeuen* a yong wenche to [a yolde] feble,
B. 9.201	But god *gyue* hem grace here to amende.
B. 9.205	To *ȝyuen* and to yemen boþe yonge and olde,
B.10.28	Thilke þat god [moost *gyueþ*] leest good þei deleþ,
B.10.48	*ȝyue* hem to hir yeresȝyue þe [value] of a grote.
B.10.206	To do good for goddes loue and *gyuen* men þat asked,
B.10.317	Litel hadde lordes to doon to *ȝyue* lond from hire heires
B.10.385	God *gaf* hym grace of wit and alle goodes after
B.10.452	Beþ noȝt [afered of þat folk], for I shal [*ȝyue* yow tonge],
B.11.196	That *ȝyueþ* hem mete or moneie [and] loueþ hem for my sake.'
B.12.17	And bidde for hem þat *ȝyueþ* þee breed, for þer are bokes y[n]owe
B.12.60	Ac grace ne groweþ noȝt [til good wil *yeue* reyn];
B.12.111	*ȝyue* mercy for hire mysdedes, if men it wole aske
B.12.145	If any frere were founde þere I *ȝyue* þee fyue shillynges!
B.12.198	Riȝt as som man *yeue* me mete and [sette me amydde þe floor];
B.12.253	That euere he gadered so grete and *gaf* þerof so litel,
B.12.272	Ac god is so good, I hope þat siþþe he *gaf* hem wittes
B.12.275	That god for his grace *gyue* hir soules reste,
B.13.170	*Yeue* þee al þat þei may yeue, as þee for best yemere:
B.13.170	*Yeue* þee al þat þei may *yeue*, as þee for best yemere;
B.13.181	'For I wol go wiþ þis gome, if god wol *yeue* me grace,
B.13.299	And if he *gyueþ* ouȝt to pouere gomes, telle what he deleþ;
B.13.340	[For] Goddes word [ne grace] *gaf* me neuere boote,
B.13.373	And if I r[o]þe ouerreche, or *yaf* hem reed þat ropen
B.13.424	And *ȝyueþ* hem mete and mede, and pouere men refuse,
B.14.9	And [siþþe] shryuen of þe preest, þat [for my synnes *gaf* me]
B.14.127	To *ȝyue* many m[e]n his [mercymonye] er he it haue deserued.
B.14.151	*ȝyueþ* hym a cote aboue his couenaunt, riȝt so crist *ȝyueþ* heuene
B.14.151	*ȝyueþ* hym a cote aboue his couenaunt, riȝt so crist *ȝyueþ* heuene
B.14.169	Of þe good þat þow hem *gyuest* ingrati ben manye;
B.14.170	Ac god, of þi goodnesse *gyue* hem grace to amende.
B.14.250	Lecherie loueþ hym noȝt for he *ȝyueþ* but litel siluer
B.14.321	Now god þat alle good *gyueþ* graunte his soule reste
B.15.222	And as gladliche he it *gaf* to gomes þat it neded.
B.15.250	And *gyue* vs grace, goode god, charite to folwe.
B.15.319	If lewed men knewe þis latyn þei wolde loke whom þei *yeue*,
B.15.323	To *ȝyue* from youre heires þat youre Aiels yow lefte,
B.15.331	And of hem þat habbeþ þei taken and *ȝyueþ* hem þat [ne] habbeþ.
B.15.337	And helpeþ hem þat helpeþ yow and *ȝyue* þer no nede is,
B.15.437	And hardie hem þat bihynde ben, and *ȝyue* hem good euidence.
B.15.482	That is god of his grace, *gyueþ* alle men blisse.
B.15.576	Bodily foode and goostly foode to] *gyue* þere it nedeþ:
B.17.271	And *gyueþ* youre good to þat god þat grace of ariseþ.
B.17.331	Cogheþ and curseþ þat crist *gyue* h[y]m sorwe
B.18.191	[At] þe bigynn[yng god] *gaf* þe doom hymselue
B.18.298	Wheiþer he were god or goddes sone; he [*g]af* me short answere;
B.18.383	Lawe wolde he *yeue* hym lif if he loked on hym.
B.19.54	For he *yaf* Adam and Eue and oþere mo blisse
B.19.60	And siþ [alle hise lele liges largely he *yeueþ*]
B.19.104	And som tyme he *gaf* good and grauntede heele boþe.
B.19.125	He made lame to lepe and *yaf* light to blynde
B.19.183	*yaf* Piers [pardon, and power] he grauntede hym,
B.19.225	Forþi', quod grace, 'er I go I wol *gyue* yow tresor
B.19.227	And *gaf* ech man a grace to gide wiþ hymseluen
B.19.229	Some [wyes] he *yaf* wit with wordes to shewe,
B.19.262	Grace *gaf* Piers a teeme, foure grete Oxen.
B.19.267	And Grace *gaf* Piers of his goodnesse foure stottes,
B.19.274	And Grace *gaf* [Piers] greynes, Cardynal[es] vertues,
B.19.319	'By god! Grace', quod Piers, 'ye moten *gyue* tymber,
B.19.321	And Grace *gaf* hym þe cros, wiþ þe [garland] of þornes,
B.19.331	And *gaf* hym caples to his carte, contricion and confession;
B.19.386	Grace, þoruȝ goddes word, [*g]af* Piers power,
B.19.454	Of gile ne of gabbyng *gyue* þei neuere tale,
B.20.58	Freres folwede þat fend for he *gaf* hem copes,
B.20.155	And [so] forȝyte sorwe and [of synne *ȝyue* noȝt].'
B.20.171	[And] *gaf* hym gold good woon þat gladede his herte,
B.20.172	And þei *gyuen* hym ageyn a glaȝene howue.
B.20.291	As sisours and executours; þei [shul] *ȝyue* þe freres
B.20.300	Ypocrisie and h[ij] an hard assaut þat [ȝeuen].
B.20.363	And gooþ gropeþ Contricion and *gaf* hym a plastre
C.Pr.74	Thus ȝe *gyue* ȝoure gold glotons to helpe
C. 1.15	To be fayful to hym [he] *ȝaf* ȝow fyue wittes
C. 2.72	That Gyle hath *gyue* to falsnesse and grauntid also mede,'
C. 2.100	Glotonye a *gyueth* hem and grete othes togederes,
C. 2.129	And thow has[t] *gyue* here as gyle tauhte, now god *ȝeue* þe sorwe!
C. 2.129	And thow has[t] *gyue* here as gyle tauhte, now god *ȝeue* þe sorwe!
C. 2.161	And bade gyle '[g]o *gyue* gold al aboute,
C. 2.165	Tho this gold was *ygyue* grete was þe thonkynge
C. 2.235	And *gaf* pardon for pans poundmele aboute.
C. 3.22	Of here grete goodnesse and *gaf* hem vchone
C. 3.176	And *gyueth* þe gaylers gold and grotes togederes
C. 3.213	Thus lereth this lady thi lond, now lord *ȝeue* here sorwe!
C. 3.228	And also gryp[en] my gold and *gyue* hit where þe liked.
C. 3.266	To *ȝeue* men mede þat meekliche hym serueth,
C. 3.272	And *ȝeuen* mede to men to meyntene here lawes;
C. 3.288	As þe sauhter sayth by such þat *ȝeueth* mede:
C. 3.290	To *ȝeue* men mede, more oþer lasse.
C. 3.293	Mede many tymes men *ȝeueth* bifore þe doynge
C. 3.303	And Gylours *gyuen* byfore and goode men at þe ende
C. 3.316	*ȝeue* lond or lordschipe [or] oþer large ȝeftes
C. 3.323	That kyng oþer kayser hem *gaf*, Catel oþer rente.
C. 3.324	For god *gaf* salomon grace vpon erthe,
C. 3.329	So god *gyueth* no [grace] þat "si" [ne] is the glose
C. 3.331	Bothe *gyue* and graunte there his grace lyketh
C. 3.339	That [is] þe gyft þat god *gyueth* to alle lele lyuynge,
C. 3.412	And *ȝaf* the kyndom to his knaue þat kept shep and lambren;
C. 3.486	That *ȝeueth* ȝeftes, taketh ȝeme, the victorie a wynneth
C. 3.499	Worschipe a wynneth þat wol *ȝeue* mede
C. 4.37	They *gyue* n[ouh]t of good fayth, woe[t] god the sothe,
C. 5.163	Lytel hadde lordes ado to *ȝeue* lond fro [here] heyres
C. 6.47	And what y *gaf* for godes loue to gossipus y tolde,
C. 6.61	'Now god for his goodnesse *gyue* the grace to amende,'
C. 6.270	And [yf] y raap ouerreche or *ȝaf* hem red þat repe
C. 6.348	For the and for many mo þat man shal *ȝeue* a rykenynge
C. 6.375	*Geuen* glotoun with glad chere good ale to hansull.
C. 6.440	Til abstinence myn aunte haue *ȝeue* me leue;
C. 7.53	And ȝede aboute in my ȝouthe and *ȝaf* me to no thedom
C. 7.84	And *ȝeueth* [hem] mede & mete and pore men refuse,
C. 8.133	And ȝelde ȝow of ȝoure Almesse þat ȝe *ȝeuen* vs here;
C. 8.177	'Haue mercy on hem, hunger,' quod [Peres], 'and lat me *ȝeue* hem benes
C. 8.187	Al for drede of here deth, such duntus *ȝaf* hunger.
C. 8.203	And *ȝaf* hem mete and money as þei myhte deserue.
C. 8.253	Byno[m] hym al þat he hadde and *ȝaf* hit to his felawe
C. 8.282	And [ȝif thow [the pore be thy] pouer, [Peres], y þe rede;
C. 9.65	And also gileth hym þat *gyueth* and taketh agayne his wille.
C. 9.66	For he þat *gyueth* for goddes loue wolde nat *gyue*, his thankes,
C. 9.66	For he þat *gyueth* for goddes loue wolde nat *gyue*, his thankes,
C. 9.68	And moste merytorie to men þat he *ȝeueth* fore.
C. 9.116	To *ȝeue* vch a wyht wyt, welthe and his hele
C. 9.133	Me [*g]yueth* hem giftes and gold for grete lordes sake.
C. 9.349	That god *gyue* vs grace here ar we go hennes
C.10.60	And *gyue* me grace on þis grounde with good ende to deye.'
C.10.179	*ȝaf* his douhter for a daunsynge in a disch þe heued
</table>

C.10.256   Ac fewe folke now folweth this for thei ȝeue her childurne
C.10.300   Bote god ȝeue hem grace her [g]oynge here to amende.
C.10.304   To ȝeue and to ȝeme bothe ȝonge and olde,
C.11.25   Tho þat god most goed ȝeueth greueth most riht and treuthe:
C.11.210   God gaf hym grace of wit and of goed aftur,
C.11.277   Beth nat aferd of þat folk for y shal ȝeue ȝow tonge,
C.12.165   Ȝef pore peple þe panes; þerof pors þou none
C.12.166   Ac ȝef hem forth to pore folk þat for my loue hit aske;
C.12.200   Yf god gyueth hym þe lyf, to haue a goed heruost,
C.12.211   How god, as þe gospelle telleth, gyueth [hym] foel to name,
C.13.83   That þe lawe ȝeueth leue such low folk to be excused,
C.14.24   Ac grace ne groweth nat til gode wil gyue reyne
C.14.56   To ȝeue mercy for mysde[de]s ȝif men hit wol aske
C.14.89   Yf eny frere we[re] founde þere y ȝeue the fyue shillynges!
C.14.137   Riht Ás sum man ȝeueth me mete and sette me Amydde þe flore;
C.14.194   Ac god is so gode, y hope þat seth he gaf þise wittes
C.14.197   That god for his grace gyue here soules reste
C.15.18   Of kynde and [of] his connynge and what connynge he ȝaf bestes
C.15.20   For alle a wisseth and ȝeueth wit þat walketh oþer crepeth.
C.15.144   Ȝef hym eft and eft, euere at his nede,
C.16.152   And sobrete ȝeueth here swete drynke and solaceth here in all
           angrys.
C.16.156   Now god þat al [good] gyueth graunte his soule reste
C.16.347   And also gladliche he hit gaf to gomes þat hit nedede.
C.17.67   He gaf goddes men goddes goodes and nat grete lordes
C.17.129   Withoute gyle and gabbyng gyue and sulle and lene.
C.19.252   And gyueth ȝoure goed to þat god þat grace of aryseth.
C.19.311   Coueth and corseth þat Crist ȝeue hym sorwe
C.20.196   At the bigynnynge god gaf the doem hymsulue
C.20.331   Where he were god or godes sone; he gaf me short answere.
C.20.425   Lawe wolde he ȝoue hym lyf and he loked on hym.
C.21.54   For he ȝaf Adam and Eue and oþere mo blisse
C.21.60   And sethe [all his lele leges largeliche he ȝeueth]
C.21.104   And som tyme he gaf goed and graunted hele bothe;
C.21.125   He made lame to lepe and ȝaf liht to blynde
C.21.183   And ȝaf [peres pardoun] and [power] he graunted [hym],
C.21.225   Forthy,' quod grace, 'or y go y wol gyue ȝow tresor
C.21.227   And gaf vch man a grace to gye with hymsuluen
C.21.229   Som [wyes] he ȝaf wyt with wordes to schewe,
C.21.262   Grace gaf [Peres] a teme, foure grete oxen.
C.21.267   And grace [gaef Peres of his goednesse] foure stottes,
C.21.274   And grace gaf Peres graynes, cardinales vertues,
C.21.319   'By god! grace,' quod [Peres], 'ȝe moet gyue tymber
C.21.321   And grace gaf hym þe cros with [the garlond] of thornes
C.21.331   And gaf hym caples to his Carte, Contrissioun & confessioun;
C.21.386   Grace thorw godes word gaf [Peres] power,
C.21.454   Of gyle ne of gabbyng[e] gyueth they neuer tale
C.22.58   Freres folewed þat fende for he ȝaf hem copes
C.22.155   And [s]o forȝete [sorwe] and [of synne ȝeue nouht].'
C.22.171   And gaef hym goelde goed woen þat gladde h[is] hert[e]
C.22.172   And they gyuen hym agayne a glasene houe.
C.22.291   As sisours and secutours; they shal ȝeue þe freres
C.22.300   Ypocrisye and [h]y an hard sawt they ȝeuen.
C.22.363   And goeth gropeth contricion and gaf hym a plastre

gyuere n *yevere n.* A 1; B 1
A. 8.71   And [ek] giliþ þe gyuere ageyns his wille.
B. 7.69   And [ek g]ileþ þe gyuere ageynes his wille.

gyues n *gives n.pl.* B 1; C 1
B.14.53   Shul neuere gyues þee greue ne gret lordes wraþe,
C.15.252   Shal neuere gyues the greue ne grete lordes wrathe,

glad adj *glad adj.* A 5 glad (3) gladdere (1) glade (1); B 10 glad (5)
gladder (2) gladdere (1) glade (2); C 8 glad (4) gladdere (1) glade (2)
gladere (1)
A. 5.167   Ȝeue glotoun wiþ glad chiere good ale to hansele.
A. 9.85   And wiþ glad wil doþ hem good for so god [hiȝte].
A.10.100   And be glad of þe grace þat god haþ Isent þe.
A.11.111   Gladdere þanne þe gleman þat gold haþ to ȝifte,
A.11.193   Sike with þe sory, singe with þe glade,
B. 3.302   That Iewes shul wene in hire wit, and wexen glade,
B. 5.91   I wolde be gladder, by god! þat Gybbe hadde meschaunce
B. 5.318   Geue Gloton wiþ glad chere good ale to hansele.
B. 8.95   And wiþ glad wille dooþ hem good for so god hoteþ.
B.10.159   Gladder þan þe gleman þat gold haþ to ȝifte,
B.15.167   And is as glad of a gowne of a gray russet
B.15.169   He is glad wiþ alle glade and good til alle wikkede
B.15.169   He is glad wiþ alle glade and good til alle wikkede
B.16.155   And gile in þi glad chere and galle is in þi laughyng.
B.20.62   Whiche foolis were wel [gladdere] to deye
C. 3.283   And glad for to grype hem, gret lord oþer pore.'
C. 3.455   That iewes shal wene in he[re] wit, & wexen so glade,
C. 6.375   Geuen glotoun with glad chere good ale to hansull.

C.11.101   Gladdere then [þe] gleman þat gold hath to ȝefte
C.16.300   And as glad of a goune of a gray russet
C.16.302   He is glad with alle glade as gurles þat lawhen alle
C.16.302   He is glad with alle glade as gurles þat lawhen alle
C.22.62   [Whiche foles] were wel gladere to deye

glade > glad,gladen

gladen v *gladen v.* A 2 glade; B 7 glade (3) gladede (1) gladen (1) gladeþ
(1) gladie (1); C 6 gladde (1) glade (1) gladeth (1) gladie (1) gladien
(1) gladyen (1)
A. 7.111   Shal no greyn þat here growiþ glade ȝow at nede;
A.10.201   And [þanne] glade ȝe god þat al good sendiþ.
B. 5.534   'Nay, so [god] glade me]', seide þe gome þanne.
B. 6.119   Shal no greyn þat [here] groweþ glade yow at nede;
B.10.44   Thei konne na moore mynstralcie ne Musik men to glade
B.17.221   And as glowynge gledes gladeþ noȝt þise werkmen
B.18.256   In alle myȝtes of man and his moder gladie,
B.19.147   And goon into Galilee and gladen hise Apostles
B.20.171   [And] gaf hym gold good woon þat gladede his herte,
C. 8.126   Shal no grayn þat here groweth gladyen ȝow at nede;
C. 9.301   And which a pardoun Peres hadde th[e] peple to glade
C.19.187   And as glowyng gledes gladeth nat this werkmen
C.20.178   And [in] here gay garnementes wham she gladie thouhte.
C.21.147   And goen into Galilee and gladien his apostlis
C.22.171   And gaef hym goelde goed woen þat gladde h[is] hert[e]

gladly adv *gladli adv.* B 2 gladly (1) gladliche (1); C 2 gladliche
B. 4.194   'I graunte [gladly]', quod kyng, 'goddes forbode [he faile]!
B.15.222   And as gladliche he it gaf to gomes þat it neded.
C. 6.105   'I am wr[a]the,' quod þat weye, 'wol gladliche smyte
C.16.347   And also gladliche he hit gaf to gomes þat hit nedede.

glase > glaȝen; glasene > glaȝene

glaȝen v *glasen v.* A 1 glase; B 2 glaȝe (1) glaȝen (1); C 2 glase
A. 3.48   Woldist þou glase þe gable, & graue þere þin name,
B. 3.49   Woldestow glaȝe þ[e] gable & graue [here] þy name
B. 3.61   Wowes do whiten and wyndowes glaȝen,
C. 3.52   Wolde ȝe glase þ[e] gable and graue ther ȝoure name
C. 3.65   Bothe wyndowes and wowes y wol amende and glase

glaȝene adj *glasen adj.* B 1; C 1 glasene
B.20.172   And þei gyuen hym ageyn a glaȝene howue.
C.22.172   And they gyuen hym agayne a glasene houe.

gle > glee

glede n *glede n.(2)* B 5 glede (2) gledes (1) gleede (2); C 3 glede (2)
gledes (1)
B. 2.12   And þeron [riche] Rubies as rede as any gleede,
B. 5.283   Nis na moore to þe mercy of god þan [amyd] þe see a gleede:
B.17.221   And as glowynge gledes gladeþ noȝt þise werkmen
B.17.227   So þat þe holy goost gloweþ but as a [glede vn]glade
B.17.235   And as wex wiþouten moore on a warm glede
C.19.187   And as glowyng gledes gladeth nat this werkmen
C.19.193   So þat the holy gost gloweth but as a glede
C.19.201   And as wex withouten more vpo[n] a warm glede

glee n *gle n.(1)* A 1 gle; B 1
A.Pr.34   And gete gold wiþ here gle giltes, I trowe.
B.Pr.34   And geten gold with hire glee [gilt]lees, I leeue.

gleede > glede

gleman n *gleman n.* A 2 gleman (1) glemans (1); B 4 gleman (3)
glemannes (1); C 2 gleman (1) glemans (1)
A. 5.194   And þanne gan he to go [lik a glemans bicche],
A.11.111   Gladdere þanne þe gleman þat gold haþ to ȝifte,
B. 5.346   And þanne gan he to go lik a glemannes bicche
B. 9.104   And goddes gleman and a game of heuene.
B. 9.106   Ne his gleman a gedelyng, a goere to tauernes.
B.10.159   Gladder þan þe gleman þat gold haþ to ȝifte,
C. 6.404   And thenne gan he go lyke a glemans byche
C.11.101   Gladdere then [þe] gleman þat gold hath to ȝefte

glide v *gliden v.* B 1; C 1 glyde
B.18.431   May no grisly goost glide þere it [shadweþ].'
C.20.475   May no grisly goest glyde þer hit shaddeweth.'

glorie n *glorie n.* A 1; B 4; C 3
A.11.70   Suche motifs þei meuen, þise maistris in here glorie
B.10.117   Swiche motyues þei meue, þise maistres in hir glorie,
B.18.265   For here comeþ wiþ crowne þat kyng is of glorie.'' '
B.18.308   Wiþ glorie and with gret light; god it is, I woot wel.
B.20.157   And geten in hir glorie a gadelyng at þe laste,
C.20.273   For here cometh with croune þe kynge of all glorie.'
C.20.342   With glorie and with [grete] lihte; god hit is ich woet wel.
C.22.157   And geten in here glorie a gadlyng at þe laste,

gloriously adv *gloriousli adv.* B 1; C 1
B.17.15   The glose was *gloriously* writen wiþ a gilt penne:
C.19.16   The glose was *gloriously* writen with a gult penne:

glosares > gloseris

glose n *glose n.* B 4; C 5
B. 5.276   And whoso leueþ [þat I liȝe] loke in þe Sauter *glose*,
B.12.294   The *glose* graunteþ vpon þat vers a greet mede to truþe.
B.15.82   Gooþ to þe *glose* of þ[e] vers, ye grete clerkes;
B.17.15   The *glose* was gloriously writen wiþ a gilt penne:
C. 3.329   So god gyueth no [grace] þat "si" [ne] is the *glose*
C. 6.301   And what lede leueth þat y lye look in þe sauter *glos[e]*,
C.10.242   Ac þe gospel is a *glose* ther and huydeth þe grayth treuthe;
C.15.81   Þat toek this for his teme and tolde hit withoute *glose*.
C.19.16   The *glose* was gloriously writen with a gult penne:

glosed(e > gloseþ

gloseris n *gloser n.* B 1; C 1 glosares
B.19.221   And false prophetes fele, flatereris and *gloseris*,
C.21.221   And false profetes fele, flateres and *glosares*,

gloseþ v *losen v.* A 2 gloside (1) yglosid (1); B 6 glosed (2) gloseþ (3) yglosed (1); C 6 glosede (1) gloseth (2) glosynge (1) yglosed (2)
A.Pr.57   *Gloside* þe gospel as h[e]m good likide;
A.11.127   And sette hire to sapience & to hire sauter *yglosid*.
B.Pr.60   *Glosed* þe gospel as hem good liked;
B.10.175   And sette hire to Sapience and to þe Sauter *glose[d]*.
B.10.197   Whoso *gloseþ* as gylours doon, go me to þe lawe.
B.11.306   The gome þat *gloseþ* so chartres for a goky is holden.
B.17.12   Wheron [was] writen two wordes on þis wise *yglosed*.
B.20.368   Thus he gooþ and gadereþ and *gloseþ* þere he shryueþ.
C.Pr.58   *Glosede* þe gospel as hem good likede;
C. 4.138   Ne gete my grace thorw eny gyfte ne *glosynge* spe[ch]e
C.11.115   And sette here to sapience and to þe sauter *yglosed*.
C.13.120   The gome þat *gloseth* so Chartres for a goky is halden.
C.19.13   Whereon was writen two wordes on this wyse *yglosed*.
C.22.368   Thus he goeth and gedereth and *gloseth* þer he shryueth

glosyng ger *glosinge ger.* &> *gloseþ* B 2 glosyng (1) glosynges (1); C 2 glosynge (1) glosynges (1)
B.13.75   Taken it for his teme and telle it wiþouten *glosyng*.
B.20.125   Wiþ *glosynges* and gabbynges he giled þe peple.
C. 6.259   And with Gyle and *glosynge* ygadered þat y haue,
C.22.125   With *glosynges* and gabbynges he gyled þe peple.

gloton n *glotoun n.* A 8 glotonis (1) glotoun (7); B 16 gloton (13) glotons (2) glotoun (1); C 11 gloton (2) glotonis (1) glotoun (8)
A.Pr.73   Þus [ȝe gyuen ȝoure] gold *glotonis* to helpe
A. 5.146   Now begynneþ *glotoun* for to [go to] shrift,
A. 5.152   'I haue good ale, gossib,' quaþ heo; '*glotoun*, wilt þou assaie?'
A. 5.154   'Ȝa, *glotoun* gossib,' quaþ heo, 'god wot, wel hote:
A. 5.157   Þanne goþ [*glotoun* in], and grete oþis aftir.
A. 5.167   Ȝeue *glotoun* wiþ glad chiere good ale to hansele.
A. 5.184   And grete sire *glotoun* wiþ a galoun ale.
A. 5.188   Til *glotoun* hadde ygulpid a galoun & a gille.
B.Pr.76   Thus [ye] gyuen [youre] gold *glotons* to [helpe]
B.Pr.139   Thanne greued hym a Goliardeis, a *gloton* of wordes,
B. 5.296   Now bigynneþ *Gloton* for to go to shrifte
B. 5.302   'I haue good Ale, gossib', quod she, '*Gloton*, woltow assaye?'
B. 5.306   Thanne goþ *Gloton* In and grete oþes after.
B. 5.318   Geue *Gloton* wiþ glad chere good ale to hanselle.
B. 5.335   And greten sire *Gloton* wiþ a Galon ale.
B. 5.339   Til *Gloton* hadde yglubbed a galon and a gille.
B. 5.353   Ac *Gloton* was a gret cherl and grym in þe liftyng;
B. 5.367   'I, *Gloton*', quod þe [gome], 'gilty me yelde
B. 5.372   That I, *Gloton*, girte it vp er I hadde gon a myle,
B. 5.379   And þanne gan *Gloton* greete and gret doel to make
B. 6.301   Wiþ good Ale as *Gloton* taȝte [þei] garte [hym to] slepe.
B. 9.62   And þat ben glotons, glubberes; hir god is hire wombe:
B.13.78   'Ac þis goddes *gloton*', quod I, 'wiþ hise grete chekes
B.13.399   [Yet *glotoun* wiþ grete oþes his [garnement] hadde soiled
C.Pr.74   Thus ȝe gyue ȝoure gold *glotons* to helpe
C. 6.350   Now bygynneth *glotoun* for to go to shryfte
C. 6.357   'Y haue good ale, gossip *Glotoun*, woltow assaye?'
C. 6.361   Thenne goth *glotoun* in and grete othes aftur.
C. 6.375   Geuen *glotoun* with glad chere good ale to hansull.
C. 6.393   And grete syre *glotoun* with a galoun ale.
C. 6.397   Til *glotoun* hadde yglobbed a galoun and a gylle.
C. 6.411   Ac *gloton* was a greet cherl and gr[ym] in þe luftynge
C. 6.425   To the, god, y *glotoun*, gulty me ȝelde
C. 8.323   And thenne *gloton* with gode ale garte hunger slepe.
C.15.85   And also a gnedy *glotoun* with two grete chekes,

glotonye n *glotonie n.* A 5; B 9 glotonie (3) glotonye (6); C 8 glotony (1) glotonye (7)
A.Pr.22   [Wonne] þat þise wastours wiþ *glotonye* destroiȝeþ.
A.Pr.43   In *glotonye*, god wot, go þei to bedde,
A. 2.64   *Glotonye* & grete oþes I gyue hem togidere;
A. 7.285   Wiþ good ale & *glotonye* h[y] gart hym to slepe.
A.11.37   *Glotonye* & grete oþis, þise arn games nowadayes.
B.Pr.22   Wonnen þat [þise] wastours with *glotonye* destruyeþ.
B.Pr.43   In *glotonye*, god woot, go þei to bedde,
B. 1.33   And þere gat in *glotonie* gerles þat were cherles.
B. 2.93   *Glotonye* he [gyueþ] hem ek and grete oþes togidere,
B.10.51   *Glotonye* and grete oþes, þis[e arn games nowadaies].
B.10.84   But in gaynesse and *glotonye* forglutten hir good
B.14.230   And if *glotonie* greue pouerte he gadereþ þe lasse
B.14.232   And þouȝ his *glotonye* be to good ale he goþ to cold beddyng
B.14.235   So for his *glotonie* and his greete sleuþe he haþ a greuous penaunce
C.Pr.24   And wonne þat þis wastors with *glotony* destrueth.
C.Pr.44   In *glotonye* þ[o] gomus goth þei to bedde
C. 1.29   In his *glotonye* bygat gurles þat were cherles
C. 2.100   *Glotonye* a gyueth hem and grete othes togederes,
C.11.64   Bote in gaynesse and *glotonye* forglotten here godes
C.16.71   And yf *glotonye* greue pouerte h[e] gadereth þe lasse
C.16.73   And thogh his *glotonye* be of gode ale he goth to a colde beddynge
C.16.76   So for his *glotonye* and his grete synne he hath a greuous penaunce

glotoun > gloton

gloue n *glove n.* A 1; B 2 gloue (1) gloues (1); C 2 gloues
A. 7.140   To peris þe plouȝman he profride his *gloue*.
B. 5.253   That payed neuere for his prentishode noȝt a peire *gloues*.'
B. 6.153   To Piers þe Plowman he profrede his *gloue*.
C. 6.251   Payed neuere for his prentished nat a payre *gloues*.
C.13.48   Oþer his hatt or his hoed or elles his *gloues*

glowe v *glouen v.(1)* B 3 glowe (1) gloweþ (1) glowynge (1); C 4 glowe (1) gloweth (2) glowyng (1)
B.17.221   And as *glowynge* gledes gladeþ noȝt þise werkmen
B.17.226   Til þe holy goost gynne to *glowe* and to blase,
B.17.227   So þat þe holy goost *gloweþ* but as a [glede vn]glade
C. 3.103   And goode mennes for here gultes *gloweth* on fuyr aftur.
C.19.187   And as *glowyng* gledes gladeth nat this werkmen
C.19.192   Til the holy goest gynne to *glowe* and [to] blase,
C.19.193   So þat the holy gost *gloweth* but as a glede

glubberes n *globber n.* B 1
B. 9.62   And þat ben glotons, *glubberes*; hir god is hire wombe:

gnawen v *ganuen v.* A 1; B 1; C 1
A.11.44   And *gnawen* god in [þe gorge] whanne here guttis fullen.
B.10.58   And *gnawen* god [in] þe gorge whanne hir guttes fullen.
C.11.39   And *gnawen* god with gorge when here gottes f[u]llen.

gnede adj *gnede adj.* C 1
C.15.85   And also a *gnedy* glotoun with two grete chekes,

go v *gon v.* A 38 go (30) gon (6) goþ (2); B 77 go (57) goynge (1) gon (2) goon (6) gooþ (7) goþ (3) ygo (1); C 79 ga (2) go (54) goen (4) goeth (2) goynge (1) gone (1) goo (2) goth (12) ygo (1)
A.Pr.43   In glotonye, god wot, *go* þei to bedde,
A.Pr.105   Goode gees & gris; *go* we dyne, go we!'
A.Pr.105   Goode gees & gris; go we dyne, *go* we!'
A. 1.44   '*Go* to þe gospel,' quaþ heo, 'þat god seide himseluen,
A. 1.179   And ek þe graiþ gate þat *goþ* into heuene.
A. 2.109   And bad gile *go* gyue gold al aboute,
A. 2.119   Þat he[o] grauntiþ to *gon* wiþ a good wille
A. 2.163   And ge[rd]iþ of giles hed; let hym *go* no ferþere;
A. 3.147   Þat feiþ may not haue his forþ, hire floreynes *go* so þikke.
A. 3.213   Mede & marchaundise mote nede *go* togidere;
A. 4.110   Þat no man *go* to galis but ȝif he go for euere;
A. 4.110   Þat no man go to galis but ȝif he *go* for euere;
A. 5.24   He bad wastour *go* werche what he best couþe
A. 5.121   Ne hadde [þe] grace of gile *gon* among my ware
A. 5.146   Now begynneþ glotoun for to [*go* to] shrift,
A. 5.157   Þanne *goþ* [glotoun in], and grete oþis aftir.
A. 5.185   Þere was lauȝing & louryng & 'lete *go* þe cuppe!'
A. 5.194   And þanne gan he to *go* [lik a glemans bicche],
A. 6.48   Ȝe mote *go* þoruȝ meknesse, boþe men & wyues,
A. 6.92   And ȝif grace graunte þe to *gon* in [on] þis wise,
A. 6.123   Þou miȝt gete grace [þere] so þou *go* be tyme.'
A. 7.31   And ȝo hunte hardily [to] har[is] & [to] fox[is],
A. 7.142   And bad hym *go* pisse wiþ his plouȝ: 'pilide shrewe!
A. 7.202   And ȝif þe [g]omes grucche bidde hem *gon* & sywnke,
A. 7.216   *Go* to genesis þe geaunt, engendrour of vs alle:
A. 7.221   He shal *go* [begge & bidde] & no man bete his hungir;

A. 8.41	Þat no gile *go* wiþ ȝow but þe graiþ treuþe.'	B.20.192	And gyued me in goutes: I may noȝt *goon* at large.
A. 8.77	And *gon* & faiten wiþ here fauntis for eueremore aftir.	B.20.273	Enuye herde þis and heet freres *go* to scole
A. 8.117	Haue þei no garner [to *go*] to, but god fynt hem alle.'	B.20.305	'*Go* salue þo þat sike ben and þoruȝ synne ywounded.'
A. 8.181	Þat god ȝiue vs grace er we *go* hennis	B.20.341	'Ye? *go* þi gate!' quod Pees, 'by god! for al þi phisik,
A. 9.49	Ac ȝif I may lyuen & loken I shal *go* lerne betere.	B.20.363	And *gooþ* gropeþ Contricion and gaf hym a plastre
A.10.21	And sire godefrey *go* wel, grete lordis alle.	B.20.368	Thus he *gooþ* and gadereþ and gloseþ þere he shryueþ
A.11.48	But hunsen hym as an hound & hoten hym *go* þenne.	C.Pr.44	In glotonye þ[o] gomus *goth* þei to bedde
A.11.52	[Mendynauntȝ] meteles miȝte *go* to bedde.	C.Pr.231	Goode gees and grys! *ga* we dyne, ga we!
A.12.36	And drow þe dore after him and bad me *go* do wel	C.Pr.231	Goode gees and grys! ga we dyne, *ga* we!'
A.12.69	'*Go* we forþ,' quod þe gom, 'I haue a gret boyste	C. 1.44	'*Go* to þe gospel,' quod she, 'and se what god sayde
A.12.76	For gronyng of my guttys I durst *gon* no ferther].	C. 2.161	And bade gyle '[g]o gyue gold al aboute,
B.Pr.43	In glotonye, god woot, *go* þei to bedde,	C. 2.171	That he graunteþ to *go* with a goode wille
B.Pr.227	Goode gees and grys! *go* we dyne, go we!'	C. 2.216	And gurdeth of gyles heed; lat hym *goo* no wyddore
B.Pr.227	Goode gees and grys! go we dyne, *go* we!'	C. 2.224	And gyle doth hym to *gone* agaste for to deye.
B. 1.46	'*Go* to þe gospel', quod she, 'þat god seide hymseluen,	C. 3.137	And ay þe lengur y late [the] *go* the lasse treuthe is with the,
B. 1.205	And also þe graiþe gate þat *goþ* into heuene.	C. 3.195	That fayth may nat haue his forth, here floreynes *goth* so thykke,
B. 2.145	And bad gile '[*go*] gyu[e] gold al aboute,	C. 3.281	Marchaundise and mede mot nede [*go*] togederes.
B. 2.155	That she graunteþ to *goon* wiþ a good wille	C. 4.100	Wrong *goth* nat so away ar y wete more.
B. 2.202	And girdeþ of Gyles heed; lat hym *go* no ferþer;	C. 4.124	So þat noon *go* to galys but yf he go for euere;
B. 2.214	And Gyle dooþ hym to *go* agast for to dye.	C. 4.124	So þat noon go to galys but yf he *go* for euere;
B. 3.157	That feiþ may noȝt haue his forþ, hire floryns *go* so þikke.	C. 5.105	Ne þe kyrke y gan *go* god to honoure;
B. 3.226	[Mede and Marchaundiȝe] mote nede *go* togideres;	C. 5.126	He bad wastoures [*g*]o wurche and wynne here sustinaunce
B. 3.245	Of god at a gret nede whan þei *gon* hennes.	C. 6.213	Ne hadde þe grace of Gyle *go* among my ware
B. 4.127	That no man *go* to Galis but if he go for euere.	C. 6.350	Now bygynneth glotoun for to *go* to shryfte
B. 4.127	That no man go to Galis but if he *go* for euere.	C. 6.361	Thenne *goth* glotoun in and grete othes aftur.
B. 5.24	He bad wastour *go* werche what he best kouþe	C. 6.394	There was leyhing and louryng and 'lat *go* the coppe!'
B. 5.205	Ne hadde þe grace of gyle *ygo* amonges my [ware]	C. 6.404	And thenne gan he *go* lyke a glemans byche
B. 5.296	Now bigynneþ Gloton for to *go* to shrifte	C. 7.157	To haue grace to *go* to treuthe; god leue þat they mote.
B. 5.306	Thanne *goþ* Gloton In and grete oþes aftir.	C. 7.206	Ȝe mote *go* thorw mekenesse, alle men and wommen,
B. 5.336	There was lauȝynge and lourynge and 'lat *go* þe cuppe!'	C. 7.254	And yf grace graunte the to *go* in [in] this wyse
B. 5.346	And þanne gan he to *go* lik a glemannes bicche.	C. 7.291	Thow myhte gete grace there so thow *go* bytymes.'
B. 5.372	That I, Gloton, girte it vp er I hadde *gon* a myle,	C. 7.296	To *goo* with a good wil and graytheliche hem dryue.
B. 5.512	To haue grace to [to] truþe, [God leue þat þei moten].	C. 8.28	And go hunte hardelyche to hares and to foxes,
B. 5.561	Ye moten þoruȝ mekenesse, boþe men and wyues,	C. 8.138	That no faytrye were founde in folk þat *goth* abeggeth.
B. 5.605	And if grace graunte þee to *go* in [in] þis wise	C. 8.151	And bad hym *go* pisse with his plogh, pyuische shrewe.
B. 5.638	Thow myȝt gete grace þere so þow *go* bityme.'	C. 8.226	And yf þe [g]omes gruche bid[d]e hem *go* and swynke
B. 5.640	I wol *go* fecche my box wiþ my breuettes & a bulle with bisshopes lettres	C. 8.238	*Go* to oure bygynnynge the god the world made,
B. 6.29	And *go* hunte hardiliche to hares and to foxes,	C. 8.245	And abribeth and abeggeth and no man beten his hungur:
B. 6.155	And bad hym *go* pissen with his plowȝ: '[pyuysshe] sherewe!	C. 9.117	And suffreth suche *go* so, it semeth to myn inwyt
B. 6.216	And if þe gomes grucche bidde hem *go* [and] swynke	C. 9.171	And *goen* and fayten with here fauntes for eueremore aftur.
B. 6.232	*Go* to Genesis þe geaunt, engendrour of vs alle:	C. 9.267	For to *go* wurye þe wolf that the wolle fou[l]leth?
B. 6.237	He shal [*go*] begge and bidde and no man bete his hunger.	C. 9.349	That god gyue vs grace here ar we *go* hennes
B. 7.95	And *goon* [and] faiten with [hire] fauntes for eueremoore after.	C.10.57	Ac yf y may lyue and loke y shal *go* lerne bettere.'
B. 7.135	Haue þei no gerner to *go* to but god fynt hem alle.'	C.10.148	And sire go[dfray] *go-wel*, grete lordes alle.
B. 7.203	That god gyue vs grace er we *go* hennes	C.10.223	And bad *go* shapen a ship of shides and bordes.
B. 8.58	Ac if I may lyue and loke I shal *go* lerne bettre.'	C.10.284	Wisely *go* wedde and war fro synne;
B. 9.22	And sire Godefray *Go-wel*, grete lordes [alle].	C.11.42	Is non so hende to haue hym [in] but hote hym *go* þer god is.
B. 9.84	A Iew wolde noȝt se a Iew *go* Ianglyng for defaute	C.11.48	Mony tym[e] mendenauntes myhte *goen* afyngred.
B. 9.94	And biddeþ þe beggere gon for his broke cloþes:	C.11.198	'*Go* y to helle or to heuene y shal nat go myn one.
B. 9.109	Grace to *go* to hem and ofgon hir liflode:	C.11.198	'Go y to helle or to heuene y shal nat *go* myn one.
B. 9.135	"Swiþe *go* shape a ship of shides and of bordes;	C.12.49	And plihte in pauci preueiliche and lette þe remenaunt *go* rome.'
B. 9.183	Wisely *go* wedde and ware [þee] fro synne,	C.12.101	For god, as þe gospel saith, *goth* ay as þe pore
B.10.62	But [hunsen] hym as an hound and hoten hym *go* þennes.	C.12.164	Al þat thow has[t] here hastly *go* and sulle hit;
B.10.66	Mendinauntȝ meteles myȝte *go* to bedde.	C.12.212	And þat his soul shal *go* and [his] goed bileue
B.10.197	Whoso gloseþ as gylours doon, *go* me to þe same,	C.13.53	The marchaunt with his marchauntdyse may nat *go* so swythe
B.10.366	And oure bakkes þat moþeeten be and seen beggeris *go* naked,	C.14.93	And bad hem *go* to Bedlem goddes berthe to honoure
B.11.54	*Go* confesse þee to som frere and shewe hym þi synnes.	C.16.73	And thogh his glotonye be of gode ale he *goth* to a colde beddynge
B.11.114	And plukked in Pauci pryueliche and leet þe remenaunt *go* rome.'	C.16.106	Here fader and alle here frendes and *goth* forth with here paramours:
B.12.16	And þow medlest þee wiþ makynges and myȝtest *go* seye þi sauter,	C.16.284	That thus *goth* here godes at þe laste ende
B.12.149	And bad hem *go* to Bethlem goddes burþe to honoure	C.17.112	*Go* now to eny degre and bote gyle be holde a maistre
B.13.32	'Welcome, wye, *go* and wassh; þow shalt sitte soone.'	C.18.121	To *go* ransake þat ragman and reue hym of his apples
B.13.181	'For I wol *go* wiþ þis gome, if god wol yeue me grace,	C.18.226	Now *go* we to godhede: in god, fader of heuene,
B.14.232	And þouȝ his glotonye be to good ale he *goþ* to cold beddyng	C.18.237	And to godhede *goth* thre and o god is all thre.
B.15.82	*Gooþ* to þe glose of þ[e] vers, ye grete clerkes;	C.19.46	*Go* thy gate!' quod y to spes; 'so me god helpe,
B.15.145	Thus *goon* hire goodes, be þe goost faren.	C.19.64	And dredfully withdrow hym and durste *go* no nerre.
B.15.357	*Go* now to any degree, and but if gile be maister,	C.19.77	'And þat more profit for his medicyne y make the good aȝeynward
B.15.436	And be gide and *go* bifore as a good Banyer,	C.19.249	To *go* semeliche ne sitte, seth holy writ techeth
B.15.444	Til Gregory garte clerkes to *go* here and preche.	C.20.284	Ar we thorw brihtnesse be b[l]ente *go* barre þe ȝates;
B.16.89	To *go* robbe þat Rageman and reue þe fruyt fro hym.	C.20.296	Bothe this lord and this lihte, ys longe *ygo* y knewe hym.
B.17.39	The gome þat *gooþ* wiþ o staf, he semeþ in gretter heele	C.20.328	'For god hath *go*,' quod gobelyne, 'in gome liknesse
B.17.40	Than he þat *gooþ* wiþ two staues to sighte of vs alle;	C.20.470	'Arise and *go* reuerense godes resureccio[n]
B.17.48	*Go* þi gate!' quod I to Spes, 'so me god helpe,	C.21.147	And *goen* into Galilee and gladien his apostlis
B.17.114	And neuere eft greue gome þat *gooþ* þis ilke gate:	C.21.158	*Goynge* toward galilee in godhede and manhede
B.18.357	Graciousliche þi gile haue quyt: *go* gile amende gile!	C.21.213	Thenne bigan grace to *go* with [Peres Plouhman]
B.19.147	And *goon* into Galilee and gladen hise Apostles	C.21.225	Forthy,' quod grace, 'or y *go* y wol gyue ȝow tresor
B.19.158	*Goynge* toward Galilee in godhede and manhede	C.21.300	For gyle *goth* so priueyly þat goed fayth oþer while
B.19.213	[Th]anne bigan grace to *go* wiþ Piers Plowman	C.21.359	To *goen* agayn pruyde bute grace were with vs.'
B.19.225	Forþi,' quod grace, 'er I *go* I wol gyue yow tresor	C.21.392	Al þat we owen eny wyhte or we *go* to hosele?'
B.19.300	For gile *gooþ* so pryuely þat good feiþ ouþer while	C.22.186	'Syre euele yt[a]uȝte Elde,' quod y, 'vnhende *go* with the!
B.19.359	To *goon* agayn Pride but Grace weere wiþ vs.'	C.22.192	And gyued me in gowtes: y may nat *go* at large.
B.19.392	Al þat we owen any wight er we *go* to housel?'	C.22.273	Enuye herde this and heete freres *go* to scole
B.20.186	'Sire yuele ytauȝt Elde!' quod I, 'vnhende *go* wiþ þe!	C.22.305	'*Go* salue tho þat syke [ben] and thorw synne ywounded.'

C.22.341 '3e? *go* thy gate!' quod pees, 'bi god! for al thi fisyk,
C.22.363 And *goeth* gropeth contricion and gaf hym a plastre
C.22.368 Thus he *goeth* and gedereth and gloseth þer he shryueth

gobelyn *gobelin n.* B 1; C 2 gobelyne
B.18.293 For god wol no3t be bigiled', quod *Gobelyn*, 'ne byiaped.
C.20.323 [For] god wol nat be [bi]gyled,' quod *gobelyne*, 'n[e] byiaped.
C.20.328 'For god hath go,' quod *gobelyne*, 'in gome liknesse

gobet n *gobet n.* C 1
C. 5.100 A *gobet* of his grace and bigynne a tyme

god n *God n.(1)* A 96 god (86) goddis (1) godes (1) godis (8); B 290 god (243) goddes (47); C 292 God (231) goddes (27) goddis (2) godes (32)
A.Pr.43 In glotonye, *god* wot, go þei to bedde,
A. 1.44 'Go to þe gospel,' quaþ heo, 'þat *god* seide himseluen,
A. 1.50 "Reddite cesari," quaþ *god*, "þat cesari befall[iþ],
A. 1.85 It is as derworþi a dreury as dere *god* hymseluen.
A. 1.88 He is a *god* be þe gospel on ground & on lofte,
A. 1.156 Of such good as *god* sent goodlyche parteþ,
A. 2.71 Þere to wone wiþ wrong while *god* is in heuene.'
A. 2.84 *God* grauntide to gyue mede to treuþe,
A. 2.85 And þou hast gyuen hire to a gilour, now *god* 3iue þe sorewe!
A. 2.92 3e shuln abigge boþe, be *god* þat me made.
A. 3.8 I wile forgyue hire þe gilt, so me *god* helpe.'
A. 3.53 Ac *god* alle good folk such grauyng defendiþ,
A. 3.58 Neiþer in si3t ne in þi soule, for *god* hymself knowiþ
A. 3.62 Oþer to grede aftir *godis* men whan 3e [g]iue dolis,
A. 3.219 Þat 3e gon of his grace gyueþ in his blisse
A. 3.224 *Godis* mede & his mercy þerwiþ mi3te þou wynne.
A. 3.229 And he þat gripiþ here giftes, so me *god* helpe,
A. 3.240 *God* sente hym to segge be samuels mouþ
A. 3.244 Samuel seide to saul, "*god* sendiþ þe & hotiþ
A. 3.254 *God* seide to samuel þat saul shulde dei3e,
A. 3.257 Þat *god* hati[de him for euere] & alle hise heires aftir.
A. 4.65 'Wiþoute gilt, *god* wot, gat I þis skaþe.'
A. 4.74 '*God* wot,' quaþ wysdom, 'þat were not þe beste.
A. 4.91 'Nay,' quaþ þe king, 'so *god* 3iue me blisse,
A. 4.124 Ne gete my grace þoru3 giftes, so me *god* helpe!
A. 4.157 'I graunte,' quaþ þe king, '*godis* forbode he faille!
A. 5.22 Ac I shal sei3e as I sai3, so me *god* helpe,
A. 5.55 To make mercy for his mysdede betwyn *god* & hym
A. 5.122 It hadde be vnsold þis seue 3er, so me *god* helpe.
A. 5.138 A galoun for a grote, *god* wot no lasse,
A. 5.154 '3a, glotoun gossib,' quaþ heo, '*god* wot, wel hote:
A. 5.221 And made auowe tofore *god* for his foule slouþe:
A. 5.254 To haue grace to seke treuþe; *god* leue þat hy moten!
A. 6.22 'Nay, so [me *god*] helpe,' seide þe [gome] þanne.
A. 6.58 A[nd] nameliche an ydel þe name of *god* almi3t;
A. 6.110 Ac whoso is sib to þis sistris, so me *god* helpe,
A. 6.117 'Wyte *god*,' quaþ a waffrer, 'wiste I þat forsoþe,
A. 7.69 Þei arn askapid good auntir, now *god* hem amende.'
A. 7.74 Let *god* worþe wiþal for so his woord techiþ.
A. 7.118 Þat *god* of his grace 3our greyn multiplie,
A. 7.131 Þei shuln ete as good as I, so me *god* helpe,
A. 7.132 Til *god* of his grace gare h[e]m to arise.
A. 7.193 And it ben my blody breþeren, for *god* bou3te vs alle.
A. 7.213 'I wolde not greue *god*,' quaþ peris, 'for al þe gold on ground.
A. 7.236 *God* 3iueþ [hem] his blissing þat here liflode so wynneþ.'
A. 7.262 'I behote *god*,' quaþ hunger, 'henis nile I wende
A. 8.23 And for þei swere be here soule, & so *god* muste hem helpe,
A. 8.56 Ne wolde neuere holy writ, *god* wot be soþe.
A. 8.58 To waxen & wanyen where þat *god* likiþ.
A. 8.98 But do wel & haue wel, & *god* shal haue þi soule,
A. 8.110 Þat louiþ *god* lelly, his liflode is þe more:
A. 8.117 Haue þei no garner [to go] to, but *god* fynt hem alle.'
A. 8.179 Forþi I counseil alle cristene [to] cri3e *god* mercy,
A. 8.181 Þat *god* 3iue vs grace er we go hennis
A. 9.47 *God* wile suffre þe to dei3e so for þiself hast þe maistrie.'
A. 9.85 And wiþ glad wil doþ hem goode for so *god* [hi3te].
A. 9.102 'Ac 3et sauouriþ me nou3t þi segging, so me *god* helpe;
A.10.29 And þat is þe grete *god* þat gynnyng had neuere,
A.10.48 Aftir þe grace of *god* [þe grettest is Inwyt].
A.10.79 And þat is dred of *god*, dowel it makiþ.
A.10.80 It is begynnyng of goodnesse *god* for to douten.
A.10.94 [And so witnesseþ *goddis* worde and holiwrit boþe]:
A.10.95 Ac 3if þou werchist be *godis* word I warne þe þe beste,
A.10.100 And be glad of þe grace þat *god* haþ Isent þe.
A.10.116 Loke þou grucche nou3t on *god* þei3 he gyue þe litel;
A.10.132 And lyuen as here law[e] wil[e]; it likeþ *god* almi3ty
A.10.160 Ageyns *godis* hest girlis hy geten
A.10.161 Þat *god* was wroþ wiþ here werkis & [suche wordis seide]:
A.10.201 And [þanne] glade 3e *god* þat al good sendiþ.

A.10.215 But 3if *god* [g]iue h[e]m grace here to amende.
A.11.31 For 3if harlotrie ne halp[e] hem betere, haue *god* my trouþe,
A.11.32 More þanne musik, or makyng of *god* almi3t,
A.11.44 And gnawen *god* in [þe gorge] whanne here guttis fullen.
A.11.53 *God* is muche in þe [gorge] of þis grete maistris,
A.11.56 Clerkis and k[ete] men carpen of *god* faste,
A.11.75 Wilneþ neuere to wyte why that *god* wolde
A.11.80 For alle þat wilneþ to wyte þe [whyes] of *god* almi3t,
A.11.82 Þat euere eft wilneþ to wyte why [þat] *god* wolde
A.11.153 And do good a[g]ens euil; *god* hymself hotiþ
A.11.173 Was neuere [gome] vpon þis ground, siþþe *god* makid heuene,
A.11.196 Be þat at euere in þe gospel grauntiþ & techiþ,
A.11.198 Prince ouer *godis* peple to prechen or to chaste.
A.11.215 *Godis* flessh, & his fet, & hise fyue woundis
A.11.240 Ac cristene men, *god* wot, comiþ not so to heuene,
A.11.243 *Godis* word witnessiþ we shuln 3iue & dele
A.11.252 To harme hem ne slen hem *god* hi3te vs neuere,
A.11.266 *God* 3af h[i]m grace & ricchesse togidere
A.11.300 For I shal graunte 3ow grace of *god* þat 3e seruen,
A.11.304 Seide þis for a sarmoun, so me *god* helpe:
A.12.19 'Dauid *godes* derling defendyþ hit also:
A.12.25 And *god* graunted hit neuere; þe gospel hit witnesseþ
A.12.26 In þe passioun, whan pilat aposed *god* almy3thi,
A.12.29 *God* gaf him non answere but gan his tounge holde.
A.12.88 'My3th I so, *god* wot, 3oure gates wolde I holden.'
A.12.111 *God* for his goudnesse gif hem swyche happes
A.12.115 *God* saue hem sound by se and by land.
B.Pr.43 In glotonye, *god* woot, go þei to bedde,
B.Pr.210 Deuyne ye, for I ne dar, by deere *god* in heuene.
B. 1.46 'Go to þe gospel', quod she, 'þat *god* seide hymseluen,
B. 1.52 "Reddite Cesari", quod *god*, "þat Cesari bifalleþ,
B. 1.87 It is as derewerþe a drury as deere *god* hymseluen.
B. 1.90 He is a *god* by þe gospel, a grounde and o lofte,
B. 1.122 Til *god* of his goodnesse [garte þe heuene to stekie]
B. 1.182 [Of] swich good as *god* sent goodliche parteþ,
B. 2.29 My fader þe grete *god* is and ground of alle graces,
B. 2.30 Oo *god* wiþouten gynnyng, and I his goode dou3ter;
B. 2.107 And with hym to wonye [in] wo while *god* is in heuene.'
B. 2.120 *God* graunte[d] to gyue Mede to truþe,
B. 2.121 And þow hast gyuen hire to a gilour, now *god* gyue þee sorwe!
B. 2.128 Ye shul abiggen boþe, by *god* þat me made!
B. 3.8 I wol forgyuen hire þ[e] gilt, so me *god* helpe.'
B. 3.64 Ac *god* alle good folk swich grauynge defendeþ,
B. 3.67 For [*god*] knoweþ þi conscience and þi kynde wille
B. 3.71 Or to greden after *goddes* men whan ye [gyue] doles
B. 3.75 For þus [bit *god* in] þe gospel goode men doon hir almesse.
B. 3.232 That oon *god* of his grace [gyueþ] in his blisse
B. 3.245 Of *god* at a gret nede whan þei gon hennes.
B. 3.250 And he þat gripeþ hir [giftes], so me *god* helpe,
B. 3.261 *God* sente to Saul by Samuel þe prophete
B. 3.264 "Forþi", seide Samuel to Saul, "*god* hymself hoteþ [þ]ee
B. 3.276 *God* seide to Samuel þat Saul sholde deye
B. 3.279 That *god* hated hym for euere and alle hise heires after.
B. 4.37 Thei ne [gy]ueþ no3t of [good feiþ, woot *god* þe so-þe]:
B. 4.79 'Wiþouten gilt, *god* woot, gat I þis scaþe.'
B. 4.87 '*God* woot', quod wisdom, 'þat were no3t þe beste.
B. 4.141 Ne gete my grace [þoru3] giftes, so me *god* [helpe]!
B. 4.194 'I graunte [gladly]', quod þe kyng, '*goddes* forbode [he faile]!
B. 5.22 Ac I shal seye as I sau3, so me *god* helpe,
B. 5.53 Moore þan gold ouþer giftes if ye wol *god* plese;
B. 5.72 To maken mercy for hi[s] mysded[e] bitwene *god* and [hym]
B. 5.91 I wolde be gladder, by *god*! þat Gybbe hadde meschaunce
B. 5.134 I wole amende þis if I may þoru3 my3t of *god* almy3ty.'
B. 5.206 It hadde ben vnsold þis seuen yer, so me *god* helpe.
B. 5.222 A galon for a grote, *god* woot no lesse,
B. 5.261 '*God* lene þee neuere grace] þi good wel to bisette,
B. 5.274 For a[l] þat ha[þ] of þi good, haue *god* my trouþe,
B. 5.283 Nis na moore to þe mercy of *god* þan [amyd] þe see a gleede:
B. 5.369 Sworen *goddes* soule [and his sydes] and "so me god helpe"
B. 5.369 Sworen goddes soule [and his sydes] and "so me *god* helpe"
B. 5.404 *Goddes* peyne and his passion [pure] selde þenke I on.
B. 5.449 And made auow tofore *god* for his foule sleuþe,
B. 5.480 *God*, þat of þi goodnesse [g]onne þe world make,
B. 5.512 To haue grace to go [to] truþe, [*God* leue þat þei moten].
B. 5.534 'Nay, so [*god* glade me]', seide þe gome þanne.
B. 5.563 That ye louen oure lord *god* leuest of alle þynges.
B. 5.571 And-nameliche-on-ydel-þe-name-of-*god*-almy3ty.
B. 5.625 A[c] who is sib to þise [sustren], so me *god* helpe,
B. 5.631 'Wite *god*', quod a waf[erer], 'wiste I þis for soþe
B. 6.77 They ben ascaped auenture, [now] *god* hem amende.'
B. 6.82 Lat-*god*-yworþe-wiþ-al-for-so-his-word-techeþ.
B. 6.126 That *god* of his grace youre greyn multiplie
B. 6.137 [Thei] shal ete [as good as I, so me *god* helpe],

B. 6.138   Til *god* of his [grace gare hem to arise].
B. 6.207   [And it] are my blody breþeren for *god* bou3te vs alle;
B. 6.225   Loue hem and lakke hem no3t; lat *god* take þe vengeaunce;
B. 6.226   Thei3 þei doon yuele lat [þow] *god* yworþe.
B. 6.227   And if þow wilt be gracious to *god* do as þe gospel techeþ
B. 6.229   'I wolde no3t greue *god*', quod Piers, 'for al þe good on grounde!
B. 6.278   '[I] bihote *god*', quod hunger, 'hennes [nil] I wende
B. 6.316   He greueþ hym ageyn *god* and gruccheþ ageyn Reson,
B. 6.331   But [if] *god* of his goodnesse graunte vs a trewe.
B. 7.21   And for þei swere by hir soule and so *god* moste hem helpe
B. 7.56   That neuere shul wexe ne wanye wiþouten *god* hymselue.
B. 7.78   For wite ye neuere who is worþi, ac *god* woot who haþ nede.
B. 7.82   For beggeres borwen eueremo and hir borgh is *god* almy3ty,
B. 7.116   But do wel and haue wel, and *god* shal haue þi soule,
B. 7.128   That loueþ *god* lelly his liflode is ful esy:
B. 7.135   Haue þei no gerner to go to but *god* fynt hem alle.'
B. 7.201   Forþi I counseille alle cristene to crie *god* mercy,
B. 7.203   That *god* gyue vs grace er we go hennes
B. 8.51   *God* wole suffre wel þi sleuþe if þiself likeþ,
B. 8.95   And wiþ glad wille dooþ hem good for so *god* hoteþ.
B. 8.112   'Ac yet sauoreþ me no3t þi seying, [so me *god* helpe!
B. 9.28   And þat is þe grete *god* þat gynnyng hadde neuere,
B. 9.45   And in þis manere was man maad þoru3 my3t of *god* almy3ty,
B. 9.47   And þus *god* gaf hym a goost [of] þe godhede of heuene
B. 9.60   For after þe grace of *god* þe gretteste is Inwit.
B. 9.62   And þat ben glotons, glubberes; hir *god* is hire wombe:
B. 9.65   And alle þat lyuen good lif are lik to *god* almy3ty:
B. 9.66   Allas þat drynke shal fordo þat *god* deere bou3te,
B. 9.67   And dooþ vs forsaken hem þat he shoop to his liknesse:
B. 9.95   He dooþ no3t wel þat dooþ þus, ne drat no3t *god* almy3ty,
B. 9.97   That dredeþ *god*, he dooþ wel; þat dredeþ hym for loue
B. 9.104   And *goddes* gleman and a game of heuene.
B. 9.119   And þus was wedlok ywro3t and *god* hymself it made.
B. 9.127   [For] *god* sente to Se[þ] and seide by an Aungel,
B. 9.132   Til *god* wraþed [wiþ] hir werkes and swich a word seide,
B. 9.157   And al for þei wro3te wedlokes ayein [þe wille of *god*].
B. 9.181   And þanne gete ye grace of *god* and good ynou3 to lyue wiþ.
B. 9.193   A[c] if þei leden þus hir lif it likeþ *god* almy3ty,
B. 9.201   But *god* gyue hem grace here to amende.
B.10.28   Thilke þat *god* [moost gyueþ] leest good þei deleþ,
B.10.38   Or daunted or drawe forþ; I do it on *god* hymselue.
B.10.46   Ne [holpe hir] harlotrye, haue *god* my trouþe.
B.10.58   And gnawen *god* [in] þe gorge whanne hir guttes fullen.
B.10.67   *God* is muche in þe gorge of þise grete maistres,
B.10.70   Clerkes and [kete] men carpen of *god* faste
B.10.79   [For *god* is def nowadayes and deyneþ [no3t vs to here],
B.10.122   Wilneþ neuere to wite why þat *god* wolde
B.10.127   For alle þat wilneþ to wite þe [whyes] of *god* almy3ty,
B.10.129   That euere [eft] wilneþ to wite why þat *god* wolde
B.10.204   And do good a[g]ein yuel; *god* hymself hoteþ.
B.10.206   To do good for *goddes* loue and gyuen men þat asked,
B.10.209   And no3t to greuen hem þat greueþ vs; *god* [þat forbedeþ]:
B.10.230   Was neuere gome vpon þis ground, siþ *god* made [heuene],
B.10.241   On þe grete *god* þat gynnyng hadde neuere,
B.10.246   For al is but oon *god* and ech is god hymselue:
B.10.246   For al is but oon *god* and ech is god hymselue:
B.10.247   *God* þe fader, god þe sone, god holy goost of boþe,
B.10.247   God þe fader, *god* þe sone, god holy goost of boþe,
B.10.247   God þe fader, god þe sone, *god* holy goost of boþe,
B.10.267   *God* in þe gospel [grymly] repreueþ
B.10.277   For *goddes* word wolde no3t be lost, for þat wercheþ euere;
B.10.280   That *goddes* word wercheþ no3t on [wis] ne on lewed
B.10.361   That is, loue þi lord *god* leuest abouen alle,
B.10.370   *God* hoteþ hei3e and lowe þat no man hurte ooþer,
B.10.385   *God* gaf hym grace of wit and alle goodes after
B.10.389   Maistres þat of *goddes* mercy techen men and prechen,
B.10.396   Thou3 hir goost be vngracious *god* for to plese.
B.10.398   In good þan in *god*; forþi hem grace failleþ—
B.10.400   Whan þei shal lif lete [a lippe of *goddes* grace]—
B.10.411   *God* lene it fare no3t so bi folk þat þe feiþ techeþ
B.10.412   Of holi chirche þat herberwe is, and *goddes* hous to saue
B.10.438   In þe hondes of almy3ty *god*, and he woot þe soþe
B.10.447   For soþest word þat euer *god* seide was þo he seide Nemo bonus.
B.10.481   The which is mannes soule to saue, as *god* seiþ in þe gospel:
B.11.38   'And Deus disponit', quod he; 'lat *god* doon his wille.
B.11.118   That vnderfonged me atte font for oon of *goddes* chosene.
B.11.139   For þei beþ, as oure bokes telleþ, aboue *goddes* werkes:
B.11.169   *God* wrou3te it and wroot it wiþ his [owene] fynger,
B.11.197   [Alle my3te haue maad riche men if he wolde],
B.11.206   Of Adames issue and Eue ay til *god* man deide.
B.11.244   Many tyme *god* haþ ben met among nedy peple,
B.11.252   And hastily *god* answerde, and eiþeres wille [lowed],
B.11.254   Ac pouerte *god* putte bifore and preised þe bettre:

B.11.264   Makeþ a man to haue mynde in *god* and a gret wille
B.11.274   And lif moost likynge to *god* as luc bereþ witnesse:
B.11.278   To beggeris þat begge and bidden for *goddes* loue.
B.11.279   For failed neuere man mete þat my3tful *god* serueþ;
B.11.281   To serue *god* goodliche, ne greueþ hym no penaunce:
B.11.288   That if þei trauaille truweliche, and truste in *god* almy3ty,
B.11.307   So is it a goky, by *god*! þat in his gospel failleþ,
B.11.312   The bisshop shal be blamed bifore *god*, as I leue,
B.11.313   That crouneþ swiche *goddes* kny3tes, þat konneþ no3t sapienter
B.11.380   Who suffre[þ] moore þan *god*?' quod he; 'no gome, as I leeue.
B.11.397   The shap ne þe shaft þat *god* shoop hymselue,
B.11.419   The wisedom and þe wit of *god*, he was put fram blisse.
B.12.12   And wiþ þise bittre baleises *god* beteþ his deere children:
B.12.68   Ac grace is a gifte of *god* and of greet loue sprynge þ;
B.12.72   For Moyses witnesseþ þat *god* wroot for to wisse þe peple
B.12.79   Giltier an afore *god*, and gretter in synne,
B.12.85   For *goddes* body my3te no3t ben of breed wiþouten clergie,
B.12.90   Ri3t so *goddes* body, breþeren, but it be worþili taken,
B.12.101   Alþou3 men made bokes [þe maister was *god*]
B.12.149   And bad hem go to Bethlem *goddes* burþe to honoure
B.12.192   The þef þat hadde grace of *god* on good fryday, as þow spek[e],
B.12.194   And grace asked of *god* þat [graiþ is hem euere]
B.12.272   Ac *god* is so good, I hope þat siþþe he gaf hem wittes
B.12.275   That *god* for his grace gyue hir soules reste,
B.12.290   Ne wolde neuere trewe *god* but [trewe] truþe were allowed.
B.13.78   'Ac þis *goddes* gloton', quod I, 'wiþ hise grete chekes
B.13.164   [And ek, haue *god* my soule, and þow wilt it craue
B.13.181   'For I wol go wiþ þis gome, if *god* wol me grace,
B.13.188   'Nay, by crist!' quod Conscience to Clergie, '*god* þee foryelde;
B.13.205   'That is soþ', [seide] Conscience, 'so me *god* helpe.
B.13.244   And I hadde neuere of hym, haue *god* my trouþe,
B.13.256   To haue þe grace of *god*, and no gilt of [þe] pope.
B.13.340   [For] *Goddes* word [ne grace] gaf me neuere boote,
B.13.356   Moore to good þan to *god* þe gome his loue caste,
B.13.384   Hadde I neuere wille, woot *god*, witterly to biseche
B.13.398   Than in þe grace of *god* and hise grete helpes:
B.13.401   As þere no nede was *goddes* name an Idel:
B.13.427   Patriarkes and prophetes, prechours of *goddes* wordes,
B.13.434   Ther wise men were, witnesseþ *goddes* wordes,
B.13.439   Haue beggeres bifore hem þe whiche ben *goddes* minstrales
B.14.8   To agulte *god* or good man by aught þat I wiste,
B.14.20   And engreynen it wiþ good wille and *goddes* grace to amende þe,
B.14.58   Ne deeþ drede [ne deuel], but deye as *god* likeþ
B.14.101   There is Charite þe chief, chaumbrere for *god* hymselue.'
B.14.119   But *god* sente hem som tyme som manere Ioye
B.14.126   Ac *god* is of [a] wonder wille, by þat kynde wit sheweþ,
B.14.128   Ri3t so fareþ *god* by som riche; ruþe me it þynkeþ,
B.14.144   It may no3t be, ye riche men, or Mathew on *god* lyeþ:
B.14.156   That *god* rewarded double reste to any riche wye.
B.14.170   Ac *god*, of þi goodnesse gyue hem grace to amende.
B.14.254   And þou3 Sleuþe suwe pouerte, and serue no3t *god* to paie,
B.14.256   That *god* is his grettest help and no gome ellis,
B.14.264   And for *goddes* loue leueþ al and lyueþ as a beggere.
B.14.273   The which is sib to *god* hymself, [so nei3 is pouerte].'
B.14.274   'Haue *god* my trouþe', quod Haukyn '[I here yow] preise faste
            pouerte.
B.14.321   Now *god* þat alle good gyueþ graunte his soule reste
B.14.328   That [euere he] dide dede þat deere *god* displesed;
B.14.332   'I were no3t worþi, woot *god*', quod haukyn, 'to werien any cloþes,
B.15.9   '*God* loke yow, lordes', ne loutede faire,
B.15.26   And whan I make mone to *god* memoria is my name;
B.15.32   Thanne am I Conscience ycalled, *goddes* clerk and his Notarie;
B.15.66   Of *god* and of hise grete my3tes, hise graces it letteþ.
B.15.93   Thoru3 lele libbynge men þat *goddes* lawe techen,
B.15.130   Wolde neuere þe wit of witty *god* but wikkede men it hadde,
B.15.135   A[c] *goddes* folk for defaute þerof forfaren and spillen.
B.15.146   Ac for goode men, *god* woot, greet doel men maken,
B.15.158   I sei3 neuere swich a man, so me *god* helpe,
B.15.216   For charite is *goddes* champion, and as a good child hende,
B.15.250   And gyue vs grace, goode *god*, charite to folwe.
B.15.255   The mooste liflode he lyueþ by is loue in *goddes* passion;
B.15.260   That þei3 þei suffrede al þis, *god* suffrede for vs moore
B.15.263   For wel may euery man wite, if *god* hadde wold hymselue,
B.15.285   And þou3 þe gome hadde a gest *god* fond hem boþe.
B.15.295   Ac moost þoru3 [meditacion] and mynde of *god* almyghty.
B.15.305   Ac *god* sente hem foode by foweles and by no fierse beestes
B.15.313   For we [by] *goddes* [behestes] abiden alwey
B.15.392   And for hir lyuynge þat lewed men be þe loþer *god* agulten.
B.15.395   And we lered and lewed [bileueþ in oon *god*]
B.15.396   Cristene and vncristene on oon *god* bileueþ].
B.15.407   That þe coluere þat com so com from *god* of heuene
B.15.442   That *goddes* salt sholde be to saue mannes soule.
B.15.482   That is *god* of his grace, gyueþ alle men blisse.

B.15.505	In [o] gre[et] *god*, and his grace asken,
B.15.580	Arn ferme as in þe feiþ, *goddes* forbode ellis,
B.15.606	Arn folk of oon feiþ; þe fader *god* þei honouren.
B.16.9	And so þoruȝ *god* and goode men groweþ þe fruyt Charite.'
B.16.13	'It groweþ in a gardyn', quod he, 'þat *god* made hymselue
B.16.38	Thoruȝ preieres and penaunces and *goddes* passion in mynde
B.16.191	So *god*, þat gynnyng hadde neuere but þo hym good þouȝte,
B.16.200	In menynge þat man moste on o *god* bileue,
B.16.217	Na moore myȝte *god* be man but if þe moder hadde.
B.16.224	Which is þe holy goost of alle, and alle is but o *god*.
B.16.271	The myght of *goddes* mercy þat myȝte vs amende.'
B.17.30	And alle þre but o *god*; þus Abraham me tauȝte;
B.17.48	Go þi gate!' quod I to Spes, 'so me *god* helpe,
B.17.130	And alle þre but o *god*? þus Abraham me tauȝte;
B.17.132	O *god* wiþ al my good, and alle gomes after
B.17.140	For *god* is after an hand; yheer now and knowe it.
B.17.170	So is þe fader a ful *god*, formour and shappere:
B.17.175	And ful *god* as is þe fader, no febler ne no bettre.
B.17.182	So is þe holy goost *god*, neiþer gretter ne lasse
B.17.184	And alle [þre] but o *god* as is myn hand and my fyngres.
B.17.201	For he prikeþ *god* as in þe pawme þat peccat in spiritu[m] sanct[um].
B.17.202	For *god* þe fader is as a fust; þe sone is as a fynger;
B.17.205	*God* þat he grypeþ wiþ, and wolde his grace quenche.
B.17.218	So is [þe] holy goost *god* and grace wiþoute mercy
B.17.252	So is þe holi goost *god* and grace wiþouten mercy
B.17.271	And gyueþ youre good to þat *god* þat grace of ariseþ.
B.17.275	The grace of þe holy goost, *goddes* owene kynde.
B.17.291	Innocence is next *god* and nyght and day it crieþ
B.17.316	Noght of þe nounpower of *god*, þat he ne is myghtful
B.17.348	That is coueitise and vnkyndenesse þat quencheþ *goddes* mercy;
B.18.68	Some seide þat he was *goddes* sone þat so faire deide:
B.18.75	Ac was no bo[y] so boold *goddes* body to touche:
B.18.132	And þat my tale be trewe I take *god* to witnesse.
B.18.184	And þat *god* haþ forgyuen and graunted me, pees, & mercy
B.18.191	[At] þe bigynn[yng *god*] gaf þe doom hymselue
B.18.212	So *god* þat bigan al of his goode wille
B.18.218	Forþi *god*, of his goodnesse, þe firste gome Adam,
B.18.222	And after *god* Auntrede hymself and took Adames kynd[e]
B.18.232	'By *goddes* body', quod þis book, 'I wol bere witnesse
B.18.238	That he was *god* þat al wroȝte þe wolkne first shewed:
B.18.242	The water witnesse[þ] þat he was *god* for he wente on it;
B.18.249	Lo! helle myȝte nat holde, but opnede þo *god* þolede,
B.18.293	For *god* wol noȝt be bigiled', quod Gobelyn, 'ne byiaped.
B.18.298	Wheiþer he were *god* or *goddes* sone; he [g]af me short answere;
B.18.298	Wheiþer he were god or *goddes* sone; he [g]af me short answere;
B.18.308	Wiþ glorie and with gret light; *god* it is, I woot wel.
B.18.355	Getest bi gile þo þat *god* louede;
B.18.427	'[Ariseþ] and reuerence[þ] *goddes* resurexion,
B.18.429	For *goddes* blissede body it bar for oure boote;
B.19.18	Anoon as men nempned þe name of *god* Iesu;
B.19.110	And þere bigan *god* of his grace to do wel:
B.19.116	Bigan *god* of his grace and goodnesse to dowel,
B.19.173	Thow art my lord, I bileue, *god* lord Iesu;
B.19.208	And comeþ fro þe grete *god*; grace is his name.
B.19.291	To suffren al þat *god* sente, siknesse and Angres.
B.19.299	Wiþ *god*, and nauȝt agast but of gile one.
B.19.319	'By *god*! Grace', quod Piers, 'ye moten gyue tymber,
B.19.385	Here is breed yblessed, and *goddes* body þervnder.
B.19.386	Grace, þoruȝ *goddes* word, [g]af Piers power,
B.19.404	Vnblessed artow, Brewere, but if þee *god* helpe.
B.19.419	Forþi', quod þis vicory, 'by verray *god* I wolde
B.19.430	A[c] wel worþe Piers þe plowman þat pursueþ *god* in doynge,
B.20.34	[*God*] gouerneþ alle goode vertues.
B.20.40	And *god* al his grete Ioye goostliche he lefte
B.20.57	And gerte gile growe þere as he a *god* weere.
B.20.226	And brode hoked arwes, *goddes* herte and hise nayles,
B.20.254	That in mesure *god* made alle manere þynges,
B.20.278	For *god* made to men a lawe and Moyses it tauȝte:
B.20.341	'Ye? go þi gate!' quod Pees, 'by *god*! for al þi phisik,
C.Pr.117	*God* was wel þe wrother and took þe raþer vengeance.
C.Pr.121	*God* shal take vengeaunce on alle suche prestis
C.Pr.221	Deuyne ȝe, for y ne dar, by dere *god* almyhten.
C. 1.26	Wykked[ly] wroghte and wrathed *god* almyhty.
C. 1.44	'Go to þe gospel,' quod she, 'and se what *god* sayde
C. 1.46	And *god* askede at hem hoes was þe koyne.
C. 1.48	"Reddite cesari," sayde *god*, "þat cesar[i] byfalleth
C. 1.83	Hit is a[s] derworthe a druerie as dere *god* hymseluen.
C. 1.86	He is a *god* by þe gospel and graunte may hele
C. 1.104	And *god* whan he bigan heuene in þat grete blisse
C. 1.108	He was an Archangel of heuene, on of *goddes* knyghtes;
C. 1.178	Of such good as *god* sent goodliche parte,
C. 2.128	And *god* graunte[de] hit were so so no gyle were,

C. 2.129	And thow has[t] gyue here as gyle tauhte, now *god* ȝeue þe sorwe!
C. 2.131	That *god* wolde were ydo withoute som deseyte.
C. 2.135	"*God* of thy grace heuene gates opene,
C. 2.137	And se[t]he man may [o]n heye mede of *god* diserue
C. 3.8	Y wol forgyue here alle gultes, so me *god* helpe.'
C. 3.68	Ac *god* to alle good folk suche grauynge defendeth,
C. 3.71	For *god* knoweth thi consience [and þy kynde wille,
C. 3.74	*God* in þe gospel suche grauynge nouȝt alloueth:
C. 3.95	That so bigileth hem of here goed, þat *god* on hem sende
C. 3.139	Ȝut y forgyue the þis gult; *godes* forb[o]de eny more
C. 3.324	For *god* gaf salomon grace vpon erthe,
C. 3.326	And as sone as *god* seyh a sewed nat his wille
C. 3.329	So *god* gyueth no [grace] þat "si" [ne] is the glose
C. 3.339	That [is] þe gyft þat *god* gyueth to alle lele lyuynge,
C. 3.354	That is *god*, the ground of al, a gracious antecedent.
C. 3.410	Agaynes *godes* comandement, god tok such a vengeaunce
C. 3.410	Agaynes godes comandement, *god* tok such a vengeaunce
C. 3.414	How *god* sente to sauel be samuel þe prophete
C. 3.417	"Sauel," quod samuel, "*god* hymsulue hoteth [the]
C. 3.428	Otherwyse þen *god* wolde and warnede hym by þe prophete,
C. 3.429	*God* sayde to samuel þat sauel sholde deye
C. 3.432	That *god* [hated hym] for euere and alle [his] eyres aftur.
C. 3.463	Spynne oþer speke of *god* and spille no tyme.
C. 4.37	They gyue n[ouh]t of good fayth, woe[t] *god* the sothe,
C. 4.39	More then for oure lordes loue oþer oure lady, *goddes* moder.'
C. 4.75	'Withouten gult, *god* wot, [ȝat y] this s[c]athe;
C. 4.83	'*God* woot,' quod [wysdom], 'þat were nat the beste.
C. 5.1	Thus y awakede, woet *god*, whan y wonede in Cornehull,
C. 5.22	'Sertes,' y sayde, 'and so me *god* helpe,
C. 5.62	/*God* and good men, as here degre asketh:
C. 5.105	And to þe kyrke y gan go *god* to honoure;
C. 6.16	Haue þe vnbuxum, y byseche *god* of mercy,
C. 6.18	*God* and goode men so gret was myn herte;
C. 6.47	And what y gaf for *godes* loue to gossipus y tolde,
C. 6.61	'Now *god* for his goodnesse gyue the grace to amende,'
C. 6.84	For *god* ne goddes word ne gras helpe me neuere
C. 6.84	For god ne *goddes* word ne gras helpe me neuere
C. 6.92	For thy synnes souereynly and biseke *god* of mercy.'
C. 6.111	On *god* when me greued auht and grochede of his sonde:
C. 6.113	But y hadde weder at my wille y witte *god* þe cause
C. 6.169	And bad hym bid to *god* be his helpe to amende.
C. 6.175	Y, gulty in gost, to *god* y me shryue
C. 6.214	Hit hadde be vnsold this seuene ȝer, so me *god* helpe.
C. 6.273	Hadde y neuere will, [woot *god*], witterly to byseche
C. 6.285	Then in the grace of *god* and in his grete myhte;
C. 6.296	For alle that hauen of thy good, haue *god* my treuthe,
C. 6.306	Then an errant vsurer, haue *god* my treuthe,
C. 6.425	To the, *god*, y glotoun, gulty me ȝelde,
C. 6.427	Sworn *godes* soule and his sides and "so helpe [me] god almyhty"
C. 6.427	Sworn godes soule and his sides and "so helpe [me] *god* almyhty"
C. 6.436	Herof, gode *god*, graunte me forȝeuenesse,
C. 6.438	For y vowe to verray *god*, for hungur or furste,
C. 7.20	*Goddes* payne and his passioun is puyre selde in my thouhte.
C. 7.63	And made [a]uowe tofore *god* for his foule sleuthe:
C. 7.87	Patriarkes and prophetes, precheours of *goddes* wordes,
C. 7.94	There wyse men were, wittnesseth *goddes* wordes,
C. 7.99	Haue beggares beþfore hem þe whiche ben *goddes* mu[n]strals
C. 7.106	And fithele the withoute flaterynge of *god* friday þe [g]este
C. 7.118	For a lythed and louede þat *goddes* lawe despiseth:
C. 7.122	*God* þat of thi goodnesse gonne þe world make
C. 7.150	That euere they gulte aȝeyn þe, *god*, in gost or in dede.'
C. 7.157	To haue grace to go to treuthe; *god* leue þat they mote.
C. 7.179	'Nay, so me *god* [h]elpe,' sayde þe gome thenne,
C. 7.207	Til ȝe come into Consience, yknowe of *god* sulue,
C. 7.218	And-nameliche-an-ydel-þe-name-of-*god*-almyhty.
C. 7.278	And ho is sib to þis seuene, so me *god* helpe
C. 7.285	'Wyte *god*,' quod a wafre[re], 'wiste y this for sothe
C. 8.79	They ben ascaped good aunter, now *god* hem amende.'
C. 8.86	Lat *god* yworthe with al, as holy wryt techeth:
C. 8.132	That *god* [of] his grace ȝoure grayn multiplye
C. 8.135	[We haue] none lymes to labory with, lord *god* we thonketh.'
C. 8.216	And hit are my blody bretherne for *god* bouhte vs alle.
C. 8.235	'Y wolde nat greue [*god*],' quod Peres, 'for al þe good on erthe!
C. 8.238	For oure bygynnynge þo *god* the world made,
C. 8.283	Alle þat gr[eden at] thy gate for *godes* loue aftur fode
C. 8.352	But yf [*god*] of his goodnesse graunte vs a trewe.
C. 9.25	And for they sw[e]re by here soule and [so] *god* mote hem helpe
C. 9.35	Fynde men for *godes* loue and fauntkynes to scole,
C. 9.66	For he þat gyueth for *goddes* loue wolde nat gyue, his thankes,
C. 9.104	Lyuen aȝen *goddes* lawe and þe lore of holi churche
C. 9.115	And to oure syhte as hit semeth; seth *god* hath þe myhte
C. 9.127	And *godes* boys, bourdyors as the book telleth:
C. 9.136	*Godes* munstrals and his mesagers and his mury bordiours

C. 9.138 For vnder *godes* secret seal here synnes ben keuered.
C. 9.158 And lyueth lyke a lollare, *goddes* lawe hym dampneth.
C. 9.179 And alle pore pacient apayed of *goddes* sonde,
C. 9.228 And vppon sonendayes to cese *goddes* seruice to here,
C. 9.290 Bote do wel and haue wel, and [*god*] shal haue thy soule
C. 9.323 Worth fayre vnderfonge byfore *god* þat tyme
C. 9.347 Forthy y consayle alle cristene to crye *god* mercy
C. 9.349 That *god* gyue vs grace here ar we go hennes
C.10.55 Oure lyf to oure lord *god* for oure lycames gultes.'
C.10.99 Ac dobest sholde drede hem nat but do as *god* hihte:
C.10.154 The which is *god* grettest [þat gynnynge hadde] neuere,
C.10.158 And semblable in soule to *god* but if synne hit make.
C.10.162 That *god* [s]eweth nat synnefole men and soffreth hem mysfare,
C.10.164 *God* wol nat of hem wyte bute lat hem yworthe,
C.10.167 Of gold and of oþer goed ac *goddes* grace hem fayleth.
C.10.176 For þat is *goddes* oune goed, his grace and his tresour,
C.10.201 For hoso loueth, leueth h[it] wel, *god* wol nat laton hym sterue
C.10.207 For *god* saith hymsulue, "shal neuere goed appel
C.10.221 And for þe synne of Caymes seed sayede *god* to Noe:
C.10.243 For *god* seid ensaumple of suche manere issue
C.10.249 And *god* sente to seth so sone he was of age
C.10.252 And seth for he soffred hit *god* sayde, "me forthynketh
C.10.287 Awrek þe þerwith on wyfyng, for *godes* werk y holde hit:
C.10.300 Bote *god* ȝeue hem grace her [g]oynge here to amende.
C.11.25 Tho þat *god* most goed ȝeueth greueth most riht and treuthe:
C.11.39 And gnawen *god* with gorge when here gottes f[u]llen.
C.11.42 Is non so hende to haue hym [in] but hote hym go þer *god* is.
C.11.44 *God* is nat in þat hoem ne his helpe nother.
C.11.50 Clerkes and knyhtes carpen of *god* ofte
C.11.59 For *god* is deef nowadayes and deyneth [nat vs] to here
C.11.109 Yf thow hit vse oþer haunte, haue *god* my treuthe,
C.11.141 And byleef lely how *goddes* [l]o[u]e alyhte
C.11.147 Ho was his Autor And hym of *god* tauhte?
C.11.152 And alle thre bote o *god*, and herof he made
C.11.201 Sholde sitte in *goddis* sihte ne se god in his blisse.
C.11.201 Sholde sitte in goddis sihte ne se *god* in his blisse.
C.11.210 *God* gaf hym grace of wit and of goed aftur,
C.11.215 Maistres þat [of *goddis* mercy techen men and prechen]
C.11.224 A[c] me were leuere, by oure lord, a lyppe of *goddes* grace
C.11.227 Thogh here gost be vngracious *god* for to plese.
C.11.229 In goed then in *god*; forthy hem grace faileth.
C.11.232 As holy writ witnesseth, *goddes* word in þe gospel:
C.11.235 Wittnesseth *godes* word þat was neuere vntrewe:
C.11.242 *God* lene hit fare nat so by folk þat þe faith techen
C.11.248 For lewed folk, *goddes* foles and his fre bestes:
C.11.283 Withoute þe gifte of *god* w[it]h grace of fortune.
C.11.304 'Et deus disponit,' quod he; 'la[t] *god* do his wille.
C.12.53 That vnderfeng me at þe fonte for on of *godes* chosene.
C.12.74 They b[e]t[h], as oure bokes telleth, [aboue] *godes* werkes:
C.12.84 *God* of his goodnesse ysei his grete will.
C.12.101 For *god*, as þe gospel saith, goth ay as þe pore
C.12.114 Of Adames issue and Eue ay til *god* man deyede;
C.12.139 And here aytheres wille [hasteliche *god* assoilede
C.12.141 Ac pouerte *god* potte byfore and preuede for þe betere:
C.12.150 Maketh man to haue mynde in *god* and his mercy to craue,
C.12.162 What *god* saide hymsulue to a segg þat he louede:
C.12.163 "Yf thow likest to lyue," quod *god*, "þe lyf þat is parfit,
C.12.178 And by þe grayn þat groweth *god* vs all techeth
C.12.185 And thorw þe grace of *god* and grayn dede [i]n erthe
C.12.200 Yf *god* gyueth hym þe lyf, to haue a goed heruost,
C.12.211 How *god*, as þe gospelle telleth, gyueth [hym] foel to name,
C.13.18 Derworthe and dere *god*, do we so mala",
C.13.92 Ther gareth *god* almsulf and vch a gome knoweth.
C.13.102 That yf th[ey] trauaile treulyche and trist in *god* almyhty
C.13.121 So [is hit] a goky, by *god*! þat in [his] gospel fayleth
C.13.124 The bishop shal be blamed before *god*, as y leue,
C.13.125 That crouneth suche *goddes* knyhtes that conne [nat] sapienter
C.13.168 Dompynges dyuede; 'dere *God*,' y sayde,
C.13.197 Ho soffreth more then *god*?' quod he; 'no gome, as y leue.
C.13.201 So is soffrance souereynliche, so hit be for *godes* loue.
C.13.227 The wisdom and the wit of *god* he was pot out of blisse.
C.14.26 Ac Ar such a wil wexe worcheth *go[d]* sulue
C.14.28 So grace withouten grace of *god* and also gode werkes
C.14.33 So grace is a gifte of *god* and kynde wit a chaunce
C.14.37 For moyses witnesseth þat *god* wroet [in stoen with his fynger;
C.14.46 [Althouh men maden bokes] *God* was here maystre
C.14.69 And do we as dauid techeth for doute of *godes* veniance.
C.14.93 And bad hem go to Bedlem *goddes* berthe to honoure
C.14.131 The thef þat hadde grace of *god* a gode fryday, As thow toldest,
C.14.133 And *god* is ay gracious to alle þat gredeth to hym
C.14.194 Ac *god* is so gode, y hope þat seth he gaf hem wittes
C.14.197 That *god* for his grace gyue here soules reste
C.14.212 Ne wolde neuere trewe *god* bote trewe treuthe were alloued.

C.14.217 For al worth as *god* wol;' and þerwith he vanschede.
C.15.139 And avowe byfore *god* and forsaken hit neuere
C.15.198 As a waf[e]rer with wafres, a[nd] welcome *godes* gestes.
C.15.226 To haue þe grace of *god* and no gulte of þe pope.
C.15.257 Ne d[e]th drede ne deuel, [but] deye as *god* liketh
C.15.277 'Where pouerte and pacience plese more *god* almyhty
C.15.295 Bote *god* sen[t]e hem som tyme sum manere ioye
C.16.94 And thow sleuthe sewe pouerte and serue nat *god* to paye
C.16.96 That *god* is his gretteste helpe and no gome elles
C.16.104 And for *goddes* loue leueth al and lyueth as a beggare.
C.16.156 Now *god* þat al [good] gyueth graunte his soule reste
C.16.186 And when y make mone to *god* Memoria y hatte;
C.16.192 Thenne am y Concience ycald, *goddes* Clerk and his notarie;
C.16.277 Wolde neuere oþerwyse *god* but wikkede men hit hadde,
C.16.308 For drede of *god* þat so goed is and thusgates vs techeth:
C.16.374 To begge or to borwe but of *god* one:
C.17.8 Withoute borwynge or beggynge bote of *god* one,
C.17.35 For wolde neuere faythfull *god* þat freres and monkes
C.17.59 For *god* bad his blessed as þe boek techeth–
C.17.67 He gaf *goddes* men goddes goodes and nat grete lordes
C.17.67 He gaf goddes men *goddes* goodes and nat grete lordes
C.17.81 That *god* coueyteth nat þe coyne þat crist hymsulue printede
C.17.91 Nat in *god* þat he ne is goed and þe grounde bothe;
C.17.131 *God* lereth no lyf to l[eu]e withouten lele cause.
C.17.134 And o *god* þat al bygan with gode herte they honoureth
C.17.141 Loue *god* for he is goed and grounde of alle treuthe;
C.17.142 Loue thyn enemye entierely *goddes* heste to fulfille;
C.17.152 Louen as by lawe of kynde oure lord *god* almyhty.
C.17.179 And sothliche þat *god* sulue in suche a coluere lyknesse
C.17.256 In þe gre[te] *god* and his grace asken
C.17.314 Thorw Moises and Macometh and myhte of *god* þat made al.
C.18.95 Shollen serue for þe lord sulue, and so fareth *god* almyhty.
C.18.148 That he was *god* or godes sone for þat grete wonder;
C.18.148 That he was god or *godes* sone for þat grete wonder;
C.18.203 *God* [that] bigynnyng hadde neuere bote tho hym goed thouhte
C.18.210 O *god* almyhty þat man made and wrouhte
C.18.215 And o *god* almyhty, yf alle men ben of Adam.
C.18.226 Now go we to godhede: in *god*, fader of heuene,
C.18.228 Wh[om] *god* wolde oute of þe wey [d]rawe.
C.18.235 So i[n] *god* [and] godes sone i[s] thre persones, the trinite.
C.18.235 So i[n] god [and] *godes* sone i[s] thre persones, the trinite.
C.18.237 And to godhede goth thre and o *god* is alle thre.
C.18.239 'Hastow ysey this,' y seyde, 'alle thre and o *god*?'
C.18.241 Where *god* [riȝt be my gate cam gangynge a thre];
C.18.242 Y roos vp and reuerensed *god* and riȝt fayre hym grette,
C.18.287 The myhte of *goddes* mercy þat myhte vs alle amende.'
C.19.31 And alle thre bote o *god*; thus abraham bereth witenesse
C.19.38 To godhede but o *god* and on god almyhty
C.19.38 To godhede but o god and on *god* almyhty
C.19.46 Go thy gate!' quod y to spes; 'so me *god* helpe,
C.19.99 And alle thre bote o *god*? thus abraham me tauhte.
C.19.100 And hope afturward of *god* more me toelde
C.19.109 And as Abraham þe olde of o *god* the tauhte
C.19.113 For *god* þat al bygan in bigynnynge of the worlde
C.19.132 So is þe fader o *god*, the fu[r]ste of hem alle
C.19.148 Thus is the holy goste *god*, noyther grettore ne lassore
C.19.150 And alle thre is bote o *god* as myn hoend and my fyngeres.
C.19.167 For he priketh *god* as in [the] paume that peccat in spiritum sanctum.
C.19.168 For [g]o[d] the fader is as þe fust; þe sone is as þe fynger;
C.19.171 *God* þ[at] he gripeth [with] and wolde his grace quenche.
C.19.184 So is þe holi gost *god* and grace withouten mercy
C.19.218 So is þe holy gost *god* and grace withouten mercy
C.19.242 For *godes* tretor he is [to]ld for al his trewe catel
C.19.252 And gyueth ȝoure goed to þat *god* þat grace of aryseth.
C.19.256 The grace of the holy goest, *godes* owene kynde.
C.19.272 Innocence is next *god* and nyht and day hit crieth
C.19.281 Confesse me and crye his grace, *god* þat al made,
C.19.296 And nat of þe nownpower of *god*, þat he ne is ful of myhte
C.19.328 That is coueytise and vnkyndenesse whiche quencheth *godes* mercy
C.20.70 Somme saide he was *godes* sone þat so fayre deyede:
C.20.77 Ac was no boie so bold *godes* body to touche;
C.20.135 And þat my tale [be] trewe y take *god* to witnesse.
C.20.187 And þat *god* hath forgyue and graunted to mankynde
C.20.196 At the bigynnynge *god* gaf the doem hymsulue
C.20.217 Ne hadde *god* ysoffred of som oþer then hymsulue
C.20.221 So *god* þat bigan al of his gode wille
C.20.227 Forthy *god*, of his goednesse, þe furste [gome] Adam,
C.20.231 And aftur *god* auntred hymsulue and toek Adames kynde
C.20.241 'By *godes* body,' quod this boek, 'y wol [b]ere witnesse
C.20.247 That he was *god* þat al wrouhte the welkene furste shewede:
C.20.251 The water witnesseth þat he was *god* for a wente on h[it];

C.20.258   Loo! helle myhte nat holde, bote opened tho *god* tholede
C.20.318   As two *godes*, with god, bothe goed and ille.
C.20.318   As two godes, with *god*, bothe goed and ille.
C.20.323   [For] *god* wol nat be [bi]gyled,' quod gobelyne, 'n[e] byiaped.
C.20.326   And as thowe bigyledest *godes* ymag[e] in goynge of an addre,
C.20.327   So hath *god* bigiled vs alle in goynge of a weye.'
C.20.328   'For *god* hath go,' quod gobelyne, 'in gome liknesse
C.20.331   Where he were *god* or godes sone; he gaf me short answere.
C.20.331   Where he were god or *godes* sone; he gaf me short answere.
C.20.342   With glorie and with [grete] lihte; *god* hit is ich woet wel.
C.20.470   'Arise and go reuerense *godes* resureccio[n]
C.20.473   For *godes* blessed body hit baer for oure bote
C.21.18   Anoon as men nemned þe name of *god* iesu;
C.21.110   And þer bigan *god* of his grace to do wel:
C.21.116   Bigan *god* of his grace and goodnesse to do wel
C.21.173   Thow art my lord, y bileue, *god* lord iesu;
C.21.208   And cometh fro the grete *god*; grace is his name.
C.21.291   To soffre al þat *god* sente, seeknesse and angeres.
C.21.299   With *god* and nat agast bote of gyle one.
C.21.319   'By *god*! grace,' quod [Peres], 'ȝe moet gyue tymber
C.21.385   Here is bred yblessed and *godes* body þervnder.
C.21.386   Grace thorw *godes* word gaf [Peres] power,
C.21.404   Vnblessed art thow, breware, but yf the *god* helpe.
C.21.419   Forthy,' quod this vicory, 'bi verray *god* y wolde
C.21.430   Ac wel worth Peres the plouhman þat pursueth *god* in doyng[e],
C.22.34   *God* gouerneth all gode vertues.
C.22.40   And *god* al his grete ioye goestliche he lefte
C.22.57   And garte gyle [growe] þere as he a *god* were.
C.22.226   And brode hokede Arwes, *goddes* herte and his nayles,
C.22.254   That in mesure *god* made alle [manere] thynges
C.22.278   For *god* made to men a lawe and Moyses hit tauhte:
C.22.341   'ȝe? go thy gate!' quod pees, 'bi *god*! for al thi fisyk,

godchildren n *godchild n.* B 2
B. 9.77   Godfad[er] and godmod[er] þat seen hire *godchildren*
B.10.330 That Gregories *godchildren* [vngodly] despended.

goddes -is > god; gode > good

godefray n prop *n.i.d.* A 1 godefrey; B 2; C 2 Godefray (1) godfray (1)
A.10.21   And sire *godefrey* go wel, grete lordis alle.
B. 5.316 *Godefray* of Garlekhiþe and Griffyn þe walshe
B. 9.22   And sire *Godefray* Go-wel, grete lordes [alle].
C. 6.373   *Godefray* þe garlekmonger and Gryffyth þe walshe
C.10.148 And sire *go[dfray]* go-wel, grete lordes alle.

godes > god,good

godfader n *godfader n.* B 1
B. 9.77   *Godfad[er]* and godmod[er] þat seen hire godchildren

godfray > godefray

godhede n *godhede n.(1)* A 1 godhed; B 3; C 6
A.10.36   ȝaf hym gost of his *godhed* & grauntide hym blisse,
B. 9.47   And þus god gaf hym a goost [of] þe *godhede* of heuene
B.19.158 Goynge toward Galilee in *godhede* and manhede
B.19.197 The goode to *godhede* and to greet Ioye,
C.18.226 Now go we to *godhede*: in god, fader of heuene,
C.18.237 And to *godhede* goth thre and o god is all thre.
C.18.238 Lo! treys encountre treys,' quod he, 'in *godhede* and in manhede.'
C.19.38   To *godhede* but o god and on god almyhty
C.21.158 Goynge toward galilee in *godhede* and manhede
C.21.197 The gode to *godhede* and to grete ioye

godis > god,good

godmoder n *godmoder n.* B 1
B. 9.77   Godfad[er] and *godmod[er]* þat seen hire godchildren

goed(- > good(-; goeld > gold; goen > go

goere n *goer n.* B 1
B. 9.106 Ne his gleman a gedelyng, a *goere* to tauernes.

goest > goost,holy_goost; goestliche > goostly

goyng ger *goinge ger. &> go* A 1 going; B 1; C 3 goynge
A.10.53   Of good speche & [*going*] he is þe begynnere;
B.14.165 Heuene after hir hennes *goyng* þat here han swich defaute.
C.10.300 Bote god ȝeue hem grace her [*g]oynge* here to amende.
C.20.326 And as thowe bigyledest godes ymag[e] in *goynge* of an addre,
C.20.327 So hath god bigiled vs alle in *goynge* of a weye.'

goky n *goki n.& adj.* B 2; C 2
B.11.306 The gome þat gloseþ so chartres for a *goky* is holden.
B.11.307 So is it a *goky*, by god! þat in his gospel failleþ,
C.13.120 The gome þat gloseth so Chartres for a *goky* is halden.
C.13.121 So [is hit] a *goky*, by god! þat in [his] gospel fayleth

gold n *gold n.* A 14; B 22 gold (17) golde (5); C 21 goelde (1) gold (17) golde (3)
A.Pr.34 And gete *gold* wiþ here gle giltes, I trowe.
A.Pr.73 Þus [ȝe gyuen ȝoure] *gold* glotonis to helpe
A. 2.13   In red scarlet robid & ribande wiþ *gold*.
A. 2.109 And bad gile go gyue *gold* al aboute,
A. 2.113 Þo þis *gold* was gyue gret was þe þonking
A. 3.21   Coupis of clene *gold* [and] pecis of siluer,
A. 3.23   Þe leste man of here mayne a mutoun of *gold*.
A. 3.127 And [g]iueþ þe gaileris *gold* & grotis togidere
A. 3.169 And ek grepe my *gold* & gyue it where þe likiþ.
A. 4.82   And profride pees a presaunt al of purid *gold*;
A. 4.113 Neiþer grotis ne *gold* ygraue wiþ kynges coyn,
A. 7.213 'I wolde not greue god,' quaþ peris, 'for al þe *gold* on ground.
A. 7.254 And ek his cloke [of] calabre & þe knoppis of *gold*,
A.11.111 Gladdere þanne þe gleman þat *gold* haþ to ȝifte,
B.Pr.34 And geten *gold* with hire glee [gilt]lees, I leeue.
B.Pr.76 Thus [ye] gyuen [youre] *gold* glotons to [helpe]
B. 2.16   Wiþ Ribanes of reed *gold* and of riche stones.
B. 2.145 And bad gile '[go] gyu[e] *gold* al aboute,
B. 2.149 Tho þis *gold* was ygyue gret was þe þonkyng
B. 3.22   Coupes of clene *gold* and coppes of siluer,
B. 3.24   The leeste man of hire meynee a moton of *golde*.
B. 3.138 And gyueþ þe Gailers *gold* and grotes togidres
B. 3.182 And [ek] griped my *gold* [and] gyue it where þee liked.
B. 4.95   And profrede Pees a present al of pure[d] *gold*,
B. 4.130 Neiþer [grotes ne *gold* ygraue wiþ kynges coyn]
B. 5.53   Moore þan *gold* ouþer giftes if ye wol god plese;
B. 5.248 And wiþ lumbardes lettres I ladde *gold* to Rome;
B. 5.268 For þe beste book in oure hous, þeiȝ brent *gold* were þe leues,
B. 6.270 And his cloke of Calabre [and] þe knappes of *golde*.
B.10.159 Gladder þan þe gleman þat *gold* haþ to ȝifte,
B.15.166 As proud of a peny as of a pound of *golde*,
B.15.543 For coueitise after cros; þe croune stant in *golde*.
B.19.76   Mirre and muche *gold* wiþouten merc[ede] askynge
B.19.88   Rightwisnesse vnder reed *gold*, Resones felawe;
B.19.89   *Gold* is likned to leautee þat laste shal euere
B.20.171 [And] gaf hym *gold* good woon þat gladede his herte,
C.Pr.74 Thus ȝe gyue ȝoure *gold* glotons to helpe
C.Pr.180 Bere beyus of bryghte *gold* aboute here nekkes
C. 2.161 And bade gyle '[g]o gyue *gold* al aboute,
C. 2.165 Tho this *gold* was ygyue grete was the thonkynge
C. 3.23   Coupes of clene *gold* [and] coppes of syluer,
C. 3.25   The leste man of here mayne a motoun of *gold*.
C. 3.176 And gyueth the gaylers *gold* and grotes togederes
C. 3.228 And also gryp[en] my *gold* and gyue hit where þe liked,
C. 4.91   And profrede pees a present al of puyre *golde*.
C. 4.127 Nother ygraue ne vngraue, of *gold* oþer of suluer,
C. 6.246 And with lumbardus lettres le[d]e *gold* to Rome;
C. 6.287 Were y a frere, in good fayth, for al þe *gold* on erthe
C. 9.133 Me [g]yueth hem giftes and *gold* for grete lordis sake.
C.10.167 Of *gold* and of oþer goed ac goddes grace hem fayleth.
C.11.101 Gladdere then [þe] gleman þat *gold* hath to ȝefte
C.16.299 As proud of a peny as of a pounde of *golde*
C.17.205 For couetyse aftur cros; the corone stand in *golde*.
C.21.76   Mirre and moche *gold* withouten merc[ede] askynge
C.21.88   Rihtwisnesse vnder reed *gold*, resones felawe;
C.21.89   *Gold* is likened to lewetee that laste shal euere
C.22.171 And gaef hym *goelde* goed woen þat gladde h[is] hert[e]

gold adj *gold adj.* B 2; C 1 golde
B. 2.11   Fetisliche hire fyngres were fretted with *gold* wyr
B.15.545 That in grotes is ygraue and in *gold* nobles.
C.17.207 That in grotes is graue and in *golde* nobles.

goliardeis n *goliardeis n.* B 1
B.Pr.139 Thanne greued hym a *Goliardeis*, a gloton of wordes,

gome n1 *gome n.(1)* A 5 gom (1) gome (2) gomes (2); B 19 gome (14) gomes (5); C 13 gome (9) gomes (2) gomus (2)
A. 2.56   Þus begynne þe *gomes* & gredde wel heiȝe:
A. 6.22   'Nay, so [me god] helpe,' seide þe [*gome*] þanne.
A. 7.202 And ȝif þe [g]*omes* grucche bidde hem gon & sywnke.
A.11.173 Was neuere [*gome*] vpon þis ground, siþþe god makid heuene,
A.12.69   'Go we forþ,' quod þe *gom*, 'I haue a gret boyste
B. 2.74   [Th]us bigynnen þ[e] *gomes* [and] greden [wel] heiȝe:
B. 5.367 'I, Gloton', quod þe [*gome*], 'gilty me yelde
B. 5.534 'Nay, so [god glade me]', seide þe *gome* þanne.
B. 6.216 And if þe *gomes* grucche bidde hem go [and] swynke
B.10.230 Was neuere vpon þis ground, siþ god made [heuene],
B.11.306 The *gome* þat gloseþ so chartres for a goky is holden.
B.11.380 Who suffre[þ] moore þan god?' quod he; 'no *gome*, as I leeue.
B.13.181 'For I wol go wiþ þis *gome*, if god wol yeue me grace,
B.13.299 And if he gyueþ ouȝt to pouere *gomes*, telle what he deleþ;

B.13.356 Moore to good þan to god þe *gome* his loue caste,
B.14.256 That god is his grettest help and no *gome* ellis,
B.15.222 And as gladliche he it gaf to *gomes* þat it neded.
B.15.285 And þouȝ þe gretteste hadde a best god fond hem boþe.
B.17.39   The *gome* þat gooþ wiþ o staf, he semeþ in gretter heele
B.17.88   And graunted hym to ben his [*gome*]; 'graunt mercy', he seide;
B.17.114 And neuere eft greue *gome* þat gooþ þis ilke gate:
B.17.132 O god wiþ al my good, and alle *gomes* after
B.18.218 Forþi god, of his goodnesse, þe firste *gome* Adam,
B.19.121 That he þoruȝ grace was gete and of no *gome* ellis.
C.Pr.44   In glotonye þ[o] *gomus* goth þei to bedde
C. 7.179 'Nay, so me god [h]elpe,' sayde þe *gome* thenne,
C. 8.226 And yf þe [g]omes gruche bid[d]e hem go and swynke
C.10.236 The gospel is hereagayn, as *gomus* may rede:
C.13.92   Ther god is gateward hymsulf and vch a *gome* knoweth.
C.13.120 The *gome* þat gloseth so Chartres for a goky is halden.
C.13.197 Ho soffreth more then god?' quod he; 'no *gome*, as y leue.
C.16.96   That god is his gretteste helpe and no *gome* elles
C.16.307 Ne þat eny *gome* wolde gyle [ne greue oþere]
C.16.347 And also gladliche he hit gaf to *gomes* þat hit nedede.
C.20.227 Forthy god, of his goodnesse, þe firste [*gome*] Adam,
C.20.328 'For god hath go,' quod gobelyne, 'in *gome* liknesse
C.21.121 That he thorw grace was gete and of no *gome* elles.

gome n2 *gome n.(4)* C 1
C.19.15   This was the tyxt trewly; y toek ful good *gome*.

gommes n *gomme n.* A 1; B 1; C 1
A. 2.188 For he coude on here craft & kneuȝ manye *gommes*.
B. 2.229 For he couþe [on] hir craft and knew manye *gommes*.
C. 2.239 For a can on here craft and knoweth manye *gommes*.

gomus > gome; gon(e > go; gonne(n > gynneþ

gonnes n *gonne v.* C 1
C.20.291 Setteth bo[w]es of brake and brasene *gonnes*

goo > go

good n *god n.(2)* A 18 good (6) goode (5) goodis (2) gode (2) godis (3); B
  60 good (31) goode (14) goodes (15); C 62 gode (11) godes (14) goed
  (21) good (11) goode (3) goodes (2)
A. 1.156 Of such *good* as god sent goodlyche parteþ,
A. 2.96   And mede is a mulere, [a maiden of *gode*];
A. 3.156 Such a maister is mede among men of *goode*.'
A. 3.210 Prestis þat preche þe peple to *goode*
A. 3.248 Loke þou kille þe king; coueite nouȝt hise *godis*;
A. 4.108 And do it in dede to drawe vs to *goode*;
A. 4.139 'Whoso wilneþ hire to wyue for welþe of hire *godis*,
A. 5.103 'Ȝis, redily,' quaþ repentaunce & redde hym to *goode*:
A. 6.119 'Ȝis,' quaþ peris þe plouȝman & pukide hym to *goode*;
A. 8.51   Counfortiþ hym in þat cas, coueitiþ nouȝt his *goodis*;
A. 9.35   Þe *goodis* of þis ground be lik þe grete wawes,
A. 9.85   And wiþ glad wil doþ hem *good* for so god [hiȝte].
A.10.52   He eggiþ eiȝe siȝt & heryng to *goode*;
A.10.188 Or wedde any wydewe for any wele of *godis*,
A.10.201 And [þanne] glade ȝe god þat al *good* sendiþ.
A.10.211 Vngracious to gete loue or any *good* ellis,
A.11.153 And do *good* a[g]ens euil; god hymself hotiþ
A.11.248 And ȝiuen hem of oure *good* as good as oureseluen,
B.Pr.182 A Mous þat muche *good* kouþe, as me [þo] þouȝte,
B. 1.182 [Of] swich *good* as god sent goodliche parteþ,
B. 2.76   That Mede is ymaried moore for hire *goodes*
B. 2.132 And Mede is muliere, a maiden of *goode*;
B. 3.169 Swich a maister is Mede among men of *goode*.'
B. 3.223 Preestes þat prechen þe peple to *goode*
B. 3.343 Wiþouten Mede doþ hem good and þe truþe helpeþ,
B. 4.163 'Whoso wilneþ hire to wif for welþe of hire *goodes*,
B. 5.43   And dooþ it in dede, it shal drawe yow to *goode*.
B. 5.126 'Ȝis! redily', quod Repentaunce and radde hym to [*goode*]:
B. 5.261 'God lene þee neuere grace] þi *good* wel to bisette,
B. 5.274 For a[l] þat ha[þ] of þi *good*, haue god my trouþe,
B. 5.287 For þe *good* þat þow hast geten bigan al wiþ falshede,
B. 5.295 And what he lente yow of oure lordes *good* to lette yow fro synne.'
B. 5.634 'Ȝis!' quod Piers þe Plowman, and poked [hym] to *goode*,
B. 6.229 'I wolde noȝt greue god,' quod Piers, 'for al þe *good* on grounde!
B. 8.39   The *goodes* of þis grounde arn like þe grete wawes,
B. 8.95   And wiþ glad wille dooþ hem *good* for so god hoteþ.
B. 9.89   Whi [ne wol] we cristene of cristes *good* be as kynde?
B. 9.163 [For] *goode* sholde wedde goode, þouȝ þei no good hadde;
B. 9.163 [For] goode sholde wedde *goode*, þouȝ þei no good hadde;
B. 9.163 [For] goode sholde wedde goode, þouȝ þei no *good* hadde;
B. 9.167 Or wedden any wodewe for [wele] of hir *goodes*
B. 9.181 And þanne gete ye grace of god and *good* ynouȝ to lyue wiþ.
B. 9.197 Vngracious to gete *good* or loue of þe peple,
B.10.28   Thilke þat god [moost gyueþ] leest *good* þei deleþ,

B.10.30   Harlotes for hir harlotrie may haue of hir *goodes*,
B.10.75   That folk is·noȝt fermed in þe feiþ ne free of hire *goodes*
B.10.84   But in gaynesse and glotonye forglutten hir *good*
B.10.87   And lordeþ in [ledes] þe lasse *good* he deleþ.
B.10.204 And do *good* a[g]ein yuel; god hymself hoteþ:
B.10.206 To do *good* for goddes loue and gyuen men þat asked,
B.10.385 God gaf hym grace of wit and alle *goodes* after
B.10.398 In *good* þan in god; forþi hem grace failleþ–
B.10.441 And be allowed as he lyued so; for by luþere men knoweþ þe
            goode.
B.11.53   'Haue no conscience', [quod she],'how þow come to *goode*;
B.11.72   That wedde none widwes but for to welden hir *goodes*.
B.11.247 And as pouere pilgrymes preyed mennes *goodes*.
B.11.382 Ac he suffreþ for som mannes *goode*, and so is oure bettre.
B.12.263 So is þe riche [reuerenced] by reson of hise *goodes*.
B.13.356 Moore to *good* þan to god þe gome his loue caste,
B.13.369 Thoruȝ gile to gaderen þe *good* þat ich haue.
B.13.386 For losse of *good*, leue me, þan for likames giltes;
B.13.397 That my mynde ne was moore on my *good* in a doute
B.14.169 Of þe *good* þat þow hem gyuest ingrati ben manye;
B.14.246 For pouerte haþ but pokes to putten in hise *goodes*
B.14.321 Now god þat alle *good* gyueþ graunte his soule reste
B.15.104 And be kynde as bifel for clerkes and curteise of cristes *goodes*,
B.15.134 So harlotes and hores arn holpe wiþ swiche *goodes*
B.15.140 And [nempneþ hym] a nygard þat no *good* myȝte aspare
B.15.145 Thus goon hire *goodes*, be þe goost faren.
B.15.175 Coueiteþ he noon erþely *good*, but heueneriche blisse.'
B.16.110 And sike and synfulle boþe so] to *goode* turnede:
B.17.132 O god wiþ al my *good*, and alle gomes after
B.17.271 And gyueþ youre *good* to þat god þat grace of ariseþ.
B.18.279 Body and soule beþ myne, boþe *goode* and ille.
B.19.104 And som tyme he gaf *good* and grauntede heele boþe.
B.19.197 The *goode* to godhede and to greet Ioye,
B.19.440 And worshiped be he þat wroȝte al, boþe *good* and wikke,
B.20.289 And maken hym murie wiþ ooþer mennes *goodes*.
C.Pr.199 A mous þat moche *good* couthe, as me tho thoughte,
C. 1.24   And drynke þat doth the *good*–a[c] drynke nat out of tyme.
C. 1.178 Of such *good* as god sent goodliche parte,
C. 2.35   Shal haue grace to *good* ynow and a good ende,
C. 2.148 And mede is moylore, [a] mayden of *gode*;
C. 3.95   That so bigileth hem of here *goed*, þat god on hem sende
C. 3.215 Such a maistre is mede among men of *goode*.'
C. 3.366 In whiche ben *gode* and nat gode, and graunte here n[eyther] will.
C. 3.366 In whiche ben gode and nat *gode*, and graunte here n[eyther] will.
C. 4.158 'Hoso wilneth here to wy[u]e for welthe of here *goodes*
C. 6.258 'With false wordes and w[ittes] haue y ywonne my *godes*
C. 6.275 For lo[s] of *good*, leef me, then for lycames gultes.
C. 6.284 That my muynde ne was more [o]n my *godes* in a doute
C. 6.296 For alle that hauen of thy *good*, haue god my treuthe,
C. 6.341 For thow hast no *good*, by good fayth, to gete the with a wastel.
C. 6.342 For the *good* that thow hast gete bygan al with falshede
C. 7.287 'Ȝus!' quod [Perus] þe [plouhman], and pokede hem alle to *gode*,
C. 8.144 Such poore,' quod [Peres], 'shal parte with my *godes*,
C. 8.235 'Y wolde nat greue [god],' quod Peres, 'for al þe *good* on erthe!
C. 8.250 And ledares for here laboryng ouer al þe lordes *godes*;
C. 9.15   Merciable to meke and mylde to þe *gode*
C. 9.31   And wyckede wayes with here *goed* amende
C. 9.135 Welcomen and worschipen and with ȝoure *goed* helpen
C.10.45   The *godes* of this grounde ar like þe grete wawes
C.10.94   And halie with þe hoked ende [i]lle men to *gode*
C.10.167 Of gold and of oþer *goed* ac goddes grace hem fayleth.
C.10.176 For þat is goddes oune *goed*, his grace and his tresour,
C.10.254 For *goode* sholde wedde goode thouh they no goode hadde
C.10.254 For goode sholde wedde *goode* thouh they no goode hadde
C.10.254 For goode sholde wedde goode thouh they no *goode* hadde
C.10.261 Bote he haue oþer *goed* haue wol here no ryche.
C.10.296 Vngracious to gete *goed* or loue of [þe] peple,
C.10.307 The more he is worthy and worth, of wyse and *goed* ypresed.'
C.11.25   Tho þat god most *goed* ȝeueth greueth most riht and treuthe:
C.11.55   That folk is nat ferme[d] in þe faith ne fre of here *godes*
C.11.64   Bote in gaynesse and glotonye forglotten here *godes*
C.11.67   And lordeth in ledes the lasse *goed* he deleth
C.11.70   And is to mene no more bote "who[so] muche *goed* wéldeth
C.11.75   Bote lythen how þey myhte lerne leest *go[e]d* spene.
C.11.210 God gaf hym grace of wit and of *goed* aftur,
C.11.229 In *goed* then in god; forthy hem grace faileth.
C.11.305 All þat treuth attacheth and testifieth for *goed*
C.12.5   [Haue no consience how þou come to *good*]; confesse the to som
            frere.
C.12.20   That wilneth nat þe wedewe bote for to welde here *godes*.
C.12.212 And þat his gost shal go and [his] *goed* bileue
C.12.238 That fals folk fecche aweye felonliche his *godes*;
C.12.242 And so is many man ymorthred for his moneye and his *godes*

C.13.4   And ay þe lengere they lyuede the lasse *goed* they hadde:
C.13.73   Tythen here *goed* tre[u]liche, a tol, as hit semeth,
C.14.164 Of *goed* and of wykke kynde was þe furste;
C.16.86   For pouerte hath bote pokes to potten in his *godes*
C.16.156 Now god þat al [*good*] gyueth graunte his soule reste
C.16.257 And be corteys and kynde of holy kyrke *godes*,
C.16.284 That thus goth here *godes* at þe laste ende
C.17.67   He gaf goddes men goddes *goodes* and nat grete lordes
C.19.252 And gyueth ȝoure *goed* to þat god þat grace of aryseth.
C.20.301 Body and soule beth myne, bothe *gode* and ille.
C.20.318 As two godes, with god, bothe *goed* and ille.
C.21.104 And som tyme he gaf *goed* and graunted hele bothe;
C.21.197 The *gode* to godhede and to grete ioye
C.21.440 And worschiped be he þat wrouhte all, bothe *gode* and wicke.
C.22.289 And maken hym murye with oþere menne *godes*.

good adj *god adj*. A 24 good (17) goode (4) gode (3); B 94 good (71)
goode (23); C 90 gode (27) goed (28) good (26) goode (9)
A.Pr.105 *Goode* gees & gris; go we dyne, go we!'
A. 1.34   Al is not *good* to þe gost þat þe gut [ask]iþ,
A. 2.32   And become a *good* man for any coueitise, I rede.'
A. 2.119 Þat he[o] grauntiþ to gon wiþ a *good* wille
A. 3.53   Ac god alle *good* folk such grauyng defendiþ,
A. 3.159 Þe king grauntide hire grace wiþ a *good* wille:
A. 4.88   I forgyue hym þ[at] gilt wiþ a *good* wille;
A. 5.78   His grace & hise *gode* happis greuide me wel sore.
A. 5.148 And Betoun þe breustere bad h[ym] *good* morewe,
A. 5.152 'I haue *good* ale, gossib,' quaþ heo; 'glotoun, wilt þou assaie?'
A. 5.167 Ȝeue glotoun wiþ glad chiere *good* ale to hansele.
A. 6.19   And souȝt *goode* seintes for my soule hele.'
A. 6.82   Grace hattiþ þe [gateward], a *good* man forsoþe,
A. 7.69   Þei arn askapid *good* auntir, now god hem amende.'
A. 7.131 Þei shuln ete as *good* as I, so me god helpe,
A. 7.285 Wiþ *good* ale & glotonye h[y] gart hym to slepe.
A. 9.52   And [g]iue þe grace on þis erþe in *good* lif to ende'.
A. 9.87   Is hokid at þat on ende to holde men in *good* lif.
A.10.53   Of *good* speche & [going] he is þe begynnere,
A.11.170 I grette þe *goode* man as þe gode wyf me tauȝte,
A.11.170 I grette þe goode man as þe *gode* wyf me tauȝte,
A.11.204 Gregory þe grete clerk, a *good* pope in his tyme,
A.11.279 A *goode* friday, I fynde, a feloun was saued
A.12.75   Þer bad me hunger haue *gode* day but I helde me stille;
B.Pr.227 *Goode* gees and grys! go we dyne, go we!'
B. 1.36   [Al is nouȝt] *good* to þe goost þat þe gut askeþ,
B. 2.30   Oo god wiþouten gynnyng, and I his *goode* douȝter;
B. 2.155 That she graunteþ to goon wiþ a *good* wille
B. 3.64   Ac god alle *good* folk swich grauynge defendeþ,
B. 3.75   For þus [bit god in] þe gospel *goode* men doon hir almesse.
B. 3.172 The kyng graunted hire grace wiþ a *good* wille.
B. 4.37   Thei ne [gy]ueþ noȝt of [*good* feiþ, woot god þe sooþe]:
B. 4.101 I forgyue hym þat gilt wiþ a *good* wille
B. 5.98   His grace and his *goode* happes greuen me [wel] soore.
B. 5.166 Seint Gregory was a *good* pope and hadde a good forwit:
B. 5.166 Seint Gregory was a good pope and hadde a *good* forwit:
B. 5.265 For were I frere of þat hous þer *good* feiþ and charite is
B. 5.273 That þow hast maad ech man *good* I may þee noȝt assoille:
B. 5.285 For þow hast no *good* ground to gete þee wiþ a wastel
B. 5.298 [Ac] Beton þe Brewestere bad hym *good* morwe
B. 5.302 'I haue *good* Ale, gossib', quod she, 'Gloton, woltow assaye?'
B. 5.318 Geue Gloton wiþ glad chere *good* ale to hanselle.
B. 5.488 On *good* fryday for mannes sake at ful tyme of þe daye;
B. 5.531 And souȝt *goode* Seintes for me soul[e] hel[e].'
B. 5.595 Grace hatte þe gateward, a *good* man for soþe;
B. 6.77   They ben ascaped *good* auenture, [now] god hem amende.'
B. 6.137 [Thei] shal ete [as *good* as I, so me god helpe],
B. 6.301 Wiþ *good* Ale as Gloton taȝte [bei] garte [hym to] slepe.
B. 7.76   Ac Gregory was a *good* man and bad vs gyuen alle
B. 8.61   And ȝyue yow grace on þis grounde *goode* men to worþe'.
B. 8.97   Is hoked [at] þat oon ende to [holde men in *good* lif].
B. 9.65   And alle þat lyuen *good* lif are lik to god almyȝty:
B.10.227 [I] grette þe *goode* man as [þe goode wif] me tauȝte,
B.10.227 [I] grette þe goode man as [þe *goode* wif] me tauȝte,
B.10.298 Gregorie þe grete clerk and þe *goode* pope
B.10.420 On *good* Friday, I fynde, a felon was ysaued
B.10.443 And who were a *good* man but if þer were som sherewe?
B.10.444 Forþi lyue we forþ wiþ [liþere] men; I leue fewe ben *goode*,
B.11.111 This was hir teme and hir text–I took ful *good* hede–
B.11.297 That haþ no lond ne lynage riche ne *good* loos of hise handes.
B.12.30   Feiþ, hope and Charite, and alle ben *goode*,
B.12.60   Ac grace ne groweþ noȝt [til *good* wil yeue reyn];
B.12.155 Why I haue told [þee] al þis, I took ful *good* hede
B.12.192 The þef þat hadde grace of god on *good* fryday, as þow spek[e],
B.12.202 So it fareþ by þat felon þat a *good* friday was saued;
B.12.272 Ac god is so *good*, I hope þat siþþe he gaf hem wittes

B.13.73   And greue þerwiþ [þat *goode* ben]–ac gramariens shul re[d]e:
B.13.192 The *goode* wil of a wight was neuere bouȝt to þe fulle,
B.13.234 I haue no *goode* giftes of þise grete lordes
B.13.361 And menged his marchaundise and made a *good* moustre:
B.13.446 And fiþele þee wiþoute flaterynge of *good* friday þe [geste],
B.13.448 To crie a largesse bifore oure lord, youre *good* loos to shewe.
B.14.8   To agulte god or *good* man by aught þat I wiste,
B.14.20   And engreynen it wiþ *good* wille and goddes grace to amende þe,
B.14.232 And þouȝ his glotonye be to *good* ale he goþ to cold beddyng
B.14.281 Thanne is it *good* by good skile, al þat agasteþ pride.
B.14.281 Thanne is it good by *good* skile, al þat agasteþ pride.
B.14.318 And sobretee swete drynke and *good* leche in siknesse.
B.15.58   And þe moore þat a man of *good* matere hereþ,
B.15.146 Ac for *goode* men, god woot, greet doel men maken,
B.15.147 And bymeneþ *goode* meteȝyueres and in mynde haueþ
B.15.169 He is glad wiþ alle glade and *good* til alle wikkede
B.15.216 For charite is goddes champion, and as a *good* child hende,
B.15.250 And gyue vs grace, *goode* god, charite to folwe.
B.15.350 The merk of þat monee is *good* ac þe metal is feble;
B.15.424 Grace sholde growe and be grene þoruȝ hir *goode* lyuynge,
B.15.434 So is mannes soule, sooþly, þat seeþ no *goo[d]* ensampl[e]
B.15.436 And be gide and go bifore as a *good* Banyer,
B.15.437 And hardie hem þat bihynde ben, and ȝyue hem *good* euidence.
B.16.9   And so þoruȝ god and *goode* men groweþ þe fruyt Charite.'
B.16.194 So god, þat gynnyng hadde neuere but þo hym *good* þouȝte,
B.17.14   This was þe txite, trewely; I took ful *good* yeme.
B.17.80   'What he spendeþ moore [for medicyne] I make þee *good* herafter,
B.17.106 And [may] ech man see and *good* mark take
B.17.242 Mercy for his mekenesse wol maken *good* þe remenaunt.
B.17.281 For euery manere *good* [man may] be likned
B.17.283 And who[so] morþereþ a *good* man, me þynkeþ, by myn Inwit,
B.17.315 *Good* hope, þat helpe sholde, to wanhope torneþ.
B.17.352 *Good* wille, good word [boþe], wisshen and willen
B.17.352 Good wille, *good* word [boþe], wisshen and willen
B.18.69   And some seide he was a wicche; '*good* is þat we assaye
B.18.108 Now youre *goode* dayes arn doon as daniel prophecied;
B.18.161 So shal grace that bigan [al] make a *good* [ende
B.18.162 And bigile þe gilour, and þat is *good*] sleighte:
B.18.212 So god þat bigan al of his *goode* wille
B.18.339 That gilours be bigiled and þat is *good* reson:
B.18.347 And þat grace gile destruye *good* feiþ it askeþ.
B.18.351 Falsliche and felonliche; *good* feiþ it tauȝte
B.19.270 Gregori þe grete clerk and [þe *goode* Ierom]:
B.19.300 For gile goþ so pryuely þat *good* feiþ ouþer while
B.19.325 And þerwiþ Grace bigan to make a *good* foundement,
B.20.28   And greue men gretter þan *good* feiþ it wolde.
B.20.34   [God] gouerneþ alle *goode* vertues.
B.20.131 And garte *good* feiþ flee and fals to abide,
B.20.167 And Elde hente *good* hope and hastiliche he shifte hym
B.20.171 [And] gaf hym gold *good* woon þat gladede his herte,
B.20.180 And in hope of his heele *good* herte he nam
B.20.223 Than I do to drynke a drauȝte of *good* ale.'
C.Pr.29   In hope to haue a *good* ende and heuenriche blisse.
C.Pr.231 *Goode* gees and grys! ga we dyne, ga we!'
C. 1.34   Al is nat *good* to þe gost þat þe gott ascuth
C. 2.35   Shal haue grace to good ynow and a *good* ende,
C. 2.171 That he graunteþ to go with a *goode* wille
C. 3.68   Ac god to alle *good* folk suche grauynge defendeth,
C. 3.92   That bygyleth *goode* men and greueth hem wrongly,
C. 3.103 And *goode* mennes for here gultes gloweth on fuyr aftur.
C. 3.218 The kyng grauntede here grace with a *goode* wille:
C. 3.303 And Gylours gyuen byfore and *goode* men at þe ende
C. 3.340 Grace of *good* ende and gret ioye aftur:
C. 4.37   They gyue n[ouh]t of *good* fayth, woe[t] god the sothe,
C. 5.62   /God and *good* men, as here degre asketh·
C. 5.192 And no grace [to] graunte til *good* loue were
C. 6.18   God and *goode* men so gret was myn herte;
C. 6.102 Graunte me, *gode* lord, grace of amendement.'
C. 6.260 Meddeled my marchaundyse and made a *good* mostre.
C. 6.287 Were y a frere, in *good* fayth, for al þe gold on erthe
C. 6.337 Of alle manere men þat [mid] *goode* wille
C. 6.341 For thow hast no good, by *good* fayth, to gete the with a wastel.
C. 6.353 By betene hous the brewestere þat bad hym *good* morwen
C. 6.357 'Y haue *good* ale, gossip Glotoun, woltow assaye?'
C. 6.375 Geuen glotoun with glad chere *good* ale to hansull.
C. 7.108 To crye a largesse tofore oure lord ȝoure *good* loos to shewe.
C. 7.176 [And] souht *gode* seyntes for my soule helthe.'\
C. 7.243 Grace hatte þe gateward, a *goed* man for sothe;
C. 7.296 To goo with a *good* wil and graytheliche hem dryue.
C. 8.79   They ben ascaped *good* aunter, now god hem amende.'
C. 8.323 And thenne gloton with *gode* ale garte hunger slepe.
C. 9.50   Shal haue grace of a *good* ende and greet ioye aftur.

C. 9.71 Ac þat most neden aren oure neyhebores and we nyme *gode* he[d]e,
C. 9.111 With a *good* will, witteles, mony wyde contreyes
C.10.60 And gyue me grace on þis grounde with *good* ende to deye.'
C.10.207 For god saith hymsulue, "shal neuere *goed* appel
C.10.260 A mayde and wel yma[ner]ed and of *gode* men yspronge,
C.11.60 And *gode* men for oure gultes he al togrynt to deth.
C.11.217 Were wonder *goed* and wisest in here tyme
C.11.252 A *gode* friday, y fynde, a feloun was ysaued
C.11.302 Lewede men in *good* bileue and lene hem at here nede.'
C.12.45 Of here teme and here tales y took ful *good* hede;
C.12.200 Yf god gyueth hym þe lyf, to haue a *goed* heruost,
C.13.29 Bothe t[w]o ben *gode*, be ȝe ful certeyn,
C.13.111 That hath n[o] lond ne lynage ryche ne *good* los of his handes.
C.14.24 Ac grace ne groweth nat til *gode* wil gyue reyne
C.14.25 And w[o]ky thorw *gode* werkes wikkede hertes.
C.14.28 So grace withouten grace of god and also *gode* werkes
C.14.99 Why y haue tolde [the] al þis, y toek ful *gode* hede
C.14.131 The thef þat hadde grace of god a *gode* fryday, As thow toldest,
C.14.141 So hit f[areth] by þe feloun þat a *goed* fryday was saued:
C.14.194 Ac god is so *gode*, y hope þat seth he gaf hem wittes
C.15.208 Y haue no *gode* giftes of thise grete lordes
C.15.214 [For] lordes and lorelles, luther and *gode*,
C.16.73 And thogh his glotonye be of *gode* ale he goth to a colde beddynge
C.16.121 Thenne is [hit] *goed* by *goed* skill, thouh hit greue a litel,
C.16.121 Thenne is [hit] *goed* by *goed* skill, thouh hit greue a litel,
C.16.193 And when y wol do or [nat do] *gode* dedes or ille
C.16.308 For drede of god þat so *goed* is and thusgates vs techeth:
C.17.58 With þat ȝoure bernes and ȝoure bloed by *goed* lawe may clayme!
C.17.74 And to a badde peny with a *gode* printe:
C.17.91 Nat in god þat he ne is *goed* and þe grounde bothe;
C.17.134 And o god þat al bygan with *gode* herte they honoureth
C.17.141 Loue god for he is *goed* and grounde of alle treuthe;
C.18.12 And þerof cometh a *goed* fruyt þe wiche men calleth werkes
C.18.83 Why groweth this fruyt in thre degres?' 'A *goed* skil,' he saide.
C.18.86 And thenne aboue is bettere fruyt, ac bothe two ben *gode*,
C.18.203 God [that] bigynnyng hadde neuere bote tho hym *goed* thouhte
C.19.15 This was the tyxt trewly; y toek ful *good* gome.
C.19.77 'And þat more goth for his medicyne y make the *good* aȝeynward
C.19.208 Mercy for his mekenesse wol maky *good* þe remenaunt.
C.19.262 For euery manere *goed* man may be likned to a torche
C.19.264 And hoso morthereth a *goed* man, me thynketh bi myn inwit,
C.19.295 For *goed* hope, that helpe scholde, to wanhope turneth
C.19.332 *Goed* wil, goed word bothe, wischen and wilnen
C.19.332 Goed wil, *goed* word bothe, wischen and wilnen
C.20.71 And somme saide, 'he can of soercerie; *goed* is þat we assaie
C.20.111 Now ben ȝoure *gode* dayes ydoen, as daniel of ȝow telleth;
C.20.164 So shal grace þat bigan al maken a *goed* ende
C.20.165 And bigile þe gilour, and þat is *goed* sleythe:
C.20.221 So god þat bigan al of his *gode* wille
C.21.270 Gregory the grete Clerk and [þe *gode* Ieroem];
C.21.300 For gyle goth so priueyly þat *goed* fayth oþer while
C.21.325 And þerwith grace bigan to make a *goode* fo[un]dement
C.22.28 And greue men grettore then *goed* faith hit w[o]lde.
C.22.34 God gouerneth all *gode* vertues.
C.22.131 And gert *goed* faith fle and fals to abyde
C.22.167 And elde hente *gode* hope and hastiliche [he] sh[ifte] hym
C.22.171 And gaef hym goelde *goed* woen þat gladde h[is] hert[e]
C.22.180 And in hope of his hele *goed* herte he hente
C.22.223 Then y do to drynke a drauht of *goed* ale.'

good adv *god adv.* A 2; B 1; C 1
A.Pr.57 Gloside þe gospel as h[e]m *good* likide;
A.11.248 And ȝiuen hem of oure good as *good* as oureseluen,
B.Pr.60 Glosed þe gospel as hem *good* liked;
C.Pr.58 Glosede þe gospel as hem *good* likede;

goodliche adv *godli adv.(2)* A 1 goodlyche; B 2; C 2 goodliche (1) goodly (1)
A. 1.156 Of such good as god sent *goodlyche* parteþ,
B. 1.182 [Of] swich good as god sent *goodliche* parteþ,
B.11.281 To serue god *goodliche*, ne greueþ hym no penaunce:
C. 1.178 Of such good as god sent *goodliche* parte,
C.11.136 Y grette hym *goodly* and graythly y hym tolde

goodnesse n *godnesse n.(2)* A 4 goodnesse (3) goudnesse (1); B 10; C 9 goednesse (2) goodnesse (7)
A. 3.20 Of here grete *goodnesse*, & [g]af hem ichone
A. 5.219 For is no [g]ilt here so gret þat his *goodnesse* nis more'.
A.10.80 It is begynnyng of *goodnesse* god for to douten.
A.12.111 God for his *goudnesse* gif hem swyche happes
B. 1.122 Til god of his *goodnesse* [garte þe heuene to stekie]
B. 3.21 Of hire grete *goodnesse*, and gaf hem echone
B. 5.447 For is no gilt here so gret þat his *goodnesse* [i]s moore.'

B. 5.480 God, þat of þi *goodnesse* [g]onne þe world make,
B. 6.331 But [if] god of his *goodnesse* graunte vs a trewe.
B.14.170 Ac god, of þi *goodnesse* gyue hem grace to amende.
B.16.62 The ground þere it groweþ, *goodnesse* it hatte;
B.18.218 Forþi god, of his *goodnesse*, þe firste gome Adam,
B.19.116 Bigan god of his grace and *goodnesse* to dowel,
B.19.267 And Grace gaf Piers of his *goodnesse* foure stottes,
C. 3.22 Of here grete *goodnesse* and gaf hem vchone
C. 6.61 'Now god for his *goodnesse* gyue the grace to amende,'
C. 7.61 For is no gult [here] so greet þat his *goodnesse* is more.'
C. 7.122 God þat of thi *goodnesse* gonne þe world make
C. 8.352 But yf [god] of his *goodnesse* graunte vs a trewe.
C.12.84 God of his *goodnesse* ysey his grete will.
C.20.227 Forthy god, of his *goodnesse*, þe furste [gome] Adam,
C.21.116 Bigan god of his grace and *goodnesse* to do wel,
C.21.267 And grace [gaef Peres of his *goednesse*] foure stottes,

goon > go

goos n *gos n.* A 3 gees; B 3 gees; C 5 gees (4) goos (1)
A.Pr.105 Goode *gees* & gris; go we dyne, go we!'
A. 4.38 'Boþe my *gees* & my gris hise gadelynges fecchen;
A. 7.265 Noþer *gees* ne gris, but two grene chesis,
B.Pr.227 Goode *gees* and grys! go we dyne, go we!'
B. 4.51 'Boþe my *gees* and my grys hise gadelynges feccheþ,
B. 6.281 Neiþer *gees* ne grys, but two grene cheses,
C.Pr.231 Goode *gees* and grys! ga we dyne, ga we!'
C. 4.49 'Bothe my *gees* and my grys and my g[r]as he taketh.
C. 5.19 Heggen or harwen or swyn or *gees* dryue
C. 8.303 Noþer *gees* ne gries but two grene cheses,
C.15.67 Brawen and bloed of *gees*, bacon and colhoppes.

goost n *gost n.* &> *holy_goost* A 2 gost; B 5; C 6 goest (1) gost (5)
A. 1.34 Al is not good to þe *gost* þat þe gut [ask]iþ,
A.10.36 ȝaf hym *gost* of his godhed & grauntide hym blisse,
B. 1.36 [Al is nouȝt] good to þe *gost* þat þe gut askeþ,
B. 9.47 And þus god gaf hym a *goost* [of] þe godhede of heuene
B.10.396 Thouȝ hir *goost* be vngracious god for to plese.
B.15.145 Thus goon hire goodes, be þe *goost* faren.
B.18.431 May no grisly *goost* glide þere it [shadweþ].'
C. 1.34 Al is nat good to þe *gost* þat þe gott ascuth
C. 6.175 Y, gulty in *gost*, to god y me shryue
C. 7.150 That euere they gulte aȝeyn þe, god, in *gost* or in dede.'
C.11.227 Thogh here *gost* be vngracious god for to plese.
C.12.212 And þat his *gost* shal go and [his] goed bileue
C.20.475 May no grisly *goest* glyde þer hit shaddeweth.'

goostly adj *gostli adj.* B 2
B.15.573 And feden hem wiþ *goostly* foode and [nedy folk to fynden]
B.15.576 Bodily foode and *goostly* foode to] gyue þere it nedeþ:

goostliche adv *gostli adv.* B 1; C 1 goestliche
B.20.40 And god al his grete Ioye *goostliche* he lefte
C.22.40 And god al his grete ioye *goestliche* he lefte

gooþ > go

gorge n *gorge n.* A 2; B 2; C 1
A.11.44 And gnawen god in [þe *gorge*] whanne here guttis fullen.
A.11.53 God is muche in þe [*gorge*] of þis grete maistris,
B.10.58 And gnawen god [in] þe *gorge* whanne hir guttes fullen.
B.10.67 God is muche in þe *gorge* of þise grete maistres,
C.11.39 And gnawen god with *gorge* when here gottes f[u]llen.

gospel n *gospel n.* A 7; B 15; C 12 gospel (10) gospell (1) gospelle (1)
A.Pr.57 Gloside þe *gospel* as h[e]m good likide;
A. 1.44 'Go to þe *gospel*,' quaþ heo, 'þat god seide himseluen,
A. 1.88 He is a god be þe *gospel* on ground & on lofte,
A. 8.113 Ne soliciti sitis he seiþ in his *gospel*,
A.11.196 Be þat god in þe *gospel* grauntiþ & techiþ:
A.11.263 Or ellis [vn]writen for wykkid as witnessiþ þe *gospel*:
A.12.45 And god graunted hit neuere; þe *gospel* hit witnesseþ
B.Pr.60 Glosed þe *gospel* as hem good liked;
B. 1.46 'Go to þe *gospel*', quod she, 'þat god seide hymseluen,
B. 1.90 He is a god by þe *gospel*, a grounde and o lofte,
B. 3.75 For þus [bit god in] þe *gospel* goode men doon hir almesse.
B. 5.54 For whoso contrarieþ truþe, he telleþ in þe *gospel*,
B. 6.227 And if þow wilt be gracious to god do as þe *gospel* techeþ
B. 7.131 Ne soliciti sitis he seiþ in þe *gospel*,
B. 9.148 The *gospel* is hera[g]ein o degre, I fynde,
B.10.113 "Of þat [ye] clerkes vs kenneþ of crist by þe *gospel*:
B.10.267 God in þe *gospel* [grymly] repreueþ
B.10.281 But in swich manere as Marc meneþ in þe *gospel*:
B.10.481 The which is mannes soule to saue, as god seiþ in þe *gospel*,
B.11.89 'They wole aleggen also', quod I, 'and by þe *gospel* preuen:
B.11.307 So is it a goky, by god! þat in his *gospel* failleþ,

B.12.63   And þoruȝ þe gifte of þe holy goost as þe *gospel* telleþ:

C.Pr.58   Glosede þe *gospel* as hem good likede;

C. 1.44   'Go to þe *gospel*,' quod she, 'and se what god sayde

C. 1.86   He is a god by þe *gospel* and graunte may hele

C. 3.74   God in þe *gospel* suche grauynge nouȝt alloueth:

C.10.236   The *gospel* is hereagayn, as gomus may rede:

C.10.242   Ac þe *gospel* is a glose ther and huydeth þe grayth treuthe;

C.11.232   As holy writ witnesseth, goddes word in þe *gospel*:

C.12.30   Thei wolle allegge also and by þe *gospel* preuen:

C.12.101   For god, as þe *gospel* saith, goth ay as þe pore

C.12.211   How god, as þe *gospelle* telleth, gyueth [hym] foel to name,

C.13.98   As þe ryche man for al his mone, and more as by þe *gospell*:

C.13.121   So [is hit] a goky, by god! þat in [his] *gospel* fayleth

gossib n *godsibbe n.* A 2; B 1; C 2 gossip (1) gossipus (1)

A. 5.152   'I haue good ale, *gossib*,' quaþ heo; 'glotoun, wilt þou assaie?'

A. 5.154   'ȝa, glotoun *gossib*,' quaþ heo, 'god wot, wel hote:

B. 5.302   'I haue good Ale, *gossib*', quod she, 'Gloton, woltow assaye?'

C. 6.47   And what y gaf for godes loue to *gossipus* y tolde,

C. 6.357   'Y haue good ale, *gossip* Glotoun, woltow assaye?'

gost > goost, holy_goost; goste > holy_goost; goth goþ > go

goþelen v *gothelen v.* B 2 goþele (1) goþelen (1); C 2 gothelen (1) gothly (1)

B. 5.340   Hise guttes bigonne to *goþelen* as two gredy sowes;

B.13.89   And þanne shullen hise guttes *goþele* and he shal galpen after.

C. 6.398   His gottes gan to *gothly* as t[w]o g[re]dy sowes,

C.15.96   And thenne shal [his gottes *gothelen*] and [he shal] galpe [after].

gott(es > gut; goudnesse > goodnesse; goune(s > gowne

goutes n *goute n.(1)* B 1; C 1 gowtes

B.20.192   And gyued me in *goutes*: I may noȝt goon at large.

C.22.192   And gyued me in *gowtes*: y may nat go at large.

gouerne v *governen v.* A 1; B 3 gouerne (2) gouerneþ (1); C 2 gouerne (1) gouerneth (1)

A. 3.261   Þat resoun shal regne & reumes *gouerne*,

B. 3.285   That Reson shal regne and Reaumes *gouerne*,

B. 5.51   And er he gyue any grace *gouerne* first hymselue.

B.20.34   [God] *gouerneþ* alle goode vertues.

C. 3.438   That resoun shal regne and reumes *gouerne*

C.22.34   God *gouerneth* all gode vertues.

gowne n *goune n.* B 2 gowne (1) gownes (1); C 2 goune (1) gounes (1)

B.13.227   [Ac] fewe robes I fonge or furrede *gownes*.

B.15.167   And is as glad of a *gowne* of a gray russet

C.15.201   And fewe robes y fonge or forrede *gounes*.

C.16.300   And as glad of a *goune* of a gray russet

gowtes > goutes

grace n *grace n.* A 31; B 108 grace (105) graces (3); C 113 grace (112) graces (1)

A. 1.77   Þanne I knelide on my knes & criȝide hire of *grace*;

A. 1.176   Þat is þe lok of loue þat letiþ out my *grace*

A. 2.1   ȝet knelide I on my knes & criȝede hire of *grace*,

A. 3.97   Ac I forgyue þe þe gilt & graunte þe [my] *grace*;

A. 3.159   Þe king grauntide hire *grace* wiþ a good wille:

A. 3.219   Þat on god of his *grace* gyueþ in his blisse

A. 4.59   For boþe þi lyf & þi lond liþ in his *grace*.'

A. 4.124   Ne gete my *grace* þoruȝ giftes, so me god helpe!

A. 5.78   His *grace* & hise gode happis greuide me wel sore.

A. 5.121   Ne hadde [þe] *grace* of gile gon among my ware

A. 5.218   And beet þiself on þe brest & bidde hym of *grace*,

A. 5.237   Þo dismas my broþer besouȝte þe of *grace*,

A. 5.254   To haue *grace* to seke treuþe; god leue þat hy moten!

A. 6.82   *Grace* hattiþ þe [gateward], a good man forsoþe,

A. 6.92   And ȝif *grace* graunte þe to gon in [on] þis wise,

A. 6.103   And geten it aȝen þoruȝ *grace* & þoruȝ no gift ellis.

A. 6.114   To gete ingang at any gate but *grace* be þe more.'

A. 6.123   Þou miȝt gete *grace* [þere] so þou go be tyme.'

A. 7.118   Þat god of his *grace* ȝour greyn multiplie,

A. 7.132   Til god of his *grace* gare h[e]m to arise.

A. 8.181   Þat god ȝiue vs *grace* er we go hennis

A. 9.52   And [g]iue þe *grace* on þis erþe in good lif to ende'.

A. 9.95   And putten hem þere in penaunce wiþoute pite or *grace*,

A.10.48   Aftir þe *grace* of god [þe grettest is Inwyt].

A.10.100   And be glad of þe *grace* þat god haþ Isent þe.

A.10.129   For loue of here louȝnesse oure lord ȝiueþ hem *grace*

A.10.215   But ȝif god [g]iue h[e]m *grace* here to amende.

A.11.99   In signe þat I shulde beseke hire of *grace*.

A.11.143   For þere þat loue is lord lakkiþ neuere *grace*.

A.11.266   God ȝaf h[i]m *grace* & ricchesse togidere

A.11.300   For I shal graunte ȝow *grace* of god þat ȝe seruen,

B. 1.79   Thanne I [kneled] on my knees and cried hire of *grace*;

B. 1.202   [Th]at is þe lok of loue [þat] leteþ out my *grace*

B. 2.1   YEt [kneled I] on my knees and cried hire of *grace*,

B. 2.29   My fader þe grete god is and ground of alle *graces*,

B. 3.108   But I forgyue þee þ[e] gilt and graunte þee my *grace*;

B. 3.172   The kyng graunted hire *grace* wiþ a good wille.

B. 3.232   That oon god of his *grace* [gyueþ] in his blisse

B. 4.73   For boþe þi lif and þi lond lyþ in his *grace*.'

B. 4.141   Ne gete my *grace* [þoruȝ] giftes, so me god [helpe]!

B. 5.51   And er he gyue any *grace* gouerne first hymselue.

B. 5.98   His *grace* and his goode happes greuen me [wel] soore.

B. 5.152   [That] I ne moste folwe this folk, for swich is my *grace*.

B. 5.205   Ne hadde þe *grace* of gyle ygo amonges my [ware]

B. 5.261   'God lene þee neuere *grace*| þi good wel to bisette,

B. 5.290   Ber it to þe Bisshop, and bid hym of his *grace*

B. 5.446   And beet þiself on þe brest and bidde hym of *grace*,

B. 5.465   Tho Dysmas my broþer bisouȝte [þee] of *grace*

B. 5.478   'I shal biseche for alle synfulle oure Saueour of *grace*

B. 5.512   To haue *grace* to go [to] truþe, [God leue þat þei moten].

B. 5.595   *Grace* hatte þe gateward, a good man for soþe;

B. 5.605   And if *grace* graunte þee to go in [in] þis wise

B. 5.617   And [gete it ayein þoruȝ] *grace* [ac þoruȝ no gifte ellis].

B. 5.629   To geten ing[o]ng at any gate but *grace* be þe moore.'

B. 5.638   Thow myȝt gete *grace* þere so þow go bityme.'

B. 6.126   That god of his *grace* youre greyn multiplie

B. 6.138   Til god of his [*grace* gare hem to arise.

B. 6.228   And biloue þee amonges [lowe] men: so shaltow lacche *grace*.'

B. 7.203   That god gyue vs *grace* er we go hennes

B. 8.61   And ȝyue yow *grace* on þis grounde goode men to worþe'.

B. 8.105   And putten hem þer in penaunce wiþoute pite or *grace*],

B. 9.48   And of his grete *grace* graunted hym blisse,

B. 9.60   For after þe *grace* of god þe gretteste is Inwit.

B. 9.103   And siþþe to spille speche þat [spire] is of *grace*

B. 9.109   *Grace* to go to hem and ofgon hir liflode:

B. 9.181   And þanne gete ye *grace* of god and good ynouȝ to lyue wiþ.

B. 9.201   But god gyue hem *grace* here to amende.

B.10.146   In signe þat I sholde bisechen hire of *grace*.

B.10.191   For þere þat loue is ledere lakke[þ] neuere *grace*.

B.10.348   Ther riche men no riȝt may cleyme but of ruþe and *grace*.'

B.10.385   God gaf hym *grace* of wit and alle goodes after

B.10.398   In good þan in god; forþi hem *grace* failleþ–

B.10.400   Whan þei shal lif lete [a lippe of goddes *grace*]–

B.10.457   Whan man was at meschief wiþoute þe moore *grace*.

B.11.149   Graunted [me worþ] *grace* [þorȝ his grete wille].

B.11.408   [Th]anne seide I to myself, '[slepyng hadde I *grace*]

B.12.59   Ac *grace* is a gras þer[for] þo greuaunces to abate.

B.12.60   Ac *grace* ne groweþ noȝt [til good wil yeue reyn];

B.12.68   Ac *grace* is a gifte of god and of greet loue spryngeþ;

B.12.112   Buxomliche and benigneliche and bidden it of *grace*.

B.12.192   The þef þat hadde *grace* of god on good fryday, as þow spek[e],

B.12.194   And *grace* asked of god þat [graiþ is hem euere]

B.12.275   That god for his *grace* gyue hir soules reste,

B.13.181   'For I wol go wiþ þis gome, if god wol yeue me *grace*,

B.13.256   To haue þe *grace* of god, and no gilt of [þe] pope.

B.13.340   [For] Goddes word [ne *grace*] gaf me neuere boote,

B.13.398   Than in þe *grace* of god and hise grete helpes:

B.14.20   And engreynen it wiþ good wille and goddes *grace* to amende þe,

B.14.63   As holy writ witnesseþ whan men seye wiþ *graces*:

B.14.170   Ac god, of þi goodnesse gyue hem *grace* to amende.

B.15.66   Of god and of hise grete myȝtes, hise *graces* it letteþ.

B.15.250   And gyue vs *grace*, goode god, charite to folwe.

B.15.424   *Grace* sholde growe and be grene þoruȝ hir goode lyuynge,

B.15.482   That is god of his *grace*, gyueþ alle men blisse.

B.15.505   In [o] gre[et] god, and his *grace* asken.

B.15.514   Men myȝte noȝt be saued but þoruȝ mercy and *grace*,

B.16.51   And palleþ adoun þe pouke pureliche þoruȝ *grace*

B.17.205   God þat he grypeþ wiþ, and wolde his *grace* quenche.

B.17.218   So is [þe] holy goost god and *grace* wiþoute mercy

B.17.225   Graunte no *grace* ne for[g]ifnesse of synnes

B.17.233   So *grace* of þe holy goost þe grete myȝt of þe Trinite

B.17.252   So is þe holi goost god and *grace* wiþouten mercy

B.17.271   And gyueþ youre good to þat god þat *grace* of ariseþ.

B.17.275   The *grace* of þe holy goost, goddes owene kynde.

B.17.301   Confesse me and crye his *grace*, [crist] þat al made,

B.17.313   [Drede of desperacion [þanne] dryueþ awey *grace*

B.18.90   For þe dede þat I haue doon I do me in youre *grace*.

B.18.130   And *grace* of þe holy goost; weex greet wiþ childe;

B.18.161   So shal *grace* that bigan [al] make a good [ende

B.18.347   And þat *grace* gile destruye good feiþ it askeþ.

B.18.353   So þat þoruȝ gile þow gete þoruȝ *grace* it is ywonne.

B.18.362   And my *grace* to growe ay gretter and widder.

B.18.386   And if lawe wole I loke on hem it liþ in my *grace*

B.19.30   Ac to be conquerour called, þat comeþ of special *grace*,

B.19.110   And þere bigan god of his *grace* to do wel:

B.19.116   Bigan god of his *grace* and goodnesse to dowel,
B.19.121   That he þoruȝ *grace* was gete and of no gome ellis.
B.19.131   And alle he heeled and halp þat hym of *grace* askede;
B.19.208   And comeþ fro þe grete god; *grace* is his name.
B.19.212   And cride wiþ Conscience, 'help vs, [crist], of *grace*!'
B.19.213   [Th]anne bigan *grace* to go wiþ Piers Plowman
B.19.215   'For I wole dele today and [dyuyde] *grace*
B.19.225   Forþi', quod *grace*, 'er I go I wol gyue yow tresor
B.19.227   And gaf ech man a *grace* to gide wiþ hymseluen
B.19.233   And by wit to wissen oþere as *grace* hem wolde teche.
B.19.252   'Thouȝ some be clenner þan some, ye se wel', quod *Grace*,
B.19.262   *Grace* gaf Piers a teeme, foure grete Oxen.
B.19.267   And *Grace* gaf Piers of his goodnesse foure stottes,
B.19.274   And *Grace* gaf [Piers] greynes, Cardynal[es] vertues,
B.19.317   'Ayeins þi greynes', quod *Grace*, 'bigynneþ for to ripe,
B.19.319   'By god! *Grace*', quod Piers, 'ye moten gyue tymber,
B.19.321   And *Grace* gaf hym þe cros, wiþ þe [garland] of þornes
B.19.325   And þerwiþ *Grace* bigan to make a good foundement,
B.19.329   And whan þis dede was doon *Grace* deuysede
B.19.359   To goon agayn Pride but *Grace* weere wiþ vs.'
B.19.386   *Grace*, þoruȝ goddes word, [g]af Piers power,
B.19.425   And *Grace* þat þow gr[e]dest so of, gyour of alle clerkes;
B.20.140   'Allas!' quod Conscience and cryde, 'wolde crist of his *grace*
B.20.386   And siþþe he gradde after *Grace* til I gan awake.
C. 1.76   Thenne y knelede on my knees and criede here of *grace*
C. 1.197   Þat is þe lok of loue [þat] vnloseth *grace*
C. 1.200   And þe graffe of *grace* and gray[th]est way to heuene.
C. 2.1   And thenne y kneled [o]n my knees and cried here of *grace*,
C. 2.35   Shal haue *grace* to good ynow and a good ende,
C. 2.135   "God of thy *grace* heuene gates opene,
C. 2.247   And putte hem thorw appeles in þe popes *grace*.
C. 3.100   Graunte gylours on erthe *grace* to amende
C. 3.135   And monye a gulte y haue þe forgyue & my *grace* graunted
C. 3.218   The kyng grauntede here *grace* with a goode wille:
C. 3.324   For god gaf salomon *grace* vpon erthe,
C. 3.329   So god gyueth no [*grace*] þat "si" [ne] is the glose
C. 3.331   Bothe gyue and graunte there his *grace* lyketh
C. 3.340   *Grace* of good ende and gret ioye aftur:
C. 4.138   Ne gete my *grace* thorw eny gyfte ne glosynge spe[ch]e
C. 5.98   Suche a wynnyng hym warth thorw w[y]rdes of *grace*:
C. 5.100   A gobet of his *grace* and bigynne a tyme
C. 5.192   And no *grace* [to] graunte til good loue were
C. 6.61   'Now god for his goodnesse gyue þe *grace* to amende,'
C. 6.83   To the soutere of southewerk, suche is his *grace*.
C. 6.102   Graunte me, gode lord, *grace* of amendement.'
C. 6.213   Ne hadde þe *grace* of Gyle go among my ware
C. 6.285   Then in the *grace* of god and in his grete myhte;
C. 6.319   Tho dysmas my brother bisouhte [þe] of *grace*
C. 6.345   Bere hit to th[e] bischop and bide hym of *grace*
C. 7.60   And bete thysulue [o]n þe breste and bidde hym of *grace*
C. 7.120   'Y shal byseke for alle synnefole oure sauiour of *grace*
C. 7.157   To haue *grace* to go to treuthe; god leue þat they mote.
C. 7.243   *Grace* hatte þe gateward, a goed man for sothe;
C. 7.248   Biddeth amende-ȝow meke [hym] to his maistre *grace*
C. 7.251   A ful leel lady vnlek hit of *grace*
C. 7.254   And yf *grace* graunte the to go in [in] this wyse
C. 7.269   And geten hit agayne thorw *grace* Ac thorw no gifte elles.
C. 7.282   To geten ingang at eny ȝate bote *grace* be þe more.'
C. 7.291   Thow myhte gete *grace* there so thow go bytymes.'
C. 8.132   That god [of] his *grace* ȝoure grayn multiplye
C. 9.50   Shal haue *grace* of a good ende and greet ioye aftur.
C. 9.55   For hit is symonye to sulle þat sent is of *grace*,
C. 9.206   And carteres knaues and Clerkes withouten *grace*,
C. 9.349   That god gyue vs *grace* here ar we go hennes
C.10.60   And gyue me *grace* on þis grounde with good ende to deye.'
C.10.167   Of gold and of oþer goed ac goddes *grace* hem fayleth
C.10.176   For þat is goddes oune goed, his *grace* and his tresour,
C.10.210   Out of matrimonye, nat moyloure, mowen nat haue þe *grace*
C.10.300   Bote god ȝeue hem *grace* her [g]oynge here to amende.
C.11.84   Semyng þat y sholde bysechen here of *grace*.
C.11.206   Or p[resci]t inparfit, pult out of *grace*,
C.11.210   God gaf hym *grace* of wit and of goed aftur,
C.11.224   A[c] me were leuere, by oure lord, a lyppe of goddes *grace*
C.11.229   In goed then in goed; forthy hem *grace* faileth.
C.11.283   Withoute þe gifte of god w[it]h *grace* of fortune.
C.12.185   And thorw þe *grace* of god and grayn dede [i]n erthe
C.13.23   As grayn þat lith in greut and thorw *grace* at the laste
C.13.216   And saide anoen to mysulue, 'slepynge bade y *grace*
C.14.2   Thogh y sete by mysulue, suche is my *grace*.
C.14.23   Ac *grace* is a graes þerfore to don hem [growe efte];
C.14.24   Ac *grace* ne groweth nat til gode wil gyue reyne
C.14.28   So *grace* withouten grace of god and also gode werkes
C.14.28   So grace withouten *grace* of god and also gode werkes

C.14.33   So *grace* is a gifte of god and kynde wit a chaunce
C.14.57   Buxumliche and benyngnelyche and bidden hit of *grace*.
C.14.131   The thef þat hadde *grace* of god a gode fryday, As thow toldest,
C.14.132   Was for A ȝeld hym creaunt to crist and his *grace* askede.
C.14.197   That god for his *grace* gyue here soules reste
C.15.226   To haue þe *grace* of god and no gulte of þe pope.
C.15.262   As witnesseth holy writ when we seggeth oure *graces*:
C.17.48   Thenne *grace* sholde growe ȝut and grene loue wexe
C.17.256   In þe gre[te] god and his *grace* asken
C.17.265   That men myhte nat be saued but thorw mercy and *grace*
C.18.52   And that is *grace* of þe holy gost; and thus gete þe maystrye.'
C.19.171   God þ[at] he gripeth [with] and wolde his *grace* quenche.
C.19.184   So is þe holi gost god and *grace* withouten mercy
C.19.191   Graunten [no] *grace* ne forgeuenesse of synnes
C.19.199   So *grace* of þe holi gost the grete myhte of þe trinite
C.19.218   So is þe holy gost god and *grace* withouten mercy
C.19.252   And gyueth ȝoure goed to þat god þat *grace* of aryseth.
C.19.256   The *grace* of the holy goest, godes owene kynde.
C.19.281   Confesse me and crye his *grace*, god þat al made,
C.19.293   Drede of disparacion thenne dryueth [away] *grace*
C.20.92   Of þe dede þat y haue do y do me in ȝoure *grace*;
C.20.133   And *grace* of the holy gost; wax grete with childe,
C.20.164   So shal *grace* þat bigan al maken a goed ende
C.20.190   Into pees and pyte of his puyr *grace*.
C.20.392   And gyle [be] bigyled thorw *grace* at þe laste:
C.20.396   So þat [thorw] gyle was gete thorw *grace* is now ywonne
C.20.400   And my *grace* to growe ay [gretter] and wyddore.
C.20.428   And if lawe wol y loke on hem hit lith in my *grace*
C.21.30   Ac to be conquerour cald, þat cometh of special *grace*
C.21.110   And þer bigan god of his *grace* to do wel:
C.21.116   Bigan god of his *grace* and goodnesse to do wel
C.21.121   That he thorw *grace* was gete and of no gome elles.
C.21.131   And all he heled and halp þat hym of *grace* asked;
C.21.208   And cometh fro þe grete god; *grace* is his name.
C.21.212   And criden with Consience, 'helpe vs, [Crist], of *grace*!'
C.21.213   Thenne bigan *grace* to go with [Peres Plouhman]
C.21.215   'For y wol dele today and deuyde *grace*
C.21.225   Forthy,' quod *grace*, 'or y go y wol gyue ȝow tresor
C.21.227   And gaf vch man a *grace* to gye with hymsuluen
C.21.233   And bi wit to wissen oþere as *grace* hem wolde teche.
C.21.252   'Thouh somme be clenner then somme, ȝe sen wel,' quod *grace*,
C.21.262   *Grace* gaf [Peres] a teme, foure grete oxen.
C.21.267   And *grace* [gaef Peres of his goednesse] foure stottes,
C.21.274   And *grace* gaf Peres graynes, cardinales vertues,
C.21.317   'Aȝeynes thy graynes,' quod *grace*, 'bigynneth for to rype,
C.21.319   'By god! *grace*,' quod [Peres], 'ȝe moet gyue tymber
C.21.321   And *grace* gaf hym þe cros with [the garlond] of thornes
C.21.325   And þerwith *grace* bigan to make a goode fo[un]dement,
C.21.329   And when this dede was doen *grace* deuysed
C.21.359   To goen agayn pruyde bute *grace* were with vs.'
C.21.386   *Grace* thorw godes word gaf [Peres] power,
C.21.425   And *grace* that thow gredest so of, gyour of all Clerkes;
C.22.140   'Allas!' quod Consience and cryede, 'wolde crist of his *grace*
C.22.386   And sethe he gradde aftur *grace* tyl y gan awake.

gracious adj *gracious adj.* B 1; C 2 gracious (1) graciouse (1)
B. 6.227   And if þow wilt be *gracious* to god do as þe gospel techeþ
C. 3.354   That is god, the ground of al, a *graciouse* antecedent.
C.14.133   And god is ay *gracious* to alle þat gredeth to hym

graciousliche adv *graciousli adv.* B 1; C 1
B.18.357   *Graciousliche* þi gile haue quyt: go gile ayein gile!
C.18.7   That hihte ymago dei, *graciousliche* hit growede.

gradde > greden; graes > gras

graffe n *graffe n.* C 1
C. 1.200   And þe *graffe* of grace and gray[th]est way to heuene.

graffen v *graffen v.* B 1
B. 5.138   And þe Couentes Gardyner for to *graffen* Impes.

gray adj *grei adj. n. &> grey* B 1; C 1
B.15.167   And is as glad of a gowne of a *gray* russet
C.16.300   And as glad of a goune of a *gray* russet

grayeth > graiþ; grayn(es > greyn

graiþ adj *greith adj.* A 2; B 2 graiþ (1) graiþe (1); C 4 grayeth (1) grayth (2) graythest (1)
A. 1.179   And ek þe *graiþ* gate þat goþ into heuene.
A. 8.41   Þat no gile go wiþ ȝow but þe *graiþ* treuþe.'
B. 1.205   And also þe *graiþe* gate þat goþ into heuene.
B.12.194   And grace asked of god þat [*graiþ* is hem euere]
C. 1.200   And þe graffe of grace and *gray[th]est* way to heuene.
C. 3.89   A grypeth þerfore a[s] gret as for þe *grayeth* treuthe.

C. 6.230   A galon for a grote, and ȝut no *grayth* mesure
C.10.242   Ac þe gospel is a glose ther and huydeth þe *grayth* treuthe;

graiþly adv *greithli adv.* B 2; C 4 graythli (3) graytheliche (1)
B.11.41   Ne shal noȝt greue þee [*graiþly*], ne bigile [þee], but þow wolt.'
B.18.292   'It is noȝt *graiþly* geten þer gile is þe roote,
C. 7.296   To goo with a good wil and *graytheliche* hem dryue.
C.11.136   Y grette hym goodly and *graythly* y hym tolde
C.11.308   Ne shal nat greue the *gr[ayth]ly* ne bigyle the, but thow wolle.'
C.20.322   'Hit is nat *graythly* ygete ther gyle is þe rote

gramariens n *gramarien n.* B 1
B.13.73   And greue þerwiþ [þat goode ben]–ac *gramariens* shul re[d]e:

grammer n *gramere n.* A 1 gramer; B 2; C 2 Gramer
A.11.132   *Gramer* for girles I garte ferst write,
B.10.180   *Grammer* for girles I garte first write,
B.15.372   *Grammer*, þe ground of al, bigileþ now children,
C.11.120   *Gramer* for gurles y gart furste write
C.17.108   *Gramer*, þe grounde of al, bigileth nouthe childrene,

grange > graunge

grant adj *graunt adj.* A 1 graunt; B 2 grant (1) graunt (1)
A.11.166   I seide '*graunt* mercy madame,' & mekly hire grette
B.10.224   I seide '*grant* mercy, madame', and mekely hir grette,
B.17.88   And graunted hym to ben his [gome]; '*graunt* mercy', he seide;

grape n *grape n.(1)* B 1
B.14.31   Thouȝ neuere greyn growed, ne *grape* vpon vyne,

gras n *gras n.* B 3; C 6 graes (1) gras (5)
B.11.366   And how among þe grene *gras* growed so manye hewes,
B.12.59   Ac grace is a *gras* þer[for] þo greuaunces to abate.
B.14.44   And bestes by *gras* and by greyn and by grene rootes,
C. 4.49   'Bothe my gees and my grys and my *g[r]as* he taketh.
C. 6.84   For god ne goddes word ne *gras* helpe me neuere
C. 6.431   And as an hound þat eet *gras* so gan y to brake
C.13.176   And how out of greeut and of *gras* gr[e]we so many hewes
C.14.23   Ac grace is a *graes* þerfore to don hem [growe efte];
C.15.242   Bestes by *gra[s]* and by grayn and by grene rotes,

graunge n *graunge n.* B 1; C 1 grange
B.17.74   And ladde hym so forþ on Lyard to lex Christi, a *graunge*
C.19.73   And ladde hym forth to lauacrum lex dei, a *grang[e]*

graunt > grant

graunte v *graunten v.* A 18 graunte (7) graunted (1) grauntid (3) grauntide (3) grauntiþ (3) ygrauntid (1); B 28 graunte (11) graunted (9) grauntede (3) graunteþ (4) ygraunted (1); C 32 graunte (17) graunted (4) grauntede (3) graunten (1) graunteth (4) graunteþ (1) grauntid (1) ygraunted (1)
A. 1.147   Þat he was miȝtful & mek & mercy gan *graunte*
A. 2.24   Gile haþ begon hire so heo *grauntiþ* alle his wille;
A. 2.84   God *grauntide* to gyue mede to treuþe,
A. 2.119   Þat he[o] *grauntiþ* to gon wiþ a good wille
A. 3.97   Ac I forgyue þe þe gilt & *graunte* þe [my] grace;
A. 3.159   Þe king *grauntide* hire grace wiþ a good wille:
A. 3.233   Shal haue mede on þis molde þat mattheu haþ *grauntid*;
A. 4.157   'I *graunte*,' quaþ þe king, 'godis forbode he faille!
A. 6.92   And ȝif grace *graunte* þe to gon in [on] þis wise,
A. 8.8   Part in þ[at] pardoun þe pope haþ hem *grauntid*.
A. 8.21   But non a pena & a culpa þe pope wolde h[e]m *graunte*,
A. 8.87   For loue of here louȝ herte oure lord haþ hem *grauntid*
A. 8.157   Now haþ þe pope power pardoun to *graunte*
A.10.36   Ȝaf hym gost of his godhed & *grauntide* hym blisse,
A.10.206   As betwyn sengle & sengle, siþþe lawe haþ *ygrauntid*
A.11.196   Be þat god in þe gospel *grauntiþ* & techiþ:
A.11.300   For I shal *graunte* ȝow grace of god þat ȝe seruen,
A.12.25   And god *graunted* hit neuere; þe gospel hit witnesseþ
B. 1.173   That he was myȝtful and meke and mercy gan *graunte*
B. 2.87   That is vsure and Auarice; al I hem *graunte*
B. 2.120   God *graunte[d]* to gyue Mede to truþe,
B. 2.155   That she *graunteþ* to goon wiþ a good wille
B. 3.108   But I forgyue þee þ[e] gilt and *graunte* þee my grace;
B. 3.172   The kyng *graunted* hire grace wiþ a good wille.
B. 3.254   [Shul haue] Mede [on þis molde þat] Mathew [haþ *graunted*]:
B. 4.194   'I *graunte* [gladly]', quod þe kyng, 'goddes forbode [he faile]!
B. 5.605   And if grace *graunte* þee to go in [in] þis wise
B. 6.331   But [if] god of his goodnesse *graunte* vs a trewe.
B. 7.8   Pardon wiþ Piers Plowman truþe haþ *ygraunted*.
B. 7.19   Ac noon A pena & a culpa þe pope [w]olde hem *graunte*
B. 7.105   For loue of hir lowe hert[e] oure lord haþ hem *graunted*
B. 7.179   Now haþ þe pope power pardon to *graunte*
B. 9.48   And of his grete grace *graunted* hym blisse,
B.11.97   If hem likeþ and lest; ech a lawe it *graunteþ*,

B.11.128   Wiþouten leue of his lord; no lawe wol it *graunte*.
B.11.149   *Graunted* [me worþ] grace [þorȝ his grete wille].
B.12.294   The glose *graunteþ* vpon þat vers a greet mede to truþe.
B.14.321   Now god þat alle good gyueþ *graunte* his soule reste
B.16.97   The maide myldeliche þo þe messager *graunted*
B.16.241   To me and to myn issue moore yet he [me] *grauntede*,
B.17.88   And *graunted* hym to ben his [gome]; '*graunt* mercy', he seide;
B.17.225   *Graunte* no grace ne for[g]ifnesse of synnes
B.18.184   And þat god haþ forgyuen and *graunted* me, pees, & mercy
B.18.338   Thefliche þow me robbedest; þe olde lawe *graunteþ*
B.19.104   And som tyme he gaf good and *grauntede* heele boþe.
B.19.183   And yaf Piers [pardon, and power] he *grauntede* hym,
C. 1.86   He is a god by þe gospel and *graunte* may hele
C. 1.169   That he was myhtfull and meke and mercy gan *graunte*
C. 2.72   That Gyle hath gyue to falsnesse and *grauntid* also mede,'
C. 2.91   The Erldom of enuye and yre he hem *graunteth*,
C. 2.128   And god *graunte[de]* hit were so so no gyle were,
C. 2.171   That he *graunteþ* to go with a goode wille
C. 3.100   *Graunte* gylours on erthe grace to amende
C. 3.135   And monye a gulte y haue the forgyue & my grace *graunted*
C. 3.218   The kyng *grauntede* here grace with a goode wille:
C. 3.252   To helpe heyliche alle his oste or elles *graunte*
C. 3.331   Bothe gyue and *graunte* there his grace lyketh
C. 3.366   In whiche ben gode and nat gode, and *graunte* here n[eyther] will.
C. 5.192   And no grace [to] *graunte* til good loue were
C. 6.102   *Graunte* me, gode lord, grace of amendement.'
C. 6.436   Herof, gode god, *graunte* me forȝeuenesse,
C. 7.254   And yf grace *graunte* the to go in [in] this wyse
C. 8.352   But yf [god] of his goodnesse *graunte* vs a trewe.
C. 9.8   Pardoun with [Peres] þe [Plouhman] perpetuelly he *graunteth*.
C. 9.19   And suche liue as þei lereth men oure lord treuthe hem *graunteth*
C. 9.23   Ac no [a] pena & a culpa treuthe wolde hem *graunte*
C. 9.59   Lellyche and lauhfollyche, oure lord treuthe hem *graunteth*
C. 9.185   For loue of here lowe hertes oure lord hath hem *ygraunted*
C. 9.278   Loke now, for thy lacchesse, what lawe wol the *graunte*:
C. 9.325   Ȝut hath þe pope power pardoun to *graunte*
C.12.63   Withouten leue of [his] lord; no lawe wol hit *graunte*.
C.16.156   Now god þat al [good] gyueth *graunte* his soule reste
C.18.130   The mayde myldeliche [tho] the messager *grauntede*
C.19.191   *Graunten* [no] grace ne forgeuenesse of synnes
C.19.289   That may no kynge mercy *graunte* til bothe men acorde
C.20.187   And þat god hath forgyue and *graunted* to mankynde
C.21.104   And som tyme he gaf goed and *graunted* hele bothe;
C.21.183   And ȝaf [peres pardoun] and [power] he *graunted* [hym],

graue n *grave n.(1)* B 3 graue (2) graues (1); C 2 graue (1) graues (1)
B.15.593   And whan he lifte vp Laȝar þat leid was in *graue*
B.16.113   Saue þo he leched laȝar þat hadde yleye in *graue*;
B.18.62   Dede men for þat dene come out of depe *graues*
C.17.302   Tho he luft vp lasar þat layde was in *graue*;
C.20.64   And dede men for þat dene cam oute of depe *graues*

graue v *graven v.(1)* A 2 graue (1) ygraue (1); B 3 graue (1) ygraue (2); C 4 graue (2) ygraue (2)
A. 3.48   Woldist þou glase þe gable, & *graue* þere þin name,
A. 4.113   Neiþer grotis ne gold *ygraue* wiþ kynges coyn,
B. 3.49   Woldestow glaȝe þ[e] gable & *graue* [þere] þy name
B. 4.130   Neiþer [grotes ne gold *ygraue* wiþ kynges coyn]
B.15.545   That in grotes is *ygraue* and in gold nobles.
C. 3.52   Wolde ȝe glase þ[e] gable and *graue* ther ȝoure name
C. 4.127   Nother *ygraue* ne vngraue, of gold oþer of suluer,
C.17.76   And ȝut is þe printe puyr trewe and parfitliche *ygraue*.
C.17.207   That in grotes is *graue* and in golde nobles.

grauynge ger *gravinge ger.* A 1 grauyng; B 1; C 2 grauynge
A. 3.53   Ac god alle good folk such *grauyng* defendiþ
B. 3.64   Ac god alle good folk swich *grauynge* defendeþ,
C. 3.68   Ac god to alle good folk suche *grauynge* defendeth,
C. 3.74   God in þe gospel suche *grauynge* nouȝt alloueth:

gre > gree

grece n *grese n.* B 1
B.13.63   Wombe cloutes and wilde brawen and egges yfryed wiþ *grece*.

greden v *greden v.* A 2 gredde (1) grede (1); B 5 gradde (2) greden (2) gredest (1); C 5 gradde (1) greden (2) gredest (1) gredeth (1)
A. 2.56   Þus begynne þe gomes & *gredde* wel heiȝe:
A. 3.62   Oþer to *grede* aftir godis men whan ȝe [g]iue dolis,
B. 2.74   [Th]us bigynnen þ[e] gomes [and] *greden* [wel] heiȝe:
B. 3.71   Or to *greden* after goddes men whan ye [gyue] doles
B.16.78   I hadde ruþe whan Piers rogged, it *gradde* so rufulliche;
B.19.425   And Grace þat þow *gr[e]dest* so of, gyour of alle clerkes;
B.20.386   And siþþe he *gradde* after Grace til I gan awake.
C. 8.283   Alle þat *gr[eden* at] thy gate for godes loue aftur fode
C. 9.76   To aglotye with here gurles that *greden* aftur fode.

C.14.133 And god is ay gracious to alle þat *gredeth* to hym
C.21.425 And grace that thow *gredest* so of, gyour of all Clerkes;
C.22.386 And sethe he *gradde* aftur grace tyl y gan awake.

gredy adj *gredi adj.* B 1 gredy; C 1 gredy
B. 5.340 Hise guttes bigonne to goþelen as two *gredy* sowes;
C. 6.398 His gottes gan to gothly as t[w]o *g[re]dy* sowes,

gredyre n *gridere n.* C 1
C. 2.133 That laurence the leuyte that lay on þe *gredyre*

gree n *gre n.(1)* B 1; C 1 gre
B.18.98 The *gree* ȝit haþ he geten for al his grete wounde,
C.20.101 The *gre* ȝut hath he geten for al his grete wound[e]

greet > gret

greete v *greten v.(3)* &> gret A 1 grete; B 1
A. 5.207 And gan *grete* grymly & gret doel ma[k]e
B. 5.379 And þanne gan Gloton *greete* and gret doel to make

greetliche > gretly

greetnesse n *gretnesse n.* B 1 greetnesse
B.16.59 And of o *greetnesse* and grene of greyn þei semen.'

greeut > greut

gregorie n prop *n.i.d.* A 1 Gregory; B 9 Gregori (1) Gregory (3) Gregorie (4) Gregories (1); C 3 Gregori (1) Gregory (2)
A.11.204 *Gregory* þe grete clerk, a good pope in his tyme,
B. 5.166 Seint *Gregory* was a good pope and hadde a good forwit:
B. 7.76 Ac *Gregory* was a good man and bad vs gyuen alle
B.10.298 *Gregorie* þe grete clerk and þe goode pope
B.10.330 That *Gregories* godchildren [vngodly] despended.
B.11.146 *Gregorie* wiste þis wel, and wilned to my soule
B.11.157 Was þat Sarsen saued, as Seint *Gregorie* bereþ witnesse.
B.11.230 And as Seint *Gregorie* seide, for mannes soule helþe
B.15.444 Til *Gregory* garte clerkes to go here and preche.
B.19.270 *Gregori* þe grete clerk and [þe goode Ierom];
C. 5.146 *Gregory* þe grete Clerk gart wryte in bokes
C.12.81 *Gregori* wiste this wel and wilned to my soule
C.21.270 *Gregory* the grete Clerk and [þe gode Ieroem];

grey n *grei n.(2) cf. gray* B 1; C 1 gray
B.15.221 Boþe in *grey* and in grys and in gilt harneis,
C.16.346 Bothe in *gray* and in grys and in gult harneys,

greyn n *grain n.* A 3 grayn (1) greyn (2); B 8 greyn (6) greynes (2); C 9 grayn (7) graynes (2)
A. 7.111 Shal no *greyn* þat here growiþ glade ȝow at nede;
A. 7.118 Þat god of his grace ȝour *greyn* multiplie,
A.11.97 I miȝte gete no *g[r]ayn* of hise grete wyttes,
B. 6.119 Shal no *greyn* þat [here] groweþ glade yow at nede;
B. 6.126 That god of his grace youre *greyn* multiplie
B.10.144 I myȝte gete no *greyn* of his grete wittes,
B.14.31 Thouȝ neuere *greyn* growed, ne grape vpon vyne,
B.14.44 And bestes by gras and by *greyn* and by grene rootes,
B.16.59 And of o greetnesse and grene of *greyn* þei semen.'
B.19.274 And Grace gaf [Piers] *greynes*, Cardynal[es] vertues,
B.19.317 'Ayeins þi *greynes*', quod Grace, 'bigynneþ for to ripe,
C. 8.126 Shal no *grayn* þat here groweth gladyen ȝow at nede;
C. 8.132 That god [of] his grace ȝoure *grayn* multiplye
C.11.82 I myhte gete no *grayn* of [his] grete wittes
C.12.178 And by þe *grayn* that groweth god vs all techeth
C.12.185 And thorw þe grace of god and *grayn* dede [i]n erthe
C.13.23 As *grayn* þat lith in greut and thorw grace at the laste
C.15.242 Bestes by gra[s] and by *grayn* and by grene rotes,
C.21.274 And grace gaf Peres *graynes*, cardinales vertues,
C.21.317 'Aȝeynes thy *graynes*,' quod grace, 'bigynneth for to rype,

grekes n prop *Grek n.* B 3
B.15.390 And so may Sarȝens be saued, Scribes and [*Grekes*].
B.15.501 And siþ þat þise Sarȝens, Scribes and [*Grekes*]
B.15.605 Ac pharisees and Sarȝens, Scribes and [*Grekes*]

grene adj *grene adj.* A 2; B 8; C 6
A. 7.265 Noþer gees ne gris, but two *grene* chesis,
A. 7.282 [*Grene* porret and pesen; to [peysen] him þei þouȝte.
B. 6.281 Neiþer gees ne grys, but two *grene* cheses,
B. 6.298 *Grene* poret and pesen; to [peisen] hym þei þoȝte.
B.11.366 And how among þe *grene* gras growed so manye hewes,
B.14.44 And bestes by gras and by greyn and by *grene* rootes,
B.15.102 Shal neuere flour ne fruyt [wexe] ne fair leef be *grene*.
B.15.424 Grace sholde growe and be *grene* þoruȝ hir goode lyuynge,
B.16.59 And of o greetnesse and *grene* of greyn þei semen.'
B.18.48 And bigan of [*grene*] þorn a garland to make,
C. 8.303 Noþer goos ne gries but two *grene* cheses,

C.15.242 Bestes by gra[s] and by grayn and by *grene* rotes,
C.16.250 Tho bowes þat bereth nat and beth nat *grene* yleued,
C.16.255 Shal neuere flour ne fruyt wexe ne fayre leue be *grene*.
C.17.48 Thenne grace sholde growe ȝut and *grene* loue wexe
C.20.48 And bigan of *grene* thorn a garlond to make

grepe > gripeþ

gret adj *gret adj.&adv.& n.* A 21 gret (9) grete (11) grettest (1); B 70 greet (11) greete (1) gret (13) grete (37) gretter (6) grettest (1) gretteste (1); C 68 greet (10) gret (8) grete (43) gretter (1) grettere (1) grettest (1) gretteste (1) grettore (3)
A.Pr.52 *Grete* lobies & longe þat loþ were to swynke
A. 2.64 Glotonye & *grete* oþes I gyue hem togidere;
A. 2.113 Þo þis gold was gyue *gret* was þe þonking
A. 3.20 Of here *grete* goodnesse, & [g]af hem ichone
A. 3.164 Þere þat meschief is *gret* mede may helpe.
A. 4.33 And wordiden a *gret* while wel wisly togidere.
A. 5.102 Ȝif shrift shulde, it shop[e] a *gret* wondir.'
A. 5.157 Þanne goþ [glotoun in], and *grete* oþis aftir.
A. 5.207 And gan grete grymly & *gret* doel ma[k]e
A. 5.219 For is no gilt here so *gret* þat his goodnesse nis more'.
A. 8.44 For he co[pie]de þus here clause þei [couden] hym *gret* mede.
A. 9.9 Maistris of þe menours, men of *gret* wyt.
A.10.21 And sire godefrey go wel, *grete* lordis alle.
A.10.29 And þat is þe *grete* god þat gynnyng had neuere,
A.10.48 Aftir þe grace of god [þe *grettest* is Inwyt].
A.11.37 Glotonye & *grete* oþis, þise arn games nowadayes.
A.11.53 God is muche in þe [gorge] of þis *grete* maistris,
A.11.97 I miȝte gete no g[r]ayn of hise *grete* wyttes,
A.11.204 Gregory þe *grete* clerk, a good pope in his tyme,
A.12.69 'Go we forþ,' quod þe gom, 'I haue a *gret* boyste
B.Pr.55 *Grete* lobies and longe þat loþe were to swynke
B. 2.29 My fader þe *grete* god is and ground of alle graces,
B. 2.70 That Gile wiþ hise *grete* oþes gaf hem togidere',
B. 2.93 Glotonye he [gyueþ] hem ek and *grete* oþes togidere,
B. 2.149 Tho þis gold was ygyue *gret* was þe þonkyng
B. 3.21 Of hire *grete* goodnesse, and gaf hem echone
B. 3.245 Of god at a *gret* nede whan þei gon hennes.
B. 4.46 And wordeden [a *gret* while wel wisely] togideres.
B. 4.159 And þe mooste peple in þe [moot] halle and manye of þe *grete*,
B. 5.306 Thanne goþ Gloton In and *grete* oþes after.
B. 5.353 Ac Gloton was a *gret* cherl and grym in þe liftyng;
B. 5.379 And þanne gan Gloton greete and *gret* doel to make
B. 5.447 For is no gilt here so *gret* þat his goodnesse [i]s moore.'
B. 8.9 Maistres of þe Menours, men of *grete* witte.
B. 8.39 The goodes of þis grounde arn like þe *grete* wawes,
B. 9.22 And sire Godefray Go-wel, *grete* lordes [alle].
B. 9.28 And þat is þe *grete* god þat gynnyng hadde neuere,
B. 9.48 And of his *grete* grace graunted hym blisse.
B. 9.60 For after þe grace of god þe *gretteste* is Inwit.
B.10.51 Glotonye and *grete* oþes, þis[e arn games nowadaies].
B.10.67 God is muche in þe gorge of þise *grete* maistres,
B.10.144 I myȝte gete no greyn of his *grete* wittes,
B.10.241 On þe *grete* god þat gynnyng hadde neuere,
B.10.298 Gregorie þe *grete* clerk and þe goode pope
B.10.310 And *gret* loue and likyng for ech [loweþ hym to] ooþer.
B.10.401 As Salomon dide and swiche oþere, þat shewed *grete* wittes
B.11.149 Graunted [me worþ] grace [þorȝ his *grete* wille].
B.11.264 Makeþ a man to haue mynde in god and a *gret* wille
B.12.68 Ac grace is a gifte of god and of *greet* loue spryngeþ;
B.12.79 Giltier as afore god, and *gretter* in synne,
B.12.253 That euere he gadered so *grete* and gaf þerof so litel,
B.12.268 [Swiche tales telleþ Aristotle þe *grete* clerk]:
B.12.291 And wheiþer it worþ [of truþe] or noȝt, [þe] worþ [of] bileue is *gret*,
B.12.294 The glose graunteþ vpon þat vers a *greet* mede to truþe.
B.13.78 'Ac þis goddes gloton', quod I, 'wiþ hise *grete* chekes
B.13.234 I haue no goode giftes of þise *grete* lordes
B.13.271 I took [*greet*] kepe, by crist! and Conscience boþe,
B.13.362 'The worste withInne was; a *greet* wit I let it.
B.13.398 Than in þe grace of god and hise *grete* helpes:
B.13.399 [Yet glotoun wiþ *grete* oþes his [garnement] hadde soiled
B.13.450 And in his deeþ deyinge þei don hym *gret* confort
B.14.37 Vitailles of *grete* vertues for alle manere beestes
B.14.53 Shul neuere gyues þee greue ne *gret* lordes wraþe,
B.14.130 And *greet* likynge to lyue wiþouten labour of bodye,
B.14.235 So for his glotonie and his *greete* sleuþe he haþ a greuous penaunce,
B.14.256 That god is his *grettest* help and no gome ellis,
B.15.66 Of god and of hise *grete* myȝtes, hise graces it letteþ.
B.15.82 Gooþ to þe glose of þ[e] vers, ye *grete* clerkes;
B.15.146 Ac for goode men, god woot, *greet* doel men maken,

B.15.505   In [o] gre[et] god, and his grace asken,
B.16.80   And gadrede hem alle togideres, boþe grete and smale,
B.17.39   The gome þat gooþ wiþ o staf, he semeþ in gretter heele
B.17.182   So is þe holy goost god, neiþer gretter ne lasse
B.17.233   So grace of þe holy goost þe grete myȝt of þe Trinite
B.17.317   To amende al þat amys is, and his mercy gretter
B.18.98   The gree ȝit haþ he geten for al his grete wounde,
B.18.122   Eiþer asked ooþer of þis grete wonder,
B.18.130   And grace of þe holy goost; weex greet wiþ childe;
B.18.308   Wiþ glorie and with gret light; god it is, I woot wel.
B.18.362   And my grace to growe ay gretter and widder.
B.19.128   Thus he confortede carefulle and caughte a gretter name
B.19.197   The goode to godhede and to greet Ioye,
B.19.208   And comeþ fro þe grete god; grace is his name.
B.19.262   Grace gaf Piers a teeme, foure grete Oxen.
B.19.270   Gregori þe grete clerk and [þe goode Ierom];
B.19.336   And gadered hym a greet Oost; greuen he þynkeþ
B.20.20   So nede at gret nede may nymen as for his owene
B.20.40   And god al his grete Ioye goostliche he lefte
B.20.113   And gaderede a greet hoost al agayn Conscience.
B.20.215   And bisegede [sikerly] wiþ seuene grete geauntȝ
C.Pr.36   Wolleth neyther swynke ne swete bote sweren grete othes,
C.Pr.53   Grete lobies and longe þat loth were to swynke
C.Pr.137   For in loue and lettrure lith þe grete eleccoun.
C.Pr.179   Sayde, 'y haue seyen grete syres in Cytees and in townes
C. 1.104   And god whan he bigan heuene in þat grete blisse
C. 2.100   Glotonye a gyueth hem and grete othes togederes,
C. 2.165   Tho this gold was ygyue grete was the thonkynge
C. 2.179   Thenne gan gyle borwen hors at many gret maystres
C. 3.22   Of here grete goodnesse and gaf hem vchone
C. 3.89   A grypeth þerfore a[s] gret as for þe grayeth treuthe.
C. 3.223   Ther þat meschief is greet mede may helpe;
C. 3.283   And glad for to grype here, gret lord oþer pore.'
C. 3.340   Grace of good ende and gret ioye aftur.
C. 5.146   Gregory þe grete Clerk gart wryte in bokes
C. 6.18   God and goode men so gret was myn herte;
C. 6.261   The worste lay withynne; a greet wit y lat hit.
C. 6.285   Then in the grace of god and in his grete myhte;
C. 6.361   Thenne goth glotoun in and grete othes aftur.
C. 6.411   Ac gloton was a greet cherl and gr[ym] in þe luftynge
C. 7.61   For is no gult [here] so greet þat his goodnesse is more.'
C. 7.110   And in his deth deynge they don hym greet confort
C. 8.87   Maystres, as mayres and grete menne, senatours,
C. 9.50   Shal haue grace of a good ende and greet ioye aftur.
C. 9.67   Bote ther he wiste were wel grete nede
C. 9.133   Me [g]yueth hem giftes and gold for grete lordes sake.
C. 9.259   Vigilare were fayrere for thow haste a greet charge.
C.10.9   Maystres of þe menore[s], men of gret witte.
C.10.45   The godes of this grounde ar like þe grete wawes
C.10.148   And sire go[dfray] go-wel, grete lordes alle.
C.10.154   The which is god grettest [þat gynnynge hadde] neuere,
C.11.82   I myhte gete no grayn of [his] grete wittes
C.11.286   Saide thus in his sarmon for ensau[m]ple of grete clerkes,
C.12.84   God of his goodnesse ysey his grete will.
C.13.8   For in greet pouerte he was put: a prince, as hit were,
C.14.213   And wher hit worth or worth nat, the bileue is gret of treuthe.
C.15.85   And also a gnedy glotoun with two grete chekes,
C.15.184   And wenten forth here way; with grete wille y folowede.
C.15.208   Y haue no gode giftes of thise grete lordes
C.15.252   Shal neuere gyues the greue ne grete lordes wrathe,
C.16.19   For al myhtest þou haue ymad men of grete welthe
C.16.76   So for his glotonye and his grete synne he hath a greuous penaunce
C.16.96   That god is his gretteste helpe and no gome elles
C.17.67   He gaf goddes men goddes goodes and nat grete lordes
C.17.166   And a cardinal of Court, a gret clerk withalle,
C.17.256   In þe gre[te] god and his grace asken
C.18.56   A[c] in thre degrees hit grewe; grete ferly me thouhte,
C.18.62   Of o kynde apples aren nat iliche grete
C.18.65   Swettore and saueriore and also more grettore
C.18.111   And gadered hem alle togyderes, bothe grete & smale,
C.18.148   That he was god or godes sone for þat grete wonder;
C.19.148   Thus is the holy goste god, noyther grettore ne lassore
C.19.199   So grace of þe holi gost the grete myhte of þe trinite
C.19.297   To amende al þat amys is and his mercy grettore
C.20.101   The gre ȝut hath he geten for al his grete wound[e]
C.20.125   Ayþer asked oþer of this grete Wonder,
C.20.133   And grace of the holy gost; wax grete with childe,
C.20.342   With glorie and with [grete] lihte; god hit is ich woet wel.
C.20.400   And my grace to growe ay [gretter] and wyddore
C.21.128   Thus he comfortede carefole and cauhte a grettere name,
C.21.197   The gode to godhede and to grete ioye
C.21.208   And cometh fro the grete god; grace is his name.
C.21.262   Grace gaf [Peres] a teme, foure grete oxen.

C.21.270   Gregory the grete Clerk and [þe gode Ieroem];
C.21.336   And gadered hym a grete oeste; greue he thenketh
C.22.20   So nede at greet nede may nyme as for his owne
C.22.40   And god al his grete ioye goestliche he lefte
C.22.113   And gaderet[h] a greet oest alle agayn Consience.
C.22.215   And biseged s[iker]ly with seuene grete geauntes

grete &> greete,gret,greten

greten v *greten v.(2)* A 4 grete (2) grette (2); B 7 grete (2) greten (1) grette (4); C 8 grete (2) grette (6)
A. 5.184   And grete sire glotoun wiþ a galoun ale.
A.11.126   And þat [I] grete wel his wyf for I wrot hire þe bible,
A.11.166   I seide 'graunt mercy madame,' & mekly hire grette
A.11.170   I grette þe goode man as þe gode wyf me tauȝte,
B. 5.335   And greten sire Gloton wiþ a Galon ale.
B.10.174   And þat I grete wel his wif, for I wroot hire [þe bible],
B.10.224   I seide 'grant mercy, madame', and mekely hir grette,
B.10.227   [I] grette þe goode man as [þe goode wif] me tauȝte,
B.16.226   I roos vp and reuerenced hym and riȝt faire hym grette.
B.18.175   And in hire gaye garnementȝ whom she grete þouȝte,
B.20.355   And cam to Conscience and curteisly hym grette.
C. 4.42   Corteyslyche þe kyng thenne cam and grette resoun
C. 6.393   And grete syre glotoun with a galoun ale.
C.11.114   And sey y gre[t]e wel his wyf, for y wrot here a bible
C.11.136   Y grette hym goodly and graythly y hym tolde
C.12.207   Angelis in here anger on this wyse hem grette:
C.18.183   'Of whennes artow?' quod y, and hendeliche hym grette.
C.18.242   Y roos vp and reuerensed god and riȝt fayre hym grette,
C.22.355   And cam to Consience and cortey[s]liche hym grette.

gretly adv *gretli adv.* B 1; C 1 greetliche
B.18.7   Of gerlis and of Gloria laus gretly me dremed,
C.20.6   Of gurles and of gloria laus greetliche me dremede

grette > greden

gretter adv *gret adj.&adv.& n. &>* gret B 1 gretter; C 2 grettere (1) grottore (1)
B.20.28   And greue men gretter þan good feiþ it wolde.
C.Pr.122   Wel hardere and grettere on suche shrewed faderes
C.22.28   And greue men grettore then goed faith hit w[o]lde.

grettere -ore > gret,gretter; grettest(e > gret

greut n *gret n.(3)* C 2 greeut (1) greut (1)
C.13.23   As grayn þat lith in greut and thorw grace at the laste
C.13.176   And how out of greeut and of gras gr[e]we so many hewes

greuaunces n *grevaunce n.* B 1
B.12.59   Ac grace is a gras þer[for] þo greuaunces to abate.

greuen v *greven v.* A 2 greue (1) greuide (1); B 24 greue (11) greued (3) greuen (4) greuest (1) greueþ (5); C 29 greue (19) greued (3) greuede (1) greuest (1) greueth (4) ygreued (1)
A. 5.78   His grace & hise gode happis greuide me wel sore.
A. 7.213   'I wolde not greue god,' quaþ peris, 'for al þe gold on ground.
B.Pr.139   Thanne greued hym a Goliardeis, a gloton of wordes,
B.Pr.153   And if we grucche of his game he wol greuen vs alle,
B.Pr.203   Shal neuere þe cat ne þe kiton by my counseil be greued,
B. 5.98   His grace and his goode happes greuen me [wel] soore.
B. 6.229   'I wolde noȝt greue god', quod Piers, 'for al þe good on grounde!
B. 6.316   He greueþ hym ageyn god and gruccheþ ageyn Reson.
B. 9.203   To loue [and to lowe þee and no lif to greue;
B.10.209   And noȝt to greuen hem þat greueþ vs; god [þat forbedeþ]:
B.10.209   And noȝt to greuen hem þat greueþ vs; god [þat forbedeþ]:
B.10.292   [Th]anne shul burel clerkes ben abasshed to blame yow or to greue,
B.11.41   Ne shal noȝt greue þee [graiþly], ne bigile [þee], but þow wolt.'
B.11.281   To serue god goodliche, ne greueþ hym no penaunce:
B.13.73   And greue þerwiþ [þat goode ben]–ac gramariens shul re[d]e;
B.14.53   Shul neuere gyues þee greue ne gret lordes wraþe,
B.14.113   And wilde wormes in wodes, þoruȝ wyntres þow hem greuest
B.14.230   And if glotonie greue pouerte he gadereþ þe lasse
B.15.47   'Ye, sire!' I seide, 'by so no man were greued
B.15.257   Misdooþ he no man ne wiþ his mouþ greueþ.
B.17.19   Shal neuere deuel hym dere ne deeþ in soule greue;
B.17.114   And neuere eft greue gome þat gooþ þis ilke gate:
B.17.204   So whoso synneþ in þe Seint Spirit, it semeþ þat he greueþ
B.19.219   For Antecrist and hise al þe world greue
B.19.336   And gadered hym a greet Oost; greuen he þynkeþ
B.20.28   And greue men gretter þan good feiþ it wolde.
C.Pr.173   'And yf we groche of his game a wol greue vs [alle],
C.Pr.211   Shal neuer þe Cat ne [þe] kytoun be my conseil be greued
C. 3.92   That bygyleth goode men and greueth hem wrongly,
C. 4.95   To haue mercy on þat man that many tymes hym greuede;
C. 5.58   Ne fyhte in no faumewarde ne his foe greue:

C. 6.111   On god when me *greued* auht and grochede of his sonde:
C. 8.235   'Y wolde nat *greue* [god],' quod Peres, 'for al þe good on erthe!
C. 8.268   Of al a woke worche nat, so oure wombe *greueth*.'
C. 8.338   Suche lawes to lerne laboreres to *greue*.
C.10.302   To louye and to loue the and no lyf to *greue*;
C.11.25   Tho þat god most goed ʒeueth *greueth* most riht and treuthe:
C.11.131   For loue is a lykyng thyng and loth for to *greue*.
C.11.308   Ne shal nat *greue* the gr[ayth]ly ne bigyle the, but thow wolle.'
C.13.60   And leueth for his lettres god ne [lede] wole hym *greue*.
C.15.163   Ne n[oþ]ere hete ne hayl ne helle pouke hym *greue*,
C.15.252   Shal neuere gyues the *greue* ne grete lordes wrathe,
C.15.289   And wilde wormes in wodes, thorw wyntres thow hem *greuest*
C.16.71   And yf glotonye *greue* pouerte h[e] gadereth þe lasse
C.16.121   Thenne is [hit] goed by good skill, thouh hit *greue* a litel,
C.16.209   'ʒe, sire!' y sayde, 'by so no man were *ygreued*,
C.16.290   Charite þat chargeth nauht ne chyt thow me *greue* hym,
C.16.307   Ne þat eny gome wolde gyle [ne *greue* oþere]
C.19.20   Shal neuere deuel hym dere ne deth in soule *greue*;
C.19.128   And þat the fynger gropeth he grypeth bote yf hit *greue* þe paume.
C.19.147   Bote [be he] *greued* with here grype the holy goost lat falle.
C.19.170   So hoso synegeth aʒeyn þe seynt spirit hit semeth þat he *greueth*
C.21.219   For Auntecrist and hise al the world shal *greue*
C.21.336   And gadered hym a grete oeste; *greue* he thenketh
C.22.28   And *greue* men grettore then goed faith hit w[o]lde.

greuous adj *grevous adj.* B 1; C 1
B.14.235   So for his glotonie and his greete sleuþe he haþ a *greuous*
                penaunce,
C.16.76   So for his glotonye and his grete synne he hath a *greuous* penaunce

grewe > growe; gries > grys

griffyn n prop *n.i.d.* B 1; C 1 Gryffyth
B. 5.316   Godefray of Garlekhiþe and *Griffyn* þe walshe;
C. 6.373   Godefray þe garlekmonger and *Gryffyth* þe walshe

grym adj *grim adj.* B 1; C 1
B. 5.353   Ac Gloton was a gret cherl and *grym* in þe liftyng;
C. 6.411   Ac gloton was a greet cherl and *gr[ym]* in þe luftynge

grymly adv *grimli adv.* A 1; B 1
A. 5.207   And gan grete *grymly* & gret doel ma[k]e
B.10.267   God in þe gospel [*grymly*] repreueþ

grype n *gripe n.(1)* &> *gripeþ* C 1
C.19.147   Bote [be he] greued with here *grype* the holy goost lat falle.

gripeþ v *gripen v.* A 2 grepe (1) gripiþ (1); B 3 griped (1) gripeþ (1)
     grypeþ (1); C 5 gripeth (1) grype (1) grypen (1) grypeth (2)
A. 3.169   And ek *grepe* my gold & gyue it where þe likiþ.
A. 3.229   And he þat *gripiþ* here giftes, so me god helpe,
B. 3.182   And [ek] *griped* my gold [and] gyue it where þee liked.
B. 3.250   And he þat *gripeþ* hir [giftes], so me god helpe,
B.17.205   God þat he *grypeþ* wiþ, and wolde his grace quenche.
C. 3.89   A *grypeth* þerfore a[s] gret as for þe grayeth treuthe.
C. 3.228   And also *gryp[en]* my gold and gyue hit where þe liked.
C. 3.283   And glad for to *grype* here, gret lord oþer pore.'
C.19.128   And þat the fynger gropeth he *grypeth* bote yf hit greue þe paume.
C.19.171   God þ[at] he *gripeth* [with] and wolde his grace quenche.

grys n1 *gris n.(1)* A 3 gris; B 3; C 3 gries (1) grys (2)
A.Pr.105   Goode gees & *gris*; go we dyne, go we!'
A. 4.38   'Boþe my gees & my *gris* hise gadelynges fecchen;
A. 7.265   Noþer gees ne *gris*, but two grene chesis,
B.Pr.227   Goode gees and *grys*! go we dyne, go we!'
B. 4.51   'Boþe my gees and my *grys* hise gadelynges feccheþ.
B. 6.281   Neiþer gees ne *grys*, but two grene cheses,
C.Pr.231   Goode gees and *grys*! ga we dyne, ga we!'
C. 4.49   'Bothe my gees and my *grys* and my g[r]as he taketh.
C. 8.303   Noþer goos ne *gries* but two grene cheses,

grys n2 *gris n.(2)* B 1; C 1
B.15.221   Boþe in grey and in *grys* and in gilt harneis,
C.16.346   Bothe in gray and in *grys* and in gult harneys,

grisly adj *grisli adj.* B 1; C 1
B.18.431   May no *grisly* goost glide þere it [shadweþ].'
C.20.475   May no *grisly* goest glyde þer hit shaddeweth.'

groche(de > gruccheþ

grone v *gronen v.* A 1; B 2 grone (1) gronede (1); C 1 groned
A. 7.242   Þei han mangid ouer muche, þat makiþ hem *grone* ofte.
B. 6.258   Ye han manged ouer muche, þat makeþ yow *grone*.
B.20.311   Sire leef-to-lyue-in-lecherie lay þere and *gronede*;
C.22.311   Sire l[ee]f-to-lyue-in-lecherye lay þer and *groned*;

gronyng ger *groninge ger.* A 1
A.12.76   For *gronyng* of my guttys I durst gon no ferther].

grope v *gropen v.* B 3 grope (2) gropeþ (1); C 4 grope (2) gropeth (2)
B.13.346   Aboute þe mouþ, or byneþe bigynneþ to *grope*,
B.19.170   And took Thomas by þe hand and tauʒte hym to *grope*
B.20.363   And gooþ *gropeþ* Contricion and gaf hym a plastre
C. 6.180   Aboute þe mouthe and bynethe bygan y to *grope*,
C.19.128   And þat the fynger *gropeth* he grypeth bote yf hit greue þe paume.
C.21.170   And toek Thomas by the hoende and tauhte hym to *grope*
C.22.363   And goeth *gropeth* contricion and gaf hym a plastre

grote n *grot n.(3)* A 5 grote (3) grotis (2); B 6 grote (3) grotes (3); C 4
     grote (2) grotes (2)
A. 3.127   And [g]iueþ þe gaileris gold & *grotis* togidere
A. 4.113   Neiþer *grotis* ne gold ygraue wiþ kynges coyn,
A. 5.31   Þat hire hed was worþ a mark & his hod not worþ a *grote*.
A.11.34   ʒiue hem to here ʒerisʒiue þe value of a *grote*.
A. 5.138   A galoun for a *grote*, god wot no lasse,
B. 3.138   And gyueþ þe Gailers gold and *grotes* togidres
B. 4.130   Neiþer [*grotes* ne gold ygraue wiþ kynges coyn]
B. 5.31   [That] hire heed was worþ [a] marc & his hood noʒt a *grote*.
B. 5.222   A galoun for a *grote*, god woot no lasse,
B.10.48   ʒyue hem to hir yeresʒyue þe [value] of a *grote*.
B.15.545   That in *grotes* is ygraue and in gold nobles.
C. 3.176   And gyueth the gaylers gold and *grotes* togederes
C. 5.133   [That] here hed was worth half marc and his hoed nat a *grote*.
C. 6.230   A galon for a *grote*, and ʒut no grayth mesure
C.17.207   That in *grotes* is graue and in golde nobles.

ground n *ground n.* A 6 ground (5) grounde (1); B 14 ground (5) grounde
     (9); C 10 ground (1) grounde (9)
A. 1.88   He is a god be þe gospel on *ground* & on lofte,
A. 5.18   Bechis & broode okis wern blowen to [þe] *grounde*,
A. 7.213   'I wolde not greue god,' quaþ peris, 'for al þe gold on *ground*.
A. 9.35   Þe goodis of þis *ground* be lik þe grete wawes,
A.11.96   Ac for no carpyng I couþe, ne knelyng to þe *ground*,
A.11.173   Was neuere [gome] vpon þis *ground*, siþþe god makid heuene,
B. 1.90   He is a god by þe gospel, a *grounde* and a lofte,
B. 2.29   My fader þe grete god is and *ground* of alle graces,
B. 5.18   Beches and brode okes were blowen to þe *grounde*
B. 5.285   For þow hast no good *ground* to gete þee wiþ a wastel
B. 6.229   'I wolde noʒt greue god', quod Piers, 'for al þe good on *grounde*!
B. 8.39   The goodes of þis *grounde* arn like þe grete wawes,
B. 8.61   And ʒyue yow grace on þis *grounde* goode men to worþe'.
B.10.143   A[c] for no carpyng I couþe, ne knelyng to þe *grounde*,
B.10.230   Was neuere gome vpon þis *ground*, siþ god made [heuene],
B.11.357   And brouʒten forþ hir briddes al aboue þe *grounde*.
B.12.201   But as a beggere bordlees by myself on þe *grounde*.
B.15.372   Grammer, þe *ground* of al, bigileþ now children,
B.16.62   The *ground* þere it groweþ, goodnesse it hatte;
B.18.45   Boþe as long and as large bi lofte and by *grounde*.'
C. 3.354   That is god, the *ground* of al, a graciouse antecedent.
C. 5.120   Beches and brode okes were blowe to þe *grounde*
C.10.45   The godes of this *grounde* ar like þe grete wawes
C.10.60   And gyue me grace on þis *grounde* with good ende to deye.'
C.13.166   And brouhte forth here briddes al aboue þe *grounde*.
C.14.140   Bote as a beggare bordles be mysulue on þe *grounde*.
C.17.91   Nat in god þat he ne is goed and þe *grounde* bothe;
C.17.108   Gramer, þe *grounde* of al, bigileth nouthe childrene,
C.17.141   Loue god for he is goed and *grounde* of alle treuthe;
C.20.44   Bothe as longe and as large aloofte and o *grounde*

grounde ptp *grinden v.(1)* A 1 ygrounde; B 2 grounde (1) ygrounde (1);
     C 2 ygrounde
A. 7.169   To abate þe barly bred & þe benis *ygrounde*,
B.13.43   Ac hir sauce was ouer sour and vnsauourly *grounde*
B.18.78   Ac þer cam forþ a knyʒt wiþ a kene spere *ygrounde*,
C.15.48   Ac here sauce was ouersour and vnsauerly *ygrounde*
C.20.80   Ac þer cam forth a knyhte with a kene spere *ygrounde*,

growe v *grouen v.* A 1 growiþ; B 16 growe (3) growed (4) growen (1)
     groweþ (8); C 16 grewe (2) growe (6) growede (2) groweth (6)
A. 7.111   Shal no greyn þat here *growiþ* glade ʒow at nede;
B. 6.119   Shal no greyn þat [here] *groweþ* glade yow at nede;
B.11.366   And how among þe grene gras *growed* so manye hewes,
B.12.60   Ac grace ne *groweþ* noʒt [til good wil yeue reyn];
B.12.61   Pacience and pouerte þe place [is] þer it *groweþ*,
B.14.31   Thouʒ neuere greyn *growed*, ne grape vpon vyne,
B.15.424   Grace sholde *growe* and be grene þoruʒ hir goode lyuynge,
B.16.9   And so þoruʒ god and goode men *groweþ* þe fruyt Charite.'
B.16.12   Lord!' quod I, 'if any wight wite whiderout it *groweþ*?'
B.16.13   'It *groweþ* in a gardyn', quod he, 'þat god made hymselue
B.16.15   Herte hightte þe herber þat it Inne *groweþ*,
B.16.56   In what wode þei woxen and where þat þei *growed*,

B.16.58   And to my mynde, as me þinkeþ, on o more þei *growed*;
B.16.62   The ground þere it *groweþ*, goodnesse it hatte;
B.18.362   And my grace to *growe* ay gretter and widder.
B.19.313   Foulen þe fruyt in þe feld þer þei *growen* togideres,
B.20.57   And gerte gile *growe* þere as he a god weere.
C. 8.126   Shal no grayn þat here *groweth* gladyen ȝow at nede;
C.10.153   Fader and formour of al þat forth *groweth*
C.10.208   Thorw no sotil sciense on sour stok *growe*";
C.12.178   And by þe grayn þat *groweth* god vs all techeth
C.12.224   On fat lond ful of donge foulest wedes *groweth*.
C.13.176   And how out of greeut and of gras *gr[e]we* so many hewes
C.14.23   Ac grace is a graes þerfore to don hem [*growe* efte];
C.14.24   Ac grace ne *groweth* nat til gode wil gyue reyne
C.17.48   Thenne grace sholde *growe* ȝut and grene loue wexe
C.18.7   That hihte ymago dei, graciousliche hit *growede*.
C.18.23   Moche merueyled me on what more thei *growede*
C.18.56   A[c] in thre degrees hit *grewe*; grete ferly me thouhte,
C.18.83   Why *groweth* this fruyt in thre degres?' 'A goed skil,' he saide.
C.20.400   And my grace to *growe* ay [gretter] and wyddore.
C.21.313   Fouleth the fruyt in the feld ther thei *growe* togyderes
C.22.57   And garte gyle [*growe*] þere as he a god were.

growel n *gruel n.* A 1
A. 7.167   And bledde into þe bodyward a bolle ful of *growel*,

gruccheþ v *grucchen v.* A 2 grucche; B 3 grucche (2) gruccheþ (1); C 4
           groche (1) grochede (1) gruche (2)
A. 7.202   And ȝif þe [g]omes *grucche* bidde hem gon & sywnke,
A.10.116   Loke þou *grucche* nouȝt on god þeiȝ he gyue þe litel;
B.Pr.153   And if we *grucche* of his gamen he wol greuen vs alle,
B. 6.216   And if þe gomes *grucche* bidde hem go [and] swynke
B. 6.316   He greueþ hym ageyn god and *gruccheþ* ageyn Reson,
C.Pr.173   'And yf we *groche* of his game a wol greue vs [alle],
C. 6.111   On god when me greued auht and *grochede* of his sonde:
C. 8.226   And yf þe [g]omes *gruche* bid[d]e hem go and swynke
C. 8.336   Aȝenes Catones consayle comseth he to *gruche*:

gult(- > gilt(-; gurdeth > girdeþ; gurles > girles

gut n *gut n.* A 3 gut (1) guttis (1) guttys (1); B 5 gut (1) guttes (4); C 5
           gott (1) gottes (4)
A. 1.34   Al is not good to þe gost þat þe *gut* [ask]iþ,
A.11.44   And gnawen god in [þe gorge] whanne here *guttis* fullen.
A.12.76   For gronyng of my *guttys* I durst gon no ferther].
B. 1.36   [Al is nouȝt] good to þe goost þat þe *gut* askeþ,
B. 4.186   'But I rule þus youre Reaume rende out my *guttes*–
B. 5.340   Hise *guttes* bigonne to goþelen as two gredy sowes;
B.10.58   And gnawen god [in] þe gorge whanne hir *guttes* fullen.
B.13.89   And þanne shullen hise *guttes* goþele and he shal galpen after.
C. 1.34   Al is nat good to þe gost þat þe *gott* ascuth
C. 6.398   His *gottes* gan to gothly as t[w]o g[re]dy sowes,
C. 8.175   [He] beet hem so bothe he barste ner her *gottes*
C.11.39   And gnawen god with gorge when here *gottes* f[u]llen.
C.15.96   And thenne shal [his *gottes* gothelen] and [he shal] galpe [after].

*ȝaf > gyuen; ȝef > gyuen,if; ȝefte(s > gifte; ȝerne(eth > rennen; ȝeue(- >
gyuen; ȝif > gyuen,if; ȝifte(s > gifte; ȝiue(- > gyuen; ȝorn > rennen; ȝoue >
gyuen. **All other forms beginning with yogh will be found under Y.**

H

habbeþ > hauen; haberion > haubergeon

habite n *habit n.* A 1 abite; B 1; C 1 abite
A.Pr.3   In *abite* as an Ermyte, vnholy of werkis,
B.Pr.3   In *habite* as an heremite, vnholy of werkes,
C.Pr.3   In abite as an heremite, vnholy of werkes,

hacches n *hacche n.* C 2
C. 5.29   Or beggest thy bylyue aboute at men *hacches*
C.16.338   Thogh y my byliue sholde begge aboute at menne *hacches*.

hachet n *hachet n.* B 1; C 1
B. 3.306   Ax ouþer *hachet* or any wepene ellis,
C. 3.459   Ax oþer *hachet* or eny kyne w[e]pne,

hackenayman > hakeneyman; hacky > hakke; had- hae- > hauen

hayl n1 *hail n.* B 2 hayl (1) Hayll (1); C 1
B.13.161   Ne neiþer hete ne *hayl* ne noon helle pouke,
B.14.172   Ne neiþer hete ne *Hayll*, haue þei hir heele;
C.15.163   Ne n[oþ]ere hete ne *hayl* ne helle pouke hym greue,

hayl n2 *heil n.* A 1
A.12.62   'Al *hayl*,' quod on þo, and I answered, 'welcome, & with whom be
                 ȝe?'

hailsed v *heilsen v.* A 4 hailside (2) hailsiden (1) halsed (1); B 3; C 2
      haylsede
A. 5.82   I *hailside* hym as hendely as I his frend were:
A. 8.144   And þe enleuene sterris *ha[i]lsiden* hym alle.
A. 9.10   I *hailside* hem hendely as I hadde ylernid,
A.12.79   He *halsed* me, and I asked him after
B. 5.102   I *hailse[d]* hym hendely as I his frend were:
B. 7.166   And þe elleuene sterres *hailsed* hym alle.
B. 8.10   I *hailsed* hem hendely as I hadde ylerned,
C. 9.310   And the eleuene s[t]erres *haylsede* hym alle;
C.10.10   Y *haylsede* hem hendly as y hadde ylered

hayre > heyre

hayward n *heiward n.* B 1; C 5 haiward (1) hayward (4)
B.19.332 And made preesthod *hayward* þe while hymself wente
C. 5.16   Or haue an horn and be *hayward* and lygge þeroute [a]nyhtes
C. 6.368   An *hayward*, an heremyte, the hangeman of tybourne,
C.13.45   Ne non *haiward* is hote his wed for to taken.
C.13.47   And þe *hayward* happe with hym for to mete,
C.21.332 And made presthoed *hayward* the while hymsulue wente

hakeneyman n *hakeneie n.* A 1; B 1; C 2 hackenayman
A. 5.161   Hikke þe *hakeneyman* & hogge þe [nede]lere,
B. 5.310   Hikke þe *hakeneyman* and hugh þe Nedlere,
C. 6.365   Hicke þe *hackenayman* and hewe þe nedlare,
C. 6.378   Hicke þe *hackenayman* hit his hod aftur

hakeneys n *hakeneie n.* C 2
C. 2.178   Ac *hakeneys* hadde thei none bote hakeneys to huyre;
C. 2.178   Ac hakeneys hadde thei none bote *hakeneys* to huyre;

hakke v *hakken v.* B 1; C 1 hacky
B.19.401 And noȝt *hakke* after holynesse; hold þi tonge, Conscience!
C.21.401 And nat *hacky* aftur holinesse; hold thy tonge, consience!

hald- > holden; halewe > halwe

half n *half n.* A 5; B 8; C 9
A. 2.5   'Loke on þi left *half*, & lo where he standis,
A. 2.7   I lokide on [my] left *half* as þat lady me tauȝte,
A. 3.168   Þou hast hongid on myn *half* enleuene tymes,
A. 6.65   Leue hem on þi left *half*, & loke nouȝt þereaftir,
A.11.119   Leue hym on þi left *half* a large myle or more,
B. 2.5   'Loke [o]n þi left *half*, and lo where he stondeþ,
B. 2.7   I loked on my left *half* as þe lady me tauȝte
B. 3.73   Lat noȝt þi left *half*, late ne raþe,
B. 3.181   Thow hast hanged on myn *half* elleuene tymes,
B. 3.341   Hadde she loked þat [left] *half* and þe leef torned
B. 5.578   Leue hem on þi lift *half* and loke noȝt þerafter.
B.10.167   Leue [hym] on þi left *half* a large myle or moore

B.13.316 What on bak, and what on body *half*, and by þe two sides
C. 2.5   'Loke [o]n thy left *half*, and loo where he standeth,
C. 2.8   Y lokede [o]n my luft *half* as þe lady me tauhte,
C. 2.58   Were beden to þe Bridale a bothe *half* þe contre,
C. 3.75   Lat nat thy lyft *ha[lf]*, oure lord techeth,
C. 3.227   Thow hast hanged on my *half* enleuene tymes
C. 3.493   Ac hadde she loked in þe luft *half* and þe lef turned
C. 7.225   And leu[e] hem [o]n þ[y] luft *ha[lf]* and loke [nat] þeraftur
C. 8.349   Shal brynge bane and batayle on bothe *half* þe mone;
C.18.66   Then tho that selde haen þe sonne and sitten in þe North *half*;

half adj *half adj.* A 5; B 8; C 10
A. 2.190 And wiþheld him *half* [a] ȝer & elleuene dayes.
A. 7.4   I haue an *half* akir to er[e]n be þe heiȝe weiȝe;
A. 7.5   Hadde y [erid] þat *half* akir
A. 7.98   To erien þis *half* akir helpen hym manye;
A. 7.108   And holpen [to] ere þe *half* akir wiþ 'hey trolly lolly'.
B. 2.231 And [wiþ]helden hym an *half* yeer and elleuene dayes.
B. 3.326 By sixe sonnes and a ship and *half* a shef of Arwes;
B. 6.4   I haue an *half* acre to erie by þe heiȝe weye;
B. 6.5   Hadde I eryed þis *half* acre and sowen it after
B. 6.106   To erie þis *half* acre holpen hym manye;
B. 6.116   And holpen ere þ[e] *half* acre wiþ 'how trolly lolly'.
B.13.151 Wiþ *half* a laumpe lyne in latyn, Ex vi transicionis,,
B.13.201 Haue pacience parfitliche þan *half* þi pak of bokes.'
C. 2.241 And [wiþ]helden hym [a] *half* ȝere and eleue dayes.
C. 3.479 Be six [s]onnes [and] a ship and *half* a shef of Arwes;
C. 5.133 [That] here hed was worth *half* marc and his hoed nat a grote.
C. 6.267 And yf y ȝede to þe plough y pynched on his *half* aker
C. 8.2   Ich haue an *half* aker to erye by þe heye [way];
C. 8.3   Haued ich yered þis *half* aker and ysowed hit aftur
C. 8.113   To erien this *half* ak[er] holpen hym monye;
C. 8.123   And holpe erye this *half* aker with 'hey trollilolly.'
C. 9.150   Loef oþer *half* loef other a lompe of chese
C.15.179 Haue pacience parfitlyche then *half* thy pak of bokes.

halfpeny n *half adj.* A 1 halpeny; B 1; C 1 halpeny
A. 7.289 Ne non *halpeny* ale in no wyse drynke,
B. 6.305 Ne noon *halfpeny* ale in none wise drynke,
C. 8.327 Ne noon *halpeny* ale in none wyse drynke

haly > holy; haly_day(es > holy_day

halie v *halen v.* C 1
C.10.94   And *halie* with þe hoked ende [i]lle men to gode

halle > hallen,moot_halle

hallen *halle n.* A 3 halle (2) hallis (1); B 7 halle (6) halles (1); C 5 halle
   (4) halles (1)
A. 2.38   Þer nas *halle* ne hous to herberwe þe peple,
A. 4.118   Whil mede haþ þe maistrie to mo[te] in þis *halle*.
A. 6.77   Alle þe housis ben helid, *hallis* & chaumbris,
B. 4.135   While Mede haþ þe maistrie [to mote in þis] *halle*.
B. 5.590   And alle þe houses ben hiled, *halles* and chambres,
B.10.97   Elenge is þe *halle*, ech day in þe wike,
B.10.101 Or in a chambre wiþ a chymenee, and leue þe chief *halle*
B.12.200 As þo þat seten at þe syde table or wiþ þe souereynes of þe *halle*,
B.13.433 Sholde noon harlot haue audience in *halle* n[e] in Chambre
B.20.133 Muche of þe wit and wisdom of westmynstre *halle*.
C. 7.93   Sholde non harlote haue audiense in *halle* ne in chaumbre
C.14.139 As tho þat sitten at þe syde table or wiþ þe souereyns [of þe] *halle*
C.15.39   Resoun stoed and s[t]yhlede as for styward of *halle*.
C.22.133 Moche of þe Wyt and Wisdoem of Westmunstre *halle*.

halp(e > helpen; halpeny > halfpeny

hals n *hals n.* A 2; B 4; C 4 hals (2) halse (2)
A. 2.157 And do hem hange be þe *hals* & alle þat hem maynteniþ.
A. 7.56   And heng his hoper at his *hals* in stede of a scrippe:
B.Pr.170 [And hangen it vpon þe cattes *hals*; þanne here we mowen]
B.Pr.179 Ne hangen it aboute [his] *hals* al Engelond to wynne;
B. 2.196 And doon hem hange by þe *hals* and alle þat hem maynteneþ.
B. 6.61   And [heng his] hoper at [his] *hals* in stede of a Scryppe:

C.Pr.187 And hongen hit aboute þe cattes *halse*; thanne here we mowe
C.Pr.196 Ne hanged it aboute his *hals* al yngelond to wynne;
C. 2.210 And do hem hange by þe *halse* and alle þat hem maynteyneth.
C. 8.60   And heng his hopur on his *hal[s]* in stede of a scryppe;

halsede v *halsen v.(1)* A 1 halside; B 1; C 1
A. 1.71   And *h[a]lside* hire on þe heiȝe name, er heo þennis ȝede,
B. 1.73   And *[halsede]* hire on þe heiȝe name, er she þennes yede,
C. 1.70   And *ha[ls]ede* here on the hey name or she thennes [ȝede]

halsyng ger *halsinge ger.(2)* C 1
C. 6.187 And handlyng and *halsyng* and also thorw kyssyng,

halt > holden

haluebreþeren n *halfbrother n.* B 1; C 1 haluebrethere
B.18.393 And my mercy shal be shewed to manye of my *[halue]breþeren*,
C.20.436 To be merciable to monye of my *haluebrethere*.

haluendele n *halfdel n.& adj.* C 1
C. 7.29   Nat twies in ten ȝer and thenne telle y nat þe *haluendele*.

halwe v *halwen v.* B 1; C 1 halewe
B.15.529 [And nauȝt to] huppe aboute in Engelond to *halwe* mennes Auteres
C.17.279 And nat in Ingelond to huppe aboute and *halewe* men auters

han > hauen

hand n *honde n.* A 9 handes (1) handis (2) hond (3) hondis (3); B 38
  hand (19) hande (2) handes (6) hond (4) hondes (7); C 37 hand (13)
  hande (1) handes (17) hoend (4) hoende (1) hondes (1)
A. 3.55   Let not þi left *hond*, late ne raþe,
A. 3.56   Be war what þi riȝt *hond* werchiþ or deliþ,
A. 7.232 Oþer wiþ teching, oþer telling, or trauaillyng of *hondis*,
A. 7.235 He þat get his fode here wiþ trauaile of his *hondis*,
A. 7.291 Laboureris þat haue no land [to] lyue on [but] here *handis*
A. 8.63   Alle libbyng laboureris þat lyuen be here *hondis*,
A. 9.72   Trewe of his tunge & of his two *handis*,
A.10.20   Sire werche wel wiþ þin *hond*, [a] wiȝt man of strengþe,
A.12.38   Þan held I vp myn *handes* to scripture þe wise
B. 5.286 But if it were wiþ þi tonge or ellis wiþ þi *hondes*.
B. 6.248 Or [wiþ tech]ynge or [tell]ynge or trauaillynge [of *hondes*],
B. 6.307 Laborers þat haue no land to lyue on but hire *handes*
B. 7.61   Alle libbynge laborers þat lyuen [by] hir *hondes*,
B. 8.81   Trewe of his tunge and of his two *handes*,
B. 9.21   Sire werch-wel-wiþ-þyn-*hand*, a wiȝt man of strengþe,
B.10.438 In þe *hondes* of almyȝty god, and he woot þe soþe
B.11.297 That haþ no lond ne lynage riche ne good loos of hise *handes*.
B.12.114 Hadde neuere lewed man leue to leggen *hond* on þat cheste
B.12.120 And leiden *hand* þeron to liften it vp loren here lif after.
B.13.297 And most sotil of song oþer sleyest of *handes*,
B.14.242 And haþ *hondes* and armes of [a long] lengþe,
B.15.122 [And beere] bedes in hir *hand* and a book vnder hir arme.
B.15.291 And wan wiþ hise *hondes* þat his wombe neded.
B.15.455 Ytouked and yteynted and vnder taillours *hande*.
B.15.472 [And by þe *hond* fedde foules [i]s folk vnderstonde
B.17.57   He myȝte neiþer steppe ne stande ne stere foot ne *handes*
B.17.67   He lighte adown of Lyard and ladde hym in his *hande*,
B.17.139 Or Eretikes wiþ argumentȝ, þyn *hond* þow hem shewe.
B.17.140 For god is after an *hand*; yheer now and knowe it.
B.17.144 The pawme is [þe piþ of] þe *hand*, and profreþ forþ þe fyngres
B.17.145 To ministren and to make þat myȝt of *hand* knoweþ;
B.17.154 Thus are þei alle but oon, as it an *hand* weere,
B.17.159 And as þe *hand* halt harde and alle þyng faste
B.17.168 Na moore [may an *hand*] meue wiþoute fyngres.
B.17.169 And as my fust is ful *hand* y[f]olden togideres
B.17.172 The fyngres formen a ful *hand* to portreye or peynten;
B.17.176 The pawme is pureliche þe *hand*, haþ power by hymselue
B.17.184 And alle [þre] but o god as is myn *hand* and my fyngres.
B.17.186 Al is but an *hand*, [howso I turne it.
B.17.187 Ac who is hurte in þe *hand*], euene in þe myddes,
B.17.192 Were þe myddel of myn *hand* ymaymed or yperissed
B.17.195 And þe myddel of myn *hand* wiþoute maleese
B.17.278 Sleeþ a man for hise moebles wiþ mouþ or with *handes*.
B.18.77   That noon harlot were so hardy to leyen *hond* vpon hym.
B.19.170 And took Thomas by þe *hand* and tauȝte hym to grope
B.19.246 He wissed hem wynne it ayein þoruȝ wightnesse of *handes*
B.20.117 He bar a bowe in his *hand* and manye brode arewes,
C.Pr.226 Webbesteres and walkeres and wynners with *handes*,
C. 1.84   For who is trewe of his tonge and of his two *handes*,
C. 3.118 'Haue reuthe on this regraters þat han riche *handes*,
C. 3.243 In his enemyes *handes* his heritage of Fraunce.
C. 3.289 Tha[t] vnlaufulliche lyuen hauen large *handes*
C. 4.143 And yf ȝe wor[c]he it in werke y wedde bothe myn *handes*
C. 6.109 The harm þat y haue do with *hand* and with tonge.
C. 8.258 Lo! what þe sauter sayth to swynkares with *handes*:

C. 8.260 Thorw eny lele labour as thorw lymes and *handes*:
C. 8.329 Laborers þat han no lond to lyue on but here *handes*
C. 9.58   Alle libbyng laborers þat lyuen with here *handes*
C. 9.199 And summe lyuede by here letterure and labour of here *handes*
C.10.78   Ho[so] is trewe of his tonge and of his two *handes*
C.10.147 Sire worch-wel-with-thyn-*hand*, a wyht man of strenghe,
C.13.111 That hath n[o] lond ne lynage ryche ne good los of his *handes*.
C.14.59   Hadde neuere lewede [man] leue to legge *hand* on þat cheste
C.14.63   And all lewede þat leide *hand* þeron loren lyf aftir.
C.16.82   And hath *hondes* and Armes of a longe lenthe
C.17.18   And wan with his *handes* al þat hym nedede.
C.19.56   For he ne myhte stepe ne stande ne stere foet ne *handes*
C.19.66   [A l]ihte a[dou]n of lyard and ladde hym in his *hand[e]*
C.19.112 Or eretikes with argumentis, thien *hoend* thow hem shewe.
C.19.118 The paume is the pethe of the *hand* and profereth [forth] the
          fyngeres
C.19.119 To ministre and to make þat myhte of *hand* knoweth
C.19.129 Thus are they alle bote oen as hit an *hand* were,
C.19.131 And as þe fuste is a ful *hand* yfolde togyderes,
C.19.136 The fyngeres is a fol *hand* for failed thei or thombe
C.19.141 The paume is puyrliche the *hand* and hath power by hymsulue
C.19.150 And alle thre is bote o god as myn *hoend* and my fyngeres.
C.19.152 Al is bote oen *hoend* howso y turne hit.
C.19.153 Ac ho is herte in the *hand* euene in þe myddes
C.19.158 Were þe myddel of myn *hand* ymaymed or ypersed
C.19.161 And þe myddel of myn *hand*] withoute maleese
C.19.259 Sleth a man for his mebles with mouthe or with *handes*.
C.21.170 And toek Thomas by the *hoende* and tauhte hym to grope
C.21.246 He wissede [h]e[m] wynne hit aȝeyn thorw whitnesse of *handes*
C.22.117 He baer a bowe in his *hoend* and many brode arwes,

handele > handle

handy_dandy n *handidandi n.* A 1; B 1; C 1
A. 4.61   For of hise penys he proffride *handy dandy* to paye.
B. 4.75   To maken [his] pees wiþ his pens, *handy dandy* payed.
C. 4.68   And for to haue here helpe *handy dandy* payde.

handle v *hondlen v.* A 1 yhandlit; B 2 handle (1) yhandled (1); C 1
  handele
A. 2.99   Lediþ hire to lundoun þere lawe is *yhandlit*
B. 2.135 Ledeþ hire to Londoun þere [lawe] is *[yhandled]*,
B.20.313 'Ther is a Surgien in þ[e] sege þat softe kan *handle*,
C.22.313 'Ther is a surgien in the sege that softe can *handele*

handlynge ger *hondlinge ger.* B 1; C 2 handlyng (1) handlynge (1)
B.14.56   In [ondynge] and in *handlynge* and in alle þi fyue wittes,
C. 6.187 And handlyng and halsyng and also thorw kyssyng,
C.15.255 In [ond]ynge and [in] *handlynge* [and] in alle thy fyue wittes,

handmaiden n *honde n.* B 1; C 1 hondmayden
B.16.98   And seide hendeliche to hym, 'lo me his *handmaiden*
C.18.131 And saide hendely to hym, 'lo me his *hondmayden*

handwhile n *honde n.* B 1; C 1
B.19.272 And harewede in an *handwhile* al holy Scripture
C.21.272 And harwed in an *handwhile* al holy scripture

hangeman n *hangman n.* C 1
C. 6.368 An hayward, an heremyte, the *hangeman* of tybourne,

hangen v *hongen v.* A 8 hange (2) hangiþ (1) heng (1) honge (1) hongid
  (1) hongide (2); B 22 hange (5) hanged (5) hangen (4) hangeþ (3)
  hangyng (1) hangynge (1) heng (1) hengen (1) honge (1); C 19 hange
  (4) hanged (5) hangeth (4) hangid (1) heng (1) hengen (1)
  honge (1) hongen (1)
A. 1.66   And siþen on an Eldir *hongide* him aftir.
A. 1.148 To hem þat *hongide* him [heiȝe] & his herte þirlide.
A. 2.157 And do hem *hange* be þe hals & alle þat hem maynteniþ.
A. 3.102 [But I be holly at ȝour heste *honge* me ellys].'
A. 3.130 And *hangiþ* hym for hattrede þat harmide neuere.
A. 3.168 Þou hast *hongid* on myn half enleuene tymes,
A. 4.20   *Hange* on hym þe heuy bridel to holde his hed lowe,
A. 7.56   And *heng* his hoper at his hals in stede of a scrippe:
B.Pr.170 [And *hangen* it vpon þe cattes hals; þanne here we mowen]
B.Pr.176 Ac þo þe belle was ybrouȝt and on þe beiȝe *hanged*
B.Pr.179 Ne *hangen* it aboute [his] hals al Engelond to wynne;
B. 1.68   And siþen on an Eller *hanged* hym [after].
B. 1.174 To hem þat *hengen* hym heiȝ and his herte þirled.
B. 2.196 And doon hem *hange* by þe hals and alle þat hem maynteneþ.
B. 3.113 But I be holly at youre heste *hange* me [ellis].'
B. 3.141 And *hangeþ* h[y]m for hatrede þat harm[e]de neuere.
B. 3.181 Thow hast *hanged* on myn half elleuene tymes,
B. 4.22   *Hange* on hym þe heuy brydel to holde his heed lowe,
B. 5.136 And neuelynge wiþ þe nose and his nekke *hangyng*,
B. 5.234 Thow haddest be bettre worþi ben *hanged* þerfore.'

B. 5.279   Thanne weex þ[e] sherewe in wanhope & wolde han *hanged*
           hym[self]
B. 5.594   Of almesdedes are þe hokes þat þe gates *hangen* on.
B. 6.61   And [*heng* his] hoper at [his] hals in stede of a Scryppe;
B.12.292   And an hope *hangynge* þerInne to haue a mede for his truþe;
B.13.390   Vpon a cruwel coueitise m[y conscience] gan *hange*.
B.15.214   Ne at Ancres þere a box *hangeþ;* alle swiche þei faiten.
B.16.66   'To [dyuyse] þe fruyt þat so faire *hangeþ'.*
B.17.6   And þat is cros and cristendom and crist þeron to *honge;*
B.18.250   And leet out Symondes sone[s] to seen hym *hange* on roode.
B.18.379   It is noȝt vsed in erþe to *hangen* a feloun
C.Pr.99   In menynge of myracles muche wex *hangeth* there;
C.Pr.187   And *hongen* hit aboute þe cattes halse; thanne here we mowe
C.Pr.193   Ac tho þe belle was ybroughte and on þe beygh *hangid*
C.Pr.196   Ne *hanged* it aboute his hals al yngelond to wynne;
C. 1.170   To hem þat *hengen* [hym] hye and [his] herte thorlede.
C. 2.210   And do hem *hange* by þe halse and alle þat hem maynteyneth;
C. 3.150   But y be holly at thyn heste; lat *hange* me elles.'
C. 3.179   And *hangeth* hym for ha[t]rede þat harmede nere.
C. 3.227   Thow hast *hanged* on my half enleuene tymes
C. 6.238   Thow wolt be *hanged* heye þerfore, here oþer in helle.
C. 7.242   The hokes aren Almesdedes þat þe ȝates *hange* on.
C. 8.60   And *heng* his hopur on his hal[s] in stede of a scryppe;
C.10.163   A[s] somme *hangeth* hemsulue and oþerwhile adrencheth.
C.10.240   For thogh þe fader be a frankeleyn and for a felon be *hanged*
C.14.214   And hope *hangeth* ay þeron to haue þat treuthe deserueth:
C.17.138   And theues louyen and leute hatien and at þe laste ben *hanged*
C.19.8   The which is Cr[oes] and cristendoem and cr[ist] þer[o]n [to]
           hang[e];
C.20.259   And lette out symondes sones to sen hym *honge* on rode:
C.20.421   Hit is nat vsed [i]n erthe to *hangen* [a] felo[n]

hangynge ger *honginge ger.* &> *hangen* C 1
C. 3.408   How he absoloun to *hangynge* brouhte;

hanselle n *hanselle n.* A 1 hansele; B 1; C 1 hansull
A. 5.167   Ȝeue glotoun wiþ glad chiere good ale to *hansele.*
B. 5.318   Geue Gloton wiþ glad chere good ale to *hanselle.*
C. 6.375   Geuen glotoun with glad chere good ale to *hansull.*

hap n *hap n.* A 2 happes (1) happis (1); B 3 hap (2) happes (1); C 3
A. 5.78   His grace & hise gode *happis* greuide me wel sore.
A.12.111   God for his goudnesse gif hem swyche *happes*
B. 5.98   His grace and his goode *happes* greuen me [wel] soore.
B.12.106   And haþ noon *hap* wiþ his ax his enemy to hitte,
B.20.385   And sende me *hap* and heele til I haue Piers þe Plowman.'
C. 3.298   Ne haue *hap* to his hele mede to deserue.
C.14.51   And hath non *hap* with his ax his enemye to hutte,
C.22.385   And s[e]nde me *hap* and hele til y haue [Peres Plouhman]'.

hapeward > apeward; hapliche > happily

happe v *happen v.(1)* A 1; B 3; C 7 happe (5) happed (1) happeth (1)
A. 3.262   And riȝt as agag hadde *happe* shal somme:
B. 3.286   And riȝt as Agag hadde *happe* shul somme.
B. 6.46   Thouȝ he be þyn vnderlyng here wel may *happe* in heuene
B.16.87   He hitte after hym, [*happe*] how it myȝte,
C. 3.439   And riht as agag hadde *happe* shal somme:
C. 5.95   And ay loste an[d] loste and at þe laste hym *happed*
C. 9.113   Ne none muracles maken; Ac many tymes hem *happeth*
C.11.111   A[c] if þow *happe*,' quod he, 'þat þou hitte on clergie
C.13.47   And þe hayward *happe* with hym for to mete,
C.15.6   And how elde man[a]ced me, so myhte *happe*
C.18.119   And hit aftur þe fende, *happe* how hit myhte.

happes > hap

happily adv *happili adv.* A 1; B 1; C 1 hapliche
A. 6.101   *Happily* an hundrit wynter er þou eft entre.
B. 5.615   *Happily* an hundred wynter er þow eft entre.
C. 7.267   *Hapliche* an hundred wynter ar thow eft entre.

happis > hap

hard adj *hard adj.* A 4 hard (3) hardere (1); B 12 hard (11) hardere (1);
C 12 hard (10) harde (1) hardore (1)
A. 1.165   Arn none *hardere* þan [hy] whanne [hy] ben auauncid,
A. 4.146   'Ac it is wel *hard*, be myn hed, herto to bringe it.
A. 6.113   It is wel *hard*, be myn hed, any of ȝow alle,
A.11.155   Astronomye is *hard* þing & euil for to knowe;
B. 1.191   Are [none *hardere*] þan hij whan þei ben auaunced,
B. 4.183   It is [wel] *hard*, by myn heed, hert[o] to brynge it,
B. 5.628   It is [wel] *hard*, by myn heed, any of yow alle,
B.10.212   Ac Astronomye is *hard* þyng and yuel for to knowe;
B.14.278   '[Al þis] in englissh', quod Pacience, 'it is wel *hard* to expounen,
B.14.325   So *hard* it is', quod haukyn, 'to lyue and to do synne.
B.17.11   [He plukkede] forþ a patente, a pece of an *hard* roche

B.17.43   Than for to techen hem two, and to *hard* to lerne þe leeste!
B.17.44   It is ful *hard* for any man on Abraham bileue
B.20.217   Sleuþe wiþ his slynge an *hard* [s]aut he made.
B.20.300   Ypocrisie and h[ij] an *hard* assaut þei [ȝeuen].
B.20.335   Ypocrisie haþ hurt hem; ful *hard* is if þei keuere.'
C. 1.187   Aren none *hardore* ne hungriore then men of holy chirche,
C. 3.400   To syke for here synnes and soffre *harde* penaunc[e]
C. 4.117   Hit is ful *hard*, by myn heued, herto to bryngen hit
C. 7.281   Hit is ful *hard*, be myn heued, eny of ȝow alle
C.12.199   But as an hosebonde hopeth aftur an *hard* wynter,
C.12.244   And he for his *hard* holdyng in helle paarautur:
C.16.119   In engelysch is ful *hard* Ac sumdel y shal telle the.
C.19.12   A pluhte forth a patente, a pece of an *hard* roche
C.20.62   The *hard* roch al toroef and riht derk nyht hit semede;
C.22.217   Sleuthe with his slynge a[n] *hard* sawt he made.
C.22.300   Ypocrisye and [h]y an *hard* sawt they ȝeuen.
C.22.335   Ypocrysye haeth her[t]e hem; ful *hard* is yf thei keuere.'

harde adv *harde adv.* &> *hard* A 3; B 9 harde (8) hardest (1); C 7 harde
(5) hardere (1) hardest (1)
A.Pr.21   In settyng & sowyng swonke ful *harde;*
A. 1.171   So [*harde*] haþ auarice haspide ȝow togideris.
A. 8.104   I shal cesse of my sowyng,' quaþ peris, '& swynke not so *harde,*
B.Pr.21   In settynge and sowynge swonken ful *harde;*
B. 1.197   So *harde* haþ Auarice yhasped [yow] togideres.
B. 7.122   I shal cessen of my sowyng', quod Piers, '& swynke noȝt so *harde,*
B.11.85   'Wherfore lourestow?' quod lewtee, and loked on me *harde.*
B.12.179   In which flood þe fend fondeþ a man *hardest.*
B.17.159   And as þe hand halt *harde* and alle þyng faste
B.20.185   So *harde* he yede ouer myn heed it wole be sene euere.
B.20.216   That wiþ Antecrist helden *harde* ayein Conscience.
B.20.301   [Ypocrisie at þe yate *harde* gan fighte]
C.Pr.23   In settynge and sowynge swonken ful *harde*
C.Pr.122   Wel *hardere* and grettere on suche shrewed faderes
C. 1.192   So *harde* haþ auaryce yhasped hem togederes.
C.14.179   In whiche floed þe fende fondeth [a] man *hardest.*
C.22.185   So *harde* he ȝede ouer myn heued hit wol be sene euere.
C.22.216   That with auntecrist helden *harde* aȝeyn Consience.
C.22.301   Ypocrisye at þe ȝate *harde* gan fyhte

hardelyche > hardiliche; hardere > hard,harde

hardy adj *hardi adj.* A 3; B 7 hardy (5) hardier (1) hardiere (1); C 11
hardy (10) hardior (1)
A. 4.47   I am not *hardy* [for hym vnneþe] to loke.'
A. 7.173   þat hunger was not *hardy* on hem for to loke.
A.12.23   "I am not *hardy*," quod he, "þat I herde with erys,
B. 4.60   I am noȝt *hardy* for hym vnneþe to loke.'
B. 6.185   That hunger was noȝt *hardy* on hem for to loke.
B.14.308   And an *hardy* man of herte among an heep of þeues;
B.17.108   For he halt hym *hardier* on horse þan he þat is [on] foote.
B.18.77   That noon harlot were so *hardy* to leyen hond vpon hym.
B.19.58   Who was *hardiere* þan he? his herte blood he shadde
B.19.290   And who[so] ete [of] þat seed *hardy* was euere
C. 3.237   Hast arwed many *hardy* man þat hadde wille to fyhte,
C. 3.299   Y halde hym ouer *hardy* or elles nat trewe
C. 3.322   Noyther [thei ne] here ayres *hardy* to claymen
C. 3.352   So of ho[l] herte cometh hope and *hardy* relacoun
C. 4.63   Y am nat *hardy* for hym vnnethe to loke.'
C. 8.181   That hunger was nat *hardy* on hem for to loke.
C. 9.266   How, herde! where is thyn ho[u]nd[e] and thyn *hardy* herte
C.13.10   And Abraham not *hardy* ones to letten hym
C.13.62   Haue hors and *hardy* men; thogh he mette theues
C.21.58   Ho was *hardior* then he? his herte bloed he she[d]de
C.21.290   And hoso ete of þa[t] seed *hardy* was euere

hardie v *hardien v.* B 1
B.15.437   And *hardie* hem þat bihynde ben, and ȝyue hem good euidence.

hardier adv *hardi adv.* &> *hardy* B 1; C 1 hardyore
B.14.262   Muche *hardier* may he asken þat here myȝte haue his wille
C.16.102   Moche *hardyore* may he aske þat here myhte haue his wille

hardiliche adv *hardili adv.* A 1 hardily; B 1; C 2 hardelyche (1)
hardiloker (1)
A. 7.31   And go hunte *hardily* [to] har[is] & [to] fox[is],
B. 6.29   And go hunte *hardiliche* to hares and to foxes,
C. 6.305   For an hore of here ers wynnynge may *hardiloker* tythe
C. 8.28   And go hunte *hardelyche* to hares and to foxes,

hardynesse n *hardinesse n.* B 1; C 2 hardinesse (1) hardynesse (1)
B.19.31   And of *hardynesse* of herte and of hendenesse,
B.20.79   That hadde no boie *hardynesse* hym to touche in deynge.
C.21.31   And of *hardinesse* of herte and of hendenesse

hardior > hardy; hardyore > hardier; hardore > hard

hare n *hare n.* A 1 haris; B 2 hare (1) hares (1); C 2 hare (1) hares (1)
A. 7.31   And go hunte hardily [to] har[is] & [to] fox[is],
B. 5.417   But I kan fynden in a feld or in a furlang an *hare*
B. 6.29   And go hunte hardiliche to *hares* and to foxes,
C. 7.32   Ac y can fynden in a feld and in a forlong an *hare*
C. 8.28   And go hunte hardelyche to *hares* and to foxes,

harewen v *harwen v.* B 4 harewe (1) harewede (1) harewen (1) hareweþ (1); C 5 harewe (1) harwed (1) harwen (2) harweth (1)
B.19.268   Al þat hise oxen eriede þei to *harewen* after.
B.19.272   And *harewede* in an handwhile al holy Scripture
B.19.309   Thise foure sedes Piers sew, and siþþe he dide hem *harewe*
B.19.315   'Harreweþ alle þat konneþ kynde wit by conseil of þise docto[urs],
C. 5.19   Heggen or *harwen* or swyn or gees dryue
C.21.268   All þat his oxes erede they t[o] harwe[n] aftur.
C.21.272   And *harwed* in an handwhile al holy scripture
C.21.309   Thise foure sedes [Peres] sewe and sennes he dede hem *harewe*
C.21.315   'Harweth alle þa[t] conneth kynde wit bi consail of [this] doctours

harlot n *harlot n.* A 2 harlotis; B 11 harlot (3) harlotes (7) harlottes (1); C 8 harlote (1) harlotes (7)
A. 4.104   And *harlotis* holynesse be holde for an [heþyng];
A. 7.47   Holde wiþ none *harlotis* ne here nouȝt here talis,
B. 4.118   And *harlottes* holynesse be holden for an [heþyng];
B. 6.52   Hold wiþ none *harlotes* ne here noȝt hir tales,
B.10.30   *Harlotes* for hir harlotrie may haue of hir goodes,
B.13.415   And if he auȝt wole here it is an *harlotes* tonge.
B.13.433   Sholde noon *harlot* haue audience in halle n[e] in Chambre
B.14.183   [To hores, to *harlotes*, to alle maner peple].
B.15.134   So *harlotes* and hores arn holpe wiþ swiche goodes
B.17.111   He was vnhardy, þat *harlot*, and hidde hym in Inferno.
B.17.279   For þat þe holy goost haþ to kepe þ[o] *harlotes* destruyeþ,
B.18.77   That noon *harlot* were so hardy to leyen hond vpon hym.
B.20.144   And armed hym [in] haste [in] *harlotes* wordes,
C. 3.301   *Harlotes* and hoores and also fals leches,
C. 4.113   And *harlotes* holynesse be an heye ferie;
C. 6.369   Dawe þe dikere with a dosoyne *harlotes*
C. 7.93   Sholde non *harlote* haue audiense in halle ne in chaumbre
C. 8.50   Hoold with non *harlotes* ne here nat here tales
C.11.26   *Harlotes* for here harlotrye aren holpe ar nedy pore;
C.19.260   For that the holy goest hath to kepe tho *harlotes* distruyeth,
C.22.144   And Armed hym in haste in *harlotes* wordes

harlotrie n *harlotrie n.* A 2; B 7 harlotrie (4) harlotrye (3); C 6 harlotrie (4) harlotrye (2)
A. 4.106   And haten [to] here *harlotrie* oþer mouþe it;
A.11.31   For ȝif *harlotrie* ne halp[e] hem betere, haue god my trouþe.
B. 4.115   And haten alle *harlotrie* to heren or to mouþen it;
B. 5.406   I haue leuere here an *harlotrye* or a Somer game of Souters,
B.10.30   Harlotes for hir *harlotrie* may haue of hir goodes,
B.10.46   Ne [holpe hir] *harlotrye*, haue god my trouþe.
B.13.353   And of hir *harlotrye* and horedom in hir elde tellen.
B.13.430   To entice men þoruȝ hir tales to synne and *harlotrie*.
B.15.106   And hatien to here *harlotrie*, and [au]ȝt to vnderfonge
C. 4.110   And hatien alle *harlotrie* to heren oþer to mouthen hit;
C. 7.22   Y hadde leuere here an *harlotrye* or a lesyng to lauhen of
C. 7.75   But *harlotrie* and horedom or elles of som wynnynge;
C. 7.90   To entise men thorw here tales to synne and *harlotrie*.
C.11.26   Harlotes for here *harlotrye* aren holpe ar nedy pore;
C.16.260   And hatien *harlotrie* and to vnderfonge þe tythes

harlottes > harlot

harm n *harm n.* A 3; B 3 harm (2) harmes (1); C 5
A. 3.69   For þise arn men of þise molde þat most *harm* werchiþ
A. 4.28   For to saue hemself from shame & from *harm*.
A. 5.83   He is douȝtiere þanne I–I dar non *harm* don hym,
B. 3.80   For þise are men on þis molde þat moost *harm* wercheþ
B. 4.31   For to saue hem[seluen] from shame and from *harmes*.
B. 5.103   He is douȝtier þan I; I dar [noon *harm* doon hym],
C. 3.81   For thyse men don most *harm* to þe mene peple,
C. 6.109   The *harm* þat y haue do with hand and with tonge.
C. 6.117   *Harm* of eny man, byhynde or bifore.
C. 9.47   That innocent and nedy is and no man *harm* wolde,
C.15.112   'Do thy neyhebore non *harm* ne thysulue nother

harme v *harmen v.* A 3 harme (1) harmid (1) harmide (1); B 3 harmed (2) harmede (1); C 2 harmed (1) harmede (1)
A. 2.166   Þat holy chirche for hem worþ *harmid* for euere;
A. 3.130   And hangiþ hym for hattrede þat *harmide* neuere.
A.11.252   To *harme* hem ne slen hem god hiȝte vs neuere.
B. 2.205   That holy chirche for hem worþ *harmed* for euere.]
B. 3.141   And hangeþ h[y]m for hatrede þat *harm[e]de* neuere.
B.13.107   For ye han *harmed* vs two in þat ye eten þe puddyng,
C. 2.251   And holy churche thorw hem worth *harmed* for euere.'

C. 3.179   And hangeth hym for ha[t]rede þat *harmede* nere.

harneis n *harneis n.* B 1; C 1 harneys
B.15.221   Boþe in grey and in grys and in gilt *harneis*,
C.16.346   Bothe in gray and in grys and in gult *harneys*,

harow > harrow

harpe n *harpe n. &> harpen* A 1
A. 1.137   And ek þe plante of pes; preche it in þin *harpe*

harpen v *harpen v.* B 2 harpeden (1) harpen (1); C 2 harpe (1) harpeden (1)
B.13.231   Farten ne fiþelen at festes ne *harpen*,
B.18.407   Manye hundred of Aungeles *harpeden* and songen,
C.15.205   Farten ne fythelen at festes ne *harpe*,
C.20.450   Many hundret of Angels *harpeden* and songen,

harpour n *harpere n.* B 1
B.14.25   Shal noon heraud ne *harpour* haue a fairer garnement

harrow exclam *harou interj.& n.* B 1; C 1 harow
B.20.88   There was 'harrow!' and 'help! here comeþ kynde
C.22.88   There was 'harow!' and 'helpe! here cometh kynde

harwe- > harewen; haspide > yhaspid; hast > hauen

haste n *haste n. &> hasteþ,hauen* A 3; B 6; C 7
A. 7.159   Hungir in *haste* þanne hente wastour be þe mawe,
A. 7.226   And ȝaf [it] hym in *haste* þat hadde ten before,
A. 7.280   Hungir [eet] þis in *haste* & askide aftir more.
B. 6.174   Hunger in *haste* þoo hente wastour by þe [mawe]
B. 6.242   And yaf [it hym in *haste* þat hadde ten bifore];
B. 6.296   [Hunger eet þis] in *haste* and axed after moore.
B.20.136   An[d] to þe Arches in *haste* he yede anoon after
B.20.144   And armed hym [in] *haste* [in] harlotes wordes,
B.20.331   And in *haste* askede what his wille were.
C. 8.171   Hunger in *haste* tho hente wastour by þe mawe
C. 8.205   And bade hunger in *haste* hye hym out of contraye
C. 8.318   Hunger eet al in *haste* and askede aftur more.
C.14.175   And haue hem [in] *haste* at þyn owen wille
C.22.136   And [t]o þe Arches in *haste* he ȝede anoen aftur
C.22.144   And Armed hym in *haste* in harlotes wordes
C.22.331   And in *haste* eschete what his wille were.

hasteliche > hastily

hasteþ v *hasten v.* A 2 hastidest (1) hastiþ (1); B 2 hastedest (1) hasteþ (1); C 2 haste (1) hasteth (1)
A. 3.181   And *hastide[st]* þe homward for hunger of þi wombe.
A. 7.303   For hungir hiderward *hastiþ* hym faste.
B. 3.194   And [*hastedest* þee] homward for hunger of þi wombe.
B. 6.322   For hunger hiderward *hasteþ* hym faste.
C. 3.419   *Haste* the with al thyn oste to þe lond of Amalek
C. 8.342   For hungur hiderwardes *hasteth* hym faste.

hastily adv *hastili adv.* B 4 hastily (1) hastiliche (2) hastilokest (1); C 5 hasteliche (1) hastiliche (2) hastilokest (1) hastly (1)
B.11.252   And *hastily* god answerde, and eiþeres wille [lowed],
B.19.356   *Hastiliche* into vnitee and holde we vs þere.
B.19.469   Ther I may *hastilokest* it haue, for I am heed of lawe;
B.20.167   And Elde hente good hope and *hastiliche* he shifte hym
C.12.139   And here aytheres wille [*hasteliche* god assoilede
C.12.164   Al þat thow has[t] here *hastly* go and sulle hit;
C.21.356   *Hastiliche* [in]to vnite and holde we vs there.
C.21.469   Ther y may *hastilokest* hit haue, for y am heed of lawe;
C.22.167   And elde hente gode hope and *hastiliche* [he] sh[ifte] hym

hastite n *hastite n.* C 1
C.17.118   That they ouerhippe nat for *hastite*, as y hope they do nat,

hastly > hastily; hastow > hauen

hat n *hat n.* A 2; B 3 hat (2) hatte (1); C 3 hat (2) hatt (1)
A. 6.8   An hundrit of ampollis on his *hat* seten,
A. 6.17   Ȝe mowe se be my signes þat sitten on myn *hat*
B. 5.194   Wiþ an hood on his heed, a *hat* aboue,
B. 5.520   An hundred of Ampulles on his *hat* seten,
B. 5.529   Ye may se by my signes þat sitten on myn *hatte*
C. 6.202   With his hood on his heued and his *hat* bothe,
C. 7.165   An hundret of Aunpolles on his *hat* se[t]e,
C.13.48   Oþer his *hatt* or his hoed or elles his gloues

hate hated(- haten > hatien

hater n *hatere n.(1)* B 1; C 1 hatur
B.14.1   'I haue but oon hool *hater*', quod haukyn, 'I am þe lasse to blame
C. 9.157   And ouermore to [a]n [*ha*]tur to hele with his bonis

haterynge ger *hateringe ger.* B 1
B.15.78　In housynge, in *haterynge*, [in] heigh clergie shewynge

hateþ > hatien; haþ > hauen

hatien v *haten v.* A 7 hate (1) haten (1) hatid (2) hatide (3); B 18 hate (1) hated (2) hatede (2) hateden (1) haten (3) hateþ (3) hatie (3) hatien (2) yhated (1); C 12 hate (1) hated (3) hatede (2) hateth (3) hatien (3)
A. 3.257　Þat god *hati[de* him for euere] & alle hise heires aftir.
A. 4.106　And *haten* [to] here harlotrie oþer mouþe it;
A. 5.81　Whanne I mette hym in market þat I most *hatide*
A. 5.212　And ȝet haue I *hatid* hire al my lif tyme.'
A. 7.45　And þat þou be trewe of [þi] tunge, & talis þou *hate*,
A.10.151　Alle þat comen of þat caym crist *hatid* aftir,
A.10.156　And alle þat couplide hem with þat kyn crist *hatide* [dedliche].
B. 3.279　That god *hated* hym for euere and alle hise heires after.
B. 4.115　And *haten* alle harlotrie to heren or to mouþen it;
B. 5.101　Whan I met[t]e hym in Market þat I moost *hate[de*
B. 5.116　Whoso vndernymeþ me herof, I *hate* hym dedly after.
B. 5.384　And yet haue I *hated* hire al my lif tyme.'
B. 6.50　And þat þow be trewe of þi tonge and tales þow *hatie*
B. 9.102　Is moost *yhated* vpon erþe of hem þat ben in heuene;
B.10.96　Homliche at oþere mennes houses and *hatien* hir owene.
B.11.183　For hem þat *haten* vs is oure merite to louye,
B.12.52　And þo men þat þei moost *haten* mynistren it at þe laste.
B.13.225　Al yde[l] ich *hatie* for of Actif is my name.
B.13.238　And þat am I, Actif, and ydelnesse *hatie*,
B.13.419　He *hateþ* to here þerof and alle þat it telleþ.
B.14.224　And eiþer *hateþ* ooþer in alle maner werkes.
B.14.280　Pouerte is þe firste point þat pride moost *hateþ*;
B.15.106　And *hatien* to here harlotrie, and [au]ȝt to vnderfonge
B.18.302　For Iewes *hateden* hym and han doon hym to deþe.
B.20.294　Enuye herfore *hatede* Conscience.
C. 3.432　That god [*hated* hym] for euere and alle [his] eyres aftur.
C. 4.110　And *hatien* alle harlotrie to heren oþer to mouthen hit;
C. 6.11　Of alle þat y haue *hated* in myn herte.'
C. 6.441　And ȝut haue y [*ha]ted* here al my lyf tyme.'
C. 7.79　He *hateth* to here thereof and alle þat þerof carpeth.
C. 9.191　Al þat holy Ermytes *hatede* and despisede,
C.15.213　And for me Actyf, his man, þat ydelnesse *ha[t]e*.
C.16.65　And ayther *hateth* oþer and may nat wone togyderes.
C.16.120　Pouerte is the furste poynte þat pruyde moest *hateth*;
C.16.260　And *hatien* harlotrie and to vnderfonge þe tythes
C.17.138　And theues louyen and leute *hatien* and at þe laste ben hanged
C.22.294　Enuye herfore *hatede* Consience.

hatrede n *hatrede n.* A 1 hattrede; B 1; C 1
A. 3.130　And hangiþ hym for *hattrede* þat harmide neuere.
B. 3.141　And hangeþ h[y]m for *hatrede* þat harm[e]de neuere.
C. 3.179　And hangeth hym for *ha[t]rede* þat harmede nere.

hatt > hat; hatte > hat,hote; hattest(ow hattiþ > hote; hattrede > hatrede; ; hatur > hater

haubergeon n *habergeoun n.* B 1; C 1 haberion
B.18.23　In his helm and in his *haubergeon*, humana natura;
C.20.22　In his helm and in his *haberion*, humana natura;

haukes n *hauk n.(1)* B 2; C 1
B. 4.125　Hire *haukes* and hire houndes help to pouere Religious;
B. 5.431　For I haue and haue had somdel *haukes* maneres;
C. 7.44　For y haue and haue yhad sumdel *haukes* maners;

haukyn n prop *n.i.d.* B 17 haukyn (16) Haukyns (1)
B.13.272　Of *haukyn* þe Actif man and how he was ycloped.
B.13.313　'By crist!' quod Conscience þo, 'þi beste cote, *Haukyn*,
B.13.315　'Ye, whoso toke hede', quod *haukyn*, 'bihynde and bifore,
B.13.457　Thus *haukyn* þe Actif man hadde ysoiled his cote
B.14.1　'I haue but oon hool hater', quod *haukyn*, 'I am þe lasse to blame
B.14.26　Than *Haukyn* þe Actif man, and þow do by my techyng,
B.14.28　Than *Hauky[n]* wi[l] þe wafrer, [which is] Actiua vita.'
B.14.34　Thanne laughed *haukyn* a litel and lightly gan swerye;
B.14.51　'Haue, *haukyn*', quod Pacience, 'and et þis whan þe hungreþ
B.14.98　'Where wonyeþ Charite?' quod *Haukyn*; 'I wiste neuere in my lyue
B.14.102　'Wheiþer paciente pouerte', quod *Haukyn*, 'be moore plesaunt to oure d[riȝte]
B.14.274　'Haue god my trouþe', quod *Haukyn* '[I here yow] preise faste pouerte.
B.14.277　'I kan noȝt construe', quod *haukyn*; 'ye moste kenne me þis on englissh.'
B.14.323　'Allas', quod *Haukyn* þe Actif man þo, 'þat after my cristendom
B.14.325　So hard it is', quod *haukyn*, 'to lyue and to do synne.'
B.14.332　'I were noȝt worþi', woot god', quod *haukyn*, 'to werien any cloþes,
B.16.2　For *Haukyns* loue þe Actif man euere I shal yow louye.

haukynge ger *hauking ger.(1)* B 1; C 1 haukyng
B. 3.313　Huntynge or *haukynge* if any of hem vse
C. 3.466　*Haukyng* or huntyng yf eny of hem hit vse

haunt n *haunt n.* B 1; C 1
B.14.253　Hadde þei no[on *haunt*] but of poore men; hir houses stoode vntyled.
C.16.93　Hadde they noen *haunt* bote of pore [men; here houses stoed vntyled].

haunteþ v *haunten v.* A 1 haunten; B 3 haunten (2) haunteþ (1); C 5 haunte (1) haunted (1) haunten (1) haunteth (2)
A.Pr.74　And leniþ it loselis þat leccherie *haunten*.
B.Pr.77　And leneþ it Losels [þat] leccherie *haunten*.
B. 3.53　While ye loue lordes þat lecherie *haunten*
B. 3.59　Haue mercy', quod Mede, 'of men þat it *haunteþ*
C.Pr.75　And leneth hit lorelles þat lecherye *haunten*.
C. 3.57　The whiles ȝe louyen lordes that lecherye *haunteth*
C. 3.63　Haueth mercy,' quod mede, 'o[f] men þat hit *haunteth*
C.11.109　Yf thow hit vse oþer *haunte*, haue god my treuthe,
C.15.196　'Hastow vsed or *haunted* al thy lyf tyme?'

hauthorn > haweþorn

hauen v *haven v.* A 253 had (3) hadde (54) hadden (1) haddist (1) han (21) hast (7) haþ (52) haue (108) hauiþ (2); B 676 habbeþ (4) had (3) hadde (177) hadden (5) haddest (3) haddestow (2) han (63) hast (13) hastow (3) hath (1) haþ (128) haue (268) hauen (1) haueþ (4) nadde (1); C 641 had (2) hadd (1) hadde (152) hadden (8) haddest (4) haddestow (1) haen (43) haeth (4) han (28) hast (15) haste (1) hastow (6) hath (112) haþ (2) haue (250) haued (2) hauede (1) hauen (2) haueth (6) yhad (1)
A.Pr.27　In hope [for] to *haue* heueneriche blisse,
A.Pr.37　And *haue* wyt at wille to wirche ȝif hem list.
A.Pr.49　And *hadde* leue to leiȝe al here lif aftir.
A.Pr.54　Shopen hem Ermytes here ese to *haue*.
A.Pr.61　Siþen charite *haþ* ben chapman & chief to shryue lordis
A.Pr.62　Manye ferlis *han* fallen in a fewe ȝeris.
A.Pr.79　Þat þe pore peple of þe parissh shulde *haue* ȝif þei ne were.
A.Pr.82　To *haue* a licence & leue at lundoun to dwelle.
A.Pr.92　Archideknes & denis þat dignites *hauen*
A. 1.8　*Haue* þei worsshipe in þis world þei kepe no betere:
A. 1.69　Þanne *hadde* I wondir in my wyt what womman it were
A. 1.95　Til treuþe *hadde* termined here trespas to þe ende.
A. 1.116　For pride þat he put out his peyne *haþ* non ende.
A. 1.127　'Ȝet *haue* I no kynde knowyng,' quaþ I, '[ȝe mote kenne me bet]
A. 1.145　To *haue* pite on þat peple þat pynede hym to deþe.
A. 1.149　Forþi I rede þe riche *haue* reuþe on þe pore;
A. 1.157　Ȝe ne *haue* no more meryt in [masse] ne in [houres]
A. 1.171　So [harde] *haþ* auarice haspide ȝow togideris.
A. 1.182　Now *haue* I told þe what treuþe is, þat no tresour is betere,
A. 2.10　Icorounid in a coroune, *haþ* þe king non betere;
A. 2.16　'þat is mede þe maide, *haþ* noiȝede me ful ofte,
A. 2.23　Fauel wiþ fair speche *haþ* forgid hem togidere;
A. 2.24　Gile *haþ* begon hire so heo grauntiþ alle his wille;
A. 2.55　And vnfolde þe feffement þat fals *haþ* ymakid;
A. 2.67　Þei to *haue* & to holde & here eires aftir
A. 2.85　And þou *hast* gyuen hire a gilour, now god ȝiue þe sorewe!
A. 2.87　Worþi is þe werkman his mede to *haue*,
A. 2.88　And þou *hast* fastnid hire wiþ fals, fy on þi law[e]!
A. 2.107　Til he *hadde* siluer for his selis & signes.
A. 2.118　For we *haue* mede amaistried wiþ oure mery speche
A. 2.131　Þ[o] *hadde* notories none; anoyed þei were
A. 2.147　I rede we nom tom to telle þe tail þat hem touchiþ
A. 2.181　Til pardoners *hadde* pite & pulden him to house,
A. 2.193　Ac he *haþ* leue to lepen out as ofte as him likiþ,
A. 3.37　'Þeiȝ lerid & lewide *hadde* leiȝe be þe ichone,
A. 3.38　And þeiȝ falshed folewid þe þis fiftene wynter,
A. 3.47　'We *haue* a wyndowe [in] werching wile stonde vs wel heiȝe;
A. 3.49　Sikir shulde þi soule be heuene *haue*'.
A. 3.63　An aunter ȝe *haue* ȝoure hire þerof h[e]re;
A. 3.89　To *haue* ȝeftis [or ȝerisȝiuys] in ȝouþe or in elde.
A. 3.95　'Vnwittily, [wy], wrouȝt *hast* þou ofte;
A. 3.99　I *haue* a kniȝt, consience, com late fro beȝonde;
A. 3.100　Ȝif he wilneþ þe to wyue wilt þou hym *haue*?'
A. 3.147　Þat feiþ may not *haue* his forþ, hire floreynes go so þikke.
A. 3.155　For pouere men mowe *haue* no power to pleyne [þeiȝ] hem smerte,
A. 3.158　To *haue* space to speke, spede ȝif she miȝte.
A. 3.168　Þou *hast* hongid on myn half enleuene tymes,
A. 3.173　And þou *hast* famid me foule before þe king here.
A. 3.179　Wendist þat wynter wolde *han* last euere;
A. 3.187　Dede hym hoppe for hope to *haue* me at wille.
A. 3.188　*Hadde* I be march[al] of his men, be marie of heuene,
A. 3.189　I durste *han* leid my lif & no lesse wed
A. 3.190　He shulde *haue* be lord of þat lond in lengþe & in brede,

A. 3.201   Þoruʒ ʒeftis han ʒonge men to [ʒerne] & to ride.
A. 3.208   Þe king haþ [m]ede of his men to make pes in londis;
A. 3.216   Mede is worþi þe maistrie to haue'.
A. 3.233   Shal haue mede on þis molde þat mattheu haþ grauntid:
A. 3.233   Shal haue mede on þis molde þat mattheu haþ grauntid:
A. 3.242   Shulde diʒe for a dede þat don hadde here eldren
A. 3.256   Such a meschef mede made þe kyng [to] haue
A. 3.262   And riʒt as agag hadde happe shal somme:
A. 4.25   Folewide hem faste for hy hadden to done
A. 4.35   How wrong aʒen his wil hadde his wyf take,
A. 4.51   And seide, 'hadde I loue of my lord þe king, litel wolde I recche
A. 4.54   For þat wrong hadde wrouʒt so wykkide a dede,
A. 4.75   And he amendis mowe make let maynprise hym haue,
A. 4.83   'Haue þis of me, man,' quaþ heo, 'to amende þi skaþe,
A. 4.86   To haue mercy on þat man þat mysdede hym ofte.
A. 4.87   'For he haþ wagid me wel as wysdom hym tauʒte
A. 4.90   For mede haþ mad my mendis; I may no more axen.'
A. 4.95   But resoun haue reuþe on hym he shal reste in þe stokkis
A. 4.97   Summe redde resoun to haue reuþe on þat shrewe,
A. 4.100   'Rede me not,' quaþ resoun, 'no reuþe to haue
A. 4.117   And ʒet,' quaþ resoun, 'be þe rode, I shal no reuþe haue
A. 4.118   Whil mede haþ þe maistrie to mo[te] in þis halle.
A. 4.125   Ne for no mede haue mercy but meknesse it made,
A. 4.145   And reherside þat resoun [hadde] riʒtfulliche shewide;
A. 5.4   Þat I ne hadde yslepe saddere & yseyn more.
A. 5.5   Er I hadde faren a furlong feyntise me h[ent]e
A. 5.12   And preyede þe peple haue pite on hemselue,
A. 5.53   Of alle þat I haue had enuye in myn herte.'
A. 5.53   Of alle þat I haue had enuye in myn herte.'
A. 5.64   As a lek þat hadde leyn longe in þe sonne,
A. 5.73   I haue a neiʒebour neiʒ me, I haue noiʒed hym ofte,
A. 5.73   I haue a neiʒebour neiʒ me, I haue noiʒed hym ofte,
A. 5.79   Betwyn hym & his meyne I haue mad wraþþe;
A. 5.84   Ac hadde I maistrie & miʒt I wolde murdre hym for euere.
A. 5.91   & beholde how heyne haþ a newe cote;
A. 5.97   And whoso haþ more þanne I, þat angriþ myn herte.
A. 5.114   'I haue [ben] coueit[ous],' quaþ [þat caitif], 'I [bi]knowe [hit] h[e]re,
A. 5.121   Ne hadde [þe] grace of gile gon among my ware
A. 5.122   It hadde be vnsold þis seue ʒer, so me god helpe.
A. 5.141   Sheo haþ yholde huxterie elleuene wynter.
A. 5.152   'I haue good ale, gossib,' quaþ heo; 'glotoun, wilt þou assaie?'
A. 5.153   'Hast þou,' quaþ he, 'any hote spices?'
A. 5.155   I haue pepir, & p[ye]nye, & a pound of garlek,
A. 5.173   Whoso hadde þe hood shulde haue amendis of þe cloke.
A. 5.173   Whoso hadde þe hood shulde haue amendis of þe cloke.
A. 5.180   Hikke þe hostiller þanne hadde þe cloke
A. 5.182   And haue hikkes hood þe hostiller, & holde hym yseruid,
A. 5.188   Til glotoun hadde ygulpid a galoun & a gille.
A. 5.192   And wisshide it hadde be wexid wiþ a wysp of firsen.
A. 5.193   He hadde no strengþe to stonde er he his staf hadde,
A. 5.193   He hadde no strengþe to stonde er he his staf hadde,
A. 5.201   And aftir al þis surfet an axesse he hadde
A. 5.208   For his liþer lif þat he lyued hadde,
A. 5.211   Er abstinence myn aunte haue ygyue me leue,
A. 5.212   And ʒet haue I hatid hire al my lif tyme.'
A. 5.226   Til I haue euesong herd, I behote [to] þe rode.
A. 5.227   And ʒet wile I ʒelde aʒen, ʒif I so muchel haue,
A. 5.228   Al þat I wykkidly wan siþen I wyt hadde,
A. 5.230   Þat iche man shal haue his er I hennis wende,
A. 5.238   And þou haddist mercy on þat man for memento sake,
A. 5.239   Þi wil w[orþ]e vpon me, as I haue wel deseruid
A. 5.240   To haue helle for euere ʒif þat hope nere.
A. 5.241   So rewe on þis robert þat red[dere] ne hauiþ,
A. 5.250   For he hadde leiʒe be latro luciferis [aunte].
A. 5.254   To haue grace to seke treuþe; god leue þat hy moten!
A. 6.12   And sen be his signes whom he souʒt hadde.
A. 6.15   At bedlem, at babiloyne, I haue ben in boþe;
A. 6.18   Þat I haue walkid wel wide in wet & in driʒe,
A. 6.30   I haue ben his folewere al þis fourty wynter,
A. 6.37   [I] haue myn here of hym [wel] & oþerwhile more;
A. 6.39   He [wiþ]halt non hyne his hire þat he ne haþ it at eue.
A. 6.91   For he haþ þe keiʒes & I þe cliket þeiʒ þe king slepe.
A. 6.96   For he haþ enuye to hym þat in þin herte sitteþ
A. 6.115   'Be crist,' quaþ a cuttepurs, 'I haue no kyn þere.'
A. 6.120   'Mercy [is] a maiden [þere], haþ miʒt ouer [hem] alle;
A. 7.1   'Þis were a wikkide weye, but whoso hadde a gide
A. 7.4   I haue an half akir to er[e]n be þe heiʒe weiʒe;
A. 7.5   Hadde y [erid] þat half akir
A. 7.10   And wyues þat han woll[e] werchiþ it faste,
A. 7.19   Þat in silk & sendel, sewiþ it whanne tyme is,
A. 7.60   Shal haue be oure lord be more here in heruist,
A. 7.72   His sone hattiþ suffre þi souereynes to hauen here wille

A. 7.75   'For [now] I am old & hor & haue of myn owene
A. 7.79   He shal haue my soule þat best haþ deseruid,
A. 7.79   He shal haue my soule þat best haþ deseruid,
A. 7.82   To haue reles & remissioun, on þat rental I leue.
A. 7.83   Þe [k]ir[k]e shal haue my caroyn & kepe my bones,
A. 7.86   He is holden, I hope, to haue me in mynde,
A. 7.88   My wyf shal haue of þat I wan wiþ treuþe, & namore,
A. 7.112   And þeiʒ ʒe deiʒe for doel þe deuil haue þat recche!'
A. 7.116   'We haue none [lymes] to laboure wiþ, lord, ygracid be ʒe;
A. 7.134   Shuln haue of myn almesse al þe while I libbe,
A. 7.139   Þanne gan wastour arise & wolde haue yfouʒte;
A. 7.143   Wilt þou, nilt þou, we wile haue oure wil
A. 7.164   N[e] hadde peris [wiþ] a pese lof preyede hym beleue,
A. 7.168   Ne hadde þ[e] fisician ferst defendite him watir
A. 7.170   Þei hadde be ded be þis day & doluen al warm.
A. 7.174   For a potel of pe[s]is þat peris hadde mad
A. 7.186   Þanne hadde piers pite & preiʒede hungir to wende
A. 7.203   And he shal soupe swettere whanne he it haþ deseruid.
A. 7.204   Ac ʒif þou fynde any frek þat fortune haþ apeirid
A. 7.209   Þat nedy ben or nakid, & nouʒt han to spende,
A. 7.223   Seruus nequam had a nam, & for he nolde it vsen.
A. 7.224   He hadde maugre of his maister eueremore aftir,
A. 7.226   And ʒaf [it] hym in haste þat hadde ten before,
A. 7.228   "He þat haþ shal haue to helpe þere nede is,
A. 7.228   "He þat haþ shal haue to helpe þere nede is,
A. 7.229   And he þat nouʒt haþ shal nouʒt haue ne no man him helpe,
A. 7.229   And he þat nouʒt haþ shal nouʒt haue ne no man him helpe,
A. 7.230   And þat he weniþ wel to haue I wile it be hym bereuid".
A. 7.242   Þei han mangid ouer muche, þat makiþ hem grone ofte.
A. 7.248   Aris vp er ap[e]ti[t] ha[ue] eten his fille;
A. 7.263   Er I haue dyned be þis day & ydronke boþe.'
A. 7.264   'I haue no peny,' quaþ piers, 'pulettis to biggen,
A. 7.268   And I seiʒe, be my soule, I haue no salt bacoun,
A. 7.270   Ac I haue persile & poret, & many cole plantis,
A. 7.274   Be þat I hope to haue heruest in my croft,
A. 7.291   Laboureris þat haue no land [to] lyue on [but] here handis
A. 8.8   Part in þ[at] pardoun þe pope haþ hem grauntid.
A. 8.11   Han þardoun þoruʒ purcatorie to passe wel sone,
A. 8.18   Han pardoun wiþ þe apostlis whanne þei passe hennis,
A. 8.20   Marchauntis in þe margyn hadde manye ʒeris,
A. 8.45   Men of lawe hadde lest for le[ttr]id þei ben alle;
A. 8.66   Hadde þe same absolucioun þat sent was to peris.
A. 8.69   For he þat beggiþ or bit, but he haue nede,
A. 8.86   Han as pleyn pardoun as þe plouʒman hymselue.
A. 8.87   For loue of here louʒ herte oure lord haþ hem grauntid
A. 8.98   But do wel & haue wel, & god shal haue þi soule,
A. 8.98   But do wel & haue wel, & god shal haue þi soule,
A. 8.99   And do euele & haue euele, & hope þou non oþer
A. 8.117   Haue þei no garner [to go] to, but god fynt hem alle.'
A. 8.131   Manye tyme þis metelis han mad me to stodie,
A. 8.142   Þe king les his lordsshipe, & lesse men it hadde.
A. 8.151   On peris þe plouʒman, whiche a pardoun he hauiþ,
A. 8.157   Now haþ þe pope power pardoun to graunte
A. 8.162   Soulis þat han ysynned seue siþes dedly.
A. 8.166   Vpon trist of ʒour tresour trienalis to haue
A. 8.169   Þat han þe [welþe of þis] world, & wise men ben holden,
A. 8.177   And haue indulgence doublefold, but dowel þe helpe
A. 9.10   I hailside hem hendely as I hadde ylernid,
A. 9.15   And euere haþ [as] I hope, & euere shal hereaftir.'
A. 9.47   God wile suffre þe to deiʒe so for þiself hast þe maistrie.'
A. 9.48   'I haue no kynde knowyng,' quaþ I, 'to conseyue þi wordis,
A. 9.66   'I haue sewide þe seuen ʒer; seiʒe þou me no raþere?'
A. 9.78   Whiles he haþ ouʒt of his owene he helpiþ þere nede is;
A. 9.79   Þe bagges & þe [bi]gerdlis, he haþ broken hem alle
A. 9.80   Þat þe Erl auerous hadde, or his eires,
A. 9.81   And wiþ mammones money he haþ mad hym frendis,
A. 9.82   And is ronne to religioun, & haþ rendrit þe bible,
A. 9.91   Þei han crounide o king to kepe hem alle,
A.10.5   Kynde haþ closid þereinne, craftily wiþalle,
A.10.7   Anima he[o] ha[tte]; to hire [haþ] enuye
A.10.11   And haþ don hire to sire dowel, duk of þise marchis.
A.10.18   And haþ fyue faire sones be his furste wyf:
A.10.25   'What calle ʒe þat castel,' quaþ I, 'þat kynde haþ ymakid?
A.10.29   And þat is þe grete god þat gynnyng had neuere,
A.10.62   Thanne haþ þe pouk power, sire princeps huius mundi,
A.10.64   Ac in fauntis ne in folis þe [fend] haþ no miʒt
A.10.71   A[c] iche wiʒt in þis world þat haþ wys vndirstonding
A.10.77   And sauiþ þe soule þat synne haþ no miʒt
A.10.100   And be glad of þe grace þat god haþ Isent þe.
A.10.103   I haue [lernid] how lewid men han [lerid] here children
A.10.103   I haue [lernid] how lewid men han [lerid] here children
A.10.169   Til fourty dayes be fulfild, þat flood haue ywasshe
A.10.170   Clene awey þe cursid blood þat caym haþ ymakid.

A.10.191 Manye peire siþen þ[e] pestilence han p[l]iȝt hem togidere.
A.10.193 *Haue* þei no children but ch[este], & choppis [betwene].
A.10.206 As betwyn sengle & sengle, siþþe lawe *hap* ygrauntid
A.10.207 Þat iche man *haue* a make in [mariage] of wedlak
A.11.1 Þanne *hadde* wyt a wyf þat hatte dame studie,
A.11.10 Among hogges þat *hauen* hawen at wille.
A.11.24 And he þat *hap* holy writ ay in his mouþ,
A.11.31 For ȝif harlotrie ne halp[e] hem betere, *haue* god my trouþe,
A.11.57 And *han* [hym] muchel in here mouþ, ac mene men in herte.
A.11.58 Freris and faitours *han* founden vp suche questiouns
A.11.106 He *hap* weddit a wif wiþinne þise woukes sixe,
A.11.111 Gladdere þanne þe gleman þat gold *hap* to ȝifte,
A.11.137 Ac theologie *hap* tenid me ten score tymes,
A.11.195 Sire dobest *hap* ben [in office], so is he best worþi
A.11.200 And *hap* possessions & pluralites for pore menis sake;
A.11.221 For I *haue* seiȝe it myself, & siþþen red it aftir,
A.11.231 *Hauen* eritage in heuene, ac riche men non.'
A.11.239 *Haue* eritage in heuene as an heiȝ cristene.
A.11.241 For cristene *han* a degre & is þe comun speche
A.11.258 –Ȝet am I neuere þe ner for nouȝt I *haue* walkid
A.11.280 Þat *hadde* lyued al his lyf wiþ lesinges & þeft[e],
A.11.282 Sonnere *hadde* he saluacioun þanne seint Ion þe baptist,
A.11.284 Þat *hadde* leyn with cumfre manye longe ȝeris;
A.11.285 A robbere *hadde* remission raþere þanne þei alle,
A.11.286 Wiþoute penaunce of purcatorie to *haue* paradis for euere.
A.11.289 Or poule þe apostil þat no pite *hadde*
A.11.293 And ȝet [*haue*] I forget[e ferþer] of fyue wyttis teching
A.11.299 For to answere hem *haue* ȝe no doute,
A.12.2 I *haue* do my deuer þe dowel to teche,
A.12.34 And when scripture þe skolde *hadde* þis [skele] ysheued
A.12.69 'Go we forþ,' quod þe gom, 'I *haue* a gret boyste
A.12.75 Þer bad me hunger *haue* gode day but I helde me stille;
A.12.83 I am masager of deþ; men *haue* I tweyne.
A.12.86 We *han* letteres of lyf, he shal his lyf ty[n]e.
A.12.105 And is closed vnder clom, crist *haue* his soule.
B.Pr.27 In hope [for] to *haue* heueneriche blisse.
B.Pr.37 And *han* wit at wille to werken if [hem liste].
B.Pr.49 And *hadden* leue to lyen al hire lif after.
B.Pr.50 I seiȝ somme þat seiden þei *hadde* ysouȝt Seintes;
B.Pr.57 Shopen hem heremytes hire ese to *haue*.
B.Pr.64 Siþ charite *hap* ben chapman and chief to shryue lordes
B.Pr.65 Manye ferlies *han* fallen in a fewe yeres.
B.Pr.82 That þe [pouere peple] of þe parisshe sholde *haue* if þei ne were.
B.Pr.85 To *haue* a licence and leue at London to dwelle,
B.Pr.88 That *han* cure vnder crist, and crownynge in tokene
B.Pr.100 I parceyued of þe power þat Peter *hadde* to kepe,
B.Pr.109 To *han* [þe] power þat Peter hadde–impugnen I nelle–
B.Pr.109 To *han* [þe] power þat Peter *hadde*–impugnen I nelle–
B.Pr.160 'I *haue* yseyen segges', quod he, 'in þe Cite of Londoun
B.Pr.178 That dorste *haue* bounden þe belle aboute þe cattes nekke,
B.Pr.185 'Thouȝ we [*hadde*] kille[d] þe cat yet sholde þer come anoþer
B.Pr.197 For may no renk þer reste *haue* for Ratons by nyȝte,]
B.Pr.201 For *hadde* ye rattes youre [raik] ye kouþe noȝt rule yowselue.
B.1.8 *Haue* þei worship in þis world þei [kepe] no bettre;
B.1.71 Thanne *hadde* I wonder in my wit what womman it weere
B.1.97 Til treuþe *hadde* ytermyned hire trespas to þe ende.
B.1.127 For pride þat he putte out his peyne *hap* noon ende.
B.1.138 'Yet *haue* I no kynde knowyng', quod I, 'ye mote kenne me bettre
B.1.154 Til it *hadde* of þe erþe [y]eten [hitselue].
B.1.155 And whan it *hadde* of þis fold flessh and blood taken
B.1.171 To *haue* pite [on] þat peple þat peyned hym to deþe;
B.1.175 Forþi I rede [þe] riche, *haueþ* ruþe [on] þe pouere;
B.1.183 Ye ne *haue* na moore merite in masse n[e] in houres
B.1.197 So harde *hap* Auarice yhasped [yow] togideres.
B.1.208 Now *haue* I told þee what truþe is, þat no tresor is bettre,
B.2.10 Ycorouned [in] a coroune, þe kyng *hap* noon bettre.
B.2.18 I *hadde* wonder what she was and whos wif she were.
B.2.20 'That is Mede þe mayde, *hap* noyed me ful ofte,
B.2.22 And bilowen h[ym] to lordes þat lawes han to kepe.
B.2.25 For Fals was hire fader þat *hap* a fikel tonge
B.2.31 And *hap* yeuen me mercy to marie wiþ myselue,
B.2.42 Fauel þoruȝ his faire speche *hap* þis folk enchaunted,
B.2.49 And *haue* power to punysshe hem; þanne put forþ þi reson.
B.2.73 And vnfoldeþ þe feffement that Fals *hath* ymaked.
B.2.102 'And þei to *haue* and to holde, and hire heires after,
B.2.121 And þow *hast* gyuen hire to a gilour, now god gyue þee sorwe!
B.2.123 For Dignus est operarius his hire to *haue*,
B.2.124 And þow *hast* fest hire [wiþ] Fals; fy on þi lawe!
B.2.143 Til he *hadde* siluer for his [seles] and [signes of] Notaries.
B.2.154 For we *haue* Mede amaistried wiþ oure murie speche
B.2.167 Tho *hadde* Notaries none; anoyed þei were
B.2.186 I *haue* no tome to telle þe tail þat [hem] folwe[þ]
B.2.222 Til Pardoners *hadde* pite and pulled hym [to] house,

B.2.234 Ac he *hap* leue to lepen out as ofte as hym likeþ,
B.3.38 'Theiȝ [lered and lewed] *hadde* leyen by þee [echone],
B.3.39 And [þeiȝ] Fals[hede] *hadde* yfolwed þee alle þise fift[ene] wynter,
B.3.48 'We *haue* a wyndow in werchynge wole [stonden] vs [wel] hye;
B.3.50 Syker sholde þi soule be heuene to *haue*'.
B.3.59 *Haue* mercy', quod Mede, 'of men þat it haunteþ
B.3.72 On auenture ye *haue* youre hire here and youre heuene als.
B.3.106 'Vnwittily, [wye], wroȝt *hastow* ofte,
B.3.110 I *haue* a knyȝt, Conscience, cam late fro biyonde;
B.3.111 If he wilneþ þee to wif wiltow hym *haue*?'
B.3.157 That feiþ may noȝt *haue* his forþ, hire floryns go so þikke.
B.3.168 For pouere men may *haue* no power to pleyne þouȝ [hem] smerte,
B.3.171 To *haue* space to speke, spede if she myȝte.
B.3.181 Thow *hast* hanged on myn half elleuene tymes,
B.3.186 Ac þow *hast* famed me foule bifore þe kyng here.
B.3.192 Wendest þat wynter wolde *han* ylasted euere;
B.3.200 And dide hem hoppe for hope to *haue* me at wille.
B.3.201 *Hadde* I ben Marchal of his men, by Marie of heuene!
B.3.202 I dorste *haue* leyd my lif and no lasse wedde
B.3.203 He sholde *haue* be lord of þat lond in lengþe and in brede,
B.3.214 [Thoruȝ] ȝiftes *han* yonge men to [yerne] and to ryde.
B.3.221 The kyng *hap* mede of his men to make pees in londe;
B.3.229 Mede is worþi, [me þynkeþ], þe maistrie to *haue*'.
B.3.239 And *han* ywroght werkes wiþ right and wiþ reson,
B.3.244 Swiche manere men, my lord, shul *haue* þis firste Mede
B.3.254 [Shul *haue*] Mede [on þis molde þat] Mathew [hap grauntid]:
B.3.254 [Shul haue] Mede [on þis molde þat] Mathew [*hap* grauntid]:
B.3.263 Sholden deye for a dede þat doon *hadde* hire eldres.
B.3.278 Swich a meschief Mede made þe kyng to *haue*
B.3.282 For so is þis world went wiþ hem þat *han* power
B.3.286 And riȝt as Agag *hadde* happe shul somme.
B.3.304 And *haue* wonder in hire hertes þat men beþ so trewe.
B.3.335 And [muche] worshipe *ha[þ]* þerwiþ as holy writ telleþ:
B.3.341 *Hadde* she loked þat [left] half and þe leef torned
B.3.342 She sholde *haue* founden fel[l]e wordes folwynge þerafter,
B.3.346 This text þat ye *han* told were [trewe] for lordes,
B.3.347 Ac yow failed a konnynge clerk þat kouþe þe leef *han* torned.
B.3.352 That þeiȝ we wynne worship and with Mede *haue* victorie,
B.4.28 Folwed h[e]m faste for þei *hadde* to doone
B.4.48 How wrong ayeins his wille *hadde* his wif taken,
B.4.65 And seide, '*hadde* I loue of my lord þe kyng litel wolde I recche
B.4.68 For þat wrong *hadde* ywroȝt so wikked a dede,
B.4.88 And he amendes mowe make lat maynprise hym *haue*,
B.4.96 '*Haue* þis [of me, man]', quod she, 'to amenden þi scaþe,
B.4.99 To *haue* mercy on þat man þat mysdide hym ofte.
B.4.100 'For he *hap* waged me wel as wisdom hym tauȝte
B.4.103 For Mede *hap* [maad myne amendes]; I may na moore axe.'
B.4.108 But Reson *hadde* ruþe on hym he shal reste in [þe] stokkes
B.4.110 Som[me] radde Reson to *haue* ruþe on þat shrewe
B.4.113 'Reed me noȝt', quod Reson, 'no ruþe to *haue*
B.4.134 And yet', quod Reson, 'by þe Rode! I shal no ruþe *haue*
B.4.135 While Mede *hap* þe maistrie [to mote in þis] halle.
B.4.142 Ne for no Mede *haue* mercy but mekenesse it ma[de],
B.4.169 'For ofte *haue* I', quod he, 'holpen yow at þe barre,
B.4.172 And recordede þat Reson *hadde* riȝtfully shewed,
B.4.174 And gan wexe wroþ with lawe for Mede almoost *hadde* shent it,
B.4.178 And deme yow, bi þis day, as ye *han* deserued.
B.4.180 I wole *haue* leaute in lawe, and lete be al youre ianglyng;
B.5.4 That I ne *hadde* slept sadder and yseiȝen moore.
B.5.5 Ac er I *hadde* faren a furlong feyntise me hente
B.5.50 And siþen he preide þe pope *haue* pite on holy chirche,
B.5.52 'And ye þat *han* lawes to [loke], lat truþe be youre coueitise
B.5.70 [Of alle þat] I *haue* [had enuye] in myn herte.'
B.5.70 [Of alle þat] I *haue* [had enuye] in myn herte.'
B.5.81 As a leek þat *hadde* yleye longe in þe sonne
B.5.91 I wolde be gladder, by god! þat Gybbe *hadde* meschaunce
B.5.92 Than þouȝ I *hadde* þis wouke ywonne a weye of Essex chese.
B.5.93 I *haue* a neȝebore [neiȝ] me, I haue anoyed hym ofte,
B.5.93 I *haue* a neȝebore [neiȝ] me, I *haue* anoyed hym ofte,
B.5.104 Ac *hadde* I maistrie and myȝt [I wolde murþere hym for euere].
B.5.111 And biholde [how H]eyne *hap* a newe cote;
B.5.118 [And] whoso *hap* moore þan I, þat angreþ [myn herte].
B.5.130 Amonges Burgeises *haue* be, [bigg]yng at Londoun,
B.5.142 And now is fallen þerof a fruyt þat folk *han* wel leuere
B.5.144 And now persons *han* parceyued þat freres parte wiþ hem
B.5.153 I *haue* an Aunte to Nonne and an Abbesse boþe;
B.5.155 He bad be cook in hir kichene and þe Couent serued
B.5.161 For she *hadde* child in chirietyme; al oure Chapitre it wiste.
B.5.165 *Hadde* þei had knyues, by crist! eiþer hadde kild ooþer.
B.5.165 Hadde þei *had* knyues, by crist! eiþer hadde kild ooþer.
B.5.165 Hadde þei *had* knyues, by crist! eiþer hadde kild ooþer.
B.5.166 Seint Gregory was a good pope and *hadde* a good forwit:
B.5.168 They *hadde* þanne ben Infamis, þei kan so yuele hele co[unseil].

B. 5.176   Forþi *haue* I no likyng, [leue me], wiþ þo leodes to wonye;
B. 5.179   [I] *haue* a flux of a foul mouþ wel fyue dayes after;
B. 5.198   'I *haue* ben coueitous', quod þis caytif, 'I biknowe it here.
B. 5.205   Ne *hadde* þe grace of gyle ygo amonges my [ware]
B. 5.206   It *hadde* ben vnsold þis seuen yer, so me god helpe.
B. 5.225   She *haþ* holden hukkerye [elleuene wynter].
B. 5.234   Thow *haddest* be bettre worþi ben hanged þerfore.'
B. 5.243   I *haue* mo Manoirs þoruȝ Rerages þan þoruȝ Miseretur & com[m]odat.
B. 5.244   I *haue* lent lordes and ladies my chaffare
B. 5.251   'Ye, I *haue* lent lordes loued me neuere after,
B. 5.252   And *haue* ymaad many a knyȝt boþe Mercer and draper
B. 5.254   'Hastow pite on pouere men þat [for pure nede] borwe?'
B. 5.255   'I *haue* as muche pite of pouere men as pedlere haþ of cattes,
B. 5.255   'I *haue* as muche pite of pouere men as pedlere *haþ* of cattes,
B. 5.259   Amonges my neȝebores namely swich a name ich *haue*.'
B. 5.262   Ne þyne heires after þee *haue* ioie of þat þow wynnest,
B. 5.267   Ne *haue* a peny to my pitaunce, [for pyne of my soule],
B. 5.273   That þow *hast* maad ech man good I may þee noȝt assoille:
B. 5.274   For a[l] þat *ha[þ]* of þi good, haue god my trouþe,
B. 5.274   For a[l] þat ha[þ] of þi good, *haue* god my trouþe,
B. 5.279   Thanne weex þ[e] sherewe in wanhope & wolde *han* hanged hym[self]
B. 5.280   Ne *hadde* repentaunce þe raþer reconforted hym in þis manere:
B. 5.281   '*Haue* mercy in þi mynde, and wiþ þi mouþ biseche it—
B. 5.284   Forþi *haue* mercy in þy mynde, and marchaundise leue it,
B. 5.285   For þow *hast* no good ground to gete þee wiþ a wastel
B. 5.287   For þe good þat þow *hast* geten bigan al wiþ falshede,
B. 5.302   'I *haue* good Ale, gossib', quod she, 'Gloton, woltow assaye?'
B. 5.303   'Hastow', quod he, 'any hote spices?'
B. 5.304   'I *haue* pepir and pion[e] and a pound of garleek,
B. 5.324   Whoso *hadde* þe hood sholde han amendes of þe cloke.
B. 5.324   Whoso *hadde* þe hood sholde *han* amendes of þe cloke.
B. 5.331   Hikke þe hostiler [þanne] *hadde* þe cloke
B. 5.333   And Hikkes hood [þe] hostiler and holden hym yserued,
B. 5.339   Til Gloton *hadde* yglubbed a galon and a gille.
B. 5.344   And wisshed it *hadde* ben wexed wiþ a wispe of firses.
B. 5.345   He [*hadde* no strengþe to] stonde er he his staf hadde,
B. 5.345   He [hadde no strengþe to] stonde er he his staf *hadde*,
B. 5.359   And after al þis excesse he *hadde* an Accidie
B. 5.365   'As þow wiþ wordes & werkes *hast* wroȝt yuele in þi lyue
B. 5.368   That I *haue* trespased with my tonge, I kan noȝt telle how ofte;
B. 5.372   That I, Gloton, girte it vp er I *hadde* gon a myle,
B. 5.380   For his luþer lif þat he lyued *hadde*,
B. 5.383   Til Abstinence myn Aunte *haue* ȝyue me leeue,
B. 5.384   And yet *haue* I hated hire al my lif tyme.'
B. 5.397   I *haue* maad auowes fourty and foryete hem on þe morwe,
B. 5.406   I *haue* leuere here an harlotrye or a Somer game of Souters,
B. 5.415   I *haue* be preest and person passynge þritty wynter,
B. 5.431   For I *haue* and haue had somdel haukes maneres;
B. 5.431   For I haue and *haue* had somdel haukes maneres;
B. 5.431   For I haue and haue *had* somdel haukes maneres;
B. 5.434   Sixty siþes I, Sleuþe, *haue* foryete it siþþe
B. 5.454   Til I *haue* euensong herd: I bihote to þe Roode.
B. 5.455   And yet wole I yelde ayein, if I so muche *haue*,
B. 5.456   Al þat I wikkedly wan siþen I wit *hadde*,
B. 5.458   That ech man shal *haue* his er I hennes wende;
B. 5.466   And *haddest* mercy on þat man for Memento sake,
B. 5.467   So rewe on þis Robbere þat Reddere ne *haue*
B. 5.476   For he *hadde* leyen by Latro, luciferis Aunte.
B. 5.477   [Th]anne *hadde* Repentaunce ruþe and redde hem alle to knele.
B. 5.499   And al þat Marc *haþ* ymaad, Mathew, Iohan and Lucas
B. 5.504   And *haue* ruþe on þise Ribaudes þat repenten hem soore
B. 5.512   To *haue* grace to go [to] truþe, [God leue þat þei moten].
B. 5.524   And se bi hise signes whom he souȝt *hadde*.
B. 5.527   [At] Bethlem, [at] Babiloyne, I *haue* ben in boþe,
B. 5.530   That I *haue* walked [wel] wide in weet and in drye
B. 5.542   I *haue* ben his folwere al þis [fourty] wynter,
B. 5.550   I *haue* myn hire [of hym] wel and ouþerwhiles moore.
B. 5.552   He wiþhalt noon hewe his hire þat he ne *haþ* it at euen.
B. 5.604   For he *haþ* þe keye and þe cliket þouȝ þe kyng slepe.
B. 5.610   [For] he *haþ* enuye to hym þat in þyn herte sitteþ
B. 5.624   Heo *haþ* holpe a þousand out of þe deueles punfolde.
B. 5.630   'By Crist!' quod a kuttepurs, 'I *haue* no kyn þere.'
B. 5.635   'Mercy is a maiden þere *haþ* myȝt ouer [hem] alle;
B. 6.1   'This were a wikkede wey but whoso *hadde* a gyde
B. 6.4   I *haue* an half acre to erie by þe heiȝe weye;
B. 6.5   *Hadde* I eryed þis half acre and sowen it after
B. 6.11   That ye *haue* silk and Sandel to sowe whan tyme is
B. 6.64   To pilgrymage as palmeres doon pardon to *haue*.
B. 6.66   Shal *haue* leue, by oure lord, to lese here in heruest
B. 6.80   His sone hiȝte Suffre-þi-Souereyns-to-*hauen*-hir-wille-
B. 6.83   'For now I am old and hoor and *haue* of myn owene

B. 6.87   He shal *haue* my soule þat best haþ deserued,
B. 6.87   He shal haue my soule þat best *haþ* deserued,
B. 6.90   To *haue* relees and remission, on þat rental I leue.
B. 6.91   The kirke shal *haue* my caroyne and kepe my bones
B. 6.94   [He is] holden, I hope, to *haue* me in [mynde]
B. 6.96   My wif shal *haue* of þat I wan wiþ truþe and na moore,
B. 6.120   And þouȝ ye deye for doel þe deuel *haue* þat recch[e]!'
B. 6.124   'We *haue* no lymes to laboure with; lord, ygraced be [y]e!
B. 6.146   And na moore er morwe, myn almesse shul þei *haue*,
B. 6.147   And catel to [cope] hem wiþ þat *han* Cloistres and chirches.
B. 6.148   Ac Robert Renaboute shal [riȝt] noȝt *haue* of myne,
B. 6.149   Ne Postles, but þei preche konne and *haue* power of þe bisshop:
B. 6.150   Thei shul *haue* payn and potage and [a pitaunce biside],
B. 6.151   For it is as vnresonable Religion þat *haþ* riȝt noȝt of certein.'
B. 6.152   [Th]anne gan wastour to wraþen hym and wolde *haue* yfouȝte;
B. 6.156   Wiltow, neltow, we wol *haue* oure wille
B. 6.179   Ne *hadde* Piers wiþ a pese loof preyed [hym bileue]
B. 6.180   They *hadde* be [dede and] doluen, ne deme þow noon ooþer.
B. 6.186   For a pot[el] of peses þat Piers *hadde* ymaked
B. 6.195   And ech a pouere man wel apaied to *haue* pesen for his hyre
B. 6.199   Thanne *hadde* Piers pite and preide hunger to wende
B. 6.217   And he shal soupe swetter whan he it *haþ* deserued.
B. 6.218   A[c] if þow fynde any freke þat Fortune *haþ* apeired
B. 6.223   That nedy ben [or naked, and nouȝt *han* to spende,
B. 6.239   Seruus nequam *hadde* a Mnam and for he [n]olde [it vse]
B. 6.240   He *hadde* maugree of his maister eueremoore after,
B. 6.242   And yaf [it hym in haste þat *hadde* ten biforn;]
B. 6.244   "He þat *haþ* shal haue and helpe þere [nede is]
B. 6.244   "He þat haþ shal *haue* and helpe þere [nede is]
B. 6.245   And he þat noȝt *haþ* shal noȝt haue and no man hym helpe,
B. 6.245   And he þat noȝt haþ shal noȝt *haue* and no man hym helpe,
B. 6.246   And þat he weneþ wel to *haue* I wole it hym bireue".
B. 6.258   Ye *han* manged ouer muche; þat makeþ yow grone.
B. 6.264   [A]rys vp er Appetit *haue* eten his fille.
B. 6.279   [Er] I *haue* dyned by þis day and ydronke boþe.'
B. 6.280   'I *haue* no peny', quod Piers, 'pulettes to bugge,
B. 6.284   And yet I seye, by my soule! I *haue* no salt bacon
B. 6.286   Ac I *haue* percile and pore[t] and manye [plaunte coles],
B. 6.290   By þat I hope to *haue* heruest in my crofte;
B. 6.307   Laborers þat *haue* no land to lyue on but hire handes
B. 6.328   And a mayde *haue* þe maistrie, and multiplie by eiȝte,
B. 7.8   Pardon wiþ Piers Plowman truþe *haþ* ygraunted.
B. 7.11   *Han* pardon þoruȝ purgatorie to passen ful liȝtly,
B. 7.18   Marchauntȝ in þe margyne *hadde* manye yeres,
B. 7.40   Men of lawe leest pardon *hadde*, [leue þow noon ooþer],
B. 7.57   Whan þei drawen on to [þe deþ] and Indulgences wolde *haue*,
B. 7.64   *Ha[dde]* þe same absolucion þat sent was to Piers.
B. 7.67   For he þat beggeþ or bit, but he *haue* nede,
B. 7.78   For wite ye neuere who is worþi, ac god woot who *haþ* nede.
B. 7.84   Forþi biddeþ noȝt, ye beggeres, but if ye *haue* nede;
B. 7.85   For whoso *haþ* to buggen hym breed, þe book bereþ witnesse,
B. 7.86   He *haþ* ynouȝ þat haþ breed ynouȝ, þouȝ he haue noȝt ellis.
B. 7.86   He haþ ynouȝ þat *haþ* breed ynouȝ, þouȝ he haue noȝt ellis.
B. 7.86   He haþ ynouȝ þat haþ breed ynouȝ, þouȝ he *haue* noȝt ellis.
B. 7.104   *Han* as pleyn pardon as þe Plowman hymselue;
B. 7.105   For loue of hir lowe hert[e] oure lord *haþ* hem graunted
B. 7.116   But do wel and *haue* wel, and god shal haue þi soule,
B. 7.116   But do wel and haue wel, and god shal *haue* þi soule,
B. 7.117   And do yuel and *haue* yuel, [and] hope þow noon ooþer
B. 7.118   [That] after þi deeþ day þe deuel shal *haue* þi soule.'
B. 7.135   *Haue* þei no gerner to go to but god fynt hem alle.'
B. 7.149   Many tyme þis metels *haþ* maked me to studie,
B. 7.152   And which a pardon Piers *hadde* þe peple to conforte,
B. 7.154   Ac I *haue* no sauour in songewarie for I se it ofte faille.
B. 7.164   The kyng lees his lordshipe and [lasse] men it *hadde*.
B. 7.179   Now *haþ* þe pope power pardon to graunte
B. 7.184   Soules þat *haue* synned seuen siþes dedly.
B. 7.188   Vpon trust of youre tresor triennals to *haue*,
B. 7.191   That *haue* þe welþe of þis world and wise men ben holden
B. 7.199   And *haue* Indulgences doublefold, but dowel [þee] helpe
B. 8.10   I hailsed hem hendely as I *hadde* ylerned,
B. 8.19   And euere *haþ* as I hope, and euere shal herafter.'
B. 8.55   Ac man *haþ* moost þerof and moost is to blame
B. 8.57   'I *haue* no kynde knowyng', quod I, 'to conceyuen [þi] wordes
B. 8.75   'I *haue* sued þee seuen yeer; seye þow me no raþer?'
B. 8.87   [Whiles he *haþ* ouȝt of his owene he helpeþ þer nede is];
B. 8.88   The bagges and þe bigirdles, he *haþ* [b]roke hem alle
B. 8.89   That þe Erl Auarous [*hadde*, or] hise heires,
B. 8.90   And wiþ Mammonaes moneie he *haþ* maad hym frendes;
B. 8.91   And is ronne to Religion, and *haþ* rendred þe bible,
B. 8.101   [Thei *han*] crowne[d a] kyng to [kepen] hem [alle],
B. 9.5   Kynde *haþ* closed þerInne, craftily wiþalle,
B. 9.7   Anima she hatte; [to hir *haþ* enuye]

B. 9.11	And [*haþ*] doo[n] hire wiþ sire dowel, duc of þise Marches.
B. 9.19	And *haþ* fyue faire sones bi his firste wyue:
B. 9.28	And þat is þe grete god þat gynnyng *hadde* neuere,
B. 9.40	Thouʒ he [wiste to] write neuer so wel, [and] he *hadde* [a] penne,
B. 9.63	For þei seruen Sathan hir soules shal he *haue*;
B. 9.71	And widewes þat *han* noʒt wherwith to wynnen hem hir foode,
B. 9.138	Til fourty daies be fulfild, þat flood *haue* ywasshen
B. 9.139	Clene awey þe corsed blood þat Caym *haþ* ymaked.
B. 9.151	That somdel þe sone shal *haue* þe sires tacches.
B. 9.155	And *haue* a Sauour after þe sire; selde sestow ooþer:
B. 9.158	Forþi *haue* þei maugre of hir mariages þat marie so hir children.
B. 9.163	[For] goode sholde wedde goode, þouʒ þei no good *hadde*;
B. 9.170	Many peire siþen þe pestilence *han* pliʒt hem togideres.
B. 9.172	*Haue* þei no children but cheeste and [choppes] bitwene.
B. 9.187	Whan ye *han* wyued beþ war and wercheþ in tyme,
B.10.1	Thanne *hadde* wit a wif was hote dame Studie,
B.10.10	Among hogges þat *han* hawes at wille,
B.10.30	Harlotes for hir harlotrie may *haue* of hir goodes,
B.10.32	Ac he þat *haþ* holy writ ay in his mouþe
B.10.46	Ne [holpe hir] harlotrye, *haue* god my trouþe,
B.10.71	And *haue* hym muche in [hire] mouþ, ac meene men in herte.
B.10.72	Freres and faitours *han* founde [vp] swiche questions
B.10.78	That preieres *haue* no power þ[ise] pestilence[s] to lette.
B.10.90	Whoso *haþ* muche spende manliche, so [meneþ] Tobye,
B.10.92	For we *haue* no lettre of oure lif how longe it shal dure.
B.10.99	Now *haþ* ech riche a rule to eten by hymselue.
B.10.104	I *haue* yherd heiʒe men etynge at þe table
B.10.154	He *haþ* wedded a wif wiþInne þise [woukes sixe],
B.10.159	Gladder þan þe gleman þat gold *haþ* to ʒifte,
B.10.185	Ac Theologie *haþ* tened me ten score tymes;
B.10.241	On þe grete god þat gynnyng *hadde* neuere,
B.10.255	For *hadde* neuere freke fyn wit þe feiþ to dispute,
B.10.256	Ne man *hadde* no merite myʒte it ben ypreued:
B.10.268	Alle þat lakkeþ any lif and lakkes *han* hemselue:
B.10.296	And al for youre holynesse; *haue* ye þis in herte.
B.10.317	Litel *hadde* lordes to doon to ʒyue lond from hire heires
B.10.318	To Religiouse þat *han* no rouþe þouʒ it reyne on hir Auters.
B.10.320	Of þe pouere *haue* þei no pite, and þat is hir [pure chartre];
B.10.332	*Haue* a knok of a kyng, and incurable þe wounde.
B.10.347	That þei *han* Eritage in heuene, and by trewe riʒte,
B.10.356	*Haue* heritage [in] heuene as [an heiʒ] cristene.
B.10.395	Ac of fele witty in feiþ litel ferly I *haue*
B.10.421	That *hadde* lyued al his lif wiþ lesynges and þefte,
B.10.425	That *hadde* yleyen wiþ lucifer many longe yeres.
B.10.430	Or Poul þe Apostle þat no pite *hadde*
B.10.446	And he þat may al amende *haue* mercy on vs alle,
B.10.448	[And yet *haue* I forgete ferþer of fyue wittes techyng
B.10.472	Ye, men knowe clerkes þat *han* corsed þe tyme
B.10.474	And principally hir paternoster; many a persone *haþ* wisshed.
B.11.12	Thanne *hadde* Fortune folwynge hire two fair damyseles:
B.11.18	And seide, 'þow art yong and yeep and *hast* yeres ynowe
B.11.23	Til þow be a lord and *haue* lond leten þee I nelle
B.11.35	'Folwe forþ þat Fortune wole; þow hast wel fer til Elde.
B.11.45	'That wit shal torne to wrecchednesse for wil to *haue* his likyng!'
B.11.49	I *hadde* no likyng, leue me, [þe leste] of hem to knowe.
B.11.53	'*Haue* no conscience', [quod she],'how þow come to goode;
B.11.57	To hir Priour prouincial a pardon for to *haue*,
B.11.74	Where my body were buryed by so ye *hadde* my siluer.
B.11.75	Ich *haue* muche merueille of yow, and so haþ many anoþer,
B.11.75	Ich haue muche merueille of yow, and so *haþ* many anoþer,
B.11.158	Wel ouʒte ye lordes þat lawes kepe þis lesson *haue* in mynde
B.11.197	[Alle myʒte god *haue* maad riche men if he wolde],
B.11.233	For in hir liknesse oure lord [lome] *haþ* ben yknowe
B.11.244	Many tyme god *haþ* ben met among nedy peple,
B.11.264	Makeþ a man to *haue* mynde in god and a gret wille
B.11.273	That parfit pouerte was no possession to *haue*,
B.11.287	Spera in deo speketh of preestes þat *haue* no spendyng siluer,
B.11.294	For made neuere kyng no knyʒt but he *hadde* catel to spende
B.11.297	That *haþ* no lond ne lynage riche ne good loos of hise handes.
B.11.299	That *han* neiþer konnynge ne kyn, but a crowne one
B.11.318	This lokynge on lewed preestes *haþ* doon me lepe from pouerte
B.11.338	As whan þei *hadde* ryde in Rotey tyme anoon [reste þei] after;
B.11.341	Ther ne was cow ne cowkynde þat conceyued *hadde*
B.11.346	*Hadde* neuere wye wit to werche þe leeste.
B.11.347	I *hadde* wonder at whom and wher þe pye
B.11.360	Muche merueilled me what maister [þei *hadde*],
B.11.374	'I *haue* wonder [in my wit], þat witty art holden,
B.11.377	Why I suffre or noʒt suffre; þiself *hast* noʒt to doone.
B.11.407	That I in metels ne myʒte moore *haue* yknowen.
B.11.408	[Th]anne seide I to myself, 'slepyng *hadde* I grace]
B.11.413	'*Haddestow* suffred', he seide, 'slepynge þo þow were,
B.11.414	Thow sholdest *haue* knowen þat clergie kan & [conceyued] moore þoruʒ Res[on],

B.11.415	For Reson wolde *haue* reherced þee riʒt as Clergie seid;
B.11.417	Adam, whiles he spak noʒt, *hadde* paradis at wille,
B.11.422	Tho *hadde* he [litel] likyng for to lere þe moore.
B.11.435	'Ye siggen sooþ', quod I, 'ich *haue* yseyen it ofte.
B.12.3	I *haue* folwed þee, in feiþ, þise fyue and fourty wynter,
B.12.4	And manye tymes *haue* meued þee to [mynne] on þyn ende,
B.12.10	Amende þee while þow myʒt; þow *hast* ben warned ofte
B.12.106	And *haþ* noon hap wiþ his ax his enemy to hitte,
B.12.114	*Hadde* neuere lewed man leue to leggen hond on þat cheste
B.12.155	Why I *haue* told [þee] al þis, I took ful good hede
B.12.181	And *haþ* no contricion er he come to shrifte; & þanne kan he litel telle
B.12.190	That *haþ* take fro Tybourne twenty stronge þeues,
B.12.192	The þef þat *hadde* grace of god on good fryday, as þow spek[e],
B.12.196	Ac þouʒ þat þeef *hadde* heuene he hadde noon heiʒ blisse,
B.12.196	Ac þouʒ þat þeef hadde heuene he *hadde* noon heiʒ blisse,
B.12.197	As Seint Iohan and oþere Seintes þat deserued *hadde* bettre.
B.12.199	[I] *hadde* mete moore þan ynouʒ, ac noʒt so muche worshipe
B.12.211	That oure lord ne *hadde* hym liʒtly out, so leue I [by] þe þef in heuene.
B.12.224	How euere beest ouþer brid *haþ* so breme wittes.
B.12.259	By þe po feet is vnderstande, as I *haue* lerned in Auynet,
B.12.292	And an hope hangynge þerInne to *haue* a mede for his truþe;
B.13.4	And of þis metyng many tyme muche þouʒt I *hadde*,
B.13.20	And whan he *hadde* seid so, how sodeynliche he passed.
B.13.57	And þanne *hadde* Pacience a pitaunce, Pro hac orabit ad te omnis
B.13.79	*Haþ* no pite on vs pouere; he parfourneþ yuele
B.13.88	He shal haue a penaunce in his paunche and puffe at ech a worde,
B.13.90	For now he *haþ* dronken so depe he wole deuyne soone
B.13.107	For ye *han* harmed vs two in þat ye eten þe puddyng,
B.13.108	Mortrews and ooþer mete, and we no morsel *hadde*.
B.13.120	'I *haue* seuene sones', he seide, seruen in a Castel
B.13.124	For oon Piers þe Plowman *haþ* impugned vs alle,
B.13.134	Pacience *haþ* be in many place, and paraunter [knoweþ]
B.13.156	And herwith am I welcome þer I *haue* it wiþ me.
B.13.164	[And ek, *haue* god my soule, and þow wilt it craue
B.13.182	And be Pilgrym wiþ pacience til I *haue* preued moore.'
B.13.191	*Haþ* meued my mood to moorne for my synnes.
B.13.194	*Hadde* noʒt [Marie] Maudeleyne moore for a box of salue
B.13.201	*Haue* pacience parfitliche þan half þi pak of bokes.'
B.13.214	Til Pacience *haue* preued þee and parfit þee maked.'
B.13.216	Thanne *hadde* Pacience, as pilgrymes han, in his poke vitailles:
B.13.216	Thanne hadde Pacience, as pilgrymes *han*, in his poke vitailles:
B.13.234	I *haue* no goode giftes of þise grete lordes
B.13.244	And I *hadde* neuere of hym, haue god my trouþe,
B.13.244	And I hadde neuere of hym, *haue* god my trouþe,
B.13.247	*Hadde* ich a clerc þat couþe write I wolde caste hym a bille
B.13.254	For siþ he *haþ* þe power þat Peter hadde he haþ þe pot wiþ þe salue:
B.13.254	For siþ he haþ þe power þat Peter *hadde* he haþ þe pot wiþ þe salue:
B.13.254	For siþ he haþ þe power þat Peter hadde he *haþ* þe pot wiþ þe salue:
B.13.256	To *haue* þe grace of god, and no gilt of [þe] pope.
B.13.260	For er I *haue* breed of mele ofte moot I swete,
B.13.261	And er þe commune *haue* corn ynouʒ many a cold morwenyng;
B.13.273	He *hadde* a cote of cristendom as holy kirke bileueþ;
B.13.278	Ooþerwise þan he *haþ* wiþ herte or siʒte shewynge hym;
B.13.289	As best for his body be to *haue* a [bold] name;
B.13.290	And entremetten hym ouer al þer he *haþ* noʒt to doone;
B.13.302	Boldest of beggeris; as bostere þat noʒt *haþ*,
B.13.309	What I suffrede and seiʒ and somtymes *hadde*,
B.13.314	*Haþ* manye moles and spottes; it moste ben ywasshe.'
B.13.333	And whan I may noʒt *haue* þe maistrie [wiþ] malencolie Itake,
B.13.341	But þoruʒ charme *hadde* I chaunce and my chief heele.'
B.13.351	Til þei myʒte na moore; and þanne [*hadde*] murye tales,
B.13.357	And ymagynede how he it myʒte *haue*
B.13.363	And if my Neghebore *hadde* a[n] hyne or any beest ellis
B.13.365	How I myʒte *haue* it al my wit I caste,
B.13.366	And but I *hadde* by ooþer wey at þe laste I stale it,
B.13.369	Thoruʒ gile to gaderen þe good þat ich *haue*.
B.13.378	And boþe to kiþ and to kyn vnkynde of þat ich *hadde*;
B.13.384	*Hadde* I neuere wille, woot god, witterly to biseche
B.13.387	As if I *hadde* dedly synne doon I dredde noʒt þat so soore
B.13.399	[Yet glotoun wiþ grete oþes his [garnement] *hadde* soiled
B.13.423	And *han* likynge to liþen hem [in hope] to do yow lauʒe–
B.13.433	Sholde noon harlot *haue* audience in halle n[e] in Chambre
B.13.439	*Haue* beggeres bifore hem þe whiche ben goddes minstrales
B.13.442	For to solace youre soules swiche minstrales to *haue*:
B.13.457	Thus haukyn þe Actif man *hadde* ysoiled his cote
B.13.459	Why he ne *hadde* [w]asshen it or wiped it wiþ a brusshe.
B.14.1	'I *haue* but oon hool hater', quod haukyn, 'I am þe lasse to blame
B.14.3	And also I *haue* an houswif, hewen and children–

B.14.5   It *haþ* be laued in lente and out of lente boþe
B.14.25   Shal noon heraud ne harpour *haue* a fairer garnement
B.14.51   '*Haue*, haukyn', quod Pacience, 'and et þis whan þe hungreþ
B.14.96   And as it neuere [n]*adde* ybe to noȝte bryngeþ dedly synne
B.14.99   [Wye] þat wiþ hym spak, as wide as I *haue* passed.'
B.14.110 To *haue* allowaunce of his lord; by þe lawe he it cleymeþ,
B.14.111 Ioye þat neuere ioye *hadde* of riȝtful Iugge he askeþ,
B.14.118 That al hir lif *han* lyued in langour and defaute.
B.14.122 Aungeles þat in helle now ben *hadden* ioye som tyme,
B.14.127 To ȝyue many m[e]n his [mercymonye] er he it *haue* deserued.
B.14.129 For þei *han* hir hire heer and heuene as it were,
B.14.134 Hewen þat *han* hir hire afore arn eueremoore nedy,
B.14.136 And til he *haue* doon his deuoir and his dayes iournee.
B.14.137 For whan a werkman *haþ* wroȝt, þan may men se þe soþe,
B.14.138 What he were worþi for his werk and what he *haþ* deserued,
B.14.141 *Haue* heuene in youre her[berw]yng and heuene þerafter
B.14.143 As he þat noon *hadde* and *haþ* hire at þe laste.
B.14.143 As he þat noon hadde and *haþ* hire at þe laste.
B.14.145 Ac if ye riche *haue* ruþe and rewarde wel þe poore,
B.14.148 And rewarden alle double richesse þat rewful hertes *habbeþ*.
B.14.149 And as an hyne þat *hadde* his hire er he bigonne,
B.14.150 And whan he *haþ* doon his deuoir wel men dooþ hym ooþer
          bountee.
B.14.153 And alle þat doon hir deuoir wel *han* double hire for hir trauaille,
B.14.165 Heuene after hir hennes goyng þat here *han* swich defaute.
B.14.166 For alle myȝtestow *haue* maad noon mener þan ooþer
B.14.167 And yliche witty and wise, if þee wel *hadde* liked.
B.14.168 [And] *haue* ruþe on þise riche men þat rewarde noȝt þi prisoners;
B.14.172 Ne neiþer hete ne Hayll, *haue* þei hir heele;
B.14.211 For þe riche *haþ* muche to rekene, and [riȝt softe] walkeþ;
B.14.217 [Or] in þe maister [or] in þe man som mansion he *haueþ*.
B.14.218 Ac in pouerte is pride *haþ* no myȝt,
B.14.220 Ne *haue* power in pouerte, if pacience [it] folwe.
B.14.225 If wraþe wrastle wiþ þe poore he *haþ* þe worse ende
B.14.235 So for his glotonie and his greete sleuþe he *haþ* a greuous
          penaunce.
B.14.242 And *haþ* hondes and armes of [a long] lengþe,
B.14.245 And þouȝ Auarice wolde angre þe poore he *haþ* but litel myȝte,
B.14.246 For pouerte *haþ* but pokes to putten in hise goodes
B.14.247 Ther Auarice *haþ* Almaries and yren bounden cofres.
B.14.253 *Hadde* þei no[on haunt] but of poore men; hir houses stoode
          vntyled.
B.14.262 Muche hardier may he asken þat here myȝte *haue* his wille
B.14.274 '*Haue* god my trouþe', quod Haukyn '[I here yow] preise faste
          pouerte.
B.14.324 I ne *hadde* be deed and doluen for dowelis sake!
B.14.330 That euere he *hadde* lond ouþer lordshipe lasse oþer moore,
B.15.11   Til reson *hadde* ruþe on me and rokked me aslepe,
B.15.123 Sir Iohan and sire Geffrey *haþ* [of siluer a girdel],
B.15.126 *Hadde* he neuere [saued] siluer þerto [for spendyng at ale];
B.15.130 Wolde neuere þe wit of witty god but wikkede men it *hadde*,
B.15.137 Lightliche þat þei leuen losels it *habbeþ*.
B.15.141 To frend ne to fremmed: "þe fend *haue* his soule!
B.15.147 And bymeneþ goode meteȝyueres and in mynde *haueþ*,
B.15.152 I *haue* lyued in londe', quod [I], 'my name is longe wille,
B.15.172 Ne no likynge *haþ* to lye ne laughe men to scorne.
B.15.176 '*Haþ* he anye rentes or richesse or any riche frendes?'
B.15.183 Ther poore men and prisons liggeþ, hir pardon to *haue*;
B.15.198 'Clerkes *haue* no knowyng', quod he, 'but by werkes and wordes.
B.15.203 And to poore peple *han* pepir in þe nose,
B.15.207 Ac it is moore to *haue* hir mete [on] swich an esy manere
B.15.220 For I *haue* seyen hym in silk and som tyme in russet,
B.15.225 I *haue* yseyen charite also syngen and reden
B.15.232 In þat secte siþþe to selde *haþ* he ben [knowe].
B.15.242 And þat Conscience and crist *haþ* yknyt faste
B.15.247 Ac auarice *haþ* þe keyes now and kepeþ for his kynnesmen
B.15.259 In alle manere angres, *haue* þis at herte
B.15.263 For wel may euery man wite, if god *hadde* wold hymselue,
B.15.264 Sholde neuere Iudas ne Iew *haue* Iesu doon on roode,
B.15.265 Ne *han* martired Peter ne Poul, ne in prison holden.
B.15.281 And day bi day *hadde* he hire noȝt his hunger for to slake,
B.15.284 *Hadde* a brid þat brouȝte hym breed þat he by lyuede,
B.15.285 And þouȝ þe gome *hadde* a gest god fond hem boþe.
B.15.286 Poul primus heremita *hadde* parroked hymselue
B.15.301 And if þei kouþe *han* ycarped, by crist! as I trowe,
B.15.302 Thei wolde *haue* yfed þat folk bifore wilde foweles;
B.15.315 For *hadde* ye potage and payn ynogh and penyale to drynke,
B.15.317 Ye *hadde* riȝt ynoȝ, ye Religiouse, and so yow rule me tolde.
B.15.322 Allas, lordes and ladies, lewed counseil *haue* ye
B.15.331 And of hem þat *habbeþ* þei taken and ȝyueþ hem þat [ne] *habbeþ*.
B.15.331 And of hem þat habbeþ þei taken and ȝyueþ hem þat [ne] *habbeþ*.
B.15.333 Fele of yow fareþ as if I a forest *hadde*
B.15.341 Hem þat *han* as ye han; hem ye make at ese.

B.15.341 Hem þat han as ye *han*; hem ye make at ese.
B.15.351 And so it fareþ by som folk now; þei *han* a fair speche,
B.15.358 *Han* no bileue to þe lifte ne to þe [lodesterre].
B.15.393 For Sarȝens *han* somwhat semynge to oure bileue,
B.15.440 Sholde alle maner men; we *han* so manye maistres,
B.15.480 So hope þei to *haue* heuene þoruȝ hir whistlyng.
B.15.487 That heuedes of holy chirche ben, þat *han* hir wil here.
B.15.495 That þei ne wente as crist wisseþ, siþen þei wille *haue* name,
B.15.502 *Han* a lippe of oure bileue, þe lightlier me þynkeþ
B.15.519 Many a seint syþen *haþ* suffred to deye
B.15.560 "Dos ecclesie þis day *haþ* ydronke venym
B.15.561 And þo þat *han* Petres power arn apoisoned alle."
B.15.575 That no man sholde be bisshop but if he *hadde* boþe
B.15.581 And *han* clerkes to kepen vs þerInne & hem þat shul come after.
B.16.11   And to *haue* my fulle of þat fruyt forsake a[l] oþ[er] saule[e].
B.16.16   And liberum arbitrium *haþ* þe lond [to] ferme,
B.16.52   And help of þe holy goost, and þus *haue* I þe maistrie.'
B.16.55   Ac I *haue* þouȝtes a þreve of þise þre piles,
B.16.63   And I *haue* told þee what hiȝte þe tree; þe Trinite it meneþ.'
B.16.67   'Heer now byneþe', quod he þo, 'if I nede *hadde*,
B.16.74   And suffre me to assaien what sauour it *hadde*.
B.16.78   I *hadde* ruþe whan Piers rogged, it gradde so rufulliche;
B.16.102 To *haue* yfouȝte wiþ þe fend er ful tyme come.
B.16.113 Saue þo he leched laȝar þat *hadde* yleye in graue;
B.16.123 For I *haue* saued yowself and youre sones after,
B.16.184 The firste *haþ* myȝt and maiestee, makere of alle þynges;
B.16.187 Wardeyn of þat wit *haþ*; was euere wiþouten gynnyng.
B.16.189 The light of al þat lif *haþ* a londe and a wane,
B.16.194 So god, þat gynnyng *hadde* neuere but þo hym good þouȝte,
B.16.206 And þe issue þat þei *hadde* it was of hem boþe,
B.16.217 Na moore myȝte god be man but if he moder *hadde*.
B.16.247 Thus *haue* I ben his heraud here and in helle
B.16.253 I *hadde* wonder of hise wordes and of hise wide cloþes
B.16.257 'What awaitestow?' quod he, 'and what woldestow *haue*?'
B.16.260 'This is a present of muche pris; what prynce shal it *haue*?'
B.16.261 'It is a precious present', quod he, 'ac þe pouke it *haþ* attached,
B.17.5   'Nay', he seide, '[I] seke hym þat *haþ* be seel to kepe,
B.17.20   For, þouȝ I seye it myself, I *haue* saued with þis charme
B.17.22   '[He seiþ] sooþ', seide þis heraud; 'I *haue* [founded] it ofte.
B.17.31   And *haþ* saued þat bileued so and sory for hir synnes,
B.17.35   And now com[s]eþ Spes and spekeþ, þat [*haþ*] aspied þe lawe,
B.17.60   Feiþ *hadde* first siȝte of hym, ac he fleiȝ aside
B.17.62   Hope cam hippynge after þat *hadde* so ybosted
B.17.63   How he wiþ Moyses maundement *hadde* many men yholpe,
B.17.64   Ac whan he *hadde* sighte of þat segge aside he gan hym drawe
B.17.66   Ac so soone so þe Samaritan *hadde* siȝte of þis leode
B.17.70   And but he *hadde* recouerer þe ra[þ]er þat rise sholde he neuere.
B.17.77   '*Haue*, kepe þis man', [quod he], 'til I come fro þe Iustes.
B.17.93   '*Haue* hem excused', quod he; 'hir help may litel auaille.
B.17.100 Til he *haue* eten al þe barn and his blood ydronke.
B.17.122 Til I *haue* salue for alle sike; and þanne shal I turne
B.17.176 The pawme is pureliche þe hand, *haþ* power by hymselue
B.17.178 For [þe pawme] *haþ* power to putte out þe ioyntes
B.17.223 As dooþ a kex or a candle þat caught *haþ* fir and blaseþ,
B.17.247 [Fro] þe fader of heuene forȝifnesse to *haue*.
B.17.249 But þow *haue* tow to take it wiþ, tonder or broches,
B.17.279 For þat þe holy goost *haþ* to kepe þ[o] harlotes destruyeþ,
B.17.298 Ne *haue* pite for any preiere þer þat he pleyneþ,
B.17.299 'I pose I *hadde* synned so and sholde [nouþe] deye,
B.17.310 And eyþer *haue* equyte, as holy writ telleþ:
B.17.344 That þei *han* cause to contrarie by kynde of hir siknesse;
B.17.346 *Haþ* mercy on swiche men þat so yuele may suffre.
B.18.66   Shal no wight wite witterly who shal *haue* þe maistrie
B.18.79   Highte Longeus as þe lettre telleþ, and longe *hadde* lore his sight;
B.18.90   For þe dede þat I *haue* doon I do me in youre grace.
B.18.91   *Haue* on me ruþe, riȝtful Iesu;' and riȝt wiþ þat he wepte.
B.18.98   The gree ȝit *haþ* he geten for al his grete wounde,
B.18.102 And ye, lurdaynes, *han* ylost for lif shal haue þe maistrye;
B.18.102 And ye, lurdaynes, han ylost for lif shal *haue* þe maistrye;
B.18.105 [Ne] *haue* lordshipe in londe ne no lond tilye,
B.18.125 'Ich *haue* ferly of þis fare, in feiþ', seide truþe,
B.18.127 '*Haue* no merueille', quod mercy; 'murþe it bitokneþ.
B.18.138 For patriarkes and prophetes *han* preched herof ofte
B.18.146 Ne *haue* hem out of helle; hold þi tonge, mercy!
B.18.153 That Adam and Eue *haue* shul bote].
B.18.169 Loue *haþ* coueited hire longe; leue I noon ooþer
B.18.184 And þat god *haþ* forgyuen and graunted me, pees, & mercy
B.18.203 'And I shal preue', quod Pees, 'hir peyne moot *haue* ende,
B.18.205 For *hadde* þei wist of no wo, wele hadde þei noȝt knowen,
B.18.205 For hadde þei wist of no wo, wele *hadde* þei noȝt knowen;
B.18.207 Ne what is hoot hunger þat *hadde* neuere defaute.
B.18.223 To [se] what he *haþ* suffred in þre sondry places,
B.18.254 [And to *haue* out of helle alle þat hym likeþ].

B.18.271	Patriarkes and prophetes *han* parled herof longe
B.18.291	And so þow *haddest* hem out and hider at þe laste.'
B.18.294	We *haue* no trewe title to hem, for þoruȝ treson were þei dampned.'
B.18.297	I *haue* assailled hym with synne and som tyme yasked
B.18.299	And þus *haþ* he trolled forþ [lik a tidy man] þise two and þritty wynter.
B.18.302	For Iewes hateden hym and *han* doon hym to deþe.
B.18.303	I wolde *haue* lengþed his lif for I leued if he deide
B.18.314	And now for þi laste lesynge ylorn we *haue* Adam,
B.18.341	And al þat man *haþ* mysdo I man wole amende.
B.18.357	Graciousliche þi gile *haue* quyt: go gile ayein gile!
B.18.363	[Þe bitternesse þat þow *hast* browe, now brouke it þiselue];
B.18.372	And *haue* out of helle alle mennes soules.
B.19.1	Thus I awaked and wroot what I *hadde* ydremed,
B.19.55	That longe *hadde* yleyen bifore as Luciferis cherles,
B.19.107	Til he *hadde* alle hem þat he for bledde.
B.19.140	[Her]of Cayphas *hadde* enuye and oþere Iewes,
B.19.188	Thus *haþ* Piers power, b[e] his pardon paied,
B.19.261	And for to tilie truþe a teeme shal he *haue*.'
B.19.273	Wiþ two [aiþes] þat þei *hadde*, an oold and a newe:
B.19.282	He þat ete of þat seed *hadde* swich a kynde:
B.19.372	Ther nas no cristene creature þat kynde wit *hadde*
B.19.384	That *han* laboured lelly al þis lenten tyme.
B.19.389	Or as ofte as þei *hadde* nede, þo þat *hadde* ypaied
B.19.389	Or as ofte as þei hadde nede, þo þat *hadde* ypaied
B.19.447	It semeþ bi so hymself *hadde* his wille
B.19.469	Ther I may hastilokest it *haue*, for I am heed of lawe;
B.19.479	[*Haue*] þow mayst [þyn askyng] as þi lawe askeþ:
B.19.480	The viker *hadde* fer hoom and faire took his leeue
B.20.10	And nede *haþ* no lawe ne neuere shal falle in dette
B.20.13	Ne wight noon wol ben his boruȝ, ne wed *haþ* noon to legge;
B.20.45	And þe fissh *haþ* fyn to flete wiþ to reste;
B.20.46	Ther nede *haþ* ynome me þat I moot nede abide
B.20.51	Whan nede *ha[dde]* vndernome me þus anoon I fil aslepe
B.20.69	Antecrist *hadde* þus soone hundredes at his baner,
B.20.86	*Hadde* ypriked and prayed polles of peple;
B.20.94	And er heraudes of Armes *hadden* discryued lordes,
B.20.170	And bisouȝte hym of socour and of his salue *hadde*;
B.20.188	*Haddestow* be hende', quod I, 'þow woldest haue asked leeue.'
B.20.188	Haddestow be hende', quod I, 'þow woldest *haue* asked leeue.'
B.20.193	And of þe wo þat I was Inne my wif *hadde* ruþe
B.20.198	So Elde and [heo] *hadden* it forbeden
B.20.202	Lo! Elde þe hoore *haþ* me biseye.
B.20.227	And *hadden* almoost vnitee and holynesse adown.
B.20.233	That þei come for coueitise, to *haue* cure of soules.
B.20.246	Holdeþ yow in vnitee, and *haueþ* noon enuye.
B.20.248	And I wol be youre boruȝ: ye shal *haue* breed and cloþes
B.20.258	*Han* Officers vnder hem, and ech of hem a certein.
B.20.265	Hir ordre and hir reule wole to *han* a certein noumbre
B.20.270	Heuene *haþ* euene noumbre and helle is wiþoute noumbre.
B.20.307	For hir mys[fetes] þat þei wroȝt *hadde*,
B.20.318	'We *han* no nede', quod Conscience; 'I woot no bettre leche
B.20.320	Saue Piers þe Plowman þat *haþ* power ouer alle
B.20.325	To a lord for a lettre leue to *haue*
B.20.327	Boldely to þe bisshop and his brief *hadde*
B.20.335	Ypocrisie *haþ* hurt hem; ful hard is if þei keuere.'
B.20.369	Til Contricion *hadde* clene foryeten to crye and to wepe
B.20.378	The frere wiþ his phisyk þis folk *haþ* enchaunted,
B.20.383	And þat freres *hadde* a fyndyng þat for nede flateren
B.20.385	And sende me hap and heele til I *haue* Piers þe Plowman.'
C.Pr.29	In hope to *haue* a good ende and heuenriche blisse,
C.Pr.38	And [*han*] wytt at wille to worche yf þei wolde.
C.Pr.50	And *hadde* leue to lye [al here lyf aftir].
C.Pr.55	And [shopen] he[m] heremites here ese to *haue*.
C.Pr.62	Ac sith charite *hath* be Chapman and [c]hief to shryue lordes
C.Pr.63	Mony ferlyes *han* falle in a fewe ȝeres.
C.Pr.80	That þe [pore] peple [of þe] parsch[e] sholde *haue* yf þei ne were.
C.Pr.83	To *haue* a licence and leue [at] Londoun to dwelle
C.Pr.86	That *han* cure vnder crist and crownyng in tokene
C.Pr.128	I parsceyued of þe power þat Peter *hadde* to kepe,
C.Pr.134	Ac of þe Cardinales at Court þat caught *han* such a name
C.Pr.136	To *haue* þe power þat Peter hadde inpugne y nelle
C.Pr.136	To haue þe power þat Peter *hadde* inpugne y nelle
C.Pr.179	Sayde, 'y *haue* seyen grete syres in Cytees and in townes
C.Pr.195	That derste *haue* ybounde þe belle aboute þe kattes nekke
C.Pr.202	'Thow we *hadde* ykuld þe Cat ȝut shulde ther come another
C.Pr.219	For *hadde* ȝe ratones ȝoure [reik] ȝe couthe nat reule ȝowsuluen.'
C. 1.8	*Ha[u]e* thei worschip in this world thei wilneth no bettere;
C. 1.68	Thenne *hadde* y wonder in my wit what woman he were
C. 1.93	Til treuthe *hadde* termyned here trespas to þe ende
C. 1.94	And halden with h[y]m and [with] here þat *han* trewe action
C. 1.111	That *hadde* [lu]st to be lyk his lord þat was almyghty:
C. 1.129	For pruyde th[at] hym pokede his payne *hath* non ende.

C. 1.132	And alle þat *han* wel ywrouhte wende þey sholle
C. 1.137	'I *haue* no kynde knowyng,' quod y, '[ȝe mot] kenne me bettere
C. 1.150	Til hit *hadde* of erthe yȝoten hitsilue.
C. 1.151	/A[nd] when hit *hadde* of þe folde flesch and blode taken
C. 1.167	To *haue* pitee on þat peple þat paynede hym to dethe.
C. 1.171	Forthy y rede ȝow riche, *haueth* reuthe [o]n þe pore;
C. 1.179	ȝe n[e] *haueth* na more meryte in masse ne in oures
C. 1.192	So harde *haþ* auaryce yhapsed hem togederes
C. 2.11	And crouned [in] a croune, þe kyng *haþ* non bettre;
C. 2.15	For to telle of here atyer no tyme *haue* y nouthe.
C. 2.19	'That is mede þe mayde, *hath* niyed me ful ofte
C. 2.21	And [ylow on] hym to lordes þat lawes han to kepe;
C. 2.25	Oon fauel was he[re] fader þat *hath* a fykel tonge
C. 2.35	Shal *haue* grace to good ynow and a good ende,
C. 2.45	Fauel thorw his flaterynge speche *hath* mede foule enchaunted,
C. 2.52	And *haue* power to p[uny]schen hem; thenne pot forth thy resoun.
C. 2.72	That Gyle *hath* gyue to falsnesse and grauntid also mede,'
C. 2.75	And vnfoldeth the feffament þat fals *hath* ymaked.
C. 2.86	And fauel þat *hath* a fals speche Feffeth hem by þis lettre
C. 2.120	And sayde to Symonye, 'now sorwe mot thow *haue*
C. 2.129	And thow *has[t]* gyue here as gyle tauhte, now god ȝeue þe sorwe!
C. 2.136	For y, man, of thy mercy mede *haue* diserued."
C. 2.140	And thow *hast* feffed here with fals; fy on suche lawe.
C. 2.159	Til he *hadde* seluer for the seel and signes of notaries.
C. 2.166	That [fals] and [fauel] *hadde* for he[re] fayre ȝeftes,
C. 2.170	For we *haue* mede amaystred [with] oure mery [speche]
C. 2.173	To be maried for mone med[e] *hath* assented.'
C. 2.178	Ac hakeneys *hadde* thei none bote hakeneys to huyre;
C. 2.199	Y *haue* no tome to telle the tayl þat hem folewe[th]
C. 2.232	Tyl Pardoners *hadde* [pyte] and polleden hym [t]o house.
C. 2.244	Ac he *hath* leue to lep out as ofte as hym liketh,
C. 3.26	[W]henne they *hadde* lauhte here leue at this lady mede
C. 3.33	And bygge ȝow benefices, [here bonchef] to *haue*,
C. 3.40	'Thow le[r]ed men and le[w]ed *haued* layn by the bothe
C. 3.51	'We *han* a wyndowe awurchynge wol stande vs [wel] heye;
C. 3.63	*Haueth* mercy,' quod mede, 'o[f] men þat hit haunteth
C. 3.86	Thei *han* no pite on the peple þat parselmele mot begge;
C. 3.101	And *haue* here penaunce on puyre erthe and nat þe peyne of helle.
C. 3.104	Al this *haue* we seyn, þat som tyme thorw a breware
C. 3.114	Be yfranchised for a fre man and *haue* a fals name.
C. 3.118	'*Haue* reuthe on this regraters þat han riche handes,
C. 3.118	'Haue reuthe on this regraters þat *han* riche handes,
C. 3.133	Til treuthe *hadde* ytolde here a tokene fram hymsulue.
C. 3.134	And saide, 'vnwittiliche, womman, wro[uh]t *hastow* ofte
C. 3.135	And monye a gulte y *haue* the forgyue & my grace graunted
C. 3.147	Y *haue* a knyght, Consience, cam late fro beȝende;
C. 3.148	Yf he wilneth the to wyue wolt thow hym *haue*?'
C. 3.165	He *hath* apoisend popes, he appeyreth holy churche.
C. 3.195	That fayth may nat *haue* his forth, here floreynes goth so thykke,
C. 3.209	*Han* almost mad, but marye the helpe,
C. 3.211	For clerkes and coueitise mede *hath* knet togederes
C. 3.217	To *haue* space to speke, spede yf a myhte.
C. 3.227	Thow *hast* hanged on my half eleuene tymes
C. 3.232	Ac thow *hast* famed me foule byfore þe kyng here
C. 3.234	Ac y *haue* saued myselue sixty thousend lyues,
C. 3.237	*Hast* arwed many hardy man þat hadde wille to fyhte,
C. 3.237	Hast arwed many hardy man þat *hadde* wille to fyhte,
C. 3.258	Ac *hadde* y, mede, ben marchel o[f] his men in Fraunce
C. 3.259	Y durste *haue* yleyd my lyf and no lasse wedde
C. 3.260	He sholde *haue* [ben] lord of þat lond alenghe and abrede
C. 3.270	Thorw ȝeftes *haen* ȝemen to ȝerne and to ryde;
C. 3.285	Mede is worthy, me thynketh, þe maistrye to *haue*.'
C. 3.289	Tha[t] vnlaufulliche lyuen *hauen* large handes
C. 3.298	Ne *haue* hap to his hele mede to deserue.
C. 3.302	They asken here huyre ar thei hit *haue* deserued
C. 3.332	And efte *haue* hit aȝeyne of hem þat don ylle.
C. 3.350	To pay hym yf he parforme and *haue* pite yf he faileth
C. 3.358	In nombre, Rotye and aryse and remissioun to *haue*,
C. 3.369	For hoso wolde to wyue *haue* my worliche douhter
C. 3.385	Thow the kyng and þe comune al the coest *hadde*.
C. 3.435	For so is the world went with hem þat *han* power
C. 3.439	And riht as agag *hadde* happe shal somme:
C. 3.493	Ac *hadde* she loked in þe luft half and þe lef turned
C. 3.494	A sholde *haue* yfonde [felle wordes folwynge] aftur:
C. 3.498	The whiche þat hatte, as y *haue* rad an[d] oþer þat can rede,
C. 4.46	How wrong wilfully *hadde* his wyf forleyn
C. 4.68	And for to *haue* here helpe handy dandy payde.
C. 4.69	'*Hadde* y loue of [my] lord lytel wolde y reche
C. 4.84	Yf he amendes may [make] lat maynprise hym *haue*
C. 4.92	'*Haue* this, man, of me,' quod she, 'to amende thy scathe
C. 4.95	To *haue* mercy on þat man that many tymes hym greuede:
C. 4.96	'For he [*hath*] waged me wel as wysdom hym tauhte,
C. 4.97	And mede *hath* made my mendes y may no more asken.

C. 4.103	Bute resoun *haue* reuth on hym he shal reste in [þe] stokkes
C. 4.105	Summe radden resoun tho to *haue* reuthe vppon þat shrewe
C. 4.108	'Rede me nat,' quod resoun, 'no reuthe to *haue*
C. 4.131	And [ʒut],' quod resoun, 'by þe rode! y shal no reuthe *haue*
C. 4.132	Whiles mede *hath* the maistrie þer motyng is at [þe] Barr[e].
C. 4.172	And deme ʒow, by this day, as ʒe *haen* deserued.
C. 4.174	Y wol *haue* leutee for my lawe and late be al ʒoure iangl[ing]
C. 5.7	In an hot heruest whenne y *hadde* myn hele
C. 5.16	Or *haue* an horn and be hayward and lygge þeroute [a]nyhtes
C. 5.26	'Thenne *hastow* londes to lyue by,' quod resoun, 'or lynage ryche
C. 5.70	Ac sythe bondemen barnes *haen* be mad bisshopes
C. 5.71	And bar[o]nes bastardus *haen* be Erchedekenes
C. 5.72	And so[p]ares and here sones for suluer *han* be knyhtes,
C. 5.80	Lyfholynesse and loue *hath* be longe hennes
C. 5.93	That y *haue* ytynt tyme and tyme myspened;
C. 5.94	Ac ʒut y hope, as he þat ofte *hath* ychaffared
C. 5.99	So hope y to *haue* of hym þat is almyghty
C. 5.157	*Haen* ryde out of aray, here reule euele yholde,
C. 5.163	Lytel *hadde* lordes ado to ʒeue lond fro [here] heyres
C. 5.164	To religious þat *haen* no reuthe thow it ryne on here auters.
C. 5.166	Of þe pore *haueth* thei no pite and þat is here puyre chartre.
C. 5.177	Shal *haue* a knok vppon here crounes and incurable þe wounde:
C. 5.191	And sethe a preyede þe pope *haue* pite on holy chirche
C. 6.11	Of alle þat y *haue* hated in myn herte.
C. 6.16	*Haue* be vnbuxum, y byseche god of mercy;
C. 6.17	And [bold *haue*] y be, nat abaschet to agulte
C. 6.31	Otherwyse then y *haue*, withynne or withouten
C. 6.57	What y soffrede and seyh and some tymes *hadde*
C. 6.66	A wroth his f[u]ste vppon wrath; *hadde* [he] wesches at wille
C. 6.77	And when y may nat *haue* þe maystrie [with] malecolie ytake,
C. 6.85	But thorw a charme *hadde* y chaunce and my chef hele.
C. 6.109	The harm þat y *haue* do with hand and with tonge.
C. 6.113	But y *hadde* weder at my wille y witte god þe cause
C. 6.114	In alle manere angres þat y *hadde* or felede.
C. 6.128	Y *haue* an Aunte to nonne and an abbesse;
C. 6.130	Y *haue* be coek in here kychene and the couent serued
C. 6.136	For he *hadde* childe in the chapun co[t]e; he worth chalenged at þe eleccioun."
C. 6.146	For she *had* haly bred ar y my herte gan change.
C. 6.158	Y *haue* no luste, lef me, to longe amonges monkes
C. 6.161	Y *haue* a flux of a foul mouth wel fyue daies aftur;
C. 6.172	That he *haue* pite on me, p[u]tou[r], of his puyr mercy,
C. 6.185	Til we myhte no more; thenne *hadde* we mery tales
C. 6.193	When y was olde and hoor and *hadde* ylore þat kynde
C. 6.194	Y *hadde* likyng to talke of lecherye tales.
C. 6.195	Now, lord, for thy lewete on lechours *haue* mercy.'
C. 6.206	'Y *haue* be couetous,' quod this kaytif, 'y biknowe hit here.
C. 6.213	Ne *hadde* þe grace of Gyle go among my ware
C. 6.214	Hit *hadde* be vnsold this seuene ʒer, so me god helpe.
C. 6.233	[He] *ha[th]* holde hokkerye this eleuene wynter.'
C. 6.249	'Y *haue* lent lordes and ladyes þat louede me neuere aftur
C. 6.250	And *haue* ymad many a knyht bothe mercer and draper
C. 6.255	Ne thyn heyres, as y hope, *haue* ioye of þat thow wonne
C. 6.258	'With false wordes and w[ittes] *haue* y ywonne my godes
C. 6.259	And with Gyle and glosynge ygadered þat y *haue*,
C. 6.262	And yf my neyhebore *hadde* an hyne or eny beste elles
C. 6.264	How y myhte *haue* hit al my wit y caste
C. 6.265	And but y *hadde* by other wey at the laste y stale hit
C. 6.273	*Hadde* y neuere will, [woot god], witterly to byseche
C. 6.286	'Now redily,'quod repentaunce, 'y *haue* reuthe of thy lyuynge.'
C. 6.293	Then *haue* my fode and my fyndynge of fals menne wynnyngus.
C. 6.295	Til thow *haue* ymad þy myhte to alle men restitucioun.
C. 6.296	For alle that *hauen* of thy good, haue god my treuthe,
C. 6.296	For alle that hauen of thy good, *haue* god my treuthe,
C. 6.304	And [what] penaunce the prest shal *haue* þat p[r]oud is of his tithes.
C. 6.306	Then an errant vsurer, *haue* god my treuthe,
C. 6.309	Hyhte ʒeuan-ʒelde-aʒeyn-yf-y-so-moche-*haue*-
C. 6.310	Al-þat-y-wikkedly-wan-sithen-y-witte-*hadde*-
C. 6.312	That eche man shal *haue* his ar y hennes wende
C. 6.320	And *haddest* mercy vppon þat man for memento sake,
C. 6.321	So rewe on Robert þat reddere ne *haue*
C. 6.330	For he *hadde* layʒe by latro, luciferes aunte.
C. 6.340	'And *haue* his mercy in thy mynde and marchaundise, leue hit,
C. 6.341	For thow *hast* no good, by good fayth, to gete the with a wastel.
C. 6.342	For the good that thow *hast* gete bygan al with falshede
C. 6.357	'Y *haue* good ale, gossip Glotoun, woltow assaye?'
C. 6.358	'*Hastow*,' quod he, 'eny hote spyces?'
C. 6.359	'Y *haue* pepur and pyonie and a pound of garlek,
C. 6.381	That hoso *hadde* the hood sholde nat haue þe cloke
C. 6.381	That hoso hadde the hood sholde nat *haue* þe cloke
C. 6.385	And there were othes an heep for on sholde *haue* þe worse.
C. 6.389	Hicke þe hostiler *hadde* þe cloke

C. 6.391	And *haue* hickes hood þe hostiler and holde hym yserued:
C. 6.397	Til glotoun *hadde* yglobbed a galoun and a gylle.
C. 6.402	And wesched hit *hadde* [be wexed] with a weps of breres.
C. 6.403	He myhte noþer steppe ne stande til he a staf *hadde*
C. 6.417	And aftur al this exces he *hadde* an accidie;
C. 6.419	Then [wakede he] wel wanne and wolde *haue* ydronke;
C. 6.423	To repentaunce ryht thus, '*haue* reuthe on me,' he saide,
C. 6.426	Of þat y *haue* trespased with tonge, y can nat telle how ofte;
C. 6.440	Til abstinence myn aunte *haue* ʒeue me leue;
C. 6.441	And ʒut *haue* y [ha]ted here al my lyf tyme.'
C. 7.13	Y *haue* [made] voues fourty and forʒeten hem amorwen
C. 7.22	Y *hadde* leuere here an harlotrye or a lesyng to lauhen of
C. 7.27	Til matynes and masse be ydo; thenne *haue* y a memorie at þe freres.
C. 7.30	I *haue* be prest and persoun passynge thritty wyntur
C. 7.38	And thus *haue* y tened trewe men ten hundrit tymes.
C. 7.44	For y *haue* and haue yhad sumdel haukes maners;
C. 7.44	For y haue and *haue* yhad sumdel haukes maners;
C. 7.44	For y haue and haue *yhad* sumdel haukes maners;
C. 7.47	Sixty sythes y, sleuthe, *haue* forʒeten hit sethe
C. 7.54	And sethe a beggare *haue* y be for my foule sleuthe:
C. 7.68	Til y *haue* euensong yherd: y bihote to þe rode.'
C. 7.74	And *hath* no likynge to lerne ne of oure lord to here
C. 7.83	And *han* lykyng to lythen hem in hope to do ʒow lawhe–
C. 7.93	Sholde non harlote *haue* audiense in halle ne in chaumbre
C. 7.99	*Haue* beggares byfore hem þe whiche ben goddes mu[n]strals
C. 7.102	For to solace ʒoure soules suche munstrals to *haue*:
C. 7.139	And al þat mark *hath* ymade, Matheu, Ion and lucas
C. 7.146	For dedes that we *han* don ylle dampned sholde we ben neuere
C. 7.149	*Haue* reuthe of alle these rybaudes þat repenten hem sore
C. 7.157	To *haue* grace to go to treuthe; god leue þat they mote.
C. 7.169	And se by [his] signes wham a souht *hadde*:
C. 7.172	In bedlem and in babiloyne y *haue* be in bothe,
C. 7.175	/[Y *haue*] ywalked ful wyde in wete and in drye
C. 7.189	[I]ch *haue* ybe his foloware al this fourty wynter
C. 7.194	Y *haue* myn huyre of hym wel and oþerwhiles more.
C. 7.252	And he *hath* þe keye and þe clycat thow þe kyng slepe
C. 7.262	For he *hath* enuye to hym þat in thyn herte setteth
C. 7.283	'By Crist!' quod a cottepors, 'y *haue* no kyn there.'
C. 7.288	'Mercy is a mayden there *hath* myhte ouer hem alle
C. 7.294	Anoþer anoen riht nede he sayde he *hadde*
C. 7.300	'Y *haue* wedded a wyf wel wantowen of maneres;
C. 7.307	Ac þe way is ful wikked but hoso *hadde* a gyde
C. 8.2	Ich *haue* an half aker to erye by þe heye [way];
C. 8.3	*Haued* ye yered þis half aker and ysowed hit aftur
C. 8.10	That ʒe [*han*] selk and sendel to sowe whan tyme is
C. 8.67	Shal *haue* leue, by oure lord, to [lese here in heruest]
C. 8.82	His sone hihte soffre-thy-souereynes-*haue*-her-wille-
C. 8.85	Ne hem þat han lawes to loke lacke hem nat, y hote;
C. 8.92	'For now y am olde and hoer and *haue* of myn owene
C. 8.96	He shal *haue* my soule þat alle soules made
C. 8.99	To *haue* re[lees] and re[missioun]; on þat rental y leue.
C. 8.100	The kyrke shal *haue* my caroyne and my bones
C. 8.103	He is holdyng, y hope, to *haue* me in his masse
C. 8.105	My wyf shal *haue* of þat y wan with treuthe and no more
C. 8.127	And thow ʒe deye for deul þe deuel *haue* þat reche!'
C. 8.135	[We maun] none lymes to labory with, lord god we thonketh.'
C. 8.149	Thenne gan wastor to wrath hym and wolde *haue* yfouhte
C. 8.153	'Wolle thow, nulle thow, we wol *haue* oure wille
C. 8.176	Ne *hadde* [Peres] with a pese loof preyede hym b[ile]ue.
C. 8.177	'*Haue* mercy on hem, hunger,' quod [Peres], 'and lat me ʒeue hem benes
C. 8.195	To be his holde hewe thow he *hadde* no more
C. 8.204	Tho *hadde* [Peres] pitee vppon alle pore peple
C. 8.227	And h[e] shal soupe swetture when [he] hit *hath* deserued.
C. 8.228	Ac yf thow fynde eny folke þat fals men *han* apayred
C. 8.234	Yf thow *hast* wonne auht wikkedliche, wiseliche despene hit:
C. 8.239	As wyse men *haen* wryten and as witnesseth Genesis
C. 8.244	In somur for his sleuthe he shal *haue* defaute
C. 8.253	Byno[m] hym al þat he *hadde* and ʒaf hit to his felawe
C. 8.254	Þat leely *hadde* ylabored and thenne the lord sayde:
C. 8.255	"He þat *hath* shal haue and helpe þer hym liketh
C. 8.255	"He þat hath shal *haue* and helpe þer hym liketh
C. 8.256	And he þat nauht *hath* shal nauht haue and no man [hym helpen]
C. 8.256	And he þat nauht hath shal nauht *haue* and no man [hym helpen]
C. 8.257	And þat he weneth wel to *haue* y wol hit hym bireue".
C. 8.270	ʒe *han* manged ouer moche; þat maketh ʒow to be syke.
C. 8.279	And ʒut *hadde* he [heyh]nam] nat for y, hungur, culde hym–
C. 8.288	Til alle thyne nedy neyhbores *haue* noen ymaked.
C. 8.299	For thow *hast* wel awroke me and also wel ytauhte me.'
C. 8.301	Ar y *haue* ydyned be þis day and ydronke bothe.'
C. 8.302	'Y *haue* no peny,' quod [Peres], 'polettes for to begge,
C. 8.306	And ʒut y say[e], be my soule! y *haue* no sal[t] bacoun

C. 8.308 Ac y *haue* poret-pl[o]ntes, parsilie and skalones,
C. 8.313 And by [t]hat y hope to *haue* heruost in my croft[e];
C. 8.329 Laborers þat *han* no lond to lyue on but here handes
C. 9.11 *Haen* pardon thorw purgatorye to passe ful lyhtly,
C. 9.22 Marchauntes in þe margine *hadde* many ȝeres
C. 9.43 Alle þe peple *hadde* pardon ynow þat parfitliche lyuede.
C. 9.44 Men of lawe *hadde* lest þat loth were to plede
C. 9.50 Shal *haue* grace of a good ende and greet ioye aftur.
C. 9.52 For whenne ȝe drawe to þe deth and indulgences wolde *haue*
C. 9.63 For he þat beg[g]eth or biddeth, but y[f he] *haue* nede,
C. 9.70 Woet no man, as y wene, who is worthy to *haue*
C. 9.89 What other byhoueth þat *hath* many childrene
C. 9.90 And *hath* no catel but his craft to clothe h[e]m and to fede
C. 9.96 These are Almusse to helpe þat *han* suche charges.
C. 9.102 For alle þat *haen* here hele and here yesyhte
C. 9.115 And to oure syhte as hit semeth; seth god *hath* þe myhte
C. 9.125 We sholde [*haue*] hem to house and helpe hem when they come:
C. 9.148 Where he may rathest *haue* a repaest or a ronde of bacoun,
C. 9.161 Ne no beggare[s] þat beggeth but yf they *haue* nede.'
C. 9.175 Þai *haue* no part of pardoun ne of preyeres ne of penaunc[e].
C. 9.185 For loue of here lowe hertes oure lord *hath* hem ygrauntud
C. 9.188 And alle holy Eremytes *haue* shal þe same;
C. 9.198 Summe *hadde* lyflode of h[ere] lynage and of no lyf elles
C. 9.200 And somme *hadde* foreynes to frendes þat hem fode sente
C. 9.207 H[e]lden ful hungry hous and *hadde* muche defaute,
C. 9.209 That faytede in frere clothinge *hadde* fatte chekes.
C. 9.259 Vigilare were fayrere for thow *haste* a greet charge.
C. 9.270 When thy lord loketh to *haue* allouaunce of his bestes
C. 9.271 And of þe moneye thow *haddest* ther[myd] his mebles to [s]aue
C. 9.274 Thyn huyre, herde, as y hope, *hath* nat to quyte thy dette
C. 9.276 But '*haue* this for þat tho þat thow toke
C. 9.290 Bote do wel and *haue* wel, and [god] shal haue thy soule
C. 9.290 Bote do wel and haue wel, and [god] shal *haue* thy soule
C. 9.291 And do yuele and *haue* euele and hope thow non oþere
C. 9.298 Mony tyme this meteles *hath* maked me to studie
C. 9.301 And which a pardoun Peres *hadde* th[e] peple to glade
C. 9.307 Of Nabugodonasor þat no pere *hadde*
C. 9.325 ȝut *hath* þe pope power pardoun to graunte
C. 9.330 Soules þat *haue* syneged seuene sythes dedly.
C. 9.334 Vp truste of ȝoure tresor trionales to *haue*,
C. 9.337 That *haen* the welthe of this world and wise men ben holde
C. 9.345 And *haue* indulgences doublefold, but dowel vs helpe
C.10.10 Y haylsede hem hendly as y *hadde* ylered
C.10.19 And euere *hath*, as y hope, and euere wol hereaftur.'
C.10.54 For rather *haue* we no reste til we restitue
C.10.56 'Y *haue* no kynde kno[w]yng,' [quod y], 'to conseyue al this speche
C.10.73 'Y *haue* sued the seuen ȝer; saw thow me nat ȝut ones?'
C.10.85 The bagges and þe bigerdeles, he *hath* [b]roken hem alle
C.10.88 And is ronne [t]o religioun and *hath* rendred þe bible
C.10.132 Kynde *hath* closed therynne, craftily withalle,
C.10.134 Anima she hatte; to here *hath* enuye
C.10.138 And *hath* do here with sire dowel, duk of this marches.
C.10.145 And *hath* fyue fayre sones by his furste wyue:
C.10.154 The which is god grettest [þat gynnynge *hadde*] neuere,
C.10.181 Euery man þat *hath* inwit and his hele bothe
C.10.182 *Hath* tresor ynow of treuthe to fynden hymsulue.
C.10.194 The catel that Crist *hadde*, thre clothes hit were;
C.10.210 Out of matrimonye, nat moyloure, mowen nat *haue* þe grace
C.10.214 Aftur þat Adam and Eue *hadden* ysyneged:
C.10.219 Þat lycame *haen* aȝen þe lawe þat oure lord ordeynede.
C.10.226 Til fourty [dayes] be fulfild and floed *haue* ywasche
C.10.241 The eritage þat þe eyer sholde *haue* is at þe kynges wille.
C.10.247 Aftur þat Caym þ[e] corsed *hadde* ykuld abel,
C.10.254 For goode sholde wedde goode thouh they no goode *hadde*
C.10.261 Bote he *haue* oþer goed haue wol here no ryche.
C.10.261 Bote he haue oþer goed *haue* wol here no ryche.
C.10.271 Many a payre sethe th[e] pestelens[e] *han* plyhte treuthe to louye;
C.10.274 *Haen* þei no childerne here mouth Ac [c]hoppes hem bitwene.
C.10.288 ȝe þat *han* wyues ben war and wo[r]cheth nat out of tyme
C.11.1 Thenne *hadde* wit a wyf was hote dame studie
C.11.8 Among hoggus þat *han* hawes at wille.
C.11.28 Helpe hym þat *hath* nauhte then tho that haen no nede.
C.11.28 Helpe hym þat hath nauhte then tho that *haen* no nede.
C.11.29 Ac he þat *hath* holy writ ay in his mouth
C.11.42 Is non so hende to *haue* hym [in] but hote hym go þer god is.
C.11.51 And *haen* [hym] muche in here mouth Ac mene [men] in herte.
C.11.52 Freres and faytours *haen* founde vp suche questions
C.11.58 That preyeres *haen* no power this pestilences to lette.
C.11.66 Ac þe more a wynneth and *hath* þe world at his wille
C.11.72 And yf thow *haue* litel, leue sone, loke by þy lyue
C.11.79 Amonges hem þat *han* hawes at wille,
C.11.101 Gladdere then [þe] gleman þat gold *hath* to ȝefte
C.11.109 Yf thow hit vse oþer haunte, *haue* god my treuthe,

C.11.112 And *hast* vnderstandyng what a wolde mene
C.11.126 Ac teologie *hath* tened me ten score tymes;
C.11.156 For *hadde* neuere frek fyn wi[t] the faith to dispute
C.11.157 Ne man mouhte *haue* mery[t]e [thereof] mouhte hit be ypreued:
C.11.171 Thenne *hadde* fortune folwyng here two fayre maydenes:
C.11.177 And saide, 'þou art ȝong and ȝep and *hast* ȝeres ynowe
C.11.182 Til thow be a lord and *haue* lond leten y the nelle
C.11.194 'Folowe forth þat fortune wole; þou *hast* [wel] fer to elde.
C.11.226 For of fele witty in faith litel ferly y *haue*
C.11.253 That vnlawefulliche *hadde* ylyued al his lyf tyme
C.11.257 That *hadde* yley with lucifer mony longe ȝeres.
C.11.266 [Or] Poul þe apostel [þat] no pite *hadde*
C.11.272 Thus y, rechelesnesse, *haue* yrad registres and bokes
C.11.298 Of al þat they *haen* had of hym þat is here maistre
C.11.298 Of al þat they *haen* had of hym þat is here maistre.
C.12.2 'That wit shal turne to wrechednesse for wil *hath* al his wille!'
C.12.5 [*Haue* no consience how þou come to good]; confesse the to som frere.
C.12.9 To here prior prouincial [a] pardon to *haue*
C.12.16 And saide he myhte [me nat] assoile but y suluer *hadde*
C.12.22 Wher my body were yber[i]ed by so ȝe *hadde* my [suluer].'
C.12.90 Wel ouhte ȝe lordes þat lawes kepeth this lesson *haue* in mynde
C.12.119 To *haue* as we haen serued, as holy chirche witnesseth:
C.12.119 To haue as we *haen* serued, as holy chirche witnesseth:
C.12.122 For in here likenesse oure lord lome *hath* be yknowe.
C.12.150 Maketh man to *haue* mynde in god and his mercy to craue,
C.12.159 He shal *haue* an hundredfold of heueneryche blisse
C.12.164 Al þat thow *has[t]* here hastly go and sulle hit;
C.12.172 Mo prouerbes y myhte *haue* of mony holy seyntes
C.12.200 Yf god gyueth hym þe lyf, to *haue* a goed heruost,
C.12.213 And asketh [hym after] ho shal hit *haue*,
C.12.218 Vpholderes on þe hulle shal *haue* hit to sulle."
C.12.228 And *haen* þe world at he[re] wille oþerwyse to leuene.
C.12.237 For if he be fer þerfro fol ofte *hath* he drede
C.13.4 And ay þe lengere they lyuede the lasse goed they *hadde*:
C.13.6 And out of nombre tho men many mebles *hadden*.
C.13.7 Abraham for his [auȝte] *hadde* moche tene
C.13.15 Iob þe gentele, what ioye *hadde* he on erthe?
C.13.25 And þe gentel Iob; here ioye *hath* non ende.
C.13.36 What oen *hath*, what [o]þer hath and what they hadde bothe,
C.13.36 What oen hath, what [o]þer *hath* and what they hadde bothe,
C.13.36 What oen hath, what [o]þer hath and what they *hadde* bothe,
C.13.62 *Haue* hors and catel of here and; thogh he mette theues
C.13.70 And *haue* reuthe and releue with his rychesse by his power
C.13.101 For spera in deo speketh of prestis þat *han* no spendynge suluer
C.13.108 For made neuere kyng no knyhte but he *hadde* catel to spene
C.13.111 That *hath* n[o] lond ne lynage ryche ne good los of his handes.
C.13.113 That [*hath*] noþer connyng ne kyn bote a croune one
C.13.128 For ignorancia non excusat as ych *haue* herd in bokes.'
C.13.146 As when þei *hadde* [ryde in] roteye[tyme] anon they reste aftur;
C.13.149 Ther ne [was] cow ne cowkynde þat conseyued *hadde*
C.13.151 Ther ne was no kyne kynde þat conseyued *hadde*
C.13.157 *Hadde* neuere weye wyt to worche þe leste.
C.13.158 Y *hadde* wonder at wh[om] and where þe pye
C.13.169 'Where *hadde* thise wilde suche wit and at what scole?'
C.13.184 'Y *haue* wonder in my wit, so wys as thow art holden,
C.13.215 That y ne *hadde* met more, so murye as y slepte,
C.13.216 And saide anoen to mysulue, 'slepynge *hadde* y grace
C.13.221 '*Haddestow* soffred,' he sayde, 'slepyng tho thow were,
C.13.222 Thow sholdest *haue* yknowe þat clergie ca[n] & conseyued mor[e] [thorw] resoun
C.13.223 For resoun wolde *haue* rehersed þe riht as clergie seide;
C.13.225 Adam, whiles he spak nat, *hadde* paradys at wille
C.13.241 'ȝe seggeth soth, be my soule,' quod y, 'I *haue* sey hit ofte.
C.14.3 Y *haue* folewed the, in fayth, mo then fourty wynter
C.14.51 And *hath* non hap with his ax his enemye to hutte,
C.14.59 *Hadde* neuere lewede [man] leue to legge hand on þat cheste
C.14.99 Why y *haue* tolde al þis, y toek ful gode hede
C.14.106 That oen *hath* connyng and can swymmen and dyuen;
C.14.121 And *hath* no contricion ar he come to shrifte; and thenne can he lytel telle,
C.14.129 Hit *hath* take fro tybourne twenty stronge theues
C.14.131 The thef þat *hadde* grace of god a gode fryday, As thow toldest,
C.14.135 Ac thogh th[at] theef *hadde* heuene he hadde noen hey blisse
C.14.135 Ac thogh th[at] theef hadde heuene he *hadde* noen hey blisse
C.14.136 A[s] seynt Ioh[a]n and oþer seyntes þat *haen* [de]serued bettere.
C.14.138 Ich *haue* mete more then ynow Ac nat [so] muche worschipe
C.14.150 That oure [lord] ne *hauede* [hym] lihtliche out, so leue y [by] þ[e] thef in heuene.
C.14.157 How creatures *han* kynde wit and how clerkes come to bokes
C.14.175 And *haue* hem [in] haste at þyn owen wille
C.14.214 And hope hangeth ay þeron to *haue* þat treuthe deserueth:
C.15.4 And many tym[e] of this meteles moche thouhte y *hadde*:

C.15.23   And when he *hadde* ysaide so, how sodeynliche he vanschede.
C.15.35   A meles mete for a pore man or moneye yf they *hadde*.
C.15.59   Thenne cam contricion þat *hadd* coked for hem all
C.15.86   *Hath* no pyte on vs pore; he parformeth euele
C.15.95   He shal *haue* a penaunce in his paunche and poffe at vch a worde
C.15.97   [For] now he *hath* dronke so depe a wol deuyne sone
C.15.123   'Y *haue* yseide,' quod þat segg, 'y can sey no bettre.
C.15.128   'Haue me excused,' quod Clergie, 'be crist, but in scole.
C.15.148   And whan he *hadde* yworded thus wiste no man aftur
C.15.154   Y wolde, and y will *hadde*, wynnen all fraunce
C.15.162   Shal neuere buyren be abasched þat *hath* this abouten hym
C.15.166   To *haue* alle londes at thy likyng and the here lord make
C.15.179   *Haue* pacience parfitlyche then half thy pak of bokes.
C.15.185   Thenne *haue* pacience, as pilgrimes haen, in h[is] poke vitayles,
C.15.185   Thenne hadde pacience, as pilgrimes *haen*, in h[is] poke vitayles,
C.15.196   'Hastow vsed or haunted al thy lyf tyme?'
C.15.208   Y *haue* no gode giftes of thise grete lordes
C.15.224   For sethe he *hath* þe power þat peter hadde he hath þe pott with þe salue:
C.15.224   For sethe he hath þe power þat peter *hadde* he hath þe pott with þe salue:
C.15.224   For sethe he hath þe power þat peter hadde he *hath* þe pott with þe salue:
C.15.226   To *haue* þe grace of god and no gulte of þe pope.
C.15.245   'Hastow,' quod actyf, 'ay such mete with the?'
C.15.250   'Haue, Actyf,' quod pacience, 'and eet this when þe hungreth
C.15.286   To *haue* allouaunce of his lord; by [þe] lawe he [hit] claymeth.
C.15.287   Ioye þat neuere ioye *hadde* of rihtfull iuge he asketh
C.15.294   That al here lyf *haen* lyued in langour and defaute.
C.15.298   Angeles þat in helle now ben *hadden* som tyme ioye
C.15.301   Many man *hath* his ioye here for al here wel dedes
C.15.302   And lordes and ladyes ben cald for ledes þat they *haue*
C.16.3   Hewen þat *haen* here huyre byfore aren eueremore pore
C.16.6   Thenne may men wyte what he is worth and what he *hath* deserued
C.16.9   *Haue* two heuenes for ȝoure her[berw]ynge.
C.16.12   And moche murthe among ryche men is þat *han* meble ynow and hele.
C.16.19   For al myhtest þou *haue* ymad men of grete welthe
C.16.22   Riht so *haue* reuthe on [thy renkes] alle
C.16.52   For þe ryche *hath* moche to rykene and riht softe walketh;
C.16.58   Or in þe maystre or in þe man som mansion he *haueth*.
C.16.59   Ac in pouerte þer pacience is pruyde *hath* no myhte
C.16.61   Ne *haue* power in pouerte yf pacience h[it] folewe.
C.16.66   Yf wrathe wrastle with þe pore he *hath* þe worse ende
C.16.76   So for his glotonye and his grete synne he *hath* a greuous penaunce
C.16.82   And *hath* hondes and Armes of a longe lenthe
C.16.85   And thogh Auaryce wolde Angry [þe] pou[r]e he *hath* bote lytel myhte
C.16.86   For pouerte *hath* bote pokes to potten in his godes
C.16.87   There Auaryce *hath* almaries and yrebounden coffres.
C.16.90   Lecherye loueth no pore for he *hath* bote litel siluer
C.16.93   *Hadde* they noen haunt bote of pore [men; here houses stoed vntyled].
C.16.102   Moche hardyore may he aske þat here myhte *haue* his wille
C.16.158   Thenne *hadde* Actyf a ledare þat hihte lib[e]rum arbitrium;
C.16.160   'He þat *hath* lond and lordschipe,' quod he, 'at þe laste ende
C.16.162   Thenne *hadde* y wonder what he was, þat l[i]berum Arbitrium.
C.16.182   And so is man þat *hath* his mynde myd liberum Arbitrium.
C.16.277   Wolde neuere oþerwyse god but wikkede men hit *hadde*,
C.16.288   Ich *haue* yleued in londone monye longe ȝeres
C.16.310   *Hath* he no lykynge to lawhe ne to likene men to scorne.
C.16.316   'H[o] fynt hym his fode,' quod y, 'or what frendes *hath* he,
C.16.319   A frende he *hath* þat fyn[t] hym þat faylede hym neuere.
C.16.330   And when he *hath* visited thus fetured folk and oþer folke pore,
C.16.345   Ych *haue* ysey hym mysulue som tyme in russet,
C.16.350   Ich *haue* yseye charite also syngen and rede,
C.16.357   In [þat] sekte sethe to selde *hath* he be [knowen].
C.17.13   Paul primus heremita *hadde* yparrokede hymsulue
C.17.39   "Wyf! be ywar," quod he; "what *haue* we herynne?
C.17.56   Allas, lordes and ladyes, lewede consayle *haue* ȝe
C.17.63   And afturward awayte ho *hath* moest nede
C.17.64   And þer helpe yf thow *has[t]*; and þat halde y charite.
C.17.88   Lewed men *han* no byleue, [so] lettred men erren;
C.17.96   *Haen* no byleue to þe lyft ne to þe lodesterr[e].
C.17.151   'Hit may be so þat sarresynes *haen* such a manere charite,
C.17.154   For þer is no man þat mynde *hath* þat ne meketh [hym] and bysecheth
C.17.161   And when kynde *hath* his cours and no contrarie fyndeth
C.17.167   And pursuede to *haue* be pope, prince of holy chirche;
C.17.172   In ayþer of his eres priueliche he *hadde*
C.17.223   "Dos ecclesie this day *hath* ydronke venym
C.17.224   And [tho] þat *haen* petres power aren apo[y]sened alle."
C.17.240   *Hadde* al surie as hymsulue wolde and sarrasines in equitee.

C.17.241   Naught thorw manslaght and mannes strenghe Macometh *hadde* þe maistrie
C.17.253   *Haen* a lyppe of oure bileue, the lihtlokour me thynketh
C.17.293   Ac we cristene conneth þe [crede] and *haen* of oure tonge
C.17.313   And haen a suspectioun to be saef, bothe sarresynes & iewes;
C.18.20   Hit *hadde* schoriares to shuyuen hit vp, thre shides of o lenghe
C.18.66   Then tho that selde *haen* þe sonne and sitten in þe North half;
C.18.75   These *haen* þe [hete] of þe holi goest as þe crop of tre [the] sonne.
C.18.84   'Here beneth y may nyme, yf y nede *hadde*,
C.18.103   Assay what sauour hit *hadde* and saide þat tyme,
C.18.110   For euere as Elde *hadde* eny down, þe deuel was redy
C.18.136   To *haue* yfouthte with þe fende Ar fol tyme come.
C.18.151   'Thenne is saton ȝoure saueour,' quod iesus, '& *hath* ysaued ȝow ofte.
C.18.191   'Su[t]he they ben suyrelepus,' quod y, 'they *haen* sondry names?'
C.18.203   God [that] bigynnyng *hadde* neuere bote tho hym goed thouhte
C.18.239   'Hastow ysey this,' y seyde, 'alle thre and o god?'
C.18.255   For hymsulue saide y sholde [haue], y and myn issue bothe,
C.18.265   Thus *haue* y ben his heraud here and in helle
C.18.269   Thenne *hadde* y wonder of his wordes and of [his] wyde clothes
C.18.273   'What [a]waytest thow,' quod fayth, 'and what wost thow *haue*?'
C.18.276   'This is a present of moche pris; what prince shal hit *haue*?'
C.18.277   'Hit is a preciouse present,' quod he, 'Ac the pouke hit *hath* atached
C.19.7   'Nay,' he saide, 'y seke hym þat *hath* þe seel to kepe,
C.19.21   For, thogh y sey hit mysulue, y *haue* saued with this charme
C.19.23   'He seyth soth,' saide fayth; 'y *haue* yfounde hit trewe.
C.19.32   And *hath* ysaued þat bileued so and sory for here synnes;
C.19.36   And now cometh this sp[es] and speketh that *hath* aspyed þe lawe,
C.19.54   In a wi[d]e wildernesse where theues *hadde* ybounde
C.19.59   Fayth [*hadde* furst siht of hym] Ac he fleyh asyde
C.19.61   Hope cam huppynge aftur þat *hadde* so ybosted
C.19.62   How he with Moyses maundement *hadde* mony men yholpe
C.19.63   Ac when he *hadde* sihte of this s[egg]e asyde he gan hym drawe
C.19.65   Ac so sone so the samaritaen *hadde* sihte of this carefole
C.19.69   And bote he *hadde* recouerre the raþer þat ryse sholde he neuere
C.19.83   'Haue hem excused,' quod [t]he samaritaen; 'here helpe may nat availe.
C.19.90   Til he *haue* eten al þ[e] barn and his bloed dronken
C.19.141   The paume is puyrliche the hand and *hath* power by hymsulue
C.19.143   For þe paume *hath* power to pu[t]te out þe ioyntes
C.19.189   A[s] doth a kix [o]r a candle þat cauht *hath* fuyr and blaseth,
C.19.213   To þe fader of heuene forȝe[ue]nesse to *haue*.
C.19.215   Bote thow *haue* tasch to take hit with, tender [or] broches,
C.19.260   For that the holy goest *hath* to kepe tho harlotes distruyeth,
C.19.265   A fordoth the lihte þat oure lord loketh to *haue* worschipe of.
C.19.279   'Y pose y *hadde* syneged so and sholde nouthe deye
C.19.290   That eyþer man equitee, as holy writ witnesseth:
C.19.324   That they *haen* cause to contrarien bi kynde of here sekness[e];
C.19.326   *Haeth* mercy on suche men þat [so] euele may soffre.
C.20.20   'Liberum dei Arbitrium for loue *hath* vndertake
C.20.68   Ac shal no wyht wyte witturlich ho shal *haue* þe maistry
C.20.79   That *hadde* no boie hardynesse hym to touche in deynge.
C.20.81   Hihte longies as þe lettre telleth, and longe *hadde* lore his sihte;
C.20.92   Of þe dede þat y *haue* do y do me in ȝoure grace;
C.20.94   *Haue* [on me reuthe], riȝtfol iesu;' and riht with þat a wepte.
C.20.101   The gre ȝut *hath* he geten for al his grete wound[e];
C.20.105   And ȝe, lordeyne[s], *haen* lost for lyf shal haue [þe] maistrie;
C.20.105   And ȝe, lordeyne[s], haen lost for lyf shal *haue* [þe] maistrie;
C.20.108   Ne *haue* lordschipe in londe ne no londe tulye
C.20.128   'Y *haue* ferly of this fare, in faith,' seide Treuthe,
C.20.130   'Haue no merueyle,' quod Mercy; 'merthe hit bitokneth.
C.20.141   For patriarkes and prophetes *haen* preched herof ofte
C.20.149   Ne *haue* hem out of helle; holde thy tonge, mercy!
C.20.156   That Adam and Eue *haue* shullen bote.
C.20.172   Loue *hath* coueyted here longe; leue y non oþere
C.20.173   Bote loue *haue* ysente her som lettre what this liht bymeneth
C.20.187   And þat god *hath* forgyue and graunted to mankynde
C.20.189   And þat Crist hadde conuerted the kynde of rihtwisnesse
C.20.208   'And y shal pre[u]e,' quod pees, 'here payne moet *haue* ende
C.20.210   For *hadde* they wist of no wo, wele hadde thay nat knowen;
C.20.210   For hadde they wist of no wo, wele *hadde* thay nat knowen;
C.20.212   Ne what is hoet hunger þat *hadde* neuere defaute.
C.20.217   Ne *hadde* god ysoffred of som oþer then hymsulue
C.20.218   He *hadde* nat wist witterly where deth were sour or swete.
C.20.232   To wyte what he *hath* soffred in thre sundry places,
C.20.263   And to *haue* out [of helle] alle þat hym liketh.
C.20.279   Patriarkes and prophetes *haen* parled herof longe
C.20.287   Astarot, hoet out and *haue* out oure knaues,
C.20.309   And sethen we *haen* ben sesed seuene thousand wynter
C.20.321   And so *haddest* hem out and hiddere at þe laste.'
C.20.324   We *haen* no trewe title to hem for thy tresoun hit maketh.'
C.20.327   So *hath* god bigiled vs alle in goynge of a weye.'
C.20.328   'For god *hath* go,' quod gobelyne, 'in gome liknesse

C.20.330 Y *haue* ass[a]yled hym with synne and som tyme ich askede
C.20.332 Thus *hath* he trolled forth lyke a tydy man this two & thritty
 wynter.
C.20.335 Y wolde *haue* lenghed his lyf for y leued, yf he deyede,
C.20.349 We *haen* ylost oure lordschipe a londe and in helle:
C.20.385 The same sore shal he *haue* þat eny so smyteth:
C.20.386 So lyf shal lyf le[t]e ther lyf *hath* lyf an[y]en[t]ed
C.20.401 The bitternesse þat thow *hast* browe, now brouk hit thysulue;
C.20.414 And *haue* out of helle alle mennes soules.
C.21.1 Thus y wakede and wrot what y *hadde* ydremed
C.21.55 That longe *hadden* leye bifore as luciferes cherles
C.21.107 Til he *hadde* all hem þat he fore bledde.
C.21.140 Hereof *hadde* Cayphas enuye and oþer iewes
C.21.188 Thus *hath* Peres power, be his pardoun payed,
C.21.261 And for to tulye treuthe a teme shal he *haue*.'
C.21.273 With two aythes þat they *hadde*, an oelde and a newe:
C.21.282 He þat eet of that seed *hadde* such a kynde:
C.21.372 Ther ne was cristene creature that kynde wit *hadde*
C.21.384 That *haen* labored lelly al this lenten tyme.
C.21.389 Or as ofte as they *hadden* nede, tho þat hadden payed
C.21.389 Or as ofte as they hadden nede, tho þat *hadden* payed
C.21.447 Hit semeth bi so hymsulue *hadde* his wille
C.21.469 Ther y may hastilokest hit *haue*, for y am heed of lawe;
C.21.479 [*Haue* þou mayst] thyn askyng as thy lawe asketh:
C.21.480 The vicory *hadde* fer hoem and [fayre] toek his leue
C.22.10 And nede *hath* no lawe ne neuere shal falle in dette
C.22.13 Ne wyht no[n] wol be his borwe ne wed *hath* [non] to legge;
C.22.45 And þe fisch *hath* fyn to flete with to reste:
C.22.46 Ther nede *hath* ynome me þat y moet nede abyde
C.22.51 Whenne nede *hadde* vndernome [me] thus anoen y ful aslepe
C.22.69 Auntecrist *hadde* thus sone hondredes at his baner
C.22.86 *Hadde* ypriked and preyede polles of peple;
C.22.94 And ar heroudes of Armes *hadden* descreued lordes,
C.22.170 And bisouhte hym of socour and of h[is] salue *hadde*
C.22.188 *Haddest* thow be hende,' quod y, 'thow wost haue asked leue.'
C.22.188 Haddest thow be hende,' quod y, 'thow wost *haue* asked leue.'
C.22.193 And of þe wo þat y was ynne my wyf *hadde* reuthe
C.22.198 So Elde and hee hit *hadde* forbete
C.22.202 Lo! Elde þe hore *hath* me byseye;
C.22.227 And *hadden* almost vnite and holynesse adowne.
C.22.233 That they cam for Couetyse, to *haue* cure of soules.
C.22.246 Holdeth ȝow in vnite and *haueth* noen enuye
C.22.248 [And] y wol be ȝoure borwh: ȝe shal *haue* breed and clothes
C.22.258 *Haen* officerys vnder hem and vch of hem a certeyne.
C.22.265 Here ordre and here reule wol to *haue* a certeyne nombre
C.22.270 [Heuene *haeth* euene nombre and helle is withoute nombre].
C.22.307 For here mys[fetes] that thei wrouht *hadde*
C.22.318 'We *haen* no nede,' quod Consience; 'y woet no bettere leche
C.22.320 Saue [Peres the Plouhman] þat *haeth* power ouer alle
C.22.325 To a lord for a lettre leue to *haue*
C.22.327 Baldly to þe bishope and his breef *hadde*
C.22.335 Ypocrysye *haeth* her[t]e hem; ful hard is yf thei keuere.'
C.22.369 Til Contricioun *hadde* clene forȝete to crye and to wepe
C.22.378 The frere with his fisyk this folk *hath* enchaunted
C.22.383 And þat freres *hadde* a fyndynge þat for nede flateren
C.22.385 And s[e]nde me hap and hele til y *haue* [Peres Plouhman]'.

hauer *n* *haver n.(2)* A 1
A. 7.266 A fewe cruddis & crem, & [a]n [*hauer*] cake,

hauylons *n* *haviloun n.* B 1
B.10.134 And þo þat vseþ þise *hauylons* [for] to blende mennes wittes,

hawes *n* *haue n.(2)* A 1 hawen; B 1; C 2
A.11.10 Among hogges þat hauen *hawen* at wille.
B.10.10 Among hogges þat han *hawes* at wille.
C.11.8 Among hoggus þat han *hawes* at wille.
C.11.79 Amonges hem þat haen *hawes* at wille,

haweþorn *n* *hauethorn n.* B 1; C 1 hauthorn
B.16.173 As hoor as an *haweþorn* and Abraham he highte.
C.18.182 As hoer as a *hauthorn*, and abraham he hihte.

he *pron* *he pron.(1)* &> heo A 763 he (247) him (39) hym (167) his (282)
hise(28); B 2138 he (891) hym (508) his (605) hise (134); C 2111 a
(112) he (762) him (1) hym (487) his (745) hise (3) is (1)

a C 112 &> a,heo
C.Pr.72, C.Pr.173, C.2.100, C.2.108, C.2.239, C.3.50, C.3.89, C.3.326, C.3.327,
C.3.426, C.3.486, C.3.499, C.4.52, C.4.58, C.4.66, C.5.96, C.5.140, C.5.180, C.5.191,
C.6.66, C.6.70, C.6.316, C.6.326, C.6.328, C.6.349, C.6.399, C.6.408, C.6.418, C.6.422,
C.7.6, C.7.77, C.7.113, C.7.118, C.7.164, C.7.169, C.7.192, C.7.204, C.8.19, C.8.173,
C.8.174, C.8.201, C.8.337, C.8.340, C.9.119, C.9.122, C.9.123, C.9.156, C.9.252, C.10.5,
C.10.18, C.10.37, C.10.306, C.11.66, C.11.112, C.11.184, C.12.41, C.12.55, C.12.82,
C.12.83, C.13.17, C.13.94, C.13.247, C.14.132, C.14.142, C.14.166, C.14.211, C.15.20,
C.15.87, C.15.93, C.15.93, C.15.97, C.15.102, C.15.176, C.15.191, C.16.98, C.16.146,

C.16.159, C.16.294, C.16.322, C.16.358, C.16.360, C.16.361, C.16.362, C.16.364,
C.16.366, C.17.5, C.17.170, C.17.246, C.17.263, C.18.108, C.18.109, C.18.141,
C.18.250, C.18.260, C.18.268, C.18.270, C.18.270, C.19.12, C.19.66, C.19.67, C.19.108,
C.19.243, C.19.265, C.19.306, C.19.335, C.20.28, C.20.30, C.20.94, C.20.251, C.20.299,
C.21.202, C.22.312

he A 247
A.Pr.65, A.Pr.71, A.1.14, A.1.17, A.1.31, A.1.47, A.1.55, A.1.60, A.1.62, A.1.63,
A.1.65, A.1.67, A.1.88, A.1.108, A.1.111, A.1.112, A.1.116, A.1.143, A.1.144, A.1.147,
A.2.5, A.2.79, A.2.104, A.2.107, A.2.112, A.2.141, A.2.168, A.2.179, A.2.188, A.2.193,
A.2.194, A.3.32, A.3.35, A.3.46, A.3.46, A.3.82, A.3.100, A.3.106, A.3.149, A.3.151,
A.3.176, A.3.190, A.3.229, A.3.251, A.4.8, A.4.9, A.4.21, A.4.36, A.4.40, A.4.42,
A.4.46, A.4.48, A.4.49, A.4.61, A.4.73, A.4.84, A.4.87, A.4.93, A.4.93, A.4.95,
A.4.110, A.4.136, A.4.140, A.4.157, A.5.24, A.5.24, A.5.25, A.5.28, A.5.30, A.5.32,
A.5.34, A.5.37, A.5.41, A.5.56, A.5.59, A.5.60, A.5.60, A.5.61, A.5.65, A.5.66, A.5.67,
A.5.67, A.5.68, A.5.83, A.5.109, A.5.149, A.5.150, A.5.153, A.5.189, A.5.193, A.5.193,
A.5.194, A.5.197, A.5.198, A.5.201, A.5.202, A.5.203, A.5.204, A.5.208, A.5.234,
A.5.246, A.5.248, A.5.250, A.6.5, A.6.7, A.6.12, A.6.13, A.6.14, A.6.33, A.6.35, A.6.38,
A.6.39, A.6.39, A.6.40, A.6.68, A.6.80, A.6.81, A.6.83, A.6.91, A.6.96, A.6.111, A.7.54,
A.7.79, A.7.84, A.7.86, A.7.130, A.7.138, A.7.140, A.7.141, A.7.162, A.7.163, A.7.163,
A.7.203, A.7.203, A.7.221, A.7.223, A.7.224, A.7.225, A.7.227, A.7.228, A.7.229,
A.7.230, A.7.235, A.7.250, A.7.296, A.7.296, A.7.297, A.7.301, A.7.304, A.8.44, A.8.49,
A.8.54, A.8.69, A.8.69, A.8.70, A.8.81, A.8.81, A.8.111, A.8.113, A.8.122, A.8.151,
A.8.156, A.8.184, A.9.5, A.9.14, A.9.20, A.9.21, A.9.28, A.9.28, A.9.29, A.9.30, A.9.40,
A.9.42, A.9.64, A.9.65, A.9.69, A.9.76, A.9.77, A.9.78, A.9.78, A.9.79, A.9.81, A.9.101,
A.9.110, A.10.6, A.10.9, A.10.17, A.10.27, A.10.33, A.10.35, A.10.40, A.10.52, A.10.53,
A.10.54, A.10.73, A.10.75, A.10.83, A.10.116, A.10.130, A.10.157, A.11.24, A.11.29,
A.11.49, A.11.61, A.11.67, A.11.85, A.11.88, A.11.89, A.11.90, A.11.91, A.11.94,
A.11.94, A.11.98, A.11.106, A.11.150, A.11.195, A.11.199, A.11.205, A.11.214,
A.11.238, A.11.253, A.11.268, A.11.270, A.11.281, A.11.282, A.11.295, A.12.3,
A.12.14, A.12.20, A.12.23, A.12.28, A.12.31, A.12.32, A.12.33, A.12.33, A.12.46,
A.12.54, A.12.79, A.12.80, A.12.86, A.12.92, A.12.107, A.12.109,
A.12.109

he B 891
B.Pr.68, B.Pr.74, B.Pr.102, B.Pr.114, B.Pr.124, B.Pr.153, B.Pr.155, B.Pr.160,
B.Pr.171, B.Pr.189, B.Pr.189, B.1.14, B.1.17, B.1.31, B.1.49, B.1.57, B.1.62, B.1.64,
B.1.65, B.1.67, B.1.69, B.1.90, B.1.110, B.1.113, B.1.113, B.1.127, B.1.150, B.1.162,
B.1.169, B.1.170, B.1.173, B.2.5, B.2.26, B.2.35, B.2.78, B.2.93, B.2.101, B.2.115,
B.2.140, B.2.143, B.2.148, B.2.180, B.2.207, B.2.220, B.2.229, B.2.234, B.2.235, B.3.33,
B.3.36, B.3.47, B.3.47, B.3.93, B.3.111, B.3.117, B.3.160, B.3.162, B.3.189, B.3.203,
B.3.240, B.3.250, B.3.273, B.3.275, B.3.307, B.4.8, B.4.9, B.4.23, B.4.49, B.4.53,
B.4.55, B.4.59, B.4.61, B.4.63, B.4.86, B.4.88, B.4.97, B.4.100, B.4.106, B.4.106,
B.4.108, B.4.127, B.4.164, B.4.169, B.4.194, B.5.13, B.5.24, B.5.24, B.5.28, B.5.30,
B.5.32, B.5.34, B.5.41, B.5.45, B.5.48, B.5.50, B.5.51, B.5.54, B.5.57, B.5.73, B.5.76,
B.5.77, B.5.77, B.5.78, B.5.82, B.5.83, B.5.84, B.5.84, B.5.85, B.5.86, B.5.89, B.5.103,
B.5.132, B.5.137, B.5.167, B.5.186, B.5.190, B.5.231, B.5.238, B.5.242, B.5.256,
B.5.258, B.5.292, B.5.294, B.5.295, B.5.299, B.5.300, B.5.303, B.5.341, B.5.345,
B.5.345, B.5.346, B.5.349, B.5.350, B.5.359, B.5.360, B.5.361, B.5.362, B.5.380,
B.5.390, B.5.441, B.5.462, B.5.472, B.5.474, B.5.476, B.5.517, B.5.519, B.5.524,
B.5.525, B.5.526, B.5.545, B.5.551, B.5.552, B.5.552, B.5.553, B.5.581, B.5.596,
B.5.604, B.5.610, B.5.626, B.6.46, B.6.47, B.6.59, B.6.87, B.6.92, B.6.94, B.6.136,
B.6.153, B.6.154, B.6.173, B.6.176, B.6.177, B.6.178, B.6.178, B.6.181, B.6.217,
B.6.217, B.6.237, B.6.239, B.6.240, B.6.241, B.6.243, B.6.244, B.6.245, B.6.246,
B.6.252, B.6.266, B.6.312, B.6.312, B.6.313, B.6.314, B.6.316, B.6.320, B.6.323, B.7.47,
B.7.52, B.7.67, B.7.67, B.7.68, B.7.70, B.7.70, B.7.70, B.7.74, B.7.80, B.7.81, B.7.86,
B.7.86, B.7.99, B.7.99, B.7.129, B.7.131, B.7.140, B.7.178, B.7.206, B.8.5, B.8.18,
B.8.24, B.8.25, B.8.32, B.8.32, B.8.33, B.8.34, B.8.44, B.8.46, B.8.52, B.8.56, B.8.59,
B.8.73, B.8.74, B.8.78, B.8.85, B.8.86, B.8.87, B.8.87, B.8.88, B.8.90, B.8.111, B.8.120,
B.8.130, B.9.6, B.9.9, B.9.15, B.9.15, B.9.18, B.9.26, B.9.32, B.9.34, B.9.36, B.9.40,
B.9.40, B.9.42, B.9.44, B.9.52, B.9.58, B.9.59, B.9.63, B.9.67, B.9.80, B.9.81, B.9.85,
B.9.93, B.9.95, B.9.97, B.9.99, B.9.154, B.9.194, B.10.32, B.10.37, B.10.63, B.10.80,
B.10.86, B.10.87, B.10.94, B.10.120, B.10.132, B.10.135, B.10.136, B.10.137, B.10.138,
B.10.141, B.10.141, B.10.145, B.10.154, B.10.199, B.10.201, B.10.232, B.10.314,
B.10.316, B.10.351, B.10.355, B.10.388, B.10.406, B.10.406, B.10.422,
B.10.423, B.10.438, B.10.441, B.10.446, B.10.447, B.10.450, B.10.450, B.10.454,
B.11.25, B.11.28, B.11.36, B.11.37, B.11.38, B.11.67, B.11.87, B.11.107, B.11.120,
B.11.124, B.11.129, B.11.147, B.11.148, B.11.177, B.11.180, B.11.197, B.11.214,
B.11.223, B.11.234, B.11.235, B.11.237, B.11.238, B.11.267, B.11.268,
B.11.269, B.11.292, B.11.294, B.11.301, B.11.380, B.11.381, B.11.382, B.11.398,
B.11.399, B.11.402, B.11.413, B.11.417, B.11.418, B.11.419, B.11.422, B.11.430,
B.11.432, B.11.434, B.11.437, B.11.439, B.11.441, B.12.1, B.12.20, B.12.21, B.12.29,
B.12.32, B.12.56, B.12.100, B.12.115, B.12.116, B.12.143, B.12.165, B.12.171,
B.12.172, B.12.174, B.12.181, B.12.181, B.12.193, B.12.196, B.12.203, B.12.206,
B.12.212, B.12.213, B.12.227, B.12.235, B.12.244, B.12.247, B.12.253, B.12.254,
B.12.269, B.12.270, B.12.272, B.12.282, B.12.284, B.12.289, B.12.297, B.13.10,
B.13.15, B.13.16, B.13.17, B.13.20, B.13.20, B.13.25, B.13.41, B.13.49, B.13.50,
B.13.51, B.13.53, B.13.62, B.13.79, B.13.80, B.13.85, B.13.87, B.13.88, B.13.89,
B.13.90, B.13.90, B.13.94, B.13.95, B.13.102, B.13.118, B.13.120, B.13.123, B.13.132,
B.13.137, B.13.146, B.13.147, B.13.147, B.13.149, B.13.195, B.13.199, B.13.222,
B.13.223, B.13.223, B.13.248, B.13.254, B.13.254, B.13.272, B.13.273, B.13.278,
B.13.279, B.13.279, B.13.280, B.13.290, B.13.295, B.13.299, B.13.304,
B.13.305, B.13.306, B.13.308, B.13.311, B.13.318, B.13.323, B.13.325, B.13.326,
B.13.344, B.13.344, B.13.345, B.13.357, B.13.377, B.13.380, B.13.406, B.13.415,
B.13.417, B.13.419, B.13.440, B.13.453, B.13.459, B.14.35, B.14.87, B.14.87, B.14.106,

B.14.107, B.14.107, B.14.110, B.14.111, B.14.121, B.14.127, B.14.131, B.14.135, B.14.135, B.14.136, B.14.138, B.14.138, B.14.143, B.14.149, B.14.150, B.14.214, B.14.217, B.14.225, B.14.227, B.14.228, B.14.230, B.14.232, B.14.234, B.14.235, B.14.236, B.14.237, B.14.245, B.14.250, B.14.257, B.14.257, B.14.258, B.14.258, B.14.262, B.14.275, B.14.295, B.14.296, B.14.307, B.14.307, B.14.312, B.14.314, B.14.315, B.14.315, B.14.315, B.14.326, B.14.328, B.14.330, B.14.334, B.15.15, B.15.16, B.15.23, B.15.44, B.15.50, B.15.52, B.15.59, B.15.126, B.15.127, B.15.142, B.15.143, B.15.149, B.15.159, B.15.160, B.15.165, B.15.169, B.15.171, B.15.171, B.15.173, B.15.174, B.15.175, B.15.176, B.15.177, B.15.180, B.15.181, B.15.182, B.15.184, B.15.184, B.15.186, B.15.186, B.15.193, B.15.193, B.15.196, B.15.198, B.15.204, B.15.213, B.15.217, B.15.222, B.15.228, B.15.230, B.15.232, B.15.233, B.15.235, B.15.236, B.15.237, B.15.239, B.15.252, B.15.255, B.15.256, B.15.257, B.15.266, B.15.281, B.15.284, B.15.289, B.15.290, B.15.349, B.15.399, B.15.400, B.15.402, B.15.403, B.15.406, B.15.446, B.15.463, B.15.465, B.15.465, B.15.483, B.15.509, B.15.512, B.15.524, B.15.527, B.15.570, B.15.575, B.15.590, B.15.592, B.15.593, B.15.596, B.15.598, B.15.601, B.15.603, B.16.4, B.16.13, B.16.25, B.16.32, B.16.41, B.16.64, B.16.67, B.16.73, B.16.77, B.16.86, B.16.87, B.16.100, B.16.101, B.16.105, B.16.107, B.16.112, B.16.112, B.16.113, B.16.115, B.16.118, B.16.120, B.16.140, B.16.141, B.16.142, B.16.143, B.16.151, B.16.160, B.16.173, B.16.174, B.16.175, B.16.175, B.16.201, B.16.217, B.16.231, B.16.232, B.16.233, B.16.233, B.16.241, B.16.243, B.16.249, B.16.252, B.16.254, B.16.254, B.16.257, B.16.259, B.16.261, B.16.265, B.16.274, B.16.275, B.16.275, B.16.275, B.17.1, B.17.5, B.17.11, B.17.17, B.17.22, B.17.28, B.17.32, B.17.39, B.17.40, B.17.54, B.17.55, B.17.57, B.17.58, B.17.60, B.17.63, B.17.64, B.17.64, B.17.67, B.17.68, B.17.69, B.17.70, B.17.70, B.17.71, B.17.72, B.17.77, B.17.78, B.17.79, B.17.80, B.17.81, B.17.84, B.17.88, B.17.93, B.17.97, B.17.99, B.17.99, B.17.100, B.17.102, B.17.102, B.17.108, B.17.108, B.17.109, B.17.111, B.17.113, B.17.131, B.17.134, B.17.147, B.17.156, B.17.158, B.17.181, B.17.188, B.17.198, B.17.199, B.17.201, B.17.203, B.17.204, B.17.205, B.17.229, B.17.259, B.17.284, B.17.289, B.17.298, B.17.316, B.17.326, B.17.326, B.17.330, B.17.351, B.17.355, B.17.355, B.18.12, B.18.19, B.18.21, B.18.29, B.18.31, B.18.43, B.18.46, B.18.68, B.18.69, B.18.70, B.18.70, B.18.76, B.18.80, B.18.81, B.18.89, B.18.91, B.18.98, B.18.155, B.18.156, B.18.156, B.18.220, B.18.223, B.18.224, B.18.238, B.18.242, B.18.242, B.18.244, B.18.247, B.18.269, B.18.276, B.18.277, B.18.277, B.18.283, B.18.296, B.18.298, B.18.298, B.18.299, B.18.303, B.18.326, B.18.380, B.18.383, B.18.383, B.19.13, B.19.29, B.19.32, B.19.44, B.19.48, B.19.50, B.19.52, B.19.53, B.19.54, B.19.57, B.19.58, B.19.58, B.19.60, B.19.62, B.19.63, B.19.67, B.19.69, B.19.71, B.19.97, B.19.102, B.19.102, B.19.103, B.19.104, B.19.105, B.19.107, B.19.107, B.19.117, B.19.119, B.19.121, B.19.122, B.19.123, B.19.123, B.19.124, B.19.125, B.19.128, B.19.129, B.19.131, B.19.132, B.19.133, B.19.182, B.19.183, B.19.192, B.19.195, B.19.202, B.19.229, B.19.234, B.19.236, B.19.238, B.19.246, B.19.248, B.19.250, B.19.261, B.19.277, B.19.278, B.19.282, B.19.293, B.19.298, B.19.304, B.19.304, B.19.305, B.19.306, B.19.308, B.19.309, B.19.323, B.19.324, B.19.327, B.19.336, B.19.350, B.19.374, B.19.413, B.19.429, B.19.436, B.19.440, B.19.448, B.19.464, B.19.464, B.20.11, B.20.12, B.20.14, B.20.15, B.20.16, B.20.19, B.20.19, B.20.22, B.20.26, B.20.29, B.20.29, B.20.32, B.20.35, B.20.40, B.20.42, B.20.43, B.20.49, B.20.56, B.20.56, B.20.57, B.20.58, B.20.76, B.20.95, B.20.96, B.20.102, B.20.103, B.20.106, B.20.111, B.20.117, B.20.119, B.20.121, B.20.125, B.20.134, B.20.136, B.20.137, B.20.138, B.20.147, B.20.149, B.20.153, B.20.167, B.20.168, B.20.175, B.20.176, B.20.180, B.20.185, B.20.189, B.20.191, B.20.217, B.20.232, B.20.238, B.20.239, B.20.277, B.20.288, B.20.288, B.20.295, B.20.312, B.20.312, B.20.314, B.20.328, B.20.334, B.20.347, B.20.350, B.20.361, B.20.368, B.20.368, B.20.370, B.20.371, B.20.377, B.20.386

he C 762 &> heo

C.Pr.66, C.Pr.113, C.Pr.114, C.Pr.115, C.Pr.123, C.Pr.130, C.Pr.141, C.Pr.175, C.Pr.188, C.1.14, C.1.15, C.1.17, C.1.27, C.1.30, C.1.53, C.1.58, C.1.61, C.1.63, C.1.65, C.1.66, C.1.86, C.1.104, C.1.108, C.1.109, C.1.112, C.1.120, C.1.121, C.1.121, C.1.158, C.1.165, C.1.166, C.1.169, C.2.5, C.2.26, C.2.31, C.2.37, C.2.85, C.2.91, C.2.93, C.2.108, C.2.119, C.2.147, C.2.156, C.2.159, C.2.164, C.2.193, C.2.219, C.2.230, C.2.244, C.2.245, C.3.36, C.3.39, C.3.50, C.3.77, C.3.110, C.3.111, C.3.121, C.3.148, C.3.154, C.3.198, C.3.200, C.3.240, C.3.250, C.3.260, C.3.282, C.3.295, C.3.297, C.3.325, C.3.328, C.3.350, C.3.350, C.3.355, C.3.356, C.3.391, C.3.392, C.3.436, C.3.460, C.3.496, C.3.500, C.4.8, C.4.9, C.4.41, C.4.47, C.4.48, C.4.49, C.4.53, C.4.55, C.4.55, C.4.56, C.4.62, C.4.64, C.4.70, C.4.82, C.4.84, C.4.93, C.4.96, C.4.101, C.4.101, C.4.103, C.4.124, C.4.159, C.5.12, C.5.66, C.5.91, C.5.94, C.5.96, C.5.126, C.5.128, C.5.130, C.5.132, C.5.134, C.5.136, C.5.143, C.5.160, C.5.162, C.5.188, C.5.189, C.6.56, C.6.66, C.6.70, C.6.71, C.6.97, C.6.168, C.6.172, C.6.198, C.6.205, C.6.235, C.6.240, C.6.300, C.6.300, C.6.303, C.6.330, C.6.347, C.6.352, C.6.354, C.6.355, C.6.358, C.6.403, C.6.403, C.6.404, C.6.407, C.6.417, C.6.419, C.6.420, C.6.423, C.7.55, C.7.79, C.7.100, C.7.162, C.7.170, C.7.171, C.7.191, C.7.195, C.7.196, C.7.197, C.7.262, C.7.277, C.7.294, C.7.294, C.7.299, C.8.43, C.8.44, C.8.58, C.8.96, C.8.101, C.8.103, C.8.121, C.8.143, C.8.166, C.8.175, C.8.175, C.8.188, C.8.189, C.8.195, C.8.227, C.8.227, C.8.244, C.8.251, C.8.253, C.8.255, C.8.256, C.8.257, C.8.279, C.8.280, C.8.334, C.8.334, C.8.335, C.8.336, C.8.343, C.9.8, C.9.46, C.9.63, C.9.63, C.9.64, C.9.66, C.9.67, C.9.68, C.9.100, C.9.147, C.9.148, C.9.155, C.9.213, C.9.216, C.9.237, C.9.239, C.9.248, C.9.250, C.9.253, C.9.292, C.9.352, C.10.25, C.10.28, C.10.29, C.10.35, C.10.36, C.10.38, C.10.39, C.10.39, C.10.42, C.10.42, C.10.43, C.10.53, C.10.58, C.10.71, C.10.72, C.10.76, C.10.82, C.10.83, C.10.84, C.10.85, C.10.107, C.10.116, C.10.133, C.10.136, C.10.144, C.10.195, C.10.195, C.10.196, C.10.249, C.10.252, C.10.267, C.10.307, C.11.19, C.11.29, C.11.32, C.11.45, C.11.60, C.11.67, C.11.69, C.11.83, C.11.93, C.11.150, C.11.150, C.11.151, C.11.152, C.11.187, C.11.195, C.11.197, C.11.202, C.11.214, C.11.237, C.11.254, C.11.255, C.11.275, C.11.279, C.11.284, C.11.303, C.11.304, C.12.6, C.12.16, C.12.25, C.12.26, C.12.59, C.12.59, C.12.64, C.12.98, C.12.123, C.12.124, C.12.126, C.12.127, C.12.128, C.12.152, C.12.154, C.12.159, C.12.162, C.12.170, C.12.214, C.12.237, C.12.237, C.12.244, C.13.1, C.13.8, C.13.12, C.13.15, C.13.16, C.13.57, C.13.62, C.13.85, C.13.87, C.13.89, C.13.97, C.13.106, C.13.108, C.13.193, C.13.195, C.13.197, C.13.198, C.13.199, C.13.210, C.13.218, C.13.221, C.13.225, C.13.226, C.13.227, C.13.236, C.13.237, C.13.239, C.13.240, C.13.240, C.13.243, C.13.245, C.14.1, C.14.18, C.14.61, C.14.109, C.14.111, C.14.112, C.14.114, C.14.121, C.14.121, C.14.134, C.14.135, C.14.145, C.14.151, C.14.152, C.14.161, C.14.182, C.14.191, C.14.194, C.14.204, C.14.206, C.14.217, C.15.12, C.15.18, C.15.19, C.15.23, C.15.23, C.15.33, C.15.46, C.15.55, C.15.56, C.15.57, C.15.69, C.15.86, C.15.94, C.15.95, C.15.96, C.15.97, C.15.101, C.15.109, C.15.111, C.15.126, C.15.126, C.15.146, C.15.147, C.15.147, C.15.148, C.15.149, C.15.153, C.15.192, C.15.192, C.15.220, C.15.224, C.15.224, C.15.281, C.15.282, C.15.282, C.15.286, C.15.287, C.15.297, C.15.300, C.15.300, C.16.4, C.16.4, C.16.6, C.16.6, C.16.53, C.16.55, C.16.58, C.16.66, C.16.68, C.16.69, C.16.71, C.16.73, C.16.75, C.16.76, C.16.77, C.16.78, C.16.85, C.16.90, C.16.97, C.16.97, C.16.98, C.16.102, C.16.115, C.16.122, C.16.130, C.16.131, C.16.143, C.16.148, C.16.149, C.16.149, C.16.149, C.16.160, C.16.160, C.16.162, C.16.164, C.16.167, C.16.174, C.16.179, C.16.206, C.16.212, C.16.214, C.16.220, C.16.221, C.16.221, C.16.293, C.16.302, C.16.303, C.16.305, C.16.306, C.16.310, C.16.311, C.16.313, C.16.314, C.16.315, C.16.316, C.16.318, C.16.319, C.16.327, C.16.330, C.16.331, C.16.331, C.16.336, C.16.336, C.16.340, C.16.342, C.16.343, C.16.343, C.16.347, C.16.353, C.16.355, C.16.357, C.16.369, C.16.372, C.16.373, C.17.2, C.17.4, C.17.16, C.17.17, C.17.38, C.17.38, C.17.39, C.17.67, C.17.91, C.17.125, C.17.141, C.17.168, C.17.169, C.17.169, C.17.171, C.17.172, C.17.173, C.17.174, C.17.242, C.17.277, C.17.301, C.17.301, C.17.302, C.17.304, C.17.311, C.18.8, C.18.9, C.18.19, C.18.25, C.18.36, C.18.45, C.18.58, C.18.83, C.18.105, C.18.133, C.18.145, C.18.148, C.18.149, C.18.168, C.18.180, C.18.182, C.18.187, C.18.190, C.18.192, C.18.195, C.18.212, C.18.212, C.18.214, C.18.238, C.18.240, C.18.244, C.18.245, C.18.247, C.18.248, C.18.257, C.18.267, C.18.275, C.18.277, C.18.281, C.18.290, C.18.291, C.18.291, C.18.291, C.19.1, C.19.4, C.19.7, C.19.18, C.19.23, C.19.29, C.19.33, C.19.52, C.19.53, C.19.56, C.19.57, C.19.59, C.19.62, C.19.63, C.19.63, C.19.68, C.19.69, C.19.69, C.19.70, C.19.71, C.19.75, C.19.78, C.19.86, C.19.89, C.19.89, C.19.90, C.19.92, C.19.121, C.19.128, C.19.134, C.19.140, C.19.147, C.19.154, C.19.164, C.19.165, C.19.167, C.19.169, C.19.170, C.19.171, C.19.195, C.19.225, C.19.236, C.19.238, C.19.241, C.19.242, C.19.244, C.19.270, C.19.296, C.19.306, C.19.310, C.19.316, C.19.316, C.19.331, C.19.335, C.20.10, C.20.17, C.20.19, C.20.42, C.20.46, C.20.54, C.20.54, C.20.70, C.20.71, C.20.72, C.20.72, C.20.78, C.20.82, C.20.83, C.20.90, C.20.91, C.20.101, C.20.158, C.20.159, C.20.159, C.20.218, C.20.229, C.20.232, C.20.233, C.20.247, C.20.251, C.20.253, C.20.256, C.20.264, C.20.277, C.20.298, C.20.299, C.20.307, C.20.307, C.20.311, C.20.331, C.20.331, C.20.332, C.20.335, C.20.352, C.20.385, C.20.420, C.20.422, C.20.425, C.20.425, C.21.13, C.21.29, C.21.32, C.21.44, C.21.48, C.21.50, C.21.52, C.21.53, C.21.54, C.21.57, C.21.58, C.21.58, C.21.60, C.21.62, C.21.63, C.21.67, C.21.69, C.21.71, C.21.97, C.21.102, C.21.102, C.21.103, C.21.104, C.21.105, C.21.107, C.21.107, C.21.117, C.21.119, C.21.121, C.21.122, C.21.123, C.21.123, C.21.124, C.21.125, C.21.128, C.21.129, C.21.131, C.21.132, C.21.133, C.21.160, C.21.182, C.21.183, C.21.192, C.21.195, C.21.229, C.21.234, C.21.236, C.21.238, C.21.246, C.21.248, C.21.250, C.21.261, C.21.277, C.21.278, C.21.282, C.21.293, C.21.298, C.21.304, C.21.304, C.21.305, C.21.306, C.21.308, C.21.309, C.21.323, C.21.324, C.21.327, C.21.336, C.21.350, C.21.374, C.21.413, C.21.429, C.21.436, C.21.440, C.21.448, C.21.464, C.21.464, C.22.11, C.22.12, C.22.14, C.22.15, C.22.16, C.22.19, C.22.19, C.22.22, C.22.26, C.22.29, C.22.29, C.22.32, C.22.35, C.22.40, C.22.42, C.22.43, C.22.49, C.22.56, C.22.56, C.22.57, C.22.58, C.22.76, C.22.95, C.22.96, C.22.102, C.22.103, C.22.106, C.22.111, C.22.117, C.22.119, C.22.121, C.22.125, C.22.134, C.22.136, C.22.137, C.22.138, C.22.147, C.22.149, C.22.153, C.22.167, C.22.168, C.22.175, C.22.176, C.22.180, C.22.185, C.22.189, C.22.191, C.22.217, C.22.232, C.22.238, C.22.239, C.22.277, C.22.288, C.22.288, C.22.295, C.22.312, C.22.314, C.22.328, C.22.334, C.22.347, C.22.350, C.22.361, C.22.368, C.22.368, C.22.370, C.22.371, C.22.377, C.22.386

him A 206 him (39) hym (167)

A.Pr.69, A.1.16, A.1.29, A.1.30, A.1.36, A.1.45, A.1.56, A.1.66, A.1.100, A.1.134, A.1.143, A.1.145, A.1.148, A.2.79, A.2.163, A.2.167, A.2.171, A.2.173, A.2.174, A.2.174, A.2.175, A.2.176, A.2.181, A.2.182, A.2.182, A.2.182, A.2.183, A.2.187, A.2.189, A.2.190, A.2.191, A.2.192, A.2.193, A.3.31, A.3.44, A.3.44, A.3.84, A.3.100, A.3.118, A.3.128, A.3.129, A.3.130, A.3.162, A.3.177, A.3.185, A.3.186, A.3.187, A.3.193, A.3.197, A.3.199, A.3.240, A.3.251, A.3.253, A.3.257, A.3.263, A.3.269, A.4.8, A.4.15, A.4.19, A.4.20, A.4.23, A.4.23, A.4.32, A.4.39, A.4.40, A.4.47, A.4.48, A.4.50, A.4.60, A.4.72, A.4.75, A.4.76, A.4.86, A.4.87, A.4.88, A.4.95, A.4.114, A.4.148, A.5.47, A.5.55, A.5.67, A.5.73, A.5.74, A.5.74, A.5.75, A.5.76, A.5.76, A.5.79, A.5.81, A.5.82, A.5.83, A.5.84, A.5.88, A.5.103, A.5.107, A.5.108, A.5.147, A.5.148, A.5.149, A.5.179, A.5.182, A.5.200, A.5.200, A.5.205, A.5.215, A.5.218, A.5.220, A.5.249, A.6.13, A.6.24, A.6.26, A.6.28, A.6.28, A.6.36, A.6.37, A.6.43, A.6.50, A.6.80, A.6.84, A.6.88, A.6.96, A.6.119, A.7.61, A.7.85, A.7.98, A.7.123, A.7.141, A.7.142, A.7.146, A.7.147, A.7.150, A.7.155, A.7.157, A.7.160, A.7.164, A.7.168, A.7.187, A.7.225, A.7.226, A.7.229, A.7.230, A.7.250, A.7.256, A.7.281, A.7.282, A.7.285, A.7.303, A.8.3, A.8.4, A.8.5, A.8.5, A.8.44, A.8.51, A.8.52, A.8.53, A.8.144, A.9.29, A.9.40, A.9.75, A.9.81, A.9.113, A.9.118, A.10.32, A.10.36, A.10.36, A.10.73, A.10.74, A.10.142, A.10.148, A.10.157, A.10.165, A.11.7, A.11.7, A.11.7, A.11.47, A.11.48, A.11.48, A.11.49, A.11.50, A.11.57, A.11.78, A.11.92, A.11.95, A.11.113, A.11.117, A.11.119, A.11.125, A.11.125, A.11.130, A.11.266, A.11.281, A.12.29, A.12.31, A.12.36, A.12.45, A.12.51, A.12.53, A.12.54, A.12.54, A.12.65, A.12.72, A.12.79, A.12.100, A.12.104, A.12.104, A.12.114

hym B 508

B.Pr.72, B.Pr.112, B.Pr.113, B.Pr.139, B.Pr.149, B.Pr.172, B.Pr.173, B.Pr.174, B.Pr.188, B.Pr.190, B.Pr.190, B.Pr.206, B.1.16, B.1.29, B.1.30, B.1.38, B.1.47, B.1.58,

B.1.68, B.1.102, B.1.116, B.1.146, B.1.149, B.1.150, B.1.169, B.1.171, B.1.174, B.2.22, B.2.27, B.2.100, B.2.106, B.2.107, B.2.115, B.2.202, B.2.206, B.2.212, B.2.214, B.2.215, B.2.215, B.2.216, B.2.217, B.2.222, B.2.223, B.2.223, B.2.223, B.2.224, B.2.228, B.2.230, B.2.231, B.2.232, B.2.233, B.2.234, B.3.32, B.3.45, B.3.45, B.3.95, B.3.111, B.3.129, B.3.139, B.3.140, B.3.141, B.3.156, B.3.175, B.3.190, B.3.206, B.3.210, B.3.212, B.3.274, B.3.279, B.3.287, B.3.294, B.3.314, B.4.8, B.4.15, B.4.21, B.4.22, B.4.25, B.4.43, B.4.45, B.4.52, B.4.53, B.4.60, B.4.61, B.4.64, B.4.85, B.4.88, B.4.89, B.4.99, B.4.100, B.4.101, B.4.108, B.4.109, B.4.131, B.4.185, B.5.11, B.5.64, B.5.72, B.5.84, B.5.89, B.5.93, B.5.94, B.5.94, B.5.95, B.5.96, B.5.96, B.5.101, B.5.102, B.5.103, B.5.104, B.5.108, B.5.116, B.5.126, B.5.188, B.5.189, B.5.280, B.5.290, B.5.297, B.5.298, B.5.299, B.5.330, B.5.333, B.5.351, B.5.352, B.5.352, B.5.358, B.5.358, B.5.363, B.5.364, B.5.443, B.5.446, B.5.448, B.5.475, B.5.482, B.5.525, B.5.536, B.5.538, B.5.540, B.5.540, B.5.549, B.5.550, B.5.556, B.5.597, B.5.601, B.5.608, B.5.610, B.5.634, B.6.20, B.6.67, B.6.93, B.6.106, B.6.131, B.6.152, B.6.155, B.6.159, B.6.160, B.6.165, B.6.170, B.6.172, B.6.175, B.6.179, B.6.200, B.6.241, B.6.242, B.6.245, B.6.246, B.6.266, B.6.272, B.6.298, B.6.301, B.6.316, B.6.322, B.7.3, B.7.4, B.7.5, B.7.5, B.7.49, B.7.50, B.7.51, B.7.79, B.7.80, B.7.85, B.7.166, B.7.172, B.8.33, B.8.44, B.8.56, B.8.84, B.8.90, B.8.123, B.8.129, B.9.31, B.9.39, B.9.42, B.9.47, B.9.48, B.9.88, B.9.97, B.9.98, B.9.99, B.9.134, B.10.7, B.10.7, B.10.7, B.10.61, B.10.62, B.10.62, B.10.63, B.10.64, B.10.71, B.10.89, B.10.91, B.10.125, B.10.139, B.10.142, B.10.161, B.10.165, B.10.167, B.10.173, B.10.173, B.10.178, B.10.236, B.10.310, B.10.316, B.10.316, B.10.316, B.10.335, B.10.385, B.10.422, B.10.455, B.11.54, B.11.70, B.11.131, B.11.131, B.11.132, B.11.132, B.11.133, B.11.134, B.11.181, B.11.208, B.11.235, B.11.239, B.11.245, B.11.281, B.11.295, B.11.373, B.11.403, B.11.426, B.11.426, B.11.428, B.11.428, B.11.428, B.11.429, B.11.429, B.11.431, B.11.432, B.11.437, B.11.437, B.11.439, B.11.440, B.12.22, B.12.56, B.12.107, B.12.116, B.12.154, B.12.173, B.12.182, B.12.186, B.12.187, B.12.188, B.12.193, B.12.193, B.12.211, B.12.214, B.12.231, B.12.249, B.13.27, B.13.27, B.13.31, B.13.60, B.13.85, B.13.101, B.13.102, B.13.136, B.13.146, B.13.158, B.13.176, B.13.218, B.13.222, B.13.237, B.13.244, B.13.247, B.13.252, B.13.255, B.13.278, B.13.290, B.13.308, B.13.308, B.13.318, B.13.412, B.13.414, B.13.450, B.13.458, B.14.85, B.14.99, B.14.107, B.14.150, B.14.151, B.14.227, B.14.234, B.14.250, B.14.251, B.14.272, B.14.311, B.15.14, B.15.59, B.15.140, B.15.160, B.15.162, B.15.178, B.15.178, B.15.179, B.15.195, B.15.197, B.15.209, B.15.218, B.15.220, B.15.227, B.15.251, B.15.251, B.15.284, B.15.287, B.15.288, B.15.378, B.15.464, B.15.571, B.15.594, B.15.595, B.15.597, B.16.30, B.16.46, B.16.65, B.16.65, B.16.83, B.16.87, B.16.89, B.16.98, B.16.104, B.16.106, B.16.114, B.16.137, B.16.144, B.16.151, B.16.152, B.16.174, B.16.179, B.16.190, B.16.194, B.16.196, B.16.201, B.16.201, B.16.213, B.16.225, B.16.226, B.16.226, B.16.232, B.16.233, B.16.244, B.16.249, B.16.250, B.16.274, B.17.5, B.17.19, B.17.36, B.17.60, B.17.61, B.17.64, B.17.67, B.17.73, B.17.73, B.17.74, B.17.76, B.17.79, B.17.82, B.17.83, B.17.84, B.17.85, B.17.85, B.17.88, B.17.90, B.17.90, B.17.108, B.17.111, B.17.142, B.17.171, B.17.179, B.17.228, B.17.245, B.17.259, B.17.270, B.17.289, B.17.307, B.17.328, B.17.331, B.17.335, B.17.351, B.18.14, B.18.26, B.18.34, B.18.39, B.18.40, B.18.50, B.18.51, B.18.53, B.18.77, B.18.84, B.18.84, B.18.85, B.18.100, B.18.131, B.18.219, B.18.220, B.18.229, B.18.244, B.18.246, B.18.250, B.18.251, B.18.253, B.18.254, B.18.274, B.18.276, B.18.285, B.18.297, B.18.302, B.18.302, B.18.325, B.18.383, B.18.383, B.18.395, B.18.403, B.18.406, B.18.406, B.18.406, B.18.414, B.18.419, B.19.11, B.19.15, B.19.15, B.19.23, B.19.28, B.19.51, B.19.57, B.19.73, B.19.77, B.19.92, B.19.102, B.19.105, B.19.131, B.19.136, B.19.137, B.19.141, B.19.142, B.19.157, B.19.170, B.19.183, B.19.193, B.19.210, B.19.210, B.19.214, B.19.224, B.19.228, B.19.283, B.19.284, B.19.293, B.19.296, B.19.321, B.19.331, B.19.336, B.19.434, B.19.437, B.20.12, B.20.17, B.20.18, B.20.35, B.20.36, B.20.59, B.20.61, B.20.116, B.20.123, B.20.126, B.20.144, B.20.152, B.20.166, B.20.167, B.20.170, B.20.171, B.20.172, B.20.175, B.20.183, B.20.218, B.20.230, B.20.230, B.20.289, B.20.297, B.20.316, B.20.352, B.20.355, B.20.358, B.20.363

him C 488 him (1) hym (487)

C.Pr.70, C.Pr.111, C.Pr.139, C.Pr.140, C.Pr.170, C.Pr.172, C.Pr.189, C.Pr.190, C.Pr.191, C.Pr.205, C.1.15, C.1.16, C.1.36, C.1.45, C.1.54, C.1.64, C.1.94, C.1.109, C.1.129, C.1.145, C.1.165, C.1.167, C.1.170, C.2.21, C.2.27, C.2.105, C.2.119, C.2.216, C.2.218, C.2.224, C.2.225, C.2.225, C.2.226, C.2.227, C.2.232, C.2.233, C.2.233, C.2.233, C.2.234, C.2.238, C.2.241, C.2.242, C.2.243, C.2.244, C.3.47, C.3.47, C.3.148, C.3.166, C.3.177, C.3.178, C.3.179, C.3.194, C.3.221, C.3.239, C.3.248, C.3.263, C.3.266, C.3.268, C.3.299, C.3.327, C.3.328, C.3.350, C.3.351, C.3.370, C.3.376, C.3.379, C.3.403, C.3.427, C.3.428, C.3.432, C.3.440, C.3.447, C.4.8, C.4.15, C.4.21, C.4.23, C.4.23, C.4.25, C.4.41, C.4.56, C.4.63, C.4.64, C.4.81, C.4.84, C.4.85, C.4.95, C.4.96, C.4.103, C.4.128, C.4.153, C.4.179, C.5.51, C.5.95, C.5.98, C.5.99, C.5.162, C.6.5, C.6.56, C.6.56, C.6.107, C.6.168, C.6.169, C.6.196, C.6.197, C.6.307, C.6.329, C.6.338, C.6.345, C.6.351, C.6.353, C.6.354, C.6.388, C.6.391, C.6.409, C.6.410, C.6.410, C.6.416, C.6.416, C.6.421, C.6.422, C.7.57, C.7.60, C.7.62, C.7.72, C.7.110, C.7.124, C.7.170, C.7.181, C.7.183, C.7.185, C.7.185, C.7.193, C.7.194, C.7.208, C.7.244, C.7.245, C.7.248, C.7.262, C.7.298, C.8.18, C.8.59, C.8.68, C.8.113, C.8.149, C.8.151, C.8.156, C.8.157, C.8.162, C.8.166, C.8.168, C.8.172, C.8.176, C.8.194, C.8.205, C.8.206, C.8.253, C.8.255, C.8.256, C.8.257, C.8.279, C.8.280, C.8.293, C.8.342, C.9.3, C.9.4, C.9.5, C.9.5, C.9.6, C.9.65, C.9.123, C.9.144, C.9.144, C.9.145, C.9.146, C.9.151, C.9.158, C.9.238, C.9.238, C.9.240, C.9.249, C.9.250, C.9.255, C.9.310, C.9.316, C.9.348, C.10.43, C.10.81, C.10.87, C.10.119, C.10.157, C.10.175, C.10.201, C.10.216, C.11.28, C.11.42, C.11.42, C.11.45, C.11.46, C.11.51, C.11.113, C.11.118, C.11.136, C.11.136, C.11.137, C.11.147, C.11.196, C.11.210, C.11.254, C.11.264, C.11.280, C.11.298, C.12.66, C.12.66, C.12.67, C.12.67, C.12.68, C.12.69, C.12.96, C.12.124, C.12.128, C.12.133, C.12.158, C.12.200, C.12.211, C.12.213, C.12.241, C.13.2, C.13.9, C.13.10, C.13.13, C.13.39, C.13.47, C.13.60, C.13.63, C.13.63, C.13.90, C.13.91, C.13.109, C.13.132, C.13.183, C.13.211, C.13.235, C.13.235, C.13.235, C.13.236, C.13.238, C.13.238, C.13.239, C.13.243, C.13.245, C.13.246, C.14.18, C.14.52, C.14.61, C.14.98, C.14.113, C.14.122, C.14.125, C.14.126, C.14.127, C.14.132, C.14.133, C.14.150, C.14.153, C.15.30, C.15.30, C.15.36, C.15.64, C.15.92, C.15.108, C.15.109, C.15.141, C.15.144, C.15.145, C.15.146, C.15.150, C.15.157, C.15.162, C.15.163, C.15.173, C.15.187, C.15.191, C.15.216, C.15.225, C.15.236, C.15.282, C.16.68, C.16.75, C.16.78, C.16.95, C.16.112, C.16.145, C.16.163, C.16.178, C.16.228, C.16.290, C.16.291, C.16.294, C.16.296, C.16.316, C.16.317, C.16.319, C.16.319, C.16.320, C.16.321, C.16.337, C.16.337, C.16.339, C.16.340, C.16.341, C.16.345, C.16.352, C.16.367, C.16.368, C.16.370, C.16.370, C.17.14, C.17.15, C.17.18, C.17.154, C.17.155, C.17.155, C.17.159, C.17.168, C.17.180, C.17.180, C.17.284, C.17.303, C.17.305, C.18.13, C.18.24, C.18.34, C.18.96, C.18.97, C.18.98, C.18.114, C.18.117, C.18.121, C.18.131, C.18.137, C.18.140, C.18.144, C.18.164, C.18.164, C.18.168, C.18.183, C.18.203, C.18.205, C.18.216, C.18.240, C.18.242, C.18.246, C.18.248, C.18.248, C.18.261, C.18.267, C.18.290, C.19.7, C.19.20, C.19.59, C.19.60, C.19.63, C.19.64, C.19.66, C.19.72, C.19.72, C.19.73, C.19.75, C.19.76, C.19.79, C.19.91, C.19.102, C.19.116, C.19.135, C.19.144, C.19.145, C.19.194, C.19.211, C.19.225, C.19.237, C.19.270, C.19.287, C.19.308, C.19.311, C.19.315, C.19.331, C.20.12, C.20.25, C.20.33, C.20.38, C.20.39, C.20.51, C.20.53, C.20.79, C.20.86, C.20.86, C.20.87, C.20.103, C.20.134, C.20.228, C.20.229, C.20.238, C.20.253, C.20.255, C.20.259, C.20.260, C.20.262, C.20.263, C.20.296, C.20.298, C.20.317, C.20.330, C.20.334, C.20.334, C.20.368, C.20.425, C.20.425, C.20.438, C.20.446, C.20.449, C.20.449, C.20.449, C.20.457, C.20.462, C.21.11, C.21.15, C.21.15, C.21.23, C.21.28, C.21.51, C.21.57, C.21.73, C.21.77, C.21.92, C.21.102, C.21.105, C.21.131, C.21.136, C.21.137, C.21.141, C.21.142, C.21.157, C.21.170, C.21.183, C.21.193, C.21.210, C.21.210, C.21.214, C.21.224, C.21.228, C.21.283, C.21.284, C.21.293, C.21.296, C.21.321, C.21.331, C.21.336, C.21.434, C.21.437, C.22.12, C.22.17, C.22.18, C.22.35, C.22.36, C.22.59, C.22.61, C.22.116, C.22.123, C.22.126, C.22.144, C.22.152, C.22.166, C.22.167, C.22.170, C.22.171, C.22.172, C.22.175, C.22.183, C.22.218, C.22.230, C.22.230, C.22.289, C.22.297, C.22.316, C.22.352, C.22.355, C.22.358, C.22.363

his A 282

A.Pr.69, A.Pr.70, A.Pr.71, A.Pr.72, A.Pr.76, A.1.13, A.1.20, A.1.27, A.1.28, A.1.64, A.1.68, A.1.80, A.1.86, A.1.102, A.1.105, A.1.106, A.1.108, A.1.112, A.1.116, A.1.135, A.1.141, A.1.148, A.1.159, A.2.24, A.2.30, A.2.51, A.2.51, A.2.53, A.2.87, A.2.103, A.2.107, A.2.151, A.2.155, A.2.179, A.3.3, A.3.104, A.3.106, A.3.147, A.3.184, A.3.186, A.3.188, A.3.191, A.3.192, A.3.194, A.3.202, A.3.208, A.3.219, A.3.219, A.3.224, A.3.239, A.3.241, A.3.243, A.3.245, A.3.255, A.3.268, A.4.14, A.4.15, A.4.17, A.4.20, A.4.22, A.4.24, A.4.32, A.4.35, A.4.35, A.4.42, A.4.50, A.4.50, A.4.52, A.4.59, A.4.64, A.4.64, A.4.70, A.4.71, A.4.76, A.4.115, A.4.141, A.5.1, A.5.30, A.5.31, A.5.38, A.5.43, A.5.44, A.5.55, A.5.59, A.5.62, A.5.66, A.5.66, A.5.67, A.5.68, A.5.74, A.5.78, A.5.79, A.5.80, A.5.80, A.5.82, A.5.93, A.5.94, A.5.110, A.5.116, A.5.116, A.5.159, A.5.160, A.5.168, A.5.170, A.5.171, A.5.193, A.5.199, A.5.199, A.5.200, A.5.203, A.5.203, A.5.205, A.5.208, A.5.214, A.5.215, A.5.219, A.5.221, A.5.230, A.5.246, A.5.247, A.5.248, A.5.249, A.5.253, A.6.7, A.6.8, A.6.10, A.6.12, A.6.25, A.6.26, A.6.27, A.6.30, A.6.31, A.6.32, A.6.34, A.6.35, A.6.39, A.6.42, A.6.83, A.6.88, A.6.102, A.7.54, A.7.55, A.7.55, A.7.56, A.7.56, A.7.71, A.7.72, A.7.74, A.7.81, A.7.87, A.7.94, A.7.102, A.7.118, A.7.123, A.7.124, A.7.126, A.7.127, A.7.128, A.7.132, A.7.136, A.7.136, A.7.140, A.7.142, A.7.149, A.7.154, A.7.155, A.7.160, A.7.162, A.7.183, A.7.187, A.7.221, A.7.224, A.7.225, A.7.227, A.7.235, A.7.235, A.7.236, A.7.246, A.7.248, A.7.251, A.7.253, A.7.253, A.7.254, A.7.255, A.8.2, A.8.5, A.8.25, A.8.43, A.8.49, A.8.51, A.8.53, A.8.59, A.8.71, A.8.76, A.8.76, A.8.76, A.8.91, A.8.108, A.8.110, A.8.113, A.8.142, A.8.145, A.8.147, A.8.173, A.8.180, A.9.71, A.9.71, A.9.72, A.9.72, A.9.73, A.9.73, A.9.73, A.9.74, A.9.74, A.9.78, A.9.80, A.9.93, A.9.111, A.9.112, A.10.18, A.10.31, A.10.34, A.10.36, A.10.37, A.10.39, A.10.50, A.10.55, A.10.72, A.10.75, A.10.97, A.10.109, A.10.121, A.10.153, A.10.158, A.10.159, A.10.167, A.10.173, A.10.179, A.10.208, A.11.23, A.11.24, A.11.47, A.11.54, A.11.66, A.11.76, A.11.79, A.11.81, A.11.81, A.11.81, A.11.83, A.11.91, A.11.93, A.11.100, A.11.100, A.11.123, A.11.126, A.11.171, A.11.176, A.11.178, A.11.204, A.11.205, A.11.214, A.11.215, A.11.216, A.11.216, A.11.238, A.11.238, A.11.253, A.11.257, A.11.267, A.11.267, A.11.269, A.11.280, A.11.295, A.12.29, A.12.44, A.12.64, A.12.86, A.12.93, A.12.93, A.12.105, A.12.111

his B 605 &> it

B.Pr.72, B.Pr.73, B.Pr.74, B.Pr.75, B.Pr.79, B.Pr.92, B.Pr.122, B.Pr.153, B.Pr.156, B.Pr.173, B.Pr.174, B.Pr.179, B.Pr.208, B.1.13, B.1.20, B.1.66, B.1.70, B.1.82, B.1.88, B.1.104, B.1.107, B.1.108, B.1.110, B.1.113, B.1.122, B.1.127, B.1.147, B.1.167, B.1.174, B.2.30, B.2.33, B.2.42, B.2.50, B.2.79, B.2.101, B.2.123, B.2.139, B.2.143, B.2.190, B.2.210, B.2.220, B.3.3, B.3.115, B.3.117, B.3.157, B.3.197, B.3.198, B.3.201, B.3.204, B.3.205, B.3.207, B.3.221, B.3.232, B.3.232, B.3.260, B.3.262, B.3.265, B.3.265, B.3.274, B.3.277, B.3.293, B.3.296, B.3.314, B.4.14, B.4.15, B.4.17, B.4.22, B.4.24, B.4.27, B.4.45, B.4.48, B.4.48, B.4.64, B.4.66, B.4.73, B.4.75, B.4.75, B.4.78, B.4.78, B.4.83, B.4.86, B.4.89, B.4.132, B.5.25, B.5.30, B.5.31, B.5.46, B.5.48, B.5.60, B.5.72, B.5.76, B.5.79, B.5.83, B.5.84, B.5.85, B.5.87, B.5.89, B.5.94, B.5.97, B.5.97, B.5.98, B.5.98, B.5.102, B.5.113, B.5.114, B.5.133, B.5.136, B.5:192, B.5.193, B.5.194, B.5.200, B.5.200, B.5.242, B.5.253, B.5.290, B.5.297, B.5.308, B.5.309, B.5.319, B.5.321, B.5.322, B.5.345, B.5.352, B.5.357, B.5.357, B.5.358, B.5.361, B.5.363, B.5.369, B.5.380, B.5.390, B.5.404, B.5.430, B.5.443, B.5.447, B.5.449, B.5.458, B.5.473, B.5.474, B.5.475, B.5.511, B.5.519, B.5.520, B.5.522, B.5.537, B.5.539, B.5.542, B.5.543, B.5.544, B.5.552, B.5.555, B.5.596, B.5.601, B.5.616, B.6.61, B.6.61, B.6.72, B.6.79, B.6.80, B.6.82, B.6.95, B.6.102, B.6.110, B.6.126, B.6.131, B.6.134, B.6.138, B.6.153, B.6.155, B.6.164, B.6.169, B.6.170, B.6.175, B.6.177, B.6.195, B.6.200, B.6.237, B.6.240, B.6.241, B.6.251, B.6.262, B.6.264, B.6.267, B.6.269, B.6.269, B.6.270, B.6.271, B.6.331, B.7.2, B.7.23, B.7.47, B.7.51, B.7.58, B.7.58, B.7.69, B.7.77, B.7.94, B.7.94, B.7.94, B.7.109, B.7.126, B.7.128, B.7.164,

B.7.168, B.7.170, B.7.172, B.7.195, B.7.202, B.8.80, B.8.80, B.8.81, B.8.81, B.8.82, B.8.82, B.8.82, B.8.83, B.8.83, B.8.87, B.8.103, B.8.121, B.8.122, B.8.131, B.9.16, B.9.19, B.9.30, B.9.33, B.9.35, B.9.44, B.9.44, B.9.46, B.9.48, B.9.49, B.9.59, B.9.61, B.9.67, B.9.94, B.9.105, B.9.106, B.9.131, B.10.32, B.10.61, B.10.68, B.10.108, B.10.123, B.10.126, B.10.128, B.10.128, B.10.128, B.10.130, B.10.138, B.10.140, B.10.144, B.10.147, B.10.147, B.10.171, B.10.174, B.10.228, B.10.233, B.10.235, B.10.248, B.10.251, B.10.288, B.10.314, B.10.315, B.10.315, B.10.331, B.10.335, B.10.355, B.10.376, B.10.409, B.10.421, B.10.440, B.11.25, B.11.38, B.11.45, B.11.121, B.11.125, B.11.127, B.11.128, B.11.135, B.11.149, B.11.150, B.11.156, B.11.169, B.11.199, B.11.207, B.11.207, B.11.236, B.11.295, B.11.300, B.11.301, B.11.307, B.11.331, B.11.371, B.11.375, B.11.399, B.11.403, B.11.430, B.11.441, B.11.441, B.12.12, B.12.21, B.12.29, B.12.41, B.12.41, B.12.42, B.12.77, B.12.93, B.12.106, B.12.106, B.12.108, B.12.117, B.12.167, B.12.182, B.12.233, B.12.234, B.12.244, B.12.245, B.12.245, B.12.247, B.12.248, B.12.249, B.12.255, B.12.256, B.12.260, B.12.269, B.12.275, B.12.284, B.12.287, B.12.288, B.12.292, B.13.15, B.13.23, B.13.48, B.13.60, B.13.69, B.13.75, B.13.83, B.13.84, B.13.88, B.13.94, B.13.126, B.13.144, B.13.145, B.13.159, B.13.216, B.13.243, B.13.248, B.13.249, B.13.252, B.13.289, B.13.291, B.13.292, B.13.343, B.13.354, B.13.356, B.13.361, B.13.367, B.13.372, B.13.399, B.13.402, B.13.450, B.13.451, B.13.457, B.14.36, B.14.48, B.14.59, B.14.60, B.14.61, B.14.62, B.14.86, B.14.107, B.14.110, B.14.127, B.14.133, B.14.136, B.14.136, B.14.138, B.14.142, B.14.147, B.14.149, B.14.150, B.14.151, B.14.207, B.14.213, B.14.215, B.14.222, B.14.222, B.14.228, B.14.231, B.14.232, B.14.233, B.14.234, B.14.235, B.14.235, B.14.237, B.14.243, B.14.256, B.14.257, B.14.257, B.14.262, B.14.311, B.14.321, B.15.16, B.15.21, B.15.32, B.15.57, B.15.61, B.15.125, B.15.141, B.15.142, B.15.159, B.15.190, B.15.196, B.15.218, B.15.229, B.15.245, B.15.247, B.15.248, B.15.248, B.15.257, B.15.281, B.15.290, B.15.291, B.15.292, B.15.292, B.15.379, B.15.402, B.15.406, B.15.409, B.15.413, B.15.464, B.15.482, B.15.484, B.15.505, B.15.511, B.15.517, B.15.526, B.15.571, B.15.571, B.15.598, B.15.602, B.16.19, B.16.84, B.16.98, B.16.99, B.16.104, B.16.105, B.16.106, B.16.140, B.16.143, B.16.179, B.16.183, B.16.185, B.16.192, B.16.193, B.16.195, B.16.221, B.16.235, B.16.245, B.16.245, B.16.247, B.16.248, B.16.250, B.16.254, B.16.255, B.16.263, B.16.265, B.17.32, B.17.67, B.17.69, B.17.73, B.17.73, B.17.88, B.17.91, B.17.100, B.17.103, B.17.109, B.17.120, B.17.125, B.17.126, B.17.128, B.17.142, B.17.205, B.17.242, B.17.245, B.17.268, B.17.269, B.17.301, B.17.302, B.17.307, B.17.317, B.17.319, B.17.320, B.17.322, B.17.325, B.17.325, B.17.327, B.17.328, B.17.351, B.17.354, B.18.22, B.18.23, B.18.23, B.18.31, B.18.49, B.18.53, B.18.79, B.18.81, B.18.86, B.18.98, B.18.195, B.18.197, B.18.198, B.18.212, B.18.218, B.18.240, B.18.243, B.18.256, B.18.257, B.18.259, B.18.259, B.18.276, B.18.287, B.18.303, B.18.304, B.18.304, B.18.310, B.18.326, B.18.344, B.18.360, B.19.13, B.19.14, B.19.35, B.19.35, B.19.43, B.19.43, B.19.58, B.19.59, B.19.63, B.19.66, B.19.70, B.19.81, B.19.108, B.19.110, B.19.116, B.19.119, B.19.124, B.19.134, B.19.143, B.19.148, B.19.171, B.19.172, B.19.188, B.19.208, B.19.239, B.19.267, B.19.287, B.19.288, B.19.308, B.19.323, B.19.326, B.19.331, B.19.339, B.19.340, B.19.352, B.19.426, B.19.447, B.19.449, B.19.465, B.19.480, B.20.11, B.20.13, B.20.15, B.20.20, B.20.32, B.20.40, B.20.43, B.20.69, B.20.81, B.20.91, B.20.92, B.20.106, B.20.117, B.20.120, B.20.124, B.20.134, B.20.135, B.20.140, B.20.142, B.20.156, B.20.158, B.20.170, B.20.171, B.20.180, B.20.217, B.20.326, B.20.327, B.20.331, B.20.340, B.20.349, B.20.351, B.20.371, B.20.378

his C 745 &> it

C.Pr.70, C.Pr.71, C.Pr.72, C.Pr.73, C.Pr.76, C.Pr.77, C.Pr.90, C.Pr.91, C.Pr.107, C.Pr.113, C.Pr.114, C.Pr.114, C.Pr.115, C.Pr.173, C.Pr.174, C.Pr.174, C.Pr.176, C.Pr.190, C.Pr.191, C.Pr.196, C.1.13, C.1.20, C.1.25, C.1.27, C.1.27, C.1.29, C.1.62, C.1.67, C.1.67, C.1.84, C.1.84, C.1.102, C.1.105, C.1.110, C.1.111, C.1.119, C.1.120, C.1.129, C.1.158, C.1.163, C.1.170, C.1.181, C.2.32, C.2.33, C.2.45, C.2.53, C.2.108, C.2.146, C.2.149, C.2.155, C.2.222, C.2.230, C.3.3, C.3.130, C.3.132, C.3.152, C.3.154, C.3.181, C.3.195, C.3.240, C.3.241, C.3.243, C.3.243, C.3.251, C.3.252, C.3.253, C.3.258, C.3.261, C.3.262, C.3.264, C.3.298, C.3.300, C.3.308, C.3.315, C.3.326, C.3.327, C.3.327, C.3.331, C.3.348, C.3.349, C.3.349, C.3.349, C.3.351, C.3.353, C.3.362, C.3.368, C.3.368, C.3.368, C.3.375, C.3.376, C.3.377, C.3.411, C.3.412, C.3.415, C.3.418, C.3.427, C.3.430, C.3.432, C.3.449, C.3.467, C.3.467, C.4.14, C.4.15, C.4.17, C.4.24, C.4.27, C.4.43, C.4.46, C.4.50, C.4.58, C.4.70, C.4.71, C.4.74, C.4.74, C.4.79, C.4.80, C.4.82, C.4.85, C.4.104, C.4.129, C.4.130, C.4.153, C.4.195, C.5.58, C.5.97, C.5.100, C.5.113, C.5.132, C.5.133, C.5.138, C.5.144, C.5.160, C.5.161, C.5.161, C.5.176, C.5.180, C.5.188, C.6.1, C.6.2, C.6.61, C.6.64, C.6.65, C.6.66, C.6.67, C.6.68, C.6.83, C.6.104, C.6.111, C.6.169, C.6.172, C.6.199, C.6.200, C.6.201, C.6.202, C.6.202, C.6.202, C.6.208, C.6.208, C.6.248, C.6.251, C.6.256, C.6.266, C.6.266, C.6.267, C.6.269, C.6.285, C.6.304, C.6.312, C.6.326, C.6.327, C.6.329, C.6.333, C.6.340, C.6.345, C.6.351, C.6.363, C.6.364, C.6.371, C.6.376, C.6.378, C.6.379, C.6.398, C.6.400, C.6.407, C.6.410, C.6.415, C.6.415, C.6.416, C.6.421, C.6.421, C.6.421, C.6.427, C.7.6, C.7.20, C.7.43, C.7.56, C.7.57, C.7.61, C.7.63, C.7.70, C.7.110, C.7.111, C.7.156, C.7.164, C.7.165, C.7.167, C.7.169, C.7.182, C.7.183, C.7.184, C.7.187, C.7.187, C.7.188, C.7.189, C.7.196, C.7.197, C.7.199, C.7.244, C.7.248, C.7.268, C.7.273, C.7.293, C.8.21, C.8.58, C.8.59, C.8.59, C.8.60, C.8.60, C.8.75, C.8.81, C.8.82, C.8.98, C.8.103, C.8.104, C.8.117, C.8.132, C.8.141, C.8.151, C.8.157, C.8.161, C.8.172, C.8.174, C.8.195, C.8.196, C.8.196, C.8.206, C.8.244, C.8.245, C.8.247, C.8.252, C.8.252, C.8.253, C.8.272, C.8.277, C.8.290, C.8.290, C.8.291, C.8.291, C.8.292, C.8.352, C.9.2, C.9.4, C.9.5, C.9.27, C.9.46, C.9.53, C.9.53, C.9.65, C.9.66, C.9.90, C.9.100, C.9.116, C.9.118, C.9.118, C.9.136, C.9.136, C.9.143, C.9.143, C.9.144, C.9.146, C.9.151, C.9.154, C.9.157, C.9.216, C.9.248, C.9.252, C.9.254, C.9.255, C.9.270, C.9.271, C.9.283, C.9.308, C.9.314, C.9.314, C.9.316, C.9.317, C.9.317, C.9.341, C.9.348, C.10.53, C.10.78, C.10.78, C.10.79, C.10.80, C.10.80, C.10.86, C.10.117, C.10.118, C.10.121, C.10.142, C.10.145, C.10.156, C.10.176, C.10.176, C.10.179, C.10.180, C.10.181, C.10.196, C.10.217, C.10.230, C.10.251, C.10.251, C.10.269, C.11.21, C.11.29, C.11.44, C.11.66, C.11.69, C.11.82, C.11.85, C.11.114, C.11.137, C.11.147, C.11.153, C.11.184, C.11.197, C.11.201, C.11.240, C.11.240, C.11.240, C.11.248, C.11.253, C.11.265, C.11.286, C.11.304, C.11.312, C.12.2, C.12.56, C.12.60, C.12.62, C.12.63, C.12.69, C.12.70, C.12.71, C.12.84, C.12.84, C.12.85, C.12.96, C.12.99, C.12.115, C.12.115, C.12.116, C.12.125, C.12.127, C.12.134, C.12.150, C.12.156, C.12.156, C.12.157, C.12.157, C.12.170, C.12.170, C.12.204, C.12.205, C.12.212, C.12.212, C.12.238, C.12.242, C.12.242, C.12.244, C.13.3, C.13.7, C.13.9, C.13.14, C.13.17, C.13.19, C.13.20, C.13.38, C.13.40, C.13.41, C.13.41, C.13.43, C.13.44, C.13.45, C.13.46, C.13.48, C.13.48, C.13.49, C.13.53, C.13.59, C.13.60, C.13.64, C.13.70, C.13.70, C.13.86, C.13.98, C.13.109, C.13.111, C.13.114, C.13.121, C.13.139, C.13.153, C.13.164, C.13.171, C.13.172, C.13.172, C.13.211, C.13.232, C.13.243, C.13.247, C.13.247, C.14.37, C.14.44, C.14.51, C.14.51, C.14.53, C.14.62, C.14.62, C.14.122, C.14.132, C.14.160, C.14.178, C.14.178, C.14.179, C.14.180, C.14.180, C.14.181, C.14.182, C.14.183, C.14.184, C.14.184, C.14.197, C.14.206, C.14.209, C.14.210, C.15.18, C.15.54, C.15.64, C.15.81, C.15.91, C.15.95, C.15.96, C.15.101, C.15.107, C.15.142, C.15.143, C.15.144, C.15.158, C.15.172, C.15.185, C.15.213, C.15.218, C.15.218, C.15.221, C.15.246, C.15.258, C.15.259, C.15.260, C.15.261, C.15.286, C.15.301, C.16.2, C.16.5, C.16.5, C.16.48, C.16.54, C.16.56, C.16.63, C.16.63, C.16.63, C.16.69, C.16.72, C.16.73, C.16.74, C.16.75, C.16.76, C.16.76, C.16.83, C.16.86, C.16.96, C.16.97, C.16.97, C.16.102, C.16.131, C.16.142, C.16.145, C.16.151, C.16.156, C.16.161, C.16.164, C.16.168, C.16.182, C.16.192, C.16.219, C.16.223, C.16.291, C.16.293, C.16.316, C.16.317, C.16.324, C.16.334, C.16.335, C.16.354, C.16.360, C.16.361, C.16.369, C.17.10, C.17.17, C.17.18, C.17.19, C.17.19, C.17.38, C.17.59, C.17.65, C.17.66, C.17.66, C.17.82, C.17.113, C.17.153, C.17.160, C.17.161, C.17.172, C.17.182, C.17.236, C.17.236, C.17.246, C.17.256, C.17.262, C.17.268, C.17.284, C.17.284, C.17.291, C.17.306, C.17.310, C.18.30, C.18.68, C.18.115, C.18.121, C.18.131, C.18.132, C.18.135, C.18.143, C.18.146, C.18.162, C.18.186, C.18.186, C.18.195, C.18.201, C.18.202, C.18.204, C.18.229, C.18.234, C.18.249, C.18.251, C.18.265, C.18.266, C.18.269, C.18.269, C.18.270, C.18.271, C.18.279, C.18.281, C.18.288, C.19.33, C.19.66, C.19.67, C.19.68, C.19.70, C.19.71, C.19.72, C.19.77, C.19.80, C.19.85, C.19.90, C.19.95, C.19.97, C.19.101, C.19.171, C.19.208, C.19.211, C.19.234, C.19.235, C.19.237, C.19.239, C.19.242, C.19.259, C.19.281, C.19.282, C.19.287, C.19.297, C.19.299, C.19.302, C.19.305, C.19.305, C.19.307, C.19.308, C.19.309, C.19.321, C.19.331, C.19.334, C.20.21, C.20.22, C.20.22, C.20.30, C.20.49, C.20.50, C.20.52, C.20.53, C.20.53, C.20.59, C.20.81, C.20.83, C.20.88, C.20.101, C.20.190, C.20.197, C.20.200, C.20.202, C.20.203, C.20.221, C.20.227, C.20.249, C.20.252, C.20.265, C.20.267, C.20.283, C.20.288, C.20.292, C.20.298, C.20.303, C.20.311, C.20.313, C.20.314, C.20.314, C.20.314, C.20.335, C.20.336, C.20.341, C.20.344, C.20.351, C.20.356, C.20.383, C.21.13, C.21.13, C.21.14, C.21.33, C.21.35, C.21.35, C.21.43, C.21.43, C.21.43, C.21.58, C.21.59, C.21.60, C.21.63, C.21.66, C.21.70, C.21.81, C.21.101, C.21.108, C.21.110, C.21.116, C.21.119, C.21.124, C.21.130, C.21.134, C.21.143, C.21.147, C.21.148, C.21.155, C.21.169, C.21.171, C.21.171, C.21.172, C.21.188, C.21.201, C.21.208, C.21.239, C.21.267, C.21.268, C.21.287, C.21.288, C.21.308, C.21.323, C.21.326, C.21.326, C.21.331, C.21.339, C.21.340, C.21.352, C.21.426, C.21.436, C.21.447, C.21.449, C.21.465, C.21.480, C.22.11, C.22.13, C.22.15, C.22.20, C.22.32, C.22.40, C.22.43, C.22.69, C.22.81, C.22.91, C.22.92, C.22.106, C.22.117, C.22.120, C.22.124, C.22.134, C.22.135, C.22.140, C.22.142, C.22.143, C.22.156, C.22.158, C.22.170, C.22.171, C.22.180, C.22.217, C.22.226, C.22.326, C.22.327, C.22.331, C.22.340, C.22.349, C.22.351, C.22.358, C.22.361, C.22.370, C.22.371, C.22.378

hise A 28

A.Pr.75, A.1.96, A.2.6, A.2.171, A.3.132, A.3.197, A.3.248, A.3.257, A.4.38, A.4.61, A.4.73, A.5.77, A.5.77, A.5.78, A.5.147, A.5.197, A.5.206, A.6.31, A.6.94, A.7.55, A.7.65, A.7.128, A.7.166, A.8.4, A.9.115, A.11.54, A.11.97, A.11.215

hise B 135

B.Pr.78, B.Pr.93, B.Pr.154, B.1.27, B.1.28, B.1.98, B.1.150, B.1.162, B.1.185, B.2.6, B.2.70, B.2.99, B.2.130, B.2.194, B.2.212, B.3.143, B.3.210, B.3.215, B.3.279, B.4.39, B.4.51, B.4.55, B.4.64, B.4.84, B.4.133, B.4.158, B.5.1, B.5.40, B.5.61, B.5.83, B.5.191, B.5.340, B.5.349, B.5.361, B.5.442, B.5.472, B.5.524, B.5.538, B.5.543, B.6.59, B.6.60, B.6.60, B.6.60, B.6.73, B.6.89, B.6.132, B.6.243, B.7.4, B.7.5, B.7.49, B.7.172, B.8.89, B.8.125, B.9.142, B.10.23, B.10.68, B.10.105, B.10.299, B.10.409, B.10.439, B.11.134, B.11.136, B.11.176, B.11.208, B.11.238, B.11.297, B.11.433, B.11.433, B.12.97, B.12.99, B.12.230, B.12.262, B.12.263, B.13.78, B.13.89, B.13.100, B.13.174, B.13.249, B.13.252, B.13.367, B.13.398, B.13.410, B.14.246, B.14.296, B.14.327, B.15.66, B.15.66, B.15.88, B.15.139, B.15.192, B.15.204, B.15.291, B.15.346, B.15.400, B.15.411, B.15.450, B.15.450, B.16.116, B.16.253, B.16.253, B.16.272, B.17.36, B.17.68, B.17.71, B.17.72, B.17.78, B.17.95, B.17.272, B.17.278, B.17.329, B.18.52, B.18.53, B.18.59, B.19.13, B.19.33, B.19.43, B.19.60, B.19.101, B.19.130, B.19.147, B.19.155, B.19.169, B.19.171, B.19.201, B.19.219, B.19.268, B.19.326, B.19.436, B.20.61, B.20.143, B.20.226, B.20.358, B.20.361, B.20.370

hise C 3

C.19.253, C.21.219, C.22.61

is C 1 &> ben

C.6.328

hed > hede,heed; ; heddere > hider; heddes > heed

hede n *hed n.(2)* A 3 hed (1) hede (1) heed (1); B 9; C 10

A. 7.14 þe nedy & þe nakid, nymeþ *hed* how þei liggen;
A. 8.78 Þere ben mo mysshapen amonges hem, whoso takiþ *hede*,
A.11.149 Ac theologie techiþ not so, who[so] takiþ *heed*;
B. 6.15 The nedy and þe naked nymeþ *hede* how þei liggeþ;
B.10.88 Tobye [techeþ] noȝt so; takeþ *hede* ye riche

B.11.111 This was hir teme and hir text—I took ful good *hede*–
B.11.322 And nempned me by my name and bad me nymen *hede*,
B.12.155 Why I haue told [þee] al þis, I took ful good *hede*
B.13.315 'Ye, whoso toke *hede*', quod haukyn, 'bihynde and bifore,
B.13.318 And he torned hym as tyd and þanne took I *hede*;
B.15.91 I shal tellen it for truþes sake; take *hede* whoso likeþ.
B.15.373 For is noon of þise newe clerkes, whoso nymeþ *hede*,
C. 9.71 Ac þat most neden aren oure neyhebores and we nyme gode *he[d]e*,
C.11.68 Tobie techeth nat so; taketh *hede*, ȝe ryche,
C.11.244 For Archa Noe, nymeth *hede*, ys no more to mene
C.12.45 Of here teme and here tales y took ful good *hede*;
C.12.219 Lo! lordes, lo! and ladyes, taketh *hede*:
C.14.99 Why y haue tolde [the] al þis, y toek ful gode *hede*
C.17.86 For is [now] noon, hoso nymeth *hede*,
C.17.239 And take *hede* [how] Macometh thorw a mylde dowue
C.18.19 And he thonkede me tho; bote thenne toek y *hede*
C.18.53 I toted vpon þ[e] tree tho and thenne toek y *hede*

hedes > heed; hee > heo

heed n *hed n.(1)* &> *hede* A 9 hed (7) heued (1) heuid (1); B 23 hed (1)
   heddes (2) heed (17) heued (1) heuedes (2); C 26 heed (2) hed (2)
   hedes (2) hefdes (1) heued (17) heuedes (2)
A. 2.163 And ge[rd]iþ of giles *hed*; let hym go no ferþere;
A. 4.20 Hange on hym þe heuy bridel to holde his *hed* lowe,
A. 4.64 Pees putte forþ his *heued* & his panne blody:
A. 4.146 'Ac it is wel hard, be myn *hed*, herto to bringe it.
A. 5.31 Þat hire *hed* was worþ a mark & his hod not worþ a grote.
A. 6.25 'Petir,' quaþ a plouȝman and putte forþ his *hed*,
A. 6.113 It is wel hard, be myn *hed*, any of ȝow alle,
A.10.49 Inwyt in þe *heuid* is, & an help to þe soule,
A.10.60 Þei helde ale in here *hed* til Inwyt be drenchit,
B. 1.164 And in þe herte þere is þe *heed* and þe heiȝe welle.
B. 2.34 And what man takeþ Mede, myn *heed* dar I legge,
B. 2.202 And girdeþ of Gyles *heed*; lat hym go no ferþer;
B. 4.22 Hange on hym þe heuy brydel to holde his *heed* lowe,
B. 4.78 Pees putte forþ his *heed*, and his panne blody:
B. 4.183 It is [wel] hard, by myn *heed*, hert[o] to brynge it,
B. 5.31 [That] hire *heed* was worþ [a] marc & his hood noȝt a grote.
B. 5.194 Wiþ an hood on his *heed*, a hat aboue,
B. 5.537 'Peter!' quod a Plowman, and putte forþ his *hed*:
B. 5.628 It is [wel] hard, by myn *heed*, any of yow alle
B. 6.327 Whan ye se þe [mone] amys and two monkes *heddes*,
B. 9.58 Ac Inwit is in þe *heed* and to þe herte he lokeþ
B.13.144 Cast coles on his *hed* of alle kynde speche;
B.14.233 And his *heued* vnheled, vnesiliche ywrye
B.15.430 The *heuedes* of holy chirche, and þei holy were,
B.15.487 That *heuedes* of holy chirche ben, þat han hir wil here,
B.17.73 Enbawmed hym and bond his *heed* and in his [barm] hym leide,
B.18.49 And sette it sore on his *heed* and seide in enuye;
B.19.469 Ther I may hastilokest it haue, for I am *heed* of lawe;
B.19.471 And siþ I am youre aller *heed* I am youre aller heele
B.20.183 And Elde after [hym]; and ouer myn *heed* yede
B.20.185 So harde he yede ouer myn *heed* it wole be sene euere.
B.20.187 Siþ whanne was þe wey ouer mennes *heddes*?
C. 1.160 And in þe herte þer is þe *hed* and þe heye welle.
C. 2.216 And gurdeth of giles *heed*; lat hym goo no wyddore
C. 3.380 Bothe *heued* and here kyng, haldyng with no parteyȝe
C. 4.74 ȝut pees put forth his *heued* and his panne blody:
C. 4.177 Hit is ful hard, by myn *heued*, herto to bryngen hit
C. 5.133 [That] here *hed* was worth half marc and his hoed nat a grote.
C. 6.150 Til bothe here *hedes* were bar and blody here chekes.
C. 6.202 With his hood on his *heued* and his hat bothe,
C. 7.182 '[Peter]! quod a [plouhman], and potte forth his *heued*,
C. 7.281 Hit is ful hard, be myn *heued*, eny of ȝow alle
C.10.174 Inwit is in þe *heued* and anima in herte
C.10.179 ȝaf his douhter for a daunsynge in a disch þe *heued*
C.12.18 'Ouh!' quod y tho and myn *heued* waggede,
C.15.142 Caste coles on his *heued* of alle kyn[de] speche,
C.16.74 And his *heued* vnheled, vnesylyche ywrye
C.17.140 The whiche is þe *heued* of charite and hele of mannes soule:
C.17.230 The *heuedes* of holy churche and tho that ben vnder hem,
C.19.72 Enbaumed hym and bond his *heued* and on bayard hym sette
C.20.49 And sette hit sore on his *heued* and saide in Enuye;
C.20.290 Al hoet on here *hedes* þat entrith ney þe walles;
C.21.469 Ther y may hastilokest hit haue, for y am *heed* of lawe;
C.21.471 And sethe y am ȝoure alere *heued* y am ȝoure alere hele
C.22.183 And Elde aftur hym; and ouer myn *heued* ȝede
C.22.185 So harde he ȝede ouer myn *heued* hit wol be sene euere.
C.22.187 Sennes whanne was þe way ouer menne *heuedes*?

heeld > holden

heele n *hele n.(1)* &> *helen* A 2 hele; B 12 heele (10) hele (2); C 19
   hele
A. 6.19 And souȝt goode seintes for my soule *hele*.'
A. 7.243 Ac I hote þe,' quaþ hunger, 'as þou þin *hele* wilnest,
B. 5.531 And souȝt goode Seintes for me soul[e] *hel[e]*.'
B. 6.259 Ac I hote þee', quod hunger, 'as þow þyn *hele* wilnest,
B.13.341 But þoruȝ a charme hadde I chaunce and my chief *heele*.'
B.14.172 Ne neiþer hete ne Hayll, haue þei hir *heele*;
B.17.39 The gome þat gooþ wiþ o staf, he semeþ in gretter *heele*
B.17.94 May no medicyne [vnder mone] þe man to *heele* bringe,
B.19.104 And som tyme he gaf good and grauntede *heele* boþe.
B.19.388 In help of hir *heele* ones in a Monþe,
B.19.471 And siþ I am youre aller heed I am youre aller *heele*
B.20.153 '*Heele* and I', quod he, 'and heighnesse of herte
B.20.180 And in hope of his *heele* good herte he hente
B.20.385 And sende me hap and *heele* til I haue Piers þe Plowman.'
C. 1.86 He is a god by þe gospel and graunte may *hele*
C. 3.298 Ne haue hap to his *hele* mede to deserue.
C. 5.7 In an hot heruest whenne y hadde myn *hele*
C. 5.10 In *hele* and [vnnit] oen me apposede;
C. 6.85 But thorw a charme hadde y chaunce and my chef *hele*.
C. 9.102 For alle þat haen here *hele* and here yesyhte
C. 9.105 A[nd] ȝut ar ther oþere beggares, in *hele* as hit semeth
C. 9.116 To ȝeue vch a wyht wyt, welthe and his *hele*
C.10.181 Euery man þat hath inwit and his *hele* bothe
C.16.12 And moche murthe among ryche men is þat han meble ynow and *hele*.
C.17.140 The whiche is þe heued of charite and *hele* of mannes soule:
C.19.84 Ne no medicyne vnder molde the man to *hele* brynge,
C.20.219 For sholde neuere riȝt riche man þat lyueth in rest and *hele*
C.21.104 And som tyme he gaf goed and graunted *hele* bothe;
C.21.388 In helpe of here *hele* ones in a monthe
C.21.471 And sethe y am ȝoure alere heued y am ȝoure alere *hele*
C.22.153 '*Hele* and y,' quod he, 'and heynesse of herte
C.22.180 And in hope of his *hele* goed herte he hente
C.22.385 And s[e]nde me hap and *hele* til y haue [Peres Plouhman].

heeled > helen

heep n *hep n.* A 4 hep; B 8; C 9 heep (5) hep (2) hepe (2)
A.Pr.50 Ermytes on an *hep*, wiþ hokide staues,
A. 5.166 Of vpholderis an *hep*, erliche be þe morewe,
A. 5.176 Þere were oþes an *hep*, [whoso it herde];
A. 7.175 [A]n *he[p]* of heremites henten hem spadis,
B.Pr.53 Heremytes on an *heep* with hoked staues,
B. 5.231 'ȝis, ones I was yherberwed', quod he, 'wiþ an *heep* of chapmen;
B. 5.317 [Of] vpholderes an *heep*, erly by þe morwe,
B. 5.327 [There were oþes an *heep*, whoso it herde];
B. 6.187 An *heep* of heremytes henten hem spades
B.10.314 An *heep* of houndes at his ers as he a lord were,
B.14.308 And an hardy man of herte among an *heep* of þeues;
B.15.43 And oþere names an *heep*, Episcopus and Pastor.'
C.Pr.51 Eremites on an *hep* with hokede staues
C. 5.160 A[n] *hep* of houndes at h[is] ers as he a lord were
C. 6.235 'ȝus! ones y was herberwed,' quod he, 'with an *heep* of chapmen;
C. 6.374 And of vphalderes an *heep*, [e]rly by þe morwe,
C. 6.385 And there were othes an *heep* for on sholde haue þe worse.
C. 8.183 An *heep* of Eremytes henten hem spades,
C.10.190 And ȝut were best to ben aboute and brynge hit to *hepe*
C.10.192 Bishope[s] sholde ben hereaboute and bryng this to *hepe*
C.16.205 And oþere names an *heep*, Episcopus and pastor.'

heer > here; heere > heren; heet- > hote

heeþ n *heth n.* B 1
B.15.459 Heþen is to mene after *heeþ* and vntiled erþe,

hefdes > heed

heggen v *heggen v.* C 1
C. 5.19 *Heggen* or harwen or swyn or gees dryue

hegges n *hegge n.* A 2 heggis; B 2; C 2
A. 3.122 To [monkis], to [mynstrelis], to myselis in *heggis*.
A. 7.32 And [to] boris & [to] bukkes þat breken þat myn *heggis*,
B. 3.133 To Monkes, to Mynstrales, to Meseles in *hegges*.
B. 6.30 To bores and to [bukkes] þat breken myne *hegges*,
C. 3.170 To Monekes, to [mynstrals, to] musels in *hegge[s]*;
C. 8.29 To bores and to bokkes þat breketh adoun myn *hegges*

hehte > hote; hey > heiȝ,how trolly lolly; heye heigh(e > heiȝ

heighnesse n *heighnesse n.* B 1; C 1 heynesse
B.20.153 'Heele and I', quod he, 'and *heighnesse* of herte
C.22.153 'Hele and y,' quod he, 'and *heynesse* of herte

hei3 adj *heigh adj.* A 15 hei3 (4) hei3e (5) hei3est (1) herre (1) hy (1) hye (1) hi3ere (1) hi3este (1); B 38 heigh (6) heighe (3) hei3 (10) hei3e (16) hei3est (1) hye (1) hyere (1); C 40 hey (16) heye (11) heyh (5) herrore (1) hy (3) hye (4)

A.Pr.13   Ac as I beheld into þe Est an *hei3* to þe sonne
A. 1.71   And h[a]lside hire on þe *hei3e* name, er heo þennis 3ede,
A. 2.21   I au3te ben *hi3ere* þanne heo for I com of a betere.
A. 5.50   'Shal neuere *hei3* herte me hente, but holde me lowe
A. 7.4   I haue an half akir to er[e]n be þe *hei3e* wei3e;
A. 7.104 At *hei3* prime peris let þe plou3 stande
A. 7.178 [Þat ley3e [blereyed] and brokelegged be þe *hye* waye];
A.10.45   Ac in þe herte is hire hom *hei3est* of alle.
A.10.101 For 3if þou comsist to clymbe, & coueitest *herre,*
A.11.112 And axide hire þe *hei3e* wey where clergie [dwell]ide,
A.11.114 'Axe a *hei3e* wey,' quaþ heo, 'from henis to suffre
A.11.239 Haue eritage in heuene as an *hei3* cristene.
A.12.27   And asked Iesu on *hy* þat herden hit an hundred.
B.Pr.13   [Ac] as I biheeld into þe Eest, an *hei3* to þe sonne
B.Pr.128 And siþen in þe Eyr an *hei3* an Aungel of heuene
B.Pr.140 And to þe Aungel an *hei3* answerde after:
B. 1.73   And [halsede] hire on þe *hei3e* name, er she þennes yede,
B. 1.158 That my3te noon Armure it lette ne none *hei3e* walles.
B. 1.164 And in þe herte þere is þe heed and þe *hei3e* welle.
B. 2.28   I ou3te ben *hyere* þan she; I kam of a bettre.
B. 2.33   Shal be my lord and I his leef in þe *hei3e* heuene.
B. 4.42   And þanne Reson rood faste þe ri3te *hei3e* gate
B. 5.67   'Shal neuere *hei3* herte me hente, but holde me lowe
B. 5.275 [Is] holden at þe *hei3e* doom to helpe þee to restitue,
B. 5.292 For he shal answere for þee at þe *hei3e* dome,
B. 6.4   I haue an half acre to erie by þe *hei3e* weye;
B. 6.112 At *hei3* prime Piers leet þe plow3 stonde
B.10.104 I haue yherd *hei3e* men etynge at þe table
B.10.160 And asked hire þe *heighe* wey where Clergie dwelte,
B.10.162 'Aske þe *heighe* wey', quod she, 'hennes to Suffre-
B.10.356 Haue heritage [in] heuene as [an *hei3*] cristene.
B.10.370 God hoteþ *hei3e* and lowe þat no man hurte ooþer,
B.10.459 Was Austyn þe olde, and *hei3est* of þe foure,
B.11.81   Thoru3 contricion [clene] come to þe *hei3e* heuene–
B.11.107 'He seiþ sooþ', quod Scripture þo, and skipte an *hei3* and preched.
B.12.37   And hold þee vnder obedience þat *heigh* wey is to heuene.
B.12.40   [Lo]! what made lucifer to lese þe *hei3e* heuene,
B.12.103 [And ri3t as si3t serueþ a man to se þe *hei3e* strete]
B.12.132 And helden it an *hei3* science hir wittes to knowe;
B.12.139 For þe *hei3e* holy goost heuene shal tocleue,
B.12.196 Ac þou3 þat þeef hadde heuene he hadde noon *hei3* blisse,
B.13.61   For þis doctour on þe *hei3e* dees drank wyn so faste:
B.13.414 Ech day is halyday with hym or an *hei3* ferye,
B.14.212 The *hei3e* wey to heueneward [ofte] Richesse letteþ:
B.15.78   In housynge, in haterynge, [in] *heigh* clergie shewynge
B.15.435 Of hem of holi chirche þat þe *heighe* wey sholde teche
B.15.511 [Whan þe *hye* kyng of heuene sente his sone to erþe
B.15.559 An Aungel men herden an *heigh* at Rome crye,
B.16.118 That he was leche of lif and lord of *heigh* heuene.
B.19.191 Anoon after an *heigh* vp into heuene
B.20.116 And armede hym in ydelnesse and in *heigh* berynge.
C. 1.70   And ha[ls]ede here on þe *hey* name or she thennes [3ede]
C. 1.154 [That my3te] non Armure hit lette ne none *heye* walles.
C. 1.160 And in þe herte þer is þe hed and þe *heye* welle.
C. 2.30   Y ouhte ben *herrore* then he; y com of a bettre.
C. 2.84   Then for holynesse oþer hendenesse oþer for *hey* kynde.
C. 2.137 And se[t]he man may [o]n *heye* mede of god diserue
C. 4.113 And harlotes holynesse be an *heye* ferie;
C. 5.186 Lo! in heuene an *heyh* was an holy comune
C. 6.8   'Shal neuere *heyh* herte me hente, but holde me lowe
C. 6.124 Til y, wrathe, wexe an *hey* and walke with hem bothe;
C. 6.182 As wel fastyng dayes and frydayes and *heye* fest[e] euenes.
C. 6.297 [Ben] haldyng at þe *heye* dome to helpe þe restitue,
C. 6.347 For he shal onswerie for þe at the *hey* dome,
C. 7.249 To opene and vndo þe *hye* gate of heuene
C. 8.2   Ich haue an half aker to erye by þe *heye* [way];
C. 8.119 At *hey* prime [Peres] leet þe plouh stande
C. 8.137 Myhte helpe, as y hope; Ac *hey* treuthe wolde
C. 9.32   And brugges tobrokene by the *heye* wayes
C. 9.189 Ac Ermytes þat inhabiten by the *heye* weye
C. 9.202 Al they holy Ermytes were of *heye* kynne,
C. 9.204 Ac thise Ermytes þat edifien thus by the *heye* weye
C.11.102 And askede here þe *hey* way whare clergie dwelle;
C.11.104 'Aske þe *hey* wey,' [quod he], 'hennes to soffre-
C.12.41   'A saith soth,' quod scripture tho, and skypte an *heyh* and prechede.
C.13.68   That holde mote þe *hey* way, euene the ten hestes,
C.14.48   And riht as syht serueth a man to se [þe *hye* strete],

C.14.76   They helden hit an *hey* science here sotiltees to knowe,
C.14.84   For the *hey* holi gost heuene shal tocleue
C.14.135 Ac thogh th[at] theef hadde heuene he hadde noen *hey* blisse
C.15.65   For [this] doctour at þe *hey* deys dranke wyn [so] faste–
C.16.33   And lereth lewed and lered, *hey* and lowe to knowe
C.16.53   The *hey* way to heueneward he halt hit nat fol euene
C.16.237 In housynge, in helynge, in *h[eyh]* clergie schewynge
C.17.222 An angel men herde an *hye* at rome crye,
C.17.247 The whiche is þe *hy* holy gost þat out of heuene descendet[h]
C.17.262 For when þe *hye* kyng of heuene sente his so[n]e til erthe
C.18.105 And anoon he hihte Elde an *hy* for to clymbe
C.18.138 Til plenitudo temporis [h]y tyme aprochede,
C.21.191 Anoon aftur an *heyh* vp into heuene
C.22.116 And armed hym in ydelnesse and in *hey* berynge.

hei3 adv *heighe adv.* A 5 hei3 (1) hei3e (4); B 9 heighe (1) hei3 (1) hei3e (5) hye (1) hyeste (1); C 7 hey (2) heye (4) hye (1)

A. 1.148 To hem þat hongide him [*hei3e*] & his herte þirlide.
A. 2.56   Þus begynne þe gomes & gredde wel *hei3e;*
A. 3.47   'We haue a wyndowe [in] werching wile stonde vs wel *hei3e;*
A. 3.74   For tok h[y] on trewely h[y] tymbride not so *hei3e,*
A. 6.66   And hold wel þin haliday *hei3* til euen.
B. 1.174 To hem þat hengen hym *hei3* and his herte þirled.
B. 2.74   [Th]us bigynnen þ[e] gomes [and] greden [wel] *hei3e:*
B. 3.48   'We haue a wyndow in werchynge wole [stonden] vs [wel] *hye;*
B. 3.85   For toke þei on trewely þei tymbred nou3t so *hei3e,*
B. 5.579 And hold wel þyn haliday *heighe* til euen.
B.11.361 And who tau3te hem on trees to tymbre so *hei3e*
B.12.144 Ne of lordes þat were lewed men, but of þe *hyeste* lettred oute:
B.12.243 They may no3t flee fer ne ful *hei3e* neiþer];
B.18.312 First þoru3 þe we fellen fro heuene so *hei3*
C. 1.64   And afterward anhengede hym *hey* vppon an hellerne.
C. 1.170 To hem þat hengen [hym] *hye* and [his] herte thorlede.
C. 3.51   'We han a wyndowe awurchynge wol stande vs [wel] *heye;*
C. 3.84   For tok thei [o]n trewely they tymbred nat so *heye*
C. 6.238 Thow wolt be hanged *heye* þerfore, here oþer in helle.
C. 7.226 And hold wel þ[in] haliday *heye* til euen.
C.14.176 For þey may nat fle fer ne ful *hey* neyther

hei3liche adv *heighli adv.* A 2 hei3liche (1) hei3ly (1); B 2; C 3 heiliche (1) heyliche (2)

A. 7.296 But he be *hei3liche* hirid ellis wile he chide,
A.11.247 We be holde *hei3ly* to herie & honoure,
B. 6.312 But he be *hei3liche* hyred ellis wole he chide;
B.15.526 Holy chirche is honoured *hei3liche* þoru3 his deying;
C. 3.252 To helpe *heyliche* alle his oste or elles graunte
C. 8.89   Al þat they hoten, y hote; *heiliche* thow soffre hem
C. 8.334 But he be *heyliche* yhuyred elles wol he chy[d]e;

heyh > hei3; heihte > hote; heiliche > hei3liche

heyne n prop *n.i.d.* A 1; B 1
A. 5.91   & beholde how *heyne* haþ a newe cote;
B. 5.111 And biholde [how *H]eyne* haþ a newe cote;

heynesse > heighnesse

heir n *heir n.* A 5 eires (3) heires (2); B 8 heir (1) heires (7); C 9 ayr (1) ayres (3) eyer (1) eyres (2) heyres (2)

A. 2.67   Þei to haue & to holde & here *eires* aftir
A. 3.257 Þat god hati[de him for euere] & alle hise *heires* aftir.
A. 8.4   For hym & for hise *heires* eueremore aftir,
A. 9.80   Þat þe Erl auerous hadde, or his *eires,*
A.10.210 And þat ben fals folk, & fals *eires* also, foundlynges & [lei3eris],
B. 2.102 'And þei to haue and to holde, and hire *heires* after,
B. 3.279 That god hated hym for euere and alle hise *heires* after.
B. 5.262 Ne þyne *heires* after þee haue ioie of þat þow wynnest,
B. 7.4   For hym and for hise *heires* eueremoore after.
B. 8.89   That þe Erl Auarous [hadde, or] hise *heires,*
B.10.317 Litel hadde lordes to doon so 3yue lond from hire *heires*
B.15.323 To 3yue from youre *heires* þat youre Aiels yow lefte,
B.16.232 Hym or Ysaak myn *heir,* þe which he hi3te me kulle,
C. 3.322 Noyther [thei ne] here *ayres* hardy to claymen
C. 3.432 That god [hated hym] for euere and alle [his] *eyres* aftur.
C. 5.59   For hit ben *eyres* of heuene alle þat ben ycrouned
C. 5.163 Lytel hadde lordes ado 3eue lond fro [here] *heyres*
C. 6.255 Ne thyn *heyres,* as y hope, haue ioye of þat thow wonne
C. 9.4   For hym and [for] his *ayres* for euere to ben assoiled.
C.10.86   Þat þe Erl Auerous held and his *ayres*
C.10.241 The eritage þat þe *eyer* sholde haue is at þe kyngys wille.
C.18.245 He bihihte vs issue and *ayr* in oure olde age;

heyre n *here n.(2)* A 1 heire; B 1; C 1 hayre
A. 5.48   Heo shulde vnsewe hire serke & sette þere an *heire*
B. 5.65   She sholde vnsowen hir serk and sette þere an *heyre*
C. 6.6   A sholde vnsowen here serk and sette þe[r] an *hayre*

held > holden

helde v *helden v. &> holden* A 1
A.10.60 Þei *helde* ale in here hed til Inwyt be drenchit,

helden > holden

hele n *hele n.(3) &> heele,helen,helien* A 2; B 2; C 1
A. 8.178 I ne wolde ȝiue for þi patent on pye *hele*.
A.11.81 I wolde his eiȝen wern in his ars & his *hele* aftir
B. 7.200 I sette youre patentes and youre pardon at one pies *hele*.
B.10.128 I wolde his eiȝe were in his ers and his [*hele*] after,
C. 9.346 Y sette nat by pardon a pese ne nat a pye *hele*.

helen v *helen v.(1)* A 1 helide; B 8 heele (2) heeled (3) hele (1) helen (1) yheeled (1); C 5 hele (3) heled (1) helen (1)
A. 7.179 Hungir hem *helide* wiþ an hot[e] cake.
B. 6.192 That seten to begge siluer soone were þei *heeled*,
B. 9.206 To *helen* and to helpen, is dobest of alle.
B.14.97 That it neuere eft is sene ne soor, but semeþ a wounde *yheeled*.'
B.16.112 Ofte [he] *heeled* swiche; he held it for no maistrie
B.17.121 And hostele hem and *heele* þoruȝ holy chirche bileue
B.19.131 And alle he *heeled* and halp þat hym of grace askede;
B.20.282 Ben Curatours called to knowe and to hele,
B.20.356 'Thow art welcome', quod Conscience; 'kanstow *heele* sike?
C. 8.224 With houndes bred and hors breed *hele* hem when þei hungren
C.10.305 *Helen* and helpen, is dobest of alle.
C.21.282 And all he *heled* and halp þat hym of grace asked;
C.22.282 Ben curatours cald to knowe and to *hele*,
C.22.356 'Thow art welcome,' quod Consience; 'can[st] thow *hele* syke?'

helid > hiled; helide > helen

helien v *helen v.(2)* B 3 hele (2) helien (1); C 4 hele (2) helede (1) yheled (1)
B. 5.168 They hadde þanne ben Infamis, þei kan so yuele *hele* co[unseil].
B.12.231 And tauȝte hym and Eue to *helien* hem wiþ leues.
B.20.339 What hattestow, I praye þee? *hele* noȝt þi name.'
C. 7.237 And alle þe hous[es] been *yheled*, halles and chaumbres,
C. 9.157 And ouermore to [a]n [ha]tur to *hele* with his bonis
C.13.163 Hudden and *helede* here egges dernely
C.22.339 What hattest thow? y praye the, *hele* nat thy name.'

helyng ger *helinge ger.(1)* B 1
B.17.118 And Hope þe Hostile[r] shal þer [an *helyng* þe man lith];

helynge ger *heilinge ger.(2)* C 1
C.16.237 In housynge, in *helynge*, in h[eyh] clergie schewynge

helle n *helle n.* A 13; B 41; C 50 hell (2) helle (48)
A. 1.113 Out of heuene into *helle* hobelide þei faste,
A. 1.114 Summe in eir, summe in erþe, summe in *helle* depe.
A. 1.162 Chastite wiþoute charite worþ cheynide in *helle*;
A. 1.168 Such chastite wiþoute charite worþ cheynid in *helle*.
A. 1.172 Þ[at] is no treuþe of trinite but treccherie of *helle*,
A. 2.68 Wiþ alle þe purtenaunce of purcatorie into þe pyne of *helle*;
A. 3.119 Betwyn heuene & *helle*, & erþe þeiȝ men souȝte.
A. 5.240 To haue *helle* for euere ȝif þat hope nere.
A. 8.100 Þat aftir þi deþ day to *helle* shalt þou wende.'
A.10.177 Ellis shal alle diȝen & to *helle* wenden."
A.11.68 Þoruȝ whiche a werk & wille þei wenten to *helle*,
A.11.256 I shal punisshen in purcatory or in þe put of *helle*
A.11.271 And al holy chirche holden hem in *helle*.
B. 1.115 Into a deep derk *helle* to dwelle þere for euere;
B. 1.125 Somme in Eyr, somme in erþe, somme in *helle* depe.
B. 1.188 Chastite wiþouten charite worþ cheyned in *helle*;
B. 1.194 Swich chastite wiþouten charite worþ cheyned in *helle*.
B. 1.198 [Th]at is no truþe of þe Trinite but tricherie of *helle*,
B. 2.104 Wiþ alle þe [p]urtinaunces of Purgatorie into þe pyne of *helle*.
B. 3.130 Bitwene heuene and *helle*, [and] erþe þouȝ men souȝte.
B. 9.184 Fo[r] lecherie in likynge is lymeyerd of *helle*.
B.10.170 Thoruȝ whic[h werk and wil] þei wente to *helle*,
B.10.375 "I shal punysshe in purgatorie or in þe put of *helle*
B.10.391 And al holy chirche holdeþ hem boþe [in *helle*]!
B.11.140 'Ye? baw for bokes!' quod oon was broken out of *helle*.
B.11.144 That al þe clergie vnder crist ne myȝte me cracche fro *helle*,
B.11.164 Yblissed be truþe þat so brak *helle* yates,
B.12.210 And riȝt as Troianus þe trewe knyȝt [tilde] noȝt depe in *helle*
B.13.161 Ne neiþer hete ne hayl ne noon *helle* pouke,
B.13.428 Sauen þoruȝ hir sermo[n] mannes soule fram *helle*;
B.14.81 [So] thei sonken into *helle*, þe Citees echone.
B.14.122 Aungeles þat in *helle* now ben hadden ioye som tyme,
B.15.75 And of þe braunches þat burioneþ of hem and bryngen men to *helle*,
B.16.247 Thus haue I ben his heraud here and in *helle*
B.17.164 Heuene and *helle* and al þat is þerInne.
B.18.124 And which a light and a leme lay bifore *helle*.

B.18.146 Ne haue hem out of *helle*; hold þi tonge, mercy!
B.18.148 For þat is ones in *helle* out comeþ [it] neuere.
B.18.171 That ouerhoueþ *helle* þus; she vs shal telle.'
B.18.178 Adam and Eue and oþere mo in *helle*.
B.18.189 Leuestow þat yond light vnlouke myȝte *helle*
B.18.224 Boþe in heuene and in erþe, and now til *helle* he þenkeþ
B.18.249 Lo! *helle* myȝte nat holde, but opnede þo god þolede,
B.18.254 [And to haue out of *helle* alle þat hym likeþ].
B.18.262 A spirit spekeþ to *helle* and biddeþ vnspere þe yates:
B.18.266 Thanne sikede Sathan and seide to he[l]le,
B.18.315 And al oure lordshipe, I leue, a londe and [in *helle*]:
B.18.321 And wiþ þat breeþ *helle* brak with Belialles barres;
B.18.332 I bihiȝte hem noȝt here *helle* for euere.
B.18.372 And haue out of *helle* alle mennes soules.
B.18.396 Ac my rightwisnesse and right shul rulen al *helle*,
B.19.52 That he naroos and regnede and rauysshed *helle*,
B.19.56 [And took [Lucifer þe loþely] þat lord was of *helle*
B.20.270 Heuene haþ euene noumbre and *helle* is wiþoute noumbre.
C. 1.121 And *helle* is þer he is and [he] þere ybounde.
C. 1.127 Summe in erthe, summe in ayr, summe in *helle* depe.
C. 1.184 Chastite withouten charite worth c[h]eyned in *helle*;
C. 2.111 With alle þe [p]urtinaunc[e] of purgatorye and þe peyne of *helle*.'
C. 3.94 Here on this erthe or elles in *helle*,
C. 3.101 And haue here penaunce on puyre erthe and nat þe peyne of *helle*.
C. 3.167 Bytwene heuene and *helle*, and erthe thogh men soughte.
C. 3.328 And [soffrede] hym lyu[e] in mysbileue; y leue he be in *helle*.
C. 6.238 Thow wolt be hanged heye þerfore, here oþer in *helle*.
C. 6.338 Confessen hem and cryen hym mercy; shal neuere come in *helle*:
C. 7.88 Sauen thorw here sarmon mannes soule fram *helle*;
C. 7.133 Feddest tho with thy [fresshe] blood oure forfadres in *helle*:
C. 9.279 Purgatorie for thy paie O[r] perpetuel *helle*
C.10.285 That lecherye is a lykyng thynge, a lymȝerd of *helle*.
C.10.299 And after her deth day dwellen shollen in *helle*
C.11.198 'Go y to *helle* or to heuene y shal nat go myn one.
C.11.218 And holi churche, as y here, haldeth bothe in *helle*!
C.12.75 'Ȝe? bawe for bokes!' quod oen was broken out of *helle*.
C.12.79 That al þe cristendoem vnde[r] Crist ne myhte me crache fro [*helle*]
C.12.244 And he for his hard holdyng in *helle* parauntur:
C.14.149 And riht as troianes þe trewe knyhte [telde] nat depe in *helle*
C.14.193 Wher þey ben in *hell* or in heuene or Aristotel þe wyse.
C.15.163 Ne n[oþ]ere hete ne hayl ne *helle* pouke hym greue,
C.15.298 Angeles þat in *helle* now ben hadden som tyme ioye
C.15.300 And now he buyth hit bittere; he is a beggare of *helle*.
C.15.305 Then aren hit puyre pore thynges in purgatorie or in *hell*.
C.18.265 Thus haue y ben his heraud here and in *helle*
C.19.243 And dampned a dwelleth with þe deuel in *helle*.
C.19.246 And is in *helle* for al þat, how wol riche nouthe
C.20.127 And which a lihte and a leem lay bifore *helle*.
C.20.149 Ne haue hem out of *helle*; holde thy tonge, mercy!
C.20.151 [For] þat ones is in *helle* out cometh hit neuere.
C.20.174 That ouerhoueth *helle* thus; he vs shal telle.'
C.20.181 Adam and Eue and other mo in *helle*.
C.20.194 Leuest thow þat ȝone lihte vnlouke myhte *helle*
C.20.233 Bothe in heuene and in erthe, and now to *helle* he thenketh
C.20.258 Loo! *helle* myhte nat holde, bote opened tho god tholede
C.20.263 And to haue out [of *helle*] alle þat hym liketh.
C.20.270 A spirit speketh to *helle* and bit vnspere þe ȝates:
C.20.274 Thenne syhed satoun and saide to *helle*,
C.20.349 We haen ylost oure lordschipe a londe and in *helle*:
C.20.364 And with þat breth *helle* braek with belialles barres;
C.20.375 Y bihihte hem nat here *helle* for euere.
C.20.407 Ac thy drynke worth deth and depe *helle* thy bolle.
C.20.414 And haue out of *helle* alle mennes soules.
C.20.420 Shal neuere in *helle* eft come be he ones oute!
C.20.420 Ac my rihtwysnesse and rihte shal r[ul]en [al] *helle*
C.21.52 That he ne aroos and regnede and rauesschede *helle*.
C.21.56 And toek lucifer the loethliche þat lord was of *helle*
C.22.270 [Heuene haeth euene nombre and *helle* is withoute nombre].

hellerne > eller

helleward adv *OED hellward, MED helle n.* B 1; C 1 hellward
B.18.114 Cam walkynge in þe wey; to *helleward* she loked.
C.20.117 Cam walkynge in þe way; to *hellward* she lokede.

helm n *helm n.* B 1; C 1
B.18.23 In his *helm* and in his haubergeon, humana natura;
C.20.22 In his *helm* and in his haberion, humana natura;

help n *help n. &> helpen* A 4 help (2) helpe (2); B 17 help (13) helpe (3) helpes (1); C 17 helpe
A. 6.122 And þoruȝ *helpe* of hem [two], hope þou non oþer,
A. 9.41 Þat is charite þe champioun, chief *helpe* aȝens synne.
A.10.49 Inwyt in þe heuid is, & an *help* to þe soule,

A.11.301 Þe *help* of þe holy gost to answere hem [alle]'.
B. 4.125 Hire haukes and hire houndes *help* to pouere Religious;
B. 5.637 And þoruȝ *help* of hem two, hope þow noon oþer,
B. 6.244 "He þat haþ shal haue and *helpe* þere [nede is]
B. 8.45   [Th]at is charite þe champion, chief *help* ayein synne.
B.10.244 Thoruȝ þe *help* of þe holy goost þe which is of boþe;
B.11.219 Thanne is bileue a lele *help*, aboue logyk or lawe.
B.13.398 Than in þe grace of god and hise grete *helpes*:
B.14.256 That god is his grettest *help* and no gome ellis,
B.15.196 'Wiþouten *help* of Piers Plowman', quod he, 'his persone sestow neuere.'
B.16.52   And *help* of þe holy goost, and þus haue I þe maistrie.'
B.17.59   And as naked as a nedle and noon *help* aboute.
B.17.93   'Haue hem excused', quod he; 'hir *help* may litel auaille.
B.18.139 That man shal man saue þoruȝ a maydenes *helpe*,
B.18.399 And nameliche at swich a nede þer nedes *help* bihoueþ:
B.19.388 In *help* of hir heele ones in a Monþe,
B.19.472 And holy chirches chief *help* and Chieftayn of þe comune,
B.20.169 And lif fleiȝ for feere to phisik after *helpe*
C. 3.245 For þat [is] conquere[d] thorw a comune *helpe*, a kyndom or ducherie,
C. 3.338 And ayther is otheres *helpe*; of hem cometh retribucoun
C. 4.68   And for to haue here *helpe* handy dandy payde.
C. 6.169 And bad hym bid to god be his *helpe* to amende.
C. 7.290 And thorw þe *help[e]* of hem two, hope þou non oþer,
C. 8.255 "He þat hath shal haue and *helpe* þer hym liketh
C.11.44   God is nat in þat hoem ne his *helpe* nother.
C.15.236 Tho[r]w the *helpe* of hym þat me hyder sente;'
C.16.96   That god is his gretteste *helpe* and no gome elles
C.17.185 Holy men, as y hope, thorw *helpe* of the holy goste
C.19.58   And as naked as an nedle and noen *helpe* abouten.
C.19.83   'Haue hem excused,' quod [t]he samaritaen; 'here *helpe* may nat availe.
C.20.142 [That man shal man saue thorw a maydenes *helpe*
C.20.442 And namliche at such a nede þat nedes *helpe* asketh:
C.21.388 In *helpe* of here hele ones in a monthe
C.21.472 And holy churche cheef *helpe* and cheuenteyn of þe comu[n]e,
C.22.169 And lyf fley for fere to fisyk aftur *helpe*

helpe > help,helpen; helpeles > helplees

helpen v *helpen* v. A 38 halpe (1) helpe (27) helpen (3) helpiþ (5) holpen (2); B 86 halp (2) help (4) helpe (56) helpen (3) helpeþ (11) holpe (4) holpen (5) yholpe (1); C 86 halp (1) halpe (1) helpe (67) helpen (4) helpeth (8) holpe (3) holpen (1) yholpe (1)

A.Pr.73   Þus [ȝe gyuen ȝoure] gold glotonis to *helpe*
A. 1.17   And þerfore he hiȝte þe erþe to *helpe* ȝow ichone
A. 3.8   I wile forgyue hire þe gilt, so me god *helpe*.'
A. 3.164 Þere þat meschief is gret mede may *helpe*.
A. 3.191 And ek king of þat kiþ his kyn for to *helpe*,
A. 3.229 And he þat gripiþ here giftes, so me god *helpe*,
A. 4.11   And counte wiþ [þe] consience, so me crist *helpe*,
A. 4.60   Wrong þanne on wysdom wepi[de] hym to *helpe*,
A. 4.124 Ne gete my grace þoruȝ giftes, so me god *helpe*!
A. 5.22   Ac I shal seiȝe as I saiȝ, so me god *helpe*,
A. 5.122 It hadde be vnsold þis seue ȝer, so me god *helpe*.
A. 6.22   'Nay, so [me god] *helpe*,' seide þe [gome] þanne.
A. 6.108 Pacience & pees mekil [peple] þei *helpen*,
A. 6.110 Ac whoso is sib to þis sistris, so me god *helpe*,
A. 7.22   *Helpiþ* hem werche wiȝtly þat wynne ȝoure foode.'
A. 7.59   And whoso *helpiþ* me to eren, or any þing swynke,
A. 7.96   And *helpe* my cultir to kerue & close þe forewis.'
A. 7.98   To erien þis half akir *helpen* hym manye;
A. 7.108 And *holpen* [to] ere þe half akir wiþ 'hey trolly lolly'.
A. 7.131 Þei shuln ete as good as I, so me god *helpe*,
A. 7.195 And *helpe* hem of alle þing [aftir] þat hem nedi[þ].
A. 7.228 "He þat haþ shal haue to *helpe* þere nede is,
A. 7.229 And he þat nouȝt haþ shal nouȝt haue ne no man him *helpe*
A. 8.6   And [alle] þat *holpen* to erien or to sowen,
A. 8.7   Or any maner mester þat miȝte peris *helpen*,
A. 8.23   And for þei swere be here soule, & so god muste hem *helpe*,
A. 8.28   And make mesonis deux þerewiþ myseis[e] to *helpe*,
A. 8.177 And haue indulgence doublefold, but dowel þe *helpe*
A. 9.40   Ac dedly synne doþ he nouȝt, for dowel hym *helpiþ*,
A. 9.78   Whiles he haþ ouȝt of his owene he *helpiþ* þere nede is;
A. 9.102 'Ac ȝet sauouriþ me nouȝt þi segging, so me god *helpe*;
A.10.69   Þanne is holichirche owyng to *helpe* hem & saue
A.10.194 Þeiȝ þei don hem to dunmowe, but ȝif þe deuil *helpe*
A.11.31   For ȝif harlotrie ne *halp[e]* hem betere, haue god my trouþe,
A.11.227 *Helpiþ* nouȝt to heuene[ward] at one ȝeris ende,
A.11.251 And siþen he[þen] to *helpe* in hope hem to amende.
A.11.304 Seide þis for a sarmoun, so me god *helpe*:
A.12.65   [To kyllyn him ȝif I can, þei kynde wit *helpe*].
B.Pr.76   Thus [ye] gyuen [youre] gold glotons to [*helpe*]

B. 1.17   And þerfore he hiȝte þe erþe to *helpe* yow echone
B. 3.8   I wol forgyuen hire þ[e] gilt, so me god *helpe*.'
B. 3.177 Ther þat meschief is [most] Mede may *helpe*.
B. 3.204 And [ek] kyng of þat kiþ his kyn for to *helpe*,
B. 3.242 And alle þat *helpen* þe Innocent and holden with þe riȝtfulle,
B. 3.243 Wiþouten Mede doþ hem good and þe truþe *helpeþ*
B. 3.250 And he þat gripeþ hir [giftes], so me god *helpe*,
B. 4.11   And acounte wiþ þee, Conscience, so me crist *helpe*,
B. 4.104 'Nay', quod þe kyng, 'so me crist *helpe*,
B. 4.141 Ne gete my grace [þoruȝ] giftes, so me god [*helpe*]!
B. 5.22   Ac I shal seye as I sauȝ, so me god *helpe*,
B. 5.206 It hadde ben vnsold þis seuen yer, so me god *helpe*.
B. 5.275 [Is] holden at þe heiȝe doom to *helpe* þee to restitue,
B. 5.369 Sworen goddes soule [and his sydes] and "so me god *helpe*"
B. 5.429 If any man dooþ me a bienfait or *helpeþ* me at nede
B. 5.622 Pacience and pees muche peple þei *helpeþ*;
B. 5.624 Heo haþ *holpe* a þousand out of þe deueles punfolde.
B. 5.625 A[c] who is sib to þise [sustren], so me god *helpe*,
B. 6.20   *Helpeþ* hym werche wiȝtliche þat wynneþ youre foode.'
B. 6.65   And whoso *helpeþ* me to erie [or any þyng swynke]
B. 6.104 And *helpe* my cultour to kerue and [close] þe furwes.'
B. 6.106 To erie þis half acre *holpen* hym manye;
B. 6.116 And *holpen* ere þ[e] half acre wiþ 'how trolly lolly'.
B. 6.137 [Thei] shal ete [as good as I, so me god *helpe*],
B. 6.142 Or *helpe* make morter or bere Muk afeld.
B. 6.209 And *helpen* hem of alle þyng [after þat] hem nedeþ.
B. 6.245 And he þat noȝt haþ shal noȝt haue and no man hym *helpe*,
B. 7.6   And alle þat *holpen* to erye or to sowe,
B. 7.7   Or any [maner] mestier þat myȝte Piers [*helpe*],
B. 7.21   And for þei swere by hir soule and so god moste hem *helpe*
B. 7.26   And [make] Mesondieux þer[wiþ] myseise [to] *helpe*,
B. 7.43   Pledours sholde peynen hem to plede for swiche and *helpe*;
B. 7.55   Thise ben truþes tresores trewe folk to *helpe*,
B. 7.71   Anoþer that were moore nedy; so þe nedieste sholde be *holpe*.
B. 7.199 And haue Indulgences doublefold, but dowel [þee] *helpe*
B. 8.44   Ac dedly synne doþ he noȝt for dowel hym [*helpeþ*],
B. 8.87   [Whiles he haþ ouȝt of his owene he *helpeþ* þer nede is];
B. 8.112 'Ac yet sauoreþ me noȝt þi seying, [so me god *helpe*!
B. 9.38   My myȝt moot *helpe* forþ wiþ my speche".
B. 9.69   [Holy chirche is owynge to *helpe* hem and saue,
B. 9.79   Shul [purchace] penaunce in purgatorie but þei hem *helpe*.
B. 9.88   Eyþer of hem *helpeþ* ooþer of þat þat h[y]m nedeþ,
B. 9.115 The wif was maad þe w[y]e for to *helpe* werche,
B. 9.173 [Th]ouȝ þei do hem to Dunmowe, but if þe deuel *helpe*
B. 9.206 To helen and to *helpen*, is dobest of alle.
B.10.46   Ne [*holpe* hir] harlotrye, haue god my trouþe,
B.10.339 *Helpeþ* noȝt to heueneward [at] oone [y]eris ende,
B.10.369 And siþen heþen to *helpe* in hope of amendement.
B.11.184 And [soureynly] pouere peple; hir preieres maye vs *helpe*.
B.11.211 And euery man *helpe* ooþer for hennes shul we alle:
B.11.221 Is litel alowaunce maad, but if bileue hem *helpe*;
B.13.10   But quik he biqueþe [hem] auȝt [or sholde *helpe*] quyte hir dettes;
B.13.12   And how þat lewed men ben lad, but oure lord hem *helpe*,
B.13.205 'That is sooþ', [seide] Conscience, 'so me god *helpe*.
B.13.389 So if I kidde any kyndenesse myn euencristen to *helpe*
B.13.407 The whiche is sleuþe so slow þat may no sleiȝtes *helpe* it,
B.14.203 The fend folweþ hem alle and fondeþ hem to *helpe*,
B.15.134 So harlotes and hores arn *holpe* wiþ swiche goodes
B.15.158 I seiȝ neuere swich a man, so me god *helpe*,
B.15.337 And *helpeþ* hem þat helpeþ yow and ȝyueþ þer no nede is,
B.15.337 And *helpeþ* hem þat *helpeþ* yow and ȝyueþ þer no nede is,
B.16.26   And in blowyng tyme abite þe floures but if þise piles *helpe*.
B.16.124 Youre bodies, youre beestes, and blynde men *holpen*,
B.17.48   Go þi gate!' quod I to Spes, 'so me god *helpe*,
B.17.58   Ne *helpe* hymself sooþly, for semyvif he semed,
B.17.63   How he wiþ Moyses maundement hadde many men *yholpe*,
B.17.196 In many kynnes maneres I myghte myself *helpe*,
B.17.258 The holy goost hereþ þee noȝt ne *helpe* may þee by reson.
B.17.289 [How myȝte he aske mercy, or any mercy hym *helpe*],
B.17.315 Good hope, þat *helpe* sholde, to wanhope torneþ.
B.18.54   And [seide], 'if þat þow sotil be [þiselue] now [þow *help*].
B.18.200 That hir peyne be perpetuel and no preiere hem *helpe*.
B.18.398 For I were an vnkynde kyng but I my kynde *helpe*,
B.19.131 And alle he heeled and *halp* þat hym of grace askede;
B.19.212 And cride wiþ Conscience, '*help* vs, [crist], of grace!'
B.19.220 And acombre þee, Conscience, but if crist þee *helpe*.
B.19.366 In *helpe* holy chirche and hem þat it kepeþ.
B.19.374 That he ne *halp* a quantite holynesse to wexe,
B.19.404 Vnblessed artow, Brewere, but if þee god *helpe*.
B.19.428 Inparfit is þat pope þat al [peple] sholde *helpe*
B.20.88   There was 'harrow!' and '*help*! here comeþ kynde
B.20.228 Conscience cryede, '*help*, Clergie or I falle

B.20.230 Freres herden hym crye and comen hym to *helpe*,
B.20.375 Conscience cryed eft [Clergie to *helpe*],
C.Pr.74 Thus ȝe gyue ȝoure gold glotons to *helpe*
C. 1.17 Wherfore he hette þe elementis to *helpe* ȝow alle tymes
C. 2.38 That *helpeth* man moste to heuene mede most letteth.
C. 3.8 Y wol forgyue here alle gultes, so me god *helpe*.'
C. 3.209 Han almest mad, but marye the *helpe*,
C. 3.223 Ther þat meschief is greet mede may *helpe*;
C. 3.352 To *helpe* heyliche alle his oste or elles graunte
C. 3.261 And also kyng of þat kuth his kyn for to *helpe*,
C. 3.445 Tho shal be maistres on molde trewe men to *helpe*.
C. 4.11 And acounte with the, Consience, so me Crist *helpe*,
C. 4.176 Quod Consience to þe kyng, 'withoute þe comune *helpe*
C. 4.192 To wage thyn and *helpe* wynne þat thow wilnest aftur
C. 5.22 'Sertes,' y sayde, 'and so me god *helpe*,
C. 5.48 Th[u]s y s[yn]ge for here soules of suche as me *helpeth*
C. 6.84 For god ne goddes word ne gras ne *helpe*
C. 6.214 Hit hadde be vnsold this seuene ȝer, so me god *helpe*.
C. 6.297 [Ben] haldyng at the heye dome to *helpe* the restitue.
C. 6.299 Shal parte with the in purgatorye and *helpe* paye thy dette
C. 6.427 Sworn godes soule and his sides and "so *helpe* [me] god almyhty"
C. 7.42 Yf eny man do[th] me a beenfeet or *helpeth* me at nede
C. 7.179 'Nay, so me god [h]*elpe*,' sayde þe gome thenne.
C. 7.274 Pacience and pees muche peple þei *helpe*,
C. 7.276 Noen of hem alle *helpe* may in betere
C. 7.278 And ho is sib to þis seuene, so me god *helpe*,
C. 8.18 *Helpeth* hym worche wi[ȝt]liche þat wynneth ȝoure fode.'
C. 8.65 And *helpe* my Coltur to kerue and cl[o]se þe forwes;
C. 8.66 And alle þat *helpen* me [to] erye or elles to wedy
C. 8.113 To erien this half ak[er] *holpen* hym monye;
C. 8.123 And *holpe* erye this half aker with 'hey trollilolly.'
C. 8.137 Myhte *helpe*, as y hope; Ac hey treuthe wolde
C. 8.218 And *helpe* hem of alle thyng ay as hem nedeth.
C. 8.232 In meschief or in malese, and thow mowe hem *helpe*,
C. 8.256 And he þat nauht hath shal nauht haue and no man [hym *helpen*]
C. 9.6 And alle þat *holpe* hym to erye, to sette or to sowe
C. 9.25 And for they sw[e]re by here soule and [so] god mote hem *helpe*
C. 9.33 Amende in som manere wyse and ma[y]dones *helpe*;
C. 9.96 These are Almusse to *helpe* þat han suche charges
C. 9.125 We sholde [haue] hem to house and *helpe* hem when they come:
C. 9.135 Welcomen and worschipen and with ȝoure goed *helpen*
C. 9.345 And haue indulgences doublefold, but dowel vs *helpe*
C.10.43 So dedly synne doth he nat for dowel hym *helpeth*.
C.10.84 And *helpeth* alle men of þat he may spare.
C.10.185 And holy churche *helpe* to, so sholde no man begge
C.10.189 Oure enemyes enterely and *helpe* hem at here nede.
C.10.275 Thogh they [do] hem to donemowe, bote þe deuel *helpe*
C.10.305 Helen and *helpen*, is dobest of alle.
C.11.26 Harlotes for here harlotrye aren *holpe* ar nedy pore;
C.11.28 *Helpe* hym þat hath nauhte men tho that haen no nede.
C.11.185 The man þat me liketh to *helpe* myhte nat myshappe.'
C.12.100 And nameliche pore peple, here preeyeres may vs *helpe*
C.12.118 And euery man *helpe* other for hennes shal we alle
C.13.131 Til þat kynde cam clergie to *helpe*
C.14.15 And þat is dobet, yf eny suche be, a blessed man þat *helpeth*
C.14.21 And holy chirche horen *helpe*, Auero[s] and coueytous,
C.14.55 To v[n]louken hit at here lykynge the lewed to *helpe*,
C.15.12 Bote quyke he byqu[e]th hem auht or wolde *helpe* quyte here
dettes;
C.15.15 And how þat lewede men ben lad, but oure lord hem *helpe*,
C.15.22 That iustus bifore iesu in die iudicij non saluabitur bote vix *helpe*;
C.15.222 And thenne wolde y be bysy and buxum to *helpe*
C.16.44 The fend followeth hem alle and fondeth hem to *helpe*
C.17.60 To *helpe* thy fader formost byfore freres or monkes
C.17.62 *Helpe* thy kyn, Crist bid, for þer [coms]eth charite
C.17.64 And þer *helpe* yf thow has[t]; and þat halde y charite.
C.18.13 Of holynesse, of hendenesse, of *helpe*-hym-þat-nedeth,
C.19.46 'Go thy gate!' quod y to spes; 'so me god *helpe*,
C.19.57 Ne *helpe* hymsulue sothly for semyuief he semede
C.19.62 How he with Moyses maundement hadde mony men *yholpe*
C.19.140 Ne holde ne *helpe* ne hente þat he louede:
C.19.162 In many kyne manere y myhte mysulfe *helpe*,
C.19.224 The holy goest hereth the nat ne *helpeth* the, be thow certeyne.
C.20.54 And saiden, 'yf he sotil be hymsulue now he wol *helpe*;'
C.20.205 That her peyne [be] perpetuel [and] no preyer hem *helpe*.
C.20.441 For y were an vnkynde kyng bote y my kyn *helpe*
C.21.131 And all he heled and *halp* þat hym of grace asked,
C.21.212 And criden with Consience, '*helpe* vs, [Crist], of grace!'
C.21.220 And acombre þe, Consience, bote yf Crist the *helpe*.
C.21.366 To *helpe* holi churche and hem þat hit kepeth.
C.21.374 That he ne *halpe* a qua[n]tite holinesse to wexe,

C.21.404 Vnblessed art thow, breware, but yf the god *helpe*.
C.21.428 Inparfit is þat pope þat all peple sholde *helpe*
C.22.88 There was 'harow!' and '*helpe*! here cometh kynde
C.22.228 Consience cryede, '*helpe*, Clergie, or y falle
C.22.230 Freres herde hym crye and comen hym to *helpe*
C.22.375 Consience cryede efte clergie [to] *helpe*

helplees adj *helples adj.* A 1 helpeles; B 3 helplees (2) helplese (1); C 1
helples
A. 8.82 Ac olde men & hore þat *helpeles* ben of strengþe,
B. 7.100 Ac olde men and hore þat *helpeles* ben of strengþe,
B. 9.72 Madde men and maydenes þat *helplese* were;
B.15.458 It is heþene as to heueneward and *helplees* to þe soule.
C. 9.176 Ac olde [men] and hore þat *helples* ben and nedy

helþe n *helthe n.* B 7; C 3 helthe
B.10.257 [So] is dobet to suffre for þ[i] soules *helþe*
B.11.230 And as Seint Gregorie seide, for mannes soule *helþe*
B.12.2 Thouȝ I sitte by myself in siknesse n[e] in *helþe*.
B.12.39 Seke þow neuere Seint ferþer for no soule *helþe*.
B.14.285 And Ioye to pacient pouere], pure spiritual *helþe*,
B.14.301 The fifte is moder of [myȝt and of mannes] *helþe*,
B.20.332 'In faiþ', quod þis frere, 'for profit and for *helþe*
C. 7.176 [And] souht gode seyntes for my soule *helthe*.'\
C.16.137 [The fifte is] moder of myhte and of mannes *helthe*
C.22.332 'In fayth,' quod this frere, 'for profyt and for *helthe*

hem > hij

hemself pron *hemself pron.* A 5 hemself (1) hemselue (3) hemseluen (1);
B 20 hemself (7) hemselue (11) hemseluen (2); C 15 hemself (1)
hemsulue (12) hemsuluen (2)
A. 4.28 For to saue *hemself* from shame & from harm.
A. 4.107 Til prestis here prechyng preue it *hemselue*,
A. 5.12 And preyede þe peple haue pite on *hemselue*,
A. 5.35 þat þei preche þe peple preue it *hemselue*,
A. 5.175 And preisiden þe peneworthis [aparte] be *hemseluen*.
B. 4.31 For to saue *hem[seluen]* from shame and from harmes.
B. 4.40 Forþi, Reson, lat hem ride þo riche by *hemselue*,
B. 4.122 And til prechours prechynge be preued on *hemselue*;
B. 5.326 And preised þ[e] penyworþes apart by *hemselue*.
B. 9.118 And siþenes by assent of *hemself* as þei two myȝte acorde;
B.10.40 Ayein þe lawe of oure lord, and lyen on *hemselue*,
B.10.268 Alle þat lakkeþ any lif and lakkes han *hemselue*:
B.10.404 As þei seyen *hemself* selde doon þerafter:
B.11.179 Loue hir eyþer ooþer, and lene hem as *hemselue*.
B.11.182 [Hir euencristene as *hemself*] and hir enemyes after.
B.11.339 Males drowen hem to males [al mornyng] by *hemselue*,
B.12.78 [For] þoruȝ caractes þat crist wroot þe Iewes knewe *hemselue*
B.12.122 Ne sette short bi hir science, whatso þei don *hemselue*.
B.14.78 For [men] mesured noȝt *hemself* of [mete] and dr[y]nke,
B.15.274 Monkes and mendinauntȝ, men by *hemselue*
B.15.303 And on *hemself* som, and swiche as ben hir laborers,
B.15.597 And studieden to struyen hym and struyden *hemselue*,
B.17.167 And aren serel[e]pes by *hemself*; asondry were þei neuere;
B.18.306 To saue men from synne if *hemself* wolde.
B.19.149 The knyghtes þat kepten it biknewe *hemseluen*
C.Pr.135 And power presumen in *hemself* a pope to make
C. 3.335 On a sad and a siker semblable to *hemsuluen*.
C. 3.384 For they wilnen and wolden as beste were for *hemsulue*
C. 5.165 In many places ther thei persones ben, be *hemsulue* at ese,
C. 6.384 And preisede th[e] penworthis apart by *hemsulue*
C. 9.77 And *hemsulue* also soffre muche hungur
C.10.163 A[s] somme hangeth *hemsulue* and oþerwhile adrencheth.
C.13.147 Males drow hem to males a[l mour]nynge by *hemsulue*
C.13.208 And if creatures cristene coude make *hemsulue*
C.14.65 Ne sette shorte by here science, whatso þei doen *hemsulue*.
C.14.72 Kynde wittede men [c]an a clergie by *hemsulue*;
C.17.7 Solitarie by *hemsulue* in here selles lyuede
C.17.132 Iewes and gentel sarresines iugen *hemsulue*
C.17.305 And studeden to struye hym and struyden *hemsulue*
C.21.149 The knyhtes þat kepten hit biknewen *hemsuluen*

hende adj *hende adj.* A 2; B 6; C 6
A. 2.52 At bedde & at boord buxum and *hende*,
A.10.19 Sire se wel, & sey wel, & here wel þe *hende*,
B. 5.258 'I am holden', quod he, 'as *hende* as hound is in kichene,
B. 9.20 Sire Se-wel, and Sey-wel, and here-wel þe *hende*,
B.15.216 For charite is goddes champion, and as a good child *hende*,
B.20.188 Haddestow be *hende*', quod I, 'þow woldest haue asked leeue.'
B.20.348 *Hende* speche heet pees, 'opene þe yates.
B.20.354 Thus þoruȝ *hende* speche [þe frere entred]
C. 8.47 Hit bicometh to the, knyhte, to be corteys and *hende*,
C.10.146 Sire se-wel and sey-wel [and] here-wel þe [h]*ende*,
C.11.42 Is non so *hende* to haue hym [in] but hote hym go þer god is.

C.22.188 Haddest thow be *hende*,' quod y, 'thow wost haue asked leue.'
C.22.348 *Hende* speche heet pees, 'opene the 3ates.
C.22.354 Thus thorw *hende* speche [the frere entred]

hendely *adv* *hendeli adv.* A 3; B 4 hendely (2) hendeliche (1) hendiliche (1); C 4 hendely (1) hendeliche (2) hendly (1)
A.3.28   *Hendely* þanne heo behi3te hem þe same,
A.5.82   I hailside hym as *hendely* as I his frend were:
A.9.10   I hailside hem *hendely* as I hadde ylernid,
B.3.29   *Hendiliche* heo þanne bihi3te hem þe same,
B.5.102   I hailse[d] hym *hendely* as I his frend were:
B.8.10   I hailsed hem *hendely* as I hadde ylerned,
B.16.98   And seide *hendeliche* to hym, 'lo me his handmaiden
C.3.30   And Mede *hendeliche* behyhte hem þe same,
C.10.10   Y haylsede hem *hendly* as y hadde ylered
C.18.131 And saide *hendely* to hym, 'lo me his hondmayden
C.18.183 'Of whennes artow?' quod y, and *hendeliche* hym grette.

hendenesse *n hendinesse n.* B 2; C 5
B.19.31   And of hardynesse of herte and of *hendenesse*,
B.20.145 And heeld holynesse a Iape and *hendenesse* a wastour,
C.2.84   Then for holynesse oþer *hendenesse* oþer for hey kynde,
C.11.13   More then holynesse or *hendenesse* or al þat seyntes techeth.
C.18.13   Of holynesse, of *hendenesse*, of helpe-hym-þat-nedeth,
C.21.31   And of hardinesse of herte and of *hendenesse*
C.22.145 And helde holinesse a iape and *hendenesse* a wastour

hendeþ *v henden v.* A 1
A.12.67   'I wolde folwe þe fayn, but fentesye me *hendeþ*;

hendiliche hendly > hendely; heng(- > hangen; henis > hennes

henne *adv henne adv.* A 2; B 1
A.4.153   Ac redily, resoun, þou shalt not [raike] *henne*,
A.8.81   Þat euere he was man wrou3t whanne he shal *henne* fare.
B.4.190   Ac redily, Reson, þow shalt no3t [raike *henne*];

hennes *adv hennes adv.* A 8 henis (3) hennes (2) hennis (3); B 21; C 20
A.1.152   3e shuln be wei3e þerwiþ whanne 3e wende *hennes*.
A.3.98   *Henis* to þi deþ day do þou so no more.
A.5.230   Þat iche man shal haue his er I *hennis* wende,
A.7.262   'I behote god,' quaþ hunger, '*henis* nile I wende
A.8.18   Han pardoun wiþ þe apostlis whanne þei passe *hennis*,
A.8.181   Þat god 3iue vs grace er we go *hennis*
A.10.1   'Sire dowel dwelliþ,' quaþ wyt, 'nou3t a day *hennes*,
A.11.114 'Axe þe hei3e wey,' quaþ heo, 'from *henis* to suffre
B.1.178   Ye shulle ben weyen þerwiþ whan ye wenden *hennes*:
B.3.109   *Hennes* to þi deeþ day do [þow] so na moore.
B.3.245   Of god at a gret nede whan þei gon *hennes*.
B.5.458   That ech man shal haue his er I *hennes* wende;
B.6.278   '[I] bihote god', quod hunger, '*hennes* [nil] I wende
B.7.58   Hi[s] pardon is [wel] petit at hi[s] partyng *hennes*
B.7.99   That euere [he was man] wro3t whan [he] shal *hennes* fare.
B.7.203   That god gyue vs grace er we go *hennes*
B.9.1   'SIre Dowel dwelleþ', quod Wit, 'no3t a day *hennes*
B.10.162 'Aske þe heighe wey', quod she, '*hennes* to Suffre-
B.10.469 And passen Purgatorie penauncelees at hir *hennes* partyng
B.11.211 And euery man helpe ooþer for *hennes* shul we alle:
B.14.165 Heuene after hir *hennes* goyng þat here han swich defaute.
B.18.164 Out of þe nyppe of þe North no3t ful fer *hennes*
B.18.272 That swich a lord and [a] light sholde lede hem alle *hennes*.'
B.18.309 I rede we fle', quod [þe fend], 'faste alle *hennes*,
B.18.400 Thus by lawe', quod oure lord, 'lede I wole fro *hennes*
B.19.61   Places in Paradis at hir partynge *hennes*
B.19.248 And some he lered to lyue in longynge to ben *hennes*,
B.19.320 And ordeyne þat hous er ye *hennes* wende.'
B.20.203 Awreke me if youre wille be for I wolde be *hennes*.'
C.1.174   3e shal be weye þerwith whenne 3e wende *hennes*:
C.4.184   Forthy, resoun, redyly thow shalt nat ryden *hennes*
C.5.35   'When y [3ut] 3ong was, many 3er *hennes*,
C.5.80   Lyfholynesse and loue hath be longe *hennes*
C.6.312   That eche man shal haue his ar y *hennes* wende
C.8.300   'Y behote the,' quod hunger, 'þat *hennes* ne wol y wende
C.9.53   His pardoun is ful petyt at his partynge *hennes*
C.9.349   That god gyue vs grace here ar we go *hennes*
C.10.128 'Sire dowel dwelleth,' quod wit, 'nat a day *hennes*
C.11.104 'Aske þe hey wey,' [quod he], '*hennes* to soffre-
C.12.118 And euery man helpe other for *hennes* shal we alle
C.16.161 Shal be porest of power at his partynge *hennes*.'
C.20.167 Out of þe nype of þe north nat ful fer *hennes*
C.20.280 That such a lord and a lihte sh[olde] lede hem alle *hennes*.
C.20.343 Y rede we flee,' quod the fende, 'faste all *hennes*
C.20.443 Thus by lawe,' quod oure lord, 'lede y wol fro *hennes*
C.21.61   Places in paradys at here partyng *hennes*
C.21.248 And somme he [l]ered to lyue in longyng to be *hennes*,
C.21.320 And ordeyne þat hous ar 3e *hennes* wende.'

C.22.203 Awreke me 3if 3oure wille be for y wolde be *hennes*.'

hente *v henten v.* A 4 hente (3) henten (1); B 10 hente (9) henten (1); C 9 hente (7) henten (2)
A.5.5   Er I hadde faren a furlong feyntise me *h[ent]e*
A.5.50   'Shal neuere hei3 herte me *hente*, but holde me lowe
A.7.159   Hungir in haste þanne *hente* wastour be þe mawe,
A.7.175   [A]n he[p] of heremites *henten* hem spadis,
B.5.5   Ac er I hadde faren a furlong feyntise me *hente*
B.5.67   'Shal neuere hei3 herte me *hente*, but holde me lowe
B.5.506   Thanne *hente* hope an horn of Deus tu conuersus viuificabis [nos]
B.6.174   Hunger in haste þoo *hente* wastour by þe [mawe]
B.6.187   An heep of heremytes *henten* hem spades
B.14.36   'No?' quod Pacience paciently, and out of his poke *hente*
B.14.48   [Th]at pacience so preisede, [and of his poke *hente*]
B.14.240 And by þe nekke namely hir noon may *hente* ooþer;
B.20.167 And Elde *hente* good hope and hastiliche he shifte hym
B.20.180 And in hope of his heele good herte he *hente*
C.6.8   'Shal neuere heyh herte me *hente*, but holde me lowe
C.7.151   Thenne *hente* [hope] an horn of deus tu conuersus viuificabis nos
C.8.171   Hunger in haste tho *hente* wastour be þe mawe
C.8.183   An heep of Eremytes *henten* hem spades,
C.15.246 '3e!' quod pacience [paciently], and oute of his poke *hente*
C.16.80   And by þe nekke namelyche here noen may *henten* other;
C.19.140 Ne holde ne helpe ne *hente* þat he louede:
C.22.167 And elde *hente* gode hope and hastiliche [he] sh[ifte] hym
C.22.180 And in hope of his hele goed herte he *hente*

heo *pron he pron.(2) cf she* A 137 he (1) heo (42) her (1) here (3) hire (86) hure (4); B 160 heo (9) here (1) hir (37) hire (113); C 223 a (12) he (44) hee (1) her (9) here (157)

a C 12 *&> he*
C.2.17, C.2.149, C.2.254, C.3.115, C.3.180, C.3.181, C.3.217, C.3.494, C.5.135, C.6.6, C.6.225, C.7.304

he A 1
A.5.113

he C 44
C.1.68, C.2.23, C.2.30, C.2.171, C.3.161, C.3.165, C.3.165, C.3.173, C.3.174, C.3.175, C.3.182, C.3.183, C.3.185, C.3.187, C.3.188, C.3.188, C.3.194, C.3.201, C.3.203, C.3.205, C.3.408, C.6.4, C.6.135, C.6.136, C.6.136, C.6.223, C.6.226, C.6.233, C.7.252, C.7.253, C.7.301, C.10.259, C.10.261, C.10.265, C.11.95, C.11.104, C.11.111, C.11.169, C.12.46, C.20.154, C.20.169, C.20.169, C.20.174, C.20.255

hee C 1
C.22.198

heo A 42
A.1.10, A.1.12, A.1.44, A.1.71, A.1.72, A.1.73, A.1.129, A.2.18, A.2.19, A.2.20, A.2.21, A.2.24, A.2.51, A.2.97, A.2.119, A.2.197, A.2.198, A.3.7, A.3.28, A.3.76, A.3.108, A.3.116, A.3.124, A.3.129, A.3.131, A.3.132, A.3.133, A.3.152, A.4.83, A.5.46, A.5.48, A.5.131, A.5.133, A.5.134, A.5.149, A.5.152, A.5.154, A.10.7, A.10.46, A.10.141, A.11.114, A.11.175

heo B 9
B.3.29, B.5.299, B.5.624, B.9.56, B.9.124, B.18.151, B.18.166, B.18.166, B.20.198

her A 1
A.12.47

her C 9
C.1.54, C.2.124, C.10.262, C.12.13, C.12.73, C.17.149, C.20.123, C.20.173, C.20.175

here A 3
A.2.11, A.12.12, A.12.42

here B 1
B.1.102

here C 157 *&> here,heren,hij*
C.1.10, C.1.54, C.1.70, C.1.76, C.1.77, C.1.94, C.1.180, C.2.1, C.2.12, C.2.14, C.2.15, C.2.16, C.2.16, C.2.17, C.2.25, C.2.37, C.2.50, C.2.67, C.2.68, C.2.83, C.2.85, C.2.85, C.2.123, C.2.124, C.2.125, C.2.126, C.2.127, C.2.127, C.2.129, C.2.140, C.2.151, C.3.4, C.3.5, C.3.6, C.3.8, C.3.10, C.3.11, C.3.16, C.3.22, C.3.25, C.3.27, C.3.28, C.3.45, C.3.46, C.3.46, C.3.48, C.3.48, C.3.50, C.3.129, C.3.129, C.3.131, C.3.133, C.3.159, C.3.159, C.3.161, C.3.163, C.3.168, C.3.171, C.3.172, C.3.193, C.3.195, C.3.196, C.3.208, C.3.213, C.3.216, C.3.218, C.3.283, C.3.370, C.3.370, C.3.377, C.3.491, C.3.500, C.4.3, C.4.10, C.4.448, C.4.48, C.4.90, C.4.111, C.4.158, C.4.158, C.4.161, C.5.51, C.5.128, C.5.129, C.5.133, C.6.3, C.6.6, C.6.7, C.6.129, C.6.130, C.6.134, C.6.178, C.6.192, C.6.225, C.6.232, C.6.305, C.6.441, C.7.289, C.7.301, C.10.134, C.10.136, C.10.137, C.10.138, C.10.139, C.10.150, C.10.261, C.10.264, C.10.267, C.10.268, C.10.268, C.11.84, C.11.102, C.11.114, C.11.115, C.11.116, C.11.117, C.11.171, C.11.191, C.12.11, C.12.20, C.12.45, C.12.45, C.12.46, C.12.50, C.13.9, C.13.11, C.13.11, C.13.159, C.13.160, C.16.105, C.16.106, C.16.106, C.16.106, C.16.151, C.16.152, C.16.152, C.17.24, C.17.171, C.17.176, C.18.125, C.19.304, C.19.304, C.19.304, C.20.120, C.20.172, C.20.176, C.20.177, C.20.178, C.20.249, C.20.254, C.20.316, C.20.317, C.20.463, C.20.464, C.22.161, C.22.197

hir B 37
B.4.50, B.5.26, B.5.65, B.5.154, B.5.155, B.5.159, B.5.224, B.9.7, B.9.57,

B.9.57, B.9.167, B.10.224, B.11.4, B.11.32, B.11.59, B.11.111, B.11.111, B.11.115,
B.11.138, B.11.349, B.12.46, B.12.48, B.12.75, B.12.77, B.12.227, B.13.139, B.14.266,
B.14.266, B.16.92, B.16.101, B.17.324, B.17.324, B.18.117, B.18.173, B.20.104,
B.20.161, B.20.197

hire A 86

A.1.10, A.1.56, A.1.56, A.1.71, A.1.77, A.1.78, A.1.100, A.1.158, A.2.1, A.2.19,
A.2.24, A.2.49, A.2.50, A.2.85, A.2.88, A.2.99, A.2.101, A.3.4, A.3.5, A.3.6, A.3.8,
A.3.10, A.3.12, A.3.15, A.3.25, A.3.26, A.3.42, A.3.43, A.3.43, A.3.45, A.3.45, A.3.46,
A.3.91, A.3.91, A.3.92, A.3.111, A.3.111, A.3.113, A.3.115, A.3.120, A.3.120, A.3.123,
A.3.145, A.3.147, A.3.148, A.3.153, A.3.154, A.3.157, A.3.159, A.4.3, A.4.10, A.4.37,
A.4.37, A.4.81, A.4.102, A.4.137, A.4.137, A.4.139, A.4.139, A.5.26, A.5.27, A.5.31,
A.5.45, A.5.48, A.5.49, A.5.133, A.5.140, A.5.212, A.6.107, A.6.121, A.10.7, A.10.9,
A.10.10, A.10.11, A.10.12, A.10.24, A.10.45, A.11.99, A.11.112, A.11.126, A.11.127,
A.11.127, A.11.128, A.11.129, A.11.166, A.11.172

hire B 113

B.1.10, B.1.58, B.1.58, B.1.73, B.1.79, B.1.80, B.1.184, B.2.1, B.2.11, B.2.15,
B.2.17, B.2.25, B.2.35, B.2.65, B.2.66, B.2.76, B.2.78, B.2.121, B.2.124,
B.2.135, B.2.137, B.3.4, B.3.5, B.3.6, B.3.8, B.3.10, B.3.12, B.3.15, B.3.21, B.3.24,
B.3.26, B.3.27, B.3.43, B.3.44, B.3.44, B.3.46, B.3.46, B.3.47, B.3.102, B.3.102,
B.3.103, B.3.122, B.3.122, B.3.124, B.3.126, B.3.131, B.3.134, B.3.155, B.3.157,
B.3.158, B.3.159, B.3.166, B.3.167, B.3.170, B.3.172, B.3.339, B.4.3, B.4.10, B.4.50,
B.4.94, B.4.116, B.4.153, B.4.161, B.4.163, B.4.163, B.4.166, B.4.167, B.5.27, B.5.31,
B.5.62, B.5.66, B.5.217, B.5.384, B.5.621, B.5.636, B.9.9, B.9.10, B.9.11, B.9.12,
B.9.24, B.9.59, B.10.146, B.10.160, B.10.174, B.10.175, B.10.176, B.10.177, B.10.229,
B.11.12, B.11.218, B.11.218, B.12.46, B.12.75, B.13.344, B.14.265, B.14.266, B.15.45,
B.15.281, B.15.401, B.15.405, B.17.324, B.18.120, B.18.169, B.18.170, B.18.173,
B.18.174, B.18.175, B.18.240, B.18.245, B.18.290, B.18.420, B.18.421

hure A 4

A.12.39, A.12.41, A.12.41, A.12.48

hep(e > heep; her > heo,here,hij

herafter adv *herafter adv.* A 2 hereaftir; B 4; C 1 hereaftur

A. 8.106   Of preyours & of penaunce my plou3 shal ben *hereaftir*,
A. 9.15   And euere haþ [as] I hope, & euere shal *hereaftir*.'
B. 7.124   Of preieres and of penaunce my plou3 shal ben *herafter*,
B. 8.19   And euere haþ as I hope, and euere shal *herafter*.'
B.17.80   'What he spendeþ moore [for medicyne] I make þee good *herafter*,
B.18.344   Adam and al his issue at my wille *herafter*;
C.10.19   And euere hath, as y hope, and euere wol *hereaftur*.'

herafterward adv *herafterward adv.* B 1

B.10.119   Ymaginatif *herafterward* shal answere to [youre] purpos.

heragein adv *herayen adv.* B 2 heragein (1) herayein (1); C 2 hereagayn
(1) herea3en (1)

B. 9.148   The gospel is *hera[g]ein* in o degre, I fynde:
B.14.189   A[c] if þe [pouke] wolde plede *herayein*, and punysshe vs in
conscience,
C.10.236   The gospel is *hereagayn*, as gomus may rede:
C.19.111   And yf kynde wit carpe *herea3en* or eny kyne thouhtes

heraud n *heraud n.* B 8 heraud (7) heraudes (1); C 4 heraud (3) heroudes
(1)

B.14.25   Shal noon *heraud* ne harpour haue a fairer garnement
B.16.177   And of Abrahames hous an *heraud* of armes;
B.16.247   Thus haue I ben his *heraud* here and in helle
B.17.22   '[He seiþ] sooþ', seide þis *heraud*; 'I haue [founded] it ofte.
B.17.55   Boþe þe *heraud* and hope and he mette atones
B.17.134   'After Abraham', quod he, 'þat *heraud* of armes,
B.18.16   As dooþ an *heraud* of armes whan Auentrous comeþ to Iustes.
B.20.94   And er *heraudes* of Armes hadden discryued lordes,
C.18.185   An *heraud* of Armes Ar any lawe were.'
C.18.265   Thus haue y ben his *heraud* here and in helle
C.20.14   As doth an *heraud* of Armes when Auntres cometh to ioustes.
C.22.94   And ar *heroudes* of Armes hadden descreued lordes,

herber n *herber n.(1)* B 1; C 1 erber

B.16.15   Herte highte þe *herber* þat it Inne groweþ,
C.18.5   *Erber* of alle pryuatees and of holynesse.

herberwe n *herberwe n.* B 1; C 1 herborw

B.10.412   Of holi chirche þat *herberwe* is, and goddes hous to saue
C.11.245   Bote holy churche, *herborw* to alle þat ben yblessed.

herberwe v *herberwen v.* A 1; B 3 herberwe (1) herberwed (1)
yherberwed (1); C 3 herberwed (1) herborwe (2)

A. 2.38   Þer nas halle ne hous to *herberwe* þe peple,
B. 5.231   '3is, ones I was *yherberwed*', quod he, 'wiþ an heep of chapmen;
B.17.76   *Herberwed* hym at an hostrie and þe hostiler called:
B.19.318   Ordeigne þee an hous, Piers, to *herberwe* Inne þi cornes.'
C. 6.235   '3us! ones y was *herberwed*,' quod he, 'with an heep of chapmen;
C. 7.258   In thyne hole herte to *herborwe* alle trewe
C.21.318   Ordeyne the an hous, [Peres], to *herborwe* in thy cornes.'

herberwyng ger *herberwinge ger.* B 1; C 1 herberwynge

B.14.141   Haue heuene in youre *her[berw]yng* and heuene þerafter
C.16.9   Haue two heuenes for 3oure *her[berw]ynge*.

herby adv *herbi adv.* C 1

C. 6.121   Withoute licence and leue, and *herby* lyueth wrathe.

herborw(e > herberwe; herd > heren

herde n *herde n.(2)* &> heren C 2

C. 9.266   How, *herde*! where is thyn ho[u]nd[e] and thyn hardy herte
C. 9.274   Thyn huyre, *herde*, as y hope, hath nat to quyte thy dette

herden > heren

here adv *her adv.* &> heo,heren,hij,hire A 21; B 74 heer (2) here (72); C
62 her (2) here (60)

A.Pr.38   Þat poule prechiþ of hem I dar not proue it *here*:
A. 1.9   Of oþer heuene þanne *here* holde þei no tale.'
A. 1.16   For to worsshipe hym þerewiþ whiles 3e ben *here*.
A. 1.146   *Here* mi3t þou sen ensaumplis in hymself one
A. 3.63   An aunter 3e haue 3oure hire þerof *h[e]re*;
A. 3.173   And þou hast famid me foule before þe king *here*.
A. 3.220   To hem þat werchen wel whiles þei ben *here*.
A. 5.114   'I haue [ben] coueit[ous],' quaþ [þat caitif], 'I [bi]knowe [hit]
h[e]re,
A. 5.219   For is no gilt *here* so gret þat his goodnesse nis more'.
A. 7.111   Shal no greyn þat *here* growiþ glade 3ow at nede;
A. 7.119   And 3elde 3ow of 3our almesse þat 3e 3iuen vs *here*,
A. 7.211   [Or with werk or with word þe while þou art here];
A. 7.235   He þat get his fode *here* wiþ trauaile of his hondis,
A. 8.173   How þou leddist þi lif *here* & his lawe keptest,
A. 8.182   Suche werkis to werche, whiles we ben *here*.
A. 9.33   Ri3t þus [it] fariþ,' quaþ þe Frere, 'be folk *here* on erþe.
A. 9.118   *Here* is wil wolde wyte 3if wit couþe hym teche.'
A.10.215   But 3if god [g]iue h[e]m grace *here* to amende.
A.11.79   And for his muchel mercy to amende vs *here*.
A.12.92   And mannes merþe w[or]þ no mor þan he deseruyþ *here*
A.12.101   And wrou3the þat *here* is wryten and oþer werkes boþe
B.Pr.38   That Poul precheþ of hem I [dar] nat preue it *here*;
B. 1.9   Of ooþer heuene þan *here* holde þei no tale.'
B. 1.16   For to worshipe hym þerwiþ while ye ben *here*.
B. 1.172   *Here* my3tow sen ensample[s] in hymself oone
B. 2.69   Thanne leep liere forþ and seide, 'lo! *here* a chartre
B. 3.72   On auenture ye haue youre hire *here* and youre heuene als.
B. 3.186   Ac þow hast famed me foule bifore þe kyng *here*.
B. 3.233   To [hem] þat [werchen wel] while þei ben *here*.
B. 5.198   'I haue ben coueitous', quod þis caytif, 'I biknowe it *here*.
B. 5.249   And took it by tale *here* and tolde hem þere lasse.'
B. 5.447   For is no gilt *here* so gret þat his goodnesse [i]s moore.
B. 6.46   Thou3 he be þyn vnderlyng *here* wel may happe in heuene
B. 6.66   Shal haue leue, by oure lord, to lese *here* in heruest
B. 6.119   Shal no greyn þat [*here*] groweþ glade yow at nede;
B. 6.127   And yelde yow [of] youre Almesse þat ye 3yue vs *here*;
B. 7.195   How þow laddest þi lif *here* and hi[s] law[e] keptest,
B. 7.204   Swiche werkes to werche, while we ben *here*,
B. 8.37   [Ri3t] þus it [fareþ]', quod þe frere, 'by folk *here* on erþe.
B. 8.129   *Here* is wil wolde wite if wit koude [hym teche];
B. 9.64   That lyuen synful lif *here* mis soule is lich þe deuel.
B. 9.146   *Here* abou3te þe barn þe belsires giltes,
B. 9.201   But god gyue hem grace *here* to amende.
B.10.112   *Here* lyeþ youre lore", þise lordes gynneþ dispute,
B.10.126   And for his muche mercy to amende [vs] *here*.
B.10.471   That inparfitly *here* knewe and ek lyuede.
B.11.10   [Siþen] she seide to me, '*here* my3tow se wondres
B.11.189   Wheiþer we loue þe lordes *here* bifore þe lord of blisse;
B.11.240   And al was ensample, [sooþliche], to vs synfulle *here*
B.11.416   Ac for þyn entremetynge *here* artow forsake?
B.12.241   Bitokneþ ri3t riche men þat reigne *here* on erþe.
B.13.52   'Here is propre seruice', quod Pacience, 'þer fareþ no Prince bettre.'
B.13.71   Holi writ bit men be war–I wol no3t write it *here*
B.13.190   Ac þe wil of þe wye and þe wil of folk *here*
B.13.275   Of pride *here* a plot, and þere a plot of vnbuxom speche,
B.13.393   To marchaunden wiþ [my] moneie and maken [*here*] eschaunges,
B.14.38   And seide, 'lo! *here* liflode ynogh, if oure bileue be trewe
B.14.120   Ouþer *here* or elliswhere, kynde wolde it neuere;
B.14.129   For þei han hir hire *heer* and heuene as it were,
B.14.154   *Here* for3ifnesse of hir synnes, and heuene blisse after.
B.14.165   Heuene after hir hennes goyng þat *here* han swich defaute.
B.14.173   Of þat þei wilne and wolde wanteþ hem no3t *here*,
B.14.176   Thoru3 derþe, þoru3 droghte, alle hir dayes *here*,
B.14.261   After hir endynge *here*, heueneriche blisse.
B.14.262   Muche hardier may he asken þat *here* my3te haue his wille
B.15.444   Til Gregory garte clerkes to go *here* and preche.
B.15.487   That heuedes of holy chirche ben, þat han hir wil *here*,

B.16.24	'Piers', quod I, 'I preie þee, whi stonde þise piles *here*?'
B.16.67	'*Heer* now byneþe', quod he þo, 'if I nede hadde,
B.16.196	To ocupie hym *here* til issue were spronge,
B.16.208	And in heuene and *here* oon singuler name.
B.16.247	Thus haue I ben his heraud *here* and in helle
B.16.252	Seide þat he seiჳ *here* þat sholde saue vs alle:
B.17.3	To rule alle Reames wiþ; I bere þe writ [riჳt] *here*.'
B.17.17	[Is *here* alle þi lordes lawes?' quod I; 'ye, leue me', he seide.
B.17.23	Lo! *here* in my lappe þat leeued on þat charme,
B.17.25	Ye! and sixti þousand biside forþ þat ben noჳt seyen *here*.'
B.17.78	And lo, *here* siluer', he seide, 'for salue to hise woundes.'
B.17.115	And þanne shal Feiþ be forster *here* and in þis Fryth walke,
B.17.200	Neiþer *here* ne elliswhere, as I herde telle:
B.18.24	That crist be noჳt [y]knowe *here* for consummatus deus
B.18.43	Edifie it eft newe–*here* he stant þat seide it–
B.18.167	'That is sooþ', seide Mercy, 'and I se *here* by Sowþe
B.18.186	Lo! *here* þe patente', quod Pees, 'In pace in idipsum,
B.18.265	For *here* comeþ wiþ crowne þat kyng is of glorie." '
B.18.278	For by right and by reson þe renkes þat ben *here*
B.18.327	And seide to Sathan, 'lo! *here* my soule to amendes
B.18.332	I bihiჳte hem noჳt *here* helle for euere.
B.18.349	But by right and by reson raunsone *here* my liges:
B.19.189	To bynde and vnbynde boþe *here* and elli[s],
B.19.385	*Here* is breed yblessed, and goddes body þervnder.
B.20.88	There was 'harrow!' and 'help! *here* comeþ kynde
B.20.317	For *here* is many a man hurt þoruჳ ypocrisye.'
B.20.350	He may se and here [*here*, so] may bifalle,
B.20.357	*Here* is Contricion', quod Conscience, 'my cosyn, ywounded.
C. 1.9	Of othere heuene then *here* [halde thei] no tale.'
C. 1.16	For to worschipe hym þerwith þe whiles ჳe lyuen *here*.
C. 1.168	*Here* myhtow se ensamples in hymself one
C. 2.71	Thenne lup lyare forth and saide, 'loo! *here* a Chartre
C. 3.94	*Here* on this erthe or elles in helle,
C. 3.232	Ac thow hast famed me foule byfore þe kyng *here*
C. 3.235	Bothe *here* and ellesswhere, in alle kyne londes.
C. 4.33	'*Here* cometh', quod Consience, 'þat Coueytise seruen.
C. 6.206	'Y haue be couetous', quod this kaytif, 'y biknowe hit *here*.
C. 6.238	Thow wolt be hanged heye þerfore, *here* oþer in helle.
C. 7.61	For is no gult [*here*] so greet þat his goodnesse is more.'
C. 8.43	Thogh he be *here* thyn vnderlynge in heuene parauntur
C. 8.67	Shal haue leue, by oure lord, to [lese *here* in heruest]
C. 8.126	Shal no grayn þat *here* groweth gladyen ჳow at nede;
C. 8.133	And ჳelde ჳow of ჳoure Almesse þat ჳe ჳeuen vs *here*;
C. 9.322	For hoso doth wel *here* at þe day of dome
C. 9.341	How we ladde oure lyf *here* and his lawes kepte
C. 9.349	That god gyue vs grace *here* ar we go hennes
C. 9.350	Suche werkes to worche the while we ben *here*
C.10.125	*Here* is oen wolde ჳwyte yf wit couthe teche;
C.10.234	*Here* aboute þe barn the belsires gultes
C.10.300	Bote god ჳeue hem grace her [g]oynge *here* to amende.
C.11.169	And senes he saide to me, '*here* myhte thow se wondres
C.11.200	Y leue neuere þat lord ne lady þat lyueth *her* [o]n erthe
C.11.269	Tho that worste wrouhten while thei *here* were.
C.12.129	And al was ensample, sothly, to vs synfole *here*
C.12.164	Al þat thow has[t] *here* hastly go and sulle hit;
C.13.224	Ac for thyn entermetynge *her* artow forsake:
C.15.114	'Sertes, sire,' thenne saide y, 'hit semeth nou[th]e *here*,
C.15.237	And saide, 'lo! *here* lyflode ynow yf oure beleue be trewe
C.15.296	Other *here* or elliswher, elles hit were reuthe;
C.15.301	Many man hath his ioye *here* for al here wel dedes
C.16.37	Elles is al an ydel al oure lyuynge *here*,
C.16.101	Aftur here endynge *here* heuenaryche blisse.
C.16.102	Moche hardyore may he aske þat *here* myhte haue his wille
C.18.84	'*Here* beneth y may nyme, yf y nede hadde,
C.18.96	Maydones and martres ministrede [hym] *here* on erthe
C.18.205	To ocupien hym *here* til issue were spronge
C.18.265	Thus haue y ben his heraud *here* and in helle
C.18.268	Saide þat a seyh *here* þat sholde saue vs alle:
C.19.4	Lo, *here* the lettre,' quod he, 'a latyn and [an] ebrew;
C.19.18	'Is *here* al thy lordes l[aw]es?' quod y; 'ჳe, leef me,' he saide,
C.19.24	Lo! *here* in my lappe þat leuede vpon þat lettre,
C.19.92	For wente neuere man this way þat he ne was *here* yruyfled
C.19.166	Noþer *here* ne ellesswhere, as y herde telle:
C.20.42	Edefien hit eft newe–*here* he stant þat saide hit–
C.20.170	'That is soth,' saide mercy, 'and y se *here* bi southe
C.20.191	Loo! *here* þe patente,' quod pees, 'In pace in idipsum,
C.20.273	For *here* cometh with croune þe kynge of all glorie.'
C.20.300	For bi riht and by resoun þ[e] renkes þat ben *here*
C.20.304	[Sh]olde deye with doel and *here* dwelle euere.
C.20.370	'Lo! me *here*, ' quod oure lord, 'lyf and soule bothe,
C.20.375	Y bihihte hem nat *here* helle for euere.
C.20.394	*Here* eny synfole soule souereynliche by maistrie,
C.20.395	Bote [by] riht and [by] resoun raunsome *here* my lege[s]:

C.20.434	And so of alle wykkede y wol *here* take veniaunce.
C.21.189	To bynde and vnbynde bothe *here* and elles
C.21.385	*Here* is bred yblessed and godes body þervnder.
C.22.88	There was 'harow!' and 'helpe! *here* cometh kynde
C.22.317	For *here* is many [a] man hert thorw ypocrisye.'
C.22.350	He may se and here *here*, so may bifalle,
C.22.357	*Here* is contricioun,' quod Consience, 'my cosyn, ywounded.

hereaboute adv *hereabouten adv.* C 1
C.10.192	Bishope[s] sholde ben *hereaboute* and bryng this to hepe

hereaftir -tur > herafter; hereagayn hereaჳen > heragein; hereynne > herinne

heremyte n *heremite n.* A 6 Ermyte (1) Ermytes (3) heremites (1) heremytes (1); B 11 heremite (1) heremyte (3) heremites (2) heremytes (5); C 19 Eremites (2) Eremytes (4) Ermites (1) Ermytes (9) heremite (1) heremites (1) heremyte (1)
A.Pr.3	In abite as an *Ermyte*, vnholy of werkis,
A.Pr.28	As ancris & *Ermytes* þat holden hem in [here] cellis,
A.Pr.50	*Ermytes* on an hep, wiþ hokide staues,
A.Pr.54	Shopen hem *Ermytes here* ese to haue.
A. 7.133	Ankeris & *heremytes* þat holde hem in here sellis,
A. 7.175	[A]n he[p] of *heremites* henten hem spadis,
B.Pr.3	In habite as an *heremite*, vnholy of werkes,
B.Pr.28	As Ancres and *heremites* þat holden hem in hire selles,
B.Pr.53	*Heremytes* on an heep with hoked staues
B.Pr.57	Shopen hem *heremytes here* ese to haue.
B. 6.145	Ac Ancres and *heremites* þat eten but at Nones
B. 6.187	An heep of *heremytes* henten hem spades,
B.13.30	And preyde mete 'p[u]r charite, for a pouere *heremyte*'.
B.13.284	Yhabited as an *heremyte*, an ordre by hymselue,
B.15.213	For he [lyueþ] noჳt in lolleris ne in londleperis *heremytes*
B.15.276	Ac neiþer Antony ne Egidie ne *heremyte* þat tyme
B.15.417	Ancres and *heremytes* and Monkes and freres
C.Pr.3	In abite as an *heremite*, vnholy of werkes,
C.Pr.30	As Ankeres and *Eremites* þat holdeth hem in here selles
C.Pr.51	*Eremites* on an hep with hokede staues
C.Pr.55	And [shopen] he[m] *heremites here* ese to haue.
C. 5.4	Amonges lollares of londone and lewede *Ermytes*,
C. 6.368	An hayward, an *heremyte*, the hangeman of tybourne,
C. 8.146	Ankerus and *Eremites* þat eten but at nones
C. 8.183	An heep of *Eremytes* henten hem spades,
C. 9.140	The whiche is lollarne lyf and lewede *Ermytes*;
C. 9.188	And alle holy *Eremytes* haue shal þe same;
C. 9.189	Ac *Ermytes* þat inhabiten by the heye weye
C. 9.191	Al þat holy *Ermytes* hatede and despisede,
C. 9.193	Thise lollares, lachedraweres, lewede *Ermytes*
C. 9.196	Noyther of lynage ne of lettrure ne lyfholy as *Ermytes*
C. 9.202	Al they holy *Ermytes* were of heye kynne,
C. 9.204	Ac thise *Ermytes* þat edifien thus by the heye weye
C. 9.218	Rihte so, sothly, such manere *Ermytes*
C. 9.241	Loke now where this lollares and lewede *Ermites*
C.17.6	Holy writ witnesseth þer were suche *eremytes*,

heren v *heren v.* A 21 here (10) herd (1) herde (8) herden (2); B 62 heere (1) herd (1) herde (20) herden (3) here (32) heren (2) hereþ (2) yherd (1); C 60 herd (1) herde (21) here (33) heren (3) hereth (1) yherd (1)
A.Pr.4	Wente wyde in þis world wondris to *here*.
A.Pr.97	I sauჳ in þat sem[b]le as ჳe shuln *here* aftir,
A. 2.79	Þanne tenide hym theologie whan he þis tale *herde*,
A. 2.169	Dreed at þe dore stood & þat doom *herde*,
A. 4.8	Comaunde hym þat he come my counseil to *here*,
A. 4.106	And haten [to] *here* harlotrie oþer mouþe it;
A. 4.138	And seide it so loude þat soþnesse it *herde*;
A. 5.2	To *here* matynes & masse, and to þe mete aftir.
A. 5.150	'To holy chirche,' quaþ he, 'for to *here* masse,
A. 5.176	Þere were oþes an hep, [whoso it *herde*];
A. 5.191	[Þat] alle þat *herden* þat horn held here nose aftir
A. 5.224	And *here* masse & matynes as I a monk were;
A. 5.226	Til I haue euesong *herd*, I behote [to] þe rode.
A. 7.47	Holde wiþ none harlotis ne *here* nouჳt here talis,
A. 7.157	And houpide aftir hungir þat *herde* hym at þe ferste:
A. 7.198	'*Here* now,' quaþ hungir, '& holde it for a wisdom:
A. 7.227	And siþen he seide, his seruaunt[s] it *h[er]de*:
A. 8.1	Treuþe *herde* telle hereof, & to peris sente
A.10.19	Sire se wel, & sey wel, & *here* wel þe hende,
A.12.23	"I am not hardy," quod he, "þat I *herde* with erys,
A.12.27	And asked Iesu on hy þat *herden* hit an hundred.
B.Pr.4	Wente wide in þis world wondres to *here*.
B.Pr.164	And ouþer while þei arn elliswhere, as I *herde* telle.
B.Pr.170	[And hangen it vpon þe cattes hals; þanne *here* we mowen]
B.Pr.193	For I *herde* my sire seyn, seuen yeer ypassed,
B.Pr.218	I seiჳ in þis assemblee, as ye shul *here* after.
B. 2.115	Thanne tened hym Theologie whan he þis tale *herde*,

B. 2.208   Drede at þe dore stood and þe doom *herde*,
B. 4.8   Comaunde hym þat he come my counseil to *here*,
B. 4.115   And haten alle harlotrie to *heren* or to mouþen it;
B. 4.162   And seid[e] it so [loude] þat [soþnesse] it *herde*:
B. 5.2   To *here* matyns [and masse and to þe mete] after.
B. 5.141   And siþen þei blosmede abrood in boure to *here* shriftes.
B. 5.300   'To holy chirche', quod he, 'for to *here* masse,
B. 5.327   [There were opes an heep, whoso it *herde*];
B. 5.343   That alle þat *herde* þat horn helde hir nos[e] after
B. 5.406   I haue leuere *here* an harlotrye or a Somer game of Souters,
B. 5.420   I kan holde louedayes and *here* a Reues rekenyng,
B. 5.427   Ruþe is to *here* rekenyng whan we shul rede acountes:
B. 5.452   And *here* matyns and masse as I a monk were;
B. 5.454   Til I haue euensong *herd*: I bihote to þe Roode.
B. 6.52   Hold wiþ none harlotes ne *here* noȝt hir tales,
B. 6.172   And houped after hunger þat *herde* hym at þe firste.
B. 6.212   '*Here* now', quod hunger, 'and hoold it for a wisdom:
B. 6.243   And [siþen] he seide–[hise seruauntȝ] it *herde*–
B. 7.1   TReuþe *herde* telle herof, and to Piers sente
B. 9.20   Sire Se-wel, and Sey-wel, and *here*-wel þe hende,
B.10.79   [For god is def nowadayes and deyneþ [noȝt vs to *here*],
B.10.93   Swiche lessons lordes sholde louye to *here*,
B.10.104   I haue *yherd* heiȝe men etynge at þe table
B.11.66   For I *herde* ones how Conscience it tolde,
B.11.392   Ne þow shalt fynde but fewe fayne [wolde] *heere*
B.12.23   And of holy men I *her[e]*', quod I, 'how þei ouþerwhile
B.12.246   And vnlouelich of ledene and looþ for to *here*.
B.13.64   Thanne seide I to myself so pacience it *herde*,
B.13.101   Coughed and carped, and Conscience hym *herde*
B.13.383   [I]n haly daies at holy chirche whan ich *herde* masse
B.13.415   And if he auȝt wole *here* it is an harlotes tonge.
B.13.417   He wexeþ wroþ, and wol noȝt *here* but wordes of murþe;
B.13.419   He hateþ to *here* þerof and alle þat it telleþ.
B.13.451   That bi his lyue liþed hem and loued hem to *here*.
B.14.163   And arated of riche men þat ruþe is to *here*.
B.14.274   'Haue god my trouþe', quod Haukyn '[I *here* yow] preise faste
             pouerte.
B.15.56   To englisshe men þis is to mene, þat mowen speke and *here*,
B.15.58   And þe moore þat a man of good matere *hereþ*,
B.15.106   And hatien to *here* harlotrie, and [au]ȝt to vnderfonge
B.15.559   An Aungel men *herden* an heigh at Rome crye,
B.16.19   That I *here* nempne his name anoon I swowned after,
B.16.130   And seide it in sighte of hem alle so þat alle *herden*:
B.16.249   And þus I seke hym', he seide, 'for I *herde* seyn late
B.17.200   Neiþer here ne elliswhere, as I *herde* telle.
B.17.258   The holy goost *hereþ* þe noȝt ne helpe may þee by reson.
B.18.261   'Suffre we', seide truþe; 'I *here* and see boþe
B.19.3   To *here* holly þe masse and to be housled after.
B.19.21   For alle derke deueles arn adrad to *heren* it,
B.19.130   For deue þoruȝ hise doynges and dombe speke [and *herde*],
B.20.80   Kynde Conscience þo *herde* and cam out of þe planetes
B.20.190   And hitte me vnder þe ere; vnneþe [may] ich *here*.
B.20.230   Freres *herden* hym crye and comen hym to helpe,
B.20.273   Enuye *herde* þis and heet freres go to scole
B.20.324   The frere herof *herde* and hiede faste
B.20.328   In contrees þer he coome confessions to *here*;
B.20.350   He may se and *here* [here, so] may bifalle,
C.Pr.4   Wente forth in þe world wondres to *here*
C.Pr.95   Consience cam and [ac]cu[s]ed hem–and þe comune *herde* hit–
C.Pr.187   And hongen hit aboute þe cattes halse; thanne *here* we mowe
C.Pr.206   For y *herde* my syre sayn, seuene ȝer ypassed,
C.Pr.224   Al y say slepynge, as ȝe shal *here* [a]ftur,
C. 2.76   Thenne saide symonye þat syuyle it *herde*:
C. 2.119   Thenne tened hym teologie when he this tal[e] *herde*,
C. 2.220   Drede stod at þe dore and [þe] d[om]e *herde*,
C. 3.98   That Innocence is *herde* in heuene amonge seyntes
C. 4.8   Comaunde hym þat he come my consayle to *here*
C. 4.110   And hatien alle harlotrie to *heren* oþer to mouthen hit;
C. 4.157   And cryede to Consience, the kyng myhte hit *here*:
C. 6.116   With lewed and lered þat leef ben to *here*
C. 6.272   In halydayes at holy churche when y *herde* masse
C. 6.332   By so hit be in thyn herte as y *here* thy tonge.
C. 6.355   'To holy churche,' quod he, 'for to *here* masse
C. 6.401   That alle þat *herde* þ[at] hor[n] helde here nose aftur
C. 6.435   Out of resoun among rybaudes here rybaudrye to *here*.
C. 7.22   Y hadde leuere *here* an harlotrye or a lesyng to lauhen of
C. 7.40   Reuthe is to *here* rekenynge when we shal rede acountes,
C. 7.66   And *here* mateynes and masse as y a monke were;
C. 7.68   Til y haue euensong *yherd*: y bihote to þe rode.
C. 7.74   And hath no likynge to lerne ne of oure lord to *here*
C. 7.77   A wexeth wroth and wol not *here* but wordes of murthe;
C. 7.79   He hateth to *here* thereof and alle þat þerof carpeth.
C. 7.111   That by his lyue l[yth]ed hem and louede hem to *here*.

C. 8.48   Treuwe of thy tonge and tales loth to *here*
C. 8.50   Hoold with non harlotes ne *here* nat here tales
C. 8.168   And houped aftur hunger þat *herde* hym at the furste.
C. 9.1   Treuthe *herde* telle herof and to [Peres] sente
C. 9.228   And vppon sonendayes to cese goddes seruice to *here*,
C. 9.230   To *heren* here euensong euery man ouhte.
C. 9.232   Vcche halyday to *here* holly þe seruise,
C. 9.243   Where se we hem on sonendayes the seruise to *here*,
C.10.109   More kynd[e] knowynge coueyte y to *here*
C.10.146   Sire se-wel and sey-wel [and] *here*-wel þe [h]ende,
C.11.59   For god is deef nowadayes and deyneth [nat vs] to *here*
C.11.74   Ac lust no lord now ne lettred man of suche lore to *here*
C.11.218   And holi churche, as y *here*, haldeth bothe in helle!
C.13.128   For ignorancia non excusat as ych haue *herd* in bokes.'
C.15.68   Thenne saide y to mysulue so pacience hit *herde*,
C.15.108   Cowhede and capede, and consience hym *herde*
C.15.176   And sethe a saide to clergie so þat y hit *herde*:
C.16.16   [And arated of] ryche men þat reuthe is to *here*.
C.16.218   To engelische men this is to mene, þat mowen speke and *here*,
C.17.38   To his wyf; when he was blynde he *herde* a la[m]be blete:
C.17.222   An angel men *herde* an hye at rome crye,
C.19.166   Noþer here ne elleswhere, as y *herde* telle:
C.19.224   The holy goest *hereth* the nat ne helpeth the, be thow certeyne.
C.20.269   'Soffre we,' sayde truthe; 'y *here* and se bothe
C.21.3   To *here* holly þe masse and to [be] hoseled aftur.
C.21.21   For alle derke deueles aren drad to *heren* hit
C.21.130   For deue thorw his doynges and dombe speke [&] *herde*
C.22.80   Kynde Consience tho *herde* and cam oute of the planetes
C.22.190   And hitte me vnder þe ere; vnnethe may ich *here*.
C.22.230   Freres *herde* hym crye and comen hym to helpe,
C.22.273   Enuye *herde* this and heete freres go to scole
C.22.324   The frere herof *herde* and hyede faste
C.22.328   In contreys þer he cam confessiones to *here*;
C.22.350   He may se and *here* here, so may bifalle,

hereof > herof; heresulue > hirself; hereto > herto

herfore adv *herfor adv.* B 1; C 1
B.20.294   Enuye *herfore* hatede Conscience,
C.22.294   Enuye *herfore* hatede Consience,

herie v *herien v.(1)* A 1; B 1 yherd; C 1 yherde
A.11.247   We be holde heiȝly to *herie* & honoure,
B.14.210   Than richesse or reautee, and raþer *yherd* in heuene.
C.16.51   Then rychesse or ryalte and rather *yherde* in heuene.

heryng ger *heringe ger.* A 1
A.10.52   He eggiþ eiȝe siȝt & *heryng* to gode;

herinne adv *herinne adv.* B 1; C 3 hereynne (1) herynne (2)
B.20.342   But þow konne [any] craft þow comest nouȝt *herInne*.
C.17.39   "Wyf! be ywar," quod he; "what haue we *herynne*?
C.17.40   Lord leue," quod þat lede, " no stole thynge be *herynne*!"
C.22.342   Bote thow conne eny craft thow comest nat *hereynne*.

heritage n *heritage n.* A 2 eritage; B 3 Eritage (1) heritage (2); C 3
     eritage (2) heritage (1)
A.11.231   Hauen *eritage* in heuene, ac riche men non.'
A.11.239   Haue *eritage* in heuene as an heiȝ cristene.
B.10.347   That þei han *Eritage* in heuene, and by trewe riȝte,
B.10.356   Haue *heritage* [in] heuene as [an heiȝ] cristene.
B.14.294   Selde is poore [riȝt] riche but of riȝtful *heritage*.
C. 3.243   In his enemyes handes his *heritage* of Fraunce.
C.10.241   The *eritage* þat þe eyer sholde haue is at þe kynges wille.
C.16.129   Selde is pore rihte ryche but of rihtfole *eritage*.

herkene v *herken v.* C 1
C. 8.222   'Now *herkene*,' quod hunger, 'and holde hit for a wysdom:

hernes n *hirne n.* A 1 hernis; B 2; C 2
A. 2.195   Alle fledden for fer & flowen into *hernis*;
B. 2.236   Alle fledden for fere and flowen into *hernes*;
B.18.404   Astroth and al þe route hidden hem in *hernes*;
C. 2.252   Alle fledde for fere and flowen into *hernes*;
C.20.447   Astarot and alle [þe route] hidden hem in *hernes*;

herodes n prop *n.i.d.* C 1
C.10.178   As lo[t] dede and Noe, and *herodes* þe daffe

herof adv *herof adv.* A 1 hereof; B 8; C 13 hereof (3) herof (10)
A. 8.1   Treuþe herde telle *hereof*, & to peris sente
B. 5.116   Whoso vndernymeþ me *herof*, I hate hym dedly after.
B. 7.1   TReuþe herde telle *herof*, and to Piers sente
B.10.249   Austyn þe olde *herof* made bokes.
B.18.138   For patriarkes and prophetes han preched *herof* ofte
B.18.237   And alle þe elementȝ', quod þe book, '*herof* beren witnesse.
B.18.271   Patriarkes and prophetes han parled *herof* longe

B.19.140 [Her]of Cayphas hadde enuye and oþere Iewes,
B.20.324 The frere herof herde and hiede faste
C. 6.436 Herof, gode god, graunte me forȝeuenesse,
C. 9.1   Treuthe herde telle herof and to [Peres] sente
C.11.144 And al þat holi churche herof can þe lere
C.11.146 Austyn þe olde herof made bokes;
C.11.152 And alle thre bote o god, and herof he made
C.16.35   And holy churche and charite herof a chartre made.
C.18.212 A thre he is þer he is and hereof bereth wittnesse
C.19.251 Vch a riche y rede reward herof take
C.20.141 For patriarkes and prophetes haen preched herof ofte
C.20.246 And all þe elementis', quod the boek, 'hereof bereth witnesse.
C.20.279 Patriarkes and prophetes haen parled herof longe
C.21.140 Hereof hadde Cayphas enuye and oþer iewes
C.22.324 The frere herof herde and hyede faste

heron adv heron adv. B 2

B.10.289 Forþi, ye Correctours, claweþ heron and correcteþ first yowselue,
B.13.131 'I kan noȝt heron', quod Conscience, 'ac I knowe Piers.

heroudes > heraud; herre -ore > heiȝ; hert > hurte

herte n herte n. &> hurte A 26 herte (24) hertis (2); B 59 herte (54)
          hertes (5); C 54 herte (50) hertes (4)

A. 1.39   [And þat] shend[iþ] þi soule; set it in þin herte;
A. 1.130 It is a kynde knowyng þat kenneþ in þin herte
A. 1.139 For in kynde knowyng in herte þer comsiþ a miȝt,
A. 1.148· To hem þat hongide him [heiȝe] & his herte þirlide.
A. 3.166 Ne to depraue þi persone wiþ a proud herte.
A. 3.186 And bateride hym on þe bak, boldite his herte,
A. 5.45   Pernel proud herte plat hire to þe erþe
A. 5.50   'Shal neuere heiȝ herte me hente, but holde me lowe
A. 5.53   Of alle þat I haue had enuye in myn herte.'
A. 5.58   Enuye wiþ heuy herte askide aftir shrift,
A. 5.93   Of his lesing I lauȝe; [it liȝtiþ] myn herte,
A. 5.97   And whoso haþ more þanne I, þat angriþ myn herte.
A. 5.101 Ne no dyapendyon dryue it fro myn herte.
A. 6.50   Þat ȝe loue hym leuere þanne þe lif in ȝoure hertis;
A. 6.93   Þou shalt se treuþe himself wel sitte in þin herte
A. 6.96   For he haþ enuye to hym þat in þin herte sitteþ
A. 7.200 Wiþ houndis bred & hors bred holde vp here hertis,
A. 8.65   And lyuen in loue & [in] lawe, for here louȝ herte
A. 8.87   For loue of here louȝ herte oure lord haþ hem grauntid
A. 8.132 And for peris loue þe plouȝman wel pensif in herte,
A.10.45   Ac in þe herte is hire hom heiȝest of alle.
A.10.78   To routen ne to resten ne ro[t]en in þin herte;
A.11.57   And han [hym] muchel in here mouþ, ac mene men in herte,
A.11.259 To wyte what is dowel witterly in herte,
A.12.48   And þanked hure a þousand syþes with þrobbant herte.
A.12.114 And alle lordes þat louyn him lely in herte,
B. 1.41   And that [shendeþ] þi soule; [set] it in þin herte.
B. 1.142 It is a kynde knowyng þat kenneþ in þin herte
B. 1.164 And in þe herte þere is þe heed and þe heiȝe welle.
B. 1.165 For in kynde knowynge in herte þer [comseþ a myȝt],
B. 1.174 To hem þat hengen hym heiȝ and his herte þirled.
B. 3.179 Ne [to] depraue þi persone wiþ a proud herte.
B. 3.199 I batred hem on þe bak and boldede hire hertes
B. 3.304 And haue wonder in hire hertes þat men beþ so trewe.
B. 3.339 Was omnia probate, and þat plesed hire herte
B. 5.62   Pernele proud-herte platte hire to þe erþe
B. 5.67   'Shal neuere heiȝ herte me hente, but holde me lowe
B. 5.70   [Of alle þat] I haue [had enuye] in myn herte.'
B. 5.75   Enuye wiþ heuy herte asked after shrifte,
B. 5.113 And of [his] lesynge I lauȝe, [it liȝteþ] myn herte;
B. 5.118 [And] whoso haþ moore þan I, þat angreþ [myn herte].
B. 5.124 Ne no Diapenidion dryue it fro myn herte,
B. 5.401 That I telle wiþ my tonge is two myle fro myn herte.
B. 5.606 Thow shalt see in þiselue truþe [sitte] in þyn herte
B. 5.610 [For] he haþ enuye to hym þat in þyn herte sitteþ
B. 6.49   Or a knyȝt from a knaue; knowe þis in þyn herte.
B. 6.214 Wiþ houndes breed and horse breed hoold vp hir hertes,
B. 7.63   And lyuen in loue and in lawe, for hir lowe hert[e]
B. 7.105 For loue of hir lowe hert[e] oure lord haþ hem graunted
B. 7.151 And for Piers [loue] þe Plowman [wel] pencif in herte,
B. 9.57   A[c] in þe herte is hir hoom and hir mooste reste.
B. 9.58   Ac Inwit is in þe heed and to þe herte he lokeþ
B.10.71   And haue hym muche in [hire] mouþ, ac meene men in herte,
B.10.296 And al for youre holynesse; haue ye þis in herte.
B.10.397 For many men on þis moolde moore setten hir hert[e]
B.10.440 Or ellis for his yuel wille and enuye of herte,
B.11.115 Al for tene of hir text trembled myn herte,
B.11.136 Mercy for hise mysdedes wiþ mouþe [or] wiþ herte.'
B.11.188 To knowen vs by oure kynde herte and castynge of oure eiȝen,
B.13.140 "Wiþ wordes and werkes", quod she, "and wil of þyn herte

B.13.278 Ooþerwise þan he haþ wiþ herte or siȝte shewynge hym;
B.14.14   Or þoruȝ werk or þoruȝ word or wille of myn herte
B.14.100 'Ther parfit truþe and poore herte is, and pacience of tonge,
B.14.148 And rewarden alle double richesse þat rewful hertes habbeþ.
B.14.195 And principalliche of al[l]e peple but þei be poore of herte.
B.14.307 And euer þe lasse þat he [lede], þe [liȝter] he is of herte:
B.14.308 And an hardy man of herte among an heep of þeues;
B.15.49   I wolde I knewe and couþe kyndely in myn herte.'
B.15.151 'Where sholde men fynde swich a frend wiþ so fre an herte?
B.15.218 The loue þat liþ in his herte makeþ hym liȝt of speche,
B.15.259 In alle manere angres, haue þis at herte
B.15.517 And baptised and bishened wiþ þe blode of his herte
B.16.8   Pacience hatte þe pure tree and [pouere] symple of herte,
B.16.15   Herte highte þe herber þat it Inne groweþ,
B.17.238 So wol þe fader forȝyue folk of mylde hertes
B.17.351 That he ne may louye, and hym like, and lene of his herte
B.18.85   But þis blynde bacheler baar hym þoruȝ þe herte.
B.19.31   And of hardynesse of herte and of hendenesse,
B.19.58   Who was hardiere þan he? his herte blood he shadde
B.19.171 And feele wiþ hise fyngres his flesshliche herte.'
B.20.2   Heuy chered I yede and elenge in herte.
B.20.153 'Heele and I', quod he, 'and heighnesse of herte
B.20.171 [And] gaf hym gold good woon þat gladede his herte,
B.20.180 And in hope of his heele good herte he hente
B.20.226 And brode hoked arwes, goddes herte and hise nayles,
C. 1.39   And þat [see]th þ[i] soule and sayth hit the in herte
C. 1.141 Hit is a kynde knowynge that kenet in thyn herte
C. 1.160 And in þe herte þer is þe hed and þe heye welle.
C. 1.161 For [in] kynde knowynge [in] herte ther comseth a myhte
C. 1.170 To hem þat hengen [hym] hye and [his] herte thorlede.
C. 2.16   Here aray with here rychesse raueschede my herte;
C. 3.225 Ne to depraue thy persone with a pro[u]d herte.
C. 3.352 So of ho[l] herte cometh hope and hardy relacoun
C. 3.491 Was omnia probate; þat plesede here herte.
C. 4.36   Ac there is loue and leutee hit lyketh nat here hertes:
C. 6.3   P[ur]nele proude herte platte here to þe erthe
C. 6.8   'Shal neuere heyh herte me hente, but holde me lowe
C. 6.11   Of alle þat y haue hated in myn herte.'
C. 6.18   God and goode men so gret was myn herte;
C. 6.63   Enuye with heuy herte asked aftur shrifte.
C. 6.89   Ne derworth drynke dryue hit fro myn herte
C. 6.146 For she had haly bred ar y my herte gan change.
C. 6.289 Ne take a meles mete of thyn and myn herte hit wiste
C. 6.332 By so hit be in thyn herte as y here thy tonge.
C. 7.17   That y telle with my tonge is t[wo] myle fro myn herte.
C. 7.255 Thow shalt se treuthe sitte in thy sulue herte
C. 7.258 In thyne hole herte to herborwe alle trewe
C. 7.262 For he hath enuye to hym þat in thyn herte setteth
C. 9.184 That taketh thise meschiefes mekeliche and myldeliche at herte
C. 9.185 For loue of here lowe hertes oure lord hath hem ygraunted
C. 9.266 How, herde! where is thyn ho[u]nd[e] and thyn hardy herte
C. 9.300 And of [Peres] the [plouhman] fol pencyf in herte
C.10.174 Inwit is in the heued and anima in herte
C.11.51   And haen [hym] muche in here mouth Ac mene [men] in herte.
C.11.228 For mony men [o]n this molde more sette here herte
C.12.50   Al for tene of here tyxst tremblede myn herte
C.12.71   Mercy for his mysdedes with mouthe and with herte.'
C.14.25   And w[o]ky thorw gode werkes wikkede hertes.
C.15.21   And y merueyle[d] in herte how ymaginatyf saide
C.15.132 Saue loue and leute and lowenesse of herte,
C.16.24   Lowe and lele and louynge and of herte pore.
C.16.29   Cordis contricio cometh of sor[w]e of herte
C.16.142 And euere þe lasse þat [eny] lede þe lihtere his herte is there,
C.16.211 Y wolde y knewe and couthe kyndeliche in myn herte.'
C.17.134 And o god þat al bygan with gode herte they honoureth
C.17.268 And baptised and bis[hin]ede with þe bloed of his herte
C.18.259 As we wilnede and wolde with mou[th]e and herte aske.
C.19.204 So wol þe fader forȝeue folke of mylde hertes
C.19.300 As sorwe of herte is satisfaccioun for suche þat may nat paye.
C.19.331 That he ne may louye, and hym lyke, and lene of his herte
C.20.87   Bote this blynde bacheler that bar hym thorw þe herte.
C.21.31   And of hardinesse of herte and of hendenesse
C.21.58   Ho was hardior then he? his herte bloed he she[d]de
C.21.171 And fele with his fyngeres his fleschliche herte.
C.22.2   Heuy chered y ȝede and [e]lyng in herte.
C.22.153 'Hele and y,' quod he, 'and heynesse of herte
C.22.171 And gaef hym goelde goed woen þat gladde h[is] hert[e]
C.22.180 And in hope of his hele goed herte he hente
C.22.226 And brode hokede Arwes, goddes herte and his nayles,

herted adj herted adj. B 2; C 1

B.15.201 For þer are [pure] proude herted men, pacient of tonge
B.20.37   [For nede makeþ nede fele nedes lowe herted].
C.22.37   For nede maketh neede fele nedes louh herted.

hertely *adv hertelie adv.* C 1
C.15.141 [*Hertely* þou hym] helpe emforth thy myhte,

herteth > hurte

hertford *n prop n.i.d.* B 1; C 1
B. 5.355 Is noon so hungry hound in *hertford* shire
C. 6.413 Ys non so hungry hound in *hertford* shyre

herto *adv herto adv.* A 2 hereto (1) herto (1); B 3; C 2 hereto (1) herto (1)
A. 2.106 *Hereto* assentiþ Cyuyle, ac symonye ne wolde
A. 4.146 'Ac it is wel hard, be myn hed, *herto* to bringe it.
B. 2.142 *Hereto* assenteþ Cyuyle, ac Symonye ne wolde
B. 4.183 It is [wel] hard, by myn heed, *hert[o]* to brynge it,
B. 9.37 As who seiþ, "moore moot *herto* þan my word oone;
C. 2.158 *Hereto* assenteth syuyle, ac symonye ne wolde
C. 4.177 Hit is ful hard, by myn heued, *herto* to bryngen hit

heruest *n hervest n.* A 4 heruest (2) heruist (2); B 4; C 7 heruest (3) heruost (4)
A. 7.60 Shal haue be oure lord þe more here in *heruist*,
A. 7.106 Shulde ben hirid þereaftir whan *heruist* tyme come.
A. 7.274 Be þat I hope to haue *heruest* in my croft,
A. 7.283 Be þat it neiȝide ner *heruest* [þat] newe corn com to chepyng.
B. 6.66 Shal haue leue, by oure lord, to lese here in *heruest*
B. 6.114 Sholde be hired þerafter whan *heruest* tyme come.
B. 6.290 By þat I hope to haue *heruest* in my crofte;
B. 6.299 By þat it neȝed neer *heruest* newe corn cam to chepyng.
C. 5.7 In an hot *heruest* whenne y hadde myn hele
C. 6.112 As som tyme in somur and also in *heruest*,
C. 8.67 Shal haue leue, by oure lord, to [lese here in *heruest*]
C. 8.124 He sholde be huyred þeraftur when *heruost* tyme come.
C. 8.313 And by [t]hat y hope to haue *heruost* in my croft[e];
C. 8.321 By that hit nyhed neyh *heruost* and newe corn cam to chepyng.
C.12.200 Yf god gyueth hym þe lyf, to haue a goed *heruost*,

heruy *n prop n.i.d.* A 1; B 1; C 1
A. 5.108 So hungirly & holewe sire *heruy* hym lokide.
B. 5.189 So hungrily and holwe sire *heruy* hym loked.
C. 6.197 So hungrily and holow sire *heruy* hym lokede.

heruist -ost > heruest

herwith *adv herwith adv.* B 1; C 2
B.13.156 And *herwith* am I welcome þer I haue it wiþ me.
C.12.161 Crist acordeth efte *herwith*; clerkes wyteth þe sothe,
C.18.28 Of o will, of o wit; and *he[r]with* y kepe

heste *n heste n.(1)* A 5 hest (2) heste (1) hestis (2); B 3 heste (1) hestes (2); C 7 heste (3) hestes (4)
A. 3.102 [But I be holly at ȝour *heste* honge me ellys].'
A. 8.167 Be þou neuere þe baldere to breke þe ten *hestis*;
A.10.142 Aȝens þe *hest* of hym þat hem of nouȝt made,
A.10.160 Ageyns godis *hest* girlis hy geten
A.11.253 For he seiþ it hymself in his ten *hestis*;
B. 2.83 Vnbuxome and bolde to breke þe ten *hestes*;
B. 3.113 But I be holly at youre *heste* hange me [ellis].'
B. 7.189 Be [þow] neuer þe bolder to breke þe x *hestes*,
C. 2.90 Vnbuxum and bold to breke þe ten *hestes*;
C. 3.150 But y be holly at thyn *heste*; lat hange me elles.'
C. 8.212 And for defaute this folk folweth myn *hestes*.
C. 9.335 Be ȝe neuere þe baldere to breke þe ten *hestes*
C.13.68 That holde mote þe hey way, euene the ten *hestes*,
C.17.142 Loue thyn enemye entierely goddes *heste* to fulfille;
C.18.249 I withsaet nat his *heste*; y hope and bileue

hete *n hete n.(1)* *&> hote* B 5; C 8
B.13.161 Ne neiþer *hete* ne hayl ne noon helle pouke
B.14.59 Or þoruȝ hunger or þoruȝ *hete*, at his wille be it;
B.14.172 Ne neiþer *hete* ne Hayll, haue þei hir heele;
B.15.271 In hunger, in *hete*, in alle manere angres.
B.17.231 Ysekeles in euesynges þoruȝ *hete* of þe sonne
C. 1.124 Hewes in þe haliday after *hete* wayten
C. 8.248 Chaffare and cheue þerwith in chele and in *hete*.
C. 9.109 Careth they for no colde ne counteth of non *hete*
C.15.163 Ne n[oþ]ere *hete* ne hayl ne helle pouke hym greue,
C.15.258 Wheþer thorw hunger or [thorw] *hete*, at his wille be hit;
C.16.181 And ayther is otheres *hete* and also of o will;
C.18.75 These haen þe [*hete*] of þe holi goest as þe crop of tre [the] sonne.
C.19.197 Isekeles in euesynges thorwe *hete* of the sonne

heþen *n hether adj.& n.* A 2 heþen (1) heþene (1); B 5 heþen (3) heþene (2); C 1 hethene
A.11.237 Þat arn vncristene in þat cas may cristene an *heþene*,
A.11.251 And siþen *he[þen]* to helpe in hope hem to amende.
B.10.354 That [arn] vncristene in þat caas may cristen an *heþen*,

B.10.369 And siþen *heþen* to helpe in hope of amendement.
B.15.458 It is *heþene* as to heueneward and helplees to þe soule.
B.15.459 *Heþen* is to mene after heeþ and vntiled erþe,
B.19.348 That Conscience shal noȝt knowe who is cristene or *heþene*,
C.21.348 That Consience shal nat knowe [ho is cristene or *hethene*]

hethynesse *n hethenesse n.* B 1
B.15.443 Al was *hethynesse* som tyme Engelond and Walis

heþyng *n hething n.* A 1; B 1
A. 4.104 And harlotis holynesse be holde for an [*heþyng*];
A. 4.118 And harlottes holynesse be holden for an [*heþyng*];

hette > hote; heued(- > heed; heueg- > heuy

heuene *n heven n.* A 24; B 90; C 80 heuene (79) heuenes (1)
A. 1.9 Of oþer *heuene* þanne here holde þei no tale.'
A. 1.109 Lucifer wiþ legionis leride it in *heuene*,
A. 1.113 Out of *heuene* into helle hobelide þei faste,
A. 1.121 Mowe be sikur þat here soule shal wende into *heuene*,
A. 1.179 And ek þe graiþ gate þat goþ into *heuene*.
A. 2.2 And seide, 'mercy madame, for marie loue of *heuene*
A. 2.71 Þere to wone wiþ wrong while god is in *heuene*.'
A. 3.49 Sikir shulde þi soule be *heuene* to haue'.
A. 3.119 Betwyn *heuene* & helle, & erþe þeiȝ men souȝte.
A. 3.188 Hadde I be march[al] of his men, be marie of *heuene*,
A. 3.223 Loue hem & le[n]e hem for oure lordis loue of *heuene*;
A. 7.17 As longe as I lyue for þe lordis loue of *heuene*.
A. 7.206 Counforte hem wiþ þi catel for cristis loue of *heuene*;
A. 8.33 Fynde suche here foode for oure lordis loue of *heuene*,
A. 8.38 Þat I ne shal sende [ȝour] soule sauf into *heuene*,
A.10.46 Heo is lyf & ledere, a lemman of *heuene*.
A.11.173 Was neuere [gome] vpon þis ground, siþþe god makid *heuene*,
A.11.229 Poul prouiþ it is vnpossible, riche men in *heuene*.
A.11.231 Hauen eritage in *heuene*, ac riche men non.'
A.11.239 Haue eritage in *heuene* as an heiȝ cristene.
A.11.240 Ac cristene men, god wot, comiþ not so to *heuene*,
A.11.276 And ȝif I shal werke be here werkis to wynne me *heuene*,
A.11.291 And arn no[ne], forsoþe, souereynes in *heuene*
A.11.312 Percen wiþ a paternoster þe paleis of *heuene*
B.Pr.106 And to opene it to hem and *heuene* blisse shewe.
B.Pr.127 And for þi riȝtful rulyng be rewarded in *heuene*'.
B.Pr.128 And siþen in þe Eyr an heiȝ an Aungel of *heuene*
B.Pr.210 Deuyne ye, for I ne dar, by deere god in *heuene*.
B. 1.9 Of ooþer *heuene* þan here holde þei no tale.'
B. 1.111 Lucifer wiþ legions lerned it in *heuene*
B. 1.120 And alle þat hoped it myȝte be so, noon *heuene* myȝte hem holde,
B. 1.122 Til god of his goodnesse [garte þe *heuene* to stekie]
B. 1.132 Mowe be siker þat hire soul[e] sh[a]l wende to *heuene*
B. 1.148 For truþe telleþ þat loue is triacle of *heuene*.
B. 1.151 And lered it Moyses for þe leueste þyng and moost lik to *heuene*,
B. 1.153 For *heuene* myȝte nat holden it, [so heuy it semed],
B. 1.159 Forþi is loue ledere of þe lordes folk of *heuene*
B. 1.205 And also þe graiþe gate þat goþ into *heuene*.
B. 2.2 And seide 'mercy, madame, for Marie loue of *heuene*
B. 2.33 Shal be my lord and I his leef in þe heiȝe *heuene*.
B. 2.107 And with hym to wonye [in] wo while god is in *heuene*.'
B. 3.50 Syker sholde þi soule be *heuene* to haue'.
B. 3.72 On auenture ye haue youre hire here and youre *heuene* als.
B. 3.130 Bitwene *heuene* and helle, [and] erþe þouȝ men souȝte.
B. 3.201 Hadde I ben Marchal of his men, by Marie of *heuene*!
B. 4.179 Mede shal noȝt maynprise yow, by þe marie of *heuene*!
B. 5.272 And siþen þat Reson rolle it in þe Registre of *heuene*
B. 6.18 As longe as I lyue, for þe lordes loue of *heuene*.
B. 6.46 Thouȝ he be þyn vnderlyng here wel may happe in *heuene*
B. 6.220 Conforte h[e]m wiþ þi catel for cristes loue of *heuene*;
B. 7.31 Fynden [swiche] hir foode [for oure lordes loue of *heuene*]
B. 7.54 Thise foure þe fader of *heuene* made to þis foold in commune;
B. 9.47 And þus god gaf hym a goost [of] þe godhede of *heuene*
B. 9.102 Is moost yhated vpon erþe of hem þat ben in *heuene*;
B. 9.104 And goddes gleman and a game of *heuene*.
B. 9.120 In erþe [þe] *heuene* [is]; hymself [was þe] witnesse.
B. 9.130 Yet [seþ], ayein þe sonde of oure Saueour of *heuene*,
B.10.230 Was neuere gome vpon þis ground, siþ god made [*heuene*],
B.10.305 For if *heuene* be on þis erþe, and ese to any soule,
B.10.341 Poule preueþ it impossible, riche men [in] *heuene*;
B.10.347 That þei han Eritage in *heuene*, and by trewe riȝte,
B.10.356 Haue heritage [in] *heuene* as [an heiȝ] cristene.
B.10.357 Ac cristene men wiþoute moore maye noȝt come to *heuene*,
B.10.392 And if I sh[al] werche by hir werkes to wynne me *heuene*,
B.10.432 And now ben [swiche] as Souereyns wiþ Seintes in *heuene*,
B.10.468 Percen wiþ a Paternoster þe paleys of *heuene*
B.11.28 'Man', quod he, 'if I mete wiþ þe, by Marie of *heuene*!
B.11.81 Thoruȝ contricion [clene] come to þe heiȝe *heuene*–
B.11.185 [For] oure Ioye and oure [Iuel], Iesu crist of *heuene*,

B.12.37   And hold þee vnder obedience þat heigh wey is to *heuene*.
B.12.40   [Lo]! what made lucifer to lese þe heiȝe *heuene*,
B.12.66   Of quod scimus comeþ Clergie, [a] konnynge of *heuene*,
B.12.126 For Clergie is kepere vnder crist of *heuene*;
B.12.139 For þe heiȝe holy goost *heuene* shal tocleue,
B.12.196 Ac þouȝ þat þeef hadde *heuene* he hadde noon heiȝ blisse,
B.12.211 That oure lord ne hadde hym liȝtly out, so leue I [by] þe þef in
            heuene.
B.12.212 For he is in þe loweste of *heuene*, if oure bileue be trewe,
B.12.284 And he is saaf, seiþ þe book, and his soule in *heuene*.
B.13.142 And so þow lere þe to louye, for [þe] lordes loue of *heuene*,
B.14.66   And in Elyes tyme *heuene* was yclosed,
B.14.129 For þei han hir hire heer and *heuene* as it were,
B.14.141 Haue *heuene* in youre her[berw]yng and heuene þerafter
B.14.141 Haue heuene in youre her[berw]yng and *heuene* þerafter
B.14.154 Here forȝifnesse of hir synnes, and *heuene* blisse after.
B.14.165 *Heuene* after hir hennes goyng þat here han swich defaute.
B.14.210 Than richesse or reautee, and raþer yherd in *heuene*.
B.15.51   For swich a lust and likyng Lucifer fel from *heuene*:
B.15.352 Crowne and cristendom, þe kynges mark of *heuene*,
B.15.407 That þe coluere þat com so com from god of *heuene*
B.15.480 So hope þei to haue *heuene* þoruȝ hir whistlyng.
B.15.511 [Whan þe hye kyng of *heuene* sente his sone to erþe
B.16.118 That he was leche of lif and lord of heigh *heuene*.
B.16.208 And in *heuene* and here oon singuler name.
B.16.213 Hym þat first formed al, þe fader of *heuene*.
B.16.222 And is noȝt but gendre of a generacion bifore Iesu crist in *heuene*:
B.17.147 The holy goost of *heuene*: he is as þe pawme.
B.17.164 *Heuene* and helle and al þat is þerInne.
B.17.166 That þre þynges bilongeþ in oure [fader] of *heuene*
B.17.203 The holy goost of *heuene* [he] is as þe pawme.
B.17.247 [Fro] þe fader of *heuene* forȝifnesse to haue.
B.18.224 Boþe in *heuene* and in erþe, and now til helle he þenkeþ
B.18.239 [The oostes] in *heuene* token stella com[a]ta
B.18.280 For hymself seide, þat Sire is of *heuene*,
B.18.312 First þoruȝ þe we fellen fro *heuene* so heiȝe:
B.18.320 That Crist may come In, þe kynges sone of *heuene*!'
B.18.356 And I in liknesse of a leode, þat lord am of *heuene*,
B.18.397 And mercy al mankynde bifore me in *heuene*.
B.19.74   Aungeles out of *heuene* come knelynge and songe,
B.19.81   For alle þe Aungeles of *heuene* at his burþe kneled[e],
B.19.191 Anoon after an heigh vp into *heuene*
B.20.194 And wisshed ful witterly þat I were in *heuene*.
B.20.270 *Heuene* haþ euene noumbre and helle is wiþoute noumbre.
B.20.276 That alle þynges vnder *heuene* ouȝte to ben in comune.
C.Pr.133 Thare Crist is in kynedom to close with *heuene*.
C.Pr.151 And for thy rightful ruylynge be rewardid in *heuene*.'
C. 1.9   Of othere *heuene* then here [halde thei] no tale.'
C. 1.104 And god whan he bigan *heuene* in þat grete blisse
C. 1.108 He was an Archangel of *heuene*, on of goddes knyghtes;
C. 1.133 Estward til *heuene*, euere to abyde
C. 1.149 For *heuene* holde hit ne myghte, so heuy hit semede,
C. 1.155 Forthi is loue ledare of [þe] lordes folk of *heuene*
C. 1.200 And þe graffe of grace and gray[th]est way to *heuene*.
C. 2.2   And sayde 'mercy, madame, for mary loue of *heuene*
C. 2.33   And y am his dere doughter, ducchesse of *heuene*.
C. 2.38   That helpeth man moste to *heuene* mede most letteth.
C. 2.135 "God of thy grace *heuene* gates opene,
C. 3.98   That Innocence is herde in *heuene* amonge seyntes.
C. 3.167 Bytwene *heuene* and helle, and erthe thogh men soughte.
C. 3.456 That here kyng be ycome fro þe Court of *heuene*,
C. 4.139 Ne thorw mede mercy, by marie of *heuene*!
C. 4.173 Mede shal nat maynprise [ȝow], by marye of *heuene*!
C. 5.59   For hit ben eyres of *heuene* alle þat ben ycrouned
C. 5.125 How resoun radde al the reume to *heuene*.
C. 5.152 For yf *heuene* be on this erthe or ese to [eny] soule
C. 5.186 Lo! in *heuene* an heyh was an holy comune
C. 6.307 And arste shal come to *heuene*, [by hym þat me made]!'
C. 6.317 Ac ȝut þ[e] synful shrewe saide to *heuene*:
C. 6.331 'Be þe rode,' quod repentaunce, 'thow romest toward *heuene*
C. 7.135 And brouhte thyne yblessed fro thennes into þe blisse of *heuene*.
C. 7.249 To opene and vndo þe hye gate of *heuene*
C. 8.16   As longe as y leue, for [þe] lordes loue of *heuene*.
C. 8.43   Thogh he be here thyn vnderlynge in *heuene* parauntur
C. 9.126 For hit aren murye mouthed men, munstrals of *heuene*
C.11.187 'Man,' quod [he], 'yf y me[t]e with the, by marie of *heuene*,
C.11.198 'Go y to helle or to *heuene* y shal nat go myn one.
C.11.219 And yf we sholde wurche aftur here werkes to wy[n]nen vs *heuene*
C.11.268 And now beth this seyntes, by that men saith, and souereynes in
            heuene,
C.11.294 Persen with a paternoster [þe paleys of] *heuene*
C.12.98   And cristis oune clergie; he cam fro *heuene* to teche hit

C.12.160 And lyf lastyng for euere byfore oure lord in *heuene*:
C.13.30   And lyues þat oure lord loueth and large weyes to *heuene*;
C.13.67   Aren alle acountable to crist and to þe kyng of *heuene*,
C.14.84   For the hey holi gost *heuene* shal tocleue
C.14.135 Ac thogh th[at] theef hadde *heuene* he hadde noen hey blisse
C.14.150 That oure [lord] ne hauede [hym] lihtliche out, so leue y [by] þ[e]
            thef in *heuene*.
C.14.151 For he is in þe loweste of *heuene*, yf oure byleue be trewe,
C.14.193 Wher þey ben in hell or in *heuene* or Aristotel þe wyse.
C.14.206 And he is saef, saith the boek, and his soule in *heuene*.
C.15.34   Crauede and cryede for cristes loue of *heuene*
C.15.265 And in Elies tyme *heuene* was yclosed
C.16.9   Haue two *heuenes* for ȝoure her[berw]ynge.
C.16.27   And satisfaccioun þe whiche folfilleth þe fader will of *heuene*;
C.16.51   Then rychesse or ryalte and rather yherde in *heuene*.
C.16.213 For such a lust and lykynge lucifer ful fram *heuene*:
C.16.312 And alle manere meschiefs as munstracie of *heuene*.
C.17.78   Cristendoem of holy kyrke, the kynges marke of *heuene*,
C.17.149 Contrarie her nat as in Consience yf thow wol[t] come to *heuene*.'
C.17.178 For Macometh to men swaer hit was a messager of *heuene*
C.17.247 The whiche is þe hy holy gost þat out of *heuene* descendet[h]
C.17.248 To make a perpetuel pees bitwene þe prince of *heuene*
C.17.262 For when þe hye kyng of *heuene* sente his so[n]e til erthe
C.18.26   Bytokeneth trewely the trinite of *heuene*,
C.18.72   The whiche þe seynt spirit seweth, the sonne of al *heuene*,
C.18.87   Wydewhode, more worthiore then wedlok, as in *heuene*,
C.18.88   Thenne is virginite, more vertuous and fayrest, as in *heuene*,
C.18.90   Hit was þe furste fruyte þat þe fader of *heuene* blessed,
C.18.97   And in *heuene* is priueoste and next hym by resoun
C.18.226 Now go we to godhede: in god, fader of *heuene*,
C.19.121 The holy goest of *heuene*: he is as þe paume.
C.19.169 The holy gost of *heuene* he is as þe paume.
C.19.213 To þe fader of *heuene* forȝe[ue]nesse to haue.
C.20.233 Bothe in *heuene* and in erthe, and now to helle he thenketh
C.20.248 Tho þat weren in *heuene* token stella comata
C.20.302 For hymsulue said, þat sire is of *heuene*,
C.20.346 And out of *heuene* hidore thy pryde made vs falle.
C.20.363 That Crist may come in, þe kynges sone of h[e]uene!'
C.20.440 And mercy a[l] mankynde bifore me in *heuene*.
C.21.74   Angele[s] out of *heuene* come knel[yng] and songe,
C.21.81   For alle þe angelis of *heuene* at his burthe knelede
C.21.191 Anoon aftur an heyh vp into *heuene*
C.22.194 And wesched wel witterly þat y were in *heuene*.
C.22.270 [*Heuene* haeth euene nombre and helle is withoute nombre].
C.22.276 That alle thynges vnder *heuene* ou[h]te to be in comune.

heueneriche n *hevenriche n.* A 1; B 3; C 3 heueneryche (2) heuenriche
(1)

A.Pr.27   In hope [for] to haue *heueneriche* blisse,
B.Pr.27   In hope [for] to haue *heueneriche* blisse.
B.14.261 After hir endynge here, *heueneriche* blisse.
B.15.175 Coueiteþ he noon erþely good, but *heueneriche* blisse.'
C.Pr.29   In hope to haue a good ende and *heuenriche* blisse,
C.12.159 He shal haue an hundredfold of *heueneryche* blisse
C.16.101 Aftur here endynge here *heueneryche* blisse.

heueneward adv *heaven n.* A 1; B 3; C 1

A.11.227 Helpiþ nouȝt to *heuene[ward]* at one ȝeris ende,
B.10.339 Helpeþ noȝt to *heueneward* [at] oone [y]eris ende,
B.14.212 The heiȝe wey to *heueneward* [ofte] Richesse letteþ:
B.15.458 It is heþene as to *heueneward* and helplees to be soule.
C.16.53   The hey way to *heueneward* he halt hit nat fol euene

heuenriche > heueneriche

heuy adj *hevi adj.* A 2; B 6 heuy (5) heuyeste (1); C 6 heuegeste (1)
heuegore (1) heuy (4)

A. 4.20   Hange on hym þe *heuy* bridel to holde his hed lowe,
A. 5.58   Enuye wiþ *heuy* herte askide aftir shrift,
B. 4.22   Hange on hym þe *heuy* brydel to holde his heed lowe,
B. 4.165 Mede mornede þo and made *heuy* chere
B. 5.75   Enuye wiþ *heuy* herte asked after shrifte,
B. 5.240 To weye pens wiþ a peis and pare þe *heuyeste*
B.11.27   Thanne was þer oon þat hiȝte Elde, þat *heuy* was of chere;
B.20.2   *Heuy* chered I yede and elenge in herte.
C. 4.160 Mede mornede tho and made *heuy* chere
C. 6.63   Enuye with *heuy* herte asked aftur shrifte
C. 6.242 To weye pans with a peyse and par[e] þe *heuegeste*
C.11.186 Thenne was [there] oen þat hihte Elde þat *heuy* was of chere;
C.14.105 And bothe naked as a nedle, here noen *heuegore* then othere.
C.22.2   *Heuy* chered y ȝede and [e]lyng in herte.

heuy adv *hevie adv.* B 1; C 1

B. 1.153 For heuene myȝte nat holden it, [so *heuy* it semed],
C. 1.149 For heuene holde hit ne myghte, so *heuy* hit semede,

heuid > *heed*

heuynesse n *hevinesse n.* B 1; C 1
B.18.247   The Erþe for *heuynesse* þat he wolde suffre
C.20.256   Þe erthe for *heuynesse* þat he wolde soffre

hewe n *heue n.(1)* B 5 hewe (1) hewen (4); C 8 hewe (4) hewen (1)
    hewes (3)
B. 4.55   He maynteneþ hise men to murþere myne *hewen*,
B. 4.107   And [ofte] þe boldere be to bete myne *hewen*.
B. 5.552   He wiþhalt noon *hewe* his hire þat he ne haþ it at euen.
B.14.3   And also I haue an houswif, *hewen* and children–
B.14.134   *Hewen* þat han hir hire afore arn eueremoore nedy,
C. 1.124   *Hewes* in þe haliday after hete wayten
C. 3.308   The huyre of his *hewe* ouer eue til amorwe:
C. 4.58   A meynteyneth his men to morthere myn *hewes*,
C. 4.102   And efte the baldore be to bete myn *hewes*.
C. 7.196   He withhalt non *hewe* his huyre ouer euen;
C. 8.195   To be his holde *hewe* thow he hadde no more
C.10.216   As an *hewe* þat erieth nat aun[t]reth hym to sowe
C.16.3   *Hewen* þat haen here huyre byfore aren eueremore pore

hewe v *heuen v.(1)* B 1; C 1
B.17.248   Ac *hewe* fir at a flynt foure hundred wynter;
C.19.214   Ac *hewe* fuyr at a flynt foure hundret wynter,

hewe & > *hugh*

hewes n *heu n. &* > *hewe* B 2; C 2
B.11.366   And how among þe grene gras growed so manye *hewes*,
B.12.221   And of þe floures in þe Fryth and of hire faire *hewes*,
C.13.176   And how out of greeut and of gras gr[e]we so many *hewes*
C.14.158   And how þe floures in þe fryth cometh to fayre *hewes*:

heȝede > *hye; hy* > *heiȝ,hij; hicke(s* > *hikke; hidde(n* > *hiden; hiddere* >
hider

hiden v *hiden v.* B 8 hidde (2) hidden (3) hide (1) hiden (1) yhudde (1); C
    7 hidden (1) hyden (1) hudde (1) hudden (1) huyde (2) huydeth (1)
B.10.437   Ther are witty and wel libbynge ac hire werkes ben *yhudde*
B.11.352   *Hidden* and hileden hir egges ful derne
B.11.354   In Mareys and moores [manye] *hidden* hir egges]
B.17.111   He was vnhardy, þat harlot, and *hidde* hym in Inferno.
B.18.404   Astroth and al þe route *hidden* hem in hernes;
B.19.102   Som tyme he suffrede, and som tyme he *hidde* hym,
B.19.457   Ech man subtileþ a sleiȝte synne to *hide*
B.20.124   His wepne was al wiles, to wynnen and to *hiden*;
C.10.242   Ac þe gospel is a glose ther and *huydeth* þe grayth treuthe;
C.13.163   *Hudden* and helede here egges dernely
C.19.127   To *huyde* and to holde as holy writ telleth–
C.20.447   Astarot and alle [þe route] *hidden* hem in hernes;
C.21.102   Som tyme he soffrede and som tyme he *hudde* hym
C.21.457   Vch man sotileth a sleythe synne to *huyde*
C.22.124   His wepne was al wyles, to wynnen and to *hyden*;

hider adv *hider adv.* A 1; B 2; C 6 heddere (1) hiddere (1) hider (2)
    hyder (1) hidore (1)
A.11.179   And I sei[d]e, 'soþliche, þei sente me *hider*
B.18.291   And so þow haddest hem out and *hider* at þe laste.'
B.20.333   Carpe I wolde wiþ contricion, and þerfore cam I *hider*.'
C.15.236   Tho[r]w the helpe of hym þat me *hyder* sente;'
C.18.17   'Y thonke ȝow a thousend s[i]the that ȝe me *hider* kende
C.20.321   And so haddest hem out and *hiddere* at þe laste.'
C.20.336   That if his soule *hider* cam hit sholde shende vs all.
C.20.346   And out of heuene *hidore* thy pryde made vs falle.
C.22.333   Karpe y wolde with Contricioun and þerfore [cam y] *heddere*.'

hiderward adv *hiderward adv.* A 1; B 2; C 2 hiderward (1) hiderwardes
    (1)
A. 7.303   For hungir *hiderward* hastiþ hym faste.
B. 6.322   For hunger *hiderward* hasteþ hym faste.
B.18.307   And now I se wher a soule comeþ [silynge *hiderward*]
C. 8.342   For hungur *hiderwardes* hasteth hym faste.
C.20.341   And now y se where his soule cometh sylinge *hid[er]ward*

hidore > *hider*

hye v *hien v. &* > *heiȝ* A 1 heȝede; B 2 hyed (1) hiede (1); C 2 hye (1)
    hyede (1)
A. 7.165   And wiþ a bene batte *he[ȝe]de* [hem] betwene,
B. 5.376   For loue of tales in Tauernes [to] drynke þe moore I [*hyed*];
B.20.324   The frere herof herde and *hiede* faste
C. 8.205   And bade hunger in haste *hye* hym out of contraye
C.22.324   The frere herof herde and *hyede* faste

hyere -este > *heiȝ; highte* > *hote; hiȝere -este* > *heiȝ; hiȝt(- hihte* > *hote*

hij pron *he pron.(3) cf þei* A 371 hem (207) here (137) hy (24) hij (1)
    hire (2); B 836 hem (462) here (1) hij (4) hir (269) hire (100); C 825
    hem (433) her (14) here (376) hy (2)

    hem A 207
    A.Pr.20, A.Pr.23, A.Pr.23, A.Pr.25, A.Pr.28, A.Pr.31, A.Pr.36, A.Pr.36, A.Pr.37,
    A.Pr.38, A.Pr.45, A.Pr.46, A.Pr.53, A.Pr.54, A.Pr.57, A.Pr.59, A.Pr.67, A.Pr.71, A.Pr.80,
    A.Pr.106, A.1.21, A.1.22, A.1.22, A.1.30, A.1.47, A.1.67, A.1.94, A.1.97, A.1.101,
    A.1.105, A.1.105, A.1.106, A.1.107, A.1.108, A.1.115, A.1.122, A.1.143, A.1.148,
    A.2.23, A.2.29, A.2.29, A.2.62, A.2.64, A.2.66, A.2.110, A.2.125, A.2.126, A.2.134,
    A.2.137, A.2.138, A.2.147, A.2.149, A.2.150, A.2.151, A.2.157, A.2.157, A.2.159,
    A.2.164, A.2.165, A.2.166, A.2.186, A.2.194, A.3.1, A.3.14, A.3.19, A.3.20, A.3.28,
    A.3.29, A.3.29, A.3.72, A.3.80, A.3.81, A.3.88, A.3.115, A.3.126, A.3.154, A.3.155,
    A.3.198, A.3.209, A.3.220, A.3.223, A.3.223, A.3.247, A.3.249, A.3.250, A.3.264,
    A.3.272, A.4.25, A.4.27, A.4.52, A.4.63, A.4.132, A.5.20, A.5.33, A.5.126, A.5.126,
    A.5.127, A.5.127, A.6.61, A.6.65, A.6.120, A.6.122, A.7.15, A.7.16, A.7.22, A.7.41,
    A.7.41, A.7.63, A.7.67, A.7.68, A.7.69, A.7.73, A.7.100, A.7.105, A.7.113, A.7.115,
    A.7.132, A.7.133, A.7.163, A.7.165, A.7.173, A.7.175, A.7.179, A.7.184, A.7.185,
    A.7.194, A.7.195, A.7.195, A.7.197, A.7.197, A.7.201, A.7.202, A.7.206, A.7.207,
    A.7.207, A.7.210, A.7.236, A.7.241, A.7.242, A.7.257, A.7.293, A.8.8, A.8.15, A.8.21,
    A.8.23, A.8.25, A.8.26, A.8.26, A.8.31, A.8.35, A.8.68, A.8.78, A.8.87, A.8.92, A.8.115,
    A.8.116, A.8.117, A.9.10, A.9.11, A.9.79, A.9.85, A.9.86, A.9.90, A.9.91, A.9.94,
    A.9.95, A.9.96, A.9.99, A.10.16, A.10.58, A.10.67, A.10.68, A.10.69, A.10.70, A.10.129,
    A.10.142, A.10.143, A.10.154, A.10.156, A.10.168, A.10.191, A.10.194, A.10.215,
    A.11.11, A.11.14, A.11.31, A.11.34, A.11.133, A.11.136, A.11.152, A.11.152, A.11.164,
    A.11.188, A.11.190, A.11.190, A.11.220, A.11.222, A.11.248, A.11.251, A.11.252,
    A.11.252, A.11.271, A.11.299, A.11.301, A.12.111, A.12.112, A.12.115

    hem B 462
    B.Pr.20, B.Pr.23, B.Pr.23, B.Pr.25, B.Pr.28, B.Pr.31, B.Pr.36, B.Pr.36, B.Pr.37,
    B.Pr.38, B.Pr.45, B.Pr.46, B.Pr.56, B.Pr.57, B.Pr.60, B.Pr.62, B.Pr.70, B.Pr.74, B.Pr.83,
    B.Pr.90, B.Pr.106, B.Pr.108, B.Pr.130, B.Pr.147, B.Pr.150, B.Pr.150, B.Pr.151, B.Pr.159,
    B.Pr.163, B.Pr.180, B.Pr.183, B.Pr.228, B.1.21, B.1.22, B.1.22, B.1.30, B.1.49, B.1.69,
    B.1.96, B.1.99, B.1.103, B.1.107, B.1.107, B.1.108, B.1.109, B.1.110, B.1.120, B.1.126,
    B.1.133, B.1.169, B.1.174, B.2.47, B.2.47, B.2.48, B.2.48, B.2.49, B.2.70, B.2.87,
    B.2.93, B.2.97, B.2.98, B.2.146, B.2.161, B.2.162, B.2.170, B.2.175, B.2.186, B.2.188,
    B.2.189, B.2.190, B.2.196, B.2.196, B.2.198, B.2.203, B.2.204, B.2.205, B.2.227,
    B.2.235, B.3.1, B.3.14, B.3.20, B.3.21, B.3.29, B.3.30, B.3.30, B.3.83, B.3.91, B.3.92,
    B.3.99, B.3.126, B.3.137, B.3.167, B.3.168, B.3.199, B.3.200, B.3.211, B.3.222, B.3.233,
    B.3.243, B.3.267, B.3.282, B.3.283, B.3.288, B.3.313, B.3.317, B.3.317, B.3.349, B.4.19,
    B.4.28, B.4.30, B.4.32, B.4.36, B.4.40, B.4.66, B.4.77, B.4.121, B.4.149, B.5.20, B.5.35,
    B.5.36, B.5.58, B.5.143, B.5.143, B.5.144, B.5.146, B.5.148, B.5.148, B.5.156, B.5.158,
    B.5.172, B.5.210, B.5.210, B.5.211, B.5.211, B.5.249, B.5.256, B.5.256, B.5.263,
    B.5.271, B.5.397, B.5.477, B.5.504, B.5.574, B.5.578, B.5.635, B.5.637, B.6.2, B.6.16,
    B.6.17, B.6.39, B.6.69, B.6.75, B.6.76, B.6.77, B.6.81, B.6.108, B.6.113, B.6.121,
    B.6.138, B.6.147, B.6.178, B.6.181, B.6.181, B.6.185, B.6.187, B.6.188, B.6.196,
    B.6.197, B.6.198, B.6.208, B.6.209, B.6.209, B.6.211, B.6.211, B.6.215, B.6.216,
    B.6.220, B.6.221, B.6.221, B.6.224, B.6.225, B.6.225, B.6.273, B.6.309, B.7.19, B.7.21,
    B.7.23, B.7.24, B.7.24, B.7.29, B.7.33, B.7.41, B.7.43, B.7.66, B.7.83, B.7.83, B.7.89,
    B.7.105, B.7.110, B.7.133, B.7.134, B.7.135, B.8.10, B.8.11, B.8.88, B.8.95, B.8.100,
    B.8.101, B.8.104, B.8.105, B.8.106, B.8.109, B.8.126, B.9.15, B.9.17, B.9.67, B.9.69,
    B.9.70, B.9.70, B.9.71, B.9.73, B.9.78, B.9.79, B.9.88, B.9.102, B.9.108, B.9.109,
    B.9.170, B.9.173, B.9.201, B.10.11, B.10.14, B.10.39, B.10.43, B.10.43, B.10.48,
    B.10.80, B.10.181, B.10.184, B.10.203, B.10.203, B.10.209, B.10.221, B.10.321,
    B.10.325, B.10.326, B.10.391, B.10.398, B.10.410, B.10.453, B.11.15, B.11.49, B.11.87,
    B.11.97, B.11.121, B.11.179, B.11.183, B.11.196, B.11.196, B.11.221, B.11.289,
    B.11.339, B.11.353, B.11.361, B.11.372, B.11.375, B.11.393, B.12.17, B.12.45, B.12.54,
    B.12.56, B.12.56, B.12.87, B.12.94, B.12.124, B.12.127, B.12.149, B.12.160, B.12.194,
    B.12.195, B.12.231, B.12.251, B.12.272, B.13.10, B.13.12, B.13.38, B.13.42, B.13.121,
    B.13.240, B.13.264, B.13.324, B.13.350, B.13.373, B.13.423, B.13.424, B.13.437,
    B.13.439, B.13.451, B.13.451, B.13.455, B.14.33, B.14.80, B.14.113, B.14.114,
    B.14.115, B.14.119, B.14.146, B.14.161, B.14.164, B.14.169, B.14.170, B.14.171,
    B.14.173, B.14.184, B.14.203, B.14.203, B.14.255, B.15.37, B.15.75, B.15.109,
    B.15.184, B.15.184, B.15.185, B.15.189, B.15.190, B.15.190, B.15.192, B.15.224,
    B.15.245, B.15.285, B.15.296, B.15.305, B.15.312, B.15.320, B.15.331, B.15.331,
    B.15.335, B.15.337, B.15.341, B.15.341, B.15.344, B.15.431, B.15.435,
    B.15.437, B.15.437, B.15.451, B.15.463, B.15.466, B.15.486, B.15.503, B.15.537,
    B.15.563, B.15.564, B.15.565, B.15.566, B.15.567, B.15.572, B.15.572, B.15.573,
    B.15.581, B.15.603, B.15.610, B.16.27, B.16.80, B.16.83, B.16.106, B.16.127, B.16.128,
    B.16.130, B.16.147, B.16.193, B.16.206, B.16.228, B.16.246, B.17.43, B.17.93,
    B.17.120, B.17.121, B.17.133, B.17.139, B.17.162, B.17.190, B.17.237, B.17.312,
    B.17.354, B.18.93, B.18.145, B.18.146, B.18.172, B.18.176, B.18.192, B.18.200,
    B.18.201, B.18.227, B.18.272, B.18.287, B.18.289, B.18.291, B.18.294, B.18.295,
    B.18.329, B.18.332, B.18.335, B.18.345, B.18.348, B.18.352, B.18.386, B.18.390,
    B.18.404, B.18.405, B.19.44, B.19.47, B.19.85, B.19.107, B.19.139, B.19.145, B.19.153,
    B.19.153, B.19.154, B.19.156, B.19.181, B.19.181, B.19.196, B.19.202, B.19.203,
    B.19.206, B.19.233, B.19.246, B.19.251, B.19.265, B.19.309, B.19.338, B.19.338,
    B.19.342, B.19.366, B.19.415, B.19.421, B.19.429, B.20.58, B.20.67, B.20.111,
    B.20.130, B.20.231, B.20.234, B.20.237, B.20.237, B.20.241, B.20.243, B.20.256,
    B.20.258, B.20.258, B.20.259, B.20.260, B.20.284, B.20.295,
    B.20.335, B.20.349, B.20.360, B.20.365

    hem C 433
    C.Pr.22, C.Pr.25, C.Pr.25, C.Pr.27, C.Pr.30, C.Pr.37, C.Pr.39, C.Pr.46, C.Pr.47,
    C.Pr.54, C.Pr.55, C.Pr.58, C.Pr.68, C.Pr.72, C.Pr.81, C.Pr.95, C.Pr.106, C.Pr.109,
    C.Pr.109, C.Pr.110, C.Pr.110, C.Pr.120, C.Pr.168, C.Pr.171, C.Pr.171, C.Pr.172,

C.Pr.197, C.Pr.200, C.Pr.215, C.Pr.232, C.1.21, C.1.22, C.1.22, C.1.28, C.1.46, C.1.92, C.1.103, C.1.128, C.1.165, C.1.170, C.1.186, C.1.192, C.2.49, C.2.49, C.2.51, C.2.51, C.2.52, C.2.57, C.2.86, C.2.91, C.2.93, C.2.100, C.2.153, C.2.162, C.2.176, C.2.177, C.2.183, C.2.191, C.2.199, C.2.202, C.2.203, C.2.204, C.2.210, C.2.210, C.2.212, C.2.217, C.2.237, C.2.245, C.2.247, C.2.248, C.2.251, C.3.1, C.3.15, C.3.21, C.3.22, C.3.30, C.3.31, C.3.31, C.3.82, C.3.87, C.3.92, C.3.93, C.3.95, C.3.95, C.3.99, C.3.119, C.3.120, C.3.123, C.3.127, C.3.163, C.3.171, C.3.175, C.3.267, C.3.321, C.3.323, C.3.332, C.3.338, C.3.376, C.3.387, C.3.387, C.3.398, C.3.435, C.3.466, C.3.470, C.3.470, C.3.497, C.4.28, C.4.32, C.4.67, C.4.73, C.4.117, C.4.146, C.5.21, C.5.122, C.5.137, C.5.148, C.5.195, C.5.199, C.6.19, C.6.22, C.6.25, C.6.69, C.6.120, C.6.124, C.6.131, C.6.133, C.6.138, C.6.148, C.6.154, C.6.218, C.6.218, C.6.219, C.6.219, C.6.254, C.6.256, C.6.270, C.6.338, C.7.13, C.7.23, C.7.25, C.7.83, C.7.84, C.7.97, C.7.99, C.7.111, C.7.111, C.7.115, C.7.119, C.7.149, C.7.221, C.7.225, C.7.276, C.7.287, C.7.288, C.7.290, C.7.296, C.8.15, C.8.70, C.8.77, C.8.78, C.8.79, C.8.83, C.8.85, C.8.85, C.8.89, C.8.120, C.8.128, C.8.145, C.8.148, C.8.148, C.8.157, C.8.175, C.8.177, C.8.177, C.8.181, C.8.183, C.8.185, C.8.197, C.8.203, C.8.217, C.8.218, C.8.218, C.8.220, C.8.224, C.8.225, C.8.226, C.8.229, C.8.230, C.8.230, C.8.232, C.8.233, C.8.261, C.8.279, C.8.284, C.8.285, C.8.287, C.8.287, C.8.331, C.9.19, C.9.21, C.9.23, C.9.25, C.9.27, C.9.28, C.9.28, C.9.35, C.9.36, C.9.49, C.9.59, C.9.62, C.9.87, C.9.90, C.9.106, C.9.113, C.9.119, C.9.125, C.9.125, C.9.129, C.9.133, C.9.185, C.9.200, C.9.211, C.9.243, C.9.247, C.9.284, C.9.308, C.10.10, C.10.11, C.10.85, C.10.92, C.10.92, C.10.96, C.10.99, C.10.122, C.10.143, C.10.162, C.10.164, C.10.164, C.10.167, C.10.184, C.10.189, C.10.274, C.10.275, C.10.300, C.11.9, C.11.62, C.11.79, C.11.121, C.11.229, C.11.241, C.11.278, C.11.302, C.12.56, C.12.95, C.12.108, C.12.117, C.12.126, C.12.166, C.12.207, C.12.236, C.12.245, C.13.22, C.13.103, C.13.147, C.13.182, C.13.191, C.14.18, C.14.18, C.14.23, C.14.62, C.14.67, C.14.93, C.14.104, C.14.175, C.14.177, C.14.194, C.15.12, C.15.15, C.15.36, C.15.43, C.15.47, C.15.59, C.15.76, C.15.77, C.15.231, C.15.289, C.15.290, C.15.291, C.15.295, C.15.303, C.15.304, C.16.14, C.16.17, C.16.44, C.16.44, C.16.132, C.16.199, C.16.263, C.16.326, C.16.326, C.16.326, C.16.332, C.16.333, C.16.334, C.16.334, C.16.335, C.16.349, C.17.11, C.17.25, C.17.29, C.17.32, C.17.54, C.17.186, C.17.198, C.17.226, C.17.227, C.17.229, C.17.230, C.17.231, C.17.232, C.17.242, C.17.245, C.17.254, C.17.285, C.17.285, C.17.285, C.17.286, C.17.311, C.17.318, C.18.31, C.18.73, C.18.111, C.18.114, C.18.141, C.18.142, C.18.155, C.18.157, C.18.202, C.18.217, C.18.230, C.18.231, C.18.243, C.19.27, C.19.83, C.19.102, C.19.107, C.19.112, C.19.132, C.19.156, C.19.174, C.19.203, C.19.247, C.19.292, C.19.334, C.20.96, C.20.148, C.20.149, C.20.179, C.20.188, C.20.205, C.20.206, C.20.236, C.20.280, C.20.294, C.20.308, C.20.313, C.20.319, C.20.320, C.20.321, C.20.324, C.20.325, C.20.334, C.20.353, C.20.372, C.20.375, C.20.377, C.20.380, C.20.380, C.20.428, C.20.432, C.20.447, C.20.448, C.21.44, C.21.47, C.21.85, C.21.107, C.21.139, C.21.145, C.21.153, C.21.153, C.21.154, C.21.156, C.21.181, C.21.181, C.21.196, C.21.202, C.21.203, C.21.206, C.21.233, C.21.246, C.21.251, C.21.265, C.21.309, C.21.338, C.21.338, C.21.342, C.21.366, C.21.415, C.21.421, C.21.429, C.22.58, C.22.67, C.22.111, C.22.130, C.22.231, C.22.234, C.22.237, C.22.237, C.22.241, C.22.243, C.22.256, C.22.258, C.22.258, C.22.259, C.22.260, C.22.261, C.22.284, C.22.292, C.22.295, C.22.335, C.22.349, C.22.360, C.22.365

her C 14

C.Pr.123, C.8.82, C.8.175, C.10.193, C.10.193, C.10.256, C.10.299, C.10.300, C.17.93, C.17.306, C.20.36, C.20.67, C.20.205, C.21.112

here A 137

A.Pr.28, A.Pr.30, A.Pr.34, A.Pr.41, A.Pr.41, A.Pr.42, A.Pr.48, A.Pr.49, A.Pr.51, A.Pr.54, A.Pr.60, A.Pr.60, A.Pr.71, A.Pr.80, A.Pr.81, A.Pr.87, A.Pr.89, A.Pr.102, A.Pr.104, A.1.95, A.1.97, A.1.118, A.1.121, A.1.166, A.1.167, A.2.67, A.2.70, A.2.114, A.2.132, A.2.136, A.2.144, A.2.175, A.2.175, A.2.187, A.2.188, A.3.20, A.3.23, A.3.30, A.3.73, A.3.125, A.3.125, A.3.140, A.3.183, A.3.203, A.3.204, A.3.205, A.3.206, A.3.207, A.3.211, A.3.212, A.3.229, A.3.234, A.3.242, A.3.252, A.4.105, A.4.107, A.5.19, A.5.32, A.5.37, A.5.177, A.5.191, A.5.252, A.6.60, A.6.61, A.6.90, A.7.47, A.7.72, A.7.114, A.7.133, A.7.163, A.7.199, A.7.200, A.7.201, A.7.236, A.7.240, A.7.258, A.7.277, A.7.291, A.7.295, A.7.300, A.8.15, A.8.15, A.8.16, A.8.17, A.8.19, A.8.22, A.8.23, A.8.24, A.8.33, A.8.44, A.8.47, A.8.63, A.8.65, A.8.77, A.8.80, A.8.84, A.8.87, A.8.88, A.8.88, A.8.127, A.9.98, A.10.60, A.10.61, A.10.63, A.10.83, A.10.103, A.10.129, A.10.132, A.10.135, A.10.145, A.10.161, A.10.167, A.10.181, A.10.214, A.11.13, A.11.15, A.11.18, A.11.34, A.11.39, A.11.43, A.11.44, A.11.57, A.11.69, A.11.69, A.11.70, A.11.71, A.11.152, A.11.185, A.11.186, A.11.274, A.11.275, A.11.275, A.11.276, A.11.277, A.11.277, A.11.313, A.12.21

here B 1

B.12.120

here C 376 &> heo,here,heren

C.Pr.30, C.Pr.32, C.Pr.42, C.Pr.42, C.Pr.43, C.Pr.49, C.Pr.50, C.Pr.52, C.Pr.55, C.Pr.61, C.Pr.61, C.Pr.72, C.Pr.82, C.Pr.109, C.Pr.120, C.Pr.144, C.Pr.164, C.Pr.166, C.Pr.180, C.Pr.182, C.Pr.183, C.Pr.197, C.Pr.198, C.Pr.228, C.Pr.230, C.1.93, C.1.103, C.1.131, C.1.189, C.1.190, C.2.7, C.2.61, C.2.78, C.2.102, C.2.109, C.2.166, C.2.196, C.2.208, C.2.209, C.2.226, C.2.226, C.2.238, C.2.239, C.3.26, C.3.33, C.3.72, C.3.83, C.3.93, C.3.95, C.3.96, C.3.101, C.3.103, C.3.174, C.3.174, C.3.189, C.3.253, C.3.272, C.3.273, C.3.274, C.3.275, C.3.276, C.3.279, C.3.280, C.3.302, C.3.317, C.3.322, C.3.366, C.3.380, C.3.400, C.3.416, C.3.426, C.3.451, C.3.455, C.3.456, C.3.465, C.3.465, C.3.470, C.4.34, C.4.36, C.4.68, C.4.115, C.4.115, C.4.116, C.5.48, C.5.62, C.5.72, C.5.73, C.5.73, C.5.77, C.5.121, C.5.126, C.5.136, C.5.143, C.5.157, C.5.163, C.5.164, C.5.166, C.5.172, C.5.173, C.5.175, C.5.175, C.5.177, C.5.195, C.6.20, C.6.21, C.6.69, C.6.99, C.6.99, C.6.120, C.6.150, C.6.150, C.6.236, C.6.271, C.6.280, C.6.386, C.6.401, C.6.435, C.7.39, C.7.88, C.7.90, C.7.97, C.7.114, C.7.220, C.7.221, C.7.253, C.7.259, C.8.50, C.8.90, C.8.91, C.8.115, C.8.129, C.8.130, C.8.178, C.8.185, C.8.187, C.8.215, C.8.221, C.8.223, C.8.225, C.8.250, C.8.259, C.8.262, C.8.262, C.8.295, C.8.316, C.8.329, C.8.333, C.8.339, C.9.17, C.9.18, C.9.24, C.9.25, C.9.31, C.9.48, C.9.54, C.9.58, C.9.76, C.9.87, C.9.98, C.9.102, C.9.102, C.9.138, C.9.170, C.9.171, C.9.174, C.9.178, C.9.182, C.9.185, C.9.186, C.9.186, C.9.198, C.9.199, C.9.199, C.9.210, C.9.230, C.9.246, C.9.264, C.9.294, C.10.65, C.10.65, C.10.66, C.10.97, C.10.97, C.10.98, C.10.105, C.10.168, C.10.189, C.10.205, C.10.215, C.10.235, C.10.272, C.11.11, C.11.15, C.11.26, C.11.39, C.11.51, C.11.55, C.11.56, C.11.64, C.11.65, C.11.133, C.11.164, C.11.216, C.11.216, C.11.217, C.11.219, C.11.220, C.11.227, C.11.228, C.11.230, C.11.295, C.11.298, C.11.302, C.12.9, C.12.100, C.12.122, C.12.126, C.12.139, C.12.176, C.12.195, C.12.196, C.12.207, C.12.228, C.13.25, C.13.51, C.13.73, C.13.116, C.13.136, C.13.163, C.13.166, C.13.175, C.13.178, C.13.178, C.14.46, C.14.55, C.14.65, C.14.66, C.14.66, C.14.74, C.14.75, C.14.76, C.14.77, C.14.78, C.14.79, C.14.81, C.14.82, C.14.82, C.14.95, C.14.97, C.14.98, C.14.105, C.14.163, C.14.169, C.14.172, C.14.173, C.14.177, C.14.190, C.14.196, C.14.197, C.14.198, C.14.200, C.14.201, C.15.11, C.15.12, C.15.48, C.15.98, C.15.166, C.15.167, C.15.167, C.15.169, C.15.169, C.15.184, C.15.291, C.15.294, C.15.301, C.15.304, C.16.3, C.16.11, C.16.18, C.16.80, C.16.93, C.16.101, C.16.207, C.16.216, C.16.233, C.16.235, C.16.240, C.16.263, C.16.279, C.16.284, C.16.325, C.16.349, C.16.358, C.16.365, C.17.7, C.17.25, C.17.36, C.17.45, C.17.70, C.17.77, C.17.97, C.17.101, C.17.106, C.17.117, C.17.122, C.17.124, C.17.133, C.17.146, C.17.195, C.17.195, C.17.227, C.17.257, C.17.257, C.17.288, C.17.312, C.18.73, C.18.76, C.18.77, C.18.80, C.18.141, C.18.156, C.18.156, C.18.219, C.18.234, C.18.243, C.19.26, C.19.32, C.19.83, C.19.147, C.19.247, C.19.291, C.19.294, C.19.322, C.19.323, C.19.324, C.19.325, C.20.67, C.20.75, C.20.76, C.20.208, C.20.235, C.20.235, C.20.290, C.20.320, C.20.382, C.20.430, C.21.49, C.21.61, C.21.79, C.21.167, C.21.217, C.21.235, C.21.239, C.21.275, C.21.316, C.21.388, C.21.414, C.21.415, C.21.421, C.21.423, C.21.450, C.21.462, C.22.59, C.22.67, C.22.68, C.22.104, C.22.128, C.22.157, C.22.231, C.22.265, C.22.265, C.22.283, C.22.284, C.22.307, C.22.353

hy A 24

A.Pr.63, A.1.165, A.1.165, A.2.25, A.2.126, A.2.185, A.3.24, A.3.74, A.3.74, A.4.25, A.5.95, A.5.254, A.6.3, A.7.125, A.7.155, A.7.190, A.7.191, A.7.192, A.7.240, A.7.277, A.7.285, A.8.73, A.10.160, A.10.213

hy C 2 &> heiȝ

C.22.261, C.22.300

hij A 1

A.3.65

hij B 4

B.Pr.66, B.1.191, B.5.115, B.20.300

hir B 269

B.Pr.180, B.1.99, B.1.129, B.2.67, B.2.95, B.2.172, B.2.229, B.3.65, B.3.75, B.3.216, B.3.218, B.3.219, B.3.220, B.3.225, B.3.250, B.3.273, B.3.317, B.4.33, B.4.120, B.5.34, B.5.45, B.5.143, B.5.256, B.5.328, B.5.343, B.5.426, B.6.52, B.6.80, B.6.122, B.6.123, B.6.188, B.6.213, B.6.214, B.6.215, B.6.274, B.6.293, B.6.311, B.6.319, B.7.20, B.7.21, B.7.22, B.7.31, B.7.61, B.7.63, B.7.82, B.7.98, B.7.105, B.7.106, B.7.106, B.7.145, B.8.108, B.9.62, B.9.63, B.9.64, B.9.71, B.9.91, B.9.109, B.9.112, B.9.132, B.9.147, B.9.158, B.9.158, B.9.193, B.9.200, B.10.13, B.10.15, B.10.18, B.10.30, B.10.30, B.10.46, B.10.48, B.10.53, B.10.57, B.10.58, B.10.82, B.10.84, B.10.96, B.10.111, B.10.111, B.10.117, B.10.203, B.10.287, B.10.318, B.10.320, B.10.325, B.10.327, B.10.328, B.10.390, B.10.390, B.10.392, B.10.393, B.10.396, B.10.397, B.10.399, B.10.402, B.10.469, B.10.470, B.10.474, B.11.56, B.11.57, B.11.61, B.11.72, B.11.179, B.11.182, B.11.182, B.11.184, B.11.187, B.11.195, B.11.233, B.11.284, B.11.286, B.11.316, B.11.328, B.11.344, B.11.352, B.11.354, B.11.357, B.11.362, B.11.365, B.11.368, B.11.368, B.12.54, B.12.110, B.12.122, B.12.123, B.12.123, B.12.131, B.12.132, B.12.133, B.12.134, B.12.135, B.12.136, B.12.137, B.12.137, B.12.151, B.12.153, B.12.154, B.12.161, B.12.219, B.12.222, B.12.240, B.12.251, B.12.274, B.12.275, B.12.276, B.12.278, B.13.9, B.13.9, B.13.10, B.13.43, B.13.91, B.13.171, B.13.236, B.13.324, B.13.353, B.13.353, B.13.374, B.13.428, B.13.430, B.13.437, B.13.454, B.14.63, B.14.80, B.14.115, B.14.118, B.14.125, B.14.125, B.14.129, B.14.134, B.14.153, B.14.153, B.14.154, B.14.159, B.14.165, B.14.172, B.14.176, B.14.240, B.14.253, B.14.261, B.15.54, B.15.72, B.15.76, B.15.81, B.15.121, B.15.121, B.15.122, B.15.122, B.15.132, B.15.183, B.15.207, B.15.233, B.15.234, B.15.240, B.15.248, B.15.300, B.15.310, B.15.311, B.15.321, B.15.330, B.15.359, B.15.364, B.15.370, B.15.384, B.15.392, B.15.424, B.15.426, B.15.427, B.15.427, B.15.480, B.15.487, B.15.506, B.15.506, B.15.522, B.15.534, B.15.534, B.15.598, B.15.604, B.16.128, B.16.138, B.16.165, B.16.228, B.17.31, B.17.93, B.17.314, B.17.342, B.17.343, B.17.344, B.17.345, B.18.37, B.18.65, B.18.65, B.18.73, B.18.74, B.18.109, B.18.200, B.18.203, B.18.226, B.18.226, B.18.388, B.18.391, B.19.49, B.19.61, B.19.79, B.19.112, B.19.167, B.19.217, B.19.235, B.19.239, B.19.275, B.19.316, B.19.388, B.19.414, B.19.415, B.19.421, B.19.423, B.19.450, B.19.462, B.20.59, B.20.67, B.20.68, B.20.128, B.20.157, B.20.231, B.20.265, B.20.265, B.20.283, B.20.284, B.20.307, B.20.353

hire A 2

A.Pr.94, A.3.252

hire B 100

B.Pr.28, B.Pr.30, B.Pr.34, B.Pr.41, B.Pr.41, B.Pr.42, B.Pr.48, B.Pr.49, B.Pr.51, B.Pr.52, B.Pr.54, B.Pr.57, B.Pr.63, B.Pr.63, B.Pr.74, B.Pr.84, B.Pr.89, B.Pr.97, B.Pr.97, B.Pr.97, B.Pr.117, B.Pr.161, B.Pr.165, B.Pr.166, B.Pr.181, B.Pr.181, B.Pr.214, B.Pr.216, B.Pr.224, B.Pr.226, B.1.97, B.1.132, B.1.192, B.1.193, B.2.59, B.2.102, B.2.106, B.2.150, B.2.168, B.2.183, B.2.216, B.2.216, B.2.228, B.3.31, B.3.84, B.3.100, B.3.136, B.3.136, B.3.151, B.3.196, B.3.199, B.3.217, B.3.224, B.3.255, B.3.263, B.3.302, B.3.304, B.4.34, B.4.125, B.4.125, B.5.19, B.5.143, B.5.162, B.5.232, B.5.245, B.5.250, B.5.573, B.5.574, B.6.178, B.6.307, B.7.17, B.7.44, B.7.95, B.7.102, B.8.67, B.9.62, B.9.77, B.10.71, B.10.75, B.10.76, B.10.118, B.10.274, B.10.317, B.10.321, B.10.409,

B.10.437, B.11.65, B.11.384, B.11.393, B.12.84, B.12.111, B.12.221, B.15.145, B.15.418, B.15.478, B.15.564, B.15.599, B.16.54, B.17.230, B.17.311

hikke n prop *Hikke n.* A 4 Hikke (3) hikkes (1); B 4 Hikke (3) Hikkes (1); C 4 Hicke (3) hickes (1)
A. 5.161   *Hikke þe* hakeneyman & hogge þe [nede]lere,
A. 5.170   *Hikke þe* hostiler hitte his hood aftir
A. 5.180   *Hikke þe* hostiller þanne hadde þe cloke
A. 5.182   And haue *hikkes* hood þe hostiller, & holde hym yseruid,
B. 5.310   *Hikke þe* hakeneyman and hugh þe Nedlere,
B. 5.321   *Hikke þe* [Hostiler] hitte his hood after
B. 5.331   *Hikke þe* hostiler [þanne] hadde þe cloke
B. 5.333   And haue *Hikkes* hood [þe] hostiler and holden hym yserued,
C. 6.365   *Hicke þe* hackenayman and hewe þe nedlare,
C. 6.378   *Hicke þe* hackenayman hit his hod aftur
C. 6.389   *Hicke þe* hostiler hadde þe cloke
C. 6.391   And haue *hickes* hood þe hostiler and holde hym yserued:

hiled v *hilen v.* A 1 helid; B 3 hiled (2) hileden (1)
A. 6.77   Alle þe housis ben *helid*, hallis & chaumbris,
B. 5.590   And alle þe houses ben *hiled*, halles and chambres,
B.11.352   Hidden and *hileden* hir egges ful derne
B.12.233   Why Adam *hiled* noȝt first his mouþ þat eet þe Appul

hilles > hulle; him > he

hymself pron *himself pron.* A 29 himself (1) himselue (1) hymself (17) hymselue (7) himseluen (1) hymseluen (2); B 85 hymself (46) hymselue (33) hymseluen (6); C 64 hymself (3) hymseluen (1) hymsulf (4) hymsulue (54) hymsuluen (2)
A.Pr.67   And seide þat *hymself* miȝte assoile hem alle
A. 1.44   'Go to þe gospel,' quaþ heo, 'þat god seide *himseluen*,
A. 1.62   Fadir of falshed, he foundi[de] it *hymselue*.
A. 1.85   It is as derworþi a dreury as dere god *hymseluen*.
A. 1.111   Til he brak buxumnesse þoruȝ bost of *hymseluen*.
A. 1.146   Here miȝt þou sen ensaumplis in *hymself* one
A. 2.136   Sire symonye *hymself* shal sitte on here bakkis;
A. 3.58   Neiþer in siȝt ne in þi soule, for god *hymself* knowiþ
A. 3.64   For oure sauiour it seide & *hymself* prechid:
A. 3.203   And mediþ men *hymself* to mayntene here lawis;
A. 4.32   And betwyn *hymself* & his sone sette hym a benche,
A. 5.135   For laboureris & louȝ folk þat lay be *h[y]mselue*;
A. 5.235   And ȝet þe synful shrewe seide to *hymselue*:
A. 6.79   Þe tour þere treuþe is *hymself* is vp to þe sonne,
A. 6.93   Þou shalt se treuþe *himself* wel sitte in þin herte
A. 7.102   Eche man on his maner made *hymself* to done,
A. 7.105   To ouersen hem *hymself*; whoso best wrouȝte
A. 8.86   Han as pleyn pardoun as þe plouȝman *hymselue*;
A. 9.32   Þere were þe manis lif lost for lacchesse of *hymselue*.
A.10.6   A lemman þat he louiþ lik to *hymselue*.
A.10.24   Til kynde come oþer sende [and] kepe hire *hymselue*.'
A.10.35   Saue man þat he made ymage to *himselue*,
A.10.72   Is chief souereyn ouer *hymself* his soule is ȝeme,
A.10.74   Saue *hymself* fro synne, for so hym behouiþ;
A.10.167   *Hymself* & his sones þre, & siþen here wyues
A.11.153   And do good a[g]ens euil; god *hymself* hotiþ
A.11.154   And seide it *hymself* in ensaumple for þe beste:
A.11.253   For he seiþ it *hymself* in his ten hestis;
A.11.295   For he seide it *hymself* to summe of his disciplis:
B.Pr.70   And seide þat *hymself* myȝte assoillen hem alle
B.Pr.206   But suffren as *hymself* wolde to [slen þat] hym likeþ,
B. 1.46   'Go to þe gospel,' quod she, 'þat god seide *hymseluen*,
B. 1.64   Fader of falshede, [he] founded it *hymselue*.
B. 1.87   It is as dereworþe a drury as deere god *hymseluen*.
B. 1.172   Here myȝtow sen ensample[s] in *hymself* oone
B. 2.172   Sire Symonye *hymself* shal sitte vpon hir bakkes.
B. 3.216   And medeþ men *h[y]mseluen* to mayntene hir lawes.
B. 3.237   And Dauid assoileþ it *hymself* as þe Sauter telleþ:
B. 3.264   "Forþi", seide Samuel to Saul, "god *hymself* hoteþ [þ]ee
B. 3.310   Spynne or sprede donge or spille *hymself* with sleuþe
B. 4.45   And bitwene *hymself* and his sone sette hym on benche,
B. 5.51   And er he gyue any grace gouerne first *hymselue*.
B. 5.219   For laborers and lowe folk þat lay by *hymselue*.
B. 5.279   Thanne weex þ[e] sherewe in wanhope & wolde han hanged *hym[self]*
B. 5.291   Bisette it *hymself* as best [be] for þi soule.
B. 5.463   Ac yet þe synfulle sherewe seide to *hymselue*:
B. 6.110   Ech man in his manere made *hymself* to doone,
B. 6.113   To ouersen hem *hymself*; whoso best wroȝte
B. 6.251   The freke þat fedeþ *hymself* wiþ his feiþful labour
B. 7.56   That neuere shul wexe ne wanye wiþouten god *hymselue*.
B. 7.81   And he þat biddeþ borweþ and bryngeþ *hymself* in dette.
B. 7.104   Han as pleyn pardon as þe Plowman *hymselue*;
B. 8.36   [There] were [þe mannes] lif lost [for] lachesse of *hymselue*.
B. 9.6   A lemman þat he loueþ lik to *hymselue*.
B. 9.24   Til kynde come or sende [and kepe] hire [*hymselue*].'
B. 9.34   [Saue man þat he made ymage] to *hymself*,
B. 9.36   For he was synguler *hymself* and seide faciamus
B. 9.119   And þus was wedlok ywroȝt and god *hymself* it made.
B. 9.120   In erþe [þe] heuene [is]; *hymself* [was þe] witnesse.
B. 9.194   For he made wedlok first and [þus] *hymself* seide:
B.10.38   Or daunted or drawe forþ; I do it on god *hymselue*.
B.10.99   Now haþ ech riche a rule to eten by *hymselue*
B.10.204   And do good a[g]ein yuel; god *hymself* hoteþ:
B.10.246   For al is but oon god and ech is god *hymselue*:
B.10.250   And *hymself* ordeyned to sadde vs in bileue.
B.10.252   And Crist cleped *hymself* so, þe [scripture] bereþ witnesse:
B.10.272   I rede ech a blynd bosard do boote to *hymselue*,
B.11.389   For is no creature vnder crist can formen *hymseluen*,
B.11.390   And if a man myȝte make [laklees] *hymself*
B.11.397   The shap ne þe shaft þat god shoop *hymselue*,
B.12.166   Or þe swymmere þat is saaf by so *hymself* like,
B.12.205   But by *hymself* as a soleyn and serued on [þe] erþe.
B.12.226   Ac kynde knoweþ þe cause *hymself*, no creature ellis.
B.13.114   And seide *hymself*, 'sire doctour, and it be youre wille,
B.13.118   And dobest doþ *hymself* so as he seiþ and precheþ:
B.13.282   And so singuler by *hymself* [as to siȝte of þe peple
B.13.283   Was noon swich as *hymself*], ne [noon] so po[pe] holy;
B.13.284   Yhabited as an heremyte, an ordre by *hymselue*.
B.13.312   Which myȝte plese þe peple and preisen *hymselue*:
B.13.440   As he seiþ *hymself*; seynt Iohan bereþ witnesse:
B.13.452   Thise solaceþ þe soule til *hymself* be falle
B.14.101   There is Charite þe chief, chaumbrere for god *hymselue*.'
B.14.201   Forþi cristene sholde be in commune riche, noon coueitous for *hymselue*,
B.14.273   The which is sib to god *hymself*, [so neiȝ is pouerte].'
B.14.283   And a sorwe of *hymself* and solace to þe soule,
B.14.317   For pacience is payn for pouerte *hymselue*,
B.14.331   Or maistrie ouer any man mo þan of *hymselue*.
B.15.219   And is compaignable and confortatif as crist bit *hymselue*:
B.15.263   For wel may euery man wite, if god hadde wold *hymselue*,
B.15.286   Poul primus heremita hadde parroked *hymselue*
B.15.497   And as *hymself* seide [so] to lyue and dye:
B.15.582   And Iewes lyuen in lele lawe; oure lord wroot it *hymselue*
B.16.13   'It groweþ in a gardyn', quod he, 'þat god made *hymselue*
B.16.96   Wheiþer sholde fonge þe fruyt, þe fend or *hymselue*.
B.16.105   That, þouȝ he were wounded with his enemy, to warisshen *hymselue*;
B.16.145   It was *hymself* sooþly and seide 'tu dicis'.
B.16.185   Pater is his propre name, a persone by *hymselue*.
B.16.188   The þridde highte þe holi goost, a persone by *hymselue*,
B.16.193   Of *hym[self]* and of his seruaunt, and what [suffreþ hem] boþe.
B.16.205   Adam, oure aller fader. Eue was of *hymselue*,
B.16.239   For *hymself* bihiȝte to me and to myn issue boþe
B.17.58   Ne helpe *hymself* sooþly, for semyvif he semed.
B.17.176   The pawme is pureliche þe hand, haþ power by *hymselue*
B.17.253   To alle vnkynde creatures; crist *hymself* witnesseþ:
B.17.354   And louye hem lik *hymself*, and his lif amende.
B.18.157   The first venymouste, þoruȝ [vertu] of *hymselue*.
B.18.191   [At] þe bigynn[yng god] gaf þe doom *hymselue*
B.18.222   And after god Auntrede *hymself* and took Adames kynd[e]
B.18.280   For *hymself* seide, þat Sire is of heuene.
B.19.67   To penaunce and to pouerte he moste puten *hymseluen*,
B.19.227   And gaf ech man a grace to gide wiþ *hymseluen*
B.19.332   And made preesthod hayward þe while *hymself* wente
B.19.436   As for *hymself* and hise seruauntȝ, saue he is first yserued.
B.19.447   It semeþ bi so *hymself* hadde his wille
C.Pr.68   [And] sayde þat *hymself* myhte assoylen hem alle
C. 1.83   Hit is a[s] derworthe a druerie as dere god *hymseluen*.
C. 1.168   Here myhtou se ensamples in *hymself* one
C. 2.41   And dauid vndoth *hymself* as þe doumbe sheweth:
C. 3.133   Til treuthe hadde ytolde here a tokene fram *hymsulue*.
C. 3.417   "Sauel," quod samuel, "god *hymsulue* hoteth [the]
C. 4.43   And bytwene *hymsulue* and his sone sette tho sire resoun
C. 5.187   Til lucifer þe lyare leued þat *hymselue*
C. 6.227   For laboreres and louh folk þat lay by *hymsulue*.
C. 6.346   To bysetten hit *hymsulue* as beste be for thy soule.
C. 7.100   As he sayth *hymsulf*; seynt Ion bereth witnesse:
C. 7.112   Thise solaseth þe soule til *hymsulue* be yfalle
C. 8.117   Vch man in his manere made *hymsulue* to done,
C. 8.120   [To] ouersey hem *hymsulue*; hoso beste wrouhte
C.10.133   A lemman þat he louyeth ylyke to *hymsulue*.
C.10.150   Til kynde come o[r] sende and kepe here *hymsulue*.'
C.10.182   Hath tresor ynow of treuthe to fynden *hymsulue*.
C.10.207   For god saith *hymsulue*, "shal neuere goed appel
C.10.238   That þe sire by *hymsulue* doth þe sone sholde be þe worse.
C.11.96   And clergi[es] wedded wyf, as wyse as *hymsulue*
C.12.162   What god saide *hymsulue* to a segg þat he louede:

295

C.12.170 He moet forsaken *hymsulue* his suster and his broþer
C.13.9 Bynoem [hym] his hosewyf [and helde here *hymsulue*]
C.13.78 As Crist *hymsulf* comaundeth alle cristene peple:
C.13.92 Ther god is gateward *hymsulf* and vch a gome knoweth.
C.13.94 In þat a wilneth and wolde vch wyht as *hymsulue*.
C.13.164 For no foul sholde hit fynde but his fere and *hymsulue*.
C.13.196 'Vch a segge for *hymsulue*, salamon vs techeth:
C.13.207 For is no creature vnder Crist þat can *hymsulue* make
C.14.41 "That seth *hymsulue* synnelees sese nat, y hote,
C.14.134 And wol no wikkede man [be] lost bote if he wol *hymsulue*:
C.14.144 Bote as a soleyn by *hymsulue* [and] yserued [o]n þe [erthe].
C.15.121 And saide *hymsulue*, 'sire doctour, [and] hit be ȝoure wille.
C.15.234 Pruyde wolde potte *hymsulf* forth thogh no plough erye.
C.16.42 Forthy cristene sholde be in comune ryche, noon coueytous for *hymsulue*.
C.16.113 The whiche is syb to crist [hym]*sulue* and semblable bothe.'
C.16.344 And compenable in companye a[s] Crist *hymsulue* techeth:
C.17.13 Paul primus heremita hadde yparrokede *hymsulue*
C.17.49 And charite þat chield is now sholde chaufen of *hymsulue*
C.17.81 That god coueyteth þe coyne þat crist *hymsulue* printede
C.17.193 And as *hymsulue* saide so to lyue and deye:
C.17.240 Hadde al surie as *hymsulue* wolde and sarrasines in equitee.
C.18.194 The thridde is þat halt al, a thyng by *hymsulue*;
C.18.202 Of *hymsulue* and his seruant, and what soffreth hem bothe.
C.18.211 Semblable to *hymsulue* ar eny synne were,
C.18.213 The werkes þat *hymsulue* wr[o]uhte and this world bothe:
C.18.227 Was þe sone in *hymsulue*, in a simile as Eue was,
C.18.255 For *hymsulue* saide y sholde [haue], y and my issue bothe,
C.19.57 Ne helpe *hymsulue* sothly for semyuief he semede.
C.19.141 The paume is puyrliche the hand and hath power by *hymsulue*
C.19.219 To alle vnkynde creatures, as Crist *hymsulue* witnesseth:
C.19.238 And *hymsulue*, sayth the boek, sotiled how he myhte
C.19.334 And louye h[e]m yliche *hymsulue* [and his lyf] amende.
C.20.54 And saiden, 'yf he sotil be *hymsulue* now he wol helpe;'
C.20.160 The [f]erste venemouste, thorw vertu of *hymsulue*.
C.20.196 At the bigynnyge god gaf the doem *hymsulue*
C.20.217 Ne hadde god ysoffred of som oþer then *hymsulue*
C.20.231 And aftur god auntred *hymsulue* and toek Adames kynde
C.20.302 For *hymsulue* said, þat sire is of heuene,
C.21.67 To penaunce and to pouerte he mot putte *hymsuluen*
C.21.227 And gaf vch man a grace to gye with *hymsuluen*
C.21.332 And made presthoed hayward the while *hymsulue* wente
C.21.436 As for *hymsulue* and his seruauntes, saue he is furste yserued.
C.21.447 Hit semeth bi so *hymsulue* hadde his wille

hynde n *hinde n.* B 1; C 1
B.15.279 Except þat Egidie after an *hynde* cride,
C.17.9 Excepte þat Egide a *hynde* oþerwhile

hyne n *hine n.* A 5 hyne (3) hynen (2); B 4; C 1
A.Pr.39 Qui loquitur turpiloquium [is] luciferis *hyne*.
A.4.42 He maynteniþ his men to murþre myne *hynen*,
A.4.94 And ofte þe boldere be to bete myn *hynen*.
A.6.39 He [wiþ]halt non *hyne* his hire þat he ne haþ it at eue.
A.7.123 And I am his [h]olde *hyne* & auȝte hym to warne.
B.Pr.39 Qui loquitur turpiloquium is luciferes *hyne*.
B.6.131 And I am his [h]olde *hyne* and [auȝte] hym to warne
B.13.363 And if my Neghebore hadde a[n] *hyne* or any beest ellis
B.14.149 And as an *hyne* þat hadde his hire er he bigonne,
C.6.262 And yf my neyhebore hadde an *hyne* or eny beste elles

hippynge > huppe; hir > heo,hij

hire n *hire n.* &> *heo,hij* A 6 here (2) hire (4); B 13 hire (10) hyre (2) huyre (1); C 10 huyre
A.3.63 An aunter ȝe haue ȝoure *hire* þerof h[e]re;
A.3.235 Is no maner of mede but a mesurable *hire*;
A.6.37 [I] haue myn *here* of hym [wel] & oþerwhile more.
A.6.39 He [wiþ]halt non *hyne* his *hire* þat he ne haþ it at eue.
A.6.43 'ȝa, leue piers,' quaþ þe pilgrimes & profride hym *hire*.
A.7.60 Shal haue be oure lord þe more *here* in heruist,
B.2.123 For Dignus est operarius his *hire* to haue,
B.3.72 On aunenture ye haue youre *hire* here and youre heuene als.
B.3.256 It is no manere Mede but a mesurable *hire*.
B.5.550 I haue myn *hire* [of hym] wel and ouþerwhiles moore.
B.5.552 He wiþhalt noon hewe his *hire* þat he ne haþ it at euen.
B.5.556 'Ye! leue Piers', quod þise pilgrimes and profred hym *huyre*.
B.6.139 Ac ye myȝte trauaille as truþe wolde and take mete and *hyre*
B.6.195 And ech a pouere man wel apaied to haue pesen for his *hyre*,
B.14.129 For þei han hir *hire* heer and heuene as it were,
B.14.134 Hewen þat han hir *hire* afore arn eueremoore nedy,
B.14.143 As he þat noon hadde and haþ *hire* at þe laste.
B.14.149 And as an hyne þat hadde his *hire* er he bigonne,
B.14.153 And alle þat doon hir deuoir wel han double *hire* for hir trauaille,
C.2.178 Ac hakeneys hadde thei none bote hakeneys to *huyre*;

C.3.302 They asken here *huyre* ar thei hit haue deserued
C.3.308 The *huyre* of his hewe ouer eue til amorwe:
C.7.194 Y haue myn *huyre* of hym wel and oþerwhiles more.
C.7.196 He withhalt non hewe his *huyre* ouer euen;
C.8.115 Therwith was [Perkyn] apayed and payede wel here *huyre*.
C.9.74 Þat they with spynnyng may spare spenen hit [i]n hous *huyre*,
C.9.274 Thyn *huyre*, herde, as y hope, hath nat to quyte thy dette
C.14.215 And þat is loue and large *huyre*, yf þe lord be trewe,
C.16.3 Hewen þat haen here *huyre* byfore aren eueremore pore

hired ptp *hiren v.* A 2 hirid; B 2 hired (1) hyred (1); C 2 huyred (1) yhuyred (1)
A.7.106 Shulde ben *hirid* þereaftir whan heruist tyme come.
A.7.296 But he be heiȝliche *hirid* ellis wole he chide,
B.6.114 Sholde be *hired* þerafter whan heruest tyme come.
B.6.312 But he be heiȝliche *hyred* ellis wole he chide;
C.8.121 He sholde be *huyred* þeraftur when heruost tyme come.
C.8.334 But he be heyliche *yhuyred* elles wol he chy[d]e;

hireself pron *hireself pron.* A 2; B 4 hireself (1) hirselue (3); C 4 heresulue
A.3.133 Heo is assoilid [as] sone as *hireself* likiþ.
A.3.137 Sire symonye & *hireself* seliþ þe bullis;
B.3.144 She is assoiled as soone as *hireself* likeþ.
B.3.148 Sire Symonie and *hirselue* seleþ [þe] bulles.
B.18.245 And lo! how þe sonne gan louke hire light in *hirselue*
B.18.289 And eggedest hem to ete, Eue by *hirselue*,
C.3.182 He is assoiled [as] sone as *heresulue* lyketh.
C.3.186 For symonye and *heresulue* seleth [þe] bulles.
C.3.208 Vnsittyng soffraunce, here suster, and *heresulue*
C.20.254 And lo! how þe sonne gan louke here lihte in *heresulue*

his(e > he,it; hit > hitte,it

hitselue pron *hitself pron.* B 1; C 1 hitsilue
B.1.154 Til it hadde of þe erþe [y]eten [*hitselue*].
C.1.150 Til hit hadde of erthe yȝoten *hitsilue*.

hitte v *hitten v.* A 2; B 7; C 8 hit (3) hitte (4) hutte (1)
A.5.170 Hikke þe hostiler *hitte* his hood aftir
A.7.166 And *hitte* hunger þerwiþ amydde hise lippes,
B.5.164 And eiþer *hit[t]e* ooþer vnder þe cheke.
B.5.321 Hikke þe [Hostiler] *hitte* his hood after
B.12.106 And haþ noon hap wiþ his ax his enemy to *hitte*,
B.16.87 He *hitte* after hym, [happe] how it myȝte,
B.20.103 That he *hitte* euene, þat euere stired after.
B.20.175 And Elde auntred hym on lyf, and at þe laste he *hitte*
B.20.190 And *hitte* me vnder þe ere; vnneþe [may] ich here.
C.6.378 Hicke þe hackenayman *hit* his hod aftur
C.11.111 A[c] if þow happe,' quod he, 'þat þou *hitte* on clergie
C.14.51 And hath non hap with his ax his enemye to *hutte*,
C.18.119 And *hit* aftur þe fende, happe how hit myhte,
C.20.383 And hoso *hit* out a mannes eye or elles his foreteth
C.22.103 That he *hi[t]te* euene, þat euere stured aftur.
C.22.175 And Elde auntered hym on lyf and at þe laste he *hitte*
C.22.190 And *hitte* me vnder þe ere; vnnethe may ich here.

ho > who

hobelide v *hobelen v.* A 1
A.1.113 Out of heuene into helle *hobelide* þei faste,

hod > hood; hode > hood,robyn_hood; hoed > hood; hoem > hoom; hoend(e > hand; hoer(- > hoor(-; hoes > who; hoet > hoot,hote

hogge n prop *Hogge n.(3)* A 1
A.5.161 Hikke þe hakeneyman & *hogge* þe [nede]lere,

hogges n *hogge n.(1)* A 1; B 2; C 1 hoggus
A.11.10 Among *hogges* þat hauen hawen at wille.
B.6.181 '[Lat] hem lyue', he seide, 'and lat hem ete wiþ *hogges*,
B.10.10 Among *hogges* þat han hawes at wille.
C.11.8 Among *hoggus* þat han hawes at wille.

hoked ptp *hoken v.* A 2 hokid (1) hokide (1); B 3; C 3 hoked (1) hokede (2)
A.Pr.50 Ermytes on an hep, wiþ *hokide* staues,
A.9.87 Is *hokid* at þat on ende to holde men in good lif.
B.Pr.53 Heremytes on an heep with *hoked* staues
B.8.97 Is *hoked* [at] þat oon ende to [holde men in good lif].
B.20.226 And brode *hoked* arwes, goddes herte and hise nayles,
C.Pr.51 Eremites on an hep with *hokede* staues
C.10.94 And halie with þe *hoked* ende [i]lle men to gode
C.22.226 And brode *hokede* Arwes, goddes herte and his nayles,

hokes n *hok n.* B 1; C 1
B.5.594 Of almesdedes are þe *hokes* þat þe gates hangen on.
C.7.242 The *hokes* aren Almesdedes þat þe ȝates hange on.

hokkerye > hukkerye; hol > hool; hold > holden

holde adj *hold adj. &> holden* A 1; B 1; C 1
A. 7.123   And I am his [h]olde hyne & au3te hym to warne.
B. 6.131   And I am his [h]olde hyne and [au3te] hym to warne
C. 8.195   To be his holde hewe thow he hadde no more

holden v *holden v.(1)* A 46 halden (1) held (3) helde (1) hold (2) holde
     (22) holden (14) holdiþ (1) yholde (1) yholden (1); B 82 halt (3) heeld
     (2) held (1) helde (1) helden (8) hold (6) holde (26) holden (23)
     holdeþ (5) hoold (2) yholde (2) yholden (1); C 87 halde (11) halden
     (3) haldeth (1) haldyng (2) halt (6) heeld (1) held (2) helde (3) helden
     (8) hold (2) holde (29) holden (6) holdeth (5) holdyng (1) hoold (1)
     yholde (6)
A.Pr.28   As ancris & Ermytes þat holden hem in [here] cellis,
A.Pr.63   But holy chirche & [hy] holden bet togidere
A. 1.9   Of oþer heuene þanne here holde þei no tale.'
A. 1.42   Ac þe mone on þis molde þat men so faste holdiþ,
A. 1.55   For husbondrie & he holden togideris.'
A. 1.82   How I may sauen my soule, þat seint art yho[ld]en.'
A. 1.100 But holde wiþ hym & wiþ hire þat aske þe treuþe,
A. 2.36   Þat fals & fauel be any fyn halden,
A. 2.67   Þei to haue & to holde & here eires aftir
A. 2.104 And 3if he fynde 3ow in defaute, & wiþ fals holden,
A. 3.140 To holde lemmanis & lotebies alle here lif dayes,
A. 3.199 Mede makiþ hym be louid & for a man holde.
A. 4.20   Hange on hym þe heuy bridel to holde his hed lowe,
A. 4.104 And harlotis holynesse be holde for an [heþyng];
A. 4.136 Þat he ne held resoun a maister & mede a muche wrecche.
A. 5.37   And siþþe he redde religioun here rewel[e] to holde
A. 5.50   'Shal neuere hei3 herte me hente, but holde me lowe
A. 5.141 Sheo haþ yholde huxterie elleuene wynter.
A. 5.182 And haue hikkes hood þe hostiller, & holde hym yseruid,
A. 5.191 [Þat] alle þat herden þat horn held here nose aftir
A. 5.225 Shal non ale aftir mete holde me þennis
A. 6.66   And hold wel þin haliday hei3 til euen.
A. 6.74   And alle þe wallis ben of wyt to holde wil þeroute;
A. 6.94   And lere þe for to loue & hise lawes holden.
A. 7.47   Holde wiþ none harlotis ne here nou3t here talis,
A. 7.68   For holy chirche is holden of hem no tiþes to asken.
A. 7.86   He is holden, I hope, to haue me in mynde,
A. 7.133 Ankeris & heremytes þat holde hem in here sellis,
A. 7.187 Hom into his owene er[d]e & holde him þere euere.
A. 7.198 'Here now,' quaþ hungir, '& holde it for a wisdom:
A. 7.200 Wiþ houndis bred & hors bred holde vp here hertis,
A. 8.5   And bad hym holde hym at hom & erien his lai3es.
A. 8.22   For þei h[o]lde nou3t here haly dayes as holy chirche techiþ,
A. 8.72   Þei lyue nou3t in loue, ne no lawe holden.
A. 8.75   And bringen forþ barnes þat bois ben holden.
A. 8.169 Þat han þe [welþe of þis] world, & wise men ben holden,
A. 9.87   Is hokid at þat on ende to holde men in good lif.
A.10.114 Hold þe stable & stedefast & strengþe þiseluen
A.10.209 Þat oþere gatis ben geten for gadelynges ben holden;
A.11.62   To tellen of þe trinite to be holden a sire,
A.11.247 We be holde hei3ly to herie & honoure,
A.11.271 And al holy chirche holden hem in helle.
A.12.29   God gaf him non answere but gan his tounge holde.
A.12.38   Þan held I vp myn handes to scripture þe wise
A.12.75   Þer bad me hunger haue gode day but I helde me stille;
A.12.88   'My3th I so, god wot, 3oure gates wolde I holden.'
B.Pr.28   As Ancres and heremites þat holden hem in hire selles,
B.Pr.66   But holy chirche and hij holde bettre togidres
B.Pr.154 Cracchen vs or clawen vs, and in hise clouches holde
B.Pr.180 [Ac] helden hem vnhardy and hir counseil feble,
B. 1.9   Of ooþer heuene þan here holde þei no tale.'
B. 1.44   Ac þe moneie [on] þis molde þat men so faste holdeþ,
B. 1.57   For housbondrie and h[e] holden togidres.'
B. 1.84   How I may saue my soule þat Seint art yholden.'
B. 1.102 But holden wiþ hym and with here þat [asken þe] truþe,
B. 1.120 And alle þat hoped it my3te be so, noon heuene my3te hem holde,
B. 1.153 For heuene my3te nat holden it, [so heuy it semed],
B. 2.102 'And þei to haue and to holde, and hire heires after,
B. 2.140 And if he fynde yow in defaute, and with [fals] holde,
B. 3.151 To [holde] lemmans and lotebies alle hire lifdaies,
B. 3.212 Mede makeþ hym biloued and for a man holden.
B. 3.242 And alle þat helpen þe Innocent and holden wiþ þe ri3tfulle,
B. 4.22   Hange on hym þe heuy brydel to holde his heed lowe,
B. 4.118 And harlottes holynesse be holden for an [heþyng];
B. 5.45   And siþen he radde Religion hir rule to holde
B. 5.67   'Shal neuere hei3 herte me hente, but holde me lowe
B. 5.225 She haþ holden hukkerye [elleuene wynter].
B. 5.258 'I am holden', quod he, 'as hende as hound is in kichene;
B. 5.275 [Is] holden at þe hei3e doom to helpe þee to restitue,
B. 5.333 And haue Hikkes hood [þe] hostiler and holden hym yserued,

B. 5.343 That alle þat herde þat horn helde hir nos[e] after
B. 5.412 Come I to Ite missa est I holde me yserued.
B. 5.420 I kan holde louedayes and here a Reues rekenyng,
B. 5.453 Shal noon ale after mete holde me þennes
B. 5.579 And hold wel þyn haliday heighe til euen.
B. 6.52   Hold wiþ none harlotes ne here no3t hir tales,
B. 6.76   For holy chirche is [holde] of hem no tiþe to [aske],
B. 6.94   [He is] holden, I hope, to haue me in [mynde]
B. 6.200 Hoom [in]to his owene [e]rd and holden hym þere [euere].
B. 6.212 'Here now', quod hunger, 'and hoold it for a wisdom:
B. 6.214 Wiþ houndes breed and horse breed hoold vp here hertes,
B. 7.5   And bad hym holde hym at home and erien hise leyes.
B. 7.20   For þei holde no3t hir halidayes as holy chirche techeþ,
B. 7.90   For [þei] lyue in no loue ne no lawe holde.
B. 7.191 That haue þe welþe of þis world and wise men ben holden
B. 8.97   Is hoked [at] þat oon ende to [holde men in good lif].
B. 9.195 [That] oþergates ben geten for gedelynges arn holden,
B.10.297 [Amonges ri3tful religious þis rule sholde be holde.
B.10.391 And al holy chirche holdeþ hem boþe [in helle]!
B.11.68   And for I seide þus to freres a fool þei me helden,
B.11.70   Ac yet I cryde on my Confessour þat [so konnyng heeld hym]:
B.11.306 The gome þat gloseþ so chartres for a goky is holden.
B.11.374 'I haue wonder [in my wit], þat witty art holden,
B.12.37   And hold þee vnder obedience þat heigh wey is to heuene.
B.12.132 And helden it an hei3 science hir wittes to knowe;
B.12.251 To alle hem þat it holdeþ til hir tail be plukked.
B.12.274 And þe bettre for hir bokes to bidden we ben holden–
B.12.296 To kepe wiþ a commune; no catel was holde bettre,
B.13.117 [That trauailleþ to teche oþere I holde it for a dobet].
B.13.413 Lyueþ ayein þe bileue and no lawe holdeþ.
B.15.10   That folk helden me a fool; and in þat folie I raued
B.15.142 For a wrecchede hous [he held] al his lif tyme,
B.15.265 Ne han martired Peter ne Poul, ne in prison holden.
B.15.570 Euery bisshop þat bereþ cros, by þat he is holden
B.16.112 Ofte [he] heeled swiche; he held it for no maistrie
B.17.108 For he halt hym hardier on horse þan he þat is [on] foote.
B.17.159 And as þe hand halt harde and alle þyng faste
B.17.162 [Halt] al þe wide world wiþInne hem þre,
B.17.191 To clucche or to clawe, to clippe or to holde.
B.18.146 Ne haue hem out of helle; hold þi tonge, mercy!
B.18.249 Lo! helle my3te nat holde, but opnede þo god þolede,
B.19.356 Hastiliche into vnitee and holde we vs þere.
B.19.370 Witynge and wilfully wiþ þe false helden,
B.19.401 And no3t hakke after holynesse; hold þi tonge, Conscience!
B.19.421 But in hir holynesse helden hem stille
B.19.460 'I holde it ri3t and reson of my Reue to take
B.20.75   Into vnite holy chirche and holde we vs þere.
B.20.128 To holden wiþ Antecrist, hir temporaltees to saue.
B.20.145 And heeld holynesse a lape and hendenesse a wastour,
B.20.205 And hold þee þere euere til I sende for þee.
B.20.216 That wiþ Antecrist helden harde ayein Conscience.
B.20.220 Coomen ayein Conscience; wiþ Coueitise þei helden.
B.20.246 Holdeþ yow in vnitee, and haueþ noon enuye
B.20.262 Alle oþere in bataille ben yholde Brybours,
B.20.280 And yuele is þis yholde in parisshes of Engelonde,
B.20.297 In vnitee holy chirche Conscience held hym
B.20.365 [And] for [hem] þat ye ben holden to al my lif tyme,
C.Pr.30   As Ankeres and Eremites þat holdeth hem in here selles
C.Pr.174 To his clees clawe vs and [in] his cloches halde
C.Pr.197 [Ac helden hem vnhardy and here conseil feble]
C. 1.9   Of othere heuene then here [halde thei] no tale.'
C. 1.53   For hosbondrye and he holdeth togederes.'
C. 1.80   How y may saue my soule, þat saynt art yholde.'
C. 1.94   And halden with h[y]m and [with] here þat han trewe action
C. 1.109 He and oþer with hym helden nat with treuthe,
C. 1.149 For heuene holde hit ne myghte, so heuy hit semede,
C. 2.156 And yf he fynde 3ow in defaute and with the fals holde,
C. 3.87   Thow thei take hem vntidy thyng no tresoun þei ne halden hit;
C. 3.189 To holde lemmanes and lotebyes al here lyfdayes
C. 3.268 Mede maketh hym byloued and for a man yholde.
C. 3.299 Y halde hym ouer hardy or elles nat trewe
C. 3.380 Bothe heued and here kyng, haldyng with no partey3e
C. 3.387 And halt hem vnstedefast for hem lakketh case.
C. 5.143 And sethe he radde religioun here reule to holde
C. 5.157 Haen ryde out of aray, here reule euele yholde,
C. 5.161 And but if his knaue knele þat shal his coppe holde
C. 5.189 Holde 3ow in vnite; and he þat oþer wolde
C. 6.8   'Shal neuere heyh herte me hente, but holde me lowe
C. 6.40   Be holden for holy and honoured by þat enchesoun;
C. 6.233 [He] ha[th] holde hokkerye this eleuene wynter.'
C. 6.297 [Ben] haldyng at the heye dome to helpe the restitue.
C. 6.391 And haue hickes hood þe hostiler and holde hym yserued:

C. 6.401   That alle þat herde þ[at] hor[n] *helde* here nose aftur
C. 6.420   The furste [word] þat he spake was '[wh]o *halt* þe bolle?'
C. 7.33   And *holden* a knyhtus Court and acounte with þe reue
C. 7.67   Shal non ale aftur m[e]te *holde* me thennes
C. 7.226   And *hold* wel þ[in] haliday heye til euen.
C. 8.50   *Hoold* with non harlotes ne here nat here tales
C. 8.74   That lollares and loseles lele men *holdeth*,
C. 8.78   For holy chirche is *ho[ld]e* of hem no tythe to aske,
C. 8.103   He is *holdyng*, y hope, to haue me in his masse
C. 8.206   Hoem [in]to his owene [e]rd and *halde* hym þere euere.
C. 8.222   'Now herkene,' quod hunger, 'and *holde* hit for a wysdom:
C. 9.5   And bad hym *holden* hym at hoem and eryen his leyes
C. 9.24   For they *holde* nat here haliday[es] as holi chirch [tech]eth
C. 9.167   For they lyue in no loue ne no lawe *holden*
C. 9.207   *H[e]lden* ful hungry hous and hadde muche defaute,
C. 9.222   Furste, Religious of religioun a reule to *holde*
C. 9.337   That haen the welthe of this world and wise men ben *holde*
C.10.86   Þat þe Erl Auerous *held* and his ayres
C.10.287   Awrek the þerwith on wyfyng, for godes werk y *holde* hit:
C.10.294   That oþergatus ben gete for gadelynges ben *holden*
C.11.218   And holi churche, as y here, *haldeth* bothe in helle!
C.11.306   Thow thei folowe þat fortune wole [no] folye ich it *holde*.
C.13.9   Bynoem [hym] his hosewyf [and *helde* here hymsulue]
C.13.68   That *holde* mote þe hey way, euene the ten hestes,
C.13.120   The gome þat gloseth so Chartres for a goky is *halden*.
C.13.184   'Y haue wonder in my wit, so wys as thow art *holden*,
C.13.238   To blame hym or to bete hym thenne y *halde* hit but synne.
C.14.76   They *helden* hit an hey science here sotiltees to knowe,
C.14.196   And þe bettere for here bokes to bidden we ben *yholde*–
C.15.124   Bote do as doctours techeth, for dowel y hit *holde*,
C.15.125   That trauayleth to teche oþere y *halde* hit for a dobet;
C.15.126   And he þat doth as he techeth y *halde* hit for þe beste:
C.16.53   The hey way to heueneward he *halt* hit nat fol euene
C.16.367   Ac auaris oþerwhiles *halt* hym withoute þe gate.
C.16.373   He *halt* hit for a vyce and a foule shame
C.17.22   Loue and lele byleue *held* lyf and soule togyderes.
C.17.64   And þer helpe yf thow has[t]; and þat *halde* y charite.
C.17.112   Go now to eny degre and bote gyle be *holde* a maistre
C.17.159   A man þat hihte Makameth for messie they hym *holdeth*
C.18.194   The thridde is þat *halt* al, a thyng by hymsulue;
C.19.39   The which alle men aren *holde* ouer al thyng to honoure
C.19.127   To huyde and to *holde* as holy writ telleth–
C.19.140   Ne *holde* ne helpe ne hente þat he louede
C.19.157   To cluche or to clawe, to clippe or to *holde*.
C.20.149   Ne haue hem out of helle; *holde* thy tonge, mercy!
C.20.258   Loo! helle myhte nat *holde*, bote opened tho god tholede
C.21.356   Hastiliche [in]to vnite and *holde* we vs there.
C.21.370   Wytyng and wilfully with the false *helden*
C.21.401   And nat hacky aftur holinesse; *hold* thy tonge, consience!
C.21.421   Bote in here holinesse *h[e]lden* hem stille
C.21.460   'Y *halde* hit riht and resoun of my reue to take
C.22.75   Into vnite holi churche and *halde* we vs there.
C.22.128   To *holde* with auntecrist, here temperaltee[s] to saue.
C.22.145   And *helde* holinesse a iape and hendenesse a wastour
C.22.205   And *halde* the there euere til y sende for the.
C.22.216   That with auntecrist *helden* harde aȝeyn Consience.
C.22.220   Comen aȝen Consience; with couetyse they *helden*.
C.22.246   *Holdeth* ȝow in vnite and haueth noen enuye
C.22.262   Alle oþere in bataile been *yholde* brybours,
C.22.280   And euele is this *yholde* in parsches of yngelond
C.22.297   In vnite holi church Consience *heeld* hym
C.22.365   And for hem þat ȝe aren *holde* to al my lyf tyme

holdyng ger *holdinge ger. &> holden* C 1
C.12.244   And he for his hard *holdyng* in helle parauntur:

hole n *hole n.(2) &> hool* B 2; C 2
B.19.399   Boþe dregges and draf and drawe at oon *hole*
B.20.44   "Boþe fox and fowel may fle to *hole* and crepe
C.21.399   Bothe dregges and draf and drawe at on *hole*
C.22.44   "Bothe fox and foule may fle to *hole* and crepe

holewe > holwe

holy adj *holi adj.(2) &>*
   holy_chirche,holy_day,holy_goost,holy_writ,pope_holy A 2; B 16 holy
   (14) holye (2); C 23 haly (1) holy (22)
A. 7.12   But ȝif it be holy day oþer euen;
A.12.13   And on clergie crieþ on cristes *holy* name
B. 3.235   Lord, who shal wonye in þi wones wiþ þyne *holy* seintes,
B. 3.236   Or resten in þyne *holy* hilles: þis askeþ Dauid.
B.10.27   "Lo!" seiþ *holy* lettrure, "whiche [lordes] beþ þise sherewes";
B.10.27   And of *holy* men I her[e]', quod I, 'how þei ouþerwhile
B.12.62   And in lele lyuynge men and in lif *holy*,
B.13.295   And noon so *holy* as he ne of lif clennere,

B.14.155   Ac it is but selde yseien, as by *holy* seintes bokes,
B.15.269   [Lo]! in legenda sanctorum, þe lif of *holy* Seintes,
B.15.272   Antony and Egidie and oþere *holy* fadres
B.15.430   The heuedes of holy chirche, and þei *holy* were,
B.15.438   Elleuene *holy* men al þe world tornede
B.15.450   As wel þoruȝ hise werkes as wiþ hise *holy* wordes
B.16.84   And made of *holy* men his hoord In limbo Inferni,
B.19.272   And harewede in an handwhile al *holy* Scripture
B.20.65   [And] þat were mylde men and *holye* þat no meschief dradden;
B.20.252   Frere Fraunceys and Domynyk, for loue to be *holye*.
C. 5.186   Lo! in heuene an heyh was an *holy* comune
C. 6.40   Be holden for *holy* and honoured by þat enchesoun;
C. 6.48   They to wene þat y were wel *holy* and almesfull
C. 6.146   For she had *haly* bred ar y my herte gan change.
C. 9.188   And alle *holy* Eremytes haue shal þe same;
C. 9.191   Al þat *holy* Ermytes hatede and despisede,
C. 9.202   Al they *holy* Ermytes were of heye kynne,
C.11.24   "Lo!" saith *holy* letrure, "whiche lordes beth this schrewes";
C.11.34   The lewed aȝen þe lered þe *holy* lore to disp[u]te
C.12.133   *Holy* seyntes hym sey Ac neuere in secte of riche.
C.12.172   Mo prouerbes y myhte haue of mony *holy* seyntes
C.13.86   Halyday or *holy* euene his mete to discerue.
C.15.73   For oure lordes loue, as *holy* lettre telleth:
C.16.241   Aȝen þe consayl of crist, as *holy* clergie witnesseth:
C.16.285   That lyuen aȝen *holy* lore and þe loue of charite.
C.17.34   Fynde honest men and *holy* men and oþer rihtfole peple.
C.17.65   Lo laurence for his largenesse, as *holy* lore telleth
C.17.185   *Holy* men, as y hope, thorw helpe of the holy goste
C.17.194   Hit is reuthe to rede how riht *holy* men lyuede,
C.18.115   And made of *holy* men his hoerd in limbo inferni
C.21.272   And harwed in an handwhile al *holy* scripture
C.22.65   And þat were mylde men and *holy* þat no meschief dradden,
C.22.252   Frere fraunceys and domynyk, for loue to be *holy*.

holy_chirche n *Holi Chirche n.* A 15 holy_cherche (1) holichirche (1)
   holy_chirche (12) holykirke (1); B 63 holi_cherches (1) holi_chirche
   (9) holy_chirche (36) holy_chirches (2) holy_kirk (1) holi_kirke (1)
   holy_kirke (13); C 89 holi_chirch (1) holi_chirche (1) holy_chirche
   (11) holi_church (1) holy_church (1) holi_churche (12) holy_churche
   (39) holy_kerke (1) holi_kirke (2) holy_kirke (10) holy_kyrke (10)
A.Pr.63   But *holy chirche* & [hy] holden bet togidere
A. 1.73   '*Holy chirche* I am,' quaþ heo, 'þou auȝtest me to knowe;
A. 2.90   Symonye & þiself shenden *holy chirche*;
A. 2.166   Þat *holy chirche* for hem worþ harmid for euere;
A. 3.117   Apoisonide popis, apeiride *holy chirche*;
A. 5.150   'To *holy chirche*,' quaþ he, 'for to here masse,
A. 7.29   In couenaunt þat þou kepe *holy[k]ir[k]e* and myself
A. 7.68   For *holy chirche* is holden of hem no tiþes to asken,
A. 8.9   Kinges & kniȝtes þat kepen *holy chirche*
A. 8.22   For þei h[o]lde nouȝt here haly dayes as *holy chirche* techiþ,
A.10.69   Þanne is *holichirche* owyng to helpe hem & saue
A.10.91   Be counseil of consience, accordyng *holy chirche*,
A.11.77   Ac beleue lelly o[n þe] lore of *holy chirche*,
A.11.271   And al *holy chirche* holden hem in helle.
A.12.17   Þat hit were boþe skaþe and sklaundre to *holy cherche*
B.Pr.66   But *holy chirche* and hij holde bettre togidres
B. 1.75   '*Holi chirche* I am', quod she, 'þow ouȝtest me to knowe.
B. 2.126   Symonye and þiself shenden *holi chirche*;
B. 2.205   That *holy chirche* for hem worþ harmed for euere.]
B. 3.128   [A]poisoned popes, [a]peired *holy chirche*.
B. 5.50   And siþen he preide þe pope haue pite on *holy chirche*,
B. 5.300   'To *holy chirche*', quod he, 'for to here masse,
B. 6.27   In couenaunt þat þow kepe *holy kirke* and myselue
B. 6.76   For *holy chirche* is [holde] of hem no tiþe to [aske],
B. 7.9   Kynges and knyȝtes þat kepen *holy chirche*
B. 7.20   For þei holde noȝt hir halidayes as *holy chirche* techeþ,
B. 9.69   [*Holy chirche* is owynge to helpe hem and saue,
B.10.124   Ac bileueþ lelly in þe loore of *holy chirche*,
B.10.128   'It is a commune lyf', quod Clergie, 'on *holy chirche* to bileue
B.10.258   Al þat þe book bit bi *holi cherches* techyng;
B.10.391   And al *holy chirche* holdeþ hem boþe [in helle]!
B.10.412   Of *holi chirche* þat herberwe is, and goddes hous to saue
B.10.416   That ben Carpenters *holy kirk* to make for cristes owene beestes:
B.10.418   Forþi I counseille yow clerkes, of *holy [kirke]* þe wriȝtes,
B.10.480   As clerkes of *holy [k]ir[k]e* þat kepen cristes tresor.
B.11.98   Excepte persons and preestes and prelates of *holy chirche*.
B.11.117   Wheiþer I were chosen or noȝt chosen; on *holi chirche* I þouȝte
B.11.160   [This matere is merk for many, ac men of *holi chirche*,
B.12.27   Wolde I neuere do werk, but wende to *holi chirche*
B.12.82   *Holy kirke* knoweþ þis þat cristes writyng saued;
B.12.213   And wel lose[l]ly he lolleþ þere by þe lawe of *holy chirche*:
B.13.273   He hadde a cote of cristendom as *holy kirke* bileueþ;
B.13.383   [I]n haly daies at *holy chirche* whan ich herde masse
B.13.421   Ye lordes and ladies and legates of *holy chirche*

B.14.87 That whiles he lyuede he bileuede in þe loore of *holy chirche*,
B.15.92 As holynesse and honeste out of *holy chirche* [spryngeþ]
B.15.94 Right so out of *holi chirche* alle yueles [spredeþ]
B.15.99 Right so persons and preestes and prechours of *holi chirche*
B.15.136 Curatours of *holy kirke*, as clerkes þat ben auarouse,
B.15.197 'Wheiþer clerkes knowen hym', quod I, 'þat kepen *holi kirke*?'
B.15.285 Wherfore I am afered of folk of *holy kirke*,
B.15.430 The heuedes of *holy chirche*, and þei holy were,
B.15.435 Of hem of *holi chirche* þat þe heighe wey sholde teche
B.15.487 That heuedes of *holy chirche* ben, þat han hir wil here,
B.15.526 *Holy chirche* is honoured heiȝliche þoruȝ þis deying;
B.15.546 For coueitise of þat cros [clerkes] of *holy kirke*
B.15.557 Whan Costantyn of curteisie *holy kirke* dowed
B.15.566 [Charite] were to deschargen hem for *holy chirches* sake,
B.16.6 The leues ben lele wordes, þe lawe of *holi chirche*;
B.16.197 That is children of charite, and *holi chirche* þe moder.
B.16.199 And Crist and cristendom and cristene *holy chirche*.
B.17.121 And hostele hem and heele þoruȝ *holy chirche* bileue
B.17.295 And siþ *holy chirche* and charite chargeþ þis so soore
B.19.223 And Pride shal be Pope, Prynce of *holy chirche*,
B.19.328 And called þat hous vnitee, *holy chirche* on englissh.
B.19.334 [And þe [lond] of bileue, þe lawe of *holy chirche*].
B.19.363 That *holy chirche* stode in [holynesse] as it a Pyl weere.
B.19.366 To helpe *holy chirche* and hem þat it kepeþ.
B.19.380 Made vnitee *holy chirche* in holynesse stonde.
B.19.410 'I am a Curatour of *holy kirke*, and cam neuere in my tyme
B.19.442 And [Piers] amende þe pope, þat pileþ *holy kirke*
B.19.467 And *holy kirke* and clergie fro cursed men to [de]fende.
B.19.472 And *holy chirches* chief help and Chieftayn of þe comune.
B.20.75 Into vnite *holy chirche* and holde we vs þere.
B.20.120 Conscience and his compaignye, of *holy [kirke]* þe techeris.
B.20.229 Thoruȝ inparfite preestes and prelates of *holy chirche*.'
B.20.245 To vnitee and *holy chirche*; ac o þyng I yow preye:
B.20.297 In vnitee *holy chirche* Conscience held hym
C.Pr.64 But *holi chirche* and charite choppe adoun suche shryuars
C.Pr.87 Ben charged with *holy chirche* charite to tylie,
C.Pr.116 And for þei were prestis and men of *holy chirche*
C.Pr.118 Forthy I sey ȝ[ow] prestes and men of *holy churche*
C.Pr.138 Contreplede hit noght,' quod Consience, 'for *holi [k]ir[k]e* sake.'
C. 1.72 '*Holy churche* y am,' quod she; 'þou oughtest me to knowe;
C. 1.187 Aren none hardore ne hungriore then men of *holy chirche*,
C. 2.143 *Holy churche*, and charite ȝe cheweth and deuoureth.
C. 2.251 And *holy churche* thorw hem worth harmed for euere.'
C. 3.165 He hath apoisened popes, he appeyreth *holy churche*.
C. 3.357 In case, credere in ecclesia, in *holy kyrke* to bileue;
C. 3.398 Sholde conforme hem to o kynde on *holy kyrke* to bileue
C. 5.179 Clerkes and *holy [kyrke]* shal be clothed newe.'
C. 5.191 And sethe a preyede þe pope haue pite on *holy chirche*
C. 6.19 Inobedient to *holy churche* and to hem þat þer serueth;
C. 6.119 And preuen inparfit prelates of *holy churche*;
C. 6.272 In halydayes at *holy churche* when y herde masse
C. 6.355 'To *holy churche*,' quod he, 'for to here masse
C. 7.81 ȝe lordes and ladies and legatus of *holy chirche*
C. 8.26 In couenant þat thow kepe *holy kerke* and mysulue
C. 8.53 Ne countreplede nat Consience ne *holy kyrke* ryhtes.'
C. 8.78 For *holy chirche* is ho[ld]e of hem no tythe to aske,
C. 8.159 They acounteth nat of corsyng[e] ne *holy kyrke* dredeth–
C. 9.9 Kyngus and knyhtus þat *holy kyrke* defenden
C. 9.24 For they holde nat here haliday[es] as *holi chirch* [tech]eth
C. 9.104 Lyuen aȝen goddes lawe and þe lore of *holi churche*.
C. 9.219 Lollen aȝen byleue and lawe of *holy churche*;
C. 9.220 For *holy churche* hoteth alle manere peple
C. 9.327 As lettrede men vs lereth and lawe of *holi churche*:
C.10.185 And *holy churche* helpe to, so sholde no man begge
C.10.197 Prelates and prestes and princes of *holy churche*
C.11.144 And al þat *holi churche* herof can þe lere
C.11.218 And *holi churche*, as y here, haldeth bothe in helle!
C.11.243 Of *holy kirke* þat sholde kepe alle cristene soules
C.11.245 Bote *holy churche*, herborw to alle þat ben yblessed.
C.11.247 That [ben] carpentares vnder Crist *holy kirke* to make
C.11.250 Worcheth, ȝe wrihtus of *holy churche*, as holy writ techeth,
C.11.301 As clerkes of *holy [k]ir[k]e* þat [kepe] sholde and saue
C.12.52 Where y were chose [or nat chose]; on *holy churche* y thouhte
C.12.119 To haue as we haen serued, as *holy churche* witnesseth:
C.13.90 Knowelecheth hym cristene and of *holy kirke* byleue,
C.14.9 Lowe the and l[y]ue forth in þe lawe of *holy chirche*;
C.14.21 And *holy chirche* horen helpe, Auerou[s] and coueytous,
C.14.139 And crist cam and confermede and *holy kyrke* made
C.14.152 And wel lo[s]liche he lolleth þere by þe lawe of *holy churche*:
C.16.35 And *holy churche* and charite herof a chartre made.
C.16.243 As holinesse and honestee out of *holy churche*
C.16.245 Thorw parfit preesthoed and prelates of *holy churche*,
C.16.246 Riht [so] oute of *holy churche* al euel spredeth

C.16.252 Riht so persones and prestes and prechours of *holy churche*
C.16.257 And be corteys and kynde of *holy kyrke* godes,
C.16.281 Curatours of *holy [kirke]* and clerkes þat ben Auerous,
C.16.298 'Charite is a childische thyng, as *holy churche* witnesseth:
C.16.339 Where clerkes knowe hym nat,' quod y, 'þat kepen *holy churche*?'
C.17.5 'A passeth cheef charite yf *holy churche* be trewe:
C.17.41 This is no more to mene bote men of *holy churche*
C.17.50 And conforte alle cristene wolde *holy [kirke]* amende.
C.17.71 Of þat þat *holy churche* of þe olde lawe claymeth
C.17.78 Cristendoem of *holy kyrke*, the kynges marke of heuene,
C.17.124 In þe lettynge of here lyf to leue on *holy churche*.
C.17.125 'What is *holy churche*, chere frende?' quod y; 'Charite,' he saide;
C.17.167 And pursuede to haue þe pope, prince of *holy chirche*;
C.17.202 To amende and to make, as with men of *holy churche*,
C.17.208 For couetyse of th[at] croes clerkes of *holi churche*
C.17.220 Whan Constantyn of cortesye *holy kirke* dowede
C.17.230 The heuedes of *holy churche* and tho that ben vnder hem,
C.17.231 Hit were charite to deschargen hem for *holy churche* sake,
C.17.275 Amonges v[n]kynde cristene in *holy [kirke]* was slawe
C.17.276 And alle *holy kirke* honoured thorw that deyng.
C.17.286 And enchaunten hem to charite on *holy churche* to bileue.
C.18.74 As monkes and monyals, men of *holy churche*;
C.18.206 The whiche aren childrene of charite and *holy church* [the] moder.
C.18.208 And Crist and cristendoem and cristene *holy churche*
C.19.276 And sethe Charite þat *holy churche* is chargeth this so sore
C.21.223 And [pryde shal] be pope, prince of *holy chirche*,
C.21.328 And calde þat hous vnite, *holy chirche* an englisch.
C.21.334 And þe londe of bileue, the lawe of *holi chirche*.
C.21.363 That *holi churche* stoede in holinesse as hit [a pyle were].
C.21.366 To helpe *holi churche* and hem þat hit kepeth.
C.21.380 Made vnite *holi churche* in holinesse stande.
C.21.410 'Ich am a Curatour of *holi [kirke]* and cam neuer in my tyme
C.21.442 And [Peres] amende þe pope þat pileth *holi churche*
C.21.467 And *holy kyrke* and clerge fro cursed men to defende.
C.21.472 And *holy churche* cheef helpe and cheuenteyn of þe comu[n]e
C.22.75 Into vnite *holi churche* and halde we vs there.
C.22.120 Consience and his companye, of *holy [kirke]* þe techares.
C.22.229 Thorw inparfit prestes and prelates of *holy churche*.'
C.22.245 To vnite and *holi churche*; ac o thyng y ȝow praye:
C.22.297 In vnite *holi church* Consience heeld hym

holy_day n *halidai n.& phr.* A 3 haliday (1)   haly_dayes (1) holy_day (1);
B 5 haliday (1) halyday (2) halidayes (1) haly_daies (1); C 7 haliday
(3) halyday (2) halidayes (1) halydayes (1)
A. 6.66 And hold wel þin *haliday* heiȝ til euen.
A. 7.12 But ȝif it be *holy day* oþer holy euen;
A. 8.22 For þei h[o]lde nouȝt here *haly dayes* as holy chirche techiþ,
B. 5.402 I am ocupied eche day, *halyday* and ooþer,
B. 5.579 And hold wel þyn *haliday* heighe til euen.
B. 7.20 For þei holde noȝt hir *halidayes* as holy chirche techeþ,
B.13.383 [I]n *haly daies* at holy chirche whan ich herde masse
B.13.414 Ech day is *halyday* with hym or an heiȝ ferye,
C. 1.124 Hewes in þe *haliday* after hete wayten
C. 6.272 In *halydayes* at holy churche when y herde masse
C. 7.18 Y am occuepied vch day, *haliday* and oþere,
C. 7.226 And hold wel þ[in] *haliday* heye til euen.
C. 9.24 For they holde nat here *haliday[es]* as holi chirch [tech]eth
C. 9.232 Vcche *halyday* to here holly þe seruise,
C.13.86 *Halyday* or holy euene his mete to discerue.

holy_goost n *Holi Gost n.* A 1 holy_goost; B 21 holi_goost (2) holy_goost
(19), C 20 holi_goest (1) holy_goest (6) holy_goest (1) holi_gost (3)
holy_gost (7) holy_goste (2)
A.11.301 Þe help of þe *holy gost* to answere hem [alle]'.
B.10.244 Thoruȝ þe help of þe *holy goost* þe which is of boþe;
B.10.247 God þe fader, god þe sone, god *holy goost* of boþe,
B.12.63 And þoruȝ þe gifte of þe *holy goost* as þe gospel telleþ:
B.12.139 For þe heiȝe *holy goost* heuene shal tocleue,
B.16.52 And help of þe *holy goost*, and þus haue I þe maistrie.'
B.16.188 The þridde highte þe *holi goost*, a persone by hymselue,
B.16.224 Which is þe *holy goost* of alle, and alle is but o god.
B.17.147 The *holy goost* of heuene: he is as þe pawme.
B.17.158 How he þat is *holy goost* sire and sone preueþ.
B.17.182 So is þe *holy goost* god, neiþer gretter ne lasse
B.17.203 The *holy goost* of heuene [he] is as þe pawme.
B.17.218 So is [þe] *holy goost* god and grace wiþoute mercy
B.17.226 Til þe *holy goost* gynne to glowe and to blase,
B.17.227 So þat þe *holy goost* gloweþ but as a [glede vn]glade
B.17.233 So grace of þe *holy goost* þe grete myȝt of þe Trinite
B.17.252 So is þe *holi goost* god and grace wiþouten mercy
B.17.258 The *holy goost* hereþ þee noȝt ne helpe may þee by reson.
B.17.275 The grace of þe *holy goost*, goddes owene kynde.
B.17.279 For þat þe *holy goost* haþ to kepe þ[o] harlotes destruyeþ,
B.17.285 A[c] yet in mo maneres men offenden þe *holy goost*;

B.18.130   And grace of þe *holy goost*; weex greet wiþ childe;
C.14.84   For the hey *holi gost* heuene shal tocleue
C.17.185   Holy men, as y hope, thorw helpe of the *holy goste*
C.17.247   The whiche is þe hy *holy gost* þat out of heuene descendet[h]
C.18.52   And that is grace of þe *holy gost*; and thus gete y the maystrye.'
C.18.75   These haen þe [hete] of þe *holi goest* as þe crop of tre [the] sonne.
C.18.195   *Holy goest* is his name and he is in all.'
C.19.121   The *holy goest* of heuene: he is as þe paume.
C.19.147   Bote [be he] greued with here grype the *holy goost* lat falle.
C.19.148   Thus is the *holy goste* god, noyther grettore ne lassore
C.19.169   The *holy gost* of heuene he is as þe paume.
C.19.184   So is þe *holi gost* god and grace withouten mercy
C.19.192   Til the *holy goest* gynne to glowe and [to] blase,
C.19.193   So þat the *holy gost* gloweth but as a glede
C.19.199   So grace of þe *holi gost* the grete myhte of þe trinite
C.19.218   So is þe *holy goost* god and grace withouten mercy
C.19.224   The *holy goest* hereth the nat ne helpeth the, be thow certeyne.
C.19.256   The grace of the *holy goest*, godes owene kynde.
C.19.260   For that the *holy goest* hath to kepe tho harlotes distruyeth,
C.19.266   And ȝut in mo maneres men [o]ffenden þe *holy gost*;
C.20.133   And grace of the *holy gost*; wax grete with childe,

holykerk -kirk > holy_chirche

holynesse n *holinesse n.(2)*   A 1; B 11; C 15 holinesse (7) holynesse (8)
A. 4.104   And harlotis *holynesse* be holde for an [heþyng];
B. 4.118   And harlottes *holynesse* be holden for an [heþyng];
B.10.296   And al for youre *holynesse*; haue ye þis in herte.
B.11.44   'Allas, eiȝe!' quod Elde and *holynesse* boþe,
B.15.92   As *holynesse* and honeste out of holy chirche [spryngeþ]
B.19.363   That holy chirche stode in [*holynesse*] as it a Pyl weere.
B.19.374   That he ne halp a quantite *holynesse* to wexe,
B.19.380   Made vnitee holy chirche in *holynesse* stonde.
B.19.401   And noȝt hakke after *holynesse*; hold þi tonge, Conscience!
B.19.421   But in hir *holynesse* helden hem stille
B.20.145   And heeld *holynesse* a Iape and hendenesse a wastour,
B.20.227   And hadden almoost vnitee and *holynesse* adown.
C. 2.84   Then for *holynesse* oþer hendenesse oþer for hey kynde.
C. 4.113   And harlotes *holynesse* be an heye ferie;
C.11.13   More then *holynesse* or hendenesse or al þat seyntes techeth.
C.12.1   'Allas, eye!' quod elde and *holynesse* bothe,
C.16.243   As *holinesse* and honeste out of holy churche
C.18.5   Erber of alle pryuatees and of *holynesse*.
C.18.13   Of *holynesse*, of hendenesse, of helpe-hym-þat-nedeth,
C.18.158   And saide, 'this is an hous of orysones and of *holynesse*
C.21.363   That holi churche stoede in *holinesse* as hit [a pyle were].
C.21.374   That he ne halpe a qua[n]tite *holinesse* to wexe,
C.21.380   Made vnite holi churche in *holinesse* stande.
C.21.401   And nat hacky aftur *holinesse*; hold thy tonge, consience!
C.21.421   Bote in here *holinesse* h[e]lden hem stille
C.22.145   And helde *holinesse* a iape and hendenesse a wastour,
C.22.227   And hadden almost vnite and *holynesse* adowne.

holy_writ n *Holi Writ n.*   A 7 holiwrit (1) holy_writ (5) holy_wryt (1); B 20 holi_writ (1) holy_writ (19); C 34 holy_writ (31) holy_wryt (3)
A. 1.70   Þat suche wise wordis of *holy writ* shewide,
A. 1.119   Ac þo þat werchen þe word þat *holy writ* techiþ,
A. 8.56   Ne wolde neuere *holy writ*, god wot þe soþe.
A.10.94   [And so witnesseþ goddis worde and *holiwrit* boþe]:
A.11.24   And he þat haþ *holy writ* ay in his mouþ,
A.11.268   De[m]de he not wel & wisly, as *holy [writ]* techiþ,
A.12.97   So þat þou werke þe word þat *holy wryt* techeþ,
B.Pr.195   That witnesseþ *holy writ*, whoso wole it rede:
B. 1.72   That swiche wise wordes of *holy writ* shewed,
B. 1.130   [Ac] þo þat werche wel as *holy writ* telleþ,
B. 3.335   And [muche] worshipe ha[þ] þerwiþ as *holy writ* telleþ:
B.10.32   Ac he þat haþ *holy writ* ay in his mouþe
B.10.382   Or ellis vnwriten for wikkednesse as *holy writ* witnesseþ:
B.10.387   He demed wel and wisely as *holy writ* telleþ;
B.10.402   Ac hir werkes, as *holy writ* seiþ, [was] euere þe contrarie.
B.11.383   [*Holy writ*', quod þat wye, 'wisseþ men to suffre:
B.11.398   For al þat he [wrouȝt] was wel ydo, as *holy writ* witnesseþ:
B.13.71   *Holi writ* bit men be war–I wol noȝt write it here
B.13.132   He wol noȝt ayein *holy writ* speken, I dar vndertake.'
B.13.431   Ac clerkes þat knowen *holy writ* sholde kenne lordes
B.14.63   As *holy writ* witnesseþ whan men seye hir graces:
B.17.310   And eyþer haue equyte, as *holy writ* telleþ:
B.17.318   Than alle oure wikkede werkes as *holy writ* telleþ–
B.17.322   For to fleen his owene [hous] as *holy writ* sheweþ.
B.18.390   And þouȝ *holy writ* wole þat I be wroke of hem þat diden ille–
B.19.109   Water into wyn turnede, as *holy writ* telleþ.
B.19.327   And of al *holy writ* he made a roof after;
C.Pr.104   That al þe world be [þe] wors, as *holy writ* telleth.
C.Pr.208   Wyttenesse at *holy wryt* whoso kan rede:

C. 1.69   That suche wyse wordes of *holy writ* shewede
C. 1.126   Wonderwyse, *holy wryt* telleth, how þei fullen,
C. 2.145   For wel ȝe wyte, wernardus, as *holy writ* telleth,
C. 3.487   And muche worschipe therwith, as *holy writ* telleth:
C. 5.37   Tyl y wyste witterly what *holy writ* menede
C. 8.86   Lat god yworthe with al, as *holy wryt* techeth:
C.10.237   *Holy writ* witnesseth þat for no wikkede dede
C.10.245   Ac why þe world was adreynt, *holy writ* telleth,
C.10.293   Bote wyues and wedded men, as *holy writ* techeth:
C.11.29   Ac he þat hath *holy writ* ay in his mouth
C.11.78   Forthy, wit,' quod she, 'be waer *holy writ* to shewe
C.11.207   Vnwriten for som wikkednesse, as *holy writ* sheweth:
C.11.232   As *holy writ* witnesseth, goddes word in þe gospel:
C.11.250   Worcheth, ȝe wrihtus of holy churche, as *holy writ* techeth,
C.12.155   *Holy [writ]* witnesseth hoso forsaketh
C.13.28   Worthiore as by *holy writ* and wyse fylosofres.
C.15.76   *Holy writ* byt men be waer and wysly hem kepe
C.15.156   Y take wittenesse,' quod [þe wy], 'of *holy writ* a partye:
C.15.262   As witnesseth *holy writ* when we seggeth oure graces:
C.16.242   Lo, what *holy writ* wittnesseth of wikkede techares:
C.17.4   'Ho is wroeth and wolde be awreke, *holy writ* preueth,' quod he,
C.17.6   *Holy writ* witnesseth þer were suche eremytes,
C.17.37   As wittnesseth *holy writ* what tobie saide
C.17.190   That they ne wente [þe wey] as *holy writ* byd:
C.19.127   To huyde and to holde as *holy writ* telleth–
C.19.249   To go semeliche ne sitte, seth *holy writ* techeth
C.19.290   That eyþer haue equitee, as *holy writ* witnesseth:
C.19.298   Thenne al oure wikkede werkes as *holy writ* telleth:
C.19.302   Out of his oune house as *holy writ* sheweth.
C.20.432   For *holy writ* wol þat y be wreke of hem þat wrouhte ille–
C.21.109   [Watur into wyn turned], As *holy writ* telleth.
C.21.327   And of all *holy writ* he made a roef aftur

holly adv *holli adv.*   A 1; B 3 holly (2) hoolly (1); C 4
A. 3.102   [But I be *holly* at ȝour heste honge me ellys].'
B. 3.113   But I be *holly* at youre heste hange me [ellis].'
B.17.28   Abraham seiþ þat he seiȝ *hoolly* þe Trinite,
B.19.3   To here *holly* þe masse and to be housled after.
C. 3.150   But y be *holly* at thyn heste; lat hange me elles.'
C. 9.232   Vcche halyday to here *holly* þe seruise,
C.19.29   Abraham saith þat he seyh *holly* þe trinitee,
C.21.3   To here *holly* þe masse and to [be] hoseled aftur.

holow > holwe; holpe- > helpen

holwe adj *holwe adj.*   A 1 holewe; B 1; C 1 holow
A. 5.108   So hungirly & *holewe* sire heruy hym lokide.
B. 5.189   So hungrily and *holwe* sire heruy hym loked.
C. 6.197   So hungrily and *holow* sire heruy hym lokede.

hom > hoom

homage n *homage n.*   B 1; C 1
B.12.154   And diden [hir] *homage* honurably to hym þat was almyȝty.
C.14.98   And deden here *homage* honerably to hym þat was almyhty.

home(s > hoom

homliche adv *homli adv.*   B 1
B.10.96   *Homliche* at oþere mennes houses and hatien hir owene.

homward adv *homward adv.*   A 1; B 1
A. 3.181   And hastide[st] þe *homward* for hunger of þi wombe.
B. 3.194   And [hastedest þee] *homward* for hunger of þi wombe.

hond(es -is > hand; hondmayden > handmayden ; hondredes > hundred ; honerably > honurably

honeste n *honeste n.*   B 1; C 1 honestee
B.15.92   As holynesse and *honeste* out of holy chirche [spryngeþ]
C.16.243   As holinesse and *honestee* out of holy churche

honeste adj *honeste adj.*   B 1; C 2 honest (1) honeste (1)
B.19.94   [Erþeliche] *honeste* þynges w[as] offred þus at ones
C.17.34   Fynde *honest* men and holy men and oþer rihtfole peple.
C.21.94   Ertheliche *honeste* thynges was offred thus at ones

honge(n > hangen; honger -ur > hunger; hongid- > hangen

hony n *honi n.*   B 2; C 2
B.15.57   The man þat muche *hony* eteþ his mawe it engleymeþ,
B.15.64   And riȝt as *hony* is yuel to defie and engleymeþ þe mawe,
C.16.219   The man þat moche *hony* eet his mawe hit engleymeth;
C.16.226   And riht as *hony* is euel to defie,

honouren v *honouren v.*   A 4 honoure (3) honouriþ (1); B 10 honoure (4) honoured (3) honouren (2) honoureþ (1); C 19 honoure (11) honoured (4) honourede (1) honouren (1) honoureth (2)
A. 3.198   To alienes, to alle men, to *honoure* hem with ȝeftis.

A. 6.54   Forto ʒe fynden a foorþe, ʒoure fadris *honouriþ*;
A. 7.20   Chesiblis for chapellis chirches to *honoure*.
A.11.247   We be holde heiʒly to herie & *honoure*,
B. 3.211   To aliens, to alle men, to *honouren* hem with ʒiftes;
B. 5.567   [Forto] ye fynden a ford, youre-fadres-*honoureþ*:
B. 6.12   Chesibles for Chapeleyns chirches to *honoure*.
B.12.149   And bad hem go to Bethlem goddes burþe to *honoure*
B.15.447   To crist and to cristendom and cros to *honoure*,
B.15.526   Holy chirche is *honoured* heiʒliche þoruʒ his deying;
B.15.532   Er cristendom [were] knowe þere, or any cros *honoured*.
B.15.544   Boþe riche and Religious, þat roode þei *honoure*
B.15.548   [Mynne] ye noʒt, wise men, how þo men *honoured*
B.15.606   Arn folk of oon feiþ; þe fader god þei *honoure*
C. 2.177   To wende with h[e]m to westminstre [the] weddyng to *honoure*.
C. 3.267   To aliens, to alle men, to *honoure* hem with ʒeftes;
C. 5.105   And to þe kyrke y gan go god to *honoure*;
C. 6.40   Be holden for holy and *honoured* by þat enchesoun;
C. 7.214   Forto ʒe fynde a ford, ʒoure-fader[s]-*honoureth*;
C. 8.11   Chesibles for chapeleynes churches to *honoure*.
C.14.43   Forthy y conseile vch a creature clergie to *honoure*
C.14.93   And bad hem go to Bedlem goddes berthe to *honoure*
C.14.179   Ac for his peynted pennes þe pecok is *honoured*
C.17.134   And o god þat al bygan with gode herte they *honoureth*
C.17.153   Hit is kyndly thyng creature his creatour to *honoure*,
C.17.206   Bothe riche and religiou[s] þat rode they *honouren*
C.17.210   Minne ʒe [nat], lettred men, how tho men *honourede*
C.17.276   And alle holy kirke *honoured* thorw that deyng.
C.17.282   Or cristendoem were knowe þere or eny croos *honoured*.
C.18.92   In menynge þat the fayrest thyng the furste thynge shold *honoure*
C.18.248   To make sacrefice of hym he heet me, hym to *honoure*.
C.19.39   The which alle men aren holde ouer al thyng to *honoure*
C.20.267   And bote they reuerense [h]is resurexioun and þe rode *honoure*

honte > hunte

honurably adv *honourabli adv.* B 1; C 1 honerably
B.12.154   And diden [hir] homage *honurably* to hym þat was almyʒty.
C.14.98   And deden here homage *honerably* to hym þat was almyhty.

hood n *hod n. &> robyn_hood* A 5 hod (1) hood (4); B 7; C 8 hod (1) hode (1) hoed (3) hood (3)
A. 5.31   Þat hire hed was worþ a mark & his *hod* not worþ a grote.
A. 5.170   Hikke þe hostiler hitte his *hood* aftir
A. 5.173   Whoso hadde þe *hood* shulde haue amendis of þe cloke.
A. 5.182   And haue hikkes *hood* þe hostiller, & holde hym yseruid,
A. 7.253   Þat fisik shal his furrid *hood* for his foode selle,
B. 5.31   [That] hire heed was worþ [a] marc & his *hood* noʒt a grote.
B. 5.194   Wiþ an *hood* on his heed, a hat aboue,
B. 5.321   Hikke þe [Hostiler] hitte his *hood* after
B. 5.324   Whoso hadde þe *hood* sholde han amendes of þe cloke.
B. 5.333   And haue Hikkes *hood* [þe] hostiler and holden hym yserued,
B. 6.269   That Phisik shal hi[s] furred *ho[od]* for his fode selle,
B.20.176   A Phisicien wiþ a furred *hood* þat he fel in a palsie,
C. 5.133   [That] here hed was worth half marc and his *hoed* nat a grote.
C. 6.202   With his *hood* on his heued and his hat bothe,
C. 6.378   Hikke þe hackenayman hit his *hod* aftur
C. 6.381   That hoso hadde the *hood* sholde nat haue þe cloke
C. 6.391   And haue hickes *hood* þe hostiler and holde hym yserued:
C. 8.290   That fysik shal his forred *hod[e]* for his fode sulle
C.13.48   Oþer his hatt or his *hood* or elles his gloues
C.22.176   A fisician with a forred *hoed* that he ful in a palesye

hool adj *hole adj.(2)* A 1 hole; B 3 hole (2) hool (1); C 3 hol (1) hole (2)
A. 7.54   He caste on his cloþis, ycloutid & *hole*,
B. 6.59   [He] caste on [hise] cloþes, yclouted and *hole*,
B.14.1   'I haue but oon *hool* hater', quod haukyn, 'I am þe lasse to blame
B.18.377   Ac alle þat beþ myne *hole* breþeren, in blood and in baptisme,
C. 3.352   So of *ho[l]* herte cometh hope and hardy relacoun
C. 7.258   In thyne *hole* herte to herborwe alle trewe
C.20.419   Ac alle þat beth myn *hole* breth[r]ene, in bloed and in baptisme,

hoold > holden; hoolly > holly

hoom n *hom n.* A 4 hom (3) home (1); B 5 hom (1) home (2) hoom (2); C 5 hoem (2) hom (1) homes (1)
A. 3.88   Þe hous and þe *hom[e]* of hem þat desiren
A. 8.5   And bad hym holde hym at *hom* & erien his laiʒes.
A. 9.20   Ergo he nis not alwey at *hom* among ʒow Freris;
A.10.45   Ac in þe herte is hire *hom* heiʒest of alle.
B. 3.99   The hou[s] and [þe] *ho[m]* of hem þat desireþ
B. 7.5   And bad hym holde hym at *home* and erien hise leyes,
B. 8.24   Ergo he nys noʒt alwey [at *hoom*] amonges yow freres;
B. 9.57   A[c] in þe herte is hir *hoom* and hir mooste reste.
B.11.129   Ac he may renne in arerage and rome fro *home*,
C. 3.127   The houses and þe *homes* of hem þat taketh ʒeftes.

C. 9.5   And bad hym holden hym at *hoem* and eryen his leyes
C.10.28   Ergo he [n]is nat alwey at *hom* amonges ʒow freres;
C.11.44   God is nat in þat *hoem* ne his helpe nother.
C.12.64   Ac he may renne in arrerage and rome fro *home*

hoom adv *hom adv.* A 4 hom; B 6 hom (2) home (1) hoom (3); C 7 hoem (6) hom (1)
A. 5.29   And fecche [*hom*] felis fro wyuene pyne.
A. 7.33   And fecche þe *hom* fauconis þe foulis to kille,
A. 7.91   I bar *hom* þat I borewide er I to bedde ʒede.
A. 7.187   *Hom* into his owene er[d]e & holde him þere euere.
A. 5.29   And fecche Felice *hom* fro wyuen pyne.
B. 6.31   And [fette þee *hoom*] faucons foweles to kille
B. 6.99   I bar *hom* þat I borwed er I to bedde yede.
B. 6.200   *Hoom* [in]to his owene [e]rd and holden hym þere [euere].
B.19.330   A cart highte cristendom to carie [*home*] Piers sheues,
B.19.480   The viker hadde fer *hoom* and faire took his leeue
C. 4.56   He borwed of me bayard a[nd] brouhte hym *hom* neuere
C. 5.131   And fette felyce *hoem* fram wyuene pyne.
C. 8.108   I bar *hoem* þat y borwed ar y to bedde ʒede.
C. 8.206   *Hoem* [in]to his owene [e]rd and halde hym þere euere.
C. 9.151   And ca[ry]eth hit *hoem* to his cote and cast hym to lyuene
C.21.330   A Cart hihte Cristendoem to carie *hoem* Peres sheues
C.21.480   The vicory hadde fer *hoem* and [fayre] toek his leue

hoor adj *hor adj.* A 2 hor (1) hore (1); B 5 hore (1) hoor (2) hoore (2); C 6 hoer (2) hore (3) hoer (1)
A. 7.75   'For [now] I am old & *hor* & haue of myn owene
A. 8.82   Ac olde men & *hore* þat helpeles ben of strengþe,
B. 6.83   'For now I am old and *hoor* and haue of myn owene
B. 7.100   Ac olde men and *hore* þat helplees ben of strengþe,
B.16.173   As *hoor* as an haweþorn and Abraham he highte.
B.20.95   Elde þe *hoore*; [he] was in þe vauntwarde
B.20.202   Lo! Elde þe *hoore* haþ me biseye.
C. 6.193   When y was olde and *hoor* and hadde ylore þat kynde
C. 8.92   'For now y am olde and *hoer* and haue of myn owene
C. 9.176   Ac olde [men] and *hore* þat helples ben and nedy
C.18.182   As *hoer* as a hauthorn, and abraham he hihte.
C.22.95   Elde þe *hore*; he was in þe Vawwarde
C.22.202   Lo! Elde þe *hore* hath me byseye;

hoord n *hord n.(1)* B 1; C 1 hoerd
B.16.84   And made of holy men his *hoord* In limbo Inferni,
C.18.115   And made of holy men his *hoerd* in limbo inferni

hoores > hore

hoost n *hoste n.(1)* A 1 ost; B 4 hoost (1) oost (2) oostes (1); C 4 oest (1) oeste (1) oste (2)
A. 3.246   Wende þidir with þin *ost* wommen to kille;
B. 3.266   Weend to Amalec with þyn *oost* & what þow fyndest þere sle it.
B.18.239   [The *oostes*] in heuene token stella com[a]ta
B.19.336   And gadered hym a greet *Oost*; greuen he þynkeþ
B.20.113   And gaderede a greet *hoost* al agayn Conscience.
C. 3.252   To helpe heyliche alle his *oste* or elles graunte
C. 3.419   Haste the with al thyn *oste* to þe lond of Amalek
C.21.336   And gadered a grete *oeste*; greue he thenketh
C.22.113   And gaderet[h] a greet *oest* alle agayn Consience.

hoot adj *hot adj.* A 4 hote; B 4 hote (3) hoot (1); C 7 hoet (2) hot (1) hote (4)
A.Pr.104   Cookis & here knaues crieþ 'hote pyes, hote!
A.Pr.104   Cookis & here knaues crieþ 'hote pyes, *hote*!
A. 5.153   'Hast þou,' quaþ he, 'any *hote* spices?'
A. 5.154   'ʒa, glotoun gossib,' quaþ heo, 'god wot, wel *hote*:
B.Pr.226   Cokes and hire knaues cryden, 'hote pies, hote!
B.Pr.226   Cokes and hire knaues cryden, 'hote pies, *hote*!
B. 5.303   'Hastow', quod he, 'any *hote* spices?'
B.18.207   Ne what is *hoot* hunger þat hadde neuere defaute.
C.Pr.230   Cokes and here knaues cryede, 'hote pyes, hote!
C.Pr.230   Cokes and here knaues cryede, 'hote pyes, *hote*!
C. 5.7   In an *hot* heruest whenne y hadde myn hele
C. 6.358   'Hastow,' quod he, 'eny *hote* spyces?'
C. 9.142   In hope to sitte at euen by þe *hote* coles,
C.20.212   Ne what is *hoet* hunger þat hadde neuere defaute.
C.20.290   Al *hoet* on here hedes þat entrith ney þe walles;

hope n *hope n.(1)* A 4; B 17; C 14
A.Pr.27   In *hope* [for] to haue heueneriche blisse,
A. 3.187   Dede hym hoppe for *hope* to haue me at wille.
A. 5.240   To haue helle for euere ʒif þat *hope* nere.
A.11.251   And siþen he[þen] to helpe in *hope* hem to amende.
B.Pr.27   In *hope* [for] to haue heueneriche blisse,
B. 3.200   And dide hem hoppe for *hope* to haue me at wille.
B. 5.506   Thanne hente *hope* an horn of Deus tu conuersus viuificabis [nos]
B.10.369   And siþen heþen to helpe in *hope* of amendement.

B.12.30 Feiþ, *hope* and Charite, and alle ben goode,
B.12.292 And an *hope* hangynge þerInne to haue a mede for his truþe;
B.13.423 And han likynge to liþen hem [in *hope*] to do yow lauȝe–
B.17.55 Boþe þe heraud and *hope* and he mette atones
B.17.62 *Hope* cam hippynge after þat hadde so ybosted
B.17.95 Neiþer Feiþ ne fyn *hope*, so festred be hise woundes,
B.17.118 And *Hope* þe Hostile[r] shal be þer [an helyng þe man lith];
B.17.120 *Hope* shal lede hem forþ with loue as his lettre telleþ,
B.17.131 And *Hope* afterward he bad me to louye
B.17.136 And as *hope* highte þee I hote þat þow louye
B.17.315 Good *hope*, þat helpe sholde, to wanhope torneþ.
B.20.167 And Elde hente good *hope* and hastiliche he shifte hym
B.20.180 And in *hope* of his heele good herte he hente
C.Pr.29 In *hope* to haue a good ende and heuenriche blisse,
C. 1.101 And neuer leue for loue in *hope* to lacche syluer.
C. 3.136 Bothe to the and to thyne in *hope* thow shost amende;
C. 3.352 So of ho[l] herte cometh *hope* and hardy relacoun
C. 7.83 And han lykyng to lythen hem in *hope* to do ȝow lawhe–
C. 7.151 Thenne hente [*hope*] an horn of deus tu conuersus viuificabis nos
C. 9.142 In *hope* to sitte at euen by þe hote coles,
C.14.214 And *hope* hangeth ay þeron to haue þat treuthe deserueth:
C.19.61 *Hope* cam huppynge aftur þat hadde so ybosted
C.19.85 Noþer faith ne fyn *hope*, so festred aren his woundes.
C.19.100 And *hope* afturward of god more me toelde
C.19.295 For goed *hope*, that helpe scholde, to wanhope turneth
C.22.167 And elde hente gode *hope* and hastiliche [he] sh[ifte] hym
C.22.180 And in *hope* of his hele goed herte he hente

hope v *hopen v.(1)* A 6; B 15 hope (13) hoped (1) hopen (1); C 24 hope (21) hopen (1) hopeth (2)
A. 6.122 And þoruȝ þe helpe of hem [two], *hope* þou non oþer,
A. 7.86 He is holden, I *hope*, to haue me in mynde,
A. 7.274 Be þat I *hope* to haue heruest in my croft,
A. 8.99 And do euele & haue euele, & *hope* þou non oþer
A. 9.15 And euere haþ [as] I *hope*, & euere shal hereaftir.'
A.11.108 Þei two, [as] I *hope*, aftir my besekyng,
B. 1.120 And alle þat *hoped* it myȝte be so, noon heuene myȝte hem holde,
B. 5.637 And þoruȝ þe help of hem two, *hope* þow noon ooþer,
B. 6.94 [He is] holden, I *hope*, to haue me in [mynde]
B. 6.290 By þat I *hope* to haue heruest in my crofte,
B. 7.117 And do yuel and haue yuel, [and] *hope* þow noon ooþer
B. 8.19 And euere haþ as I *hope*, and euere shal herafter.'
B.10.156 They two, as I *hope*, after my [bis]echyng
B.12.272 Ac god is so good, I *hope* þat siþþe he gaf hem wittes
B.15.387 [Ac] if þei ouerhuppe, as I *hope* noȝt, oure bileue suffiseþ,
B.15.480 So *hope* þei to haue heuene þoruȝ hir whistlyng.
B.15.603 And *hopen* þat he be to come þat shal hem releue;
B.16.237 Bledden blood for þat lordes loue and *hope* to blisse þe tyme.
B.17.272 For þat ben vnkynde to hise, *hope* I noon ooþer
B.18.151 'Thoruȝ experience', quod [heo], 'I *hope* þei shul be saued;
B.19.382 The lord of lust shal be letted al þis lente, I *hope*.
C. 5.94 Ac ȝut y *hope*, as he þat ofte hath ychaffared
C. 5.99 So *hope* y to haue of hym þat is almyghty
C. 6.255 Ne thyn heyres, as y *hope*, haue ioye of þat thow wonne
C. 7.290 And thorw þe help[e] of hem two, *hope* þou non oþer,
C. 8.103 He is holdyng, y *hope*, to haue me in his masse
C. 8.137 Myhte helpe, as y *hope*; Ac hey treuthe wolde
C. 8.313 And by [t]hat y *hope* to haue heruost in my croft[e];
C. 9.274 Thyn huyre, herde, as y *hope*, hath nat to quyte thy dette
C. 9.291 And do yuele and haue euele and *hope* thow non oþere
C.10.19 And euere hath, as y *hope*, and euere wol hereaftur.'
C.12.199 But as an hosebonde *hopeth* aftur an hard wynter,
C.14.11 Clerkes þat conne al, y *hope* they can do bettere.
C.14.194 Ac god is so gode, y *hope* þat seth he gaf hem wittes
C.16.21 Ac for þe beste, as y *hope*, aren som pore and ryche.
C.17.118 That they ouerhippe nat for hastite, as y *hope* they do nat,
C.17.146 And ay *hopeth* eft to be with here body at þe laste
C.17.185 Holy men, as y *hope*, thorw helpe of the holy goste
C.17.311 And *hopen* þat he be to come þat shal hem releue;
C.18.1 'Leue liberum Arbitrium,' quod y, 'y leue, as y *hope*,
C.18.249 I withsaet nat his heste; y *hope* and bileue
C.18.253 Bledden bloed for þat lordes loue [and] *hope* to blisse þ[e] tyme.
C.19.253 For þat ben vn[k]ynde to hise, *hope* ȝe noen oþer
C.20.154 'Thorw experiense,' quod me, 'y *hope* they shal ben saued;
C.21.382 The lord of lust shal be ylette al this lente, y *hope*.

hoper n *hoppere n.* A 1; B 1; C 1 hopur
A. 7.56 And heng his *hoper* at his hals in stede of a scrippe:
B. 6.61 And [heng his] *hoper* at [his] hals in stede of a Scryppe:
C. 8.60 And heng his *hopur* on his hal[s] in stede of a scryppe;

hoppe v *hoppen v.* A 1; B 1
A. 3.187 Dede hym *hoppe* for hope to haue me at wille.
B. 3.200 And dide hem *hoppe* for hope to haue me at wille.

hopur > hoper; hor > hoor

hore n *hore n.(2) &> hoor* B 4 hore (1) hores (2) hoores (1); C 6 hore (3) horen (1) hores (1) hoores (1)
B. 4.166 For þe mooste commune of þat court called hire an *hore*.
B.14.183 [To *hores*, to harlotes, to alle maner peple].
B.15.85 Of vsurers, of *hoores*, of Auarouse chapmen,
B.15.134 So harlotes and *hores* arn holpe wiþ swiche goodes,
C. 3.301 Harlotes and *hoores* and also fals leches,
C. 4.161 For þe comune calde here queynte comune *hore*.
C. 6.149 Tyl ayþer clepede oþer "*hore*!" and o[f] with the clothes
C. 6.305 For an *hore* of here ers wynnynge may hardiloker tythe
C.14.21 And holy chirche *horen* helpe, Auerou[s] and coueytous,
C.16.261 Of vsererus, of *hores*, of alle euel wynnynges,

horedom n *horedom n.* B 1; C 1
B.13.353 And of hir harlotrye and *horedom* in hir elde tellen.
C. 7.75 But harlotrie and *horedom* or elles of som wynnynge;

horen > hore

horn n *horn n.* A 1; B 2; C 3
A. 5.191 [Þat] alle þat herden þat *horn* held here nose aftir
B. 5.343 That alle þat herde þat *horn* helde hir nos[e] after
B. 5.506 Thanne herde me an *horn* of Deus tu conuersus viuificabis [nos]
C. 5.16 Or haue an *horn* and be hayward and lygge þeroute [a]nyhtes
C. 6.401 That alle þat herde þ[at] *hor[n]* helde here nose aftur
C. 7.151 Thenne hente [hope] an *horn* of deus tu conuersus viuificabis nos

hors n *hors n.* A 1; B 4 hors (1) horse (3); C 3
A. 7.200 Wiþ houndis bred & *hors* bred holde vp here hertis,
B. 6.214 Wiþ houndes breed and *horse* breed hoold vp hir hertes,
B.11.343 Boþe *hors* and houndes and alle oþere beestes
B.17.107 Who is bihynde and who bifore and who ben on *horse*;
B.17.108 For he halt hym hardier on *horse* þan he þat is [on] foote.
C. 2.179 Thenne gan gyle borwen *hors* at many gret maystres
C. 8.224 With houndes bred and *hors* breed hele hem when þei hungren
C.13.62 Haue *hors* and hardy men; thogh he mette theues

hosbande > hosebonde; hosbondrye > housbondrie

hosebonde n *housbonde n.* A 1 husbondis; C 3 hosbande (1) hosebonde (2)
A.11.183 Actif it is hoten; [*husbondis*] it vsen,
C. 7.299 Thenne was oen hihte actif; an *hosbande* he semede.
C.10.267 That he ne wol bowe to þat bonde to beden here an *hosebonde*
C.12.199 But as an *hosebonde* hopeth aftur an hard wynter,

hosele(- > housel,-sled; hosewyf > houswif; hoso > whoso

hostele v *hostelen v.* B 1
B.17.121 And *hostele* hem and heele þoruȝ holy chirche bileue

hostiele n *hostel n.* C 1
C.13.64 And as safly as þe messager and a[s] sone at his *hostiele*.

hostiler n *hostiler n.* A 3 hostiler (1) hostiller (2); B 5; C 3
A. 5.170 Hikke þe *hostiler* hitte his hood aftir
A. 5.180 Hikke þe *hostiller* þanne hadde þe cloke
A. 5.182 And haue hikkes hood þe *hostiller*, & holde hym yseruid,
B. 5.321 Hikke þe [*Hostiler*] hitte his hood after
B. 5.331 Hikke þe *hostiler* [þanne] hadde þe cloke
B. 5.333 And haue Hikkes hood [þe] *hostiler* and holden hym yserued,
B.17.76 Herberwed hym at an hostrie and þe *hostiler* called:
B.17.118 And Hope þe *Hostile[r]* shal be þer [an helyng þe man lith];
C. 6.389 Hicke þe *hostiler* hadde þe cloke
C. 6.391 And haue hickes hood þe *hostiler* and holde hym yserued:
C.19.76 And toek two pans the *hostiler* to take kepe to hym;

hostrie n *hostrie n.* B 1
B.17.76 Herberwed hym at an *hostrie* and þe hostiler called:

hot > hoot

hote v *hoten v.(1) &> hoot,otes* A 42 hatte (9) hattiþ (7) hete (1) hyȝt (1) hiȝte (9) hyȝth (1) hote (7) hoten (3) hotiþ (2) yhote (1) yhoten (1); B 74 hatte (13) hattestow (1) heet (2) highte (18) hiȝte (19) hote (10) hoten (3) hoteþ (6) yhote (2); C 72 hatte (13) hattest (1) heet (2) heete (1) hehte (1) heihte (1) hette (1) hihte (26) hyhte (3) hoet (1) hote (11) hoten (2) hoteth (7) ihote (1) yhote (1)
A. 1.17 And þerfore he *hiȝte* þe erþe to helpe ȝow ichone
A. 1.61 Þereinne woniþ a wy þat wrong is *yhoten*;
A. 2.140 Shuln serue myself þat cyuyle *hatte*;
A. 2.161 To atache þis tiraunt[is] 'for any tresour, I *hote*;
A. 2.168 Er he be put on þe pillorie, for any preyour, I *hote*.'
A. 2.180 Oueral yhuntid & *yhote* trusse,
A. 3.9 Curteisliche þe clerk þanne, as þe king *hiȝte*,
A. 3.244 Samuel seide to saul, "god sendiþ þe & *hotiþ*
A. 4.3 Kisse hire,' quaþ þe king, 'consience, I *hote*!'

A. 5.120	Wiþ many maner marchaundise as my maister me *hiȝte*.	
A. 6.33	Dyke[d] & d[o]luen & do what he *hiȝte*,	
A. 6.60	Þ[e] croft *hattiþ* coueite nouȝt menis catel ne here wyues,	
A. 6.64	Þei *hote* stele nouȝt, ne sle nouȝt; strik forþ be boþe.	
A. 6.82	Grace *hattiþ* þe [gateward], a good man forsoþe,	
A. 6.83	His man *hattiþ* amende ȝow, for many man he knowiþ,	
A. 6.106	Þat on *hattiþ* abstinence, and [humylite] anoþer,	
A. 7.43	In a wel perilous place þat purcatorie *hattiþ*;	
A. 7.70	Dame werche whanne tyme is piers wyf *hatte*;	
A. 7.71	His douȝter *hattiþ* do riȝt [so] or þi damme shal þe bete;	
A. 7.72	His sone *hattiþ* suffre þi souereynes to hauen here wille	
A. 7.215	'Ȝe, I *hote* þe,' quaþ hungir, 'oþer ellis þe bible leiȝeþ.	
A. 7.218	& labouren for þi liflode, & so oure lord *hiȝte*;	
A. 7.243	Ac I *hote* þe,' quaþ hunger, 'as þou þin hele wilnest,	
A. 7.245	And ete nouȝt, I *hote* þe, er hunger be take	
A. 8.184	Þat at þe day of dome we dede as he *hiȝte*.	
A. 9.85	And wiþ glad wil doþ hem good for so god [*hiȝte*].	
A.10.7	Anima he[o] *ha[tte]*; to hire [haþ] enuye	
A.10.17	Is a wys kniȝt withalle, sire [inwit] he *hatte*,	
A.10.38	Þat is þe castel þat kynde made, caro it *hatte*,	
A.10.143	An aungel in angir *hiȝte* h[e]m to wende	
A.11.1	Þanne hadde wyt a wyf þat *hatte* dame studie,	
A.11.48	But hunsen hym as an hound & *hoten* hym go þenne.	
A.11.105	I shal kenne þe to my cosyn þat clergie is *hoten*.	
A.11.118	And ek þe longe launde þat leccherie *hatte*,	
A.11.153	And do good a[g]ens euil; god hymself *hotiþ*	
A.11.183	Actif it is *hoten*; [husbondis] it vsen,	
A.11.187	Diken or deluen, dowel it *hatte*.	
A.11.252	To harme hem ne slen hem god *hiȝte* vs neuere,	
A.12.50	*Hyȝt* omnia probate, a pore þing withalle;	
A.12.53	Ken him to my cosenes hous þat kinde wit *hyȝth*.	
A.12.63	'I am dwellyng with deth, and hunger I *hatte*.	
A.12.74	[But ete as hunger me *hete* til my belly swellyd.	
B.Pr.102	How he it lefte wiþ loue as oure lord *hiȝte*	
B. 1.17	And þerfore he *hiȝte* þe erþe to helpe yow echone	
B. 1.63	TherInne wonyeþ a [wye] þat wrong is *yhote*,	
B. 2.21	And ylakked my lemman þat leautee is *hoten*,	
B. 2.200	To attachen þo Tyrauntȝ 'for any [tresor], I *hote*;	
B. 2.207	Er he be put on þe Pillory for any preyere I *hote*.'_	
B. 2.221	Ouer al yhonted and *yhote* trusse,	
B. 3.9	Curteisly þe clerk þanne, as þe kyng *hiȝte*,	
B. 3.264	"Forþi", seide Samuel to Saul, "god hymself *hoteþ* [þ]ee	
B. 4.3	Kis hire', quod þe kyng, 'Conscience, I *hote*!'	
B. 5.204	Wiþ many manere marchaundise as my maister me *hiȝte*.	
B. 5.398	I parfournede neuere penaunce as þe preest me *hiȝte*,	
B. 5.545	Idyke[d] and Id[o]lue, Ido þat [he] *hoteþ*.	
B. 5.548	I weue and I wynde and do what truþe *hoteþ*.	
B. 5.573	Th[e] croft *hatte* Coueite-noȝt-mennes-catel-ne-hire-wyues-	
B. 5.577	Thei *hiȝte* Stele-noȝt-[ne]-Sle-noȝt; strik forþ by boþe.	
B. 5.595	Grace *hatte* þe gateward, a good man for soþe;	
B. 5.596	His man *hatte* amende-yow, for many m[a]n h[e] knoweþ.	
B. 5.620	That oon *hatte* Abstinence, and humilite anoþer;	
B. 6.44	In a [wel] perilous place [þat] Purgatorie *hatte*.	
B. 6.78	Dame werch-whan-tyme-is Piers wif *hiȝte*;	
B. 6.79	His douȝter *hiȝte* do-riȝt-so-or-þi-dame-shal-þee-bete;	
B. 6.80	His sone *hiȝte* Suffre-þi-Souereyns-to-hauen-hir-wille-	
B. 6.231	'Ye I [h]ote þee', quod hunger, 'or ellis þe bible lieþ.	
B. 6.234	And laboure for þi liflode, and so oure lord *hiȝte*.	
B. 6.259	Ac I *hote* þee', quod hunger, 'as þow þyn hele wilnest,	
B. 6.261	Ete noȝt, I *hote* þee, er hunger þee take	
B. 7.206	At þe day of dome we dide as he *hiȝte*.	
B. 8.95	And wiþ glad wille dooþ hem good for so god *hoteþ*.	
B. 9.7	Anima she *hatte*; [to hir haþ enuye]	
B. 9.18	Is a wis knyȝt wiþalle, sire Inwit he *hatte*,	
B. 9.50	[Th]at is þe Castel þat kynde made; caro it *hatte*,	
B.10.1	Thanne hadde wit a wif was *hote* dame Studie,	
B.10.62	But [hunsen] hym as an hound and *hoten* hym go þennes.	
B.10.153	I shal kenne þee to my Cosyn þat Clergie is *hoten*.	
B.10.166	And also þe [longe] launde [þat] lecherie *hatte*,	
B.10.204	And do good a[g]ein yuel; god hymself *hoteþ*:	
B.10.370	God *hoteþ* heiȝe and lowe þat no man hurte ooþer,	
B.11.9	And in a Mirour þat *hiȝte* middelerþe she made me biholde.	
B.11.27	Thanne was þer oon þat *hiȝte* Elde, þat heuy was of chere;	
B.11.37	'Homo proponit', quod a poete, and Plato he *hiȝte*,	
B.11.324	And on a mountaigne þat myddelerþe *hiȝte*, as me [þo] þouȝte,	
B.15.24	And whan I wilne and wolde animus ich *hatte*;	
B.15.36	Thanne am I spirit spechelees; Spiritus þanne ich *hatte*.	
B.15.415	How englisshe clerkes a coluere fede þat coueitise *hiȝte*,	
B.15.491	What pope or prelat now parfourneþ þat crist *hiȝte*,	
B.16.8	Pacience *hatte* þe pure tree and [pouere] symple of herte,	
B.16.15	Herte *hiȝte* þe herber þat it Inne groweþ,	
B.16.61	I shal telle þee as tid what þis tree *hiȝte*.	
B.16.62	The ground þere it groweþ, goodnesse it *hatte*;	

B.16.63	And I haue told þee what *hiȝte* þe tree; þe Trinite it meneþ.'	
B.16.91	To a maide þat *hiȝte* Marie, a meke þyng wiþalle,	
B.16.134	As euere it was and as wid; wherfor I *hote* yow	
B.16.173	As hoor as an haweþorn and Abraham he *highte*.	
B.16.188	The þridde *highte* þe holi goost, a persone by hymselue,	
B.16.232	Hym or Ysaak myn heir, þe which he *hiȝte* me kulle	
B.16.275	What he *highte* & whider he wolde, and wightly he tolde.	
B.17.110	On my Capul þat *highte* caro–of mankynde I took it–	
B.17.136	And as hope *highte* þee I hote þat þow louye	
B.17.136	And as hope highte þee I *hote* þat þow louye	
B.18.79	*Highte* Longeus as þe lettre telleþ, and longe hadde lore his sight;	
B.18.115	Mercy *highte* þat mayde, a meke þyng wiþ alle,	
B.18.119	A comely creature [and a clene]; truþe she *highte*.	
B.18.128	A maiden þat *highte* Marie, and moder wiþouten felyng	
B.18.231	Book *highte* þat beaupeere, a bold man of speche,	
B.18.392	In my prisone Purgatorie til parce it *hote*.	
B.19.269	Oon *highte* Austyn and Ambrose anoþer,	
B.19.276	Spiritus prudencie þe firste seed *highte*,	
B.19.281	The seconde seed *highte* Spiritus temperancie.	
B.19.324	He made a manere morter, and mercy it *highte*.	
B.19.330	A cart *highte* cristendom to carie [home] Piers sheues,	
B.20.273	Enuye herde þis and *heet* freres go to scole	
B.20.339	What *hattestow*, I praye þee? hele noȝt þi name.'	
B.20.348	Hende speche *heet* pees, 'opene þe yates.	
C. 1.17	Wherfore he *hette* þe elementis to helpe ȝow alle tymes	
C. 1.59	Therynne wonyeth a wyghte þat wrong is [*ihote*];	
C. 2.20	And [lakked] my lemman þat leute is *hoten*	
C. 2.31	The fader þat me forth brouhte filius dei he *hoteth*,	
C. 2.214	[T]o atache tho tyrauntes, 'for eny tresor, y *hote*;	
C. 2.219	Ar he be put on þe pylorye for eny preyere ich *hote*.'	
C. 2.231	Oueral yhonted and *yhote* trusse,	
C. 3.9	Cortesliche þe Clerk thenne, as þe kyng *hyhte*,	
C. 3.417	"Sauel," quod samuel, "god hymsulue *hoteth* [the]	
C. 3.498	The whiche þat *hatte*, as y haue rad an[d] oþer þat can rede,	
C. 4.3	Kusse here,' quod þe kyng, 'Consience, y *hote*!'	
C. 6.212	With many manere marchandise as my maistre *hyhte*;	
C. 6.309	*Hyhte* ȝeuan-ȝelde-aȝeyn-yf-y-so-moche-haue-	
C. 7.14	Y parfourmede neuere penaunc[e] þat þe prest me *hihte*	
C. 7.220	The croft *hatte* coueite-nat-menne-catel-ne-here-wyues-	
C. 7.224	Thei *hatte* stele-nat and sle-nat; stryk forth by bothe	
C. 7.240	The Brygge *hatte* b[id]-wel-the-bet-may-th[ow]-spede;	
C. 7.243	Grace *hatte* þe gateward, a goed man for sothe;	
C. 7.244	His man *hatte* amende-ȝow, many man hym knoweth.	
C. 7.247	And parformed þe penaunce þat þe prest me *hihte*."	
C. 7.272	That on *hatte* a[b]stinence and vmbletee a[n]oþer,	
C. 7.299	Thenne was oen *hihte* actif; an hosbande he semede.	
C. 8.80	Dame worch-when-tyme-is [Peres] wyf *hehte*;	
C. 8.81	His douhter *hihte* do-rihte-so-or-thy-dame-shal-þe-bete;	
C. 8.82	His sone *hihte* soffre-thy-souereynes-haue-her-wille-	
C. 8.85	Ne hem þat han lawes to loke lacke hem nat, y *hote*;	
C. 8.89	Al þat they *hoten*, y hote; heiliche thow soffre hem	
C. 8.89	Al þat they hoten, y *hote*; heiliche thow soffre hem	
C. 8.271	Ac ete nat, y *hote*, Ar hungur the take	
C. 9.220	For holy churche *hoteth* alle manere peple	
C.10.99	Ac dobest sholde drede hem nat but do as god *hihte*:	
C.10.134	Anima she *hatte*; to here hath enuye	
C.10.144	Is a wise knyhte withalle, sire inwit he *hatte*,	
C.11.1	Thenne hadde wit a wyf was *hote* dame studie,	
C.11.42	Is non so hende to haue hym [in] but *hote* hym go þer god is.	
C.11.65	And breketh nat here bred to þe pore as þe boke *hoteth*:	
C.11.168	And in a myrrour þat *hihte* myddelerd she made me to loke.	
C.11.186	Thenne was [there] oen þat *hihte* Elde þat heuy was of chere;	
C.11.303	'Homo pr[o]ponit,' quod a poete tho, and plato he *hihte*,	
C.13.45	Ne non haiward is *hote* his wed for to taken.	
C.14.41	"That seth hymsulue synnelees sese nat, y *hote*,	
C.16.158	Thenne hadde Actyf a ledare þat *hihte* lib[e]rum arbitrium;	
C.16.184	And when y wilne and wolde Animus y *hatte*,	
C.16.186	And when y make mone to god Memoria y *hatte*;	
C.16.198	Thenne am [y] spirit specheles; spiritus then y *hote*.	
C.17.159	A man þat *hihte* Makameth for messie they hym holdeth	
C.18.4	Til we cam into a contre, cor hominis hit *heihte*,	
C.18.7	That *hihte* ymago dei, graciousliche hit growede.	
C.18.8	Thenne gan y aske what hit *hihte* and he me sone tolde:	
C.18.9	'The tree *hatte* trewe loue,' quod he, 'þe trinite hit sette.	
C.18.18	And sethen þat ȝe fouchen saef to sey me as hit *hoteth*.'	
C.18.105	And anoon he *hihte* Elde an hy for to clymbe	
C.18.124	To a mayde þat *hihte* marie, a meke thyng withalle,	
C.18.182	As hoer as a hauthorn, and abraham he *hihte*.	
C.18.190	And, sondry to se vpon, solus deus he *hoteth*.'	
C.18.192	'That is soth,' saide he thenne, 'the syre pater	
C.18.248	To make sacrefice of hym he *heet* me, hym to honoure.	
C.18.291	What he *hihte* and whoder he wolde & whithliche he tolde.	
C.20.81	*Hihte* longies as þe lettre telleth, and longe hadde lore his sihte;	

C.20.118   Mercy *hihte* þat mayde, a mylde thynge with alle,
C.20.122   A comely creature and a clene; Treuthe she *hihte*.
C.20.131   A mayde þat *hoteth* Marie, a[nd] moder withouten velynge
C.20.240   Boek *hihte* þat beaupere, a bolde man of speche.
C.20.287   Astarot, *hoet* out and haue our oure knaues,
C.21.269   Oen *hihte* Austyn and Ambros[e] anoþer,
C.21.276   Spiritus prudencie the furste seed *hihte*
C.21.281   The seconde se[d]e *hihte* Spiritus temperancie.
C.21.324   He made a manere morter and mercy hit *hihte*.
C.21.330   A Cart *hihte* Cristendoem to carie hoem Peres sheues
C.22.273   Enuye herde this and *heete* freres go to scole
C.22.339   What *hattest* thow? y praye the, hele nat thy name.'
C.22.348   Hende speche *heet* pees, 'opene the ʒates.

hou > how; houe(s > howue

hound n *hound n.*   A 2 hound (1) houndis (1); B 8 hound (3) houndes (5); C 5 hound (2) hounde (1) houndes (2)
A. 7.200   Wiþ *houndis* bred & hors bred holde vp here hertis,
A.11.48   But hunsen hym as an *hound* & hoten hym go þenne.
B. 4.125   Hire haukes and hire *houndes* help to pouere Religious;
B. 5.258   'I am holden', quod he, 'as hende as *hound* is in kichene;
B. 5.355   Is noon so hungry *hound* in hertford shire
B. 6.214   Wiþ *houndes* breed and horse breed hoold vp hir hertes,
B.10.62   But [hunsen] hym as an *hound* and hoten hym go þennes.
B.10.293   And carpen noʒt as þei carpe now, [and] calle yow doumbe *houndes*:
B.10.314   An heep of *houndes* at his ers as he a lord were,
B.11.343   Boþe hors and *houndes* and alle oþere beestes
C. 5.160   A[n] hep of *houndes* at h[is] ers as he a lord were
C. 6.413   Ys non so hungry *hound* in hertford shyre
C. 6.431   And as an *hound* þat eet gras so gan y to brake
C. 8.224   With *houndes* bred and hors breed hele hem when þei hungren
C. 9.266   How, herde! where is thyn *ho[u]nd[e]* and thyn hardy herte

houped v *houpen v.*   A 1 houpide; B 1; C 1
A. 7.157   And *houpide* aftir hungir þat herde hym at þe ferste:
B. 6.172   And *houped* after hunger þat herde hym at þe firste.
C. 8.168   And *houped* aftur hunger þat herde hym at the furste.

houre n *houre n.*   A 1 houres; B 4 houre (1) houres (3); C 2 oures
A. 1.157   ʒe ne haue no more meryt in [masse] ne in [houres]
B.Pr.97   Hire messe & hire matyns and many of hire *houres*
B. 1.183   Ye ne haue na moore merite in masse n[e] in *houres*
B.14.12   And kouþe I neuere, by crist! kepen it clene an *houre*
B.15.386   Lest þei ouerhuppen as ooþere doon in office and in *houres*.
C.Pr.125   ʒoure masse and [ʒoure] matynes and many of [ʒoure] *oures*
C. 1.179   ʒe n[e] haueth na more meryte in masse ne in *oures*

hous n *hous n.*   A 9 hous (6) house (2) housis (1); B 20 hous (14) house (2) houses (4); C 20 hous (12) house (3) houses (5)
A. 2.38   Þer nas halle ne *hous* to herberwe þe peple,
A. 2.181   Til pardoners hadde pite & pulden hit to *house*,
A. 3.52   Þat iche segge shal se I am sistir of ʒour *hous*.'
A. 3.88   Þe *hous* and þe hom[e] of hem þat desiren
A. 6.32   And kepide his corn, & cariede it to *house*,
A. 6.77   Alle þe *housis* ben helid, hallis & chaumbris,
A.11.176   Þat I was of wyttis *hous* & wiþ his wyf dame stodie.
A.12.53   Ken him to my cosenes *hous* þat kinde wit hyʒth.
A.12.84   Þat on is called cotidian, a courrour of oure *hous*;
B. 2.222   Til Pardoners hadde pite and pulled hym [to] *house*,
B. 3.63   That [ech] segge shal [see] I am suster of youre *house*.'
B. 3.99   The *hou[s]* and [þe] ho[m] of hem þat desireþ
B. 5.265   For were I frere of þat *hous* þer good feiþ and charite is
B. 5.268   For þe beste book in oure *hous*, þeiʒ brent gold were þe leues,
B. 5.590   And alle þe *houses* ben hiled, halles and chambres,
B.10.96   Homliche at oþere mennes *houses* and hatien hir owene.
B.10.233   That I was of wittes *hous* and wiþ his wif dame Studie.
B.10.412   Of holi chirche þat herberwe is, and goddes *hous* to saue
B.11.65   Be buried at hire *hous* but at my parisshe chirche;
B.14.253   Hadde þei no[on haunt] but of poore men; hir *houses* stoode vntyled.
B.15.142   For a wrecchede *hous* [he held] al his lif tyme,
B.15.423   To lyue by litel and in lowe *houses* by lele mennes almesse.
B.16.177   And of Abrahames *hous* an heraud of armes;
B.17.322   For to fleen his owene [hous] as holy writ sheweþ.
B.17.325   And if his *hous* be vnhiled and reyne on his bedde
B.19.167   In an *hous* al bishet and hir dore ybarred
B.19.318   Ordeigne þee an *hous*, Piers, to herberwe Inne þi cornes.'
B.19.320   And ordeyne þat *hous* er ye hennes þede.'
B.19.328   And called þat *hous* vnitee, holy chirche on englissh.
C. 2.232   Tyl Pardoners hadde [pyte] and polleden hym [t]o *house*.
C. 3.96   Feuer or foul[e] euel other fuyr on here *houses*,
C. 3.102   And thenne falleth ther fuyr on fals men *houses*
C. 3.127   The *houses* and þe homes of hem þat taketh ʒeftes.

C. 6.353   By betene *hous* the brewestere þat bad hym good morwen
C. 7.52   Forsleuthed in my seruice and set [hous] afuyre
C. 7.237   And alle þe *hous*[es] been yheled, halles and chaumbres,
C. 9.74   Þat they with spynnyng may spare spenen hit [i]n *hous* huyre,
C. 9.125   We sholde [haue] hem to *house* and helpe hem when they come:
C. 9.207   H[e]lden ful hungry *hous* and hadde muche defaute,
C.14.90   Ne in no cote ne Caytyfs *hous* [crist was ybore
C.14.91   Bote in a burgeises *hous*], the beste of þe toune.
C.16.93   Hadde they noen haunt bote of pore [men; here *houses* stoed vntyled].
C.18.158   And saide, 'this is an *hous* of orysones and of holynesse
C.19.302   Out of his oune *house* as holy writ sheweth.
C.19.305   And if his *hous* be vnheled and reyne on his bedde
C.21.167   In an *hous* al bishut and here dore ybarred
C.21.318   Ordeyne the an *hous*, [Peres], to herberwe in thy cornes.'
C.21.320   And ordeyne þat *hous* ar ʒe hennes wende.'
C.21.328   And calde þat *hous* vnite, holy chirche an englisch.

housbondrie n *husbondrie n.*   A 1 husbondrie; B 1; C 1 hosbondrye
A. 1.55   For *husbondrie* & he holden togideris.'
B. 1.57   For *housbondrie* and h[e] holden togidres.'
C. 1.53   For *hosbondrye* and he holdeth togederes.'

housel n *housel n.(1)*   B 1; C 1 hosele
B.19.392   Al þat we owen any wight er we go to *housel*?'
C.21.392   Al þat we owen eny wyhte or we go to *hosele*?'

housynge ger *housinge ger.*   B 1; C 1
B.15.78   In *housynge*, in haterynge, [in] heigh clergie shewynge
C.16.237   In *housynge*, in helynge, in h[eyh] clergie schewynge

housled ptp *houselen v.*   B 3 houseled (1) housled (2); C 3 hoseled
B.19.3   To here holly þe masse and to be *housled* after.
B.19.395   And so to ben assoilled and siþþen ben *houseled*.'
B.19.475   So I may boldely be *housled* for I borwe neuere,
C.21.3   To here holly þe masse and to [be] *hoseled* aftur.
C.21.395   And so to ben assoiled and sennes be *hoseled*.'
C.21.475   So y may boldely be *hoseled* for y borwe neuere

houswif n *houswif n.*   B 1; C 1 hosewyf
B.14.3   And also I haue an *houswif*, hewen and children–
C.13.9   Bynoem [hym] his *hosewyf* [and helde here hymsulue]

houue -is > howue

houed v *hoven v.(1)*   A 1 houide; B 3; C 3
A.Pr.84   Þere *houide* an hundrit in houuis of silk,
B.Pr.211   Yet *houed* þer an hundred in howues of selk,
B.18.80   Bifore Pilat and ooþer peple in þe place he *houed*.
B.18.83   For alle þei were vnhardy þat *houed* [þer] or stode
C.Pr.161   Where *houed* an hundrid in houes of selke,
C.20.82   Bifore pilatus and oþere peple in þe place he *houed*.
C.20.85   For alle [they were] vnhardy þat *houed* þer or stode

how adv *hou interrog. adv.*   B 5; C 5
B. 2.36   *How* construeþ David þe kyng of men þat [caccheþ] Mede,
B. 2.38   And *how* ye shul saue yourself? þe Sauter bereþ witnesse:
B.17.289   [How myʒte he aske mercy, or any mercy hym helpe],
B.19.391   'How?' quod al þe comune; 'þow conseillest vs to yelde
B.20.209   'How shal I come to catel so to cloþe me and to feede?'
C. 9.266   *How*, herde! where is thyn ho[u]nd[e] and thyn hardy herte
C.19.246   And is in helle for al þat, *how* wol riche nouthe
C.19.270   How myhte he aske mercy or eny mercy hym defende
C.21.391   'How?' quod alle þe comune; 'thow conseylest vs to ʒelde
C.22.209   'How shal y come to catel so to clothe me and to fede?'

how conj *hou conjunctive adv.*   A 22; B 85; C 92 hou (3) how (89)
     A.1.6, A.1.82, A.4.12, A.4.35, A.4.36, A.5.23, A.5.91, A.7.14, A.7.197, A.8.17, A.8.136, A.8.143, A.8.152, A.8.173, A.9.23, A.9.104, A.10.103, A.10.119, A.11.40, A.11.93, A.11.178, A.11.222
     B.Pr.102, B.1.6, B.1.84, B.2.53, B.2.209, B.4.12, B.4.48, B.4.49, B.5.11, B.5.23, B.5.111, B.5.368, B.6.15, B.6.123, B.6.211, B.7.153, B.7.158, B.7.165, B.7.174, B.7.195, B.8.27, B.8.114, B.10.54, B.10.89, B.10.92, B.10.94, B.10.140, B.10.235, B.11.53, B.11.66, B.11.142, B.11.213, B.11.334, B.11.351, B.11.359, B.11.366, B.12.5, B.12.23, B.12.69, B.12.156, B.12.157, B.12.175, B.12.177, B.12.191, B.12.224, B.13.5, B.13.6, B.13.7, B.13.11, B.13.12, B.13.14, B.13.15, B.13.16, B.13.19, B.13.20, B.13.272, B.13.352, B.13.357, B.13.365, B.14.180, B.14.199, B.15.39, B.15.76, B.15.185, B.15.335, B.15.415, B.15.462, B.15.462, B.15.533, B.15.534, B.15.539, B.15.548, B.15.590, B.16.87, B.17.63, B.17.91, B.17.158, B.18.8, B.18.37, B.18.123, B.18.245, B.19.69, B.20.121, B.20.150, B.20.199
     C.Pr.130, C.1.6, C.1.80, C.1.126, C.2.56, C.3.393, C.3.408, C.3.414, C.4.12, C.4.46, C.4.47, C.4.65, C.5.125, C.6.39, C.6.145, C.6.264, C.6.426, C.7.293, C.8.130, C.8.220, C.9.302, C.9.306, C.9.309, C.9.319, C.9.341, C.9.342, C.10.31, C.11.35, C.11.69, C.11.75, C.11.137, C.11.141, C.11.263, C.12.5, C.12.6, C.12.77, C.12.105, C.12.211, C.12.235, C.12.246, C.13.16, C.13.21, C.13.142, C.13.162, C.13.170, C.13.171, C.13.176, C.14.100, C.14.101, C.14.115, C.14.117, C.14.130, C.14.157, C.14.157, C.14.158, C.15.5, C.15.6, C.15.9, C.15.13, C.15.15, C.15.17, C.15.19, C.15.21,

C.15.23, C.15.72, C.16.40, C.16.201, C.16.235, C.17.169, C.17.180, C.17.194, C.17.195, C.17.200, C.17.210, C.17.212, C.17.239, C.18.119, C.18.161, C.18.197, C.18.247, C.19.62, C.19.81, C.19.238, C.20.7, C.20.36, C.20.126, C.20.254, C.20.333, C.21.69, C.22.121, C.22.150, C.22.199

howso *adv* *houso adv.* A 1; B 1; C 1
A.11.260 For *howso* I werche in þis world, [wrong] oþer ellis,
B.17.186 Al is but an hand, [*howso* I turne it.
C.19.152 Al is bote oen hoend *howso* y turne hit.

how_trolly_lolly *exclam* *hou interj., trolli lolli interj.* A 1 hey_trolly_lolly; B 1; C 1 hey_trollilolly
A. 7.108 And holpen [to] ere þe half akir wiþ '*hey trolly lolly*'.
B. 6.116 And holpen ere þ[e] half acre wiþ '*how trolly lolly*'.
C. 8.123 And holpe erye this half aker with '*hey trollilolly*.'

howue *n* *houve n.* A 2 houue (1) houuis (1); B 3 howue (2) howues (1); C 3 houe (2) houes (1)
A.Pr.84 Þere houide an hundrit in *houuis* of silk,
A. 3.270 Shal no seriaunt for þat seruyse were a silk *houue*,
B.Pr.211 Yet houed þer an hundred in *howues* of selk,
B. 3.295 Shal no sergeant for [þat] seruice were a silk *howue*,
B.20.172 And þei gyuen hym ageyn a glaȝene *howue*.
C.Pr.161 Where houed an *hundrid* in houes of selke,
C. 3.448 Shal no ser[i]aunt for [þat] seruic[e] werie a selk *houe*
C.22.172 And they gyuen hym agayne a glasene *houe*.

hucche *n* *huche n.* A 1; B 1; C 1 whicche
A. 4.102 And pernelis purfile be put in hire *hucche*;
B. 4.116 Til pernelles purfill be put in hire *hucche*,
C. 4.111 Tyl purnele porfiel be putte in here *whicche*

hudde(n > hiden

huge *adj* *huge adj.* B 2; C 2
B.11.250 Martha on Marie Maudeleyne an *huge* pleynt made
B.17.308 For þer þat partie pursueþ þe [peel] is so *huge*
C.12.136 Marthe on marie maudelene an *huge* pleynte made
C.19.288 The[r] þat partye pursueth the apeel is so *huge*

hugh *n prop* *n.i.d.* B 1; C 1 hewe
B. 5.310 Hikke þe hakeneyman and *hugh* þe Nedlere,
C. 6.365 Hicke þe hackenayman and *hewe* þe nedlare,

huyde(th > hiden; huyre(- > hire(-

hukkerye *n* *hukkerie n.* A 1 huxterie; B 1; C 1 hokkerye
A. 5.141 Sheo haþ yholde *huxterie* elleuene wynter.
B. 5.225 She haþ holden *hukkerye* [elleuene wynter].
C. 6.233 [He] ha[th] holde *hokkerye* this eleuene wynter.'

hulle *n* *hille n.* A 5 hilles; B 6 hilles (4) hulles (2); C 7 hulle (1) hulles (6)
A.Pr.5 But on a may morwenyng on maluerne *hilles*
A.Pr.88 Tho[u] miȝtest betere mete myst on maluerne *hilles*
A. 6.2 But blustrid forþ as bestis ouer [baches] & *hilles*
A. 8.129 Metel[es and money]les on maluerne *hilles*.
A.10.173 Alle shuln deiȝe for his dedis be dounes & *hilles*,
B.Pr.5 Ac on a May morwenynge on Maluerne *hilles*
B.Pr.215 Thow myȝtest bettre meete myst on Maluerne *hilles*
B. 3.236 Or resten in þyne holy *hilles*; þis askeþ Dauid.
B. 5.514 But blustreden forþ as beestes ouer [baches] and *hilles*
B. 7.147 Metelees and moneilees on Maluerne *hulles*.
B. 9.142 Alle shul deye for hise dedes by [dounes] and *hulles*,
C.Pr.6 Ac on a May mornyng on maluerne *hulles*
C. 5.110 Of þe matere þat me mette furste on Maluerne *hulles*.
C. 7.159 But blostrede forth as bestes ouer baches and *hulles*
C. 9.296 Meteles and moneyles on Maluerne *hulles*.
C.10.230 Alle sholle deye for his dedis by dales and *hulles*
C.12.218 Vpholderes on þe *hulle* shal haue hit to sulle."

humilite *n* *humilite n.* A 1 humylite; B 1; C 1 vmbletee
A. 6.106 Þat on hattiþ abstinence, and [*humylite*] anoþer,
B. 5.620 That oon hatte Abstinence, and *humilite* anoþer,
C. 7.272 That on hatte a[b]stinence and *vmbletee* a[n]oþer,

hundred *num* *hundred card. num.* A 4 hundred (1) hundrit (3); B 14 hundred (13) hundredes (1); C 10 hondredes (1) hundred (3) hundret (4) hundrid (1) hundrit (1)
A.Pr.84 Þere houide an *hundrit* in houuis of silk,
A. 6.8 An *hundrit* of ampollis on his hat seten,
A. 6.101 Happily an *hundrit* wynter er þou eft entre.
A.12.27 And asked Iesu on hy þat herden hit an *hundred*.
B.Pr.211 Yet houed þer an *hundred* in howues of selk,
B. 5.370 There no nede was nyne *hundred* tymes;
B. 5.425 And þus tene I trewe men ten *hundred* tymes,
B. 5.520 An *hundred* of Ampulles on his hat seten,

B. 5.615 Happily an *hundred* wynter er þow eft entre.
B.13.269 A thousand and þre *hundred*, twies [þritty] and ten,
B.14.69 Seuene slepe, as seiþ þe book, seuene *hundred* wynter
B.15.375 [Ne] nauȝt oon among an *hundred* þat an Auctour kan construwe,
B.16.10 'I wolde trauaille', quod I, 'þis tree to se twenty *hundred* myle,
B.17.248 Ac hewe fir at a flynt foure *hundred* wynter;
B.18.407 Manye *hundred* of Aungeles harpeden and songen,
B.19.211 Þanne song I þat song; so dide manye *hundred*,
B.20.69 Antecrist hadde þus soone *hundredes* at his baner,
B.20.218 Proude preestes coome with hym; [passynge an *hundred*]
C.Pr.161 Where houed an *hundrid* in houes of selke,
C. 7.38 And thus haue y tened trewe men ten *hundrit* tymes,
C. 7.165 An *hundret* of Aunpolles on his hat se[t]e,
C. 7.267 Hapliche an *hundred* wynter ar thow eft entre.
C.12.175 Aristotel, Ennedy, enleuene *hundred*,
C.19.214 Ac hewe fuyr at a flynt foure *hundret* wynter,
C.20.450 Many *hundret* of Angels harpeden and songen,
C.21.211 [Þanne] sang [y] þat song; so dede many *hundret*
C.22.69 Auentecrist hadde thus sone *hondredes* at his baner
C.22.218 Proute prestes cam with hym; passyng an *hundred*

hundredfold *n* *hundredfold adj.,adv.,n.* C 1
C.12.159 He shal haue an *hundredfold* of heueneryche blisse

hundret -rid -rit > hundred

hunger *n* *hunger n.* A 26 hunger (13) hungir (13); B 26; C 33 honger (1) hongur (1) hunger (22) hungur (9)
A. 3.181 And hastide[st] þe homward for *hunger* of þi wombe.
A. 5.209 And auowide to faste, for *hungir* or þrist.
A. 7.157 And houpide aftir *hungir* þat herde hym at þe ferste:
A. 7.159 *Hungir* in haste þanne hente wastour be þe mawe,
A. 7.166 And hitte *hunger* þerwiþ amydde hise lippes,
A. 7.173 Þat *hunger* was not hardy on hem for to loke.
A. 7.176 And doluen drit & dung to ditte out *hunger*.
A. 7.179 *Hungir* hem helide wiþ an hot[e] cake.
A. 7.183 Al for coueitise of his corn to [cacche] awey *hungir*.
A. 7.186 Þanne hadde piers pite & preiȝede *hungir* to wende
A. 7.198 'Here now,' quaþ *hungir*, '& holde it for a wisdom:
A. 7.215 'Ȝe, I hote þe,' quaþ *hungir*, 'oþer ellis þe bible leiȝeþ.
A. 7.221 He shal go [begge & bidde] & no man bete his *hungir*;
A. 7.241 'I wot wel,' quaþ *hunger*, 'what seknesse hem eileþ.
A. 7.243 Ac I hote þe,' quaþ *hunger*, 'as þou þin hele wilnest,
A. 7.245 And ete nouȝt, I hote þe, er *hunger* þe take
A. 7.262 'I behote god,' quaþ *hunger*, 'henis nile I wende
A. 7.279 And profride peris [þis] present to plese þerewiþ *hungir*.
A. 7.280 *Hungir* [eet] þis in haste & askide aftir more.
A. 7.284 Þanne was folk fayn, & fedde *hunger* with þe beste;
A. 7.300 Ac while *hunger* was here maister wolde þere non chide,
A. 7.303 For *hungir* hiderward hastiþ hym faste.
A.11.46 Boþe for *hungir* & for þrest, & for chele quak[e];
A.12.63 'I am dwellyng with deth, and *hunger* I hatte.
A.12.74 [But ete as *hunger* me hete til my belly swellyd.
A.12.75 Þer bad me *hunger* haue gode day but I helde me stille.
B. 3.194 And [hastedest þee] homward for *hunger* of þi wombe.
B. 5.381 And auowed to faste for *hunger* or þurste:
B. 6.172 And houped after *hunger* þat herde hym at þe firste.
B. 6.174 *Hunger* in haste þoo hente wastour by þe [mawe]
B. 6.185 That *hunger* was noȝt hardy on hem for to loke.
B. 6.190 And doluen [drit] [and] [dung] to [ditte out] *hunger*.
B. 6.199 Thanne hadde Piers pite and preide *hunger* to wende
B. 6.202 Ac I preie þee, er þow passe', quod Piers to *hunger*,
B. 6.212 'Here now', quod *hunger*, 'and hoold it for a wisdom:
B. 6.231 'Ye I [h]ote þee', quod *hunger*, 'or ellis þe bible lieþ.
B. 6.237 He shal [go] begge and bidde and no man bete his *hunger*.
B. 6.257 'I woot wel', quod *hunger*, 'what siknesse yow eyleþ.
B. 6.259 Ac I hote þee', quod *hunger*, 'as þow þyn hele wilnest,
B. 6.261 Ete noȝt, I hote þee, er *hunger* þee take
B. 6.278 '[I] bihote god', quod *hunger*, 'hennes [nil] I wende
B. 6.295 And profrede Piers þis present to plese wiþ *hunger*.
B. 6.296 [*Hunger* eet þis] in haste and axed after moore.
B. 6.297 Thanne pouere folk for fere fedden *hunger* yerne
B. 6.300 Thanne was folk fayn and fedde *hunger* wiþ þe beste;
B. 6.319 Ac whiles *hunger* was hir maister þer wolde noon chide
B. 6.322 For *hunger* hiderward hasteþ hym faste.
B. 6.330 And Dawe þe dykere deye for *hunger*
B.14.59 Or þoruȝ *hunger* or þoruȝ hete, at his wille be it;
B.15.271 In *hunger*, in hete, in alle manere angres.
B.15.281 And day bi day hadde he hire noȝt his *hunger* for to slake,
B.18.207 Ne what is hoot *hunger* þat hadde neuere defaute.
C. 6.438 For y vowe to verray god, for *hungur* or furste,
C. 8.168 And houped aftur *hunger* þat herde hym at the furste.
C. 8.169 'Y preye the,' quod [Perus] tho, 'pur charite, sire *hunger*,
C. 8.171 *Hunger* in haste tho hente wastour by þe mawe

C. 8.177   'Haue mercy on hem, *hunger*,' quod [Peres], 'and lat me ȝeue hem
            benes
C. 8.181   That *hunger* was nat hardy on hem for to loke.
C. 8.184   Sp[it]teden and spradden donge in dispit of *hunger*.
C. 8.187   Al for drede of here deth, such duntus ȝaf *hunger*.
C. 8.191   And freres of alle þe fyue ordres, alle for fere of *hunger*.
C. 8.202   Þat durste withsitte þat [Peres] sayde for fere of syre *hunger*
C. 8.205   And bade *hunger* in haste hye hym out of contraye
C. 8.208   Ac y preye the,' quod [Peres], '*hunger*, ar thow wende,
C. 8.221   For here lyflode, lere me now, sire *hunger*.'
C. 8.222   'Now herkene,' quod *hunger*, 'and holde hit for a wysdom:
C. 8.237   'Ȝe, y bihote the,' quod *hunger*, 'or elles þe bible lyeth.
C. 8.245   And go abribeth and abeggeth and no man beten his *hungur*:
C. 8.261   This aren euidences,' quod *hunger*, 'for hem þat wolle nat swynke
C. 8.265   Ac ȝut y praye ȝow,' quod [Peres], 'pur charite, syre *hungur*,
C. 8.269   'Y wot wel,' quod *hungur*, 'what sekenesse ȝow ayleth.
C. 8.271   Ac ete nat, y hote, Ar *hungur* the take
C. 8.279   And ȝut hadde he [hem] nat for y, *hungur*, culde hym–
C. 8.300   'Y behote the,' quod *hunger*, 'þat hennes ne wol y wende
C. 8.317   And profrede [Peres] this present to plese with *hongur*.
C. 8.318   *Hunger* eet al in haste and askede aftur more.
C. 8.319   Pore folk for fere tho fedde *honger* ȝerne
C. 8.322   Thenne [was] folke fayn and fedde *hunger* dentie[f]liche
C. 8.323   And thenne gloton with gode ale garte *hunger* slepe.
C. 8.339   Ac whiles *hungur* was here maistre ther wolde non chyde
C. 8.342   For *hungur* hiderwardes hasteth hym faste.
C. 9.77   And hemsulue also soffre muche *hungur*
C.15.235 Hit am y þat fynde alle folke and fram *hunger* saue
C.15.258 Wheþer thorw *hunger* or [thorw] hete, at his wille be hit;
C.20.212 Ne what is hoet *hunger* þat hadde neuere defaute.

hungirly > hungrily

hungreþ v *hungren v.* B 1; C 2 hungren (1) hungreth (1)
B.14.51   'Haue, haukyn', quod Pacience, 'and et þis whan þe *hungreþ*
C. 8.224 With houndes bred and hors breed hele hem when þei *hungren*
C.15.250 'Haue, Actyf,' quod pacience, 'and eet this when þe *hungreth*

hungry adj *hungrie adj.* B 5; C 5 hungry (4) hungriore (1)
B. 5.355 Is noon so *hungry* hound in hertford shire
B. 5.373 And yspilt þat myȝte be spared and spended on som *hungry*;
B. 6.193 For þat was bake for bayard was boote for many *hungry*;
B.13.219 There vnkyndenesse and coueitise is, *hungry* contrees boþe.
B.18.394 For blood may suffre blood boþe *hungry* and acale
C. 1.187 Aren none hardore ne *hungriore* then men of holy chirche,
C. 6.413 Ys non so *hungry* hound in hertford shyre
C. 8.192 For þat was bake for bayard was bote for many *hungry*,
C. 9.207 H[e]lden ful *hungry* hous and hadde muche defaute,
C.15.188 There vnkyndenesse and coueytise [is], *hungry* contreys bothe.

hungrily adv *hungriliche adv.* A 1 hungirly; B 2 hungrily (1) hungriliche
  (1); C 2 hungrily (1) hungriliche (1)
A. 5.108 So *hungirly* & holewe sire heruy hym lokide.
B. 5.189 So *hungrily* and holwe sire heruy hym loked.
B.20.123 And armed hym in Auarice and *hungriliche* lyuede.
C. 6.197 So *hungrily* and holow sire heruy hym lokede.
C.22.123 And Armed hym in Auarice and *hungriliche* lyuede.

hungur > hunger

hunsen v *honishen v.* A 1; B 1
A.11.48   But *hunsen* hym as an hound & hoten hym go þenne.
B.10.62   But [*hunsen*] hym as an hound and hoten hym go þennes.

hunte v *huntern v.* A 2 hunte (1) yhuntid (1); B 3 hunte (2) yhonted (1);
  C 3 honte (1) hunte (1) yhonted (1)
A. 2.180 Oueral *yhuntid* & yhote trusse,
A. 7.31   And go *hunte* hardily [to] har[is] & [to] fox[is],
B. 2.221 Ouer al *yhonted* and yhote trusse,
B. 3.311 Preestes and persons wiþ Placebo to *hunte*
B. 6.29   And go *hunte* hardiliche to hares and to foxes,
C. 2.231 Oueral *yhonted* and yhote trusse,
C. 8.28   And go *hunte* hardelyche to hares and to foxes,
C. 9.224 Lewede men to labory; lordes to *honte*

huntynge ger *huntinge ger.* B 1; C 1 huntyng
B. 3.313 *Huntynge* or haukynge if any of hem vse
C. 3.466 Haukyng or *huntyng* yf eny of hem hit vse

huppe v *hippen v.* B 2 hippynge (1) huppe (1); C 2 huppe (1) huppynge
  (1)
B.15.529 [And nauȝt to] *huppe* aboute in Engelond to halwe mennes Auteres
B.17.62 Hope cam *hippynge* after þat hadde so ybosted
C.17.279 And nat in Ingelond to *huppe* aboute and halewen men auters
C.19.61 Hope cam *huppynge* aftur þat hadde so ybosted

hure > heo

hurte v *hurten v.* B 4 hurt (2) hurte (2); C 4 hert (1) herte (2) herteth (1)
B.10.370 God hoteþ heiȝe and lowe þat no man *hurte* ooþer,
B.17.187 Ac who is *hurte* in þe hand], euene in þe myddes,
B.20.317 For here is many a man *hurt* þoruȝ ypocrisye.'
B.20.335 Ypocrisie haþ *hurt* hem; ful hard is if þei keuere.'
C.19.153 Ac ho is *herte* in the hand euene in þe myddes
C.20.384 Or eny manere membre maymeth oþer *herteth*,
C.22.317 For here is many [a] man *hert* thorw ypocrisye.'
C.22.335 Ypocrysye haeth *her[t]e* hem; ful hard is yf thei keuere.'

husbondis > hosebonde; husbondrie > housbondrie; hutte > hitte; huxterie >
hukkerye

I

i pron *ich pron.* A 757 I (461) y (1) ich (1) me (139) mi (1) my (127) myn (25) myne (2); B 1856 I (1113) ich (15) ik (1) me (365) my (304) myn (40) myne (18); C 1790 I (31) y (1035) ich (14) ych (3) me (353) my (303) myen (1) myn (46) myne (4)

I A 462 I (461) y (1)

A.Pr.2, A.Pr.2, A.Pr.7, A.Pr.9, A.Pr.10, A.Pr.11, A.Pr.12, A.Pr.12, A.Pr.13, A.Pr.14, A.Pr.17, A.Pr.34, A.Pr.38, A.Pr.55, A.Pr.90, A.Pr.97, A.Pr.109, A.1.2, A.1.10, A.1.21, A.1.40, A.1.41, A.1.56, A.1.58, A.1.69, A.1.73, A.1.74, A.1.77, A.1.80, A.1.82, A.1.84, A.1.120, A.1.123, A.1.123, A.1.127, A.1.127, A.1.133, A.1.149, A.1.175, A.1.180, A.1.180, A.1.182, A.1.183, A.2.1, A.2.7, A.2.15, A.2.21, A.2.21, A.2.26, A.2.31, A.2.31, A.2.32, A.2.58, A.2.62, A.2.64, A.2.66, A.2.147, A.2.154, A.2.156, A.2.161, A.2.165, A.2.168, A.3.3, A.3.5, A.3.8, A.3.18, A.3.31, A.3.32, A.3.39, A.3.43, A.3.50, A.3.51, A.3.52, A.3.60, A.3.84, A.3.97, A.3.99, A.3.102, A.3.107, A.3.110, A.3.160, A.3.165, A.3.171, A.3.171, A.3.174, A.3.175, A.3.184, A.3.188, A.3.189, A.3.214, A.3.236, A.3.258, A.3.259, A.3.260, A.4.1, A.4.3, A.4.5, A.4.6, A.4.13, A.4.16, A.4.18, A.4.39, A.4.41, A.4.47, A.4.51, A.4.51, A.4.57, A.4.65, A.4.84, A.4.88, A.4.89, A.4.90, A.4.92, A.4.96, A.4.109, A.4.117, A.4.119, A.4.119, A.4.120, A.4.121, A.4.122, A.4.129, A.4.149, A.4.151, A.4.154, A.4.154, A.4.155, A.4.156, A.4.157, A.4.158, A.5.3, A.5.4, A.5.5, A.5.6, A.5.7, A.5.8, A.5.9, A.5.9, A.5.10, A.5.10, A.5.21, A.5.22, A.5.22, A.5.51, A.5.52, A.5.53, A.5.61, A.5.69, A.5.70, A.5.71, A.5.72, A.5.73, A.5.73, A.5.75, A.5.79, A.5.81, A.5.81, A.5.82, A.5.82, A.5.83, A.5.83, A.5.84, A.5.84, A.5.85, A.5.88, A.5.90, A.5.92, A.5.93, A.5.94, A.5.95, A.5.95, A.5.96, A.5.97, A.5.98, A.5.105, A.5.105, A.5.106, A.5.107, A.5.112, A.5.114, A.5.114, A.5.115, A.5.117, A.5.119, A.5.123, A.5.125, A.5.132, A.5.133, A.5.142, A.5.142, A.5.142, A.5.151, A.5.152, A.5.155, A.5.212, A.5.217, A.5.223, A.5.224, A.5.226, A.5.226, A.5.227, A.5.227, A.5.228, A.5.228, A.5.229, A.5.230, A.5.232, A.5.232, A.5.239, A.5.242, A.5.243, A.5.244, A.5.245, A.5.246, A.6.15, A.6.18, A.6.23, A.6.26, A.6.29, A.6.30, A.6.36, A.6.36, A.6.37, A.6.42, A.6.45, A.6.85, A.6.86, A.6.87, A.6.87, A.6.115, A.6.116, A.6.116, A.6.117, A.6.118, A.7.4, A.7.5, A.7.6, A.7.16, A.7.17, A.7.24, A.7.25, A.7.27, A.7.36, A.7.37, A.7.38, A.7.49, A.7.50, A.7.52, A.7.58, A.7.58, A.7.63, A.7.67, A.7.75, A.7.76, A.7.77, A.7.77, A.7.78, A.7.80, A.7.81, A.7.82, A.7.85, A.7.86, A.7.88, A.7.90, A.7.91, A.7.91, A.7.91, A.7.93, A.7.121, A.7.122, A.7.123, A.7.131, A.7.134, A.7.151, A.7.152, A.7.152, A.7.156, A.7.188, A.7.190, A.7.196, A.7.197, A.7.213, A.7.214, A.7.215, A.7.219, A.7.230, A.7.237, A.7.241, A.7.243, A.7.245, A.7.252, A.7.262, A.7.262, A.7.263, A.7.264, A.7.268, A.7.268, A.7.270, A.7.273, A.7.274, A.7.275, A.7.302, A.8.36, A.8.38, A.8.40, A.8.59, A.8.61, A.8.89, A.8.90, A.8.92, A.8.97, A.8.104, A.8.107, A.8.127, A.8.130, A.8.133, A.8.146, A.8.160, A.8.165, A.8.178, A.8.179, A.9.1, A.9.3, A.9.5, A.9.6, A.9.8, A.9.10, A.9.10, A.9.15, A.9.16, A.9.18, A.9.22, A.9.24, A.9.48, A.9.48, A.9.49, A.9.49, A.9.50, A.9.53, A.9.54, A.9.56, A.9.60, A.9.63, A.9.65, A.9.66, A.9.67, A.9.101, A.9.103, A.9.107, A.9.113, A.9.114, A.10.25, A.10.95, A.10.103, A.10.164, A.10.182, A.10.185, A.10.197, A.11.13, A.11.81, A.11.91, A.11.96, A.11.97, A.11.99, A.11.100, A.11.100, A.11.101, A.11.105, A.11.108, A.11.109, A.11.110, A.11.113, A.11.125, A.11.126, A.11.126, A.11.128, A.11.129, A.11.130, A.11.131, A.11.132, A.11.134, A.11.135, A.11.136, A.11.138, A.11.139, A.11.142, A.11.146, A.11.163, A.11.165, A.11.165, A.11.166, A.11.168, A.11.169, A.11.169, A.11.170, A.11.171, A.11.176, A.11.179, A.11.218, A.11.219, A.11.221, A.11.224, A.11.225, A.11.226, A.11.232, A.11.232, A.11.256, A.11.258, A.11.258, A.11.260, A.11.261, A.11.262, A.11.266, A.11.278, A.11.278, A.11.279, A.11.293, A.11.300, A.12.2, A.12.5, A.12.5, A.12.7, A.12.10, A.12.11, A.12.14, A.12.20, A.12.20, A.12.23, A.12.23, A.12.30, A.12.33, A.12.37, A.12.38, A.12.39, A.12.46, A.12.47, A.12.54, A.12.57, A.12.59, A.12.60, A.12.61, A.12.62, A.12.63, A.12.63, A.12.65, A.12.66, A.12.67, A.12.68, A.12.69, A.12.71, A.12.72, A.12.73, A.12.75, A.12.76, A.12.79, A.12.81, A.12.82, A.12.83, A.12.83, A.12.88, A.12.88

I B 1113

B.Pr.2, B.Pr.2, B.Pr.7, B.Pr.9, B.Pr.10, B.Pr.11, B.Pr.12, B.Pr.12, B.Pr.13, B.Pr.14, B.Pr.17, B.Pr.34, B.Pr.38, B.Pr.50, B.Pr.58, B.Pr.100, B.Pr.109, B.Pr.111, B.Pr.160, B.Pr.164, B.Pr.187, B.Pr.193, B.Pr.202, B.Pr.202, B.Pr.205, B.Pr.208, B.Pr.210, B.Pr.218, B.Pr.231, B.1.2, B.1.10, B.1.21, B.1.42, B.1.43, B.1.58, B.1.60, B.1.71, B.1.75, B.1.76, B.1.79, B.1.82, B.1.84, B.1.86, B.1.131, B.1.134, B.1.134, B.1.138, B.1.138, B.1.145, B.1.175, B.1.201, B.1.206, B.1.206, B.1.208, B.1.209, B.2.1, B.2.7, B.2.17, B.2.18, B.2.19, B.2.28, B.2.30, B.2.33, B.2.34, B.2.50, B.2.62, B.2.87, B.2.186, B.2.193, B.2.195, B.2.200, B.2.204, B.2.207, B.3.3, B.3.5, B.3.8, B.3.19, B.3.32, B.3.33, B.3.40, B.3.44, B.3.51, B.3.51, B.3.60, B.3.63, B.3.69, B.3.95, B.3.108, B.3.110, B.3.113, B.3.118, B.3.121, B.3.173, B.3.178, B.3.184, B.3.184, B.3.187, B.3.188, B.3.197, B.3.198, B.3.199, B.3.201, B.3.202, B.3.227, B.3.257, B.3.280, B.3.281, B.3.284, B.3.332, B.3.337, B.4.1, B.4.3, B.4.5, B.4.6, B.4.13, B.4.16, B.4.19, B.4.20, B.4.41, B.4.52, B.4.54, B.4.60, B.4.65, B.4.65, B.4.71, B.4.79, B.4.97, B.4.101, B.4.102, B.4.103, B.4.105, B.4.109, B.4.126, B.4.134, B.4.136, B.4.136, B.4.137, B.4.138, B.4.139, B.4.146, B.4.152, B.4.155, B.4.156, B.4.169, B.4.175, B.4.175, B.4.177, B.4.180, B.4.186, B.4.188, B.4.191, B.4.192, B.4.193, B.4.194, B.4.195, B.5.3, B.5.4, B.5.5, B.5.6, B.5.7, B.5.8, B.5.9, B.5.10, B.5.10, B.5.21, B.5.22, B.5.22, B.5.68, B.5.69, B.5.70, B.5.78, B.5.90, B.5.90, B.5.91, B.5.92, B.5.93, B.5.93, B.5.99, B.5.101, B.5.101, B.5.102, B.5.102, B.5.103, B.5.103, B.5.104, B.5.104, B.5.105, B.5.108, B.5.110, B.5.112, B.5.113, B.5.114, B.5.115, B.5.115, B.5.116, B.5.117, B.5.118, B.5.119, B.5.121, B.5.128, B.5.128, B.5.129, B.5.130, B.5.132, B.5.132, B.5.134, B.5.134, B.5.137, B.5.137, B.5.139, B.5.148, B.5.151, B.5.152, B.5.153, B.5.155, B.5.157, B.5.162, B.5.169, B.5.169, B.5.172, B.5.174, B.5.176, B.5.177, B.5.178, B.5.179, B.5.180, B.5.181, B.5.188, B.5.196, B.5.196, B.5.198, B.5.198, B.5.199, B.5.201, B.5.203, B.5.207, B.5.209, B.5.216, B.5.217, B.5.226, B.5.226, B.5.231, B.5.232, B.5.235, B.5.235, B.5.236, B.5.239, B.5.242, B.5.243, B.5.244, B.5.246, B.5.248, B.5.251, B.5.255, B.5.258, B.5.265, B.5.266, B.5.269, B.5.270, B.5.273, B.5.276, B.5.277, B.5.301, B.5.302, B.5.304, B.5.367, B.5.368, B.5.368, B.5.372, B.5.372, B.5.375, B.5.376, B.5.384, B.5.386, B.5.386, B.5.387, B.5.388, B.5.389, B.5.393, B.5.393, B.5.394, B.5.395, B.5.397, B.5.398, B.5.399, B.5.399, B.5.400, B.5.401, B.5.402, B.5.404, B.5.405, B.5.406, B.5.409, B.5.412, B.5.412, B.5.413, B.5.414, B.5.415, B.5.416, B.5.417, B.5.420, B.5.421, B.5.422, B.5.423, B.5.424, B.5.425, B.5.428, B.5.430, B.5.431, B.5.432, B.5.434, B.5.439, B.5.445, B.5.451, B.5.452, B.5.454, B.5.454, B.5.455, B.5.455, B.5.456, B.5.456, B.5.457, B.5.458, B.5.460, B.5.460, B.5.468, B.5.469, B.5.470, B.5.471, B.5.472, B.5.478, B.5.483, B.5.527, B.5.530, B.5.535, B.5.538, B.5.541, B.5.542, B.5.546, B.5.546, B.5.548, B.5.548, B.5.549, B.5.549, B.5.550, B.5.555, B.5.558, B.5.598, B.5.599, B.5.600, B.5.600, B.5.630, B.5.631, B.5.631, B.5.632, B.5.633, B.5.639, B.5.640, B.5.641, B.5.642, B.5.642, B.6.4, B.6.5, B.6.6, B.6.14, B.6.17, B.6.18, B.6.22, B.6.23, B.6.25, B.6.34, B.6.35, B.6.36, B.6.36, B.6.37, B.6.54, B.6.55, B.6.57, B.6.63, B.6.63, B.6.69, B.6.75, B.6.83, B.6.84, B.6.85, B.6.85, B.6.86, B.6.88, B.6.89, B.6.90, B.6.93, B.6.94, B.6.96, B.6.98, B.6.99, B.6.99, B.6.99, B.6.101, B.6.129, B.6.130, B.6.131, B.6.137, B.6.166, B.6.167, B.6.167, B.6.171, B.6.201, B.6.202, B.6.204, B.6.210, B.6.211, B.6.229, B.6.230, B.6.231, B.6.235, B.6.246, B.6.253, B.6.257, B.6.259, B.6.261, B.6.268, B.6.278, B.6.278, B.6.279, B.6.280, B.6.284, B.6.284, B.6.286, B.6.289, B.6.290, B.6.291, B.6.321, B.7.34, B.7.60, B.7.107, B.7.108, B.7.110, B.7.115, B.7.122, B.7.125, B.7.145, B.7.150, B.7.154, B.7.154, B.7.169, B.7.182, B.7.187, B.7.200, B.7.201, B.8.1, B.8.3, B.8.5, B.8.6, B.8.8, B.8.10, B.8.10, B.8.19, B.8.20, B.8.22, B.8.26, B.8.28, B.8.57, B.8.57, B.8.58, B.8.58, B.8.59, B.8.60, B.8.62, B.8.63, B.8.65, B.8.69, B.8.72, B.8.74, B.8.75, B.8.76, B.8.111, B.8.113, B.8.117, B.8.123, B.8.124, B.9.25, B.9.41, B.9.74, B.9.76, B.9.76, B.9.91, B.9.122, B.9.128, B.9.133, B.9.148, B.9.150, B.9.159, B.9.162, B.9.164, B.9.164, B.9.176, B.10.13, B.10.38, B.10.104, B.10.128, B.10.138, B.10.143, B.10.144, B.10.146, B.10.147, B.10.147, B.10.148, B.10.149, B.10.153, B.10.156, B.10.157, B.10.158, B.10.161, B.10.173, B.10.174, B.10.174, B.10.176, B.10.177, B.10.178, B.10.179, B.10.180, B.10.182, B.10.183, B.10.184, B.10.186, B.10.187, B.10.190, B.10.194, B.10.220, B.10.224, B.10.226, B.10.226, B.10.227, B.10.228, B.10.233, B.10.236, B.10.236, B.10.272, B.10.306, B.10.336, B.10.337, B.10.338, B.10.349, B.10.349, B.10.372, B.10.375, B.10.377, B.10.377, B.10.380, B.10.381, B.10.383, B.10.392, B.10.394, B.10.395, B.10.405, B.10.418, B.10.420, B.10.436, B.10.444, B.10.448, B.10.452, B.10.460, B.10.475, B.11.4, B.11.5, B.11.7, B.11.22, B.11.23, B.11.24, B.11.28, B.11.49, B.11.59, B.11.60, B.11.63, B.11.64, B.11.66, B.11.68, B.11.70, B.11.71, B.11.83, B.11.84, B.11.86, B.11.86, B.11.89, B.11.109, B.11.111, B.11.116, B.11.117, B.11.117, B.11.123, B.11.141, B.11.142, B.11.148, B.11.151, B.11.161, B.11.195, B.11.225, B.11.226, B.11.232, B.11.256, B.11.298, B.11.301, B.11.312, B.11.319, B.11.321, B.11.325, B.11.327, B.11.331, B.11.333, B.11.335, B.11.345, B.11.347, B.11.349, B.11.356, B.11.359, B.11.363, B.11.364, B.11.365, B.11.373, B.11.373, B.11.374, B.11.377, B.11.380, B.11.387, B.11.405, B.11.407, B.11.408, B.11.408, B.11.410, B.11.411, B.11.435, B.11.438, B.11.438, B.11.440, B.12.1, B.12.1, B.12.2, B.12.3, B.12.20, B.12.22, B.12.22, B.12.23, B.12.23, B.12.27, B.12.49, B.12.92, B.12.94, B.12.98, B.12.121, B.12.145, B.12.155, B.12.155, B.12.169, B.12.199, B.12.211, B.12.217, B.12.223, B.12.254, B.12.257, B.12.259, B.12.272, B.12.277, B.13.1, B.13.2, B.13.4, B.13.21, B.13.21, B.13.23, B.13.24, B.13.25, B.13.25, B.13.35, B.13.60, B.13.64, B.13.71, B.13.74, B.13.78, B.13.80, B.13.84, B.13.86, B.13.99, B.13.103, B.13.106, B.13.111, B.13.111, B.13.117, B.13.120, B.13.122, B.13.123, B.13.131, B.13.131, B.13.132, B.13.152, B.13.156, B.13.156, B.13.181, B.13.182, B.13.185, B.13.189, B.13.200, B.13.211, B.13.212, B.13.212, B.13.224, B.13.227, B.13.228, B.13.228, B.13.230, B.13.234, B.13.235, B.13.238, B.13.240, B.13.243, B.13.244, B.13.247, B.13.250, B.13.252, B.13.260, B.13.262, B.13.263, B.13.271, B.13.307, B.13.309, B.13.310, B.13.310, B.13.318, B.13.332, B.13.333, B.13.334, B.13.336, B.13.338, B.13.341, B.13.342, B.13.362, B.13.364, B.13.365, B.13.365, B.13.366, B.13.366, B.13.370, B.13.370, B.13.371, B.13.373, B.13.374, B.13.377, B.13.379, B.13.381, B.13.384, B.13.385, B.13.387, B.13.387, B.13.388, B.13.389, B.13.391, B.13.405, B.13.425, B.13.441, B.14.1, B.14.1, B.14.2, B.14.3, B.14.8, B.14.12, B.14.13, B.14.15, B.14.16, B.14.29, B.14.32, B.14.35, B.14.47, B.14.98, B.14.99, B.14.106, B.14.140, B.14.252, B.14.274, B.14.277, B.14.279, B.14.324, B.14.332, B.14.335, B.15.2, B.15.3, B.15.10, B.15.12, B.15.13, B.15.14, B.15.14, B.15.16, B.15.19, B.15.22, B.15.23, B.15.23, B.15.24, B.15.25, B.15.25, B.15.26, B.15.27, B.15.29, B.15.31, B.15.32, B.15.33, B.15.35, B.15.36, B.15.40,

B.15.44, B.15.47, B.15.49, B.15.49, B.15.80, B.15.83, B.15.87, B.15.89, B.15.91, B.15.149, B.15.152, B.15.152, B.15.153, B.15.158, B.15.162, B.15.163, B.15.164, B.15.195, B.15.195, B.15.195, B.15.197, B.15.220, B.15.225, B.15.227, B.15.249, B.15.296, B.15.301, B.15.333, B.15.334, B.15.335, B.15.344, B.15.383, B.15.385, B.15.387, B.15.414, B.15.489, B.15.489, B.15.549, B.16.1, B.16.2, B.16.3, B.16.10, B.16.10, B.16.12, B.16.18, B.16.19, B.16.19, B.16.23, B.16.24, B.16.24, B.16.30, B.16.36, B.16.39, B.16.39, B.16.52, B.16.53, B.16.55, B.16.61, B.16.63, B.16.64, B.16.67, B.16.68, B.16.73, B.16.78, B.16.123, B.16.131, B.16.134, B.16.142, B.16.154, B.16.158, B.16.167, B.16.169, B.16.171, B.16.172, B.16.174, B.16.176, B.16.178, B.16.178, B.16.179, B.16.180, B.16.212, B.16.214, B.16.225, B.16.225, B.16.226, B.16.227, B.16.229, B.16.231, B.16.234, B.16.235, B.16.243, B.16.247, B.16.249, B.16.249, B.16.253, B.16.255, B.16.258, B.16.258, B.16.259, B.16.265, B.16.270, B.16.272, B.16.272, B.16.274, B.17.1, B.17.3, B.17.4, B.17.5, B.17.7, B.17.10, B.17.14, B.17.17, B.17.18, B.17.20, B.17.20, B.17.22, B.17.26, B.17.48, B.17.77, B.17.80, B.17.81, B.17.86, B.17.86, B.17.90, B.17.90, B.17.110, B.17.112, B.17.117, B.17.122, B.17.122, B.17.127, B.17.127, B.17.136, B.17.186, B.17.193, B.17.193, B.17.196, B.17.198, B.17.200, B.17.261, B.17.264, B.17.270, B.17.272, B.17.296, B.17.299, B.17.299, B.17.300, B.17.302, B.17.333, B.17.355, B.17.356, B.18.1, B.18.4, B.18.5, B.18.18, B.18.21, B.18.27, B.18.90, B.18.90, B.18.111, B.18.112, B.18.132, B.18.147, B.18.151, B.18.152, B.18.158, B.18.163, B.18.167, B.18.169, B.18.177, B.18.180, B.18.183, B.18.199, B.18.203, B.18.208, B.18.216, B.18.217, B.18.232, B.18.255, B.18.261, B.18.273, B.18.274, B.18.284, B.18.285, B.18.286, B.18.295, B.18.296, B.18.297, B.18.300, B.18.300, B.18.303, B.18.303, B.18.307, B.18.308, B.18.309, B.18.315, B.18.329, B.18.332, B.18.336, B.18.341, B.18.343, B.18.348, B.18.356, B.18.365, B.18.366, B.18.367, B.18.370, B.18.371, B.18.384, B.18.386, B.18.389, B.18.390, B.18.398, B.18.398, B.18.400, B.18.401, B.18.425, B.19.1, B.19.1, B.19.5, B.19.9, B.19.10, B.19.115, B.19.173, B.19.181, B.19.204, B.19.211, B.19.215, B.19.225, B.19.225, B.19.258, B.19.358, B.19.373, B.19.381, B.19.382, B.19.396, B.19.398, B.19.410, B.19.413, B.19.419, B.19.460, B.19.466, B.19.468, B.19.469, B.19.470, B.19.471, B.19.471, B.19.473, B.19.473, B.19.474, B.19.475, B.19.475, B.19.481, B.20.1, B.20.1, B.20.2, B.20.3, B.20.4, B.20.46, B.20.51, B.20.74, B.20.153, B.20.178, B.20.186, B.20.188, B.20.192, B.20.193, B.20.194, B.20.197, B.20.199, B.20.199, B.20.200, B.20.203, B.20.205, B.20.207, B.20.209, B.20.212, B.20.213, B.20.222, B.20.222, B.20.223, B.20.228, B.20.245, B.20.248, B.20.271, B.20.277, B.20.318, B.20.322, B.20.333, B.20.333, B.20.336, B.20.337, B.20.338, B.20.339, B.20.343, B.20.344, B.20.362, B.20.362, B.20.364, B.20.380, B.20.385, B.20.386

I C 1066 I (31) y (1035)

C.Pr.2, C.Pr.2, C.Pr.8, C.Pr.8, C.Pr.9, C.Pr.11, C.Pr.13, C.Pr.13, C.Pr.14, C.Pr.15, C.Pr.16, C.Pr.17, C.Pr.19, C.Pr.39, C.Pr.56, C.Pr.103, C.Pr.118, C.Pr.128, C.Pr.136, C.Pr.179, C.Pr.204, C.Pr.206, C.Pr.210, C.Pr.210, C.Pr.213, C.Pr.221, C.Pr.224, C.Pr.235, C.1.2, C.1.10, C.1.21, C.1.41, C.1.54, C.1.56, C.1.68, C.1.72, C.1.73, C.1.76, C.1.80, C.1.82, C.1.115, C.1.116, C.1.123, C.1.137, C.1.137, C.1.144, C.1.171, C.1.196, C.1.201, C.1.201, C.1.203, C.2.1, C.2.8, C.2.14, C.2.15, C.2.18, C.2.30, C.2.30, C.2.33, C.2.36, C.2.39, C.2.53, C.2.56, C.2.64, C.2.132, C.2.136, C.2.186, C.2.199, C.2.207, C.2.209, C.2.214, C.3.3, C.3.5, C.3.8, C.3.20, C.3.35, C.3.36, C.3.42, C.3.46, C.3.56, C.3.64, C.3.65, C.3.67, C.3.129, C.3.135, C.3.137, C.3.139, C.3.141, C.3.147, C.3.150, C.3.155, C.3.158, C.3.219, C.3.224, C.3.230, C.3.230, C.3.233, C.3.234, C.3.254, C.3.256, C.3.257, C.3.258, C.3.259, C.3.299, C.3.313, C.3.328, C.3.341, C.3.368, C.3.370, C.3.394, C.3.433, C.3.434, C.3.437, C.3.489, C.3.498, C.4.1, C.4.3, C.4.5, C.4.6, C.4.13, C.4.16, C.4.19, C.4.20, C.4.50, C.4.52, C.4.53, C.4.54, C.4.57, C.4.63, C.4.69, C.4.69, C.4.75, C.4.93, C.4.97, C.4.100, C.4.104, C.4.131, C.4.133, C.4.133, C.4.134, C.4.135, C.4.136, C.4.143, C.4.169, C.4.169, C.4.171, C.4.174, C.4.180, C.4.183, C.4.187, C.4.190, C.4.191, C.4.196, C.5.1, C.5.1, C.5.2, C.5.5, C.5.6, C.5.6, C.5.7, C.5.22, C.5.23, C.5.35, C.5.37, C.5.39, C.5.40, C.5.42, C.5.43, C.5.43, C.5.44, C.5.45, C.5.48, C.5.49, C.5.50, C.5.51, C.5.82, C.5.83, C.5.83, C.5.86, C.5.89, C.5.92, C.5.92, C.5.93, C.5.94, C.5.99, C.5.102, C.5.105, C.5.106, C.5.108, C.5.109, C.5.111, C.5.123, C.5.124, C.5.124, C.5.153, C.5.182, C.6.9, C.6.10, C.6.11, C.6.14, C.6.15, C.6.16, C.6.17, C.6.22, C.6.24, C.6.28, C.6.31, C.6.32, C.6.39, C.6.46, C.6.47, C.6.47, C.6.48, C.6.51, C.6.51, C.6.53, C.6.55, C.6.57, C.6.58, C.6.58, C.6.59, C.6.60, C.6.77, C.6.78, C.6.80, C.6.82, C.6.85, C.6.86, C.6.93, C.6.93, C.6.94, C.6.95, C.6.97, C.6.97, C.6.99, C.6.100, C.6.101, C.6.105, C.6.107, C.6.108, C.6.108, C.6.109, C.6.113, C.6.113, C.6.114, C.6.124, C.6.126, C.6.127, C.6.128, C.6.130, C.6.132, C.6.139, C.6.140, C.6.143, C.6.145, C.6.146, C.6.148, C.6.151, C.6.151, C.6.154, C.6.156, C.6.156, C.6.158, C.6.159, C.6.160, C.6.161, C.6.162, C.6.163, C.6.173, C.6.175, C.6.175, C.6.178, C.6.178, C.6.179, C.6.180, C.6.192, C.6.193, C.6.194, C.6.196, C.6.204, C.6.204, C.6.206, C.6.206, C.6.207, C.6.209, C.6.211, C.6.215, C.6.217, C.6.224, C.6.225, C.6.235, C.6.236, C.6.241, C.6.243, C.6.244, C.6.245, C.6.249, C.6.253, C.6.255, C.6.258, C.6.259, C.6.261, C.6.263, C.6.264, C.6.264, C.6.265, C.6.265, C.6.267, C.6.267, C.6.268, C.6.270, C.6.271, C.6.272, C.6.273, C.6.274, C.6.276, C.6.276, C.6.277, C.6.278, C.6.286, C.6.287, C.6.288, C.6.290, C.6.291, C.6.294, C.6.298, C.6.301, C.6.309, C.6.310, C.6.310, C.6.311, C.6.312, C.6.322, C.6.323, C.6.324, C.6.325, C.6.326, C.6.332, C.6.357, C.6.359, C.6.425, C.6.426, C.6.426, C.6.431, C.6.432, C.6.432, C.6.438, C.6.441, C.7.2, C.7.2, C.7.3, C.7.4, C.7.5, C.7.9, C.7.9, C.7.10, C.7.11, C.7.13, C.7.14, C.7.15, C.7.16, C.7.17, C.7.18, C.7.21, C.7.22, C.7.25, C.7.27, C.7.28, C.7.29, C.7.30, C.7.31, C.7.32, C.7.34, C.7.35, C.7.36, C.7.37, C.7.38, C.7.41, C.7.43, C.7.44, C.7.45, C.7.47, C.7.54, C.7.59, C.7.65, C.7.66, C.7.68, C.7.68, C.7.85, C.7.101, C.7.120, C.7.125, C.7.172, C.7.175, C.7.180, C.7.183, C.7.186, C.7.193, C.7.193, C.7.194, C.7.199, C.7.202, C.7.203, C.7.246, C.7.246, C.7.283, C.7.284, C.7.284, C.7.285, C.7.286, C.7.292, C.7.297, C.7.298, C.7.300, C.7.301, C.7.302, C.7.303, C.7.304, C.7.305, C.7.306, C.8.4, C.8.7, C.8.15, C.8.16, C.8.20, C.8.21, C.8.21, C.8.22, C.8.24, C.8.33, C.8.34, C.8.35, C.8.54, C.8.56, C.8.62, C.8.62, C.8.70, C.8.77, C.8.85, C.8.89, C.8.92, C.8.93, C.8.94, C.8.94, C.8.95, C.8.98, C.8.99, C.8.102, C.8.103, C.8.105, C.8.107, C.8.108, C.8.108, C.8.108, C.8.110, C.8.137, C.8.139, C.8.148, C.8.163, C.8.164, C.8.164, C.8.167, C.8.169, C.8.207, C.8.208, C.8.210, C.8.219, C.8.220, C.8.235, C.8.236, C.8.237, C.8.257, C.8.263, C.8.265, C.8.269, C.8.271, C.8.279, C.8.280, C.8.282, C.8.289, C.8.297, C.8.300, C.8.300, C.8.301, C.8.302, C.8.306, C.8.306, C.8.308, C.8.313, C.8.314, C.8.341, C.9.37, C.9.39, C.9.70, C.9.88, C.9.239, C.9.247, C.9.268, C.9.274, C.9.281, C.9.282, C.9.284, C.9.289, C.9.294, C.9.297, C.9.299, C.9.313, C.9.328, C.9.333, C.9.346, C.9.347, C.10.1, C.10.3, C.10.5, C.10.6, C.10.8, C.10.10, C.10.10, C.10.19, C.10.20, C.10.25, C.10.30, C.10.32, C.10.56, C.10.56, C.10.57, C.10.57, C.10.58, C.10.59, C.10.61, C.10.64, C.10.70, C.10.72, C.10.72, C.10.73, C.10.74, C.10.107, C.10.109, C.10.112, C.10.113, C.10.119, C.10.120, C.10.151, C.10.239, C.10.253, C.10.255, C.10.278, C.10.287, C.10.289, C.11.11, C.11.49, C.11.82, C.11.84, C.11.85, C.11.85, C.11.86, C.11.87, C.11.91, C.11.100, C.11.103, C.11.103, C.11.114, C.11.114, C.11.116, C.11.117, C.11.118, C.11.119, C.11.120, C.11.122, C.11.125, C.11.127, C.11.128, C.11.130, C.11.134, C.11.135, C.11.136, C.11.136, C.11.150, C.11.164, C.11.165, C.11.166, C.11.181, C.11.182, C.11.183, C.11.187, C.11.198, C.11.198, C.11.200, C.11.203, C.11.204, C.11.208, C.11.218, C.11.222, C.11.223, C.11.226, C.11.236, C.11.252, C.11.272, C.11.273, C.11.277, C.11.312, C.12.11, C.12.12, C.12.15, C.12.16, C.12.18, C.12.19, C.12.23, C.12.24, C.12.26, C.12.27, C.12.27, C.12.43, C.12.45, C.12.51, C.12.52, C.12.52, C.12.58, C.12.76, C.12.77, C.12.83, C.12.86, C.12.107, C.12.108, C.12.142, C.12.172, C.12.173, C.12.176, C.13.26, C.13.27, C.13.39, C.13.50, C.13.91, C.13.112, C.13.124, C.13.134, C.13.139, C.13.141, C.13.143, C.13.156, C.13.158, C.13.160, C.13.165, C.13.168, C.13.170, C.13.173, C.13.174, C.13.180, C.13.183, C.13.183, C.13.184, C.13.187, C.13.195, C.13.197, C.13.205, C.13.213, C.13.215, C.13.215, C.13.216, C.13.218, C.13.219, C.13.238, C.13.241, C.13.241, C.13.244, C.13.246, C.14.1, C.14.1, C.14.2, C.14.3, C.14.11, C.14.12, C.14.41, C.14.43, C.14.64, C.14.89, C.14.99, C.14.99, C.14.109, C.14.150, C.14.156, C.14.166, C.14.166, C.14.194, C.14.199, C.15.1, C.15.2, C.15.4, C.15.7, C.15.21, C.15.24, C.15.26, C.15.27, C.15.40, C.15.64, C.15.68, C.15.78, C.15.80, C.15.84, C.15.91, C.15.106, C.15.110, C.15.113, C.15.114, C.15.123, C.15.123, C.15.124, C.15.125, C.15.126, C.15.138, C.15.138, C.15.151, C.15.154, C.15.154, C.15.156, C.15.175, C.15.176, C.15.177, C.15.178, C.15.182, C.15.183, C.15.184, C.15.197, C.15.200, C.15.201, C.15.202, C.15.202, C.15.204, C.15.208, C.15.209, C.15.211, C.15.211, C.15.215, C.15.216, C.15.218, C.15.222, C.15.232, C.15.235, C.15.248, C.15.281, C.15.283, C.16.8, C.16.21, C.16.36, C.16.92, C.16.115, C.16.117, C.16.119, C.16.162, C.16.163, C.16.165, C.16.167, C.16.170, C.16.173, C.16.179, C.16.183, C.16.183, C.16.184, C.16.184, C.16.185, C.16.185, C.16.186, C.16.186, C.16.187, C.16.189, C.16.191, C.16.192, C.16.193, C.16.194, C.16.195, C.16.197, C.16.198, C.16.198, C.16.202, C.16.206, C.16.209, C.16.211, C.16.211, C.16.239, C.16.286, C.16.289, C.16.292, C.16.297, C.16.316, C.16.337, C.16.337, C.16.337, C.16.338, C.16.339, C.16.352, C.16.371, C.17.1, C.17.25, C.17.64, C.17.69, C.17.118, C.17.125, C.17.150, C.17.168, C.17.185, C.17.211, C.18.1, C.18.1, C.18.1, C.18.8, C.18.16, C.18.17, C.18.19, C.18.28, C.18.34, C.18.40, C.18.42, C.18.50, C.18.52, C.18.53, C.18.53, C.18.59, C.18.81, C.18.84, C.18.84, C.18.100, C.18.102, C.18.152, C.18.152, C.18.159, C.18.171, C.18.175, C.18.178, C.18.180, C.18.180, C.18.181, C.18.183, C.18.184, C.18.186, C.18.191, C.18.196, C.18.197, C.18.197, C.18.214, C.18.218, C.18.239, C.18.240, C.18.240, C.18.242, C.18.244, C.18.246, C.18.249, C.18.249, C.18.250, C.18.251, C.18.255, C.18.255, C.18.260, C.18.264, C.18.265, C.18.267, C.18.269, C.18.271, C.18.274, C.18.274, C.18.275, C.18.281, C.18.286, C.18.288, C.18.288, C.18.290, C.19.1, C.19.5, C.19.6, C.19.7, C.19.9, C.19.11, C.19.15, C.19.18, C.19.19, C.19.21, C.19.21, C.19.23, C.19.26, C.19.27, C.19.46, C.19.77, C.19.78, C.19.81, C.19.93, C.19.96, C.19.104, C.19.106, C.19.107, C.19.108, C.19.114, C.19.133, C.19.137, C.19.152, C.19.159, C.19.159, C.19.162, C.19.164, C.19.166, C.19.227, C.19.230, C.19.231, C.19.251, C.19.277, C.19.279, C.19.279, C.19.280, C.19.282, C.19.313, C.19.335, C.19.336, C.20.1, C.20.4, C.20.5, C.20.16, C.20.19, C.20.26, C.20.90, C.20.92, C.20.92, C.20.114, C.20.115, C.20.128, C.20.135, C.20.150, C.20.154, C.20.155, C.20.161, C.20.166, C.20.170, C.20.172, C.20.180, C.20.183, C.20.186, C.20.204, C.20.208, C.20.215, C.20.225, C.20.226, C.20.241, C.20.264, C.20.269, C.20.283, C.20.295, C.20.296, C.20.307, C.20.312, C.20.325, C.20.329, C.20.330, C.20.333, C.20.333, C.20.333, C.20.335, C.20.335, C.20.341, C.20.343, C.20.351, C.20.357, C.20.358, C.20.358, C.20.372, C.20.375, C.20.389, C.20.393, C.20.403, C.20.404, C.20.405, C.20.408, C.20.412, C.20.413, C.20.426, C.20.428, C.20.431, C.20.432, C.20.434, C.20.441, C.20.441, C.20.443, C.20.444, C.20.468, C.21.1, C.21.1, C.21.5, C.21.9, C.21.10, C.21.115, C.21.173, C.21.181, C.21.204, C.21.211, C.21.215, C.21.225, C.21.225, C.21.258, C.21.358, C.21.373, C.21.381, C.21.382, C.21.396, C.21.398, C.21.413, C.21.419, C.21.460, C.21.466, C.21.468, C.21.469, C.21.469, C.21.470, C.21.471, C.21.471, C.21.473, C.21.473, C.21.474, C.21.475, C.21.475, C.21.481, C.22.1, C.22.1, C.22.2, C.22.3, C.22.4, C.22.46, C.22.51, C.22.74, C.22.153, C.22.178, C.22.186, C.22.188, C.22.192, C.22.193, C.22.194, C.22.197, C.22.199, C.22.199, C.22.200, C.22.203, C.22.205, C.22.207, C.22.209, C.22.212, C.22.213, C.22.222, C.22.222, C.22.223, C.22.228, C.22.245, C.22.248, C.22.271, C.22.277, C.22.318, C.22.322, C.22.333, C.22.333, C.22.336, C.22.337, C.22.338, C.22.339, C.22.343, C.22.344, C.22.362, C.22.362, C.22.364, C.22.380, C.22.385, C.22.386

ich A 1

A.9.65

ich B 15

B.5.259, B.7.148, B.11.75, B.11.435, B.12.28, B.13.225, B.13.247, B.13.368, B.13.369, B.13.378, B.13.383, B.15.24, B.15.36, B.18.125, B.20.190

ich C 17 ich (14) ych (3)

C.2.219, C.7.189, C.8.2, C.8.3, C.11.306, C.13.128, C.14.138, C.15.87, C.15.193, C.15.216, C.16.288, C.16.345, C.16.350, C.20.330, C.20.342, C.21.410, C.22.190

ik B 1

B.5.226

me A 139

A.Pr.2, A.Pr.6, A.Pr.6, A.Pr.7, A.1.4, A.1.41, A.1.43, A.1.72, A.1.73, A.1.75, A.1.76, A.1.79, A.1.80, A.1.81, A.1.81, A.1.127, A.2.4, A.2.7, A.2.16, A.2.92, A.2.164, A.3.8, A.3.102, A.3.109, A.3.110, A.3.118, A.3.170, A.3.173, A.3.187, A.3.215, A.3.229, A.3.259, A.3.260, A.4.2, A.4.4, A.4.5, A.4.9, A.4.11, A.4.16, A.4.40, A.4.45, A.4.46, A.4.83, A.4.87, A.4.91, A.4.100, A.4.124, A.5.5, A.5.8, A.5.22, A.5.50, A.5.50, A.5.52, A.5.73, A.5.78, A.5.106, A.5.106, A.5.120, A.5.122, A.5.123, A.5.145, A.5.211, A.5.223, A.5.225, A.5.239, A.5.244, A.6.22, A.6.27, A.6.28, A.6.46, A.6.85, A.6.110, A.7.25, A.7.30, A.7.52, A.7.57, A.7.59, A.7.66, A.7.66, A.7.81, A.7.86, A.7.87, A.7.131, A.7.158, A.7.194, A.7.238, A.8.107, A.8.118, A.8.120, A.8.121, A.8.131, A.8.149, A.8.163, A.9.6, A.9.13, A.9.18, A.9.55, A.9.56, A.9.58, A.9.59, A.9.61, A.9.62, A.9.66, A.9.67, A.9.68, A.9.101, A.9.102, A.9.102, A.10.26, A.10.164, A.10.186, A.11.103, A.11.113, A.11.137, A.11.139, A.11.170, A.11.172, A.11.177, A.11.179, A.11.276, A.11.304, A.12.5, A.12.9, A.12.14, A.12.16, A.12.33, A.12.36, A.12.37, A.12.40, A.12.42, A.12.49, A.12.58, A.12.59, A.12.67, A.12.68, A.12.74, A.12.75, A.12.75, A.12.79

me B 365

B.Pr.2, B.Pr.6, B.Pr.6, B.Pr.7, B.Pr.165, B.Pr.167, B.Pr.182, B.Pr.202, B.Pr.204, B.Pr.205, B.1.4, B.1.43, B.1.45, B.1.74, B.1.75, B.1.77, B.1.78, B.1.81, B.1.82, B.1.83, B.1.83, B.1.138, B.2.4, B.2.7, B.2.17, B.2.20, B.2.31, B.2.32, B.2.52, B.2.53, B.2.64, B.2.128, B.2.203, B.3.8, B.3.113, B.3.120, B.3.121, B.3.129, B.3.183, B.3.186, B.3.200, B.3.228, B.3.229, B.3.250, B.3.281, B.3.284, B.3.322, B.4.2, B.4.4, B.4.5, B.4.9, B.4.11, B.4.16, B.4.18, B.4.53, B.4.58, B.4.59, B.4.96, B.4.100, B.4.104, B.4.113, B.4.141, B.4.170, B.5.5, B.5.8, B.5.9, B.5.22, B.5.37, B.5.67, B.5.67, B.5.69, B.5.93, B.5.98, B.5.116, B.5.129, B.5.129, B.5.173, B.5.176, B.5.186, B.5.187, B.5.204, B.5.206, B.5.207, B.5.229, B.5.251, B.5.278, B.5.367, B.5.369, B.5.371, B.5.377, B.5.383, B.5.389, B.5.393, B.5.398, B.5.412, B.5.423, B.5.429, B.5.429, B.5.433, B.5.439, B.5.451, B.5.453, B.5.470, B.5.531, B.5.534, B.5.539, B.5.540, B.5.559, B.5.598, B.5.625, B.6.23, B.6.28, B.6.57, B.6.62, B.6.65, B.6.74, B.6.74, B.6.89, B.6.94, B.6.95, B.6.137, B.6.173, B.6.208, B.6.254, B.7.72, B.7.125, B.7.136, B.7.138, B.7.139, B.7.149, B.7.173, B.7.185, B.8.6, B.8.13, B.8.22, B.8.64, B.8.67, B.8.68, B.8.70, B.8.71, B.8.75, B.8.76, B.8.77, B.8.111, B.8.112, B.8.112, B.9.25, B.9.91, B.9.133, B.9.153, B.9.165, B.9.204, B.10.151, B.10.161, B.10.185, B.10.187, B.10.197, B.10.227, B.10.229, B.10.234, B.10.392, B.11.1, B.11.2, B.11.2, B.11.6, B.11.7, B.11.8, B.11.9, B.11.10, B.11.16, B.11.17, B.11.25, B.11.42, B.11.46, B.11.47, B.11.48, B.11.49, B.11.52, B.11.62, B.11.62, B.11.68, B.11.69, B.11.79, B.11.84, B.11.85, B.11.118, B.11.144, B.11.149, B.11.153, B.11.177, B.11.318, B.11.320, B.11.322, B.11.322, B.11.324, B.11.351, B.11.360, B.11.367, B.11.369, B.11.371, B.11.376, B.11.406, B.11.410, B.11.438, B.12.14, B.12.15, B.12.20, B.12.20, B.12.25, B.12.94, B.12.198, B.12.198, B.13.5, B.13.6, B.13.14, B.13.22, B.13.23, B.13.48, B.13.86, B.13.96, B.13.109, B.13.113, B.13.139, B.13.156, B.13.158, B.13.181, B.13.189, B.13.200, B.13.204, B.13.205, B.13.221, B.13.248, B.13.253, B.13.307, B.13.329, B.13.331, B.13.332, B.13.336, B.13.340, B.13.374, B.13.375, B.13.382, B.13.386, B.13.394, B.13.425, B.13.438, B.14.7, B.14.9, B.14.128, B.14.277, B.14.319, B.15.5, B.15.10, B.15.11, B.15.11, B.15.13, B.15.15, B.15.19, B.15.21, B.15.38, B.15.39, B.15.46, B.15.83, B.15.84, B.15.120, B.15.158, B.15.161, B.15.317, B.15.379, B.15.439, B.15.502, B.16.20, B.16.21, B.16.22, B.16.49, B.16.58, B.16.64, B.16.74, B.16.98, B.16.230, B.16.231, B.16.232, B.16.233, B.16.239, B.16.241, B.16.241, B.16.243, B.16.245, B.16.246, B.16.259, B.16.262, B.17.2, B.17.17, B.17.30, B.17.41, B.17.48, B.17.86, B.17.89, B.17.109, B.17.128, B.17.130, B.17.131, B.17.283, B.17.301, B.18.5, B.18.6, B.18.7, B.18.21, B.18.89, B.18.90, B.18.91, B.18.111, B.18.113, B.18.163, B.18.182, B.18.184, B.18.270, B.18.277, B.18.277, B.18.286, B.18.295, B.18.298, B.18.329, B.18.338, B.18.351, B.18.367, B.18.368, B.18.373, B.18.374, B.18.397, B.19.2, B.19.2, B.19.5, B.19.9, B.19.23, B.19.180, B.19.200, B.19.200, B.19.411, B.19.411, B.19.462, B.19.468, B.19.481, B.20.5, B.20.5, B.20.46, B.20.51, B.20.74, B.20.184, B.20.189, B.20.190, B.20.191, B.20.192, B.20.195, B.20.200, B.20.201, B.20.202, B.20.203, B.20.207, B.20.209, B.20.268, B.20.337, B.20.384, B.20.384, B.20.385

me C 353 &> me pron indef

C.Pr.2, C.Pr.7, C.Pr.9, C.Pr.182, C.Pr.184, C.Pr.199, C.Pr.210, C.Pr.212, C.Pr.213, C.Pr.222, C.1.4, C.1.41, C.1.43, C.1.71, C.1.72, C.1.74, C.1.75, C.1.75, C.1.77, C.1.78, C.1.79, C.1.79, C.1.137, C.1.194, C.1.204, C.2.4, C.2.8, C.2.19, C.2.31, C.2.34, C.2.55, C.2.66, C.2.217, C.3.8, C.3.108, C.3.140, C.3.149, C.3.150, C.3.157, C.3.158, C.3.166, C.3.229, C.3.232, C.3.284, C.3.285, C.3.434, C.3.437, C.3.475, C.4.2, C.4.4, C.4.5, C.4.9, C.4.11, C.4.16, C.4.18, C.4.54, C.4.54, C.4.56, C.4.61, C.4.62, C.4.92, C.4.96, C.4.108, C.4.180, C.5.3, C.5.5, C.5.10, C.5.11, C.5.22, C.5.24, C.5.36, C.5.41, C.5.48, C.5.49, C.5.53, C.5.82, C.5.109, C.5.110, C.5.178, C.6.8, C.6.8, C.6.10, C.6.27, C.6.28, C.6.32, C.6.54, C.6.55, C.6.74, C.6.80, C.6.84, C.6.94, C.6.94, C.6.100, C.6.102, C.6.111, C.6.142, C.6.155, C.6.158, C.6.171, C.6.172, C.6.175, C.6.214, C.6.215, C.6.247, C.6.249, C.6.271, C.6.275, C.6.281, C.6.288, C.6.292, C.6.307, C.6.313, C.6.324, C.6.423, C.6.425, C.6.427, C.6.434, C.6.436, C.6.440, C.7.5, C.7.9, C.7.14, C.7.42, C.7.42, C.7.46, C.7.53, C.7.65, C.7.67, C.7.85, C.7.98, C.7.179, C.7.184, C.7.185, C.7.192, C.7.204, C.7.247, C.7.278, C.7.293, C.7.295, C.7.302, C.7.304, C.8.56, C.8.66, C.8.76, C.8.76, C.8.103, C.8.104, C.8.158, C.8.170, C.8.177, C.8.217, C.8.221, C.8.299, C.8.299, C.8.314, C.9.239, C.9.298, C.9.318, C.9.331, C.10.6, C.10.13, C.10.60, C.10.63, C.10.66, C.10.67, C.10.68, C.10.69, C.10.73, C.10.74, C.10.75, C.10.107, C.10.108, C.10.108, C.10.151, C.10.252, C.10.303, C.11.3, C.11.89, C.11.103, C.11.126, C.11.128, C.11.135, C.11.137, C.11.160, C.11.161, C.11.162, C.11.162, C.11.165, C.11.166, C.11.167, C.11.168, C.11.169, C.11.174, C.11.175, C.11.176, C.11.184, C.11.185, C.11.196, C.11.224, C.11.309, C.11.311, C.12.3, C.12.14, C.12.14, C.12.15, C.12.16, C.12.25, C.12.25, C.12.26, C.12.53, C.12.79, C.12.88, C.12.167, C.13.153, C.13.161, C.13.162, C.13.177, C.13.179, C.13.181, C.13.192, C.13.194, C.13.214, C.13.244, C.14.137, C.14.137, C.15.5, C.15.6, C.15.7, C.15.17, C.15.24, C.15.26, C.15.54, C.15.74, C.15.78, C.15.103, C.15.109, C.15.117, C.15.120, C.15.128, C.15.129, C.15.157, C.15.178, C.15.190, C.15.210, C.15.213, C.15.236, C.16.153, C.16.164, C.16.166, C.16.170, C.16.172, C.16.178, C.16.200, C.16.201, C.16.208, C.16.290, C.16.296, C.17.113, C.17.184, C.17.243, C.17.253, C.18.2, C.18.2, C.18.3, C.18.8, C.18.17, C.18.18, C.18.19, C.18.21, C.18.23, C.18.56, C.18.131, C.18.184, C.18.196, C.18.247, C.18.248, C.18.250, C.18.257, C.18.257, C.18.260, C.18.275, C.18.278, C.19.2, C.19.18, C.19.46, C.19.55, C.19.97, C.19.99, C.19.100, C.19.101, C.19.107, C.19.264, C.19.281, C.20.5, C.20.6, C.20.19, C.20.91, C.20.92, C.20.94, C.20.114, C.20.116, C.20.166, C.20.185, C.20.188, C.20.278, C.20.281, C.20.299, C.20.299, C.20.312, C.20.325, C.20.331, C.20.370, C.20.372, C.20.379, C.20.408, C.20.410, C.20.415, C.20.440, C.21.2, C.21.2, C.21.5, C.21.9, C.21.23, C.21.180, C.21.200, C.21.200, C.21.411, C.21.411, C.21.462, C.21.468, C.21.481, C.22.5, C.22.5, C.22.46, C.22.51, C.22.74, C.22.184, C.22.189, C.22.190, C.22.191, C.22.192, C.22.195, C.22.200, C.22.201, C.22.202, C.22.203, C.22.207, C.22.209, C.22.268, C.22.337, C.22.384, C.22.384, C.22.385

my A 128 mi (1) my (127)

A.1.69, A.1.75, A.1.77, A.1.78, A.1.82, A.1.128, A.1.176, A.2.1, A.2.7, A.2.17, A.2.112, A.3.7, A.3.80, A.3.97, A.3.169, A.3.176, A.3.184, A.3.189, A.3.218, A.3.222, A.4.8, A.4.9, A.4.18, A.4.18, A.4.38, A.4.38, A.4.43, A.4.43, A.4.44, A.4.44, A.4.46, A.4.51, A.4.90, A.4.123, A.4.123, A.4.124, A.4.140, A.4.147, A.4.149, A.4.151, A.4.152, A.5.3, A.5.7, A.5.8, A.5.70, A.5.72, A.5.75, A.5.77, A.5.80, A.5.88, A.5.89, A.5.89, A.5.96, A.5.99, A.5.99, A.5.118, A.5.120, A.5.121, A.5.123, A.5.129, A.5.136, A.5.139, A.5.144, A.5.210, A.5.212, A.5.217, A.5.229, A.5.237, A.6.17, A.6.19, A.6.44, A.6.86, A.7.28, A.7.34, A.7.34, A.7.36, A.7.36, A.7.51, A.7.77, A.7.79, A.7.81, A.7.83, A.7.83, A.7.84, A.7.84, A.7.85, A.7.88, A.7.89, A.7.89, A.7.90, A.7.93, A.7.95, A.7.95, A.7.96, A.7.156, A.7.193, A.7.238, A.7.239, A.7.255, A.7.267, A.7.268, A.7.272, A.7.274, A.8.39, A.8.104, A.8.105, A.8.106, A.8.146, A.9.22, A.9.62, A.9.63, A.11.31, A.11.87, A.11.102, A.11.105, A.11.108, A.11.167, A.12.2, A.12.43, A.12.47, A.12.53, A.12.56, A.12.64, A.12.70, A.12.74, A.12.76, A.12.82, A.12.91

my B 304

B.Pr.193, B.Pr.203, B.1.71, B.1.77, B.1.79, B.1.80, B.1.84, B.1.139, B.1.202, B.2.1, B.2.7, B.2.21, B.2.29, B.2.33, B.2.148, B.3.7, B.3.91, B.3.108, B.3.182, B.3.189, B.3.197, B.3.202, B.3.231, B.3.244, B.4.8, B.4.9, B.4.20, B.4.20, B.4.51, B.4.51, B.4.56, B.4.56, B.4.57, B.4.57, B.4.59, B.4.65, B.4.140, B.4.140, B.4.141, B.4.155, B.4.164, B.4.186, B.4.188, B.4.189, B.5.3, B.5.7, B.5.8, B.5.37, B.5.37, B.5.59, B.5.95, B.5.97, B.5.100, B.5.108, B.5.109, B.5.109, B.5.117, B.5.120, B.5.120, B.5.123, B.5.125, B.5.133, B.5.148, B.5.150, B.5.152, B.5.170, B.5.187, B.5.202, B.5.204, B.5.205, B.5.207, B.5.213, B.5.220, B.5.223, B.5.228, B.5.238, B.5.244, B.5.259, B.5.267, B.5.267, B.5.274, B.5.368, B.5.371, B.5.382, B.5.384, B.5.388, B.5.394, B.5.399, B.5.401, B.5.407, B.5.410, B.5.419, B.5.426, B.5.428, B.5.438, B.5.440, B.5.445, B.5.457, B.5.465, B.5.529, B.5.557, B.5.599, B.5.640, B.5.640, B.6.26, B.6.32, B.6.32, B.6.34, B.6.34, B.6.56, B.6.85, B.6.87, B.6.89, B.6.91, B.6.91, B.6.92, B.6.92, B.6.93, B.6.96, B.6.97, B.6.97, B.6.98, B.6.101, B.6.103, B.6.103, B.6.104, B.6.117, B.6.163, B.6.171, B.6.206, B.6.207, B.6.254, B.6.255, B.6.271, B.6.283, B.6.284, B.6.288, B.6.290, B.7.37, B.7.122, B.7.123, B.7.124, B.7.169, B.8.26, B.8.71, B.8.72, B.9.37, B.9.38, B.9.38, B.9.202, B.10.46, B.10.150, B.10.153, B.10.156, B.10.225, B.10.380, B.11.16, B.11.26, B.11.43, B.11.51, B.11.61, B.11.65, B.11.69, B.11.70, B.11.71, B.11.74, B.11.74, B.11.145, B.11.146, B.11.147, B.11.152, B.11.196, B.11.322, B.11.326, B.11.369, B.11.374, B.11.378, B.11.388, B.12.15, B.12.28, B.12.169, B.13.5, B.13.111, B.13.164, B.13.191, B.13.191, B.13.212, B.13.224, B.13.225, B.13.241, B.13.244, B.13.262, B.13.263, B.13.270, B.13.341, B.13.363, B.13.365, B.13.372, B.13.379, B.13.385, B.13.390, B.13.391, B.13.392, B.13.392, B.13.393, B.13.397, B.13.397, B.13.404, B.14.4, B.14.9, B.14.11, B.14.26, B.14.98, B.14.274, B.14.323, B.14.334, B.15.1, B.15.3, B.15.4, B.15.20, B.15.26, B.15.28, B.15.29, B.15.34, B.15.39, B.15.83, B.15.152, B.16.11, B.16.40, B.16.45, B.16.49, B.16.58, B.16.225, B.16.227, B.16.233, B.16.234, B.16.235, B.16.236, B.16.238, B.16.269, B.17.9, B.17.23, B.17.110, B.17.132, B.17.169, B.17.184, B.17.185, B.17.185, B.17.194, B.17.194, B.17.197, B.17.265, B.18.3, B.18.88, B.18.132, B.18.158, B.18.176, B.18.182, B.18.183, B.18.277, B.18.327, B.18.335, B.18.344, B.18.345, B.18.349, B.18.350, B.18.362, B.18.365, B.18.368, B.18.374, B.18.375, B.18.386, B.18.389, B.18.389, B.18.392, B.18.393, B.18.393, B.18.396, B.18.398, B.18.401, B.18.426, B.18.426, B.19.173, B.19.253, B.19.258, B.19.258, B.19.260, B.19.260, B.19.355, B.19.393, B.19.400, B.19.410, B.19.460, B.19.461, B.19.462, B.19.476, B.19.476, B.20.191, B.20.193, B.20.345, B.20.345, B.20.346, B.20.357, B.20.365

my C 303

C.Pr.206, C.Pr.211, C.1.68, C.1.74, C.1.76, C.1.80, C.1.138, C.2.1, C.2.8, C.2.16, C.2.20, C.2.22, C.2.34, C.2.36, C.2.164, C.2.186, C.3.119, C.3.135, C.3.143, C.3.227, C.3.228, C.3.256, C.3.257, C.3.259, C.3.367, C.3.369, C.3.418, C.4.8, C.4.9, C.4.12, C.4.20, C.4.20, C.4.49, C.4.49, C.4.49, C.4.59, C.4.59, C.4.60, C.4.60, C.4.62, C.4.69, C.4.97, C.4.98, C.4.137, C.4.137, C.4.138, C.4.159, C.4.174, C.4.175, C.4.180, C.4.185, C.4.186, C.4.191, C.5.13, C.5.17, C.5.17, C.5.36, C.5.36, C.5.40, C.5.46, C.5.47, C.5.47, C.5.49, C.5.52, C.5.83, C.5.101, C.5.106, C.5.106, C.5.107, C.5.107, C.5.200, C.6.21, C.6.21, C.6.26, C.6.35, C.6.42, C.6.46, C.6.52, C.6.52, C.6.85, C.6.88, C.6.90, C.6.100, C.6.113, C.6.115, C.6.118, C.6.125, C.6.127, C.6.140, C.6.146, C.6.176, C.6.190, C.6.210, C.6.212, C.6.213, C.6.215, C.6.221, C.6.228, C.6.228, C.6.231, C.6.240, C.6.252, C.6.258, C.6.260, C.6.262, C.6.264, C.6.269, C.6.274, C.6.278, C.6.279, C.6.279, C.6.280, C.6.284, C.6.284, C.6.293, C.6.293, C.6.296, C.6.306, C.6.311, C.6.319, C.6.429, C.6.430, C.6.433, C.6.433, C.6.437, C.6.437, C.6.439, C.6.441, C.7.4, C.7.10, C.7.15, C.7.17, C.7.20, C.7.26, C.7.39, C.7.41, C.7.52, C.7.53, C.7.54, C.7.59, C.7.174, C.7.174, C.7.176, C.7.201, C.7.246, C.8.25, C.8.31, C.8.31, C.8.33, C.8.33, C.8.55, C.8.64, C.8.64, C.8.65, C.8.91, C.8.94, C.8.96, C.8.97, C.8.98, C.8.100, C.8.100, C.8.101, C.8.101, C.8.102, C.8.105, C.8.106, C.8.106, C.8.107, C.8.110, C.8.144, C.8.145, C.8.145, C.8.216, C.8.267, C.8.292, C.8.305, C.8.306, C.8.311, C.8.313, C.9.40, C.9.277, C.9.313, C.10.30, C.10.69, C.10.70, C.10.212, C.10.301, C.11.43, C.11.88,

C.11.91, C.11.95, C.11.109, C.11.113, C.11.125, C.11.134, C.11.175, C.11.203, C.11.310, C.12.13, C.12.19, C.12.22, C.12.22, C.12.80, C.12.81, C.12.82, C.12.87, C.12.166, C.12.169, C.12.171, C.13.134, C.13.179, C.13.184, C.13.241, C.14.2, C.15.5, C.15.8, C.15.8, C.15.74, C.15.193, C.15.195, C.15.199, C.16.171, C.16.176, C.16.188, C.16.189, C.16.196, C.16.201, C.16.338, C.18.43, C.18.159, C.18.176, C.18.240, C.18.241, C.18.244, C.18.247, C.18.251, C.18.252, C.18.254, C.18.285, C.19.24, C.19.133, C.19.133, C.19.150, C.19.160, C.19.160, C.19.163, C.19.231, C.20.3, C.20.90, C.20.93, C.20.93, C.20.135, C.20.161, C.20.179, C.20.185, C.20.186, C.20.188, C.20.299, C.20.358, C.20.378, C.20.380, C.20.381, C.20.381, C.20.390, C.20.395, C.20.400, C.20.403, C.20.410, C.20.416, C.20.417, C.20.428, C.20.431, C.20.435, C.20.435, C.20.435, C.20.436, C.20.439, C.20.441, C.20.444, C.20.469, C.20.469, C.21.173, C.21.253, C.21.258, C.21.258, C.21.260, C.21.260, C.21.355, C.21.393, C.21.400, C.21.410, C.21.460, C.21.461, C.21.462, C.21.476, C.21.476, C.22.191, C.22.193, C.22.345, C.22.345, C.22.346, C.22.357, C.22.365

myen C 1
C.18.254

myn A 25
A.3.51, A.3.168, A.4.94, A.4.146, A.4.150, A.5.53, A.5.90, A.5.92, A.5.93, A.5.97, A.5.101, A.5.132, A.5.211, A.6.17, A.6.37, A.6.113, A.7.32, A.7.75, A.7.134, A.7.252, A.8.36, A.8.120, A.9.54, A.11.261, A.12.38

myn B 40
B.2.34, B.3.181, B.4.183, B.4.187, B.5.70, B.5.112, B.5.113, B.5.118, B.5.124, B.5.216, B.5.383, B.5.401, B.5.433, B.5.529, B.5.550, B.5.628, B.6.83, B.6.146, B.7.34, B.7.138, B.8.63, B.10.371, B.11.115, B.13.330, B.13.364, B.13.389, B.14.14, B.15.49, B.15.120, B.16.232, B.16.238, B.16.239, B.16.241, B.17.184, B.17.192, B.17.195, B.17.283, B.19.461, B.20.183, B.20.185

myn C 46
C.4.58, C.4.102, C.4.143, C.4.177, C.5.7, C.6.11, C.6.18, C.6.75, C.6.89, C.6.98, C.6.106, C.6.152, C.6.224, C.6.263, C.6.289, C.6.440, C.7.17, C.7.26, C.7.46, C.7.194, C.7.281, C.8.29, C.8.92, C.8.148, C.8.212, C.8.289, C.9.37, C.9.117, C.10.61, C.11.198, C.12.18, C.12.50, C.16.208, C.16.211, C.18.49, C.18.255, C.18.257, C.19.150, C.19.158, C.19.161, C.19.264, C.20.419, C.20.431, C.21.461, C.22.183, C.22.185

myne A 2
A.4.42, A.4.129

myne B 18
B.4.55, B.4.103, B.4.107, B.4.146, B.5.110, B.5.410, B.6.30, B.6.148, B.6.268, B.11.410, B.15.46, B.16.45, B.16.159, B.16.167, B.18.279, B.18.329, B.18.350, B.18.377

myne C 4
C.4.62, C.6.41, C.20.301, C.20.372

yarmed > armed; yarn > rennen; yasked > asken v; ybake(n > bake; ybaptised > baptiƺe

ybarred ptp *barren v.* B 1; C 1
B.19.167   In an hous al bishet and hir dore *ybarred*
C.21.167   In an hous al bishut and here dore *ybarred*

ybe > ben; ybedded > bedden; yberied > burye; ybet(e > beten v2; yblamed > blame; yblessed > blesse; yblissed > blesse; yblissid > blesse; yblowe(n > blowe; ybore yborn > beren v2; yborwed > borwe; ybosted > bosten; ibotrased > botrased; ybouƺt > buggen; ybounde > bynden; ybrent > brennen; ybroke(n -ne > breke; ybroughte ybrouƺt ybrouhte > brynge; ycald > callen; ycalde > callen v

ycalled adj *called adj. &> callen* B 1; C 1
B.15.229   *Ycalled* and ycrymyled and his crowne yshaue.
C.16.354   *Ycalled* and ycrimyled and his croune yshaue.

ycarped > carpen; ich > i; ychaffared > chaffare; ychaunged > chaunge; ich > I; iche > ech; ycheueled > hyueled; ichone > echone; ychose > chese; yclansed > clanse; yclepid > clepe; ycliketed > cliketted; yclosed > close; yclothed > cloþen; yclouted > cloute; ycome > comen; ycongeyed > congeien; ycoped > cope; ycorouned > croune

ycouped ptp *coupen v.(2)* B 1; C 1
B.18.14   To geten hym gilte spores [and] galoches *ycouped*.
C.20.12   To geten h[ym] gult spores and galoches *ycouped*.

ycoupled > coupleþ

ycrammed ptp *crammen v.* A 1 ycrammid; B 1; C 1
A.Pr.41   Til here bely & here bagge were bratful *ycrammid*;
B.Pr.41   [Til] hire bel[y] and hire bagg[e were] bret]ful *ycrammed*
C.Pr.42   Til here [bely] and here [bagge] w[ere] bretful *ycrammed*,

ycrymyled ptp *crimplen v.* B 1; C 1 ycrimyled
B.15.229   Ycalled and *ycrymyled* and his crowne yshaue.
C.16.354   Ycalled and *ycrimyled* and his croune yshaue.

ycristened > cristen; ycrouned > croune; ycursed > curseþ; ydampned > dampneþ

ydel n *idel n.* A 1; B 6 Idel (1) ydel (5); C 5
A. 6.58   A[nd] nameliche an *ydel* þe name of god almiƺt;
B. 5.571   And-nameliche-on-*ydel*-þe-name-of-god-almyƺty.
B.13.225   Al *yde[l]* ich hatie for of Actif is my name.

B.13.401   As þere no nede was goddes name an *Idel*:
B.14.196   Ellis is al on *ydel*, al þat euere [we diden],
B.19.402   Of Spiritus Iusticie þow spekest muche on *ydel*.'
B.20.299   Of alle taletelleris and titeleris in *ydel*.
C. 7.218   And-nameliche-an-*ydel*-þe-name-of-god-almyhty.
C.14.7   Ne to spille speche, As to speke an *ydel*,
C.16.37   Elles is al an *ydel* al oure lyuynge here,
C.21.402   Of spiritus Iusticie thow spekest moche an *ydel*.'
C.22.299   Of all taletellares and titerares an *ydel*.

ydel adj *idel adj.* B 5; C 4 ydel (3) ydele (1)
B. 2.91   And in we[n]es and in wisshynges and wiþ *ydel* þouƺtes
B. 5.403   Wiþ *ydel* tales at þe Ale and ouþerwhile [in] chirche[s];
B.12.1   'I am ymaginatif,' quod he; '*ydel* was I neuere
B.14.13   That I ne soiled it wiþ siƺte or som *ydel* speche,
B.15.127   [He syngeþ seruice bokelees], seiþ it with *ydel* wille.
C. 2.98   In w[e]des and in weschynges and with *ydel* thouhtes
C. 5.27   That fynde[th] the thy fode–for an *ydel* man þow semest,
C. 7.19   With *ydele* tales at þe ale and oþerwhile in chirches;
C.14.1   'I am ymagenatyf,' quod he; '*ydel* was y neuere

ydelnesse n *idelnesse n.* B 4; C 6 idelnesse (1) ydelnesse (5)
B.13.238   And þat am I, Actif, þat *ydelnesse* hatie,
B.19.228   That *ydelnesse* encombre hym noƺt, enuye ne pride:
B.19.286   Waste word of *ydelnesse* ne wikked speche moeue;
B.20.116   And armede hym in *ydelnesse* and in heigh berynge.
C. 2.104   With spiserye, speke *ydelnesse* in vayne spe[ch]e and spene
C. 9.152   In *idelnesse* and in ese and by otheres trauayle.
C.15.213   And for me Actyf, his man, þat *ydelnesse* ha[t]e.
C.21.228   That *ydelnesse* encombre h[y]m nat, enuye ne pryde:
C.21.286   Wast[e] word of *ydelnesse* ne wikede speche meue;
C.22.116   And armed hym in *ydelnesse* and in hey berynge.

ydyademed > diademed; idyked > diken; ydyned > dyne

ydiot n *idiote n.* B 1
B.16.170   And yede forþ as an *ydiot* in contree to aspie

ydiotes adj *idiotes adj.* B 1
B.11.317   Non excusat episcopos nec *ydiotes* preestes'.

ydo(en > doon

ydolatrie n *idolatrie n.* C 1
C.Pr.96   And seide, '*ydolatrie* ƺe soffren in sondrye places manye

idolue > deluen; ydrawe > drawe; ydremed > dremeþ; ydronke > drynken; yerne > rennen; yentred > entreþ; yered > erien; yes > eiƺe n1

yesyhte n *eiesight n.* C 1
C. 9.102   For alle þat haen here hele and here *yesyhte*

if conj *if conj.* A 84 ƺef (1) ƺif (83); B 242; C 202 if (19) yf (175) ƺef (1) ƺif (7)
A.Pr.37, A.Pr.79, A.1.46, A.1.138, A.1.155, A.1.161, A.2.27, A.2.29, A.2.30, A.2.93, A.2.97, A.2.100, A.2.101, A.2.104, A.2.120, A.2.167, A.3.7, A.3.100, A.3.107, A.3.124, A.3.138, A.3.158, A.3.160, A.3.167, A.4.58, A.4.69, A.4.110, A.4.129, A.4.150, A.5.102, A.5.112, A.5.227, A.5.240, A.6.41, A.6.92, A.6.112, A.7.12, A.7.16, A.7.73, A.7.121, A.7.196, A.7.202, A.7.204, A.7.237, A.7.252, A.7.294, A.8.61, A.8.68, A.8.111, A.8.133, A.9.4, A.9.12, A.9.30, A.9.49, A.9.92, A.9.118, A.10.9, A.10.55, A.10.68, A.10.88, A.10.93, A.10.95, A.10.101, A.10.113, A.10.194, A.10.196, A.10.212, A.10.215, A.11.31, A.11.38, A.11.115, A.11.117, A.11.133, A.11.144, A.11.162, A.11.276, A.12.1, A.12.10, A.12.14, A.12.37, A.12.39, A.12.45, A.12.65, A.12.91
B.Pr.37, B.Pr.82, B.Pr.153, B.Pr.172, B.Pr.174, B.1.48, B.1.181, B.1.187, B.2.45, B.2.47, B.2.129, B.2.136, B.2.137, B.2.140, B.2.156, B.2.206, B.3.7, B.3.111, B.3.118, B.3.135, B.3.149, B.3.171, B.3.173, B.3.180, B.3.307, B.3.313, B.3.348, B.4.72, B.4.82, B.4.127, B.4.146, B.4.177, B.4.187, B.5.33, B.5.49, B.5.53, B.5.134, B.5.172, B.5.196, B.5.242, B.5.256, B.5.286, B.5.289, B.5.388, B.5.393, B.5.400, B.5.400, B.5.413, B.5.422, B.5.422, B.5.423, B.5.429, B.5.455, B.5.502, B.5.554, B.5.575, B.5.605, B.5.627, B.6.17, B.6.51, B.6.81, B.6.129, B.6.136, B.6.170, B.6.210, B.6.216, B.6.218, B.6.227, B.6.268, B.6.310, B.6.331, B.7.13, B.7.36, B.7.60, B.7.66, B.7.70, B.7.79, B.7.84, B.7.129, B.7.150, B.8.4, B.8.12, B.8.34, B.8.51, B.8.56, B.8.58, B.8.102, B.8.129, B.9.9, B.9.39, B.9.150, B.9.152, B.9.154, B.9.173, B.9.186, B.9.193, B.9.198, B.10.52, B.10.163, B.10.165, B.10.181, B.10.192, B.10.219, B.10.305, B.10.309, B.10.315, B.10.372, B.10.392, B.10.442, B.10.443, B.11.24, B.11.28, B.11.39, B.11.58, B.11.86, B.11.91, B.11.97, B.11.108, B.11.119, B.11.135, B.11.197, B.11.204, B.11.221, B.11.223, B.11.257, B.11.283, B.11.288, B.11.304, B.11.350, B.11.378, B.11.390, B.11.441, B.12.25, B.12.33, B.12.35, B.12.38, B.12.58, B.12.100, B.12.111, B.12.145, B.12.173, B.12.174, B.12.212, B.12.247, B.12.289, B.13.45, B.13.98, B.13.109, B.13.157, B.13.181, B.13.186, B.13.206, B.13.218, B.13.255, B.13.257, B.13.299, B.13.307, B.13.363, B.13.370, B.13.373, B.13.387, B.13.389, B.13.391, B.13.415, B.14.38, B.14.60, B.14.71, B.14.72, B.14.90, B.14.145, B.14.167, B.14.186, B.14.189, B.14.200, B.14.220, B.14.225, B.14.226, B.14.227, B.14.230, B.14.239, B.15.15, B.15.46, B.15.83, B.15.119, B.15.121, B.15.160, B.15.180, B.15.236, B.15.240, B.15.263, B.15.301, B.15.319, B.15.328, B.15.333, B.15.377, B.15.383, B.15.387, B.15.403, B.15.553, B.15.565, B.15.568, B.15.575, B.15.609, B.16.12, B.16.26, B.16.67, B.16.107, B.16.212, B.16.214, B.16.217, B.16.231, B.17.84, B.17.138, B.17.241,

B.17.325, B.18.54, B.18.55, B.18.194, B.18.208, B.18.269, B.18.277, B.18.281,
B.18.303, B.18.306, B.18.331, B.18.381, B.18.383, B.18.386, B.19.209, B.19.220,
B.19.303, B.19.404, B.19.468, B.20.18, B.20.32, B.20.203, B.20.204, B.20.253,
B.20.259, B.20.310, B.20.321, B.20.335
    C.Pr.38, C.Pr.80, C.Pr.173, C.Pr.189, C.Pr.191, C.1.177, C.1.183, C.2.18, C.2.26,
C.2.49, C.2.132, C.2.156, C.2.172, C.2.218, C.3.7, C.3.148, C.3.155, C.3.173, C.3.217,
C.3.219, C.3.226, C.3.318, C.3.350, C.3.350, C.3.355, C.3.460, C.3.466, C.3.477, C.4.30,
C.4.54, C.4.78, C.4.84, C.4.124, C.4.143, C.4.171, C.5.42, C.5.66, C.5.135, C.5.152,
C.5.161, C.6.22, C.6.55, C.6.154, C.6.204, C.6.262, C.6.267, C.6.270, C.6.278, C.6.300,
C.6.309, C.6.344, C.7.4, C.7.9, C.7.16, C.7.16, C.7.28, C.7.35, C.7.35, C.7.36, C.7.42,
C.7.142, C.7.147, C.7.222, C.7.254, C.7.260, C.7.297, C.8.15, C.8.83, C.8.143, C.8.201,
C.8.226, C.8.228, C.8.234, C.8.266, C.8.289, C.8.352, C.9.13, C.9.16, C.9.63, C.9.161,
C.9.213, C.9.237, C.9.299, C.10.4, C.10.12, C.10.35, C.10.57, C.10.125, C.10.136,
C.10.158, C.10.290, C.11.72, C.11.105, C.11.107, C.11.109, C.11.111, C.11.121,
C.11.132, C.11.139, C.11.183, C.11.187, C.11.219, C.12.10, C.12.42, C.12.54, C.12.70,
C.12.112, C.12.143, C.12.163, C.12.180, C.12.200, C.12.237, C.13.2, C.13.33, C.13.46,
C.13.87, C.13.102, C.13.118, C.13.161, C.13.208, C.13.247, C.14.15, C.14.45, C.14.56,
C.14.71, C.14.89, C.14.113, C.14.114, C.14.134, C.14.151, C.14.211, C.14.215, C.15.35,
C.15.50, C.15.105, C.15.187, C.15.225, C.15.227, C.15.237, C.15.259, C.15.270,
C.15.271, C.16.41, C.16.61, C.16.66, C.16.67, C.16.68, C.16.71, C.16.166, C.16.208,
C.16.220, C.16.221, C.16.294, C.16.360, C.16.361, C.16.365, C.17.5, C.17.15, C.17.54,
C.17.64, C.17.122, C.17.123, C.17.149, C.17.216, C.17.228, C.17.229, C.17.250,
C.17.317, C.18.84, C.18.215, C.19.75, C.19.111, C.19.128, C.19.145, C.19.207,
C.19.305, C.20.54, C.20.55, C.20.199, C.20.214, C.20.215, C.20.277, C.20.299,
C.20.305, C.20.335, C.20.336, C.20.374, C.20.423, C.20.428, C.21.209, C.21.220,
C.21.404, C.21.468, C.22.18, C.22.32, C.22.203, C.22.204, C.22.253, C.22.259,
C.22.310, C.22.321, C.22.335

*yfalle(n > falle; yfed > feden; yfolde(n > folde; yfolled > follen; yfolwed >
folwen; yfonde > fynden; yfou3te yfouhte > fi3te; yfounde(n > fynden; yfouthte
> fi3te*

yfranchised ptp *fraunchisen v.* C 1
C. 3.114   Be *yfranchised* for a fre man and haue a fals name.

yfryed ptp *frien v.(3)* A 1 yfried; B 2; C 1 yfried
A. 7.294   But 3if it be fressh flessh oþer fissh *yfried*,
B. 6.310   But if it be fressh flessh ouþer fissh *[y]fryed*,
B.13.63   Wombe cloutes and wilde brawen and egges *yfryed* wiþ grece.
C. 8.332   But hit be [fresh] flesch or fisch *yfried* or ybake

yfruyted ptp *fruiten v.* B 1
B.16.39   I saue it til I se it ripen and somdel *yfruyted*.

*yfulled > follen; ygadered > gaderen; ygete > geten; ygyue > gyuen;
yglobbed > yglubbed; yglosed > glose þ*

yglubbed ptp *globben v.* B 1; C 1 yglobbed
B. 5.339   Til Gloton hadde *yglubbed* a galon and a gille.
C. 6.397   Til glotoun hadde *yglobbed* a galoun and a gylle.

ygo > go

ygraced ptp *gracen v.* A 1 ygracid; B 1
A. 7.116   'We haue none [lymes] to laboure wiþ, lord, *ygracid* be 3e;
B. 6.124   'We haue no lymes to laboure with; lord, *ygraced* be [y]e!

*ygraue > graue; ygraunted > graunte; ygraue > graue; ygreued > greuen;
ygrounde > grounde*

ygulpid ptp *gulpen v.* A 1
A. 5.188   Til glotoun hadde *ygulpid* a galoun & a gille.

yhabited ptp *habiten v.* B 1
B.13.284   *Yhabited* as an heremyte, an ordre by hymselue,

yhad > hauen; yhandled -lit > handle

yhasped ptp *haspen v.* A 1 haspide; B 1; C 1 yhapsed
A. 1.171   So [harde] haþ auarice *haspide* 3ow togideris.
B. 1.197   So harde haþ Auarice *yhasped* [yow] togideres.
C. 1.192   So harde haþ auaryce *yhapsed* hem togederes.

yhated > hatien; yheeled > helen

yheer v *iheren v.* B 1; C 1 yhere
B.17.140   For god is after an hand; *yheer* now and knowe it.
C. 4.187   'Y assente,' sayde resoun, 'by so 3owsulue *yhere*

*yheled > helien; yherberwed > herberwe; yherd > heren,herie; yherde >
herie; yhere > yheer; iherusalem > ierusalem; yholde(n > holden; yholpe >
helpen; yhonted > hunte; yhote(n > hote; yhudde > hiden; yhuyred > hired;
yhuntid > hunte; ik > i; ykald > callen; ykeyed ikei3id > keyed; ykyuered >
couere; yknyt > knytten*

yknowe v *iknouen v. &> knowen* C 1
C. 7.168   And þe vernicle bifore for men sholde *yknowe*

*yknowen > knowen; ykud > kidde; ykuld > killen; ylabored > labouren;
ylakked : lakke; ylasted > laste*

ile n *ile n.(1)* A 1
A. 2.63   And al þe *Ile* of vsurie, & auarice þe faste,

*ylefte > leuen; yley > ligge; yleyd > leggen v2; yleye(n > ligge; ylered >
leren; ylerned > lerne; ylet > leten,lette; ylette > lette*

ylettrede adj *ilettred ppl.* B 1; C 1 ylettred
B.10.403   Forþi wise witted men and wel *ylettrede* clerkes
C.11.233   Wel ywitted men and wel *ylettred* clerkes,

yleued > leued,lyuen; ylich > ylik; yliche > ylik,ylike

ylik adj *ilich adj.* B 3 yliche (1) ylik (2); C 8 ilych (1) yliche (2) ylik (1)
ylyk (1) ylike (2) ylyke (1)
B. 1.91   And [ek] *ylik* to oure lord by Seint Lukes wordes.
B. 5.486   And madest þiself wiþ þi sone vs synfulle *yliche*:
B.18.337   Thus *ylik* a Lusard wiþ a lady visage
C. 7.128   And madest thysulue with thy sone oure soule & body *ilych*:
C.10.68   A muche man, me thoghte, *ylike* to mysulue,
C.10.116   He was long and lene, *ylyk* to noon other;
C.10.133   A lemman þat he louyeth *ylyke* to hymsulue.
C.13.192   And þerfore merueileth me, for man is moste *yliche* the,
C.18.70   Summe litel, somme large, *ylik* apples of kynde,
C.19.334   And louye h[e]m *yliche* hymsulue [and his lyf] amende.
C.20.3   And 3ede forth *ylike* a lorel al my lyf tyme

ylike adv *iliche adv. &> ylik* A 1 ilike; B 6 ylike (2) yliche (4); C 8
iliche (1) yliche (3) ylyche (2) ilyke (1) ylyke (1)
A. 1.48   And þe [Image *ilike*], þat þereinne standis.
B. 1.50   And þe ymage *[y]lik[e]* þat þerInne stondeþ.
B.12.209   It were neiþer reson ne ri3t to rewarde boþe *yliche*.
B.13.349   And as [lef] in lente as out of lente, alle tymes *yliche*.
B.14.167   And *yliche* witty and wise, if þee wel hadde liked.
B.14.303   And for þe [lewde] euere [*yliche*] a lemman of alle clennesse:
B.19.439   As for a trewe tidy man alle tymes *ylike*.
C. 6.183   As leef in lente as out of lente, alle tymes *ylyche*,
C.14.148   Hit were no resoun ne riht to rewarde bothe *ylyche*.
C.15.33   *Ilyk[e* peres] the [ploghman], as he a palmere were,
C.16.20   And *yliche* witty and wys and lyue withoute nede;
C.18.22   Alle thre *yliche* long and yliche large.
C.18.22   Alle thre yliche long and *yliche* large.
C.18.62   Of o kynde apples aren nat *iliche* grete
C.21.439   As for a trewe tydy man alle tymes *ylyke*.

ylikned > likne; ylyued > lyuen

ilke adj *ilke pron.* A 1; B 2; C 3
A. 1.81   'Teche me to no tresour but tel me þis *ilke*,
B. 1.83   'Teche me to no tresor, but tel me þis *ilke*,
B.17.114   And neuere eft greue gome þat gooþ þis *ilke* gate.
C. 1.79   'Teche me to [no] tresor but telle me this *ilke*,
C.16.314   Ne mysliked thogh he lore or lened þat *ilke*
C.18.264   I leue þat *ilke* lord thenketh a newe lawe to make:

ille n *ille n.* A 5; B 8; C 8 ille (4) ylle (4)
A. 1.51   Et que sunt dei deo oþer ellis 3e don *ille*."
A. 1.63   Adam & Eue he eggide to *ille*,
A. 1.87   Doþ þe werkis þerwiþ & wilneþ no man *ille*,
A. 9.93   And were vnbuxum at his bidding, and bold to don *ille*,
A.10.68   And 3if þei ben pore & cateles, to kepe hem fro *ille*,
B. 1.53   Et que sunt dei deo or ellis ye don *ille*."
B. 1.65   Adam and Eue he egged to *ille*,
B. 1.89   Dooþ þe werkes þerwiþ and wilneþ no man *ille*,
B. 8.103   [And were vnbuxum at his biddyng, and bold to don *ille*],
B.10.26   The Sauter seiþ þe same by swiche þat doon *ille*:
B.18.279   Body and soule beþ myne, boþe goode and *ille*.
B.18.387   Wheiþer þei deye or deye no3t for þat þei diden *ille*.
B.18.390   And þou3 holy writ wole þat I be wroke of hem þat diden *ille*–
C.Pr.109   And for here syre sey hem synne and suffred hem do *ille*
C. 1.49   Et que sunt dei deo or [elles] 3e don *ylle*."
C. 1.61   Adam and Eue he eggede to *ylle*,
C. 1.85   And doth þe werkes þerwith and wilneth no man *ylle*,
C. 3.332   And efte haue hit a3eyne of hem þat don *ille*
C.20.301   Body and soule beth myne, bothe gode and *ille*.
C.20.318   As two godes, with god, bothe goed and *ille*.
C.20.432   For holy writ wol þat y be wreke of hem þat wrouhte *ille*–

ille adj *ille adj.* C 2
C.10.94   And halie with þe hoked ende [*i]lle* men to gode
C.16.193   And when y wol do or [nat do] gode dedes or *ille*

ille adv *ille adv.* A 5; B 5; C 5 ille (2) ylle (3)
A.Pr.102   As dikeris & delueris þat doþ here dede *ille*
A. 2.156   I wolde be wroken of þise wrecchis þat werchen so *ille*,
A. 5.95   I deme men þere [hy] don *ille*, & 3et I do wers;
A. 5.244   Dampne me nou3t at domisday for þat I dede so *ille*.'
A. 7.190   For I wot wel, be þou ywent, hy wile werche *ille*;

B.Pr.224   As dykeres and delueres þat doon hire ded[e] *ille*
B. 2.195   I wolde be wroken of þo wrecches þat wercheþ so *ille*,
B. 5.115   [I] deme [men þere hij] doon *ille*, [and yet] I do werse;
B. 5.470   Dampne me noȝt at domesday for þat I dide so *ille*.'
B. 6.204   For I woot wel, be þow went þei wol werche *ille*;
C.Pr.228   As dykers and deluers þat doth here dedis *ylle*
C. 6.324   Dampne me nat at domesday for þat y dede so *ylle*.'
C. 7.146   For dedes that we han don *ylle* dampned sholde we ben neuere
C. 8.210   For y woet wel, be [thow] went, worche þei wol ful *ille*;
C.20.429   Where they deye or dey nat, dede they neuere so *ille*.

ylope > lepen; ilore ylorn ylost > lesen; ylow > lyen; ymaad ymad > maken

imade v *imaken v.* C 1
C. 5.77   *Imade* here kyn knyhtes and knyhtes fees ypurchased,

imaed > maken

ymage n *image n.* A 2 Image (1) ymage (1); B 2; C 1
A. 1.48   And þe [*Image* ilike], þat þereinne standis.
A.10.35   Saue man þat he made *ymage* to himselue,
B. 1.50   And þe *ymage* [y]lik[e] þat þerInne stondeþ.
B. 9.34   [Saue man þat he made *ymage*] to hymself,
C.20.326   And as thowe bigyledest godes *ymag[e]* in goynge of an addre,

imagenatyf > imaginatif; imageny > imagynen

ymaginacion n *imaginacioun n.* B 1; C 1 ymaginacioun
B.20.33   Wenynge is no wysdom, ne wys *ymaginacion*:
C.22.33   Wenyng is no wisdoem ne wyse *ymaginacioun*:

ymaginatif adj *imaginatif adj.& n.* B 5; C 4 ymagenatyf (1) ymaginatyf
    (2) ymagynatif (1)
B.10.119   *Ymaginatif* herafterward shal answere to [youre] purpos.
B.12.1   'I am *ymaginatif*', quod he; 'ydel was I neuere
B.12.280   'Contra!' quod *Ymaginatif* þoo and comsed to loure,
B.13.14   And how þat *Ymaginatif* in dremels me tolde
B.13.19   And siþen how *ymaginatif* seide 'vix saluabitur [iustus]',
C.14.1   'I am *ymagenatyf*,' quod he; 'ydel was y neuere
C.14.202   'Contra!' quod *ymagynatif* tho and comesed to loure
C.15.17   And how þat *ymaginatyf* in dremeles me tolde
C.15.21   And y merueyle[d] in herte how *ymaginatyf* saide

ymagynen v *imaginen v.* B 3 ymagynede (1) ymagynen (2); C 1 ymageny
B.13.288   Wiþ Inwit and wiþ outwit *ymagynen* and studie
B.13.357   And *ymagynede* how he it myȝte haue
B.19.277   And whoso ete þat *ymagynen* he sholde,
C.21.277   [And] hoso ete þat *ymageny* he sholde,

ymaymed > maymeth; ymaked > maken; ymanered > manered; ymaried > marien; ymartired > martre; ymedled > medle; ymorthred > murþere

ympe n *impe n.* B 1 Impes; C 1
B. 5.138   And þe Couentes Gardyner for to graffen *Impes*.
C.18.6   Euene in þe myddes an *ympe*, as hit were,

impe v *impen v.* B 2 impe (1) ymped (1)
B. 5.139   On lymitours and listres lesynges I *ymped*
B. 9.152   *Impe* on an Ellere, and if þyn appul be swete

impossible adj *impossible adj.* B 2 impossible (1) inpossible (1); C 1
    inposible
B.10.341   Poule preueþ it *impossible*, riche men [in] heuene;
B.18.419   For *inpossible* is no þyng to hym þat is almyghty.'
C.20.462   For *inposible* is no thynge to hym þat is almyhty.'

impugnen v *impugnen v.* A 1 inpugnid; B 4 impugned (1) impugnen (1)
    impugneþ (1) inpugned (1); C 4 enpugneth (1) inpugne (1) inpugnede
    (2)
A. 8.152   And how þe prest *inpugnid* it al be [pu]re resoun,
B.Pr.109   To han [þe] power þat Peter hadde–*impugnen* I nelle–
B. 7.153   And how þe preest *inpugned* it wiþ two propre wordes.
B.11.304   If fals latyn be in þat lettre þe lawe it *impugneþ*,
B.13.124   For oon Piers þe Plowman haþ *impugned* vs alle,
C.Pr.136   To haue þe power þat Peter hadde *inpugne* y nelle
C. 9.302   And how þe prest *inpugnede* hit thorw two propre wordes.
C.13.118   Yf fals latyn be in þat lettre þe lawe hit *enpugneth*,
C.15.130   For Peres loue þe palmare ȝent, þat *inpugnede* ones

in adv *in adv.* A 8; B 19; C 18
A. 4.31   Curteisliche þe king þanne com *in* to resoun,
A. 5.139   Whanne it com *in* cuppemel; þat craft my wyf vside.
A. 5.157   Þanne goþ [glotoun *in*], and grete oþis aftir.
A. 6.68   He is fre[þ]id *in* wiþ Floreynes & oþere [fees] manye.
A. 6.92   And ȝif grace graunte þe to gon *in* [on] þis wise,
A. 6.109   Largenesse þe lady let *in* wel manye.
A. 7.287   Ne no beggere ete bred þat benis *in* come,
A.11.47   Is non to nymen hym *In* ne his [noye] amende,
B. 4.44   Curteisly þe kyng þanne com [*in* to] Reson,

B. 5.223   [Whan] it cam *In* cuppemele, þis craft my wif vsed.
B. 5.306   Thanne goþ Gloton *In* and grete oþes after.
B. 5.581   He is fryþed *In* wiþ floryns and oþere fees manye;
B. 5.605   And if grace graunte þee to go *in* [in] þis wise
B. 5.623   Largenesse þe lady let *in* [wel] manye;
B.10.61   Is noon to nyme hym [*in*, ne] his [n]oy amende,
B.11.114   And plukked *in* Pauci pryueliche and leet þe remenaunt go rome.'
B.11.217   Crist to a commune womman seide, in [comen] at a feste,
B.13.31   Conscience called hym *In* and curteislche seide
B.15.530   And crepe [*in*] amonges curatours, confessen ageyn þe lawe:
B.17.332   That sholde brynge *in* bettre wode or blowe it til it brende.
B.18.269   If þis kyng come *In* mankynde wole he fecche
B.18.320   That crist may come *In*, þe kynges sone of heuene!'
B.19.7   And com *in* wiþ a cros bifore þe comune peple,
B.19.168   Crist cam *In*, and al closed boþe dore and yates,
B.20.243   And curteisliche conforted hem and called *in* alle freres,
B.20.344   Coom *in* þus ycoped at a Court þere I dwelde,
B.20.349   Lat *in* þe frere and his felawe, and make hem fair cheere.
C. 6.231   When hit cam *in* coppemele; this crafte my wyf vsede.
C. 6.361   Thenne goth glotoun *in* and grete othes aftur.
C. 7.228   Is frithed *in* with floreynes and othere fees monye;
C. 7.253   And may lede *in* þat he loueth as here lef lyketh.
C. 7.254   And yf grace graunte the to go *in* [in] this wyse
C. 7.275   Largenesse þ[e] lady lat *in* ful monye,
C. 7.276   Noen of hem alle helpe may *in* betere
C.11.42   Is non so hende to haue hym [*in*] but hote hym go þer god is.
C.12.49   And plihte *in* pauci preueiliche and lette þe remenaunt go rome.'
C.17.280   And crepe *in* amonges curatours and confessen aȝeyn þe lawe:
C.19.312   That sholde brynge *in* bettere wode or blowen hit til hit brente.
C.20.277   Yf this kyng come *in* mankynde wol he fecche
C.20.286   That no liht lepe *in* at louer ne at loupe.
C.20.363   That Crist may come *in*, the kynges sone of h[e]uene!'
C.21.7   And cam *in* with a cros bifore þe comune peple
C.21.168   Crist cam *in*, and al closed bothe dore and ȝates,
C.22.243   And cortey[s]liche confortede hem and calde *in* all freres
C.22.349   Lat *in* þe frere and his felawe and make hem fayere chiere.

in prep *in prep* A 293; B 987; C 982
A.Pr.1   *IN* a somer sesoun whanne softe was the sonne
A.Pr.3   *In* abite as an Ermyte, vnholy of werkis,
A.Pr.4   Wente wyde *in* þis world wondris to here,
A.Pr.12   þat I was *in* a wildernesse, wiste I neuere where;
A.Pr.21   *In* settyng & sowyng swonke ful harde;
A.Pr.24   *In* cuntenaunce of cloþing comen disgisid.
A.Pr.25   *In* preyours & penaunce putten hem manye,
A.Pr.27   *In* hope [for] to haue heueneriche blisse,
A.Pr.28   As ancris & Ermytes þat holden hem *in* [here] cellis,
A.Pr.29   Coueite not *in* cuntre to cairen aboute
A.Pr.43   *In* glotonye, god wot, go þei to bedde,
A.Pr.48   Wenten forþ *in* here wey wiþ many wise talis,
A.Pr.53   Cloþide hem *in* copis to be knowen from oþere;
A.Pr.62   Manye ferlis han fallen *in* a fewe ȝeris.
A.Pr.84   Þere houide an hundrit *in* houuis of silk,
A.Pr.97   I sauȝ *in* þat sem[b]le as ȝe shuln here aftir,
A. 1.3   A louely lady of lire *in* lynene ycloþid
A. 1.8   Haue þei worsshipe *in* þis world þei kepe no betere:
A. 1.19   *In* mesurable maner to make ȝow at ese;
A. 1.20   And comaundite of his curteisie *in* comoun þre þinges;
A. 1.22   And rekne hem *in* resoun; reherse þou hem aftir.
A. 1.27   For loth, *in* his lyf dayes, for lykyng of drink
A. 1.29   [Delyted hym *in* drynke as the deuyl wolde],
A. 1.39   [And þat] shend[iþ] þi soule; set it *in* þin herte;
A. 1.45   Þo þe peple hym aposide with a peny *in* þe temple
A. 1.57   'Þe dungeon *in* þe dale þat dredful is of siȝt:
A. 1.69   Þanne hadde I wondir *in* my wyt what womman it were
A. 1.93   And riden & rappe doun *in* reaumes aboute,
A. 1.96   For dauid, *in* hise dayes, dubbide kniȝtes,
A. 1.99   And nouȝt to fasten a friday *in* fyue score wynter,
A. 1.102   And whoso passiþ þat poynt is apostata *in* his ordre,
A. 1.105   Ȝaf hem miȝt *in* his mageste, þe meryere hem þouȝte,
A. 1.109   Lucifer wiþ legionis leride it *in* heuene,
A. 1.114   Summe *in* eir, summe in erþe, summe in helle depe.
A. 1.114   Summe in eir, summe *in* erþe, summe in helle depe.
A. 1.114   Summe in eir, summe in erþe, summe *in* helle depe.
A. 1.120   And enden as I er seide, *in* perfite werkis,
A. 1.122   Þere treuþe is *in* trinite & tron[iþ] h[e]m alle.
A. 1.128   Be what craft *in* my cors it compsiþ, & where.'
A. 1.130   It is a kynde knowyng þat kenneþ *in* þin herte
A. 1.137   And ek þe plante of pes; preche it *in* þin harpe
A. 1.139   For *in* kynde knowyng in herte þer comsiþ a miȝt,
A. 1.139   For in kynde knowyng *in* herte þer comsiþ a miȝt,
A. 1.146   Here miȝt þou sen ensaumplis *in* hymself one
A. 1.154   And ek as chast as a child þat *in* chirche wepiþ,
A. 1.157   Ȝe ne haue no more meryt *in* [masse] ne in [houres]

A. 1.157   ȝe ne haue no more meryt in [masse] ne *in* [houres]
A. 1.159   For Iames þe ientil ioynide *in* his bokis
A. 1.162   Chastite wiþoute charite worþ cheynide in helle;
A. 1.168   Such chastite wiþoute charite worþ cheynid *in* helle.
A. 1.174   For þise arn þe wordis writen *in* þe Euaungelie:
A. 2.10   Icorounid *in* a coroune, þe king haþ non betere;
A. 2.13   *In* red scarlet robid & ribande wiþ gold.
A. 2.18   *In* þe popis paleis heo is preuy as myselue;
A. 2.30   ȝif þou wilnest to wone wiþ treuþe *in* his blisse.
A. 2.37   And feffe mede þer[myd] *in* mariage for euere.
A. 2.40   *In* myddis a mounteyne at mydmorewe tide
A. 2.47   *In* what maner þat mede in mariage was feffid;
A. 2.47   In what maner þat mede *in* mariage was feffid;
A. 2.50   *In* foreward þat falshed shal fynde hire for euere,
A. 2.59   To be present *in* pride for pouere [or for] riche,
A. 2.61   Wiþ alle þe lordsshipe of leccherie in lengþe & in brede;
A. 2.61   Wiþ alle þe lordsshipe of leccherie in lengþe & *in* brede;
A. 2.66   *In* al þe signiure of slouþe I se[se] hem togidere;
A. 2.70   Here soulis to sathanas to synken *in* pyne,
A. 2.71   Þere to wone wiþ wrong while god is *in* heuene.'
A. 2.72   *In* witnesse of whiche þing wrong was þe furste,
A. 2.77   *In* þe date of þe deuil þe dede is asselid
A. 2.104   And ȝif he fynde ȝow *in* defaute, & wiþ fals holden,
A. 2.121   Iuggen ȝow ioyntly *in* ioye for euere'.
A. 2.123   And let somoune alle þe segges [*in* shires abouten],
A. 2.135   'And let apparaille þise prouisours *in* palfreis wise;
A. 2.139   Paulynes peple, for pleyntes *in* constorie,
A. 2.146   And mede *in* þe myddis, & al þis mene aftir.
A. 2.175   Besshette hym *in* here shoppis to shewen here ware;
A. 2.182   Wysshen hym & wypide him & wounde hym *in* cloþis,
A. 3.30   And *in* constory at court callen here names.
A. 3.36   And seide [wel] softely, *in* shrifte as it were,
A. 3.47   'We haue a wyndowe [*in*] werching wile stonde vs wel heiȝe;
A. 3.58   Neiþer *in* siȝt ne in þi soule, for god hymself knowiþ
A. 3.58   Neiþer in siȝt ne *in* þi soule, for god hymself knowiþ
A. 3.61   To writen *in* wyndowis of ȝoure wel dedis,
A. 3.73   Of þat þe pore peple shulde putte *in* here wombe.
A. 3.89   To haue ȝeftis [or ȝerisȝiuys] *in* ȝouþe or in elde.
A. 3.89   To haue ȝeftis [or ȝerisȝiuys] in ȝouþe or *in* elde.
A. 3.113   *In* trist of hire tresour she teniþ [wel] manye;
A. 3.122   To [monkis], to [mynstrelis], to myselis *in* heggis.
A. 3.131   To be cursid *in* constorie heo countiþ not a risshe;
A. 3.134   She may neiȝ as muche do *in* a moneþ ones
A. 3.135   As ȝoure secre sel *in* seue score dayes.
A. 3.144   Barouns & burgeis she bringeþ *in* sorewe;
A. 3.176   *In* normandie was he nouȝt anoyed for my sake,
A. 3.190   He shulde haue be lord of þat lond in lengþe & in brede,
A. 3.190   He shulde haue be lord of þat lond in lengþe & *in* brede,
A. 3.208   Þe king haþ [m]ede of his men to make pes *in* londis;
A. 3.219   Þat on god of his grace gyueþ *in* his blisse.
A. 3.221   Þe prophet prechiþ it & put it *in* þe sauter:
A. 3.227   And þerof sei[þ] þe sauter *in* a salmis ende
A. 3.236   *In* marchaundie is no mede, I may it wel auowe;
A. 4.14   And riȝt renneþ to resoun & rouniþ *in* his ere;
A. 4.26   *In* cheker & in chauncerie, to be dischargid of þinges,
A. 4.26   In cheker & *in* chauncerie, to be dischargid of þinges,
A. 4.43   Forstalliþ my feiris, fiȝteþ *in* my chepyng,
A. 4.59   For boþe þi lyf & þi lond liþ *in* his grace.'
A. 4.72   & comaundid a cunstable to caste hym *in* yrens]:
A. 4.95   But resoun haue reuþe on hym he shal reste *in* þe stokkis
A. 4.102   And pernelis purfile be put *in* hire hucche;
A. 4.108   And do it *in* dede to drawe vs to goode;
A. 4.118   Whil mede haþ þe maistrie to mo[te] *in* þis halle.
A. 4.122   Shulde neuere wrong *in* þis world þat I wyte miȝte
A. 4.129   And ȝif þou werche [it *in*] werk I wedde myne eris
A. 4.135   Þere nas man *in* þe mothalle, more ne lesse,
A. 5.17   *In* ensaumple, se[gges], þat ȝe shulde do þe betere;
A. 5.19   And turnide vpward here tail *in* toknyng of drede
A. 5.27   And kep[e] it *in* hire coffre for catel at nede.
A. 5.53   Of alle þat I haue had enuye *in* myn herte.'
A. 5.60   He was as pale as a p[e]let, [*in*] þe palesie he semide,
A. 5.61   He was cloþid *in* a caurymaury, I [couþe] it nouȝt descryue;
A. 5.64   As a lek þat hadde leyn longe *in* þe sonne,
A. 5.70   Walewiþ *in* my wombe & waxiþ as I wene.
A. 5.72   Such wynd *in* my wombe wexiþ er I dyne.
A. 5.74   And blamide hym behynde his bak to bringe hym *in* fame;
A. 5.81   Whanne I mette hym *in* market þat I most hatide
A. 5.111   *In* a torn tabbard of twelue wynter age,
A. 5.127   Putte hem *in* a pressour, & pynnede hem þereinne
A. 5.136   Þe beste *in* my bedchaumbre lay be þe wouȝ.
A. 5.174   Þo risen vp *in* rape & ro[wn]eden togideris,
A. 5.181   *In* couenaunt þat clement [shulde þe cuppe felle],
A. 5.189   He pisside a potel *in* a paternoster while,

A. 5.210   'Shal neuere fissh on þe Friday defie *in* my wombe
A. 6.4   Aparailid as a paynym *in* pilgrim[ys] wyse.
A. 6.6   *In* a [weþewindes] wyse [ywounden] aboute;
A. 6.15   At bedlem, at babiloyne, I haue ben *in* boþe;
A. 6.16   *In* armonye, in alisaundre, in manye oþere places.
A. 6.16   In armonye, *in* alisaundre, in manye oþere places.
A. 6.16   In armonye, in alisaundre, *in* manye oþere places.
A. 6.18   Þat I haue walkid wel wide in wet & in driȝe,
A. 6.18   Þat I haue walkid wel wide in wet & *in* driȝe,
A. 6.24   Axen aftir hym, er now *in* þis place.'
A. 6.35   Þere is no labourer *in* þis lordsshipe þat he louiþ beter
A. 6.50   Þat ȝe loue hym leuere þanne þe lif *in* ȝoure hertis;
A. 6.51   And þanne ȝoure neiȝebours next *in* none wise apeir[e]
A. 6.55   Wadiþ *in* þat watir & wasshiþ ȝow wel þere,
A. 6.93   Þou shalt se treuþe himself wel sitte *in* þin herte
A. 6.96   For he haþ enuye to hym þat *in* þin herte sitteþ
A. 7.7   'Þis were a long lettyng,' quaþ a lady *in* a scleire;
A. 7.29   *In* couenaunt þat þou kepe holy[k]ir[k]e and myself
A. 7.43   *In* a wel perilous place þat purcatorie hattiþ;
A. 7.52   'And I shal apparaille me,' quaþ perkyn, '*in* pilgrym[ys] wyse,
A. 7.56   And heng his hoper at his hals *in* stede of a scrippe;
A. 7.60   Shal haue be oure lord þe more here *in* heruist;
A. 7.62   And alle kyne crafty men þat conne lyue *in* treuþe,
A. 7.86   He is holden, I hope, to haue me *in* mynde,
A. 7.87   And monewe me *in* his memorie among alle cristene.
A. 7.93   I wile worsshipe þerewiþ treuþe *in* my lyue,
A. 7.109   'Be þe prince of paradis!' quaþ piers þo *in* wraþþe,
A. 7.124   Suche wastours *in* þis world his werkmen distroyeþ;
A. 7.133   Ankeris & heremytes þat holde hem *in* here sellis
A. 7.159   Hungir *in* haste þanne hente wastour be þe mawe,
A. 7.184   And pieris was proud þerof, & putte hem *in* office,
A. 7.219   And sapience seiþ þe same, I saiȝ it *in* þe bible:
A. 7.226   And ȝaf [it] hym *in* haste þat hadde ten before,
A. 7.234   The sauter seiþ *in* þe salme of Beati omnes:
A. 7.274   Be þat I hope to haue heruest *in* my croft,
A. 7.277   Benes & [b]ake applis hy brouȝte *in* here lappe[s],
A. 7.280   Hungir [eet] þis *in* haste & askide aftir more.
A. 7.289   Ne non halpeny ale *in* no wyse drynke,
A. 8.8   Part *in* þ[at] pardoun þe pope haþ hem grauntid.
A. 8.10   And r[iȝt]fulliche *in* reaum rewliþ þe peple
A. 8.12   Wiþ patriarkes *in* paradis to pleiȝe þereaftir.
A. 8.20   Marchauntis *in* þe margyn hadde manye ȝeris,
A. 8.51   Counfortiþ hym *in* þat cas, coueitiþ nouȝt his goodis,
A. 8.59   His pardoun *in* purcatorie wel [petit] is, I trowe,
A. 8.65   And lyuen in loue & [*in*] lawe, for here louȝ herte
A. 8.65   And lyuen in loue & [*in*] lawe, for here louȝ herte
A. 8.67   Beggeris & bidderis ben not *in* þe bulle
A. 8.72   Þei lyue nouȝt *in* loue, ne no lawe holden,
A. 8.76   Or his bak or his bon þei breken *in* his ȝouþe,
A. 8.93   *In* two lynes it lay & nouȝt o lettre more,
A. 8.94   And was writen riȝt þus *in* witnesse of treuþe:
A. 8.108   Þe prophet his p[a]yn e[et] *in* penaunce & in wepyng
A. 8.108   Þe prophet his p[a]yn e[et] in penaunce & *in* wepyng
A. 8.113   Ne soliciti sitis he seiþ *in* his gospel,
A. 8.115   Þe foulis *in* þe firmament, who fynt hem a wynter?
A. 8.132   And for peris loue þe plouȝman wel pensif *in* herte,
A. 8.141   As daniel deui[n]ide *in* dede it fel aftir:
A. 8.147   It befel as his fadir seide *in* faraos tyme.
A. 8.176   Þeiȝ þou be founde *in* þe fraternite among þe foure ordris,
A. 9.1   Thus, yrobid *in* rosset, I rombide aboute
A. 9.25   Let bringe a man *in* a bot amydde a brood watir;
A. 9.28   For stande he neuere so stif he stumbliþ *in* þe waggyng,
A. 9.39   Synnes þe sad man seuene [siþes] *in* þe day.
A. 9.43   Þat, þeiȝ þi body bowe as bot doþ *in* þe watir,
A. 9.52   And [g]iue þe grace on þis erþe *in* good lif to ende'.
A. 9.60   Þat euere dremide driȝt *in* doute, as I wene.
A. 9.87   Is hokid at þat on ende to holde men *in* good lif.
A. 9.88   A pik is *in* þat potent to pungen adoun þe wykkide,
A. 9.94   Þanne shulde þe kyng come & casten hem *in* presoun,
A. 9.95   And putten hem *in* penaunce wiþoute pite or grace,
A. 9.116   Þanne þouȝt, *in* þat tyme, seide þis wordis:
A. 9.117   'Where þat dowel, & dobet, & dobest beþ *in* londe,
A.10.2   *In* a castel þat kynde made of foure skenis þinges.
A.10.4   Þat is Anima, þat oueral *in* þe body wandriþ,
A.10.45   Ac *in* þe herte is hire hom heiȝest of alle.
A.10.49   Inwyt *in* þe heuid is, & an help to þe soule,
A.10.51   *In* rewele & in resoun, but reccheles it make.
A.10.51   In rewele & *in* resoun, but reccheles it make.
A.10.54   *In* manis brayn is he most & miȝtiest to knowe.
A.10.58   *In* ȝonge fauntes & folis, wiþ hem failiþ Inwyt,
A.10.59   And ek *in* sottis þou miȝt se, þat sitten at þe nale.
A.10.60   Þei helde ale *in* here hed til Inwyt be drenchit,
A.10.63   Ouer suche maner of men miȝt *in* here soulis.

A.10.64	Ac *in* fauntis ne in folis þe [fend] haþ no miȝt
A.10.64	Ac in fauntis ne *in* folis þe [fend] haþ no miȝt
A.10.71	A[c] iche wiȝt *in* þis world þat haþ wys vndirstonding
A.10.78	To routen ne to resten ne ro[t]en *in* þin herte;
A.10.84	And alle kynde scoleris *in* scole to lerne.
A.10.89	Wilne þou neuere *in* þis world, [wy], for to do betere,
A.10.109	Poule þe apostel *in* his pistil wrot it
A.10.110	*In* ensaumple [þat] suche shulde not renne aboute,
A.10.111	And for wisdom is writen & witnessid *in* chirches:
A.10.118	Þus *in* dred liþ dowel, [and] dobet to suffre,
A.10.140	Ben conseyuid *in* cursid tyme as kaym was on Eue.
A.10.143	An aungel *in* angir hiȝte h[e]m to wende
A.10.145	*In* tene & trauaille to here lyues ende;
A.10.146	*In* þat curside constellacioun þei knewe togideris,
A.10.148	Caym þei hym callide, *in* cursid tyme engendrit.
A.10.176	Þat *in* þe [shynglid] ship shal ben ysauid:
A.10.189	Þat neuere shal bere [barne] but it be *in* armes.
A.10.190	*In* gelosie, ioyeles, & ianglyng [a] bedde,
A.10.202	For [vn]tyme, treweliche, betwyn m[a]n & womm[a]n
A.10.207	Þat iche man haue a make *in* [mariage] of wedlak
A.11.12	Þanne al þe precious perrie þat *in* paradis wexiþ.
A.11.23	Iob þe ientile *in* his gestis seide it:
A.11.24	And he þat haþ holy writ ay *in* his mouþ,
A.11.39	At mete [*in* here] merþe, whanne mynstralis ben stille,
A.11.44	And gnawen god *in* [þe gorge] whanne here guttis fullen.
A.11.51	Nere mercy *in* mene men more þan in riche
A.11.51	Nere mercy in mene men more þan *in* riche
A.11.53	God is muche *in* þe [gorge] of þis grete maistris,
A.11.55	And so seiþ þe sauter, se[ke] it *in* Memento:
A.11.57	And han [hym] muchel *in* here mouþ, ac mene men in herte.
A.11.57	And han [hym] muchel in here mouþ, ac mene men *in* herte.
A.11.66	"Why wolde oure sauiour suffre such a worm *in* his blisse
A.11.70	Suche motifs þei meuen, þise maistris *in* here glorie,
A.11.78	And preye hym of pardoun & penaunce [*in*] þi lyue,
A.11.81	I wolde his eiȝen wern *in* his ars & his hele aftir
A.11.90	But he lyue *in* þe leste degre þat longiþ to dowel
A.11.99	*In* signe þat I shulde beseke hire of grace.
A.11.123	Þat iche wiȝt be *in* wille his wyt þe to shewen;
A.11.146	*In* oþer science it seiþ, I saiȝ it in catoun,
A.11.146	In oþer science it seiþ, I saiȝ it *in* catoun,
A.11.154	And seide it hymself *in* ensaumple for þe beste.
A.11.189	Counforte þe carful þat *in* castel ben fetterid,
A.11.195	Sire dobest haþ ben [*in* office], so is he best worþi
A.11.196	Be þat god *in* þe gospel grauntiþ & techiþ:
A.11.204	Gregory þe grete clerk, a good pope *in* his tyme,
A.11.205	Of religioun þe rewele he reherside *in* his morals,
A.11.206	And seide it *in* ensaumple þat þei shulde do þe betere:
A.11.216	Arn more *in* his mynde þan þe memorie of his foundours.
A.11.229	Poul prouiþ it is vnpossible, riche men *in* heuene.
A.11.230	Ac pore men *in* pacience & penaunce togidere
A.11.231	Hauen eritage *in* heuene, ac riche men non.'
A.11.237	Þat arn vncristene *in* þat cas may cristene an heþene,
A.11.239	Haue eritage *in* heuene as an heiȝ cristene.
A.11.251	And siþen he[þen] to helpe *in* hope hem to amende.
A.11.253	For he seiþ it hymself *in* his ten hestis;
A.11.256	I shal punisshen *in* purcatory or in þe put of helle
A.11.256	I shal punisshen in purcatory or *in* þe put of helle
A.11.259	To wyte what is dowel witterly *in* herte,
A.11.260	For howso I werche *in* þis world, [wrong] oþer ellis,
A.11.262	*In* þe legende of lif longe er I were,
A.11.269	Boþe enden, as I er seide, *in* world in his tyme?
A.11.269	Boþe in werk & in woord, *in* world in his tyme?
A.11.269	Boþe in werk & in woord, in world *in* his tyme?
A.11.269	Boþe in werk & *in* woord, in world in his tyme?
A.11.271	And al holy chirche holden hem *in* helle.
A.11.272	And was þere neuere *in* þis world to wysere of werkis,
A.11.274	Taken ensampl[e] of here sawis *in* sarmonis þat þei maken,
A.11.291	And arn no[ne], forsoþe, souereynes *in* heuene
A.11.292	As þise þat wrouȝte wykkidly *in* world whanne þei were.
A.11.306	And is to mene *in* oure mouþ, more ne lesse,
A.12.15	Of þe kynde cardinal wit, and cristned *in* a font,
A.12.21	Til þo wrecches ben *in* wil here synne to lete."
A.12.26	*In* þe passioun, whan pilat aposed god almyȝthi,
A.12.42	Þat lady þan low and lauȝthe me *in* here armes
A.12.58	Many ferlys me byfel *in* a fewe ȝeris.
A.12.61	I stode stille *in* a stodie and stared abowte,
A.12.64	To lyf *in* his lordshepe longyt my weye
A.12.66	I shal felle þat freke *in* a fewe dayes.'
A.12.95	Þat þi play be plentevous *in* paradys with aungelys.
A.12.112	To lyue as þat lord lykyþ þat lyf in hem putte:
A.12.114	And alle lordes þat louyn him lely *in* herte,
B.Pr.1	*IN* a somer seson whan softe was þe sonne
B.Pr.3	*In* habite as an heremite, vnholy of werkes,
B.Pr.4	Wente wide *in* þis world wondres to here.
B.Pr.12	That I was *in* a wildernesse, wiste I neuere where.
B.Pr.21	*In* settynge and sowynge swonken ful harde;
B.Pr.24	*In* contenaunce of cloþynge comen d[is]gised.
B.Pr.25	*In* preieres and penaunc[e] putten hem manye,
B.Pr.27	*In* hope [for] to haue heueneriche blisse.
B.Pr.28	As Ancres and heremites þat holden hem *in* hire selles,
B.Pr.29	Coueiten noȝt *in* contree to [cairen] aboute
B.Pr.43	*In* glotonye, god woot, go þei to bedde,
B.Pr.48	Wenten forþ *in* hire wey wiþ many wise tales,
B.Pr.56	Cloþed hem *in* copes to ben knowen from oþere;
B.Pr.65	Manye ferlies han fallen *in* a fewe yeres.
B.Pr.88	That han cure vnder crist, and crownynge *in* tokene
B.Pr.91	Liggen at Londoun *in* Lenten and ellis.
B.Pr.93	*In* Cheker and in Chauncelrie chalangen hise dettes
B.Pr.93	In Cheker and *in* Chauncelrie chalangen hise dettes
B.Pr.96	And *in* stede of Stywardes sitten and demen.
B.Pr.99	Lest crist *in* Consistorie acorse ful manye.
B.Pr.105	There [crist is *in*] kyngdom, to close and to shette,
B.Pr.108	And power presumed *in* hem a pope to make
B.Pr.110	For *in* loue and lettrure þe eleccion bilongeþ;
B.Pr.127	And for þi riȝtful rulyng be rewarded *in* heuene'.
B.Pr.128	And siþen *in* þe Eyr an heiȝ an Aungel of heuene
B.Pr.129	Lowed to speke *in* latyn, for lewed men ne koude
B.Pr.143	Thanne [comsed] al þe commune crye *in* vers of latyn
B.Pr.154	Cracchen vs or clawen vs, and *in* hise clouches holde
B.Pr.160	'I haue yseyen segges', quod he, '*in* þe Cite of Londoun
B.Pr.163	Boþe *in* wareyne and in waast where hem [leue] like[þ];
B.Pr.163	Boþe in wareyne and *in* waast where hem [leue] like[þ];
B.Pr.173	And peeren *in* his presence þe while hym pleye likeþ,
B.Pr.177	Ther ne was Raton *in* þe route, for al þe Reaume of Fraunce,
B.Pr.210	Deuyne ye, for I ne dar, by deere god *in* heuene.
B.Pr.211	Yet houed þer an hundred *in* howues of selk,
B.Pr.218	I seiȝ *in* þis assemblee, as ye shul here after.
B.Pr.221	Taillours, Tynkers and Tollers *in* Markettes,
B. 1.3	A louely lady of leere *in* lynnen ycloþed
B. 1.8	Haue þei worship *in* þis world þei [kepe] no bettre;
B. 1.19	*In* mesurable manere to make yow at ese;
B. 1.20	And comaunded of his curteisie *in* commune þree þynges;
B. 1.27	For Lot, *in* hise lifdayes, for likynge of drynke,
B. 1.29	Delited hym *in* drynke as þe deuel wolde,
B. 1.33	And þere gat *in* glotonie gerles þat were cherles.
B. 1.41	And that [shendeþ] þi soule; [set] it *in* þin herte.
B. 1.47	Tho þe poeple hym apposede wiþ a peny *in* þe temple
B. 1.59	'Th[e] dongeon *in* þe dale þat dredful is of siȝte–
B. 1.71	Thanne hadde I wonder *in* my wit what womman it weere
B. 1.95	Riden and rappen doun *in* Reaumes aboute,
B. 1.98	/For Dauid *in* hise dayes dubbed knyȝtes,
B. 1.101	And nauȝt to fasten o friday *in* fyue score wynter,
B. 1.104	And whoso passe[þ] þat point [is] Apostata *in* [his] ordre.
B. 1.107	Yaf hem myȝt *in* his maiestee, þe murier hem þouȝte,
B. 1.111	Lucifer wiþ legions lerned it *in* heuene
B. 1.114	And fel fro þat felawshipe *in* a fendes liknesse
B. 1.117	Lopen out wiþ Lucifer *in* loþliche forme
B. 1.118	For þei leueden vpon [Lucifer] þat lyed *in* þis manere:
B. 1.121	But fellen out *in* fendes liknesse [ful] nyne dayes togideres
B. 1.123	And [stable and stynte] and stonden *in* quiete.
B. 1.125	Somme *in* Eyr, somme in erþe, somme in helle depe.
B. 1.125	Somme in Eyr, somme *in* erþe, somme in helle depe.
B. 1.125	Somme in Eyr, somme in erþe, somme *in* helle depe.
B. 1.131	And enden, as I er seide, *in* truþe þat is þe beste.
B. 1.133	Ther Treuþe is *in* Trinitee and troneþ hem alle,
B. 1.139	By what craft *in* my cors it comseþ, and where.'
B. 1.141	To litel latyn þow lernedest, leode, *in* þi youþe:
B. 1.142	It is a kynde knowyng þat kenneþ *in* þyn herte
B. 1.164	And *in* þe herte þere is þe heed and þe heiȝe welle.
B. 1.165	For *in* kynde knowynge in herte þer [comseþ a myȝt],
B. 1.165	For in kynde knowynge *in* herte þer [comseþ a myȝt],
B. 1.172	Here myȝtow sen ensample[s] *in* hymself oone
B. 1.180	And as chaste as a child þat *in* chirche wepeþ,
B. 1.183	Ye ne haue na moore merite *in* masse n[e] in houres
B. 1.183	Ye ne haue na moore merite in masse n[e] *in* houres
B. 1.185	For Iames þe gentile [Ioyned] *in* hise bokes
B. 1.188	Chastite wiþouten charite worþ cheyned *in* helle;
B. 1.194	Swich chastite wiþouten charite worþ cheyned *in* helle.
B. 1.200	Fo[r] þise [ben wordes] writen *in* þe [euauangelie]:
B. 2.10	Ycorouned [*in*] a coroune, þe kyng haþ noon bettre.
B. 2.23	*In* þe popes Paleis she is pryuee as myselue,
B. 2.33	Shal be my lord and I his leef *in* þe heiȝe heuene.
B. 2.53	And how Mede was ymaried *in* Metels me þouȝte;
B. 2.80	To be Princes *in* pride and pouerte to despise,
B. 2.88	*In* bargaynes and brocages wiþ þe Burgh of þefte,
B. 2.89	[Wiþ] al þe lordshipe of leccherie *in* lengþe and in brede,

B. 2.89   [Wiþ] al þe lordshipe of leccherie in lengþe and *in* brede,
B. 2.90   As *in* werkes and in wordes and waityn[g] with eiȝes
B. 2.90   As in werkes and *in* wordes and waityn[g] with eiȝes
B. 2.91   And in we[n]es and in wisshynges and wiþ ydel þouȝtes
B. 2.91   And in we[n]es and *in* wisshynges and wiþ ydel þouȝtes
B. 2.96   And *in* fastynge dayes to frete er ful tyme were.
B. 2.107   And with hym to wonye [*in*] wo while god is in heuene.'
B. 2.107   And with hym to wonye [in] wo while god is *in* heuene.'
B. 2.108   *In* witnesse of which þyng wrong was þe firste,
B. 2.113   'In þe date of þe deuel þ[e] dede [is asseled]
B. 2.130   That Fals is fe[ynt]lees and fikel *in* hise werkes,
B. 2.140   And if he fynde yow *in* defaute, and with [fals] holde,
B. 2.157   Iuggen yow ioyntly *in* ioie for euere'.
B. 2.159   And leten somone alle segges *in* shires aboute,
B. 2.171   'And late apparaille þise prouisours *in* palfreyes wise;
B. 2.177   To bere Bisshopes aboute abrood *in* visitynge.
B. 2.178   Paulynes pryuees for pleintes in Consistorie
B. 2.185   And Mede *in* þe myddes and [al þis meynee] after.
B. 2.216   And bishetten hym *in* hire shoppes to shewen hire ware;
B. 2.223   Wesshen hym & wiped hym & wounden hym *in* cloutes,
B. 3.31   And *in* Consistorie at court callen hire names.
B. 3.37   And seide [wel] softely, *in* shrift as it were,
B. 3.48   'We haue a wyndow *in* werchynge wole [stonden] vs [wel] hye;
B. 3.55   It is a freletee of flessh–ye fynden it *in* bokes–
B. 3.65   To writen *in* wyndowes of hir wel dedes,
B. 3.70   To writen *in* wyndowes of youre wel dedes
B. 3.75   For þus [bit god *in*] þe gospel goode men doon hir almesse.
B. 3.84   [Of] þat þe pouere peple sholde putte *in* hire wombe.
B. 3.124   [*In*] trust of hire tresor [she teneþ wel] manye.
B. 3.133   To Monkes, to Mynstrales, to Meseles *in* hegges.
B. 3.142   To be corsed *in* Consistorie she counteþ noȝt a [risshe];
B. 3.145   [She] may neiȝ as muche do *in* a Monþe one[s]
B. 3.146   As youre secret seel *in* sixe score dayes.
B. 3.163   Barons and Burgeises she bryngeþ *in* sorwe,
B. 3.164   And al þe comune *in* care þat coueiten lyue in truþe.
B. 3.164   And al þe comune in care þat coueiten lyue *in* truþe.
B. 3.189   *In* Normandie was he noȝt noyed for my sake,
B. 3.203   He sholde haue be lord of þat lond *in* lengþe and in brede,
B. 3.203   He sholde haue be lord of þat lond in lengþe and *in* brede,
B. 3.221   The kyng haþ mede of his men to make pees *in* londe;
B. 3.232   That oon god of his grace [gyueþ] *in* his blisse
B. 3.234   The prophete precheþ [it] and putte it *in* þe Sauter:
B. 3.235   Lord, who shal wonye *in* þi wones wiþ þyne holy seintes,
B. 3.236   Or resten *in* þyne holy hilles: þis askeþ Dauid.
B. 3.248   And þerof seiþ þe Sauter *in* a Salmes ende:
B. 3.257   *In* marchaundise is no Mede, I may it wel auowe;
B. 3.296   Ne no pelure *in* his [panelon] for pledynge at þe barre;
B. 3.302   That Iewes shul wene *in* hire wit, and wexen glade,
B. 3.304   And haue wonder *in* hire hertes þat men beþ so trewe.
B. 3.317   Ne putte hem *in* panel to doon hem pliȝte hir truþe;
B. 3.331   Also wroþ as þe wynd weex Mede *in* a while.
B. 3.333   Se what Salomon seiþ *in* Sapience bokes!
B. 3.345   Tho ye [souȝte] Sapience sittynge *in* youre studie.
B. 4.14   And [riȝt renneþ] to Reson and rouneþ *in* his ere;
B. 4.29   *In* [c]heker and in Chauncerye, to ben descharged of þynges.
B. 4.29   In [c]heker and *in* Chauncerye, to ben descharged of þynges.
B. 4.34   'Ther are wiles *in* hire wordes, and with Mede þei dwelleþ;
B. 4.56   Forstalleþ my feires, fiȝteþ *in* my Chepyng,
B. 4.73   For boþe þi lif and þi lond lyþ *in* his grace.'
B. 4.85   And comaundede a Constable to casten hym *in* Irens:
B. 4.108   But Reson haue ruþe on hym he shal reste *in* [þe] stokkes
B. 4.116   Til pernelles purfill be put *in* hire hucche,
B. 4.120   And Religiouse Romeris Recordare *in* hir cloistres
B. 4.135   While Mede haþ þe maistrie [to mote *in* þis] halle.
B. 4.139   Sholde neuere wrong *in* þis world þat I wite myȝte
B. 4.146   And if [þow] werch[e] it *in* werk I wedde myne eris
B. 4.152   For I seiȝ Mede *in* þe [moot] halle on men of lawe wynke
B. 4.156   I falle *in* floryns', quod þat freke, 'and faile speche ofte.'
B. 4.159   And þe mooste peple *in* þe [moot] halle and manye of þe grete,
B. 4.180   I wole haue leaute *in* lawe, and lete be al youre ianglyng;
B. 5.17   *In* ensample, [segges, þat ye] sholden do þe bettre:
B. 5.19   [And] turned vpward hire tai[l] *in* tokenynge of drede
B. 5.27   And kepe it *in* hire cofre for catel at nede.
B. 5.43   And dooþ it *in* dede, it shal drawe yow to goode.
B. 5.54   For whoso contrarieþ truþe, he telleþ *in* þe gospel,
B. 5.70   [Of alle þat] I haue [had enuye] *in* myn herte.'
B. 5.77   He was as pale as a pelet, *in* þe palsy he semed.
B. 5.78   [He was] cloþed *in* a kaurymaury–I kouþe it nouȝt discryue–
B. 5.81   As a leek þat hadde yleye longe *in* þe sonne
B. 5.94   [And blamed hym bihynde his bak to brynge hym *in* fame;
B. 5.101   Whan I met[t]e hym *in* Market þat I moost hate[de]
B. 5.141   And siþen þei blosmede abrood *in* boure to here shriftes.
B. 5.146   And freres fyndeþ hem *in* defaute, as folk bereþ witnesse,

B. 5.147   That whan þei preche þe peple *in* many places aboute
B. 5.155   I haue be cook *in* hir kichene and þe Couent serued
B. 5.161   For she hadde child *in* chirietyme; al oure Chapitre it wiste.
B. 5.174   And am chalanged *in* þe Chapitrehous as I a child were
B. 5.181   I cou[ȝ]e it [vp] *in* oure Cloistre þat al [þe] Couent woot it.'
B. 5.195   *In* a [torn] tabard of twelf wynter age;
B. 5.211   Putte hem *in* a press[our] and pyn[ned] hem þerInne
B. 5.220   The beste lay [*in* my bedchambre] lay [by þe walle],
B. 5.236   And I kan no frenssh *in* feiþ but of þe ferþest ende of Northfolk.'
B. 5.237   'Vsedestow euere vsurie', quod Repentaunce, '*in* al þi lif tyme?'
B. 5.238   'Nay, soþly', he seide, 'saue *in* my youþe.
B. 5.258   'I am holden', quod he, 'as hende as hound is *in* kichene;
B. 5.268   For þe beste book *in* oure hous, þeiȝ brent gold were þe leues,
B. 5.272   And siþen þat Reson rolle it *in* þe Registre of heuene
B. 5.276   And whoso leueþ [þat I liȝe] loke *in* þe Sauter glose,
B. 5.277   *In* Miserere mei deus, wher I mene truþe:
B. 5.279   Thanne weex þ[e] sherewe *in* wanhope & wolde han hanged
           hym[self]
B. 5.280   Ne hadde repentaunce þe raþer reconforted hym *in* þis manere:
B. 5.281   'Haue mercy *in* þi mynde, and wiþ þi mouþ biseche it–
B. 5.282   And al þe wikkednesse *in* þis world þat man myȝte werche or
           þynke
B. 5.284   Forþi haue mercy *in* þy mynde, and marchaundise leue it,
B. 5.294   What he lerned yow *in* lente, leue þow noon ooþer,
B. 5.325   T[h]o risen vp *in* Rape and rouned togideres
B. 5.332   *In* couenaunt þat Clement sholde þe cuppe fille,
B. 5.341   He pissed a potel *in* a paternoster while,
B. 5.353   Ac Gloton was a gret cherl and grym *in* þe liftyng;
B. 5.354   And kouȝed vp a cawdel *in* Clementes lappe.
B. 5.355   Is noon so hungry hound *in* hertford shire
B. 5.365   'As þow wiþ wordes & werkes hast wroȝt yuele *in* þi lyue
B. 5.376   For loue of tales *in* Tauernes [to] drynke þe moore I [hyed;
B. 5.382   'Shal neuere fyssh on [þe] Fryday defyen *in* my wombe
B. 5.400   And if I bidde any bedes, but if it be *in* wraþe,
B. 5.403   Wiþ ydel tales at þe Ale and ouþerwhile [*in*] chirche[s];
B. 5.405   I visited neuere feble men ne fettred [men] *in* puttes.
B. 5.410   And ligge abedde *in* lenten and my lemman in myne armes
B. 5.410   And ligge abedde in lenten and my lemman *in* myne armes
B. 5.414   Nouȝt twyes *in* two yer, and þanne [telle I vp gesse].
B. 5.417   But I kan fynden *in* a feld or in a furlang an hare
B. 5.417   But I kan fynden in a feld or *in* a furlang an hare
B. 5.418   Bettre þan *in* Beatus vir or in Beati omnes
B. 5.418   Bettre þan in Beatus vir or *in* Beati omnes
B. 5.421   Ac *in* Canoun nor in decretals I kan noȝt rede a lyne.
B. 5.421   Ac in Canoun nor *in* decretals I kan noȝt rede a lyne.
B. 5.435   *In* speche and in sparynge of speche; yspilt many a tyme
B. 5.435   In speche and *in* sparynge of speche; yspilt many a tyme
B. 5.438   Forsleuþeþ *in* my seruice til it myȝte serue no man.
B. 5.439   I [yarn] aboute *in* youþe and yaf me nauȝt to lerne,
B. 5.487   And siþþe wiþ þi selue sone *in* oure s[u]te deidest
B. 5.489   Ther þiself ne þi sone no sorwe *in* deeþ feledest,
B. 5.490   But *in* oure secte was þe sorwe and þi sone it ladde:
B. 5.493   Feddest wiþ þi fresshe blood oure forefadres *in* derknesse:
B. 5.496   The þridde day [þer]after þow yedest *in* oure sute;
B. 5.500   Of þyne douȝ[tiest] dedes was doon *in* oure armes:
B. 5.505   That euere þei wraþed þee *in* þis world in word, þouȝt or dedes.'
B. 5.505   That euere þei wraþed þee in þis world *in* word, þouȝt or dedes.'
B. 5.516   Apparailled as a paynym *in* pilgrymes wise.
B. 5.518   *In* a wiþwynde[s] wise ywounden aboute.
B. 5.527   [At] Bethlem, [at] Babiloyne, I haue ben *in* boþe,
B. 5.528   *In* Armonye, in Alisaundre, in manye oþere places.
B. 5.528   In Armonye, *in* Alisaundre, in manye oþere places.
B. 5.528   In Armonye, in Alisaundre, *in* manye oþere places.
B. 5.530   That I haue walked [wel] wide *in* weet and in drye
B. 5.530   That I haue walked [wel] wide in weet and *in* drye
B. 5.536   Asken after hym er now is *in* þis place.'
B. 5.547   *In* taillours craft and tynkeris craft, what truþe kan deuyse,
B. 5.564   And þanne youre neȝebores next *in* none wise apeire
B. 5.568   Wadeþ *in* þat water and wasshe yow wel þer
B. 5.584   *In*-[no]-manere-ellis-noȝt-for-no-mannes-biddyng.
B. 5.605   And if grace graunte þee to go *in* [in] þis wise
B. 5.606   Thow shalt see *in* þiselue truþe [sitte] in þyn herte
B. 5.606   Thow shalt see in þiselue truþe [sitte] *in* þyn herte
B. 5.607   *In* a cheyne of charite as þow a child were,
B. 5.610   [For] he haþ enuye to hym þat *in* þyn herte sitteþ
B. 6.7   'This were a long lettyng', quod a lady *in* a Scleyre.
B. 6.27   *In* couenaunt þat þow kepe holy kirke and myselue
B. 6.44   *In* a [wel] perilous place [þat] Purgatorie hatte.
B. 6.46   Thouȝ he be þyn vnderlyng here wel may happe *in* heuene
B. 6.48   For *in* Charnel at chirche cherles ben yuel to knowe,
B. 6.49   Or a knyȝt from a knaue; knowe þis *in* þyn herte.
B. 6.57   'And I shal apparaille me', quod Perkyn, '*in* pilgrymes wise
B. 6.61   And [heng his] hoper at [his] hals *in* stede of a Scryppe:

B. 6.66	Shal haue leue, by oure lord, to lese here *in* heruest
B. 6.68	And alle kynne crafty men þat konne lyuen *in* truþe,
B. 6.94	[He is] holden, I hope, to haue me *in* [mynde]
B. 6.95	And mengen [me] *in* his memorie amonges alle cristene.
B. 6.110	Ech man *in* his manere made hymself to doone,
B. 6.117	'Now by þe peril of my soule!' quod Piers al *in* pure tene,
B. 6.132	Whiche þei were *in* þis world hise werkmen apeired.
B. 6.140	To kepe kyen *in* þe feld, þe corn fro þe beestes,
B. 6.143	*In* lecherie and in losengerie ye lyuen, and *in* Sleuþe,
B. 6.143	In lecherie and *in* losengerie ye lyuen, and *in* Sleuþe,
B. 6.143	In lecherie and in losengerie ye lyuen, and *in* Sleuþe,
B. 6.174	Hunger in haste þoo hente wastour by þe [mawe]
B. 6.197	And [Piers was proud þerof] and putte hem [*in* office]
B. 6.235	And Sapience seiþ þe same—I seiȝ it *in* þe bible:
B. 6.242	And yaf [it hym in haste þat hadde ten bifore];
B. 6.250	The Sauter seiþ, *in* þe psalme of Beati omnes,
B. 6.252	He is blessed by þe book *in* body and in soule:
B. 6.252	He is blessed by þe book in body and *in* soule:
B. 6.290	By þat I hope to haue heruest *in* my crofte;
B. 6.293	Benes and baken apples þei broȝte *in* hir lappes,
B. 6.296	[Hunger eet þis] *in* haste and axed after moore.
B. 6.305	Ne noon halfpeny ale *in* none wise drynke,
B. 7.10	And riȝtfully *in* Rem[e] rulen þe peple
B. 7.12	Wiþ Patriarkes and prophetes *in* paradis to be felawe.
B. 7.15	And *in* as muche as þei mowe amenden alle synfulle,
B. 7.18	Marchauntȝ *in* þe margyne hadde manye yeres,
B. 7.30	Pouere peple [bedredene] and prisons [*in* stokkes]
B. 7.35	That no deuel shal yow dere ne [*in* youre deying fere yow],
B. 7.37	And sende youre soules *in* saufte to my Seintes Ioye.'
B. 7.37	And sende youre soules in saufte to my Seintes Ioye.'
B. 7.49	Conforteþ hym *in* þat caas, [coueiteþ noȝt hise] ȝiftes,
B. 7.54	Thise foure þe fader of heuene made to þis foold *in* commune;
B. 7.63	And lyuen *in* loue and in lawe, for hir lowe hert[e]
B. 7.63	And lyuen in loue and *in* lawe, for hir lowe hert[e]
B. 7.65	Beggeres [and] bidderes beþ noȝt *in* þe bulle
B. 7.74	And *in* þe stories he techeþ to bistowe þyn almesse:
B. 7.79	*In* hym þat takeþ þe trecherie if any treson walke,
B. 7.81	And he þat biddeþ borweþ and bryngeþ hymself *in* dette.
B. 7.89	The book banneþ beggerie and blameþ hem *in* þis manere:
B. 7.90	For [þei] lyue *in* no loue ne no lawe holde.
B. 7.94	Or [his] bak or [his] boon [þei] brekeþ *in* his youþe
B. 7.111	*In* two lynes it lay and noȝt a [lettre] moore,
B. 7.112	And was writen riȝt þus *in* witnesse of truþe:
B. 7.126	The prophete his payn eet *in* penaunce and in sorwe
B. 7.126	The prophete his payn eet in penaunce and *in* sorwe
B. 7.131	Ne soliciti sitis he seiþ *in* þe gospel,
B. 7.133	The foweles *in* þe [firmament], who fynt hem at wynter?
B. 7.141	As diuinour *in* diuinite, wiþ Dixit inspiens to þi teme.'
B. 7.151	And for Piers [loue] þe Plowman [wel] pencif *in* herte,
B. 7.154	Ac I haue no sauour *in* songewarie for I se it ofte faille.
B. 7.156	To sette sadnesse *in* Songewarie for sompnia ne cures.
B. 7.163	As Daniel diuined *in* dede it fel after:
B. 7.170	It bifel as his fader seide *in* Pharaoes tyme
B. 7.198	Theiȝ [þow] be founde *in* þe fraternite [among] þe foure ordres
B. 8.1	Thus, yrobed *in* russet, I romed aboute
B. 8.29	Lat brynge a man *in* a boot amydde [a] bro[od] watre;
B. 8.32	For stonde he neuer so stif, he stumbleþ [*in* þe waggyng],
B. 8.47	[That], þouȝ þ[i] body bowe as boot dooþ *in* þe watre,
B. 8.69	That euer dremed [driȝt] *in* [doute], as I wene.
B. 8.97	Is hoked [at] þat oon ende to [holde men *in* good lif].
B. 8.98	A pik is [*in*] þat potente to [punge] adown þe wikked
B. 8.104	Thanne [sholde] þe kyng come and casten hem *in* [prison,
B. 8.105	And putten hem þer *in* penaunce wiþoute pite or grace],
B. 8.127	Thanne þoȝt *in* þat tyme seide þise wordes:
B. 8.128	'Wher dowel [and] dobet and dobest ben *in* londe
B. 9.2	*In* a Castel þat kynde made of foure kynnes þynges.
B. 9.42	And so it semeþ by hym [þere he seide *in* þe bible
B. 9.45	And *in* þis manere was man maad þoruȝ myȝt of god almȝty,
B. 9.56	Ouer al *in* mannes body he[o] walkeþ and wandreþ,
B. 9.57	A[c] *in* þe herte is hir hoom and hir mooste reste.
B. 9.58	Ac Inwit is *in* þe heed and to þe herte he lokeþ
B. 9.79	Shul [purchace] penaunce *in* purgatorie but þei hem helpe.
B. 9.102	Is moost yhated vpon erþe of hem þat ben *in* heuene;
B. 9.110	[Dowel *in* þis world is trewe wedded libbynge folk],
B. 9.120	*In* erþe [þe] heuene [is]; hymself [was þe] witnesse.
B. 9.123	Conceyued ben *in* [cursed] tyme as Caym was on Eue
B. 9.128	"Thyn issue *in* þyn issue, I wol þat þei be wedded,
B. 9.145	That *in* [þe] shyngled ship shul ben ysaued."
B. 9.148	The gospel is hera[g]ein *in* a degre, I fynde.
B. 9.168	That neuere shal barn bere but it be *in* armes.
B. 9.169	[*In* Ielousie, ioyelees, and ianglynge on bedde,
B. 9.184	Fo[r] lecherie *in* likynge is lymeyerd of helle.
B. 9.187	Whan ye han wyued beþ war and wercheþ *in* tyme,
B. 9.189	For *in* vntyme, trewely, bitwene man and womman
B.10.12	Than al þe precious perree þat *in* paradis wexeþ.
B.10.23	Iob þe gentile *in* hise gestes witnesseþ
B.10.32	Ac he þat haþ holy writ ay *in* his mouþe
B.10.53	At mete *in* hir murþe whan Mynstrals beþ stille,
B.10.58	And gnawen god [*in*] þe gorge whanne hir guttes fullen.
B.10.65	Ne were mercy *in* meene men moore þan in riche
B.10.65	Ne were mercy in meene men moore þan *in* riche
B.10.67	God is muche *in* þe gorge of þise grete maistres,
B.10.69	And so seiþ þe Sauter; [seke it *in* memento]:
B.10.71	And haue hym muche *in* [hire] mouþ, ac meene men in herte.
B.10.71	And haue hym muche in [hire] mouþ, ac meene men *in* herte.
B.10.75	That folk is noȝt fermed *in* þe feiþ ne free of hire goodes
B.10.77	*In* Religion and in al þe Reme amonges riche and pouere
B.10.77	In Religion and *in* al þe Reme amonges riche and pouere
B.10.84	But *in* gaynesse and glotonye forglutten hir good
B.10.87	And lordeþ *in* [ledes] þe lasse good he deleþ.
B.10.97	Elenge is þe halle, ech day *in* þe wike,
B.10.100	*In* a pryuee parlour for pouere mennes sake,
B.10.101	Or *in* a chambre wiþ a chymenee, and leue þe chief halle
B.10.108	"Why wolde oure Saueour suffre swich a worm *in* his blisse
B.10.117	Swiche motyues þei meue, þise maistres *in* hir glorie,
B.10.118	And maken men *in* mys bileue þat muse on hire wordes.
B.10.124	Ac bileueþ lelly *in* þe loore of holy chirche,
B.10.125	And preie hym of pardon and penaunce *in* þi lyue,
B.10.128	I wolde his eiȝe were *in* his ers and his [hele] after,
B.10.137	But he lyue *in* þe [leeste degre] þat longeþ to dowel
B.10.146	*In* signe þat I sholde bisechen hire of grace.
B.10.171	That ech wight be *in* wille his wit þee to shewe.
B.10.177	And alle [þe] Musons *in* Musik I made hire to knowe.
B.10.194	*In* ooþer Science it seiþ, I seiȝ it in Catoun,
B.10.194	In ooþer Science it seiþ, I seiȝ it *in* Catoun,
B.10.216	Yet ar þer fibicches *in* [forelles] of fele mennes [wittes],
B.10.245	Thre [propre] persones, ac noȝt *in* plurel nombre,
B.10.250	And hymself ordeyned to sadde vs *in* bileue.
B.10.260	Loke þow werche it *in* werk þat þi word sheweþ;
B.10.261	Swich as þow semest *in* siȝte be in assay yfounde:
B.10.261	Swich as þow semest in siȝte be *in* assay yfounde.
B.10.263	But be swich *in* þi soule as þow semest wiþoute:
B.10.265	Syþenes þow seest þiself as *in* soule clene;
B.10.267	God *in* þe gospel [grymly] repreueþ
B.10.269	Why meuestow þi mood for a mote *in* þi broþeres eiȝe,
B.10.270	Siþen a beem [is] *in* þyn owene ablyndeþ þiselue—
B.10.281	But *in* swich manere as Marc meneþ in þe gospel:
B.10.281	But in swich manere as Marc meneþ *in* þe gospel:
B.10.282	Lewed men may likne yow þus, þat þe beem liþ *in* youre eiȝen.
B.10.284	*In* alle maner men þoruȝ mansede preestes.
B.10.294	And drede to wraþe yow *in* any word youre werkmanship to lette,
B.10.296	And al for youre holynesse; haue ye þis *in* herte.
B.10.299	Of religion þe rule reherseþ *in* hise morales,
B.10.300	And seiþ it *in* ensample [þat] þei sholde do þerafter:
B.10.306	It is *in* cloistre or in scole, by manye skiles I fynde.
B.10.306	It is in cloistre or *in* scole, by manye skiles I fynde.
B.10.307	For cloistre comeþ [no] man to [carpe] ne to fiȝte
B.10.309	*In* scole þere is scorn but if a clerk wol lerne,
B.10.319	*In* many places þer þei [persons ben, be þei purely] at ese,
B.10.328	And þanne Freres *in* hir fraytour shul fynden a keye
B.10.341	Poule preueþ it impossible, riche men [*in*] heuene;
B.10.347	That þei han Eritage *in* heuene, and by trewe riȝte,
B.10.354	That [arn] vncristene *in* þat caas may cristen an heþen.
B.10.356	Haue heritage [*in*] heuene as [an heiȝ] cristene.
B.10.362	And after alle cristene creatures, *in* commune ech man ooþer;
B.10.364	And but we do þus *in* dede, [er] þe day of dome,
B.10.367	Or delit *in* wyn and wildefowel and wite any in defaute.
B.10.367	Or delit in wyn and wildefowel and wite any *in* defaute.
B.10.369	And siþen heþen to helpe *in* hope of amendement.
B.10.375	"I shal punysshe *in* purgatorie or in þe put of helle
B.10.375	"I shal punysshe in purgatorie or *in* þe put of helle
B.10.381	*In* þe legende of lif longe er I were,
B.10.390	Of hir wordes þei wissen vs for wisest as *in* hir tyme,
B.10.391	And al holy chirche holdeþ hem boþe [*in* helle]!
B.10.393	That for hir werkes and wit now wonyeþ *in* pyne,
B.10.395	Ac of fele witty *in* feiþ litel ferly I haue
B.10.398	*In* good þan in god; forþi hem grace failleþ—
B.10.398	In good þan *in* god; forþi hem grace failleþ—
B.10.405	Ac I wene it worþ of manye as was *in* Noes tyme
B.10.432	And now ben [swiche] as Souereyns wiþ Seintes *in* heuene,
B.10.433	Tho þat wrouȝte wikkedlokest *in* world þo þei were;
B.10.438	In hondes of almyȝty god, and he woot þe soþe
B.10.460	Seide þus *in* a sermon—I seigh it writen ones—
B.10.476	That seruauntȝ þat seruen lordes selde fallen *in* arerage,
B.10.479	Selden falle so foule and so fer *in* synne
B.10.481	The which is mannes soule to saue, as god seiþ *in* þe gospel:

B.11.2	And lakked me *in* latyn and li3t by me sette,
B.11.5	And *in* a wynkynge [worþ til I weex] aslepe.
B.11.9	And *in* a Mirour þat hi3te middelerþe she made me biholde.
B.11.20	And *in* þis Mirour þow my3t se [myrþes] ful manye
B.11.34	'Ye? recche þee neuere', quod Rechelesnesse, stood forþ *in* raggede cloþes;
B.11.50	Coueitise of ei3es com ofter *in* mynde
B.11.56	And [festne] þee [*in*] hir Fraternitee and for þe biseke
B.11.94	And *in* þe Sauter also seiþ dauid þe prophete
B.11.102	To reden it *in* Retorik to arate dedly synne?
B.11.116	And *in* a weer gan I wexe, and wiþ myself to dispute
B.11.129	Ac he may renne *in* arerage and rome fro home,
B.11.132	And conscience acounte wiþ hym] and casten hym *in* arerage,
B.11.133	And putten hym after *in* prison in purgatorie to brenne;
B.11.133	And putten hym after in prison *in* purgatorie to brenne;
B.11.142	How [I] was ded and dampned to dwellen *in* pyne
B.11.147	Sauacion for sooþnesse þat he sei3 *in* my werkes.
B.11.152	By loue and by lernyng of my lyuynge *in* truþe;
B.11.155	That was an vncristene creature, as clerkes fyndeþ *in* bokes:
B.11.158	Wel ou3te ye lordes þat lawes kepe þis lesson haue *in* mynde
B.11.162	Ac þus leel loue and lyuyng *in* truþe
B.11.177	Whoso loueþ no3t, leue me, he lyueþ *in* deeþ deyinge.
B.11.186	*In* a pouere mannes apparaille pursue[þ] vs euere,
B.11.187	And lokeþ on vs *in* hir liknesse and þat wiþ louely chere
B.11.205	*In* þe olde lawe, as [þe] lettre telleþ, mennes sones men calle[d] vs
B.11.220	Of logyk [ne] of lawe *in* legenda sanctorum
B.11.233	For *in* hir liknesse oure lord [lome] haþ ben yknowe.
B.11.234	Witnesse *in* þe Pask wyke, whan he yede to Emaus;
B.11.243	And *in* þe apparaille of a pouere man and pilgrymes liknesse
B.11.245	Ther neuere segge hym sei3 *in* secte of þe riche.
B.11.246	Seint Iohan and oþere seintes were seyen *in* poore cloþyng,
B.11.264	Makeþ a man to haue mynde *in* god and a gret wille
B.11.268	And lasse he dredeþ deeþ and *in* derke to ben yrobbed
B.11.270	Alþou3 Salomon seide, as folk seeþ *in* þe bible,
B.11.280	As Dauid seiþ *in* þe Sauter: to swiche þat ben in wille
B.11.280	As Dauid seiþ in þe Sauter: to swiche þat ben *in* wille
B.11.286	And þei hir deuoir dide as Dauid seiþ *in* þe Sauter:
B.11.288	That if þei trauaille truweliche, and truste *in* god almy3ty,
B.11.304	If fals latyn be *in* þat lettre þe lawe it impugneþ,
B.11.307	So is it a goky, by god! þat *in* his gospel failleþ,
B.11.308	Or *in* masse or in matyns makeþ any defaute:
B.11.308	Or in masse or *in* matyns makeþ any defaute:
B.11.310	And also *in* þe Sauter seiþ Dauid to ouerskipperis,
B.11.320	Ac muche moore *in* metynge þus wiþ me gan oon dispute,
B.11.329	Wilde wormes *in* wodes, and wonderful foweles
B.11.336	*In* etynge, in drynkynge and in engendrynge of kynde.
B.11.336	In etynge, *in* drynkynge and in engendrynge of kynde.
B.11.336	In etynge, in drynkynge and *in* engendrynge of kynde.
B.11.338	As whan þei hadde ryde *in* Rotey tyme anoon [reste þei] after;
B.11.345	Briddes I biheld þat *in* buskes made nestes;
B.11.348	Lerned to legge þe stikkes *in* whiche she leyeþ and bredeþ.
B.11.354	*In* Mareys and moores [manye] hidden hir egges]
B.11.365	I sei3 floures *in* þe fryth and hir faire colours
B.11.374	'I haue wonder [*in* my wit], þat witty art holden,
B.11.381	He my3te amende *in* a Minute while al þat mysstandeþ,
B.11.394	The wise and þe witty wroot þus *in* þe bible,
B.11.399	Euery creature *in* his kynde encreesse [he bad]
B.11.401	*In* fondynge of þe flessh and of þe fend boþe,
B.11.407	That I *in* metels ne my3te moore haue yknowen.
B.11.427	For lat a dronken daffe *in* a dyk falle,
B.12.2	Thou3 I sitte by myself *in* siknesse n[e] in helþe.
B.12.2	Thou3 I sitte by myself in siknesse n[e] *in* helþe.
B.12.3	I haue folwed þee, *in* feiþ, þise fyue and fourty wynter,
B.12.7	To amende it *in* þi myddel age, lest my3t þe faill[e]
B.12.8	*In* þyn olde elde, þat yuele kan suffre
B.12.13	And Dauid *in* þe Sauter seiþ, of swiche þat loueþ Iesus,
B.12.24	[*In* manye places pleyden þe parfiter to ben].
B.12.29	'Poul *in* his pistle', quod he, 'preueþ what is dowel:
B.12.48	The beaute of hir body; *in* baddenesse she despended.
B.12.62	And *in* lele lyuynge men and in lif holy,
B.12.62	And in lele lyuynge men and *in* lif holy,
B.12.73	*In* þe olde lawe as þe lettre telleþ, þat was þe lawe of Iewes
B.12.74	That what womman were *in* auoutrye taken, whe[r] riche or poore,
B.12.79	Giltier as afore god, and gretter *in* synne,
B.12.105	And as a blynd man *in* bataille bereþ wepne to fi3te
B.12.113	Archa dei, *in* þe olde lawe, leuytes it kepten;
B.12.119	That wiþ archa dei [wenten] *in* [worship and reuerence]
B.12.146	Ne *in* none [beggers] cote [n]as þat barn born,
B.12.147	But *in* a Burgeises place, of Bethlem þe beste:
B.12.151	[Riche men rutte þo and *in* hir reste were
B.12.159	And þow seidest sooþ of somme, ac se *in* what manere.
B.12.160	Tak two stronge men and *in* Themese cast hem,
B.12.164	Which trowestow of þo two [*in* Themese] is in moost drede,
B.12.164	Which trowestow of þo two [in Themese] is *in* moost drede,
B.12.168	And is *in* drede to drenche, þat neuere dide swymme?'
B.12.176	As þow seest *in* þe Sauter in Salmes oon or tweyne
B.12.176	As þow seest in þe Sauter *in* Salmes oon or tweyne
B.12.179	*In* which flood þe fend fondeþ a man hardest.
B.12.195	[Th]at buxomliche biddeþ it and ben *in* wille to amenden hem.
B.12.206	For he þat is ones a þef is eueremoore *in* daunger,
B.12.210	And ri3t as Troianus þe trewe kny3t [tilde] no3t depe *in* helle
B.12.211	That oure lord ne hadde hym li3tly out, so leue I [by] þe þef *in* heuene.
B.12.212	For he is *in* þe loweste of heuene, if oure bileue be trewe,
B.12.221	And of þe floures *in* þe Fryth and of hire faire hewes,
B.12.227	He is þe pies patron and putteþ it *in* hir ere
B.12.229	And kynde kenned þe pecok to cauken *in* swich a [wise.
B.12.249	Ri3t as þe pennes of þe pecok peyneþ hym *in* his fli3t,
B.12.255	His ledene þe trewe lordes ere lik a pies chiteryng;
B.12.256	And whan his caroyne shal come *in* caue to be buryed
B.12.259	By þe po feet is vnderstande, as I haue lerned *in* Auynet,
B.12.269	Thus he likneþ *in* his logik þe leeste fowel oute.
B.12.278	Seyen *in* hir Sermons þat neiþer Sarsens ne Iewes
B.12.284	And he is saaf, seiþ þe book, and his soule *in* heuene.
B.12.285	[Ac] þer is fullynge of Font and fullynge *in* blood shedyng
B.12.289	And if þer were he wolde amende, and *in* swich wille deieþ–
B.13.3	*In* manere of a mendynaunt many yer after.
B.13.9	And no corps *in* hir kirk3erd n[e] in hir kirk was buryed
B.13.9	And no corps in hir kirk3erd n[e] *in* hir kirk was buryed
B.13.14	And how þat Ymaginatif *in* dremels me tolde
B.13.21	I lay doun longe *in* þis þo3t and at þe laste I slepte,
B.13.29	A[c] Pacience *in* þe Paleis stood in pilgrymes cloþes
B.13.29	A[c] Pacience in þe Paleis stood *in* pilgrymes cloþes
B.13.44	*In* a morter, Post mortem, of many bitter peyne
B.13.55	*In* a dissh of derne shrifte, Dixi & confitebor tibi.
B.13.69	That Poul *in* his Pistle to al þe peple tolde:
B.13.72	*In* englissh on auenture it sholde be reherced to ofte,
B.13.83	Were molten leed *in* his mawe and Mahoun amyddes.
B.13.88	He shal haue a penaunce *in* his paunche and puffe at ech a worde,
B.13.95	What he fond *in* a [forel of] a freres lyuyng,
B.13.106	'By þis day, sire doctour', quod I, 'þanne [*in* dowel be ye no3t]!
B.13.107	For ye han harmed vs two *in* þat ye eten þe puddyng,
B.13.109	And if ye fare so *in* youre Fermerye, ferly me þynkeþ
B.13.111	I wolde permute my penaunce with youre, for I am *in* point to dowel.'
B.13.120	'I haue seuene sones', he seide, seruen *in* a Castel
B.13.133	'Thanne passe we ouer til Piers come and preue þis *in* dede.
B.13.134	Pacience haþ be *in* many place, and paraunter [knoweþ]
B.13.143	Thyn enemy *in* alle wise eueneforþ wiþ þiselue.
B.13.151	Wiþ half a laumpe lyne *in* latyn, Ex vi transicionis,,
B.13.152	I bere þer, [*in* a bouste] faste ybounde, dowel.
B.13.153	*In* a signe of þe Saterday þat sette first þe kalender,
B.13.199	And siþen softeliche me seide *in* clergies ere,
B.13.207	Ther nys wo *in* þis world þat we ne sholde amende;
B.13.216	Thanne hadde Pacience, as pilgrymes han, *in* his poke vitailles:
B.13.218	To conforte hym and Conscience if þei come *in* place
B.13.268	*In* þe date of oure dri3te, in a drye Aprill,
B.13.268	In þe date of oure dri3te, *in* a drye Aprill,
B.13.274	Ac it was moled *in* many places wiþ manye sondry plottes,
B.13.277	As *in* apparaill and in porte proud amonges þe peple;
B.13.277	As in apparaill and *in* porte proud amonges þe peple;
B.13.287	*In* likynge of lele lif and a liere in soule;
B.13.287	In likynge of lele lif and a liere *in* soule;
B.13.300	Pouere of possession *in* purs and in cofre;
B.13.300	Pouere of possession in purs and *in* cofre;
B.13.303	*In* towne and in Tauernes tales to telle
B.13.303	In towne and *in* Tauernes tales to telle
B.13.335	Or an Ague *in* swich an Angre and som tyme a Feuere
B.13.349	And as [lef] *in* lente as out of lente, alle tymes yliche.
B.13.353	And of hir harlotrye and horedom *in* hir elde telleþ.
B.13.383	[I]*n* haly daies at holy chirche whan ich herde masse
B.13.394	Mi3te neuere me conforte *in* þe mene [tyme]
B.13.397	That my mynde ne was moore on my good *in* a doute
B.13.398	Than *in* þe grace of god and hise grete helpes:
B.13.405	And þanne I dradde to deye *in* dedlich synne',
B.13.423	And han likynge to liþen hem [*in* hope] to do yow lau3e–
B.13.425	*In* youre deeþ deyinge I drede me soore
B.13.433	Sholde noon harlot haue audience *in* halle n[e] in Chambre
B.13.433	Sholde noon harlot haue audience in halle n[e] *in* Chambre
B.13.450	And *in* his deeþ deyinge þei don hym gret confort
B.13.453	*In* a welhope, [for he wrou3te so], amonges worþi seyntes],
B.13.458	Til conscience acouped hym þerof *in* a curteis manere.
B.14.5	It haþ be laued *in* lente and out of lente boþe
B.14.11	Al for coueitise of my cristendom *in* clennesse to kepen it.
B.14.24	Ne fend ne fals man defoulen it *in* þi lyue.
B.14.42	Fissh to lyue *in* þe flood and in þe fir þe Criket,

B.14.42	Fissh to lyue in þe flood and *in* þe fir þe Criket,
B.14.45	*In* menynge þat alle men myȝte þe same
B.14.56	*In* [ondynge] and in handlynge and in alle þi fyue wittes,
B.14.56	In [ondynge] and *in* handlynge and in alle þi fyue wittes,
B.14.56	In [ondynge] and in handlynge and *in* alle þi fyue wittes,
B.14.66	And *in* Elyes tyme heuene was yclosed
B.14.67	That no reyn ne roon; þus rede men *in* bokes,
B.14.87	That whiles he lyuede he bileuede *in* þe loore of holy chirche.
B.14.94	As Dauid seiþ *in* þe Sauter: et quorum tecta sunt peccata.
B.14.98	'Where wonyeþ Charite?' quod Haukyn; 'I wiste neuere *in* my lyue
B.14.108	And þat at þe rekenyng *in* Arrerage fel raþer þan out of dette.
B.14.113	And wilde wormes *in* wodes, þoruȝ wyntres þow hem greuest
B.14.118	That al hir lif han lyued *in* langour and defaute.
B.14.122	Aungeles þat *in* helle now ben hadden ioye som tyme
B.14.123	And diues *in* deyntees lyuede and in douce vie;
B.14.123	And diues in deyntees lyuede and *in* douce vie;
B.14.125	And hir [ladies] also lyuede hir lif *in* murþe.
B.14.131	And whan he dyeþ ben disalowed, as Dauid seiþ *in* þe Sauter:
B.14.141	Haue heuene *in* youre her[berw]yng and heuene þerafter
B.14.157	For muche murþe is amonges riche, as *in* mete and cloþyng,
B.14.158	And muche murþe *in* May is amonges wilde beestes;
B.14.174	Ac poore peple, þi prisoners, lord, *in* þe put of meschief,
B.14.177	Wo *in* wynter tymes for wantynge of cloþes,
B.14.178	And *in* somer tyme selde soupen to þe fulle.
B.14.179	Conforte þi carefulle, crist, *in* þi rich[e],
B.14.184	Thou tauȝtest hem *in* þe Trinite to taken bapteme
B.14.186	And if vs fille þoruȝ folie to falle *in* synne after
B.14.189	A[c] if þe [pouke] wolde plede herayein, and punysshe vs *in* conscience,
B.14.200	*In* fenestres at þe freres–if fals be þe foundement.
B.14.201	Forþi cristene sholde be *in* commune riche, noon coueitous for hymselue.
B.14.206	And þat is plesaunt to pride *in* poore and in riche.
B.14.206	And þat is plesaunt to pride in poore and *in* riche.
B.14.210	Than richesse or reautee, and raþer yherd *in* heuene.
B.14.216	A[c] pride *in* richesse regneþ raþer þan in pouerte;
B.14.216	A[c] pride in richesse regneþ raþer þan *in* pouerte;
B.14.217	[Or] *in* þe maister [or] in þe man som mansion he haueþ.
B.14.217	[Or] in þe maister [or] *in* þe man som mansion he haueþ.
B.14.218	Ac *in* pouerte þer pacience is pride haþ no myȝte,
B.14.220	Ne haue power *in* pouerte, if pacience [it] folwe.
B.14.224	And eiþer hateþ ooþer *in* alle maner werkes.
B.14.246	For pouerte haþ but pokes to putten *in* hise goodes
B.14.259	And *in* þat secte oure saueour saued al mankynde.
B.14.263	*In* lond and in lordshipe and likynge of bodie
B.14.263	In lond and *in* lordshipe and likynge of bodie
B.14.278	'[Al þis] *in* englissh', quod Pacience, 'it is wel hard to expounen,
B.14.302	A frend *in* alle fondynges, [of foule yueles leche],
B.14.314	Than he may [soþly] deserue, *in* somer or in wynter;
B.14.314	Than he may [soþly] deserue, in somer or *in* wynter;
B.14.318	And sobretee swete drynke and good leche *in* siknesse.
B.15.7	As persons *in* pelure wiþ pendauntȝ of siluer;
B.15.10	That folk helden me a fool; and *in* þat folie I raued
B.15.17	*In* cristes court yknowe wel and of [cristene in many a place].
B.15.17	In cristes court yknowe wel and of [cristene *in* many a place].
B.15.22	'What are ye called', quod I, '*in* þat court among cristes peple?'
B.15.34	Thanne is lele loue my name, and *in* latyn Amor;
B.15.49	I wolde I knewe and kouþe kyndely *in* myn herte.'
B.15.67	For *in* þe likynge liþ a pride and licames coueitise
B.15.76	And how þat folk *in* folies [hir fyue wittes mysspenden],
B.15.78	*In* housynge, in haterynge, [in] heigh clergie shewynge
B.15.78	In housynge, *in* haterynge, [in] heigh clergie shewynge
B.15.78	In housynge, in haterynge, [*in*] heigh clergie shewynge
B.15.96	[And] se it by ensample *in* somer tyme on trowes:
B.15.98	Ther is a meschief *in* þe more of swiche manere [stokkes].
B.15.111	[For ypocrisie] *in* latyn is likned to a [loþly] dongehill
B.15.122	[And beere] bedes *in* hir hand and a book vnder hir arme.
B.15.143	And þat he spared and bisperede [s]pende we *in* murþe."
B.15.147	And bymeneþ goode meteȝyueres and *in* mynde haueþ
B.15.148	*In* preieres and in penaunces, and in parfit charite.'
B.15.148	In preieres and *in* penaunces, and in parfit charite.'
B.15.148	In preieres and in penaunces, and *in* parfit charite.'
B.15.152	I haue lyued *in* londe', quod [I], 'my name is longe wille,
B.15.161	Clerkes kenne me þat crist is *in* alle places
B.15.162	Ac I seiȝ hym neuere sooþly but as myself *in* a Mirour;
B.15.173	Al þat men seyn, he leet it sooþ and *in* solace takeþ,
B.15.174	And alle manere meschiefs *in* myldenesse he suffreþ.
B.15.187	Labouren *in* [a] lauendrye wel þe lengþe of a Mile,
B.15.203	And to poore peple han pepir *in* þe nose,
B.15.213	For he [lyueþ] noȝt *in* lolleris ne in londleperis heremytes
B.15.213	For he [lyueþ] noȝt in lolleris ne *in* londleperis heremytes
B.15.218	The loue þat liþ *in* his herte makeþ hym liȝt of speche,
B.15.220	For I haue seyen hym *in* silk and som tyme in russet,

B.15.220	For I haue seyen hym in silk and som tyme *in* russet,
B.15.221	Boþe *in* grey and in grys and in gilt harneis,
B.15.221	Boþe in grey and *in* grys and in gilt harneis,
B.15.221	Boþe in grey and in grys and *in* gilt harneis,
B.15.226	Riden and rennen *in* raggede wedes
B.15.228	Ac *in* riche robes raþest he walkeþ,
B.15.230	And *in* a freres frokke he was yfounden ones,
B.15.231	Ac it is fern [and fele yeer *in*] Fraunceis tyme;
B.15.232	*In* þat secte siþþe to selde haþ he ben [knowe].
B.15.235	*In* kynges court he comeþ ofte þer þe counseil is trewe,
B.15.237	*In* court amonges [þe commune] he comeþ but selde
B.15.239	*In* þe Consistorie bifore þe Commissarie he comeþ noȝt ful ofte
B.15.255	The mooste liflode he lyueþ by is loue *in* goddes passion;
B.15.259	*In* alle manere angres, haue þis at herte
B.15.261	*In* ensample we sholde do so, and take no vengeaunce
B.15.265	Ne han martired Peter ne Poul, ne *in* prison holden.
B.15.266	Ac he suffrede *in* ensample þat we sholde suffren also,
B.15.269	[Lo]! *in* legenda sanctorum, þe lif of holy Seintes,
B.15.271	*In* hunger, in hete, in alle manere angres;
B.15.271	In hunger, *in* hete, in alle manere angres.
B.15.271	In hunger, in hete, *in* alle manere angres.
B.15.273	Woneden *in* wildernesse among wilde beestes.
B.15.275	*In* spekes and spelonkes; selde speken togideres.
B.15.278	But of foweles þat fleeþ; þus fyndeþ men *in* bokes.
B.15.304	*In* likkyng and in lowynge, þer þei on laundes yede].
B.15.304	In likkyng and *in* lowynge, þer þei on laundes yede].
B.15.306	*In* menynge þat meke þyng mylde þyng sholde fede.
B.15.329	For þat þei beggen aboute *in* buyldynge þei spende,
B.15.347	Ac þer is a defaute *in* þe folk þat þe feiþ kepeþ,
B.15.349	As *in* lussheburwes is a luþer alay, and yet lokeþ he lik a sterlyng;
B.15.359	Astronomiens alday *in* hir Art faillen
B.15.376	Ne rede a lettre *in* any langage but in latyn or englissh.
B.15.376	Ne rede a lettre in any langage but *in* latyn or englissh.
B.15.384	Thei sholde faillen of hir Philosophie and Phisik boþe.
B.15.386	Lest þei ouerhuppen as ooþere doon *in* office and in houres.
B.15.386	Lest þei ouerhuppen as ooþere doon in office and *in* houres.
B.15.388	As clerkes *in* Corpus Christi feeste syngen and reden
B.15.394	For þei loue and bileue *in* o [lord] almyghty
B.15.395	And we lered and lewed [bileueþ *in* oon god;
B.15.397	A[c] oon Makometh, a man, *in* mysbileue
B.15.398	Brouȝte Sarȝens of Surree, and see *in* what manere.
B.15.402	The corn þat she croppede he caste it *in* his ere,
B.15.403	And if he among þe peple preched, or *in* places come,
B.15.406	And dide folk þanne falle on knees; for he swoor *in* his prechyng
B.15.410	Makometh *in* mysbileue men and wommen brouȝte,
B.15.413	Thoruȝ a cristene clerk acorsed *in* his soule–
B.15.423	To lyue by litel and *in* lowe houses by lele mennes almesse.
B.15.425	And folkes sholden [fynde], þat ben *in* diuerse siknesse,
B.15.426	The bettre for hir biddynges *in* body and in soule.
B.15.426	The bettre for hir biddynges in body and *in* soule.
B.15.453	Til it be fulled vnder foot or *in* fullyng stokkes,
B.15.457	Til it be cristned *in* cristes name and confermed of þe bisshop
B.15.460	As *in* wildernesse wexeþ wilde beestes
B.15.466	The calf bitokneþ clennesse in hem þat kepeþ lawes,
B.15.474	Riȝt as capons *in* a court comeþ to mennes whistlyng,
B.15.475	*In* menyng after mete folweþ men þat whistlen
B.15.498	And seide it *in* saluacion of Sarȝens and oþere;
B.15.505	*In* [o] gre[et] god, and his grace asken,
B.15.507	Thus *in* a feiþ leue þat folk, and in a fals mene,
B.15.507	Thus in a feiþ leue þat folk, and *in* a fals mene,
B.15.508	And þat is rouþe for riȝtful men þat *in* þe Reawme wonyen,
B.15.513	*In* ensaumple þat men sholde se by sadde reson
B.15.520	Al for to enforme þe feith; *in* fele contrees deyeden,
B.15.521	*In* ynde, in alisaundre, in ermonye and spayne,
B.15.521	In ynde, *in* alisaundre, in ermonye and spayne,
B.15.521	In ynde, in alisaundre, *in* ermonye and spayne,
B.15.522	*In* dolful deþ deyeden for hir faith.
B.15.523	*In* sauacion of [mannes soule] seint [Thomas] was ymartired;
B.15.529	[And nauȝt to] huppe aboute *in* Engelond to halwe mennes Auteres
B.15.543	For coueitise after cros; þe croune stant *in* golde.
B.15.545	That *in* grotes is ygraue and in gold nobles.
B.15.545	That in grotes is ygraue and *in* gold nobles.
B.15.580	Arn ferme as *in* þe feiþ, goddes forbode ellis,
B.15.582	And Iewes lyuen *in* lele lawe; oure lord wroot it hymselue
B.15.583	*In* stoon for it stedefast was and stonde sholde euere.
B.15.593	And whan he lifte vp Laȝar þat leid was *in* graue
B.16.3	Ac ȝit I am *in* a weer what charite is to mene.'
B.16.13	'It groweþ *in* a gardyn', quod he, 'þat god made hymselue
B.16.20	And lay doun *in* a louedreem; and at þe laste me þouȝte
B.16.26	And *in* blowyng tyme abite þe floures but if þise piles helpe.
B.16.31	The flessh is a fel wynd, and *in* flouryng tyme,
B.16.38	Thoruȝ preieres and penaunces and goddes passion *in* mynde
B.16.56	*In* what wode þei woxen and where þat þei growed,

B.16.90 And þanne spak spiritus sanctus *in* Gabrielis mouþe
B.16.92 That oon Iesus a Iustices sone moste Iouke *in* hir chambre
B.16.100 And *in* þe wombe of þat wenche was he fourty woukes
B.16.111 Boþe meseles and mute and *in* þe menyson blody,
B.16.113 Saue þo he leched laʒar þat hadde yleye *in* graue;
B.16.129 That *in* chirche chaffareden or chaungeden any moneie;
B.16.130 And seide it *in* sighte of hem alle so þat alle herden:
B.16.132 And *in* þre daies after edifie it newe,
B.16.133 And maken it as muche ouþer moore *in* alle manere poyntes
B.16.136 Enuye and yuel wil [arne] *in* þe Iewes.
B.16.154 'Falsnesse I fynde *in* þi faire speche
B.16.155 And gile in þi glad chere and galle is in þi laughyng.
B.16.155 And gile in þi glad chere and galle is *in* þi laughyng.
B.16.159 Suffreþ myne Apostles in [pays] and in [pees] gange.'
B.16.159 Suffreþ myne Apostles in [pays] and *in* [pees] gange.'
B.16.160 On a þursday *in* þesternesse þus was he taken;
B.16.163 Iusted *in* Iherusalem, a ioye to vs alle.
B.16.170 And yede forþ as an ydiot *in* contree to aspie
B.16.181 'Thre leodes *in* oon lyth, noon lenger þan ooþer,
B.16.182 Of oon muchel and myght *in* mesure and lengþe.
B.16.200 *In* menynge þat man moste on o god bileue.
B.16.201 And þere hym likede and [he] louede, *in* þre persones hym
shewede.
B.16.204 *In* tokenynge of þe Trinite, was [taken out of a man],
B.16.207 And eiþer is oþeres ioye *in* þre sondry persones,
B.16.208 And *in* heuene and here oon singuler name.
B.16.211 Migh[t] is [*in*] matrimoyne þat multiplieþ þe erþe
B.16.220 Thus are þre persones in parfitliche [pure] manhede,
B.16.222 And is noʒt but gendre of a generacion bifore Iesu crist *in* heuene:
B.16.225 Thus in a somer I hym seiʒ as I sat in my porche;
B.16.225 Thus in a somer I hym seiʒ as I sat *in* my porche;
B.16.234 I am ful siker *in* soule þerof, and my sone boþe.
B.16.238 Myn affiaunce and my feiþ is ferme *in* þis bileue
B.16.247 Thus haue I ben his heraud here and *in* helle
B.16.251 That to patriarkes & prophetes and ooþer peple *in* derknesse
B.16.254 For *in* his bosom he bar a þyng þat he blissed euere.
B.16.255 And I loked in his lappe; a laʒar lay þerInne
B.16.258 'I wolde wite', quod I þo, 'what is *in* youre lappe.'
B.16.269 Lollynge *in* my lappe til swich a lord vs fecche.'
B.17.19 Shal neuere deuel hym dere ne deeþ *in* soule greue;
B.17.23 Lo! here *in* my lappe þat leeued on þat charme,
B.17.29 Thre persones *in* parcelles departable fro ooþer
B.17.32 He kan noʒt siggen þe somme, and some arn *in* his lappe.
B.17.37 To bileeue and louye *in* o lord almyghty
B.17.39 The gome þat gooþ wiþ o staf, he semeþ *in* gretter heele
B.17.46 It is lighter to leeue *in* þre louely persones
B.17.50 And as we wenten þus *in* þe wey wordynge togideres
B.17.54 To a Iustes *in* Ierusalem he [I]aced awey faste.
B.17.67 He lighte adown of Lyard and ladde hym *in* his hande,
B.17.69 And parceyued bi his pous he was *in* peril to dye
B.17.73 Enbawmed hym and bond his heed and *in* his [barm] hym leide,
B.17.97 And [he be] baþed *in* þat blood, baptised as it were,
B.17.101 For wente neuere wye *in* þis world þoruʒ þat wildernesse
B.17.105 For [an] Outlaw[e is] *in* þe wode and vnder bank lotieþ,
B.17.115 And þanne shal Feiþ be forster here and *in* þis Fryth walke,
B.17.125 For þe barn was born *in* Bethleem þat with his blood shal saue
B.17.126 Alle þat lyuen *in* Feiþ and folwen his felawes techynge.'
B.17.129 *In* þre persones departable þat perpetuele were euere,
B.17.155 And þre sondry sightes [shewynge *in* oon],
B.17.166 That þre þynges bilongeþ *in* oure [fader] of heuene
B.17.171 Al þe myʒt myd hym is *in* makynge of þynges.
B.17.183 Than is þe sire [or] þe sone and *in* þe same myghte,
B.17.187 Ac who is hurte in þe hand], euene in þe myddes,
B.17.187 Ac who is hurte *in* þe hand], euene *in* þe myddes,
B.17.196 *In* many kynnes maneres I myghte myself helpe,
B.17.199 That whoso synneþ *in* þe Seint Spirit assoilled worþ he neuere,
B.17.201 For he prikeþ god as *in* þe pawme þat peccat in spiritu[m]
sanct[um].
B.17.204 So whoso synneþ *in* þe Seint Spirit, it semeþ þat he greueþ
B.17.217 Wiþouten leye or light [liþ fir *in* þe macche]–
B.17.222 That werchen and waken *in* wyntres nyʒtes
B.17.230 And melteþ hire myʒt into mercy, as men may se *in* wyntre
B.17.231 Ysekeles *in* euesynges þoruʒ hete of þe sonne
B.17.232 Melte in a Mynut while to myst and to watre.
B.17.237 And solacen hem þat mowe [noʒt] se, þat sitten *in* derknesse,
B.17.240 *In* as muche as þei mowen amenden and paien;
B.17.241 And if it suffise noʒt for assetʒ, þat *in* swich a wille deyeþ,
B.17.244 For to murþen men [wiþ] þat *in* [m]erke sitten,
B.17.285 A[c] yet *in* mo maneres men offenden þe holy goost;
B.17.314 That mercy *in* hir mynde may noʒt þanne falle];
B.17.327 And whan smoke and smolder smyt *in* his sighte
B.17.330 Til he be blereighed or blynd and [þe borre] *in* þe þrote;
B.17.342 And þouʒ þat men make muche doel *in* hir angre

B.17.343 And ben inpacient *in* hir penaunce, pure reson knoweþ
B.17.347 Ac þe smoke and þe smolder þat smyt *in* oure eighen,
B.18.15 Thanne was feiþ *in* a fenestre and cryde 'a! fili dauid!'
B.18.19 And who sholde Iuste *in* Ierusalem. 'Iesus', he seide,
B.18.21 'Is Piers *in* þis place?' quod I, and he preynte on me.
B.18.22 'This Iesus of his gentries wol Iuste *in* Piers armes,
B.18.23 *In* his helm and in his haubergeon, humana natura,
B.18.23 In his helm and *in* his haubergeon, humana natura;
B.18.25 *In* Piers paltok þe Plowman þis prikiere shal ryde,
B.18.30 Al þat lyueþ [or] lokeþ *in* londe [or] in watre.
B.18.30 Al þat lyueþ [or] lokeþ in londe [or] *in* watre.
B.18.42 To fordoon it on o day, and *in* þre dayes after
B.18.44 And ʒit maken it as muche *in* alle manere poyntes,
B.18.49 And sette it sore on his heed and seide *in* enuye;
B.18.65 'Lif and deeþ, *in* þis derknesse hir oon fordooþ hir ooþer.
B.18.80 Bifore Pilat and ooþer peple *in* þe place he houed.
B.18.90 For þe dede þat I haue doon I do me *in* youre grace.
B.18.103 And youre fraunchise þat fre was fallen is *in* þraldom;
B.18.105 [Ne] haue lordshipe *in* londe ne no lond tilye,
B.18.107 Which is lif þat oure lord *in* alle lawes acurseþ.
B.18.111 I drow me *in* þat derknesse to descendit ad inferna
B.18.114 Cam walkynge *in* þe wey; to helleward she loked.
B.18.125 'Ich haue ferly of þis fare, *in* feiþ', seide truþe,
B.18.136 *In* menynge þat man shal fro merknesse be drawe
B.18.144 Patriarkes and prophetes þat *in* peyne liggen,
B.18.148 For þat is ones *in* helle out comeþ [it] neuere.
B.18.168 Where pees comeþ pleyinge *in* pacience ycloþed.
B.18.172 Whan Pees in Pacience ycloþed approched ner hem tweyne
B.18.175 And hire gaye garnementʒ whom she grete þouʒte.
B.18.178 Adam and Eue and oþere mo *in* helle.
B.18.193 Sholden deye downrighte and dwelle *in* pyne after
B.18.210 Sholde neuere riʒt riche man þat lyueþ *in* reste and ese
B.18.219 Sette hym in solace and in souereyn murþe,
B.18.219 Sette hym in solace and *in* souereyn murþe,
B.18.223 To [se] what he haþ suffred *in* þre sondry places,
B.18.224 Boþe in heuene and in erþe, and now til helle he þenkeþ
B.18.224 Boþe in heuene and *in* erþe, and now til helle he þenkeþ
B.18.234 That alle þe wise of þis world *in* o wit acor[de]den
B.18.235 That swich a barn was ybore *in* Bethleem þe Citee
B.18.239 [The oostes] *in* heuene token stella com[a]ta
B.18.245 And lo! how þe sonne gan louke hire light *in* hirselue
B.18.256 *In* alle myʒtes of man and his moder gladie,
B.18.263 A vois loude *in* þat light to lucifer crieþ,
B.18.288 And in semblaunce of a serpent sete vpon þe Appultree
B.18.304 That his soule wolde suffre no synne *in* his sighte;
B.18.315 And al oure lordshipe, I leue, a londe and [*in* helle]:
B.18.335 For *in* my paleis, Paradis, in persone of an Addre
B.18.335 For in my paleis, Paradis, *in* persone of an Addre
B.18.345 And þat deeþ *in* hem fordide my deeþ shal releue
B.18.350 Thow fettest myne *in* my place [maugree] alle resoun,
B.18.354 Thow, lucifer, *in* liknesse of a luþer Addere
B.18.356 And I *in* liknesse of a leode, þat lord am of heuene
B.18.360 And gile is bigiled and *in* his gile fallen:
B.18.369 Til þe vendage falle *in* þe vale of Iosaphat,
B.18.376 For we beþ breþeren of blood, [ac] noʒt *in* baptisme alle.
B.18.377 Ac alle þat beþ myne hole breþeren, in blood and in baptisme,
B.18.377 Ac alle þat beþ myne hole breþeren, *in* blood and *in* baptisme,
B.18.379 It is noʒt vsed *in* erþe to hangen a feloun
B.18.381 And if þe kyng of þat kyngdom come *in* þat tyme
B.18.386 And if lawe wole I loke on hem it liþ *in* my grace
B.18.392 *In* my prisone Purgatorie til parce it hote.
B.18.397 And mercy al mankynde bifore me *in* heuene.
B.18.401 Tho [ledes] þat [I] lou[e], and leued *in* my comynge;
B.18.404 Astroth and al þe route hidden hem *in* hernes;
B.18.413 Was neuere werre *in* þis world ne wikkednesse so kene
B.18.417 Clippe we *in* couenaunt, and ech of vs [kisse] ooþer,
B.18.423 And þanne lutede [loue] *in* a loud note:
B.19.4 *In* myddes of þe masse þo men yede to offryng
B.19.8 And riʒt lik *in* alle [lymes] to oure lord Ies[u].
B.19.47 And from fendes þat *in* hem [was] and false bileue.
B.19.61 Places *in* Paradis at hir partynge hennes.
B.19.68 And muche wo *in* þis world willen and suffren.
B.19.71 Tho he was born *in* Bethleem, as þe book telleþ,
B.19.82 And al þe wit of þe world was *in* þo þre kynges.
B.19.98 *In* þe manere of a man and þat by muchel sleighte,
B.19.101 And so dide Iesu *in* hise dayes, whoso [dorste] telle it.
B.19.108 *In* his Iuuentee þis Iesus at Iewene feeste
B.19.124 And whan he [was woxen] moore, *in* his moder absence,
B.19.132 And þo was he called *in* contre of þe comune peple,
B.19.134 For dauid was doghtiest of dedes *in* his tyme;
B.19.158 Goynge toward Galilee *in* godhede and manhede
B.19.160 *In* ech a compaignie þer she cam, Christus resurgens.
B.19.167 *In* an hous al bishet and hir dore ybarred

B.19.179 And blessed mote þei be, *in* body and in soule,
B.19.179 And blessed mote þei be, in body and *in* soule,
B.19.180 That neuere shul se me *in* sighte as þow [seest] nowþe,
B.19.186 *In* couenaunt þat þei come and knewelich[e] to paie
B.19.198 And wikkede to wonye *in* wo wiþouten ende.'
B.19.202 *In* liknesse of a lightnynge he lighte on hem alle
B.19.205 And was afered [for] þe light, for *in* fires [lik]nesse
B.19.248 And some he lered to lyue *in* longynge to ben hennes,
B.19.249 *In* pouerte and in [pacience] to preie for alle cristene.
B.19.249 In pouerte and *in* [pacience] to preie for alle cristene.
B.19.272 And harewede *in* an handwhile al holy Scripture
B.19.275 And sew [it] *in* mannes soule and siþen tolde hir names.
B.19.288 Ne no mete *in* his mouþ þat maister Iohan Spicede.
B.19.293 Maken hym, for any mournynge, þat he nas murie *in* soule,
B.19.303 And to correcte [þ]e kyng if [þe kyng] falle *in* gilt.
B.19.304 For counteþ he no kynges wraþe whan he *in* Court sitteþ;
B.19.312 'For comunliche *in* contrees cammokes and wedes
B.19.313 Foulen þe fruyt *in* þe feld þer þei growen togideres,
B.19.344 'And Piers bern worþ ybroke; and þei þat ben *in* vnitee
B.19.353 'To wasten on welfare and *in* wikked [kepyng]
B.19.354 Al þe world *in* a while þoruȝ oure wit', quod Pryde.
B.19.357 Praye we þat a pees weere *in* Piers berne þe Plowman.
B.19.363 That holy chirche stode *in* [holynesse] as it a Pyl weere.
B.19.380 Made vnitee holy chirche *in* holynesse stonde.
B.19.388 *In* help of hir heele ones in a Monþe,
B.19.388 In help of hir heele ones *in* a Monþe,
B.19.410 'I am a Curatour of holy kirke, and cam neuere *in* my tyme
B.19.421 But *in* hir holynesse helden hem stille
B.19.423 Or *in* Rome as hir rule wole þe relikes to kepe;
B.19.424 And þow Conscience *in* kynges court, and sholdest neuere come
                                                                                þennes,
B.19.430 A[c] wel worþe Piers þe plowman þat pursueþ god *in* doynge,
B.19.477 '*In* condicion', quod Conscience, 'þat þow [þe comune] defende
B.19.478 And rule þi reaume *in* reson [as right wol and] truþe
B.20.2 Heuy chered I yede and elenge *in* herte.
B.20.10 And nede haþ no lawe ne neuere shal falle *in* dette
B.20.14 And he [cacche] *in* þat caas and come þerto by sleighte
B.20.31 And Spiritus prudencie *in* many a point shal faille
B.20.42 So [he was nedy], as seiþ þe book *in* manye sondry places,
B.20.43 That he seide *in* his sorwe on þe selue roode:
B.20.52 And mette ful merueillously þat *in* mannes forme
B.20.56 *In* ech a contree þer he cam he kutte awey truþe
B.20.95 Elde þe hoore; [he] was *in* þe vauntwarde
B.20.116 And armede hym *in* ydelnesse and in heigh berynge.
B.20.116 And armede hym in ydelnesse and *in* heigh berynge.
B.20.117 He bar a bowe *in* his hand and manye brode arewes,
B.20.123 And armed hym *in* Auarice and hungriliche lyuede.
B.20.130 And [knokked] Conscience *in* Court afore hem alle;
B.20.134 He logged to a Iustice and Iusted *in* his eere.
B.20.136 An[d] to þe Arches *in* haste he yede anoon after
B.20.144 And armed hym [*in*] haste [in] harlotes wordes,
B.20.144 And armed hym [in] haste [*in*] harlotes wordes,
B.20.157 And geten *in* hir glorie a gadelyng at þe laste,
B.20.176 A Phisicien wiþ a furred hood þat he fel *in* a palsie,
B.20.180 And *in* hope of his heele good herte he hente
B.20.192 And gyued me *in* goutes: I may noȝt goon at large.
B.20.194 And wisshed ful witterly þat I were *in* heuene.
B.20.197 I ne myghte *in* no manere maken it at hir wille,
B.20.199 And as I seet *in* þis sorwe I sauȝ how kynde passede
B.20.219 *In* paltokes and pyked shoes, [purses and] longe knyues,
B.20.246 Holdeþ yow *in* vnitee, and haueþ noon enuye
B.20.254 That *in* mesure god made alle manere þynges,
B.20.259 And if þei wage men to werre þei write hem *in* noumbre;
B.20.261 [But þei ben nempned *in* þe noumbre of hem þat ben ywaged].
B.20.262 Alle oþere *in* bataille ben yholde Brybours,
B.20.263 Pylours and Pykeharneys, *in* ech a [parissche] ycursed._
B.20.271 Forþi I wolde witterly þat ye were *in* þe Registre
B.20.276 That alle þynges vnder heuene ouȝte to ben *in* comune.
B.20.280 And yuele is þis yholde *in* parisshes of Engelonde,
B.20.284 And [be] ashamed *in* hir shrift; ac shame makeþ hem wende
B.20.288 Ac while he is *in* westmynstre he wol be bifore
B.20.293 And suffre þe dede *in* dette to þe day of doome.
B.20.297 *In* vnitee holy chirche Conscience yeld hym
B.20.299 Of alle taletelleris and titeleris *in* ydel.
B.20.310 If any surgien were [*in*] þe seg[e] þat softer koude plastre.
B.20.311 Sire leef-to-lyue-*in*-lecherie lay þere and gronede;
B.20.313 'Ther is a Surgien *in* þ[e] sege þat softe kan handle,
B.20.328 *In* contrees þer he coome confessions to here;
B.20.331 And *in* haste askede what his wille were.
B.20.332 '*In* faiþ', quod þis frere, 'for profit and for helþe
B.20.366 And make [of] yow [memoria] *in* masse and in matyns
B.20.366 And make [of] yow [memoria] in masse and *in* matyns
C.Pr.1 *In* a somur sesoun whan softe was þe sonne

C.Pr.3 *In* abite as an heremite, vnholy of werkes,
C.Pr.4 Wente forth *in* þe world wondres to here
C.Pr.8 And *in* a launde as y lay lened y and slepte
C.Pr.16 Westward y waytede *in* a while aftir
C.Pr.18 Woned *in* tho wones and wikkede spiritus.
C.Pr.23 *In* settynge and sowynge swonken ful harde
C.Pr.26 *In* continance [of] clothyng in many kyne gyse.
C.Pr.26 In continance [of] clothyng *in* many kyne gyse.
C.Pr.27 *In* preiers and penaunc[e] potten hem mony,
C.Pr.29 *In* hope to haue a good ende and heuenriche blisse,
C.Pr.30 As Ankeres and Eremites þat holdeth hem *in* here selles
C.Pr.31 Coueyten noȝt in contre[y] to cayren aboute
C.Pr.44 *In* glotonye þ[o] gomus goth þei to bedde
C.Pr.49 Wenten forth [*i*]*n* here way with many wyse tales
C.Pr.54 Clothed hem *in* copis to be knowe fram othere
C.Pr.63 Mony ferlyes han falle *in* a fewe ȝeres.
C.Pr.77 His seel sholde nouȝt be ysent *in* deseyte of þe peple.
C.Pr.86 That han cure vnder crist and crownyng *in* tokene
C.Pr.89 Leyen [at] Londoun *in* lenton and elles.
C.Pr.91 *In* Cheker and in Chancerye chalengen his dettes
C.Pr.91 In Cheker and *in* Chancerye chalengen his dettes
C.Pr.94 And ben *in* stede of stewardus and sitten and demen.
C.Pr.96 And seide, 'ydolatrie ȝe soffren *in* sondrye places manye
C.Pr.99 *In* menynge of myracles muche wex hangeth there;
C.Pr.102 That lewed men *in* mysbileue lyuen and dyen.
C.Pr.108 Thei were discomfited *in* batayle and losten Archa domini
C.Pr.112 Were disconfit *in* batayle and Archa domini lorn
C.Pr.127 Lest crist *in* constorie acorse of [ȝow] manye.
C.Pr.133 Thare Crist is *in* kynedom to close with heuene.
C.Pr.135 And power presumen *in* hemself a pope to make
C.Pr.137 For *in* loue and lettrure lith þe grete eleccoun.
C.Pr.151 And for thy rightful ruylynge be rewardid *in* heuene.'
C.Pr.161 Where houed an hundrid *in* houes of selke,
C.Pr.174 To his clees clawe vs and [*in*] his cloches halde
C.Pr.179 Sayde, 'y haue seyen grete syres *in* Cytees and in townes
C.Pr.179 Sayde, 'y haue seyen grete syres in Cytees and *in* townes
C.Pr.190 And apere *in* his presence þe while hym pleye lyketh
C.Pr.194 Ther ne was [raton *in*] þe route, for al þe reame of Fraunce,
C. 1.3 A louely lady of [lere] *in* lynnene [y]clothed
C. 1.8 Ha[u]e thei worschip *in* this world thei wilneth no bettere;
C. 1.19 And, *in* mesure thow muche were, to make ȝow attese
C. 1.20 And comaundede of his cortesye *in* comune thre thynges.
C. 1.25 Loot *in* his lyue thorw likerous drynke
C. 1.27 *In* his dronkenesse aday his doughteres he dighte
C. 1.29 *In* his glotonye bygat gurles þat were cherles
C. 1.39 And þat [see]th þ[i] soule and sayth hit the *in* herte
C. 1.45 Whenne þe peple aposed hym of a peny *in* þe temple
C. 1.66 That tristeth *in* tresor of erthe he bytrayeth sonest.
C. 1.68 Thenne hadde y wonder *in* my wit what woman he were
C. 1.91 Rydon and rappe adoun *in* reumes aboute
C. 1.101 And neuer leue for loue *in* hope to lacche syluer.
C. 1.102 Dauid *in* his daies dobbed knyghtes,
C. 1.104 And god whan he bigan heuene *in* þat grete blisse
C. 1.105 Made knyghtes *in* his Couert creatures tene,
C. 1.110 Lepen out *in* lothly forme for his [luþer] wille
C. 1.114 Thenne sitten *in* þe sonne syde þere þe day roweth?'
C. 1.118 Then *in* þe north by many notes, no man leue other.
C. 1.124 Hewes *in* þe haliday after hete wayten
C. 1.127 Summe *in* erthe, summe in ayr, summe in helle depe.
C. 1.127 Summe in erthe, summe *in* ayr, summe in helle depe.
C. 1.127 Summe in erthe, summe in ayr, summe *in* helle depe.
C. 1.140 To lyte [Latyn þow] lernedest, [leode], *in* thy ȝowthe:
C. 1.141 Hit is a kynde knowynge that kenet *in* thyn herte
C. 1.160 And *in* þe herte þer is þe hed and þe heye welle.
C. 1.161 For [*in*] kynde knowynge [in] herte ther comseth a myhte
C. 1.161 For [in] kynde knowynge [*in*] herte ther comseth a myhte
C. 1.168 Here myhtow se ensaumples *in* hymself one
C. 1.172 Thow ȝe be myhty to mote beth meke *in* ȝoure werkes,
C. 1.179 ȝe n[e] haueth na more meryte *in* masse ne in oures
C. 1.179 ȝe n[e] haueth na more meryte in masse ne *in* oures
C. 1.181 For Iames þe gentele iuge[d] *in* his bokes
C. 1.184 Chastite withouten charite worth c[h]eyned *in* helle;
C. 1.195 For this aren wordes ywryten *in* þe ewangelie:
C. 2.11 And crouned [*in*] a croune, þe kyng haþ non bettre;
C. 2.22 *In* kynges court, in comune court contra[r]ieth my techynge.
C. 2.22 In kynges court, *in* comune court contra[r]ieth my techynge.
C. 2.23 *In* þe popes palays he is pryue as mysulue,
C. 2.32 That neuere lyede ne lauhede *in* al his lyf tyme;
C. 2.87 To ben pr[inces] *in* pruyde and pouert to dispice,
C. 2.95 *In* bargaynes and Brocages with the borw of thefte,
C. 2.96 With al þe lordschip of leccherye *in* lenghe and in Brede,
C. 2.96 With al þe lordschip of leccherye in lenghe and *in* Brede,
C. 2.97 As *in* werkes and in wordes and waytyng[e] of yes,

C. 2.97	As in werkes and *in* wordes and waytyng[e] of yes,
C. 2.98	*In* w[e]des and in weschynges and with ydel thouhtes
C. 2.98	In w[e]des and *in* weschynges and with ydel thouhtes
C. 2.104	With spiserye, speke ydelnesse *in* vayne spe[ch]e and spene
C. 2.106	And sue forth suche felawschipe til they ben falle *in* Slewthe
C. 2.110	*In* lordschip with lucifer, as this lettre sheweth,
C. 2.112	*In* wittenesse of [which] thyng wrong was the furste,
C. 2.117	'In þe date of the deuel th[e] dede is aseled
C. 2.156	And yf he fynde ʒow *in* defaute and with the fals holde,
C. 2.175	And leten somne alle seggus in vche syde aboute,
C. 2.181	Softliche *in* s[am]b[u]re fram syse [to] syse,
C. 2.189	And on pore prouisores and appeles *in* þe Arches.
C. 2.198	And mede *in* þe myddes and al this me[y]n[e] aftur.
C. 2.226	And byschytten hym *in* here shoppe[s] to shewen here ware;
C. 2.233	Thei woschen hym and wypeden hym and wonden hym *in* cloutes,
C. 2.247	And putte hem thorw appeles *in* þe popes grace.
C. 3.34	And *in* constorie at court do calle ʒoure names.
C. 3.53	*In* masse and in mataynes for mede we shal synge
C. 3.53	In masse and *in* mataynes for mede we shal synge
C. 3.59	Hit is but frelete of fleysche–ʒe fyndeth [hit *in*] bokes–
C. 3.69	To writen [i/n] wyndowes of eny wel dedes,
C. 3.74	God *in* þe gospel suche grauynge nouʒt alloueth:
C. 3.83	With that þe pore peple sholde potte *in* here wombe.
C. 3.90	Many sondry sorwes *in* Citees falleth ofte
C. 3.94	Here on this erthe or elles *in* helle,
C. 3.98	That Innocence is herde *in* heuene amonge seyntes
C. 3.106	And thorw a candle clemynge *in* [a] cursed place
C. 3.111	Ar he were vnderfonge fre and felawe in ʒoure rolles.
C. 3.112	Hit is nat seemely, forsothe, *in* Citee [ne] in borw toun
C. 3.112	Hit is nat seemely, forsothe, in Citee [ne] *in* borw toun
C. 3.122	*In* amendement of mayres and oþer stywardes
C. 3.136	Bothe to the and to thyne *in* hope thow shost amende;
C. 3.141	*In* the Castel of Corf y shal do close the,
C. 3.142	Or *in* a wel wors, wo[en ther as an ancre,
C. 3.161	*In* trist of here tresor he teneth fol monye,
C. 3.170	To Monekes, to [mynstrals, to] musels *in* hegge[s];
C. 3.180	To be cursed *in* constorie a counteth nat a rusche;
C. 3.183	He may ny as muche do *in* a monthe ones
C. 3.184	As ʒoure secrete seel *in* sixe score dayes.
C. 3.202	And al þe comune *in* care and in coueytise
C. 3.202	And al þe comune in care and *in* coueytise;
C. 3.235	Bothe here and elleswhere, *in* alle kyne londes.
C. 3.239	*In* contrees there the kyng cam, consience hym lette
C. 3.243	*In* his enemyes handes his heritage of Fraunce.
C. 3.258	Ac hadde y, mede, ben marchel o[f] his men *in* Fraunce
C. 3.294	And þat is nother resoun ne ryhte ne [i/n] no rewme lawe
C. 3.313	*In* Marchandise is no mede, y may hit wel avowe;
C. 3.328	And [soffrede] hym lyu[e] in mysbileue; y leue he be in helle.
C. 3.328	And [soffrede] hym lyu[e] in mysbileue; y leue he be *in* helle.
C. 3.337	Acordaunce *in* kynde, in case and in nombre
C. 3.337	Acordaunce in kynde, *in* case and in nombre
C. 3.337	Acordaunce in kynde, in case and *in* nombre
C. 3.347	*In* kynde and in case and in cours of nombre.
C. 3.347	In kynde and *in* case and in cours of nombre.
C. 3.347	In kynde and in case and *in* cours of nombre.
C. 3.349	*In* his pay and in his pite and in his puyr treuthe,
C. 3.349	In his pay and *in* his pite and in his puyr treuthe,
C. 3.349	In his pay and in his pite and *in* his puyr treuthe,
C. 3.356	He acordeth with crist *in* kynde, verbum caro factum est;
C. 3.357	*In* case, credere in ecclesia, in holy kyrke to bileue;
C. 3.357	In case, credere in ecclesia, in holy kyrke to bileue;
C. 3.358	In nombre, Rotye and aryse and remissioun to haue,
C. 3.362	Acordeth in alle kyndes with his antecedent.
C. 3.366	*In* whiche ben gode and nat gode, and graunte here n[eyther] will.
C. 3.372	To acorde *in* alle kynde and in alle kyn nombre,
C. 3.372	To acorde in alle kynde and *in* alle kyn nombre,
C. 3.381	Bote standynge as a stake þat stikede *in* a mere
C. 3.395	That is vnite, acordaun[c]e *in* case, in gendre and in noumbre,
C. 3.395	That is vnite, acordaun[c]e in case, in gendre and in noumbre,
C. 3.395	That is vnite, acordaun[c]e in case, in gendre and *in* noumbre,
C. 3.396	And is to [mene] *in* oure mouth more n[e] mynne
C. 3.402	And coueytede oure kynde and be kald *in* oure name–
C. 3.404	Thus is man and mankynde in maner of [a] sustantyf,
C. 3.413	As me ret *in* regum [of þe reuthe] of kynges,
C. 3.449	Ne no pelure *in* his panelon for pledyng at þe barre.
C. 3.455	That iewes shal wene *in* he[re] wit, & wexen so glade,
C. 3.470	Ne potte [hem] *in* panele [to] do [hem] plihte here treuthe;
C. 3.485	'Loo what salamon sayth,' quod she, '*in* sapiense in þe bible!
C. 3.485	'Loo what salamon sayth,' quod she, 'in sapiense *in* þe bible!
C. 3.493	Ac hadde she loked *in* þe luft half and þe lef turned
C. 4.13	'Y am fayn of that foreward, *in* fayth,' tho quod Consience,
C. 4.14	And rood forth to resoun and rouned *in* his ere
C. 4.50	Y dar nat for his felawschipe, *in* fayth,' pees sayde,
C. 4.59	Forstalleth my fayres and fyhteth *in* my chepyng[e]
C. 4.81	And comaundede a Constable to caste [hym] *in* yrones
C. 4.82	Ther he sholde nat *in* seuene ʒer see his feet [ones].
C. 4.103	Bute resoun haue reuth on hym he shal reste *in* [þe] stokkes
C. 4.111	Tyl purnele porfiel be putte *in* here whicche
C. 4.116	And religious outryderes be reclused *in* here Cloistres
C. 4.123	*In* prisones and in pore cotes be pilgrimages to Rome
C. 4.123	In prisones and *in* pore cotes be pilgrimages to Rome
C. 4.125	And alle Rome rennares for ruyflares *in* Fraunce
C. 4.136	Shulde neuere wrong in this worlde þat y wyte myhte
C. 4.137	Be vnpunisched *in* my power for perel of [my] soule
C. 4.142	Lat thy Confessour, syre kyng, construe this *in* englische
C. 4.143	And yf ʒe wor[c]he it *in* werke y wedde bothe myn handes
C. 4.148	Mede *in* the mothalle tho on men of lawe gan wynke
C. 4.149	*In* signe þat thei sholde with som sotil speche
C. 4.185	But be my cheef Chaunceller *in* Cheker and in parlement
C. 4.185	But be my cheef Chaunceller in Cheker and *in* parlement
C. 4.186	And Consience *in* alle my Courtes be a[s] kynges Iustice.'
C. 5.1	Thus y awakede, woet god, whan y wonede *in* Cornehull,
C. 5.2	[K]ytte and y *in* a cote, yclothed as a lollare
C. 5.7	*In* an hot heruest whenne y hadde myn hele
C. 5.10	*In* hele and [unnit] oen me apposede;
C. 5.11	Romynge *in* remembraunce thus resoun me aratede:
C. 5.12	'Can thow seruen,' he sayde, 'or syngen *in* a churche
C. 5.17	And kepe my corn *in* my croft f[or] pykares and theues
C. 5.30	Or faytest vppon frydayes or festeday[es] *in* churches,
C. 5.33	Or thow art broke, so may be, *in* body or in membre
C. 5.33	Or thow art broke, so may be, in body or *in* membre
C. 5.40	And foen[d y] nere, *in* fayth, seth my frendes deyede
C. 5.41	Lyf þat me [l]ykede but *in* this longe clothes.
C. 5.44	And so y leue in london and [vp] lond[on] bothe.
C. 5.50	To be welcome when y come oþerwhile *in* a monthe.
C. 5.58	Ne fyhte *in* no faumewarde ne his foe greue:
C. 5.60	And *in* quoer and in kyrkes Cristes mynistres:
C. 5.60	And in quoer and *in* kyrkes Cristes mynistres:
C. 5.75	*In* confort of the comune and the kynges worschipe;
C. 5.83	For *in* my Consience y knowe what Crist w[o]lde y wrouhte.
C. 5.90	Ac it semeth no sad parfitnesse *in* Citees to b[e]gge
C. 5.119	*In* ensau[m]ple, seggus, þat we sholde do þe bettere;
C. 5.121	And turned vpward here tayl *in* tokenynge of drede
C. 5.129	And kepe hit *in* here cofre for catel at nede.
C. 5.146	Gregory þe grete Clerk gart wryte *in* bokes
C. 5.148	Ryht as fysches *in* floed whan hem fayleth water
C. 5.153	Hit is in C[l]oystre or in scole, by many skilles y fynde.
C. 5.153	Hit is in C[l]oystre or *in* scole, by many skilles y fynde.
C. 5.154	For *in* C[l]oystre cometh no man to chyde ne to fyhte;
C. 5.155	*In* scole is loue and louhnesse and lykyng to lerne.
C. 5.165	*In* many places ther thei persones ben, be hemsulue at ese,
C. 5.173	Freres *in* here fraytour shal fynde þat tyme
C. 5.183	And comuners [to] acorde *in* alle kyn treuthe.
C. 5.186	Lo! *in* heuene an heyh was an holy comune.
C. 5.189	Holde ʒow *in* vnite; and he þat oþer wolde
C. 5.198	Seketh seynt treuthe *in* sauac[ioun] of ʒoure soules
C. 6.11	Of alle þat y haue hated *in* myn herte.'
C. 6.26	*In* alle [manere] maneres my name to be knowe;
C. 6.30	Proud of aparayle *in* port amongus þe peple
C. 6.32	Me wilnynge þat men wen[t]e y were as *in* auer
C. 6.38	Summe tyme *in* o sekte, summe tyme in another,
C. 6.38	Summe tyme in o sekte, summe tyme *in* another,
C. 6.39	*In* alle kyne couent contreuede how y myhte
C. 6.50	Tales to telle *in* tauernes and in stretes,
C. 6.50	Tales to telle in tauernes and *in* stretes,
C. 6.76	Aʒeyn þe consayl of Crist, as clerkes fyndeth *in* bokes:
C. 6.79	Or an ague *in* suche [an] angre and som tyme a feuere
C. 6.96	Amongus marchauntes many tymes and nameliche *in* londone.
C. 6.100	Now hit athynketh me *in* my thouhte þat euere y so wrouhte.
C. 6.110	Inpacient *in* alle penaunc[e] and pleyned, as hit were,
C. 6.112	As som tyme *in* somur and also in heruest,
C. 6.112	As som tyme in somur and also *in* heruest,
C. 6.114	*In* alle manere angres þat y hadde or felede.
C. 6.130	Y haue be coek *in* here kychene and the couent serued
C. 6.136	For he hadde childe *in* the chapun co[t]e; he worth chalenged at þe eleccioun."
C. 6.144	Yparroke[d] *in* pues; the persone hit knoweth
C. 6.156	ʒut am y chalenged *in* oure chapitrehous as y a childe were
C. 6.163	Y cou[ʒ]e hit vp *in* oure Cloystre þat al þe couent woet hit.'
C. 6.175	Y, gulty *in* gost, to god y me shryue
C. 6.176	As *in* likynge of lecherye my lycames gultes
C. 6.177	*In* word, in wedes, in waytynge of eyes.
C. 6.177	In word, *in* wedes, in waytynge of eyes.
C. 6.177	In word, in wedes, *in* waytynge of eyes.
C. 6.183	As leef *in* lente as out of lente, alle tymes ylyche,
C. 6.203	*In* a tore tabard of twelue wynter age;

C. 6.219	Potte hem *in* [a] pressou[r] and pynne[d] hem þerynne
C. 6.228	Þe beste ale lay *in* m[y] bour and in my bed chau[m]bre
C. 6.228	Þe beste ale lay in m[y] bour and *in* my bed chau[m]bre
C. 6.238	Thow wolt be hanged heye þerfore, here oþer *in* helle.
C. 6.239	Vsedest [thow] euere vsurye *in* al thy lyf tyme?'
C. 6.240	'Nay, sothly,' he saide, 'saue *in* my 3outhe.
C. 6.272	*In* halydayes at holy churche when y herde masse
C. 6.281	Myhte neuere me comforte *in* the mene tyme
C. 6.284	That my muynde ne was more [o]n my godes *in* a doute
C. 6.285	Then *in* the grace of god and in his grete myhte;
C. 6.285	Then in the grace of god and *in* his grete myhte;
C. 6.287	Were y a frere, *in* good fayth, for al þe gold on erthe
C. 6.299	Shal parte with the *in* purgatorye and helpe paye thy dette
C. 6.301	And what lede leueth þat y lye look *in* þe sauter glos[e],
C. 6.313	For me is leuere *in* this lyue as a lorel begge
C. 6.314	Then *in* lysse to lyue and lese lyf and soule.'
C. 6.332	By so hit be *in* thyn herte as y here thy tonge.
C. 6.333	[T]rist *in* his mechel mercy and 3ut þou myhte be saued.
C. 6.338	Confessen hem and cryen hym mercy; shal neuere come *in* helle:
C. 6.340	'And haue his mercy *in* thy mynde and marchaundise, leue hit,
C. 6.383	Tho rysen vp [*in*] rape and rounned togyderes
C. 6.390	*In* couenaunt þat clement sholde the coppe fulle
C. 6.399	A pissede a potel *in* a paternoster whyle
C. 6.411	Ac gloton was a greet cherl and gr[ym] *in* þe luftynge
C. 6.412	And cowed vp a caudel *in* Clementis lappe.
C. 6.413	Ys non so hungry hound *in* hertford shyre
C. 6.437	Of my luyther ly[uynge] *in* al my lyf tyme.
C. 6.439	Shal neuere fysch [o]n þe fryday defyen *in* my wombe
C. 7.16	And yf y bidde eny bedes, but yf hit be *in* wrath,
C. 7.19	With ydele tales at þe ale and oþerwhile *in* chirches;
C. 7.20	Goddes payne and his passioun is puyre selde *in* my thouhte.
C. 7.21	Y visitede neuere feble man ne fetered man *in* prisone.
C. 7.23	Or lacke men or likene hem *in* vnlikyng manere
C. 7.26	And ligge abedde *in* lente and my lemman in myn armus
C. 7.26	And ligge abedde in lente and my lemman *in* myn armus
C. 7.29	Nat twies *in* ten 3er and thenne telle y nat þe haluendele.
C. 7.32	Ac y can fynden *in* a feld and in a forlong an hare
C. 7.32	Ac y can fynden in a feld and *in* a forlong an hare
C. 7.48	*In* speche and in sparyng of speche; yspilde many a tyme
C. 7.48	In speche and *in* sparyng of speche; yspilde many a tyme
C. 7.52	Forsleuthed *in* my seruice and set [hous] afuyre
C. 7.53	And 3ede aboute *in* my 3outhe and 3af me to no thedom
C. 7.83	And han lykyng to lythen hem *in* hope to do 3ow lawhe–
C. 7.85	*In* 3oure deth deynge y drede me sore
C. 7.93	Sholde non harlote haue audiense *in* halle ne in chaumbre
C. 7.93	Sholde non harlote haue audiense in halle ne *in* chaumbre
C. 7.110	And *in* his deth deynge they don hym greet confort
C. 7.113	*In* a welhope for a wrouhte so amongus worthy seyntes
C. 7.129	And sethe *in* oure secte, as hit semed, deyedest,
C. 7.130	On a friday *in* fourme of man feledest oure sorwe:
C. 7.133	Feddest tho with thy [fresshe] blood oure forfadres *in* helle:
C. 7.136	The thridde day þeraftur thow 3edest i[*n*] oure sekte;
C. 7.140	Of thy douhtiokest dedes was don *in* oure sekte.
C. 7.150	That euere they gulte a3eyn þe, god, *in* gost or in dede.'
C. 7.150	That euere they gulte a3eyn þe, god, in gost or *in* dede.'
C. 7.161	[A]parayled as a paynyem *in* pilgrimes wyse.
C. 7.163	*In* a wethewynde wyse ywrithe al aboute;
C. 7.172	*In* bedlem and in babiloyne y haue be in bothe,
C. 7.172	In bedlem and *in* babiloyne y haue be in bothe,
C. 7.172	In bedlem and in babiloyne y haue be *in* bothe,
C. 7.173	*In* Armonye, in Alisaundre [and in damaske].
C. 7.173	In Armonye, *in* Alisaundre [and in damaske].
C. 7.173	In Armonye, in Alisaundre [and *in* damaske].
C. 7.175	/[Y haue] ywalked ful wyde *in* wete and in drye
C. 7.175	/[Y haue] ywalked ful wyde in wete and *in* drye
C. 7.181	Axen aftur hym [er] now *in* þis place.'
C. 7.191	*In* alle kyne craftes þat he couthe deuise
C. 7.211	And thenne 3oure neyhebores nexst *in* none wyse apayre
C. 7.215	Wadeth *in* þat water and wascheth 3ow wel there
C. 7.231	*In*-none-manere-elles-nat-for-no-mannes-preeyre.
C. 7.233	The mote is of mercy, the manere *in* þe myddes
C. 7.254	And yf grace graunte the to go in [*in*] this wyse
C. 7.255	Thow shalt se treuthe sitte *in* thy sulue herte
C. 7.258	*In* thyne hole herte to herborwe alle trewe
C. 7.262	For he hath enuye to hym þat *in* thyn herte setteth
C. 7.277	For he payeth for prisones *in* places and in peynes.
C. 7.277	For he payeth for prisones in places and *in* peynes.
C. 8.5	'Th[is] were a long lettyng,' quod [a] lady *in* a slayre;
C. 8.26	*In* couenant þat thow kepe holy kerke and mysulue
C. 8.34	To defende þe *in* fayth, fyhte thow y sholde.'
C. 8.43	Thogh he be here thyn vnderlynge *in* heuene worthy parauntur
C. 8.45	At churche *in* the Charnel cherles Aren euele to knowe
C. 8.56	'And [y] shal [ap]parayle me,' quod Perkyn, '*in* pilgrimes wyse

C. 8.57	And wende with alle tho þat wolden lyue *in* treuthe.'
C. 8.60	And heng his hopur on his hal[s] *in* stede of a scryppe;
C. 8.67	Shal haue leue, by oure lord, to [lese here *in* heruest]
C. 8.69	And alle kyne crafty men þat conne lyue *in* treuthe,
C. 8.103	He is holdyng, y hope, to haue me *in* his masse
C. 8.104	And men[g]e me in his memorie amongus alle cristene.
C. 8.117	Vch man *in* his manere made hymsulue to done
C. 8.124	Quod [Peres] þe [plouhman] al *in* puyre tene:
C. 8.138	That no faytrye were founde *in* folk þat goth abeggeth.
C. 8.163	'Or y shal bete the by the lawe and brynge þe *in* stokkes.'
C. 8.171	Hunger *in* haste hye hente wastour by þe mawe
C. 8.184	Sp[it]teden and spradden donge *in* dispit of hunger.
C. 8.198	*In* daubynge and in deluynge, in donge afeld berynge,
C. 8.198	In daubynge and *in* deluynge, in donge afeld berynge,
C. 8.198	In daubynge and in deluynge, *in* donge afeld berynge,
C. 8.199	*In* threschynge, in thekynge, in thwytinge of pynnes,
C. 8.199	In threschynge, *in* thekynge, in thwytinge of pynnes,
C. 8.199	In threschynge, in thekynge, *in* thwytinge of pynnes,
C. 8.200	*In* alle kyne trewe craft þat man couthe deuyse.
C. 8.205	And bade hunger *in* haste hye hym out of contraye
C. 8.214	But for fere of famyen, *in* fayth,' sayde [Peres].
C. 8.232	*In* meschief or in malese, and thow mowe hem helpe,
C. 8.232	In meschief or *in* malese, and thow mowe hem helpe,
C. 8.244	*In* somur for his sleuthe he shal haue defaute
C. 8.247	His suluer to thre maner men [*in*] menyng they sholden
C. 8.248	Chaffare and cheue þerwith *in* chele and in hete.
C. 8.248	Chaffare and cheue þerwith in chele and *in* hete.
C. 8.281	*In* al manere ese in Abrahammus lappe.
C. 8.281	In al manere ese *in* Abrahammus lappe.
C. 8.313	And by [t]hat y hope to haue heruost *in* my croft[e];
C. 8.316	Benes and bake aples they brouhten *in* here lappe
C. 8.318	Hunger eet al *in* haste and askede aftur more.
C. 8.327	Ne noon halpeny ale *in* none wyse drynke
C. 9.10	And ryhtfulliche *in* reumes ruylen þe comune
C. 9.12	With patriarkes and prophetes *in* paradis to sitton.
C. 9.16	And bitynge *in* badde men but yf they wol amende,
C. 9.22	Marchauntes *in* þe margine hadde many 3eres
C. 9.33	Amende *in* som manere wyse and ma[y]dones helpe;
C. 9.34	Pore peple bedredene and prisones *in* stokkes
C. 9.38	That no deuel shal 3ow dere ne despeyre *in* 3oure d[e]ynge
C. 9.40	And abyde þer *in* my blisse body and soule for euere.'
C. 9.48	That conforteth suche *in* eny caes and coueyteth nat he[re] 3iftes
C. 9.61	Beggares and Biddares beth nat *in* þ[e] bulle
C. 9.72	As prisones *in* puttes and pore folk in cotes,
C. 9.72	As prisones in puttes and pore folk *in* cotes,
C. 9.74	Þat they with spynnyng may spare spenen hit [*i*]*n* hous huyre,
C. 9.75	Bothe *in* mylke and in mele to make with papelotes
C. 9.75	Bothe in mylke and *in* mele to make with papelotes
C. 9.78	And wo *in* wynter tym[e] and wakynge on nyhtes
C. 9.82	That reuthe is to rede or *in* ryme shewe
C. 9.83	The wo of this wommen þat wonyeth *in* cotes
C. 9.105	A[nd] 3ut ar ther oþere beggares, *in* hele as hit semeth
C. 9.119	For a sent hem forth seluerles *in* a somur garnement
C. 9.131	Men suffreth al þat suche sayen and *in* solace taketh
C. 9.142	*In* hope to sitte at euen by þe hote coles,
C. 9.152	*In* idelnesse and in ese and by otheres trauayle.
C. 9.152	In idelnesse and *in* ese and by otheres trauayle.
C. 9.155	And can eny craft *in* caes he wolde hit vse,
C. 9.159	'Forthy lollares þat lyuen *in* sleuthe and ouer land strikares
C. 9.160	Buth nat *in* this bulle,' quod [Peres], 'til they ben amended
C. 9.162	The boek banneth beggarie and blameth hit *in* this manere:
C. 9.167	For they lyue *in* no loue ne no lawe holden
C. 9.180	As mesels and mendenantes, men yfalle *in* meschief
C. 9.190	And *in* borwes among brewesteres and beggen in churches–
C. 9.190	And in borwes among brewesteres and beggen *in* churches–
C. 9.197	That wonede whilom *in* wodes with beres and lyons.
C. 9.209	That faytede *in* frere clothinge hadde fatte chekes.
C. 9.211	And clothed hem *in* copes, clerkes as hit were
C. 9.217	Or ymaymed *in* som membre, for to meschief hit souneth,
C. 9.225	*In* frithes and in forestes for fox and other bestes
C. 9.225	In frithes and *in* forestes for fox and other bestes
C. 9.226	That *in* wilde wodes been or in waste places,
C. 9.226	That in wilde wodes been or *in* waste places,
C. 9.229	Bothe matynes and masse; and aftir mete *in* churches
C. 9.248	[C]o[m]e *in* his cope as he a Clerk were;
C. 9.252	Ac while a wrouhte *in* þe world and wan his mete with treuthe
C. 9.254	Cam no wyn *in* his wombe thorw þe woke longe
C. 9.264	Here salue is of supersedeas *in* sumnoures boxes;
C. 9.273	Redde racionem villicacionis or *in* arrerage fall!
C. 9.285	*In* two lynes hit lay and nat a lettre more
C. 9.286	And was ywryte ryhte thus *in* witnesse of treuthe:
C. 9.295	And seyh the sonne *in* the sou[t]he sitte þat tyme,
C. 9.300	And of [Peres] the [plouhman] fol pencyf *in* herte

C. 9.314	Hit biful as his fadur saide *in* farao his tyme
C. 9.344	Thow we be founden *in* the fraternite of alle fyue ordres
C.10.1	Thus, yrobed *in* russet, y romede aboute
C.10.33	Lat bryng a man *in* a boet amydde a brood water;
C.10.39	Thow he falle falleth nat but [as] hoso ful *in* a boet
C.10.112	Elles knowe y noen þat can *in* none kynneryche.'
C.10.123	Thenne thouht *in* þat tyme sayde this wordes:
C.10.124	'Whare dowel and dobet And dobest ben *in* londe
C.10.129	*In* a Castel þat kynde made of foure kyne thynges:
C.10.158	And semblable *in* soule to god but if synne hit make.
C.10.174	Inwit is *in* the heued and anima in herte
C.10.174	Inwit is in the heued and anima *in* herte
C.10.179	ʒaf his douhter for a daunsynge *in* a disch þe heued
C.10.191	That alle landes loueden and *in* on lawe bileuede.
C.10.202	*In* meschief for defaute of mete ne for myssyng of clothes:
C.10.203	Hoso lyueth *in* lawe and in loue doth wel
C.10.203	Hoso lyueth in lawe and *in* loue doth wel
C.10.213	Caym þe corsede creature conseyued was *in* synne
C.10.233	That *in* thi [s]hingled ship shal be with þe ysaued."
C.10.266	Ther ne is squier ne knyhte *in* contreye aboute
C.10.270	*In* ielosyne, ioyles and iangelynge abedde,
C.10.279	For coueytise of catel *in* none kyne wyse;
C.10.291	Clene of lyf and *in* loue of soule and in lele wedlok.
C.10.291	Clene of lyf and in loue of soule and *in* lele wedlok.
C.10.299	And after her deth day dwellen shollen *in* helle
C.11.21	Iob þe gentele *in* his g[e]stes witnesseth
C.11.29	Ac he þat hath holy writ ay *in* his mouth
C.11.44	God is nat *in* þat hoem ne his helpe nother.
C.11.47	Ne were mercy *in* m[e]ne men more then in riht riche
C.11.47	Ne were mercy in m[e]ne men more then *in* riht riche
C.11.49	And so saith þe sauter; y say hit [*in*] memento:
C.11.51	And haen [hym] muche *in* here mouth Ac mene [men] in herte.
C.11.51	And haen [hym] muche in here mouth Ac mene [men] *in* herte.
C.11.55	That folk is nat ferme[d] *in* þe faith ne fre of here godes
C.11.57	*In* religion and in al þe reume amongus riche and pore
C.11.57	In religion and *in* al þe reume amongus riche and pore
C.11.64	Bote *in* gaynesse and glotonye forglotten here godes
C.11.67	And lordeth *in* ledes the lasse goed he deleth.
C.11.69	How he tolde *in* a tyme and tauhte his sone dele:
C.11.117	And alle þe musons *in* musyk y made here to knowe.
C.11.162	And lakkede [me *in*] latyn and lyhte by me sette
C.11.165	And *in* a wynkynge y warth and wonderliche me mette
C.11.168	And *in* a myrrour þat hihte myddelerd she made me to loke.
C.11.179	And *in* þis myrrour thow myhte se murthes fol monye
C.11.193	'ʒe? reche þe neuere,' quod rechelesnesse, stod forth *in* ragged clothes;
C.11.197	For rechelesnesse *in* his rybaud[i]e riht thus he saide:
C.11.201	Sholde sitte *in* goddis sihte ne se god in his blisse:
C.11.201	Sholde sitte in goddis sihte ne se god *in* his blisse:
C.11.202	For clergie saith þat he seyh *in* þe seynt euaungelie
C.11.204	*In* þe legende of lyf longe ar y were.
C.11.217	Were wonder goed and wisest *in* here tyme
C.11.218	And holi churche, as y here, haldeth bothe *in* helle!
C.11.220	That for here werkes and wyt wonyeth now *in* payne,
C.11.226	For of fele witty *in* faith litel ferly y haue
C.11.229	*In* goed then in god; forthy hem grace faileth.
C.11.229	In goed then *in* god; forthy hem grace faileth.
C.11.232	As holy writ witnesseth, goddes word *in* þe gospel:
C.11.236	Ac y wene hit worth of monye as was *in* noes tyme
C.11.262	As *in* likyng of lecherye no lyf denyede!
C.11.268	And now beth this seyntes, by that men saith, and souereynes *in* heuene,
C.11.273	And fonde y neuere *in* faith, for to telle treuthe,
C.11.280	And myhte no kyng ouercome hym as *in* connynge of speche.
C.11.286	Saide thus *in* his sarmon for ensau[m]ple of grete clerkes,
C.11.290	Comuneliche then clerkes most knowyng *in* konnyng
C.11.291	Ne none sanere ysa[u]eth then *in* bileue
C.11.296	Selde falleth þe seruant so depe *in* arrerage
C.11.300	Selde falleth so foule and so depe *in* synne
C.11.302	Lewede men *in* good bileue and lene hem at here nede.'
C.12.8	And festene the *in* ther f[r]aternite and for the byseche
C.12.46	He saide *in* here sarmon selcouthe wordes:
C.12.51	And *in* a wer gan y wex and with mysulue to despute
C.12.64	Ac he may renne *in* arrerage and rome fro home
C.12.67	And consience acounte with hym and casten hym *in* arrerag[e]
C.12.68	And potten hym aftur *in* prisoun in purgatorie to brenne
C.12.68	And potten hym aftur in prisoun *in* purgatorie to brenne
C.12.77	How y was ded and dampned to dwellen *in* [pyne]
C.12.80	Bote onlyche loue and leaute as *in* my lawes demynge.
C.12.82	Sauacion for soethnesse [þat] a sey *in* my werkes.
C.12.90	Wel ouhte ʒe lordes þat lawes kepeth this lesson haue *in* mynde
C.12.91	And on Troianus treuthe to thenke alle tyme[s] *in* ʒoure lyue
C.12.113	*In* þe olde lawe, as þe lettre telleth, mennes sones me calde vs

C.12.122	For *in* here likenesse oure lord lome hath be yknowe.
C.12.123	Witnesse *in* þe paske woke when he ʒede to Emaux:
C.12.132	*In* þe parail of a pilgrime and in pore likenesse
C.12.132	In þe parail of a pilgrime and *in* pore likenesse
C.12.133	Holy seyntes hym sey Ac neuere *in* secte of riche.
C.12.150	Maketh man to haue mynde *in* god and his mercy to craue,
C.12.153	And lasse drat [dethe] or *in* derke to ben yrobbed
C.12.157	Or eny welthe *in* this world, his wyf or his childrene,
C.12.160	And lyf lastyng for euere byfore oure lord *in* heuene:
C.12.168	ʒut conseileth Crist *in* commen vs all:
C.12.180	Bote if þe seed þat sowen is *in* the sloo sterue
C.12.183	[And] oþer sedes also *in* þe same wyse
C.12.184	That ben layd *in* louhe erthe, ylore as hit were,
C.12.185	And thorw þe grace of god and grayn dede [*i*]n erthe
C.12.189	Then sedes þat [*in* somer] sowe ben and mowen nat with forstes
C.12.190	Ne wynde ne wederes as *in* wynter tym[e],
C.12.193	*In* þe feld with þe forst and hit frese longe.
C.12.203	Bitokeneth treuly *in* tyme comyng aftur
C.12.207	Angelis *in* here anger on this wyse hem grette:
C.12.214	Þe catel þat he kepeth so *in* coffres and in bernis,
C.12.214	Þe catel þat he kepeth so in coffres and *in* bernis,
C.12.217	That many mothe was maistre ynne *in* A myntewhyle;
C.12.229	Riht as wedes waxeth *in* wose and in donge
C.12.229	Riht as wedes waxeth in wose and *in* donge
C.12.244	And he for his hard holdyng *in* helle parauntur:
C.13.2	Among Pilours *in* pees yf pacience hym folowe.
C.13.8	For *in* greet pouerte he was put: a prince, as hit were,
C.13.17	And for a song *in* his sorwe, "si bona accepimus a domino &c,
C.13.22	And brouhte hem all aboue þat *in* bale rotede!
C.13.23	As grayn þat lith *in* greut and thorw grace at the laste
C.13.51	Marchauntʒ for here marchaundyse *in* many place to tolle.
C.13.57	And dredeth to be ded þerfore and he *in* derke mette
C.13.71	Alle maner men [*in*] meschief yfalle,
C.13.85	Ne *in* none enquestes to come ne cont[u]max thogh he worche
C.13.94	*In* þat a wilneth and wolde vch wyht as hymsulue.
C.13.102	That yf th[ey] trauaile treulyche and trist *in* god almyhty
C.13.118	Yf fals latyn be *in* þat lettre þe lawe hit enpugneth,
C.13.121	So [is hit] a goky, by god! þat in [his] gospel fayleth
C.13.122	Or *in* masse or in matynes maketh eny defaute:
C.13.122	Or in masse or *in* matynes maketh eny defaute:
C.13.123	[To] ouerskippperes also *in* þe sauter sayth dauid:
C.13.128	For ignorancia non excusat as ych haue herd *in* bokes.'
C.13.129	Thus rechelesnesse *in* a rage aresenede clergie
C.13.132	And *in* þe myrour of mydelerthe made him efte to loke,
C.13.137	Wilde wormes *in* wodes and wondurfol foules
C.13.144	*In* etynge, [in] drynkyng [and] in engend[eryng] of kynde.
C.13.144	In etynge, [*in*] drynkyng [and] in engend[eryng] of kynde.
C.13.144	In etynge, [in] drynkyng [and] *in* engend[eryng] of kynde.
C.13.146	As when þei hadde [ryde *in*] roteye[tyme] anon they reste aftur;
C.13.155	As *in* derne dedes, bothe drynkyng and elles.
C.13.156	Briddes y beheld [þat] *in* bosches made nestes;
C.13.167	*In* mareys and in mores, in myres and in watres,
C.13.167	In mareys and *in* mores, in myres and in watres,
C.13.167	In mareys and in mores, *in* myres and in watres,
C.13.167	In mareys and in mores, in myres and *in* watres,
C.13.184	'Y haue wonder *in* my wit, so wys as thow art holden,
C.13.188	*In* mete out of mesure and mony tymes in drynke,
C.13.188	In mete out of mesure and mony tymes *in* drynke,
C.13.189	*In* wommen, in wedes and in wordes bothe
C.13.189	In wommen, *in* wedes and in wordes bothe
C.13.189	In wommen, in wedes and *in* wordes bothe
C.13.198	He myhte amende *in* a myntewhile al þat [mys]standeth
C.13.199	Ac he soffreth *in* ensaumple þat we sholde soffren alle.
C.13.234	For lat a dronkene daffe *in* a dykke falle,
C.14.3	Y haue folewed the, *in* fayth, mo then fourty wynter
C.14.9	Lowe the and l[y]ue forth *in* þe lawe of holy chirche;
C.14.31	As to be bore or bygete *in* such a constillacioun;
C.14.37	For moyses witnesseth þat god wroet [*in* stoen with his fynger;
C.14.40	And *in* soend a signe wroet and saide to þe iewes,
C.14.50	And as a blynde man *in* bataile bereth wepene to fyhte
C.14.58	Arca dei *in* þe olde lawe leuytes hit kepte;
C.14.74	And markede hit *in* here manere and mused þeron to knowe.
C.14.90	Ne *in* no cote ne Caytyfs hous [crist was ybore
C.14.91	Bote *in* a burgeises hous], the beste of þe toune.
C.14.95	Ryche men rotte tho and *in* here reste were
C.14.103	And thow saidest sothe of somme, Ac [yse] *in* what manere.
C.14.104	Take two stronge men and *in* temese cast hem,
C.14.108	Which trowest [þou] of tho two *in* temese [is] in moste drede?'
C.14.108	Which trowest [þou] of tho two in temese [is] *in* moste drede?'
C.14.116	As we seen *in* þe sauter in psalmes oen or tweyne
C.14.116	As we seen in þe sauter *in* psalmes oen or tweyne
C.14.119	*In* whiche floed þe fende fondeth [a] man hardest.
C.14.145	For he þat is ones a thef is eueremore *in* daunger

C.14.149	And riht as troianes þe trewe knyhte [telde] nat depe *in* helle
C.14.150	That oure [lord] ne hauede [hym] lihtliche out, so leue y [by] þ[e] thef *in* heuene.
C.14.151	For he is *in* þe loweste of heuene, yf oure byleue be trewe,
C.14.158	And how þe floures *in* þe fryth cometh to fayre hewes:
C.14.175	And haue hem [*in*] haste at þyn owen wille
C.14.184	And þe ryche for his rentes or for rychesse *in* his shopp[e].
C.14.190	Likneth *in* here logik þe leste foul out[e].
C.14.193	Wher þey ben *in* hell or in heuene or Aristotel þe wyse.
C.14.193	Wher þey ben in hell or *in* heuene or Aristotel þe wyse.
C.14.200	Segen [*in*] here sarmons þat noþer saresynes ne iewes
C.14.206	And he is saef, saith the boek, and his soule *in* heuene.
C.14.207	Ac þer is follyng of fonte and follyng *in* bloed [s]hedyng
C.14.211	And yf þer were a wolde [amende], and *in* suche a wille deyeth–
C.15.3	*In* manere of [a] mendenaunt mony ʒer aftur.
C.15.11	Ne no cors of pore comine *in* here kyrkeʒerde most lygge
C.15.17	And how þat ymaginatyf *in* dremeles me tolde
C.15.21	And y merueyle[d] *in* herte how ymaginatyf saide
C.15.49	*In* a morter, post mortem, of many bittere peynes
C.15.74	Ac me wondreth *in* my wyt why þat they ne preche
C.15.89	Þat *in* þ[e] mawe of þat maystre alle þo metes were,
C.15.95	He shal haue a penaunce *in* his paunche and poffe at vch a worde
C.15.102	What a fond *in* a forel of a frere[s] lyuynge,
C.15.115	*In* þat ʒe parteth nat with vs pore, þat ʒe passeth dowel
C.15.128	'Haue me excused,' quod Clergie, 'be crist, but *in* scole.
C.15.160	And bere hit *in* thy bosom aboute where þou wendest
C.15.161	*In* þe corner of a car[t]whel with a crow croune.
C.15.165	Þer [n]is wyht *in* this world þat wolde the lette
C.15.185	Thenne hadde pacience, as pilgrimes haen, *in* h[is] poke vitayles,
C.15.187	To conforte hym and Consience yf they come *in* place
C.15.221	*In* his mouthe mercy and amende vs all:
C.15.240	Þe worm and wonte vnder erthe and *in* water fisches,
C.15.243	*In* menynge þat alle men myhte be same
C.15.255	*In* [ond]ynge and [*in*] handlynge [and] in alle thy fyue wittes,
C.15.255	In [ond]ynge and [*in*] handlynge [and] in alle thy fyue wittes,
C.15.255	In [ond]ynge and [in] handlynge [and] *in* alle thy fyue wittes,
C.15.265	And *in* Elies tyme heuene was yclosed
C.15.266	That no reyn ne roen; thus [r]at men [*i*]n bokes,
C.15.284	Hit are but fewe folk of this ryche that ne falleth *in* arrerage
C.15.289	And wilde wormes *in* wodes, thorw wyntres thow hem greuest
C.15.294	That al here lyf haen lyued *in* langour and defaute.
C.15.298	Angeles þat *in* helle now ben hadden som tyme ioye
C.15.299	And dyues *in* deyntees lyuede and [*in*] douce vie
C.15.299	And dyues in deyntees lyuede and [*in*] douce vie
C.15.305	Then aren hit puyre pore thynges *in* purgatorie or in hell.
C.15.305	Then aren hit puyre pore thynges in purgatorie or *in* hell.
C.15.306	Dauid *in* þe sauter of suche maketh mynde and sayth: dormierunt
C.16.10	Muche murthe is *in* may amonge wilde bestes
C.16.18	That al here lyf leden *in* lownesse and in pouerte.
C.16.18	That al here lyf leden in lownesse and *in* pouerte.
C.16.41	*In* fenestres at þe freres–yf fals be þe fondement.
C.16.42	Forthy cristene sholde be *in* comune ryche, noon coueytous for hymsulue.
C.16.47	And þat is plesant to pruyde *in* pore and in ryche.
C.16.47	And þat is plesant to pruyde in pore and *in* ryche.
C.16.51	Then rychesse or ryalte and rather yherde *in* heuene.
C.16.57	And pruyde *in* rychesse regneth rather then in pouerte;
C.16.57	And pruyde in rychesse regneth rather then *in* pouerte;
C.16.58	Or *in* þe maystre or in þe man som mansion he haueth.
C.16.58	Or in þe maystre or *in* þe man som mansion he haueth.
C.16.59	Ac *in* pouerte þer pacience is pruyde hath no myhte
C.16.61	Ne haue power *in* pouerte yf pacience h[it] folewe.
C.16.86	For pouerte hath bote pokes to potten *in* his godes
C.16.99	And *in* þat secte oure saueour saued al mankynde.
C.16.103	*In* lond and in lordschipe [and] lykynge of body
C.16.103	In lond and *in* lordschipe [and] lykynge of body
C.16.119	*In* engelysch is ful hard Ac sumdel y shal telle the.
C.16.122	Al þat may potte of pruyde *in* place þer he regneth;
C.16.138	And frende *in* alle fondynges and of foule eueles leche:
C.16.148	Then he may sothly deserue *in* Somur or in wynter;
C.16.148	Then he may sothly deserue in Somur or *in* wynter;
C.16.152	And sobrete ʒeueth here swete drynke and solaceth here *in* all angrys.
C.16.167	'Y am cristes creature,' quod he, 'and cristene *in* mony a place
C.16.168	And *in* cristes court yknowe wel and of his kynne a party.
C.16.196	Thenne is lele loue my name and *in* latyn Amor;
C.16.211	Y wolde y knewe and couthe kyndeliche *in* myn herte.'
C.16.235	And [ho]w that folk [*in* folies] here fyue wittes myspen[en],
C.16.237	*In* housynge, in helynge, in h[eyh] clergie schewynge
C.16.237	In housynge, *in* helynge, in h[eyh] clergie schewynge
C.16.237	In housynge, in helynge, *in* h[eyh] clergie schewynge
C.16.248	And s[e] hit by ensample *In* somur tyme on trees
C.16.251	There is a meschief *in* þe more of suche manere stokkes.
C.16.266	And is ylikned *in* latyn to a lothly donghep
C.16.288	Ich haue yleued *in* londone monye longe ʒeres
C.16.289	And fonde y neuere *in* faith, as freres hit precheth,
C.16.291	As poul *in* his pistul of hym bereth wittenesse
C.16.315	That neuere payed peny aʒeyn *in* places þer he borwede.'
C.16.327	What sorwe he soffrede *in* ensaumple of vs alle
C.16.333	And laueth hem *in* þe lauendrie, labora[ui] in gemitu meo,
C.16.344	And compenable *in* companye a[s] Crist hymsulue techeth:
C.16.345	Ych haue ysey hym mysulue som tyme *in* russet,
C.16.346	Bothe *in* gray and in grys and in gult harneys,
C.16.346	Bothe in gray and *in* grys and in gult harneys,
C.16.346	Bothe in gray and in grys and *in* gult harneys,
C.16.351	Ryden and rennen *in* raggede clothes
C.16.353	Ac *in* riche robes rathest he walketh,
C.16.355	And *in* a frere f[r]okke he was founde ones
C.16.356	Ac hit is fer and fele ʒer *in* franceys tyme;
C.16.357	*In* [þat] sekte sethe to selde hath he be [knowen].
C.16.360	*In* kynges Court a cometh yf his consaile be trewe
C.16.362	Amongus þe comune *in* Court a cometh bote selde
C.16.364	*In* constorie bifore [þe] commissarie a cometh nat ful ofte
C.17.7	Solitarie by hemsulue *in* here selles lyuede
C.17.11	Elles foules fedde hem *in* frythes þer they wonede,
C.17.23	Marie Egipciaca eet *in* thritty wynter
C.17.28	And woneden *in* wildernesses amonges wilde bestes.
C.17.33	*In* tokenynge þat trewe man alle tymes sholde
C.17.36	Toke lyflode of luyther wynnynges *in* all here lyf tyme.
C.17.68	And fedde þat afyn[g]red were and *in* defaute lyuede.
C.17.87	May no preyere pees make *in* no place hit semeth.
C.17.90	As they ywoned were; *in* wham is defaute?
C.17.91	Nat *in* god þat he ne is goed and þe grounde bothe;
C.17.97	Astronomiens alday *in* here arte faylen
C.17.116	Bo[t]e they fayle *in* philosophie and philosoferes lyuede.
C.17.120	As Clerkes *in* corpus cristi feste syngen and reden
C.17.124	*In* þe lettynge of here lyf to leue on holy churche.'
C.17.126	'[Lif *in*] loue and leutee in o byleue a[nd] lawe,
C.17.126	'[Lif in] loue and leutee *in* o byleue a[nd] lawe,
C.17.135	And ayther loueth and byleueth *in* o [lord] almyhty.
C.17.144	For when alle frendes faylen and fleen away *in* deynge
C.17.147	*In* murthe or in mournynge and neuere[more] to departe.
C.17.147	In murthe or *in* mournynge and neuere[more] to departe.
C.17.149	Contrarie her nat as *in* Consience yf thow wol[t] come to heuene.'
C.17.164	Ne kynde sanʒ cortesie *in* no contreye is preysed.
C.17.172	*In* ayþer of his eres pr=iueliche he hadde
C.17.173	Corn [þat þe] coluere eet when he come *in* places
C.17.174	And *in* what place he prechede and the peple tauhte
C.17.179	And sothliche þat god sulue *in* suche a coluere lyknesse
C.17.181	Thus macumeth *in* misbileue man & womman brouhte
C.17.205	For couetyse aftur cros; the corone stand *in* golde.
C.17.207	That *in* grotes is graue and in golde nobles.
C.17.207	That in grotes is graue and *in* golde nobles.
C.17.228	Yf the kynges coueyte *in* cristes pees to lyuene.
C.17.237	Alle londes into loue And þat *in* lytel tyme;
C.17.240	Hadde al surie as hymsulue wolde and sarrasines *in* equitee.
C.17.243	*In* such manere me thynketh moste þe pope,
C.17.256	*In* þe gre[te] god and his grace asken
C.17.258	Thus *in* a fayth l[e]ueth þat folk and in a fals mene,
C.17.258	Thus in a fayth l[e]ueth þat folk and *in* a fals mene,
C.17.259	And þat is reuthe for rihtfole men þat *in* þ[e] reume wonyeth
C.17.264	*In* ensaumple þat men sholde se by sad resoen
C.17.272	*In* ynde, in alisandre, in Armonye [and] spayne
C.17.272	In ynde, *in* alisandre, in Armonye [and] spayne
C.17.272	In ynde, in alisandre, *in* Armonye [and] spayne
C.17.274	*In* sauacioun of mannes soule seynte Thomas of Canterbury
C.17.275	Amonges v[n]kynde cristene *in* holy [kirke] was slawe
C.17.279	And nat *in* Ingelond to huppe aboute and halewe men auters
C.17.288	And amonges here enemyes *in* mortel batayles
C.17.295	Iewes lyuen *in* þe lawe þat oure lord tauhte
C.17.302	Tho he luft vp lasar þat layde was *in* graue;
C.18.2	Thow couthest telle me and teche me [*in*] charite [to] leue.'
C.18.6	Euene *in* þe myddes an ympe, as hit were,
C.18.15	And solaceth alle soules sorwful *in* purgatory.'
C.18.35	Thenne is þe flesch a fel wynde and *in* flouryng tyme
C.18.56	A[c] *in* thre degrees hit grewe; grete ferly me thouhte,
C.18.64	Tho that sitten *in* þe sonne syde sannore aren rype,
C.18.66	Then tho that selde haen þe sonne and sitten *in* þe North half;
C.18.73	And conforteth hem *in* here continence þat lyuen in contemplacioun,
C.18.73	And conforteth hem in here continence þat lyuen *in* contemplacioun,
C.18.80	That [lyf Actiua] lettred men *in* here langage calleth.'
C.18.83	Why groweth this fruyt *in* thre degres?' 'A goed skil,' he saide.
C.18.87	Wydewhode, more worthiore then wedlok, as *in* heuene;
C.18.88	Thenne is virginite, more vertuous and fayrest, as *in* heuene,

C.18.92	*In* menynge þat the fayrest thyng the furste thynge shold honoure
C.18.94	*In* kynges Court and in knyhtes, the clenneste men and fayreste
C.18.94	In kynges Court and *in* knyhtes, the clenneste men and fayreste
C.18.97	And *in* heuene is priueoste and next hym by resoun
C.18.123	And thenne spak spiritus sanctus *in* gabrieles mouthe
C.18.125	That oen Iesus, a Iustices sone, most iouken *in* here chaumbre
C.18.133	And *in* þe wombe of þat wenche was he fourty wokes
C.18.135	Byg and abydyng, and bold *in* his barnhoed
C.18.143	And luft vp laȝar þat lay *in* his tombe;
C.18.156	And ouerturnede *in* þe temple here tables and here stalles
C.18.163	Enuye and euel wil ern *in* þe iewes
C.18.171	'Falsnesse y fynde *in* thy fayre speche
C.18.172	And kene care *in* thy kissyng and combraunce to thysulue
C.18.176	Soffreth my postles *in* pays and in pees gange.'
C.18.176	Soffreth my postles in pays and *in* pees gange.'
C.18.179	*In* inwit and in alle wittes aftur liberum Arbitrium
C.18.179	In inwit and *in* alle wittes aftur liberum Arbitrium
C.18.186	'What is his [conn]esaunc[e],' quod y, '*in* his cote Armure?'
C.18.187	'Thre persones *in* o pensel,' quod he, 'departable fram oþere.
C.18.195	Holy goest is his name and he is *in* all.'
C.18.197	How o lord myhte lyue [*in*] thre; y leue hit nat,' y sayde.
C.18.219	And abel here issue, aren bote oen *in* manhede.
C.18.226	Now go we to godhede: *in* god, fader of heuene,
C.18.227	Was þe sone *in* hymsulue, in a simile as Eue was,
C.18.227	Was þe sone in hymsulue, in a simile as Eue was,
C.18.235	So i[n] god [and] godes sone i[s] thre persones, the trinite.
C.18.236	*In* matrimonie aren thre and of o man cam alle thre
C.18.238	Lo! treys encountre treys,' quod he, '*in* godhede and in manhede.'
C.18.238	Lo! treys encountre treys,' quod he, 'in godhede and *in* manhede.'
C.18.240	'*In* a somur y hym seyh,' quod he, 'as y saet in my porche,
C.18.240	'In a somur y hym seyh,' quod he, 'as y saet *in* my porche,
C.18.245	He bihihte vs issue and ayr *in* oure olde age;
C.18.250	Where y walke *in* this worlde a wol hit me allowe.
C.18.254	Myen affiaunce and my faith is ferme *in* [t]his bileue
C.18.262	At ones on an auter *in* worschipe of th[e] trinite
C.18.265	Thus haue y ben his heraud here and *in* helle
C.18.270	For *in* his bosome a baer [a] thyng þat [a] blessede [euere].
C.18.271	And y lokede *in* his lappe; a laȝar lay þerynne
C.18.274	'I wolde ywyte,' quod y tho, 'what is *in* thy lappe.'
C.18.285	Lollyng *in* my lappe til suche a lord vs feche.'
C.19.3	To reule alle reumes þerwith *in* riȝhte and in resoun.
C.19.3	To reule alle reumes þerwith in riȝhte and *in* resoun.
C.19.20	Shal neuere deuel hym dere ne deth *in* soule greue;
C.19.24	Lo! here *in* my lappe þat leuede vpon þat lettre,
C.19.33	He can no certeyn somme telle and somme aren *in* his lappe.
C.19.42	And for to louye and bileue *in* o lord almyhty
C.19.44	Ac for to bileue in o lord þat lyueth *in* thre persones
C.19.44	Ac for to bileue *in* o lord þat lyueth in thre persones
C.19.48	And as we wenten *in* þe way thus wordyng this matere
C.19.52	To ioust *in* Ierusalem he Iaced awey faste.
C.19.54	*In* a wi[d]e wildernesse where theues hadde ybounde
C.19.66	[A l]ihte a[dou]n of lyard and ladde hym *in* his hand[e]
C.19.68	And parseued by his poues he was *in* perel to deye
C.19.98	*In* thre persones, a parceles departable fram oþere,
C.19.104	Eny wikkedere *in* þe worlde then y were mysulue
C.19.113	For god þat al bygan *in* bigynnynge of the worlde
C.19.153	Ac ho is herte *in* the hand euene in þe myddes
C.19.153	Ac ho is herte in the hand euene *in* þe myddes
C.19.162	*In* many kyne manere y myhte mysulfe helpe,
C.19.165	That hoso synegeth *in* þe seynt spirit assoiled worth he neuere,
C.19.167	For he priketh god as *in* [the] paume that peccat in spiritum sanctum.
C.19.183	Withouten leye [or] lihte lith fuyr *in* þe mache–
C.19.188	That worchen and waken *in* wynteres nyhtes
C.19.197	Isekeles *in* euesynges thorwe hete of the sonne
C.19.198	Melteth in a myntwhile to myst and to water.
C.19.203	And solacen [hem] þat mowen nat se, sittynge *in* derkeness[e],
C.19.206	*In* as moche as they mowen amenden and payen;
C.19.207	And yf hit suffic[e] nat for ase[t]h þat *in* suche a will deyeth
C.19.210	For to murthe men with þat *in* merke sitten,
C.19.243	And dampned a dwelleth with þe deuel *in* helle.
C.19.246	And is *in* helle for al þat, how wol riche nouthe
C.19.266	And ȝut *in* mo maneres men [o]ffenden þe holy gost;
C.19.294	That mercy *in* here mynde may nat thenne falle;
C.19.307	Ac when smoke and smolder [smyt *in* his sihte
C.19.310	Til he be blereyede or blynde and þe borre *in* [the] throte,
C.19.321	As Paul þe apostel *in* his episteles techeth:
C.19.322	And thogh that men make moche deul *in* here anger
C.19.323	And be inpacient *in* here penaunc[e], puyr resoun knoweth
C.19.327	Ac þe smoke and þe smolder þat smyt *in* oure yes,
C.20.13	Thenne was faith *in* a fenestre and criede 'a! fil[i] dauid!'
C.20.17	And ho sholde iouste *in* Ierusalem. 'Iesus,' he saide,
C.20.19	'Is Peres *in* this place?' quod y, and he printe on me.
C.20.21	That this iesus of his gentrice shal iouste *in* Pers Armes,
C.20.22	*In* his helm and in his haberion, humana natura;
C.20.22	In his helm and *in* his haberion, humana natura;
C.20.24	*In* [Pers paltok] the [plouhman] this prikiare shal ryde
C.20.41	To fordoen hit on a day, and *in* thre dayes aftur
C.20.43	And ȝut maken hit as moche *in* alle manere poyntes,
C.20.49	And sette hit sore on his heued and saide *in* Enuye;
C.20.67	'Lyf & deth, *in* this derkenesse here oen fordoth her oþer.
C.20.79	That hadde no boie hardynesse hym to touche *in* deynge.
C.20.82	Bifore pilatus and oþere peple *in* þe place he houed.
C.20.92	Of þe dede þat y haue do y do me *in* ȝoure grace;
C.20.106	And ȝoure franchise þat fre was yfallen i[n] thraldoem;
C.20.108	Ne haue lordschipe *in* londe ne no londe tulye
C.20.110	The which is lif þat oure lord *in* all lawes defendeth.
C.20.114	Y [d]row [me] *in* þat derkenesse to descendit ad inferna
C.20.117	Cam walkynge *in* þe way; to hellward she lokede.
C.20.128	'Y haue ferly of this fare, *in* faith,' seide Treuthe,
C.20.139	*In* menynge þat man shal fro me[r]kenesse be ydrawe
C.20.147	Patriarkes and prophetes þat *in* peyne liggen,
C.20.151	[For] þat ones is *in* helle out cometh hit neuere.
C.20.171	Where cometh pees pleiynge *in* pacience yclothed.
C.20.175	Whenne pees *in* pacience yclothed aproched her ayþer oþer
C.20.176	Rihtwisnesse reuerenced pees *in* here rich clothyng
C.20.178	And [*in*] here gay garnementes wham she gladie thouhte.
C.20.181	Adam and Eue and other mo *in* helle.
C.20.198	Sholde deye downriht and d[welle] *in* payne euere
C.20.219	For sholde neuere riȝt riche man þat lyueth *in* rest and hele
C.20.228	Sette hym *in* solace and in souereyne merthe
C.20.228	Sette hym in solace and *in* souereyne merthe
C.20.232	To wyte what he hath soffred *in* thre sundry places,
C.20.233	Bothe *in* heuene and in erthe, and now to helle he thenketh
C.20.233	Bothe in heuene and *in* erthe, and now to helle he thenketh
C.20.243	That alle þe wyse of th[is] world *in* o wit acordede
C.20.244	That such a barn was ybore *in* Bethleem þe Citee
C.20.248	Tho þat weren *in* heuene token stella comata
C.20.254	And lo! how þe sonne gan louke here lihte *in* heresulue
C.20.271	A vois loude þat liht to lucifer saide,
C.20.315	Not *in* fourme of a fende bote in fourme of an Addre
C.20.315	Not in fourme of a fende bote *in* fourme of an Addre
C.20.326	And as thowe bigyledest godes ymag[e] *in* goynge of an addre,
C.20.327	So hath god bigiled vs alle *in* goynge of a weye.'
C.20.328	'For god hath go,' quod gobelyne, '*in* gome liknesse
C.20.344	For vs were bettere nat be then abyde *in* his sihte.
C.20.349	We haen ylost oure lordschipe a londe and *in* helle:
C.20.356	Witnesseth *in* his writyng[e] what is lyares mede:
C.20.378	For *in* my palays, paradys, in persone of an addere
C.20.378	For in my palays, paradys, *in* persone of an addere
C.20.382	That gylours [beth] bigiled and [*in*] here gyle falle
C.20.411	Til þe ventage valle *in* þe vale of Iosophat
C.20.418	For we beth brethrene of bloed Ac nat *in* baptisme alle.
C.20.419	Ac alle þat beth myn hole breth[r]ene, *in* bloed and in baptisme,
C.20.419	Ac alle þat beth myn hole breth[r]ene, in bloed and *in* baptisme,
C.20.420	Shal neuere *in* helle eft come be he ones oute:
C.20.421	Hit is nat vsed [i]n erthe to hangen [a] felo[n]
C.20.423	And yf þe kynge of þe kyngdoem come *in* þe tyme
C.20.428	And if lawe wol y loke on hem hit lith *in* my grace
C.20.435	A[c] ȝut my kynde [*in*] my kene ire shal constrayne my will–
C.20.440	And mercy a[l] mankynde bifore me *in* heuene.
C.20.444	Tho [ledes] þat y louye and leued *in* my comynge;
C.20.447	Astarot and alle [þe route] hidden hem *in* hernes;
C.20.456	Was neuere werre *in* this world ne wikkedere enuye
C.20.460	Cluppe we *in* couenaunt and vch of vs kusse oþere.'
C.20.466	And thenne lutede loue *in* a loude note:
C.21.4	*In* myddes of þe masse tho men ȝede to offrynge
C.21.8	And riht lyke *in* alle lymes to oure lord iesu.
C.21.47	And fro fendes þat *in* hem was and false bileue.
C.21.61	Places *in* paradys at here partyng hennes
C.21.68	And moche wo *in* this world wilnen and soffren.
C.21.71	Tho he was bore *in* Bedlehem, as þe boek telleth,
C.21.82	And al þe wit of the world was *in* [þo] thre kynges.
C.21.98	*In* þe manere of a man and þat by moche sleythe.
C.21.101	And so dede iesu *in* his dayes, whoso durste tellen hit.
C.21.108	*In* his iuuentee this iesus at iewene feste
C.21.124	And when he was wexen more, *in* his moder absence,
C.21.132	And tho was he cald *in* contreye of þe comune peple,
C.21.134	For dauid was douhtiest of dedes *in* his tyme
C.21.158	Goynge toward galilee *in* godhede and manhede
C.21.160	*In* vch a companye he cam, christus resurgens.
C.21.167	*In* an hous al bishut and here dore ybarred
C.21.179	And yblessed mote they be, *in* body and in soule,
C.21.179	And yblessed mote they be, in body and *in* soule,
C.21.180	Tha[t] neuere shal se me *in* sihte as thowe seste nowthe
C.21.186	*In* couenaunt þat they come and knolech[e] to pay

C.21.198 And wikked to wonye *in* wo withouten ende.'
C.21.202 *In* liknesse of a lihtnynge a lyhte on hem alle
C.21.205 And was afered for the lihte, for *in* fuyres liknesse
C.21.248 And somme he [l]ered to lyue *in* longyng to be hennes,
C.21.249 *In* pouerte and *in* pacience to preye for alle cristene;
C.21.249 In pouerte and *in* pacience to preye for alle cristene;
C.21.272 And harwed *in* an handwhile al holy scripture
C.21.275 And sewe hit *in* mannes soule and sethe toelde here names.
C.21.288 Ne no mete *in* his mouth þat maistre iohann spyced.
C.21.293 Makyn hym, for eny mornynge, þat he ne was murye *in* soule
C.21.303 And to corecte the kyng and the kyng falle *in* [g]ulte.
C.21.304 For counteth he no kynges wreth when he *in* Court sitteth;
C.21.312 'For cominliche *in* Contrayes cammokes and wedes
C.21.313 Fouleth the fruyt *in* the feld ther thei growe togyderes
C.21.318 Ordeyne the an hous, [Peres], to herborwe *in* thy cornes.'
C.21.344 'And Peres berne worth broke and þei þat ben *in* vnite
C.21.353 'To waston on welfare and *in* wikked kepynge
C.21.354 Alle the world *in* a while thorw oure wit,' quod pruyde.
C.21.357 Preye we þat a pees were *in* [Peres] berne [þe Plouhman]
C.21.363 That holi churche stoede *in* holinesse as hit [a pyle were].
C.21.380 Made vnite holi churche *in* holinesse stande.
C.21.388 *In* helpe of here hele ones *in* a monthe
C.21.388 In helpe of here hele ones *in* a monthe
C.21.410 'Ich am a Curatour of holi [kirke] and cam neuer *in* my tyme
C.21.421 Bote *in* here holinesse h[e]lden hem stille
C.21.423 Or *in* Rome, as here reule wo[l], þe relikes to kepe;
C.21.424 And thow, Consience, *in* kynges Court and sholdest neuer come thennes;
C.21.430 Ac wel worth Peres the plouhman þat pursueth god *in* doyng[e],
C.21.477 '*In* condicioun,' quod Consience, 'þat þou [þe] comune defende
C.21.478 And rewle thy rewme *in* resoun [as] riht w[o]l and treuthe,
C.22.2   Heuy chered y ȝede and [e]lyng *in* herte.
C.22.10   And nede hath no lawe ne neuere shal falle *in* dette
C.22.14   And he cacche *in* þat caes and come therto by sleithe
C.22.31   And spiritus Prudencie *in* many a poynt shal faile
C.22.42   So he was nedy, as saith the boek *in* mony sondry places,
C.22.43   That he saide *in* his sorwe on þe sulue note:
C.22.52   And mette ful merueylousely þat *in* mannes fourme
C.22.56   *In* vch a Contrey ther he cam [he] kutte awey treuthe
C.22.95   Elde þe hore; he was *in* þe Vawwarde
C.22.116 And armed hym *in* ydelnesse and *in* hey berynge.
C.22.116 And armed hym in ydelnesse and *in* hey berynge.
C.22.117 He baer a bowe *in* his hoend and many brode arwes,
C.22.123 And Armed hym *in* Auarice and hungriliche lyuede.
C.22.130 And knokked Consience *in* Court bifore hem alle;
C.22.134 He iogged til a iustice and iustede *in* his ere
C.22.136 And [t]o þe Arches *in* haste he ȝede anoen aftur
C.22.144 And Armed hym *in* haste in harlotes wordes
C.22.144 And Armed hym in haste *in* harlotes wordes
C.22.157 And geten *in* here glorie a gadlyng at þe laste,
C.22.176 A fisician with a forred hoed that he ful *in* a palesye
C.22.180 And *in* hope of his hele goed herte he hente
C.22.192 And gyued me *in* gowtes: y may nat go at large.
C.22.194 And wesched wel witterly þat y were *in* heuene.
C.22.197 Y ne myhte *in* none manere maken hit at here wille
C.22.199 And as y saet *in* this sorwe y say how kynde passede
C.22.219 *In* paltokes and pikede shoes, [purses and] longe knyues
C.22.246 Holdeth ȝow *in* vnite and haueth noen enuye
C.22.254 That *in* mesure god made alle [manere] thynges
C.22.259 And yf thei wage men to werre thei writen hem *in* nombre;
C.22.261 Bote hy ben nempned *in* þe nombre of hem þat been ywaged.
C.22.262 Alle oþere *in* bataile been yholde brybours,
C.22.263 Pilours and pikeharneys *in* vch a parsch acorsed.
C.22.271 Forthy y wolde witterly þat ȝe were *in* [þe] registre
C.22.276 That alle thynges vnder heuene ou[h]te to be *in* comune.
C.22.280 And euele is this yholde *in* parsches of yngelond
C.22.284 And be aschamed *in* here shryft; ac shame maketh [hem] wende
C.22.288 Ac while he is *in* Westmynstre he wol be bifore
C.22.293 And soffren þe dede *in* dette to þe day of dome.
C.22.297 *In* vnite holi church Consience heeld hym
C.22.310 Yf eny surgien were *in* þe sege that softur couthe plastre
C.22.311 Sire I[ee]f-to-lyue-*in*-lecherye lay þer and groned;
C.22.313 'Ther is a surgien *in* the sege that softe can handele
C.22.328 *In* contreys þer he cam confessions to here;
C.22.331 And *in* haste eschete what his wille were.
C.22.332 '*In* fayth,' quod this frere, 'for profyt and for helthe
C.22.366 And make [of] ȝow [memoria] *in* masse and in matynes
C.22.366 And make [of] ȝow [memoria] in masse and *in* matynes

incurable adj *incurable adj.* B 2; C 2
B.10.332 Haue a knok of a kyng, and *incurable* þe wounde.
B.13.13   Thoruȝ vnkonnynge curatours to *incurable* peynes;
C. 5.177 Shal haue a knok vppon here crounes and *incurable* þe wounde:
C.15.16   Thorw vnkunynge curatours to *incurable* peynes;

ynde n prop *Inde n.(1)* B 2 Inde (1) ynde (1); C 2
B.15.521 In *ynde*, in alisaundre, in ermonye and spayne,
B.19.165 Thaddee and ten mo wiþ Thomas of *Inde*.
C.17.272 In *ynde*, in alisandre, in Armonye [and] spayne
C.21.165 Taddee and ten mo with Thomas of *ynde*.

indepartable adj *indepartable adj.* C 1
C.18.27   Thre persones *indepartable*, perpetuel were euere,

indirect adj *indirect adj.* C 6
C. 3.334 Rect and *indirect*, reninde bothe
C. 3.342 What is relacion rect and *indirect* aftur,
C. 3.363 *Indirect* thyng is as hoso coueytede
C. 3.371 So *indirect* is inlyche to coueyte
C. 3.383 Ac þe moste partie of peple puyr *indirect* semeth
C. 3.388 As rela[tifs] *indirect* re[cc]heth the[y] neuere

indulgence n *indulgence n.* A 2; B 5 Indulgence (1) Indulgences (4); C 5 indulgence (1) indulgences (4)
A. 8.153 And [dem]ide þat dowel *indulgence* passiþ,
A. 8.177 And haue *indulgence* doublefold, but dowel þe helpe
B. 7.57   Whan þei drawen on to [þe deþ] and *Indulgences* wolde haue,
B. 7.175 And demed þat dowel *Indulgences* passe[þ],
B. 7.199 And haue *Indulgences* doublefold, but dowel [þee] helpe
B.17.257 And *Indulgences* ynowe, and be ingratus to þi kynde,
B.20.321 And *Indulgence* may do but if dette lette it.
C. 9.52   For whenne ȝe drawe to þe deth and *indulgences* wolde haue
C. 9.320 And demede þat dowel *indulgences* passeth,
C. 9.345 And haue *indulgences* doublefold, but dowel vs helpe
C.19.223 And *indulgences* ynowe and be ingrat[u]s to thy kynde,
C.22.321 And *indulgence* may do but yf dette lette hit.

ynempned > *nempne*

infamis adj *infamis adj.* B 1
B. 5.168 They hadde þanne ben *Infamis*, þei kan so yuele hele co[unseil].

infinites n *infinite n.* B 2
B.13.128 And [demeþ] þat dowel and dobet arn two *Infinites*,
B.13.129 Whiche *Infinites* wiþ a feiþ fynden out dobest,

infirmite n *infirmite n.* C 1
C. 9.234 And fulfille th[e] fastyng[e] but *infirmite* hit made,

ingang > *ingong*; *ingelond* > *engelond*

ingong n *ingang n.* A 1 ingang; B 1; C 1 ingang
A. 6.114 To gete *ingang* at þe gate but grace be þe more.'
B. 5.629 To geten *ing[o]ng* at any gate but grace be þe moore.'
C. 7.282 To geten *ingang* at eny ȝate bote grace be þe more.'

inhabiten v *enhabiten v.* C 1
C. 9.189 Ac Ermytes þat *inhabiten* by the heye weye

ynliche adv *inli adv.* B 1; C 1 inlyche
B.14.90   Ac shrift of mouþ moore worþi is if man be *y[n]liche* contrit,
C. 3.371 So indirect is *inlyche* to coueyte

inne n *in n.* A 1; B 1; C 1 ynne
A. 9.4   Ȝif any wiȝt wiste where dowel was at *Inne*;
B. 8.4   If any wiȝt wiste wher dowel was at *Inne*;
C.10.4   Yf eny wiht wiste where dowel was at *ynne*;

inne adv *inne adv.* B 5; C 2 ynne
B.10.102 That was maad for meles men to eten *Inne*,
B.10.188 It is no Science forsoþe for to sotile *Inne*;
B.10.329 Of Costantyns cofres [þer þe catel is *Inne*]
B.15.537 Ne no richesse but þe roode to reioisse men *Inne*:
B.19.318 Ordeigne þee an hous, Piers, to herberwe *Inne* þi cornes.'
C.17.198 Ne no rychesse but þe rode to reioysen hem *ynne*:
C.22.344 Kam *ynne* thus ycoped at a Court þer y dwelte

inne prep *inne prep.* A 2; B 5; C 6 ynne
A. 1.163 It is as lewid as a laumpe þat no liȝt is *inne*.
A.12.41   Kynde [wit] hure confessour, hure cosyn was *Inne*.
B. 1.189 It is as lewed as a lampe þat no liȝt is *Inne*.
B. 6.303 Ne no beggere ete breed þat benes *Inne* [come],
B.16.15   Herte highte þe herber þat it *Inne* groweþ,
B.19.147 "The contree is þe corseder þat Cardinals come *Inne*,
B.20.193 And of þe wo þat I was *Inne* my wif hadde ruþe
C. 1.134 There treuthe is, þe tour that trinite *ynne* sitteth.
C. 1.185 Hit is as lewed as a laumpe þat no liht is *ynne*.
C. 8.325 Ne no beggare eten bred þat benes *ynne* were
C.12.217 That many mothe was maistre *ynne* in A myntewhyle;
C.21.417 "The contreye is þe corsedore þat cardinals cometh *ynne*
C.22.193 And of þe wo þat y was *ynne* my wyf hadde reuthe

innocence n *innocence n.* B 1; C 2
B.17.291 *Innocence* is next god and nyght and day it crieþ

C. 3.98   That *Innocence* is herde in heuene amonge seyntes
C.19.272   *Innocence* is next god and nyht and day hit crieth

innocent adj *innocent adj.* A 1; B 3 Innocent (2) Innocentȝ (1); C 1
A. 8.50   Þat is *Innocent* & nedy, & no man apeiriþ,
B. 3.242   And alle þat helpen þe *Innocent* and holden with þe riȝtfulle,
B. 7.42   And nameliche of *Innocentȝ* þat noon yuel konneþ:
B. 7.48   That is *Innocent* and nedy and no man apeireþ,
C. 9.47   That *innocent* and nedy is and no man harm wolde,

inobedient adj *inobedient adj.* B 1; C 1
B.13.281   And *inobedient* to ben vndernome of any lif lyuynge;
C. 6.19   *Inobedient* to holy churche and to hem þat þer serueth;

inogh ynoȝ > ynouȝ; ynome > nymen

ynouȝ n *inough n.* A 1 inouȝ; B 4 ynogh (2) ynoȝ (1) ynouȝ (1); C 1
ynow
A. 7.135   *Inouȝ* iche day at non, ac no more til on þe morewe
B. 7.86   He haþ *ynouȝ* þat haþ breed ynouȝ, þouȝ he haue noȝt ellis:
B.14.33   And þat *ynogh*; shal noon faille of þyng þat hem nedeþ:
B.15.317   Ye hadde riȝt *ynoȝ*, ye Religiouse, and so youre rule me tolde.
B.18.217   Woot no wight, as I wene, what [is *ynogh*] to mene.
C.20.226   Ne woet no wyht, as y wene, what is *ynow* to mene.

ynouȝ adj *inough adj.* A 3 ynouȝ (1) ynowe (2); B 13 ynogh (2) ynoȝ (1)
ynouȝ (4) ynowe (6); C 14 ynow (8) ynowe (6)
A. 2.108   Þanne fette fauel forþ floreynes *ynowe*,
A. 2.111   And feffe false wytnesse wiþ floreynes *ynowe*,
A. 7.137   Ones at noon is *ynouȝ* þat no werk vsiþ;
B. 2.144   Thanne fette Fauel forþ floryns *ynowe*
B. 2.147   And feffe fal[s] witness[e] wiþ floryns *ynowe*,
B. 7.86   He haþ *ynouȝ* þat haþ breed *ynouȝ*, þouȝ he haue noȝt ellis:
B. 9.181   And þanne gete ye grace of god and good *ynouȝ* to lyue wiþ.
B.11.18   And seide, 'þow art yong and yeep and hast yeres *ynowe*
B.11.36   A man may stoupe tyme *ynoȝ* whan he shal tyne þe crowne.'
B.12.17   And bidde for hem þat ȝyueþ þee breed, for þer are bokes *y[n]owe*
B.12.199   [I] hadde mete moore þan *ynouȝ*, ac noȝt so muche worshipe
B.13.261   And er þe commune haue corn *ynouȝ* many a cold morwenyng;
B.14.38   And seide, 'lo! here liflode *ynogh*, if oure bileue be trewe.
B.15.315   For hadde ye potage and payn *ynogh* and penyale to drynke,
B.17.257   And Indulgences *ynowe*, and be ingratus to þi kynde,
B.20.249   And oþere necessaries *ynowe*; ȝow shal no þyng [lakke]
C. 2.35   Shal haue grace to good *ynow* and a good ende,
C. 2.160   T[h]o fette fauel forth floreynes *ynowe*
C. 2.163   And feffe fals witnesse with floreynes *ynowe*,
C. 9.43   Alle þe peple hadde pardon *ynow* þat parfitliche lyuede.
C.10.182   Hath tresor *ynow* of treuthe to fynden hymsulue.
C.11.177   And saide, 'þou art ȝong and ȝep and hast ȝeres *ynowe*
C.11.195   A man may stoupe tyme *ynowe* when he shal tyne þe croune.'
C.14.138   Ich haue mete more then *ynow* Ac nat [so] muche worschipe
C.15.237   And saide, 'lo! here lyflode *ynow* yf oure beleue be trewe
C.16.12   And moche murthe among ryche men is þat han meble *ynow* and
hele.
C.18.256   Lond and lordschip *ynow* and lyf withouten ende.
C.19.223   And indulgences *ynowe* and be ingrat[u]s to thy kynde,
C.20.292   And sheteth out shot *ynow* his sheltrom to blende;
C.22.249   And oþere necessaries *ynowe*; ȝow shal no thyng lakke

inpacient adj *impacient adj.* B 1; C 2
B.17.343   And ben *inpacient* in hir penaunce, pure reson knoweþ
C. 6.110   *Inpacient* in alle penaunc[e] and pleyned, as hit were,
C.19.323   And be *inpacient* in here penaunc[e], puyr resoun knoweth

inparfit adj *imparfit adj.* B 6 inparfit (3) inparfite (3); C 12 inparfit (9)
inparfyt (2) inparfite (1)
B.15.50   'Thanne artow *inparfit*', quod he, 'and oon of prides knyȝtes.
B.15.95   There *inparfit* preesthode is, prechours and techeris.
B.15.131   The whiche arn preestes *inparfite* and prechours after siluer,
B.15.565   If possession be poison and *inparfite* hem make,
B.19.428   *Inparfit* is þat pope þat al [peple] sholde helpe
B.20.229   Thoruȝ *inparfite* preestes and prelates of holy chirche.'
C. 3.386   Such *inparfit* peple repreueth alle resoun
C. 6.119   And preuen *inparfit* prelates of holy churche;
C.11.206   Or p[resci]t *inparfit*, pult out of grace,
C.15.135   And preueth by puyre skile *inparfyt* alle thynges–
C.16.212   'Thenne artow *inparfit*,' quod he, 'and oen of pruydes knyhtes.
C.16.247   There *inparfit* preesthoed is, prechares and techares.
C.16.278   As *inparfite* prestes and prechours aftur suluer,
C.17.229   For if possession be poysen and *inparfit* hem make,
C.18.102   Bothe parfit and *inparfit*.' Puyr fayn y wolde
C.19.105   And moest *inparfyt* of alle persones; and pacientliche soffre
C.21.428   *Inparfit* is þat pope þat all peple sholde helpe
C.22.229   Thorw *inparfit* prestes and prelates of holy churche.'

inparfitly adv *imparfitlich adv.* B 1
B.10.471   That *inparfitly* here knewe and ek lyuede.

inposible inpossible > impossible; inpugn > impugnen

insolibles adj *insolible adj.* C 1
C.16.232   Mouen motyues, mony tymes *insolibles* and falaes,

intestate adj *intestate adj.* B 1
B.15.138   Or [endeþ] *intestate* and þanne [entreþ þe bisshop]

intil prep *intil prep.* B 1
B.13.210   Turne into þe trewe feiþ and *intil* oon bileue.'

into prep *into prep.* A 19; B 43; C 41
A.Pr.2   I shop me *into* a shroud as I a shep were;
A.Pr.10   I slomeride *into* a slepyng, it swiȝede so merye.
A.Pr.13   Ac as I beheld *into* þe Est an heiȝ to þe sonne
A. 1.113   Out of heuene *into* helle hobelide þei faste,
A. 1.121   Mowe be sikur þat here soule shal wende *into* heuene,
A. 1.179   And ek þe graiþ gate þat goþ *into* heuene.
A. 2.68   Wiþ alle þe purtenaunce of purcatorie *into* þe pyne of helle;
A. 2.195   Alle fledden for fer & flowen *into* hernis;
A. 3.178   Crope *into* a caban for cold of þi nailes;
A. 4.34   Þanne com pes *into* þe parlement & putte vp a bille
A. 6.49   Til ȝe come *into* consience þat crist wyte þe soþe,
A. 7.167   And bledde *into* þe bodyward a bolle ful of growel,
A. 7.171   Faitours for fer flowen *into* bernis
A. 7.187   Hom *into* his owene er[d]e & holde him þere euere.
A. 8.38   Þat I ne shal sende [ȝour] soule sauf *into* heuene,
A.10.144   *Into* þis wrecchide world to wonen & to libben
A.11.313   Wiþoute penaunce at here partyng, *into* [þe] heiȝe blisse.
A.12.35   Clergie *into* a caban crepte anon after,
A.12.96   Þou shalt be lauȝth by lyȝth with loking of an eye
B.Pr.2   I shoop me *into* [a] shrou[d] as I a sheep weere;
B.Pr.10   I slombred *into* a slepyng, it sweyed so murye.
B.Pr.13   [Ac] as I biheeld *into* þe Eest, an heiȝ to þe sonne,
B. 1.115   *Into* a deep derk helle to dwelle þere for euere;
B. 1.205   And also þe graiþe gate þat goþ *into* heuene.
B. 2.104   Wiþ alle þe [p]urtinaunces of Purgatorie *into* þe pyne of helle.
B. 3.10   Took Mede bi þe myddel and broȝte hire *into* chambre.
B. 3.191   Crope *into* a Cabane for cold of þi nayles;
B. 3.303   That Moyses or Messie be come *into* [myddel]erþe,
B. 3.308   *Into* sikel or to siþe, to Shaar or to kultour:
B. 4.47   [Th]anne com pees *into* [þe] parlement and putte [vp] a bille
B. 5.495   And blewe alle þi blessed *into* þe blisse of Paradys.
B. 5.562   Til ye come *into* Conscience þat crist wite þe soþe,
B. 6.183   Faitours for fere flowen *into* Bernes
B. 6.200   Hoom [in]to his owene [e]rd and holden hym þere [euere].
B.10.470   *Into* þe [parfit] blisse of Paradis for hir pure bileue,
B.11.8   And *into* þe lond of longynge [and] loue she me brouȝte
B.11.60   Til I for[yede] youþe and yarn *into* Elde.
B.12.140   And loue shal lepen out after *into* þ[is] lowe erþe,
B.13.197   Than alle þo þat offrede *into* Gaȝophilacium?'
B.13.210   Turne *into* þe trewe feiþ and intil oon bileue.'
B.13.392   Or *into* Prucelond my Prentis my profit to waiten,
B.13.406   That *into* wanhope he [worþ] and wende nauȝt to be saued.
B.14.81   [So] thei sonken *into* helle, þe Citees echone.
B.14.93   Ther contricion dooþ but dryueþ it doun *into* a venial synne
B.15.188   And yerne *into* youþe and yepeliche [seche]
B.15.400   *Into* Surrie he souȝte, and þoruȝ hise sotile wittes
B.15.439   *Into* lele bileue; þe lightloker me þinkeþ
B.17.230   And melteþ hire myȝt *into* mercy, as men may se in wyntre
B.18.131   Wiþouten [wommene] wem *into* þis world broȝte hym.
B.18.204   And wo *into* wele mowe wenden at þe laste.
B.18.241   The light folwede þe led doun *into* þe lowe erþe.
B.18.326   And þo þat oure lord louede *into* his light he laughte.
B.19.65   Therwith to fiȝte and [f]enden vs fro fallynge *in[to]* synne,
B.19.79   *Into* hir kyngene kiþ by counseil of Aungeles.
B.19.109   Water *into* wyn turnede, as holy writ telleþ.
B.19.147   And goon *into* Galilee and gladen hise Apostles
B.19.191   Anoon after an heigh vp *into* heuene
B.19.356   Hastiliche *into* vnitee and holde we vs þere.
B.20.75   *Into* vnite holy chirche and holde we vs þere
B.20.113   And tornede Cyuyle *into* Symonye, and siþþe he took þe Official.
B.20.204   'If þow wolt be wroken wend *into* vnitee
C.Pr.2   Y shope me *into* [a] shroud[e] as y a shep were;
C.Pr.101   A[c] for it profiteþ ȝow *into* pursward ȝe prelates soffren
C.Pr.160   Consience and þe kynge *into* Court wente
C. 2.252   Alle fledde for fere and flowen *into* hernes;
C. 3.11   *Into* Boure with blisse and by here gan sitte.
C. 3.212   That al þe witt of the world is woxe *into* Gyle.
C. 3.403   And nyme hym *into* oure noumbre, now and eueremore:
C. 3.461   *Into* sykel or [t]o sythe, to shar oþer to colter:

C. 4.45   Thenne cam p[ees] *into* [þe] parlement and putte vp a bille
C. 6.279   Or *in[to]* pruyslond my prenties my profit to awayte,
C. 7.135   And brouhte thyne yblessed fro thennes *into* þe blisse of heuene.
C. 7.207   Til ȝe come *into* Consience, yknowe of god sulue,
C. 8.179   Tho were faytours afered and flowen *into* [Peres] bernes
C. 8.206   Hoem *[in]to* his owene [e]rd and halde hym þere euere.
C. 9.183   Or thorw fuyr or thorw floed yfalle *into* pouerte,
C. 9.260   For many wakere wolues ar wr[iþ]en *into* thy foldes;
C. 9.326   To peple withouten penaunce to passe *into* ioye,
C.11.18   That coueite can and caste thus ar cleped *into* consayle:
C.11.167   And *into* þe lond of longyng [and loue] she me brouhte
C.12.12   Til y forȝet ȝouthe and ȝorn *into* elde.
C.12.208   Ȝoure sorwe *into* solace shal turne at þe laste
C.12.209   And out of wo *into* wele ȝoure wirdes shal chaunge."
C.14.85   And loue shal lepe out aftur *into* þis lowe erthe
C.16.331   Thenne ȝerneth he *into* ȝouthe and ȝeepliche he secheth
C.17.169   Forthy souhte [he] *into* surie and sotiled how he myhte
C.17.237   Alle londes *into* loue And þat in lytel tyme;
C.18.4   Til we cam *into* a contre, cor hominis hit heihte,
C.19.196   And melteth myhte *into* mercy, as we may se a wynter
C.20.134   Withouten wommane wem *into* this world brouhte hym,
C.20.190   *Into* pees and pyte of his puyr grace.
C.20.209   And wo *into* wele moet wende at þe laste.
C.20.250   The lihte folewede þe lord *into* þe lowe erthe.
C.21.65   Therwith to fihte and fende vs fro fallyng *into* synne
C.21.79   *Into* here kyngene kuth by consail of Angelis.
C.21.109   [Watur *into* wyn turned], As holy writ telleth.
C.21.147   And goen *into* Galilee and gladien his apostlis
C.21.191   Anoon aftur an heyh vp *into* heuene
C.21.356   Hastiliche [*in*]to vnite and holde we vs there.
C.22.75   *Into* vnite holi churche and halde we vs there.
C.22.137   And turnede syuyle *into* symonye and sethe he toek þe official.
C.22.204   'Yf thow wol[t] be wreke wende *into* vnite

inwit n *inwit* n.   A 9 inwit (4) Inwyt (5); B 10; C 12 inwit (11) inwyt (1)
A.10.17   Is a wys kniȝt withalle, sire [*inwit*] he hatte,
A.10.42   *Inwit* & alle wyttes enclosid ben þerinne,
A.10.47   *Inwyt* is þe [allie] þat anima desiriþ,
A.10.48   Aftir þe grace of god [þe grettest is *Inwyt*].
A.10.49   *Inwyt* in þe heuid is, & an help to þe soule,
A.10.56   For whan blood is bremere þanne brayn, þan is *Inwit* bounde,
A.10.58   In ȝonge fauntes & folis, wiþ hem failiþ *Inwyt*,
A.10.60   Þei helde ale in here hed til *Inwyt* be drenchit,
A.12.99   Wille þurgh *inwit* [wiste] wel þe soþe,
B. 9.18   Is a wis knyȝt wiþalle, sire *Inwit* he hatte,
B. 9.54   *Inwit* and alle wittes [en]closed ben þerInne,
B. 9.58   Ac *Inwit* is in þe heed and to þe herte he lokeþ
B. 9.60   For after þe grace of god þe gretteste is *Inwit*.
B. 9.61   Muche wo worþ þat man þat mysruleþ his *Inwit*,
B. 9.68   [Fauntes and] fooles þat fauten *Inwit*,
B. 9.73   Alle þise lakken *Inwit* and loore [hem] bihoueþ.
B.13.288   Wiþ *Inwit* and wiþ outwit ymagynen and studie
B.15.518   Alle þat wilned and wolde wiþ *Inwit* bileue it.
B.17.283   And who[so] morþereþ a good man, me þynkeþ, by myn *Inwit*,
C. 6.421   His wyf and his *inwit* Edwitede hym of his synne;
C. 9.117   And suffreth suche go so, it semeth to myn *inwyt*
C.10.144   Is a wise knyhte withalle, sire *inwit* he hatte,
C.10.171   *Inwit* and alle wittes closed been þerynne:
C.10.173   And lyf lyueth by *inwit* and leryng of kynde.
C.10.174   *Inwit* is in the heued and anima in herte
C.10.175   And moche wo worth hym þat *inwit* myspeneth
C.10.181   Euery man þat hath *inwit* and his hele bothe
C.10.183   Ac fauntokynes and foles þat fauten *inwit*
C.17.269   Alle þat wilnede and wolde with *inwit* bileue hit.
C.18.179   In *inwit* and in alle wittes aftur liberum Arbitrium
C.19.264   And hoso morthereth a goed man, me thynketh bi myn *inwit*,

iotten > yeden; ypayd ypaied > paien; yparroked(e > parroked; ypassed > passen; yperissed ypersed > percen; ypliȝt yplyht > pliȝten

ypocras n prop *n.i.d.*   B 1
B.12.43   Aristotle and oþere mo, *ypocras* and virgile,

ypocrisie n *ipocracie* n.   B 6 ypocrisie (5) ypocrisye (1); C 6 ypocrisye (5) ypocrysye (1)
B.15.110   Than for to prechen and preuen it noȝt–*ypocrisie* it semeþ.
B.15.111   [For *ypocrisie*] in latyn is likned to a [loþly] dongehill
B.20.300   *Ypocrisie* and h[ij] an hard assaut þei [ȝeuen].
B.20.301   [*Ypocrisie* at þe yate harde gan fighte]
B.20.317   For here is many a man hurt þoruȝ *ypocrisye*.'
B.20.335   *Ypocrisie* haþ hurt hem; ful hard is if þei keuere.'
C.16.264   Then for to prechen and preue hit nat–*ypocrisye* hit semeth.
C.16.265   *Ypocrysye* is a braunche of pruyde and most amonges clerkes
C.22.300   *Ypocrisye* and [h]y an hard sawt they ȝeuen.
C.22.301   *Ypocrisye* at þe ȝate harde gan fyhte

C.22.317   For here is many [a] man hert thorw *ypocrisye*.'
C.22.335   *Ypocrysye* haeth her[t]e hem; ful hard is yf thei keuere.'

ypot > putten; ypresed > preisen; ypreued > preuen; ypriked > prikeþ; ypurchaced ypurchased > purchase; ipurfilid > purfiled; yput > putten; yquited > quyte; yrad > reden; irael > israel; yraunsomed yraunsoned > raunsone; yraueschid yraussshed > rauyssshed

ire n *ire* n.   &> iren   B 1; C 2 ire (1) yre (1)
B. 2.84   And þe Erldom of Enuye and [*Ire*] togideres,
C. 2.91   The Erldom of enuye and *yre* he hem graunteth,
C.20.435   A[c] ȝut my kynde [in] my kene *ire* shal constrayne my will–

yrebounden > yren; yrebuked > rebuken; ireland > irlonde

yren n *iren* n.   A 1 yrens; B 5 yren (2) yrene (1) Irens (2); C 6 yre (1) yren (2) yrebounden (2) yrones (1)
A. 4.72   & comaundid a cunstable to caste hym in *yrens*]:
B. 4.85   And comaundede a Constable to casten hym in *Irens*:
B. 6.136   But if he be blynd or brokelegged or bolted wiþ *Irens*,
B.14.247   Ther Auarice haþ Almaries and *yren* bounden cofres.
B.14.249   A beggeris bagge þan an *yren* bounde cofre.
B.19.57   And bond [hym] as [he is bounde] wiþ bondes of *yrene*.
C.Pr.97   And boxes ben yset forth ybounde with *yren*
C. 4.81   And comaundede a Constable to caste [hym] in *yrones*
C. 8.143   But yf he be blynde or brokelegged or bolted with *yren*,
C.16.87   There Auaryce hath almaries and *yrebounden* coffres.
C.16.89   A beggares bagge then an *yrebounden* coffre.
C.21.57   And bonde [hym] as he is bounde with bondes of *yre*.

yrented > renten

yreuestede ptp *revesten* v.   C 1
C. 5.112   And resoun *yreuestede* ryht as a pope

yrynged ptp *ringen* v.(1)   C 1
C. 2.12   On alle here fyue fyngeres ful richeliche *yrynged*,

irlonde n prop *Irlond* n.   B 1; C 1 Ireland
B.20.221   'By [þe] Marie!' quod a mansed preest, [was] of þe March of [*Irlonde*],
C.22.221   'By þe Marie!' quod a mansed prest, was of þe march of *Ireland*,

yrobbed > robbe; yrobed > robeþ; yrones > yren; yruyfled > rifled; yruled > rulen; is > ben,he

ysaak n prop *n.i.d.*   B 1; C 1
B.16.232   Hym or *Ysaak* myn heir, þe which he hiȝte me kulle
C.18.247   How he fondede me furste; my fayre sone *ysaak*

ysaide > siggen

ysaye n prop *n.i.d.*   &> seen   A 1; B 3 ysaie (1) Ysaye (2); C 2
A.11.283   Or adam, or *ysaye*, or any of þe prophetis
B.10.424   Or Adam or *Ysaye* or any of þe prophetes
B.15.574   Ac *ysaie* of yow spekeþ and oȝias boþe,
B.16.81   Adam and Abraham and *Ysaye* þe prophete,
C.11.256   And ar Adam oþer *ysaye* oþer eny of þe profetes
C.18.112   Adam and Abraham and *ysaye* þe prophete.

ysamme adv *isame* adv.   A 1; B 1
A.10.199   But maidenis & maidenis macche ȝow *ysamme*;
B. 9.178   Ac maidenes and maydenes macche yow [*ysamme*];

ysaued > sauen; yschape > shape

yse v *isen* v.(1)   C 5 yse (3) ysey (1) yseye (1)
C. 2.69   When simonye and syuile *ysey[e]* þer bothe wille
C.12.84   God of his goodnesse *ysey* his grete will.
C.14.103   And thow saidest sothe of somme, Ac [*yse*] in what manere.
C.17.150   'Where sarresynes,' y saide, '*yse* nat what is charite?'
C.19.6   'Is hit asseled?' y saide; 'may men *yse* th[e] lettres?'

ysey(e > yse,seen; yseide > siggen; yseyen yseyn yseiȝe(n > seen

ysekeles n *isikle* n.   B 1; C 1 Isekeles
B.17.231   *Ysekeles* in euesynges þoruȝ hete of þe sonne
C.19.197   *Isekeles* in euesynges thorwe hete of the sonne

isent(e > sende; yserued > seruen; yset > sette

yshaue ptp *shaven* v.   B 2; C 2
B. 5.193   And as a bondeman[nes] bacon his berd was [*yshaue*].
B.15.229   Ycalled and ycrymyled and his crowne *yshaue*.
C. 6.201   And as a bondemannes bacoun his berd was *yshaue*,
C.16.354   Ycalled and ycrimyled and his croune *yshaue*.

ysherewed v *shreuen* v.   B 1
B.13.330   As a shepsteres shere *ysherewed* [myn euencristen]:

yssheued > shewen; yshryue > shryuen; ysyneged ysynned > synnen; yslepe > slepe; ysoden > soden

ysodorus n prop *n.i.d.* B 1; C 1
B.15.37   Austyn and *Ysodorus*, eiþer of hem boþe
C.16.199   Austyn and *ysodorus*, either of hem bothe

ysoffred > suffren; ysoiled > soiled; ysouȝt > seken; ysowed en > sowe;
yspened > spende; yspilde yspilt > spille

yspoused ptp *spousen v.* B 1
B. 9.129   And noȝt þi kynde wiþ Caymes ycoupled n[e] *yspoused*'.

yspronge > sprynge

israel n prop *Israel n.* A 1; B 1; C 3 Irael (2) Israel (1)
A. 3.243   [Aȝens *isra[e]l* and aaron and moyses his broþer].
B.10.285   The bible bereþ witnesse þat al[le] þe [barnes] of *Israel*
C.Pr.105   What cheste and meschaunce to þe children of *Irael*
C.Pr.111   Anon as it was tolde hym that þe children of *Irael*
C. 9.317   And his fadur *Is[rael]* and also his dame.

issue n *issue n.* B 9; C 10
B. 9.128   "Thyn *issue* in þyn issue, I wol þat þei be wedded,
B. 9.128   "Thyn issue in þyn *issue*, I wol þat þei be wedded,
B.10.331   And þanne shal þe Abbot of Abyngdoun and al his *issue* for euere
B.11.206   Of Adames *issue* and Eue ay til god man deide;
B.16.196   To ocupie hym here til *issue* were spronge,
B.16.206   And þe *issue* þat þei hadde it was of hem boþe,
B.16.239   For hymself bihiȝte to me and to myn *issue* boþe
B.16.241   To me and to myn *issue* moore yet he [me] grauntede,
B.18.344   Adam and al his *issue* at my wille herafter;
C.10.243   For god seid ensaumple of suche manere *issue*
C.12.114   Of Adames *issue* and Eue ay til god man deyede;
C.18.205   To ocupien hym here til *issue* were spronge
C.18.219   And abel here *issue*, aren bote oen in manhede.
C.18.234   The which is man and his make and moilere here *issue*,
C.18.245   He bihihte vs *issue* and ayr in oure olde age;
C.18.255   For hymsulue saide y sholde [haue], y and myn *issue* bothe,
C.18.257   To me and [to] myn *issue* more he me bihihte,
C.20.197   That Adam and Eue and al his *issue*
C.20.303   That Adam and Eue and all his *issue*

it pron *hit pron.* A 192 it (177) hit (15); B 642 his (2) hise (1) it (639); C
611 his (2) it (33) hit (575) hyt (1)

> **his B 2 &> he**
> B.12.258, B.17.251
> **his C 2 &> he**
> C.19.217, C.21.216
> **hise B 1**
> B.19.216
> **hit A 15**
> A.5.114, A.11.294, A.12.1, A.12.7, A.12.14, A.12.17, A.12.18, A.12.19, A.12.22,
> A.12.22, A.12.24, A.12.25, A.12.25, A.12.27, A.12.71

> **hit C 576 hit (575) hyt (1)**
> C.Pr.11, C.Pr.11, C.Pr.39, C.Pr.75, C.Pr.95, C.Pr.100, C.Pr.138, C.Pr.186,
> C.Pr.187, C.Pr.213, C.Pr.213, C.1.39, C.1.56, C.1.60, C.1.83, C.1.88, C.1.90, C.1.115,
> C.1.117, C.1.125, C.1.135, C.1.135, C.1.141, C.1.149, C.1.149, C.1.150, C.1.151,
> C.1.154, C.1.159, C.1.159, C.1.185, C.1.203, C.2.39, C.2.70, C.2.73, C.2.78, C.2.128,
> C.2.138, C.2.157, C.2.206, C.3.59, C.3.59, C.3.62, C.3.63, C.3.87, C.3.97, C.3.112,
> C.3.149, C.3.157, C.3.228, C.3.236, C.3.240, C.3.265, C.3.295, C.3.302, C.3.306,
> C.3.313, C.3.314, C.3.321, C.3.332, C.3.420, C.3.423, C.3.423, C.3.423, C.3.425,
> C.3.425, C.3.434, C.3.460, C.3.466, C.3.477, C.4.19, C.4.22, C.4.36, C.4.76, C.4.110,
> C.4.157, C.4.177, C.4.177, C.4.183, C.5.59, C.5.61, C.5.81, C.5.124, C.5.129, C.5.141,
> C.5.153, C.5.161, C.6.70, C.6.71, C.6.89, C.6.100, C.6.110, C.6.144, C.6.163, C.6.163,
> C.6.205, C.6.206, C.6.214, C.6.216, C.6.222, C.6.225, C.6.229, C.6.231, C.6.261,
> C.6.264, C.6.265, C.6.276, C.6.277, C.6.277, C.6.289, C.6.332, C.6.340, C.6.345,
> C.6.346, C.6.377, C.6.402, C.6.414, C.7.4, C.7.10, C.7.16, C.7.28, C.7.35, C.7.36,
> C.7.36, C.7.37, C.7.43, C.7.47, C.7.50, C.7.50, C.7.57, C.7.64, C.7.129, C.7.134,
> C.7.141, C.7.142, C.7.152, C.7.193, C.7.203, C.7.222, C.7.230, C.7.234, C.7.251,
> C.7.269, C.7.281, C.7.293, C.7.303, C.8.3, C.8.22, C.8.40, C.8.40, C.8.41, C.8.41,
> C.8.47, C.8.52, C.8.62, C.8.68, C.8.76, C.8.83, C.8.88, C.8.95, C.8.97, C.8.102, C.8.211,
> C.8.213, C.8.213, C.8.216, C.8.222, C.8.227, C.8.234, C.8.253, C.8.257, C.8.295,
> C.8.297, C.8.321, C.8.332, C.9.29, C.9.55, C.9.57, C.9.74, C.9.105, C.9.114, C.9.115,
> C.9.118, C.9.126, C.9.151, C.9.155, C.9.162, C.9.164, C.9.166, C.9.195, C.9.211,
> C.9.217, C.9.231, C.9.234, C.9.239, C.9.258, C.9.282, C.9.285, C.9.299, C.9.302,
> C.9.303, C.9.304, C.9.314, C.9.332, C.10.8, C.10.38, C.10.41, C.10.130, C.10.158,
> C.10.190, C.10.194, C.10.194, C.10.201, C.10.252, C.10.276, C.10.287, C.10.306, C.11.11,
> C.11.15, C.11.43, C.11.49, C.11.71, C.11.76, C.11.77, C.11.109, C.11.127, C.11.128,
> C.11.129, C.11.130, C.11.145, C.11.155, C.11.157, C.11.161, C.11.183, C.11.199,
> C.11.208, C.11.236, C.11.241, C.11.242, C.11.270, C.12.6, C.12.28, C.12.32, C.12.36,
> C.12.39, C.12.40, C.12.42, C.12.57, C.12.61, C.12.63, C.12.98, C.12.99, C.12.112,
> C.12.126, C.12.143, C.12.145, C.12.164, C.12.166, C.12.174, C.12.184, C.12.193,
> C.12.213, C.12.218, C.12.220, C.12.232, C.12.234, C.12.235, C.12.235, C.12.236,
> C.12.239, C.12.241, C.13.8, C.13.16, C.13.27, C.13.73, C.13.110, C.13.114, C.13.118,
> C.13.121, C.13.152, C.13.164, C.13.178, C.13.190, C.13.201, C.13.238, C.13.241,
> C.14.12, C.14.36, C.14.45, C.14.55, C.14.56, C.14.57, C.14.58, C.14.60, C.14.74,
> C.14.76, C.14.83, C.14.86, C.14.86, C.14.87, C.14.96, C.14.109, C.14.110, C.14.117,
> C.14.129, C.14.141, C.14.148, C.14.160, C.14.165, C.14.165, C.14.165, C.14.167,
> C.14.213, C.15.68, C.15.69, C.15.81, C.15.98, C.15.113, C.15.114, C.15.121, C.15.124,
> C.15.125, C.15.126, C.15.139, C.15.160, C.15.174, C.15.176, C.15.210, C.15.225,
> C.15.235, C.15.248, C.15.249, C.15.258, C.15.263, C.15.284, C.15.286, C.15.296,
> C.15.300, C.15.303, C.15.305, C.16.4, C.16.8, C.16.53, C.16.61, C.16.84, C.16.88,
> C.16.92, C.16.111, C.16.114, C.16.115, C.16.121, C.16.121, C.16.135, C.16.214,
> C.16.219, C.16.248, C.16.264, C.16.264, C.16.277, C.16.282, C.16.283, C.16.287,
> C.16.289, C.16.294, C.16.305, C.16.311, C.16.323, C.16.329, C.16.347, C.16.347,
> C.16.356, C.16.373, C.17.77, C.17.87, C.17.100, C.17.119, C.17.130, C.17.151,
> C.17.153, C.17.163, C.17.178, C.17.194, C.17.217, C.17.231, C.17.269, C.17.297,
> C.17.304, C.17.310, C.17.320, C.17.320, C.18.4, C.18.6, C.18.7, C.18.8, C.18.9, C.18.10,
> C.18.11, C.18.18, C.18.20, C.18.20, C.18.30, C.18.32, C.18.37, C.18.42, C.18.42,
> C.18.47, C.18.47, C.18.47, C.18.56, C.18.57, C.18.58, C.18.59, C.18.67, C.18.90,
> C.18.91, C.18.99, C.18.100, C.18.103, C.18.104, C.18.106, C.18.107, C.18.108,
> C.18.109, C.18.119, C.18.159, C.18.160, C.18.184, C.18.197, C.18.199, C.18.214,
> C.18.250, C.18.263, C.18.276, C.18.277, C.18.277, C.19.6, C.19.9, C.19.21, C.19.23,
> C.19.34, C.19.43, C.19.47, C.19.117, C.19.117, C.19.128, C.19.129, C.19.144, C.19.152,
> C.19.154, C.19.170, C.19.207, C.19.215, C.19.217, C.19.235, C.19.250, C.19.255,
> C.19.272, C.19.273, C.19.274, C.19.285, C.19.291, C.19.299, C.19.308, C.19.312,
> C.19.312, C.19.316, C.20.33, C.20.41, C.20.42, C.20.42, C.20.43, C.20.45, C.20.49,
> C.20.62, C.20.63, C.20.90, C.20.91, C.20.93, C.20.98, C.20.99, C.20.116, C.20.120,
> C.20.130, C.20.143, C.20.150, C.20.151, C.20.195, C.20.201, C.20.207, C.20.225,
> C.20.230, C.20.235, C.20.251, C.20.260, C.20.275, C.20.278, C.20.289, C.20.322,
> C.20.324, C.20.333, C.20.336, C.20.337, C.20.337, C.20.339, C.20.340, C.20.342,
> C.20.376, C.20.387, C.20.389, C.20.393, C.20.401, C.20.404, C.20.417, C.20.421,
> C.20.428, C.20.430, C.20.471, C.20.473, C.20.474, C.20.475, C.21.11, C.21.21, C.21.42,
> C.21.99, C.21.101, C.21.144, C.21.145, C.21.149, C.21.152, C.21.156, C.21.161,
> C.21.172, C.21.177, C.21.195, C.21.246, C.21.247, C.21.275, C.21.324, C.21.326,
> C.21.326, C.21.335, C.21.363, C.21.366, C.21.371, C.21.387, C.21.408,
> C.21.447, C.21.453, C.21.458, C.21.460, C.21.464, C.21.468, C.21.469, C.21.473,
> C.22.4, C.22.28, C.22.54, C.22.66, C.22.68, C.22.70, C.22.96, C.22.147, C.22.182,
> C.22.185, C.22.197, C.22.198, C.22.239, C.22.255, C.22.269, C.22.275, C.22.278,
> C.22.286, C.22.292, C.22.321, C.22.330, C.22.362

> **it A 177**
> A.Pr.10, A.Pr.32, A.Pr.38, A.Pr.58, A.Pr.74, A.Pr.77, A.Pr.85, A.1.25, A.1.31,
> A.1.39, A.1.54, A.1.58, A.1.62, A.1.69, A.1.84, A.1.85, A.1.90, A.1.90, A.1.91, A.1.92,
> A.1.109, A.1.125, A.1.125, A.1.128, A.1.130, A.1.134, A.1.137, A.1.163, A.2.105,
> A.2.153, A.3.36, A.3.57, A.3.64, A.3.109, A.3.136, A.3.169, A.3.175, A.3.196, A.3.221,
> A.3.221, A.3.230, A.3.236, A.3.237, A.3.259, A.4.57, A.4.57, A.4.58, A.4.96, A.4.106,
> A.4.107, A.4.108, A.4.115, A.4.120, A.4.120, A.4.125, A.4.128, A.4.129, A.4.138,
> A.4.138, A.4.146, A.4.146, A.4.150, A.5.27, A.5.35, A.5.61, A.5.92, A.5.93, A.5.100,
> A.5.101, A.5.102, A.5.112, A.5.113, A.5.122, A.5.124, A.5.130, A.5.133, A.5.137,
> A.5.139, A.5.169, A.5.176, A.5.192, A.5.215, A.5.222, A.6.32, A.6.36, A.6.39, A.6.57,
> A.6.62, A.6.70, A.6.103, A.6.113, A.7.10, A.7.11, A.7.12, A.7.19, A.7.42, A.7.46,
> A.7.49, A.7.58, A.7.61, A.7.66, A.7.73, A.7.78, A.7.80, A.7.121, A.7.121, A.7.191,
> A.7.193, A.7.198, A.7.203, A.7.219, A.7.223, A.7.226, A.7.227, A.7.230, A.7.233,
> A.7.238, A.7.258, A.7.260, A.7.283, A.7.294, A.8.27, A.8.62, A.8.90, A.8.93, A.8.101,
> A.8.114, A.8.133, A.8.134, A.8.141, A.8.142, A.8.147, A.8.152, A.8.164, A.9.8, A.9.33,
> A.10.3, A.10.38, A.10.51, A.10.55, A.10.79, A.10.80, A.10.81, A.10.107, A.10.109,
> A.10.132, A.10.133, A.10.149, A.10.164, A.10.186, A.10.189, A.10.195, A.11.18,
> A.11.23, A.11.55, A.11.138, A.11.140, A.11.141, A.11.142, A.11.142, A.11.146,
> A.11.146, A.11.154, A.11.175, A.11.182, A.11.183, A.11.183, A.11.187, A.11.206,
> A.11.209, A.11.221, A.11.221, A.11.229, A.11.233, A.11.253, A.11.257, A.11.295

> **it B 639**
> B.Pr.10, B.Pr.32, B.Pr.38, B.Pr.52, B.Pr.61, B.Pr.77, B.Pr.80, B.Pr.102, B.Pr.106,
> B.Pr.169, B.Pr.170, B.Pr.179, B.Pr.195, B.Pr.205, B.Pr.205, B.Pr.212, B.1.25, B.1.31,
> B.1.41, B.1.56, B.1.60, B.1.64, B.1.71, B.1.86, B.1.87, B.1.92, B.1.92, B.1.93, B.1.94,
> B.1.111, B.1.120, B.1.136, B.1.136, B.1.139, B.1.142, B.1.146, B.1.151, B.1.153,
> B.1.153, B.1.154, B.1.155, B.1.158, B.1.163, B.1.163, B.2.71, B.2.141, B.2.192,
> B.3.37, B.3.55, B.3.55, B.3.58, B.3.59, B.3.120, B.3.147, B.3.182, B.3.188, B.3.209,
> B.3.234, B.3.234, B.3.237, B.3.251, B.3.256, B.3.257, B.3.258, B.3.266, B.3.270,
> B.3.270, B.3.270, B.3.271, B.3.272, B.3.272, B.3.281, B.3.307, B.4.71, B.4.71, B.4.72,
> B.4.115, B.4.132, B.4.137, B.4.142, B.4.145, B.4.146, B.4.162, B.4.162,
> B.4.174, B.4.183, B.4.183, B.5.27, B.5.42, B.5.43, B.5.43, B.5.49, B.5.78, B.5.112,
> B.5.113, B.5.124, B.5.161, B.5.181, B.5.181, B.5.197, B.5.198, B.5.206, B.5.208,
> B.5.214, B.5.217, B.5.221, B.5.223, B.5.241, B.5.241, B.5.245, B.5.249, B.5.272,
> B.5.281, B.5.284, B.5.286, B.5.290, B.5.291, B.5.320, B.5.327, B.5.344, B.5.356,
> B.5.366, B.5.372, B.5.388, B.5.394, B.5.400, B.5.413, B.5.419, B.5.422, B.5.423,
> B.5.423, B.5.424, B.5.430, B.5.434, B.5.438, B.5.443, B.5.450, B.5.490, B.5.494,
> B.5.498, B.5.501, B.5.502, B.5.507, B.5.549, B.5.552, B.5.570, B.5.575, B.5.583,
> B.5.617, B.5.628, B.6.5, B.6.42, B.6.42, B.6.43, B.6.51, B.6.54, B.6.63, B.6.67, B.6.74,
> B.6.81, B.6.86, B.6.88, B.6.129, B.6.129, B.6.205, B.6.207, B.6.212, B.6.217,
> B.6.235, B.6.239, B.6.242, B.6.243, B.6.246, B.6.249, B.6.254, B.6.274, B.6.276,
> B.6.299, B.6.310, B.7.25, B.7.70, B.7.108, B.7.111, B.7.119, B.7.150, B.7.153, B.7.154,
> B.7.163, B.7.164, B.7.170, B.7.172, B.7.186, B.8.8, B.8.37, B.9.3, B.9.42, B.9.50,
> B.9.85, B.9.119, B.9.133, B.9.165, B.9.174, B.9.193, B.10.18, B.10.38, B.10.69,
> B.10.92, B.10.116, B.10.186, B.10.188, B.10.189, B.10.190, B.10.190, B.10.194,
> B.10.194, B.10.238, B.10.254, B.10.256, B.10.260, B.10.278, B.10.278, B.10.279,
> B.10.300, B.10.303, B.10.306, B.10.318, B.10.341, B.10.343, B.10.350, B.10.365,
> B.10.376, B.10.376, B.10.405, B.10.410, B.10.411, B.10.449, B.10.460,
> B.11.24, B.11.39, B.11.66, B.11.91, B.11.96, B.11.97, B.11.99, B.11.100, B.11.102,
> B.11.104, B.11.104, B.11.105, B.11.106, B.11.106, B.11.108, B.11.122, B.11.126,
> B.11.128, B.11.169, B.11.169, B.11.170, B.11.176, B.11.204, B.11.210, B.11.213,

B.11.222, B.11.257, B.11.259, B.11.277, B.11.296, B.11.304, B.11.307, B.11.350,
B.11.368, B.11.396, B.11.431, B.11.435, B.12.7, B.12.15, B.12.19, B.12.52, B.12.61,
B.12.69, B.12.90, B.12.100, B.12.110, B.12.111, B.12.112, B.12.113, B.12.120,
B.12.132, B.12.138, B.12.141, B.12.141, B.12.152, B.12.153, B.12.169, B.12.170,
B.12.177, B.12.195, B.12.202, B.12.209, B.12.218, B.12.220, B.12.227, B.12.248,
B.12.251, B.12.257, B.12.258, B.12.261, B.12.291, B.13.64, B.13.65, B.13.71, B.13.72,
B.13.75, B.13.75, B.13.91, B.13.114, B.13.117, B.13.123, B.13.148, B.13.156, B.13.157,
B.13.163, B.13.164, B.13.172, B.13.177, B.13.215, B.13.253, B.13.255, B.13.264,
B.13.274, B.13.304, B.13.314, B.13.319, B.13.319, B.13.320, B.13.323, B.13.325,
B.13.326, B.13.342, B.13.357, B.13.362, B.13.365, B.13.366, B.13.381, B.13.382,
B.13.388, B.13.388, B.13.400, B.13.407, B.13.415, B.13.419, B.13.459, B.13.459,
B.14.2, B.14.4, B.14.5, B.14.11, B.14.12, B.14.13, B.14.15, B.14.18, B.14.18, B.14.19,
B.14.19, B.14.20, B.14.21, B.14.22, B.14.23, B.14.23, B.14.24, B.14.47, B.14.50,
B.14.59, B.14.64, B.14.75, B.14.84, B.14.91, B.14.93, B.14.96, B.14.97, B.14.110,
B.14.120, B.14.127, B.14.128, B.14.129, B.14.135, B.14.140, B.14.144, B.14.155,
B.14.190, B.14.220, B.14.244, B.14.248, B.14.252, B.14.271, B.14.278, B.14.279,
B.14.281, B.14.299, B.14.325, B.15.1, B.15.4, B.15.12, B.15.52, B.15.57, B.15.59,
B.15.66, B.15.73, B.15.91, B.15.96, B.15.110, B.15.110, B.15.127, B.15.130, B.15.137,
B.15.160, B.15.163, B.15.173, B.15.181, B.15.205, B.15.207, B.15.222, B.15.222,
B.15.231, B.15.243, B.15.312, B.15.312, B.15.328, B.15.351, B.15.355, B.15.383,
B.15.402, B.15.432, B.15.433, B.15.453, B.15.456, B.15.457, B.15.458, B.15.498,
B.15.518, B.15.533, B.15.554, B.15.576, B.15.582, B.15.583, B.15.585, B.15.586,
B.15.589, B.15.602, B.15.612, B.15.612, B.16.4, B.16.12, B.16.13, B.16.15, B.16.17,
B.16.17, B.16.23, B.16.23, B.16.25, B.16.33, B.16.39, B.16.39, B.16.47, B.16.60,
B.16.62, B.16.62, B.16.63, B.16.72, B.16.74, B.16.75, B.16.76, B.16.77, B.16.78,
B.16.87, B.16.112, B.16.116, B.16.130, B.16.132, B.16.133, B.16.134, B.16.139,
B.16.145, B.16.176, B.16.202, B.16.202, B.16.206, B.16.233, B.16.260, B.16.261,
B.16.261, B.17.4, B.17.7, B.17.9, B.17.20, B.17.22, B.17.33, B.17.42, B.17.44, B.17.46,
B.17.49, B.17.97, B.17.110, B.17.124, B.17.124, B.17.140, B.17.143, B.17.143,
B.17.154, B.17.157, B.17.165, B.17.179, B.17.186, B.17.188, B.17.204, B.17.241,
B.17.249, B.17.251, B.17.269, B.17.274, B.17.291, B.17.292, B.17.293, B.17.305,
B.17.311, B.17.328, B.17.332, B.17.332, B.17.336, B.17.336, B.17.336, B.18.34,
B.18.42, B.18.43, B.18.43, B.18.44, B.18.49, B.18.88, B.18.89, B.18.95, B.18.96,
B.18.117, B.18.127, B.18.140, B.18.147, B.18.148, B.18.190, B.18.196, B.18.202,
B.18.216, B.18.221, B.18.226, B.18.242, B.18.251, B.18.267, B.18.270, B.18.292,
B.18.300, B.18.305, B.18.308, B.18.333, B.18.347, B.18.348, B.18.351, B.18.353,
B.18.363, B.18.375, B.18.379, B.18.386, B.18.388, B.18.392, B.18.403, B.18.428,
B.18.429, B.18.430, B.18.431, B.19.11, B.19.21, B.19.42, B.19.90, B.19.99, B.19.101,
B.19.144, B.19.145, B.19.149, B.19.152, B.19.156, B.19.161, B.19.172, B.19.177,
B.19.195, B.19.246, B.19.247, B.19.275, B.19.324, B.19.326, B.19.326, B.19.335,
B.19.363, B.19.366, B.19.371, B.19.387, B.19.387, B.19.408, B.19.447, B.19.453,
B.19.458, B.19.460, B.19.464, B.19.468, B.19.469, B.19.473, B.20.4, B.20.28, B.20.54,
B.20.66, B.20.68, B.20.70, B.20.96, B.20.147, B.20.182, B.20.185, B.20.197, B.20.198,
B.20.239, B.20.255, B.20.269, B.20.275, B.20.278, B.20.286, B.20.290, B.20.321,
B.20.330, B.20.362

it **C 33**
C.Pr.34, C.Pr.78, C.Pr.101, C.Pr.111, C.Pr.130, C.Pr.162, C.Pr.196, C.1.30,
C.1.52, C.1.82, C.1.88, C.1.89, C.1.107, C.1.138, C.2.56, C.2.76, C.3.185, C.3.343,
C.4.129, C.4.134, C.4.134, C.4.143, C.4.147, C.5.90, C.5.164, C.6.59, C.7.138, C.7.217,
C.9.117, C.11.306, C.12.27, C.12.40, C.21.90

ytailed ptp *taillen v.* **B 1; C 1** ytayled
B. 5.422　　If I bigge and borwe auȝt, but if it be *ytailed*,
C. 7.35　　Yf y b[y]gge and borwe [ouh]t, but yf hit be *ytayled*,

ytake > taken; ytauȝt(e ytauhte > techen

yteynted ptp *tenten v.(2)* **B 1**
B.15.455　　Ytouked and *yteynted* and vnder taillours hande.

ytempted > tempted

ytermyned ptp *terminen v.* **A 1** termined; **B 1; C 1** termyned
A. 1.95　　Til treuþe hadde *termined* here trespas to þe ende.
B. 1.97　　Til treuþe hadde *ytermyned* hire trespas to þe ende.
C. 1.93　　Til treuthe hadde *termyned* here trespas to þe ende

ythryueth v *cf. thriven v.* **C 1**
C.Pr.34　　As it semeþ to oure sighte that suche men *ythryueth*.

ytilied > tilien; ytynt > tyne; ytolde > tellen; ytouked > toke; yvysed yvsed > vsen

yuel n *ivel n.* **A 4** euele (3) euil (1); **B 13** yuel (9) yueles (4); **C 11** euel
(4) euele (2) eueles (3) yuel (1) yuele (1)
A. 8.99　　And do euele & haue euele, & hope þou non oþer
A. 8.99　　And do euele & haue *euele*, & hope þou non oþer
A.10.213　　Aȝens dowel hy don *euele*, & þe deuil plesen,
A.11.153　　And do good a[g]ens *euil*; god hymself hotiþ
B. 7.42　　And nameliche of Innocentȝ þat noon *yuel* konneþ:
B. 7.117　　And do *yuel* and haue euele, [and] hope þow non ooþer
B. 7.117　　And do yuel and haue *yuel*, [and] hope þow non ooþer
B. 9.199　　Ayeins dowel þei doon *yuel* and þe deuel [plese],
B.10.204　　And do good a[g]ein *yuel*; god hymself hoteþ:
B.11.104　　Thouȝ þow se *yuel* seye it noȝt first; be sory it nere amended.
B.13.105　　'Do noon *yuel* to þyn euencristen, nouȝt by þi power.'

B.14.302　　A frend in alle fondynges, [of foule *yueles* leche],
B.15.94　　Right so out of holi chirche alle *yueles* [spredeþ]
B.18.156　　Til he be deed and do þerto; þe *yuel* he destruyeþ,
B.19.46　　And defended from foule *yueles*, feueres and Fluxes,
B.19.340　　And his Spye Spille-loue, oon Spek-*yuel*-bihynde.
B.20.85　　Frenesies and foule *yueles*; forageres of kynde
C. 3.96　　Feuer or foul[e] *euel* other fuyr on here houses,
C. 3.450　　Muchel [*euel*] is thorw mede mony tymes ysoffred
C. 9.291　　And do *yuele* and haue euele and hope thow non oþere
C. 9.291　　And do yuele and haue *euele* and hope thow non oþere
C.16.138　　And frende in alle fondynges and of foule *eueles* leche:
C.16.246　　Riht [so] oute of holy churche al *euel* spredeth
C.19.107　　Y sholde tholye and thonken hem þat me *euel* wolden.'
C.20.159　　Til he [be] ded [and] ydo þerto; [þe *yuel*] he destruyeth,
C.21.46　　And fended fro foule *eueles*, feueres and fluxes
C.21.340　　And his spye spille-loue, oen speke-*euele*-bihynde.
C.22.85　　Freneseyes and foule *eueles*; forageres of kynde

yuel adj *ivel adj.* **A 1** euil; **B 9; C 8** euel (5) euele (1) euyl (1) vuel (1)
A.11.155　　Astronomye is hard þing & *euil* for to knowe;
B. 5.122　　For enuye and *yuel* wil is yuel to defie.
B. 5.122　　For enuye and yuel wil is *yuel* to defie.
B. 6.48　　For in Charnel at chirche cherles ben *yuel* to knowe,
B. 9.126　　And alle þat come of þat Caym come to *yuel* tende,
B.10.212　　Ac Astronomye is hard þyng and *yuel* for to knowe,
B.10.440　　Or ellis for his *yuel* wille and enuye of herte,
B.13.321　　Wiþ enuye and *yuel* speche entisynge to fighte,
B.15.64　　And riȝt as hony is *yuel* to defie and engleymeþ þe mawe,
B.16.116　　Enuye and *yuel* wil [arne] in þe Iewes
C. 6.20　　Demed for here *vuel* vices and exitede oþere
C. 6.21　　Thorw my word and my witt here *euel* werkes to shewe;
C. 6.87　　For enuye and *euyl* wil is euel to defye.
C. 6.87　　For enuye and euyl wil is *euel* to defye.
C. 8.45　　At churche in the Charnel cherles Aren *euele* to knowe
C.16.226　　And riht as hony is *euel* to defie,
C.16.261　　Of vsererus, of hores, of alle *euel* wynnynges,
C.18.163　　Enuye and *euel* wil ern in þe iewes

yuele adv *ivele adv.* **A 1** euele; **B 14; C 16** euel (1) euele (14) yuele (1)
A. 9.19　　[Þat] dowel & do *euele* mowe not dwelle togidere.
B. 5.168　　They hadde þanne ben Infamis, þei kan so *yuele* hele co[unseil].
B. 5.365　　'As þow wiþ wordes & werkes hast wroȝt *yuele* in þi lyue
B. 6.226　　Theiȝ þei doon *yuele* lat [þow] god yworþe:
B. 8.17　　And dowel and do *yuele*, wher þei dwelle boþe.'
B. 8.23　　[That] dowel and do *yuele* mowe noȝt dwelle togideres.
B.12.8　　In þyn olde elde, þat *yuele* kan suffre
B.12.87　　And deeþ and dampnacion to hem þat deyeþ *yuele*,
B.13.79　　Haþ no pite on vs pouere; he parfourneþ *yuele*
B.13.411　　[Ac] penaunce þat þe preest enioyneþ parfourneþ *yuele*;
B.15.535　　Fer fro kyth and fro kyn *yuele* ycloþed yeden,
B.17.312　　*Yuele* lyuen and leten noȝt til lif hem forsake.
B.17.346　　Haþ mercy on swiche men þat so *yuele* may suffre.
B.20.186　　'Sire *yuele* ytauȝt Elde!' quod I, 'vnhende go wiþ þe!
B.20.280　　And *yuele* is þis yholde in parisshes of Engelonde,
C. 1.188　　Auerous and *euel* willed when þei ben avaunsed,
C. 5.157　　Haen ryde out of aray, here reule *euele* yholde,
C. 7.71　　The penauns[e] þat þe prest enioyneth parformeth *euele*,
C. 9.292　　Bote he þat *euele* lyueth euele shal ende.'
C. 9.292　　Bote he þat euele lyueth *euele* shal ende.'
C.10.17　　And dowel and do *euele*, where þei dwellen bothe.'
C.10.26　　For hoso synegeth sicurly doth *euele*
C.10.27　　And dowel and do *euele* may nat dwelle togyderes.
C.10.298　　Aȝen dowel they do *yuele* and þe deuel serue
C.13.115　　*Euele* beth thei ysoffred, suche þat [shenden] þe masse
C.15.86　　Hath no pyte on vs pore; he parformeth *euele*
C.17.196　　Fer fro [k]uthe and fro kyn *euele* yclothed ȝeden,
C.19.292　　That *euele* lyuen and leten nat t[il lif] hem forsake.
C.19.326　　Haeth mercy on suche men þat [so] *euele* may soffre.
C.22.186　　'Syre *euele* yt[a]uȝte Elde,' quod I, 'vnhende go with the!
C.22.280　　And *euele* is this yholde in parsches of yngelond

yvenquisshed ptp *venquishen v.* **B 1; C 1** yvenkused
B.18.101　　For be þis derknesse ydo deeþ worþ [*yvenquisshed*];
C.20.104　　For be this derkenesse ydo deth worth *yvenkused*;

ywaer > ywar; ywaged > wage; ywalked > walken

ywar adj *iwar adj.* **A 2; B 4; C 11** ywaer (2) ywar (9)
A. 9.109　　Ac er we *ywar* were wiþ wyt gonne we mete.
A.10.85　　Þanne is dobet to ben *ywar* for betyng of þe ȝarde,
B. 1.42　　And for þow sholdest ben *ywar* I wisse þee þe beste.'
B.10.81　　And yet þe wrecches of þis world is noon *ywar* by ooþer,
B.10.140　　And whan þat wit was *ywar* [how his wif] tolde
B.10.275　　This text was told yow to ben *ywar* er ye tauȝte
C. 1.40　　And wysseth þe to ben *ywar* what wolde þe desseyue.'

C. 2.154 Ȝut beth *ywar* of þe weddynge; for witty is treuthe
C. 7.80 This beth þe branches, beth *ywar*, þat bryngeth a man to wanhope.
C. 9.51 Beth *ywar*, ȝe wis men and witty of þe lawe,
C.10.115 And ar we *ywar* were with wit gan we mete.
C.11.61 And ȝut th[e] wrechus of this world is noen *ywar* by oþer
C.11.81 And when wit was *ywar* what studie menede
C.17.39 "Wyf! be *ywar*," quod he; "what haue we herynne?
C.19.228 Forthy beth *ywar*, ȝe wyse men þat with the world deleth,
C.20.354 Beth *ywaer*, ȝe wyse clerkes and ȝe witty of lawe,
C.21.243 Bothe of wele and of wo and be *ywaer* bifore,

ywasche ywasshe(n > wasshen; ywedded > wedden

ywende v *iwenden v.* C 1
C. 5.104 'Ȝe! and contynue,' quod Consience, 'and to þe kyrke *ywen[d]e.*'

ywent > wenden; ywete > ywyte; ywhitlymed > whitlymed

ywis adv *iwis adv.& adj.& n.* B 1; C 1
B.11.411 '[What is dowel?' quod þat wiȝt]; '*ywis*, sire', I seide,
C.13.219 'What is dowel?' quod þat wyhte; '*ywis*, sire,' y saide,

ywyte v *iwiten v.(1)* C 6 ywete (1) ywyte (5)
C.Pr.183 Men Myghte *ywete* where þei wente and here [way roume].
C. 3.76 *Ywyte* what thow delest with thi ryhte syde.
C.10.125 Here is oen wolde *ywyte* yf wit couthe teche;
C.18.274 'I wolde *ywyte*,' quod y tho, 'what is in thy lappe.'
C.20.216 Sholde *ywyte* witterly what day is to mene.
C.20.220 *Ywyte* what wo is ne were þe deth of kynde.

ywitted > witted; ywoned > woned

ywonne v *iwinnen v. &> wynnen* C 1
C.19.247 Excuse hem þat ben vnkynde and ȝut here [catel] *ywonne*

yworded > wordeden; yworshiped yworsshipid > worshipen

yworþe v *iworthen v.* B 2 yworþe; C 3 yworthe
B. 6.82 Lat-god-*yworþe*-wiþ-al-for-so-his-word-techeþ.
B. 6.226 Theiȝ þei doon yuele lat [þow] god *yworþe*:
C.Pr.204 Forthy y conseile for oure comune profit lat þe Cat *yworthe*
C. 8.86 Lat god *yworthe* with al, as holy wryt techeth:
C.10.164 God wol nat of hem wyte bute lat hem *yworthe*,

ywounded > wownde; ywounden > wounden

ywrye ptp *wrien v.(1)* 1; C 1
B.14.233 And his heued vnheled, vnesiliche *ywrye*
C.16.74 And his heued vnheled, vnesylyche *ywrye*

ywrite(n > writen; ywrithe > wroþ v; ywroght ywroȝt ywrouȝt ywrouhte > werchen; yȝoten > yeten

J

iaced v *jacen v.* B 1; C 1
B.17.54   To a Iustes in ierusalem he [I]*aced* awey faste.
C.19.52   To ioust in Ierusalem he *Iaced* awey faste.

iacke > iakke

iacob n prop *n.i.d.* B 1; C 1
B. 7.167   Thanne *Iacob* iugged Iosephes sweuene:
C. 9.311   Thenne *Iacob* iuged Iosepes sweuene:

iakke n prop *jakke n.(1)* A 1; B 1; C 1 Iacke
A. 7.64   Saue *Iakke* þe Iugelour & Ionete of þe stewis,
B. 6.70   Saue *Ia[kk]e* þe Iogelour and Ionette of þe Stuwes
C. 8.71   Saue *Iacke* þe iogelour and ionet of þe stuyues

iames n prop *Jame n.* A 6 Iame (4) Iames (2); B 6 Iame (2) Iames (4); C 5 Iame (1) Iames (4)
A.Pr.47   For to seke seint *Iame* & seintes at rome;
A. 1.159   For *Iames* þe ientil ioynide in his bokis
A. 4.109   Til seint *Iame* be souȝt þere I shal assigne,
A. 5.40   And ȝe þat seke seint *Iame* & seintes at rome,
A. 7.50   'I assente, be seint *Iame*,' seide þe kniȝt þanne,
A.12.108   By *Iames* and by Ierom, by Iop and by oþere,
B.Pr.47   For to seken Seint *Iame* and Seintes at Rome;
B. 1.185   For *Iames* þe gentile [Ioyned] in hise bokes
B. 4.126   And til Seint *Iames* be souȝt þere I shal assigne,
B. 5.56   And ye þat seke Seynt *Iames* and Seyntes [at] Rome,
B. 6.55   'I assente, by Seint *Iame*', seide þe knyȝt þanne,
B.19.164   Boþe *Iames* and Iohan, Iesu to seke,
C.Pr.48   To seke seynt *Iame* and seyntes [at] Rome;
C. 1.181   For *Iames* þe gentele iuge[d] in his bokes
C. 4.122   And til saynt *Iames* be souhte there pore sykke lyggen,
C. 5.197   And ȝe þat seketh seynt *Iames* and seyntes [at] Rome,
C.21.164   Bothe *Iames* and Iohann, iesu to seke,

iangele(de > iangle

iangeleres n *janglere n.* A 1 iangleris; B 2 Iangeleres (1) Iangleris (1)
A.Pr.35   Ac Iaperis & *iangleris*, Iudas children,
B.Pr.35   Ac Iaperes and *Iangeleres*, Iudas children,
B.10.31   And Iaperis and Iogelours and *Iangleris* of gestes,

iangelyng(e > ianglyng

iangle v *janglen v.* A 1; B 9 Iangle (6) iangled (2) ianglyng (1); C 4 iangele (1) iangelede (1) iangle (2)
A. 9.113   I durste meue no mater to make hym to *iangle*,
B.Pr.130   *Iangle* ne Iugge þat Iustifie hem sholde,
B. 2.95   And þere to *Iangle* and Iape and Iugge hir euencristen,
B. 4.155   And seide, 'madame, I am youre man what so my mouþ *Iangle*.
B. 6.314   Ayeins Catons counseil comseþ he to *Iangle*:
B. 8.123   I dorste meue no matere to maken hym to *Iangle*,
B. 9.84   A Iew wolde noȝt se a Iew go *Ianglyng* for defaute
B.13.84   'I shal *Iangle* to þis Iurdan wiþ his Iuste wombe
B.16.119   Iewes *iangled* þerayein [þat] Iuggede lawes,
B.16.144   Iudas *iangled* þerayein, ac Iesus hym tolde
C. 2.102   And there to *iangele* and iape and iuge here Emcristene,
C. 9.293   The prest thus and perkyn of þe pardon *iangelede*
C.10.119   Y durste meue no matere to maken hym to *iangle*
C.15.91   'Y schal *iangle* to þis iurdan with his iuyste wombe

iangleris > iangeleres

ianglyng ger *janglinge ger.* &> *iangle* A 1; B 4 ianglyng (2) ianglynge (2); C 4 iangelyng (1) iangelynge (2) iangling (1)
A.10.190   In gelosie, ioyeles, & *ianglyng* [a] bedde,
B. 4.180   I wole haue leaute in lawe, and lete be al youre *ianglyng*;
B. 5.158   And maad hem Ioutes of *Ianglyng* þat dame Iohane was a bastard,
B. 9.169   [In Ielousie, ioyelees, and *ianglynge* on bedde,
B.19.397   By Iesu! for al youre *Ianglynge*, wiþ Spiritus Iusticie.
C. 4.174   Y wol haue leutee for my lawe and late be al ȝoure *iangl[ing]*
C. 6.133   And made hem ioutes of *iangelynge*: "dame Ione was a bastard
C.10.270   In ielosye, ioyles and *iangelynge* abedde,
C.21.397   By iesu! for al ȝoure *iangelyng*, [with] spiritus Iusticie

iapare > iaper

iape n *jape n.* B 1; C 1
B.20.145   And heeld holynesse a *Iape* and hendenesse a wastour,
C.22.145   And helde holinesse a *iape* and hendenesse a wastour

iape v *japen v.* A 1 iapide; B 5 Iape (2) iaped (2) Iapen (1); C 3 iape (2) iaped (1)
A. 1.65   Iudas he *iapide* wiþ Iewene siluer,
B. 1.67   Iudas he *iaped* wiþ Iewen siluer
B. 2.95   And þere to Iangle and *Iape* and Iugge hir euencristen,
B.13.232   *Iape* ne Iogele ne gentilliche pipe,
B.13.352   And how þat lecchours louye laughen and *Iapen*,
B.18.41   'This Iesus of oure Iewes temple *Iaped* and despised,
C. 2.102   And there to iangele and *iape* and iuge here Emcristene,
C.15.206   *Iape* ne i[o]gele ne genteliche pipe,
C.20.40   'This iesus of oure iewene temple *iaped* and despised,

iaper n *japere n.* A 1 Iaperis; B 3 Iaper (1) Iaperes (1) Iaperis (1); C 1 iapare
A.Pr.35   Ac *Iaperis* & iangleris, Iudas children,
B.Pr.35   Ac *Iaperes* and Iangeleres, Iudas children,
B. 9.93   He is [Iugged wiþ] Iudas þat ȝyueþ a *Iaper* siluer
B.10.31   And *Iaperis* and Iogelours and Iangleris of gestes,
C.17.308   That iesus was bote a iogelour, a *iapare* amonges þe comune,

ielousie n *jelousie n.* A 1 gelosie; B 1; C 1 ielosye
A.10.190   In *gelosie*, ioyeles, & ianglyng [a] bedde,
B. 9.169   [In *Ielousie*, ioyelees, and ianglynge on bedde,
C.10.270   In *ielosye*, ioyles and iangelynge abedde,

ientel > gentil; ientil(e > gentile; ientily > gentilliche

ierico n prop *OED Jerico* B 1; C 1
B.17.53   Comynge from a contree þat men called *Ierico*;
C.19.51   Comynge fram a contraye þat men callide *Ierico*;

ierom n prop *n.i.d.* A 1; B 1; C 1 Ieroem
A.12.108   By Iames and by *Ierom*, by Iop and by oþere,
B.19.270   Gregori þe grete clerk and [þe goode *Ierom*];
C.21.270   Gregory the grete Clerk and [þe gode *Ieroem*];

ierusalem n prop *OED Jerusalem* B 6 Ierusalem (5) Iherusalem (1); C 4
B.16.163   Iusted in *Iherusalem*, a ioye to vs alle.
B.17.54   To a Iustes in *Ierusalem* he [I]aced awey faste.
B.17.82   And raped hym to [ryde þe riȝte wey to *Ierusalem*].
B.17.117   Which is þe wey þat I wente and wher forþ to *Ierusalem*;
B.18.17   Olde Iewes of *Ierusalem* for ioye þei songen,
B.18.19   And who sholde Iuste in *Ierusalem*. 'Iesus', he seide,
C.19.52   To ioust in *Ierusalem* he Iaced awey faste.
C.19.79   And rapede hym to ryde the rihte way to *Ierusalem*.
C.20.15   Olde iewes of *Ierusalem* for ioye they songen,
C.20.17   And ho sholde iouste in *Ierusalem*. 'Iesus,' he saide,

iesus n prop *Jesu n.* A 4 Iesu; B 62 Iesu (26) Iesus (36); C 56 iesu (22) iesus (34)
A. 3.145   Be *Iesu*, wiþ hire Iuelx ȝoure Iustice she shendiþ,
A.11.27   To *iesu* þe gentil þat Iewis todrowe
A.11.84   [O]r Iudas þe Iew *Iesu* betraye[n].
A.12.27   And asked *Iesu* on hy þat herden hit an hundred.
B.Pr.165   Were þer a belle on hire beiȝe, by *Iesu*, as me þynkeþ,
B. 3.155   By *Iesus*! wiþ hire Ieweles youre Iustices she shendeþ
B.10.35   To *Iesu* þe gentile þat Iewes todrowe
B.10.131   Or Iudas [þe Iew] *Iesu* bitraye.
B.11.185   [For] oure Ioye and oure [Iuel], *Iesu* crist of heuene,
B.11.238   So bi hise werkes þei wisten þat he was *Iesus*.
B.11.248   *Iesu* crist on a Iewes doȝter liȝte, gentil womman þouȝ she were,
B.12.13   And Dauid in þe Sauter seiþ, of swiche þat loueþ *Iesus*,
B.12.89   The womman þat þe Iewes [iugged] þat *Iesus* þouȝte to saue:
B.14.181   Thus in genere of gentries *Iesu* crist seide
B.15.87   Ayein youre rule and Religion; I take record at *Iesus*
B.15.264   Sholde neuere Iudas ne Iew haue *Iesu* doon on roode,
B.15.496   To be pastours and preche þe passion of *Iesus*,
B.16.37   That is þe passion and þe power of oure prince *Iesu*.
B.16.92   That oon *Iesus* a Iustices sone moste Iouke in hir chambre
B.16.95   And þanne sholde *Iesus* Iuste þerfore bi Iuggement of armes
B.16.121   'Thanne are ye cherles', [chidde *Iesus*], 'and youre children boþe,

B.16.144 Iudas iangled þerayein, ac *Iesus* hym tolde
B.16.147 And tolde hem a tokne to knowe wiþ *Iesus*;
B.16.150 And [þus] was wiþ Iudas þo þat *Iesus* bitrayed:
B.16.153 Thanne *Iesus* to Iudas and to þe Iewes seide,
B.16.161 Thoru3 Iudas and Iewes *Iesus* was [ynome]
B.16.222 And is no3t but gendre of a generacion bifore *Iesu* crist in heuene:
B.18.19 And who sholde Iuste in Ierusalem. '*Iesus*', he seide,
B.18.22 'This *Iesus* of his gentries wol Iuste in Piers armes,
B.18.27 'Who shal Iuste wiþ *Iesus*', quod I, 'Iewes or Scrybes?'
B.18.38 The Iewes and þe Iustice ayeins *Iesu* þei weere,
B.18.41 'This *Iesus* of oure Iewes temple Iaped and despised,
B.18.82 To [Iusten wiþ *Iesus*, þis blynde Iew Longeus].
B.18.87 Thanne fil þe kny3t vpon knees and cryde [*Iesu*] mercy:
B.18.91 Haue on me ruþe, ri3tful *Iesu*;' and ri3t wiþ þat he wepte.
B.18.100 3ilt hym recreaunt re[m]yng, ri3t at *Iesus* wille.
B.18.181 For *Iesus* Iustede wel Ioye bigynneþ dawe:
B.18.252 For [*Iesus* as a] geaunt wiþ a gyn [comeþ yonde]
B.18.255 And I, book, wole be brent but *Iesus* rise to lyue
B.18.301 To warne Pilates wif what done man was *Iesus*,
B.18.416 'Trewes', quod Truþe, 'þow tellest vs sooþ, by *Iesus*!
B.19.8 And ri3t lik in alle [lymes] to oure lord *Ies[u]*.
B.19.10 'Is þis *Iesus* þe Iustere', quod I, 'þat Iewes dide to deþe?
B.19.15 'Why calle [ye] hym crist, siþen Iewes calle[d] hym *Iesus*?
B.19.18 Anoon as men nempned þe name of god *Iesu*;
B.19.19 Ergo is no name to þe name of *Iesus*,
B.19.25 Than *Iesu* or Iesus þat al oure Ioye com of?'
B.19.25 Than *Iesu* or Iesus þat al oure Ioye com of?'
B.19.34 The Iewes þat were gentil men, *Ies[u]* þei despised,
B.19.40 And gentil men wiþ *Iesu*, for Iesu[s] was yfulled
B.19.40 And gentil men wiþ *Iesu*, for Iesu[s] was yfulled
B.19.44 And so dide *Iesus* þe Iewes; he Iustified and tau3te hem
B.19.48 Tho was he *Iesus* of Iewes called, gentile prophete,
B.19.70 Faithly for to speke, his firste name was *Iesus*.
B.19.91 The þridde kyng þo kam knelynge to *Iesu*
B.19.95 Thoru3 þre kynne kynges knelynge to *Iesu*.
B.19.96 Ac for alle þise preciouse present3 oure lord [prynce] *Iesus*
B.19.101 And so dide *Iesu* in hise dayes, whoso [dorste] telle it.
B.19.106 As kynde is of a Conquerour, so comsede *Iesu*
B.19.108 In his Iuuentee þis *Iesus* at Iewene feeste
B.19.117 And þanne was he [cleped and] called no3t [oonly] crist but *Iesu*,
B.19.136 Forþi þe contree þer *Iesu* cam called hym fili dauid,
B.19.139 Ne ouer Iewes Iustice, as *Iesus* was, hem þou3te.
B.19.164 Boþe Iames and Iohan, *Iesu* to seke,
B.19.173 Thow art my lord, I bileue, god lord *Iesu*;
B.19.397 By *Iesu*! for al youre Ianglynge, wiþ Spiritus Iusticie,
C.Pr.182 Wer ther a belle on here beygh, by *iesu*, as me thynketh,
C. 3.193 By *iesu*! with here ieweles the Iustices she shendeth;
C.10.22 Fallyng fro ioye, *iesu* woet þe sothe!
C.12.127 So by [h]is werkes thei wisten þat he was *iesu*
C.13.3 Oure prince *iesu* pouerte chees and his apostles alle
C.15.22 That iustus bifore *iesu* in die iudicij non saluabitur bote vix helpe;
C.17.192 To be p[astor]s and preche the passioun of *iesu*
C.17.308 That *iesus* was bote a iogelour, a iapare amonges þe comune,
C.18.41 The which is þe passioun & þe penaunce & þe parfitnesse of *iesus*
C.18.125 That oen *Iesus*, a Iustices sone, most iouken in here chaumbre
C.18.128 That *iesus* sholde iouste þerfore by iugement of Armes
C.18.129 Who sholde fecche this fruyt, the fende or *iesus* suluen.
C.18.151 'Thenne is saton 3oure saueour,' quod *iesus*, '& hath ysaued 3ow
⠀⠀⠀⠀⠀⠀ofte.
C.18.161 The iewes tolde þe iustice how þat *iesus* saide;
C.18.165 Of Ieudas þe iew, *iesus* oune disciple.
C.18.167 That Iudas and iewes *iesus* thei mette.
C.18.169 And kuste *iesus* to be knowe þerby and cauht of þe iewes.
C.18.170 Thenne riste to Iudas and to þe iewes sayde,
C.18.177 This iewes to þe iustices *iesus* they ladde.
C.20.17 And ho sholde iouste in Ierusalem. '*Iesus*,' he seide,
C.20.21 That this *iesus* of his gentrice shal iouste in Pers Armes,
C.20.26 'Who shal iouste with *iesus*,' quod y, 'iewes or scrib3?'
C.20.37 The iewes and þe iustic[e] a3eyns *iesus* þey were
C.20.40 'This *iesus* of oure iewene temple iaped and despised,
C.20.84 [To] iouste with *iesus*, this blynde iewe longies.
C.20.89 Tho ful the knyhte vppon knees and criede *iesu* mercy:
C.20.94 Haue [on me reuthe], ri3tful *iesu*;' and riht with þat a wepte.
C.20.103 3elde hym [re]creaunt remyng, riht at *iesu[s]* wille.
C.20.184 For *iesus* ioustede wel ioy bigynneth dawe:
C.20.261 For *iesus* as a geaunt with a gyn cometh 3ende
C.20.459 'Trewes,' quod treuthe; 'thow tellest vs soeth, by *iesus*!
C.21.8 And riht lyke in alle lymes to oure lord *iesu*.
C.21.10 'Is this *iesus* the ioustare,' quod y, 'þat iewes dede to dethe?
C.21.15 'Whi calle 3e hym Crist sennes iewes callede hym *iesus*?
C.21.18 Anoon as men nemned þe name of god *iesu*;
C.21.19 Ergo is no name to þe name of *iesus*
C.21.25 Then *iesu* or *iesus* þat all oure ioye cam of ?'

C.21.25 Then iesu or *iesus* þat all oure ioye cam of ?'
C.21.34 The iewes þat were gentel men *iesu* thei dispisede,
C.21.40 And Ientel men with *iesu* for iesu[s] was yfolled
C.21.40 And Ientel men with iesu for *iesu[s]* was yfolled
C.21.44 And so dede *iesus* þe iewes; he iustified and tauhte hem
C.21.48 Tho was he *iesu[s]* of iewes [cald], gentel profete.
C.21.70 Faythly for to speke his furste name was *iesus*.
C.21.91 The thridde kyng cam [þo] knel[ynge] to *iesu*
C.21.95 Thorw thre kyne kynges knelyng to *iesu*.
C.21.96 Ac for all this precíouse presentes oure lord prince *iesu[s]*
C.21.101 And so dede *iesu* in his dayes, whoso durste tellen hit.
C.21.106 As kynde is of a conquerour, so comesede *iesu*
C.21.108 In his iuuentee this *iesus* at iewene feste
C.21.117 And tho was he cleped and calde not [onl]y Crist but *iesu*,
C.21.136 Forthy þe contre þer *iesu* cam calde hym fili dauid
C.21.139 Ne ouer Iewes Iustice as *iesus* was, hem thouhte.
C.21.164 Bothe Iames and Iohann, *iesu* to seke,
C.21.173 Thow art my lord, y bileue, god lord *iesu*,
C.21.397 By *iesu*! for al 3oure iangelyng, [with] spiritus Iusticie

ieudas > *iudas*; *ieudith* > *iudith*

iew n prop *Jeu n.* A 4 Iew (1) Iewene (1) Iewis (2); B 53 Iew (6) Iewen (2) iewene (3) Iewes (42); C 43 iew (1) iewe (1) iewene (4) iewes (37)
A. 1.65 Iudas he iapide wiþ *Iewene* siluer,
A.11.27 To iesu þe gentil þat *Iewis* todrowe
A.11.84 [O]r Iudas þe *Iew* Iesu betraye[n].
A.11.235 'þat is in extremis,' quaþ scripture, 'as sarisines & *Iewis*
B. 1.67 Iudas he iaped wiþ *Iewen* siluer,
B. 3.302 That *Iewes* shul wene in hire wit, and wexen glade,
B. 3.327 And þe myddel of a Moone shal make þe *Iewes* torne,
B. 5.239 I lerned among lumbardes [a lesson and of *Iewes*],
B. 9.84 A *Iew* wolde no3t se a Iew go Ianglyng for defaute
B. 9.84 A Iew wolde no3t se a *Iew* go Ianglyng for defaute
B. 9.87 Syn *Iewes*, þat we Iugge Iudas felawes,
B. 9.90 [So] *Iewes* [shul] ben oure loresmen, shame to vs alle!
B.10.35 To Iesu þe gentile þat *Iewes* todrowe
B.10.131 Or Iudas [þe *Iew*] Iesu bitraye.
B.10.352 'That is in extremis', quod Scripture, '[as] Sar3ens & *Iewes*
B.11.120 Sar3ens and scismatikes and so he dide þe *Iewes*:
B.11.248 Iesu crist on a *Iewes* do3ter li3te, gentil womman þou3 she were,
B.12.42 Iob þe *Iew* his ioye deere abou3te;
B.12.73 þe olde lawe as þe lettre telleþ, þat was þe lawe of *Iewes*,
B.12.78 [For] þoru3 caractes þat crist wroot þe *Iewes* knewe hemselue
B.12.89 The womman þat þe *Iewes* [iugged] þat Iesus þou3te to saue:
B.12.91 Dampneþ vs at þe day of dome as [dide þe caractes] þe *Iewes*.
B.12.278 Seyen in hir Sermons þat neiþer Sarsens ne *Iewes*
B.13.209 Sarsens and Surre, and so forþ alle þe *Iewes*,
B.15.264 Sholde neuere Iudas ne *Iew* haue Iesu doon on roode,
B.15.582 And *Iewes* lyuen in lele lawe; oure lord wroot it hymselue
B.15.584 Dilige deum & proximum is parfit *Iewen* lawe;
B.15.595 Dide hym rise and rome ri3t bifore þe *Iewes*.
B.15.607 And siþen þat þe Sar3ens and also þe *Iewes*
B.16.119 *Iewes* iangled þerayein [bat] Iuggede lawes,
B.16.127 And mysseide þe *Iewes* manliche and manaced hem to bete
B.16.136 Enuye and yuel wil [arne] in þe *Iewes*.
B.16.146 Thanne wente forþ þat wikked man and wiþ þe *Iewes* mette
B.16.152 And kiste hym to be caught þerby and kulled of þe *Iewes*.
B.16.153 Thanne Iesus to Iudas and to þe *Iewes* seide,
B.16.158 Thou3 I bi treson be take [to] youre [*iewene*] wille
B.16.161 Thoru3 Iudas and *Iewes* Iesus was [ynome]
B.18.17 Olde *Iewes* of Ierusalem for ioye þei songen,
B.18.27 'Who shal Iuste wiþ Iesus', quod I, '*Iewes* or Scrybes?'
B.18.38 The *Iewes* and þe Iustice ayeins Iesu þei weere,
B.18.41 'This Iesus of oure *Iewes* temple Iaped and despised,
B.18.82 To [Iusten wiþ Iesus, þis blynde *Iew* Longeus].
B.18.92 Thanne gan Feiþ felly þe false *Iewes* despise;
B.18.110 What for feere of þis ferly and of þe false *Iewes*
B.18.258 And al þe *Iewene* Ioye vnioynen and vnlouken;
B.18.302 For *Iewes* hateden hym and han doon hym to deþe.
B.19.10 'Is þis Iesus þe Iustere', quod I, 'þat *Iewes* dide to deþe?
B.19.15 'Why calle [ye] hym crist, siþen *Iewes* calle[d] hym Iesus?
B.19.34 The *Iewes* þat were gentil men, Ies[u] þei despised,
B.19.41 And vpon Caluarie on cros ycrouned kyng of *Iewes*.
B.19.44 And so dide Iesus þe *Iewes*; he Iustified and tau3te hem
B.19.48 Tho was he Iesus of *Iewes* called, gentile prophete,
B.19.108 In his Iuuentee þis Iesus at *Iewene* feeste
B.19.139 Ne ouer *Iewes* Iustice, as Iesus was, hem þou3te.
B.19.140 [Her]of Cayphas hadde enuye and oþere *Iewes*,
B.19.154 The *Iewes* preide hem pees, and [preide] þe knyghtes
B.19.422 At Auynoun among *Iewes*–Cum sancto sanctus eris &c–
C. 1.63 Iudas he byiapede thorw *iewene* suluer
C. 3.455 That *iewes* shal wene in he[re] wit, & wexen so glade,

C. 3.480	And the [myddell] of [a] mone shal make þe *iewes* turne
C. 4.194	Or lumbardus of lukes þat leuen by lone as *iewes*.'
C. 6.241	Y lernede among lumbardus a lessoun and of *iewes*,
C.12.55	Sarrasynes and sismatikes and so a ded þe *iewes*:
C.14.40	And in soend a signe wroet and saide to þe *iewes*,
C.14.200	Segen [in] here sarmons þat noþer saresynes ne *iewes*
C.17.132	*Iewes* and gentel sarresines iugen hemsulue
C.17.156	Ac many manere men þer ben, as sarresynes and *iewes*,
C.17.252	For sethe þat this sarrasines, Scribȝ and this *iewes*
C.17.295	*Iewes* lyuen in þe lawe þat oure lord tauhte
C.17.304	*Iewes* sayde þat hit seye with soercerye he wrouhte,
C.17.313	And haen a suspectioun to be saef, bothe sarresynes & *iewes*,
C.17.315	And sethe þat th[e] sarresynes and also þe *iewes*
C.18.149	And some *iewes* saide with sorserie he wrouhte
C.18.161	The *iewes* tolde þe iustice how þat iesus saide;
C.18.163	Enuye and euel wil ern in þe *iewes*
C.18.165	Of Ieudas þe *iew*, iesus oune disciple.
C.18.167	That Iudas and *iewes* iesus thei mette.
C.18.169	And kuste iesus to be knowe þerby and cauht of þe *iewes*.
C.18.170	Thenne iesus to Iudas and to þe *iewes* sayde,
C.18.175	Sethe y be tresoun am take and to ȝoure will, *iewes*,
C.18.177	This *iewes* to þe iustices iesus they ladde.
C.20.15	Olde *iewes* of Ierusalem for ioye they songen,
C.20.26	'Who shal iouste with iesus,' quod y, '*iewes* or scribȝ?'
C.20.37	The *iewes* and þe iustic[e] aȝeyns iesus þey were
C.20.40	'This iesus of oure *iewene* temple iaped and despised,
C.20.84	[To] iouste with iesus, this blynde *iewe* longies.
C.20.95	Thenne gan faith f[el]ly þe false *iewes* dispice,
C.20.113	What for fere of this ferly and of þe false *iewes*
C.20.266	And alle þe *iewene* ioye vnioynen and vnlouken:
C.21.10	'Is this iesus the ioustare,' quod y, 'þat *iewes* dede to dethe?
C.21.15	'Whi calle ȝe hym Crist sennes *iewes* callede hym iesus?
C.21.34	The *iewes* þat were gentel men iesu thei dispisede,
C.21.41	And vpon Caluarie on cros ycrouned kyng of *iewes*.
C.21.44	And so dede iesus þe *iewes*; he iustified and tauhte hem
C.21.48	Tho was he iesu[s] of *iewes* [cald], gentel profete,
C.21.108	In his iuuentee this iesus at *iewene* feste
C.21.139	Ne ouer *Iewes* Iustice as iesus was, hem thouhte.
C.21.140	Hereof hadde Cayphas enuye and oþer *iewes*
C.21.154	The *iewes* preyed hem pees and preyede th[e] knyhtes
C.21.422	At Auenon among *iewes*–cum sancto sanctus eris &c–

iewel(es > iuwel; iewen(e > iew; iewyse > iuwise

iob n prop *OED Job* A 2 Iob (1) Iop (1); B 3; C 7 Iob (5) Iop (2)

A.11.23	*Iob* þe ientile in his gestis seide it:
A.12.108	By Iames and by Ierom, by *Iop* and by oþere,
B.10.23	*Iob* þe gentile in hise gestes witnesseþ
B.12.42	*Iob* þe Iew his ioye deere abouȝte;
B.18.149	*Iob* þe [parfit] patriark repreueþ þi sawes:
C.11.21	*Iob* þe gentele in his g[e]stes witnesseth
C.13.5	Ȝut ret me þat abraham and *Iob* weren wonder ryche
C.13.15	*Iob* þe gentele, what ioye hadde he on erthe?
C.13.20	And *Iob* bykam as a iolyf man and al his ioye newe.
C.13.25	And þe gentel *Iob*; here ioye hath non ende.
C.17.51	*Iop* þe parfite patriarke this prouerbe wroet and tauhte
C.20.152	*Iop* þe parfite patriarke repreueth thy sawes:

iogele v *jogelen v.* B 1; C 1

B.13.232	Iape ne *Iogele* ne gentilliche pipe,
C.15.206	Iape ne i[o]gele ne genteliche pipe,

iogelour n *jogelour n.* A 1 Iugelour; B 2 Iogelour (1) Iogelours (1); C 2

A. 7.64	Saue Iakke þe *Iugelour* & Ionete of þe stewis,
B. 6.70	Saue Ia[kk]e þe *Iogelour* and Ionette of þe Stuwes
B.10.31	And Iaperis and *Iogelours* and Iangleris of gestes,
C. 8.71	Saue Iacke þe *iogelour* and ionet of þe stuyues
C.17.308	That iesus was bote a *iogelour*, a iapare amonges þe comune,

iogged v *jaggen v.* B 1; C 1

B.20.134	He *Iogged* to a Iustice and Iusted in his eere
C.22.134	He *iogged* til a iustice and iustede in his ere

iohan n prop *cf. Jon n.* A 1 Ion; B 17 Iohan (16) Iohanes (1); C 13 Iohan (2) Iohann (5) Iohannes (1) Iohn (2) Ion (3)

A.11.282	Sonnere hadde he saluacioun þanne seint *Ion* þe baptist,
B. 5.408	Than al þat euere Marc made, Mathew, *Iohan* and Lucas.
B. 5.499	And al þat Marc haþ ymaad, Mathew, *Iohan* and Lucas
B. 7.45	Ac many a Iustice and Iurour wolde for *Iohan* do moore
B.10.423	He was sonner ysaued þan seint *Iohan* þe Baptist
B.11.176	For Seint *Iohan* seide it, and soþe arn hise wordes:
B.11.227	That saued synful men as Seint *Iohan* bereþ witnesse:
B.11.246	Seint *Iohan* and oþere seintes were seyen in poore cloþyng,
B.12.197	As Seint *Iohan* and oþere Seintes þat deserued hadde bettre.
B.12.203	He sit neiþer wiþ Seint *Iohan*, Symond ne Iude,
B.13.440	As he seiþ hymself; seynt *Iohan* bereþ witnesse:
B.15.123	Sir *Iohan* and sire Geffrey haþ [of siluer a girdel],
B.16.82	Sampson and Samuel and Seint *Iohan* þe Baptist,
B.16.250	Of a [buyrn] þat baptised hym–*Iohan* Baptist was his name–
B.18.324	Songen seint *Iohanes* song, Ecce agnus dei.
B.19.164	Boþe Iames and *Iohan*, Iesu to seke,
B.19.265	And Ioyned to hem oon *Iohan*, moost gentil of alle,
B.19.288	Ne no mete in his mouþ þat maister *Iohan* Spicede.
C. 7.24	Th[en] al þat euere Mark made, Matheu, *Iohn* or lucas.
C. 7.100	As he sayth hymsulf; seynt *Ion* bereth witnesse:
C. 7.139	And al þat mark hath ymade, Matheu, *Ion* and lucas
C.11.255	He was sunnere ysaued then seynt *Iohn* þe baptiste
C.12.99	And seynt *Ion* sethen saide hit of his techyng:
C.14.136	A[s] seynt *Ioh[a]n* and oþer seyntes þat haen [de]serued bettere.
C.14.142	A sit noþer with seynte *Iohan*, simond ne Iude,
C.18.113	Sampson and samuel and seynt *Iohann* þe Baptiste,
C.18.267	Forthy y seke hym,' he saide, 'for seynt *Iohann* þe Baptiste
C.20.367	Songen seynt *Iohann[es* songe], ecce agnus dei.
C.21.164	Bothe Iames and *Iohann*, iesu to seke,
C.21.265	And ioyned til hem oen *iohann*, most gentill of all,
C.21.288	Ne no mete in his mouth þat maistre *iohann* spyced.

iohan_but n prop *n.i.d.* A 1

A.12.106	And so bad *Iohan but* busily wel ofte

iohane n prop *n.i.d.* B 1; C 1 Ione

B. 5.158	And maad hem Ioutes of Ianglyng þat dame *Iohane* was a bastard,
C. 6.133	And made hem ioutes of iangelynge: "dame *Ione* was a bastard

iohann > iohan

iohannes_crisostomus n prop *n.i.d.* &> iohan B 1; C 1

B.15.117	*Iohannes Crisostomus* of clerkes [carpeþ] and preestes:
C.16.272	*Iohannes Crisostomus* carpeth thus of clerkes [and prestes]:

iohn > iohan

ioye n *joie n.* A 6; B 32 ioie (2) ioye (30); C 33 ioy (1) ioye (32)

A. 2.121	Iuggen ȝow ioyntly in *ioye* for euere'.
A. 3.13	Ientily wiþ *ioye* þe Iustices so[mm]e
A. 3.92	And brouȝte hire to bo[ure] wiþ blisse & wiþ *ioye*.
A. 8.42	Þanne were marchauntis merye; many wepe for *ioye*,
A. 8.112	[By foules, þat are not] besy aboute þe bely *ioye*:
A. 8.158	Þe peple wiþoute penaunce [to passe to *Ioye*]?
B. 2.157	Iuggen yow ioyntly in *ioie* for euere'.
B. 3.13	Gentilliche wiþ *ioye* þe Iustices somme
B. 3.103	And brouȝte hire to boure wiþ blisse and wiþ *ioye*.
B. 5.262	Ne þyne heires after þee haue *ioie* of þat þow wynnest,
B. 7.37	And sende youre soules in saufte to my Seintes in *Ioye*.'
B. 7.38	Thanne were Marchauntȝ murie; manye wepten for *ioye*
B. 7.130	By foweles [þat are] noȝt bisy aboute þe [bely *ioye*];
B. 7.180	[Th]e peple wiþouten penaunce to passen [to *ioye*]?
B.11.168	For þat is þe book blissed of blisse and of *ioye*;
B.11.185	[For] oure *Ioye* and oure [Iuel], Iesu crist of heuene,
B.12.42	Iob þe Iew his *ioye* deere abouȝte;
B.12.134	Ne broȝt by hir bokes to blisse ne to *ioye*,
B.14.111	*Ioye* þat neuere ioye hadde of riȝtful Iugge he askeþ,
B.14.111	Ioye þat neuere *ioye* hadde of riȝtful Iugge he askeþ,
B.14.115	And after þow sendest hem somer þat is hir souereyn *ioye*
B.14.119	But god sente hem som tyme som manere *Ioye*
B.14.121	For to wroþerhele was he wroȝt þat neuere was *Ioye* shapen.
B.14.122	Aungeles þat in helle now ben hadden *ioye* som tyme,
B.14.164	Now, lord, sende hem somer, and som maner of *ioye*,
B.14.285	And *Ioye* to pacient pouerte], pure spiritual helþe,
B.16.18	'Piers þe Plowman!' quod I þo, and al for pure *Ioye*
B.16.163	Iusted in Iherusalem, a *ioye* to vs alle.
B.16.207	And eiþer is oþeres *ioye* in þre sondry persones,
B.18.17	Olde Iewes of Ierusalem for *ioye* þei songen,
B.18.181	For Iesus Iustede wel *Ioye* bigynneþ dawe:
B.18.225	To wite what alle wo is [þat woot of] alle *ioye*.
B.18.258	And al þe Iewene *Ioye* vnioynen and vnlouken;
B.19.25	Than Iesu or Iesus þat al oure *Ioye* com of?'
B.19.66	And se bi his sorwe þat whoso loueþ *ioye*
B.19.197	The goode to godhede and to greet *Ioye*,
B.20.40	And god al his grete *Ioye* goostliche he lefte
B.20.47	And suffre sorwes ful soure, þat shal to *Ioye* torne."
C. 3.14	Genteliche with *ioye* the Iustices somme
C. 3.340	Grace of good ende and gret *ioye* aftur
C. 6.255	Ne thyn heyres, as y hope, haue *ioye* of þat thow wonne
C. 9.41	Tho were Marchauntes mury; many wopen for *ioye*
C. 9.50	Shal haue grace of a good ende and greet *ioye* aftur.
C. 9.326	To peple withouten penaunce to passe into *ioye*,
C.10.22	Fallyng fro *ioye*, iesu woet þe sothe!
C.13.15	Iob þe gentele, what *ioye* hadde he on erthe?
C.13.20	And Iob bykam as a iolyf man and al his *ioye* newe.
C.13.25	And þe gentel Iob; here *ioye* hath non ende.
C.14.78	Ne brouhte by here bokes to blisse ne to *ioye*,

C.15.71   Alle þat coueyte[d] to come to eny kyne *ioye*,
C.15.287   *Ioye* þat neuere ioye hadde of rihtfull iuge he asketh
C.15.287   Ioye þat neuere *ioye* hadde of rihtfull iuge he asketh
C.15.291   [And] aftur thow sendest hem somer þat is here souereyne *ioye*
C.15.295   Bote god sen[t]e hem som tyme sum manere *ioye*
C.15.297   For to wroþerhele was he wrouht þat neuere was *ioye* yschape.
C.15.298   Angeles þat in helle now hen hadden som tyme *ioye*
C.15.301   Many man hath his *ioye* here for al here wel dedes
C.16.17   Now, lord, sende hem somur som tyme to solace and to *ioye*
C.16.56   For his pouerte and pacience perpetuel *ioye*.
C.17.145   Thenne seweth the [thy] soule to sorwe or to *ioye*
C.18.16   'Now, certes,' y sayde, and siȝte for *ioye*,
C.20.15   Olde iewes of Ierusalem for *ioye* they songen,
C.20.184   For iesus iousted wel *ioy* bigynneth dawe:
C.20.234   To wyte what al wo is þat woet of alle *ioye*:
C.20.266   And alle þe iewene *ioye* vnioynen and vnlouken;
C.20.345   For thy lesinges, lucifer, we losten furst oure *ioye*
C.21.25   Then iesu or iesus þat all oure *ioye* cam of ?'
C.21.66   And se bi his sorwe þat hoso loueth *ioye*
C.21.197   The gode to godhede and to grete *ioye*
C.22.40   And god al his grete *ioye* goestliche he lefte
C.22.47   And soffre sorwes ful soure þat shal to *ioye* torne."

ioyelees adj *joieles adj.* A 1 ioyeles; B 1; C 1 ioyls
A.10.190   In gelosie, *ioyeles*, & ianglyng [a] bedde,
B. 9.169   [In Ielousie, *ioyelees*, and ianglynge on bedde,
C.10.270   In ielosye, *ioyls* and iangelynge abedde,

ioyned v1 *joinen v.(1)* A 1; B 2; C 1
A. 2.101   And ȝif þe iustice iugge hire to be *ioyned* with fals,
B. 2.137   And [if þe] Iustic[e] Iugg[e] hire to be *Ioyned* [wiþ] Fals
B.19.265   And *Ioyned* to hem oon Iohan, moost gentil of alle,
C.21.265   And *ioyned* til hem oen iohann, most gentill of all,

ioyned v2 *joinen v.(2)* A 1 ioynide; B 1
A. 1.159   For Iames þe ientil *ioynide* in his bokis
B. 1.185   For Iames þe gentile [*Ioyned*] in hise bokes

ioynte n *jointe n.(1)* B 1 ioyntes; C 2 ioynte (1) ioyntes (1)
B.17.178   For [þe pawme] haþ power to putte out þe *ioyntes*
C. 9.216   He þat lolleth is lame or his leg out of *ioynte*
C.19.143   For þe paume hath power to pu[t]te out þe *ioyntes*

ioyntly adv *jointlie adv.* A 1; B 1
A. 2.121   Iuggen ȝow *ioyntly* in ioye for euere'.
B. 2.157   Iuggen yow *ioyntly* in ioie for euere'.

iolyf adj *joli adj.* C 1
C.13.20   And Iob bykam as a *iolyf* man and al his ioye newe.

ion > iohan; ione > iohane

ionette n prop *Jonete-of-the-steues n.* A 1 Ionete; B 1; C 1 ionet
A. 7.64   Saue Iakke þe Iugelour & *Ionete* of þe stewis,
B. 6.70   Saue Ia[kk]e þe Iogelour and *Ionette* of þe Stuwes
C. 8.71   Saue Iacke þe iogelour and *ionet* of þe stuyues

ionettes n *jonette n.* C 1
C.12.221   As pesecoddes, pere *ionettes*, plommes and cheries;

ionettes > pere_ionettes; iop > iob

iosaphat n prop *n.i.d.* B 1; C 1 Iosophat
B.18.369   Til þe vendage falle in þe vale of *Iosaphat*,
C.20.411   Til þe ventage valle in þe vale of *Iosaphat*

ioseph n prop *OED Joseph* A 2 Iosep; B 3 Ioseph (2) Iosephes (1); C 3
              Iosepes (1) Ioseph (2)
A. 8.143   And *Iosep* mette merueillously how þe mone & þe sonne
A. 8.148   Þat *Iosep* was Iustice Egipt to kepe–
B. 7.165   And *Ioseph* mette merueillously how þe moone and þe sonne
B. 7.167   Thanne Iacob iugged *Iosephes* sweuene:
B. 7.171   That *Ioseph* was Iustice Egipte to loke;
C. 9.309   And *Ioseph* mette merueilously how þe mone and þe sonne
C. 9.311   Thenne Iacob iuged *Iosepes* sweuene:
C. 9.315   That *Ioseph* was Iustice Egipte to saue;

iosophat > iosaphat

iosue n prop *n.i.d.* B 1; C 1
B.17.24   *Iosue* and Iudith and Iudas Macabeus,
C.19.25   Bothe *Iosue* and Ieudith and Iudas Macabeus,

iottis > iuttes

iouke v *jouken v.* B 1; C 1 iouken
B.16.92   That oon Iesus a Iustices sone moste *Iouke* in hir chambre
C.18.125   That oen Iesus, a Iustices sone, most *iouken* in here chaumbre

iournee n *journei n.* B 1; C 1 iourne
B.14.136   And til he haue doon his deuoir and his dayes *iournee*,
C.16.5   When his d[eu]er is doen and his dayes *iourne*

ioust(- > iust-

ioutes n *joute n.* B 1; C 1
B. 5.158   And maad hem *Ioutes* of Ianglyng þat dame Iohane was a bastard,
C. 6.133   And made hem *ioutes* of iangelynge: "dame Ione was a bastard

iuda n prop *Jude n.* B 1; C 1
B.19.138   To be kaiser or kyng of þe kyngdom of *Iuda*,
C.21.138   To be Cayser or kyng of the kyngdoem of *Iuda*

iudas n prop *OED Judas* A 3; B 11; C 5 Ieudas (1) Iudas (4)
A.Pr.35   Ac Iaperis & iangleris, *Iudas* children,
A. 1.65   *Iudas* he iapide wiþ Iewene siluer,
A.11.84   [O]r *Iudas* þe Iew Iesu betraye[n].
B.Pr.35   Ac Iaperes and Iangeleres, *Iudas* children,
B. 1.67   *Iudas* he iaped wiþ Iewen siluer
B. 9.87   Syn Iewes, þat we Iugge *Iudas* felawes,
B. 9.93   He is [Iugged wiþ] *Iudas* þat ȝyueþ a Iaper siluer
B.10.131   Or *Iudas* [þe Iew] Iesu bitraye.
B.15.264   Sholde neuere *Iudas* ne Iew haue Iesu doon on roode,
B.16.144   *Iudas* Iangled þerayein, ac Iesus hym tolde
B.16.150   And [þus] was wiþ *Iudas* þo þat Iesus bitrayed:
B.16.153   Thanne Iesus to *Iudas* and to þe Iewes seide,
B.16.161   Thoruȝ *Iudas* and Iewes Iesus was [ynome]
B.17.24   Iosue and Iudith and *Iudas* Macabeus,
C. 1.63   *Iudas* he byiapede thorw iewene suluer
C.18.165   Of *Ieudas* þe iew, iesus oune disciple.
C.18.167   That *Iudas* and iewes iesus thei mette.
C.18.170   Thenne iesus to *Iudas* and to þe iewes sayde,
C.19.25   Bothe Iosue and Ieudith and *Iudas* Macabeus,

iude n prop *n.i.d.* B 1; C 1
B.12.203   He sit neiþer wiþ Seint Iohan, Symond ne *Iude*,
C.14.142   A sit noþer with seynte Iohan, simond ne *Iude*,

iudith n prop *n.i.d.* B 1; C 1 Ieudith
B.17.24   Iosue and *Iudith* and Iudas Macabeus,
C.19.25   Bothe Iosue and *Ieudith* and Iudas Macabeus,

iuel iuelx > iuwel; iuge > iugge,iuggen; iuged > iuggen; iugelour > iogelour;
iugement > iuggement; iugen > iuggen

iugge n *juge n. &> iuggen* A 1 iuggis; B 2 Iugge (1) Iugges (1); C 2
              iuge (1) iuges (1)
A. 8.168   And nameliche ȝe maistris, as meiris & *iuggis*,
B. 7.190   And namely ye maistres, Meires and *Iugges*,
B.14.111   Ioye þat neuere ioye hadde of riȝtful *Iugge* he askeþ,
C. 9.336   And manliche ȝe maistres, mayres and *iuges*,
C.15.287   Ioye þat neuere ioye hadde of rihtfull *iuge* he asketh

iuggement n *jugement n.* B 1; C 1 iugement
B.16.95   And þanne sholde Iesus Iuste þerfore bi *Iuggement* of armes
C.18.128   That iesus sholde iouste þerfore by *iugement* of Armes

iuggen v *jugen v.* A 2 iugge (1) iuggen (1); B 12 Iugge (6) iugged (3)
              Iuggede (1) Iuggen (2); C 8 iuge (3) iuged (2) iugen (2) iugge (1)
A. 2.101   And ȝif þe iustice *iugge* hire to be ioyned with fals,
A. 2.121   *Iuggen* ȝow ioyntly in ioye for euere'.
B.Pr.130   Iangle ne *Iugge* þat Iustifie hem sholde,
B. 2.95   And þere to Iangle and Iape and *Iugge* hir euencristen,
B. 2.137   And [if þe] Iustic[e] *Iugg[e]* hire to be Ioyned [wiþ] Fals
B. 2.157   *Iuggen* yow ioyntly in ioie for euere'.
B. 7.167   Thanne Iacob *iugged* Iosephes sweuene:
B. 9.87   Syn Iewes, þat we *Iugge* Iudas felawes,
B. 9.93   He is [*Iugged* wiþ] Iudas þat ȝyueþ a Iaper siluer
B.12.89   The womman þat þe Iewes [*iugged*] þat Iesus þouȝte to saue:
B.14.289   [O]r as Iustice to *Iugge* men enioyned is no poore,
B.16.119   Iewes iangled þerayein [þat] *Iuggede* lawes,
B.19.474   Of Spiritus Iusticie for I *Iugge* yow alle.
B.20.29   And Spiritus Iusticie shal *Iuggen*, wole he, nel he,
C. 1.181   For Iames þe gentele *iuge[d]* in his bokes
C. 2.102   And there to iangele and iape and *iuge* here Emcristene,
C. 2.172   To londone to loke yf lawe wille *iugge*,
C. 9.311   Thenne Iacob *iuged* Iosepes sweuene:
C.16.124   Or a[s] iustice to *iuge* men, me enioyneth þerto no pore,
C.17.132   Iewes and gentel sarresines *iugen* hemsulue
C.21.474   Of spiritus iusticie for y *iuge* ȝow alle.
C.22.29   And spiritus iusticie shal *iugen*, wol he, nel he,

iuyste > iuste

iurdan n prop *n.i.d.* B 1; C 1
B.13.84   'I shal Iangle to þis *Iurdan* wiþ his Iuste wombe
C.15.91   'Y schal iangle to þis *iurdan* with his iuyste wombe

iurour n *jurour n.* B 1; C 1 Iuroures
B. 7.45   Ac many a Iustice and *Iurour* wolde for Iohan do moore
C. 2.153   And thow Iustices enioynen hem thorw *I[u]roures* othes

iuste adj *juste n. &> iusten* B 1; C 1 iuyste
B.13.84   'I shal Iangle to þis Iurdan wiþ his *Iuste* wombe
C.15.91   'Y schal iangle to þis iurdan with his *iuyste* wombe

iusten v *justen v.* B 8 Iuste (4) Iusted (2) Iustede (1) Iusten (1); C 8
    iustede (1) ioust (1) iouste (5) ioustede (1)
B.16.95   And þanne sholde Iesus *Iuste* þerfore bi Iuggement of armes
B.16.163 *Iusted* in Iherusalem, a ioye to vs alle.
B.18.19   And who sholde *Iuste* in Ierusalem. 'Iesus', he seide,
B.18.22   'This Iesus of his gentries wol *Iuste* in Piers armes,
B.18.27   'Who shal *Iuste* wiþ Iesus', quod I, 'Iewes or Scrybes?'
B.18.82   To [*Iusten* wiþ þis blynde Iew Longeus].
B.18.181 For Iesus *Iustede* wel Ioye bigynneþ dawe:
B.20.134 He Iogged to a Iustice and *Iusted* in his eere
C.18.128 That iesus sholde *iouste* þerfore by iugement of Armes
C.19.52   To *ioust* in Ierusalem he Iaced awey faste.
C.20.17   And ho sholde *iouste* in Ierusalem. 'Iesus,' he seide,
C.20.21   That this iesus of his gentrice shal *iouste* in Pers Armes,
C.20.26   'Who shal *iouste* with iesus,' quod y, 'iewes or scrib3?'
C.20.84   [To] *iouste* with iesus, this blynde iewe longies.
C.20.184 For iesus *ioustede* wel ioy bigynneth dawe:
C.22.134 He iogged til a iustice and *iustede* in his ere

iustere n *justere n.* B 1; C 1 ioustare
B.19.10   'Is þis Iesus þe *Iustere*', quod I, 'þat Iewes dide to deþe?
C.21.10   'Is this iesus the *ioustare*,' quod y, 'þat iewes dede to dethe?

iustes n *justes n.pl.* B 3; C 1 ioustes
B.17.54   To a *Iustes* in Ierusalem he [I]aced awey faste.
B.17.77   'Haue, kepe þis man', [quod he], 'til I come fro þe *Iustes*.
B.18.16   As dooþ an heraud of armes whan Auentrous comeþ to *Iustes*.
C.20.14   As doth an heraud of Armes when Auntres cometh to *ioustes*.

iustice n *justice n.* A 4 iustice (3) Iustices (1); B 15 Iustice (12) Iustices
   (3); C 18 iustice (12) iustices (6)
A. 2.101 And 3if þe *iustice* iugge hire to be ioyned with fals,
A. 3.13   Ientily wiþ ioye þe *Iustices* so[mm]e
A. 3.145 Be Iesu, wiþ hire Iuelx 3oure *Iustice* she shendiþ,
A. 8.148 Þat Iosep was *Iustice* Egipt to kepe–
B. 2.48   And lakke hem no3t but lat hem worþe til leaute be *Iustice*
B. 2.137 And [if þe] *Iustic[e]* Iugg[e] hire to be Ioyned [wiþ] Fals
B. 3.13   Gentilliche wiþ ioye þe *Iustices* somme
B. 3.155 By Iesus! wiþ hire Ieweles youre *Iustices* she shendeþ
B. 3.321 Al shal be but oon court, and oon [burn] be *Iustice*,
B. 6.329 Thanne shal deeþ wiþdrawe and derþe be *Iustice*,
B. 7.45   Ac many a *Iustice* and Iurour wolde for Iohan do moore
B. 7.171 That Ioseph was *Iustice* Egipte to loke;
B.11.303 A chartre is chalangeable bifore a chief *Iustice*;
B.14.289 [O]r as *Iustice* to Iugge men enioyned is no poore,
B.16.92   That oon Iesus a *Iustices* sone moste Iouke in hir chambre
B.17.306 Any creature [be] coupable afore a kynges *Iustice*
B.18.38   The Iewes and þe *Iustice* ayeins Iesu þei weere,
B.19.139 Ne ouer Iewes *Iustice*, as Iesus was, hem þou3te.
B.20.134 He Iogged to a *Iustice* and Iusted in his eere
C. 2.51   Lacke hem nat but lat hem worthe til leutee be *Iustice*
C. 2.153 And thow *Iustices* enioynen hem thorw I[u]roures othes
C. 3.14   Genteliche with ioye the *Iustices* somme
C. 3.193 By iesu! with here ieweles the *Iustices* she shendeth;
C. 3.474 Al shal be but [o] couert and o [buyrne] be *Iustice*;
C. 4.186 And Consience in alle my Courtes be a[s] kynges *Iustice*.'
C. 8.337 And thenne a corseth þe kyng and alle þe kynges *Iustices*
C. 8.350 And thenne shal deth withdrawe and derthe be *Iustice*
C. 9.315 That Ioseph was *Iustice* Egipte to saue;
C.13.117 A Chartre is chaleniable byfore a chief *Iustice*;
C.16.124 Or a[s] *iustice* to iuge men, me enioyneth þerto no pore,
C.18.125 That oen Iesus, a *Iustices* sone, most iouken in here chaumbre
C.18.161 The iewes tolde þe *iustice* how þat iesus saide;
C.18.177 This iewes to þe *iustices* iesus they ladde.
C.19.286 Eny creature be coupable bifore a kynges *iustice*
C.20.37   The iewes and þe *iustic[e]* a3eyns iesus þey were,
C.21.139 Ne ouer Iewes *Iustice* as iesus was, hem thouhte.
C.22.134 He iogged til a *iustice* and iustede in his ere

iustifie v *justifien v.* B 2 Iustifie (1) Iustified (1); C 1 iustified
B.Pr.130 Iangle ne Iugge þat *Iustifie* hem sholde,
B.19.44   And so dide Iesus þe Iewes; he *Iustified* and tau3te hem
C.21.44   And so dede iesus þe iewes; he *iustified* and tauhte hem

iuttes n *jot n.* A 1 iottis; B 1
A.11.311 Souteris & seweris; suche lewide *iottis*
B.10.467 Souteres and shepherdes; [swiche] lewed *Iuttes*

iuuentee n *juvente n.(2)* B 1; C 1
B.19.108 In his *Iuuentee* þis Iesus at Iewene feeste
C.21.108 In his *iuuentee* this iesus at iewene feste

iuwel n *jeuel n.* A 1 Iuelx; B 3 Ieweles (1) Iuel (1) Iuwel (1); C 2 iewel
   (1) ieweles (1)
A. 3.145 Be Iesu, wiþ hire *Iuelx* 3oure Iustice she shendiþ,
B. 3.155 By Iesus! wiþ hire *Ieweles* youre Iustices she shendeþ
B.11.185 [For] oure Ioye and oure [*Iuel*], Iesu crist of heuene,
B.18.428 And crepe[þ] to þe cros on knees and kisse[þ] it for a *Iuwel*
C. 3.193 By iesu! with here *ieweles* the Iustices she shendeth;
C.20.471 And crepe to þe croes on knees and kusse hit for a *iewel*

iuwise n *juwise n.* B 1; C 1 iewyse
B.18.382 There [a] feloun þole sholde deeþ ooþer *Iuwise*
C.20.424 Ther a thief tholie sholde deth oþer *iewyse*

K

kaes > caas

kaylewey n *calewei n.* B 1
B.16.69   Thanne Continence is neer þe crop as *kaylewey* bastard.

kaym(es > caym; kaires -eþ > cairen

kaiser n *caiser n.* A 1 caiseris; B 3 kaiser (1) kaysers (2); C 5 Cayser (3)
    Caysers (1) kayser (1)
A.11.219   'I wende þat kinghed, & kni3thed, & *caiseris* wiþ Erlis
B. 9.113   Kynges and kny3tes, *kaysers* and [clerkes];
B.19.138   To be *kaiser* or kyng of þe kyngdom of Iuda,
B.20.101   Kynges and knyghtes, *kaysers* and popes.
C. 3.315   And thow the kyng of his cortesye, *Cayser* or pope,
C. 3.319   Bothe kyng and *Cayser* and þe crouned pope
C. 3.323   That kyng oþer *kayser* hem gaf, Catel oþer rente.
C.21.138   To be *Cayser* or kyng of þe kyngdoem of Iuda
C.22.101   Kynges and knyhtes, *Caysers* and popes.

kaytif > caytif; kalculed > calculed; kald(e > callen

kalender n *calender n.* B 1
B.13.153   In a signe of þe Saterday þat sette first þe *kalender,*

kalketrappes n *calketrappe n.* C 1
C.20.294   [With] crokes and *kalketrappes* [a]cloye we hem vchone.'

kam > comen; kan(- > konne; karpe > carpen; kattes > cat; kau3te > cacchen

kaurymaury n *caurimauri n.* A 1 caurymaury; B 1
A. 5.61   He was cloþid in a *caurymaury*, I [couþe] it nou3t descryue;
B. 5.78   [He was] cloþed in a *kaurymaury*–I kouþe it nou3t discryue–

kayes> keye; keep > kepen; kei3es > keye

kele v *kelen v.* B 1; C 1
B.19.280   [That] caste for to ke[l]e a crokke to saue þe fatte aboue.
C.21.280   That caste for to *kele* a crok [to] saue þe fatte aboue.

kembe v *kemben v.* C 2 kembe (1) kemben (1)
C. 9.80   Bothe to carde and to *kembe*, to cloute and to wasche,
C.11.15   Bote hit be cardet with coueytise as clotheres *kemben* here wolle.

ken(de > kennen

kene adj *kene adj.* B 11; C 13
B. 9.185   Whiles þow art yong [and yeep] and þi wepene [yet] *kene*
B.12.254   Thou3 he crye to crist þanne wiþ *kene* wil, I leue
B.13.347   Til eiþeres wille wexeþ *kene* and to þe werke yeden,
B.14.241   For men knowen wel þat Coueitise is of [a] *kene* wille
B.18.47   'Tolle, tolle!' quod anoþer, and took of *kene* þornes
B.18.78   Ac þer cam forþ a kny3t wiþ a *kene* spere ygrounde,
B.18.413   Was neuere werre in þis world ne wikkednesse so *kene*
B.20.97   Kynde cam after wiþ many *kene* soores,
B.20.129   And cam to þe kynges counseille as a *kene* baroun
B.20.141   That Coueitise were cristene þat is so *kene* [to fighte],
B.20.374   And comen wiþ a *kene* wille Conscience to assaille.
C. 2.29   Ne on a croked *kene* thorn kynde fyge wexe.
C. 6.65   His clothes were of corsemen[t] and of *kene* wordes.
C. 6.140   And thenne y crye and crache with my *kene* nayles,
C.10.286   And whil þou art 3ong an[d] 3ep and thy wepene *kene*
C.16.81   For men knowen wel þat coueytise is of a *kene* will
C.18.172   And *kene* care in thy kissyng and combraunce to thysulue.
C.20.47   'Tolle, tolle!' quod another, and toek of *kene* thornes
C.20.80   Ac þer cam forth a knyhte with a *kene* spere ygrounde,
C.20.435   A[c] 3ut my kynde [in] my *kene* ire shal constrayne my will–
C.22.97   Kynde cam aftur with many *k[e]ne* sores,
C.22.129   And cam to þe kynges consail as a *kene* Baroun
C.22.141   That couetyse were cristene þat is so *kene* to fihte
C.22.374   And comen with a *kene* wil Consience to assaile.

kenet > kennen; kenis > kyn; kenne > kennen,kyn

kennen v *kennen v.(1)* A 19 ken (1) kende (1) kenne (11) kenneþ (2)
    kennide (1) kennist (1) kenniþ (1); B 31 kenne (15) kenned (6)
    kennede (1) kennen (2) kennest (1) kenneþ (6); C 19 kende (2) kenet
    (1) kenne (10) kenned (1) kennede (1) kennen (1) kenneth (3)
A. 1.79   And ek *kenne* me kyndely on crist to beleue,

A. 1.90   Þe clerkis þat knowe it shulde *kenne* it aboute,
A. 1.127   '3et haue I no kynde knowyng,' quaþ I, '[3e mote *kenne* me bet]
A. 1.130   It is a kynde knowyng þat *kenneþ* in þin herte
A. 2.4   *Kenne* me be sum craft to k[now]e þe false'.
A. 3.209   Men þat [*kenne*] clerkis crauen of h[e]m mede;
A. 6.27   Clene consience & wyt *kende* me to his place,
A. 7.23   'Be crist,' quaþ a kni3t þo, 'þou [*kenn]ist* vs þe beste;
A. 7.25   Ac *kenne* me,' quaþ þe kni3t, '& I wile [conne] eren.'
A. 7.237   '3et I preye þe,' quaþ peris, 'pur charite, 3if þou *kenne*
A. 8.13   Bisshopis þat blissen, & boþe lawes *kenne*,
A. 8.90   For I shal construe iche clause & *kenne* it þe on englissh.'
A. 8.121   And consience com aftir & *kennide* me betere.'
A.11.103   [To] *kenne* me kyndely to knowe what is dowel'.
A.11.105   I shal *kenne* þe to my cosyn þat clergie is hoten.
A.11.135   Of carpenteris & kerueris; [I] *kende* ferst masons,
A.11.150   He *kenniþ* vs þe contrarie, a3ens catonis wordis,
A.11.222   How crist counseilliþ þe comune & *kenneþ* hem þis tale:
A.12.53   *Ken* him to my cosenes hous þat kinde wil hy3th.
B. 1.81   And [ek] *kenne* me kyndely on crist to bileue,
B. 1.92   The clerkes þat knowen [it] sholde *kennen* it aboute
B. 1.138   'Yet haue I no kynde knowyng', quod I, 'ye mote *kenne* me bettre
B. 1.142   It is a kynde knowyng þat *kenneþ* in þyn herte
B. 2.4   *Kenne* me by som craft to knowe þe false'.
B. 3.222   Men þat [*kenne* clerkes] crauen [of hem] Mede;
B. 4.43   As Conscience hym *kenned* til þei come to þe kynge.
B. 5.419   Construe clause[m]el[e] and *kenne* it to my parisshens.
B. 5.539   Conscience and kynde wit *kenned* me to his place
B. 6.14   Makeþ cloþ, I counseille yow, and *kenneþ* so youre dou3tres.
B. 6.21   'By crist!' quod a kny3t þoo, '[þow] *kenne[st* vs þe beste,
B. 6.23   [Ac] *kenne* me', quod þe kny3t, 'and [I wole konne erie].'
B. 7.72   Caton *kenneþ* me þus and þe clerc of stories.
B. 7.108   For I [shal] construe ech clause and *kenne* it þee on englissh.'
B. 7.139   And Conscience cam afte[r] and *kenned* me [bettre].'
B.10.113   "Of þat [ye] clerkes vs *kenneþ* of crist by þe gospel:
B.10.151   [To] *kenne* me kyndely to knowe what is dowel
B.10.153   I shal *kenne* þee to my Cosyn þat Clergie is hoten.
B.10.183   Of Carpent[ers and] kerueres; [I *kenned* first] Masons
B.10.201   He *kenneþ* vs þe contrarie ayein Catons wordes,
B.10.343   And Caton *kenneþ* vs to coueiten it nau3t but as nede techeþ:
B.12.229   And kynde *kenned* þe pecok to cauken in swich a [wise.
B.12.230   Kynde] *kenned* Adam to knowe hise pryue membres,
B.13.431   Ac clerkes þat knowen holy writ sholde *kenne* lordes
B.14.16   'And I shal *kenne* þee', quod Conscience, 'of Contricion to make
B.14.277   'I kan no3t construe', quod haukyn; 'ye moste *kenne* me þis on
            englissh.'
B.15.161   Clerkes *kenne* me þat crist is in alle places
B.17.116   And *kennen* outcom[en] men þat knowen no3t þe contree
B.19.9   And þanne called I Conscience to *kenne* me þe soþe:
B.19.234   And some he *kennede* craft and konnynge of sighte,
B.19.240   And some to deuyne and diuide, [figures] to *kenne*;
C. 1.78   And also *kenne* me kyndly on crist to bileue.
C. 1.88   Clerkes þat knowen hit sholde *kenne* it aboute
C. 1.137   'I haue no kynde knowyng,' quod y, '[3e mot] *kenne* me bettere
C. 1.141   Hit is a kynde knowynge that *kenet* in thyn herte
C. 2.4   *Kenne* me by sum craft to knowe þe false.'
C. 3.277   Maistres þat *kenneth* clerkes craueth therfore mede;
C. 3.360   And lyue as oure crede vs *kenneth* with crist withouten ende.
C. 4.41   Bute dede as Consience hym *kennede* til he þe kyng mette.
C. 7.91   Clerkes þat knoweth this sholde *kenne* lordes
C. 7.184   Consience and kynde wit *kende* me to his place
C. 8.19   'By Crist!' quod a knyhte tho, 'a *kenneth* vs þe beste
C. 9.282   For y can construe vch a word and *kennen* hit the an englische.'
C.11.89   With þat 3e *kenne* me kyndeliche to knowe what is dowel.'
C.11.91   Y shal *kenne* þe to clergie, my cosyn, þat knoweth
C.11.138   To *kenne* and to knowe kyndeliche dowel.
C.18.17   'Y thonke 3ow a thousand s[i]the that 3e me hider *kende*
C.21.9   And thenne calde y Consience to *kenne* me þe sothe:
C.21.234   And somme he *kende* craft and konnynge of syhte,
C.21.240   And somme to deuyne and deuyde, [figu]res to *kenne*;

kennyng ger *kenninge ger.* B 1
B.10.199   This is Catons *kennyng* to clerkes þat he lereþ.

kep > kepe,kepen; kepar(- > kepere

kepe n *kep n. &> kepen* A 1 kep; B 5; C 6
A.10.97 Catoun counseilliþ–tak *kep* of his teching–
B.11.337 And after cours of concepcion noon took *kepe* of ooþer,
B.11.356 And some troden, [I took *kepe*], and on trees bredden.
B.11.359 And some caukede; I took *kepe* how pecokkes bredden.
B.13.271 I took [greet *kepe*, by crist! and Conscience boþe,
B.20.358 Conforte hym', quod Conscience, 'and tak *kepe* to hise soores.
C.13.145 Aftur cors of concepcion noon toek *kepe* of oþer,
C.13.165 And som treden, y toke *kepe*, and on trees bredde
C.13.170 And how þe pocok caukede [y toke *kepe* þerof],
C.15.175 Ac Concience, y toek *kepe*, coniey[e]d sone this doctour
C.19.76 And toek two pans the hostiler to take *kepe* to hym;
C.22.358 Conforte hym,' quod Consience, 'and taek *kepe* to his sores.

kepen v *kepen v.* A 34 kep (2) kepe (22) kepen (3) kepide (1) kepiþ (4) kept (1) keptest (1); B 57 keep (1) kepe (28) kepen (17) kepeþ (8) kepten (2) keptest (1); C 57 kepe (35) kepen (6) kepeth (11) kept (1) kepte (3) kepten (1)
A. 1.8 Haue þei worsshipe in þis world þei *kepe* no betere:
A. 1.53 And kynde wyt be wardeyn ȝoure welþe to *kepe*,
A. 1.92 Kinges & kniȝtes shulde *kepe* it be resoun,
A. 1.169 Ȝe curatours þat *kepe* ȝow clene of ȝour body,
A. 2.29 Knowe hem þere ȝif þou canst and *kep* þe from hem alle
A. 3.66 Betwyn þe king & þe comunes, to *kepe* þe lawis,
A. 3.83 For to amende [meiris and] men þat *kepiþ* þe lawis,
A. 3.196 It becom[iþ] a king þat *kepiþ* a reaume
A. 3.258 Þe culorum of þis [cas] *kepe* I not to shewe;
A. 3.265 And o cristene king *kepe* vs ichone.
A. 4.121 Þat I were king wiþ croune to *kepe* a reaume,
A. 4.156 So consience be of ȝour counseil, *kepe* I no betere.'
A. 5.27 And *kep[e]* it in hire coffre for catel at nede.
A. 6.32 And *kepide* his corn, & cariede it to house,
A. 6.100 Ikeiȝid & ycliket to *kepe* þe þeroute
A. 7.29 In couenaunt þat þou *kepe* holy[k]ir[k]e and myself
A. 7.83 Þe [k]ir[k]e shal haue my caroyn & *kepe* my bones,
A. 7.128 [Cacche cowes] from his corn, [and] *kepen* hise bestis,
A. 7.147 To *kepen* hym as couenaunt was fro curside shrewis,
A. 7.181 And become knaues to *kepe* peris bestis,
A. 7.247 And *kep* sum [til] soper tyme, & sit nouȝt to longe;
A. 8.9 Kinges & kniȝtes þat *kepen* holy chirche
A. 8.148 Þat Iosep was Iustice Egipt to *kepe*–
A. 8.173 How þou leddist þi lif here & his lawe *keptest*,
A. 9.91 Þei han crounide o king to *kepe* hem alle,
A.10.10 Ac kynde knowiþ [þis] wel and *kepiþ* hire þe betere,
A.10.15 Beþ maistris of þis maner þis maide to *kepe*,
A.10.16 Ac þe cunstable of þe castel, þat *kepiþ* hem alle,
A.10.23 To *kepe* þise womman þise wise men ben chargid,
A.10.24 Til kynde come oþer sende [and] *kepe* hire hymselue.'
A.10.50 For þoruȝ þis connyng is *kept* caro & anima
A.10.68 And ȝif þei ben pore & cateles, to *kepe* hem fro ille,
A.10.158 To *kepe* his kynrede fro kaymes, þei couplide nouȝt togideris;
A.11.120 Til þou come to a court, *kepe* wel þi tunge
B.Pr.100 I parceyued of þe power þat Peter hadde to *kepe*,
B.Pr.125 'Crist *kepe* þee, sire kyng, and þi kyngryche,
B. 1.8 Haue þei worship in þis world þei [*kepe*] no bettre;
B. 1.55 And kynde wit be wardeyn youre welþe to *kepe*
B. 1.94 Kynges and knyȝtes sholde *kepen* it by reson,
B. 1.195 [Ye] curatours [þat] *kepen* [yow] clene of [youre] bod[y],
B. 2.22 And bilowen h[ym] to lordes þat lawes han to *kepe*.
B. 2.47 Knowe hem þere if þow kanst and *kepe* [þee from hem alle],
B. 3.77 The kyng and þe comune to *kepe* þe lawis,
B. 3.94 For to amenden Maires and men þat *kepen* [þe] lawes,
B. 3.209 It bicomeþ a kyng þat *kepeþ* a Reaume
B. 3.280 The culorum of þis cas *kepe* I noȝt to [shewe];
B. 3.289 And oon cristene kyng *kepe* [vs echone].
B. 4.138 That I were kyng with coroune to *kepe* a Reaume,
B. 4.193 So Conscience be of [y]oure counseil [*kepe* I] no bettre.'
B. 5.27 And *kepe* it in hire coffre for catel at nede.
B. 5.614 Keyed and cliketted to *kepe* þee wiþouten
B. 6.27 In couenaunt þat þow *kepe* holy kirke and myselue
B. 6.91 The kirke shal haue my caroyne and *kepe* my bones
B. 6.140 To *kepe* kyen in þe feld, þe corn fro þe beestes,
B. 6.160 To *kepen* hym as couenaunt was fro cursede sherewes,
B. 6.263 And *keep* som til soper tyme and sitte noȝt to longe;
B. 7.9 Kynges and knyȝtes þat *kepen* holy chirche
B. 7.195 How þow laddest þi lif here and hi[s] law[e] *keptest*,
B. 8.101 [Thei han] crowne[d a] kyng to [*kepen*] hem [alle],
B. 9.10 Ac kynde knoweþ þis wel and *kepeþ* hire þe bettre,
B. 9.17 Ac þe Constable of [þe] Castel þat *kepeþ* [hem alle]
B. 9.24 Til kynde come or sende [and *kepe*] hire [hymselue].'
B.10.168 Til þow come to a court, *kepe*-wel-þi-tunge-
B.10.365 It shal bisitten vs ful soure þe siluer þat we *kepen*,

B.10.477 But þo þat *kepen* þe lordes catel, clerkes and Reues.
B.10.480 As clerkes of holy [k]ir[k]e þat *kepen* cristes tresor,
B.11.158 Wel ouȝte ye lordes þat lawes *kepe* þis lesson haue in mynde
B.11.424 That Clergie þi compaignye *kepeþ* noȝt to suwe.
B.12.109 Which is þe cofre of cristes tresor, and clerkes *kepe* þe keyes
B.12.113 Archa dei, in þe olde lawe, leuytes it *kepten*;
B.12.247 Right so þe riche, if he his richesse *kepe*
B.12.296 To *kepe* wiþ a commune; no catel was holde bettre,
B.14.11 Al for coueitise of my cristendom in clennesse to *kepen* it.
B.14.12 And kouþe I neuere, by crist! *kepen* it clene an houre
B.14.22 Dobest [shal *kepe* it clene from vnkynde werkes].
B.15.197 'Wheiþer clerkes knowen hym', quod I, 'þat *kepen* holi kirke?'
B.15.247 Ac auarice haþ þe keyes now and *kepeþ* for his kynnesmen
B.15.347 Ac þer is a defaute in þe folk þat þe feiþ *kepeþ*,
B.15.466 The calf bitokneþ clennesse in hem þat *kepeþ* lawes,
B.15.581 And han clerkes to *kepen* vs þerInne as þei shul come after.
B.17.5 'Nay', he seide, '[I] seke hym þat haþ þe seel to *kepe*,
B.17.77 'Haue, *kepe* þis man', [quod he], 'til I come fro þe Iustes.
B.17.279 For þat þe holy goost haþ to *kepe* þ[o] harlotes destruyeþ,
B.19.42 It bicomeþ to a kyng to *kepe* and to defende,
B.19.144 *Kepen* it fro nyghtcomeris wiþ knyghtes yarmed
B.19.149 The knyghtes þat *kepten* it biknewe hemseluen
B.19.366 To helpe holy chirche and hem þat it *kepeþ*.
B.19.423 Or in Rome as hir rule wole þe relikes to *kepe*;
B.20.92 'Alarme! alarme!' quod þat lord, 'ech lif *kepe* his owene!'
B.20.257 Kynges and knyghtes þat *kepen* and defenden
B.20.376 And [bad] Contricion [come] to *kepe* þe yate.
C.Pr.128 I parsceyued of þe power that Peter hadde to *kepe*,
C.Pr.149 'Crist *kepe* þe, [sire] kynge, and thy kyneriche
C. 1.42 Ac þe moneye of þis molde þat men so faste *kepen*,
C. 1.51 And kynde witte be wardeyn ȝoure welthe to *kepe*
C. 1.90 Kynges and knyghtes sholde *kepen* hit by resoun,
C. 2.21 And [ylow on] hym to lordes þat lawes han to *kepe*;
C. 2.49 Knowe hem wel yf þou kanst and *kepe* the fro hem alle
C. 3.78 Bothe Schyreues and seriauntes and suche as *kepeth* lawes,
C. 3.265 Hit bycometh for a kyng þat shal *kepe* a reume
C. 3.412 And ȝaf þe kyndom to his knaue þat *kept* shep and lambren;
C. 3.433 The culorum of this kaes *kepe* y nat to shewe;
C. 3.442 And o cristene kyng *kepe* vs echone.
C. 4.135 That y were kyng with c[r]oune to *kepe* [a] reume,
C. 5.17 And *kepe* my corn in my croft f[or] pykares and theues
C. 5.18 Or shap shon or cloth or shep and kyne *kepe*,
C. 5.79 And taken Symondus sones seyntwarie to *kepe*,
C. 5.129 And *kepe* hit in here cofre for catel at nede.
C. 5.185 That o wit and o wil al ȝoure wardes *kepe*.
C. 7.49 Bothe flesch and fysch and vitailes *kepte* so longe
C. 7.73 Lyueth aȝen þe bileue and no lawe *kepeth*
C. 7.266 Ykeyed and yclyketed to [*kepe*] the withouten,
C. 8.26 In couenant þat thow *kepe* holy kerke and mysulue
C. 8.100 The kyrke shal haue my caroyne and *kepe* my bones
C. 8.145 Bothe of my corn and of my cloth to *kepe* hem fram defaute.
C. 8.157 To *kepe* hym and his catel as couenant was bitwene hem:
C. 8.273 And *kepe* som til soper tyme and site nat to longe;
C. 9.341 How we ladde oure lyf here and his lawes *kepte*
C.10.104 Crounede oen to be a kyng to *kepen* vs alle
C.10.137 A[c] kynde knoweth this wel and *kepeth* here þe betere
C.10.143 Ac þe constable of þ[e] Castel þat *kepeth* hem alle
C.10.150 Til kynde come o[r] sende and *kepe* here hymsulue.'
C.10.184 Frendes shal fynde hem and fram folye *kepe*
C.11.140 *Kepe* þe ten comaundementis and *kepe* þe fro synne
C.11.140 Kepe þe ten comaundementis and *kepe* þe fro synne
C.11.243 Of holy kirke þat sholde *kepe* alle cristene soules
C.11.301 As clerkes of holy [k]ir[k]e þat [*kepe*] sholde and saue
C.12.90 Wel ouhte ȝe lordes þat lawes *kepeth* this lesson haue in mynde
C.12.214 Þe catel þat he *kepeth* so in coffres and in bernis,
C.12.236 Worldly wele y[s] wykked thyng to hem þat hit *kepeth*.
C.12.241 For coueytyse of catel to culle hym þat hit *kepeth*.
C.13.232 Ne clergie of his connynge *kepeth* [t]he nat shewe.
C.14.54 Whiche [is the] coffre of cristis tresor, and clerkes *kepeth* þe keyes
C.14.58 Arca dei in þe olde lawe leuytes hit *kepte*;
C.15.76 Holy writ byt men be waer and wysly hem *kepe*
C.16.339 Where clerkes knowe hym nat,' quod y, 'þat *kepen* holy churche?'
C.17.69 Y dar nat carpe of clerkes now þat cristes [tresor] *kepe*
C.18.28 Of o will, of o wit; and he[r]with y *kepe*
C.19.7 'Nay,' he saide, 'y seke hym þat hath þe seel to *kepe*,
C.19.260 For that the holy goest hath to *kepe* tho harlotes distruyeth,
C.21.42 Hit bicometh [to] a kyng to *kepe* and to defende
C.21.144 *Kepen* hit fro nyhtecomares with knyhtes y[ar]med
C.21.149 The knyhtes þat *kepten* hit biknewen hemsuluen
C.21.366 To helpe holi churche and hem þat hit *kepeth*.
C.21.423 Or in Rome, as here reule wo[l], þe relikes to *kepe*;
C.22.92 'Alarme! alarme!' quod þat lord, 'vch lyf *kepe* his owene!'
C.22.257 Kynges and knyhtes þat *ke[p]en* and defenden

C.22.376 And baed contricioun come to *kepe* þe ʒate.

kepere n *kepere n.* B 4 kepere (3) keperes (1); C 4 kepar (1) kepare (1)
kepares (2)
B.12.126 For Clergie is *kepere* vnder crist of heuene;
B.15.461 Rude and vnresonable, rennynge wiþouten [*keperes*].
B.19.443 And cleymeþ bifore þe kyng to be *kepere* ouer cristene,
B.20.72 That kam ayein conscience þat *kepere* was and gyour
C.14.88 Bote of clennesse of clerkes and *kepares* of bestes:
C.16.275 Vnk[ynd]e curatours to be *kepares* of ʒoure soules.
C.21.443 And claymeth bifore þe kynge to be *kepare* ouer cristene
C.22.72 That cam aʒen Consience þat *kepar* was and gyour

kepyng ger *kepinge ger.* B 1; C 1 kepynge
B.19.353 'To wasten on welfare and in wikked [*kepyng*]
C.21.353 'To waston on welfare and in wikked *kepynge*

kept(- > kepen; kerke > holy_chirche; kerke > chirche

kerne v *kirnen v.* C 1
C.12.181 Shal neuere spir sprynge vp ne spiek on straw *kerne*;

kernel n *kirnel n.* B 2 kernel (1) kernell (1); C 2 cornel
B.11.262 Is a *kernel* of confort kynde to restore.
B.11.266 Of which crist is a *kernell* to conforte þe soule.
C.12.148 Is a *cornel* of confort kynde to restore,
C.12.151 The which is þe *cornel* of confort for alle cristene soules.

kerneles n *carnel n.(1)* A 1 kirnelis; B 1; C 1 carneles
A. 6.75 þe *kirnelis* ben of cristendom þat kynde to saue,
B. 5.588 [The] *kernele[s* ben of] cristendom [þat] kynde to saue,
C. 7.235 The *carneles* ben of cristendom þat kynde to saue,

kertil > kirtel

kerue v *kerven v.* A 1; B 2; C 3 curuen (1) kerue (2)
A. 7.96 And helpe my cultir to *kerue* & close þe forewis.'
B. 6.104 And helpe my cultour to *kerue* and [close] þe furwes.'
B.19.241 And some to [*kerue* and compace], and colours to make;
C. 8.65 And helpe my Coltur to *kerue* and cl[o]se þe forwes;
C. 8.185 They *curuen* here copes and courtepies hem made
C.21.241 [And somme to *kerue* a]nd compace and coloures to make;

kerueres n *kervere n.* A 1 kerueris; B 1; C 1 keruers
A.11.135 Of carpenteris & *kerueris*; [I] kende ferst masons,
B.10.183 Of Carpent[ers and] *kerueres*; [I kenned first] Masons
C.11.123 Of carpent[ers and] *keruers*, and contreuede þe compas

keruynge ger *kervinge ger.* B 1
B.17.173 *Keruynge* and compasynge [i]s craft of þe fyngres.

kete adj *kete adj.* A 2; B 2
A.11.56 Clerkis and *k[ete*] men carpen of god faste,
A.11.308 þanne arn þise [*k*]*ete* clerkis þat conne many bokis,
B.10.70 Clerkes and [*kete*] men carpen of god faste
B.10.464 Than are þise [*kete*] clerkes þat konne manye bokis,

keuere v *coveren v.(2)* B 2 keuere (1) keuered (1); C 1
B.18.391 They shul be clensed clerliche and [*keuered*] of hir synnes
B.20.335 Ypocrisie haþ hurt hem; ful hard is if þei *keuere*.'
C.22.335 Ypocrysye haeth her[t]e hem; ful hard is yf thei *keuere*.'

keuered > couere,keuere; keuereth > couere

kex n *kexe n.* B 1; C 1 kix
B.17.223 As dooþ a *kex* or a candle þat caught haþ fir and blaseþ,
C.19.189 A[s] doth a *kix* [o]r a candle þat cauht hath fuyr and blaseth,

keye n *keye n.(1)* A 2 keiʒes; B 5 keye (2) keyes (3); C 3 kayes (1) keye (1) keyes (1)
A. 6.10 And many crouch [o]n his cloke, & *keiʒes* of rome,
A. 6.91 For he haþ þe *keiʒes* & þe cliket þeiʒ þe king slepe.
B. 5.522 And many crouch on his cloke and *keyes* of Rome,
B. 5.604 For he haþ þe *keye* and þe cliket þouʒ þe kyng slepe.
B.10.328 And þanne Freres in hir fraytour shul fynden a *keye*
B.12.109 Which is þe cofre of cristes tresor, and clerkes kepe þe *keyes*
B.15.247 Ac auarice haþ þe *keyes* now and kepeþ for his kynnesmen
C. 7.167 And many crouch on his cloke [and] *kayes* of Rome
C. 7.252 And he hath þe *keye* and þe clycat thow þe kyng slepe.
C.14.54 Whiche [is the] coffre of cristis tresor, and clerkes kepeth þe *keyes*

keyed ptp *keied ppl.* A 1 ikeiʒid; B 1; C 1 ykeyed
A. 6.100 *Ikeiʒid* & ycliket to kepe þe þeroute
B. 5.614 *Keyed* and clicketted to kepe þee wiþouten
C. 7.266 *Ykeyed* and yclyketed to [kepe] the withouten,

kichene n *kichene n.* B 2; C 1 kychene
B. 5.155 I haue be cook in hir *kichene* and þe Couent serued
B. 5.258 'I am holden', quod he, 'as hende as hound is in *kichene*;
C. 6.130 Y haue be coek in here *kychene* and the couent serued

kidde v *kithen v.* A 2 couden (1) couþe (1); B 4 kidde (3) kouþe (1); C 2 kud (1) ykud (1)
A. 8.44 For he co[pie]de þus here clause þei [*couden*] hym gret mede.
A.11.96 Ac for no carping I *couþe*, ne knelyng to þe ground,
B. 5.433 The kyndenesse þat myn euencristene *kidde* me fernyere,
B.10.143 A[c] for no carpyng I *kouþe*, ne knelyng to þe grounde,
B.13.389 So if I *kidde* any kyndenesse myn euencristen to helpe
B.15.303 [For al þe curteisie þat beestes konne þei *kidde* þat folk ofte,
C. 7.46 The kyndenesse þat myn emcristen *kud* me ferneʒer,
C.12.197 Or for a confessour *ykud* þat counteth nat a ruche

kyen > cow

kyke v *kiken v.(1)* C 1
C. 4.22 For hit is þe wone of wil to wynse and to *kyke*

killen v *killen v.* A 9 kilde (3) kille (4) kyllyn (1) kiln (1); B 14 kild (1) kilde (1) kille (4) killed (3) killeden (1) killen (1) kulle (2) kulled (1); C 15 culd (2) culden (1) culle (4) cullen (1) kulde (2) kull (1) kulle (1) ykuld (2)
A. 1.64 Counseilid kaym to *kiln* his broþer,
A. 3.174 For *kilde* I neuere no king ne counseilide þeraftir,
A. 3.246 Wende þidir with þin ost wommen to *kille*;
A. 3.248 Loke þou *kille* þe kyng; coueite nouʒt hise godis;
A. 3.251 And for he *kilde* not þe king as crist [him] bode sente,
A. 3.252 Coueitide here catel, *kilde* nouʒt hire bestis,
A. 7.33 And fecche þe hom fauconis þe foulis to *kille*,
A.11.290 Cristene kynde to *kille* to deþe?
A.12.65 [To *kyllyn* him ʒif I can, þei kynde wit helpe].
B.Pr.185 'Thouʒ we [hadde] *kille*[d] þe cat yet sholde þer come anoþer
B. 1.66 Counseilled Kaym to *killen* his broþer,
B. 3.187 For *killed* I neuere no kyng, ne counseiled þerafter,
B. 5.165 Hadde þei had knyues, by crist! eiþer hadde *kild* ooþer.
B. 5.256 That wolde *kille* hem if he cacche hem myʒte for coueitise of hir skynnes
B. 6.31 And [fette þee hoom] faucons foweles to *kille*
B.10.431 Cristene kynde to *kille* to deþe?
B.16.137 Thei casten and contreueden to *kulle* hym whan þei myʒte;
B.16.152 And kiste hym to be caught þerby and *kulled* of þe Iewes.
B.16.232 Hym or Ysaak myn heir, þe which he hiʒte me *kulle*.
B.19.142 *Killeden* hym on cros wise at Caluarie on Friday,
B.19.444 And counteþ noʒt þouʒ cristene ben *killed* and robbed,
B.20.99 So kynde þoruʒ corrupcions *kilde* ful manye.
B.20.151 And *kille* a[l] erþely creatur[e] saue conscience oone.
C.Pr.202 'Thow we hadde *ykuld* þe Cat ʒut shulde ther come another
C. 1.62 Conseylede Caym to *cullen* his brother,
C. 3.233 For *kulde* y neuere no kyng ne conseilede so to done;
C. 8.30 And afayte thy faucones [wylde foules to *culle*]
C. 8.279 And ʒut hadde he [hem] nat for y, hungur, *culde* hym–
C.10.101 And crounede oen to be kyng to *kull* withoute synne
C.10.247 Aftur þat Caym þ[e] corsed hadde *ykuld* abel,
C.11.267 Cristene [kynde] to *culle* to dethe?
C.12.241 For coueytyse of catel to *culle* hym þat hit kepeth.
C.16.26 And confessioun to *kulle* alle kyne synnes
C.17.289 To be *culd* and ouercome the comune to defende,
C.21.142 *Culden* hym on cros wyse at Caluarie on fryday
C.21.444 And counteth nat thow cristene be *culde* and yrobbed
C.22.99 So kynde thorw corupcions *kulde* fol mony.
C.22.151 And *culle* all erthely creature saue Consience one.

kyn n *kin n.* A 17 kenis (2) kenne (1) kyn (6) kyne (3) kynne (2) skenis (1) skynes (2); B 40 kyn (11) kynne (11) kynnes (18); C 72 kyn (21) kyne (40) kynes (1) kynne (7) kynnes (1) skynes (2)
A. 1.166 Vnkynde to here *kyn* & ek to alle cristene,
A. 2.162 Feteriþ falsnesse faste for any *skynes* ʒeftis,
A. 3.191 And ek king of þat kiþ his *kyn* for to helpe,
A. 3.212 Alle *kyn* crafty men craue mede for here prentis;
A. 6.115 'Be crist,' quaþ a cuttepurs, 'I haue no *kyn* þere.'
A. 7.62 And alle *kyne* crafty men þat conne lyue in treuþe,
A. 8.34 Sette scoleris to scole or [to] summe *skynes* craftis,
A.10.2 In a castel þat kynde made of foure *skenis* þinges.
A.10.26 [And what [*kenis*] þing is kynde, conne ʒe me telle]?'
A.10.27 'Kynde,' quaþ he, 'is creatour of alle *kenis* bestis,
A.10.137 Kinges & kniʒtes, & alle *kyne* clerkis,
A.10.154 For þei mariede hem wiþ curside men of caymes *kyn*.
A.10.156 And alle þat couplide hem with þat *kyn* crist hatide [dedliche].
A.11.134 [Of] alle *kynne* craftis I contreuide tolis,
A.11.185 And alle *kyne* crafty men þat cunne here foode wynne,
A.11.246 Alle *kynne* creatures þat to crist be[n] l[yche]
A.12.110 Now alle *kenne* creatures þat cristene were euere
B.Pr.223 Of alle *kynne* lybbynge laborers lopen forþ somme,
B. 1.192 Vnkynde to hire *kyn* and to alle cristene,
B. 2.131 And [as] a Bastard ybore of Belsabubbes *kynne*.
B. 2.201 Fettreþ [Falsnesse faste] for any *kynnes* ʒiftes,
B. 3.204 And [ek] kyng of þat kiþ his *kyn* for to helpe,

B. 3.225	Alle *kynne* craft[y] men crauen Mede for hir Prentices;
B. 5.630	'By Crist!' quod a kuttepurs, 'I haue no *kyn* þere.'
B. 6.68	And alle *kynne* crafty men þat konne lyuen in truþe,
B. 7.32	Sette Scolers to scole or to som [*kynnes*] craftes,
B. 8.15	And knowen contrees and courtes and many *kynnes* places,
B. 9.2	In a Castel þat kynde made of foure *þynges*.
B. 9.25	'What *kynnes* þyng is kynde?' quod I; 'kanstow me telle?'
B. 9.26	'Kynde', quod [he], 'is creatour of alle *kynnes* [beestes],
B.10.182	Of alle *kynne* craftes I contreued tooles,
B.11.191	We sholde noȝt clepe oure *kyn* þerto ne none kynnes riche:
B.11.191	We sholde noȝt clepe oure *kyn* þerto ne none *kynnes* riche:
B.11.299	That han neiþer konnynge ne *kyn*, but a crowne one
B.12.93	For kynde wit is of his *kyn* and neiȝe Cosynes boþe
B.12.128	Ac kynde wit comeþ of alle *kynnes* siȝtes,
B.13.208	And conformen kynges to pees; and alle *kynnes* londes,
B.13.310	And what I kouþe and knew and what *kyn* I com of.
B.13.378	And boþe to kiþ and to *kyn* vnkynde of þat ich hadde;
B.14.17	That shal clawe þi cote of alle *kynnes* filþe:
B.14.185	And be clene þoruȝ þat cristnyng of alle *kynnes* synne.
B.15.16	'I am cristes creature', quod he, 'and [of his *kyn* a party],
B.15.52	It were ayeins kynde', quod he, 'and alle *kynnes* reson
B.15.381	That sholde konne and knowe alle *kynnes* clergie
B.15.535	Fer fro kyth and fro *kyn* yuele ycloþed yeden,
B.17.196	In many *kynnes* maneres I myghte myself helpe,
B.17.214	That alle *kynne* cristene clenseþ of synnes
B.17.288	For coueitise of any *kynnes* þyng þat crist deere bouȝte.
B.17.349	For vnkyndenesse is þe contrarie of alle *kynnes* reson.
B.18.18	Of any *kynnes* creature, conceyued þoruȝ speche
B.18.257	And conforte al his *kyn* and out of care brynge,
B.19.17	That alle *kynne* creatures sholden knelen and bowen
B.19.77	Or any *kynnes* catel; but knowelich[ede] hym souereyn
B.19.95	Thoruȝ þre *kynne* kynges knelynge to hym.
B.19.203	And made hem konne and knowe alle *kynne* langages.
B.19.216	To alle *kynne* creatures þat [k]an hi[se] fyue wittes,
B.19.367	Thanne alle *kynne* cristene saue comune wommen
C.Pr.26	In continance [of] clothyng in many *kyne* gyse.
C. 1.189	Vnkynde to here *kyn* and to alle cristene,
C. 2.44	To oon fals faythlesse of þe fendes *kynne.*
C. 2.59	Of many manere men þat of mede[s] *kynne* were,
C. 2.215	Lat fetere falsnesse faste for eny *skynes* ȝeftes,
C. 3.113	That vsurers oþer regraters for eny *skynes* ȝeftes
C. 3.235	Bothe here and elleswhere, in alle *kyne* londes.
C. 3.261	And also kyng of þat kuth his *kyn* for to helpe,
C. 3.280	Alle *kyn* crafty men crauen mede for here prentises;
C. 3.364	Alle *kyn* kynde to knowe and to folowe
C. 3.372	To acorde in alle kynde and in alle *kyn* nombre,
C. 3.373	Withouten coest and care and alle *kyn* trauayle.
C. 3.378	So comune claymeth of a kyng thre *kyne* thynges,
C. 3.459	Ax oþer hachet or eny *kyne* w[e]pne,
C. 5.20	Or eny other *kynes* craft þat to þe comune nedeth,
C. 5.69	Thyse bylongeth to labory and lordes *kyn* to serue.
C. 5.77	Imade here *kyn* knyhtes and knyhtes fees ypurchased,
C. 5.183	And comuners [to] acorde in alle *kyn* treuthe.
C. 5.184	Lat no *kyne* consayl ne couetyse ȝow parte,
C. 5.193	Amonges alle *kyne* kynges ouer cristene peple.
C. 6.39	In alle *kyne* couent contreuede how y myhte
C. 6.58	And what y couthe and knewe and what *kyn* y cam of."
C. 7.191	In alle *kyne* craftes þat he couthe deuise
C. 7.283	'By Crist!' quod a cottepors, 'y haue no *kyn* there.'
C. 8.58	[He] caste on his clothes of alle *kyn* craftes,
C. 8.69	And alle *kyne* crafty men þat conne lyue in treuthe,
C. 8.200	In alle *kyne* trewe craft þat man couthe deuyse.
C. 8.266	Yf ȝe can or knowe eny *kyne* thyng[e] of fisyk
C. 9.202	Al they holy Ermytes were of heye *kynne*,
C.10.15	And knowen contrees and Courtes and many *kynne* plases,
C.10.129	In a Castel þat kynde made of foure *kynne* þynges.
C.10.151	'What *kynne* thyng is kynde?' quod y; 'canst thow me telle?'
C.10.152	'Kynde is creatour,' quod wit, 'of [alle] *kyne* thynges,
C.10.169	On catel more then on kynde that alle *kyne* thynges wrouhte,
C.10.250	That for no *kyne* catel ne no kyne byheste
C.10.250	That for no kyne catel ne no *kyne* byheste
C.10.258	Of *kyn* ne of kynrede counteth men bote litel.
C.10.279	For coueytise of catel in none *kyne* wyse;
C.11.92	Alle *kynne* kunnynges and comsynges of dowel,
C.11.122	Of alle *kyne* craftes y contreuede toles,
C.12.103	We sholde nat clepie knyhtes þerto ne none *kyne* ryche:
C.13.56	Ther þe marchaunt l[et] a male with many *kyne* thynges
C.13.113	That [hath] noþer connyng ne *kyn* bote a croune one
C.13.151	Ther ne was no *kyne* kynde þat conseyued hadde
C.14.182	Then for eny *kyn* he come of or for his kynde wittes.
C.15.13	And how þis coueytyse ouercome al *kyne* sectes,
C.15.71	Alle þat coueyte[d] to come to eny *kyne* ioye,
C.15.131	Alle *kyne* connynges and alle kyne craftes

C.15.131	Alle kyne connynges and alle *kyne* craftes
C.15.223	Vch a *kyne* creature þat on crist leueth.
C.16.26	And confessioun to kulle alle *kyne* synnes
C.16.168	And in cristes court yknowe wel and of his *kynne* a party.
C.16.214	Hit were aȝeyns kynde,' quod he, 'and alle *kyne* resoun
C.17.62	Helpe thy *kyn*, Crist bid, for þer [coms]eth charite
C.17.128	Alle *kyne* cristene cleuynge on o will,
C.17.196	Fer fro [k]uthe and fro *kyn* euele yclothed ȝeden,
C.18.21	And of o *kyne* colour & kynde, as me thoghte,
C.19.111	And yf kynde wit carpe hereaȝen or eny *kyne* thouhtes
C.19.162	In many *kyne* manere y myhte mysulfe helpe,
C.19.180	That alle *kyne* cristene clanseth of synne[s].
C.19.269	For coueytise of eny *kyne* thynge þat Crist dere bouhte.
C.19.329	For vnkyndenesse is þe contrarie of alle *kyne* resoun.
C.20.132	Of eny *kyne*[nes] creature, conceyued thorw speche
C.20.265	And comforte alle his *kyn* and out of care brynge
C.20.288	Coltyng and al his *kyn*, the car to saue.
C.20.441	For y were an vnkynde kyng bote y my *kyn* helpe
C.21.17	T[hat] alle *kyn* creatures sholde knelen and bowen
C.21.77	Or eny *kyne* catel; bote knoweleched hym souereyn
C.21.95	Thorw thre *kyne* kynges knelyng to iesu.
C.21.203	And made hem konne & knowe alle *kyne* langages.
C.21.216	To alle *kyne* creatures þat can his fyue wittes,
C.21.367	Thenne alle *kyne* cristene saue commune wommen

kynde n *kinde* n. A 15; B 76; C 104 kynde (103) kyndes (1)

A. 2.95	[And] as a bastard yborn of belsab[ubb]is *kynde*;
A. 6.75	Þe kirnelis ben of cristendom þat *kynde* to saue,
A. 7.149	Curteisliche þe kniȝt þanne as his *kynde* wolde
A. 7.207	Loue hem & lene hem & so þe lawe of *kynde* wolde.
A. 9.37	Þe boot is lik[nid] to þe body þat britel is of *kynde*,
A.10.2	In a castel þat *kynde* made of foure skenis þinges.
A.10.5	*Kynde* haþ closid þereinne, craftily wiþalle,
A.10.10	Ac *kynde* knowiþ [þis] wel and kepiþ hire þe betere,
A.10.24	Til *kynde* come or sende [and] kepe hire himselue.'
A.10.25	'What calle ȝe þat castel,' quaþ I, 'þat *kynde* haþ ymakid?'
A.10.26	[And what [kenis] þing is *kynde*, conne ȝe me telle]?'
A.10.27	'Kynde,' quaþ he, 'is creatour of alle kenis bestis,
A.10.38	Þat is þe castel þat *kynde* made, caro it hatte,
A.10.135	For of here *kynde* þei comen þat confessours ben nempnid,
A.11.290	Cristene *kynde* to kille to deþe?
B.Pr.186	To c[r]acchen vs & al oure *kynde* þouȝ we cropen vnder benches;
B. 2.27	And Mede is manered after hym [as men of] *kynde* [carpeþ]:
B. 2.77	Than for any vertue or fairnesse or any free *kynde*.
B. 3.56	And a cours of *kynde* wherof we comen alle;
B. 5.588	[The] kernele[s ben of] cristendom [þat] *kynde* to saue,
B. 6.164	Curteisly þe knyȝt þanne, as his *kynde* wolde,
B. 6.221	Loue hem and lene hem [and] so [þe] lawe of [*kynde* wolde]:
B. 8.41	The boot is likned to [þe] body þat brotel is of *kynde*,
B. 9.2	In a Castel þat *kynde* made of foure kynnes þynges.
B. 9.5	*Kynde* haþ closed þerInne, craftily wiþalle,
B. 9.10	Ac *kynde* knoweþ þis wel and kepeþ hire þe bettre,
B. 9.24	Til *kynde* come or sende [and kepe] hire [hymselue].'
B. 9.25	'What kynnes þyng is *kynde*?' quod I; 'kanstow me telle?'
B. 9.26	'Kynde', quod [he], 'is creatour of alle kynnes [beestes],
B. 9.50	[Th]at is þe Castel þat *kynde* made; caro it hatte,
B. 9.112	For of hir *kynde* þei come þat Confessours ben nempned,
B. 9.129	And noȝt þi *kynde* wiþ Caymes ycoupled n[e] yspoused".
B. 9.131	Caymes *kynde* and his kynde coupled togideres,
B. 9.131	Caymes kynde and his *kynde* coupled togideres,
B. 9.144	Excepte oonliche of ech *kynde* a couple
B.10.431	Cristene *kynde* to kille to deþe?
B.11.67	[At kirke] þere a man were cristned by *kynde* he sholde be buryed.
B.11.262	Is a kernel of confort *kynde* to restore.
B.11.321	And slepynge I seiȝ al þis, and siþen cam *kynde*
B.11.326	Thorugh ech a creature *kynde* my creatour to louye.
B.11.336	In etynge, in drynkynge and in engendrynge of *kynde*.
B.11.368	Of hir *kynde* and hir colour to carpe it were to longe.
B.11.399	Euery creature in his *kynde* encreesse [he bad]
B.11.403	That som tyme hym bitit to folwen his *kynde*;
B.12.226	Ac *kynde* knoweþ þe cause hymself, no creature ellis.
B.12.229	And *kynde* kenned þe pecok to cauken in swich a [wise.
B.12.230	*Kynde*] kenned Adam to knowe hise pryue membres,
B.12.235	*Kynde* knoweþ whi he dide so, ac no clerk ellis.
B.13.15	Of *kynde* and of his konnynge, and how curteis he is to bestes,
B.13.18	[For alle] creatures þat crepen [or walken] of *kynde* ben engendred;
B.13.403	And moore mete eet and dronk þan *kynde* myȝte defie,
B.14.43	The Corlew by *kynde* of þe Eyr, moost clennest flessh of briddes,
B.14.120	Ouþer here or elliswhere, *kynde* wolde it neuere;
B.15.14	And wherof I cam & of what *kynde*. I coniured hym at þe laste
B.15.52	It were ayeins kynde', quod he, 'and alle kynnes reson
B.15.316	And a mees þermyd of o maner *kynde*,
B.17.251	For may no fir flaumbe make, faille it [h]is *kynde*.
B.17.257	And Indulgences ynowe, and be ingratus to þi *kynde*,

B.17.275	The grace of þe holy goost, goddes owene *kynde*.
B.17.276	For þat *kynde* dooþ vnkynde fordooþ, as þise corsede þeues,
B.17.335	For *kynde* clyueþ on hym euere to contrarie þe soule;
B.17.344	That þei han cause to contrarie by *kynde* of hir siknesse;
B.18.13	As is þe *kynde* of a knyght þat comeþ to be dubbed,
B.18.76	For he was knyȝt and kynges sone *kynde* foryaf þat [þrowe]
B.18.211	Wite what wo is, ne were þe deeþ of *kynde*.
B.18.222	And after god Auntrede hymself and took Adames *kynd[e]*
B.18.375	A[c] to be merciable to man þanne my *kynde* [it] askeþ
B.18.398	For I were an vnkynde kyng but I my *kynde* helpe,
B.19.106	As *kynde* is of a Conquerour, so comsede Iesu
B.19.123	After þe *kynde* þat he cam of; þere comsede he do wel.
B.19.282	He þat ete of þat seed hadde swich a *kynde*:
B.19.400	Thikke ale and þynne ale; þat is my *kynde*,
B.19.476	Ne craue of my comune but as my *kynde* askeþ.'
B.20.18	And if hym list for to lape þe lawe of *kynde* wolde
B.20.76	And crye we to *kynde* þat he come and defende vs
B.20.80	*Kynde* Conscience þo herde and cam out of þe planetes
B.20.85	Frenesies and foule yueles; forageres of *kynde*
B.20.88	There was 'harrow!' and 'help! here comeþ *kynde*
B.20.97	*Kynde* cam after wiþ many kene soores
B.20.99	So *kynde* þoruȝ corrupcions kilde ful manye.
B.20.106	Conscience of his curteisie [þo] *kynde* he bisouȝte
B.20.109	And *kynde* cessede [sone] to se þe peple amende.
B.20.150	Ne careþ noȝt how *Kynde* slow and shal come at þe laste
B.20.199	And as I seet in þis sorwe I sauȝ how *kynde* passede
B.20.201	And cryde to *kynde*: 'out of care me brynge!
B.20.207	'Counseille me, *kynde*', quod I, 'what craft is best to lerne?'
B.20.208	'Lerne to loue', quod *kynde*, 'and leef alle oþere.'
B.20.212	And [I] by conseil of *kynde* comsed to rome
B.20.253	And if ye coueite cure, *kynde* wol yow [telle]
B.20.372	That is þe souerayn[e] salue for alle [synnes of *kynde*].
B.20.384	And countrepledeþ me, Conscience; now *kynde* me avenge,
C.Pr.203	To crache vs and alle oure *kynde* thogh we crope vnder benches;
C. 1.67	To combre men with coueytise, þat is his *kynde* and his lore.'
C. 2.27	And mede is manered aftur hym as men of *kynde* carpeth:
C. 2.84	Then for holynesse oþer hendenesse oþer for hey *kynde*.
C. 2.250	Thy kynedom thorw Coueytise wol out of *kynde* wende,
C. 3.60	And [a] cours of *kynde* wherof we comen alle.
C. 3.130	Corteisliche þe kynge, as his *kynde* wolde,
C. 3.251	And þat is þe *kynde* of a kyng þat conquereth on his enemys,
C. 3.337	Acordaunce in *kynde*, in case and in nombre
C. 3.347	In *kynde* and in case and in cours of nombre.
C. 3.356	He acordeth with crist in *kynde*, verbum caro factum est;
C. 3.362	Acordeth in alle *kyndes* with his antecedent.
C. 3.364	Alle kyn *kynde* to knowe and to folowe
C. 3.372	To acorde in alle *kynde* and in alle kyn nombre,
C. 3.398	Sholde confourme hem to o *kynde* on holy kyrke to bileue
C. 3.402	And coueytede oure *kynde* and be kald in oure name–
C. 6.193	When y was olde and hoor and hadde ylore þat *kynde*
C. 6.430	More then my *kynde* myhte deffye
C. 7.235	The carneles ben of cristendom þat *kynde* to saue.
C. 8.161	Courteisliche þe knyhte thenne, as his *kynde* wolde,
C. 8.230	Loue hem and lene hem and so lawe of *kynde* wolde:
C. 9.169	Bringeth forth bastardus, beggares of *kynde*,
C.10.47	The boet is liknet to oure body þat bretil is of *kynde*,
C.10.129	In a Castel þat *kynde* made of foure kyne thynges.
C.10.132	*Kynde* hath closed therynne, craftily withalle,
C.10.137	A[c] *kynde* knoweth this wel and kepeth here þe betere
C.10.150	Til *kynde* come o[r] sende and kepe here hymsulue.'
C.10.151	'What kynne thyng is *kynde*?' quod y; 'canst thow me telle?'
C.10.152	'*Kynde* is creatour,' quod wit, 'of [alle] kyne thynges,
C.10.169	On catel more then on *kynde* that alle kyne thynges wrouhte,
C.10.173	And lyf lyueth by inwit and leryng of *kynde*.
C.10.205	For of here *kynde* þey come, bothe confessours and martres,
C.10.232	Excepte onliche of vch *kynde* a payre
C.10.244	That *kynde* folweth kynde and contrarieth neuere:
C.10.244	That kynde folweth *kynde* and contrarieth neuere:
C.10.246	Was for mariages ma[ugre *kynd]e* þat men made þat tyme.
C.11.267	Cristene [*kynde*] to culle to dethe?
C.12.148	Is a cornel of confort *kynde* to restore,
C.13.131	Til þat *kynde* cam clergie to helpe
C.13.133	To knowe by vch a creature *kynde* to louye.
C.13.144	In etynge, [in] drynkyng [and] in engend[eryng] of *kynde*.
C.13.151	Ther ne was no kynne *kynde* þat conseyued hadde
C.13.171	How vncortey[s]liche þat cok his *kynde* for[th] strenede
C.13.178	Of here *kynde* and here colour to carpe hit were to longe.
C.14.160	Bote *kynde* þat contreuede hit furst of his corteyse wille.
C.14.163	A cantel of kynde wyt here *kynde* to saue.
C.14.164	Of goed and of wykke *kynde* was þe furste;
C.15.18	Of *kynde* and [of] his connynge and what connynge he ȝaf bestes
C.15.241	The Cryket by *kynde* of þe fuyr and corleu by þe wynde,

C.16.214	Hit were aȝeyns *kynde*,' quod he, 'and alle kyne resoun
C.16.370	And hoso coueyteth to knowe [hym] such a *kynde* hym foloweth
C.17.152	Louen as by lawe of *kynde* oure lord god almyhty.
C.17.160	And aftur his leryng they lyue and by lawe of *kynde*
C.17.161	And when *kynde* hath his cours and no contrarie fyndeth
C.17.164	Ne *kynde* sanȝ cortesie in no contreye is preysed.
C.17.287	For as þe *kynde* of a knyhte or [of] a kynge to be take
C.17.290	So is þe *kynde* of a curatour for criste[s] loue to preche
C.18.21	And of o kyne colour & *kynde*, as me thoghte,
C.18.57	And askede efte tho where hit were all [of] o *kynde*.
C.18.59	Hit is al of o *kynde*, and þat shal y preuen,
C.18.62	Of o *kynde* apples aren nat iliche grete
C.18.67	And so hit fareth sothly, sone, by oure *kynde*.
C.18.70	Summe litel, somme large, ylik apples of *kynde*,
C.18.78	And more lykynde to oure lord then lyue as *kynde* asketh
C.18.217	And Abel of hem bothe and alle thre o *kynde*;
C.18.222	That acorsede alle couples þat no *kynde* forth brouhte:
C.18.223	And man withoute a make myhte nat wel of *kynde*
C.19.217	For may no fuyr flaume make, faile hit his *kynde*,
C.19.223	And indulgences ynowe and be ingrat[u]s to thy *kynde*,
C.19.256	The grace of the holy goest, godes owene *kynde*.
C.19.257	For þat *kynde* doth vnkynde fordoth, as this corsede theues,
C.19.315	For *kynde* cleueth on hym euere to contrarie þe soule;
C.19.324	That they haen cause to contrarien bi *kynde* of here seknes[e];
C.20.11	As is þe *kynde* of a knyhte þat cometh to be dobbet,
C.20.78	For he was knyht and kynges sone *kynde* forȝaf þat [þrowe]
C.20.189	And þat Crist hath conuerted the *kynde* of rihtwisnesse
C.20.220	Ywyte what wo is ne were þe deth of *kynde*.
C.20.231	And aftur god auntred hymsulue and toek Adames *kynde*
C.20.417	Ac to be merciable to man thenne my *kynde* [hit] asketh
C.20.435	A[c] ȝut my *kynde* [in] my kene ire shal constrayne my will–
C.21.106	As *kynde* is of a Conquerour, so comsede iesu
C.21.123	Aftur þe *kynde* þat he cam of; þer comsede he do wel.
C.21.282	He þat eet of that seed hadde such a *kynde*:
C.21.400	Thikke ale [&] thynne ale; þat is my *kynde*
C.21.476	Ne craue of my comune bote as my *kynde* asketh.'
C.22.18	And yf [hym] lust for to lape þe lawe of *kynde* wolde
C.22.76	And crye we to *kynde* þat he come and defende vs
C.22.80	*Kynde* Consience tho herde and cam oute of the planetes
C.22.85	Freneseyes and foule eueles; forageres of *kynde*
C.22.88	There was 'harow!' and 'helpe! here cometh *kynde*
C.22.97	*Kynde* cam aftur with many k[e]ne sores,
C.22.99	So *kynde* thorw corupcions kulde fol mony.
C.22.106	Concience of his cortesye tho *kynde* he bisouhte
C.22.109	And *kynde* sesede [sone] to se þe peple amende.
C.22.150	Ne careth nat how *kynde* slowh and shal come at þe laste
C.22.199	And as y saet in this sorwe y say how *kynde* passede
C.22.201	And cryede to *kynde*: 'out of care me brynge!
C.22.207	'Consaileth me, *kynde*,' quod y, 'what craft be beste to lere?'
C.22.208	'Lerne to loue,' quod *kynde*, 'and leef all othere.'
C.22.212	And y bi conseil of *kynde* comsed to Rome
C.22.253	And yf ȝe coueiteth cure *kynde* wol ȝow telle
C.22.372	That is þe souereyne salue for alle [synnes of *kynde*].
C.22.384	And countrepledeth me, Consience; now *kynde* me avenge

kynde adj. *kinde adj.* A 20 kinde (1) kynde (19); B 46; C 48

A. 1.53	And *kynde* wyt be wardeyn ȝoure welþe to kepe,
A. 1.127	'Ȝet haue I no *kynde* knowyng,' quaþ I, '[ȝe mote kenne me bet]
A. 1.130	It is a *kynde* knowyng þat kenneþ in þin herte
A. 1.139	For in *kynde* knowyng in herte þer comsiþ a miȝt,
A. 3.59	Who is curteis or *kynde* or coueitous, or ellis.
A. 3.260	[I] consience knowe þis, for *kynde* [w]it me tauȝte,
A. 3.275	Ac *kynde* wyt shal come ȝet, & consience togidere,
A. 7.231	*kynde* wyt wolde þat iche wiȝt wrouȝte
A. 9.48	'I haue no *kynde* knowyng,' quaþ I, 'to conseyue þi wordis,
A. 9.62	Com & callide me be my *kynde* name.
A. 9.103	More *kynde* knowyng I coueyte to lere,
A.10.84	And alle *kynde* scoleris in scole to lerne.
A.10.128	Among men of þis molde þat mek ben & *kynde*.
A.11.250	Þat is, iche cristene [creature] be *kynde* to oþer,
A.11.254	Ne mecaberis, ne sle nouȝt, is þe *kynde* englissh;
A.12.15	Of þe *kynde* cardinal wit, and cristned in a font,
A.12.41	*Kynde* [wit] hure confessour, hure cosyn was Inne.
A.12.43	And sayde, 'my cosyn *kynde* wit knowen is wel wide,
A.12.53	Ken him to my cosenes hous þat *kinde* wit hyȝth.
A.12.65	[To kyllyn him ȝif I can, þat *kynde* wit helpe].
B.Pr.114	And þanne cam *kynde* wit and clerkes he made
B.Pr.118	The commune contreued of *kynde* wit craftes,
B.Pr.121	The kyng and þe commune and *kynde* wit þe þridde
B. 1.55	And *kynde* wit be wardeyn youre welþe to kepe
B. 1.138	'Yet haue I no *kynde* knowyng', quod I, 'ye mote kenne me bettre
B. 1.142	It is a *kynde* knowyng þat kenneþ in þyn herte
B. 1.165	For in *kynde* knowynge in herte þer [comseþ a myȝt],
B. 3.67	For [god] knoweþ þi conscience and þi *kynde* wille

B. 3.284   I, Conscience, knowe þis for *kynde* wit me tauȝte
B. 3.299   Ac *kynde* loue shal come ȝit and Conscience togideres
B. 4.158   [*Kynde*] wit acorded þerwiþ and comendede hise wordes,
B. 5.539   Conscience and *kynde* wit kenned me to his place
B. 6.247   *Kynde* wit wolde þat ech wiȝt wroȝte,
B. 8.57   'I haue no *kynde* knowyng', quod I, 'to conceyuen [þi] wordes
B. 8.71   Cam and called me by my *kynde* name.
B. 8.113   More *kynde* knowynge] I coueite to lerne,
B. 9.89   Whi [ne wol] we cristene of cristes good be as *kynde*?
B.10.368   For euery cristene creature sholde be *kynde* til ooþer,
B.11.188   To knowen vs by oure *kynde* herte and castynge of oure eiȝen,
B.12.45   Catel and *kynde* wit was combraunce to hem alle.
B.12.55   [So catel and *kynde* wit acombreþ ful manye;
B.12.64   Clergie and *kynde* wit comeþ of siȝte and techyng
B.12.67   And of quod vidimus comeþ *kynde* wit, of siȝte of diuerse peple.
B.12.69   Knew neuere clerk how it comeþ forþ, ne *kynde* wit þe weyes:
B.12.70   Ac yet is Clergie to comende and *kynde* wit boþe,
B.12.93   For *kynde* wit is of his kyn and neiȝe Cosynes boþe
B.12.107   Na moore kan a *kynde* witted man, but clerkes hym teche,
B.12.108   Come for al his *kynde* wit to cristendom and be saued;
B.12.128   Ac *kynde* wit comeþ of alle kynnes siȝtes,
B.12.135   For alle hir *kynde* knowyn[g] co[m] but of diuerse siȝtes.
B.12.158   Than clerkes or *kynde* witted men of cristene peple.
B.12.225   Clergie ne *kynde* wit ne knew neuere þe cause,
B.13.144   Cast coles on his heed of alle *kynde* speche;
B.13.150   *Kynde* loue coueiteþ noȝt no catel but speche.
B.14.126   Ac god is of [a] wonder wille, by þat *kynde* wit sheweþ,
B.14.270   Moore for coueitise of [catel] þan *kynde* loue of boþe–
B.15.104   And be *kynde* as bifel for clerkes and curteise of cristes goodes,
B.15.467   For as þe Cow þoruȝ *kynde* mylk þe calf norisseþ til an Oxe,
B.15.553   If knyghthod and *kynde* wit and þe commune [and] conscience
B.16.70   Thanne bereþ þe crop *kynde* fruyt and clennest of alle,
B.17.138   And if Conscience carpe þerayein, or *kynde* wit eyþer,
B.19.315   'Hareweþ alle þat konneþ *kynde* wit by conseil of þise docto[urs],
B.19.360   And þanne kam *Kynde* wit Conscience to teche,
B.19.372   Ther nas no cristene creature þat *kynde* wit hadde
B.20.73   Ouer *kynde* cristene and Cardynale vertues.
B.20.268   Forþi', quod Conscience, 'by crist! *kynde* wit me telleþ

C.Pr.141   And thenne cam *kynde* wytt [& clerkus he made
C.Pr.143   Conscience & *kynde* wit] and knyghthed togideres
C.Pr.145   *Kynde* wytt and þe comune contreued alle craftes
C.Pr.148   Thenne *kynde* witt to þe kynge and to þe comune saide:
C. 1.51   And *kynde* witte be wardeyn ȝoure welthe to kepe
C. 1.137   'I haue no *kynde* knowyng', quod y, '[ȝe mot] kenne me bettere
C. 1.141   Hit is a *kynde* knowynge þat kenet in thyn herte
C. 1.161   For [in] *kynde* knowynge [in] herte ther comseth a myhte
C. 2.29   Ne on a croked kene thorn *kynde* fyge wexe:
C. 3.71   For god knoweth thi consience [and þy *kynde* wille,
C. 3.437   [I], Consience,knowe this for *kynde* me tauhte
C. 3.452   A[c] *kynde* loue shal come ȝut and Consience togyderes
C. 4.152   And *kynde* [wit] and Consience corteysliche thonkede
C. 5.56   Clerkes ycrouned, of *kynde* vnderstondynge,
C. 7.184   Consience and *kynde* wit kenned me to his place
C. 8.59   His cokeres and his coffes, as *kynde* wit hym tauhte,
C.10.56   'Y haue no *kynde* kno[w]yng,' [quod y], 'to conseyue al this speche
C.10.69   Cam and calde me be my *kynde* name.
C.10.109   More *kynd[e]* knowynge coueyte y to here
C.11.225   Thenne al þe *kynde* wyt þat ȝe can bothe and kunnyng of ȝoure
            bokes.
C.13.13   That the *kynde* [kyng] criede hym mercy.
C.13.237   Of clergie ne of *kynde* wyt counteth he nat a rusche.
C.14.14   Is ycalde Caritas, *kynde* loue an engelysche,
C.14.17   Ac catel and *kynde* wit acombreth fol monye;
C.14.30   Ac clergie cometh bote of syhte and *kynde* wit of sterres,
C.14.33   So clergie is a gifte of god and *kynde* wit a chaunce
C.14.34   And clergie a connynge of *kynde* wittes techyng
C.14.36   Then eny connyng of *kynde* wit but clergi hit reule.
C.14.52   No more can a *kynde* witted man, but clerkes hym teche,
C.14.53   Come for al his *kynde* wit thorw cristendoem to be saued;
C.14.72   *Kynde* wittede men [c]an a clergie by hemsulue;
C.14.79   For al here *kynde* knowyng cam bote of diuerse syhtes.
C.14.102   The[n] connynge clerkes of *kynde* vnderstondynge.
C.14.157   How creatures han *kynde* wit and how clerkes come to bokes
C.14.163   A cantel of kynde wyt here *kynde* to saue.
C.14.182   Then for eny kyn he come of or for his *kynde* wittes.
C.15.142   Caste coles on his heued of alle *kyn[de]* speche,
C.15.145   Conforte hym with thy catel and with thy *kynde* speche.
C.15.181   That they knoweth nat,' quod Concience, 'what is *kynde* pacience.
C.16.110   More for coueytise of catel then *kynde* loue of þe mariage.
C.16.257   And be corteys and *kynde* of holy kyrke godes,
C.17.216   Ȝif knyhthoed and *kynde* wit and þe comune and consience
C.19.111   And yf *kynde* wit carpe hereaȝen or eny kyne thouhtes
C.21.315   'Harweth alle þa[t] conneth *kynde* wit bi consail of [this] doctours

C.21.360   And thenne cam *kynde* wit Consience to teche
C.21.372   Ther ne was cristene creature that *kynde* wit hadde
C.22.73   Ouer *kynde* cristene and cardinale vertues.
C.22.268   For[thy],' quod Consience, 'bi Crist! *kynde* wit me telleth

kyndely adv *kindeli adv. &> kyndly adj* A 4; B 10 kyndely (8) kyndeliche
            (2); C 12 kyndeliche (8) kyndely (1) kyndelyche (1) kyndly (2)
A. 1.79   And ek kenne me *kyndely* on crist to beleue,
A. 3.15   Counforti[de] hire *kyndely* be clergie[s] leue,
A. 6.26   'I knowe hym as *kyndely* as clerk doþ his bokis.
A.11.103   [To] kenne me *kyndely* to knowe what is dowel'.
B. 1.81   And [ek] kenne me *kyndely* on crist to bileue,
B. 1.163   And for to knowen it *kyndely*, it comseþ by myght,
B. 3.15   Conforte[d] hire *kyndely* by clergies leue,
B. 5.538   'I knowe hym as *kyndely* as clerc doþ hise bokes.
B.10.151   [To] kenne me *kyndely* to knowe what is dowel.'
B.10.223   To counseille þee *kyndely* to knowe what is dowel.'
B.14.88   Ergo contricion, feiþ and conscience is *kyndeliche* dowel,
B.15.2   Er I koude *kyndely* knowe what was dowel.
B.15.49   I wolde I knewe and kouþe *kyndely* in myn herte.'
B.18.221   To wite what wele was, *kyndeliche* [to] knowe it.
C. 1.78   And also kenne me *kyndly* on crist to bileue.
C. 1.159   And for to knowe hit *kyndly*, hit comeseth by myhte,
C. 4.147   To construe this c[l]ause, *kyndeliche* what it meneth.
C. 7.183   'I knowe hym as *kyndely* as Clerk doth his bokes.
C. 9.214   *Kyndeliche*, by Crist, ben suche ycald lollares.
C.11.89   With þat ȝe kenne me *kyndeliche* to knowe what is dowel.'
C.11.99   Thow shalt kunne and knowe *kyndeliche* dowel.'
C.11.138   To kenne and to knowe *kyndeliche* dowel.
C.16.211   Y wolde y knewe and couthe *kyndeliche* in myn herte.'
C.17.111   Ne [can] construe *kyndelyche* þat poetes made.
C.20.213   Ho couthe *kyndeliche* whit colour descreue
C.20.230   To wyte what wele [was], *kyndeliche* to knowe [hit].

kyndenesse n *kindenesse n.* A 1; B 2; C 1
A. 3.274   Vnkyndenesse is comaundour, & *kyndenesse* is banisshit.
B. 5.433   The *kyndenesse* þat myn euencristene kidde me fernyere,
B.13.389   So if I kidde any *kyndenesse* myn euencristen to helpe
C. 7.46   The *kyndenesse* þat myn emcristen kud me ferneȝer,

kyndly adj *kindeli adj. &> kyndely adv* C 1
C.17.153   Hit is *kyndly* thyng creature his creatour to honoure,

*kyndoem -dom > kyngdom; kyne > cow,kyn; kynedom > kyngdom; kyneriche
> kyngryche; kynes > kyn*

kyng n *king n.* A 72 king (58) kyng (7) kingene (1) kinges (5) kynges (1);
            B 148 kyng (105) kynge (5) kyngene (2) kynges (36); C 163 kyng
            (102) kynge (17) kyngene (1) kynges (41) kyngus (2)
A.Pr.91   Become clerkis of acountis þe *king* for to serue;
A.Pr.95   And ben clerkis of þe *kinges* bench þe cuntre to shende.
A. 1.46   Ȝif þei [shulde] worsshipe þerwiþ cesar þe *king*.
A. 1.92   *Kinges* & kniȝtes shulde kepe it be resoun,
A. 1.103   And crist, *king[ene]* kin[g], kniȝtide tene,
A. 1.103   And crist, *king[ene]* kin[g], kniȝtide tene,
A. 2.10   Icorounid in a coroune, þe *king* haþ non betere;
A. 2.97   She miȝte kisse þe *king* for cosyn ȝif he[o] wolde.
A. 2.152   And come to þe *kinges* court & consience tolde,
A. 2.153   And consience to þe *king* carpide it aftir.
A. 2.154   'Be crist,' quaþ þe *king*, '& I miȝte cacche
A. 3.2   Wiþ bedelis & baillifs ybrouȝt to þe *king*.
A. 3.3   Þe *king* calliþ a clerk–I can not his name–
A. 3.9   Curteisliche þe clerk þanne, as þe *king* hiȝte,
A. 3.17   For we wile wisse þe *king* & þi wey [shape]
A. 3.66   Betwyn þe *king* & þe comunes, to kepe þe lawis,
A. 3.90   Þe *king* fro counseil com & callide aftir mede
A. 3.93   [Curteisly] þe *king* compsiþ to telle:
A. 3.104   Before þe *kyng* & his counseil, clerkis & oþere.
A. 3.105   Knelynge, consience to þe *kyng* loutide,
A. 3.109   Quaþ consience to þe *kyng*, 'crist it [me] forbede!
A. 3.142   Þere she is wel wiþ þe *king* wo is þe reaume,
A. 3.157   Þanne mournide mede & menide hire to þe *king*
A. 3.159   Þe *king* grauntide hire grace wiþ a good wille:
A. 3.173   And þou hast famid me foule before þe *king* here.
A. 3.174   For kilde I neuere no *king* ne counseilide þeraftir,
A. 3.175   Ne dide as þou demist; I do it on þe *king*.
A. 3.191   And ek *king* of þat kiþ his kyn for to helpe,
A. 3.196   It becom[iþ] a *king* þat kepiþ a reaume
A. 3.208   Þe *king* haþ [m]ede of his men to make pes in londis;
A. 3.215   Quaþ þe *king* to consience, 'be crist, as me þinkiþ,
A. 3.217   'Nay,' quaþ consience to þe *king* & knelide to þe erþe,
A. 3.248   Loke þou kille þe *king*; coueite nouȝt hise godis;
A. 3.251   And for he kilde not þe *king* as crist [him] bode sente,
A. 3.256   Such a meschef mede made þe *kyng* [to] haue
A. 3.265   And o cristene *king* kepe vs ichone.

A. 4.1	'Sessiþ,' seide þe *king*, 'I suffre ȝow no lengere.
A. 4.3	Kisse hire,' quaþ þe *king*, 'consience, I hote!'
A. 4.6	'And I comaunde þe,' quaþ þe *king* to consience þanne,
A. 4.15	Sende hym as þe *king* sente & siþþe tok his leue.
A. 4.30	And rombide forþ wiþ resoun riȝt to þe *king*.
A. 4.31	Curteisliche þe *king* þanne com in to resoun,
A. 4.48	[Þe *king* kneuȝ] he seide soþ for consience hym tolde.
A. 4.51	And seide, 'hadde I loue of my lord þe *king*, litel wolde I recche
A. 4.66	Consience & þe *king* kneuȝ wel þe soþe,
A. 4.69	To ouercome þe *king* wiþ catel ȝif þei miȝte.
A. 4.70	Þe *king* swor be crist & be his croune boþe
A. 4.85	Pees þanne pitousliche preyede to þe *king*
A. 4.91	'Nay,' quaþ þe *king*, 'so god ȝiue me blisse,
A. 4.98	And to counseile þe *king* & consience boþe;
A. 4.112	Bere no siluer ouer se þat signe of *king* shewi[þ],
A. 4.113	Neiþer grotis ne gold ygraue wiþ *kynges* coyn,
A. 4.121	Þat I were *king* wiþ croune to kepe a reaume,
A. 4.128	Let þi confessour, sire *king*, construe it þe on englissh,
A. 4.144	Þe *king* acordite, be crist, to resonis sawis
A. 4.148	'Be hym þat [rauȝte] on þe rode,' quaþ resoun to þe *king*,
A. 4.151	'And I assente,' quaþ þe *king*, 'be seinte marie my lady,
A. 4.157	'I graunte,' quaþ þe *king*, 'godis forbode he faille!
A. 5.1	Þe *king* & [his] kniȝtes to þe [k]ir[k]e wente
A. 5.38	'Lest þe *king* & his counseil ȝoure comunes apeir[e]
A. 6.91	For he haþ þe keiȝes & þe cliket þeiȝ þe *king* slepe.
A. 7.298	And þanne curse þe *king* & alle þe counseil aftir
A. 8.9	*Kinges* & kniȝtes þat kepen holy chirche
A. 8.136	How Dani[el] deui[n]ide þe drem[is] of a *king*
A. 8.138	Daniel seide, 'sire *king*, þi sweuene is to mene
A. 8.142	Þe *king* les his lordsshipe, & lesse men it hadde.
A. 9.91	Þei han crounide o *king* to kepe hem alle,
A. 9.94	Þanne shulde þe *kyng* come & casten hem in presoun,
A. 9.98	Corounid on to be *kyng* & be h[ere] counseil werchen,
A.10.137	*Kinges* & kniȝtes, & alle kyne clerkis,
A.11.33	Wolde neuere *king*, ne kniȝt, ne canoun of seint poulis
A.12.113	Furst to rekne Richard, *kyng* of þis rewme,
B.Pr.92	Somme seruen þe *kyng* and his siluer tellen
B.Pr.112	Thanne kam þer a *kyng*; knyȝthod hym ladde,
B.Pr.115	For to counseillen þe *kyng* and þe commune saue.
B.Pr.116	The *kyng* and knyȝthod and clergie boþe
B.Pr.121	The *kyng* and þe commune and kynde wit þe þridde
B.Pr.124	And knelynge to þe *kyng* clergially he seide,
B.Pr.125	'Crist kepe þee, sire *kyng*, and þi kyngryche,
B.Pr.144	To þe *kynges* counseil, construe whoso wolde,
B. 1.48	[If] þei sholde [worshipe þerwiþ Cesar þe *kyng*].
B. 1.94	*Kynges* and knyȝtes sholde kepen it by reson,
B. 1.105	[And] crist, *kyngene* kyng, knyȝted ten,
B. 1.105	[And] crist, kyngene *kyng*, knyȝted ten,
B. 1.160	And a meene, as þe Mair is, bitwene þe [commune] & þe [*kyng*];
B. 2.10	Ycorouned [in] a coroune, quod þe kyng haþ noon bettre.
B. 2.36	How construeþ David þe *kyng* of men þat [caccheþ] Mede,
B. 2.133	[She] myȝte kisse þe *kyng* for cosyn and she wolde.
B. 2.191	And com to þe *kynges* court and Conscience tolde,
B. 2.192	And Conscience to þe *kyng* carped it after.
B. 2.193	'By crist!' quod þe *kyng*, 'and I cacche myȝte
B. 2.209	And how þe *kyng* comaunded Constables and sergeauntȝ
B. 3.2	Wiþ Bedeles and baillies brouȝt [to] þe *kyng*.
B. 3.3	The *kyng* called a clerk–[I kan] noȝt his name–
B. 3.9	Curteisly þe clerk þanne, as þe *kynge* hiȝte,
B. 3.17	For we wol wisse þe *kyng* and þi wey shape
B. 3.77	The *kyng* and þe comune to kepe þe lawes,
B. 3.101	The *kyng* fro conseil cam and called after Mede
B. 3.104	Curteisly þe *kyng* comse[þ] to telle;
B. 3.115	Bifore þe *kyng* and his conseil, clerkes and oþere.
B. 3.116	Knelynge, Conscience to þe *kyng* louted,
B. 3.120	Quod Conscience to þe *kyng*, 'crist it me forbede!
B. 3.153	Ther she is wel wiþ þe *kyng* wo is þe Reaume,
B. 3.170	Thanne mournede Mede and mened hire to þe *kynge*
B. 3.172	The *kyng* graunted hire grace wiþ a good wille.
B. 3.186	Ac þow hast famed me foule bifore þe *kyng* here.
B. 3.187	For killed I neuere no *kyng*, ne counseiled þerafter,
B. 3.188	Ne dide as þow demest; I do it on þe *kynge*.
B. 3.204	And [ek] *kyng* of þat kiþ his kyn for to helpe,
B. 3.209	It bicomeþ a *kyng* þat kepeþ a Reaume,
B. 3.221	The *kyng* haþ mede of his men to make pees in londe,
B. 3.228	Quod þe *kyng* to Conscience, 'by crist, as me þynkeþ,
B. 3.230	'Nay', quod Conscience to þe *kyng* and kneled to þe erþe.
B. 3.273	And for he coueited hir catel and þe *kyng* spared,
B. 3.278	Swich a meschief Mede makeþ be *kyng* to haue
B. 3.289	And oon cristene *kyng* kepen [vs echone].
B. 3.315	Shal neiþer *kyng* ne knyght, Constable ne Meire
B. 3.320	*Kynges* Court and commune Court, Consistorie and Chapitle,
B. 4.1	'CEsseþ', sei[de] þe *kyng*, 'I suffre yow no lenger.

B. 4.3	Kis hire', quod þe *kyng*, 'Conscience, I hote!'
B. 4.6	'And I comaunde þee', quod þe *kyng* to Conscience þanne,
B. 4.15	[Seide hym] as þe *kyng* [sente] and siþen took his leue.
B. 4.43	As Conscience hym kenned til þei come to þe *kynge*.
B. 4.44	Curteisly þe *kyng* þanne com [in to] Reson.
B. 4.61	The *kyng* knew he seide sooþ, for Conscience hym tolde
B. 4.65	And seide, 'hadde I loue of my lord þe *kyng* litel wolde I recche
B. 4.82	To ouercomen þe *kyng* wiþ catel if þei myȝte.
B. 4.83	The *kyng* swor by crist and by his crowne boþe
B. 4.98	[Pees þanne pitously] preyde to þe *kynge*
B. 4.104	'Nay', quod þe *kyng*, 'so me crist helpe,
B. 4.111	And to counseille þe *kyng* and Conscience [boþe]
B. 4.123	Til þe *kynges* counseil be þe commune profit;
B. 4.129	Bere no siluer ouer see þat signe of *kyng* sheweþ,
B. 4.130	Neiþer [grotes ne gold ygraue wiþ *kynges* coyn]
B. 4.138	That I were *kyng* with coroune to kepen a Reaume,
B. 4.145	Late [þi] Confessour, sire *kyng*, construe [it þee on englissh],
B. 4.150	Al to construe þis clause for þe *kynges* profit,
B. 4.151	Ac noȝt for confort of þe commune ne for þe *kynges* soule.
B. 4.171	The *kyng* callede Conscience and afterward Reson
B. 4.173	And modiliche vpon myȝt þe *kyng* loked,
B. 4.182	Quod Conscience to þe *kyng*, 'but þe commune wole assente
B. 4.185	'By hym þat rauȝte on þe Rode!' quod Reson to þe *kynge*,
B. 4.188	'And I assente', seiþ þe *kyng*, 'by Seinte Marie my lady,
B. 4.194	'I graunte [gladly]', quod þe *kyng*, 'goddes forbode [he faile]!
B. 5.1	The *kyng* and hise knyȝtes to þe kirke wente
B. 5.12	And wiþ a cros afore þe *kyng* comsede þus to techen.
B. 5.46	'Lest þe *kyng* and his conseil youre comunes apeire
B. 5.48	And siþen he counseiled þe *kyng* his commune to louye:
B. 5.604	For he haþ þe keye and þe cliket þouȝ þe *kyng* slepe.
B. 6.317	And þanne corseþ þe *kyng* and al [þe] counseil after
B. 7.9	*Kynges* and knyȝtes þat kepen holy chirche
B. 7.158	How Daniel diuined þe dre[mes] of a *kyng*
B. 7.160	Daniel seide, 'sire *kyng*, þi [sweuene is to mene]
B. 7.164	The *kyng* lees his lordshipe and [lasse] men it hadde.
B. 8.101	[Thei han] crowne[d a] *kyng* to [kepen] hem [alle],
B. 8.104	Thanne [sholde] þe *kyng* come and casten hem in [prison,
B. 8.108	Crouned oon to be *kyng*, [and by hir counseil werchen],
B. 9.113	*Kynges* and knyȝtes, kaysers and [clerkes];
B.10.47	[W]olde neuere *kyng* ne knyȝt ne [c]anon of Seint Poules
B.10.322	Ac þer shal come a *kyng* and confesse yow Religiouses,
B.10.332	Haue a knok of a *kyng*, and incurable þe wounde.
B.10.334	Ac er þat *kyng* come Caym shal awake,
B.10.451	Thouȝ ye come bifore *kynges* and clerkes of þe lawe
B.10.454	Dauid makeþ mencion, he spak amonges *kynges*,
B.10.455	And myȝte no *kyng* ouercomen hym as by konnynge of speche.
B.11.294	For made neuere *kyng* no knyȝt but he hadde catel to spende
B.11.296	It is a careful knyȝt, and of a caytif *kynges* makyng,
B.12.127	Was þer neuere [*kyng* ne] knyȝt but clergie hem made.
B.13.169	Do poyse and quene and alle þe comune after
B.13.175	Ne bitwene two cristene *kynges* kan no wiȝt pees make
B.13.208	And conformen *kynges* to pees; and alle kynnes londes,
B.13.436	[Clerkes and kniȝtes welcomeþ *kynges* minstrales,
B.14.290	Ne to be Mair aboue men ne Mynystre vnder *kynges*;
B.15.223	Edmond and Edward, [eiþer] were *kynges*
B.15.235	In *kynges* court he comeþ ofte þer þe counseil is trewe,
B.15.352	Crowne and cristendom, þe *kynges* mark of heuene,
B.15.445	Austyn [þe *kyng*] cristnede at Caunterbury),
B.15.511	[Whan þe hye *kyng* of heuene sente his sone to erþe
B.17.306	Any creature [be] coupable afore a *kynges* Iustice
B.17.309	That þe *kyng* may do no mercy til boþe men acorde
B.18.55	If þow be crist and *kynges* sone com down of þe roode:
B.18.76	For he was knyȝt and *kynges* sone kynde foryaf þat [þrowe]
B.18.265	For here comeþ wiþ crowne þat *kyng* is of glorie." '
B.18.269	If þis *kyng* come In mankynde wole he fecche
B.18.320	That crist may come In, þe *kynges* sone of heuene!'
B.18.371	And þanne shal I come as a *kyng*, crouned, wiþ Aungeles,
B.18.381	And if þe *kyng* of þat kyngdom come in þat tyme
B.18.384	And I þat am *kyng* of kynges shal come swich a tyme
B.18.384	And I þat am kyng of *kynges* shal come swich a tyme
B.18.398	For I were an vnkynde *kyng* but I my kynde helpe,
B.19.27	That knyght, *kyng*, conquerour may be o persone.
B.19.29	To be called a *kyng* is fairer for he may knyghtes make.
B.19.41	And vpon Caluarie on cros ycrouned *kyng* of Iewes.
B.19.42	It bicomeþ to a *kyng* to kepe and to defende,
B.19.49	And *kyng* of hir kyngdom and croune bar of þornes,
B.19.72	And cam to take mankynde *kynges* and Aungeles,
B.19.75	*Kynges* come after, knelede and offrede [sense],
B.19.79	Into hir kyngene kiþ by counseil of Aungeles.
B.19.82	And al þe wit of þe world was in þo þre *kynges*.
B.19.86	That o *kyng* cam wiþ Reson couered vnder sense.
B.19.87	The seconde *kyng* siþþe sooþliche offrede
B.19.91	The þridde *kyng* þo kam knelynge to Iesu

B.19.95	Thoru3 þre kynne *kynges* knelynge to Iesu.
B.19.97	Was neiþer *kyng* ne conquerour til he [comsed] wexe
B.19.138	To be kaiser or *kyng* of þe kyngdom of Iuda,
B.19.222	Shullen come and be curatours ouer *kynges* and Erles;
B.19.256	And crouneþ Consience *kyng* and makeþ craft youre Stiward,
B.19.303	And to correcte [þ]e *kyng* if [þe kyng] falle in gilt.
B.19.303	And to correcte [þ]e kyng if [þe *kyng*] falle in gilt.
B.19.304	For counteþ he no *kynges* wraþe whan he in Court sitteþ;
B.19.424	And þow Consience in *kynges* court, and sholdest neuere come þennes;
B.19.443	And cleymeþ bifore þe *kyng* to be kepere ouer cristene,
B.19.465	And þanne can þe *kyng* a and by his croune seide,
B.19.466	'I am *kyng* wiþ croune þe comune to rule,
B.20.6	'[Coudes]tow no3t excuse þee as dide þe *kyng* and oþere:
B.20.30	After þe *kynges* counseil and þe comune like.
B.20.67	And what *kyng* þat hem conforted, knowynge [hir gile],
B.20.101	*Kynges* and knyghtes, kaysers and popes.
B.20.129	And cam to þe *kynges* counseille as a kene baroun
B.20.257	*Kynges* and knyghtes þat kepen and defenden
C.Pr.90	Summe seruen þe *kynge* and his siluer tellen,
C.Pr.139	Thenne cam the[r] a *kyng*; knygh[t]hede hym la[dd]e;
C.Pr.142	For to conseillen þe *kyng* and þe commune saue.
C.Pr.148	Thenne kynde witt to þe *kynge* and to þe comune saide:
C.Pr.149	'Crist kepe þe, [sire] *kynge*, and thy kyneriche
C.Pr.152	Consience to Clergie and to þe *kynge* sayde:
C.Pr.160	Consience and þe *kynge* into Court wente
C. 1.90	*Kynges* and knyghtes sholde kepen hit by resoun,
C. 1.156	And a mene, as þe Mayre is, bitwene þe *kyng* and þe comune;
C. 2.11	And crouned [in] a croune, þe *kyng* haþ non bettre;
C. 2.22	In *kynges* court, in comune court contra[r]ieth my techynge.
C. 2.149	A myhte kusse the *kyng* as for his kyn[nes] womman.
C. 2.205	And kam to þe *kynges* Court and Consience tolde,
C. 2.206	And consience to þe *kyng* carpede hit aftur.
C. 2.207	'Now, by crist!' quod þe *kyng*, 'and y cacche myhte
C. 2.221	What was þe *kynges* wille and wyghtliche wente
C. 2.248	Ac Consience to þe *kyng* accused hem bothe
C. 2.249	And sayde, 'syre *kyng*, by crist! but clerkes amende,
C. 3.2	[With] Bedeles and Baylifs ybrouhte byfor þe *kyng*.
C. 3.3	The *kyng* callede a clerke–y can nat his name–
C. 3.9	Cortesliche þe Clerk thenne, as þe *kyng* hyhte,
C. 3.18	For we w[o]l wisse the *kyng* and thy wey shape
C. 3.44	Amonge *kynges* and knyhtes and clerkes and the lyke.'
C. 3.128	The *kyng* fram conseyl come [and] calde aftur mede
C. 3.130	Corteisliche þe *kynge*, as his kynde wolde,
C. 3.152	Byfore þe *kyng* and his consayl, clerkes and oþere.
C. 3.153	Knelyng, consience to þe *kyng* loutede,
C. 3.157	Quod Consience to the *kyng*, 'Crist hit me forbede!
C. 3.191	Ther she is wel with eny *kyng* wo is þ[e] rewme
C. 3.216	Thenne mournede mede and menede here to þe *kyng*
C. 3.218	The *kyng* grauntede here grace with a goode wille:
C. 3.232	Ac thow hast famed me foule byfore þe *kyng* here
C. 3.233	For kulde y neuere no *kyng* ne conseilede so to done;
C. 3.239	In contrees there the *kyng* cam, consience hym lette
C. 3.242	Caytifliche thow, Consience, conseiledest þe *kyng* leten
C. 3.247	Of folk þat fauht þerfore and folwede þe *kynges* wille.
C. 3.251	And þat is þe kynde of a *kyng* þat conquereth on his enemys,
C. 3.254	Forthy y consayl no *kynge* eny conseyl aske
C. 3.256	For sholde neuere Consience be my constable were y a *kyng*,' quod mede,
C. 3.261	And also *kyng* of þat kuth his kyn for to helpe,
C. 3.265	Hit bycometh for a *kyng* þat shal kepe a reume
C. 3.284	Quod þe *kyng* to Consience, 'by crist, as me thynketh,
C. 3.286	'Nay,' quod Consience to þe *kyng*, 'clerkes witeth þe sothe,
C. 3.315	And thow the *kyng* of his cortesye, Cayser or pope,
C. 3.319	Bothe *kyng* and Cayser and þe crouned pope
C. 3.323	That *kyng* oþer kayser hem gaf, Catel oþer rente.
C. 3.330	And ryhte so, sothly, may *kyng* and pope
C. 3.341	Quod the *kyng* to Consience, 'knowen y wolde
C. 3.375	As a *kyng* to clayme the comune at his wille
C. 3.378	So comune claymeth of a *kyng* thre kyne thynges,
C. 3.380	Bothe heued and here *kyng*, haldyng with no partey3e
C. 3.385	Thow the *kyng* and þe comune al the coest hadde.
C. 3.409	And se[t]he, for sauel saued a *kyng* fo[r] mede
C. 3.413	As me ret in regum [of þe reuthe] of *kynges*,
C. 3.426	And for a coueytede mere catel plod alle *kynges* sparede,
C. 3.431	Thus was *kyng* sauel ouercome thorw coueytise of mede.
C. 3.442	And o cristene *kyng* kepe vs echone.
C. 3.456	That here *kyng* be ycome fro þe Court of heuene,
C. 3.468	Shal nother *kyng* ne knyght, Constable ne Mayre
C. 3.473	*Kyngus* Court and comune Court, constorie and [c]hap[itre],
C. 4.1	'[Cesseth],' saide þe *kynge*, 'y soffre 3ow no lengore.
C. 4.3	Kusse here,' quod the *kyng*, 'Consience, y hote!'
C. 4.6	'And y comaunde [the],' quod the *kyng* to Consience thenne,
C. 4.15	And sayde hym as þe *kyng* sayde and sennes took his leue.
C. 4.30	Byfore þe *kyng* an[d] Consience yf þe comune playne
C. 4.41	Bute dede as Consience hym kennede til he þe *kyng* mette.
C. 4.42	Corteyslyche þe *kyng* thenne cam and grette resoun
C. 4.64	[The *kyng* knew he sayde soth for Consience hym tolde.
C. 4.78	To ouercome þe *kyng* [with] catel y[f] they myhte.
C. 4.79	The *kyng* [s]wor by Crist and by his croune bothe
C. 4.94	Pitousliche pees tho preyede the *kyng*
C. 4.98	So alle my claymes ben quyt by so þe *kyng* assente.'
C. 4.99	'Nay, by crist!' quod þe *kyng*, 'for Consiences sake
C. 4.106	And for to consayle þe *kynge* on Consience thei lokede;
C. 4.119	And til þe *kynges* consayl be alle comune profit
C. 4.126	Bere no seluer ouer see þat sygne of *kyng* sheweth,
C. 4.135	That y were *kyng* with c[r]oune to kepe [a] reume,
C. 4.142	Lat thy Confessour, syre *kyng*, construe this in englische
C. 4.157	And cryede to Consience, the *kyng* myhte hit here
C. 4.166	The *kyng* to consayl tho toek Consience and resoun
C. 4.176	Quod Consience to þe *kyng*, 'withoute þe comune helpe
C. 4.179	'By hym þat rauhte [on] þe rode,' quod resoun to the *kyng*,
C. 4.183	'Y wolde hit were,' quod the *kynge*, 'wel al aboute.
C. 4.186	And Consience in alle my Courtes be a[s] *kynges* Iustice.'
C. 4.195	The *kyng* comaundede Consience tho to congeye alle his offeceres
C. 5.75	In confort of the comune and the *kynges* worschipe,
C. 5.113	And Consience his crocer byfore þe *kyng* stande.
C. 5.144	'Laste þe *kyng* and his consayl 3oure comunes apayre
C. 5.168	Ac þer shal come a *kyng* and confesse 3ow alle
C. 5.178	Ac ar þat *kyng* come, as cronicles me tolde,
C. 5.180	And sethe a consailede þe *kyng* his comine to louie:
C. 5.181	'For þe comune is þe *kynges* tresor, Consience woet wel.
C. 5.193	Amonges alle kyne *kynges* ouer cristene peple.
C. 5.194	'Comaunde þat alle confessours þat eny *kyng* shryueth
C. 7.96	Clerkes and knyhtes welcometh *kynges* munstrals
C. 7.252	And he hath þe keye and þe clycat thow þe *kyng* slepe
C. 8.84	'Consayle nat þe comune þe *kyng* to desplese
C. 8.88	What þei comaunde as by þe *kyng* countreplede hit neuere;
C. 8.337	And thenne a corseth þe *kyng* and alle þe kynges Iustices
C. 8.337	And thenne a corseth þe kyng and alle þe *kynges* Iustices
C. 9.9	*Kyngus* and knyhtus þat holy kyrke defenden
C. 9.306	How danyel deuynede and vndede þe dremes of *kynges*,
C.10.101	And crounede oen to be *kyng* to kull withoute synne
C.10.104	Crounede oen to be a *kyng* to kepen vs alle
C.10.241	The eritage þat þe eyer sholde haue is at þe *kynges* wille.
C.11.276	Thogh 3e come bifore *kynges* and clerkes of þe law[e]
C.11.279	Dauid maketh mensioun he spake among *kynges*
C.11.280	And myhte no *kyng* ouercome hym as in connynge of speche.
C.13.13	That the kynde [*kyng*] criede hym mercy
C.13.67	Aren alle acountable to crist and to þe *kyng* of heuene,
C.13.108	For made neuere *kyng* no knyhte but he hadde catel to spene
C.13.110	For hit is a carfol knyhte and of a Caytif *kynges* makynge
C.15.168	The *kyng* and alle þe comune and clergie to þe loute
C.16.125	Ne to be mair ouer men ne mynistre vnder *kynges*;
C.16.360	In *kynges* Court a cometh yf his consaile be trewe
C.16.368	*Kynge*[s] and Cardynals kn[o]wen hym sum tyme
C.17.78	Cristendoem of holy kyrke, the *kynges* marke of heuene,
C.17.228	Yf the *kynges* coueyte in cristes pees to lyuene.
C.17.262	For when þe hye *kyng* of heuene sente his so[n]e til erthe
C.17.287	For as þe kynde is of a knyhte or [of] a *kynge* to be take
C.18.94	In *kynges* Court and in knyhtes, the clennest men and fayreste
C.19.286	Eny creature be coupable bifore a *kynges* iustice
C.19.289	That may no *kynge* mercy graunte til bothe men acorde.
C.20.55	And 'yf thow be Crist and [*kynges*] sone come adoun of th[e] rode;
C.20.78	For he was knyht and *kynges* sone kynde for3af þat [browe]
C.20.273	For here cometh with croune þe *kynge* of all glorie.'
C.20.277	Yf this *kyng* come in mankynde wol he fecche
C.20.363	That Crist may come in, the *kynges* sone of h[e]uene!'
C.20.413	And thenne shal y come as [a] *kynge*, croune[d], with angeles
C.20.423	And yf þe *kynge* of þe kyngdoem come in þe tyme
C.20.426	And y þat am *kynge* o[f] kynges shal come such a tyme
C.20.426	And y þat am kynge o[f] *kynges* shal come such a tyme
C.20.441	For y were an vnkynde *kyng* bote y my kyn helpe
C.21.27	That knyht, *kyng*, conquerour may be o persone.
C.21.29	To be cald a *kyng* is fairor for he may knyhtes make;
C.21.41	And vpon Caluarie on cros ycrouned *kyng* of iewes.
C.21.42	Hit bicometh [to] a *kyng* to kepe and to defende
C.21.49	And *kyng* of here kyngdoem and croune baer of thornes.
C.21.72	And cam to take mankynde *kynges* and angeles
C.21.75	*Kynges* cam aftur, knelede and offrede [sense],
C.21.79	Into here *kyngene* kuth by consail of Angelis.
C.21.82	And al þe wit of the world was in [þo] thre *kynges*.
C.21.86	That [o] *kyng* cam with reson ykyuered vnder ensense.
C.21.87	The seconde *kyng* seth soethliche offrede]
C.21.91	The thridde *kyng* cam [þo] knel[ynge] to iesu
C.21.95	Thorw thre kyne *kynges* knelyng to iesu.

C.21.97   Was noþer *kyng* ne conquerour til he comsed wexe
C.21.138   To be Cayser or *kyng* of the kyngdoem of Iuda
C.21.222   Shal come and be curatours ouer *kynges* and Erles;
C.21.256   And crouneth Consience *kyng* and maketh craft ȝoure styward
C.21.303   And to corecte the *kyng* and the kyng falle in [g]ulte.
C.21.303   And to corecte the kyng and the *kyng* falle in [g]ulte.
C.21.304   For counteth he no *kynges* wreth when he in Court sitteth;
C.21.424   And thow, Consience, in *kynges* Court and sholdest neuer come
            thennes;
C.21.443   And claymeth bifore þe *kynge* to be kepare ouer cristene
C.21.465   And thenne cam þer a *kyng* and bi his corone saide,
C.21.466   'Y am *kyng* with croune the comune to reule
C.22.6   'Couthest thow nat excuse the as dede the *kyng* and oþere:
C.22.30   Aftur þe *kynges* conseyl and þe comune lyke.
C.22.67   And what *kyng* þat hem conforted, knowynge here gyle,
C.22.101 *Kynges* and knyhtes, Caysers and popes.
C.22.129 And cam to þe *kynges* consail as a kene Baroun
C.22.257 *Kynges* and knyhtes þat ke[p]en and defenden

kyngdom n *kingdom n.* A 2 kingdom; B 6; C 9 kyndoem (1) kyndom (3) kynedom (2) kyngdoem (3)
A. 2.62   Wiþ þe *kingdom* of coueitise I croune hem togidere;
A. 8.139 Þat [vncouþe] kniȝt[is] shal come þi *kingdom* to cleyme;
B.Pr.105 There [crist in is] *kyngdom*, to close and to shette,
B. 7.161 That vnkouþe knyȝtes shul come þi *kyngdom* to cleyme;
B.18.109 Whan crist cam hir *kyngdom* þe crowne sholde [!ese]:
B.18.381 And if þe kyng of þat *kyngdom* come in þat tyme
B.19.49   And kyng of hir *kyngdom* and croune bar of þornes.
B.19.138 To be kaiser or kyng of þe *kyngdom* of Iuda,
C.Pr.133 Thare Crist is in *kynedom* to close with heuene.
C. 2.250 Thy *kynedom* thorw Coueytise wol out of kynde wende,
C. 3.244 Vnconnynge is þat Consience a *kyndom* to sulle
C. 3.245 For þat [is] conquere[d] thorw a comune helpe, a *kyndom* or
            ducherie,
C. 3.412 And ȝaf the *kyndom* to his knaue þat kept shep and lambren;
C.20.112 When Crist thorw croos ouercam ȝoure *kyndoem* sholde tocleue:
C.20.423 And yf þe kynge of þe *kyngdoem* come in þe tyme
C.21.49   And kyng of here *kyngdoem* and croune baer of thornes.
C.21.138 To be Cayser or kyng of the *kyngdoem* of Iuda

kyngene > kyng

kynghod n *kinghod n.* A 2 kinghed (1) kinghod (1); B 1
A.11.219 'I wende þat *kinghed*, & kniȝthed, & caiseris wiþ Erlis
A.11.226 *Kinghod* & kniȝthod, for auȝt I can aspie,
B.10.338 *Kynghod* [and] knyȝthod, [for auȝt] I kan awayte,

kyngryche n *kingriche n.* B 1; C 3 kyneriche (2) kynneryche (1)
B.Pr.125 'Crist kepe þee, sire kyng, and þi *kyngryche*,
C.Pr.149 'Crist kepe þe, [sire] kynge, and thy *kyneriche*
C.10.112 Elles knowe y noen þat can in none *kynneryche*.'
C.12.169 "Hoso coueiteth to come to my *kyneriche*

kyngus > kyng; kynne(s > kyn; kynneryche > kyngryche; kynnes > kyn,kynnes_womman

kynnes_womman n *kinneswomman n.* C 1
C. 2.149 A myhte kusse the kyng as for his *kyn[nes] womman.*

kynnesmen n *kinnesman n.* B 1
B.15.247 Ac auarice haþ þe keyes now and kepeþ for his *kynnesmen*

kynrede n *kinrede n.* A 2; B 1; C 1
A.10.158 To kepe his *kynrede* fro kaymes, þei couplide nouȝt togideris;
A.10.198 For coueitise of catel or of *kynrede* riche,
B. 9.177 For coueitise of catel ne of *kynrede* riche;
C.10.258 Of kyn ne of *kynrede* counteth men bote litel.

kirk(e > chirche, holy_chirche; kyrkeȝerd > kirkȝerd

kirkeward adv *chircheward adv.* A 1; B 1; C 1 kyrkeward
A. 5.147 And ca[iriþ] hym to [k]ir[k]eward hise [coupe] to shewe.
B. 5.297 And [kaireþ] hym to *kirkeward* his coupe to shewe.
C. 6.351 And kayres hym to *kyrkeward* his coup[e] to shewe.

kirkȝerd n *chircheyerd n.* B 1; C 1 kyrkeȝerde
B.13.9   And no corps in hir *kirkȝerd* n[e] in hir kirk was buryed
C.15.11 Ne no cors of pore comine in here *kyrkeȝerde* most lygge

kirnelis > kernel

kirtel n *kirtel n.* A 1 kertil; B 2
A. 5.62   A *kertil* & a courtepy, a knyf be his side,
B. 5.79   [A] *kirtel* and [a] Courtepy, a knyf by his syde,
B.11.285 Ne neiþer *kirtel* ne cote, þeiȝ þei for cold sholde deye,

kissen v *kissen v.* A 5 kisse (2) kissen (1) kiste (1) kyste (1); B 9 kis (1) kisse (3) kissen (1) kisseþ (1) kiste (3); C 8 custe (1) kyssen (1) kusse (5) kuste (1)
A.Pr.70 Comen vp knelynge to *kissen* his bulle.
A. 2.97 She miȝte *kisse* þe king for cosyn ȝif he[o] wolde.
A. 4.3   *Kisse* hire,' quaþ þe king, 'consience, I hote!'
A.11.177 Curteisliche clergi[e] c[o]llide me & *kiste*,
A.12.47 And þanne I kneled on my knes and *kyste* her [fete] sone,
B.Pr.73 Comen vp knelynge to *kissen* hi[s] bull[e].
B. 2.133 [She] myȝte *kisse* þe kyng for cosyn and she wolde.
B. 4.3   *Kis* hire', quod þe kyng, 'Conscience, I hote!'
B.10.234 [Curteisly clergie collede me and *kiste*,
B.16.152 And *kiste* hym to be caught þerby and kulled of þe Iewes.
B.18.417 Clippe we in couenaunt, and ech of vs [*kisse*] ooþer,
B.18.420 'Thow seist sooþ', [seyde] Rightwisnesse, and reuerentliche hire
            kiste:
B.18.428 And crepe[þ] to þe cros on knees and *kisse[þ]* it for a Iuwel
B.20.353 And acorde wiþ Conscience and *kisse* hir eiþer ooþer.'
C.Pr.71 Comen [vp] knel[yng] to *kyssen* his bull[e].
C. 2.149 A myhte *kusse* the kyng as for his kyn[nes] womman.
C. 4.3   *Kusse* here,' quod the kyng, 'Consience, y hote!'
C.18.169 And *kuste* iesus to be knowe þerby and cauht of þe iewes.
C.20.460 Cluppe we in couenaunt and vch of vs *kusse* oþere.'
C.20.463 'Thowe saiste soeth,' saide rihtwisnesse, and reuerentlich here
            custe,
C.20.471 And crepe to þe croes on knees and *kusse* hit for a iewel
C.22.353 And acorde with Consience and *kusse* here ayther oþer.'

kissynge ger *kissinge ger.* B 1; C 2 kissyng (1) kyssyng (1)
B.16.149 That is *kissynge* and fair contenaunce and vnkynde wille.
C. 6.187 And handlyng and halsyng and also thorw *kyssyng*,
C.18.172 And kene care in thy *kissyng* and combraunce to thysulue.

kiþ n *kitthe n.* A 1; B 4 kyth (1) kiþ (3); C 3 kuth (2) kuthe (1)
A. 3.191 And ek king of þat *kiþ* his kyn for to helpe,
B. 3.204 And [ek] kyng of þat *kiþ* his kyn for to helpe,
B.13.378 And boþe to *kiþ* and to kyn vnkynde of þat ich hadde,
B.15.535 Fer fro *kyth* and fro kyn yuele ycloþed yeden,
B.19.79 Into hir kyngene *kiþ* by counseil of Aungeles.
C. 3.261 And also kyng of þat *kuth* his kyn for to helpe,
C.17.196 Fer fro [k]uthe and fro kyn euele yclothed ȝeden,
C.21.79 Into here kyngene *kuth* by consail of Angelis.

kitoun n *kitoun n.* B 2 kiton (1) kitoun (1); C 3 kitones (1) kytoun (2)
B.Pr.194 Ther þe cat is a *kitoun* þe court is ful elenge;
B.Pr.203 Shal neuere þe cat ne þe *kiton* by my counseil be greued,
C.Pr.207 Ther þe Cat [is] a *kytoun* þe Court is ful elynge.
C.Pr.211 Shal neuer þe Cat ne [þe] *kytoun* be my conseil be greued
C.Pr.218 Ne were þe Cat of þe Court and ȝonge *kitones* toward;

kytte n prop *Kitte n.(2) &> kutte* B 1; C 3 kitte (2) Kytte (1)
B.18.426 And callede *kytte* my wif and Calote my doghter:
C. 5.2   [K]*ytte* and y in a cote, yclothed as a lollare
C. 7.304 I may nat come for a *kitte*, so a cleueth on me:
C.20.469 And calde *kitte* my wyf and Calote my douhter.

kitten > kutte; kix > kex

knappes n *knappe n.(1)* A 1 knoppis; B 1
A. 7.254 And ek his cloke [of] calabre & þe *knoppis* of gold,
B. 6.270 And his cloke of Calabre [and] þe *knappes* of golde,

knaue n *knave n.(1)* A 8 knaue (4) knaues (4); B 8 knaue (5) knaues (3); C 16 knaue (6) knaues (10)
A.Pr.44 And risen vp wiþ ribaudrie as robertis *knaues*;
A.Pr.104 Cookis & here *knaues* crieþ 'hote pyes, hote!
A. 3.121 As comoun as þe cartweye to *knaue* & to [alle],
A. 4.17 And calde catoun his *knaue*, curteis of speche:
A. 5.96 I wolde þat iche wiȝt were my *knaue*;
A. 5.160 [T]ymme þe tynkere & tweyne of his *knaues*,
A. 7.181 And become *knaues* to kepe peris bestis,
A.12.77 With þat cam a *knaue* with a confessoures face,
B.Pr.44 And risen [vp] wiþ ribaudie [as] Roberdes *knaues*;
B.Pr.226 Cokes and hire *knaues* cryden, 'hote pies, hote!
B. 3.132 As commune as [þe] Cartwey to [*knaue* and to alle],
B. 4.17 And called Caton his *knaue*, curteis of speche,
B. 5.117 I wolde þat ech wight were my *knaue*.
B. 5.309 Tymme þe Tynkere and tweyne of his [*knaues*],
B. 6.49 Or a knyȝt from a *knaue*; knowe þis in þyn herte.
B.10.315 And but if his *knaue* knele þat shal his coppe brynge
C.Pr.40 Qui turpiloquium loquitur [is] luciferes *knaue*.
C.Pr.45 And ryseþ with rybaudrye, þo robardus *knaues*;
C.Pr.230 Cokes and here *knaues* cryede, 'hote pyes, hote!
C. 1.125 Ac thei caren nat thow hit be cold, *knaues*, when þe[i] worche.
C. 3.169 As comyn as þe cartway to *knaues* and to alle,
C. 3.412 And ȝaf the kyndom to his *knaue* þat kept shep and lambren;

C. 4.17   And kalde Catoun his *knaue*, Corteys of speche,
C. 5.54   Me sholde constrayne no Cler[k] to no *knaues* werkes,
C. 5.65   And *knaue*[s] vncrouned to carte and to worche.
C. 5.161   And but if his *knaue* knele þat shal his coppe holde
C. 6.364   Tymme þe Tynekare and tweyne of his *knaues*,
C. 6.371   A rybibour, a ratoner, a rakeare and his *knaue*,
C. 8.46   Or a knyhte [fram] a *knaue* or a quene fram a queene.
C. 9.206   And Clerkes *knaues* withouten grace,
C. 9.210   Forthy lefte they here labour, thise lewede *knaues*,
C.20.287 Astarot, hoet out and haue out oure *knaues*,

knees n *kne n.* A 4 knes; B 7 knees (6) knowes (1); C 7

A. 1.77   Þanne I knelide on my *knes* & cri3ide hire of grace;
A. 2.1   3et knelide I on my *knes* & cri3ede hire of grace,
A. 5.88   Þanne I cri3e on my *knes* þat crist gyue hym sorewe
A.12.47   And þanne I kneled on my *knes* and kyste her [fete] sone,
B. 1.79   Thanne I [kneled] on my *knees* and cried hire of grace;
B. 2.1   YEt [kneled I] on my *knees* and cried hire of grace,
B. 5.108   Thanne I crye on my *knees* þat crist 3yue h[y]m sorwe
B. 5.352   For to liften hym o lofte and leyde hym on his *knowes*.
B.15.406 And dide folk þanne falle on *knees*; for he swoor in his prechyng
B.18.87   Thanne fil þe kny3t vpon *knees* and cryde [Iesu] mercy:
B.18.428 And crepe[þ] to þe cros on *knees* and kisse[þ] it for a Iuwel
C. 1.76   Thenne y knelede on my *knees* and criede here of grace
C. 2.1   And thenne y kneled [o]n my *knees* and cried here of grace,
C. 3.93   The whiche crien on here *knees* þat crist hem auenge,
C. 5.106   Byfore þe cross on my *knees* knokked y my brest,
C. 6.410   For to lyfte hym aloft [and] leyde hym on his *knes*.
C.20.89   Tho ful þe knyhte vppon *knees* and criede iesu mercy:
C.20.471 And crepe to þe croes on *knees* and kusse hit for a iewel

knelen v *knelen v.* A 9 knele (2) kneled (1) knelide (4) knelynge (2); B 24 knele (8) kneled (5) knelede (3) knelen (1) knelynge (7); C 21 knele (6) kneled (1) knelede (7) knelen (1) knelyng (5) knelynge (1)

A.Pr.70   Comen vp *knelynge* to kissen his bulle.
A. 1.77   Þanne I *knelide* on my knes & cri3ide hire of grace;
A. 2.1   3et *knelide* I on my knes & cri3ede hire of grace,
A. 3.42   Þanne mede for hire mysdedis þat man *knelide*,
A. 3.105   *Knelynge*, consience to þe kyng loutide,
A. 3.217   'Nay,' quaþ consience to þe king & *knelide* to þe erþe.
A. 5.85   Whanne I come to þe [k]ir[k]e & *knel*[e] to þe rode,
A.11.100 And whanne I was war of his wil to his wif gan I *knele*,
A.12.47   And þanne I *kneled* on my knes and kyste her [fete] sone,
B.Pr.73   Comen vp *knelynge* to kissen hi[s] bull[e].
B.Pr.124 And *knelynge* to þe kyng clergially he seide,
B. 1.79   Thanne I [*kneled*] on my knees and cried hire of grace;
B. 2.1   YEt [*kneled* I] on my knees and cried hire of grace,
B. 3.43   Thanne Mede for hire mysdedes to þat man *kneled*
B. 3.116   *Knelynge*, Conscience to þe kyng louted,
B. 3.230   'Nay', quod Conscience to þe kyng and *kneled* to þe erþe.
B. 5.105   Whan I come to þe kirk and *knele* to þe Roode
B. 5.387   I may no3t stonde ne stoupe ne wiþoute stool *knele*.
B. 5.477   [Th]anne hadde Repentaunce ruþe and redde hem alle to *knele*.
B.10.147 And whan I was war of his wille to his wif gan I [*knele*]
B.10.315 And but if his knaue *knele* þat shal his coppe brynge
B.19.12 Quod Conscience and *kneled* þo, 'þise arn Piers armes,
B.19.17 That alle kynne creatures sholden *knelen* and bowen
B.19.28 To be called a knyght is fair for men shul *knele* to hym.
B.19.74 Aungeles out of heuene come *knelynge* and songe,
B.19.75 Kynges come after, *knelede* and offrede [sense],
B.19.81 For alle þe Aungeles of heuene at his burþe *knelede*,
B.19.91 The þridde kyng þo kam *knelynge* to Iesu
B.19.95 Thoru3 þre kynne kynges *knelynge* to Iesu.
B.19.151 Come *knelynge* to þe corps and songen
B.19.200 And counseiled me to *knele* þerto; and þanne cam, me þou3te,
B.19.207 Quod Conscience and *knelede*, 'þis is cristes messager
B.19.209 *Knele* now', quod Conscience, 'and if þow kanst synge
C.Pr.71   Comen [vp] *knel*[*yng*] to kyssen his bull[e].
C. 1.76   Thenne y *knelede* on my knees and criede here of grace
C. 2.1   And thenne y *kneled* [o]n my knees and cried here of grace,
C. 3.45   Thenne mede for here mysdedes to th[at] man *knelede*
C. 3.153   *Knelyng*, consience to þe kyng loutede,
C. 5.161   And but if his knaue *knele* þat shal his coppe holde
C. 7.3   Y may nat stande ne stoupe ne withouten stool *knele*.
C. 7.119   Tho was repentaunce aredy and redde hem alle to *knele*:
C.17.177 And when þe coluer ca[m] th[us] then *knelede* þe peple
C.21.12 Quod Conciense and *knelede* tho, 'this aren [Peres] Armes,
C.21.17 T[hat] alle kyn creatures sholde *knelen* and bowen
C.21.28 To be cald a knyht is fayr for men shal *knele* to hym;
C.21.74 Angele[s] out of heuene come *knel*[*yng*] and songe,
C.21.75 Kynges cam aftur, *knelede* and offrede [sense],
C.21.81 For alle þe angelis of heuene at his burthe *knelede*
C.21.91 The thridde kyng cam [þo] *knel*[*ynge*] to iesu
C.21.95 Thorw thre kyne kynges *knelyng* to iesu.

C.21.151 Comen *knelyng* to þ[e] Cors and songen
C.21.200 And conseyled me to *knele* þerto; and thenne cam, me thouhte,
C.21.207 Quod Consience and *knelede*, 'this is Cristes messager
C.21.209 *Knele* now,' quod Consience, 'and yf thow canst synge,

knelyng ger *knelinge ger.* &> *knelen* A 1; B 1

A.11.96   Ac for no carping I couþe, ne *knelyng* to þe ground,
B.10.143 A[c] for no carpyng I kouþe, ne *knelyng* to þe grounde,

knelynge > knelen,knelyng; knes > knees; knet > knytten; kneu3 knew(- > know-

knyf n *knif n.* A 1; B 3 knyf (1) knyues (2); C 1 knyues

A. 5.62   A kertil & a courtepy, a *knyf* be his side,
B. 5.79   [A] kirtel and [a] Courtepy, a *knyf* by his syde,
B. 5.165   Hadde þei had *knyues*, by crist! eiþer hadde kild ooþer.
B.20.219 In paltokes and pyked shoes, [purses and] longe *knyues*,
C.22.219 In paltokes and pikede shoes, [purses and] longe *knyues*

knight(- > kni3t(-

kny3t n *knight n.* A 20 kni3t (10) kni3tes (9) kni3tis (1); B 50 knyght (7) knyghtes (6) kny3t (20) kny3te (2) kni3tes (1) kny3tes (14); C 60 knyght (2) knyghtes (7) kny3te (1) knyht (8) knyhte (21) knyhtes (19) knyhtus (2)

A. 1.92   Kinges & *kni3tes* shulde kepe it be resoun,
A. 1.96   For dauid, in hise dayes, dubbide *kni3tes*,
A. 1.98   Þat is þe profession apertly þat apendiþ to *kni3tes*,
A. 2.43   Of *kni3tes* of cuntr[e], of comeres aboute,
A. 3.41   Among clerkis & *kni3tes* consience to felle'.
A. 3.99   I haue a *kni3t*, consience, com late fro be3onde;
A. 4.105   Til clerkis & *kni3tes* be curteis of here mouþes,
A. 5.1   Þe king & [his] *kni3tes* to þe [k]ir[k]e wente
A. 7.23   'Be crist,' quaþ a *kni3t* þo, 'þou [kenn]ist vs þe beste;
A. 7.25   Ac kenne me,' quaþ þe *kni3t*, '& I wile [conne] eren.'
A. 7.35   Curteisliche þ[e] *kni3t* [conseyuede] þise wordis,
A. 7.50   'I assente, be seint Iame', seide þe *kni3t* þanne,
A. 7.146   Þanne peris þe plou3man pleynede hym to þe *kni3t*
A. 7.149   Curteisliche þe *kni3t* þanne as his kynde wolde
A. 7.153   And let li3t of þe lawe & lesse of þe *kni3t*,
A. 8.9   Kinges & *kni3tes* þat kepen holy chirche
A. 8.139   Þat [vncouþe] *kni3t*[is] shal come þi kingdom to cleyme;
A.10.17   Is a wys *kni3t* withalle, sire [inwit] he hatte,
A.10.137 Kinges & *kni3tes*, & alle kyne clerkis,
A.11.33   Wolde neuere king, ne *kni3t*, ne canoun of seint poulis
B. 1.94   Kynges and *kny3tes* sholde kepen it by reson,
B. 1.98   /For Dauid in hise dayes dubbed *kny3tes*,
B. 1.100   [That] is [þe] profession apertli þat apendeþ to *kny3tes*,
B. 2.58   Of *kny3tes* and of clerkes and ooþer commune peple,
B. 3.42   Amonges [clerkes] and [*kny3tes*] Conscience to [felle]'.
B. 3.110   I haue a *kny3t*, Conscience, cam late fro biyonde;
B. 3.315   Shal neiþer kyng ne *knyght*, Constable ne Meire
B. 5.1   The kyng and hise *kny3tes* to þe kirke wente
B. 5.159   And dame Clarice a *kny3tes* dou3ter ac a cokewold was hir sire,
B. 5.252   And haue ymaad many a *kny3t* boþe Mercer and draper
B. 6.21   'By crist!' quod a *kny3t* þoo, '[þow] kenne[st] vs þe beste;
B. 6.23   [Ac] kenne me', quod þe *kny3t*, 'and [I wole konne erie].'
B. 6.33   Curteisly þe *kny3t* [conseyued] þise wordes,
B. 6.49   Or a *kny3t* from a knaue; knowe þis in þyn herte.
B. 6.55   'I assente, by Seint Iame', seide þe *kny3t* þanne,
B. 6.159   Thanne Piers þe plowman pleyned hym to þe *kny3te*
B. 6.164   Curteisly þe *kny3t* þanne, as his kynde wolde,
B. 6.168   And leet li3t of þe lawe and lasse of þe *kny3te*,
B. 7.9   Kynges and *kny3tes* þat kepen holy chirche
B. 7.161   That vnkouþe *kny3tes* shul come þi kyngdom to cleyme;
B. 9.18   Is a wis *kny3t* wiþalle, sire Inwit he hatte,
B. 9.113   Kynges and *kny3tes*, kaysers and [clerkes];
B.10.47   [W]olde neuere kyng ne *kny3t* ne [c]anon of Seint Poules
B.11.141 '[I] Troianus, a trewe *kny3t*, [take] witnesse at a pope
B.11.294 For made neuere kyng no *kny3t* but he hadde catel to spende
B.11.295 As bifel for a *kny3t*, or foond hym for his strengþe.
B.11.296 It is a careful *kny3t*, and of a caytif kynges makyng,
B.11.313 That crouneþ swiche goddes *kny3tes*, þat konneþ no3t sapienter
B.12.127 Was þer neuere [kyng ne] *kny3t* but clergie hem made.
B.12.210 And ri3t as Troianus þe trewe *kny3t* [tilde] no3t depe in helle
B.12.283 "Troianus was a trewe *knyght* and took neuere cristendom
B.13.436 [Clerkes and *kni3tes*] welcomeþ kynges minstrales,
B.15.50   'Thanne artow inparfit', quod he, 'and oon of prides *kny3tes*.
B.15.332 Ac clerkes and *kny3tes* and communers þat ben riche,
B.17.1   'I am Spes, [a spie', quod he], 'and spire after a *Knyght*
B.18.13   As is þe kynde of a *knyght* þat comeþ to be dubbed,
B.18.76   For he was *kny3t* and kynges sone kynde foryaf þat [þrowe]
B.18.78   Ac þer cam forþ a *kny3t* wiþ a kene spere ygrounde,
B.18.87   Thanne fil þe *kny3t* vpon knees and cryde [Iesu] mercy:
B.18.99   For youre champion chiualer, chief *kny3t* of yow alle,

B.19.27 That *knyght*, kyng, conquerour may be o persone.
B.19.28 To be called a *knyght* is fair for men shul knele to hym.
B.19.29 To be called a kyng is fairer for he may *knyghtes* make.
B.19.144 Kepen it fro nyghtcomeris wiþ *knyghtes* yarmed
B.19.149 The *knyghtes* þat kepten it biknewe hemseluen
B.19.154 The Iewes preide hem pees, and [preide] þe *knyghtes*
B.20.91 After Confort a *knyght* to come and bere his baner:
B.20.101 Kynges and *knyghtes*, kaysers and popes.
B.20.104 Manye a louely lady and [hir] lemmans *kny3tes*
B.20.257 Kynges and *knyghtes* þat kepen and defenden
C.Pr.181 And colers of crafty werk, bothe *knyghte[s]* and squieres.
C. 1.90 Kynges and *knyghtes* sholde kepen hit by resoun,
C. 1.97 Is þe professioun and puyr ordre that apendeth to *knyghtes*
C. 1.102 Dauid in his daies dobbed *knyghtes*,
C. 1.105 Made *knyghtes* in his Couert creatures tene,
C. 1.108 He was an Archangel of heuene, on of goddes *knyghtes*;
C. 2.60 Of *knyghtes*, of clerkes [and] other comune peple,
C. 3.44 Amonge kynges and *knyhtes* and clerkes and the lyke.'
C. 3.49 Among *knyhtes* and clerkes consience to turne.
C. 3.147 Y haue a *knyght*, Consience, cam late fro be3ende;
C. 3.468 Shal nother kyng ne *knyght*, Constable vs be Mayre
C. 5.72 And so[p]ares and here sones for suluer han be *knyhtes*,
C. 5.77 Imade here kyn *knyghtes* and knyhtes fees ypurchased,
C. 5.77 Imade here kyn knyhtes and *knyhtes* fees ypurchased,
C. 6.134 And dame clarice a *knyhtes* douhter, a cokewolde was here syre,
C. 6.250 · And haue ymad many a *knyht* bothe mercer and draper
C. 7.33 And holden a *knyhtus* Court and acounte with þe reue
C. 7.96 Clerkes and *knyhtes* welcometh kynges munstrals
C. 8.19 'By Crist!' quod a *knyhte* tho, 'a kenneth vs þe beste
C. 8.21 Y wolde y couthe,' quod the *knyhte*, 'by Crist and his moder!
C. 8.23 'Sikerliche, sire *knyhte*,' sayde [Peris] thenne,
C. 8.32 Courteisliche the *knyhte* thenne co[nseyu]ed thise wordes:
C. 8.46 Or a *knyhte* [fram] a knaue or a quene fram a queene.
C. 8.47 Hit bicometh to the, *knyhte*, to be corteys and hende,
C. 8.54 'Y assente, by seynt Gyle,' sayde the *knyht* thenne,
C. 8.156 [Peres] the [plouhman] tho pleynede hym to þe *knyhte*
C. 8.161 Courteisliche the *knyhte* thenne, as his kynde wolde,
C. 8.165 And leet lyhte of þe lawe and lasse of the *knyhte*
C. 8.170 Awreke [me] of this wastors for þe *knyhte* wil nat.'
C. 9.9 Kyngus and *knyhtus* þat holy kyrke defenden
C.10.144 Is a wise *knyhte* withalle, sire inwit he hatte,
C.10.266 Ther ne is squier ne *knyhte* in contreye aboute
C.11.50 Clerkes and *knyhtes* carpen of god ofte
C.12.76 'I troianes, a trewe *knyht*, take witnesse of a pope
C.12.103 We sholde nat clepie *knyhtes* þerto ne none kyne ryche:
C.13.108 For made neuere kyng no *knyhte* but he hadde catel to spene
C.13.109 As byful for a *knyht* or fond hym for his strenthe
C.13.110 For hit is a carfol *knyhte* and of a Caytif kynges makynge
C.13.125 That crouneth suche goddes *knyhtes* that conne [nat] sapienter
C.14.149 And riht as troianes þe trewe *knyhte* [telde] nat depe in helle
C.14.205 Troianes was a trewe *knyhte* and toek neuere cristendoem
C.16.212 'Thenne artow inparfit,' quod he, 'and oen of pruydes *knyhtes*.
C.17.287 For as þe kynde is of a *knyhte* or [of] a kynge to be take
C.18.94 In kynges Court and in *knyhtes*, the clenneste men and fayreste
C.19.1 'I am spes, a spie,' quod he, 'and spere aftur a *kny3te*
C.20.11 As is þe kynde of a *knyhte* þat cometh to be dobbet,
C.20.78 For he was *knyht* and kynges sone kynde for3af þat [þrowe]
C.20.80 Ac þer cam forth a *knyhte* with a kene spere ygrounde,
C.20.89 Tho ful the *knyhte* vppon knees and criede iesu mercy:
C.20.102 For 3oure chaumpioun Chiualer, chief *knyht* of 3ow alle,
C.21.27 That *knyht*, kyng, conquerour may be o persone.
C.21.28 To be cald a *knyht* is fayr for men shal knele to hym;
C.21.29 To be cald a kyng is fairor for he may *knyhtes* make.
C.21.144 Kepen hit fro nyhtecomares with *knyhtes* y[ar]med
C.21.149 The *knyhtes* þat kepten hit biknewen hemsuluen
C.21.154 The iewes preyed hem pees and preyede th[e] *knyhtes*
C.22.91 Aftur conforte, a *knyhte*, [to] come and beer his baner:
C.22.101 Kynges and *knyhtes*, Caysers and popes.
C.22.104 Many a louly lady and here lemmanes *knyhtes*
C.22.257 Kynges and *knyhtes* þat ke[p]en and defenden

kny3ted v *knighten v.* A 1 kni3tide; B 1
A. 1.103 And crist, king[ene] kin[g], *kni3tide* tene,
B. 1.105 [And] crist, kyngene kyng, *kny3ted* ten,

kny3thod n *knighthode n.* A 2 kni3thed (1) kni3thod (1); B 6 knyghthod (1) knyghthood (1) kny3thod (3) kny3thode (1); C 5 knyghthed (2) knyghthede (1) knyhthoed (2)
A.11.219 'I wende þat kinghed, & *kni3thed*, & caiseris wiþ Erlis
A.11.226 Kinghod & *kni3thod*, for au3t I can aspie,
B.Pr.112 Thanne kam þer a kyng; *kny3thod* hym ladde;
B.Pr.116 The kyng and *kny3thod* and clergie boþe
B.10.336 'Thanne is dowel and dobet', quod I, 'dominus and *kny3thode*?'
B.10.338 Kynghod [and] *kny3thod*, [for au3t] I kan awayte,

B.15.553 If *knyghthod* and kynde wit and þe commune [and] conscience
B.18.96 Cursede cayt[yues]! *knyghthood* was it neuere
C.Pr.139 Thenne cam the[r] a kyng; *knygh[t]hede* hym la[dd]e;
C.Pr.143 Conscience & kynde wit] and *knyghthed* togedres
C. 1.98 And hoso passeth þat poynt is appostata of *knyghthed*.
C.17.216 3if *knyhthoed* and kynde wit and þe comune and consience
C.20.99 Corsede Caytifues! *knyhthoed* was hit neuere

kni3tide > kny3ted; knyht(- > kni3t(-

knytten v *knitten v.* B 2 knytten (1) yknyt (1); C 2 knet (1) knytten (1)
B.Pr.169 And *knytten* it on a coler for oure commune profit
B.15.242 And þat Conscience and crist haþ *yknyt* faste
C.Pr.186 And *knytten* hit on a coler for oure comune profyt
C. 3.211 For clerkes and coueitise mede hath *knet* togederes

knyues > knyf; knocke > knokked

knok n *knokke n.* B 1; C 1
B.10.332 Haue a *knok* of a kyng, and incurable þe wounde.
C. 5.177 Shal haue a *knok* vppon here crounes and incurable þe wounde:

knokked v *knokken v.* B 4; C 5 knocke (1) knokked (3) knokkede (1)
B. 5.390 He bigan Benedicite with a bolk and his brest *knokked*,
B.16.128 And *knokked* on hem wiþ a corde, and caste adoun hir stalles
B.20.130 And [*knokked*] Conscience in Court afore hem alle;
B.20.329 And cam þere Conscience was and *knokked* at þe yate.
C. 5.106 Byfore þe cross on my knees *knokked* y my brest,
C. 7.6 A bigan benedicite with a bolk and his breste *knokkede*,
C. 8.286 And thouh lyares and l[a]chdraweres and lollares *knocke*
C.22.130 And *knokked* Consience in Court bifore hem alle;
C.22.329 And cam þer Consience was and *knokked* at þe 3ate.

knowleche(de > knoweliched; knoppis > knappes

knoweliched v *knoulechen v.* A 1 knowelechide; B 4 kneweliche (1) knewliched (1) knoweliched (1) knowelechede (1); C 5 knoleche (1) knolechede (1) knoweleched (1) Knowelecheth (1) knowelechede (1)
A. 5.247 And *knowelechide* his [coupe] to crist 3et eftsones,
B. 5.473 And *knoweliched* his [coupe] to crist yet eftsones,
B.12.193 Was for he yald hym creaunt to crist & *knewliched* hym gilty,
B.19.77 Or any kynnes catel; but *knowelich[ede]* hym sowereyn
B.19.186 In couenaunt þat þei come and *knewelich[e]* to paie
C. 6.327 And *knolechede* [his coupe to Crist] 3ut eftsones,
C. 7.147 Yf we *knowelechede* and cryde Crist þerfore mercy:
C.13.90 *Knowelecheth* hym cristene and of holy kirke byleue,
C.21.77 Or eny kyne catel; bote *knoweleched* hym sowereyn
C.21.186 In couenaunt þat they come and *knolech[e]* to pay

knowen v *knouen v.* A 36 kneu3 (4) knewe (1) knewen (1) knowe (15) knowen (5) knowist (4) knowiþ (6); B 128 knew (14) knewe (11) knewen (2) knowe (55) knowen (12) knowest (6) knowestow (1) knoweþ (22) knowynge (1) yknowe (3) yknowen (1); C 122 knew (1) knewe (20) knowe (51) knowen (8) knowest (7) knoweth (26) knowyng (1) knowynge (1) yknowe (7)
A.Pr.53 Cloþide hem in copis to be *knowen* from oþere;
A. 1.73 'Holy chirche I am,' quaþ heo, 'þou au3test me to *knowe*;
A. 1.90 Þe clerkis þat *knowe* it shulde kenne it aboute,
A. 1.107 Tau3te hem þoru3 þe trinite þe trouþe to *knowe*:
A. 1.125 Leriþ it þus lewide men, for lettrid it *knowiþ*,
A. 2.4 Kenne me be sum craft to *k[now]e* þe false'.
A. 2.29 *Knowe* hem þere 3if þou canst and kep þe from hem alle
A. 2.103 For consience is of his counseil & *knowiþ* 3ow ichone,
A. 2.188 For he coude on here craft & *kneu3* manye gommes.
A. 3.58 Neiþer in si3t ne in þi soule, for god hymself *knowiþ*
A. 3.136 She is preuy wiþ þe pope, prouisours it *knowiþ*;
A. 3.165 And þou *knowist*, consience, I ca[m] nou3t to chide,
A. 3.172 And maynteyne þi manhod more þan þou *knowist*;
A. 3.260 [I] consience *knowe* þis, for kynde [w]it me tau3te,
A. 4.48 [Þe king *kneu3*] he seide soþ for consience hym tolde.
A. 4.66 Consience & þe king *kneu3* wel þe soþe,
A. 6.11 And þe vernicle beforn for men shulde *knowe*
A. 6.20 '*Knowist* þou ou3t a corseint,' quaþ þei, 'þat men callen treuþe?
A. 6.26 'I *knowe* hym as kyndely as clerk doþ his bokis.
A. 6.38 He is þe presteste payere þat pore men *knowen*;
A. 6.83 His man hattiþ amende 3ow, for many man he *knowiþ*.
A. 6.116 'Ne I,' quaþ an apeward, 'be au3t þat I *knowe*.'
A. 7.205 Wiþ fuyr or wiþ false men, fond suche [to] *knowen*;
A. 9.12 3if þei *knewen* any cuntre or costis aboute
A. 9.63 'What art þou,' quaþ I þo, 'þat my name *knowist*?'
A.10.10 Ac kynde *knowiþ* [þis] wel and kepiþ hire þe betere,
A.10.54 In manis brayn is he most & mi3tiest to *knowe*.
A.10.133 Þat þoru3 wedlak þe world stant, whoso wile it *knowen*.
A.10.146 In þat curside constellacioun þei *knewe* togideris,
A.11.43 Þus þei dryuelen at here deis þe deite to *knowe*.
A.11.103 [To] kenne me kyndely to *knowe* what is dowel'.
A.11.129 And alle þe musons of musik I made hire [to] *knowe*.

A.11.155 Astronomye is hard þing & euil for to *knowe*;
A.11.281 And for he *kneuȝ* on þe crois & to crist shr[o]f hym,
A.12.1 'Crist wot,' quod clergie, '*knowe* hit ȝif þe lyke,
A.12.43 And sayde, 'my cosyn kynde wit *knowen* is wel wide,
B.Pr.56 Cloþed hem in copes to ben *knowen* from oþere;
B.Pr.122 Shopen lawe and leaute, ech [lif] to *knowe* his owene.
B. 1.75 'Holi chirche I am', quod she; 'þow ouȝtest me to *knowe*.
B. 1.92 The clerkes þat *knowen* [it] sholde kennen it aboute
B. 1.109 Tauȝte hem [þoruȝ] þe Trinitee [þe] treuþe to *knowe*:
B. 1.136 Lereþ it þ[us] lewed men, for lettred it *knoweþ*,
B. 1.163 And for to *knowen* it kyndely, it comseþ by myght,
B. 2.4 Kenne me by som craft to *knowe* þe false'.
B. 2.47 *Knowe* hem þere if þow kanst and kepe [þee from hem alle],
B. 2.139 [For] Conscience is of his counseil and *knoweþ* yow echone;
B. 2.229 For he kouþe [on] hir craft and *knew* manye gommes.
B. 3.67 For [god] *knoweþ* þi conscience and þi kynde wille
B. 3.147 She is pryuee wiþ þe pope, prouisours it *knoweþ*,
B. 3.178 And þow *knowest*, Conscience, I kam noȝt to chide,
B. 3.185 And mayntene þi manhode moore þan þow *knowest*;
B. 3.284 I, Conscience, *knowe* þis for kynde wit me tauȝte
B. 4.32 A[c] Conscience *knew* hem wel, þei loued coueitise,
B. 4.41 For Conscience *know[e* þei] noȝt, ne crist, as I trowe.'
B. 4.61 The kyng *knew* he seide sooþ, for Conscience hym tolde
B. 4.80 Conscience and þe commune *kn[e]wen* [wel] þe soþe,
B. 4.164 But he be *knowe* for a Cokewold kut of my nose.'
B. 5.183 Counseil þat þow *knowest* by contenaunce ne by [speche];
B. 5.523 And þe vernycle bifore, for men sholde *knowe*
B. 5.532 '*Knowestow* auȝt a corsaint', [quod þei], 'þat men calle truþe?
B. 5.538 'I *knowe* hym as kyndely as clerc doþ hise bokes.
B. 5.551 He is þe presteste paiere þat pouere men *knoweþ*;
B. 5.596 His man hatte amende-yow, for many m[a]n h[e] *knoweþ*.
B. 5.631 'Nor I', quod an Apeward, 'by auȝt þat I *knowe*.'
B. 5.639 'Bi seint Poul!' quod a pardoner, 'parauenture I be noȝt *knowe* þere;
B. 6.48 For in Charnel at chirche cherles ben yuel to *knowe*,
B. 6.49 Or a knyȝt from a knaue; *knowe* þis in þyn herte.
B. 6.219 [Wiþ fir or wiþ] false men, fonde swiche to *knowe*.
B. 8.12 If þei *knewe* any contree or costes [aboute]
B. 8.15 And *knowen* contrees and courtes and many kynnes places,
B. 8.72 'What art [þ]ow', quod I þo, 'þat my name *knowest*?'
B. 9.10 Ac kynde *knoweþ* þis wel and kepeþ hire þe bettre,
B. 9.80 For moore bilongeþ to þe litel barn er he þe lawe *knowe*
B.10.57 Thus þei dryuele at hir deys þe deitee to *knowe*,
B.10.151 [To] kenne me kyndely to *knowe* what is dowel.'
B.10.177 And alle [þe] Musons in Musik I made hire to *knowe*.
B.10.212 Ac Astronomye is hard þyng and yuel for to *knowe*;
B.10.223 To counseille þee kyndely to *knowe* what is dowel.'
B.10.239 Wiþ alle þe articles of þe feiþ þat falleþ to be *knowe*.
B.10.441 And be allowed as he lyued so; for by luþere men *knoweþ* þe goode.
B.10.471 That inparfitly here *knewe* and ek lyuede.
B.10.472 Ye, men *knowe* clerkes þat han corsed þe tyme
B.11.11 And *knowe* þat þow coueitest and come þerto paraunter'.
B.11.32 Coueitise of eiȝe, þat euere þow hir *knewe*–
B.11.49 I hadde no likyng, leue me, [þe leste] of hem to *knowe*.
B.11.108 Ac þe matere þat she meued, if lewed men it *knewe*,
B.11.188 To *knowen* vs by oure kynde herte and castynge of oure eiȝen,
B.11.214 Forþi lakke no lif ooþer þouȝ he moore latyn *knowe*,
B.11.233 For in hir liknesse oure lord [lome] haþ ben *yknowe*.
B.11.235 Cleophas ne *knew* hym noȝt þat he crist were
B.11.239 Ac by cloþyng þei *knewe* hym noȝt, [so caitifliche he yede].
B.11.302 [Moore þan cure] for konnyng or '*knowen* for clene [of] berynge'.
B.11.325 I was fet forþ by [forbisenes] to *knowe*
B.11.407 That I in metels ne myȝte moore haue *yknowen*.
B.11.414 Thow sholdest haue *knowen* þat clergie kan & [conceyued] moore þoruȝ Res[on],
B.11.418 Ac whan he mamelede about mete, and entremetede to *knowe*
B.12.69 *Knew* neuere clerk how it comeþ forþ, ne kynde wit þe weyes:
B.12.78 [For] þoruȝ caractes þat crist wroot þe Iewes *knewe* hemselue
B.12.82 Holy kirke *knoweþ* þis þat cristes writyng saued;
B.12.132 And helden it an heiȝ science hir wittes to *knowe*;
B.12.153 Clerkes *knewen* it wel and comen wiþ hir presentȝ
B.12.171 That he þat *knoweþ* clergie kan sonner arise
B.12.174 For if þe clerk be konnynge he *knoweþ* what is synne,
B.12.219 /And willest of briddes & beestes and of hir bredyng *knowe*,
B.12.225 Clergie ne kynde wit ne *knew* neuere þe cause,
B.12.226 Ac kynde *knoweþ* þe cause hymself, no creature ellis.
B.12.230 Kynde] kenned Adam to *knowe* hise pryue membres,
B.12.235 Kynde *knoweþ* whi he dide so, ac no clerk ellis.
B.13.27 Conscience *knew* hym wel and welcomed hym faire.
B.13.115 What is dowel and dobet? ye dyuynours *knoweþ*.'
B.13.131 'I kan noȝt heron', quod Conscience, 'ac I *knowe* Piers.
B.13.134 Pacience haþ be in many place, and paraunter [*knoweþ*]
B.13.186 And lere yow if yow like þe leeste point to *knowe*

B.13.187 That Pacience þe pilgrym parfitly *knew* neuere.'
B.13.310 And what I kouþe and *knew* and what kyn I com of'.
B.13.431 Ac clerkes þat *knowen* holy writ sholde kenne lordes
B.14.112 And seiþ, 'lo! briddes and beestes þat no blisse ne *knoweþ*
B.14.241 For men *knowen* wel þat Coueitise is of [a] kene wille
B.15.2 Er I koude kyndely *knowe* what was dowel,
B.15.17 In cristes court *yknowe* wel and of [cristene in many a place].
B.15.20 At mydnyght, at mydday, my vois so is *knowe*
B.15.25 And for þat I kan [and] *knowe* called am I mens;
B.15.39 How þow coueitest to calle me, now þow *knowest* [alle] my names.
B.15.45 Thow woldest *knowe* and konne þe cause of alle [hire] names,
B.15.49 I wolde I *knewe* and kouþe kyndely in myn herte.'
B.15.62 Coueitise to konne and to *knowe* scienc[e]
B.15.65 Right so þat þoruȝ reson wolde þe roote *knowe*
B.15.195 'By crist! I wolde I *knewe* hym', quod I, 'no creature leuere.'
B.15.197 'Wheiþer clerkes *knowen* hym', quod I, 'þat kepen holi kirke?'
B.15.209 Therfore by colour ne by clergie *knowe* shaltow [hym] neuere,
B.15.211 And þat *knoweþ* no clerk ne creature on erþe.
B.15.232 In þat secte siþþe to selde haþ he ben [*knowe*].
B.15.319 If lewed men *knewe* þis latyn þei wolde loke whom þei yeue,
B.15.369 Neiþer þei konneþ ne *knoweþ* oon cours bifore anoþer.
B.15.381 That sholde konne and *knowe* alle kynnes clergie
B.15.532 Er cristendom [were] *knowe* þere, or any cros honoured.
B.15.587 And ȝit *knewe* þei crist þat cristendom tauȝte,
B.16.147 And tolde men a tokne to *knowe* wiþ Iesus;
B.16.179 A ful bold bacheler; I *knew* hym by his blasen.'
B.16.192 Might and [a] mene [his owene myȝte to *knowe*],
B.16.215 That is, creatour weex creature to *knowe* what was boþe.
B.16.229 Calues flessh and Cakebreed; and *knewe* what I þouȝte.
B.17.9 [And þus my lettre meneþ; [ye] mowe *knowe* it al].'
B.17.10 'Lat se þi lettres', quod I, 'we myghte þe lawe *knowe*.'
B.17.42 It is lighter to lewed men o lesson to *knowe*
B.17.116 And kennen outcom[en] men þat *knowen* noȝt þe contree
B.17.140 For god is after an hand; yheer now and *knowe* it.
B.17.145 To ministren and to make þat myȝt of hand *knoweþ*;
B.17.263 That riche ben and reson *knoweþ* ruleþ wel youre soule;
B.17.343 And ben inpacient in hir penaunce, pure reson *knoweþ*
B.18.24 That crist be noȝt [y]knowe here for consummatus deus
B.18.205 For hadde þei wist of no wo, wele hadde þei noȝt *knowen*,
B.18.221 To wite what wele was, kyndeliche [to] *knowe* it.
B.18.244 And as he wente on þe water wel hym *knew* and seide,
B.18.273 'Listneþ!' quod lucifer, 'for I þis lord knowe;
B.18.274 Boþe þis lord and þis light, is longe ago I *knew* hym.
B.19.26 'Thow *knowest* wel', quod Conscience, 'and þow konne reson,
B.19.203 And made hem konne and *knowe* alle kynne langages.
B.19.348 That Conscience shal noȝt *knowe* who is cristene or heþene,
B.19.413 I *knew* neuere Cardynal þat he ne cam fro þe pope.
B.20.67 And what kyng þat hem conforted, *knowynge* [hir gile],
B.20.282 Ben Curatours called to *knowe* and to hele,
B.20.337 Conscience *knoweþ* me wel and what I kan boþe.'
B.20.343 I *knew* swich oon ones, noȝt eighte wynter [passed],
C.Pr.54 Clothed hem in copis to be *knowe* fram othere
C. 1.47 "Sesares," thei sayde, "sothliche we *knoweth*."
C. 1.72 'Holy churche y am', quod she; 'þou oughtest me to *knowe*;
C. 1.88 Clerkes þat *knowen* hit sholde kenne hit aboute
C. 1.135 Lere hit thus lewed men, for lettred hit *knoweth*:
C. 1.159 And for to *knowe* hit kyndly, hit comeseth by myhte
C. 2.4 Kenne me by sum craft to *knowe* þe false.
C. 2.18 'Leue lady,' quod y tho,'layn nought yf ȝe *knowen*.'
C. 2.49 *Knowe* hem wel yf þou kanst and kepe the fro hem alle
C. 2.132 Y, Theo[lo]gie, þe tixt *knowe* yf trewe doom wittenesseth,
C. 2.155 And Consience is of his consayl and *knoweth* ȝow [echone];
C. 2.239 For a can on here craft and *knoweth* manye gommes.
C. 3.71 For god *knoweth* thi consience [and þy kynde wille],
C. 3.185 He is priue with þe pope, prouysours it *knoweth*,
C. 3.224 And þ[ou] *knowe[st]*, Consience, y cam nat to chyde
C. 3.231 And maynteyne thi manhede more then thow *knowest*,
C. 3.341 Quod the kyng to Consience, '*knowen* y wolde,
C. 3.364 Alle kyn kynde to *knowe* and to folowe
C. 3.437 [I], Consience,*knowe* this for kynde wit me tauhte
C. 4.32 Ac Consience *knewe* hem wel and carped to resoun;
C. 4.64 [The kyng *knew* he sayde soth for Consience hym tolde
C. 4.71 Thorw wrong and his werkes there was mede *yknowe*
C. 4.76 Consience *knoweth* hit wel and al þe Comune trewe.'
C. 4.159 But he be *knowe* for a cokewold kut of my nose.'
C. 5.83 For in my Consience y *knowe* what Crist w[o]lde y wrouhte.
C. 6.26 In alle [manere] maneres my name to be *knowe*;
C. 6.58 And what y couthe and *knewe* and what kyn y cam of."
C. 6.144 Yparroke[d] in pues; the persone hit *knoweth*
C. 6.165 Consayl þat thow *knowest* by continaunce ne by speche;
C. 6.322 Ne neuere wene to wynne with craft þat y *knowe*;
C. 7.91 Clerkes þat *knoweth* this sholde kenne lordes
C. 7.177 '*Knowest* thow auht a corsent,' quod they, 'þat men calleth treuthe?

C. 7.183   'I *knowe* hym as kyndely as Clerk doth his bokes.
C. 7.195   He is þe presteste payere þat eny pore man *knoweth*;
C. 7.207   Til ȝe come into Consience, *yknowe* of god sulue,
C. 7.244   His man hatte amende-ȝow, many man hym *knoweth*.
C. 7.284   'Ne y,' quod an hapeward, 'by auht þat y *knowe*.'
C. 8.45   At churche in the Charnel cherles Aren euele to *knowe*
C. 8.266   Yf ȝe can or *knowe* eny kyne thyng[e] of fisyk
C. 9.233   Vigilies and fastyngdays forthermore to *knowe*
C.10.12   Yf they *knewe* eny contre oþer costes aboute
C.10.15   And *knowen* contrees and Courtes and many kynne plases,
C.10.70   'What art thow,' quod y [þo], 'þat my name *knowest*?'
C.10.75   Where þat dowel dwelleth And do me to *knowe*.'
C.10.112   Elles *knowe* y noen þat can in none kynneryche.'
C.10.137   A[c] kynde *knoweth* this wel and kepeth here þe betere
C.10.264   That no cortesye can, bute [*knowe* late here be]
C.11.38   Thus they dreuele a[t] the deyes the deite to *knowe*
C.11.89   With þat ȝe kenne me kyndeliche to *knowe* what is dowel.'
C.11.91   Y shal kenne þe to clergie, my cosyn, þat *knoweth*
C.11.93   Of dobet [and] of dobest–for doctour he is *knowe*
C.11.99   Thow shalt kunne and *knowe* kyndeliche dowel.'
C.11.110   To clergie shaltow neuere come ne *knowe* what is dowel.
C.11.117   And alle þe musons in musyk y made here to *knowe*.
C.11.138   To kenne and to *knowe* kyndeliche dowel.
C.11.170   And *knowe* þat þou coueytest and come þerto parauntur.'
C.11.191   Coueytes-of-yes þat euere thow here *knewe*–
C.11.290   Comuneliche then clerkes most *knowyng* in konnyng
C.12.42   Ac þe matere þat she meuede, if lewede men hit *knewe*,
C.12.122   For in here likenesse oure lord lome hath be *yknowe*.
C.12.124   Cleophas ne *knewe* hym nat þat he Crist were
C.12.128   Ac by clothyng they *knewe* hym nat, so caytifliche ȝede.
C.13.92   Ther god is gateward hymsulf and vch a gome *knoweth*.
C.13.133   To *knowe* by vch a creature kynde to louye.
C.13.222   Thow sholdest haue *yknowe* þat clergie ca[n] & conseyued mor[e]
         [thorw] resoun
C.13.226   Ac when he mamelede aboute mete and musede to *knowe*
C.14.74   And markede hit in here manere and mused þeron to *knowe*.
C.14.76   They helden hit an hey science here sotiltees to *knowe*,
C.14.97   Clerkes *kn[e]we* [þe] comet and comen with here presentes
C.14.111   Þat he þat *knoweth* clergie conne sonnore aryse
C.14.114   For yf þe clerke be connynge [he] *knoweth* what is synne
C.14.159   Was neuere creature vnder crist þat *knewe* wel þe bygynnyng
C.15.30   Concience *knewe* hym [wel and] welcomede hym fayre.
C.15.36   Concience *knewe* h[y]m wel and welcomede hem all;
C.15.78   Ac me thynketh loth, thogh y latyn *knowe*, to lacken eny secte
C.15.122   What is dowel and dobet? ȝe deuynours *knoweth*.'
C.15.181   That they *knoweth* nat,' quod Concience, 'what is kynde pacience.'
C.15.288   And saith, "loo! briddes and bestes þat no blisse ne *knoweth*
C.16.33   And lereth lewed and lered, hey and lowe to *knowe*
C.16.81   For men *knowen* wel þat coueytise is of a kene will
C.16.159   A *knewe* Consience ful wel and clergie bothe.
C.16.168   And in cristes court *yknowe* wel and of his kynne a party.
C.16.171   At mydnyhte, at myddday, my vois is so *yknowe*
C.16.185   And [for] þat y can and *knowe* ycald am y [mens];
C.16.201   How þou coueytest to calle me, now þou *knowest* al my namus.
C.16.207   Thow woldest *knowe* and conne þe cause of all here names
C.16.211   Y wolde y *knewe* and couthe kyndeliche in myn herte.'
C.16.224   Coueytyse to conne and to *knowe* scienc[e]
C.16.292   I *knewe* neuere, by Crist, clerk noþer lewed
C.16.339   Where clerkes *knowe* hym nat,' quod y, 'þat kepen holy churche?'
C.16.340   'Peres the plouhman,' quod he, 'moste parfitlyche hym *knoweth*:
C.16.341   By clothyng ne by carpynge *knowe* shaltow hym neuere
C.16.357   In [þat] sekte sethe to selde hath he be [*knowen*].
C.16.368   Kynge[s] and Cardynals *kn[o]wen* hym sum tyme
C.16.370   And hoso coueyteth to *knowe* [hym] such a kynde hym foloweth
C.17.54   Yf lewede men *knewe* this latyn a litel they wolden auysen hem
C.17.105   Noþer they [*conn*]eth ne [*know*]eth a cours by[fore] anoþer.
C.17.282   Or cristendoem were *knowe* þere or eny croos honoured.
C.17.292   And nameliche þer þat lewede lyuen and no lawe *knoweth*.
C.17.298   And ȝut *knewe* they crist þat cristendoem tauhte
C.18.93   And þe clennest creature furste creat[our].
C.18.169   And kuste iesus to be *knowe* þerby and cauht of þe iewes.
C.18.198   'Muse nat to moche þeron,' quod faith, 'til thow more *knowe*
C.19.11   'Let se thy lettres,' quod y, 'we myhte þe lawe *knowe*.'
C.19.119   To ministre and to make þat myhte of hand *knoweth*
C.19.229   That riche ben and resoun *knoweth*; reule wel ȝoure soul[e];
C.19.323   And be inpacient in here penaunc[e], puyr resoun *knoweth*
C.20.23   That Crist be nat *yknowe* for consumm[a]tus deus
C.20.210   For hadde they wist of no wo, wele hadde thay nat *knowen*;
C.20.230   To wyte what wele [was], kyndeliche to *knowe* [hit].
C.20.253   And as he wente on þe watur wel hym *knewe* and saide.
C.20.295   'Lustneth!' quod lucifer, 'for y this lord *knowe*;
C.20.296   Bothe this lord and this lihte, ys longe ygo y *knewe* hym.
C.20.317   And byhihtest here and hym aftur to *knowe*

C.21.26   'Thow *knowest* wel,' quod Concience, 'and þou kunne resoun,
C.21.203   And made hem konne & *knowe* alle kyne langages.
C.21.348   That Consience shal nat *knowe* [ho is cristene or hethene]
C.21.413   Y *knewe* neuere cardinale þat he ne cam fro þe pope
C.22.67   And what kyng þat hem confortede, *knowynge* here gyle,
C.22.282   Ben curatours cald to *knowe* and to hele,
C.22.337   Consience *knoweth* me wel and what y can bothe.'
C.22.343   Y *knewe* such oen ones, nat eyhte wynter passed,

knowes > knees

knowyng ger *knouinge ger. &> knowen* A 6 knowing (1) knowyng (5); B
    10 knowyng (6) knowynge (4); C 8 knowyng (5) knowynge (3)
A. 1.127   'ȝet haue I no kynde *knowyng*,' quaþ I, '[ȝe mote kenne me bet]
A. 1.130   It is a kynde *knowyng* þat kenneþ in þin herte
A. 1.139   For in kynde *knowyng* in herte þer comsiþ a miȝt,
A. 2.192   F[or] *knowing* of comeris copide hym as a Frere.
A. 9.48   'I haue no kynde *knowyng*,' quaþ I, 'to conseyue þi wordis,
A. 9.103   More kynde *knowyng* I coueyte to lere,
B. 1.138   'Yet haue I no kynde *knowyng*', quod I, 'ye mote kenne me bettre
B. 1.142   It is a kynde *knowyng* þat kenneþ in þyn herte
B. 1.165   For in kynde *knowynge* in herte þer [comseþ a myȝt],
B. 2.233   For *knowynge* of comeres coped hym as a Frere.
B. 8.57   'I haue no kynde *knowyng*', quod I, 'to conceyuen [þi] wordes
B. 8.113   More kynde *knowyng*] I coueite to lerne,
B.10.478   Right so lewed [laborers] and of litel *knowyng*
B.12.135   For alle hir kynde *knowyn[g]* co[m] but of diuerse siȝtes,
B.15.198   'Clerkes haue no *knowyng*', quod he, 'but by werkes and wordes.
B.19.308   He dide equyte to alle eueneforþ his [*knowynge*].
C. 1.137   'I haue no kynde *knowyng*,' quod y, '[ȝe mot] kenne me bettere
C. 1.141   Hit is a kynde *knowynge* that kenet in thyn herte
C. 1.161   For [in] kynde *knowynge* [in] herte ther comseth a myhte
C. 2.243   For *knowyng* of co[mere]s copeden hym as a frere.
C.10.56   'Y haue no kynde *kno[w]yng*,' [quod y], 'to conseyue al this speche
C.10.109   More kynd[e] *knowynge* coueyte ye to haue
C.14.79   For al here kynde *knowyng* cam bote of diuerse syhtes,
C.21.308   He dede equite to alle eueneforth his *knowyng*.

knowynge > knowen,knowyng; *knowlechede* > knoweliched

knowlichynge ger *knoulechinge ger.* B 1; C 1 knowlechyng
B.14.187   Confession and *knowlichynge* [and] craungye þi mercy
C.16.30   And oris confessio cometh of [*knowlechyng* and] shrifte of mouthe

koyne > coyn; *koke* > coke

konne v *connen v.* A 44 can (16) canst (3) conne (8) coude (3) couþe (10)
    couþest (1) cunne (2) konne (1); B 142 can (1) coudestow (1) couþe
    (3) kan (68) kanst (4) kanstow (3) konne (23) konneþ (6) koude (8)
    koudest (1) kouþe (24); C 135 can (70) canst (5) conne (12) conneth
    (5) coude (1) couthe (27) couthest (3) kan (6) kanst (2)
    konne (1) kunne (2)
A.Pr.33   And somme merþis to make as mynstrals *conne*,
A. 1.133   Þis I trowe be treuþe; who *can* teche þe betere,
A. 1.170   ȝe ben acumbrid wiþ coueitise, ȝe [*conne*] not out crepe
A. 2.29   Knowe hem þere ȝif þou *canst* and kep þe from hem alle
A. 2.188   For he *coude* on here craft & kneuȝ manye gommes.
A. 3.3   Þe king calliþ a clerk–I *can* not his name–
A. 3.160   'Excuse þe ȝif þou *canst*; I can no more seiȝe.
A. 3.160   'Excuse þe ȝif þou canst; I *can* no more seiȝe,
A. 4.41   Ne no ferþing þerfore for nouȝt I *couþe* plete.
A. 4.89   So [þat] ȝe assente I *can* sey no more,
A. 4.142   *Couþe* nouȝt warpen a word to wiþsigge resoun,
A. 5.24   He bad wastour go werche what he best *couþe*
A. 5.61   He was cloþid in a caurymaury, I [*couþe*] it nouȝt descryue;
A. 5.107   Þanne com coueitise; I *can* hym nouȝt descryue,
A. 5.112   But ȝif a lous *couþe* lepe, I may it nouȝt leue
A. 5.177   Þei *couþe* [not] be here consience acorden togidere
A. 5.245   Ac what befel of þis feloun I *can* not faire shewe;
A. 6.1   Ac þere w[ere] fewe men so wys þat þe [wey] þider *couþe*,
A. 6.21   *Canst* þou wisse vs þe wey where þat wy dwelliþ?'
A. 7.25   Ac kenne me,' quaþ þe kniȝt, '& I wile [*conne*] eren.'
A. 7.62   And alle kyne crafty men þat *conne* lyue in treuþe,
A. 7.114   Somme leide here leg alery as suche lorellis *cunne*,
A. 8.97   'Petir,' quaþ þe prest þo, 'I *can* no pardoun fynde
A. 9.6   Was neuere wiȝt as I wen[t]e þat me wisse *couþe*
A. 9.67   'Art þou þouȝt, þo?' quaþ I; 'þou *coupest* me telle
A. 9.105   'But wyt *can* wisse þe,' quaþ þouȝt, 'where þo þre dwellen,
A. 9.118   Here is wil wolde wyte ȝif wit *couþe* hym teche.'
A.10.26   [And what [kenis] þing is kynde, *conne* ȝe me telle]?'
A.10.107   Ne men þat *conne* manye craftis, clergie [it telliþ],
A.11.19   Þat *can* construe deseites, & conspire wrongis,
A.11.21   Þat suche craftis *conne* [to counseil ben yclepid]
A.11.25   And *can* telle of tobie & of þe twelue apostlis,
A.11.94   He beco[m] so confus he *couþe* nouȝt mele,
A.11.124   So shalt þou come to clergie þat *can* many wyttes.

349

A.11.165	I bekenne þe crist,' quaþ she, 'I *can* teche þe no betere.'
A.11.169	And er I com to clergie *coude* I neuere stynte.
A.11.185	And alle kyne crafty men þat *cunne* here foode wynne,
A.11.226	Kinghod & kniȝthod, for auȝt I *can* aspie,
A.11.232	'Contra,' quaþ I, 'be crist! þat *can* I þe wi[þsigg]e,
A.11.308	Þanne arn þise [k]ete clerkis þat *conne* many bokis,
A.12.7	Þou woldest *konne* þat I can and carpen hit after;
A.12.7	Þou woldest konne þat I *can* and carpen hit after;
A.12.65	[To kyllyn him ȝif I *can*, þei kynde wit helpe]
A.12.73	For þe myssyng of mete no mesour I *coude*,
B.Pr.33	And somme murþes to make as Mynstralles *konne*,
B.Pr.111	Forþi I *can* & kan nauȝt of court speke moore.
B.Pr.111	Forþi I kan & *kan* nauȝt of court speke moore.
B.Pr.129	Lowed to speke in latyn, for lewed men ne *koude*
B.Pr.182	A Mous þat muche good *kouþe*, as me [þo] þouȝte,
B.Pr.200	Nere þe cat of þ[e] court þat kan yow ouerlepe;
B.Pr.201	For hadde ye rattes youre [raik] ye *kouþe* noȝt rule yowselue.
B.1.116	And mo þousandes myd hym þan man *kouþe* nombre
B.1.145	This I trowe be truþe; who *kan* teche þee bettre,
B.1.196	[Ye] ben acombred wiþ coueitise; [ye] *konne* noȝt [out crepe],
B.2.47	Knowe hem þere if þow *kanst* and kepe [þee from hem alle],
B.2.62	I *kan* noȝt rekene þe route þat ran aboute Mede.
B.2.229	For he *kouþe* [on] hir craft and knew manye gommes.
B.3.3	The kyng called a clerk–[I *kan*] noȝt his name–
B.3.173	'Excuse þee if þow *kanst*; I kan na moore seggen,
B.3.173	'Excuse þee if þow kanst; I *kan* na moore seggen,
B.3.332	'I *kan* no latyn?' quod she, 'clerkes wite þe soþe!
B.3.344	And so [mys]ferde ye, madame; ye *kouþe* na moore fynde
B.3.347	Ac yow failed a konnynge clerk þat *kouþe* þe leef han torned.
B.4.54	Ne no ferþyng þerfore for [n]ouȝt I *koude* plede.
B.4.102	So þat [ye] assente I *kan* seye no [moore],
B.5.24	He bad wastour go werche what he best *kouþe*
B.5.78	[He was] cloþed in a kaurymaury–I *kouþe* it nouȝt discryue–
B.5.168	They hadde þanne ben Infamis, þei *kan* so yuele hele co[unseil].
B.5.188	[Th]anne cam Coueitise; [I *kan*] hym naȝt discryue,
B.5.196	But if a lous *couþe* [lepe, I leue and I trowe],
B.5.236	And I *kan* no frenssh in feiþ but of þe ferþest ende of Northfolk.'
B.5.270	Thow art an vnkynde creature; I *kan* þee noȝt assoille
B.5.328	Thei *kouþe* noȝt, by hir Conscience, acorden [togideres]
B.5.368	That I haue trespased with my tonge, I *kan* noȝt telle how ofte;
B.5.394	I *kan* noȝt parfitly my Paternoster as þe preest it syngeþ,
B.5.395	But I *kan* rymes of Robyn hood and Randolf Erl of Chestre,
B.5.416	Yet kan I neyþer solue ne synge ne seintes lyues rede;
B.5.417	But I *kan* fynden in a feld or in a furlang an hare
B.5.420	I *kan* holde louedayes and here a Reues rekenyng,
B.5.421	Ac in Canoun nor in decretals I *kan* noȝt rede a lyne.
B.5.430	I am vnkynde ayeins [his] curteisie and *kan* nouȝt vnderstonden it,
B.5.471	What bifel of þis feloun I *kan* noȝt faire shewe.
B.5.513	Ac þere was [wye] noon so wys þe wey þider *kouþe*,
B.5.533	[*Kanstow*] wissen vs þe wey wher þat wye dwelleþ?'
B.5.547	In taillours craft and tynkeris craft, what truþe *kan* deuyse,
B.6.23	[Ac] kenne me', quod þe knyȝt, 'and [I wole *konne* erie].'
B.6.68	And alle kynne crafty men þat *konne* lyuen in truþe,
B.6.122	Somme leide hir le[g] aliry as swiche lo[r]els *konneþ*
B.6.149	Ne Postles, but þei preche *konne* and haue power of þe bisshop:
B.6.253	'Yet I preie [þee]', quod Piers, 'p[u]r charite, and [þow] *konne*
B.7.42	And nameliche of Innocentȝ þat noon yuel *konneþ*:
B.7.115	'Peter!' quod þe preest þoo, 'I *kan* no pardon fynde
B.8.6	Was neuere wiȝt as I wente þat me wisse *kouþe*
B.8.76	'Artow þouȝt?' quod I þoo; 'þow *koudest* me [telle]
B.8.115	'But wit *konne* wisse þee', quod þoȝt, 'where þo þre dwelle
B.8.129	Here is wil wolde wite if wit *koude* [hym teche];
B.9.25	'What kynnes þyng is kynde?' quod I; '*kanstow* me telle?'
B.10.19	[That] *kan* con[strue] deceites and conspire wronges
B.10.21	[That] swiche craftes k[*onne*] to counseil [are] cleped;
B.10.33	And *kan* telle of Tobye and of [þe] twelue Apostles
B.10.44	Thei *konne* na moore mynstralcie ne Musik men to glade
B.10.141	He bicom so confus he *kouþe* noȝt [mele],
B.10.172	[So] shaltow come to Clergie þat *kan* manye [wittes,
B.10.226	And [er] I com to clergie [*koude* I] neuere stynte.
B.10.253	Alle þe clerkes vnder crist ne *koude* þis assoille,
B.10.338	Kynghod [and] knyȝthod, [for auȝt] I *kan* awayte,
B.10.349	'Contra!' quod I, 'by crist! þat *kan* I [wiþseye],
B.10.464	Than are þise [kete] clerkes þat *konne* manye bokes,
B.10.473	That euere þe[i] *kouþe* [konne on book] moore þan Credo in deum patrem,
B.10.473	That euere þe[i] kouþe [*konne* on book] moore þan Credo in deum patrem,
B.11.166	Ther no clergie ne *kouþe*, ne konnyng of lawes.
B.11.256	And alle þe wise þat euere were, by auȝt I *kan* aspye,
B.11.313	That crouneþ swiche goddes knyȝtes, þat *konneþ* noȝt sapienter
B.11.389	For is no creature vnder crist *can* formen hymseluen,
B.11.414	Thow sholdest haue knowen þat clergie *kan* & [conceyued] moore þoruȝ Res[on],
B.12.8	In þyn olde elde, þat yuele *kan* suffre
B.12.65	As þe book bereþ witnesse to burnes þat *kan* rede:
B.12.100	Na moore *kan* no Clerk but if he cauȝte it first þoruȝ bokes.
B.12.107	Na moore *kan* a kynde witted man, but clerkes hym teche,
B.12.162	That oon [*kan*] konnynge and kan swymmen and dyuen;
B.12.162	That oon [kan] konnynge and *kan* swymmen and dyuen;
B.12.165	He þat neuere ne dyued ne noȝt *kan* of swymmyng,
B.12.169	'That swymme *kan* noȝt', I seide, 'it semeþ to my wittes.'
B.12.171	That he þat knoweþ clergie *kan* sonner arise
B.12.181	And haþ no contricion er he come to shrifte; & þanne *kan* he litel telle
B.12.216	Alle þe clerkes vnder crist ne *kouþe* þe skile assoille:
B.12.271	Ne of Sortes ne of Salomon no scripture *kan* telle.
B.13.131	'I *kan* noȝt heron', quod Conscience, 'ac I knowe Piers.
B.13.135	That no clerk ne *kan*, as crist bereþ witnesse:
B.13.174	*Kan* noȝt [parfournen] a pees bitwene [þe pope] and hise enemys,
B.13.175	Ne bitwene two cristene kynges *kan* no wiȝt pees make
B.13.178	That Pacience þ[o] most passe, 'for pilgrymes *konne* wel lye'.
B.13.223	To Conscience what craft he *kouþe*, and to what contree he wolde.
B.13.228	*Couþe* I lye [and] do men lauȝe, þanne lacchen I sholde,
B.13.230	Ac for I *kan* neiþer taboure ne trompe ne telle no gestes,
B.13.247	Hadde ich a clerc þat *couþe* write I wolde caste hym a bille
B.13.308	Askeþ at hym or at hym and he yow *kan* telle.
B.13.310	And what I *kouþe* and knew and what kyn I com of'.
B.13.338	And seye þat no clerc ne *kan*, ne crist as I leue,
B.14.12	And *kouþe* I neuere, by crist! kepen it clene an houre
B.14.208	Ther þe poore is put bihynde, and parauenture moore
B.14.277	'I *kan* noȝt construe', quod haukyn; 'ye moste kenne me þis on englissh.'
B.15.2	Er I *koude* kyndely knowe what was dowel
B.15.25	And for þat I *kan* [and] knowe called am I mens;
B.15.45	Thow woldest knowe and *konne* þe cause of alle [hire] names,
B.15.49	I wolde I knewe and *kouþe* kyndely in myn herte.'
B.15.53	That any creature sholde *konne* al except crist oone.
B.15.62	Coueitise to *konne* and to knowe scienc[e]
B.15.171	Corseþ he no creature ne he *kan* bere no wraþe,
B.15.181	He *kan* portreye wel þe Paternoster and peynte it with Aues
B.15.301	And if þei *kouþe* han ycarped, by crist! as I trowe,
B.15.303	[For al þe curteisie þat beestes *konne* ne kidde þat folk ofte,
B.15.369	Neiþer þei *konneþ* ne knoweþ oon cours bifore anoþer.
B.15.374	[That *kan* versifie faire ne formaliche enditen],
B.15.375	[Ne] nauȝt oon among an hundred þat an Auctour *kan* construwe,
B.15.381	That sholde *konne* and knowe alle kynnes clergie
B.15.476	Riȝt so rude men þat litel reson *konneþ*
B.15.608	*Konne* þe firste clause of oure bileue, Credo in deum patrem omnipotentem,
B.15.611	Til þei *kouþe* speke and spelle et in Spiritum sanctum,
B.16.41	Wiþ alle þe wiles þat he *kan*, and waggeþ þe roote
B.16.101	Til he weex a faunt þoruȝ hir flessh and of fightyng *kouþe*
B.17.32	He *kan* noȝt siggen þe somme, and some arn in his lappe.
B.17.254	Be vnkynde to þyn euenecristene and al þat þow *kanst* bidde,
B.17.259	For vnkyndenesse quencheþ hym þat he *kan* noȝt shyne
B.18.32	That, for al þat deeþ *kan* do, wiþInne þre daies to walke
B.18.46	'Crucifige!' quod a Cachepol, '[he *kan* of wicchecraft]!'
B.19.26	'Thow knowest wel', quod Conscience, 'and þow *konne* reson,
B.19.99	As it bicomeþ a conquerour to *konne* manye sleightes,
B.19.203	And made hem *konne* and knowe alle kynne langages.
B.19.209	Knele now', quod Conscience, 'and if þow *kanst* synge
B.19.216	To alle kynne creatures þat [k]*an* hi[se] fyue wittes,
B.19.255	And who þat moost maistries *kan* he myldest of berynge.
B.19.315	'Hareweþ alle þat *konneþ* kynde wit by conseil of þise docto[urs],
B.19.398	Ne after Conscience, by crist! while I *kan* selle
B.19.411	Man to me þat me *kouþe* telle of Cardinale vertues,
B.20.6	'[*Coudes*]tow noȝt excuse þee as dide þe kyng and oþere;
B.20.16	And þouȝ he come so to a clooþ and *kan* no bettre cheuyssaunce
B.20.206	And loke þow *konne* som craft er þow come þennes.'
B.20.231	Ac for þei *kouþe* noȝt wel hir craft Conscience forsook hem.
B.20.304	Conscience called a leche þat *koude* wel shryue:
B.20.310	If any surgien were [in] þe seg[e] þat softer *koude* plastre.
B.20.313	'Ther is a Surgien in þ[e] sege þat softe *kan* handle,
B.20.336	'I am a Surgien', seide þe [frere], 'and salues *kan* make.
B.20.337	Conscience knoweþ me wel and what I *kan* boþe.'
B.20.342	But þow *konne* [any] craft þow comest nouȝt herInne.
B.20.356	'Thow art welcome', quod Conscience; '*kanstow* heele sike?
C.Pr.35	And summe murthes to make, as mynstrels *conneth*,
C.Pr.199	A mous þat moche good *couthe*, as me tho thoughte,
C.Pr.208	Wyttenesse at holy wryt whoso *kan* rede:
C.Pr.219	For hadde ȝe ratones ȝoure [reik] ȝe *couthe* nat reule ȝowsuluen.'
C.1.144	And this y trowe be treuth; [ho] *kan* tecche þe bettre
C.1.191	And ben acombred with coueytise: thei *can* nouȝt [out crepe]
C.2.14	Here robynge was rychere þen y rede *couthe*;

C. 2.49   Knowe hem wel yf þou *kanst* and kepe the fro hem alle
C. 2.64   Y *kan* nouȝt rykene þe route þat ran aboute mede.
C. 2.239   For a *can* on here craft and knoweth manye gommes.
C. 3.3   The kyng callede a clerke–y *can* nat his name–
C. 3.16   Confortede here as they *couthe* by the clerkes leue
C. 3.219   'Excuce the yf thow *kanst*,' y can no more segge
C. 3.219   'Excuce the yf thow kanst,' y *can* no more segge
C. 3.399   And coueyte þe case, when thei *couthe* vnderstande,
C. 4.57   Ne [no] ferthyng therfore, for nouhte y *couthe* plede.
C. 5.12   'Can thow seruen,' he sayde, 'or syngen in a churche
C. 5.89   Quod Consience, 'by Crist, y *can* nat se this lyeth;
C. 6.56   Ascuth at hym or at h[ym] and he ȝow *can* telle
C. 6.58   And what y *couthe* and knewe and what kyn y cam of."
C. 6.82   And segge þat no clerk ne *can*, ne Crist as y leue,
C. 6.196   Thenne cam couetyse; y *can* hym nat descreue;
C. 6.204   But yf a lous *couthe* lepe, y leue [and] y trowe,
C. 6.294   Thow art an vnkynde creature; y *can* the nat assoile
C. 6.325   What byful of this feloun y *can* nat fayre shewe;
C. 6.386   They *couthe* nat by here Consience acorden for treuthe
C. 6.426   Of þat y haue trespased with tonge, y *can* nat telle how ofte;
C. 6.432   And spilde þat y aspele myhte; y *kan* nat speke for shame
C. 7.10   Y *can* nat parfitly my paternoster as þe prest hit syngeth;
C. 7.11   Y *can* rymes of robyn hode and of randolf Erle of Chestre
C. 7.25   Vigilies and fastyngdayes y *can* forȝeten hem alle
C. 7.31   ȝut *kan* y nother solfe ne synge ne a seyntes lyf rede;
C. 7.32   Ac y *can* fynden in a feld and in a forlong an hare
C. 7.34   Ac y *can* nat construe catoun ne clergialiche reden.
C. 7.43   Y am vnkynde aȝen his cortesie [and] *can* nat vnderstande hit
C. 7.158   Ac þer was wye non so wys þat the way thider *couthe*
C. 7.178   [Can]st [thow] wissen vs [þe w]ay whoderout treuth woneth?'
C. 7.191   In alle kyne craftes þat he *couthe* deuise
C. 8.21   Y wolde y *couthe*,' quod the knyhte, 'by Crist and his moder!
C. 8.69   And alle kyne crafty men þat *conne* lyue in treuthe,
C. 8.129   [Somme] leyde here legges alery as suche lorelles *conneth*
C. 8.200   In alle kyne trewe craft þat man *couthe* deuyse.
C. 8.266   Yf ȝe *can* or knowe eny kyne thyng[e] of fisyk
C. 9.155   And *can* eny craft in caes he wolde hit vse,
C. 9.156   Thorw which craft a *couthe* come to bred and to ale
C. 9.282   For y *can* construe vch a word and kennen hit the an englische.'
C. 9.289   'Peter!' quod the prest tho, 'y *kan* no pardoun fynde
C.10.6   Was neuere wihte [as y wente] þat me wisse *couthe*
C.10.74   'Art thow thouht?' quod y tho; 'thow *couthest* me wisse
C.10.112   Elles knowe y noen þat *can* in none kynneryche.'
C.10.125   Here is oen wolde ywyte yf wit *couthe* teche;
C.10.151   'What kynne thyng is kynde?' quod y; '*canst* thow me telle?'
C.10.264   That no cortesye *can*, bute [knowe late here be]
C.11.16   Ho *can* caste and contreue to disseyue þe ri[gh]tfole,
C.11.18   That coueite *can* and caste thus ar cleped into consayle:
C.11.19   He is reuerensed and yrobed þat *can* robbe þe peple
C.11.30   And *can* telle of treuthe and of þe twelue aposteles
C.11.98   So with þat clergie *can* and consail of scripture
C.11.99   Thow shalt *kunne* and knowe kyndeliche dowel.'
C.11.144   And al þat holi churche herof *can* þe lere
C.11.154   Alle þe Clerkes vnder Crist ne *couthe* this assoile
C.11.211   Neuere to man so moche þat man *can* of telle,
C.11.225   Thenne al þe kynde wyt þat ȝe *can* bothe and kunnyng of ȝoure bokes.
C.12.142   And alle þe wyse þat euere were, by auhte y *can* aspye,
C.12.176   Tulius, tolomeus–y *can* nat tel here names–
C.13.125   That crouneth suche goddes knyhtes þat *conne* [nat] sapienter
C.13.207   For is no creature vnder Crist þat *can* hymsulue make
C.13.208   And if creatures cristene *couth* make hemsulue
C.13.222   Thow sholdest haue yknowe þat clergie *ca[n]* & conseyued mor[e] [thorw] resoun
C.14.10   And thenne dost thow wel, withoute drede; ho *can* do bet no force.
C.14.11   Clerkes þat *conne* al, y hope they can do bettere;
C.14.11   Clerkes þat conne al, y hope they *can* do bettere;
C.14.45   No more *can* no clerk but if hit come of bokes.
C.14.52   No more *can* a kynde witted man, but clerkes hym teche,
C.14.72   Kynde wittede men [c]*an* a clergie by hemsulue;
C.14.106   That oen hath connyng and *can* swymmen and dyuen;
C.14.109   'He þat *can* nat swymmen,' y sayde, 'hit semeth he alle wittes.'
C.14.111   Þat he þat knoweth clergie *conne* sonnore aryse
C.14.121   And hath no contricion ar he come to shrifte; and thenne *can* he lytel telle,
C.14.155   Alle þe Clerkes vnder Crist ne *couthe* [þe skyle] assoile:
C.14.192   Ne of sortes ne of salamon n[o] scripture *can* telle
C.15.123   'Y haue yseide,' quod þat segg, 'y *can* sey no bettre.
C.15.151   Saue Concience and clergie y *couthe* no mo aspye.
C.15.172   *Can* nat parfourme a pees of the pope and his enemyes
C.15.192   What craft þat he *couthe* and cortey[s]liche he saide:
C.15.197   'Munstracye *can* y nat moche bote make men merye,

C.15.202   [Cou]de y lye and do men lawhe thenne lacchen y scholde
C.15.204   [Ac for] y *can* nat tabre ne trompy ne telle [no] gestes,
C.16.49   There þe pore is potte behynde and parauntur *can* more
C.16.117   'Y *can* nat construe al this,' quod Actiua vita.
C.16.185   And [for] þat y *can* and knowe ycald am y [mens];
C.16.207   Thow woldest knowe and *conne* þe cause of all here names
C.16.211   Y wolde y knewe and *couthe* kyndeliche in myn herte.'
C.16.215   That eny creature sholde *conne* al excepte crist one.
C.16.224   Coueytyse to *conne* and to knowe scienc[e]
C.16.322   And also a *can* clergie, credo in deum patrem,
C.17.25   Y *can* nat rykene hem riȝt now ne reherse here names
C.17.105   Noþer they [conn]*eth* ne [know]eth a cours by[fore] anoþer.
C.17.110   Þat *can* versifye vayre or formallych endite
C.17.111   Ne [*can*] construe kyndelyche þat poetes made.
C.17.115   That sholde þe seuene ars *conne* and assoile a quodlibet
C.17.293   Ac we cristene *conneth* þe [crede] and haen of oure tonge
C.17.316   *Conne* þe furste clause of oure bileue, credo in deum patrem,
C.17.319   Til they *couthe* speke and spele et in spiritum sanctum,
C.18.2   Thow *couthest* telle me and teche me [in] charite [to] leue.'
C.18.45   And with alle þe wyles þat he *can* waggeth þe tayl
C.19.26   And six thousand mo,' quod fayth; 'y [*can*] nat seyn here names.'
C.19.33   He *can* no certeyn somme telle and somme aren in his lappe.
C.19.220   Be vnkynde to thyn emcristene and al þat thow *canst* bidde,
C.19.225   For vnkyndenesse quencheth hym þat he *can* nat shine
C.20.31   That for al þat deth *can* do, withynne thre dayes to walke
C.20.46   'Crucifige!' q[uo]d a cachepol, 'he *can* of wycchecrafte!'
C.20.71   And somme saide, 'he *can* of soercerie; goed is þat we assaie
C.20.213   Ho *couthe* kyndeliche whit colour descreue
C.21.26   'Thow knowest wel,' quod Concience, 'and þou *kunne* resoun,
C.21.99   As hit bicometh a conquerour to *conne* mony sleythes
C.21.203   And made hem *konne* & knowe alle kyne langages.
C.21.209   Knele now,' quod Consience, 'and yf thow *canst* synge,
C.21.216   To alle kyne creatures þat *can* his fyue wittes,
C.21.255   And [ho] þat moest maistries *can* be myldest of berynge.
C.21.315   'Harweth alle þa[t] *conneth* kynde wit bi consail of [this] doctours
C.21.398   Ne aftur Consience, bi Crist! [while] y *c[an]* sulle
C.21.411   Man to me þat me *couthe* telle of cardinal[e] vertues
C.22.6   'Couthest thow nat excuse the as dede the kyng and oþere:
C.22.16   And thow he come so to a cloth and *can* no bettere cheuesaunce
C.22.206   And loke thow *conne* som craft ar thow come thennes.'
C.22.231   A[c] for they *couthe* nat wel here crafte Consience forsoek hem.
C.22.304   Consience calde a leche þat *couthe* wel shryue:
C.22.310   Yf eny surgien were in þe sege that softur *couthe* plastre.
C.22.313   'Ther is a surgien in the sege that softe *can* handele
C.22.336   'Y am a surgien,' saide the frere, 'and salues can make.
C.22.337   Consience knoweth me wel and what y *can* bothe.'
C.22.342   Bote thow *conne* eny craft thow comest nat hereynne.
C.22.356   'Thow art welcome,' quod Consience; '*can[st]* thow hele syke?

konnyng *adj* conning *ppl.* A 2 cunnyng; B 4 konnyng (1) konnynge (3);
    C 5 connynge (4) connyngest (1)

A. 3.33   Þere *cunnyng* clerkis shuln clokke behynde.'
A.11.273   For alle *cunnyng* clerkis siþþe crist ȝede on erþe
B. 3.34   Ther *konnynge* clerkes shul clokke bihynde.'
B. 3.347   Ac yow failed a *konnynge* clerk þat kouþe þe leef han torned.
B.11.70   And yet I cryde on my Confessour þat [so *konnyng*] heeld hym]:
B.12.174   For if þe clerk be *konnynge* he knoweþ what is synne,
C. 3.37   There *connynge* clerkes shal clokke byhynde.'
C. 6.42   And *connyngest* of my craft, Clerkysh oþer other,
C.10.257   For coueytise of catel and *connynge* chapmen;
C.14.102   The[n] *connynge* clerkes of kynde vnderstondynge.
C.14.114   For yf þe clerke be *connynge* [he] knoweth what is synne

konnyng *ger* conninge *ger.* A 1 connyng; B 13 konnyng (5) konnynge (8);
    C 18 connyng (7) connynge (6) connynges (1) konnyng (1) konnynge
    (1) kunnyng (1) kunnynges (1)

A.10.50   For þoruȝ his *connyng* is kept caro & anima
B.10.453   *Konnyng* [and] clergie] to conclude hem alle".
B.10.455   And myȝte no kyng ouercomen hym as by *konnynge* of speche.
B.11.166   Ther no clergie ne kouþe, ne *konnyng* of lawes.
B.11.212   And be we noȝt vnkynde of oure catel, ne of oure *konnyng* neiþer,
B.11.299   That han neiþer *konnynge* ne kyn, but a crowne one
B.11.302   [Moore þan cure] for *konnyng* or 'knowen for clene [of] berynge'.
B.12.66   Of quod scimus comeþ Clergie, [a] *konnynge* of heuene,
B.12.162   That oon [kan] *konnynge* and kan swymmen and dyuen;
B.13.15   Of kynde and of his *konnynge*, and how curteis he is to bestes.
B.13.292   [Or for his crafty *konnynge* or of clerkes þe wisest,
B.19.234   And some he kennede craft and *konnynge* of sighte,
B.19.253   '[That al craft and *konnyng* come] of my ȝifte.
B.19.458   And coloureþ it for a *konnynge* and a clene lyuynge'.
C.11.92   Alle kynne *kunnynges* and comsynges of dowel.
C.11.222   Ac y countresegge the nat, clergie, ne thy *connyng*, scripture;
C.11.225   Thenne al þe kynde wyt þat ȝe can bothe and *kunnyng* of ȝoure bokes.

C.11.278   *Connyng* and clergie to conclude [hem] alle".
C.11.280   And myhte no kyng ouercome hym as in *connynge* of speche.
C.11.290   Comuneliche then clerkes most knowyng in *konnyng*
C.13.113   That [hath] noþer *connyng* ne kyn bote a croune one
C.13.232   Ne clergie of his *connynge* kepeth [t]he nat shewe.
C.14.19   Ac comunlyche *connynge* and vnkynde ryche[sse],
C.14.34   And clergie a *connynge* of kynde wittes techyng.
C.14.36   Then eny *connyng* of kynde wit but clergi hit reule.
C.14.106   That oen hath *connyng* and can swymmen and dyuen;
C.15.18   Of kynde and [of] his *connynge* and what connynge he ȝaf bestes
C.15.18   Of kynde and [of] his connynge and what *connynge* he ȝaf bestes
C.15.131   Alle kyne *connynges* and alle kyne craftes
C.21.234   And somme he kende craft and *konnynge* of syhte,
C.21.253   'That all craft and *connyng* c[o]m[e] of my ȝefte.
C.21.458   And coloureth hit for a *connyng* and a clene lyuynge.'

koude(st > konne; kouȝed > cogheþ; kouþe > kidde,konne; kud > kidde; kulde
kull(e -ed > killen; kultour > cultour; kunne > konne; kunnyng(es > konnyng;
kusse kuste > kissen; kut > kutte; kuth(e > kiþ

kutte v *cutten v.* A 1 kitte; B 4 kitten (1) kut (1) kutte (2); C 3 kut (1)
       kutte (2)
A. 4.140   But he be cokewald ycald, *kitte* of my nose.'
B. 4.164   But he be knowe for a Cokewold *kut* of my nose.'
B. 5.32   [He] bad Bette *kutte* a bouȝ ouþer tweye
B. 6.188   And *kitten* hir copes and courtepies hem maked
B.20.56   In ech a contree þer he cam he *kutte* awey truþe
C. 4.159   But he be knowe for a cokewold *kut* of my nose.'
C. 5.134   He bad b[e]tte *kutte* a bo[u]he or twene
C.22.56   In vch a Contrey ther he cam [he] *kutte* awey treuthe

kuttepurs n *cuttepurs n.* A 1 cuttepurs; B 1; C 1 cottepors
A. 6.115   'Be crist,' quaþ a *cuttepurs*, 'I haue no kyn þere.'
B. 5.630   'By Crist!' quod a *kuttepurs*, 'I haue no kyn þere.'
C. 7.283   'By Crist!' quod a *cottepors*, 'y haue no kyn there.'

L

labor(ed) > labouren

laborer n *labourer n.* A 9 labourer (3) laboureris (6); B 11 laborer (2) laborers (9); C 12 laborer (4) laboreres (5) laborers (3)

A. 2.45   For lerid, for lewid, for *laboureris* of þropis,
A. 3.234   Þat *laboreris* & louȝ folk taken of here maistris
A. 3.276   And make of lawe a *labourer*, such loue shal arise.'
A. 4.130   Þat lawe shal ben a *labourer* & lede afeld donge,
A. 5.135   For *laboureris* & louȝ folk þat lay be h[y]mselue;
A. 6.35   Þere is no *labourer* in his lordsshipe þat he louiþ beter
A. 7.291   *Laboureris* þat haue no land [to] lyue on [but] here handis
A. 7.299   Suche lawis to loke *laboureris* to chast[e].
A. 8.63   Alle libbyng *laboureris* þat lyuen be here hondis,
B.Pr.223   Of alle kynne lybbynge *laborers* lopen forþ somme,
B. 3.255   That *laborers* and lowe [lewede] folk taken of hire maistres
B. 3.300   And make of lawe a *laborer*; swich loue shal arise
B. 4.147   That lawe shal ben a *laborer* and lede afeld donge,
B. 5.219   For *laborers* and lowe folk þat lay by hymselue.
B. 6.307   *Laborers* þat haue no land to lyue on but hire handes
B. 6.318   Swiche lawes to loke *laborers* to [chaste].
B. 7.61   Alle libbyng *laborers* þat lyuen [by] hir hondes,
B.10.466   Than Plowmen and pastours and [pouere] commune *laborers*,
B.10.478   Right so lewed [*laborers*] and of litel knowyng
B.15.330   And on hemself som, and swiche as ben hir *laborers*;
C. 3.310   That bothe the lord and the *laborer* be leely yserued.
C. 3.348   As a leel *laborer* byleueth [with] his maister
C. 3.453   And maky of lawe [a] *laborer*; suche loue shal aryse
C. 4.144   That lawe shal ben a *laborer* and lede afelde donge
C. 5.73   And lordes sones here *laboreres* and leyde here rentes to wedde
C. 6.227   For *laboreres* and louh folk þat lay by hymsulue.
C. 8.329   *Laborers* þat han no lond to lyue on but here handes
C. 8.338   Suche lawes to lerne *laboreres* to greue.
C. 9.58   Alle libbyng *laborers* þat lyuen with here handes
C.11.251   Laste ȝe be loste as þe *laboreres* were þat lab[o]red vnder Noe.
C.11.293   Lewed lele *laboreres* and land tulyng peple
C.11.299   Ac lewede *laborers* of litel vnderstondyng

laboreth labory > labouren

laboryng ger *labouringe ger.* C 1

C. 8.250   And ledares for here *laboryng* ouer al þe lordes godes;

labour n *labour n.* A 1; B 10; C 18 labor (1) labour (15) laboure (2)

A. 9.73   And þoruȝ his *labour* or his lond his liflode wynneþ,
B.Pr.181   And leten hire *labour* lost and al hire longe studie.
B. 6.251   The freke þat fedeþ hymself wiþ his feiþful *labour*
B. 8.82   And þoruȝ his *labour* or his land his liflode wynneþ,
B.12.163   That ooþer is lewed of þat *labour*, lerned neuere swymme.
B.14.130   And greet likynge to lyue wiþouten *labour* of bodye,
B.14.199   Ellis is al youre *labour* lost–lo, how men writeþ
B.14.313   The eighteþe is a lele *labour* and looþ to take moore
B.17.250   Al þi *labour* is lost and al þi long trauaille;
B.19.232   They lelly to lyue by *labour* of tonge,
B.19.237   And lyue, by þat *labour*], a lele lif and a trewe.
C.Pr.147   With lele *labour* to lyue while lif on londe lasteth.
C.Pr.198   And leten here *labour* ylost and al here longe study.
C. 5.42   Yf y be *labour* sholde lyuen and lyflode deseruen,
C. 5.43   That *laboure* þat y lerned beste þerwith lyuen y sholde:
C. 5.85   Is the leuest *labour* þat oure lord pleseth.
C. 8.196   But lyflode for his *la[b]our* and his loue at nones.
C. 8.260   Thorw eny lele *labour* as thorw lymes and handes:
C. 9.199   And summe lyuede by here letterure and *labour* of here handes
C. 9.208   Long *labour* and litte wynnynge and at the laste they aspyde
C. 9.210   Forthy lefte they here *labour*, thise lewede knaues,
C.10.79   And thorw lele *labour* lyueth and loueth his emcristene
C.14.107   That oþer is lewed of þat *labour*, lerned neuere swymme.
C.15.199   Of [m]y *labour* th[ey] lauhe, þe lasse and þe more;
C.16.40   Elles is alle oure *labour* loest–loo how men writeth
C.16.147   The eyȝte is a lel *labour* and loeth to take more
C.19.216   Al thy *labor* is loste and al thy longe trauaile;
C.21.232   They leely to lyue bi *labour* of tonge
C.21.237   And lyue by þat *laboure* a leele lyf and a trewe.

laboure > labour, labouren

labouren v *labouren v.* A 5 laboure (3) labouren (1) laboureþ (1); B 8 laboure (5) laboured (1) labouren (1) laboureþ (1); C 17 labore (2) labored (3) laboreth (1) labory (9) laboure (1) ylabored (1)

A. 7.13   Lokiþ forþ ȝoure lynen & *laboureþ* þeron faste.
A. 7.28   A[nd] ek *laboure* for þi loue al my lif tyme,
A. 7.116   'We haue none [lymes] to *laboure* wiþ, lord, ygracid be ȝe;
A. 7.218   & *labouren* for þi liflode, & so oure lord hiȝte;
A. 7.256   And lerne to *laboure* wiþ lond lest liflode hym faile.
B. 6.26   And [ek] *labour[e]* for þi loue al my lif tyme,
B. 6.124   'We haue no lymes to *laboure* with; lord, ygraced be [y]e!
B. 6.234   And *laboure* for þi liflode, and so oure lord hiȝte;
B. 6.272   And lerne to *laboure* wiþ lond [lest] liflode [hym faille].
B.15.187   *Labouren* in [a] lauendrye wel þe lengþe of a Mile,
B.19.236   And some he lered to *laboure* [on lond and on watre
B.19.384   That han *laboured* lelly al þis lenten tyme.
B.20.239   Than he þat *laboureþ* for liflode and leneþ it beggeris.
C. 5.8   And lymes to *labory* with and louede wel fare
C. 5.45   The lomes þat y *labore* with and lyflode deserue.
C. 5.69   Thyse bylongeth to *labory* and lordes kyn to serue.
C. 8.25   And *labory* for tho thow louest al my lyf tyme,
C. 8.135   [We haue] none lymes to *labory* with, lord god we thonketh.'
C. 8.213   Hit is nat for loue, leue hit, thei *labore* thus faste
C. 8.220   How y myhte amaystre hem to louye and *labory*
C. 8.249   And þat best *labored* best was alloued
C. 8.254   Þat leely hadde *ylabored* and thenne the lord sayde:
C. 8.293   And lerne to *labory* with lond lest lyflode h[y]m fayle.
C. 9.103   And lymes to *labory* with and lollares lyf vsen
C. 9.224   Lewede men to *labory*; lordes to honte
C. 9.246   Or *labory* for here lyflode as þe lawe wolde?
C.11.251   Laste ȝe be loste as þe *laboreres* were þat lab[o]red vnder Noe.
C.21.236   And som he lered to *laboure* a londe and a watre
C.21.384   That haen *labored* lelly al this lenten tyme.
C.22.239   Then he þat *laboreth* for lyflode and leneth hit beggares.

labouris > laborer

lacchen v *lacchen v.(1)* A 7 lacche (2) lauȝte (2) lauȝth (1) lauȝthe (1) lauȝþe (1); B 15 lacche (5) lacchen (2) laccheþ (1) laughte (1) lauȝte (6); C 14 lacche (4) lacchen (3) lache (1) laghte (1) lauhte (5)

A. 1.30   And leccherie h[i]m *lauȝte* & lay be hem boþe;
A. 2.167   And ȝif ȝe *lacche* leiȝere let him not askape
A. 3.24   Þanne *lauȝte* hy leue, þise lordis at mede.
A. 5.196   As whoso leide lynes to *lacche* wiþ [foules].
A.12.42   Þat lady þan low and *lauȝthe* me in here armes
A.12.55   Þus we *lauȝþe* oure leue, lowtyng at onys,
A.12.96   Þou shalt be *lauȝth* into lyȝth with loking of an eye
B.Pr.150   And ouerleep hem liȝtliche and *lauȝte* hem at wille
B. 1.30   And Leccherie hym *lauȝte*, and lay by hem boþe;
B. 2.206   And if ye *lacche* lyere lat hym noȝt ascapen
B. 3.25   Thanne *lauȝte* þei leue, þise lordes, at Mede.
B. 5.348   As whoso leiþ lynes to *lacche* [wiþ] foweles.
B. 6.228   And biloue þee amonges [lowe] men: so shaltow *lacche* grace.'
B.11.223   And lawe is looþ to louye but if he *lacche* siluer.
B.11.301   He [ouȝte no] bileue, as I leue, to *lacche* þoruȝ his croune
B.13.228   Couþe I lye [and] do men lauȝe, þanne *lacchen* I sholde
B.15.240   For hir lawe dureþ ouerlonge but if þei *lacchen* siluer,
B.16.50   Thanne liberum arbitrium *laccheþ* þe [bridde] plan[k]e
B.16.86   And Piers for pure tene þat a pil he [*l]auȝte*,
B.17.151   Seinte Marie, a mayde, and mankynde *lauȝte*:
B.18.326   And þo þat oure lord louede into his light he *laughte*,
B.20.152   Lyf lepte aside and *lauȝte* hym a lemman.
C.Pr.171   And ouerlep hem lightliche and *laghte* hem at wille
C. 1.101   And neuer leue for loue in hope to *lacche* syluer.
C. 1.204   To lere the what loue is;' and leue at me she *lauhte*.
C. 2.141   For by lesynges ȝe *lacchen* largeliche mede.
C. 2.218   And yf ȝe *lacchen* lyare lat hym nat askape
C. 3.26   [W]henne they hadde *lauhte* here leue at this lady mede
C. 3.391   He þat mede may *lacche* maketh lytel tale;
C. 6.406   As hoso layth lynes for to *lacche* foules.
C. 9.141   Loken louhliche to *lacche* men Almesse,
C.15.202   [Cou]de y lye and do men lawhe thenne *lacchen* y scholde
C.16.365   For ouerlong is here lawe but yf þay *lacche* siluer.

353

C.18.118 That libera voluntas dei *lauhte* þe myddel Shoriare
C.19.125 Seynte marie, a mayden, and mankynde *lauhte*:
C.22.152 Lyf lepte asyde and *lauhte* hym a lemman.

lacchesse > lachesse

lacchynge ger *lacching ger.(1)* A 1 lacching; B 1
A. 1.101 And neuere leue h[e]m for loue ne *lacching* of ȝeftis;
B. 1.103 And neuere leue hem for loue ne *lacchynge* of [yiftes];_

lachdraweres n *lacche n.* C 2 lachdraweres (1) lachedraweres (1)
C. 8.286 And thouh lyares and *l[a]chdraweres* and lollares knocke
C. 9.193 Thise lollares, *lachedraweres*, lewede Ermytes

lache > lacchen; lachedraweres > lachdrawere

lachesse n *lachesse n.* A 1 lacchesse; B 1; C 3 lacchesse (2) lachesse (1)
A. 9.32 Þere were þe manis lif lost for *lacchesse* of hymselue.
B. 8.36 [There] were [þe mannes] lif lost [for] *lachesse* of hymselue.
C. 8.252 The lord for his *lachesse* and his luther sleuthe
C. 9.268 Y leue, for thy *lacchesse*, thow lesest many wetheres
C. 9.278 Loke now, for thy *lacchesse*, what lawe wol the graunte:

lack- > lakke; lacles > laklees; lad > leden

ladde n *ladde n.(1) &> leden* B 1 laddes; C 3 ladde (2) laddes (1)
B.19.32 To make lordes of *laddes* of lond þat he wynneþ
C. 3.248 The leste *ladde* þat longeth with hym, be þe londe ywonne
C. 8.194 There was no *ladde* þat lyuede þat ne lowede hym to Peres
C.21.32 To make lordes of *laddes* of lond þat he wynneth

laddere > laddre; laddest > leden

laddre n *laddere n.* B 1; C 1 laddere
B.16.44 And leiþ a *laddre* þerto, of lesynges are þe ronges,
C.18.44 And leyth a *laddere* þerto, of lesynges ben þe ronges,

ladel n *ladel n.* B 1; C 1
B.19.279 And lerned men a *ladel* bugge wiþ a long stele
C.21.279 And lered men a *ladel* bugge with a longe stale

lady n *ladie n.* A 16 lady (13) ladies (3); B 35 lady (22) ladies (13); C 43 ladies (3) lady (29) ladyes (11)
A. 1.3 A louely *lady* of lire in lynene ycloþid
A. 2.7 I lokide on [my] left half as þat *lady* me tauȝte,
A. 3.80 'For my loue,' quaþ þat *lady*, 'loue hem ichone,
A. 3.101 'Ȝa lord,' quaþ þat *lady*, 'lord forbede ellis;
A. 3.153 Þis is þe lif of þat *lady*, now lord ȝif hire sorewe!
A. 3.162 'Nay lord,' quod þat *lady*, 'leu[iþ] him þe wers
A. 4.101 Til lordis & *ladies* louen alle treuþe,
A. 4.151 'And I assente,' quaþ þe king, 'be seinte marie my *lady*,
A. 5.54 Lecchour seide 'allas!' & to oure *lady* criede
A. 6.109 Largenesse þe *lady* let in wel manye.
A. 7.7 'Þis were a long lettyng,' quaþ a *lady* in a scleire;
A. 7.18 And ȝe loueliche *ladies* wiþ ȝour [longe] fyngris,
A.10.13 And seruiþ þis *lady* lelly boþe late and raþe.
A.10.43 For loue of þat *lady* þat lif is ynempnid.
A.11.203 Ne no leperis ouer lond *ladies* to shryue.
A.12.42 Þat *lady* þan low and lauȝthe me in here armes
B.Pr.95 And somme seruen as seruauntȝ lordes and *ladies*,
B. 1.3 A louely *lady* of leere in lynnen ycloþed
B. 2.7 I loked on my left half as þe *lady* me tauȝte
B. 2.43 And al is lieres ledynge þat [*lady*] is þus ywedded.
B. 2.52 Thus lefte me þat *lady* liggynge aslepe,
B. 3.54 And lakkeþ noȝt *ladies* þat louen wel þe same.
B. 3.91 'For my loue', quod þat *lady*, 'loue hem echone,
B. 3.112 'Ye, lord,' quod þat *lady*, 'lord forbede ellis!
B. 3.166 This is þe lif of þat *lady*, now lord ȝyue hire sorwe,
B. 3.175 'Nay lord', quod þat *lady*, 'leueþ hym þe werse
B. 3.337 'I leue wel, *lady*', quod Conscience, 'þat þi latyn be trewe.
B. 3.338 Ac þow art lik a *lady* þat radde a lesson ones
B. 4.114 Til lordes and *ladies* louen alle truþe
B. 4.188 'And I assente', seiþ þe kyng, 'by Seinte Marie my *lady*,
B. 5.71 Lechour seide 'allas!' and [to] oure *lady* cryde
B. 5.157 I was þe Prioresse potager and oþere pouere *ladies*,
B. 5.244 I haue lent lordes and *ladies* my chaffare
B. 5.396 Ac neiþer of oure lord ne of oure *lady* þe leeste þat euere was maked.
B. 5.623 Largenesse þe *lady* let in [wel] manye;
B. 6.7 'This were a long lettyng', quod a *lady* in a Scleyre.
B. 6.10 And ye louely *ladies* wiþ youre longe fyngres,
B. 9.13 To seruen þis *lady* leelly, boþe late and raþe.
B. 9.16 [By his leryng is lad þat *lady* Anima].
B. 9.23 Thise [sixe] ben set to [saue] þis *lady* anima
B. 9.55 For loue of þe *lady* anima þat lif is ynempned.
B.10.98 Ther þe lord ne þe *lady* likeþ noȝt to sitte.
B.11.19 For to lyue longe and *ladies* to louye,
B.13.421 Ye lordes and *ladies* and legates of holy chirche

B.14.125 And hir [*ladies*] also lyuede hir lif in murþe.
B.15.6 Lordes or *ladies* or any lif ellis,
B.15.309 And þanne wolde lordes and *ladies* be looþ to agulte,
B.15.322 Allas, lordes and *ladies*, lewed counseil haue ye
B.18.337 Thus ylik a Lusard wiþ a *lady* visage
B.20.104 Manye a louely *lady* and [hir] lemmans knyȝtes
B.20.345 And was my lordes leche and my *ladies* boþe.
C. 1.3 A louely *lady* of [lere] in lynnene [y]clothed
C. 1.116 Ac y wol lacky no lyf,' quod þat *lady* sothly;
C. 1.203 Loue hit,' quod þat *lady*; 'lette may y no lengore
C. 2.8 Y lokede [o]n my luft half as þe *lady* me tauhte
C. 2.18 'Leue *lady*,' quod y tho,'layn nought yf ȝe knowen.'
C. 2.46 And al is lyares ledynge th[at] *lady* is thus ywedded.
C. 2.55 Thus le[f]te me that *lady* lyggynge as aslepe,
C. 3.26 [W]henne they hadde lauhte here leue at this *lady* mede
C. 3.55 Loueliche þat *lady* laghynge sayde,
C. 3.58 And lacketh nat *ladyes* þat louyeth [wel] þe same.
C. 3.99 That louten for hem to oure lord and to oure *lady* bothe
C. 3.119 Loue hem for my loue,' quod this *lady* mede,
C. 3.143 [And marre þe with myschef], be seynte mary my *lady*,
C. 3.149 'Ȝe, lord,' quod that *lady*, 'lord hit me forbede
C. 3.213 Thus lereth this *lady* thi lond, now lord ȝeue here sorwe!
C. 3.221 'Nay, lord,' quod þat *lady*, 'leueth hym þe worse
C. 3.489 'I leue the, *lady*,' quod Consience, 'for þat latyn is trewe.
C. 3.490 Thow art lyk a *lady* þat a lessoun radde
C. 4.39 More then for oure lordes loue oþer oure *lady*, goddes moder.'
C. 4.109 Til lordes and *ladies* louen alle treuthe
C. 6.132 I was the Prioresse potager and oþer pore *ladies*
C. 6.138 Til "thow lixt!" and "thow lixt!" be *lady* ouer hem alle;
C. 6.142 That alle *ladyes* me lot[h]eth þat louyet[h] eny worschipe.
C. 6.170 Thenne seyde lecherye 'alas!' and to oure *lady* cryede,
C. 6.171 '*Lady*, to thy leue sone loute for me nouthe
C. 6.249 'Y haue lent lordes and *ladyes* þat louede me neuere aftur
C. 7.12 Ac of oure lord ne of oure *lady* þe leste þat euere was maked.
C. 7.81 Ȝe lordes and *ladies* and legatus of holy churche
C. 7.251 A ful leel *lady* vnlek hit of grace
C. 7.275 Largenesse þ[e] *lady* lat in ful monye,
C. 8.5 'Th[is] were a long lettyng,' quod [a] *lady* in a slayre;
C. 8.7 'Y preye ȝow for ȝoure profit,' quod Peres to þe *ladyes*,
C. 9.130 For þe lordes loue or þe *ladyes* þat they with longen.
C.10.140 To serue þat *lady* leely bot[h] late and rathe.
C.10.142 And by his leryng is lad þat *lady* Anima.
C.11.178 For to lyue longe and *ladyes* to louye
C.11.200 Y leue neuere þat lord ne *lady* þat lyueth her [o]n erthe
C.12.219 Lo! lordes, lo! and *ladyes*, taketh hede:
C.15.302 And lordes and *ladyes* ben cald for ledes þat they haue
C.17.44 Thenne wolde lordes and *ladyes* be loth to agulte
C.17.56 Allas, lordes and *ladyes*, lewede consayle haue ȝe
C.22.104 Many a louly *lady* and here lemmanes knyhtes
C.22.345 And was my lordes leche and my *ladyes* bothe.

lafte > leuen; laghynge > lauȝen; laghte > lacchen

lay n *lai n.(2) &> ligge* A 1 laies; B 2 lay (1) layes (1); C 2 lay (1) layes (1)
A. 9.57 To lerne þe *laies* þat louely [foulis] maden.
B. 8.66 To [lerne] þe *layes* [þat] louely foweles made.
B.13.456 Wiþ turpiloquio, a *l[a]y* of sorwe, and luciferis fiþele.
C. 7.116 With turpiloquio, a *lay* of sorwe and luciferes fythele,
C.10.65 To lythen here *layes* and here louely notes.

layd(e > leggen

layes n *lei n. &> lay, cf. lawe* C 1
C.21.43 And conquerour of his conqueste his *layes* and his large.

layk n *leik n. &> laike* B 1; C 1
B.14.244 And louely *layk* was it neuere bitwene þe longe and þe shorte.
C.16.84 And louely *layk* was hit neuere bytwene a longe and a short.

laike v *leiken v.* B 1; C 2 layk (1) layke (1)
B.Pr.172 And if hym list for to *laike* þanne loke we mowen
C.Pr.189 And yf [hym] lust for to *layke* than loke we mowe
C.16.176 *Layk* or leue, at my lykyng chese

layn v *leinen v. &> ligge* C 1
C. 2.18 'Leue lady,' quod y tho,'*layn* nought yf ȝe knowen.'

layth > leggen; layȝe > ligge; laiȝes > leyes

lakke v *lakken v.* A 3 lakke (1) lakkide (1) lakkiþ (1); B 34 lakke (14) lakked (2) lakkede (2) lakkedest (1) lakken (4) lakkeþ (9) lakkynge (1) ylakked (1); C 24 lacke (11) lacked (1) lacken (1) lacketh (1) lacky (1) lakke (3) lakked (2) lakkede (1) lakken (1) lakketh (2)
A. 2.17 And *lakkide* my lore to lordis aboute.
A. 5.229 [And] þeiȝ my liflode *lakke* leten I nille
A.11.143 For þere þat loue is lord *lakkiþ* neuere grace.

B. 2.21   And *ylakked* my lemman þat leautee is hoten,
B. 2.48   And *lakke* hem noȝt but lat hem worþe til leaute be Iustice
B. 3.54   And *lakkeþ* noȝt ladies þat louen wel þe same.
B. 5.133   To lye and to loure on my neȝebore and to *lakke* his chaffare.
B. 5.457   And þouȝ my liflode *lakke* leten I nelle
B. 6.225   Loue hem and *lakke* hem noȝt; lat god take þe vengeaunce;
B. 9.39   Right as a lord sholde make lettres; [if] hym *lakked* parchemyn,
B. 9.73   Alle þise *lakken* Inwit and loore [hem] bihoueþ.
B.10.191   For þere þat loue is ledere *lakke[þ]* neuere grace.
B.10.208   And alle þat *lakkeþ* vs or lyeþ oure lord techeþ vs to louye,
B.10.268   Alle þat *lakkeþ* any lif and lakkes han hemselue:
B.10.316   He loureþ on hym and [*lakkeþ*] hym: who [lered] hym curteisie?
B.11.2   And *lakked* me in latyn and liȝt by me sette,
B.11.106   Neiþer for loue [looue] it noȝt ne *lakke* it for enuye:
B.11.214   Forþi *lakke* no lif ooþer þouȝ he moore latyn knowe,
B.11.282   Ne *lakkeþ* neuere liflode, lynnen ne wollen.
B.11.289   Hem sholde *lakke* no liflode, neyþer lynnen ne wollen.
B.11.388   And er þow *lakke* my lif loke [þyn] be to preise.
B.11.396   For be a man fair or foul it falleþ noȝt to *lakke*
B.11.421   *Lakkedest* and losedest þyng þat longed noȝt to doone:
B.12.97   Forþi *lakke* þow neuere logik, lawe ne hise custumes,
B.13.264   And louren whan þei *lakken* hem; it is noȝt longe ypassed
B.13.286   *Lakkynge* lettrede men and lewed men boþe;
B.15.4   And some *lakkede* my lif–allowed it fewe–
B.15.204   And as a lyoun he lokeþ þer men *lakken* hise werkes.
B.15.249   Ac I ne *lakke* no lif, but lord amende vs alle,
B.15.253   *Lakkeþ* ne loseþ ne lokeþ vp sterne,
B.15.602   And þat his loore be lesynges, and *lakken* it alle,
B.17.297   Wol loue [þat lif] þat [*lakkeþ* charite],
B.19.112   And lawe *lakkede* þo for men louede noȝt hir enemys,
B.19.254   Lokeþ þat no[on] *lakke* ooþer, but loueþ as breþeren;
B.19.468   And if me *lakkeþ* to lyue by þe lawe wole I take it
B.20.210   'And þow loue lelly *lakke* shal þee neuere
B.20.249   And oþere necessaries ynowe; yow shal no þyng [*lakke*]
C. 1.116   Ac y wol *lacky* no lyf,' quod þat lady sothly;
C. 2.20   And [*lakked*] my lemman þat leute is hoten
C. 2.51   *Lacke* hem nat but lat hem worthe til leutee be Iustice
C. 3.58   And *lacketh* nat ladyes þat louyeth [wel] þe same.
C. 3.131   *Lacked* here a litel w[iht] for þat she louede gyle
C. 3.387   And halt hem vnstedefast for hem *lakketh* case.
C. 6.98   To lye and to loure and to *lakke* myn neyhebores,
C. 6.311   'And thow m[y] lyflode *lakke* leten y nelle
C. 7.23   Or *lacke* men or likene hem in vnlikyng manere
C. 8.85   Ne hem þat han lawes to loke *lacke* hem nat, y hote;
C.11.162   And *lakkede* [me in] latyn and lyhte by me sette
C.12.40   Nother for loue [loue] it [nat] ne *lacke* hit for enuye:
C.13.26   Ac leueth nat, lewede men, þat y *lacke* rychesse
C.13.103   Hem sholde neuere *lacke* lyflode, noþer lynnen ne wollene
C.13.206   And ar thow *lacke* eny lyf loke ho is to preyse.
C.14.6   Noþer to lye ne to *lacke* ne lere þat is defended
C.15.78   Ac me thynketh loth, thogh y latyn knowe, to *lacken* eny secte
C.17.310   And that his lore was lesynges and *lakken* hit alle
C.19.103   Noþer *lacke* ne alose ne leue þat per were
C.21.112   And lawe *lakked* tho for men loued nat her enemyes
C.21.254   Loke þat noen *lacke* oþere bute loueth as bretherne
C.21.468   And yf me *lakketh* to lyue by þe lawe wol y take hit
C.22.210   'And thow loue lelly *lacke* shal þe neuere
C.22.249   And oþere necessaries ynowe; ȝow shal no thyng *lakke*

lakkes n *lak* n. B 1
B.10.268   Alle þat *lakkeþ* any lif and *lakkes* han hemselue:

lakkyng ger *lakkinge* ger. B 2 lakkyng (1) lakkynge (1); C 1
B.13.322   Lyinge and *la[kk]ynge* and leue tonge to chide;
B.20.36   And as lowe as a lomb for *lakkyng* þat hym nedeþ;
C.22.36   And as louh as a lamb for *lakkyng* þat hym nedeth;

lakkynge > lakke, lakkyng

laklees adj *lakles* adj. B 2; C 1 lacles
B.11.390   And if a man myȝte make [*laklees*] hymself
B.11.391   Ech a lif wolde be *laklees*, leue þow noon oþer.
C.13.209   Vch a lede wolde be *lacles*, leef thow non other.

lamasse > lammesse; lamb(- > lomb

lame adj *lame* adj. A 1; B 1; C 3
A. 7.180   And *lame* menis lymes wern li[þ]id þat tyme,
B.19.125   He made *lame* to lepe and yaf light to blynde
C. 8.189   And *lame* men he lechede with longes of bestes.
C. 9.216   He þat lolleth is *lame* or his leg out of ioynte
C.21.125   He made *lame* to lepe and ȝaf liht to blynde

lammesse n *lammasse* n. A 1 lammasse; B 1; C 1 lamasse
A. 7.273   Be þis liflode I mote lyue til *lammasse* tyme;
B. 6.289   By þis liflode [I moot] lyue til *lammesse* tyme,

C. 8.312   By this lyflode we mote lyue til *l[a]masse* tyme

lampe n *laumpe* n. A 1 laumpe; B 2 lampe (1) laumpe (1); C 1 laumpe
A. 1.163   It is as lewid as a *laumpe* þat no liȝt is inne.
B. 1.189   It is as lewed as a *lampe* þat no liȝt is Inne.
B.13.151   Wiþ half a *laumpe* lyne in latyn, Ex vi transicionis,,
C. 1.185   Hit is as lewed as a *laumpe* þat no liht is ynne.

land(es > lond; lane > cokkeslane

lanes n *lane* n. A 1; B 1; C 1
A. 2.178   Lurkyng þoruȝ *lanes*, toluggid of manye.
B. 2.219   Lurkynge þoruȝ *lanes*, tolugged of manye.
C. 2.229   Lorkyng thorw *lanes*, tologged of moneye.

lang > long

langage n *langange* n. B 2 langage (1) langages (1); C 2 langage (1) langages (1)
B.15.376   Ne rede a lettre in any *langage* but in latyn or englissh.
B.19.203   And made hem konne and knowe alle kynne *langages*.
C.18.80   That [lyf Actiua] lettred men in here *langage* calleth.'
C.21.203   And made hem konne & knowe alle kyne *langages*.

langour n *langour* n. B 2; C 3
B.14.118   That al hir lif han lyued in *langour* and defaute.
B.18.227   Shal lere hem what *langour* is and lisse wiþouten ende.
C.15.294   That al here lyf haen lyued in *langour* and defaute.
C.18.141   A lechede hem of here *langour*, bothe lasares and blynde,
C.20.236   Shal lere hem what *l[angour]* is and lisse withouten ende.

lanterne n *lanterne* n. A 1; B 1; C 1
A. 7.162   Þat he lokide lik a *lanterne* al his lif aftir;
B. 6.177   That he loked lik a *lanterne* al his lif after.
C. 8.174   Þat a lokede lyke a *l[a]nterne* al his lyf aftur;

lape v *lapen* v. B 2; C 2
B. 5.356   Dorste *lape* of þat leuynges, so vnlouely [it] smauȝte.
B.20.18   And if hym list for to *lape* þe lawe of kynde wolde
C. 6.414   Durste *lape* of þat lyuynge, so vnlouely hit smauhte.
C.22.18   And yf [hym] lust for to *lape* the lawe of kynde wolde

lappe n *lappe* n. A 1 lappes; B 7 lappe (6) lappes (1); C 8
A. 7.277   Benes & [b]ake applis hy brouȝte in here *lappe[s]*,
B. 5.354   And kouȝed vp a cawdel in Clementes *lappe*.
B. 6.293   Benes and baken apples þei broȝte in hir *lappes*,
B.16.255   And I loked in his *lappe*; a laȝar lay þerInne
B.16.258   'I wolde wite', quod I þo, 'what is in youre *lappe*.'
B.16.269   Lollynge in my *lappe* til swich a lord vs fecche.'
B.17.23   Lo! here in my *lappe* þat leeued on þat charme,
B.17.32   He kan noȝt siggen þe somme, and some arn in his *lappe*.
C. 6.412   And cowed vp a caudel in Clementis *lappe*.
C. 8.281   In al manere ese in Abrahammus *lappe*.
C. 8.316   Benes and bake aples they brouhten in here *lappe*
C.18.271   And y lokede in his *lappe*; a laȝar lay þerynne
C.18.274   'I wolde ywyte,' quod y tho, 'what is in þy *lappe*.'
C.18.285   Lollyng in my *lappe* til suche a lord vs feche.'
C.19.24   Lo! here in my *lappe* þat leuede vpon þat lettre,
C.19.33   He can no certeyn somme telle and somme aren in his *lappe*.

large n *large* n. B 2; C 2
B.19.43   And conquerour of [his] conquest hise lawes and his *large*.
B.20.192   And gyued me in goutes: I may noȝt goon at *large*.
C.21.43   And conquerour of his conqueste his layes and his *large*.
C.22.192   And gyued me in gowtes: y may nat go at *large*.

large adj *large* adj. A 1; B 4; C 11
A.11.119   Leue hym on þi left half a *large* myle or more,
B.10.167   Leue [hym] on þi left half a *large* myle or moore,
B.13.298   And *large* to lene, [loos] þerby to cacche'.
B.18.45   Boþe as long and as *large* bi lofte and by grounde.'
B.19.263   That oon was Luk, a *large* beest and a lowe chered,
C. 3.249   Loketh aftur lordschipe or oþer *large* mede
C. 3.289   Tha[t] vnlaufulliche lyuen hauen *large* handes
C. 3.316   Ȝeue lond or lordschipe [or] oþer *large* ȝeftes
C. 3.451   And letteth the lawe thorw here *large* ȝeftes
C.11.71   Be *large* þerof whil hit lasteth to ledes þat ben nedy
C.13.30   And lyues þat oure lord loueth and *large* weyes to heuene;
C.14.215   And þat is loue and *large* huyre, yf þe lord be trewe,
C.18.22   Alle thre yliche long and yliche *large*.
C.18.70   Summe litel, somme *large*, ylik apples of kynde,
C.20.44   Bothe as longe and as *large* aloofte and o grounde.
C.21.263   That oen was luc, a *large* beste and a lou chered,

largely adv *largelie* adv. B 2 largely (1) largeliche (1); C 5 largeliche (4) largelyche (1)
B.19.60   And siþ [alle hise lele liges *largely* he yeueþ]
B.20.87   *Largeliche* a legion loste [þe] lif soone.

C. 2.141   For by lesynges ȝe lacchen *largeliche* mede.
C. 4.67   On men of lawe wrong lokede and *largelyche* hem profered
C.12.108   That louieth and leneth hem *largeliche* shal y quyte."
C.21.60   And sethe [all his lele leges *largeliche* he ȝeueth]
C.22.87   *Largeliche* a legioun lees the lyf sone.

largenesse n *largenesse n.*   A 1; B 1; C 2
A. 6.109   *Largenesse* þe lady let in wel manye.
B. 5.623   *Largenesse* þe lady let in [wel] manye;
C. 7.275   *Largenesse* þ[e] lady lat in ful monye,
C.17.65   Lo laurence for his *largenesse*, as holy lore telleth

largere adv *large adv.*   B 1
B.11.161   The legend[a] sanctorum yow lereþ more *largere* þan I yow telle.

largesse n *largesse n.*   B 1; C 1
B.13.448   To crie a *largesse* bifore oure lord, youre good loos to shewe.
C. 7.108   To crye a *largesse* tofore oure lord ȝoure good loos to shewe.

larke n *larke n.*   B 2; C 2
B.12.264   The *larke* þat is a lasse fowel is moore louelich of ledene,
B.12.267   To lowe libbynge men þe *larke* is resembled.
C.14.185   The *larke* þat is a lasse foul is loueloke[re] of ledene
C.14.187   To lowe lyuynge men þe *larke* is resembled

lasar(es > laȝar

lasse n *lesse n.(2)*   A 2; B 6 lasse (5) lesse (1); C 6
A. 2.28   Þat longiþ to þ[at] lordsshipe, þe *lasse* & þe more.
A. 5.138   A galoun for a grote, god wot no *lasse*,
B. 2.46   That longen to þat lordshipe, þe *lasse* and þe moore.
B. 5.222   A galon for a grote, god woot no *lesse*,
B. 5.249   And took it by tale here and tolde hem þere *lasse*.'
B.13.17   Leneþ he no lif *lasse* ne moore–
B.14.230   And if glotonie greue pouerte he gadereþ þe *lasse*
B.14.307   And euer þe *lasse* þat he [lede], þe [liȝter] he is of herte:
C. 2.50   That loueth here lordschipe, *lasse* other more.
C. 8.285   Lene hem som of thy loef thouh thow þe *lasse* chewe.
C. 9.304   Caton counteth hit at nauht and Canonistres *at lasse*.
C.15.199   Of [m]y labour th[ey] lauhe, þe *lasse* and þe more;
C.16.71   And yf glotonye greue pouerte h[e] gadereth þe *lasse*
C.16.142   And euere þe *lasse* þat [eny] lede þe lihtere his herte is there,

lasse adj *lesse adj.comp.*   A 3 lesse; B 9; C 8 lasse (7) lassore (1)
A. 3.189   I durste han leid my lif & no *lesse* wed
A. 4.135   Þere nas man in þe mothalle, more ne *lesse*,
A. 8.142   Þe king les his lordsshipe, & *lesse* men it hadde.
B. 3.202   I dorste haue leyd my lif and no *lasse* wedde
B. 7.164   The kyng lees his lordship and [*lasse*] men it hadde.
B.10.87   And lordeþ in [ledes] þe *lasse* good he deleþ.
B.12.264   The larke þat is a *lasse* fowel is moore louelich of ledene,
B.14.248   And wheiþer be liȝter to breke? *lasse* boost [it] makeþ
B.14.330   That euere he hadde lond ouþer lordshipe *lasse* oþer moore,
B.16.57   For alle are þei aliche longe, noon *lasse* þan ooþer,
B.17.182   So is þe holy goost god, neiþer gretter ne *lasse*
B.20.272   And youre noumbre vnder Notaries signe and neiþer mo ne *lasse*.'
C. 3.137   And ay the lengur y late [the] go the *lasse* treuthe is with the,
C. 3.259   Y durste haue yleyd my lyf and no *lasse* wedde
C.11.67   And lordeth in ledes the *lasse* goed he deleth.
C.13.4   And ay þe lengere they lyuede the *lasse* goed they hadde.
C.14.185   The larke þat is a *lasse* foul is loueloke[re] of ledene
C.16.88   And where be [lyh]tere to breke? *lasse* boest hit maketh
C.19.148   Thus is the holy goste god, noyther grettore ne *lassore*
C.22.272   And ȝoure nombre vnde[r] notarie sygne and noþer mo ne *lasse*.'

lasse adv *lesse adv.*   A 3 lesse; B 10 lasse (9) lesse (1); C 8
A. 7.153   And let liȝt of þe lawe & *lesse* of þe kniȝt,
A. 9.7   Where þis lede lengide, *lesse* ne more,
A.11.306   And is to mene in oure mouþ, more ne *lesse*,
B. 4.161   Loue leet of hire liȝt and leaute yet *lasse*,
B. 5.559   Truþe wolde loue me þe *lasse* a long tyme after.
B. 6.168   And leet liȝt of þe lawe and *lasse* of þe knyȝte,
B. 8.7   Where þis leode lenged, *lasse* ne moore,
B.10.271   Which letteþ þee to loke, *lasse* ouþer moore?
B.10.462   And is to mene to [Englissh] men, moore ne *lesse*,
B.11.69   And loued me þe *lasse* for my lele speche.
B.11.109   Þe *lasse*, as I leue, louyen þei wolde
B.11.268   And *lasse* he dredeþ deeþ and in derke to ben yrobbed
B.14.1   'I haue but oon hool hater', quod haukyn, 'I am þe *lasse* to blame
C. 3.290   To ȝeue men mede, more oþer *lasse*.
C. 4.156   Loue l[et]te of mede lyhte and leutee ȝut *lasse*
C. 7.204   A wolde loue me þe *lasse* a long tyme aftur.
C. 8.165   And leet lyhte of þe lawe and *lasse* of the knyhte
C. 9.108   And madden as þe mone sit, more other *lasse*;
C.10.7   Where this [lede] l[e]nged, *lasse* ne more,
C.12.43   The *lasse*, as y leue, louyon þey wolde

C.12.153   And *lasse* drat [dethe] or in derke to ben yrobbed

laste adj *laste adj.sup.*   A 2; B 25; C 33
A. 2.105   It shal besette ȝoure soulis wel sore at þe *laste*.'
A. 3.87   Þat fuyr shal falle & forbrenne at þe *laste*
B.Pr.98   Arn doon vndeuoutliche; drede is at þe *laste*
B. 2.101   For he leueþ be lost, þis is [his] *laste* ende.
B. 2.141   It shal bisitte youre soules [wel] soure at þe *laste*.'
B. 3.98   That fir shal falle & [forbrenne at þe *laste*]
B. 5.391   Raxed and [remed] and rutte at þe *laste*.
B.11.131   A[c] reson shal rekene wiþ hym [and rebuken hym at þe *laste*,
B.12.26   What were dowel and dobet and dobest at þe *laste*,
B.12.52   And þo men þat þei moost haten mynistren it at þe *laste*;
B.13.21   I lay doun longe in þis þoȝt and at þe *laste* I slepte,
B.13.366   And but I hadde by ooþer wey at þe *laste* I stale it,
B.14.70   And lyueden wiþouten liflode and at þe *laste* þei woken.
B.14.133   Fram þe loue of oure lord at his *laste* ende!
B.14.143   As he þat noon hadde and haþ hire at þe *laste*.
B.14.147   Crist of his curteisie shal conforte yow at þe *laste*,
B.15.14   And wherof I cam & of what kynde. I coniured hym at þe *laste*
B.16.20   And lay longe in a louedreem; and at þe *laste* me þouȝte
B.17.296   Leue I neuere þat oure lord [at þe *laste*]
B.18.204   And wo into wele mowe wenden at þe *laste*.
B.18.291   And so þow haddest hem out and hider at þe *laste*.'
B.18.314   And now for þi *laste* lesynge] ylorn we haue Adam,
B.19.192   He wente, and wonyeþ þere, and wol come at þe *laste*
B.20.150   Ne careþ noȝt how Kynde slow and shal come at þe *laste*
B.20.157   And geten in hir glorie a gadelyng at þe *laste*,
B.20.175   And Elde auntred hym on lyf, and at þe *laste* he hitte
B.20.346   And at þe *laste* þis lymytour, þo my lord was oute,
C.Pr.126   Ar don vndeuouteliche; drede is at þe *laste*
C. 2.78   Leueth hit le[l]ly this worth here *laste* mede
C. 2.157   Hit shal [bi]sitte ȝoure soules ful so[u]re at þe *laste*.'
C. 4.155   That mekenesse worth maystre ouer mede at þe *laste*.'
C. 5.95   And ay loste an[d] loste and at þe *laste* hym happed
C. 5.97   And sette his los at a leef at the *laste* ende
C. 6.265   And but y hadde by other wey at the *laste* y stale hit
C. 7.7   R[a]xlede and r[e]mede and rotte at þe *laste*.
C. 9.208   Long labour and litte wynnynge and at þe *laste* they aspyde
C.12.66   A[c] reson shal rekene with hym and rebuken hym at þe *laste*
C.12.186   At the *laste* launceth vp whereby we lyuen all.
C.12.195   Worth allowed of oure lord at here *laste* ende
C.12.208   ȝoure sorwe into solace shal turne at þe *laste*
C.13.23   As grayn þat lith in greut and thorw grace at the *laste*
C.15.269   [And] lyuede withouten lyflode and [at] the *laste* awakede.
C.16.2   Fro þe loue of oure lord at his *laste* ende.
C.16.160   'He þat hath lond and lordschipe,' quod he, 'at þe *laste* ende
C.16.284   That thus goth here godes at þe *laste* ende
C.17.137   For lechours louyen aȝen þe lawe and at þe *laste* ben dampned
C.17.138   And theues louyen and leute hatien and at þe *laste* ben hanged
C.17.146   And ay hopeth eft to hele with here body at þe *laste*
C.19.95   That his lycame shal lechen at þe *laste* vs alle.'
C.19.277   Leue y neuere þat oure lord at þe *laste* ende
C.20.209   And wo into wele moet wende at þe *laste*.
C.20.321   And so haddest hem out and hiddere at þe *laste*.'
C.20.352   Bote oure lord at þe *laste* lyares h[e] rebuke[th]
C.20.355   That ȝe belyen nat this lewed men for at the *laste* dauid
C.20.392   And gyle [be] bigyled thorw grace at þe *laste*:
C.21.192   He wente and woneth there and wol come at þe *laste*
C.22.150   Ne careth nat how kynde slowh and shal come at þe *laste*
C.22.157   And geten in here glorie a gadlyng at þe *laste*,
C.22.175   And Elde auntered hym on lyf and at þe *laste* he hitte
C.22.346   And at þe *laste* this lymytour, tho my lord was oute,

laste v *lasten v.(1)*   A 6 last (1) laste (2) lastiþ (2) lesten (1); B 14 laste (7) lasteþ (5) lastynge (1) ylasted (1); C 16 last (1) laste (5) lasteth (9) lastyng (1)
A. 2.60   Wiþ þe Erldom of enuye for euere to *laste*,
A. 3.27   For to werche þi wil while þi lif *lastiþ*.'
A. 3.179   Wendist þat wynter wolde han *last* euere;
A. 7.272   To drawe on feld my dong while þe drouȝt *lastiþ*.
A.10.37   Lif þat ay shal *laste*, & al his lynage aftir.
A.12.93   Whil his lyf and his lykhame *lesten* togedere.
B. 3.28   For to werche þi wille [while þi lif *lasteþ*].'
B. 3.192   Wendest þat wynter wolde han *ylasted* euere;
B. 6.288   To drawe afeld my donge while þe droȝte *lasteþ*.
B. 9.46   Wiþ his word and werkmanshipe and wiþ lif to *laste*.
B. 9.49   Lif þat ay shal *laste*, [and] al his lynage after.
B.13.331   Ther is no lif þat me loueþ *lastynge* any while.
B.14.159   And so forþ while somer *lasteþ* hir solace dureþ.
B.15.258   Amonges cristene men þis myldenesse sholde *laste*
B.17.8   That Luciferis lordshipe *laste* shal no lenger.
B.19.45   The lawe of lif þat *laste* shal euere,
B.19.89   Gold is likned to leautee þat *laste* shal euere

B.19.175 And now art lyuynge and lokynge and *laste* shalt euere."
B.20.142 And boold and bidynge while his bagge *lasteþ*.'
B.20.211 [Weede] ne worldly [mete] while þi lif *lasteþ*.'
C.Pr.147 With lele labour to lyue while lif on londe *lasteth*.
C. 3.32 'And purchace ȝow prouendres while ȝoure panes *lasteth*
C. 3.205 Ther he is alowed and ylet by þat *laste* shal eny while
C. 8.311 To drawe afeld my donge þe while þe drouthe *lasteth*.
C.10.170 The which is loue and lyf þat *last* withouten ende.
C.11.71 Be large þerof whil hit *lasteth* to ledes þat ben nedy
C.12.121 And pore peple fayle we nat while eny peny vs *lasteth*
C.12.160 And lyf *lastyng* for euere byfore oure lord in heuene:
C.12.220 Hit *lasteth* nat longe þat is lycour-swete,
C.16.11 And so forth whiles somur *laste*[th] here solace duyreth
C.17.66 That his mede and his manhede for eueremore shal *laste*:
C.21.45 The lawe of lyf that *laste* shal euere
C.21.89 Gold is likened to lewetee that *laste* shal euere
C.21.175 And now art lyuynge and lokynge and *laste* shalt euere."
C.22.142 And bolde and [b]ydynge while his bagge *lasteth*.'
C.22.211 Wede ne worldly mete while thy lif *lasteth*.'

laste &> lest; lat > leden,leten

late adv *late adv. &> leten* A 6 late (5) lattere (1); B 9 late (8) latter (1);
 C 7
A. 1.173 And a lering to lewide men þe *lattere* to dele.
A. 3.55 Let not þi left hond, *late* ne raþe,
A. 3.99 I haue a kniȝt, consience, com *late* fro beȝonde;
A. 6.3 Til *late* & longe þat hy a lede mette,
A.10.13 And seruiþ þis lady lelly boþe *late* & raþe.
A.11.157 Þat þinkeþ werche wiþ þo þre þriueþ wel *late*,
B. 1.199 And lernynge to lewed men þe *latter* to deele.
B. 3.73 Lat noȝt þi left half, *late* ne raþe,
B. 3.110 I haue a knyȝt, Conscience, cam *late* fro biyonde;
B. 5.515 Til *late* and longe, þat þei a leode mette
B. 9.13 To seruen þis lady lelly, boþe *late* and raþe.
B.10.149 As longe as I lyue, boþe *late* and raþe,
B.10.214 [That] þynkeþ werche with þo [þre] þryueþ [wel] *late*,
B.15.19 That wole defende me þe dore, dynge I neuer so *late*.
B.16.249 And þus I seke hym', he seide, 'for I herde seyn *late*
C. 3.147 Y haue a knyght, Consience, cam *late* fro beȝende.
C. 4.48 And margarete of here maydenhod as he mette here *late*.
C. 6.160 Ac other while when wyn cometh and when y drynke *late* at euen
C. 7.160 Til *late* was and longe þat thei a lede mette
C.10.140 To serue þat lady leely bot[h] *late* and rathe,
C.11.87 As longe as y lyue, bothe *late* and rathe,
C.16.170 That wol defende me [þe] dore, dynge y neuere so *late*.

later adj *late adj.* C 1
C.20.348 And now for a *later* lesynge] þat thow lowe til Eue

laþered ptp *letheren v.* B 1
B.14.7 And [*laþered*] wiþ þe losse of catel [forto me] looþ [were]

latyn n *Latin* A 1; B 16; C 14
A. 3.86 Among þise lettride lordis þis *latyn* amountiþ
B.Pr.129 Lowed to speke in *latyn*, for lewed men ne koude
B.Pr.143 Thanne [comsed] al þe commune crye in vers of *latyn*
B. 1.141 To litel *latyn* þow lernedest, leode, in þi youþe:
B. 3.97 Among þise lettrede l[or]des þis *latyn* [amounteþ]
B. 3.332 'I kan no *latyn*?' quod she, 'clerkes wite þe soþe!
B. 3.337 'I leue wel, lady', quod Conscience, 'þat þi *latyn* be trewe.
B.11.2 And lakked me in *latyn* and liȝt by me sette,
B.11.214 Forþi lakke no lif ooþer þouȝ he moore *latyn* knowe,
B.11.304 If fals *latyn* be in þat lettre þe lawe it impugneþ,
B.12.282 Ergo saluabitur', quod he and seide na moore *latyn*.
B.13.151 Wiþ half a laumpe lyne in *latyn*, Ex vi transicionis,,
B.15.34 Thanne is lele loue my name, and in *latyn* Amor;
B.15.111 [For ypocrisie] in *latyn* is likned to a [loþly] dongehill
B.15.119 If lewed [ledes] wiste what þis *latyn* meneþ,
B.15.319 If lewed men knewe þis *latyn* þei wolde loke whom þei yeue,
B.15.376 Ne rede a lettre in any langage but in *latyn* or englissh.
C. 1.140 To lyte [*Latyn* þow] lernedest, [leode], in thy ȝowthe:
C. 3.125 Amonge thise lettred lordes þis *latin* is to mene
C. 3.489 'I leue the, lady,' quod Consience, 'for þat *latin* is trewe.
C. 9.165 And lere this lewede men what þis *latyn* meneth
C. 9.213 Aȝen þe lawe he lyueth yf *latyn* be trewe:
C.10.92 Lene hem and loue hem", this *latyn* is to mene.
C.11.162 And lakkede [me in] *latyn* and lyhte by me sette
C.13.118 Yf fals *latyn* be in þat lettre þe lawe hit enpugneth,
C.14.204 Ergo saluabitur,' quod he and saide no more *latyn*.
C.15.78 Ac me thynketh loth, thogh y *latyn* knowe, to lacken eny secte
C.16.196 Thenne is lele loue my name and in *latyn* Amor;
C.16.266 And is ylikned in *latyn* to a lothly donghep
C.17.54 Yf lewede men knewe this *latyn* a litel they wolden auysen hem
C.19.4 Lo, here the lettre,' quod he, 'a *latyn* and [an] ebrew;

laton > leten; latter(e > late; laughe(d -en > lauȝen

laughyng ger *laughinge ger.* A 1 lauȝing; B 3 laughyng (1) laughynge (1)
 lauȝynge (1); C 2 lauhynge (1) leyhing (1)
A. 5.185 Þere was *lauȝing* & louryng & 'lete go þe cuppe!'
B. 5.336 There was *lauȝynge* and lourynge and 'lat go þe cuppe!'
B.16.155 And gile in þi glad chere and galle is in þi *laughyng*.
B.18.414 That loue, and hym liste, to *laughynge* ne brouȝte;
C. 6.394 There was *leyhing* and louryng and 'lat go the coppe!'
C.20.457 That loue, and hym luste, to *l[a]u[h]ynge* [ne] brouhte;

laughynge > laughyng,lauȝen; laughte > lacchen

lauȝen v *laughen v.* A 5 lauȝe (1) lauȝen (1) lauȝinge (1) louȝ (1) low (1);
 B 19 laughe (3) laughed (1) laughen (1) laughynge (1) lauȝe (5) lauȝen
 (3) lauȝynge (2) lough (1) louȝ (2); C 22 laghynge (1) lauhe (4)
 lauhede (1) lauhen (1) lauhyng (1) lauhynge (1) lawen (1) lawhe (5)
 lawhen (1) lawheth (1) louh (1) louhe (1) lowh (2)
A. 4.93 Le[þe] he so liȝtly awey, *lauȝen* he wolde,
A. 4.137 Loue let of hire liȝt & *louȝ* hire to scorne,
A. 5.93 Of his lesing I *lauȝe* [it liȝtiþ] myn herte,
A.11.98 But al *lauȝinge* he loutide & lokide vpon studie
A.12.42 Þat lady þan *low* and lauȝthe me in here armes
B. 4.19 Ne-lesynge-to-*lauȝen*-of-for-I-loued-hem-neuere.
B. 4.106 Lope he so liȝtly [awey], *lauȝen* he wolde,
B. 4.153 And þei *lauȝynge* lope to hire and lefte Reson manye,
B. 5.113 And of [his] lesynge I *lauȝe*, [it liȝteþ] myn herte,
B. 5.407 Or lesynge[s] to *lauȝen* [of] and bilye my neȝebores,
B.10.145 But al *lauȝynge* he louted and loked vpon Studie
B.11.84 And lewte [*louȝ*] on me [for] I loured [on þe frere]
B.11.209 Forþi loue we as leue [children shal], and ech man *laughe* of ooþer,
B.13.146 And leye on hym þus with loue til he *lauȝe* on þe.
B.13.228 Couþe I lye [and] do men *lauȝe*, þanne lacchen I sholde
B.13.352 And how þat lecchours louye *laughen* and Iapen,
B.13.423 And han likynge to liþen hem [in hope] to do yow *lauȝe*–
B.13.449 Thise þre maner minstrales makeþ a man to *lauȝe*,
B.14.34 Thanne *laughed* haukyn a litel and lightly gan swerye;
B.15.172 Ne no likynge haþ to lye ne *laughe* men to scorne.
B.19.459 Thanne *louȝ* þer a lord and, 'by þis light!' seide,
B.20.114 This lecherie leide on wiþ [*laughynge*] chiere
B.20.143 And þanne *lough* lyf and leet daggen hise cloþes,
B.20.143 Conscience of þis counseil þo comsede for to *laughe*,
C. 2.32 That neuere lyede ne *lauhede* in al his lyf tyme;
C. 3.55 Loueliche þat lady *laghynge* sayde,
C. 4.19 Ne-lesynges-to-*lauhe*-of-for-y-louede-hit-neuere.
C. 4.101 Lope he so lihtliche [awey], *lawen* he wolde
C. 6.23 *Lauhyng* al aloude for lewede men sholde
C. 7.22 Y hadde leuere here an harlotrye or a lesyng to *lauhen* of
C. 7.83 And han lykyng to lythen hem in hope to do ȝow *lawhe*–
C. 7.109 Thise thre manere munstrals maketh a man to *lauhe*
C.11.83 But al *lauhynge* he louted and loked vppon stud[i]e,
C.12.23 And thenne *louhe* leaute for y loured on þe frere:
C.15.146 And ley on hym thus with loue til he *lauhe* on þe.
C.15.199 Of [m]y labour th[ey] *lauhe*, þe lasse and þe more;
C.15.202 [Cou]the y lye and do men *lawhe* thenne lacchen y scholde
C.16.302 He is glad with alle glade as gurles þat *lawhen* alle
C.16.304 *Lawhe* þer men lawheth and loure þer oþere louren.
C.16.304 Lawhe þer men *lawheth* and loure þer oþere louren.
C.16.310 Hath no lykynge to *lawhe* ne to likene men to scorne.
C.18.3 Thenne *louh* liberum Arbitrium and ladde me forth with tales
C.21.459 Thenne *lowh* ther a lord and 'bi this lihte!' saide,
C.22.114 This lecherye leyde [o]n with *lauhyng* chere
C.22.143 And thenne *lowh* lyf and lette dagge his clothes
C.22.242 Con[s]ience of this con[s]ail tho comesed for to *lawhe*

lauȝing > laughyng; lauȝynge > laughyng,lauȝen; lauȝt- lauȝþe > lacchen;
lauhe(- > lauȝen

lauhfollyche adv *lauefulli adv.* C 1
C. 9.59 Lellyche and *lauhfollyche*, oure lord treuthe hem graunteth

lauhyng > lauȝen; lauhynge > laughyng,lauȝen; lauhte > lacchen; laumpe >
lampe

launce n *launce n.* B 1; C 1
B. 3.305 Alle þat beren baselard, brood swerd or *launce*,
C. 3.458 For alle þat bereth baslard, br[ode] swerd oþer *launce*,

launceth > launseth

launde n *launde n.* A 2; B 4 launde (2) laundes (2); C 2
A. 9.56 And vndir a lynde vpon a *launde* lenide I me a stounde
A.11.118 And ek þe longe *launde* þat leccherie hatte,
B. 8.65 And vnder a lynde vpon a *launde* lened I a stounde
B.10.166 And also þe [longe] *launde* þat lecherie hatte,
B.15.298 Ac þer ne was leoun ne leopard þat on *laundes* wenten,
B.15.304 In likkyng and in lowynge, þer þei on *laundes* yede].

C.Pr.8   And in a *launde* as y lay lened y and slepte
C.10.64   And vnder lynde vpon a *launde* lened y a stounde

launseth v *launcen v.* C 3 launceth (1) launseth (2)
C.12.186 At the laste *launceth* vp whereby we lyuen all.
C.12.222 That lihtlich *launseth* vp litel while dureth
C.18.10   Thorw louely lokyng[e] hit lyueth and *launseth* vp blosmes,

laurence n prop *n.i.d.* C 2
C. 2.133 That *laurence* the leuyte that lay on þe gredyre
C.17.65   Lo *laurence* for his largenesse, as holy lore telleth

laued > laueth

lauendrye n *lavendrie n.* B 1; C 1 lauendrie
B.15.187 Labouren in [a] *lauendrye* wel þe lengþe of a Mile,
C.16.333 And laueth hem in þe *lauendrie*, labora[ui] in gemitu meo,

laueth v *laven v.* B 1 laued; C 1
B.14.5   It haþ be *laued* in lente and out of lente boþe
C.16.333 And *laueth* hem in þe lauendrie, labora[ui] in gemitu meo,

lawe n *laue n. cf. layes* A 34 lawe (27) lawes (2) lawis (5); B 122 law (1)
          lawe (102) lawes (19); C 149 lawe (135) lawes (14)
A.Pr.86   Pleten for penis & [poundide] þe *lawe*
A. 2.88   And þou hast fastnid hire wiþ fals, fy on þi *law[e]*!
A. 2.99   Lediþ hire to lundoun þere *lawe* is yhandlit
A. 2.120 To lundoun to loke 3if þat *lawe* wolde
A. 2.159 But ri3t as þe *lawe* lokis let falle on hem alle.'
A. 3.66   Betwyn þe king & þe comunes, to kepe þe *lawis*,
A. 3.83   For to amende [meiris and] men þat kepiþ þe *lawis*,
A. 3.141 And bringen forþ barnes a3ens forboden *lawis*.
A. 3.146 And leiþ a3en þe *lawe* & lettiþ þe treuþe
A. 3.148 She let *lawe* as hire list & louedaies makiþ;
A. 3.150 *Lawe* is so lordlich & loþ to make ende,
A. 3.203 And mediþ men hymself to mayntene here *lawis*;
A. 3.269 Leaute shal do hym *lawe* [and no] lif ellis.
A. 3.273 Þat *lawe* is lord waxen & lewte & louedaies
A. 3.276 And make of *lawe* a labourer, such loue shal arise.'
A. 4.130 Þat *lawe* shal ben a labourer & lede afeld donge,
A. 6.94   And lere þe for to loue & hise *lawes* holden.
A. 7.151 'Or þou shalt abigge be þe *lawe*, be þe ordre þat I bere'.
A. 7.153 And let li3t of þe *lawe* & lesse of þe kni3t,
A. 7.207 Loue hem & lene hem & so þe *lawe* of kynde wolde.
A. 7.299 Suche *lawis* to loke laboureris to chast[e].
A. 8.13   Bisshopis þat blissen, & boþe *lawes* kenne,
A. 8.14   Loke on þat o *lawe*, & lere men þat oþer,
A. 8.45   Men of *lawe* hadde lest for le[ttr]id þei ben alle;
A. 8.52   Ac for oure lordis loue *lawe* for hym shewiþ,
A. 8.65   And lyuen in loue & [in] *lawe*, for here lou3 herte
A. 8.72   Þei lyue nou3t in loue, ne no *lawe* holden.
A. 8.173 How þou leddist þi lif here & his *lawe* keptest,
A.10.132 And lyuen as here *law[e]* wil[e]; it likeþ god almi3ty
A.10.180 A3en þe *lawe* of oure lord le[i3en] togideris,
A.10.204 Of lif & of loue & of *lawe* also
A.10.206 As betwyn sengle & sengle, siþþe *lawe* haþ ygrauntid
A.11.128 Logik I lerid hire, & al þe *lawe* aftir,
A.11.298 'Wh[anne] 3e ben aposid of princes or of prestis of þe *lawe*
B.Pr.122 Shopen *lawe* and leaute, ech [lif] to knowe his owene.
B.Pr.213 Pleteden for penyes and pounde[d] þe *lawe*
B. 1.161 Right so is loue a ledere and þe *lawe* shapeþ;
B. 2.22   And bilowen h[ym] to lordes þat *lawes* han to kepe.
B. 2.124 And þow hast fest hire [wiþ] Fals; fy on þi *lawe*!
B. 2.135 Ledeþ hire to Londoun þere [*lawe*] is [yhandled],
B. 2.156 To london to loken if [þat] *lawe* wolde
B. 2.198 But ri3t as þe *lawe* [lokeþ] lat falle on hem alle.'
B. 3.77   The kyng and þe comune to kepe þe *lawes*,
B. 3.94   For to amenden Maires and men þat kepen [þe] *lawes*,
B. 3.152 And bryngeþ forþ barnes ayein forbode *lawes*.
B. 3.156 And liþ ayein þe *lawe* and letteþ hym þe gate
B. 3.158 She ledeþ *lawe* as hire list and louedaies makeþ,
B. 3.159 And doþ men lese þoru3 hire loue þat *lawe* my3te wynne;
B. 3.161 *Lawe* is so lordlich and looþ to maken ende;
B. 3.216 And medeþ men h[y]mseluen to mayntene hir *lawes*.
B. 3.294 Leaute shal don hym *lawe* and no lif ellis.
B. 3.298 And ouer lordes *lawes* [ledeþ] þe Reaumes.
B. 3.300 And make of *lawe* a laborer; swich loue shal arise
B. 4.147 That *lawe* shal ben a laborer and lede afeld donge,
B. 4.152 For I sei3 Mede in þe moot halle on men of *lawe* wynke
B. 4.174 And gan wexe wroþ with *lawe* for Mede almoost hadde shent it,
B. 4.175 And seide, 'þoru3 [youre] *lawe*, as I leue, I lese manye eschetes;
B. 4.176 Mede ouermaistreþ *lawe* and muche truþe letteþ.
B. 4.180 I wole haue leaute in *lawe*, and lete be al youre ianglyng;
B. 5.52   'And ye þat han *lawes* to [loke], lat truþe be youre coueitise
B. 6.166 'Or þow shalt abigge by þe *lawe*, by þe ordre þat I bere!'
B. 6.168 And leet li3t of þe *lawe* and lasse of þe kny3te,

B. 6.221 Loue hem and lene hem [and] so þe *lawe* of [kynde wolde]:
B. 6.318 Swiche *lawes* to loke laborers to [chaste].
B. 7.14   Legistres of boþe *lawes* þe lewed þerwiþ to preche,
B. 7.40   Men of *lawe* leest pardon hadde, [leue þow noon ooþer],
B. 7.50   [Ac] for oure lordes loue [*lawe* for hym sheweþ],
B. 7.63   And lyuen in loue and in *lawe*, for hir lowe hert[e]
B. 7.90   For [þei] lyue in no loue ne no *lawe* holde.
B. 7.195 How þow laddest þi lif here and hi[s] *law[e]* keptest,
B. 9.80   For moore bilongeþ to þe litel barn er he þe *lawe* knowe
B. 9.191 Of lif and of [loue] and [of *lawe* also]
B. 9.202 Dowel, my [deere], is to doon as *lawe* techeþ:
B.10.25   And þat þei ben lordes of ech a lond þat out of *lawe* libbeþ:
B.10.40   Ayein þe *lawe* of oure lord, and lyen on hemselue,
B.10.176 Logyk I lerned hire, and [al þe *lawe* after],
B.10.358 For þat crist for cristene men deide, and confermed þe *lawe*
B.10.360 He sholde louye and lene and þe *lawe* fulfille.
B.10.451 Thou3 ye come bifore kynges and clerkes of þe *lawe*
B.11.91   'And wherof serueþ *law*', quod lewtee, 'if no lif vndertoke it
B.11.97   If hem likeþ and lest; ech a *lawe* it graunteþ.
B.11.128 Wiþouten leue of his lord; no *lawe* wol it graunte.
B.11.158 Wel ou3te ye lordes þat *lawes* kepe þis lesson haue in mynde,
B.11.166 Ther no clergie ne kouþe, ne konnyng of *lawes*.
B.11.171 '*Lawe* wiþouten loue', quod Troianus, 'ley þer a bene!'
B.11.205 In þe olde *lawe*, as [þe] lettre telleþ, mennes sones men calle[d] vs
B.11.219 Thanne is bileue a lele help, aboue logyk or *lawe*.
B.11.222 Of logyk [ne] of *lawe* in legenda sanctorum
B.11.223 And *lawe* is looþ to louye but if he lacche siluer,
B.11.224 Boþe logyk and *lawe*, þat loueþ no3t to lye,
B.11.229 Forþi lerne we þe *lawe* of loue as oure lord tau3te;
B.11.304 If fals latyn be in þat lettre þe *lawe* it impugneþ,
B.12.34   And lyue forþ as *lawe* wole while ye lyuen boþe.
B.12.73   In þe olde *lawe* as þe lettre telleþ, þat was þe *lawe* of Iewes,
B.12.73   In þe olde lawe as þe lettre telleþ, þat was þe *lawe* of Iewes,
B.12.97   Forþi lakke þow neuere logik, *lawe* ne hise custumes,
B.12.113 Archa dei, in þe olde *lawe*, leuytes it kepten;
B.12.207 And as *lawe* likeþ to lyue or to deye:
B.12.213 And wel lose[l]y he lolleþ þere by þe *lawe* of holy chirche:
B.12.287 Ac truþe þat trespased neuere ne trauersed ayeins his *lawe*,
B.12.288 But lyueþ as his *lawe* techeþ and leueþ þer be no bettre,
B.13.185 I shal brynge yow a bible, a book of þe olde *lawe*,
B.13.413 Lyueþ ayein þe bileue and no *lawe* holdeþ.
B.14.110 To haue allowaunce of his lord; by þe *lawe* he it cleymeþ.
B.14.146 And lyuen as *lawe* techeþ, doon leaute to hem alle,
B.15.93   Thoru3 lele libbynge men þat goddes *lawe* techen,
B.15.240 For hir *lawe* dureþ ouerlonge but if þei lacchen siluer,
B.15.243 Thei vndoon it vn[digne]ly, þo doctours of *lawe*.
B.15.411 That [lered] þere and [lewed] 3it leeuen on hise *lawes*.
B.15.466 The calf bitokneþ clennesse in hem þat kepeþ *lawes*,
B.15.530 And crepe [in] amonges curatours, confessen ageyn þe *lawe*:
B.15.569 That contrarien cristes *lawe* and cristendom dispise.
B.15.582 And Iewes lyuen in lele *lawe*; oure lord wroot it hymselue
B.15.584 Dilige deum & proximum is parfit Iewen *lawe*;
B.15.586 And on þat *lawe* þei l[e]ue and leten it þe beste.
B.16.6   The leues ben lele wordes, þe *lawe* of holy chirche;
B.16.119 Iewes iangled þerayein [þat] Iuggede *lawes*,
B.17.10   'Lat se þi lettres', quod I, 'we myghte þe *lawe* knowe.'
B.17.17   [Is] here alle þi lordes *lawes*?' quod I; 'ye, leue me', he seide.
B.17.33   What neded it [now] a newe *lawe* to [brynge]
B.17.35   And now com[s]eþ Spes and spekeþ, þat [haþ] aspied þe *lawe*,
B.17.149 Tho þat lernen þi *lawe* wol litel while vsen it.'
B.18.72   Vpon a croos bisides crist; so was þe comune *lawe*.
B.18.107 Which is lif þat oure lord in alle *lawes* acurseþ.
B.18.260 And bileue on a newe *lawe* be lost, lif and soule.'
B.18.285 I leeue þat *lawe* nyl no3t lete hym þe leeste.'
B.18.338 Thefliche þow me robbedest; þe olde *lawe* graunteþ
B.18.342 Membre for membre [was amendes by þe olde *lawe*],
B.18.343 And lif for lif also, and by þat *lawe* I clayme
B.18.348 So leue [it] no3t, lucifer, ayein þe *lawe* I fecche hem,
B.18.383 *Lawe* wolde he yeue hym lif if he loked on hym.
B.18.386 And if *lawe* wole I loke on hem it liþ in my grace
B.18.400 Thus by *lawe*', quod oure lord, 'lede I wole fro hennes
B.19.33   And fre men foule þralles þat folwen no3t hise *lawes*.
B.19.35   Boþe his loore and his *lawe*; now are þei lowe cherles.
B.19.43   And conquerour of [his] conquest hise *lawes* and his large.
B.19.45   The *lawe* of lif þat laste shal euere,
B.19.59   To maken alle folk free þat folwen his *lawe*].
B.19.111 For wyn is likned to *lawe* and lifholynesse,
B.19.112 And *lawe* lakkede þo for men louede no3t hir enemys,
B.19.231 As prechours and preestes and Prentices of *lawe*:
B.19.247 And fecchen it fro false men wiþ Foluyles *lawes*.
B.19.306 Neiþer of duc ne of deeþ, þat he ne dide *lawe*
B.19.310 Wiþ olde *lawe* and newe lawe þat loue my3te wexe
B.19.310 Wiþ olde lawe and newe *lawe* þat loue my3te wexe

B.19.334   [And þe [lond] of bileue, þe *lawe* of holy chirche].
B.19.446   Ayein þe olde *lawe* and newe lawe, as Luc [bereþ] witness[e]:
B.19.446   Ayein þe olde lawe and newe *lawe*, as Luc [bereþ] witness[e]:
B.19.468   And if me lakkeþ to lyue by þe *lawe* wole I take it
B.19.469   Ther I may hastilokest it haue, for I am heed of *lawe*;
B.19.479   [Haue] þow mayst [þyn askyng] as þi *lawe* askeþ:
B.20.10   And nede haþ no *lawe* ne neuere shal falle in dette
B.20.18   And if hym list for to lape þe *lawe* of kynde wolde
B.20.266   Of lewed and of lered; þe *lawe* wole and askeþ
B.20.274   And lerne logyk and *lawe* and ek contemplacion,
B.20.278   For god made to men a *lawe* and Moyses it tauȝte:
C.Pr.163   Plededen for penyes and pounde[d] þe *lawe*
C. 1.157   Ryht so is loue [a] ledare and þe *lawe* shapeth;
C. 2.21   And [ylow on] hym to lordes þat *lawes* han to kepe;
C. 2.140   And thow hast feffed here with fals; fy on suche *lawe*.
C. 2.151   And ledeth here to londone there *lawe* may declare
C. 2.172   To londone to loke yf *lawe* wille iugge;
C. 2.212   But riht as þe *lawe* loketh lat falle on hem alle.'
C. 3.78   Bothe Schyreues and seriauntes and suche as kepeth *lawes*,
C. 3.88   And [t]how thei fillen nat ful þat for *lawe* is seled
C. 3.120   'And soffre hem som tyme to selle aȝeyne þe *lawe*.'
C. 3.190   And bringeth forth bar[n]es aȝenes forbodene *lawes*:
C. 3.194   He lyth aȝeyn þe *lawe* and le[tte]th hym þe gate
C. 3.196   And le[deth] þe *lawe* as here luste and louedayes maketh,
C. 3.199   *Lawe* is so lordliche and loth to make ende;
C. 3.206   Withouten werre oþer wo oþer wickede *lawe*
C. 3.272   And ȝeuen mede to men to meyntene here *lawes*;
C. 3.294   And þat is nother resoun ne ryhte ne [i]n no rewme *lawe*
C. 3.377   That here loue to his *lawe* Thorw al þe lond acorde.
C. 3.379   *Lawe*, l[o]ue and lewete and hym lord antecedent,
C. 3.447   Lewete shal do hym *lawe* and no lyf elles.
C. 3.451   And letteth the *lawe* thorw here large ȝeftes.
C. 3.453   And maky of *lawe* [a] laborer; suche loue shal aryse
C. 4.67   On men of *lawe* wrong lokede and largelyche hem profered
C. 4.144   That *lawe* shal ben a laborer and lede afelde donge
C. 4.148   Mede in the mothalle tho on men of *lawe* gan wynke
C. 4.168   And lourede vppon men of *lawe* and lyhtlych sayde:
C. 4.169   'Thorw ȝoure *lawe*, as y leue, y lese many chetes;
C. 4.174   Y wol haue leutee for my *lawe* and late be al ȝoure iangl[ing]
C. 4.175   And by lele and lyfholy my *lawe* shal be demed.'
C. 5.55   For by þe *lawe* of leuyticy þat oure lord ordeynede,
C. 6.45   And likynge of such a lyf þat no *lawe* preiseth,
C. 7.73   Lyueth aȝen þe bileue and no *lawe* kepeth
C. 7.118   For a lythed and louede þat godes *lawe* despiseth:
C. 7.260   ȝef loue and leute and oure *lawe* [be] trewe:
C. 8.85   Ne hem þat han *lawes* to loke lacke hem nat, y hote;
C. 8.163   'Or y shal bete the by the *lawe* and brynge þe in stokkes.'
C. 8.165   And leet lyhte of þe *lawe* and lasse of the knyhte
C. 8.230   Loue hem and lene hem and so *lawe* of kynde wolde:
C. 8.338   Suche *lawes* to lerne laboreres to greue.
C. 9.44   Men of *lawe* hadde lest þat loth were to plede
C. 9.49   And for þe loue of oure lord *lawe* for hem declareth
C. 9.51   Beth ywar, ȝe wis men and witty of þe *lawe*,
C. 9.104   Lyuen aȝen goddes *lawe* and þe lore of holi churche.
C. 9.158   And lyueth lyke a lollare, goddes *lawe* hym dampneth.
C. 9.167   For they lyue in no loue ne no *lawe* holden
C. 9.213   Aȝen þe *lawe* he lyueth yf latyn be trewe:
C. 9.219   Lollen aȝen þe byleue and *lawe* of holy churche.
C. 9.221   Vnder obedience to be and buxum to þe *lawe*:
C. 9.246   Or labory for here lyflode as þe *lawe* wolde?
C. 9.277   Mercy for mede and my *lawe* breke.'
C. 9.278   Loke now, for thy lacchesse, what *lawe* wol the graunte:
C. 9.327   As lettrede men vs lereth and *lawe* of holi churche:
C. 9.341   How we ladde oure lyf here and his *lawes* kepte
C.10.96   Lordes þat lyuen as hem lust and no *lawe* acounten,
C.10.126   And what lyues they lyue and what *lawe* þei vsen
C.10.191   That alle landes loueden and in on *lawe* bileuede,
C.10.196   And seth [he les] his lyf for *lawe* sholde loue wexe.
C.10.203   Hoso lyueth in *lawe* and in loue doth wel
C.10.211   That lele legityme by þe *lawe* may claymen.
C.10.219   þat lycame haen aȝen þe *lawe* þat oure lord ordeynede.
C.10.239   Ac Westm[in]stre *lawe*, y woet wel, worcheth þe contra[r]ye.
C.10.301   And thus is dowel, my frende, to do as *lawe* techeth:
C.11.97   Of lore and of lettrure, of *lawe* and of resoun.
C.11.116   Logyk y lerned here and al þe *lawe* aftur
C.11.276   Thogh ȝe come bifore kynges and clerkes of þe *law[e]*
C.12.32   'And wherof serueth *lawe*,' quod leaute, ' and no lyf vndertoke
           [hit],
C.12.63   Withouten leue of [his] lord; no *lawe* wol hit graunte.
C.12.80   Bote onlyche loue and leaute as in my *lawes* demynge.
C.12.87   Loue withoute lele bileue a[nd] my *lawe* riht[ful]
C.12.90   Wel ouhte ȝe lordes þat *lawes* kepeth this lesson haue in mynde
C.12.93   For *lawe* withouten leutee, ley þer a bene!

C.12.113   In þe olde *lawe*, as þe lettre telleth, mennes sones me calde vs
C.12.120   Forthy lerne we t[he] *lawe* of loue as oure lord tauhte.
C.13.50   And ȝut he ylette, as y leue, for the *lawe* asketh
C.13.80   Beth nat ybounde, as beth [þ]e ryche, to [bothe two] *lawes*,
C.13.83   That þe *lawe* ȝeueth leue such low folk to be excused,
C.13.87   For if he loueth and byleueth as the *lawe* techeth–
C.13.91   Ther is no *lawe*, as y leue, wol lette hym þe gate
C.13.93   So þe pore of puyr reuthe may parforme þe *lawe*
C.13.118   Yf fals latyn be in þat lettre þe *lawe* hit enpugneth,
C.14.9   Lowe the and l[y]oue forth in þe *lawe* of holy chirche;
C.14.38   *Lawe* of loue oure lord wrouht] long ar crist were.
C.14.58   Arca dei in þe olde *lawe* leuytes hit kepte;
C.14.146   And as þe *lawe* lyketh to lyue oþer to dye:
C.14.152   And wel lo[s]liche he lolleth þere by þe *lawe* of holy churche:
C.14.209   Ac treuth þat trespassed neuere ne trauersede aȝens his *lawe*
C.14.210   Bote lyue[th] as his *lawe* t[echeth] and leueth þer be no bettere,
C.15.286   To haue allouaunce of his lord; by [þe] *lawe* he [hit] claymeth.
C.16.365   For ouerlong is here *lawe* but yf þay lacche suluer.
C.17.46   And marchauntȝ merciable wolde be and men of *lawe* bothe
C.17.58   With þat ȝoure bernes and ȝoure bloed by goed *lawe* may clayme!
C.17.71   Of þat þat holy churche of þe olde *lawe* claymeth
C.17.126   '[Lif in] loue and leutee in o byleue a[nd] *lawe*,
C.17.130   Loue *lawe* withoute leutee? allouable was hit neuere!
C.17.133   That lelyche they byleue, and ȝut here *lawe* diuerseth,
C.17.136   Ac oure lord aloueth no loue but *lawe* be to pause:
C.17.137   For lechours louyen aȝen þe *lawe* and at þe laste ben dampned
C.17.139   And lele men lyue as *lawe* techeth and loue þerof aryseth
C.17.152   Louen as by *lawe* of kynde oure lord god almyhty.
C.17.160   And aftur his leryng they lyue and by *lawe* of kynde
C.17.162   Thenne is *lawe* ylefte and leute vnknowe.
C.18.185   An heraud of Armes Ar eny *lawe* were.'
C.18.221   As þe bible bereth witnesse, A boek of þe olde *lawe*,
C.18.264   I leue þat ilke lord thenketh a newe *lawe* to make:
C.19.11   'Let se thy lettres,' quod y, 'we myhte þe *lawe* knowe.'
C.19.18   'Is here al thy lordes l[aw]es?' quod y; 'ȝe, leef me,' he saide,
C.19.34   What nedede hit thanne a newe *lawe* to brynge
C.19.36   And now cometh this sp[es and speketh] that hath aspyed þe *lawe*,
C.19.47   Tho þat lerneth thy *lawe* wollen litel while hit vse.'
C.20.74   Vppon cros bisyde Crist; so was þe comune *lawe*.
C.20.110   The which is lif þat oure lord in all *lawes* defendeth.
C.20.268   And bile[u]e on a newe *lawe* be ylost, lyf and soule.'
C.20.306   Thus this lord of liht such a *lawe* made
C.20.339   The which lyf and *lawe*, be hit longe yvysed,
C.20.354   Beth ywaer, ȝe wyse clerkes and ȝe witty of *lawe*,
C.20.381   Aȝeyne my loue and my leue: þe olde *lawe* techeth
C.20.387   So þat lyf quyte lyf; þe olde *lawe* hit asketh.
C.20.393   So leue hit nat, lucifer, aȝeyne þe *lawe* y feche
C.20.425   *Lawe* wolde he ȝoue hym lyf and he loked on hym.
C.20.428   And if *lawe* wol y loke on hem hit lith in my grace
C.20.443   Thus by *lawe*,' quod oure lord, 'lede y wol fro hennes
C.21.33   And fre men foule thralles þat followeth nat his *lawes*.
C.21.35   Bothe his lore and his *lawe*; now are they lowe cherles.
C.21.45   The *lawe* of lyf that laste shal euere
C.21.59   To make alle folk fre þat folweth his *lawe*.
C.21.111   For wyn is likned to *lawe* and lyfholinesse
C.21.112   And *lawe* lakked tho for men loued nat her enemyes
C.21.231   As prechours and prestes and prentises of *lawe*;
C.21.247   And fechen hit fro false men with foleuiles *lawes*;
C.21.306   Noþer of deuk ne of deth þat he ne dede *lawe*
C.21.310   With olde and newe [*lawe*] that loue myhte wexe
C.21.310   With olde lawe and newe [*lawe*] that loue myhte wexe
C.21.334   And þe londe of bileu, the *lawe* of holi churche.
C.21.446   Aȝen þe olde *lawe* and newe lawe, as Luk bereth witnesse:
C.21.446   Aȝen þe olde lawe and newe *lawe*, as Luk bereth witnesse:
C.21.468   And yf me lakketh to lyue by þe *lawe* wol y take hit
C.21.469   Ther y may hastilokest hit haue, for y am heed of *lawe*;
C.21.479   [Haue þou mayst] thyn askyng as thy *lawe* asketh:
C.22.10   And nede hath no *lawe* ne neuere shal falle in dette
C.22.18   And yf [hym] lust for to lape the *lawe* of kynde wolde
C.22.266   Of lewed and of lered; the *lawe* wol and asketh
C.22.274   And lerne logyk and *lawe* and eke contemplacioun,
C.22.278   For god made to men a *lawe* and Moyses hit tauhte:

laweful adj *laueful adj.* B 2 laweful (1) lawefulle (1)
B.11.145   But oonliche loue and leautee and my *laweful* domes.
B.15.308   And *lawefulle* men to lifholy men liflode brynge;

lawen lawhe(- > lauȝen

lawieres n *lauiere n.* A 1 lawieris; B 1
A. 8.61   ȝe legistris & *lawi[er]is*, [ȝe] wyten ȝif I leiȝe;
B. 7.60   Ye legistres and *lawieres*, [if I lye witeþ Mathew]:

laȝar n *laser n.(1)* B 5; C 7 laȝar (5) lasar (1) lasares (1)
B.15.593   And whan he lifte vp *Laȝar* þat leid was in graue
B.16.113   Saue þo he leched *laȝar* þat hadde yleye in graue;
B.16.255   And I loked in his lappe; a *laȝar* lay þerInne
B.18.267   'Swich a light, ayeins oure leue *laȝar* [i]t fette.
B.18.270   And lede it þer [*laȝar* is] and lightliche me bynde.
C. 8.278   And *laȝar* þe lene beggare þat longede aftur crommes–
C.17.302   Tho he luft vp *lasar* þat layde was in graue;
C.18.141   A lechede hem of here langour, bothe *lasares* and blynde,
C.18.143   And luft vp *laȝar* þat lay in his tombe;
C.18.271   And y lokede in his lappe; a *laȝar* lay þerynne
C.20.275   'Such a lyht aȝenes oure leue *laȝar* hit fette;
C.20.278   And lede hit þer *laȝar* is and lihtliche me bynde.

leaute n *leaute n.* A 4 leaute (3) leute (1); B 22 leaute (8) leautee (7)
      Leute (1) lewte (3) lewtee (3); C 32 leaute (4) leautee (2) leute (12)
      leutee (8) lewete (4) lewetee (1) lewte (1)
A. 2.100   ȝif any *Leaute* wile loke þei ligge togidere;
A. 3.267   But loue & louȝnesse & *leaute* togideris;
A. 3.269   *Leaute* shal do hym lawe [and no] lif ellis.
A. 3.273   þat lawe is lord waxen & *leute* is pore,
B.Pr.122   Shopen lawe and *leaute*, ech [lif] to knowe his owene.
B.Pr.126   And lene þee lede þi lond so *leaute* þee louye,
B. 2.21   And ylakked my lemman þat *leautee* is hoten,
B. 2.48   And lakke hem noȝt but lat hem worþe til *leaute* be Iustice
B. 2.136   If any [*lewte*] wol loke þei ligge togideres,
B. 3.291   Ac loue and lowenesse and *leautee* togideres;
B. 3.294   *Leaute* shal don hym lawe and no lif ellis.
B. 4.36   Ac [þ]ere is loue and *leautee* [hem likeþ] noȝt come þere:
B. 4.161   Loue leet of hire liȝt and *leaute* yet lasse,
B. 4.180   I wole haue *leaute* in lawe, and lete be al youre ianglyng;
B.11.84   And *lewte* [louȝ] on me [for] I loured [on þe frere];
B.11.85   'Wherfore lourestow?' quod *lewtee*, and loked on me harde.
B.11.91   'And wherof serueþ law', quod *lewtee*, 'if no lif vndertoke it
B.11.145   But oonliche loue and *leautee* and my laweful domes.
B.11.154   Lo! ye lordes, what *leautee* dide by an Emperour of Rome
B.11.167   Loue and *lewtee* is a leel science,
B.12.32   For he dooþ wel, wiþouten doute, þat dooþ as *lewte* techeþ
B.14.146   And lyuen as lawe techeþ, doon *leaute* to hem alle,
B.15.468   So loue and *leaute* lele men susteneþ.
B.19.89   Gold is likned to *leautee* þat laste shal euere
B.20.63   [Th]an to lyue lenger siþ [*Leute*] was so rebuked
B.20.146   And leet *leautee* a cherl and lyere a fre man.
C.Pr.150   And lene [þe] lede þy londe [so] *lewte* þe louye
C. 2.20   And [lakked] my lemman þat *leute* is hoten,
C. 2.51   Lacke hem nat but lat hem worthe til *leutee* be Iustice
C. 3.197   Thorw which loueday is loste þat *leute* myhte wynne
C. 3.379   Lawe, l[o]ue and *lewete* and hym lord antecedent,
C. 3.444   Ac loue and lownesse and *lewete* togyderes;
C. 3.447   *Lewete* shal do hym lawe and no lyf elles.
C. 4.36   Ac there is loue and *leutee* hit lyketh nat here hertes:
C. 4.156   Loue l[et]te of mede lyhte and *leutee* ȝut lasse
C. 4.174   Y wol haue *leutee* for my lawe and late be al ȝoure iangl[ing]
C. 6.195   Now, lord, for thy *lewete* on lechours haue mercy.'
C. 7.260   ȝef loue and *leute* and oure lawe [be] trewe:
C.10.172   By loue and by *leute*, þerby lyueth anima
C.11.158   Thus bileue and *le[ute]*, and loue is the thridde
C.12.23   And thenne louhe *leaute* for y loured on þe frere:
C.12.24   'Why lourest [thou]?' quod *leaute*; 'leue sire,' y saide,
C.12.32   'And wherof serueth lawe,' quod *leaute*, ' and no lyf vndertoke
             [hit]
C.12.80   Bote onlyche loue and *leaute* as in my lawes demynge.
C.12.89   'Lo! lordes, what *leute* dede and leele dome yvsed.
C.12.92   And louye for oure lordes loue and do *leute* euermore.
C.12.93   For lawe withouten *leutee*, ley þer a bene!
C.12.95   Bote loue and *leute* hem lede ylost is al þe tyme
C.12.97   So loue and *leute* ben oure lordes bokes
C.15.132   Saue loue and *leute* and lowenesse of herte,
C.17.126   '[Lif in] loue and *leute* in o byleue a[nd] lawe,
C.17.127   A loueknotte of *leutee* and of lele byleue,
C.17.130   Loue lawe withoute *leutee*? allouable was hit neuere!
C.17.138   And theues louyen and *leute* hatien and at þe laste ben hanged
C.17.162   Thenne is lawe ylefte and *leute* vnknowe.
C.21.89   Gold is likened to *lewetee* that laste shal euere
C.22.63   Then to lyue lengere sethe *leautee* was so rebuked
C.22.146   And leet *leautee* a cherl and lyare a fre man.

lecch- > lech-

leche n *leche n.(3)* &> *lechen* A 2 lechis; B 10 leche (8) leches (2); C 10
      lecche (1) leche (5) leches (4)
A. 2.185   Þanne louride *lechis* & lettris [hy] sente
A. 7.257   Þere arn mo liȝeris þan *lechis*, lord hem amende.
B. 1.204   Loue is *leche* of lif and next oure lord selue,
B. 2.226   Thanne lourede *leches*, and lettres þei sente
B. 6.273   [Ther are mo lieres þan] *leches*; lord hem amende!
B.14.302   A frend in alle fondynges, [of foule yueles *leche*],
B.14.318   And sobretee swete drynke and good *leche* in siknesse.
B.16.118   That he was *leche* of lif and lord of heigh heuene.
B.20.304   Conscience called a *leche* þat koude wel shryue:
B.20.309   Some liked noȝt þis *leche* and lettres þei sente
B.20.318   'We han no nede', quod Conscience; 'I woot no bettre *leche*
B.20.345   And was my lordes *leche* and my ladies boþe.
C. 1.199   So loue is *lecche* of lyf and lysse of alle payne
C. 2.236   Thenne lourede *leches* and lettre[s] thei sente
C. 3.301   Harlotes and hoores and also fals *leches*,
C. 8.294   Ther ar many luther *leches* Ac lele leches fewe
C. 8.294   Ther ar many luther leches Ac lele *leches* fewe;
C.16.138   And frende in alle fondynges and of foule eueles *leche*:
C.22.304   Consience calde a *leche* þat couthe wel shryue:
C.22.309   Somme liked nat this *leche* and letteres they sente
C.22.318   'We haen no nede,' quod Consience; 'y woet no bettere *leche*
C.22.345   And was my lordes *leche* and my ladyes bothe.

lechecraft n *lechecraft n.* A 1; B 4; C 3 lechecraeft (1) lechecraft (2)
A. 7.238   Eny l[e]f of *lechecraft* lere it me, my dere,
B. 6.254   Any leef of *lechecraft* lere it me, my deere,
B.13.337   *Lechecraft* of oure lord and leue on a wicche,
B.16.104   And lered hym *lechecraft* his lif for to saue
B.20.173   Lyf leeued þat *lechecraft* lette sholde Elde
C. 6.81   *Lechecraft* of oure lord and leue on a wycche
C.18.137   Ac liberum Arbitrium *lechecraeft* hym tauhte
C.22.173   Lyf leuede þat *lechecraft* lette sholde Elde

lechen n *lechen v.(2)* B 2 leched (1) lechen (1); C 4 leche (1) lechede (2)
      lechen (1)
B.13.253   Miȝte *lechen* a man as [me þynkeþ] it sholde.
B.16.113   Saue þo he *leched* laȝar þat hadde yleye in graue;
C. 8.189   And lame men he *lechede* with longes of bestes.
C.15.219   Lette this luythere [eir] and *leche* þe sike–
C.18.141   A *lechede* hem of here langour, bothe lasares and blynde,
C.19.95   That his lycame shal *lechen* at þe laste vs alle.'

lecherie n *lecherie n.* A 6 leccherie; B 16 leccherie (3) lecherie (13); C
      20 leccherye (3) lecherie (1) lechery (1) lecherye (15)
A.Pr.74   And leniþ it loselis þat *leccherie* haunten.
A. 1.30   And *leccherie* h[i]m lauȝte & lay be hem boþe;
A. 2.61   Wiþ alle þe lordsshipe of *leccherie* in lengþe & in brede;
A. 3.115   Leri[þ] hem *leccherie* þat loui[þ] hire ȝeftis.
A.11.36   *Leccherie* & losengerie & loselis talis.
A.11.118   And ek þe longe launde þat *leccherie* hatte.
B.Pr.77   And leneþ it Losels [þat] *leccherie* haunten.
B. 1.30   And *Leccherie* hym lauȝte, and lay by hem boþe;
B. 2.89   [Wiþ] al þe lordshipe of *leccherie* in lengþe and in brede,
B. 3.53   While ye loue lordes þat *lecherie* haunten.
B. 3.126   Lereþ hem *lecherie* þat loueþ hire ȝiftes.
B. 6.143   In *lecherie* and in losengerie ye lyuen, and in Sleuþe,
B. 9.184   Fo[r] lecherie in likynge is lymeyerd of helle.
B.10.50   *Lecherie*, losengerye and losels tales;
B.10.166   And also þe [longe] launde þat *lecherie* hatte,
B.13.343   Wiþ likynge of *lecherie* as by lokynge of his eiȝe.
B.14.250   *Lecherie* loueþ hym noȝt for he ȝyueþ but litel siluer
B.15.103   Forþi wolde ye lettrede leue þe *lecherie* of cloþyng,
B.19.418   And þer þei ligge and lenge moost *lecherie* þere regneþ".
B.20.111   And bihighte hem long lif, and *lecherie* he sente
B.20.114   This *lecherie* leide on wiþ [laughynge] chiere
B.20.311   Sire leef-to-lyue-in-*lecherie* lay þere and gronede;
C.Pr.75   And leneth hit lorelles þat *lecherye* haunten.
C. 2.96   With al þe lordschip of *leccherye* in lenghe and in Brede,
C. 2.191   On hem þat loueth *leccherye* lyppeth vp and rydeth,
C. 3.57   The whiles ȝe louyen lordes þat *lecherye* haunteth
C. 3.163   And lereth hem *lecherye* þat louyeth here ȝeftes.
C. 6.170   Thenne seyde *lecherye* 'alas!' and to oure lady cryede,
C. 6.176   As in likynge of *lecherye* my lycames gultes
C. 6.194   Y hadde likyng to lythe of *lecherye* tales.
C. 9.18   *Lechery* amonges lordes and here luyther custumes
C.10.161   So let *lecherye* and other luther synnes
C.10.285   That *lecherye* is a lykyng thynge, a lymȝerd of helle.
C.11.262   As in likyng of *lecherye* no lyf denyede!
C.16.90   *Lecherye* loueth no pore for he hath bote litel siluer
C.16.256   For wolde ȝe lettered leue þ[e] *lecherye* of clothyng
C.17.80   Is alayed with *leccherye* and oþer lustes of synne
C.18.36   Thorw *lecherie* and lustes so loude he gynneth blowe

C.21.418 And þer they lygge and lenge moest *lecherye* þer regneth".
C.22.111 And bihihte hem long lyf and *lecherye* he sente
C.22.114 This *lecherye* leyde [o]n with lauhyng chere
C.22.311 Sire l[ee]f-to-lyue-in-*lecherye* lay þer and groned;

lecherouse adj *lecherous adj.* A 1 leccherous; B 1
A. 2.89 For al be lesinges þou lyuest, & *leccherous* werkis;
B. 2.125 For al bi lesynges þow lyuest and *lecherouse* werkes;

lechyng ger *lechinge ger.* C 1
C.19.75 And lefte hym þere a *lechyng* to lyue yf he myhte

lechour n *lechour n.* A 2 lecchour; B 3 lecchours (1) lechour (2); C 2
lechours
A. 5.54 *Lecchour* seide 'allas!' & to oure lady criede
A. 7.250 L[o]ue hym nou3t, for he is a *lecchour* & likerous of tunge,
B. 5.71 *Lechour* seide 'allas!' and [to] oure lady cryde
B. 6.266 L[o]ue hym no3t for he is [a] *lech[our]* and likerous of tunge,
B.13.352 And how þat *lecchours* louye laughen and Iapen,'
C. 6.195 Now, lord, for thy lewete on *lechours* haue mercy.'
C.17.137 For *lechours* louyen a3en þe lawe and at þe laste ben dampned

led > leed; ledare(s > ledere; leddist > leden; lede > leden,leode

leden v *leden v.(1)* A 8 leddist (1) lede (4) leden (1) lediþ (1) let (1); B
31 lad (2) ladde (5) laddest (1) lede (13) leden (4) ledeþ (5) let (1); C
32 lad (2) ladde (7) lat (1) lede (15) leden (3) ledest (1) ledeth (2) let
(1)
A. 2.99 *Lediþ* hire to lundoun þere þe lawe is yhandlit
A. 2.143 And makiþ of lyere a lang carte to *leden* al þis oþere,
A. 3.148 She *let* lawe as hire list & louedaies makiþ;
A. 4.130 Þat lawe shal ben a labourer & *lede* afeld donge,
A. 4.131 And loue shal *lede* þi land as þe lef likeþ.'
A. 4.147 And alle my lige ledis to *lede* þus euene.'
A. 8.173 How þou *leddist* þi lif here & his lawe keptest,
A.11.20 And *lede* forþ a loueday to lette þe treuþe,
B.Pr.112 Thanne kam þer a kyng; kny3thod hym *ladde*;
B.Pr.126 And lene þee *lede* þi lond so leaute þee louye,
B. 2.135 *Ledeþ* hire to London þere [lawe] is [yhandled],
B. 2.182 And makeþ a lyere a lang cart to *leden* alle þise oþere,
B. 3.158 She *ledeþ* lawe as hire list and louedaies makeþ,
B. 3.298 And ouer lordes lawes [*ledeþ*] þe Reaumes.
B. 4.147 That lawe shal ben a laborer and *lede* afeld donge,
B. 4.148 And loue shal *lede* þi lond as þe leef likeþ.'
B. 4.184 [And] alle youre lige leodes to *lede* þus euene'.
B. 5.248 And wiþ lumbardes lettres I *ladde* gold to Rome;
B. 5.490 But in oure secte was þe sorwe and þi sone it *ladde*;
B. 7.195 How þow *laddest* þi lif here and hi[s] law[e] keptest,
B. 9.16 [By his leryng is *lad* þat lady Anima].
B. 9.59 What anima is leef or looþ; he l[e]t hire at his wille,
B. 9.193 A[c] if þei *leden* þus hir lif it likeþ god almy3ty,
B.10.20 And *lede* forþ a loueday to lette [þe] truþe,
B.10.22 Thei *lede* lordes wiþ lesynges and bilieþ truþe.
B.11.21 That *leden* þee wole to likynge al þi lif tyme'.
B.13.12 And how þat lewed men ben *lad*, but oure lord hem helpe,
B.13.455 *Leden* þo þat [liþed] hem to Luciferis feste
B.14.307 And euer þe lasse þat he [*lede*], þe [li3ter] he is of herte:
B.15.83 If I lye on yow to my lewed wit, *ledeþ* me to brennyng!
B.15.234 That wiþouten wiles *ledeþ* [wel] hir lyues:
B.17.67 He lighte adown of Lyard and *ladde* hym in his hande,
B.17.74 And *ladde* hym so forþ on Lyard to lex Christi, a graunge
B.17.120 Hope shal *lede* hem forþ with loue as his lettre telleþ,
B.18.270 And *lede* it þer [la3ar is] and lightliche me bynde.
B.18.272 That swich a lord and [a] light sholde *lede* hem alle hennes.'
B.18.400 Thus by lawe', quod oure lord, '*lede* I wole fro hennes
B.18.406 But leten hym *lede* forþ [what] hym liked and lete [what] hym
liste.
B.19.224 Coueitise and vnkyndenesse Cardinals hym to *lede*.
C.Pr.139 Thenne cam the[r] a kyng; knygh[t]hede hym *la[dd]e*;
C.Pr.150 And lene [þe] *lede* þy londe [so] lewte þe louye
C. 2.151 And *ledeth* here to londone there lawe may declare
C. 2.195 And maketh of lyare a lang cart to *lede* al this othere,
C. 3.129 And sente to se here; y myhte nat se þat *ladde* here.
C. 3.196 And le[*deth*] þe lawe as here luste and louedayes maketh,
C. 4.12 How thow *ledest* my peple, lered and lewed.'
C. 4.144 That lawe shal ben a laborer and *lede* afeld donge
C. 4.145 And loue shal *lede* thi land as þe leef lyketh.'
C. 4.178 And alle 3oure lege l[e]des to *lede* thus euene.'
C. 6.246 And with lumbardus lettres le[*d*]e gold to Rome;
C. 7.115 *Leden* tho þat lythed hem to luciferes feste
C. 7.253 And may *lede* in þat he loueth as here lef lyketh.
C. 9.341 How we *ladde* oure lyf here and his lawes kepte
C.10.142 And by his leryng is *lad* þat lady Anima.
C.11.180 That *lede* þe wol to lykynge Al thy lyf tyme.'
C.12.95 Bote loue and leute hem *lede* ylost is al þe tyme

C.13.56 Ther þe marchaunt l[et] a male with many kyne thynges
C.15.15 And how þat lewede men ben *lad*, but oure lord hem helpe,
C.15.274 The whiche wil loue *lat* to oure lordes place
C.16.18 That al here lyf *leden* in lownesse and in pouerte.
C.16.142 And euere þe lasse þat [eny] *lede* þe lihtere his herte is there,
C.18.3 Thenne louh liberum Arbitrium and *ladde* me forth with tales
C.18.77 And chaste *leden* here lyf, is lyf of contemplacioun,
C.18.177 This iewes to þe iustices iesus they *ladde*.
C.19.66 [A l]ihte a[dou]n of lyard and *ladde* hym in his hand[e]
C.19.73 And *ladde* hym forth to lauacrum lex dei, a grang[e]
C.20.278 And *lede* hit þer la3ar is and lihtliche me bynde.
C.20.280 That such a lord and a lihte sh[olde] *lede* hem alle hennes.
C.20.443 Thus by lawe,' quod oure lord, '*lede* y wol fro hennes
C.20.449 Bote leten hym *lede* forth which hym luste and leue which hym
likede.
C.21.224 Coueytise and vnkyndenesse Cardynales hym [to] *lede*.

ledene n *leden n.* B 3; C 3
B.12.246 And vnlouelich of *ledene* and looþ for to here.
B.12.255 His *ledene* be in oure lordes ere lik a pies chiteryng;
B.12.264 The larke þat is a lasse fowel is moore louelich of *ledene*,
C.13.172 And ferlyede of his fayrenesse and of his foul le[*den*]e.
C.14.178 His le[*d*]ene is vnloueliche and lothliche his careyne
C.14.185 The larke þat is a lasse foul is loueloke[re] of *ledene*

ledere n *ledere n.(1)* A 2; B 6 ledere (5) lederes (1); C 7 ledare (5)
ledares (2)
A.10.46 Heo is lyf & *ledere*, a lemman of heuene.
A.11.212 A *ledere* of l[oue]d[a]ies & a lond biggere;
B. 1.159 Forþi is loue *ledere* of þe lordes folk of heuene
B. 1.161 Right so is loue a *ledere* and þe lawe shapeþ;
B.10.191 For þere þat loue is *ledere* lakke[þ] neuere grace.
B.10.312 A *ledere* of louedayes and a lond buggere.
B.12.96 And *lederes* for lewed men and for lettred boþe.
B.19.100 And manye wiles and wit þat wole ben a *ledere*.
C. 1.155 Forthi is loue *ledare* of [þe] lordes folk of heuene.
C. 1.157 Ryht so is loue [a] *ledare* and þe lawe shapeth;
C. 5.158 *Ledares* of l[ou]edays, and londes ypurchaced
C. 8.250 And *ledares* for here laboryng ouer al þe lordes godes;
C.15.169 As for here lord and here *ledare* and l[y]ue as thow techest.'
C.16.158 Thenne hadde Actyf a *ledare* þat hihte lib[e]rum arbitrium;
C.21.100 And many wyles and wyt þat wol be a *ledare*.

ledes > leode

ledynge ger *ledinge ger.(1)* A 1 ledyng; B 1; C 1
A. 2.25 And al is li3eris *ledyng* þat hy li3en togideris.
B. 2.43 And al is lieres *ledynge* þat [lady] is þus ywedded.
C. 2.46 And al is lyares *ledynge* th[at] lady is thus ywedded.

ledis > leode

leed n *led n.* A 1 led; B 3; C 1
A. 6.78 Wiþ no *led* but [wiþ] loue & lou3nesse, as breþeren of o wombe.
B. 5.591 Wiþ no *leed* but wiþ loue and lowe[nesse] as breþeren [of o
wombe].
B.13.83 Were molten *leed* in his mawe and Mahoun amyddes.
B.13.246 Saue a pardon wiþ a peis of *leed* and two polles amyddes.
C. 7.238 With no *leed* but with loue and with lele speche;

leef n1 *lef n.(1)* A 3 lef; B 16 leef (8) leues (8); C 10 leef (3) lef (2) leue
(1) leues (4)
A. 5.117 Ferst I lernide to lei3e a *lef* oþer twei3e;
A. 7.238 Eny l[e]f of lechecraft lere it me, my dere,
A. 8.159 Þis is [a] l[e]f of oure beleue, as lettrid men vs [tech]iþ,
B. 1.156 Was neuere *leef* vpon lynde lighter þerafter,
B. 3.340 For þat lyne was no lenger at þe *leues* ende.
B. 3.341 Hadde she loked þat [left] half and þe *leef* torned
B. 3.347 Ac yow failed a konnynge clerk þat kouþe þe *leef* han torned.
B. 5.140 Til þei beere *leues* of lowe speche lordes to plese,
B. 5.201 First I lerned to lye a *leef* ouþer tweyne;
B. 5.268 For þe beste book in oure hous, þei3 brent gold were þe *leues*,
B. 6.254 Any l[e]f of lechecraft lere me, my dere;
B. 7.181 This is [a *leef*] of oure bileue, as lettred men vs techeþ:
B.12.231 And tau3te hym and Eue to helien hem wiþ *leues*.
B.13.96 And but [þe] first [*leef*] be lesyng leue me neuere eft.
B.15.102 Shal neuere flour ne fruyt [wexe] ne fair *leef* be grene.
B.15.287 That no man my3te hym se for mosse and for *leues*.
B.16.6 The *leues* ben lele wordes, þe lawe of holy chirche;
B.16.28 Coueitise comþ of þat wynd and crepeþ among þe *leues*
B.16.35 And forbiteþ þe blosmes ri3t to be bare *leues*.
C. 1.152 Was neuer *lef* vppon lynde lyhtere theraftur\
C. 3.492 That l[yne] was no lengur at þe *leues* ende
C. 3.493 Ac hadde she loked in þe luft half and þe *lef* turned
C. 5.97 And sette his los at a *leef* at the laste ende,
C. 6.209 Furste y lerned to lye a *leef* oþer tweye;

C.15.103　And bote þe furste *leef* be lesyng[e] leue me neuere aftur.
C.16.249　Þere som bowes bereth *leues* and som bereth none:
C.16.255　Shal neuere flour ne fruyt wexe ne fayre *leue* be grene.
C.17.14　That no man myhte se hym for moes and for *leues*.
C.18.48　So this lordeynes lithereth þerto þat alle þe *leues* falleth

leef n2 *lef n.(2)* B 1
B. 2.33　Shal be my lord and I his *leef* in þe hei3e heuene.

leef adj *lef adj.& adv.* A 8 lef (2) leue (1) leuere (2) leuest (1) leueste (1) leuist (1); B 20 leef (4) leeue (1) leue (3) leuer (1) leuere (8) leuest (2) leueste (1); C 26 leef (3) lef (1) leue (11) leuer (2) leuere (5) leuest (2) leuore (2)

A. 1.35　Ne liflode to þe lykam þat *lef* is to þe soule.
A. 1.136　Þat loue is þe *leuest* þing þat oure lord askiþ,
A. 1.178　Loue is þe *leueste* þing þat oure lord askiþ,
A. 3.6　What man of þis world þat hire were *leuist*;
A. 6.43　'3a, *leue* piers,' quaþ þe pilgrimes & profride hym hire.
A.11.11　Þei do but drauele þeron; draf were hem *leuere*
A.11.14　Þat hem were *leuere* lond, & lordsshipe on erþe,
A.12.6　Þe were *lef* to lerne but loþ for to stodie;
B. 1.37　Ne liflode to þ[e] likame [þat *lef* is to þ[e] soule.
B. 1.151　And lered it Moyses for þe *leueste* þyng and moost lik to heuene,
B. 3.6　What man of þis [world] þat hire were *leuest*.
B. 4.39　Moore þan for] loue of oure lord or alle hise *leeue* Seintes.
B. 5.38　"[Lo], þe *leuere* child þe moore loore bihoueþ";
B. 5.142　And now is fallen þerof a fruyt þat folk han wel *leuere*
B. 5.154　Hir [were] *leuere* swowe or swelte þan suffre any peyne.
B. 5.406　I haue *leuere* here an harlotrye or a Somer game of Souters,
B. 5.556　'Ye! *leue* Piers', quod þise pilgrimes and profred hym huyre.
B. 9.59　What anima is *leef* or looþ; he l[e]t hire at his wille,
B.10.11　Thei doon but dr[a]uele þeron; draf were hem *leuere*
B.10.14　That hem were *leuere* lond and lordshipe on erþe,
B.11.209　Forþi loue we as *leue* [children shal], and ech man laughe of ooþer,
B.13.200　'Me were *leuere*, by oure lord, and I lyue sholde,
B.13.322　Lyinge and la[kk]ynge and *leue* tonge to chide;
B.17.284　He fordooþ *leuest* lyght þat oure lord louyeþ.
B.18.411　Ne no loue *leuere*, ne leuer frendes,
B.18.411　Ne no loue leuere, ne *leuer* frendes,
B.20.195　For þe lyme þat she loued me fore and *leef* was to feele
B.20.311　Sire *leef*-to-lyue-in-lecherie lay þere and gronede;
C. 1.35　Ne liflode to þe lycame þat *lef* is [to] þe soule.
C. 2.18　'*Leue* lady,' quod y tho,'layn nought yf 3e knowen'.
C. 3.6　What man of this world þat here [were *leuest*].
C. 3.73　Forthy, l[e]*ue* lordes, leueth suche writynges;
C. 5.85　Is the *leuest* labour þat oure lord pleseth.
C. 6.116　With lewed and lered þat *leef* ben to here
C. 6.129　Here were *leuer* swowe or swelte then soffre eny payne.
C. 6.171　'Lady, to thy *leue* sone loute for me nouthe
C. 6.292　3ut were me *lauer*, by oure lord, lyue al by wellecresses
C. 6.313　For me is *leuere* in this lyue as a lorel begge
C. 7.22　Y hadde *leuere* here an harlotrye or a lesyng to lauhen of
C. 7.200　'3e! *leue* Peres,' quod thise pilgrimes and profrede Peres mede.
C.11.9　They do bote dr[a]uele þeron; draf were hem *leuere*
C.11.72　And yf thow haue litel, *leue* sone, loke by þy lyue
C.11.224　A[c] me were *leuere*, by oure lord, a lyppe of goddes grace
C.12.24　'Why lourest [thou]?' quod leaute; '*leue* sire,' y saide,
C.12.117　Forthy loue we as *leue* childerne, lene hem þat nedeth
C.15.178　Me were *leuere*, by oure lord, and y leue sholde,
C.16.165　'*Leue* liberum arbitrium,' quod y, 'of what lond ar 3e?
C.17.148　And þat is charite, *leue* chield, to be cher ouer thy soule;
C.18.1　'*Leue* liberum Arbitrium,' quod y, 'y leue, as y hope,
C.18.104　'*Leue* liberum Arbitrium, lat some lyf hit shake.'
C.20.454　Ne no loue *leuore* ne leuore frendes
C.20.454　Ne no loue leuore ne *leuore* frendes
C.22.195　For þe lyme þat she loued me fore and *leef* was to fele
C.22.311　Sire l[ee]*f*-to-lyue-in-lecherye lay þer and groned;

leef adv *lef adj.& adv.* A 3 lef (1) leuere (2); B 8 leef (2) lef (1) leue (1) leuere (2) leuest (2); C 5 leef (3) lef (1) leuest (1)

A. 1.131　For to loue þi lord *leuere* þanne þiselue;
A. 4.131　And loue shal lede þi land as þe *lef* likeþ.'
A. 6.50　Þat 3e loue hym *leuere* þanne þe lif in 3oure hertis;
B.Pr.163　Boþe in wareyne and in waast where hem [*leue*] like[þ];
B. 1.143　For to louen þi lord *leuere* þan þiselue.
B. 3.18　To be wedded at þi wille and wher þee *leef* likeþ
B. 4.148　And loue shal lede þi lond as þe *leef* likeþ.'
B. 5.563　That ye louen oure lord god *leuest* of alle þynges,
B.10.361　That is, loue þi lord god *leuest* abouen alle,
B.13.349　And as [*lef*] in lente as out of lente, alle tymes yliche.
B.15.195　'By crist! I wolde I knewe hym', quod I, 'no creature *leuere*.'
C. 1.142　For to louye thy lord *leuest* of alle,
C. 3.19　For to wedde at thy wille [and] where the *leef* li[k]leth
C. 4.145　And loue shal lede thi land as the *leef* lyketh.'

C. 6.183　As *leef* in lente as out of lente, alle tymes ylyche,
C. 7.253　And may lede in þat he loueth as here *lef* lyketh.

leef &> leue(n; leege > lige

leek n *lek n.* A 1 lek; B 1
A. 5.64　As a *lek* þat hadde leyn longe in þe sonne,
B. 5.81　As a *leek* þat hadde yleye longe in þe sonne

leel(e > lele; leely(- leelli- > lelly; leem > leme; leene > lene; leep > lepen

leere n *ler n.* A 1 lire; B 1; C 1 lere
A. 1.3　A louely lady of *lire* in lynene ycloþid
B. 1.3　A louely lady of *leere* in lynnen ycloþed
C. 1.3　A louely lady of [*lere*] in lynnene [y]clothed

lees > lesen

leest adj *leste adj.(1) cf. lasse* A 5 lest (1) leste (4); B 13 leest (2) leeste (10) leste (1); C 10 leest (1) leeste (1) lest (1) leste (7)

A. 2.158　Shal neuere man of þis molde meynprise þe [*l*]*este*,
A. 3.23　Þe *leste* man of here mayne a mutoun of gold.
A. 3.192　Þe *leste* brol of his blood a barouns pere.
A. 8.45　Men of lawe hadde *lest* for le[ttr]id þei ben alle;
A.11.90　But he lyue in þe *leste* degre þat longiþ to dowel
B. 2.197　Shal neuere man of þis molde meynprise þe *leeste*,
B. 3.24　The *leeste* man of hire meynee a moton of golde.
B. 3.205　The *leeste* brol of his blood a Barones piere.
B. 5.396　Ac neiþer of oure lord ne of oure lady þe *leeste* þat euere was maked.
B. 7.40　Men of lawe *leest* pardon hadde, [leue þow noon ooþer],
B.10.28　Thilke þat god [moost gyueþ] *leest* good þei deleþ,
B.10.137　But he lyue in þe [*leeste* degree] þat longeþ to dowel
B.11.49　I hadde no likyng, leue me, [þe *leste*] of hem to knowe.
B.11.346　Hadde neuere wye wit to werche þe *leeste*.
B.12.269　Thus he likneþ in his logik þe *leeste* fowel oute.
B.13.186　And lere yow if yow like þe *leeste* point to knowe
B.17.43　Than for to techen hem two, and to hard to lerne þe *leeste*!
B.18.405　They dorste no3t loke on oure lord, þe [*leeste*] of hem alle,
C. 2.211　Shal neuere man on þis molde maynpryse þe *leste*,
C. 3.25　The *leste* man of here mayne a motoun of gold.
C. 3.248　The *leste* ladde þat longeth with hym, be þe londe ywonne,
C. 3.262　The *leste* brolle of his blod a Barones pere.
C. 7.12　Ac of oure lord ne of oure lady þe *leste* þat euere was maked.
C. 9.44　Men of lawe hadde *lest* þat loth were to plede
C.11.75　Bote lythen how þey myhte lerne *leest* go[e]d spene.
C.13.157　Hadde neuere weye wyt to worche þe *leste*.
C.14.190　Likneth in here logik þe *leste* foul out[e].
C.20.448　They dorste nat loke on oure lord, the *leste* of hem alle,

leeste adv *leste adv. cf. lasse* B 1; C 1
B.18.285　I leeue þat lawe nyl no3t lete hym þe *leeste*.'
C. 3.210　That no lond ne loueth the and 3ut *leeste* thyn owene.

leet(e > leten; leeue > leef,leue; leeued -en > leue; lef > leef,leue

left adj *lift adj.* A 5; B 7 left (5) lift (1) luft (1); C 5 left (1) lyft (1) luft (3)

A. 2.5　'Loke on þi *left* half, & lo where he standis,
A. 2.7　I lokide on [my] *left* half as þat lady me tau3te,
A. 3.55　Let not þi *left* hond, late ne raþe,
A. 6.65　Leue hem on þi *left* half, & loke nou3t þereaftir,
A.11.119　Leue hym on þi *left* half a large myle or more,
B. 2.5　'Loke [o]n þi *left* half, and lo where he stondeþ,
B. 2.7　I loked on my *left* half as þe lady me tau3te
B. 3.73　Lat no3t þi *left* half, late ne raþe,
B. 3.341　Hadde she loked þat [*left*] half and þe leef torned
B. 4.62　That wrong was a wikked *luft* and wro3te muche sorwe.
B. 5.578　Leue hem on þi *lift* half and loke no3t þerafter.
B.10.167　Leue [hym] on þi *left* half a large myle or more
C. 2.5　'Loke [o]n thy *left* half, and loo where he standeth,
C. 2.8　Y lokede [o]n my *luft* half as þe lady me tauhte
C. 3.75　Lat nat thy *lyft* ha[lf], oure lord techeth,
C. 3.493　Ac hadde she loked in þe *luft* half and þe lef torned
C. 7.225　And leu[e] hem [o]n þ[y] *luft* ha[lf] and loke [nat] þeraftur

lefte > leuen

leg n *leg n.* A 2 leg (1) leggys (1); B 2 leg (1) legges (1); C 4 leg (1) legges (3)
A. 7.114　Somme leide here *leg* alery as suche lorellis cunne,
A.12.78　[Lene & rewlyche, with *leggys* ful smale].
B. 6.122　Somme leide hir *le[g]* aliry as swiche lo[r]els konneþ
B.18.73　A Cachepol cam forþ and craked boþe hir *legges*
C. 8.129　[Somme] leyde here *legges* alery as suche lorelles conneth
C. 9.143　Vnlouke his *legges* abrood or ligge at his ese,
C. 9.216　He þat lolleth is lame or his *leg* out of ioynte,
C.20.75　A cachepol cam [forth] a[nd] craked ato he[re] *legges*

legates n *legate n.* B 1; C 1 legatus
B.13.421 Ye lordes and ladies and *legates* of holy chirche
C. 7.81 Ʒe lordes and ladies and *legatus* of holy churche

lege > leggen,lige

legende n *legende n.* A 1; B 1; C 2
A.11.262 In þe *legende* of lif longe er I were,
B.10.381 In þe *legende* of lif longe er I were,
C.11.204 In þe *legende* of lyf longe ar y were.
C.17.157 Louyeth nat þat lord aryht as by þe *legende* sanctorum

leges > lige

legge v1 *leggen v.(1) &> leggen* B 1
B.11.96 It is licitum for lewed men to [*legge*] þe soþe

leggen v2 *leien v.(1)* A 4 ley (1) leid (1) leide (2); B 26 legge (7) leggen
(2) ley (1) leid (1) leyd (1) leide (4) leyde (2) leiden (1) leyden (1)
leye (1) leyen (1) leieþ (1) leyeþ (1) leiþ (2); C 24 layd (1) layde (1)
layth (1) lege (1) legge (7) leggeth (1) leide (2) ley (2) leyde (5) leyeth
(1) leyth (1) yleyd (1)
A. 3.189 I durste han *leid* my lif & no lesse wed
A. 5.196 As whoso *leide* lynes to lacche wiþ [foules].
A. 7.114 Somme *leide* here leg alery as suche lorellis cunne,
A. 7.252 And ʒif þou diʒete þe þus I dar *ley* myn armes
B. 2.34 And what man takeþ Mede, myn heed dar I *legge*,
B. 3.202 I dorste haue *leyd* my lif and no lasse wedde
B. 5.241 And lene it for loue of þe cros, to *legge* a wed and lese it.
B. 5.348 As whoso *leiþ* lynes to lacche [wiþ] foweles.
B. 5.352 For to liften hym o lofte and *leyde* hym on his knowes.
B. 6.122 Somme *leide* hir le[g] aliry as swiche lo[r]els konneþ
B. 6.268 And if þow diete þee þus I dar *legge* myne [armes]
B.10.106 And *leyden* fautes vpon þe fader þat formede vs alle,
B.11.171 'Lawe wiþouten loue', quod Troianus, '*ley* þer a bene!'
B.11.348 Lerned to *legge* þe stikkes in whiche she *leyeþ* and bredeþ.
B.11.348 Lerned to *legge* þe stikkes in whiche she *leyeþ* and bredeþ.
B.12.114 Hadde neuere lewed man leue to *leggen* hond on þat cheste
B.12.120 And *leiden* hand þeron to liften it vp loren here lif after.
B.13.146 And *leye* on hym þus with loue til he lauʒe on þe.
B.15.191 And *leggen* on longe wiþ Laboraui in gemitu meo,
B.15.593 And whan he lifte vp Laʒar þat *leid* was in graue.
B.16.44 And *leiþ* a laddre þerto, of lesynges are þe ronges,
B.17.73 Enbawmed hym and bond his heed and in his [barm] hym *leide*,
B.18.31 Lif seiþ þat he lieþ and *leieþ* his lif to wedde
B.18.34 And *legge* it þer hym likeþ, and Lucifer bynde,
B.18.59 The lord of lif and of light þo *leide* hise eighen togideres.
B.18.77 That noon harlot were so hardy to *leyen* hond vpon hym.
B.18.158 So shal þis deeþ fordo, I dar my lif *legge*,
B.20.13 Ne wight noon wol ben his boruʒ, ne wed haþ noon to *legge*;
B.20.114 This lecherie *leide* on wiþ [laughynge] chiere
B.20.189 'Ye, leue, lurdeyn?' quod he, and *leyde* on me wiþ Age,
C. 3.259 Y durste haue *yleyd* my lyf and no lasse wedde
C. 4.191 'And y dar *lege* my lyf þat loue wol lene þe seluer
C. 5.73 And lordes sones here laboreres and *leyde* here rentes to wedde
C. 6.406 As hoso *layth* lynes for to lacche foules.
C. 6.410 For to lyfte hym aloft [and] *leyde* hym on his knees.
C. 8.129 [Somme] *leyde* here legges alery as suche lorelles conneth
C. 8.289 And yf thow dyete the thus y dar *legge* myn eres
C. 8.291 And his cloke of callabre for his comune[s] *legge*
C.12.93 For lawe withouten leutee, *ley* þer a bene!
C.12.184 That ben *layd* in louhe erthe, ylore as hit were,
C.13.159 Lernede to [*l*]*egge* stikkes þat ley on here neste.
C.14.59 Hadde neuere lewede [man] leue to *legge* hand on þat cheste
C.14.63 And all lewede þat *leide* hand þeron loren lyf aftir.
C.15.146 And *ley* on hym thus with loue til he lauhe on þe.
C.16.145 For lordes alloueth hym litel or *leggeth* ere to his resoun;
C.17.302 Tho he luft vp lasar þat *layde* was in graue;
C.18.44 And *leyth* a laddere þerto, of lesynges ben þe ronges,
C.20.30 Lyf saith þat a lyeth and [*leyeth*] his lyf to wedde,
C.20.33 And *legge* hit þere hym liketh and lucifer bynde
C.20.59 The lord of lyf and of lihte tho *leyde* his eyes togederes.
C.20.161 And so shal this deth fordo, y dar my lyf *legge*,
C.22.13 Ne wyht no[n] wol be his borwe ne wed hath [non] to *legge*;
C.22.114 This lecherye *leyde* [o]n with lauhyng chere
C.22.189 'Ʒe, leue, lordeyne?' quod he, and *leide* on me with age

legges > leg

legion n *legioun n.* A 1 legionis; B 2 legion (1) legions (1); C 1 legioun
A. 1.109 Lucifer wiþ *legionis* leride it in heuene,
B. 1.111 Lucifer wiþ *legions* lerned it in heuene
B.20.87 Largeliche a *legion* loste [þe] lif soone.
C.22.87 Largeliche a *legioun* lees the lyf sone.

legistres n *legistre n.* A 1 legistris; B 2
A. 8.61 Ʒe *legistris* & lawi[er]is, [ʒe] wyten ʒif I leiʒe;
B. 7.14 *Legistres* of boþe lawes þe lewed þerwiþ to preche,
B. 7.60 Ye *legistres* and lawieres, [if I lye witeþ Mathew]:

legityme adj *legitime adj.* C 1
C.10.211 That lele *legityme* by þe lawe may claymen.

lei > leye; ley > leggen,ligge

leiaunce n *liaunce n.* C 1
C.18.200 Thre bilongeth to a lord þat *leiaunce* claymeth,

leid- > leggen

leye n *leie n.(2)* B 3 leye; C 3 leye (2) lye (1)
B.17.210 Fostren forþ a flawmbe and a fair *leye*
B.17.217 Wiþouten *leye* or light [liþ fir in þe macche]–
B.17.280 The which is lif and loue, þe *leye* of mannes body.
C.19.176 Fostren forth a flaume and a feyr *lye*
C.19.183 Withouten *leye* [or] lihte lith fuyr in þe mache–
C.19.261 The which is lyf and loue, the *leye* of mannes body.

leye adj *leie adj.* C 2 lei (1) leye (1)
C.10.217 On a *leye* land aʒeynes his lordes wille,
C.10.272 Ac they lyen *le[i]*, here neyther lyketh other.

leye(n &> leggen,ligge

leyes n *leie n.(3)* A 1 laiʒes; B 1; C 1
A. 8.5 And bad hym holde hym at hom & erien his *laiʒes*.
B. 7.5 And bad hym holde hym at home and erien hise *leyes*,
C. 9.5 And bad hym holden hym at hoem and eryen his *leyes*

leieþ > leggen; leighe > lyen; leiʒe > lyen,ligge; leyhing > laughyng; leyn > ligge; leiþ > leggen,lyen; leiʒe > ligge,lyen; leiʒede > lyen; leiʒen > ligge; leiʒer(- > liere; leiʒeþ > lyen; lek > leek

leksed n *lek n.* C 1
C.12.191 As lynsed, *leksed* and lentesedes all

lele adj *lel adj.& n.* A 2; B 27 leel (3) lele (22) lelest (2); C 44 leel (4)
leele (4) lel (1) lele (35)
A.11.182 'It is a wel *lel[e]* lif,' quaþ she, 'among þe lewide peple;
A.11.238 And for his *lele* beleue, whanne he his lif tyneþ,
B.10.355 And for his *lele* bileue, whan he þe lif tyneþ,
B.10.439 Wher fo[r] loue] a man worþ allowed þere and hise *lele* werkes,
B.11.69 And loued me þe lasse for my *lele* speche.
B.11.162 Ac þus *leel* loue and lyuyng in truþe
B.11.167 Loue and lewtee is a *leel* science,
B.11.219 Thanne is bileue a *lele* help, aboue logyk or lawe.
B.11.241 That we sholde be lowe and loueliche, [and *lele* ech man to oþer],
B.12.62 And in *lele* lyuynge men and in lif holy,
B.13.287 In likynge of *lele* lif and a liere in soule;
B.13.294 And louelokest to loken on and *lelest* of werkes,
B.14.46 Lyue þoruʒ *leel* bileue, [as oure lord] witnesseþ:
B.15.34 Thanne is *lele* loue my name, and in latyn Amor;
B.15.93 Thoruʒ *lele* libbynge men þat goddes lawe techen,
B.15.423 To lyue by litel and in lowe houses by *lele* mennes almesse.
B.15.439 Into *lele* bileue; þe lightloker me þinkeþ
B.15.468 So loue and leaute *lele* men susteneþ.
B.15.582 And Iewes lyuen in *lele* lawe; oure lord wroot it hymselue
B.16.6 The leues ben *lele* wordes, þe lawe of holy chirche;
B.17.27 And *lelest* to leue [on] for lif and for soule?
B.17.47 Than for to louye and lene as wel lorels as *lele*.
B.17.220 *Lele* loue or lif þat oure lord shapte.
B.17.228 Til þat *lele* loue ligge on hym and blowe.
B.19.60 And siþ [alle hise *lele* liges largely he yeueþ]
B.19.237 And lyue, by þat labour], a *lele* lif and a trewe,
B.19.250 And alle he lered to be *lele*, and ech a craft loue ooþer,
B.20.138 For a [Meneuer Mantel he] made *lele* matrymoyne
C.Pr.88 That is *lele* loue and lyf among lered and lewed,
C.Pr.147 With *lele* labour to lyue while lif on londe lasteth.
C. 3.317 To here [*lele*] and lege, loue [is] the cause;
C. 3.318 And yf th[e] *lele* and lege be luyther men aftur
C. 3.339 That [is] þe gyft þat god gyueth to alle *lele* lyuynge,
C. 3.348 As a *leel* laborer byleueth [with] his maister
C. 4.175 And by *lele* and lyfholy my lawe shal be demed.'
C. 5.103 The l[y]f þat is louable and *leele* to thy soule.'
C. 7.197 He is as louh as a lombe and *leel* of his tonge.
C. 7.238 With no leed but with loue and with *lele* speche;
C. 7.251 A ful *leel* lady vnlek hit of grace
C. 8.74 That lollares and loseles *lele* men holdeth,
C. 8.140 That *lele* land tilynge men leely byswynken.
C. 8.260 Thorw eny *lele* labour as thorw lymes and handes:
C. 8.294 Ther ar many luther leches Ac *lele* leches fewe;
C. 9.14 *Lele* and fol of loue and no lord drede,

C.10.79   And thorw *lele* labour lyueth and loueth his emcristene
C.10.211   That *lele* legityme by þe lawe may claymen.
C.10.291   Clene of lyf and in loue of soule and in *lele* wedlok.
C.11.293   Lewed *lele* laboreres and land tulyng peple
C.12.87   Loue withoute *lele* bileue a[nd] my lawe riht[ful]
C.12.89   'Lo! lordes, what leute dede and *leele* dome yvsed.
C.12.130   That we sholde be low and louelich and *lele* vch man til oþer
C.13.69   Bothe louye and lene le[l]e and vnlele
C.14.188   And to *lele* and lyfholy þat louyeth alle treuthe.
C.15.136   Bote *lele* loue and treuthe that loth is to be founde.'
C.15.244   Leue thorw *lele* bileue, As oure lord wittenesseth:
C.16.24   Lowe and *lele* and louynge and of herte pore.
C.16.147   The eyȝte is a *lel* labour and loeth to take more
C.16.196   Thenne is *lele* loue my name and in latyn Amor;
C.17.22   Loue and *lele* byleue held lyf and soule togyderes.
C.17.127   A loueknotte of leutee and of *lele* byleue,
C.17.131   God lereth no lyf to l[eu]e withouten *lele* cause.
C.17.139   And *lele* men lyue as lawe techeth and loue þerof aryseth
C.17.158   And lyuen oute of *lele* byleue for they l[e]ue on a mene.
C.19.28   And *lele* to bileue on for [lif and] for soule?
C.19.45   And lereth þat we louye sholde as wel lyares as *lele*.
C.19.186   *Leel* lycame and lyf þat oure lord shupte.
C.20.307   And sethe he is a *lele* lord y leue þat he wol nat
C.20.338   To lere men to [be] *lele* and vch man to louye oþer;
C.21.60   And sethe [all his *lele* leges largeliche he ȝeueth]
C.21.237   And lyue by þat laboure a *leele* lyf and a trewe.
C.21.250   And al he lered to be *lele*, and vch a craft loue oþere,
C.22.138   For a meneuer man[t]el he made *leele* matrimonye

lelly adv *lelli adv.* A 9 lely (1) lelly (8); B 19 leelly (9) lelly (9) lelliche
    (1); C 27 leeliche (2) leely (6) leelyche (1) leelliche (1) lelelyche (2)
    leliche (1) lely (3) lelyche (1) lelly (9) lellyche (1)
A. 1.76   To loue me *lelly* whiles þi lif duriþ.'
A. 1.155   But ȝif ȝe loue *lelly* & lene þe pore,
A. 3.29   To loue hem *lelly* & lordis hem make,
A. 8.110   Þat louiþ god *lelly*, his liflode is þe more:
A. 8.160   And so I leue *lelly*, lord forbede ellis.
A.10.13   And seruiþ þis lady *lelly* boþe late & raþe.
A.11.77   Ac beleue *lelly* o[n þe] lore of holy chirche,
A.11.144   Leue *lelly* þeron ȝif þou þenke do wel,
A.12.114   And alle lordes þat louyn him *lely* in herte,
B. 1.78   To louen me *leelly* while þi lif dureþ.'
B. 1.181   But if ye louen *leelly* and lene þe pouere,
B. 2.32   And what man be merciful and *leelly* me loue
B. 3.30   To louen hem *lelly* and lordes [hem] make
B. 7.128   That loueþ god *lelly* his liflode is ful esy:
B. 7.182   And so I leue *leelly*, lor[d] forb[e]de ellis,
B. 9.13   To seruen þis lady *leelly*, boþe late and raþe.
B.10.124   Ac bileueþ *lelly* in þe loore of holy chirche,
B.10.192   Loke þow loue *lelly* if þee likeþ dowel,
B.10.240   And þat is to bileue *lelly*, boþe lered and lewed,
B.13.141   Thow loue *leelly* þi soule al þi lif tyme.
B.13.149   For he þat loueþ þee *leelly* litel of þyne coueiteþ.
B.15.33   And whan I loue *leelly* oure lord and alle oþere
B.15.155   And wollen lene þer þei leue *lelly* to ben paied.
B.15.554   Togideres loue *leelly*, leueþ it wel, ye bisshopes,
B.19.181   And *lelliche* bileue al þis; I loue hem and blesse hem:
B.19.232   They *lely* to lyue by labour of tonge,
B.19.384   That han laboured *lelly* al þis lenten tyme.
B.20.210   'And þow loue *lelly* lakke shal þee neuere
C. 1.177   But yf ȝe louye *leeliche* and lene þe pore,
C. 2.78   Leueth hit le[l]ly this worth here laste mede
C. 3.31   To louye hem *leeliche* and lordes [hem] make,
C. 3.310   That bothe the lord and the laborer be *leely* yserued.
C. 7.208   That ȝe louye hym [as] lord *leely* aboue alle.
C. 8.140   That lele land tilynge men *leely* byswynken.
C. 8.254   Þat *leely* hadde ylabored and thenne the lord sayde:
C. 8.297   And *leelyche* sayst, as y leue; lord hit þe forȝeld!
C. 9.59   *Lellyche* and lauhfollyche, oure lord treuthe hem graunteth
C. 9.328   And so y leue *lely*—lord forbede elles–
C.10.140   To serue þat lady *leely* bot[h] late and rathe.
C.11.141   And byleef *lely* how goddes [l]o[u]e alyhte
C.11.145   Leue hit *lelly* and loke þou do þeraftur.
C.11.265   *Lelly* as by his lokes, with a le[tt]re of gyle?
C.15.153   'That loueth *lely*,' quod he, 'bote litel thyng coueyteth.
C.16.195   And when y louye *lelly* oure lord and alle oþere
C.16.359   Of tho that *lelelyche* lyuen and louen and byleuen:
C.17.117   Lord lete þat this prestes *lelly* seien here masse,
C.17.133   That *lelyche* they byleue, and ȝut here lawe diuerseth,
C.17.217   Togederes louyen *lelelyche*, l[e]ueth hit [wel], bisshopes,
C.18.199   Ac leue hit *lelly* al thy lyftyme.
C.19.94   And ȝut bote they l[e]ue *lelly* vpon þat litel baby,
C.19.194   Til þat loue and bileue *leliche* to hym blowe.
C.21.181   And *leelliche* bileuen al this; y loue hem and blesse hem:

C.21.232   They *leely* to lyue bi labour of tonge,
C.21.384   That haen labored *lelly* al this lenten tyme.
C.22.210   'And thow loue *lelly* lacke shal þe neuere

leme n *leme n.* B 2; C 2 leem (1) leme (1)
B.18.124   And which a light and a *leme* lay bifore helle.
B.18.137   The while þis light and þis *leme* shal Lucifer ablende.
C.20.127   And which a lihte and a *leem* lay bifore helle.
C.20.140   The while this lihte and this l[em]e shal lucifer ablende.

lemman n *lemman n.* A 3 lemman (2) lemmanis (1); B 11 lemman (8)
    lemmannes (1) lemmans (1); C 9 lemman (6) lemmanes (3)
A. 3.140   To holde *lemmanis* & lotebies alle here lif dayes,
A.10.6   A *lemman* þat he louiþ lik to hymselue.
A.10.46   Heo is lyf & ledere, a *lemman* of heuene.
B. 2.21   And ylakked my *lemman* þat leautee is hoten,
B. 3.151   To [holde] *lemmans* and lotebies alle hire lifdaies,
B. 5.410   And ligge abedde in lenten and my *lemman* in myne armes
B. 9.6   A *lemman* þat he loueþ lik to hymselue.
B.13.139   [Th]us [lerede] me ones a *lemman*, loue was hir name.
B.14.303   And for þe [lewde] euere [yliche] a *lemman* of alle clennesse:
B.15.132   Executours and Sodenes, Somonours and hir *lemmannes*.
B.18.182   Loue þat is my *lemman* swiche lettres me sente
B.20.104   Manye a louely lady and [hir] *lemmans* knyȝtes
B.20.152   Lyf lepte aside and lauȝte hym a *lemman*.
B.20.156   This likede lif and his *lemman* fortune
C. 2.20   And [lakked] my *lemman* þat leute is hoten
C. 3.189   To holde *lemmanes* and lotebyes al here lyfdayes
C. 7.26   And ligge abedde in lente and my *lemman* in myn armus
C.10.133   A *lemman* þat he louyeth ylyke to hymsulue.
C.16.279   Seketours and sodenes, somnours and here *lemmanes*
C.20.185   Loue þat is my *lemman* such lettres me sente
C.22.104   Many a louly lady and here *lemmanes* knyhtes
C.22.152   Lyf lepte asyde and lauhte hym a *lemman*.
C.22.156   This likede lyf and his *lemman* fortune

lene adj *lene adj.(1)* &> lenen A 4; B 4 leene (1) lene (3); C 4
A. 5.65   So lokide he wiþ *lene* chekis, lourande foule.
A. 9.110   He was long & *lene*, lyk to non oþer,
A.11.2   Þat *lene* was of lich & of lo[uȝ] chere.
A.12.78   [*Lene* & rewlyche, with leggys ful smale].
B.Pr.123   Thanne loked vp a lunatik, a *leene* þyng wiþalle,
B. 5.82   So loked he wiþ *lene* chekes, lourynge foule.
B. 8.120   He was long and *lene*, lik to noon ooþer,
B.10.2   That *lene* was of [liche] and of [lowe chere].
C. 8.262   That here lyflode be *lene* and lyte worth here clothes.'
C. 8.278   And laȝar þe *lene* beggare þat longede aftur crommes–
C.10.116   He was long and *lene*, ylyk to noon other;
C.11.2   That ful *lene* lokede and lyfholy semede.

lened v1 *lenen v.(1)* &> lenen A 2 lenide; B 4 lened (2) lenede (1)
    leneden (1); C 3
A.Pr.9   And as I lay & *lenide* & lokide on þe watris
A. 9.56   And vndir a lynde vpon a launde *lenide* I me a stounde
B.Pr.9   And as I lay and *lenede* and loked on þe watres
B. 8.65   And vnder a lynde vpon a launde *lened* I a stounde
B.16.246   And defende hem fro þe fend, folk þat on me *leneden*.
B.18.5   And *lened* me to a lenten, and longe tyme I slepte;
C.Pr.8   And in a launde as y lay *lened* y and slepte
C.10.64   And vnder lynde vpon a launde *lened* y a stounde
C.20.5   And *lened* me to lenten: and long tyme y slepte.

lenede > lened,lenen

lenen v2 *lenen v.(3)* A 7 lene (4) lenen (1) leniþ (2); B 33 lene (16) lened
    (2) lenen (1) leneþ (7) lent (5) lente (1) lentestow (1); C 32 lene (19)
    lened (1) lenede (2) lenedest (1) leneth (4) lent (1) lente (4)
A.Pr.74   And *leniþ* it loselis þat leccherie haunten.
A. 1.155   But ȝif ȝe loue lelly & *lene* þe pore,
A. 3.223   Loue hem & le[n]e þe pore for oure lordis loue of heuene:
A. 7.16   For I shal *lene* hem lyflode, but ȝif þe lond faile,
A. 7.207   Loue hem & *lene* hem & so þe lawe of kynde wolde.
A.11.49   Litel louiþ he þat lord þat *leniþ* hym al þat blisse,
A.11.152   And louen hem þat liȝen on vs, & *lenen* hem at here nede,
B.Pr.77   And *leneþ* it Losels [þat] leccherie haunten.
B.Pr.126   And *lene* þee lede þi lond so leaute þee louye,
B. 1.181   But if ye louen leelly and *lene* þe pouere,
B. 5.241   And *lene* it for loue of þe cros, to legge a wed and lese it.
B. 5.244   I haue *lent* lordes and ladies my chaffare
B. 5.247   And *lene* folk þat lese wole a lippe at euery noble.
B. 5.250   '*Lentestow* euere lordes for loue of hire mayntenaunce?'
B. 5.251   'Ye, I haue *lent* lordes loued me neuere after,
B. 5.261   'God *lene* þee neuere grace] þi good wel to bisette,
B. 5.295   And what he *lente* yow of oure lordes good to lette yow fro synne.'
B. 6.17   For I shal *lenen* hem liflode but if þe lond faille
B. 6.221   Loue hem and *lene* hem [and] so [þe] lawe of [kynde wolde]:

B. 7.77   That askeþ for his loue þat vs al *leneþ:*
B. 9.108   Oure lord loueþ hem and *lent,* loude ouþer stille,
B. 9.204   Ac to loue and to *lene],* leue me, þat is dobet;
B.10.43   Likne men and lye on hem þat *leneþ* hem no ʒiftes,
B.10.63   Litel loueþ he þat lord þat *lent* hym al þat blisse
B.10.203   And louen hem þat lyen on vs and *lene* hem [at hir nede]
B.10.360   He sholde louye and *lene* and þe lawe fulfille.
B.10.411   God *lene* it fare noʒt so bi folk þat þe feiþ techeþ
B.11.179   Loue hir eyþer ooþer, and *lene* hem as hemselue.
B.11.180   Whoso *leneþ* noʒt he loueþ noʒt, [lord] woot þe soþe,
B.13.17   *Leneþ* he no lif lasse ne moore–
B.13.298   And large to *lene,* [loos] þerby to cacche].
B.13.359   *Lened* for loue of þe wed and looþ to do truþe;
B.13.388   As whan I *lened* and leued it lost or longe er it were paied.
B.14.39   For *lent* neuere was lif but liflode were shapen,
B.15.86   And louten to þise lordes þat mowen *lene* yow nobles
B.15.155   And wollen *lene* þer þei leue lelly to ben paied.
B.15.170   And *leneþ* and loueþ alle þat oure lord made.
B.17.47   Than for to louye and *lene* as wel lorels as lele.
B.17.351   That he ne may louye, and hym like, and *lene* of his herte
B.20.239   Than he þat laboureþ for liflode and *leneþ* it beggeris.
C.Pr.75   And *leneth* hit lorelles þat lecherye haunten.
C.Pr.150   And *lene* [þe] lede þy londe [so] lewte þe louye
C. 1.177   But yf ʒe louye leeliche and *lene* þe pore,
C. 4.191   'And y dar lege my lyf þat loue wol *lene* þe seluer
C. 6.243   And *len[e]* for loue of þe wed the whych y lette bettere
C. 6.244   And more worth then the moneye or men þat y *lenede.*
C. 6.245   Y *lene* folk þat lese wole a lyppe [at] vch a noble
C. 6.248   '*Lenedest* [thow] euere eny lord for loue of his mayntenaunce?'
C. 6.249   'Y haue *lent* lordes and ladyes þat louede me neuere aftur
C. 6.277   As whenne y *lenede* and leuede hit lost or longe or hit were payed.
C. 8.15   For y shal *lene* hem lyflode but [yf] þe lond faylle
C. 8.230   Loue hem and *lene* hem and so lawe of kynde wolde:
C. 8.246   Mathew maketh mencioun of a man þat *lente*
C. 8.285   *Lene* hem som of thy loef thouh thow þe lasse chewe.
C.10.92   *Lene* hem and loue hem", this latyn is to mene.
C.10.303   Ac to louye and to *l[e]ne,* leef me, þat is dobet;
C.11.45   Lytel loueth he þat lord þat *lent* hym al þat blisse
C.11.242   God *lene* hit fare nat so by folk þat þe faith techen
C.11.302   Lewede men in good bileue and *lene* hem at here nede.'
C.12.108   That louieth and *leneth* hem largeliche shal y quyte."
C.12.117   Forþi loue we as leue childerne, *lene* hem þat nedeth
C.13.69   Bothe louye and *lene* le[l]e and vnlele
C.13.81   To *lene* ne to lerne ne lentones to faste
C.14.13   Ac to louye and *lene* and lyue wel and byleue
C.15.238   For *lente* neuere was lyf but lyflode were shape,
C.16.132   And me *leneth* lyhtly fewe men and me wene hem pore:
C.16.314   Ne mysliked thogh he lore or *lened* þat ilke
C.17.129   Withoute gyle and gabbyng gyue and sulle and *lene.*
C.17.155   To þat lord þat hym lyf *lente* lyflode hym sende.
C.19.40   And seth to louye and to *lene* for þat lordes sake
C.19.331   That he ne may louye, and hym lyke, and *lene* of his herte
C.22.239   Then he þat laboreth for lyflode and *leneth* hit beggares.

lenge v *lengen v.* A 3 lenge (1) lengen (1) lengide (1); B 4 lenge (3) lenged (1); C 2 lenge (1) lenged (1)

A. 1.183   I may no lengere *lenge;* now loke þe oure lord.'
A. 9.7   Where þis lede *lengide,* lesse ne more,
A.11.209   Þei diʒe for þe drouʒte, whanne þei dreiʒe *lengen;*
B. 1.209   I may no lenger *lenge;* now loke þee oure lord.'
B. 8.7   Where þis leode *lenged,* lasse ne moore,
B.10.302   Thei deyen for drouʒte, whan þei drie [*lenge*];
B.19.418   And þer þei ligge and *lenge* moost lecherie þere regneþ".
C.10.7   Where this [lede] *l[e]nged,* lasse ne more,
C.21.418   And þer they lygge and *lenge* moest lecherye þer regneth".

lenger(e > long(e; lenghe(d > lengþe; lengide > lenge; lengore > long(e

lengþe n *lengthe n.* A 2; B 6; C 5 lenghe (4) lenthe (1)

A. 2.61   Wiþ alle þe lordsshipe of leccherie in *lengþe* & in brede;
A. 3.190   He shulde haue be lord of þat lond in *lengþe* & in brede,
B. 2.89   [Wiþ] al þe lordshipe of leccherie in *lengþe* and in brede,
B. 3.203   He sholde haue be lord of þat lond in *lengþe* and in brede,
B.14.242   And haþ hondes and armes of [a long] *lengþe,*
B.15.187   Labouren in [a] lauendrye wel þe *lengþe* of a Mile,
B.16.182   Of oon muchel and myght in mesure and *lengþe*
B.17.61   And nolde noʒt neghen hym by nyne londes *lengþe.*
C. 2.96   With al þe lordschip of leccherye in *lenghe* and in Brede,
C.13.39   Wol lette hym, as y leue, the *lenghe* of a myle
C.16.82   And hath hondes and Armes of a longe *lenthe*
C.18.20   Hit hadde schoriares to shuyuen hit vp, thre shides of o *lenghe*
C.19.60   And [n]olde nat neyhele hym by nyne londes *lenghe.*

lengþe v *lengthen v.* B 2 lengþe (1) lengþed (1); C 2 lenghe (1) lenghed (1)

B.18.53   And beden hym drynken his deeþ [to lette and] hise daies [*lengþe*],
B.18.303   I wolde haue *lengþed* his lif for I leued if he deide
C.20.53   And beden hym drynke his deth to lette and his dayes *lenghe*
C.20.335   Y wolde haue *lenghed* his lyf for y leued, yf he deyede,

lengur > long(e; lent > lenen; lente > lenen,lenten

lenten n *lenten n.* B 13 lente (7) lenten (6); C 11 lente (7) lenten (2) lenton (1) lentones (1)

B.Pr.91   Liggen at Londoun in *Lenten* and ellis.
B. 5.294   What he lerned yow in *lente,* leue þow noon ooþer,
B. 5.410   And ligge abedde in *lenten* and my lemman in myne armes
B.12.180   Ther þe lewed liþ stille and lokeþ after *lente,*
B.13.349   And as [lef] in *lente* as out of lente, alle tymes yliche.
B.13.349   And as [lef] in lente as out of *lente,* alle tymes yliche.
B.14.5   It haþ be laued in *lente* and out of lente boþe
B.14.5   It haþ be laued in lente and out of *lente* boþe
B.18.5   And lened me to a *lenten,* and longe tyme I slepte;
B.19.382   The lord of lust shal be letted al þis *lente,* I hope.
B.19.384   That han labored lelly al þis *lenten* tyme.
B.20.361   Fro *lenten* to lenten he lat hise plastres bite.'
B.20.361   Fro lenten to *lenten* he lat hise plastres bite.'
C.Pr.89   Leyen [at] Londoun in *lenton* and elles.
C. 6.183   As leef in *lente* as out of lente, alle tymes ylyche,
C. 6.183   As leef in lente as out of *lente,* alle tymes ylyche,
C. 7.26   And ligge abedde in *lente* and my lemman in myn armes
C.13.81   To lene ne to lerne ne *lentones* to faste
C.14.13   There þe lewede lyth stille and loketh aftur *lente*
C.20.5   And lened me to *lenten:* and long tyme y slepte.
C.21.382   The lord of lust shal be ylette al this *lente,* y hope.
C.21.384   That haen labored lelly al this *lenten* tyme.
C.22.361   Fro *lente* to lente he lat his plastres byte.'
C.22.361   Fro lente to *lente* he lat his plastres byte.'

lentesedes n *lenten n.* C 1

C.12.191   As lynsed, lekseed and *lentesedes* all

lentestow > lenen; lenthe > lengþe lenton(es > lenten

leode n *lede n.(2)* A 4 lede (3) ledis (1); B 14 ledes (4) leode (7) leodes (3); C 17 lede (10) ledes (6) leode (1)

A. 3.31   'Shal no lewidnesse hym lette, þe *lede* þat I louye,
A. 4.147   And alle my lige *ledis* to lede þus euene.'
A. 6.3   Til late & longe þat hy a *lede* mette,
A. 9.7   Where þis *lede* lengide, lesse ne more,
B. 1.141   To litel latyn þow lernedest, *leode,* in þi youþe:
B. 3.32   'Shal no lewednesse [hym] lette, þe *leode* þat I louye,
B. 4.184   [And] alle youre lige *leodes* to lede þus euene'.
B. 5.174   Forþi haue I no likyng, [leue me], wiþ þo *leodes* to wonye;
B. 5.515   Til late and longe, þat þei a *leode* mette
B. 8.7   Where þis *leode* lenged, lasse ne moore,
B.10.87   And lordeþ in [*ledes*] þe lasse good he deleþ.
B.15.119   If lewed [*ledes*] wiste what þis latyn meneþ,
B.15.558   Wiþ londes and *ledes,* lordshipes and rentes,
B.16.181   'Thre *leodes* in oon lyth, noon lenger þan ooþer,
B.17.66   Ac so soone so þe Samaritan hadde siʒte of þis *leode*
B.17.81   For I may noʒt lette', quod þat *Leode* and lyard he bistrideþ
B.18.356   And I in liknesse of a *leode,* þat lord am of heuene,
B.18.401   Tho [*ledes*] þat [I] lou[e], and leued in my comynge;
C. 1.140   To lyte [Latyn þow] lernedest, [*leode*], in thy ʒowthe:
C. 3.35   Shal no lewedenesse lette þe [*lede*] þat y louye
C. 3.82   Is no *lede* þat leueth þat he ne loueth mede
C. 4.178   And alle ʒoure lege *l[e]des* to lede thus euene.'
C. 6.301   And what *lede* leueth þat y lye look in þe sauter glos[e],
C. 7.160   Til late was and longe þat thei a *lede* mette
C.10.7   Where this [*lede*] l[e]nged, lasse ne more,
C.10.177   That many *lede* leseth thorw lykerous drynke,
C.11.67   And lordeth in *ledes* the lasse goed he deleth.
C.11.71   Be large þerof whil hit lasteth to *ledes* þat ben nedy
C.13.60   And leueth for his lettres þat no [*lede*] wole hym greue.
C.13.209   Vch a *lede* wolde be lacles, leef thow non other.
C.15.302   And lordes and ladyes ben cald for *ledes* þat they haue
C.17.40   Lord leue," quod þat *lede,* " no stole thynge be herynne!"
C.17.221   With londes and *ledes,* lordschipes and rentes,
C.19.78   For y may nat lette,' quod that *lede;* and lyard he bystrideth
C.20.444   Tho [*ledes*] þat y louye and leued in my comynge;

leons > lyoun

leopard n *leopard n.* B 2 leopard (1) leopardes (1)

B.15.277   Of leons ne of *leopardes* no liflode ne toke,
B.15.298   Ac þer ne was leoun ne *leopard* þat on laundes wenten,

leoun > lyoun; lep > lepen; lepares > leperis

lepen v *lepen v.* A 7 lep (1) lepe (4) lepen (1) ylope (1); B 17 leep (2) lepe (6) lepen (2) lepte (1) lope (2) lopen (4); C 15 lep (2) lepe (6) lepen (1) lepte (1) lyppeth (1) lope (1) lup (2) luppen (1)

A.Pr.94   Ben *ylope* to lundoun þe leue of hire bisshop,
A. 2.177   Liȝtliche liȝere *lep* awey þennes,
A. 2.193   Ac he haþ leue to *lepen* out as ofte as him likiþ,
A. 4.93   *Le[pe]* he so liȝtly awey, lauȝen he wolde,
A. 5.112   But ȝif a lous couþe *lepe*, I may it nouȝt leue
A. 5.249   And *lepe* with hym ouer lond al his lif tyme,
A. 6.56   And ȝe shuln *lepe* þe liȝtliere al ȝoure lif tyme;
B.Pr.223   Of alle kynne lybbynge laborers *lopen* forþ somme,
B. 1.117   *Lopen* out wiþ Lucifer in loþliche forme
B. 2.69   Thanne *leep* liere forþ and seide, 'lo! here a chartre
B. 2.218   Liȝtliche Lyere *leep* awey þanne,
B. 2.234   Ac he haþ leue to *lepen* out as ofte as hym likeþ,
B. 4.106   *Lope* he so liȝtly [awey], lauȝen he wolde,
B. 4.153   And þei lauȝynge *lope* to hire and lefte Reson manye.
B. 5.163   Til "þow lixt!" and "þow lixt!" *lopen* out at ones
B. 5.196   But if a lous couþe [*lepe*, I leue and I trowe],
B. 5.475   And *lepe* wiþ hym ouer lond al his lif tyme,
B. 5.494   [Th]e liȝt þat *lepe* out of þee, Lucifer [it] blent[e]
B. 5.569   And ye shul *lepe* þe liȝtloker al youre lif tyme.
B.11.318   This lokynge on lewed preestes haþ doon me *lepe* from pouerte
B.12.140   And loue shal *lepen* out after into þ[is] lowe erþe,
B.18.313   For we leued þi lesynges [we *lopen* out alle;
B.19.125   He made lame to *lepe* and yaf light to blynde
B.20.152   Lyf *lepte* aside and lauȝte hym a lemman.
C. 1.110   *Lepen* out in lothly forme for his [luþer] wille
C. 1.113   *Luppen* alofte [in lateribus Aquilonis],
C. 2.71   Thenne *lup* lyare forth and saide, 'loo! here a Chartre
C. 2.191   On hem þat loueth leccherye *lyppeth* vp and rydeth,
C. 2.228   Lyhtliche lyare *lep* away thenne,
C. 2.244   Ac he hath leue to *lep* out as ofte as hym liketh,
C. 4.101   *Lope* he so lihtliche [awey], lawen he wolde,
C. 6.204   But yf a lous couthe *lepe*, y leue [and] y trowe,
C. 6.329   [And *lepe* wiþ hym ouer lond al his lif tyme]
C. 7.134   The lihte þat *lup* oute of the, lucifer hit blente
C. 7.216   And ȝe shal *lepe* þe lihtloker al ȝoure lyf tyme:
C.14.85   And loue shal *lepe* out aftur into þis lowe erthe.
C.21.125   He made lame to *lepe* and ȝaf liht to blynde
C.20.286   That no liht *lepe* in at louer ne at loupe.
C.22.152   Lyf *lepte* asyde and lauhte hym a lemman.

leperis n *lepere n.* A 1; C 2 lepares
A.11.203   Ne no *leperis* ouer lond ladies to shryue.
C. 9.107   The whiche aren lunatyk lollares and *lepares* aboute
C. 9.137   The whiche [arn] lunatyk loreles and *lepares* aboute

lepte > lepen; lere > leere,leren

leren v *leren v.* A 21 lere (10) lerid (5) leride (1) lerist (1) leriþ (4); B 42 lere (12) lered (18) lerede (1) leren (3) lereþ (7) ylered (1); C 59 lere (15) lered (27) lerede (2) lereth (13) ylered (2)

A. 1.109   Lucifer wiþ legionis *leride* it in heuene,
A. 1.125   *Leriþ* it þus lewide men, for lettrid it knowiþ,
A. 1.134   Loke þou suffre hym to seyn & siþþe *lere* it aftir.
A. 2.45   For *lerid*, for lewid, for laboureris of þropis,
A. 3.37   'Þeiȝ *lerid* & lewide men leiȝe be þe ichone,
A. 3.60   Forþi I *lere* ȝow lordis, leuiþ such wrytyng,
A. 3.115   *Leri[þ]* hem leccherie þat loui[þ] hire ȝeftis.
A. 4.12   How þou *lerist* þe peple, þe lerid & þe lewid.'
A. 4.12   How þou lerist þe peple, þe lerid & þe lewid.'
A. 5.36   'And libbe as ȝe *lere* vs, we wile leue ȝow þe betere'.
A. 5.123   Þanne drouȝ I me among drapers my donet to *lere*,
A. 6.94   And *lere* þe for to loue & hise lawes holden.
A. 7.238   Eny l[e]f of lechecraft *lere* it me, my dere,
A. 8.14   Loke on þat o lawe, & *lere* men þat oþer,
A. 8.111   And but ȝif luk leiȝe he *leriþ* vs anoþer,
A. 9.103   More kynde knowyng I coueyte to *lere*,
A.10.103   I haue [lernid] how lewid men han [*lerid*] here children
A.10.120   And so *leriþ* vs luk þat leiȝede neuere:
A.11.128   Logik I *lerid* hire, & al þe lawe aftir,
A.11.180   To *lere* at ȝow dowel & dobet þereaftir,
A.11.278   Þanne wrouȝte I vnwisly wiþ alle þe wyt þat I *lere*.
B. 1.136   *Lereþ* it þ[us] lewed men, for lettred it knoweþ,
B. 1.146   Loke þow suffre hym to seye and siþen *lere* it after.
B. 1.151   And *lered* it Moyses for þe leueste þyng and moost lik to heuene,
B. 3.38   'Theiȝ [*lered* and lewed] hadde leyen by þee [echone],
B. 3.69   Forþi I *lere* yow lordes, leueþ swic[h writynge],
B. 3.126   *Lereþ* hem lecherie þat loueþ hire ȝiftes.
B. 4.12   How þow lernest þe peple, þe *lered* and þe lewed.'
B. 5.44   [Lyue] as ye *leren* vs; we shul leue yow þe bettre.'
B. 6.254   Any leef of lechecraft *lere* it me, my deere;
B. 7.129   And but if luc lye he *lereþ* vs [anoþer]

B. 9.76   And þat I lye noȝt of þat I *lere* þee, luc bereþ witnesse.
B.10.199   This is Catons kennyng to clerkes þat he *lereþ*.
B.10.240   And þat is to bileue lelly, boþe *lered* and lewed,
B.10.316   He loureþ on hym and [lakkeþ] hym: who [*lered*] hym curteisie?
B.11.161   The legend[a] sanctorum yow *lereþ* more largere þan I yow telle.
B.11.170   And took it moises vpon þe mount alle men to *lere*].
B.11.422   Tho hadde he [litel] likyng for to *lere* þe moore.
B.12.104   Riȝt so [*lereþ*] lettrure lewed men to Reson.
B.12.182   But as his loresman *lereþ* hym bileueþ and troweþ,
B.12.184   To *lere* lewed men as luc bereþ witnesse:
B.13.121   Ther þe lord of lif wonyeþ, to *leren* [hem] what is dowel.
B.13.139   [Th]us [*lerede*] me ones a lemman, loue was hir name.
B.13.142   And so þow *lere* þe to louye, for [þe] lordes loue of heuene,
B.13.186   And *lere* yow if yow like þe leeste point to knowe
B.13.213   And confermen fauntekyns ooþer folk *ylered*
B.13.444   And a *lered* man to lere þee what our lord suffred
B.13.444   And a lered man to *lere* þee what our lord suffred
B.14.319   Thus *lered* me a lettred man for oure lordes loue, Seint Austyn:
B.15.144   By *lered*, by lewed, þat looþ is to [s]pende
B.15.391   Allas, þanne, but oure looresmen lyue as þei *leren* vs,
B.15.395   And we *lered* and lewed [bileueþ in oon god;
B.15.411   That [*lered*] þere and [lewed] ȝit leeuen on hise lawes.
B.15.610   *Lere* hem litlum and litlum et in Iesum Christum filium,
B.16.104   And *lered* hym lechecraft his lif for to saue
B.18.227   Shal *lere* hem what langour is and lisse wiþouten ende.
B.19.114   [Boþe] to *lered* and to lewede, to louyen oure enemys.
B.19.236   And some he *lered* to laboure [on lond and on watre
B.19.248   And some he *lered* to lyue in longynge to ben hennes,
B.19.250   And alle he *lered* to be lele, and ech a craft loue ooþer,
B.20.102   *Lered* [ne] lewed he leet no man stonde,
B.20.247   To *lered* ne to lewed, but lyueþ after youre reule.
B.20.266   Of lewed and of *lered*; þe lawe wole and askeþ
C.Pr.88   That is lele loue and lyf among *lered* and lewed,
C. 1.135   *Lere* hit thus lewed men, for lettred hit knoweth:
C. 1.204   To *lere* the what loue is;' and leue at me she lauhte.
C. 3.40   'Thow *le[r]ed* men and le[w]ed haued layn by the bothe
C. 3.163   And *lereth* hem lecherye þat louyeth here ȝeftes.
C. 3.171   Lyggeth by here, when hem lust, *lered* and lewed.
C. 3.213   Thus *lereth* this lady thi lond, now lord ȝeue here sorwe!
C. 4.12   How thow ledest my peple, *lered* and lewed.'
C. 4.118   Til þat *lerede* men lyue as thei lere and teche
C. 4.118   Til þat lerede men lyue as thei *lere* and teche
C. 5.142   Lyue as ȝe *lereth* vs; we shall leue ȝow þe bettere.'
C. 6.116   With lewed and *lered* þat leef ben to here
C. 6.215   Thenne drow y me amonge drapers my donet to *lere*,
C. 6.349   What a *lered* ȝow to lyue with and to lette ȝow fram thefte.'
C. 7.104   With a *lered* man to lere the what oure lord suffrede
C. 7.104   With a lered man to *lere* the what oure lord suffrede
C. 8.221   For here lyflode, *lere* me now, sire hunger.'
C. 9.19   And suche liue as þei *lereth* men oure lord treuthe hem graunteth
C. 9.165   And *lere* this lewede men what þis latyn meneth
C. 9.231   Thus hit bylongeth for lord[e], for *lered* and for lewed
C. 9.327   As lettrede men vs *lereth* and lawe of holi churche:
C.10.10   Y haylsede hem hendly as y hadde *ylered*
C.11.34   The lewed aȝen þe *lered* þe holy lore to disp[u]te
C.11.125   Thus thorw my lore ben men *ylered* thogh y loke demme.
C.11.130   Ac for hit *lered* men to louie y beleue þeron þ[e] bettere
C.11.144   And al þat holi churche herof can þe *lere*
C.11.234   Seldom ar they seyen so lyue as they *lere*;
C.14.6   Noþer to lye ne to lacke ne *lere* þat is defended
C.14.49   Riht so *lereth* lettrure lewed men to resoun.
C.14.71   Bothe lewede and *lerede* were lost yf clergie ne were.
C.14.122   But as his loresman [*lereth* hym] byleueth and troweth,
C.14.124   To *lere* lewede men As luk bereth witnesse:
C.15.14   As wel *lered* as lewede and lorde as þe [b]oende;
C.15.93   And why a lyueth nat as a *lereth*.' 'lat be,' quod pacience.
C.15.116   Ne l[yu]eth as ȝe *lereth*, as oure lord wolde.
C.16.33   And *lereth* lewed and lered, hey and lowe to knowe
C.16.33   And lereth lewed and *lered*, hey and lowe to knowe
C.16.153   Thus *lered* me a le[tte]red man for oure lordes loue, seynt Austyn:
C.16.228   And doth hym to be deynous and deme þat beth nat *lered*.
C.16.233   That bothe *le[r]ed* and le[w]ed of here beleue douten.
C.16.283   Leueth hit wel, lordes, both lewed and *lered*,
C.17.131   God *lereth* no lyf to l[eu]e withouten lele cause.
C.17.182   And on his lore thei l[e]uen ȝut, as wel *lered* as lewed.
C.17.318   *Lere* hem littelum and littelum [et] in iesum christum filium
C.18.82   That oure lord alloweth, as *lered* men vs techeth,
C.19.43   Hit is liht for lewed and for *lered* bothe
C.19.45   And *lereth* þat we louye sholde as wel lyares as lele.
C.19.101   And *lered* me for his loue to louye al mankynde
C.20.236   Shal *lere* hem what l[angour] is and lisse withouten ende.
C.20.338   To *lere* men to [be] lele and vch man to louye oþer;
C.21.114   Bothe to *lered* and to lewed, to louye oure enemyes.

C.21.236 And som he *lered* to laboure a londe and a watre
C.21.248 And somme he [*l*]*ered* to lyue in longyng to be hennes,
C.21.250 And al he *lered* to be lele, and vch a craft loue oþere,
C.21.279 And *lered* men a ladel bugge with a longe stale
C.22.102 *Lered* ne lewed he lefte no man stande,
C.22.207 'Consaileth me, kynde,' quod y, 'what craft be beste to *lere*?'
C.22.247 To *lered* ne to lewed, but lyueth aftur ʒoure reule.
C.22.266 Of lewed and of *lered*; the lawe wol and asketh

leryng ger *leringe n.* A 1 lering; B 1; C 3
A. 1.173 And a *lering* to lewide men þe lattere to dele.
B. 9.16 [By his *leryng* is lad þat lady Anima].
C.10.142 And by his *leryng* is lad þat lady Anima.
C.10.173 And lyf lyueth by inwit and *leryng* of kynde.
C.17.160 And aftur his *leryng* they lyue and by lawe of kynde

lerne v *lernen v.* A 13 lerne (8) lernid (1) lernide (3) ylernid (1); B 35 lerne (16) lerned (13) lernedest (1) lernen (1) lernest (1) lerneþ (2) ylerned (1); C 24 lerne (15) lerned (4) lernede (2) lernedest (1) lerneth (2)
A. 5.117 Ferst I *lernide* to leiʒe a lef oþer tweiʒe;
A. 7.256 And *lerne* to laboure wiþ lond lest liflode hym faile.
A. 8.119 Þou art le[*ttr*]id a litel; who *lernide* þe on boke?'
A. 9.10 I hailside hem hendely as I hadde *ylernid*,
A. 9.49 Ac ʒif I may lyuen & loken I shal go *lerne* betere.
A. 9.57 To *lerne* þe laies þat louely [foulis] maden.
A.10.84 And alle kynde scoleris in scole to *lerne*.
A.10.103 I haue [*lernid*] how lewid men han [*lerid*] here children
A.11.115 Boþe wele & wo ʒif þat þou wile *lerne*,
A.11.133 And bet hem wiþ a baleis but ʒif þei wolde *lerne*.
A.11.136 And *lernide* h[*e*]m lyuel & lyne þeiʒ I loke dymme.
A.12.6 Þe were lef to *lerne* but loþ for to stodie;
A.12.32 For he cam not by cause to *lerne* to dowel
B. 1.111 Lucifer wiþ legions *lerned* it in heuene
B. 1.141 To litel latyn þow *lernedest*, leode, in þi youþe:
B. 4.12 How þow *lernest* þe peple, þe lered and þe lewed.'
B. 5.201 First I *lerned* to lye a leef ouþer tweyne;
B. 5.207 Thanne drouʒ I me among drapiers my donet to *lerne*,
B. 5.235 'I wende riflynge were restitucion for I *lerned* neuere rede on boke,
B. 5.239 I *lerned* among lumbardes [a lesson and of Iewes],
B. 5.294 What he *lerned* yow in lente, leue þow noon ooþer,
B. 5.439 I [*yarn*] aboute in youþe and yaf me nauʒt to *lerne*,
B. 6.272 And *lerne* to laboure wiþ lond [lest] liflode [hym faille].
B. 7.137 Thow art lettred a litel; who *lerned* þee on boke?'
B. 8.10 I hailsed hem hendely as I hadde *ylerned*,
B. 8.58 Ac if I may lyue and loke I shal go *lerne* bettre.'
B. 8.66 To [*lerne*] þe layes [þat] louely foweles made.
B. 8.113 More kynde knowynge I coueite to *lerne*,
B.10.163 Boþe-wele-and-wo if þat þow wolt *lerne*;
B.10.176 Logyk I *lerned* hire, and [al þe lawe after],
B.10.181 And bette hem wiþ a baleys but if þei wolde *lerne*.
B.10.184 And *lerned* hem leuel and lyne þouʒ I loke dymme.
B.10.237 Dowel and dobet and dobest to *lerne*.
B.10.308 But al is buxomnesse þere and bokes, to rede and to *lerne*].
B.10.309 In scole þere is scorn but if a clerk wol *lerne*,
B.10.379 Manye tales ʒe tellen þat Theologie *lerneþ*,
B.11.173 But þei ben *lerned* for oure lordes loue, lost is al þe tyme,
B.11.229 Forþi *lerne* we þe lawe of loue as oure lord tauʒte;
B.11.348 *Lerned* to legge þe stikkes in whiche she leyeþ and bredeþ.
B.12.163 That ooþer is lewed of þat labour, *lerned* neuere swymme.
B.12.259 By þe po feet is vnderstande, as I haue *lerned* in Auynet,
B.17.43 Than for to techen hem two, and to hard to *lerne* þe leeste!
B.17.49 Tho þat *lernen* þi lawe wol litel while vsen it.'
B.19.279 And *lerned* men a ladel bugge wiþ a long stele
B.20.207 'Counseille me, kynde,' quod I, 'what craft is best to *lerne*?'
B.20.208 '*Lerne* to loue', quod kynde, 'and leef alle oþere.'
B.20.250 Wiþ þat ye leue logik and *lerneþ* for to louye.
B.20.274 And *lerne* logyk and lawe and ek contemplacioun
C. 1.140 To lyte [Latyn þow] *lernedest*, [leode], in thy ʒowthe:
C. 1.145 Lok þow soffre hym to seye and so thow myht *lerne*.
C. 5.43 That laboure þat y *lerned* beste þerwith lyuen y sholde:
C. 5.155 In scole is loue and louhnesse and lykyng to *lerne*.
C. 6.209 Furste y *lerned* to lye a leef oþer tweye;
C. 6.241 Y *lernede* among lumbardus a lessoun and of iewes,
C. 7.74 And hath no likynge to *lerne* ne of oure lord to here
C. 7.192 Profitable as for þe plouh a potte me to *lerne*
C. 8.293 And *lerne* to labory with lond lest lyflode h[*y*]m fayle.
C. 8.338 Suche lawes to *lerne* laboreres to greue.
C.10.57 Ac yf y may lyue and loke y shal go *lerne* bettere.'
C.11.75 Bote lythen how þey myhte *lerne* leest go[*e*]d spene.
C.11.105 Bothe-wele-and-wo yf þou wilt *lerne*;
C.11.116 Logyk y *lerned* here and al þe lawe aftur
C.11.121 And be[*t*] hem with a baleyse bute yf þei wolde *lerne*.
C.11.132 *Lerne* for to louie yf þe lik[*e*] dowel

C.12.120 Forthy *lerne* we t[*he*] lawe of loue as oure lord tauhte
C.13.81 To lene ne to *lerne* ne lentones to faste
C.13.159 *Lernede* to [*l*]*egge* stikkes þat ley on here neste.
C.14.107 That oþer is lewed of þat labour, *lerned* neuere swymme.
C.19.47 Tho þat *lerneth* thy lawe wollen litel while hit vse.'
C.22.208 '*Lerne* to loue,' quod kynde, 'and leef all othere.'
C.22.250 With þat ʒe l[*e*]ue logyk and *lerneth* for to louye.
C.22.274 And *lerne* logyk and lawe and eke contemplacioun

lernyng ger *lerninge ger.* B 3 lernyng (2) lernynge (1)
B. 1.199 And *lernynge* to lewed men þe latter to dele.
B.11.152 By loue and by *lernyng* of my lyuynge in truþe;
B.15.473 That loþ ben to louye wiþouten *lernyng* of ensaumples.

les > lesen

lese v1 *lesen b.(1)* &> *lesen* B 1; C 1
B. 6.66 Shal haue leue, by oure lord, to *lese* here in heruest
C. 8.67 Shal haue leue, by oure lord, to [*lese* here in heruest]

lesen v2 *lesen v.(4)* A 7 les (1) lese (4) lost (2); B 33 lees (2) lese (11) lesen (2) lore (1) loren (1) lost (13) loste (1) ylorn (1) ylost (1); C 43 lees (3) les (1) lese (8) lesen (2) lesest (1) leseth (1) loest (1) lore (2) loren (1) lorn (1) lost (7) loste (5) losten (3) ylore (2) ylost (5)
A. 3.125 She doþ men *lese* here land & here lif boþe;
A. 5.76 And belowen hym to lordis to don hym *lese* siluer,
A. 5.80 Boþe his lyme & his lif was *lost* þoruʒ my tunge.
A. 6.102 Þus miʒt þou riȝt to lete wel be þiselue,
A. 8.142 Þe king *les* his lordsshipe, & lesse men it hadde.
A. 9.32 Þere were þe manis lif *lost* for lacchesse of hymselue.
A.10.102 Þou miʒtest *lese* þi louʒnesse for a litel pride.
B.Pr.187 And lerne hire labour *lost* and al hire longe studie.
B. 2.35 That he shal *lese* for hire loue a l[*i*]ppe of Caritatis.
B. 3.136 She dooþ men *lese* hire lond and hire lif boþe.
B. 3.159 And doþ men *lese* þoruʒ hire loue þat lawe myʒte wynne,
B. 4.175 And seide, 'þoruʒ [youre] lawe, as I leue, I *lese* manye eschetes;
B. 5.96 And [bilowen] hym to lordes to doon hym *lese* siluer,
B. 5.100 That boþe lif and lyme is *lost* þoruʒ my speche.
B. 5.241 And lene it for loue of þe cros, to legge a wed and *lese* it.
B. 5.247 And lene folk þat *lese* wole a lippe at euery noble.
B. 5.491 The sonne for sorwe þerof *lees* [*s*]iʒt [for] a tyme.
B. 5.616 Thus myʒtestow *lesen* his loue, to lete wel by þiselue,
B. 7.164 The kyng *lees* his lordshipe and [lasse] men it hadde.
B. 8.36 [There] were [þe mannes] lif *lost* [for] lachesse of hymselue.
B.10.277 For goddes word wolde noʒt be *lost*, for þat wercheþ euere;
B.11.173 But þei ben lerned for oure lordes loue, *lost* is al þe tyme,
B.12.40 [Lo]! what made lucifer to *lese* þe heiʒe heuene,
B.12.54 And loue hem noʒt as oure lord bit, *lesen* hir soules:
B.12.120 And leiden hand þeron to liften it vp *loren* here lif after.
B.13.388 As whan I lened and leued it *lost* or longe er it were paied.
B.14.199 Ellis is al oure labour *lost*–lo, how men writeþ
B.15.128 Allas, ye lewed men, muche *lese* ye on preestes!
B.15.555 The lordshipe of londes [*lese* ye shul for euere],
B.17.250 Al þi labour is *lost* and al þi long trauaille;
B.18.79 Highte Longeus as þe lettre telleþ, and longe hadde *lore* his sight;
B.18.102 And ye, lurdaynes, han *ylost* for lif shal haue þe maistrye;
B.18.109 Whan crist cam hir kyngdom þe crowne sholde [*lese*]:
B.18.260 And bileue on a newe lawe be *lost*, lif and soule.'
B.18.311 For þi lesynges, Lucifer, *lost* is al oure praye.
B.18.314 And now for þi laste lesynge] *ylorn* we haue Adam,
B.19.408 Leue it wel [þow art] *ylost*, boþe lif and soule.'
B.19.409 'Thanne is many a [lif] *lost*', quod a lewed vicory.
B.20.87 Largeliche a legion *loste* [þe] lif soone.
C.Pr.112 Thei were discomfited in batayle and *losten* Archa domini
C.Pr.112 Were disconfit in batayle and Archa domini *lorn*
C.Pr.198 And leten here labour *ylost* and al here longe study.
C. 2.37 He shal *lese* for here loue [a] lippe of trewe charite;
C. 2.108 For a leueth be *lost* when he his lyf leteth,\
C. 3.174 For he doth men *lesen* here lond and here lyf bothe;
C. 3.197 Thorw which loueday is *loste* þat leute myhte wynne;
C. 3.467 Shal *lese* þerfore his lyflode and his lyf parauntur.
C. 4.169 'Thorw ʒoure lawe, as y leue, y *lese* many chetes;
C. 5.95 And ay *loste* an[*d*] loste and at þe laste hym happed
C. 5.95 And ay *loste* an[*d*] *loste* and at þe laste hym happed
C. 6.193 When y was olde and hoor and hadde *ylore* þat kynde
C. 6.245 Y lene folk þat *lese* wole a lyppe [at] vch a noble.
C. 6.277 As whenne y lenede and leuede hit *lost* or longe or hit were payed.
C. 6.314 Then in lysse to lyue and *lese* lyf and soule.'
C. 7.131 The sonne for sorwe þerof *lees* [*s*]iht for a tyme.
C. 7.268 Thus myhte thow *lesen* his loue, to lete wel by thysulue,
C. 9.182 Or bylowe thorw luther men and *lost* here catel aftur
C. 9.268 Y leue, for thy lacchesse, thow *lesest* many wetheres
C.10.177 That many lede *leseth* thorw lykerous drynke,
C.10.193 For to *lese* þerfore her lond and her lyf aftur.

C.10.196 And seth [he *les*] his lyf for lawe sholde loue wexe.
C.11.251 Laste ȝe be *loste* as þe laboreres were þat lab[o]red vnder Noe.
C.12.95 Bote loue and leute hem lede *ylost* is al þe tyme
C.12.184 That ben layd in louhe erthe, *ylore* as hit were,
C.13.152 That ne *lees* the lykynge of lost of flesch, as hit were,
C.14.63 And all lewede þat leide hand þeron *loren* lyf aftir.
C.14.71 Bothe lewede and lerede were *lost* yf clergie ne were.
C.14.134 And wol no wikkede man [be] *lost* bote if he wol hymsulue:
C.16.40 Elles is alle oure labour *loest*–loo how men writeth
C.16.274 Allas! lewed men, moche *lese* ȝe þat fynde
C.16.314 Ne mysliked thogh he *lore* or lened þat ilke
C.17.218 The lordschipe of londes *lese* ȝe shal for euer
C.19.216 Al thy labor is *loste* and al thy longe trauaile;
C.20.81 Hihte longies as þe lettre telleth, and longe hadde *lore* his sihte;
C.20.105 And ȝe, lordeyne[s], haen *lost* for lyf shal haue [þe] maistrie;
C.20.268 And bile[u]e on a newe lawe be *ylost*, lyf and soule.'
C.20.345 For thy lesinges, lucifer, we *losten* furst oure ioye
C.20.347 For we leued on thy lesynges [there *losten* we blisse;
C.20.349 We haen *ylost* oure lordschipe a londe and in helle:
C.21.408 Leue hit [wel thou] be[st] *lost*, bothe lyf and soule.'
C.21.409 'Thenne is many [a lyf] *ylost*,' quod a lewed vicory.
C.22.87 Largeliche a legioun *lees* the lyf sone.

lesynge n *lesinge ger.(3)* A 1 lesing; B 1

A. 5.93 Of his *lesing* I lauȝe; [it liȝtiþ] myn herte,
B. 5.113 And of [his] *lesynge* I lauȝe, [it liȝteþ] myn herte;

lesynge ger *lesinge ger.(2)* A 3 lesinges; B 15 lesyng (1) lesynge (3) lesynges (11); C 13 lesinges (1) lesyng (1) lesynge (3) lesynges (8)

A. 2.89 For al þe *lesinges* þou lyuest, & leccherous werkis;
A.11.121 F[ro] *lesinges* & li[þer] speche & likerous drinkes.
A.11.280 Þat hadde lyued al his lyf wiþ *lesinges* & þeft[e],
B. 2.125 For al bi *lesynges* þow lyuest and lecherouse werkes;
B. 4.19 Ne-*lesynge*-to-lauȝen-of-for-I-loued-hem-neuere.
B. 5.139 On lymitours and listres *lesynges* I ymped
B. 5.407 Or *lesynge*[s] to lauȝen [of] and bilye my neȝebores,
B.10.22 Thei lede lordes wiþ *lesynges* and bilieþ truþe.
B.10.169 Fro-*lesynges*-and-liþer-speche-and-likerouse-drynkes.
B.10.421 That hadde lyued al his lif wiþ *lesynges* and þefte,
B.13.96 And but [þe] first [leef] be *lesyng* leue me neuere after.
B.15.602 And þat his loore be *lesynges*, and lakken it alle,
B.16.44 And leiþ a laddre þerto, of *lesynges* are þe ronges,
B.18.311 For þi *lesynges*, Lucifer, lost is al oure praye.
B.18.313 For we leued þi *lesynges* [we lopen out alle;
B.18.314 And now for þi laste *lesynge* ylorn we haue Adam,
B.18.402 And for þi *lesynge*, lucifer, þat þow leighe til Eue
B.19.292 Mighte no [lyere wiþ *lesynges*] ne los of worldly catel
C. 2.141 For by *lesynges* [a] lacchen largeliche mede.
C. 4.19 Ne-*lesynges*-to-lauhe-of-for-y-louede-hit-neuere.
C. 7.22 Y hadde leuere here an harlotrye or a *lesyng* to lauhen of
C.15.103 And bote þe furste leef be *lesyng*[e] leue me neuere aftur.
C.17.310 And that his lore was *lesynges* and lakken hit alle
C.18.44 And leyth a laddere þerto, of *lesynges* ben þe ronges,
C.20.345 For thy *lesinges*, lucifer, we losten furst oure ioye
C.20.347 For we leued on thy *lesynges* [there losten we blisse;
C.20.348 And now for a laste *lesynge* [þat thow lowe til Eue
C.20.351 Lucifer for his *lesynges*, leue y noen oþer.
C.20.357 (A litel y ouerleep for *lesynges* sake,
C.20.445 Ac for þe *lesynge* þat thow low, lucifer, til eue
C.21.292 Myhte no lyare with *lesynge*[s] ne losse of worldly catel

lesse > lasse

lesson n *lessoun n.* A 4 lessoun; B 11 lesson (10) lessons (1); C 5 lesson (1) lessoun (3) lessounn (1)

A. 5.118 Wykkidly to weiȝe was my ferste *lessoun*.
A. 5.125 Among þe riche rayes I rendrit a *lessoun*;
A. 7.260 Þis is a louely *lessoun*, lord it þe forȝelde.
A.11.29 Litel is he louid or lete by þat suche a *lessoun* techiþ,
B. 3.338 Ac þow art lik a lady þat radde a *lesson* ones
B. 5.202 Wikkedly to weye was my firste *lesson*.
B. 5.209 Among þe riche Rayes I rendred a *lesson*;
B. 5.239 I lerned among lumbardes [a *lesson* and of Iewes],
B. 6.276 /[Th]is is a louely *lesson*; lord it þee foryelde.
B.10.37 Litel is he loued [or lete by] þat swich a *lesson* [techeþ],
B.10.93 Swiche *lessons* lordes sholde louye to here,
B.10.377 'This is a long *lesson*', quod I, 'and litel am I þe wiser;
B.11.158 Wel ouȝte ye lordes þat lawes kepe þis *lesson* haue in mynde
B.11.222 For it is ouerlonge er logyk any *lesson* assoille.
B.17.42 It is lighter to lewed men o *lesson* to knowe
C. 3.490 Thow art lyk a lady þat a *lessoun* radde
C. 6.210 Wykkedliche to waye was my furste *lessounn*.
C. 6.217 Amongus the ryche rayes y rendrede a *lessoun*,
C. 6.241 Y lernede among lumbardus a *lessoun* and of iewes,
C.12.90 Wel ouhte ȝe lordes þat lawes kepeth this *lesson* haue in mynde

lest conj *leste conj. &> leest,list* A 3; B 10; C 9 laste (7) lest (2)

A. 5.38 '*Lest* þe king & his counseil ȝour comunes apeir[e]
A. 7.136 *Lest* his flessh & þe fend foulide his soule.
A. 7.256 And lerne to laboure wiþ lond *lest* liflode hym faile.
B.Pr.99 *Lest* crist in Consistorie acorse ful manye.
B. 5.46 '*Lest* þe kyng and his conseil youre comunes apeire
B. 6.272 And lerne to laboure wiþ lond [*lest*] liflode [hym faille].
B.10.419 Wercheþ ye as ye sen ywrite, *lest* ye worþe noȝt þerInne.
B.11.432 Ac whan nede nymeþ hym vp for [nede] *lest* he sterue,
B.12.7 To amende it in þi myddel age, *lest* myȝt þe faill[e]
B.12.125 *Lest* cheste cha[fe] vs to choppe ech man oþer:
B.13.426 *Lest* þo þre maner men to muche sorwe yow brynge:
B.15.386 *Lest* þei ouerhuppen as oþere doon in office and in houres.
B.18.295 'Certes I drede me', quod þe deuel, '*lest* truþe [do] hem fecche.
C.Pr.127 *Lest* crist in constorie acorse of [ȝow] manye.
C. 5.144 '*Laste* þe kyng and his consayl ȝoure comunes apayre
C. 7.86 *Laste* tho manere men to muche sorwe ȝow brynge:
C. 8.293 And lerne to labory with lond *lest* lyflode h[y]m fayle.
C.11.251 *Laste* ȝe be loste as þe laboreres were þat lab[o]red vnder Noe.
C.14.68 *Laste* cheste chauf[e] vs to [c]hoppe vch man oþer.
C.16.229 "Non plus sapere," saide þe wyse, [*laste* synne of pruyde wexe,]
C.20.325 'Forthy y drede me,' quod þe deuel, '*laste* treuthe wol hem fecche.
C.20.334 Lette hem þat louede hym nat *laste* they wolde hym martre.

leste > leest; lesten > laste; let > leden,leten,lette

leten v *leten v.* A 31 lat (1) let (20) lete (6) leten (2) letiþ (2); B 79 lat (35) late (6) leet (11) let (2) lete (11) leten (9) leteþ (5); C 82 lat (38) late (7) laton (1) leet (4) leete (1) let (3) lete (6) leten (11) leteth (1) lette (8) ylet (2)

A. 1.141 Lokide on vs wiþ loue, & *let* his sone deiȝe
A. 1.176 Þat is þe lok of loue þat *letiþ* out my grace
A. 2.123 And *let* somoune alle þe segges [in shires abouten],
A. 2.135 'And *let* apparaille þise prouisours in palfreis wise;
A. 2.141 And *let* cartesaidl þe Comissare, oure carte shal he drawe,
A. 2.159 But riȝt as þe lawe lokis *let* falle on hem alle.'
A. 2.163 And ge[rd]iþ of giles hed; *let* hym go no ferþere;
A. 2.167 And ȝif ȝe lacche leiȝere *let* him not askape
A. 3.55 *Let* not þi left hond, late ne raþe,
A. 3.126 And *letiþ* passe prisoners & paieþ for hem ofte,
A. 4.19 And *let* warroke hym wel wiþ [wy]tful gerþis.
A. 4.75 And he amendis mowe make *let* maynprise hym haue,
A. 4.128 *Let* þi confessour, sire king, construe it þe on englissh,
A. 4.137 Loue *let* of hire liȝt & louȝ hire to scorne,
A. 4.154 For as longe as I lyue *l[et]*e þe I [n]ile.'
A. 5.33 '*Let* no wynnyng forwanye hem whiles þei ben ȝonge'.
A. 5.142 Ac I swere now, so þ[e I], þat synne shal I *lete*,
A. 5.185 Þere was lauȝing & louryng & '*lete* go þe cuppe!'
A. 5.229 [And] þeiȝ my liflode lakke *leten* I nille
A. 6.102 Þus miȝt þou lese his loue, to *lete* wel be þiselue,
A. 6.109 Largenesse þe lady *let* in wel manye.
A. 7.74 *Let* god worþe wiþal for so his woord techiþ.
A. 7.104 At heiȝ prime peris *let* þe plouȝ stande
A. 7.153 And *let* liȝt of þe lawe & lesse of þe kniȝt,
A. 7.210 Wiþ mete or [wiþ] mone *let* make hem [fare þe betere],
A. 7.249 *Let* nouȝt sire surfet sitten at þi bord;
A. 7.255 And be fayn be my feiþ his fesik to *leten*,
A. 9.25 *Let* bringe a man in a bot amydde a brood watir;
A.11.29 Litel is he louid or *lete* by þat suche a lessoun techiþ,
A.11.142 Ac for it *lat* best be loue I loue it þe betere,
A.12.21 Til þo wrecches ben in wil here synne to *lete*."
B.Pr.155 That vs loþeþ þe lif er he *late* vs passe.
B.Pr.181 And *leten* hire labour lost and al hire longe studie.
B.Pr.187 Forþi I counseille al þe commune to *late* þe cat worþe,
B. 1.167 Loked on vs wiþ loue and *leet* his sone dye
B. 1.202 [Th]at is þe lok of loue [þat] *leteþ* out my grace
B. 2.48 And lakke hem noȝt but *lat* hem worþe til leaute be Iustice
B. 2.51 And *lat* no conscience acombre þee for coueitise of Mede.'
B. 2.159 And *leten* somoune alle segges in shires aboute,
B. 2.171 'And *late* apparaille þise prouisours in palfreyes wise;
B. 2.175 *Lat* sadle hem wiþ siluer oure synne to suffre,
B. 2.180 And [*lat*] Cartsadle þe Commissarie; oure cart shal he [drawe]
B. 2.198 But riȝt as þe lawe [lokeþ] *lat* falle on hem alle.'
B. 2.202 And girdeþ of Gyles heed; *lat* hym go no ferþer:
B. 2.206 And if ye lacche lyere *lat* hym noȝt ascapen
B. 3.73 *Lat* noȝt þi left half, late ne raþe,
B. 3.137 [And] *leteþ* passe prisoners and paieþ for hem ofte,
B. 4.21 And *lat* warroke hym wel wiþ wit[ful] gerþes.
B. 4.40 Forþi, Reson, *lat* hem ride þo riche by hemselue,
B. 4.88 And he amendes mowe make *lat* maynprise hym haue,
B. 4.145 *Late* [þi] Confessour, sire kyng, construe [it þee on englissh],
B. 4.160 And *leten* Mekenesse a maister and Mede a mansed sherewe.
B. 4.161 Loue *leet* of hire liȝt and leaute yet lasse,
B. 4.180 I wole haue leaute in lawe, and *lete* be al youre ianglyng;

B. 4.191 For as longe as I lyue *lete* þee I nelle.'
B. 5.35 'Late no wynnyng [forwanye hem] while þei be yonge,
B. 5.52 'And ye þat han lawes to [loke], *lat* truþe be youre coueitise
B. 5.226 Ac I swere now, so thee ik, þat synne wol I *lete*
B. 5.336 There was lauȝynge and lourynge and '*lat* go þe cuppe!'
B. 5.409 Vigilies and fastyng dayes, alle þise *late* I passe,
B. 5.457 And þouȝ my liflode lakke *leten* I nelle
B. 5.616 Thus myȝtestow lesen his loue, to *lete* wel by þiselue,
B. 5.623 Largenesse þe lady *let* in [wel] manye;
B. 6.39 And þouȝ [þow] mowe amercy hem *lat* mercy be taxour
B. 6.82 *Lat*-god-yworþe-wiþ-al-for-so-his-word-techeþ.
B. 6.112 At heiȝ prime Piers *leet* þe plowȝ stonde
B. 6.168 And *leet* liȝt of þe lawe and lasse of þe knyȝte,
B. 6.181 '[*Lat*] hem lyue', he seide, 'and lat hem ete wiþ hogges,
B. 6.181 '[*Lat*] hem lyue', he seide, 'and *lat* make hem fare be bettre].
B. 6.224 Wiþ mete or wiþ mone *lat* make hem fare be bettre].
B. 6.225 Loue hem and lakke hem noȝt; *lat* god take þe vengeaunce;
B. 6.226 Theiȝ þei doon yuele *lat* [þow] god yworþe:
B. 6.265 *Lat* noȝt sire Surfet sitten at þi borde;
B. 6.271 And be fayn, by my feiþ, his Phisik to *lete*,
B. 7.88 *Lat* vsage be youre solas of seintes lyues redyng.
B. 8.29 *Lat* brynge a man in a boot amydde [a] bro[od] watre;
B.10.37 Litel is he loued [or *lete* by] þat swich a lesson [techeþ],
B.10.190 Ac for it *leteþ* best bi loue I loue it þe bettre,
B.10.262 And *lat* no body be by þi beryng bigiled
B.10.321 Ac þei *leten* hem as lordes, hire lon[d liþ] so brode.
B.10.400 Whan þei shal lif *lete* [a lippe of goddes grace]–
B.11.23 Til þow be a lord and haue *leten* þee I nelle
B.11.38 'And Deus disponit', quod he; '*lat* god doon his wille.
B.11.114 And plukked in Pauci pryueliche and *leet* þe remenaunt go rome.'
B.11.427 For *lat* a dronken daffe in a dyk falle,
B.11.428 *Lat* hym ligge, loke noȝt on hym til hym list aryse.
B.13.157 Vndo it; *lat* þis doctour deme if dowel be þerInne.
B.13.362 'The worste withInne was; a greet wit I *let* it.
B.15.5 And *lete* me for a lorel and looþ to reuerencen
B.15.173 Al þat men seyn, he *leet* it sooþ and in science takeþ,
B.15.564 Takeþ hire landes, ye lordes, and *leteþ* hem lyue by dymes;
B.15.586 And on þat lawe þei l[e]ue and *leten* it þe beste.
B.16.259 'Loo!' quod he and *leet* me see; 'lord, mercy!' I seide,
B.17.10 '*Lat* se þi lettres', quod I, 'we myghte þe lawe knowe.'
B.17.312 Yuele lyuen and *leten* noȝt til lif hem forsake.
B.18.56 Thanne shul we leue þat lif þee loueþ and wol noȝt *lete* þee deye.'
B.18.201 Forþi *lat* hem chewe as þei chosen and chide we noȝt, sustres,
B.18.250 And *leet* out Symondes sone[s] to seen hym hange on roode.
B.18.285 I leeue þat lawe nyl noȝt *lete* hym þe leeste.'
B.18.406 But *leten* hym lede forþ [what] hym liked and lete [what] hym liste.
B.18.406 But leten hym lede forþ [what] hym liked and *lete* [what] hym liste.
B.18.418 And *leteþ* no peple', quod pees, 'parceyue þat we chidde;
B.20.102 Lered [ne] lewed he *leet* no man stonde,
B.20.143 And þanne lough lyf and *leet* daggen hise cloþes,
B.20.146 And *leet* leautee a cherl and lyere a fre man.
B.20.237 *Lat* hem chewe as þei chose and charge hem with no cure.
B.20.241 *Lat* hem be as beggeris or lyue by Aungeles foode.'
B.20.349 *Lat* in þe frere and his felawe, and make hem fair cheere.
B.20.360 [And] *lat* hem ligge ouerlonge and looþ is to chaunge;
B.20.361 Fro lenten to lenten he *lat* hise plastres bite.'
C.Pr.175 That vs loteth þe lyf ar he *lette* vs passe.
C.Pr.198 And *leten* here labour ylost and al here longe study.
C.Pr.204 Forthy y conseile for oure comune profit *lat* þe Cat yworthe
C. 1.163 Lokede on vs with loue [and] *let* hys sone deye
C. 2.51 Lacke hem nat but *lat* hem worthe til leutee be Iustice
C. 2.108 For a leueth be lost when he his lyf *leteth*,\
C. 2.175 And *leten* somne alle seggus in vche syde aboute,
C. 2.193 And *lat* cop[l]e þe commissarie; oure cart shal he drawe
C. 2.212 But riht as þe lawe loketh *lat* falle on hem alle.'
C. 2.215 *Lat* fetere falsnesse faste for eny skynes ȝeftes,
C. 2.216 And gurdeth of gyles heed; *lat* hym goo no wyddore
C. 2.218 And yf ȝe lacchen lyare *lat* hym nat askape
C. 3.75 *Lat* nat thy lyft ha[lf], oure lord techeth,
C. 3.137 And ay the lengur y *late* [the] go the lasse treuthe is with the,
C. 3.150 But y be holly at thyn heste; *lat* hange me elles.'
C. 3.175 He *lat* passe prisones [and] paieth for hem ofte
C. 3.205 Ther he is alowed and *ylet* by þat laste shal eny while
C. 3.242 Caytifliche thow, Consience, conseiledest þe kyng *leten*
C. 3.264 To *lete* so his lordschipe for a litel mone.
C. 4.21 And *lat* warrokye [hym] w[e]ll with auys[e]-þe-byfore;
C. 4.23 *Lat* peytrele [hym] and pole hym with peynted wittes.'
C. 4.84 Yf he amendes may [make] *lat* maynprise hym haue
C. 4.142 *Lat* thy Confessour, syre kyng, construe this in englische
C. 4.156 Loue l[et]te of mede lyhte and leutee ȝut lasse
C. 4.174 Y wol haue leutee for my lawe and *late* be al ȝoure iangl[ing]

C. 5.3 And lytel *ylet* by, leueth me for sothe,
C. 5.137 '*Late* no wynnynge forwanyen hem while thei ben ȝonge,
C. 5.167 Ac ȝe *leten* ȝow alle as lordes, ȝoure lond lyth so brode.
C. 5.184 *Lat* no kyne consayl ne couetyse ȝow parte,
C. 6.101 Lord, ar y lyf *lete*, for loue of thysulue
C. 6.243 And len[e] for loue of þe wed the whych y *lette* bettere
C. 6.261 The worste lay withynne; a greet wit y *lat* hit.
C. 6.311 'And thow m[y] lyflode lakke *leten* y nelle
C. 6.394 There was leyhyng and louryng and '*lat* go the coppe!'
C. 7.268 Thus myhte thow lesen his loue, to *lete* wel by thysulue,
C. 7.275 Largenesse þ[e] lady *lat* in ful monye,
C. 8.37 And when ȝe mersyen eny man *late* mercy be taxour,
C. 8.86 *Lat* god yworthe with al, as holy wryt techeth:
C. 8.119 At hey prime [Peres] *leet* þe plouh stande
C. 8.165 And *leet* lyhte of þe lawe and lasse of the knyhte
C. 8.177 'Haue mercy on hem, hunger,' quod [Peres], 'and *lat* me ȝeue hem benes
C. 8.233 Loke by thy lyue *lat* hem nat forfare.
C. 8.275 *Lat* nat sire sorfeet sitt[en] at thy borde;
C. 8.287 *Lat* hem abyde til the bord be drawe; Ac bere hem none crommes
C. 8.292 And be fayn, be my fayth, his fysik to *leete*
C.10.33 *Lat* bryng a man in a boet amydde a brood water;
C.10.164 God wol nat of hem wyte bute *lat* hem yworthe,
C.10.201 For hoso loueth, leueth h[it] wel, god wol nat *laton* hym sterue
C.10.262 Ac *lat* he[r] be vnlouely and vnlofsum abedde,
C.10.264 That no cortesye can, bute [knowe *late* here be]
C.11.22 What shal worthen of suche when þei lyf *leten*?
C.11.32 Litel is he loued or *leet* [by] among lordes at festes.
C.11.76 And þat loueth lordes now and *leten* hit a dowel
C.11.182 Til thow be a lord and haue lond *leten* y the nelle
C.11.304 'Et deus disponit,' quod he; '*la[t]* god do his wille.
C.12.49 And plihte in pauci preueiliche and *lette* þe remenaunt go rome.'
C.12.215 "And art so loth to leue that *lete* shal thow nedes:
C.13.234 For *lat* a dronkene daffe in a dykke falle,
C.13.235 *Lat* hym lygge, lok nat on hym til hym luste [a]ryse.
C.15.93 And why a lyueth nat as a lereth.' '*lat* be,' quod pacience,
C.17.117 Lord *lete* þat this prestes lelly seien here masse.
C.17.168 Ac for he was lyk a lossheborw y leue oure lord hym *lette*.
C.17.227 Taketh here londe[s], ȝe lordes, and *lat* hem lyue by dymes
C.17.297 And on þat lawe they leue and *leten* hit for þe reste.
C.18.104 'Leue liberum Arbitrium, *lat* some lyf hit shake.'
C.18.275 'Loo!' quod he and *lette* me see: 'lord, mercy!' y saide,
C.19.11 '*Let* se thy lettres,' quod y, 'we myhte þe lawe knowe.'
C.19.147 Bote [be he] greued with here grype the holy goost *lat* falle.
C.19.292 That euele lyuen and *leten* nat t[il lif] hem forsake.
C.20.56 Thenne shal we leue that lyf þe loueth and wol nat *late* the deye.'
C.20.206 Forthy [*let*] hem che[w]e as they chose and chyde we nat, sustres,
C.20.259 And *lette* out symondes sones to sen hym honge on rode:
C.20.386 So lyf shal lyf *le[t]e* ther lyf hath an[y]en[t]ed
C.20.449 Bote *leten* hym lede forth which hym luste and leue which hym likede.
C.20.461 'And *lat* no peple,' quod pees, 'perseyue þat we chydde;
C.22.143 And thenne lowh lyf and *lette* dagge his clothes
C.22.146 And *leet* leautee a cherl and lyare a fre man.
C.22.237 *Late* hem chewe as thei chose and charge hem with no cure.
C.22.241 *Lat* hem be as beggares or lyue by angeles fode.'
C.22.349 *Lat* in þe frere and his felawe and make hem fayere chiere.
C.22.360 And *lat* hem lygge ouerlonge and loeth is to chaungen;
C.22.361 Fro lente to lente he *lat* his plastres byte.'

leþeren adj *letheren adj.* A 1 leþerene; B 1; C 1 letherne
A. 5.110 [And] as a l[e]þerene purs lollide his chekis.
B. 5.191 And [lik] a leþeren purs lolled hise chekes.
C. 6.199 And as a letherne pors lollede his chekes

letyse n prop *n.i.d.* C 1
C. 6.145 How lytel y louye *letyse* at þe style.

letrede > lettred; letrure > lettrure

lette v *letten v. &> leten* A 5 lette (4) lettiþ (1); B 24 lette (15) letted (2) letteþ (7); C 33 let (1) lette (21) letten (1) letteth (7) ylet (1) ylette (2)
A. 2.31 I may no lengere *lette*, lord I þe bekenne.
A. 3.31 'Shal no lewidnesse hym *lette*, þe lede þat I louye,
A. 3.146 And leiþ aȝen þe lawe & *lettiþ* þe treuþe.
A.10.165 And com to noe anon, and bad hym nouȝt *lette*
A.11.20 And lede forþ a loueday to *lette* þe treuþe.
B. 1.158 That myȝte noon Armure it *lette* ne none heiȝe walles.
B. 3.32 'Shal no lewednesse [hym] *lette*, þe leode þat I louye,
B. 3.156 And liþ ayein þe lawe and *letteþ* hym þe gate
B. 3.198 I made his me[ynee] murye and mournynge *lette*;
B. 4.176 Mede ouermaistreþ lawe and muche truþe *letteþ*.
B. 5.295 And what he lente yow of oure lordes good to *lette* yow fro synne.'
B. 9.134 And com to Noe anon and bad hym noȝt *lette*:
B.10.20 And lede forþ a loueday to *lette* [þe] truþe,

B.10.78   That preieres haue no power þ[ise] pestilence[s] to *lette*.
B.10.271   Which *letteþ* þee to loke, lasse ouþer moore?
B.10.294   And drede to wraþe yow in any word youre werkmanship to *lette*,
B.11.137   'That is sooþ', seide Scripture; 'may no synne *lette*
B.14.212   The heiȝe wey to heueneward [ofte] Richesse *letteþ*:
B.15.66   Of god and of hise grete myȝtes, hise graces it *letteþ*.
B.15.563   That sholden preie for þe pees, possession hem *letteþ*;
B.16.46   Ac liberum arbitrium *letteþ* hym som tyme,
B.16.83   Bar hem forþ bo[lde]ly–no body hym *letted*–
B.16.270   'Allas!' I seide, 'þat synne so longe shal *lette*
B.17.81   For I may noȝt *lette*', quod þat Leode and lyard he bistrideþ
B.17.355   I may no lenger *lette*', quod he, and lyard he prikede
B.18.53   And beden hym drynken his deeþ [to *lette* and] hise daies [lengþe],
B.19.382   The lord of lust shal be *letted* al þis lente, I hope.
B.20.173   Lyf leeued þat lechecraft *lette* sholde Elde
B.20.321   And Indulgence may do but if dette *lette* it.
C. 1.154   [That myȝte] non Armure hit *lette* ne none heye walles,
C. 1.203   Loue hit,' quod þat lady; '*lette* may y no lengore
C. 2.38   That helpeth man moste to heuene mede most *letteth*.
C. 3.35   Shal no lewedenesse *lette* þe [lede] þat y louye
C. 3.194   He lyth aȝeyn þe lawe and *le[tte]th* hym þe gate
C. 3.239   In contrees there the kyng cam, consience hym *lette*
C. 3.451   And *letteth* the lawe thorw here large ȝeftes.
C. 4.170   Mede and men of ȝsource craft muche treuthe *letteth*.
C. 6.349   What a lered ȝow to lyue with and to *lette* ȝow fram thefte.'
C.10.161   So *let* lecherye and other luther synnes
C.11.17   And *lette* with a loueday [lewed] treuthe and bigile
C.11.58   That preyeres haen no power þis pestilences to *lette*.
C.12.72   'That is soth,' saide scripture; ' may no synne *lette*
C.13.10   And Abraham not hardy ones to *letten* hym
C.13.37   The marchaunt mote nede be *ylet* lenger then the messager
C.13.39   Wol *lette* hym, as y leue, the lenghe of a myle
C.13.50   And ȝut be *ylette*, as y leue, for the lawe asketh
C.13.91   Ther is no lawe, as y leue, wol *lette* hym þe gate
C.14.177   For here fetheres þat fayre beth to fle fer hem *letteth*.
C.15.165   Þer [n]is wyht in this world þat wolde the *lette*
C.15.180   Lettrure and longe studie *letteth* fol monye
C.15.219   *Lette* this luythere [eir] and leche þe sike–
C.17.226   That sholde preye for þe pees possession hem *letteth*;
C.18.114   Baer hem forth baldly–no body hym *lette*–
C.18.286   'Allas!' y saide, 'þat synne so longe shal *lette*
C.19.78   For y may nat *lette*,' quod that lede; and lyard he bystrideth
C.19.335   Y may no lengore *lette*,' quod he, and lyard a prikede
C.20.53   And beden hym drynke his deth to *lette* and his dayes lenghe
C.20.283   And [y] shal *lette* this loerd and his lint stoppe.
C.20.334   *Lette* hem þat louede hym nat laste they wolde hym martre.
C.21.382   The lord of lust shal be *ylette* al this lente, y hope.
C.22.173   Lyf leuede þat lechecraft *lette* sholde Elde
C.22.321   And indulgence may do but yf dette *lette* hit.

lettere n *lettere n.(1)* A 1; B 1; C 1
A. 1.67   He is *lettere* of loue, leiȝeþ hem alle;
B. 1.69   He is *lettere* of loue, lieþ hem alle;
C. 1.65   He is *lettere* of loue and lyeth alle tymes;

lettered > lettred; letteres > lettre; letterure > lettrure

lettyng ger1 *lettinge ger.* A 2; B 2; C 2 lettyng (1) lettynge (1)
A. 7.7   'Þis were a long *lettyng*,' quaþ a lady in a scleire;
A.11.167   And wente wiȝtly my wey wiþoute more *lettyng*,
B. 6.7   'This were a long *lettyng*', quod a lady in a Scleyre.
B.10.225   And wente wightly [my w]ey wiþoute moore *lettyng*,
C. 8.5   'Th[is] were a long *lettyng*,' quod [a] lady in a slayre;
C.11.134   Tho wente y my way withouten more *lettynge*

lettynge ger2 *letinge ger. &>* lettyng C 1
C.17.124   In þe *lettynge* of here lyf to leue on holy churche.'

lettre n *lettre n.* A 8 letteres (1) lettre (3) lettres (3) lettris (1); B 28 lettre (15) lettres (13); C 29 letteres (1) lettre (16) lettres (12)
A. 1.47   And he askide of hem of whom spak þe *lettre*,
A. 2.185   Þanne louride lechis & *lettris* [hy] sente
A. 4.115   But it be marchaunt, oþer his man, oþer messang[er] with *lettres*,
A. 8.25   Ac vndir his secre sel treuþe sente h[e]m a *lettre*,
A. 8.93   In two lynes it lay & nouȝt o *lettre* more,
A. 8.154   Bienalis & trienalis & bisshopis *lettres*.
A. 8.175   A pokeful of pardoun þere, ne þe prouincialis *lettres*,
A.12.86   We han *letteres* of lyf, he shal his lyf ty[n]e.
B. 1.49   And [he] asked of h[e]m of whom spak þe *lettre*,
B. 2.226   Thanne louride leches, and *lettres* þei sente
B. 4.132   But it be Marchaunt or his man or Messager wiþ *lettres*,
B. 5.248   And wiþ lumbardes *lettres* I ladde gold to Rome
B. 5.640   I wol go fecche my box wiþ my breuettes & a bulle with bisshopes *lettres*
B. 7.23   Ac vnder his secret seel truþe sente hem a *lettre*,

B. 7.111   In two lynes it lay and noȝt a [*lettre*] moore,
B. 7.176   Biennals and triennals and Bisshopes *lettres*.
B. 7.197   A pokeful of pardon þere, ne prouincials *lettres*,
B. 9.39   Right as a lord sholde make *lettres*; [if] hym lakked parchemyn,
B. 9.41   The *lettre*, for al þe lordshipe, I leue, were neuere ymaked.
B.10.92   For we haue no *lettre* of oure lif how longe it shal dure.
B.11.205   In þe olde lawe, as [þe] *lettre* telleþ, mennes sones men calle[d] vs
B.11.304   If fals latyn be in þat *lettre* þe lawe it impugneþ,
B.12.73   In þe olde lawe as þe *lettre* telleþ, þat was þe lawe of Iewes,
B.15.376   Ne rede a *lettre* in any langage but in latyn or englissh.
B.17.4   'Is it enseled?' I seide; 'may men see þ[e] *lettres*?'
B.17.9   [And þus my *lettre* meneþ; [ye] mowe knowe it al].'
B.17.10   'Lat se þi *lettres*', quod I, 'we myghte þe lawe knowe.'
B.17.36   And telleþ noȝt of þe Trinite þat took hym hise *lettres*,
B.17.120   Hope shal lede hem forþ with loue as his *lettre* telleþ,
B.17.79   Highte Longeus as þe *lettre* telleþ, and longe hadde lore his sight;
B.18.170   But [loue] sente hire som *lettre* what þis light bymeneþ
B.18.182   Loue þat is my lemman swiche *lettres* me sente
B.19.307   For present or for preiere or any Prynces *lettres*.
B.20.309   Some liked noȝt þis leche and *lettres* þei sente
B.20.325   To a lord for a *lettre* leue to haue
B.20.326   To curen as a Curatour; and cam with hi[s] *lettr[e]*
C. 2.86   And fauel þat hath a fals speche Feffeth hem by þis *lettre*
C. 2.110   In lordschip with lucifer, as this *lettre* sheweth,
C. 2.236   Thenne lourede leches and *lettre[s]* thei sente
C. 4.129   But [it] be marchaunt or his man or messager [with] *lettres*,
C. 4.189   And þat vnsittynge suffraunce ne sele ȝoure priue *lettres*
C. 6.246   And with lumbardus *lettres* le[d]e gold to Rome;
C. 9.27   Ac vnder his secrete seal treuthe sente hem a *lettre*
C. 9.280   For shal no pardon preye for ȝow there ne no princes *lettres*.
C. 9.285   In two lynes hit lay and nat a *lettre* more
C. 9.321   Bionales and trionales and bisshopes *lettres*.
C. 9.343   A pouhe ful of pardon there ne prouinciales *lettres*,
C.11.265   Lelly as by his lokes, with a *le[tt]re* of gyle?
C.12.113   In þe olde lawe, as þe *lettre* telleth, mennes sones me calde vs
C.13.41   His erende and his *lettre* sheweth and is anoon delyuered.
C.13.60   And leueth for his *lettres* þat no [lede] wole hym greue.
C.13.89   And sheweth be seel and seth by *lettre* with what lord he dwelleth,
C.13.118   Yf fals latyn be in þat *lettre* þe lawe hit enpugneth,
C.15.73   For oure lordes loue, as holy *lettre* telleth:
C.19.4   Lo, here the *lettre*,' quod he, 'a latyn and [an] ebrew;
C.19.6   'Is hit asseled?' y saide; 'may men yse th[e] *lettres*?'
C.19.11   'Let se thy *lettres*,' quod y, 'we myhte þe lawe knowe.'
C.19.24   Lo! here in my lappe þat leuede vpon þat *lettre*,
C.20.81   Hihte longies as þe *lettre* telleth, and longe hadde lore his sihte;
C.20.173   Bote loue haue ysente her som *lettre* what this liht bymeneth
C.20.185   Loue þat is my lemman such *lettres* me sente
C.21.307   For presente or for preyere or eny prinses *lettres*.
C.22.309   Somme liked nat þis leche and *letteres* they sente
C.22.325   To a lord for a *lettre* leue to haue
C.22.326   To curen as a curatour; and kam with his *lettre*

lettred adj *lettred adj.* A 5 lettrid (4) lettride (1); B 16 lettred (12) lettrede (4); C 14 letrede (1) lettered (2) lettred (10) lettrede (1)
A. 1.125   Leriþ it þus lewide men, for *lettrid* it knowiþ,
A. 3.86   Among þise *lettride* lordis þis latyn amountiþ
A. 8.45   Men of lawe hadde lest for *le[ttr]id* þei ben alle;
A. 8.119   Þou art *le[ttr]id* a litel; who lernide þe on boke?'
A. 8.159   Þis is [a] l[e]f of oure beleue, as *lettrid* men vs [tech]iþ;
B. 1.136   Lereþ it þ[us] lewed men, for *lettred* it knoweþ,
B. 3.97   Among þise *lettrede* l[or]des þis latyn [amounteþ]
B. 7.137   Thow art *lettred* a litel; who lerned þee on boke?'
B. 7.181   This is [a leef of] oure bileue, as *lettred* men vs techeþ:
B.11.83   Loke, ye *lettred* men, wheiþer I lye or noȝt.'
B.11.110   [The bileue [of oure] lord þat *lettred* men techeþ].
B.12.96   And lederes for lewed men and for *lettred* boþe.
B.12.144   Ne of lordes þat were lewed men, but of þe hyeste *lettred* oute:
B.12.157   How þat lewed men liȝtloker þan *lettrede* were saued,
B.12.276   For *lettred* men were lewed yet ne were loore of hir bokes.'
B.13.286   Lakkynge *lettrede* men and lewed men boþe;
B.14.319   Thus lered me a *lettred* man for oure lordes loue, Seint Austyn:
B.15.103   Forþi wolde ye *lettrede* leue þe lecherie of cloþyng,
B.15.354   Boþe *lettred* and lewed beþ alayed now wiþ synne
B.15.477   Louen and bileuen by *lettred* mennes doynges,
B.19.85   Maistres and *lettred* men, Magi hem callede.
C. 1.135   Lere hit thus lewed men, for *lettred* hit knoweth:
C. 3.125   Amonge thise *lettred* lordes this latyn is to mene
C. 9.327   As *lettrede* men vs lereth and lawe of holi churche:
C.11.74   Ac lust no lord now ne *lettred* man of suche lore to here
C.12.44   The bileue of oure lord þat *lettred* men techeth.
C.14.198   For *letrede* men were lewede ȝut ne were lore of [here bokes].'
C.16.153   Thus lered me a *le[tte]red* man for oure lordes loue, seynt Austyn:
C.16.194   Thenne am y liberum Arbitrium, as *le[tt]red* men telleth;
C.16.256   For wolde ȝe *lettered* leue þ[e] lecherye of clothyng

C.17.73   Me may now likene *lettred* men to a loscheborw oþer worse
C.17.88   Lewed men han no byleue, [so] *lettred* men erren;
C.17.210 Minne ȝe [nat], *lettred* men, how tho men honourede
C.18.80   That [lyf Actiua] *lettred* men in here langage calleth.'
C.21.85   Maistres & *lettred* men, Magi hem calde.

lettrure n *lettrure n.*   A 1;   B 5;   C 9   leture (1)   letterure (1)   lettrure (7)
A.11.264 And I leue on oure lord & on no *lettrure* betere.
B.Pr.110 For in loue and *lettrure* þe eleccion bilongeþ;
B.10.27   "Lo!" seiþ holy *lettrure*, "whiche [lordes] beþ þise sherewes";
B.10.383 I leue it wel by oure lord and on no *lettrure* bettre.
B.12.104 Riȝt so [lereþ] *lettrure* lewed men to Reson.
B.12.188 That lyuynge after *lettrure* saue[d] hym lif and soule.
C.Pr.137 For in loue and *lettrure* lith þe grete eleccoun.
C. 9.196 Noyther of lynage ne of *lettrure* ne lyfholy as Ermytes
C. 9.199 And summe lyuede by here *letterure* and labour of here handes
C.11.24   "Lo!" saith holy *letrure*, "whiche lordes beth this schrewes";
C.11.97   Of lore and of *lettrure*, of lawe and of resoun.
C.11.208 Y leue hit wel by oure lord and on no *lettrure* bettere.
C.14.49   Riht so lereth *lettrure* lewed men to resoun.
C.14.127 That lyuynge Aftur *lettrure* saued hy[m] lyf and soule.
C.15.180 *Lettrure* and longe studie letteth fol monye

leute(e > leaute

leue n *leve n.(2) &> leef*   A 10;   B 18   leeue (4)   leue (14);   C 24
A.Pr.49   And hadde *leue* to leiȝe al here lif aftir.
A.Pr.82   To haue a licence & *leue* at lundoun to dwelle,
A.Pr.94   Ben ylope to lundoun be *leue* of hire bisshop,
A. 2.193 Ac he haþ *leue* to lepen out as ofte as him likiþ,
A. 3.15   Counforti[de] hire kyndely be clergie[s] *leue*,
A. 3.24   Þanne lauȝte hy *leue*, þise lordis at mede.
A. 3.218 'Þere arn to maner of medis, my lord, be ȝour *leue*.
A. 4.15   Seide hym as þe king sente & siþþe tok his *leue*.
A. 5.211 Er abstinence myn aunte haue ygyue me *leue*,
A.12.55   Þus we lauȝþe oure *leue*, lowtyng at onys,
B.Pr.49   And hadden *leue* to lyen al hire lif after.
B.Pr.85   To haue a licence and *leue* at London to dwelle,
B. 2.114 By siȝte of sire Symonie and Cyuyles *leeue*.'
B. 2.234 Ac he haþ *leue* to lepen out as ofte as hym likeþ,
B. 3.15   Conforte[d] hire kyndely by clergies *leue*,
B. 3.25   Thanne lauȝte þei *leue*, þise lordes, at Mede.
B. 3.231 'Ther are two manere of Medes, my lord, [bi] youre *leue*.
B. 4.15   [Seide hym] as þe kyng [sente] and siþen took his *leue*.
B. 5.383 Til Abstinence myn Aunte haue ȝyue me *leeue*,
B. 6.66   Shal haue *leue*, by oure lord, to lese here in heruest
B.11.128 Wiþouten *leue* of his lord; no lawe wol it graunte.
B.12.114 Hadde neuere lewed man *leue* to leggen hond on þat cheste
B.16.47   That is lieutenaunt to loken it wel bi *leue* of myseluie:
B.18.267 'Swich a light, ayeins oure *leue* laȝar [i]t fette.
B.19.480 The viker hadde fer hoom and faire took his *leeue*
B.20.188 Haddestow be hende', quod I, 'þow woldest haue asked *leeue*.'
B.20.189 'Ye, *leue*, lurdeyn?' quod he, and leyde on me wiþ Age,
B.20.325 To a lord for a lettre *leue* to haue
C.Pr.50   And hadde *leue* to lye [al here lyf aftir].
C.Pr.83   To haue a licence and *leue* [at] Londoun to dwelle,
C. 1.204 To lere the what loue is;' and *leue* at me she lauhte.
C. 2.118 By syhte of sire Simonye and syuyles *leue*.'
C. 2.244 Ac he hath *leue* to lep out as ofte as hym liketh,
C. 3.16   Confortede here as they couthe by the clerkes *leue*
C. 3.26   [W]henne they hadde lauhte here *leue* at this lady mede
C. 3.132 And wilned to be wedded withouten his *leue*,
C. 4.15   And sayde hym as þe kyng sayde and sennes took his *leue*.
C. 6.121 Withoute licence and *leue*, and herby lyueth wrathe.
C. 6.440 Til abstinence myn aunte haue ȝeue me *leue*;
C. 7.293 To loke how me liketh hit,' and toek his *leue* at Peres.
C. 8.67   Shal haue *leue*, by oure lord, to [lese here in heruest]
C. 9.146 And whenne hym lyketh and luste, his *leue* is to ryse
C.12.63   Withouten *leue* of [his] lord; no lawe wol hit graunte.
C.13.83   That þe lawe ȝeueth *leue* such low folk to be excused,
C.14.59   Hadde neuere lewede [man] *leue* to legge hand on þat cheste
C.20.275 'Such a lyht aȝenes oure *leue* laȝar hit fette;
C.20.314 Aȝeyne his loue and his *leue* on his londe ȝedest,
C.20.381 Aȝeyne my loue and my *leue*: þe olde lawe techeth
C.21.480 The vicory hadde fer hoem and [fayre] toek his *leue*
C.22.188 Haddest thow be hende,' quod y, 'thow wost haue asked *leue*.'
C.22.189 'Ȝe, *leue*, lordeyne?' quod he, and leide on me with age
C.22.325 To a lord for a lettre *leue* to haue

leue v1 *leven v.(4)*   A 9   leue (7)   leuide (1)   leuiþ (1);   B 70   leeue (5)   leeued
(2)   leeuen (1)   lef (1)   leue (46)   leued (5)   leueden (1)   leuen (1)
leuestow (1)   leueþ (7);   C 90   leef (6)   lef (2)   leue (57)   leued (5)   leuede
(3)   leuen (2)   leuest (1)   leueth (14)
A.Pr.69   Lewide men *leuide* [hym] wel & likide his speche;
A. 1.36   *Leue* not þi lycam for a li[ȝ]er hym techiþ,

A. 3.162 'Nay lord,' quod þat lady, '*leu[iþ]* him þe wers
A. 5.36   'And libbe as ȝe lere vs, we wile *leue* ȝow þe betere'.
A. 5.112 But ȝif a lous couþe lepe, I may it nouȝt *leue*.
A. 7.82   To haue reles & remissioun, on þat rental I *leue*.
A. 8.160 And so I *leue* lelly, lord forbede ellis,
A.11.144 *Leue* lelly þeron ȝif þou þenke do wel,
A.11.264 And I *leue* on oure lord & on no lettrure betere.
B.Pr.34   And geten gold with hire glee [gilt]lees, I *leeue*.
B.Pr.72   Lewed men *leued* [hym] wel and liked hi[s] speche;
B. 1.38   *Lef* nauȝt þi licame] for a liere hym techeþ,
B. 1.118 For þei *leueden* vpon [Lucifer] þat lyed in þis manere:
B. 2.101 For he *leueþ* be lost, þis is [his] laste ende.
B. 3.175 'Nay lord', quod þat lady, '*leueþ* hym þe werse
B. 3.337 'I *leue* wel, lady', quod Conscience, 'þat þi latyn be trewe.
B. 4.175 And seide, 'þoruȝ [youre] lawe, as I *leue*, I lese manye eschetes;
B. 5.44   [Lyue] as ye leren vs; we shul *leue* yow þe bettre.'
B. 5.176 Forþi haue I no likyng, [*leue* me], wiþ þo leodes to wonye;
B. 5.196 But if a lous couþe [lepe, I *leue* and I trowe],
B. 5.276 And whoso *leueþ* [þat I liȝe] loke in þe Sauter glose,
B. 5.294 What he lerned yow in lente, *leue* þow noon ooþer,
B. 6.90   To haue relees and remission, on þat rental I *leue*.
B. 7.40   Men of lawe leest pardon hadde, [*leue* þow noon ooþer],
B. 7.182 And so I *leue* leelly, lor[d] forb[e]de ellis,
B. 9.41   The lettre, for al þe lordshipe, I *leue*, were neuere ymaked.
B. 9.204 Ac to loue and to lene], *leue* me, þat is dobet;
B.10.363 And þus bilongeþ to louye þat *leueþ* [to] be saued.
B.10.383 I *leue* it wel by oure lord and on no lettrure bettre.
B.10.444 Forþi lyue we forþ wiþ [liþere] men; I *leue* fewe ben goode,
B.11.49   I hadde no likyng, *leue* me, [þe leste] of hem to knowe.
B.11.109 Þe lasse, as I *leue*, louyen þei wolde
B.11.177 Whoso *loueþ* noȝt, *leue* me, he lyueþ in deeþ deyinge.
B.11.301 He [ouȝte no] bileue, as I *leue*, to lacche þoruȝ his croune
B.11.312 The bisshop shal be blamed bifore god, as I *leue*,
B.11.380 Who suffre[þ] moore þan god?' quod he; 'no gome, as I *leeue*.
B.11.391 Ech a lif wolde be laklees, *leue* þow noon oþer.
B.12.94   To oure lord, *leue* me; forþi loue hem, I rede.
B.12.211 That oure lord ne hadde hym liȝtly out, so *leue* I [by] þe þef in
          heuene.
B.12.223 And of þe stones and of þe sterres; þow studiest, as I *leue*,
B.12.254 Thouȝ he crye to crist þanne wiþ kene wil, I *leue*
B.12.257 I *leue* it flawme ful foule be fold al aboute,
B.12.277 'Alle þise clerkes', quod I þo, "þat [o]n crist *leuen*"
B.12.288 But lyueþ as his lawe techeþ and *leueþ* þer be no bettre,
B.13.96   And but [þe] first [leef] be lesyng *leue* me neuere after.
B.13.263 Al londoun, I *leue*, likeþ wel my wafres,
B.13.307 'Lo! if ye *leue* me noȝt, or þat I lye wenen,
B.13.337 Lechecraft of oure lord and *leue* on a wicche,
B.13.338 And seye þat no clerc ne kan, ne crist as I *leue*,
B.13.386 For losse of good, *leue* me, þan for likames giltes;
B.13.388 As whan I lened and *leued* it lost or longe er it were paied.
B.14.35   'Whoso *leueþ* yow, by oure lord! I leue noȝt he be blessed.'
B.14.35   'Whoso *leueþ* yow, by oure lord! I *leue* noȝt he be blessed.'
B.15.155 And wollen lene þer þei *leue* lelly to ben paied.
B.15.411 That [lered] þere and [lewed] ȝit *leeuen* on hise lawes.
B.15.507 Thus in a feiþ *leue* þat folk, and in a fals mene,
B.15.554 Togideres loue leelly, *leueþ* it wel, ye bisshopes,
B.15.586 And on þat lawe þei l[e]ue and leten it be beste.
B.17.17   [Is] here alle þi lordes lawes?' quod I; 'ye, *leue* me', he seide.
B.17.23   Lo! here in my lappe þat *leeued* on þat charme,
B.17.27   And lelest to *leue* [on] for lif and for soule?
B.17.46   It is lighter to *leeue* in þre louely persones
B.17.296 *Leue* I neuere þat oure lord [at þe laste ende]
B.18.56   Thanne shul we *leue* þat lif þee loueþ and wol noȝt lete þee deye.'
B.18.145 *Leue* þow neuere þat yon light hem alofte brynge
B.18.169 Loue haþ coueited hire longe; *leue* I noon ooþer.
B.18.189 *Leuestow* þat yond light vnlouke myȝte helle
B.18.208 If no nyȝt ne weere, no man as I *leeue*
B.18.251 And now shal Lucifer *leue* it, þouȝ hym looþ þynke.
B.18.285 I *leeue* þat lawe nyl noȝt lete hym þe leeste.'
B.18.303 I wolde haue lengþed his lif for I *leued* if he deide
B.18.313 For we *leued* þi lesynges [we lopen out alle];
B.18.315 And al oure lordshipe, I *leue*, a londe and [in helle]:
B.18.348 So *leue* [it] noȝt, lucifer, ayein þe lawe I fecche hem,
B.18.401 Tho [ledes] þat [I] lou[e], and *leued* in my comynge;
B.19.408 *Leue* it wel [þow art] lost, boþe lif and soule.
B.20.173 Lyf *leeued* þat lechecraft lette sholde Elde
B.20.277 He lyeþ, as I *leue*, þat to þe lewed so precheþ,
B.20.362 'That is ouerlonge', quod þis Lymytour, 'I *leue*. I shal amende it!'
C.Pr.17   And seigh a depe dale; deth, as y *leue*,
C.Pr.70   Lewed men *leued* hym wel and lykede his wordes;
C.Pr.103 I *leue*, by oure lord, for loue of ȝoure coueytise
C. 1.36   *Leef* nat thy lycame for a lyare hym techeth;
C. 1.75   [To] *leue* on me and loue me al thy lyf tyme.'

C. 1.118 Then in þe north by many notes, no man *leue* other.
C. 1.194 And a luther ensau[m]ple, *leef* me, [to] þe lewed peple.
C. 2.78   *Leueth* hit le[l]ly this worth here laste mede
C. 2.105 /This lyf to folowe falsnesse and folk þat on hym *leueth*,
C. 2.108 For a *leueth* be lost when he his lyf leteth,\
C. 3.221 'Nay, lord,' quod þat lady, '*leueth* hym þe worse
C. 3.328 And [soffrede] hym lyu[e] in mysbileue; y *leue* he be in helle.
C. 3.489 'I *leue* the, lady,' quod Consience, 'for þat latyn is trewe.
C. 4.169 'Thorw ȝoure lawe, as y *leue*, y lese many chetes;
C. 5.3   And lytel ylet by, *leueth* me for sothe,
C. 5.24   And to long, *lef* me, lowe to stoupe,
C. 5.142 Lyue as ȝe lereth vs; we shall *leue* ȝow þe bettere.'
C. 5.187 Til lucifer þe lyare *leued* þat hymsulue
C. 6.55   "Lo! yf ȝe *leue* me nat or þat y lye wenen
C. 6.81   Lechecraft of oure lord and *leue* on a wycche
C. 6.82   And segge þat no clerk ne can, ne Crist as y *leue*,
C. 6.158 Y haue no luste, *lef* me, to longe amonges monkes
C. 6.204 But yf a lous couthe lepe, y *leue* [and] y trowe,
C. 6.253 'Now redily,' quod repentaunce, 'and by þe rode, y *leue*,
C. 6.275 For lo[s] of good, *leef* me, then for lycames gultes.
C. 6.277 As whenne y lenede and *leuede* hit lost or longe or hit were payed.
C. 6.301 And what lede *leueth* þat y lye look in þe sauter glos[e],
C. 8.99   To haue re[lees] and re[missioun]; on þat rental y *leue*.
C. 8.213 Hit is nat for loue, *leue* hit, thei labore thus faste
C. 8.297 And leelyche sayst, as y *leue*; lord hit þe forȝeld!
C. 9.174 Tho þat lyueth thus here lyf, *leue* ȝe non other,
C. 9.268 Y *leue*, for thy lacchesse, thow lesest many wetheres
C. 9.328 And so y *leue* lely–lord forbede elles–
C.10.201 For hoso loueth, *leueth* h[it] wel, god wol nat laton hym sterue
C.10.303 Ac to louye and to l[e]ne, *leef* me, þat is dobet;
C.11.145 *Leue* hit lelly and loke þou do þeraftur.
C.11.200 Y *leue* neuere þat lord ne lady þat lyueth her [o]n erthe
C.11.208 Y *leue* hit wel by oure lord and on no lettrure bettere.
C.11.223 That hoso doth by ȝoure doctrine doth wel, y *leue*,
C.12.43   The lasse, as y *leue*, louyon þey wolde
C.13.26   Ac *leueth* nat, lewede men, þat y lacke rychesse
C.13.39   Wol lette hym, as y *leue*, the lenghe of a myle
C.13.50   And ȝut be ylette, as y *leue*, for the lawe asketh
C.13.60   And *leueth* for his lettres þat no [lede] wole hym greue.
C.13.91   Ther is no lawe, as y *leue*, wol lette hym þe gate
C.13.124 The bishop shal be blamed before god, as y *leue*,
C.13.197 Ho soffreth more then god?' quod he; 'no gome, as y *leue*.
C.13.209 Vch a lede wolde be lacles, *leef* thow non other.
C.14.150 That oure [lord] ne hauede [hym] lihtliche out, so *leue* y [by] þ[e] thef in heuene.
C.14.166 Ac why a wolde þat wykke were, y wene and y *leue*
C.14.199 'Alle thise clerkes,' quod y tho, 'þat [o]n crist *leuen*
C.14.210 Bote lyue[th] as his lawe t[echeth] and *leueth* þer be no bettere,
C.15.103 And bote þe furste leef be lesyngh[e] *leue* me neuere aftur.
C.15.223 Vch a kyne creature þat on crist *leueth*.
C.16.283 *Leueth* hit wel, lordes, both lewed and lered,
C.17.124 In þe lettynge of here lyf to *leue* on holy churche.'
C.17.158 And lyuen oute of lele byleue for they *l[e]ue* on a mene.
C.17.168 Ac for he was lyk a losshehorw y *leue* oure lord hym lette.
C.17.182 And on his lore thei *l[e]uen* ȝut, as wel lered as lewed.
C.17.217 Togederes louyen lelelyche, *l[e]ueth* hit [wel], bisshopes.
C.17.258 Thus in a fayth *l[e]ueth* þat folk and in a fals mene,
C.17.297 And on þat lawe they *leue* and leten hit for þe beste.
C.18.1   'Leue liberum Arbitrium,' quod y, 'y *leue*, as y hope,
C.18.58   'Ȝe, sertes,' he sayde, 'and sothliche *leue* hit.
C.18.197 How o lord myhte lyue [in] thre; y *leue* hit nat,' y sayde.
C.18.199 Ac *leue* hit lelly al thy lyftyme.
C.18.264 I *leue* þat ilke lord thenketh a newe lawe to make:
C.19.18   'Is here al thy lordes l[aw]es?' quod y; 'ȝe, *leef* me,' he saide,
C.19.24   Lo! here in my lappe þat *leuede* vpon þat baby,
C.19.94   And ȝut bote they *l[e]ue* lelly vpon þat litel baby,
C.19.103 Noþer lacke ne alose ne *leue* þat þer were
C.19.114 Ferde furste as a f[u]ste, and ȝut is, as y *leue*,
C.19.137 Portrey ne peynte parfitliche, y *leue*,
C.19.277 *Leue* y neuere þat oure lord at þe laste ende
C.20.56   Thenne shal we *leue* that lyf þe loueth and wol nat late the deye.'
C.20.148 *Leue* [þou] neuere þat ȝone liht hem alofte brynge
C.20.172 Loue hath coueyted here longe; *leue* y won oþere
C.20.194 *Leuest* thow þat ȝone lihte vnlouke myhte helle
C.20.215 Yf no nyht ne were no man, [as] y *leue*,
C.20.260 And now shal lucife[r] *leue* [hit], thogh hym loeth thynk.
C.20.307 And sethe he is a lele lord y *leue* þat he wol nat
C.20.335 Y wolde haue lenghed his lyf for y *leued*, yf he deyede,
C.20.347 For we *leued* on thy lesynges [there losten we blisse;
C.20.351 Lucifer for his lesynges, *leue* y noen oþer
C.20.393 So *leue* hit nat, lady, aȝeyne þe lawe y feche
C.20.444 Tho [ledes] þat y louye and *leued* in my comynge;
C.21.408 *Leue* hit [wel thou] be[st] lost, bothe lyf and soule.'

C.22.173 Lyf *leuede* þat lechecraft lette sholde Elde
C.22.277 He lyeth, as y *leue*, þat to þe lewed so precheth,
C.22.362 'That is ouerlonge,' quod this lymitour, 'y *leue*; y schal amenden hit!'

leue v2 *leven v.(3)* A 1; B 1; C 2
A. 5.254 To haue grace to seke treuþe; god *leue* þat hy moten!
B. 5.512 To haue grace to go [to] truþe, [God *leue* þat þei moten].
C. 7.157 To haue grace to go to treuthe; god *leue* þat they mote.
C.17.40   Lord *leue*," quod þat lede, " no stole thynge be herynne!"

leue &> leef,leuen,lyuen

leued ptp *leven v.(2)* &> *leue v1* B 1; C 1 yleued
B.15.97   Ther some bowes ben *leued* and some bereþ none
C.16.250 Tho bowes þat bereth nat and beth nat grene *yleued*,

leuede(n > leue v1

leuel n *level n.* A 1 lyuel; B 1; C 1 leuele
A.11.136 And lernide h[e]m *lyuel* & lyne þeiȝ I loke dymme.
B.10.184 And lerned hem *leuel* and lyne þouȝ I loke dymme.
C.11.124 And caste [mette] by squire bothe lyne and *leuele*.

leuen v *leven v.(1)* &> *leue v1,lyuen* A 8 lefte (1) leue (5) leuen (1) leuiþ (1); B 28 lafte (3) leef (1) lefte (6) leue (12) leuen (2) leuest (1) leueþ (2) lyue (1); C 31 leef (1) lefte (9) leue (17) leuest (1) leueth (2) ylefte (1)
A. 1.101 And neuere *leue* h[e]m for loue ne lacching of ȝeftis;
A. 3.60   Forþi I lere ȝow lordis, *leuiþ* such wrytyng,
A. 3.184 Þere I *lefte* wiþ my lord his lif for to saue,
A. 3.185 And made hym merþe mournyng to *leue*,
A. 3.194 To *leuen* his lordsshipe for a litel siluer,
A. 5.26   And preyede pernel hire purfil to *leue*
A. 6.65   *Leue* hem on þi left half, & loke nouȝt þereaftir,
A.11.119 *Leue* hym on þi left half a large myle or more,
B.Pr.102 How he it *lefte* wiþ loue as oure lord hiȝte
B. 1.103 And neuere *leue* hem for loue ne lacchynge of [yiftes];_
B. 2.52   Thus *lefte* me þat lady liggynge aslepe,
B. 3.69   Forþi I lere yow lordes, *leueþ* swic[h writynge],
B. 3.197 Ther I *lafte* wiþ my lord his lif to saue.
B. 3.207 To *leuen* his lordshipe for a litel siluer,
B. 4.153 And þei lauȝynge lope to hire and *lefte* Reson manye.
B. 4.195 Als longe as [I lyue] *lyue* we togideres.'
B. 5.26   [And] preide Pernele hir purfil to *le[u]e*
B. 5.263 Ne þyne executours wel bisette þe siluer þat þow hem *leuest*;
B. 5.284 Forþi haue mercy in þy mynde, and marchaundise *leue* it,
B. 5.578 *Leue* hem on þi lift half and loke noȝt þeraftur.
B. 7.155 Caton and Canonistres counseillen vs to *leue*
B.10.101 Or in a chambre wiþ a chymenee, and *leue* þe chief halle
B.10.167 *Leue* [hym] on þi left half a large myle or moore
B.14.264 And for goddes loue *leueþ* al and lyueþ as a beggere.
B.15.103 Forþi wolde ye lettrede *leue* þe lecherie of cloþyng,
B.15.137 Lightliche þat þei *leuen* losels it habbeþ,
B.15.323 To ȝyue from youre heires þat youre Aiels yow *lefte*,
B.15.366 And what to *leue* and to lyue by; þe lond was so trewe.
B.16.126 And *lefte* baskettes ful of broke mete, bere awey whoso wolde.'
B.20.40   And god al his grete Ioye goostliche he *lefte*
B.20.108 *Leue* pride pryuely and be parfite cristene.
B.20.208 'Lerne to loue', quod kynde, 'and *leef* alle oþere.'
B.20.250 Wiþ þat ye *leue* logik and lerneþ for to louye.
B.20.251 For loue *lafte* þei lordshipe, boþe lond and scole,
B.20.351 That lif þoruȝ his loore shal *leue* coueitise
B.20.371 For confort of his confessour Contricion he *lafte*,
C.Pr.130 Hou he it *lefte* with loue as oure lord wolde
C. 1.95   And for no lordene loue *leue* þe trewe partie
C. 1.101 And neuer *leue* for loue in hope to lacche syluer.
C. 2.55   Thus *le[f]te* me that lady lyggynge as aslepe,
C. 3.73   Forthy, l[e]ue lordes, *leueth* suche writynges;
C. 5.128 He p[ra]yde p[ur]nele here purfyel to *leue*
C. 6.254 Shal neuere seketoure[s] wel bysette þe syluer þat thow hem *leuest*
C. 6.340 'And haue his mercy in thy mynde and marchaundise, *leue* hit,
C. 7.225 And *leu[e]* hem [o]n þ[y] luft ha[lf] and loke [nat] þeraftur
C. 9.210 Forthy *lefte* they here labour, thise lewede knaues,
C.12.215 "And art so loth to *leue* that lete shal thow nedes:
C.15.7   That y lyuede longe, *leue* me byhynde
C.16.104 And for goddes loue *leueth* al and lyueth as a beggare.
C.16.176 Layk or *leue*, at my lykyng chese
C.16.197 And when y fle fro þe [flessh] and feye *leue* þe caroyne
C.16.256 For wolde ȝe lettered *leue* þ[e] lecherye of clothyng
C.16.258 Parte with þe pore and ȝoure pruyde *leue*
C.16.282 Lihtliche þat they *leue* loseles hit deuoureth.
C.17.103 And what lyue by and *leue*, the londe was so trewe.
C.17.162 Thenne is lawe *ylefte* and leute vnknowe.
C.18.154 And *lefte* basketes ful of Broke mete, bere awey hoso wolde.

C.19.75 And *lefte* hym þere a lechyng to lyue yf he myhte

C.20.449 Bote leten hym lede forth which hym luste and *leue* which hym
likede.

C.22.40 And god al his grete ioye goestliche he *lefte*

C.22.102 Lered ne lewed he *lefte* no man stande,

C.22.108 *Leue* pruyde priueyliche and be parfyt cristene.

C.22.208 'Lerne to loue,' quod kynde, 'and *leef* all othere.'

C.22.250 With þat ȝe l[e]ue logyk and lerneth for to louye.

C.22.251 For loue *lefte* they lordshipe, bothe lond and scole,

C.22.351 That lyf thorw his lore shal *leue* Couetyse

C.22.371 For confort of his confessour Contricioun he *lefte*

leuene > lyuen; *leuer(e* > leef; *leues* > leef n1; *leuest* > leef,leue v1,leuen;
leueste > leef; *leuestow* > leue v1; *leueth* > leue v1,leuen,lyuen; *leueþ* > leue
v1,leuen; *leuide* > leue v1

leuynges ger *levinge ger.(1)* B 1; C 1 lyuynge

B. 5.356 Dorste lape of þat *leuynges*, so vnlouely [it] smauȝte.

C. 6.414 Durste lape of þat *lyuynge*, so vnlouely hit smauhte.

leuist > leef

leuyte n *levite n.* B 2 leuites (1) leuytes (1); C 2 leuyte (1) leuytes (1)

B.12.113 Archa dei, in þe olde lawe, *leuytes* it kepten;

B.12.118 And manye mo oþer men, þat were no *leuites*,

C. 2.133 That laurence the *leuyte* that lay on þe gredyre

C.14.58 Arca dei in þe olde lawe *leuytes* hit kepte;

leuiþ > leue v1,leuen; *leuore* > leef

lewed adj *leued adj.* A 15 lewid (8) lewide (7); B 62 lewde (1) lewed (59)
lewede (2); C 69 lewed (37) lewede (32)

A.Pr.69 *Lewide* men leuide [hym] wel & likide his speche;

A. 1.125 Leriþ it þus *lewide* men, for lettrid it knowiþ,

A. 1.163 It is as *lewid* as a laumpe þat no liȝt is inne.

A. 1.173 And a lering to *lewide* men þe lattere to dele.

A. 2.45 For lerid, for *lewid*, for laboureris of þropis,

A. 3.37 'Þeiȝ lerid & *lewide* hadde leiȝe be þe ichone,

A. 3.138 She blissiþ þise bisshopis ȝif þei be *lewid*;

A. 4.12 How þou lerist þe peple, þe lerid & þe *lewid*.'

A. 8.124 '*Lewide* lorel,' quaþ peris, 'litel lokest þou on þe bible;

A.10.103 I haue [lernid] how *lewid* men han [lerid] here children

A.11.38 Ac ȝif þei carpen of crist, þise clerkis & þise *lewid*,

A.11.141 Ne were þe loue þat liþ þerein a wel *lewid* þing it were.

A.11.182 'It is a wel lel[e] lif,' quaþ she, 'among þe *lewide* peple;

A.11.297 And is as muche to mene, to men þat ben *lewid*,

A.11.311 Souteris & seweris; suche *lewide* iottis

B.Pr.72 *Lewed* men leued [hym] wel and liked hi[s speche];

B.Pr.129 Lowed to speke in latyn, for *lewed* men ne koude

B. 1.136 Lereþ it þ[us] *lewed* men, for lettred it knoweþ,

B. 1.189 It is as *lewed* as a lampe þat no liȝt is Inne.

B. 1.199 And lernynge to *lewed* men þe latter to deele.

B. 3.38 'Theiȝ [lered and *lewed*] hadde leyen by þee [echone],

B. 3.149 She blesseþ þise Bisshopes [if] þei be *lewed*;

B. 3.255 That laborers and lowe [*lewede*] folk taken of hire maistres

B. 4.12 How þow lernest þe peple, þe lered and þe *lewed*.'

B. 7.14 Legistres of boþe lawes þe *lewed* þerwiþ to preche,

B. 7.142 '*Lewed* lorel!' quod Piers, 'litel lokestow on þe bible;

B.10.52 Ac if þei carpen of crist, þise clerkes and þise *lewed*,

B.10.189 [Ne were þe loue þat liþ þerinne a wel *lewed* þyng it were].

B.10.240 And þat is to bileue lelly, boþe lered and *lewed*,

B.10.254 But þus it bilongeþ to bileue to *lewed* þat willen dowel.

B.10.280 That goddes word wercheþ noȝt on [wis] ne on *lewed*

B.10.282 *Lewed* men may likne yow þus, þat þe beem liþ in youre eiȝen,

B.10.467 Souteres and shepherdes; [swiche] *lewed* Iuttes

B.10.478 Right so *lewed* [laborers] and of litel knowyng

B.11.96 It is licitum for *lewed* men to [legge] þe soþe

B.11.108 Ac þe matere þat she meued, if *lewed* men it knewe,

B.11.318 This lokynge on *lewed* preestes haþ doon me lepe from pouerte

B.12.96 And lederes for *lewed* men and for lettred boþe.

B.12.104 Riȝt so [lereþ] lettrure *lewed* men to Reson.

B.12.110 To vnloken it at hir likyng, and to þe *lewed* peple

B.12.114 Hadde neuere *lewed* man leue to leggen hond on þat cheste

B.12.144 Ne of lordes þat were *lewed* men, but of þe hyeste lettred oute:

B.12.157 How þat *lewed* men liȝtloker þan lettrede were saued,

B.12.163 That ooþer is *lewed* of þat labour, lerned neuere swymme.

B.12.173 If hym likeþ and lest, þan any *lewed* [sooþly].

B.12.180 Ther þe *lewed* liþ stille and lokeþ after lente,

B.12.184 To lere *lewed* men as luc bereþ witnesse:

B.12.186 Wo was hym marked þat wade moot wiþ þe *lewed*!

B.12.191 Ther *lewed* þeues ben lolled vp; loke how þei be saued!

B.12.232 *Lewed* men many tymes maistres þei apposen

B.12.234 Raþer þan his likame alogh; *lewed* asken þus clerkes.

B.12.276 For lettred men were *lewed* yet ne were loore of hir bokes.'

B.13.12 And how þat *lewed* men ben lad, but oure lord hem helpe,

B.13.286 Lakkynge lettrede men and *lewed* men boþe;

B.14.303 And for þe [*lewde*] euere [yliche] a lemman of alle clennesse:

B.15.70 Freres and fele oþere maistres þat to [þe] *lewed* [folk] prechen,

B.15.72 That [lome] þe *lewed* peple of hir bileue doute.

B.15.83 If I lye on yow to my *lewed* wit, ledeþ me to brennyng!

B.15.108 Loþe were *lewed* men but þei youre loore folwede

B.15.119 If *lewed* [ledes] wiste what þis latyn meneþ,

B.15.128 Allas, ye *lewed* men, muche lese ye on preestes!

B.15.144 By lered, by *lewed*, þat looþ is to [s]pende

B.15.319 If *lewed* men knewe þis latyn þei wolde loke whom þei yeue,

B.15.322 Allas, lordes and ladies, *lewed* counseil haue ye

B.15.354 Boþe lettred and *lewed* beþ alayed now wiþ synne

B.15.389 That sola fides sufficit to saue wiþ *lewed* peple.

B.15.392 And for hir lyuynge þat *lewed* men be þe loþer god agulten.

B.15.395 And we lered and *lewed* [bileueþ] in oon god;

B.15.395 That [lered] þere and [*lewed*] ȝit leeuen on hise lawes.

B.17.42 It is lighter to *lewed* men o lesson to knowe

B.19.114 [Boþe] to lered and to *lewede*, to louyen oure enemys.

B.19.409 'Thanne is many a [lif] lost', quod a *lewed* vicory.

B.20.68 They cursed and hir conseil, were it clerk or *lewed*.

B.20.102 Lered [ne] *lewed* he leet no man stonde,

B.20.247 To lered ne to *lewed*, but lyueþ after youre reule.

B.20.266 Of *lewed* and of lered; þe lawe wole and askeþ

B.20.277 He lyeþ, as I leue, þat to þe *lewed* so precheþ,

C.Pr.70 *Lewed* men leued hym wel and lykede his wordes;

C.Pr.88 That is lele loue and lyf among lered and *lewed*,

C.Pr.102 That *lewed* men in mysbileue lyuen and dyen.

C. 1.135 Lere hit thus *lewed* men, for lettred hit knoweth:

C. 1.185 Hit is as *lewed* as a laumpe þat no liht is ynne.

C. 1.194 And a luther ensau[m]ple, leef me, [to] þe *lewed* peple.

C. 3.40 'Thow le[r]ed men and le[w]ed haued layn by the bothe

C. 3.171 Lyggeth by here, when hem lust, lered and *lewed*.

C. 3.187 He blesseth this bischopes thow thei ben *lewede*;

C. 4.12 How thow ledest my peple, lered and *lewed*.'

C. 5.4 Amonges lollares of londone and *lewede* Ermytes

C. 6.23 Lauhyng al aloude for *lewede* men sholde

C. 6.29 To carpe and to consayle then eny Clerk or *lewed*;

C. 6.116 With *lewed* and lered þat leef ben to here

C. 9.140 The whiche is lollarne lyf and *lewede* Ermytes;

C. 9.165 And lere this *lewede* men what þis latyn meneth

C. 9.193 Thise lollares, lachedraweres, *lewede* Ermytes

C. 9.210 Forthy lefte they here lande, thise *lewede* knaues,

C. 9.224 *Lewede* men to labory; lordes to honte

C. 9.231 Thus hit bylongeth for lord[e], for lered and for *lewed*

C. 9.241 Loke now where this lollares and *lewede* Ermites

C.11.11 And lette with a loueday [*lewed*] treuthe and bigile

C.11.34 The *lewed* aȝen þe lered þe holy lore to disp[u]te

C.11.248 For *lewed* folk, goddes foles and his fre bestes;

C.11.288 And is to mene no more to men þat beth *lewed*:

C.11.293 *Lewed* lele laboreres and land tulyng peple

C.11.299 Ac *lewede* laborers of litel vnderstondyng

C.11.302 *Lewede* men in good bileue and lene hem at here nede.'

C.12.42 Ac þe matere þat she meuede, if *lewede* men hit knewe,

C.13.26 Ac leueth nat, *lewede* men, þat y lacke rychesse

C.13.116 Thorw here luyther lyuynge and *lewede* vnderstondynge.

C.14.20 As loreles to be lordes and *lewede* men techares,

C.14.49 Riht so lereth lettrure *lewed* men to resoun.

C.14.55 To v[n]louken hit at here lykynge the *lewed* to helpe,

C.14.59 Hadde neuere *lewede* [man] leue to legge hand on þat cheste

C.14.63 And all *lewede* þat leide hand þeron loren lyf aftir.

C.14.71 Bothe *lewede* and lerede were lost yf clergie ne were.

C.14.101 That is, how *lewede* men and luythere lyhtloker were ysaued

C.14.107 That oþer is *lewed* of þat labour, lerned neuere swymme.

C.14.113 Yf hym liketh and luste, then eny *lewede* sothly.

C.14.120 There þe *lewede* lyth stille and loketh aftur lente,

C.14.123 And þat is aftur person other parsche preest, and parauntur bothe
lewede

C.14.124 To lere *lewede* men As luk bereth witnesse:

C.14.125 Muchel wo was hym marked þat wade shal with þe *lewede*!

C.14.130 There *lewede* theues ben lolled vp; loke how þei ben saued!

C.14.198 For letrede men were *lewede* ȝut ne were lore of [here bokes].'

C.15.14 As wel lered as *lewede* and lorde as þe [b]oende;

C.15.15 And how þat *lewede* men ben lad, but oure lord hem helpe,

C.16.33 And lereth *lewede* and lered, hey and lowe to knowe

C.16.233 That bothe le[r]ed and le[w]ed of here beleue douten.

C.16.262 Loeth were *lewed* [men] bote they ȝoure lore folwede[n]

C.16.274 Allas! *lewed* men, moche lese ȝe þat fynde

C.16.283 Leueth hit wel, lordes, both *lewed* and lered,

C.16.292 I knewe neuere, by Crist, clerk noþer *lewed*,

C.17.54 Yf *lewede* men knewe this latyn a litel they wolden auysen hem

C.17.56 Allas, lordes and ladyes, *lewede* consayle haue ȝe

C.17.88 *Lewed* men han no byleue, [so] lettred men erren;

C.17.121 That sola fides sufficit to saue with *lewede* peple.

C.17.182 And on his lore thei l[e]uen ȝut, as wel lered as *lewed*.

C.17.292 And nameliche þer þat *lewede* lyuen and no lawe knoweth.
C.19.43   Hit is liht for *lewed* and for lered bothe.
C.20.355 That ʒe belyen nat this *lewed* men for at the laste dauid
C.21.114 Bothe to lered and to *lewed*, to louye oure enemyes.
C.21.409 'Thenne is many [a lyf] ylost,' quod a *lewed* vicory.
C.22.68   Thei corsede and here consail, were hit Clerk or *lewed*.
C.22.102 Lered ne *lewed* he lefte no man stande,
C.22.247 To lered ne to *lewed*, but lyueth aftur ʒoure reule.
C.22.266 Of *lewed* and of lered; the lawe wol and asketh
C.22.277 He lyeth, as y leue, þat to þe *lewed* so precheth,

lewednesse n *leuednesse n.* A 1 lewidnesse; B 1; C 1 lewedenesse
A. 3.31   'Shal no *lewidnesse* hym lette, þe lede þat I louye,
B. 3.32   'Shal no *lewednesse* [hym] lette, þe leode þat I louye,
C. 3.35   Shal no *lewedenesse* lette þe [lede] þat y louye

lewete(e > leaute; lewid(- > lewed(-; lewte(e > leaute; leye(n > legge,ligge

lyard n *liard adj.& n.* B 4; C 3
B.17.67   He lighte adown of *Lyard* and ladde hym in his hande,
B.17.74   And ladde hym so forþ on *Lyard* to lex Christi, a graunge
B.17.81   For I may noʒt lette', quod þat Leode and *lyard* he bistrideþ
B.17.355 I may no lenger lette', quod he, and *lyard* he prikede
C.19.66   [A l]ihte a[dou]n of *lyard* and ladde hym in his hand[e]
C.19.78   For y may nat lette,' quod that lede; and *lyard* he bystrideth
C.19.335 Y may no lengore lette,' quod he, and *lyard* a prikede

lyare(s > liere; libb- > lyuen

liberal adj *liberal adj.* B 1
B.15.150 Wiþouten fauntelte or folie a fre *liberal* wille.'

licam(e -es > likame

licence n *license n.* A 1; B 1; C 2
A.Pr.82   To haue a *licence* & leue at lundoun to dwelle,
B.Pr.85   To haue a *licence* and leue at London to dwelle,
C.Pr.83   To haue a *licence* and leue [at] Londoun to dwelle
C. 6.121 Withoute *licence* and leue, and herby lyueth wrathe.

lich > liche,lik

liche n *lich n. &> lik* A 1 lich; B 1
A.11.2   Þat lene was of *lich* & of lo[uʒ] chere.
B.10.2   That lene was of [*liche*] and of [lowe chere].

lycour n *licour n.* C 1
C.12.220 Hit lasteth nat longe þat is *lycour*-swete,

lye > leye,lyen

lyen v *lien v.(2) &> ligge* A 13 leiʒe (6) leiʒede (1) leiʒeþ (2) leiþ (1) liʒe (1) liʒen (1) liʒeþ (1); B 38 leighe (1) lie (1) lye (18) lyed (1) lyen (4) lieþ (4) lyeþ (5) liʒe (1) liþ (1) lixt (2); C 28 lye (13) lyed (1) lyede (1) lyen (1) lyeth (6) lyth (1) lixt (1) low (1) lowe (1) ylow (1)
A.Pr.49   And hadde leue to *leiʒe* al here lif aftir.
A. 1.67   He is lettere of loue, *leiʒeþ* hem alle;
A. 3.146 And *leiþ* aʒen þe lawe & lettiþ þe treuþe
A. 3.167 Wel þou wost, consience, but ʒif þou wilt *leiʒe*,
A. 3.230 Shal abiʒe it bitterly or þe bok *liʒeþ*.
A. 5.117 Ferst I lernide to *leiʒe* a lef oþer tweiʒe;
A. 6.71   [And] loke þat þou *leiʒe* nouʒt for no manis biddyng.
A. 7.215 'ʒe, I hote þe,' quaþ hungir, 'oþer ellis þe bible *leiʒeþ*.
A. 8.61   ʒe legistris & lawi[er]is, [ʒe] wyten ʒif I *leiʒe*;
A. 8.111 And but ʒif luk *leiʒe* he leriþ vs anoþer,
A.10.120 And so leriþ vs luk þat *leiʒede* neuere:
A.11.152 And louen hem þat *liʒen* on vs, & lenen hem at here nede,
A.11.225 'I nile not scorne,' quaþ scripture, 'but scryueyns *liʒe*,
B.Pr.49   And hadden leue to *lyen* al hire lif aftir.
B.Pr.51   To ech a tale þat þei tolde hire tonge was tempred to *lye*
B. 1.69   He is lettere of loue, *lieþ* hem alle;
B. 1.118 For þei leueden vpon [Lucifer] þat *lyed* in þis manere:
B. 3.156 And *liþ* ayein þe lawe and letteþ hym þe gate
B. 3.180 Wel þow woost, [Conscience], but if þow wolt [*lie*],
B. 3.251 Shal abien it bittre or þe book *lieþ*.
B. 5.133 To *lye* and to loure on my neʒebore and to lakke his chaffare.
B. 5.163 Til "þow *lixt*!" and "þow lixt!" lopen out at ones
B. 5.163 Til "þow lixt!" and "þow *lixt*!" lopen out at ones
B. 5.201 First I lerned to *lye* a leef ouþer tweyne;
B. 5.276 That whoso leueþ [þat I *liʒe*] loke in þe Sauter glose,
B. 6.231 'ʒe I [h]ote þee,' quod hunger, 'or ellis þe bible *lieþ*.
B. 7.60   Ye legistres and lawieres, [if I *lye* witeþ Mathew]:
B. 7.129 And but if luc *lye* he lereþ vs [anoþer]
B. 9.76   And þat I *lye* nouʒt of þat I lere þee, luc bereþ witnesse.
B.10.40   Ayein þe lawe of oure lord, and *lyen* on hemselue,
B.10.43   Likne men and *lye* on hem þat leneþ hem no ʒiftes,
B.10.112 Here *lyeþ* youre lore", þise lordes gynneþ dispute,
B.10.203 And louen hem þat *lyen* on vs and lene hem [at hir nede]

B.10.208 And alle þat lakkeþ vs or *lyeþ* oure lord techeþ vs to louye,
B.10.337 'I nel noʒt scorne', quod Scripture; 'but scryueynes *lye*,
B.11.83   Loke, ye lettred men, wheiþer I *lye* or noʒt.'
B.11.224 Boþe logyk and lawe, þat loueþ noʒt to *lye*,
B.13.178 That Pacience þ[o] most passe, 'for pilgrymes konne wel *lye*'.
B.13.228 Couþe I *lye* [and] do men lauʒe, þanne lacchen I sholde
B.13.307 'Lo! if ye leue me noʒt, or þat I *lye* wenen,
B.14.144 It may noʒt be, ye riche men, or Mathew on god *lyeþ*:
B.15.80   That I *lye* noʒt, loo! for lordes ye plesen
B.15.83   If I *lye* on yow to my lewed wit, ledeþ me to brennyng!
B.15.172 No no likynge haþ to *lye* ne laughe men to scorne.
B.15.289 Til he foundede freres of Austynes ordre, [or ellis freres *lyen*].
B.16.176 'I am feiþ', quod þat freke, 'it falleþ noʒt to *lye*,
B.17.261 Poul þe Apostel preueþ wheiþer I *lye*:
B.18.31   Lif seiþ þat he *lieþ* and leieþ his lif to wedde
B.18.402 And for þi lesynge, lucifer, þat þow *leighe* til Eue
B.20.238 For lomere he *lyeþ* þat liflode moot begge
B.20.277 He *lyeþ*, as I leue, þat to þe lewed so precheþ,
C.Pr.50   And hadde leue to *lye* [al here lyf aftir].
C. 1.65   He is lettere of loue and *lyeth* alle tymes;
C. 2.21   And [*ylow* on] hym to lordes þat lawes han to kepe;
C. 2.32   That neuere *lyede* ne lauhede in al his lyf tyme;
C. 2.39   Y do hit vppon dauyd; the doumbe wil noʒt *lyen*:
C. 3.194 He *lyth* aʒeyn þe lawe and le[tte]th hym þe gate
C. 6.52   And *lyed* o my lycame and on my lyf bothe;
C. 6.55   "Lo! yf ʒe leue me nat or þat y *lye* wenen
C. 6.98   To *lye* and to loure and to lakke myn neyhebores.
C. 6.138 Til "thow *lixt*!" and "thow lixt!" be lady ouer hem alle;
C. 6.138 Til "thow lixt!" and "thow *lixt*!" be lady ouer hem alle;
C. 6.209 Furste y lerned to *lye* a leef oþer tweye;
C. 6.301 And what lede leueth þat y *lye* look in þe sauter glos[e],
C. 8.237 'ʒe, y bihote the,' quod hunger, 'or elles þe bible *lyeth*.
C.14.6   Noþer to *lye* ne to lacke ne lere þat is defended
C.15.177 'By Crist!' quod Consience, 'clergie, y wol nat *lye*;
C.15.202 [Cou]de y *lye* and do men lawhe thenne lacchen y scholde
C.16.239 That y *lye* nat; loo! for lordes ʒe plese
C.16.306 Weneth he þat no wyhte wolde *lye* and swerie
C.17.27   Withoute borwynge or beggynge, or þe boek *lyeth*,
C.18.184 'I am with fayth,' quod þat freke, 'hit falleth nat me to *lye*,
C.19.227 Paul the apostel preueth where y *lye*:
C.19.231 For mony of ʒow riche men, by my soule y *lye* nat,
C.20.30   Lyf saith þat a *lyeth* and [leyeth] his lyf to wedde,
C.20.348 And now for a later lesynge] þat thow *lowe* til Eue
C.20.445 Ac for þe lesynge þat thow *low*, lucifer, til eue
C.22.238 For lomere he *lyeth* þat lyflode moet begge
C.22.277 He *lyeth*, as y leue, þat to þe lewed so precheth,

liere n *liere n.(1)* A 8 leiʒere (1) leiʒeris (2) lyere (1) liʒer (1) liʒere (1) liʒeris (2); B 13 liere (3) lyere (5) lieres (3) lyeres (1) lieris (1); C 20 lyare (13) lyares (7)
A. 1.36   Leue not þi lycam for a *li[ʒ]er* hym techiþ,
A. 2.25   And al is *liʒeris* ledyng þat hy liʒen togideris.
A. 2.143 And makiþ of *lyere* a lang carte to leden al þis oþere,
A. 2.167 And ʒif ʒe lacche *leiʒere* let him not askape
A. 2.177 Liʒtliche *liʒere* lep awey þennes,
A. 7.257 Þere arn mo *liʒeris* þan lechis, lord hem amende
A.10.139 Ac fals folk & feiþles, þeuis & *leiʒeris*,
A.10.210 And þat ben fals folk, & fals eires also, foundlynges & [*leiʒeris*],
B. 1.38   Lef nauʒt þi licame] for a *liere* hym techeþ,
B. 2.43   And al is *lieres* ledynge þat [lady] is þus ywedded.
B. 2.69   Thanne leep *liere* forþ and seide, 'lo! here a chartre
B. 2.182 And makeþ of *lyere* a lang cart to leden alle þise oþere,
B. 2.206 And if ye lacche *lyere* lat hym noʒt ascapen
B. 2.218 Liʒtliche *Lyere* leep awey þanne,
B. 6.273 [Ther are mo *lieres* þan] leches; lord hem amende!
B. 9.121 Ac fals folk, feiþlees, þeues and *lyeres*,
B. 9.196 As fals folk, fondlynges, faitours and *lieres*,
B.13.287 In likynge of lele lif and *lyere* in soule;
B.13.422 That fedeþ fooles sages, flatereris and *lieris*,
B.19.292 Mighte no [*lyere* wiþ lesynges] ne los of worldly catel
B.20.146 And leet leautee a cherl and *lyere* a fre man.
C. 1.36   Leef nat thy lycame for a *lyare* hym techeth
C. 2.6   [Boþe] fals and fauel and fikel tonge *lyare*
C. 2.46   And al is *lyares* ledynge th[at] lady is thus ywedded.
C. 2.71   Thenne lup *lyare* forth and saide, 'loo! here a Chartre
C. 2.79   That foleweth falsnesse, Fauel and *lyare*,
C. 2.195 And maketh of *lyare* a lang cart to lede al this othere,
C. 2.208 Fals or fauel or here felawe *lyare*
C. 2.218 And yf ʒe lacchen *lyare* lat hym nat askape
C. 2.228 Lyhtliche *lyare* lep awey thenne,
C. 2.237 That *lyare* sholde wonye with hem watres to loke.
C. 2.240 Ac mynstrals and mesagers mette with *lyare* ones
C. 5.187 Til lucifer þe *lyare* leued þat hymsulue
C. 7.82   That feden foel sages, flateres and *lyares*

C. 8.286   And thouh *lyares* and l[a]chdraweres and lollares knocke
C.10.295   And fals folk and fondlynges, faytors and *lyares*,
C.19.45   And lereth þat we louye sholde as wel *lyares* as lele.
C.20.352   Bote oure lord at þe laste *lyares* h[e] rebuke[th]
C.20.356   Witnesseth in his writyng[e] what is *lyares* mede:
C.21.292   Myhte no *lyare* with lesynge[s] ne losse of worldly catel
C.22.146   And leet leautee a cherl and *lyare* a fre man.

lyeth > *lyen,ligge*

lieutenaunt n *lieutenaunt n.* B 1
B.16.47   That is *lieutenaunt* to loken it wel bi leue of myselue:

lif n *lif n. &> lif_tyme* A 46 lif (29) lyf (12) lyue (4) lyues (1); B 128 lif
(108) lyf (6) lyue (9) lyues (5); C 136 lif (7) lyf (112) lyue (10) lyues
(7)
A.Pr.49   And hadde leue to leiȝe al here *lif* aftir.
A. 1.27   For loth, in his *lyf* dayes, for lykyng of drink
A. 1.76   To loue me lelly whiles þi *lif* duriþ.'
A. 2.14   Þere nis no quen queyntere þat quyk is o *lyue*.
A. 3.27   For to werche þi wil while þi *lif* lastiþ.'
A. 3.125   She doþ men lese here land & here *lif* boþe;
A. 3.140   To holde lemmanis & lotebies alle here *lif* dayes,
A. 3.153   Þis is þe *lif* of þat lady, now lord ȝif hire sorewe!
A. 3.184   Þere I lefte wiþ my lord his *lif* for to saue.
A. 3.189   I durste han leid my *lif* & no lesse wed
A. 3.269   Leaute shal do hym lawe [and no] *lif* ellis.
A. 4.59   For boþe þi *lyf* & þi lond lyþ in his grace.'
A. 5.80   Boþe his lyme & his *lif* was lost þoruȝ my tunge.
A. 5.208   For his liþer *lif* þat he lyued hadde,
A. 6.50   Þat ȝe loue hym leuere þanne þe *lif* in ȝoure hertis;
A. 7.51   'For to werche be þi *lyf* while my *lif* duriþ.'
A. 7.93   I wile worsshipe þerewiþ treuþe in my *lyue*,
A. 7.162   Þat he lokide lik a lanterne al his *lif* aftir;
A. 7.233   Actif *lif* oþer contemplatif; crist wolde it alse.
A. 8.80   Þo þat lyuen þus here *lif* mowe loþe þe tyme
A. 8.173   How þou leddist þi *lif* here & his lawe keptest.
A. 9.32   Þere were þe manis *lif* lost for lacchesse of hymselue.
A. 9.52   And [g]iue þe grace on þis erþe in good *lif* to ende'.
A. 9.87   Is hokid at þat on ende to holde men in good *lif*.
A. 9.106   Ellis wot no man þat now is o *lyue*.'
A.10.30   Þe lord of *lif* & of li[ȝt], of lisse & of peyne.
A.10.37   *Lif* þat ay shal laste, & al his lynage aftir.
A.10.43   For loue of þat lady þat *lif* is ynempnid.
A.10.46   Heo is *lyf* & ledere, a lemman of heuene.
A.10.145   In tene & trauaille to here *lyues* ende.
A.10.204   Of *lif* & of loue & of lawe also
A.11.78   And preye hym of pardoun & penaunce [in] þi *lyue*,
A.11.102   For to werche ȝour wil [while] my *lif* duriþ.
A.11.182   'It is a wel lel[e] *lif*,' quaþ she, 'among þe lewide peple;
A.11.217   Þis is þe *lif* of þis lordis þat lyuen shulde wiþ dobet,
A.11.238   And for his lele beleue, whanne he his *lif* tyneþ,
A.11.262   In þe legende of *lif* longe er I were,
A.11.280   Þat hadde lyued al his *lyf* wiþ lesinges & þeft[e],
A.12.4   He passeþ þe apostolis *lyf*, and [peryth] to aungelys.
A.12.44   And his loggyng is with *lyf* þat lord is of erþe,
A.12.64   To *lyf* in his lordshepe longyt my weye
A.12.86   We han letteres of *lyf*, he shal his lyf ty[n]e.
A.12.86   We han letteres of lyf, he shal his *lyf* ty[n]e.
A.12.90   But lyue as þis *lyf* is ordeyned for the.
A.12.93   Whil his *lyf* and his lykhame lesten togedere.
A.12.112   To lyue as þat lord lykyþ þat *lyf* in hem putte:
B.Pr.49   And hadden leue to lyen al hire *lif* after.
B.Pr.120   To tilie and to trauaille as trewe *lif* askeþ.
B.Pr.122   Shopen lawe and leaute, ech [*lif*] to knowe his owene.
B.Pr.155   That vs loþeþ þe *lif* er he late vs passe.
B. 1.78   To louen me leelly while þi *lif* dureþ.'
B. 1.204   Loue is leche of *lif* and next oure lord selue,
B. 3.28   For to werche þi wille [while þi *lif* lasteþ].'
B. 3.136   She dooþ men lese hire lond and hire *lyf* boþe;
B. 3.166   This is þe *lif* of þat lady, now lord ȝyue hire sorwe,
B. 3.197   Ther I lafte wiþ my lord his *lif* for to saue.
B. 3.202   I dorste haue leyd my *lif* and no lasse wedde
B. 3.240   And he þat vseþ noȝt þe *lyf* of vsurie,
B. 3.294   Leaute shal don hym lawe and no *lif* ellis.
B. 4.73   For boþe þi *lif* and þi lond lyþ in his grace.'
B. 5.100   That boþe *lif* and lyme is lost þoruȝ my speche.
B. 5.365   'As þow wiþ wordes & werkes hast wroȝt yuele in þi *lyue*
B. 5.380   For his luþer *lif* þat he lyued hadde,
B. 5.416   Yet kan I neyþer solue ne synge ne seintes *lyues* rede;
B. 6.56   'For to werche by þi wor[d] while my *lif* dureþ.'
B. 6.101   I wol worshipe þerwiþ truþe by my *lyue*,
B. 6.177   That he loked lik a lanterne al his *lif* after.
B. 6.249   Contemplatif *lif* or Actif lif; crist wolde [it als].

B. 6.249   Contemplatif lif or Actif *lif*; crist wolde [it als].
B. 7.88   Lat vsage be youre solas of seintes *lyues* redyng.
B. 7.98   [Tho] þat lyue þus hir *lif* mowe loþe þe tyme
B. 7.195   How þow laddest þi *lif* here and hi[s] law[e] keptest,
B. 8.36   [There] were [þe mannes] *lif* lost [for] lachesse of hymselue.
B. 8.97   Is hoked [at] þat oon ende to [holde men in good *lif*].
B. 9.29   Lord of *lif* and of liȝt, of lisse and of peyne.
B. 9.46   Wiþ his word and werkmanshipe and wiþ *lif* to laste.
B. 9.49   *Lif* þat ay shal laste, [and] al his lynage after.
B. 9.55   For loue of þe lady anima þat *lif* is ynempned.
B. 9.64   That lyuen synful *lif* here hir soule is lich þe deuel.
B. 9.65   And alle þat lyuen good *lif* are lik to god almyȝty:
B. 9.191   Of *lif* and of [loue] and [of lawe also]
B. 9.193   A[c] if þei leden þus hir *lif* it likeþ god almyȝty,
B. 9.203   To loue [and to lowe] þee and no *lif* to greue;
B.10.92   For we haue no lettre of oure *lif* how longe it shal dure
B.10.125   And preie hym of pardon and penaunce in þi *lyue*,
B.10.150   For to werche youre wille while my *lif* dureþ,
B.10.238   'It is a commune *lyf*', quod Clergie, 'on holy chirche to bileue
B.10.268   Alle þat lakkeþ any *lif* and lakkes han hemselue:
B.10.355   And for his lele bileue, whan he his *lif* tyneþ,
B.10.381   In þe legende of *lif* longe er I were,
B.10.400   Whan þei shal *lif* lete [a lippe of goddes grace]–
B.10.421   That hadde lyued al his *lif* wiþ lesynges and þefte,
B.11.91   'And wherof serueþ law', quod lewtee, 'if no *lif* vndertoke it
B.11.135   But if Contricion wol come and crye by his *lyue*
B.11.214   Forþi lakke no *lif* ooþer þouȝ he moore latyn knowe,
B.11.257   Preise[n] pouerte for best *lif* if Pacience it folw[e],
B.11.274   And *lif* moost likynge to god as luc bereþ witnesse:
B.11.388   And er þow lakke my *lif* loke [þyn] be to preise.
B.11.391   Ech a *lif* wolde be laklees, leue þow noon oþer.
B.12.62   And in lele lyuynge men and in *lif* holy,
B.12.120   And leiden hand þeron to liften it vp loren here *lif* after.
B.12.188   That lyuynge after lettrure saue[d] hym *lif* and soule.
B.13.16   And how louynge he is to [ech *lif*] on londe and on watre–
B.13.17   Leneþ he no *lif* lasse ne moore–
B.13.51   'As longe', quod [he], 'as [*lif*] and lycame may dure'.
B.13.121   Ther þe lord of *lif* wonyeþ, to leren [hem] what is dowel
B.13.281   And inobedient to ben vndernome of any *lif* lyuynge;
B.13.287   In likynge of lele *lif* and a liere in soule;
B.13.295   And noon so holy as he ne of *lif* clennere,
B.13.331   Ther is no *lif* þat me loueþ lastynge any while.
B.13.451   That bi his *lyue* liþed hem and loued hem to here.
B.14.24   Ne fend ne fals man defoulen it in þi *lyue*.
B.14.39   For lent neuere was *lif* but liflode were shapen,
B.14.60   For if þow lyue after his loore, þe shorter *lif* þe bettre:
B.14.98   'Where wonyeþ Charite?' quod Haukyn; 'I wiste neuere in my *lyue*
B.14.118   That al hir *lif* han lyued in langour and defaute.
B.14.145   And hir [ladies] also lyuede hir *lif* in murþe.
B.14.320   A blessed *lif* wiþouten bisynesse for body and soule:
B.15.4   And some lakkede my *lif*–allowed it fewe–
B.15.6   Lordes or ladies or any *lif* ellis,
B.15.234   That wiþouten wiles ledeþ [wel] hir *lyues*:
B.15.249   Ac I ne lakke no *lif*, but lord amende vs alle,
B.15.269   [Lo]! in legenda sanctorum, þe *lif* of holy Seintes,
B.15.355   That no *lif* loueþ ooþer, ne oure lord as it semeþ.
B.16.104   And lered hym lechecraft his *lif* for to saue
B.16.118   That he was leche of *lif* and lord of heigh heuene.
B.16.189   The light of al þat *lif* haþ a londe and a watre,
B.16.240   Lond and lordshipe and *lif* wiþouten ende.
B.16.268   That is for *lif*; or ligge þus euere
B.16.268   That is *lif* for lif; or ligge þus euere
B.17.27   And lelest to leue [on] for *lif* and for soule?
B.17.220   Lele loue or *lif* þat oure lord shapte.
B.17.280   The which is *lif* and loue, þe leye of mannes body.
B.17.297   Wol loue [þat *lif*] þat [lakkeþ charite];
B.17.312   Yuele lyuen and leten noȝt til *lif* hem forsake.
B.17.345   And lightliche oure lord at hir *lyues* ende
B.17.354   And louye hem lik hymself, and his *lif* amende.
B.18.31   *Lif* seiþ þat he lieþ and leieþ his lif to wedde
B.18.31   Lif seiþ þat he lieþ and leieþ his *lif* to wedde
B.18.56   Thanne shul we leue þat *lif* þee loueþ and wol noȝt lete þee deye.'
B.18.59   The lord of *lif* and of light þo leide hise eighen togideres.
B.18.65   '*Lif* and deeþ, in þis derknesse hir oon fordooþ hir ooþer.
B.18.102   And ye, lurdaynes, han ylost for *lif* shal haue þe maistrye;
B.18.107   Which is *lif* þat oure lord in alle lawes acurseþ.
B.18.158   So shal þis deeþ fordo, I dar my *lif* legge,
B.18.255   And I, book, wole be brent but Iesus rise to *lyue*
B.18.260   And bileue on a newe lawe be lost, *lif* and soule.'
B.18.303   I wolde haue lengþed his *lif* for I leued if he deide
B.18.343   And *lif* for lif also, and by þat lawe I clayme
B.18.343   And lif for *lif* also, and by þat lawe I clayme
B.18.359   Adam and alle þoruȝ a tree shul turne to *lyue*,

B.18.365	For I þat am lord of *lif*, loue is my drynke,	C.13.30	And *lyues* þat oure lord loueth and large weyes to heuene;
B.18.383	Lawe wolde he yeue hym *lif* if he loked on hym.	C.13.74	That oure lord loketh aftur of vch a *lyf* þat wynneth
B.19.45	The lawe of *lif* þat laste shal euere,	C.13.99	So pore and pacient parfitest *lyf* is of alle.
B.19.105	*Lif* and lyme as hym liste he wroȝte.	C.13.206	And ar thow lacke eny *lyf* loke ho is to preyse.
B.19.217	Tresour to lyue by to hir *lyues* ende,	C.14.63	And all lewede þat leide hand þeron loren *lyf* aftir.
B.19.237	And lyue, by þat labour], a lele *lif* and a trewe.	C.14.127	That lyuynge Aftur lettrure saued hy[m] *lyf* and soule.
B.19.408	Leue it wel [þow art] lost, boþe *lif* and soule.'	C.15.19	And how louyng he is to vch *lyf* a londe and o watere
B.19.409	'Thanne is many a [*lif*] lost', quod a lewed vicory.	C.15.57	'As longe,' quod he, ' as *lyf* and lycame may duyre.'
B.20.11	For þre þynges he takeþ his *lif* for to saue.	C.15.238	For lente neuere was *lyf* but lyflode were shape,
B.20.87	Largeliche a legion loste [þe] *lif* soone.	C.15.259	For if thow lyu[e] aftur his lore the shortere *lyf* þe betere:
B.20.92	'Alarme! alarme!' quod þat lord, 'ech *lif* kepe his owene!'	C.15.294	That al here *lyf* haen lyued in langour and defaute.
B.20.111	And bihighte hem long *lif*, and lecherie he sente	C.16.18	That al here *lyf* leden in lownesse and in pouerte.
B.20.143	And þanne lough *lyf* and leet daggen hise cloþes,	C.16.155	A blessed *lyf* withoute bisinesse bote onelyche for þe soule:
B.20.148	Thus relyede *lif* for a litel fortune	C.16.349	And cheef charite with hem and chaste all here *lyu[e]*.
B.20.152	*Lyf* lepte aside and lauȝte hym a lemman.	C.17.22	Loue and lele byleue held *lyf* and soule togyderes.
B.20.156	This likede *lif* and his lemman fortune	C.17.124	In þe lettynge of here *lyf* to leue on holy churche.'
B.20.168	And wayued awey wanhope and wiþ *lif* he fighteþ.	C.17.126	'[*Lif* in] loue and leutee in o byleue a[nd] lawe,
B.20.169	And *lif* fleiȝ for feere to phisik after helpe	C.17.131	God lereth no *lyf* to l[eu]e withouten lele cause.
B.20.173	*Lyf* leeued þat lechecraft lette sholde Elde	C.17.155	To þat lord þat hym *lyf* lente lyflode hym sende.
B.20.175	And Elde auntred hym on *lyf*, and at þe laste he hitte	C.18.77	And chaste leden here *lyf*, is lyf of contemplacioun,
B.20.178	'Now I se', seide *lif*, 'þat Surgerie ne phisik	C.18.77	And chaste leden here lyf, is *lyf* of contemplacioun,
B.20.211	[Weede] ne worldly [mete] while þi *lif* lasteþ.'	C.18.80	That [*lyf* Actiua] lettred men in here langage calleth.'
B.20.351	That *lif* þoruȝ his loore shal leue coueitise	C.18.81	'ȝe, sire,' I sayde, 'and sethen þer aren but tweyne *lyues*
C.Pr.50	And hadde leue to lye [al here *lyf* aftir].	C.18.104	'Leue liberum Arbitrium, lat some *lyf* hit shake.'
C.Pr.88	That is lele loue and *lyf* among lered and lewed,	C.18.256	Lond and lordschip ynow and *lyf* withouten ende.
C.Pr.147	With lele labour to lyue while *lif* on londe lasteth.	C.18.284	And þat is *lyf* for lyf or ligge thus euere
C.Pr.175	That vs lotheth þe *lyf* ar he lette vs passe.	C.18.284	And þat is lyf for *lyf* or ligge thus euere
C.1.25	Loot in his *lyue* thorw likerous drynke	C.19.28	And lele to bileue on for [*lif* and] for soule?
C.1.116	Ac y wol lacky no *lyf*,' quod þat lady sothly;	C.19.186	Leel lycame and *lyf* þat oure lord shupte.
C.1.199	So loue is lecche of *lyf* and lysse of alle payne	C.19.261	The which is *lyf* and loue, the leye of mannes body.
C.2.36	And what [man] mede loueth, my *lyf* [dar y] wedde,	C.19.278	Wol louye þat *lyf* þat loue and Charite destruyeth.'
C.2.105	/This *lyf* to folowe falsnesse and folk þat on hym leueth,	C.19.292	That euele lyuen and leten nat t[il *lif*] hem forsake.
C.2.108	For a leueth be lost when he his *lyf* leteth,\	C.19.325	And lihtliche oure lord at here *lyues* ende
C.3.174	For he doth men lesen here lond and here *lyf* bothe;	C.19.334	And louye h[e]m yliche hymsulue [and his *lyf*] amende.
C.3.234	Ac y haue saued myselue sixty thousend *lyues*,	C.20.30	*Lyf* saith þat a lyeth and [leyeth] his lyf to wedde,
C.3.259	Y durste haue yleyd my *lyf* and no lasse wedde	C.20.30	Lyf saith þat a lyeth and [leyeth] his *lyf* to wedde,
C.3.447	Lewete shal do hym lawe and no *lyf* elles.	C.20.56	Thenne shal we leue that *lyf* þe loueth and wol nat late the deye.'
C.3.467	Shal lese þerfore his lyflode and his *lyf* parauntur.	C.20.59	The lord of *lyf* and of liht tho leyde his eyes togederes.
C.4.191	'And y dar lege my *lyf* þat loue wol lene þe seluer	C.20.67	'*Lyf* & deth, in this derkenesse here oen fordoth her oþer.
C.5.31	The whiche is lollarne *lyf* þat lytel is preysed	C.20.105	And ȝe, lordeyne[s], haen lost for *lyf* shal haue [þe] maistrie;
C.5.41	*Lyf* þat me [l]ykede but in this longe clothes.	C.20.110	The which is *lif* þat oure lord in all lawes defendeth.
C.5.103	The l[y]f þat is louable and leele to thy soule.'	C.20.161	And so shal this deth fordo, y dar my *lyf* legge,
C.6.45	And likynge of such a *lyf* þat no lawe preiseth,	C.20.268	And bile[u]e on a newe lawe be ylost, *lyf* and soule.'
C.6.52	And lyed o my lycame and on my *lyf* bothe;	C.20.335	Y wolde haue lenghed his *lyf* for y leued, yf he deyede,
C.6.67	Sholde no *lyf* lyue þat on his lond pissede	C.20.339	The which *lyf* and lawe, be hit longe yvysed,
C.6.101	Lord, ar y *lyf* lete, for loue of thysulue	C.20.370	'Lo! me here, ' quod oure lord, '*lyf* and soule bothe,
C.6.313	For me is leuere in this *lyue* as a lorel begge	C.20.386	So *lyf* shal lyf le[t]e ther lyf hath lyf an[y]en[t]ed
C.6.314	Then in lysse to lyue and lese *lyf* and soule.'	C.20.386	So lyf shal *lyf* le[t]e ther lyf hath lyf an[y]en[t]ed
C.6.424	'Thow lord [þat] aloft art and alle *lyues* shope.	C.20.386	So lyf shal lyf le[t]e ther *lyf* hath lyf an[y]en[t]ed
C.7.31	ȝut kan y nother solfe ne synge ne a seyntes *lyf* rede;	C.20.386	So lyf shal lyf le[t]e ther lyf hath lyf *lyf* an[y]en[t]ed
C.7.50	Til eche *lyf* hit lothed to loke þeron or smylle hit;	C.20.387	So þat *lyf* quyte lyf; þe olde lawe hit asketh.
C.7.111	That by his *lyue* l[yth]e]d hem and louede hem to here.	C.20.387	So þat lyf quyte *lyf*; þe olde lawe hit asketh.
C.8.110	Y wol worschipe þerwith treuthe al my *lyue*	C.20.398	Adam and alle thorw a tre shal turne to *lyue*.
C.8.174	Þat a lokede lyke a l[a]nterne al his *lyf* aftur;	C.20.403	For y þat am lord of *lyf*, loue is my drynke,
C.8.233	Loke by thy *lyue* lat hem nat forfare.	C.20.425	Lawe wolde he ȝoue hym *lyf* and he loked on hym.
C.8.277	Thenk þat [diues] for his delicat *lyf* to þe deuel wente	C.21.45	The lawe of *lyf* that laste shal euere
C.9.103	And lymes to labory with and lollares [*lyf* vsen	C.21.105	*Lyf* and lyme as hym luste he wrouhte.
C.9.140	The whiche is lollarne *lyf* and lewede Ermytes;	C.21.217	Tresor to lyue by to here *lyues* ende
C.9.174	Tho þat lyueth thus here *lyf*, leue ȝe non other,	C.21.237	And lyue by þat laboure a leele *lyf* and a trewe.
C.9.198	Summe hadde lyflode of h[ere] lynage and of no *lyf* elles.	C.21.408	Leue hit [wel thou] be[st] lost, bothe *lyf* and soule.'
C.9.341	How we ladde oure *lyf* here and his lawes kepte	C.21.409	'Thenne is many [a *lyf*] ylost,' quod a lewed vicory.
C.10.50	And lyf[holie]st of *lyf* þat lyueth vnder sonne.	C.22.11	For thre thynges he taketh [h]is *lyf* for to saue.
C.10.55	Oure *lyf* to oure lord god for oure lycames gultes.'	C.22.87	Largeliche a legioun lees the *lyf* sone.
C.10.126	And what *lyues* they lyue and what lawe þei vsen	C.22.92	'Alarme! alarme!' quod þat lord, 'vch *lyf* kepe his owene!'
C.10.155	Lord of *lyf* and of lyht, of lisse and of payne.	C.22.111	And bihihte hem long *lyf* and lecherye he sente
C.10.170	The which is loue and *lyf* þat last withouten ende.	C.22.143	And thenne lowh *lyf* and lette dagge his clothes
C.10.173	And *lyf* lyueth by inwit and leryng of kynde.	C.22.148	Thus relyed *lyf* for a litel fo[rtune]
C.10.193	For to lese þerfore her lond and her *lyf* aftur.	C.22.152	*Lyf* lepte asyde and lauhte hym a lemman.
C.10.196	And seth [he les] his *lyf* for lawe sholde loue wexe.	C.22.156	This likede *lyf* and his lemman fortune
C.10.291	Clene of *lyf* and in loue of soule and in lele wedlok.	C.22.168	And wayued away wanhope and with *lyf* he fihteth.
C.10.302	To louye and to loue the and no *lyf* to greue;	C.22.169	And *lyf* fley for fere to fisyk aftur helpe
C.11.22	What shal worthen of suche when þei *lyf* leten:	C.22.173	*Lyf* leuede þat lechecraft lette sholde Elde
C.11.72	And yf thow haue litel, leue sone, loke by þy *lyue*	C.22.175	And Elde auntered hym on *lyf* and at þe laste he hitte
C.11.88	For to worche ȝoure wille while my *lyf* duyreth	C.22.178	'Now y see,' saide *lyf*, ' that surgerie ne fysyke
C.11.204	In þe legende of *lyf* longe ar y were.	C.22.211	Wede ne worldly mete while thy *lif* lasteth.'
C.11.262	As in likyng of lecherye no *lyf* denyede!	C.22.351	That *lyf* thorw his lore shal leue Couetyse
C.12.32	'And wherof serueth lawe,' quod leaute, ' and no *lyf* vndertoke [hit],		
C.12.70	Bote yf contricioun and confessioun crye by his *lyue*	**lif_tyme** n *liftime n.* A 4; B 10; C 17 lyftyme (2) lif_tyme (1) lyf_tyme (14)
C.12.91	And on Troianus treuthe to thenke alle tyme[s] in ȝoure *lyue*	
C.12.143	Preise[n] pouerte for beste [*lif*] if pacience hit folowe	A. 5.212	And ȝet haue I hatid hire al my *lif tyme*.'
C.12.160	And *lyf* lastyng for euere byfore oure lord in heuene:	A. 5.249	And lepe with hym ouer lond al his *lif tyme*,
C.12.163	"Yf thow likest to lyue," quod god, "þe *lyf* þat is parfit	A. 6.56	And ȝe shuln lepe þe liȝtliere al ȝoure *lif tyme*;
C.12.200	Yf god gyueth hym þe *lyf*, to haue a goed heruost,	A. 7.28	A[nd] ek laboure for þi loue al my *lif tyme*,
		B. 5.237	'Vsedestow euere vsurie', quod Repentaunce, 'in al þi *lif tyme*?'

B. 5.384   And yet haue I hated hire al my *lif tyme*.'
B. 5.475   And lepe wiþ hym ouer lond al his *lif tyme*,
B. 5.569   And ye shul lepe þe liȝtloker al youre *lif tyme*.
B. 6.26   And [ek] labour[e] for þi loue al my *lif tyme*,
B.11.21   That leden þee wole to likynge al þi *lif tyme*'.
B.13.141   Thow loue leelly þi soule al þi *lif tyme*.
B.15.142   For a wrecchede hous [he held] al his *lif tyme*,
B.18.3   And yede forþ lik a lorel al my *lif tyme*
B.20.365   [And] for [hem] þat ye ben holden to al my *lif tyme*,
C. 1.75   [To] leue on me and loue me al thy *lyf tyme*.'
C. 2.32   That neuere lyede ne lauhede in al his *lyf tyme*;
C. 6.239   Vsedest [thow] euere vsurye in al thy *lyf tyme*?'
C. 6.329   [And lepe wiþ hym ouer lond al his *lif tyme*]
C. 6.437   Of my luyther ly[uynge] in al my *lyf tyme*.
C. 6.441   And ȝut haue y [ha]ted here al my *lyf tyme*.'
C. 7.216   And ȝe shal lepe þe lihtloker al ȝoure *lyf tyme*:
C. 8.25   And labory for tho thow louest al my *lyf tyme*,
C.10.168   For they louyeth and bylyueth al here *lyf tyme*
C.11.180   That lede þe wol to lykynge Al thy *lyf tyme*.'
C.11.253   That vnlawefulliche hadde ylyued al his *lyf tyme*
C.15.196   'Hastow vsed or haunted al thy *lyf tyme*?'
C.17.36   Toke lyflode of luyther wynnynges in all here *lyf tyme*.
C.18.199   Ac leue hit lelly al thy *lyftyme*.
C.19.110   Loke thow louye and bileue al thy *lyftyme*.
C.20.3   And ȝede forth ylike a lorel al my *lyf tyme*
C.22.365   And for hem þat ȝe aren holde to al my *lyf tyme*

lifdayes n *lif dai n.* B 2 lifdaies (1) lifdayes (1); C 1 lyfdayes
B. 1.27   For Lot, in hise *lifdayes*, for likynge of drynke,
B. 3.151   To [holde] lemmans and lotebies alle hire *lifdaies*,
C. 3.189   To holde lemmanes and lotebyes al here *lyfdayes*

lifholy adj *lifholi adj.* B 2; C 5 lyfholy (4) lyfholiest (1)
B.15.206   Loken as lambren and semen [*lif*]*holy*,
B.15.308   And lawefulle men to *lifholy* men liflode brynge;
C. 4.175   And by lele and *lyfholy* my lawe shal be demed.'
C. 9.196   Noyther of lynage ne of lettrure ne *lyfholy* as Ermytes
C.10.50   And *lyf[holie]st* of lyf þat lyueth vnder sonne.
C.11.2   That ful lene lokede and *lyfholy* semede.
C.14.188   And to lele and *lyfholy* þat louyeth alle treuthe.

lifholynesse n *lifholinesse n.* B 1; C 2 lifholynesse (1) lyfholynesse (1)
B.19.111   For wyn is likned to lawe and *lifholynesse*,
C. 5.80   *Lyfholynesse* and loue hath be longe hennes.
C.21.111   For wyn is likned to lawe and *lyfholinesse*

liflode n *liflode n.* A 12 liflode (11) lyflode (1); B 28; C 29 liflode (2) lyflode (27)
A.Pr.30   For no likerous *liflode* here likam to plese.
A. 1.18   Of [woll]ene, of [lyn]ene, of *liflode* at nede
A. 1.35   Ne *liflode* to þe lykam þat lef is to þe soule.
A. 5.229   [And] þeiȝ my *liflode* lakke leten I nille
A. 7.16   For I shal lene hem *lyflode*, but ȝif þe lond faile,
A. 7.218   & labouren for þi *liflode*, & so oure lord hiȝte,
A. 7.236   God ȝiueþ [hem] his blissing þat here *liflode* so wynneþ.'
A. 7.256   And lerne to laboure wiþ lond lest *liflode* hym faile.
A. 7.273   Be þis *liflode* I mote lyue til lammasse tyme;
A. 8.107   And beloure þat I [be]louȝ er þeiȝ *liflode* me faile.
A. 8.110   Þat louiþ god lelly, his *liflode* is þe more:
A. 9.73   And þoruȝ his labour or his lond his *liflode* wynneþ,
B.Pr.30   For no likerous *liflode* hire likame to plese.
B. 1.18   Of wollene, of lynnen, of *liflode* at nede
B. 1.37   Ne *liflode* to þ[e] likame [þat leef is to þ[e] soule.
B. 5.87   Of chidynge and chalangynge was his chief *liflode*,
B. 5.457   And þouȝ my *liflode* lakke leten I nille
B. 6.17   For I shal lenen hem *liflode* but if þe lond faille
B. 6.234   And labouren for þi *liflode*, and so oure lord hiȝte.
B. 6.272   And lerne to laboure wiþ lond [lest] *liflode* [hym faille].
B. 6.289   By þis *liflode* [I moot] lyue til lammasse tyme,
B. 7.128   That loueþ god lelly his *liflode* is ful esy:
B. 8.82   And þoruȝ his labour or his lond his *liflode* wynneþ,
B. 9.109   Grace to go to hem and ofgon hir *liflode*:
B.11.282   Ne lakkeþ neuere *liflode*, lynnen ne wollen:
B.11.289   Hem sholde lakke no *liflode*, neyþer lynnen ne wollen.
B.11.300   And a tale, a tale of noȝt, to his *liflode* at meschief.
B.14.32   All þat lyueþ and lokeþ *liflode* wolde I fynde
B.14.38   And seide, 'lo! here *liflode* ynogh, if oure bileue be trewe.
B.14.39   For lent neuere was lif but *liflode* were shapen,
B.14.47   But I [listnede and] lokede what *liflode* it was
B.14.70   And lyueden wiþouten *liflode* and at þe laste þei woken.
B.15.184   Thouȝ he bere hem no breed he bereþ hem swetter *liflode*,
B.15.255   The mooste *liflode* he lyueþ by is loue in goddes passion;
B.15.277   Of leons ne of leopardes no *liflode* ne toke,
B.15.308   And lawefulle men to lifholy men *liflode* brynge;
B.17.79   And he took hym two pens to *liflode* and seide,

B.19.239   To wynne wiþ hir *liflode* bi loore of his techynge;
B.20.238   For lomere he lyeþ þat *liflode* moot begge
B.20.239   Than he þat laboureþ for *liflode* and leneþ it beggeris.
C.Pr.32   For no likerous *liflode* here lycame to plese.
C. 1.35   Ne *liflode* to þe lycame þat lef is [to] þe soule.
C. 3.467   Shal lese þerfore his *lyflode* and his lyf parauntur.
C. 4.115   And here pelure and here palfrayes pore menne *lyflode*
C. 5.42   Yf y be labour sholde lyuen and *lyflode* deseruen,
C. 5.45   The lomes þat y labore with and *lyflode* deserue
C. 6.68   Chidynge and chalengynge was his cheef *lyflode*
C. 6.311   'And thow m[y] *lyflode* lakke leten y nelle
C. 8.15   For y shal lene hem *lyflode* but [yf] þe lond faylle
C. 8.196   But *lyflode* for his la[b]our and his loue at nones.
C. 8.221   For here *lyflode*, lere me now, sire hunger.'
C. 8.241   Bytu[lye] and bytrauayle trewely [ȝ]oure *lyflode*:
C. 8.262   That here *lyflode* be lene and lyte worth here clothes.'
C. 8.293   And lerne to labory with lond lest *lyflode* h[y]m fayle.
C. 8.312   By this *lyflode* we mote lyue til l[a]masse tyme
C. 9.100   Thouh he falle for defaute þat fayteth for his *lyflode*
C. 9.198   Summe hadde *lyflode* of h[ere] lynage and of no lyf elles
C. 9.246   Or labory for here *lyflode* as þe lawe wolde?
C.13.103   Hem sholde neuere lacke *lyflode*, noþer lynnen ne wollene.
C.13.114   And a title, a tale of nauht, to his *lyflode* as hit were.
C.15.237   And saide, 'lo! here *lyflode* ynow yf oure beleue be trewe.
C.15.238   For lente neuere was lyf but *lyflode* were shape,
C.15.248   And y lystnede and lokede what *lyflode* hit were
C.15.269   [And] lyuede withouten *lyflode* and [at] þe laste awakede.
C.17.36   Toke *lyflode* of luyther wynnynges in all here lyf tyme.
C.17.155   To þat lord þat hym lyf lente *lyflode* hym sende.
C.21.239   To wynne with here *lyflode* bi lore of his techynge];
C.22.238   For lomere he lyeth þat *lyflode* moet begge
C.22.239   Then he þat laboreth for *lyflode* and leneth hit beggares.

lyft > left,lifte

lifte n *lift n.(1)* &> *liften* B 1; C 1 lyft
B.15.358   Han no bileue to þe *lifte* ne to þe [lodesterre].
C.17.96   Haen no byleue to þe *lyft* ne to þe lodesterr[e].

liften v *liften v.* B 3 lifte (1) liften (2); C 3 lyfte (1) luft (2)
B. 5.352   For to *liften* hym o lofte and leyde hym on his knowes.
B.12.120   And leiden hand þeron to *liften* it vp loren here lif after.
B.15.593   And whan he *lifte* vp Laȝar þat leid was in graue
C. 6.410   For to *lyfte* hym aloft [and] leyde hym on his knees.
C.17.302   Tho he *luft* vp lasar þat layde was in graue;
C.18.143   And *luft* vp laȝar þat lay in his tombe;

liftyme > lif_tyme

liftyng ger *liftinge ger.* B 1; C 1 luftynge
B. 5.353   Ac Gloton was a gret cherl and grym in þe *liftyng*;
C. 6.411   Ac gloton was a greet cherl and gr[ym] in þe *luftynge*

lige adj *lege adj.* A 1; B 3 lige (1) liges (2); C 6 leege (1) lege (3) leges (2)
A. 4.147   And alle my *lige* ledis to lede þus euene.'
A. 4.184   [And] alle youre *lige* leodes to lede þus euene'.
B.18.349   But by right and by reson raunsone here my *liges*:
B.19.60   And siþ [alle hise lele *liges* largely he yeueþ]
C. 3.317   To here [lele] and *lege*, loue [is] the cause;
C. 3.318   And yf th[e] lele and *lege* be luyther men aftur
C. 3.415   That agag of amalek and alle his *leege* peple
C. 4.178   And alle ȝoure *lege* l[e]des to lede thus euene.'
C.20.395   Bote [by] riht and [by] resoun raunsome here my *lege[s]*:
C.21.60   And sethe [all his lele *leges* largeliche he ȝeueth]

lygge adj *cf. OED ledger n. and a. B.2.5.b* C 1
C.12.232   Whete þat þeron wexeth worth *lygge* ar hit rype;

ligge v *lien v.(1)* A 22 lay (6) leiȝe (2) leiȝen (1) leyȝe (1) leyn (2) ligge (2) liggen (1) liggeþ (1) liȝen (1) liþ (5); B 46 lay (11) leiȝe (1) ligge (8) liggeþ (4) liggynge (1) lith (2) liþ (9) lyþ (3) yleye (2) yleyen (2); C 47 lay (13) layȝe (1) layn (1) ley (1) leye (1) leyen (1) lyen (1) lyeth (2) ligge (3) lygge (9) liggen (1) lyggen (1) liggeth (1) lyggeth (1) lyggynge (1) lith (5) lyth (3) yley (1)
A.Pr.9   And as I *lay* & lenide & lokide on þe watris
A. 1.30   And leccherie h[i]m lauȝte & *lay* be hem boþe;
A. 1.115   A[c] lucifer lowest *liþ* of hem alle;
A. 2.25   And al is liȝeris ledyng þat hy *liȝen* togideris.
A. 2.100   ȝif þe Leaute wile loke þei *ligge* togidere.
A. 3.37   'Þeiȝ lerid & lewide hadde *leiȝe* be þe ichone,
A. 3.163   Whanne ȝe wyte wytterly where þe wrong *liggeþ*;
A. 4.46   And ȝet he betiþ me þerto & *liþ* be my maiden.
A. 4.59   For boþe þi lyf & þi lond *liþ* in his grace.
A. 5.46   And *lay* longe er heo lokide, & 'lord mercy' criede,
A. 5.64   As a lek þat hadde *leyn* longe in þe sonne,

A. 5.135 For laboureris & lou3 folk þat *lay* be h[y]mselue;
A. 5.136 Þe beste in my bedchaumbre *lay* be þe wou3.
A. 5.250 For he hadde *lei3e* be latro luciferis [aunte].
A. 7.14 Þe nedy & þe nakid, nymeþ hed how þei *liggen*;
A. 7.130 But he be blynd, or brokesshankid, or beddrede *ligge*:
A. 7.178 [Þat *ley3e* [blereyed] and brokelegged by þe hye waye];
A. 8.93 In two lynes it *lay* & nou3t o lettre more,
A.10.118 Þus in dred *liþ* dowel, [and] dobet to suffre,
A.10.180 A3en þe lawe of oure lord *le[i3en]* togideris,
A.11.141 Ne were þe loue þat *liþ* þerein a wel lewid þing it were.
A.11.284 Þat hadde *leyn* with lucifer manye longe 3eris;
B.Pr.9 And as I *lay* and lenede and loked on þe watres
B.Pr.91 *Liggen* at Londoun in Lenten and ellis.
B. 1.30 And Leccherie hym lau3te, and *lay* by hem boþe;
B. 1.126 Ac Lucifer lowest *liþ* of hem alle;
B. 2.52 Thus lefte me þat lady *liggynge* aslepe,
B. 2.136 If any [lewte] wol loke þei *ligge* togideres.
B. 3.38 'Thei3 [lered and lewed] hadde *leyen* by þee [echone],
B. 3.176 Whan ye witen witterly wher þe wrong *liggeþ*.
B. 4.59 And yet he beteþ me þerto and *lyþ* by my mayde.
B. 4.73 For boþe þi lif and þi lond *lyþ* in his grace.'
B. 5.63 And *lay* longe er she loked, and 'lord, mercy!' cryde,
B. 5.81 As a leek þat hadde *yleye* longe in þe sonne
B. 5.219 For laborers and lowe folk þat *lay* by hymselue.
B. 5.220 The beste [in my bedchambre] *lay* [by þe walle].
B. 5.410 And *ligge* abedde in lenten and my lemman in myne armes
B. 5.432 I am no3t lured wiþ loue but þer *ligge* au3t vnder þe þombe.
B. 5.476 For he hadde *leyen* by Latro, luciferis Aunte.
B. 6.15 The nedy and þe naked nymeþ hede how þei *liggeþ*;
B. 6.163 Plentee among þe peple þe while my plow3 *liggeþ*'.
B. 7.111 In two lynes it *lay* and no3t a [lettre] moore,
B.10.189 [Ne were þe loue þat *liþ* þerinne a wel lewed þyng it were].
B.10.282 Lewed men may likne yow þus, þat þe beem *liþ* in youre ei3en,
B.10.321 Ac þei leten hem as lordes, hire lon[d *liþ*] so brode.
B.10.425 That hadde *yleyen* wiþ lucifer many longe yeres.
B.11.428 Lat hym *ligge*, loke no3t on hym til hym list aryse.
B.12.180 Ther þe lewed *liþ* stille and lokeþ after lente,
B.12.258 And alle þe oþere þer it *lith* enuenymeþ þoru3 his attre.
B.13.21 I *lay* doun longe in þis þo3t and at þe laste I slepte,
B.15.67 For in þe likynge *liþ* a pride and licames coueitise
B.15.183 Ther poore men and prisons *liggeþ*, hir pardon to haue;
B.15.218 The loue þat *liþ* in his herte makeþ hym li3t of speche,
B.16.20 And *lay* longe in a louedreem; and at þe laste me þou3te
B.16.113 Saue þo he leched la3ar þat hadde *yleye* in graue;
B.16.255 And I loked in his lappe; a la3ar *lay* þerInne
B.16.268 That is lif for lif; or *ligge* þus euere
B.17.118 And Hope þe Hostile[r] shal be þer [an helyng þe man *lith*];
B.17.217 Wiþouten leye or light [*liþ* fir in þe macche]–
B.17.228 Til þat lele loue *ligge* on hym and blowe.
B.18.124 And which a light and a leme *lay* bifore helle.
B.18.144 Patriarkes and prophetes þat in peyne *liggen*,
B.18.386 And if lawe wole I loke on hem it *liþ* in my grace
B.19.55 That longe hadde *yleyen* bifore as Luciferis cherles,
B.19.418 And þer þei *ligge* and lenge moost lecherie þere regneþ".
B.20.311 Sire leef-to-lyue-in-lecherie *lay* þere and gronede;
B.20.360 [And] lat hem *ligge* ouerlonge and looþ is to chaunge;
B.20.377 'He *lyþ* [adreynt] and dremeþ', seide Pees, 'and so do manye oþere.
C.Pr.8 And in a launde as y *lay* lened y and slepte
C.Pr.89 *Leyen* [at] Londoun in lenton and elles.
C.Pr.137 For in loue and lettrure *lith* þe grete eleccoun.
C. 1.28 And *lay* by hem bothe as þe boke telleth;
C. 1.128 Ac lucifer lowest *lith* of hem alle;
C. 2.55 Thus le[f]te me that lady *lyggynge* as aslepe,
C. 2.133 That laurence the leuyte that *lay* on þe gredyre
C. 3.40 'Thow le[r]ed men and le[w]ed haued *layn* by the bothe
C. 3.171 *Lyggeth* by here, when hem lust, lered and lewed.
C. 3.222 When 3e [wyten] witterly [where] þe wrong *liggeth*.
C. 4.62 And 3ut he manes[c]heth me and myne and *lyth* be my mayde.
C. 4.122 And til saynt Iames be souhte there pore sykke *lyggen*,
C. 5.16 Or haue an horn and be hayward and *lygge* þeroute [a]nyhtes
C. 5.89 Quod Consience, 'by Crist, y can nat se this *lyeth*;
C. 5.149 Dyen for drouthe whenne they drye *lygge*,
C. 5.167 Ac 3e leten 3ow alle as lordes, 3oure lond *lyth* so brode.
C. 6.4 And [*lay*] long ar he lokede and 'lord, mercy!' cryede
C. 6.192 Y *lay* by þe louelokest and louede here neuere aftur.
C. 6.227 For laboreres and louh folk þat *lay* by hymsulue.
C. 6.228 Þe beste ale *lay* in m[y] bour and in my bed chau[m]bre
C. 6.261 The worste *lay* withynne; a greet wit y lat hit.
C. 6.330 For he hadde *lay3e* by latro, luciferes aunte.
C. 7.26 And *ligge* abedde in lente and my lemman in myn armus
C. 7.45 Y am nat luyred with loue but þer *lygge* ouht vnder þe t[h]umbe.
C. 8.160 For ther worth no plente,' quod [Perus], 'and þe plouh *lygge*.'
C. 9.143 Vnlouke his legges abroad or *ligge* at his ese,

C. 9.285 In two lynes hit *lay* and nat a lettre more
C.10.272 Ac they *lyen* le[i], here neyther lyketh other.
C.11.257 That hadde *yley* with lucifer mony longe 3eres.
C.13.23 As grayn þat *lith* in greut and thorw grace at the laste
C.13.159 Lernede to [l]egge stikkes þat *ley* on here neste.
C.13.235 Lat hym *lygge*, lok nat on hym til hym luste [a]ryse.
C.14.120 There þe lewede *lyth* stille and loketh aftur lente
C.15.11 Ne no cors of pore comine in here kyrke3erde most *lygge*
C.18.143 And luft vp la3ar þat *lay* in his tombe.
C.18.271 And y lokede in his lappe; a la3ar *lay* þerynne
C.18.284 And þat is lyf for lyf or *ligge* thus euere
C.19.10 That luciferes lordschipe lowe sholde *lygge*.'
C.19.183 Withouten leye [or] lihte *lith* fuyr in þe mache–
C.20.127 And which a lihte and a leem *lay* bifore helle.
C.20.147 Patriarkes and prophetes þat in peyne *liggen*,
C.20.428 And if lawe wol y loke on hem hit *lith* in my grace
C.21.55 That longe hadden *leye* bifore as luciferes cherles
C.21.418 And þer they *lygge* and lenge moest lecherye þer regneth".
C.22.311 Sire l[ee]f-to-lyue-in-lecherye *lay* þer and groned;
C.22.360 And lat hem *lygge* ouerlonge and loeth is to chaungen;
C.22.377 'He *lyeth* adreint [and dremeth],' saide pees, 'and so doth mony oþere.

light n *light n.* A 3 li3t (2) ly3th (1); B 28 light (23) li3t (5); C 28 liht (12) lihte (14) lyht (2)

A. 1.163 It is as lewid as a laumpe þat no *li3t* is inne.
A.10.30 Þe lord of lif & of *li[3t]*, of lisse & of peyne.
A.12.96 Þou shalt be lau3th into *ly3th* with loking of an eye
B. 1.112 [And was þe louelokest of *li3t* after oure lord
B. 1.189 It is as lewed as a lampe þat no *li3t* is Inne.
B. 5.492 Aboute mydday, whan moost *li3t* is and meel tyme of Seintes,
B. 5.494 [Th]e *li3t* þat lepe out of þee, Lucifer [it] blent[e]
B. 9.29 Lord of lif and of *li3t*, of lisse and of peyne.
B.16.189 The *light* of al þat lif haþ a londe and a watre,
B.17.217 Wiþouten leye or *light* [*liþ* fir in þe macche]–
B.17.284 He fordooþ þe leuest *light* þat oure lord louyeþ.
B.18.59 The lord of lif and of *light* þo leide hise eighen togideres.
B.18.124 And which a *light* and a leme lay bifore helle.
B.18.137 The while þis *light* and þis leme shal Lucifer ablende.
B.18.145 Leue þow neuere þat yon *light* hem alofte brynge
B.18.170 But [loue] sente hire som lettre what þis *light* bymeneþ
B.18.189 Leuestow þat yond *light* vnlouke my3te helle
B.18.241 The *light* folwede þe lord into þe lowe erþe.
B.18.245 And lo! how þe sonne gan louke hire *light* in hirselue
B.18.263 A vois loude in þat *light* to lucifer crieþ,
B.18.267 'Swich a *light*, ayeins oure leue la3ar [i]t fette.
B.18.272 That swich a lord and [a] *light* sholde lede hem alle hennes.'
B.18.274 Boþe þis lord and þis *light*, is longe ago I knew hym.
B.18.308 Wiþ glorie and with gret *light*; god it is, I woot wel.
B.18.316 Eft þe *light* bad vnlouke and Lucifer answerde
B.18.317 What lord artow?' quod Lucifer; þe *light* soone seide
B.18.325 Lucifer loke ne my3te, so *light* hym ablente.
B.18.326 And þo þat oure lord louede into his *light* he laughte,
B.19.125 He made lame to lepe and yaf *light* to blynde
B.19.205 And was afered [for] þe *light*, for in fires [lik]nesse
B.19.459 Thanne lou3 þer a lord and, 'by þis *light*!' seide,
C. 1.185 Hit is as lewed as a laumpe þat no *liht* is ynne.
C. 7.132 Aboute mydday, whan most *liht* is and meel tyme of sayntes,
C. 7.134 The *lihte* þat lup oute of the, lucifer hit blente
C.10.155 Lord of lyf and of *lyht*, of lisse and of payne.
C.19.183 Withouten leye [or] *lihte* lith fuyr in þe mache–
C.19.265 A fordoth þe *lihte* þat oure lord loketh to haue worschipe of.
C.20.59 The lord of lyf and of *liht* tho leyde his eyes togederes.
C.20.127 And which a *lihte* and a leem lay bifore helle.
C.20.140 The while this *lihte* and this l[em]e shal lucifer ablende.
C.20.148 Leue [þou] neuere þat 3one *liht* hem alofte brynge
C.20.173 Bote loue haue ysente her som lettre what this *liht* bymeneth
C.20.194 Leuest thow þat 3one *lihte* vnlouke myhte helle
C.20.250 The *lihte* folewede þe lord into þe lowe erthe.
C.20.254 And lo! how þe sonne gan louke here *lihte* in heresulue
C.20.271 A vois loude in þat *liht* to lucifer saide,
C.20.275 'Such a *lyht* a3enes oure leue la3ar hit fette;
C.20.280 That such a lord and a *lihte* sh[olde] lede hem alle hennes.
C.20.283 And [y] shal lette this loerd and his *liht* stoppe.
C.20.286 That no *liht* lepe in at louer ne at loupe.
C.20.296 Bothe this lord and this *lihte*, ys longe ygo y knewe hym.
C.20.306 Thus this lord of *liht* such a lawe made
C.20.342 With glorie and with [grete] *lihte*; god hit is ich woet wel.
C.20.359 For efte þat *lihte* bade vnlouke [and lucifer answerede].
C.20.368 Lucifer loke ne myhte, so *liht* hym ablen[t]e,
C.20.369 And tho that oure lord louede forth with þat *liht* flowen.
C.21.125 He made lame to lepe and 3af *liht* to blynde
C.21.205 And was afered for the *lihte*, for in fuyres liknesse
C.21.459 Thenne lowh ther a lord and 'bi this *lihte*!' saide,

lighte > liʒteþ; lighter > liʒt; lightl- > liʒtly

lightnynge *ger* **lightninge** *ger.* B 1; C 1 lihtnynge
B.19.202   In liknesse of a *lightnynge* he lighte on hem alle
C.21.202   In liknesse of a *lihtnynge* a lyhte on hem alle

liʒe > lyen; liʒen > lyen,ligge; liʒer(- > liere; liʒeþ > lyen

liʒt adj **light** *adj.(2)* B 6 lighter (3) liʒt (1) liʒter (2); C 4 liht (1) lihtere (1) lyhtere (2)
B. 1.156   Was neuere leef vpon lynde *lighter* þerafter,
B.14.248   And wheiþer be *liʒter* to breke? lasse boost [it] makeþ
B.14.307   And euer þe lasse þat he [lede], þe [*liʒter*] he is of herte:
B.15.218   The loue þat liþ in his herte makeþ hym *liʒt* of speche,
B.17.42   It is *lighter* to lewed men o lesson to knowe
B.17.46   It is *lighter* to leeue in þre louely persones
C. 1.152   Was neuer lef vppon lynde *lyhtere* theraftur\
C.16.88   And where be [*lyh]tere* to breke? lasse boest hit maketh
C.16.142   And euere þe lasse þat [eny] lede þe *lihtere* his herte is there,
C.19.43   Hit is *liht* for lewed and for lered bothe.

liʒt adv **lighte** *adv.* A 2; B 4 liʒt (3) liʒte (1); C 4 lihte (1) lyhte (3)
A. 4.137   Loue let of hire *liʒt* & louʒ hire to scorne,
A. 7.153   And let *liʒt* of þe lawe & lesse of þe kniʒt,
B. 4.161   Loue leet of hire *liʒt* and leaute yet lasse,
B. 6.168   And leet *liʒt* of þe lawe and lasse of þe knyʒte,
B.11.2   And lakked me in latyn and *liʒt* by me sette,
B.11.16   And bad me for my contenaunce acounten Clergie *liʒte*.
C. 4.156   Loue l[et]te of mede *lyhte* and leutee ʒut lasse
C. 8.165   And leet *lyhte* of þe lawe and lasse of the knyhte
C.11.162   And lakkede [me in] latyn and *lyhte* by me sette
C.11.175   And bade me for my contin[au]nce counte cler[gie] *lihte*.

liʒt &> light; liʒte > liʒt,liʒteþ

liʒteþ v **lighten** *v.(2)* A 1 liʒtiþ; B 4 lighte (2) liʒte (1) liʒteþ (1); C 2 lihte (1) lyhte (1)
A. 5.93   Of his lesing I lauʒe, [it *liʒtiþ*] myn herte,
B. 5.113   And of [his] lesynge I lauʒe, [it *liʒteþ*] myn herte;
B.11.248   Iesu crist on a Iewes doʒter *liʒte*, gentil womman þouʒ she were,
B.17.67   He *lighte* adown of Lyard and ladde hym in his hande,
B.19.202   In liknesse of a lightnynge he *lighte* on hem alle
C.19.66   [A *l]ihte* a[dou]n of lyard and ladde hym in his hand[e]
C.21.202   In liknesse of a lihtnynge a *lyhte* on hem alle

lyʒth > light

liʒtly adv **lightli** *adv.* A 3 liʒtliche (1) liʒtliere (1) liʒtly (1); B 14 lightly (2) lightliche (3) lightlier (1) lightloker (1) liʒtly (3) liʒtliche (2) liʒtloker (2); C 16 lihtliche (1) lihtly (1) lyhtly (2) lihtlich (1) lyhtlych (1) lihtliche (6) lyhtliche (1) lihtloker (1) lyhtloker (1) lihtlokour (1)
A. 2.177   *Liʒtliche liʒere* lep awey þennes,
A. 4.93   Le[pe] he so *liʒtly* awey, lauʒen he wolde,
A. 6.56   And ʒe shuln lepe þe *liʒtliere* al ʒoure lif tyme;
B.Pr.150   And ouerleep hem *liʒtliche* and lauʒte hem at wille
B. 2.218   *Liʒtliche* Lyere leep awey þanne,
B. 4.106   Lope he so *liʒtly* [awey], lauʒen he wolde,
B. 5.569   And ye shul lepe þe *liʒtloker* al youre lif tyme.
B. 7.11   Han pardon þoruʒ purgatorie to passen ful *liʒtly*,
B.12.157   How þat lewed men *liʒtloker* þan lettrede were saued,
B.12.211   That oure lord ne hadde hym *liʒtly* out, so leue I [by] þe þef in heuene.
B.14.34   Thanne laughed haukyn a litel and *lightly* gan swerye;
B.15.137   *Lightliche* þat þei leuen losels it habbeþ,
B.15.439   Into lele bileue; þe *lightloker* me þinkeþ
B.15.502   Han a lippe of oure bileue, þe *lightlier* me þynkeþ
B.17.337   And "þat is *lightly* forʒyuen and forʒeten boþe
B.17.345   And *lightliche* oure lord at hir lyues ende
B.18.270   And lede it þer [laʒar is] and *lightliche* me bynde.
C.Pr.171   And ouerlep hem *lightliche* and laghte hem at wille
C. 2.228   *Lyhtliche* lyare lep awey thenne,
C. 4.101   Lope he so *lihtliche* [awey], lawen he wolde\
C. 4.168   And lourede vppon men of lawe and *lyhtlych* sayde:
C. 7.216   And ʒe shal lepe þe *lihtloker* al ʒoure lyf tyme:
C. 7.302   And loure on me and *lihtly* chyde and sygge y louede another.
C. 9.11   Haen pardon thorw purgatorye to passe ful *lyhtly*,
C.12.222   That *lihtlich* launseth vp litel while dureth
C.14.101   That is, how lewede men and luythere *lyhtloker* were ysaued
C.14.150   That oure [lord] ne hauede [hym] *lihtliche* out, so leue y [by] þ[e] thef in heuene.
C.16.132   And me leneth *lyhtly* fewe men and me wene hem pore;
C.16.282   *Lihtliche* þat they leue loseles hit deuoureth.
C.17.253   Haen a lyppe of oure bileue, the *lihtlokour* me thynketh
C.19.317   And "þat is *lihtliche* forʒeue and forʒete bothe
C.19.325   And *lihtliche* oure lord at here lyues ende
C.20.278   And lede hit þer laʒar is and *lihtliche* me bynde.

liht > light,liʒt; lyhte > light,liʒt,liʒteþ; lihtere > liʒt; lihtl- > liʒtly; lihtnynge > lightnynge

lyinge *ger* **liinge** *ger.(2)* B 1
B.13.322   *Lyinge* and la[kk]ynge and leue tonge to chide;

lik adj **lik** *adj.* A 6 lyche (1) lik (3) lyk (2); B 8; C 3 lyk (2) lyke (1)
A. 1.89   And ek *lyk* to oure lord be seint lukis wordis.
A. 9.61   A muchel man, me þouʒte, *lik* to myselue,
A. 9.110   He was long & lene, *lyk* to non oþer,
A.10.6   A lemman þat he louiþ *lik* to hymselue.
A.10.32   Ac man is hym most *lik* of mark & of shap.
A.11.246   Alle kynne creatures þat to crist be[n] *l[yche*]
B. 1.151   And lered it Moyses for þe leueste þyng and moost *lik* to heuene,
B. 5.481   And of nauʒt madest auʒt and man moost *lik* to þiselue,
B. 8.70   A muche man me þouʒte, *lik* to myselue,
B. 8.120   He was long and lene, *lik* to noon ooþer;
B. 9.6   A lemman þat he loueþ *lik* to hymselue.
B. 9.31   Ac man is hym moost *lik* of marc and of [shape].
B. 9.65   And alle þat lyuen good lif are *lik* to god almyʒty:
B.19.8   And riʒt *lik* in alle [lymes] to oure lord Ies[u].
C. 1.87   And also *lyk* [to] oure lord by saynt Lukes wordes.
C.10.157   Man is hym most *lyk* of membres and of face
C.21.8   And riht *lyke* in alle lymes to oure lord iesu.

lik prep **like** *prep.* A 4 lik (3) lyk (1); B 14 lich (1) lik (12) like (1); C 12 liche (1) lyk (4) like (1) lyke (6)
A. 5.98   Þus I lyue loueles, [*lyk*] a lyþer dogge,
A. 5.194   And þanne gan he to go [*lik* a glemans bicche],
A. 7.162   Þat he lokide *lik* a lanterne al his lif aftir;
A. 9.35   Þe goodis of þis ground be *lik* þe grete wawes,
B. 3.338   Ac þow art *lik* a lady þat radde a lesson ones
B. 5.119   [Th]us I lyue louelees *lik* a luþer dogge
B. 5.191   And [*lik*] a leþeren purs lolled hise chekes
B. 5.346   And þanne gan he to go *lik* a glemannes bicche
B. 6.177   That he loked *lik* a lanterne al his lif after.
B. 8.39   The goodes of þis grounde arn *like* þe grete wawes,
B. 9.64   That lyuen synful lif here hir soule is *lich* þe deuel.
B.11.71   'By my feiþ! frere, quod I, 'ye faren *lik* þise woweris
B.12.255   His ledene be in oure lordes ere *lik* a pies chiteryng;
B.15.349   As in lussheburwes is a luþer alay, and yet lokeþ he *lik* a sterlyng;
B.17.133   Louye hem *lik* myselue, ac oure lord abouen alle.'
B.17.354   And louye hem *lik* hymself, and his lif amende.
B.18.3   And yede forþ *lik* a lorel al my lif tyme
B.18.299   And þus haþ he trolled forþ [*lik* a tidy man] þise two and þritty wynter.
C. 1.111   That hadde [lu]st to be *lyk* his lord þat was almyghty:
C. 3.490   Thow art *lyk* a lady þat a lessoun radde
C. 6.75   *Lyke* a schupestares sharre and shrewed myn euencristene
C. 6.440   And thenne gan he go *lyke* a glemans byche
C. 7.123   And [of nauhte madest] auhte and man *liche* thysulue
C. 8.174   Þat a lokede *lyke* a l[a]nterne al his lyf aftur;
C. 9.158   And lyueth *lyke* a lollare, goddes lawe hym dampneth.
C.10.45   The godes of this grounde ar *like* þe grete wawes
C.12.19   'By my faith! frere,' quod y, 'ʒe fare *lyke* þe woware
C.15.29   And metten with a maystre, a man *lyk* a frere.
C.17.168   Ac for he was *lyk* a lossheborw y leue oure lord hym lette.
C.20.332   Thus hath he trolled forth *lyke* a tydy man this two & thritty wynter.

likame n **lichame** *n.* A 4 lycam (1) likam (1) lykam (1) lykhame (1); B 7 licame (1) lycame (1) licames (1) likame (3) likames (1); C 13 licame (1) lycame (9) lycames (3)
A.Pr.30   For no likerous liflode here *likam* to plese.
A. 1.35   Ne liflode to þe *lykam* þat lef is to þe soule.
A. 1.36   Leue not þi *lycam* for a li[ʒ]er hym techiþ,
A.12.93   Whil his lyf and his *lykhame* lesten togedere.
B.Pr.30   For no likerous liflode hire *likame* to plese.
B. 1.37   Ne liflode to þ[e] *likame* [þat leef is to þ[e] soule.
B. 1.38   Lef nauʒt þi *licame*] for a liere hym techeþ,
B.12.234   Raþer þan his *likame* alogh; lewed asken þus clerkes
B.13.51   'As longe', quod [he], 'as [lif] and *lycame* may dure'.
B.13.386   For losse of good, leue me, þan for *likames* giltes;
B.15.67   For in þe likynge liþ a pride and *licames* coueitise
C.Pr.32   For no likerous liflode here *lycame* to plese.
C. 1.35   Ne liflode to þe *lycame* þat lef is [to] þe soule.
C. 1.36   Leef nat thy *lycame* for a lyare hym techeth,
C. 6.52   And lyed o my *lycame* and on my lyf bothe;
C. 6.176   As in likynge of lecherye my *lycames* gultes
C. 6.275   For lo[s] of good, leef me, then for *lycames* gultes.
C.10.55   Oure lyf to oure lord god for oure *lycames* gultes.'
C.10.219   Þat *lycame* haen aʒen þe lawe þat oure lord ordeynede.
C.15.57   'As longe,' quod he, 'as lyf and *lycame* may duyre.'
C.19.95   That his *lycame* shal lechen at þe laste vs alle.
C.19.186   Leel *lycame* and lyf þat oure lord shupte.

C.19.239   Moste lordliche lyue and 3ut [on] his *lycame* werie
C.20.93   Bothe my lond and my *licame* at 3oure likynge taketh hit.

like adv *like adv.* &> *lik,likeþ* B 1; C 1 lyke
B.20.30   After þe kynges counseil and þe comune *like*.
C.22.30   Aftur þe kynges conseyl and þe comune *lyke*.

liked- > *likeþ*; *liken-* > *likn-*

likerous adj *likerous adj.* A 3; B 3 likerous (2) likerouse (1); C 3
   likerous (2) lykerous (1)
A.Pr.30   For no *likerous* liflode here likam to plese.
A. 7.250 L[o]ue hym nou3t, for he is a lecchour & *likerous* of tunge,
A.11.121 F[ro] lesinges & li[þer] speche & *likerous* drinkes.
B.Pr.30   For no *likerous* liflode hire likame to plese.
B. 6.266 L[o]ue hym no3t for he is [a] lech[our] and *likerous* of tunge,
B.10.169 Fro-lesynges-and-liþer-speche-and-*likerouse*-drynkes.
C.Pr.32   For no *likerous* liflode here lycame to plese.
C. 1.25   Loot in his lyue thorw *likerous* drynke
C.10.177 That many lede leseth thorw *lykerous* drynke,

likeþ v *liken v.(1)* A 21 lyke (1) lyked (1) likeþ (5) likide (3) lykide (1)
   likiþ (7) lykiþ (1) lykyþ (2); B 46 like (4) liked (11) likede (3) likeþ
   (28); C 44 like (3) lyke (3) liked (2) likede (6) lykede (3) likest (1)
   liketh (17) lyketh (11)
A.Pr.57   Gloside þe gospel as h[e]m good *likide*;
A.Pr.69   Lewide men leuide [hym] wel & *likide* his speche;
A. 1.28   Dede be his dou3ter[n] þat þe deuil *lykide*,
A. 1.41   'A madame mercy,' quaþ I, 'me *likiþ* wel 3oure wordis.
A. 2.193 Ac he haþ leue to lepen out as ofte as him *likiþ*,
A. 3.128 To vnfetere þe fals, fle where hym *lykiþ*.
A. 3.133 Heo is assoilid [as] as hireself *likiþ*.
A. 3.169 And ek grepe my gold & gyue it where þe *likiþ*.
A. 4.131 And loue shal lede þi land as þe lef *likeþ*.'
A. 6.80   He may do wiþ þe day sterre what hym dere *likiþ*;
A. 7.144 Of þ[i] flour, and þi flessh fecche whanne vs *likeþ*,
A. 7.275 Þanne may I di3te þi dyner as he dere *likeþ*.'
A. 8.26   And bad h[e]m begge boldely what [hem best] *likeþ*.
A. 8.58   To waxen & wanyen where þat god *likiþ*.
A. 8.122 'Were þou a prest, piers,' quaþ he, 'þou mi3test preche wh[an] þe
            liki[de];
A.10.132 And lyuen as here law[e] wil[e]; it *likeþ* god almi3ty
A.10.149 And so seiþ þe sauter, se it whanne þe *likiþ*:
A.12.1   'Crist wot,' quod clergie, 'knowe wit 3if þe *lyke*,
A.12.37   Or wycke 3if I wolde, wheþer me *lyked*.
A.12.51   'Þou shalt wende with wil,' quod she, 'whiles þat him *lykyþ*,
A.12.112 To lyue as þat lord *lykyþ* þat lyf in hem putte:
B.Pr.60   Glosed þe gospel as hem good *liked*;
B.Pr.72   Lewed men leued [hym] wel and *liked* hi[s speche];
B.Pr.149 For a cat of a [court] cam whan hym *liked*
B.Pr.163 Boþe in wareyne and in waast where hem [leue] *like[þ]*;
B.Pr.173 And peeren in his presence þe while hym pleye *likeþ*,
B.Pr.206 But suffren as hymself wolde to [slen þat] hym *likeþ*,
B. 1.28   Dide by hise dou3tres þat þe deuel *liked*;
B. 1.43   '[A] madame, mercy', quod I, 'me *likeþ* wel youre wordes.
B. 2.234 Ac he haþ leue to lepen out as ofte as hym *likeþ*,
B. 3.18   To be wedded at þi wille and wher þee leef *likeþ*
B. 3.139 To vnfettre þe fals, fle where hym *likeþ*.
B. 3.144 She is assoiled as soone as hireself *likeþ*.
B. 3.182 And [ek] griped my gold [and] gyue it where þee *liked*.
B. 4.36   Ac [þ]ere is loue and leautee [hem *likeþ*] no3t come þere:
B. 4.148 And loue shal lede þi lond as þe leef *likeþ*.'
B. 6.157 Of þi flour and þi flessh, fecche whanne vs *likeþ*,
B. 6.291 [Th]anne may I di3te þi dyner as [þee] deere *likeþ*.'
B. 7.24   [And bad hem] buggen boldely [what] hem best *liked*
B. 7.140 'Were þow a preest, [Piers]', quod he, 'þow my3test preche [whan
            þee *liked*]
B. 8.51   God wole suffre wel þi sleuþe if þiself *likeþ*,
B. 9.193 A[c] if þei leden þus hir lif it *likeþ* god almy3ty,
B.10.98   Ther þe lord ne þe lady *likeþ* no3t to sitte.
B.10.192 Loke þow loue lelly if þee *likeþ* dowel,
B.11.24   That I ne shal folwe þi felawship, if Fortune it *like*.'
B.11.97   If hem *likeþ* and lest; ech a lawe it graunteþ,
B.12.166 Or þe swymmere þat is saaf by so hymself *like*,
B.12.167 Ther his felawe fleteþ forþ as þe flood *likeþ*
B.12.173 If hym *likeþ* and lest, þan any lewed [sooþly].
B.12.207 And as lawe *likeþ* to lyue or to deye:
B.13.186 And lere yow if yow *like* þe leeste point to knowe
B.13.263 Al londoun, I, leue, *likeþ* wel my wafres,
B.14.58   Ne deeþ drede [ne deuel], but deye as god *likeþ*
B.14.79   Diden dedly synne þat þe deuel *liked*,
B.14.167 And yliche witty and wise, yif þee wel hadde *liked*.
B.15.91   I shal tellen it for truþes sake; take hede whoso *likeþ*.
B.16.201 And þere hym *likede* and [he] louede, in þre persones hym
            shewede.

B.16.230 Ful trewe toknes bitwene vs is to telle whan me *likeþ*.
B.17.142 Til hym [*likede*] and liste to vnlosen his fynger,
B.17.146 And bitokneþ trewely, telle whoso *likeþ*,
B.17.351 That he ne may louye, and hym *like*, and lene of his herte
B.18.34   And legge it þer hym *likeþ*, and Lucifer bynde,
B.18.254 [And to haue out of helle alle þat hym *likeþ*].
B.18.374 And be at my biddyng wherso [best] me *likeþ*.
B.18.406 But leten hym lede forþ [what] hym *liked* and lete [what] hym
            liste.
B.20.156 This *likede* lif and his lemman fortune
B.20.309 Some *liked* no3t þis leche and lettres þei sente
C.Pr.58   Glosede þe gospel as hem good *likede*;
C.Pr.70   Lewed men leued hym wel and *lykede* his wordes.
C.Pr.170 For a Cat of a Court cam whan hym *likede*
C.Pr.172 And playde with somme perilously and potte hem þer hym *lykede*.
C.Pr.190 And apere in his presence þe while hym pleye *lyketh*
C. 1.22   And rekene hem by rewe: reherse hem wher þe *liketh*.
C. 1.41   'A madame, mercy,' [quod I], 'me *lyketh* wel 3oure wordes.
C. 2.244 Ac he hath leue to lep out as ofte as hym *liketh*,
C. 3.19   For to wedde at thy wille [and] where the leef *li[k]eth*
C. 3.44   Amonge kynges and knyhtes and clerkes and the *lyke*.'
C. 3.177 To vnfetere the fals, fle wher hym *liketh*,
C. 3.182 He is assoiled [as] sone as heresulue *lyketh*.
C. 3.228 And also gryp[en] my gold and gyue hit where þe *liked*.
C. 3.331 Bothe gyue and graunte there his grace *lyketh*
C. 4.36   Ac there is loue and leutee hit *lyketh* nat here hertes:
C. 4.145 And loue shal lede thi land as the leef *lyketh*.'
C. 5.41   Lyf þat me [*l]ykede* but in this longe clothes.
C. 7.253 And may lede in þat he loueth as here lef *lyketh*.
C. 7.293 To loke how me *liketh* hit,' and toek his leue at Peres.
C. 8.154 [Of] thy flour and thy flesch, feche whenne vs *liketh*
C. 8.255 "He þat hath shal haue and helpe þer hym *liketh*
C. 8.314 Thenne may y dyhte [þ]y dyner as me dere *lyketh*.'
C. 9.28   [And] bad hem bugge boldly what hem best *likede*
C. 9.146 And whenne hym *lyketh* and luste, his leue is to ryse
C.10.272 Ac they lyen le[i], here neyther *lyketh* other.
C.11.132 Lerne for to louie yf þe *lik[e]* dowel.
C.11.155 Bote thus hit bilongeth to bileue alle þat *liketh* dowel.
C.11.183 That y ne shal folowe thy felowschipe yf fortune [hit] *lyke*.'
C.11.185 'The man þat me *liketh* to helpe myhte nat myshappe.'
C.12.163 "Yf thow *likest* to lyue," quod god, "þe lyf þat is parfit,
C.14.113 Yf hym *liketh* and luste, thene eny lewede sothly.
C.14.146 And as þe lawe *lyketh* to lyue oþer to dye:
C.15.257 Ne d[e]th drede ne deuel, [but] deye as god *liketh*
C.16.178 And may nat be withoute a body to bere me where hym *liketh*.'
C.19.5   That that y sey is soeth se hoso *liketh*.'
C.19.116 Til hym *likede* and luste to vnlose that fynger
C.19.120 And bitokeneth trewly, telle hoso *liketh*,
C.19.145 And receue þat the fyngeres recheth and refuse, yf h[y]m *liketh*,
C.19.331 That he ne may louye, and hym *lyke*, and lene of his herte
C.20.33   And legge hit þere hym *liketh* and lucifer bynde
C.20.263 And to haue out [of helle] alle þat hym *liketh*.
C.20.449 Bote leten hym lede forth which hym luste and leue which hym
            likede.
C.22.156 This *likede* lyf and his lemman fortune
C.22.309 Somme *liked* nat this leche and letteres they sente

lykhame > *likame*; *likynde* > *likynge adj*

likyng ger1 *likinge ger.(1)* &> *likynge* A 2 lyking (1) lykyng (1); B 20
   likyng (10) likynge (10); C 20 likyng (4) lykyng (5) likynge (3)
   lykynge (8)
A.Pr.59   Manye of þise maistris may cloþe hem at *lyking*
A. 1.27   For loth, in his lyf dayes, for *lykyng* of drink
B.Pr.62   Manye of þise maistre[s mowe] cloþen hem at *likyng*
B. 1.27   For Lot, in hise lifdayes, for *likynge* of drynke,
B. 5.176 Forþi haue I no *likyng*, [leue me], wiþ þo leodes to wonye;
B. 9.184 Fo[r] lecherie in likynge is lymeyerd of handes,
B.10.310 And gret loue and *likynge* for ech [loweþ hym to] ooþer.
B.11.21   That leden þee wole to *likynge* al þi lif tyme'.
B.11.45   'That wit shal torne to wrecchednesse for wil to haue his *likyng*!'
B.11.49   I hadde no *likyng*, leue me, [þe leste] of hem to knowe.
B.11.422 Tho hadde he [litel] *likyng* for to lere þe moore.
B.12.110 To vnloken it at hir *likyng*, and to þe lewed peple
B.12.220 Why some be alou3 & some aloft, þi *likyng* it were;
B.13.343 Wiþ *likynge* of lecherie as by lokynge of his ei3e.
B.13.423 And han *likynge* to liþen hem [in hope] to do yow lau3e–
B.14.130 And greet *likynge* to lyue wiþouten labour of bodye,
B.14.263 In lond and in lordshipe and *likynge* of bodie
B.15.51   For swich a lust and *likyng* Lucifer fel from heuene:
B.15.67   For in þe *likynge* liþ a pride and licames coueitise
B.15.172 Ne no *likynge* haþ to lye ne laughe men to scorne.
B.16.32   Thoru3 *likynge* and lustes so loude he gynneþ blowe
B.20.71   Wiþ a lord þat lyueþ after *likyng* of body,

C. 2.77   'Al þat loueth and byleueth vp *lykyng* of mede,
C. 5.155 In scole is loue and louhnesse and *lykyng* to lerne.
C. 6.176 As in *likynge* of lecherye my lycames gultes
C. 6.194 Y hadde *likyng* to lythe of lecherye tales.
C. 7.74   And hath no *likynge* to lerne ne of oure lord to here
C. 7.83   And han *lykyng* to lythen hem in hope to do ȝow lawhe–
C. 9.203 Forsoken lond and lordschipe and *lykyng[*e*]* of body.
C.11.12 Þat [they] louyen lond and lordschipe and *lykynge* of body
C.11.80 The which is a *lykyng* and luste, þe loue of þe world.'
C.11.180 That lede þe wol to *lykynge* Al thy lyf tyme.'
C.11.262 As in *likyng* of lecherye no lyf denyede!
C.13.152 That ne lees the *lykynge* of lost of flesch, as hit were,
C.14.55 To v[n]louken hit at here *lykynge* the lewed to helpe,
C.15.166 To haue alle londes at thy *likyng* and the here lord make
C.16.103 In lond and in lordschipe [and] *lykynge* of body
C.16.176 Layk or leue, at my *lykyng* chese
C.16.213 For such a lust and *lykynge* lucifer ful fram heuene:
C.16.310 Hath he no *lykynge* to lawhe ne to likene men to scorne.
C.20.93 Bothe my lond and my licame at ȝoure *likynge* taketh hit.
C.22.71 With a lord þat lyueth aftur *likyng* of body

likynge ger2 *likinge ger.(2)*   B 1
B.13.287 In *likynge* of lele lif and a liere in soule;

likynge adj *likinge ppl.adj.*   B 1; C 4 lykynde (1) lykyng (2) lykyngest (1)
B.11.274 And lif moost *likynge* to god as luc bereþ witnesse:
C. 6.44   And louelokest to loke vppon a[nd] *lykyngest* abedde
C.10.285 That lecherye is a *lykyng* thynge, a lymȝerd of helle.
C.11.131 For loue is a *lykyng* thyng and loth for to greue.
C.18.78   And more *lykynde* to oure lord then lyue as kynde asketh

likynge prp *liken v.(2)*   C 1
C. 6.45   And *likynge* of such a lyf þat no lawe preiseth,

lykyngliche adv *likyngli adv.*   C 1
C.19.245 Lordliche for to lyue and *lykyngliche* be clothed

likkyng ger *likkinge ger.*   B 1
B.15.304 In *likkyng* and in lowynge, þer þei on laundes yede].

likne v *liknen v.(2)*   A 2 liknid; B 10 likne (2) likned (7) likneþ (1); C 13 likne (3) likened (1) lykened (1) likned (4) liknet (1) likneth (1) ylikned (2)
A. 9.34   Þe watir is *liknid* to þe world þat waniþ & waxiþ;
A. 9.37   Þe boot is *lik[nid]* to þe body þat britel is of kynde,
B. 8.38   The water is *likned* to þe world þat wanyeþ and wexeþ;
B. 8.41   The boot is *likned* to [þe] body þat britel is of kynde,
B.10.43 *Likne* men and lye on hem þat leneþ hem no ȝiftes.
B.10.282 Lewed men may *likne* yow þus, þat þe beem liþ in youre eiȝen,
B.12.269 Thus he *likneþ* in his logik þe leeste fowel oute.
B.15.111 [For ypocrisie] in latyn ys *likned* to a [loþly] dongehill
B.17.206 [For] to a torche or a tapur þe Trinite is *likned*,
B.17.281 For euery manere good [man may] be *likned*
B.19.89 Gold is *likned* to leautee þat laste shal euere
B.19.111 For wyn is *likned* to lawe and lifholynesse,
C. 7.23   Or lacke men or *likene* hem in vnlikyng manere
C.10.44 The water is *likned* to þe wor[l]d þat wanyeth and waxeth;
C.10.47 The boet is *liknet* to oure body þat bretil is of kynde,
C.14.168 Ac longe lybbynge men *lykened* men[nes] lyuynge
C.14.190 *Likneth* in here logik þe leste foul out[e].
C.16.266 And is *ylikned* in latyn to a lothly donghep
C.16.310 Hath he no lykynge to lawhe ne to *likene* men to scorne.
C.17.73 Me may now *likene* lettred men to a lasheborw oþer worse
C.17.83 Thus ar ȝe luyþer *ylikned* to lossheborw[e] sterlynges
C.19.172 For to a torche or a taper þe trinite is *likned*,
C.19.262 For euery manere goed man may be *likned* to a torche
C.21.89 Gold is *likened* to lewetee that laste shal euere
C.21.111 For wyn is *likned* to lawe and lyfholinesse

liknesse n *liknesse n.*   B 12; C 6 likenesse (2) liknesse (3) lyknesse (1)
B. 1.114 And fel fro þat felawshipe in a fendes *liknesse*
B. 1.121 But fellen out in fendes *liknesse* [ful] nyne dayes togideres
B. 9.67   And dooþ god forsaken hem þat he shoop to his *liknesse*:
B.10.371 And seiþ "slee noȝt þat semblable is to myn owene *liknesse*
B.11.187 And lokeþ on vs in hir *liknesse* and þat wiþ louely chere
B.11.233 For in hir *liknesse* oure lord [lome] haþ ben yknowe
B.11.243 And in þe apparaille of a pouere man and pilgrymes *liknesse*
B.12.279 Ne no creature of cristes *liknesse* withouten cristendom worþ saued.'
B.18.354 Thow, lucifer, in *liknesse* of a luþer Addere
B.18.356 And I in *liknesse* of a leode, þat lord am of heuene,
B.19.202 In *liknesse* of a lightnynge he lighte on hem alle
B.19.205 And was afered [for] þe light, for in fires *[lik]nesse*
C.12.122 For in here *likenesse* oure lord lome hath yknowe.
C.12.132 In þe parail of a pilgrime and in pore *likenesse*
C.17.179 And sothliche þat god sulue in suche a coluere *lyknesse*

C.20.328 'For god hath go,' quod gobelyne, 'in gome *liknesse*
C.21.202 In *liknesse* of a lihtnynge a lyhte on hem alle
C.21.205 And was afered for the lihte, for in fuyres *liknesse*

liknet > likne

lyme n *lim n.(1)*   A 3 lyme (1) lymes (2); B 6 lyme (3) lymes (3); C 8 lyme (2) lymes (6)
A. 5.80   Boþe his *lyme* & his lif was lost þoruȝ my tunge.
A. 7.116 'We haue none *[lymes]* to laboure wiþ, lord, ygracid be ȝe;
A. 7.180 And lame menis *lymes* wern li[þ]id þat tyme,
B. 5.100 That boþe lif and *lyme* is lost þoruȝ my speche.
B. 6.124 'We haue no *lymes* to laboure with; lord, ygraced be [y]e!
B.19.8   And riȝt lik in alle *[lymes]* to oure lord Ies[u].
B.19.105 Lif and *lyme* as hym liste he wroȝte.
B.20.77 Fooles fro þise fendes *lymes*, for Piers loue þe Plowman.
B.20.195 For þe *lyme* þat she loued me fore and leef was to feele
C. 8.8   And *lymes* to labory with and louede wel fare
C. 8.135 [We haue] none *lymes* to labory with, lord god we thonketh.'
C. 8.260 Thorw eny lele labour as thorw *lymes* and handes:
C. 9.103 And *lymes* to labory with and lollares lyf vsen
C.21.8   And riht lyke in alle *lymes* to oure lord iesu.
C.21.105 Lyf and *lyme* as hym luste he wrouhte.
C.22.77 Foles fro this fendes *lymes* for [Peres] loue the [plouhman].
C.22.195 For þe *lyme* þat she loued me fore and leef was to fele

lymeyerd n *lim n.(2)*   B 1; C 1 lymȝerd
B. 9.184 Fo[r] lecherie in likynge is *lymeyerd* of helle.
C.10.285 That lecherye is a lykyng thynge, a *lymȝerd* of helle.

lymytour n *limitour n.*   B 3 lymytour (2) lymitours (1); C 2 limitour (1) lymytour (1)
B. 5.139 On *lymitours* and listres lesynges I ymped
B.20.346 And at þe laste þis *lymytour*, þo my lord was oute,
B.20.362 'That is ouerlonge', quod þis *Lymytour*, 'I leue. I shal amende it!'
C.22.346 And at þe laste this *lymytour*, tho my lord was oute,
C.22.362 'That is ouerlonge,' quod this *lymitour*, 'y leue; y schal amenden hit!'

limȝerd > limeyerd

lynage n *linage n.*   A 1; B 2; C 4
A.10.37 Lif þat ay shal laste, & al his *lynage* aftir.
B. 9.49   Lif þat ay shal laste, [and] al his *lynage* after.
B.11.297 That haþ no lond ne *lynage* riche ne good loos of hise handes.
C. 5.26   'Thenne hastow londes to lyue by,' quod resoun, 'or *lynage* ryche
C. 9.196 Noyther of *lynage* ne of lettrure ne lyfholy as Ermytes
C. 9.198 Summe hadde lyflode of h[ere] *lynage* and of no lyf elles
C.13.111 That hath n[o] lond ne *lynage* ryche ne good los of his handes.

lynde n *linde n.*   A 1; B 2; C 2
A. 9.56   And vndir a *lynde* vpon a launde lenide I me a stounde
B. 1.156 Was neuere leef vpon *lynde* lighter þerafter,
B. 8.65   And vnder a *lynde* vpon a launde lened I a stounde
C. 1.152 Was neuer lef vppon *lynde* lyhtere theraftur\
C.10.64 And vnder a *lynde* vpon a launde lened y a stounde

lyne n *line n.(1)*   A 3 lyne (1) lynes (2); B 6 lyne (4) lynes (2); C 4 lyne (2) lynes (2)
A. 5.196 As whoso leide *lynes* to lacche wiþ [foules].
A. 8.93   In two *lynes* it lay & nouȝt o lettre more,
A.11.136 And lernide h[e]m lyuel & *lyne* þeiȝ I loke dymme.
B. 3.340 For þat *lyne* was no lenger at þe leues ende.
B. 5.348 As whoso leiþ *lynes* to lacche [wiþ] foweles.
B. 5.421 Ac in Canoun nor in decretals I kan noȝt rede a *lyne*.
B. 7.111 In two *lynes* it lay and noȝt a [lettre] moore,
B.10.184 And lerned hem leuel and *lyne* þouȝ I loke dymme.
B.13.151 Wiþ half a laumpe *lyne* in latyn, Ex vi transicionis,,
C. 3.492 That l[yne] no lengur aut at þe leues ende
C. 6.406 As hoso layth *lynes* for to lacche foules.
C. 9.285 In two *lynes* hit lay and nat a lettre more
C.11.124 And caste [mette] by squire bothe *lyne* and leuele.

lynnen n *linen n.*   A 4 lynen (2) lynene (2); B 5; C 3 lynnen (2) lynnene (1)
A.Pr.99 Wollene websteris and weueris of *lynen*,
A. 1.3   A louely lady of lire in *lynene* ycloþid
A. 1.18 Of [woll]ene, of *[lyn]ene*, of liflode at nede
A. 7.13 Lokiþ forþ ȝoure *lynen* & laboureþ þeron faste.
B.Pr.220 Wollen webbesters and weueres of *lynnen*,
B. 1.3   A louely lady of leere in *lynnen* ycloþed
B. 1.18 Of wollene, of *lynnen*, of liflode at nede
B.11.282 Ne lakkeþ neuere liflode, *lynnen* ne wollen:
B.11.289 Hem sholde lakke no liflode, neyþer *lynnen* ne wollen.
C. 1.3   A louely lady of [lere] in *lynnene* [y]clothed
C. 1.18 And brynge forth ȝoure bilyue, bothe *lynnen* and wollene,
C.13.103 Hem sholde neuere lacke lyflode, noþer *lynnen* ne wollen.

lynsed n *linsed n.* C 1
C.12.191   As *lynsed*, leksed and lentesedes all

lyoun n *lioun n.(1)* B 4 leons (1) leoun (1) lyoun (2); C 1 lyons
B.13.301   And as a *lyoun* on to loke and lordlich of speche;
B.15.204   And as a *lyoun* he lokeþ þer men lakken hise werkes.
B.15.277   Of *leons* ne of leopardes no liflode ne toke,
B.15.298   Ac þer ne was *leoun* ne leopard þat on laundes wenten,
C. 9.197   That wonede whilom in wodes with beres and *lyons*.

lippe n *lippe n.(2)* B 4; C 4 lippe (1) lyppe (3)
B. 2.35   That he shal lese for hire loue a *l[i]ppe* of Caritatis.
B. 5.247   And lene folk þat lese wole a *lippe* at euery noble.
B.10.400   Whan þei shal lif lete [a *lippe* of goddes grace]–
B.15.502   Han a *lippe* of oure bileue, þe lightlier me þynkeþ
C. 2.37   He shal lese for here loue [a] *lippe* of trewe charite.
C. 6.245   Y lene folk þat lese wole a *lyppe* [at] vch a noble.
C.17.253   Haen a *lyppe* of oure bileue, the lihtlokour me thynketh

lippes n *lippe n.(1)* A 4; B 4; C 4 lippes (2) lyppes (2)
A.Pr.87   A[c] nou3t for loue of oure lord vnlose here *lippes* ones.
A. 5.66   His body was bolnid for wr[aþþe] þat he bot his *lippe[s]*,
A. 7.166   And hitte hunger þerwiþ amydde hise *lippes*,
A. 7.246   And sende þe of his saus to sauoure þi *lippes*,
B.Pr.214   [Ac] no3t for loue of oure lord vnlose hire *lippes* ones.
B. 5.83   His body was [b]ollen for wraþe þat he boot hise *lippes*,
B. 6.262   And sende þee of his Sauce to sauore þi *lippes*,
B.18.52   And poison on a poole þei putte vp to hise *lippes*
C.Pr.164   And nat for loue of oure lord vnlose here *lyppes* ones.
C. 6.104   And with a niuilyng[e] nose, nippynge his *lippes*.
C. 8.272   And sende the of his sauce [t]o sauery with thy *lyppes*
C.20.52   And with a pole poysen potten vp to his *lippes*

lyppeth > lepen; lire > leere

lisse n *lisse n.* A 1; B 2; C 4 lisse (2) lysse (2)
A.10.30   Þe lord of lif & of li[3t], of *lisse* & of peyne.
B. 9.29   Lord of lif and of li3t, of *lisse* and of peyne.
B.18.227   Shal lere hem what langour is and *lisse* wiþouten ende.
C. 1.199   So loue is lecche of lyf and *lysse* of alle payne
C. 6.314   Then in *lysse* to lyue and lese lyf and soule.'
C.10.155   Lord of lyf and of lyht, of *lisse* and of payne.
C.20.236   Shal lere hem what l[angour] is and *lisse* withouten ende.

list n *liste n.(2)* A 2; B 2 list (1) liste (1); C 2 lyst (1) liste (1)
A. 5.124   To drawe þe *list* along, þe lengere it semide;
A. 6.5   He bar a burdoun ybounde wiþ a brood *list*,
B. 5.208   To drawe þe [*list*] along, þe lenger it semed;
B. 5.517   He bar a burdoun ybounde wiþ a brood *liste*,
C. 6.216   To drawe the *lyst* along the lengur hit semede;
C. 7.162   He bar a bordoun ybounde with a brood *liste*,

list v *listen v.(1)* A 2; B 12 lest (2) list (4) liste (6); C 15 lust (6) luste (9)
A.Pr.37   And haue wyt at wille to wirche 3if hem *list*.
A. 3.148   She let lawe as hire *list* & louedaies makiþ;
B.Pr.37   And han wit at wille to werken if [hem *liste*].
B.Pr.172   And if hym *list* for to laike þanne loke we mowen
B. 1.150   And alle hise werkes he wrou3te with loue as hym *liste*.
B. 3.158   She ledeþ lawe as hire *list* and louedaies makeþ,
B.11.97   If hem likeþ and *lest*; ech a lawe it graunteþ,
B.11.428   Lat hym ligge, loke no3t on hym til hym *list* aryse.
B.12.173   If hym likeþ and *lest*, þan any lewed [sooþly].
B.17.142   Til hym [likede] and *liste* to vnlosen his fynger,
B.18.406   But leten hym lede forþ [what] hym liked and lete [what] hym *liste*.
B.18.414   That loue, and hym *liste*, to laughynge ne brou3te;
B.19.105   Lif and lyme as hym *liste* he wro3te.
B.20.18   And if hym *list* for to lape þe lawe of kynde wolde
C.Pr.177   We myhte be lordes alofte and lyue as vs *luste*.'
C.Pr.189   And yf [hym] *lust* for to layke than loke we mowe
C. 3.171   Lyggeth by here, when hem *lust*, lered and lewed.
C. 3.196   And le[deth] þe lawe as here *luste* and louedayes maketh,
C. 9.146   And whenne hym lyketh and *luste*, his leue is to ryse
C.10.96   Lordes þat lyuen as hem *lust* and no lawe acounten,
C.11.74   Ac *lust* no lord now ne lettred man of suche lore to here
C.13.235   Lat hym lygge, lok nat on hym til hym *luste* [a]ryse.
C.14.113   Yf hym liketh and *luste*, then eny lewede sothly.
C.15.24   And so y musede vppon þis matere þat me *lust* to slepe.
C.19.116   Til hym likede and *luste* to vnlose that fynger
C.20.449   Bote leten hym lede forth which hym *luste* and leue which hym likede.
C.20.457   That loue, and hym *luste*, to l[a]u[h]ynge [ne] brouhte;
C.21.105   Lyf and lyme as hym *luste* he wrouhte.
C.22.18   And yf [hym] *lust* for to lape the lawe of kynde wolde

listneþ v *listen v.(2)* B 3 listnede (1) listneþ (2); C 2 lystnede (1) lustneth (1)
B.14.47   But I [*listnede* and] lokede what liflode it was
B.14.311   [For] lordes alloweþ hym litel or *listneþ* to his reson;
B.18.273   '*Listneþ*!' quod lucifer, 'for I þis lord knowe;
C.15.248   And y *lystnede* and lokede what lyflode hit were
C.20.295   '*Lustneth*!' quod lucifer, 'for y this lord knowe;

listres n *lister n.* B 1
B. 5.139   On lymitours and *listres* lesynges I ymped

lite adj *lite adj.(1)* B 1; C 3 lyte (2) litte (1)
B.13.267   And werkmen were agast a *lite*; þis wole be þou3t longe:
C. 1.140   To *lyte* [Latyn þow] lernedest, [leode], in thy 3owthe:
C. 8.262   That here lyflode be lene and *lyte* worth here clothes.'
C. 9.208   Long labour and *litte* wynnynge and at the laste they aspyde

litel adj *litel adj.* A 4; B 22; C 23 litel (17) lytel (5) litle (1)
A. 2.150   Soþnesse sei3 hem wel & seide but *litel*,
A. 3.194   To leuen his lordsshipe for a *litel* siluer,
A.10.102   Þou mi3test lese þi lou3nesse for a *litel* pride.
A.10.116   Loke þou grucche nou3t on god þei3 he gyue þe *litel*;
B.Pr.191   For bettre is a *litel* los þan a long sorwe.
B. 1.141   To *litel* latyn þow lernedest, leode, in þi youþe:
B. 2.189   Sothnesse sei3 hem wel and seide but *litel*,
B. 3.207   To leuen his lordshipe for a *litel* siluer,
B. 9.80   For moore bilongeþ to þe *litel* barn er he þe lawe knowe
B.10.91   And whoso *litel* weldeþ [wisse] hym þerafter,
B.10.317   *Litel* hadde lordes to doon to 3yue lond from hire heires
B.10.395   Ac of fele witty in feiþ *litel* ferly I haue
B.10.478   Right so lewed [laborers] and of *litel* knowyng
B.11.221   Is *litel* alowaunce maad, but if bileue hem helpe;
B.11.422   Tho hadde he [*litel*] likyng for to lere þe moore.
B.12.181   And haþ no contricion er he come to shrifte; & þanne kan he *litel* telle
B.12.253   That euere he gadered so grete and gaf þerof so *litel*,
B.13.8   And [peple] þat was pouere at *litel* pris þei sette,
B.13.149   For he þat loueþ þee leelly *litel* of þyne coueiteþ.
B.14.245   And þou3 Auarice wolde angre þe poore he haþ but *litel* my3te,
B.14.250   Lecherie loueþ hym no3t for he 3yueþ but *litel* siluer.
B.15.423   To lyue by *litel* and in lowe houses by lele mennes almesse.
B.15.476   Ri3t so rude men þat *litel* reson konneþ
B.17.49   Tho þat lernen þi lawe wol *litel* while vsen it.'
B.20.148   Thus relyede lif for a *litel* fortune
B.20.367   As frere[s] of oure Fraternytee, for a *litel* siluer'.
C. 1.107   Lucifer, louelokest tho, ac *litel* while it duyred.
C. 2.203   Sothnesse seyh hem [wel] and sayde but *litel*,
C. 3.131   Lacked here a *litel* w[iht] for þat she louede gyle
C. 3.264   To lete so his lordschipe for a *litel* mone.
C. 3.391   He þat mede may lacche maketh *lytel* tale;
C.11.72   And yf thow haue *litel*, leue sone, loke þo þy lyue
C.11.226   For of fele witty in faith *litel* ferly y haue
C.11.299   Ac lewede laborers of *litel* vnderstondyng
C.12.26   And now y am pore and penyles at *litel* pris he sette[th] me.
C.12.222   That lihtlich launseth vp *litel* while dureth
C.14.121   And hath no contricion ar he come to shrifte; and thenne can he *lytel* telle,
C.15.10   And peple þat was pore at *litel* pris [þei] setten
C.15.153   'That loueth lely,' quod he, 'bote *litel* thyng coueyteth.
C.16.85   And thogh Auaryce wolde Angry [þe] pou[r]e he hath bote *lytel* myhte
C.16.90   Lecherye loueth no pore for he hath bote *litel* siluer
C.16.371   As y tolde þe with tonge a *litel* tyme ypassed;
C.17.24   Bote thre *litle* loues and loue was here soule.
C.17.237   Alle londes into loue And þat in *lytel* tyme;
C.18.70   Summe *litel*, somme large, ylik apples of kynde,
C.19.47   Tho þat lerneth thy lawe wollen *litel* while hit vse.'
C.19.94   And 3ut bote they l[e]ue lelly vpon þat *litel* baby,
C.22.148   Thus relyed lyf for a *litel* fo[rtune].
C.22.367   [As] freres of oure fraternite for a *litel* suluer'.

litel adv *litel adv.* A 5; B 13; C 17 litel (11) lytel (6)
A. 4.51   And seide, 'hadde I loue of my lord þe king, *litel* wolde I recche
A. 8.119   Þou art le[ttr]id a *litel*; who lernide þe on boke?'
A. 8.124   'Lewide lorel,' quaþ peris, '*litel* lokest þou on þe bible.
A.11.29   *Litel* is he louid or lete by þat suche a lessoun techiþ,
A.11.49   *Litel* louiþ he þat lord þat leniþ hym al þat blisse,
B. 4.65   And seide, 'hadde I loue of my lord þe kyng *litel* wolde I recche
B. 7.137   Thow art lettred a *litel*; who lerned þee on boke?'
B. 7.142   'Lewed lorel!' quod Piers, '*litel* lokestow on þe bible.
B.10.37   *Litel* is he loued [or lete by] þat swich a lesson [techeþ],
B.10.63   *Litel* loueþ he þat lord þat lent hym al þat blisse
B.10.37   'This is a long lesson', quod I, 'and *litel* am I þe wiser;
B.13.189   For al þat Pacience me profreþ proud am I *litel*.
B.14.34   Thanne laughed haukyn a *litel* and lightly gan swerye;

B.14.311 [For] lordes alloweþ hym *litel* or listneþ to his reson;
B.16.139 Til it bifel on a friday, a *litel* bifore Pasqe,
B.17.93 'Haue hem excused', quod he; 'hir help may *litel* auaille.
B.19.451 For þe comune', quod þis Curatour, 'counten ful *litel*
B.20.27 And bete men ouer bittre, and so[m body] to *litel*,
C. 3.393 How þat cliauntes acorde acounteth mede *litel*.
C. 4.69 'Hadde y loue of [my] lord *litel* wolde y reche
C. 5.3 And *lytel* ylet by, leueth me for sothe,
C. 5.31 The whiche is lollarne lyf þat *lytel* is preysed
C. 5.163 *Lytel* hadde lordes ado to 3eue lond fro [here] heyres
C. 6.145 How *lytel* y louye letyse at þe style.
C.10.258 Of kyn ne of kynrede counteth men bote *litel*.
C.11.32 *Litel* is he loued or leet [by] among lordes at festes.
C.11.45 *Lytel* loueth he þat lord þat lente hym al þat blisse
C.11.312 Clergie [and] his conseile y counted ful *litel*.
C.16.121 Thenne is [hit] goed by goed skill, thouh hit greue a *litel*,
C.16.145 For lordes alloueth hym *litel* or leggeth ere to his resoun;
C.17.54 Yf lewede men knewe this latyn a *litel* they wolden auysen hem
C.18.166 This biful on a fryday, a *litel* bifore Pasche,
C.20.357 (A *litel* y ouerleep for lesynges sake,
C.21.451 [For] the comune,' quod this curatour, 'counteth ful *litel*
C.22.27 And bete men ouer bitere and som body to *litel*

lyth n *lith n.(3)* &> *lyen,ligge* B 1
B.16.181 'Thre leodes in oon *lyth*, noon lenger þan ooþer,

lithe(d > liþen,liþeþ

liþen v *lithen v.(3)* &> *liþeþ* B 2 liþed (1) liþen (1); C 5 lythe (1) lythed (1) lythen (3)
B.13.423 And han likynge to *liþen* hem [in hope] to do yow lau3e–
B.13.455 Leden þat [*liþed*] hem to Luciferis feste
C. 6.194 Y hadde likyng to *lythe* of lecherye tales.
C. 7.83 And han lykyng to *lythen* hem in hope to do 3ow lawhe–
C. 7.115 Leden tho that *lythed* hem to luciferes feste
C.10.65 To *lythen* here layes and here louely notes.
C.11.75 Bote *lythen* how þey myhte lerne leest go[e]d spene.

lyther adv *lithere adv. cf. luþer* C 1
C.10.166 Such *lyther* lyuyng men lome been ryche

lithereth v *litheren v.(1)* C 1
C.18.48 So this lordeynes *lithereth* þerto þat alle þe leues falleth

liþeþ v *lithen v.(2) cf. liþen* A 1 liþid; B 2 liþed (1) liþeþ (1); C 4 lithe (1) lythed (2) lytheth (1)
A. 7.180 And lame menis lymes wern *li[þ]id* þat tyme,
B.13.437 And for loue of [hir] lorde *liþeþ* hem at festes;
B.13.451 That bi his lyue *liþed* hem and loued hem to here.
C. 7.97 And for loue of here lord *ly[th]eth* hem at festes;
C. 7.111 That by his lyue *l[yth]ed* hem and louede hem to here.
C. 7.118 For a *lythed* and louede þat godes lawe despiseth:
C.19.71 With wyn and with oyle his woundes he gan *li[th]e*,

litle > litel

litlum adv *litlum adv.* B 2; C 2 littelum
B.15.610 Lere hem *litlum* and litlum et in Iesum Christum filium,
B.15.610 Lere hem litlum and *litlum* et in Iesum Christum filium,
C.17.318 Lere hem *littelum* and littelum [et] in iesum christum filium
C.17.318 Lere hem littelum and *littelum* [et] in iesum christum filium

litte > lite; littelum > litlum; lyue > leuen,lif,lyuen; lyuel > leuel

lyuen v *liven v.(1)* A 33 libbe (5) libben (2) libbeþ (2) libbyng (1) libbiþ (1) lyue (12) lyued (2) lyuede (1) lyuen (6) lyuest (1); B 116 libbe (4) libben (2) libbeth (1) libbeþ (6) libbynge (5) lybbynge (1) lyue (42) lyued (7) lyuede (11) lyueden (4) lyuen (15) lyuest (2) lyueþ (12) lyuynge (4); C 151 leue (6) leuen (1) leuene (1) leueth (3) libbe (2) lybbe (1) libbeth (3) libbyng (1) lybbynge (1) liue (1) lyue (52) lyued (1) lyuede (21) lyueden (2) lyuen (20) lyuene (3) lyuest (1) lyueth (24) lyuyng (1) lyuynge (4) yleued (1) ylyued (1)
A.Pr.26 Al for loue of oure lord *lyuede* wel streite
A. 2.89 For al þe lesinges þou *lyuest*, & leccherous werkis;
A. 2.148 Of many maner of m[e]n þat on þis molde *libbeþ*.
A. 3.214 No wi3t as I wene wiþoute mede mi3te *libbe*.'
A. 4.96 As longe as I *lyue* but more loue it make.'
A. 4.154 For as longe as I *lyue* l[et]e þe I [n]ile.'
A. 4.158 As longe as I *lyue* libbe we togideris.'
A. 4.158 As longe as I lyue *libbe* we togideris.'
A. 5.36 'And *libbe* as 3e lere vs, we wile leue 3ow þe betere'.
A. 5.98 Þus I *lyue* loueles, [lyk] a lyþer dogge,
A. 5.208 For his liþer lif þat he *lyued* hadde,
A. 7.17 As longe as I *lyue* for þe lordis loue of heuene.
A. 7.21 And alle maner of men þat be þe mete *libbiþ*,
A. 7.62 And alle kyne crafty men þat conne *lyue* in treuþe,
A. 7.63 I shal fynde hem foode þat feiþfulliche *libbeþ*,

A. 7.134 Shuln haue of myn almesse al þe while I *libbe*,
A. 7.273 Be þis liflode I mote *lyue* til lammasse tyme;
A. 7.291 Laboureris þat haue no land [to] *lyue* on [but] here handis
A. 8.63 Alle *libbyng* laboureris þat lyuen be here hondis,
A. 8.63 Alle libbyng laboureris þat *lyuen* be here hondis,
A. 8.65 And *lyuen* in loue & [in] lawe, for here lou3 herte
A. 8.72 Þei *lyue* nou3t in loue, ne no lawe holden.
A. 8.80 Þo þat *lyuen* þus here lif mowe loþe þe tyme
A. 9.49 Ac 3if I may *lyuen* & loken I shal go lerne betere.
A. 9.84 [3]e wise suffriþ þe vnwise with 3ow to *libbe*,
A.10.132 And *lyuen* as here law[e] wil[e]; it likeþ god almi3ty
A.10.144 Into þis wrecchide world to wonen & to *libben*
A.11.90 But he *lyue* in þe leste degre þat longiþ to dowel
A.11.210 Þat out of couent & cloistre coueiten to *libben*".
A.11.217 Þis is þe lif of þis lordis þat *lyuen* shulde wiþ dobet,
A.11.280 Þat hadde *lyued* al his lyf wiþ lesinges & þeft[e],
A.12.90 But *lyue* as þis lyf is ordeyned for the.
A.12.112 To *lyue* as þat lord lykyþ þat lyf in hem putte:
B.Pr.26 Al for loue of oure lord *lyueden* [wel] streyte
B.Pr.157 We my3te be lordes o lofte and *lyuen* at oure ese.'
B.Pr.223 Of alle kynne *lybbynge* laborers lopen forþ somme,
B. 2.125 For al þi lesynges þow *lyuest* and lecherouse werkes;
B. 2.187 [Of many maner man þat on þis molde *libbeth*],
B. 3.164 And al þe comune in care þat coueiten *lyue* in truþe.
B. 3.227 No wi3t, as I wene, wiþouten Mede may *libbe*.'
B. 4.109 As longe as [I *lyue*], but lowenesse hym borwe.'
B. 4.191 For as longe as I *lyue* lete þee I nelle.'
B. 4.195 Als longe as [I *lyue*] leue we togideres.'
B. 5.44 [*Lyue*] as ye leren vs; we shul leue yow þe bettre.'
B. 5.119 [Th]us I *lyue* louelees lik a luþer dogge
B. 5.150 Til þei be boþe beggers and by my spiritualte *libben*,
B. 5.288 And as longe as þow *lyuest* þerwith þow yeldest no3t but borwest;
B. 5.380 For his luþer lif þat he *lyued* hadde,
B. 6.18 As longe as I *lyue*, for þe lordes loue of heuene.
B. 6.19 And alle manere of men þat [by þe] mete *libbeþ*,
B. 6.36 Als longe as I *lyue* I shal þee mayntene.'
B. 6.68 And alle kynne crafty men þat konne *lyuen* in truþe,
B. 6.69 I shal fynden hem fode þat feiþfulliche *libbeþ*,
B. 6.143 In lecherie and in losengerie ye *lyuen*, and in Sleuþe,
B. 6.181 '[Lat] hem *lyue*', he seide, 'and lat hem ete wiþ hogges,
B. 6.289 By þis liflode [I moot] *lyue* til lammesse tyme,
B. 6.307 Laborers þat haue no land to *lyue* on but hire handes
B. 7.61 Alle *libbynge* laborers þat lyuen [by] hir hondes,
B. 7.61 Alle libbynge laborers þat *lyuen* [by] hir hondes,
B. 7.63 And *lyuen* in loue and in lawe, for hir loue hert[e]
B. 7.90 For [þei] *lyue* in no loue ne no lawe holde.
B. 7.98 [Tho] þat *lyue* þus hir lif mowe loþe þe tyme
B. 8.58 Ac if I may *lyue* and loke I shal go lerne bettre.'
B. 8.94 [Ye wise] suffreþ þe vnwise wiþ yow to *libbe*,
B. 9.64 That *lyuen* synful lif here hir soule is lich þe deuel.
B. 9.65 And alle þat *lyuen* good lif are lik to god almy3ty:
B. 9.110 [Dowel in þis world is trewe wedded *libbynge* folk],
B. 9.181 And þanne gete ye grace of god and good ynou3 to *lyue* wiþ.
B.10.25 And þat þei ben lordes of ech a lond þat out of lawe *libbeþ*:
B.10.39 But þoo þat feynen hem foolis, and wiþ faityng *libbeþ*
B.10.137 But he *lyue* in þe [leeste degre] þat longeþ to dowel
B.10.149 As longe as I *lyue*, boþe late and raþe,
B.10.304 That out of couent and cloistre coueiten to *libbe*.
B.10.421 That hadde *lyued* al his lif wiþ lesynges and þefte,
B.10.437 Ther are witty and wel *libbynge* ac hire werkes ben yhudde
B.10.441 And be allowed as he *lyued* so; for by luþere men knoweþ þe goode.
B.10.444 Forþi *lyue* we forþ wiþ [liþere] men; I leue fewe ben goode,
B.10.471 That inparfitly here knewe and ek *lyuede*.
B.11.19 For to *lyue* longe and ladies to louye,
B.11.177 Whoso loueþ no3t, leue me, he *lyueþ* in deeþ deyinge.
B.11.275 And is to mene to men þat on þis moolde *lyuen*,
B.12.34 And *lyue* forþ as lawe wole while ye lyuen boþe.
B.12.34 And lyue forþ as lawe wole while ye *lyuen* boþe.
B.12.62 And in lele *lyuynge* men and in lif holy,
B.12.188 That *lyuynge* after lettrure saue[d] hym lif and soule.
B.12.207 And as lawe likeþ to *lyue* or to deye:
B.12.267 To lowe *libbynge* men þe larke is resembled.
B.12.288 But *lyueþ* as his lawe techeþ and leueþ þer be no bettre,
B.13.200 'Me were leuere, by oure lord, and I *lyue* sholde,
B.13.281 And inobedient to ben vndernome of any lif *lyuynge*;
B.13.413 *Lyueþ* ayein þe bileue and no lawe holdeþ.
B.14.32 All þat *lyueþ* and lokeþ liflode wolde I fynde
B.14.40 Wherof or wherfore or wherby to *libbe*:
B.14.42 Fissh to *lyue* in þe flood and in þe fir þe Criket,
B.14.46 *Lyue* þoru3 leel bileue, [as oure lord] witnesseþ:
B.14.60 For if þow *lyue* after his loore, þe shorter lif þe bettre:
B.14.62 Ergo þoru3 his breeþ [boþe] men and beestes *lyuen*,

B.14.64	It is founden þat fourty wynter folk *lyuede* withouten tulying,
B.14.68	That manye wyntres men *lyueden* and no mete ne tulieden.
B.14.70	And *lyueden* wiþouten liflode and at þe laste þei woken.
B.14.71	And if men *lyuede* as mesure wolde sholde neuere moore be defaute
B.14.87	That whiles he *lyuede* he bileuede in þe loore of holy chirche.
B.14.118	That al hir lif han *lyued* in langour and defaute.
B.14.123	And diues in deyntees *lyuede* and in douce vie;
B.14.125	And hir [ladies] also *lyuede* hir lif in murþe.
B.14.130	And greet likynge to *lyue* wiþouten labour of bodye,
B.14.146	And *lyuen* as lawe techeþ, doon leaute to hem alle,
B.14.152	Boþe to riche and to noȝt riche þat rewfulliche *libbeþ*;
B.14.264	And for goddes loue leueþ al and *lyueþ* as a beggere.
B.14.325	So hard it is', quod haukyn, 'to *lyue* and to do synne.
B.15.93	Thoruȝ lele *libbynge* men þat goddes lawe techen,
B.15.152	And I haue *lyued* in londe', quod [I], 'my name is longe wille,
B.15.213	For he [*lyueþ*] noȝt in lolleris ne in londleperis heremytes
B.15.255	The mooste liflode he *lyueþ* by is loue in goddes passion;
B.15.284	Hadde a brid þat brouȝte hym breed þat he by *lyuede*,
B.15.293	Som þei solde and som þei soden, and so þei *lyued boþe*.
B.15.294	And also Marie Maudeleyne by mores *lyuede* and dewes,
B.15.297	That *lyueden* þus for oure lordes loue many longe yeres.
B.15.314	Til briddes brynge vs [wherby] we sholde *lyue*.
B.15.326	Who parfourneþ þis prophecie of þe peple þat now *libbeþ*,
B.15.366	And what to leue and to *lyue* by; þe lond was so trewe.
B.15.391	Allas, þanne, but oure looresmen *lyue* as þei leren vs,
B.15.423	To *lyue* by litel and in lowe houses by lele mennes almesse.
B.15.497	And as hymself seide [so] to *lyue* and dye:
B.15.533	It is ruþe to rede how riȝtwise men *lyuede*,
B.15.556	And *lyuen* as Leuitici as oure lord [yow] techeþ:
B.15.564	Takeþ hire landes, ye lordes, and leteþ hem *lyue* by dymes.
B.15.582	And Iewes *lyuen* in lele lawe; oure lord wroot it hymselue
B.17.126	Alle þat *lyuen* in Feiþ and folwen his felawes techynge.'
B.17.312	Yuele *lyuen* and leten noȝt til lif hem forsake.
B.18.30	Al þat *lyueþ* [or] lokeþ in londe [or] in watre.
B.18.106	But [as] barayne be and [by] vsurie [*libben*],
B.18.210	Sholde neuere riȝt riche man þat *lyueþ* in reste and ese
B.19.161	Thus cam it out þat crist ouercoom, recouerede and *lyuede*:
B.19.175	And now art *lyuynge* and lokynge and laste shalt euere."
B.19.217	Tresour to *lyue* by to hir lyues ende,
B.19.232	They lelly to *lyue* by labour of tonge,
B.19.237	And *lyue*, by þat labour], a lele lif and a trewe.
B.19.248	And some he lered to *lyue* in longynge to ben hennes,
B.19.352	Wiþ þe lord þat *lyueþ* after þe lust of his body,
B.19.405	But þow *lyue* by loore of Spiritus Iusticie,
B.19.468	And if me lakkeþ to *lyue* by þe lawe wole I take it
B.20.63	[Th]an to *lyue* lenger siþ [Leute] was so rebuked
B.20.71	Wiþ a lord þat *lyueþ* after likyng of body,
B.20.90	The lord þat *lyued* after lust þe peple aloud cryde
B.20.123	And armed hym in Auarice and hungriliche *lyuede*.
B.20.241	Lat hem be as beggeris or *lyue* by Aungeles foode.'
B.20.247	To lered ne to lewed, but *lyueþ* after youre reule.
B.20.311	Sire leef-to-*lyue*-in-lecherie lay þere and gronede;
C.Pr.28	Al for loue of oure lord *lyueden* [ful streyte]
C.Pr.102	That lewed men in mysbileue *lyuen* and dyen.
C.Pr.147	With lele labour to *lyue* while lif on londe lasteth.
C.Pr.177	We myhte be lordes alofte and *lyue* as vs luste.'
C. 1.16	For to worschipe hym þerwith þe whiles ȝe *lyuen* here.
C. 3.203	Religioun he al toreueth and oute of reule to *lybbe*.
C. 3.250	Wherby he may as a man for eueremore *lyue* aftur.
C. 3.282	Is no lede þat *leueth* þat he ne loueth mede
C. 3.289	Tha[t] vnlaufulliche *lyuen* haueth large handes
C. 3.297	And wot neuere witterly where he *lyue* so longe
C. 3.325	Richesse and resoun the while he ryhte *lyuede*
C. 3.328	And [soffrede] hym *lyu[e]* in mysbileue; y leue he be in helle.
C. 3.339	That [is] þe gyft þat god gyueth to alle lele *lyuynge*,
C. 3.360	And *lyue* as oure crede vs kenneth with crist withouten ende.
C. 3.420	And alle þat *leueth* on þat lond oure [lord] wol þat thow sle hit;
C. 4.104	As longe as y *lyue* for his luther werkes.'
C. 4.118	Til þat lerede men *lyue* as thei lere and teche
C. 4.194	Or lumbardus of lukes þat *leuen* by lone as iewes.'
C. 5.26	'Thenne hastow londes to *lyue* by,' quod resoun, 'or lynage ryche
C. 5.42	Yf y be labour sholde *lyuen* and lyflode deseruen,
C. 5.43	That laboure þat y lerned beste þerwith *lyuen* y sholde:
C. 5.44	And so y *leue* in london and [vp] lond[on] bothe.
C. 5.142	*Lyue* as ȝe lereth vs; we shall leue ȝow þe bettere.'
C. 5.174	Bred withouten beggynge to *lyue* by euere aftur
C. 6.67	Sholde no lyf *lyue* þat on his lond pissede.
C. 6.121	Withoute licence and leue, and herby *lyueth* wrathe.
C. 6.125	Or til they bothe be beggares and by [my] spiritual[t]e *libbe*
C. 6.292	Ȝut were me leuer, by oure lord, *lyue* al by wellecresses
C. 6.314	Then in lysse to *lyue* and lese lyf and soule.'
C. 6.343	And as longe as thow *lyuest* therwith þou ȝeldest nat bote borwest;

C. 6.349	What a lered ȝow to *lyue* with and to lette ȝow fram thefte.'
C. 7.73	*Lyueth* aȝen þe bileue and no lawe kepeth
C. 8.16	As longe as y *leue*, for [þe] lordes loue of heuene.
C. 8.57	And wende with alle tho þat wolden *lyue* in treuthe.'
C. 8.69	And alle kyne crafty men þat conne *lyue* in treuthe,
C. 8.70	Y shal fynde hem fode þat fayfulleche *libbeth*.
C. 8.194	There was no ladde þat *lyuede* þat ne lowede hym to Peres
C. 8.312	By this lyflode we mote *lyue* til l[a]masse tyme
C. 8.329	Laborers þat han no lond to *lyue* on but here handes
C. 9.19	And suche *liue* as þei lereth men oure lord treuthe hem graunteth
C. 9.43	Alle þe peple hadde pardon ynow þat parfitliche *lyuede*.
C. 9.58	Alle *libbyng* laborers þat lyuen with here handes
C. 9.58	Alle libbyng laborers þat *lyuen* with here handes
C. 9.104	*Lyuen* aȝen goddes lawe and þe lore of holi churche.
C. 9.151	And ca[rry]eth hit hoem to his cote and cast hym to *lyuene*
C. 9.158	And *lyueth* lyke a lollare, goddes lawe hym dampneth.
C. 9.159	'Forthy lollares þat *lyuen* in sleuthe and ouer land strikares
C. 9.167	For they *lyue* in no loue ne no lawe holden
C. 9.174	Tho þat *lyueth* thus here lyf, leue ȝe non other,
C. 9.194	Coueyten þe contrarye for as coterelles they *libbeth*.
C. 9.199	And summe *lyuede* by here letterure and labour of here handes
C. 9.201	And briddes brouhte somme bred þat they by *lyuede*.
C. 9.213	Aȝen þe lawe he *lyueth* yf latyn be trewe:
C. 9.292	Bote he þat euele *lyueth* euele shal ende.'
C.10.50	And lyf[holie]st of lyf þat *lyueth* vnder sonne.
C.10.57	Ac yf y may *lyue* and loke y shal go lerne bettere.'
C.10.79	And thorw lele labour *lyueth* and loueth his emcristene
C.10.96	Lordes þat *lyuen* as hem lust and no laue acounten,
C.10.126	And what lyues they *lyue* and what lawe þei vsen
C.10.166	Such lyther *lyuyng* men lome been ryche
C.10.172	By loue and by leute, þerby *lyueth* anima
C.10.173	And lyf *lyueth* by inwit and leryng of kynde.
C.10.203	Hoso *lyueth* in lawe and in loue doth wel
C.11.87	As longe as y *lyue*, bothe late and rathe,
C.11.178	For to *lyue* longe and ladyes to louye
C.11.200	Y leue neuere þat lord ne lady þat *lyueth* her [o]n erthe
C.11.234	Seldom ar they seyen so *lyue* as they lere;
C.11.253	That vnlawefulliche hadde *ylyued* al his lyf tyme
C.12.163	"Yf thow likest to *lyue*," quod god, "þe lyf þat is parfit,
C.12.186	At the laste launceth vp whereby we *lyuen* all.
C.12.228	And haen þe world at he[re] wille oþerwyse to *leuene*.
C.13.4	And ay þe lengere they *lyuede* the lasse goed they hadde:
C.13.79	The messager aren th[e] mendenantȝ þat *lyuen* by menne almesse,
C.13.193	Why he ne loueth thy lore and *leueth* as þou techest.'
C.14.9	Lowe the and *l[y]ue* forth in þe lawe of holy chirche;
C.14.13	Ac to louye and lene and *lyue* wel and byleue
C.14.127	That *lyuynge* Aftur lettrure saued hy[m] lyf and soule.
C.14.146	And as þe lawe lyketh to *lyue* oþer to dye:
C.14.168	Ac longe *lybbynge* men lykened men[nes] lyuynge
C.14.187	To lowe *lyuynge* men þe larke is resembled
C.14.210	Bote *lyue[th]* as his lawe t[echeth] and leueth þer be no bettere,
C.15.7	That y *lyuede* longe, leue me byhynde
C.15.93	And why a lereth nat as a lereth.' 'lat be,' quod pacience,
C.15.116	Ne *l[yu]eth* as ȝe lereth, as oure lord wolde:
C.15.169	As for here lord and here ledare and *l[y]ue* as thow techest.'
C.15.178	Me were leuere, by oure lord, and y *leue* sholde,
C.15.229	Wherof or wherfore [or] wherwith to *lyuene*:
C.15.244	*Leue* thorw lele bileue, As oure lord wittenesseth:
C.15.259	For if thow *lyu[e]* aftur his lore the shortere lyf þe betere:
C.15.261	Ergo thorw his breth bestes *lyueth*, bothe men and fisches,
C.15.263	Hit is founde þat fourty wynter folke *lyuede* and tylde nat
C.15.267	That manye wynter men *lyuede* and no mete ne tylede.
C.15.269	[And] *lyuede* withouten lyflode and [at] the laste awakede.
C.15.270	And yf men *lyuede* as mesure wolde sholde neuere[more] be defaute
C.15.294	That al here lyf haen *lyued* in langour and defaute.
C.15.299	And dyues in deyntees *lyuede* and [in] douce vie;
C.16.20	And yliche witty and wys and *lyue* withoute nede;
C.16.104	And for goddes loue leueth al and *lyueth* as a beggare.
C.16.271	And as lambes they loke and *ly[u]en* as wolues.
C.16.285	That *lyuen* aȝen holy lore and þe loue of charite.'
C.16.288	Ich haue *yleued* in londone monye longe ȝeres
C.16.359	Of tho that lelelyche *lyuen* and louen and byleuen:
C.17.7	Solitarie by hemsulue in here selles *lyuede*
C.17.20	Som they so[l]de and som they s[o]de and so they *lyuede* bothe.
C.17.21	Marie Maudeleyne by mores *lyuede* and dewes;
C.17.26	That *lyueden* thus for oure lordes loue monye longe ȝeres.
C.17.68	And fedde þat afyn[g]red were and in defaute *lyuede*.
C.17.103	And what *lyue* by and leue, the londe was so trewe.
C.17.116	Bo[t]e they fayle in philosophie and philosoferes *lyuede*.
C.17.131	God lereth no lyf to *l[eu]e* withouten lele cause.
C.17.139	And lele men *lyue* as lawe techeth and loue þerof aryseth
C.17.158	And *lyuen* oute of lele byleue for they l[e]ue on a mene.

C.17.160　And aftur his leryng they *lyue* and by lawe of kynde
C.17.193　And as hymsulue saide so to *lyue* and deye:
C.17.194　Hit is reuthe to rede how riht holy men *lyuede*,
C.17.219　And *lyuen* as leuitici, as oure lord ȝow techeth:
C.17.227　Taketh here londe[s], ȝe lordes, and lat hem *lyue* by dymes
C.17.228　Yf the kynges coueyte in cristes pees to *lyuene*.
C.17.249　And alle maner men þat on this molde *libbeth*.
C.17.292　And nameliche þer þat lewede *lyuen* and no lawe knoweth.
C.17.295　Iewes *lyuen* in þe lawe þat oure lord tauhte
C.18.2　　Thow couthest telle me and teche me [in] charite [to] *leue*.'
C.18.10　Thorw louely lokyng[e] hit *lyueth* and launseth vp blosmes,
C.18.73　And conforteth hem in here continence þat *lyuen* in
　　　　　　contemplacioun,
C.18.78　And more lykynde to oure lord then *lyue* as kynde asketh
C.18.197　How o lord myhte *lyue* [in] thre; y leue hit nat,' y sayde.
C.19.44　Ac for to bileue in o lord þat *lyueth* in thre persones
C.19.75　And lefte hym þere a lechyng to *lyue* yf he myhte
C.19.239　Moste lordliche *lyue* and ȝut [on] his lycame werie
C.19.245　Lordliche for to *lyue* and lykyngliche be clothed
C.19.292　That euele *lyuen* and leten nat t[il lif] hem forsake.
C.20.29　Alle þat *lyueth* or loketh a londe or a watre.
C.20.109　[But] as bareyne be and by vsure *libbe*,
C.20.219　For sholde neuere riȝt riche man þat *lyueth* in rest and hele
C.20.264　And y, boek, wol be brente bote he aryse to *lyue*
C.21.161　Thus cam hit out þat Crist ouerkam, rekeuerede and *lyuede*:
C.21.175　And now art *lyuynge* and lokynge and laste shalt euere."
C.21.217　Tresor to *lyue* by to here lyues ende
C.21.232　They leely to *lyue* bi labour of tonge
C.21.237　And *lyue* by þat laboure a leele lyf and a trewe.
C.21.248　And somme he [l]ered to *lyue* in longyng to be hennes,
C.21.352　With the lord þat *lyueth* aftur the lust of his body,
C.21.405　Bote thow *lyue* bi lore of spiritus Iusticie,
C.21.468　And yf me lakketh to *lyue* by þe lawe wol y take hit
C.22.63　Then to *lyue* lengere sethe leautee was so rebuked
C.22.71　With a lord þat *lyueth* aftur likyng of body
C.22.90　The lord þat *lyuede* aftur lust tho aloud cryede
C.22.123　And Armed hym in Auarice and hungriliche *lyuede*,
C.22.241　Lat hem be as beggares or *lyue* by angeles fode.'
C.22.247　To lered ne to lewed, but *lyueth* aftur ȝoure reule.
C.22.311　Sire l[ee]f-to-*lyue*-in-lecherye lay þer and groned;

lyues adj *lives adj. &> lif* B 1; C 1
B.19.159　And *lyues* and lokynge and aloud cride
C.21.159　And *lyues* and lokynge and aloude criede

lyuyng ger *livinge ger. &> lyuen* B 10 lyuyng (2) lyuynge (8); C 15
　　lyuynge
B.11.15　Pride of parfit *lyuynge* pursued hem boþe
B.11.33　And pride of parfit *lyuynge* to muche peril þee brynge.'
B.11.152　By loue and by lernyng of my *lyuynge* in truþe;
B.11.162　Ac þus leel loue and *lyuyng* in truþe
B.13.95　What he fond in a [forel of] a freres *lyuyng*,
B.15.392　And for hir *lyuynge* þat lewed men be þe loþer god agulten.
B.15.418　Peeren to Apostles þoruȝ hire parfit *lyuynge*.
B.15.424　Grace sholde growe and grene þoruȝ hir goode *lyuynge*,
B.19.379　Clennesse [of þe] comune and clerkes clene *lyuynge*
B.19.458　And coloureþ it for a konnynge and a clene *lyuynge*.'
C.2.57　Al þe riche retenaunce þat ro[t]eth hem o fals *lyuynge*
C.6.33　Ryche, and resonable and ryhtful of *lyuynge*;
C.6.286　'Now redily,'quod repentaunce, 'y haue reuthe of thy *lyuynge*.'
C.6.437　Of my luyther *ly[uynge]* in al my lyf tyme.
C.11.174　And pruyde-of-parfit-*lyuynge* pursuede me faste
C.11.192　And pruyde-of-parfit-*lyuynge* to moche perel the brynge.'
C.12.96　Of hym þat trauaileth [t]heron bote treuthe be his *lyuynge*.
C.13.116　Thorw here luyther *lyuynge* and lewede vnderstondynge.
C.13.230　[For] pruyde or presumpcioun of thy parfit *lyuynge*,
C.14.168　Ac longe lybbynge men lykened men[nes] *lyuynge*
C.15.102　What he fond in a forel of a frere[s] *lyuynge*,
C.16.37　Elles is al an ydel al oure *lyuynge* here,
C.16.154　That puyre pouerte and pacience was a louh *lyuynge* on erthe,
C.21.379　Clannesse of þe comune and clerkes clene *lyuynge*
C.21.458　And coloureth hit for a connyng and a clene *lyuynge*.'

*lyuynge > leuynges,lyuen,lyuyng; lixt > lyen; liȝe > lyen; liȝen > lyen,ligge;
liȝer(- > liere; liȝeþ > lyen*

lo exclam *lo interj.* A 1; B 21 lo (19) loo (2); C 29 lo (20) loo (9)
A.2.5　　'Loke on þi left half, & *lo* where he standis,
B.2.5　　'Loke [o]n þi left half, and *lo* where he stondeþ,
B.2.69　Thanne leep liere forþ and seide, '*lo*! here a chartre
B.5.38　"[*Lo*], þe leuere child þe moore loore bihoueþ";
B.10.27　"*Lo*!" seiþ holy lettrure, "whiche [lordes] beþ þise sherewes";
B.11.154　*Lo*! ye lordes, what leautee dide by an Emperour of Rome
B.12.40　[*Lo*]! what made lucifer to lese þe heiȝe heuene,
B.13.307　'*Lo*! if ye leue me noȝt, or þat I lye wenen,

B.14.38　And seide, '*lo*! here liflode ynogh, if oure bileue be trewe
B.14.112　And seiþ, "*lo*! briddes and beestes þat no blisse ne knoweþ
B.14.199　Ellis is al oure labour lost–*lo*, how men writeþ
B.15.80　That I lye noȝt, *loo*! for lordes ye plesen
B.15.269　[*Lo*]! in legenda sanctorum, þe lif of holy Seintes,
B.16.98　And seide hendeliche to hym, '*lo* me his handmaiden
B.16.259　'*Loo*!' quod he and leet me see; 'lord, mercy!' I seide.
B.17.23　*Lo*! here in my lappe þat leeued on þat charme,
B.17.78　And *lo*, here siluer', he seide, 'for salue to hise woundes.'
B.18.186　*Lo*! here þe patente', quod Pees, 'In pace in idipsum,
B.18.245　And *lo*! how þe sonne gan louke hire light in hirselue
B.18.249　*Lo*! helle myȝte nat holde, but opnede þo god þolede,
B.18.327　And seide to Sathan, '*lo*! here my soule to amendes
B.20.202　*Lo*! Elde þe hoore haþ me biseye.
C.2.5　　'Loke [o]n thy left half, and *loo* where he standeth,
C.2.71　Thenne lup lyare forth and saide, '*loo*! here a Chartre
C.3.485　'*Loo* what salamon sayth,' quod she, 'in sapiense in þe bible!
C.5.186　*Lo*! in heuene an heyh was an holy comune
C.6.55　"*Lo*! yf ȝe leue me nat or þat y lye wenen
C.8.258　*Lo*! what þe sauter sayth to swynkares with handes:
C.11.24　"*Lo*!" saith holy letrure, "whiche lordes beth this schrewes";
C.12.89　'*Lo*! lordes, what leute dede and leele dome yvsed.
C.12.219　*Lo*! lordes, lo! and ladyes, taketh hede:
C.12.219　Lo! lordes, *lo*! and ladyes, taketh hede:
C.12.231　*Lo*! lond ouerleyd with marl and with donge,
C.12.246　*Lo*, how pans purchaseth fayre places and d[r]ede,
C.13.21　*Lo*, how pacience and pouerte thise patriarkes releuede
C.15.237　And saide, '*lo*! here lyflode ynow yf oure beleue be trewe
C.15.288　And saith, "*loo*! briddes and bestes þat no blisse ne knoweth
C.16.40　Elles is alle oure labour loest–*loo* how men writeth
C.16.239　That y lye nat; *loo*! for lordes ȝe plese
C.16.242　*Lo*, what holy writ wittnesseth of wikkede techares:
C.17.65　*Lo* laurence for his largenesse, as holy lore telleth
C.18.131　And saide hendely to hym, '*lo* me his hondmayden
C.18.238　*Lo*! treys encountre treys,' quod he, 'in godhede and in manhede.'
C.18.275　'*Loo*!' quod he and lette me see: 'lord, mercy!' y saide,
C.19.4　　*Lo*, here the lettre,' quod he, 'a latyn and [an] ebrew;
C.19.24　*Lo*! here in my lappe þat leuede vpon þat lettre,
C.20.191　*Loo*! here þe patente,' quod pees, 'In pace in idipsum,
C.20.254　And *lo*! how þe sonne louke here lihte in heresulue
C.20.258　*Loo*! helle myhte nat holde, bote opened þo god tholede
C.20.370　'*Lo*! me here, ' quod oure lord, 'lyf and soule bothe,
C.22.202　*Lo*! Elde þe hore hath me byseye;

lobies n *lob n.* A 1; B 1; C 1
A.Pr.52　Grete *lobies* & longe þat loþ were to swynke
B.Pr.55　Grete *lobies* and longe þat loþe were to swynke
C.Pr.53　Grete *lobies* and longe þat loth were to swynke

lodesterre n *lodesterre n.* B 1; C 1
B.15.358　Han no bileue to þe lifte ne to þe [*lodesterre*].
C.17.96　Haen no byleue to þe lyft ne to þe *lodesterr[e]*.

*loef > loof; loerd > lord; loes > losse; loest > lesen; loeth > looþ; loethliche
> loþly; lof > loof*

lofte n *loft n.* A 1; B 4
A.1.88　He is a god be þe gospel on ground & on *lofte*,
B.Pr.157　We myȝte be lordes o *lofte* and lyuen at oure ese.'
B.1.90　He is a god by þe gospel, a grounde and o *lofte*,
B.5.352　For to liften hym o *lofte* and leyde hym on his knowes.
B.18.45　Boþe as long and as large bi *lofte* and by grounde.'

loggyng ger *logginge ger.* A 1
A.12.44　And his *loggyng* is with lyf þat lord is of erþe,

logh > lowe

logyk n *logike n.* A 1 logik; B 9 logik (3) logyk (6); C 4 logik (1) logyk
　　(3)
A.11.128　*Logik* I lerid hire, & al þe lawe aftir,
B.10.176　*Logyk* I lerned hire, and [al þe lawe after],
B.11.219　Thanne is bileue a lele help, aboue *logyk* or lawe.
B.11.220　Of *logyk* [ne] of lawe in legenda sanctorum
B.11.222　For it is ouerlonge er *logyk* any lesson assoille,
B.11.224　Boþe *logyk* and lawe, þat loueþ noȝt to lye,
B.12.97　Forþi lakke þow neuere *logik*, lawe ne hise custumes,
B.12.269　Thus he likneþ in his *logik* þe leeste fowel oute.
B.20.250　Wiþ þat ye leue *logik* and lerneþ for to louye
B.20.274　And lerne *logyk* and lawe and ek contemplacion,
C.11.116　*Logyk* y lerned here and al þe lawe aftur
C.14.190　Likneth in here *logik* þe leste foul out[e].
C.22.250　With þat ȝe l[e]ue *logyk* and lerneth for to louye.
C.22.274　And lerne *logyk* and lawe and eke contemplacioun

lok n *lok n.(2)* &> *loken* A 1; B 2 lok (1) lokes (1); C 2 lok (1) lokes (1)

A. 1.176   Þat is þe *lok* of loue þat letiþ out my grace
B. 1.202   [Th]at is þe *lok* of loue [þat] leteþ out my grace
B.13.367   Or pryueliche his purs shook, vnpikede hise *lokes*.
C. 1.197   Þat is þe *lok* of loue [þat] vnloseth grace
C. 6.266   Or priueliche his pors shoke, vnpiked his *lokes*.

loken v *loken v.(2)* A 34 loke (20) loken (1) lokest (1) lokide (10) lokis (1) lokiþ (1); B 80 loke (37) loked (21) lokede (3) loken (4) lokestow (1) lokeþ (12) lokynge (2); C 74 lok (2) loke (36) loked (3) lokede (18) loken (3) loketh (9) lokynge (2) look (1)

A.Pr.9   And as I lay & lenide & *lokide* on þe watris
A. 1.134   *Loke* þou suffre hym to seyn & siþþe lere it aftir.
A. 1.141   *Lokide* on vs wiþ loue, & let his sone deiȝe
A. 1.183   I may no lengere lenge; now *loke* þe oure lord.'
A. 2.5   'Loke on þi left half, & lo where he standis,
A. 2.7   I *lokide* on [my] left half as þat lady me tauȝte,
A. 2.100   Ȝif any Leaute wile *loke* þei ligge togidere.
A. 2.120   To lundoun to *loke* ȝif þat lawe wolde
A. 2.159   But riȝt as þe lawe *lokis* let falle on hem alle.'
A. 2.186   For to wone wiþ hem, watris to *loke*.
A. 3.248   *Loke* þou kille þe king; coueite nouȝt hise godis;
A. 4.47   I am not hardy [for hym vnneþe] to *loke*.'
A. 5.46   And lay longe er heo *lokide*, & 'lord mercy' criede,
A. 5.65   So *lokide* he wiþ lene chekis, lourande foule.
A. 5.108   So hungirly & holewe sire heruy hym *lokide*.
A. 5.116   And was his prentis ypliȝt his profit to *loke*.
A. 5.233   Robert þe robbour on reddite *lokide*,
A. 6.62   *Loke* þou breke no bowis þere but it be þin owene.
A. 6.65   Leue hem on þi left half, & *loke* nouȝt þereaftir.
A. 6.69   *Loke* þou plukke no plant[e] þere for peril of þi soule.
A. 6.71   [And] *loke* þat þou leiȝe nouȝt for no manis biddyng.
A. 7.13   *Lokiþ* forþ ȝoure lynen & laboureþ þeron faste.
A. 7.39   *Loke* þou tene no tenaunt but treuþe wile assent,
A. 7.162   Þat he *lokide* lik a lanterne al his lif aftir.
A. 7.173   Þat hunger was not hardy on hem for to *loke*.
A. 7.299   Suche lawis to *loke* laboureris to chast[e].
A. 7.301   Ne stryue aȝen þe statut, so sternely he *lokide*.
A. 8.14   *Loke* on þat o lawe, & lere men þat oþer,
A. 8.124   'Lewide lorel,' quaþ peris, 'litel *lokest* þou on þe bible;
A. 9.49   Ac ȝif I may lyuen & *loken* I shal go lerne betere.
A.10.92   *Loke* þou wisse þi wyt & þi werkis aftir;
A.10.116   *Loke* þou grucche nouȝt on god þeiȝ he gyue þe litel;
A.11.98   But al lauȝinge he loutide & *lokide* vpon studie
A.11.136   And lernide h[e]m lyuel & lyne þeiȝ I *loke* dymme.
B.Pr.9   And as I lay and lenede and *loked* on þe watres
B.Pr.123   Thanne *loked* vp a lunatik, a leene þyng wiþalle,
B.Pr.152   'For doute of diuerse d[e]des we dar noȝt wel *loke*,
B.Pr.172   And if hym list for to laike þanne *loke* we mowen
B. 1.146   *Loke* þow suffre hym to seye and siþen lere it after.
B. 1.167   *Loked* on vs wiþ loue and leet his sone dye
B. 1.209   I may no lenger lenge; now *loke* þee oure lord.'
B. 2.5   'Loke [o]n þi left half, and lo where he stondeþ,
B. 2.7   I *loked* on my left half as þe lady me tauȝte
B. 2.136   If any [lewte] wol *loke* þei ligge togideres.
B. 2.156   To london to *loken* if [þat] lawe wolde
B. 2.198   But riȝt as þe lawe [*lokeþ*] lat falle on hem alle.'
B. 2.227   [For to] wonye with hem watres to *loke*.
B. 3.271   For Mede ne for monee *loke* þow destruye it.
B. 3.341   Hadde she *loked* þat [left] half and þe leef torned
B. 4.60   I am noȝt hardy for hym vnneþe to *loke*.'
B. 4.173   And modiliche vpon Mede wiþ myȝt þe kyng *loked*,
B. 5.52   'And ye þat han lawes to [*loke*], lat truþe be youre coueitise
B. 5.63   And lay longe er she *loked*, and 'lord, mercy!' cryde,
B. 5.82   So *loked* he wiþ lene chekes, lourynge foule.
B. 5.189   So hungrily and holwe sire heruy hym *loked*.
B. 5.200   And was his prentice ypliȝt his profit to [*loke*].
B. 5.276   And whoso leueþ [þat I liȝe] *loke* in þe Sauter glose,
B. 5.461   Roberd þe Robbere on Reddite *loked*,
B. 5.575   *Loke* [þow] breke no bowes þere but if it be [þyn] owene.
B. 5.578   Leue hem on þi lift half and *loke* noȝt þerafter.
B. 5.582   *Loke* þow plukke no plaunte þere for peril of þi soule.
B. 6.38   *Loke* [þow] tene no tenaunt but truþe wole assente,
B. 6.177   That he *loked* lik a lanterne al his lif after.
B. 6.185   That hunger was noȝt hardy on hem for to *loke*.
B. 6.318   Swiche lawes to *loke* laborers to [chaste].
B. 6.320   Ne stryuen ayeins [þe] statut, so sterneliche he *loked*.
B. 7.142   'Lewed lorel!' quod Piers, 'litel *lokestow* on þe bible;
B. 7.171   That Ioseph was Iustice Egipte to *loke*;
B. 8.58   Ac if I may lyue and *loke* I shal go lerne bettre.'
B. 9.58   Ac Inwit is in þe heed and to þe herte he *lokeþ*
B. 9.180   For no londes, but for loue, *loke* ye be wedded
B.10.145   But al lauȝynge he louted and *loked* vpon Studie

B.10.184   And lerned hem leuel and lyne þouȝ I *loke* dymme.
B.10.192   *Loke* þow loue lelly if þee likeþ dowel,
B.10.210   Forþi *loke* þow louye as longe as þow durest,
B.10.260   *Loke* þow werche it in werk þat þi word sheweþ;
B.10.271   Which letteþ þee to *loke*, lasse ouþer moore?
B.11.83   *Loke*, ye lettred men, wheiþer I lye or noȝt.'
B.11.85   'Wherfore lourestow?' quod lewtee, and *loked* on me harde.
B.11.187   And *lokeþ* on vs in hir liknesse and þat wiþ louely chere
B.11.363   And siþen I *loked* on þe see and so forþ on þe sterres;
B.11.388   And er þow lakke my lif [þyn] be to preise.
B.11.410   And as I caste vp myne eiȝen oon *loked* on me.
B.11.428   Lat hym ligge, *loke* noȝt on hym til hym list aryse.
B.12.180   Ther þe lewed liþ stille and *lokeþ* after lente,
B.12.191   Ther lewed þeues ben lolled vp; *loke* how þei be saued!
B.13.102   And tolde hym of a Trinite, and toward vs he *loked*.
B.13.294   And louelokest to *loken* on and lelest of werkes,
B.13.301   And as a lyoun on to *loke* and lordlich of speche;
B.14.32   All þat lyueþ and *lokeþ* liflode wolde I fynde
B.14.47   But I [listnede and] *lokede* what liflode it was
B.14.228   [For lowliche he *lokeþ*, and louelich is his speche
B.15.9   'God *loke* yow, lordes', ne loutede faire,
B.15.185   Loueþ hem as oure lord biddeþ and *lokeþ* how þei fare.
B.15.204   And as a lyoun he *lokeþ* þer men lakken hise werkes.
B.15.206   *Loken* as lambren and semen [lif]holy,
B.15.253   Lakkeþ ne loseþ ne *lokeþ* vp sterne,
B.15.319   If lewed men knewe þis latyn þei wolde *loke* whom þei yeue,
B.15.343   As in lussheburwes is a luþer alay, and yet *lokeþ* he lik a sterlyng;
B.16.47   That is lieutenaunt to *loken* it wel bi leue of myselue;
B.16.64   And egreliche he *loked* on me and þerfore I spared
B.16.255   And I *loked* in his lappe; a laȝar lay þerInne
B.18.12   Wiþouten spores oþer spere; spakliche he *lokede*
B.18.30   Al þat lyueþ [or] *lokeþ* in londe [or] in watre.
B.18.114   Cam walkynge in þe wey; to helleward she *loked*.
B.18.118   Euene out of þe Est and westward she *lokede*,
B.18.325   Lucifer *loke* ne myȝte, so light hym ablente.
B.18.383   Lawe wolde he yeue hym lif if he *loked* on hym.
B.18.386   And if lawe wole I *loke* on hem it liþ in my grace
B.18.405   They dorste noȝt *loke* on oure lord, þe [leeste] of hem alle,
B.19.159   And lyues and *lokynge* and aloud cride
B.19.175   And now art lyuynge and *lokynge* and laste shalt euere."
B.19.254   *Lokeþ* þat no[on] lakke ooþer, but loueþ as breþeren;
B.20.206   And *loke* þow konne som craft er þow come þennes.'
C.Pr.189   And yf [hym] lust for to layke than *loke* we mowe
C. 1.145   *Lok* þow soffre hym to seye and so thow myht lerne.
C. 1.163   *Lokede* on vs with loue [and] let his sone deye
C. 2.5   'Loke [o]n thy left half, and loo where he standeth,
C. 2.8   Y *lokede* [o]n my luft half as þe lady me tauhte
C. 2.134   *Lokede* vp to oure lord and alowed sayde:
C. 2.172   To londone to *loke* yf lawe wille iugge;
C. 2.212   But riht as þe lawe *loketh* lat falle on hem alle.'
C. 2.237   That lyare sholde wonye with hem watres to *loke*.
C. 3.249   *Loketh* aftur lordschipe or oþer large mede
C. 3.493   Ac hadde she *loked* in þe luft half and þe lef turned
C. 4.63   Y am nat hardy for hym vnnethe to *loke*.'
C. 4.67   On men of lawe wrong *lokede* and largelyche hem profered
C. 4.106   And for to consayle þe kynge on Consience thei *lokede*;
C. 4.167   And modiliche vppon mede many tym[e] *lokede*
C. 5.162   He *loketh* al lourynge and lordeyne hym calleth.
C. 6.4   And [lay] long ar he *lokede* and 'lord, mercy!' cryede,
C. 6.44   And louelokest to *loke* vppon a[nd] lykyngest abedde
C. 6.197   So hungrily and holow sire heruy hym *lokede*.
C. 6.301   And what lede leueth þat y lye *look* in þe sauter glos[e],
C. 6.315   Robert the ruyflare on reddite *lokede*
C. 7.50   Til eche lyf hit lothed to *loke* þeron or smylle hit;
C. 7.222   *Loke* þou bere n[ouht] þere away but yf hit be thyn owene.
C. 7.225   And leu[e] hem [o]n þ[y] luft ha[lf] and *loke* [nat] þeraftur
C. 7.229   *Loke* thow plokke no plonte þere for perel of thy soule.
C. 7.293   To *loke* how me liketh hit,' and toek his leue at Peres.
C. 8.36   *Loke* ȝe tene no tenaunt but treuthe wol assente
C. 8.85   Ne hem þat han lawes to *loke* lacke hem nat, y hote;
C. 8.174   Þat a *lokede* lyke a l[a]nterne al his lyf aftur;
C. 8.181   That hunger was nat hardy on hem for to *loke*.
C. 8.233   *Loke* by thy lyue lat hem nat forfare.
C. 8.276   And *loke* þou drynke no day ar thow dyne sumwhat.
C. 8.340   Ne stryue aȝeynes [þe] statuyt, [so sturnliche a *lokede*].
C. 9.141   *Loken* louhliche to lache men Almesse,
C. 9.241   *Loke* now where this lollares and lewede Ermites
C. 9.270   When thy lord *loketh* to haue allouaunce of his bestes
C. 9.278   *Loke* now, for thy lacchesse, what lawe wol the graunte:
C.10.57   Ac yf y may lyue and *loke* y shal go lerne bettere.'
C.10.259   And thogh he be louelich to *loke*[n] on and lossum abedde,
C.10.282   And *loke* þat loue be more þe cause then lond oþer nobles.
C.11.2   That ful lene *lokede* and lyfholy semede.

C.11.72   And yf thow haue litel, leue sone, *loke* by þy lyue
C.11.83   But al lauhynge he louted and *loked* vppon stud[i]e,
C.11.125   Thus thorw my lore ben men ylered thogh y *loke* demme.
C.11.145   Leue lelli and *loke* þou do þeraftur.
C.11.168   And in a myrrour þat hihte myddelerd she made me to *loke*.
C.13.74   That oure lord *loketh* aftur of vch a lyf þat wynneth
C.13.132   And in þe myrour of mydelerthe made him efte to *loke*,
C.13.173   And sethe y *lokede* on þe see and so forth on [þe] sterres;
C.13.206   And ar thow lacke eny lyf *loke* ho is to preyse.
C.13.235   Lat hym lygge, *lok* nat on hym til hym luste [a]ryse.
C.14.120   There þe lewede lyth stille and *loketh* aftur lente
C.14.130   There lewede theues ben lolled vp; *loke* how þei ben saued!
C.15.109   And tolde hym of a trinite, and toward me he *lokede*.
C.15.248   And y lystnede and *lokede* what lyflode hit were
C.16.69   For lo[w]lyche he *loketh* and lo[uelych]e is his speche
C.16.271   And as lambes they *loke* and ly[u]en as woluos.
C.18.54   Where þe fruyt were fayre or foul for to *loke* on.
C.18.266   And conforted many a carfol þere þat aftur his comyng *loke*[n].
C.18.271   And y *lokede* in his lappe; a laȝar lay þerynne
C.19.110   *Loke* thow louye and bileue al thy lyftyme.
C.19.265   A fordoth the lihte þat oure lord *loketh* to haue worschipe of.
C.20.10   Withouten spores oþer spere; sp[a]keliche he *lokede*
C.20.29   Alle þat lyueth or *loketh* a londe or a watre.
C.20.117   Cam walkynge in þe way; to hellward she *lokede*.
C.20.368   Lucifer *loke* ne myhte, so liht hym ablen[t]e,
C.20.379   Falsliche [thow] fettest there þat me biful to *loke*,
C.20.425   Lawe wolde he ȝoue hym lyf and he *loked* on hym.
C.20.428   And if lawe wol y *loke* on hem hit lith in my grace.
C.20.448   They dorste nat *loke* on oure lord, þe leste of hem alle,
C.21.159   And lyues and *lokynge* and aloude criede
C.21.175   And now art lyuynge and *lokynge* and laste shalt euere."
C.21.254   *Loke* þat noen lacke oþere bute loueth as bretherne
C.22.206   And *loke* thow conne som craft ar thow come thennes.'

lokes n *lok* n.(4) &> *lok* C 1
C.11.265   Lelly as by his *lokes*, with a le[tt]re of gyle?

lokynge ger *lokinge* ger. &> *loken* A 1 loking; B 3; C 2
A.12.96   Þou shalt be lauȝth into lyȝth with *loking* of an eye
B.11.318   This *lokynge* on lewed preestes haþ doon me lepe from pouerte
B.13.343   Wiþ likynge of lecherie as by *lokynge* of his eiȝe.
B.16.7   The blosmes beþ buxom speche and benigne *lokynge*.
C.2.125   Amendes was here moder by trewe menne *lokynge*,
C.18.10   Thorw louely *lokyng[e]* hit lyueth and launseth vp blosmes,

lokis > *loken*

lollare n *lollere* n. B 1 lolleris; C 13 lollare (2) lollares (9) lollarne (2)
B.15.213   For he [lyueþ] noȝt in *lolleris* ne in londleperis heremytes
C.5.2   [K]ytte and y in a cote, yclothed as a *lollare*
C.5.4   Amonges *lollares* of londone and lewede Ermytes,
C.5.31   The whiche is *lollarne* lyf þat lytel is preysed
C.8.74   That *lollares* and loseles lele men holdeth,
C.8.286   And thouh lyares and l[a]chdraweres and *lollares* knocke
C.9.103   And lymes to labory with and *lollares* lyf vsen
C.9.107   The whiche aren lunatyk *lollares* and lepares aboute
C.9.140   The whiche is *lollarne* lyf and lewede Ermytes;
C.9.158   And lyueth lyke a *lollare*, goddes lawe hym dampneth.
C.9.159   'Forthy *lollares* þat lyuen in sleuthe and ouer land strikares
C.9.193   Thise *lollares*, lachedraweres, lewede Ermytes
C.9.214   Kyndeliche, by Crist, ben suche ycald *lollares*.
C.9.241   Loke now where this *lollares* and lewede Ermites

lolleþ v *lollen* v. A 1 lollide; B 4 lolled (2) lolleþ (1) lollynge (1); C 6 lolled (1) lollede (1) lollen (1) lolleth (2) lollyng (1)
A.5.110   [And] as a l[e]þerene purs *lollide* his chekis.
B.5.191   And [lik] a leþeren purs *lolled* hise chekes
B.12.191   Ther lewed þeues ben *lolled* vp; loke how þei be saued!
B.12.213   And wel lose[l]ly he *lolleþ* þere by þe lawe of holy chirche
B.16.269   *Lollynge* in my lappe til swich a lord vs fecche.'
C.6.199   And as a letherne pors *lollede* his chekes
C.9.216   He þat *lolleth* is lame or his leg out of ioynte
C.9.219   *Lollen* aȝen þe byleue and lawe of holy churche.
C.14.130   There lewede theues ben *lolled* vp; loke how þei ben saued!
C.14.152   And wel lo[s]liche he *lolleth* þere by þe lawe of holy churche:
C.18.285   *Lollyng* in my lappe til suche a lord vs feche.'

lolly > *how_trolly_lolly*

lomb n *lomb* n. A 2; B 4 lambren (1) lomb (3); C 7 lamb (1) lambe (1) lambes (1) lambren (1) lomb (1) lombe (1) lombren (1)
A.6.40   He is as louȝ as a *lomb* & loueliche of speche.
A.9.77   He is as louȝ as a *lomb*, louelich of speche.
B.5.553   He is as lowe as a *lomb* and louelich of speche.
B.8.86   He is as lowe as a *lomb*, louelich of speche;
B.15.206   Loken as *lambren* and semen [lif]holy,

B.20.36   And as lowe as a *lomb* for lakkyng þat hym nedeþ;
C.3.412   And ȝaf the kyndom to his knaue þat kept shep and *lambren*;
C.7.197   He is as louh as a *lombe* and leel of his tonge.
C.9.261   Thy berkeres aren a[l] blynde that bringeth forth thy *lombren*:
C.10.83   He is [as] logh as a *lomb* and loueliche of speche.
C.16.271   And as *lambes* they loke and ly[u]en as woluos.
C.17.38   To his wyf; when he was blynde he herde a *la[m]be* blete:
C.22.36   And as louh as a *lamb* for lakkyng þat hym nedeth;

lome adv *lome* adv. B 3 lome (2) lomere (1); C 3 lome (2) lomere (1)
B.11.233   For in hir liknesse oure lord [*lome*] haþ ben yknowe.
B.15.72   That [*lome*] þe lewed peple of hir bileue doute.
B.20.238   For *lomere* he lyeþ þat liflode moot begge
C.10.166   Such lyther lyuyng men *lome* been ryche
C.12.122   For in here likenesse oure lord *lome* hath be yknowe.
C.22.238   For *lomere* he lyeth þat lyflode moet begge

lomes n *lome* n. C 1
C.5.45   The *lomes* þat y labore with and lyflode deserue

lompe n *lumpe* n. C 1
C.9.150   Loef oþer half loef other a *lompe* of chese

lond n *lond* n. A 16 land (4) lond (9) londe (1) londis (2); B 45 land (2) landes (1) lond (29) londe (8) londes (5); C 61 land (5) landes (1) lond (32) londe (13) londes (10)
A.3.125   She doþ men lese here *land* & here lif boþe;
A.3.190   He shulde haue be lord of þat *lond* in lengþe & in brede,
A.3.208   Þe king haþ [m]ede of his men to make pes in *londis*;
A.4.59   For boþe þi lyf & þi *lond* liþ in his grace.'
A.4.131   And loue shal lede þi *land* as þe lef likeþ.'
A.5.249   And lepe with hym ouer *land* al his lif tyme,
A.7.16   For I shal lene hem lyflode, but ȝif þe *lond* faile
A.7.256   And lerne to laboure wiþ *lond* lest liflode hym faile.
A.7.291   Laboureris þat haue no *land* [to] lyue on [but] here handis
A.8.140   Among l[ower]e lordis þi *londis* shuln be departid'.
A.9.73   And þoruȝ his labour or his *lond* his liflode wynneþ,
A.9.117   'Where þat dowel, & dobet, & dobest beþ in *londe*,
A.11.14   Þat hem were leuere *lond*, & lordsshipe on erþe,
A.11.203   Ne no leperis ouer *land* ladies to shryue.
A.11.212   A ledere of l[oue]d[a]ies & a *lond* biggere;
A.12.115   God saue hem sound by se and by *land*.
B.Pr.126   And lene þee lede þi *lond* so leaute þee louye,
B.3.136   She dooþ men lese here *lond* and hire lif boþe;
B.3.203   He sholde haue be lord of þat *lond* in lengþe and in brede,
B.3.221   The kyng haþ mede of his men to make pees in *londe*;
B.4.73   For boþe þi lif and þi *lond* lyþ in his grace.'
B.4.148   And loue shal lede þi *lond* as þe leef likeþ.'
B.5.475   And lepe wiþ hym ouer *lond* al his lif tyme,
B.6.17   For I shal lenen hem liflode but if þe *lond* faille
B.6.272   And lerne to laboure wiþ *lond* [lest] liflode [hym faille].
B.6.307   Laborers þat haue no *land* to lyue on but hire handes
B.7.162   Amonges lower lordes þi *lond* shal be departed.
B.8.82   And þoruȝ his labour or his *land* his liflode wynneþ,
B.8.128   'Wher dowel [and] dobet and dobest ben in *londe*
B.9.180   For no *londes*, but for loue, loke ye be wedded
B.10.14   That hem were leuere *lond* and lordshipe on erþe,
B.10.25   And þat þei ben lordes of ech a *lond* þat out of lawe libbeþ,
B.10.312   A ledere of louedayes and a *lond* buggere,
B.10.317   Litel hadde lordes to doon to ȝyue *lond* from hire heires
B.10.321   Ac þei leten hem as lordes, hire *lon[d* liþ] so brode,
B.11.8   And into þe *lond* of longynge [and] loue she me brouȝte
B.11.23   Til þow be a lord and haue *lond* leten þee I nelle
B.11.297   That haþ no *lond* ne lynage riche ne good loos of hise handes.
B.13.16   And how louynge he is to [ech lif] on *londe* and on watre–
B.13.208   And conformen kynges to pees; and alle kynnes *londes*,
B.13.371   That a foot *lond* or a forow fecchen I wolde
B.14.263   In *lond* and in lordshipe and likynge of bodie
B.14.330   That euere he hadde *lond* ouþer lordshipe lasse oþer moore.
B.15.152   I haue lyued in *londe*', quod [I], 'my name is longe wille,
B.15.366   And what to leue and to lyue by; þe *lond* was so trewe.
B.15.367   Now faileþ þe folk of þe flood and of þe *lond* boþe,
B.15.555   The lordshipe of *londes* [lese ye shul for euere],
B.15.558   Wiþ *londes* and ledes, lordshipes and rentes,
B.15.564   Takeþ hire *landes*, ye lordes, and leteþ hem lyue by dymes.
B.16.16   And liberum arbitrium haþ þe *lond* [to] ferme,
B.16.189   The light of al þat lif haþ a *londe* and a watre,
B.16.240   *Lond* and lordshipe and lif wiþouten ende.
B.17.61   And nolde noȝt neghen hym by nyne *londes* lengþe.
B.18.30   Al þat lyueþ [or] lokeþ in *londe* [or] in watre.
B.18.105   [Ne] haue lordshipe in *londe* ne no lond tilye,
B.18.105   [Ne] haue lordshipe in londe ne no *lond* tilye,
B.18.315   And al oure lordshipe, I leue, a *londe* and [in helle]:
B.19.32   To make lordes of laddes of *lond* þat he wynneþ
B.19.236   And some he lered to laboure [on *lond* and on watre

B.19.334 [And þe [*lond*] of bileue, þe lawe of holy chirche].
B.20.251 For loue lafte þei lordschip, boþe *lond* and scole,
C.Pr.147 With lele labour to lyue while lif on *londe* lasteth.
C.Pr.150 And lene [þe] lede þy *londe* [so] lewte þe louye
C. 3.174 For he doth men lesen here *lond* and here lyf bothe;
C. 3.210 That no *lond* ne loueth the and зut leeste thyn owene.
C. 3.213 Thus lereth this lady thi *lond*, now lord зeue here sorwe!
C. 3.235 Bothe here and elleswhere, in alle kyne *londes*.
C. 3.248 The leste ladde þat longeth with hym, be þe *londe* ywonne,
C. 3.260 He sholde haue [ben] lord of þat *lond* alenghe and abrede
C. 3.316 зeue *lond* or lordschipe [or] oþer large зeftes
C. 3.377 That here loue to his lawe Thorw al þe *lond* acorde,
C. 3.382 Bytwene two *lo[n]des* for a trewe marke.
C. 3.419 Haste the with al thyn oste to þe *lond* of Amalek
C. 3.420 And alle þat leueth on þat *lond* oure [lord] þat thow sle hit;
C. 4.145 And loue shal lede thi *land* as the leef lyketh.'
C. 5.26 'Thenne hastow *londes* to lyue by,' quod resoun, 'or lynage ryche
C. 5.158 Ledares of l[ou]edays, and *londes* ypurchaced
C. 5.163 Lytel hadde lordes ado to зeue *lond* fro [here] heyres
C. 5.167 Ac зe leten зow alle as lordes, зoure *lond* lyth so brode.
C. 6.67 Sholde no lyf lyue þat on his *lond* pissede.
C. 6.268 That a faet *lond* or a forw fecchen y wolde
C. 6.329 [And lepe wiþ hym ouer *lond* al his lif tyme]
C. 8.15 For y shal lene hem lyflode but [yf] þe *lond* faylle
C. 8.140 That lele *land* tilynge men leely byswynken.
C. 8.293 And lerne to labory with *lond* lest lyflode h[y]m fayle.
C. 8.329 Laborers þat han no *lond* to lyue on but here handes
C. 9.159 'Forthy lollares þat lyuen in sleuthe and ouer *land* strikares
C. 9.203 Forsoken *lond* and lordschipe and lykyng[e] of body
C.10.124 'Whare dowel and dobet And dobest ben in *londe*
C.10.191 That alle *landes* loueden and in on lawe bileuede.
C.10.193 For to lese þerfore her *lond* and her lyf aftur.
C.10.217 On a leye *land* aзeynes his lordes wille,
C.10.282 And loke þat loue be more þe cause then *lond* oþer nobles.
C.11.12 Þat [they] louyen *lond* and lordschipe and lykynge of body
C.11.167 And into þe *lond* of longyng [and loue] she me brouhte
C.11.182 Til thow be a lord and haue *lond* leten y the nelle
C.11.293 Lewed lele laboreres and *land* tulyng peple
C.12.224 On fat *lond* ful of donge foulest wedes groweth.
C.12.231 Lo! lord ouerleyd with marl and with donge,
C.13.111 That hath n[o] *lond* ne lynage ryche ne good los of his handes.
C.15.19 And how louyng he is to vch lyf a *londe* and o watere
C.15.166 To haue alle *londes* at thy likyng and the here lord make
C.16.103 In *lond* and in lordschipe [and] lykynge of body
C.16.160 'He þat hath *lond* and lordschipe,' quod he, 'at þe laste ende
C.16.165 'Leue liberum arbitrium,' quod y, 'of what *lond* ar зe?
C.17.103 And what lyue by and leue, the *londe* was so trewe.
C.17.218 The lordschipe of *londes* lese зe shal for euer
C.17.221 With *londes* and ledes, lordschipes and rentes,
C.17.227 Taketh here *londe[s]*, зe lordes, and lat hem lyue by dymes
C.17.237 Alle *londes* into loue And þat in lytel tyme;
C.18.256 *Lond* and lordschip ynow and lyf withouten ende.
C.19.60 And [n]olde nat neyhele hym by nyne *londes* lenghe.
C.20.29 Alle þat lyueth or loketh a *londe* or a watre.
C.20.93 Bothe my *lond* and my licame at зoure likynge taketh hit.
C.20.108 Ne haue lordschipe in *londe* ne no londe tulye
C.20.108 Ne haue lordschipe in londe ne no *londe* tulye
C.20.314 Aзeyne his loue and his leue on his *londe* зedest,
C.20.349 We haen ylost oure lordschipe a *londe* and in helle.
C.21.32 To make lordes of laddes of *lond* þat he wynneth
C.21.236 And som he lered to laboure a *londe* and a watre
C.21.334 And þe *londe* of bileue, the lawe of holi churche.
C.22.251 For loue lefte they lordschipe, bothe *lond* and scole,

londleperis n *londlepere n.* B 1
B.15.213 For he [lyueþ] noзt in lolleris ne in *londleperis* heremytes

londoun n prop *London n.* A 4 lundoun; B 7 London (2) Londoun (5); C 9 london (2) londone (5) londoun (2)
A.Pr.82 To haue a licence & leue at *lundoun* to dwelle,
A.Pr.94 Ben ylope to *lundoun* be leue of hire bisshop,
A. 2.99 Lediþ hire to *lundoun* þere lawe is yhandlit
A. 2.120 To *lundoun* to loke зif þat lawe wolde
B.Pr.85 To haue a licence and leue at *London* to dwelle,
B.Pr.91 Liggen at *Londoun* in Lenten and ellis.
B.Pr.160 'I haue yseyen segges', quod he, 'in þe Cite of *Londoun*
B. 2.135 Ledeþ hire to *Londoun* þere [lawe] is [yhandled],
B. 2.156 To *london* to loken if [þat] lawe wolde
B. 5.130 Amonges Burgeises haue I be, [bigg]yng at *Londoun*,
B.13.263 Al *londoun*, I leue, likeþ wel my wafres,
C.Pr.83 To haue a licence and leue at [*Londoun* to dwelle,
C.Pr.89 Leyen [at] *Londoun* in lenton and elles.
C. 2.151 And ledeth here to *londone* there lawe may declare
C. 2.172 To *londone* to loke yf lawe wille iugge;

C. 5.4 Amonges lollares of *londone* and lewede Ermytes,
C. 5.44 And so y leue in *london* and [vp] lond[on] bothe.
C. 5.44 And so y leue in london and [vp] *lond[on]* bothe.
C. 6.96 Amongus marchauntes many tymes and nameliche in *londone*.
C.16.288 Ich haue yleued in *londone* monye longe зeres

lone > loone

long adj *long adj.(1)* &> *longe* A 11 lang (1) lengere (1) long (3) longe (6); B 34 lang (1) long (12) longe (17) lenger (4); C 32 lang (1) lengore (1) lengur (2) long (8) longe (20)
A.Pr.52 Grete lobies & *longe* þat loþ were to swynke
A.Pr.103 And driueþ forþ þe *longe* day wiþ dieu saue dame emme;
A. 2.143 And makiþ of lyere a *lang* carte to leden al þis oþere,
A. 5.124 To drawe þe list along, þe *lengere* it semide;
A. 6.3 Til late & *longe* þat hy a lede mette,
A. 6.46 For treuþe wolde loue me þe wers a *long* tyme aftir.
A. 7.7 'Þis were a *long* lettyng,' quaþ a lady in a scleire;
A. 7.18 And зe loueliche ladies wiþ зour [*longe*] fyngris,
A. 9.110 He was *long* & lene, lyk to non oþer,
A.11.118 And ek þe *longe* launde þat leccherie hatte,
A.11.284 Þat hadde leyn with lucifer manye *longe* зeris;
B.Pr.55 Grete lobies and *longe* þat loþe were to swynke
B.Pr.181 And leten hire labour lost and al hire *longe* studie.
B.Pr.191 For bettre is a litel los þan a *long* sorwe.
B.Pr.225 And dryueþ forþ þe *longe* day with 'Dieu saue dame Emme'.
B. 2.182 And makeþ of lyere a *lang* cart to leden alle þise oþere,
B. 3.340 For þat lyne was no *lenger* at þe leues ende.
B. 5.208 To drawe þe [list] along, þe *lenger* it semed;
B. 5.515 Til late and *longe*, þat þei a leode mette
B. 5.559 Truþe wolde loue me þe lasse a *long* tyme after.
B. 6.7 'This were a *long* lettyng', quod a lady in a Scleyre.
B. 6.10 And ye louely ladies wiþ youre *longe* fyngris,
B. 8.120 He was *long* and lene, lik to noon ooþer;
B. 9.74 Of þis matere I myзte make a *long* tale
B.10.166 And also þe [*longe*] launde þat lecherie hatte,
B.10.377 'This is a *long* lesson', quod I, 'and litel am I þe wiser;
B.10.425 That hadde yleyen wiþ lucifer many *longe* yeres.
B.11.368 Of hir kynde and hir colour to carpe it were to *longe*.
B.13.388 As whan I lened and leued it lost or *longe* er it were paied.
B.14.242 And haþ hondes and armes of [a *long*] lengþe,
B.14.244 And loueth layk was it neuere bitwene þe *longe* and þe shorte.
B.15.1 AC after my wakynge it was wonder *longe*
B.15.89 Of þis matere I myзte make a *long* bible,
B.15.152 I haue lyued in londe', quod [I], 'my name is *longe* wille,
B.15.297 That lyueden þus for oure lordes loue many *longe* yeres.
B.16.57 For alle are þei aliche *longe*, noon lasse þan ooþer,
B.16.181 'Thre leodes in oon lyth, noon *lenger* þan ooþer,
B.17.250 Al þi labour is lost and al þi *long* trauaille;
B.18.5 And lened me to a lenten, and *longe* tyme I slepte.
B.18.45 Boþe as *long* and as large bi lofte and by grounde.'
B.18.63 And tolde why þat tempeste so *longe* tyme durede:
B.19.279 And lerned men a ladel bugge wiþ a *long* stele
B.20.111 And bihighte hem *long* lif, and lecherie he sente
B.20.219 In paltokes and pyked shoes, [purses and] *longe* knyues,
B.20.287 Yerne of forзifnesse or *lenger* yeres loone.
C.Pr.53 Grete lobies and *longe* þat loth were to swynke
C.Pr.198 And leten here labour ylost and al here *longe* study.
C.Pr.229 And dryueth forth [þe *longe*] da[y] with 'd[ieu] saue dame Emme.'
C. 2.195 And maketh of lyare a *lang* cart to lede al this othere,
C. 3.492 That l[yne] was no *lengur* and at þe leues ende
C. 4.44 And speke wyse wordes a *longe* while togederes.
C. 5.24 And to *long*, lef me, lowe to stoupe,
C. 5.41 Lyf þat me [l]ykede but in this *longe* clothes.
C. 6.216 To drawe the lyst along the *lengur* hit semede;
C. 6.277 As whenne y lenede and leuede hit lost or *longe* or hit were payed.
C. 7.160 Til late was and *longe* þat þei a lede mette
C. 7.204 A wolde loue me þe lasse a *long* tyme aftur.
C. 8.5 'Th[is] were a *long* lettyng,' quod [a] lady in a slayre;
C. 8.9 And зe worthily wymmen with зoure *longe* fyngris,
C. 9.208 *Long* labour and litte wynnynge and at the laste they aspyde
C.10.116 He was *long* and lene, ylyk to noon other;
C.11.257 That hadde yley with lucifer mony *longe* зeres.
C.13.178 Of here kynde and here colour to carpe hit were to *longe*.
C.15.180 Lettrure and *longe* studie letteth fol monye
C.16.82 And hath hondes and Armes of a *longe* lenthe
C.16.84 And louely layk was hit neuere bytwene a *longe* and a short.
C.16.288 Ich haue yleued in londone monye *longe* зeres
C.17.26 That lyueden thus for oure lordes loue monye *longe* зeres
C.18.22 Alle thre yliche *long* and yliche large.
C.19.216 Al thy labor is loste and al thy *longe* trauaile;
C.20.5 And lened me to lenten: and *long* tyme y slepte.
C.20.44 Bothe as *longe* and as large aloofte and o grounde
C.20.65 And tolde why þ[at] tempest so *longe* tyme durede:

C.21.279 And lered men a ladel bugge with a *longe* stale
C.22.111 And bihihte hem *long* lyf and lecherye he sente
C.22.219 In paltokes and pikede shoes, [purses and] *longe* knyues
C.22.287 ȝerne of forȝeuenesse or *lengore* ȝeres l[on]e.

longe n *long n.* C 1
C. 9.254 Cam no wyn in his wombe thorw þe woke *longe*

longe adv *longe adv. &> long* A 12 lengere (3) longe (9); B 36 longe (31) lenger (5); C 35 lenger (1) lengere (2) lengore (3) lengur (1) long (2) longe (26)
A. 1.183 I may no *lengere* lenge; now loke þe oure lord.'
A. 2.31 I may no *lengere* lette, lord I þe bekenne,
A. 4.1 'Sessiþ,' seide þe king, 'I suffre ȝow no *lengere*.
A. 4.96 As *longe* as I lyue but more loue it make.'
A. 4.154 For as *longe* as I lyue l[et]e þe I [n]ile.'
A. 4.158 As *longe* as I lyue libbe we togideris.'
A. 5.21 Of þis mater I miȝte mamele wel *longe*,
A. 5.46 And lay *longe* er heo lokide, & 'lord mercy' criede,
A. 5.64 As a lek þat hadde leyn *longe* in þe sonne,
A. 7.17 As *longe* as I lyue for þe lordis loue of heuene.
A. 7.247 And kep sum [til] soper tyme, & sit nouȝt to *longe*;
A.11.262 In þe legende of lif *longe* er I were,
B. 1.209 I may no *lenger* lenge; now loke þee oure lord.'
B. 4.1 'CEsseþ', sei[de] þe kyng, 'I suffre yow no *lenger*.
B. 4.109 As *longe* as [I lyue], but lowenesse hym borwe.'
B. 4.191 For as *longe* as I lyue lete þee I nelle.'
B. 4.195 Als *longe* as [I lyue] lyue we togideres.'
B. 5.21 Of þis matere I myȝte mamelen [wel] *longe*,
B. 5.63 And lay *longe* er she loked, and 'lord, mercy!' cryde,
B. 5.81 As a leek þat hadde yleye *longe* in þe sonne
B. 5.288 And as *longe* as þow lyuest þerwith þow yeldest noȝt but borwest;
B. 5.375 And sat som tyme so *longe* þere þat I sleep and eet at ones.
B. 6.18 As *longe* as I lyue, for þe lordes loue of heuene.
B. 6.36 Als *longe* as I lyue I shal þee mayntene.
B. 6.263 And keep som til soper tyme and sitte noȝt to *longe*;
B.10.92 For we haue no lettre of oure lif how *longe* it shal dure.
B.10.149 As *longe* as I lyue, boþe late and raþe,
B.10.210 Forþi loke þow louye as *longe* as þow durest,
B.10.381 In þe legende of lif *longe* er I were,
B.11.19 For to lyue *longe* and ladies to louye,
B.13.21 I lay doun *longe* in þis þoȝt and at þe laste I slepte,
B.13.51 'As *longe*', quod [he], 'as [lif] and lycame may dure'.
B.13.264 And louren whan þei lakken hem; it is noȝt *longe* ypassed
B.13.267 And werkmen were agast a lite; þis wole be þouȝt *longe*:
B.14.219 Ne none of þe seuene synnes sitten ne mowe þer *longe*,
B.15.191 And leggen on *longe* wiþ Laboraui in gemitu meo,
B.15.492 Allas, þat men no *longe* [sholde bileue on Makometh]!
B.15.551 Right so, ye clerkes, for youre coueitise er [come auȝt] *longe*
B.16.20 And lay *longe* in a louedreem; and at þe laste me þouȝte
B.16.270 'Allas!' I seide, 'þat synne so *longe* shal lette
B.17.8 That Luciferis lordshipe laste shal no *lenger*.
B.17.355 I may no *lenger* lette', quod he, and lyard he prikede
B.18.79 Highte Longeus as þe lettre telleþ, and *longe* hadde lore his sight;
B.18.169 Loue haþ coueited hire *longe*; leue I noon ooþer
B.18.271 Patriarkes and prophetes han parled herof *longe*
B.18.274 Boþe þis lord and þis light, is *longe* ygo y knewe hym.
B.19.55 That *longe* hadde yleyen bifore as Luciferis cherles,
B.20.63 [Th]an to lyue *lenger* siþ [Leute] was so rebuked
C. 1.203 Loue hit,' quod þat lady; 'lette may y no *lengore*
C. 3.137 And ay the *lengur* y late [the] go the lasse treuthe is with the,
C. 3.297 And wot neuere witterly where he lyue so *longe*
C. 4.1 '[Cesseth],' saide þe kynge, 'y soffre ȝow no *lengore*.
C. 4.104 As *longe* as y lyue for his luther werkes.'
C. 5.80 Lyfholynesse and loue hath be *longe* hennes
C. 5.123 Of this mater y myhte mamele [wel] *longe*
C. 6.4 And [lay] *long* ar he lokede and 'lord, mercy!' cryede
C. 6.343 And as *longe* as thow lyuest therwith þou ȝeldest nat bote borwest;
C. 7.49 Bothe flesch and fysch and vitailes kepte so *longe*
C. 8.16 As *longe* as y leue, for [þe] lordes loue of heuene.
C. 8.273 And kepe som til soper tyme and site nat to *longe*;
C.11.87 As *longe* as y lyue, bothe late and rathe,
C.11.178 For to lyue *longe* and ladyes to louye
C.11.204 In þe legende of lyf *longe* ar y were.
C.12.193 In þe feld with þe forst and hit frese *longe*.
C.12.220 Hit lasteth nat *longe* þat is lycour-swete,
C.13.4 And ay þe *lengere* they lyuede the lasse goed they hadde:
C.13.37 The marchaunt mote nede be ylet *lenger* then the messager
C.14.38 Lawe of loue oure lord wrouht] *long* ar crist were.
C.14.168 Ac *longe* lybbynge men lykened men[nes] lyuynge
C.15.7 That y lyuede *longe*, leue me byhynde
C.15.57 'As *longe*,' quod he, ' as lyf and lycame may duyre.'
C.16.60 Ne none of þe seuene synnes sitte ne may þer *longe*
C.17.187 Allas, þat men so *longe* on Macometh bileueth!

C.17.214 Riht so, ȝe clerkes, ȝoure coueytise ar come auht *longe*
C.18.286 'Allas!' y saide, 'þat synne so *longe* shal lette
C.19.335 Y may no *lengore* lette,' quod he, and lyard a prikede
C.20.81 Hihte longies as þe lettre telleth, and *longe* hadde lore his sihte;
C.20.172 Loue hath coueyted here *longe*; leue y non oþere
C.20.279 Patriarkes and prophetes haen parled herof *longe*
C.20.296 Bothe this lord and this lihte, ys *longe* ygo y knewe hym.
C.20.339 The which lyf and lawe, be hit *longe* yvysed,
C.21.55 That *longe* hadden leye bifore as luciferes cherles
C.22.63 Then to lyue *lengere* sethe leautee was so rebuked

longe v1 *longen v.(3)* A 5 longiþ (4) longyt (1); B 5 longed (1) longen (1) longeþ (3); C 3 longe (1) longen (1) longeth (1)
A. 2.28 þat *longiþ* to þ[at] lordsshipe, þe lasse & þe more.
A. 6.105 And ben porteris to þe posternis þat to þe place *longiþ*:
A.11.90 But he lyue in þe leste degre þat *longiþ* to dowel
A.11.158 For sorcerie is þe souerayn bok þat to þat science *longiþ*.
A.12.64 To lyf in his lordshepe *longyt* my weye
B. 2.46 That *longen* to þat lordshipe, þe lasse and þe moore.
B. 5.619 And arn porters of þe Posternes þat to þe place *longeþ*.
B.10.137 But he lyue in þe [leeste degre] þat *longeþ* to dowel
B.10.215 For sorcerie is þe Souereyn book þat to [þat] Scienc[e] [*l*]ongeþ.
B.11.421 Lakkedest and losedest þyng þat *longed* noȝt to doone:
C. 3.248 The leste ladde þat *longeth* with hym, be þe londe ywonne,
C. 6.158 Y haue no luste, lef me, to *longe* amonges monkes
C. 9.130 For þe lordes loue or þe ladyes þat they with *longen*.

longede v2 *longen v.(1)* C 1
C. 8.278 And laȝar þe lene beggare þat *longede* aftur crommes–

longen > longe v1

longes n *longe n.* C 1
C. 8.189 And lame men he lechede with *longes* of bestes.

longeth > longe v1

longeus n prop *n.i.d.* B 2; C 2 longies
B.18.79 Highte *Longeus* as þe lettre telleþ, and longe hadde lore his sight;
B.18.82 To [Iusten wiþ Iesus, þis blynde Iew *Longeus*].
C.20.81 Hihte *longies* as þe lettre telleth, and longe hadde lore his sihte;
C.20.84 [To] iouste with iesus, this blynde iewe *longies*.

longynge ger *longinge ger.* B 2; C 2 longyng
B.11.8 And into þe lond of *longynge* [and] loue she me brouȝte
B.19.248 And some he lered to lyue in *longynge* to ben hennes,
C.11.167 And into þe lond of *longyng* [and loue] she me brouhte
C.21.248 And somme he [l]ered to lyue in *longyng* to be hennes,

longyt -iþ > longe v1; loo > lo

loof n *lof n.(2)* A 2 lof; B 7 lof (1) loof (2) loues (4); C 8 loef (4) loof (1) loues (3)
A. 7.164 N[e] hadde peris [wiþ] a pese *lof* preyede hym beleue,
A. 7.267 A *lof* of benis & bren ybake for my children;
B. 6.179 Ne hadde Piers wiþ a pese *loof* preyed [hym bileue]
B. 6.283 [A *lof*] of benes and bran ybake for my fauntes.
B.13.49 He sette a sour *loof* toforn vs and seide 'Agite penitenciam',
B.14.222 And buxom at hi[s] biddyn[g] for his broke *loues*,
B.15.591 Wiþ two fisshes and fyue *loues* fyue þousand peple,
B.16.125 And fed yow wiþ two fisshes and wiþ fyue *loues*,
B.19.126 And fedde wiþ two fisshes and with fyue *loues*
C. 8.176 Ne hadde [Peres] with a pese *loof* preyede hym b[ile]ue.
C. 8.285 Lene hem som of thy *loef* thouh thow þe lasse chewe.
C. 9.150 *Loef* oþer half loef other a lompe of chese
C. 9.150 Loef oþer half *loef* other a lompe of chese
C.15.55 He sette a sour *loef* and saide, 'Agite penitenciam',
C.17.24 Bote thre litle *loues* and loue was here soule.
C.18.153 With [two] fisches and [fyue] *loues*, fyue thousen[d] at ones,
C.21.126 And fedde with two fisches and with fyue *loues*

look > loken

loone n *lone n.(1)* B 1; C 2 lone
B.20.287 Yerne of forȝifnesse or lenger yeres *loone*.
C. 4.194 Or lumbardus of lukes þat leuen by *lone* as iewes.'
C.22.287 ȝerne of forȝeuenesse or lengore ȝeres l[on]e.

loore n *lore n.(2)* A 2 lore; B 14 loore (13) lore (1); C 20 lore
A. 2.17 And lakkide my *lore* to lordis aboute.
A.11.77 Ac beleue lelly o[n þe] *lore* of holy chirche,
B. 5.38 "[Lo], þe leuere child þe moore *loore* bihoueþ";
B. 9.73 Alle þise lakken Inwit and *loore* [hem] bihoueþ.
B.10.112 Here lyeþ youre *lore*", þise lordes gynneþ dispute,
B.10.124 Ac bileueþ lelly in þe *loore* of holy chirche,
B.12.276 For lettred men were lewed yet ne were *loore* of hir bokes.'
B.14.60 For if þow lyue after his *loore*, þe shorter lif þe bettre:
B.14.87 That whiles he lyuede he bileuede in þe *loore* of holy chirche,

B.15.108	Loþe were lewed men but þei youre *loore* folwede
B.15.602	And þat his *loore* be lesynges, and lakken it alle,
B.18.197	The loue of oure lord and his *loore* boþe,
B.19.35	Boþe his *loore* and his lawe; now are þei lowe cherles.
B.19.239	To wynne wiþ hir liflode bi *loore* of his techynge;
B.19.405	But þow lyue by *loore* of Spiritus Iusticie,
B.20.351	That lif þoruȝ his *loore* shal leue coueitise
C. 1.67	To combre men with coueytise, þat is his kynde and his *lore*.'
C. 9.104	Lyuen aȝen goddes lawe and þe *lore* of holi churche.
C.11.34	The lewed aȝen þe lered þe holy *lore* to disp[u]te
C.11.74	Ac lust no lord now ne lettred man of suche *lore* to here
C.11.97	Of *lore* and of lettrure, of lawe and of resoun.
C.11.125	Thus thorw my *lore* ben men ylered thogh y loke demme.
C.13.193	Why he ne loueth thy *lore* and leueth as þou techest.'
C.14.198	For letrede men were lewede ȝut ne were *lore* of [here bokes].'
C.15.259	For if thow lyu[e] aftur his *lore* the shortere lyf þe betere:
C.16.262	Loeth were lewed [men] bote they ȝoure *lore* folwede[n]
C.16.285	That lyuen aȝen holy *lore* and þe loue of charite.'
C.17.65	Lo laurence for his largenesse, as holy *lore* telleth
C.17.182	And on his *lore* thei l[e]uen ȝut, as wel lered as lewed.
C.17.235	Aȝen þe *lore* of oure lord as seynt luk witnesseth–
C.17.310	And that his *lore* was lesynges and lakken hit alle
C.20.202	The loue of oure lord and his *lore* bothe
C.21.35	Bothe his *lore* and his lawe; now are they lowe cherles.
C.21.239	To wynne with here lyflode bi *lore* of his techynge];
C.21.405	Bote thow lyue bi *lore* of spiritus Iusticie,
C.22.351	That lyf thorw his *lore* shal leue Couetyse

looresmen > loresman

loos n *los n.(2)* B 3; C 2 loos (1) los (1)

B.11.297	That haþ no lond ne lynage riche ne good *loos* of hise handes.
B.13.298	And large to lene, [*loos*] þerby to cacche].
B.13.448	To crie a largesse bifore oure lord, youre good *loos* to shewe.
C. 7.108	To crye a largesse tofore oure lord ȝoure good *loos* to shewe.
C.13.111	That hath n[o] lond ne lynage ryche ne good *los* of his handes.

loot > lot

looþ adj *loth adj.* A 3 loþ; B 16 looþ (12) loþ (1) loþe (2) loþer (1); C 14 loeth (4) loth (10)

A.Pr.52	Grete lobies & longe þat *loþ* were to swynke
A. 3.150	Lawe is so lordlich & *loþ* to make ende,
A.12.6	Þe were lef to lerne but *loþ* for to stodie;
B.Pr.55	Grete lobies and longe þat *loþe* were to swynke
B. 3.161	Lawe is so lordlich and *looþ* to maken ende;
B. 9.59	What anima is leef or *looþ*; he l[e]t hire at his wille,
B.11.223	And lawe is *looþ* to louye but if he lacche siluer.
B.12.246	And vnlouelich of ledene and *looþ* for to here.
B.13.359	Lened for loue of þe wed and *looþ* to do truþe;
B.14.7	And [laþered] wiþ þe losse of catel [forto me] *looþ* [were]
B.14.313	The eighteþe is a lele labour and *looþ* to take moore
B.15.5	And lete me for a lorel and *looþ* to reuerencen
B.15.108	*Loþe* were lewed men but þei youre loore folwede
B.15.144	By lered, by lewed, þat *looþ* is to [s]pende
B.15.309	And þanne wolde lordes and ladies be *looþ* to agulte,
B.15.392	And for hir lyuynge þat lewed men be þe *loþ*er god agulten.
B.15.473	That *loþ* ben to louye wiþouten lernyng of ensaumples.
B.18.251	And now shal Lucifer leue it, þouȝ hym *looþ* þynke.
B.20.360	[And] lat hem ligge ouerlonge and *looþ* is to chaunge;
C.Pr.53	Grete lobies and longe þat *loth* were to swynke
C. 3.199	Lawe is so lordliche and *loth* to make ende;
C. 8.48	Treuwe of thy tonge and tales *loth* to here
C. 8.264	To beggares and to boys þat *loth* ben to worche
C. 9.44	Men of lawe hadde lest þat *loth* were to plede
C.11.131	For loue is a lykyng thyng and *loth* her to greue.
C.12.215	"And art so *loth* to leue that lete shal thow nedes:
C.15.78	Ac me thynketh *loth*, thogh y latyn knowe, to lacken eny secte
C.15.136	Bote lele loue and treuthe that *loth* is to be founde.'
C.16.147	The eyȝte is a lel labour and *loeth* to take more
C.16.262	*Loeth* were lewed [men] bote they ȝoure lore folwede[n]
C.17.44	Thenne wolde lordes and ladyes be *loth* to agulte,
C.20.260	And now shal lucife[r] leue [hit], thogh hym *loeth* thynk.
C.22.360	And lat hem lygge ouerlonge and *loeth* is to chaungen;

looue n *love n.(2)* &> *loue v2* A 1 loue; B 1

A. 4.36	And how he rauisshide rose, reynaldis *loue*,
B. 4.49	And how he rauysshede Rose, Reignaldes *looue*,

lope(n > lepen

lord n *lord n.* A 54 lord (36) lordes (1) lordis (17); B 180 lord (112) lorde (1) lordes (67); C 210 loerd (1) lord (140) lorde (3) lordene (1) lordes (65)

A.Pr.26	Al for loue of oure *lord* lyuede wel streite
A.Pr.61	Siþen charite haþ ben chapman & chief to shryue *lordis*

A.Pr.87	A[c] nouȝt for loue of oure *lord* vnlose here lippes ones.
A. 1.89	And ek lyk to oure *lord* be seint lukis wordis.
A. 1.110	And was þe louelokest [of siȝt] aftir oure *lord*
A. 1.131	For to loue þi *lord* leuere þanne þiselue;
A. 1.136	Þat loue is þe leuest þing þat oure *lord* askiþ,
A. 1.178	Loue is þe leueste þing þat oure *lord* askiþ,
A. 1.183	I may no lengere lenge; now loke þe oure *lord*.'
A. 2.17	And lakkide my lore to *lordis* aboute.
A. 2.31	I may no lengere lette, *lord* I þe bekenne.
A. 3.24	Þanne lauȝte hy leue, þise *lordis* at mede.
A. 3.29	To loue hem lelly & *lordis* hem make,
A. 3.60	Forþi I lere ȝow *lordis*, leuiþ such wrytyng,
A. 3.86	Among þise lettride *lordis* þis latyn amountiþ
A. 3.101	'Ȝa *lord*,' quaþ þat lady, '*lord* forbede ellis;
A. 3.101	'Ȝa *lord*,' quaþ þat lady, '*lord* forbede ellis;
A. 3.153	Þis is þe lif of þat lady, now *lord* ȝif hire sorewe!
A. 3.162	'Nay *lord*,' quod þat lady, 'leu[iþ] him þe wers
A. 3.184	Þere I lefte wiþ my *lord* his lif for to saue,
A. 3.190	He shulde haue þe *lord* of þat lond in lengþe & in brede,
A. 3.200	Emperours & Erlis & alle maner *lordis*
A. 3.218	'Þere arn to maner of medis, my *lord*, be ȝour leue.
A. 3.222	Tak no mede, my *lord*, of [men] þat ben trewe;
A. 3.223	Loue hem & le[n]e hem for oure *lordis* loue of heuene.
A. 3.273	Þat lawe is *lord* waxen & leute is pore,
A. 4.51	And seide, 'hadde I loue of my *lord* þe king, litel wolde I recche
A. 4.101	Til *lordis* & ladies louen alle treuþe,
A. 5.46	And lay longe er heo lokide, & '*lord* mercy' criede,
A. 5.76	And belowen hym to *lordis* to don hym lese siluer,
A. 7.17	As longe as I lyue for þe *lordis* loue of heuene.
A. 7.60	Shal haue þe more here in heruist,
A. 7.116	'We haue none [lymes] to laboure wiþ, *lord*, ygracid be ȝe;
A. 7.218	& labouren for þi liflode, & so oure *lord* hiȝte;
A. 7.257	Þere arn mo liȝeris þan lechis, *lord* hem amende.
A. 7.260	Þis is a louely lessoun, *lord* it þe forȝelde.
A. 8.33	Fynde suche here foode for oure *lordis* loue of heuene.
A. 8.52	Ac for oure *lordis* loue lawe for hym shewiþ,
A. 8.87	For loue of here louȝ herte oure *lord* haþ hem grauntid
A. 8.140	Among l[ower]e *lordis* þi londis shuln be departid'.
A. 8.160	And so I leue lelly, *lord* forbede ellis,
A.10.21	And sire godefrey go wel, grete *lordis* alle.
A.10.30	Þe *lord* of lif & of li[ȝt], of lisse & of peyne.
A.10.129	For loue of here louȝnesse oure *lord* ȝiueþ hem grace
A.10.180	Aȝen þe lawe of oure *lord* le[iȝen] togideris,
A.11.49	Litel louiþ he þat *lord* þat leniþ hym al þat blisse,
A.11.85	–Al was as he wolde; *lord* yworsshipid be þou,
A.11.143	For þere þat loue is *lord* lakkiþ neuere grace.
A.11.217	Þis is þe lif of þis *lordis* þat lyuen shulde wiþ dobet,
A.11.228	Ne ricchesse, ne rentis, ne realte of *lordis*.
A.11.264	And I leue on oure *lord* & on no lettrure betere.
A.12.44	And his loggyng is with lyf þat *lord* is of erþe,
A.12.112	To lyue as þat *lord* lykyþ þat lyf in hem putte:
A.12.114	And alle *lordes* þat louyn him lely in herte,
B.Pr.26	Al for loue of oure *lord* lyueden [wel] streyte
B.Pr.64	Siþ charite haþ ben chapman and chief to shryue *lordes*
B.Pr.95	And somme seruen as seruauntȝ *lordes* and ladies,
B.Pr.102	How he it lefte wiþ loue as oure *lord* hiȝte
B.Pr.157	We myȝte be *lordes* o lofte and lyuen at oure ese.'
B.Pr.214	[Ac] noȝt for loue of oure *lord* vnlose hire lippes ones.
B. 1.91	And [ek] ylik to oure *lord* by Seint Lukes wordes.
B. 1.112	[And was þe louelokest of liȝt] after oure *lord*
B. 1.143	For to louen þi *lord* leuere þan þiselue;
B. 1.159	Forþi is loue ledere of þe *lordes* folk of heuene
B. 1.204	Loue is leche of lif and next oure *lord* selue,
B. 1.209	I may no lenger lenge; now loke þee oure *lord*.'
B. 2.22	And bilowen h[ym] to *lordes* þat lawes han to kepe.
B. 2.33	Shal be my *lord* and I his leef in þe heiȝe heuene.
B. 3.25	Thanne lauȝte þei leue, þise *lordes*, at Mede.
B. 3.30	To louen hem lelly and *lordes* [hem] make
B. 3.53	While ye loue *lordes* þat lecherie haunten
B. 3.69	Forþi I lere yow *lordes*, leueþ swic[h writynge],
B. 3.97	Among þise lettrede l[or]des þis latyn [amounteþ]
B. 3.112	'Ye, *lord*', quod þat lady, '*lord* forbede ellis!
B. 3.112	'Ye, *lord*', quod þat lady, '*lord* forbede ellis!
B. 3.166	This is þe lif of þat lady, now *lord* ȝyue hire sorwe,
B. 3.175	'Nay *lord*', quod þat lady, 'leueþ hym þe werse
B. 3.197	Ther I lafte wiþ my *lord* his lif for to saue.
B. 3.203	He sholde haue þe *lord* of þat lond in lengþe and in brede,
B. 3.213	Emperours and Erles and alle manere *lordes*
B. 3.231	'Ther are two manere of Medes, my *lord*, [bi] youre leue.
B. 3.235	*Lord*, who shal wonye in þi wones wiþ þyne holy seintes,
B. 3.244	Swiche manere men, my *lord*, shul haue þis firste Mede
B. 3.297	Mede of mysdoeres makeþ manye *lordes*,
B. 3.298	And ouer *lordes* lawes [ledeþ] þe Reaumes.

B. 3.346 This text þat ye han told were [trewe] for *lordes*,
B. 4.39 Moore þan for] loue of oure *lord* or alle hise leeue Seintes.
B. 4.65 And seide, 'hadde I loue of my *lord* þe kyng litel wolde I recche
B. 4.114 Til *lordes* and ladies louen alle truþe
B. 5.63 And lay longe er she loked, and '*lord*, mercy!' cryde,
B. 5.96 And [bilowen] hym to *lordes* to doon hym lese siluer,
B. 5.140 Til þei beere leues of lowe speche *lordes* to plese,
B. 5.244 I haue lent *lordes* and ladies my chaffare
B. 5.250 'Lentestow euere *lordes* for loue of hire mayntenaunce?'
B. 5.251 'Ye, I haue lent *lordes* loued me neuere after,
B. 5.295 And what he lente yow of oure *lordes* good to lette yow fro synne.'
B. 5.396 Ac neiþer of oure *lord* ne of oure lady þe leeste þat euere was
　　　　　maked.
B. 5.563 That ye louen oure *lord* god leuest of alle þynges.
B. 6.18 As longe as I lyue, for þe *lordes* loue of heuene.
B. 6.66 Shal haue leue, by oure *lord*, to lese here in heruest
B. 6.124 'We haue no lymes to laboure with; *lord*, ygraced be [y]e!
B. 6.234 And laboure for þi liflode, and so oure *lord* hiȝte.
B. 6.273 [Ther are mo lieres þan] leches; *lord* hem amende!
B. 6.276 /[Th]is is a louely lesson; *lord* it þee foryelde.
B. 7.31 Fynden [swiche] hir foode [for oure *lordes* loue of heuene],
B. 7.50 [Ac] for oure *lord* loue [lawe for hym sheweþ],
B. 7.105 For loue of hir lowe hert[e] oure *lord* haþ hem graunted
B. 7.162 Amonges lower *lordes* þi lond shal be departed.'
B. 7.182 And so I leue leelly, *lor[d]* forb[e]de ellis,
B. 9.22 And sire Godefray Go-wel, grete *lordes* [alle].
B. 9.29 *Lord* of lif and of liȝt, of lisse and of peyne.
B. 9.39 Right as a *lord* sholde make lettres; [if] hym lakked parchemyn,
B. 9.108 Oure *lord* loueþ hem and lent, loude ouþer stille,
B.10.22 Thei lede *lordes* wiþ lesynges and bilieþ truþe.
B.10.25 And þat þei ben *lordes* of ech a lond þat out of lawe libbeþ:
B.10.27 "Lo!" seiþ holy lettrure, "whiche [*lordes*] beþ þise sherewes";
B.10.40 Ayein þe lawe of oure *lord*, and lyen on hemselue,
B.10.63 Litel loueþ he þat *lord* þat lent hym al þat blisse
B.10.93 Swiche lessons *lordes* sholde louye to here,
B.10.98 Ther þe *lord* ne þe lady likeþ noȝt to sitte.
B.10.112 Here lyeþ youre lore", þise *lordes* gynneþ dispute,
B.10.132 Al was as [he] wold[e]–*lord*, yworshiped be þ[ow],
B.10.208 And al þat lakkeþ vs or lyeþ oure *lord* techeþ vs to louye,
B.10.314 An heep of houndes at his ers as he a *lord* were,
B.10.317 Litel hadde *lordes* to doon to ȝyue lond from hire heires
B.10.321 Ac þei leten hem as *lordes*, hire lon[d liþ] so brode.
B.10.340 Ne richesse [ne rentes] ne Reautee of *lordes*.
B.10.361 That is, loue þi *lord* god leuest abouen alle,
B.10.383 I leue it wel by oure *lord* and on no lettrure bettre.
B.10.476 That seruauntȝ þat seruen *lordes* selde fallen in arerage,
B.10.477 But þo þat kepen þe *lordes* catel, clerkes and Reues.
B.11.23 Til þow be a *lord* and haue lond leten þee I nelle
B.11.110 [The bileue [of oure] *lord* þat lettred men techeþ].
B.11.128 Wiþouten leue of his *lord*; no lawe wol it graunte.
B.11.154 Lo! ye *lordes*, what leautee dide by an Emperour of Rome
B.11.158 Wel ouȝte ye *lordes* þat lawes kepe þis lesson haue in mynde
B.11.173 But þei ben lerned for oure *lordes* loue, lost is al þe tyme,
B.11.175 But al for loue of oure *lord* and þe bet to loue þe peple.
B.11.180 Whoso leneþ noȝt he loueþ noȝt, [*lord*] woot þe soþe,
B.11.189 Wheiþer we loue þe *lordes* here bifore þe lord of blisse;
B.11.189 Wheiþer we loue þe *lordes* here bifore þe *lord* of blisse;
B.11.229 Forþi lerne we þe lawe of loue as oure *lord* tauȝte;
B.11.233 For in hir liknesse oure *lord* [lome] haþ ben yknowe.
B.12.54 And loue hem noȝt as oure *lord* bit, lesen hir soules:
B.12.94 To oure *lord*, leue me; forþi loue hem, I rede.
B.12.144 Ne of *lordes* þat were lewed men, but of þe hyeste lettred oute:
B.12.211 That oure *lord* ne hadde hym liȝtly out, so leue I [by] þe þef in
　　　　　heuene.
B.12.255 His ledene be in oure *lordes* ere lik a pies chiteryng;
B.13.12 And how þat lewed men ben lad, but oure *lord* hem helpe,
B.13.121 Ther þe *lord* of lif wonyeþ, to leren [hem] what is dowel.
B.13.142 And so þow lere þe to louye, for [þe] *lordes* loue of heuene,
B.13.200 'Me were leuere, by oure *lord*, and I lyue sholde,
B.13.226 A wafrer, wol ye wite, and serue manye *lordes*,
B.13.229 Ouþer mantel or moneie amonges *lordes* Mynstrals.
B.13.234 I haue no goode giftes of þise grete *lordes*
B.13.337 Lechecraft of oure *lord* and leue on a wicche,
B.13.421 Ye *lordes* and ladies and legates of holy chirche
B.13.431 Ac clerkes þat knowen holy writ sholde kenne *lordes*
B.13.435 Ne no mysproud man amonges *lordes* ben allowed.
B.13.437 And for loue of [hir] *lorde* liþeþ hem at festes,
B.13.444 And a lered man to lere þee what our *lord* suffred
B.13.448 To crie a largesse bifore oure *lord*, youre good loos to shewe.
B.14.35 'Whoso leueþ yow, by oure *lord*! I leue noȝt he be blessed.'
B.14.46 Lyue þoruȝ leel bileue, [as oure *lord*] witnesseþ:
B.14.53 Shul neuere gyues þee greue ne gret *lordes* wraþe,
B.14.110 To haue allowaunce of his *lord*; by þe lawe he it cleymeþ.

B.14.124 Right so reson sheweþ þat [þo renkes] þat were [*lordes*]
B.14.133 Fram þe loue of oure *lord* at his laste ende!
B.14.164 Now, *lord*, sende hem somer, and som maner ioye,
B.14.174 Ac poore peple, þi prisoners, *lord*, in þe put of meschief,
B.14.311 [For] *lordes* alloweþ hym litel or listneþ to his reson;
B.14.319 Thus lered me a lettred man for oure *lordes* loue, Seint Austyn:
B.15.6 *Lordes* or ladies or any lif ellis,
B.15.9 'God loke yow, *lordes*', ne loutede faire,
B.15.33 And whan I loue leelly oure *lord* and alle oþere
B.15.80 That I lye noȝt, loo! for *lordes* ye plesen
B.15.86 And louten to þise *lordes* þat mowen lene yow nobles
B.15.170 And leneþ and loueþ alle þat oure *lord* made.
B.15.185 Loueþ hem as oure *lord* biddeþ and lokeþ how þei fare.
B.15.202 And buxome as of berynge to burgeises and to *lordes*,
B.15.249 Ac I ne lakke no lif, but *lord* amende vs alle,
B.15.297 That lyueden þus for oure *lordes* loue many longe yeres.
B.15.309 And þanne wolde *lordes* and ladies be looþ to agulte,
B.15.322 Allas, *lordes* and ladies, lewed counseil haue ye
B.15.355 That no lif loueþ ooþer, ne oure *lord* as it semeþ.
B.15.394 For þei loue and bileue in o [*lord*] almyghty
B.15.556 And lyuen as Leuitici as oure *lord* [yow] techeþ:
B.15.564 Takeþ hire landes, ye *lordes*, and leteþ hem lyue by dymes.
B.15.582 And Iewes lyuen in lele lawe; oure *lord* wroot it hymselue
B.16.12 *Lord*!' quod I, 'if any wight wite whiderout it groweþ?'
B.16.118 That he was leche of lif and *lord* of heigh heuene.
B.16.191 So þre bilongeþ for a *lord* þat lordshipe cleymeþ:
B.16.237 Bledden blood for þat *lordes* loue hadde to blisse þe tyme.
B.16.259 'Loo!' quod he and leet me see; '*lord*, mercy!' I seide.
B.16.269 Lollynge in my lappe til swich a *lord* vs fecche.'
B.17.17 [Is] here alle þi *lordes* lawes?' quod I; 'ye, leue me', he seide.
B.17.37 To bileeue and louye in o *lord* almyghty
B.17.133 Louye hem lik myselue, ac oure *lord* abouen alle.'
B.17.220 Lele loue or lif þat oure *lord* shapte.
B.17.284 He fordooþ þe leuest light þat oure *lord* louyeþ.
B.17.296 Leue I neuere þat oure *lord* [at þe laste ende]
B.17.345 And lightliche oure *lord* at hir lyues ende
B.18.59 The *lord* of lif and of light þo leide hise eighen togideres.
B.18.88 'Ayein my wille it was, *lord*, to wownde yow so soore.'
B.18.107 Which is lif þat oure *lord* in alle lawes acurseþ:
B.18.197 The loue of oure *lord* and his loore boþe,
B.18.241 The light folwede þe *lord* into þe lowe erþe.
B.18.272 That swich a *lord* and [a] light sholde lede hem alle hennes.'
B.18.273 'Listneþ!' quod lucifer, 'for I þis lord knowe;
B.18.274 Boþe þis *lord* and þis light, is longe ago I knew hym.
B.18.275 May no deeþ [þis *lord*] dere, ne no deueles queyntise,
B.18.317 What *lord* artow?' quod Lucifer; þe light soone seide
B.18.318 [The] *lord* of myght and of ma[y]n and alle manere vertues,
B.18.326 And þo þat oure *lord* louede into his light he laughte,
B.18.356 And I in liknesse of a leode, þat *lord* am of heuene,
B.18.365 For I þat am *lord* of lif, loue is my drynke,
B.18.400 Thus by lawe', quod oure *lord*, 'lede I wole fro hennes
B.18.405 They dorste noȝt loke on oure *lord*, þe [leeste] of hem alle,
B.19.8 And riȝt lik in alle [lymes] to oure *lord* Ies[u].
B.19.32 To make *lordes* of laddes of lond þat he wynneþ
B.19.56 [And took [Lucifer þe loþely] þat *lord* was of helle
B.19.96 Ac for alle þise preciouse presentȝ oure *lord* [prynce] Iesus
B.19.173 Thow art my *lord*, I bileue, god lord Iesu;
B.19.173 Thow art my lord, I bileue, god *lord* Iesu;
B.19.352 Wiþ þe *lord* þat lyueþ after þe lust of his body,
B.19.382 The *lord* of lust shal be letted al þis lente, I hope.
B.19.459 Thanne louȝ þer a *lord* and, 'by þis light!' seide,
B.20.71 Wiþ a *lord* þat lyueþ after likyng of body,
B.20.90 The *lord* þat lyued after lust þo aloud cryde
B.20.92 'Alarme! alarme!' quod þat *lord*, 'ech lif kepe his owene!'
B.20.94 And er heraudes of Armes hadden discryued *lordes*,
B.20.325 To a *lord* for a lettre leue to haue
B.20.345 And was my *lordes* leche and my ladies boþe.
B.20.346 And at þe laste þis lymytour, [þo my *lord* was oute,
C.Pr.28 Al for loue of oure *lord* lyueden [ful streyte]
C.Pr.62 Ac sith charite hath be Chapman and [c]hief to shryue *lordes*
C.Pr.93 And summe aren as seneschalles and seruen oþer *lordes*
C.Pr.103 I leue, by oure *lord*, for loue of ȝoure coueytise
C.Pr.130 Hou he it lefte with loue as oure *lord* wolde
C.Pr.164 And nat for loue of oure *lord* vnlose here lyppes ones.
C.Pr.177 We myhte be *lordes* alofte and lyue as vs luste.'
C. 1.87 And also lyk [to] oure *lord* by saynt Lukes wordes.
C. 1.95 And for no *lordene* loue leue þe trewe partie.
C. 1.111 That hadde [lu]st to be lyk his *lord* þat was almyghty:
C. 1.112 '*Lord*! why wolde he tho, þat wykkede lucifer,
C. 1.142 For to louye thy *lord* leuest of alle,
C. 1.155 Forthi is loue ledare of [þe] *lordes* folk of heuene
C. 2.21 And [ylow on] hym to *lordes* þat lawes han to kepe;
C. 2.134 Lokede vp to oure *lord* and alowed sayde:

C. 3.31	To louye hem leeliche and *lordes* [hem] make,
C. 3.57	The whiles ʒe louyen *lordes* that lecherye haunteth
C. 3.73	Forthy, l[e]ue *lordes*, leueth suche writynges;
C. 3.75	Lat nat thy lyft ha[lf], oure *lord* techeth,
C. 3.99	That louten for hem to oure *lord* and to oure lady bothe
C. 3.125	Amonge thise lettred *lordes* this latyn is to mene
C. 3.149	'ʒe, *lord*,' quod that lady, '*lord* hit me forbede
C. 3.149	'ʒe, *lord*,' quod that lady, '*lord* hit me forbede
C. 3.213	Thus lereth this lady thi lond, now *lord* ʒeue here sorwe!
C. 3.221	'Nay, *lord*,' quod þat lady, 'leueth hym þe worse
C. 3.241	And as his wyrdus were ordeyned at þe wille of oure *lorde*.
C. 3.260	He sholde haue [ben] *lord* of þat lond alenghe and abrede
C. 3.269	Emperours and Erles and alle manere *lordes*
C. 3.283	And glad for to grype here, gret *lord* oþer pore.'
C. 3.310	That bothe the *lord* and the laborer be leely yserued.
C. 3.379	Lawe, l[o]ue and lewete and hym *lord* antecedent,
C. 3.401	For þat *lordes* loue that for oure loue deyede
C. 3.420	And alle þat leueth on þat lond oure [*lord*] wol þat thow sle hit;
C. 4.39	More then for oure *lordes* loue oþer oure lady, goddes moder.'
C. 4.69	'Hadde y loue of [my] *lord* lytel wolde y reche
C. 4.109	Til *lordes* and ladies louen alle treuthe
C. 5.55	For by þe lawe of leuyticy þat oure *lord* ordeynede,
C. 5.69	Thyse bylongeth to labory and *lordes* kyn to serue.
C. 5.73	And *lordes* sones here laboreres and leyde here rentes to wedde
C. 5.85	Is the leuest labour þat oure *lord* pleseth.
C. 5.160	A[n] hep of houndes at h[is] ers as he a *lord* were
C. 5.163	Lytel hadde *lordes* ado to ʒeue lond fro [here] heyres
C. 5.167	Ac ʒe leten ʒow alle as *lordes*, ʒoure lond lyth so brode.
C. 6.4	And [lay] long ar he lokede and '*lord*, mercy!' cryede
C. 6.81	Lechecraft of oure *lord* and leue on a wycche
C. 6.101	*Lord*, ar y lyf lete, for loue of thysulue
C. 6.102	Graunte me, gode *lord*, grace of amendement.'
C. 6.195	Now, *lord*, for thy lewete on lechours haue mercy.'
C. 6.248	'Lenedest [thow] euere eny *lord* for loue of his mayntenaunce?'
C. 6.249	'Y haue lent *lordes* and ladyes þat louede me neuere aftur
C. 6.292	ʒut were me leuer, by oure *lord*, lyue al by wellecresses
C. 6.424	'Thow *lord* [þat] aloft art and alle lyues shope.
C. 7.12	Ac of oure *lord* ne of oure lady þe leste þat euere was maked.
C. 7.74	And hath no likynge to lerne ne of oure *lord* to here
C. 7.81	ʒe *lordes* and ladies and legatus of holy churche
C. 7.91	Clerkes þat knoweth this sholde kenne *lordes*
C. 7.95	Ne no mysproud man amongus *lordes* be [alow]ede.
C. 7.97	And for loue of here ly[th]eth hem at festes;
C. 7.104	With a lered man to lere the what oure *lord* suffrede
C. 7.108	To crye a largesse tofore oure *lord* ʒoure good loos to shewe.
C. 7.208	That ʒe louye hym [as] *lord* leely aboue alle.
C. 8.16	As longe as y leue, for [þe] *lordes* loue of heuene.
C. 8.67	Shal haue leue, by oure *lord*, to [lese here in heruest]
C. 8.135	[We haue] none lymes to labory with, *lord* god we thonketh.'
C. 8.250	And ledares for here laboryng ouer al þe *lordes* godes;
C. 8.252	The *lord* for his lachesse and his luther sleuthe
C. 8.254	Þat leely hadde ylabored and thenne the *lord* sayde:
C. 8.297	And leelyche sayst, as y leue; *lord* hit þe forʒeld!
C. 9.14	Lele and fol of loue and no *lord* drede,
C. 9.18	Lechery amonges *lordes* and here luyther custumes,
C. 9.19	And suche liue as þei lereth men oure *lord* treuthe hem graunteth
C. 9.49	And for þe loue of oure *lord* lawe for hem declareth
C. 9.59	Lellyche and lauhfollyche, oure *lord* treuthe hem graunteth
C. 9.73	Charged with childrene and chief *lordes* rente.
C. 9.130	For þe *lordes* loue or þe ladyes þat they with longen.
C. 9.133	Me [g]yueth hem giftes and gold for grete *lordes* sake.
C. 9.185	For loue of here lowe hertes oure *lord* hath hem ygraunted
C. 9.224	Lewede men to labory; *lordes* to honte
C. 9.231	Thus hit bylongeth for *lord[e]*, for lered and for lewed
C. 9.270	When thy *lord* loketh to haue allouaunce of his bestes
C. 9.328	And so y leue lely–*lord* forbede elles–
C. 10.55	Oure lyf to oure *lord* god for oure lycames gultes.'
C. 10.96	*Lordes* þat lyuen as hem lust and no lawe acounten,
C. 10.148	And sire go[dfray] go-wel, grete *lordes* alle.
C. 10.155	*Lord* of lyf and of lyht, of lisse and of payne.
C. 10.217	On a leye land aʒeynes his *lordes* wille,
C. 10.219	Þat lycame haen aʒen þe law þat oure *lord* ordeynede.
C. 11.24	"Lo!" saith holy leture, "whiche *lordes* beth this schrewes";
C. 11.32	Litel is he loued or leet [by] among *lordes* at festes.
C. 11.45	Lytel loueth he þat *lord* þat lente hym al þat blisse
C. 11.74	Ac lust no *lord* now ne lettred man of suche lore to here
C. 11.76	And þat loueth *lordes* now and leten hit a dowel
C. 11.182	Til thow be a *lord* and haue lond leten y þe nelle
C. 11.200	Y leue neuere þat *lord* ne lady þat lyueth her [o]n erthe
C. 11.208	Y leue hit wel by oure *lord* and on no letture bettere.
C. 11.224	A[c] me were leuere, by oure *lord*, a lyppe of goddes grace
C. 12.44	The bileue of oure *lord* þat lettred men techeth.
C. 12.63	Withouten leue of [his] *lord*; no lawe wol hit graunte.
C.12.89	'Lo! *lordes*, what leute dede and leele dome yvsed.
C.12.90	Wel ouhte ʒe *lordes* þat lawes kepeth this lesson haue in mynde
C.12.92	And louye for oure *lordes* loue and do leute euermore.
C.12.97	So loue and leute ben oure *lordes* bokes
C.12.116	And we his blody bretherne, as wel beggares as *lordes*.
C.12.120	Forthy lerne we t[he] lawe of loue as oure *lord* tauhte
C.12.122	For in here likenesse oure *lord* lome hath be yknowe.
C.12.158	For þe loue of oure *lord* lo[w]eth hym to be pore,
C.12.160	And lyf lastyng for euere byfore oure *lord* in heuene:
C.12.195	Worth allowed of oure *lord* at here laste ende
C.12.219	Lo! *lordes*, lo! and ladyes, taketh hede:
C.13.12	And for he soffrede and saide nauht oure *lord* sente tookene
C.13.30	And lyues þat oure *lord* loueth and large weyes to heuene;
C.13.74	That oure *lord* loketh aftur of vch a lyf þat wynneth
C.13.88	Telleth þe *lord* a tale as a trewe messager
C.13.89	And sheweth be seel and seth by lettre with what *lord* he dwelleth,
C.14.20	As loreles to be *lordes* and lewede men techares,
C.14.38	Lawe of loue oure *lord* wrouhte] long ar crist were
C.14.87	Hit speketh þer of ryche men riht nouht ne of ryche *lordes*
C.14.150	That oure [*lord*] ne hauede [hym] lihtliche out, so leue y [by] þ[e]
	thef in heuene.
C.14.215	And þat is loue and large huyre, yf þe *lord* be trewe,
C.15.14	As wel lered as lewede and *lorde* as þe [b]oende,
C.15.15	And how þat lewede men ben lad, but oure *lord* hem helpe,
C.15.73	For oure *lordes* loue, as holy lettre telleth:
C.15.116	Ne l[yu]eth as ʒe lereth, as oure *lord* wolde:
C.15.166	To haue alle londes at thy likyng and the here *lord* make
C.15.169	As for here *lord* and here ledare and l[y]ue as thow techest.'
C.15.178	Me were leuere, by oure *lord*, and y leue sholde,
C.15.203	Or mantel or mone amonges *lordes* munstrals.
C.15.208	Y haue no gode giftes of thise grete *lordes*
C.15.209	For no breed þat y betrauaile to [brynge] byfore *lordes*.
C.15.214	[For] *lordes* and lorelles, luther and gode,
C.15.244	Leue thorw lele bileue, As oure *lord* wittenesseth:
C.15.252	Shal neuere gyues the greue ne grete *lordes* wrathe,
C.15.274	The whiche wil loue lat to oure *lordes* place
C.15.286	To haue allouaunce of his *lord*; by [þe] lawe he [hit] claymeth.
C.15.302	And *lordes* and ladyes ben cald for ledes þat they haue
C.16.2	Fro þe loue of oure *lord* at his laste ende.
C.16.17	Now, *lord*, sende hem somur som tyme to solace and to ioye
C.16.145	For *lordes* alloueth hym litel or leggeth ere to his resoun;
C.16.153	Thus lered me a le[tte]red man for oure *lordes* loue, seynt Austyn;
C.16.195	And when y louye lelly oure *lord* and alle oþere
C.16.239	That y lye nat; loo! for *lordes* ʒe plese
C.16.283	Leueth hit wel, *lordes*, both lewed and lered,
C.17.26	That lyueden thus for oure *lordes* loue monye longe ʒeres
C.17.40	*Lord* leue," quod my lede, " no stole thynge be herynne!"
C.17.44	Thenne wolde *lordes* and ladyes be loth to agulte
C.17.56	Allas, *lordes* and ladyes, lewede consayle haue ʒe
C.17.67	He gaf goddes men goddes goodes and nat grete *lordes*
C.17.117	*Lord* lete þat this prestes lelly seien here masse,
C.17.135	And ayther loueth and byleueth in o [*lord*] almyhty.
C.17.136	Ac oure *lord* aloueth no loue but lawe be þe cause:
C.17.152	Louen as by lawe of kynde oure *lord* god almyhty.
C.17.155	To þat *lord* þat hym lyf lente lyflode hym sende.
C.17.157	Loueth nat þat *lord* aryht as by þe legende sanctorum
C.17.168	Ac for he was lyk a lossheborw y leue oure *lord* hym lette.
C.17.219	And lyuen as leuitici, as oure *lord* ʒow techeth:
C.17.227	Taketh here londe[s], ʒe *lordes*, and lat hem lyue by dymes
C.17.235	Aʒen þe lore of oure *lord* as seynt luk witnesseth–
C.17.295	Iewes lyuen in þe lawe þat oure *lord* tauhte
C.18.78	And more lykynde to oure *lord* then lyue as kynde asketh
C.18.82	That oure *lord* alloweth, as lered men vs techeth,
C.18.95	Shollen serue for þe *lord* sulue, and so fareth god almyhty.
C.18.197	How o *lord* myhte lyue [in] thre; y leue hit nat,' y sayde.
C.18.200	Thre bilongeth to a *lord* þat leiaunce claymeth,
C.18.253	Bledden bloed for þat *lordes* loue [and] hope to blisse þ[e] tyme.
C.18.264	I leue þat ilke *lord* thenketh a newe lawe to make:
C.18.275	'Loo!' quod he and lette me see: '*lord*, mercy!' y saide,
C.18.285	Lollyng in my lappe til suche a *lord* vs feche.'
C.19.18	'Is here al thy *lordes* l[aw]es?' quod y; 'ʒe, leef me,' he saide,
C.19.40	And seth to louye and to lene for þat *lordes* sake
C.19.42	And for to louye and bileue in o *lord* almyhty
C.19.44	Ac for to bileue in o *lord* þat lyueth in thre persones
C.19.186	Leel lycame and lyf þat oure *lord* shupte.
C.19.265	A fordoth the lihte þat oure *lord* loketh to haue worschipe of.
C.19.277	Leue y neuere þat oure *lord* at þe laste ende
C.19.325	And lihtliche oure *lord* at here lyues ende
C.20.59	The *lord* of lyf and of liht tho leyde his eyes togederes.
C.20.110	The which is lif þat oure *lord* in all lawes defendeth.
C.20.202	The loue of oure *lord* and his lore bothe
C.20.250	The lihte folewede þe *lord* into þe lowe erthe.
C.20.280	That such a *lord* and a lihte sh[olde] lede hem alle hennes.

C.20.283   And [y] shal lette this *loerd* and his liht stoppe.
C.20.295   'Lustneth!' quod lucifer, 'for y this *lord* knowe;
C.20.296   Bothe this *lord* and this lihte, ys longe ygo y knewe hym.
C.20.297   May no deth this *lord* dere ne [n]o deueles quentyse
C.20.306   Thus this *lord* of liht such a lawe made
C.20.307   And sethe he is a lele *lord* y leue þat he wol nat
C.20.352   Bote oure *lord* at þe laste lyares h[e] rebuke[th]
C.20.360   'What *lord* artow?' quod lucifer; a voys aloude saide:
C.20.361   'The *lord* of myhte and of mayne þat lord alle thynges.
C.20.369   And tho that oure *lord* louede forth with þat liht flowen.
C.20.370   'Lo! me here, ' quod oure *lord*, 'lyf and soule bothe,
C.20.403   For y þat am *lord* of lyf, loue is my drynke,
C.20.443   Thus by lawe,' quod oure *lord*, 'lede y wol fro hennes
C.20.448   They dorste nat loke on oure *lord*, þe leste of hem alle,
C.21.8   And riht lyke in alle lymes to oure *lord* iesu.
C.21.32   To make *lordes* of laddes of lond þat he wynneth
C.21.56   And toek lucifer the loethliche þat *lord* was of helle
C.21.96   Ac for all this preciouse presentes oure *lord* prince iesu[s]
C.21.173   Thow art my *lord*, y bileue, god lord iesu,
C.21.173   Thow art my lord, y bileue, god *lord* iesu,
C.21.352   With the *lord* þat lyueth aftur the lust of his body,
C.21.382   The *lord* of lust shal be ylette al this lente, y hope.
C.21.459   Thenne lowh ther a *lord* and 'bi this lihte!' saide:
C.22.71   With a *lord* þat lyueth aftur likyng of body
C.22.90   The *lord* þat lyuede aftur lust tho aloud cryede
C.22.92   'Alarme! alarme!' quod þat *lord*, 'vch lyf kepe his owene!'
C.22.94   And ar heroudes of Armes hadden descreued *lordes*,
C.22.325   To a *lord* for a lettre leue to haue
C.22.345   And was my *lordes* leche and my ladyes bothe.
C.22.346   And at þe laste this lymytour, tho my *lord* was oute,

lordeyne(s > lurdeyn; lordene > lord

lordeþ v *lorden v.* B 1; C 1 lordeth
B.10.87   And *lordeþ* in [ledes] þe lasse good he deleþ.
C.11.67   And *lordeth* in ledes the lasse goed he deleth.

lordlich adj *lordli adj.* A 1; B 2; C 1 lordliche
A. 3.150   Lawe is so *lordlich* & loþ to make ende.
B. 3.161   Lawe is so *lordlich* and looþ to maken ende.
B.13.301   And as a lyoun on to loke and *lordlich* of speche;
C. 3.199   Lawe is so *lordliche* and loth to make ende;

lordliche adv *lordli adv. &> lordlich* C 2
C.19.239   Moste *lordliche* lyue and ʒut [on] his lycame werie
C.19.245   *Lordliche* for to lyue and lykyngliche be clothed

lordshipe n *lordshipe n.* A 7 lordshepe (1) lordsshipe (6); B 16 lordshipe
        (15) lordshipes (1); C 17 lordschipe (3) lordschipe (13) lordschipes (1)
A. 2.28   Þat longiþ to þ[at] *lordsshipe*, þe lasse & þe more.
A. 2.61   Wiþ alle þe *lordsshipe* of leccherie in lengþe & in brede;
A. 3.194   To leuen his *lordsshipe* for a litel siluer,
A. 6.35   Þere is no labourer in his *lordsshipe* þat he louiþ beter
A. 8.142   Þe king lees his *lordsshipe*, & lesse men it hadde.
A.11.14   Þat hem were leuere lond, & *lordsshipe* on erþe,
A.12.64   To lyf in his *lordshepe* longyt my weye
B. 2.46   That longen to þat *lordshipe*, þe lasse and þe moore.
B. 2.89   [Wiþ] al þe *lordshipe* of leccherie in lengþe and in brede,
B. 3.207   To leuen his *lordshipe* for a litel siluer,
B. 7.164   The kyng lees his *lordshipe* and [lasse] men it hadde.
B. 9.41   The lettre, for al þe *lordshipe*, I leue, were neuere ymaked.
B.10.14   That hem were leuere lond and *lordshipe* on erþe,
B.14.263   In lond and in *lordshipe* and likynge of bodie
B.14.330   That euere he hadde lond ouþer *lordshipe* lasse oþer moore,
B.15.555   The *lordshipe* of londes [lese ye shul for euere],
B.15.558   Wiþ londes and ledes, *lordshipes* and rentes,
B.16.191   So þre bilongeþ for a lord þat *lordshipe* cleymeþ;
B.16.240   Lond and *lordshipe* and lif wiþouten ende.
B.17.8   That Luciferis *lordshipe* laste shal no lenger.
B.18.105   [Ne] haue *lordshipe* in londe ne no lond tilye,
B.18.315   And al oure *lordshipe*, I leue, a londe and [in helle]:
B.20.251   For loue lafte þei *lordshipe*, boþe lond and scole,
C. 2.50   That loueth here *lordschipe*, lasse other more.
C. 2.96   With al þe *lordschip* of leccherye in lenghe and in Brede,
C. 2.110   In *lordschip* with lucifer, as this lettre sheweth,
C. 3.249   Loketh aftur *lordschipe* or oþer large mede
C. 3.264   To lete so his *lordschipe* for a litel mone.
C. 3.316   ʒeue lond or *lordschipe* [or] oþer large ʒeftes
C. 9.203   Forsoken lond and *lordschipe* and lykyng[e] of body.
C.11.12   Þat [they] louyen lond and *lordschipe* and lykynge of body
C.16.103   In lond and in *lordschipe* [and] lykynge of body
C.16.160   'He þat hath lond and *lordschipe*,' quod he, 'at þe laste ende
C.17.218   The *lordschipe* of londes lese ʒe shal for euer
C.17.221   With londes and ledes, *lordschipes* and rentes,
C.18.256   Lond and *lordschip* ynow and lyf withouten ende.

C.19.10   That luciferes *lordschipe* lowe sholde lygge.'
C.20.108   Ne haue *lordschipe* in londe ne no londe tulye
C.20.349   We haen ylost oure *lordschipe* a londe and in helle:
C.22.251   For loue lefte they *lordschipe*, bothe lond and scole,

lore > lesen, loore

lorel n *lorel n.* A 2 lorel (1) lorellis (1); B 5 lorel (3) lorels (2); C 8 lorel
        (2) loreles (2) lorelles (4)
A. 7.114   Somme leide here leg alery as suche *lorellis* cunne,
A. 8.124   'Lewide *lorel*,' quaþ peris, 'litel lokest þou on þe bible;
B. 6.122   Somme leide hir le[g] aliry as swiche *lo[r]els* konneþ
B. 7.142   'Lewed *lorel*!' quod Piers, 'litel lokestow on þe bible;
B.15.5   And lete me for a *lorel* and looþ to reuerencen
B.17.47   Than for to louye and lene as wel *lorels* as lele.
B.18.3   And yede forþ lik a *lorel* al my lif tyme
C.Pr.75   And leneth hit *lorelles* þat lecherye haunten.
C. 6.313   For me is leuere in this lyue as a *lorel* begge
C. 8.129   [Somme] leyde here legges alery as suche *lorelles* conneth
C. 9.101   Reche ʒe neuere, ʒe riche, Thouh suche *lo[rell]es* sterue.
C. 9.137   The whiche [arn] lunatyk *loreles* and lepares aboute
C.14.20   As *loreles* to be lordes and lewede men techares,
C.15.214   [For] lordes and *lorelles*, luther and gode,
C.20.3   And ʒede forth ylike a *lorel* al my lyf tyme

loren > lesen

loresman n *loresman n.* B 3 looresmen (1) loresman (1) loresmen (1); C 1
B. 9.90   [So] Iewes [shul] ben oure *loresmen*, shame to vs alle!
B.12.182   But as his *loresman* lereþ hym bileueþ and troweþ,
B.15.391   Allas, þanne, but oure *looresmen* lyue as þei leren vs,
C.14.122   But as his *loresman* [lereth hym] byleueth and troweth,

*lorkyng > lurkynge; lorn > lesen; los > loos, losse; loscheborw >
lussheburwes; losedest > loseþ; loseles > losels*

losely adv *loslie adv.* B 1; C 1 loslich
B.12.213   And wel *lose[l]y* he lolleþ þere by þe lawe of holy chirche.
C.14.152   And wel *lo[s]liche* he lolleth þere by þe lawe of holy churche:

losels n *losel n.* A 2 loselis; B 3; C 2 loseles
A.Pr.74   And leniþ it *loselis* þat leccherie haunten.
A.11.36   Leccherie & losengerie & *loselis* talis;
B.Pr.77   And leneþ it *Losels* [þat] leccherie haunten.
B.10.50   Lecherie, losengerye and *losels* tales.
B.15.137   Lightliche þat þei leuen *losels* it habbeþ.
C. 8.74   That lollares and *loseles* lele men holdeth,
C.16.282   Lihtliche þat they leue *loseles* hit deuoureth.

losengerie n *losengerie n.* A 1; B 2 losengerie (1) losengerye (1)
A.11.36   Leccherie & *losengerie* & loselis talis;
B. 6.143   In lecherie and in *losengerie* ye lyuen, and in Sleuþe,
B.10.50   Lecherie, *losengerye* and losels tales.

loseþ v *losen v.(1)* B 2 losedest (1) loseþ (1)
B.11.421   Lakkedest and *losedest* þyng þat longed noʒt to doone;
B.15.253   Lakkeþ ne *loseþ* ne lokeþ vp sterne,

losliche > losely

losse n *los n.(1)* B 5 los (2) losse (3); C 4 loes (1) los (2) losse (1)
B.Pr.191   For bettre is a litel *los* þan a long sorwe.
B.13.386   For *losse* of good, leue me, þan for likames giltes;
B.14.7   And [laþered] wiþ þe *losse* of catel [forto me] looþ [were]
B.14.315   And [þouʒ] he chaffareþ he chargeþ no *losse*, mowe he charite
        wynne;
B.19.292   Mighte no [lyere wiþ lesynges] ne *los* of worldly catel
C. 5.97   And sette his *los* at a leef at the laste ende,
C. 6.275   For *lo[s]* of good, leef me, then for lycames gultes.
C.16.149   And thogh he chaffare he chargeth no *loes* may he charite wynne
C.21.292   Myhte no lyare with lesynge[s] ne *losse* of worldly catel

lossheborw n *lusheburgh n.& adj.* B 1 lussheburwes; C 3 loscheborw (1)
        lossheborw (1) lossheborwe (1)
B.15.349   As in *lussheburwes* is a luþer alay, and yet lokeþ he lik a sterlyng;
C.17.73   Me may now likene lettred men to a *loscheborw* oþer worse
C.17.83   Thus ar ʒe luyþer ylikned to *lossheborw*[e] sterlynges
C.17.168   Ac for he was lyk a *lossheborw* y leue oure lord hym lette.

lossum adj *lofsom adj.* C 1
C.10.259   And thogh he be louelich to loke[n] on and *lossum* abedde,

lost > lesen, lust; loste(n > lesen

lot n prop *n.i.d.* A 1 loth; B 2 Lot (1) loth (1); C 3 loot (2) lot (1)
A. 1.27   For *loth*, in his lyf dayes, for lykyng of drink
B. 1.27   For *Lot*, in hise lifdayes, for likynge of drynke,
B. 1.32   Thoruʒ wyn and þoruʒ wommen þer was *loth* acombred,
C. 1.25   *Loot* in his lyue thorw likerous drynke

C. 1.31   Thorw wyn and thorw wom[e]n there was *loot* acombred;
C.10.178   As *lo[t]* dede and Noe, and herodes þe daffe

lotebies n *lotebi n.*   A 1; B 1; C 1 lotebyes
A. 3.140   To holde lemmanis & *lotebies* alle here lif dayes,
B. 3.151   To [holde] lemmans and *lotebies* alle hire lifdaies,
C. 3.189   To holde lemmanes and *lotebyes* al here lyfdayes

loth > loþ,lot; loþ > loþe

loþe v *lothen v.* &> loþe A 1 loþe; B 2 loþe (1) loþeþ (1); C 3 lothed (1) lotheth (2)
A. 8.80   Þo þat lyuen þus here lif mowe *loþe* þe tyme
B.Pr.155   That vs *loþeþ* þe lif er he late vs passe.
B. 7.98   [Tho] þat lyue þus hir life mowe *loþe* þe tyme
C.Pr.175   That vs *lotheth* þe lyf ar he lette vs passe.
C. 6.142   That alle ladyes me *lot[h]eth* þat louyet[h] eny worschipe.
C. 7.50   Til eche lyf hit *lothed* to loke þeron or smylle hit;

loþely > loþly; loþer > loþe

loþly adj *lothli adj.*   B 3 loþely (1) loþly (1) loþliche (1); C 4 loethliche (1) lothliche (1) lothly (2)
B. 1.117   Lopen out wiþ Lucifer in *loþliche* forme
B.15.111   [For ypocrisie] in latyn is likned to a [*loþly*] dongehill
B.19.56   [And took [Lucifer þe *loþely*] þat lord was of helle
C. 1.110   Lepen out in *lothly* forme for his [luþer] wille
C.14.178   His le[d]ene is vnloueliche and *lothliche* his careyne
C.16.266   And is ylikned in latyn to a *lothly* dongheþ
C.21.56   And toek lucifer the *loethliche* þat lord was of helle

lotieþ v *loten v.(1)*   B 1
B.17.105   For [an] Outlaw[e is] in þe wode and vnder bank *lotieþ,*

lotus n *lote n.*   C 1
C.15.8   And vansche alle my vertues and my fayre *lotus;*

lou > lowe

louable adj *louable adj.*   C 1
C. 5.103   The l[y]f þat is *louable* and leele to thy soule.'

loud adj *loud adj.*   B 1; C 1 loude
B.18.423   And þanne lutede [loue] in a *loud* note:
C.20.466   And thenne lutede loue in a *loude* note:

loude adv *loude adv.* &> loud A 2; B 5; C 2
A. 4.138   And seide it so *loude* þat soþnesse it herde:
A.12.16   And seyde so *loude* þat shame me thou3the,
B. 4.162   And seid[e] it so [*loude*] þat [soþnesse] it herde:
B. 9.108   Oure lord loueþ hem and lent, *loude* ouþer stille,
B.13.179   Ac Conscience carped *loude* and curteisliche seide,
B.16.32   Thoru3 likynge and lustes so *loude* he gynneþ blowe
B.18.263   A vois *loude* in þat light to lucifer crieþ,
C.18.36   Thorw lecherie and lustes so *loude* he gynneth blowe
C.20.271   A vois *loude* in þat liht to lucifer saide,

loue n *loue n.(2)* &> lowe C 1
C.Pr.103   I leue, by oure lord, for *loue* of 3oure coueytise

lough > lau3en; lou3 > lau3en,lowe; lou3nesse > lowenesse; louh(e >
lau3en,lowe; louhliche > lowliche; louhnesse > lowenesse

louke v *louken v.(1)*   B 1; C 1
B.18.245   And lo! how þe sonne gan *louke* hire light in hirselue
C.20.254   And lo! how þe sonne gan *louke* here lihte in heresulue

loupe n *loupe n.(2)*   C 1
C.20.286   That no liht lepe in at louer ne at *loupe.*

loure v *louren v.*   A 2 lourande (1) louride (1); B 8 loure (2) loured (1) lourede (1) louren (1) lourestow (1) loureþ (1) lourynge (1); C 10 loure (4) loured (1) lourede (2) louren (1) lourest (1) lourynge (1)
A. 2.185   Þanne *louride* lechis & lettris [hy] sente
A. 5.65   So lokide he wiþ lene chekis, *lourande* foule.
B. 2.226   Thanne *lourede* leches, and lettres þei sente
B. 5.82   So loked he wiþ lene chekes, *lourynge* foule.
B. 5.133   To lye and to *loure* on my ne3ebore and to lakke his chaffare.
B.10.316   He *loureþ* on hym and [lakkeþ] hym: who [lered] hym curteisie?
B.11.84   And lewte [lou3] on me [for] I *loured* [on þe frere];
B.11.85   'Wherfore *lourestow*?' quod lewtee, and loked on me harde.
B.12.280   'Contra!' quod Ymaginatif þoo and comsed to *loure,*
B.13.264   And *louren* whan þei lakken hem; it is no3t longe ypassed
C. 2.236   Thenne *lourede* leches and lettre[s] þei sente
C. 4.168   And *lourede* vppon men of lawe and lyhtlych sayde:
C. 5.162   He loketh al *lourynge* and lordeyne hym calleth.
C. 6.98   To lye and to *loure* and to lakke myn neyhebores,
C. 7.302   And *louren* on me and lihtly chyde and sygge y louede another.
C.12.23   And thenne louhe leaute for y *loured* on þe frere:
C.12.24   'Why *lourest* [thou]?' quod leaute; 'leue sire,' y saide,

C.14.202   'Contra!' quod ymagynatif tho and comesed to *loure*
C.16.304   Lawhe þer men lawheth and *loure* þer oþere louren.
C.16.304   Lawhe þer men lawheth and loure þer oþere *louren.*

lourynge ger *louringe ger.* &> louren A 1 louryng; B 1; C 1 louryng
A. 5.185   Þere was lau3ing & *louryng* & 'lete go þe cuppe!'
B. 5.336   There was lau3ynge and *lourynge* and 'lat go þe cuppe!'
C. 6.394   There was leyhing and *louryng* and 'lat go þe coppe!'

lous n *louse n.*   A 1; B 1; C 1
A. 5.112   But 3if a *lous* couþe lepe, I may it nou3t leue
B. 5.196   But if a *lous* couþe [lepe, I leue and I trowe],
C. 6.204   But yf a *lous* couthe lepe, y leue [and] y trowe,

louten v *louten v.(1)*   A 4 loutide (3) lowtyng (1); B 6 louted (3) loutede (2) louten (1); C 6 loute (2) louted (1) loutede (1) louten (2)
A. 3.35   To mede þe maiden mekeliche he *loutide,*
A. 3.105   Knelynge, consience to þe kyng *loutide,*
A.11.98   But al lau3inge he *loutide* & lokide vpon studie
A.12.55   Þus we lau3þe oure leue, *lowtyng* at onys,
B. 3.36   To Mede þe mayde [mekeliche he *loutede*]
B. 3.116   Knelynge, Conscience to þe kyng *louted,*
B.10.145   But al lau3ynge he *louted* and loked vpon Studie
B.13.26   That lowe *louted* and loueliche to scripture.
B.15.9   'God loke yow, lordes', ne *loutede* faire,
B.15.86   And *louten* to þise lordes þat mowen lene yow nobles
C. 3.99   That *louten* for hem to oure lord and to oure lady bothe
C. 3.153   Knelyng, consience to þe kyng *loutede,*
C. 6.171   'Lady, to thy leue sone *loute* for me nouthe
C.11.83   But al lauhynge he *louted* and loked vppon stud[i]e,
C.11.85   And when y was war of his wille to þat womman gan y *louten*
C.15.168   The kyng and alle þe comune and clergie to þe *loute*

loue n1 *love n.(1)*   A 36 loue (35) louis (1); B 108 loue (107) loues (1); C 139
A.Pr.26   Al for *loue* of oure lord lyuede wel streite
A.Pr.87   A[c] nou3t for *loue* of oure lord vnlose here lippes ones.
A. 1.67   He is lettere of *loue*, lei3eþ hem alle;
A. 1.101   And neuere leue h[e]m for *loue* ne lacching of 3eftis;
A. 1.136   Þat *loue* is þe leuest þing þat oure lord askiþ,
A. 1.141   Lokide on vs wiþ *loue*, & let his sone dei3e
A. 1.176   Þat is þe lok of *loue* þat letiþ out my grace
A. 1.178   *Loue* is þe leueste þing þat oure lord askiþ,
A. 2.2   And seide, 'mercy madame, for marie *loue* of heuene
A. 3.80   'For my *loue*,' quaþ þat lady, 'loue hem ichone,
A. 3.223   Loue hem & le[n]e hem for oure lordis *loue* of heuene;
A. 3.267   But *loue* & lou3nesse & leaute togideris;
A. 3.276   And make of lawe a labourer, such *loue* shal arise.'
A. 4.51   And seide, 'hadde I *loue* of my lord þe king, litel wolde I recche
A. 4.96   As longe as I lyue but more *loue* it make.'
A. 4.131   And *loue* shal lede þi land as þe lef likeþ.'
A. 4.137   *Loue* let of hire li3t & lou3 hire to scorne.
A. 6.78   Wiþ no led but [wiþ] *loue* & lou3nesse, as breþeren of o wombe.
A. 6.102   Þus mi3t þou lese his *loue*, to lete wel be þiselue,
A. 7.17   As longe as I lyue for þe lordis *loue* of heuene.
A. 7.28   A[nd] ek laboure for þi *loue* al my lif tyme,
A. 7.206   Counforte hem wiþ þi catel for cristis *loue* of heuene;
A. 8.33   Fynde suche here foode for oure lordis *loue* of heuene,
A. 8.52   Ac for oure lordis *loue* lawe for hym shewiþ,
A. 8.65   And lyuen in *loue* & [in] lawe, for here lou3 herte
A. 8.72   Þei lyue nou3t in *loue*, ne no lawe holden.
A. 8.87   For *loue* of here lou3 herte oure lord haþ hem grauntid
A. 8.132   And for peris *loue* þe plou3man wel pensif in herte,
A.10.43   For *loue* of þat lady þat lif is ynempnid.
A.10.129   For *loue* of here lou3nesse oure lord 3iueþ hem grace
A.10.204   Of lif & of *loue* & of lawe also
A.10.21   Vngracious to gete *loue* or any good ellis,
A.11.141   Ne were þe *loue* þat liþ þerein a wel lewid þing it were.
A.11.142   Ac for it lat best be *loue* I loue it þe betere,
A.11.143   For þere þat *loue* is lord lakkiþ neuere grace.
A.11.145   For dobet & dobest ben drawen of *louis* s[co]le.
B.Pr.26   Al for *loue* of oure lord lyueden [wel] streye
B.Pr.102   How he it lefte wiþ *loue* as oure lord hi3te
B.Pr.110   For in *loue* and lettrure þe eleccion bilongeþ;
B.Pr.214   [Ac] no3t for *loue* of oure lord vnlose hire lippes ones.
B. 1.69   He is lettere of *loue*, lieþ hem alle;
B. 1.103   And neuere leue hem for *loue* ne lacchynge of [3iftes];_
B. 1.148   For truþe telleþ þat *loue* is triacle of heuene:
B. 1.150   And alle hise werkes he wrou3te with *loue* as hym liste;
B. 1.159   Forþi is *loue* ledere of þe lordes folk of heuene
B. 1.161   Right so is *loue* a ledere and þe lawe shapeþ;
B. 1.167   Loked on vs wiþ *loue* and leet his sone dye
B. 1.202   [Th]at is þe lok of *loue* [þat] leteþ out my grace
B. 1.204   *Loue* is leche of lif and next oure lord selue,
B. 2.2   And seide 'mercy, madame, for Marie *loue* of heuene

B. 2.35	That he shal lese for hire *loue* a l[i]ppe of Caritatis.
B. 3.91	'For my *loue*', quod þat lady, '*loue* hem echone,
B. 3.159	And doþ men lese þoruȝ hire *loue* þat lawe myȝte wynne;
B. 3.291	Ac *loue* and lowenesse and leautee togideres;
B. 3.299	Ac kynde *loue* shal come ȝit and Conscience togideres
B. 3.300	And make of lawe a laborer; swich *loue* shal arise
B. 4.36	Ac [þ]ere is *loue* and leautee [hem likeþ] noȝt come þere.
B. 4.39	Moore þan for] *loue* of oure lord or alle hise leeue Seintes.
B. 4.65	And seide, 'hadde I *loue* of my lord þe kyng litel wolde I recche
B. 4.148	And *loue* shal lede þi lond as þe leef likeþ.'
B. 4.161	*Loue* leet of hire liȝt and leaute yet lasse,
B. 5.241	And lene it for *loue* of þe cros, to legge a wed and lese it.
B. 5.250	'Lentestow euere lordes for *loue* of hire mayntenaunce?'
B. 5.376	For *loue* of tales in Tauernes [to] drynke þe moore I [hyed;
B. 5.432	I am noȝt lured wiþ *loue* but þer ligge auȝt vnder þe þombe.
B. 5.591	Wiþ no leed but wiþ *loue* and lowe[nesse] as breþeren [of o wombe.]
B. 5.616	Thus myȝtestow lesen his *loue*, to lete wel by þiselue,
B. 6.18	As longe as I lyue, for þe lordes *loue* of heuene.
B. 6.26	And [ek] labour[e] for þi *loue* al my lif tyme,
B. 6.220	Conforte h[e]m wiþ þi catel for cristes *loue* of heuene;
B. 7.31	Fynden [swiche] hir foode [for oure lordes *loue* of heuene],
B. 7.50	[Ac] for oure lordes *loue* [lawe for hym sheweþ],
B. 7.63	And lyuen in *loue* and in lawe, for hir lowe hert[e]
B. 7.77	That askeþ for his *loue* þat vs al leneþ
B. 7.90	For [þei] lyue in no *loue* ne no lawe holde.
B. 7.105	For *loue* of hir lowe hert[e] oure lord haþ hem graunted
B. 7.151	And for Piers [*loue*] þe Plowman [wel] pencif in herte,
B. 9.55	For *loue* of þe lady anima þat lif is ynempned.
B. 9.97	That dredeþ god, he dooþ wel; þat dredeþ hym for *loue*
B. 9.180	For no londes, but for *loue*, loke ye be wedded
B. 9.191	Of lif and of [*loue*] and [of lawe also]
B. 9.197	Vngracious to gete good or *loue* of þe peple;
B.10.189	[Ne were þe *loue* þat liþ þerinne a wel lewed þyng it were].
B.10.190	Ac for it leteþ best bi *loue* I loue it þe bettre,
B.10.191	For þere þat *loue* is ledere lakke[þ] neuere grace.
B.10.193	For dobet and dobest ben [drawen] of *loues* [scole].
B.10.206	To do good for goddes *loue* and gyuen men þat asked,
B.10.310	And gret *loue* and likyng for ech [loweþ hym to] ooþer.
B.10.439	Wher fo[r *loue*] a man worþ allowed þere and hise lele werkes.
B.11.8	And into þe lond of longynge [and] *loue* she me brouȝte
B.11.106	Neiþer for *loue* [looue] it noȝt ne lakke it for enuye:
B.11.145	But oonliche *loue* and leautee and my laweful domes.
B.11.152	By *loue* and by lernyng of my lyuynge in truþe;
B.11.162	Ac þus leel *loue* and lyuyng in truþe
B.11.167	*Loue* and lewtee is a leel science,
B.11.171	'Lawe wiþouten *loue*', quod Troianus, 'ley þer a bene!'
B.11.229	Forþi lerne we þe lawe of *loue* as oure lord tauȝte;
B.11.278	To beggeris þat begge and bidden for goddes *loue*.
B.12.68	Ac grace is a gifte of god and of greet *loue* spryngeþ;
B.12.71	And namely Clergie for cristes *loue*, þat of Clergie is roote.
B.12.140	And *loue* shal lepen out after into þ[is] lowe erþe,
B.13.125	And set alle sciences at a sop saue *loue* one;
B.13.139	[Th]us [lerede] me ones a lemman, *loue* was hir name.
B.13.142	And so þow lere þe to louye, for [þe] lordes *loue* of heuene.
B.13.145	Boþe wiþ wer[k] and with wor[d] fonde his *loue* to wynne;
B.13.146	And leye on hym þus with *loue* til he lauȝe on þe.
B.13.150	Kynde *loue* coueiteþ noȝt no catel but speche.
B.13.356	Moore to good þan to god þe gome his *loue* caste,
B.13.359	Lened for *loue* of þe wed and looþ to do truþe;
B.13.437	And for *loue* of [hir] lorde liþeþ hem at festes;
B.14.133	Fram þe *loue* of oure lord at his laste ende!
B.14.264	And for goddes *loue* leueþ al and lyueþ as a beggere.
B.14.265	And as a mayde for mannes *loue* hire moder forsakeþ,
B.14.270	Moore for coueitise of [catel] þan kynde *loue* of boþe–
B.14.319	Thus lered me a lettred man for oure lordes *loue*, Seint Austyn:
B.15.15	If he were cristes creature [for cristes *loue*] me to tellen.
B.15.34	Thanne is lele *loue* my name, and in latyn Amor;
B.15.218	The *loue* þat liþ in his herte makeþ hym liȝt of speche,
B.15.255	The mooste liflode he lyueþ by is *loue* in goddes passion;
B.15.297	That lyueden þus for oure lordes *loue* many longe yeres.
B.15.468	So *loue* and leaute lele men susteneþ.
B.15.524	Amonges vnkynde cristene for cristes *loue* he deyede,
B.15.531	Many man for cristes *loue* was martired [amonges] Romayne[s]
B.16.2	For Haukyns *loue* þe Actif man euere I shal yow louye.
B.16.237	Bledden blood for þat lordes *loue* and hope to blisse þe tyme.
B.17.120	Hope shal lede hem forþ with *loue* as his lettre telleþ,
B.17.213	[Fostren forþ amonges folk *loue* and bileue]
B.17.220	Lele *loue* or lif þat oure lord shapte.
B.17.228	Til þat lele *loue* ligge on hym and blowe.
B.17.280	The which is lif and *loue*, þe leye of mannes body.
B.18.169	*Loue* haþ coueited hire longe; leue I noon ooþer
B.18.170	But [*loue*] sente hire som lettre what þis light bymeneþ
B.18.182	*Loue* þat is my lemman swiche lettres me sente
B.18.197	The *loue* of oure lord and his loore boþe,
B.18.365	For I þat am lord of lif, *loue* is my drynke,
B.18.411	Ne no *loue* leuere, ne leuer frendes,
B.18.412	Than after werre and wo whan *loue* and pees ben maistres.
B.18.414	That *loue*, and hym liste, to laughynge ne brouȝte;
B.18.423	And þanne lutede [*loue*] in a loud note:
B.19.310	Wiþ olde lawe and newe lawe þat *loue* myȝte wexe
B.19.340	And his Spye Spille-*loue*, oon Spek-yuel-bihynde.
B.20.77	Fooles fro þise fendes lymes, for Piers *loue* þe Plowman.
B.20.251	For *loue* lafte þei lordshipe, boþe lond and scole,
B.20.252	Frere Fraunceys and Domynyk, for *loue* to be holye.
C.Pr.28	Al for *loue* of oure lord lyueden [ful streyte]
C.Pr.88	That is lele *loue* and lyf among lered and lewed,
C.Pr.130	Hou he it lefte with *loue* as oure lord wolde
C.Pr.137	For in *loue* and lettrure lith þe grete eleccoun.
C.Pr.164	And nat for *loue* of oure lord vnlose here lyppes ones.
C. 1.65	He is lettere of *loue* and lyeth alle tymes;
C. 1.95	And for no lordene *loue* leue þe trewe partie.
C. 1.101	And neuer leue for *loue* in hope to lacche syluer.
C. 1.136	Tha[n] treuthe and trewe *loue* is no tresor bettre.'
C. 1.146	For treuthe telleth þat *loue* ys triacle [for] synne
C. 1.148	*Loue* is [þe] plonte of pees, most precious of vertues,
C. 1.155	Forthi is *loue* ledare of [þe] lordes folk of heuene
C. 1.157	Ryht so is *loue* [a] ledare and þe lawe shapeth;
C. 1.163	Lokede on vs with *loue* [and] let his sone deye
C. 1.197	Þat is þe lok of *loue* [þat] vnloseth grace,
C. 1.199	So *loue* is lecche of lyf and lysse of alle payne
C. 1.204	To lere the what *loue* is;' and leue at me she lauhte.
C. 2.2	And sayde 'mercy, madame, for mary *loue* of heuene
C. 2.37	He shal lese for here *loue* [a] lippe of trewe charite.
C. 3.119	Loue hem for my *loue*,' quod this lady mede,
C. 3.317	To here [lele] and lege, *loue* [is] the cause;
C. 3.377	That here *loue* to his lawe Thorw al þe lond acorde.
C. 3.379	Lawe, l[o]ue and lewete and hym lord antecedent,
C. 3.401	For þat lordes *loue* that for oure loue deyede
C. 3.401	For þat lordes loue that for oure *loue* deyede
C. 3.444	Ac *loue* and lownesse and lewete togyderes;
C. 3.452	A[c] kynde *loue* shal come ȝut and Consience togyderes
C. 3.453	And maky of lawe [a] laborer; suche *loue* shal aryse
C. 4.36	Ac there is *loue* and leutee hit lyketh nat here hertes:
C. 4.39	More then for oure lordes *loue* oþer oure lady, goddes moder.'
C. 4.69	'Hadde y *loue* of [my] lord lytel wolde y reche
C. 4.145	And *loue* shal lede thi land as the leef lyketh.'
C. 4.156	*Loue* l[et]te of mede lyhte and leutee ȝut lasse
C. 4.191	'And y dar lege my lyf þat *loue* wol lene þe seluer
C. 5.80	Lyfholynesse and *loue* hath be longe hennes
C. 5.155	In scole is *loue* and louhnesse and lykyng to lerne.
C. 5.192	And no grace [to] graunte til good *loue* were
C. 6.47	And what y gaf for goddes *loue* to gossipus y tolde,
C. 6.101	Lord, ar y lyf lete, for *loue* of thysulue
C. 6.173	With þat y shal,' quod þat shrewe, 'saturdayes for thy *loue*
C. 6.243	And len[e] for *loue* of þe wed the whych y lette bettere
C. 6.248	'Lenedest [thow] euere eny lord for *loue* of his mayntenaunce?'
C. 7.45	Y am nat luyred with *loue* but þer lygge ouht vnder þe t[h]umbe.
C. 7.97	And for *loue* of here lord ly[th]eth hem at festes;
C. 7.148	And for [that] muchel mercy and marie *loue* thi moder
C. 7.238	With no leed but with *loue* and with lele speche;
C. 7.260	Ȝef *loue* and leute and oure lawe [be] trewe:
C. 7.268	Thus myhte thow lesen his *loue*, to lete wel by thysulue,
C. 8.16	As longe as y leue, for [þe] lordes *loue* of heuene.
C. 8.213	Hit is nat for *loue*, leue hit, thei labore thus faste
C. 8.215	'Ther is no fi[al] *loue* with this folk for al here fayre speche
C. 8.283	Alle þat gr[eden at] thy gate for godes *loue* aftur fode
C. 9.14	Lele and fol of *loue* and no lord drede,
C. 9.35	Fynde hem for godes *loue* and fauntkynes to scole,
C. 9.49	And for þe *loue* of oure lord lawe for hem declareth
C. 9.66	For he þat gyueth for goddes *loue* wolde nat gyue, his thankes,
C. 9.130	For þe lordes *loue* or þe ladyes þat they with longen.
C. 9.167	For they lyue in no *loue* ne no lawe holden
C. 9.185	For *loue* of here lowe hertes oure lord hath hem ygraunted
C.10.170	The which is *loue* and lyf þat last withouten ende.
C.10.172	By *loue* and by leute, þerby lyueth anima
C.10.196	And seth [he les] his lyf for lawe sholde *loue* wexe.
C.10.203	Hoso lyueth in lawe and in *loue* doth wel
C.10.282	And loke þat *loue* be more þe cause then lond oþer nobles.
C.10.291	Clene of lyf and in *loue* of soule and in lele wedlok.
C.10.296	Vngracious to gete goed or *loue* of [þe] peple,
C.11.73	Get þe *loue* þerwith thogh thow worse fare".
C.11.80	The which is a lykyng and luste, *loue* of þe world.'
C.11.131	For *loue* is a lykyng thyng and loth for to greue.
C.11.133	For of dobet and dobest here doctour is dere *loue*.'
C.11.141	And byleef lely how goddes [l]o[u]e alyhte

C.11.158	Thus bileue and le[ute], and *loue* is the thridde
C.11.167	And into þe lond of longyng [and *loue*] she me brouhte
C.12.40	Nother for *loue* [loue] it [nat] ne lacke hit for enuye:
C.12.80	Bote onlyche *loue* and leaute as in my lawes demynge.
C.12.87	*Loue* withoute lele bileue a[nd] my lawe riht[ful]
C.12.92	And louye for oure lordes *loue* and do leute euermore.
C.12.95	Bote *loue* and leute hem lede ylost is al þe tyme
C.12.97	So *loue* and leute ben oure lordes bokes
C.12.120	Forthy lerne we t[he] lawe of *loue* as oure lord tauhte
C.12.158	For þe *loue* of oure lord lo[w]eth hym to be pore,
C.12.166	Ac 3ef hem forth to pore folk þat for my *loue* hit aske;
C.13.201	So is soffrance souereynliche, so hit be for godes *loue*.
C.14.14	Is ycalde Caritas, kynde *loue* an engelysche,
C.14.27	And sent forth the seynt espirit to do *loue* sprynge:
C.14.35	And 3ut is clergie to comende for cristes *loue* more
C.14.38	Lawe of *loue* oure lord wrouht] long ar crist were.
C.14.85	And *loue* shal lepe out aftur into þis lowe erthe
C.15.34	Crauede and cryede for cristes *loue* of heuene
C.15.73	For oure lordes *loue*, as holy lettre telleth:
C.15.130	For Peres *loue* þe palmare 3ent, þat inpugnede ones
C.15.132	Saue *loue* and leute and lowenesse of herte,
C.15.136	Bote lele *loue* and treuthe that loth is to be founde.'
C.15.143	Fond [with] wit & word his *loue* to wynne,
C.15.146	And ley on hym thus with *loue* til he lauhe on þe.
C.15.217	That pestilenc[e] to pees and parfyt *loue* turn[e].
C.15.274	The whiche wil *loue* lat to oure lordes place
C.16.2	Fro þe *loue* of oure lord at his laste ende.
C.16.104	And for goddes *loue* leueth al and lyueth as a beggare.
C.16.105	As a mayde for mannes *loue* here moder fors[a]ke[th],
C.16.110	More for coueytise of catel then kynde *loue* of þe mariage.
C.16.153	Thus lered me a le[tte]red man for oure lordes *loue*, seynt Austyn:
C.16.166	And yf thow be cristes creature, for cristes *loue* telle me.'
C.16.196	Thenne is lele *loue* my name and in latyn Amor;
C.16.285	That lyuen a3en holy lore and þe *loue* of charite.'
C.17.22	*Loue* and lele byleue held lyf and soule togyderes.
C.17.24	Bote thre litle loues and *loue* was here soule.
C.17.26	That lyueden thus for oure lordes *loue* monye longe 3eres
C.17.48	Thenne grace sholde growe 3ut and grene *loue* wexe
C.17.126	'[Lif in] *loue* and leutee in o byleue a[nd] lawe,
C.17.136	Ac oure lord aloueth no *loue* but lawe be þe cause:
C.17.139	And lele men lyue as lawe techeth and *loue* þerof aryseth
C.17.237	Alle londes into *loue* And þat in lytel tyme;
C.17.281	Many man for cristes *loue* was martired amonges Romaynes
C.17.290	So is þe kynde of a curatour for criste[s] *loue* to preche
C.18.9	'The tree hatte trewe *loue*,' quod he, 'the trinite hit sette.
C.18.253	Bledden bloed for þat lordes *loue* [and] hope to blisse þ[e] tyme.
C.19.101	And lered me for his *loue* to louye al mankynde
C.19.179	Fostren forth amongus folke *loue* and bileue
C.19.194	Til þat *loue* and bileue leliche to hym blowe.
C.19.261	The which is lyf and *loue*, the leye of mannes body.
C.19.278	Wol louye þat lyf þat *loue* and Charite destruyeth.'
C.20.20	'Liberum dei Arbitrium for *loue* hath vndertake
C.20.172	*Loue* hath coueyted here longe; leue y non oþere
C.20.173	Bote *loue* haue ysente her som lettre what this liht bymeneth
C.20.185	*Loue* þat is my lemman such lettres me sente
C.20.202	The *loue* of oure lord and his lore bothe
C.20.314	A3eyne his *loue* and his leue on his londe 3edest,
C.20.381	A3eyne my *loue* and my leue: þe olde lawe techeth
C.20.403	For y þat am lord of lyf, *loue* is my drynke,
C.20.454	Ne no *loue* leuore ne leuore frendes
C.20.455	Then aftur werre and wrake when *loue* and pees ben maistres.
C.20.457	That *loue*, and hym luste, to l[a]u[h]ynge [ne] brouhte;
C.20.466	And thenne lutede *loue* in a loude note:
C.21.310	With olde lawe and newe [lawe] that *loue* myhte wexe
C.21.340	And his spye spille-*loue*, oen speke-euele-bihynde.
C.22.77	Foles fro this fendes lymes for [Peres] *loue* the [plouhman].
C.22.251	For *loue* lefte they lordschipe, bothe lond and scole,
C.22.252	Frere fraunceys and domynyk, for *loue* to be holy.

loue *n2* *lof n.(1) cf. n1* B 2; C 2

B.11.173	But þei ben lerned for oure lordes *loue*, lost is al þe tyme
B.11.175	But al for *loue* of oure lord and þe bet to loue þe peple.
C.8.196	But lyflode for his la[b]our and his *loue* at nones.
C.14.215	And þat is *loue* and large huyre, yf þe lord be trewe,

loue *v1* *loven v.(1) cf. v2* A 21 loue (12) louen (1) louid (1) louye (1) louyn (1) louiþ (5); B 100 loue (27) loued (6) louede (9) louen (9) loueþ (19) louye (28) louyen (1) louyeþ (1); C 107 loue (14) loued (2) louede (15) loueden (1) louen (3) louest (1) loueth (20) louie (3) louye (35) louyen (5) louieth (1) louyeth (7)

A.1.76	To *loue* me lelly whiles þi lif duriþ.'
A.1.131	For to *loue* þi lord leuere þanne þiselue;
A.1.155	But 3if 3e *loue* lelly & lene þe pore,
A.3.29	To *loue* hem lelly & lordis hem make,

A.3.31	'Shal no lewidnesse hym lette, þe lede þat I *louye*,
A.3.80	'For my *loue*,' quaþ þat lady, '*loue* hem ichone,
A.3.115	Leri[þ] hem leccherie þat *loui[þ]* hire 3eftis.
A.3.199	Mede makiþ hym be *louid* & for a man holde.
A.3.223	*Loue* hem & le[n]e hem for oure lordis loue of heuene:
A.6.35	Þere is no labourer in his lordsshipe þat he *louiþ* beter
A.6.46	For treuþe wolde *loue* me þe wers a long tyme aftir.
A.6.50	Þat 3e *loue* hym leuere þanne þe lif in 3oure hertis;
A.6.94	And lere þe for to *loue* & hise lawes holden.
A.7.194	Treuþe tau3te me ones to *loue* hem ichone
A.7.207	*Loue* hem & lene hem & so þe lawe of kynde wolde.
A.7.250	*L[o]ue* hym nou3t, for he is a lecchour & likerous of tunge,
A.8.110	Þat *louiþ* god lelly, his liflode is þe more:
A.10.6	A lemman þat he *louiþ* lik to hymselue.
A.11.49	Litel *louiþ* he þat lord þat leniþ hym al þat blisse,
A.11.152	And *louen* hem þat li3en on vs, & lenen hem at here nede,
A.12.114	And alle lordes þat *louyn* him lely in herte,
B.1.78	To *louen* me leelly while þi lif dureþ.'
B.1.143	For to *louen* þi lord leuere þan þiselue,
B.1.181	But if ye *louen* leelly and lene þe pouere,
B.2.32	And what man be merciful and leelly me *loue*
B.3.30	To *louen* hem lelly and lordes [hem] make
B.3.32	'Shal no lewednesse [hym] lette, þe leode þat I *louye*,
B.3.53	While ye *loue* lordes þat lecherie haunten
B.3.54	And lakkeþ no3t ladies þat *louen* wel þe same.
B.3.91	'For my *loue*', quod þat lady, '*loue* hem echone,
B.3.126	Lereþ hem lecherie þat *loueþ* hire 3iftes.
B.4.19	Ne-lesynge-to-lau3en-of-for-I-*loued*-hem-neuere.
B.4.32	A[c] Conscience knew hem wel, þei *loued* coueitise,
B.5.48	And siþen he counseiled þe kyng his commune to *louye*:
B.5.251	'Ye, I haue lent lordes *loued* me neuere after,
B.5.559	Truþe wolde *loue* me þe lasse a long tyme after.
B.5.563	That ye *louen* oure lord god leuest of alle þynges.
B.6.208	Truþe tau3te me ones to *louen* hem ech one,
B.6.221	*Loue* hem and lene hem [and] so [þe] lawe of [kynde wolde]
B.6.225	*Loue* hem and lakke hem no3t; lat god take þe vengeaunce;
B.6.266	*L[o]ue* hym no3t for he is [a] lech[our] and likerous of tunge,
B.7.118	That *loueþ* god lelly his liflode is ful esy:
B.9.6	A lemman þat he *loueþ* lik to hymselue.
B.9.108	Oure lord *loueþ* hem and lent, loude ouþer stille,
B.9.203	To *loue* [and to lowe þee and no lif to greue;
B.9.204	Ac to *loue* and to lene], leue me, þat is dobet;
B.10.63	Litel *loueþ* he þat lord þat lent hym al þat blisse
B.10.93	Swiche lessons lordes sholde *louye* to here,
B.10.192	Loke þow *loue* lelly if þee likeþ dowel,
B.10.203	And *louen* hem þat lyen on vs and lene hem [at hir nede].
B.10.205	Poul preched þe peple, þat parfitnesse *louede*,
B.10.208	And alle þat lakkeþ vs or lyeþ oure lord techeþ vs to *louye*,
B.10.210	Forþi loke þow *louye* as longe as þow durest,
B.10.342	Salomon seiþ also þat siluer is worst to *louye*:
B.10.360	He sholde *louye* and lene and þe lawe fulfille.
B.10.361	That is, *loue* þi lord god leuest abouen alle,
B.10.363	And þus bilongeþ to *louye* þat leueþ [to] be saued.
B.10.450	For he seide to Seint Peter and to swiche as he *louede*,
B.11.19	For to lyue longe and ladies to *louye*,
B.11.55	For whiles Fortune is þi frend freres wol þee *louye*,
B.11.69	And *loued* me þe lasse for my lele speche.
B.11.175	But al for loue of oure lord and þe bet to *loue* þe peple.
B.11.177	Whoso *loueþ* no3t, leue me, he lyueþ in deeþ deyinge.
B.11.179	*Loue* hir eyþer oþer, and lene hem as hemselue.
B.11.180	Whoso leneþ no3t he *loueþ* no3t, [lord] woot þe soþe,
B.11.181	[And] comaundeþ ech creature to conformen hym to *louye*
B.11.183	For hem þat haten vs is oure merite to *louye*,
B.11.189	Wheiþer we *loue* þe lordes here bifore be lord of blisse;
B.11.196	That 3yueþ hem mete or moneie [and] *loueþ* hem for my sake.'
B.11.209	Forþi *loue* we as leue [children shal], and ech man laughe of ooþer,
B.11.223	And lawe is looþ to *louye* but if he lacche siluer.
B.11.224	Boþe logyk and lawe, þat *loueþ* no3t to lye,
B.11.326	Thorugh ech a creature kynde my creatour to *louye*.
B.12.13	And Dauid in þe Sauter seiþ, of swiche þat *loueþ* Iesus,
B.12.33	That is, if þow be man maryed þi make þow *louye*
B.12.54	And *loue* hem no3t as oure lord bit, lesen hir soules:
B.13.141	Thow *loue* leelly þi soule al þi lif tyme.
B.13.142	And so þow lere þe to *louye*, for [þe] lordes loue of heuene.
B.13.149	For he þat *loueþ* þee leelly litel of þyne coueiteþ.
B.13.331	Ther is no lif þat me *loueþ* lastynge any while.
B.13.352	And how þat lecchours *louye* laughen and Iapen,
B.13.451	That bi his lyue liþed hem and *loued* hem to here.
B.14.250	Lecherie *loueþ* hym no3t for he 3yueþ but litel siluer
B.14.267	Muche is [þat maide] to *loue* of [a man] þat swich oon takeþ
B.15.33	And whan I *loue* leelly oure lord and alle oþere
B.15.170	And leneþ and *loueþ* alle þat oure lord made.
B.15.185	*Loueþ* hem as oure lord biddeþ and lokeþ how þei fare.

B.15.355	That no lif *loueþ* ooþer, ne oure lord as it semeþ.
B.15.394	For þei *loue* and bileue in o [lord] almyghty
B.15.465	And wiþ calues flessh he fedde þe folk þat he *louede*.
B.15.473	That loþ ben to *louye* wiþouten lernyng of ensaumples.
B.15.477	*Louen* and bileuen by lettred mennes doynges,
B.15.554	Togideres *loue* leelly, leueþ it wel, ye bisshopes,
B.16.2	For Haukyns loue þe Actif man euere I shal yow *louye*.
B.16.201	And þere hym likede and [he] *louede*, in þre persones hym shewede.
B.16.231	First he fonded me if I, [feiþ], *louede* bettre
B.17.37	To bileeue and *louye* in o lord almyghty
B.17.38	And siþþe riȝt as myself so *louye* alle peple.
B.17.45	And wel awey worse ȝit for to *loue* a sherewe.
B.17.47	Than for to *louye* and lene as wel lorels as lele.
B.17.131	And Hope afterward he bad me to *louye*
B.17.133	*Louye* hem lik myselue, ac oure lord abouen alle.'
B.17.136	And as hope highte þee I hote þat þow *louye*
B.17.284	He fordooþ þe leuest light þat oure lord *louyeþ*.
B.17.297	Wol *loue* [þat lif] þat [lakkeþ charite],
B.17.351	That he ne may *louye*, and hym, like, and lene of his herte
B.17.354	And *louye* hem lik hymself, and his lif amende.
B.18.56	Thanne shul we leue þat lif þee *loueþ* and wol noȝt lete þee deye.'
B.18.326	And þo þat oure lord *louede* into his light he laughte,
B.18.336	Falsliche þow fettest þyng þat I *louede*.
B.18.355	Getest bi gile þo þat god *louede*;
B.18.401	Tho [ledes] þat [I] *lou[e]*, and leued in my comynge;
B.19.66	And se bi his sorwe þat whoso *loueþ* ioye
B.19.112	And lawe lakkede þo for men *louede* noȝt hir enemys,
B.19.114	[Boþe] to lered and to lewede, to *louyen* oure enemys.
B.19.181	And lelliche bileue al þis; I *loue* hem and blesse hem:
B.19.254	Lokeþ þat no[on] lakke ooþer, but *loueþ* as breþeren;
B.20.195	For þe lyme þat she *loued* me fore and leef was to feele
B.20.208	'Lerne to *loue*', quod kynde, 'and leef alle oþere.'
B.20.210	'And þow *loue* lelly lakke shal þee neuere
B.20.250	Wiþ þat ye leue logik and lerneþ for to *louye*.
C. 1.75	[To] leue on me and *loue* me al thy lyf tyme.'
C. 1.142	For to *louye* thy lord leuest of alle,
C. 1.177	But yf ȝe *loue* leeliche and lene þe pore,
C. 1.203	*Loue* hit,' quod þat lady; 'lette may y no lengore
C. 2.34	[W]hat man [that] me *louyeth* and my wille foleweth
C. 2.36	And what [man] mede *loueth*, my lyf [dar y] wedde.
C. 2.50	That *loueth* here lordschipe, lasse other more.
C. 2.77	'Al þat *loueth* and byleueth vp lykyng of mede,
C. 2.191	On hem þat *loueth* leccherye lyppeth vp and rydeth,
C. 3.31	To *louye* hem leeliche and lordes [hem] make,
C. 3.35	Shal no lewednesse lette þe [lede] þat y *louye*
C. 3.57	The whiles ȝe *louyen* lordes that lecherye haunteth
C. 3.58	And lacketh nat ladyes þat *louyeth* [wel] þe same.
C. 3.119	*Loue* hem for my loue,' quod this lady mede,
C. 3.131	Lacked here a litel w[iht] for þat she *louede* gyle.
C. 3.146	And teche the to *louye* treuthe and take consail of resoun.
C. 3.163	And lereth hem lecherye þat *louyeth* here ȝeftes.
C. 3.210	That no lond ne *loueth* and þe ȝut leeste thyn owene.
C. 3.282	Is no lede þat leueth þat he ne *loueth* mede
C. 4.19	Ne-lesynges-to-lauhe-of-for-y-*louede*-hit-neuere.
C. 4.109	Til lordes and ladies *louen* alle treuthe
C. 4.196	And receyue tho that resoun *louede*; and riht with þat y wakede
C. 5.8	And lymes to labory with and *louede* wel fare
C. 5.180	And sethe a consailede þe kyng his comine to *louie*:
C. 5.196	Of alle maner actions and eche man *loue* other.
C. 6.142	That alle ladyes me lot[h]eth þat *louyet[h]* eny worschipe.
C. 6.145	How lytel y *louye* letyse at þe style.
C. 6.192	Y lay by þe louelokest and *louede* here neuere aftur.
C. 6.249	'Y haue lent lordes and ladyes þat *louede* me neuere aftur
C. 7.111	That by his lyue l[yth]ed hem and *louede* hem to here.
C. 7.118	For a lythed and *louede* þat godes lawe despiseth:
C. 7.204	A wolde *loue* me þe lasse a long tyme aftur.
C. 7.208	That ȝe *louye* hym [as] lord leely aboue alle.
C. 7.253	And may lede in þat he *loueth* as here lef lyketh.
C. 7.302	And louue on me and lihtly chyde and sygge y *louede* another.
C. 8.25	And labory for tho thow *louest* al my lyf tyme.
C. 8.217	Treuthe tauhte me ones to *louye* hem vchone
C. 8.220	How y myhte amaystre hem to *louye* and labory
C. 8.232	*Loue* hem and lene hem and so lawe of kynde wolde
C.10.79	And thorw lele labour lyueth and *loueth* his emcristene
C.10.92	Lene hem and *loue* hem", this latyn is to mene.
C.10.133	A lemman þat he *louyeth* ylyke to hymsulue.
C.10.168	For they *louyeth* and bylyueth al here lyf tyme
C.10.188	Ac thenne dede we alle wel, and wel bet ȝut, to *louye*
C.10.191	That alle landes *loueden* and in on lawe bileuede.
C.10.200	To tulie þe erthe with tonge and teche men to *louye*.
C.10.201	For hoso *loueth*, leueth h[it] wel, god wol nat laton hym sterue
C.10.271	Many a payre sethe th[e] pestelens[e] han plyhte treuthe to *louye*;

C.10.302	To *louye* and to loue the and no lyf to greue;
C.10.303	Ac to *louye* and to l[e]ne, leef me, þat is dobet;
C.11.12	þat [they] *louyen* lond and lordschipe and lykynge of body
C.11.45	Lytel *loueth* he þat lord þat lente hym al þat blisse
C.11.130	Ac for hit lereth men to *louie* y beleue þeron þ[e] bettere
C.11.132	Lerne for to *louie* yf þe lik[e] dowel
C.11.178	For to *lyue* longe and ladyes to *louye*
C.11.275	For Crist saide to sayntes and to suche as he *louede*,
C.12.7	For while fortune is thy frende freres wol þe *louye*
C.12.92	And *louye* for oure lordes loue and do leute euermore.
C.12.108	That *louieth* and leneth hem largeliche shal y quyte."
C.12.117	Forthy *loue* we as leue childerne, lene hem þat nedeth
C.12.162	What god saide hymsulue to a segg þat he *louede*:
C.13.30	And lyues þat oure lord *loueth* and large weyes to heuene;
C.13.69	Bothe *louye* and lene le[l]e and vnlele
C.13.87	For if he *loueth* and byleueth as the lawe techeth–
C.13.133	To knowe by vch a creature kynde to *louye*.
C.13.193	Why he ne *loueth* thy lore and leueth as þou techest.'
C.14.13	Ac to *louye* and lene and lyue wel and byleue
C.15.153	'That *loueth* lely,' quod he, 'bote litel thyng coueyteth.
C.16.90	Lecherye *loueth* no pore for he hath bote litel siluer
C.16.107	Moche is [þat] mayde to *louye* of a man þat such oen taketh,
C.16.172	That vch a creature þat *loueth* crist welcometh me faire.'
C.16.195	And when y *louye* lelly oure lord and alle oþere
C.16.359	Of tho that lelelyche lyuen and *louen* and byleuen:
C.17.135	And ayther *loueth* and byleueth in o [lord] almyhty.
C.17.137	For lechours *louyen* aȝen þe lawe and at þe laste ben dampned
C.17.138	And theues *louyen* and leute hatien and at þe laste ben hanged
C.17.141	*Loue* god for he is goed and grounde of alle treuthe
C.17.142	*Loue* thyn enemye entierely goddes heste to fulfille;
C.17.143	*Loue* thy frende þat folleweth thy wille, that is thy fayre soule.
C.17.152	*Louen* as by lawe of kynde oure lord god almyhty.
C.17.157	*Louyeth* nat þat lord aryht as by þe legende sanctorum
C.17.217	Togederes *louyen* lelelyche, l[e]ueth hit [wel], bisshopes,
C.18.224	Multiplie ne moreouer withoute a make *louye*
C.19.40	And seth to *louye* and to lene for þat lordes sake
C.19.42	And for to *louye* and bileue in o lord almyhty
C.19.45	And lereth þat we *louye* sholde as wel lyares as lele.
C.19.93	Saue mysulue soethly and such as y *louede*–
C.19.101	And lered me for his loue to *louye* al mankynde
C.19.110	Loke thow *louye* and bileue al thy lyftyme.
C.19.140	Ne holde ne helpe ne hente þat he *louede*:
C.19.278	Wol *louye* þat lyf þat loue and Charite destruyeth.'
C.19.331	That he ne may *louye*, and hym lyke, and lene of his herte
C.19.334	And *louye* h[e]m yliche hymsulue [and his lyf] amende.
C.20.56	Thenne shal we leue that lyf þe *loueth* and wol nat late the deye.'
C.20.334	Lette hem þat *louede* hym nat laste they wolde hym martre.
C.20.338	To lere men to [be] lele and vch man to *louye* oþer;
C.20.369	And tho that oure lord *louede* forth with þat liht flowen.
C.20.444	Tho [ledes] þat y *louye* and leued in my comynge;
C.21.66	And se bi his sorwe þat hoso *loueth* ioye
C.21.112	And lawe lakked tho for men *loued* nat her enemyes
C.21.114	Bothe to lered and to lewed, to *louye* oure enemys.
C.21.181	And leelliche bileuen al this; y *loue* hem and blesse hem:
C.21.254	Loke þat noen lacke oþere bute *loueth* as bretherne
C.22.195	For þe lyme þat she *loued* me fore and leef was to fele
C.22.208	'Lerne to *loue*,' quod kynde, 'and leef all othere.'
C.22.210	'And thow *loue* lelly lacke shal the neuere
C.22.250	With þat ȝe l[e]ue logyk and lerneth for to *louye*.

loue v2 *loven v.(2), cf. louen v.(4) cf. v1* A 3 loue (1) louen (1) louid (1); B 11 looue (1) loue (3) loued (1) loueþ (1) louye (2) louyen (1) louen (1) lowed (1); C 10 loue (3) loued (1) louede (1) loueth (1) louye (2) louyeth (1) louyon (1)

A. 4.101	Til lordis & ladies *louen* alle treuþe,
A.11.29	Litel is he *louid* or lete by þat suche a lessoun techiþ,
A.11.142	Ac for it lat best be loue I *loue* it þe betere,
B.Pr.126	And lene þee lede þi lond so leaute þe *louye*,
B. 4.114	Til lordes and ladies *louen* alle truþe
B. 9.96	[Ne] *loueþ* noȝt Salomons sawes þat Sapience tauȝte:
B.10.37	Litel is he *loued* [or lete by] þat swich a lesson [techeþ],
B.10.190	Ac for it leteþ best bi loue I *loue* it þe bettre,
B.11.106	Neiþer for loue [looue] it noȝt ne lakke it for enuye:
B.11.109	Þe lasse, as I leue, *louyen* þei wolde
B.11.252	And hastily god answerde, and eiþeres wille [lowed],
B.12.9	Forþi I counseille þee for cristes sake clergie þat þow *louye*;
B.12.94	To oure lord, leue me; forþi *loue* hem, I rede.
B.19.250	And alle he lered to be lele, and ech a craft *loue* oþer,
C.Pr.150	And lene [þe] lede þy londe [so] lewte þe *louye*
C. 4.153	Resoun for his ryhtful speche; ryche and pore hym *louede*
C.11.32	Litel is he *loued* or leet [by] among lordes at festes.
C.11.76	And þat *loueth* lordes now and leten hit a dowel
C.12.40	Nother for loue [loue] it [nat] ne lacke hit for enuye:
C.12.43	The lasse, as y leue, *louyon* þey wolde

C.14.188   And to lele and lyfholy þat *louyeth* alle treuthe.
C.17.52   To make men *louye* mesure þat monkes ben and freres:
C.17.130   *Loue* lawe withoute leutee? allouable was hit neuere!
C.21.250   And al he lered to be lele, and vch a craft *loue* oþere,

loue &> loue n,looue,lowe; loued > loue v1,v2

loueday n *lovedai n.* A 3 louedaies (2) loueday (1); B 4 loueday (1)
   louedaies (1) louedayes (2); C 4 loueday (2) louedayes (1) louedays (1)
A. 3.148   She let lawe as hire list & *louedaies* makiþ;
A.11.20   And lede forþ a *loueday* to lette þe treuþe,
A.11.212   A ledere of *l[oue]d[a]ies* & a lond biggere;
B. 3.158   She ledeþ lawe as hire list and *louedaies* makeþ,
B. 5.420   I kan holde *louedayes* and here a Reues rekenyng,
B.10.20   And lede forþ a *loueday* to lette [þe] truþe,
B.10.312   A ledere of *louedayes* and a lond buggere,
C. 3.196   And le[deth] þe lawe as here luste and *louedayes* maketh,
C. 3.197   Thorw which *loueday* is loste þat leute myhte wynne;
C. 5.158   Ledares of *l[ou]edays*, and londes ypurchaced
C.11.17   And lette with a *loueday* [lewed] treuthe and bigile

louede > loue v1,v2

louedreem n *love n.(1)* B 1
B.16.20   And lay longe in a *louedreem*; and at þe laste me þou3te

loueknotte n *love n.(1)* C 1
C.17.127   A *loueknotte* of leutee and of lele byleue,

louelees adj *loveles adj.* A 1 loueles; B 1
A. 5.98   Þus I lyue *loueles*, [lyk] a lyþer dogge,
B. 5.119   [Th]us I lyue *louelees* lik a luþer dogge

louely adj *loveli adj.* A 7 louely (3) louelich (1) loueliche (2) louelokest
   (1); B 15 louely (8) louelich (4) loueliche (1) louelokest (2); C 13
   louely (4) louelich (2) loueliche (1) louelyche (1) louelokere (1)
   louelokest (3) louly (1)
A. 1.3   A *louely* lady of lire in lynene ycloþid
A. 1.110   And was þe *louelokest* [of si3t] aftir oure lord
A. 6.40   He is as lou3 as a lomb & *loueliche* of speche.
A. 7.18   And 3e *loueliche* ladies wiþ 3our [longe] fyngris,
A. 7.260   Þis is a *louely* lessoun, lord it þe for3elde.
A. 9.57   To lerne þe laies þat *louely* [foulis] maden.
A. 9.77   He is as lou3 as a lomb, *louelich* of speche,
B. 1.3   A *louely* lady of leere in lynnen ycloþed
B. 1.112   [And was þe *louelokest* of li3t after oure lord
B. 5.553   He is as lowe as a lomb and *louelich* of speche.
B. 6.10   And ye *louely* ladies wiþ youre longe fyngres,
B. 6.276   /[Th]is is a *louely* lesson; lord it þee foryelde.
B. 8.66   To [lerne] þe layes [þat] *louely* foweles made.
B. 8.86   He is as lowe as a lomb, *louelich* of speche;
B.11.187   And lokeþ on vs in hir liknesse and þat wiþ *louely* chere
B.11.241   That we sholde be lowe and *loueliche*, [and lele ech man to oþer],
B.12.264   The larke þat is a lasse fowel is moore *louelich* of ledene,
B.13.294   And *louelokest* to loken on and lelest of werkes,
B.14.228   [For lowliche he lokeþ, and *louelich* is his speche
B.14.244   And *louely* layk was it neuere bitwene þe longe and þe shorte.
B.17.46   It is lighter to leeue in þre *louely* persones
B.20.104   Manye a *louely* lady and [hir] lemmans kny3tes
C. 1.3   A *louely* lady of [lere] in lynnene [y]clothed
C. 1.107   Lucifer, *louelokest* tho, ac litel while it duyred.
C. 6.44   And *louelokest* to loke vppon a[nd] lykyngest abedde
C. 6.192   Y lay by þe *louelokest* and louede here neuere aftur.
C.10.65   To lythen here layes and here *louely* notes.
C.10.83   He is [as] logh as a lomb and *loueliche* of speche
C.10.259   And thogh he be *louelich* to loke[n] on and lossum abedde,
C.12.130   That we sholde be low and *louelich* and lele vch man til oþer
C.14.185   The larke þat is a lasse foul is *loueloke[re]* of ledene
C.16.69   For lo[w]lyche he loketh and *lo[uelych]e* is his speche
C.16.84   And *louely* layk was hit neuere bytwene a longe and a short.
C.18.10   Thorw *louely* lokyng[e] hit lyueth and launseth vp blosmes,
C.22.104   Many a *louly* lady and here lemmanes knyhtes

loueliche adv *loveli adv. &> louely* B 1; C 1
B.13.26   That lowe louted and *loueliche* to scripture.
C. 3.55   *Loueliche* þat lady laghynge sayde,

loueloke- > louely

louer n *lovere n.(1)* C 1
C.20.286   That no liht lepe in at *louer* ne at loupe.

loues > loof,loue n1; loueth louid louye(n > loue v1,v2

louynge adj *loue v.(1)* B 1; C 2 louyng (1) louynge (1)
B.13.16   And how *louynge* he is to [ech lif] on londe and on watre–
C.15.19   And how *louyng* he is to vch lyf a londe and o watere
C.16.24   Lowe and lele and *louynge* and of herte pore.

---

louyon > loue v2; louly > louely; low > lau3en,lyen,lowe

lowe adj *loue adj.* A 8 lou3 (7) lowere (1); B 18 lowe (16) lower (1)
   loweste (1); C 17 logh (1) louh (4) louhe (1) low (2) lowe (8) loweste
   (1)
A. 3.234   Þat laboureris & *lou3* folk taken of here maistris
A. 5.135   For laboureris & *lou3* folk þat lay be h[y]mselue;
A. 6.40   He is as *lou3* as a lomb & loueliche of speche.
A. 8.65   And lyuen in loue & [in] lawe, for here *lou3* herte
A. 8.87   For loue of here *lou3* herte oure lord haþ hem grauntid
A. 8.140   Among *l[ower]e* lordis þi londis shuln be departid'.
A. 9.77   He is as *lou3* as a lomb, louelich of speche.
A.11.2   Þat lene was of lich & of *lo[u3]* chere.
B. 3.255   That laborers and *lowe* [lewede] folk taken of hire maistres
B. 5.140   Til þei beere leues of *lowe* speche lordes to plese,
B. 5.219   For laborers and *lowe* folk þat lay by hymselue,
B. 5.553   He is as *lowe* as a lomb and louelich of speche.
B. 6.228   And biloue þee amonges [*lowe*] men: so shaltow lacche grace.'
B. 7.63   And lyuen in loue and in lawe, for hir *lowe* hert[e]
B. 7.105   For loue of hir *lowe* hert[e] oure lord haþ hem graunted
B. 7.162   Amonges *lower* lordes þi lond shal be departed.'
B. 8.86   He is as *lowe* as a lomb, louelich of speche;
B.10.2   That lene was of [liche] and of [*lowe* chere].
B.10.370   God hoteþ hei3e and *lowe* þat no man hurte ooþer,
B.11.241   That we sholde be *lowe* and loueliche, [and lele ech man to oþer],
B.12.140   And loue shal lepen out after into þ[is] *lowe* erþe,
B.12.212   For he is in þe *loweste* of heuene, if oure bileue be trewe,
B.15.423   To lyue by litel and in *lowe* houses by lele mennes almesse.
B.18.241   The light folwede þe lord into þe *lowe* erþe.
B.19.35   Boþe his loore and his lawe; now are þei *lowe* cherles.
B.20.36   And as *lowe* as a lomb for lakkyng þat hym nedeþ
C. 6.227   For laboreres and *louh* folk þat lay by hymsulue.
C. 7.197   He is as *louh* as a lombe and leel of his tonge.
C. 9.185   For loue of here *lowe* hertes oure lord hath hem ygraunted
C.10.83   He is [as] *logh* as a lomb and loueliche of speche
C.12.14   And pouerte pursuede me and potte me to be *lowe*.
C.12.130   That we sholde be *low* and louelich and lele vch man til oþer
C.12.184   That ben layd in *louhe* erthe, ylore as hit were,
C.13.83   That þe lawe 3eueth leue such *low* folk to be excused,
C.14.85   And loue shal lepe out aftur into þis *lowe* erthe
C.14.151   For he is in þe *loweste* of heuene, yf oure byleue be trewe,
C.16.24   *Lowe* and lele and louynge and of herte pore.
C.16.33   And lereth lewed and lered, hey and *lowe* to knowe
C.16.154   That puyre pouerte and pacience was a *louh* lyuynge on erthe,
C.17.30   Bote myldelyche when þey metten maden *louh* [c]here
C.20.250   The lihte folewede þe lord into þe *lowe* erthe.
C.21.35   Bothe his lore and his lawe; now are they *lowe* cherles.
C.22.36   And as *louh* as a lamb for lakkyng þat hym nedeth;

lowe adv *loue adv.* A 4 lowe (3) lowest (1); B 9 lowe (8) lowest (1); C 7
   lou (1) louh (1) lowe (4) lowest (1)
A. 1.115   A[c] lucifer *lowest* liþ of hem alle;
A. 4.20   Hange on hym þe heuy bridel to holde his hed *lowe*,
A. 5.50   'Shal neuere hei3 herte me hente, but holde me *lowe*
A. 7.26   'Be seint poule,' quaþ perkyn, 'for þou profrist þe so *lowe*
B. 1.126   Ac Lucifer *lowest* liþ of hem alle;
B. 4.22   Hange on hym þe heuy brydel to holde his heed *lowe*,
B. 5.67   'Shal neuere hei3 herte me hente, but holde me *lowe*
B. 6.24   'By Seint Poul!' quod Perkyn, '[for þow profrest þee so *lowe*]
B.11.62   And pouerte pursued me and putte me *lowe*.
B.12.267   To *lowe* libbynge men þe larke is resembled.
B.13.26   That *lowe* louted and loueliche to scripture.
B.19.263   That oon was Luk, a large beest and a *lowe* chered,
B.20.37   [For nede makeþ nede fele nedes *lowe* herted].
C. 1.128   Ac lucifer *lowest* lith of hem alle;
C. 5.24   And to long, lef me, *lowe* to stoupe,
C. 6.8   'Shal neuere heyh herte me hente, but holde me *lowe*
C.14.187   To *lowe* lyuynge men þe larke is resembled
C.19.10   That luciferes lordschipe *lowe* sholde lygge.'
C.21.263   That oen was luc, a large beste and a *lou* chered,
C.22.37   For nede maketh neede fele nedes *louh* herted.

lowe v *louen v.(1)* B 3 lowe (1) lowed (1) loweþ (1); C 4 loue (1) lowe
   (1) lowede (1) loweth (1)
B.Pr.129   *Lowed* to speke in latyn, for lewed men ne koude
B. 9.203   To loue [and to *lowe*] þee and no lif to greue;
B.10.310   And gret loue and likyng for ech [*loweþ* hym to] ooþer.
C. 8.194   There was no ladde þat lyuede þat ne *lowede* hym to Peres
C.10.302   To louye and to *loue* the and no lyf to greue;
C.12.158   For þe loue of oure lord *lo[w]eth* hym to be pore,
C.14.9   *Lowe* the and l[y]ue forth in þe lawe of holy chirche;

lowe &> lyen; lowed > loue v2,lowe v

lowenesse n *lounesse n.* A 4 louʒnesse; B 3; C 4 louhnesse (1) lowenesse (1) lownesse (2)
A. 3.267   But loue & *louʒnesse* & leaute togideris;
A. 6.78   Wiþ no led but [wiþ] loue & *louʒnesse*, as breþeren of o wombe.
A.10.102   Þou miʒtest lese þi *louʒnesse* for a litel pride.
A.10.129   For loue of here *louʒnesse* oure lord ʒiueþ hem grace
B. 3.291   Ac loue and *lowenesse* and leautee togideres;
B. 4.109   As longe as [I lyue], but *lowenesse* hym borwe.'
B. 5.591   Wiþ no leed but wiþ loue and *lowe[nesse]* as breþeren [of o wombe].
C. 3.444   Ac loue and *lownesse* and lewete togyderes;
C. 5.155   In scole is loue and *louhnesse* and lykyng to lerne.
C.15.132   Saue loue and leute and *lowenesse* of herte.
C.16.18   That al here lyf leden in *lownesse* and in pouerte.

lowh > lauʒen

lowynge ger *louinge ger.(1)* B 1
B.15.304   In likkyng and in *lowynge*, þer þei on laundes yede].

lowliche adv *louli adv.* B 1; C 2 louhliche (1) lowlyche (1)
B.14.228   [For *lowliche* he lokeþ, and louelich is his speche
C. 9.141   Loken *louhliche* to lache men Almesse,
C.16.69   For *lo[w]lyche* he loketh and lo[uelych]e is his speche

lownesse > lowenesse; lowtyng > louten

luc n prop *n.i.d.* A 3 luk (2) lukis (1); B 9 luc (5) Lucas (2) Luk (1) Lukes (1); C 7 luc (1) lucas (2) luk (3) lukes (1)
A. 1.89   And ek lyk to oure lord be seint *lukis* wordis.
A. 8.111   And but ʒif *luk* leiʒe he leriþ vs anoþer,
A.10.120   And so leriþ vs *luk* þat leiʒede neuere:
B. 1.91   And [ek] ylik to oure lord by Seint *Lukes* wordes.
B. 5.408   Than al þat euere Marc made, Mathew, Iohan and *Lucas*.
B. 5.499   And al þat Marc haþ ymaad, Mathew, Iohan and *Lucas*.
B. 7.129   And but if *luc* lye he lereþ vs [anoþer]
B. 9.76   And þat I lye noʒt of þat I lere þee, *luc* bereþ witnesse.
B.11.274   And lif moost likynge to god as *luc* bereþ witnesse:
B.12.184   To lere lewed men as *luc* bereþ witnesse:
B.19.263   That oon was *Luk*, a large beest and a lowe chered,
B.19.446   Ayein þe olde lawe and newe lawe, as *Luc* [bereþ] witness[e]:
C. 1.87   And also lyk [to] oure lord by saynt *Lukes* wordes.
C. 7.24   Th[en] al þat euere Mark made, Matheu, Iohn or *lucas*.
C. 7.139   And al þat mark hath ymade, Matheu, Ion and *lucas*
C.14.124   To lere lewede men As *luk* bereth witnesse:
C.17.235   Aʒen þe lore of oure lord as seynt *luk* witnesseth–
C.21.263   That oen was *luc*, a large beste and a lou chered,
C.21.446   Aʒen þe olde lawe and newe lawe, as *Luk* bereth witnesse:

lucifer n prop *Lucifer n.* A 5 lucifer (3) luciferis (2); B 27 Lucifer (21) luciferes (1) luciferis (5); C 27 lucifer (21) luciferes (6)
A.Pr.39   Qui loquitur turpiloquium [is] *luciferis* hyne.
A. 1.109   *Lucifer* wiþ legionis leride it in heuene,
A. 1.115   A[c] *lucifer* lowest liþ of hem alle;
A. 5.250   For he hadde leiʒe be latro *luciferis* [aunte].
A.11.284   þat hadde leyn with *lucifer* manye longe ʒeris;
B.Pr.39   Qui loquitur turpiloquium is *luciferes* hyne.
B. 1.111   *Lucifer* wiþ legions lerned it in heuene
B. 1.117   Lopen out wiþ *Lucifer* in loþliche forme
B. 1.118   For þei leueden vpon [*Lucifer*] þat lyed in þis manere:
B. 1.126   Ac *Lucifer* lowest liþ of hem alle;
B. 5.476   For he hadde leyn by Latro, *luciferis* Aunte.
B. 5.494   [Th]e liʒt þat lepe out of þee, *Lucifer* [it] blent[e]
B.10.425   That hadde yleyen wiþ *lucifer* many longe yeres.
B.12.40   [Lo]! what made *lucifer* to lese þe heiʒe heuene,
B.13.455   Leden þo þat [liþed] hem to *Luciferis* feste
B.13.456   Wiþ turpiloquio, a l[a]y of sorwe, and *luciferis* fiþele,
B.15.51   For swich a lust and likyng *Lucifer* fel from heuene:
B.17.8   That *Luciferis* lordshipe laste shal no lenger.
B.18.34   And legge it þer hym likeþ, and *Lucifer* bynde,
B.18.137   The while þis light and þis leme shal *Lucifer* ablende.
B.18.251   And now shal *Lucifer* leue it, þouʒ hym looþ þynke.
B.18.263   A vois loude in þat light to *lucifer* crieþ,
B.18.273   'Listneþ!' quod *lucifer*, 'for I þis lord knowe;
B.18.311   For þi lesynges, *Lucifer*, lost is al oure praye.
B.18.316   Eft þe light bad vnlouke and *Lucifer* answerde
B.18.317   What lord artow?' quod *Lucifer*; þe light soone seide
B.18.325   *Lucifer* loke ne myʒte, so light hym ablente.
B.18.348   So leue [it] noʒt, *lucifer*, ayein þe lawe I fecche hem,
B.18.354   Thow, *lucifer*, in liknesse of a luþer Addere
B.18.402   And for þi lesynge, *lucifer*, þat þow leighe til Eue
B.19.55   That longe hadde yleyen bifore as *Luciferis* cherles,
B.19.56   [And took [*Lucifer* þe loþely] þat lord was of helle
C.Pr.40   Qui turpiloquium loquitur [is] *luciferes* knaue.
C. 1.107   *Lucifer*, louelokest tho, ac litel while it duyred.
C. 1.112   'Lord! why wolde he tho, þat wykkede *lucifer*,

C. 1.128   Ac *lucifer* lowest lith of hem alle;
C. 2.110   In lordschip with *lucifer*, as this lettre sheweth,
C. 5.187   Til *lucifer* þe lyare leued þat hymsulue
C. 6.330   For he hadde layʒe by latro, *luciferes* aunte.
C. 7.115   Leden tho that lythed hem to *luciferes* feste
C. 7.116   With turpiloquio, a lay of sorwe and *luciferes* fythele,
C. 7.134   The lihte þat lup oute of the, *lucifer* hit blente
C.11.257   That hadde yley with *lucifer* mony longe ʒeres.
C.16.213   For such a lust and lykynge *lucifer* ful fram heuene:
C.19.10   That *luciferes* lordschipe lowe sholde lygge.'
C.20.33   And legge hit þere hym liketh and *lucifer* bynde
C.20.140   The while this lihte and this l[em]e shal *lucifer* ablende.
C.20.260   And now shal *lucife[r]* leue [hit], thogh hym loeth thynk.
C.20.271   A vois loude in þat liht to *lucifer* saide,
C.20.295   'Lustneth!' quod *lucifer*, 'for y this lord knowe;
C.20.345   For thy lesinges, *lucifer*, we losten furst oure ioye
C.20.351   *Lucifer* for his lesynges, leue y noen oþer
C.20.359   For efte þat lihte bade vnlouke [and *lucifer* answerede].
C.20.360   'What lord artow?' quod *lucifer*; a voys aloude saide:
C.20.368   *Lucifer* loke ne myhte, so liht hym ablen[t]e.
C.20.393   So leue hit nat, *lucifer*, aʒeyne þe lawe y feche
C.20.445   Ac for þe lesynge þat thow low, *lucifer*, til eue
C.21.55   That longe hadden leye bifore as *luciferes* cherles
C.21.56   And toek *lucifer* the loethliche þat lord was of helle

luft > left,liften; luftynge > liftyng; luyred > lured; luyther(e > luþer; luk > luc

lukes n prop *OED Luke n.2* &> *luc* B 1; C 2
B. 6.100   And wiþ þe residue and þe remenaunt, by þe Rode of *Lukes*!
C. 4.194   Or lumbardus of *lukes* þat leuen by lone as iewes.'
C. 8.109   And with þe res[i]due and þe remenant, by the rode of *lukes*!

lumbardes n prop *Lombard n.& adj.* B 2; C 3 lumbardus
B. 5.239   I lerned among *lumbardes* [a lesson and of Iewes],
B. 5.248   And wiþ *lumbardes* lettres I ladde gold to Rome
C. 4.194   Or *lumbardus* of lukes þat leuen by lone as iewes.'
C. 6.241   Y lernede among *lumbardus* a lessoun and of iewes,
C. 6.246   And with *lumbardus* lettres le[d]e gold to Rome;

lunatik n *lunatik n.* B 1; C 2 lunatyk
B.Pr.123   Thanne loked vp a *lunatik*, a leene þyng wiþalle,
C. 9.107   The whiche aren *lunatyk* lollares and lepares aboute
C. 9.137   The whiche [arn] *lunatyk* loreles and lepares aboute

lundoun > londoun; lup(pen > lepen

lurdeyn n *lurden n.* B 2 lurdaynes (1) lurdeyn (1); C 4 lordeynes (2) lordeyne (2)
B.18.102   And ye, *lurdaynes*, han ylost for lif shal haue þe maistrye,
B.20.189   'Ye, leue, *lurdeyn*?' quod he, and leyde on me wiþ Age,
C. 5.162   He loketh al lourynge and *lordeyne* hym calleth.
C.18.18   So this *lordeynes* lithereth þerto þat alle þe leues falleth
C.20.105   And ʒe, *lordeyne[s]*, haen lost for lyf shal haue [þe] maistrie,
C.22.189   'ʒe, leue, *lordeyne*?' quod he, and leide on me with age

lured ptp *luren v.(1)* B 1; C 1 luyred
B. 5.432   I am noʒt *lured* wiþ loue but þer ligge auʒt vnder þe þombe.
C. 7.45   Y am nat *luyred* with loue but þer lygge ouht vnder þe t[h]umbe.

lurkynge prp *lurken v.* A 1 lurkyng; B 1; C 1 lorkyng
A. 2.178   *Lurkyng* þoruʒ lanes, toluggid of manye.
B. 2.219   *Lurkynge* þoruʒ lanes, tolugged of manye.
C. 2.229   *Lorkyng* thorw lanes, tologged of moneye.

lusard n *lesarde n.* B 1
B.18.337   Thus ylik a *Lusard* wiþ a lady visage

lussheburwes > lossheborw

lust n *lust n.* &> *list* A 1; B 5 lust (4) lustes (1); C 10 lost (1) lust (5) luste (2) lustes (2)
A. 2.65   Wiþ alle þe delites of *lust* þe deuil for to serue,
B.15.51   For swich a *lust* and likyng Lucifer fel from heuene:
B.16.32   Thoruʒ likynge and *lustes* so loude he gynneþ blowe
B.19.352   Wiþ þe lord þat lyueþ after þe *lust* of his body,
B.19.382   The lord of *lust* shal be letted al þis lente, I hope.
B.20.90   The lord þat lyued after *lust* þo aloud cryde
C. 1.111   That hadde [lu]st to be lyk his lord þat was almyghty:
C. 6.158   Y haue no *luste*, lef me, to longe amonges monkes
C.11.80   The which is a lykyng and *luste*, þe loue of þe world.'
C.13.152   That ne lees the lykynge of *lost* of flesch, as hit were,
C.16.213   For such a *lust* and lykynge lucifer ful fram heuene:
C.17.80   Is alayed with leccherye and oþer *lustes* of synne
C.18.36   Thorw lecherie and *lustes* so loude he gynneth blowe
C.21.352   With the lord þat lyueth aftur the *lust* of his body,
C.21.382   The lord of *lust* shal be ylette al this lente, y hope.
C.22.90   The lord þat lyuede aftur *lust* tho aloud cryede

luste > list,lust; lustneth > listneþ

lutede v *luten v.(1)* B 1; C 1
B.18.423   And þanne *lutede* [loue] in a loud note:
C.20.466   And thenne *lutede* loue in a loude note:

luþer adj *lithere adj.* A 3 liþer (2) lyþer (1); B 7 liþer (1) liþere (1) luþer
    (4) luþere (1); C 17 luyther (6) luythere (2) luyþer (1) luther (7) luþer
    (1)
A. 5.98   Þus I lyue loueles, [lyk] a *lyþer* dogge,
A. 5.208   For his *liþer* lif þat he lyued hadde,
A.11.121   F[ro] lesinges & *li[þer]* speche & likerous drinkes.
B. 5.119   [Th]us I lyue louelees lik a *luþer* dogge
B. 5.380   For his *luþer* lif þat he lyued hadde,
B.10.169   Fro-lesynges-and-*liþer*-speche-and-likerouse-drynkes.
B.10.441   And be allowed as he lyued so; for by *luþere* men knoweþ þe
                goode.
B.10.444   Forþi lyue we forþ wiþ [*liþere*] men; I leue fewe ben goode,
B.15.349   As in lussheburwes is a *luþer* alay, and yet lokeþ he lik a sterlyng;
B.18.354   Thow, lucifer, in liknesse of a *luþer* Addere
C. 1.110   Lepen out in lothly forme for his [*luþer*] wille
C. 1.194   And a *luther* ensau[m]ple, leef me, [to] þe lewed peple.
C. 3.318   And yf th[e] lele and lege be *luyther* men aftur
C. 4.104   As longe as y lyue for his *luther* werkes.'
C. 6.437   Of my *luyther* ly[uynge] in al my lyf tyme.
C. 8.252   The lord for his lachesse and his *luther* sleuthe
C. 8.294   Ther ar many *luther* leches Ac lele leches fewe;
C. 9.18   Lechery amonges lordes and here *luyther* custumes,
C. 9.182   Or bylowe thorw *luther* men and lost here catel aftur
C.10.161   So let lecherye and other *luther* synnes
C.13.116   Thorw here *luyther* lyuynge and lewede vnderstondynge.
C.14.101   That is, how lewede men and *luythere* lyhtloker were ysaued
C.15.214   [For] lordes and lorelles, *luther* and gode,
C.15.219   Lette this *luythere* [eir] and leche þe sike–
C.17.36   Toke lyflode of *luyther* wynnynges in all here lyf tyme.
C.17.83   Thus ar ȝe *luyþer* ylikned to lossheborw[e] sterlynges
C.19.248   With wyles and with *luyther* whitus and ȝut wollen nat atymye

M

ma > mo; maad > maken

macabeus n prop *n.i.d.* B 1; C 1
B.17.24 Iosue and Iudith and Iudas *Macabeus*,
C.19.25 Bothe Iosue and Ieudith and Iudas *Macabeus*,

macche n *mecche n.* B 1; C 1 mache
B.17.217 Wiþouten leye or light [liþ fir in þe *macche*]--
C.19.183 Withouten leye [or] lihte lith fuyr in þe *mache*–

macche v *macchen v.* A 1; B 1
A.10.199 But maidenis & maidenis *macche* ȝow ysamme;
B. 9.178 Ac maidenes and maydenes *macche* yow [ysamme];

maceres n *macere n.* A 1 maceris; B 1
A. 3.65 Meiris & *ma[ce]ris*, hij þat ben mene
B. 3.76 Maires and *Maceres* þat menes ben bitwene

*machameth > makometh; mache > macche; macometh macumeth >
makometh; mad > maken*

madame n *madame n.& phr.* A 6; B 8; C 5
A. 1.11 And seide 'mercy *madame*, what is þis to mene?'
A. 1.41 'A *madame* mercy,' quaþ I, 'me likiþ wel ȝoure wordis.
A. 1.58 What may it [be]mene, *madame* I þe biseche?'
A. 2.2 And seide, 'mercy *madame*, for marie loue of heuene
A.11.101 And seide, 'mercy *madame*, ȝour man shal I worþe
A.11.166 I seide 'graunt mercy *madame*,' & mekly hire grette
B. 1.11 And seide, 'mercy *madame*, what [may] þis [by]meene?'
B. 1.43 '[A] *madame*, mercy', quod I, 'me likeþ wel youre wordes.
B. 1.60 What may it [by]meene, *madame*, I [þee] biseche?'
B. 2.2 And seide 'mercy, *madame*, for Marie loue of heuene
B. 3.344 And so [mys]ferde ye, *madame*; ye kouþe na moore fynde
B. 4.155 And seide, '*madame*, I am youre man what so my mouþ Iangle,
B.10.148 And seide, 'mercy, *madame*; youre man shal I worþe
B.10.224 I seide 'grant mercy, *madame*', and mekely hir grette,
C. 1.11 And sayde, 'mercy, *madame*, what may this [by]meene?'
C. 1.41 'A *madame*, mercy,' [quod I], 'me lyketh wel ȝoure wordes.
C. 1.56 What may hit bymene, *madame*, y [þe] byseche?'
C. 2.2 And sayde 'mercy, *madame*, for mary loue of heuene
C.11.86 And saide, 'mercy, *madame*; ȝoure man shal y worthen

madde adj *mad adj.* B 1
B. 9.72 *Madde* men and maydenes þat helplese were;

madden v *madden v.* C 1
C. 9.108 And *madden* as þe mone sit, more other lasse;

made(- maed > maken

mageste n *mageste n.* A 2 mageste (1) maieste (1); B 4 mageste (2)
maiestee (2)
A. 1.105 ȝaf hem miȝt in his *mageste*, þe meryere hem þouȝte,
A.10.41 Þoruȝ miȝt of þe *maieste* man was ymakid:
B. 1.107 Yaf hem myȝt in his *maiestee*, þe murier hem þouȝte,
B. 9.53 Thorgh myȝt of þe *mageste* man was ymaked:
B.15.481 And by þe man þat made þe feste þe *mageste* bymeneþ
B.16.184 The firste haþ myȝt and *maiestee*, makere of alle þynges;

magi n *mages n.* B 1; C 1
B.19.85 Maistres and lettred men, *Magi* hem callede.
C.21.85 Maistres & lettred men, *Magi* hem calde.

mahoun n prop *Mahoun n.* B 1; C 2 Mahond
B.13.83 Were molten leed in his mawe and *Mahoun* amyddes.
C.18.150 And thorw the myhte of *Mahond* and thorw misbileue:
C.20.293 Set *Mahond* at þe mang[n]el and mullestones throweth;

may n1 *mai n.(2)* A 1; B 2; C 2
A.Pr.5 But on a *may* morwenyng on maluerne hilles
B.Pr.5 Ac on a *May* morwenynge on Maluerne hilles
B.14.158 And muche murþe in *May* is amonges wilde beestes;
C.Pr.6 Ac on a *May* mornyng on maluerne hulles
C.16.10 Muche murthe is in *may* amonge wilde bestes

may n2 *mai n.(1)* A 1
A.12.116 Marie moder and *may*, for man þou byseke

may v *mouen v.(3)* A 81 may (26) miȝt (6) miȝte (29) myȝte (1) miȝtest
(3) myȝth (1) myȝthe (1) mowe (14); B 281 may (125) maye (2)
mayst (1) myght (1) mighte (2) myghte (7) myȝt (8) miȝte (4) myȝte
(93) myȝtest (4) myȝtestow (2) myȝtow (2) mow (1) mowe (22)
mowen (6); C 290 may (146) mayst (1) myghte (4) myghtest (1)
myȝte (1) myht (2) myhte (110) myhtest (3) myhtow (1) mouhte (3)
mowe (11) mowen (7)
A.Pr.59 Manye of þise maistris *may* cloþe hem at lyking
A.Pr.67 And seide þat hymself *miȝte* assoile hem alle
A.Pr.88 Tho[u] *miȝtest* betere mete myst on maluerne hilles
A. 1.58 What *may* it [be]mene, madame I þe biseche?'
A. 1.60 *May* banne þat he born was to body or to soule.
A. 1.80 Þat I *miȝte* werchen his wil þat wrouȝte me to man:
A. 1.82 How I *may* sauen my soule, þat seint art yho[ld]en.'
A. 1.121 *Mowe* be sikur þat here soule shal wende into heuene,
A. 1.146 Here *miȝt* þou sen ensaumplis in hymself one
A. 1.183 I *may* no lengere lenge; now loke þe oure lord.'
A. 2.27 Þere *miȝte* þou wyte ȝif þou wilt whiche þei ben alle
A. 2.31 I *may* no lengere lette, lord I þe bekenne.
A. 2.97 She *miȝte* kisse þe king for cosyn ȝif he[o] wolde.
A. 2.112 For he *may* mede amaistrien and maken at my wille'.
A. 2.154 'Be crist,' quaþ þe king, '& I *miȝte* cacche
A. 3.134 She *may* neiȝ as muche do in a moneþ ones
A. 3.147 Þat feiþ *may* not haue his forþ, hire floreynes go so þikke.
A. 3.155 For pouere men *mowe* haue no power to pleyne [þeiȝ] hem smerte,
A. 3.158 To haue space to speke, spede ȝif she *miȝte*.
A. 3.164 Þere þat meschief is gret mede *may* helpe.
A. 3.171 ȝet I *may*, as I miȝte, [menske] þe wiþ ȝeftis,
A. 3.171 ȝet I may, as I *miȝte*, [menske] þe wiþ ȝeftis
A. 3.205 Takiþ mede of here maistris as þei *mowe* accorde;
A. 3.214 No wiȝt as I wene wiþoute mede *miȝte* libbe.'
A. 3.224 Godis mede & his mercy þerwiþ *miȝte* þou wynne.
A. 3.236 In marchaundie is no mede, I *may* it wel auowe;
A. 4.69 To ouercome þe king wiþ catel ȝif þei *miȝte*.
A. 4.75 And he amendis *mowe* make let maynprise hym haue,
A. 4.90 For mede haþ mad my mendis; I *may* no more axen.'
A. 4.119 Ac I *may* shewe ensaumplis as I se [oþer],
A. 4.122 Shulde neuere wrong in þis world þat I wyte *miȝte*
A. 5.6 Þat I ne *miȝte* ferþere a fote for defaute of slepyng.
A. 5.21 Of þis mater I *miȝte* mamele wel longe,
A. 5.41 Sekiþ seint treuþe for he *may* saue ȝou alle
A. 5.71 I *miȝte* not many day do as a man [au]ȝte,
A. 5.100 *May* no sugre ne swet þing swage it an vnche,
A. 5.106 And þat makiþ me so ma[t] for I ne *may* me venge.'
A. 5.112 But ȝif a lous couþe lepe, I *may* it nouȝt leue
A. 6.17 ȝe *mowe* se be my signes þat sitten on myn hat
A. 6.29 Boþe sowe [and sette] while I swynke *miȝte*.
A. 6.61 Ne none of here seruauntis, þat noiȝe hem *miȝte*;
A. 6.80 He *may* do wiþ þe day sterre what hym dere likiþ.
A. 6.102 Þus *miȝt* þou lese his loue, to lete wel be þiselue,
A. 6.123 Þou *miȝt* gete grace [þere] so þou go be tyme.'
A. 7.2 Þat *miȝte* folewe vs iche fote [forto] we were þere.'
A. 7.37 To fulfille þe foreward whiles I *may* stande!
A. 7.41 Nyme hem nouȝt, an aunter þou *mowe* hem nouȝt deserue.
A. 7.120 For we *mowe* no[þer] swynke ne swete, such seknesse vs eileþ'.
A. 7.185 And ȝaf hem mete & monie as þei *miȝte* asserue.
A. 7.197 And how I *miȝte* amaistrie hem & make hem to werche.'
A. 7.199 Bolde beggeris & bigge, þat *mowe* here breed beswynken,
A. 7.208 And alle maner of men þat þou *miȝte* aspien,
A. 7.214 *Miȝte* I synneles do as þou seist?' seide peris þanne.
A. 7.275 Þanne *may* I diȝte þi dyner as þe dere likeþ.'
A. 7.293 *May* no penyale men paye, ne no pece of bacoun,
A. 7.302 I warne ȝow werkmen, wynneþ while ȝe *mowe*,
A. 8.7 Or any maner mester þat *miȝte* peris helpen,
A. 8.80 Þo þat lyuen þus here lif *mowe* loþe þe tyme
A. 8.83 And wommen wiþ childe þat werche ne *mowe*,
A. 8.122 'Were þou a prest, piers,' quaþ he, 'þou *miȝtest* preche wh[an] þe
liki[de];
A. 8.123 Quoniam literaturam non cognoui, þat *miȝte* be þi teme.'
A. 8.133 For þat I saiȝ slepyng ȝif it so be *miȝte*.
A. 9.5 And what man he *miȝte* be of many man I askide.

401

A. 9.19	[Þat] dowel & do euele *mowe* not dwelle togidere.
A. 9.49	Ac ȝif I *may* lyuen & loken I shal go lerne betere.
A.10.9	And wolde wynne hire awey with wyles ȝif he *miȝte*.
A.10.59	And ek in sottis þou *miȝt* se, þat sitten at þe nale.
A.10.86	And þerof seiþ þe sauter, þe salme þou *miȝt* rede:
A.10.102	Þou *miȝtest* lese þi louȝnesse for a litel pride.
A.10.119	For þoruȝ suffraunce se þou *miȝt* how soueraynes ariseþ,
A.10.212	But wandriþ [as wolues] & wastiþ [ȝif] þei *mowe*;
A.11.45	Ac þe carful *may* criȝen & carpe at þe ȝate,
A.11.52	[Mendynauntȝ] meteles *miȝte* go to bedde.
A.11.97	I *miȝte* gete no g[r]ayn of hise grete wyttes,
A.11.236	*Mowe* be sauid so, & so is oure beleue.
A.11.237	Þat arn vncristene in þat cas *may* cristene an heþene,
A.11.287	Þanne marie þe maudeleyn who *miȝte* do wers?
A.12.9	That *myȝthe* turne m[e] to tene & theologie boþe.
A.12.68	Me folweþ such a fentyse, I *may* no ferþer walke.
A.12.88	'*Myȝth* I so, god wot, ȝoure gates wolde I holden.'
A.12.103	And whan þis werk was wrouȝt, ere wille *myȝte* aspie,
B.Pr.62	Manye of þise maistre[s *mowe*] cloþen hem at likyng
B.Pr.70	And seide þat hymself *myȝte* assoillen hem alle
B.Pr.156	*Miȝte* we wiþ any wit his wille wiþstonde
B.Pr.157	We *myȝte* be lordes o lofte and lyuen at oure ese.'
B.Pr.166	Men *myȝte* witen wher þei wente and [hire] wey r[oum]e.
B.Pr.170	[And hangen it vpon þe cattes hals; þanne here we *mowen*]
B.Pr.172	And if hym list for to laike þanne loke we *mowen*
B.Pr.197	For *may* no renk þer reste haue for Ratons by nyȝte,]
B.Pr.207	Coupled and vncoupled to cacche what þei *mowe*.
B.Pr.215	Thow *myȝtest* bettre meete myst on Maluerne hilles
B. 1.11	And seide, 'mercy, madame, what [*may*] þis [by]meene?'
B. 1.60	What *may* it [by]meene, madame, I [þee] biseche?'
B. 1.62	*May* þanne þat he born was to bodi or to soule.
B. 1.82	That I *myȝte* werchen his wille þat wroȝte me to man.
B. 1.84	How I *may* saue my soule þat Seint art yholden.'
B. 1.120	And alle þat hoped it *myȝte* be so, noon heuene myȝte hem holde,
B. 1.120	And alle þat hoped it myȝte be so, noon heuene *myȝte* hem holde,
B. 1.132	*Mowe* be siker þat hire soul[e] sh[a]l wende to heuene
B. 1.149	*May* no synne be on hym seene þat vseþ þat spice,
B. 1.153	For heuene *myȝte* nat holden it, [so heuy it semed],
B. 1.158	That *myȝte* noon Armure it lette ne none heiȝe walles.
B. 1.172	Here *myȝtow* sen ensample[s] in hymself oone
B. 1.209	I *may* no lenger lenge; now loke þee oure lord.'
B. 2.45	[There] *myȝtow* witen if þow wilt whiche þei ben alle
B. 2.133	[She] *myȝte* kisse þe kyng for cosyn and she wolde.
B. 2.148	For [he] *may* Mede amaistrye and maken at my wille'.
B. 2.193	'By crist!' quod þe kyng, 'and I cacche *myȝte*
B. 3.57	Who *may* scape [þe] sclaundre, þe scaþe is soone amended;
B. 3.145	[She] *may* neiȝ as muche do in a Monþe one[s]
B. 3.157	That feiþ *may* noȝt haue his forþ, hire floryns go so þikke.
B. 3.159	And doþ men lese þoruȝ hire loue þat lawe *myȝte* wynne;
B. 3.168	For pouere men *may* haue no power to pleyne þouȝ [hem] smerte,
B. 3.171	To haue grace to speke, spede if she *myȝte*.
B. 3.177	Ther þat meschief is [most] Mede *may* helpe.
B. 3.184	Yet I *may*, as I myȝte, menske þee wiþ ȝiftes,
B. 3.184	Yet I may, as I *myȝte*, menske þee wiþ ȝiftes,
B. 3.218	Taken Mede of hir maistres as þei *mowe* acorde;
B. 3.227	No wiȝt, as I wene, wiþouten Mede *may* libbe.'
B. 3.257	In marchaundise is no Mede, I *may* it wel auowe;
B. 3.269	Moebles and vnmoebles, and al þow *myȝt* fynde,
B. 3.319	Mercy or no mercy as Truthe [*may*] acorde.
B. 4.82	To ouercomen þe kyng wiþ catel if þei *myȝte*.
B. 4.88	And he amendes *mowe* make lat maynprise hym haue,
B. 4.103	For Mede haþ [maad myne amendes]; I *may* na moore axe.'
B. 4.136	Ac I *may* shewe ensamples as I se ouþ[er].
B. 4.139	Sholde neuere wrong in þis world þat I wite *myȝte*
B. 5.6	That I ne *myȝte* ferþer a foot for defaute of slepynge.
B. 5.21	Of þis matere I *myȝte* mamelen [wel] longe,
B. 5.57	Sekeþ Seynt Truþe, for he *may* saue yow alle
B. 5.121	I *myȝte* noȝt ete many yeres as a man ouȝte
B. 5.123	*May* no sugre ne swete þyng aswage my swellyng,
B. 5.129	And þat makeþ me [so mat], for I ne *may* me venge.
B. 5.134	I wole amende þis if I *may* þoruȝ myȝt of god almyȝty.'
B. 5.169	Among Monkes I *myȝte* be ac many tyme I shonye
B. 5.185	That þi wille [ne þi wit] to wraþe *myȝte* turne:
B. 5.256	That wolde kille hem if he cacche hem *myȝte* for coueitise of hir skynnes
B. 5.273	That þow hast maad ech man good I *may* þee noȝt assoille:
B. 5.282	And al þe wikkednesse in þis world þat man *myȝte* werche or þynke
B. 5.373	And yspilt þat *myȝte* be spared and spended on som hungry;
B. 5.387	I *may* noȝt stonde ne stoupe ne wiþoute stool knele.
B. 5.438	Forsleuþed in my seruice til it *myȝte* serue no man.
B. 5.501	And by so muche [it] semeþ þe sikerer we *mowe*
B. 5.529	Ye *may* se by my signes þat sitten on myn hatte
B. 5.541	Boþe sowe and sette while I swynke *myȝte*.
B. 5.574	Ne-noon-of-hire-seruauntȝ-þat-noyen-hem-*myȝte*;
B. 5.592	The brugg[e] is of bidde-wel-þe-bet-*may*-þow-spede';
B. 5.616	Thus *myȝtestow* lesen his loue, to lete wel by þiselue,
B. 5.638	Thow *myȝt* gete grace þere so þow go bityme.
B. 6.2	That [*myȝt*] folwen vs ech foot': þus þis folk hem mened.
B. 6.39	And þouȝ [þow] *mowe* amercy hem lat mercy be taxour
B. 6.42	Nyme it noȝt an auenture [þow] *mowe* it noȝt deserue.
B. 6.46	Thouȝ he be þyn vnderlyng here wel *may* happe in heuene
B. 6.123	And made hir mone to Piers [how þei *myȝte* noȝt werche]:
B. 6.128	For we *may* [neiþer] swynke ne swete, swich siknesse vs eyleþ.'
B. 6.139	Ac ye *myȝte* trauaille as truþe wolde and take mete and hyre
B. 6.198	And yaf hem mete [and money as þei] *myȝte* [asserue].
B. 6.211	And how I *myȝte* amaistren hem and make hem to werche.'
B. 6.213	Bolde beggeris and bigge þat *mowe* hir breed biswynke,
B. 6.222	And alle manere of men þat þow *myȝt* aspie
B. 6.230	*Miȝte* I synnelees do as þow seist?' seide Piers þanne.
B. 6.291	[Th]anne *may* I diȝte þi dyner as [þee] deere likeþ.'
B. 6.309	*May* no peny ale hem paie, ne no pece of bacoun,
B. 6.321	Ac I warne yow werkmen, wynneþ whil ye *mowe*
B. 7.7	Or any [maner] mestier þat *myȝte* Piers [helpe],
B. 7.15	And in as muche as þei *mowe* amenden alle synfulle,
B. 7.98	[Tho] þat lyue þus hir lif *mowe* loþe þe tyme
B. 7.101	And wommen wiþ childe þat werche ne *mowe*,
B. 7.140	'Were þow a preest, [Piers]', quod he, 'þow *myȝtest* preche [whan þee liked]
B. 7.150	Of þat I seiȝ slepynge, if it so be *myȝte*,
B. 8.5	And what man he *myȝte* be of many man I asked.
B. 8.23	[That] dowel and do yuele *mowe* noȝt dwelle togidere.
B. 8.58	Ac if I *may* lyue and loke I shal go lerne bettre.'
B. 9.9	And wolde wynne hire awey wiþ wiles [if] he *myȝte*.
B. 9.74	Of þis matere I *myȝte* make a long tale
B. 9.78	At myseise and at myschief and *mowe* hem amende
B. 9.85	For alle þe mebles on þis moolde and he amende it *myȝte*.
B. 9.118	And siþenes by assent of hemself as þei two *myȝte* acorde;
B. 9.164	"I am via & veritas", seiþ crist, "I *may* auaunce alle."
B. 9.182	And euery maner seculer [man] þat *may* noȝt continue
B. 9.198	Wandren [as wolues] and wasten [if þei] *mowe*;
B.10.30	Harlotes for hir harlotrie *may* haue of hir goodes,
B.10.59	Ac þe carefulle *may* crie and carpen at þe yate
B.10.66	Mendinauntȝ meteles *myȝte* go to bedde.
B.10.94	And how he *myȝte* moost meynee manliche fynde,
B.10.144	I *myȝte* gete no greyn of his grete wittes,
B.10.256	Ne man hadde no merite *myȝte* it ben ypreued:
B.10.278	[Thouȝ] it auailleþ noȝt þe commune it *myȝte* auaille yowselue.
B.10.282	Lewed men *may* likne yow þus, þat þe beem liþ in youre eiȝen,
B.10.290	And þanne *mowe* ye [manly] seye, as Dauid made þe Sauter,
B.10.348	Ther riche men no riȝt *may* cleyme but of ruþe and grace.'
B.10.353	*Mowen* be saued so, and [so] is oure bileue.
B.10.354	That [arn] vncristene in þat caas *may* cristen an heþen,
B.10.357	Ac cristene men wiþoute moore *maye* noȝt come to heuene,
B.10.428	Than Marie Maudeleyne [who *myȝte* do] werse?
B.10.446	And he þat *may* al amende haue mercy on vs alle,
B.10.455	And my kyng ouercomen hym as by konnynge of speche.
B.10.475	I se ensamples myself and so *may* manye oþer,
B.11.10	[Siþen] she seide to me, 'here *myȝtow* se wondres
B.11.20	And in þis Mirour þow *myȝt* se [myrþes] ful manye
B.11.36	A man *may* stoupe tyme ynoȝ whan he shal tyne þe crowne.'
B.11.80	For a baptiȝed man *may*, as maistres telleþ,
B.11.82	Ac [a] barn wiþouten bapteme *may* noȝt be saued:
B.11.122	And drynke boote for bale, brouke it whoso *myȝte*.
B.11.123	'Thanne *may* alle cristene come', quod I, 'and cleyme þere entree
B.11.127	For *may* no cherl chartre make ne his c[h]atel selle
B.11.129	Ac he *may* renne in arerage and rome fro home,
B.11.137	'That is sooþ', seide Scripture; '*may* no synne lette
B.11.144	That al þe clergie vnder crist ne *myȝte* me cracche fro helle,
B.11.151	And I saued as ye [*may*] see, wiþouten syngynge of masses,
B.11.153	Brouȝte me fro bitter peyne þer no biddyng *myȝte*.'
B.11.184	And [souereynly] pouere peple; hir preieres *maye* vs helpe.
B.11.197	[Alle *myȝte* god haue riche men if he wolde],
B.11.220	And of þat ech man *may* forbere amende þere it nedeþ,
B.11.331	Man and his make I *myȝte* [se] boþe.
B.11.362	Ther neiþer burn ne beest *may* hir briddes rechen.
B.11.378	Amende þow, if þow *myȝt*, for my tyme is to abide.
B.11.381	He *myȝte* amende in a Minute while al þat mysstandeþ,
B.11.390	And if a man *myȝte* make [laklees] hymself
B.11.402	For man was maad of swich a matere he *may* noȝt wel asterte
B.11.407	That I in metels ne *myȝte* moore haue yknowen.
B.12.10	Amende þee while þow *myȝt*; þow hast ben warned ofte
B.12.16	And þow medlest þee wiþ makynges and *myȝtest* go seye þi sauter,
B.12.38	And if þow be maiden to marye and *myȝt* wel continue,
B.12.49	Of manye swiche I *may* rede, of men and of wommen,
B.12.85	For goddes body *myȝte* noȝt ben of breed wiþouten clergie,

B.12.99	For as a man *may* noȝt see þat mysseþ hise eiȝen,
B.12.187	Wel *may* þe barn blesse þat hym to book sette,
B.12.243	They *may* noȝt flee fer ne ful heiȝe neiþer];
B.13.6	And how þat Elde manaced me, *myȝte* we euere mete;
B.13.51	'As longe', quod [he], 'as [lif] and lycame *may* dure'.
B.13.87	And seide, 'þow shalt see þus soone, whan he *may* na moore,
B.13.158	For, by hym þat me made, *myȝte* neuere pouerte,
B.13.170	Yeue þee al þat þei *may* yeue, as þee for best yemere;
B.13.249	And þat his blessynge and hise bulles bocches *myȝte* destruye:
B.13.253	*Miȝte* lechen a man as [me þynkeþ] it sholde.
B.13.257	For *may* no blessynge doon vs boote but if we wile amende,
B.13.312	Which *myȝte* plese þe peple and preisen hymselue:
B.13.333	And whan I *may* noȝt haue þe maistrie [wiþ] malencolie Itake,
B.13.351	Til þei *myȝte* na moore; and þanne [hadde] murye tales,
B.13.357	And ymagynede how he it *myȝte* haue
B.13.365	How I *myȝte* haue it al my wit I caste,
B.13.394	*Miȝte* neuere me conforte in þe mene [tyme]
B.13.403	And moore mete eet and dronk þan kynde *myȝte* defie,
B.13.407	The whiche is sleuþe so slow þat *may* no sleiȝtes helpe it,
B.14.45	In menynge þat alle men *myȝte* þe same
B.14.75	[Ac] mesure is [so] muche worþ it *may* noȝt be to deere.
B.14.85	And þouȝ a man *myȝte* noȝt speke contricion myȝte hym saue
B.14.85	And þouȝ a man myȝte noȝt speke contricion *myȝte* hym saue
B.14.117	Thanne *may* beggeris, as beestes, after boote waiten
B.14.137	For whan a werkman haþ wroȝt, þan *may* men be soþe,
B.14.144	It *may* noȝt be, ye riche men, or Mathew on god lyeþ:
B.14.166	For alle *myȝtestow* haue maad noon mener þan ooþer
B.14.171	For *may* no derþe hem deere, droghte ne weet,
B.14.219	Ne none of þe seuene synnes sitten ne *mowe* þer longe,
B.14.234	And if Coueitise cacche þe poore þei *may* noȝt come togideres,
B.14.240	And by þe nekke namely hir noon *may* hente ooþer;
B.14.260	Forþi [al] poore þat pacient is [of pure riȝt] *may* cleymen,
B.14.262	Muche hardier *may* he asken þat here myȝte haue his wille
B.14.262	Muche hardier may he asken þat here *myȝte* haue his wille
B.14.296	Ne borweþ of hise neighebores but þat he *may* wel paie;
B.14.305	Pouerte *myȝte* passe wiþouten peril of robbyng.
B.14.314	Than he *may* [soþly] deserue, in somer or in wynter;
B.14.315	And [þouȝ] he chaffareþ he chargeþ no losse, *mowe* he charite wynne.
B.15.38	Nempnede me þus to name; now þow *myȝt* chese
B.15.46	And of [myne] if þow *myȝtest*, me þynkeþ by þi speche.'
B.15.56	To englisshe men þis is to mene, þat *mowen* speke and here,
B.15.86	And louten to þise lordes þat *mowen* lene yow nobles
B.15.89	Of þis matere I *myȝte* make a long bible,
B.15.140	And [nempneþ hym] a nygard þat no good *myȝte* aspare
B.15.160	Thyng þat neded hym noȝt and nyme it if he *myȝte*.
B.15.251	For whoso *myȝte* meete [wiþ] hym swiche maneres hym eileþ:
B.15.263	For wel *may* euery man wite, if god hadde wold hymselue,
B.15.287	That no man *myȝte* hym se for mosse and for leues.
B.15.335	How I *myȝte* mo þerInne amonges hem sette.
B.15.365	By þe seed þat þei sewe what þei sel[l]e *myȝte*,
B.15.390	And so *may* Sarȝens be saued, Scribes and [Grekes].
B.15.446	And þoruȝ miracles, as men *mow* rede, al þat marche he tornede
B.15.514	Men *myȝte* noȝt be saued but þoruȝ mercy and grace,
B.15.562	A medicyne moot þerto þat *may* amende prelates.
B.15.592	And by þat mangerie [þei] *myȝte* wel se þat Messie he semede;
B.15.609	Prelates of cristene prouinces sholde preue if þei *myȝte*
B.16.60	'That is sooþ', [seide] Piers, 'so it *may* bifalle.
B.16.68	Matrimoyne I *may* nyme, a moiste fruyt wiþalle.
B.16.87	He hitte after hym, [happe] how it *myȝte*;
B.16.137	Thei casten and contreueden to kulle hym whan þei *myȝte*;
B.16.202	And þat it *may* be so and sooþ [sheweþ] it manhode]:
B.16.217	Na moore *myȝte* god be man but if he moder hadde.
B.16.218	So widewe withouten wedlok *may* noȝt wel stande,
B.16.262	And me þer[wiþ]', quod þat [wye]; '*may* no wed vs quyte,
B.16.264	Out of þe poukes pondfold no maynprise *may* vs fecche–
B.16.271	The myght of goddes mercy þat *myȝte* vs alle amende.'
B.17.4	'Is it enseled?' I seide; '*may* men see þ[e] lettres?'
B.17.9	[And þus my lettre meneþ; [ye] *mowe* knowe it al].'
B.17.10	'Lat se þi lettres', quod I, 'we *myȝte* þe lawe knowe.'
B.17.57	He *myȝte* neiþer steppe ne stande ne stere foot ne handes
B.17.81	For I *may* noȝt lette', quod þat Leode and lyard he bistrideþ
B.17.84	And Spes spakliche hym spedde, spede if he *myȝte*,
B.17.93	'Haue hem excused', quod he; 'hir help *may* litel auaille.
B.17.94	*May* no medicyne [vnder mone] þe man to heele bringe,
B.17.106	And [*may*] ech man see and good mark take
B.17.119	And alle þat feble and feynte be, þat Feiþ *may* noȝt teche,
B.17.168	Na moore [*may* an hand] meue wiþoute fyngres.
B.17.188	He *may* receyue riȝt noȝt; reson it sheweþ;
B.17.193	I sholde receyue riȝt noȝt of þat I reche *myȝte*;
B.17.196	In many kynnes maneres I *myghte* myself helpe,
B.17.230	And melteþ hire myȝt into mercy, as men *may* se in wyntre
B.17.237	And solacen hem þat *mowe* [noȝt] se, þat sitten in derknesse,

B.17.240	In as muche as þei *mowen* amenden and paien;
B.17.251	For *may* no fir flaumbe make, faille it [h]is kynde.
B.17.258	The holy goost hereþ þee noȝt ne helpe *may* þee by reson.
B.17.281	For euery manere good [man *may*] be likned
B.17.286	Ac þis is þe worste wise þat any wight *myghte*
B.17.289	[How *myȝte* he aske mercy, or any mercy hym helpe],
B.17.302	And myldeliche his mercy aske; *myghte* I noȝt be saued?'
B.17.303	'ȝis', seide þe Samaritan, 'so þow *myght* repente
B.17.304	That rightwisnesse þoruȝ repentaunce to ruþe *myȝte* turne.
B.17.309	That þe kyng *may* do no mercy til boþe men acorde
B.17.314	That mercy in hir mynde *may* noȝt þanne falle];
B.17.320	His sorwe is satisfaccion for [swich] þat *may* noȝt paie.
B.17.346	Haþ mercy on men þat so yuele *may* suffre.
B.17.351	That he ne *may* louye, and hym like, and lene of his herte
B.17.355	I *may* no lenger lette', quod he, and lyard he prikede
B.18.155	*May* no medicyne [amende] þe place þer he styngeþ
B.18.177	That many day *myȝte* I noȝt se for merknesse of synne,
B.18.189	Leuestow þat yond light vnlouke *myȝte* helle.
B.18.204	And wo into wele *mowe* wenden at þe laste.
B.18.216	For til modicum mete with vs, I *may* it wel auowe,
B.18.249	Lo! helle *myȝte* nat holde, but opnede þo god þolede,
B.18.275	*May* no deeþ [þis lord] dere, ne no deueles queyntise,
B.18.320	That crist *may* come In, þe kynges sone of heuene!'
B.18.325	Lucifer loke ne *myȝte*, so light hym ablente.
B.18.329	Myne þei ben and of me; I *may* þe bet hem cleyme.
B.18.368	*May* no drynke me moiste, ne my þurst slake,
B.18.389	I [*may*] do mercy þoruȝ [my] rightwisnesse and alle my wordes trewe;
B.18.394	For blood *may* suffre blood boþe hungry and acale
B.18.395	Ac blood *may* noȝt se blood blede but hym rewe.
B.18.431	*May* no grisly goost glide þere it [shadweþ].'
B.19.27	That knyght, kyng, conquerour *may* be o persone.
B.19.29	To be called a kyng is fairer for he *may* knyghtes make.
B.19.51	*Mighte* no deeþ hym fordo ne adoun brynge
B.19.62	He *may* [be wel] called conquerour, and þat is crist to mene.
B.19.162	For þat womm[a]n witeþ *may* noȝt wel be counseille.
B.19.292	*Mighte* no [lyere wiþ lesynges] ne los of worldly catel
B.19.310	Wiþ olde lawe and newe lawe þat loue *myȝte* wexe
B.19.365	And make a muche moot þat *myghte* ben a strengþe
B.19.469	Ther I *may* hastilokest it haue, for I am heed of lawe;
B.19.475	So I *may* boldely be housled for I borwe neuere,
B.19.479	[Haue] þow *mayst* [þyn askyng] as þi lawe askeþ:
B.20.20	So nede at gret nede *may* nymen as for his owene
B.20.44	"Boþe fox and fowel *may* fle to hole and crepe,
B.20.93	[Th]anne mette þise men, er Mynstrals *myȝte* pipe,
B.20.121	Thanne cam Coueitise and caste how he *myȝte*
B.20.179	*May* noȝt a myte auaille to med[l]e ayein Elde.'
B.20.190	And hitte me vnder þe ere; vnneþe [*may*] ich here.
B.20.192	And gyued me in goutes: I *may* noȝt goon at large.
B.20.197	I ne *myghte* in no manere maken it at hir wille,
B.20.321	And Indulgence *may* do but if dette lette it.
B.20.322	I *may* wel suffre', seide Conscience, 'syn ye desiren,
B.20.350	He *may* se and here [here, so] may bifalle,
B.20.350	He may se and here [here, so] *may* bifalle,
B.20.382	To seken Piers þe Plowman, þat pryde [*myȝte*] destruye,
C.Pr.9	And merueylousliche me mette, as y *may* [ȝow] telle.
C.Pr.39	Tha[t] Poule preche[þ] of hem preue hit y *myhte*;
C.Pr.68	[And] sayde þat hymself *myhte* assoylen hem alle
C.Pr.100	Al þe world wol hit *myghte* nouȝt be trewe
C.Pr.165	Thow *myghtest* betre meten myst on maluerne hulles
C.Pr.176	*Myghte* [we] with eny wyt his wille w[i]thsytte
C.Pr.177	We *myhte* be lordes alofte and lyue as vs luste.'
C.Pr.183	Men *Myghte* ywete where þei wente and here [wey roume].
C.Pr.187	And hongen hit aboute þe cattes halse; thanne here we *mowe*
C.Pr.189	And yf [hym] lust for to layke than loke we *mowe*
C. 1.11	And sayde, 'mercy, madame, what *may* this [be]mene?'
C. 1.56	What *may* hit bymene, madame, y [þe] byseche?'
C. 1.58	*May* banne þat he born was [to] body [or to] soule.
C. 1.80	How y *may* saue my soule, þat saynt art yholde.'
C. 1.86	He is a god by þe gospel and graunte *may* hele
C. 1.145	Lok þow soffre hym to seye and so thow *myht* lerne.
C. 1.149	For heuene holde hit ne *myghte*, so heuy hit semede,
C. 1.154	[That *myȝte*] non Armure hit lette ne none heye walles.
C. 1.168	Here *myhtow* se ensaumples in hymself one
C. 1.201	Forthi y *may* seye, as y saide eer, by s[ih]t of this tex[t]es:
C. 1.203	Loue hit', quod þat lady; 'lette *may* y no lengore
C. 2.121	Suche a weddyng to wurche þat wrathe *myhte* treuthe;
C. 2.126	And withouten here moder amendes mede *may* [nat] be wedded.
C. 2.137	And se[t]he man *may* [o]n heye mede of god diserue
C. 2.139	That mede *may* be wedded to no man bot treuthe,
C. 2.149	A *myhte* kusse the kyng as for his kyn[nes] womman.
C. 2.151	And ledeth here to londone there lawe *may* declare
C. 2.152	Where matrymonye *may* be of mede and of falshede.

C. 2.164 For he *may* mede amaystrye [and maken at my wille].'
C. 2.207 'Now, by crist!' quod þe kyng, 'and y cacche *myhte*
C. 3.29 For to worche thy wille the while þou *myhte* dure.'
C. 3.61 Ho *may* askape þe sclaundre, þe skathe myhte sone be mended;
C. 3.61 Ho may askape þe sclaundre, þe skathe *myhte* sone be mended;
C. 3.129 And sente to se here; y *myhte* nat se þat ladde here.
C. 3.140 Thow tene me and treuthe: and thow *mowe* be atake
C. 3.183 He *may* ny as muche do in a monthe ones
C. 3.195 That fayth *may* nat haue his forth, here floreynes goth so thykke,
C. 3.197 Thorw which loueday is loste þat leute *myhte* wynne;
C. 3.217 To haue space to speke, spede yf a *myhte*.
C. 3.223 Ther þat meschief is greet mede *may* helpe;
C. 3.230 Ʒut y *may*, as y myhte, menske þe with ʒeftes
C. 3.230 Ʒut y may, as y *myhte*, menske þe with ʒeftes
C. 3.246 *May* nat be sold sothliche, so many part asketh
C. 3.250 Wherby he *may* as a man for eueremore lyue aftur.
C. 3.253 Al þat his men *may* wynne, do ther[mid] here beste.
C. 3.274 Taken mede of here maistres as þei *mowen* acorde;
C. 3.295 That eny man Mede toke but he hi[t] *myhte* deserue,
C. 3.313 In Marchandise is no mede, y *may* hit wel avowe;
C. 3.320 *May* desa[u]owe that thei dede and do[uwe] þerwith another
C. 3.330 And ryhte so, sothly, *may* kyng and pope
C. 3.391 He þat mede *may* lacche maketh lytel tale;
C. 3.407 Ac hoso rat of regum rede me *may* of mede,
C. 3.424 For eny mede of money al that thow *myhte* [fynde],
C. 4.78 To ouercome þe kyng [with] catel y[f] they *myhte*.
C. 4.84 Yf he amendes *may* [make] lat maynprise hym haue
C. 4.97 And mede hath made my mendes y *may* no more asken.
C. 4.107 That mede *myhte* be maynpernour [resoun] thei bysouhte.
C. 4.133 Ac y *may* s[hew]en ensaumples as y see othere.
C. 4.136 Shulde neuere wrong in this worlde þat y wyte *myhte*
C. 4.150 Reherce the[r] anon ryhte þat *myhte* resoun stoppe.
C. 4.157 And cryede to Consience, the kyng *myhte* hit here:
C. 5.33 Or thow art broke, so *may* be, in body or in membre
C. 5.34 Or ymaymed thorw som myshap whereby thow *myhte* be excused?'
C. 5.123 Of this mater y *myhte* mamele [wel] longe
C. 6.39 In alle kyne couent contreuede how y *myhte*
C. 6.77 And when y *may* nat haue þe maystrie [with] malecolie ytake,
C. 6.86 Y *myhte* nat ete many ʒer as a man ouhte
C. 6.88 *May* no sugre ne swete thyng aswage my swellynge
C. 6.94 And þat maketh me so megre for y ne *may* me venge.
C. 6.151 Amonges monkes y *myhte* be Ac mony tyme y spare
C. 6.167 That thy wil ne thy wit to wr[at]he *myhte* turne.
C. 6.185 Til we *myhte* no more; thenne hadde we mery tales
C. 6.264 How y *myhte* haue hit al my wit y caste
C. 6.281 *Myhte* neuere me comforte in the mene tyme
C. 6.305 For an hore of here ers wynnynge *may* hardiloker tythe
C. 6.333 [T]rist in his mechel mercy and ʒut þou *myhte* be saued.
C. 6.403 He *myhte* noþer steppe ne stande til he a staf hadde
C. 6.430 More then my kynde *myhte* deffye
C. 6.432 And spilde þat y aspele *myhte*; y kan nat speke for shame
C. 7.3 Y *may* nat stande ne stoupe ne withouten stoel knele.
C. 7.141 And by so muche hit semeth the sykerloker we *mowe*
C. 7.174 Ʒe *may* se be [my] signes þat sitten on my cappe
C. 7.186 Bothe to sowe and to sette þe while y swynke *myhte*
C. 7.221 Ne-none-of-here-seruauntes-þat-nuye-hem-*myhte*;
C. 7.240 The Brygge hatte b[id]-wel-the-bet-may-th[ow]-spede;
C. 7.253 And may lede in þat he loueth as here lef lyketh.
C. 7.268 Thus *myhte* thow lesen his loue, to lete wel by thysulue,
C. 7.276 Noen of hem alle helpe *may* in betere
C. 7.291 Thow *myhte* gete grace there so thow go bytymes.'
C. 7.304 I *may* nat come for a kitte, so a cleueth on me:
C. 7.308 That *myhte* folowe vs vch fote for drede of mysturnynge.'
C. 8.40 Nym hit nat an auntur thow *mowe* hit nauht deserue
C. 8.41 For thow shalt ʒelden hit, so *may* be, or sumdel abuggen hit.
C. 8.42 Misbede nat thy bondeman, the bette *may* th[ow] spede;
C. 8.130 And maden me mone to [Peres] how þei m[/yht] nat worche,
C. 8.134 We *may* nother swynke ne swete, suche sekenes vs ayleth;
C. 8.137 *Myhte* helpe, as y hope; Ac hey treuthe wolde
C. 8.178 And þat was bake for bayard *may* be here bote.'
C. 8.203 And ʒaf hem mete and money as þei *myhte* deserue.
C. 8.220 How y *myhte* amaystre hem to louye and labory
C. 8.223 Bolde beggares and bygge þat *mowe* here breed byswynke,
C. 8.231 And alle manere [of] men þat thow *myhte* aspye
C. 8.232 In meschief or in malese, and thow *mowe* hem helpe,
C. 8.236 *Myhte* y synneles do as thow sayst?' sayde Peres þe plouhman.
C. 8.314 Thenne *may* y dyhte [þ]y dyner as me dere lyketh.'
C. 8.331 *May* no peny ale hem pay ne no pece of bacoun
C. 8.341 Ac y warne ʒow werkmen, wynneth whiles ʒe *mowe*
C. 9.7 Or eny manere mester þat *myhte* [Peres] auayle
C. 9.74 Þat they with spynnyng *may* spare spenen hit [i]n hous huyre,
C. 9.148 Where he *may* rathest haue a repaest or a ronde of bacoun,
C. 9.177 And wymmen with childe þat worche ne *mowe*,

C. 9.275 Ther as mede ne mercy *may* nat a myte availle
C. 9.299 Of that y seyh slepynge, if hit so be *myhte*,
C.10.5 And what man a *myhte* be of mony m[a]n y askede.
C.10.27 And dowel and do euele *may* nat dwelle togyderes.
C.10.57 Ac yf y *may* lyue and loke y shal go lerne bettere.'
C.10.84 And helpeth alle men of þat he *may* spare.
C.10.136 And wol[d]e wynne here awaye with wyles [ʒif] he *myhte*.
C.10.160 *May* nat shyne ne shewe on schalkes on erthe,
C.10.210 Out of matrimonye, nat moyloure, *mowen* nat haue þe grace
C.10.211 That lele legityme by þe lawe *may* claymen.
C.10.236 The gospel is hereagayn, as gomus *may* rede:
C.10.255 For y am via & veritas and *may* avauncen alle."
C.10.283 And euery maner seculer man þat *may* nat contynue
C.10.297 Awayten and wasten alle þat they cacche *mowe*;
C.10.306 For þe more a man *may* do, by so þat a do hit,
C.11.40 Ac þe carfole *may* crye and quake at þe ʒate,
C.11.48 Mony tym[e] mendenauntes *myhte* goen afyngred.
C.11.75 Bote lythen how þey *myhte* lerne leest go[e]d spene.
C.11.82 I *myhte* gete no grayn of [his] grete wittes
C.11.157 Ne man *mouhte* haue mery[t]e [thereof] mouhte hit be ypreued:
C.11.157 Ne man mouhte haue mery[t]e [thereof] *mouhte* hit be ypreued:
C.11.169 And senes he saide to me, 'here *myhte* thow se wondres
C.11.179 And in þis myrrour thow *myhte* se murthes fol monye
C.11.185 'The man þat me liketh to helpe *myhte* nat myshappe.'
C.11.195 A man may stoupe tyme ynowe when he shal tyne þe croune.'
C.11.261 Then marie maudelene who *myhte* do worse?
C.11.264 *Mouhte* sleylokeste be slawe and sente hym to w[e]rre,
C.11.280 And *myhte* no kyng ouercome hym as in connynge of speche.
C.12.16 And saide he *myhte* [me nat] assoile but y suluer hadde
C.12.57 And drynke bote for bale, brouke hit hoso *myhte*.\
C.12.58 'Thenne *may* alle cristene come,' [quod y], 'and clayme þer entre
C.12.62 For *may* no cherl chartre make ne his chatel sulle
C.12.64 Ac he *may* renne in arrerage and rome fro home
C.12.72 'That is soth,' saide scripture; ' *may* no synne lette
C.12.79 That al þe cristendoem vnde[r] Crist ne *myhte* me crache fro [helle]
C.12.86 And y saued, as ʒe *may* se, withoute syngynge of masses.
C.12.100 And namelyche pore peple, here preeyeres *may* vs helpe
C.12.107 Ac for þe pore nat paye y wol pay mysulue;
C.12.172 Mo prouerbes y *myhte* haue of mony holy seyntes
C.12.187 A[c] sedes þat ben sowen and *mowen* soffre wyntres
C.12.189 Then sedes þat [in somer] sowe ben and *mowen* nat with forstes
C.12.192 Aren nat so worthy as whete ne so wel mowen
C.12.194 Riht so, sothly, þat soffry *may* penaunc[e]
C.12.210 Ac hoso rat of th[e] ryche the reuers *may* fynde,
C.13.1 Ac wel worth pouerte for he *may* walke vnrobbed
C.13.53 The marchaunt with his marchauntdyse *may* nat go so swythe
C.13.54 As þe messager *may* ne with so moche ese.
C.13.61 Ac ʒut *myhte* þe marchaunt thorw moneye and other ʒeftes
C.13.93 So þe pore of puyr reuthe *may* parforme þe lawe
C.13.96 As al þat þe ryche *may* rayme and rihtfuly dele
C.13.139 Man and his make y *myhte* se bothe;
C.13.198 He *myhte* amende in a myntewhile al þat [mys]standeth
C.13.210 Man was made of such [a] matere he *may* nat wel asterte
C.14.29 *May* nat be, [be] þ[ow] syker, thogh we bidde euere.
C.14.44 For as a man *may* nat se þat misseth his yes,
C.14.126 Wel *may* þe barne blesse þat hym to boek sette,
C.14.167 Was neuere man vppon molde þat *myhte* hit aspie.
C.14.176 For þey *may* nat fle fer ne ful hey neyther
C.15.6 And how elde man[a]ced me, so *myhte* happe
C.15.45 Ac of this mete þat maystre *myhte* nat we[l c]hewe;
C.15.57 'As longe,' quod he, ' as lyf and lycame *may* duyre.'
C.15.94 And saide, 'Thow shalt se thus sone, when he *may* no more,
C.15.157 For, by hym þat me made, *myhte* neuere pouerte,
C.15.218 For founde y þat his blessynge and his bulle [bocches] *myhte*
         [destruye],
C.15.220 As þe boek bereth witnesse þat he bere *myhte*
C.15.227 For *may* no blessynge doen vs bote but yf we wol amende
C.15.243 In menynge þat alle men *myhte* þe same
C.15.293 Thenne *may* beggares, as bestes, aftur blisse aske
C.16.6 Thenne *may* men wyte what he is worth and what he hath deserued
C.16.19 For al *myhtest* þou haue ymad men of grete welthe
C.16.60 Ne none of þe seuene synnes sitte ne *may* þer longe
C.16.65 And ayther hateth oþer and *may* nat wone togyderes.
C.16.79 And thogh coueytyse [cacche] þe pore they *may* nat come
         togyderes
C.16.80 And by þe nekke namelyche here noen *may* henten other;
C.16.100 Forthy alle pore þat pacient is of puyr rihte *may* claymen
C.16.102 Moche hardyore *may* he aske þat here myhte haue his wille
C.16.102 Moche hardyore may he aske þat here *myhte* haue his wille
C.16.122 Al þat *may* potte of pruyde in place þer he regneth;
C.16.131 Ne boreweth of his neyhebore but þat he *may* wel paye
C.16.140 Pouerte *myhte* passe withoute perel of robbynge.
C.16.148 Then he *may* sothly deserue in Somur or in wynter;

C.16.149 And thogh he chaffare he chargeth no loes *may* he charite wynne:
C.16.178 And *may* nat be withoute a body to bere me where hym liketh.'
C.16.200 Nempned me thus to name; now þou *myhte* chese
C.16.208 And of myn yf thow *myhtes[t]*, me thynketh by thy speche.'
C.16.218 To engelische men this is to mene, þat *mowen* speke and here,
C.16.287 That maistres commenden moche. Where *may* hit be yfounde?
C.16.294 Thyng that nedede hym nauhte and nyme hit yf a *myhte*.
C.16.329 Worth moche meryte to þat man þat hit *may* soffre.
C.16.342 Ac thorw werkes thow *myhte* wyte wher forth he walketh:
C.17.14 That no man *myhte* se hym for moes and for leues.
C.17.58 With þat ȝoure bernes and ȝoure bloed by goed lawe *may* clayme!
C.17.70 That pore peple by puyre riht here part *myhte* aske.
C.17.73 Me *may* now likene lettred men to a loscheborw oþer worse
C.17.87 *May* no preyere pees make in no place hit semeth.
C.17.102 By the seed þat they sewe what þey sulle *myhte*
C.17.123 For sarrasynes *may* be saued so yf they so byleued
C.17.151 'Hit *may* be so þat sarresynes haen such a manere charite,
C.17.169 Forthy souhte [he] into surie and sotiled how he *myhte*
C.17.225 A medecyne moste þerto þat *m[ay]* amende prelates.
C.17.265 That men *myhte* nat be saued but thorw mercy and grace
C.17.317 Prelates and prestes sholde proue yf they *myhte*
C.18.55 And þe fruyt was fayre, non fayrere be *myhte*,
C.18.61 Me *may* se on an appul tree monye tyme and ofte
C.18.84 'Here beneth y *may* nyme, yf y nede hadde,
C.18.119 And hit aftur þe fende, happe how hit *myhte*.
C.18.197 How o lord *myhte* lyue [in] thre; y leue hit nat,' y sayde.
C.18.223 And man withoute a make *myhte* nat wel of kynde
C.18.278 And me þerwith', quod the weye; 'may no wed vs quyte
C.18.280 Fro þe poukes pondefold no maynprise *may* vs feche–
C.18.287 The myhte of goddes mercy þat *myhte* vs alle amende.'
C.19.6 'Is hit asseled?' y saide; 'may men yse th[e] lettres?'
C.19.11 'Let se thy lettres,' quod y, 'we *myhte* þe lawe knowe.'
C.19.56 For he ne *myhte* stepe ne stande ne stere foet ne handes
C.19.75 And lefte hym þere a lechyng to lyue yf he *myhte*
C.19.78 For y *may* nat lette,' quod that lede; and lyard he bystrideth
C.19.83 'Haue hem excused,' quod [t]he samaritaen; 'here helpe *may* nat availe.
C.19.106 Alle manere men and thogh y *myhte* venge
C.19.139 Riht so failed þe sone, the syre be ne *myhte*
C.19.154 He *may* resceyue riht nauhte; resoun hit sheweth.
C.19.159 Y sholde receyue ryht nouht of þat y reche *myhte*;
C.19.162 In many kyne manere y *myhte* mysulfe helpe,
C.19.196 And melteth myhte into mercy, as we *may* se a wynter
C.19.203 And solacen [hem] þat *mowen* nat se, sittynge in derkeness[e],
C.19.206 In as moche as they *mowen* amenden and payen;
C.19.217 For *may* no fuyr flaume make, faile hit his kynde.
C.19.238 And hymsulue, sayth the boek, sotiled how he *myhte*
C.19.244 Sethe he withoute wyles wan and wel *myhte* atymye
C.19.262 For euery manere goed man *may* be likned to a torche
C.19.267 Ac this is the worste wyse þat eny wiht *myhte*
C.19.270 How *myhte* he aske mercy or eny mercy hym defende
C.19.282 And myldeliche his mercy aske; *myhte* y nat be saued?'
C.19.283 'Þus,' saide þe samaritaen, 'so thow *myhtest* repente
C.19.284 That rihtwisnesse thorw repentaunce to reuthe *myhte* turne.
C.19.289 That *may* no kynge mercy graunte til bothe men acorde
C.19.294 That mercy in here mynde *may* nat thenne falle;
C.19.300 As sorwe of herte is satisfaccioun for suche þat *may* nat paye
C.19.326 Haeth mercy on suche men þat [so] euele *may* soffre.
C.19.331 That he ne *may* louye, and hym lyke, and lene of his herte
C.19.335 Y *may* no lengore lette,' quod he, and lyard a prikede
C.20.158 *May* no medecyne amende the place there he styngeth
C.20.180 That many day *myhte* y nat se for merkenesse of synne,
C.20.194 Leuest thow þat ȝone lihte vnlouke *myhte* helle
C.20.225 For til [modicum] mete with vs, y *may* hit wel avowe,
C.20.258 Loo! helle *myhte* nat holde, bote opened tho god tholede
C.20.297 *May* no deth this lord dere ne [n]o deueles quentyse
C.20.333 And when y seyh hit was so, y sotiled how y *myhte*
C.20.363 That Crist *may* come in, the kynges sone of h[e]uene!'
C.20.368 Lucifer loke ne *myhte*, so liht hym ablen[t]e,
C.20.372 Myne they [be] and of me; y *may* þe bet hem clayme.
C.20.409 *May* no pyement ne pomade ne precious drynkes
C.20.431 [Y] *may* do mercy of my rihtwysnesse and alle myn wordes trewe
C.20.437 For bloed *may* s[uffr]e bloed brothe afurst and acale
C.20.438 Ac bloed *may* nat se bloed blede bote hym rewe:
C.20.475 *May* no grisly goest glyde þer hit shaddeweth.'
C.21.27 That knyht, kyng, conquerour *may* be o persone.
C.21.29 To be cald a kyng is fairor for he *may* knyhtes make;
C.21.51 *Myhte* no deth hym fordo ne adown brynge
C.21.62 He *may* be wel called conquerour and that is Crist to mene.
C.21.162 For þat womman witeth [may] nat [wel be] conseyl.
C.21.292 *Myhte* no lyare with lesynge[s] ne losse of worldly catel
C.21.310 With olde lawe and newe [lawe] that loue *myhte* wexe
C.21.365 And make a moche moet þat *myhte* be a strenghe

C.21.469 Ther y *may* hastilokest hit haue, for y am heed of lawe;
C.21.475 So y *may* boldely be hoseled for y borwe neuere
C.21.479 [Haue þou *mayst*] thyn askyng as thy lawe asketh:
C.22.20 So nede at greet nede *may* nyme as for his owne
C.22.44 "Bothe fox and foule *may* fle to hole and crepe
C.22.93 Thenne mette thise men, ar muinstrals *myhte* pype
C.22.121 Thenne cam couetyse and caste how he *myhte*
C.22.179 *May* nat a myte avayle to medlen aȝen Elde.'
C.22.190 And hitte me vnder þe ere; vnnethe *may* ich here.
C.22.192 And gyued me in gowtes: y *may* nat go at large.
C.22.197 Y ne *myhte* in none manere maken hit at here wille
C.22.321 And indulgence *may* do but yf dette lette hit.
C.22.322 Y *may* wel soffre,' sayde Consience, 'sennes ȝe desiren,
C.22.350 He *may* se and here here, so may bifalle,
C.22.350 He may se and here here, so *may* bifalle,
C.22.382 To seke [Peres the Plouhman], þat pruyde *myhte* destruye,

mayde n *maide n.& adj.* A 16 maide (6) maiden (5) maidenes (1) maidenis (4); B 39 maide (8) mayde (15) maiden (5) maidenes (3) maydenes (8); C 42 maide (6) mayde (22) mayden (3) maydenes (5) maydones (6)
A. 2.16 'Þat is mede þe *maide*, haþ noiȝede me ful ofte,
A. 2.96 And mede is a mulere, [a *maiden* of gode];
A. 2.196 Saue mede þe *maiden* no mo durste abide.
A. 3.1 Now is mede þe *maide*, & no mo of hem alle,
A. 3.4 To take mede þe *maide* & make hire at ese.
A. 3.35 To mede þe *maiden* mekeliche he loutide,
A. 3.76 Ac mede þe *maide* þe mair heo besouȝte
A. 3.94 To mede þe *maide* melis þise wordis:
A. 4.46 And ȝet he betiþ me þerto & liþ be my *maiden*.
A. 6.107 Charite & chastite beþ hire chief *maidenes*,
A. 6.110 'Mercy [is] a *maiden* [þere], haþ miȝt ouer [hem] alle;
A. 8.31 Marie *maidenis* also [or] maken hem nonnes,
A.10.15 Beþ maistris of þis maner þis *maide* to kepe.
A.10.136 Boþe *maidenis* & [mynchons], monkes & ancris,
A.10.199 But *maidenis* & maidenis macche ȝow ysamme;
A.10.199 But maidenis & *maidenis* macche ȝow ysamme;
B. 2.20 'That is Mede þe *mayde*, haþ noyed me ful ofte,
B. 2.44 Tomorwe worþ ymaked þe *maydenes* bridale;
B. 2.57 To marien þis *mayde* [was] many m[a]n assembled,
B. 2.132 And Mede is muliere, a *maiden* of goode;
B. 2.237 Saue Mede þe *mayde* na mo dorste abide.
B. 3.1 NOw is Mede þe *mayde* and na mo of hem alle
B. 3.4 To take Mede þe *maide* and maken hire at ese.
B. 3.36 To Mede þe *mayde* [mekeliche he loutede]
B. 3.87 Ac Mede þe *mayde* þe Mair [she] bisouȝt[e]
B. 3.105 To Mede þe *mayde* [melleþ] þise wordes:
B. 4.59 And yet he beteþ me þerto and lyþ by my *mayde*.
B. 5.485 And bicam man of a *maide* mankynde to saue,
B. 5.621 Charite and Chastite ben hi[r]e chief *maidenes*;
B. 5.635 'Mercy is a *maiden* þere haþ myȝt ouer [hem] alle;
B. 6.328 And a *mayde* haue þe maistrie, and multiplie by eiȝte,
B. 7.29 Marien *maydenes* or maken hem Nonnes,
B. 9.72 Madde men and *maydenes* þat helplese were;
B. 9.114 *Maidenes* and martires out of o man come.
B. 9.178 Ac *maidenes* and maydenes macche yow [ysamme];
B. 9.178 Ac maidenes and *maydenes* macche yow [ysamme];
B.11.13 Concupiscencia carnis men called þe elder *mayde*
B.11.249 Was a pure pouere *maide* and to a pouere man ywedded.
B.12.38 And if þow be *maiden* to marye and myȝt wel continue,
B.12.204 Ne wiþ maydenes ne with martires [ne wiþ mylde] wydewes,
B.13.344 For ech a *maide* þat he mette he made hire a signe
B.14.265 And as a *mayde* for mannes loue hire moder forsakeþ,
B.14.267 Muche is [þat *maide*] to loue of [a man] þat swich oon takeþ,
B.14.268 [Moore] þan [a *maide* is] þat is maried þoruȝ brocage
B.15.469 And *maidenes* and mylde men mercy desiren
B.15.516 And bicam man of a *maide* and metropolitanus,
B.16.91 To a *maide* þat hiȝte Marie, a meke þyng wiþalle,
B.16.97 The *maide* myldeliche þo þe messager graunted
B.17.96 Wiþouten þe blood of a barn born of a *mayde*.
B.17.151 Seinte Marie, a *mayde*, and mankynde lauȝte:
B.18.115 Mercy highte þat *mayde*, a meke þyng wiþ alle,
B.18.121 Whan þise *maydenes* mette, mercy and truþe,
B.18.128 A *maiden* þat highte Marie, and moder wiþouten felyng
B.18.139 That man shal man saue þoruȝ a *maydenes* helpe,
B.18.213 Bicam man of a *mayde* mankynde to saue
C. 2.19 'That is mede þe *mayde*, hath niyed me ful ofte,
C. 2.148 And mede is moylore, [a] *mayden* of gode;
C. 2.253 Saue mede þe *mayde* no ma durste abyde.
C. 3.1 Now is mede þe *mayde* and na mo of hem alle
C. 3.4 To take mede þe *mayde* and maken here at ese.
C. 3.39 To mede þe *mayde* myldeliche he sayde,
C. 3.115 Ac Mede þe *mayde* þe mayre a bisowte
C. 3.155 'Woltow wedde this *m[ai]de* yf y wol assente?

C. 4.62   And ʒut he manes[c]heth me and myne and lyth be my *mayde*.
C. 4.163 With mede þe *mayde* out of þe moethalle.
C. 6.178 For eche *mayde* þat y mette y made here a signe
C. 7.127 And bicam man of a *mayde* mankynde to amende
C. 7.273 Charite and chastite ben his chief *maydenes*,
C. 7.288 'Mercy is a *mayden* there hath myhte ouer hem alle
C. 9.33   Amende in som manere wyse and *ma[y]dones* helpe;
C.10.206 Prophetus and patriarkes, popes and *maydenes*.
C.10.260 A *mayde* and wel yma[ner]ed and of gode men yspronge,
C.10.280 Bote *maydones* and maydones marie ʒow togyderes:
C.10.280 Bote maydones and *maydones* marie ʒow togyderes:
C.11.142 On þe *maide* Marie for mankynde sake
C.11.143 And bycam man of þat *maide* withoute mankynde.
C.11.171 Thenne hadde fortune folwyng here two fayre *maydenes*:
C.11.172 Concupiscencia carnis men calde þ[e] eldre *maide*
C.12.135 Was a puyre pore *mayde* and to a pore man ywedded.
C.14.143 Ne with *maydenes* ne with martires ne with mylde weddewes,
C.16.105 As a *mayde* for mannes loue here moder fors[a]ke[th],
C.16.107 Moche is [þat] *mayde* to louye of a man þat such oen taketh,
C.16.108 More then þat *mayde* is þat is maried by brocage,
C.17.267 And bicam man of a *mayde* and metropol[it]anus
C.18.71   As weddede men and wedewes and riht worthy *maydones*
C.18.91   And bad hit be, of a bat of erthe, a man and a *maide*,
C.18.96   *Maydones* and martres ministrede [hym] here on erthe
C.18.124 To a *mayde* þat hihte marie, a meke thynge withalle,
C.18.130 The *mayde* myldeliche [tho] the messager grauntede
C.18.134 And bycam man of þat *maide* mankynde to saue,
C.19.87   The whiche barn mote nedes be born of a *mayde*,
C.19.125 Seynte marie, a *mayden*, and mankynde lauhte:
C.20.118 Mercy hihte þat *mayde*, a mylde thynge with alle,
C.20.124 When this *maydones* metten, Mercy and treuthe,
C.20.131 A *mayde* þat hoteth Marie, a[nd] moder withouten velynge
C.20.142 [That man shal man saue thorw a *maydenes* helpe
C.20.222 Bycam man of a *mayde* mankynde to saue

maydenhede n *maidenhede* n. A 2 maidenhed (1) maydenhed (1); B 3
   maydenhede (2) maydenhode (1); C 2 maydenheed (1) maydenhod (1)
A. 1.158 Þanne malkyn of hire *maidenhed* þat no man desiriþ.
A. 4.37   And margerete of hire *maydenhed* maugre hire chekis.
B. 1.184 Than Malkyn of hire *maydenhede* þat no man desireþ.
B. 4.50   And Margrete of hir *maydenhede* maugree hire chekes.
B.16.71   *Maidenhode*, Aungeles peeris, and [erst] wole be ripe
C. 1.180 Then malkyn of here *maydenheed* [þat] no man [desir]eth.
C. 4.48   And margarete of here *maydenhod* as he mette here late.

maydenis -ones > mayde; maieste(e > mageste

maymeth v *maimen* v. B 1 ymaymed; C 4 maymeth (1) ymaymed (3)
B.17.192 Were þe myddel of myn hand *ymaymed* or yperissed
C. 5.34   Or *ymaymed* thorw som myshap whereby thow myhte be excused?'
C. 9.217 Or *ymaymed* in som membre, for to meschief hit souneth,
C.19.158 Were þe myddel of myn hand [*ymaymed*] or ypersed
C.20.384 Or eny manere membre *maymeth* oþer herteth,

mayn n *main* n. B 1; C 1 mayne
B.18.318 [The] lord of myght and of *ma[y]n* and alle manere vertues,
C.20.361 'The lord of myhte and of *mayne* þat made alle thynges.

mayne > mayn,meynee

maynpernour n *mainpernour* n. A 1 meynpernour; B 2 maynpernour (1)
   meynpernour (1); C 1
A. 4.99   Þat mede muste be *meynpernour* resoun þei besouʒte.
B. 4.112 That Mede moste be *maynpernour* Reson þei bisouʒte.
B.18.185 To be mannes *meynpernour* for eueremoore after.
C. 4.107 That mede myhte be *maynpernour* [resoun] thei bysouhte.

maynprise n *mainprise* n. A 1; B 3; C 3
A. 4.75   And he amendis mowe make let *maynprise* hym haue,
B. 4.88   And he amendes mowe make lat *maynprise* hym haue,
B.16.264 Out of þe poukes pondfold no *maynprise* may vs fecche–
B.20.17   Nede anoon righte nymeþ hym vnder *maynprise*.
C. 4.84   Yf he amendes may [make] lat *maynprise* hym haue
C.18.280 Fro þe poukes pondfold no *maynprise* may vs feche–
C.22.17   Nede anoen riht nymeth hym vnder *maynprise*.

maynprise v *mainprisen* v. A 1 meynprise; B 2 maynprise (1) meynprise
   (1); C 3 maynprise (1) maynprisen (1) maynpryse (1)
A. 2.158 Shal neuere man of þis molde *meynprise* þe [l]este,
B. 2.197 Shal neuere man of þis molde *meynprise* þe leeste,
B. 4.179 Mede shal noʒt *maynprise* yow, by [þe marie of heuene!
C. 2.211 Shal neuere man on þis molde *maynpryse* þe leste,
C. 4.173 Mede shal nat *maynprise* [ʒow], by marye of heuene!
C.20.188 Mercy, [my sustur], and me to *maynprisen* hem alle

maynteyne(- > maintene

mayntenaunce n *maintenaunce* n. B 1; C 1
B. 5.250 'Lentestow euere lordes for loue of hire *mayntenaunce*?'
C. 6.248 'Lenedest [thow] euere eny lord for loue of his *mayntenaunce*?'

mayntene v *maintenen* v. A 8 maynteyne (1) mayntene (2) maynteniþ (3)
   meynteyne (1) meynteniþ (1); B 11 mayntene (6) maynteneþ (5); C 6
   maynteyne (1) maynteneth (2) mainteneth (1) meynteyneth (1)
   meyntene (1)
A. 2.157 And do hem hange be þe hals & alle þat hem *mayntenip*.
A. 3.79   Ryng[es] or oþer richesse, þ[ise] regratour[is] to *meynteyne*.
A. 3.139 Prouendrours, [persones], & [prestis] she *maynteniþ*
A. 3.154 And alle þat *meyntenib* hire men meschaunce hem betide!
A. 3.172 And *maynteyne* þi manhod more þan þou knowist;
A. 3.203 And mediþ men hymself to *maynteyne* here lawis;
A. 3.226 To *maynteyne* mysdoeris mede þei taken,
A. 4.42   He *mayntenib* his men to murþre myne hynen,
B. 2.37   And men of þis moolde þat *maynteneþ* truþe,
B. 2.196 And doon hem hange by þe hals and alle þat hem *maynteneþ*.
B. 3.90   Rynges or ooþer richesse þ[ise] Regratiers to *maynteene*.
B. 3.150 Prouendre[s], persones and preestes [she] *maynteneþ*
B. 3.167 And alle þat *maynteneþ* hire men, meschaunce hem bitide!
B. 3.185 And *maynteene* þi manhode moore þan þow knowest;
B. 3.216 And medeþ men h[y]mseluen to *maynteene* hir lawes.
B. 3.247 To *maynteene* mysdoers Mede þei take;
B. 4.55   He *mayntenep* hise men to murþere myne hewen,
B. 6.36   Als longe as I lyue I shal þee *maynteene*.'
B.13.126 And no text ne takeþ to *maynteene* his cause
C. 2.210 And do hem hange by þe halse and alle þat hem *maynteyneth*.
C. 3.188 He prouendreth persones and prestes he *maynteneth*
C. 3.231 And *maynteyne* thi manhede more then thow knowest.
C. 3.272 And ʒeuen mede to men to *meyntene* here lawes;
C. 4.58   A *meynteyneth* his men to morthere myn hewes,
C.17.234 That with moneye *maynteyneth* men [t]o werre vppon cristene

mayntenour n *maintenour* n. C 1
C. 3.287 That mede [is] euermore a *mayntenour* of Gyle,

mair n *maire* n. A 4 mair (1) meiris (3); B 8 Mair (3) Maire (1) Maires
   (2) Meire (1) Meires (1); C 10 mair (1) Mayr (1) mayre (4) mayres
   (4)
A. 3.65   *Meiris* & ma[ce]ris, hij þat ben mene
A. 3.76   Ac mede þe maide þe *mair* heo besouʒte
A. 3.83   For to amende [*meiris* and] men þat kepiþ þe lawis,
A. 8.168 And nameliche ʒe maistris, as *meiris* & iuggis,
B. 1.160 And a meene, as þe *Mair* is, bitwene þe [commune] & þe [kyng];
B. 3.76   *Maires* and Maceres þat menes ben bitwene
B. 3.87   Ac Mede þe mayde þe *Mair* [she] bisouʒt[e]
B. 3.94   For to amenden *Maires* and men þat kepen [þe] lawes,
B. 3.315 Shal neiþer kyng ne knyght, Constable ne *Meire*
B. 7.190 And namely ye maistres, *Meires* and Iugges,
B.13.270 My wafres were gesene whan Chichestre was *Maire*.'
B.14.290 Ne to be *Mair* aboue men ne Mynystre vnder kynges;
C. 1.156 And a mene, as þe *Mayre* is, bitwene þe kyng and þe comune;
C. 3.77   ʒut mede the *Mayr* myldeliche he bysouhte,
C. 3.108 Forthy *mayres* þat maketh fre men, me thynketh þat ʒe ouhten
C. 3.115 Ac Mede þe mayde þe *mayre* a bisowte
C. 3.122 In amendement of *mayres* and oþer stywardes
C. 3.468 Shal nother kyng ne knyght, Constable ne *Mayre*
C. 8.87   Maystres, as *mayres* and grete menne, senatours,
C. 9.122 And thauh a mete with þe *mayre* ameddes þe strete
C. 9.336 And manliche ʒe maistres, *mayres* and iuges,
C.16.125 Ne to be *mair* ouer men ne mynistre vnder kynges;

mayst > may

maister n *maister* n. A 18 maister (8) maistris (10); B 40 maister (19)
   maistres (21); C 40 maister (4) maistre (13) maystre (7) maistres (10)
   maystres (6)
A.Pr.59   Manye of þise *maistris* may cloþe hem at lyking
A. 3.156 Such a *maister* is mede among men of goode.'
A. 3.205 Takiþ mede of here *maistris* as þei mowe accorde;
A. 3.225 Þere is a mede mesurles þat *maistris* desiriþ;
A. 3.234 Þat laboureris & lou3 folk taken of here *maistris*
A. 3.266 Shal no more mede þe *maister* on erþe;
A. 4.136 Þat he ne held resoun a *maister* & mede a muche wrecche.
A. 5.120 Wiþ many maner marchaundise as my *maister* me hiʒte.
A. 6.88   Biddiþ amende ʒow meke hym to his *maister* ones
A. 7.224 He hadde maugre of his *maister* eueremore aftir,
A. 7.300 Ac while hunger was here *maister* wolde þere non chide,
A. 8.168 And nameliche ʒe *maistris*, as meiris & iuggis,
A. 9.9   *Maistris* of þe menours, men of gret wyt.
A. 9.14   'Marie,' quaþ þe *maistris*, 'among vs he dwelliþ,
A.10.15   Beþ *maistris* of þis maner þis maide to kepe.
A.10.82   For doute men doþ þe bet; dred is such a *maister*
A.11.53   God is muche in þe [gorge] of þis grete *maistris*,

A.11.70 Suche motifs þei meuen, þise *maistris* in here glorie,
B.Pr.62 Manye of þise *maistre[s* mowe] cloþen hem at likyng
B.Pr.87 Bisshopes and Bachelers, boþe *maistres* and doctours,
B. 3.169 Swich a *maister* is Mede among men of goode.'
B. 3.218 Taken Mede of hir *maistres* as þei mowe acorde;
B. 3.246 Ther is [a] Mede mesurelees þat *maistres* desireþ;
B. 3.255 That laborers and lowe [lewede] folk taken of hire *maistres*
B. 3.290 Shal na moore Mede be *maister* [on erþe],
B. 3.292 Thise shul ben *Maistres* on moolde [trewe men] to saue.
B. 4.160 And leten Mekenesse a *maister* and Mede a mansed sherewe.
B. 5.204 Wiþ many manere marchaundise as my *maister* me hiȝte.
B. 5.601 Biddeþ amende-yow meke hym til his *maister* ones
B. 6.40 And mekenesse þi *maister* maugree Medes chekes;
B. 6.240 He hadde maugree of his *maister* eueremoore after,
B. 6.319 Ac whiles hunger was hir *maister* þer wolde noon chide
B. 7.190 And namely ye *maistres*, Meires and Iugges,
B. 8.9 *Maistres* of þe Menours, men of grete witte.
B. 8.18 '[Marie]', quod þe [*maistres*, 'amonges vs he dwelleþ],
B.10.67 God is muche in þe gorge of þise grete *maistres*,
B.10.117 Swiche motyues þei meue, þise *maistres* in hir glorie,
B.10.389 *Maistres* þat of goddes mercy techen men and prechen,
B.11.80 For a baptiȝed man may, as *maistres* telleþ,
B.11.174 For no cause to cacche siluer þerby, ne to be called a *maister*,
B.11.360 Muche merueilled me what *maister* [þei hadde],
B.12.101 Alþouȝ men made bokes [þe *maister* was god]
B.12.232 Lewed men many tymes *maistres* þei apposen
B.13.25 And þere I [mette] a *maister*, what man he was I nyste,
B.13.33 This *maister* was maad sitte as for þe mooste worþi,
B.13.40 Ac þis *maister* [of þise men] no maner flessh [eet],
B.13.167 *Maister* of alle þo men þoruȝ myȝt of þis redels,
B.14.217 [Or] in þe *maister* [or] in þe man som mansion he haueþ.
B.15.70 Freres and fele oþere *maistres* þat to [þe] lewed [folk] prechen,
B.15.364 Tilieris þat tiled þe erþe tolden hir *maistres*
B.15.377 Go now to any degree, and but if gile be *maister*,
B.15.380 Doctours of decrees and of diuinite *maistres*,
B.15.440 Sholde alle maner men; we han so manye *maistres*,
B.15.604 Moyses eft or Messie hir *maistres* deuyneþ.
B.16.85 There is derknesse and drede and þe deuel *maister*.
B.18.412 Than after werre and wo whan loue and pees ben *maistres*.
B.19.85 *Maistres* and lettred men, Magi hem callede.
B.19.288 Ne no mete in his mouþ þat *maister* Iohan Spicede.
C.Pr.60 Mony of þise *maistres* of mendenant freres
C.Pr.85 Bischopes and bachelers, bothe *maystres* and doctours,
C. 2.179 Thenne gan gyle borwen hors at many gret *maystres*
C. 3.215 Such a *maistre* is mede among men of gode.'
C. 3.274 Taken mede of here *maistres* as þei mowen acorde;
C. 3.277 *Maistres* þat kenneth clerkes craueth therfore mede;
C. 3.348 As a leel laborer byleueth [with] his *maister*
C. 3.443 Shal no mede be *maistre* neueremore aftur
C. 3.445 Tho shal be *maistres* on molde trewe men to helpe.
C. 4.26 Whiche a *maistre* mede was amonges pore and ryche.
C. 4.155 That mekenesse worth *maystre* ouer mede at þe laste.'
C. 5.188 Were wittiore and worthiore then he þat was his *maister*.
C. 6.212 With many manere marchaundise as my *maistre* hyhte,
C. 7.248 Biddeth amende-ȝow meke [hym] to his *maistre* grace
C. 8.38 And Mekenesse thy *maystre* maugre mede chekes
C. 8.87 *Maystres*, as mayres and grete menne, senatours,
C. 8.339 Ac whiles hungur was here *maistre* ther wolde non chyde
C. 9.336 And manliche ȝe *maistres*, mayres and iuges,
C.10.9 *Maystres* of þe menore[s], men of gret witte.
C.11.215 *Maistres* þat [of goddis mercy techen men and prechen]
C.11.289 Of al þat they haen had of hym þat is here *maistre*.
C.12.217 That many mothe was *maistre* ynne in A myntewhyle;
C.14.46 [Althouh men maden bokes] God was here *maystre*
C.15.29 And metten with a *maystre*, a man lyk a frere.
C.15.38 The *maistre* was maed sitte As for þe moste worthy;
C.15.45 Ac of this mete þat *maystre* myhte nat we[l c]hewe;
C.15.89 Þat in þ[e] mawe of þat *maystre* alle þo metes were,
C.15.167 And *maistre* of alle here mebles and of here moneye aftur,
C.16.58 Or in þe *maystre* or in þe man som mansion he haueth.
C.16.287 That *maistres* commenden moche. Where may hit be yfounde?
C.17.101 Tilyares þat tilede þe erthe tolden here *maystres*
C.17.112 Go now to eny degre and bote gyle be holde a *maistre*
C.17.114 Doctours of decre[s] and of diuinite *maistres*,
C.17.170 Be *maistre* ouer alle tho men and on this manere a wrouhte:
C.17.296 Moises be *maistre* þerof til messie come
C.17.312 Moises oþer Macometh here *maystres* deuyneth.
C.18.116 There is derknesse and drede and þe deuel *maister*.
C.20.455 Then aftur werre and wrake when loue and pees ben *maistres*.
C.21.85 *Maistres* & lettred men, Magi hem calde.
C.21.288 Ne no mete in his mouth þat *maistre* iohann spyced.

maistrie n *maistrie n.* A 4; B 15 maistrie (12) maistrye (1) maistries (2);
    C 12 maistre (1) maistrie (6) maystrie (1) maystrye (1) maistries (1)
    maistry (1) maistrye (1)
A. 3.216 Mede is worþi þe *maistrie* to haue'.
A. 4.118 Whil mede haþ þe *maistrie* to mo[te] in þis halle.
A. 5.84 Ac hadde I *maistrie* & miȝt I wolde murdre hym for euere.
A. 9.47 God wile suffre þe to deiȝe so for þiself hast þe *maistrie*.'
B. 3.229 Mede is worþi, [me þynkeþ], þe *maistrie* to haue'.
B. 4.26 Whiche *maistries* Mede makeþ on þis erþe.
B. 4.135 While Mede haþ þe *maistrie* [to mote in þis] halle.
B. 5.104 Ac hadde I *maistrie* and myȝt [I wolde murþere hym for euere].
B. 6.328 And a mayde haue þe *maistrie*, and multiplie by eiȝte,
B.10.456 But wit [ne] wisedom wan neuere þe *maistrie*
B.13.333 And whan I may noȝt haue þe *maistrie* [wiþ] malencolie Itake,
B.14.331 Or *maistrie* ouer any man mo þan of hymselue.
B.16.52 And help of þe holy goost, and þus haue I þe *maistrie*.'
B.16.112 Ofte [he] heeled swiche; he held it for no *maistrie*
B.16.115 Ac [er] he made þe *maistrie* mestus cepit esse
B.18.66 Shal no wight wite witterly who shal haue þe *maistrie*
B.18.102 And ye, lurdaynes, han ylost for lif shal haue þe *maistrye*;
B.18.277 If he reu[e] me my riȝt he robbeþ me by *maistrie*.
B.19.255 And who þat moost *maistries* kan be myldest of berynge.
C. 3.285 Mede is worthy, me thynketh, þe *maistrye* to haue.'
C. 4.132 Whiles mede hath the *maistrie* þer motyng is at [þe] Barr[e].
C. 6.77 And when y may nat haue þe *maystrie* [with] malecolie ytake,
C. 6.191 By sorserie sum tyme and sum tyme by *maystrie*,
C.11.282 That wit ne witnesse wan neuere þe *maistre*
C.17.241 Naught thorw manslaght and mannes strenghe Macometh hadde þe
    maistrie
C.18.52 And that is grace of þe holy gost; and thus gete y the *maystrye*.'
C.20.68 Ac shal no wyht wyte witturlich ho shal haue þe *maistry*
C.20.105 And ȝe, lordeyne[s], haen lost for lyf shal haue [þe] *maistrie*;
C.20.299 Yf he reue me my rihte A robbeth me [by] *maistrie*
C.20.394 Here eny synfole soule souereynliche by *maistrie*,
C.21.255 And [ho] þat moest *maistries* can be myldest of berynge.

maistris > maister; makameth > makometh

make n *make n.(1)* &> *maken* A 2; B 10 make (9) makes (1); C 7
A. 3.108 For heo is fayn of þi Felasshipe, for to be þi *make*.'
A.10.207 Þat iche man haue a *make* in [mariage] of wedlak
B. 3.119 For she is fayn of þi felaweshipe, for to be þi *make*.'
B.10.248 Makere of man [and his *make*] and of beestes boþe.
B.11.328 And where þat briddes and beestes by hir *mak[e* þei] yeden,
B.11.331 Man and his *make* I myȝte [se] boþe.
B.11.344 Medled noȝt wiþ hir *makes*, [saue man allone].
B.11.371 Saue man and his *make*; many tyme [me þouȝte],
B.11.375 Why þow ne sewest man and his *make* þat no mysfeet hem folwe.'
B.12.33 That is, if þow be man maryed þi *make* þow louye
B.14.266 Hir fader and alle hire frendes, and folweþ hir *make*–
B.16.221 That is man and his *make* and mulliere children;
C. 3.156 For she is fayn of thy felawschipe, for to be thy *make*.'
C.13.136 And where þat briddes and bestis by here *make* þei ȝeden,
C.13.139 Man and his *make* y myhte se bothe;
C.13.153 Saue man and his *make*; and þerof me wondrede,
C.18.223 And man withoute a *make* myhte nat wel of kynde
C.18.224 Multiplie ne moreouer withoute a *make* louye
C.18.234 The which is man and his *make* and moilere here issue,

maken v *maken v.(1)* A 91 mad (8) made (24) maden (1) make (32)
    maken (4) makeþ (1) makid (1) makide (1) makiþ (13) ymad (1)
    Imakid (1) ymakid(4); B 244 maad (16) made (86) maden (2) madest
    (4) make (62) maked (4) makede (1) maken (25) makest (1) makeþ
    (34) ymaad (2) ymaked (7); C 224 mad (3) made (88) maden (4)
    madest (4) maed (2) make (62) maked (2) maken (15) makest (1)
    maketh (31) maky (3) makyn (1) ymad (3) ymade (1) ymaed (1)
    ymaked (1)
A.Pr.14 I saiȝ a tour on a toft triȝely *Imakid*;
A.Pr.33 And somme merþis to *make* as mynstralis conne,
A.Pr.36 Fonden hem fantasies & foolis hem *make*,
A. 1.19 In mesurable maner to *make* ȝow at ese;
A. 1.56 Þanne I fraynide hire faire for him þat hire *made*,
A. 1.106 And ouer his meyne *made* hem archaungelis;
A. 2.22 Tomorewe worþ þe mariage *mad* of mede & of fals;
A. 2.26 Tomorewe worþ þe mariage *ymad* as I þe telle;
A. 2.55 And vnfolde þe feffement þat fals haþ *ymakid*;
A. 2.92 Ȝe shuln abigge boþe, be god þat me *made*.
A. 2.112 For he may mede amaistrien and *maken* at my wille'.
A. 2.143 And *makiþ* of lyere a lang carte to leden al þis oþere,
A. 2.174 Ac marchauntis mette wiþ hym & *made* him abide;
A. 3.4 To take mede þe maide & *make* hire at ese.
A. 3.16 And seide, 'mourne nouȝt, mede, ne *make* þou no sorewe,
A. 3.29 To loue hem lelly & lordis hem *make*,
A. 3.51 Þat I ne shulde *make* or mende, & myn name writen

A. 3.82	Salamon þe sage a sarmon he *made*
A. 3.112	She *makiþ* men mysdo manye score tymes;
A. 3.118	I[s] not a betere baude, be hym þat me *made*,
A. 3.148	She let lawe as hire list & louedaies *makiþ*;
A. 3.150	Lawe is so lordlich & loþ to *make* ende,
A. 3.185	And *made* hym merþe mournyng to leue,
A. 3.199	Mede *makiþ* hym so louid & for a man holde.
A. 3.208	Þe king haþ [m]ede of his men to *make* þes in londis;
A. 3.256	Such a meschef mede *made* þe kyng [to] haue
A. 3.259	An aunter it [noiȝide me non] ende wile I *make*.
A. 3.272	Mede of mysdoeris *makiþ* hem so riche
A. 3.276	And *make* of lawe a labourer, such loue shal arise.'
A. 4.21	And ȝet wile [h]e *make* many wehe er we come þere.'
A. 4.50	To *make* his pes with his panis & profride hym manye,
A. 4.56	'Whoso werchiþ be wil wraþþe *makiþ* ofte.
A. 4.58	But ȝif mede it *make* [þi] meschief is vppe,
A. 4.75	And he amendis mowe *make* let maynprise hym haue,
A. 4.90	For mede haþ *mad* my mendis; I may no more axen.'
A. 4.96	As longe as I lyue but more loue it *make*.'
A. 4.125	Ne for no mede haue mercy but meknesse it *made*,
A. 5.44	And *made* wil to wepe watir wiþ his eiȝen.
A. 5.47	And behiȝte to hym þat vs alle *made*
A. 5.55	To *make* mercy for his mysdede betwyn god & hym
A. 5.79	Betwyn hym & his meyne I haue *mad* wraþþe,
A. 5.106	And þat *makiþ* me so ma[t] for I ne may me venge.'
A. 5.129	My wyf was a wynstere & wollene cloþ *made*,
A. 5.143	Ne neuere wykkidly weiȝe ne wykkide chaffare *make*,
A. 5.207	And gan grete grymly & gret doel *ma[k]e*
A. 5.221	And made auowe tofore god for his foule slouþe:
A. 5.222	'Shal no sonneday be þis seue ȝer, but seknesse it *make*,
A. 6.98	Þe boldnesse of þi bienfait *makiþ* þe blynd þanne,
A. 7.61	And *make* hym mery wiþ þe corn whoso it begrucchiþ.
A. 7.78	In dei nomine Amen I *make* it myseluen:
A. 7.102	Eche man on his maner *made* hymself to done,
A. 7.145	And *make* vs merye þerwiþ maugre þi chekis'.
A. 7.174	For a potel of pe[s]is þat peris hadde *mad*
A. 7.191	Meschief it *makiþ* h[y] ben so mek nouþe,
A. 7.197	And how I miȝte amaistrie hem & *make* hem to werche.'
A. 7.210	Wiþ mete or [wiþ] mone let *make* hem [fare þe betere],
A. 7.212	*Make* þe Frendis þermi[d] for so matheu vs techiþ:
A. 7.242	Þei han mangid ouer muche, þat *makiþ* hem grone ofte.
A. 7.269	Ne no cokenay, be crist, colopis to *maken*.
A. 8.28	And *make* mesonis deux þerewiþ myseis[e] to helpe,
A. 8.31	Marie maidenis also [or] *maken* hem nonnes,
A. 8.131	Manye tyme þis metelis han *mad* me to stodie,
A. 8.149	Al þis *makiþ* me on metelis to þinke
A. 9.27	*Makeþ* þe man many tymes to falle & to stande.
A. 9.55	Blisse of þe briddis *made* me abide,
A. 9.57	To lerne þe laies þat louely [foulis] *maden*.
A. 9.81	And wiþ mammones money he haþ *mad* hym frendis,
A. 9.113	I durste meue no mater to *make* hym to iangle,
A.10.2	In a castel þat kynde *made* of foure skenis þinges.
A.10.3	Of erþe & eir it is *mad*, medlit togideris;
A.10.25	'What calle ȝe þat castel,' quaþ I, 'þat kynde haþ *ymakid*?
A.10.35	Saue man þat he *made* ymage to himselue,
A.10.38	Þat is þe castel þat kynde *made*, caro it hatte,
A.10.41	Þoruȝ miȝt of þe maieste man was *ymakid*,
A.10.51	In rewele & in resoun, but reccheles it *make*.
A.10.55	Þere is his bour bremest but ȝif blod it *make*;
A.10.79	And þat is dred of god, dowel it *makiþ*.
A.10.83	Þat he *makiþ* men meke & mylde of here speche,
A.10.142	Aȝens þe hest of hym þat hem of nouȝt *made*,
A.10.164	"Þat I man *makide* now it me forþinkeþ".
A.10.170	Clene awey þe cursid blood þat caym haþ *ymakid*.
A.11.64	And [ek] defame þe fadir þat vs alle *made*,
A.11.71	And *make* men to mysbeleue þat musen on here wordis.
A.11.129	And alle þe musons of musik I *made* hire [to] knowe.
A.11.173	Was neuere [gome] vpon þis ground, siþþe god *makid* heuene,
A.11.174	Fairere vndirfonge ne frendliere *mad* at ese
A.11.257	Eche man for his misdede but mercy it *make*.'
A.11.265	For salamon þe sage, þat sapience *made*,
A.11.274	Taken ensaumpl[e] of here sawis in sarmonis þat þei *maken*,
A.12.59	The fyrste ferly I fond afyngrid me *made*;
A.12.109	And for he medleþ of makyng he *maketh* þis ende.
B.Pr.14	I seiȝ a tour on a toft trieliche *ymaked*,
B.Pr.33	And somme murþes to *make* as Mynstralles konne,
B.Pr.36	[Fonden] hem fantasies and fooles hem *makeþ*,
B.Pr.108	And power presumed in hem a pope to *make*
B.Pr.113	Might of þe communes *made* hym to regne.
B.Pr.114	And þanne cam kynde wit and clerkes he *made*
B. 1.19	In mesurable manere to *make* yow at ese;
B. 1.58	Thanne I frayned hire faire for hym þat [hire] *made*,
B. 1.108	And ouer his meynee *made* hem Archangeles;

B. 2.44	Tomorwe worþ *ymaked* þe maydenes bridale;
B. 2.73	And vnfoldeþ þe feffement that Fals hath *ymaked*.
B. 2.82	To scorne and to scolde and sclaundre to *make*;
B. 2.128	Ye shul abiggen boþe, by god þat me *made*!
B. 2.148	For [he] may Mede amaistrye and *maken* at my wille'.
B. 2.182	And *makeþ* of lyere a lang cart to leden alle þise oþere,
B. 2.215	Ac Marchauntȝ metten with hym and *made* hym abyde
B. 3.4	To take Mede þe maide and *maken* hire at ese.
B. 3.16	And seiden, 'mourne noȝt, Mede, ne *make* þow no sorwe,
B. 3.30	To louen hem lelly and lordes [hem] *make*
B. 3.60	And I shal couere youre kirk, youre cloistre do *maken*,
B. 3.93	Salomon þe sage a sermon he *made*
B. 3.123	[She] *makeþ* men mysdo many score tymes.
B. 3.129	Is noȝt a bettre baude, by hym þat me *made*,
B. 3.158	She ledeþ lawe as hire list and louedaies *makeþ*,
B. 3.161	Lawe is so lordlich and looþ to *maken* ende;
B. 3.198	I *made* his me[ynee] murye and mournynge lette;
B. 3.212	Mede *makeþ* hym biloued and for a man holden.
B. 3.221	The kyng haþ mede of his men to *make* pees in londe;
B. 3.278	Swich a meschief Mede *made* þe kyng to haue
B. 3.281	On auenture it noyed m[e] noon ende wol I *make*,
B. 3.297	Mede of mysdoeres *makeþ* manye lordes,
B. 3.300	And *make* of lawe a laborer; swich loue shal arise
B. 3.327	And þe myddel of a Moone shal *make* þe Iewes torne,
B. 3.343	Quod bonum est tenete; truþe þat text *made*.
B. 4.23	For he wol *make* wehee twies er [we] be þere.'
B. 4.26	Whiche maistries Mede *makeþ* on þis erþe.
B. 4.64	To *maken* [his] pees with hise pens and profred hym manye,
B. 4.70	'Whoso wercheþ by wille wraþe *makeþ* ofte.
B. 4.72	But if Mede it *make* þi meschief is vppe,
B. 4.75	To *maken* [his] pees wiþ his pens, handy dandy payed.
B. 4.88	And he amendes mowe *make* lat maynprise hym haue,
B. 4.103	For Mede haþ [*maad* myne amendes]; I may *maken* no moore axe.'
B. 4.142	Ne for no Mede haue mercy but mekenesse it *ma[de]*,
B. 4.165	Mede mornede þo and *made* heuy chere
B. 5.39	And Salomon seide þe same þat Sapience *made*,
B. 5.61	And [*made*] wille to wepe water wiþ hise eiȝen.
B. 5.64	And bihiȝte to hym þat vs alle *made*
B. 5.72	To *maken* mercy for hi[s] mysded[e] bitwene god and [hym]
B. 5.99	Bitwene [meyne and meyne] I *make* debate ofte
B. 5.129	And *maad* hem [so mat], for I ne may me venge.
B. 5.158	And *maad* hem Ioutes of Ianglyng þat dame Iohane was a bastard,
B. 5.162	Of wikkede wordes I, wraþe, hire wortes *made*
B. 5.213	My wif was a [wynnestere] and wollen cloþ *made*,
B. 5.230	'Repentedestow euere', quod Repentaunce, 'or restitucion *madest*?'
B. 5.252	And haue *ymaad* many a knyȝt boþe Mercer and draper
B. 5.271	Til þow *make* restitucion', [quod Repentaunce], 'and rekene wiþ hem alle;
B. 5.273	That þow hast *maad* ech man good I may þee noȝt assoille:
B. 5.379	And þanne gan Gloton greete and gret doel to *make*
B. 5.388	Were I brouȝt abedde, but if my tailende it *made*,
B. 5.396	Ac neiþer of oure lord ne of oure lady þe leeste þat euere was *maked*.
B. 5.397	I haue *maad* auowes fourty and foryete hem on þe morwe,
B. 5.408	Than al þat euere Marc *made*, Mathew, Iohan and Lucas.
B. 5.413	I [a]m noȝt shryuen som tyme but if siknesse it *make*
B. 5.449	And *made* auow tofore god for his foule sleuþe:
B. 5.450	'Shal no Sonday be þis seuen yer, but siknesse it [*make*],
B. 5.480	God, þat of þi goodnesse [g]onne þe world *make*,
B. 5.481	And of nauȝt *madest* auȝt and man moost lik to þiselue,
B. 5.486	And *madest* þiself wiþ þi sone vs synfulle yliche:
B. 5.499	And al þat Marc haþ *ymaad*, Mathew, Iohan and Lucas
B. 5.612	The boldnesse of þi bienfe[et] *makeþ* þee blynd þanne,
B. 6.14	*Makeþ* cloþ, I counseille yow, and kenneþ so youre douȝtres.
B. 6.67	And *make* h[y]m murie þermyd, maugree whoso bigruccheþ it.
B. 6.86	In dei nomine, amen. I *make* it myselue.
B. 6.110	Ech man in his manere *made* hymself to doone,
B. 6.123	And *made* hir mone to Piers [how þei myȝte noȝt werche]:
B. 6.142	Or helpe *make* morter or bere Muk afeld.
B. 6.158	And *maken* vs murye þer[wiþ] maugree þi chekes.'
B. 6.161	'And fro þise wastours wolueskynnes þat *makeþ* þe world deere,
B. 6.186	For a pot[el] of peses þat Piers hadde *ymaked*
B. 6.188	And kitten hir copes and courtepies hem *maked*
B. 6.205	Meschief it *makeþ* þei be so meke nouþe,
B. 6.211	And how I myȝte amaistren hem and *make* hem to werche.'
B. 6.224	Wiþ mete or wiþ mone lat *make* hem fare þe bettre].
B. 6.258	Ye han manged ouer muche; þat *makeþ* yow grone.
B. 6.285	Ne no cokeney, by crist! coloppes to *maken*.
B. 7.26	And [*make*] Mesondieux þer[wiþ] myseise [to] helpe,
B. 7.29	Marien maydenes or *maken* hem Nonnes,
B. 7.54	Thise foure þe fader of heuene *made* to þis foold in commune;
B. 7.149	Many tyme þis metels haþ *maked* me to studie
B. 7.173	Al þis *makeþ* me on metels to þynke,

B. 8.31	*Makeþ* þe man many tyme to falle and to stonde.
B. 8.64	Blisse of þe briddes [abide me *made*],
B. 8.66	To [lerne] þe layes [þat] louely foweles *made.*
B. 8.67	Murþe of hire mouþes *made* me to slep[e];
B. 8.90	And wiþ Mammonaes moneie he haþ *maad* hym frendes;
B. 8.123	I dorste meue no matere to *maken* hym to langle,
B. 9.2	In a Castel þat kynde *made* of foure kynnes þynges.
B. 9.3	Of erþe and Eyr [it is] *maad,* medled togideres,
B. 9.34	[Saue man þat he *made* ymage] to hymself,
B. 9.39	Right as a lord sholde *make* lettres; [if] hym lakked parchemyn,
B. 9.41	The lettre, for al þe lordshipe, I leue, were neuere *ymaked.*
B. 9.45	And in þis manere was man *maad* þoru3 my3t of god almy3ty,
B. 9.50	[Th]at is þe Castel þat kynde *made*; caro hatte,
B. 9.53	Thorgh my3t of þe mageste man was *ymaked.*
B. 9.74	Of þis matere I my3te *make* a long tale
B. 9.115	The wif was *maad* þe w[y]e for to helpe werche,
B. 9.119	And þus was wedlok ywro3t and god hymself it *made.*
B. 9.125	Of swiche synfulle sherewes þe Sauter *makeþ* mynde:
B. 9.133	"That I [man *makede* now] it me forþynkeþ":
B. 9.139	Clene awey þe corsed blood þat Caym haþ *ymaked.*
B. 9.194	For he *made* wedlok first and [þus] hymself seide:
B.10.102	That was *maad* for meles men to eten Inne,
B.10.118	And *maken* men in mys bileue þat muse on hire wordes.
B.10.177	And alle [þe] Musons in Musik I *made* hire to knowe.
B.10.230	Was neuere gome vpon þis ground, siþ god *made* [heuene],
B.10.249	Austyn þe olde herof *made* bokes,
B.10.290	And þanne mowe ye [manly] seye, as Dauid *made* þe Sauter,
B.10.376	Ech man for hi[s] mysded[e] but mercy it [*make*]." '
B.10.380	And þat I man *maad* was, and my name yentred
B.10.384	For Salomon þe sage þat Sapience [*made*],
B.10.386	[To rule þe reume and riche to *make*];
B.10.414	And men þat *maden* it amydde þe flood adreynten.
B.10.416	That ben Carpenters holy kirk to *make* for cristes owene beestes:
B.10.454	Dauid *makeþ* mencion, he spak amonges kynges,
B.11.9	And in a Mirour þat hi3te middelerþe she *made* me biholde.
B.11.127	For may no cherl chartre *make* ne his c[h]atel selle
B.11.190	And exciteþ vs by þe Euaungelie þat, whan we *maken* festes,
B.11.197	[Alle my3te god haue *maad* riche men if he wolde].
B.11.204	No beggere ne boye amonges vs but if it synne *made*:
B.11.221	Is litel alowaunce *maad,* but if bileue hem helpe;
B.11.250	Martha on Marie Maudeleyne an huge pleynt *made*
B.11.264	*Makeþ* a man to haue mynde in god and a gret wille
B.11.294	For *made* neuere kyng no kny3t but he hadde catel to spende
B.11.308	Or in masse or in matyns *makeþ* any defaute:
B.11.345	Briddes I biheld þat in buskes *made* nestes;
B.11.350	If any Mason *made* a molde þerto muche wonder it were.
B.11.390	And if a man my3te *make* [laklees] hymself
B.11.402	For man was *maad* of swich a matere he may no3t wel asterte
B.12.22	To solacen hym som tyme; [so] I do whan I *make*:
B.12.40	[Lo]! what *made* lucifer to lese þe hei3e heuene,
B.12.101	Alþou3 men *made* bokes [þe maister was god]
B.12.127	Was þer neuere [kyng ne] kny3t but clergie hem *made.*
B.13.33	This maister was *maad* sitte as for þe mooste worþi,
B.13.42	Of þat men myswonne þei *made* hem wel at ese,
B.13.60	And *made* hym murþe wiþ his mete, ac I mornede euere
B.13.112	Than Conscience curteisly a contenaunce *made*,
B.13.158	For, by hym þat me *made*, my3te neuere pouerte,
B.13.166	Pope ne patriark, þat pure reson ne shal [þee] *make*
B.13.175	Ne bitwene two cristene kynges kan no wi3t pees *make*
B.13.214	Til Pacience haue preued þee and parfit þee *maked.*'
B.13.250	And þanne wolde I be prest to þe peple paast for to *make*,
B.13.258	Ne mannes masse *make* pees among cristene peple
B.13.327	And *made* of frendes foes þoru3 a fals tonge.
B.13.344	For ech a maide þat he mette he *made* hire a signe
B.13.361	And menged his marchaundise and *made* a good moustre:
B.13.364	Moore profitable þan myn, manye slei3tes I *made.*
B.13.393	To marchaunden wiþ [my] moneie and *maken* [here] eschaunges,
B.13.410	[Is whan men] moorneþ no3t for hise mysdedes, ne *makeþ* no sorwe;
B.13.441	Forþi I rede yow riche, reueles whan ye *makeþ*,
B.13.449	Thise þre maner minstrales *makeþ* a man to lau3e,
B.14.16	'And I shal kenne þee', quod Conscience, 'of Contricion to *make*
B.14.73	Ac vnkyndenesse caristiam *makeþ* amonges cristen peple,
B.14.74	[Oþer] plentee *makeþ* pryde amonges poore and riche.
B.14.82	Forþi mesure we vs wel and *make* [we] feiþ oure sheltrom;
B.14.114	And *makest* hem wel nei3 meke and mylde for defaute,
B.14.166	For alle my3testow haue *maad* noon mener þan ooþer
B.14.248	And wheiþer be li3ter to breke? lasse boost [it] *makeþ*
B.14.255	Meschief is [ay a mene] and *makeþ* hem to þynke
B.15.26	And whan I *make* mone to god memoria is my name;
B.15.89	Of þis matere I my3te *make* a long bible,
B.15.139	And *makeþ* murþe þer[wiþ] and hise me[yne] boþe;
B.15.146	Ac for goode men, god woot, greet doel men *maken*,

B.15.170	And leneþ and loueþ alle þat oure lord *made.*
B.15.218	The loue þat liþ in his herte *makeþ* hym li3t of speche,
B.15.241	And matrimoyne for moneie *maken* and vnmaken,
B.15.290	Poul after his prechyng paniers he *made*
B.15.341	Hem þat han as ye han; hem ye *make* at ese.
B.15.462	Ye mynnen wel how Mathew seiþ, how a man *made* a feste.
B.15.481	And by þe man þat *made* þe feste þe mageste bymeneþ
B.15.493	So manye prelates to preche as þe Pope *makeþ*,
B.15.506	And *make* hir mone to Makometh hir message to shewe.
B.15.509	And a peril to þe pope and prelates þat he *makeþ*
B.15.565	If possession be poison and inparfite hem *make*
B.16.13	'It groweþ in a gardyn', quod he, 'þat god *made* hymselue
B.16.77	And whan [he] meued matrimoyne it *made* a foul noise.
B.16.84	And *made* of holy men his hoord In limbo Inferni,
B.16.115	Ac [er] he *made* þe maistrie mestus cepit esse
B.16.133	And *maken* it as muche ouþer moore in alle manere poyntes
B.16.140	The þursday bifore, þere he *made* his [cene],
B.16.166	Deide and dee[þ] fordide, and day of ny3t *made.*
B.16.227	Thre men, to my si3te, I *made* wel at ese,
B.17.80	'What he spendeþ moore [for medicyne] I *make* þee good herafter,
B.17.145	To ministren and to *make* þat my3t of hand knoweþ;
B.17.189	For þe fyngres þat folde sholde and þe fust *make*,
B.17.239	That rufully repenten and restitucion *make*,
B.17.242	Mercy for his mekenesse wol *maken* good þe remenaunt.
B.17.243	And as þe weke and fir wol *maken* a warm flaumbe
B.17.251	For may no fir flaumbe *make*, faille it [h]is kynde.
B.17.301	Confesse me and crye his grace, [crist] þat al *made*,
B.17.336	And þou3 it falle it fynt skiles þat "frelete it *made*",
B.17.342	And þou3 þat men *make* muche doel in hir angre
B.18.44	And 3it *maken* it as muche in alle manere poyntes,
B.18.48	And bigan of [grene] þorn a garland to *make*,
B.18.81	Maugree his manye teeþ he was *maad* þat tyme
B.18.161	So shal grace þat bigan [al] *make* a good [ende
B.18.246	Whan she sei3 hym suffre þat sonne and see *made.*
B.18.282	And dwelle wiþ vs deueles; þis þretynge [dri3ten] *made.*
B.18.333	For þe dede þat þei dide, þi deceite it *made*;
B.18.364	That art doctour of deeþ drynk þat þow *madest.*
B.19.29	To be called a kyng is fairer for he may knyghtes *make.*
B.19.32	To *make* lordes of laddes of lond þat he wynneþ
B.19.59	To *maken* alle folk free þat folwen his lawe].
B.19.119	For bifore his moder Marie *made* he þat wonder
B.19.125	He *made* lame to lepe and yaf light to blynde
B.19.203	And *made* hem konne and knowe alle kynne langages.
B.19.241	And some to [kerue and compace], and colours to *make*;
B.19.256	And crouneþ Conscience kyng and *makeþ* craft youre Stiward,
B.19.258	For I *make* Piers þe Plowman my procuratour and my reue,
B.19.283	Sholde neuere mete ne [meschief] *make* hym to swelle,
B.19.293	*Maken* hym, for any mournynge, þat he nas murie in soule,
B.19.324	He *made* a manere morter, and mercy it highte.
B.19.325	And þerwiþ Grace bigan to *make* a good foundement,
B.19.327	And of al holy writ he *made* a roof after;
B.19.332	And *made* preesthod hayward þe while hymself wente
B.19.365	And *make* a muche moot þat myghte ben a strengþe
B.19.380	*Made* vnitee holy chirche in holynesse stonde.
B.19.387	[My3t] to *maken* it and men to ete it after
B.20.37	[For nede *makeþ* nede fele nedes lowe herted].
B.20.55	And [*made*] fals sprynge and sprede and spede mennes nedes.
B.20.127	And [pressed on] þe [pope] and prelates þei *maden*
B.20.138	For a [Meneuer Mantel he] *made* lele matrymoyne
B.20.163	This Sleuþe [wex slei3] of werre and a slynge *made,*
B.20.184	And *made* me balled bifore and bare on þe croune;
B.20.197	I ne myghte in no manere *maken* it at hir wille,
B.20.217	Sleuþe wiþ his slynge an hard [s]aut he *made.*
B.20.254	That in mesure god *made* alle manere þynges,
B.20.278	For god *made* to men a lawe and Moyses it tau3te:
B.20.284	And [be] ashamed in hir shrift; ac shame *makeþ* hem wende
B.20.289	And *maken* hym murie wiþ ooþer mennes goodes.
B.20.298	And *made* pees porter to pynne þe yates
B.20.306	Shrift shoop sharp salue and *made* men do penaunce
B.20.336	'I am a Surgien', seide þe [frere], 'and salues kan *make.*
B.20.349	Lat in þe frere and his felawe, and *make* hem fair cheere.
B.20.366	And *make* [of] yow [memoria] in masse and in matyns
C.Pr.35	And summe murthes to *make*, as mynstrels conneth,
C.Pr.37	Fyndeth out foule fantasyes and foles hem *maketh*
C.Pr.135	And power presumen in himself a pope to *make*
C.Pr.140	Myght of tho men *made* hym to regne.
C.Pr.141	And thenne cam kynde wytt [& clerkus he *made*
C.Pr.146	And for most profi[t to þe peple] a plogh gonne þei *make*,
C. 1.19	And, in mesure thouhe were, to *make* 3ow attese
C. 1.54	[Thanne] y fraynede hym fayr for hym þat here *made*
C. 1.73	Y vndirfenge þe formeste and fre man the *made.*
C. 1.105	*Made* knyghtes in his Couert creatures tene,
C. 2.75	And vnfoldeth the feffament þat fals hath *ymaked.*

C. 2.89   To skorne and to skolde and sklaundre to *make*;
C. 2.164   For he may mede amaystrye [and *maken* at my wille].'
C. 2.195   And *maketh* of lyare a lang cart to lede al this othere,
C. 2.225   A[c] marchauntes mette with hym and *made* hym abyde
C. 3.4   To take mede þe mayde and *maken* here at ese.
C. 3.17   And sayden, 'mourne nat, mede, ne *make* thow no sorwe
C. 3.31   To louye hem leeliche and lordes [hem] *make*,
C. 3.64   And y shal cuuere ȝoure kyrke and ȝoure clo[i]stre *make*;
C. 3.108   Forthy mayres þat *maketh* fre men, me thynketh þat ȝe ouhten
C. 3.121   Salamon þe sage a sarmon he *made*
C. 3.160   And *maketh* men mysdo manye score tymes.
C. 3.166   Is nat a bettere baud, by hym þat me *made*,
C. 3.196   And le[deth] þe lawe as here luste and louedayes *maketh*,
C. 3.199   Lawe is so lordliche and loth to *make* ende;
C. 3.209   Han almest mad, but marye the helpe,
C. 3.268   Mede *maketh* hym byloued and for a man yholde.
C. 3.391   He þat mede may lacche *maketh* lytel tale;
C. 3.434   An Auntur hit nuyede me noen ende wol y *make*,
C. 3.453   And *maky* of lawe [a] laborer; suche loue shal aryse
C. 3.480   And the [myddell] of [a] mone shal *make* þe iewes turne
C. 4.84   Yf he amendes may [*make*] lat maynprise hym haue
C. 4.97   And mede hath *made* my mendes y may no more asken.
C. 4.160   Mede mornede tho and *made* heuy chere
C. 5.5   For y *made* of tho men as resoun me tauhte.
C. 5.14   Mowen or mywen or *make* bond to sheues,
C. 5.70   Ac sythe bondemen barnes haen be *mad* bisshopes
C. 6.2   And *made* will to wepe water with his eyes
C. 6.5   And bihyhte to hym þat vs alle *made*
C. 6.72   And *made* of frendes foes thorw fikel and fals tonge.
C. 6.94   And þat *maketh* me so megre for y ne may me venge.
C. 6.133   And *made* hem ioutes of iangelynge: "dame Ione was a bastard
C. 6.178   For eche mayde þat y mette y *made* here a signe
C. 6.221   My wyf was a webbe and wollone cloth *made*
C. 6.234   'Repentedest [thow e]uere,' quod repentaunce, '[or] Restitucioun
           madest?'
C. 6.250   And haue *ymad* many a knyht bothe mercer and draper
C. 6.260   Meddeled my marchaundyse and *made* a good mostre.
C. 6.263   More profitable then myn, y *made* many wentes.
C. 6.280   To marchaunde with my moneye and *maken* here eschaunges,
C. 6.295   Til thow haue *ymad* by thy myhte to alle men restitucioun.
C. 6.307   And arste shal come to heuene, [by hym þat me *made*]!'
C. 7.4   Were y brouhte [o]n bed, but yf my taylende hit *made*,
C. 7.12   Ac of oure lord ne of oure lady þe leste þat euere was *maked*.
C. 7.13   Y haue [*made*] voues fourty and forȝeten hem amorwen.
C. 7.24   Th[en] al þat euere Mark *made*, Matheu, Iohn or lucas.
C. 7.28   Y am nat shryue som tyme but yf seknesse hit *make*
C. 7.63   And *made* [a]uowe tofore god for his foule sleuthe:
C. 7.64   'Shal no sonday be this seuene ȝere, but seknesse hit *make*,
C. 7.101   Forthy y rede ȝow ryche, reueles when ȝe *maketh*,
C. 7.109   Thise thre manere munstrals *maketh* a man to lauhe
C. 7.122   God þat of thi goodnesse gonne þe world *make*
C. 7.123   And [of nauhte *madest*] auhte and man liche thysulue
C. 7.128   And *madest* thysulue with thy sone oure soule & body ilych:
C. 7.139   And al þat mark hath *ymade*, Matheu, Ion and lucas
C. 7.185   And *maden* me sykere[n hym] sethen to seruen hym for euere,
C. 7.257   And charge charite a churche to *make*
C. 7.264   The boldenesse of thy beenfet[e] *maketh* the blynd thenne;
C. 8.13   Consience conseyleth ȝow cloth for to *make*
C. 8.68   And *m[a]ken* hym merye þermy[d], maugrey ho[so] bigruchen hit;
C. 8.95   In dei nomine, Amen: y *make* hit mysulue.
C. 8.96   He shal haue my soule þat alle soules *made*
C. 8.117   Vch man in his manere *made* hymsulue to done
C. 8.130   And *maden* here mone to [Peres] how þei m[yht] nat worche;
C. 8.155   And *maken* vs murye þer[with] maugreye h[o] begrucheth.'
C. 8.158   'Awreke me of this wastors þat *maketh* this world dere—
C. 8.182   For a potte ful of potage þat [Peres] wyf *made*
C. 8.185   They curuen here copes and courtepies hem *made*
C. 8.211   Meschef hit *maketh* they ben so meke nouthe
C. 8.238   Go to oure bygynnynge tho god the world *made*,
C. 8.246   Mathew *maketh* mencioun of a man þat lente
C. 8.270   Ȝe han manged ouer moche; þat *maketh* ȝow to be syke.
C. 8.288   Til alle thyne nedy neyhbores haue noen *ymaked*.
C. 8.307   Ne no cokeney, be Crist! colloppes to *make*.
C. 9.75   Bothe in mylke and in mele to *make* with papelotes
C. 9.113   Ne none muracles *maken*; Ac many tymes hem happeth
C. 9.234   And fulfille th[e] fastyng[e] but infirmite hit *made*,
C. 9.298   Mony tyme this meteles hath *maked* me to studie
C. 9.318   Al this *maketh* me on meteles to studie
C. 10.35   *Maketh* þe man many tyme to stomble yf he stande.
C. 10.63   Blisse of þe briddes abyde me *made*
C. 10.66   Murthe of here mouthes *made* me to slepe
C. 10.87   And of mammonaus mone *ymaked* hym many frendes
C. 10.119 Y durste meue no matere to *maken* hym to iangle

C. 10.129 In a Castel þat kynde *made* of foure kyne thynges.
C. 10.130 Of erthe and ayer [hit is] *maed*, ymedled togyderes,
C. 10.158 And semblable in soule to god but if synne hit *make*.
C. 10.246 Was for mariages ma[ugre kynd]e þat men *made* þat tyme.
C. 10.253 Þat y man *made* or matrimonye soffrede
C. 11.117 And alle þe musons in musyk y *made* here to knowe.
C. 11.146 Austyn þe olde herof *made* bokes;
C. 11.152 And alle thre bote o god, and herof he *made*
C. 11.161 And continaunce *made* on clergie, to congeie me hit semede,
C. 11.168 And in a myrrour þat hihte myddelerd she *made* me to loke.
C. 11.203 That y man *ymaed* was and my name yentred
C. 11.209 For salomon þe sage sayde of sapience *made*,
C. 11.212 To reule [þe] reum[e] and ryche to *make*
C. 11.247 That [ben] carpentares vnder Crist holy kirke to *make*
C. 11.279 Dauid *maketh* mensioun he spake among kynges
C. 12.62   For may no cherl chartre *make* ne his chatel sulle
C. 12.102 And, as þe euaungelie witnesseth, when we *maken* festes
C. 12.112 No beggare ne boy among vs but [yf] hit synne ma[d]e:
C. 12.136 Marthe on marie maudelene an huge pleynte *made*
C. 12.150 *Maketh* man to haue mynde in god and his mercy to craue,
C. 12.239 And ȝut more hit *ymaketh* men mony tymes & ofte
C. 13.43   Thogh the messager *make* his way amydde the fayre whete
C. 13.46   Ac if þe marchaunt *make* his way ouer menne corne
C. 13.76   And ȝut more, to *maken* pees and quyten menne dettes
C. 13.108 For made neuere kyng no knyhte but he hadde catel to spene
C. 13.122 Or in masse or in matynes *maketh* eny defaute:
C. 13.132 And in þe myrour of mydelerthe *made* him efte to loke,
C. 13.156 Briddes y beheld [þat] in bosches *made* nestes;
C. 13.161 Yf eny mason *made* a molde þerto moche wonder me thynketh.
C. 13.207 For is no creature vnder Crist þat can hymsulue *make*
C. 13.208 And if creatures cristene couth *make* hemsulue
C. 13.210 Man was *made* of such [a] matere he may nat wel asterte
C. 14.39   And crist cam and confermede and holy kyrke *made*
C. 14.46   [Althouh men *maden* bokes] God was here maystre
C. 15.38   The maistre was *maed* sitte As for þe moste worthy;
C. 15.47   Of þat men myswonne they *made* hem wel at ese
C. 15.64   And *made* [hym] mer[þe] with [h]is mete Ac y mournede euere
C. 15.119 Thenne consience corteyslyche a continaunce *made*
C. 15.157 For, by hym þat me *made*, myhte neuere pouerte,
C. 15.166 To haue alle londes at thy likyng and the here lord *make*
C. 15.197 'Munstracye can y nat moche bote *make* men merye,
C. 15.228 Ne mannes prayere *maky* pees amonges cristene peple
C. 15.231 And reste and ryche metes, rebaudes hem *made*.'
C. 15.290 And *makest* hem wel neyh meke and mylde for defaute
C. 15.306 Dauid in þe sauter of suche *maketh* mynde and sayth: dormierunt
C. 16.19   For al myhtest þou haue *ymad* men of grete welthe
C. 16.23   And amende vs [of] thy mercy and *make* vs alle meke,
C. 16.35   And holy churche and charite herof a chartre *made*.
C. 16.88   And where be [lygh]tere to breke? lasse boest hit *maketh*
C. 16.95   Meschief is ay a mene and *maketh* hym to thenke
C. 16.186 And when y *make* mone to god Memoria y hatte;
C. 17.17   Paul aftur his prechyng paniars he *made*
C. 17.30   Bote myldelyche when þey metten *maden* lowe [c]here
C. 17.52   To *make* men louye mesure þat monkes ben and freres:
C. 17.87   May no preyere pees *make* in no place hit semeth.
C. 17.111 Ne [can] construe kyndelyche þat poetes *made*.
C. 17.188 So manye prelates to preche as þe pope *maketh*,
C. 17.202 To amende and to *make*, as with men of holy churche,
C. 17.229 For if possession be poysen and inparfit hem *make*,
C. 17.238 The pope with alle prestes pax vobis sholde *make*
C. 17.248 To *make* a perpetuel pees bitwene þe prince of heuene
C. 17.257 And *maken* here message to Macometh here message to shewe.
C. 17.260 And a perel for prelates þat þe pope *maketh*
C. 17.301 By þe myracles þat he *made* messie he semede
C. 17.314 Thorw Moises and Macometh and myhte of god þat *made* al.
C. 18.109 A meued matrimonye; þat *made* a fo[u]le noyse.
C. 18.115 And *made* of holy men his hoerd in limbo inferni
C. 18.145 Ac ar he *made* þat miracle mestus cepit esse
C. 18.210 O god almyhty þat man *made* and wrouhte
C. 18.248 To *make* sacrefice of hym he heet me, hym to honoure.
C. 18.263 And ma[k]e sacrefice so: somwhat hit bitokneth;
C. 18.264 I leue þat ilke lord thenketh a newe lawe to *make*:
C. 19.77   'And þat more goth for his medicyne y *make* the good aȝeynward
C. 19.119 To ministre and to *make* þat myhte of hand knoweth
C. 19.155 For þe fyngeres þat folde sholde and þe fust *make*
C. 19.205 That reufulliche repenten and restitucion *make*,
C. 19.208 Mercy for his mekenesse wol *maky* good þe remenaunt.
C. 19.209 And as þe wyke and [fuyr wol *make* a warm] flaume
C. 19.217 For may no fuyr flaume *make*, faile hit his kynde.
C. 19.250 [That that wickedliche is wonne to wasten hit and *make* frendes?]
C. 19.281 Confesse me and crye his grace, god þat al *made*,
C. 19.299 Ac ar [h]is rihtwisnesse to reuthe turne rest[i]t[uci]on hit *maketh*,
C. 19.316 And thogh he falle he fynte skiles þat "freelete hit *made*"

C.19.322   And thogh that men *make* moche deul in here anger
C.20.43   And ʒut *maken* hit as moche in alle manere poyntes,
C.20.48   And bigan of grene thorn a garlond he *made*
C.20.83   Maugre his mony teth he was *mad* þat tyme
C.20.90   'Aʒeyn my will hit was,' quod he, 'þat y ʒow wounde *made*.'
C.20.164   So shal grace þat bigan al *maken* a goed ende
C.20.255   When he sye hym soffre þat sonne and se *made*.
C.20.306   Thus this lord of liht such a lawe *made*
C.20.324   We haen no trewe title to hem for thy tresoun hit *maketh*.'
C.20.346   And out of heuene hidore thy pryde *made* vs falle.
C.20.361   'The lord of myhte and of mayne þat *made* alle thynges,
C.20.376   For the [dede] that they dede, thi deseite hit *made*;
C.20.402   That art doctour of deth drynke þat thow *madest*.
C.21.29   To be cald a kyng is fairor for he may knyhtes *make*;
C.21.32   To *make* lordes of laddes of lond þat he wynneth
C.21.59   To *make* alle folk fre þat folweth his lawe.
C.21.119   For bifore his moder Marie *made* he þat wonder
C.21.125   He *made* lame to lepe and ʒaf liht to blynde
C.21.203   And *made* hem konne & knowe alle kyne langages.
C.21.241   [And somme to kerue a]nd compace and coloures to *make*;
C.21.256   And crouneth Consience kyng and *maketh* craft ʒoure styward
C.21.258   For y *make* [Peres the plouhman] my proc[ur]atour and my reue
C.21.283   Sholde neuere mete ne meschief *maken* hym to swelle
C.21.293   *Makyn* hym, for eny mornynge, þat he ne was murye in soule
C.21.324   He *made* a manere morter and mercy hit hihte.
C.21.325   And þerwith grace bigan to *make* a goode fo[un]dement
C.21.327   And of all holy writ he *made* a roef aftur
C.21.332   And *made* presthoed hayward the while hymsulue wente
C.21.365   And *make* a moche moet þat myhte be a strenghe
C.21.380   *Made* vnite holi churche in holinesse stande.
C.21.387   Myhte to *make* hit and men to eten hit [aftur]
C.22.37   For nede *maketh* neede fele nedes louh herted.
C.22.55   And *made* fals sprynge and sprede and spe[d]e menne nedes.
C.22.127   And presed on þe pope and prelates thei *made*
C.22.138   For a meneuer man[t]el he *made* leele matrimonye
C.22.163   This sleuthe wa[x] sley of werre and a slynge *made*
C.22.184   And *made* me balled bifore and baer on þe crowne;
C.22.197   Y ne myhte in none manere *maken* hit at here wille
C.22.217   Sleuthe with his slynge a[n] hard sawt he *made*.
C.22.254   That in mesure god *made* alle [manere] thynges
C.22.278   For god *made* to men a lawe and Moyses hit tauhte:
C.22.284   And be aschamed in here shryft; ac shame *maketh* [hem] wende
C.22.289   And *maken* hym murye with oþere menne godes.
C.22.298   And *made* pees porter to pynne þe ʒates
C.22.306   Shrift schupte scharp salue and *made* men do penauns[e]
C.22.336   'Y am a surgien,' saide the frere, 'and salues can *make*.
C.22.349   Lat in þe frere and his felawe and *make* hem fayere chiere.
C.22.366   And *make* [of] ʒow [memoria] in masse and in matynes

makere n *makere n.* B 2
B.10.248   *Makere* of man [and his make] and of beestes boþe.
B.16.184   The firste haþ myʒt and maiestee, *makere* of alle þynges;

maky(n > maken

makyng ger *makinge ger.* A 3; B 6 makyng (2) makynge (3) makynges
        (1); C 3 makyng (1) makynge (2)
A.11.32   More þanne musik, or *makyng* of god almiʒt,
A.11.160   Experimentis of alkenemye of albertis *makyng*,
A.12.109   And for he medleþ of *makyng* he made þis ende.
B. 3.62   Do peynten and portraye [who] paie[d] for þe *makynge*
B.10.217   Experimentʒ of Alkenamye of Albertes *makynge*,
B.11.296   It is a careful knyʒt, and of a caytif kynges *makyng*,
B.12.16   And þow medlest þee wiþ *makynges* and myʒtest go seye þi sauter,
B.13.53   /And he brouʒte vs of Beati quorum of Beatus virres *makyng*,
B.17.171   Al þe myʒt myd hym is in makynge of þynges.
C. 3.66   And [do] peynten and purtrayen ho payede for þe *makyng*
C. 3.495   Quod bonum est tenete, a tixst of treuthe [m]akynge.
C.13.110   For hit is a carfol knyhte and of a Caytif kynges *makynge*

makometh n prop *Makomete n.* B 9; C 12 Makameth (1) Machameth (1)
        Macometh (8) macumeth (2)
B. 3.329   For *Makometh* and Mede myshappe shul þat tyme;
B.15.397   A[c] oon *Makometh*, a man, in mysbileue
B.15.399   This *Makometh* was cristene [man], and for he moste noʒt ben
                    pope
B.15.405   Menynge as after mete; þus *Makometh* hire enchauntede,
B.15.408   As messager to *Makometh*, men for to teche.
B.15.410   *Makometh* in mysbileue men and wommen brouʒte,
B.15.416   And ben manered after *Makometh* þat no man vseþ troube.
B.15.492   Allas, þat men so longe [sholde bileue on *Makometh*]!
B.15.506   And make hir mone to *Makometh* hir message to shewe.
C. 3.482   For *Machameth* and mede [shal] mishap þat tyme;
C.17.159   A man þat hihte *Makameth* for messie they hym holdeth
C.17.165   Me fynde[th] þat *Macometh* was a man ycristened

C.17.176   Menyng as aftur mete; thus *macumeth* here enchauntede,
C.17.178   For *Macometh* to men swaer hit was a messager of heuene
C.17.181   Thus *macumeth* in misbileue man & womman brouhte
C.17.187   Allas, þat men so longe on *Macometh* bileueth!
C.17.239   And take hede [how] *Macometh* thorw a mylde dowue
C.17.241   Naught thorw manslaght and mannes strenghe *Macometh* hadde þe
                    maistrie
C.17.257   And maken here mone to *Macometh* here message to shewe.
C.17.312   Moises oþer *Macometh* here maystres deuyneth
C.17.314   Thorw Moises and *Macometh* and myhte of god þat made al.

male n *male n.(2)* B 1 males; C 2 male (1) males (1)
B. 5.232   I roos whan þei were areste and riflede hire *males*.'
C. 6.236   Y roes and ryflede here *males* when the[y] areste were.'
C.13.56   Ther þe marchaunt l[et] a *male* with many kyne thynges

male adj *male adj.(2)* B 1; C 1
B.16.236   Myself and my meynee; and alle þat *male* weere
C.18.252   Mysulue and my mayne; and alle þat *male* were

malecolie > malencolie

maleese n *malese n.& phr.* B 2; C 3 maleese (2) malese (1)
B.13.77   And what meschief and *maleese* crist for man þolede,
B.17.195   And þe myddel of myn hand wiþoute *maleese*,
C. 8.232   In meschief or in *malese*, and thow mowe hem helpe,
C.15.83   And what meschief and *maleese* crist for man tholede,
C.19.161   And þe myddel of myn hand] withoute *maleese*

malencolie n *malencolie n.* B 1; C 1 malecolie
B.13.333   And whan I may noʒt haue þe maistrie [wiþ] *malencolie* Itake,
C. 6.77   And when y may nat haue þe maystrie [with] *malecolie* ytake,

males n *male n.(1)* &> male B 2; C 2
B.11.339   *Males* drowen hem to males [al mornyng] by hemselue,
B.11.339   Males drowen hem to *males* [al mornyng] by hemselue,
C.13.147   *Males* drow hem to males a[l mour]nynge by hemsulue
C.13.147   Males drow hem to *males* a[l mour]nynge by hemsulue

malese > maleese

malkyn n prop *malkin n.* A 1; B 1; C 1
A. 1.158   Þanne *malkyn* of hire maidenhed þat no man desiriþ.
B. 1.184   Than *Malkyn* of hire maydenhede þat no man desireþ.
C. 1.180   Then *malkyn* of here maydenheed [þat] no man [desir]eth.

malt n *malt n.* B 1; C 1
B.Pr.198   [And] many m[a]nnes *malt* we mees wolde destruye,
C.Pr.216   For many mannys *malt* we muys wolde distruye

maluerne n prop *n.i.d.* A 3; B 3; C 4
A.Pr.5   But on a may morwenyng on *maluerne* hilles
A.Pr.88   Tho[u] miʒtest betere mete myst on *maluerne* hilles
A. 8.129   Metel[es and money]les on *maluerne* hilles.
B.Pr.5   Ac on a May morwenynge on *Maluerne* hilles
B.Pr.215   Thow myʒtest bettre meete myst on *Maluerne* hilles
B. 7.147   Metelees and moneilees on *Maluerne* hilles.
C.Pr.6   Ac on a May mornyng on *maluerne* hulles
C.Pr.165   Thow myghtest betre meten myst on *maluerne* hulles.
C. 5.110   Of þe matere þat me mette furste on *Maluerne* hulles.
C. 9.296   Meteles and moneyles on *Maluerne* hulles.

mamelen v *mamelen v.* A 1 mamele; B 2 mamelede (1) mamelen (1); C 2
        mamele (1) mamelede (1)
A. 5.21   Of þis mater I miʒte *mamele* wel longe,
A. 5.21   Of þis matere I myʒte *mamelen* [wel] longe,
B.11.418   Ac whan he *mamelede* about mete, and entremetede to knowe
C. 5.123   Of this mater y myhte *mamele* [wel] longe
C.13.226   Ac when he *mamelede* aboute mete and musede to knowe

mammonaes n *Mammon n.* A 1 mammones; B 1; C 1 mammonaus
A. 9.81   And wiþ *mammones* money he haþ mad hym frendis,
B. 8.90   And wiþ *Mammonaes* moneie he haþ maad hym frendes;
C.10.87   And of *mammonaus* mone ymaked hym many frendes

man n *man n. cf. me pron indef* A 150 man (53) manis (5) mannes (1)
        men (87) menis (4); B 580 man (208) mannes (32) men (319) mennes
        (21); C 568 man (194) mannes (21) mannys (1) mannus (1) men (328)
        menne (17) mennes (6)
A.Pr.18   Of alle maner of *men*, þe mene & þe riche,
A.Pr.32   As it semiþ to oure siʒt þat suche *men* þriuen.
A.Pr.69   Lewide *men* leuide [hym] wel & likide his speche;
A.Pr.93   To preche þe peple & pore *men* to fede
A. 1.42   Ac þe mone on þis molde þat *men* so faste holdiþ,
A. 1.80   Þat I miʒte werchen his wil þat wrouʒte me to *man*:
A. 1.87   Doþ þe werkis þerwiþ & wilneþ no *man* ille,
A. 1.125   Leriþ it þus lewide *men*, for lettrid it knowiþ,
A. 1.138   [Þer] þou art m[er]y at mete, ʒif *men* bidde þe ʒedde.

A. 1.158   Þanne malkyn of hire maidenhed þat no *man* desiriþ.
A. 1.173   And a lering to lewide *men* þe lattere to dele.
A. 2.32   And become a good *man* for any coueitise, I rede.'
A. 2.148   Of many maner of *m[e]n* þat on þis molde libbeþ.
A. 2.158   Shal neuere *man* of þis molde meynprise þe [l]este,
A. 3.6   What *man* of þis world þat hire were leuist;
A. 3.23   Þe leste *man* of here mayne a mutoun of gold.
A. 3.42   Þanne mede for hire mysdedis to þat *man* knelide.
A. 3.62   Oþer to grede aftir godis *men* whan ʒe [g]iue dolis,
A. 3.69   For þise arn *men* of þise molde þat most harm werchiþ
A. 3.83   For to amende [meiris and] *men* þat kepiþ þe lawis,
A. 3.112   She makiþ *men* mysdo manye score tymes;
A. 3.119   Betwyn heuene & helle, & erþe þeiʒ *men* souʒte.
A. 3.123   Sisours & sompnours, suche *men* hire preisiþ;
A. 3.125   She doþ *men* lese here land & here lif boþe;
A. 3.149   Þe mase for a mene *man* þeiʒ he mote euere.
A. 3.154   And alle þat meynteniþ hire *men* meschaunce hem betide!
A. 3.155   For pouere *men* mowe haue no power to pleyne [þeiʒ] hem smerte,
A. 3.156   Such a maister is mede among *men* of goode.'
A. 3.182   Wiþoute pite, pilour, pore þou robb[ed]est,
A. 3.188   Hadde I be march[al] of his *men*, be marie of heuene,
A. 3.197   To ʒiuen hise *men* mede þat mekly hym seruen,
A. 3.198   To alienes, to alle *men*, to honoure hem wiþ ʒeftis.
A. 3.199   Mede makiþ hym be louid & for a *man* holde.
A. 3.201   Þoruʒ ʒeftis han ʒonge *men* to [ʒerne] & to ride.
A. 3.203   And mediþ *men* hymself to mayntene here lawis;
A. 3.206   Beggeris for here bidding biddiþ of *men* mede;
A. 3.208   Þe king haþ [m]ede of his *men* to make pes in londis;
A. 3.209   *Men* þat [kenne] clerkis crauen of h[e]m mede;
A. 3.212   Alle kyn crafty *men* craue mede for here prentis;
A. 3.222   Tak no mede, my lord, of [men] þat ben trewe;
A. 4.10   Of mede & of mo oþere, what *man* shal hire wedde,
A. 4.42   He maynteniþ his *men* to murþre myne hynen,
A. 4.83   'Haue þis of me, *man*,' quaþ heo, 'to amende þi skaþe,
A. 4.86   To haue mercy on þat *man* þat mysdede hym ofte:
A. 4.110   Þat no *man* go to galis but ʒif he go for euere;
A. 4.115   But it be marchaunt, oþer his *man*, oþer messang[er] with lettres,
A. 4.126   For nullum malum [þ]e *ma[n]* met[t]e with Inpunitum
A. 4.135   Þere nas *man* in þe mothalle, more ne lesse,
A. 5.71   I miʒte not many day do as a *man* [au]ʒte,
A. 5.95   I deme *men* þere [hy] don ille, & ʒet I do wers;
A. 5.230   Þat iche *man* shal haue his er I hennis wende,
A. 5.238   And þou haddist mercy on þat *man* for memento sake,
A. 5.251   [A] þousand of *men* þ[o þ]rong[en] togideris,
A. 6.1   Ac þere w[ere] fewe *men* so wys þat þe [wey] þider couþe,
A. 6.11   And þe vernicle beforn for *men* shulde knowe
A. 6.20   'Knowist þou ouʒt a corseint,' quaþ þei, 'þat *men* callen treuþe?
A. 6.38   He is þe presteste payere þat pore *men* knowen;
A. 6.48   Ʒe mote go þoruʒ meknesse, boþe *men* & wyues,
A. 6.52   Oþerwise þanne þou woldist *men* wrouʒte to þiselue;
A. 6.60   Þ[e] croft hattiþ coueite nouʒt *menis* catel ne here wyues,
A. 6.71   [And] loke þat þou leiʒe nouʒt for no *manis* biddyng.
A. 6.82   Grace hattiþ þe [gateward], a good *man* forsoþe,
A. 6.83   His *man* hattiþ amende ʒow, for many man he knowiþ.
A. 6.83   His man hattiþ amende ʒow, for many *man* he knowiþ.
A. 7.21   And alle maner of *men* þat be þe mete libbiþ,
A. 7.30   Fro wastours [and wikkide men] þat wolde me destroye,
A. 7.40   And þei pore *men* profre þe presauntis or ʒeftis
A. 7.48   And nameliche at mete suche *men* eschew[e],
A. 7.62   And alle kyne crafty *men* þat conne lyue in treuþe,
A. 7.94   And ben his pilgrym at þe plouʒ for pore *menis* sake.
A. 7.102   Eche *man* on his maner made hymself to done,
A. 7.155   And manacide hym & his *men* whanne h[y] next metten.
A. 7.180   And lame *menis* lymes wern li[þ]id þat tyme,
A. 7.205   Wiþ fuyr or wiþ false *men*, fond suche [to] knowen;
A. 7.208   And alle maner of *men* þat þou miʒte aspien,
A. 7.221   He shal go [begge & bidde] & no *man* bete his hungir;
A. 7.222   Matheu wiþ þe *manis* face [mouþ]iþ þise wordis:
A. 7.229   And he þat nouʒt haþ shal nouʒt haue ne no *man* him helpe,
A. 7.258   Þei do *men* diʒe þoruʒ here drynkes er destenye it wolde.'
A. 8.14   Loke on þat o lawe, & lere *men* þat oþer,
A. 8.45   *Men* of lawe hadde lest for le[ttr]id þei ben alle;
A. 8.50   Þat is Innocent & nedy, & no *man* apeiriþ,
A. 8.60   Þat any mede of mene *men* for motyng resceyueþ.
A. 8.79   Þanne of alle oþer maner *men* þat on þis molde wandriþ.
A. 8.81   Þat euere he was *man* wrouʒt whanne he shal henne fare.
A. 8.82   Ac olde *men* & hore þat helpeles ben of strengþe,
A. 8.142   Þe king les his lordsshipe, & lesse *men* it holde.
A. 8.150   Manye tymes at mydniʒt whan *men* shulde slepe,
A. 8.159   Þis is [a] l[e]f of oure beleue, as lettrid *men* vs [tech]iþ:
A. 8.169   Þat han þe [welþe of þis] world, & wise *men* ben holden,
A. 9.5   And what *man* he miʒte be of many man I askide.
A. 9.5   And what man he miʒte be of many *man* I askide.

A. 9.9   Maistris of þe menours, *men* of gret wyt.
A. 9.23   'How seue siþes þe sadde *man* synneþ on þe day;
A. 9.25   Let bringe a *man* in a bot amydde a brood watir;
A. 9.27   Makeþ þe *man* many tymes to falle & to stande.
A. 9.32   Þere were þe *manis* lif lost for lacchesse of hymselue.
A. 9.39   Synnes þe sad *man* seuene [siþes] in þe day.
A. 9.61   A muchel *man*, me þouʒte, lik to myselue.
A. 9.87   Is hokid at þat on ende to holde *men* in good lif.
A. 9.106   Ellis wot no *man* þat now is o lyue.'
A. 10.20   Sire werche wel wiþ þin hond, [a] wiʒt *man* of strengþe,
A. 10.23   To kepe þise womman þise wise *men* ben chargid,
A. 10.32   Ac *man* is hym most lik of mark & of shap.
A. 10.35   Saue *man* þat he made ymage to himselue,
A. 10.39   As muche to mene [as] *man* with his soule,
A. 10.41   Þoruʒ miʒt of þe maieste *man* was ymakid:
A. 10.54   In *manis* brayn is he most & miʒtiest to knowe.
A. 10.63   Ouer suche maner of *men* miʒt in here soulis.
A. 10.82   For doute *men* doþ þe bet; dred is such a maister
A. 10.83   Þat he makiþ *men* meke & mylde of here speche,
A. 10.96   Whatso *men* worden of þe wraþþe be more.
A. 10.103   I haue [lernid] how lewid *men* han [lerid] here children
A. 10.104   Þat selde m[os]seþ þe marbil þat *men* ofte [t]reden,
A. 10.107   Ne *men* þat conne manye craftis, clergie [it telliþ],
A. 10.113   Ʒif þou be *man* maried, monk, oþer chanoun,
A. 10.128   Among *men* of þis molde þat mek ben & kynde.
A. 10.152   And manye mylions mo of *men* & of wommen
A. 10.154   For þei mariede hem wiþ curside *men* of caymes kyn.
A. 10.164   "Þat I *man* makide now it me forþinkeþ".
A. 10.181   And [were] marie[d] at meschief as *men* do now here children.
A. 10.202   For in [vn]tyme, treweliche, betwyn *m[a]n* & womm[a]n
A. 10.205   Þat dede derne do no *man* ne shulde.
A. 10.207   Þat iche *man* haue a make in [mariage] of wedlak
A. 11.9   And seide, 'Nolite mittere, *Man*, margerie perlis
A. 11.35   Menstralsie & merþe among *men* is nouþe
A. 11.51   Nere mercy in mene *men* more þan in riche
A. 11.54   Ac among [mene] *men* hise mercy & his werkis,
A. 11.56   Clerkis and k[ete] *men* carpen of god faste,
A. 11.57   And han [hym] muchel in here mouþ, ac mene *men* in herte,
A. 11.59   To pleise wiþ proude *men*, siþen þe pestilence tyme,
A. 11.71   And make *men* to mysbeleue þat musen on here wordis.
A. 11.101   And seide, 'mercy madame, ʒour *man* shal I worþe
A. 11.104   'For þi meknesse, *man*,' quaþ she, 'and for þi mylde speche,
A. 11.159   Ʒet arn þere febicchis of Forellis of many *manis* wittes,
A. 11.170   I grette þe goode *man* as þe gode wyf me tauʒte,
A. 11.185   And alle kyne crafty *men* þat cunne here foode wynne,
A. 11.200   And haþ possessions & pluralites for pore *menis* sake;
A. 11.201   For mendynauntʒ at meschief þ[o] *men* were dewid,
A. 11.229   Poul prouiþ it is vnpossible, riche *men* in heuene.
A. 11.230   Ac pore *men* in pacience & penaunce togidere
A. 11.231   Hauen eritage in heuene, ac riche *men* non.'
A. 11.240   Ac cristene *men*, god wot, comiþ not so to heuene.
A. 11.244   Oure enemys and alle *men* þat arn nedy & pore,
A. 11.257   Eche *man* for his misdede but mercy it make.'
A. 11.297   And is as muche to mene, to *men* þat ben lewid,
A. 12.39   To be hure *man* ʒif I most for eueremore after,
A. 12.83   I am masager of deþ; *men* haue I tweyne:
A. 12.92   And *mannes* merþe w[or]þ no mor þan he deseruyþ here
A. 12.116   Marie moder and may, for *man* þou byseke
B.Pr.18   Of alle manere of *men*, þe meene and þe riche,
B.Pr.32   As it semeþ to oure siʒt þat swiche *men* þryueþ.
B.Pr.72   Lewed *men* leued [hym] wel and liked hi[s speche];
B.Pr.129   Lowed to speke in latyn, for lewed *men* ne koude
B.Pr.166   *Men* myʒte witen wher þei wente and [hire] wey r[oum]e.
B.Pr.198   [And] many *m[a]nnes* malt we mees wolde destruye,
B.Pr.199   And also ye route of Ratons rende *mennes* cloþes,
B.Pr.209   What þis metels bymeneþ, ye *men* þat ben murye,
B. 1.44   Ac þe moneie [on] þis molde þat *men* so faste holdeþ,
B. 1.82   That I myʒte werchen his wille þat wroʒte me to *man*.
B. 1.89   Dooþ þe werkes þerwiþ and wilneþ no *man* ille,
B. 1.116   And mo þousandes myd hym þan *man* kouþe nombre
B. 1.136   Lereþ it þ[us] lewed *men*, for lettred it knoweþ,
B. 1.162   Vpon *man* for hise mysdedes þe mercyment he taxeþ.
B. 1.184   Than Malkyn of hire maydenhede þat no *man* desireþ.
B. 1.199   And lernynge to lewed *men* þe latter to deele.
B. 2.27   And Mede is manered after hym [as *men* of] kynde [carpeþ]:
B. 2.32   And what *man* be merciful and leelly me loue
B. 2.34   And what *man* takeþ Mede, myn heed dar I legge,
B. 2.36   How construeþ David þe kyng of *men* þat [caccheþ] Mede,
B. 2.37   And *men* of þis moolde þat maynteneþ truþe,
B. 2.56   Of alle manere of *men*, þe meene and þe riche,
B. 2.57   To marien þis mayde [was] many *m[a]n* assembled,
B. 2.64   Were moost pryuee with Mede of any *men* me þouʒte.
B. 2.187   [Of many maner *man* þat on þis molde libbeth],

B. 2.197	Shal neuere *man* of þis molde meynprise þe leeste,
B. 3.6	What *man* of þis [world] þat hire were leuest.
B. 3.24	The leeste of hire meynee a moton of golde.
B. 3.43	Thanne Mede for hire mysdedes to þat *man* kneled
B. 3.59	Haue mercy', quod Mede, 'of *men* þat it haunteþ
B. 3.71	Or to greden after goddes *men* whan ye [gyue] doles
B. 3.75	For þus [bit god in] þe gospel goode *men* doon hir almesse.
B. 3.80	For þise are *men* on þis molde þat moost harm wercheþ
B. 3.94	For to amenden Maires and *men* þat kepen [þe] lawes,
B. 3.123	[She] makeþ *men* mysdo many score tymes.
B. 3.130	Bitwene heuene and helle, [and] erþe þou3 *men* sou3te.
B. 3.134	Sisours and Somonours, swiche *men* hire preiseþ;
B. 3.136	She dooþ *men* lese hire lond and hire lif boþe;
B. 3.159	And doþ *men* lese þoru3 hire loue þat lawe my3te wynne;
B. 3.160	The ma3e for a mene þat þou3 he mote euere!
B. 3.167	And alle þat maynteneþ hire *men*, meschaunce hem bitide!
B. 3.168	For pouere *men* may haue no power to pleyne þou3 [hem] smerte,
B. 3.169	Swich a maister is Mede among *men* of goode.'
B. 3.195	Wiþouten pite, Pilour, pouere *men* þow robbedest
B. 3.201	Hadde I ben Marchal of his *men*, by Marie of heuene!
B. 3.210	To yeue [hise *men* mede] þat mekely hym serueþ,
B. 3.211	To aliens, to alle *men*, to honouren hem with 3iftes;
B. 3.212	Mede makeþ hym biloued and for a *man* holden.
B. 3.214	[Thoru3] 3iftes han yonge *men* to [yerne] and to ryde.
B. 3.216	And medeþ *men* h[y]mseluen to mayntene hir lawes.
B. 3.219	Beggeres for hir biddynge bidden [of] *men* Mede;
B. 3.221	The kyng haþ mede of his *men* to make pees in londe;
B. 3.222	*Men* þat [kenne clerkes] crauen [of hem] Mede;
B. 3.225	Alle kynne craft[y] *men* crauen Mede for hir Prentices;
B. 3.244	Swiche manere *men*, my lord, shul haue þis firste Mede
B. 3.292	Thise shul ben Maistres on moolde [trewe *men*] to saue.
B. 3.304	And maner *men* in hire hertes þat *men* beþ so trewe.
B. 3.309	Ech *man* to pleye with a plow, Pykoise or spade,
B. 3.322	Tha[t] worþ Trewe-tonge, a tidy *man* þat tened me neuere.
B. 3.323	Batailles shul none be, ne no *man* bere wepene.
B. 3.325	And er þis fortune falle fynde *men* shul þe worste
B. 4.10	[Of Mede and of mo oþere, what *man* shal hire wedde],
B. 4.55	He maynteneþ hise *men* to murþere myne hewen,
B. 4.96	'Haue þis [of me, *man*]', quod she, 'to amenden þi scaþe,
B. 4.99	To haue mercy on þat *man* þat mysdide hym ofte:
B. 4.127	That no *man* go to Galis but if he go for euere.
B. 4.132	But it be Marchaunt or his *man* or Messager wiþ lettres,
B. 4.143	For Nullum malum þe *man* mette wiþ inpunitum
B. 4.152	For I sei3 Mede in þe moot halle on *men* of lawe wynke
B. 4.155	And seide, 'madame, I am youre *man* what so my mouþ Iangle.
B. 5.115	[I] deme [men þere hij] doon ille, [and yet] I do werse;
B. 5.121	I my3te no3t ete many yeres as a *man* ou3te
B. 5.131	And gart bakbityng be a brocour to blame *mennes* ware.
B. 5.254	'Hastow pite on pouere *men* þat [for pure nede] borwe?'
B. 5.255	'I haue as muche pite of pouere *men* as pedlere haþ of cattes,
B. 5.264	And þat was wonne wiþ wrong wiþ wikked *men* be despended.
B. 5.273	That þow hast maad ech *man* good I may þee no3t assoille:
B. 5.282	And al þe wikkednesse in þis world þat *man* my3te werche or þynke
B. 5.293	For þee and for many mo þat *man* shal yeue a rekenyng:
B. 5.405	I visited neuere feble *men* ne fettred [men] in puttes.
B. 5.405	I visited neuere feble *men* ne fettred [men] in puttes.
B. 5.423	I foryete it as yerne, and if *men* me it axe
B. 5.425	And þus tene I trewe *men* ten hundred tymes,
B. 5.429	If any *man* dooþ me a bienfait or helpeþ me at nede
B. 5.438	Forsleuþed in my seruice til it my3te serue no *man*.
B. 5.458	That ech *man* shal haue his er I hennes wende.
B. 5.466	And haddest mercy on þat *man* for Memento sake,
B. 5.481	And of nau3t madest au3t and *man* moost lik to þiselue,
B. 5.485	And bicam *man* of a maide mankynde to saue,
B. 5.488	On good fryday for *mannes* sake at ful tyme of þe daye;
B. 5.510	A þousand of *men* þo þrungen togideres,
B. 5.523	And þe vernycle bifore, for *men* sholde knowe
B. 5.532	'Knowestow au3t a corsaint', [quod þei], 'þat *men* calle truþe?
B. 5.551	He is þe presteste paiere þat pouere *men* knoweþ;
B. 5.561	Ye moten go þoru3 mekenesse, boþe *men* and wyues,
B. 5.565	Oþerwise þan þow woldest [men] wrou3te to þiselue.
B. 5.573	Th[e] croft hatte Coueite-no3t-*mennes*-catel-ne-hire-wyues-
B. 5.584	In-[no]-manere-ellis-no3t-for-no-*mannes*-biddyng.
B. 5.595	Grace hatte þe gateward, a good *man* for soþe;
B. 5.596	His *man* hatte amende-yow, for many m[a]n h[e] knoweþ.
B. 5.596	His man hatte amende-yow, for many *m[a]n* h[e] knoweþ.
B. 6.19	And alle manere of *men* þat [by þe] lande libbeþ,
B. 6.28	Fro wastours and wikked *men* þat [wolde me destruye],
B. 6.41	And þou3 pouere *men* profre [þee] presentes and 3iftes
B. 6.53	And namely at mete swiche *men* eschuwe,
B. 6.68	And alle kynne crafty *men* þat konne lyuen in truþe,
B. 6.102	And ben his pilgrym atte plow for pouere *mennes* sake.
B. 6.110	Ech *man* in his manere made hymself to doone,
B. 6.133	Ye wasten þat *men* wynnen wiþ trauaille and tene.
B. 6.170	And manaced [hym] and his *men* if þei mette eftsoone.
B. 6.195	And ech a pouere *man* wel apaied to haue pesen for his hyre,
B. 6.219	[Wiþ fir or wiþ] false *men*, fonde swiche to knowe.
B. 6.222	And alle manere of *men* þat þow my3t aspie,
B. 6.228	And biloue þee amonges [lowe] *men*: so shaltow lacche grace.'
B. 6.237	He shal [go] begge and bidde and no *man* bete his hunger.
B. 6.238	Mathew wiþ *mannes* face mouþe[þ] þise wordes:
B. 6.245	And he þat no3t haþ shal no3t haue and no *man* hym helpe,
B. 6.274	They do *men* deye þoru3 hir drynkes er destynee it wolde.'
B. 7.40	*Men* of lawe leest pardon hadde, [leue þow noon ooþer],
B. 7.48	That is Innocent and nedy and no *man* apeireþ,
B. 7.59	That any Mede of mene *men* for motyng takeþ
B. 7.76	Ac Gregory was a good *man* and bad vs gyuen alle
B. 7.93	And bryngen forþ barnes þat bastardes *men* calleþ;
B. 7.97	Than of alle [oþere] manere *men* þat on þis moolde [wandreþ].
B. 7.99	That euere [he was *man*] wro3t whan [he] shal hennes fare.
B. 7.100	Ac olde *men* and hore þat helplees ben of strengþe,
B. 7.164	The kyng lees his lordshipe and [lasse] *men* it hadde.
B. 7.181	This is [a leef of] oure bileue, as lettred *men* vs techeþ:
B. 7.191	That haue þe welþe of þis world and wise *men* ben holden
B. 8.5	And what *man* he my3te be of many man I asked.
B. 8.5	And what man he my3te be of many *man* I asked.
B. 8.9	Maistres of þe Menours, *men* of grete witte.
B. 8.14	For [ye] be *men* of þis moolde þat moost wide walken,
B. 8.16	Boþe princes paleises and pouere *mennes* cotes,
B. 8.27	'How seuen siþes þe sadde *man* [synneþ on þe day].
B. 8.29	Lat brynge a *man* in a boot amydde [a] bro[od] watre;
B. 8.31	Makeþ þe *man* many tyme to falle and to stonde.
B. 8.36	[There] were [þe *mannes*] lif lost [for] lachesse of hymselue.
B. 8.43	Synneþ þe sadde *man* [seuen siþes a day].
B. 8.55	Ac *man* haþ moost þerof and moost is to blame
B. 8.61	And 3yue yow grace on þis grounde goode *men* to worþe'.
B. 8.70	A muche *man* me þou3te, lik to myselue,
B. 8.97	Is hoked [at] þat oon ende to [holde *men* in good lif].
B. 8.116	Ellis [n]oot [no *man*] þat now is alyue.'
B. 8.130	And wheiþer he be *man* or [no man] þis man wolde aspie,
B. 8.130	And wheiþer he be man or [no *man*] þis man wolde aspie,
B. 8.130	And wheiþer he be man or [no man] þis *man* wolde aspie,
B. 9.21	Sire werch-wel-wiþ-þyn-hand, a wi3t *man* of strengþe,
B. 9.31	Ac *man* is hym moost lik of marc and of [shape].
B. 9.34	[Saue *man* þat he made ymage] to hymself,
B. 9.45	And in þis manere was *man* maad þoru3 my3t of god almy3ty,
B. 9.51	As muche to mene as *man* wiþ a Soule.
B. 9.53	Thorgh my3t of þe mageste *man* was ymaked.
B. 9.56	Ouer al in *mannes* body he[o] walkeþ and wandreþ,
B. 9.61	Muche wo worþ þat *man* þat mysruleþ his Inwit,
B. 9.72	Madde *men* and maydenes þat helplese were;
B. 9.107	To alle trewe tidy *men* þat trauaille desiren,
B. 9.114	Maidenes and martires out of o *man* come.
B. 9.133	"That I [*man* makede now] it me forþynkeþ":
B. 9.182	And euery maner seculer [*man*] þat may no3t continue
B. 9.189	For in vntyme, trewely, bitwene *man* and womman
B. 9.192	That [dede derne] do no *man* ne sholde.
B.10.9	And seide, 'noli[te] mittere, *man*, margery perles
B.10.24	That wikked *men* þei welden þe welþe of þis worlde,
B.10.42	Drynken and dreuelen and do *men* for to gape,
B.10.43	Likne *men* and lye on hem þat leneþ hem no 3iftes,
B.10.44	Thei konne na moore mynstralcie ne Musik *men* to glade,
B.10.49	Ac [mynstralcie and murþe] amonges *men* is nouþe
B.10.65	Ne were mercy in meene *men* moore þan in riche
B.10.68	Ac amonges meene *men* his mercy and hise werkes.
B.10.70	Clerkes and [kete] *men* carpen of god faste
B.10.71	And haue hym muche in [hire] mouþ, ac meene *men* in herte.
B.10.73	To plese wiþ proude *men* syn þe pestilence tyme;
B.10.96	Homliche at oþere *mennes* houses and hatien hir owene.
B.10.100	In a pryuee parlour for pouere *mennes* sake,
B.10.102	That was maad for meles *men* to eten Inne,
B.10.104	I haue yherd hei3e *men* etynge at þe table
B.10.118	And maken *men* in mys bileue þat muse on hire wordes.
B.10.134	And þo þat vseþ þise hauylons [for] to blende *mennes* wittes,
B.10.148	And seide, 'mercy, madame; youre *man* shal I worþe
B.10.152	'For þi mekenesse, *man*', quod she, 'and for þi mylde speche
B.10.206	To do good for goddes loue and gyuen *men* þat asked,
B.10.216	Yet ar þer fibicches in [forelles] of fele *mennes* [wittes],
B.10.227	[I] grette þe goode *man* as [þe goode wif] me tau3te,
B.10.248	Makere of *man* [and his make] and of beestes boþe.
B.10.256	Ne *man* hadde no merite my3te it ben ypreued:
B.10.259	And þat is, *man*, bi þy my3t, for mercies sake,
B.10.274	Alle maner *men* to amenden bi hire my3tes;
B.10.282	Lewed *men* may likne yow þus, þat þe beem liþ in youre ei3en,
B.10.284	In alle maner *men* þoru3 mansede preestes.

B.10.307	For in cloistre comeþ [no] *man* to [carpe] ne to fiȝte	B.12.96	And lederes for lewed *men* and for lettred boþe.
B.10.341	Poule preueþ it impossible, riche *men* [in] heuene;	B.12.99	For as a *man* may noȝt see þat mysseþ hise eiȝen,
B.10.348	Ther riche *men* no riȝt may cleyme but of ruþe and grace.'	B.12.101	Alþouȝ *men* made bokes [þe maister was god]
B.10.357	Ac cristene *men* wiþoute moore maye noȝt come to heuene,	B.12.102	And seint Spirit þe Samplarie, & seide what *men* sholde write.
B.10.358	For þat crist for cristene *men* deide, and conformed þe lawe	B.12.103	[And riȝt as siȝt serueþ a *man* to se þe heiȝe strete]
B.10.362	And after alle cristene creatures, in commune ech *man* ooþer;	B.12.104	Riȝt so [lereþ] lettrure lewed *men* to Reson.
B.10.370	God hoteþ heiȝe and lowe þat no *man* hurte ooþer,	B.12.105	And as a blynd *man* in bataille bereþ wepne to fiȝte
B.10.376	Ech *man* for hi[s] mysded[e] but mercy it [make]." '	B.12.107	Na moore kan a kynde witted *man*, but clerkes hym teche,
B.10.380	And þat I *man* maad was, and my name yentred	B.12.111	Ȝyue mercy for hire mysdedes, if *men* it wole aske
B.10.388	Aristotle and he, who wissed *men* bettre?	B.12.114	Hadde neuere lewed *man* leue to leggen hond on þat cheste
B.10.389	Maistres þat of goddes mercy techen *men* and prechen,	B.12.118	And manye mo oþer *men*, þat were no leuites,
B.10.397	For many *men* on þis moolde moore setten hir hert[e]	B.12.125	Lest cheste cha[fe] vs to choppe ech *man* ooþer;
B.10.403	Forþi wise witted *men* and wel ylettrede clerkes	B.12.143	He spekeþ þere of riche *men* riȝt noȝt, ne of riȝt witty,
B.10.414	And *men* þat maden it amydde þe flood adreynten.	B.12.144	Ne of lordes þat were lewed *men*, but of þe hyeste lettred oute:
B.10.439	Wher fo[r loue] a *man* worþ allowed þere and hise lele werkes,	B.12.151	[Riche *men* rutte þo and in hir reste were
B.10.441	And be allowed as he lyued so; for by luþere *men* knoweþ þe goode.	B.12.157	How þat lewed *men* liȝtloker þan lettrede were saued,
B.10.442	And wherby wiste *men* which [is] whit if alle þyng blak were,	B.12.158	Than clerkes or kynde witted *men* of cristene peple.
B.10.443	And who were a good *man* but if þer were som sherewe?	B.12.160	Tak two stronge *men* and in Themese cast hem,
B.10.444	Forþi lyue we forþ wiþ [liþere] *men*; I leue lewe ben goode,	B.12.179	In which flood þe fend fondeþ a *man* hardest.
B.10.457	Whan *man* was at meschief wiþoute þe moore grace.	B.12.184	To lere lewed *men* as luc bereþ witnesse:
B.10.462	And is to mene to [Englissh] *men*, moore ne lesse,	B.12.198	Riȝt as som *man* yeue me mete and [sette me amydde þe floor];
B.10.472	Ye, *men* knowe clerkes þat han corsed þe tyme	B.12.232	Lewed *men* many tymes maistres þei apposen
B.10.481	The which is *mannes* soule to saue, as god seiþ in þe gospel:	B.12.236	Ac of briddes and of beestes *men* by olde tyme
B.11.13	Concupiscencia carnis *men* called þe elder mayde	B.12.241	Bitokneþ riȝt riche *men* þat reigne here on erþe.
B.11.28	'*Man*', quod he, 'if I mete wiþ þe, by Marie of heuene!	B.12.267	To lowe libbynge *men* þe larke is resembled.
B.11.36	A *man* may stoupe tyme ynoȝ whan he shal tyne þe crowne.'	B.12.276	For lettred *men* were lewed yet ne were loore of hir bokes.'
B.11.67	[At kirke] þere a *man* were cristned by kynde he sholde be buryed.	B.13.12	And how þat lewed *men* ben lad, but oure lord hem helpe,
B.11.80	For a baptiȝed *man* may, as maistres telleþ,	B.13.25	And þere I [mette] a maister, what *man* he was I nyste,
B.11.83	Loke, ye lettred *men*, wheiþer I lye or noȝt.'	B.13.40	Ac þis maister [of þise *men*] no maner flessh [eet],
B.11.86	'If I dorste', quod I, 'amonges *men* þis metels auowe!'	B.13.42	Of þat *men* myswonne þei made hem wel at ese,
B.11.96	It is licitum for lewed *men* to [legge] þe soþe	B.13.71	Holi writ bit *men* be war–I wol noȝt write it here
B.11.108	Ac þe matere þat she meued, if lewed *men* it knewe,	B.13.74	Ac I wiste neuere freke þat as a frere yede bifore *men* on englissh
B.11.110	[The bileue [of oure] lord þat lettred *men* techeþ].	B.13.77	And what meschief and maleese crist for *man* þolede,
B.11.125	For þouȝ a cristen *man* coueited his cristendom to reneye,	B.13.130	Which shal saue *mannes* soule; þus seiþ Piers þe Plowman.'
B.11.160	[This matere is merk for many, ac *men* of holy chirche,	B.13.136	'A[t] youre preiere', quod Pacience þo, 'so no *man* displese hym;
B.11.170	And took it moises vpon þe mount alle *men* to lere].	B.13.159	Misese ne meschief ne *man* wiþ his tonge,
B.11.178	And þat alle manere *men*, enemyes and frendes,	B.13.167	Maister of alle þo *men* þoruȝ myȝt of þis redels,
B.11.186	In a pouere *mannes* apparaille pursue[þ] vs euere,	B.13.173	Al þe wit of þis world and wiȝt *mennes* strengþe
B.11.197	[Alle myȝte god haue maad riche *men* if he wolde],	B.13.224	'I am a Mynstrall', quod þat *man*, 'my name is Actiua vita.
B.11.203	As quasi modo geniti gentil *men* echone,	B.13.228	Couþe I lye [and] do *men* lauȝe, þanne lacchen I sholde
B.11.205	In þe olde lawe, as [þe] lettre telleþ, *mennes* sones men calle[d] vs	B.13.253	Miȝte lechen a *man* as [me þynkeþ] it sholde.
B.11.205	In þe olde lawe, as [þe] lettre telleþ, mennes sones *men* calle[d] vs	B.13.255	Ac if myȝt of myracle hym faille it is for *men* ben noȝt worþi
B.11.206	Of Adames issue and Eue ay til god *man* deide;	B.13.258	Ne *mannes* masse make pees among cristene peple.
B.11.209	Forþi loue we as leue [children shal], and ech *man* laughe of ooþer,	B.13.272	Of haukyn þe Actif *man* and how he was ycloþed.
B.11.210	And of þat ech *man* may forbere amende þere it nedeþ,	B.13.279	Willyng þat alle *men* wende he were þat he is noȝt,
B.11.211	And euery *man* helpe ooþer for hennes shul we alle:	B.13.286	Lakkynge lettrede *men* and lewed men boþe;
B.11.213	For woot no *man* how neiȝ it is to ben ynome fro boþe.	B.13.286	Lakkynge lettrede men and lewed *men* boþe;
B.11.227	That saued synful *men* as Seint Iohan bereþ witnesse:	B.13.291	Willynge þat *men* wende his wit were þe beste,
B.11.230	And as Seint Gregorie seide, for *mannes* soule helþe	B.13.311	Al he wolde þat *men* wiste of werkes and wordes
B.11.241	That we sholde be lowe and loueliche, [and lele ech *man* to oþer],	B.13.317	*Men* sholde fynde manye frounces and manye foule plottes.'
B.11.243	And in þe apparaille of a pouere *man* and pilgrymes liknesse	B.13.324	And blame *men* bihynde hir bak and bidden hem meschaunce;
B.11.247	And as pouere pilgrymes preyed *mennes* goodes.	B.13.328	'Or wiþ myȝt [of] mouþ or þoruȝ m[a]nnes strengþe
B.11.249	Was a pure pouere maide and to a pouere *man* ywedded.	B.13.332	For tales þat I telle no *man* trusteþ to me,
B.11.264	Makeþ a *man* to haue mynde in god and a gret wille	B.13.408	Ne no mercy amenden þe *man* þat so deieþ].
B.11.275	And is to mene to *men* þat on þis moolde lyuen,	B.13.409	[Ac] whiche ben þe braunches þat bryngen a *man* to sleuþe?
B.11.279	For failed neuere *man* mete þat myȝtful god serueþ;	B.13.410	[Is whan *men*] moorneþ noȝt for hise mysdedes, ne makeþ no sorwe]
B.11.331	*Man* and his make I myȝte [se] boþe.	B.13.416	Whan *men* carpen of crist or clennesse of soul[e]
B.11.334	And how *men* token Mede and Mercy refused.	B.13.418	Penaunce [and] pouere *men* and þe passion of Seintes,
B.11.344	Medled noȝt wiþ hir makes, [saue *man* allone].	B.13.420	Thise ben þe braunches, beþ war, þat bryngen a *man* to wanhope.
B.11.353	[For *man* sholde hem noȝt fynde whan þei þerfro wente;	B.13.424	And ȝyueþ hem mete and mede, and pouere *men* refuse,
B.11.371	Saue *man* and his make; many tyme [me þouȝte]	B.13.426	Lest þo þre maner *men* to muche sorwe yow brynge:
B.11.375	Why þow ne sewest *man* and his make þat no mysfeet hem folwe.'	B.13.428	Sauen þoruȝ hir sermo[n] *mannes* soule fro helle:
B.11.382	Ac he suffreþ for som *mannes* goode, and so is oure bettre.	B.13.430	To entice *men* þoruȝ hir tales to synne and harlotrie.
B.11.383	[Holy writ', quod þat wye, 'wisseþ *men* to suffre:	B.13.432	What Dauid seiþ of swiche *men* as þe Sauter telleþ:
B.11.384	Frenche *men* and fre men affaiteþ þus hire children:	B.13.434	Ther wise *men* were, witnesseþ goddes wordes,
B.11.384	Frenche men and fre *men* affaiteþ þus hire children:	B.13.435	Ne no mysproud *man* amonges lordes ben allowed.
B.11.390	And if a *man* myȝte make [laklees] hymself	B.13.438	Muche moore, me þynkeþ, riche *men* sholde
B.11.396	For be a *man* fair or foul it falleþ noȝt to lakke	B.13.444	And a lered *man* to lere þee what our lord suffred
B.11.400	Al to murþe wiþ *man* þat moste wo þolie.	B.13.447	And a blynd *man* for a bourdeour, or a deurede womman
B.11.402	For *man* was maad of swich a matere he may noȝt wel asterte	B.13.449	Thise þre maner minstrales makeþ a *man* to lauȝe,
B.11.425	Shal neuere chalangynge ne chidynge chaste a *man* so soone	B.13.457	Thus haukyn þe Actif *man* hadde ysoiled his cote
B.11.437	As shame: þere he sheweþ hym, [hym shonyeþ euery *man*].	B.14.8	To agulte god or good *man* by aught þat I wiste,
B.12.18	To telle *men* what dowel is, dobet and dobest boþe.	B.14.10	To penaunce pacience and pouere *men* to fede,
B.12.23	And of holy *men* I her[e]', quod I, 'how þei ouþerwhile	B.14.24	Ne fend ne fals *man* defoulen it in þi lyue.
B.12.31	And sauen *men* sondry tymes, ac noon so soone as Charite.	B.14.26	Than Haukyn þe Actif *man*, and þow do by my techyng,
B.12.33	That is, if þow be *man* maryed þi make þow louye	B.14.45	In menynge þat alle *men* myȝte þe same
B.12.49	Of manye swiche I may rede, of *men* and of wommen,	B.14.62	Ergo þoruȝ his breeþ [boþe] *men* and beestes lyuen,
B.12.52	And þo *men* þat þei moost haten mynistren it at þe laste;	B.14.63	As holy writ witnesseþ whan *men* seye hir graces,
B.12.57	Sapience, seiþ þe bok, swelleþ a *mannes* soule:	B.14.67	That no reyn ne roon; þus rede *men* in bokes,
B.12.62	And in lele lyuynge *men* and in lif holy,	B.14.68	That manye wyntres *men* lyueden and no mete ne tulieden.
B.12.75	Wiþ stones *men* sholde hir strike and stone hire to deþe,	B.14.71	And if *men* lyuede as mesure wolde sholde neuere moore be defaute
B.12.84	And to mansede *men* meschief at hire ende.		

B.14.76   For þe meschief and þe meschaunce amonges *men* of Sodome
B.14.78   For [*men*] mesured noȝt hemself of [*mete*] and dr[y]nke,
B.14.85   And þouȝ a *man* myȝte noȝt speke contricion myȝte hym saue
B.14.90   Ac shrift of mouþ moore worþi is if *man* be y[n]liche contrit,
B.14.105   Thouȝ *men* rede of richesse riȝt to þe worldes ende,
B.14.127   To ȝyue many *m[e]n* his [mercymonye] er he it haue deserued.
B.14.132   Allas þat richesse shal reue and robbe *mannes* soule
B.14.137   For whan a werkman haþ wroȝt, þan may *men* se þe soþe,
B.14.144   It may noȝt be, ye riche *men*, or Mathew on god lyeþ:
B.14.150   And whan he haþ doon his deuoir wel *men* dooþ hym ooþer
           bountee,
B.14.163   And arated of riche *men* þat ruþe is to here.
B.14.168   [And] haue ruþe on þise riche *men* þat rewarde noȝt þi prisoners;
B.14.188   Shulde amenden vs as manye siþes as *man* wolde desire.
B.14.199   Ellis is al oure labour lost–lo, how *men* writeþ
B.14.204   Ac wiþ richesse þ[o] Ribaud[es] raþest *men* bigileþ.
B.14.217   [Or] in þe maister [or] in þe *man* som mansion he haueþ.
B.14.229   That mete or money of oþere *men* moot asken.
B.14.241   For *men* knowen wel þat Coueitise is of [a] kene wille
B.14.253   Hadde þei no[on haunt] but of poore *men*; hir houses stoode
           vntyled.
B.14.265   And as a mayde for *mannes* loue hire moder forsakeþ,
B.14.267   Muche is [þat maide] to loue of [a *man*] þat swich oon takeþ,
B.14.289   [O]r as Iustice to lugge *men* enioyned is no poore,
B.14.290   Ne to be Mair aboue *men* ne Mynystre vnder kynges;
B.14.292   /Ergo pouerte and poore *men* parfournen þe comaundement
B.14.301   The fifte is moder of [myȝt and of *mannes*] helþe,
B.14.308   And an hardy *man* of herte among an heep of þeues;
B.14.319   Thus lered me a lettred *man* for oure lordes loue, Seint Austyn:
B.14.322   That þ[u]s first wroot to wissen *men* what Pouerte was to mene.'
B.14.323   'Allas', quod Haukyn þe Actif *man* þo, 'þat after my cristendom
B.14.331   Or maistrie ouer any *man* mo þan of hymselue.
B.15.47   'Ye, sire!' I seide, 'by so no *man* were greued
B.15.56   To englisshe *men* þis is to mene, þat mowen speke and here,
B.15.57   The *man* þat muche hony eteþ his mawe it engleymeþ,
B.15.58   And þe moore þat a *man* of good matere hereþ,
B.15.74   And tellen *men* of þe ten comaundementȝ, and touchen þe seuene
           synnes,
B.15.75   And of þe braunches þat burioneþ of hem and bryngen *men* to
           helle,
B.15.84   For as [me þynkeþ] ye forsakeþ no *mannes* almesse,
B.15.93   Thoruȝ lele libbynge *men* þat goddes lawe techen,
B.15.108   Loþe were lewed *men* but þei youre loore folwede
B.15.128   Allas, ye lewed *men*, muche lese ye on preestes!
B.15.130   Wolde neuere þe wit of witty god but wikkede *men* it hadde,
B.15.146   Ac for goode *men*, god woot, greet doel men maken,
B.15.146   Ac for goode men, god woot, greet doel *men* maken,
B.15.151   'Where sholde *men* fynde swich a frend wiþ so fre an herte?
B.15.154   *Men* þe merciable to mendinauntȝ and to poore,
B.15.158   I seiȝ neuere swich a *man*, so me god helpe,
B.15.163   And so I trowe trewely, by þat *men* telleþ of [it,
B.15.172   Ne no likynge haþ to lye ne laughe *men* to scorne.
B.15.173   Al þat *men* seyn, he leet it sooþ and in solace takeþ,
B.15.183   Ther poore *men* and prisons liggeþ, hir pardon to haue;
B.15.201   For þer are [pure] proude herted *men*, pacient of tonge
B.15.204   And as a lyoun he lokeþ þer *men* lakken hise werkes.
B.15.233   Riche *men* he recomendeþ, and of hir robes takeþ
B.15.257   Misdooþ he no *man* ne wiþ his mouþ greueþ.
B.15.258   Amonges cristene *men* þis myldenesse sholde laste
B.15.263   For wel may euery *man* wite, if god hadde wold hymselue,
B.15.274   Monkes and mendinauntȝ, *men* by hemselue
B.15.278   But of foweles þat fleeþ; þus fyndeþ *men* in bokes.
B.15.280   And þoruȝ þe mylk of þat mylde beest þe *man* was sustened;
B.15.287   That no *man* myȝte hym se for mosse and for leues.
B.15.307   [Riȝt so] Religiouses rightfulle *men* sholde [fynde],
B.15.308   And lawefulle *men* to lifholy liflode brynge;
B.15.308   And lawefulle men to lifholy *men* liflode brynge;
B.15.319   If lewed *men* knewe þis latyn þei wolde loke whom þei yeue,
B.15.353   Ac þe metal, þat is *mannes* soule, [myd] synne is foule alayed.
B.15.363   As of wedres and wyndes þei warned *men* ofte.
B.15.392   And for hir lyuynge þat lewed *men* be þe loþer god agulten.
B.15.397   A[c] oon Makometh, a *man*, in mysbileue
B.15.399   This Makometh was cristene [*man*], and for he moste noȝt ben
           pope
B.15.408   As messager to Makometh, *men* for to teche.
B.15.410   Makometh in mysbileue *men* and wommen brouȝte,
B.15.416   And ben manered after Makometh þat no *man* vseþ trouþe.
B.15.420   Of tirauntȝ þat teneþ trewe *men* taken any almesse,
B.15.423   To lyue by litel and in lowe houses by lele *mennes* almesse,
B.15.434   So is *mannes* soule, sooþly, þat seeþ no goo[d] ensampl[e]
B.15.438   Elleuene holy *men* al þe world tornede
B.15.440   Sholde alle maner *men*; we han so manye maistres,
B.15.442   That goddes salt sholde be to saue *mannes* soule.

B.15.446   And þoruȝ miracles, as *men* mow rede, al þat marche he tornede
B.15.462   Ye mynnen wel how Mathew seiþ, how a *man* made a feste.
B.15.468   So loue and leaute lele *men* susteneþ.
B.15.469   And maidenes and mylde *men* mercy desiren
B.15.471   So [menen] riȝtfulle *men* [after] mercy and truþe.
B.15.474   Riȝt as capons in a court comeþ to *mennes* whistlyng,
B.15.475   In menyng after mete folweþ *men* þat whistlen;
B.15.476   Riȝt so rude *men* þat litel reson konneþ
B.15.477   Louen and bileuen by lettred *mennes* doynges,
B.15.481   And by þe *man* þat made þe feste þe mageste bymeneþ,
B.15.482   That is god of his grace, gyueþ alle *men* blisse.
B.15.488   Wiþouten trauaille þe tiþe deel þat trewe *men* biswynken?
B.15.492   Allas, þat *men* so longe [sholde bileue on Makometh]!
B.15.508   And þat is rouþe for riȝtful *men* þat in þe Reawme wonyen,
B.15.512   Many myracles wrouȝte *m[e]n* for to turne,
B.15.513   In ensaumple þat *men* sholde se by sadde reson
B.15.514   *Men* myȝte noȝt be saued but þoruȝ mercy and grace,
B.15.516   And bicam *man* of a maide and metropolitanus,
B.15.523   In sauacion of [*mannes* soule] seint [Thomas] was ymartired;
B.15.529   [And nauȝt to] huppe aboute in Engelond to halwe *mennes* Auteres
B.15.531   Many *man* for cristes loue was martired [amonges] Romayne[s]
B.15.533   It is ruþe to rede how riȝtwise *men* lyuede,
B.15.548   [Mynne] ye noȝt, wise *men*, how þo men honoured
B.15.548   [Mynne] ye noȝt, wise men, how þo *men* honoured
B.15.559   An Aungel *men* herden an heigh at Rome crye,
B.15.575   That no *man* sholde be bisshop but if he hadde boþe
B.15.585   And took it Moyses to teche *men* til Messie coome,
B.15.590   Boþe of miracles and merueilles, and alle þise *men* festede,
B.16.2   For Haukyns loue þe Actif *man* euere I shal yow louye.
B.16.9   And so þoruȝ god and goode *men* groweþ þe fruyt Charite.'
B.16.14   Amyddes *mannes* body; þe more is of þat stokke.
B.16.84   And made of holy *men* his hoord In limbo Inferni,
B.16.124   Youre bodies, youre beestes, and blynde *men* holpen,
B.16.146   Thanne wente forþ þat wikked *man* and wiþ þe Iewes mette
B.16.156   Thow shalt be myrour to many *men* to deceyue,
B.16.172   And þanne mette I wiþ a *man*, a mydlenten sonday,
B.16.200   In menynge þat *man* moste on o god bileue,
B.16.204   In tokenynge of þe Trinite, was [taken out of a *man*],
B.16.217   Na moore myȝte god be *man* but if he moder hadde.
B.16.221   That is *man* and his make and mulliere children;
B.16.227   Thre *men*, to my siȝte, I made wel at ese,
B.17.4   'Is it enseled?' I seide; 'may *men* see þ[e] lettres?'
B.17.21   Of *men* and of wommen many score þousand.'
B.17.42   It is lighter to lewed *men* o lesson to knowe
B.17.44   It is ful hard for any *man* on Abraham bileue
B.17.53   Comynge from a contree þat *men* called Ierico;
B.17.56   Where a *man* was wounded and wiþ þeues taken.
B.17.63   How he wiþ Moyses maundement hadde many *men* yholpe,
B.17.77   'Haue, kepe þis *man*', [quod he], 'til I come fro þe Iustes.
B.17.94   May no medicyne [vnder mone] þe *man* to heele bringe,
B.17.106   And [may] ech *man* see and good mark take
B.17.116   And kennen outcom[en] *men* þat knowen noȝt þe contree
B.17.118   And Hope þe Hostile[r] shal be þer [an helyng þe *man* lith];
B.17.165   Thus it is–nedeþ no *man* trowe noon ooþer–
B.17.230   And melteþ hire myȝt into mercy, as *men* may se in wyntre
B.17.244   For to murþen *men* [wiþ] þat in [m]erke sitten,
B.17.245   So wole crist of his curteisie, and *men* crye hym mercy,
B.17.262   Forþi beþ war, ye wise *men* þat wiþ þe world deleþ;
B.17.265   For manye of yow riche *men*, by my soule, men telleþ,
B.17.265   For manye of yow riche men, by my soule, *men* telleþ,
B.17.267   [Mynne ye noȝt, riche *men*, to whiche a myschaunce
B.17.269   Of his mete and moneie to *men* þat it nedede?
B.17.277   Vnkynde cristene *men*, for coueitise and enuye
B.17.278   Sleeþ a *man* for hise moebles wiþ mouþ or with handes.
B.17.280   The which is lif and loue, þe leye of *mannes* body.
B.17.281   For euery manere good [*man* may] be likned
B.17.283   And who[so] morþereþ a good *man*, me þynkeþ, by myn Inwit,
B.17.285   A[c] yet in mo maneres *men* offenden þe holy goost;
B.17.309   That þe kyng may do no mercy til boþe *men* acorde
B.17.321   Thre þynges þer ben þat doon a *man* by strengþe
B.17.338   To *man* þat mercy askeþ and amende þenkeþ".
B.17.342   And þouȝ þat *men* make muche doel in hir angre
B.17.346   Haþ mercy on swiche *men* þat so yuele may suffre.
B.17.353   Alle manere *men* mercy and forȝifnesse.
B.18.62   Dede *men* for þat dene come out of depe graues.
B.18.136   In menynge þat *man* shal fro merknesse be drawe
B.18.139   That *man* shal man saue þoruȝ a maydenes helpe,
B.18.139   That man shal *man* saue þoruȝ a maydenes helpe,
B.18.160   And riȝt as [þe gilour] þoruȝ gile [bigiled *man* formest]
B.18.185   To be *mannes* meynpernour for eueremoore after.
B.18.190   And saue *mannes* soule? suster, wene it neuere.
B.18.208   If no nyȝt ne weere, no *man* as I leeue
B.18.210   Sholde neuere riȝt riche *man* þat lyueþ in reste and ese

B.18.213	Bicam *man* of a mayde mankynde to saue
B.18.231	Book highte þat beaupeere, a bold *man* of speche.
B.18.236	That *mannes* soule sholde saue and synne destroye.
B.18.256	In alle my3tes of *man* and his moder gladie,
B.18.299	And þus haþ he trolled forþ [lik a tidy *man*] þise two and þritty wynter.
B.18.301	To warne Pilates wif what done *man* was Iesus,
B.18.306	To saue *men* from synne if hemself wolde.
B.18.341	And al þat *man* haþ mysdo I man wole amende.
B.18.341	And al þat man haþ mysdo I *man* wole amende.
B.18.367	I fau3t so me þursteþ 3it for *mannes* soule sake;
B.18.372	And haue out of helle alle *mennes* soules.
B.18.375	A[c] to be merciable to *man* þanne my kynde [it] askeþ
B.18.425	That *men* rongen to þe resurexion, and ri3t wiþ þat I wakede
B.19.4	In myddes of þe masse þo *men* yede to offryng
B.19.18	Anoon as *men* nempned þe name of god Iesu;
B.19.28	To be called a knyght is fair for *men* shul knele to hym.
B.19.33	And fre *men* foule þralles þat folwen no3t hise lawes.
B.19.34	The Iewes þat were gentil *men*, Ies[u] þei despised,
B.19.39	Aren frankeleyns, free *men* þoru3 fullynge þat þei toke
B.19.40	And gentil *men* wiþ Iesu, for Iesu[s] was yfulled
B.19.84	Wherfore and why wise *men* þat tyme,
B.19.85	Maistres and lettred *men*, Magi hem callede.
B.19.98	In þe manere of a *man* and þat by muchel sleighte,
B.19.112	And lawe lakkede þo for *men* louede no3t hir enemys,
B.19.137	And nempned hym of Na3areth; and no *man* so worþi
B.19.143	And siþen buriede his body, and beden þat *men* sholde
B.19.148	And his moder Marie; þus *men* bifore de[uyn]ede,
B.19.153	Verray *m[a]n* bifore hem alle and forþ wiþ hem yede.
B.19.184	[Myght [*men*] to assoille of alle manere synne[s],
B.19.185	To alle maner *men* mercy and for3ifnesse]
B.19.190	And assoille *men* of alle synnes saue of dette one.
B.19.227	And gaf ech *man* a grace to gide wiþ hymseluen
B.19.247	And fecchen it fro false *men* wiþ Foluyles lawes.
B.19.275	And sew [it] in *mannes* soule and siþen tolde hir names.
B.19.279	And lerned *men* a ladel bugge wiþ a long stele
B.19.378	Egreliche ernynge out of *mennes* eighen.
B.19.387	[My3t] to maken it and *men* to ete it after
B.19.394	[Or] ech *man* for3yue ooþer, and þat wole þe Paternoster:
B.19.411	*Man* to me þat me kouþe telle of Cardinale vertues,
B.19.416	The comune clamat cotidie, ech a *man* til ooþer,
B.19.427	Emperour of al þe world, þat alle *men* were cristene.
B.19.432	And sent þe sonne to saue a cursed *mannes* tilþe
B.19.433	As brighte as to þe beste *man* or to þe beste womman.
B.19.439	As for a trewe tidy *man* alle tymes ylike.
B.19.457	Ech *man* subtileþ a slei3te synne to hide
B.19.467	And holy kirke and clergie fro cursed *men* to [de]fende.
B.20.12	That is mete whan *men* hym werneþ and he no moneye weldeþ,
B.20.27	And bete *men* ouer bittre, and so[m body] to litel,
B.20.28	And greue *men* gretter þan good feiþ it wolde.
B.20.52	And mette ful merueillously þat in *mannes* forme
B.20.55	And [made] fals sprynge and sprede and spede *mennes* nedes.
B.20.65	[And] þat were mylde *men* and holye þat no meschief dradden;
B.20.93	[Th]anne mette þise *men*, er Mynstrals my3te pipe,
B.20.102	Lered [ne] lewed he leet no *man* stonde,
B.20.112	Amonges alle manere *men*, wedded and vnwedded,
B.20.146	And leet leautee a cherl and lyere a fre *man*.
B.20.182	The compaigyne of confort *men* cleped it som tyme
B.20.187	Siþ whanne was þe wey ouer *mennes* heddes?
B.20.259	And if þei wage *men* to werre þei write hem in noumbre;
B.20.264	Monkes and Moniales and alle *men* of Religion,
B.20.275	And preche *men* of Plato, and preue it by Seneca
B.20.278	For god made to *men* a lawe and Moyses it tau3te:
B.20.289	And maken hym murie wiþ ooþer *mennes* goodes.
B.20.306	Shrift shoop sharp salue and made *men* do penaunce
B.20.317	For here is many a *man* hurt þoru3 ypocrisye.'
B.20.379	And [doþ *men* drynke dwale]; þei drede no synne.'
C.Pr.20	Of alle manere [of] *men*, þe mene and þe [riche],
C.Pr.34	As it semeþ to oure sighte that suche *men* ythryueth.
C.Pr.70	Lewed *men* leued hym wel and lykede his wordes;
C.Pr.102	That lewed *men* in mysbileue lyuen and dyen.
C.Pr.116	And for þei were prestis and *men* of holy chirche
C.Pr.118	Forthy y sey 3[ow] prestes and *men* of holy churche
C.Pr.119	That soffreth *men* do sacrefyce and worschipe maumettes
C.Pr.140	Myght of tho *men* made hym to regne.
C.Pr.183	*Men* Myghte ywete where þei wente and here [way roume].
C.Pr.215	Til þat meschief amende hem þat many *man* chasteth.
C.Pr.216	For many *mannys* malt we muys wolde distruye
C.Pr.217	And [3]e route of ratones of reste *men* awake
C.Pr.220	What þis meteles bymeneth, 3e *men* þat ben merye,
C.1.42	Ac þe moneye of þis molde þat *men* so faste kepen,
C.1.67	To combre *men* with coueytise, þat is his kynde and his lore.'
C.1.73	Y vndirfenge þe formeste and fre *man* the made.

C.1.85	And doth þe werkes þerwith and wilneth no *man* ylle,
C.1.115	'Nere hit for northerne *men* anon y wolde 3ow telle
C.1.118	Then in þe north by many notes, no *man* leue other.
C.1.135	Lere hit thus lewed *men*, for lettred hit knoweth.
C.1.158	Vp *man* for his mysdedes the mercement he taxeth.
C.1.180	Then malkyn of here maydenheed [þat] no *man* [desir]eth.
C.1.187	Aren none hardore ne hungriore then *men* of holy chirche,
C.2.7	And mony mo of here maners, of *men* and of wymmen.
C.2.27	And mede is manered aftur hym as *men* of kynde carpeth:
C.2.34	[W]hat *man* [that] me louyeth and my wille foleweth
C.2.36	And what [*man*] mede loueth, my lyf [dar y] wedde,
C.2.38	That helpeth *man* moste to heuene mede most letteth.
C.2.59	Of many manere *men* þat of mede[s] kynne were,
C.2.66	Were most pryue with mede of eny *men* [me] thoghte.
C.2.80	Mede and suche *men* þat aftur mede wayten.
C.2.125	Amendes was here moder by trewe *men* lokynge,
C.2.136	For y, *man*, of thy mercy mede haue diserued."
C.2.137	And se[t]he *man* may [o]n heye mede of god diserue
C.2.139	That mede may be wedded to no *man* bot treuthe,
C.2.187	Wol Ryde vppon Rectores and ryche *men* deuoutours,
C.2.192	On secatours and such *men* cometh softly aftur.
C.2.200	Of many maner *men* for mede sake seude aftur.
C.2.211	Shal neuere *man* on þis molde maynpryse þe leste,
C.3.6	What *man* of this world þat here [were leuest].
C.3.7	And yf she worche wysely and by wys *men* consayl
C.3.25	The leste *man* of here mayne a motoun of gold.
C.3.40	'Thow le[r]ed *men* and le[w]ed haued layn by the bothe
C.3.45	Thenne mede for here mysdedes to th[at] *man* knelede
C.3.63	Haueth mercy,' quod mede, 'o[f] *men* þat hit haunteth
C.3.81	For thyse *men* don most harm to þe mene peple,
C.3.92	That bygyleth goode *men* and greueth hem wrongly,
C.3.102	And thenne falleth ther fuyr on fals *men* houses
C.3.103	And goode *mennes* hous for here gultes gloweth on fuyr aftur.
C.3.108	Forthy mayres þat maketh fre *men*, me thynketh þat 3e ouhten
C.3.114	Be yfranchised for a fre *man* and haue a fals name.
C.3.160	And maketh *men* mysdo manye score tymes.
C.3.167	Bytwene heuene and helle, and erthe thogh *men* soughte.
C.3.172	Sysores and somnours, suche *men* he[re] preiseth;
C.3.174	For he doth *men* lesen here lond and here lyf bothe;
C.3.198	The mase for a mene *man* thow he mote euere!
C.3.214	For pore *men* dar nat pleyne ne no pleynt shewe,
C.3.215	Such a maistre is mede among *men* of gode.'
C.3.237	Hast arwed many hardy *man* þat hadde wille to fyhte,
C.3.250	Wherby he may as a *man* for eueremore lyue aftur.
C.3.253	Al þat his *man* may wynne, do ther[mid] here beste.
C.3.257	'Ne be Marschal ouer my *men* there y moste fyhte.
C.3.258	Ac hadde y, mede, ben marchel o[f] his *men* in Fraunce
C.3.266	To 3eue *men* mede þat meekliche hym serueth,
C.3.267	To aliens, to alle *men*, to honoure hem with 3eftes;
C.3.268	Mede maketh hym byloued and for a *man* yholde.
C.3.272	And 3euen mede to *men* to meyntene here lawes;
C.3.280	Alle kyn crafty *men* crauen mede for here prentises;
C.3.290	To 3eue *men* mede, more oþer lasse.
C.3.291	Ac ther is mede and mercede and bothe *men* demen
C.3.293	Mede many tymes *men* 3eueth bifore þe doynge
C.3.295	That eny *man* Mede toke but he hi[t] myhte deserue,
C.3.303	And Gylours gyuen byfore and goode *men* at þe ende
C.3.318	And yf th[e] lele and lege be luyther *men* aftur
C.3.355	And *man* is relatif rect yf he be rihte trewe:
C.3.397	But þat alle maner *men*, wymmen and childrene
C.3.404	Thus is *man* and mankynde in maner of [a] sustantyf,
C.3.421	*Man*, womman and wyf, childe, wedewe and bestes,
C.3.422	Mebles and vnmebles, *man* and alle [thynges],
C.3.436	That he þat sayth *men* sothe[s] is sonnest yblamed.
C.3.445	Tho shal be maistres on molde trewe *men* to helpe.
C.3.457	Moises or messie, þat *man* ben so trewe.
C.3.462	Vche *man* to pley with a plogh, a pikois oþer a spade,
C.3.475	Þat worth trewe-tonge, a tydy *man* þat tened me neuere.
C.3.476	Batailes sholle neuere eft be ne *man* bere eg toel
C.4.10	Of mede and of mo othere and what *man* shal here wedde
C.4.40	Thenne resoun rood forth Ac took reward of no *man*
C.4.58	A meynteyneth his *men* to morthere myn hewes,
C.4.65	How wrong was a wykked *man* and muche wo wrouhte.
C.4.67	On *men* of lawe wrong lokede and largelyche hem profered
C.4.92	'Haue this, *man*, of me,' quod she, 'to amende thy scathe
C.4.95	To haue mercy on þat *man* that many tymes hym greuede:
C.4.115	And here pelur and here palfrayes pore *menne* lyflode
C.4.118	Til þat lerede *men* lyue as thei lere and teche
C.4.121	For alle manere *men* þat me fynt neodefole;
C.4.129	But [it] be marchaunt or his *man* or messager [with] lettres,
C.4.140	For nullum malum [þe] *man* mette with inpunitum
C.4.148	Mede in the mothalle tho on *men* of lawe gan wynke
C.4.168	And lourede vppon *men* of lawe and lyhtlych sayde:

C. 4.170   Mede and *men* of ʒoure craft muche treuthe letteth.
C. 4.181   And brynge alle *men* to bowe withouten bittere wounde,
C. 5.5   For y made of tho *men* as resoun me tauhte.
C. 5.27   That fynde[th] the thy fode–for an ydel *man* þow semest,
C. 5.29   Or beggest thy bylyue aboute at *men* hacches
C. 5.32   There ryhtfulnesse rewardeth ryht as *men* deserueth–
C. 5.62   /God and good *men*, as here degre asketh:
C. 5.67   Of frankeleynes and fre*men* and of folke ywedded.
C. 5.84   Preeyeres of a parfit *man* and penaunce d[iscret]e
C. 5.154   For in C[l]oystre cometh no *man* to chyde ne to fyhte;
C. 5.156   Ac mony day, *men* telleth, bothe monkes and chanons
C. 5.196   Of alle maner actions and eche *man* loue other.
C. 6.18   God and goode *men* so gret was myn herte;
C. 6.23   Lauhyng al aloude for lewede *men* sholde
C. 6.32   Me wilnynge þat *men* wen[t]e y were as in auer
C. 6.41   Wilnynge þat *men* wen[d]e myne werkes weren þe beste
C. 6.59   Al [y] wolde þat *men* wiste when it to pruyde souneth,
C. 6.69   And blame *men* byhynde here bak and bidde hem meschaunce;
C. 6.73   'Or thorw myhte of mouthe or thorw *mannes* sleythes
C. 6.86   Y myhte nat ete many ʒer as a *man* ouhte
C. 6.95   ʒut am y brokour of bakbytynge to blame *menne* w[a]re
C. 6.115   Amonges alle manere *men* my dwellyng is som tyme,
C. 6.117   Harm of eny *man*, byhynde or bifore.
C. 6.244   And more worth then the moneye or *men* þat y lenede
C. 6.293   Then haue my fode and my fyndynge of fals *menne* wynnyngus.
C. 6.295   Til thow haue ymad by thy myhte to alle *men* restitucioun.
C. 6.312   That eche *man* shal haue his ar y hennes wende
C. 6.320   And haddest mercy vppon þat *man* for memento sake,
C. 6.337   Of alle manere *men* þat [mid] goede wille
C. 6.348   For the and for many mo þat *man* shal ʒeue a rykenynge
C. 7.21   Y visitede neuere feble *man* ne fetered man in prisone.
C. 7.21   Y visitede neuere feble man ne fetered *man* in prisone.
C. 7.23   Or lacke men or likene hem in vnlikyng *manere*
C. 7.36   Y forʒete hit as ʒerne and yf eny *man* hit aske
C. 7.38   And thus haue y tened trewe *men* ten hundrit tymes.
C. 7.42   Yf eny *man* do[th] me a beenfeet or helpeth me at nede
C. 7.69   Ac wheche been þe braunches þat bryngeth *men* to sleuthe?
C. 7.70   Is when *men* mourneth not for his mysdedes,
C. 7.78   Penaunse and pore *men* and the passioun of seyntes,
C. 7.80   This beth þe branches, beth ywar, þat bryngeth a *man* to wanhope.
C. 7.84   And ʒeueth [hem] mede & mete and pore *men* refuse,
C. 7.86   Laste this manere *men* to muche sorwe ʒow brynge:
C. 7.88   Sauen thorw here sarmon *mannes* soule fram helle;
C. 7.90   To entise *men* thorw here tales to synne and harlotrie.
C. 7.92   Wh[at] dauid sayth of such *men* as þe sauter telleth:
C. 7.94   There wyse *men* were, wittnesseth goddes wordes,
C. 7.95   Ne no mysproud *man* amongus lordes be [alow]ede.
C. 7.98   Muche more, me thynketh, riche *men* ouhte
C. 7.104   With a lered *man* to lere the what oure lord suffrede
C. 7.107   And a blynd *man* for a bordor or a bedredene womman
C. 7.109   Thise thre manere munstrals maketh a *man* to lauhe
C. 7.123   And [of nauhte madest] auhte and *man* liche thysulue
C. 7.127   And bicam *man* of a mayde mankynde to amende
C. 7.130   On a friday in fourme of *man* feledest oure sorwe:
C. 7.145   That what tyme we synnefole *men* wolden be sory
C. 7.155   A thousand of *men* tho throngen togyderes,
C. 7.168   And þe vernicle bifore for *men* sholde yknowe
C. 7.177   'Knowest thow auht a corsent,' quod they, 'þat *men* calleth treuthe?
C. 7.195   He is þe presteste payere þat eny pore *man* knoweth;
C. 7.206   ʒe mote go thorw mekenesse, alle *men* and wommen,
C. 7.220   The croft hatte coueyte-nat-*menne*-catel-ne-here-wyues-
C. 7.231   In-none-manere-elles-nat-for-no-*mannes*-preeyre.
C. 7.243   Grace hatte þe gateward, a goed *man* for sothe;
C. 7.244   His *man* hatte amende-ʒow, many man hym knoweth.
C. 7.244   His man hatte amende-ʒow, many *man* hym knoweth.
C. 8.17   And alle manere *men* þat by þe molde is susteyned
C. 8.27   Fro wastores and wikked *men* þat þis world struyen
C. 8.37   And when ʒe mersyen eny *man* late mercy be taxour,
C. 8.39   And thogh pore *men* profre ʒow presentes and ʒyftes
C. 8.51   Ac [manliche] at mete suche *men* eschewe
C. 8.52   For hit beeþ þe deueles dysors to drawe *men* to synne;
C. 8.69   And alle kyne crafty *men* þat conne lyue in treuthe,
C. 8.74   That lollares and loseles lele *men* holdeth,
C. 8.87   Maystres, as mayres and grete *menne*, senatours,
C. 8.117   Vch *man* in his manere made hymsulue to done
C. 8.140   That lele land tilynge *men* leely byswynken.
C. 8.189   And lame *men* he lechede with longes of bestes.
C. 8.200   In alle kyne trewe craft þat *man* couthe deuyse
C. 8.228   Ac yf thow fynde eny folke þat fals *men* han apayred
C. 8.231   And alle manere [of] *men* þat thow myhte aspye
C. 8.239   As wyse *men* haen wryten and as wittnesseth Genesis
C. 8.245   And go abribeth and abeggeth and no *man* beten his hungur:
C. 8.246   Mathew maketh mencioun of a *man* þat lente

C. 8.247   His suluer to thre maner *men* [in] menyng they sholden
C. 8.256   And he þat nauht hath shal nauht haue and no *man* [hym helpen]
C. 8.295   They don *men* deye thorw here drynkes Ar destyne hit wolde.'
C. 9.16   And bitynge in badde *men* but yf they wol amende,
C. 9.19   And suche liue as þei lereth *men* oure lord treuthe hem graunteth
C. 9.30   Amende mesondewes þerwith and myseyse *men* fynde
C. 9.44   *Men* of lawe hadde lest þat loth were to plede
C. 9.47   That innocent and nedy is and no *man* harm wolde,
C. 9.51   Beth ywar, ʒe wis *men* and witty of þe lawe,
C. 9.54   That mede of mene *men* for here motynge taken.
C. 9.68   And moste merytorie to *men* þat he ʒeueth fore.
C. 9.70   Woet no *man*, as y wene, who is worthy to haue
C. 9.84   And of monye oþer *men* þat moche wo soffren,
C. 9.97   And to conforte suche coterelles and crokede *men* and blynde.
C. 9.106   Ac hem wanteth wyt, *men* and women bothe,
C. 9.121   Barfoot and bredles, beggeth they of no *man*
C. 9.124   Suche manere *men*, Matheu vs techeth,
C. 9.126   For hit aren murye mouthed *men*, munstrals of heuene
C. 9.131   *Men* suffreth al þat suche sayen and in solace taketh
C. 9.132   And ʒut more to suche *men* me doth ar they passe;
C. 9.141   Loken louhliche to lache *men* Almesse,
C. 9.165   And lere this lewede *men* what þis latyn meneth
C. 9.173   Then of many oþere *men* þat [o]n this molde walken
C. 9.176   Ac olde [*men*] and hore þat helples ben and nedy
C. 9.180   As mesels and mendenantes, *men* yfalle in meschief
C. 9.181   As prisones and pilgrimes and parauntur *men* yrobbed
C. 9.182   Or bylowe thorw luther *men* and lost here catel aftur
C. 9.192   As rychesses and reuerences and ryche *menne* Almesse,
C. 9.215   As by þe engelisch of oure eldres of olde *mennes* techynge.
C. 9.224   Lewede *men* to labory; lordes to honte
C. 9.227   As wolues þat wuryeth *men*, wymmen and childrene
C. 9.230   To heren here euensong euery *man* soynge.
C. 9.303   Ac *men* setteth nat by sowngewarie for me seth hit often fayle;
C. 9.327   As lettrede *men* vs lereth and lawe of holi churche:
C. 9.337   That haen the welthe of this world and wise *men* ben holde
C.10.5   And what *man* a myhte be of mony m[a]n y askede.
C.10.5   And what man a myhte be of mony m[a]n y askede.
C.10.9   Maystres of þe menore[s], *men* of gret witte.
C.10.14   For ʒe ar *men* of this molde þat moste wyde walken
C.10.16   Bothe princes paleis and pore *menne* cotes
C.10.31   'How seuene sithes þe sad *man* synegeth on þe day.
C.10.33   Lat bryng a *man* in a boet amydde a brood water;
C.10.35   Maketh þe *man* many tyme to stomble yf he stande.
C.10.41   So hit fareth,' quod þe frere, 'by þe ryhtful *mannus* fallynge.
C.10.49   Synegeth seue sithe þe saddest *man* on erthe
C.10.51   Ac fre wil and fre wit foleweth *man* euere
C.10.68   A muche *man*, me thoghte, ylike to mysulue,
C.10.84   And helpeth alle *men* of þat he may spare.
C.10.94   And halie with þe hoked ende [i]lle *men* to gode
C.10.97   For here mok and here mebles suche *men* thenketh
C.10.147   Sire worch-wel-with-thyn-hand, a wyht *man* of strenghe,
C.10.157   *Man* is hym most lyk of membres and of face
C.10.162   That god [s]eweth nat synnefole *men* and soffreth hem mysfare,
C.10.166   Such lyther lyuyng *men* lome been ryche
C.10.181   Euery *man* þat hath inwit and his hele bothe
C.10.185   And holy churche helpe to, so sholde no *man* begge
C.10.200   To tulie þe erthe with tonge and teche *men* to louye;
C.10.204   As this wedded *men* þat this world susteyneth,
C.10.209   And is no more to mene but *men* þat ben bygeten
C.10.246   Was for mariages ma[ugre kynd]e þat *men* made þat tyme.
C.10.253   Þat y *man* made or matrimonye soffrede
C.10.258   Of kyn ne of kynrede counteth *men* bote litel.
C.10.260   A mayde and wel yma[ner]ed and of gode *men* yspronge,
C.10.283   And euery maner seculer *man* þat may nat contynue
C.10.292   For þat dede derne do no *man* sholde
C.10.293   Bote wyues and wedded *men*, as holy writ techeth:
C.10.306   For þe more a *man* may do, by so þat a do hit,
C.11.7   And sayde, 'nolite mittere, ʒe *men*, Margerie perles
C.11.47   Ne were mercy in m[e]ne *men* more then in riht riche
C.11.51   And haen [hym] muche in here mouth Ac mene [*men*] in herte.
C.11.53   To plese with proude *men* senes th[e] pestelenc[e tyme]
C.11.60   And gode *men* for oure gultes he al togrynt to deth.
C.11.74   Ac lust no lord now ne lettred *man* of suche lore to here
C.11.86   And saide, 'mercy, madame; ʒoure *man* shal y worthen
C.11.90   'For thy mekenesse, [*man*],' quod she, 'and for thy mylde speche
C.11.125   Thus thorw my lore ben *men* ylered thogh y loke demme.
C.11.130   Ac for hit lereth *men* to louie y beleue þeron þ[e] bettere
C.11.143   And bycam *man* of þat maide witoute mankynde,
C.11.157   Ne *man* mouhte haue mery[t]e [thereof] mouhte hit be ypreued:
C.11.159   That [doth] *men* dowel, dobet and dobest.'
C.11.172   Concupiscencia carnis *men* calde þ[e] eldre maide
C.11.185   'The *man* þat me liketh to helpe myhte nat myshappe.'
C.11.187   '*Man*,' quod [he], 'yf y me[t]e with the, by marie of heuene,

C.11.195 A *man* may stoupe tyme ynowe when he shal tyne þe croune.'
C.11.196 Sir wanhope was sib to hym, as som *men* me tolde,
C.11.203 That y *man* ymaed was and my name yentred
C.11.211 Neuere to *man* so moche þat man can of telle,
C.11.211 Neuere to man so moche þat *man* can of telle,
C.11.214 Aristotel and he, ho tauhte *men* bettere?
C.11.215 Maistres þat [of goddis mercy techen *men* and prechen]
C.11.228 For mony *men* [o]n this molde more sette here herte
C.11.233 Wel ywitted *men* and wel ylettred clerkes,
C.11.268 And now beth this seyntes, by that *men* saith, and souereynes in
          heuene,
C.11.285 Was Austyn þe oelde þat euere *man* wiste,
C.11.288 And is to mene no more to *men* þat beth lewed:
C.11.302 Lewede *men* in good bileue and lene hem at here nede.'
C.12.28   The sauter sayth hit is no synne for suche *men* þat ben trewe
C.12.42   Ac þe matere þat she meuede, if lewede *men* hit knewe,
C.12.44   The bileue of oure lord þat lettred *men* techeth.
C.12.60   For thogh a cristene *man* coueitede his cristendom to renoye
C.12.106 Meles and manschipes, vch *man* oþer.
C.12.111 As quasi modo geniti gentel *men* vchone,
C.12.113 In þe olde lawe, as þe lettre telleth, *mennes* sones me calde vs
C.12.114 Of Adames issue and Eue ay til god *man* deyede;
C.12.118 And euery *man* helpe other for hennes shal we alle
C.12.130 That we sholde be low and louelich and lele vch *man* til oþer
C.12.135 Was a puyre pore mayde and to a pore *man* ywedded.
C.12.150 Maketh *man* to haue mynde in god and his mercy to craue,
C.12.188 Aren tidiore and touore to *mannes* byhofte
C.12.198 Fere ne famyne ne fals *mennes* tonges.
C.12.239 And ȝut more hit maketh *men* mony tymes & ofte
C.12.242 And so is many *man* ymorthred for his moneye and his godes
C.13.6   And out of nombre tho *men* many mebles hadden.
C.13.20   And Iob bykam as a iolyf *man* and al his ioye newe.
C.13.26   Ac leueth nat, lewede *men*, þat y lacke rychesse
C.13.44   Wol no wys *man* be wroth ne his wed take–
C.13.46   Ac if þe marchaunt make his way ouer *menne* corne
C.13.58   With robbares and reuares þat ryche *men* despoilen
C.13.62   Haue hors and hardy *men*; thogh he mette theues
C.13.65   Ȝe wyte, ȝe wyse *men*, what this is to mene:
C.13.66   The marchaunt is no more to mene but *men* þat ben ryche
C.13.71   Alle maner *men* [in] meschief yfalle,
C.13.76   And ȝut more, to maken pees and quyten *menne* dettes
C.13.79   The messager aren th[e] mendenantȝ þat lyuen by *menne* almesse,
C.13.98   As þe ryche *man* for al his mone, and more as by þe gospell:
C.13.139 *Man* and his make y myhte se bothe;
C.13.142 And how þat [men] mede toke and mercy refusede
C.13.153 Saue *man* and his make; and þerof me wondrede.
C.13.181 Saue *man* and mankynde; mony tymes me thouhte
C.13.192 And þerfore merueileth me, for *man* is moste yliche the,
C.13.210 *Man* was made of such [a] matere he may nat wel asterte
C.13.243 As shame: ther he sheweth hym vch *man* shoneth his companye.
C.14.15   And þat is dobet, yf eny suche be, a blessed *man* þat helpeth
C.14.20   As loreles to be lordes and lewede *men* techares,
C.14.44   For as a *man* may nat se þat misseth his yes,
C.14.46   [Althouh *men* maden bokes] God was here maystre
C.14.47   And seynt spirit þe saumplarie and said what *men* sholde wryte.
C.14.48   And riht as syht serueth a *man* to se [þe hye strete],
C.14.49   Riht so lereth lettrure lewed men to resoun.
C.14.50   And as a blynde *man* in bataile bereth wepene to fyhte
C.14.52   No more can a kynde witted *man*, but clerkes hym teche,
C.14.56   To ȝeue mercy for mysde[de]s ȝif *men* hit wol aske
C.14.59   Hadde neuere lewede [*man*] leue to legge hand on þat cheste
C.14.68   Laste cheste chauf[e] vs to [c]hoppe vch *man* oþer.
C.14.72   Kynde wittede *men* [c]an a clergie by hemsulue;
C.14.87   Hit speketh þer of ryche *men* riht nouht ne of ryche lordes
C.14.95   Ryche *men* rotte tho and in here reste reste
C.14.101 That is, how lewede *men* and luythere lyhtloker were ysaued
C.14.104 Take two stronge *men* and in temese cast hem,
C.14.119 In whiche floed þe fende fondeth [a] *man* hardest.
C.14.124 To lere lewede *men* As luk bereth witnesse:
C.14.134 And wol now wikkede *man* [be] lost bote if he wol hymsulue:
C.14.137 Riht As sum *man* ȝeueth me mete and sette me Amydde þe flore;
C.14.167 Was neuere *man* vppon molde þat myhte hit aspie.
C.14.168 Ac longe lybbynge *men* lykened men[nes] lyuynge
C.14.168 Ac longe lybbynge men lykened *men[nes]* lyuynge
C.14.173 Bytokenen riht ryche *men* þat reygne here on erthe.
C.14.181 Riht so *men* reuerence[th] more þe ryche for h[is] mebles
C.14.187 To lowe lyuynge *men* þe larke is resembled
C.14.198 For letrede *men* were lewede ȝut ne were lore of [here bokes].'
C.15.15   And how þat lewede *men* ben lad, but oure lord hem helpe,
C.15.29   And metten with a maystre, a *man* lyk a frere.
C.15.35   A meles mete for a pore *man* or moneye yf they hadde.
C.15.47   Of þat *men* myswonne they made hem wel at ese
C.15.76   Holy writ byt *men* be waer and wysly hem kepe

C.15.83   And what meschief and maleese crist for *man* tholede.
C.15.148 And whan he hadde yworded thus wiste no *man* aftur
C.15.158 Meseyse ne meschief ne *man* with his tonge
C.15.171 Al th[e] wit of this world and wyhte *menne* strenghe
C.15.193 'Ich am a mynstral,' quod this *man*, 'my name is actiua vita,
C.15.197 'Munstracye can y nat moche bote make *men* merye,
C.15.202 [Cou]de y lye and do *men* lawhe thenne lacchen y scholde
C.15.213 And for me Actyf, his *man*, þat ydelnesse ha[t]e.
C.15.225 Ac yf myhte of myracle hym fayle hit is for *men* beth nat worthy
C.15.228 Ne *mannes* prayere maky pees amonges cristene peple
C.15.243 In menynge þat alle *men* myhte þe same
C.15.261 Ergo thorw his breth bestes lyueth, bothe *men* and fisches.
C.15.266 That no reyn ne roen; thus [r]at *men* [i]n bokes,
C.15.267 That manye wynter *men* lyuede and no mete ne tylede.
C.15.270 And yf *men* lyuede as mesure wolde sholde neuere[more] be
          defaute
C.15.273 'Meeknesse and mylde speche and *men* of o will,
C.15.280 Thogh *men* rede of rychesse rihte to þe worldes ende
C.15.301 Many *man* hath his ioye here for al here wel dedes
C.16.1   Allas þat rychesse shal reue and robbe *mannes* soule
C.16.6   Thenne may *men* wyte what he is worth and what he hath deserued
C.16.12   And moche murthe among ryche *men* is þat han meble ynow and
          hele.
C.16.16   [And arated of] ryche *men* þat reuthe is to here.
C.16.19   For al myhtest þou haue ymad *men* of grete welthe
C.16.40   Elles is alle oure labour loest–loo how *men* writeth
C.16.45   Ac with rychesse tho rybaudes rathest *men* bigileth.
C.16.58   Or in þe maystre or in þe *man* som mansion he haueth.
C.16.70   That mete or moneye of straunge *men* moet begge.
C.16.81   For *men* knowen wel þat coueytise is of a kene will
C.16.91   Ne doth *men* dyne delicatlyche ne drynke wyne ofte.
C.16.93   Hadde they noen haunt bote of pore [*men*; here houses stoed
          vntyled].
C.16.105 As a mayde for *mannes* loue here moder fors[a]ke[th],
C.16.107 Moche is [þat] mayde to louye of a *man* þat such oen taketh,
C.16.124 Or a[s] iustice to iuge *men*, me enioyneth þerto no pore,
C.16.125 Ne to be mair ouer *men* ne mynistre vnder kynges;
C.16.127 Ergo pouerte and pore *men* parforme þe comandement
C.16.132 And me leneth lyhtly fewe *men* and me wene hem pore:
C.16.137 [The fifte is] moder of myhte and of *mannes* helthe
C.16.153 Thus lered me a le[tte]red *man* for oure lordes loue, seynt Austyn:
C.16.157 That wroet thus to wisse *men* what pouerte was to mene.'
C.16.182 And so is *man* þat hath his mynde myd liberum Arbitrium.
C.16.194 Thenne am y liberum Arbitrium, as le[tt]red *men* telleth;
C.16.209 'Ȝe, sire!' y sayde, 'by so no *man* were ygreued,
C.16.218 To engelische *men* this is to mene, þat mowen speke and here,
C.16.219 The *man* þat moche hony eet his mawe hit engleymeth;
C.16.227 Riht so sothly scienc[e] swelleth a *mannes* soule
C.16.262 Loeth were lewed [*men*] bote they ȝoure lore folwede[n]
C.16.277 Wolde neuere oþerwyse god but wikkede *men* hit hadde,
C.16.303 And sory when he seth *men* sory, as thow seest childerne
C.16.304 Lawhe þer *men* lawheth and loure þer oþere louren.
C.16.305 And when a *man* swereth "forsoth" for sooth he hit troweth.
C.16.310 Hath he no lykynge to lawhe ne to likene *men* to scorne;
C.16.325 There pore *men* and prisones ben and paye for here fode,
C.16.329 Worth moche meryte to þat *man* þat hit may soffre.
C.16.338 Thogh y my byliue sholde begge aboute at *menne* hacches.
C.16.358 Riche *men* a recomendeth, and of [here] robes taketh,
C.17.14   That no *man* myhte se hym for moes and for leues.
C.17.31   And faire byfore tho *men* faunede with þe tayles.
C.17.33   In tokenynge þat trewe *man* alle tymes sholde
C.17.34   Fynde honest *men* and holy men and oþer rihtfole peple.
C.17.34   Fynde honest men and holy *men* and oþer rihtfole peple.
C.17.41   This is no more to mene bote *men* of holy churche
C.17.46   And marchauntȝ merciable wolde be and of lawe bothe
C.17.52   To make *men* louye mesure þat monkes ben and freres:
C.17.54   Yf lewede *men* knewe this latyn a litel they wolden auysen hem
C.17.67   He gaf goddes *men* goddes goodes and nat grete lordes
C.17.73   Me may now likene lettred *men* to a loscheborwe oþer worse
C.17.79   Ac þe metal þat is *mannes* soule of [many of] this techares
C.17.88   Lewed *men* han no byleue, [so] lettred men erren;
C.17.88   Lewed men han no byleue, [so] lettred *men* erren;
C.17.139 And lele *men* lyue as lawe techeth and loue þerof aryseth
C.17.140 The whiche is þe heued of charite and hele of *mannes* soule:
C.17.154 For þer is no *man* þat mynde hath þat ne meketh [hym] and
          byseceth
C.17.156 Ac many manere *men* þer ben, as sarresynes and iewes,
C.17.159 A *man* þat hihte Makameth for messie they hym holdeth
C.17.165 Me fynde[th] þat Macometh was a *man* ycristened
C.17.170 Be maistre ouer alle tho *men* and on this manere a wrouhte:
C.17.178 For Macometh to *men* swaer hit was a messager of heuene
C.17.181 Thus macumeth in misbileue *man* & womman brouhte

C.17.185 Holy *men*, as y hope, thorw helpe of the holy goste
C.17.187 Allas, þat *men* so longe on Macometh bileueth!
C.17.194 Hit is reuthe to rede how riht holy *men* lyuede,
C.17.202 To amende and to make, as with *men* of holy churche,
C.17.210 Minne ȝe [nat], lettred *men*, how tho men honourede
C.17.210 Minne ȝe [nat], lettred men, how tho *men* honourede
C.17.222 An angel *men* herde an hye at rome crye,
C.17.234 That with moneye maynteyneth *men* [t]o werre vppon cristene
C.17.241 Naught thorw manslaght and *mannes* strenghe Macometh hadde þe maistrie
C.17.249 And alle maner *men* þat on this molde libbeth.
C.17.259 And þat is reuthe for rihtfole *men* þat in þ[e] reume wonyeth
C.17.263 Mony myracles a wrouhte *men* for to torne,
C.17.264 In ensaumple þat *men* sholde se by sad resoen
C.17.265 That men myhte nat be saued but thorw mercy and grace
C.17.267 And bicam *man* of a mayde and metropol[it]anus
C.17.273 And fro mysbileue mony *men* turnede.
C.17.274 In sauacioun of *mannes* soule seynte Thomas of Canterbury
C.17.279 And nat in Ingelond to huppe aboute and halewe *men* auters
C.17.281 Many *man* for cristes loue was martired amonges Romaynes
C.17.300 And of selcouthe sores saued *men* fol ofte.
C.18.12 And þerof cometh a goed fruyt þe wiche *men* calleth werkes
C.18.71 As weddede *men* and wedewes and riht worthy maydones
C.18.74 As monkes and monyals, *men* of holy churche;
C.18.80 That [lyf Actiua] lettred *men* in here langage calleth.'
C.18.82 That oure lord alloweth, as lered *men* vs techeth,
C.18.91 And bad hit be, of a bat of erthe, a *man* and a maide,
C.18.94 In kynges Court and in knyhtes, the clenneste *men* and fayreste
C.18.115 And made of holy *men* his hoerd in limbo inferni
C.18.122 That thorw fals biheste and fruyt furste *man* disseyued.
C.18.134 And bycam *man* of þat maide mankynde to saue,
C.18.173 Thow shalt be myrrour to monye *men* to disceue.
C.18.181 And thenne mette y with a *man* a myddelento[n] sonenday,
C.18.210 O god almyhty þat *man* made and wrouhte
C.18.215 And o god almyhty, yf alle *men* ben of Adam.
C.18.223 And *man* withoute a make myhte nat wel of kynde
C.18.234 The which is *man* and his make and moilere here issue,
C.18.236 In matrimonie aren thre and of o *man* cam alle thre
C.19.6 'Is hit asseled?' y saide; 'may *men* yse th[e] lettres?'
C.19.22 Of *men* and of wommen meny score thousend.'
C.19.39 The which alle *men* aren holde ouer al thyng to honoure
C.19.41 Alle manere *men* as moche as ouresulue.
C.19.51 Comynge fram a contraye þat *men* callide Ierico;
C.19.55 A *man*, as me tho thouhte, to moche care they brouhte
C.19.62 How he with Moyses maundement hadde mony *men* yholpe
C.19.82 Were afered and flowe fram þe *man* ywounded.
C.19.84 Ne no medicyne vnder molde the *man* to hele brynge,
C.19.92 For wente neuere *man* this way þat he ne was here yruyfled
C.19.106 Alle manere *men* and thogh y myhte venge
C.19.210 For to murthe *men* with þat in merke sitten,
C.19.211 So wol Crist of his cortesye, and *men* crien hym mercy,
C.19.228 Forthy beth ywar, ȝe wyse *men* þat with the world deleth,
C.19.231 For mony of ȝow riche *men*, by my soule y lye nat,
C.19.233 Minne ȝe nat, riche *men*, to which a myschaunce
C.19.235 Of his mete and mone to *men* þat hit nedede?
C.19.237 Bute riȝtfulliche, as *men* [r]at, al his richesse cam hym
C.19.258 Vnkynde cristene *men*, for coueytise and enuye
C.19.259 Sleth a *man* for his mebles with mouthe or with handes.
C.19.261 The which is lyf and loue, the leye of *mannes* body.
C.19.262 For euery manere goed *man* may be likned to a torche
C.19.264 And hoso morthereth a goed *man*, me thynketh bi myn inwit,
C.19.266 And ȝut in mo maneres *men* [o]ffenden þe holy gost;
C.19.289 That may no kynge mercy graunte til bothe *men* acorde
C.19.301 Thre thynges ther ben þat doth a *man* to sterte
C.19.318 To *man* þat mercy asketh and amende thenketh."
C.19.322 And thogh that *men* make moche deul in here anger
C.19.326 Haeth mercy on suche *men* þat [so] euele may soffre.
C.19.333 Alle manere *men* mercy and forȝeuenesse
C.20.64 And dede *men* for þat dene cam oute of depe graues
C.20.139 In menynge þat *man* shal fro me[r]kenesse be ydrawe
C.20.142 [That *man* shal man saue thorw a maydenes helpe
C.20.142 [That man shal *man* saue thorw a maydenes helpe
C.20.163 And riht as the gylour thorw gyle bigiled *man* formost
C.20.195 And saue *mannes* soule? suster, wene hit neuere.
C.20.215 Yf no nyht ne were no *man*, [as] y leue,
C.20.219 For sholde neuere riȝt riche *man* þat lyueth in rest and hele
C.20.222 Bycam *man* of a mayde mankynde to saue
C.20.240 Boek hihte þat beaupere, a bolde *man* of speche.
C.20.245 That *mannes* soule sholde saue and synne distruye.
C.20.332 Thus hath he trolled forth lyke a tydy *man* this two & thritty wynter.
C.20.338 To lere *men* to [be] lele and vch man to louye oþer,
C.20.338 To lere men to [be] lele and vch *man* to louye oþer,

C.20.355 That ȝe belyen nat this lewed *men* for at the laste dauid
C.20.383 And hoso hit out a *mannes* eye or elles his foreteth
C.20.389 And al þat m[a]n mysdede, y *man* to amenden hit
C.20.389 And al þat *m[a]n* mysdede, y man to amenden hit
C.20.408 Y fauht so me fursteth ȝut for *mannes* soule sake:
C.20.414 And haue out of helle alle *mennes* soules.
C.20.417 Ac to be merciable to *man* thenne my kynde [hit] asketh
C.20.468 That *men* rang to þe resureccioun and riht with þat y wakede
C.21.4 In myddes of þe masse tho *men* ȝede to offrynge
C.21.18 Anoon as *men* nemned þe name of god iesu;
C.21.28 To be cald a knyht is fayr for *men* shal knele to hym;
C.21.33 And fre *men* foule thralles þat folleweth nat his lawes.
C.21.34 The iewes þat were gentel *men* iesu thei dispisede,
C.21.39 Aren frankeleynes, fre *men* Thorw follyng þat they toke
C.21.40 And Ientel *men* with iesu for iesu[s] was yfolled
C.21.84 [Wherefore & why wyse *men* þat tyme,
C.21.85 Maistres & lettred *men*, Magi hem calde.
C.21.98 In þe manere of a *man* and þat by moche sleythe,
C.21.112 And lawe lakked tho for *men* loued nat her enemyes
C.21.137 And nempned hym of naȝareth; and no *man* so worthy
C.21.143 And sethen bur[ie]den his body and beden þat *men* sholde
C.21.148 And his moder marie; thus *men* bifore deuyned.
C.21.153 Verray *man* bifore [hem] alle, and forth with hem ȝede
C.21.184 /Myhte *men* to assoyle of alle manere synnes,
C.21.185 To alle manere *men* mercy and forȝeuenesse\
C.21.190 And assoile *men* of alle synnes saue of dette one.
C.21.227 And gaf vch *man* a grace to gye with hymsuluen
C.21.247 And fechen hit fro false *men* with foleuiles lawes;
C.21.275 And sewe hit in *mannes* soule and sethe toelde here names.
C.21.279 And lered *men* a ladel bugge with a longe stale
C.21.378 Egrelich ernynge oute [of] *menne* yes.
C.21.387 Myhte to make hit and *men* to eten hit [aftur]
C.21.394 Or vch *man* forȝeue oþer, and þat wol þe paternost[er]:
C.21.411 *Man* to me þat me couthe telle of cardinal[e] vertues
C.21.416 The comu[n]e clamat cotidie, vch a *man* to oþer,
C.21.427 Emperour of al þe world, þat all *men* were cristene.
C.21.432 And sente þe so[nn]e to saue a corsed *mannes* tulthe
C.21.433 As brihte as to þe beste *man* or to þe beste womman.
C.21.439 As for a trewe tydy *man* alle tymes ylyke.
C.21.457 Vch *man* sotileth a sleythe synne to huyde
C.21.467 And holy kyrke and clerge fro cursed *men* to defende.
C.22.12 That is mete when *men* hym werneth [and] he no money weldeth
C.22.27 And bete *men* ouer bitere and som body to litel
C.22.28 And greue *men* grettore then goed faith hit w[o]lde.
C.22.52 And mette ful merueylousely þat in *mannes* fourme
C.22.55 And made fals sprynge and sprede and spe[d]e *menne* nedes.
C.22.65 And þat were mylde *men* and holy þat no meschief dradden,
C.22.93 Thenne mette thise *men*, ar muinstrals myhte pype
C.22.102 Lered ne lewed he lefte no *man* stande,
C.22.112 Amonges alle manere *men*, wedded and vnwedded,
C.22.146 And leet leautee a cherl and lyare a fre *man*.
C.22.182 The compeny of comfort *men* clepede hit som tyme.
C.22.187 Sennes whanne was þe way ouer *menne* heuedes?
C.22.259 And yf thei wage *men* to werre thei writen hem in nombre;
C.22.264 Monkes and monyales and alle *men* of religioun,
C.22.275 And preche *men* of plato and preuen hit by seneca
C.22.278 For god sopede *men* to a lawe and Moyses hem tauhte:
C.22.289 And maken hym murye with oþere *menne* godes.
C.22.306 Shrift schupte scharp salue and made *men* do penauns[e]
C.22.317 For here is many [a] *man* hert thorw ypocrisye.'
C.22.379 And doth *men* drynke dwale; [they] drat no synne.'

manacen v *manacen* v. A 1 manacide; B 4 manaced (3) manacen (1); C 2 manaced (1) manescheth (1)
A. 7.155 And *manacide* hym & his men whanne h[y] next metten.
B. 6.170 And *manaced* [hym] and his men if þei mette eftsoone.
B.13.6 And how þat Elde *manaced* me, myȝte we euere mete;
B.16.49 *Manacen* bihynde me, my fruyt for to fecche,
B.16.127 And mysseide þe Iewes manliche and *manaced* hem to bete
C. 4.62 And ȝut he *manes[c]heth* me and myne and lyth be my mayde.
C.15.6 And how elde *man[a]ced* me, so myhte happe

maner n *manere* n. &> *manoir* A 16; B 64 maner (17) manere (43) maneres (4); C 70 maner (11) manere (55) maneres (2) maners (2)
A.Pr.18 Of alle *maner* of men, þe mene & þe riche,
A. 1.19 In mesurable *maner* to make ȝow at ese;
A. 2.47 In what *maner* þat mede in mariage was feffid;
A. 2.148 Of many *maner* of m[e]n þat on þis molde libbeþ.
A. 3.200 Emperours & Erlis & alle *maner* lordis
A. 3.218 'Þere arn to *maner* of medis, my lord, be ȝour leue.
A. 3.235 Is no *maner* of mede but a mesurable hire;
A. 5.25 And wynne þat he wastide wiþ sum *maner* craft,
A. 5.120 Wiþ many *maner* marchaundise as my maister me hiȝte.
A. 7.21 And alle *maner* of men þat be þe mete libbiþ,

A. 7.102	Eche man on his *maner* made hymself to done,
A. 7.208	And alle *maner* of men þat þou miȝte aspien,
A. 7.251	And aftir many *maner* metis his mawe is alongid.
A. 8.7	Or any *maner* mester þat miȝte peris helpen,
A. 8.79	Þanne of alle oþer *maner* men þat on þis molde wandriþ.
A.10.63	Ouer suche *maner* of men miȝt in here soulis.
B.Pr.18	Of alle *manere* of men, þe meene and þe riche,
B. 1.19	In mesurable *manere* to make yow at ese;
B. 1.118	For þei leueden vpon [Lucifer] þat lyed þis *manere*:
B. 2.13	And Diamaundes of derrest pris and double *manere* Saphires,
B. 2.56	Swiche *manere* men, my lord, shul haue þis firste Mede
B. 2.187	[Of many *manere* man þat on þis molde libbeth],
B. 3.213	Emperours and Erles and alle *manere* lordes
B. 3.231	'Ther are two *manere* of Medes, my lord, [bi] youre leue.
B. 3.244	Swiche *manere* men, my lord, shul haue þis firste Mede
B. 3.256	It is no *manere* Mede but a mesurable hire.
B. 5.25	And wynnen his wastyng wiþ som *maner* crafte.
B. 5.204	Wiþ many *manere* marchaundise as my maister me hiȝte.
B. 5.280	Ne hadde repentaunce þe raþer reconforted hym in þis *manere*:
B. 5.431	For I haue and haue had somdel haukes *maneres*;
B. 5.584	In-[no]-*manere*-ellis-noȝt-for-no-mannes-biddyng.
B. 6.19	And alle *manere* of men þat [by þe] mete libbeþ,
B. 6.110	Ech man in his *manere* made hymself to doone,
B. 6.222	And alle *manere* of men þat þow myȝt aspie,
B. 6.267	And after many *maner* metes his mawe is [alonged].
B. 7.7	Or any [*maner*] mestier þat myȝte Piers [helpe],
B. 7.89	The book banneþ beggerie and blameþ hem in þis *manere*:
B. 7.97	Than of alle [oþere] *manere* men þat on þis moolde [wandreþ].
B. 9.45	And in þis *manere* was man maad þoruȝ myȝt of god almyȝty,
B. 9.182	And euery *maner* seculer [man] þat may noȝt continue
B.10.274	Alle *maner* men to amenden bi hire myȝtes;
B.10.281	But in swich *manere* as Marc meneþ in þe gospel:
B.10.284	In alle *maner* men þoruȝ mansede preestes.
B.11.178	And þat alle *manere* men, enemyes and frendes,
B.12.159	And þow seidest sooþ of somme, ac se in what *manere*.
B.13.3	In *manere* of a mendynaunt many ȝer after.
B.13.40	Ac þis maister [of þise men] no *maner* flessh [eet],
B.13.395	Neiþer masse ne matynes, ne none *maner* siȝtes;
B.13.426	Lest þo þre *maner* men to muche sorwe yow brynge:
B.13.458	Thise þre *maner* minstrales makeþ a man to lauȝe,
B.13.458	Til conscience acouped hym þerof in a curteis *manere*,
B.14.37	Vitailles of grete vertues for alle *manere* beestes
B.14.119	But god sente hem som tyme som *manere* Ioye
B.14.164	Now, lord, sende hem somer, and som *maner* ioye,
B.14.183	[To hores, to harlotes, to alle *maner* peple]
B.14.224	And eiþer hateþ ooþer in alle *maner* werkes.
B.15.98	Ther is a meschief in þe more of swiche *maner* [stokkes].
B.15.174	And alle *manere* meschiefs in myldenesse he suffreþ.
B.15.207	Ac it is moore to haue hir mete [on] swich an esy *manere*
B.15.251	For whoso myȝte meete [wiþ] hym swiche *maneres* hym eileþ:
B.15.259	In alle *manere* angres, haue þis at herte
B.15.271	In hunger, in hete, in alle *manere* angres.
B.15.316	And a mees þermyd of o *maner* kynde,
B.15.398	Brouȝte Sarȝens of Surree, and see in what *manere*.
B.15.440	Sholde alle *maner* men; we han so manye maistres,
B.16.133	And maken it as muche ouþer moore in alle *manere* poyntes
B.17.196	In many kynnes *maneres* I myghte myself helpe,
B.17.281	For euery *manere* good [man may] be likned
B.17.285	A[c] yet in mo *maneres* men offenden þe holy goost;
B.17.353	Alle *manere* men mercy and forȝifnesse,
B.18.44	And ȝit maken it as muche in alle *manere* poyntes,
B.18.318	[The] lord of myght and of ma[y]n and alle *manere* vertues,
B.19.98	In þe *manere* of a man and þat by muchel sleighte,
B.19.184	[Myght [men] to assoille of alle *manere* synne[s],
B.19.185	To alle *maner* men mercy and forȝifnesse]
B.19.324	He made a *manere* morter, and mercy it highte.
B.19.349	Ne no *manere* marchaunt þat wiþ moneye deleþ
B.20.112	Amonges alle *manere* men, wedded and vnwedded,
B.20.197	I ne myghte in no *manere* maken it at hir wille,
B.20.254	That in mesure god made alle *manere* þynges,
C.Pr.20	Of alle *manere* [of] men, þe mene and þe [riche],
C. 2.7	And mony mo of here *maners*, of men and of wymmen.'
C. 2.59	Of many *manere* men þat of mede[s] kynne were,
C. 2.200	Of many *maner* men for mede sake seude aftur.
C. 3.110	What *maner* muster oþer marchandise he vsed
C. 3.269	Emperours and Erles and alle *manere* lordes
C. 3.305	And þat is no mede but a mercede, a *manere* dewe dette,
C. 3.333	Thus is mede and mercede as two *maner* relacions,
C. 3.397	But þat alle *maner* men, wymmen and childrene
C. 3.404	Thus is man and mankynde in *maner* of [a] sustantyf,
C. 4.121	For alle *manere* men þat me fynt neodefole,
C. 5.196	Of alle *maner* actions and eche man loue other.
C. 6.26	In alle [*manere*] maneres my name to be knowe;

C. 6.114	In alle *manere* angres þat y hadde or felede.
C. 6.115	Amonges alle *manere* men my dwellyng is som tyme,
C. 6.212	With many *manere* marchandise as my maistre hyhte;
C. 6.282	Nother matynes ne masse ne no *maner* syhtus;
C. 6.337	Of alle *manere* men þat [mid] goode wille
C. 7.23	Or lacke men or likene hem in vnlikyng *manere*;
C. 7.44	For y haue and haue yhad sumdel haukes *maners*;
C. 7.86	Laste tho *manere* men to muche sorwe ȝow brynge:
C. 7.109	Thise thre *manere* munstrals maketh a man to lauhe
C. 7.231	In-none-*manere*-elles-nat-for-no-mannes-preeyre.
C. 7.259	And fynde alle *manere* folk fode to here soules
C. 7.300	'Y haue wedded a wyf wel wantowen of *maneres*;
C. 8.17	And alle *manere* men þat by þe molde is susteyned
C. 8.117	Vch man in his *manere* made hymsulue to done,
C. 8.231	And alle *manere* [of] men þat thow myhte aspye
C. 8.247	His suluer to thre *maner* men [in] menyng they sholden
C. 8.281	In al *manere* ese in Abrahammus lappe.
C. 9.7	Or eny *manere* mester þat myhte [Peres] auayle
C. 9.33	Amende in som *manere* wyse and ma[y]dones helpe;
C. 9.124	Suche *manere* men, Matheu vs techeth,
C. 9.128	And alle *manere* munstrals, me woet wel þe sothe,
C. 9.162	The boek banneth beggarie and blameth hit in this *manere*:
C. 9.218	Rihte so, sothly, such *manere* Ermytes
C. 9.220	For holy churche hoteth alle *manere* peple
C.10.243	For god seid ensaumple of suche *manere* issue
C.10.283	And euery *maner* seculer man þat may nat contynue
C.11.33	Nowe is þe *manere* at mete when munstrals ben stille
C.11.176	Concupiscencia Carnis confortede me o[n] this *manere*
C.13.71	Alle *maner* men [in] meschief yfalle,
C.14.74	And markede hit in here *manere* and mused þeron to knowe.
C.14.103	And thow saidest sothe of somme, Ac [yse] in what *manere*.
C.15.3	In *manere* of [a] mendenaunt mony ȝer aftur.
C.15.195	'What *manere* munstracye, my dere frende,' quod Concience.
C.15.295	Bote god sen[t]e hem som tyme sum *manere* ioye
C.16.251	There is a meschief in þe more of suche *manere* stokkes.
C.16.312	And alle *manere* meschiefs as munstracie of heuene.
C.17.151	'Hit may be so þat sarresynes haen such a *manere* charite,
C.17.156	Ac many *manere* men þer ben, as sarresynes and iewes,
C.17.170	Be maistre ouer alle tho men and on this *manere* a wrouhte:
C.17.243	In such *manere* me thynketh moste þe pope,
C.17.249	And alle *maner* men þat on this molde libbeth.
C.19.41	Alle *manere* men as moche as ouresulue.
C.19.106	Alle *manere* men and thogh y myhte venge
C.19.162	In many kyne *manere* y myhte mysulfe helpe,
C.19.262	For euery *manere* goed man may be likned to a torche
C.19.266	And ȝut in mo *maneres* men [o]ffenden þe holy gost;
C.19.333	Alle *manere* men mercy and forȝeuenesse
C.20.43	And ȝut maken hit as moche in alle *manere* poyntes,
C.20.384	Or eny *manere* membre maymeth oþer herteth,
C.21.98	In þe *manere* of a man and þat by moche sleythe,
C.21.184	/Myhte men to assoyle of alle *manere* synnes,
C.21.185	To alle *manere* men mercy and forȝeuenesse\
C.21.324	He made a *manere* morter and mercy hit hihte.
C.21.349	Ne no *manere* Marchaunt þat with moneye deleth
C.22.112	Amonges alle *manere* men, wedded and vnwedded,
C.22.197	Y ne myhte in none *manere* maken hit at here wille
C.22.254	That in mesure god made alle [*manere*] thynges

manere(s > maner,manoir

manered ptp *maneren v.* B 2; C 2 manered (1) ymanered (1)

B. 2.27	And Mede is *manered* after hym [as men of] kynde [carpeþ]:
B.15.416	And ben *manered* after Makometh þat no man vseþ trouþe.
C. 2.27	And mede is *manered* aftur hym as men of kynde carpeth:
C.10.260	A mayde and wel *yma[ner]ed* and of gode men yspronge,

manescheth > manacen

manged v *maungen v.* A 2 mangid (1) maunged (1); B 1; C 1

A. 7.242	Þei han *mangid* ouer muche, þat makiþ hem grone ofte.
A.12.72	Than *maunged* I wit[h him] vp at þe fulle;
B. 6.258	Ye han *manged* ouer muche; þat makeþ yow grone.
C. 8.270	Ȝe han *manged* ouer moche; þat maketh ȝow to be syke.

mangerie n *maungerie n.* B 2; C 1 mangerye

B.11.112	'Multi to a *mangerie* and to þe mete were sompned,
B.15.592	And by þat *mangerie* [þei] myȝte wel se þat Messie he semede;
C.12.47	'Multi to a *mangerye* and to þe mete were sompned

mangnel n *mangonel n.* C 1

C.20.293	Set Mahond at þe *mang[n]el* and mullestones throweth;

manhede n *manhede n.* A 1 manhod; B 6 manhede (3) manhod (1) manhode (2); C 5

A. 3.172	And mayntene þi *manhod* more þan þou knowist;
B. 3.185	And mayntene þi *manhode* moore þan þow knowest;

B.12.297 And muche murþe and *manhod*;' and riȝt wiþ þat he vanysshed.
B.16.202 And þat it may be so and sooþ [sheweþ it *manhode*]:
B.16.209 And þus is mankynde and *manhede* of matrimoyne ysprenge
B.16.220 Thus in þre persones is parfitliche [pure] *manhede*,
B.19.158 Goynge toward Galilee in godhede and *manhede*
C. 3.231 And maynteyne thi *manhede* more then thow knowest.
C.17.66 That his mede and his *manhede* for eueremore shal laste:
C.18.219 And abel here issue, aren bote oen in *manhede*.
C.18.238 Lo! treys encountre treys,' quod he, 'in godhede and in *manhede*.'
C.21.158 Goynge toward galilee in godhede and *manhede*

many adj *many adj.& n.* A 50 many (18) *manye* (32); B 155 many (73)
manye (82); C 162 many (92) *manye* (9) meny (1) *moneye* (1) mony
(38) monye (21)

A.Pr.25 In preyours & penaunce putten hem *manye*,
A.Pr.48 Wenten forþ in here wey wiþ *many* wise talis,
A.Pr.59 *Manye* of þise maistris may cloþe hem at lyking
A.Pr.62 *Manye* ferlis han fallen in a fewe ȝeris.
A.Pr.98 Baxteris & bocheris & breusteris *manye*,
A.Pr.101 Masonis, mynours, & *oþere* craftis,
A. 1.164 *Manye* chapelleins arn chast ac charite is aweye;
A. 2.6 Boþe fals & fauel & hise feris *manye*.'
A. 2.20 Out of wrong heo wex to wroþerhele *manye*.
A. 2.76 Munde þe myllere, & *manye* mo oþere.
A. 2.148 Of *many* maner of m[e]n þat on þis molde libbeþ.
A. 2.178 Lurkyng þoruȝ lanes, toluggid of *manye*.
A. 2.179 He was nowhere welcome for his *many* talis,
A. 2.188 For he coude on here craft & kneuȝ *manye* gommes.
A. 3.22 Rynges wiþ rubies & ricchesse *manye*;
A. 3.112 She makiþ men mysdo *manye* score tymes;
A. 3.113 In trist of hire tresour she teniþ [wel] *manye*.
A. 4.21 And ȝet wile [h]e make *many* wehe er we come þere.'
A. 4.50 To make his pes with his panis & profride hym *manye*,
A. 5.71 I miȝte not *many* day do as a man [au]ȝte,
A. 5.104 'Sorewe for synne sauiþ wel *manye*.'
A. 5.120 Wiþ *many* maner marchaundise as my maister me hiȝte.
A. 6.10 And *many* crouch [o]n his cloke, & keiȝes of rome,
A. 6.16 In armonye, in alisaundre, in *manye* oþere places.
A. 6.68 He is fre[þ]id in wiþ Floreynes & oþere [fees] *manye*.
A. 6.83 His man hattiþ amende ȝow, for *many* man he knowiþ.
A. 6.109 Largenesse þe lady let in wel *manye*.
A. 7.98 To erien þis half akir helpen hym *manye*;
A. 7.251 And aftir *many* maner metis his mawe is alongid.
A. 7.270 Ac I haue persile & poret, & *many* cole plantis,
A. 7.278 Chibollis, & chiriuellis, & ri[p]e chiries *manye*,
A. 7.281 Þanne þise folk for fer fetten hym *manye*
A. 8.20 Marchauntis in þe margyn hadde *manye* ȝeris,
A. 8.42 Þanne were marchauntis merye; *many* wepe for ioye,
A. 8.109 Be þat þe sauter vs seiþ, & so dede oþere *manye*.
A. 8.131 *Manye* tyme þis metelis han mad me to stodie,
A. 8.150 *Manye* tymes at mydniȝt whan men shulde slepe,
A. 9.5 And what man he miȝte be of *many* man I askide.
A. 9.27 Makeþ þe man *many* tymes to falle & to stande.
A.10.107 Ne men þat conne *manye* craftis, clergie [it telliþ],
A.10.152 And *manye* mylions mo of men & of wommen
A.10.191 *Manye* peire siþen þ[e] pestilence han p[l]iȝt hem togidere.
A.10.192 Þe fruyt þat þei bringe forþ arn *manye* foule wordis.
A.10.218 And þat is wykkide wil þat *many* werk shendiþ.'
A.11.124 So shalt þou come to clergie þat can *many* wyttes.
A.11.159 Ȝet arn þere febicchis of Forellis of *many* manis wittes,
A.11.284 Þat hadde leyn with lucifer *manye* longe ȝeris;
A.11.308 Þanne arn þise [k]ete clerkis þat conne *many* bokis,
A.12.8 Presumptuowsly, parauenture, apose so *manye*
A.12.58 *Many* ferlys me byfel in a fewe ȝeris.
B.Pr.25 In preieres and penaunc[e] putten hem *manye*,
B.Pr.48 Wenten forþ in hire wey wiþ *many* wise tales,
B.Pr.62 *Manye* of þise maistre[s mowe] cloþen hem at likyng
B.Pr.65 *Manye* ferlies han fallen in a fewe yeres.
B.Pr.97 Hire messe & hire matyns and *many* of hire houres
B.Pr.99 Lest crist in Consistorie acorse ful *manye*.
B.Pr.198 [And] *many* m[a]nnes malt we mees wolde destruye,
B.Pr.219 Baksteres and Brewesteres and Bochiers *manye*,
B.Pr.222 Masons, Mynours and *many* oþere craftes;
B. 1.180 *Manye* Chapeleyns arn chaste ac charite is aweye;
B. 2.6 Boþe Fals and Fauel and hi[s]e feeres *manye*.'
B. 2.57 To marien þis mayde [was] *many* m[a]n assembled,
B. 2.112 [Munde] þe Millere and *many* mo oþere:
B. 2.187 [Of *many* maner man þat on þis molde libbeth],
B. 2.219 Lurkynge þoruȝ lanes, tolugged of *manye*.
B. 2.220 He was nowher welcome for his *manye* tales,
B. 2.229 For he couþe [on] hir craft and knew *manye* gommes.
B. 3.23 Rynges wiþ Rubies and richesses *manye*,
B. 3.123 [She] makeþ men mysdo *many* score tymes.
B. 3.124 [In] trist of hire tresor [she teneþ] wel *manye*.

B. 3.297 Mede of mysdoeres makeþ *manye* lordes,
B. 4.64 To maken [his] pees with hise pens and profred hym *manye*,
B. 4.153 And þei lauȝynge lope to hire and lefte Reson *manye*.
B. 4.159 And þe mooste peple in þe [moot] halle and *manye* of þe grete,
B. 4.175 And seide, 'þoruȝ [youre] lawe, as I leue, I lese *manye* eschetes;
B. 5.121 I myȝte noȝt ete *many* yeres as a man ouȝte
B. 5.147 That whan þei preche þe peple in *many* places aboute
B. 5.156 *Manye* Monþes wiþ hem, and wiþ Monkes boþe.
B. 5.169 Among Monkes I myȝte be ac *many* tyme I shonye
B. 5.170 For þere ben *manye* felle frekes my feeris to aspie,
B. 5.204 Wiþ *many* manere marchaundise as my maister me hiȝte.
B. 5.252 And haue ymaad *many* a knyȝt boþe Mercer and draper
B. 5.293 For þee and for *many* mo þat man shal ȝaue a rekenyng:
B. 5.435 In speche and in sparynge of speche; yspilt *many* a tyme
B. 5.436 Boþe flessh and fissh and *manye* oþere vitailles;
B. 5.522 And *many* crouch on his cloke and keyes of Rome,
B. 5.528 In Armonye, in Alisaundre, in *manye* oþere places.
B. 5.581 He is fryþed In wiþ floryns and oþere fees *manye*;
B. 5.596 His man hatte amende-yow, for *many* m[a]n h[e] knoweþ.
B. 5.623 Largenesse þe lady let in [wel] *manye*;
B. 6.106 To erie þis half acre holpen hym *manye*;
B. 6.193 For þat was bake for bayard was boote for *many* hungry;
B. 6.194 And *many* a beggere for benes buxum was to swynke,
B. 6.267 And after *many* maner metes his mawe is [alonged].
B. 6.286 Ac I haue percile and pore[t] and *manye* [plaunte coles],
B. 6.294 Chibolles and Cheruelles and ripe chiries *manye*;
B. 7.18 Marchaunȝ in þe margyne hadde *manye* yeres,
B. 7.38 Thanne were Marchaunȝ murie; *manye* wepten for ioye
B. 7.45 Ac *many* a Iustice and Iurour wolde for Iohan do moore
B. 7.127 By þat þe Sauter [vs] seith, [and] so dide othere *manye*.
B. 7.149 *Many* tyme þis metels haþ maked me to studie
B. 8.5 And what man he myȝte be of *many* man I asked.
B. 8.15 And knowen contrees and courtes and *many* kynnes places,
B. 8.31 Makeþ þe man *many* tyme to falle and to stonde.
B. 9.170 *Many* peire siþen þe pestilence han pliȝt hem togideres.
B. 9.171 The fruyt þat [þei] brynge forþ arn [*manye*] foule wordes;]
B. 9.209 And þat is wikked wille þat *many* werk shendeþ,
B.10.172 [So] shaltow come to Clergie þat kan *manye* [wittes].
B.10.306 It is in cloistre or in scole, by *manye* skiles I fynde.
B.10.319 In *many* places þer þei [persons ben, be þei purely] at ese,
B.10.379 *Manye* tales ye tellen þat Theologie lerneþ,
B.10.397 For *many* men on þis moolde moore setten hir hert[e]
B.10.405 Ac I wene it worþ of *manye* as was in Noes tyme
B.10.425 That hadde yleyen wiþ lucifer *many* longe yeres.
B.10.434 And þo þat wisely worededen and writen *manye* bokes
B.10.464 Than are þise [kete] clerkes þat konne *manye* bokes,
B.10.474 And principally hir paternoster; *many* a persone haþ wisshed.
B.10.475 I se ensamples myself and so may *manye* oþer,
B.11.20 And in þis Mirour þow myȝt se [myrþes] ful *manye*
B.11.75 Ich haue muche merueille of yow, and so haþ *many* anoþer,
B.11.160 [This matere is merk for *many*, ac men of holy chirche,
B.11.244 *Many* tyme god haþ be boden amonge nedy peple,
B.11.258 And boþe bettre and blesseder by *many* fold þan Richesse.
B.11.351 Ac yet me merueilled moore how *many* oþere briddes
B.11.354 In Mareys and moores [*manye*] hidden hir egges]
B.11.364 *Manye* selkouþes I seiȝ ben noȝt to seye nouþe.
B.11.366 And how among þe grene gras growed so *manye* hewes,
B.11.371 Saue man and his make; *many* tyme [me þouȝte]
B.12.4 And *manye* tymes haue meued þee to [mynne] on þyn ende,
B.12.19 And prechours to preuen what it is of *many* a peire freres.'
B.12.24 [In *manye* places pleyden þe parfiter to ben].
B.12.49 Of *manye* swiche I may rede, of men and of wommen,
B.12.53 And for þei suffren and see so *manye* nedy folkes
B.12.55 [So catel and kynde wit acombreþ ful *manye*;
B.12.118 And *manye* mo oþer men, þat were no leuites,
B.12.232 Lewed men *many* tymes maistres þei apposen
B.13.3 In manere of a mendynaunt *many* yer after.
B.13.4 And of þis metyng *many* tyme muche þouȝt I hadde,
B.13.38 Ac serued hem þus soone of sondry metes *manye*,
B.13.44 In a morter, Post mortem, of *many* bitter peyne
B.13.62 He eet *manye* sondry metes, mortrews and puddynges,
B.13.134 Pacience haþ be in *many* place, and paraunter [knoweþ]
B.13.226 A wafrer, wol ye wite, and serue *manye* lordes,
B.13.261 And er þe commune haue corn ynouȝ *many* a cold morwenyng;
B.13.274 Ac it was moled in *many* places wiþ manye sondry plottes,
B.13.274 Ac it was moled in many places wiþ *manye* sondry plottes,
B.13.280 Forwhy he bosteþ and braggeþ wiþ *manye* bolde oþes;
B.13.314 Haþ *manye* moles and spottes; it moste ben ywasshe.'
B.13.317 Men sholde fynde *manye* frounces and manye foule plottes.'
B.13.317 Men sholde fynde manye frounces and *manye* foule plottes.'
B.13.364 Moore profitable þan myn, *manye* sleiȝtes I made.
B.13.382 That it coste me muche moore; swoor *manye* oþes.
B.14.4 That wollen bymolen it *many* tyme maugree my chekes.

B.14.68	That *manye* wyntres men lyueden and no mete ne tulieden.
B.14.127	To ʒyue *many* m[e]n his [mercymonye] er he it haue deserued.
B.14.169	Of þe good þat þow hem gyuest ingrati ben *manye*;
B.14.188	Shulde amenden vs as *manye* siþes as man wolde desire.
B.14.299	It afaiteþ þe flessh fram folies ful *manye*,
B.15.17	In cristes court yknowe wel and of [cristene in *many* a place].
B.15.41	'For bisshopes yblessed bereþ *manye* names,
B.15.73	Bettre it were [by] *manye* doctours to [bi]leuen swich techyng
B.15.114	Right so [preestes, prechours and prelates *manye*],
B.15.121	But if *many* preest [forbeere] hir baselardes and hir broches
B.15.200	What is þe wille and wherfore þat *many* wight suffreþ:
B.15.268	Pacientes Vincunt verbi gracia, and [verred] ensamples *manye*.
B.15.297	That lyueden þus for oure lordes loue *many* longe yeres.
B.15.346	And *many* a prison fram purgatorie þoruʒ hise preieres deliuereþ.
B.15.440	Sholde alle maner men; we han so *manye* maistres,
B.15.493	So *manye* prelates to preche as þe Pope makeþ,
B.15.512	*Many* myracles he wrouʒte m[e]n for to turne,
B.15.519	*Many* a seint syþen haþ suffred to deye
B.15.531	*Many* man for cristes loue was martired [amonges] Romayne[s]
B.16.29	And forfreteþ neiʒ þe fruyt þoruʒ *manye* faire sightes.
B.16.116	And wepte water with hise eiʒen; þer seiʒen it *manye*.
B.16.156	Thow shalt be myrour to *many* men to deceyue,
B.16.171	After Piers þe Plowman; *many* a place I souʒte.
B.16.242	Mercy for oure mysdedes as *many* tyme as we asken:
B.16.248	And conforted *many* a careful þat after his comynge waite[n],
B.17.21	Of men and of wommen *many* score þousand.'
B.17.63	How he wiþ Moyses maundement hadde *many* men yholpe,
B.17.196	In *many* kynnes maneres I myghte myself helpe,
B.17.265	For *manye* of yow riche men, by my soule, men telleþ,
B.18.81	Maugree his *manye* teeþ he was maad þat tyme
B.18.177	That *many* day myʒte I noʒt se for merknesse of synne,
B.18.179	Moyses and *many* mo mer[ye] shul [synge];
B.18.393	And my mercy shal be shewed to *manye* of my [halue]breþeren,
B.18.407	*Manye* hundred of Aungeles harpeden and songen,
B.19.99	As it bicomeþ a conquerour to konne *manye* sleightes,
B.19.100	And *manye* wiles and wit þat wole ben a ledere.
B.19.211	Thanne song I þat song; so dide *manye* hundred,
B.19.409	'Thanne is *many* a [lif] lost', quod a lewed vicory.
B.20.26	He shal do moore þan mesure *many* tyme and ofte,
B.20.31	And Spiritus prudencie in *many* a point shal faille
B.20.42	So [he was nedy], as seiþ þe book in *manye* sondry places,
B.20.97	Kynde cam after wiþ *many* kene soores
B.20.99	So kynde þoruʒ corrupcions kilde ful *manye*.
B.20.104	*Manye* a louely lady and [hir] lemmans knyʒtes
B.20.117	He bar a bowe in his hand and *manye* brode arewes,
B.20.118	Weren feþered wiþ fair biheste and *many* a fals truþe.
B.20.132	And boldeliche bar adoun wiþ *many* a bright Noble
B.20.225	And shotten ayein wiþ shot, *many* a sheef of oþes,
B.20.302	And woundede wel wikkedly *many* a wys techere
B.20.317	For here is *many* a man hurt þoruʒ ypocrisye.'
B.20.334	'He is sik', seide Pees, 'and so are *manye* oþere.
B.20.377	'He lyþ [adreynt] and dremeþ', seide Pees, 'and so do *manye* oþere.
C.Pr.5	And say *many* selles and selkouthe thynges.
C.Pr.26	In continance [of] clothyng in *many* kyne gyse.
C.Pr.27	In preiers and penaunc[e] potten hem *mony*,
C.Pr.49	Wenten forth [i]n here way with *many* wyse tales
C.Pr.60	*Mony* of þise maistres of mendenant freres
C.Pr.63	*Mony* ferlyes han falle in a fewe ʒeres.
C.Pr.96	And seide, 'ydolatrie ʒe soffren in sondrye places *manye*
C.Pr.125	ʒoure masse and [ʒoure] matynes and *many* of [ʒoure] oures
C.Pr.127	Lest crist in constorie acorse of [ʒow] *manye*.
C.Pr.215	Til þat meschief amende here þat *man* chasteth.
C.Pr.216	For *many* mannys malt we muys wolde distruye
C. 1.118	Then in þe north by *many* notes, no man leue other.
C. 1.186	*Mony* chapeleynes aren chaste ac charite hem fayleth;
C.2.7	And *mony* mo of here maners, of men and of wymmen.'
C.2.59	Of *many* manere men þat of mede[s] kynne were,
C.2.115	Raynald þe reue and redyngkynges *manye*,
C.2.116	Munde þe mullere and *monye* mo othere:
C.2.179	Thenne gan gyle borwen hors at *many* gret maystres
C.2.200	Of *many* maner men for mede sake seude aftur.
C.2.229	Lorkyng thorw lanes, tologged of *moneye*;
C.2.230	He was nawher welcome for his *many* tales,
C.2.239	For a can on here craft and knoweth *manye* gommes.
C.3.13	That wendeth to Westmynstre worsch[e]ip[th] here *monye*.
C.3.90	*Many* sondry sorwes in Citees falleth ofte
C.3.97	Morreyne or other meschaunc[e]: and *mony* tymes hit falleth
C.3.105	*Many* burgages ybrent and bodies þerynne
C.3.135	And *monye* a gulte y haue the forgyue & my grace graunted
C.3.160	And maketh men mysdo *manye* score tymes.
C.3.161	In trist of here tresor he teneth fol *monye*,
C.3.237	Hast arwed *many* hardy man þat hadde wille to fyhte,
C.3.246	May nat be sold sothliche, so *many* part asketh

C. 3.293	Mede *many* tymes men ʒeueth bifore þe doynge
C. 3.311	The mede þat *many* prest[es] taken for masses þat thei syngen,
C. 3.450	Muchel [euel] is thorw mede *mony* tymes ysoffred
C. 4.95	To haue mercy on þat man þat *many* tymes hym greuede:
C. 4.167	And modiliche vppon mede *many* tym[e] lokede
C. 4.169	'Thorw ʒoure lawe, as y leue, y lese *many* chetes;
C. 5.35	'When y [ʒut] ʒong was, *many* ʒer hennes,
C. 5.153	Hit is in C[l]oystre or in scole, by *many* skilles y fynde.
C. 5.156	Ac *mony* day, men telleth, bothe monkes and chanons
C. 5.165	In *many* places ther thei persones ben, be hemsulue at ese,
C. 6.34	Bostyng and braggynge with *many* bolde othes,
C. 6.86	Y myhte nat ete *many* ʒer as a man ouhte
C. 6.96	Amongus marchauntes *many* tymes and nameliche in londone.
C. 6.131	*Mony* monthes with hem and with monkes bothe.
C. 6.151	Amonges monkes y myhte be Ac *mony* tyme y spare
C. 6.152	For there aren *many* felle frekes myn aferes to aspye,
C. 6.212	With *many* manere marchandise as my maistre hyhte;
C. 6.250	And haue ymad *many* a knyht bothe mercer and draper
C. 6.263	More profitable then myn, y made *many* wentes.
C. 6.348	For the and for *many* mo þat man shal ʒeue a rykenynge
C. 6.428	There no nede ne was, *many* sythe falsly;
C. 7.48	In speche and in sparyng of speche; yspilde *many* a tyme
C. 7.167	And *many* crouch on his cloke [and] kayes of Rome
C. 7.228	Is frithed in with floreynes and othere fees *monye*;
C. 7.244	His man hatte amende-ʒow, *many* man hym knoweth.
C. 7.275	Largenesse þ[e] lady lat in ful *monye*,
C. 8.113	To erien this half ak[er] holpen hym *monye*;
C. 8.192	For þat was bake for bayard was bote for *many* hungry,
C. 8.193	Drosenes and dregges drynke for *many* beggares.
C. 8.294	Ther ar *many* luther leches Ac lele leches fewe;
C. 9.22	Marchauntes in þe margine hadde *many* ʒeres
C. 9.41	Tho were Marchauntes mury; *many* wopen for ioye
C. 9.84	And of *monye* oþer men þat moche wo soffren,
C. 9.89	What other byhoueth þat hath *many* childrene
C. 9.111	With a good will, witteles, *mony* wyde contreyes
C. 9.113	Ne none muracles maken; Ac *many* tymes hem happeth
C. 9.173	Then of *many* oþere men þat [o]n this molde walken.
C. 9.256	The cause of al this caytiftee cometh of *many* bischopes
C. 9.260	For *many* wakere wolues ar wr[iþ]en into thy foldes;
C. 9.268	Y leue, for thy lacchesse, thow lesest *many* wetheres
C. 9.269	And *many* a fayre flees falsliche is ywasche!
C. 9.298	*Mony* tyme this meteles hath maked me to studie
C.10.5	And what man a myhte be of *mony* m[a]n y askede.
C.10.15	And knowen contrees and Courtes and *many* kynne plases,
C.10.35	Maketh þe man *many* tyme to stomble yf he stande.
C.10.87	And of mammonaus mone ymaked *mony* frendes
C.10.177	That *many* lede leseth thorw lykerous drynke.
C.10.271	*Many* a payre sethe th[e] pestelens[e] han plyhte treuthe to louye;
C.10.273	The fruyt þat they brynge forth aren *many* foule wordes;
C.11.48	*Mony* tym[e] mendenauntes myhte goen afyngred.
C.11.160	Thenne scripture scorned me and *mony* skiles shewed
C.11.179	And in þis myrrour thow myhte se murthes fol *monye*
C.11.228	For *mony* men [o]n this molde more sette here herte
C.11.236	Ac y wene hit worth of *monye* as was in *mony* tyme
C.11.257	That hadde yley with lucifer *mony* longe ʒeres.
C.11.281	Sothly,' saide rechelesnesse, 'ʒe se by *many* euydences
C.12.144	And bothe bettere and blessedere by *many* fold then richesse.
C.12.172	Mo prouerbes y myhte haue of *mony* holy seyntes
C.12.202	Mescheues and myshappes and *many* tribulac[ion]s
C.12.217	That *many* mothe was maistre ynne in A myntewhyle;
C.12.239	And ʒut more hit maketh men *mony* tymes & ofte
C.12.242	And so is *many* man ymorthred for his moneye and his godes
C.13.6	And out of nombre tho men *many* mebles hadden.
C.13.51	Marchauntʒ for here marchaundyse in *many* place to tolle.
C.13.56	Ther þe marchaunt l[et] a male with *many* kyne thynges
C.13.130	And scripture scornede þat *many* skilles shewede,
C.13.162	And ʒut me merueylede more [how] *many* [other] briddes
C.13.174	*Mony* selcouthes y seyh aren nat to segge nouthe
C.13.176	And how out of greeut and of gras gr[e]we so *many* hewes
C.13.181	Saue man and mankynde; *mony* tymes me thouhte
C.13.188	In mete out of mesure and *mony* tymes in drynke,
C.14.17	Ac catel and kynde wit acombreth fol *monye*;
C.14.73	Of cloudes and of costumes they contreuede *mony* thynges
C.14.189	Thus porfirie and plato and poetes *monye*
C.15.3	In manere of [a] mendenaunt *mony* ʒer aftur.
C.15.4	And *many* tym[e] of this meteles moche thouhte y hadde:
C.15.43	And serued hem thus sone of sondry metes *monye*,
C.15.49	In a morter, post mortem, of *many* bittere peynes
C.15.66	And ete *manye* sondry metes, mortreues and poddynges,
C.15.180	Lettrure and longe studie letteth fol *monye*
C.15.267	That *manye* wynter men lyueden and no mete ne tylede.
C.15.301	*Many* man hath his ioye here for al here wel dedes
C.16.135	Hit defendeth þe flesche fram folies ful *monye*,

C.16.167   'Y am cristes creature,' quod he, 'and cristene in *mony* a place
C.16.203   'For bisshopes yblessed bereth *many* names,
C.16.232   Mouen motyues, *mony* tymes insolibles and falaes,
C.16.269   Riht so *many* prestes, prechours and prelates,
C.16.288   Ich haue yleued in londone *monye* longe ʒeres
C.17.12   Bothe Antony and arseny and oþer fol *monye*.
C.17.26   That lyueden thus for oure lordes loue *monye* longe ʒeres
C.17.79   Ac þe metal þat is mannes soule of [*many* of] this techares
C.17.156   Ac *many* manere men þer ben, as sarresynes and iewes,
C.17.188   So *manye* prelates to preche as þe pope maketh,
C.17.263   *Mony* myracles a wrouhte men for to torne,
C.17.270   *Mony* [a] seynte sethe soffrede deth also,
C.17.273   And fro mysbileue *mony* men turnede.
C.17.281   *Many* man for cristes loue was martired amonges Romaynes
C.18.33   And forfret þat fruyt thorw *many* fayre s[ih]tus.
C.18.38   And *manye* wikkede werkes, wormes of synne,
C.18.61   Me may se on an appul tree *monye* tyme and ofte
C.18.173   Thow shalt be myrrour to *monye* men to disceue.
C.18.196   'This is myrke thyng for me,' quod y, 'and for *many* anoþer,
C.18.258   Mercy for oure mysdedes as *many* tymes
C.18.266   And conforted *many* a carfol þere þat aftur his comyng loke[n].
C.19.22   Of men and of wommen *meny* score thousand.'
C.19.62   How he with Moyses maundement hadde *mony* men yholpe
C.19.162   In *many* kyne manere y myhte mysulfe helpe,
C.19.231   For *mony* of ʒow riche men, by my soule y lye nat,
C.20.83   Maugre his *mony* teth he was mad þat tyme
C.20.180   That *many* day myhte y nat se for merkenesse of synne,
C.20.182   Moises and *many* moo Mer[y] shal synge;
C.20.436   To be merciable to *monye* of my haluebretherne.
C.20.450   *Many* hundret of Angels harpeden and songen,
C.21.99   As hit bicometh a conquerour to conne *mony* sleythes
C.21.100   And *many* wyles and wyt þat wol be a ledare.
C.21.211   [Thanne] sang [y] þat song; so dede *many* hundret
C.21.409   'Thenne is *many* [a lyf] ylost,' quod a lewed vicory.
C.22.26   He shal do more þe[n] mesure *mony* tymes and often
C.22.31   And spiritus Prudencie in *many* a poynt shal faile
C.22.42   So he was nedy, as saith the boek in *mony* sondry places,
C.22.97   Kynde cam aftur with *many* k[e]ne sores,
C.22.99   So kynde thorw corupcions kulde fol *mony*.
C.22.104   *Many* a louly lady and here lemmanes knyhtes
C.22.117   He baer a bowe in his hoend and *many* brode arwes,
C.22.118   Weren fythered with fayre biheste and *many* a fals treuthe,
C.22.132   And baldeliche baer adoun with *many* a brihte noble
C.22.225   And shoten aʒeyn[e with] shotte *many* a shef of othes
C.22.302   And wounded wel wykkedly *many* a wys techare
C.22.317   For here is *many* [a] man hert thorw ypocrisye.'
C.22.334   'He is syke,' saide Pees, 'and so ar *many* other.
C.22.377   'He lyeth adreint [and dremeth],' saide pees, 'and so doth *mony*
           oþere.

mankynde n *mankinde n.* B 14 mankynde (13) mankyndes (1); C 20
B. 5.485   And bicam man of a maide *mankynde* to saue,
B.10.242   And on þe sooþfast sone þat saued *mankynde*
B.14.259   And in þat secte oure saueour saued al *mankynde*.
B.16.162   That on þe friday folwynge for *mankyndes* sake
B.16.209   And þus is *mankynde* and manhede of matrimoyne yspronge
B.17.110   On my Capul þat highte caro--of *mankynde* I took it--
B.17.151   Seinte Marie, a mayde, and *mankynde* lauʒte;
B.18.183   That mercy, my suster, and I *mankynde* sholde saue,
B.18.213   Bicam man of a mayde *mankynde* to saue
B.18.269   If þis kyng come In *mankynde* wole he fecche
B.18.397   And mercy al *mankynde* bifore me in heuene.
B.19.72   And cam to take *mankynde* kynges and Aungeles
B.19.322   That crist vpon Caluarie for *mankynde* on pyned.
B.20.41   And cam and took *mankynde* and bicam nedy.
C. 3.404   Thus is man and *mankynde* in maner of a[s] sustantyf,
C. 7.127   And bicam man of a mayde *mankynde* to amende
C.11.142   On þe maide Marie for *mankynde* sake
C.11.143   And bycam man of þat maide withoute *mankynde*;
C.13.181   Saue man and *mankynde*; mony tymes me thouhte
C.13.187   Y se non so ofte forfeten sothly so *mankynde*.
C.16.99   And in þat secte oure saueour saued al *mankynde*.
C.18.134   And bycam man of þat maide *mankynde* to saue,
C.18.214   That he is thre persones departable y preue hit by *mankynde*,
C.18.233   And as thre persones palpable is puy[r]lich bote o *mankynde*,
C.19.101   And lered me for his loue to louye al *mankynde*
C.19.125   Seynte marie, a mayden, and *mankynde* lauhte:
C.20.187   That mercy, my sustur, and y *mankynde* sh[olde] saue
C.20.187   And þat god hath forgyue and graunted to *mankynde*
C.20.222   Bycam man of a mayde *mankynde* to saue
C.20.277   Yf this kyng come in *mankynde* wol he fecche
C.20.440   And mercy a[l] *mankynde* bifore me in heuene.
C.21.72   And cam to take *mankynde* kynges and angeles
C.21.322   That Crist vpon Caluary for *mankynde* on peyned.

C.22.41   And cam and toek *mankynde* and bicam nedy.

manly > manliche

manlich adj *manli adj.* B 1
B. 5.257   'Artow *manlich* among þi neʒebores of þi mete and drynke?'

manliche adv *manli adv.(1)* B 4 manly (1) manliche (3); C 2
B.10.90   Whoso haþ muche spende *manliche*, so [meneþ] Tobye,
B.10.94   And how he myʒte moost meynee *manliche* fynde;
B.10.290   And þanne mowe ye [*manly*] seye, as Dauid made þe Sauter,
B.16.127   And mysseide þe Iewes *manliche* and manaced hem to bete
C. 8.51   Ac [*manliche*] at mete suche men eschewe
C. 9.336   And *manliche* ʒe maistres, mayres and iuges,

mannes -us > man

manoir n *maner n.(1)* A 2 maner; B 3 manere (1) Manoir (1) Manoirs
           (1); C 3 manere (1) maneres (2)
A. 6.73   Þe mot is of mercy þe *Maner* al aboute,
A.10.15   Beþ maistris of þis *maner* þis maide to kepe.
B. 5.243   I haue mo *Manoirs* þoruʒ Rerages þan þoruʒ Miseretur &
           com[m]odat.
B. 5.586   The moot is of mercy þe *Manoir* aboute;
B.10.313   A prikere on a palfrey fro [place] to *Manere*,
C. 5.159   And pryked aboute on palfrayes fram places to *maneres*,
C. 6.26   In alle [*manere*] *maneres* my name to be knowe;
C. 7.233   The mote is of mercy, the *manere* in þe myddes

manschipes n *manshipe n.* C 1
C.12.106   Meles and *manschipes*, vch man oþer.

mansed ptp *mansen v.* B 5 mansed (3) mansede (2); C 2
B. 2.40   And now worþ þis Mede ymaried [t]o a *mansed* sherewe,
B. 4.160   And leten Mekenesse a maister and Mede a *mansed* sherewe.
B.10.284   In alle maner men þoruʒ *mansede* preestes.
B.12.84   And to *mansede* men meschief at hire ende.
B.20.221   'By [þe] Marie!' quod a *mansed* preest, [was] of þe March of
           [Irlonde],
C. 2.43   Tomorwe worth mede ymaried to a *mansed* wrecche,
C.22.221   'By þe Marie!' quod a *mansed* prest, was of þe march of Ireland,

mansion n *mansion n.(1)* B 1; C 1
B.14.217   [Or] in þe maister [or] in þe man som *mansion* he haueþ.
C.16.58   Or in þe maystre or in þe man som *mansion* he haueth.

manslauht n *manslaught n.* C 2 manslaght (1) manslauht (1)
C. 4.182   Withouten mercement or *manslauht* amende alle reumes.'
C.17.241   Naught thorw *manslaght* and mannes strenghe Macometh hadde þe
           maistrie

mantel n *mantel n.* B 2; C 2
B.13.229   Ouþer *mantel* or moneie amonges lordes Mynstrals.
B.20.138   For a [Meneuer *Mantel* he] made lele matrymoyne
C.15.203   Or *mantel* or mone amonges lordes munstrals.
C.22.138   For a meneuer *man[t]el* he made leele matrimonye

marbil n *marbel n.* A 1
A.10.104   Þat selde m[os]seþ þe *marbil* þat men ofte [t]reden,

marc n prop *n.i.d.* B 5 marc (4) mark (1); C 3 marc (1) mark (2)
B. 5.408   Than al þat euere *Marc* made, Mathew, Iohan and Lucas.
B. 5.499   And al þat *Marc* haþ ymaad, Mathew, Iohan and Lucas.
B.10.281   But in swich manere as *Marc* meneþ in þe gospel:
B.15.490   Boþe Mathew and *Marc* and Memento domine dauid:
B.19.264   And *Mark*, and Mathew þe þridde, myghty beestes boþe;
C. 7.24   Th[en] al þat euere *Mark* made, Matheu, Iohn or lucas.
C. 7.139   And al þat *mark* hath ymade, Matheu, Ion and lucas
C.21.264   And *Marc* and Mathewe the thridde, myhty bestes bothe;

marc n *marke n.(2)* A 1 mark; B 1; C 1
A. 5.31   Þat hire hed was worþ a *mark* & his hod not worþ a grote.
B. 5.31   [That] hire heed was worþ [a] *marc* & his hood noʒt a grote.
C. 5.133   [That] here hed was worth half *marc* and his hoed nat a grote.

marc &> mark; marcat > market

march n *marche n.(2)* A 1 marchis; B 3 March (1) marche (1) Marches
           (1); C 2 march (1) marches (1)
A.10.11   And haþ don hire to sire dowel, duk of þise *marchis*.
B. 9.11   And [haþ] doo[n] hire wiþ sire dowel, duc of þise *Marches*.
B.15.446   And þoruʒ miracles, as men mow rede, al þat *marche* he tornede
B.20.221   'By [þe] Marie!' quod a mansed preest, [was] of þe *March* of
           [Irlonde],
C.10.138   And hath do here with sire dowel, duk of this *marches*.
C.22.221   'By þe Marie!' quod a mansed prest, was of þe *march* of Ireland,

marchal n *marshal n.* A 1; B 1; C 2 marchel (1) Marschal (1)
A. 3.188   Hadde I be *march[al]* of his men, be marie of heuene,
B. 3.201   Hadde I ben *Marchal* of his men, by Marie of heuene!

C. 3.257　'Ne be *Marschal* ouer my men there y moste fyhte.
C. 3.258　Ac hadde y, mede, ben *marchel* o[f] his men in Fraunce

marchandise > *marchaundise*; *marchant* > *marchaunt*

marchaunden v *marchaunden v.* B 1; C 1 marchaunde
B.13.393　To *marchaunden* wiþ [my] moneie and maken [here] eschaunges,
C. 6.280　To *marchaunde* with my moneye and maken here eschaunges,

marchaundise n *marchaundise n.* A 4 marchaundie (1) marchaundise (3);
　　B 6 marchaundise (4) marchaundiȝe (2); C 9 marchandise (4)
　　marchaundise (2) marchaundyse (2) marchauntdyse (1)
A.Pr.60　For here mony & here *marchaundise* meten togidere.
A. 3.213　Mede & *marchaundise* mote nede go togidere;
A. 3.236　In *marchaundie* is no mede, I may it wel auowe;
A. 5.120　Wiþ many maner *marchaundise* as my maister me hiȝte.
B.Pr.63　For hire moneie and hire *marchaundise* marchen togideres.
B. 3.226　[Mede and *Marchaundiȝe*] mote nede go togideres;
B. 3.257　In *marchaundise* is no Mede, I may it wel auowe;
B. 5.204　Wiþ many manere *marchaundise* as my maister me hiȝte.
B. 5.284　Forþi haue mercy in þy mynde, and *marchaundise* leue it,
B.13.361　And menged his *marchaundise* and made a good moustre:
C.Pr.61　Here moneye and [here] *marchandise* ma[rch]en togyderes.
C. 3.110　What maner muster oþer *marchandise* he vsed
C. 3.281　*Marchaundise* and mede mot nede [go] togederes.
C. 3.313　In *Marchandise* is no mede, y may hit wel avowe;
C. 6.212　With many manere *marchandise* as my maistre hyhte;
C. 6.260　Meddeled my *marchaundyse* and made a good mostre.
C. 6.340　'And haue his mercy in thy mynde, and *marchaundise*, leue hit,
C.13.51　*Marchauntȝ* for here *marchaundyse* in many place to tolle.
C.13.53　The marchaunt with his *marchauntdyse* may nat go so swythe

marchaunt n *marchaunt n.* A 4 marchaunt (1) marchauntis (3); B 5
　　marchaunt (2) marchauntȝ (3); C 17 marchant (1) marchaunt (9)
　　marchauntes (5) marchauntȝ (2)
A. 2.174　Ac *marchauntis* mette wiþ hym & made him abide.
A. 4.115　But it be *marchaunt*, oþer his man, oþer messang[er] with lettres,
A. 8.20　*Marchauntis* in þe margyn hadde manye ȝeris,
A. 8.42　Þanne were *marchauntis* merye; many wepe for ioye,
B. 2.215　Ac *Marchauntȝ* metten with hym and made hym abyde
B. 4.132　But it be *Marchaunt* or his man or Messager wiþ lettres,
B. 7.18　*Marchauntȝ* in þe margyne hadde manye yeres,
B. 7.38　Thanne were *Marchauntȝ* murie; manye wepten for ioye
B.19.349　Ne no manere *marchaunt* þat wiþ moneye deleþ
C. 2.225　A[c] *marchauntes* mette with hym and made hym abyde
C. 4.129　But [it] be *marchaunt* or his man or messager [with] lettres,
C. 4.193　More then alle thy *marchauntes* or thy mytrede Bysshopes
C. 6.96　Amongus *marchauntes* many tymes and nameliche in londone.
C. 9.22　*Marchauntes* in þe margine hadde many ȝeres
C. 9.41　Tho were *Marchauntes* mury; many wopen for ioye
C.13.33　For yf a *marchant* and [a] mesager metten togyderes
C.13.37　The *marchaunt* mote nede be ylet lenger then the messager
C.13.46　Ac if þe *marchaunt* make his way ouer menne corne
C.13.49　The *marchaunt* mote forgo or moneye of his porse
C.13.51　*Marchauntȝ* for here marchaundyse in many place to tolle.
C.13.53　The *marchaunt* with his marchauntdyse may nat go so swythe
C.13.56　Ther þe *marchaunt* l[et] a male with many kyne thynges
C.13.61　Ac ȝut myhte þe *marchaunt* thorw moneye and other ȝeftes
C.13.66　The *marchaunt* is no more to mene but men þat ben ryche
C.17.46　And *marchauntȝ* merciable wolde be and men of lawe bothe
C.21.349　Ne no manere *Marchaunt* þat with moneye deleth

marchauntdyse > *marchaundise*; *marchel* > *marchal*

marchen v *marchen v.(2)* B 1; C 1
B.Pr.63　For hire moneie and hire marchaundiȝe *marchen* togideres.
C.Pr.61　Here moneye and [here] marchandise *ma[rch]en* togyderes.

mare n *mere n.(1)* &> *moore* A 1; B 1; C 1
A. 7.271　And ek a cow & a calf, & a carte *mare*
B. 6.287　And ek a cow and a calf, and a cart *mare*
C. 8.310　And a cow with a calf and a cart *m[a]re*

mareys n *mareis n.sg.& pl.* B 1; C 1
B.11.354　In *Mareys* and moores [manye] hidden hir egges]
C.13.167　In *mareys* and in mores, in myres and in watres,

margarete margerete > *margrete*

margery n *margerie n.* A 1 margerie; B 1; C 1 Margerie
A.11.9　And seide, 'Nolite mittere, Man, *margerie* perlis
B.10.9　And seide, 'noli[te] mittere, man, *margery* perles
C.11.7　And sayde, 'nolite mittere, ȝe men, *Margerie* perles

margyne n *margine n.* A 1 margyn; B 1; C 1 margine
A. 8.20　Marchauntis in þe *margyn* hadde manye ȝeris,
B. 7.18　Marchauntȝ in þe *margyne* hadde manye yeres,
C. 9.22　Marchauntes in þe *margine* hadde many ȝeres

margrete n prop *OED Margaret* A 1 margerete; B 1; C 1 margarete
A. 4.37　And *margerete* of hire maydenhed maugre hire chekis.
B. 4.50　And *Margrete* of hir maydenhede maugree hire chekes.
C. 4.48　And *margarete* of here maydenhod as he mette here late.

mary > *marie*

mariage n *mariage n.* A 5; B 1 mariages; C 2 mariage (1) mariages (1)
A. 2.22　Tomorewe worþ þe *mariage* mad of mede & of fals;
A. 2.26　Tomorewe worþ þe *mariage* ymad as I þe telle.
A. 2.37　And feffe mede þer[myd] in *mariage* for euere.
A. 2.47　In what maner þat mede in *mariage* was feffid;
A.10.207　Þat iche man haue a make in [*mariage*] of wedlak
B. 9.158　Forþi haue maugre of hir *mariages* þat marie so hir children.
C.10.246　Was for *mariages* ma[ugre kynd]e þat men made þat tyme.
C.16.110　More for coueytise of catel then kynde loue of þe *mariage*.

marie n prop *Marie n.* &> *marien* A 7; B 21 Marie (20) Maries (1); C
　　23 mary (2) marie (18) marye (3)
A. 2.2　And seide, 'mercy madame, for *marie* loue of heuene
A. 3.188　Hadde I be march[al] of his men, be *marie* of heuene,
A. 4.151　'And I assente,' quaþ þe king, 'be seinte *marie* my lady,
A. 8.180　And *marie* his modir to be mene betwene,
A. 9.14　'*Marie*,' quaþ þe maistris, 'among vs he dwelliþ,
A.11.287　Þanne *marie* þe maudeleyn who miȝte do wers?
A.12.116　*Marie* moder and may, for man þou byseke
B. 2.2　And seide 'mercy, madame, for *Marie* loue of heuene
B. 3.201　Hadde I ben Marchal of his men, by *Marie* of heuene!
B. 4.179　Mede shal noȝt maynprise yow, by þe *marie* of heuene!
B. 4.188　'And I assente', seiþ þe kyng, 'by Seinte *Marie* my lady,
B. 5.497　A synful *Marie* þe seiȝ er seynte Marie þi dame,
B. 5.497　A synful Marie þe seiȝ er seynte *Marie* þi dame,
B. 7.202　And *Marie* his moder be meene bitwene,
B. 8.18　'[*Marie*]', quod þe [maistres, 'amonges vs he dwelleþ,
B.10.428　Than *Marie* Maudeleyne [who myȝte do] werse?
B.11.28　'Man', quod he, 'if I mete wiþ þe, by *Marie* of heuene!
B.11.250　Martha on *Marie* Maudeleyne an huge pleynt made
B.11.253　Boþe Marthaes and *Maries*, as Mathew bereþ witnesse.
B.13.194　Hadde noȝt [*Marie*] Maudeleyne moore for a box of salue
B.15.294　And also *Marie* Maudeleyne by mores lyuede and dewes,
B.16.91　To a maide þat hiȝte *Marie*, a meke þyng wiþalle,
B.17.151　Seinte *Marie*, a mayde, and mankynde lauȝte,
B.18.128　A maiden þat highte *Marie*, and moder wiþouten felyng
B.19.119　For bifore his moder *Marie* made he þat wonder
B.19.148　And his moder *Marie*; þus men bifore de[uyn]ede.
B.19.157　Ac *Marie* Maudeleyne mette hym by þe weye
B.20.221　'By [þe] *Marie*!' quod a mansed preest, [was] of þe March of
　　　　　　[Irlonde]
C. 2.2　And sayde 'mercy, madame, for *mary* loue of heuene
C. 3.143　[And marre þe with myschef], be seynte *mary* my lady,
C. 3.209　Han almest mad, but *marye* the helpe,
C. 4.139　Ne thorw mede mercy, by *marie* of heuene!
C. 4.173　Mede shal nat maynprise [ȝow], by *marye* of heuene!
C. 7.137　A synful *marie* þe sey ar seynte marye þy dame
C. 7.137　A synful marie þe sey ar seynte *marye* þy dame
C. 7.148　And for [that] muchel mercy and *marie* loue thi moder
C. 9.348　And *marie* his moder be oure mene to hym
C.11.142　On þe maide *Marie* for mankynde sake
C.11.187　'Man,' quod [he], 'yf y me[t]e with the, by *marie* of heuene,
C.11.261　Then *marie* maudelene who myhte do worse?
C.12.134　And seynt *marie* his moder, as Mathew bereth witnesse,
C.12.136　Marthe on *marie* maudelene an huge pleynte made
C.17.21　*Marie* Maudeleyne by mores lyuede and dewes;
C.17.23　*Marie* Egipciaca eet in thritty wynter
C.18.124　To a mayde þat hihte *marie*, a meke thyng withalle,
C.19.125　Seynte *marie*, a mayden, and mankynde lauhte:
C.20.131　A mayde þat hoteth *Marie*, a[nd] moder withouten velynge
C.21.119　For bifore his moder *Marie* made he þat wonder
C.21.148　And his moder *marie*; thus men bifore deuyned.
C.21.157　Ac *Marie* Maudeleyne mette hym by þe weye
C.22.221　'By þe *Marie*!' quod a mansed prest, was of þe march of Ireland,

marien v *marien v.* A 5 marie (1) maried (3) mariede (1); B 11 marie (2)
　　marye (1) maryed (1) marien (2) ymaried (3); C 7 marie
　　(1) maried (4) ymaried (2)
A. 8.31　*Marie* maidenis also [or] maken hem nonnes,
A.10.113　Ȝif þou be man *maried*, monk, oþer chanoun,
A.10.154　For þei *mariede* hem wiþ curside men of caymes kyn.
A.10.181　And [were] *marie[d]* at meschief as men do now here children.
A.10.183　For coueitise of catel vnkyndely be *maried*.
B. 2.31　And haþ yeuen me mercy to *marie* wiþ myselue,
B. 2.40　And now worþ þis Mede *ymaried* [t]o a mansed sherewe,
B. 2.53　And how Mede was *ymaried* in Metels me þouȝte;
B. 2.57　To *marien* þis mayde [was] many m[a]n assembled,
B. 2.76　That Mede is *ymaried* moore for hire goodes

B. 7.29   *Marien* maydenes or maken hem Nonnes,
B. 9.158   Forþi haue þei maugre of hir mariages þat *marie* so hir children.
B. 9.160   For coueitise of catel vnkyndely ben [*maried*].
B.12.33   That is, if þow be man *maryed* þi make þow louye
B.12.38   And if þow be maiden to *marye* and myȝt wel continue,
B.14.268   [Moore] þan [a maiden is] þat is *maried* þoruȝ brocage
C. 2.43   Tomorwe worth mede *ymaried* to a mansed wrecche,
C. 2.48   That mede is thus *ymaried*; tomorwe þou shalt aspye.
C. 2.56   And y say how mede was *maried*, metyng as it were.
C. 2.83   That mede is *maried* more for here richesse
C. 2.173   To be *maried* for mone med[e] hath assented.'
C.10.280   Bote maydones and maydones *marie* ȝow togyderes:
C.16.108   More then þat mayde is þat is *maried* by brocage,

mark n *marke n.(1) &> marc n,marc n prop* A 1; B 4 marc (1) mark (2)
    merk (1); C 2 marke
A.10.32   Ac man is hym most lik of *mark* & of shap.
B. 9.31   Ac man is hym moost lik of *marc* and of [shape].
B.15.350   The *merk* of þat monee is good ac þe metal is feble;
B.15.352   Crowne and cristendom, þe kynges *mark* of heuene,
B.17.106   And [may] ech man see and good *mark* take
C. 3.382   Bytwene two lo[n]des for a trewe *marke*.
C.17.78   Cristendoem of holy kyrke, the kynges *marke* of heuene,

markeden v *marken v.(1)* A 1 markid; B 2 marked (1) markeden (1); C 2
    marked (1) markede (1)
A.11.261   I was *markid* wiþoute mercy, & myn name entrid
B.12.130   [Dyuyneris] toforn vs [viseden and *markeden*]
B.12.186   Wo was hym *marked* þat wade moot wiþ þe lewed!
C.14.74   And *markede* hit in here manere and mused þeron to knowe.
C.14.125   Muchel wo was hym *marked* þat wade shal with þe lewede!

market n *market n.(1)* A 1; B 3 Market (2) Markettes (1); C 1 marcat
A. 5.81   Whanne I mette hym in *market* þat I most hatide
B.Pr.221   Taillours, Tynkers and Tollers in *Markettes*,
B. 5.101   Whan I met[t]e hym in *Market* þat I moost hate[de]
B.17.75   Wel sixe Mile or seuene biside þe newe *Market*;
C.19.74   Is syxe myle or seuene bisyde þe newe *marcat*,

markid > markeden

marl n *marle n.* C 1
C.12.231   Lo! lond ouerleyd with *marl* and with donge,

marre v *merren v.* C 1
C. 3.143   [And *marre* þe with myschef], be seynte mary my lady,

marschal > marchal

martha n prop *OED Martha* B 2 Martha (1) Marthaes (1); C 1 Marthe
B.11.250   *Martha* on Marie Maudeleyne an huge pleynt made
B.11.253   Boþe *Marthaes* and Maries, as Mathew bereþ witnesse.
C.12.136   *Marthe* on marie maudelene an huge pleynte made

martir n *martir n.* B 2 martires; C 4 martir (1) martires (1) martres (2)
B. 9.114   Maidenes and *martires* out of o man come.
B.12.204   Ne wiþ maydenes ne with *martires* [ne wiþ mylde] wydewes,
C.10.205   For of here kynde þey come, bothe confessours and *martres*,
C.12.196   And for here pacience be ypressed as for puyr *martir*
C.14.143   Ne with maydenes ne with *martires* ne with mylde weddewes,
C.18.96   Maydones and *martres* ministrede [hym] here on erthe

martre v *martiren v.* B 3 martired (2) ymartired (1); C 2 martre (1)
    martired (1)
B.15.265   Ne han *martired* Peter ne Poul, ne in prison holden.
B.15.523   In sauacion of [mannes soule] seint [Thomas] was *ymartired*;
B.15.531   Many man for cristes loue was *martired* [amonges] Romayne[s]
C.17.281   Many man for cristes loue was *martired* amonges Romaynes
C.20.334   Lette hem þat louede hym nat laste they wolde hym *martre*.

martres > martir; mas > massepens; masager > messager; mase > maȝe

mason n *masoun n.* A 2 masonis (1) masons (1); B 3 Mason (1) Masons
    (2); C 1
A.Pr.101   *Masonis*, mynours, & manye oþere craftis,
A.11.135   Of carpenteris & kerueris; [I] kende ferst *masons*,
B.Pr.222   *Masons*, Mynours and many oþere craftes;
B.10.183   Of Carpent[ers and] kerueres; [I kenned first] *Masons*
B.11.350   If any *Mason* made a molde þerto muche wonder it were.
C.13.161   Yf eny *mason* made a molde þerto moche wonder me thynketh.

masse n *messe n.(1)* A 5 masse (4) massis (1); B 18 masse (13) masses
    (4) messe (1); C 22 masse (18) masses (4)
A. 1.157   Ȝe ne haue no more meryt in [*masse*] ne in [houres]
A. 3.232   þat take mede & money for *massis* þat þei synge,
A. 5.2   To here matynes & *masse*, and to þe mete aftir.
A. 5.150   'To holy chirche', quaþ he, 'for to here *masse*,
A. 5.224   And here *masse* & matynes as I a monk were;

B.Pr.97   Hire *messe* & hire matyns and many of hire houres
B. 1.183   Ye ne haue na moore merite in *masse* n[e] in houres
B. 3.253   That taken Mede and moneie for *masses* þat þei syngeþ,
B. 5.2   To here matyns [and *masse* and to þe mete] after.
B. 5.300   'To holy chirche', quod he, 'for to here *masse*,
B. 5.411   Til matyns and *masse* be do, and þanne [moste] to þe freres;
B. 5.452   And here matyns and *masse* as I a monk were;
B.11.151   And I saued as ye [may] see, wiþouten syngynge of *masses*,
B.11.284   For *masses* ne for matyns, noȝt hir mete of vsureres,
B.11.291   Thanne nedeþ yow noȝt to [nyme] siluer for *masses* þat ye syngen,
B.11.308   Or in *masse* or in matyns makeþ any defaute:
B.11.314   Synge ne psalmes rede ne seye a *masse* of þe day.
B.13.258   Ne mannes *masse* make pees among cristene peple
B.13.383   [I]n haly daies at holy chirche whan ich herde *masse*
B.13.395   Neiþer *masse* ne matynes, ne none maner siȝtes;
B.19.3   To here holly þe *masse* and to be houseled after.
B.19.4   In myddes of þe *masse* þo men yede to offryng
B.20.366   And make [of] yow [memoria] in *masse* and in matyns
C.Pr.125   Ȝoure *masse* and [ȝoure] matynes and many of [ȝoure] oures
C. 1.179   Ȝe n[e] haueth na more meryte in *masse* ne in oures
C. 3.53   In *masse* and in matayne for mede we shal synge
C. 3.311   The mede þat many prest[es] taken for *masses* þat thei syngen,
C. 5.63   Somme to synge *masses* or sitten and wryten,
C. 6.272   In halydayes at holy churche when y herde *masse*
C. 6.282   Nother matynes ne *masse* ne no maner syhtus;
C. 6.355   'To holy churche,' quod he, 'for to here *masse*
C. 7.27   Til matynes and *masse* be ydo; thenne haue y a memorie at þe
                freres.
C. 7.66   And here mateynes and *masse* as y a monke were;
C. 8.103   He is holdyng, y hope, to haue me in his *masse*
C. 9.229   Bothe matynes and *masse*; and aftir mete in churches
C. 9.244   As matynes by þe morwe til *masse* bygynne,
C.12.86   And y saued, as ȝe may se, withoute syngynge of *masses*.
C.13.105   And nedeth [ȝow] nat to nyme siluer for *masses* þat ȝe synge
C.13.115   Euele beth thei ysoffred, suche þat [shenden] þe *masse*
C.13.122   Or in *masse* or in matynes maketh eny defaute:
C.13.126   Syng ne [psalmes] rede [ne sey a *masse* of þe daye].
C.17.117   Lord lete þat this prestes lelly seien here *masse*,
C.21.3   To here holly þe *masse* and to [be] hoseled aftur.
C.21.4   In myddes of þe *masse* tho men ȝede to offrynge
C.22.366   And make [of] ȝow [memoria] in *masse* and in matynes

massepens n *messe n.(1)* A 1 messe_penis; B 1; C 1 mas_pans
A. 3.211   Asken mede & *messe penis* & here mete alse;
B. 3.224   Asken Mede and *massepens* and hire mete [als];
C. 3.279   Asken mede and *mas pans* and here mete bothe;

mat adj *mat adj.* A 1; B 1
A. 5.106   And þat makiþ me so *ma[t]* for I ne may me venge.'
B. 5.129   And þat makeþ me [so *mat*], for I ne may me venge.

mataynes mateynes > matyns

matere n *matere n.* A 2 mater; B 10 matere (9) materes (1); C 8 mater
    (1) matere (7)
A. 5.21   Of þis *mater* I miȝte mamele wel longe,
A. 9.113   I durste meue no *mater* to make hym to iangle,
B. 5.21   Of þis *matere* I myȝte mamelen [wel] longe,
B. 8.123   I dorste meue no *matere* to maken hym to Iangle,
B. 9.74   Of þis *matere* I myȝte make a long tale
B.11.108   Ac þe *matere* þat she meued, if lewed men it knewe,
B.11.160   [This *matere* is merk for many, ac men of holy chirche,
B.11.232   Why I meue þis *matere* is moost for þe pouere;
B.11.402   For man was maad of swich a *matere* he may noȝt wel asterte
B.15.58   And þe moore þat a man of good *matere* hereþ,
B.15.71   Ye moeuen *materes* vnmesurable to tellen of þe Trinite
B.15.89   Of þis *matere* I myȝte make a long bible,
C. 1.123   Ac of þis *matere* no more [meu]en y nelle.
C. 5.110   Of þe *matere* þat me mette furste on Maluerne hulles.
C. 5.123   Of this *mater* y myhte mamele [wel] longe
C.10.119   Y durste meue no *matere* to maken hym to iangle,
C.12.42   Ac þe *matere* þat she meuede, if lewede men hit knewe,
C.13.210   Man was maad of such [a] *matere* he may nat wel asterte
C.15.24   And so y musede vppon þis *matere* þat me lust to slepe.
C.19.48   And as we wenten in þe way thus wordyng of this *matere*

mathew n prop *n.i.d.* A 3 matheu (2) mattheu (1); B 10; C 7 Matheu (4)
    Mathew (2) Mathewe (1)
A. 3.233   Shal haue mede on þis molde þat *mattheu* haþ grauntid:
A. 7.212   Make þe Frendis þermi[d] for so *matheu* vs techiþ:
A. 7.222   *Matheu* wiþ þe manis face [mouþ]iþ þise wordis:
B. 3.254   [Shul haue] Mede [on þis molde þat] *Mathew* [haþ graunted]:
B. 5.408   Than al þat euere Marc made, *Mathew*, Iohan and Lucas.
B. 5.499   And al þat Marc haþ ymaad, *Mathew*, Iohan and Lucas
B. 6.238   *Mathew* wiþ mannes face mouþe[þ] þise wordes:

B. 7.60   Ye legistres and lawieres, [if I lye witeþ *Mathew*]:
B.11.253   Boþe Marthaes and Maries, as *Mathew* bereþ witnesse.
B.14.144   It may noȝt be, ye riche men, or *Mathew* on god lyeþ:
B.15.462   Ye mynnen wel how *Mathew* seiþ, how a man made a feste.
B.15.490   Boþe *Mathew* and Marc and Memento domine dauid:
B.19.264   And Mark, and *Mathew* þe þridde, myghty beestes boþe;
C. 3.312   Amen Amen, *Matheu* seyth, Mercedem suam rec[e]p[er]unt.
C. 7.24   Th[en] al þat euere Mark made, *Matheu*, Iohn or lucas.
C. 7.139   And al þat mark hath ymade, *Matheu*, Ion and lucas
C. 8.246   *Mathew* maketh mencioun of a man þat lente
C. 9.124   Suche manere men, *Matheu* vs techeth,
C.12.134   And seynt marie his moder, as *Mathew* bereth witnesse,
C.21.264   And Marc and *Mathewe* the thridde, myhty bestes bothe;

matyns n *matin n.* A 2 matynes; B 8 matynes (1) matyns (7); C 9
    mataynetwork (1) mateynes (1) matynes (7)

A. 5.2   To here *matynes* & masse, and to þe mete aftir.
A. 5.224   And here masse & *matynes* as I a monk were;
B.Pr.97   Hire messe & hire *matyns* and many of hire houres
B. 5.2   To here *matyns* [and masse and to þe mete] after.
B. 5.411   Til *matyns* and masse be do, and þanne [moste] to þe freres;
B. 5.452   And here *matyns* and masse as I a monk were;
B.11.284   For masses ne for *matyns*, noȝt hir mete of vsureres,
B.11.308   Or in masse or in *matyns* makeþ any defaute:
B.13.395   Neiþer masse ne *matynes*, ne none maner siȝtes;
B.20.366   And make [of] yow [memoria] in masse and in *matyns*
C.Pr.125   ȝoure masse and [ȝoure] *matynes* and many of [ȝoure] oures
C. 3.53   In masse and in *matayines* for mede we shal synge
C. 6.282   Nother *matynes* ne masse ne no maner syhtus;
C. 7.27   Til *matynes* and masse be ydo; thenne haue y a memorie at þe
                freres.
C. 7.66   And here *mateynes* and masse as y a monke were;
C. 9.229   Bothe *matynes* and masse; and aftir mete in churches
C. 9.244   As *matynes* by þe morwe til masse bygynne,
C.13.122   Or in masse or in *matynes* maketh any defaute:
C.22.366   And make [of] ȝow [memoria] in masse and in *matynes*

matrimoyne n *matrimoine n.* B 7 matrimoyne (6) matrymoyne (1); C 8
    matrimonie (1) matrimonye (6) matrymonye (1)

B.15.241   And *matrimoyne* for moneie maken and vnmaken,
B.16.68   *Matrimoyne* I may nyme, a moiste fruyt wiþalle.
B.16.77   And whan [he] meued *matrimoyne* it made a foul noise.
B.16.209   And þus is mankynde and manhede of *matrimoyne* ysprongge
B.16.211   Migh[t] is [in] *matrimoyne* þat multiplieþ þe erþe
B.16.219   Ne *matrimoyne* withouten Mul[eri]e is noȝt muche to preise:
B.20.138   For a [Meneuer Mantel he] made lele *matrymoyne*
C. 2.152   Where *matrymonye* may be of mede and of falshede.
C.10.210   Out of *matrimonye*, nat moyloure, mowen nat haue þe grace
C.10.253   Þat y man made or *matrimonye* soffrede
C.18.85   *Matrimonye*, a moist fruyt þat multiplieth þe peple;
C.18.109   A meued *matrimonye*; hit made a fo[u]le noyse.
C.18.220   *Matrimonye* withoute moylere is nauht moche to preyse
C.18.236   In *matrimonie* aren thre and of o man cam alle thre
C.22.138   For a meneuer man[t]el he made leele *matrimonye*

mattheu > *mathew*

maudeleyne n prop *Maudelaine n.* A 1 maudeleyn; B 5; C 4 Maudeleyne
    (2) maudelene (2)

A.11.287   Þanne marie þe *maudeleyn* who miȝte do wers?
B.10.428   Than Marie *Maudeleyne* [who myȝte do] werse?
B.11.250   Martha on Marie *Maudeleyne* an huge pleynt made
B.13.194   Hadde noȝt [Marie] *Maudeleyne* moore for a box of salue
B.15.294   And also Marie *Maudeleyne* by mores lyuede and dewes,
B.19.157   Ac Marie *Maudeleyne* mette hym by þe weye
C.11.261   Then marie *maudelene* who myhte do worse?
C.12.136   Marthe on marie *maudelene* an huge pleynte made
C.17.21   Marie *Maudeleyne* by mores lyuede and dewes;
C.21.157   Ac Marie *Maudeleyne* mette hym by þe weye

maugree n *maugre n.* A 1 maugre; B 2 maugre (1) maugree (1)

A. 7.224   He hadde *maugre* of his maister eueremore aftir,
B. 6.240   He hadde *maugre* of his maister eueremoore after,
B. 9.158   Forþi haue þei *maugre* of hir mariages þat marie so hir children.

maugree prep *maugre prep.* A 3 maugre; B 8; C 6 maugre (3) maugrey
    (2) maugreye (1)

A. 2.164   And bringeþ mede to me *maugre* hem alle.
A. 4.37   And margerete of hire maydenhed *maugre* hire chekis.
A. 7.145   And make vs merye þerwiþ *maugre* þi chekis'.
B. 2.203   /And bryngeþ Mede to me *maugree* hem alle.
B. 4.50   And Margrete of hir maydenhede *maugree* hire chekes.
B. 6.40   And mekenesse þi maister *maugree* Medes chekes;
B. 6.67   And make h[y]m murie þermyd, *maugree* whoso bigruccheþ it.
B. 6.158   And maken vs murye þer[wiþ] *maugree* þi chekes.'
B.14.4   That wollen bymolen it many tyme *maugree* my chekes.

B.18.81   *Maugree* his manye teeþ he was maad þat tyme
B.18.350   Thow fettest myne in my place [*maugree*] alle resoun,
C. 2.217   And bryngeth mede to me *maugrey* hem alle.
C. 8.38   And Mekenesse thy maystre *maugre* mede chekes
C. 8.68   And m[a]ken hym merye þermy[d], *maugrey* ho[so] bigruchen hit;
C. 8.155   And maken vs murye þer[with] *maugreye* h[o] begrucheth.'
C.10.246   Was for mariages *ma[ugre* kynd]e þat men made þat tyme.
C.20.83   *Maugre* his mony teth he was mad þat tyme

maumettes n *maumet n.* C 1

C.Pr.119   That soffreth men do sacrefyce and worschipe *maumettes*

maundement n *maundement n.* B 2; C 2

B.17.2   That took me a *maundement* vpon þe mount of Synay
B.17.63   How he wiþ Moyses *maundement* hadde many men yholpe,
C.19.2   That toek me a *maundement* vpon þe mont of synay
C.19.62   How he with Moyses *maundement* hadde mony men yholpe

maunged > *manged*

mawe n *maue n.* A 4 mawe (3) mawis (1); B 8 mawe (7) mawes (1); C 6

A. 7.159   Hungir in haste þanne hente wastour be þe *mawe*,
A. 7.163   He beet hem so boþe he brast ner here *mawis*.
A. 7.251   And aftir many maner metis his *mawe* is alongid.
A. 7.295   And chaud, & pluys chaud, for chillyng of h[ere] *mawe*.
B. 5.125   Ne neiþer shrifte ne shame, but whoso shrape my *mawe*?'
B. 6.174   Hunger in haste þoo hente wastour by þe [*mawe*]
B. 6.178   He bette hem so boþe he brast ner hire [*mawes*]
B. 6.267   And after many maner metes his *mawe* is [alonged].
B. 6.311   And þat chaud and plus chaud for chillynge of hir *mawe*.
B.13.83   Were molten leed in his *mawe* and Mahoun amyddes.
B.15.57   The man þat muche hony eteþ his *mawe* it engleymeþ,
B.15.64   And riȝt as hony is yuel to defie and engleymeþ þe *mawe*,
C. 6.90   Ne noþer shame ne shryfte but hoso shrap[e] my *mawe*?'
C. 6.433   The vilony of my foule mouthe and of my foule *mawe*:
C. 8.171   Hunger in haste þo hente wastour by þe *mawe*
C. 8.333   And þat chaut and pluchaut for chillyng of h[ere] *mawe*.
C.15.89   Þat in þ[e] *mawe* of þat maystre alle þo metes were,
C.16.219   The man þat moche hony eet his *mawe* hit engleymeth;

maȝe n *mase n.* A 2 mase; B 3; C 2 mase

A. 1.6   How besy þei ben aboute þe *mase*?
A. 3.149   Þe *mase* for a mene man þeiȝ he mote euere.
B.Pr.192   The *maȝe* among vs alle þeiȝ we mysse a sherewe,
B. 1.6   How bisie þei ben aboute þe *maȝe*?
B. 3.160   The *maȝe* for a mene man þouȝ he mote euere!
C. 1.6   Hou bisy þei ben aboute þe *mase*?
C. 3.198   The *mase* for a mene man thow he mote euere!

me pron indef *me pron.(1) &> i, cf. man* C 21

C. 3.407   Ac hoso rat of regum rede *me* may of mede,
C. 3.413   As *me* ret in regum [of þe reuthe] of kynges,
C. 3.478   Ac ar this fortune falle fynde *me* shal the worste
C. 4.121   For alle manere men þat *me* fynt neodefole;
C. 5.54   *Me* sholde constrayne no Cler[k] to no knaues werkes,
C. 7.76   When *me* carpeth of Crist or clannesse of soule
C. 9.128   And alle manere munstrals, *me* woet wel þe sothe,
C. 9.132   And ȝut more to suche men *me* doth ar they passe;
C. 9.133   *Me* [g]yueth hem giftes and gold for grete lordes sake.
C. 9.303   Ac men setteth nat by sowngewarie for *me* seth hit often fayle;
C.11.27   And þat is no riht ne resoun for rather *me* sholde
C.12.113   In þe olde lawe, as þe lettre telleth, mennes sones *me* calde vs
C.13.5   ȝut ret *me* þat abraham and Iob weren wonder ryche
C.16.124   Or a[s] iustice to iuge men, *me* enioyneth þerto no pore,
C.16.132   And *me* leneth lyhtly fewe men and me wene hem pore:
C.16.132   And me leneth lyhtly fewe men and *me* wene hem pore:
C.16.295   For thogh *me* souhte alle þe sektes of susturne and brethurne
C.16.297   And so y trowe truely, by þat *me* telleth of charite.'
C.17.73   *Me* may now likene lettred men to a loscheborw oþer worse
C.17.165   *Me* fynde[th] þat Macometh was a man ycristened
C.18.61   *Me* may se on an appul tree monye tyme and ofte

meble n *moeble n.* B 3 mebles (1) moebles (2); C 9 meble (2) mebles (7)

B. 3.269   *Moebles* and vnmoebles, and al þow myȝt fynde,
B. 9.85   For alle þe *mebles* on þis moolde and he amende it myȝte.
B.17.278   Sleeþ a man for hise *moebles* wiþ mouþ or with handes.
C. 3.422   *Mebles* and vnmebles, man and alle [thynges],
C. 9.271   And of þe moneye thow haddest ther[myd] his *mebles* to [s]aue
C.10.97   For here mok and here *mebles* suche men thenketh
C.10.187   *Meble* ne vnmeble, mete noþer drynke.
C.13.6   And out of nombre tho men many *mebles* hadden.
C.14.181   Riht so men reuerence[th] more þe ryche for h[is] *mebles*
C.15.167   And maistre of alle here *mebles* and of here moneye aftur,
C.16.12   And moche murthe among ryche men is þat han *meble* ynow and
                hele.
C.19.259   Sleth a man for his *mebles* with mouthe or with handes.

mechel > *muche*; *meddeled* > *medle*

mede n *mede n.(4)* A 67 mede (66) medis (1); B 90 Mede (88) Medes (2);
    C 125 mede (124) medes (1)

A. 2.16	'Þat is *mede* þe maide, haþ noiȝede me ful ofte,
A. 2.22	Tomorewe worþ þe mariage mad of *mede* & of fals;
A. 2.37	And feffe *mede* þer[myd] in mariage for euere.
A. 2.47	In what maner þat *mede* in mariage was feffid;
A. 2.58	Þat I, fauel, feffe falsnesse to *mede*,
A. 2.83	For *mede* is molere of [m]endis engendrit
A. 2.84	God grauntide to gyue *mede* to treuþe,
A. 2.87	Worþi is þe werkman his *mede* to haue,
A. 2.96	And *mede* is a mulere, [a maiden of gode];
A. 2.112	For he may *mede* amaistrien and maken at my wille'.
A. 2.117	Til *mede* be þi weddit wyf þoruȝ wyt of vs alle,
A. 2.118	For we haue *mede* amaistried wiþ oure mery speche
A. 2.128	Sette *mede* on a shirreue shod al newe,
A. 2.146	And *mede* in þe myddis, & al þis mene aftir.
A. 2.164	And bringeþ *mede* to me maugre hem alle.
A. 2.196	Saue *mede* þe maiden no mo durste abide.
A. 3.1	Now is *mede* þe maide, & no mo of hem alle,
A. 3.4	To take *mede* þe maide & make hire at ese.
A. 3.10	Tok *mede* be þe myddel & brouȝte hire to chaumbre.
A. 3.11	Ac þere was merþe & mynstralcie *mede* to plese;
A. 3.16	And seide, 'mourne nouȝt, *mede*, ne make þou no sorewe,
A. 3.19	Mildeliche *mede* þanne merciede hem alle
A. 3.24	Þanne lauȝte hy leue, þise lordis at *mede*.
A. 3.35	To *mede* þe maiden mekeliche he loutide,
A. 3.42	Þanne *mede* for hire mysdedis to þat man knelide,
A. 3.76	Ac *mede* þe maide þe mair heo besouȝte
A. 3.90	Þe king fro counseil com & callide aftir *mede*
A. 3.94	To *mede* þe maide melis þise wordis:
A. 3.156	Such a maister is *mede* among men of goode'.
A. 3.157	Þanne mournide *mede* & menide hire to þe king
A. 3.164	Þere þat meschief is gret *mede* may helpe.
A. 3.197	To ȝiuen hise men *mede* þat mekly hym seruen,
A. 3.199	*Mede* makiþ hym be louid & for a man holde.
A. 3.205	Takiþ *mede* of here maistris as þei mowe accorde;
A. 3.206	Beggeris for here bidding biddiþ of men *mede*;
A. 3.207	Mynstralis for here merþis þei asken;
A. 3.208	Þe king haþ [m]ede of his men to make pes in londis;
A. 3.209	Men þat [kenne] clerkis crauen of h[e]m *mede*;
A. 3.211	Asken *mede* & messe penis & here mete alse;
A. 3.212	Alle kyn crafty men craue *mede* for here prentis;
A. 3.213	*Mede* & marchaundise mote nede go togidere;
A. 3.214	No wiȝt as I wene wiþoute *mede* miȝte libbe'.
A. 3.216	*Mede* is worþi þe maistrie to haue'.
A. 3.218	'Þere arn to maner of *medis*, my lord, be ȝour leue.
A. 3.222	Tak no *mede*, my lord, of [men] þat ben trewe;
A. 3.224	Godis *mede* & his mercy þerwiþ miȝte þou wynne.
A. 3.225	Þere is a *mede* mesurles þat maistris desiriþ;
A. 3.226	To mayntene mysdoeris *mede* þei taken,
A. 3.232	Þat take *mede* & money for massis þat þei synge,
A. 3.233	Shal haue *mede* on þis molde þat mattheu haþ grauntid,
A. 3.235	Is no maner of *mede* but a mesurable hire;
A. 3.236	In marchaundie is no *mede*, I may it wel auowe;
A. 3.238	Ac reddist þou neuere Regum, þou recreiȝede *mede*,
A. 3.256	Such a meschef *mede* made þe kyng [to] haue
A. 3.266	Shal no more *mede* be maister on erþe,
A. 3.272	*Mede* of mysdoeris makiþ hem so riche
A. 4.10	Of *mede* & of mo oþere, what man shal hire wedde,
A. 4.58	But ȝif *mede* it make [þi] meschief is vppe,
A. 4.63	And tok *mede* wiþ hem mercy to wynne.
A. 4.81	Þanne gan *mede* to meke hire, & mercy besouȝte,
A. 4.90	For *mede* haþ mad my mendis; I may no more axen'.
A. 4.99	Þat *mede* muste be meynpernour resoun þei besouȝte.
A. 4.118	Whil *mede* haþ þe maistrie to mo[te] in þis halle.
A. 4.125	Ne for no *mede* haue mercy but meknesse it made,
A. 4.136	Þat he ne held resoun a maister & *mede* a muche wrecche.
A. 8.44	For he co[pie]de þus here clause þei [couden] hym gret *mede*.
A. 8.60	Þat any *mede* of mene men for motyng resceyueþ.
B. 2.20	'That is *Mede* þe mayde, haþ noyed me ful ofte,
B. 2.27	And *Mede* is manered after hym [as men of] kynde [carpeþ]:
B. 2.34	And what man takeþ *Mede*, myn heed dar I legge,
B. 2.36	How construeþ David þe kyng of men þat [caccheþ] *Mede*,
B. 2.40	And now worþ þis *Mede* ymaried [t]o a mansed sherewe,
B. 2.51	And lat no conscience acombre þee for coueitise of *Mede*.'
B. 2.53	And how *Mede* was ymaried in Metels me þouȝte;
B. 2.62	I kan noȝt rekene þe route þat ran aboute *Mede*.
B. 2.64	Were moost pryuee with *Mede* of any men me þouȝte.
B. 2.76	That *Mede* is ymaried moore for hire goodes
B. 2.119	For *Mede* is muliere of Amendes engendred
B. 2.120	God graunte[d] to gyue *Mede* to truþe,
B. 2.132	And *Mede* is muliere, a maiden of goode;
B. 2.148	For [he] may *Mede* amaistrye and maken at my wille'.
B. 2.153	Til *Mede* be þi wedded wif þoruȝ wi[t] of vs alle,
B. 2.154	For we haue *Mede* amaistried wiþ oure murie speche
B. 2.164	Sette *Mede* vpon a Sherreue shoed al newe,
B. 2.185	And *Mede* in þe myddes and [al þis meynee] after.
B. 2.203	/And bryngeþ *Mede* to me maugree hem alle.
B. 2.237	Saue *Mede* þe mayde na mo dorste abide.
B. 3.1	NOw is *Mede* þe mayde and na mo of hem alle
B. 3.4	To take *Mede* þe maide and maken hire at ese.
B. 3.10	Took *Mede* bi þe myddel and broȝte hire into chambre.
B. 3.11	A[c] þer was murþe & Mynstralcie *Mede* to plese;
B. 3.16	And seiden, 'mourne noȝt, *Mede*, ne make þow no sorwe,
B. 3.20	Mildely *Mede* þanne merciede hem alle
B. 3.25	Thanne lauȝte þei leue, þise lordes, at *Mede*.
B. 3.36	To *Mede* þe mayde [mekeliche he loutede]
B. 3.43	Thanne *Mede* for hire mysdedes to þat man kneled
B. 3.59	Haue mercy', quod *Mede*, 'of men þat it haunteþ
B. 3.87	Ac *Mede* þe mayde þe Mair [she] bisouȝt[e]
B. 3.101	The kyng fro conseil cam and called after *Mede*
B. 3.105	To *Mede* þe mayde [melleþ] þise wordes:
B. 3.169	Swich a maister is *Mede* among men of goode.'
B. 3.170	Thanne mournede *Mede* and mened hire to þe kynge
B. 3.177	Ther þat meschief is [most] *Mede* may helpe.
B. 3.210	To yeue [hise men *mede*] þat mekely hym serueþ,
B. 3.212	*Mede* makeþ hym biloued and for a man holden.
B. 3.218	Taken *Mede* of hir maistres as þei mowe acorde;
B. 3.219	Beggeres for hir biddynge bidden [of] men *Mede*;
B. 3.220	Mynstrales for hir myrþe *Mede* þei aske;
B. 3.221	The kyng haþ *mede* of his men to make pees in londe;
B. 3.222	Men þat [kenne clerkes] crauen [of hem] *Mede*;
B. 3.224	Asken *Mede* and massepens and hire mete [als];
B. 3.225	Alle kynne craft[y] men crauen *Mede* for hir Prentices;
B. 3.226	[*Mede* and Marchaundiȝe] mote nede go togideres;
B. 3.227	No wiȝt, as I wene, wiþouten *Mede* may libbe.'
B. 3.229	*Mede* is worþi, [me þynkeþ], þe maistrie to haue'.
B. 3.231	'Ther are two manere of *Medes*, my lord, [bi] youre leue.
B. 3.243	Wiþouten *Mede* doþ hem good and þe truþe helpeþ.
B. 3.244	Swiche manere men, my lord, shul haue þis firste *Mede*
B. 3.246	Ther is [a] *Mede* mesurelees þat maistres desireþ;
B. 3.247	To mayntene mysdoers *Mede* þei take;
B. 3.253	That taken *Mede* and moneie for masses þat þei syngeþ,
B. 3.254	[Shul haue] *Mede* [on þis molde þat] Mathew [haþ graunted]:
B. 3.256	It is no manere *Mede* but a mesurable hire.
B. 3.257	In marchaundise is no *Mede*, I may it wel auowe;
B. 3.259	Ac reddestow neuere Regum, þow recrayed *Mede*,
B. 3.271	For *Mede* ne for monee loke þow destruye it.
B. 3.278	Swich a meschief *Mede* made þe kyng to haue
B. 3.290	Shal na moore *Mede* be maister [on erþe],
B. 3.297	*Mede* of mysdoeres makeþ manye lordes,
B. 3.329	For Makometh and *Mede* myshappe shul þat tyme;
B. 3.331	Also wroþ as þe wynd weex *Mede* in a while.
B. 3.349	A ful teneful text to hem þat takeþ *Mede*:
B. 3.352	That þeiȝ we wynne worship and with *Mede* haue victorie,
B. 4.10	[Of *Mede* and of mo oþere, what man shal hire wedde],
B. 4.26	Whiche maistries *Mede* makeþ on þis erþe.
B. 4.34	'Ther are wiles in hire wordes, and with *Mede* þei dwelleþ;
B. 4.72	But if *Mede* it make þi meschief is vppe,
B. 4.77	And token *Mede* myd hem mercy to wynne.
B. 4.94	[Th]anne gan *Mede* to me[k]en hire, and mercy bisouȝte,
B. 4.103	For *Mede* haþ [maad myne amendes]; I may na moore axe.'
B. 4.112	That *Mede* moste be maynpernour Reson þei bisouȝte.
B. 4.135	While *Mede* haþ þe maistrie [to mote in þis] halle.
B. 4.142	Ne for no *Mede* haue mercy but mekenesse it ma[de],
B. 4.152	For I seiȝ *Mede* in þe moot halle on men of lawe wynke
B. 4.154	Waryn wisdom wynked vpon *Mede*
B. 4.160	And leten Mekenesse a maister and *Mede* a mansed sherewe.
B. 4.165	*Mede* mornede þo and made heuy chere
B. 4.173	And modiliche vpon *Mede* wiþ myȝt þe kyng loked,
B. 4.174	And gan wexe wroþ with lawe for *Mede* almoost hadde shent it,
B. 4.176	*Mede* ouermaistreþ lawe and muche truþe letteþ.
B. 4.179	*Mede* shal noȝt maynprise yow, by þe marie of heuene!
B. 6.40	And mekenesse þi maister maugree *Medes* chekes;
B. 7.59	That any *Mede* of mene men for motyng takeþ.
B.11.334	And how men token *Mede* and Mercy refused.
B.12.292	And an hope hangynge þerInne to haue a *mede* for his truþe;
B.12.294	The glose graunteþ vpon þat vers a greet *mede* to truþe.
B.13.424	And ȝyueþ hem mete and *mede*, and pouere men refuse,
C. 2.19	'That is *mede* þe mayde, hath niyed me ful ofte
C. 2.27	And *mede* is manered aftur hym as men of kynde carpeth:
C. 2.36	And what [man] *mede* loueth, my lyf [dar y] wedde,
C. 2.38	That helpeth man moste to heuene *mede* most letteth.
C. 2.43	Tomorwe worth *mede* ymaried to a mansed wrecche,
C. 2.45	Fauel thorw his flaterynge speche hath *mede* foule enchaunted,

C. 2.48   That *mede* is thus ymaried; tomorwe þou shalt aspye.
C. 2.54   Acombre neuere thy Consience for coueityse of *mede*.'
C. 2.56   And y say how *mede* was maried, metyng as it were.
C. 2.59   Of many manere men þat of *mede[s]* kynne were,
C. 2.64   Y kan nouȝt rykene þe route þat ran aboute *mede*.
C. 2.66   Were most pryue with *mede* of eny men [me] thoghte.
C. 2.72   That Gyle hath gyue to falsnesse and grauntid also *mede*,'
C. 2.77   'Al þat loueth and byleueth vp lykyng of *mede*,
C. 2.78   Leueth hit le[l]ly this worth here laste *mede*
C. 2.80   *Mede* and suche men þat aftur mede wayten.
C. 2.80   Mede and suche men þat aftur *mede* wayten.
C. 2.83   That *mede* is maried more for here richesse
C. 2.123   For *mede* is moilere, amendes was here dame;
C. 2.126   And withouten here moder amendes *mede* may [nat] be wedded.
C. 2.136   For y, man, of thy mercy *mede* haue diserued."
C. 2.137   And se[t]he man may [o]n heye *mede* of god diserue
C. 2.139   That *mede* may be wedded to no man bot treuthe.
C. 2.141   For by lesynges ȝe lacchen largeliche *mede*.
C. 2.148   And *mede* is moylore, [a] mayden of gode;
C. 2.152   Where matrymonye may be of *mede* and of falshede.
C. 2.164   For he may *mede* amaystrye [and maken at my wille].'
C. 2.169   Til *mede* be thy wedded wyf wolle we nat stunte,
C. 2.170   For we haue *mede* amaystred [with] oure mery [speche]
C. 2.173   To be maried for mone *med[e]* hath assented.'
C. 2.180   And shop þat a shereue sholde bere *mede*
C. 2.183   And ryde on hem and on reue[s] righte faste by *mede*.
C. 2.198   And *mede* in þe myddes and al this me[y]n[e] aftur.
C. 2.200   Of many maner men for *mede* sake seude aftur.
C. 2.202   For to wisse hem þe way and with *mede* abyde.
C. 2.217   And bryngeth *mede* to me maugrey hem alle.
C. 2.253   Saue *mede* þe mayde no ma durste abyde.
C. 3.1   Now is *mede* þe mayde and na mo of hem alle
C. 3.4   To take *mede* þe mayde and maken here at ese.
C. 3.10   Took *mede* by þe myddel and myldeliche here brouhte
C. 3.12   Ac there was myrthe and mynstracie *mede* to plese;
C. 3.17   And sayden, 'mourne nat, *mede*, ne make thow no sorwe
C. 3.21   Myldeliche *mede* thenne mercyede hem alle
C. 3.26   [W]henne they hadde lauhte here leue at this lady *mede*
C. 3.30   And *Mede* hendeliche behyhte hem þe same,
C. 3.39   To *mede* þe mayde myldeliche he sayde,
C. 3.45   Thenne *mede* for here mysdedes to th[at] man knelede
C. 3.53   In masse and in mataynes for *mede* we shal synge
C. 3.63   Haueth mercy,' quod *mede*, 'o[f] men þat hit haunteth
C. 3.77   Ȝut *mede* the Mayr myldeliche he bysouhte,
C. 3.115   Ac *Mede* þe mayde þe mayre a bisowte
C. 3.119   Loue hem for my loue,' quod this lady *mede*,
C. 3.123   And wittenesseth what worth of hem þat wolleth take *mede*:
C. 3.128   The kyng fram conseyl come [and] calde aftur *mede*
C. 3.211   For clerkes and coueitise hath knet togederes
C. 3.215   Such a maistre is *mede* among men of gode.'
C. 3.216   Thenne mournede *mede* and menede here to þe kyng
C. 3.223   Ther þat meschief is greet *mede* may helpe;
C. 3.249   Loketh aftur lordschipe or oþer large *mede*
C. 3.256   For sholde neuere Consience be my constable were y a kyng,' quod *mede*,
C. 3.258   Ac hadde y, *mede*, ben marchel o[f] his men in Fraunce
C. 3.266   To ȝeue men *mede* þat meekliche hym serueth,
C. 3.268   *Mede* maketh hym byloued and for a man yholde.
C. 3.272   And ȝeuen *mede* to men to meyntene here lawes;
C. 3.274   Taken *mede* of here maistres as þei mowen acorde;
C. 3.275   Bothe Beg[g]eres and bedemen crauen *mede* for here preyeres;
C. 3.276   Munstrals for here m[yrth]e *mede* thei asken;
C. 3.277   Maistres þat kenneth clerkes craueth therfore *mede*;
C. 3.279   Asken *mede* and mas pans and here mete bothe;
C. 3.280   Alle kyn crafty men crauen *mede* for here prentises;
C. 3.281   Marchaundise and *mede* mot nede [go] togederes,
C. 3.282   Is no lede þat leueth þat he ne loueth *mede*
C. 3.285   *Mede* is worthy, me thynketh, þe maistrye to haue.'
C. 3.287   That *mede* [is] euermore a mayntenour of Gyle,
C. 3.288   As þe sauhter sayth by such þat ȝeueth *mede*:
C. 3.290   To ȝeue men *mede*, more oþer lasse.
C. 3.291   Ac ther is *mede* and mercede and bothe men demen
C. 3.293   *Mede* many tymes men ȝeueth bifore þe doynge
C. 3.295   That eny man *Mede* toke but he hi[t] myhte deserue,
C. 3.298   Ne haue hap to his hele *mede* to deserue
C. 3.305   And þat is no *mede* but a mercede, a manere dewe dette.
C. 3.311   The *mede* þat many prest[es] taken for masses þat thei syngen,
C. 3.313   In Marchandise is no *mede*, y may hit wel avowe;
C. 3.333   Thus is *mede* and mercede as two maner relacions,
C. 3.391   He þat *mede* may lacche maketh lytel tale;
C. 3.393   How þat cliauntes acorde acounteth *mede* litel.
C. 3.407   Ac hoso rat of regum rede me may of *mede*,
C. 3.409   And se[t]he, for sauel saued a kyng fo[r] *mede*

C. 3.424   For eny *mede* of money al that thow myhte [fynde],
C. 3.431   Thus was kyng sauel ouercome thorw coueytise of *mede*,
C. 3.443   Shal no *mede* be maistre neueremore aftur
C. 3.450   Muchel [euel] is thorw *mede* mony tymes ysoffred
C. 3.482   For Machameth and *mede* [shal] mishap þat tyme;
C. 3.484   As wroth as [þe] wynd wax *mede* þeraftur:
C. 3.497   A ful teneful tyxst to hem þat taketh *mede*,
C. 3.499   Worschipe a wynneth þat y wol ȝeue *mede*
C. 4.10   Of *mede* and of mo othere and what man shal here wedde
C. 4.26   Whiche a maistre *mede* was amonges pore and ryche.
C. 4.71   Thorw wrong and his werkes there was *mede* yknowe
C. 4.73   And token *mede* [myd] hem mercy to wynne.
C. 4.90   Then gan *mede* to m[e]ken here and mercy bisouhte
C. 4.97   And *mede* hath made my mendes y may no more asken.
C. 4.107   That *mede* myhte be maynpernour [resoun] thei bysouhte.
C. 4.132   Whiles *mede* hath the maistrie þer motyng is at [þe] Barr[e].
C. 4.139   Ne thorw *mede* mercy, by marie of heuene!
C. 4.148   *Mede* in the mothalle tho on men of lawe gan wynke
C. 4.155   That mekenesse worth maystre ouer *mede* at þe laste.'
C. 4.156   Loue l[et]te of *mede* lyhte and leutee ȝut lasse
C. 4.160   *Mede* mornede tho and made heuy chere
C. 4.163   With *mede* þe mayde out of þe moethalle
C. 4.164   A shyreues Clerk cryede, 'a! capias *mede*
C. 4.167   And modiliche vppon *mede* many tym[e] lokede
C. 4.170   *Mede* and men of ȝoure craft muche treuthe letteth.
C. 4.173   *Mede* shal nat maynprise [ȝow], by marye of heuene!
C. 7.84   And ȝeueth [hem] *mede* & mete and pore men refuse,
C. 7.200   "Ȝe! leue Peres,' quod thise pilgrimes and profrede Peres *mede*.
C. 7.203   Were hit itolde treuthe þat y toke *mede*
C. 8.38   And Mekenesse thy maystre maugre *mede* chekes
C. 9.54   That *mede* of mene men for here motynge taken.
C. 9.275   Ther as *mede* ne mercy may nat a myte availle
C. 9.277   Mercy for *mede* and my lawe breke.'
C.13.97   And as moche *mede* for a myte þer he offreth
C.13.142   And how þat [men] *mede* toke and mercy refusede.
C.17.66   That his *mede* and his manhede for eueremore shal laste:
C.20.356   Witnesseth in his writyng[e] what is lyares *mede*:

medecyne > medicyne

medeþ v *meden v.* A 1 mediþ; B 1
A. 3.203   And mediþ men hymself to mayntene here lawis;
B. 3.216   And medeþ men h[y]mseluen to mayntene hir lawes.

medicyne n *medicine n.* A 1 medicine; B 5 medicine (1) medicyne (4); C 5 medecyne (3) medicyne (2)
A. 1.33   Mesure is *medicine* þeiȝ þou muche ȝerne.
B. 1.35   Mesure is *medicine* þouȝ þow muchel yerne.
B.15.562   A *medicyne* moot þerto þat may amende prelates.
B.17.80   'What he spendeþ moore [for *medicyne*] y make þee good herafter,
B.17.94   May no *medicyne* [vnder mone] þe man to heele bringe,
B.18.155   May no *medicyne* [amende] þe place þer he styngeþ
C. 1.33   Mesure is *medecyne* thogh þow muche ȝerne;
C.17.225   A *medecyne* moste þerto þat m[ay] amende prelates.
C.19.77   'And þat more goth for his *medicyne* y make the good aȝeynward
C.19.84   Ne no *medicyne* vnder molde the man to hele brynge,
C.20.158   May no *medecyne* amende the place there he styngeth

meditacion n *meditacioun n.* B 1
B.15.295   Ac moost þoruȝ [*meditacion*] and mynde of god almyghty.

medle v *medlen v.* A 2 medleþ (1) medlit (1); B 5 medle (2) medled (2) medlest (1); C 4 meddeled (1) medle (1) medlen (1) ymedled (1)
A.10.3   Of erþe & eir it is mad, *medlit* togideris;
A.12.109   And for he *medleþ* of makyng he made þis ende.
B. 9.3   Of erþe and Eyr [it is] maad, *medled* togideres,
B.11.344   *Medled* noȝt wiþ hir makes, [saue man allone].
B.12.16   And þow *medlest* þee wiþ makynges and myȝtest go seye þi sauter,
B.12.124   And *medle* noȝt muche wiþ hem to meuen any wraþe
B.20.179   May noȝt a myte auaille to *med[l]e* ayein Elde.'
C. 6.260   *Meddeled* my marchaundyse and made a good mostre.
C.10.130   Of erthe and ayer [hit is] maed, *ymedled* togyderes,
C.14.67   And *medle* we nat moche with hem to meuen eny wrathe
C.22.179   May nat a myte avayle to *medlen* aȝen Elde.'

meek- > meke-

meel n *mel n.(2)* A 1; B 3 meel (2) meles (1); C 5 mel (1) mele (1) meles (3)
A. 1.24   Þat oþer is mete at *meel* for myseise of þiselue;
B. 1.24   [That oþer is] mete at *meel* for mysese of þiselue;
B. 5.492   Aboute mydday, whan moost liȝt is and *meel* tyme of Seintes,
B.10.102   That was maad for *meles* men to eten Inne,
C. 6.289   Ne take a *meles* mete of thyn and myn herte hit wiste
C. 7.132   Aboute mydday, when most liht is and *mel* tyme of sayntes,
C. 9.247   Ac aboute mydday at *mele* tyme y mette with hem ofte,

C.12.106   *Meles* and manschipes, vch man oþer.
C.15.35   A *meles* mete for a pore man or moneye yf they hadde.

meene > *mene*

mees n *mes n.(2)* &> *mous* B 2
B.13.54   And þanne a *mees* of ooþer mete of Miserere mei deus,_
B.15.316   And a *mees* þermyd of o maner kynde,

meete > *mete*

megre adj *megre adj.* C 1
C. 6.94   And þat maketh me so *megre* for y ne may me venge.

meynee n *meine n.* A 4 mayne (1) meyne (2) mene (1); B 9 meyne (3) meynee (6); C 3 mayne (2) meyne (1)
A. 1.106   And ouer his *meyne* made hem archaungelis;
A. 2.146   And mede in þe myddis, & al þis *mene* aftir.
A. 3.23   Þe leste man of here *mayne* a mutoun of gold.
A. 5.79   Betwyn hym & his *meyne* I haue mad wraþþe;
B. 1.108   And ouer his *meynee* made hem Archangeles;
B. 2.185   And Mede in þe myddes and [al þis *meynee*] after.
B. 3.24   The leeste man of hire *meynee* a moton of golde.
B. 3.198   I made his *me[ynee]* murye and mournynge lette;
B. 5.99   Bitwene [*meyne* and meyne] I make debate ofte
B. 5.99   Bitwene [meyne and *meyne*] I make debate ofte
B.10.94   And how he my3te moost *meynee* manliche fynde;
B.15.183   And makeþ murþe þer[wiþ] and hise *me[yne]* boþe;
B.16.236   Myself and my *meynee*; and alle þat male weere
C. 2.198   And mede in þe myddes and al this *me[y]n[e]* aftur.
C. 3.25   The leste man of here *mayne* a motoun of gold.
C.18.252   Mysulue and my *mayne*; and alle þat male were

meynp- > *maynp-; meynt-* > *mayntene; meire(s* > *mair*

meke adj *mek adj.* &> *meken* A 6 mek (5) meke (1); B 8; C 7
A. 1.147   Þat he was mi3tful & *mek* & mercy gan graunte
A. 1.150   Þei3 3e ben mi3ty to mote beþ *mek* of 3our werkis;
A. 7.191   Meschief it makiþ h[y] ben so *mek* nouþe,
A. 9.71   Whoso is *mek* of his mouþ, mylde of his speche,
A.10.83   Þat he makiþ men *meke* & mylde of here speche,
A.10.128   Among men of þis molde þat *mek* ben & kynde.
B. 1.173   That he was mi3tful and *meke* and mercy gan graunte
B. 1.176   Thou3 ye be my3t[y] to mote beeþ *meke* [of] youre werkes,
B. 6.205   Meschief it makeþ þei be so *meke* nouþe,
B. 8.80   Whoso is [*meke* of his mouþ, milde of his speche],
B.14.114   And makest hem wel nei3 *meke* and mylde for defaute,
B.15.306   In menynge þat *meke* þyng mylde þyng sholde fede.
B.16.91   To a maide þat hi3te Marie, a *meke* þyng wiþalle,
B.18.115   Mercy hi3te þat mayde, a *meke* þyng wiþ alle,
C. 1.169   That he was myhtfull and *meke* and mercy gan graunte
C. 1.172   Thow 3e be myhty to mote beth *meke* in 3oure werkes,
C. 8.211   Meschef hit maketh they ben so *meke* nouthe
C. 9.15   Merciable to *meke* and mylde to þe gode
C.15.290   And makest hem wel neyh *meke* and mylde for defaute
C.16.23   And amende vs [of] thy mercy and make vs alle *meke*,
C.18.124   To a mayde þat hihte marie, a *meke* thyng withalle,

mekel > *muche*

mekely adv *mekli adv.* A 6 mekeliche (1) mekliche (2) mekly (3); B 6 mekely (4) mekeliche (2); C 6 meekliche (1) mekeliche (5)
A. 1.142   *Mekliche* for oure misdedis to amende vs alle.
A. 1.144   But *mekly* wiþ mouþe mercy he besou3te
A. 3.35   To mede þe maiden *mekeliche* he loutide,
A. 3.197   To 3iuen hise men mede þat *mekly* hym seruen,
A. 8.85   Þat takiþ [þ]is meschief *mekliche* as myselis & oþere,
A.11.166   I seide 'graunt mercy madame,' & *mekly* hire grette
B. 1.168   *Mekely* for oure mysdedes to amenden vs alle.
B. 1.170   But *mekely* wiþ mouþe mercy [he] bisou3te
B. 3.36   To Mede þe mayde [*mekeliche* he loutede]
B. 3.210   To yeue [hise men mede] þat *mekely* hym serueþ,
B. 7.103   That taken þi[s] myschie[f] *mekeliche* as Mesels and oþere,
B.10.224   I seide 'grant mercy, madame', and *mekely* hir grette,
C. 1.164   *Mekeliche* for oure mysdedes to amende vs alle.
C. 1.166   Bote *mekeliche* with mouth mercy he bysoughte
C. 3.266   To 3eue men mede þat *meekliche* hym serueth,
C. 9.184   That taketh thise meschiefes *mekeliche* and myldeliche at herte
C. 9.238   Amend[e] hym and mercy aske and *mekeliche* hym shryue,
C.12.179   Mesc[h]iefes on molde *mekeliche* to soffren:

meken v *meken v.* A 3 meke; B 4 meke (2) meken (1) mekeþ (1); C 5 meke (2) meken (1) meketh (2)
A. 4.81   Þanne gan mede to *meke* hire, & mercy besou3te,
A. 5.52   But now wile I *meke* me & mercy beseke
A. 6.88   Biddiþ amende 3ow *meke* hym to his maister ones
B. 4.94   [Th]anne gan Mede to *me[k]en* hire, and mercy bisou3te,

B. 5.69   But now [wole I] *meke* me and mercy biseche
B. 5.601   Biddeþ amende-yow *meke* hym til his maister ones
B.20.35   Ac nede is next hym for anoon he *mekeþ*
C. 4.90   Then gan mede to *m[e]ken* here and mercy bisouhte
C. 6.10   But now wol y *meke* me and mercy byseche
C. 7.248   Biddeth amende-3ow *meke* [hym] to his maistre grace
C.17.154   For þer is no man þat mynde hath þat ne *meketh* [hym] and bysecheth
C.22.35   A[c] nede is nexst hym for anoen he *meketh*

mekenesse n *meknesse n.* A 3 meknesse; B 7; C 7 meeknesse (1) mekenesse (6)
A. 4.125   Ne for no mede haue mercy but *meknesse* it made,
A. 6.48   3e mote go þoru3 *meknesse*, boþe men & wyues,
A.11.104   'For þi *mekenesse*, man,' quaþ she, 'and for þi mylde speche
B. 4.142   Ne for no Mede haue mercy but *mekenesse* it ma[de],
B. 4.160   And leten *Mekenesse* a maister and Mede a mansed sherewe.
B. 5.561   Ye moten go þoru3 *mekenesse*, boþe men and wyues,
B. 6.40   And *mekenesse* þi maister maugree Medes chekes;
B.10.152   'For þi *mekenesse*, man', quod she, 'and for þi mylde speche
B.11.138   Mercy al to amende and *Mekenesse* hir folwe;
B.17.242   Mercy for his *mekenesse* wol maken good þe remenaunt.
C. 4.155   That *mekenesse* worth maystre ouer mede at þe laste.'
C. 7.206   3e mote go thorw *mekenesse*, alle men and wommen,
C. 8.38   And *Mekenesse* thy maystre maugre mede chekes
C.11.90   'For thy *mekenesse*, [man],' quod she, 'and for thy mylde speche
C.12.73   Mercy al [to] amende and *mekenesse* her folowe;
C.15.273   '*Meeknesse* and mylde speche and men of o will,
C.19.208   Mercy for his *mekenesse* wol maky good þe remenaunt.

mekil > *muche; mekly -liche* > *mekely; meknesse* > *mekenesse; mel* > *meel*

mele n *mele n.(1)* &> *meel* B 1; C 1
B.13.260   For er I haue breed of *mele* ofte moot I swete,
C. 9.75   Bothe in mylke and in *mele* to make with papelotes

mele v *melen v.* A 2 mele (1) melis (1); B 2 mele (1) melleþ (1)
A. 3.94   To mede þe maide *melis* þise wordis:
A.11.94   He beco[m] so confus he couþe nou3t *mele*,
B. 3.105   To Mede þe mayde [*melleþ*] þise wordes:
B.10.141   He bicom so confus he couþe no3t [*mele*],

meles > *meel*

melk n *milk n.* B 4 melk (2) mylk (2); C 2 mylke
B. 5.437   Boþ[e] bred and ale, buttre, *melk* and chese
B.15.280   And þoru3 þe *mylk* of þat mylde beest þe man was sustened;
B.15.467   For as þe Cow þoru3 kynde *mylk* þe calf norisseþ til an Oxe,
B.15.470   Right as þe cow calf coueiteþ [swete *melk*];
C. 7.51   Bothe Bred and ale, Botere, *mylke* and chese
C. 9.75   Bothe in *mylke* and in mele to make with papelotes

melleþ > *mele v*

melteþ v *melten v.* B 4 melte (1) melteþ (2) molten (1); C 3 melteth
B.13.83   Were *molten* leed in his mawe and Mahoun amyddes.
B.17.230   And *melteþ* hire my3t into mercy, as men may se in wyntre
B.17.232   *Melte* in a Mynut while to myst and to watre.
B.17.234   *Melteþ* to mercy, to merciable and to [noon] oþere.
C.19.196   And *melteth* myhte into mercy, as we may se a wynter
C.19.198   *Melteth* in a myntwhile to myst and to water.
C.19.200   *Melteth* to mercy, to merciable and to non oþere.

membre n *membre n.* A 1 membris; B 5 membre (2) membres (3); C 6 membre (3) membres (3)
A. 8.84   Blynde & bedrede, & broken here *membris*,
B. 7.102   Blynde and bedreden and broken hire *membres*
B.12.230   Kynde] kenned Adam to knowe hise pryue *membres*,
B.18.342   *Membre* for membre [was amendes by þe olde lawe],
B.18.342   Membre for *membre* [was amendes by þe olde lawe],
B.19.470   Ye ben but *membres* and I aboue alle.
C. 5.33   Or thow art broke, so may be, in body or in *membre*
C. 9.178   Blynde and bedredne and broken here *membres*,
C. 9.217   Or ymaymed in som *membre*, for to meschief hit souneth,
C.10.157   Man is hym most lyk of *membres* and of face
C.20.384   Or eny manere *membre* maymeth oþer herteth,
C.21.470   3e ben bote *membres* and y aboue alle.

memento n *memento n.* A 2; B 2; C 2
A. 5.238   And þou haddist mercy on þat man for *memento* sake,
A.11.55   And so sei3 þe sauter, se[ke] it in *Memento*:
B. 5.466   And haddest mercy on þat man for *Memento* sake,
B.10.69   And so sei3 þe Sauter; [seke it in *memento*]:
C. 6.320   And haddest mercy vppon þat man for *memento* sake,
C.11.49   And so saith þe sauter; y say hit [in] *memento*:

memorie n *memorie n.* A 2; B 1; C 2
A. 7.87   And monewe me in his *memorie* among alle cristene.

A.11.216 Arn more in his mynde þan þe *memorie* of his foundours.
B. 6.95 And mengen [me] in his *memorie* amonges alle cristene.
C. 7.27 Til matynes and masse be ydo; thenne haue y a *memorie* at þe freres.
C. 8.104 And men[g]e me in his *memorie* amongus alle cristene.

men > man

mencion n *mencioun n.* B 1; C 2 mencioun (1) mensioun (1)
B.10.454 Dauid makeþ *mencion*, he spak amonges kynges,
C. 8.246 Mathew maketh *mencioun* of a man þat lente
C.11.279 Dauid maketh *mensioun* he spake among kynges

mende v *menden v.* A 1; C 2 mende (1) mended (1)
A. 3.51 Þat I ne shulde make or *mende*, & myn name writen
C. 3.61 Ho may askape þe sclaundre, þe skathe myhte sone be *mended*;
C. 6.288 Y ne wolde cope me with thy catel ne oure kyrke *mende*

mendenant(- mendenaunt(- > mendynaunt; mendes > mendis

mendynaunt n *mendinaunt n.* A 2 mendynaunt3; B 4 mendynaunt (1) mendinaunt3 (3); C 7 mendenant (1) mendenantes (2) mendenant3 (1) mendenaunt (1) mendenauntes (1) mendynant3 (1)
A.11.52 [*Mendynaunt3*] meteles mi3te go to bedde.
A.11.201 For *mendynaunt3* at meschief þ[o] men were dewid,
B.10.66 *Mendinaunt3* metelees my3te go to bedde.
B.13.3 In manere of a *mendynaunt* many yer after.
B.15.154 Men beþ merciable to *mendinaunt3* and to poore,
B.15.274 Monkes and *mendinaunt3*, men by hemselue
C.Pr.60 Mony of þise maistres of *mendenant* freres
C. 5.76 And monkes and moniales þat *mendenant[es]* sholde fynde
C. 9.180 As mesels and *mendenantes*, men yfalle in meschief
C.11.48 Mony tym[e] *mendenauntes* myhte goen afyngred.
C.13.79 The messager aren th[e] *mendenant3* þat lyuen by menne almesse,
C.15.3 In manere of [a] *mendenaunt* mony 3er aftur.
C.15.80 Ac y wiste neuere freke þat frere is ycald of þe fyue *mendynant3*

mendis n *mende n. cf. amendes* A 2; C 1 mendes
A. 2.83 For mede is molere of [m]*endis* engendrit
A. 4.90 For mede haþ mad my *mendis*; I may no more axen.'
C. 4.97 And mede hath made my *mendes* y may no more asken.

mene n *mene n.(3)* A 3; B 8 meene (2) mene (5) menes (1); C 7
A. 3.65 Meiris & ma[ce]ris, hij þat ben *mene*
A. 8.180 And marie his modir to be *mene* betwene,
A. 9.114 But as I bad þou3t þo be *mene* betwene,
B. 1.160 And a *meene*, as þe Mair is, bitwene þe [commune] & þe [kyng];
B. 3.76 Maires and Maceres þat *menes* ben bitwene
B. 7.202 And Marie his moder be *meene* bitwene,
B. 8.124 But as I bad þo3t þoo be *mene* bitwene,
B. 9.35 And Eue of his ryb bon wiþouten any *mene*.
B.14.255 Meschief is [ay a *mene*] and makeþ hem to þynke
B.15.507 Thus in a feiþ leue þat folk, and in a fals *mene*,
B.16.192 Might and [a] *mene* [his owene my3te to knowe],
C. 1.156 And a *mene*, as þe Mayre is, bitwene þe kyng and þe comune;
C. 9.348 And marie his moder be oure *mene* to hym
C.10.120 Bote as y bad thouht þo be *mene* betwene
C.16.95 Meschief is ay a *mene* and maketh hym to thenke
C.17.158 And lyuen oute of lele byleue for they l[e]ue on a *mene*.
C.17.258 Thus in a fayth l[e]ueth þat folk and in a fals *mene*,
C.18.201 Mi3te and a *mene* to se his owne myhte,

mene adj1 *mene adj.(1)* A 6; B 8 meene (5) mene (2) mener (1); C 7
A.Pr.18 Of alle maner of men, þe *mene* & þe riche,
A. 3.149 Þe mase for a *mene* man þei3 he mote euere.
A. 8.60 Þat any mede of *mene* men for motyng resceyueþ.
A.11.51 Nere mercy in *mene* men more þan in riche
A.11.54 Ac among [*mene*] men hise mercy & his werkis,
A.11.57 And han [hym] muchel in herte mouþ, ac *mene* men in herte.
B.Pr.18 Of alle manere of men, þe *meene* and þe riche,
B. 2.56 Of alle manere of men, þe *meene* and þe riche.
B. 3.160 The ma3e for a *mene* man þou3 he mote euere!
B. 7.59 That any Mede of *mene* men for motyng takeþ.
B.10.65 Ne were mercy in *meene* men moore þan in riche
B.10.68 Ac amonges *meene* men his mercy and hise werkes.
B.10.71 And haue hym muche in [hire] mouþ, ac *meene* men in herte.
B.14.166 For alle my3testow haue maad noon *mener* þan ooþer
C.Pr.20 Of alle manere [of] men, þe *mene* and þe [riche],
C.Pr.222 3ut mette me more of *mene* and of riche,
C. 3.81 For thyse men don most harm to þe *mene* peple,
C. 3.198 The mase for a *mene* man thow he mote euere!
C. 9.54 That mede of *mene* men for here motynge taken.
C.11.47 Ne were mercy in *m[e]ne* men more then in riht riche
C.11.51 And haen [hym] muche in here mouth Ac *mene* [men] in herte.

mene adj2 *mene adj.(2)* B 2; C 1
B. 9.116 And þus was wedlok ywro3t wiþ a *mene* persone,

B.13.394 Mi3te neuere me conforte in þe *mene* [tyme]
C. 6.281 Myhte neuere me comforte in the *mene* tyme

mene v *menen v.(1)* A 6; B 25 meene (1) mene (15) menen (1) menest (1) meneþ (6) menynge (1); C 26 mene (20) menede (2) meneth (3) menyng (1)
A. 1.11 And seide 'mercy madame, what is þis to *mene*?'
A. 8.138 Daniel seide, 'sire king, þi sweuene is to *mene*
A.10.39 As muche to *mene* [as] man with his soule,
A.10.163 And is as muche to *mene*, among vs alle,
A.11.297 And is as muche to *mene*, to men þat ben lewid,
A.11.306 And is to *mene* in oure mouþ, more ne lesse,
B. 5.277 In Miserere mei deus, wher I *mene* truþe:
B. 7.160 Daniel seide, 'sire kyng, þi [sweuene is to *mene*]
B. 9.51 As muche to *mene* as man wiþ a Soule.
B.10.90 Whoso haþ muche spende manliche, so [*meneþ*] Tobye,
B.10.281 But in swich manere as Marc *meneþ* in þe gospel:
B.10.415 The culorum of þis clause curatours is to *mene*,
B.10.462 And is to *mene* to [Englissh] men, moore ne lesse,
B.11.275 And is to *mene* to men þat on þis moolde lyuen,
B.13.211 'That is sooþ', [seide] Clergie, 'I se what þow *menest*.
B.14.275 What is Pouerte, pacience', quod he, 'properly to *mene*?'
B.14.322 That þ[u]s first wroot to wissen men what Pouerte was to *mene*.'
B.15.56 To englisshe men þis is to *mene*, þat mowen speke and here,
B.15.119 If lewed [ledes] wiste what þis latyn *meneþ*,
B.15.405 *Menynge* as after mete; þus Makometh hire enchauntede,
B.15.451 [Enformed] hem what fullynge and feiþ was to *mene*.
B.15.459 Heþen is to *mene* after heeþ and vntiled erþe,
B.15.471 So [*menen*] ri3tfulle men [after] mercy and truþe.
B.16.3 Ac 3it I am in a weer what charite is to *mene*.'
B.16.63 And I haue told þee what hi3te þe tree; þe Trinite it *meneþ*.'
B.17.9 [And þus my lettre *meneþ*; [ye] mowe knowe it al].'
B.18.126 'And am wendynge to wite what þis wonder *meneþ*.
B.18.209 Sholde wite witterly what day is to *meene*.
B.18.217 Woot no wight, as I wene, what [is ynogh] to *mene*.
B.19.62 He may [be wel] called conquerour, and þat is crist to *mene*.
B.19.93 For Mirre is mercy to *mene* and mylde speche of tonge.
C. 3.125 Amonge thise lettred lordes this latyn is to *mene*
C. 3.396 And is to [*mene*] in oure mouth more n[e] mynne
C. 4.147 To construe this c[l]ause, kyndeliche what it *meneth*.
C. 5.37 Tyl y wyste witterly what holy writ *menede*
C. 6.303 There shal he wite witturly what vsure is to *mene*
C. 9.165 And lere this lewede men what þis latyn *meneth*
C.10.92 Lene hem and loue hem", this latyn is to *mene*.
C.10.209 And is no more to *mene* but men þat ben bygeten
C.11.70 And is to *mene* no more bote "who[so] muche goed weldeth
C.11.81 And when wit was ywar what studie *menede*
C.11.112 And hast vnderstandyng what a wolde *mene*
C.11.244 For Archa Noe, nymeth hede, ys no more to *mene*
C.11.246 The culorum of this clause curatores is to *mene*
C.11.288 And is to *mene* no more to men þat beth lewed:
C.13.65 3e wyte, 3e wyse men, what this is to *mene*:
C.13.66 The marchaunt is no more to *mene* but men þat ben ryche
C.14.4 And wissed the [wel] ofte what dowel was to *mene*
C.16.157 That wroet thus to wisse men what pouerte was to *mene*.'
C.16.218 To engelische men this is to *mene*, þat mowen speke and here,
C.17.41 This is no more to *mene* bote men of holy churche
C.17.176 *Menyng* as aftur mete; thus macumeth here enchauntede.
C.20.129 'And am wendynge to wyte what þis wonder *meneth*.'
C.20.216 Sholde ywyte witterly what day is to *mene*.
C.20.226 Ne woet no wyht, as y wene, what is ynow to *mene*.
C.21.62 He may be wel called conquerour and that is Crist to *mene*.
C.21.93 For Mirre is mercy to *mene* and mylde speche of tonge.

mene &> meynee

mened v *menen v.(2)* A 1 menide; B 2; C 1 menede
A. 3.157 Þanne mournide mede & *menide* hire to þe king
B. 3.170 Thanne mournede Mede and *mened* hire to þe kynge
B. 6.2 That [my3te] folwen vs ech foot': þus þis folk hem *mened*.
C. 3.216 Thenne mournede mede and *menede* here to þe kyng

menede > mene v, mened; menen > mene v

meneuer adj *meniver n.* B 1; C 1
B.20.138 For a [*Meneuer* Mantel he] made lele matrymoyne
C.22.138 For a *meneuer* man[t]el he made leele matrimonye

menge > mengen

menged v *mengen v.* B 1
B.13.361 And *menged* his marchaundise and made a good moustre:

mengen v *mingen v.* A 1 monewe; B 1; C 1 menge
A. 7.87 And *monewe* me in his memorie among alle cristene
B. 6.95 And *mengen* [me] in his memorie amonges alle cristene.
C. 8.104 And *men[g]e* me in his memorie amongus alle cristene.

meny > *many; menide* > *mened*

menyng ger *meninge ger.(1)* &> *mene v* B 5 menyng (1) menynge (4); C
  6 menyng (1) menynge (4) menynges (1)
B.14.45   In *menynge* þat alle men my3te þe same
B.15.306 In *menynge* þat meke þyng mylde þyng sholde fede.
B.15.475 In *menynge* after mete folweþ men þat whistlen;
B.16.200 In *menynge* þat man moste on o god bileue,
B.18.136 In *menynge* þat man shal fro merknesse be drawe
C.Pr.99   In *menynge* of myracles muche wex hangeth there;
C. 1.138 By what wey it wexeth and wheder out of my *menynges*.'
C. 8.247 His suluer to thre maner men [in] *menyng* they sholden
C.15.243 In *menynge* þat alle men myhte þe same
C.18.92   In *menynge* þat the fayrest thyng the furste thynge shold honoure
C.20.139 In *menynge* þat man shal fro me[r]kenesse be ydrawe

menynge > *mene v, menyng; menis* > *man*

menyson n *menisoun n.* B 1
B.16.111 Boþe meseles and mute and in þe *menyson* blody,

menne(s > *man*

menours n *Menour n.& adj.* A 1; B 1; C 1 menores
A. 9.9   Maistris of þe *menours*, men of gret wyt.
B. 8.9   Maistres of þe *Menours*, men of grete witte.
C.10.9   Maystres of þe *menore[s]*, men of gret witte.

mension > *mencion*

menske v *mensken v.* A 1; B 1; C 1
A. 3.171 3et I may, as I mi3te, [*menske*] þe wiþ 3eftis,
B. 3.184 Yet I may, as I my3te, *menske* þee wiþ 3iftes,
C. 3.230 3ut y may, as y myhte, *menske* þe with 3eftes

menstralsie > *mynstralcie*

mercede n *mercede n.* B 1; C 4
B.19.76 Mirre and muche gold wiþouten *merc[ede]* askynge
C. 3.291 Ac ther is mede and *mercede* and bothe men demen
C. 3.305 And þat is no mede but a *mercede*, a manere dewe dette,
C. 3.333 Thus is mede and *mercede* as two maner relacions,
C.21.76 Mirre and moche gold withouten *merc[ede]* askynge

mercement > *mercyment*

mercer n *mercer n.* B 1; C 1
B. 5.252 And haue ymaad many a kny3t boþe *Mercer* and draper
C. 6.250 And haue ymad many a knyht bothe *mercer* and draper

mercy n *merci n.* A 25; B 85 mercy (84) mercies (1); C 85
A. 1.11   And seide '*mercy* madame, what is þis to mene?'
A. 1.41   'A madame *mercy*,' quaþ I, 'me likiþ wel 3oure wordis.
A. 1.144   But mekly wiþ mouþe *mercy* he besou3te
A. 1.147   Þat he was mi3tful & mek & *mercy* gan graunte
A. 2.2   And seide, '*mercy* madame, for marie loue of heuene
A. 3.224   Godis mede & his *mercy* þerwiþ mi3te þou wynne.
A. 4.63   And tok mede wiþ hem *mercy* to wynne.
A. 4.81   Þanne gan mede to meke hire, & *mercy* besou3te,
A. 4.86   To haue *mercy* on þat man þat mysdede hym ofte:
A. 4.125   Ne for no mede haue *mercy* but meknesse it made,
A. 5.46   And lay longe er heo lokide, & 'lord *mercy*' criede,
A. 5.52   But now wile I meke me & *mercy* beseke
A. 5.55   To make *mercy* for his mysdede betwyn god & hym
A. 5.238   And þou haddist *mercy* on þat man for memento sake,
A. 5.243   But for þi muchel *mercy* mytygacioun I beseche,
A. 6.73   Þe mot is of *mercy* þe Maner al aboute,
A. 6.120   '*Mercy* [is] a maiden [þere], haþ mi3t ouer [hem] alle;
A. 8.179   Forþi I counseil alle cristene [to] cri3e god *mercy*,
A.11.51   Nere *mercy* in meene men more þan in riche
A.11.54   Ac among [mene] men hise *mercy* & his werkis,
A.11.79   And for his muchel *mercy* to amende vs here.
A.11.101 And seide, '*mercy* madame, 3our man shal I worþe
A.11.166 I seide 'graunt *mercy* madame,' & mekly hire grette
A.11.257 Eche man for his misdede but *mercy* it make.'
A.11.261 I was markid wiþoute *mercy*, & myn name entrid
B. 1.11   And seide, '*mercy*, madame, what [may] þis [by]meene?'
B. 1.43   '[A] madame, *mercy*', quod I, 'me likeþ wel youre wordes.
B. 1.170   But mekely wiþ mouþe *mercy* he [he] bisou3te
B. 1.173   That he was my3tful and meke and *mercy* gan graunte
B. 2.2   And seide '*mercy*, madame, for Marie loue of heuene
B. 2.31   And haþ yeuen me *mercy* to marie wiþ myselue,
B. 3.59   Haue *mercy*', quod Mede, 'of men þat it haunteþ
B. 3.319   *Mercy* or no mercy as Truthe [may] acorde.
B. 3.319   Mercy or no *mercy* as Truthe [may] acorde.
B. 4.77   And token Mede myd hem *mercy* to wynne.
B. 4.94   [Th]anne gan Mede to me[k]en hire, and *mercy* bisou3te,
B. 4.99   To haue *mercy* on þat man þat mysdide hym ofte:

B. 4.142   Ne for no Mede haue *mercy* but mekenesse it ma[de],
B. 5.63   And lay longe er she loked, and 'lord, *mercy*!' cryde,
B. 5.69   But now [wole I] meke me and *mercy* biseche
B. 5.72   To maken *mercy* for hi[s] mysded[e] bitwene god and [hym]
B. 5.281   'Haue *mercy* in þi mynde, and wiþ þi mouþ biseche it–
B. 5.283   Nis na moore to þe *mercy* of god þan [amyd] þe see a gleede:
B. 5.284   Forþi haue *mercy* in þy mynde, and marchaundise leue it,
B. 5.466   And haddest *mercy* on þat man for Memento sake,
B. 5.469   But for þi muchel *mercy* mitigacion I biseche:
B. 5.586   The moot is of *mercy* þe Manoir aboute;
B. 5.635   '*Mercy* is a maiden þere haþ my3t ouer [hem] alle;
B. 6.39   And þou3 [þow] mowe amercy hem lat *mercy* be taxour
B. 7.201   Forþi I counseille alle cristene to crie god *mercy*,
B.10.65   Ne were *mercy* in meene men moore þan in riche
B.10.68   Ac amonges meene men his *mercy* and hise werkes
B.10.126 And for his muche *mercy* to amende [vs] here.
B.10.148 And seide, '*mercy*, madame; youre man shal I worþe
B.10.224 I seide 'grant *mercy*, madame', and mekely hir grette,
B.10.259 And þat is, man, bi þy my3t, for *mercies* sake,
B.10.376 Ech man for hi[s] mysded[e] but *mercy* it [make]." '
B.10.389 Maistres þat of goddes *mercy* techen men and prechen,
B.10.399 [Ac] at hir mooste meschief [*mercy* were þe beste].
B.10.446 And he þat may al amende haue *mercy* on vs alle,
B.11.136 *Mercy* for hise mysdedes wiþ mouþe [or] wiþ herte.'
B.11.138 *Mercy* al to amende and Mekenesse hir folwe;
B.11.265 To wepe and to wel bidde, wherof wexeþ *Mercy*
B.11.334 And how men token Mede and *Mercy* refused.
B.12.111 3yue *mercy* for hire mysdedes, if men it wole aske
B.13.385 *Mercy* for my mysdedes, þat I ne moorned moore
B.13.408 Ne no *mercy* amenden þe man þat so deieþ].
B.14.187 Confession and knowlichynge [and] crauynge þi *mercy*
B.14.334 To couere my careyne', quod he, and cride *mercy* faste
B.15.469 And maidenes and mylde men *mercy* desiren
B.15.471 So [menen] ri3tfulle men [after] *mercy* and truþe.
B.15.514 Men my3te no3t be saued but þoru3 *mercy* and grace,
B.16.5   *Mercy* is þe more þerof; þe myddul stok is ruþe;
B.16.242 *Mercy* for oure mysdedes as many tyme as we asken:
B.16.259 'Loo!' quod he and leet me see; 'lord, *mercy*!' I seide,
B.16.271 The myght of goddes *mercy* þat my3te vs alle amende.'
B.17.88   And grauntede hym to ben his [gome]; 'graunt *mercy*', he seide;
B.17.218 So is [þe] holy goost god and grace wiþoute *mercy*
B.17.230 And melteþ hire my3t into *mercy*, as men may se in wyntre
B.17.234 Melteþ to *mercy*, to merciable and to [noon] oþere.
B.17.242 *Mercy* for his mekenesse wol maken good þe remenaunt.
B.17.245 So wole crist of his curteisie, and men crye hym *mercy*,
B.17.252 So is þe holi goost god and grace wiþouten *mercy*
B.17.289 [How my3te he aske *mercy*, or any mercy hym helpe],
B.17.289 [How my3te he aske mercy, or any *mercy* hym helpe],
B.17.290 That wikkedliche and wilfulliche wolde *mercy* aniente?
B.17.302 And myldeliche his *mercy* aske; myghte I no3t be saued?'
B.17.309 That þe kyng may do no *mercy* til boþe men acorde
B.17.314 That *mercy* in hir mynde may no3t þanne falle];
B.17.317 To amende al þat amys is, and his *mercy* gretter
B.17.338 To man þat *mercy* askeþ and amende þenkeþ".
B.17.346 Haþ *mercy* on swiche men þat so yuele may suffre
B.17.348 That is coueitise and vnkyndenesse þat quencheþ goddes *mercy*;
B.17.353 Alle manere men *mercy* and for3ifnesse,
B.18.87   Thanne fil þe kny3t vpon knees and cryde [Iesu] *mercy*:
B.18.115 *Mercy* highte þat mayde, a meke þyng wiþ alle,
B.18.121 Whan þise maydenes mette, *mercy* and truþe,
B.18.127 'Haue no merueille', quod *mercy*; 'murþe it bitokneþ.
B.18.146 Ne haue hem out of helle; hold þi tonge, *mercy*!
B.18.150 Thanne *Mercy* ful myldely mouþed þise wordes,
B.18.167 'That is sooþ', seide *Mercy*, 'and I se here by Sowþe
B.18.183 That *mercy*, my suster, and I mankynde sholde saue,
B.18.184 And þat god haþ forgyuen and grauntede me, pees, & *mercy*
B.18.389 I [may] do *mercy* þoru3 [my] rightwisnesse and alle my wordes
            trewe;
B.18.393 And my *mercy* shal be shewed to manye of my [halue]breþeren,
B.18.397 And *mercy* al mankynde bifore me in heuene.
B.19.93   For Mirre is *mercy* to mene and mylde speche of tonge.
B.19.185 To alle maner men *mercy* and for3ifnesse]
B.19.324 He made a manere morter, and *mercy* it highte.
C. 1.11   And sayde, '*mercy*, madame, what may this [be]mene?'
C. 1.41   'A madame, *mercy*,' [quod I], 'me lyketh wel 3oure wordes.
C. 1.166   Bote mekeliche with mouth *mercy* he bysoughte
C. 1.169   That he was myhtfull and meke and *mercy* gan graunte
C. 2.2   And sayde '*mercy*, madame, for mary loue of heuene
C. 2.136   For y, man, of thy *mercy* mede haue diserued."
C. 3.63   Haueth *mercy*,' quod mede, 'o[f] men þat hit haunteth
C. 3.472   *Mercy* or no mercy as most trewe acorden.
C. 3.472   Mercy or no *mercy* as most trewe acorden.

C. 4.73   And token mede [myd] hem *mercy* to wynne.
C. 4.90   Then gan mede to m[e]ken here and *mercy* bisouhte
C. 4.95   To haue *mercy* on þat man that many tymes hym greuede:
C. 4.139   Ne thorw mede *mercy*, by marie of heuene!
C. 6.4   And [lay] long ar he lokede and 'lord, *mercy*!' cryede
C. 6.10   But now wol y meke me and *mercy* byseche
C. 6.16   Haue be vnbuxum, y byseche god of *mercy*;
C. 6.92   For thy synnes souereynly and biseke god of *mercy*.'
C. 6.172   That he haue pite on me, p[u]tou[r], of his puyr *mercy*,
C. 6.195   Now, lord, for thy lewete on lechours haue *mercy*.'
C. 6.274   *Mercy* for my mysdedes þat y ne mourned [o]ftur
C. 6.320   And haddest *mercy* vppon þat man for memento sake.
C. 6.323   For thy mochel *mercy* mitigacioun y biseche:
C. 6.333   [T]rist in his mechel *mercy* and ȝut þou myhte be saued.
C. 6.338   Confessen hem and cryen hym *mercy*; shal neuere come in helle:
C. 6.340   'And haue his *mercy* in thy mynde and marchaundise, leue hit,
C. 7.121   To Amende vs of oure mysdedes, do *mercy* to vs alle.
C. 7.147   Yf we knowlechede and cryde Crist þerfore *mercy*:
C. 7.148   And for [that] muchel *mercy* and marie loue thi moder
C. 7.233   The mote is of *mercy*, the manere in þe myddes
C. 7.288   '*Mercy* is a mayden there hath myhte ouer hem alle
C. 8.37   And when ȝe mersyen eny man late *mercy* be tauour,
C. 8.177   'Haue *mercy* on hem, hunger,' quod [Peres], 'and lat me ȝeue hem benes
C. 9.238   Amend[e] hym and *mercy* aske and mekeliche hym shryue,
C. 9.275   Ther as mede ne *mercy* may nat a myte availle
C. 9.277   *Mercy* for mede and my lawe breke.'
C. 9.347   Forthy y consayle alle cristene to crye god *mercy*
C.11.47   Ne were *mercy* in m[e]ne men more then in riht riche
C.11.86   And saide, '*mercy*, madame; ȝoure man shal y worthen
C.11.215   Maistres þat [of goddis *mercy*] techen men and prechen]
C.11.230   [Ac] at he[re] moste meschef *mercy* were þe beste
C.11.231   And *mercy* of mercy nedes moet aryse
C.11.231   And mercy of *mercy* nedes moet aryse
C.12.71   *Mercy* for his mysdedes with mouthe and with herte.'
C.12.73   *Mercy* al [to] amende and mekenesse her folowe;
C.12.150   Maketh man to haue mynde in god and his *mercy* to craue,
C.13.13   That the kynde [kyng] criede hym *mercy*
C.13.142   And how þat [men] mede toke and *mercy* refusede.
C.14.56   To ȝeue *mercy* for mysde[de]s ȝif men hit wol aske
C.15.221   In his mouthe *mercy* and amende vs all:
C.16.23   And amende vs [of] thy *mercy* and make vs alle meke,
C.17.265   That men myhte nat be saued but thorw *mercy* and grace
C.18.258   *Mercy* for oure mysdedes as many tymes
C.18.275   'Loo!' quod he and lette me see: 'lord, *mercy*!' y saide,
C.18.287   The myhte of goddes *mercy* that myhte vs alle amende.'
C.19.184   So is þe holi gost god and grace withouten *mercy*
C.19.196   And melteth myhte into *mercy*, as we may se a wynter
C.19.200   Melteth to *mercy*, to merciable and to non oþere.
C.19.208   *Mercy* for his mekenesse wol maky good þe remenaunt.
C.19.211   So wol Crist of his cortesye, and men crien hym *mercy*,
C.19.218   So is þe holy gost god and grace withouten *mercy*
C.19.270   How myhte he aske *mercy* or eny mercy hym defende
C.19.270   How myhte he aske mercy or eny *mercy* hym defende
C.19.271   That wikkedliche and wilfulliche wolde *mercy* anyente?
C.19.282   And myldeliche his *mercy* aske; myhte y nat be saued?'
C.19.289   That may no kynge *mercy* graunte til bothe men acorde
C.19.294   That *mercy* in here mynde may nat thenne falle;
C.19.297   To amende al þat amys is and his *mercy* grettore
C.19.318   To man þat *mercy* asketh and amende thenketh."
C.19.326   Haeth *mercy* on suche men þat [so] euele may soffre.
C.19.328   That is coueytise and vnkyndenesse whiche quencheth godes *mercy*
C.19.333   Alle manere men *mercy* vppon and forȝeuenesse
C.20.89   Tho ful the knyhte vppon knees and criede iesu *mercy*:
C.20.118   *Mercy* hihte þat mayde, a mylde thynge with alle,
C.20.124   When this maydones metten, *Mercy* and treuthe,
C.20.130   'Haue no merueyle,' quod *Mercy*; 'merthe hit bitokneth.
C.20.149   Ne haue hem out of helle; holde thy tonge, *mercy*!
C.20.153   Thenne *mercy* fol myldely mouthed this wordes,
C.20.170   'That is soth,' saide *mercy*, 'and y se here bi southe
C.20.186   That *mercy*, my sustur, and y mankynde sh[olde] saue
C.20.188   *Mercy*, [my sustur], and me to maynprisen hem alle
C.20.431   [Y] may do *mercy* of my rihtwysnesse and alle myn wordes trewe
C.20.440   And *mercy* a[l] mankynde bifore me in heuene.
C.21.93   For Mirre is *mercy* to mene and mylde speche of tonge.
C.21.185   To alle manere men *mercy* and forȝeuenesse\
C.21.324   He made a manere morter and *mercy* hit hihte.

merciable adj *merciable adj.* B 4; C 5
B. 5.503   That art oure fader and oure broþer, be *merciable* to vs,
B.15.154   Men beþ *merciable* to mendinauntȝ and to poore,
B.17.234   Melteþ to mercy, to *merciable* and to [noon] oþere.
B.18.375   A[c] to be *merciable* to man þanne my kynde [it] askeþ

C. 9.15   *Merciable* to meke and mylde to þe gode
C.17.46   And marchauntȝ *merciable* wolde be and men of lawe bothe
C.19.200   Melteth to mercy, to *merciable* and to non oþere.
C.20.417   Ac to be *merciable* to man thenne my kynde [hit] asketh
C.20.436   To be *merciable* to monye of my haluebretherne.

merciede v *mercien v.(1)* A 1; B 1; C 1 mercyede
A. 3.19   Mildeliche mede þanne *merciede* hem alle
B. 3.20   Mildely Mede þanne *merciede* hem alle
C. 3.21   Myldeliche mede thenne *mercyede* hem alle

merciful adj *merciful adj.* B 1
B. 2.32   And what man be *merciful* and leelly me loue

mercyment n *merciment n.* B 1; C 2 mercement
B. 1.162   Vpon man for hise mysdedes þe *mercyment* he taxeþ.
C. 1.158   Vp man for his mysdedes the *mercement* he taxeth.
C. 4.182   Withouten *mercement* or manslauht amende alle reumes.'

mercymonye n *mercimonie n.* B 1
B.14.127   To ȝyue many m[e]n his [*mercymonye*] er he it haue deserued.

mere n *mere n.(3)* C 1
C. 3.381   Bote standynge as a stake þat stikede in a *mere*

mery(e- > murye

merite n *merite n.* A 1 meryt; B 4 meryt (1) merite (3); C 3 meryte
A. 1.157   ȝe ne haue no more *meryt* in [masse] ne in [houres]
B. 1.183   Ye ne haue na moore *merite* in masse n[e] in houres
B. 5.378   'This shewynge shrift', quod Repentaunce, 'shal be *meryt* to þe.'
B.10.256   Ne man hadde no merite myȝte it ben ypreued:
B.11.183   For hem þat haten vs is oure *merite* to louye,
C. 1.179   ȝe n[e] haueth na more *meryte* in masse ne in oures
C.11.157   Ne man mouhte haue *mery[t]e* [thereof] mouhte hit be ypreued:
C.16.329   Worth moche *meryte* to þat man þat hit may soffre.

meritorie adj *meritorie adj.* B 1; C 1 merytorie
B.11.79   Ac muche moore *meritorie*, me þynkeþ, is to baptiȝe,
C. 9.68   And moste *merytorie* to men þat he ȝeueth fore.

merk adj *mirke adj. &> mark* A 1 merke; B 3 merk (1) merke (2); C 3 merke (2) myrke (1)
A. 1.1   What þe mounteyne [be]meniþ, & ek þe [m]erke dale,
B. 1.1   What þ[e] Mountaigne bymeneþ and þe *merke* dale
B.11.160   [This matere is *merk* for many, ac men of holy chirche,
B.17.244   For to murþen men [wiþ] þat in [m]erke sitten,
C. 1.1   What the montaigne bymeneth and þe *merke* dale
C.18.196   'This is *myrke* thyng for me,' quod y, 'and for many anoþer,
C.19.210   For to murthe men with þat in *merke* sitten,

merknesse n *mirkenesse n.* B 2; C 2 merkenesse
B.18.136   In menynge þat man shal fro *merknesse* be drawe
B.18.177   That many day myȝte I noȝt se for *merknesse* of synne,
C.20.139   In menynge þat man shal fro *me[r]kenesse* be ydrawe
C.20.180   That many day myhte y nat se for *merkenesse* of synne,

mersyen v *mercien v.(2)* C 1
C. 8.37   And when ȝe *mersyen* eny man late mercy be taxour,

merþe > murþe

merueille n *merveille n.* B 4 merueille (3) merueilles (1); C 1 merueyle
B. 9.153   Muchel *merueille* me þynkeþ; and moore of a sherewe
B.11.75   Ich haue muche *merueille* of yow, and so haþ many anoþer,
B.15.590   Boþe of miracles and *merueilles*, and how he men festede,
B.18.127   'Haue no *merueille*', quod mercy; 'murþe it bitokneþ.
C.20.130   'Haue no *merueyle*,' quod Mercy; 'merthe hit bitokneth.

merueilled v *merveillen v.* B 2; C 4 merueyled (2) merueylede (1) merueileth (1)
B.11.351   Ac yet me *merueilled* moore how many oþere briddes
B.11.360   Muche *merueilled* me what maister [þei hadde],
C.13.162   And ȝut me *merueylede* more [how] mony [other] briddes
C.13.192   And þerfore *merueileth* me, for man is moste yliche the,
C.15.21   And y *merueyle[d]* in herte how ymaginatyf saide
C.18.23   Moche *merueyled* me on what more thei growede

merueillous adj *merveillous adj.* A 2 merueilleste (1) merueillous (1); B 3 merueillous (2) merueillouseste (1)
A.Pr.11   Þanne gan I mete a *merueillous* sweuene,
A. 9.59   Þe *merueilleste* metyng mette me þanne
B.Pr.11   Thanne gan I meten a *merueillous* sweuene,
B. 8.68   The *merueillouseste* metels mette me þanne
B.11.6   A *merueillous* metels mette me þanne,

merueillously adv *merveillousli adv.* A 1; B 2; C 4 merueilously (1) merueylousely (1) merueilousliche (1) merueylousliche (1)
A. 8.143   And Iosep mette *merueillously* how þe mone & þe sonne

B. 7.165 And Ioseph mette *merueillously* how þe moone and þe sonne
B.20.52 And mette ful *merueillously* þat in mannes forme
C.Pr.9 And *merueylousliche* me mette, as y may [ʒow] telle.
C. 9.309 And Ioseph mette *merueilously* how þe mone and þe sonne
C.10.67 And *merueilousliche* me mette amyddes al þat blisse.
C.22.52 And mette ful *merueylousely* þat in mannes fourme

mesager(s > messager

meschaunce n *mischaunce n.* A 2 meschaunce (1) myschaunce (1); B 6
  meschaunce (4) myschaunce (2); C 5 meschaunce (4) myschaunce (1)
A. 3.154 And alle þat meynteniþ hire men *meschaunce* hem betide!
A. 9.51 And þei seide, 'þe same saue yow fro *myschaunce*,
B. 3.167 And alle þat maynteneþ hire men, *meschaunce* hem bitide!
B. 5.91 I wolde be gladder, by god! þat Gybbe hadde *meschaunce*
B. 8.60 And I seide 'þe same saue yow fro *myschaunce*,
B.13.324 And blame men bihynde hir bak and bidden hem *meschaunce*;
B.14.76 For þe meschief and þe *meschaunce* amonges men of Sodome
B.17.267 [Mynne ye noʒt, riche men, to whiche a *myschaunce*
C.Pr.105 What cheste and *meschaunce* to þe children of Irael
C. 3.97 Morreyne or other *meschaunc[e]*: and mony tymes hit falleth
C. 6.69 And blame men byhynde here bak and bidde hem *meschaunce*;
C.10.59 And y sayde, 'þe same saue ʒow fro *meschaunce*
C.19.233 Minne ʒe nat, riche men, to which a *myschaunce*

meschief n *mischef n.* A 8 meschef (1) meschief (7); B 21 meschief (18)
  meschiefs (1) myschief (2); C 22 meschef (2) mescheues (1) meschief
  (15) meschiefes (2) meschiefs (1) myschef (1)
A.Pr.64 þe moste *meschief* on molde is mountyng vp faste.
A. 3.164 þere þat *meschief* is gret mede may helpe.
A. 3.256 Such a *meschef* mede made þe kyng [to] haue
A. 4.58 But ʒif mede it make [þi] *meschief* is vppe,
A. 7.191 *Meschief* it makiþ h[y] ben so mek nouþe,
A. 8.85 þat takiþ [þ]is *meschief* mekeliche as myselis & oþere,
A.10.181 And [were] marie[d] at *meschief* as men do now here children.
A.11.201 For mendynaun.ʒ *meschief* þ[o] men were dewid,
B.Pr.67 The mooste *meschief* on Molde is mountynge [vp] faste.
B. 3.177 Ther þat *meschief* is [most] Mede may helpe.
B. 3.278 Swich a *meschief* Mede made þe kyng to haue
B. 4.72 But if Mede it make þi *meschief* is vppe,
B. 6.205 *Meschief* it makeþ þei be so meke nouþe,
B. 7.103 That taken þi[s] *myschie[f]* mekeliche as Mesels and oþere,
B. 9.78 At myseise and at *myschief* and mowe hem amende
B.10.399 [Ac] at hir mooste *meschief* [mercy were þe beste],
B.10.457 Whan man was at *meschief* wiþoute þe moore grace.
B.11.300 And a title, a tale of noʒt, to his liflode at *meschief*.
B.12.84 And to mansede men *meschief* at hire ende.
B.13.77 And what *meschief* and maleese crist for man þolede,
B.13.159 Misese ne *meschief* ne man wiþ his tonge,
B.14.76 For þe *meschief* and þe meschaunce amonges men of Sodome
B.14.174 Ac poore peple, þi prisoners, lord, in þe put of *meschief*,
B.14.238 Wiþoute mournynge amonge, and *meschief* to bote].
B.14.255 *Meschief* is [ay a mene] and makeþ hem to þynke
B.15.98 Ther is a *meschief* in þe more of swiche manere [stokkes].
B.15.174 And alle manere *meschiefs* in myldenesse he suffreþ.
B.19.283 Sholde neuere mete ne [*meschief*] make hym to swelle;
B.20.65 [And] þat were mylde men and holye þat no *meschief* dradden,
C.Pr.65 The moste *meschief* on molde mounteth vp faste.
C.Pr.215 Til þat *meschief* amende hem þat many man chasteth.
C. 3.143 [And marre þe with *myschef*], be seynte mary my lady,
C. 3.223 Ther þat *meschief* is greet mede may helpe.
C. 8.211 *Meschef* hit maketh they ben so meke nouthe,
C. 8.232 In *meschief* or in malese, and thow mowe hem helpe,
C. 9.180 As mesels and mendenantes, men yfalle in *meschief*
C. 9.184 That taketh thise *meschiefes* mekeliche and myldeliche at herte
C. 9.217 Or ymaymed in som membre, for to *meschief* hit souneth,
C.10.202 In *meschief* for defaute of mete ne for myssyng of clothes:
C.11.230 [Ac] at he[re] moste *meschef* mercy were þe beste
C.12.179 *Mesc[h]iefes* on molde mekeliche to soffren:
C.12.202 *Mescheues* and myshappes and many tribulac[ion]s
C.13.71 Alle maner men [in] *meschief* yfalle,
C.15.83 And what *meschief* and maleese crist for man tholede.
C.15.158 Meseyse ne *meschef* ne man with his tonge
C.16.78 So he is neuere[more ful] merye, so *meschef* hym followeth
C.16.95 *Meschief* is ay a mene and maketh hym to thenke
C.16.251 There is a *meschief* in þe more of suche manere stokkes.
C.16.312 And alle manere *meschiefs* as munstracie of heuene.
C.21.283 Sholde neuere mete ne *meschief* maken hym to swelle
C.22.65 And þat were mylde men and holy þat no *meschief* dradden,

meseyse > myseise

meseles n *mesel n.* A 2 myselis; B 3 Meseles (2) Mesels (1); C 2 mesels
  (1) musels (1)
A. 3.122 To [monkis], to [mynstrelis], to *myselis* in heggis.

A. 8.85 þat takiþ [þ]is meschief mekliche as *myselis* & oþere,
B. 3.133 To Monkes, to Mynstrales, to *Meseles* in hegges.
B. 7.103 That taken þi[s] myschie[f] mekeliche as *Mesels* and oþere,
B.16.111 Boþe *meseles* and mute and in þe menyson blody,
C. 3.170 To Monekes, to [mynstrals, to] *musels* in hegge[s];
C. 9.180 As *mesels* and mendenantes, men yfalle in meschief

mesondieux n *mesondeu n.* A 1 mesonis_deux; B 1; C 1 mesondewes
A. 8.28 And make *mesonis deux* þerewiþ myseis[e] to helpe,
B. 7.26 And [make] *Mesondieux* þer[wiþ] myseise [to] helpe,
C. 9.30 Amende *mesondewes* þerwith and myseyse men fynde

mesour > mesure

message n *message n.* B 1; C 1
B.15.506 And make hir mone to Makometh hir *message* to shewe.
C.17.257 And maken here mone to Macometh here *message* to shewe.

messager n *messager n.* A 3 masager (1) messanger (1) messangeris (1); B
  5 Messager (4) Messagers (1); C 15 mesager (1) mesagers (2)
  messager (12)
A. 2.189 Mynstralis & *messangeris* mette wiþ him ones,
A. 4.115 But it be marchaunt, oþer his man, oþer *messang[er]* with lettres,
A.12.83 I am *masager* of deþ; men haue I tweyne:
B. 2.230 A[c] Mynstrales and *Messagers* mette with hym ones,
B. 4.132 But it be Marchaunt or his man or *Messager* wiþ lettres,
B.15.408 As *messager* to Makometh, men for to teche.
B.16.97 The maide myldeliche þo þe *messager* graunted
B.19.207 Quod Conscience and knelede, 'þis is cristes *messager*
C. 2.240 Ac mynstrals and *mesagers* mette with lyare ones
C. 4.129 But [it] be marchaunt or his man or *messager* [with] lettres,
C. 9.136 Godes munstrals and his *mesagers* and his mury bordiours
C.13.33 For yf a marchant and [a] *mesager* metten togyderes
C.13.37 The marchaunt mote nede be ylet lenger then the *messager*
C.13.40 Ther þe *messager* doth no more but with his mouth telleth
C.13.43 Thogh the *messager* make his way amydde the fayre whete
C.13.54 As þe *messager* may ne with so moche ese.
C.13.59 Ther þe *messager* is ay merye and his mouth ful of songes
C.13.64 And as safly as þe *messager* and a[s] sone at his hostiele.
C.13.79 The *messager* aren th[e] mendenant.ʒ þat lyuen by menne almesse,
C.13.88 Telleth þe lord a tale as a trewe *messager*
C.17.178 For Macometh to men swaer hit was a *messager* of heuene
C.18.130 The mayde myldeliche [tho] the *messager* grauntede
C.21.207 Quod Consience and knelede, 'this is Cristes *messager*

messe(- > masse(-

messie n *Messias n.* B 4; C 4
B. 3.303 That Moyses or *Messie* be come into [myddel]erþe,
B.15.585 And took it Moyses to teche men til *Messie* coome,
B.15.592 And by þat mangerie [þei] myʒte wel se þat *Messie* he semede;
B.15.604 Moyses eft or *Messie* hir maistres deuyneþ.
C. 3.457 Moises or *messie*, þat men ben so trewe.
C.17.159 A man þat hihte Makameth for *messie* they hym holdeth
C.17.296 Moises to be maister þerof til *messie* come
C.17.301 By þe myracles þat he made *messie* he semede

mestier n *mister n.* A 1 mester; B 1; C 1 mester
A. 8.7 Or any maner *mester* þat miʒte peris helpen,
B. 7.7 Or any [maner] *mestier* þat myʒte Piers [helpe],
C. 9.7 Or eny manere *mester* þat myhte [Peres] auayle

mesurable adj *mesurable adj.* A 2; B 2
A. 1.19 In *mesurable* maner to make ʒow at ese;
A. 3.235 Is no maner of mede but a *mesurable* hire;
B. 1.19 In *mesurable* manere to make yow at ese;
B. 3.256 It is no manere Mede but a *mesurable* hire.

mesure n *mesure n.* A 3 mesour (2) mesure (1); B 9 mesure (7) mesures
  (2); C 10 mesure (9) mesures (1)
A. 1.33 *Mesure* is medicine þeiʒ þou muche ʒerne.
A. 1.151 For þe same *mesour* ʒe mete, amys oþer ellis,
A.12.73 For þe myssyng of mete no *mesour* I coude,
B. 1.35 *Mesure* is medicine þouʒ þow muchel yerne.
B. 1.177 For þe same *mesur[e]* þat ye mete, amys ouþer ellis,
B.13.358 [Thoruʒ] false *mesures* and met, and wiþ fals witnesse;
B.14.71 And if men lyuede as *mesure* wolde sholde neuere moore be
          defaute
B.14.75 [Ac] *mesure* is [so] muche worþ it may noʒt be to deere.
B.14.295 Wynneþ he noʒt wiþ wiʒtes false ne wiþ vnseled *mesures*,
B.16.182 Of oon muchel and myght in *mesure* and lengþe.
B.20.26 He shal do moore þan *mesure* many tyme and ofte,
B.20.254 That in *mesure* god made alle manere þynges,
C. 1.19 And, in *mesure* thow muche were, to make ʒow attese
C. 1.33 *Mesure* is medecyne thogh þow muche ʒerne.
C. 1.173 For þe same *mesure* þat ʒe meteth, amis other elles,
C. 6.230 A galon for a grote, and ʒut no grayth *mesure*

C.13.188 In mete out of *mesure* and mony tymes in drynke,
C.15.270 And yf men lyuede as *mesure* wolde sholde neuere[more] be
          defaute
C.16.130 Wynneth he nat with w[ih]tus false ne with vnselede *mesures*
C.17.52   To make men louye *mesure* þat monkes ben and freres:
C.22.26   He shal do more þe[n] *mesure* mony tymes and often
C.22.254 That in *mesure* god made alle [manere] thynges

mesure v *mesuren v.* B 2 mesure (1) mesured (1)
B.14.78   For [men] *mesured* noȝt hemself of [mete] and dr[y]nke,
B.14.82   Forþi *mesure* we vs wel and make [we] feiþ oure sheltrom;

mesurelees adj *mesureles adj.* A 1 mesurles; B 1
A. 3.225 Þere is a mede *mesurles* þat maistris desiriþ;
B. 3.246 Ther is [a] Mede *mesurelees* þat maistres desireþ;

met n *met n.* &> mete v2,meten B 1; C 1 mette
B.13.358 [Thoruȝ] false mesures and *met*, and wiþ fals witnesse;
C.11.124 And caste [*mette*] by squire bothe lyne and leuele.

metal n *metal n.* B 2; C 2
B.15.350 The merk of þat monee is good ac þe *metal* is feble;
B.15.353 Ac þe *metal*, þat is mannes soule, [myd] synne is foule alayed.
C.17.75   Of moche [m]one þe *metal* is nauhte
C.17.79   Ac þe *metal* þat is mannes soule of [many of] this techares

mete n *mete n.* A 13 mete (12) metis (1); B 47 mete (43) metes (4); C 45
mete (40) metes (5)
A. 1.24   Þat oþer is *mete* at meel for myseise of þiselue;
A. 1.138 [Þer] þou art m[er]y at *mete*, ȝif men bidde þe ȝedde.
A. 3.211 Asken mede & messe penis & here *mete* alse;
A. 5.2   To here matynes & masse, and to þe *mete* aftir.
A. 5.225 Shal non ale aftir *mete* holde me þennis
A. 7.21   And alle maner of men þat be þe *mete* libbiþ,
A. 7.48   And nameliche at *mete* suche men eschew[e],
A. 7.185 And ȝaf hem *mete* & monie as þei miȝte asserue.
A. 7.210 Wiþ *mete* or [wiþ] mone let make hem [fare þe betere],
A. 7.217 In sudore & swynke þou shalt þi *mete* tilen
A. 7.251 And aftir many maner *metis* his mawe is alongid.
A.11.39   At *mete* [in here] merþe, whanne mynstralis ben stille,
A.12.73   For þe myssyng of *mete* no mesour I coude,
B. 1.24   [That oþer is] *mete* at meel for mysese of þiselue;
B. 3.224 Asken Mede and massepens and hire *mete* [als];
B. 5.2   To here matyns [and masse and to þe *mete*] after.
B. 5.257 'Artow manlich among þi neȝebores of þi *mete* and drynke?'
B. 5.453 Shal noon ale after *mete* holde þe þennes
B. 6.19   And alle manere of men þat [by þe] *mete* libbeþ,
B. 6.53   And namely at *mete* swiche men eschuwe,
B. 6.139 Ac ye myȝte trauaille as truþe wolde and take *mete* and hyre
B. 6.198 And yaf hem *mete* [and money as þei] myȝte [asserue].
B. 6.224 Wiþ *mete* or wiþ mone lat make hem fare þe bettre].
B. 6.233 In sudore and swynk þow shalt þi *mete* tilie
B. 6.267 And after many maner *metes* his mawe is [alonged].
B.10.53   At *mete* in hir murþe whan Mynstrals beþ stille,
B.11.112 'Multi to a mangerye and to þe *mete* were sompned,
B.11.196 That ȝyueþ hem *mete* or moneie [and] loueþ hem for my sake.'
B.11.279 For failed neuere man *mete* þat myȝtful god serueþ;
B.11.284 For masses ne for matyns, noȝt hir *mete* of vsureres,
B.11.418 Ac whan he mamelede about *mete*, and entremetede to knowe
B.12.198 Riȝt as som man yeue me *mete* and [sette me amydde þe floor];
B.12.199 [I] hadde *mete* moore þan ynouȝ, ac noȝt so muche worshipe
B.13.30   And preyde *mete* 'p[u]r charite, for a pouere heremyte'.
B.13.37   Conscience called after *mete* and þanne cam Scripture
B.13.38   And serued hem þus soone of sondry *metes* manye,
B.13.41   Ac [he eet] *mete* of moore cost, mortrews and potages.
B.13.48   And me þat was his [mette oþer *mete* boþe].
B.13.54   And þanne a mees of oþer *mete* of Miserere mei deus,_
B.13.60   And made hym murþe wiþ his *mete*, ac I mornede euere
B.13.62   He eet manye sondry *metes*, mortrews and puddynges,
B.13.108 Mortrews and ooþer *mete*, and we no morsel hadde.
B.13.403 And moore *mete* eet and dronk þan kynde myȝte defie,
B.13.424 And ȝyueþ hem *mete* and mede, and pouere men refuse,
B.14.68   That manye wyntres men lyueden and no *mete* ne tulieden.
B.14.78   For [men] mesured noȝt hemself of [*mete*] and dr[y]nke,
B.14.157 For muche murþe is amonges riche, as in *mete* and cloþyng,
B.14.229 That many of oþere men moot asken.
B.14.231 For his rentes ne wol nauȝt reche no riche *metes* to bigge;
B.15.207 Ac it is moore to haue hir *mete* [on] swich an esy manere
B.15.217 And þe murieste of mouþ at *mete* where he sitteþ.
B.15.475 Menynge as after *mete*; þus Makometh hire enchauntede,
B.15.475 In menyng after *mete* folweþ men þat whistlen.
B.16.126 And lefte baskettes ful of broke *mete*, bere awey whoso wolde.'
B.17.269 Of his *mete* and moneie to men þat it nedede?
B.19.283 Sholde neuere *mete* ne [meschief] make hym to swelle;
B.19.288 Ne no *mete* in his mouþ þat maister Iohan Spicede.

B.19.415 For hir pelure and palfreyes *mete* and pilours þat hem folweþ.
B.20.12   That is *mete* whan men hym werneþ and he no moneye weldeþ,
B.20.211 [Weede] ne worldly [*mete*] while þi lif lasteþ.'
C. 3.279 Asken mede and mas pans and here *mete* bothe;
C. 6.147 [Afturward, aftur *mete*], she and she chydde
C. 6.289 Ne take a meles *mete* of thyn and myn herte hit wiste
C. 7.67   Shal non ale aftur m[e]te holde me thennes
C. 7.84   And ȝeueth [hem] mede & *mete* and pore men refuse,
C. 8.51   Ac [manliche] at *mete* suche men eschewe
C. 8.203 And ȝaf hem *mete* and money as þei myhte deserue.
C. 9.149 Suluer or sode *mete* and sum tyme bothe,
C. 9.229 Bothe matynes and masse; and aftir *mete* in churches
C. 9.252 Ac while a wrouhte in þe world and wan his *mete* with treuthe
C.10.187 Meble ne vnmeble, *mete* noþer drynke.
C.10.202 In meschief for defaute of *mete* ne for myssyng of clothes:
C.11.33   Nowe is þe manere at *mete* when munstrals ben stille,
C.12.47   'Multi to a mangerye and to þe *mete* were sompned
C.13.86   Halyday or holy euene his *mete* to discerue.
C.13.188 In *mete* out of mesure and mony tymes in drynke,
C.13.226 Ac when he mamelede aboute *mete* and musede to knowe
C.14.137 Riht As sum man ȝeueth me *mete* and sette me Amydde þe flore;
C.14.138 Ich haue *mete* more then ynow Ac nat [so] muche worschipe
C.15.32   [Pacience as a pore thyng cam] and preeyede *mete* pur charite;
C.15.35   A meles *mete* for a pore man or moneye yf they hadde.
C.15.42   Clergie cald aftur *mete* and thenne cam scripture
C.15.43   And serued hem thus sone of sondry *metes* monye,
C.15.45   Ac of this *mete* þat maystre myhte nat we[l c]hewe;
C.15.46   Forthy eet he *mete* of more cost, mortrewes and potages.
C.15.54   And to me þat was his mette tho, and oþer *mete* bothe.
C.15.64   And made [hym] mer[þe] with [h]is *mete* Ac y mournede euere
C.15.66   And ete manye sondry *metes*, mortrewes and poddynges,
C.15.89   þat in þ[e] mawe of þat maystre alle þo *metes* were,
C.15.215 Fro Mihelmasse to Mihelmasse y fynde *mete* and drynke,
C.15.231 And reste and ryche *metes*, rebaudes hem made.'
C.15.245 'Hastow,' quod actyf, 'ay such *mete* with the?'
C.15.267 That manye wynter men lyuede and no *mete* ne tylede.
C.16.70   That *mete* or moneye of straunge men moet begge;
C.16.72   For his rentes wol nat reche ryche *metes* to bugge;
C.16.343 He is þe murieste of mouthe at *mete* þer he sitteth
C.17.32   Ac bestes brouhte hem no *mete* bute onliche þe foules
C.17.176 Menyng as aftur *mete*; thus macumeth here enchauntede.
C.18.154 And lefte basketes ful of Broke *mete*, bere awey hoso wolde.
C.19.235 Of his *mete* and mone to men þat hit nedede?
C.21.283 Sholde neuere *mete* ne meschief maken hym to swelle
C.21.288 Ne no *mete* in his mouth þat maistre iohann spyced.
C.22.12   That is *mete* when men hym werneth [and] he no money weldeth
C.22.211 Wede ne worldly *mete* while thy lif lasteth.'

mete v1 *meten v.(1)* A 4 mete (2) meten (1) mette (1); B 4 meete (1)
mete (2) mette (1); C 4 meten (1) meteth (1)
A.Pr.60   For here mony & here marchaundise *meten* togidere.
A.Pr.88   Tho[u] miȝtest betere *mete* myst on maluerne hilles
A. 1.151 For þe same mesour ȝe *mete*, amys oþer ellis,
A. 4.126 For nullum malum [þ]e ma[n] *met[t]e* with Inpunitum
B.Pr.215 Thow myȝtest bettre *meete* myst on Maluerne hilles
B. 1.177 For þe same mesur[e] þat ye *mete*, amys ouþer ellis,
B. 4.143 For Nullum malum þe man *mette* wiþ inpunitum
B.17.83   Feiþ folwede after faste and fondede to *meete* hym,
C.Pr.165 Thow myghtest betre *meten* myst on maluerne hulles
C. 1.173 For þe same mesure þat ȝe *meteth*, amis other elles,
C. 4.41   Bute dede as Consience hym kennede til he þe kyng *mette*.
C. 4.140 For nullum malum [þe] man *mette* with inpunitum

mete v2 *meten v.(4)* A 8 mete (1) mette (6) metten (1); B 23 meete (1)
met (1) mete (4) mette (16) metten (1); C 31 mete (6) meten (1) mette
(20) metten (4)
A. 2.174 Ac marchauntis *mette* wiþ hym & made him abide;
A. 2.189 Mynstralis & messangeris *mette* wiþ him ones,
A. 5.81   Whanne I *mette* hym in market þat I most hatide
A. 6.3   Til late & longe þat hy a lede *mette*,
A. 7.155 And manacide hym & his men whanne h[y] next *metten*.
A. 9.3   And fraynide ful ofte of folk þat I *mette*
A. 9.8   Til it befel on a Friday two Freris I *mette*,
A. 9.109 Ac er we ywar were wiþ wyt gonne we *mete*.
B. 2.215 Ac Marchauntȝ *metten* with hym and made hym abyde
B. 2.230 A[c] Mynstrales and Messagers *mette* with hym ones,
B. 5.101 Whan I *met[t]e* hym in Market þat I moost hate[de]
B. 5.515 Til late and longe, þat þei a lede *mette*
B. 6.170 And manaced [hym] and his men if þei *mette* eftsoone.
B. 8.3   And frayned ful ofte of folk þat I *mette*
B. 8.8   Til it bifel on a Friday two freres I *mette*,
B. 8.119 A[c] er we [war were] wiþ wit gonne we *mete*.
B.11.28   'Man', quod he, 'if I *mete* wiþ þe, by Marie of heuene!

B.11.244 Many tyme god haþ ben *met* among nedy peple,
B.13.6 And how þat Elde manaced me, my3te we euere *mete*;
B.13.25 And þere I [*mette*] a maister, what man he was I nyste,
B.13.221 Thei *mette* wiþ a Mynstral, as me þo þou3te.
B.13.344 For ech a maide þat he *mette* he made hire a signe
B.15.251 For whoso my3te *meete* [wiþ] hym swiche maneres hym eileþ:
B.16.146 Thanne wente forþ þat wikked man and wiþ þe Iewes *mette*
B.16.172 And þanne *mette* I wiþ a man, a mydlenten sonday,
B.17.55 Boþe þe heraud and hope and he *mette* atones
B.18.121 Whan þise maydenes *mette*, mercy and truþe,
B.18.216 For til modicum *mete* with vs, I may it wel auowe,
B.19.157 Ac Marie Maudeleyne *mette* hym by þe weye
B.20.4 And it neghed nei3 þe noon and wiþ nede I *mette*
B.20.93 [Th]anne *mette* þise men, er Mynstrals my3te pipe,
C. 2.225 A[c] marchauntes *mette* with hym and made hym abyde
C. 2.240 Ac mynstrals and mesagers *mette* with lyare ones
C. 4.48 And margarete of here maydenhod as he *mette* here late.
C. 5.6 For as y cam by Consience with resoun y *mette*
C. 6.178 For eche mayde þat y *mette* y made here a signe
C. 7.160 Til late was and longe þat hit was a lede mette
C. 7.297 Forthy y pray 3ow, [Peres], parauntur 3if 3e *m[e]ten*
C. 9.122 And thauh a *mete* with the mayre ameddes þe strete
C. 9.247 Ac aboute myddday at mele tyme y *mette* with hem ofte,
C.10.3 And fraynede ful ofte of folke þat y mette
C.10.8 Til hit biful [o]n [a] fryday two freres y *mette*,
C.10.115 And ar we ywar were with wit gan we *mete*.
C.11.187 'Man,' quod [he], 'yf y *me[t]e* with the, by marie of heuene,
C.13.33 For yf a marchant and [a] mesager *metten* togyderes
C.13.47 And þe hayward happe with hym for to *mete*,
C.13.57 And dredeth to be ded þerfore and he in derke *mette*
C.13.62 Haue hors and hardy men; thogh he *mette* theues
C.15.27 And y aroos and romede forth and with resoun we *mette*.
C.15.29 And *metten* with a maystre, a man lyk a frere.
C.15.190 They *mette* with a mynstral, as me tho thouhte.
C.16.143 As he þat woet neuere with wham on nyhtes tyme to *mete*:
C.17.30 Bote myldelyche when þey *metten* maden lowe [c]here
C.18.167 That Iudas and iewes iesus thei *mette*.
C.18.181 And thenne *mette* y with a man a myddelento[n] sonenday,
C.18.246 Fol trewe tokenes bitwene vs is wh[at] tyme þat y *met[t]e* hym,
C.19.53 Bothe abraham and sp[e]s and he *mette* at ones
C.20.124 When this maydone *metten*, Mercy and treuthe,
C.20.225 For til [modicum] *mete* with vs, y may it wel avowe,
C.21.157 Ac Marie Maudeleyne *mette* hym by þe weye
C.22.4 And hit neyhed neyh þe noen and with nede y *mette*
C.22.93 Thenne *mette* thise men, ar muinstrals myhte pype,

mete &> meten

metelees adj *meteles adj.* A 2 meteles; B 2; C 1 meteles
A. 8.129 *Metel[es* and money]les on maluerne hilles.
A.11.52 [Mendynaunt3] *meteles* mi3te go to bedde.
B. 7.147 *Metelees* and moneilees on Maluerne hulles.
B.10.66 Mendinaunt3 *metelees* my3te go to bedde.
C. 9.296 *Meteles* and moneyles on Maluerne hulles.

meteles > metelees,metels

metels n *metels n.(2)* A 3 metelis; B 9; C 5 meteles
A. 8.130 Musyng on þis *metelis* a myle wey I 3ede;
A. 8.131 Manye tyme þis *metelis* han mad me to stodie,
A. 8.149 Al þis makiþ me on *metelis* to þinke
B.Pr.209 What þis *metels* bymeneþ, ye men þat ben murye,
B. 2.53 And how Mede was ymaried in *Metels* me þou3te;
B. 7.148 Musynge on þis *metels* [a myle] wey ich yede.
B. 7.149 Many tyme þis *metels* haþ maked me to studie
B. 7.173 Al þis makeþ me on *metels* to þynke.
B. 8.68 The merueillouseste *metels* mette me þanne
B.11.6 A merueillous *metels* mette me þanne,
B.11.86 'If I dorste', quod I, 'amonges men þis *metels* auowe!'
B.11.407 That I in *metels* ne my3te moore haue yknowen.
C.Pr.220 What þis *meteles* bymeneth, 3e men þat ben merye,
C. 9.297 Musyng on this *meteles* A myle way y 3ede.
C. 9.298 Mony tyme this *meteles* hath maked me to studie
C. 9.318 Al þis maketh me on *meteles* to studie
C.15.4 And many tym[e] of this *meteles* moche thouhte y hadde:

meten v *meten v.(3) &> mete* A 3 mete (1) mette (2); B 8 meten (1)
mette (7); C 12 met (1) mette (10) metyng (1)
A.Pr.11 Þanne gan I *mete* a merueillous sweuene,
A. 8.143 And Iosep *mette* merueillously how þe mone & þe sonne
A. 9.59 Þe merueillesthe metyng *mette* me þanne
B.Pr.11 Thanne gan I *meten* a merueillous sweuene,
B. 5.9 [Th]anne [*mette* me] muche moore þan I bifore tolde,
B. 7.165 And Ioseph *mette* merueillously how þe moone and þe sonne
B. 8.68 The merueillouseste metels *mette* me þanne

B.11.6 A merueillous metels *mette* me þanne,
B.19.5 I fel eftsoones aslepe, and sodeynly me *mette*
B.19.481 And I awakned þerwiþ and wroot as me *mette*
B.20.52 And *mette* ful merueillously þat in mannes forme
C.Pr.9 And merueylousliche me *mette*, as y may [3ow] telle.
C.Pr.222 3ut *mette* me more of mene and of riche,
C. 2.56 And y say how mede was maried, *metyng* as it were.
C. 5.109 Thenne *mette* me muche more then y byfore tolde
C. 5.110 Of þe matere þat me *mette* furste on Maluerne hulles.
C. 9.309 And Ioseph *mette* merueilously how þe mone and þe sonne
C.10.67 And merueilousliche me *mette* amyddes al þat blisse.
C.11.165 And in a wynkynge y warth and wonderliche me *mette*
C.13.215 That y ne hadde *met* more, so murye as y slepte,
C.21.5 Y ful eftesones aslepe and sodeynliche me *mette*
C.21.481 And y [a]wakned þerwith and wroet as [me] *mette*.
C.22.52 And *mette* ful merueylousely þat in mannes fourme

mete3yueres n *meteyever n.* B 1
B.15.147 And bymeneþ goode *mete3yueres* and in mynde haueþ

metyng ger *metinge ger.(3) &> meten* A 1; B 2 metyng (1) metynge (1)
A. 9.59 Þe merueilleste *metyng* mette me þanne
B.11.320 Ac muche moore in *metynge* þus wiþ me gan oon dispute,
B.13.4 And of þis *metyng* many tyme muche þou3t I hadde,

mette n *mette n. &> met,mete,meten* B 2 mette (1) mettes (1); C 2 mette
(1) mettes (1)
B.13.35 Pacience and I [prestly] were put to be [*mettes*],
B.13.48 And me þat was his [*mette* oþer mete boþe].
B.15.40 Pacience and y [prestly weren] pot to be *mettes*
C.15.54 And to me þat was his *mette* tho, and oþer mete bothe.

metten > mete v2

meuen v *meven v.* A 2 meue (1) meuen (1); B 14 meue (5) meued (5)
meuen (1) meuestow (1) moeue (1) moeuen (1); C 12 meue (3) meued
(2) meuede (2) meuen (2) meuynge (1) moued (1) mouen (1)
A. 9.113 I durste *meue* no mater to make hym to iangle,
A.11.70 Suche motifs þei *meuen*, þise maistris in here glorie,
B. 8.123 I dorste *meue* no matere to maken hym to Iangle,
B.10.117 Swiche motyues þei *meue*, þise maistres in hir glorie,
B.10.269 Why *meuestow* þi mood for a mote in þi broþeres ei3e,
B.11.108 Ac þe matere þat she *meued*, if lewed men it knewe,
B.11.232 Why I *meue* þis matere is moost for þe pouere,
B.11.369 Ac þat moost *meued* me and my mood chaunged,
B.12.4 And manye tymes haue *meued* þee to [mynne] on þyn ende,
B.12.124 And medle no3t muche wiþ hem to *meuen* any wraþe
B.13.191 Haþ *meued* my mood to moorne for my synnes.
B.15.71 Ye *moeuen* materes vnmesurable to tellen of þe Trinite
B.16.77 And whan [he] *meued* matrimoyne it made a foul noise.
B.17.168 Na moore [may an hand] *meue* wiþoute fyngres.
B.17.197 Boþe *meue* and amende, þou3 alle my fyngres oke.
B.19.286 Waste word of ydelnesse ne wikked speche *moeue*;
C. 1.123 Ac of þis matere no more [*meu]en* y nelle.
C. 9.110 And aren *meuynge* aftur þe mone; moneyeles þey walke
C.10.119 Y durste *meue* no matere to maken hym to iangle
C.12.42 Ac þe matere þat she *meuede*, if lewede men hit knewe,
C.13.179 Ac þat most *meuede* me and my moed chaungede
C.14.67 And medle we nat moche with hem to *meuen* eny wrathe
C.15.129 Shal no such motyef be *meued* for me bote [þ]ere
C.16.232 *Mouen* motyues, mony tymes insolibles and falaes,
C.18.109 A *meued* matrimonye; hit made a fo[u]le noyse.
C.18.117 Thenne *moued* hym moed [in] magestate dei
C.19.163 Bothe *meue* and amende, thogh alle my fyngeres oke.
C.21.286 Wast[e] word of ydelnesse ne wikede speche *meue*;

my > i

michel n prop *Mighel n.* A 1; B 1; C 1 Mihel
A. 8.36 '[And] I shal sende myself seynt *Michel* myn aungel
B. 7.34 'And I shal sende myselue Seint *Michel* myn [a]ngel
C. 9.37 'And y shal sende 3ow mysulue seynt *Mihel* myn Angel

myd prep *mid prep.(1)* A 1 mid; B 5; C 4 mid (2) myd (2)
A.10.174 Boþe fisshis & foulis, forþ *mi[d]* oþere bestis,
B.Pr.147 And smale mees *myd* hem; mo þan a þousand
B. 1.116 And mo þousandes *myd* hym þan man kouþe nombre
B. 4.77 And token Mede *myd* hem mercy to wynne.
B.15.353 Ac þe metal, þat is mannes soule, [*myd*] synne is foule alayed.
B.17.171 Al þe my3t *myd* hym is in makynge of þynges.
C.Pr.168 And smale muys [*mid*] hem; mo then a thousend
C. 4.73 And token mede [*myd*] hem mercy to wynne.
C. 6.337 Of alle manere men þat [*mid*] goode wille
C.16.182 And so is man þat hath his mynde *myd* liberum Arbitrium.

mydday n *middai n.,adj.,& adv.* B 3; C 4
B. 5.492 Aboute *mydday*, whan moost li3t is and meel tyme of Seintes,

B.15.20   At mydnyght, at *mydday*, my vois so is knowe
B.18.134   Which deide and deeþ þoled þis day aboute *mydday*,
C. 7.132   Aboute *mydday*, when most liht is and mel tyme of sayntes,
C. 9.247   Ac aboute *mydday* at mele tyme y mette with hem ofte,
C.16.171   At mydnyhte, at *mydday*, my vois is so yknowe
C.20.137   [Which] deyede and deth tholede this day aboute *mydday*

myddel n *middel n.* A 1; B 6; C 5 myddel (4) myddell (1)
A. 3.10   Tok mede be þe *myddel* & brouȝte hire to chaumbre.
B. 3.10   Took Mede bi þe *myddel* and broȝte hire into chambre.
B. 3.327   And þe *myddel* of a Moone shal make þe Iewes torne,
B. 5.351   Clement þe Cobelere kauȝte hym by þe *myddel*
B.13.155   The *myddel* of þe Moone [i]s þe [m]yght of boþe.
B.17.192   Were þe *myddel* of myn hand ymaymed or yperissed
B.17.195   And þe *myddel* of myn hand wiþoute maleese
C. 3.10   Took mede by þe *myddel* and myldeliche here brouhte
C. 3.480   And the [*myddell*] of [a] mone shal make þe iewes turne
C. 6.409   Clement þe coblere cauhte hym by þe *myddel*
C.19.158   Were þe *myddel* of myn hand [ymaymed or ypersed
C.19.161   And þe *myddel* of myn hand] withoute maleese

myddel adj *middel adj.* B 2 myddel (1) myddul (1); C 1
B.12.7   To amende it in þi *myddel* age, lest myȝt þe faill[e]
B.16.5   Mercy is þe more þerof; þe *myddul* stok is ruþe;
C.18.118   That libera voluntas dei lauhte þe *myddel* Shoriare

myddelenton > mydlenten

myddelerþe n *middelerthe n.* B 3 middelerþe (1) myddelerþe (2); C 2
    myddelerd (1) mydelerthe (1)
B. 3.303   That Moyses or Messie be come into [*myddel*]erþe,
B.11.9   And in a Mirour þat hiȝte *middelerþe* she made me biholde.
B.11.324   And on a mountaigne þat *myddelerþe* hiȝte, as me [þo] þouȝte,
C.11.168   And in a myrrour þat hihte *myddelerd* she made me to loke.
C.13.132   And in þe myrour of *mydelerthe* made him efte to loke,

myddes n *middes n.* A 2 myddis; B 3; C 5
A. 2.40   In *myddis* a mounteyne at mydmorewe tide
A. 2.146   And mede in þe *myddis*, & al þis mene aftir.
B. 2.185   And Mede in þe *myddes* and [al þis meynee] after.
B.17.187   Ac who is hurte in þe hand], euene in þe *myddes*,
B.19.4   In *myddes* of þe masse þo men yede to offryng
C. 2.198   And mede in þe *myddes* and al this me[y]n[e] aftur.
C. 7.233   The mote is of mercy, the manere in þe *myddes*
C.18.6   Euene in þe *myddes* an ympe, as hit were,
C.19.153   Ac ho is herte in the hand euene in þe *myddes*
C.21.4   In *myddes* of þe masse tho men ȝede to offrynge

mydelerthe > myddelerþe

mydlenten adj *midlenten n.* B 1; C 1 myddelenton
B.16.172   And þanne mette I wiþ a man, a *mydlenten* sonday,
C.18.181   And thenne mette y with a man a *myddelento[n]* sonenday,

mydmorewe adj *midmorwe n.* A 1
A. 2.40   In *myddis* a mounteyne at *mydmorewe* tide

mydnyght n *midnight n.* A 1 mydniȝt; B 1; C 1 mydnyhte
A. 8.150   Manye tymes at *mydniȝt* whan men shulde slepe,
B.15.20   At *mydnyght*, at mydday, my vois so is knowe
C.16.171   At *mydnyhte*, at mydday, my vois is so yknowe

midsomer n *midsomer n.* B 1; C 1 myssomur
B.14.160   Ac beggeris aboute *Midsomer* bredlees þei [soupe],
C.16.13   Ac beggares aboute *myssomur* bredles they soupe

myen > i

mighelmesse n *Mighelmesse n.* B 2; C 2 Mihelmasse
B.13.240   Fro *Mighelmesse* to Mighelmesse I fynde hem wiþ wafres.
C.13.240   Fro *Mighelmesse* to Mighelmesse I fynde hem wiþ wafres.
C.15.215   Fro *Mihelmasse* to Mihelmasse y fynde mete and drynke.
C.15.215   Fro Mihelmasse to *Mihelmasse* y fynde mete and drynke.

might(e > may,miȝt n; myghtest > may; myghtful > myȝtful; mighty > myȝty

myȝt n *might n.* &> may A 8 miȝt; B 45 might (3) myght (6) myghte (1)
    myȝt (22) myȝte (8) myȝtes (5); C 31 myght (1) myhte (29) miȝte (1)
A. 1.105   Ȝaf hem *miȝt* in his mageste, þe meryere hem þouȝte,
A. 1.139   For in kynde knowyng in herte þer comsiþ a *miȝt*,
A. 5.84   Ac hadde I maistrie & *miȝt* I wolde murdre hym for euere;
A. 6.120   'Mercy [is] a maiden [þere], haþ *miȝt* ouer [hem] alle;
A.10.41   Þoruȝ *miȝt* of þe maieste man was ymakid:
A.10.63   Ouer suche maner of men *miȝt* in here soulis.
A.10.64   Ac in fauntis ne in folis ne be [fend] haþ no *miȝt*
A.10.77   And sauiþ þe soule þat synne haþ no *miȝt*
B.Pr.113   *Might* of þe communes made hym to regne.
B. 1.107   Yaf hem *myȝt* in his maiestee, þe murier hem þouȝte,
B. 1.163   And for to knowen it kyndely, it comseþ by *myght*,

B. 1.165   For in kynde knowynge in herte þer [comseþ a *myȝt*],
B. 4.173   And modiliche vpon Mede wiþ *myȝt* þe kyng loked,
B. 5.104   Ac hadde I maistrie and *myȝt* [I wolde murþere hym for euere].
B. 5.134   I wole amende þis if I may þoruȝ *myȝt* of god almyȝty.'
B. 5.635   'Mercy is a maiden þere haþ *myȝt* ouer [hem] alle;
B. 6.201   'I am wel awroke of wastours þoruȝ þy *myȝte*.
B. 9.38   My *myȝt* moot helpe forþ wiþ my speche".
B. 9.45   And in þis manere was man maad þoruȝ *myȝt* of god almyȝty,
B. 9.53   Thorgh *myȝt* of þe mageste man was ymaked.
B.10.105   Carpen as þei clerkes were of crist and of hise *myȝtes*,
B.10.259   And þat is, man, bi þy *myȝt*, for mercies sake,
B.10.274   Alle maner men to amenden bi hire *myȝte*;
B.10.335   [Ac] dowel shal dyngen hym adoun and destruye his *myȝte*.'
B.12.7   To amende it in þi myddel age, lest *myȝt* þe faill[e]
B.13.155   The myddel of þe Moone [i]s þe [m]yght of boþe.
B.13.167   Maister of alle þo men þoruȝ *myȝt* of þis redels,
B.13.255   Ac if *myȝt* of myracle hym faille it is for men ben noȝt worþi
B.13.328   'Or wiþ *myȝt* [of] mouþ or þoruȝ m[a]nnes strengþe,
B.14.218   Ac in pouerte þer pacience is pride haþ no *myȝte*,
B.14.245   And þouȝ Auarice wolde angre þe poore he haþ but litel *myȝte*,
B.14.301   The fifte is moder of [*myȝt* and of mannes] helpe,
B.15.66   Of god and of hise grete *myȝtes*, hise graces it letteþ.
B.16.54   The power of þise postes and hire propre *myȝt*[e].
B.16.120   And seide he wroȝte þoruȝ wichecraft & wiþ þe deueles *myȝte*:
B.16.165   Ayeins deeþ and þe deuel: destruyed hir boþeres *myȝtes*,
B.16.182   Of oon muchel and *myght* in mesure and lengþe.
B.16.184   The firste haþ *myȝt* and maiestee, makere of alle þynges;
B.16.192   *Might* and [a] mene [his owene myȝte to knowe],
B.16.192   Might and [a] mene [his owene *myȝte* to knowe],
B.16.211   *Migh[t]* is [in] matrimoyne þat multiplieþ þe erþe
B.16.271   The *myght* of goddes mercy þat myȝte vs alle amende.'
B.17.145   To ministren and to make þat *myȝt* of hand knoweþ;
B.17.171   Al þe *myȝt* myd hym is in makynge of þynges.
B.17.183   Than is þe sire [or] þe sone and in þe same *myghte*,
B.17.230   And melteþ hire *myȝt* into mercy, as men may se in wyntre
B.17.233   So grace of þe holy goost þe grete *myȝt* of þe Trinite
B.18.256   In alle *myȝtes* of man and his moder gladie,
B.18.318   [The] lord of *myght* and of ma[y]n and alle manere vertues,
B.18.430   And it afereþ þe fend, for swich is þe *myȝte*
B.19.24   Is crist moore of *myȝt* and moore worþi name
B.19.184   [*Myght* [men] to assoille of alle manere synne[s],
B.19.387   [*Myȝt*] to maken it and men to ete it after
C.Pr.140   *Myght* of tho men made hym to regne.
C. 1.159   And for to knowe hit kyndly, hit comeseth by *myhte*
C. 1.161   For [in] kynde knowynge [in] herte þer comseth a *myhte*
C. 6.73   'Or thorw *myhte* of mouthe or thorw mannes sleythes
C. 6.285   Then in the grace of god and in his grete *myhte*;
C. 6.295   Til thow haue ymad by thy *myhte* to alle men restitucioun.
C. 7.288   'Mercy is a mayden there hath *myhte* ouer hem alle
C. 8.207   'Y am wel awroke of wastours thorw thy *myhte*
C. 9.115   And to oure syhte as hit semeth; seth god hath þe *myhte*
C.15.141   [Hertely þou hym] helpe emforth thy *myhte*,
C.15.225   Ac yf *myracle* hym fayle hit is for men beth nat worthy
C.16.59   Ac in pouerte þer pacience is pruyde hath no *myhte*
C.16.85   And thogh Auaryce wolde Angry [þe] pou[r]e he hath bote lytel
           myhte
C.16.137   [The fifte is] moder of *myhte* and of mannes helthe
C.17.314   Thorw Moises and Macometh and *myhte* of god þat made al.
C.18.30   [And fro fallynge the stok; hit fayle nat of his *myhte*].
C.18.150   And thorw the *myhte* of Mahond and thorw misbileue:
C.18.201   *Miȝte* and a mene to se his owne myhte,
C.18.201   Miȝte and a mene to se his owne *myhte*,
C.18.287   The *myhte* of goddes mercy that myhte vs alle amende.'
C.19.119   To ministre and to make þat *myhte* of hand knoweth
C.19.135   And al þe *myhte* with hym is, was and worth euere.
C.19.149   Then is the syre or the sone and of þe same *myhte*
C.19.196   And melteth *myhte* into mercy, as we may sea wynter
C.19.199   So grace of þe holi gost the grete *myhte* of þe trinite
C.19.296   And nat of þe nownpower of god, þat he ne is ful of *myhte*
C.20.361   'The lord of *myhte* and of mayne þat made alle thynges.
C.20.474   And hit afereth th[e] fende, for such is þe *myhte*
C.21.24   Is Crist more of *myhte* and more worth[y] name
C.21.184   /*Myhte* men to assoyle of alle manere synnes,
C.21.387   *Myhte* to make hit and men to eten hit [aftur]

miȝte > may,myȝt n; myȝtest -estow > may

myȝtful adj *mightful adj.* A 1 miȝtful; B 3 myghtful (1) myȝtful (2); C 1
    myhtfull
A. 1.147   Þat he was *miȝtful* & mek & mercy gan graunte
B. 1.173   That he was *myȝtful* and meke and mercy gan graunte
B.11.279   For failed neuere man mete þat *myȝtful* god serueþ;
B.17.316   Noght of þe nounpower of god, þat he ne is *myghtful*
C. 1.169   That he was *myhtfull* and meke and mercy gan graunte

436

my3th(e > may

my3ty *adj mighti adj.* A 2 mi3tiest (1) mi3ty (1); B 2 myghty (1) my3ty (1); C 2 myhty
A. 1.150 Þei3 3e ben *mi3ty* to mote beþ mek of 3our werkis;
A.10.54 In manis brayn is he most & *mi3tiest* to knowe.
B. 1.176 Thou3 ye be *my3t[y]* to mote beeþ meke [of] youre werkes,
B.19.264 And Mark, and Mathew þe þridde, *myghty* beestes boþe;
C. 1.172 Thow 3e be *myhty* to mote beth meke in 3oure werkes,
C.21.264 And Marc and Mathewe the thridde, *myhty* bestes bothe;

my3tow > may; mihel > michel; mihelmasse > mighelmesse; myht > may; myhte > may,my3t n; myhtest > may; myhtfull > my3tful; myhty > my3ty; myhtow > may

mylde *adj milde adj.* A 3; B 11 milde (1) mylde (9) myldest (1); C 11 mylde (10) myldest (1)
A. 9.71 Whoso is mek of his mouþ, *mylde* of his speche,
A.10.83 Þat he makiþ men meke & *mylde* of here speche,
A.11.104 'For þi meknesse, man,' quaþ she, 'and for þi *mylde* speche,
B. 8.80 Whoso is [meke of his mouþ, *milde* of his speche],
B.10.152 'For þi mekenesse, man', quod she, 'and for þi *mylde* speche
B.12.204 Ne wiþ maydenes ne with martires [ne wiþ *mylde*] wydewes,
B.14.114 And makest hem wel nei3 meke and *mylde* for defaute,
B.15.280 And þoru3 þe mylk of þat *mylde* beest þe man was sustened;
B.15.306 In menynge þat meke þyng sholde fede.
B.15.469 And maidenes and *mylde* men mercy desiren
B.17.238 So wol þe fader for3yue folk of *mylde* hertes
B.19.93 For Mirre is mercy to mene and *mylde* speche of tonge.
B.19.255 And who þat moost maistries kan be *myldest* of berynge.
B.20.65 [And] þat were *mylde* men and holye þat no meschief dradden;
C. 9.15 Merciable to meke and *mylde* to þe gode
C.11.90 'For thy mekenesse, [man],' quod she, 'and for thy *mylde* speche
C.14.143 Ne with maydenes ne with martires ne with *mylde* weddewes,
C.15.273 'Meeknesse and *mylde* speche and men of o will,
C.15.290 And makest hem wel neyh meke and *mylde* for defaute
C.17.239 And take hede [how] Macometh thorw a *mylde* dowue
C.19.204 So wol þe fader for3eue folke of *mylde* hertes
C.20.118 Mercy hihte þat mayde, a *mylde* thynge with alle,
C.21.93 For Mirre is mercy to mene and *mylde* speche of tonge.
C.21.255 And [ho] þat moest maistries can be *myldest* of berynge.
C.22.65 And þat were *mylde* men and holy þat no meschief dradden,

myldely *adv mildeli adv* A 1 mildeliche; B 4 mildely (1) myldely (1) myldeliche (2); C 9 myldeliche (7) myldely (1) myldelyche (1)
A. 3.19 *Mildeliche* mede þanne merciede hem alle
B. 3.20 *Mildely* Mede þanne merciede hem alle
B.16.97 The maide *myldeliche* þo þe messager graunted
B.17.302 And *myldeliche* his mercy aske; myghte I no3t be saued?'
B.18.150 Thanne Mercy ful *myldely* mouþed þise wordes,
C. 3.10 Took mede by þe myddel and *myldeliche* here brouhte
C. 3.21 *Myldeliche* mede thenne mercyede hem alle
C. 3.39 To mede þe mayde *myldeliche* he sayde,
C. 3.77 3ut mede the Mayr *myldeliche* he bysouhte,
C. 9.18 That taketh thise mescheliche mekeliche and *myldeliche* at herte
C.17.30 Bote *myldelyche* when þey metten maden lowe [c]here
C.18.130 The mayde *myldeliche* [tho] the messager grauntede
C.19.282 And *myldeliche* his mercy aske; myhte y nat be saued?'
C.20.153 Thenne mercy fol *myldely* mouthed this wordes,

myldenesse *n mildenesse n.* B 2
B.15.174 And alle manere meschiefs in *myldenesse* he suffreþ.
B.15.258 Amonges cristene men þis *myldenesse* sholde laste

myle *n mile n.(1)* A 3; B 8 Mile (2) myle (6); C 5
A. 4.29 Ac consience com arst to court be a *myle* wey
A. 8.130 Musyng on þis metelis a *myle* wey I 3ede;
A.11.119 Leue hym on þi left half a large *myle* or more,
B. 5.372 That I, Gloton, girte it vp er I hadde gon a *myle*,
B. 5.401 That I telle wiþ my tonge is two *myle* fro myn herte.
B. 7.148 Musynge on þis metels [a *myle*] wey ich yede.
B.10.167 Leue [hym] on þi left half a large *myle* or moore
B.15.187 Labouren in [a] lauendrye wel þe lengþe of a *Mile*,
B.16.10 'I wolde trauaille', quod I, 'þis tree to se twenty hundred *myle*,
B.17.75 Wel sixe *Mile* or seuene biside þe newe Market;
B.20.164 And threw drede of dispair a do3eyne *myle* aboute.
C. 7.17 That y telle with my tonge is t[wo] *myle* fro myn herte.
C. 9.297 Musyng on this meteles A *myle* way y 3ede.
C.13.39 Wol lette hym, as y leue, the lenghe of a *myle*
C.19.74 Is syxe *myle* or seuene bisyde þe newe marcat,
C.22.164 And th[re]w drede of dispayr a doysayne *myle* aboute.

mylionis *n milioun num.* A 2 mylionis (1) mylions (1)
A. 3.249 For any *mylionis* of mone murdre hem ichone;
A.10.152 And manye *mylions* mo of men & of wommen

mylk(e > melk

mylked *ptp milken v.* C 1
C.17.10 To his selle selde cam and soffred be *mylked*.

millere *n milnere n.* A 1 myllere; B 2; C 1 mullere
A. 2.76 Munde þe *myllere*, & manye mo oþere.
B. 2.112 [Munde] þe *Millere* and many mo oþere:
B.10.45 Than Munde þe *Millere* of Multa fecit deus.
C. 2.116 Munde þe *mullere* and monye mo othere:

myn(e > i

mynchons *n minchen n.* A 1
A.10.136 Boþe maidenis & [*mynchons*], monkes & ancris,

mynde *n minde n.* A 2; B 13; C 9 mynde (8) muynde (1)
A. 7.86 He is holden, I hope, to haue me in *mynde*,
A.11.216 Arn more in his *mynde* þan þe memorie of his foundours.
B. 5.281 'Haue mercy in þi *mynde*, and wiþ þi mouþ biseche it–
B. 5.284 Forþi haue mercy in þy *mynde*, and marchaundise leue it,
B. 6.94 [He is] holden, I hope, to haue me in [*mynde*]
B. 9.125 Of swiche synfulle sherewes þe Sauter makeþ *mynde*:
B.11.50 Coueitise of ei3es com ofter in *mynde*
B.11.158 Wel ou3te ye lordes þat lawes kepe þis lesson haue in *mynde*
B.11.264 Makeþ a man to haue *mynde* in god and a gret wille
B.13.397 That my *mynde* ne was moore on my good in a doute
B.15.147 And bymeneþ goode mete3yueres and in *mynde* haueþ
B.15.295 Ac moost þoru3 [meditacion] and *mynde* of god almyghty.
B.16.38 Thoru3 preieres and penaunces and goddes passion in *mynde*
B.16.58 And to my *mynde*, as me þinkeþ, on o more þei growed:
B.17.314 That mercy in hir *mynde* may no3t þanne falle];
C. 3.327 A refte hym of his richesse and of his ryhte *mynde*
C. 6.284 That my *muynde* ne was more [o]n my godes in a doute
C. 6.340 'And haue his mercy in thy *mynde* and marchaundise, leue hit,
C.12.90 Wel ouhte 3e lordes þat lawes kepeth this lesson haue in *mynde*
C.12.150 Maketh man to haue *mynde* in god and his mercy to craue,
C.15.306 Dauid in þe sauter of suche maketh *mynde* and sayth: dormierunt
C.16.182 And so is man þat hath his *mynde* myd liberum Arbitrium.
C.17.154 For þer is no man þat *mynde* hath þat ne meketh [hym] and
bysecheth
C.19.294 That mercy in here *mynde* may nat thenne falle;

mynystre *n ministre n.* B 2 Mynystre (1) Ministres (1); C 3 ministre (2) ministres (1)
B.14.290 Ne to be Mair aboue men ne *Mynystre* vnder kynges;
B.15.419 Wolde neuere þe feiþful fader þat [þ]ise *Ministres* sholde
C. 5.60 And in quoer and in kyrkes Cristes *ministres*:
C. 5.91 But he be obediencer to prior or to *ministre*.'
C.16.125 Ne to be mair ouer men ne *ministre* vnder kynges;

mynistren *v ministren v.* B 2 ministren (1) mynistren (1); C 2 ministre (1) ministrede (1)
B.12.52 And þo men þat þei moost haten *mynistren* it at þe laste;
B.17.145 To *ministren* and to make þat my3t of hand knoweþ;
C.18.96 Maydones and martres *ministrede* [hym] here on erthe
C.19.119 To *ministre* and to make þat myhte of hand knoweth

mynne *adj minne adj.* C 1
C. 3.396 And is to [mene] in oure mouth more n[e] *mynne*

mynne *v minnen v.(1)* B 4 mynne (3) mynnen (1); C 2 minne
B.12.4 And manye tymes haue meued þee to [*mynne*] on þyn ende,
B.15.462 Ye *mynnen* wel how Mathew seiþ, how a man made a feste.
B.15.548 [*Mynne*] ye no3t, wise men, how þo men honoured
B.17.267 [*Mynne* ye no3t, riche men, to whiche a myschaunce
C.17.210 *Minne* 3e [nat], lettred men, how tho men honourede
C.19.233 *Minne* 3e nat, riche men, to which a myschaunce

mynours *n minour n.* A 1; B 1
A.Pr.101 Masonis, *mynours*, & manye oþere craftis,
B.Pr.222 Masons, *Mynours* and many oþere craftes;

mynstracie > mynstralcie

mynstral *n minstral n.* A 5 mynstralis (4) mynstrelis (1); B 14 Mynstral (1) minstrales (4) Mynstrales (3) Mynstrall (2) Mynstralles (1) Mynstrals (3); C 16 mynstral (2) mynstrals (2) mynstrels (1) muinstrals (1) munstrals (10)
A.Pr.33 And somme merþis to make as *mynstralis* conne,
A. 2.189 *Mynstralis* & messangeris mette wiþ him ones,
A. 3.122 To [monkis], to [*mynstrelis*], to myselis in heggis.
A. 3.207 *Mynstralis* for here merþis mede þei asken;
A.11.39 At mete [in here] merþe, whanne *mynstralis* ben stille,
B.Pr.33 And somme murþes to make as *Mynstralles* konne,
B. 2.230 A[c] *Mynstrales* and Messagers mette with hym ones,
B. 3.133 To Monkes, to *Mynstrales*, to Meseles in hegges.
B. 3.220 *Mynstrales* for hir myrþe Mede þei aske;

B.10.53 At mete in hir murþe whan *Mynstrals* beþ stille,
B.13.221 Thei mette wiþ a *Mynstral*, as me þo þou3te.
B.13.224 'I am a *Mynstrall*', quod þat man, 'my name is Actiua vita.
B.13.229 Ouþer mantel or moneie amonges lordes *Mynstrals*.
B.13.436 [Clerkes and kni3tes welcomeþ kynges *minstrales*,
B.13.439 Haue beggeres bifore hem þe whiche ben goddes *minstrales*
B.13.442 For to solace youre soules swiche *minstrales* to haue:
B.13.449 Thise þre maner *minstrales* makeþ a man to lau3e,
B.14.27 Ne no *Mynstrall* be moore worþ amonges pouere and riche
B.20.93 [Th]anne mette þise men, er *Mynstrals* my3te pipe,
C.Pr.35 And summe murthes to make, as *mynstrels* conneth,
C. 2.240 Ac *mynstrals* and mesagers mette with lyare ones
C. 3.170 To Monekes, to [*mynstrals*, to] musels in hegge[s];
C. 3.276 *Munstrals* for here m[yrth]e mede thei asken;
C. 7.96 Clerkes and knyhtes welcometh kynges *munstrals*
C. 7.99 Haue beggares byfore hem þe whiche ben goddes *mu[n]strals*
C. 7.102 For to solace 3oure soules suche *munstrals* to haue:
C. 7.109 Thise thre manere *munstrals* maketh a man to lauhe
C. 9.126 For hit aren murye mouthed men, *munstrals* of heuene
C. 9.128 And alle manere *munstrals*, me woet wel þe sothe,
C. 9.136 Godes *munstrals* and his mesagers and his mury bordiours
C.11.33 Nowe is þe manere at mete when *munstrals* ben stille,
C.15.190 They mette with a *mynstral*, as me tho thouhte.
C.15.193 'Ich am a *mynstral*,' quod this man, 'my name is actiua vita,
C.15.203 Or mantel or mone amonges lordes *munstrals*.
C.22.93 Thenne mette thise men, ar *muinstrals* myhte pype

mynstralcie n *minstralsie* n. A 2 menstralsie (1) mynstralcie (1); B 3; C 4
   mynstracie (1) munstracie (1) munstracye (2)
A. 3.11 Ac þere was merþe & *mynstralcie* mede to plese;
A.11.35 *Menstralsie* & merþe among men is nouþe
B. 3.11 A[c] þer was murþe & *Mynstralcie* Mede to plese;
B.10.44 Thei konne na moore *mynstralcie* ne Musik men to glade
B.10.49 Ac [*mynstralcie* and murþe] amonges men is nouþe
C. 3.12 Ac there was myrthe and *mynstracie* mede to plese;
C.15.195 'What manere *munstracye*, my dere frende,' quod Concience,
C.15.197 '*Munstracye* can y nat moche bote make men merye,
C.16.312 And alle manere meschiefs as *munstracie* of heuene.

mynstrel(i)s > mynstral

myntewhile n *mintwhile* n. cf. minute C 3 myntewhile (1) myntewhyle (1)
   myntwhile (1)
C.12.217 That many mothe was maistre ynne in A *myntewhyle*;
C.13.198 He myhte amende in a *myntewhile* al þat [mys]standeth
C.19.198 Melteth in a *myntwhile* to myst and to water.

minute n *minute* n.(1) cf. mintwhile B 2 Mynut (1) Minute (1)
B.11.381 He my3te amende in a *Minute* while al þat mysstandeþ,
B.17.232 Melte in a *Mynut* while to myst and to watre.

myracle n *miracle* n. B 5 myracle (1) miracles (3) myracles (1); C 6
   miracle (1) myracle (1) myracles (3) muracles (1)
B.13.255 Ac if my3t of *myracle* hym faille it is for men ben no3t worþi
B.15.446 And þoru3 *miracles*, as men mow rede, al þat marche he tornede
B.15.449 Moore þoru3 *miracles* þan þoru3 muche prechyng;
B.15.512 Many *myracles* he wrou3te m[e]n for to turne,
B.15.590 Boþe of *miracles* and merueilles, and how he men festede,
C.Pr.99 In menynge of *myracles* muche wex hangeth there;
C. 9.113 Ne none *muracles* maken; Ac many tymes hem happeth
C.15.225 Ac yf myhte of *myracle* hym fayle hit is for men beth nat worthy
C.17.263 Mony *myracles* a wrouhte men for to torne,
C.17.301 By þe *myracles* þat he made messie he semede
C.18.145 Ac ar he made þat *miracle* mestus cepit esse

myres n *mire* n.(1) C 1
C.13.167 In mareys and in mores, in *myres* and in watres,

myrke > merk

mirour n *mirour* n. B 6 Mirour (3) myrour (2) Mirours (1); C 5 myrour
   (1) myrrour (4)
B.11.9 And in a *Mirour* þat hi3te middelerþe she made me biholde.
B.11.20 And in þis *Mirour* þow my3t se [myrþes] ful manye
B.12.95 For boþe ben as *Mirours* to amenden [by] defautes
B.15.162 Ac I sei3 hym neuere sooþly but as myself in a *Mirour*:
B.15.527 He is a forbisene to alle bisshopes and a bri3t *myrour*,
B.16.156 Thow shalt be *myrour* to many men to deceyue,
C.11.168 And in a *myrrour* þat hihte myddelerd she made me to loke.
C.11.179 And in þis *myrour* thow myhte se murthes fol monye
C.13.132 And in þe *myrour* of mydelerthe made him efte to loke,
C.17.277 He is a forbisene to alle bisshopis and a briht *myrrour*
C.18.173 Thow shalt be *myrrour* to monye men to disceue.

mirre n *mirre* n. B 3; C 3
B.19.76 *Mirre* and muche gold wiþouten merc[ede] askynge

B.19.92 And presented hym wiþ pitee apperynge by *Mirre*;
B.19.93 For *Mirre* is mercy to mene and mylde speche of tonge.
C.21.76 *Mirre* and moche gold withouten merc[ede] askynge
C.21.92 And presented hym with pyte apperynge bi *Mirre*
C.21.93 For *Mirre* is mercy to mene and mylde speche of tonge.

myrrour > mirour; myrþe(s > murþe

mys n *mis* n. cf. mysbeleue B 1
B.10.118 And maken men in *mys* bileue þat muse on hire wordes.

mysbede v *misbeden* v. A 1; B 1; C 1 misbede
A. 7.44 And *mysbede* nou3t þi bondemen, þe bet shalt þou spede;
B. 6.45 And *mysbede* no3t þi bondem[a]n, þe bettre [shalt] þow spede;
C. 8.42 *Misbede* nat thy bondeman, the bette may th[ow] spede;

mysbeleue v *misbileven* v. A 1
A.11.71 And make men to *mysbeleue* þat musen on here wordis.

mysbileue n *misbileve* n. cf. mys B 2; C 5 misbileue (2) mysbileue (3)
B.15.397 A[c] oon Makometh, a man, in *mysbileue*
B.15.410 Makometh in *mysbileue* men and wommen brou3te,
C.Pr.102 That lewed men in *mysbileue* lyuen and dyen.
C. 3.328 And [soffrede] hym lyu[e] in *mysbileue*; y leue he be in helle.
C.17.181 Thus macumeth in *misbileue* man & womman brouhte
C.17.273 And fro *mysbileue* mony men turnede.
C.18.150 And thorw the myhte of Mahond and thorw *misbileue*:

myschaunce > meschaunce; myschef > meschief

myscheued v *mischeven* v. B 1
B.12.117 And his sones also for þat synne *myscheued*,

myschief > meschief

mysdede n *misdede* n. &> mysdo A 5 misdede (1) mysdede (2) misdedis
   (1) mysdedis (1); B 12 mysdede (3) mysdedes (9); C 10 mysdedes
A. 1.142 Mekliche for oure *misdedis* to amende vs alle.
A. 3.42 Þanne mede for hire *mysdedis* to þat man knelide,
A. 4.77 Amende þat *mysdede*, & eueremore þe betere.'
A. 5.55 To make mercy for his *mysdede* betwyn god & hym
A.11.257 Eche man for his *misdede* but mercy it make.'
B. 1.162 Vpon man for hise *mysdedes* þe mercyment he taxeþ.
B. 1.168 Mekely for oure *mysdedes* to amenden vs alle.
B. 3.43 Thanne Mede for hire *mysdedes* to þat man kneled
B. 4.90 Amenden þat [*mysdede*] and eueremoore þe bettre.'
B. 5.72 To maken mercy for hi[s] *mysded[e]* bitwene god and [hym]
B. 5.479 To amenden vs of oure *mysdedes*: do mercy to vs alle,
B.10.376 Ech man for hi[s] *mysded[e]* but mercy it [make]." '
B.11.136 Mercy for hise *mysdedes* wiþ mouþe [or] wiþ herte.'
B.12.111 3yue mercy for hire *mysdedes*, if men it wole aske
B.13.385 Mercy for my *mysdedes*, þat I ne moorned moore
B.13.410 [Is whan men] moorneþ no3t for hise *mysdedes*, ne makeþ no
                   sorwe;
B.16.242 Mercy for oure *mysdedes* as many tyme as we asken:
C. 1.158 Vp man for his *mysdedes* the mercyment he taxeth.
C. 1.164 Mekeliche for oure *mysdedes* to amende vs alle.
C. 3.45 Thenne mede for here *mysdedes* to th[at] man knelede,
C. 6.274 Mercy for my *mysdedes* þat y ne mourned [o]ftur
C. 7.70 Is when men mourneth not for his *mysdedes*,
C. 7.121 To Amende vs of oure *mysdedes*, do mercy to vs alle.
C.12.71 Mercy for his *mysdedes* with mouthe and with herte.'
C.14.56 To 3eue mercy for *mysde[de]s* 3if men hit wol aske
C.16.263 And amenden [hem] of here *mysdedes* more for [3oure]
                   ensaumples
C.18.258 Mercy for oure *mysdedes* as many tymes

mysdo v *misdon* v. A 2 mysdede (1) mysdo (1); B 5 mysdide (1) mysdo
   (2) mysdoon (1) misdooþ (1); C 3 mysdede (1) mysdo (2)
A. 3.112 She makiþ men *mysdo* manye score tymes;
A. 4.86 To haue mercy on þat man þat *mysdede* hym ofte:
B. 3.123 [She] makeþ men *mysdo* many score tymes.
B. 4.99 To haue mercy on þat man þat *mysdide* hym ofte:
B.15.109 And amende[n] hem þat [þei] *mysdoon* moore for youre
                   ensaumples
B.15.257 *Misdoþ* he no man ne wiþ his mouþ greueþ.
B.18.341 And al þat man haþ *mysdo* I man wole amende.
C. 3.160 And maketh men *mysdo* manye score tymes.
C. 4.86 And amende þat is *mysdo* and eueremore þe betere.'
C.20.389 And al þat m[a]n *mysdede*, y man to amenden hit

mysdoers n *misdoere* n. A 2 mysdoeris; B 2 mysdoeres (1) mysdoers (1)
A. 3.226 To mayntene *mysdoeris* mede þei taken,
A. 3.272 Mede of *mysdoeris* makiþ hem so riche
B. 3.247 To mayntene *mysdoers* Mede þei take,
B. 3.297 Mede of *mysdoeres* makeþ manye lordes,

myseise n *misese n.* A 1; B 3 myseise (1) misese (1) mysese (1); C 1 meseyse
A. 1.24   þat oþer is mete at meel for *myseise* of þiselue;
B. 1.24   [That oþer is] mete at meel for *mysese* of þiselue;
B. 9.78   At *myseise* and at myschief and mowe hem amende
B.13.159   *Misese* ne meschief ne man wiþ his tonge,
C.15.158   *Meseyse* ne meschief ne man with his tonge

myseise adj *misese adj.* A 1; B 1; C 1 myseyse
A. 8.28   And make mesonis deux þerewiþ *myseis[e]* to helpe,
B. 7.26   And [make] Mesondieux þer[wiþ] *myseise* [to] helpe,
C. 9.30   Amende mesondewes þerwith and *myseyse* men fynde

myself pron *miself pron.* A 16 myself (13) myselue (2) myseluen (1); B 35 myself (23) myselue (12); C 33 myself (1) myselue (1) mysulf (4) mysulfe (1) mysulue (26)
A. 2.18   In þe popis paleis heo is preuy as *myselue*;
A. 2.140   Shuln serue *myself* þat cyuyle hatte;
A. 3.5   'I wile assaie hire *myself*, and soþly apose
A. 3.39   I shal assoile þe *myself* for a sem of whete,
A. 4.57   I sey it be *myself*, þou shalt it sone fynde,
A. 4.120   For I seiȝe it be *myself*, & it so were
A. 6.36   For, þeiȝ I sey it *myself*, I serue hym to pay.
A. 7.29   In couenaunt þat þou kepe holy[k]ir[k]e and *myself*
A. 7.58   For I wile sowe it *myself*, & siþþe wile I wende.
A. 7.78   In dei nomine Amen I make it *myseluen*:
A. 8.36   '[And] I shal sende *myself* seynt Michel myn aungel
A. 8.146   I *myself* & my sones, seke þe for nede.'
A. 9.61   A muchel man, me þouȝte, lik to *myselue*,
A.11.163   Alle þise sciences, sikir, I *myself*
A.11.175   Þanne *myself* soþly so sone [as] heo it wiste
A.11.221   For I haue seiȝe it *myself*, & siþþen red it aftir,
B. 2.23   In þe popes Paleis she is pryuee as *myselue*,
B. 2.31   And haþ yeuen me mercy to marie wiþ *myselue*,
B. 2.179   Shul seruen *myself* þat Cyuyle is nempned.
B. 3.5   'I [wol] assayen hire *myself* and sooþliche appose
B. 3.40   I shal assoille þee *myself* for a seem of whete,
B. 4.71   I seye it by *myself*, þow shalt it wel fynde,
B. 4.137   I seye it by *myself* and it so were
B. 5.245   And ben hire brocour after and bouȝt it *myselue*.
B. 5.549   For þouȝ I seye it *myself* I serue hym to paye;
B. 6.27   In couenaunt þat þow kepe holy kirke and *myselue*
B. 6.63   For I wol sowe it *myself*, and siþenes wol I wende
B. 6.86   In dei nomine, amen. I make it *myselue*.
B. 6.255   For some of my seruauntȝ and *myself* boþe
B. 7.34   'And I shal sende *myselue* Seint Michel myn [a]ngel
B. 7.169   I *myself* and my sones, seche þee for nede.'
B. 8.70   A muche man me þouȝte, lik to *myselue*,
B.10.220   Alle þise Sciences I *myself* sotilede and ordeynede,
B.10.232   Than *myself* sooþly soone so he wiste
B.10.475   I se ensamples *myself* and so may manye oþer,
B.11.116   And in a weer gan I wexe, and wiþ *myself* to dispute
B.11.408   [Th]anne seide I to *myself*, '[slepyng hadde I grace]
B.12.2   Thouȝ I sitte by *myself* in siknesse n[e] in helpe.
B.12.201   But as a beggere bordlees by *myself* on þe grounde.
B.13.64   Thanne seide I to *myself* so pacience it herde,
B.13.122   Til I se þo seuene and *myself* acorde
B.13.329   Auenge me fele tymes, oþer frete *myselue* wiþInne;
B.15.162   Ac I seiȝ hym neuere sooþly but as *myself* in a Mirour:
B.16.47   That is lieutenaunt to loken it wel bi leue of *myselue*:
B.16.236   *Myself* and my meynee; and alle þat male weere
B.17.20   For, þouȝ I seye it *myself*, I haue saued with þis charme
B.17.38   And siþþe riȝt as *myself* so louye alle peple.
B.17.103   Saue feiþ and [*myselue* and] Spes [his felawe],
B.17.133   Louye hem lik *myselue*, ac oure lord abouen alle.'
B.17.196   In many kynnes maneres I myghte *myself* helpe,
B.18.330   [Al]þouȝ Reson recorde, and riȝt of *myselue*,
C. 2.23   In þe popes palays he is pryue as *mysulue*,
C. 2.186   'And y *mysulue*, syuyle, and symonye my felawe
C. 3.5   'Y shal asaye here *mysulue* and sothliche appose
C. 3.42   Y shal assoyle the *mysulue* for a seem [of] whete
C. 3.234   Ac y haue saued *myselue* sixty thousend lyues,
C. 4.134   Y sey it [by] *mysulf*,' quod resoun, 'and it so were
C. 6.36   And ȝut so synguler be *mysulue* as to syhte of [þe] peple
C. 6.37   Was non such as [*my]sulue* ne non so popholy;
C. 6.74   Venged me vele tymes other vrete *myself* withynne
C. 7.193   And thow y sey hit *mysulf* y serue hym to paye;
C. 8.26   In couenant þat thow kepe holy kerke and *mysulue*
C. 8.62   'For y wol sowen hit *mysulf* and sethe wol y wende
C. 8.95   In dei nomine, Amen: y make hit *mysulue*.
C. 8.267   For somme of my seruauntes and *mysulf* bothe
C. 9.37   'And y shal sende ȝow *mysulue* seynt Mihel myn Angel
C. 9.39   And sende ȝoure soules þer y *mysulue* dwelle

C. 9.313   Y *mysulue* and my sones, seche the for nede.'
C.10.68   A muche man, me thoghte, ylike to *mysulue*,
C.12.51   And in a wer gan y wex and with *mysulue* to despute
C.12.107   Ac for þe pore may nat paye y wol pay *mysulue*;
C.13.216   And saide anoen to *mysulue*, 'slepynge hadde y grace
C.14.2   Thogh y sete by *mysulue*, suche is my grace.
C.14.140   Bote as a beggare bordles be *mysulue* on þe grounde.
C.15.68   Thenne saide y to *mysulue* so pacience hit herde,
C.15.211   Y am sory þat y sowe or sette but for *mysulue*.
C.16.345   Ych haue ysey hym *mysulue* som tyme in russet,
C.18.252   *Mysulue* and my mayne; and alle þat male were
C.19.21   For, thogh y sey hit *mysulue*, y haue saued with this charme
C.19.93   Saue *mysulue* soethly and such as y louede–
C.19.102   And hym aboue alle and hem as *mysulue*;
C.19.104   Eny wikkedere in þe worlde then y were *mysulue*
C.19.162   In many kyne manere y myhte *mysulfe* helpe,
C.20.373   Althouh resoun record[e], and rihte of *mysulue*,

myselis > meseles; misese > myseise

mysfare v *misfaren v.* B 1 mysferde; C 1
B. 3.344   And so [*mys]ferde* ye, madame; ye kouþe na moore fynde
C.10.162   That god [s]eweth nat synnefole men and soffreth hem *mysfare*,

mysfeet n *misfait n.* B 2 mysfeet (1) mysfetes (1); C 1 mysfetes
B.11.375   Why þow ne sewest man and his make þat no *mysfeet* hem folwe.'
B.20.307   For hir *mys[fetes]* þat þei wroȝt hadde,
C.22.307   For here *mys[fetes]* that thei wrouht hadde,

mysferde > mysfare; mysfetes > mysfeet

myshap n *mishap n. &>* myshappe C 2 myshap (1) myshappes (1)
C. 5.34   Or ymaymed thorw som *myshap* whereby thow myhte be excused?'
C.12.202   Mescheues and *myshappes* and many tribulac[ion]s

myshappe v *mishappen v.* B 2 myshappe (1) myshapped (1); C 2 mishap (1) myshappe (1)
B. 3.329   For Makometh and Mede *myshappe* shul þat tyme;
B.10.288   Archa dei *myshapped* and Ely brak his nekke.
C. 3.482   For Machameth and mede [shal] *mishap* þat tyme;
C.11.185   'The man þat me liketh to helpe myhte nat *myshappe*.'

myshappes > myshap

mysliked v *misliken v.(1)* C 1
C.16.314   Ne *mysliked* thogh he lore or lened þat ilke

myspen- > mysspenden

mysproud adj *misproude adj.& n.* B 1; C 1
B.13.435   Ne no *mysproud* man amonges lordes ben allowed.
C. 7.95   Ne no *mysproud* man amongus lordes be [alow]ede.

mysruleþ v *misreulen v.* B 1
B. 9.61   Muche wo worþ þat man þat *mysruleþ* his Inwit,

myssaide > mysseyd; mysse > mysseþ

mysseyd v *misseien v.* A 1 misseid; B 2 mysseide (1) mysseyd (1); C 2 myssaide (1) mysseyde (1)
A. 5.51   And suffre to be *misseid*, & so dide I neuere.
B. 5.68   And suffre to be *mysseyd*, and so dide I neuere.
B.16.127   And *mysseide* þe Iewes manliche and manaced hem to bete
C. 6.9   And soffre to be *mysseyde*, and so dyde y neuere.
C.20.350   Sethe þat satan *myssaide* thus foule

mysseþ v *missen v.(1)* B 2 mysse (1) mysseþ (1); C 1 misseth
B.Pr.192   The maȝe among vs alle þeiȝ we *mysse* a sherewe,
B.12.99   For as a man may noȝt see þat *mysseþ* hise eiȝen,
C.14.44   For as a man may nat se þat *misseth* his yes,

mysshapen ptp *misshapen ppl.* A 1; B 1; C 1 mysshape
A. 8.78   Þere ben mo *mysshapen* amonges hem, whoso takiþ hede,
B. 7.96   Ther is moore *mysshapen* amonges þise beggeres
C. 9.172   Ther aren mo *mysshape* amonges suche beggares

myssyng ger *missinge ger.* A 1; C 1
A.12.73   For þe *myssyng* of mete no mesour I coude,
C.10.202   In meschief for defaute of mete ne for *myssyng* of clothes:

myssomur > midsomer

mysspenden v *misspenden v.* B 1; C 4 myspende (1) myspened (1) myspenen (1) myspeneth (1)
B.15.76   And how þat folk in folies [hir fyue wittes *mysspenden*],
C. 5.93   That y haue ytynt tyme and tyme *myspened*;
C.10.175   And moche wo worth hym þat inwit *myspeneth*
C.10.186   Ne spille speche ne tyme ne *myspende* noyther
C.16.235   And [ho]w that folk [in folies] here fyue wittes *myspen[en]*,

mysstandeþ v *misstanden v.* B 1; C 1 mysstandeth
B.11.381 He myȝte amende in a Minute while al þat *mysstandeþ*,
C.13.198 He myhte amende in a myntewhile al þat *[mys]standeth*

myst n *mist n.(1)* A 1; B 2; C 2
A.Pr.88 Tho[u] miȝtest betere mete *myst* on maluerne hilles
B.Pr.215 Thow myȝtest bettre meete *myst* on Maluerne hilles
B.17.232 Melte in a Mynut while to *myst* and to watre.
C.Pr.165 Thow myghtest betre meten *myst* on maluerne hulles
C.19.198 Melteth in a myntwhile to *myst* and to water.

mystier adj *misti adj.(1)* A 1 mistlokere; B 1; C 1 mystiloker
A.11.138 For þe more I muse þeron þe *mistlokere* it semiþ,
B.10.186 The moore I muse þerInne þe *mystier* it semeþ,
C.11.127 Þe more y muse þer[i]n the *mystiloker* hit semeth

mysturnynge ger *misturning ger.* C 1
C. 7.308 That myhte folowe vs vch fote for drede of *mysturnynge*.'

mysulf(e mysulue > myself

myswonne v *miswinnen v.* B 1; C 1
B.13.42 Of þat men *myswonne* þei made hem wel at ese,
C.15.47 Of þat men *myswonne* they made hem wel at ese

myte n *mite n.(2)* A 1; B 3 myte (2) mytes (1); C 3
A. 8.53 Shal no deuil at his deþ day derie hym a *myte*
B. 7.51 Shal no deuel at his deeþ day deren hym a *myte*
B.13.196 And þe poore widewe [purely] for a peire of *mytes*
B.20.179 May noȝt a *myte* auaille to med[l]e ayein Elde.'
C. 9.275 Ther as mede ne mercy may nat a *myte* availle
C.13.97 And as moche mede for a *myte* þer he offreth
C.22.179 May nat a *myte* avayle to medlen aȝen Elde.'

mitigacion n *mitigacioun n.* A 1 mytygacioun; B 1; C 1 mitigacioun
A. 5.243 But for þi muchel mercy *mytygacioun* I beseche;
B. 5.469 But for þi muchel mercy *mitigacion* I biseche:
C. 6.323 For thy mochel mercy *mitigacioun* y biseche:

mytrede ptp *mitren v.* C 1
C. 4.193 More then alle thy marchauntes or thy *mytrede* Bysshopes

mywen v *mowen v.(4)* C 1
C. 5.14 Mowen or *mywen* or make bond to sheues,

myx n *mix n.* B 1
B.14.23 Shal neuere [*myx*] bymolen it, ne moþe after biten it,

mnam n *mnam n.* A 2 nam; B 2
A. 7.223 Seruus nequam had a *nam*, & for he nolde it vsen,
A. 7.225 And benom hym his *nam* for he nolde werche,
B. 6.239 Seruus nequam hadde a *Mnam* and for he [n]olde [it vse]
B. 6.241 And bynam hym his *Mnam* for he [n]olde werche

mo n *mo n. cf. moore* A 4; B 9; C 12 mo (11) moo (1)
A. 2.76 Munde þe myllere, & manye *mo* oþere.
A. 3.1 Now is mede þe maide, & no *mo* of hem alle,
A. 4.10 Of mede & of *mo* oþere, what man shal hire wedde,
A. 8.78 Þere ben *mo* mysshapen amonges hem, whoso takiþ hede,
B.Pr.147 And smale mees myd hem; *mo* þan a þousand
B. 2.112 [Munde] þe Millere and many *mo* oþere:
B. 3.1 NOw is Mede þe mayde and na *mo* of hem alle
B. 4.10 [Of Mede and of *mo* oþere, what man shal hire wedde],
B. 5.293 For þee and for many *mo* þat man shal yeue a rekenyng:
B.15.335 How I myȝte *mo* þerInne amonges hem sette.
B.18.179 Moyses and many *mo* mer[ye] shul [synge];
B.19.127 Sore afyngred folk, *mo* þan fyue þousand.
B.19.165 Thaddee and ten *mo* wiþ Thomas of Inde.
C.Pr.168 And smale muys [mid] hem; *mo* then a thousand
C. 2.7 And mony *mo* of here maners, of men and of wymmen.'
C. 2.116 Munde þe mullere and monye *mo* othere:
C. 3.1 Now is mede þe mayde and na *mo* of hem alle
C. 4.10 Of mede and of *mo* othere and what man shal here wedde
C. 6.348 For the and for many *mo* þat man shal ȝeue a rykenynge
C. 9.172 Ther aren *mo* mysshape amonges suche beggares
C.15.151 Saue Concience and clergie y couthe no *mo* aspye.
C.19.26 And six thousand *mo*,' quod fayth; 'y [can] nat seyn here names.'
C.20.182 Moises and many *moo* Mer[y] shal synge;
C.21.127 Sore afyngered folk, *mo* then fyue thousand.
C.21.165 Taddee and ten *mo* with Thomas of ynde.

mo adj *mo adj. cf. moore* A 1; B 6; C 4
A. 7.257 Þere arn *mo* liȝeris þan lechis, lord hem amende!
B. 1.116 And *mo* þousandes myd hym þan man kouþe nombre
B. 5.243 I haue *mo* Manoirs þoruȝ Rerages þan þoruȝ Miseretur & com[m]odat.
B. 6.273 [Ther are *mo* lieres þan] leches; lord hem amende!
B.12.118 And manye *mo* oþer men, þat were no leuites,

B.17.285 A[c] yet in *mo* maneres men offenden þe holy goost;
B.20.272 And youre noumbre vnder Notaries signe and neiþer *mo* ne lasse.'
C.12.172 *Mo* prouerbes y myhte haue of mony holy seyntes
C.19.37 That of no trinite ne telleth ne taketh *mo* persones
C.19.266 And ȝut in *mo* maneres men [o]ffenden þe holy gost;
C.22.272 And ȝoure nombre vnde[r] notarie sygne and noþer *mo* ne lasse.'

mo adv *mo adv. cf. moore* A 3; B 6; C 5 ma (1) mo (4)
A. 2.196 Saue mede þe maiden no *mo* durste abide.
A.10.152 And manye mylions *mo* of men & of wommen
A.11.131 Aristotel & oþere *mo* to arguen I tauȝte;
B. 2.237 Saue Mede þe mayde na *mo* dorste abide.
B.10.179 Aristotle and oþere *mo* to argue I tauȝte;
B.12.43 Aristotle and oþere *mo*, ypocras and virgile,
B.14.331 Or maistrie ouer any man *mo* þan of hymselue.
B.18.178 Adam and Eue and oþere *mo* in helle.
B.19.54 For he yaf Adam and Eue and oþere *mo* blisse
C. 2.253 Saue mede þe mayde no *ma* durste abyde.
C.11.119 Aristotel and oþere [*mo*] to Arguen y tauhte;
C.14.3 Y haue folewed the, in fayth, *mo* then fourty wynter
C.20.181 Adam and Eue and other *mo* in helle.
C.21.54 For he ȝaf Adam and Eue and oþere *mo* blisse

moche(l > much

moder n *moder n.* A 3 moder (1) modir (2); B 12; C 17
A. 5.253 Criede vpward to crist & to his [clene] *modir*
A. 8.180 And marie his *modir* to be mene betwene,
A.12.116 Marie *moder* and may, for man þou byseke
B. 2.50 Now I bikenne þee crist', quod she, 'and his clene *moder*,
B. 5.511 Cride vpward to Crist and to his clene *moder*
B. 7.202 And Marie his *moder* be meene bitwene,
B.14.265 And as a mayde for mannes loue hire *moder* forsakeþ,
B.14.301 The fifte is *moder* of [myȝt and of mannes] helþe,
B.16.197 That is children of charite, and holi chirche þe *moder*.
B.16.217 Na moore myȝte god be man but if he *moder* hadde.
B.18.128 A maiden þat highte Marie, and *moder* wiþouten felyng
B.18.256 In alle myȝtes of man and his *moder* gladie,
B.19.119 For bifore his *moder* Marie made he þat wonder
B.19.124 And whan he [was woxen] moore, in his *moder* absence,
B.19.148 And his *moder* Marie; þus men bifore de[uyn]ede,
C. 2.53 For y bykenne the crist,' quod she, 'and his clene *moder*,
C. 2.125 Amendes was here *moder* by trewe menne lokynge,
C. 2.126 And withouten here *moder* amendes mede may [nat] be wedded.
C. 4.39 More then for oure lordes loue oþer oure lady, goddes *moder*.'
C. 6.15 For y, formost and furste, to fader and *moder*
C. 7.148 And for [that] muchel mercy and marie loue thi *moder*
C. 7.156 Criede vpward to Crist and to his clene *moder*
C. 8.21 Y wolde y couthe,' quod the knyhte, 'by Crist and his *moder*!
C. 9.348 And marie his *moder* be oure mene to hym
C.12.134 And seynt marie his *moder*, as Mathew bereth witnesse,
C.16.105 As a mayde for mannes loue here *moder* fors[a]ke[th],
C.16.137 [The fifte is] *moder* of myhte and mannes helthe
C.18.206 The whiche aren childrene of charite and holy church [the] *moder*.
C.20.131 A mayde þat hoteth Marie, a[nd] *moder* withouten velynge
C.21.119 For bifore his *moder* Marie made he þat wonder
C.21.124 And when he was wexen more, in his *moder* absence,
C.21.148 And his *moder* marie; thus men bifore deuyned.

mody adj *modi adj.* A 1; B 1
A.10.217 And so comiþ dobest aboute, and bringeþ doun *mody*,
B. 9.208 And so comeþ dobest [aboute] and bryngeþ adoun *mody*,

modiliche adv *modili adv.* B 1; C 1
B. 4.173 And *modiliche* vpon Mede wiþ myȝt þe kyng loked,
C. 4.167 And *modiliche* vppon mede many tym[e] lokede

modir > moder; moeble(s > meble; moed > mood; moes > mosse; moest > moost; moet > moot; moethalle > moot_halle; moeue(n > meuen; moylere > mulerie,muliere; moylore moyloure > muliere

moyses n prop *Moises n.* A 1; B 9 moises (1) Moyses (8); C 8 Moises (5) moyses (3)
A. 3.243 [Aȝens isra[e]l and aaron and *moyses* his broþer].
B. 1.151 And lered it *Moyses* for þe leueste þyng and moost lik to heuene.
B. 3.303 That *Moyses* or Messie be come into [myddel]erþe,
B.11.170 And took it *moises* vpon þe mount alle men to lere].
B.12.72 For *Moyses* witnesseþ þat god wroot for to wisse þe peple
B.15.585 And took it *Moyses* to teche men til Messie coome,
B.15.604 *Moyses* eft or Messie hir maistres deuyneþ.
B.17.63 How he wiþ *Moyses* maundement hadde many men yholpe,
B.18.179 *Moyses* and many mo mer[ye] shul [synge];
B.20.278 For god made to men a lawe and *Moyses* it tauȝte:
C. 3.457 *Moises* or messie, þat men ben so trewe.
C.14.37 For *moyses* witnesseth þat god wroet [in stoen with his fynger;
C.17.296 *Moises* to be maister þerof til messie come

C.17.312   *Moises* oþer Macometh here maystres deuyneth
C.17.314   Thorw *Moises* and Macometh and myhte of god þat made al.
C.19.62   How he with *Moyses* maundement hadde mony men yholpe
C.20.182   *Moises* and many moo Mer[y] shal synge;
C.22.278   For god made to men a lawe and *Moyses* hit tauhte:

moiste adj *moiste adj.* B 1; C 1 moist
B.16.68   Matrimoyne I may nyme, a *moiste* fruyt wiþalle.
C.18.85   Matrimonye, a *moist* fruyt þat multiplieth þe peple;

moiste v *moisten v.* B 1; C 1
B.18.368   May no drynke me *moiste*, ne my þurst slake,
C.20.410   *Moiste* me to þe fulle ne my furste slokke

mok > muk

molde n1 *molde n.(1)* A 8; B 13 molde (6) moolde (7); C 12
A.Pr.64   þe moste meschief on *molde* is mountyng vp faste.
A. 1.42   Ac þe mone on þis *molde* þat men so faste holdiþ,
A. 2.148   Of many maner of m[e]n þat on þis *molde* libbeþ,
A. 2.158   Shal neuere man of þis *molde* meynprise þe [l]este,
A. 3.69   For þise arn men of þise *molde* þat most harm werchiþ.
A. 3.233   Shal haue mede on þis *molde* þat mattheu haþ grauntid:
A. 8.79   Þanne of alle oþer maner men þat on þis *molde* wandriþ.
A.10.128   Among men of þis *molde* þat mek ben & kynde.
B.Pr.67   The mooste meschief on *Molde* is mountynge [vp] faste.
B. 1.44   Ac þe moneie [on] þis *molde* þat men so faste holdeþ,
B. 2.37   And men of þis *moolde* þat maynteneþ truþe,
B. 2.187   [Of many maner man þat on þis *molde* libbeth],
B. 2.197   Shal neuere man of þis *molde* meynprise þe leeste,
B. 3.80   For þise are men on þis *molde* þat moost harm wercheþ.
B. 3.324   [Shul haue] Mede [on þis *molde* þat] Mathew [haþ graunted]:
B. 3.292   Thise shul ben Maistres on *moolde* [trewe men] to saue.
B. 7.97   Than of alle [oþere] manere men þat on þis *moolde* [wandreþ].
B. 8.14   For [ye] be men of þis *moolde* þat moost wide walken,
B. 9.85   For alle þe mebles on þis *moolde* and he amende it my3te.
B.10.397   For many men on þis *moolde* moore setten hir hert[e]
B.11.275   And is to mene to men þat on þis *moolde* lyuen,
C.Pr.65   The moste meschief on *molde* mounteth vp faste.
C. 1.42   Ac þe moneye of þis *molde* þat men so faste kepen,
C. 2.211   Shal neuere man of þis *molde* maynpryse þe leste,
C. 3.445   Tho shal be maistres on *molde* trewe men to helpe.
C. 8.17   And alle manere men þat by þe *molde* is susteyned
C. 9.173   Then of many oþere men þat [o]n this *molde* walken.
C.10.14   For 3e ar men of þis *molde* þat moost wyde walken
C.11.228   For mony men [o]n this *molde* more sette here herte
C.12.179   Mesc[h]iefes on *molde* mekeliche to soffren:
C.14.167   Was neuere man vppon *molde* þat myhte hit aspie.
C.17.249   And alle maner men þat on this *molde* libbeth.
C.19.84   Ne no medicyne vnder *molde* the man to hele brynge,

molde n2 *molde n.(3)* B 1; C 1
B.11.350   If any Mason made a *molde* þerto muche wonder it were.
C.13.161   Yf eny mason made a *molde* þerto moche wonder me thynketh.

moled ptp *moled ppl.* B 1
B.13.274   Ac it was *moled* in many places wiþ manye sondry plottes,

molere > muliere

moles n *mol n.(3)* B 1
B.13.314   Haþ manye *moles* and spottes; it moste ben ywasshe.'

molten > melteþ

mom n *mom n.* A 1; B 1; C 1 Mum
A.Pr.89   Þanne gete a *mom* of here mouþ til mony be shewid.
B.Pr.216   Than gete a *mom* of hire mouþ til moneie be shewed.
C.Pr.166   Than gete a *Mum* of here mouth [til] moneye [be] shewed.

mone n *mon n.(1) &> moneie,moone* B 3; C 3
B. 6.123   And made hir *mone* to Piers [how þei my3te no3t werche]:
B.15.26   And whan I make *mone* to god memoria is my name;
B.15.506   And make hir *mone* to Makometh hir message to shewe.
C. 8.130   And maden here *mone* to [Peres] how þei m[yht] nat worche;
C.16.186   And when y make *mone* to god Memoria y hatte;
C.17.257   And maken here *mone* to Macometh here message to shewe.

moneie n *moneie n.* A 8 mone (3) money (2) mony (2) monie (1); B 18 mone (1) monee (2) money (2) moneie (11) moneye (2); C 24 mone (7) money (3) moneye (14)
A.Pr.60   For here *mony* & here marchaundise meten togidere.
A.Pr.89   Þanne gete a mom of here mouþ til *mony* be shewid.
A. 1.42   Ac þe *mone* on þis molde þat men so faste holdiþ,
A. 3.232   Þat take mede & *money* for massis þat þei synge,
A. 3.249   For any mylionis of *mone* murdre hem ichone;
A. 7.185   And 3af hem mete & *monie* as þei mi3te asserue.
A. 7.210   Wiþ mete or [wiþ] *mone* let make hem [fare þe betere],

A. 9.81   And wiþ mammones *money* he haþ mad hym frendis,
B.Pr.63   For hire *moneie* and hire marchaundi3e marchen togideres.
B.Pr.216   Than gete a mom of hire mouþ til *moneie* be shewed.
B. 1.44   Ac þe *moneie* [on] þis molde þat men so faste holdeþ,
B. 3.253   That taken Mede and *moneie* for masses þat þei syngeþ,
B. 3.271   For Mede ne for *monee* loke þow destruye it.
B. 6.198   And yaf hem mete [and *money* as þei] my3te [asserue].
B. 6.224   Wiþ mete or wiþ *mone* lat make hem fare þe bettre.
B. 8.90   And wiþ Mammonaes *moneie* he haþ maad hym frendes;
B.11.196   That 3yueþ hem mete or *moneie* [and] loueþ hem for my sake.'
B.13.229   Ouþer mantel or *moneie* amonges lordes Mynstrals.
B.13.393   To marchaunden wiþ [my] *moneie* and maken [here] eschaunges,
B.14.229   That mete or *money* of oþere men moot asken.
B.15.241   And matrimoyne for *moneie* maken and vnmaken,
B.15.350   The merk of þat *moneie* is good ac þe metal is feble;
B.16.129   That in chirche chaffareden or chaungeden any *moneie*;
B.17.269   Of his mete and *moneie* to men þat it nedede?
B.19.349   Ne no manere marchaunt þat wiþ *moneye* deleþ
B.20.12   That is mete whan men hym werneþ and he no *moneye* weldeþ,
C.Pr.61   Here *moneye* and [here] marchandise ma[rch]en togyderes.
C.Pr.166   Than gete a Mum of here mouth [til] *moneye* [be] shewed.
C. 1.42   Ac þe *moneye* of þis molde þat men so faste kepen,
C. 2.173   To be maried for *mone* med[e] hath assented.'
C. 3.264   To lete so his lordschipe for a litel *mone*.
C. 3.424   For eny mede of *money* al that thow myhte [fynde],
C. 6.244   And more worth then the *moneye* or men þat y lenede.
C. 6.280   To marchaunde with my *moneye* and maken here eschaunges,
C. 8.203   And 3af hem mete and *money* as þei myhte deserue.
C. 9.271   And of þe *moneye* thow haddest ther[myd] his mebles to [s]aue
C.10.87   And of mammonaus *mone* ymaked hym many frendes
C.12.242   And so is many man ymorthred for his *moneye* and his godes
C.13.49   The marchaunt mote forgo or *moneye* of his carte
C.13.61   Ac 3ut myhte þe marchaunt thorw *moneye* and other 3eftes
C.13.98   As þe ryche man for al his *mone*, and more as by þe gospell:
C.15.35   A meles mete for a pore man or *moneye* yf they hadde.
C.15.167   And maistre of alle here mebles and of here *moneye* aftur,
C.15.203   Or mantel or *mone* amonges lordes munstrals.
C.16.70   That mete or *moneye* of straunge men moet begge.
C.17.75   Of moche [m]one þe metal is nauhte
C.17.234   That with *moneye* maynteyneth men [t]o werre vppon cristene
C.19.235   Of his mete and *mone* to men þat hit nedede?
C.21.349   Ne no manere Marchaunt þat with *moneye* deleth
C.22.12   That is mete when men hym werneth [and] he no *money* weldeth

moneye > many,moneie

moneiless adj *moneiles adj.* A 1 moneyles; B 1 moneilees; C 2 moneyeles (1) moneyles (1)
A. 8.129   Metel[es and *money]les* on maluerne hilles.
B. 7.147   Metelees and *moneilees* on Maluerne hulles.
C. 9.110   And aren meuynge aftur þe mone; *moneyeles* þey walke
C. 9.296   Meteles and *moneyles* on Maluerne hulles.

monekes > monk; moneþ > monþe; monewe > mengen; mony > many,moneie

monyals n *moniale n.* B 3 Monyals (1) Moniales (1) monyales (1); C 4 moniales (2) monyales (1) monyals (1)
B.10.324   And amende *Monyals*, Monkes and Chanons,
B.15.321   Er þei amortisede to monkes or [*monyales*] hir rente[s].
B.20.264   Monkes and *Moniales* and alle men of Religion,
C. 5.76   And monkes and *moniales* þat mendenant[es] sholde fynde
C. 5.170   And amende 3ow monkes, *moniales* and chanons,
C.18.74   As monkes and *monyals*, men of holy churche;
C.22.264   Monkes and *monyales* and alle men of religioun,

monie > moneie; monye > many

monk n *monk n.* A 4 monk (2) monkes (1) monkis (1); B 10 monk (1) Monkes (9); C 14 monekes (1) monke (1) monkes (12)
A. 3.122   To [*monkis*], to [mynstrelis], to myselis in heggis.
A. 5.224   And here masse & matynes as I a *monk* were.
A.10.113   3if þou be man maried, *monk*, oþer chanoun,
A.10.136   Boþe maidenis & [mynchons], *monkes* & ancris,
B. 3.133   To *Monkes*, to Mynstrales, to Meseles in heggis.
B. 5.156   Manye *Monþes* wiþ hem, and wiþ Monkes boþe.
B. 5.169   Among *Monkes* I my3te be ac many tyme I shonye
B. 5.452   And here matyns and masse as I a *monk* were;
B. 6.327   Whan ye se þe [mone] amys and two *monkes* heddes,
B.10.324   And amende Monyals, *Monkes* and Chanons,
B.15.274   *Monkes* and mendinaunt3, men by hemselue
B.15.321   Er þei amortisede to *monkes* or [monyales] hir rente[s].
B.15.417   Ancres and heremytes and *Monkes* and freres
B.20.264   *Monkes* and Moniales and alle men of Religion,
C. 3.170   To *Monekes*, to [mynstrals, to] musels in hegge[s];
C. 5.76   And *monkes* and moniales þat mendenant[es] sholde fynde
C. 5.156   Ac mony day, men telleth, bothe *monkes* and chanons

C. 5.170 And amende ʒow *monkes*, moniales and chanons,
C. 6.131 Mony monthes with hem and with *monkes* bothe.
C. 6.151 Amonges *monkes* y myhte be Ac mony tyme y spare
C. 6.158 Y haue no luste, lef me, to longe amonges *monkes*
C. 7.66   And here mateynes and masse as y a *monke* were;
C.17.35   For wolde neuere faythfull god þat freres and *monkes*
C.17.52   To make men louye mesure þat *monkes* ben and freres:
C.17.55   Ar they amorteysed eny more for *monkes* or for Chanoun[s].
C.17.60   To helpe thy fader formost byfore freres or *monkes*
C.18.74   As *monkes* and monyals, men of holy churche;
C.22.264 *Monkes* and monyales and alle men of religioun,

mont > mount; montaigne > mountaigne

monþe n *month* n. A 1 moneþ; B 3 Monþe (2) Monþes (1); C 4 monthe
(3) monthes (1)
A. 3.134 She may neiʒ as muche do in a *moneþ* ones
B. 3.145 [She] may neiʒ as muche do in a *Monþe* one[s]
B. 5.156 Manye *Monþes* wiþ hem, and wiþ Monkes boþe.
B.19.388 In help of hir heele ones in a *Monþe*,
C. 3.183 He may ny as muche do in a *monthe* ones
C. 5.50   To be welcome when y come oþerwhile in a *monthe*
C. 6.131 Mony *monthes* with hem and with monkes bothe.
C.21.388 In helpe of here hele ones in a *monthe*

moo > mo

mood n *mod* n. B 3; C 2 moed
B.10.269 Why meuestow þi *mood* for a mote in þi broþeres eiʒe,
B.11.369 Ac þat moost meued me and my *mood* chaunged,
B.13.191 Haþ meued my *mood* to moorne for my synnes.
C.13.179 Ac þat most meuede me and my *moed* chaungede
C.18.117 Thenne moued hym *moed* [in] magestate dei

moolde > molde

moone n *mone* n.(1) A 1 mone; B 5 mone (2) Moone (3); C 6 mone
A. 8.143 And Iosep mette merueillously how þe *mone* & þe sonne
B. 3.327 And þe myddel of a *Moone* shal make þe Iewes torne,
B. 6.637 Whan ye se þe [*mone*] amys and two monkes heddes.
B. 7.165 And Ioseph mette merueillously how þe *mone* and þe sonne
B.13.155 The myddel of þe *Moone* [i]s þe [m]yght of boþe.
B.17.94   May no medicyne [vnder *mone*] þe man to heele bringe,
C. 3.480 And the [myddell] of [a] *mone* shal make þe iewes turne
C. 8.349 Shal brynge bane and batayle on bothe half þe *mone*;
C. 9.108 And madden as þe *mone* sit, more other lasse;
C. 9.110 And aren meuynge aftur þe *mone*; moneyeles þey walke
C. 9.309 And Ioseph mette merueilously how þe *mone* and þe sonne
C.17.92   And þe se and the seed, þe sonne and þe *mone*

moore n *more* n.(3) cf. mo, moost A 16 mor (1) more (15); B 50 moore
(49) more (1); C 44 more
A.Pr.109 Al þis I sauʒ slepyng & seue siþes *more*.
A. 1.167 Chewen here charite & chiden aftir *more*.
A. 2.28   Þat longiþ to þ[at] lordsshipe, þe lasse & þe *more*.
A. 3.160 'Excuse þe ʒif þou canst; I can no more seiʒe,
A. 4.89   So [þat] ʒe assente I can sey no *more*,
A. 4.90   For mede haþ mad my mendis; I may no *more* axen.'
A. 4.92   Wrong wendiþ not so awey er I wyte *more*.
A. 5.4   Þat I ne hadde yslepe saddere & yseyn *more*
A. 5.9   Þanne sauʒ I meke[l] *more* þan I before tolde,
A. 5.97   And whoso haþ *more* þanne I, þat angriþ myn herte.
A. 6.37   [I] haue myn here of hym [wel] & oþerwhile *more*;
A. 7.88   My wyf shal haue of þat I wan wiþ treuþe, & na*more*,
A. 7.135 Inouʒ iche day at non, ac no *more* til on þe morewe
A. 7.280 Hungir [eet] þis in haste & askide aftir *more*.
A. 9.76   Dobet þus doþ, ac he doþ muche *more*.
A.12.92   And mannes merþe w[or]þ no *mor* þan he deseruyþ here
B.Pr.111 Forþi I kan & kan nauʒt of court speke *more*
B.Pr.231 [Al þis I seiʒ slepyng and seuene sythes *more*].
B. 1.193 Chewen hire charite and chiden after *moore*.
B. 2.46   That longen to þat lordshipe, þe lasse and þe *moore*.
B. 3.173 'Excuse þee if þow kanst; I kan na *moore* seyen,
B. 3.344 And so [mys]ferde ye, madame; ye kouþe na *moore* fynde
B. 4.39   *Moore* þan for] loue of oure lord or alle hise leeue Seintes.
B. 4.102 So þat [ye] assente I kan seye no [*moore*],
B. 4.103 For Mede haþ [maad myne amendes]; I may na *moore* axe.'
B. 4.105 Wrong wendeþ noʒt so awey [er] I wite *moore*.
B. 5.4   That I ne hadde slept saddere and yseiʒen *moore*.
B. 5.9   [Th]anne [mette me] muche *moore* þan I bifore tolde,
B. 5.118 [And] whoso haþ *moore* þan I, þat angreþ [myn herte].
B. 5.550 I haue myn hire [of hym] wel and ouþerwhiles *moore*.
B. 6.96   My wif shal haue of þat I wan wiþ truþe and na *moore*,
B. 6.146 And na *moore* er morwe, myn almesse shul þei haue,
B. 6.296 [Hunger eet þis] in haste and axed after *moore*.

B. 7.45   Ac many a Iustice and Iuruor wolde for Iohan do *moore*
B. 8.85   Dobet [þus dooþ], ac he dooþ muche *moore*.
B. 9.37   As who seiþ, "*moore* moot herto þan my word oone;
B. 9.80   For *moore* bilongeþ to þe litel barn er he þe lawe knowe
B.10.357 Ac cristene men wiþoute *moore* maye noʒt come to heuene,
B.10.473 That euere þe[i] kouþe [konne on book] *moore* þan Credo in deum
          patrem,
B.11.320 Ac muche *moore* in metynge þus wiþ me gan oon dispute,
B.11.380 Who suffre[þ] *moore* þan god?' quod he; 'no gome, as I leeue.
B.11.407 That I in metels ne myʒte *moore* haue yknowen.
B.11.412 'To se muche and suffre *moore*, certes, is dowel.'
B.11.414 Thow sholdest haue knowen þat clergie kan & [conceyued] *moore*
          þoruʒ Res[on],
B.11.422 Tho hadde he [litel] likyng for to lere þe *moore*.
B.12.100 Na *moore* kan no Clerk but if he cauʒte it first þoruʒ bokes.
B.12.199 [I] hadde mete *moore* þan ynouʒ, ac noʒt so muche worshipe
B.13.17   Leneþ he no lif lasse ne *moore*–
B.13.182 And be Pilgrym wiþ pacience til I haue preued *moore*.'
B.13.194 Hadde noʒt [Marie] Maudeleyne *moore* for a box of salue
B.13.381 *Moore* þan it was worþ, and yet wolde I swere
B.13.382 That it coste me muche *moore*; swoor manye oþes.
B.14.142 Riʒt as a seruaunt takeþ his salarie bifore, & siþþe wolde clayme
          moore
B.14.208 Ther þe poore is put bihynde, and parauenture kan *moore*
B.14.313 The eighteþe is a lele labour and looþ to take *moore*
B.15.254 Craueþ ne coueiteþ ne crieþ after *moore*:
B.15.260 That þeiʒ þei suffrede al þis, god suffrede for vs *moore*
B.15.310 And to taken of hir tenauntʒ *moore* þan trouþe wolde,
B.16.65   To asken hym any *moore* þerof, and bad hym ful faire
B.16.241 To me and to myn issue *moore* yet he [me] graunted,
B.17.235 And as wex wiþouten *moore* on a warm glede
B.18.166 For he[o] woot *moore* þan we; he[o] was er we boþe.'
B.19.69   Ac to carpe *moore* of crist and how he com to þat name,
B.20.9   And þow nome na *moore* þan nede þee tauʒte?
B.20.26   He shal do *moore* þan mesure many tyme and ofte,
B.20.314 And *moore* of phisik bi fer, and fairer he plastreþ;
C.Pr.222 Ʒut mette me *more* of mene and of riche,
C.Pr.235 [Al þis y say slepynge and seuene sythes *more*].
C. 1.123 Ac of þis matere no *more* [meu]en y nelle.
C. 1.190 [C]hewen here charite and chiden aftur *more*
C. 2.50   That loueth here lordschipe, lasse other *more*.
C. 3.219 'Excuce the yf thow kanst; y can no *more* segge
C. 4.39   *More* then for oure lordes loue oþer oure lady, goddes moder.'
C. 4.97   And mede hath made my mendes y may no *more* asken.
C. 4.100 Wrong goth nat so away ar y wete *more*.
C. 5.109 Thenne mette me muche *more* then y byfore tolde
C. 7.194 Y haue myn huyre of hym wel and oþerwhiles *more*.
C. 8.35   '[Ye], and ʒut a poynt,' quod [Peres], 'y praye ʒow of *more*:
C. 8.105 My wyf shal haue of þat y wan with treuthe and no *more*
C. 8.195 To be his holde hewe thow he hadde no *more*
C. 8.318 Hunger eet al in haste and askede aftur *more*.
C. 9.132 And ʒut *more* to suche men me doth ar they passe;
C.10.82   Dobet doth al this Ac ʒut he doth *more*.
C.10.29   And is no *more* bote men þat ben bygeten
C.10.306 For þe *more* a man may do, by so þat a do hit,
C.11.70   And is to mene no *more* bote "who[so] muche goed weldeth
C.11.244 For Archa Noe, nymeth hede, ys no *more* to mene
C.11.288 And is to mene no *more* to men þat beth lewed:
C.13.40   Ther þe messager doth no *more* but with his mouth telleth
C.13.66   The marchaunt is no *more* to mene but men þat ben ryche
C.13.197 Ho soffreth *more* then god?' quod he; 'no gome, as y leue.
C.13.215 That y ne hadde met *more*, so murye as y slepte,
C.13.222 Thow sholdest haue yknowe þat clergie ca[n] & conseyued *mor[e]*
          [thorw] resoun
C.14.45   No *more* can no clerk but if hit come of bokes.
C.14.138 Ich haue mete *more* then ynow Ac nat [so] muche worschipe
C.15.199 Of [m]y labour th[ey] lauhe, þe lasse and þe *more*
C.16.49   There þe pore is potte behynde and parauntur can *more*
C.16.147 The eyʒte is a lel labour and loeth to take *more*
C.17.41   This is no *more* to mene bote men of holy churche
C.17.45   And to take of here tenauntes *more* then treuthe wolde
C.17.55   Ar they amorteysed eny *more* for monkes or for Chanoun[s].
C.18.198 'Muse nat to moche þeron,' quod faith, 'til thow *more* knowe
C.18.257 To me and [to] myn issue *more* he me bihihte,
C.19.77   'And þat *more* goth for his medicyne y make the good aʒeynward
C.19.100 And hope afturward of god *more* me toelde
C.19.201 And as wex withouten *more* vpo[n] a warm glede
C.20.169 For he woet *more* then we; he was ar we bothe.'
C.21.69   Ac to carpe *more* of Crist and how he cam to þat name;
C.22.9   And thow nome no *more* then nede the tauhte?
C.22.26   He shal do *more* þe[n] mesure mony tymes and often
C.22.314 And *more* of fysyk bi fer, and fayror he plastereth;

moore adj *more adj.comp.* A 11 more; B 25 moore (24) more (1); C 15 more

A. 1.157	3e ne haue no *more* meryt in [masse] ne in [houres]
A. 4.96	As longe as I lyue but *more* loue it make.'
A. 4.135	Þere nas man in þe mothalle, *more* ne lesse,
A. 5.131	Þe pound þat heo [payede] by peisid a quarter *more*
A. 5.219	For is no gilt here so gret þat his goodnesse nis *more*'.
A. 6.114	To gete ingang at any gate but grace be þe *more*.'
A. 7.60	Shal haue be oure lord þe *more* here in heruist,
A. 8.93	In two lynes it lay & nou3t o lettre *more*,
A. 8.110	Þat louiþ god lelly, his lifloode is þe *more*:
A. 9.103	*More* kynde knowyng I coueyte to lere,
A.11.167	And wente wi3tly my wey wiþoute *more* lettyng,
B. 1.183	Ye ne haue na *more* merite in masse n[e] in houres
B. 5.38	"[Lo], þe leuere child þe *moore* loore bihoueþ";
B. 5.215	[Th]e pound þat she paied by peised a quartron *moore*
B. 5.283	Nis na *moore* to þe mercy of god þan [amyd] þe see a gleede:
B. 5.447	For is no gilt here so gret þat his goodnesse [i]s *moore*.'
B. 5.629	To geten ing[o]ng at any gate but grace be þe *moore*.'
B. 6.47	That he worþ worþier set and wiþ *moore* blisse:
B. 7.83	To yelden hem þat yeueþ hem and yet vsure *moore*:
B. 7.96	Ther is *moore* mysshapen amonges þise beggeres
B. 7.111	In two lynes it lay and no3t a [lettre] *moore*,
B. 8.113	*More* kynde knowynge] I coueite to lerne,
B. 9.153	Muchel merueille me þynkeþ; and *moore* of a sherewe
B.10.44	Thei konne na *moore* mynstralcie ne Musik men to glade
B.10.225	And wente wightly [my w]ey wiþoute *moore* lettyng,
B.10.457	Whan man was at meschief wiþoute þe *moore* grace.
B.11.214	Forþi lakke no lif ooþer þou3 he *moore* latyn knowe,
B.12.282	Ergo saluabitur', quod he and seide na *moore* latyn.
B.13.41	Ac [he eet] mete of *moore* cost, mortrews and potages.
B.13.403	And *moore* mete eet and dronk þan kynde my3te defie,
B.14.330	That euere he hadde lond ouþer lordshipe lasse oþer *moore*,
B.15.549	*Moore* tresor þan trouþe? I dar no3t telle þe soþe;
B.15.567	And purgen hem of poison er *moore* peril falle.
B.16.133	And maken it as muche ouþer *moore* in alle manere poyntes
B.19.24	Is crist *moore* of my3t and moore worþi name
B.19.124	And whan he [was woxen] *moore*, in his moder absence,
C. 1.179	3e n[e] haueth na *more* meryte in masse ne in oures
C. 6.159	For y ete *more* fysch then flesche there and feble ale drynke.
C. 6.223	The pound th[at] he payede by peysed a quarter *more*
C. 7.61	For is no gult [here] so greet þat his goodnesse is *more*.'
C. 7.282	To geten ingang at eny 3ate bote grace be þe *more*.'
C. 9.285	In two lynes hit lay and nat a lettre *more*
C.10.109	*More* kynd[e] knowynge coueyte y to here
C.11.134	Tho wente y my way withouten *more* lettynge
C.14.204	Ergo saluabitur,' quod he and saide no *more* latyn.
C.14.216	And a cortesye *more* þen couenant was, what so clerkes carpe,
C.15.46	Forthy eet he mete of *more* cost, mortrewes and potages.
C.17.211	*More* tresor then treuthe? Y dar nat telle þe sothe
C.17.232	And purge hem of þe olde poysyn Ar *more* perel falle.
C.21.24	Is Crist *more* of myhte and more worth[y] name
C.21.124	And when he was wexen *more*, in his moder absence,

moore adv *more adv.* A 14 more; B 53 moore (52) more (1); C 49 mare (1) more (48)

A. 3.98	Henis to þi deþ day do þou so no *more*.
A. 3.172	And mayntene þi manhod *more* þan þou knowist;
A. 3.266	Shal no *more* mede be maister on erþe;
A. 4.84	For I wile wage for wrong, he [wile] do so no *more*.'
A. 5.151	And siþen I wile be shriuen & synne no *more*.'
A. 7.38	'3a, & 3et a poynt,' quaþ perkyn, 'I preye þe *more*:
A. 8.105	Ne aboute my [belyue] so besy be na*more*;
A. 9.7	Where þis lede lengide, lesse ne *more*,
A.11.32	*More* þanne musik, or makyng of god almi3t,
A.11.51	Nere mercy in mene men *more* þan in riche
A.11.119	Leue hym on þi left half a large myle or *more*,
A.11.138	For þe *more* I muse þeron þe mistlokere it semiþ,
A.11.216	Arn *more* in his mynde þan þe memorie of his foundours.
A.11.306	And is to mene in oure mouþ, *more* ne lesse,
B.Pr.52	*Moore* þan to seye sooþ, it semed bi hire speche.
B. 2.76	That Mede is ymaried *moore* for hire goodes
B. 3.109	Hennes to þi deeþ day do [þow] so na *moore*.
B. 3.185	And mayntene þi manhode *moore* þan þow knowest;
B. 3.290	Shal na *moore* Mede be maister [on erþe],
B. 4.97	For I wol wage for wrong, he wol do so na *moore*.'
B. 5.53	*Moore* þan gold ouþer giftes if ye wol god plese;
B. 5.301	And siþen I wole be shryuen and synne na *moore*.'
B. 5.376	For loue of tales in Tauernes [to] drynke þe *moore* I [hyed;
B. 6.37	'Ye, and yet a point', quod Piers, 'I preye [þee] of *moore*:
B. 7.71	Anoþer that were nedy; so þe nedieste sholde be holpe.
B. 7.123	Ne aboute my [bilyue] so bisy be na *moore*;
B. 8.7	Where þis leode lenged, lasse ne *moore*,

B.10.65	Ne were mercy in meene men *moore* þan in riche
B.10.86	And þe *moore* he wynneþ and welt welþes and richesse
B.10.167	Leue [hym] on þi left half a large myle or *moore*
B.10.186	The *moore* I muse þerInne þe mystier it semeþ,
B.10.271	Which letteþ þee to loke, lasse ouþer *moore*?
B.10.397	For many men on þis moolde *moore* setten hir hert[e]
B.10.462	And is to mene to [Englissh] men, *moore* ne lesse,
B.11.47	And folwed me fourty wynter and a fifte *moore*,
B.11.79	Ac muche *moore* meritorie, me þynkeþ, is to bapti3e,
B.11.161	The legend[a] sanctorum yow lereþ *moore* largere þan I yow telle.
B.11.302	[*Moore* þan cure] for konnyng or 'knowen for clene [of] berynge'.
B.11.319	The which I preise, þer pacience is, *moore* parfit þan richesse.
B.11.351	Ac yet me merueilled *moore* how many oþere briddes
B.12.107	Na *moore* kan a kynde witted man, but clerkes hym teche,
B.12.264	The larke þat is a lasse fowel is *moore* louelich of ledene,
B.13.87	And seide, 'þow shalt see þus soone, whan he may na *moore*,
B.13.351	Til þei my3te na *moore*; and þanne [hadde] murye tales,
B.13.356	*Moore* to good þan to god gome his loue caste,
B.13.364	*Moore* profitable þan myn, manye slei3tes I made.
B.13.385	Mercy for my mysdedes, þat I ne moorned *moore*
B.13.397	That my mynde ne was *moore* on my good in a doute
B.13.438	Muche *moore*, me þynkeþ, riche men sholde
B.14.27	Ne no Mynstrall be *moore* worþ amonges pouere and riche
B.14.90	Ac shrift of mouþ *moore* worþi is if man be y[n]liche contrit,
B.14.102	'Wheiþer paciente pouerte', quod Haukyn, 'be *moore* plesaunt to oure d[ri3te]
B.14.268	[*Moore*] þan [a maiden is] þat is maried þoru3 brocage
B.14.270	*Moore* for coueitise of [catel] þan kynde loue of boþe—
B.14.298	Wiþ sobretee fram alle synne and also 3it *moore*;
B.15.58	And þe *moore* þat a man of good matere hereþ,
B.15.79	*Moore* for pompe þan for pure charite; þe peple woot þe soþe.
B.15.109	And amende[n] hem þat [þei] mysdoon *moore* for youre ensaumples
B.15.199	Ac Piers þe Plowman parceyueþ *moore* depper
B.15.207	Ac it is *moore* to haue hir mete [on] swich an esy manere
B.15.449	*Moore* þoru3 miracles þan þoru3 muche prechyng;
B.16.217	Na *moore* my3te god be man but if he moder hadde.
B.17.80	'What he spendeþ *moore* [for medicyne] I make þee good herafter,
B.17.168	Na *moore* [may an hand] meue wiþoute fyngres.
B.17.224	Na *moore* dooþ sire ne sone ne seint spirit togidres
B.19.24	Is crist moore of my3t and *moore* worþi name
B.20.222	'I counte na *moore* Conscience by so I cacche siluer
C. 2.83	That mede is maried *more* for here richesse
C. 3.139	3ut y forgyue þe þis gult; godes forb[o]de eny *more*
C. 3.231	And maynteyne thi manhede *more* then thow knowest.
C. 3.290	To 3eue men mede, *more* oþer lasse.
C. 3.396	And is to [mene] in oure mouth *more* n[e] mynne
C. 4.93	For y wol wage for wrong; he wol do so no *mare*.'
C. 4.193	*More* then alle thy marchauntes or thy mytrede Bysshopes
C. 6.185	Til we myhte no *more*; thenne hadde we mery tales
C. 6.244	And *more* worth then the moneye or men þat y lenede.
C. 6.263	*More* profitable then myn, y made manye wentes.
C. 6.284	That my muynde ne was *more* [o]n my godes in a doute
C. 6.356	And sennes sitte and be shryue and synege no *more*.'
C. 6.430	*More* then my kynde myhte deffye
C. 7.98	Muche *more*, me thynketh, riche men ouhte
C. 8.35	'[Ye], and 3ut a poynt,' quod [Peres], 'y praye 3ow of *more*:
C. 9.108	And madden as þe mone sit, *more* other lasse.
C.10.7	Where this [lede] l[e]nged, lasse ne *more*,
C.10.169	On catel *more* then on kynde that alle kyne thynges wrouhte,
C.10.282	And loke þat loue be *more* þe cause then lond oþer nobles.
C.10.307	The *more* he is worthy, and worth of wyse and goed ypresed.'
C.11.13	*More* then holynesse or hendenesse or al þat seyntes techeth.
C.11.47	Ne were mercy in m[e]ne men *more* then in riht riche
C.11.66	Ac þe *more* a wynneth and hath þe world at his wille
C.11.127	Þe *more* y muse þer[i]n the mystiloker hit semeth
C.11.228	For mony men [o]n this molde *more* sette here herte
C.12.239	And 3ut *more* hit maketh men mony tymes & ofte
C.13.76	And 3ut *more*, to maken pees and quyten menne dettes
C.13.98	As þe ryche man for al his mone, and *more* as by þe gospell:
C.13.162	And 3ut me merueylede *more* [how] mony [other] briddes
C.14.35	And 3ut is clergie to comende for cristes loue *more*
C.14.52	No *more* can a kynde witted man, but clerkes hym teche,
C.14.180	*More* þan for his fayre flesch or for his merye note.
C.14.181	Riht so men reuerence[th] *more* þe ryche for h[is] mebles
C.15.94	And saide, 'Thow shalt se thus sone, when he may no *more*,
C.15.268	Seuene slepen, as saith þe boek, *more* then syxty wynter
C.15.277	'Where pouerte and pacience plese *more* god almyhty
C.16.108	*More* then þat mayde is þat is maried by brocage,
C.16.110	*More* for coueytise of catel then kynde loue of þe mariage.
C.16.134	With sobrete fro alle synnes and also 3ut *more*;
C.16.238	*More* for pompe and pruyde, as þe peple woet wel

C.16.263 And amenden [hem] of here mysdedes *more* for [ȝoure]
          ensaumples
C.17.233 For were presthode *more* parfyte, that is, þe pope formost
C.18.65   Swettore and saueriore and also *more* grettore
C.18.78   And *more* lykynde to oure lord then lyue as kynde asketh
C.18.87   Wydewhode, *more* worthiore then wedlok, as in heuene;
C.18.88   Thenne is virginite, *more* vertuous and fayrest, as in heuene.
C.19.190 No *more* doth sire ne sone ne seynt spirit togyderes
C.21.24   Is Crist more of myhte and *more* worth[y] name
C.22.222 'Y counte no *more* Consience bi so y cache suluer

moore &> neuermoore

moores n *mor n.(1)* B 1; C 1 mores
B.11.354 In Mareys and *moores* [manye] hidden hir egges]
C.13.167 In mareys and in *mores*, in myres and in watres,

moorne n *morn n.* A 2 mourne (1) mournide (1); B 8 moorne (1)
          moorned (1) moorneþ (1) mornede (2) mornyng (1) mourne (1)
          mournede (1); C 7 mornede (1) mourne (1) mourned (1) mournede (2)
          mourneth (1) mournynge (1)
A.3.16   And seide, '*mourne* nouȝt, mede, ne make þou no sorewe,
A.3.157   Þanne *mournide* mede & menide hire to þe king
B.3.16   And seiden, '*mourne* noȝt, Mede, ne make þow no sorwe,
B.3.170   Thanne *mournede* Mede and mened hire to þe kynge
B.4.165   Mede *mornede* þo and made heuy chere
B.11.339 Males drowen hem to males [al *mornyng*] by hemselue,
B.13.60   And made hym murþe wiþ his mete, ac I *mornede* euere
B.13.191 Haþ meued my mood to *moorne* for my synnes.
B.13.385 Mercy for my mysdedes, þat I ne *moorned* moore
B.13.410 [Is whan men] *moorneþ* noȝt for hise mysdedes, ne makeþ no
          sorwe;
C.3.17   And sayden, '*mourne* nat, mede, ne make thow no sorwe
C.3.216   Thenne *mournede* mede and menede here to þe kyng
C.4.160   Mede *mornede* tho and made heuy chere
C.6.274   Mercy for my mysdedes þat y ne *mourned* [o]ftur
C.7.70   Is when men *mourneth* not for his mysdedes,
C.13.147 Males drow hem to males a[l *mour]nynge* by hemsulue
C.15.64   And made [hym] mer[þe] with [h]is mete Ac y *mournede* euere

moost adj *most adj.sup.& n. cf. moore* A 4 most (2) moste (2); B 18
          moost (9) most (1); C 17 moest (4) most (6) moste (7)
A.Pr.64   Þe *moste* meschief on molde is mountyng vp faste.
A.1.7   Þe *moste* partie of þis peple þat passiþ on þis erþe,
A.3.69   For þise arn men of þise molde þat *most* harm werchiþ
A.10.54   In manis brayn is he *most* & miȝtiest to knowe.
B.Pr.67   The *mooste* meschief on Molde is mountynge [vp] faste.
B.1.7   The *mooste* partie of þis peple þat passeþ on þis erþe,
B.3.80   For þise are men on þis molde þat *moost* harm wercheþ
B.3.177   Ther þat meschief is [*most*] Mede may helpe.
B.4.159   And þe *mooste* peple in þe [moot] halle and manye of þe grete,
B.4.181   And as *moost* folk witnesseþ wel wrong shal be demed.'
B.5.492   Aboute mydday, whan *moost* liȝt is and meel tyme of Seintes,
B.8.55   Ac man haþ *moost* þerof and moost is to blame
B.9.57   A[c] in þe herte is his hoom and hir *moost* reste.
B.10.28   Thilke þat god [*moost* gyueþ] leest good þei deleþ,
B.10.29   And moost vnkynde to þe commune þat *moost* catel weldeþ:
B.10.94   And how he myȝte *moost* meynee manliche fynde;
B.10.399 [Ac] at hir *mooste* meschief [mercy were þe beste],
B.11.29   Thow shalt fynde Fortune þee faille at þi *mooste* nede
B.13.5   First how Fortune me failed at my *mooste* nede;
B.15.255 The *mooste* liflode he lyueþ by is loue in goddes passion;
B.19.255 And who þat *moost* maistries kan be myldest of berynge,
B.19.418 And þer þei ligge and lenge *moost* lecherie þere regneþ".
C.Pr.65   The *moste* meschief on molde mounteth vp faste.
C.Pr.146 And for *most* profi[t to þe peple] a plogh gonne þei make,
C.1.7   The *moste* partie of þis peple þat passeth on þis erthe,
C.3.81   For thyse men don *most* harm to þe mene peple,
C.3.383   Ac þe *moste* partie of peple puyr indirect semeth
C.3.472   Mercy or no mercy as *most* trewe acorden.
C.7.132   Aboute mydday, when *most* liht is and mel tyme of sayntes,
C.11.25   Tho þat god *most* goed ȝeueth greueth most riht and treuthe:
C.11.188 Thow shalt fynde fortune þe fayle At thy *moste* nede
C.11.230 [Ac] at he[re] *moste* meschef mercy were þe beste
C.11.284 For he þat *most* se[y]h and saide of the sothfaste trinite
C.14.108 Which trowest [þou] of tho two in temese [is] in *moste* drede?'
C.15.5   Furste how fortune me faylede At my *moste* nede;
C.17.63   And afturward awayte ho hath *moest* nede
C.19.240 Clothes of *moest* cost, as clerkes bereth witnesse:
C.21.255 And [ho] þat *moest* maistries can be myldest of berynge,
C.21.418 And þer they lygge and lenge *moest* lecherye þer regneth".

moost adv *most adv.sup. cf. moore* A 2 most; B 26 moost (22) mooste (2)
          most (2); C 24 moest (2) most (14) moste (8)
A.5.81   Whanne I mette hym in market þat I *most* hatide

A.10.32   Ac man is hym *most* lik of mark & of shap.
B.Pr.103 Amonges foure vertues, [*most* vertuous of alle],
B.Pr.158 A Raton of renoun, *moost* renable of tonge,
B.1.151   And lered it Moyses for þe leueste þyng and *moost* lik to heuene,
B.1.152   And [ek] þe pl[ante] of pees, *moost* precious of vertues.
B.2.64   Were *moost* pryuee with Mede of any men me þouȝte,
B.4.166   For þe *mooste* commune of þat court called hire an hore.
B.5.101   Whan I met[t]e hym in Market þat I *moost* hate[de]
B.5.481   And of nauȝt madest auȝt and man *moost* lik to þiselue,
B.8.14   For [ye] be men of þis moolde þat *moost* wide walken,
B.8.55   Ac man haþ moost þerof and *moost* is to blame
B.9.31   Ac man is hym *moost* lik of marc and of [shape].
B.9.102   Is *moost* yhated vpon erþe of hem þat ben in heuene;
B.10.29   And moost vnkynde to þe commune þat *moost* catel weldeþ:
B.11.232 Why I meue þis matere is *moost* for þe pouere;
B.11.274 And lif *moost* likynge to god as luc bereþ witnesse:
B.11.369 Ac þat *moost* meued me and my mood chaunged,
B.12.52   And þo men þat þei *moost* haten mynistren it at þe laste;
B.12.164 Which trowestow of þo two [in Themese] is in *moost* drede,
B.13.33   This maister was maad sitte as for þe *mooste* worþi,
B.13.297 And *most* sotil of song oþer sleyest of hondes,
B.14.43   The Corlew by kynde of þe Eyr, *moost* clennest flessh of briddes,
B.14.280 Pouerte is þe firste point þat pride *moost* hateþ;
B.15.156 Ac charite þat Poul preiseþ best, and *moost* plesaunt to oure
          [Saueour]–
B.15.295 Ac *moost* þoruȝ [meditacion] and mynde of god almyghty.
B.18.40   'After sharpe shoures', quod pees, '*moost* shene is þe sonne;
B.19.265 And Ioyned to hem oon Iohan, *moost* gentil of alle,
C.Pr.131 Amonge foure vertues, *most* vertuous of vertues,
C.Pr.178 A ratoun of renown, *moste* resonable of tounge,
C.1.147   And *most* souerayne salue for soule and for body.
C.1.148   Loue is [þe] plonte of pees, *most* precious of vertues,
C.2.38   That helpeth man *moste* to heuene mede most letteth.
C.2.38   That helpeth man moste to heuene mede *most* letteth.
C.2.66   Were *most* pryue with mede of eny men [me] thoghte,
C.9.68   And *moste* merytorie to men þat he ȝeueth fore.
C.9.71   Ac þat *most* neden aren oure neyhebores and we nyme gode
          he[d]e,
C.10.14   For ȝe ar men of this molde þat *moste* wyde walken
C.10.157 Man is hym *most* lyk of membres and of face
C.11.25   Tho þat god most goed ȝeueth greueth *most* riht and treuthe:
C.11.290 Comuneliche then clerkes *most* knowyng in konnyng
C.12.223 And þat rathest rypeth rotieth *most* sonnest;
C.13.179 Ac þat *most* meuede me and my moed chaungede
C.13.192 And þerfore merueileth me, for man is *moste* yliche the,
C.15.38   The maistre was maed sitte As for þe *moste* worthy;
C.16.120 Pouerte is þe furste poynte þat pruyde *moest* hateth;
C.16.265 Ypocrisye is a braunche of pruyde and *most* amonges clerkes
C.16.340 'Peres the plouhman,' quod he, '*moste* parfitlyche hym knoweth:
C.19.105 And *moest* inparfyt of alle persones; and pacientliche soffre
C.19.239 *Moste* lordliche lyue and ȝut [on] his lycame werie
C.20.452 'Aftur sharp[e] shoures,' quod pees, '*most* shene is þe sonne;
C.21.265 And ioyned til hem oen iohann, *most* gentill of all,

moot n *mote n.(1)* A 1 mot; B 2; C 2 moet (1) mote (1)
A.6.73   Þe *mot* is of mercy þe Maner al aboute,
B.5.586   The *moot* is of mercy þe Manoir aboute;
B.19.365 And make a muche *moot* þat myghte ben a strengþe
C.7.233   The *mote* is of mercy, the manere in þe myddes
C.21.365 And make a moche *moet* þat myhte be a strenghe

moot v *moten v.(2)* A 11 most (1) mote (6) moten (1) muste (3); B 38
          moot (12) most (1) moste (15) mote (7) moten (3); C 37 moet (9)
          most (2) moste (7) mosten (1) mot (7) mote (11)
A.1.127   'Ȝet haue I no kynde knowyng,' quaþ I, '[ȝe *mote* kenne me bet]
A.3.213   Mede & marchaundise *mote* nede go togidere;
A.4.99   Þat mede *muste* be meynpernour resoun þei besouȝte.
A.5.42   Qui cum patre & filio; Faire *mote* ȝow befalle.'
A.5.254   To haue grace to seke treuþe; god leue þat hy *moten*!
A.6.48   Ȝe *mote* go þoruȝ meknesse, boþe men & wyues,
A.7.273   Be þis liflode I *mote* lyue til lammasse tyme;
A.8.23   And for þei swere be here soule, & so god *muste* hem helpe,
A.8.89   'Piers,' quaþ a prest [þo], 'þi pardon *muste* I rede,
A.11.88   What is dowel fro dobet; now def *mote* he worþe,
A.12.39   To be hure man ȝif I *mot* for eueremore after,
B.1.138   'Yet haue I no kynde knowyng', quod I, 'ye *mote* kenne me bettre
B.3.226   [Mede and Marchaundiȝe] *mote* nede go togideres;
B.4.112   That Mede *moste* be maynpernour Reson þei bisouȝte.
B.5.152   [That] I ne *mote* folwe this folk, my grace.
B.5.386   'I *moste* sitte [to be shryuen] or ellis sholde I nappe;
B.5.411   Til matyns and masse be do, and þanne [*moste*] to þe freres;
B.5.512   To haue grace to go [to] truþe, [God leue þat þei *moten*].
B.5.561   Ye *moten* go þoruȝ mekenesse, boþe men and wyues,
B.6.289   By þis liflode [I *moot*] lyue til lammesse tyme,

B. 7.21 And for þei swere by hir soule and so god *moste* hem helpe
B. 7.107 'Piers', quod a preest þoo, 'þi pardon *moste* I rede,
B. 9.15 That he bit *moot* be do; he [boldeþ] hem alle;
B. 9.37 As who seiþ, "moore *moot* herto þan my word oone;
B. 9.38 My myȝt *moot* helpe forþ wiþ my speche".
B. 9.44 He *moste* werche wiþ his word and his wit shewe.
B. 9.111 For þei *mote* werche and wynne and þe world sustene;
B.10.135 What is dowel fro dobet, [now] deef *mote* he worþe,
B.11.276 Whoso wole be pure parfit *moot* possession forsake
B.11.400 Al to murþe wiþ man þat *moste* wo þolie,
B.12.186 Wo was hym marked þat wade *moot* wiþ þe lewed!
B.13.147 And but he bowe for þis betyng blynd *mote* he worþe!"
B.13.178 That Pacience þ[o] *most* passe, 'for pilgrymes konne wel lye'.
B.13.260 For er I haue breed of mele ofte *moot* I swete,
B.13.314 Haþ manye moles and spottes; it *moste* ben ywasshe.'
B.14.192 Ac þe parchemyn of þis patente of pouerte be *moste*,
B.14.229 That mete or money of oþere men *moot* asken.
B.14.277 'I kan noȝt construe', quod haukyn; 'ye *moste* kenne me þis on englissh.'
B.15.399 This Makometh was cristene [man], and for he *moste* noȝt ben pope
B.15.562 A medicyne *moot* þerto þat may amende prelates.
B.16.92 That oon Iesus a Iustices sone *moste* Iouke in hir chambre
B.16.200 In menynge þat man *moste* on o god bileue,
B.18.203 'And I shal preue', quod Pees, 'hir peyne *moot* haue ende,
B.19.67 To penaunce and to pouerte he *moste* puten hymseluen,
B.19.178 Blessed *mote* þow be, and be shalt for euere.
B.19.179 And blessed *mote* þei be, in body and in soule,
B.19.319 'By god! Grace', quod Piers, 'ye *moten* gyue tymber
B.20.46 Ther nede haþ ynome me þat I *moot* nede abide
B.20.238 For lomere he lyeþ þat liflode *moot* begge
C. 1.137 'I haue no kynde knowyng,' quod y, '[ȝe *mot*] kenne me bettere
C. 2.120 And sayde to Symonye, 'now sorwe *mot* thow haue
C. 3.86 Thei han no pite on þe peple þat parselmele *mot* begge;
C. 3.257 'Ne be Marschal ouer my men there y *moste* fyhte.
C. 3.281 Marchaundise and mede *mot* nede [go] togederes.
C. 5.28 A spendour þat spene *mot* or a spilletyme–
C. 6.127 That y ne *mot* folowe this folk: my fortune is non oþer.
C. 7.2 'Y *moste* sitte to be shryue or elles sholde y nappe;
C. 7.157 To haue grace to go to treuthe; god leue þat they *mote*.
C. 7.206 Ȝe *mote* go thorw mekenesse, alle men and wommen,
C. 7.292 'Ȝe! villam emi,' quod oen, 'and now y *moste* thedre
C. 8.312 By this lyflode we *mote* lyue til l[a]masse tyme
C. 9.25 And for they sw[e]re by here soule and [so] god *mote* hem helpe
C. 9.281 '[Peres],' quod a prest tho, 'thy pardon *moste* y rede
C.11.231 And mercy of mercy nedes *moot* aryse
C.11.297 As doth the reue or Conturrollor þat rykene *moet* and acounten
C.12.170 He *moet* forsaken hymsulue his suster and his broþer
C.13.34 And sholden wende o wey where bothe *mosten* reste
C.13.37 The marchaunt *mote* nede be ylet lenger then the messager
C.13.49 The marchaunt *mote* forgo or moneye of his porse
C.13.68 That holde *mote* þe hey way, euene the ten hestes,
C.15.11 Ne no cors of pore comine in here kyrkeȝerde *most* lygge
C.15.147 And bote he bowe for this betynge blynde *mote* he worthen.'
C.16.70 That mete or moneye of straunge men *moet* begge.
C.16.163 And preyde pacience þat y apose hym *moste*.
C.17.225 A medecyne *moste* þerto þat m[ay] amende prelates.
C.17.243 In such manere me thynketh *moste* þe pope,
C.18.125 That oen Iesus, a Iustices sone, *most* iouken in here chaumbre
C.19.87 The whiche barn *mote* nedes be born of a mayde,
C.20.208 'And y shal pre[u]e,' quod pees, 'here payne *moet* haue ende
C.20.209 And wo into wele *moet* wende at þe laste.
C.21.67 To penaunce and to pouerte he *mot* putte hymsuluen
C.21.178 Yblessed *mote* thow be and be shalt for euere.
C.21.179 And yblessed *mote* they be, in body and in soule,
C.21.319 'By god! grace,' quod [Peres], 'ȝe *moet* gyue tymber
C.22.46 Ther nede hath ynome me þat y *moet* nede abyde
C.22.238 For lomere he lyeth þat lyflode *moet* begge

moot_halle n *mothalle n.* A 1 mothalle; B 2; C 2 moethalle (1) mothalle (1)
A. 4.135 Þere nas man in þe *mothalle*, more ne lesse,
B. 4.152 For I seiȝ Mede in þe *moot halle* on men of lawe wynke
B. 4.159 And þe mooste peple in þe [*moot*] halle and manye of þe grete,
C. 4.148 Mede in the *mothalle* tho on men of lawe gan wynke
C. 4.163 With mede þe mayde out of þe *moethalle*.

mor > moore

morales n prop *moral n.* A 1 morals; B 1
A.11.205 Of religioun þe rewele he reherside in his *morals*,
B.10.299 Of religion þe rule reherseþ in hise *morales*,

more n *more n.(1)* &> moore B 6 more (4) mores (2); C 4 more (2) mores (2)
B.15.98 Ther is a meschief in þe *more* of swiche manere [stokkes].
B.15.294 And also Marie Maudeleyne by *mores* lyuede and dewes,
B.16.5 Mercy is þe *more* þerof; þe myddul stok is ruþe;
B.16.14 Amyddes mannes body; þe *more* is of þat stokke.
B.16.58 And to my mynde, as me þinkeþ, on o *more* þei growed;
B.19.338 Blowe hem doun and breke hem and bite atwo þe *mores*.
C.16.251 There is a meschief in þe *more* of suche manere stokkes.
C.17.21 Marie Maudeleyne by *mores* lyuede and dewes;
C.18.23 Moche merueyled me on what *more* thei growede
C.21.338 Blowe hem doun and B[r]eke hem and b[y]te ato þe *mores*.

moreouer adv *moreover adv.* C 2
C. 5.53 And also *moreouer* me [sem]eth, syre resoun,
C.18.224 Multiplie ne *moreouer* withoute a make louye

mores > moores,more; morewe(n > morwe; mornede > moorne; mornyng > moorne,morwenyng,mournynge; mornynge > mournynge

morreyne n *moreine n.* C 1
C. 3.97 *Morreyne* or other meschaunc[e]: and mony tymes hit falleth

morsel n *morsel n.* B 1
B.13.108 Mortrews and ooþer mete, and we no *morsel* hadde.

mortel adj *mortal adj.* C 1
C.17.288 And amonges here enemyes in *mortel* batayles

morter n1 *morter n.(1)* B 1; C 1
B.13.44 In a *morter*, Post mortem, of many bitter peyne
C.15.49 In a *morter*, post mortem, of many bittere peynes

morter n2 *morter n.(2)* B 2; C 1
B. 6.142 Or helpe make *morter* or bere Muk afeld.
B.19.324 He made a manere *morter*, and mercy it highte.
C.21.324 He made a manere *morter* and mercy hit hihte.

morthere(th > murþere

mortrews n *mortreues n.* B 4; C 3 mortrewes
B.13.41 Ac [he eet] mete of moore cost, *mortrews* and potages.
B.13.62 He eet manye sondry metes, *mortrews* and puddynges,
B.13.92 That neiþer bacon ne braun, blancmanger ne *mortrews*,
B.13.108 *Mortrews* and ooþer mete, and we no morsel hadde.
C.15.46 Forthy eet he mete of more cost, *mortrewes* and potages.
C.15.66 And ete manye sondry metes, *mortrewes* and poddynges,
C.15.99 That noþer bacon ne brawn, blaunmanger ne *mortrewes*

morþereþ > murþere

morwe n *morwe n.* A 5 morewe (4) morewen (1); B 7; C 6 morwe (3) morwen (3)
A. 5.148 And Betoun þe breustere bad h[ym] good *morewe*,
A. 5.166 Of vpholderis an hep, erliche be þe *morewe*,
A. 7.135 Inouȝ iche day at non, ac no more til on þe *morewe*
A. 7.172 And fla[ppid]e on wiþ flailes fro *morewe* til eue,
A.11.110 Þanne was I [as] fayn as foul of fair *morewen*,
B. 5.298 [Ac] Beton þe Brewestere bad hym good *morwe*
B. 5.317 [Of] vpholderes an heep, erly by þe *morwe*,
B. 5.397 I haue maad auowes fourty and foryete hem on þe *morwe*;
B. 6.146 And na moore er *morwe*, myn almesse shul þei haue,
B. 6.184 And flapten on wiþ flailes fro *morwe* til euen
B.10.158 Thanne was [I] also fayn as fowel of fair *morwe*,
B.14.15 That I ne flobre it foule fro *morwe* til euen.'
C. 6.353 By betene hous the brewestere þat bad hym good *morwen*
C. 6.374 And of vphalderes an heep, [e]rly by þe *morwe*,
C. 8.180 And flapton on with f[lay]les fro *morwen* til euen
C. 9.244 As matynes by þe *morwe* til masse bygynne,
C.10.268 And wedden here for here welthe and weschen on þe *morwe*
C.11.100 Thenne was y as fayn as foul of faire *morwen*,

morwenyng n *morninge n.* A 1; B 2 morwenyng (1) morwenynge (1); C 1 mornyng
A.Pr.5 But on a may *morwenyng* on maluerne hilles
B.Pr.5 Ac on a May *morwenynge* on Maluerne hilles
B.13.261 And er þe commune haue corn ynouȝ many a cold *morwenyng*;
C.Pr.6 Ac on a May *mornyng* on maluerne hulles

moskeles n *muscle n.(1)* C 1
C. 9.94 Fridays and fastyngdays a ferthingworth of *moskeles*

mosse n *mos n.(1)* B 1; C 1 moes
B.15.287 That no man myȝte hym se for *mosse* and for leues.
C.17.14 That no man myhte se hym for *moes* and for leues.

mosseþ v *mossen v.* A 1
A.10.104 Þat selde m[os]seþ þe marbil þat men ofte [t]reden,

445

most > moost,moot,must; moste > moost,moot; mosten > moot; mostre >
moustre; mot > moot

mote n *mot n.(1)* B 1
B.10.269   Why meuestow þi mood for a *mote* in þi broþeres eiȝe,

mote v *moten v.(3)* A 3; B 3; C 2
A. 1.150   Þeiȝ ȝe ben miȝty to *mote* beþ mek of ȝour werkis;
A. 3.149   Þe mase for a mene man þeiȝ he *mote* euere.
A. 4.118   Whil mede haþ þe maistrie to *mo[te]* in þis halle.
B. 1.176   Thouȝ ye be myȝt[y] to *mote* beeþ meke [of] youre werkes,
B. 3.160   The maȝe for a mene man þouȝ he *mote* euere!
B. 4.135   While Mede haþ þe maistrie [to *mote* in þis] halle.
C. 1.172   Thow ȝe be myhty to *mote* beth meke in ȝoure werkes,
C. 3.198   The mase for a mene man thow he *mote* euere!

mote &> moot; moten > moot; mothalle > moot_halle

moþe n *motthe n.* B 1; C 1 mothe
B.14.23   Shal neuere [myx] bymolen it, ne *moþe* after biten it,
C.12.217   That many *mothe* was maistre ynne in A myntewhyle;

moþeeten adj *motthe n.* B 1
B.10.366   And oure bakkes þat *moþeeten* be and seen beggeris go naked,

motyef n *motif n.* A 1 motifs; B 1 motyues; C 2 motyef (1) motyues (1)
A.11.70   Suche *motifs* þei meuen, þise maistris in here glorie,
B.10.117   Swiche *motyues* þei meue, þise maistres in hir glorie,
C.15.129   Shal no such *motyef* be meued for me bote [þ]ere
C.16.232   Mouen *motyues*, mony tymes insolibles and falaes,

motyng ger *motinge ger.* A 1; B 1; C 2 motyng (1) motynge (1)
A. 8.60   Þat any mede of mene men for *motyng* resceyueþ,
B. 7.59   That any Mede of mene men for *motyng* takeþ.
C. 4.132   Whiles mede hath the maistrie þer *motyng* is at [þe] Barr[e].
C. 9.54   That mede of mene men for here *motynge* taken.

motyues > motyef

moton n *motoun n.* A 1 mutoun; B 1; C 1 motoun
A. 3.23   Þe leste man of here mayne a *mutoun* of gold.
B. 3.24   The leeste man of hire meynee a *moton* of golde.
C. 3.25   The leste man of here mayne a *motoun* of gold.

mouhte > may

mount n *mount n.(1)* B 2; C 1 mont
B.11.170   And took it moises vpon þe *mount* alle men to lere].
B.17.2   That took me a maundement vpon þe *mount* of Synay
C.19.2   That toek me a maundement vpon þe *mont* of synay

mountaigne n *mountaine n.* A 2 mounteyne; B 2; C 1 montaigne
A. 1.1   What þe *mounteyne* [be]meniþ, & ek þe [m]erke dale,
A. 2.40   In myddis a *mounteyne* at mydmorewe tide
B. 1.1   What þ[e] *Mountaigne* bymeneþ and þe merke dale
B.11.324   And on a *mountaigne* þat myddelerþe hiȝte, as me [þo] þouȝte,
C. 1.1   What the *montaigne* bymeneth and þe merke dale

mounteth v *mounten v.* A 1 mountyng; B 1 mountynge; C 1
A.Pr.64   Þe moste meschief on molde is *mountyng* vp faste.
B.Pr.67   The mooste meschief on Molde is *mountynge* [vp] faste.
C.Pr.65   The moste meschief on molde *mounteth* vp faste.

mourne(- > moorne

mournynge ger *morninge ger. &> moorne* A 1 mournyng; B 3; C 3
   mornyng (1) mornynge (1) mournynge (1)
A. 3.185   And made hym merþe *mournyng* to leue,
B. 3.198   I made his me[ynee] murye and *mournynge* lette;
B.14.238   Wiþoute *mournynge* amonge, and meschief to bote].
B.19.293   Maken hym, for any *mournynge*, þat he nas murie in soule,
C.12.204   Murthe for his *mornyng*, and þat muche plentee.
C.17.147   In murthe or in *mournynge* and neuere[more] to departe.
C.21.293   Makyn hym, for eny *mornynge*, þat he ne was murye in soule

mous n *mous n.* B 4 mees (2) Mous (2); C 4 mous (2) muys (2)
B.Pr.147   And smale *mees* myd hem; mo þan a þousand
B.Pr.182   A *Mous* þat muche good kouþe, as me [þo] þouȝte,
B.Pr.198   [And] many m[a]nnes malt we *mees* wolde destruye,
B.Pr.202   I seye for me', quod þe *Mous*, 'I se so muchel after,
C.Pr.168   And smale *muys* [mid] hem; mo þan a thousend
C.Pr.199   A *mous* þat moche good couthe, as me tho thoughte,
C.Pr.210   Y seye for me,' quod þe *mous*, 'y se so muche aftur,
C.Pr.216   For many mannys malt we *muys* wolde distruye

moustre n *moustre n.* B 1; C 2 mostre (1) muster (1)
B.13.361   And menged his marchaundise and made a good *moustre*:
C. 3.110   What maner *muster* oþer marchandima he vsed
C. 6.260   Meddeled my marchaundyse and made a good *mostre*.

mouþ n *mouth n.* A 9 mouþ (7) mouþe (1) mouþes (1); B 24 mouþ (16)
   mouþe (7) mouþes (1); C 22 mouth (9) mouthe (12) mouthes (1)
A.Pr.89   Þanne gete a mom of here *mouþ* til mony be shewid.
A. 1.144   But mekly wiþ *mouþe* mercy he besouȝte
A. 3.240   God sente hym to segge be samuels *mouþ*
A. 4.105   Til clerkis & kniȝtes be curteis of here *mouþes*,
A. 9.71   Whoso is [meke] of his *mouþ*, mylde of his speche,
A.11.24   And he þat haþ holy writ ay in his *mouþ*,
A.11.57   And han [hym] muchel in here *mouþ*, ac mene men in herte.
A.11.294   Þat clergie of cristis *mouþ* comendite [was hit] neuere,
A.11.306   And is to mene in oure *mouþ*, more ne lesse,
B.Pr.216   Than gete a mom of hire *mouþ* til moneie be shewed.
B. 1.170   But mekely wiþ *mouþe* mercy [he] bisouȝte
B. 4.155   And seide, 'madame, I am youre man what so my *mouþ* Iangle.
B. 5.179   [I] haue a flux of a foul *mouþ* wel fyue dayes after;
B. 5.281   'Haue mercy in þi mynde, and wiþ þi *mouþ* biseche it–
B. 5.366   Shryue þee and be shamed þerof and shewe it with þi *mouþe*.'
B. 8.67   Murþe of hire *mouþes* made me to slep[e];
B. 8.80   Whoso is [meke of his *mouþ*, milde of his speche],
B.10.32   Ac he þat haþ holy writ ay in his *mouþe*
B.10.71   And haue hym muche in [hire] *mouþ*, ac meene men in herte.
B.10.449   That] Clergie of cristes *mouþ* comended was it [neuere],
B.11.136   Mercy for hise mysdedes wiþ *mouþe* [or] wiþ herte.'
B.12.233   Why Adam hiled noȝt first his *mouþ* þat eet þe Appul
B.13.328   'Or wiþ myȝt [of] *mouþ* or þoruȝ m[a]nnes strengþe
B.13.346   Aboute þe *mouþ*, or byneþe bigynneþ to grope,
B.14.89   And surgiens for dedly synnes whan shrift of *mouþe* failleþ.
B.14.90   Ac shrift of *mouþ* moore worþi is if man be y[n]liche contrit,
B.14.91   For shrift of *mouþe* sleeþ synne be it neuer so dedly–
B.15.217   And þe murieste of *mouþ* at mete where he sitteþ
B.15.257   Misdooþ he no man ne wiþ his *mouþ* greueþ.
B.16.90   And þanne spak spiritus sanctus in Gabrielis *mouþe*
B.17.278   Sleeþ a man for hise moebles wiþ *mouþ* or with handes.
B.19.288   Ne no mete in his *mouþ* þat maister Iohan Spicede.
B.20.191   He buffetted me aboute þe *mouþ* [and bette out my wangteeþ];
C.Pr.166   Than gete a Mum of here *mouth* [til] moneye [be] shewed.
C. 1.166   Bote mekeliche with *mouth* mercy he bysoughte
C. 3.396   And is to [mene] in oure *mouth* more n[e] mynne
C. 6.73   'Or thorw myhte of *mouthe* or thorw mannes sleythes
C. 6.161   Y haue a flux of a foul *mouth* wel fyue daies aftur;
C. 6.180   Aboute þe *mouthe* and bynethe bygan y to grope
C. 6.433   The vilony of my foule *mouthe* and of my foule mawe:
C.10.66   Murthe of here *mouthes* made me to slepe
C.11.29   Ac he þat hath holy writ ay in his *mouth*
C.11.51   And haen [hym] muche in here *mouth* Ac mene [men] in herte.
C.11.274   That clergie of cristes *mouthe* com[e]nded was euere.
C.12.71   Mercy for his mysdedes with *mouthe* and with herte.'
C.13.40   Ther þe messager doth no more but with his *mouth* telleth
C.13.59   Ther þe messager is ay merye and his *mouth* ful of songes
C.15.221   In his *mouthe* mercy and amende vs all:
C.16.30   And oris confessio cometh of [knowlechyng and] shrifte of *mouthe*
C.16.343   He is þe murieste of *mouthe* at mete þer he sitteth
C.18.123   And thenne spak spiritus sanctus in gabrielis *mouthe*
C.18.259   As we wilnede and wolde with *mou[th]e* and herte aske.
C.19.259   Sleth a man for his mebles with *mouthe* or with handes.
C.21.288   Ne no mete in his *mouth* þat maistre iohann spyced.
C.22.191   He boffeted me aboute þe *mouthe* and beet out my wangteeth

mouþe > mouþ,mouþen

mouþen v *mouthen v.* A 2 mouþe (1) mouþiþ (1); B 3 mouþed (1)
   mouþen (1) mouþeþ (1); C 3 mouthed (2) mouthen (1)
A. 4.106   And haten [to] here harlotrie oþer *mouþe* it;
A. 7.222   Matheu wiþ þe manis face [*mouþ]iþ* þise wordis:
B. 4.115   And haten alle harlotrie to heren or to *mouþen* it;
B. 6.238   Mathew wiþ mannes face *mouþe[þ]* þise wordes:
B.18.150   Thanne Mercy ful myldely *mouþed* þise wordes,
C. 4.110   And hatien alle harlotrie to heren oþer to *mouthen* hit;
C. 9.126   For hit aren murye *mouthed* men, munstrals of heuene
C.20.153   Thenne mercy fol myldely *mouthed* this wordes,

moue- > meuen; mow(e > may

mowen v *mouen v.(1) &> may* C 1
C. 5.14   *Mowen* or mywen or make bond to sheues,

mowynge ger *mouinge ger.(1)* B 1; C 1
B. 6.189   And wente as werkmen [to wedynge] and [*mowynge*]
C. 8.186   And wenten as werkemen to wedynge and *mowynge*

muche n *muche n.* A 5 muche (4) muchel (1); B 14 muche (13) muchel
   (1); C 13 moche (10) muche (3)
A. 3.134   She may neiȝ as *muche* do in a moneþ ones
A. 5.227   And ȝet wile I ȝelde aȝen, ȝif I so *muchel* haue,
A.10.39   As *muche* to mene [as] man with his soule,
A.10.163   And is as *muche* to mene, among vs alle,

A.11.297 And is as *muche* to mene, to men þat ben lewid,
B.Pr.202 I seye for me', quod þe Mous, 'I se so *muchel* after,
B. 3.145 [She] may neiȝ as *muche* do in a Monþe one[s]
B. 3.353 The soule þat þe soude takeþ by so *muche* is bounde.'
B. 5.455 And yet wole I yelde ayein, if I so *muche* haue,
B. 5.501 And by so *muche* [it] semeþ þe sikerer we mowe
B. 7.15 And in as *muche* as þei mowe amenden alle synfulle,
B. 9.51 As *muche* to mene as man wiþ a Soule.
B.10.90 Whoso haþ *muche* spende manliche, so [meneþ] Tobye,
B.11.412 'To se *muche* and suffre moore, certes, is dowel.'
B.14.211 For þe riche haþ *muche* to rekene, and [riȝt softe] walkeþ;
B.16.133 And maken it as *muche* ouþer moore in alle manere poyntes
B.17.240 In as *muche* as þei mowen amenden and paien;
B.19.402 Of Spiritus Iusticie þow spekest *muche* on ydel.'
B.20.133 *Muche* of þe wit and wisdom of westmynstre halle.
C.Pr.210 Y seye for me,' quod þe mous, 'y se so *muche* aftur,
C. 3.183 He may ny as *muche* do in a monthe ones
C. 6.309 Hyhte ȝeuan-ȝelde-aȝeyn-yf-y-so-*moche*-haue-
C. 7.141 And by so *muche* hit semeth the sykerloker we mowe
C. 8.270 ȝe han manged ouer *moche*; þat maketh ȝow to be syke.
C.11.211 Neuere to man so *moche* þat man can of telle,
C.13.220 'To se *moche* and soffre al, certes, is dowel.'
C.16.52 For þe ryche hath *moche* to rykene and riht softe walketh;
C.16.274 Allas! lewed men, *moche* leese ȝe þat fynde
C.19.206 In as *moche* as they mowen amenden and payen;
C.20.43 And ȝut maken hit as *moche* in alle manere poyntes,
C.21.402 Of spiritus Iusticie thow spekest *moche* an ydel.'
C.22.133 *Moche* of þe Wyt and Wisdoem of Westmunstre halle.

muche *adj* *muche adj.* A 8 mechel (1) mekil (1) muche (3) muchel (3); B
    38 muche (34) muchel (4); C 47 mechel (1) moche (29) mochel (1)
    muche (13) muchel (3)
A. 4.136 Þat he ne held resoun a maister & mede a *muche* wrecche.
A. 5.243 But for þi *muchel* mercy mytygacioun I beseche;
A. 6.108 Pacience & pees *mekil* [peple] þei helpen,
A. 7.242 Þei han mangid ouer *muche*, þat makiþ hem grone ofte.
A. 9.61 A *muchel* man, me þouȝte, lik to myselue,
A.10.147 And brouȝt forþ a barn þat *muche* bale wrouȝte;
A.11.79 And for his *muchel* mercy to amende vs here.
A.12.102 Of peres þe plowman and *mechel* puple also.
B.Pr.182 A Mous þat *muche* good kouþe, as me [þo] þouȝte,
B. 3.335 And [*muche*] worshipe ha[þ] þerwiþ as holy writ telleþ:
B. 4.62 That wrong was a wikked luft and wroȝte *muche* sorwe.
B. 5.255 'I haue as *muche* pite of pouere men as pedlere haþ of cattes,
B. 5.469 But for þi *muchel* mercy mitigacion I biseche:
B. 5.622 Pacience and pees *muche* peple þei helpeþ;
B. 6.258 Ye han manged ouer *muche*; þat makeþ yow grone.
B. 8.70 A *muche* man me þou3te, lik to myselue,
B. 9.61 *Muche* wo worþ þat man þat mysruleþ his Inwit,
B. 9.153 *Muchel* merueille me þynkeþ; and moore of a sherewe
B.10.126 And for his *muche* mercy to amende [vs] here.
B.11.33 And pride of parfit lyuynge to *muche* peril þee brynge.'
B.11.75 Ich haue *muche* merueille of yow, and so haþ many anoþer,
B.11.350 If any Mason made a molde þerto *muche* wonder it were.
B.12.199 [I] hadde mete moore þan ynouȝ, ac noȝt so *muche* worshipe
B.12.297 And murþe and manhod;' and riȝt wiþ þat he vanysshed.
B.13.4 And of þis metyng many tyme *muche* þouȝt I hadde,
B.13.262 So er my wafres be ywroȝt *muche* wo I þolye.
B.13.426 Lest þo þre maner men to *muche* sorwe yow brynge:
B.14.157 For *muche* murþe is amonges riche, as in mete and cloþyng,
B.14.158 And *muche* murþe in May is amonges wilde beestes.
B.14.175 Conforte þo creatures þat *muche* care suffren
B.15.57 The man þat *muche* hony eteþ his mawe it engleymeþ,
B.15.120 And who was myn Auctour, *muche* wonder me þinkeþ
B.15.449 Moore þoruȝ miracles þan þoruȝ *muche* prechyng;
B.15.588 [And] for a parfit prophete þat *muche* peple sauede
B.16.182 Of oon *muchel* and myght in mesure and lengþe.
B.16.260 'This is a present of *muche* pris; what prynce shal it haue?'
B.17.342 And þouȝ þat men make *muche* doel in hir angre
B.18.36 Thanne cam Pilatus with *muche* peple, sedens pro tribunali,
B.18.44 And ȝit maken it as *muche* in alle manere poyntes,
B.19.68 And *muche* wo in þis world wilnen and suffren.
B.19.76 Mirre and *muche* gold wiþouten merc[ede] askynge
B.19.98 In þe manere of a man and þat by *muchel* sleighte,
B.19.365 And make a *muche* moot þat myghte ben a strengþe
B.20.98 As pokkes and pestilences, and *muche* peple shente;
B.20.158 Oon þat *muche* wo wroȝte, Sleuþe was his name.
B.20.290 And so it fareþ with *muche* folk þat to freres shryueþ,
C.Pr.99 In menynge of myracles *muche* wex hangeth there;
C.Pr.199 A mous þat *moche* good couthe, as me tho thoughte,
C. 1.19 And, in mesure thow *muche* were, to make ȝow attese
C. 3.450 *Muchel* [euel] is thorw mede mony tymes ysoffred
C. 3.487 And *muche* worschipe therwith, as holy writ telleth:
C. 4.65 How wrong was a wykked man and *muche* wo wrouhte.

C. 6.323 For thy *mochel* mercy mitigacioun y biseche:
C. 6.333 [T]rist in his *mechel* mercy and ȝut þou myhte be saued
C. 7.86 Laste tho manere men to *muche* sorwe ȝow brynge:
C. 7.148 And for [that] *muchel* mercy and marie loue thi moder
C. 7.274 Pacience and pees *muche* peple þei helpe,
C. 8.347 Pruyde and pestilences shal *moche* peple feche;
C. 9.77 And hemsulue also soffre *muche* hungur
C. 9.84 And of monye oþer men þat *moche* wo soffren,
C. 9.207 H[e]lden ful hungry hous and hadde *muche* defaute,
C.10.68 A *muche* man, me thoghte, ylike to mysulue,
C.10.175 And *moche* wo worth hym þat inwit myspeneth
C.11.70 And is to mene no more bote "who[so] *muche* goed weldeth
C.11.192 And pruyde-of-parfit-lyuynge to *moche* perel the brynge.'
C.12.204 Murthe for his mornyng, and þat *muche* plentee.
C.13.7 Abraham for his [auȝte] hadde *moche* tene
C.13.14 And delyuerede the weye his wyf with *moche* welthe aftur.
C.13.54 As þe messager may ne with so *moche* ese.
C.13.97 And as *moche* mede for a myte þer he offreth
C.13.161 Yf eny mason made a molde þerto *moche* wonder me thynketh
C.14.125 *Muchel* wo was hym marked þat wade shal with þe lewede!
C.14.138 Ich haue mete more then ynow Ac nat [so] *muche* worschipe
C.15.4 And many tym[e] of this meteles *moche* thouhte y hadde:
C.15.197 'Munstracye can y nat amonge *moche* bote make men merye,
C.16.10 *Muche* murthe is in may amonge wilde bestes
C.16.12 And *moche* murthe among ryche men is þat han meble ynow and
        hele.
C.16.219 The man þat *moche* hony eet his mawe hit engleymeth;
C.16.329 Worth *moche* meryte to þat man þat hit may soffre.
C.17.75 Of *moche* [m]one þe metal is nauhte
C.17.299 And for a parfit profete that *moche* peple sauede
C.18.178 With *moche* noyse þat nyhte nere frentyk y wakede;
C.18.276 'This is a present of *moche* pris; what prince shal hit haue?'
C.19.55 A man, as me tho thouhte, to *moche* care they brouhte
C.19.322 And thogh that men make *moche* deul in here anger
C.20.35 Thenne cam Pilatus with *moche* peple, sedens pro tribunali,
C.21.68 And *moche* wo in this world wilnen and soffren.
C.21.76 Mirre and *moche* gold withouten merc[ede] askynge
C.21.98 In þe manere of a man and þat by *moche* sleythe,
C.21.365 And make a *moche* moet þat myhte be a strenghe
C.22.98 As pokkes and pestilences, and *moche* peple shente;
C.22.158 Oen þat *moche* wo wrouhte, sleuthe was his name.
C.22.290 And so hit fareth with *moche* folke þat to freres shryuen,

muche *adv* *muche adv.* A 5 mekel (1) muche (3) muchel (1); B 19 muche
    (18) muchel (1); C 15 moche (10) muche (5)
A. 1.33 Mesure is medicine þeiȝ þou *muche* ȝerne.
A. 5.9 Þanne sauȝ I *meke[l]* more þan I before tolde,
A. 9.76 Dobet þus doþ, ac he doþ *muche* more.
A.11.53 God is *muche* in þe [gorge] of þis grete maistris,
A.11.57 And han [hym] *muchel* in here mouþ, ac mene men in herte.
B. 1.35 Mesure is medicine þouȝ þow *muchel* yerne.
B. 4.176 Mede ouermaistreþ lawe and *muche* truþe letteþ.
B. 5.9 [Th]anne [mette me] *muche* moore þan I bifore tolde,
B. 8.85 Dobet [þus dooþ], ac he dooþ *muche* moore.
B.10.67 God is *muche* in þe gorge of þise grete maistres,
B.10.71 And haue hym *muche* in [hire] mouþ, ac meene men in herte.
B.11.79 Ac *muche* moore meritorie, me þynkeþ, is to baptiȝe,
B.11.320 Ac *muche* moore in metynge þus wiþ me gan oon dispute,
B.11.360 *Muche* merueilled me what maister [þei hadde],
B.12.124 And medle vs nat wiþ hem to meuen any wraþe
B.13.382 That it coste me *muche* moore; swoor manye oþes.
B.13.438 *Muche* moore, me þynkeþ, riche men sholde
B.14.75 [Ac] mesure is [so] *muche* worþ it may noȝt be to deere.
B.14.262 *Muche* hardier may he asken þat here myȝte haue his wille
B.14.267 *Muche* is [þat maide] to loue of [a man] þat swich oon takeþ,
B.15.128 Allas, ye lewed men, *muche* lese ye on preestes!
B.16.148 And which tokne to þis day to *muche* is yvsed,
B.16.219 Ne matrimoyne wiþouten Mul[eri]e is noȝt *muche* to preise:
B.17.350 For þer nys sik ne sory, ne noon so *muche* wrecche
C. 1.33 Mesure is medecyne thogh þow *muche* ȝerne;
C. 4.170 Mede and men of ȝoure craft *muche* treuthe letteth.
C. 5.109 Thenne mette me *muche* more then y byfore tolde
C. 7.98 *Muche* more, me thynketh, riche men ouhte
C.11.51 And haen [hym] *muche* in here mouth Ac mene [men] in herte.
C.13.95 For þe wil is as *moche* worthe of a wrecche beggare
C.14.67 And medle we nat *moche* with hem to meuen eny wrathe
C.16.102 *Moche* hardyore may he aske þat here myhte haue his wille
C.16.107 *Moche* is [þat] mayde to louye of a man þat such oen taketh,
C.16.287 That maistres commenden *moche*. Where may hit be yfounde?
C.18.23 *Moche* merueyled me on what more thei growede
C.18.198 'Muse nat to *moche* þeron,' quod faith, 'til thow more knowe
C.18.220 Matrimonye withoute moylere is nauht *moche* to preyse
C.19.41 Alle manere men as *moche* as ouresulue.
C.19.330 For þer ne is sike ne sory ne non so *moche* wrecche

muyle > mule; muynde > mynde; muinstrals > mynstral; muys > mous

muk n *muk n.* B 1; C 1 mok
B. 6.142   Or helpe make morter or bere *Muk* afeld.
C.10.97   For here *mok* and here mebles suche men thenketh

mule n *mule n.(1)* B 1; C 1 muyle
B.17.51   Thanne sei3e we a Samaritan sittynge on a *Mule*,
C.19.49   Thenne sey we a samaritaen cam sittynge on a *muyle*,

mulerie n *muliere n.& adj.* B 1; C 1 moylere
B.16.219   Ne matrimoyne withouten *Mul[eri]e* is no3t muche to preise:
C.18.220   Matrimonye withoute *moylere* is nauht moche to preyse

muliere adj *muliere n.& adj.* A 2 molere (1) mulere (1); B 3 muliere (2)
    mulliere (1); C 4 moilere (2) moylore (1) moyloure (1)
A. 2.83   For mede is *molere* of [m]endis engendrit
A. 2.96   And mede is a *mulere*, [a maiden of gode];
B. 2.119   For Mede is *muliere* of Amendes engendred
B. 2.132   And Mede is *muliere*, a maude of goode;
B.16.221   That is man and his make and *mulliere* children;
C. 2.123   For mede is *moilere*, amendes was here dame;
C. 2.148   And mede is *moylore*, [a] mayden of gode;
C.10.210   Out of matrimonye, nat *moyloure*, mowen nat haue þe grace
C.18.234   The which is man and his make and *moilere* here issue,

mullere > millere

mullestones n *milneston n.* C 1
C.20.293   Set Mahond at þe mang[n]el and *mullestones* throweth;

mulliere > muliere

multiplieþ *multiplien v.* A 1 multiplie; B 3 multiplie (2) multiplieþ (1); C
    3 multiplie (1) multiplieth (1) multiplye (1)
A. 7.118   Þat god of his grace 3our greyn *multiplie*,
B. 6.126   That god of his grace youre greyn *multiplie*
B. 6.328   And a mayde haue þe maistrie, and *multiplie* by ei3te,
B.16.211   Migh[t] is [in] matrimoyne þat *multiplieþ* þe erþe
C. 8.132   That god [of] his grace 3oure grayn *multiplye*
C.18.85   Matrimonye, a moist fruyt þat *multiplieth* þe peple;
C.18.224   *Multiplie* ne moreouer withoute a make louye

mum > mom

munde n prop *n.i.d.* A 1; B 2; C 1
A. 2.76   *Munde* þe myllere, & manye mo oþere.
B. 2.112   [*Munde*] þe Millere and many mo oþere:
B.10.45   Than *Munde* þe Millere of Multa fecit deus.
C. 2.116   *Munde* þe mullere and monye mo othere:

*munstracie > mynstralcie; munstrals > mynstral; muracles > myracle;
murdre > murþere*

murye adj *mirie adj.* A 6 mery (3) merye (2) meryere (1); B 15 murie (6)
    murye (7) murier (1) murieste (1); C 17 mery (2) merye (7) mury (2)
    murye (5) murieste (1)
A. 1.105   3af hem mi3t in his mageste, þe *meryere* hem þou3te,
A. 1.138   [Þer] þou art *m[er]y* at mete, a3if men blinde þe 3edde.
A. 2.118   For we haue mede amaistried wiþ oure *mery* speche
A. 7.61   And make hym *mery* wiþ þe corn whoso it begrucchiþ.
A. 7.145   And make vs *merye* þerwiþ maugre þi chekis'.
A. 8.42   Þanne were marchauntis *merye*; many wepe for ioye,
B.Pr.209   What þis metels bymeneþ, ye men þat ben *murye*,
B. 1.107   Yaf hem my3t in his maiestee, þe *murier* hem þou3te,
B. 2.154   For we haue Mede amaistried wiþ oure *murie* speche
B. 3.198   I made his me[ynee] *murye* and mournynge lette;
B. 6.67   And make h[y]m *murie* þermyd, maugree whoso bigruccheþ it.
B. 6.158   And maken vs *murye* þer[wiþ] maugree þi chekes.'
B. 7.38   Thanne were Marchaunt3 *murie*; manye wepten for ioye,
B.12.189   Dominus pars hereditatis mee is a *murye* verset
B.13.58   And Conscience conforted vs and carped vs *murye* tales:
B.13.351   Til þei my3te na moore; and þanne [hadde] *murye* tales,
B.14.237   And som tyme for his synnes; so he is neuere *murie*
B.15.217   And þe *murieste* of mouþ at mete where he sitteþ,
B.19.293   Maken hym, for any mournynge, þat he nas *murie* in soule,
B.20.181   And rood [so to] reuel, a ryche place and a *murye*,
B.20.289   And maken hym *murie* wiþ ooþer mennes goodes.
C.Pr.220   What þis meteles bymeneth, 3e men þat ben *merye*,
C. 2.170   For we haue mede amaystred [with] oure *mery* [speche]
C. 6.185   Til we myhte no more; thenne hadde we *mery* tales
C. 8.68   And m[a]ken hym *merye* þermy[d], maugrey ho[so] bigruchen hit.
C. 8.155   And maken vs *murye* þer[with] maugreye h[o] begrucheth.'
C. 9.41   Tho were Marchauntes *mury*; many wopen for ioye
C. 9.126   For hit aren *murye* mouthed men, munstrals of heuene
C. 9.136   Godes munstrals and his mesagers and his *mury* bordiours
C.13.59   Ther þe messager is ay *merye* and his mouth ful of songes
C.14.128   Dominus pars hereditatis [mee] is A *merye* verset;

C.14.180   More þan for his fayre flesch or for his *merye* note.
C.15.197   'Munstracye can y nat moche bote make men *merye*,
C.16.78   So he is neuere[more ful] *merye*, so meschief hym followeth.
C.16.343   He is þe *murieste* of mouthe at mete þer he sitteth
C.21.293   Makyn hym, for eny mornynge, þat he ne was *murye* in soule
C.22.181   And roed so to reuel, a ryche place and a *murye*:
C.22.289   And maken hym *murye* with oþere menne godes.

murye adv *mirie adv.* A 1 merye; B 2 merye (1) murye (1); C 2 mery
    (1) murye (1)
A.Pr.10   I slomeride into a slepyng, it swi3ede so *merye*.
B.Pr.10   I slombred into a slepyng, it sweyed so *murye*.
B.18.196   Moyses and many mo *mer[ye]* shul [synge];
C.13.215   That y ne hadde met more, so *murye* as y slepte,
C.20.182   Moises and many moo *Mer[y]* shal synge;

murthe > murþe,murþen

murþe n *mirthe n. &> murþen* A 7 merþe (5) merþis (2); B 18 myrþe (1)
    myrþes (1) murþe (15) murþes (1); C 13 merthe (2) merþe (1) myrthe
    (2) murthe (6) murthes (2)
A.Pr.33   And somme *merþis* to make as mynstralis conne,
A. 3.11   Ac þere was *merþe* & mynstralcie mede to plese;
A. 3.185   And made hym *merþe* mournyng to leue,
A. 3.207   Mynstralis for here *merþis* mede þei asken;
A.11.35   Menstralsie & *merþe* among men is nouþe
A.11.39   At mete [in here] *merþe*, whanne mynstralis ben stille,
A.12.92   And mannes *merþe* w[or]þ no mor þan he deseruyþ here
B.Pr.33   And somme *murþes* to make as Mynstralles konne,
B. 3.11   A[c] þer was *murþe* & Mynstralcie Mede to plese;
B. 3.220   Mynstrales for hir *myrþe* Mede þei aske;
B. 8.67   *Murþe* of hire mouþes made me to slep[e];
B.10.49   Ac [mynstralcie and *murþe*] amonges men is nouþe
B.10.53   At mete in hir *murþe* whan Mynstrals beþ stille,
B.11.20   And in þis Mirour þow my3t se [*myrþes*] ful manye
B.12.15   It is but *murþe* as for me to amende my soule.
B.12.297   And muche *murþe* and manhod;' and ri3t wiþ þat he vanysshed.
B.13.60   And made hym *murþe* wiþ his mete, ac I mornede euere
B.13.417   He wexeþ wroþ, and wol no3t here but wordes of *murþe*;
B.14.125   And hir [ladies] also lyuede hir lif in *murþe*.
B.14.157   For muche *murþe* is amonges riche, as in mete and cloþyng,
B.14.158   And muche *murþe* in May is amonges wilde beestes;
B.15.139   And makeþ *murþe* þer[wiþ] and hise me[yne] boþe;
B.15.143   And þat he spared and bisperede [s]pende ne in *murþe*."
B.18.127   'Haue no meruueille', quod mercy; '*murþe* it bitokneþ.
B.18.219   Sette hym in solace and in souereyn *murþe*,
C.Pr.35   And summe *murthes* to make, as mynstrels conneth,
C. 3.12   Ac there was *myrthe* and mynstracie mede to plese;
C. 3.276   Munstrals for here *m[yrth]e* mede thei asken;
C. 7.77   A wexeth wroth and wol not here but wordes of *murthe*;
C.10.66   *Murthe* of here mouthes made me to slepe
C.11.179   And in þis myrrour thow myhte se *murthes* fol monye
C.12.204   *Murthe* for his mornyng, and þat muche plentee.
C.15.64   And made [hym] *mer[þe]* with [h]is mete Ac y mournede euere
C.16.10   Muche *murthe* is in may amonge wilde bestes
C.16.12   And moche *murthe* among ryche men is þat han meble ynow and
        hele.
C.17.147   In *murthe* or in mournynge and neuere[more] to departe.
C.20.130   'Haue no meruueyle,' quod Mercy; '*merthe* hit bitokneth.
C.20.228   Sette hym in solace and in souereyne *merthe*

murþen v *mirthen v.* B 2 murþe (1) murþen (1); C 1 murthe
B.11.400   Al to *murþe* wiþ man þat moste wo þolie.
B.17.244   For to *murþen* men [wiþ] þat in [m]erke sitten,
C.19.210   For to *murthe* men with þat in merke sitten,

murþere n *mortherer n.* A 3 murdre (2) murþre (1); B 3 morþereþ (1)
    murþere (2); C 3 morthere (1) morthereth (1) ymorthred (1)
A. 3.249   For any mylionis of mone *murdre* hem ichone;
A. 4.42   He mayteniþ his men to *murþre* myne hynen,
A. 5.84   Ac hadde I maistrie & mi3t I wolde *murdre* hym for euere.
B. 4.55   He mayteneþ hise men to *murþere* myne hewen,
B. 5.104   Ac hadde I maistrie and my3t [I wolde *murþere* hym for euere].
B.17.283   And who[so] *morþereþ* a good man, me þynkeþ, by myn Inwit,
C. 4.58   A meynteyneth his men to *morthere* myn hewes,
C.12.242   And so is many man *ymorthred* for his moneye and his godes
C.19.264   And hoso *morthereth* a goed man, me thynketh bi myn inwit,

muse v *musen v.* A 3 muse (1) musen (1) musyng (1); B 3 muse (2)
    musynge (1); C 6 muse (2) mused (1) musede (2) musyng (1)
A. 8.130   *Musyng* on þis metelis a myle wey I 3ede;
A.11.71   And make men to mysbeleue þat *musen* on here wordis.
A.11.138   For þe more I *muse* þeron þe mistlokere it semiþ,
B. 7.148   *Musynge* on þis metels [a myle] wey ich yede.
B.10.118   And maken men in mys bileue þat *muse* on hire wordes.
B.10.186   The moore I *muse* þerInne þe mystier it semeþ,

C. 9.297 *Musyng* on this meteles A myle way y ȝede.
C.11.127 Þe more y *muse* þer[i]n the mystiloker hit semeth
C.13.226 Ac when he mamelede aboute mete and *musede* to knowe
C.14.74 And markede hit in here manere and *mused* þeron to knowe.
C.15.24 And so y *musede* vppon þis matere þat me lust to slepe.
C.18.198 '*Muse* nat to moche þeron,' quod faith, 'til thow more knowe

musels > meseles

musik n *musike n.* A 2; B 2; C 1 musyk
A.11.32 More þanne *musik*, or makyng of god almiȝt,
A.11.129 And alle þe musons of *musik* I made hire [to] knowe.
B.10.44 Thei konne na moore mynstralcie ne *Musik* men to glade
B.10.177 And alle [þe] Musons in *Musik* I made hire to knowe.
C.11.117 And alle þe musons in *musyk* y made here to knowe.

musyng(e > muse

musons n *moisoun n.* A 1; B 1; C 1
A.11.129 And alle þe *musons* of musik I made hire [to] knowe.
B.10.177 And alle [þe] *Musons* in Musik I made hire to knowe.
C.11.117 And alle þe *musons* in musyk y made here to knowe.

must n *must n.* B 1; C 1 most
B.18.370 That I drynke riȝt ripe *Must*, Resureccio mortuorum.
C.20.412 And [y] drynke riht rype *m[o]st*, resureccio mortuorum.

muste > moot; muster > moustre

mute adj *muet adj.* B 1
B.16.111 Boþe meseles and *mute* and in þe menyson blody,

mutoun > moton

N

nabugodonosor n prop *Nabugodonosor n.* A 1; B 1; C 1 Nabugodonasor
A. 8.137   Þat *nabugodonosor* nempne þise clerkis–
B. 7.159   That *Nabugodonosor* nempne[þ þise] clerkes–
C. 9.307   Of *Nabugodonosor* þat no pere hadde

nacion n *nacioun n.* C 1
C.18.101   And bryngeth forth fruyt, folk of alle *nacion,*

nay adv *nai adv.,interj.* A 8; B 10; C 10
A. 3.162   'Nay lord,' quod þat lady, 'leu[iþ] him þe wers
A. 3.217   'Nay,' quaþ consience to þe king & knelide to þe erþe,
A. 4.4   'Nay be [Crist],' quaþ consience, 'cunge me raþere!
A. 4.91   'Nay,' quaþ þe king, 'so god ȝiue me blisse,
A. 6.22   'Nay, so [me god] helpe,' seide þe [gome] þanne.
A. 6.44   'Nay, be þe peril of my soule!' quaþ piers & gan to swere:
A. 8.134   Ac catoun construiþ it [*nay*] & canonistris boþe:
A.12.89   'Nay, wil,' quod þat wyȝth, 'wend þou no ferther,
B. 3.175   'Nay lord', quod þat lady, 'leueþ hym þe werse
B. 3.230   'Nay', quod Conscience to þe kyng and kneled to þe erþe.
B. 4.4   'Nay, by crist!' quod Conscience; 'congeye me [raþer]!
B. 4.104   'Nay', quod þe kyng, 'so me crist helpe,
B. 5.238   'Nay, soþly,' he seide, 'saue in my youþe.
B. 5.534   'Nay, so [god glade me]', seide þe gome þanne.
B. 5.557   'Nay, by [þe peril of] my soul[e]!' quod Piers and gan to swere:
B.13.188   'Nay, by crist!' quod Conscience to Clergie, 'god þee foryelde;
B.17.5   'Nay', he seide, '[I] seke hym þat haþ þe seel to kepe,
B.18.28   'Nay', quod [feiþ, 'but] þe fend and fals doom [to deye].
C. 3.221   'Nay, lord,' quod þat lady, 'leueth hym þe worse
C. 3.286   'Nay,' quod Consience to þe kyng, 'clerkes witeth þe sothe,
C. 4.4   'Nay, by Crist!' quod Consience, 'congeie me [rather]!
C. 4.99   'Nay, by crist!' quod þe kyng, 'for Consiences sake
C. 6.240   'Nay, sothly,' he saide, 'saue in my ȝouthe.
C. 7.179   'Nay, so me god [h]elpe,' sayde þe gome thenne,
C. 7.201   'Nay, bi þe perel of my soule!' Peres gan to swerie,
C.16.179   'Thenne is þat body bettere þen þou?' quod y. 'Nay,' quod he, 'no
           bettere,
C.19.7   'Nay,' he saide, 'y seke hym þat hath þe seel to kepe,
C.20.27   'Nay,' quod faith, 'bote the fende and fals doem to deye.

nailed v *nailen v.* B 1; C 1 nayled
B.18.51   *Nailed* hym with þre nailes naked on [a] roode;
C.20.51   [Thei] *nayled* hym with thre nayles naked vpon a rode

nayles n *nail n.* A 2 nailes; B 4 nailes (2) nayles (2); C 3
A. 3.178   Crope into a caban for cold of þi *nailes;*
A. 7.55   Hise cokeris & his cuffis for cold of his *nailes,*
B. 3.191   Crope into a Cabane for cold of þi *nayles;*
B. 6.60   [Hise] cokeres and [hise] coffes for cold of [hise] *nailes,*
B.18.51   Nailed hym with þre *nailes* naked on [a] roode;
B.20.226   And brode hoked arwes, goddes herte and hise *nayles,*
C. 6.140   And thenne y crye and crache with my kene *nayles,*
C.20.51   [Thei] nayled hym with thre *nayles* naked vpon a rode
C.22.226   And brode hokede Arwes, goddes herte and his *nayles,*

naked adj *naked adj.* A 2 nakid; B 7; C 5 naked (4) nakede (1)
A. 7.14   Þe nedy & þe *nakid,* nymeþ hed how þei liggen;
A. 7.209   Þat nedy ben or *nakid,* & nouȝt han to spende,
B. 6.15   The nedy and þe *naked* nymeþ hede how þei liggeþ;
B. 6.223   That nedy ben [or *naked,* and nouȝt han to spende,
B.10.366   And oure bakkes þat moþeeten be and seen beggeris go *naked,*
B.12.161   And boþe *naked* as a nedle, hir noon [sadder] þan ooþer.
B.17.59   And as *naked* as a nedle and noon help aboute.
B.18.51   Nailed hym with þre nailes *naked* on [a] roode;
B.20.196   On nyghtes namely, whan we *naked* weere,
C.13.84   As none tythes to tythe ne to clothe the *nakede*
C.14.105   And bothe *naked* as a nedle, here noen heuegore then othere.
C.19.58   And as *naked* as an nedle and noen helpe abouten.
C.20.51   [Thei] nayled hym with thre nayles *naked* vpon a rode
C.22.196   Anyhtes nameliche, when we *naked* were,

name n *name n.* A 12 name (11) names (1); B 52 name (44) names (8); C 52 name (41) names (10) namus (1)
A. 1.71   And h[a]lside hire on þe heiȝe *name,* er heo þennis ȝede,
A. 3.3   Þe king calliþ a clerk–I can not his *name*–
A. 3.30   And in constory at court callen here *names.*
A. 3.48   Woldist þou glase þe gable, & graue þere þin *name,*
A. 3.51   Þat I ne shulde make or mende, & myn *name* writen
A. 5.140   Rose þe regratour was hire riȝte *name;*
A. 6.58   A[nd] nameliche an ydel þe *name* of god almiȝt;
A. 9.62   Com & callide me be my kynde *name.*
A. 9.63   'What art þou,' quaþ I þo, 'þat my *name* knowist?'
A.11.261   I was markid wiþoute mercy, & myn *name* entrid
A.12.13   And on clergie crieþ on cristes holy *name*
A.12.82   Mi *name* is feuere on þe ferþe day; I am aþrest euere.
B.Pr.107   Ac of þe Cardinals at court þat kauȝte of þat *name,*
B. 1.73   And [halsede] hire on þe heiȝe *name,* er she þennes yede,
B. 3.3   The kyng called a clerk–[I kan] noȝt his *name*–
B. 3.31   And in Consistorie at court callen hire *names.*
B. 3.49   Woldestow glaȝe þ[e] gable & graue [þere] þy *name*
B. 5.224   Rose þe Regrater was hir riȝte *name;*
B. 5.259   Amonges my neȝebores namely swich a *name* ich haue.'
B. 5.571   And-nameliche-on-ydel-þe-*name*-of-god-almyȝty.
B. 8.71   Cam and called me by my kynde *name.*
B. 8.72   'What art [þ]ow', quod I þo, 'þat my *name* knowest?'
B. 9.81   Than nempnynge of a *name* and he neuer þe wiser.
B.10.380   And þat I man maad was, and my *name* yentred
B.11.207   And after his resurexcion Redemptor was his *name,*
B.11.322   And nempned me by my *name* and bad me nymen hede,
B.11.441   And if his wille were he wolde his *name* telle)
B.13.139   [Th]us [lerede] me ones a lemman, loue was hir *name.*
B.13.224   'I am a Mynstrall', quod þat man, 'my *name* is Actiua vita.
B.13.225   Al yde[l] ich hatie for of Actif is my *name.*
B.13.289   As best for his body be to haue a [bold] *name;*
B.13.401   As þere no nede was goddes *name* an Idel:
B.15.26   And whan I make mone to god memoria is my *name;*
B.15.28   Thanne is Racio my riȝte *name,* reson on englissh;
B.15.29   And whan I feele þat folk telleþ my firste *name* is sensus,
B.15.34   Thanne is lele loue my *name,* and in latyn Amor;
B.15.38   Nempnede me þus to *name;* now þow myȝt chese
B.15.39   How þow coueitest to calle me, now þow knowest [alle] my
           name,
B.15.41   'For bisshopes yblessed bereþ manye *names,*
B.15.43   And oþere *names* an heep, Episcopus and Pastor.'
B.15.45   Thow woldest knowe and konne þe cause of alle [hire] *names,*
B.15.152   I haue lyued in londe', quod [I], 'my *name* is longe wille,
B.15.457   Til it be cristned in cristes *name* and confermed of þe bisshop
B.15.495   That þei ne wente as crist wisseþ, siþen þei wille haue *name,*
B.15.510   That bere bisshopes *names* of Bethleem and Babiloigne.
B.15.528   And souereynliche to swiche þat of surrye bereþ þe *name*],
B.16.19   That I herde nempne his *name* anoon I swowned after,
B.16.185   Pater is his propre *name,* a persone by hymselue.
B.16.208   And in heuene and here oon singuler *name.*
B.16.250   Of a [buyrn] þat bare hym–Iohan Baptist was his *name*–
B.16.265   Til he come þat I carpe of; crist is his *name.*
B.19.18   Anoon as men nempned þe *name* of god Iesu;
B.19.19   Ergo is no *name* to þe name of Iesus,
B.19.19   Ergo is no name to þe *name* of Iesus,
B.19.22   And synfulle aren solaced and saued by þat *name,*
B.19.24   Is crist moore of myȝt and moore worþi *name*
B.19.69   Ac to carpe moore of crist and how he com to þat *name,*
B.19.70   Faithly for to speke, his firste *name* was Iesus.
B.19.128   Thus he confortede carefulle and caughte a gretter *name,*
B.19.208   And comeþ fro þe grete god; grace is his *name.*
B.19.275   And sew [it] in mannes soule and siþen tolde hir *names.*
B.20.158   Oon þat muche wo wroȝte, Sleuþe was his *name.*
B.20.256   And nempnede [hem *names*], and noumbrede þe sterres:
B.20.339   What hattestow, I praye þee? hele noȝt þi *name.*'
C.Pr.134   Ac of þe Cardinales at Court þat caught han such a *name*
C. 1.4   Cam doun fro þe castel and calde me by *name*
C. 1.70   And ha[ls]ede here on the hey *name* or she thennes [ȝede]

C. 2.17 [Wh]os wyf a were and what was here *name*,
C. 3.3 The kyng callede a clerke–y can nat his *name*–
C. 3.34 And in constorie at court do calle ȝoure *names*.
C. 3.52 Wolde ȝe glase þ[e] gable and graue ther ȝoure *name*
C. 3.114 Be yfranchised for a fre man and haue a fals *name*.
C. 3.145 And bitterliche banne the and alle þat bereth thy *name*
C. 3.367 Þat is nat resonable ne rect to refuse my syre *name*.
C. 3.402 And coueytede oure kynde and be kald in oure *name*–
C.10.69 Cam and calde me be my kynde *name*.
C.10.70 'What art thow,' quod y [þo], 'þat my *name* knowest?'
C.11.203 That y man ymaed was and my *name* yentred
C.12.115 And aftur his resureccoun redemptor was his *name*
C.12.176 Tulius, tolomeus–y can nat tell here *names*–
C.12.211 How god, as þe gospelle telleth, gyueth [hym] foel to *name*,
C.13.247 And yf his wille were A wolde his *name* telle.
C.15.193 'Ich am a mynstral,' quod this man, 'my *name* is actiua vita,
C.16.164 And he soffrede me and saide, 'assay his oþer *name*.'
C.16.188 Thenne ys racio my rihte *name*, reson an englische;
C.16.189 And when y fele þat folke telleth my furste *name* is sensus
C.16.196 Thenne is lele loue my *name* and in latyn Amor;
C.16.200 Nempned me thus to *name*; now þou myhte chese
C.16.201 How þou coueytest to calle me, now þou knowest al my *namus*.
C.16.203 'For bisshopes yblessed bereth many *names*,
C.16.205 And oþere *names* an heep, Episcopus and pastor.'
C.16.207 Thow woldest knowe and conne þe cause of all here *names*
C.17.25 Y can nat rykene hem riȝt now ne reherse here *names*
C.17.191 Ite in vniuersum mundum, sethe ȝe wilne þe *name*
C.17.261 That bereth *name* of Neptalym, of Niniue [and] of damaske.
C.17.278 And souereynliche [to] suche þat of surie bereth þe *name*
C.18.191 'Su[t]he they ben suyrelepus,' quod y, 'they haen sondry *names*?'
C.18.195 Holy goest is his *name* and he is in all.'
C.18.281 Til he come þat y carpe of; Crist is his *name*
C.19.26 And six thousand mo,' quod fayth; 'y [can] nat seyn here *names*.'
C.21.18 Anoon as men nemnede þe *name* of god iesu;
C.21.19 Ergo is no *name* to þe name of iesus
C.21.19 Ergo is no name to þe *name* of iesus
C.21.22 And synfole ben solaced and saued by þat *name*.
C.21.24 Is Crist more of myhte and more worth[y] *name*
C.21.69 Ac to carpe more of Crist and how he cam to þat *name*;
C.21.70 Faythly for to speke his furste *name* was iesus.
C.21.128 Thus he comfortede carefole and cauhte a grettere *name*,
C.21.208 And cometh fro the grete god; grace is his *name*.
C.21.275 And sewe hit in mannes soule and sethe toelde here *names*.
C.22.158 Oen þat moche wo wrouhte, sleuthe was his *name*.
C.22.256 And nempned hem *names* and nombred þe sterres:
C.22.339 What hattest thow? y praye the, hele nat thy *name*.'

namely adv *nameli adv.* A 4 *nameliche*; B 10 *namely (7) nameliche (3)*;
C 9 *nameliche (7) namelyche (1) namliche (1)*

A. 2.110 'And *nameliche* to þe notories, þat hem non fail[e];
A. 6.58 A[nd] *nameliche* an ydel þe name of god almiȝt;
A. 7.48 And *nameliche* at mete suche men eschew[e],
A. 8.168 And *nameliche* ȝe maistris, as meiris & iuggis,
B. 2.146 And *namely* to þe Notaries þat hem noon faille.
B. 5.259 Amonges my neȝebores *namely* swich a name ich haue.'
B. 5.571 And–*nameliche*–on–ydel–þe–name–of–god–almyȝty.
B. 6.53 And *namely* at mete swiche men eschuwe,
B. 7.42 And *nameliche* of Innocentȝ þat noon yuel konneþ:
B. 7.190 And *namely* ye maistres, Meires and Iugges,
B.12.71 And *namely* Clergie for cristes loue, þat of Clergie is roote.
B.14.240 And by þe nekke *namely* hir noon may hente ooþer;
B.18.399 And *nameliche* at swich a nede þer nedes help bihoueþ:
B.20.196 On nyghtes *namely*, whan we naked weere,
C. 2.162 And [*name*]liche [to] the notaries þat [hem] noon fayle.
C. 6.96 Amongus marchauntes many tymes and *nameliche* in londone.
C. 7.218 And–*nameliche*–an–ydel–þe–name–of–god–almyhty.
C. 8.274 At noon ne at no tyme and *nameliche* at sopere
C.12.100 And *nameliche* pore peple, here preeyeres may vs helpe
C.16.80 And by þe nekke *namelyche* here noen may henten other;
C.17.292 And *nameliche* þer þat lewede lyuen and no lawe knoweth.
C.20.442 And *namliche* at such a nede þat nedes helpe asketh:
C.22.196 Anyhtes *nameliche*, when we naked were,

namore > no,moore; namus > name

nappe v *nappen v.* B 1; C 1

B. 5.386 'I moste sitte [to be shryuen] or ellis sholde I *nappe*;
C. 7.2 'Y moste sitte to be shryue or elles sholde y *nappe*;

naroos > arise

narwe adv *narwe adv* B 1

B.13.370 If I yede to þe Plowȝ I pynched so *narwe*

nas > ben; nasareth > naȝareth; nat > noȝt; naught nauȝt nauht > noȝt

nauhte adj *nought adj. &> noȝt* C 1

C.17.75 Of moche [m]one þe metal is *nauhte*

nauht > noȝt

nauele n *navele n.* B 1; C 1

B.14.243 And Pouerte nys but a petit þyng, apereþ noȝt to his *nauele*,
C.16.83 And pouerte is bote a pety thyng, appereth nat to his *nauele*,

nawher > nowher

naȝareth n prop *n.i.d.* B 2; C 2 *nasareth (1) naȝareth (1)*

B.15.494 Of *Naȝareth*, of Nynyue, of Neptalym and Damaske,
B.19.137 And nempned hym of *Naȝareth*; and no man so worþi
C.17.189 Of *nasareth*, of [n]yneue, of neptalym [and] damaske,
C.21.137 And nempned hym of *naȝareth*; and no man so worthy

ne adv *ne adv.* A 27; B 81; C 89

A.Pr.79 þat þe pore peple of þe parissh shulde haue ȝif þei *ne* were.
A. 1.157 ȝe *ne* haue no more meryt in [masse] ne in [houres]
A. 2.106 Hereto assentiþ Cyuyle, ac symonye *ne* wolde
A. 3.32 Þat he *ne* worþ ferst auauncid for I am beknowe
A. 3.51 Þat I *ne* shulde make or mende, & myn name writen
A. 3.124 Shirreues of shires were shent ȝif heo *ne* were.
A. 4.136 Þat he *ne* held resoun a maister & mede a muche wrecche.
A. 5.4 Þat I *ne* hadde yslepe saddere & yseyn more.
A. 5.6 Þat I *ne* miȝte ferþere a fote for defaute of slepyng.
A. 5.106 And þat makiþ me so ma[t] for I *ne* may me venge.'
A. 5.223 Þat I *ne* shal do me er day to þe dere chirche
A. 5.241 So rewe oþ þis robert þat red[dere] *ne* hauiþ,
A. 6.39 He [wiþ]halt non hyne his hire þat he *ne* haþ it at eue.
A. 7.164 *N[e]* hadde peris [wiþ] a pese lof preyede hym beleue,
A. 7.168 *Ne* hadde þ[e] fisician ferst defendite him watir
A. 8.38 Þat I *ne* shal sende [ȝour] soule sauf into heuene,
A. 8.54 Þat he *ne* worþ sauf sykirly, & so seiþ þe sautir.
A. 8.56 *Ne* wolde neuere holy writ, god wot þe soþe.
A. 8.83 And wommen wiþ childe þat werche *ne* mowe,
A. 8.178 I *ne* wolde ȝiue for þi patent on pye hele.
A. 9.30 For ȝif he *ne* arise þe raþere & [rauȝte þe stere],
A.10.205 Þat dede derne do no man *ne* shulde.
A.11.31 For ȝif harlotrie *ne* halp[e] hem betere, haue god my trouþe,
A.11.141 *Ne* were þe loue þat liþ þerein a wel lewid þing it were.
A.11.254 *Ne* mecaberis, ne sle nouȝt, is þe kynde englissh;
A.11.254 Ne mecaberis, *ne* sle nouȝt, is þe kynde englissh;
A.12.14 That he shewe me hit *ne* sholde but ȝif [I schriuen] were
B.Pr.82 That þe [pouere peple] of þe parisshe sholde haue if þei *ne* were.
B.Pr.129 Lowed to speke in latyn, for lewed men *ne* koude
B.Pr.177 Ther *ne* was Raton in þe route, for al þe Reaume of Fraunce,
B.Pr.210 Deuyne ye, for I *ne* dar, by deere god in heuene.
B. 1.183 Ye *ne* haue na moore merite in masse n[e] in houres
B. 2.142 Herto assenteþ Cyuyle, ac Symonye *ne* wolde
B. 3.33 That he *ne* worþ first auaunced, for I am biknowen
B. 3.135 Sherreues of Shires were shent if she *ne* were.
B. 4.37 Thei *ne* [gy]ueþ noȝt of [good feiþ, woot god þe sooþe]:
B. 5.4 That I *ne* hadde slept sadder and yseiȝen moore.
B. 5.6 That I *ne* myȝte ferþer a foot for defaute of slepynge.
B. 5.49 'It is þi [tresor if treson *ne* were], and tryacle at þy nede.'
B. 5.129 And þat makeþ me [so mat], for I *ne* may me venge.
B. 5.152 [That] I *ne* moste folwe this folk, for swich is my grace.
B. 5.205 *Ne* hadde þe grace of gyle ygo amonges my [ware]
B. 5.280 *Ne* hadde repentaunce þe raþer reconforted hym in þis manere:
B. 5.451 That I *ne* shal do me er day to þe deere chirche
B. 5.467 So rewe on þis Robbere þat Reddere *ne* hauiþ,
B. 5.535 'I [*ne*] seiȝ neuere Palmere wiþ pyk ne wiþ scrippe
B. 5.552 He wiþhalt noon hewe his hire þat he *ne* haþ it at euen.
B. 5.642 Thow shalt seye I am þi Suster.' I *ne* woot where þei bicome.
B. 6.14 And al is þoruȝ suffraunce þat vengeaunce yow *ne* takeþ,
B. 6.179 *Ne* hadde Piers wiþ a pese loof preyed [hym bileue]
B. 6.180 They hadde be [dede and] doluen, *ne* deme þow noon ooþer.
B. 7.52 That he *ne* worþ saaf [sikerly]; þe Sauter bereþ witnesse:
B. 7.101 And wommen wiþ childe þat werche *ne* mowe,
B. 8.34 For if he *ne* arise þe raþer and rauȝte þe steere
B. 9.83 *Ne* faille payn ne potage and prelates dide as þei sholden.
B. 9.192 That [dede derne] do no man *ne* sholde.
B.10.65 *Ne* were mercy in meene men moore þan in riche
B.10.189 [*Ne* were þe loue þat liþ þerinne a wel lewed þyng it were].
B.10.253 Alle þe clerkes vnder crist *ne* koude þis assoille,
B.11.24 That I *ne* shal folwe þi felawship, if Fortune it like.'
B.11.144 That al þe clergie vnder crist *ne* myȝte me cracche fro helle,
B.11.166 Ther no clergie *ne* kouþe, ne konnyng of lawes.
B.11.235 Cleophas *ne* knew hym noȝt þat he crist were

B.11.341   Ther *ne* was cow ne cowkynde þat conceyued hadde
B.11.375   Why þow *ne* sewest man and his make þat no mysfeet hem folwe.'
B.11.407   That I in metels *ne* myȝte moore haue yknowen
B.12.60   Ac grace *ne* groweþ noȝt [til good wil yeue reyn];
B.12.211   That oure lord *ne* hadde hym liȝtly out, so leue I [by] þe þef in
            heuene.
B.12.216   Alle þe clerkes vnder crist *ne* kouþe þe skile assoille:
B.12.225   Clergie ne kynde wit *ne* knew neuere þe cause,
B.12.276   For lettred men were lewed yet *ne* were loore of hir bokes.'
B.12.290   *Ne* wolde neuere trewe god but [trewe] truþe were allowed.
B.13.126   And no text *ne* takeþ to mayntene his cause
B.13.135   That no clerk *ne* kan, as crist bereþ witnesse:
B.13.166   Pope ne patriark, þat pure reson *ne* shal [þee] make
B.13.175   *Ne* bitwene two cristene kynges kan no wiȝt pees make
B.13.207   Ther nys wo in þis world þat we *ne* sholde amende;
B.13.338   And seye þat no clerc *ne* kan, ne crist as I leue,
B.13.385   Mercy for my mysdedes, þat I *ne* moorned moore
B.13.397   That my mynde *ne* was moore on my good in a doute
B.14.13   That I *ne* soiled it wiþ siȝte or som ydel speche,
B.14.15   That I *ne* flobre it foule fro morwe til euen.'
B.14.67   That no reyn *ne* roon; þus rede men in bokes,
B.14.68   That manye wyntres men lyueden and no mete *ne* tulieden.
B.14.107   Whan he drogh to his deeþ day þat he *ne* dredde hym soore,
B.14.112   And seiþ, "lo! briddes and beestes þat no blisse *ne* knoweþ
B.14.231   For his rentes *ne* wol nauȝt reche no riche metes to bigge;
B.14.324   I *ne* hadde be deed and doluen for dowelis sake!
B.15.159   That he *ne* wolde aske after his, and ouþerwhile coueite
B.15.249   Ac I *ne* lakke no lif, but lord amende vs alle,
B.15.277   Of leons ne of leopardes no liflode *ne* toke,
B.15.298   Ac þer *ne* was leoun ne leopard þat on laundes wenten,
B.15.300   That *ne* fil to hir feet and fawned wiþ þe tailles;
B.15.331   And of hem þat habbeþ þei taken and ȝyueþ hem þat [*ne*] habbeþ.
B.15.495   That þei *ne* wente as crist wisseþ, siþen þei wille haue name,
B.17.316   Noght of þe nounpower of god, þat he *ne* is myghtful
B.17.351   That he *ne* may louye, and hym like, and lene of his herte
B.18.208   If no nyȝt *ne* weere, no man as I leeue
B.18.211   Wite what wo is, *ne* were þe deeþ of kynde.
B.18.325   Lucifer loke *ne* myȝte, so light hym ablente.
B.18.414   That loue, and hym liste, to laughynge *ne* brouȝte;
B.19.251   [*Ne* no boost ne] debat [be] among hem [alle].
B.19.306   Neiþer of duc ne of deeþ, þat he *ne* dide lawe
B.19.374   That he *ne* halp a quantite holynesse to wexe,
B.19.413   I knew neuere Cardynal þat he *ne* cam fro þe pope.
B.20.3   I *ne* wiste wher to ete ne at what place,
B.20.32   Of þat he weneþ wolde falle if his wit *ne* weere;
B.20.197   I *ne* myghte in no manere maken it at hir wille,
C.Pr.80   That þe [pore] peple [of þe] parsch[e] sholde haue yf þei *ne* were.
C.Pr.194   Ther *ne* was [raton in] þe route, for al þe reame of Fraunce,
C.Pr.213   And thow hit costed m[e] catel byknowen [hit] y *ne* wolde
C.Pr.218   *Ne* were þe Cat of þe Court and ȝonge kitones toward;
C.Pr.221   Deuyne ȝe, for y *ne* dar, by dere god almyhten.
C. 1.149   For heuene holde hit *ne* myghte, so heuy hit semede,
C. 1.179   Ȝe *n[e]* haueth na more meryte in masse ne in oures
C. 2.158   Hereto assenteth syuyle, ac symonye *ne* wolde
C. 3.36   That he *ne* worth furste vaunsed, for y am byknowe
C. 3.87   Thow thei take hem vntidy thyng no tresoun þei *ne* halden hit;
C. 3.204   Ther *ne* is Cite vnder sonne ne noon so ryche reume
C. 3.210   That no lond *ne* loueth the and ȝut leeste thyn owene:
C. 3.282   Is no lede þat leueth þat he *ne* loueth mede
C. 3.329   So god gyueth no [grace] þat "si" [*ne*] is the glose
C. 4.189   And þat vnsittynge suffrraunce *ne* sele ȝoure priue lettres
C. 6.82   And segge þat no clerk *ne* can, ne Crist as I leue,
C. 6.94   And þat maketh me so megre for y *ne* may me venge.
C. 6.127   That y *ne* mot folowe this folk: my fortune is non oþer.
C. 6.213   *Ne* hadde þe grace of Gyle go among my ware
C. 6.274   Mercy for my mysdedes þat y *ne* mourned [o]ftur
C. 6.284   That my muynde *ne* was more [o]n my godes in a doute
C. 6.288   Y *ne* wolde cope me with thy catel ne oure kyrke mende
C. 6.321   So rewe on Robert þat reddere *ne* haue
C. 6.428   There no nede *ne* was, many sythe falsly;
C. 7.65   That y *ne* shal do me ar day to þe dere chirche
C. 7.180   'I [*ne*] saw neuere palmere with pyk ne with scrip[p]e
C. 7.234   And al þe wallyng is of wyt for wil *ne* sholde hit wynne;
C. 8.53   *Ne* countreplede nat Consience ne holy kyrke ryhtes.'
C. 8.176   *Ne* hadde [Peres] with a pese loof preyede hym b[ile]ue.
C. 8.194   There was no ladde þat lyuede þat *ne* lowede hym to Peres
C. 8.300   'Y behote the,' quod hunger, 'þat hennes *ne* wol y wende
C. 9.177   And wymmen with childe þat worche *ne* mowe,
C.10.266   Ther *ne* is squier ne knyhte in contreye aboute
C.10.267   That he *ne* wol bowe to þat bonde to beden here an hosebonde
C.11.47   *Ne* were mercy in m[e]ne men more then in riht riche
C.11.154   Alle þe Clerkes vnder Crist *ne* couthe this assoile
C.11.183   That y *ne* shal folowe thy felowschipe yf fortune [hit] lyke.'

C.12.79   That al þe cristendoem vnde[r] Crist *ne* myhte me crache fro
            [helle]
C.12.124   Cleophas *ne* knewe hym nat þat he Crist were
C.13.149   Ther *ne* [was] cow ne cowkynde þat conseyued hadde
C.13.151   Ther *ne* was no kyne kynde þat conseyued hadde
C.13.152   That *ne* lees the lykynge of lost of flesch, as hit were,
C.13.186   That thow *ne* reul[e]st rather renkes then other bestes.
C.13.193   Why he *ne* loueth thy lore and leueth as þou techest.'
C.13.215   That y *ne* hadde met more, so murye as y slepte,
C.14.24   Ac grace *ne* groweth nat til gode wil gyue reyne
C.14.71   Bothe lewede and lerede were lost yf clergie *ne* were.
C.14.150   That oure [lord] *ne* hauede [hym] lihtliche out, so leue y [by] þ[e]
            thef in heuene.
C.14.155   Alle þe Clerkes vnder Crist *ne* couthe [þe skyle] assoile:
C.14.198   For letrede men were lewede ȝut *ne* were lore of [here bokes].'
C.14.212   *Ne* wolde neuere trewe god bote trewe treuthe were alloued.
C.15.74   Ac me wondreth in my wit why þat they *ne* preche
C.15.133   And no tixst *ne* taketh to preue this for trewe
C.15.266   That no reyn *ne* roen; thus [r]at men [i]n bokes,
C.15.267   That manye wynter men lyuede and no mete *ne* tylede.
C.15.282   When he drow to þe deth that he *ne* dradd hym sarrore
C.15.284   Hit are but fewe folk of this ryche that *ne* falleth in arrerage
C.15.288   And saith, "loo! briddes and bestes þat no blisse *ne* knoweth
C.16.60   Ne none of þe seuene synnes sitte *ne* may þer longe
C.16.293   That he *ne* askede aftur his and oþerewhiles coueytede
C.17.1   'There is no such,' y sayde, 'þat som tyme *ne* borweth
C.17.91   Nat in god þat he *ne* is goed and þe grounde bothe;
C.17.154   For þer is no man þat mynde hath þat *ne* meketh [hym] and
            byseketh
C.17.190   That they *ne* wente [þe wey] as holy writ byd:
C.18.47   And shaketh hit; *ne* were hit vndershored hit sholde nat stande.
C.18.180   Y waytede witterly; Ac whoder he wende y *ne* wiste.
C.19.37   That of no trinite *ne* telleth ne taketh mo persones
C.19.56   For he *ne* myhte stepe ne stande ne stere foet ne handes
C.19.92   For wente neuere man this way þat he *ne* was here yruyfled
C.19.139   Riht so failed þe sone, the syre be me *ne* myhte
C.19.296   And nat of þe nownpower of god, þat he *ne* is ful of myhte
C.19.330   For þer *ne* is sike ne sory ne non so moche wrecche
C.19.331   That he *ne* may louye, and hym lyke, and lene of his herte
C.20.215   Yf no nyht *ne* were no man, [as] y leue,
C.20.217   *Ne* hadde god ysoffred of som oþer then hymsulue
C.20.220   Ywyte what wo is *ne* were þe deth of kynde.
C.20.226   *Ne* woet no wyht, as y wene, what is ynow to mene.
C.20.358   That y *ne* sygge as y syhe, suynde my teme).
C.20.368   Lucifer loke *ne* myhte, so liht hym ablen[t]e,
C.20.457   That loue, and hym luste, to l[a]u[h]ynge [*ne*] brouhte;
C.21.52   That he *ne* aroos and regnede and raueschede helle.
C.21.251   *Ne* no boest ne debaet be among hem alle.
C.21.293   Makyn hym, for eny mornynge, þat he *ne* was murye in soule
C.21.306   Noþer of deuk ne of deth þat he *ne* dede lawe
C.21.372   Ther *ne* was cristene creature that kynde wit hadde
C.21.374   That he *ne* halpe a qua[n]tite holinesse to wexe,
C.22.3   Y *ne* wiste where to ete ne at what place
C.22.32   Of þat he weneth wolde falle yf his wit *ne* were;
C.22.197   Y *ne* myhte in none manere maken hit at here wille

ne conj *ne conj.*   A 65; B 352; C 346

A.1.35, A.1.101, A.1.157, A.2.38, A.3.16, A.3.50, A.3.55, A.3.58, A.3.75,
A.3.166, A.3.174, A.3.175, A.3.271, A.4.39, A.4.41, A.4.113, A.4.124, A.4.125, A.4.135,
A.4.141, A.5.100, A.5.101, A.5.121, A.5.143, A.5.143, A.5.242, A.6.23, A.6.60, A.6.61,
A.6.64, A.6.116, A.7.47, A.7.120, A.7.229, A.7.265, A.7.269, A.7.287, A.7.289, A.7.293,
A.7.301, A.8.55, A.8.55, A.8.72, A.8.105, A.8.175, A.9.7, A.9.75, A.9.111, A.10.64,
A.10.78, A.10.78, A.10.107, A.11.33, A.11.33, A.11.47, A.11.96, A.11.174, A.11.203,
A.11.228, A.11.228, A.11.228, A.11.252, A.11.306, A.11.309, A.11.309

B.Pr.130, B.Pr.179, B.Pr.203, B.Pr.204, B.1.37, B.1.103, B.1.158, B.1.183,
B.3.16, B.3.73, B.3.86, B.3.179, B.3.187, B.3.188, B.3.271, B.3.296, B.3.315, B.3.315,
B.3.316, B.3.317, B.3.323, B.4.19, B.4.41, B.4.52, B.4.54, B.4.130, B.4.141, B.4.142,
B.4.151, B.5.36, B.5.123, B.5.124, B.5.125, B.5.183, B.5.184, B.5.185, B.5.227,
B.5.262, B.5.263, B.5.266, B.5.267, B.5.289, B.5.387, B.5.387, B.5.396, B.5.399,
B.5.405, B.5.416, B.5.416, B.5.468, B.5.489, B.5.535, B.5.573, B.5.574, B.5.577, B.6.52,
B.6.128, B.6.149, B.6.281, B.6.285, B.6.303, B.6.305, B.6.309, B.6.320, B.7.35, B.7.53,
B.7.53, B.7.53, B.7.56, B.7.90, B.7.123, B.7.197, B.8.7, B.8.84, B.8.121, B.9.83, B.9.89,
B.9.95, B.9.96, B.9.106, B.9.129, B.9.177, B.10.44, B.10.46, B.10.47, B.10.47, B.10.61,
B.10.75, B.10.76, B.10.82, B.10.83, B.10.98, B.10.143, B.10.231, B.10.256, B.10.280,
B.10.307, B.10.340, B.10.340, B.10.340, B.10.407, B.10.456, B.10.462, B.10.465,
B.10.465, B.11.40, B.11.41, B.11.41, B.11.48, B.11.92, B.11.106, B.11.127, B.11.166,
B.11.174, B.11.191, B.11.204, B.11.212, B.11.215, B.11.220, B.11.281, B.11.282,
B.11.282, B.11.284, B.11.285, B.11.285, B.11.297, B.11.297, B.11.299,
B.11.314, B.11.314, B.11.315, B.11.341, B.11.342, B.11.362, B.11.372, B.11.392,
B.11.397, B.11.425, B.11.430, B.11.436, B.12.2, B.12.36, B.12.69, B.12.97, B.12.98,
B.12.122, B.12.127, B.12.134, B.12.134, B.12.137, B.12.143, B.12.146,
B.12.165, B.12.165, B.12.203, B.12.204, B.12.204, B.12.204, B.12.209, B.12.225,
B.12.243, B.12.271, B.12.271, B.12.278, B.12.279, B.12.287, B.13.9, B.13.17, B.13.92,
B.13.92, B.13.93, B.13.159, B.13.159, B.13.160, B.13.160, B.13.161, B.13.161,

B.13.161, B.13.162, B.13.162, B.13.162, B.13.165, B.13.165, B.13.166, B.13.230,
B.13.230, B.13.231, B.13.231, B.13.232, B.13.232, B.13.233, B.13.233, B.13.233,
B.13.245, B.13.258, B.13.283, B.13.295, B.13.338, B.13.340, B.13.395, B.13.395,
B.13.396, B.13.396, B.13.408, B.13.410, B.13.433, B.13.435, B.13.459, B.14.23,
B.14.24, B.14.24, B.14.25, B.14.27, B.14.31, B.14.53, B.14.54, B.14.57, B.14.57,
B.14.58, B.14.58, B.14.97, B.14.171, B.14.172, B.14.172, B.14.219, B.14.219, B.14.220,
B.14.251, B.14.251, B.14.290, B.14.290, B.14.295, B.14.296, B.14.333, B.14.333,
B.15.8, B.15.9, B.15.18, B.15.102, B.15.102, B.15.141, B.15.153, B.15.164, B.15.165,
B.15.165, B.15.165, B.15.171, B.15.172, B.15.172, B.15.177, B.15.209, B.15.210,
B.15.211, B.15.213, B.15.214, B.15.252, B.15.252, B.15.253, B.15.253, B.15.254,
B.15.254, B.15.256, B.15.256, B.15.257, B.15.264, B.15.265, B.15.265, B.15.265,
B.15.276, B.15.276, B.15.277, B.15.298, B.15.299, B.15.299, B.15.355, B.15.358,
B.15.369, B.15.374, B.15.375, B.15.376, B.15.463, B.15.537, B.16.219, B.16.263,
B.16.263, B.17.19, B.17.57, B.17.57, B.17.57, B.17.58, B.17.95, B.17.102, B.17.175,
B.17.182, B.17.200, B.17.224, B.17.224, B.17.225, B.17.258, B.17.260, B.17.260,
B.17.298, B.17.350, B.17.350, B.18.105, B.18.105, B.18.146, B.18.207, B.18.229,
B.18.275, B.18.293, B.18.368, B.18.411, B.18.411, B.18.413, B.19.20, B.19.20, B.19.51,
B.19.97, B.19.139, B.19.228, B.19.251, B.19.283, B.19.284, B.19.285, B.19.285,
B.19.286, B.19.288, B.19.292, B.19.306, B.19.349, B.19.398, B.19.454, B.19.476,
B.20.3, B.20.10, B.20.13, B.20.13, B.20.24, B.20.33, B.20.50, B.20.50, B.20.102,
B.20.150, B.20.154, B.20.178, B.20.211, B.20.247, B.20.272
          C.Pr.36, C.Pr.196, C.Pr.211, C.Pr.212, C.1.35, C.1.99, C.1.154, C.1.176, C.1.179,
C.1.187, C.2.29, C.2.32, C.3.17, C.3.85, C.3.112, C.3.204, C.3.214, C.3.225, C.3.233,
C.3.240, C.3.257, C.3.294, C.3.294, C.3.298, C.3.322, C.3.367, C.3.396, C.3.449,
C.3.468, C.3.468, C.3.469, C.3.470, C.3.476, C.4.19, C.4.57, C.4.127, C.4.138, C.4.138,
C.4.139, C.4.190, C.5.57, C.5.57, C.5.58, C.5.58, C.5.154, C.5.184, C.6.37, C.6.82,
C.6.84, C.6.84, C.6.88, C.6.89, C.6.90, C.6.90, C.6.165, C.6.166, C.6.167, C.6.255,
C.6.282, C.6.282, C.6.283, C.6.283, C.6.288, C.6.289, C.6.322, C.6.344, C.6.403, C.7.3,
C.7.3, C.7.12, C.7.15, C.7.21, C.7.31, C.7.31, C.7.34, C.7.74, C.7.93, C.7.95, C.7.180,
C.7.220, C.7.221, C.7.284, C.8.50, C.8.53, C.8.85, C.8.134, C.8.159, C.8.274, C.8.303,
C.8.307, C.8.325, C.8.327, C.8.331, C.8.340, C.9.38, C.9.109, C.9.113, C.9.139, C.9.161,
C.9.167, C.9.168, C.9.175, C.9.175, C.9.196, C.9.196, C.9.255, C.9.275, C.9.275,
C.9.280, C.9.343, C.9.346, C.10.7, C.10.81, C.10.106, C.10.117, C.10.160, C.10.186,
C.10.186, C.10.186, C.10.187, C.10.198, C.10.202, C.10.250, C.10.258, C.10.266,
C.11.27, C.11.44, C.11.55, C.11.56, C.11.62, C.11.63, C.11.74, C.11.110, C.11.157,
C.11.200, C.11.201, C.11.222, C.11.238, C.11.282, C.11.291, C.11.291, C.11.307,
C.11.308, C.11.308, C.11.311, C.12.33, C.12.40, C.12.62, C.12.103, C.12.112, C.12.181,
C.12.190, C.12.190, C.12.192, C.12.198, C.12.198, C.13.11, C.13.44, C.13.45, C.13.54,
C.13.81, C.13.81, C.13.84, C.13.85, C.13.85, C.13.103, C.13.111, C.13.111, C.13.113,
C.13.126, C.13.126, C.13.127, C.13.149, C.13.150, C.13.175, C.13.182, C.13.200,
C.13.200, C.13.232, C.13.237, C.13.242, C.14.6, C.14.6, C.14.7, C.14.8, C.14.8, C.14.65,
C.14.78, C.14.78, C.14.82, C.14.87, C.14.90, C.14.90, C.14.142, C.14.143, C.14.143,
C.14.143, C.14.148, C.14.176, C.14.192, C.14.192, C.14.200, C.14.209, C.15.11,
C.15.99, C.15.99, C.15.100, C.15.112, C.15.116, C.15.158, C.15.158, C.15.163,
C.15.163, C.15.163, C.15.164, C.15.164, C.15.204, C.15.204, C.15.205, C.15.205,
C.15.206, C.15.206, C.15.207, C.15.207, C.15.207, C.15.228, C.15.233, C.15.252,
C.15.253, C.15.256, C.15.256, C.15.257, C.15.257, C.16.60, C.16.61, C.16.91, C.16.91,
C.16.125, C.16.125, C.16.130, C.16.131, C.16.169, C.16.255, C.16.255, C.16.290,
C.16.307, C.16.307, C.16.310, C.16.313, C.16.314, C.16.318, C.16.341, C.16.372,
C.16.372, C.17.25, C.17.29, C.17.89, C.17.89, C.17.96, C.17.105, C.17.111, C.17.164,
C.17.198, C.18.63, C.18.63, C.18.140, C.18.224, C.18.225, C.18.279, C.18.279, C.19.20,
C.19.37, C.19.56, C.19.56, C.19.56, C.19.57, C.19.84, C.19.85, C.19.103, C.19.103,
C.19.137, C.19.140, C.19.140, C.19.140, C.19.148, C.19.166, C.19.190, C.19.190,
C.19.191, C.19.224, C.19.226, C.19.226, C.19.236, C.19.249, C.19.330, C.19.330,
C.20.108, C.20.108, C.20.149, C.20.212, C.20.238, C.20.286, C.20.297, C.20.323,
C.20.405, C.20.409, C.20.409, C.20.410, C.20.454, C.20.454, C.20.456, C.21.20,
C.21.20, C.21.51, C.21.97, C.21.139, C.21.228, C.21.251, C.21.283, C.21.284, C.21.285,
C.21.285, C.21.286, C.21.288, C.21.292, C.21.306, C.21.349, C.21.398, C.21.413,
C.21.454, C.21.476, C.22.3, C.22.10, C.22.13, C.22.13, C.22.24, C.22.33, C.22.50,
C.22.50, C.22.102, C.22.150, C.22.154, C.22.178, C.22.211, C.22.247, C.22.272

necessaries n *necessarie n.* B 1; C 1
B.20.249 And oþere *necessaries* ynowe; yow shal no þyng [lakke]
C.22.249 And oþere *necessaries* ynowe; ȝow shal no thyng lakke

neddres n *naddre n. cf. addre* B 1
B. 5.86 Ech a word þat he warp was of a *Neddres* tonge;

nede n *nede n.(1)* A 10; B 43 nede (42) nedes (1); C 39 nede (38) nedes (1)
A. 1.18 Of [woll]ene, of [lyn]ene, of liflode at *nede*
A. 1.54 And tutour of ȝour tresour, & take it ȝow at *nede*;
A. 5.27 And kep[e] it in hire coffre for catel at *nede*.
A. 6.57 So shalt þou se swere nouȝt but it be for *nede*,
A. 7.111 Shal no greyn þat here growiþ glade ȝow at *nede*;
A. 7.228 "He þat haþ shal haue to helpe þere *nede* is,
A. 8.69 For he þat beggiþ or bit, but he haue *nede*,
A. 8.146 I myself & my sones, seke þe for *nede*.'
A. 9.78 Whiles he haþ ouȝt of his owene he helpiþ þere *nede* is;
A.11.152 And louen þat liȝen on vs, & lenen hem at here *nede*,
B. 1.18 Of wollene, of lynnen, of liflode at *nede*
B. 1.56 And tutour of youre tresor, and take it yow at *nede*;
B. 3.245 Of god at a gret *nede* whan þei gon hennes.
B. 5.27 And kepe it in hire cofre for catel at *nede*.

B. 5.49 'It is þi [tresor if treson ne were], and tryacle at þy *nede*.'
B. 5.254 'Hastow pite on pouere men þat [for pure *nede*] borwe?'
B. 5.370 There no *nede* was nyne hundred tymes;
B. 5.429 If any man dooþ me a bienfait or helpeþ me at *nede*
B. 5.570 So shaltow se swere-noȝt-but-it-be-for-*nede*-
B. 6.119 Shal no greyn þat [here] groweþ glade yow at *nede*;
B. 6.244 "He þat haþ shal haue and helpe þere [*nede* is]
B. 7.67 For he þat beggeþ or bit, but he haue *nede*,
B. 7.78 For wite ye neuere who is worþi, ac god woot who haþ *nede*.
B. 7.84 Forþi biddeþ noȝt, ye beggeres, but if ye haue *nede*;
B. 7.169 I myself and my sones, seche þee for *nede*.'
B. 8.87 [Whiles he haþ ouȝt of his owene he helpeþ þer *nede* is];
B.10.203 And louen hem þat lyen on vs and lene hem [at hir *nede*]
B.10.343 And Caton kenneþ vs to coueiten it nauȝt but as *nede* techeþ:
B.11.29 Thow shalt fynde Fortune þee faille at þi mooste *nede*
B.11.432 Ac whan *nede* nymeþ hym vp for [nede] lest he sterue,
B.11.432 Ac whan nede nymeþ hym vp for [*nede*] lest he sterue,
B.13.5 First how Fortune me failed at my mooste *nede*;
B.13.401 As þere no *nede* was goddes name an Idel'
B.15.178 For a frend þat fyndeþ hym failed hym neuere at *nede*:
B.15.337 And helpeþ hem þat helpeþ yow and ȝyueþ þer no *nede* is,
B.16.67 'Heer now byneþe', quod he þo, 'if I *nede* hadde,
B.17.89 'Ac þi frend and þi felawe þow fyndest me at *nede*.'
B.18.399 And nameliche at swich a *nede* þer nedes help bihoueþ:
B.19.389 Or as ofte as þei hadde *nede*, þo þat hadde ypaied
B.20.4 And it neghehed neiȝ þe noon and wiþ *nede* I mette
B.20.9 And þow nome na moore þan *nede* þee tauȝte?
B.20.10 And *nede* haþ no lawe ne neuere shal falle in dette
B.20.17 *Nede* anoon righte nymeþ hym vnder maynprise.
B.20.20 So *nede* at gret nede may nymen as for his owene
B.20.20 So nede at gret *nede* may nymen as for his owene
B.20.35 Ac *nede* is next hym for anoon he mekeþ
B.20.37 [For *nede* makeþ nede fele nedes lowe herted].
B.20.46 Ther *nede* haþ ynome me þat I moot nede abide
B.20.51 Whan *nede* ha[dde] vndernome me þus anoon I fil aslepe
B.20.55 And [made] fals sprynge and sprede and spede mennes *nedes*.
B.20.232 *Nede* neghede þo neer and Conscience he tolde
B.20.318 'We han no *nede*', quod Conscience; 'I woot no bettre leche
B.20.383 And þat freres hadde a fyndyng þat for *nede* flateren
C. 1.52 And tutor of ȝoure tresor and take it ȝow at *nede*;
C. 5.129 And kepe hit in here cofre for catel at *nede*.
C. 6.428 There no *nede* ne was, many sythe falsly;
C. 7.42 Yf eny man do[th] me a beenfeet or helpeth me at *nede*
C. 7.217 [So] shalt thow se swere-nat-but-it-be-for-*nede*-
C. 7.294 Anoþer anoen riht *nede* he sayde he hadde
C. 8.126 Shal no grayn þat here groweth gladyen ȝow at *nede*;
C. 9.63 For he þat beg[g]eth or biddeth, but y[f he] haue *nede*,
C. 9.67 Bote ther he wiste were wel grete *nede*
C. 9.161 Ne no beggare[s] þat beggeth but yf they haue *nede*.'
C. 9.313 Y mysulue and my sones, seche the for *nede*.'
C. 9.316 His eleuene bretherne hym for *nede* souhte
C.10.189 Oure enemyes enterely and helpe hem at here *nede*.
C.11.28 Helpe hym þat hath nauhte then tho that haen no *nede*.
C.11.188 Thow shalt fynde fortune þe fayle At thy moste *nede*
C.11.302 Lewede men in good bileue and lene hem at here *nede*.'
C.13.239 Ac when *nede* nymeth hym vp anoen he is aschamed
C.15.5 Furste how fortune me faylede At my moste *nede*;
C.15.144 Ȝef hym eft and eft, euere at his *nede*,
C.16.20 And yliche witty and wys and lyue withoute *nede*;
C.16.317 [Rentes or other richesse to releue hym at his *nede*]?'
C.17.63 And afturward awayte no hath moest *nede*
C.18.84 'Here beneth y may nyme, yf y *nede* hadde,
C.20.442 And namliche at such a *nede* þat nedes helpe asketh:
C.21.389 Or as ofte as they hadden *nede*, tho þat hadden payed
C.22.4 And hit neyhed neyh þe noen and with *nede* y mette
C.22.9 And thow nome no more then *nede* the tauhte?
C.22.10 And *nede* hath no lawe ne neuere shal falle in dette
C.22.17 *Nede* anoen riht nymeth hym vnder maynprise.
C.22.20 So *nede* at greet nede may nyme as for his owene
C.22.20 So nede at greet *nede* may nyme as for his owene
C.22.35 A[c] *nede* is nexst hym for anoen he meketh
C.22.37 For *nede* maketh neede fele nedes louh herted.
C.22.46 Ther *nede* hath ynome me þat y moet nede abyde
C.22.51 Whenne *nede* hadde vndernome [me] thus anoen y ful aslepe
C.22.55 And made fals sprynge and sprede and spe[d]e menne *nedes*.
C.22.232 *Nede* neyhede tho ner and Consience he toelde
C.22.318 'We haen no *nede*,' quod Consience; 'y woet no bettere leche
C.22.383 And þat freres hadde a fyndynge þat for *nede* flateren

nede adv *nede adv.* A 1; B 2; C 3
A. 3.213 Mede & marchaundise mote *nede* go togidere;
B. 3.226 [Mede and Marchaundiȝe] mote *nede* go togideres;
B.20.46 Ther nede haþ ynome me þat I moot *nede* abide
C. 3.281 Marchaundise and mede mot *nede* [go] togederes.

C.13.37   The marchaunt mote *nede* be ylet lenger then the messager
C.22.46   Ther nede hath ynome me þat y moet *nede* abyde

nede &> nedy; nede(e > nedeþ

nedeful adj *nedeful adj.* A 1 nedful; B 3 nedeful (1) nedefulle (1)
   nedfulle (1); C 5 nedfol (1) nedfole (1) neodefole (1) nidefole (1)
   niedfol (1)

A. 1.21   Arn none *nedful* but þo & nempne hem I þenke,
B. 1.21   Are none *nedfulle* but þo; and nempne hem I þynke
B.11.78   Baptiȝynge and buryinge boþe beþ ful *nedefulle*;
B.19.20   Ne noon so *nedeful* to nempne by nyȝte ne by daye.
C. 1.21   Aren non [ni]*defole* but tho and nemne hem y thenke
C. 4.121   For alle manere men þat me fynt *neodefole*;
C.13.77   And spele and spare to spene vppon þe *nedfole*
C.19.241 And for he was a nygard and a nythynge to the *nedfol* pore,
C.21.20   Ne noen so *niedfol* to nemnie by nyhte ne by day

nedelere > nedlere

nedes adv *nedes adv.* &> *nede n* B 2; C 5

B.18.399 And nameliche at swich a tyme þer *nedes* help bihoueþ:
B.20.37   [For nede makeþ nede fele *nedes* lowe herted].
C.11.231 And mercy of mercy *nedes* moet aryse
C.12.215 "And art so loth to leue that lete shal thow *nedes*:
C.19.87   The whiche barn mote *nedes* be born of a mayde,
C.20.442 And namliche at such a nede þat *nedes* helpe asketh:
C.22.37   For nede maketh neede fele *nedes* louh herted.

nedeþ v *neden v.(2)* A 3 nediþ; B 14 neded (4) nedede (1) nedeþ (9); C
   17 nedede (5) neden (1) nedeth (11)

A. 7.195 And helpe hem of alle þing [aftir] þat hem *nedi[þ]*.
A.11.50   Þat þus partiþ wiþ þe poore a parcel whanne hym *nediþ*.
A.11.190 And seken out þe seke & sende hem þat hem *nediþ*,
B. 6.209 And helpen hem of alle þyng [after þat] hem *nedeþ*.
B. 9.88   Eyþer of hem helpeþ ooþer of þat hat h[y]m *nedeþ*,
B.10.64   That þus parteþ wiþ þe pouere a parcell whan hym *nedeþ*.
B.11.210 And of þat ech man may forbere amende þere it *nedeþ*,
B.11.291 Thanne *nedeþ* yow noȝt to [nyme] siluer for masses þat ye syngen,
B.14.33   And þat ynogh; shal noon faille of þyng þat hem *nedeþ*:
B.15.160 Thyng þat *neded* hym noȝt and nyme it if he myȝte.
B.15.222 And as gladliche he it gaf to gomes þat it *neded*.
B.15.291 And wan wiþ hise hondes þat his wombe *neded*.
B.15.576 Bodily foode and goostly foode to] gyue þere it *nedeþ*:
B.17.33   What *neded* it [now] a newe lawe to [brynge]
B.17.165 Thus it is–*nedeþ* no man trowe noon ooþer–
B.17.269 Of his mete and moneie to men þat it *nedede*?
B.20.36   And as lowe as a lomb for lakkyng þat hym *nedeþ*;
C. 5.20   Or eny other kynes craft þat to þe comune *nedeth*,
C. 8.148 What! y and myn wolle fynde hem what hem *nedeth*.'
C. 8.218 And helpe hem of alle thyng ay as hem *nedeth*.
C. 9.57   Thise foure sholde be fre to alle folk þat hit *nede[th]*.
C. 9.71   Ac þat most *neden* aren oure neyhebores and we nyme gode
         he[d]e,
C. 9.87   What h[e]m *nede[th]* at here neyhebores at noon and at eue.
C. 9.164 Hit *nedeth* nat nouthe anoon for to preche
C.11.46   That so parteth with þe pore a parsel when hym *nedeth*.
C.12.117 Forthy loue we as leue childerne, lene hem þat *nedeth*
C.13.105 And *nedeth* [ȝow] nat to nyme siluer for masses þat ȝe synge
C.16.294 Thyng that *nedede* hym nauhte and nyme hit yf a myhte.
C.16.347 And also gladliche he hit gaf to gomes þat hit *nedede*.
C.17.18   And wan with his handes al þat hym *nedede*.
C.18.13   Of holynesse, of hendenesse, of helpe-hym-þat-*nedeth*,
C.19.34   What *nedede* hit thanne a newe lawe to brynge
C.19.235 Of his mete and mone to men þat hit *nedede*?
C.22.36   And as louh as a lamb for lakkyng þat hym *nedeth*;

nedfol(e nedful(le > nedeful

nedy adj *nedi adj.* A 5; B 18 nede (1) nedy (16) nedieste (1); C 13 neede
   (1) nedy (12)

A. 7.14   Þe *nedy* & þe nakid, nymeþ hed how þei liggen,
A. 7.209 Þat *nedy* ben or nakid, & nouȝt han to spende,
A. 8.50   Þat is Innocent & *nedy*, & no man apeiriþ,
A. 8.70   He is fals wiþ þe fend & [defraudiþ] þe *nedy*,
A.11.244 Oure enemys and alle men þat arn *nedy* & pore,
B. 6.15   The *nedy* and þe naked nymeþ hede how þei liggeþ;
B. 6.223 That *nedy* ben [or naked, and nouȝt han to spende,
B. 7.48   That is Innocent and *nedy* and no man apeireþ,
B. 7.68   He is fals wiþ þe feend and defraudeþ þe *nedy*,
B. 7.70   For if he wiste he were noȝt *nedy* he wolde [it ȝyue]
B. 7.71   Anoþer that were moore *nedy*; so þe nedieste sholde be holpe.
B. 7.71   Anoþer that were moore *nedy*; so þe *nedieste* sholde be holpe.
B.11.244 Many tyme god haþ ben met among *nedy* peple,
B.12.53   And for þei suffren and see so manye *nedy* folkes
B.14.134 Hewen þat han hir hire afore arn eueremoore *nedy*,

B.15.573 And feden hem wiþ goostly foode and [*nedy* folk to fynden.
B.20.37   [For nede makeþ *nede* fele nedes lowe herted].
B.20.38   [Philosophres] forsoke wele for þei wolde be *nedy*
B.20.41   And cam and took mankynde and bicam *nedy*.
B.20.42   So [he was *nedy*], as seiþ þe book in manye sondry places,
B.20.48   Forþi be noȝt abasshed to bide and to be *nedy*
B.20.49   Siþ he þat wroȝte al þe world was wilfulliche *nedy*,
B.20.50   Ne neuere noon so *nedy* ne pouerer deide.
C. 8.288 Til alle thyne *nedy* neyhbores haue noen ymaked.
C. 9.47   That innocent and *nedy* is and no man harm wolde,
C. 9.64   He is fals and faytour and defraudeth the *nedy*
C. 9.176 Ac olde [men] and hore þat helples ben and *nedy*
C.11.26   Harlotes for here harlotrye aren holpe ar *nedy* pore;
C.11.71   Be large þerof whil hit lasteth to ledes þat ben *nedy*
C.22.37   For nede maketh neede fele nedes louh herted.
C.22.38   Philosopheres forsoke wel[e] for they wolde be *nedy*
C.22.41   And cam and toek mankynde and bicam *nedy*.
C.22.42   So he was *nedy*, as saith the boek in mony sondry places,
C.22.48   Forthy be nat abasched to byde and to be *nedy*
C.22.49   Sethe [he] þat wrouhte al þe worlde was willefolliche *nedy*
C.22.50   Ne neuere noen so *nedy* ne porore deyede.'

nedlare > nedlere

nedle n *nedle n.* &> *paknedle* B 3; C 3 nedle (2) nelde (1)

B. 1.157 And portatif and persaunt as þe point of a *nedle*
B.12.161 And boþe naked as a *nedle*, hir noon [sadder] þan ooþer.
B.17.59   And as naked as a *nedle* and noon help aboute.
C. 1.153 [And] portatif and persaunt as þe poynt of a *nelde*
C.14.105 And bothe naked as a *nedle*, here noen heuegore then othere.
C.19.58   And as naked as an *nedle* and noen helpe abouten.

nedlere n *nedlere n.* A 1 nedelere; B 1; C 1 nedlare

A. 5.161 Hikke þe hakeneyman & hogge þe [*nede*]*lere*,
B. 5.310 Hikke þe hakeneyman and hugh þe *Nedlere*,
C. 6.365 Hicke þe hackenayman and hewe þe *nedlare*,

neede > nedy

neer adv *ner adv.(2) cf. ner,neiȝ,next* A 1 ner; B 2 neer (1) ner (1); C 5
   ner (3) nere (1) nerre (1)

A. 7.163 He beet hem so boþe he brast *ner* here mawis.
B. 6.178 He bette hem so boþe he brast *ner* hire [mawes].
B.20.232 Nede neghede þo *neer* and Conscience he tolde
C. 8.175 [He] beet hem so bothe he barste *ner* her gottes
C. 9.265 Thy shep ben *ner* al shabbede; the wolf shyt wolle:
C.18.178 With moche noyse þat nyhte *nere* frentyk y wakede;
C.19.64   And dredfully withdrow hym and durste go no *nerre*.
C.22.232 Nede neyhede tho *ner* and Consience he toelde

neer prep *ner prep.* A 1 ner; B 3 neer (2) ner (1)

A. 7.283 Be þat it neiȝide *ner* heruest [þat] newe corn com to chepyng.
B. 6.299 By þat it neȝed *ner* heruest newe corn cam to chepyng.
B.16.69   Thanne Continence is *neer* þe crop as kaylewey bastard.
B.18.172 Whan Pees in Pacience ycloþed approched *ner* hem tweyne

neet n *net n.(2)* B 1; C 1

B.19.266 The pris *neet* of Piers plow, passynge alle oþere.
C.21.266 The pris *neet* of [Peres plouh], passynge alle oþere.

neghebore > neȝbore

neghen v *neighen v.(1)* A 1 neiȝide; B 4 neghed (1) neghede (1) neghen
   (1) neȝed (1); C 3 neyhed (1) neyhede (1) nyhed (1)

A. 7.283 Be þat it *neiȝide* ner heruest [þat] newe corn com to chepyng.
B. 6.299 By þat it *neȝed* ner heruest newe corn cam to chepyng.
B.17.61   And nolde noȝt *neghen* hym by nyne londes lengþe.
B.20.4   And it *neghed* neiȝ þe noon and wiþ nede I mette
B.20.232 Nede *neghede* þo neer and Conscience he tolde
C. 8.331 By that hit *nyhed* neyh heruost and newe corn cam to chepyng.
C.22.4   And hit *neyhed* neyh þe noen and with nede y mette
C.22.232 Nede *neyhede* tho ner and Consience he toelde

neȝebore n *neighbor n.* A 2 neiȝebour (1) neiȝebours (1); B 10 Neghebore
   (2) neȝebore (2) neȝebores (4) neighebores (2); C 9 neyhbores (1)
   neyhebore (4) neyhebores (4)

A. 5.73   I haue a *neiȝebour* neiȝ me, I haue noiȝed hym ofte,
A. 6.51   And þanne ȝoure *neiȝebours* next in none wise apeir[e]
B. 5.93   I haue a *neȝebore* [neiȝ] me, I haue anoyed hym ofte,
B. 5.133 To lye and to loure on my *neȝebore* and to lakke his chaffare.
B. 5.257 'Artow manlich among þi *neȝebores* of þi mete and drynke?'
B. 5.259 Amonges my *neȝebores* namely swich a name ich haue.'
B. 5.407 Or lesynge[s] to lauȝen [of] and bilye my *neȝebores*,
B. 5.564 And þanne youre *neȝebores* next in none wise apeire
B.13.363 And if my *Neghebore* hadde a[n] hyne or any beest ellis
B.13.372 Of my nexte *Neghebore*, nymen of his erþe:
B.14.296 Ne borweþ of hise *neighebores* but þat he may wel paie:

B.16.42   And casteþ vp to þe crop vnkynde *Neighebores*,
C. 6.98   To lye and to loure and to lakke myn *neyhebores*,
C. 6.262 And yf my *neyhebore* hadde an hyne or eny beste elles
C. 6.269 Of my *neyhebore* nexst, nymen of his erthe;
C. 7.211 And thenne 3oure *neyhebores* nexst in none wyse apayre
C. 8.288 Til alle thyne nedy *neyhbores* haue noen ymaked.
C. 9.71   Ac þat most neden aren oure *neyhebores* and we nyme gode
          he[d]e,
C. 9.87   What h[e]m nede[th] at here *neyhebores* at noon and at eue.
C.15.112 'Do thy *neyhebore* non harm ne thysulue nother
C.16.131 Ne boreweth of his *neyhebore* but þat he may wel paye

ne3ed > neghen; ney > nei3; neighebores > ne3ebore

nei3 adj *neigh adj.* cf. *neer,next* A 1; B 4 nei3 (3) nei3e (1)
A. 5.73   I haue a nei3ebour *nei3* me, I haue noi3ed hym ofte,
B. 5.93   I haue a ne3ebore [*nei3*] me, I haue anoyed hym ofte,
B.11.213 For woot no man how *nei3* it is to ben ynome fro boþe.
B.12.93   For kynde wit is of his kyn and *nei3e* Cosynes boþe
B.14.273 The which is sib to god hymself, [so *nei3* is pouerte].'

nei3 adv *neigh adv.* A 1; B 3; C 2 neyh (1) ny (1)
A. 3.134 She may *nei3* as muche do in a moneþ ones
B. 3.145 [She] may *nei3* as muche do in a Monþe one[s]
B.14.114 And makest hem wel *nei3* meke and mylde for defaute,
B.16.29   And forfreteþ *nei3* þe fruyt þoru3 manye faire sightes.
C. 3.183 He may *ny* as muche do in a monthe ones
C.15.290 And makest hem wel *neyh* meke and mylde for defaute

nei3 prep *neigh prep.* B 2; C 5 ney (2) neyh (3)
B.20.4   And it neghed *nei3* þe noon and wiþ nede I mette
B.20.200 And deeþ drogh *nei3* me; for drede gan I quake,
C. 8.296 'By seynte Poul!' quod Peres, 'thow poyntest *neyh* þe treuthe
C. 8.321 By that hit nyhed *neyh* heruost and newe corn cam to chepyng.
C.20.290 Al hoet on here hedes þat entrith *ney* þe walles;
C.22.4   And hit neyhed *neyh* be noen and with nede y mette
C.22.200 And deth drow *ney* me; for drede gan y quaken

nei3ebour > ne3ebore; nei3ide > neghen; neyh > nei3; neyh(e)bore(s >
ne3ebore; neyhed(e > neghen

neyhele v *neighlen v.* C 1
C.19.60   And [n]olde nat *neyhele* hym by nyne londes lenghe.

neiþer pron *neither pron.* B 2; C 3 neyther (2) noþer (1)
B. 4.33   And bad Reson ryde faste and recche of hir *neiþer*.
B.11.315 A[c] neuer *neiþer* is blamelees, þe bisshop ne þe Chapeleyn;
C. 3.366 In whiche ben gode and nat gode, and graunte here *n[eyther]* will.
C.10.272 Ac they lyen le[i], here *neyther* lyketh other.
C.13.127 Ac neuer *noþer* is blameles, the bischop ne þe chapeleyn,

neiþer adv *neither adv.* A 1 noþer; B 4; C 6 neyther (2) noyther (1)
          noythere (1) nother (2)
A. 9.111 Was no pride on his apparail ne no pouert *noþer*,
B. 5.184 And drynk nat ouer delicatly, ne to depe *neiþer*,
B. 8.121 Was no pride on his apparele ne pouerte *noþer*;
B.11.212 And be we no3t vnkynde of oure catel, ne of oure konnyng *neiþer*,
B.12.243 They may no3t flee fer ne ful hei3e *neiþer*];
C. 6.166 And drynke nat ouer delycaty n[e] to depe *neyther*
C.10.117 Was no pruyde on his parail ne pouerte *noythere*;
C.10.186 Ne spille speche ne tyme ne myspende *noyther*
C.11.44   God is nat in þat hoem ne his helpe *nother*.
C.14.176 For þey may nat fle fer ne ful hey *neyther*
C.15.112 'Do thy neyhebore non harm ne thysulue *nother*

neiþer conj *neither conj.* A 4 neiþer (2) noþer (2); B 43 neiþer (41)
          neyþer (2); C 42 neyther (1) noyther (4) nother (9) noþer (27) noþere
          (1)
A. 3.58   *Neiþer* in si3t ne in þi soule, for god hymself knowiþ
A. 4.113 *Neiþer* grotis ne gold ygraue wiþ kynges coyn,
A. 7.120 For we mowe *no[þer]* swynke ne swete, such seknesse vs eileþ'.
A. 7.265 *Noþer* gees ne gris, but two grene chesis,
B. 3.315 Shal *neiþer* kyng ne knyght, Constable ne Meire
B. 4.130 *Neiþer* [grotes ne gold ygraue wiþ kynges coyn]
B. 5.125 Ne *neiþer* shrifte ne shame, but whoso shrape my mawe?'
B. 5.396 Ac *neiþer* of oure lord ne of oure lady þe leeste þat euere was
          maked.
B. 5.416 Yet kan I *neyþer* solue ne synge ne seintes lyues rede;
B. 6.128 For we may [*neiþer*] swynke ne swete, swich siknesse vs eyleþ'.
B. 6.281 *Neiþer* gees ne grys, but two grene cheses,
B.11.106 *Neiþer* for loue [looue] it no3t ne lakke it for enuye:
B.11.285 Ne *neiþer* kirtel ne cote, þei3 þei for cold sholde deye,
B.11.289 Hem sholde lakke no liflode, *neyþer* lynnen ne wollen.
B.11.311 That han *neiþer* konnynge ne kyn, but a crowne one
B.11.362 Ther *neiþer* burn ne beest may hir briddes rechen
B.11.372 No Reson hem [ruled, *neiþer* riche ne pouere].
B.12.203 He sit *neiþer* wiþ Seint Iohan, Symond ne Iude,

B.12.209 It were *neiþer* reson ne ri3t to rewarde boþe yliche.
B.12.278 Seyen in hir Sermons þat *neiþer* Sarsens ne Iewes
B.13.92   That *neiþer* bacon ne braun, blancmanger ne mortrews,
B.13.93   Is *neiþer* fissh n[e] flessh, but fode for a penaunt.
B.13.161 Ne *neiþer* hete ne hayl ne noon helle pouke
B.13.162 Ne [*neiþer*] fuyr ne flood ne feere of þyn enemy
B.13.165 There nys *neiþer* emperour ne emperesse, erl ne baroun,
B.13.230 Ac for I kan *neiþer* taboure ne trompe ne telle no gestes,
B.13.233 Ne *neiþer* saille ne [sautrie] ne synge wiþ þe gyterne,
B.13.245 *Neiþer* prouendre ne personage yet of [þe] popes 3ifte;
B.13.395 *Neiþer* masse ne matynes, ne none maner si3tes;
B.14.172 Ne *neiþer* hete ne Hayll, haue þei hir heele;
B.14.333 Ne *neiþer* sherte ne shoon, saue for shame one
B.15.18   Is *neiþer* Peter þe Porter ne Poul wiþ [þe] fauchon
B.15.210 *Neiþer* þoru3 wordes ne werkes, but þoru3 wil oone,
B.15.252 *Neiþer* he blameþ ne banneþ, bosteþ ne preiseþ,
B.15.256 *Neiþer* he biddeþ ne beggeþ ne borweþ to yelde.
B.15.276 Ac *neiþer* Antony ne Egidie ne heremyte þat tyme
B.15.299 *Neiþer* bere ne boor ne ooþer beest wilde,
B.15.369 *Neiþer* þei konneþ ne knoweþ oon cours bifore anoþer.
B.17.57   He my3te *neiþer* steppe ne stande ne stere foot ne handes
B.17.95   *Neiþer* Feiþ ne fyn hope, so festred be hise woundes.
B.17.182 So is þe holy goost god, *neiþer* gretter ne lasse
B.17.200 *Neiþer* here ne elliswhere, as I herde telle:
B.19.97   Was *neiþer* kyng ne conquerour til he [comsed] wexe
B.19.306 *Neiþer* of duc ne of deeþ, þat he ne dide lawe
B.20.24   *Ne[iþer]* Spiritus Iusticie ne Spiritus fortitudinis.
B.20.154 Shal do þee no3t drede, *neiþer* deeþ ne elde,
B.20.272 And youre noumbre vnder Notaries signe and *neiþer* mo ne lasse.'
C.Pr.36   Wolleth *neyther* swynke ne swete bote sweren grete othes,
C. 1.99   For thei sholde *nother* faste ne forbere the serk
C. 1.176 And ben as chast as a child þat chyht *noþer* ne fyhteth,
C. 3.294 And þat is *nother* resoun ne ryhte ne [i]n no rewme lawe
C. 3.322 *Noyther* [thei ne] here ayres hardy to claymen
C. 3.468 Shal *nother* kyng ne knyght, Constable ne Mayre
C. 4.127 *Nother* ygraue ne vngraue, of gold oþer of suluer,
C. 5.57   Sholde *nother* swynke ne swete ne swerien at enquestes
C. 6.90   Ne *noþer* shame ne shryfte but hoso shrap[e] my mawe?'
C. 6.282 *Nother* matynes ne masse ne no maner syhtus;
C. 6.403 He myhte *noþer* steppe ne stande til he a staf hadde
C. 7.31   3ut kan y *nother* solfe ne synge ne a seyntes lyf rede;
C. 8.134 We may *nother* swynke ne swete, suche sekenes vs ayleth;
C. 8.303 *Noþer* goos ne gries but two grene chesis
C. 9.196 *Noyther* of lynage ne of lettrure ne lyfholy as Ermytes
C.10.187 Meble ne vnmeble, mete *noþer* drynke.
C.12.40   *Nother* for loue [loue] it [nat] ne lacke hit for enuye:
C.13.103 Hem sholde neuere lacke lyflode, *noþer* lynnen ne wollene.
C.13.113 That [hath] *noþer* connyng ne kyn bote a croune one
C.13.182 Resoun re[ul]ede hem nat, *noþer* ryche ne pore.
C.14.6   *Noþer* to lye ne to lacke ne lere þat is defended
C.14.142 A sit *noþer* with seynte Iohan, simond ne Iude,
C.14.200 Segen [in] here sarmons þat *noþer* saresynes ne iewes
C.15.99   That *noþer* bacon ne brawn, blaunmanger ne mortrewes
C.15.100 Is *noþer* fische ne flesche but fode for [a] penant[e].
C.15.163 Ne *n[oþ]ere* hete ne hayl ne helle pouke hym greue,
C.15.164 *Noþer* fuyr ne floed ne be aferd of enemye:
C.15.207 Ne *noþer* sayle ne sautrien ne syngen with þe geterne,
C.16.169 Is *noþer* Peter the porter ne poul with the fauchen
C.16.292 I knewe neuere, by Crist, clerk *noþer* lewed
C.16.372 For *noþer* he beggeth ne biddeth ne borweth to 3elde.
C.17.89   *Noþer* see ne s[o]nd ne þe seed 3eldeth
C.17.105 *Noþer* they [conn]eth ne [know]eth a cours by[fore] anoþer.
C.19.85   *Noþer* faith ne fyn hope, so festred aren his woundes.
C.19.103 *Noþer* lacke ne alose ne leue þat þer were
C.19.148 Thus is the holy goste god, *noyther* grettore ne lassore
C.19.166 *Noþer* here ne elleswhere, as y herde telle:
C.21.97   Was *noþer* kyng ne conquerour til he comsed wexe
C.21.306 For deuk ne of deth þat he ne dede lawe
C.22.24   *Noythe[r]* spiritus iusticie ne spiritus fortitudinis.
C.22.154 Shal do the nat drede, *noþer* deth ne elde,
C.22.272 And 3oure nombre vnde[r] notarie sygne and *noþer* mo ne lasse.'

nekke n *nekke n.* B 6 nekke (5) nekkes (1); C 4 nekke (3) nekkes (1)
B.Pr.161 Beren bei3es ful bri3te abouten hire *nekkes*,
B.Pr.178 That dorste haue bounden þe belle aboute þe cattes *nekke*,
B. 5.136 And neuelynge wiþ þe nose and his *nekke* hangyng.
B.10.288 Archa dei myshapped and Ely brak his *nekke*.
B.11.17   Concupiscencia carnis colled me aboute þe *nekke*
B.14.240 And by þe *nekke* namely hir noon may hente ooþer;
C.Pr.114 Fro his chayere þer he sat and brake his *nekke* atwene.
C.Pr.180 Bere beyus of bryghte gold aboute here *nekkes*
C.Pr.195 That derste haue ybounde þe belle aboute þe kattes *nekke*
C.16.80   And by þe *nekke* namelyche here noen may henten other;

nel > willen; nelde > nedle; nelle neltow > willen

nempne v *nemnen v.* A 8 nempne (2) nempnid (3) nempnide (2) ynempnid (1); B 19 nempne (3) nempned (10) nempnede (2) nempneþ (2) ynempned (2); C 9 nemne (1) nemned (1) nemnie (1) nempned (5) nempnede (1)

A. 1.21   Arn none nedful but þo & *nempne* hem I þenke,
A. 5.169   And at þe newe feire *nempnide* it to selle.
A. 5.179   And *nempnide* hym for a noumpere þat no debate nere.
A. 8.137   Þat nabugodonosor *nempne* þise clerkis–
A.10.43   For loue of þat lady þat lif is *ynempnid*,
A.10.135   For of here kynde þei comen þat confessours ben *nempnid*
A.11.107   Is sib to þe seuene ars þat scripture is *nempnid*,
A.11.233   And prouen it be þe pistil þat petir is *nempnid*:
B. 1.21   Are none nedfulle but þo; and *nempne* hem I þynke
B. 2.179   Shul seruen myself þat Cyuyle is *nempned*.
B. 5.320   And at þe newe feire *nempned* it to selle.
B. 5.330   And *nempned* hym for a nounpere þat no debat nere.
B. 7.159   That Nabugodonosor *nempne[þ* þise] clerkes–
B. 9.55   For loue of þe lady anima þat lif is *ynempned*.
B. 9.112   For of hir kynde þei come þat Confessours ben *nempned*,
B.10.155   Is sib to [þe] seuen art3, [þat] Scripture is [*nempned*].
B.10.350   And preuen it by [þe pistel þat Peter is *nempned*]:
B.11.322   And *nempned* me by my name and bad me nymen hede,
B.15.38   *Nempnede* me þus to name; now þow my3t chese
B.15.140   And [*nempneþ* hym] a nygard þat no good my3te aspare
B.16.19   That I herde *nempne* his name anoon I swowned after,
B.16.203   Wedlok and widwehode wiþ virginite *ynempned*,
B.19.18   Anoon as men *nempned* þe name of god Iesu;
B.19.20   Ne noon so nedeful to *nempne* by ny3te ne by daye.
B.19.137   And *nempned* hym of Na3areth; and no man so worþi
B.20.256   And *nempned* [hem names], and noumbrede þe sterres:
B.20.261   [But þei ben *nempned* in þe noumbre of hem þat ben ywaged].
C. 1.21   Aren non [ni]defole but tho and *nemne* hem y thenke
C. 6.377   And to þe newe fayre *nempnede* [hit] to sull;
C. 6.388   And *nempned* hym for a noumper þat no debat were.
C.16.200   *Nempned* me thus to name; now þou myhte chese
C.21.18   Anoon as men *nemned* þe name of god iesu;
C.21.20   Ne noen so niedfol to *nemnie* by nyhte ne by day
C.21.137   And *nempned* hym of na3areth; and no man so worthy
C.22.256   And *nempned* hem names and nombred þe sterres:
C.22.261   Bote hy ben *nempned* in þe nombre of hem þat been ywaged.

nempnynge ger *nemninge ger.* B 1
B. 9.81   Than *nempnynge* of a name and he neuer þe wiser.

neodefole > nedeful

neptalym n prop *n.i.d.* B 1; C 2
B.15.494   Of Na3areth, of Nynyue, of *Neptalym* and Damaske,
C.17.189   Of nasareth, of [n]yneue, of *neptalym* [and] damaske,
C.17.261   That bereth name of *Neptalym*, of Niniue [and] of damaske,

ner adj *nerer adj. &> neer; cf. neer,nei3,next* A 1
A.11.258   –3et am I neuere þe *ner* for nou3t I haue walkid

nere > ben,neer,neuere

nerhande adv *nerhonde adv.* B 1; C 1
B.13.1   And I awaked þerwiþ, witlees *nerhande*,
C.15.1   And y awakede þerwith, witteles *nerhande*,

nerre > neer

nese n *nece n.* C 1
C. 5.176   For þe abbot of engelonde and the abbesse his *nese*

nest n *nest n.* B 2 nest (1) nestes (1); C 3 neste (2) nestes (1)
B.11.345   Briddes I biheld þat in buskes made *nestes*;
B.11.349   Ther nys wri3te, as I wene, sholde werche hir *nes[t]* to paye;
C.13.156   Briddes y beheld [þat] in bosches made *nestes*;
C.13.159   Lernede to [l]egge stikkes þat ley on here *neste*.
C.13.160   Ther is no wriht, as y wene, sholde worch here *neste* to paye;

neste > nest,witen

neuelynge prp *nivelen v.* B 1; C 1 niuilynge
B. 5.136   And *neuelynge* wiþ þe nose and his nekke hangyng.
C. 6.104   And with a *niuilyng[e]* nose, nippynge his lippes.

neuere adv *never adv. &> neueremoore* A 42; B 181 neuer (10) neuere (171); C 163 nere (3) neuer (10) neuere (150)

       A.Pr.12, A.1.101, A.2.116, A.2.158, A.3.96, A.3.130, A.3.174, A.3.238, A.4.40, A.4.80, A.4.122, A.5.50, A.5.51, A.5.143, A.5.210, A.5.242, A.6.23, A.6.118, A.7.24, A.8.56, A.8.167, A.9.6, A.9.28, A.10.29, A.10.89, A.10.96, A.10.120, A.10.189, A.10.195, A.11.33, A.11.75, A.11.91, A.11.117, A.11.143, A.11.162, A.11.169, A.11.173, A.11.252, A.11.258, A.11.272, A.11.294, A.12.25

       B.Pr.12, B.Pr.188, B.Pr.190, B.Pr.203, B.Pr.204, B.1.103, B.1.156, B.2.17, B.2.26, B.2.152, B.2.197, B.3.52, B.3.107, B.3.141, B.3.187, B.3.259, B.3.270, B.3.322,
B.4.19, B.4.53, B.4.93, B.4.139, B.4.170, B.5.67, B.5.68, B.5.151, B.5.160, B.5.182, B.5.227, B.5.235, B.5.251, B.5.253, B.5.261, B.5.289, B.5.382, B.5.398, B.5.399, B.5.405, B.5.468, B.5.535, B.5.633, B.6.22, B.6.162, B.7.56, B.7.78, B.7.189, B.8.6, B.8.32, B.9.28, B.9.40, B.9.41, B.9.81, B.9.105, B.9.168, B.9.174, B.10.47, B.10.116, B.10.122, B.10.138, B.10.165, B.10.191, B.10.219, B.10.226, B.10.230, B.10.241, B.10.255, B.10.266, B.10.407, B.10.449, B.10.456, B.11.26, B.11.34, B.11.73, B.11.105, B.11.245, B.11.279, B.11.282, B.11.294, B.11.315, B.11.346, B.11.376, B.11.409, B.11.425, B.11.429, B.12.1, B.12.27, B.12.35, B.12.39, B.12.69, B.12.97, B.12.114, B.12.127, B.12.133, B.12.163, B.12.165, B.12.168, B.12.225, B.12.283, B.12.287, B.12.290, B.13.74, B.13.96, B.13.158, B.13.187, B.13.192, B.13.244, B.13.304, B.13.305, B.13.340, B.13.350, B.13.374, B.13.384, B.13.394, B.13.396, B.14.12, B.14.23, B.14.31, B.14.39, B.14.53, B.14.57, B.14.91, B.14.96, B.14.97, B.14.98, B.14.106, B.14.111, B.14.120, B.14.121, B.14.237, B.14.244, B.15.19, B.15.102, B.15.126, B.15.130, B.15.153, B.15.158, B.15.162, B.15.177, B.15.178, B.15.196, B.15.209, B.15.227, B.15.264, B.15.419, B.16.72, B.16.194, B.16.216, B.17.19, B.17.70, B.17.99, B.17.101, B.17.114, B.17.167, B.17.199, B.17.292, B.17.296, B.18.96, B.18.104, B.18.120, B.18.145, B.18.148, B.18.190, B.18.206, B.18.207, B.18.210, B.18.413, B.19.180, B.19.218, B.19.283, B.19.305, B.19.406, B.19.410, B.19.413, B.19.424, B.19.454, B.19.475, B.20.10, B.20.50, B.20.161, B.20.210, B.20.260

       C.Pr.205, C.Pr.211, C.Pr.212, C.1.101, C.1.152, C.2.28, C.2.32, C.2.54, C.2.147, C.2.168, C.2.211, C.3.56, C.3.138, C.3.179, C.3.233, C.3.256, C.3.343, C.3.388, C.3.423, C.3.475, C.3.476, C.4.19, C.4.56, C.4.89, C.4.236, C.5.40, C.6.8, C.6.9, C.6.51, C.6.84, C.6.135, C.6.164, C.6.184, C.6.192, C.6.249, C.6.251, C.6.254, C.6.271, C.6.273, C.6.281, C.6.283, C.6.322, C.6.338, C.6.344, C.6.439, C.7.14, C.7.15, C.7.21, C.7.146, C.7.180, C.7.286, C.8.20, C.8.88, C.9.101, C.9.335, C.10.6, C.10.36, C.10.154, C.10.207, C.10.244, C.10.276, C.10.278, C.11.107, C.11.110, C.11.156, C.11.193, C.11.200, C.11.211, C.11.235, C.11.238, C.11.273, C.11.282, C.12.4, C.12.21, C.12.39, C.12.133, C.12.181, C.12.182, C.13.103, C.13.108, C.13.127, C.13.157, C.13.194, C.13.217, C.13.233, C.13.236, C.14.1, C.14.59, C.14.77, C.14.107, C.14.159, C.14.167, C.14.205, C.14.209, C.14.212, C.15.80, C.15.103, C.15.139, C.15.157, C.15.162, C.15.233, C.15.238, C.15.252, C.15.281, C.15.287, C.15.297, C.16.84, C.16.143, C.16.170, C.16.255, C.16.277, C.16.289, C.16.292, C.16.313, C.16.315, C.16.318, C.16.319, C.16.337, C.16.341, C.16.352, C.17.35, C.17.130, C.17.163, C.18.99, C.18.139, C.18.189, C.18.203, C.19.20, C.19.69, C.19.89, C.19.92, C.19.165, C.19.273, C.19.277, C.20.99, C.20.107, C.20.123, C.20.148, C.20.151, C.20.195, C.20.211, C.20.212, C.20.219, C.20.310, C.20.420, C.20.429, C.20.456, C.21.180, C.21.218, C.21.283, C.21.305, C.21.406, C.21.410, C.21.413, C.21.424, C.21.454, C.21.475, C.22.10, C.22.50, C.22.161, C.22.210, C.22.260

neueremoore adv *nevermore adv.* B 2 neueremoore (1) neuere_moore (1); C 6 neueremoore
B.11.103   Ac be [þow] *neueremoore* þe firste [þe] defaute to blame;
B.14.71   And if men lyuede as mesure wolde sholde *neuere moore* be defaute
C. 3.321   And bynyme hit hem anone and *neueremore* aftur
C. 3.443   Shal no mede be maistre *neueremore* aftur
C.12.37   Ac be [thow] *neueremore* þe furste the defaute to blame;
C.15.270   And yf men lyuede as mesure wolde sholde *neuere[more]* be defaute
C.16.78   So he is *neuere[more* ful] merye, so meschief hym followeth.
C.17.147   In murthe or in mournynge and *neuere[more]* to departe.

newe adj *neue adj.* A 3; B 11; C 11
A. 5.91   & beholde how heyne haþ a *newe* cote;
A. 5.169   And at þe *newe* feire nempnide it to selle.
A. 7.283   Be þat it nei3ide ner heruest [þat] *newe* corn com to chepyng.
B. 5.111   And biholde [how H]eyne haþ a *newe* cote;
B. 5.320   And at þe *newe* feire nempned it to selle.
B. 6.299   By þat it ne3ed neer heruest *newe* corn cam to chepyng.
B.15.373   For is noon of þise *newe* clerkes, whoso nymeþ hede,
B.17.33   What neded it [now] a *newe* lawe to [brynge]
B.17.75   Wel sixe Mile or seuene biside þe *newe* Market;
B.18.260   And bileue on a *newe* lawe be lost, lif and soule.'
B.19.273   Wiþ two [aiþes] þat þei hadde, an oold and a *newe*:
B.19.310   Wiþ olde lawe and *newe* lawe þat loue my3te wexe
B.19.426   And Piers [þe Plowman] wiþ his *newe* plow and [þe] olde
B.19.446   Ayein þe olde lawe and *newe* lawe, as Luc [bereþ] witness[e]:
C. 6.377   And to þe *newe* fayre nempnede [hit] to sull;
C. 8.321   By that hit nyhed neyh heruost and *newe* corn cam to chepyng.
C.13.20   And Iob bykam as a iolyf man and al his ioye neuer
C.18.264   I leue þat ilke lord thenketh a *newe* lawe to make:
C.19.34   What nedede hit thanne a *newe* lawe to brynge
C.19.74   Is syxe myle or seuene bisyde þe *newe* marcat,
C.20.268   And bile[u]e on a *newe* lawe be ylost, lyf and soule.'
C.21.273   With two aythes þat they hadde, an oelde and a *newe*:
C.21.310   With olde lawe and *newe* [lawe] that loue myhte wexe
C.21.426   And [Peres the Plowman] with his *newe* [plouh] and [þe] olde
C.21.446   A3en þe olde lawe and *newe* lawe, as Luk bereth witnesse:

newe adv *neue adv.* A 2; B 4; C 4
A. 2.128   Sette mede on a shirreue shod al *newe*,
A. 5.248   Þat penitencia his pik he shulde pulsshe *newe*
B. 2.164   Sette Mede vpon a Sherreue shoed al *newe*,
B. 5.474   That penitencia his pik he sholde polshe *newe*

B.16.132 And in þre daies after edifie it *newe*,
B.18.43 Edifie it eft *newe*–here he stant þat seide it–
C. 5.179 Clerkes and holy [kyrke] shal be clothed *newe*.'
C. 6.328 That [penitencia] is pykstaff a wolde polesche *newe*
C.18.160 And ar thre dayes aftur edefye hit *newe*.'
C.20.42 Edefien hit eft *newe*–here he stant þat saide hit–

next adj *nexte adj. cf. neer,neiʒ* A 1; B 3 next (1) nexte (2); C 2 nexst
A. 6.51 And þanne ʒoure neiʒebours *next* in none wise apeir[e]
B. 5.564 And þanne youre neʒebores *next* in none wise apeire
B.13.154 And al þe wit of þe wodnesday of þe *nexte* wike after;
B.13.372 Of my *nexte* Neghebore, nymen of his erþe:
C. 6.269 Of my neyhebore *nexst*, nymen of his erthe;
C. 7.211 And thenne ʒoure neyhebores *nexst* in none wyse apayre

next adv *nexte adv.* A 1
A. 7.155 And manacide hym & his men whanne h[y] *next* metten.

next prep *nexte prep.* B 3; C 3 next (2) nexst (1)
B. 1.204 Loue is leche of lif and *next* oure lord selue,
B.17.291 Innocence is *next* god and nyght and day it crieþ
B.20.35 Ac nede is *next* hym for anoon he mekeþ
C.18.97 And in heuene is priueoste and *next* hym by resoun
C.19.272 Innocence is *next* god and nyht and day hit crieth
C.22.35 A[c] nede is *nexst* hym for anoen he meketh

ny > neiʒ

nyce adj *nice adj.* B 1; C 1 nise
B.16.33 That it norisseþ *nyce* sightes and [anoþer] tyme wordes
C.18.37 That hit norischeth *nise* s[ih]tus and som tyme wordes

nidefole niedfol > nedeful

nygard n *nigard n.* B 1; C 1
B.15.140 And [nempneþ hym] a *nygard* þat no good myʒte aspare
C.19.241 And for he was a *nygard* and a nythynge to the nedfol pore,

nyght(es > nyʒt

nyghtcomeris n *night n.* B 1; C 1 nyhtecomares
B.19.144 Kepen it fro *nyghtcomeris* wiþ knyghtes yarmed
C.21.144 Kepen hit fro *nyhtecomares* with knyhtes y[ar]med

nigromancie n *nigromancie n.* A 1; B 1
A.11.161 *Nigromancie* & per[i]mansie þe pouke to reisen;
B.10.218 *Nigromancie* and perimansie þe pouke to raise];

nyʒt n *night n.* A 2 niʒt (1) nyʒtes (1); B 16 nyght (2) nyghtes (1) nyʒt (5) nyʒte (4) nyʒtes (4); C 22 nyghtes (1) nyht (4) nyhte (11) nyhtes (6)
A. 7.292 Deyneþ nouʒt to dyne a day *niʒt* olde wortis.
A.12.81 'With deþ I duelle,' quod he, 'dayes and *nyʒtes*.
B.Pr.197 For may no renk þer reste haue for Ratons by *nyʒte*,]
B. 6.308 Deyne[þ] noʒt to dyne a day *nyʒt* olde wortes.
B. 9.99 He dooþ best þat wiþdraweþ hym by daye and by *nyʒte*
B.11.31 Bittrely shaltow banne þanne, boþe dayes and *nyʒtes*,
B.13.348 As wel fastyng dayes [as] Fridaies [and] forboden *nyʒtes*,
B.13.368 Or by *nyʒte* or by daye aboute was ich euere.
B.14.2 Thouʒ it be soiled and selde clene: I slepe þerInne o *nyʒtes*;
B.15.401 Daunted a dowue and day and *nyʒt* hire fedde.
B.16.166 Deide and dee[þ] fordide, and day of *nyʒt* made.
B.17.222 That werchen and waken in wyntres *nyʒtes*
B.17.255 Delen and do penaunce day and *nyght* euere,
B.17.291 Innocence is next god and *nyght* and day it crieþ
B.18.208 If no *nyʒt* ne weere, no man as I leeue
B.19.20 Ne noon so nedeful to nempne by *nyʒte* ne by daye.
B.19.141 And for to doon hym to deþe day and *nyʒt* þei casten.
B.20.196 On *nyghtes* namely, whan we naked weere,
C. 1.32 Forthy drede delitable drynke bothe day and *nyghtes*.
C. 4.47 And how he raueschede Rose the ryche wydewe by *nyhte*
C. 7.301 Were y seuen *nyhte* fro here syhte s[ynnen] he wolde
C. 8.330 Deyne[th noght] to dyne a day *nyhte* olde wortes;
C. 9.78 And wo in wynter tym[e] and wakynge on *nyhtes*
C. 9.223 And vnder obedience be by dayes and by *nyhtes*;
C.11.190 Bitterliche shaltow banne thenne, bothe dayes and *nyhtes*,
C.13.190 They ouerdoen hit day and *nyhte* and so doth nat oþer bestes;
C.16.143 As he þat woet neuere with wham on *nyhtes* tyme to mete:
C.17.29 Ac durste no beste byte hem by day ne by *nyhte*
C.17.93 Doen her deuer day and *nyhte*; dede we so alse
C.17.171 He endaunted a douue and day and *nyhte* here fedde;
C.17.245 Deuouteliche day and *nyhte*, withdrawe hem fro synne
C.18.178 With moche noyse þat *nyhte* nere frentyk y wakede;
C.19.177 That serueth this swynkares to [see] by a *nyhtes*,
C.19.188 That worchen and waken in wynteres *nyhtes*
C.19.221 Dele and do penaunce day and *nyhte* euere
C.19.272 Innocence is next god and *nyht* and day hit crieth
C.20.62 The hard roch al toroef and riht derk *nyht* hit semede;
C.20.215 Yf no *nyht* ne were no man, [as] y leue,

C.21.20 Ne noen so niedfol to nemnie by *nyhte* ne by day
C.21.141 And for to do hym to dethe day and *nyhte* they casten,

nyhed > neghen; nyht(e -es > nyʒt; nyhtcomares > nyghtcomeris; nil(e nille nilt > willen

nymen v *nimen v.* A 3 nyme (1) nymen (1) nymeþ (1); B 16 nyme (5) nymen (3) nymeþ (4) nome (1) ynome (3); C 16 nym (1) nyme (7) nymen (5) nymeth (5) nome (1) ynome (1)
A. 7.14 Þe nedy & þe nakid, *nymeþ* hed how þei liggen;
A. 7.41 *Nyme* hem nouʒt, an aunter þou mowe hem nouʒt deserue.
A.11.47 Is non to *nymen* hym In ne his [noye] amende,
B. 6.15 The nedy and þe naked *nymeþ* hede how þei liggeþ,
B. 6.42 *Nyme* it noʒt an auenture [þow] mowe it noʒt deserue.
B.10.61 Is noon to *nyme* hym [in, ne] his [n]oy amende,
B.11.213 For woot no man how neiʒ it is to ben *ynome* fro boþe.
B.11.291 Thanne nedeþ yow noʒt to [*nyme*] siluer for masses þat ye syngen,
B.11.322 And nempned me by my name and bad me *nymen* hede,
B.11.432 Ac whan nede *nymeþ* hym vp for [nede] lest he sterue,
B.13.372 Of my nexte Neghebore, *nymen* of his erþe:
B.15.160 Thyng þat neded hym noʒt and *nyme* it if he myʒte.
B.15.373 For is noon of þise newe clerkes, whoso *nymeþ* hede,
B.16.68 Matrimoyne I may *nyme*, a moiste fruyt wiþalle.
B.16.161 Thoruʒ Iudas and Iewes Iesus was [*ynome*]
B.20.9 And þow *nome* na moore þan nede þee tauʒte?
B.20.17 Nede anoon righte *nymeþ* hym vnder maynprise.
B.20.20 So nede at gret nede may *nymen* as for his owene
B.20.46 Ther nede haþ *ynome* me þat I moot nede abide
C. 2.142 That ʒe *nymeth* [and] notaries to nauhte gynneth brynge
C. 3.392 *Nyme* he a noumbre of nobles or of shillynges,
C. 3.403 And *nyme* hym into oure noumbre, now and eueremore:
C. 6.269 Of my neyhebore nexst, *nymen* of his erthe;
C. 8.40 *Nym* hit nat an auntur thow mowe hit nauht deserue
C. 9.71 Ac þat most neden aren oure neyhebores and we *nyme* gode he[d]e,
C.11.244 For Archa Noe, *nymeth* hede, ys no more to mene
C.13.105 And nedeth [ʒow] nat to *nyme* siluer for masses þat ʒe synge
C.13.239 Ac when nede *nymeth* hym vp anoen he is aschamed
C.16.294 Thyng that nedede hym nauhte and *nyme* hit yf a myhte.
C.17.109 For is [now] noon, hoso *nymeth* hede,
C.18.84 'Here beneth y may *nyme*, yf y nede hadde,
C.22.9 And thow *nome* no more then nede the tauhte?
C.22.17 Nede anoen riht *nymeth* hym vnder maynprise.
C.22.20 So nede at greet nede may *nyme* as for his owne
C.22.46 Ther nede hath *ynome* me þat y moet nede abyde

nyne num *nin num.* B 3; C 1
B. 1.121 But fellen out in fendes liknesse [ful] *nyne* dayes togideres
B. 5.370 There no nede was *nyne* hundred tymes;
B.17.61 And nolde noʒt neghen hym by *nyne* londes lengþe.
C.19.60 And [n]olde nat neyhele hym by *nyne* londes lenghe.

nynyue n prop *n.i.d.* B 1; C 2 Niniue (1) nyneue (1)
B.15.494 Of Naʒareth, of *Nynyue*, of Neptalym and Damaske,
C.17.189 Of nasareth, of [*n*]*yneue*, of neptalym [and] damaske,
C.17.261 That bereth name of Neptalym, of *Niniue* [and] of damaske,

nynþe num *ninthe num.* B 1; C 1 nythe
B.14.316 The *nynþe* is swete to þe soule, no sugre swetter,
C.16.150 The *nythe* is swete to [þe] soul[e], no sucre swettore,

nyppe n *nippe n.* B 1; C 1 nype
B.18.164 Out of þe *nyppe* of þe North noʒt ful fer hennes
C.20.167 Out of þe *nype* of the north nat ful fer hennes

nippynge prp *nippen v.* C 1
C. 6.104 And with a niuilyng[e] nose, *nippynge* his lippes.

nis > ben; nise > nyce; nyste > witen; nythe > nynþe

nythynge n *nithing n.* C 1
C.19.241 And for he was a nygard and a *nythynge* to the nedfol pore,

niuilynge > neuelynge; niyed > noyen

no adj *no adj.* A 95; B 289; C 300
A.Pr.30 For *no* likerous liflode here likam to plese.
A. 1.9 Of oþer heuene þanne here holde þei *no* tale.'
A. 1.81 'Teche me to *no* tresour but tel me þis ilke,
A. 1.87 Doþ þe werkis þerwiþ & wilneþ *no* man ille,
A. 1.127 'Ʒet haue I *no* kynde knowyng,' quaþ I, '[ʒe mote kenne me bet]
A. 1.132 *No* dedly synne to do, diʒe þeiʒ þou shuldist.
A. 1.143 And ʒet wolde he hem *no* woo þat wrouʒte him þat pyne.
A. 1.158 Þanne malkyn of hire maidenhed þat *no* man desiriþ.
A. 1.163 It is as lewid as a laumpe þat *no* liʒt is inne.
A. 1.182 Þ[at] is *no* treuþe of trinite but treccherie of helle,
A. 1.182 Now haue I told þe what treuþe is, þat *no* tresour is betere,
A. 2.14 Þere nis *no* quen queyntere þat quyk is o lyue.
A. 2.147 I haue *no* tom to telle þe tail þat hem folewiþ

A. 3.16	And seide, 'mourne nouȝt, mede, ne make þou *no* sorewe,
A. 3.31	'Shal *no* lewidnesse hym lette, þe lede þat I louye,
A. 3.155	For pouere men mowe haue *no* power to pleyne [þeiȝ] hem smerte,
A. 3.174	For kilde I neuere *no* king ne counseilide þeraftir,
A. 3.214	*No* wiȝt as I wene wiþoute mede miȝte libbe.'
A. 3.222	Tak *no* mede, my lord, of [men] þat ben trewe;
A. 3.235	Is *no* maner of mede but a mesurable hire;
A. 3.236	In marchaundie is *no* mede, I may it wel auowe;
A. 3.269	Leaute shal do hym lawe [and *no*] lif ellis.
A. 3.270	Shal *no* seriaunt for þat seruyse were a silk houue,
A. 3.271	Ne *no* ray robe [wiþ] riche pelure.
A. 4.41	Ne *no* ferþing þerfore for nouȝt I couþe plete.
A. 4.100	'Rede me not,' quaþ resoun, '*no* reuþe to haue
A. 4.110	Þat *no* man go to galis but ȝif he go for euere;
A. 4.112	Bere *no* siluer ouer se þat signe of king shewi[þ],
A. 4.117	And ȝet,' quaþ resoun, 'by þe rode, I shal *no* reuþe haue
A. 4.125	Ne for *no* mede haue mercy but meknesse it made,
A. 5.15	Was apertly for pride & for *no* poynt ellis.
A. 5.33	'Let *no* wynnyng forwanye hem whiles þei ben ȝonge'.
A. 5.100	May *no* sugre ne swet þing swage it an vnche,
A. 5.101	Ne *no* dyapendyon dryue it fro myn herte,
A. 5.179	And nempnide hym for a noumpere þat *no* debate nere.
A. 5.193	He hadde *no* strengþe to stonde er he his staf hadde.
A. 5.219	For is *no* gilt here so gret þat his goodnesse nis more'.
A. 5.222	'Shal *no* sonneday be þis seue ȝer, but seknesse it make,
A. 6.35	Þere is *no* labourer in his lordsshipe þat he louiþ beter
A. 6.62	Loke þou breke *no* bowis þere but it be þin owene.
A. 6.67	Þanne shalt þou blenche at a b[erw]e, bere þe fals wytnesse;
A. 6.69	Loke þou plukke *no* plant[e] þere for peril of þi soule.
A. 6.71	[And] loke þat þou leiȝe nouȝt for *no* manis biddyng.
A. 6.78	Wiþ *no* led but [wiþ] loue & louȝnesse, as breþeren of o wombe.
A. 6.103	And geten it aȝen þoruȝ grace & þoruȝ *no* gift ellis.
A. 6.115	'Be crist,' quaþ a cuttepurs, 'I haue *no* kyn þere.'
A. 6.118	Shulde I neuere ferþere a foote for *no* freris preching.'
A. 7.39	Loke þou tene *no* tenaunt but treuþe wile assent,
A. 7.68	For holy chirche is holden of hem *no* tiþes to asken,
A. 7.111	Shal *no* greyn þat here growiþ glade ȝow at nede;
A. 7.137	Ones at noon is ynouȝ þat *no* werk vsiþ;
A. 7.220	Piger propter frigus *no* feld wolde tilie;
A. 7.221	He shal go [begge & bidde] & *no* man bete his hungir;
A. 7.229	And he þat nouȝt haþ shal nouȝt haue ne *no* man him helpe,
A. 7.244	Þat þou drynke *no* day er þou dyne sumwhat,
A. 7.264	'I haue *no* peny,' quaþ piers, 'pulettis to biggen,
A. 7.268	And I seiȝe, be my soule, I haue *no* salt bacoun,
A. 7.269	Ne *no* cokenay, be crist, colopis to maken.
A. 7.287	Ne *no* beggere ete bred þat benis in come,
A. 7.289	Ne non halpeny ale in *no* wyse drynke,
A. 7.291	Laboureris þat haue *no* land [to] lyue on [but] here handis
A. 7.293	May *no* penyale hem paye, ne *no* pece of bacoun,
A. 7.293	May *no* penyale hem paye, ne *no* pece of bacoun,
A. 8.37	Þat *no* deuil shal ȝow dere, diȝe whan ȝe diȝe,
A. 8.41	Þat *no* gile go wiþ ȝow but þe graiþ treuþe.'
A. 8.48	And of no pore peple no peny[worþ] to take.
A. 8.48	And of no pore peple *no* peny[worþ] to take.
A. 8.50	Þat is Innocent & nedy, & *no* man apeiriþ,
A. 8.53	Shal *no* deuil at his deþ day derie hym a myte
A. 8.72	Þei lyue nouȝt in loue, ne *no* lawe holden.
A. 8.73	Þei wedde *no* womman þat hy wiþ delen
A. 8.97	'Petir,' quaþ þe prest þo, 'I can *no* pardoun fynde
A. 8.117	Haue þei *no* garner [to go] to, but god fynt hem alle.'
A. 9.48	'I haue *no* kynde knowyng,' quaþ I, 'to conseyue þi wordis,
A. 9.64	'Þat þou wost wel,' quaþ he, '& *no* wiȝt betere.'
A. 9.106	Ellis wot *no* man þat now is o lyue.'
A. 9.111	Was no pride on his apparail ne no pouert noþer,
A. 9.111	Was *no* pride on his apparail ne *no* pouert noþer,
A. 9.113	I durste meue *no* mater to make hym to iangle,
A.10.64	Ac in fauntis ne in folis þe [fend] haþ *no* miȝt
A.10.65	For *no* werk þat þei werche, wykkide oþer ellis.
A.10.77	And sauiþ þe soule þat synne haþ *no* miȝt
A.10.193	Haue þei *no* children but ch[este], & choppis [betwene].
A.10.203	Shulde *no* bedbourd be; but þei were boþe clene
A.10.205	Þat dede derne do *no* man ne shulde.
A.10.208	And [werche] on his wyf & on *no* womman ellis,
A.11.96	Ac for *no* carping I couþe, ne knelyng to þe ground,
A.11.97	I miȝte gete *no* g[r]ayn of hise grete wyttes,
A.11.140	It is *no* science forsoþe for to sotile þereinne.
A.11.203	Ne *no* leperis ouer lond ladies to shryue.
A.11.264	And I leue on oure lord & on *no* lettrure betere.
A.11.289	Or poule þe apostil þat *no* pite hadde
A.11.299	For to answere hem haue ȝe *no* doute,
A.12.20	"I saw synful," he seyde, "þerfore I seyde *no* þing
A.12.73	For þe myssyng of mete *no* mesour I coude,
B.Pr.30	For *no* likerous liflode hire likame to plese.
B.Pr.197	For may *no* renk þer reste haue for Ratons by nyȝte,]
B. 1.9	Of ooþer heuene þan here holde þei *no* tale.'
B. 1.83	'Teche me to *no* tresor, but tel me þis ilke,
B. 1.89	Dooþ þe werkes þerwiþ and wilneþ *no* man ille,
B. 1.138	'Yet haue I *no* kynde knowyng', quod I, 'ye mote kenne me bettre
B. 1.144	*No* dedly synne to do, deye þeiȝ þow sholdest,
B. 1.149	May *no* synne be on hym seene þat vseþ þat spice,
B. 1.169	And yet wolde he hem *no* wo þat wrouȝte hym þat peyne,
B. 1.184	Than Malkyn of hire maydenhede þat *no* man desireþ.
B. 1.189	It is as lewed as a lampe þat *no* liȝt is Inne.
B. 1.198	[Th]at is *no* truþe of þe Trinite but tricherie of helle,
B. 1.208	Now haue I told þee what truþe is, þat *no* tresor is bettre,
B. 2.51	And lat *no* conscience acombre þee for coueitise of Mede.'
B. 2.100	And þanne wanhope to awaken h[y]m so wiþ *no* wil to amende
B. 2.186	I haue *no* tome to telle þe tail þat [hem] folwe[þ]
B. 3.16	And seiden, 'mourne noȝt, Mede, ne make þow *no* sorwe,
B. 3.32	'Shal *no* lewednesse [hym] lette, þe leode þat I louye,
B. 3.168	For pouere men may haue *no* power to pleyne þouȝ [hem] smerte,
B. 3.187	For killed I neuere *no* kyng, ne counseiled þerafter,
B. 3.227	*No* wiȝt, as I wene, wiþouten Mede may libbe.'
B. 3.256	It is *no* manere Mede but a mesurable hire;
B. 3.257	In marchaundise is *no* Mede, I may it wel auowe;
B. 3.294	Leaute shal don hym lawe and *no* lif ellis.
B. 3.295	Shal *no* sergeant for [þat] seruice were a silk howue,
B. 3.296	Ne *no* pelure in his [panelon] for pledynge at þe barre;
B. 3.319	Mercy or *no* mercy as Truthe [may] acorde.
B. 3.323	Batailles shul none be, ne *no* man bere wepene,
B. 3.332	'I kan *no* latyn?' quod she, 'clerkes wite þe soþe!
B. 4.18	And also Tomme trewe-tonge-tel-me-no-tales-
B. 4.54	Ne *no* ferþyng þerfore for [n]ouȝt I koude plede.
B. 4.113	'Reed me noȝt', quod Reson, '*no* ruþe to haue
B. 4.127	That *no* man go to Galis but if he go for euere;
B. 4.129	Bere *no* siluer ouer see þat signe of kyng sheweþ,
B. 4.134	And yet', quod Reson, 'by þe Rode! I shal *no* ruþe haue
B. 4.142	Ne for *no* Mede haue mercy but mekenesse it ma[de],
B. 5.15	Was pertliche for pride and for *no* point ellis.
B. 5.35	'Late *no* wynnyng [forwanye hem] while þei be yonge,
B. 5.36	Ne for *no* poustee of pestilence plese hem noȝt out of reson.
B. 5.123	May *no* sugre ne swete þyng aswage my swellyng,
B. 5.124	Ne *no* Diapenidion dryue it fro myn herte,
B. 5.167	That *no* Priouresse were preest, for þat he [purueiede];
B. 5.175	And baleised on þe bare ers and *no* brech bitwene.
B. 5.176	Forþi haue I *no* likyng, [leue me], wiþ þo leodes to wonye;
B. 5.233	'That was *no* restitucion', quod Repentaunce, 'but a robberis þefte;
B. 5.236	And I kan *no* frenssh in feiþ but of þe ferþest ende of Northfolk.'
B. 5.285	For þow hast *no* good ground to gete þee wiþ a wastel
B. 5.330	And nempned hym for a nounpere þat *no* debat nere.
B. 5.345	He [hadde *no* strengþe to] stonde er he his staf hadde,
B. 5.370	There *no* nede was nyne hundred tymes;
B. 5.389	Sholde *no* ryngynge do me ryse er I were ripe to dyne.'
B. 5.438	Forsleuþed in my seruice til it myȝte serue *no* man.
B. 5.447	For is *no* gilt here so gret þat his goodnesse [i]s moore.'
B. 5.450	'Shal *no* Sonday be þis seuen yer, but siknesse it [make],
B. 5.489	Ther þiself ne þi sone *no* sorwe in deeþ feledest,
B. 5.575	Loke [þow] breke *no* bowes þere but if it be [þyn] owene.
B. 5.580	Thanne shaltow blenche at a Bergh, bere-*no*-fals-witnesse;
B. 5.582	Loke þow plukke *no* plaunte þere for peril of þi soule.
B. 5.584	In-[*no*]-manere-ellis-noȝt-for-no-mannes-biddyng.
B. 5.584	In-[no]-manere-ellis-noȝt-for-*no*-mannes-biddyng.
B. 5.591	Wiþ *no* leed but wiþ loue and lowe[nesse] as breþeren [of o wombe].
B. 5.617	And [gete it ayein þoruȝ] grace [ac þoruȝ *no* gifte ellis].
B. 5.630	'By Crist!' quod a kuttepurs, 'I haue *no* kyn þere.'
B. 5.633	Sholde I neuere ferþer a foot for *no* freres prechyng.'
B. 6.38	Loke [þow] tene *no* tenaunt but truþe wole assente,
B. 6.76	For holy chirche is [holde] of hem *no* tiþe to [aske],
B. 6.119	Shal *no* greyn þat [here] groweþ glade yow at nede;
B. 6.124	'We haue *no* lymes to laboure with; lord, ygraced be [y]e!
B. 6.236	Piger [propter frigus] *no* feeld [w]olde tilie;
B. 6.237	He shal [go] begge and bidde and *no* man bete his hunger.
B. 6.245	And he þat noȝt haþ shal noȝt haue and *no* man hym helpe,
B. 6.260	That þow drynke *no* day er þow dyne somwhat.
B. 6.280	'I haue *no* peny', quod Piers, 'pulettes to bugge,
B. 6.284	And yet I seye, by my soule! I haue *no* salt bacon
B. 6.285	Ne *no* cokeney, by crist! coloppes to maken.
B. 6.303	Ne *no* beggere ete breed þat benes Inne [come],
B. 6.307	Laborers þat haue *no* land to lyue on but hire handes
B. 6.309	May no peny ale hem paie, ne no pece of bacoun,
B. 6.309	May *no* peny ale hem paie, ne *no* pece of bacoun,
B. 7.35	That *no* deuel shal yow dere ne [in youre deying fere yow],
B. 7.48	That is Innocent and nedy and *no* man apeireþ,
B. 7.51	Shal *no* deuel at his deeþ day deren hym a myte
B. 7.90	For [þei] lyue in *no* loue ne no lawe holde.

B. 7.90   For [þei] lyue in no loue ne *no* lawe holde.
B. 7.91   [Thei] wedde [*no*] womman þat [þei] wiþ deele
B. 7.115 'Peter!' quod þe preest þoo, 'I kan *no* pardon fynde
B. 7.135 Haue þei *no* gerner to go to but gyf fynt hem alle.'
B. 7.154 Ac I haue no sauour in songewarie for I se it ofte faille.
B. 7.174 And how þe preest preued *no* pardon to dowel
B. 8.57   'I haue *no* kynde knowyng', quod I, 'to conceyuen [þi] wordes
B. 8.73   'That þow woost wel', quod he, 'and *no* wiȝt bettre.'
B. 8.116 Ellis [n]oot [*no* man] þat now is alyue:
B. 8.121 Was *no* pride on his apparaill ne pouerte neiþer;
B. 8.123 I dorste meue *no* matere to maken hym to Iangle,
B. 8.130 And wheiþer he be man or [*no* man] þis man wolde aspie,
B. 9.82   Sholde *no* cristene creature cryen at þe yate
B. 9.163 [For] goode sholde wedde goode, þouȝ þei *no* good hadde;
B. 9.172 Haue þei *no* children but cheeste and [choppes] bitwene.
B. 9.180 For *no* londes, but for loue, loke ye be wedded
B. 9.190 Sholde *no* [bedbourde] be; but þei boþe were clene
B. 9.192 That [dede derne] do *no* man ne sholde.
B. 9.203 To loue [and to lowe þee and *no* lif to greue;
B.10.43   Likne men and lye on hem þat leneþ hem *no* ȝiftes,
B.10.78   That preieres haue *no* power þ[ise] pestilence[s] to lette.
B.10.92   For we haue *no* lettre of oure lif how longe it shal dure.
B.10.143 A[c] for *no* carpyng I couþe, ne knelyng to þe grounde,
B.10.144 I myȝte gete *no* greyn of his grete wittes,
B.10.188 It is *no* Science forsoþe for to sotile Inne:
B.10.211 For is *no* science vnder sonne so souereyn for þe soule
B.10.256 Ne man hadde *no* merite myȝte it ben ypreued:
B.10.262 And lat *no* body be by þi beryng bigiled
B.10.307 For in cloistre comeþ [*no*] man to [carpe] ne to fiȝte
B.10.318 To Religiouse þat han *no* rouþe þouȝ it reyne on hir Auters.
B.10.320 Of þe pouere haue þei *no* pite, and þat is hir [pure chartre];
B.10.345 Writen to wissen vs to wilne *no* richesse,
B.10.348 Ther riche men *no* riȝt may cleyme but of ruþe and grace.'
B.10.370 God hoteþ heiȝe and lowe þat *no* man hurte ooþer,
B.10.383 I leue it wel by oure lord and on *no* lettrure bettre.
B.10.430 Or Poul þe Apostle þat *no* pite hadde
B.10.455 And myȝte *no* kyng ouercomen hym as by konnynge of speche.
B.11.48   That of dowel ne dobet ne deyntee me þouȝte;
B.11.49   I hadde *no* likyng, leue me, [þe leste] of hem to knowe.
B.11.53   'Haue *no* conscience', [quod she],'how þow come to goode;
B.11.91   'And wherof serueþ law', quod lewtee, 'if *no* lif vndertoke it
B.11.99   It falleþ noȝt for þat folk *no* tales to telle
B.11.126 Riȝtfully to reneye *no* reson it wolde.
B.11.127 For may *no* cherl chartre make ne his c[h]atel selle
B.11.128 Wiþouten leue of his lord; *no* lawe wol it graunte.
B.11.137 'That is sooþ', seide Scripture; 'may *no* synne lette
B.11.153 Brouȝte me fro bitter peyne þer *no* biddyng myȝte.'
B.11.166 Ther *no* clergie ne couþe, ne konnyng of lawes.
B.11.174 For *no* cause to cacche siluer þerby, ne to be called a maister,
B.11.204 *No* beggere ne boye amonges vs but if it synne made:
B.11.213 For woot *no* man how neiȝ it is to ben ynome fro boþe.
B.11.214 Forþi lakke *no* lif ooþer þouȝ he moore latyn knowe,
B.11.273 That parfit pouerte was *no* possession to haue,
B.11.281 To serue god goodliche, ne greueþ hym *no* penaunce:
B.11.283 If preestes weren [wise] þei wolde *no* siluer take
B.11.287 Spera in deo spekeþ of preestes þat haue *no* spendyng siluer,
B.11.289 Hem sholde lakke *no* liflode, neyþer lynnen ne wollen.
B.11.294 For made neuere kyng *no* knyȝt but he hadde catel to spende
B.11.297 That haþ *no* lond ne lynage riche ne good loos of hise handes.
B.11.301 He [ouȝte *no*] bileue, as I leue, to lacche þoruȝ his croune
B.11.372 *No* Reson hem [ruled, neiþer riche ne pouere].
B.11.375 Why þow ne sewest man and his make þat *no* mysfeet hem folwe.'
B.11.380 Who suffre[þ] moore þan god?' quod he; '*no* gome, as I leeue.
B.11.389 For is *no* creature vnder crist can formen hymseluen,
B.11.436 Ther smyt *no* þyng so smerte, ne smelleþ so [foule]
B.12.39   Seke þow neuere Seint ferþer for *no* soule helþe.
B.12.100 Na moore kan *no* Clerk but if he cauȝte it first þoruȝ bokes.
B.12.118 And manye mo oþer men, þat were *no* leuites.
B.12.121 Forþi I conseille alle creatures *no* clergie to dispise
B.12.181 And haþ *no* contricion er he come to shrifte; & þanne kan he litel
          telle
B.12.226 Ac kynde knoweþ þe cause hymself, *no* creature ellis.
B.12.235 Kynde knoweþ whi he dide so, ac *no* clerk ellis.
B.12.270 And wheiþer he be saaf or noȝt saaf, þe soþe woot *no* clergie,
B.12.271 Ne of Sortes ne of Salomon *no* scripture kan telle.
B.12.279 Ne *no* creature of cristes liknesse withouten cristendom worþ
          saued.'
B.12.296 To kepe wiþ a commune; *no* catel was holde bettre,
B.13.9   And *no* corps in hir kirkȝerd n[e] in hir kirk was buryed
B.13.17   Leneþ he *no* lif lasse ne moore–
B.13.40   Ac þis maister [of þise men] *no* maner flessh [eet],
B.13.52   'Here is propre seruice', quod Pacience, 'þer fareþ *no* Prince bettre.'
B.13.79   Haþ *no* pite on vs pouere; he parfourneþ yuele

B.13.108 Mortrews and ooþer mete, and we *no* morsel hadde.
B.13.126 And *no* text ne takeþ to mayntene his cause
B.13.135 That *no* clerk ne kan, as crist bereþ witnesse:
B.13.136 'A[t] youre preiere', quod Pacience þo, 'so *no* man displese hym:
B.13.150 Kynde loue coueiteþ noȝt *no* catel but speche.
B.13.175 Ne bitwene two cristene kynges kan *no* wiȝt pees make
B.13.193 For þer [is] *no* tresour [þerto] to a trewe wille.
B.13.202 Clergie of Conscience *no* congie wolde take,
B.13.230 Ac for I kan neiþer taboure ne trompe ne telle *no* gestes,
B.13.234 I haue *no* goode giftes of þise grete lordes
B.13.235 For *no* breed þat I brynge forþ, saue a benyson on þe sonday
B.13.256 To haue þe grace of god, and *no* gilt of [þe] pope.
B.13.257 For may *no* blessynge doon vs boote but if we wile amende,
B.13.265 There was a careful commune whan *no* cart com to towne
B.13.331 Ther is *no* lif þat me loueþ lastynge any while.
B.13.332 For tales þat I telle *no* man trusteþ to me.
B.13.338 And seye þat *no* clerc ne kan, ne crist as I leue,
B.13.401 As þere *no* nede was goddes name an Idel:
B.13.407 The whiche is sleuþe so slow þat may *no* sleiȝtes helpe it,
B.13.408 Ne *no* mercy amenden þe man þat so deieþ].
B.13.410 [Is whan men] moorneþ noȝt for hise mysdedes, ne makeþ *no*
          sorwe:
B.13.412 Dooþ noon almes[dede]; dred hym of *no* synne;
B.13.413 Lyueþ ayein þe bileue and *no* lawe holdeþ.
B.13.435 Ne *no* mysproud man amonges lordes ben allowed–
B.14.27   Ne *no* Mynstrall be moore worþ amonges pouere and riche
B.14.29   'And I shal purueie þee paast', quod Pacience, 'þouȝ *no* plouȝ erye,
B.14.67   That *no* reyn ne roon; þus rede men in bokes,
B.14.68   That manye wyntres men [faille] ne mete ne tulieden:
B.14.112 And seiþ, "lo! briddes and beestes þat *no* blisse ne knoweþ
B.14.171 For may *no* derþe hem deere, droghte ne weet,
B.14.218 Ac in pouerte þer pacience is pride haþ *no* myȝte,
B.14.231 For his rentes ne wol nauȝt reche *no* riche metes to bigge;
B.14.256 That god is his grettest help and *no* gome ellis,
B.14.289 [O]r as Iustice to Iugge men enioyned is *no* poore,
B.14.312 He tempreþ þe tonge to truþeward [þat] *no* tresor coueiteþ:
B.14.315 And [þouȝ] he chaffareþ he chargeþ *no* losse, mowe he charite
          wynne:
B.14.316 The nynþe is swete to þe soule, *no* sugre swetter,
B.15.47   'Ye, sire!' I seide, 'by so *no* man were greued
B.15.84   For as [me þynkeþ] ye forsakeþ *no* mannes almesse,
B.15.140 And [nempneþ hym] a nygard þat *no* good myȝte aspare
B.15.171 Corseþ he *no* creature ne he kan bere no wraþe,
B.15.171 Corseþ he no creature ne he kan bere *no* wraþe,
B.15.172 Ne *no* likynge haþ to lye ne laughe men to scorne.
B.15.184 Thouȝ he bere hem *no* breed he bereþ hem swetter liflode;
B.15.195 'By crist! I wolde I knewe hym', quod I, '*no* creature leuere.'
B.15.198 'Clerkes haue *no* knowyng', quod he, 'but by werkes and wordes.
B.15.211 And þat knoweþ *no* clerk ne creature on erþe
B.15.249 Ac I ne lakke no lif, but lord amende vs alle,
B.15.257 Misdooþ he *no* man ne wiþ his mouþ greueþ.
B.15.261 In ensample we sholde do so, and take *no* vengeaunce
B.15.277 Of leons ne of leopardes *no* liflode ne toke,
B.15.287 Ne *no* man myȝte hym ete for mosse and for leues.
B.15.305 Ac god sente hem foode by foweles and by *no* fierse beestes
B.15.337 And helpeþ hem þat helpeþ yow and ȝyueþ þer *no* nede is,
B.15.355 That *no* lif loueþ ooþer, ne oure lord as it semeþ.
B.15.358 Han *no* bileue to þe lifte ne to þe [lodesterre].
B.15.416 And ben manered after Makometh þat *no* man vseþ trouþe.
B.15.434 So is mannes soule, sooþly, þat seeþ *no* goo[d] ensampl[e]
B.15.463 He fedde hem wiþ *no* venyson ne fesauntȝ ybake
B.15.536 Baddely ybedded, *no* book but conscience,
B.15.537 Ne *no* richesse but þe roode to reioisse hem Inne:
B.15.575 That *no* man sholde be bisshop but if he hadde boþe
B.16.83   Bar hem forþ bo[lde]ly–*no* body hym letted–
B.16.112 Ofte [he] heeled swiche; he held it for *no* maistrie
B.16.262 And me þer[wiþ]', quod þat [wye]; 'may *no* wed vs quyte,
B.16.263 Ne *no* buyrn be oure borgh, ne brynge vs fram his daunger–
B.16.264 Out of þe poukes pondfold *no* maynprise may vs fecche–
B.17.94   May *no* medicyne [vnder mone] þan to heele bringe,
B.17.165 Thus it is–nedeþ *no* man trowe noon ooþer–
B.17.225 Graunte *no* grace ne for[g]ifnesse of synnes
B.17.251 For may *no* fir flaumbe make, faille it [h]is kynde.
B.17.309 That þe kyng may do *no* mercy til boþe men acorde
B.18.2   As a recchelees renk þat [reccheþ of *no* wo],
B.18.26   For *no* dynt shal hym dere as in deitate patris.'
B.18.66   Shal *no* wight wite witterly who shal haue þe maistrie
B.18.75   Ac was *no* bo[y] so boold goddes body to touche;
B.18.105 [Ne] haue lordshipe in londe ne *no* lond tilye,
B.18.127 'Haue *no* merueille', quod mercy; 'murþe it bitokneþ.
B.18.155 May *no* medicyne [amende] þe place þer he styngeþ
B.18.200 That hir peyne be perpetuel and *no* preiere hem helpe.
B.18.205 For hadde þei wist of *no* wo, wele hadde þei noȝt knowen;

B.18.206	For *no* wight woot what wele is þat neuere wo suffrede,
B.18.208	If *no* ny3t ne weere, no man as I leeue
B.18.208	If no ny3t ne weere, *no* man as I leeue
B.18.217	Woot *no* wight, as I wene, what [is ynogh] to mene.
B.18.228	Woot *no* wight what werre is þer þat pees regneþ,
B.18.275	May no deeþ [þis lord] dere, ne no deueles queyntise,
B.18.275	May no deeþ [þis lord] dere, ne *no* deueles queyntise,
B.18.294	We haue *no* trewe title to hem, for þoru3 treson were þei dampned.'
B.18.304	That his soule wolde suffre *no* synne in his sighte;
B.18.352	To recouere hem þoru3 raunsoun and by *no* reson ellis,
B.18.368	May *no* drynke me moiste, ne my þurst slake,
B.18.410	Is *no* weder warmer þan after watry cloudes;
B.18.411	Ne *no* loue leuere, ne leuer frendes.
B.18.418	And leteþ *no* peple', quod pees, 'parceyue þat we chidde;
B.18.419	For inpossible is *no* þyng to hym þat is almyghty.'
B.18.431	May *no* grisly goost glide here it [shadweþ].'
B.19.19	Ergo is *no* name to þe name of Iesus.
B.19.51	Mighte *no* deeþ hym fordo ne adoun brynge
B.19.121	That he þoru3 grace was gete and of *no* gome ellis.
B.19.122	He wro3te þat by *no* wit but þoru3 word one,
B.19.137	And nempned hym of Na3areth; and *no* man so worþi
B.19.145	For *no* fren[d] sholde [it] fecche; for prophetes hem tolde
B.19.251	[Ne *no* boost ne] debat [be] among hem [alle].
B.19.284	Ne [sholde] *no* scornere out of skile hym brynge;
B.19.287	Sholde *no* curious clooþ comen on his rugge,
B.19.288	Ne *no* mete in his mouþ þat maister Iohan Spicede.
B.19.292	Mighte *no* [lyere wiþ lesynges] ne los of worldly catel
B.19.304	For counteþ he *no* kynges wraþe whan he in Court sitteþ;
B.19.349	Ne *no* manere marchaunt þat wiþ moneye deleþ
B.19.372	Ther nas *no* cristene creature þat kynde wit hadde
B.19.420	That *no* Cardynal coome among þe comune peple,
B.20.10	And nede haþ *no* lawe ne neuere shal falle in dette
B.20.12	That is mete whan men hym werneþ and he *no* moneye weldeþ,
B.20.23	For is *no* vertue bi fer to Spiritus temperancie,
B.20.33	Wenynge is *no* wysdom, ne wys ymaginacion:
B.20.65	[And] þat were mylde men and holye þat *no* meschief dradden;
B.20.102	Lered [ne] lewed he leet *no* man stonde,
B.20.149	And prike[d] forþ wiþ pride; preiseþ he *no* vertue,
B.20.197	I ne myghte in *no* manere maken it at hir wille,
B.20.237	Lat hem chewe as þei chose and charge hem with *no* cure
B.20.249	And oþere necessaries ynowe; yow shal *no* þyng [lakke]
B.20.260	/Wol *no* [tresorer take] hem [wages], trauaille þei neuer so soore,
B.20.318	'We han *no* nede', quod Conscience; 'I woot no bettre leche
B.20.379	And [doþ men drynke dwale]; þei drede *no* synne.'
C.Pr.32	For *no* likerous liflode here lycame to plese.
C. 1.9	Of othere heuene then here [halde þei] *no* tale.'
C. 1.79	'Teche me to [*no*] tresor but telle me this ilke,
C. 1.85	And doth þe werkes þerwith and wilneth *no* man ylle,
C. 1.95	And for *no* lordene loue leue þe trewe partie.
C. 1.116	Ac y wol lacky *no* lyf,' quod þat lady sothly;
C. 1.118	Then in þe north by many notes, *no* man leue other.
C. 1.136	Tha[n] treuthe and trewe loue is *no* tresor bettre.'
C. 1.137	'I haue *no* kynde knowyng,' quod y, '[3e mot] kenne me bettere
C. 1.165	And 3ut wolde [he] hem *no* wo bat wrouhte hym þat [p]e[y]ne
C. 1.180	Then malkyn of here maydenheed [þat] *no* man [desir]eth.
C. 1.185	Hit is as lewed as a laumpe þat *no* liht is ynne.
C. 1.193	And þat is *no* treuthe of þe trinite but triccherye [and] synne
C. 2.15	For to telle of here atyer *no* tyme haue y nouthe.
C. 2.107	And awake with wanhope and *no* wille to amende.
C. 2.128	And god graunte[de] hit were so so *no* gyle were,
C. 2.139	That mede may be wedded to *no* man bot treuthe,
C. 2.199	Y haue *no* tome to telle the tayl þat hem folewe[th]
C. 3.17	And sayden, 'mourne nat, mede, ne make thow *no* sorwe
C. 3.35	Shal *no* lewedenesse lette þe [lede] þat y louye
C. 3.86	Thei han *no* pite on the peple þat parselmele mot begge;
C. 3.87	Thow thei take mem vntidy thyng *no* tresoun þei ne halden hit;
C. 3.210	That *no* lond ne loueth the and 3ut leeste thyn owene.
C. 3.214	For pore men dar nat pleyne ne *no* pleynt shewe,
C. 3.233	For kulde y neuere *no* kyng ne conseilede so to done;
C. 3.254	Forthy y consayl *no* kynge eny conseyl aske
C. 3.282	Is *no* lede þat leueth þat he ne loueth mede
C. 3.294	And þat is nother resoun ne ryhte ne [i]n *no* rewme lawe
C. 3.305	And þat is *no* mede but a mercede, a manere dewe dette,
C. 3.307	As by the book þat byt *nobody* withholde
C. 3.313	In Marchandise is *no* mede, y may hit wel avowe;
C. 3.329	So god gyueth *no* [grace] þat "si" [ne] is the glose
C. 3.380	Bothe heued and here kyng, haldyng with *no* partey3e
C. 3.443	Shal *no* mede be maistre neueremore aftur
C. 3.447	Lewete shal do hym lawe and *no* lyf elles.
C. 3.448	Shal *no* ser[i]aunt for [þat] seruic[e] werie a selk houe
C. 3.449	Ne *no* pelure in his panelon for pledyng at þe barre.
C. 3.463	Spynne oþer speke of god and spille *no* tyme.
C. 3.472	Mercy or *no* mercy as most trewe acorden.
C. 4.18	And also th[omm]e trewe-tonge-telle-me-*no*-tales-
C. 4.40	Thenne resoun rood forth Ac took reward of *no* man
C. 4.57	Ne [*no*] ferthyng therfore, for nouhte y couthe plede.
C. 4.108	'Rede me nat,' quod resoun, '*no* reuthe so haue
C. 4.126	Bere *no* seluer ouer see þat sygne of kyng sheweth,
C. 4.131	And [3ut],' quod resoun, 'by þe rode! y shal *no* reuthe haue
C. 4.190	Ne *no* supersedias sende but y assente,' quod resoun.
C. 5.9	And *no* dede to do but drynke and slepe.
C. 5.54	Me sholde constrayne *no* Cler[k] to no knaues werkes,
C. 5.54	Me sholde constrayne no Cler[k] to *no* knaues werkes,
C. 5.58	Ne fyhte in *no* faumewarde ne his foe greue:
C. 5.66	For sholde *no* clerke be crouned but yf he come were
C. 5.90	Ac it semeth *no* sad parfitnesse in Citees to b[e]gge
C. 5.117	Was pertliche for pruyde and for *no* poynt elles.
C. 5.127	Thorw som trewe trauail and *no* tyme spille.
C. 5.137	'Late *no* wynnynge forwanyen hem while thei ben 3onge
C. 5.154	For in C[l]oystre cometh *no* man to chyde ne to fyhte;
C. 5.164	To religious þat haen *no* reuthe thow it ryne on here auters.
C. 5.166	Of þe pore haueth thei *no* pite and þat is here puyre chartre.
C. 5.184	Lat *no* kyne consayl ne couetyse 3ow parte,
C. 5.192	And *no* grace [to] graunte til good loue were
C. 6.45	And likynge of such a lyf þat *no* lawe preiseth,
C. 6.67	Sholde *no* lyf lyue þat on his lond pissede.
C. 6.82	And segge þat *no* clerk ne can, ne Crist as y leue,
C. 6.88	May *no* sugre ne swete thyng aswage my swellynge
C. 6.157	And balayshed on þe bare ers and *no* brech bytwene.
C. 6.158	Y haue *no* luste, lef me, to longe amonges monkes
C. 6.230	A galon for a grote, and 3ut *no* grayth mesure
C. 6.282	Nother matynes ne masse ne *no* maner syhtus;
C. 6.291	Y rede *no* faythful frere at thy feste to sytte.
C. 6.341	For thow hast *no* good, by good fayth, to gete the with a wastel.
C. 6.388	And nempned hym for a noumper þat *no* debat were.
C. 6.428	There *no* nede ne was, many sythe falsly;
C. 7.5	Sholde *no* ryngyng do me ryse til y were rype to dyne.'
C. 7.53	And 3ede aboute in my 3outhe and 3af me to *no* thedom
C. 7.61	For is *no* gult [here] so greet þat his goodnesse is more.'
C. 7.64	'Shal *no* sonday be this seuene 3ere, but seknesse hit make,
C. 7.73	Lyueth a3en þe bileue and *no* lawe kepeth
C. 7.74	And hath *no* likynge to lerne ne of oure lord to here
C. 7.95	Ne *no* mysproud man amongus lordes be [alow]ede.
C. 7.227	Thenne shaltow blenche at a berw, bere-*no*-fals-witnesse,
C. 7.229	Loke thow plokke *no* plonte þere for perel of thy soule.
C. 7.231	In-none-manere-elles-nat-for-*no*-mannes-preeyre.
C. 7.238	With *no* leed but with loue and with lele speche;
C. 7.269	And geten hit agayne thorw grace Ac thorw *no* gifte elles.
C. 7.283	'By Crist!' quod a cottepors, 'y haue *no* kyn there.'
C. 7.286	[Sh]olde y neuere forthere [a] foet for *no* frere prechynge.'
C. 8.36	Loke 3e tene *no* tenaunt but treuthe wol assente.
C. 8.78	For holy chirche is ho[ld]e of hem *no* tythe to aske,
C. 8.126	Shal *no* grayn þat here groweth gladyen 3ow at nede;
C. 8.138	That *no* faytrye were founde in folk þat goth abeggeth.
C. 8.160	For ther worth *no* plente,' quod [Perus], 'and þe plouh lygge.'
C. 8.194	There was *no* ladde þat lyuede þat ne lowede hym to Peres
C. 8.201	Was *no* beggare so bold, but yf a blynd were,
C. 8.215	'Ther is *no* fi[al] loue with this folk for al here fayre speche
C. 8.243	"The slowe Caytif for colde wolde *no* corn tylye;
C. 8.245	And go abribeth and abeggeth and *no* man beten his hungur:
C. 8.256	And he þat nauht hath shal nauht haue and *no* man [hym helpen]
C. 8.274	At noon ne at *no* tyme and nameliche at sopere
C. 8.276	And loke þou drynke *no* day ar thow dyne sumwhat.
C. 8.302	'Y haue *no* peny,' quod [Peres], 'polettes for to begge,
C. 8.306	And 3ut y say[e], be my soule! y haue *no* sal[t] bacoun
C. 8.307	Ne *no* cokeney, be Crist! colloppes to make.
C. 8.325	Ne *no* beggare eten bred þat benes ynne were
C. 8.329	Laborers þat han *no* lond to lyue on but here handes
C. 8.331	May *no* peny ale hem pay ne no pece of bacoun
C. 8.331	May no peny ale hem pay ne *no* pece of bacoun
C. 9.14	Lele and fol of loue and *no* lord drede,
C. 9.17	Drede nat for *no* deth to distruye by here power
C. 9.23	Ac *no* [a] pena & a culpa treuthe wolde hem graunte
C. 9.38	That *no* deuel shal 3ow dere ne despeyre in 3oure d[e]ynge
C. 9.47	That innocent and nedy is and *no* man harm wolde,
C. 9.70	Woet *no* man, as y wene, who is worthy to haue
C. 9.90	And hath *no* catel but his craft to clothe h[e]m and to fede
C. 9.109	Careth they for *no* colde ne counteth of non hete
C. 9.121	Barfoot and bredles, beggeth they of *no* man
C. 9.161	Ne *no* beggare[s] þat beggeth but yf they haue nede.'
C. 9.167	For they lyue in *no* loue ne no lawe holden
C. 9.167	For they lyue in no loue ne *no* lawe holden
C. 9.175	Þai haue *no* part of pardoun ne of preyeres ne of penaunc[e].
C. 9.198	Summe hadde lyflode of h[ere] lynage and of *no* lyf elles.
C. 9.254	Cam *no* wyn in his wombe thorw þe woke longe
C. 9.255	Ne *no* blanke[t] on his bed ne whyte bred byfore hym.

C. 9.280   For shal *no* pardon preye for ʒow there ne no princes lettres.
C. 9.280   For shal no pardon preye for ʒow there ne *no* princes lettres.
C. 9.289   'Peter!' quod the prest tho, 'y kan *no* pardoun fynde
C. 9.307   Of Nabugodonasor þat *no* pere hadde
C. 9.319   And how þe prest preuede *no* pardon to do wel
C.10.54   For rather haue we *no* reste til we restitue
C.10.56   'Y haue *no* kynde kno[w]yng,' [quod y], 'to conseyue al this speche
C.10.71   'That þou [wost] w[el],' quod he, 'and *no* wyht bettere.'
C.10.96   Lordes þat lyuen as hem lust and *no* lawe acounten,
C.10.98   Sholde *no* bisshop be here biddynges to withsite.
C.10.117   Was *no* pruyde on his parail ne pouerte noythere;
C.10.119   Y durste meue *no* matere to maken hym to iangle
C.10.185   And holy churche helpe to, so sholde *no* man begge
C.10.198   Sholde doute *no* deth ne no dere ʒeres
C.10.198   Sholde doute no deth ne *no* dere ʒeres
C.10.208   Thorw *no* sotil sciense on sour stok growe";
C.10.237   Holy writ witnesseth þat for *no* wikkede dede
C.10.250   That for *no* kyne catel ne no kyne byheste
C.10.250   That for no kyne catel ne *no* kyne byheste
C.10.254   For goode sholde wedde goode thouh they *no* goode hadde
C.10.261   Bote he haue oþer goed haue wol here *no* ryche.
C.10.264   That *no* cortesye can, bute [knowe late here be]
C.10.274   Haen þei *no* childerne bute cheste and [c]hoppes hem bitwene.
C.10.290   For sholde *no* bedbourde be bote yf they bothe were
C.10.292   For þat dede derne do *no* man sholde
C.10.302   To louye and to loue the and *no* lyf to greue;
C.11.27   And þat is *no* riht ne resoun for rather me sholde
C.11.28   Helpe hym þat hath nauhte then tho that haen *no* nede.
C.11.58   That preyeres haen *no* power this pestilences to lette.
C.11.74   Ac lust *no* lord now ne lettred man of suche lore to here
C.11.77   For is *no* wit worth now but hit of wynnynge soune.
C.11.82   I myhte gete *no* grayn of [his] grete wittes
C.11.129   Hit is *no* science sothly bote a sothfaste bileue
C.11.208   Y leue hit wel by oure lord and on *no* lettrure bettere.
C.11.262   As in likyng of lecherye *no* lyf denyede!
C.11.266   [Or] Poul þe apostel [þat] *no* pite hadde
C.11.270   By that þat salamon saith hit semeth þat *no* wyht woet
C.11.280   And myhte *no* kyng ouercome hym as in connynge of speche.
C.11.306   Thow thei folowe þat fortune wole [*no*] folye ich it holde.
C.11.311   Of dowel ne of dobet *no* deynte me thouhte;
C.12.5   [Haue *no* consience how þou come to good]; confesse the to som
           frere.
C.12.27   Y wolde it were *no* synne,' y saide, 'to seien þat were treuthe.
C.12.28   The sauter sayth hit is *no* synne for suche men þat ben trewe
C.12.32   'And wherof serueth lawe,' quod leaute, ' and *no* lyf vndertoke
           [hit],
C.12.61   Rihtfolliche to renoye *no* resoun hit wolde.
C.12.62   For may *no* cherl chartre make ne his chatel sulle
C.12.63   Withouten leue of [his] lord; *no* lawe wol hit graunte.
C.12.72   'That is soth,' saide scripture; ' may *no* synne lette
C.12.112   *No* beggare ne boy among vs but [yf] hit synne ma[d]e:
C.13.44   Wol *no* wys man be wroth ne his wed take–
C.13.60   And leueth his lettres þat *no* [lede] wole hym greue.
C.13.91   Ther is *no* lawe, as y leue, wol lette hym þe gate
C.13.101   For spera in deo speketh of prestis þat han *no* spendynge suluer
C.13.108   For made neuere kyng *no* knyhte but he hadde catel to spene
C.13.111   That hath n[*o*] lond ne lynage ryche ne good los of his handes.
C.13.151   Ther ne was no kyne kynde þat conseyued hadde
C.13.160   Ther is *no* wriht, as y wene, sholde worch here neste to paye;
C.13.164   For *no* foul sholde hit fynde but his fere and hymsulue.
C.13.197   Ho soffreth more then god?' quod he; '*no* gome, as y leue.
C.13.200   Is *no* vertue so fair ne of valewe ne profit
C.13.207   For is *no* creature vnder Crist þat can hymsulue make
C.13.242   Ther smyt *no* thyng so smerte ne smelleth so foule
C.14.5   And conseyled the for cristes sake *no* creature to bygile,
C.14.8   Ne *no* tyme to tyne ne treuye thyng tene,
C.14.10   And thenne dost thow wel, withoute drede; ho can do bet *no* force.
C.14.45   No more can *no* clerk but if hit come of bokes.
C.14.64   Forthy y conseyle all creatures *no* cler[gie] to despice
C.14.90   Ne in *no* cote ne Caytyfs hous [crist was ybore
C.14.121   And hath *no* contricion ar he come to shrifte; and thenne can he
           lytel telle,
C.14.134   And wol *no* wikkede man [be] lost bote if he wol hymsulue:
C.14.148   Hit were *no* resoun ne riht to rewarde bothe ylyche.
C.14.191   And wher he be saef or nat saef þe sothe woet *no* clergie
C.14.192   Ne of sortes ne of salamon *n*[*o*] scripture can telle
C.15.11   Ne *no* cors of pore comine in here kyrkeʒerde most lygge
C.15.77   That *no* fals frere thorw flaterynge men bygyle;
C.15.86   Hath *no* pyte on vs pore; he parformeth euele
C.15.129   Shal *no* such motyef be meued for me bote [þ]ere
C.15.133   And no tixst ne taketh to preue this for trewe
C.15.148   And whan he hadde yworded thus wiste *no* man aftur
C.15.204   [Ac for] y can nat tabre ne trompy ne telle [*no*] gestes,

C.15.208   Y haue *no* gode giftes of thise grete lordes
C.15.209   For *no* breed þat y betrauaile to [brynge] byfore lordes.
C.15.226   To haue þe grace of god and *no* gulte of þe pope.
C.15.227   For may *no* blessynge doen vs bote but yf we wol amende
C.15.234   Pruyde wolde potte hymsulf forth thogh *no* plough erye.
C.15.256   Dar þe nat care for *no* corn ne for cloth ne for drynke
C.15.266   That *no* reyn ne roen; thus [r]at men [i]n bokes,
C.15.267   That manye wynter men lyuede and *no* mete ne tylede.
C.15.288   And saith, "loo! briddes and bestes þat *no* blisse ne knoweth
C.16.59   Ac in pouerte þer pacience is pruyde hath *no* myhte
C.16.90   Lecherye loueth *no* pore for he hath bote litel siluer
C.16.96   That god is his gretteste helpe and *no* gome elles
C.16.124   Or a[s] iustice to iuge men, me enioyneth þerto *no* pore,
C.16.146   A trempeth þe tonge to treuthward þat *no* tresor coueyteth:
C.16.149   And thogh he chaffare he chargeth no loes may he charite wynne:
C.16.150   The nythe is swete to [þe] soul[e], *no* sucre swettore,
C.16.209   'ʒe, sire!' y sayde, 'by so *no* man were ygreued,
C.16.306   Weneth he þat *no* wyhte wolde lye and swerie
C.16.310   Hath he *no* lykynge to lawhe ne to likene men to scorne.
C.17.1   'There is *no* such,' y sayde, 'þat som tyme ne borweth
C.17.14   That *no* man myhte se hym for moes and for leues.
C.17.29   Ac durste *no* beste byte hem by day ne by nyhte
C.17.32   Ac bestes brouhte hem *no* mete bute onliche þe foules
C.17.40   Lord leue," quod þat lede, " *no* stole thynge be herynne!"
C.17.87   May *no* preyere pees make in no place hit semeth.
C.17.87   May no preyere pees make in *no* place hit semeth.
C.17.88   Lewed men han *no* byleue, [so] lettred men erren;
C.17.96   Haen *no* byleue to þe lyft ne to þe lodesterr[e];
C.17.131   God lereth *no* lyf to l[eu]e withouten lele cause.
C.17.136   Ac oure lord aloueth *no* loue but lawe be þe cause:
C.17.154   For þer is *no* man þat mynde hath þat ne meketh [hym] and
           bysecheth
C.17.161   And when kynde hath his cours and *no* contrarie fyndeth
C.17.164   Ne kynde sanʒ cortesie in *no* contreye is preysed.
C.17.197   Baddeliche ybedded, *no* boek but Consience
C.17.198   Ne *no* rychesse but þe rode to reioysen hem ynne:
C.17.292   And nameliche þer þat lewede lyuen and *no* lawe knoweth.
C.18.114   Baer hem forth baldly–*no* body hym lette–
C.18.222   That acorsede alle couples þat *no* kynde forth brouhte:
C.18.278   And me þerwith', quod the weye; 'may *no* wed vs quyte
C.18.280   Fro þe poukes pondefold *no* maynprise may vs feche–
C.19.33   He can *no* certeyn somme telle and somme aren in his lappe.
C.19.37   That of *no* trinite ne telleth ne taketh mo persones
C.19.84   Ne *no* medicyne vnder molde the man to hele brynge,
C.19.138   Sholde n[*o*] wri[h]t worche were they awey.
C.19.191   Graunten [*no*] grace ne forgeuenesse of synnes
C.19.217   For may *no* fuyr flaume make, faile hit his kynde.
C.19.289   That may *no* kynge mercy graunte til bothe men acorde
C.20.25   For *no* d[yn]t shal hym dere as in deitate patris.'
C.20.68   Ac shal *no* wyht wyte witturlich ho shal haue þe maistry
C.20.77   Ac was *no* boie so bold godes body to touche;
C.20.79   That hadde *no* boie hardynesse hym to touche in deynge.
C.20.108   Ne lawe lordschipe in londe ne *no* londe tulye
C.20.130   'Haue *no* merueyle,' quod Mercy; 'merthe hit bitokneth.
C.20.158   May *no* medecyne amende the place there he styngeth
C.20.205   That her peyne [be] perpetuel [and] *no* preyer hem helpe.
C.20.210   For badde they wist of *no* wo, wele hadde thay nat knowen;
C.20.211   For *no* wiht woet what wele is þat neuere wo soffrede
C.20.215   Yf *no* nyht ne were no man, [as] y leue,
C.20.215   Yf no nyht ne were *no* man, [as] y leue,
C.20.226   Ne woet *no* wyht, as y wene, what is ynow to mene.
C.20.237   For woet *no* wiht what werre is þer [þat] pees regneth
C.20.286   That *no* liht lepe in at louer ne at loupe.
C.20.297   May *no* deth this lord dere ne [n]o deueles quentyse
C.20.297   May no deth this lord dere ne [*n*]o deueles quentyse
C.20.324   We haen *no* trewe title to hem for thy tresoun hit maketh.'
C.20.405   Ac y wol drynke of *no* dische ne of deep clergyse
C.20.409   May *no* pyement ne pomade ne preciouse drynkes
C.20.453   Is *no* wedore warmore then aftur watri cloudes;
C.20.454   Ne *no* loue leuore ne leuore frendes
C.20.461   'And lat *no* peple,' quod pees, 'perseyue þat we chydde;
C.20.462   For inposible is *no* thynge to hym þat is almyhty.'
C.20.475   May *no* grisly goest glyde þer hit shaddeweth.'
C.21.19   Ergo is *no* name of iesus
C.21.51   Myhte *no* deth hym fordo ne adown brynge
C.21.121   That he thorw grace was gete and of *no* gome elles.
C.21.122   He wrouhte þat by *no* wyt bote thorw word one,
C.21.137   And nempned hym of naʒareth; and *no* man so worthy
C.21.145   For *no* frende sholde hit fecche; for profetes hem tolde
C.21.251   Ne *no* boest ne debaet be among hem alle.
C.21.284   Ne sholde *no* scornare out of skille hym brynge
C.21.287   Sholde *no* curious cloth comen on his rugge
C.21.288   Ne *no* mete in his mouth þat maistre iohann spyced.

C.21.292   Myhte *no* lyare with lesynge[s] ne losse of worldly catel
C.21.304   For counteth he *no* kynges wreth when he in Court sitteth;
C.21.349   Ne *no* manere Marchaunt þat with moneye deleth
C.21.420   That *no* cardinal come among þe comune peple
C.22.10   And nede hath *no* lawe ne neuere shal falle in dette
C.22.12   That is mete when men hym werneth [and] he *no* money weldeth
C.22.23   [For is *no* vertue by fer to spiritus temperancie],
C.22.33   Wenyng is *no* wisdoem ne wyse ymaginacioun:
C.22.65   And þat were mylde men and holy þat *no* meschief dradden,
C.22.102   Lered ne lewed he lefte *no* man stande,
C.22.149   And prike[d] forth with pruyde; preyseth he *no* vertue
C.22.237   Late hem chewe as thei chose and charge hem with *no* cure.
C.22.249   And oþere necessaries yknowe; 3ow shal *no* thyng lakke
C.22.260   Wol *no* tresorer taken hem wages, trauayle they neuere so sore,
C.22.318   'We haen *no* nede,' quod Consience; 'y woet no bettere leche
C.22.379   And doth men drynke dwale; [they] drat *no* synne.'

no adv *no adv.* A 30 na (2) no (28); B 43 na (25) no (18); C 41 na (2)
no (39)

          A.1.8, A.1.157, A.1.183, A.2.31, A.2.163, A.2.196, A.3.1, A.3.98, A.3.160,
A.3.189, A.3.266, A.4.1, A.4.84, A.4.89, A.4.90, A.4.156, A.5.138, A.5.151, A.7.88,
A.7.135, A.8.105, A.9.66, A.10.99, A.11.165, A.12.30, A.12.31, A.12.68, A.12.76,
A.12.89, A.12.92

          B.1.8, B.1.183, B.1.209, B.2.202, B.2.237, B.3.1, B.3.109, B.3.173, B.3.202,
B.3.290, B.3.340, B.3.344, B.4.1, B.4.97, B.4.102, B.4.103, B.4.193, B.5.222, B.5.283,
B.5.301, B.6.96, B.6.146, B.7.123, B.8.75, B.10.44, B.12.100, B.12.107, B.12.282,
B.12.288, B.13.87, B.13.351, B.14.36, B.16.217, B.17.8, B.17.168, B.17.175, B.17.175,
B.17.224, B.17.355, B.20.9, B.20.16, B.20.222, B.20.318

          C.1.8, C.1.123, C.1.179, C.1.203, C.2.216, C.2.253, C.3.1, C.3.219, C.3.259,
C.3.492, C.4.1, C.4.93, C.4.97, C.6.185, C.6.356, C.8.105, C.8.195, C.9.123, C.10.73,
C.10.209, C.11.70, C.11.244, C.11.288, C.13.40, C.13.66, C.14.45, C.14.52, C.14.204,
C.14.210, C.15.94, C.15.123, C.15.151, C.16.179, C.17.41, C.19.64, C.19.190, C.19.335,
C.22.9, C.22.16, C.22.222, C.22.318

noble n *noble n.(2)* A 1; B 8 noble (4) nobles (4); C 8 noble (4) nobles
(4)
A. 3.44   Tolde hym a tale, & tok hym a *noble*
B. 3.45   Tolde hym a tale and took hym a *noble*
B. 5.247   And lene folk þat lese wole a lippe at euery *noble*.
B.10.295   And be prester at youre preiere þan for a pound of *nobles*,
B.12.250   So is possession peyne of pens and of *nobles*
B.15.86   And louten to þise lordes þat mowen lene yow *nobles*
B.15.539   And now is rouþe to rede how þe rede *noble*
B.15.545   That in grotes is ygraue and in gold *nobles*.
B.20.132   And boldeliche bar adoun wiþ many a bright *Noble*
C. 3.47   Tolde hym a tale and toke hym a *noble*
C. 3.392   Nyme he a noumbre of *nobles* or of shillynges,
C. 6.245   Y lene folk þat lese wole a lyppe [at] vch a *noble*
C.10.269   That his wyf were wexe or a walet ful of *nobles*.
C.10.282   And loke þat loue be more þe cause then lond oþer *nobles*.
C.17.200   And now is reuthe to rede how þe rede *noble*
C.17.207   That in grotes is graue and in golde *nobles*.
C.22.132   And baldeliche baer adoun with many a brihte *noble*

noble adj *noble adj.* B 1; C 1
B.19.50   And þo conquered he on cros as conquerour *noble*;
C.21.50   And tho conquerede he on cros as conquerour *noble*;

nobody > no,body

noe n prop *Noe n.* A 1; B 4 Noe (2) Noes (2); C 5 Noe (4) noes (1)
A.10.165   And com to *noe* anon, and bad hym nou3t lette
B. 9.134   And com to *Noe* anon and bad hym nou3t lette:
B.10.405   Ac I wene it worþ of manye as was in *Noes* tyme
B.10.408   But briddes and beestes and þe blissed *Noe*
B.10.413   And shilden vs from shame þerinne, as *Noes* ship dide beestes;
C.10.178   As lo[t] dede and *Noe*, and herodes þe daffe
C.10.221   And for þe synne of Caymes seed sayede god to *Noe*:
C.11.236   Ac y wene hit worth of monye as was in *noes* tyme
C.11.239   Bote briddes and bestis and þe blessed *Noe*
C.11.251   Laste 3e be loste as þe laboreres were þat lab[o]red vnder *Noe*.

noen > noon

no3t n *nought n.* A 1 nou3t; B 4 nau3t (1) no3t (2) no3te (1); C 5 nauht
(2) nauhte (3)
A.10.142   A3enes þe hest of hym þat hem of *nou3t* made,
B. 5.481   And of *nau3t* madest au3t and man moost lik to þiselue,
B.11.300   And a title, a tale of *no3t*, to his liflode at meschief.
B.14.96   And as it neuere [n]adde ybe to *no3te* bryngeþ dedly synne
B.15.598   And þoru3 his pacience hir power to pure *no3t* he brou3te:
C. 2.142   That 3e nymeth [and] notaries to *nauhte* gynneth brynge
C. 3.201   Trewe Burgeys and bonde he bryngeth to *nauhte* ofte
C. 7.123   And [of *nauhte* madest] auhte and man liche thysulue
C.13.114   And a title, a tale of *nauht*, to his lyflode as hit were.
C.17.306   And her power thorw his pacience to puyr *nauht* brouhte

no3t pron *nought pron.* A 8 nou3t; B 21 no3t (17) nou3t (4); C 18 nat (4)
nauht (6) nauhte (2) nautht (1) nou3t (1) nouht (3) nouhte (1)
A. 1.108   To be buxum at his bidding; he bad hem *nou3t* ellis.
A. 1.160   Þat feiþ wiþoute fait is feblere þan *nou3t*,
A. 4.41   Ne no ferþing þerfore for *nou3t* I couþe plete.
A. 5.234   Ac for þere was *nou3t* wherwith he wepte swiþe sore.
A. 7.209   Þat nedy ben or nakid, & *nou3t* han to spende,
A. 7.229   And he þat *nou3t* haþ shal nou3t haue ne no man him helpe,
A. 7.229   And he þat nou3t haþ shal *nou3t* haue ne no man him helpe,
A.11.258   –3et am I neuere þe ner for *nou3t* I haue walkid
B. 1.110   To be buxom at his biddyng, he bad hem *nou3t* ellis.
B. 1.186   That Feiþ wiþouten feit is [feblere þan *nou3t*],
B. 4.37   Thei ne [gy]ueþ *no3t* of [good feiþ, woot god þe sooþe]:
B. 4.54   Ne no ferþyng þerfore for [n]*ou3t* I koude plede.
B. 5.462   And for þer was *no3t* wher[wiþ] he wepte swiþe soore.
B. 6.148   Ac Robert Renaboute shal [ri3t] *no3t* haue of myne,
B. 6.151   For it is an vnresonable Religion þat haþ ri3t *no3t* of certein.'
B. 6.223   That nedy ben [or naked, and *nou3t* han to spende,
B. 6.245   And he þat *no3t* haþ shal no3t haue and no man hym helpe,
B. 6.245   And he þat no3t haþ shal *no3t* haue and no man hym helpe,
B. 7.86   He haþ ynou3 þat haþ breed ynou3, þou3 he haue *no3t* ellis:
B. 9.71   And widewes þat han *no3t* wherwith to wynnen hem hir foode,
B.12.165   He þat neuere ne dyued ne *no3t* kan of swymmyng,
B.13.131   'I kan *no3t* heron', quod Conscience, 'ac I knowe Piers.
B.16.222   And is *no3t* but gendre of a generacion bifore Iesu crist in heuene:
B.17.36   And telleþ *no3t* of þe Trinite þat took hym hise lettres,
B.17.188   He may receyue ri3t *no3t*; reson it sheweþ.
B.17.193   I sholde receyue ri3t *no3t* of þat I reche myghte;
B.19.448   He reccheþ ri3t *no3t* of þe remenaunt.
B.20.154   Shal do þee *no3t* drede, neiþer deeþ ne elde,
B.20.155   And [so] for3yte sorwe and [of synne 3yue *no3t*].'
C.Pr.214   But soffre and sey *nou3t*; and [so] is þe beste
C. 1.182   That fayth withouten feit is feblore then *nautht*
C. 4.37   They gyue n[ouh]t of good fayth, woe[t] god the sothe,
C. 4.57   Ne [no] ferthyng therfore, for *nouhte* y couthe plede.
C. 6.316   And for þer was *nat* wherwith a wep swythe sore.
C. 8.159   They acounteth *nat* of corsyng[e] ne holy kyrke dredeth–
C. 8.256   And he þat *nauht* hath shal nauht haue and no man [hym helpen]
C. 8.256   And he þat nauht hath shal *nauht* haue and no man [hym helpen]
C. 9.303   Ac men setteth *nat* by sowngewarie for me seth hit often fayle;
C. 9.304   Caton counteth hit at *nauht* and Canonistres at lasse.
C.11.28   Helpe hym þat hath *nauhte* then tho that haen no nede.
C.13.12   And for he soffrede and saide *nauht* oure lord sente tookene
C.17.42   Sholde reseue riht *nauht* but þat riht wolde
C.19.154   He may resceyue riht *nauhte*; resoun hit sheweth.
C.19.159   Y sholde receyue ryht *nouht* of þat y reche myhte;
C.21.448   He rekketh riht *nauht* of þe remenaunt.
C.22.154   Shal do the *nat* drede, noþer deth ne elde,
C.22.155   And [s]o for3ete [sorwe] and [of synne 3eue *nouht*].'

no3t adv *nought adv.* A 105 not (58) nou3t (47); B 343 na3t (1) nat (4)
nau3t (10) noght (1) no3t (314) nou3t (13); C 367 nat (337) naught (1)
nauht (4) nauhte (2) noght (5) no3t (2) not (7) nought (1) nou3t (6)
nouht (2)

          A.Pr.29, A.Pr.38, A.Pr.76, A.Pr.77, A.Pr.87, A.1.25, A.1.34, A.1.36, A.1.99,
A.1.170, A.2.19, A.2.86, A.2.167, A.3.3, A.3.16, A.3.55, A.3.57, A.3.74, A.3.118,
A.3.131, A.3.147, A.3.165, A.3.176, A.3.248, A.3.251, A.3.252, A.3.258, A.4.39, A.4.47,
A.4.73, A.4.74, A.4.92, A.4.100, A.4.142, A.4.153, A.5.31, A.5.61, A.5.71, A.5.107,
A.5.112, A.5.177, A.5.244, A.6.57, A.6.59, A.6.60, A.6.63, A.6.64, A.6.64, A.6.64,
A.6.65, A.6.71, A.6.76, A.6.81, A.7.11, A.7.41, A.7.41, A.7.44, A.7.47, A.7.67, A.7.73,
A.7.138, A.7.152, A.7.152, A.7.173, A.7.213, A.7.240, A.7.245, A.7.247, A.7.249,
A.7.250, A.7.286, A.7.292, A.8.22, A.8.33, A.8.67, A.8.72, A.8.93, A.8.104,
A.8.112, A.8.164, A.9.19, A.9.20, A.9.40, A.9.70, A.9.75, A.9.100, A.9.102, A.10.1,
A.10.110, A.10.116, A.10.158, A.10.165, A.10.197, A.11.17, A.11.94, A.11.116,
A.11.149, A.11.225, A.11.227, A.11.240, A.11.254, A.11.268, A.12.23, A.12.32

          B.Pr.29, B.Pr.38, B.Pr.79, B.Pr.80, B.Pr.111, B.Pr.152, B.Pr.189, B.Pr.201,
B.Pr.214, B.1.25, B.1.36, B.1.38, B.1.101, B.1.153, B.1.196, B.2.24, B.2.48, B.2.62,
B.2.122, B.2.206, B.3.3, B.3.16, B.3.51, B.3.54, B.3.73, B.3.85, B.3.129, B.3.142,
B.3.157, B.3.178, B.3.189, B.3.240, B.3.270, B.3.272, B.3.280, B.4.36, B.4.41, B.4.52,
B.4.60, B.4.86, B.4.87, B.4.105, B.4.113, B.4.151, B.4.179, B.4.190, B.5.31, B.5.36,
B.5.78, B.5.121, B.5.132, B.5.184, B.5.188, B.5.197, B.5.253, B.5.270, B.5.273, B.5.288,
B.5.328, B.5.368, B.5.387, B.5.394, B.5.413, B.5.414, B.5.421, B.5.430, B.5.432,
B.5.439, B.5.441, B.5.470, B.5.471, B.5.570, B.5.572, B.5.573, B.5.576, B.5.577,
B.5.577, B.5.578, B.5.584, B.5.589, B.5.608, B.5.639, B.6.42, B.6.42, B.6.45, B.6.52,
B.6.75, B.6.81, B.6.123, B.6.162, B.6.167, B.6.167, B.6.185, B.6.225, B.6.229, B.6.256,
B.6.261, B.6.263, B.6.265, B.6.266, B.6.302, B.6.308, B.7.20, B.7.41, B.7.49, B.7.65,
B.7.70, B.7.84, B.7.111, B.7.122, B.7.130, B.7.186, B.8.23, B.8.24, B.8.44, B.8.79,
B.8.84, B.8.110, B.8.112, B.9.1, B.9.76, B.9.84, B.9.95, B.9.95, B.9.96, B.9.98, B.9.129,
B.9.134, B.9.176, B.9.182, B.9.188, B.10.17, B.10.75, B.10.70, B.10.82, B.10.85,
B.10.88, B.10.95, B.10.98, B.10.141, B.10.164, B.10.200, B.10.209, B.10.245, B.10.277,
B.10.278, B.10.280, B.10.293, B.10.337, B.10.339, B.10.343, B.10.357, B.10.371,
B.10.373, B.10.411, B.10.419, B.10.452, B.11.41, B.11.82, B.11.83, B.11.99, B.11.104,
B.11.106, B.11.117, B.11.156, B.11.177, B.11.180, B.11.180, B.11.191, B.11.212,

B.11.215, B.11.224, B.11.225, B.11.235, B.11.239, B.11.284, B.11.291, B.11.313,
B.11.344, B.11.353, B.11.364, B.11.377, B.11.377, B.11.396, B.11.402, B.11.417,
B.11.421, B.11.424, B.11.428, B.11.430, B.12.54, B.12.60, B.12.85, B.12.99, B.12.124,
B.12.143, B.12.169, B.12.199, B.12.210, B.12.233, B.12.243, B.12.248, B.12.260,
B.12.270, B.12.291, B.13.65, B.13.71, B.13.80, B.13.105, B.13.106, B.13.132, B.13.150,
B.13.168, B.13.174, B.13.194, B.13.255, B.13.264, B.13.279, B.13.290, B.13.302,
B.13.307, B.13.333, B.13.377, B.13.387, B.13.406, B.13.410, B.13.417, B.14.35,
B.14.75, B.14.78, B.14.85, B.14.139, B.14.140, B.14.144, B.14.152, B.14.168, B.14.173,
B.14.231, B.14.239, B.14.243, B.14.250, B.14.251, B.14.252, B.14.254, B.14.258,
B.14.277, B.14.295, B.14.332, B.15.8, B.15.31, B.15.80, B.15.110, B.15.160, B.15.164,
B.15.165, B.15.213, B.15.236, B.15.239, B.15.281, B.15.296, B.15.348, B.15.375,
B.15.383, B.15.387, B.15.399, B.15.414, B.15.452, B.15.514, B.15.529, B.15.548,
B.15.549, B.16.176, B.16.218, B.16.219, B.17.25, B.17.32, B.17.61, B.17.81, B.17.86,
B.17.116, B.17.119, B.17.221, B.17.237, B.17.241, B.17.258, B.17.259, B.17.264,
B.17.266, B.17.267, B.17.302, B.17.312, B.17.314, B.17.316, B.17.320, B.17.323,
B.17.334, B.18.24, B.18.56, B.18.70, B.18.164, B.18.177, B.18.201, B.18.205, B.18.249,
B.18.285, B.18.292, B.18.293, B.18.310, B.18.332, B.18.348, B.18.376, B.18.378,
B.18.379, B.18.387, B.18.395, B.18.405, B.19.33, B.19.112, B.19.117, B.19.162,
B.19.195, B.19.228, B.19.299, B.19.301, B.19.302, B.19.348, B.19.358, B.19.381,
B.19.396, B.19.401, B.19.444, B.20.6, B.20.15, B.20.39, B.20.48, B.20.150, B.20.179,
B.20.192, B.20.231, B.20.309, B.20.339, B.20.342, B.20.343

C.Pr.31, C.Pr.77, C.Pr.78, C.Pr.100, C.Pr.110, C.Pr.110, C.Pr.115, C.Pr.138,
C.Pr.164, C.1.24, C.1.34, C.1.36, C.1.109, C.1.125, C.1.191, C.2.18, C.2.24,
C.2.39, C.2.51, C.2.64, C.2.126, C.2.169, C.2.218, C.3.3, C.3.17, C.3.58, C.3.74, C.3.75,
C.3.84, C.3.88, C.3.101, C.3.112, C.3.129, C.3.166, C.3.180, C.3.195, C.3.214, C.3.224,
C.3.240, C.3.246, C.3.299, C.3.326, C.3.366, C.3.367, C.3.423, C.3.425, C.3.433, C.4.34,
C.4.36, C.4.50, C.4.63, C.4.82, C.4.83, C.4.100, C.4.108, C.4.173, C.4.184, C.5.82,
C.5.89, C.5.133, C.6.17, C.6.55, C.6.77, C.6.86, C.6.97, C.6.108, C.6.126, C.6.166,
C.6.196, C.6.205, C.6.251, C.6.276, C.6.294, C.6.324, C.6.325, C.6.343, C.6.381,
C.6.386, C.6.426, C.6.432, C.7.3, C.7.10, C.7.28, C.7.29, C.7.29, C.7.34, C.7.43, C.7.45,
C.7.55, C.7.70, C.7.72, C.7.77, C.7.217, C.7.219, C.7.220, C.7.222, C.7.223, C.7.224,
C.7.225, C.7.231, C.7.236, C.7.280, C.7.304, C.8.40, C.8.42, C.8.50,
C.8.53, C.8.77, C.8.83, C.8.84, C.8.85, C.8.91, C.8.130, C.8.147, C.8.164, C.8.164,
C.8.170, C.8.181, C.8.213, C.8.233, C.8.235, C.8.251, C.8.261, C.8.268, C.8.271,
C.8.273, C.8.275, C.8.279, C.8.324, C.8.330, C.9.17, C.9.24, C.9.48, C.9.61, C.9.66,
C.9.86, C.9.112, C.9.123, C.9.160, C.9.164, C.9.262, C.9.274, C.9.275, C.9.285, C.9.332,
C.9.346, C.9.346, C.10.25, C.10.27, C.10.28, C.10.39, C.10.42, C.10.43, C.10.77,
C.10.81, C.10.99, C.10.102, C.10.106, C.10.108, C.10.128, C.10.160, C.10.162,
C.10.164, C.10.201, C.10.210, C.10.210, C.10.216, C.10.283, C.10.288, C.11.14,
C.11.44, C.11.55, C.11.59, C.11.65, C.11.68, C.11.106, C.11.185, C.11.198, C.11.222,
C.11.242, C.11.277, C.11.308, C.12.16, C.12.20, C.12.38, C.12.40, C.12.52, C.12.103,
C.12.107, C.12.121, C.12.124, C.12.128, C.12.176, C.12.189, C.12.192, C.12.197,
C.12.220, C.13.10, C.13.26, C.13.53, C.13.80, C.13.105, C.13.125, C.13.174, C.13.182,
C.13.190, C.13.195, C.13.210, C.13.225, C.13.231, C.13.232, C.13.235, C.13.237,
C.14.24, C.14.29, C.14.41, C.14.44, C.14.67, C.14.87, C.14.109, C.14.138, C.14.149,
C.14.176, C.14.191, C.14.201, C.14.213, C.15.45, C.15.69, C.15.87, C.15.93, C.15.115,
C.15.172, C.15.177, C.15.181, C.15.197, C.15.204, C.15.225, C.15.256, C.15.263,
C.16.7, C.16.8, C.16.53, C.16.65, C.16.72, C.16.79, C.16.83, C.16.92, C.16.94, C.16.98,
C.16.117, C.16.130, C.16.178, C.16.193, C.16.228, C.16.239, C.16.250,
C.16.250, C.16.264, C.16.290, C.16.294, C.16.339, C.16.361, C.16.364, C.17.25,
C.17.67, C.17.69, C.17.81, C.17.85, C.17.91, C.17.118, C.17.118, C.17.149, C.17.150,
C.17.157, C.17.210, C.17.211, C.17.241, C.17.265, C.17.279, C.18.30, C.18.47, C.18.62,
C.18.184, C.18.197, C.18.198, C.18.220, C.18.223, C.18.249, C.19.26, C.19.60, C.19.78,
C.19.83, C.19.86, C.19.96, C.19.187, C.19.203, C.19.207, C.19.224, C.19.225, C.19.230,
C.19.231, C.19.232, C.19.233, C.19.236, C.19.248, C.19.282, C.19.292, C.19.294,
C.19.296, C.19.300, C.19.303, C.19.314, C.20.2, C.20.23, C.20.56, C.20.72, C.20.167,
C.20.180, C.20.206, C.20.210, C.20.218, C.20.258, C.20.307, C.20.315, C.20.322,
C.20.323, C.20.334, C.20.344, C.20.355, C.20.375, C.20.393, C.20.418, C.20.421,
C.20.429, C.20.438, C.20.448, C.21.33, C.21.112, C.21.117, C.21.162, C.21.195,
C.21.228, C.21.299, C.21.301, C.21.302, C.21.348, C.21.358, C.21.381, C.21.396,
C.21.401, C.21.444, C.22.15, C.22.6, C.22.15, C.22.39, C.22.48, C.22.150, C.22.179, C.22.192,
C.22.231, C.22.309, C.22.339, C.22.342, C.22.343

noise n *noise n.* B 1; C 2 noyse
B.16.77 And whan [he] meued matrimoyne it made a foul *noise*.
C.18.109 A meued matrimonye; hit made a fo[u]le *noyse*.
C.18.178 With moche *noyse* þat nyhte nere frentyk y wakede;

noyther(e > neiþer; noi3e(- > noyen

nok n *nok n.* A 1; B 1
A. 5.115 For sum tyme I seruide symme at þe *nok*
B. 5.199 For som tyme I serued Symme atte [*Nok*]

nolde > willen

nombre v *nombren v.* &> noumbre B 2 nombre (1) noumbrede (1); C 1
  nombred
B. 1.116 And mo þousandes myd hym þan man kouþe *nombre*
B.20.256 And nempnede [hem names], and *noumbrede* þe sterres:
C.22.256 And nempned hem names and *nombred* þe sterres:

nome > nymen; non(e > noon

nones n1 *nones n.(1)* A 1
A. 2.41 Was pi3t vp a pauyloun proud for þe *nones*,

nones n2 *nones n.(2)* B 2; C 3
B. 5.371 And ouerseyen me at my soper and som tyme at *Nones*
B. 6.145 Ac Ancres and heremites þat eten but at *Nones*
C. 6.429 And ouersopped at my soper and som tyme at *nones*
C. 8.146 Ankerus and Eremytes þat eten but at *nones*
C. 8.196 But lyflode for his la[b]our and his loue at *nones*.

nonne n *nonne n.* A 1 nonnes; B 2 Nonne (1) Nonnes (1); C 1
A. 8.31 Marie maidenis also [or] maken hem *nonnes*,
B. 5.153 I haue an Aunte to *Nonne* and an Abbesse boþe;
B. 7.29 Marien maydenes or maken hem *Nonnes*,
C. 6.128 Y haue an Aunte to *nonne* and an abbesse;

noon n *non n.(1)* A 2 non (1) noon (1); B 3; C 6 noen (3) noon (2)
  noone (1)
A. 7.135 Inou3 iche day at *non*, ac no more til on þe morewe
A. 7.137 Ones at *noon* is ynou3 þat no werk vsiþ;
B. 5.377 Fedde me bifore] *noon* whan fastyng dayes were.'
B.15.283 Antony adayes aboute *noon* tyme
B.20.4 And it neghed nei3 þe *noon* and wiþ nede I mette
C. 2.103 And fastyng dayes to frete byfore *noone* and drynke
C. 6.434 [On] fastyng dayes bifore *noen* fedde me with ale,
C. 8.274 At *noon* ne at no tyme and nameliche at sopere
C. 8.288 Til alle thyne nedy neyhbores haue *noen* ymaked,
C. 9.87 What h[e]m nede[th] at here neyhebores at *noon* and at eue.
C.22.4 And hit neyhed neyh þe *noen* and with nede y mette

noon pron *non pron.* A 13 non (6) none (7); B 36 none (8) noon (28); C
  35 noen (10) non (11) none (7) noon (7)
A. 1.21 Arn *none* nedful but þo & nempne hem I þenke,
A. 1.165 Arn *none* hardere þan [hy] whanne [hy] ben auauncid,
A. 2.10 Icorounid in a coroune, þe king haþ *non* betere;
A. 2.110 'And nameliche to þe notories, þat hem *non* fail[e];
A. 2.131 Þ[o] hadde notories *none*; anoyed þei were
A. 6.61 Ne *none* of here seruauntis, þat noi3e hem mi3te;
A. 7.300 Ac while hunger was here maister wolde þere *non* chide,
A. 8.21 But *non* a pena & a culpa þe pope wolde h[e]m graunte,
A.11.47 Is *non* to nymen hym In ne his [noye] amende,
A.11.231 Hauen eritage in heuene, ac riche men *non*.'
A.11.291 And arn *no[ne]*, forsoþe, souereynes in heuene
A.11.307 Arn *none* raþere yrauisshid fro þe ri3te beleue
A.11.309 Ne *none* sonnere ysauid, ne saddere of consience,
B. 1.21 Are *none* nedfulle but þo; and nempne hem I þynke
B. 1.191 Are [*none* hardere] þan hij whan þei ben auaunced,
B. 2.10 Ycorouned [in] a coroune, þe kyng haþ *noon* bettre.
B. 2.146 And namely to þe Notaries þat hem *noon* faille.
B. 2.167 Tho hadde Notaries *none*; anoyed þei were
B. 3.323 Batailles shul *none* be, ne no man bere wepene,
B. 5.574 Ne-*noon*-of-hire-seruaunt3-þat-noyen-hem-my3te;
B. 6.319 Ac whiles hunger was hir maister þer wolde *noon* chide
B. 7.19 Ac *noon* A pena & a culpa þe pope [w]olde hem graunte
B.10.61 Is *noon* to nyme hym [in, ne] his [n]oy amende,
B.10.81 And yet þe wrecches of þis world is *noon* ywar by ooþer,
B.10.410 Of w[r]ightes þat it wro3te was *noon* of hem ysaued
B.10.463 Arn *none* raþer yrauysshed fro þe ri3te bileue
B.10.465 Ne *none* sonner saued, ne sadder of bileue,
B.11.215 Ne vndernyme no3t foule, for is *noon* wiþoute defaute.
B.11.337 And after cours of concepcion *noon* took kepe of ooþer,
B.12.31 And sauen men sondry tymes, ac *noon* so soone as Charite.
B.12.161 And boþe naked as a nedle, hir *noon* [sadder] þan ooþer.
B.13.283 Was *noon* swich as hymself], ne [noon] so po[pe] holy;
B.13.283 Was noon swich as hymself], ne [*noon*] so po[pe] holy;
B.13.295 And *noon* so holy as he ne of lif clennere.
B.14.33 And þat ynogh; shal *noon* faille of þyng þat hem nedeþ:
B.14.143 As he þat *noon* hadde and haþ hire at þe laste.
B.14.166 For alle my3testow haue maad *noon* mener þan ooþer
B.14.201 Forþi cristene sholde be in commune riche, *noon* coueitous for
  hymselue.
B.14.219 Ne *none* of þe seuene synnes sitten ne mowe þer longe,
B.14.240 And by þe nekke namely hir *noon* may hente ooþer;
B.15.97 Ther some bowes ben leued and some bereþ *none*
B.15.373 For is *noon* of þise newe clerkes, whoso nymeþ hede,
B.16.57 For alle are þei aliche longe, *noon* lasse þan ooþer,
B.16.181 'Thre leodes in oon lyth, *noon* lenger þan ooþer.
B.17.350 For þer nys sik ne sory, ne *noon* so muche wrecche
B.19.20 Ne *noon* so nedeful to nempne by ny3te ne by daye.
B.19.36 As wide as þe world is [wonyeþ] þer *noon*?
B.19.254 Lokeþ þat *no[on]* lakke ooþer, but loueþ as breþeren;
B.20.50 Ne neuere *noon* so nedy ne pouerer deide.
C. 1.21 Aren *non* [ni]defole but tho and nemne hem y thenke
C. 1.187 Aren *none* hardere ne hungriore then men of holy chirche,
C. 2.10 She was purfiled [with] pelure, *non* puyrere on erthe,
C. 2.11 And crouned [in] a croune, þe kyng haþ *non* bettre;
C. 2.162 And [name]liche [to] the notaries þat [hem] *noon* fayle.

C. 3.62   Hit is synne as of seuene *noon* sannour relesed.
C. 4.124   So þat *noon* go to galys but yf he go for euere;
C. 6.37   Was *non* such as [my]sulue ne non so popholy;
C. 6.37   Was *non* such as [my]sulue ne *non* so popholy;
C. 6.49   And *non* so bolde a beggare to bidde and to craue,
C. 7.221   Ne-*none*-of-here-seruauntes-þat-nuye-hem-myhte;
C. 7.276   *Noen* of hem alle helpe may in betere
C. 8.339   Ac whiles hungur was here maistre ther wolde *non* chyde
C.10.112 Elles knowe y *noen* þat can in none kynneryche.'
C.11.42   Is non so hende to haue hym [in] but hote hym go þer god is.
C.11.61   And ȝut th[e] wrechus of this world is *noen* ywar by oþer
C.11.241   Of wryhtes þat hit wrouhte was *noen* of hem ysaued.
C.11.289   Aren *noen* rather yrraueschid fro þe rihte bileue
C.11.291   Ne *none* sanere ysa[u]ed ne saddere in bileue
C.12.165   Ȝef pore peple þe panes; þerof pors þou *none*
C.13.145   Aftur cors of concepcion *noon* toek kepe of oþer,
C.13.187   Y se *non* so ofte forfeten sothly so mankynde;
C.14.105   And bothe naked as a nedle, here *noen* heuegore then othere.
C.16.42   Forthy cristene sholde be in comune ryche, *noon* coueytous for
             hymsulue.
C.16.60   Ne *none* of þe seuene synnes sitte ne may þer longe
C.16.80   And by þe nekke namelyche here *non* may henten other;
C.16.249   Þere som bowes bereth leues and som bereth *none*:
C.17.109   For is [now] *noon*, hoso nymeth hede,
C.18.55   And þe fruyt was fayre, *non* fayrere be myhte,
C.19.330   For þer ne is sike ne sory ne *non* so moche wrecche
C.20.472   And rihtfollokest A relyk, *noon* richore on erthe.
C.21.20   Ne *noen* so niedfol to nemnie by nyhte ne by day
C.21.36   As wyd[e] as þe worlde is wonyeth þer *none*
C.21.254   Loke þat *noen* lacke oþere bute loueth as bretherne
C.22.50   Ne neuere *noen* so nedy ne porore deyede.'

noon adj *non adj.* A 16 non (11) none (5); B 46 none (9) noon (37); C
    54 noen (8) non (24) none (17) noon (5)
A. 1.86   For whoso is trewe of his tunge, telliþ *non* oþer,
A. 1.116   For pride þat he put out his peyne haþ *non* ende.
A. 3.75   Ne bouȝte *none* burgages, be ȝe wel certayn.
A. 3.259   An aunter it [noiȝide me *non*] ende wile I make.
A. 5.83   He is douȝtiere þanne I–I dar *non* harm don hym,
A. 5.225   Shal *non* ale aftir mete holde me þennis
A. 6.39   He [wiþ]halt *non* hyne his hire þat he ne haþ it at eue
A. 6.51   And þanne ȝoure neiȝebours next in none wise apeir[e]
A. 6.122   And þoruȝ þe helpe of hem [two], hope þou *non* oþer.
A. 7.47   Holde wiþ *none* harlotis ne here nouȝt here talis,
A. 7.116   'We haue *none* [lymes] to laboure wiþ, lord, ygracid be ȝe;
A. 7.289   Ne *non* halpeny ale in no wyse drynke,
A. 8.99   And do euele & haue euele, & hope þou *non* oþer
A. 9.110   He was long & lene, lyk to *non* oþer,
A.11.202 And þat is riȝtful religioun, *none* renneris aboute,
A.12.29   God gaf him *non* answere but gan his tounge holde.
B. 1.88   [For] who is trewe of his tunge, telleþ *noon* ooþer,
B. 1.120   And alle þat hoped it myȝte be so, *noon* heuene myȝte hem holde,
B. 1.127   For pride þat he putte out his peyne haþ *noon* ende.
B. 1.158   That myȝte *noon* Armure it lette ne none heiȝe walles.
B. 1.158   That myȝte noon Armure it lette ne *none* heiȝe walles.
B. 3.86   Ne bouȝte *none* burgages, be ye [wel] certeyne.
B. 3.281   On auenture it noyed m[e] *noon* ende wol I make,
B. 5.103   He is douȝtier þan I; I dar [*noon* harm doon hym],
B. 5.294   What he lerned yow in lente, leue þow *noon* ooþer,
B. 5.355   Is *noon* so hungry hound in hertford shire
B. 5.453   Shal *noon* ale after mete holde me þennes
B. 5.513   Ac þere was [wye] *noon* so wys þe wey þider kouþe
B. 5.552   He wiþhalt *noon* hewe his hire þat he ne haþ it at euen.
B. 5.564   And þanne youre neȝebores next in *none* wise apeire
B. 5.637   And þoruȝ þe help of hem two, hope þow *noon* ooþer,
B. 6.52   Hold wiþ *none* harlotes ne here noȝt hir tales,
B. 6.180   They hadde be [dede and] doluen, ne deme þow *noon* ooþer.
B. 6.305   Ne *noon* halfpeny ale in none wise drynke,
B. 6.305   Ne noon halfpeny ale in *none* wise drynke,
B. 7.40   Men of lawe leest pardon hadde, [leue þow *noon* ooþer],
B. 7.42   And nameliche of Innocentȝ þat *noon* yuel konneþ;
B. 7.117   And do yuel and haue yuel, [and] hope þow *noon* ooþer
B. 8.120   He was long and lene, lik to *noon* ooþer;
B.11.72   That wedde *none* widwes but for to welden hir goodes.
B.11.191 We sholde noȝt clepe oure kyn þerto ne none kynnes riche:
B.11.391 Ech a lif wolde be laklees, leue þow *noon* oþer.
B.12.106 And haþ *noon* hap wiþ his ax his enemy to hitte,
B.12.146 Ne in *none* [beggers] cote [n]as þat barn born,
B.12.196 Ac þouȝ þat þeef hadde heuene he hadde *noon* heiȝ blisse,
B.13.105 'Do *noon* yuel to þyn euencristen, nouȝt by þi power.'
B.13.161 Ne neiþer hete ne hayl ne *noon* helle pouke,
B.13.395 Neiþer masse ne matynes, ne *none* maner siȝtes;
B.13.412 Dooþ *noon* almes[dede]; dred hym of no synne,
B.13.433 Sholde *noon* harlot haue audience in halle n[e] in Chambre

B.14.25   Shal *noon* heraud ne harpour haue a fairer garnement
B.14.253 Hadde þei *no[on* haunt] but of poore men; hir houses stoode
             vntyled.
B.15.175 Coueiteþ he *noon* erþely good, but heueneriche blisse.'
B.17.59   And as naked as a nedle and *noon* help aboute.
B.17.165 Thus it is–nedeþ no man trowe *noon* ooþer
B.17.234 Melteþ to mercy, to merciable and to [*noon*] oþere.
B.17.272 For þat ben vnkynde to hise, hope I *noon* ooþer
B.18.77   That *noon* harlot were so hardy to leyen hond vpon hym.
B.18.169 Loue haþ coueited hire longe; leue I *noon* ooþer
B.20.13   Ne wight *noon* wol ben his boruȝ, ne wed haþ noon to legge;
B.20.13   Ne wight noon wol ben his boruȝ, ne wed haþ *noon* to legge;
B.20.246 Holdeþ yow in vnitee, and haueþ *noon* enuye
C. 1.129   For pruyde th[at] hym pokede his payne hath *non* ende.
C. 1.154   [That myȝte] non Armure hit lette ne none heye walles.
C. 1.154   [That myȝte] non Armure hit lette ne *none* heye walles.
C. 2.178   Ac hakeneys hadde thei *none* bote hakeneys to huyre;
C. 3.85   Ne bouhte *none* burgages, be ȝe ful certayn.
C. 3.204   Ther ne is Cite vnder sonne ne *noon* so ryche reume
C. 3.434   An Auntur hit nuyede me *noen* ende wol y make,
C. 6.127   That y ne mot folowe this folk: my fortune is *non* oþer.
C. 6.298   Ȝe! þe prest þat thy tythe t[a]k[eth], trowe y *non* other,
C. 6.413   Ys *non* so hungry hound in hertford shyre
C. 7.67   Shal *non* ale aftur m[e]te holde me thennes
C. 7.72   Doth *non* Almesdede, drat hym nat of synne,
C. 7.93   Sholde *non* harlote haue audiense in halle ne in chaumbre
C. 7.158   Ac þer was wye *non* so wys þat the way thider couthe
C. 7.196   He withhalt *non* hewe his huyre ouer euen;
C. 7.211   And thenne ȝoure neyhebores nexst in *none* wyse apayre
C. 7.231   In-*none*-manere-elles-nat-for-no-mannes-preeyre.
C. 7.290   And thorw þe help[e] of hem two, hope þou *non* oþer,
C. 8.50   Hoold with *non* harlotes ne here nat here tales
C. 8.135   [We haue] *none* lymes to labory with, lord god we thonketh.'
C. 8.287   Lat hem abyde til the bord be drawe; Ac bere hem *none* crommes
C. 8.327   Ne *noon* halpeny ale in none wyse drynke
C. 8.327   Ne noon halpeny ale in *none* wyse drynke
C. 9.109   Careth they for no colde ne counteth of *non* hete
C. 9.113   Ne *none* muracles maken; Ac many tymes hem happeth
C. 9.139   For they bereth *none* bagges ne boteles vnder clokes,
C. 9.168   Ne weddeth *none* wymmen þat they with deleth,
C. 9.174   Tho þat lyueth thus here lyf, leue ȝe *non* other,
C. 9.291   And do yuele and haue euele and hope thow *non* oþere
C.10.112 Elles knowe y noen þat can in *none* kynneryche.'
C.10.116 He was long and lene, ylyk to *noon* other;
C.10.279 For coueytise of catel in *none* kyne wyse;
C.12.103 We sholde nat clepie knyhtes þerto ne *none* kyne ryche:
C.13.25   And þe gentel Iob; here ioye hath *non* ende.
C.13.45   Ne *non* haiward is hote his wed for to taken.
C.13.63   Wolde *noon* suche assailen hym for such as hym foloweth
C.13.84   As *none* tythes to tythe ne to clothe the nakede
C.13.85   Ne in *none* enquestes to come ne cont[u]max thogh he worche
C.13.209 Vch a lede wolde be lacles, leef thow *non* other.
C.14.51   And hath *non* hap with his ax his enemye to hutte,
C.14.135 Ac thogh th[at] theef hadde heuene he hadde *noen* hey blisse
C.15.112 'Do thy neyhebore *non* harm ne thysulue nother
C.16.93   Hadde they *noen* haunt bote of pore [men; here houses stoed
             vntyled.
C.18.140 Ne *noon* so faythfol fisciscyen, for all þat bysouhte hym
C.18.279 Ne *noen* bern ben oure borw ne bryngen vs [fro his] daunger–
C.19.58   And as naked as an nedle and *noen* helpe abouten.
C.19.200 Melteth to mercy, to merciable and to *non* oþere.
C.19.253 For þat ben vn[k]ynde to hise, hope ȝe *noen* oþer
C.20.172 Loue hath coueyted here longe; leue y *non* oþere
C.20.351 Lucifer for his lesynges, leue y *noen* oþer
C.22.13   Ne wyht *no[n]* wol be his borwe ne wed hath [non] to legge;
C.22.13   Ne wyht no[n] wol be his borwe ne wed hath [*non*] to legge;
C.22.197 Y ne myhte in *none* manere maken hit at here wille
C.22.246 Holdeth ȝow in vnite and haueth *noen* enuye

noot > witen

nor conj *nor conj.* B 2
B. 5.421   Ac in Canoun *nor* in decretals I kan noȝt rede a lyne.
B. 5.631   '*Nor* I', quod an Apeward, 'by auȝt þat I knowe.'

norisseþ v *norishen v.* B 2; C 2 norischeth
B.15.467 For as þe Cow þoruȝ kynde mylk þe calf *norisseþ* til an Oxe,
B.16.33   That it *norisseþ* nyce sightes and [anoþer] tyme wordes
C.12.234 Ouerplente pruyde *norischeth* þer pouerte hit distrueth.
C.18.37   That hit *norischeth* nise s[ih]tus and som tyme wordes

normandie n prop *Normandie n.& adj.* A 1; B 1
A. 3.176   In *normandie* was he nouȝt anoyed for my sake,
B. 3.189   In *Normandie* was he noȝt noyed for my sake,

north n *north n.* B 1; C 2
B.18.164 Out of þe nyppe of þe *North* noȝt ful fer hennes
C. 1.118 Then in þe *north* by many notes, no man leue other.
C.20.167 Out of þe nype of þe *north* nat ful fer hennes

north adj *north adj.* C 1
C.18.66 Then tho that selde haen þe sonne and sitten in þe *North* half;

northerne adj *northerne adj.* C 1
C. 1.115 'Nere hit for *northerne* men anon y wolde ȝow telle

northfolk n prop *Norfolk n.* B 1
B. 5.236 And I kan no frenssh in feiþ but of þe ferþest ende of *Northfolk*.'

nose n *nose n.(1)* A 2; B 4; C 3
A. 4.140 But he be cokewald ycald, kitte of my *nose*.'
A. 5.191 [Þat] alle þat herden þat horn held here *nose* aftir
B. 4.164 But he be knowe for a Cokewold kut of my *nose*.'
B. 5.136 And neuelynge wiþ þe *nose* and his nekke hangyng.
B. 5.343 That alle þat herde þat horn helde hir *nos[e]* after
B.15.203 And to poore peple han pepir in þe *nose*,
C. 4.159 But he be knowe for a cokewold kut of my *nose*.'
C. 6.104 And with a niuilyng[e] *nose*, nippynge his lippes.
C. 6.401 That alle þat herde þ[at] hor[n] helde here *nose* aftur

not > noȝt

notarie n *notarie n.* A 4 notories; B 6 Notarie (1) Notaries (5); C 6 notarie (2) notaries (4)
A. 2.78 Be siȝte of sire symonye & signes of *notories*.
A. 2.91 Ȝe & þe *notories* noye þe peple;
A. 2.110 'And nameliche to þe *notories*, þat hem non fail[e];
A. 2.131 Þ[o] hadde *notories* none; anoyed þei were
B. 2.127 The *Notaries* and ye noyen þe peple.
B. 2.143 Til he hadde siluer for his [seles] and [signes of] *Notaries*.
B. 2.146 And namely to þe *Notaries* þat hem noon faille.
B. 2.167 Tho hadde *Notaries* none; anoyed þei were
B.15.32 Thanne am I Conscience ycalled, goddes clerk and his *Notarie*;
B.20.272 And youre noumbre vnder *Notaries* signe and neiþer mo ne lasse.'
C. 2.142 That ȝe nymeth [and] *notaries* to nauhte gynneth brynge
C. 2.159 Til he hadde seluer for the seel and signes of *notaries*.
C. 2.162 And [name]liche [to] the *notaries* þat [hem] noon fayle.
C. 2.188 And *notaries* [vp]on persones þat permuten ofte
C.16.192 Thenne am y Concience ycald, goddes Clerk and his *notarie*;
C.22.272 And ȝoure nombre vnde[r] *notarie* sygne and noþer mo ne lasse.'

note n *note n.(3)* B 2; C 5 note (3) notes (2)
B.18.408 Thanne pipede pees of Poesie a *note*:
B.18.423 And þanne lutede [loue] in a loud *note*:
C. 1.118 Then in þe north by many *notes*, no man leue other.
C.10.65 To lythen here layes and here louely *notes*.
C.14.180 More þan for his fayre flesch or for his merye *note*.
C.20.451 Thenne piped pees of poe[sie] a *note*:
C.20.466 And thenne lutede loue in a loude *note*:

nother(e > neiþer; notories > notarie; nought nouȝt nouht(e > noȝt

noumbre n *nombre n.* B 9 nombre (2) noumbre (7); C 17 nombre (13) nombres (1) noumbre (3)
B.10.245 Thre [propre] persones, ac noȝt in plurel *nombre*,
B.20.255 And sette [it] at a certain and [at] a siker *nombre*.
B.20.259 And if þei wage men to werre þei write hem in *noumbre*;
B.20.261 [But þei ben nempned in þe *noumbre* of hem þat ben ywaged].
B.20.265 Hir ordre and hir reule wole to han a certein *noumbre*
B.20.269 It is wikked to wage yow; ye wexen out of *noumbre*.
B.20.270 Heuene haþ euene *noumbre* and helle is wiþoute noumbre.
B.20.270 Heuene haþ euene noumbre and helle is wiþoute *noumbre*.
B.20.272 And youre *noumbre* vnder Notaries signe and neiþer mo ne lasse.'
C. 3.337 Acordaunce in kynde, in case and in *nombre*,
C. 3.347 In kynde and in case and in cours of *nombre*.
C. 3.358 In *nombre*, Rotye and aryse and remissioun to haue,
C. 3.365 And withoute ca[s]e to cache [to] and come to bothe *nombres*,
C. 3.372 To acorde in alle kynde and in alle kyn *nombre*,
C. 3.392 Nyme he a *noumbre* of nobles or of shillynges,
C. 3.395 That is vnite, acordaun[c]e in case, in gendre and in *noumbre*,
C. 3.403 And nyme hym into oure *noumbre*, now and eueremore:
C.13.6 And out of *nombre* tho men many mebles hadden.
C.22.255 And sette hit at a serteyne and at a syker *nombre*
C.22.259 And yf thei wage men to werre thei writen hem in *nombre*;
C.22.261 Bote hy ben nempned in þe *nombre* of hem þat been ywaged.
C.22.265 Here ordre and here reule wol to haue a certeyne *nombre*
C.22.269 Hit is wikked to wage ȝow; ȝe wexeth out of *nombre*.
C.22.270 [Heuene haeth euene *nombre* and helle is withoute nombre].
C.22.270 [Heuene haeth euene nombre and helle is withoute *nombre*].
C.22.272 And ȝoure nombre vnde[r] notarie sygne and noþer mo ne lasse.'

noumbrede > nombre

nounpere n *noumpere n.* A 1 noumpere; B 1; C 1 noumper
A. 5.179 And nempnide hym for a *noumpere* þat no debate nere.
B. 5.330 And nempned hym for a *nounpere* þat no debat nere.
C. 6.388 And nempned hym for a *noumper* þat no debat were.

nounpower n *nonpouer n.* B 1; C 1 nownpower
B.17.316 Noght of þe *nounpower* of god, þat he ne is myghtful
C.19.296 And nat of þe *nownpower* of god, þat he ne is ful of myhte

nouþe adv *nouthe adv.* A 2; B 7 nouþe (6) nowþe (1); C 12 nouthe (11) nowthe (1)
A. 7.191 Meschief it makiþ h[y] ben so mek *nouþe*,
A.11.35 Menstralsie & merþe among men is *nouþe*
B. 6.205 Meschief it makeþ þei ben so meke *nouþe*,
B.10.49 Ac [mynstralcie and murþe] amonges men is *nouþe*
B.11.364 Manye selkouþes I seiȝ ben noȝt to seye *nouþe*,
B.13.183 'What!' quod Clergie to Conscience, 'ar ye coueitous *nouþe*
B.17.299 'I pose I hadde synned so and sholde [*nouþe*] deye,
B.19.180 That neuere shul se me in sighte as þow [seest] *nowþe*,
B.19.381 'I care noȝt', quod Conscience, 'þouȝ pride come *nouþe*.
C. 2.15 For to telle of here atyer no tyme haue y *nouthe*.
C. 6.171 'Lady, to thy leue sone loute for me *nouthe*
C. 8.211 Meschef hit maketh they ben so meke *nouthe*
C. 8.298 Wende *nouthe* when thow wol[t] and wel [be thow] euere
C. 9.164 Hit nedeth nat *nouthe* anoon for to preche
C.13.174 Mony selcouthes y seyh aren nat to segge *nouthe*
C.15.114 'Sertes, sire,' thenne saide y, 'hit semeth nou[th]e here,
C.17.108 Gramer, þe grounde of al, bigileth *nouthe* childrene,
C.19.246 And is in helle for al þat, how wol riche *nouthe*
C.19.279 'Y pose y hadde syneged so and sholde *nouthe* deye
C.21.180 Tha[t] neuere shal se me in sihte as thowe seste *nowthe*
C.21.381 'Y care nat,' quod Consience, 'thow pryde come *nouthe*;

now n *nou n.* A 1; B 1; C 1
A. 6.24 Axen aftir hym, er *now* in þis place.'
B. 5.536 Asken after hym er *now* in þis place.'
C. 7.181 Axen aftur hym [er] *now* in þis place.'

now adv *nou adv.* A 31; B 84; C 81 now (80) nowe (1)
A. 1.182 *Now* haue I told þe what treuþe is, þat no tresour is betere,
A. 1.183 I may no lengere lenge; *now* loke þe oure lord.'
A. 2.80 And seide to cyuyle, '*now* sorewe on þi bokes,
A. 2.85 And þou hast gyuen hire to a gilour, *now* god ȝiue þe sorewe!
A. 3.1 *Now* is mede þe maide, & no mo of hem alle,
A. 3.153 Þis is þe lif of þat lady, *now* lord ȝif hire sorewe!
A. 3.170 Why þou wraþþest þe *now* wondir me þinkiþ.
A. 5.52 But *now* wile I meke me & mercy beseke
A. 5.142 Ac I swere *now*, so þ[e I], þat synne shal I lete,
A. 5.146 *Now* begynneþ glotoun for to [go to] shrift,
A. 7.69 Þei arn askapid good auntir, *now* god hem amende.'
A. 7.75 'For [*now*] I am old & hor & haue of myn owene
A. 7.97 *Now* is peris & þe pilgrimes to þe plouȝ faren.
A. 7.152 'I was not wonid to werche,' quaþ wastour, '*now* wile I not begynne,'
A. 7.156 '*Now* be þe peril of my soule!' quaþ peris, 'I shal appeire ȝow alle,'
A. 7.196 [*Now* wolde I] wite, ȝif þou wistest, what were þe beste,
A. 7.198 'Here *now*,' quaþ hungir, '& holde it for a wisdom:
A. 7.261 Wende *now* whanne þi wille is, þat wel be þou euere.'
A. 8.157 *Now* haþ þe pope power pardoun to graunte
A. 9.106 Ellis wot no man þat *now* is o lyue.'
A.10.164 "Þat I man makide *now* it me forþinkeþ".
A.10.171 "Bestis þat *now* shuln banne þe tyme
A.10.181 And [were] marie[d] at meschief as men do *now* here children,
A.10.182 For summe, as I se *now*, soþ for to telle,
A.11.17 Wisdom and wyt *now* is not worþ a risshe
A.11.61 For *now* is iche boy bold, & he be riche,
A.11.87 And *now* comiþ a conyon & wolde cacche of my wittes
A.11.88 What is dowel fro dobet; *now* def mote he worþe,
A.11.211 Ac *now* is religioun a ridere & a rennere [be stretis],
A.12.5 But I se *now* as I seye, as me soþ thinkyȝt,
A.12.110 *Now* alle kenne creatures þat cristene were euere
B. 1.208 *Now* haue I told þee what truþe is, þat no tresor is bettre,
B. 1.209 I may no longer lenge; *now* loke þee oure lord.'
B. 2.40 And *now* worþ þis Mede ymaried [t]o a mansed sherewe!
B. 2.50 *Now* I bikenne þee crist,' quod she, 'and his clene moder,
B. 2.116 And seide [to] Cyuyle, '*now* sorwe [on] þi bokes]
B. 2.121 And þow hast gyuen hire to a gilour, *now* god gyue þee sorwe!
B. 3.1 *NOw* is Mede þe mayde and na mo of hem alle
B. 3.166 This is þe lif of þat lady, *now* lord ȝyue hire sorwe,
B. 3.183 Whi þow wraþest þee *now* wonder me þynkeþ.
B. 5.69 But *now* [wole I] meke me and mercy biseche
B. 5.135 *Now* awakeþ Wraþe wiþ two white eiȝen,
B. 5.142 And *now* is fallen a fruyt þat folk han wel leuere
B. 5.144 And *now* persons han parceyued þat freres parte wiþ hem
B. 5.182 '*Now* repente', quod Repentaunce, 'and reherce neuere
B. 5.226 Ac I swere *now*, so thee ik, þat synne wol I lete

B. 5.260 'Now [but þow repente þe raþer', quod Repentaunce,
B. 5.296 Now bigynneþ Gloton for to go to shrifte
B. 6.77 They ben ascaped good auenture, [now] god hem amende.'
B. 6.83 'For now I am old and hoor and haue of myn owene
B. 6.105 Now is Perkyn and [þe] pilgrimes to þe plow faren.
B. 6.117 'Now by þe peril of my soule!' quod Piers al in pure tene,
B. 6.167 'I was noȝt wont to werche', quod Wastour, 'now wol I noȝt bigynne!'
B. 6.171 'Now by þe peril of my soule!' quod Piers, 'I shal apeire yow alle',
B. 6.210 Now wolde I wite, [if þow wistest], what were þe beste,
B. 6.212 'Here now', quod hunger, 'and hoold it for a wisdom:
B. 6.277 Wend now whan [þi wil is], þat wel be þow euere.'\
B. 7.179 Now haþ þe pope power pardon to graunte
B. 8.116 Ellis [n]oot [no man] þat now is alyue.'
B. 9.133 "That I [man makede now] it me forþynkeþ":
B. 9.140 Beestes þat now ben shul banne þe tyme
B. 9.159 For some, as I se now, sooþ for to telle,
B.10.17 Wisdom and wit now is noȝt worþ a [risshe]
B.10.99 Now haþ ech riche a rule to eten by hymselue
B.10.115 Why sholde we þat now ben for þe werkes of Adam
B.10.135 What is dowel fro dobet, [now] deef mote he worþe,
B.10.279 Ac it semeþ now sooþly, to [siȝte of þe worlde],
B.10.293 And carpen noȝt as þei carpe now, [and] calle yow doumbe houndes:
B.10.311 Ac now is Religion a rydere, a [rennere by stretes],
B.10.393 That for hir werkes and wit now wonyeþ in pyne,
B.10.432 And now ben [swiche] as Souereyns wiþ Seintes in heuene,
B.11.423 Pryde now and presumpcion, parauenture, wol þee appele
B.13.90 For now he haþ dronken so depe he wole deuyne soone
B.13.119 'Now þow, Clergie', quod Conscience, 'carp[e] what is dowel.'
B.14.122 Aungeles þat in helle now ben hadden ioye som tyme
B.14.164 Now, lord, sende hem somer, and som maner ioye,
B.14.321 Now god þat alle good gyueþ graunte his soule reste
B.15.38 Nempnede me þus to name; now þow myȝt chese
B.15.39 How þow coueitest to calle me, now þow knowest [alle] my names.
B.15.44 'That is sooþ', seide he; 'now I se þi wille.
B.15.247 Ac auarice haþ þe keyes now and kepeþ for his kynnesmen
B.15.326 Who parfourneþ þis prophecie of þe peple þat now libbeþ,
B.15.351 And so it fareþ by som folk now; þei han a fair speche,
B.15.354 Boþe lettred and lewed beþ alayed now wiþ synne
B.15.367 Now faileþ þe folk of þe flood and of þe lond boþe,
B.15.372 Grammer, þe ground of al, bigileþ now children,
B.15.377 Go now to any degree, and but if gile be maister,
B.15.491 What pope or prelat now parfourneþ þat crist highte,
B.15.539 And now is rouþe to rede how þe rede noble
B.15.542 And now is werre and wo, and whoso why askeþ:
B.16.1 'NOw faire falle yow', quod I þo, 'for youre faire shewyng!
B.16.53 'Now faire falle yow, Piers', quod I, 'so faire ye discryuen
B.16.67 'Heer now byneþe', quod he þo, 'if I nede hadde,
B.16.122 And Sathan youre Saueour; [youre]self now ye witnessen.
B.17.33 What neded it [now] a newe lawe to [brynge]
B.17.35 And now com[s]eþ Spes and spekeþ, þat [haþ] aspied þe lawe,
B.17.104 And þiself now and swiche as suwen oure werkes.
B.17.140 For god is after an hand; yheer now and knowe it.
B.17.300 And now am sory þat I so þe Seint Spirit agulte,
B.18.54 And [seide], 'if þat þow sotil be [þiselue] now [þow help].
B.18.108 Now youre goode dayes arn doon as daniel prophecied;
B.18.135 And þat is cause of þis clips þat closeþ þe sonne,
B.18.163 'Now soffre we', seide Truþe; 'I se, as me þynkeþ,
B.18.224 Boþe in heuene and in erþe, and now til helle he þenkeþ
B.18.251 And now shal Lucifer leue it, þouȝ hym looþ þynke.
B.18.307 And now I se wher a soule comeþ [silynge hiderward]
B.18.314 And now for þi laste lesynge] ylorn we haue Adam,
B.18.361 Now bigynneþ þi gile ageyn þee to turne
B.18.363 [Þe bitternesse þat þow hast browe, now brouke it þiselue];
B.19.35 Boþe his loore and his lawe; now are þei lowe cherles.
B.19.175 And now art lyuynge and lokynge and laste shalt euere."
B.19.209 Knele now', quod Conscience, 'and if þow kanst synge,
B.19.335 Now is Piers to þe plow; pride it aspide
B.20.178 'Now I se', seide lif, 'þat Surgerie ne phisik
B.20.384 And countrepledeþ me, Conscience; now kynde me avenge,
C. 2.120 And sayde to Symonye, 'now sorwe mot þow haue
C. 2.129 And thow has[t] gyue here as gyle tauhte, now god ȝeue þe sorwe!
C. 2.207 'Now, by crist!' quod þe kyng, 'and y cacche myhte
C. 3.1 Now is mede þe mayde and na mo of mankynde
C. 3.213 Thus lereth this lady thi lond, now lord ȝeue here sorwe!
C. 3.229 Why thow wrathest þe now wonder me thynketh!
C. 3.403 And nyme hym into oure noumbre, now and eueremore:
C. 5.51 Now with hym, now with here: on this wyse y begge
C. 5.51 Now with hym, now with here: on this wyse y begge
C. 6.10 But now wol y meke me and mercy byseche
C. 6.61 'Now god for his goodnesse gyue the grace to amende,'
C. 6.100 Now hit athynketh me in my thouhte þat euere y so wrouhte.
C. 6.164 'Now repente,' quod repentaunce, 'and reherce neuere
C. 6.195 Now, lord, for thy lewete on lechours haue mercy.'

C. 6.253 'Now redily,' quod repentaunce, 'and by þe rode, y leue,
C. 6.286 'Now redily,'quod repentaunce, 'y haue reuthe of thy lyuynge.'
C. 6.350 Now bygynneth glotoun for to go to shryfte
C. 7.292 'ȝe! villam emi,' quod oen, 'and now y moste thedre
C. 8.79 They ben ascaped good aunter, now god hem amende.'
C. 8.92 'For now y am olde and hoer and haue of myn owene
C. 8.112 Now is perkyn and þ[e] pilgrimes to þe plouh faren.
C. 8.164 'I was nat woned to worche,' quod wastour, 'now wol y nat bygynne!'
C. 8.167 'Now, by Crist!' quod [Peres] the [plouhman], 'y shal apayre ȝow alle,'
C. 8.219 Now wolde y wyte, ar thow wendest, what were þe beste;
C. 8.221 For here lyflode, lere me now, sire hunger.'
C. 8.222 'Now herkene,' quod hunger, 'and holde hit for a wysdom:
C. 9.241 Loke now where this lollares and lewede Ermites
C. 9.278 Loke now, for thy lacchesse, what lawe wol the graunte:
C.10.228 Bestes þat now beth shal banne þe tyme
C.10.256 Ac fewe folke now folweth this for thei ȝeue her childurne
C.11.14 Wysdom and wit now is nat worth a carse
C.11.33 Nowe is þe manere at mete when munstrals ben stille
C.11.74 Ac lust no lord now ne lettred man of suche lore to here
C.11.76 And þat loueth lordes now and leten hit a dowel
C.11.77 For is no wit worth now but hit of wynnynge soune.
C.11.220 That for here werkes and wyt wonyeth now in payne,
C.11.268 And now beth this seyntes, by that men saith, and souereynes in heuene,
C.12.26 And now y am pore and penyles at litel pris he sette[th] me.
C.15.97 [For] now he hath dronke so depe a wol deuyne sone
C.15.127 'Now þou, Clergie,' quod Consience, 'carpe what is dowel.'
C.15.298 Angeles þat in helle now ben hadden som tyme ioye
C.15.300 And now he buyth hit bittere; he is a beggare of helle.
C.16.17 Now, lord, sende hem somur som tyme to solace and to ioye
C.16.156 Now god þat al [good] gyueth graunte his soule reste
C.16.200 Nempned me thus to name; now þou myhte chese
C.16.201 How þou coueytest to calle me, now þou knowest al my namus.
C.16.206 'That is soth,' he sayde; 'now y se thy wille.
C.17.25 Y can nat rykene hem riȝt now ne reherse here names
C.17.49 And charite þat chield is now sholde chaufen of hymsulue
C.17.69 Y dar nat carpe of clerkes now þat cristes [tresor] kepe
C.17.72 Prestes on aparayl and on purnele now spene.
C.17.73 Me may now likene lettred men to a loscheborw oþer worse
C.17.95 Wedurwyse shipmen now and oþer witty peple
C.17.104 Now failleth this folk, bothe follwares and shipmen;
C.17.109 For is [now] noon, hoso nymeth hede,
C.17.112 Go now to eny degre and bote gyle be holde a maistre
C.17.200 And now is reuthe to rede how þe rede noble
C.17.204 And now is werre and wo and whoso why asketh:
C.17.251 That contra[r]ryen now cristes law[e] and cristendoem dispisen,
C.18.16 'Now, certes,' y sayde, and siȝte for ioye,
C.18.226 Now go we to godhede: in god, fader of heuene,
C.19.36 And now cometh this sp[es and speketh] that hath aspyed þe lawe,
C.19.280 And now am sory þat y so the seynte spirit agulte,
C.20.54 And saiden, 'yf he sotil be hymsulue now he wol helpe;'
C.20.111 Now ben ȝoure gode dayes ydoen, as daniel of ȝow telleth;
C.20.138 And þat is cause of this clips þat [c]loseth now þe sonne,
C.20.166 'Now soffre we,' saide Treuthe; 'y se, as me thynketh,
C.20.233 Bothe in heuene and in erthe, and now to helle he thenketh
C.20.260 And now shal lucife[r] leue [hit], thogh hym loeth thynk.
C.20.310 And neuere [n]as þeraȝeyne and now wolde bigynne,
C.20.341 And now y se where his soule cometh sylinge hid[er]ward
C.20.348 And now for a later lesynge] þat thow lowe til Eue
C.20.396 So þat [thorw] gyle was gete thorw grace is now ywonne
C.20.399 And now bygynneth thy gyle agayne the to turne
C.20.401 The bitternesse þat thow hast browe, now brouk hit thysulue;
C.21.35 Bothe his lore and his lawe; now are they lowe cherles.
C.21.175 And now art lyuynge and lokynge and laste shalt euere."
C.21.209 Knele now,' quod Consience, 'and yf thow canst synge,
C.21.335 Now is [Peres] the [plouh]; Pryde hit aspiede
C.22.178 'Now y see,' saide lyf, ' that surgerie ne fysyke
C.22.384 And countrepledeth me, Consience; now kynde me avenge

nowadaies adv nouadaies adv. A 1 nowadayes; B 2 nowadaies (1) nowadayes (1); C 1 nowadayes
A.11.37 Glotonye & grete oþis, þise arn games nowadayes.
B.10.51 Glotonye and grete oþes, þis[e arn games nowadaies].
B.10.79 [For god is def nowadayes and deyneþ [noȝt vs to here],
C.11.59 For god is deef nowadayes and deyneth [nat vs] to here

nowher adv nowher adv. A 1 nowhere; B 1; C 1 nawher
A. 2.179 He was nowhere welcome for his many talis,
B. 2.220 He was nowher welcome for his manye tales,
C. 2.230 He was nawher welcome for his many tales,

nownpower > nounpower; nowþe > nouþe

noy n *noi n.* A 1 noye; B 1
A.11.47 Is non to nymen hym In ne his [*noye*] amende,
B.10.61 Is noon to nyme hym [in, ne] his [*n]oy* amende,

noyen v *noien v.* A 5 noye (1) noiȝe (1) noiȝed (1) noiȝede (1) noiȝide (1);
 B 5 noyed (3) noyen (2); C 3 niyed (1) nuye (1) nuyede (1)
A. 2.16 'Þat is mede þe maide, haþ *noiȝede* me ful ofte,
A. 2.91 Ȝe & þe notories *noye* þe peple;
A. 3.259 An aunter it [*noiȝide* me non] ende wile I make.
A. 5.73 I haue a neiȝebour neiȝ me, I haue *noiȝed* hym ofte,
A. 6.61 Ne none of here seruauntis, þat *noiȝe* hem miȝte;
B. 2.20 'That is Mede þe mayde, haþ *noyed* me ful ofte,
B. 2.127 The Notaries and ye *noyen* þe peple.
B. 3.189 In Normandie was he noȝt *noyed* for my sake,
B. 3.281 On auenture it *noyed* m[e] noon ende wol I make,
B. 5.574 Ne-noon-of-hire-seruauntȝ-þat-*noyen*-hem-myȝte;
C. 2.19 'That is mede þe mayde, hath *niyed* me ful ofte
C. 3.434 An Auntur hit *nuyede* me noen ende wol y make,
C. 7.221 Ne-none-of-here-seruauntes-þat-*nuye*-hem-myhte;

null(e > willen

O

o > on,oon

obedience n *obedience n.* B 2; C 4
B.12.37   And hold þee vnder *obedience* þat heigh wey is to heuene.
B.13.285 Religion saunȝ rule [and] resonable *obedience*;
C. 9.221 Vnder *obedience* to be and buxum to þe lawe;
C. 9.223 And vnder *obedience* be by dayes and by nyhtes;
C. 9.236 Vnder this *obedience* ar we vchone
C. 9.242 Breke þis *obedience* þat beth so fer fram chirche.

obediencer n *obediencer n.* C 1
C. 5.91 Buthe be *obediencer* to prior or to mynistre.'

obedient adj *obedient adj.* A 1; C 1
A.11.191 *Obedient* as breþeren & sustren to oþere,
C. 5.147 The reule of alle religious rihtful and *obedient*:

ocupie v *occupien v.* B 2 ocupie (1) ocupied (1); C 2 occuepied (1) ocupien (1)
B. 5.402 I am *occupied* eche day, halyday and ooþer,
B.16.196 To *ocupie* hym here til issue were spronge,
C. 7.18   Y am *occupied* vch day, haliday and oþere,
C.18.205 To *ocupien* hym here til issue were spronge

oelde > old; oen(- > oon(-; oest(e > hoost

of adv *of adv.* A 3; B 4; C 6
A. 2.163 And ge[rd]iþ *of* giles hed; let hym go no ferþere;
A. 4.140 But he be cokewald ycald, kitte *of* my nose.'
A. 5.168 Clement þe cobeler cast *of* his cloke
B. 2.202 And girdeþ *of* Gyles heed; lat hym go no ferþer;
B. 4.164 But he be knowe for a Cokewold kut *of* my nose.'
B. 5.319 Clement þe Cobelere caste *of* his cloke
B.14.191 And putten *of* so þe pouke, and preuen vs vnder borwe.
C. 2.216 And gurdeth *of* gyles heed; lat hym goo no wyddore
C. 4.159 But he be knowe for a cokewold kut *of* my nose.'
C. 6.13   And shryue the sharpeliche and shak *of* alle pruyde.'
C. 6.149 Tyl ayþer clepede oþer "hore!" and *o[f]* with the clothes
C. 6.376 Clement þe Coblere cast *of* his cloke
C.16.122 Al þat may potte *of* pruyde in place þer he regneth;

of prep *of prep.* &> out_of A 462; B 1461; C 1443
A.Pr.3   In abite as an Ermyte, vnholy *of* werkis,
A.Pr.6   Me befel a ferly, *of* fairie me þouȝte:
A.Pr.16   Wiþ depe dikes & derke & dredful *of* siȝt.
A.Pr.17   A fair feld ful *of* folk fand I þere betwene
A.Pr.18   *Of* alle maner of men, þe mene & þe riche,
A.Pr.18   Of alle maner *of* men, þe mene & þe riche,
A.Pr.24   In cuntenaunce *of* cloþing comen disgisid.
A.Pr.26   Al for loue *of* oure lord lyuede wel streite
A.Pr.38   Þat poule prechiþ *of* hem I dar not proue it here:
A.Pr.56   Prechinge þe peple for profit *of* þe wombe;
A.Pr.58   For coueitise *of* copis construide it as þei wolde.
A.Pr.59   Manye *of* þise maistris may cloþe hem at lyking
A.Pr.68   *Of* falsnesse of fastyng & of auowes broken.
A.Pr.68   Of falsnesse *of* fastyng & of auowes broken.
A.Pr.68   Of falsnesse of fastyng & *of* auowes broken.
A.Pr.79   Þat þe pore peple *of* þe parissh shulde haue ȝif þei ne were.
A.Pr.84   Þere houide an hundrit in houuis *of* silk,
A.Pr.87   A[c] nouȝt for loue *of* oure lord vnlose here lippes ones.
A.Pr.89   Þanne gete a mom *of* here mouþ til mony be shewid.
A.Pr.90   I sauȝ bisshopis bolde & bacheleris *of* deuyn
A.Pr.91   Become clerkis *of* acountis þe king for to serue;
A.Pr.94   Ben ylope to lundoun be leue *of* hire bisshop,
A.Pr.95   And ben clerkis *of* þe kinges bench to cuntre to shende.
A.Pr.99   Wollene websteris and weueris *of* lynen,
A.Pr.107 'W[hit] wyn *of* osay, & wyn of gascoyne,
A.Pr.107 'W[hit] wyn of osay, & wyn *of* gascoyne,
A.Pr.108 *Of* þe ryn & of þe rochel, þe rost to defie!'
A.Pr.108 Of þe ryn & *of* þe rochel, þe rost to defie!'
A. 1.2   And ek þe feld ful *of* folk I shal ȝow faire shewe.
A. 1.3   A louely lady *of* lire in lynene ycloþid
A. 1.7   Þe moste partie *of* þis peple þat passiþ on þis erþe,
A. 1.9   *Of* oþer heuene þanne here holde þei no tale.'
A. 1.10   I was aferd *of* hire face þeiȝ heo fair were,
A. 1.14   For he is fadir *of* feiþ & fourmide ȝow alle
A. 1.18   *Of* [woll]ene, of [lyn]ene, of liflode at nede
A. 1.18   Of [woll]ene, *of* [lyn]ene, of liflode at nede
A. 1.18   Of [woll]ene, of [lyn]ene, *of* liflode at nede
A. 1.20   And comaundite *of* his curteisie in comoun þre þinges;
A. 1.24   Þat oþer is mete at meel for myseise *of* þiselue;
A. 1.27   For loth, in his lyf dayes, for lykyng *of* drink
A. 1.47   And he askide *of* hem of whom spak þe lettre,
A. 1.47   And he askide of hem *of* whom spak þe lettre,
A. 1.54   And tutour *of* ȝour tresour, & take it ȝow at nede;
A. 1.57   'Þe dungeon in þe dale þat dredful is *of* siȝt:
A. 1.59   'Þ[at] is þe castel *of* care; who[so] comiþ þereinne
A. 1.62   Fadir *of* falshed, he foundi[de] it hymselue.
A. 1.67   He is lettere *of* loue, leiȝeþ hem alle;
A. 1.70   Þat suche wise wordis *of* holy writ shewide,
A. 1.77   Þanne I knelide on my knes & criȝide hire *of* grace;
A. 1.86   For whoso is trewe *of* his tunge, telliþ non oþer,
A. 1.101 And neuere leue h[e]m for loue ne lacching *of* ȝeftis;
A. 1.110 And was þe louelokest [*of* siȝt] aftir oure lord
A. 1.111 Til he brak buxumnesse þoruȝ bost *of* hymseluen.
A. 1.115 A[c] lucifer lowest liþ *of* hem alle;
A. 1.123 Forþi I seye as I seide er, be siȝte *of* þise textis:
A. 1.137 And ek þe plante *of* pes; preche it in þin harpe
A. 1.150 Þeiȝ ȝe ben miȝty to mote beþ mek *of* ȝour werkis;
A. 1.153 For þ[ei]ȝ ȝe be trewe *of* ȝoure tunge & treweliche wynne,
A. 1.156 *Of* such good as god sent goodlyche parteþ,
A. 1.158 Þanne malkyn *of* hire maidenhed þat no man desiriþ.
A. 1.169 Ȝe curatours þat kepe ȝow clene *of* ȝour body,
A. 1.172 Þ[at] is no treuþe *of* trinite but treccherie of helle,
A. 1.172 Þ[at] is no treuþe of trinite but treccherie *of* helle,
A. 1.176 Þat is þe lok *of* loue þat letiþ out my grace
A. 1.180 Forþi I seiȝe as I seide er be siȝte *of* þise tixtes:
A. 2.1   Ȝet knelide I on my knes & criȝede hire *of* grace,
A. 2.2   And seide, 'mercy madame, for marie loue *of* heuene
A. 2.8   And was war *of* a womman wondirliche cloþide,
A. 2.12   *Of* þe pureste perreiȝe þat prince werde euere;
A. 2.21   I auȝte ben hiȝere þanne heo for I com *of* a betere.
A. 2.22   Tomorewe worþ þe mariage mad *of* mede & of fals;
A. 2.22   Tomorewe worþ þe mariage mad of mede & *of* fals;
A. 2.39   Þat iche feld nas ful *of* folk al aboute.
A. 2.42   And ten þousand *of* tentis teldit beside
A. 2.43   *Of* kniȝtes of cuntr[e], of comeres aboute,
A. 2.43   Of kniȝtes *of* cuntr[e], of comeres aboute,
A. 2.43   Of kniȝtes of cuntr[e], *of* comeres aboute,
A. 2.45   For lerid, for lewid, for laboureris *of* þropis,
A. 2.60   Wiþ þe Erldom *of* enuye for euere to laste,
A. 2.61   Wiþ alle þe lordsshipe *of* leccherie in lengþe & in brede,
A. 2.62   Wiþ þe kingdom *of* coueitise I croune hem togidere;
A. 2.63   And al þe Ile *of* vsurie, & auarice þe faste,
A. 2.65   Wiþ alle þe delites *of* lust þe deuil for to serue,
A. 2.66   In al þe signiure *of* slouþe I se[se] hem togidere;
A. 2.68   Wiþ alle þe purtenaunce *of* purcatorie into þe pyne of helle;
A. 2.68   Wiþ alle þe purtenaunce of purcatorie into þe pyne *of* helle;
A. 2.72   In witnesse *of* whiche þing wrong was þe furste,
A. 2.74   Bette þe bedel *of* bukyngham shire,
A. 2.75   Randolf þe reue *of* rutelondis sokne,
A. 2.77   In þe date *of* þe deuil þe dede is asselid
A. 2.78   Be siȝte *of* sire symonye & signes of notories.
A. 2.78   Be siȝte of sire symonye & signes *of* notories.
A. 2.83   For mede is molere *of* [m]endis engendrit
A. 2.94   Þat fals is a faitour [and] feyntles *of* werkis,
A. 2.95   [And] as a bastard yborn *of* belsab[ubb]is kynde;
A. 2.96   And mede is a mulere, [a maiden *of* gode];
A. 2.102 Ȝet be war *of* þe weddyng for witty is treuþe.
A. 2.103 For consience is *of* his counseil & knowiþ ȝow ichone,
A. 2.117 Til mede be þi weddit wyf þoruȝ wyt *of* vs alle,
A. 2.127 Þanne fette fauel folis *of* þe beste,
A. 2.142 And fetten oure vitailes [*of*] fornicatouris;
A. 2.143 And makiþ *of* lyere a lang carte to leden al þis oþere,
A. 2.148 *Of* many maner of m[e]n þat on þis molde libbeþ.
A. 2.148 Of many maner *of* m[e]n þat on þis molde libbeþ.

A. 2.155	Fals oþer fauel oþer any *of* his feris,
A. 2.156	I wolde be wroken *of* þise wrecchis þat werchen so ille,
A. 2.158	Shal neuere man *of* þis molde meynprise þe [l]este,
A. 2.178	Lurkynge þoruȝ lanes, toluggid *of* manye.
A. 2.192	F[or] knowing *of* comeris copide hym as a Frere.
A. 3.1	Now is mede þe maide, & no mo *of* hem alle,
A. 3.6	What man *of* þis world þat hire were leuist;
A. 3.20	*Of* here grete goodnesse, & [g]af hem ichone
A. 3.21	Coupis *of* clene gold [and] pecis *of* siluer,
A. 3.21	Coupis *of* clene gold [and] pecis *of* siluer,
A. 3.23	Þe leste man *of* here mayne a mutoun of gold.
A. 3.23	Þe leste man *of* here mayne a mutoun of gold.
A. 3.39	I shal assoile þe myself for a sem *of* whete,
A. 3.43	And shrof hire *of* hire shrewidnesse shameles I trowe;
A. 3.52	Þat iche segge shal se I am sistir *of* ȝoure hous.'
A. 3.61	To writen in wyndowis *of* ȝoure wel dedis,
A. 3.69	For þise arn men *of* þise molde þat most harm werchiþ
A. 3.73	*Of* þat þe pore peple shulde putte in here wombe.
A. 3.77	*Of* alle suche selleris siluer to take,
A. 3.78	Or presauntis wiþoute panis as pecis *of* siluer,
A. 3.88	Þe hous and þe hom[e] *of* hem þat desiren
A. 3.108	For heo is fayn *of* þi Felasshipe, for to be þi make.'
A. 3.111	She is freel *of* hire feiþ, fikel of hire speche;
A. 3.111	She is freel *of* hire feiþ, fikel of hire speche;
A. 3.113	In trist *of* hire tresour she teniþ [wel] manye;
A. 3.120	She is tykil *of* hire tail, talewys of hire tunge,
A. 3.120	She is tykil *of* hire tail, talewys of hire tunge,
A. 3.124	Shirreues *of* shires were shent ȝif heo ne were.
A. 3.153	Þis is þe lif *of* þat lady, now lord ȝif hire sorewe!
A. 3.156	Such a maister is mede among men *of* goode.'
A. 3.178	Crope into a caban for cold *of* þi nailes;
A. 3.181	And hastide[st] þe homward for hunger *of* þi wombe.
A. 3.188	Hadde I be march[al] *of* his men, be marie of heuene,
A. 3.188	Hadde I be march[al] *of* his men, be marie of heuene,
A. 3.190	He shulde haue be lord *of* þat lond in lengþe & in brede,
A. 3.191	And ek king *of* þat kiþ his kyn for to helpe,
A. 3.192	Þe leste brol *of* his blood a barouns pere.
A. 3.205	Takiþ mede of here maistris as þei mowe accorde;
A. 3.206	Beggeris for here bidding biddiþ *of* men mede;
A. 3.208	Þe king haþ [m]ede *of* his men to make pes in londis;
A. 3.209	Men þat [kenne] clerkis crauen *of* h[e]m mede;
A. 3.218	'Þere arn to maner *of* medis, my lord, þe ȝoure leue.
A. 3.219	Þat on god *of* his grace gyueþ in his blisse
A. 3.222	Tak no mede, my lord, *of* [men] þat ben trewe;
A. 3.223	Loue hem & le[n]e hem for oure lordis loue *of* heuene;
A. 3.234	Þat laboureris & louȝ folk taken *of* here maistris
A. 3.235	Is no maner *of* mede but a mesurable hire;
A. 3.241	Þat agag *of* amaleg & [al] his peple aftir
A. 3.249	For any mylionis *of* mone murdre hem ichone;
A. 3.258	Þe culorum *of* þis [cas] kepe I not to shewe;
A. 3.272	Mede *of* mysdoeris makiþ hem so riche
A. 3.276	And make *of* lawe a labourer, such loue shal arise.'
A. 4.10	*Of* mede & of mo oþere, what man shal hire wedde,
A. 4.10	*Of* mede & of mo oþere, what man shal hire wedde,
A. 4.13	'I am fayn *of* þat foreward,' seiþ þe frek þanne,
A. 4.17	And calde catoun his knaue, curteis *of* speche:
A. 4.26	In cheker & in chauncerie, to be dischargid *of* þinges,
A. 4.37	And margerete *of* hire maydenhed maugre hire chekis.
A. 4.39	I dar not for fer *of* hym fiȝte ne chide.
A. 4.40	He borewide *of* me bayard & brouȝte him neuere aȝen.
A. 4.51	And seide, 'hadde I loue *of* my lord þe king, litel wolde I recche
A. 4.61	For *of* hise penys he proffride handy dandy to paye.
A. 4.82	And profride pees a presaunt al *of* purid gold;
A. 4.83	'Haue þis *of* me, man,' quaþ heo, 'to amende þi skaþe,
A. 4.105	Til clerkis & kniȝtes be curteis *of* here mouþes,
A. 4.111	And alle rome renneris, for robberis *of* beȝonde,
A. 4.112	Bere no siluer ouer se þat signe *of* king shewi[þ],
A. 4.114	Vpe forfaiture *of* þat fe, who fynt hym [at douere],
A. 4.123	Be vnpunisshit at my power for peril *of* my soule,
A. 4.137	Loue let *of* hire liȝt & louȝ hire to scorne,
A. 4.139	'Whoso wilneþ to wyue for welþe *of* hire godis,
A. 4.152	Be my counseil ycome *of* clerkes and Erlis.
A. 4.156	So consience be *of* ȝour counseil, kepe I no betere.'
A. 5.3	Þanne wakide I *of* my wynkyng, & wo was wiþalle
A. 5.6	Þat I ne miȝte ferþere a fote for defaute *of* slepyng.
A. 5.10	[For I sauȝ] þe feld ful *of* folk þat I before tolde],
A. 5.19	And turnide vpward here tail in toknyng *of* drede
A. 5.21	*Of* þis mater I miȝte mamele wel longe,
A. 5.39	And be steward *of* ȝoure stede til ȝe be stewid betere.
A. 5.53	*Of* alle þat I haue had enuye in myn herte.'
A. 5.63	*Of* a Freris frokke were þe foresleuys.
A. 5.93	*Of* his lesing I lauȝe; [it liȝtiþ] myn herte,
A. 5.94	Ac *of* his wynnyng I wepe and weile þe tyme.

A. 5.99	[Þat] al my brest bolniþ for bittir *of* my galle.
A. 5.111	In a torn tabbard *of* twelue wynter age,
A. 5.121	Ne hadde [þe] grace *of* gile gon among my ware
A. 5.145	And bidde þe rode *of* bromholm bringe me out of dette.'
A. 5.149	And heo askide *of* hym whidirward he wolde.
A. 5.155	I haue pepir, & p[ye]nye, & a pound *of* garlek,
A. 5.156	And a [ferþingworþ] *of* [fenelsed] for fastyng dayes.'
A. 5.160	[T]ymme þe tynkere & tweyne *of* his knaues,
A. 5.162	Claris *of* cokkislane & þe clerk of þe chirche,
A. 5.162	Claris *of* cokkislane & þe clerk of þe chirche,
A. 5.164	A ribibour, a ratoner, & a rakiere *of* chepe,
A. 5.166	*Of* vpholderis an hep, erliche be þe morewe,
A. 5.173	Whoso hadde þe hood shulde haue amendis *of* þe cloke.
A. 5.192	And wisshide it hadde be wexid wiþ a wysp *of* firsen.
A. 5.199	Þat wiþ al þe wo *of* þe world his wyf & his wenche
A. 5.203	Þanne wakide he *of* his wynkyng & wypide his eiȝen;
A. 5.205	His wyf [wit]ide hym þanne *of* wykkidnesse & synne,
A. 5.218	And beet þiself on þe brest & bidde hym *of* grace,
A. 5.231	And wiþ þe residue & þe remenaunt, be þe roode *of* chestre,
A. 5.237	Þo dismas my broþer besouȝte þe *of* grace,
A. 5.245	Ac what befel *of* þis feloun I can not faire shewe;
A. 5.251	[A] þousand *of* men þ[o þ]rong[en] togideris,
A. 6.8	An hundrit *of* ampollis on his hat seten,
A. 6.9	Signes *of* synay, & shilles of galis,
A. 6.9	Signes *of* synay, & shilles of galis,
A. 6.10	And many crouch [o]n his cloke, & keiȝes *of* rome,
A. 6.37	[I] haue myn here *of* hym [wel] & oþerwhile more;
A. 6.40	He is as louȝ as a lomb & loueliche *of* speche.
A. 6.44	'Nay, be þe peril *of* my soule!' quaþ piers & gan to swere,
A. 6.53	And so bo[wiþ] forþ be a [brok], be buxum *of* speche,
A. 6.58	A[nd] nameliche an ydel þe name *of* god almiȝt;
A. 6.61	Ne none *of* here seruauntis, þat noiȝe hem miȝte;
A. 6.69	Loke þou plukke no plant[e] þere for peril *of* þi soule.
A. 6.73	Þe mot is *of* mercy þe Maner al aboute;
A. 6.74	And alle þe wallis ben *of* wyt to holde wil þeroute;
A. 6.75	Þe kirnelis ben *of* cristendom þat kynde to saue,
A. 6.78	Wiþ no led but [wiþ] loue & louȝnesse, as breþeren *of* o wombe.
A. 6.95	Ac be war þanne *of* wraþþe, þat wykkide shrewe;
A. 6.98	Þe boldnesse *of* þi bienfait makiþ þe blynd þanne,
A. 6.112	But ȝif ȝe be sibbe to summe *of* þis seuene
A. 6.113	It is wel hard, be myn hed, any *of* ȝow alle,
A. 6.122	And þoruȝ þe helpe *of* hem [two], hope þou non oþer,
A. 7.9	'Summe shal sewe þe sak for shedyng *of* þe whete;
A. 7.17	As longe as I lyue for þe lordis loue *of* heuene.
A. 7.21	And alle maner *of* men þat þe mete libbiþ,
A. 7.45	And þat þou be trewe of [þi] tunge, & talis þou hate;
A. 7.46	But it be *of* wysdom or of wyt þi werkmen to chaste;
A. 7.46	But it be of wysdom or *of* wyt þi werkmen to chaste;
A. 7.55	Hise cokeris & his cuffis for cold *of* his nailes,
A. 7.56	And heng his hoper at his hals in stede *of* a scrippe:
A. 7.57	'A busshel *of* breed corn br[yng m]e þereinne,
A. 7.64	Saue Iakke þe Iugelour & Ionete *of* þe stewis,
A. 7.68	For holy chirche is holden *of* hem no tiþes to asken,
A. 7.75	'For [now] I am old & haue *of* myn owene
A. 7.84	For *of* my corn & my catel [he] crauide þe tiþ[e];
A. 7.85	[I] payede hym prestly for peril *of* my soule;
A. 7.88	My wyf shal haue *of* þat I wan wiþ treuþe, & namore,
A. 7.92	And wiþ þe residue & þe remenaunt, be þe rode *of* chestre,
A. 7.109	'Be þe prince *of* paradis!' quaþ piers þo in wraþþe,
A. 7.118	Þat god *of* his grace ȝour greyn multiplie,
A. 7.119	And ȝelde ȝow *of* ȝour almesse þat ȝe ȝiuen vs here,
A. 7.129	Or ȝe shuln ete barly bred & *of* þe bro[k] drynke;
A. 7.132	Til god *of* his grace gare h[e]m to arise.
A. 7.134	Shuln haue *of* myn almesse al þe while I libbe,
A. 7.144	*Of* þ[i] flour, and þi flessh fecche whanne vs likeþ,
A. 7.153	And let liȝt *of* þe lawe & lesse of þe kniȝt,
A. 7.153	And let liȝt of þe lawe & lesse *of* þe kniȝt,
A. 7.156	'Now be þe peril *of* my soule!' quaþ peris, 'I shal appeire ȝow alle,'
A. 7.167	And bledde into þe bodyward a bolle ful *of* growel,
A. 7.174	For a potel *of* pe[s]is þat peris hadde mad
A. 7.175	[A]n he[p] *of* heremites henten hem spadis,
A. 7.183	Al for coueitise *of* his corn to [cacche] awey hungir.
A. 7.189	*Of* beggeris & bidderis what best is to done.
A. 7.192	And for defaute *of* foode þus faste hy werchiþ.
A. 7.195	And helpe hem *of* alle þing [aftir] hem nedi[þ].
A. 7.201	And [a]baue hem wiþ b[e]nes for bollnyng *of* here wombe,
A. 7.206	Counforte hem wiþ þi catel for cristis loue *of* heuene;
A. 7.207	Loue hem & lene hem & so þe lawe *of* kynde wolde.
A. 7.208	And alle maner *of* men þat þou miȝte aspien,
A. 7.216	Go to genesis þe geaunt, engendrour *of* vs alle:
A. 7.224	He hadde maugre *of* his maister eueremore aftir,
A. 7.232	Oþer wiþ teching, oþer telling, or trauaillyng *of* hondis,
A. 7.234	The sauter seiþ in þe salme *of* Beati omnes:

A. 7.235	He þat get his fode here wiþ trauaile *of* his hondis,
A. 7.238	Eny l[e]f *of* lechecraft lere it me, my dere,
A. 7.239	For summe *of* my seruauntis ben seke oþer while;
A. 7.240	*Of* alle þe wyke [hy] werkiþ nou3t, so here wombe akiþ.'
A. 7.246	And sende þe *of* his saus to sauoure þi lippes,
A. 7.250	L[o]ue hym nou3t, for he is a lecchour & likerous *of* tunge,
A. 7.254	And ek his cloke [*of*] calabre & þe knoppis of gold,
A. 7.254	And ek his cloke [of] calabre & þe knoppis *of* gold,
A. 7.267	A lof *of* benis & bren ybake for my children;
A. 7.288	But coket, or clermatyn, or *of* clene whete,
A. 7.290	But *of* þe beste & þe brunneste þat breusteris sellen.
A. 7.293	May no penyale hem paye, ne no pece *of* bacoun,
A. 7.295	And chaud, & pluys chaud, for chillyng *of* h[ere] mawe.
A. 8.16	And prechen here personis þe periles *of* synne,
A. 8.19	At þe day *of* dom at here deis to sitten.
A. 8.33	Fynde suche here foode for oure lordis loue *of* heuene,
A. 8.39	And before þe face *of* my fadir fourme 3oure setis,
A. 8.45	Men *of* lawe hadde lest for le[ttr]id þei ben alle;
A. 8.47	*Of* princes & prelatis here pencioun shulde arise,
A. 8.48	And *of* no pore peple no peny[worþ] to take.
A. 8.60	Þat any mede *of* mene men for motyng resceyueþ.
A. 8.79	Þanne *of* alle oþer maner men þat on þis molde wandriþ.
A. 8.82	Ac olde men & hore þat helpeles ben *of* strengþe,
A. 8.87	For loue *of* here lou3 herte oure lord haþ hem grauntid
A. 8.94	And was writen ri3t þus in witnesse *of* treuþe.
A. 8.104	I shal cesse *of* my sowyng,' quaþ peris, '& swynke not so harde,
A. 8.106	*Of* preyours & of penaunce my plou3 shal ben hereaftir,
A. 8.106	Of preyours & *of* penaunce my plou3 shal ben hereaftir,
A. 8.136	How Dani[el] deui[n]ide þe drem[is] *of* a king
A. 8.155	Dowel at þe day *of* dome is digneliche vndirfongen;
A. 8.156	He passiþ al þe pardoun [*of*] seint petris chirche.
A. 8.159	Þis is [a] l[e]f *of* oure beleue, as lettrid men vs [tech]iþ:
A. 8.166	Vpon trist *of* 3our tresour trienalis to haue
A. 8.169	Þat han þe [welþe *of*] þis world, & wise men ben holden.
A. 8.175	A pokeful *of* pardoun þere, ne þe prouincialis lettres,
A. 8.184	Þat at þe day *of* dome we dede as he hi3te.
A. 9.3	And fraynide ful ofte *of* folk þat I mette
A. 9.5	And what man he mi3te be *of* many man I askide.
A. 9.9	Maistris *of* þe menours, men of gret wyt.
A. 9.9	Maistris of þe menours, men *of* gret wyt.
A. 9.26	Þe wynd, & þe watir, & þe waggyng *of* þe boot,
A. 9.32	Þere were þe manis lif lost for lacchesse *of* hymselue.
A. 9.35	Þe goodis *of* þis ground be lik þe grete wawes,
A. 9.37	Þe boot is lik[nid] to þe body þat britel is *of* kynde,
A. 9.55	Blisse *of* þe briddis made me abide,
A. 9.58	Blisse *of* þ[e] briddis brou3te me a slepe;
A. 9.71	Whoso is mek *of* his mouþ, mylde of his speche,
A. 9.71	Whoso is mek of his mouþ, mylde *of* his speche,
A. 9.72	Trewe *of* his tunge & of his two handis,
A. 9.72	Trewe of his tunge & *of* his two handis,
A. 9.74	Trusty *of* his tailende, takiþ but his owene,
A. 9.77	He is as lou3 as a lomb, louelich *of* speche,
A. 9.78	Whiles he haþ ou3t *of* his owene he helpiþ þere nede is;
A. 9.99	And rewele þe reaum be red *of* hem alle,
A. 9.112	Sad *of* his semblaunt & of a softe speche,
A. 9.112	Sad of his semblaunt & *of* a softe speche,
A. 10.2	In a castel þat kynde made *of* foure skenis þinges.
A. 10.3	*Of* erþe & eir it is mad, medlit togideris,
A. 10.8	A proud prikere *of* Fraunce, Princeps huius mundi,
A. 10.11	And haþ don hire to sire dowel, duk *of* þise marchis.
A. 10.15	Beþ maistris *of* þis maner þis maide to kepe.
A. 10.16	Ac þe cunstable *of* þe castel, þat kepiþ hem alle,
A. 10.20	Sire werche wel wiþ þin hond, [a] wi3t man *of* strengþe,
A. 10.27	'Kynde,' quaþ he, 'is creatour *of* alle kenis bestis,
A. 10.28	Fadir & fourmour, þe ferste *of* alle þing.
A. 10.30	Þe lord of lif & *of* li[3t], of lisse & of peyne.
A. 10.30	Þe lord of lif & of li[3t], of lisse & *of* peyne.
A. 10.30	Þe lord *of* lif & of li[3t], of lisse & of peyne.
A. 10.30	Þe lord of lif & of li[3t], *of* lisse & of peyne.
A. 10.32	Ac man is hym most lik *of* mark & of shap.
A. 10.32	Ac man is hym most lik of mark & *of* shap.
A. 10.36	3af hym gost *of* his godhed & grauntide hym blisse.
A. 10.41	Þoru3 mi3t *of* þe maieste man was ymakid:
A. 10.43	For loue *of* þat lady þat lif is ynempnid.
A. 10.45	Ac in þe herte is hire hom hei3est *of* alle.
A. 10.46	Heo is lyf & ledere, a lemman *of* heuene.
A. 10.48	Aftir þe grace *of* god [þe grettest is Inwyt].
A. 10.53	*Of* good speche & [going] he is þe begynnere;
A. 10.63	Ouer suche maner *of* men mi3t in here soulis.
A. 10.79	And þat is dred *of* god, dowel it makiþ.
A. 10.80	It is begynnyng *of* goodnesse god for to douten.
A. 10.83	Þat he makiþ men meke & mylde *of* here speche,
A. 10.85	Þanne is dobet to ben ywar for betyng *of* þe 3arde,

A. 10.91	Be counseil *of* consience, accordyng holy chirche,
A. 10.96	Whatso men worden *of* þe wraþþe þe neuere;
A. 10.97	Catoun counseilliþ–tak kep *of* his teching–
A. 10.100	And be glad *of* þe grace þat god haþ Isent þe.
A. 10.121	And þus *of* dred & h[is] dede dobest arisiþ,
A. 10.122	Which is þe flour & þe fruyt fostrid *of* boþe.
A. 10.128	Among men *of* þis molde þat mek ben & kynde.
A. 10.129	For loue *of* here lou3nesse oure lord 3iueþ hem grace
A. 10.134	Þei be þe riccheste *of* reaumes & þe rote of dowel.
A. 10.134	Þei be þe riccheste of reaumes & þe rote *of* dowel.
A. 10.135	For *of* here kynde þei comen þat confessours ben nempnid,
A. 10.138	Barouns & burgeis, *of* bondemen of tounes.
A. 10.142	A3ens þe hest *of* hym þat hem of nou3t made,
A. 10.142	A3ens þe hest of hym þat hem *of* nou3t made,
A. 10.151	Alle þat comen *of* þat caym crist hatid aftir,
A. 10.152	And manye mylions mo *of* men & of wommen
A. 10.152	And manye mylions mo of men & *of* wommen
A. 10.153	[Þat] *of* seth & his sistir siþþe forþ come
A. 10.154	For þei mariede hem wiþ curside men *of* caymes kyn.
A. 10.155	For alle þat comen *of* þat caym acursid þei were,
A. 10.166	Swiþe to shapen a sship *of* shidis & bordis;
A. 10.175	Outtake þe ei3te soulis, & *of* iche beste a couple
A. 10.180	A3en þe lawe *of* oure lord le[i3en] togideris,
A. 10.183	For coueitise *of* catel vnkyndely be maried.
A. 10.184	A carful concepcioun comiþ *of* such weddyng
A. 10.185	As fel *of* þe folk [þat I] before shewide.
A. 10.188	Or wedde any wydewe for any wele *of* godis,
A. 10.198	For coueitise *of* catel or of kynrede riche,
A. 10.198	For coueitise of catel or *of* kynrede riche,
A. 10.204	*Of* lif & of loue & of lawe also
A. 10.204	Of lif & *of* loue & of lawe also
A. 10.204	Of lif & of loue & *of* lawe also
A. 10.207	Þat iche man haue a make in [mariage] *of* wedlak
A. 11.2	Þat lene was *of* lich & of lo[u3] chere.
A. 11.2	Þat lene was of lich & *of* lo[u3] chere.
A. 11.6	To flatereris or to folis þat frentyk ben *of* wittis,'
A. 11.25	And can telle *of* tobie & of þe twelue apostlis,
A. 11.25	And can telle of tobie & *of* þe twelue apostlis,
A. 11.26	Or prechen *of* þe penaunce þat pilat[u]s wrou3te
A. 11.32	More þanne musik, or makyng *of* god almi3t,
A. 11.33	Wolde neuere king, ne kni3t, ne canoun *of* seint poulis
A. 11.34	3iue hem to here 3eris3iue þe value *of* a grote.
A. 11.38	Ac 3if þei carpen *of* crist, þise clerkis & þise lewid,
A. 11.40	Þanne telle þei *of* þe trinite how two slowe þe þridde,
A. 11.53	God is muche in þe [gorge] *of* þis grete maistris,
A. 11.56	Clerkis & k[ete] men carpen *of* god faste,
A. 11.62	To tellen *of* þe trinite to be holden a sire,
A. 11.77	Ac beleue lelly o[n þe] lore *of* holy chirche,
A. 11.78	And preye hym *of* pardoun & penaunce [in] þi lyue,
A. 11.80	For alle þat wilneþ to wyte þe [whyes] *of* god almi3t,
A. 11.87	And now comiþ a conyon & wolde cacche *of* my wittes,
A. 11.97	I mi3te gete no g[r]ayn *of* hise grete wyttes,
A. 11.99	In signe þat I shulde beseke hire *of* grace.
A. 11.100	And whanne I was war *of* his wil to his wif gan I knele,
A. 11.110	Þanne was I [as] fayn as foul *of* fair morewen,
A. 11.122	Þanne shalt þou se sobirte, & simplite *of* speche,
A. 11.129	And alle þe musons *of* musik I made hire [to] knowe.
A. 11.134	[*Of*] alle kynne craftis I contreuide tolis,
A. 11.135	*Of* carpenteris & kerueris; [I] kende ferst masons,
A. 11.145	For dobet & dobest ben drawen *of* louis s[co]le.
A. 11.156	Geometrie & geomesie is gynful *of* speche;
A. 11.159	3et arn þere febicchis *of* Forellis of many manis wittes,
A. 11.159	3et arn þere febicchis of Forellis *of* many manis wittes,
A. 11.160	Experimentis *of* alkenemye of albertis makyng,
A. 11.160	Experimentis of alkenemye *of* albertis makyng,
A. 11.176	Þat I was *of* wyttis hous & wiþ his wyf dame stodie.
A. 11.181	And siþen aftirward to se sumwhat *of* dobest'.
A. 11.205	*Of* religioun þe rewele he reherside in his morals,
A. 11.212	A ledere *of* l[oue]d[a]ies & a lond biggere;
A. 11.216	Arn more in his mynde þan þe memorie *of* his foundours.
A. 11.217	Þis is þe lif *of* þis lordis þat lyuen shulde wiþ dobet,
A. 11.220	Wern dowel, & dobet, & dobest *of* hem alle,
A. 11.224	Forþi I wende þat þo wyes wern dobest *of* alle.'
A. 11.228	Ne ricchesse, ne rentis, ne realte *of* lordis.
A. 11.248	And 3iuen hem *of* oure good as good as oureseluen,
A. 11.256	I shal punisshen in purcatory or in þe put *of* helle
A. 11.262	In þe legende *of* lif longe er I were,
A. 11.272	And was þere neuere in þis world to wysere *of* werkis,
A. 11.274	Taken ensaumpl[e] *of* here sawis in sarmonis þat þei maken,
A. 11.283	Or adam, or ysaye, or any *of* þe prophetis.
A. 11.286	Wiþoute penaunce *of* purcatorie to haue paradis for euere.
A. 11.293	And 3et [haue] I forget[e ferþer] *of* fyue wyttis teching
A. 11.294	Þat clergie *of* cristis mouþ comendite [was hit] neuere,

A.11.295	For he seide it hymself to summe *of* his disciplis:
A.11.298	'Wh[anne] ȝe ben aposid *of* princes or of prestis of þe lawe
A.11.298	'Wh[anne] ȝe ben aposid of princes or *of* prestis of þe lawe
A.11.298	'Wh[anne] ȝe ben aposid of princes or of prestis *of* þe lawe
A.11.300	For I shal graunte ȝow grace *of* god þat ȝe seruen,
A.11.301	Þe help *of* þe holy gost to answere hem [alle]'.
A.11.302	Þe douȝtiest doctour or dyuynour *of* þe trinite.
A.11.303	Þat [was] austyn þe olde, & hiȝeste *of* þe foure,
A.11.309	Ne none sonnere ysauid, ne saddere *of* consience,
A.11.310	Þanne pore peple, as plouȝmen, and pastours *of* bestis,
A.11.312	Percen wiþ a paternoster þe paleis *of* heuene
A.12.15	*Of* þe kynde cardinal wit, and cristned in a font,
A.12.31	*Of* þat he wolde wite wis him no betere;
A.12.44	And his loggyng is with lyf þat lord is *of* erþe,
A.12.70	At my bak *of* broke bred þi bely for to fylle,
A.12.71	A bagge ful *of* a beggere.' I bouȝþe hit at onys.
A.12.73	For þe myssyng *of* mete no mesour I coude,
A.12.76	For gronyng *of* my guttys I durst gon no ferther].
A.12.80	*Of* when þat he were, and wheder þat he wolde.
A.12.83	I am masager *of* deþ; men haue I tweyne.
A.12.84	Þat on is called cotidian, a courrour *of* oure hous;
A.12.86	We han letteres *of* lyf, he shal his lyf ty[n]e.
A.12.96	Þou shalt be lauȝth into lyȝth with loking *of* an eye
A.12.102	*Of* peres þe plowman and mechel peple also.
A.12.109	And for he medleþ *of* makyng he made þis ende.
A.12.113	Furst to rekne Richard, kyng *of* þis rewme,
B.Pr.3	In habite as an heremite, vnholy *of* werkes,
B.Pr.6	Me bifel a ferly, *of* Fairye me þoȝte.
B.Pr.16	Wiþ depe diches and derke and dredfulle *of* siȝte.
B.Pr.17	A fair feeld ful *of* folk fond I þer bitwene
B.Pr.18	*Of* alle manere of men, þe meene and þe riche,
B.Pr.18	Of alle manere *of* men, þe meene and þe riche,
B.Pr.24	In contenaunce *of* cloþynge comen d[is]gised.
B.Pr.26	Al for loue *of* oure lord lyueden [wel] streyte
B.Pr.38	That Poul precheþ *of* hem I [dar] nat preue it here;
B.Pr.59	Prechynge þe peple for profit *of* [þe wombe];
B.Pr.61	For coueitise *of* copes construed it as þei wolde.
B.Pr.62	Manye *of* þise maistre[s mowe] cloþen hem at likyng
B.Pr.71	*Of* falshede of fastynge [and] of Auowes ybroken.
B.Pr.71	Of falshede *of* fastynge [and] of Auowes ybroken.
B.Pr.71	Of falshede of fastynge [and] *of* Auowes ybroken.
B.Pr.82	That þe [pouere peple] *of* þe parisshe sholde haue if þei ne were.
B.Pr.94	*Of* wardes and of wardemotes, weyues and streyves.
B.Pr.94	Of wardes and *of* wardemotes, weyues and streyves.
B.Pr.96	And in stede *of* Stywardes sitten and demen.
B.Pr.97	Hire messe & hire matyns and many *of* hire houres
B.Pr.100	I parceyued *of* þe power þat Peter hadde to kepe,
B.Pr.103	Amonges foure vertues, [most vertuous *of* alle],
B.Pr.107	Ac *of* þe Cardinals at court þat kauȝte of þat name,
B.Pr.107	Ac of þe Cardinals at court þat kauȝte *of* þat name,
B.Pr.111	Forþi I kan & kan nauȝt *of* court speke moore.
B.Pr.113	Might *of* þe communes made hym to regne.
B.Pr.118	The commune contreued *of* kynde wit craftes,
B.Pr.119	And for profit *of* al þe peple Plowmen ordeyned
B.Pr.128	And siþen in þe Eyr an heiȝ an Aungel *of* heuene
B.Pr.139	Thanne greued hym a Goliardeis, a gloton *of* wordes,
B.Pr.143	Thanne [comsed] al þe commune crye in vers *of* latyn
B.Pr.146	Wiþ þat ran þer a route *of* Ratons at ones
B.Pr.149	For a cat *of* a [court] cam whan hym liked
B.Pr.152	'For doute *of* diuerse d[e]des we dar noȝt wel loke,
B.Pr.153	And if we grucche *of* his gamen he wol greuen vs alle,
B.Pr.158	A Raton *of* renoun, moost renable of tonge,
B.Pr.158	A Raton of renoun, moost renable *of* tonge,
B.Pr.160	'I haue yseyen segges', quod he, 'in þe Cite *of* Londoun
B.Pr.162	And somme colers *of* crafty werk; vncoupled þei wen[d]en
B.Pr.168	To bugge a belle *of* bras or of briȝt siluer
B.Pr.168	To bugge a belle of bras or *of* briȝt siluer
B.Pr.175	Al þ[e] route *of* Ratons to þis reson assented.
B.Pr.177	Ther ne was Raton in þe route, for al þe Reaume *of* Fraunce,
B.Pr.184	And to þe route *of* Ratons reherced þise wordes:
B.Pr.199	And also ye route *of* Ratons rende mennes cloþes
B.Pr.200	Nere þe cat *of* þ[e] court þat kan yow ouerlepe;
B.Pr.204	[Ne] carpynge *of* þis coler þat costed me neuere;
B.Pr.211	Yet houed þer an hundred in howues *of* selk,
B.Pr.214	[Ac] noȝt for loue *of* oure lord vnlose hire lippes ones.
B.Pr.216	Than gete a mom *of* hire mouþ til moneie be shewed.
B.Pr.220	Wollen webbesters and weueres *of* lynnen,
B.Pr.223	*Of* alle kynne lybbynge laborers lopen forþ somme,
B.Pr.229	'Whit wyn *of* Oseye and wyn of Gascoigne,
B.Pr.229	'Whit wyn of Oseye and wyn *of* Gascoigne,
B.Pr.230	*Of* þe Ryn and of þe Rochel þe roost to defie!'
B.Pr.230	Of þe Ryn and *of* þe Rochel þe roost to defie!'
B. 1.2	And þe feld ful *of* folk I shal yow faire shewe.

B. 1.3	A louely lady *of* leere in lynnen ycloþed
B. 1.7	The mooste partie *of* þis peple þat passeþ on þis erþe,
B. 1.9	*Of* ooþer heuene þan here holde þei no tale.'
B. 1.10	I was afered *of* hire face þeiȝ she fair weere
B. 1.14	For he is fader *of* feiþ, and formed yow alle
B. 1.18	*Of* wollene, of lynnen, of liflode at nede
B. 1.18	Of wollene, *of* lynnen, of liflode at nede
B. 1.18	Of wollene, of lynnen, *of* liflode at nede
B. 1.20	And comaunded *of* his curteisie in commune þree þynges;
B. 1.24	[That oþer is] mete at meel for mysese *of* þiselue;
B. 1.27	For Lot, in hise lifdayes, for likynge *of* drynke,
B. 1.49	And [he] asked *of* h[e]m of whom spak þe lettre,
B. 1.49	And [he] asked of h[e]m *of* whom spak þe lettre,
B. 1.56	And tutour *of* youre tresor, and take it yow at nede;
B. 1.59	'Th[e] dongeon in þe dale þat dredful is *of* siȝte—
B. 1.61	'That is þe castel *of* care; whoso comþ þerInne
B. 1.64	Fader *of* falshede, [he] founded it hymselue.
B. 1.69	He is lettere *of* loue, lieþ hem alle;
B. 1.72	That swiche wise wordes *of* holy writ shewed,
B. 1.79	Thanne I [kneled] on my knees and cried hire *of* grace;
B. 1.88	[For] who is trewe *of* his tonge, telleþ noon ooþer,
B. 1.103	And neuere leue hem for loue ne lacchynge *of* [yiftes];_
B. 1.112	[And was þe louelokest *of* liȝt after oure lord
B. 1.122	Til god *of* his goodnesse [garte þe heuene to stekie]
B. 1.126	Ac Lucifer lowest liþ *of* hem alle;
B. 1.134	Forþi I seye, as I seyde er, by siȝte *of* þise textes:
B. 1.148	For truþe telleþ þat loue is triacle *of* heuene:
B. 1.152	And [ek] þe pl[ante] *of* pees, moost precious of vertues.
B. 1.152	And [ek] þe pl[ante] of pees, moost precious *of* vertues.
B. 1.154	Til it hadde *of* þe erþe [y]eten [hitselue].
B. 1.155	And whan it hadde *of* þis fold flessh and blood taken
B. 1.157	And portatif and persaunt as þe point *of* a nedle
B. 1.159	Forþi is loue ledere *of* þe lordes folk of heuene
B. 1.159	Forþi is loue ledere of þe lordes folk *of* heuene
B. 1.176	Thouȝ ye be myȝt[y] to mote beeþ meke [*of*] youre werkes,
B. 1.179	For þouȝ ye be trewe *of* youre tonge and treweliche wynne,
B. 1.182	[*Of*] swich good as god sent goodliche parteþ,
B. 1.184	Than Malkyn *of* hire maydenhede þat no man desireþ.
B. 1.195	[Ye] curatours [þat] kepen [yow] clene *of* [youre] bod[y],
B. 1.198	[Th]at is no truþe *of* þe Trinite but tricherie of helle,
B. 1.198	[Th]at is no truþe of þe Trinite but tricherie *of* helle,
B. 1.202	[Th]at is þe lok *of* loue [þat] leteþ out my grace,
B. 1.204	Loue is leche *of* lif and next oure lord selue,
B. 1.206	Forþi I seye as I seide er by [siȝte *of* þise] textes:
B. 2.1	YEt [kneled I] on my knees and cried hire *of* grace,
B. 2.2	And seide 'mercy, madame, for Marie loue *of* heuene
B. 2.8	And was war *of* a womman [wonder]liche ycloþed,
B. 2.13	And Diamaundes *of* derrest pris and double manere Saphires,
B. 2.15	Hire Robe was ful riche, *of* reed scarlet engreyned,
B. 2.16	Wiþ Ribanes *of* reed gold and of riche stones,
B. 2.16	Wiþ Ribanes of reed gold and *of* riche stones.
B. 2.27	And Mede is manered after hym [as men *of*] kynde [carpeþ]:
B. 2.28	I ouȝte ben hyere þan she; I kam *of* a bettre.
B. 2.29	My fader þe grete god is and ground *of* alle graces,
B. 2.35	That he shal lese for hire loue a l[i]ppe *of* Caritatis.
B. 2.36	How construeþ David þe kyng *of* men þat [caccheþ] Mede,
B. 2.37	And men *of* þis moolde þat mayntneþ truþe,
B. 2.51	And lat no conscience acombre þee for coueitise *of* Mede.'
B. 2.56	*Of* alle manere of men, þe meene and þe riche.
B. 2.56	Of alle manere *of* men, þe meene and þe riche.
B. 2.58	As *of* knyȝtes and of clerkes and ooþer commune peple,
B. 2.58	As of knyȝtes and *of* clerkes and ooþer commune peple,
B. 2.60	Bedelles and baillifs and Brocours *of* chaffare,
B. 2.61	Forgoers and vitaillers and [v]okettes *of* þe Arches;
B. 2.63	Ac Symonie and Cyuylle and Sisours *of* courtes,
B. 2.64	Were moost pryuee with Mede *of* any men me þouȝte.
B. 2.78	Falsnesse is fayn *of* hire for he woot hire riche;
B. 2.84	And þe Erldom *of* Enuye and [Ire] togideres,
B. 2.85	Wiþ þe Chastilet *of* cheste and chaterynge out of reson,
B. 2.86	The Countee *of* Coueitise and alle þe costes aboute,
B. 2.88	In bargaynes and brocages wiþ þe Burgh *of* þefte,
B. 2.89	[Wiþ] al þe lordshipe *of* leccherie in lengþe and in brede,
B. 2.104	Wiþ alle þe [p]urtinaunces *of* Purgatorie into þe pyne of helle.
B. 2.104	Wiþ alle þe [p]urtinaunces of Purgatorie into þe pyne *of* helle.
B. 2.108	In witnesse *of* which þyng wrong was þe firste,
B. 2.109	And Piers þe Pardoner *of* Paulynes doctrine,
B. 2.110	Bette þe Bedel *of* Bokynghamshire,
B. 2.111	Reynald þe Reue *of* Rutland Sokene,
B. 2.113	'In þe date *of* þe deuel þ[e] dede [is asseled]
B. 2.114	By siȝte *of* sire Symonie and Cyuyles leeue.'
B. 2.119	For Mede is muliere *of* Amendes engendred
B. 2.131	And [as] a Bastard ybore *of* Belsabubbes kynne.
B. 2.132	And Mede is muliere, a maiden *of* goode;

B. 2.138 Yet be war *of* [þe] weddynge; for witty is truþe,
B. 2.139 [For] Conscience is *of* his counseil and knoweþ yow echone;
B. 2.143 Til he hadde siluer for his [seles] and [signes *of*] Notaries.
B. 2.153 Til Mede be þi wedded wif þoru3 wi[t] *of* vs alle,
B. 2.163 [Thanne fette Fauel] foles [*of* þe beste],
B. 2.182 And makeþ *of* lyere a lang cart to leden alle þise oþere,
B. 2.187 [*Of* many maner man þat on þis molde libbeth],
B. 2.194 Fals or Fauel or any *of* hise feeris
B. 2.195 I wolde be wroken *of* þo wrecches þat wercheþ so ille,
B. 2.197 Shal neuere man *of* þis molde meynprise þe leeste,
B. 2.219 Lurkynge þoru3 lanes, tolugged *of* manye.
B. 2.233 For knowynge *of* comeres coped hym as a Frere.
B. 3.1   NOw is Mede þe mayde and na mo *of* hem alle
B. 3.6   What man *of* þis [world] þat hire were leuest.
B. 3.21   *Of* hire grete goodnesse, and gaf hem echone
B. 3.22   Coupes *of* clene gold and coppes of siluer,
B. 3.22   Coupes of clene gold and coppes *of* siluer,
B. 3.24   The leeste man *of* hire meynee a moton of golde.
B. 3.24   The leeste man of hire meynee a moton *of* golde.
B. 3.40   I shal assoille þee myself for a seem *of* whete,
B. 3.44   And shrof hire *of* hire sherewednesse, shamelees I trowe;
B. 3.55   It is a freletee *of* flessh–ye fynden it in bokes–
B. 3.56   And a cours *of* kynde wherof we comen alle;
B. 3.58   It is synne *of* þe seuene sonnest relessed.
B. 3.59   Haue mercy', quod Mede, '*of* men þat it haunteþ
B. 3.63   That [ech] segge shal [see] I am suster *of* youre house.'
B. 3.65   To writen in wyndowes *of* hir wel dedes,
B. 3.66   An auenture pride be peynted þere and pomp *of* þe world;
B. 3.70   To writen in wyndowes *of* youre wel dedes
B. 3.84   [*Of*] þat þe pouere peple sholde putte in hire wombe.
B. 3.88   *Of* alle swiche Selleris siluer to take,
B. 3.89   Or present3 wiþouten pens as pieces *of* siluer,
B. 3.99   The hou[s] and [þe] ho[m] *of* hem þat desireþ
B. 3.100 Yiftes or yeresyeues bycause *of* hire Offices.
B. 3.119 For she is fayn *of* þi felaweshipe, for to be þi make.'
B. 3.122 She is frele *of* hire feiþ, fikel of hire speche;
B. 3.122 She is frele of hire feiþ, fikel *of* hire speche;
B. 3.124 [In] trust *of* hire tresor [she teneþ wel] manye.
B. 3.131 She is tikel *of* hire tail, talewis of tonge,
B. 3.131 She is tikel of hire tail, talewis *of* tonge,
B. 3.135 Sherreues *of* Shires were shent if she ne were.
B. 3.166 This is þe lif *of* þat lady, now lord 3yue hire sorwe,
B. 3.169 Swich a maister is Mede among men *of* goode.'
B. 3.191 Crope into a Cabane for cold *of* þi nayles;
B. 3.194 And [hastedest þee] homward for hunger *of* þi wombe.
B. 3.201 Hadde I ben Marchal *of* his men, by Marie of heuene!
B. 3.201 Hadde I ben Marchal of his men, by Marie *of* heuene!
B. 3.203 He sholde haue be lord *of* þat lond in lengþe and in brede,
B. 3.204 And [ek] kyng *of* þat kiþ his kyn for to helpe,
B. 3.205 The leeste brol *of* his blood a Barones piere.
B. 3.218 Taken Mede *of* hir maistres as þei mowe acorde;
B. 3.219 Beggeres for hir biddynge bidden [*of*] men Mede;
B. 3.221 The kyng haþ mede *of* his men to make pees in londe;
B. 3.222 Men þat [kenne clerkes] crauen [*of* hem] Mede;
B. 3.231 'Ther are two manere *of* Medes, my lord, [bi] youre leue.
B. 3.232 That oon god *of* his grace [gyueþ] in his blisse
B. 3.238 Tho þat entren *of* o colour and of one wille
B. 3.238 Tho þat entren of o colour and *of* one wille
B. 3.240 And he þat vseþ no3t þe lyf *of* vsurie,
B. 3.245 *Of* god at a gret nede whan þei gon hennes.
B. 3.255 That laborers and lowe [lewede] folk taken *of* hire maistres
B. 3.262 That Agag *of* Amalec and al his peple after
B. 3.275 Ooþerwise þan he was warned *of* þe prophete,
B. 3.280 The culorum *of* þis cas kepe I no3t to [shewe];
B. 3.297 Mede *of* mysdoeres makeþ manye lordes,
B. 3.300 And make *of* lawe a laborer; swich loue shal arise
B. 3.313 Huntynge or haukynge if any *of* hem vse
B. 3.314 His boost *of* his benefice worþ bynomen hym after.
B. 3.326 By sixe sonnes and a ship and half a shef *of* Arwes,
B. 3.327 And þe myddel *of* a Moone shal make þe Iewes torne,
B. 3.351 And þat is þe tail *of* þe text of þat [teme ye] shewed,
B. 3.351 And þat is þe tail of þe text *of* þat [teme ye] shewed,
B. 4.10   [*Of* Mede and of mo oþere, what man shal hire wedde],
B. 4.10   [Of Mede and *of* mo oþere, what man shal hire wedde],
B. 4.13   'I am fayn *of* þat foreward', seide þe freke þanne,
B. 4.17   And called Caton his knaue, curteis *of* speche,
B. 4.19   Ne-lesynge-to-lau3en-*of*-for-I-loued-hem-neuere.
B. 4.29   In [c]heker and in Chauncerye, to ben discharged *of* þynges.
B. 4.33   And bad Reson ryde faste and recche *of* hir neiþer.
B. 4.37   Thei ne [gy]ueþ no3t *of* [good feiþ, woot god þe sooþe]:
B. 4.39   Moore þan for] loue *of* oure lord or alle hise leeue Seintes.
B. 4.50   And Margrete *of* hir maydenhede maugree hire chekes.
B. 4.52   I dar no3t for fere *of* h[y]m fi3te ne chide.

B. 4.53   He borwed *of* me bayard [and] brou3te hym [neuere ayein],
B. 4.65   And seide, 'hadde I loue *of* my lord þe kyng litel wolde I recche
B. 4.95   And profrede Pees a present al *of* pure[d] golde.
B. 4.96   'Haue þis [*of* me, man]', quod she, 'to amenden þi scaþe,
B. 4.128 And alle Rome renneres, for Robberes [*of*] biyonde,
B. 4.129 Bere no siluer ouer see þat signe *of* kyng sheweþ,
B. 4.131 V[p] forfeture *of* þat fee, wh[o] fynt [hym] at Douere,
B. 4.140 Ben vnpunysshed [at] my power for peril *of* my soule,
B. 4.151 Ac no3t for confort *of* þe commune ne for þe kynges soule.
B. 4.152 For I sei3 Mede in þe moot halle on men *of* lawe wynke
B. 4.159 And þe mooste peple in þe [moot] halle and manye *of* þe grete,
B. 4.161 Loue leet *of* hire li3t and leaute yet lasse,
B. 4.163 'Whoso wilneþ hire to wif for welþe *of* hire goodes,
B. 4.166 For þe mooste commune *of* þat court called hire an hore.
B. 4.170 And yet yaue ye me neuere þe worþ *of* a risshe.'
B. 4.179 Mede shal no3t maynprise yow, by þe marie *of* heuene!
B. 4.187 If ye bidden buxomnesse be *of* myn assent.'
B. 4.189 [Be] my counseil co[men] *of* clerkes and of Erles.
B. 4.189 [Be] my counseil co[men] of clerkes and *of* Erles.
B. 4.193 So Conscience *of* [y]oure counseil I knew I no bettre.'
B. 5.3   Thanne waked I *of* my wynkyng and wo was withalle
B. 5.6   That I ne my3te ferþer a foot for defaute *of* slepynge.
B. 5.10   For I sei3 þe feld ful *of* folk þat I before [tolde],
B. 5.19   [And] turned vpward hire tai[l] in tokenynge *of* drede
B. 5.21   *Of* þis matere I my3te mamelen [wel] longe,
B. 5.36   Ne for no poustee *of* pestilence plese hem no3t out of reson.
B. 5.47   And be Stywar[d] *of* youre sted[e] til ye be [stewed] bettre'.
B. 5.70   [*Of* alle þat] I haue [had enuye] in myn herte.'
B. 5.80   *Of* a Freres frokke were þe foresleues.
B. 5.86   Ech a word þat he warp was *of* a Neddres tonge;
B. 5.87   *Of* chidynge and chalangynge was his chief liflode,
B. 5.88   Wiþ bakbitynge and bismere and berynge *of* fals witnesse;
B. 5.92   Than þou3 I hadde þis wouke ywonne a weye *of* Essex chese.
B. 5.113 And *of* [his] lesynge I lau3e, [it li3teþ] myn herte.
B. 5.114 [Ac *of* his] wynnynge I wepe and waille þe tyme.
B. 5.120 That al my [brest] bolneþ for bitter *of* my galle.
B. 5.127 'Sorwe [for] synn[e] is sauacion *of* soules.'
B. 5.134 I wole amende þis if I may þoru3 my3t *of* god almy3ty.'
B. 5.140 Til þei beere leues *of* lowe speche lordes to plese,
B. 5.148 I, wraþe, walke wiþ hem and wisse hem *of* my bokes.
B. 5.149 Thus þey speken *of* spiritualte þat eiþer despiseþ ooþer
B. 5.158 And maad hem Ioutes *of* Ianglyng þat dame Iohane was a bastard,
B. 5.162 *Of* wikkede wordes I, wraþe, hire wortes made
B. 5.179 [I] haue a flux *of* a foul mouþ wel fyue dayes after;
B. 5.180 Al þe wikkednesse þat I woot by any *of* oure breþeren,
B. 5.195 In a [torn] tabard *of* twelf wynter age;
B. 5.205 Ne hadde þe grace *of* gyle ygo amonges my [ware]
B. 5.229 And bidde þe Roode *of* Bromholm brynge me out of dette.'
B. 5.231 '3is, ones I was yherberwed', quod he, 'wiþ an heep *of* chapmen;
B. 5.236 And I kan no frenssh in feiþ but *of* þe ferþest ende of Northfolk.'
B. 5.236 And I kan no frenssh in feiþ but of þe ferþest ende *of* Northfolk.'
B. 5.239 I lerned among lumbardes [a lesson and *of* Iewes],
B. 5.241 And lene it for loue *of* þe cros, to legge a wed and lese it.
B. 5.250 'Lentestow euere lordes for loue *of* hire mayntenaunce?'
B. 5.255 'I haue as muche pite *of* pouere men as pedlere haþ of cattes,
B. 5.255 'I haue as muche pite of pouere men as pedlere haþ *of* cattes,
B. 5.256 That wolde kille hem if he cacche hem my3te for coueitise *of* hir skynnes
B. 5.257 'Artow manlich among þi ne3ebores *of* þi mete and drynke?'
B. 5.262 Ne þyne heires after þee haue ioie *of* þat þow wynnest,
B. 5.265 For were I frere *of* þat hous þer good feiþ and charite is
B. 5.267 Ne haue a peny to my pitaunce, [for pyne *of* my soule],
B. 5.272 And siþen þat Reson rolle it in þe Registre *of* heuene
B. 5.274 For a[l] þat ha[þ] *of* þi good, haue god my trouþe,
B. 5.283 Nis na moore to be mercy *of* god þan [amyd] þe see a gleede:
B. 5.290 Ber it to þe Bisshop, and bid hym *of* his grace
B. 5.295 And what he lente yow *of* oure lordes good to lette yow fro synne.'
B. 5.299 And [heo] asked [*of* hym] whiderward he wolde.
B. 5.304 'I haue pepir and pion[e] and a pound *of* garleek,
B. 5.305 A ferþyngworþ *of* fenel seed for fastynge dayes.'
B. 5.309 Tymme þe Tynkere and tweyne *of* his [knaues],
B. 5.311 Clarice *of* Cokkeslane and þe Clerk of þe chirche,
B. 5.311 Clarice of Cokkeslane and þe Clerk *of* þe chirche,
B. 5.312 [Sire Piers *of* Pridie and Pernele of Flaundres,
B. 5.312 [Sire Piers of Pridie and Pernele *of* Flaundres,
B. 5.314 A Ribibour, a Ratoner, a Rakiere *of* Chepe,
B. 5.316 Godefray *of* Garlekhiþe and Griffyn þe walshe;
B. 5.317 [*Of*] vpholderes an heep, erly by þe morwe,
B. 5.324 Whoso hadde þe hood sholde han amendes *of* þe cloke.
B. 5.344 And wisshed it hadde ben wexed wiþ a wispe *of* firses.
B. 5.356 Dorste lape *of* þat leuynges, so vnlouely [it] smau3te.
B. 5.357 Wiþ al þe wo *of* þ[e] world his wif and his wenche
B. 5.361 Thanne waked he *of* his wynkyng and wiped hise ei3en;

B. 5.363	His wif [edwyted] hym þo [*of* wikkednesse and synne],
B. 5.376	For loue *of* tales in Tauernes [to] drynke þe moore I [hyed;
B. 5.395	But I kan rymes *of* Robyn hood and Randolf Erl of Chestre,
B. 5.395	But I kan rymes of Robyn hood and Randolf Erl *of* Chestre,
B. 5.396	Ac neiþer[*of*] oure lord ne of oure lady þe leeste þat euere was maked.
B. 5.396	Ac neiþer of oure lord ne *of* oure lady þe leeste þat euere was maked.
B. 5.406	I haue leuere here an harlotrye or a Somer game *of* Souters,
B. 5.407	Or lesynge[s] to lauȝen [*of*] and bilye my neȝebores,
B. 5.435	In speche and in sparynge *of* speche; yspilt many a tyme
B. 5.440	And euere siþþe be beggere [by cause *of*] my] sleuþe:
B. 5.446	And beet þiself on þe brest and bidde hym *of* grace,
B. 5.459	And wiþ þe residue and þe remenaunt, bi þe Rode *of* Chestre,
B. 5.465	Tho Dysmas my broþer bisouȝte [þee] *of* grace
B. 5.471	What bifel *of* þis feloun I kan noȝt faire shewe.
B. 5.478	'I shal biseche for alle synfulle oure Saueour *of* grace
B. 5.479	To amenden vs *of* oure mysdedes: do mercy to vs alle,
B. 5.480	God, þat *of* þi goodnesse [g]onne þe world make,
B. 5.481	And *of* nauȝt madest auȝt and man moost lik to þiselue,
B. 5.485	And bicam man *of* a maide mankynde to saue,
B. 5.488	On good fryday for mannes sake at ful tyme *of* þe daye;
B. 5.492	Aboute mydday, whan moost liȝt is and meel tyme *of* Seintes,
B. 5.495	And blewe alle þi blessed into þe blisse *of* Paradys.
B. 5.500	*Of* þyne douȝt[iest] dedes was doon in oure armes:
B. 5.506	Thanne hente hope an horn *of* Deus tu conuersus viuificabis [nos]
B. 5.510	A þousand *of* men þo þrungen togideres,
B. 5.520	An hundred *of* Ampulles on his hat seten,
B. 5.521	Signes *of* Synay and shelles of Galice,
B. 5.521	Signes of Synay and shelles *of* Galice,
B. 5.522	And many crouch on his cloke and keyes *of* Rome,
B. 5.550	I haue myn hire [*of* hym] wel and ouþerwhiles moore.
B. 5.553	He is as lowe as a lomb and louelich *of* speche.
B. 5.557	'Nay, by [þe peril *of*] my soul[e]!' quod Piers and gan to swere:
B. 5.563	That ye louen oure lord god leuest *of* alle þynges.
B. 5.566	And so boweþ forþ by a brook, beþ-buxom-*of*-speche,
B. 5.571	And-nameliche-on-ydel-þe-name-*of*-god-almyȝty;
B. 5.574	Ne-noon-*of*-hire-seruauntȝ-þat-noyen-hem-myȝte;
B. 5.582	Loke þow plukke no plaunte þere for peril *of* þi soule.
B. 5.586	The moot is *of* mercy þe Manoir aboute;
B. 5.587	And alle þe walles ben *of* wit to holden wil oute;
B. 5.588	[The] kernele[s ben *of*] cristendom [þat] kynde to saue,
B. 5.591	Wiþ no leed but wiþ loue and lowe[nesse] as breþeren [*of* o wombe].
B. 5.592	The brugg[e] is *of* bidde-wel-þe-bet-may-þow-spede;
B. 5.593	Ech piler is *of* penaunce, of preieres-to-Seyntes;
B. 5.593	Ech piler is of penaunce, *of* preieres-to-Seyntes;
B. 5.594	*Of* almesdedes are þe hokes þat þe gates hangen on.
B. 5.607	In a cheyne *of* charite as þow a child were,
B. 5.609	A[c] be war þanne *of* Wraþe, þat wikked sherewe,
B. 5.612	The boldnesse *of* þi bienfe[et] makeþ þee blynd þanne,
B. 5.619	And arn porters *of* þe Posternes þat to þe place longeþ.
B. 5.627	But if ye be sibbe to some *of* þise seuene,
B. 5.628	It is [wel] hard, by myn leeue, any *of* yow alle
B. 5.637	And þoruȝ þe help *of* hem two, hope þow noon ooþer,
B. 6.3	Quod Perkyn þe Plowman, 'by Seint Peter *of* Rome!
B. 6.9	'Somme shul sowe þe sak for shedyng *of* þe Whete.
B. 6.18	As longe as I lyue, for þe lordes loue *of* heuene.
B. 6.19	And alle manere *of* men þat [by þe] mete libbeþ,
B. 6.37	'Ye, and yet a point', quod Piers, 'I preye [þee] *of* moore:
B. 6.50	And þat þow be trewe *of* þi tonge and tales þow hatie
B. 6.51	But if [it be] *of* wisdom or of wit þi werkmen to chaste;
B. 6.51	But if [it be] of wisdom or of wit þi werkmen to chaste;
B. 6.60	[Hise] cokeres and [hise] coffes for cold *of* [hise] nailes,
B. 6.61	And [heng his] hoper at [his] hals in stede *of* a Scryppe:
B. 6.62	'A busshel *of* bredcorn brynge me þerInne,
B. 6.70	Saue Ia[kk]e þe Iogelour and Ionette *of* þe Stuwes
B. 6.72	And frere faitour and folk *of* hi[s] ordre,
B. 6.76	For holy chirche is [holde] *of* hem no tiþe to [aske],
B. 6.83	'For now I am old and hoor and haue *of* myn owene
B. 6.92	For *of* my corn and [my] catel [h]e craued þe tiþe;
B. 6.93	I paide [hym] prestly for peril *of* my soule.
B. 6.96	My wif shal haue *of* þat I wan wiþ truþe and na moore,
B. 6.100	And wiþ þe residue and þe remenaunt, by þe Rode *of* Lukes!
B. 6.117	'Now by þe peril *of* my soule!' quod Piers al in pure tene,
B. 6.126	That god *of* his grace youre greyn multiplie
B. 6.127	And yelde yow [*of*] youre Almesse þat ye ȝyue vs here;
B. 6.135	Or ye shul eten barly breed and *of* þe broke drynke;
B. 6.138	Til god *of* his [grace gare hem to arise].
B. 6.148	Ac Robert Renaboute shal [riȝt] noȝt haue *of* myne,
B. 6.149	Ne Postles, but þei preche konne and haue power *of* þe bisshop.
B. 6.151	For it is an vnresonable Religion þat haþ riȝt noȝt *of* certein.'
B. 6.157	*Of* þi flour and þi flessh, fecche whanne vs likeþ,
B. 6.168	And leet liȝt *of* þe lawe and lasse of þe knyȝte,
B. 6.168	And leet liȝt of þe lawe and lasse *of* þe knyȝte,
B. 6.171	'Now by þe peril *of* my soule!' quod Piers, 'I shal apeire yow alle',
B. 6.173	'Awreke me *of* wastours', and lo, 'þat þis world shendeþ.'
B. 6.186	For a pot[el] *of* peses þat Piers hadde ymaked
B. 6.187	An heep *of* heremytes henten hem spades
B. 6.201	'I am wel awroke *of* wastours þoruȝ þy myȝte.
B. 6.203	'*Of* beggeris and bidderis what best be doone.
B. 6.206	And for defaute *of* foode þis folk is at my wille.
B. 6.209	And helpen hem *of* alle þyng [after þat] hem nedeþ.
B. 6.215	[And] aba[u]e hem wiþ benes for bollynge *of* hir womb[e];
B. 6.220	Conforte h[e]m wiþ þi catel for cristes loue *of* heuene;
B. 6.221	Loue hem and lene hem [and] so [þe] lawe *of* [kynde wolde].
B. 6.222	And alle manere *of* men þat þow myȝt aspie
B. 6.232	Go to Genesis þe geaunt, engendrour *of* vs alle:
B. 6.240	He hadde maugree *of* his maister eueremoore after,
B. 6.248	Or [wiþ tech]ynge or [tell]ynge or trauaillynge [*of* hondes],
B. 6.250	The Sauter seiþ, in þe psalme *of* Beati omnes,
B. 6.254	Any leef *of* lechecraft lere it me, my deere;
B. 6.255	For some *of* my seruauntȝ and myself boþe
B. 6.256	*Of* al a wike werche noȝt, so oure wombe akeþ.'
B. 6.262	And sende þee *of* his Sauce to sauore þi lippes,
B. 6.266	L[o]ue hym noȝt for he is [a] lech[our] and likerous *of* tunge,
B. 6.270	And his cloke *of* Calabre [and] þe knappes of golde,
B. 6.270	And his cloke of Calabre [and] þe knappes *of* golde,
B. 6.282	A fewe cruddes and creme and [a cake *of* otes],
B. 6.283	[A lof] *of* benes and bran ybake for my fauntes.
B. 6.304	But Coket [or] clermatyn or *of* clene whete,
B. 6.306	But *of* þe beste and þe brunneste þat [brewesteres] selle.
B. 6.309	May no peny ale hem paie, ne no pece *of* bacoun,
B. 6.311	And þat chaud and plus chaud for chillynge *of* hir mawe.
B. 6.331	But [if] god *of* his goodnesse graunte vs a trewe.
B. 7.14	Legistres of boþe lawes þe lewed þerwiþ to preche,
B. 7.17	At þe day *of* dome at [hire] deys [to] sitte.
B. 7.31	Fynden [swiche] hir foode [for oure lordes loue *of* heuene],
B. 7.40	Men *of* lawe leest pardon hadde, [leue þow noon ooþer],
B. 7.42	And nameliche *of* Innocentȝ þat noon yuel konneþ.
B. 7.54	Thise foure þe fader *of* heuene made to þis foold in commune;
B. 7.59	That any Mede *of* mene men for motyng takeþ.
B. 7.72	Caton kenneþ me þus and þe clerc *of* stories.
B. 7.88	Lat vsage be youre solas *of* seintes lyues redyng.
B. 7.97	Than *of* alle [oþere] manere men þat on þis moolde [wandreþ].
B. 7.100	Ac olde men and hore þat helplees ben *of* strengþe,
B. 7.105	For loue *of* hir lowe hert[e] oure lord haþ hem graunted
B. 7.112	And was writen riȝt þus in witnesse *of* truþe:
B. 7.122	I shal cessen *of* my sowyng', quod Piers, '& swynke noȝt so harde,
B. 7.124	*Of* preieres and of penaunce my plouȝ shal ben herafter,
B. 7.124	Of preieres and *of* penaunce my plouȝ shal ben herafter,
B. 7.150	*Of* þat I seiȝ slepynge, if it so be myȝte,
B. 7.158	How Daniel diuined þe dre[mes] *of* a kyng
B. 7.177	Dowel at þe day *of* dome is digneliche vnderfongen;
B. 7.178	[He] passeþ al þe pardon *of* Seint Petres cherche.
B. 7.181	This is [a leef *of*] oure bileue, as lettred men vs techeþ:
B. 7.188	Vpon trust *of* youre tresor triennals to haue,
B. 7.191	That haue þe welþe *of* þis world and wise men ben holden
B. 7.197	A pokeful *of* pardon þere, ne prouincials lettres,
B. 7.206	At þe day *of* dome we dide as he hiȝte.
B. 8.3	And frayned ful ofte *of* folk þat I mette
B. 8.5	And what man he myȝte be *of* many man I asked.
B. 8.9	Maistres *of* þe Menours, men of grete witte.
B. 8.9	Maistres of þe Menours, men *of* grete witte.
B. 8.14	For [ye] men *of* þis moolde þat moost wide walken,
B. 8.30	The wynd and þe water and þe [waggyng *of* þe boot]
B. 8.36	[There] were [þe mannes] lif lost [for] lachesse *of* hymselue.
B. 8.39	The goodes *of* þis grounde arn like þe grete wawes,
B. 8.41	The boot is likned to [þe] body þat brotel is *of* kynde,
B. 8.64	Blisse *of* þe briddes [abide me made],
B. 8.67	Murþe *of* hire mouþes made me to slep[e];
B. 8.80	Whoso is [meke *of* his mouþ, milde of his speche],
B. 8.80	Whoso is [meke of his mouþ, milde *of* his speche],
B. 8.81	Trewe *of* his tunge and of his two handes,
B. 8.81	Trewe of his tunge and *of* his two handes,
B. 8.83	Trusty *of* his tailende, takeþ but his owene,
B. 8.86	He is as lowe as a lomb, louelich *of* speche,
B. 8.87	[Whiles he haþ ouȝt *of* his owene he helpeþ þer nede is];
B. 8.109	And rule þe Reme by [rede *of* hem alle],
B. 8.122	Sad *of* his semblaunt and of [a] softe [speche].
B. 8.122	Sad of his semblaunt and *of* [a] softe [speche].
B. 9.2	In a Castel þat kynde made *of* foure kynnes þynges,
B. 9.3	*Of* erþe and Eyr [it is] maad, medled togideres,
B. 9.8	A proud prikere *of* Fraunce, Princeps huius mundi,
B. 9.11	And [haþ] doo[n] hire wiþ sire dowel, duc *of* þise Marches.
B. 9.17	Ac þe Constable *of* [þe] Castel þat kepeþ [hem alle]

B. 9.21 Sire werch-wel-wiþ-þyn-hand, a wiȝt man *of* strengþe,
B. 9.26 'Kynde', quod [he], 'is creatour *of* alle kynnes [beestes],
B. 9.27 Fader and formour, [þe first *of* alle þynges].
B. 9.29 Lord *of* lif and of liȝt, of lisse and of peyne,
B. 9.29 Lord of lif and *of* liȝt, of lisse and of peyne.
B. 9.29 Lord of lif and of liȝt, *of* lisse and of peyne.
B. 9.29 Lord of lif and of liȝt, of lisse and *of* peyne.
B. 9.31 Ac man is hym moost lik *of* marc and of [shape].
B. 9.31 Ac man is hym moost lik of marc and *of* [shape].
B. 9.35 And Eue *of* his ryb bon wiþouten any mene.
B. 9.45 And in þis manere was man maad þoruȝ myȝt *of* god almyȝty,
B. 9.47 And þus god gaf hym a goost [*of*] þe godhede of heuene
B. 9.47 And þus god gaf hym a goost [of] þe godhede *of* heuene
B. 9.48 And *of* his grete grace graunted hym blisse,
B. 9.53 Thorgh myȝt *of* þe mageste man was ymaked.
B. 9.55 For loue *of* þe lady anima þat lif is ynempned.
B. 9.60 For after þe grace *of* god þe gretteste is Inwit.
B. 9.74 *Of* þis matere I myȝte make a long tale
B. 9.76 And þat I lye noȝt *of* þat I lere þee, luc bereþ witnesse.
B. 9.81 Than nempnynge *of* a name and he neuer þe wiser.
B. 9.88 Eyþer of hem helpeþ ooþer *of* þat þat h[y]m nedeþ,
B. 9.88 Eyþer *of* hem helpeþ ooþer of þat þat h[y]m nedeþ,
B. 9.89 Whi [ne wol] we cristene *of* cristes good be as kynde?
B. 9.98 And [dredeþ hym] noȝt for drede *of* vengeaunce dooþ þerfore þe bettre;
B. 9.100 To spille any speche or any space *of* tyme:
B. 9.101 [Tynynge] *of* tyme, truþe woot þe soþe,
B. 9.102 Is moost yhated vpon erþe *of* hem þat ben in heuene;
B. 9.103 And siþþe to spille speche þat [spire] is *of* grace
B. 9.104 And goddes gleman and a game *of* heuene.
B. 9.112 For *of* hir kynde þei come þat Confessours ben nempned,
B. 9.118 And siþenes by assent of hemself as þei two myȝte acorde;
B. 9.125 *Of* swiche synfulle sherewes þe Sauter makeþ mynde;
B. 9.126 And alle þat come *of* þat Caym come to yuel ende,
B. 9.130 Yet [seþ], ayein þe sonde *of* oure Saueour of heuene,
B. 9.130 Yet [seþ], ayein þe sonde of oure Saueour *of* heuene,
B. 9.135 "Swiþe go shape a ship *of* shides and of bordes;
B. 9.135 "Swiþe go shape a ship of shides and *of* bordes;
B. 9.144 Excepte oonliche *of* ech kynde a couple
B. 9.153 Muchel merueille me þynkeþ; and moore *of* a sherewe
B. 9.157 And al for þei wroȝte wedlokes ayein [þe wille *of* god].
B. 9.158 Forþi haue þei maugre *of* hir mariages þat marie so hir children.
B. 9.160 For coueitise *of* catel vnkyndely ben [maried].
B. 9.161 [A] careful concepcion comeþ *of* [swich weddynge]
B. 9.162 As bifel *of* þe folk þat I bifore [shewed].
B. 9.167 Or wedden any wodewe for [wele] *of* hir goodes
B. 9.177 For coueitise *of* catel ne of kynrede riche;
B. 9.177 For coueitise of catel ne *of* kynrede riche;
B. 9.181 And þanne gete ye grace *of* god and good ynouȝ to lyue wiþ.
B. 9.184 Fo[r] lecherie in likynge is lymeyerd *of* helle.
B. 9.191 *Of* lif and of [loue] and [of lawe also]
B. 9.191 Of lif and *of* [loue] and [of lawe also]
B. 9.191 Of lif and of [loue] and [*of* lawe also]
B. 9.197 Vngracious to gete good or loue *of* þe peple;
B. 9.206 To helen and to helpen, is dobest *of* alle.
B.10.2 That lene was *of* [liche] and of [lowe chere].
B.10.2 That lene was of [liche] and *of* [lowe chere].
B.10.6 To flatereres or to fooles þat frenetike ben *of* wittes',
B.10.24 That wikked men þei welden þe welþe *of* þis worlde,
B.10.25 And þat þei ben lordes *of* ech a lond þat out of lawe libbeþ:
B.10.30 Harlotes for hir harlotrie may haue *of* hir goodes,
B.10.31 And Iaperis and Iogelours and Iangleris *of* gestes,
B.10.33 And kan telle *of* Tobye and of [þe] twelue Apostles
B.10.33 And kan telle of Tobye and *of* [þe] twelue Apostles
B.10.34 Or prechen *of* þe penaunce þat Pilat wroȝte
B.10.40 Ayein þe lawe *of* oure lord, and lyen on hemselue,
B.10.45 Than Munde þe Millere *of* Multa fecit deus.
B.10.47 [W]olde neuere kyng ne knyȝt ne [c]anon *of* Seint Poules
B.10.48 ȝyue hem to hir yeresȝyue þe [value] *of* a grote.
B.10.52 Ac if þei carpen *of* crist, þise clerkes and þise lewed,
B.10.54 Than telleþ þei *of* þe Trinite [how two slowe þe þridde],
B.10.67 God is muche in þe gorge *of* þise grete maistres,
B.10.70 Clerkes and [kete] men carpen *of* god faste
B.10.74 And prechen at Seint Poules, for pure enuye *of* clerkes,
B.10.75 That folk is noȝt fermed in þe feiþ ne free *of* hire goodes
B.10.81 And yet þe wrecches *of* þis world is noon ywar by ooþer,
B.10.82 Ne for drede *of* þe deeþ wiþdrawe noȝt hir pride,
B.10.89 How þe book bible *of* hym bereþ witnesse.
B.10.92 For we haue no lettre *of* oure lif how longe it shal dure.
B.10.105 Carpen as þei clerkes were *of* crist and of hise myȝtes,
B.10.105 Carpen as þei clerkes were of crist and *of* hise myȝtes,
B.10.113 "*Of* þat [ye] clerkes vs kenneþ of crist by þe gospel:
B.10.113 "Of þat [ye] clerkes vs kenneþ *of* crist by þe gospel:

B.10.115 Why sholde we þat now ben for þe werkes *of* Adam
B.10.124 Ac bileueþ lelly in þe loore *of* holy chirche,
B.10.125 And preie hym *of* pardon and penaunce in þi lyue,
B.10.127 For alle þat wilneþ to wite þe [whyes] *of* god almyȝty,
B.10.144 I myȝte gete no greyn *of* his grete wittes,
B.10.146 In signe þat I sholde bisechen hire *of* grace.
B.10.147 And whan I was war *of* his wille to his wif gan I [knele]
B.10.158 Thanne was [I] also fayn as fowel *of* fair morwe,
B.10.170 Thanne shaltow se Sobretee and Sympletee-*of*-speche,
B.10.182 *Of* alle kynne craftes I contreued tooles,
B.10.183 *Of* Carpent[ers and] kerueres; [I kenned first] Masons
B.10.193 For dobet and dobest ben [drawen] *of* loues [scole].
B.10.213 Geometrie and Geomesie [is] gynful *of* speche,
B.10.216 Yet ar þer fibicches in [forelles] *of* fele mennes [wittes],
B.10.217 Experimentȝ *of* Alkenamye [of Albertes makynge,
B.10.217 Experimentȝ of Alkenamye [*of* Albertes makynge,
B.10.233 That I was *of* wittes hous and wiþ his wif dame Studie.
B.10.239 Wiþ alle þe articles *of* þe feiþ þat falleþ to be knowe.
B.10.244 Thoruȝ þe help *of* þe holy goost þe which is of boþe;
B.10.244 Thoruȝ þe help of þe holy goost þe which is *of* boþe;
B.10.247 God þe fader, god þe sone, god holy goost *of* boþe,
B.10.248 Makere *of* man [and his make] and of beestes boþe.
B.10.248 Makere of man [and his make] and *of* beestes boþe.
B.10.279 Ac it semeþ now sooþly, to [siȝte *of* þe worlde],
B.10.285 The bible bereþ witnesse þat al[le] þe [barnes] *of* Israel
B.10.286 Bittre abouȝte þe giltes *of* two badde preestes,
B.10.295 And be prester at youre preiere þan for a pound *of* nobles,
B.10.299 *Of* religion þe rule reherseþ in hise morales,
B.10.312 A ledere *of* louedayes and a lond buggere,
B.10.314 An heep *of* houndes at his ers as he a lord were,
B.10.320 *Of* þe pouere haue þei no pite, and þat is hir [pure chartre];
B.10.323 And bete yow, as þe bible telleþ, for brekynge *of* youre rule,
B.10.329 *Of* Costantyns cofres [þer þe catel is Inne]
B.10.331 And þanne shal þe Abbot *of* Abyngdoun and al his issue for euere
B.10.332 Haue a knok *of* a kyng, and incurable þe wounde.
B.10.340 Ne richesse [ne rentes] ne Reautee *of* lordes.
B.10.348 Ther riche men no riȝt may cleyme but *of* ruþe and grace.'
B.10.364 And but we do þus in dede, [er] þe day *of* dome,
B.10.369 And siþen heþen to helpe in hope *of* amendement.
B.10.375 "I shal punyssshe in purgatorie or in þe put *of* helle
B.10.381 In þe legende *of* lif longe er I were,
B.10.385 God gaf hym grace *of* wit and alle goodes after
B.10.389 Maistres þat *of* goddes mercy techen men and prechen,
B.10.390 *Of* hir wordes þei wissen vs for wisest as in hir tyme,
B.10.395 Ac *of* fele witty in feiþ litel ferly I haue
B.10.400 Whan þei shal lif lete [a lippe *of* goddes grace]—
B.10.405 Ac I wene it worþ *of* manye as was in Noes tyme
B.10.406 Tho he shoop þat ship *of* shides and bordes:
B.10.410 *Of* w[r]ightes þat it wroȝte was noon of hem ysaued.
B.10.410 Of w[r]ightes þat it wroȝte was noon *of* hem ysaued.
B.10.412 *Of* holi chirche þat herberwe is, and goddes hous to saue
B.10.415 The culorum *of* þis clause curatours is to mene,
B.10.417 [At domesday þe deluuye worþ *of* deþ and fir at ones;
B.10.418 Forþi I counseille yow clerkes, *of* holy [kirke] þe wriȝtes,
B.10.424 Or Adam or Ysaye or any *of* þe prophetes
B.10.427 Wiþouten penaunce *of* purgatorie, to perpetuel blisse.
B.10.435 *Of* wit and of wisedom wiþ dampned soules wonye.
B.10.435 Of wit and *of* wisedom wiþ dampned soules wonye.
B.10.436 That Salomon seiþ I trowe be sooþ and certein *of* vs alle:
B.10.438 In þe hondes *of* almyȝty god, and he woot þe soþe
B.10.440 Or ellis for his yuel wille and enuye *of* herte,
B.10.448 [And yet haue I forgete ferþer *of* fyue wittes techyng
B.10.449 That] Clergie *of* cristes mouþ comended was it [neuere],
B.10.451 Thouȝ ye come bifore kynges and clerkes *of* þe lawe
B.10.452 Beþ noȝt [afered *of* þat folk], for I shal [ȝyue yow tonge],
B.10.455 And myȝte no kyng ouercomen hym as by konnynge *of* speche.
B.10.458 The douȝtieste doctuor and deuinour *of* þe trinitee
B.10.459 Was Austyn þe olde, and heiȝest *of* þe foure,
B.10.465 Ne none sonner saued, ne sadder *of* bileue,
B.10.468 Percen wiþ a Paternoster þe paleys *of* heuene
B.10.470 Into þe [parfit] blisse *of* Paradis for hir pure bileue,
B.10.478 Right so lewed [laborers] and *of* litel knowyng
B.10.480 As clerkes *of* holy [k]ir[k]e þat kepen cristes tresor,
B.11.4 Tho wepte I for wo and wraþe *of* hir speche
B.11.8 And into þe lond *of* longynge [and] loue she me brouȝte
B.11.14 And Coueitise *of* eiȝes [þat ooþer was ycalled].
B.11.15 Pride *of* parfit lyuynge pursued hem boþe
B.11.27 Thanne was þer oon þat hiȝte Elde, þat heuy was *of* chere;
B.11.28 'Man', quod he, 'if I mete wiþ þe, by Marie *of* heuene!
B.11.32 Coueitise *of* eiȝe, þat euere þow hir knewe—
B.11.33 And pride *of* parfit lyuynge to muche peril þee brynge.'
B.11.40 Concupiscencia carnis ne Coueitise *of* eiȝes
B.11.46 Coueitise *of* eiȝes conforted me anoon after

B.11.48	That *of* dowel ne dobet no deyntee me þou3te;
B.11.49	I hadde no likyng, leue me, [þe leste] *of* hem to knowe.
B.11.50	Coueitise *of* ei3es com ofter in mynde
B.11.52	Coueitise *of* ei3es [ofte me conforted];
B.11.59	By wissynge *of* þis wenche I [dide], hir wordes were so swete,
B.11.75	Ich haue muche merueille *of* yow, and so haþ many anoþer,
B.11.98	Excepte persons and preestes and prelates *of* holy chirche.
B.11.110	[The bileue [*of*] oure] lord þat lettred men techeþ].
B.11.115	Al for tene *of* hir text trembled myn herte,
B.11.118	That vnderfonged me atte font for oon *of* goddes chosene.
B.11.128	Wiþouten leue *of* his lord; no lawe wol it graunte.
B.11.134	For hise arerages rewarden hym þere [ri3t] to þe day *of* dome,
B.11.151	And I saued as ye [may] see, wiþouten syngynge *of* masses,
B.11.152	By loue and by lernyng *of* my lyuynge in truþe;
B.11.154	Lo! ye lordes, what leautee dide by an Emperour *of* Rome
B.11.156	Nou3t þoru3 preiere *of* a pope but for his pure truþe
B.11.160	[This matere is merk for many, ac men *of* holy chirche].
B.11.163	Pulte out of pyne a paynym *of* rome.
B.11.166	Ther no clergie ne kouþe, ne konnyng *of* lawes.
B.11.168	For þat is þe book blissed *of* blisse and of ioye;
B.11.168	For þat is þe book blissed of blisse and *of* ioye;
B.11.175	But al for loue *of* oure lord and þe bet to loue þe peple.
B.11.185	[For] oure Ioye and oure [Iuel], Iesu crist *of* heuene,
B.11.188	To knowen vs by oure kynde herte and castynge *of* oure ei3en,
B.11.189	Wheiþer we loue þe lordes here bifore þe lord *of* blisse;
B.11.199	For alle are we cristes creatures and *of* his cofres riche,
B.11.200	And breþeren as *of* oo blood, as wel beggeres as Erles.
B.11.201	For [at] Caluarie *of* cristes blood cristendom gan sprynge,
B.11.202	And blody breþeren we bicome þere *of* o body ywonne,
B.11.206	*Of* Adames issue and Eue ay til god man deide;
B.11.209	Forþi loue we as leue [children shal], and ech man laughe *of* ooþer,
B.11.210	And *of* þat ech man may forbere amende þere it nedeþ,
B.11.212	And be we no3t vnkynde *of* oure catel, ne of oure konnyng neiþer,
B.11.212	And be we no3t vnkynde of oure catel, ne *of* oure konnyng neiþer,
B.11.216	For whateuere clerkes carpe *of* cristendom or ellis,
B.11.218	That Fides sua sholde sauen hire and saluen hire *of* synnes.
B.11.220	*Of* logyk [ne] of lawe in legenda sanctorum
B.11.220	Of logyk [ne] *of* lawe in legenda sanctorum
B.11.226	For some wordes I fynde writen, were *of* Feiþes techyng,
B.11.229	Forþi lerne we þe lawe *of* loue as oure lord tau3te;
B.11.243	And in þe apparaille *of* a pouere man and pilgrymes liknesse
B.11.245	Ther neuere segge hym sei3 in secte *of* þe riche.
B.11.262	Is a kernel *of* confort kynde to restore.
B.11.266	*Of* which crist is a kernell to conforte þe soule.
B.11.284	For masses ne for matyns, no3t hir mete *of* vsureres,
B.11.287	Spera in deo spekeþ *of* preestes þat haue no spendyng siluer,
B.11.296	It is a careful kny3t, and *of* a caytif kynges makyng,
B.11.297	That haþ no lond ne lynage riche ne good loos *of* hise handes.
B.11.300	And a title, a tale *of* no3t, to his liflode at meschief.
B.11.302	[Moore þan cure] for konnyng or 'knowen for clene [*of*] berynge'.
B.11.314	Synge ne psalmes rede ne seye a masse *of* þe day.
B.11.316	For hir eiþer is endited, and that [*of*] 'Ignorancia
B.11.323	And þoru3 þe wondres *of* þis world wit for to take.
B.11.330	Wiþ fleckede feþeres and *of* fele colours.
B.11.336	In etynge, in drynkynge and in engendrynge *of* kynde.
B.11.337	And after cours *of* concepcion noon took kepe of ooþer,
B.11.337	And after cours of concepcion noon took kepe *of* ooþer,
B.11.355	For fere *of* oþere foweles and for wilde beestes.
B.11.368	*Of* hir kynde and hir colour to carpe it were to longe.
B.11.393	*Of* hire defautes foule bifore hem reherced].
B.11.401	In fondynge *of* þe flessh and of þe fend boþe,
B.11.401	In fondynge of þe flessh and *of* þe fend boþe,
B.11.402	For man was maad *of* swich a matere he may no3t wel asterte
B.11.419	The wisedom and þe wit *of* god, he was put fram blisse.
B.11.430	*Of* clergie ne of his counseil he counteþ no3t a risshe.
B.11.430	Of clergie ne *of* his counseil he counteþ no3t a risshe.
B.12.6	And *of* þi wilde wantownesse [whiles] þow yong were
B.12.11	Wiþ poustees *of* pestilences, wiþ pouerte and with angres;
B.12.13	And Dauid in þe Sauter seiþ, *of* swiche þat loueþ Iesus,
B.12.19	And prechours to preuen what it is *of* many a peire freres.'
B.12.23	And *of* holy men I her[e]', quod I, 'how þei ouþerwhile
B.12.48	The beaute *of* hir body; in baddenesse she despended.
B.12.49	*Of* manye swiche I may rede, of men and of wommen,
B.12.49	Of manye swiche I may rede, *of* men and of wommen,
B.12.49	Of manye swiche I may rede, of men and *of* wommen,
B.12.63	And þoru3 þe gifte *of* þe holy goost as þe gospel telleþ:
B.12.64	Clergie and kynde wit comeþ *of* si3te and techyng
B.12.66	*Of* quod scimus comeþ Clergie, [a] konnynge of heuene,
B.12.66	Of quod scimus comeþ Clergie, [a] konnynge *of* heuene,
B.12.67	And *of* quod vidimus comeþ kynde wit, of si3te of diuerse peple.
B.12.67	And of quod vidimus comeþ kynde wit, *of* si3te of diuerse peple.
B.12.67	And of quod vidimus comeþ kynde wit, of si3te *of* diuerse peple.
B.12.68	Ac grace is a gifte of god and of greet loue spryngeþ;

B.12.68	Ac grace is a gifte *of* god and of greet loue spryngeþ;
B.12.71	And namely Clergie for cristes loue, þat *of* Clergie is roote.
B.12.73	In þe olde lawe as þe lettre telleþ, þat was þe lawe *of* Iewes,
B.12.76	A womman, as [we] fynde[n], was gilty *of* þat dede,
B.12.77	Ac crist *of* his curteisie þoru3 clergie hir saued.
B.12.85	For goddes body my3te no3t ben *of* breed wiþouten clergie,
B.12.91	Dampneþ vs at þe day *of* dome as [dide þe caractes] þe Iewes.
B.12.93	For kynde wit is *of* his kyn and nei3e Cosynes boþe
B.12.109	Which is þe cofre *of* cristes tresor, and clerkes kepe þe keyes
B.12.112	Buxomliche and benigneliche and bidden it *of* grace.
B.12.126	For Clergie is kepere vnder crist *of* heuene,
B.12.128	Ac kynde wit comeþ *of* alle kynnes si3tes,
B.12.129	*Of* briddes and of beestes, [by] tastes of truþe.
B.12.129	Of briddes and of beestes, [by] tastes *of* truþe.
B.12.129	Of briddes and *of* beestes, [by] tastes of truþe.
B.12.135	For alle hir kynde knowyn[g] co[m] but *of* diuerse si3tes.
B.12.138	A[s] to þe clergie *of* crist counted it but a trufle:
B.12.143	He spekeþ þere *of* riche men ri3t no3t, ne of ri3t witty,
B.12.143	He spekeþ þere of riche men ri3t no3t, ne *of* ri3t witty,
B.12.144	Ne *of* lordes þat were lewed men, but of þe hyeste lettred oute:
B.12.144	Ne of lordes þat were lewed men, but *of* þe hyeste lettred oute:
B.12.147	But in a Burgeises place, *of* Bethlem þe beste:
B.12.150	And songe a song *of* solas, Gloria in excelsis deo.
B.12.152	Tho it shon to shepherdes, a shewer *of* blisse].
B.12.158	Than clerkes or kynde witted men *of* cristene peple.
B.12.159	And þow seidest sooþ *of* somme, ac se in what manere.
B.12.163	That ooþer is lewed [*of*] þat labour, lerned neuere swymme.
B.12.164	Which trowestow þo two [in Themese] is in moost drede,
B.12.165	He þat neuere ne dyued ne no3t kan *of* swymmyng,
B.12.192	The þef þat hadde grace *of* god on good fryday, as þow spek[e],
B.12.194	And grace asked *of* god [graiþ is hem euere]
B.12.200	As þo þat seten at þe syde table or wiþ þe souereynes *of* þe halle,
B.12.212	For he is in þe loweste *of* heuene, if oure bileue be trewe,
B.12.213	And wel lose[l]y he lolleþ þere by þe lawe *of* holy chirche:
B.12.219	/And willest *of* briddes & beestes and of hir bredyng knowe,
B.12.219	/And willest of briddes & beestes and *of* hir bredyng knowe,
B.12.221	And *of* þe floures in þe Fryth and of hire faire hewes,
B.12.221	And of þe floures in þe Fryth and *of* hire faire hewes,
B.12.223	And *of* þe stones and of þe sterres; þow studiest, as I leue,
B.12.223	And of þe stones and *of* þe sterres; þow studiest, as I leue,
B.12.236	Ac *of* briddes and of beestes men by olde tyme
B.12.236	Ac of briddes and *of* beestes men by olde tyme
B.12.239	And feblest fowel *of* fli3t is þat fleeþ or swymmeþ.
B.12.244	For þe trailynge *of* his tail ouertaken is he soone.
B.12.246	And vnlouelich *of* ledene and looþ for to here.
B.12.248	And deleþ it no3t til his deeþ day, þe tail[le is al *of*] sorwe.
B.12.249	Ri3t as þe pennes *of* þe pecok peyneþ hym in his fli3t,
B.12.250	So is possession peyne *of* pens and of nobles
B.12.250	So is possession peyne of pens and *of* nobles
B.12.263	So is þe riche [reuerenced] by reson *of* hise goodes.
B.12.264	The larke þat is a lasse fowel is moore louelich *of* ledene,
B.12.265	And wel awey *of* wynge swifter þan þe Pecock,
B.12.266	And *of* flessh by fele fold fatter and swetter;
B.12.271	Ne *of* Sortes ne of Salomon no scripture kan telle.
B.12.271	Ne of Sortes ne *of* Salomon no scripture kan telle.
B.12.276	For lettred men were lewed yet ne were loore *of* hir bokes.'
B.12.279	Ne no creature *of* cristes liknesse withouten cristendom worþ saued.'
B.12.285	[Ac] þer is fullynge *of* Font and fullynge in blood shedyng
B.12.291	And wheiþer it worþ [*of* truþe] or no3t, [þe] worþ [of] bileue is gret,
B.12.291	And wheiþer it worþ [of truþe] or no3t, [þe] worþ [*of*] bileue is gret,
B.13.3	In manere *of* a mendynaunt many yer after.
B.13.4	And *of* þis metyng many tyme muche þou3t I hadde,
B.13.15	*Of* kynde and of his konnynge, and how curteis he is to bestes,
B.13.15	Of kynde and *of* his konnynge, and how curteis he is to bestes,
B.13.18	[For alle] creatures þat crepen [or walken] *of* kynde ben engendred;
B.13.24	And for Conscience *of* Clergie spak I com wel þe raþer.
B.13.38	And serued hem þus soone *of* sondry metes manye,
B.13.39	*Of* Austyn, of Ambrose, of [alle] þe foure Euangelistes:
B.13.39	Of Austyn, *of* Ambrose, of [alle] þe foure Euangelistes:
B.13.39	Of Austyn, of Ambrose, *of* [alle] þe foure Euangelistes:
B.13.40	Ac þis maister [*of*] þise men] no maner flessh [eet],
B.13.41	Ac [he eet] mete *of* moore cost, mortrews and potages.
B.13.42	*Of* þat men myswonne þei made hem wel at ese,
B.13.44	In a morter, Post mortem, *of* many bitter peyne
B.13.53	/And he brou3te vs *of* Beati quorum of Beatus virres makyng,
B.13.53	/And he brou3te vs of Beati quorum *of* Beatus virres makyng,
B.13.54	And þanne a mees *of* ooþer mete of Miserere mei deus,_
B.13.54	And þanne a mees of ooþer mete *of* Miserere mei deus,_
B.13.55	In a dissh *of* derne shrifte, Dixi & confitebor tibi.
B.13.59	Pacience was proud *of* þat propre seruice

B.13.65	'It is noȝt foure dayes þat þis freke, bifore þe deen *of* Poules,
B.13.66	Preched *of* penaunces þat Poul þe Apostle suffrede
B.13.67	In fame & frigore and flappes *of* scourges:
B.13.85	[And appose hym] what penaunce is, *of* which he preched raþer.'
B.13.91	And preuen it by hir Pocalips and passion *of* Seint Auereys
B.13.94	And þanne shal he testifie *of* [a] Trinite, and take his felawe to witnesse
B.13.95	What he fond in a [forel *of*] a freres lyuyng,
B.13.98	*Of* dowel and dobet, and if do[best] be any penaunce.'
B.13.102	And tolde hym *of* a Trinite, and toward vs he loked.
B.13.121	Ther þe lord *of* lif wonyeþ, to leren [hem] what is dowel.
B.13.140	"Wiþ wordes and werkes", quod she, "and wil *of* þyn herte
B.13.142	And so þow lere þe to louye, for [þe] lordes loue *of* heuene,
B.13.144	Cast coles on his heed *of* alle kynde speche;
B.13.149	For he þat loueþ þee leelly litel *of* þyne coueiteþ.
B.13.153	In a signe *of* þe Saterday þat sette first þe kalender,
B.13.154	And al þe wit *of* þe wodnesday of þe nexte wike after;
B.13.154	And al þe wit of þe wodnesday *of* þe nexte wike after;
B.13.155	The myddel *of* þe Moone [i]s þe [m]yght of boþe.
B.13.155	The myddel of þe Moone [i]s þe [m]yght *of* boþe.
B.13.160	Coold ne care ne compaignye *of* þeues,
B.13.162	Ne [neiþer] fuyr ne flood ne feere *of* þyn enemy
B.13.167	Maister *of* alle þo men þoruȝ myȝt of þis redels,
B.13.167	Maister of alle þo men þoruȝ myȝt *of* þis redels,
B.13.173	Al þe wit *of* þis world and wiȝt mennes strengþe
B.13.185	I shal brynge yow a bible, a book *of* þe olde lawe,
B.13.190	Ac þe wil *of* þe wye and þe wil of folk here
B.13.190	Ac þe wil of þe wye and þe wil *of* folk here
B.13.192	The goode wil *of* a wight was neuere bouȝt to þe fulle,
B.13.194	Hadde noȝt [Marie] Maudeleyne moore for a box *of* salue
B.13.196	And þe poore widewe [purely] for a peire *of* mytes
B.13.201	Haue pacience parfitliche þan half þi pak *of* bokes.'
B.13.202	Clergie *of* Conscience no congie wolde take,
B.13.220	And as þe[i] wente by þe weye–of dowel þei carped–
B.13.225	Al yde[l] ich hatie for *of* Actif is my name.
B.13.234	I haue no goode giftes *of* þise grete lordes
B.13.239	For alle trewe trauaillours and tiliers *of* þe erþe
B.13.241	Beggeris and bidderis *of* my breed crauen,
B.13.244	And I hadde neuere *of* hym, haue god my trouþe,
B.13.245	Neiþer prouendre ne personage yet *of* [þe] popes ȝifte,
B.13.246	Saue a pardon wiþ a peis *of* leed and two polles amyddes.
B.13.255	Ac if myȝt *of* myracle hym faille it is for men ben noȝt worþi
B.13.256	To haue þe grace *of* god, and no gilt of [þe] pope.
B.13.256	To haue þe grace of god, and no gilt *of* [þe] pope.
B.13.260	For er I haue breed *of* mele ofte moot I swete,
B.13.268	In þe date *of* oure driȝte, in a drye Aprill,
B.13.272	*Of* haukyn þe Actif man and how he was ycloþed.
B.13.273	He hadde a cote *of* cristendom as holy kirke bileueþ.
B.13.275	*Of* pride here a plot, and þere a plot of vnbuxom speche,
B.13.275	Of pride here a plot, and þere a plot *of* vnbuxom speche,
B.13.276	*Of* scornyng and of scoffyng and of vnskilful berynge;
B.13.276	Of scornyng and *of* scoffyng and of vnskilful berynge;
B.13.276	Of scornyng and of scoffyng and *of* vnskilful berynge;
B.13.281	And inobedient to ben vndernome *of* any lif lyuynge;
B.13.282	And so singuler by hymself [as to siȝte *of* þe peple
B.13.287	In likynge *of* lele lif and a liere in soule;
B.13.292	[Or for his crafty konnynge or *of* clerkes þe wisest,
B.13.294	And louelokest to loken on and lelest *of* werkes,
B.13.295	And noon so holy as he ne *of* lif clennere,
B.13.296	Or feirest *of* feitures of forme and of shafte,
B.13.296	Or feirest of feitures *of* forme and of shafte,
B.13.296	Or feirest of feitures of forme and *of* shafte,
B.13.297	And most sotil *of* song oþer sleyest of hondes,
B.13.297	And most sotil of song oþer sleyest *of* hondes,
B.13.300	Pouere *of* possession in purs and in cofre,
B.13.301	And as a lyoun on to loke and lordlich *of* speche;
B.13.302	Boldest *of* beggeris; a bostere þat noȝt haþ,
B.13.305	*Of* dedes þat he neuere dide demen and bosten;
B.13.306	And *of* werkes þat he wel dide witnesse and siggen,
B.13.310	And what I kouþe and knew and what kyn I com *of*.
B.13.311	Al he wolde þat men wiste *of* werkes and wordes
B.13.327	And made *of* frendes foes þoruȝ a fals tonge.
B.13.328	'Or wiþ myȝt [*of*] mouþ or þoruȝ m[a]nnes strengþe
B.13.337	Lechecraft *of* oure lord and leue on a wicche,
B.13.339	To þe Soutere *of* Southwerk or of Shordych dame Emme;
B.13.339	To þe Soutere of Southwerk or *of* Shordych dame Emme;
B.13.343	Wiþ likynge *of* lecherie as by lokynge of his eiȝe.
B.13.343	Wiþ likynge of lecherie as by lokynge *of* his eiȝe.
B.13.353	And *of* hir harlotrye and horedom in hir elde tellen.
B.13.354	Thanne Pacience parceyued *of* pointes [his] cote
B.13.359	Lened for loue *of* þe wed and looþ to do truþe,
B.13.372	*Of* my nexte Neghebore, nymen of his erþe;
B.13.372	Of my nexte Neghebore, nymen *of* his erþe;

B.13.375	And [what body] borwed *of* me abouȝte þe tyme
B.13.378	And boþe to kiþ and to kyn vnkynde *of* þat ich hadde;
B.13.386	For losse *of* good, leue me, þan for likames giltes;
B.13.398	Than in þe grace *of* god and hise grete helpes;
B.13.412	Dooþ noon almes[dede]; dred hym *of* no synne;
B.13.416	Whan men carpen *of* crist or clennesse of soul[e
B.13.416	Whan men carpen of crist or clennesse *of* soul[e
B.13.417	He wexeþ wroþ, and wol noȝt here but wordes *of* murþe,
B.13.418	Penaunce [and] pouere men and þe passion *of* Seintes,
B.13.421	Ye lordes and ladies and legates *of* holy chirche
B.13.427	Patriarkes and prophetes, prechours *of* goddes wordes,
B.13.432	What Dauid seiþ *of* swiche men as þe Sauter telleþ:
B.13.437	And for loue *of* [hir] lorde liþeþ hem at festes;
B.13.446	And fiþele þee wiþoute flaterynge *of* good friday þe [geste],
B.13.456	Wiþ turpiloquio, a l[a]y *of* sorwe, and luciferis fiþele.
B.14.6	Wiþ þe sope *of* siknesse þat sekeþ wonder depe,
B.14.7	And [laþered] wiþ þe losse *of* catel [forto me] looþ [were]
B.14.9	And [siþþe] shryuen *of* þe preest, þat [for my synnes gaf me]
B.14.11	Al for coueitise *of* my cristendom in clennesse to kepen it.
B.14.14	Or þoruȝ werk or þoruȝ word or wille *of* myn herte
B.14.16	'And I shal kenne þee', quod Conscience, '*of* Contricion to make
B.14.17	That shal clawe þi cote *of* alle kynnes filþe:
B.14.33	And þat ynogh; shal noon faille *of* þyng þat hem nedeþ:
B.14.37	Vitailles *of* grete vertues for alle manere beestes
B.14.43	The Corlew by kynde *of* þe Eyr, moost clennest flessh of briddes,
B.14.43	The Corlew by kynde of þe Eyr, moost clennest flessh *of* briddes,
B.14.48	[Th]at pacience so preisede, [and *of* his poke hente]
B.14.49	A pece *of* þe Paternoster [and profrede vs alle];
B.14.55	By so þat þow be sobre *of* siȝte and of tonge,
B.14.55	By so þat þow be sobre of siȝte and *of* tonge,
B.14.76	For þe meschief and þe meschaunce amonges men *of* Sodome
B.14.77	Weex þoruȝ plentee *of* payn and of pure sleuþe
B.14.77	Weex þoruȝ plentee of payn and *of* pure sleuþe:
B.14.78	For [men] mesured noȝt hemself of [mete] and dr[y]nke,
B.14.87	That whiles he lyuede he bileuede in þe loore *of* holy chirche.
B.14.89	And surgiens *of* mouþ synnes whan shrift *of* mouþe failleþ.
B.14.90	Ac shrift *of* mouþ moore worþi is if man be y[n]liche contrit,
B.14.91	For shrift *of* mouþe sleeþ synne be it neuer so dedly–
B.14.100	'Ther parfit truþe and poore herte is, and pacience *of* tonge,
B.14.105	Thouȝ men rede *of* richesse riȝt to þe worldes ende,
B.14.110	To haue allowaunce *of* his lord; by þe lawe he it cleymeþ.
B.14.111	Ioye þat neuere ioye hadde *of* riȝtful Iugge he askeþ,
B.14.126	Ac god is *of* [a] wonder wille, by þat kynde wit sheweþ,
B.14.130	And greet likynge to lyue wiþouten labour *of* bodye,
B.14.133	Fram þe loue *of* oure lord at his laste ende!
B.14.139	And noȝt to fonge bifore for drede *of* disalowyng.
B.14.147	Crist *of* his curteisie shal conforte yow at þe laste,
B.14.154	Here forȝifnesse *of* hir synnes, and heuene blisse after.
B.14.163	And arated *of* riche men þat ruþe is to here.
B.14.169	*Of* þe good þat þow hem gyuest ingrati ben manye;
B.14.170	Ac god, *of* þi goodnesse gyue hem grace to amende.
B.14.173	*Of* þat þei wilne and wolde wanteþ hem noȝt here.
B.14.174	Ac poore peple, þi prisoners, lord, in þe put *of* meschief,
B.14.177	Wo in wynter tymes for wantynge *of* cloþes,
B.14.181	Thus in genere *of* gentries Iesu crist seide
B.14.185	And be clene þoruȝ þat cristnyng *of* alle kynnes synne.
B.14.192	Ac þe parchemyn *of* þis patente of pouerte be moste,
B.14.192	Ac þe parchemyn of þis patente *of* pouerte be moste,
B.14.193	And *of* pure pacience and parfit bileue.
B.14.194	*Of* pompe and of pride þe parchemyn decourreþ,
B.14.194	Of pompe and *of* pride þe parchemyn decourreþ,
B.14.195	And principalliche *of* al[l]e peple but þei be poore of herte.
B.14.195	And principalliche of al[l]e peple but þei be poore *of* herte.
B.14.198	But oure spences and spendynge sprynge *of* a trewe w[e]lle;
B.14.207	[Ac] þe riche is reuerenced by reson *of* his richesse
B.14.209	*Of* wit and of wisdom, þat fer awey is bettre
B.14.209	Of wit and *of* wisdom, þat fer awey is bettre
B.14.219	Ne none *of* þe seuene synnes sitten ne mowe þer longe,
B.14.229	That mete or money *of* oþere men moot asken.
B.14.241	For men knowen wel þat Coueitise is *of* [a] kene wille
B.14.242	And haþ hondes and armes *of* [a long] lengþe,
B.14.253	Hadde þei no[on haunt] but *of* poore men; hir houses stoode vntyled.
B.14.257	And he his seruaunt, as he seiþ, and *of* his sute boþe.
B.14.258	And wheiþer he be or be noȝt, he bereþ þe signe *of* pouerte
B.14.260	Forþi [al] poore þat pacient is [*of* pure riȝt] may cleymen,
B.14.263	In lond and in lordshipe and likynge *of* bodie
B.14.267	Muche is [þat maide] to loue *of* [a man] þat swich oon takeþ,
B.14.269	As by assent *of* sondry parties and siluer to boote,
B.14.270	Moore for coueitise *of* [catel] þan kynde loue of boþe–
B.14.270	Moore for coueitise of [catel] þan kynde loue *of* boþe–
B.14.283	And a sorwe *of* hymself and solace to þe soule,
B.14.294	Selde is poore [riȝt] riche but *of* riȝtful heritage.

B.14.296 Ne borweþ *of* hise neighebores but þat he may wel paie:
B.14.301 The fifte is moder *of* [my3t and of mannes] helþe,
B.14.301 The fifte is moder of [my3t and *of* mannes] helþe,
B.14.302 A frend in alle fondynges, [*of* foule yueles leche],
B.14.303 And for þe [lewde] euere [yliche] a lemman *of* alle clennesse:
B.14.304 The sixte is a path *of* pees; ye! þoru3 þe paas of Aultoun
B.14.304 The sixte is a path of pees; ye! þoru3 þe paas *of* Aultoun
B.14.305 Pouerte my3te passe wiþouten peril *of* robbyng.
B.14.307 And euer þe lasse þat he [lede], þe [li3ter] he is *of* herte:
B.14.308 And an hardy man *of* herte among an heep of þeues;
B.14.308 And an hardy man of herte among an heep *of* þeues;
B.14.310 The seuenþe is welle *of* wisedom and fewe wordes sheweþ
B.14.331 Or maistrie ouer any man mo þan *of* hymselue.
B.15.7 As persons in pelure wiþ pendaunt3 *of* siluer;
B.15.14 And wherof I cam & *of* what kynde. I coniured hym at þe laste
B.15.16 'I am cristes creature', quod he, 'and [*of* his kyn a party],
B.15.17 In cristes court yknowe wel and *of* [cristene in many a place].
B.15.21 That ech a creature *of* his court welcomeþ me faire.'
B.15.30 And þat is wit and wisdom, þe welle *of* alle craftes;
B.15.37 Austyn and Ysodorus, eiþer *of* hem boþe
B.15.45 Thow woldest knowe and konne þe cause *of* alle [hire] names,
B.15.46 And *of* [myne] if þow my3test, me þynkeþ by þi speche.'
B.15.50 'Thanne artow inparfit', quod he, 'and oon *of* prides kny3tes.
B.15.58 And þe moore þat a man *of* good matere hereþ,
B.15.66 *Of* god and of hise grete my3tes, hise graces it letteþ.
B.15.66 Of god and *of* hise grete my3tes, hise graces it letteþ.
B.15.71 Ye moeuen materes vnmesurable to tellen *of* þe Trinite
B.15.72 That [lome] þe lewed peple *of* hir bileue doute.
B.15.74 And tellen men *of* þe ten comaundement3, and touchen þe seuene synnes,
B.15.75 And *of* þe braunches þat burioneþ of hem and bryngen men to helle,
B.15.75 And of þe braunches þat burioneþ *of* hem and bryngen men to helle,
B.15.82 Gooþ to þe glose *of* þ[e] vers, ye grete clerkes;
B.15.85 *Of* vsurers, of hoores, of Auarouse chapmen,
B.15.85 Of vsurers, *of* hoores, of Auarouse chapmen,
B.15.85 Of vsurers, of hoores, *of* Auarouse chapmen,
B.15.89 *Of* þis matere I my3te make a long bible,
B.15.90 Ac *of* curatours of cristen peple, as clerkes bereþ witnesse,
B.15.90 Ac of curatours *of* cristen peple, as clerkes bereþ witnesse,
B.15.98 Ther is a meschief in þe more *of* swiche manere [stokkes].
B.15.99 Right so persons and preestes and prechours *of* holi chirche
B.15.100 [Is þe] roote *of* þe right feiþ to rule þe peple;
B.15.103 Forþi wolde ye lettrede leue þe lecherie *of* cloþyng,
B.15.104 And be kynde as bifel for clerkes and curteise *of* cristes goodes,
B.15.105 Trewe *of* youre tonge and of youre tail boþe,
B.15.105 Trewe of youre tonge and *of* youre tail boþe,
B.15.117 Tiþes [*of* vn]trewe þyng ytilied or chaffared,
B.15.117 Iohannes Crisostomus *of* clerkes [carpeþ] and preestes:
B.15.123 Sir Iohan and sire Geffrey haþ [*of* siluer a girdel],
B.15.130 Wolde neuere þe wit *of* witty god but wikkede men it hadde,
B.15.136 Curatours *of* holy kirke, as clerkes þat ben auarouse,
B.15.163 And so I trowe trewely, by þat men telleþ *of* [it,
B.15.166 As proud *of* a peny as of a pound of golde,
B.15.166 As proud of a peny as *of* a pound of golde,
B.15.166 As proud of a peny as of a pound *of* golde,
B.15.167 And is as glad *of* a gowne of a gray russet
B.15.167 And is as glad of a gowne *of* a gray russet
B.15.168 As *of* a tunycle of tarse or of trie scarlet.
B.15.168 As of a tunycle *of* tarse or of trie scarlet.
B.15.168 As of a tunycle of tarse or *of* trie scarlet.
B.15.177 'Of rentes n[e] of richesse rekkeþ he neuere,
B.15.177 'Of rentes n[e] *of* richesse rekkeþ he neuere,
B.15.180 And if he soupeþ eteþ but a sop *of* Spera in deo.
B.15.186 And whan he is wery *of* þat werk þan wole he som tyme
B.15.187 Labouren in [a] lauendrye wel þe lengþe *of* a Mile,
B.15.196 'Wiþouten help *of* Piers Plowman', quod he, 'his persone sestow neuere.'
B.15.201 For þer are [pure] proude herted men, pacient *of* tonge
B.15.202 And buxome as *of* beryinge to burgeises and to lordes,
B.15.217 And þe murieste *of* mouþ at mete where he sitteþ.
B.15.218 The loue þat liþ in his herte makeþ hym li3t *of* speche,
B.15.233 Riche men he recomendeþ, and *of* hir robes takeþ
B.15.236 Ac if coueitise be *of* þe counseil he wol no3t come þerInne,
B.15.238 For braulynge and bakbitynge and berynge *of* fals witnesse.
B.15.243 Thei vndoon it vn[digne]ly, þo doctours *of* lawe.
B.15.262 *Of* oure foes þat dooþ vs falsnesse; þat is oure fadres wille.
B.15.269 [Lo]! in legenda sanctorum, þe lif *of* holy Seintes,
B.15.277 *Of* leons ne of leopardes no liflode ne toke,
B.15.277 Of leons ne *of* leopardes no liflode ne toke,
B.15.278 But *of* foweles þat fleeþ; þus fyndeþ men in bokes.
B.15.280 And þoru3 þe mylk *of* þat mylde beest þe man was sustened;

B.15.289 Til he foundede freres *of* Austynes ordre, [or ellis freres lyen].
B.15.295 Ac moost þoru3 [meditacion] and mynde *of* god almyghty.
B.15.310 And to taken *of* hir tenaunt3 moore þan trouþe wolde,
B.15.316 And a mees þermyd *of* o maner kynde.
B.15.326 Who parfourneþ þis prophecie *of* þe peple þat now libbeþ,
B.15.331 And *of* hem þat habbeþ þei taken and 3yueþ hem þat [ne] habbeþ.
B.15.333 Fele *of* yow fareþ as if I a forest hadde
B.15.334 That were ful *of* faire trees, and I fondede and caste
B.15.338 As whoso filled a tonne [ful] *of* a fressh ryuer
B.15.348 Wherfore folk is þe febler and no3t ferm *of* bileue.
B.15.350 The merk *of* þat monee is good ac þe metal is feble;
B.15.352 Crowne and cristendom, þe kynges mark *of* heuene,
B.15.363 As *of* wedres and wyndes þei warned men ofte.
B.15.367 Now faileþ þe folk *of* þe flood and of þe lond boþe,
B.15.367 Now faileþ þe folk of þe flood and *of* þe lond boþe,
B.15.371 *Of* þat was calculed of þe element þe contrarie þei fynde.
B.15.371 Of þat was calculed *of* þe element þe contrarie þei fynde.
B.15.372 Grammer, þe ground *of* al, bigileþ now children,
B.15.373 For is noon *of* þise newe clerkes, whoso nymeþ hede,
B.15.380 Doctours *of* decrees and of diuinite maistres,
B.15.380 Doctours of decrees and *of* diuinite maistres,
B.15.384 Thei sholde faillen *of* hir Philosophie and in Phisik boþe.
B.15.385 Wherfore I am afered *of* folk of holy kirke,
B.15.385 Wherfore I am afered of folk *of* holy kirke,
B.15.398 Brou3te Sar3ens *of* Surree, and see in what manere.
B.15.407 That þe coluere þat com so com from god *of* heuene
B.15.409 And þus þoru3 wiles *of* his wit and a whit Dowue
B.15.414 [Ac] for drede *of* þe deeþ I dar no3t telle truþe,
B.15.420 *Of* tiraunt3 þat teneþ trewe men taken any almesse,
B.15.430 The heuedes *of* holy chirche, and þei holy were,
B.15.435 *Of* hem of holi chirche þat þe heighe wey sholde teche
B.15.435 Of hem *of* holi chirche þat þe heighe wey sholde teche
B.15.456 [And] so it fareþ by a barn þat born is *of* wombe;
B.15.457 Til it be cristned in cristes name and confermed *of* þe bisshop
B.15.473 That loþ ben to louye wiþouten lernyng *of* ensaumples.
B.15.482 That is god *of* his grace, gyueþ alle men blisse.
B.15.487 That heuedes *of* holy chirche ben, þat han hir wil here,
B.15.494 *Of* Na3areth, of Nynyue, of Neptalym and Damaske,
B.15.494 Of Na3areth, *of* Nynyue, of Neptalym and Damaske,
B.15.494 Of Na3areth, of Nynyue, *of* Neptalym and Damaske,
B.15.496 To be pastours and preche þe passion *of* Iesus,
B.15.498 And seide it in saluacion *of* Sar3ens and oþere;
B.15.502 Han a lippe *of* oure bileue, þe lightlier me þynkeþ
B.15.503 Thei sholde turne, whoso trauail[e wolde] to teche hem *of* þe Trinite.
B.15.510 That bere bisshopes names *of* Bethleem and Babiloigne.
B.15.511 [Whan þe hye kyng *of* heuene sente his sone to erþe
B.15.516 And bicam man *of* a maide and metropolitanus,
B.15.517 And baptised and bishined wiþ þe blode *of* his herte
B.15.523 In sauacion *of* [mannes soule] seint [Thomas] was ymartired;
B.15.525 And for þe ri3t *of* al þis reume and alle reumes cristene.
B.15.528 And souereynliche to swiche þat *of* surrye bereþ þe name],
B.15.546 For coueitise *of* þat cros [clerkes] of holy kirke
B.15.546 For coueitise of þat cros [clerkes] *of* holy kirke
B.15.555 The lordshipe *of* londes [lese ye shul for euere],
B.15.557 Whan Costantyn *of* curteisie holy kirke dowed
B.15.567 And purgen hem *of* poison er moore peril falle.
B.15.574 Ac ysaie *of* yow spekeþ and o3ias boþe,
B.15.589 *Of* selkouþe sores; þei sei3en it ofte,
B.15.590 Boþe *of* miracles and merueilles, and how he men festede,
B.15.599 Daniel *of* hire vndoynge deuyned and seide
B.15.606 Arn folk *of* oon feiþ; þe fader god þei honouren.
B.15.608 Konne þe firste clause *of* oure bileue, Credo in deum patrem omnipotentem,
B.15.609 Prelates *of* cristene prouinces sholde preue if þei my3te
B.16.6 The leues ben lele wordes, þe lawe *of* holy chirche;
B.16.8 Pacience hatte þe pure tree and [pouere] symple *of* herte,
B.16.11 And to haue my fulle *of* þat fruyt forsake a[l] oþ[er] saule[e].
B.16.14 Amyddes mannes body; þe more is *of* þat stokke.
B.16.28 Coueitise comþ *of* þat wynd and crepeþ among þe leues
B.16.34 And wikkede werkes þerof, wormes *of* synne,
B.16.37 That is þe passion and þe power *of* oure prince Iesu.
B.16.44 And leiþ a laddre þerto, *of* lesynges are þe ronges,
B.16.47 That is lieutenaunt to loken it wel bi leue *of* myselue:
B.16.52 And help þe holy goost, and þus haue I þe maistrie.'
B.16.54 The power *of* þise postes and hire propre my3t[e].
B.16.55 Ac I haue þou3tes a þreue *of* þise þre piles,
B.16.59 And *of* o greetnesse and grene of greyn þei semen.'
B.16.59 And of o greetnesse and grene *of* greyn þei semen.'
B.16.70 Thanne bereþ þe crop kynde fruyt and clennest *of* alle,
B.16.84 And made *of* holy men his hoord In limbo Inferni,
B.16.88 Filius by þe fader wille and frenesse *of* spiritus sancti
B.16.95 And þanne sholde Iesus Iuste þerfore bi Iuggement *of* armes

B.16.100	And in þe wombe *of* þat wenche was he fourty woukes
B.16.101	Til he weex a faunt þoruȝ hir flessh and *of* fightyng kouþe
B.16.109	And commune wommen conuertede and clensed *of* synne,
B.16.118	That he was leche *of* lif and lord of heigh heuene.
B.16.118	That he was leche of lif and lord *of* heigh heuene.
B.16.126	And lefte baskettes ful *of* broke mete, bere awey whoso wolde.'
B.16.130	And seide it in sighte *of* hem alle so hadde herden:
B.16.135	*Of* preieres and of parfitnesse þis place þat ye callen:
B.16.135	Of preieres and *of* parfitnesse þis place þat ye callen:
B.16.142	'I am sold þoruȝ [som] *of* yow; he shal þe tyme rewe
B.16.152	And kiste hym to be caught þerby and kulled *of* þe Iewes.
B.16.166	Deide and dee[þ] fordide, and day *of* nyȝt made.
B.16.175	And *of* whennes he were and whider þat he [þ]ouȝte.
B.16.177	And *of* Abrahames hous an heraud of armes;
B.16.177	And of Abrahames hous an heraud *of* armes;
B.16.182	*Of* oon muchel and myght in mesure and lengþe.
B.16.184	The firste haþ myȝt and maiestee, makere *of* alle þynges;
B.16.186	The secounde *of* þa[t] sire is Sothfastnesse filius,
B.16.187	Wardeyn *of* þat wit haþ; was euere wiþouten gynnyng.
B.16.189	The light *of* al þat lif haþ a londe and a watre,
B.16.190	Confortour *of* creatures; of hym comeþ alle blisse.
B.16.190	Confortour of creatures; *of* hym comeþ alle blisse.
B.16.193	*Of* hym[self] and of his seruaunt, and what [suffreþ hem] boþe.
B.16.193	Of hym[self] and *of* his seruaunt, and what [suffreþ hem] boþe.
B.16.197	That is children *of* charite, and holi chirche þe moder.
B.16.204	In tokenynge *of* þe Trinite, was [taken out of a man],
B.16.205	Adam, oure aller fader. Eue was *of* hymselue.
B.16.206	And þe issue þat þei hadde it was *of* hem boþe,
B.16.209	And þus is mankynde and manhede *of* matrimoyne yspronge
B.16.213	Hym þat first formed al, þe fader *of* heuene.
B.16.222	And is noȝt but gendre *of* a generacion bifore Iesu crist in heuene:
B.16.223	So is þe fader forþ with þe sone and fre wille *of* boþe,
B.16.224	Which is þe holy goost *of* alle, and alle is but o god.
B.16.245	And called me foot *of* his feiþ, his folk for to saue
B.16.250	*Of* a [buyrn] þat baptised hym–Iohan Baptist was his name–
B.16.253	I hadde wonder of hise wordes and *of* hise wide cloþes
B.16.253	I hadde wonder *of* hise wordes and of hise wide cloþes
B.16.260	'This is a present *of* muche pris; what prynce shal it haue?'
B.16.265	Til he come þat I carpe *of*; crist is his name
B.16.271	The myght *of* goddes mercy þat myȝte vs alle amende.'
B.17.2	That took me a maundement vpon þe mount *of* Synay
B.17.11	[He plukkede] forþ a patente, a pece *of* an hard roche
B.17.21	*Of* men and of wommen many score þousand.'
B.17.21	Of men and *of* wommen many score þousand.'
B.17.26	'Youre wordes arn wonderfulle', quod I, 'which *of* yow is trewest
B.17.36	And telleþ noȝt *of* þe Trinite þat took hym hise lettres,
B.17.40	Than he þat gooþ wiþ two staues to sighte *of* vs alle;
B.17.60	Feiþ hadde first siȝte *of* hym, ac he fleiȝ aside
B.17.64	Ac whan he hadde sighte *of* þat segge aside he gan hym drawe
B.17.66	Ac so soone so þe Samaritan hadde siȝte *of* þis leode
B.17.67	He lighte adown *of* Lyard and ladde hym in his hande,
B.17.87	And suwed þat Samaritan þat was so ful *of* pite,
B.17.92	For sighte *of* þ[e] sorweful [segge] þat robbed was with þeues.
B.17.96	Wiþouten þe blood *of* a barn born of a mayde.
B.17.96	Wiþouten þe blood of a barn born *of* a mayde.
B.17.98	And þanne plastred wiþ penaunce and passion *of* þat baby,
B.17.110	On my Capul þat highte caro–*of* mankynde I took it–
B.17.134	'After Abraham', quod he, 'þat heraud *of* armes,
B.17.144	The pawme is [þe piþ *of*] þe hand, and profreþ forþ þe fyngres
B.17.145	To ministren and to make þat myȝt *of* hand knoweþ;
B.17.147	The holy goost *of* heuene: he is as þe pawme.
B.17.150	That touched and tastede at techynge *of* þe pawme
B.17.166	That þre þynges bilongeþ in oure [fader] *of* heuene
B.17.171	Al þe myȝt myd hym is in makynge *of* þynges.
B.17.173	Keruynge and compassynge [i]s craft *of* þe fyngres.
B.17.174	Right so is þe sone þe Science *of* þe fader
B.17.177	Oþerwise þan þe wriþen fust or werkmanshipe *of* fyngres.
B.17.190	For peyne *of* þe pawme power hem failleþ
B.17.192	Were þe myddel *of* myn hand ymaymed or yperissed
B.17.193	I sholde receyue riȝt noȝt *of* þat I reche myghte;
B.17.195	And þe myddel *of* myn hand wiþoute maleese,
B.17.203	The holy goost *of* heuene [he] is as þe pawme.
B.17.214	That alle kynne cristene clenseþ *of* synnes.
B.17.225	Graunte no grace ne for[g]ifnesse *of* synnes
B.17.231	Ysekeles in euesynges þoruȝ hete *of* þe sonne
B.17.233	So grace *of* þe holy goost þe grete myȝt of þe Trinite
B.17.233	So grace of þe holy goost þe grete myȝt *of* þe Trinite
B.17.238	So wol þe fader forȝyue folk *of* mylde hertes
B.17.245	So wole crist *of* his curteisie, and men crye hym mercy,
B.17.247	[Fro] þe fader *of* heuene forȝifnesse to haue.
B.17.256	And purchace al þe pardon *of* Pampilon and Rome.
B.17.260	Ne brenne ne blase clere, fo[r] blowynge *of* vnkyndenesse.
B.17.265	For manye *of* yow riche men, by my soule, men telleþ,
B.17.269	*Of* his mete and moneie to men þat it nedede?
B.17.271	And gyueþ youre good to þat god þat grace *of* ariseþ.
B.17.275	The grace *of* þe holy goost, goddes owene kynde.
B.17.280	The which is lif and loue, þe leye *of* mannes body.
B.17.288	For coueitise *of* any kynnes þyng þat crist deere bouȝte.
B.17.313	[Drede *of* desperacion [þanne] dryueþ awey grace
B.17.316	Noght *of* þe nounpower of god, þat he ne is myghtful
B.17.316	Noght of þe nounpower *of* god, þat he ne is myghtful
B.17.324	Hir feere fleeþ hire for feere *of* hir tonge.
B.17.333	Thise þre þat I telle *of* ben þus to vnderstonde:
B.17.344	That þei han cause to contrarie by kynde *of* hir siknesse;
B.17.349	For vnkyndenesse is þe contrarie *of* alle kynnes reson.
B.17.351	That he ne may louye, and hym like, and lene *of* his herte
B.18.2	As a recchelees renk þat [reccheþ *of* no wo],
B.18.4	Til I weex wery *of* þe world and wilned eft to slepe
B.18.7	*Of* gerlis and of Gloria laus gretly me dremed,
B.18.7	Of gerlis and *of* Gloria laus gretly me dremed,
B.18.9	And *of* cristes passion and penaunce, þe peple þat ofrauȝte.
B.18.13	As is þe kynde *of* a knyght þat comeþ to be dubbed,
B.18.16	As dooþ an heraud *of* armes whan Auentrous comeþ to Iustes.
B.18.17	Olde Iewes *of* Ierusalem for ioye þei songen,
B.18.22	'This Iesus *of* his gentries wol Iuste in Piers armes,
B.18.41	'This Iesus *of* oure Iewes temple Iaped and despised,
B.18.46	'Crucifige!' quod a Cachepol, '[þe kan *of* wicchecraft]!'
B.18.47	'Tolle, tolle!' quod anoþer, and took *of* kene þornes
B.18.48	And bigan *of* [grene] þorn a garland to make,
B.18.55	If þow be crist and kynges sone com down *of* þe roode;
B.18.59	The lord *of* lif and of light þo leide hise eighen togideres.
B.18.59	The lord of lif and *of* light þo leide hise eighen togideres.
B.18.74	And [hir] armes after *of* eiþer of þo þeues.
B.18.74	And [hir] armes after of eiþer *of* þo þeues.
B.18.84	To touchen hym or to tasten hym or taken doun *of* roode,
B.18.99	For youre champion chiualer, chief knyȝt *of* yow alle,
B.18.110	What for feere *of* þis ferly and of þe false Iewes
B.18.110	What for feere of þis ferly and *of* þe false Iewes
B.18.116	A ful benigne burde and Buxom *of* speche.
B.18.122	Eiþer asked ooþer *of* þis grete wonder,
B.18.123	*Of* þe dyn and þe derknesse and how þe day rowed,
B.18.125	'Ich haue ferly *of* þis fare, in feiþ', seide truþe,
B.18.129	*Of* any kynnes creature, conceyued þoruȝ speche
B.18.130	And grace *of* þe holy goost; weex greet wiþ childe;
B.18.135	And þat is cause *of* þis clips þat closeþ now þe sonne,
B.18.142	'That þow tellest', quod Truþe, 'is but a tale *of* waltrot!
B.18.154	For *of* alle venymes foulest is þe scorpion;
B.18.157	The first venymmouste, þoruȝ [vertu] *of* hymselue.
B.18.164	Out of þe nyppe *of* þe North noȝt ful fer hennes
B.18.177	That many day myȝte I noȝt se for merknesse *of* synne,
B.18.196	Freet *of* þat fruyt and forsook, as it weere,
B.18.197	The loue *of* oure lord and his loore boþe,
B.18.205	For hadde þei wist *of* no wo, wele hadde þei noȝt knowen;
B.18.211	Wite what wo is, ne were þe deeþ *of* kynde.
B.18.212	So god þat bigan al *of* his goode wille
B.18.213	Bicam man *of* a mayde mankynde to saue
B.18.214	And suffrede to be sold to se þe sorwe *of* deying,
B.18.215	The which vnknytteþ alle care and comsynge is *of* reste.
B.18.218	Forþi god, *of* his goodnesse, þe firste gome Adam,
B.18.225	To wite what alle wo is [þat woot of] alle ioye.
B.18.231	Book highte þat beaupeere, a bold man *of* speche.
B.18.234	That alle þe wise *of* þis world in o wit acor[de]den
B.18.256	In alle myȝtes *of* man and his moder gladie,
B.18.264	"Prynces *of* þis place, vnpynneþ and vnloukeþ,
B.18.265	For here comeþ wiþ crowne þat kyng is *of* glorie." '
B.18.276	And where he wole is his wey; ac ware hym *of* þe perils:
B.18.280	For hymself seide, þat Sire is *of* heuene,
B.18.288	And in semblaunce *of* a serpent sete vpon þe Appultree
B.18.290	And toldest hire a tale, *of* treson were þe wordes;
B.18.318	[The] lord *of* myght and of ma[y]n and alle manere vertues,
B.18.318	[The] lord of myght and *of* ma[y]n and alle manere vertues,
B.18.319	Dukes *of* þis dymme place, anoon vndo þise yates
B.18.320	That crist may come In, þe kynges sone *of* heuene!'
B.18.329	Myne þei ben and *of* me; I may þe bet hem cleyme.
B.18.330	[Al]þouȝ Reson recorde, and riȝt *of* myselue,
B.18.335	For in my paleis, Paradis, in persone *of* an Addre
B.18.354	Thow, lucifer, in liknesse *of* a luþer Addere
B.18.356	And I in liknesse *of* a leode, þat lord am of heuene,
B.18.356	And I in liknesse of a leode, þat lord am *of* heuene,
B.18.364	That art doctour *of* deeþ drynk þat þow madest.
B.18.365	For I þat am lord *of* lif, loue is my drynke,
B.18.369	Til þe vendage falle in þe vale *of* Iosaphat,
B.18.376	For we beþ breþeren *of* blood, [ac] noȝt in baptisme alle.
B.18.381	And if þe kyng *of* þat kyngdom come in þat tyme
B.18.384	And I þat am kyng *of* kynges shal come swich a tyme
B.18.388	Be it any þyng abouȝt, þe boldnesse *of* hir synnes,

B.18.390   And þou3 holy writ wole þat I be wroke *of* hem þat diden ille–
B.18.391   They shul be clensed clerliche and [keuered] *of* hir synnes
B.18.393   And my mercy shal be shewed to manye *of* my [halue]breþeren,
B.18.405   They dorste no3t loke on oure lord, þe [leeste] *of* hem alle,
B.18.407   Manye hundred *of* Aungeles harpeden and songen,
B.18.408   Thanne pipede pees *of* Poesie a note:
B.18.417   Clippe we in couenaunt, and ech *of* vs [kisse] ooþer,
B.19.4   In myddes *of* þe masse þo men yede to offryng
B.19.14   Is crist wiþ his cros, conquerour *of* cristene.'
B.19.18   Anoon as men nempned þe name *of* god Iesu;
B.19.19   Ergo is no name to þe name *of* Iesus,
B.19.24   Is crist moore *of* my3t and moore worþi name
B.19.25   Than Iesu or Iesus þat al oure Ioye com *of*?'
B.19.30   Ac to be conquerour called, þat comeþ *of* special grace,
B.19.31   And *of* hardynesse of herte and of hendenesse,
B.19.31   And of hardynesse *of* herte and of hendenesse,
B.19.31   And of hardynesse of herte and *of* hendenesse,
B.19.32   To make lordes *of* laddes of lond þat he wynneþ
B.19.32   To make lordes of laddes *of* lond þat he wynneþ
B.19.38   And þo þat bicome cristene bi counseil *of* þe baptis[t]e
B.19.41   And vpon Caluarie on cros ycrouned kyng *of* Iewes.
B.19.43   And conquerour *of* [his] conquest hise lawes and his large.
B.19.45   The lawe *of* lif þat laste shal euere,
B.19.48   Tho was he Iesus *of* Iewes called, gentile prophete,
B.19.49   And kyng *of* hir kyngdom and croune bar of þornes.
B.19.49   And kyng of hir kyngdom and croune bar *of* þornes.
B.19.53   And þo was he conquerour called *of* quyke and of dede,
B.19.53   And þo was he conquerour called of quyke and *of* dede,
B.19.56   [And took [Lucifer þe loþely] þat lord was *of* helle
B.19.57   And bond [hym] as [he is bounde] wiþ bondes *of* yrene.
B.19.63   Ac þe cause þat he comeþ þus wiþ cros *of* his passion
B.19.69   Ac to carpe moore *of* crist and how he com to þat name,
B.19.73   Reuerenced hym [ri3t] faire wiþ richesses *of* erþe.
B.19.78   Boþe *of* [s]ond, sonne and see, and siþenes þei wente
B.19.79   Into hir kyngene kiþ by counseil *of* Aungeles.
B.19.80   And þere was þat word fulfilled þe which þow *of* speke,
B.19.81   For alle þe Aungeles *of* heuene at his burþe knelede,
B.19.82   And al þe wit *of* þe world was in þo þre kynges.
B.19.93   For Mirre is mercy to mene and mylde speche *of* tonge.
B.19.98   In þe manere *of* a man and þat by muchel sleighte,
B.19.106   As kynde is *of* a Conquerour, so comsede Iesu
B.19.110   And þere bigan god *of* his grace to do wel,
B.19.116   Bigan god *of* his grace and goodnesse to dowel,
B.19.118   A faunt[ek]yn ful *of* wit, filius Marie.
B.19.121   That he þoru3 grace was gete and *of* no gome ellis.
B.19.123   After þe kynde þat he cam *of*; þere comsede he do wel,
B.19.131   And alle he heeled and halp þat hym *of* grace askede;
B.19.132   And þo was he called in contre *of* þe comune peple,
B.19.134   For dauid was doghtiest *of* dedes in his tyme;
B.19.137   And nempned hym *of* Na3areth; and no man so worþi
B.19.138   To be kaiser or kyng *of* þe kyngdom of Iuda,
B.19.138   To be kaiser or kyng of þe kyngdom *of* Iuda,
B.19.146   That þat blissede body *of* burieles [sholde risen]
B.19.155   Telle þe comune þat þer cam a compaignie *of* hise Apostles
B.19.165   Thaddee and ten mo wiþ Thomas *of* Inde.
B.19.184   [Myght [men] to assoille *of* alle manere synne[s],
B.19.190   And assoille men *of* alle synnes saue of dette one.
B.19.190   And assoille men of alle synnes saue *of* dette one.
B.19.199   Thus Conscience *of* crist and of þe cros carpede
B.19.199   Thus Conscience of crist and *of* þe cros carpede
B.19.202   In liknesse *of* a lightnynge he lighte on hem alle
B.19.212   And cride wiþ Conscience, 'help vs, [crist], *of* grace!'
B.19.223   And Pride shal be Pope, Prynce *of* holy chirche,
B.19.231   As prechours and preestes and Prentices *of* lawe:
B.19.232   They lelly to lyue by labour *of* tonge,
B.19.234   And some he kennede craft and konnynge *of* sighte,
B.19.239   To wynne wiþ hir liflode bi loore *of* his techynge;
B.19.243   Boþe *of* wele and of wo [and be ware bifore],
B.19.243   Boþe of wele and *of* wo [and be ware bifore],
B.19.246   He wissed hem wynne it ayein þoru3 wightnesse *of* handes
B.19.253   '[That al craft and konnyng come] *of* my 3ifte.
B.19.255   And who þat moost maistries kan be myldest *of* berynge.
B.19.265   And Ioyned to hem oon Iohan, moost gentil *of* alle,
B.19.266   The pris men *of* Piers plow, passynge alle oþere.
B.19.267   And Grace gaf Piers *of* his goodnesse foure stottes,
B.19.282   He þat ete *of* þat seed hadde swich a kynde:
B.19.285   Ne wynnynge ne wele *of* worldliche richesse,
B.19.286   Waste word *of* ydelnesse ne wikked speche moeue;
B.19.290   And who[so] ete [*of*] þat seed hardy was euere
B.19.292   Mighte no [lyere wiþ lesynges] ne los *of* worldly catel
B.19.296   And couered hym vnder conseille *of* Caton þe wise:
B.19.298   And he þat ete *of* þat seed sholde be [euene] trewe
B.19.299   Wiþ god, and nau3t agast but *of* gile one.

B.19.306   Neiþer *of* duc ne of deeþ, þat he ne dide lawe
B.19.306   Neiþer of duc ne *of* deeþ, þat he ne dide lawe
B.19.315   'Hareweþ alle þat konneþ kynde wit by conseil *of* þise docto[urs],
B.19.321   And Grace gaf hym þe cros, wiþ þe [garland] *of* þornes,
B.19.323   And *of* his baptisme and blood þat he bledde on roode
B.19.327   And *of* al holy writ he made a roof after;
B.19.334   [And þe [lond] *of* bileue, þe lawe of holy chirche].
B.19.334   [And þe [lond] of bileue, þe lawe *of* holy chirche].
B.19.339   And sente forþ Surquidous, his sergeaunt *of* Armes,
B.19.352   Wiþ þe lord þat lyueþ after þe lust *of* his body,
B.19.358   For witterly, I woot wel, we beþ no3t *of* strengþe
B.19.373   Saue sherewes one swiche as I spak *of*,
B.19.379   Clennesse [*of* þe] comune and clerkes clene lyuynge
B.19.382   The lord *of* lust shal be letted al þis lente, I hope.
B.19.388   In help *of* hir heele ones in a Monþe,
B.19.402   *Of* Spiritus Iusticie þow spekest muche on ydel.'
B.19.405   But þow lyue by loore *of* Spiritus Iusticie,
B.19.410   'I am a Curatour *of* holy kirke, and cam neuere in my tyme
B.19.411   Man to me þat me kouþe telle *of* Cardinale vertues,
B.19.425   And Grace þat þow gr[e]dest so *of*, gyour of alle clerkes;
B.19.425   And Grace þat þow gr[e]dest so of, gyour *of* alle clerkes;
B.19.427   Emperour *of* al þe world, þat alle men were cristene.
B.19.435   As wel for a wastour and wenches *of* þe stewes
B.19.448   He reccheþ ri3t no3t *of* þe remenaunt
B.19.449   And crist his curteisie þe Cardinals saue
B.19.450   And torne hir wit to wisdom and to welþe *of* soule.
B.19.452   The counseil *of* Conscience or Cardinale vertues
B.19.454   *Of* gile ne of gabbyng gyue þei neuere tale,
B.19.454   Of gile ne *of* gabbyng gyue þei neuere tale,
B.19.460   'I holde it ri3t and reson *of* my Reue to take
B.19.469   Ther I may hastilokest it haue, for I am heed *of* lawe;
B.19.472   And holy chirches chief help and Chieftayn *of* þe comune,
B.19.473   And what I take *of* yow two, I take it at þe techynge
B.19.474   *Of* Spiritus Iusticie for I Iugge yow alle.
B.19.476   Ne craue *of* my comune but as my kynde askeþ.'
B.20.8   [Was] by techynge and by tellynge *of* Spiritus temperancie,
B.20.18   And if hym list for to lape þe lawe *of* kynde wolde
B.20.21   Wiþouten conseil *of* Conscience or Cardynale vertues,
B.20.32   *Of* þat he weneþ wolde falle if his wit ne weere;
B.20.53   Antecrist cam þanne, and al þe crop *of* truþe
B.20.71   Wiþ a lord þat lyueþ after likyng *of* body,
B.20.85   Frenesies and foule yueles; forageres *of* kynde
B.20.86   Hadde ypriked and prayed polles *of* peple;
B.20.94   And er heraudes *of* Armes hadden discryued lordes,
B.20.105   Swowned and swelted for sorwe *of* [deþes] dyntes
B.20.106   Conscience *of* his curteisie [þo] kynde he bisou3te
B.20.120   Conscience and his compaignye, *of* holy [kirke] þe techeris.
B.20.133   Muche *of* þe wit and wisdom of westmynstre halle.
B.20.133   Muche of þe wit and wisdom *of* westmynstre halle.
B.20.140   'Allas!' quod Conscience and cryde, 'wolde crist *of* his grace
B.20.153   'Heele and I', quod he, 'and heighnesse *of* herte
B.20.155   And [so] for3yte sorwe and [*of* synne 3yue no3t].'
B.20.159   Sleuþe wax wonder yerne and soone was *of* age
B.20.160   And wedded oon wanhope, a wenche *of* þe Stuwes
B.20.163   This Sleuþe [wex slei3] *of* werre and a slynge made,
B.20.164   And threw drede *of* dispair a do3eyne myle aboute.
B.20.170   And bisou3te hym *of* socour and his salue hadde.
B.20.170   And bisou3te hym of socour and *of* his salue hadde;
B.20.180   And in hope *of* his heele good herte he hente
B.20.182   The compaignye *of* confort men cleped it som tyme
B.20.193   And *of* þe wo þat I was Inne my wif hadde ruþe
B.20.212   And [I] by conseil *of* kynde comsed to rome
B.20.221   'By [þe] Marie!' quod a mansed preest, [was] *of* þe March of [Irlonde],
B.20.221   'By [þe] Marie!' quod a mansed preest, [was] of þe March *of* [Irlonde],
B.20.223   Than I do to drynke a drau3te *of* good ale.'
B.20.224   And so seiden sixty *of* þe same contree,
B.20.225   And shotten ayein wiþ shot, many a sheef *of* oþes,
B.20.229   Thoru3 inparfite preestes and prelates *of* holy chirche.'
B.20.233   That þei come for coueitise, to haue cure *of* soules.
B.20.240   And siþen freres forsoke þe felicite *of* erþe
B.20.242   Conscience *of* þis counseil þo comsede for to laughe,
B.20.258   Han Officers vnder hem, and ech *of* hem a certein.
B.20.261   [But þei ben nempned in þe noumbre *of* hem þat ben ywaged].
B.20.264   Monkes and Moniales and alle men *of* Religion,
B.20.266   *Of* lewed and of lered; þe lawe wole and askeþ
B.20.266   Of lewed and *of* lered; þe lawe wole and askeþ
B.20.267   A certein for a certein, saue oonliche *of* freres.
B.20.275   And preche men *of* Plato, and preue it by Seneca
B.20.280   And yuele is þis yholde in parisshes *of* Engelonde,
B.20.287   Yerne *of* for3ifnesse or lenger yeres loone.
B.20.293   And suffre þe dede in dette to þe day *of* doome.

B.20.299	*Of* alle taletelleris and titeleris in ydel.
B.20.312	For fastynge *of* a fryday he ferde as he wolde deye.
B.20.314	And moore *of* phisik bi fer, and fairer he plastreþ;
B.20.330	Pees vnpynned it, was Porter *of* vnitee.
B.20.352	And be adrad *of* deeþ and wiþdrawe hym fram pryde
B.20.359	The plastres *of* þe person and poudres biten to soore;
B.20.364	*Of* 'a pryuee paiement and I shal praye for yow
B.20.366	And make [*of*] yow [memoria] in masse and in matyns
B.20.367	As frere[s] *of* oure Fraternytee, for a litel siluer'.
B.20.371	For confort *of* his confessour Contricion he lafte,
B.20.372	That is þe souerayn[e] salue for alle [synnes *of* kynde].
C.Pr.3	In abite as an heremite, vnholy *of* werkes.
C.Pr.10	Al þe welthe *of* the world and þe wo bothe,
C.Pr.12	*Of* treuthe and tricherye, tresoun and gyle
C.Pr.19	A fair feld ful *of* folk fond y þer bytwene
C.Pr.20	*Of* alle manere [of] men, þe mene and þe [riche],
C.Pr.20	Of alle manere [*of*] men, þe mene and þe [riche],
C.Pr.26	In continance [*of*] clothyng in many kyne gyse.
C.Pr.28	Al for loue *of* oure lord lyueden [ful streyte]
C.Pr.39	Tha[t] Poule preche[þ] *of* hem preue hit y myhte;
C.Pr.57	Prechyng þe pepel for profyt *of* þe wombe;
C.Pr.59	For coueytise *of* copis contraryed somme doctours.
C.Pr.60	Mony *of* þise maistres of mendenant freres
C.Pr.60	Mony of þise maistres *of* mendenant freres
C.Pr.69	*Of* falsness[e of] fastyng[e and] of vowes ybrokene.
C.Pr.69	Of falsness[e *of*] fastyng[e and] of vowes ybrokene.
C.Pr.69	Of falsness[e of] fastyng[e and] *of* vowes ybrokene.
C.Pr.77	His seel sholde nou3t be ysent in deseyte *of* þe peple.
C.Pr.80	That þe [pore] peple [*of* þe] parsch[e] sholde haue yf þei ne were.
C.Pr.92	*Of* wardus and of wardemotis, wayues and strayues.
C.Pr.92	Of wardus and *of* wardemotis, wayues and strayues.
C.Pr.94	And ben in stede *of* stewardus and sitten and demen.
C.Pr.98	To vndertake þe tol *of* vntrewe sacrefice.
C.Pr.99	In menynge *of* myracles muche wex hangeth there;
C.Pr.103	I leue, by oure lord, for loue *of* 3oure coueytise
C.Pr.105	What cheste and meschaunce to þe children *of* Irael
C.Pr.111	Anon as it was tolde hym that þe children *of* Irael
C.Pr.116	And for þei were prestis and men *of* holy chirche
C.Pr.118	Forthy y sey 3[ow] prestes and men *of* holy churche
C.Pr.125	3oure masse and [3oure] matynes and many *of* [3oure] oures
C.Pr.127	Lest crist in constorie acorse *of* [3ow] manye.
C.Pr.128	I parsceyued *of* þe power that Peter hadde to kepe,
C.Pr.131	Amonge foure vertues, most vertuous *of* vertues,
C.Pr.134	Ac *of* þe Cardinales at Court þat caught han such a name
C.Pr.140	Myght *of* tho men made hym to regne.
C.Pr.161	Where houed an hundrid in houes *of* selke,
C.Pr.164	And nat for loue *of* oure lord vnlose here lyppes ones.
C.Pr.166	Than gete a Mum *of* here mouth [til] moneye [be] shewed.
C.Pr.167	Than ran þer a route *of* ratones [at ones]
C.Pr.170	For a Cat *of* a Court cam whan hym likede
C.Pr.173	'And yf we groche *of* his game a wol greue vs [alle],
C.Pr.178	A ratoun *of* renown, moste resonable of tounge,
C.Pr.178	A ratoun of renown, moste resonable *of* tounge,
C.Pr.180	Bere beyus *of* bryghte gold aboute here nekkes
C.Pr.181	And colers *of* crafty werk, bothe knyghte[s] and squieres.
C.Pr.185	A belle to byggen *of* bras oþer of] bryghte syluer
C.Pr.185	A belle to byggen of bras oþer of] *of* bryghte syluer
C.Pr.192	Alle th[e] route *of* ratones to þis resoun assentide;
C.Pr.194	Ther ne was [raton in] þe route, for al þe reame *of* Fraunce,
C.Pr.201	And to þe route *of* ratones rehersede thise wordes:
C.Pr.212	Ne carp[ynge] of [þis] cole[r] þat costede me neuere.
C.Pr.217	And [3]e route *of* ratones of reste men awake
C.Pr.217	And [3]e route of ratones *of* reste men awake
C.Pr.218	Ne were þe Cat *of* þe Court and 3onge kitones toward;
C.Pr.222	3ut mette me more *of* mene and of riche,
C.Pr.222	3ut mette me more of mene and *of* riche,
C.Pr.223	As Barones and Burgeys and bondemen *of* thorpus.
C.Pr.227	As taylers and tanners and tulyers [*of*] þe erthe,
C.Pr.233	'Whit wyn *of* Oseye and wyn of gascoyne,
C.Pr.233	'Whit wyn of Oseye and wyn *of* gascoyne,
C.Pr.234	*Of* þe r[yn]e and of þe rochele the roost [to] defye!'
C.Pr.234	Of þe r[yn]e and *of* þe rochele the roost [to] defye!'
C.1.2	And þe feld ful *of* folk y shal 3ou fair shewe.
C.1.3	A louely lady *of* [lere] in lynnene [y]clothed
C.1.7	The moste party *of* this peple þat passeth on þis erthe,
C.1.9	*Of* othere heuene then here [halde thei] no tale.'
C.1.10	Y was afeerd *of* here face thow she fayre were
C.1.14	For he is fader *of* fayth and formor of alle;
C.1.14	For he is fader of fayth and formor *of* alle;
C.1.20	And comaundede *of* his cortesye in comune thre thynges.
C.1.42	Ac þe moneye *of* þis molde þat men so faste kepen,
C.1.45	Whenne þe peple aposed hym *of* a peny in þe temple
C.1.52	And tutor *of* 3oure tresor and take it 3ow at nede;

C.1.57	'That is þe Castel *of* care; whoso cometh þerynne
C.1.60	Fader *of* falshede fond hit firste of alle.
C.1.60	Fader of falshede fond hit firste *of* alle.
C.1.65	He is lettere *of* loue and lyeth alle tymes;
C.1.66	That tristeth in tresor *of* erthe he bytrayeth sonest.
C.1.69	That suche wyse wordes *of* holy writ shewede
C.1.76	Thenne y knelede on my knees and criede here *of* grace
C.1.84	For who is trewe *of* his tonge and of his two handes
C.1.84	For who is trewe of his tonge and *of* his two handes
C.1.98	And hoso passeth þat poynt is appostata *of* knyghthed.
C.1.108	He was an Archangel *of* heuene, on of goddes knyghtes;
C.1.108	He was an Archangel of heuene, on *of* goddes knyghtes;
C.1.123	Ac *of* þis matere no more [meu]en y nelle.
C.1.128	Ac lucifer lowest lith *of* hem alle;
C.1.142	For to louye thy lord leuest *of* alle,
C.1.148	Loue is [þe] plonte of pees, most precious of vertues,
C.1.148	Loue is [þe] plonte *of* pees, most precious of vertues,
C.1.150	Til hit hadde *of* erthe y3oten hitsilue.
C.1.151	/A[nd] when hit hadde *of* þe folde flesch and blode taken
C.1.153	[And] portatif and persaunt as þe poynt *of* a nelde
C.1.155	Forthi is loue ledare of [þe] lordes folk of heuene
C.1.155	Forthi is loue ledare *of* [þe] lordes folk *of* heuene
C.1.175	For thow 3e ben trewe *of* 3oure tong[e] and treweliche wynne
C.1.178	*Of* such good as god sent goodliche parte,
C.1.180	Then malkyn *of* here maydenheed [þat] no man [desir]eth.
C.1.187	Aren none hardore ne hungriore then men *of* holy chirche,
C.1.193	And þat is no treuthe *of* þe trinite but triccherye [and] synne
C.1.197	Þat is þe lok *of* loue [þat] vnloseth grace
C.1.199	So loue is lecche *of* lyf and lysse of alle payne
C.1.199	So loue is lecche of lyf and lysse *of* alle payne
C.1.200	And þe graffe *of* grace and gray[th]est way to heuene.
C.1.201	Forthi y may seye, as y saide eer, by s[ih]t *of* this tex[t]es:
C.2.1	And thenne y kneled [o]n my knees and cried here *of* grace,
C.2.2	And sayde 'mercy, madame, for mary loue *of* heuene
C.2.7	And mony mo *of* here maners, of men and of wymmen.'
C.2.7	And mony mo of here maners, *of* men and of wymmen.'
C.2.7	And mony mo of here maners, of men and *of* wymmen.'
C.2.9	And [was war *of*] a womman wonderly yclothed.
C.2.15	For to telle *of* here atyer no tyme haue y nouthe.
C.2.27	And mede is manered aftur hym as men *of* kynde carpeth:
C.2.30	Y ouhte ben herrore then he; y com *of* a bettere.
C.2.33	And y am his dere doughter, ducchesse *of* heuene.
C.2.37	He shal lese for here loue [a] lippe *of* trewe charite;
C.2.44	To oon fals faythlesse *of* þe fendes kynne.
C.2.54	Acombre neuere thy Consience for coueityse *of* mede.'
C.2.59	*Of* many manere men þat of mede[s] kynne were,
C.2.59	Of many manere men þat *of* mede[s] kynne were,
C.2.60	*Of* knyghtes, of clerkes [and] other comune peple,
C.2.60	Of knyghtes, *of* clerkes [and] other comune peple,
C.2.62	Bydels and bailifs and brokeres *of* chaffar[e],
C.2.63	Vorgoers and vitalers and voketes *of* the Arches;
C.2.65	Ac simonye and syuile and sysores *of* contrees
C.2.66	Were most pryue with mede *of* eny men [me] thoghte.
C.2.77	'Al þat loueth and byleueth vp lykyng *of* mede,
C.2.85	Falsnesse is fayn *of* here for he wot here ryche;
C.2.91	The Erldom *of* enuye and yre he hem graunteth,
C.2.92	With [þe] chastel *of* cheste and chaterynge out of resoun;
C.2.93	Th[e] count[e] *of* coueytise [he] consenteth to hem bothe,
C.2.95	In bargaynes and Brocages with the borw *of* thefte,
C.2.96	With al þe lordschip *of* leccherye in lenghe and in Brede,
C.2.97	As in werkes and in wordes and waytyng[e] *of* yes,
C.2.111	With alle þe [p]urtinaunc[e] *of* purgatorye and þe peyne of helle.'
C.2.111	With alle þe [p]urtinaunc[e] of purgatorye and þe peyne *of* helle.'
C.2.112	In wittenesse *of* [which] thyng wrong was the furste,
C.2.113	And Peres þe Pardoner *of* paulines queste,
C.2.114	Butte þe Bedel *of* Bannebury sokene,
C.2.117	'In þe date *of* the deuel th[e] dede is aseled
C.2.118	By syhte *of* sire Simonye and syuyles leue.'
C.2.127	For treuthe plyhte here treuthe to wedde on *of* here douhteres,
C.2.135	"God *of* thy grace heuene gates opene,
C.2.136	For y, man, *of* thy mercy mede haue diserued."
C.2.137	And se[t]he man may [o]n heye mede *of* god diserue
C.2.148	And mede is moylore, [a] mayden *of* gode;
C.2.152	Where matrymonye may be *of* mede and of falshede.
C.2.152	Where matrymonye may be of mede and *of* falshede.
C.2.154	3ut beth ywar *of* þe weddynge; for witty is treuthe
C.2.155	And Consience is *of* his consayl and knoweth 3ow [echone];
C.2.159	Til he hadde seluer for the seel and signes *of* notaries.
C.2.195	And maketh *of* lyare a lang cart to lede al this othere,
C.2.200	*Of* many maner men for mede sake seude aftur.
C.2.229	Lorkyng thorw lanes, tologged *of* moneye.
C.2.243	For knowyng *of* co[mere]s copeden hym as a frere.
C.3.1	Now is mede þe mayde and na mo *of* hem alle

C. 3.6	What man *of* this world þat here [were leuest].
C. 3.22	*Of* here grete goodnesse and gaf hem vchone
C. 3.23	Coupes *of* clene gold [and] coppes of syluer,
C. 3.23	Coupes of clene gold [and] coppes *of* syluer,
C. 3.25	The leste man *of* here mayne a motoun of gold.
C. 3.25	The leste man of here mayne a motoun *of* gold.
C. 3.42	Y shal assoyle the mysulue for a seem [*of*] whete
C. 3.46	[And] shrofe here *of* here synne, shameles y [trowe];
C. 3.54	Solempneliche and softlyche as for a suster *of* oure ordre.'
C. 3.59	Hit is but frelete *of* fleysche–ȝe fyndeth [hit in] bokes–
C. 3.60	And [a] cours *of* kynde wherof we comen alle.
C. 3.62	Hit is synne as *of* seuene noon sannour relesed.
C. 3.63	Haueth mercy,' quod mede, '*o[f]* men þat hit haunteth
C. 3.67	That euery seg shal se y am sustre *of* ȝoure ordre.'
C. 3.69	To writen [i]n wyndowes *of* eny wel dedes,
C. 3.70	An Auntur pruyde be paynted there and pomp *of* the world,
C. 3.95	That so bigileth hem *of* here goed, þat god on hem sende
C. 3.101	And haue here penaunce on puyre erthe and nat þe peyne *of* helle.
C. 3.109	For to spyre and to aspye, for eny speche *of* suluer,
C. 3.116	*Of* alle suche sullers seluer to take
C. 3.122	In amendement *of* mayres and oþer stywardes
C. 3.123	And wittenesseth what worth *of* hem þat wolleth take mede:
C. 3.127	The houses and þe homes *of* hem þat taketh ȝeftes.
C. 3.141	In the Castel *of* Corf y shal do close the,
C. 3.146	And teche the to louye treuthe and take consail *of* resoun.
C. 3.156	For she is fayn *of* thy felawschipe, for to be thy make.'
C. 3.159	For she [is] frele *of* here fayth, fikel of here speche
C. 3.159	For she [is] frele of here fayth, fikel *of* here speche
C. 3.161	In trist *of* here tresor he teneth ful monye,
C. 3.168	For she is tikel *of* here tayl, talewys of tonge,
C. 3.168	For she is tikel of here tayl, talewys *of* tonge,
C. 3.173	Shyreues *of* shyres were shent yf he nere,
C. 3.207	And custumes *of* coueytise þe comune to destruye.
C. 3.212	That al þe witt *of* the world is woxe into Gyle.
C. 3.215	Such a maistre is mede among men *of* gode.'
C. 3.241	And as his wyrdus were ordeyned at þe wille *of* oure lorde.
C. 3.243	In his enemyes handes his heritage *of* Fraunce.
C. 3.247	*Of* folk þat fauht þerfore and folwede þe kynges wille.
C. 3.251	And þat is þe kynde *of* a kyng þat conquereth on his enemys,
C. 3.258	Ac hadde y, mede, ben marchel *o[f]* his men in Fraunce
C. 3.260	He sholde haue [ben] lord *of* þat lond alenghe and abrede
C. 3.261	And also kyng *of* þat kuth his kyn for to helpe,
C. 3.262	The leeste brolle *of* his blod a Barones pere.
C. 3.274	Taken mede *of* here maistres as þei mowen acorde;
C. 3.287	That mede [is] euermore a mayntenour *of* Gyle,
C. 3.308	The huyre *of* his hewe ouer eue til amorwe:
C. 3.315	And thow the kyng *of* his cortesye, Cayser or pope,
C. 3.327	A refte hym *of* his richesse and of his ryhte mynde
C. 3.327	A refte hym of his richesse and *of* his ryhte mynde
C. 3.332	And efte haue hit aȝeyne *of* hem þat doth ylle.
C. 3.338	And ayther is otheres helpe; *of* hem cometh retribucoun
C. 3.340	Grace *of* good ende and gret ioye aftur:
C. 3.344	'Relacioun rect,' quod Consience, 'is a record *of* treuthe–
C. 3.345	Folowynge and fyndynge out þe fundement *of* a strenghe,
C. 3.347	In kynde and in case and in cours *of* nombre.
C. 3.352	So *of* ho[l] herte cometh hope and hardy relacoun
C. 3.354	That is god, the ground *of* al, a graciouse antecedent.
C. 3.359	*Of* oure sory synnes to be assoiled and yclansed
C. 3.378	So comune claymeth *of* a kyng thre kyne thynges.
C. 3.383	Ac þe moste partie *of* peple puyr indirect semeth
C. 3.389	*Of* the cours of case so thei cache suluer.
C. 3.389	Of the cours *of* case so thei cache suluer.
C. 3.392	Nyme he a noumbre *of* nobles or of shillynges,
C. 3.392	Nyme he a noumbre of nobles or *of* shillynges,
C. 3.404	Thus is man and mankynde in maner *of* [a] sustantyf,
C. 3.406	*Of* thre trewe termisonus, trinitas vnus deus:
C. 3.407	Ac hoso rat *of* regum rede me may of mede,
C. 3.407	Ac hoso rat of regum rede me may *of* mede,
C. 3.413	As me ret in regum [*of* þe reuthe] of kynges,
C. 3.413	As me ret in regum [of þe reuthe] *of* kynges,
C. 3.415	That agag *of* amalek and alle his leege peple
C. 3.416	Sholde deye der[f]ly for dedes *of* here eldres.
C. 3.419	Haste the with al thyn oste to þe lond *of* Amalek
C. 3.424	For eny mede *of* money al that thow myhte [fynde],
C. 3.431	Thus was kyng sauel ouercome thorw coueytise *of* mede,
C. 3.433	The culorum *of* this kaes kepe y nat to shewe:
C. 3.453	And maky *of* lawe [a] laborer; suche loue shal aryse
C. 3.456	That here kyng be ycome fro þe Court *of* heuene,
C. 3.463	Spynne oþer speke *of* god and spille no tyme.
C. 3.466	Haukyng or huntyng yf eny *of* hem hit vse
C. 3.479	Be sixe [s]onnes [and] a ship and half a shef *of* Arwes;
C. 3.480	And the [myddell] *of* [a] mone shal make þe iewes turne
C. 3.495	Quod bonum est tenete, a tixst *of* treuthe [m]akynge.
C. 3.500	Ac he þat resceyueth or rec[ett]eth here is rescetour *of* Gyle.'
C. 4.10	*Of* mede and of mo othere and what man shal here wedde
C. 4.10	Of mede and *of* mo othere and what man shal here wedde
C. 4.13	'Y am fayn *of* that forward, in fayth,' tho quod Consience,
C. 4.17	And kalde Catoun his knaue, Corteys *of* speche,
C. 4.19	Ne-lesynges-to-lauhe-*of*-for-y-louede-hit-neuere.
C. 4.22	For hit is þe wone *of* wil to wynse and to kyke
C. 4.29	To take reed *of* resoun þat recorde sholde
C. 4.34	Ryde forth, syre resoun, and rech nat *of* here tales
C. 4.37	They gyue n[ouh]t *of* good fayth, woe[t] god the sothe,
C. 4.40	Thenne resoun rood forth Ac took reward *of* no man
C. 4.48	And margarete *of* here maydenhod as he mette here late.
C. 4.56	He borwed *of* me bayard a[nd] brouhte hym hom neuere
C. 4.67	On men *of* lawe wrong lokede and largelyche hem profered
C. 4.69	'Hadde y loue *of* [my] lord lytel wolde y reche
C. 4.70	*Of* pees and his power thow he pleyne euere.'
C. 4.91	And profrede pees a present al *of* puyre golde.
C. 4.92	'Haue this, man, *of* me,' quod she, 'to amende thy scathe
C. 4.126	Bere no seluer ouer see þat sygne *of* kyng sheweth,
C. 4.127	Nother ygraue ne vngraue, *of* gold oþer of suluer,
C. 4.127	Nother ygraue ne vngraue, of gold oþer *of* suluer,
C. 4.128	Vp forfeture *of* þat fee, ho fyndeth h[y]m ouerward,
C. 4.137	Be vnpunisched in my power for perel of [my] soule
C. 4.139	Ne thorw mede mercy, by marie *of* heuene!
C. 4.148	Mede in the mothale tho on men *of* lawe gan wynke
C. 4.156	Loue l[et]te *of* mede lyhte and leutee ȝut lasse
C. 4.158	'Hoso wilneth here to wy[u]e for welthe *of* here goodes
C. 4.168	And lourede vppon men *of* lawe and lyhtlych sayde:
C. 4.170	Mede and men *of* ȝoure craft muche treuthe letteth.
C. 4.173	Mede shal nat maynprise [ȝow], by marye *of* heuene!
C. 4.194	Or lumbardus *of* lukes þat leuen by lone as iewes.'
C. 5.4	Amonges lollares *of* londone and lewede Ermytes,
C. 5.5	For y made *of* tho men as resoun me tauhte.
C. 5.48	Th[u]s y s[yn]ge for here soules *of* suche as me helpeth
C. 5.55	For by þe lawe *of* leuyticy þat oure lord ordeynede,
C. 5.56	Clerkes ycrouned, *of* kynde vnderstondynge,
C. 5.59	For hit ben eyres *of* heuene alle þat ben ycrouned
C. 5.67	*Of* frankeleynes and fremen and of folke ywedded.
C. 5.67	Of frankeleynes and fremen and *of* folke ywedded.
C. 5.74	For the ryhte *of* this reume ryden aȝeyn oure enemyes
C. 5.75	In confort *of* the comune and the kynges worschipe,
C. 5.84	Preeyeres *of* a parfit man and penaunce d[iscret]e
C. 5.98	Suche a wynnyng hym warth thorw w[y]rdes *of* grace:
C. 5.99	So hope y to haue *of* hym þat is almyghty
C. 5.100	A gobet *of* his grace and bigynne a tyme
C. 5.101	That alle tymes *of* my tyme to profit shal turne.'
C. 5.110	*Of* þe matere þat me mette furste on Maluerne hulles
C. 5.111	Y saw þe felde ful *of* folk fram ende til oþer
C. 5.121	And turned vpward here tayl in tokenynge *of* drede
C. 5.123	*Of* this mater y myhte mamele [wel] longe
C. 5.145	And be stewar[d] *of* ȝoure stedes til ȝe be stewed bettere.'
C. 5.147	The reule *of* alle religious rihtful and obedient:
C. 5.158	Ledares *of* l[ou]edays, and londes ypurchaced
C. 5.160	A[n] hep *of* houndes at h[is] ers as he a lord were
C. 5.166	*Of* þe pore haueth thei no pite and þat is here puyre chartre.
C. 5.169	And bete ȝow, as þe bible telleth, for brekynge *of* ȝoure reule
C. 5.175	And constantyn shal be here cook and coueerour *of* here churches,
C. 5.176	For þe abbot *of* engelonde and the abbesse his nese
C. 5.190	Is cause *of* alle combraunc[e] to confounde a reume.'
C. 5.196	*Of* alle maner actions and eche man loue other.
C. 5.198	Seketh seynt treuthe in sauac[ioun] *of* ȝoure soules
C. 6.11	*Of* alle þat y haue hated in myn herte.
C. 6.16	Haue be vnbuxum, y byseche god *of* mercy;
C. 6.30	Proud *of* aparayle in port amongus þe peple
C. 6.33	Ryche, and resonable and ryhtful *of* lyuynge;
C. 6.36	And ȝut so synguler be mysulue as to syhte *of* [þe] peple
C. 6.42	And connyngest *of* my craft, Clerkysh oþer other,
C. 6.45	And likynge *of* such a lyf þat no lawe preiseth,
C. 6.46	Prout *of* my fayre fetures and for y song shille;
C. 6.53	*Of* werkes þat y wel dede witnesses take
C. 6.58	And what y couthe and knewe and what kyn y cam *of*."
C. 6.65	His clothes were *of* corsemen[t] and of kene wordes.
C. 6.65	His clothes were of corsemen[t] and *of* kene wordes.
C. 6.72	And made *of* frendes foes thorw fikel and fals tonge.
C. 6.73	'Or thorw myhte *of* mouthe or thorw mannes sleythes
C. 6.76	Aȝeyn þe consayl *of* Crist, as clerkes fyndeth in bokes:
C. 6.81	Lechecraft *of* oure lord and leue on a wycche
C. 6.83	To the soutere *of* southewerk, suche is his grace.
C. 6.92	For thy synnes souereynly and biseke god *of* mercy.'
C. 6.95	ȝut am y brokour *of* bakbytynge to blame menne w[a]re
C. 6.101	Lord, ar y lyf lete, for loue *of* thysulue
C. 6.102	Graunte me, gode lord, grace *of* amendement.'
C. 6.111	On god when me greued auht and grochede *of* his sonde:

C. 6.117	Harm *of* eny man, byhynde or bifore.
C. 6.119	And preuen inparfit prelates *of* holy churche;
C. 6.133	And made hem ioutes *of* iangelynge: "dame Ione was a bastard
C. 6.161	Y haue a flux *of* a foul mouth wel fyue daies aftur;
C. 6.162	Al þat y wiste wykked by eny *of* oure couent
C. 6.172	That he haue pite on me, p[u]tou[r], *of* his puyr mercy,
C. 6.176	As in likynge *of* lecherye my lycames gultes
C. 6.177	In word, in wedes, in waytynge *of* eyes.
C. 6.186	*Of* put[rie] and of paramours and proueden thorw speche
C. 6.186	Of put[rie] and *of* paramours and proueden thorw speche
C. 6.194	Y hadde likyng to lythe *of* lecherye tales.
C. 6.203	In a tore tabard *of* twelue wynter age;
C. 6.213	Ne hadde þe grace *of* Gyle go among my ware
C. 6.235	'Ʒus! ones y was herberwed,' quod he, 'with an heep *of* chapmen;
C. 6.241	Y lernede among lumbardus a lessoun and *of* iewes,
C. 6.243	And len[e] for loue *of* þe wed the whych y lette bettere
C. 6.247	So what buyrn *of* me borewede abouhte the tyme.'
C. 6.248	'Lenedest [thow] euere eny lord for loue *of* his mayntenaunce?'
C. 6.255	Ne thyn heyres, as y hope, haue ioye *of* þat thow wonne
C. 6.257	To assoyle the *of* th[y] synne sine restitucion[e]:
C. 6.269	*Of* my neyhebore nexst, nymen of his erthe;
C. 6.269	Of my neyhebore nexst, nymen *of* his erthe;
C. 6.275	For lo[s] *of* good, leef me, then for lycames gultes.
C. 6.285	Then in the grace *of* god and in his grete myhte;
C. 6.286	'Now redily,'quod repentaunce, 'y haue reuthe *of* thy lyuynge.'
C. 6.289	Ne take a meles mete *of* thyn and myn herte hit wiste
C. 6.293	Then haue my fode and my fyndynge *of* fals menne wynnyngus.
C. 6.296	For alle that hauen *of* thy good, haue god my treuthe,
C. 6.304	And [what] penaunce the prest shal haue þat p[r]oud is *of* his tithes.
C. 6.305	For an hore *of* here ers wynnynge may hardiloker tythe
C. 6.319	Tho dysmas my brother bisouhte [þe] *of* grace
C. 6.325	What byful *of* this feloun y can nat fayre shewe;
C. 6.334	For al the wrecchednesse *of* this world and wikkede dedes
C. 6.335	Fareth as flo[nke] *of* fuyr þat ful amydde Temese
C. 6.337	*Of* alle manere men þat [mid] goode wille
C. 6.345	Bere hit to th[e] bischop and bide hym *of* his grace
C. 6.359	'Y haue pepur and pyonie and a pound *of* garlek,
C. 6.360	A ferthyngworth [*of*] fenkel sed[e] for fastyng dayes.'
C. 6.364	Tymme þe Tynekare and tweyne *of* his knaues,
C. 6.366	Claryce *of* cockes lane and the clerc of þe churche,
C. 6.366	Claryce of cockes lane and the clerc *of* þe churche,
C. 6.367	Syre [Peres] *of* prydie and purnele of Flaundres,
C. 6.367	Syre [Peres] of prydie and purnele *of* Flaundres,
C. 6.368	An hayward, an heremyte, the hangeman *of* tybourne,
C. 6.370	*Of* portours and of pikeporses and of pilede tothdraweres,
C. 6.370	Of portours and *of* pikeporses and of pilede tothdraweres,
C. 6.370	Of portours and of pikeporses and *of* pilede tothdraweres,
C. 6.374	And *of* vphalderes an heep, [e]rly by þe morwe,
C. 6.402	And wesched hit hadde [be wexed] with a weps *of* breres.
C. 6.414	Durste lape *of* þat lyuynge, so vnlouely hit smauhte.
C. 6.415	With alle þe wo *of* th[e] world his wyf and his wenche
C. 6.421	His wyf and his inwit Edwitede hym *of* his synne;
C. 6.426	*Of* þat y haue trespased with tonge, y can nat telle how ofte;
C. 6.433	The vilony *of* my foule mouthe and of my foule mawe:
C. 6.433	The vilony of my foule mouthe and *of* my foule mawe:
C. 6.437	*Of* my luyther ly[uynge] in al my lyf tyme.
C. 7.11	Y can rymes *of* robyn hode and of randolf Erle of Chestre
C. 7.11	Y can rymes of robyn hode and *of* randolf Erle of Chestre
C. 7.11	Y can rymes of robyn hode and of randolf Erle *of* Chestre
C. 7.12	Ac *of* oure lord ne of oure lady þe leste þat euere was maked.
C. 7.12	Ac of oure lord ne *of* oure lady þe leste þat euere was maked.
C. 7.22	Y hadde leuere here an harlotrye or a lesyng to lauhen *of*
C. 7.48	In speche and in sparyng *of* speche; yspilde many a tyme
C. 7.60	And bete thysulue [o]n þe breste and bidde hym *of* grace
C. 7.72	Doth non Almesdede, drat hym nat *of* synne,
C. 7.74	And hath no likynge to lerne ne *of* oure lord to here
C. 7.75	But harlotrie and horedom or elles *of* som wynnynge;
C. 7.76	When me carpeth *of* Crist or clannesse of soule
C. 7.76	When me carpeth of Crist or clannesse *of* soule
C. 7.77	A wexeth wroth and wol not here but wordes *of* murthe;
C. 7.78	Penaunse and pore men and the passioun *of* seyntes,
C. 7.81	Ʒe lordes and ladies and legatus *of* holy churche
C. 7.87	Patriarkes and prophetes, precheours *of* goddes wordes,
C. 7.92	Wh[at] dauid sayth *of* such men as þe sauter telleth:
C. 7.97	And for loue *of* here lord ly[th]eth hem at festes;
C. 7.106	And fithele the withoute flaterynge *of* god friday þe [g]este
C. 7.116	With turpiloquio, a lay *of* sorwe and luciferes fythele,
C. 7.120	'Y shal byseke for alle synnefole oure sauiour *of* grace
C. 7.121	To Amende vs *of* oure mysdedes, do mercy to vs alle.
C. 7.122	God þat *of* thi goodnesse gonne þe world make
C. 7.123	And [*of* nauhte madest] auhte and man liche thysulue
C. 7.127	And bicam man *of* a mayde mankynde to amende
C. 7.130	On a friday in fourme *of* man feledest oure sorwe:
C. 7.132	Aboute mydday, when most liht is and mel tyme *of* sayntes,
C. 7.135	And brouhte thyne yblessed fro thennes into þe blisse *of* heuene.
C. 7.140	*Of* thy douhtiokest dedes was don in oure sekte:
C. 7.143	That art furste oure fadur and *of* flesch oure broþer
C. 7.149	Haue reuthe *of* alle these rybaudes þat repenten hem sore
C. 7.151	Thenne hente [hope] an horn *of* deus tu conuersus viuificabis nos
C. 7.155	A thousend *of* men tho throngen togyderes,
C. 7.165	An hundret *of* Aunpolles on his hat se[t]e,
C. 7.166	Signes *of* syse and shelles of galys
C. 7.166	Signes of syse and shelles *of* galys
C. 7.167	And many crouch on his cloke [and] kayes *of* Rome
C. 7.194	Y haue myn huyre *of* hym wel and oþerwhiles more.
C. 7.197	He is as louh as a lombe and leel *of* his tonge.
C. 7.201	'Nay, bi þe perel *of* my soule!' Peres gan to swerie,
C. 7.207	Til ʒe come into Consience, yknowe *of* god sulue,
C. 7.213	And so [boweth] forth by [a] brok, [beth-buxum-*of*-speche].
C. 7.218	And-nameliche-an-ydel-þe-name-*of*-god-almyhty.
C. 7.221	Ne-none-*of*-here-seruauntes-þat-nuye-hem-myhte;
C. 7.229	Loke thow plokke no plonte þere for perel *of* thy soule.
C. 7.233	The mote is *of* mercy, the manere in þe myddes
C. 7.234	And al þe wallyng is *of* wyt for wil ne sholde hit wynne;
C. 7.235	The carneles ben *of* cristendom þat kynde to saue,
C. 7.239	The barres aren *of* buxumnesse as bretherne of o wombe;
C. 7.239	The barres aren of buxumnesse as bretherne *of* o wombe;
C. 7.241	Vche piler is *of* penaunc[e] and preyeres to seyntes;
C. 7.249	To opene and vndo þe hye gate *of* heuene
C. 7.251	A ful leel lady vnlek hit *of* grace
C. 7.261	Ac be war thenne *of* wrath, þat wikkede shrewe,
C. 7.264	The boldenesse *of* thy beenfet[e] maketh the blynd thenne;
C. 7.276	Noen *of* hem alle helpe may in betere
C. 7.281	Hit is ful hard, be myn heued, eny *of* ʒow alle
C. 7.290	And thorw þe help[e] *of* hem two, hope þou non oþer,
C. 7.300	'Y haue wedded a wyf wel wantowen *of* maneres;
C. 7.308	That myhte folowe vs vch fote for drede *of* mysturnynge.'
C. 8.1	Qvod [perkyn] þe [plouhman], 'be seynt petur *of* Rome!
C. 8.8	'That somme sowe þe sak for shedynge *of* the whete,
C. 8.14	For profit *of* the pore and plesaunce of ʒowsuluen.
C. 8.14	For profit of the pore and plesaunce *of* ʒowsuluen.
C. 8.16	As longe as y leue, for [þe] lordes loue *of* heuene.
C. 8.35	'[Ye], and ʒut a poynt,' quod [Peres], 'y praye ʒow *of* more:
C. 8.48	Treuwe *of* thy tonge and tales loth to here
C. 8.49	Bute they be *of* bounte, of batayles or of treuthe.
C. 8.49	Bute they be of bounte, *of* batayles or of treuthe.
C. 8.49	Bute they be of bounte, of batayles or *of* treuthe.
C. 8.58	[He] caste on his clothes *of* alle kyn craftes,
C. 8.60	And heng his hopur on his hal[s] in stede *of* a scryppe;
C. 8.61	A buschel *of* breedcorn brouht was þerynne.
C. 8.71	Saue Iacke þe iogelour and ionet *of* þe stuyues
C. 8.73	And frere faytour and folk *of* þat ordre,
C. 8.78	For holy chirche is ho[ld]e *of* hem no tythe to aske,
C. 8.92	'For now y am olde and hoer and haue *of* myn owene
C. 8.101	Of my corn and my catel he craued [þe] tythe.
C. 8.102	Y payede hit prestly for perel *of* my soule;
C. 8.105	My wyf shal haue *of* þat y wan with treuthe and no more
C. 8.109	And with þe res[i]due and þe remenant, by the rode *of* lukes!
C. 8.132	That god [*of*] his grace ʒoure grayn multiplye
C. 8.133	And ʒelde ʒow *of* ʒoure Almesse þat ʒe ʒeuen vs here;
C. 8.142	Or ʒe shal ete barly breed and *of* þe broke drynke.
C. 8.145	Bothe *of* my corn and of my cloth to kepe hem fram defaute.
C. 8.145	Bothe of my corn and *of* my cloth to kepe hem fram defaute.
C. 8.154	[*Of*] thy flour and thy flesch, feche whenne vs liketh
C. 8.158	'Awreke me *of* this wastors þat maketh this world dere–
C. 8.159	They acounteth nat *of* corsyng[e] ne holy kyrke dredeth–
C. 8.165	And leet lyhte *of* þe lawe and lasse of the knyhte
C. 8.165	And leet lyhte of þe lawe and lasse *of* the knyhte
C. 8.170	Awreke [me] *of* this wastors for þe knyhte wil nat.'
C. 8.182	For a potte ful *of* potage þat [Peres] wyf made
C. 8.183	An heep *of* Eremytes henten hem spades,
C. 8.184	Sp[it]teden and spradden donge in dispit *of* hunger.
C. 8.187	Al for drede *of* here deth, such duntus ʒaf hunger.
C. 8.189	And lame men he lechede with longes *of* bestes.
C. 8.191	And freres *of* alle þe fyue ordres, alle for fere of hunger.
C. 8.191	And freres of alle þe fyue ordres, alle for fere *of* hunger.
C. 8.199	In threschynge, in thekynge, in thwytynge *of* pynnes,
C. 8.202	Þat durste withsitte þat [Peres] sayde for fere *of* syre hunger
C. 8.207	'Y am wel awroke *of* wastours thorw thy myhte
C. 8.209	*Of* beggares and biddares what beste de to be done.
C. 8.214	But for fere *of* famyen, in fayth,' sayde [Peres].
C. 8.218	And helpe hem *of* alle thyng ay as hem nedeth.
C. 8.225	And [a]baue hem with benes for bollyng *of* here wombe;
C. 8.230	Loue hem and lene hem and so lawe *of* kynde wolde:
C. 8.231	And alle manere [*of*] men þat thow myhte aspye

C. 8.246	Mathew maketh mencioun *of* a man þat lente
C. 8.266	Yf ȝe can or knowe eny kyne thyng[e] *of* fisyk
C. 8.267	For somme *of* my seruauntes and mysulf bothe
C. 8.268	*Of* al a woke worche nat, so oure wombe greueth.'
C. 8.272	And sende the *of* his sauce [t]o sauery with thy lyppes
C. 8.284	Part with hem *of* thy payne, of potage or of sowl;
C. 8.284	Part with hem of thy payne, *of* potage or of sowl;
C. 8.284	Part with hem of thy payne, of potage or *of* sowl;
C. 8.285	Lene hem som *of* thy loef thouh thow þe lasse chewe.
C. 8.291	And his cloke *of* callabre for his comune[s] legge
C. 8.304	A fewe croddes and craym and a cake *of* otes
C. 8.305	And bred for my barnes *of* benes and of peses.
C. 8.305	And bred for my barnes of benes and *of* peses.
C. 8.326	Bote clermatyn and coket and *of* clene whete
C. 8.328	Bote *of* the beste and þe brouneste þat brewestares sullen.
C. 8.331	May no peny ale hem pay ne no pece *of* bacoun
C. 8.333	And þat chaut and pluchaut for chillyng *of* h[ere] mawe.
C. 8.352	But yf [god] *of* his goodnesse graunte vs a trewe.
C. 9.14	Lele and fol *of* loue and no lord drede,
C. 9.26	Aȝen clene Consience for couetyse *of* wynnynge.
C. 9.44	Men *of* lawe hadde lest þat loth were to plede
C. 9.49	And for þe loue *of* oure lord lawe for hem declareth
C. 9.50	Shal haue grace *of* a good ende and greet ioye aftur.
C. 9.51	Beth ywar, ȝe wis men and witty *of* þe lawe,
C. 9.54	That mede *of* mene men for here motynge taken.
C. 9.55	For hit is symonye to sulle þat sent is *of* grace,
C. 9.83	The wo *of* this wommen þat wonyeth in cotes
C. 9.84	And *of* monye oþer men þat moche wo soffren,
C. 9.94	Fridays and fastyngdays a ferthingworth *of* moskeles
C. 9.104	Lyuen aȝen goddes lawe and þe lore *of* holi churche.
C. 9.109	Careth they for no colde ne counteth *of* non hete
C. 9.114	To profecye *of* þe peple, pleinge as hit were
C. 9.121	Barfoot and bredles, beggeth they *of* no man
C. 9.126	For hit aren murye mouthed men, munstrals *of* heuene
C. 9.148	Where he may rathest haue a repaest or a ronde *of* bacoun,
C. 9.150	Loef oþer half loef other a lompe *of* chese
C. 9.169	Bringeth forth bastardus, beggares *of* kynde,
C. 9.170	Or þe bak or som bon þey breke *of* he[re] children
C. 9.173	Then *of* many oþere men þat [o]n this molde walken.
C. 9.175	Þai haue no part *of* pardoun ne of preyeres ne of penaunc[e].
C. 9.175	Þai haue no part of pardoun ne *of* preyeres ne of penaunc[e].
C. 9.175	Þai haue no part of pardoun ne of preyeres ne *of* penaunc[e].
C. 9.179	And alle pore pacient apayed *of* goddes sonde,
C. 9.185	For loue *of* here lowe hertes oure lord hath hem ygraunted
C. 9.196	Noyther *of* lynage ne of lettrure ne lyfholy as Ermytes
C. 9.196	Noyther of lynage ne *of* lettrure ne lyfholy as Ermytes
C. 9.198	Summe hadde lyflode *of* h[ere] lynage and of no lyf elles
C. 9.198	Summe hadde lyflode of h[ere] lynage and *of* no lyf elles
C. 9.199	And summe lyuede by here letterure and labour *of* here handes
C. 9.202	Al they holy Ermytes were *of* heye kynne,
C. 9.203	Forsoken lond and lordschipe and lykyng[e] *of* body.
C. 9.212	Or oen *of* som ordre or elles a profete.
C. 9.215	As by þe engelisch *of* oure eldres of olde mennes techynge
C. 9.215	As by þe engelisch of oure eldres *of* olde mennes techynge
C. 9.219	Lollen aȝen þe byleue and lawe *of* holy churche.
C. 9.222	Furste, Religious *of* religioun a reule to holde
C. 9.256	The cause *of* al this caytiftee cometh of many bischopes
C. 9.256	The cause of al this caytiftee cometh *of* many bischopes
C. 9.264	Here salue is *of* supersedeas in sumnoures boxes;
C. 9.270	When thy lord loketh to haue allouaunce *of* his bestes
C. 9.271	And *of* þe moneye thow haddest ther[myd] his mebles to [s]aue
C. 9.286	And was ywryte ryhte thus in witnesse *of* treuthe:
C. 9.293	The prest thus and perkyn *of* þe pardon iangelede
C. 9.299	*Of* that y seyh slepynge, if hit so be myhte,
C. 9.300	And *of* [Peres] the [plouhman] fol pencyf in herte
C. 9.306	How danyel deuynede and vndede þe dremes *of* kynges,
C. 9.307	*Of* Nabugodonasor þat no pere hadde
C. 9.322	For hoso doth wel here at þe day *of* dome
C. 9.327	As lettrede men vs lereth and lawe *of* holi churche:
C. 9.334	Vp truste *of* ȝoure tresor trionales to haue,
C. 9.337	That haen the welthe *of* this world and wise men ben holde
C. 9.343	A pouhe ful *of* pardon there ne prouinciales lettres,
C. 9.344	Thow we be founden in the fraternite *of* alle fyue ordres
C. 9.352	At þe day *of* dome we dede as he tauhte.
C.10.3	And fraynede ful ofte *of* folke þat y mette
C.10.5	And what man a myhte be *of* mony m[a]n y askede.
C.10.9	Maystres *of* þe menore[s], men of gret witte.
C.10.9	Maystres of þe menore[s], men *of* gret witte.
C.10.14	For ȝe ar men *of* this molde þat moste wyde walken
C.10.34	The wynde and þe water and [þe] wag[g]yng *of* the bote
C.10.36	For stonde he neuere so stifliche, thorw steryng *of* þe bote
C.10.45	The godes *of* this grounde ar like þe grete wawes
C.10.47	The boet is liknet to oure body þat bretil is *of* kynde,
C.10.50	And lyf[holie]st *of* lyf þat lyueth vnder sonne.
C.10.63	Blisse *of* þe briddes abyde me made
C.10.66	Murthe *of* here mouthes made me to slepe
C.10.78	Ho[so] is trewe *of* his tonge and of his two handes
C.10.78	Ho[so] is trewe of his tonge and *of* his two handes
C.10.80	And therto trewe *of* his tayl, [taketh but his owne]
C.10.83	He is [as] logh as a lomb and loueliche *of* speche
C.10.84	And helpeth alle men *of* þat he may spare.
C.10.87	And *of* mammonaus mone ymaked hym many frendes
C.10.110	*Of* dowel and dobet and ho doth best of alle.'
C.10.110	Of dowel and dobet and ho doth best *of* alle.'
C.10.118	Sad *of* his semblant and with a softe speche.
C.10.129	In a Castel þat kynde made *of* foure kyne thynges.
C.10.130	*Of* erthe and ayer [hit is] maed, ymedled togyderes,
C.10.135	A proued prikeare *of* fraunce, princeps huius mundi,
C.10.138	And hath do here with sire dowel, duk *of* this marches.
C.10.143	Ac þe constable *of* þ[e] Castel þat kepeth hem alle
C.10.147	Sire worch-wel-with-thyn-hand, a wyht man *of* strenghe,
C.10.152	'Kynde is creatour,' quod wit, *'of* [alle] kyne thynges,
C.10.153	Fader and formour *of* al þat forth groweth
C.10.155	Lord *of* lyf and of lyht, of lisse of payne.
C.10.155	Lord of lyf and *of* lyht, of lisse of payne.
C.10.155	Lord of lyf and of lyht, *of* lisse of payne.
C.10.155	Lord of lyf and of lyht, of lisse *of* payne.
C.10.157	Man is hym most lyk *of* membres and of face
C.10.157	Man is hym most lyk of membres and *of* face
C.10.164	God wol nat *of* hem wyte bute lat hem yworthe,
C.10.167	*Of* gold and of oþer goed ac goddes grace hem fayleth.
C.10.167	Of gold and *of* oþer goed ac goddes grace hem fayleth.
C.10.173	And lyf lyueth by inwit and leryng *of* kynde.
C.10.180	*Of* þ[e] blessed baptist bifore alle his gestes.
C.10.182	Hath tresor ynow *of* treuthe to fynden hymsulue.
C.10.197	Prelates and prestes and princes *of* holy churche
C.10.202	In meschief for defaute *of* mete ne for myssyng of clothes:
C.10.202	In meschief for defaute of mete ne for myssyng *of* clothes:
C.10.205	For *of* here kynde þey come, bothe confessours and martres,
C.10.215	Withouten repentaunce *of* here rechelesnesse a rybaud þei engendrede.
C.10.220	Alle þat come *of* Caym Caytyue[s] were euere
C.10.221	And for þe synne *of* Caymes seed sayede god to Noe:
C.10.223	And bad go shapen a ship *of* shides and bordes.
C.10.227	Clene awey þe corsed bloed þat *of* Caym spronge.
C.10.232	Excepte onliche *of* vch kynde a payre
C.10.243	For god seid ensaumple *of* suche manere issue
C.10.249	And god sente to seth so sone he was *of* age
C.10.257	For coueytise *of* catel and connynge chapmen;
C.10.258	*Of* kyn ne of kynrede counteth men bote litel.
C.10.258	Of kyn ne *of* kynrede counteth men bote litel.
C.10.260	A mayde and wel yma[ner]ed and *of* gode men yspronge,
C.10.269	That his wyf were wexe or a walet ful *of* nobles.
C.10.279	For coueytise *of* catel in none kyne wyse;
C.10.285	That lecherye is a lykyng thynge, a lymȝerd *of* helle.
C.10.291	Clene *of* lyf and in loue of soule and in lele wedlok.
C.10.291	Clene of lyf and in loue *of* soule and in lele wedlok.
C.10.296	Vngracious to gete goed or loue *of* [þe] peple,
C.10.305	Helen and helpen, is dobest *of* alle.
C.10.307	The more he is worthy and worth, *of* wyse and goed ypresed.'
C.11.12	Þat [they] louyen lond and lordschipe and lykynge *of* body
C.11.22	What shal worthen *of* suche when þei lyf leten:
C.11.23	The sauter saith þe same *of* alle suche ryche:
C.11.30	And can telle *of* treuthe and of þe twelue aposteles
C.11.30	And can telle of treuthe and *of* þe twelue aposteles
C.11.31	Or *of* þe passioun of Crist or of purgatorie þe peynes,
C.11.31	Or of þe passioun *of* Crist or of purgatorie þe peynes,
C.11.31	Or of þe passioun of Crist or *of* purgatorie þe peynes,
C.11.35	And tellen *of* þe trinite how t[w]o slowe þe thridde
C.11.50	Clerkes and knyhtes carpen *of* god ofte
C.11.54	And prech[en] at seynt poules, [for] puyr enuye *of* clerkes,
C.11.55	That folk is nat ferme[d] in þe faith ne fre *of* here godes
C.11.61	And ȝut th[e] wrechus *of* this world is noen ywar by oþer
C.11.62	Ne for drede *of* eny deth withdraweth h[e]m fro pruyde
C.11.74	Ac lust no lord now ne lettred man *of* suche lore to here
C.11.77	For is no wit worth now but hit *of* wynnynge soune.
C.11.80	The which is a lykyng and luste, þe loue *of* þe world.'
C.11.82	I myhte gete no grayn *of* [his] grete wittes
C.11.84	Semyng þat y sholde bysechen here *of* grace.
C.11.85	And when y was war *of* his wille to þat womman gan y louten
C.11.92	Alle kynne kunnynges and comsynges *of* dowel,
C.11.93	*Of* dobet [and] of dobest–for doctour he is knowe
C.11.93	Of dobet [and] *of* dobest–for doctour he is knowe
C.11.97	*Of* lore and of lettrure, of lawe and of resoun.
C.11.97	Of lore and *of* lettrure, of lawe and of resoun.
C.11.97	Of lore and of lettrure, *of* lawe and of resoun.

C.11.97   Of lore and of lettrure, of lawe and of resoun.
C.11.98   So with þat clergie can and consail of scripture
C.11.100   Thenne was y as fayn as foul of faire morwen,
C.11.122   Of alle kyne craftes y contreuede toles,
C.11.123   Of carpent[ers and] keruers, and contreuede þe compas
C.11.133   For of dobet and dobest here doctour is dere loue.'
C.11.143   And bycam man of þat maide withoute mankynde;
C.11.147   Ho was his Autor And hym of god tauhte?
C.11.164   Tho wepte y for wo and wrathe of here wordes
C.11.167   And into þe lond of longyng [and loue] she me brouhte
C.11.173   And coueytise-of-yes ycalde was þat oþer.
C.11.174   And pruyde-of-parfit-lyuynge pursuede me faste
C.11.186   Thenne was [there] oen þat hihte Elde þat heuy was of chere;
C.11.187   'Man,' quod [he], 'yf y me[t]e with the, by marie of heuene,
C.11.191   Couetyse-of-yes euere thow here knewe–
C.11.192   And pruyde-of-parfit-lyuynge to moche perel the brynge.'
C.11.204   In þe legende of lyf longe ar y were.
C.11.210   God gaf hym grace of wit and of goed aftur,
C.11.210   God gaf hym grace of wit and of goed aftur,
C.11.211   Neuere to man so moche þat man can of telle,
C.11.215   Maistres þat [of goddis mercy techen men and prechen]
C.11.224   A[c] me were leuere, by oure lord, a lyppe of goddes grace
C.11.225   Thenne al þe kynde wyt þat 3e can bothe and kunnyng of 3oure
           bokes.
C.11.226   For of fele witty in faith litel ferly y haue
C.11.231   And mercy of mercy nedes moet aryse
C.11.236   Ac y wene hit worth of monye as was in noes tyme
C.11.237   Tho he shoop þe ship of shides and bordes;
C.11.241   Of wryhtes þat hit wrouhte was noen of hem ysaued.
C.11.241   Of wryhtes þat hit wrouhte was noen of hem ysaued.
C.11.243   Of holy kirke þat sholde kepe alle cristene soules
C.11.246   The culorum of this clause curatores is to mene
C.11.249   At domesday a deluuye worth of deth and fuyr at ones.
C.11.250   Worcheth, 3e wrihtus of holy churche, as holy writ techeth,
C.11.256   And ar Adam oþer ysaye oþer eny of the profetes
C.11.262   As in likyng of lecherye no lyf denyede!
C.11.265   Lelly as by his lokes, with a le[tt]re of gyle?
C.11.274   That clergie of cristes mouthe com[e]nded was euere.
C.11.276   Thogh 3e come bifore kynges and clerkes of þe law[e]
C.11.277   Beth nat aferd of þat folk for y shal 3 eue 3ow tonge,
C.11.280   And myhte no kyng ouercome hym as in connynge of speche.
C.11.283   Withoute þe gifte of god w[it]h grace of fortune.
C.11.283   Withoute þe gifte of god w[it]h grace of fortune.
C.11.284   For he þat most se[y]h and saide of the sothfaste trinite
C.11.286   Saide thus in his sarmon for ensau[m]ple of grete clerkes,
C.11.294   Persen with a paternoster [þe paleys of] heuene
C.11.298   Of al þat they haen had of hym þat is here maistre.
C.11.298   Of al þat they haen had of hym þat is here maistre.
C.11.299   Ac lewede laborers of litel vnderstondyng
C.11.301   As clerkes of holy [k]ir[k]e þat [kepe] sholde and saue
C.11.307   Concupiscencia carnis [ne coueytise-of-yes]
C.11.311   Of dowel ne of dobet no deynte me thouhte;
C.11.311   Of dowel ne of dobet no deynte me thouhte;
C.12.3   Couetyse-of-yes conforted me [anon] aftur and saide,
C.12.11   By wissyng of this wenche y dede, here wordes were so swete,
C.12.44   The bileue of oure lord þat lettred men techeth.
C.12.45   Of here teme and here tales y took ful good hede;
C.12.50   Al for tene of here tyxst tremblede myn herte
C.12.53   That vnderfeng me at þe fonte for on of godes chosene.
C.12.63   Withouten leue of [his] lord; no lawe wol hit graunte.
C.12.69   And for his rechelesnes rewarde hym þere riht to þe day of dome
C.12.76   'I troianes, a trewe knyht, take witnesse of a pope
C.12.84   God of his goodnesse ysey his grete will.
C.12.86   And y saued, as 3e may se, withoute syngynge of masses.
C.12.96   Of hym þat trauaileth [t]heron bote treuthe be his lyuynge.
C.12.99   And seynt Ion sethen saide hit of his techyng.
C.12.109   A[t] Caluarie of cristis bloed cristendoem gan sprynge
C.12.110   And blody bretherne we bycome there of o body ywonne,
C.12.114   Of Adames issue and Eue ay til god man deyede;
C.12.120   Forthy lerne we t[he] lawe of loue as oure lord tauhte
C.12.132   In þe parail of a pilgrime and in pore likenesse
C.12.133   Holy seyntes hym sey Ac neuere in secte of riche.
C.12.148   Is a cornel of confort kynde to restore,
C.12.151   The which is þe cornel of confort for alle cristene soules
C.12.158   For þe loue of oure lord lo[w]eth hym to be pore,
C.12.159   He shal haue an hundredfold of heueneryche blisse
C.12.172   Mo prouerbes y myhte haue of mony holy seyntes
C.12.177   Preueth pacient pouerte prince of alle vertues.
C.12.185   And thorw þe grace of god and grayn dede [i]n erthe
C.12.195   Worth allowed of oure lord at here laste ende
C.12.206   Pouerte and penaunce and persecucoun of body.
C.12.210   Ac hoso rat of th[e] ryche the reuers may fynde,
C.12.224   On fat lond ful of donge foulest wedes groweth.

C.12.230   So of rychesse ope rychesse ariste alle vices.
C.12.240   To synege and to souche sotiltees of Gyle,
C.12.241   For coueytyse of catel to culle hym þat hit kepeth.
C.12.245   So coueytise of catel was combraunce to hem alle.
C.12.247   That rote is of robbares, the rychess[e] withynne!
C.13.11   Ne for brihtnesse of here beaute here spouse to be byknowe.
C.13.38   For þe parcel[s] of his pauper and oþer pryue dettes
C.13.39   Wol lette hym, as y leue, the lenghe of a myle
C.13.49   The marchaunt mote forgo or moneye of his porse
C.13.59   Ther þe messager is ay merye and his mouth ful of songes
C.13.67   Aren alle acountable to crist and to þe kyng of heuene,
C.13.74   That oure lord loketh aftur of vch a lyf þat wynneth
C.13.90   Knowelecheth hym cristene and of holy kirke byleue,
C.13.93   So þe pore of puyr reuthe may parforme þe lawe
C.13.95   For þe wil is as moche worthe of a wrecche beggare
C.13.99   So pore and pacient parfitest lyf is of alle.
C.13.101   For spera in deo speketh of prestis þat han no spendynge suluer
C.13.110   For hit is a carfol knyhte and of a Caytif kynges makynge
C.13.111   That hath n[o] lond ne lynage ryche ne good los of his handes.
C.13.114   And a title, a tale of nauht, to his lyflode as hit were.
C.13.126   Syng ne [psalmes] rede [ne sey a masse of the daye].
C.13.132   And in þe myrour of mydelerthe made him efte to loke,
C.13.138   With flekede fetheres and of fele colours.
C.13.144   In etynge, [in] drynkyng [and] in engend[eryng] of kynde.
C.13.145   Aftur cors of concepcion noon toek kepe of oþer,
C.13.145   Aftur cors of concepcion noon toek kepe of oþer,
C.13.152   That ne lees the lykynge of lost of flesch, as hit were,
C.13.152   That ne lees the lykynge of lost of flesch, as hit were,
C.13.172   And ferlyede of his fayrenesse and of his foul le[den]e.
C.13.172   And ferlyede of his fayrenesse and of his foul le[den]e.
C.13.175   Ne what o[f] floures on felde and of here fayre coloures
C.13.175   Ne what o[f] floures on felde and of here fayre coloures
C.13.176   And how out of greeut and of gras gr[e]we so many hewes
C.13.178   Of here kynde and here colour to carpe hit were to longe.
C.13.200   Is no vertue so fair ne of valewe ne profit
C.13.210   Man was made of such [a] matere he may nat wel asterte
C.13.227   The wisdom and the wit of god he was pot out of blisse.
C.13.230   [For] pruyde or presumpcioun of thy parfit lyuynge,
C.13.232   Ne clergie of his connynge kepeth [t]he nat shewe.
C.13.237   Of clergie ne of kynde wyt counteth he nat a rusche.
C.13.237   Of clergie ne of kynde wyt counteth he nat a rusche.
C.14.9   Lowe the and l[y]ue forth in þe lawe of holy chirche;
C.14.28   So grace withouten grace of god and also gode werkes
C.14.30   Ac clergie cometh bote of syhte and kynde wit of sterres,
C.14.30   Ac clergie cometh bote of syhte and kynde wit of sterres,
C.14.33   So grace is a gifte of god and kynde wit a chaunce
C.14.34   And clergie a connynge of kynde wittes techyng.
C.14.36   Then eny connyng of kynde wit but clergi hit reule.
C.14.38   Lawe of loue oure lord wrouht] long ar crist were.
C.14.45   No more can no clerk but if hit come of bokes.
C.14.54   Whiche [is the] coffre of cristis tresor, and clerkes kepeth þe keyes
C.14.57   Buxumliche and benyngnelyche and bidden hit of grace.
C.14.69   And do we as dauid techeth for doute of godes veniance:
C.14.73   Of cloudes and of costumes they contreuede mony thynges
C.14.73   Of cloudes and of costumes they contreuede mony thynges
C.14.75   And of the selcouthes þat þei sye here sones þerof þei tauhten;
C.14.79   For al here kynde knowyng cam bote of diuerse syhtes,
C.14.80   Of briddes and of bestes, of blisse and of sorwe.
C.14.80   Of briddes and of bestes, of blisse and of sorwe.
C.14.80   Of briddes and of bestes, of blisse and of sorwe.
C.14.80   Of briddes and of bestes, of blisse and of sorwe.
C.14.83   As to þe clergie of crist thei counted hit but a tryfle:
C.14.87   Hit speketh þer of ryche men riht nouht ne of ryche lordes
C.14.87   Hit speketh þer of ryche men riht nouht ne of ryche lordes
C.14.88   Bote of clennesse of clerkes and kepares of bestes:
C.14.88   Bote of clennesse of clerkes and kepares of bestes:
C.14.88   Bote of clennesse of clerkes and kepares of bestes:
C.14.91   Bote in a burgeises hous], the beste of þe toune.
C.14.94   And song a song of solace, Gloria in excelcis deo.
C.14.96   Tho hit shoen to shepherdes, a sheware of blisse.
C.14.102   The[n] connynge clerkes of kynde vnderstondynge.
C.14.103   And thow saidest sothe of somme, Ac [yse] in what manere.
C.14.107   That oþer is lewed of þat labour, lerned neuere swymme.
C.14.108   Which trowest [þou] of tho two in temese [is] in moste drede?'
C.14.131   The thef þat hadde grace of god a gode fryday, As thow toldest,
C.14.139   As tho þat sitten at þe syde table or with þe souereyns [of þe] halle
C.14.151   For he is in þe loweste of heuene, yf oure byleue be trewe,
C.14.152   And wel lo[s]liche þere by þe lawe of holy churche:
C.14.160   Bote kynde þat contreuede hit furst of his corteyse wille.
C.14.163   A cantel of kynde wyt here kynde to saue
C.14.164   Of goed and of wykke kynde was þe furste;
C.14.164   Of goed and of wykke kynde was þe furste;
C.14.171   And feblest foul of flyh[t is] þat fleeth oþer swym[m]eth:

C.14.182	Then for eny kyn he come *of* or for his kynde wittes.
C.14.185	The larke þat is a lasse foul is loueloke[re] *of* ledene
C.14.186	And swettore *of* sauour and swyftore of weng[e].
C.14.186	And swettore of sauour and swyftore *of* weng[e].
C.14.192	Ne *of* sortes ne of salamon n[o] scripture can telle
C.14.192	Ne of sortes ne *of* salamon n[o] scripture can telle
C.14.198	For letrede men were lewede ȝut ne were lore *of* [here bokes].'
C.14.207	Ac þer is follyng *of* fonte and follyng in bloed [s]hedyng
C.14.213	And wher hit worth or worth nat, the bileue is gret *of* treuthe
C.15.3	In manere *of* [a] mendenaunt mony ȝer aftur.
C.15.4	And many tym[e] *of* this meteles moche thouhte y hadde:
C.15.11	Ne no cors *of* pore comine in here kyrkeȝerde most lygge
C.15.18	*Of* kynde and [of] his connynge and what connynge he ȝaf bestes
C.15.18	Of kynde and [*of*] his connynge and what connynge he ȝaf bestes
C.15.34	Crauede and cryede for cristes loue *of* heuene
C.15.39	Resoun stoed and s[t]yhlede as for styward *of* halle.
C.15.43	And serued hem thus sone *of* sondry metes monye,
C.15.44	*Of* Austyn, of Ambrose, of alle þe foure euaungeli[st]es:
C.15.44	Of Austyn, *of* Ambrose, of alle þe foure euaungeli[st]es:
C.15.44	Of Austyn, of Ambrose, *of* alle þe foure euaungeli[st]es:
C.15.45	Ac *of* this mete þat maystre myhte nat we[l c]hewe;
C.15.46	Forthy eet he mete *of* more cost, mortrewes and potages.
C.15.47	*Of* þat men myswonne they made hem wel at ese
C.15.49	In a morter, post mortem, *of* many bittere peynes
C.15.63	Pacience was wel apayed *of* this propre seruice
C.15.67	Brawen and bloed *of* gees, bacon and colhoppes.
C.15.80	Ac y wiste neuere freke þat frere is ycald *of* þe fyue mendynantȝ
C.15.84	'A[c] this doctour and dyuynour,' quod y, 'and decretistre *of* Canoen,
C.15.89	Þat in þ[e] mawe *of* þat maystre alle þo metes were,
C.15.98	And prouen hit by here pocalips and þe passioun *of* seynt Aueroy
C.15.101	And [thenne shal he testifie *of*] a trinite and take his felowe [t]o witnesse
C.15.102	What a fond in a forel *of* a frere[s] lyuynge,
C.15.105	*Of* dowel and dobet and yf dobe[s]t [be] eny penaunce.'
C.15.109	And tolde hym *of* a trinite, and toward me he lokede.
C.15.132	Saue loue and leute and lowenesse *of* herte,
C.15.142	Caste coles on his heued *of* alle kyn[de] speche,
C.15.155	Withoute brutteny[n]ge *of* buyren or eny bloed shedynge.
C.15.156	Y take wittenesse,' quod [þe wy], '*of* holy writ a partye:
C.15.161	In þe corner of a car[t]whel with a crow croune.
C.15.164	Noþer fuyr ne floed ne be aferd *of* enemye:
C.15.167	And maistre *of* alle here mebles and of here moneye aftur,
C.15.167	And maistre of alle here mebles and *of* here moneye aftur,
C.15.171	Al th[e] wit *of* this world and wyhte menne strenghe
C.15.172	Can nat parfourme a pees *of* the pope and his enemyes
C.15.179	Haue pacience parfitlyche then half thy pak *of* bokes.
C.15.189	And as they wente by the way–*of* dowel can they carpe–
C.15.199	*Of* [m]y labour th[ey] lauhe, þe lasse and þe more;
C.15.208	Y haue no gode giftes *of* thise grete lordes
C.15.225	Ac yf myhte *of* myracle hym fayle hit is for men beth nat worthy
C.15.226	To haue þe grace *of* god and no gulte of þe pope.
C.15.226	To haue þe grace of god and no gulte *of* þe pope.
C.15.230	Plente *of* payn the peple of sodoume,
C.15.230	Plente of payn the peple *of* sodoume,
C.15.233	For þoȝ nere payn [*of*] plouh ne potage were
C.15.236	Tho[r]w the helpe *of* hym þat me hyder sente;'
C.15.241	The Cryket by helpe *of* þe fuyr and corleu by þe wynde,
C.15.247	A pece *of* þe paternoster and profred vs all.
C.15.254	By so þat þou be sobre *of* syhte and of tonge,
C.15.254	By so þat þou be sobre of syhte and *of* tonge,
C.15.273	'Meeknesse and mylde speche and men *of* o will,
C.15.275	And þat is charite, chaumpion chief *of* all vertues,
C.15.280	Thogh men rede *of* rychesse rihte to þe worldes ende
C.15.284	Hit are but fewe folk *of* this ryche that ne falleth in arrerage
C.15.286	To haue allouaunce *of* his lord; by [þe] lawe he [hit] claymeth.
C.15.287	Ioye þat neuere ioye hadde *of* rihtfull iuge he asketh
C.15.300	And now he buyth hit bittere; he is a beggare *of* helle.
C.15.304	Ac when deth awaketh hem *of* here we[le] þat were er so ryche
C.15.306	Dauid in þe sauter *of* suche maketh mynde and sayth: dormierunt
C.16.2	Fro þe loue *of* oure lord at his laste ende.
C.16.7	A[nd] nat to fonge byfore for drede [*of*] dessallouwynge.
C.16.16	[And arated *of*] ryche men þat reuthe is to here.
C.16.19	For al myhtest þou haue ymad men *of* grete welthe
C.16.23	And amende vs [*of*] thy mercy and make vs alle meke,
C.16.24	Lowe and lele and louynge and *of* herte pore.
C.16.27	And satisfaccioun þe whiche folfilleth þe fader will *of* heuene;
C.16.28	And these ben dowel and dobet and dobest *of* alle.
C.16.29	Cordis contricio cometh *of* sor[w]e of herte
C.16.29	Cordis contricio cometh of sor[w]e *of* herte
C.16.30	And oris confessio cometh *of* [knowlechyng and] shrifte of mouthe
C.16.30	And oris confessio cometh of [knowlechyng and] shrifte *of* mouthe
C.16.36	And bote these thre þat y spak *of* at domesday vs defende

C.16.39	Bote oure spensis and spendyng sprynge *of* a trewe welle
C.16.48	A[c] þe ryche is reuerenced by resoun *of* his rychesse
C.16.50	*Of* wit and of wisdoem þat fer way is bettere
C.16.50	Of wit and *of* wisdoem þat fer way is bettere
C.16.60	Ne none *of* þe seuene synnes sitte ne may þer longe
C.16.70	That mete or moneye *of* straunge men moet begge.
C.16.73	And thogh his glotonye be *of* gode ale he goth to a colde beddynge
C.16.81	For men knowen wel þat coueytise is *of* a kene will
C.16.82	And hath hondes and Armes *of* a longe lenthe
C.16.93	Hadde they noen haunt bote *of* pore [men; here houses stoed vntyled]
C.16.97	And he [h]is seruant, a[s] he saith, and *of* his se[u]te bothe.
C.16.98	And where he be or be nat, a bereth þe signe *of* pouerte
C.16.100	Forthy alle pore þat pacient is *of* puyr rihte may claymen
C.16.103	In lond and in lordschipe [and] lykynge *of* body
C.16.107	Moche is [þat] mayde to louye *of* a man þat such oen taketh,
C.16.109	As by assente *of* sondry p[arti]es and suluer to bote,
C.16.110	More for coueytise *of* catel then kynde loue of þe mariage.
C.16.110	More for coueytise of catel then kynde loue *of* þe mariage.
C.16.129	Selde is pore rihte ryche but *of* rihtfole eritage.
C.16.131	Ne boreweth *of* his neyhebore but þat he may wel paye
C.16.137	[The fifte is] moder *of* myhte and of mannes helthe
C.16.137	[The fifte is] moder of myhte and *of* mannes helthe
C.16.138	And frende in alle fondynges and *of* foule eueles leche:
C.16.139	The sixte is a path *of* pees; ȝe! thorwe þe pase of Aultoun
C.16.139	The sixte is a path of pees; ȝe! thorwe þe pase *of* Aultoun
C.16.140	Pouerte myhte passe withoute perel *of* robbynge.
C.16.144	The seuethe is a welle *of* wysdoem and fewe wordes sheweth
C.16.161	Shal be porest *of* power at his partynge hennes.'
C.16.165	'Leue liberum arbitrium,' quod y, '*of* what lond ar ȝe?
C.16.168	And in cristes court yknowe wel and *of* his kynne a party.
C.16.174	'*Of* [fele] tyme to fihte,' quod he, 'falsnesse to destruye
C.16.181	And ayther is otheres hete and also *of* o will;
C.16.190	And þat is wit and wysdoem, the welle *of* alle craftes;
C.16.199	Austyn and ysodorus, either *of* hem bothe
C.16.207	Thow woldest knowe and conne þe cause *of* all here names
C.16.208	And *of* myn yf thow myhtes[t], me thynketh by thy speche.'
C.16.212	'Thenne artow inparfit,' quod he, 'and oen *of* pruydes knyhtes.
C.16.229	"Non plus sapere," saide þe wyse, [laste synne *of* pruyde wexe,]
C.16.233	That bothe le[r]ed and le[w]ed *of* here beleue douten.
C.16.241	Aȝen þe consayl *of* crist, as holy clergie witnesseth:
C.16.242	Lo, what holy writ wittnesseth *of* wikkede techares:
C.16.245	Thorw parfit preesthoed and prelates *of* holy churche,
C.16.251	There is a meschief in þe more *of* suche manere stokkes.
C.16.252	Riht so persones and prestes and prechours *of* holy churche
C.16.253	Is þe rote *of* [the] rihte fayth to reule þe peple;
C.16.256	For wolde ȝe lettered leue þ[e] lecherye *of* clothyng
C.16.257	And be corteys and kynde *of* holy kyrke godes,
C.16.259	And þerto trewe *of* ȝoure tonge and of ȝoure tayl also
C.16.259	And þerto trewe of ȝoure tonge and *of* ȝoure tayl also
C.16.261	*Of* vsererus, of hores, of alle euel wynnynges,
C.16.261	Of vsererus, *of* hores, of alle euel wynnynges,
C.16.261	Of vsererus, of hores, *of* alle euel wynnynges,
C.16.263	And amenden [hem] *of* here mysdedes more for [ȝoure] ensaumples
C.16.265	Ypocrisye is a braunche *of* pruyde and most amonges clerkes
C.16.272	Iohannes Crisostomus carpeth thus *of* clerkes [and prestes]:
C.16.275	Vnk[ynd]e curatours to be kepares *of* ȝoure soules.
C.16.281	Curatours *of* holy [kirke] and clerkes þat ben Auerous,
C.16.285	That lyuen aȝen holy lore and þe loue *of* charite.'
C.16.291	As poul in his pistul *of* hym bereth wittenesse:
C.16.295	For thogh me sounhte alle þe sektes *of* susturne and brethurne
C.16.297	And so y trowe truly, by þat me telleth *of* charite.'
C.16.299	As proud *of* a peny as of a pounde of golde
C.16.299	As proud of a peny as *of* a pounde of golde
C.16.299	As proud of a peny as of a pounde *of* golde
C.16.300	And as glad *of* a goune of a gray russet
C.16.300	And as glad of a goune *of* a gray russet
C.16.301	As *of* a cote of ca[mm]aca or of clene scarlet.
C.16.301	As of a cote *of* ca[mm]aca or of clene scarlet.
C.16.301	As of a cote of ca[mm]aca or *of* clene scarlet.
C.16.308	For drede *of* god þat so goed is and thusgates vs techeth:
C.16.312	And alle manere meschiefs as munstracie *of* heuene.
C.16.313	*Of* deth ne of derthe drad he neuere
C.16.313	Of deth ne *of* derthe drad he neuere
C.16.318	'*Of* rentes ne of rychesse reccheth he neuere;
C.16.318	'Of rentes ne *of* rychesse reccheth he neuere;
C.16.326	Clotheth hem and conforteth hem and *of* Crist precheth hem,
C.16.327	What sorwe he soffrede in ensaumple *of* vs alle
C.16.335	And with warm water *of* his yes woketh h[em] til [t]he[y] white:
C.16.343	He is þe murieste *of* mouthe at mete þer he sitteth
C.16.358	Riche men a recomendeth, and *of* [here] robes taketh,
C.16.359	*Of* tho that lelelyche lyuen and louen and byleuen:

C.16.361 Ac yf couetyse be *of* his consaile a wol nat come þerynne.
C.16.363 For braulyng and bacbitynge and berynge *of* fals witnesse.
C.16.374 To begge or to borwe but *of* god one:
C.17.8   Withoute borwynge or beggynge bote *of* god one,
C.17.36   Toke lyflode *of* luyther wynnynges in all here lyf tyme.
C.17.41   This is no more to mene bote men *of* holy churche
C.17.45   And to take *of* here tenauntes more then treuthe wolde
C.17.46   And marchaunt₃ merciable wolde be and men *of* lawe bothe
C.17.49   And charite þat chield is now sholde chaufen *of* hymsulue
C.17.69   Y dar nat carpe *of* clerkes now þat cristes [tresor] kepe
C.17.71   *Of* þat þat holy churche of þe olde lawe claymeth
C.17.71   *Of* þat þat holy churche *of* þe olde lawe claymeth
C.17.75   *Of* moche [m]one þe metal is nauhte
C.17.78   Cristendoem *of* holy kyrke, the kynges marke of heuene,
C.17.78   Cristendoem of holy kyrke, the kynges marke *of* heuene,
C.17.79   Ac þe metal þat is mannes soule *of* [many of] this techares
C.17.79   Ac þe metal þat is mannes soule of [many *of*] this techares
C.17.80   Is alayed with leccherye and oþer lustes *of* synne
C.17.82   And for þe synne *of* þe soule forsaketh his oune coyne.
C.17.107 *Of* þat was kalculed of þe clymat the contrarie þey fynde.
C.17.107 Of þat was kalculed *of* þe clymat the contrarie þey fynde.
C.17.108 Gramer, þe grounde *of* al, bigileth nouthe childrene,
C.17.114 Doctours *of* decre[s] and of diuinite maistres
C.17.114 Doctours of decre[s] and *of* diuinite maistres
C.17.124 In þe lettynge *of* here lyf to leue on holy churche.'
C.17.127 A loueknotte *of* leutee and of lele byleue,
C.17.127 A loueknotte of leutee and *of* lele byleue,
C.17.140 The whiche is þe heued *of* charite and hele of mannes soule:
C.17.140 The whiche is þe heued of charite and hele *of* mannes soule:
C.17.141 Loue god for he is goed and grounde *of* alle treuthe;
C.17.152 Louen as by lawe *of* kynde oure lord god almyhty.
C.17.160 And aftur his leryng they lyue and by lawe *of* kynde
C.17.166 And a cardinal *of* Court, a gret clerk withalle,
C.17.167 And pursuede to haue be pope, prince *of* holy chirche;
C.17.172 In ayþer *of* his eres priueliche he hadde
C.17.178 For Macometh to men swaer hit was a messager *of* heuene
C.17.185 Holy men, as y hope, thorw helpe *of* the holy goste
C.17.189 *Of* nasareth, of [n]yneue, of neptalym [and] damaske,
C.17.189 Of nasareth, *of* [n]yneue, of neptalym [and] damaske,
C.17.189 Of nasareth, of [n]yneue, *of* neptalym [and] damaske,
C.17.192 To be p[astor]s and preche the passioun *of* iesus
C.17.202 To amende and to make, as with men *of* holy churche,
C.17.208 For couetyse *of* th[at] croes clerkes of holi churche
C.17.208 For couetyse of th[at] croes clerkes *of* holi churche
C.17.218 The lordschipe *of* londes lese ȝe shal for euer
C.17.220 Whan Constantyn *of* cortesye holy kirke dowede
C.17.230 The heuedes *of* holy churche and tho that ben vnder hem,
C.17.232 And purge hem *of* þe olde poysen Ar more perel falle.
C.17.235 Aȝen þe lore *of* oure lord as seynt luk witnesseth–
C.17.248 To make a perpetuel pees bitwene þe prince *of* heuene
C.17.253 Haen a lyppe *of* oure bileue, the lihtlokour me thynketh
C.17.254 They sholde [turne], hoso trauayle wolde and *of* þe trinite teche hem.
C.17.261 That bereth name *of* Neptalym, of Niniue [and] of damaske.
C.17.261 That bereth name of Neptalym, *of* Niniue [and] of damaske.
C.17.261 That bereth name of Neptalym, of Niniue [and] *of* damaske.
C.17.262 For when þe hye kyng *of* heuene sente his so[n]e til erthe
C.17.267 And bicam man *of* a mayde and metropol[it]anus
C.17.268 And baptised and bis[hin]ede with þe bloed *of* his herte
C.17.274 In sauacioun *of* mannes soule seynte Thomas of Canterbury
C.17.274 In sauacioun of mannes soule seynte Thomas *of* Canterbury
C.17.278 And souereynliche [to] suche þat *of* surie bereth þe name
C.17.287 For as þe kynde is *of* a knyhte or [of] a kynge to be take
C.17.287 For as þe kynde is of a knyhte or [*of*] a kynge to be take
C.17.290 So is þe kynde *of* a curatour for criste[s] loue to preche
C.17.293 Ac we cristene conneth þe [crede] and haen *of* oure tonge
C.17.300 And *of* selcouthe sores saued men fol ofte.
C.17.309 And a sofistre *of* soercerie and seudopropheta
C.17.314 Thorw Moises and Macometh and myhte *of* god þat made al.
C.17.316 Conne þe furste clause *of* oure bileue, credo in deum patrem,
C.18.5   Erber of alle pryuatees and *of* holynesse.
C.18.5   Erber of alle pryuatees and *of* holynesse.
C.18.13   *Of* holynesse, of hendenesse, of helpe-hym-þat-nedeth,
C.18.13   Of holynesse, *of* hendenesse, of helpe-hym-þat-nedeth,
C.18.13   Of holynesse, of hendenesse, *of* helpe-hym-þat-nedeth,
C.18.20   Hit hadde schoriares to shuyuen hit vp, thre shides *of* o lenghe
C.18.21   And *of* o kyne colour & kynde, as me thoghte,
C.18.24   And askede [e]fte *of* hym of what wode they were.
C.18.24   And askede [e]fte of hym *of* what wode they were.
C.18.26   Bytokeneth trewely the trinite *of* heuene,
C.18.28   *Of* o will, of o wit; and he[r]with y kepe
C.18.28   Of o will, *of* o wit; and he[r]with y kepe
C.18.29   The fruyt *of* this fayre tre fro thre wikkede wyndes

C.18.30   [And fro fallynge the stok; hit fayle nat *of* his myhte].
C.18.32   Couetyse cometh *of* þat wynde and Caritas hit abiteth
C.18.38   And manye wikkede werkes, wormes *of* synne,
C.18.41   The which is þe passioun & þe penaunce & þe parfitnesse *of* iesus
C.18.44   And leyth a laddere þerto, *of* lesynges ben þe ronges,
C.18.52   And that is grace *of* þe holy gost; and thus gete y the maystrye.'
C.18.57   And askede efte tho where hit were all [*of*] o kynde.
C.18.59   Hit is al *of* o kynde, and þat shal y preuen,
C.18.62   *Of* o kynde apples aren nat iliche grete
C.18.63   Ne suynge smale ne *of* [o] swettenesse swete.
C.18.69   Somme *of* vs soethfaste and somme variable,
C.18.70   Summe litel, somme large, ylik apples *of* kynde,
C.18.72   The whiche þe seynt spirit seweth, the sonne *of* al heuene,
C.18.74   As monkes and monyals, men *of* holy churche;
C.18.75   These haen þe [hete] *of* þe holi goest as þe crop of tre [the] sonne.
C.18.75   These haen þe [hete] of þe holi goest as þe crop *of* tre [the] sonne.
C.18.77   And chaste leden here lyf, is lyf *of* contemplacioun,
C.18.90   Hit was þe furste fruyte þat þe fader *of* heuene blessed,
C.18.91   And bad hit be, *of* a bat of erthe, a man and a maide,
C.18.91   And bad hit be, of a bat *of* erthe, a man and a maide,
C.18.98   And for þe fayrest fruyte byfore hym, as *of* erthe,
C.18.101 And bryngeth forth fruyt, folk *of* alle nacion,
C.18.115 And made *of* holy men his hoerd in limbo inferni
C.18.121 To go ransake þat ragman and reue hym *of* his apples
C.18.128 That iesus sholde iouste þerfore by iugement *of* Armes
C.18.133 And in þe wombe *of* þat wenche was he fourty wokes
C.18.134 And bycam man *of* þat maide mankynde to saue,
C.18.141 A lechede hem *of* here langour, bothe lasares and blynde,
C.18.142 And comen wommen conuertede and clansed hem *of* synne
C.18.150 And thorw the myhte *of* Mahond and thorw misbileue:
C.18.154 And lefte basketes ful *of* Broke mete, bere awey hoso wolde.
C.18.158 And saide, 'this is an hous *of* orysones and of holynesse
C.18.158 And saide, 'this is an hous of orysones and *of* holynesse
C.18.162 Ac þe ouerturnynge *of* the temple bitokened his resureccioun.
C.18.165 *Of* Ieudas þe iew, iesus oune disciple.
C.18.169 And kuste iesus to be knowe þerby and cauht *of* þe iewes.
C.18.183 '*Of* whennes artow?' quod y, and hendeliche hym grette.
C.18.185 An heraud *of* Armes Ar eny lawe were.'
C.18.189 *Of* o wit and o will, [they] were neuere atwynne
C.18.193 And þe seconde is a sone *of* þe sire, filius;
C.18.202 *Of* hymsulue and his seruant, and what soffreth hem bothe
C.18.206 The whiche aren childrene *of* charite and holy church [the] moder.
C.18.215 And o god almyhty, yf alle men ben *of* Adam.
C.18.216 Eue *of* Adam was and out of hym ydrawe
C.18.217 And Abel *of* hem bothe and alle thre o kynde;
C.18.218 And thise thre þat y Carp *of*, Adam and Eue
C.18.221 As þe bible bereth witnesse, A boek *of* þe olde lawe,
C.18.223 And man withoute a make myhte nat wel *of* kynde
C.18.226 Now go we to godhede: in god, fader *of* heuene,
C.18.229 And as abel *of* Adam and of his wyf Eue
C.18.229 And as abel of Adam and *of* his wyf Eue
C.18.230 Sprang forth and spak, a spyer *of* hem tweyne,
C.18.231 So oute *of* þe syre and of þe sone þe seynt spirit of hem bothe
C.18.231 So oute of þe syre and *of* þe sone þe seynt spirit of hem bothe
C.18.234 In matrimonie aren thre and *of* o man cam alle thre
C.18.248 To make sacrefice *of* hym he heet me, hym to honoure.
C.18.262 At ones on an auter in worschipe *of* th[e] trinite
C.18.269 Thenne hadde y wonder *of* his wordes and of [his] wyde clothes
C.18.269 Thenne hadde y wonder of his wordes and *of* [his] wyde clothes
C.18.276 'This is a present *of* moche pris; what prince shal hit haue?'
C.18.281 Til he come þat y carpe *of*; Crist is his name
C.18.287 The myhte *of* goddes mercy þat myhte vs alle amende.'
C.19.2   That toek me a maundement vpon þe mont *of* synay
C.19.12   A pluhte forth a patente, a pece *of* an hard roche
C.19.22   *Of* men and of wommen meny score thousend.'
C.19.22   Of men and *of* wommen meny score thousend.'
C.19.27   'Ȝoure wordes aren wonderfol,' quod y; 'where eny *of* [hem] be trewe
C.19.37   That *of* no trinite ne telleth ne taketh mo persones
C.19.48   And as we wenten in þe way thus wordyng *of* this matere
C.19.59   Fayth [hadde furst siht *of* hym] Ac he fleyh asyde
C.19.63   Ac when he hadde sihte *of* this s[egg]e asyde he gan hym drawe
C.19.65   Ac so sone so the samaritaen hadde sihte *of* this carefole
C.19.66   [A l]ihte a[dou]n *of* lyard and ladde hym in his hand[e]
C.19.86   Withoute þe bloed *of* a barn he beth nat ysaued,
C.19.87   The whiche barn mote nedes be born *of* a mayde,
C.19.88   And with þe bloed *of* þat barn enbaumed and ybaptised.
C.19.100 And hope afturward *of* god more me toelde
C.19.105 And moest inparfyt *of* alle persones; and pacientliche soffre
C.19.109 And as Abraham þe olde *of* o god the tauhte
C.19.113 For god þat al bygan in bigynnynge *of* the worlde
C.19.118 The paume is the pethe *of* the hand and profereth [forth] the fyngeres

C.19.119 To ministre and to make þat myhte *of* hand knoweth
C.19.121 The holy goest *of* heuene: he is as þe paume.
C.19.124 Touchede and tastede at techyng *of* the paume
C.19.132 So is þe fader a fol god, the fu[r]ste *of* hem alle
C.19.134 And he fader and for[m]eour, þe furste *of* alle thynges–
C.19.142 Oþerwyse then þe writhen f[u]ste or werkmanschupe *of* fyngres.
C.19.149 Then is the syre or the sone and *of* þe same myhte
C.19.156 For peyne *of* þe paume power hem fayleth
C.19.158 Were þe myddel *of* myn hand [ymaymed or ypersed
C.19.159 Y sholde receyue ryht nouht *of* þat y reche myhte;
C.19.161 And þe myddel *of* myn hand] withoute maleese
C.19.169 The holy gost *of* heuene he is as þe paume.
C.19.174 And thenne [a fuyr flaumynge] forth *of* hem bothe.
C.19.180 That alle kyne cristene clanseth *of* synne[s].
C.19.181 And as thow seest som tyme sodeynliche *of* a torche
C.19.191 Graunten [no] grace ne forgeuenesse *of* synnes
C.19.197 Isekeles in euesynges thorwe hete *of* the sonne
C.19.199 So grace *of* þe holi gost the grete myhte *of* þe trinite
C.19.199 So grace of þe holi gost the grete myhte *of* þe trinite
C.19.204 So wol þe fader forзeue folke *of* mylde hertes
C.19.211 So wol Crist *of* his cortesye, and men crien hym mercy,
C.19.213 To þe fader *of* heuene forзe[ue]nesse to haue.
C.19.222 And purchase al the pardoun *of* pampilon and Rome
C.19.226 Ne brenne ne blase clere for blowynge *of* vnkyndenesse.
C.19.231 For mony *of* зowe riche men, by my soule y lye nat,
C.19.235 *Of* his mete and mone to men þat hit nedede?
C.19.240 Clothes *of* moest cost, as clerkes bereth witnesse:
C.19.252 And gyueth зoure goed to þat god þat grace *of* aryseth.
C.19.256 The grace *of* the holy goest, godes owene kynde.
C.19.261 The which is lyf and loue, the leye *of* mannes body.
C.19.265 A fordoth the lihte þat oure lord loketh to haue worschipe *of*.
C.19.269 For coueytise *of* eny kyne thynge þat Crist dere bouhte.
C.19.293 Drede *of* disparacion thenne dryueth [away] grace
C.19.296 And nat *of* þe nownpower of god, þat he ne is ful of myhte
C.19.296 And nat of þe nownpower *of* god, þat he ne is ful of myhte
C.19.296 And nat of þe nownpower of god, þat he ne is ful *of* myhte
C.19.300 As sorwe *of* herte is satisfaccioun for suche þat may nat paye.
C.19.304 Here f[e]re fleeth here for fere *of* here tonge.
C.19.313 Thise thre that y telle *of* thus ben [to] vnderstande:
C.19.324 That they haen cause to contrarien bi kynde *of* here sekness[e];
C.19.329 For vnkyndenesse is þe contrarie *of* alle kyne resoun.
C.19.331 That he may louye, and hym lyke, and lene *of* his herte
C.20.2 As a recheles renk þat recheth nat *of* sorwe
C.20.4 Til y waxe wery *of* the world and wilnede eefte to slepe
C.20.6 *Of* gurles and of gloria laus greetliche me dremede
C.20.6 Of gurles and *of* gloria laus greetliche me dremede
C.20.11 As is þe kynde *of* a knyhte þat cometh to be dobbet,
C.20.14 As doth an heraud *of* Armes when Auntres cometh to ioustes.
C.20.15 Olde iewes *of* Ierusalem for ioye they songen,
C.20.21 That this iesus *of* his gentrice shal iouste in Pers Armes,
C.20.40 'This iesus *of* oure iewene temple iaped and despised,
C.20.46 'Crucifige!' q[uo]d a cachepol, 'he can *of* wycchecrafte!'
C.20.47 'Tolle, tolle!' quod another, and toek *of* kene thornes
C.20.48 And bigan a garland of grene thorn *of* rode;
C.20.55 And 'yf thow be Crist and [kynges] sone come adoun *of* th[e] rode;
C.20.59 The lord *of* lyf and of liht tho leyde his eyes togederes.
C.20.59 The lord of lyf and *of* liht tho leyde his eyes togederes.
C.20.61 The wal *of* the temple tocleyef euene [a] to peces;
C.20.71 And somme saide, 'he can *of* soercerie; goed is þat we assaie
C.20.76 And here arme[s] aftur of e[ither] *of* tho theues
C.20.76 And here arme[s] aftur *of* e[ither] of tho theues.
C.20.86 To touchen hym or to t[ast]en hym or taken down [*of* rode]
C.20.92 *Of* þe dede þat y haue do y do me in зoure grace;
C.20.102 For зoure chaumpioun Chiualer, chief knyht *of* зow alle,
C.20.111 Now ben зoure gode dayes ydoen, as daniel *of* зow telleth;
C.20.113 What for fere *of* this ferly and of þe false iewes
C.20.113 What for fere of this ferly and *of* þe false iewes
C.20.119 A fol benyngne buyrde and buxum *of* speche.
C.20.125 Ayþer asked oþer *of* this grete Wonder,
C.20.126 *Of* the dene and the derkenesse and how þe day roued
C.20.128 'Y haue ferly *of* this fare, in faith,' seide Treuthe,
C.20.132 *Of* eny kyn[nes] creature, conceyued thorw speche
C.20.133 And grace *of* the holy gost; wax grete with childe,
C.20.138 And þat is cause *of* this clips þat [c]loseth now þe sonne,
C.20.145 'That thow tellest,' quod treuthe, 'is boute a tale *of* walterot!
C.20.157 For *of* alle venymes [fou]lest is the scorpioun;
C.20.160 The [f]erste venemouste, thorw vertu *of* hymsulue.
C.20.167 Out *of* þe nype *of* þe north nat ful fer hennes
C.20.180 That many day myhte y nat se for merkenesse *of* synne,
C.20.189 And þat Crist hath conuerted the kynde *of* rihtwisnesse
C.20.190 Into pees and pyte *of* his puyr grace.
C.20.199 Yf that thei touche[d a] tre and *of* þe [trees] fruyt eten.
C.20.201 Freet *of* th[at] fruyt and forsoke, as hit were,

C.20.202 The loue *of* oure lord and his lore bothe
C.20.210 For hadde they wist *of* no wo, wele hadde thay nat knowen;
C.20.217 Ne hadde god ysoffred *of* som oþer then hymsulue
C.20.220 Ywyte what wo is ne were þe deth *of* kynde.
C.20.221 So god þat bigan al *of* his gode wille
C.20.222 Bycam man *of* a mayde mankynde to saue
C.20.223 And soffred to be sold to se þe sorwe *of* deynge,
C.20.224 The which vnknytteth alle care and comsyng is *of* reste.
C.20.227 Forthy god, *of* his goodnesse, þe furste [gome] Adam,
C.20.234 To wyte what al wo is þat woet *of* alle ioye:
C.20.240 Boek hihte þat beaupere, a bolde man *of* speche.
C.20.243 That alle þe wyse *of* th[is] world in o wit acordede
C.20.272 'Princ[i]pes *of* this place, prest vndo this gates
C.20.273 For here cometh with croune þe kynge *of* all glorie.'
C.20.291 Setteth bo[w]es *of* brake and brasene gonnes
C.20.298 And where he wol is his way, ac waer hym *of* þe perelles:
C.20.302 For hymsulue said, þat sire is *of* heuene,
C.20.306 Thus this lord *of* liht such a lawe made
C.20.308 Reuen vs *of* oure riht sethe resoun hem dampnede.
C.20.311 Thenne were he vnwrast *of* his word þat witnesse is of treuthe.'
C.20.311 Thenne were he vnwrast of his word þat witnesse is *of* treuthe.'
C.20.315 Not in fourme *of* a fende bote in fourme of an Addre
C.20.315 Not in fourme of a fende bote in fourme *of* an Addre
C.20.326 And as thowe bigyledest godes ymag[e] in goynge *of* an addre,
C.20.327 So hath god bigiled vs alle in goynge *of* a weye.'
C.20.354 Beth ywaer, зe wyse clerkes and зe witty *of* lawe,
C.20.361 'The lord *of* myhte and of mayne þat made alle thynges.
C.20.361 'The lord of myhte and *of* mayne þat made alle thynges.
C.20.362 Dukes *of* this demme place, anoen vndoth this зates
C.20.363 That Crist may come in, the kynges sone *of* h[e]uene!'
C.20.372 Myne they [be] and *of* me; y may þe bet hem clayme.
C.20.373 Althouh resoun record[e], and rihte *of* mysulue,
C.20.378 For in my palays, paradys, in persone *of* an addere
C.20.402 That art doctour *of* deth drynke þat thow madest.
C.20.403 For y þat am lord *of* lyf, loue is my drynke,
C.20.405 Ac y wol drynke *of* no dische ne of deep clergyse
C.20.405 Ac y wol drynke of no dische ne *of* deep clergyse
C.20.406 Bote *of* comune coppes, alle cristene soules;
C.20.411 Til þe ventage valle in þe vale *of* Iosophat
C.20.418 For we beth brethrene *of* bloed Ac nat in baptisme alle.
C.20.423 And yf þe kynge *of* þe kyngdoem come in þe tyme
C.20.426 And y þat am kynge *of*[f] kynges shal come such a tyme
C.20.430 Be hit eny thyng abouhte, the boldenesse *of* here synne[s],
C.20.431 [Y] may do mercy *of* my rihtwysnesse and alle myn wordes trewe
C.20.432 For holy writ wol þat y be wreke *of* hem þat wrouhte ille–
C.20.434 And so *of* alle wykkede y wol here take veniaunce.
C.20.436 To be merciable to monye *of* my haluebretherne.
C.20.448 They dorste nat loke on oure lord, the leste *of* hem alle,
C.20.450 Many hundret *of* Angels harpeden and songen,
C.20.451 Thenne piped pees *of* poe[sie] a note:
C.20.460 Cluppe we in couenaunt and vch *of* vs kusse oþere.'
C.21.4 In myddes *of* þe masse tho men зede to offrynge
C.21.14 Is Crist with his croes, conquerour *of* Cristene.'
C.21.18 Anoon as men nemned þe name *of* god iesu;
C.21.19 Ergo is no name to þe name *of* iesus
C.21.24 Is Crist more *of* myhte and more worth[y] name
C.21.25 Then iesu or iesus þat all oure ioye cam *of*?'
C.21.30 Ac to be conquerour cald, þat cometh *of* special grace
C.21.31 And *of* hardinesse of herte and of hendenesse
C.21.31 And of hardinesse *of* herte and of hendenesse
C.21.31 And of hardinesse of herte and *of* hendenesse
C.21.32 To make lordes *of* laddes of lond þat he wynneth
C.21.32 To make lordes of laddes *of* lond þat he wynneth
C.21.38 And tho þat bycome cristene bi consail *of* þe baptist
C.21.41 And vpon Caluarie on cros ycrouned kyng *of* iewes.
C.21.43 And conquerour *of* his conqueste his layes and his large.
C.21.45 The lawe *of* lyf that laste shal euere
C.21.48 Tho was he iesu[s] *of* iewes [cald], gentel profete,
C.21.49 And kyng *of* here kyngdoem and croune baer of thornes.
C.21.49 And kyng of here kyngdoem and croune baer *of* thornes.
C.21.53 And tho was he conquerour cald *of* quyke and of dede
C.21.53 And tho was he conquerour cald of quyke and *of* dede
C.21.56 And toek lucifer the loethliche þat lord was *of* helle
C.21.57 And bonde [hym] as he is bounde with bondes *of* yre.
C.21.63 Ac the cause þat he cometh thus with cros [*of*] his passioun
C.21.16 Ac to carpe more *of* Crist and how he cam to þat name;
C.21.73 Reuerensed hym riht fayre with richesses *of* erthe.
C.21.78 Bothe *of* sand, sonne and see and sennes þei wente
C.21.79 Into here kyngene kuth by consail *of* Angelis.
C.21.80 And þer was þat word fulfuld þe which þou *of* speke,
C.21.81 For alle þe angelis *of* heuene at his burthe knelede
C.21.82 And al þe wit *of* the world was in [þo] thre kynges.
C.21.93 For Mirre is mercy to mene and mylde speche *of* tonge.

C.21.98   In þe manere *of* a man and þat by moche sleythe,
C.21.106   As kynde is *of* a conquerour, so comesede iesu
C.21.110   And þer bigan god *of* his grace to do wel:
C.21.116   Bigan god *of* his grace and goodnesse to do wel
C.21.118   A fauntekyn ful *of* wyt, filius Marie.
C.21.121   That he thorw grace was gete and *of* no gome elles.
C.21.123   Aftur þe kynde þat he cam *of*; þer comsede he do wel.
C.21.131   And all he heled and halp þat hym *of* grace asked;
C.21.132   And þo was he cald in contreye *of* þe comune peple,
C.21.134   For dauid was douhtiest *of* dedes in his tyme
C.21.137   And nempned hym *of* naȝareth; and no man so worthy
C.21.138   To be Cayser or kyng *of* the kyngdoem of Iuda
C.21.138   To be Cayser or kyng *of* the kyngdoem of Iuda
C.21.146   That þat blessed body *of* buyrielles sholde ryse
C.21.155   Telle þe comune þat þer cam a companie *of* his apostles
C.21.165   Taddee and ten mo with Thomas *of* ynde.
C.21.184   /Myhte men to assoyle *of* alle manere synnes,
C.21.190   And assoile men of alle synnes saue *of* dette one.
C.21.190   And assoile men of alle synnes saue *of* dette one.
C.21.199   Thus Consience *of* Crist and of þe cros carpede
C.21.199   Thus Consience of Crist and *of* þe cros carpede
C.21.202   In likenesse *of* a lihtnynge a lyhte on hem alle
C.21.212   And criden with Consience, 'helpe vs, [Crist], *of* grace!'
C.21.223   And [pryde shal] be pope, prince *of* holy chirche,
C.21.231   As prechours and prestes and prentises *of* lawe:
C.21.232   They leely to lyue bi labour *of* tonge
C.21.234   And somme he kende craft and konnynge *of* syhte,
C.21.239   To wynne with here lyflode bi lore *of* his techynge];
C.21.243   Bothe *of* wele and of wo and be ywaer bifore,
C.21.243   Bothe of wele and *of* wo and be ywaer bifore,
C.21.246   He wissede [h]e[m] wynne hit aȝeyn thorw whitnesse *of* handes
C.21.253   'That all craft and connyng c[o]m[e] *of* my ȝefte.
C.21.255   And [ho] þat moest maistries can be myldest *of* berynge.
C.21.265   And ioyned til hem oen iohann, most gentill *of* all,
C.21.266   The pris neet *of* [Peres plouh], passynge alle oþere,
C.21.267   And grace [gaef Peres *of* his goednesse] foure stottes,
C.21.282   He þat eet *of* that seed hadde such a kynde:
C.21.285   Ne wynnynge ne wel[e] *off*] wordliche richesse,
C.21.286   Wast[e] word *of* ydelnesse ne wikede speche meue;
C.21.290   And hoso ete *of* þa[t] seed hardy was euere
C.21.292   Myhte no lyare with lesynge[s] ne losse *of* worldly catel
C.21.296   And keuered hym vnder consayl *of* Caton the wyse:
C.21.298   And he þat ete *of* þat seed sholde be euene trewe
C.21.299   With god and nat agast bote *of* gyle one.
C.21.306   Noþer *of* deuk ne of deth þat he ne dede lawe
C.21.306   Noþer of deuk ne *of* deth þat he ne dede lawe
C.21.315   'Harweth alle þa[t] conneth kynde wit bi consail *of* [this] doctours
C.21.321   And grace gaf hym þe cros with [the garlond] *of* thornes
C.21.323   And *of* his bapteme and bloed þat he bledde on rode
C.21.327   And *of* all holy writ he made a roef aftur
C.21.334   And þe londe *of* bileue, the lawe of holi churche.
C.21.334   And þe londe of bileue, the lawe *of* holi churche.
C.21.339   And sente forth surquido[us], his seriaunt[e] *of* Armes,
C.21.352   With the lord þat lyueth aftur the lust *of* his body,
C.21.358   For witterly, y woet wel, we be nat *of* strenghe
C.21.373   [Saue shrewes one swiche as y spak *of*],
C.21.379   Clannesse *of* þe comune and clerkes clene lyuynge
C.21.382   The lord *of* lust shal be ylette al this lente, y hope.
C.21.388   In helpe *of* here hele ones in a monthe
C.21.402   *Of* spiritus Iusticie thow spekest moche an ydel.'
C.21.405   Bote thow lyue bi lore *of* spiritus Iusticie,
C.21.410   'Ich am a Curatour *of* holi [kirke] and cam neuer in my tyme
C.21.411   Man to me þat me couthe telle *of* cardinal[e] vertues
C.21.425   And grace that thow gredest so *of*, gyour of all Clerkes;
C.21.425   And grace that thow gredest so of, gyour *of* all Clerkes;
C.21.427   Emperour *of* al þe world, þat all men were cristene.
C.21.435   As wel for a wastour [and] wenche[s] *of* the stuyues.
C.21.448   He rekketh riht nauht *of* þe remenaunt.
C.21.449   And Crist *of* his cortesye þe cardinals saue
C.21.450   And turne here wi[t] to wisdoem and to wel[th]e [*of*] soule.
C.21.452   The conseyl *of* Consience or cardinal[e] vertues
C.21.454   *Of* gyle ne of gabbyng[e] gyueth they neuer tale
C.21.454   Of gyle ne *of* gabbyng[e] gyueth they neuer tale
C.21.460   'Y halde hit riht and resoun *of* my reue to take
C.21.469   Ther y may hastilokest hit haue, for y am heed *of* lawe;
C.21.472   And holy churche cheef helpe and cheuenteyn *of* þe comu[n]e
C.21.473   And what y take *of* ȝow two y take hit at þe techynge
C.21.474   *Of* spiritus iusticie for y iuge ȝow alle.
C.21.476   Ne craue *of* my comune bote as my kynde asketh.'
C.22.8   Was bi techyng and tellyng *of* spiritus temperancie
C.22.18   And yf [hym] lust for to lape the lawe *of* kynde wolde
C.22.21   Withouten consail *of* Consience or cardinale vertues
C.22.32   *Of* þat he weneth wolde falle yf his wit ne were;

C.22.53   Auntecrist cam thenne and al the crop *of* treuthe
C.22.71   With a lord þat lyueth aftur likyng *of* body
C.22.85   Freneseyes and foule eueles; forageres *of* kynde
C.22.86   Hadde ypriked and preyede polles *of* peple;
C.22.94   And ar heroudes *of* Armes hadden descreued lordes,
C.22.105   Swowened and swel[t]e for sorwe *of* dethus duntes.
C.22.106   Concience *of* his cortesye tho kynde he bisouhte
C.22.120   Consience and his companye, *of* holy [kirke] þe techares.
C.22.133   Moche *of* þe Wyt and Wisdoem of Westmunstre halle.
C.22.133   Moche of þe Wyt and Wisdoem *of* Westmunstre halle.
C.22.140   'Allas!' quod Consience and cryede, 'wolde crist *of* his grace
C.22.153   'Hele and y,' quod he, 'and heynesse *of* herte
C.22.155   And [s]o forȝete [sorwe] and [*of* synne ȝeue nouht].'
C.22.159   Sleuthe wax wonder ȝerne and sone was *of* age
C.22.160   And wedded oen wanhope, a wenche *of* þe stuyves.
C.22.163   This sleuthe wa[x] sley *of* werre and a slynge made
C.22.164   And th[re]w drede *of* dispayr a doysayne mile aboute.
C.22.170   And bisouhte hym *of* socour and of h[is] salue hadde
C.22.170   And bisouhte hym of socour and *of* h[is] salue hadde
C.22.180   And in hope *of* his hele goed herte he hente
C.22.182   The compeny *of* comfort men clepede hit som tyme.
C.22.193   And *of* þe wo þat y was ynne my wyf hadde reuthe
C.22.212   And y bi conseil *of* kynde comsed to Rome
C.22.221   'By þe Marie!' quod a mansed prest, was *of* þe march of Ireland,
C.22.221   'By þe Marie!' quod a mansed prest, was of þe march *of* Ireland,
C.22.223   Then y do to drynke a drauht *of* goed ale.'
C.22.224   And so sayde syxty *of* þe same contreye
C.22.225   And shoten aȝeyn[e with] shotte many a shef *of* othes
C.22.229   Thorw inparfit prestes and prelates *of* holy churche.'
C.22.233   That they cam for Coueityse, to haue cure *of* soules.
C.22.240   And senne freres forsoke the felic[it]e *of* erthe
C.22.242   Con[s]ience *of* this con[s]ail tho comesed for to lawhe
C.22.258   Haen officerys vnder hem and vch *of* hem a certeyne.
C.22.261   Bote hy ben nempned in þe nombre *of* hem þat been ywaged.
C.22.266   *Of* lewed and of lered; the lawe wol and asketh
C.22.266   Of lewed and *of* lered; the lawe wol and asketh
C.22.267   A certeyne for a certeyne saue oenliche *of* freres.
C.22.275   And preche men *of* plato and preuen hit by seneca
C.22.280   And euele is this yholde in parsches *of* yngelond
C.22.287   Ȝerne *of* forȝeuenesse or lengore ȝeres l[on]e.
C.22.293   And soffren þe dede in dette to þe day *of* dome.
C.22.299   *Of* all taletellares and titerares an ydel.
C.22.312   For fastyng *of* a fryday a feerde as he wolde deye.
C.22.314   And more *of* fysyk bi fer, and fayror he plastereth;
C.22.330   Pees vnpynned hyt, was porter *of* vnite,
C.22.352   And be adrad *of* deth and withdrawe hym fro pruyde
C.22.359   The plasteres *of* the persoun and poudres b[it]en to sore;
C.22.364   *Of* 'a pryue payement and y shal preye for ȝow
C.22.366   And make [*of*] ȝow [memoria] in masse and in matynes
C.22.367   [As] freres *of* oure fraternite for a litel suluer'.
C.22.371   For confort *of* his confessour Contricioun he lefte
C.22.372   That is the souereyne salue for alle [synnes *of* kynde].

offeceres > officers

offenden v *offenden v.* B 1; C 1
B.17.285   A[c] yet in mo maneres men *offenden* þe holy goost;
C.19.266   And ȝut in mo maneres men [*o*]*ffenden* þe holy gost;

office n *office n.* A 2; B 3 office (2) Offices (1)
A. 7.184   And pieris was proud þerof, & putte hem in *office*,
A.11.195   Sire dobest haþ ben [in *office*], so is he best worþi
B. 3.100   Yiftes or yeresyeues bycause of hire *Offices*.
B. 6.197   And [Piers was proud þerof] and putte hem [in *office*]
B.15.386   Lest þei ouerhuppen as ooþere doon in *office* and in houres.

officers n *officer n.* B 1; C 2 offeceres (1) officerys (1)
B.20.258   Han *Officers* vnder hem, and ech of hem a certein.
C. 4.195   The kyng comaundede Consience tho to congeye alle his *offeceres*
C.22.258   Haen *officerys* vnder hem and vch of hem a certeyne.

official n *official n.* B 2 Official (1) Officials (1); C 1
B. 2.174   Erchedekenes and *Officials* and alle youre Registrers,
B.20.137   And tornede Cyuyle into Symonye, and siþþe he took þe *Official*.
C.22.137   And turnede syuyle into symonye and sethe he toek þe *official*.

offyn n prop *n.i.d.* B 1; C 2 Offin (1) Offines (1)
B.10.287   *Offyn* and Fynes; for hir coueitise
C.Pr.107   For *Offines* s[yn]ne and fines his brother
C.Pr.123   Than euere he dede on *Offi[n]* and Fines [or on her] fader.

offreth v *offren v.* B 5 offred (1) offrede (4); C 5 offred (1) offrede (3) offreth (1)
B.13.197   Than alle þo þat *offrede* into Gaȝophilacium?'
B.19.75   Kynges come after, knelede and *offrede* [sense],

B.19.83 Reson and Rightwisnesse and Ruþe þei *offrede*;
B.19.87 The seconde kyng siþþe sooþliche *offrede*
B.19.94 [Erþeliche] honeste þynges w[as] *offred* þus at ones
C.13.97 And as moche mede for a myte þer he *offreth*
C.21.75 Kynges cam aftur, knelede and *offrede* [sense],
C.21.83 Resoun and riht[wis]nesse and reuthe thei *offrede*;
C.21.87 The seconde kyng seth soethliche *offrede*]
C.21.94 Ertheliche honeste thynges was *offred* thus at ones

offryng ger *offringe ger.* B 1; C 3 offrynge (2) offrynges (1)
B.19.4 In myddes of þe masse þo men yede to *offryng*
C. 6.300 Yf he wiste thow were such when he resseyued thyn *offrynge*.
C.17.43 And refuse reuerences and raue[n]ers *offrynges*.
C.21.4 In myddes of þe masse tho men ȝede to *offrynge*

ofgon v *ofgon v.* B 1
B. 9.109 Grace to go to hem and *ofgon* hir liflode:

ofrauȝte v *ofrechen v.* B 1
B.18.9 And of cristes passion and penaunce, þe peple þat *ofrauȝte*.

ofsente v *ofsenden v.* A 1; B 1
A. 3.91 And *ofsente* hire as swiþe; seriauntis hire fe[tt]e
B. 3.102 And *ofsente* hire as swiþe; [sergeauntȝ hire fette]

ofte adj *ofte adj.* B 1
B.13.404 'And kauȝte siknesse somtyme for my [surfetes] *ofte*

ofte adv *ofte adv.* A 19 ofte (18) often (1); B 45 ofte (43) ofter (2); C 39
ofte (35) often (2) oftur (2)
A. 2.16 'Þat is mede þe maide, haþ noiȝede me ful *ofte*,
A. 2.193 Ac he haþ leue to lepen out as *ofte* as him likiþ,
A. 2.194 And is welcome whanne he wile & woniþ wiþ hem *ofte*.
A. 3.71 For þei poisone þe peple preuyly wel *ofte*,
A. 3.95 'Vnwittily, [wy] wrouȝt hast þou *ofte*;
A. 3.126 And letiþ passe prisoners & paieþ for hem *ofte*,
A. 3.143 For she is fauourable to fals & fouliþ treuþe *ofte*;
A. 3.177 Ac þou þiself, soþly, asshamidest hym *ofte*;
A. 4.56 'Whoso werchiþ be wil wraþþe makiþ *ofte*.
A. 4.86 To haue mercy on þat man þat mysdede hym *ofte*:
A. 4.94 And *ofte* þe boldere be to bete myn hynen.
A. 5.73 I haue a neiȝebour neiȝ me, noiȝed hym *ofte*,
A. 5.75 To apeire hym be my power I pursuide wel *ofte*,
A. 7.138 He abideþ wel þe betere þat bummiþ nouȝt to *ofte*.'
A. 7.242 Þei han mangid ouer muche, þat makiþ hem grone *ofte*.
A. 9.3 And fraynide ful *ofte* of folk þat I mette
A.10.104 Þat selde m[os]seþ þe marbil þat men *ofte* [t]reden,
A.12.22 And poul precheþ hit *often*, prestes hit redyn:
A.12.106 And so bad Iohan but busily wel *ofte*
B. 2.20 'That is Mede þe mayde, haþ noyed me ful *ofte*,
B. 2.234 Ac he haþ leue to lepen out as *ofte* as hym likeþ,
B. 2.235 And is welcome whan he wile and woneþ with hem *ofte*.
B. 3.82 For þei [p]oisone þe peple pryueliche [wel] *ofte*
B. 3.106 'Vnwittily, [wye], wroȝt hastow *ofte*,
B. 3.137 [And] leteþ passe prisoners and paieþ for hem *ofte*,
B. 3.154 For she is fauourable to fals and [f]ouleþ truþe *ofte*.
B. 3.190 Ac þow þiself sooþly shamedest hym *ofte*;
B. 4.70 'Whoso wercheþ by wille wraþe makeþ *ofte*.
B. 4.99 To haue mercy on þat man þat mysdide hym *ofte*:
B. 4.107 And [*ofte*] þe boldere be to bete myne hewen.
B. 4.156 I falle in floryns', quod þat freke, 'and faile speche *ofte*.'
B. 4.169 'For *ofte* haue I', quod he, 'holpen yow at þe barre,
B. 5.93 I haue a neȝebore [neiȝ] me, I haue anoyed hym *ofte*,
B. 5.95 To apeire hym bi my power pursued wel *ofte*],
B. 5.99 Bitwene [meyne and meyne] I make debate *ofte*
B. 5.368 That I haue trespased with my tonge, I kan noȝt telle how *ofte*;
B. 7.154 Ac I haue no sauour in songewarie for I se it *ofte* faille.
B. 8.3 And frayned ful *ofte* of folk þat I mette
B.10.333 That þis worþ sooþ, seke ye þat *ofte* ouerse þe bible:
B.11.50 Coueitise of eiȝes com *ofter* in mynde
B.11.52 Coueitise of eiȝes [*ofte* me conforted]
B.11.435 'Ye siggen sooþ', quod I, 'ich haue yseyen it *ofte*.
B.12.10 Amende þee while þow myȝt; þow hast ben warned *ofte*
B.12.172 Out of synne and be saaf, þouȝ he synne *ofte*,
B.13.72 In englissh on auenture it sholde be rehercced to ofte;
B.13.260 For er I haue breed of mele *ofte* moot I swete,
B.13.402 Swoor þerby swiþe *ofte* and al biswatte his cote;
B.14.212 The heiȝe wey to heueneward [*ofte*] Richesse letteþ:
B.14.251 Ne dooþ hym noȝt dyne delicatly ne drynke wyn *ofte*.
B.14.329 Swouned and sobbed and siked ful *ofte*
B.15.235 In kynges court he comeþ *ofte* þer þe counseil is trewe,
B.15.239 In þe Consistorie bifore þe Commissarie he comeþ noȝt ful *ofte*
B.15.303 [For al þe curteisie þat beestes konne þei kidde þat folk *ofte*,
B.15.363 As of wedres and wyndes þei warned men *ofte*.
B.15.589 Of selkouþe sores; þei seiȝen it *ofte*,

B.16.112 *Ofte* [he] heeled swiche; he held it for no maistrie
B.17.22 '[He seiþ] sooþ', seide þis heraud; 'I haue [founded] it *ofte*.
B.18.138 For patriarkes and prophetes han preched herof *ofte*
B.18.380 *Ofter* þan ones þouȝ he were a tretour.
B.19.369 And [a sisour and a somonour] þat were forsworen *ofte*;
B.19.389 Or as *ofte* as þei hadde nede, þo þat hadde ypaied
B.20.25 For Spiritus fortitudinis forfeteþ [wel] *ofte*;
B.20.26 He shal do moore þan mesure many tyme and *ofte*,
B.20.119 Wiþ vntidy tales he tened ful *ofte*
C. 2.19 'That is mede þe mayde, hath niyed me ful *ofte*
C. 2.188 And notaries [vp]on persones þat permuten *ofte*
C. 2.244 Ac he hath leue to lep out as *ofte* as hym liketh,
C. 2.245 And is welcome when he cometh and woneth with hem *ofte*.
C. 3.90 Many sondry sorwes in Citees falleth *ofte*
C. 3.134 And saide, 'vnwittiliche, womman, wro[uh]t hastow *ofte*
C. 3.175 He lat passe prisones [and] paieth for hem *ofte*
C. 3.201 Trewe Burgeys and bonde he bryngeth to nauhte *ofte*
C. 5.94 Ac ȝut y hope, as he þat *ofte* hath ychaffared
C. 6.118 Freres folewen my [f]ore fele tyme and *ofte*
C. 6.123 Thus Beggares and Barones at debat aren *ofte*
C. 6.274 Mercy for my mysdedes þat y ne mourned [o]*ftur*
C. 6.426 Of þat y haue trespased with tonge, y can nat telle how *ofte*;
C. 7.62 Thenne sat sleuthe vp and seynede hym *ofte*
C. 9.247 Ac aboute mydday at mele tyme y mette with hem *ofte*,
C. 9.303 Ac men setteth nat by sowngewarie for me seth hit *often* fayle.
C.10.3 And fraynede ful *ofte* of folke þat y mette
C.11.50 Clerkes and knyhtes carpen of god *ofte*
C.12.237 For if he be fer þerfro fol *ofte* hath he drede
C.12.239 And ȝut more hit maketh men mony tymes & *ofte*
C.13.187 Y se non so *ofte* forfeten sothly so mankynde;
C.13.241 'Ȝe seggeth soth, be my soule,' quod y, 'I haue sey hit *ofte*.
C.14.4 And wissed the [wel] *ofte* what dowel was to mene
C.14.112 Out of synne and be saef, thogh he synege *ofte*,
C.15.75 A[s] poul þe apostle prechede to þe peple *ofte*:
C.16.91 Ne doth men dyne delicatlyche ne drynke wyne *ofte*.
C.16.334 Bouketh hem at his breste and beteth h[em] *ofte*
C.16.364 In constorie bifore [þe] commissarie a cometh nat ful *ofte*
C.16.369 Ac thorw Coueytyse and his consaile ycongeyed is he *ofte*.
C.17.300 And of selcouthe sores saued men fol *ofte*
C.18.61 Me may se on an appul tree monye tyme and *ofte*
C.18.151 'Thenne is saton ȝoure saueour,' quod iesus, '& hath ysaued ȝow *ofte*.
C.20.141 For patriarkes and prophetes haen preched herof *ofte*
C.20.422 *Oftur* then ones thogh [he] were [a] tretou[r].
C.21.369 And a sisour and [a] sompnour þat weren forsworen *ofte*;
C.21.389 Or as *ofte* as they hadden nede, tho þat hadden payed
C.22.25 For spiritus fortitudinis forfeteth wel *ofte*;
C.22.26 He shal do more þe[n] mesure mony tymes and *often*
C.22.119 With vntidy tales he tened ful *ofte*

ofwalked ptp *ofwalked ppl.* C 1
C.Pr.7 Me biful for to slepe, for werynesse *ofwalked*,

oille n *oile n.* B 1; C 1 oyle
B.17.72 Wiþ wyn and with *oille* hise woundes he wasshed,
C.19.71 With wyn and with *oyle* his woundes he gan li[th]e,

oke > akeþ

okes n *oke n.* A 1 okis; B 1; C 1
A. 5.18 Bechis & broode *okis* wern blowen to [þe] grounde,
B. 5.18 Beches and brode *okes* were blowen to þe grounde
C. 5.120 Beches and brode *okes* were blowe to þe grounde

old adj *olde adj.* A 6 old (2) olde (4); B 20 old (1) olde (18) oold (1); C
25 oelde (3) olde (22)
A. 7.75 'For [now] I am *old* & hor & haue of myn owene
A. 7.292 Deyneþ nouȝt to dyne a day niȝt *olde* wortis.
A. 8.82 Ac *olde* men & hore þat helpeles ben of strengþe,
A.10.187 To ȝiuen a ȝong wenche to an *old* feble,
A.11.72 Ac austyn þe *olde* for alle suche prechide,
A.11.303 Þat [was] austyn þe *olde*, & hiȝeste of þe foure,
B. 6.83 'For now I am *old* and hoor and haue of myn owene
B. 6.308 Deyne[þ] noȝt to dyne a day nyȝt *olde* wortes.
B. 7.100 Ac *olde* men and hore þat helplees ben of strengþe,
B. 9.205 To ȝyuen and to yemen boþe yonge and *olde*,
B.10.249 Austyn þe *olde* herof made bokes.
B.10.459 Was Austyn þe *olde*, and heiȝest of þe foure,
B.11.205 In þe *olde* lawe, as [þe] lettre telleþ, mennes sones men calle[d] vs
B.12.8 In þyn *olde* elde, þat yuele kan suffre
B.12.73 In þe *olde* lawe as þe lettre telleþ, þat was þe lawe of Iewes,
B.12.113 Archa dei, in þe *olde* lawe, leuytes it kepten;
B.12.236 Ac of briddes and of beestes men by *olde* tyme
B.13.185 I shal brynge yow a bible, a book of þe *olde* lawe,
B.18.8 And how Osanna by Organye *olde* folk songen,

B.18.17	*Olde* Iewes of Ierusalem for ioye þei songen,
B.18.338	Thefliche þow me robbedest; þe *olde* lawe graunteþ
B.18.342	Membre for membre [was amendes by þe *olde* lawe],
B.19.273	Wiþ two [aiþes] þat þei hadde, an *oold* and a newe:
B.19.310	Wiþ *olde* lawe and newe lawe þat loue myȝte wexe
B.19.426	And Piers [þe Plowman] wiþ his newe plow and [þe] *olde*
B.19.446	Ayein þe *olde* lawe and newe lawe, as Luc [bereþ] witness[e]:
C. 6.188	Exited either oþer til oure *olde* synne;
C. 6.189	Sotiled songes and sente out *olde* baudes
C. 6.193	When y was *olde* and hoor and hadde ylore þat kynde
C. 8.92	'For now y am *olde* and hoer and haue of myn owene
C. 8.330	Deyne[th noght] to dyne a day nyhte *olde* wortes;
C. 9.176	Ac *olde* [men] and hore þat helples ben and nedy
C. 9.215	As by þe engelisch of oure eldres of *olde* mennes techynge
C.10.304	To ȝeue and to ȝeme bothe ȝonge and *olde*,
C.11.146	Austyn þe *olde* herof made bokes;
C.11.285	Was Austyn þe *oelde* þat euere man wiste,
C.12.113	In þe *olde* lawe, as þe lettre telleth, mennes sones me calde vs
C.14.58	Arca dei in þe *olde* lawe leuytes hit kepte;
C.17.71	Of þat þat holy churche of þe *olde* lawe claymeth
C.17.232	And purge hem of þe *olde* poysen Ar more perel falle.
C.18.221	As þe bible bereth witnesse, A boek of þe *olde* lawe,
C.18.245	He bihihte vs issue and ayr in oure *olde* age;
C.19.109	And as Abraham þe *olde* of o god the tauhte
C.20.7	And how osanna þy orgene *oelde* folke songe.
C.20.15	*Olde* iewes of Ierusalem for ioye they songen,
C.20.381	Aȝeyne my loue and my leue: þe *olde* lawe techeth
C.20.387	So þat lyf quyte lyf; þe *olde* lawe hit asketh.
C.21.273	With two aythes þat þey hadde, an *oelde* and a newe:
C.21.310	With *olde* lawe and newe [lawe] that loue myhte wexe
C.21.426	And [Peres the Plowman] with his newe [plouh] and [þe] *olde*
C.21.446	Aȝen þe *olde* lawe and newe lawe, as Luk bereth witnesse:

on *adv. on adv.(1)* A 3; B 9; C 9

A. 3.74	For tok h[y] *on* trewely h[y] tymbride not so heiȝe,
A. 7.54	He caste *on* his cloþis, ycloutid & hole,
A. 7.172	And fla[ppid]e *on* wiþ flailes fro morewe til eue,
B. 3.85	For toke þei *on* trewely þei tymbred nouȝt so heiȝe,
B. 6.59	[He] caste *on* [hise] cloþes, yclouted and hole,
B. 6.184	And flapten *on* wiþ flailes fro morwe til euen
B. 7.57	Whan þei drawen *on* to [þe deþ] and Indulgences wolde haue,
B.13.294	And louelokest to loken *on* and lelest of werkes,
B.13.301	And as a lyoun *on* to loke and lordlich of speche;
B.15.191	And leggen *on* longe wiþ Laboraui in gemitu meo,
B.17.27	And lelest to leue [*on*] for lif and for soule?
B.20.114	This lecherie leide *on* wiþ [laughynge] chiere
C. 3.84	For tok thei [*o*]*n* trewely they tymbred nat so heye,
C. 8.58	[He] caste *on* his clothes of alle kyn craftes,
C. 8.180	And flapton *on* with f[lay]les fro morwen til euen
C. 8.329	Laborers þat han no lond to lyue *on* but here handes
C.10.259	And thogh he be louelich to loke[n] *on* and lossum abedde,
C.13.154	For out of resoun they ryde and rechelesliche t[a]ken *on*
C.18.54	Where þe fruyt were fayre or foul for to loke *on*.
C.19.28	And lele to bileue *on* for [lif and] for soule?
C.22.114	This lecherye leyde [*o*]*n* with lauhyng chere

on *prep. on prep.* A 137 o (2) on (135); B 292 o (4) on (288); C 264 o (4) on (260)

A.Pr.5	But *on* a may morwenyng on maluerne hilles
A.Pr.5	But on a may morwenyng *on* maluerne hilles
A.Pr.9	And as I lay & lenide & lokide *on* þe watris
A.Pr.14	I saiȝ a tour *on* a toft triȝely Imakid;
A.Pr.50	Ermytes *on* an hep, wiþ hokide staues,
A.Pr.64	Þe moste meschief *on* molde is mountyng vp faste,
A.Pr.88	Tho[u] miȝtest betere mete myst *on* maluerne hilles
A. 1.7	Þe moste partie of þis peple þat passiþ *on* þis erþe,
A. 1.12	'Þe tour [*on*] þe toft,' quaþ heo, 'treuþe is þereinne,
A. 1.42	Ac þe mone *on* þis molde sal me no faste holdiþ,
A. 1.66	And siþen *on* an Eldir hongide him aftir.
A. 1.68	Þat tresten *on* his tresour betraid arn sonnest.'
A. 1.71	And h[a]lside hire *on* þe heiȝe name, er heo þennis ȝede,
A. 1.77	Þanne I knelide *on* my knes & criȝide hire of grace;
A. 1.79	And ek kenne me kyndely *on* crist to beleue,
A. 1.84	I do it *on* Deus caritas to deme þe soþe.
A. 1.88	He is a god be þe gospel *on* ground & on lofte,
A. 1.88	He is a god be þe gospel on ground & *on* lofte,
A. 1.97	[Di]de hem swere *on* h[ere] swerd to serue treuþe euere.
A. 1.126	Þat treuþe is þe tresour triȝest *on* erþe.'
A. 1.141	Lokide *on* vs wiþ loue, & let his sone deiȝe
A. 1.145	To haue pite *on* þat peple þat pynede hym to deþe.
A. 1.149	Forþi I rede *on* þe riche haue reuþe *on* þe pore,
A. 2.1	Ȝet knelide I *on* my knes & criȝede hire of grace,
A. 2.3	Þat bar þe blisside barn þat bouȝte vs *on* þe rode,
A. 2.5	'Loke *on* þi left half, & lo where he standis,

A. 2.7	I lokide *on* [my] left half as þat lady me tauȝte,
A. 2.9	Ipurfilid wiþ pelure, þe pureste [*o*]*n* erþe,
A. 2.14	Þere nis no quen queyntere þat quyk is *o* lyue.
A. 2.34	Were beden to þe b[ri]dale *on* boþe two sides.
A. 2.80	And seide to cyuyle, 'now sorewe *on* þi bokes,
A. 2.88	And þou hast fastnid hire wiþ fals, fy *on* þi law[e]!
A. 2.128	Sette mede *on* a shirreue shod al newe,
A. 2.129	And fals sat *on* a sisour þat softeliche trottide,
A. 2.132	Þat symonye & cyuyle shulde *on* here fet gange
A. 2.136	Sire symonye hymself shal sitte *on* here bakkis;
A. 2.144	As fo[bb]is & faitours þat *on* here feet iotten.'
A. 2.148	Of many maner of m[e]n þat *on* þis molde libbeþ.
A. 2.151	But prikede forþ *on* his palfray & passide hem alle,
A. 2.159	But riȝt as þe lawe lokis let falle *on* hem alle.'
A. 2.168	Er he be put *on* þe pillorie, for any preyour, I hote.'
A. 2.183	And senten hym *on* sundais wiþ selis to chirche,
A. 2.188	For he coude *on* here craft & kneuȝ manye gommes.
A. 3.67	As to punisshen *on* pillories & on py[n]yng stolis
A. 3.67	As to punisshen on pillories & *on* py[n]yng stolis
A. 3.168	Þou hast hongid *on* myn half enleuene tymes,
A. 3.175	Ne dide as þou demist; I do it *on* þe king.
A. 3.183	And bar here bras *on* þi bak to caleis to selle,
A. 3.186	And bateride hym *on* þe bak, boldite his herte,
A. 3.233	Shal haue mede *on* þis molde þat mattheu haþ grauntid:
A. 3.239	Why þe vengeaunce fel *on* saul & on his children?
A. 3.239	Why þe vengeaunce fel on saul & *on* his children?
A. 3.266	Shal no more mede be maister *on* erþe,
A. 4.20	Hange *on* hym þe heuy bridel to holde his hed lowe,
A. 4.22	Þanne consience *on* his capil cairiþ forþ faste,
A. 4.60	Wrong þanne *on* wysdom wepi[de] hym to helpe,
A. 4.86	To haue mercy *on* þat man þat mysdede hym ofte:
A. 4.95	But resoun haue reuþe *on* hym he shal reste in þe stokkis
A. 4.97	Summe redde resoun to haue reuþe *on* þat shrewe,
A. 4.128	Let þi confessour, sire king, construe it þe *on* englissh,
A. 4.148	'Be hym þat [rauȝte] *on* þe rode,' quaþ resoun to þe king,
A. 5.8	And so I babelide *on* my bedis þei brouȝte me aslepe.
A. 5.12	And preyede þe peple haue pite *on* hemselue,
A. 5.14	And þe southwestryne wynd *on* satirday at eue
A. 5.88	Þanne I criȝe *on* my knes þat crist gyue hym sorewe
A. 5.113	He shulde wandre *on* þat walsshe, so was it þredbare.
A. 5.158	Cisse þe so[wes]tere sat *on* þe bench.
A. 5.171	And bed bette þe bocher be *on* his side.
A. 5.198	He [þr]umblide *on* þe presshewold & [þrew] to þe erþe
A. 5.210	'Shal neuere fissh *on* þe Friday defie in my wombe
A. 5.215	And flattide it *on* his face & faste on him criede
A. 5.215	And flattide it on his face & faste *on* him criede
A. 5.218	And beet þiself *on* þe brest & bidde hym of grace,
A. 5.233	Robert þe robbour *on* reddite lokide,
A. 5.236	'Crist, þat *on* caluarie vpon þe [cros] diȝedist,
A. 5.238	And þou haddist mercy *on* þat man for memento sake,
A. 5.241	So rewe *on* þis robert þat red[dere] ne hauiþ,
A. 6.8	An hundrit of ampollis *on* his hat seten,
A. 6.10	And many crouch [*o*]*n* his cloke, & keiȝes of rome,
A. 6.17	Ȝe mowe se be my signes þat sitten *on* myn hat
A. 6.65	Leue hem *on* þi left half, & loke nouȝt þereaftir,
A. 6.92	And ȝif grace graunte þe to gon in [*on*] þis wise,
A. 7.24	Ac *on* þe tem trewely tauȝt was I neuere.
A. 7.82	To haue reles & remissioun, *on* þat rental I leue.
A. 7.102	Eche man *on* his maner made hymself to done,
A. 7.135	Inouȝ iche day at non, ac no more til *on* þe morewe
A. 7.158	'Awreke me *on* wasto[urs],' quaþ peris, 'þat þis world [shend]iþ.'
A. 7.173	Þat hunger was not hardy *on* hem for to loke.
A. 7.213	'I wolde not greue god,' quaþ peris, 'for al þe gold *on* ground,
A. 7.272	To drawe *on* feld my dong while þe drouȝt lastiþ.
A. 7.291	Laboureris þat haue no land [to] lyue *on* [but] here handis
A. 8.14	Loke *on* þat o lawe, & lere men þat oþer,
A. 8.15	And bere men *on* here bak as here baner shewiþ,
A. 8.79	Þanne of alle oþer maner men þat *on* þis molde wandriþ.
A. 8.90	For I shal construe iche clause & kenne it þe *on* englissh.'
A. 8.119	Þou art le[ttr]id a litel; who lernide þe *on* boke?'
A. 8.124	'Lewide lorel,' quaþ peris, 'litel lokest þou *on* þe bible;
A. 8.125	*On* salamonis sawis [seldom] þou beholdis;
A. 8.129	Metel[es and money]les *on* maluerne hilles.
A. 8.130	Musyng *on* þis metelis a myle wey I ȝede;
A. 8.149	Al þis makiþ me *on* metelis to þinke
A. 8.151	*On* peris þe plouȝman, whiche a pardoun he hauiþ,
A. 8.163	A[c] to triste *on* þis trionalis, trewely, me þinkeþ,
A. 8.165	Forþi I rede ȝow renkes þat riche ben *on* erþe
A. 9.8	Til it befel *on* a Friday two Freris I mette,
A. 9.23	'How seue siþes þe sadde man synneþ *on* þe day;
A. 9.33	Riȝt þus [it] fariþ,' quaþ þe Frere, 'be folk here *on* erþe.
A. 9.50	I bekenne [ȝow] crist þat *on* þe crois deiȝede.'
A. 9.52	And [g]iue þe grace *on* þis erþe in good lif to ende'.

A. 9.104	How dowel, dobet & dobest don *on* þis erþe.'
A. 9.106	Ellis wot no man þat now is *o* lyue.'
A. 9.108	Disputyng *on* dowel day aftir oþer,
A.10.116	Loke þou grucche nouȝt *on* god þeiȝ he gyue þe litel;
A.10.140	Ben conseyuid in cursid tyme as kaym was *on* Eue:
A.10.172	Þat euere curside caym com *on* þis erþe;
A.10.208	And [werche] *on* his wyf & on no womman ellis,
A.10.208	And [werche] on his wyf & *on* no womman ellis,
A.11.14	Þat hem were leuere lond, & lordsshipe *on* erþe,
A.11.28	*On* crois vpon caluarie, as clerkis vs techiþ,
A.11.71	And make men to mysbeleue þat musen *on* here wordis.
A.11.77	Ac beleue lelly *o[n* þe] lore of holy chirche,
A.11.92	Þeiȝ dobest drawe *on* hym day aftir oþer.
A.11.119	Leue hym *on* þi left half a large myle or more,
A.11.152	And louen hem þat liȝen *on* vs, & lenen hem at here nede,
A.11.184	Trewe tilieris *on* erþe, taillours & souteris
A.11.213	Poperiþ *on* a palfrey [fro] toune to toune;
A.11.264	And I leue *on* oure lord & on no lettrure betere.
A.11.264	And I leue on oure lord & *on* no lettrure betere.
A.11.273	For alle cunnyng clerkis siþþe crist ȝede *on* þe
A.11.281	And for he kneuȝ *on* þe crois & to crist shr[o]f hym,
A.12.13	And *on* clergie crieþ on cristes holy name
A.12.13	And on clergie crieþ *on* cristes holy name
A.12.27	And asked Iesu *on* hy þat herden hit an hundred.
A.12.47	And þanne I kneled *on* my knes and kyste her [fete] sone,
A.12.56	And wente forþ *on* my way with omnia probate,
A.12.82	Mi name is feuere *on* þe ferþe day; I am aþrest euere.
B.Pr.5	Ac *on* a May morwenynge on Maluerne hilles
B.Pr.5	Ac on a May morwenynge *on* Maluerne hilles
B.Pr.9	And as I lay and lenede and loked *on* þe watres
B.Pr.14	I seiȝ a tour *on* a toft trieliche ymaked,
B.Pr.53	Heremytes *on* an heep with hoked staues
B.Pr.67	The mooste meschief *on* Molde is mountynge [vp] faste.
B.Pr.157	We myȝte be lordes *o* lofte and lyuen at oure ese.'
B.Pr.165	Were þer a belle *on* hire beiȝe, by Iesu, as me þynkeþ,
B.Pr.169	And knytten it *on* a coler for oure commune profit
B.Pr.176	Ac þo þe belle was ybrouȝt and *on* þe beiȝe hanged
B.Pr.215	Thow myȝtest bettre meete myst *on* Maluerne hilles
B. 1.7	The mooste partie of þis peple þat passeþ *on* þis erþe,
B. 1.12	'The tour *on* þe toft', quod she, 'truþe is þerInne.
B. 1.44	Ac þe moneie [on] þis molde þat men so faste holdeþ,
B. 1.68	And siþen an Eller hanged hym [after].
B. 1.70	That trusten *on* his tresour bitraye[d are] sonnest.'
B. 1.73	And [halsede] hire *on* þe heiȝe name, er she þennes yede,
B. 1.79	Thanne I [kneled] *on* my knees and cried hire of grace;
B. 1.81	And [ek] kenne me kyndely *on* crist to bileue,
B. 1.86	I do it *on* Deus caritas to deme þe soþe.
B. 1.90	He is a god by þe gospel, a grounde and *o* lofte,
B. 1.99	Dide hem sweren *on* hir swerd to seruen truþe euere.
B. 1.137	That Treuþe is tresor þe trieste *on* erþe.'
B. 1.149	May no synne be *on* hym seene þat vseþ þat spice.
B. 1.167	Loked *on* vs wiþ loue and leet his sone dye
B. 1.171	To haue pite [on] þat peple þat peyned hym to deþe.
B. 1.175	Forþi I rede [þe] riche, haueþ ruþe [on] þe pouere;
B. 2.1	YEt [kneled I] *on* my knees and cried hire of grace,
B. 2.3	That bar þ[e] blis[sed] barn þat bouȝte vs *on* þe Rode,
B. 2.5	'Loke [o]n þi left half, and lo where he stondeþ,
B. 2.7	I loked *on* my left half as þe lady me tauȝte
B. 2.9	Purfiled wiþ Pelure, þe [pureste on] erþe,
B. 2.55	Were boden to þe bridale *on* boþe two sides,
B. 2.116	And seide [to] Cyuyle, 'now sorwe [on þi bokes]
B. 2.124	And þow hast fest hire [wiþ] Fals; fy *on* þi lawe!
B. 2.165	And Fals sat *on* a Sisour þat softeli trotted,
B. 2.166	And Fauel *on* [Fair Speche] fe[ynt]ly atired.
B. 2.168	For Symonye and Cyuylle sholde *on* hire feet gange.
B. 2.183	As [fobbes] and Faitours þat *on* hire feet [iotten].'
B. 2.187	[Of many maner man þat *on* þis molde libbeth],
B. 2.190	And priked [forþ *on*] his palfrey and passed hem alle
B. 2.198	But riȝt as þe lawe [lokeþ] lat falle *on* hem alle.'_
B. 2.207	Er he be put *on* þe Pillory for any preyere I hote.'_
B. 2.224	And senten hym [on Sondayes wiþ seles] to chirch[e],
B. 2.229	For he kouþe [on] hir craft and knew manye gommes.
B. 3.72	*On* auenture ye haue youre hire here and youre heuene als.
B. 3.78	[As] to punysshe *on* Pillories and [on] pynynge stooles
B. 3.78	[As] to punysshe on Pillories and [*on*] pynynge stooles
B. 3.80	For þise are men *on* þis molde þat moost harm wercheþ
B. 3.181	Thow hast hanged *on* myn half elleuene tymes,
B. 3.188	Ne dide as þow demest; I do it *on* þe kynge.
B. 3.199	I batred hem *on* þe bak and boldede hire hertes
B. 3.254	[Shul haue] Mede [*on* þis molde þat] Mathew [haþ graunted]:
B. 3.260	Whi þ[at] vengeaunce fel *on* Saul and on his children?
B. 3.260	Whi þ[at] vengeaunce fel on Saul and *on* his children?

B. 3.281	*On* auenture it noyed m[e] noon ende wol I make,
B. 3.290	Shal na moore Mede be maister [*on* erþe],
B. 3.292	Thise shul ben Maistres *on* moolde [trewe men] to saue.
B. 4.22	Hange *on* hym þe heuy brydel to holde his heed lowe,
B. 4.24	Thanne Conscience [*o*]n his capul [caireþ] forþ faste,
B. 4.26	Whiche maistries Mede makeþ *on* þis erþe.
B. 4.45	And bitwene hymself and his sone sette hym *on* benche,
B. 4.99	To haue mercy *on* þat man þat mysdide hym ofte:
B. 4.108	But Reson haue ruþe *on* hym he shal reste in [þe] stokkes
B. 4.110	Som[me] radde Reson to haue ruþe *on* þat shrewe;
B. 4.122	And til prechours prechynge be preued *on* hemselue;
B. 4.145	Late [þi] Confessour, sire kyng, construe [it þee *on* englissh],
B. 4.152	For I seiȝ Mede in þe moot halle *on* men of lawe wynke
B. 4.185	'By hym þat rauȝte *on* þe Rode!' quod Reson to þe kynge,
B. 5.8	And so I bablede *on* my bedes þei brouȝte me aslepe.
B. 5.14	And þe Southwestrene wynd *on* Saterday at euen
B. 5.50	And siþen he preide þe pope haue pite *on* holy chirche,
B. 5.108	Thanne I crye *on* my knees þat crist ȝyue h[y]m sorwe
B. 5.133	To lye and to loure *on* my neȝebore and to lakke his chaffare.
B. 5.139	*On* lymitours and listres lesynges I ymped
B. 5.175	And baleised *on* þe bare ers and no brech bitwene.
B. 5.194	Wiþ an hood *on* his heed, a hat aboue,
B. 5.197	She sholde noȝt [wandre] *on* þat wel[ch]e, so was it þredbare.
B. 5.235	'I wende riflynge were restitucion for I lerned neuere rede *on* boke,
B. 5.254	'Hastow pite *on* pouere men þat [for pure nede] borwe?'
B. 5.278	Cum sancto sanctus eris: construwe me þis *on* englissh.'
B. 5.307	Cesse þe [sowestere] sat *on* þe benche,
B. 5.322	And bad Bette þe Bocher ben *on* his syde.
B. 5.350	He [þr]umbled *on* þe þresshfold and þrew to þe erþe.
B. 5.352	For to liften hym *o* lofte and leyde hym on his knowes.
B. 5.352	For to liften hym o lofte and leyde hym *on* his knowes.
B. 5.373	And yspilt þat myȝte be spared and spended *on* som hungry;
B. 5.374	Ouer delicatly *on* [feeste] dayes dronken and eten boþe,
B. 5.382	'Shal neuere fyssh *on* [þe] Fryday defyen in my wombe
B. 5.397	I haue maad auowes fourty and foryete hem *on* þe morwe,
B. 5.404	Goddes peyne and his passion [pure] selde þenke I *on*.
B. 5.443	And flatte it *on* his face and faste on hym cryde
B. 5.443	And flatte it on his face and faste *on* hym cryde
B. 5.446	And beet þiself *on* þe brest and bidde hym of grace,
B. 5.461	Roberd þe Robbere *on* Reddite loked,
B. 5.464	'Crist, þat *on* Caluarie vpon þe cros deidest,
B. 5.466	And haddest mercy *on* þat man for Memento sake,
B. 5.467	So rewe *on* þis Robbere þat Reddere ne haue
B. 5.488	*On* good fryday for mannes sake at ful tyme of þe daye;
B. 5.504	And haue ruþe *on* þise Ribaudes þat repenten hem soore
B. 5.520	An hundred of Ampulles *on* his hat seten,
B. 5.522	And many crouch *on* his cloke and keyes of Rome,
B. 5.529	Ye may se by my signes þat sitten *on* myn hatte
B. 5.571	And-nameliche-*on*-ydel-þe-name-of-god-almyȝty.
B. 5.578	Leue hem *on* þi lift half and loke noȝt þerafter.
B. 5.594	Of almesdedes are þe hokes þat þe gates hangen *on*.
B. 6.22	Ac *on* þe teme trewely tauȝt was I neuere.
B. 6.90	To haue relees and remission, *on* þat rental I leue.
B. 6.185	That hunger was noȝt hardy *on* hem for to loke.
B. 6.229	'I wolde noȝt greue god', quod Piers, 'for al þe good *on* grounde!
B. 6.307	Laborers þat haue no land to lyue *on* but hire handes
B. 7.97	Than of alle [oþere] manere men þat *on* þis moolde [wandreþ].
B. 7.108	For I [shal] construe ech clause and kenne it þee *on* englissh.'
B. 7.137	Thow art lettred a litel; who lerned þee *on* boke?'
B. 7.142	'Lewed lorel!' quod Piers, 'litel lokestow *on* þe bible;
B. 7.143	*On* Salomons sawes selden þow biholdest:
B. 7.147	Metelees and moneilees *on* Maluerne hulles
B. 7.148	Musynge *on* þis metels [a myle] wey ich yede.
B. 7.173	Al þis makeþ me *on* metels to þynke,
B. 7.185	Ac to truste [*on*] þise triennals, trewely, me þynkeþ
B. 7.187	Forþi I rede yow renkes þat riche ben *on* erþe
B. 8.8	Til it bifel *on* a Friday two freres I mette,
B. 8.27	'How seuen siþes þe sadde man [synneþ *on* þe day].
B. 8.37	[Riȝt] þus it [fareþ]', quod þe frere, 'by folk here *on* erþe.
B. 8.59	'I bikenne þee crist', quod he, 'þat *on* [þe] cros deyde.'
B. 8.61	And ȝyue yow grace *on* þis grounde goode men to worþe'.
B. 8.118	Disputyng [*o*]n dowel day after ooþer,
B. 8.121	Was no pride *on* his apparaill ne pouerte neiþer;
B. 9.85	For alle þe mebles *on* þis moolde and he amende it myȝte.
B. 9.123	Conceyued ben in [cursed] tyme as Caym was *on* Eue
B. 9.141	That euere cursed Caym coom *on* þis erþe.
B. 9.152	Impe *on* an Ellere, and if þyn appul be swete
B. 9.169	[In Ielousie, ioyelees, and ianglynge *on* bedde,
B.10.14	That hem were leuere lond and lordshipe *on* erþe,
B.10.36	[*On* cros vpon caluarye as clerkes vs techeþ],
B.10.38	Or daunted or drawe forþ; I do it *on* god hymselue.
B.10.40	Ayein þe lawe of oure lord, and lyen *on* hemselue,
B.10.43	Likne men and lye *on* hem þat leneþ hem no ȝiftes,

B.10.118 And maken men in mys bileue þat muse *on* hire wordes.
B.10.139 Theiȝ dobest drawe *on* hym day after ooþer.'
B.10.167 Leue [hym] *on* þi left half a large myle or moore
B.10.203 And louen hem þat lyen *on* vs and lene hem [at hir nede]
B.10.238 'It is a commune lyf', quod Clergie, '*on* holy chirche to bileue
B.10.241 *On* þe grete god þat gynnyng hadde neuere,
B.10.242 And *on* þe soþfast sone þat saued mankynde
B.10.280 That goddes word wercheþ noȝt *on* [wis] ne on lewed
B.10.280 That goddes word wercheþ noȝt on [wis] ne *on* lewed
B.10.305 For if heuene be *on* þis erþe, and ese to any soule,
B.10.313 A prikere *on* a palfrey fro [place] to Manere,
B.10.316 He loureþ *on* hym and [lakkeþ] hym: who [lered] hym curteisie?
B.10.318 To Religiouse þat han no rouþe þouȝ it reyne *on* hir Auters.
B.10.383 I leue it wel by oure lord and *on* no lettrure bettre.
B.10.397 For many men *on* þis moolde moore setten hir hert[e]
B.10.420 *On* good Friday, I fynde, a felon was ysaued
B.10.422 And for he bekne[w *on*] þe cros and to crist shrof hym
B.10.446 And he þat may al amende haue mercy *on* vs alle,
B.10.473 That euere þe[i] couþe [konne *on* book] moore þan Credo in deum patrem,
B.11.70 Ac yet I cryde *on* my Confessour þat [so konnyng heeld hym]:
B.11.84 And lewte [louȝ] *on* me [for] I loured [on þe frere];
B.11.84 And lewte [louȝ] on me [for] I loured [*on* þe frere];
B.11.85 'Wherfore lourestow?' quod lewtee, and loked *on* me harde.
B.11.117 Wheiþer I were chosen or noȝt chosen; *on* holi chirche I þouȝte
B.11.159 And *on* Troianus truþe to þenke, and do truþe to þe peple.
B.11.187 And lokeþ *on* vs in hir liknesse and þat wiþ louely chere
B.11.248 Iesu crist *on* a Iewes doȝter liȝte, gentil womman þouȝ she were,
B.11.250 Martha *on* Marie Maudeleyne an huge pleynt made
B.11.260 As *on* a walnote wiþoute is a bitter barke,
B.11.275 And is to mene to men þat *on* þis moolde lyuen,
B.11.318 This lokynge *on* lewed preestes haþ doon me lepe from pouerte
B.11.324 And *on* a mountaigne þat myddelerþe hiȝte, as me [þo] þouȝte,
B.11.356 And some troden, [I took kepe], and *on* trees bredden,
B.11.361 And who tauȝte hem *on* trees to tymbre so heiȝe
B.11.363 And siþen I loked *on* þe see and so forþ on þe sterres;
B.11.363 And siþen I loked on þe see and so forþ *on* þe sterres;
B.11.410 And as I caste vp myne eiȝen oon loked *on* me.
B.11.428 Lat hym ligge, loke noȝt *on* hym til hym list aryse.
B.12.4 And manye tymes haue meued þee to [mynne] *on* þyn ende,
B.12.114 Hadde neuere lewed man leue to leggen hond *on* þat cheste
B.12.192 The þef þat hadde grace of god *on* good fryday, as þow spek[e],
B.12.201 But as a beggere bordlees by myself *on* þe grounde.
B.12.205 But by hymself as a soleyn and serued *on* [þe] erþe.
B.12.214 A[c] why þat oon þeef *on* þe cros creaunt hym yald
B.12.241 Bitokneþ riȝt riche men þat reigne here *on* erþe.
B.12.277 'Alle þise clerkes', quod I þo, "þat [*o*]n crist leuen
B.13.16 And how louynge he is to [ech lif] *on* londe and on watre–
B.13.16 And how louynge he is to [ech lif] on londe and *on* watre–
B.13.61 For þis doctour *on* þe heiȝe dees drank wyn so faste;
B.13.72 In englissh *on* auenture it sholde be reherced to ofte,
B.13.74 Ac I wiste neuere freke þat as a frere yede bifore men *on* englissh
B.13.79 Haþ no pite *on* vs pouere; he parfourneþ yuele
B.13.86 Pacience parceyued what I þouȝte and [preynte] *on* me to be stille
B.13.144 Cast coles *on* his heed of alle kynde speche;
B.13.146 And leye *on* hym þus with loue til he lauȝe on þe.
B.13.146 And leye on hym þus with loue til he lauȝe *on* þe.
B.13.235 For no breed þat I brynge forþ, saue a benyson *on* þe sonday
B.13.293 Or strengest *on* stede, or styuest vnder girdel,
B.13.316 What *on* bak, and what on body half, and by þe two sides
B.13.316 What on bak, and what *on* body half, and by þe two sides
B.13.337 Lechecraft of oure lord and leue *on* a wicche,
B.13.397 That my mynde ne was neuere *on* my good in a doute
B.14.2 Thouȝ it be soiled and selde clene: I slepe þerInne *o* nyȝtes;
B.14.144 It may noȝt be, ye riche men, or Mathew *on* god lyeþ:
B.14.168 [And] haue ruþe *on* þise riche men þat rewarde noȝt þi prisoners;
B.14.196 Ellis is al *on* ydel, al þat euere [we diden],
B.14.277 'I kan noȝt construe', quod haukyn; 'ye moste kenne me þis *on* englissh.'
B.15.11 Til reson hadde ruþe *on* me and rokked me aslepe,
B.15.28 Thanne is Racio my riȝt name, reson *on* englissh;
B.15.83 If I lye *on* yow to my lewed wit, ledeþ me to brennyng!
B.15.96 [And] se it by ensaumple in somer tyme *on* trowes:
B.15.128 Allas, ye lewed men, muche lese ye *on* preestes!
B.15.182 And ouþerwhile he is woned to wenden *on* pilgrymages
B.15.207 Ac it is moore to haue hir mete [*on*] swich an esy manere
B.15.211 And þat knoweþ no clerk ne creature *on* erþe
B.15.215 Fy *on* faitours and in fautores suos!
B.15.264 Sholde neuere Iudas ne Iew haue Iesu doon *on* roode,
B.15.298 Ac þer ne was leoun ne leopard þat *on* laundes wenten,
B.15.304 In likkyng and in lowynge, þer þei *on* laundes yede].
B.15.330 And *on* hemself som, and swiche as ben hir laborers;
B.15.396 Cristene and vncristene *on* oon god bileueþ].

B.15.406 And dide folk þanne falle *on* knees; for he swoor in his prechyng
B.15.411 That [lered] þere and [lewed] ȝit leeuen *on* hise lawes.
B.15.492 Allas, þat men so longe [sholde bileue *on* Makometh]!
B.15.572 Tellen hem and techen hem *on* þe Trinite to bileue,
B.15.579 Ac we cristene creatures *on* þe cros bileuen
B.15.586 And *on* þat lawe þei l[e]ue and leten it þe beste.
B.16.22 And bad me toten *on* þe tree, on top and on roote.
B.16.22 And bad me toten on þe tree, *on* top and on roote.
B.16.22 And bad me toten on þe tree, on top and *on* roote.
B.16.58 And to my mynde, as me þinkeþ, *on* o more þei growed;
B.16.64 And egreliche he loked *on* me and þerfore I spared
B.16.106 And dide hym assaie his surgenrie *on* hem þat sike were
B.16.128 And knokked *on* hem wiþ a corde, and caste adoun hir stalles
B.16.139 Til it bifel *on* a friday, a litel bifore Pasqe.
B.16.160 *On* a þursday in þesternesse þus was he taken;
B.16.162 That *on* þe friday folwynge for mankyndes sake
B.16.164 *On* cros vpon Caluarie crist took þe bataille
B.16.200 In menynge þat man moste *on* o god bileue,
B.16.246 And defende hem fro þe fend, folk þat *on* me leneden.
B.17.12 Wheron [was] writen two wordes *on* þis wise yglosed.
B.17.23 Lo! here in my lappe þat leeued *on* þat charme,
B.17.44 It is ful hard for any man *on* Abraham bileue
B.17.51 Thanne seiȝe we a Samaritan sittynge *on* a Mule,
B.17.74 And ladde hym so forþ *on* Lyard to lex Christi, a graunge
B.17.107 Who is bihynde and who bifore and who ben *on* horse;
B.17.108 For he halt hym hardier *on* horse þan he þat is [on] foote.
B.17.108 For he halt hym hardier on horse þan he þat is [*on*] foote.
B.17.110 *On* my Capul þat highte caro–of mankynde I took it–
B.17.228 Til þat lele loue ligge *on* hym and blowe.
B.17.229 And þanne flawmeþ he as fir *on* fader and on filius
B.17.229 And þanne flawmeþ he as fir on fader and *on* filius
B.17.235 And as wex wiþouten moore *on* a warm glede
B.17.325 And if his hous be vnhiled and reyne *on* his bedde
B.17.335 For kynde clyueþ *on* hym euere to contrarie þe soule;
B.17.346 Haþ mercy *on* swiche men þat so yuele may suffre.
B.18.11 Barefoot *on* an Asse bak bootles cam prikye
B.18.21 'Is Piers in þis place?' quod I, and he preynte *on* me.
B.18.39 And al þe court *on* hym cryde 'crucifie!' sharpe.
B.18.42 To fordoon it *on* o day, and in þre dayes after
B.18.49 And sette it sore *on* his heed and seide in enuye;
B.18.51 Nailed hym with þre nailes naked *on* [a] roode;
B.18.52 And poison *on* a poole þei putte vp to hise lippes
B.18.91 Haue *on* me ruþe, riȝtful Iesu;' and riȝt wiþ þat he wepte.
B.18.242 The water witnesse[þ] þat he was god for he wente *on* it;
B.18.244 And as he wente *on* þe water wel hym knew and seide,
B.18.250 And leet out Symondes sone[s] to seen hym hange *on* roode.
B.18.260 And bileue *on* a newe lawe be lost, lif and soule.'
B.18.305 For þe body, while it *on* bones yede, aboute was euere
B.18.383 Lawe wolde he yeue hym lif if he loked *on* hym.
B.18.386 And if lawe wole I loke *on* hem it liþ in my grace
B.18.405 They dorste noȝt loke *on* oure lord, þe [leeste] of hem alle,
B.18.428 And crepe[þ] to þe cros *on* knees and kisse[þ] it for a Iuwel.
B.19.41 And vpon Caluarie *on* cros ycrouned kyng of Iewes.
B.19.50 And þo conquered he *on* cros as conquerour noble;
B.19.142 Killeden hym *on* cros wise at Caluarie on Friday,
B.19.142 Killeden hym on cros wise at Caluarie *on* Friday,
B.19.202 In liknesse of a lightnynge he lighte *on* hem alle
B.19.236 And some he lered to laboure [*on* lond and on watre
B.19.236 And some he lered to laboure [on lond and *on* watre
B.19.260 My prowor and my Plowman Piers shal ben *on* erþe,
B.19.287 Sholde no curious clooþ comen *on* his rugge,
B.19.322 That crist vpon Caluarie for mankynde *on* pyned.
B.19.323 And of his baptisme and blood þat he bledde *on* roode
B.19.328 And called þat hous vnitee, holy chirche *on* englissh.
B.19.353 'To wasten *on* welfare and in wikked [kepyng]
B.19.402 Of Spiritus Iusticie þow spekest muche *on* ydel.'
B.20.43 That he seide in his sorwe *on* þe selue tyme:
B.20.78 And crye we [*on*] al þe comune þat þei come to vnitee
B.20.127 And [pressed *on*] þe [pope] and prelates þei maden
B.20.175 And Elde auntred hym *on* lyf, and at þe laste he hitte
B.20.184 And made me balled bifore and bare *on* þe croune:
B.20.189 'Ye, leue, lurdeyn?' quod he, and leyde *on* me wiþ Age,
B.20.196 *On* nyghtes namely, whan we naked weere,
C.Pr.6 Ac *on* a May mornyng on maluerne hulles
C.Pr.6 Ac on a May mornyng *on* maluerne hulles
C.Pr.51 Eremites *on* an hep with hokede staues
C.Pr.65 The moste meschief *on* molde mounteth vp faste.
C.Pr.106 Ful *on* hem þat fre were thorwe two fals prestis!
C.Pr.121 God shal take vengeaunce *on* alle suche prestis
C.Pr.122 Wel hardere and grettere *on* suche shrewed faderes
C.Pr.123 Than euere he dede *on* Offi[n] and Fines [or on her] fader.
C.Pr.123 Than euere he dede on Offi[n] and Fines [or *on* her] fader.
C.Pr.147 With lele labour to lyue while lif *on* londe lasteth.

C.Pr.165	Thow myghtest betre meten myst *on* maluerne hulles
C.Pr.182	Wer ther a belle *on* here beygh, by iesu, as me thynketh,
C.Pr.186	And knytten hit *on* a coler for oure comune profyt
C.Pr.193	Ac tho þe belle was ybroughte and *on* þe beygh hangid
C. 1.7	The moste party of this peple þat passeth *on* þis erthe,
C. 1.70	And ha[ls]ede here *on* the hey name or she thennes [ȝede]
C. 1.75	[To] leue *on* me and loue me al thy lyf tyme.'
C. 1.76	Thenne y knelede *on* my knees and criede here of grace
C. 1.78	And also kenne me kyndly *on* crist to bileue.
C. 1.82	I do it [*o*]n deus caritas to deme þe sothe.
C. 1.103	Dede hem swere *on* here swerd to serue treuthe euere.
C. 1.163	Lokede *on* vs with loue [and] let his sone deye
C. 1.167	To haue pitee *on* þat peple þat paynede hym to dethe.
C. 1.171	Forthy y rede ȝow riche, haueth reuthe [*o*]n þe pore;
C. 2.1	And thenne y kneled [*o*]n my knees and cried here of grace,
C. 2.3	That bar þ[e] blessid bar[n] þat bouhte [vs] *on* þe rode,
C. 2.5	'Loke [*o*]n thy left half, and loo where he standeth,
C. 2.8	Y lokede [*o*]n my luft half as þe lady me tauhte
C. 2.10	She was purfiled [with] pelure, non puyrere *on* erthe,
C. 2.12	*On* alle here fyue fyngeres ful richeliche yrynged,
C. 2.21	And [ylow *on*] hym to lordes þat lawes han to kepe;
C. 2.29	Ne *on* a croked kene thorn kynde fyge wexe:
C. 2.57	Al þe riche retenaunce þat ro[t]eth hem *o* fals lyuynge
C. 2.82	Wyten and witnessen þat wonyen *on* erthe
C. 2.105	/This lyf to folowe falsnesse and folk þat *on* hym leueth,
C. 2.133	That laurence the leuyte that lay *on* þe gredyre
C. 2.137	And se[t]he man may [*o*]n heye mede of god diserue
C. 2.138	Hit semeth sothly riȝt so *on* erthe
C. 2.140	And thow hast feffed here with fals; fy *on* suche lawe.
C. 2.183	And ryde *on* hem and on reue[s] righte faste by mede.
C. 2.183	And ryde on hem and on reue[s] righte faste by mede.
C. 2.189	And *on* pore prouisores and appeles in þe Arches.
C. 2.191	*On* hem þat loueth leccherye lyppeth vp and rydeth,
C. 2.192	*On* secatours and such men cometh softly aftur.
C. 2.196	As fobbes and faytours þat *on* here feet rennen.'
C. 2.204	And prykede forth *on* pacience and passed hem alle
C. 2.209	Y wolde be awreke [*o*]n tho wreches and on here werkes alle,
C. 2.209	Y wolde be awreke [o]n tho wreches and *on* here werkes alle,
C. 2.211	Shal neuere man *on* þis molde maynpryse þe leste,
C. 2.212	But riht as þe lawe loketh lat falle *on* hem alle.'
C. 2.219	Ar he be put *on* þe pylorye for eny preyere ich hote.'
C. 2.234	And senten hym *on* sonendayes with seeles to churche.
C. 2.239	For a can *on* here craft and knoweth manye gommes.
C. 3.79	To punischen [*o*]n pilories and [o]n pynyng stoles
C. 3.79	To punischen [o]n pilories and [*o*]n pynyng stoles
C. 3.86	Thei han no pite *on* the peple þat parselmele mot begge;
C. 3.93	The whiche crien *on* here knees þat crist hem auenge,
C. 3.94	Here *on* this erthe or elles in helle,
C. 3.95	That so bigileth hem of here goed, þat god *on* hem sende
C. 3.96	Feuer or foul[e] euel other fuyr *on* here houses,
C. 3.100	Graunte gylours *on* erthe grace to amende
C. 3.101	And haue here penaunce *on* puyre erthe and nat þe peyne of helle.
C. 3.102	And thenne falleth ther fuyr *on* fals men houses
C. 3.103	And goode mennes fuyr here gultes gloweth *on* fuyr aftur.
C. 3.118	'Haue reuthe *on* this regraters þat han riche handes,
C. 3.227	Thow hast hanged *on* my half enleuene tymes
C. 3.251	And þat is þe kynde of a kyng þat conquereth *on* his enemys,
C. 3.335	*On* a sad and a siker semblable to hemsuluen.
C. 3.398	Sholde confourme hem to *o* kynde *on* holy kyrke to bileue.
C. 3.420	And alle þat leueth *on* þat lond oure [lord] wol þat thow sle hit;
C. 3.445	Tho shal be maistres *on* molde trewe men to helpe.
C. 4.24	Thenne Consience *on* his capel comesed to pryke
C. 4.31	[*O*]n wilyman and wittyman and wareyne wrynglawe.
C. 4.67	*On* men of lawe wrong lokede and largelyche hem profered
C. 4.95	To haue mercy *on* þat man that many tymes hym greuede:
C. 4.103	Bute resoun haue reuth *on* hym he shal reste in [þe] stokkes
C. 4.106	And for to consayle þe kynge *on* Consience thei lokede;
C. 4.148	Mede in the mothalle tho *on* men of lawe gan wynke
C. 4.179	'By hym þat rauhte [*on*] þe rode,' quod resoun to the kyng,
C. 5.51	Now with hym, now with here: *on* this wyse y begge
C. 5.106	Byfore þe cross *on* my knees knokked y my brest,
C. 5.110	Of þe matere þat me mette furste *on* Maluerne hulles.
C. 5.116	And the southweste wynde *on* saturday At euene
C. 5.152	For yf heuene be *on* this erthe or ese to [eny] soule
C. 5.159	And pryked aboute *on* palfrayes fram places to maneres,
C. 5.164	To religious þat haen no reuthe thow it ryne *on* here auters.
C. 5.191	And sethe a preyede þe pope haue pite *on* holy chirche
C. 6.52	And lyed *o* my lycame and on my lyf bothe;
C. 6.52	And lyed o my lycame and *on* my lyf bothe;
C. 6.67	Sholde no lyf lyue þat *on* his lond pissede.
C. 6.81	Lechecraft of oure lord and leue *on* a wycche
C. 6.111	*On* god when me greued auht and grochede of his sonde:
C. 6.120	And prelates pleyneth *on* hem for they here parschiens shryuen

C. 6.148	And y, wrath, was war and w[o]rthe *on* hem bothe
C. 6.157	And balayshed *on* þe bare ers and no brech bytwene.
C. 6.172	That he haue pite *on* me, p[u]tou[r], of his puyr mercy,
C. 6.195	Now, lord, for thy lewete *on* lechours haue mercy.'
C. 6.202	With his hood *on* his heued and his hat bothe,
C. 6.205	He sholde [nat] wandre [*o*]n þat walch, so was hit thredbare.
C. 6.267	And yf y ȝede to þe plough y pynched *on* his half aker
C. 6.284	That my muynde ne was more [*o*]n my godes in a doute
C. 6.287	Were y a frere, in good fayth, for al þe gold *on* erthe
C. 6.302	*On* Ecce enim veritatem dilexisti.
C. 6.315	Robert the ruyflare *on* reddite lokede
C. 6.318	'Crist, þat on Caluarie on þe crosse deyedest
C. 6.318	'Crist, þat on Caluarie *on* þe crosse deyedest
C. 6.321	So rewe *on* Robert þat reddere ne haue
C. 6.352	Fastyng *on* a friday forth gan he wende
C. 6.362	Sesse þe [sywestere] saet *on* þe benche,
C. 6.379	And bade b[et]te þe bochere ben *on* his syde.
C. 6.410	For to lyfte hym aloft [and] leyde hym *on* his knees.
C. 6.423	To repentaunce ryht thus, 'haue reuthe *on* me,' he saide,
C. 6.434	[*On*] fastyng dayes bifore noen fedde me with ale,
C. 6.439	Shal neuere fysch [*o*]n þe fryday defyen in my wombe
C. 7.4	Were y brouhte [*o*]n bed, but yf my taylende hit made,
C. 7.57	And flatte hit *on* his face and faste on hym cryede
C. 7.57	And flatte hit on his face and faste *on* hym cryede
C. 7.60	And bete thysulue [*o*]n þe breste and bidde hym of grace
C. 7.130	*On* a friday in fourme of man feledest oure sorwe:
C. 7.165	An hundret of Aunpolles *on* his hat se[t]e,
C. 7.167	And many crouch [and] kayes of Rome
C. 7.174	Ȝe may se be [my] signes þat sitten *on* my cappe
C. 7.225	And leu[e] hem [*o*]n þ[y] luft ha[lf] and loke [nat] þeraftur
C. 7.242	The hokes aren Almesdedes þat þe ȝates hange *on*.
C. 7.302	And loure *on* me and lihtly chyde and sygge y louede another.
C. 7.304	I may nat come for a kitte, so a cleueth *on* me:
C. 8.20	Ac [*on*] þe t[ee]me treuely ytauhte was y neuere.
C. 8.60	And heng his hopur *on* his hal[s] in stede of a scryppe;
C. 8.99	To haue re[lees] and re[missioun]; *on* þat rental y leue.
C. 8.177	'Haue mercy *on* hem, hunger,' quod [Peres], 'and lat me ȝeue hem benes
C. 8.181	That hunger was nat hardy *on* hem for to loke.
C. 8.235	'Y wolde nat greue [god],' quod Peres, 'for al þe good *on* erthe!
C. 8.349	Shal brynge bane and batayle *on* bothe half þe mone;
C. 9.78	And wo in wynter tym[e] and wakynge *on* nyhtes
C. 9.153	And what freke *on* this folde fiscuth aboute
C. 9.173	Then of many oþere men þat [*o*]n this molde walken.
C. 9.243	Where se we hem *on* sonendayes the seruise to here,
C. 9.255	Ne no blanke[t] *on* his bed ne whyte bred byfore hym.
C. 9.296	Meteles and moneyles *on* Maluerne hulles.
C. 9.297	Musyng *on* this meteles A myle way y ȝede.
C. 9.318	Al this maketh me *on* meteles to studie
C. 9.333	Forthy y rede ȝow renkes þat riche ben *on* this erthe
C.10.8	Til hit biful [*o*]n [a] fryday two freres y mette,
C.10.24	The rihtfulluste ren[k] þat regneth [*o*]n erthe.
C.10.31	'How seuene sithes þe sad man synegeth *on* þe day.
C.10.49	Synegeth seue sithe þe saddest man *on* erthe
C.10.58	'Y bykenne the Crist,' quod he, 'þat *on* þe cross deyede.'
C.10.60	And gyue me grace *on* þis grounde with good ende to deye.'
C.10.117	Was no pruyde *on* his parail ne pouerte noythere;
C.10.160	May nat shyne ne shewe *on* schalkes on erthe,
C.10.160	May nat shyne ne shewe on schalkes *on* erthe,
C.10.169	*On* catel more then on kynde that alle kyne thynges wrouhte,
C.10.169	On catel more then *on* kynde that alle kyne thynges wrouhte,
C.10.195	The[r]of was he robbed and ruyfled or he *on* rode deyede
C.10.208	Thorw no sotil sciense *on* sour stok growe";
C.10.217	*On* a leye land aȝeynes his lordes wille,
C.10.229	That euere corsed Caym cam *on* þis erthe.
C.10.268	And wedden here for here welthe and weschen *on* þe morwe
C.10.287	Awrek þerwith *on* wyfyng, for godes werk y holde hit:
C.11.111	A[c] if þow happe,' quod he, 'þat þou hitte *on* clergie
C.11.142	*On* þe maide Marie for mankynde sake
C.11.161	And continaunce made *on* clergie, to congeie me hit semede,
C.11.176	Concupiscencia Carnis confortede me *o*[n] this manere
C.11.200	Y leue neuere þat lord ne lady þat lyueth her [*o*]n erthe
C.11.208	Y leue hit wel by oure lord and *on* no lettrure bettere.
C.11.228	For many men [*o*]n this molde more sette here herte
C.11.254	And for he biknewe *on* þe croes and to crist shrof hym
C.12.23	And thenne louhe leaute for y loured *on* þe frere:
C.12.52	Where y were chose [or nat chose]; *on* holy churche y thouhte
C.12.91	And *on* Troianus treuthe to thenke alle tyme[s] in ȝoure lyue
C.12.136	Marthe *on* marie maudelene an huge pleynte made
C.12.146	As *on* a walnote withoute is a bittere barke
C.12.179	Mesc[h]iefes *on* molde mekeliche to soffren:
C.12.181	Shal neuere spir sprynge vp ne spiek *on* straw kerne;
C.12.207	Angelis in here anger *on* this wyse hem grette:

C.12.218 Vpholderes *on* þe hulle shal haue hit to sulle."
C.12.224 *On* fat lond ful of donge foulest wedes groweth.
C.13.15   Iob þe gentele, what ioye hadde he *on* erthe?
C.13.159 Lernede to [l]egge stikkes þat ley *on* here neste.
C.13.165 And som treden, y toke kepe, and *on* trees bredde
C.13.173 And sethe y lokede *on* þe see and so forth on [þe] sterres;
C.13.173 And sethe y lokede on þe see and so forth *on* [þe] sterres;
C.13.175 Ne what o[f] floures *on* felde and of here fayre coloures
C.13.235 Lat hym lygge, lok nat *on* hym til hym luste [a]ryse.
C.14.59   Hadde neuere lewede [man] leue to legge hand *on* þat cheste
C.14.140 Bote as a beggare bordles be mysulue *on* þe grounde.
C.14.144 Bote as a soleyn by hymsulue [and] yserued [o]n þe [erthe].
C.14.173 Bytokenen riht ryche men þat reygne here *on* erthe.
C.14.199 'Alle thise clerkes,' quod y tho, 'þat [o]n crist leuen
C.15.19   And how louyng he is to vch lyf a londe and *o* watere
C.15.86   Hath no pyte *on* vs pore; he parformeth euele
C.15.92   And apose hym what penaunce is and purgatorie *on* erthe
C.15.142 Caste coles *on* his heued of alle kyn[de] speche,
C.15.146 And ley *on* hym thus with loue til he lauhe on þe.
C.15.146 And ley on hym thus with loue til he lauhe *on* þe.
C.15.210 Nere hit þat þe parsche [prest] preyeth for me *on* sonendayes,
C.15.223 Vch a kyne creature þat *on* crist leueth.
C.16.22   Riht so haue reuthe *on* [thy renkes] alle
C.16.143 As he þat woet neuere with wham *on* nyhtes tyme to mete:
C.16.154 That puyre pouerte and pacience was a louh lyuynge *on* erthe,
C.16.248 And s[e] hit by ensample In somur tyme *on* trees
C.16.324 And oþerwhile his wone is to w[e]nde [o]n pilgrimages
C.17.72   Prestes *on* aparayl and on purnele now spene.
C.17.72   Prestes on aparayl and *on* purnele now spene.
C.17.124 In þe lettynge of here lyf to leue *on* holy churche.'
C.17.128 Alle kyne cristene cleuynge *on* o will,
C.17.158 And lyuen oute of laboure for they l[e]ue *on* a mene.
C.17.170 Be maistre ouer alle tho men and *on* this manere a wrouhte:
C.17.182 And *on* his lore thei l[e]uen ʒut, as wel lered as lewed.
C.17.187 Allas, þat men so longe *on* Macometh bileueth!
C.17.249 And alle maner men þat *on* this molde libbeth.
C.17.286 And enchaunten hem to charite *on* holy churche to bileue.
C.17.297 And *on* þat lawe they leue and leten hit for þe beste.
C.18.23   Moche meruelyed me *on* what more thei growede
C.18.61   Me may se *on* an appul tree monye tyme and ofte
C.18.96   Maydones and martres ministrede [hym] here *on* erthe
C.18.166 This biful *on* a fryday, a litel bifore Pasche,
C.18.262 At ones *on* an auter in worschipe of th[e] trinite
C.19.13   Whereon was writen two wordes *on* this wyse yglosed:
C.19.49   Thenne sey we a samaritaen cam sittynge *on* a muyle,
C.19.72   Enbaumed hym and boend his heued and *on* bayard hym sette
C.19.195 And thenne flaumeth he as fuyr *on* fader and on filius
C.19.195 And thenne flaumeth he as fuyr on fader and *on* filius
C.19.239 Moste lordliche lyue and ʒut [on] his lycame werie
C.19.305 And if his hous be vnheled and reyne *on* his bedde
C.19.315 For kynde cleueth *on* hym euere to contrarie þe soule;
C.19.326 Haeth mercy *on* suche men þat [so] euele may soffre.
C.20.9   Barfoet *on* an asse baue boetles cam priky[e]
C.20.19   'Is Peres in this place?' quod y, and he printe *on* me.
C.20.38   And alle þe Court [*on* hym] cryede 'crucifige!' [sharpe].
C.20.41   To fordoen hit *on* a day, and in thre dayes aftur
C.20.44   Bothe as longe and as large aloofte and *o* grounde
C.20.49   And sette hit sore *on* his heued and saide in Enuye;
C.20.94   Haue [*on* me reuthe], riʒtful iesu;' and riht with þat a wepte.
C.20.251 The water witnesseth þat he was god for a wente *on* h[it];
C.20.253 And as he wente *on* þe watur wel hym knewe and saide,
C.20.259 And lette out symondes sones to sen hym honge *on* rode:
C.20.268 And bile[u]e *on* a newe lawe be ylost, lyf and soule.'
C.20.290 Al hoet *on* here hedes þat entrith ney þe walles;
C.20.314 Aʒeyne his loue and his leue *on* his londe ʒedest,
C.20.337 For þe body, whiles hit *on* bones ʒede, aboute was hit euere
C.20.347 For we leued *on* thy lesynges [there losten we blisse;
C.20.353 And wyte[th] hem al þe wrechednesse þat wrouhte is *on* erthe.
C.20.425 Lawe wolde he ʒoue hym lyf and he loked *on* hym.
C.20.428 And if lawe wol y loke *on* hem hit lith in my grace
C.20.448 They dorste nat loke *on* oure lord, the leste of hem alle,
C.20.471 And crepe to þe croes *on* knees and kusse hit for a iewel
C.20.472 And rihtfollokest A relyk, noon richore *on* erthe.
C.21.41   And vpon Caluarie *on* cros ycrouned kyng of iewes.
C.21.50   And tho conquerede he *on* cros as conquerour noble;
C.21.142 Culden hym *on* cros wyse at Caluarie on fryday
C.21.142 Culden hym on cros wyse at Caluarie *on* fryday
C.21.202 In liknesse of a lihtnynge a lyhte *on* hem alle
C.21.260 My prowour and my [plouhman Peres] shal ben *on* erthe
C.21.287 Sholde no curious cloth comen *on* his rugge
C.21.322 That Crist vpon Caluary for mankynde *on* peyned.
C.21.323 And of his bapteme and bloed þat he bledde *on* rode
C.21.353 'To waston *on* welfare and in wikked kepynge

C.22.43   That he saide in his sorwe *on* þe sulue rode:
C.22.78   And crye we *on* al þe comune þat thei come to vnite
C.22.127 And presed *on* þe pope and prelates thei made
C.22.175 And Elde auntered hym *on* lyf and at þe laste he hitte
C.22.184 And made me balled bifore and baer *on* þe crowne;
C.22.189 'ʒe, leue, lordeyne?' quod he, and leide *on* me with age

on &> oon

ondynge *ger cf. onden v.(1)* B 1; C 1
B.14.56   In [*ondynge*] and in handlynge and in alle þi fyue wittes,
C.15.255 In [*ond]ynge* and [in] handlynge [and] in alle thy fyue wittes,

one > echone,oon,oone; onelich(e > oonliche

ones *adv ones adv.* A 11 ones (9) onys (2); B 30 ones (29) oones (1); C 26
A.Pr.87   A[c] nouʒt for loue of oure lord vnlose here lippes *ones*.
A. 2.189 Mynstralis & messangeris mette wiþ him *ones*,
A. 3.134 She may neiʒ as muche do in a moneþ *ones*
A. 4.73   'He sh[al] not þis seue ʒer se hise feet *ones*!'
A. 5.57   Drinke but wiþ þe doke & dyne but *ones*.
A. 6.88   Biddiþ amende ʒow meke hym to his maister *ones*
A. 7.66   Treuþe tolde me *ones* & bad me telle it forþ:
A. 7.137 *Ones* at noon is ynouʒ þat no werk vsiþ;
A. 7.194 Treuþe tauʒte me *ones* to loue hem ichone
A.12.55   Þus we lauʒþe oure leue, lowtyng at *onys*,
A.12.71   A bagge ful of a beggere.' I bouʒþe hit at *onys*.
B.Pr.146 Wiþ þat ran þer a route of Ratons at *ones*
B.Pr.214 [Ac] noʒt for loue of oure lord vnlose hire lippes *ones*.
B. 2.230 A[c] Mynstrales and Messagers mette with hym *ones*
B. 3.145 [She] may neiʒ as muche do in a Monþe *one[s]*
B. 3.338 Ac þow art lik a lady þat radde a lesson *ones*
B. 4.86   [He shal] noʒt þise seuen yer seen his feet *ones*!'
B. 5.74   Drynke but [wiþ] þe doke and dyne but *ones*.
B. 5.163 Til "þow lixt!" and "þow lixt!" lopen out at *ones*
B. 5.231 'ʒis, *ones* I was yherberwed', quod he, 'wiþ an heep of chapmen;
B. 5.375 And sat som tyme so longe þere þat I sleep and eet at *ones*.
B. 5.508 That alle Seintes [for synful] songen at *ones*
B. 5.601 Biddeþ amende-yow meke hym til his maister *ones*
B. 6.74   Truþe tolde me *ones* and bad me telle it [forþ]:
B. 6.208 Truþe tauʒte me *ones* to louen hem ech one,
B.10.417 [At domesday þe deluuye worþ of deþ and fir at *ones*;
B.10.460 Seide þus in a sermon—I seigh it writen *ones*–
B.11.66   For I herde *ones* how Conscience it tolde,
B.11.333 Blisse and bale boþe I seiʒ at *ones*,
B.12.206 For he þat is *ones* a þef is eueremoore in daunger;
B.13.139 [Th]us [lerede] me *ones* a lemman, loue was hir name.
B.15.8   To sergeauntʒ ne to swiche seide noʒt *ones*,
B.15.230 And in a freres frokke he was yfounden *ones*,
B.15.485 And feden vs and festen vs for eueremoore at *oones*].
B.16.178 [I] seke after a segge þat I seiʒ *ones*,
B.18.148 For þat is *ones* in helle out comeþ [it] neuere.
B.18.380 Ofter þan *ones* þouʒ he were a tretour.
B.19.94   [Erþeliche] honeste þynges w[as] offred þus at *ones*
B.19.388 In help of hir heele *ones* in a Monþe,
B.19.431 Qui pluit super Iustos & iniustos at *ones*
B.20.343 I knew swich oon *ones*, noʒt eighte wynter [passed],
C.Pr.164 And nat for loue of oure lord vnlose here lyppes *ones*.
C.Pr.167 Than ran þer a route of ratones [at *ones*]
C. 2.240 Ac mynstrals and mesagers mette with lyare *ones*
C. 3.183 He may ny as muche do in a monthe *ones*
C. 4.82   Ther he sholde nat in seuene ʒer see his feet [*ones*].
C. 6.174 Drynke but with þe doke and dyne but *ones*.
C. 6.235 'ʒus! *ones* y was herberwed,' quod he, 'with an heep of chapmen;
C. 8.76   Treuthe t[o]lde me *ones* and bad me telle it fort[h]:
C. 8.217 Treuthe tauhte me *ones* to louye hem vchone
C.11.249 At domesday a deluuye worth of deth and fuyr at *ones*.
C.13.10   And Abraham not hardy *ones* to letten hym
C.13.32   Rather then þe ryche thogh they renne at *ones*.
C.13.141 Blisse and bale bothe y sey at *ones*
C.14.145 For he þat is *ones* a þef is eueremore in daunger
C.15.130 For Peres loue þe palmare ʒent, þat inpugnede *ones*
C.16.355 And in a frere f[r]okke he was founde *ones*
C.18.153 With [two] fisches and [fyue] loues, fyue thousen[d] at *ones*,
C.18.262 At *ones* on an auter in worschipe of th[e] trinite
C.19.53   Bothe abraham and sp[e]s and he mette at *ones*
C.20.151 [For] þat *ones* is in helle out cometh hit neuere.
C.20.420 Shal neuere in helle eft come be he *ones* oute:
C.20.422 Oftur then *ones* thogh [he] were [a] tretou[r].
C.21.94   Ertheliche honeste thynges was offred thus at *ones*
C.21.388 In helpe of here hele *ones* in a monthe
C.21.431 Qui pluit super iustos & iniustos at *ones*
C.22.343 Y knewe such oen *ones*, nat eyhte wynter passed,

only onliche > oonliche; onswerie > answere; oo ooen > oon; oold > old

oon num *on num. &> a numeral* A 10 o (5) on (3) one (2); B 63 o (27)
  oo (2) one (5) oon (29); C 69 o (50) oen (11) on (5) ooen (1) oon (2)
A. 2.69	ȝeldinge for þis þing at *o* ȝeris ende
A. 3.265	And *o* cristene king kepe vs ichone.
A. 4.24	Ac [*o*]n wary[n] wisdom, and witty his fere
A. 6.78	Wiþ no led but [wiþ] loue & louȝnesse, as breþeren of *o* wombe.
A. 7.42	For þou shalt ȝelde it aȝen at *one* ȝeris ende
A. 8.14	Loke on þat *o* lawe, & lere men þat oþer,
A. 8.93	In two lynes it lay & nouȝt *o* lettre more,
A. 8.178	I ne wolde ȝiue for þi patent *on* pye hele.
A. 9.87	Is hokid at þat *on* ende to holde men in good lif.
A.11.227	Helpiþ nouȝt to heuene[ward] at *one* ȝeris ende,
B. 1.101	And nauȝt to fasten *o* friday in fyue score wynter,
B. 2.30	*Oo* god wiþouten gynnyng, and I his goode douȝter;
B. 2.41	To *oon* fals fikel-tonge, a fendes biyete.
B. 2.105	Yeldynge for þis þyng at *one* [yeres ende]
B. 3.238	Tho þat entren of *o* colour and of one wille
B. 3.238	Tho þat entren of *o* colour and of *one* wille
B. 3.289	And *oon* cristene kyng kepen [vs echone].
B. 3.318	But after þe dede þat is doon *oon* doom shal rewarde
B. 3.321	Al shal be but *oon* court, and oon [burn] be Iustice,
B. 3.321	Al shal be but oon court, and *oon* [burn] be Iustice,
B. 4.27	*Oon* waryn wisdom and witty his feere
B. 5.591	Wiþ no leed but wiþ loue and lowe[nesse] as breþeren [of *o* wombe].
B. 6.43	For þow shalt yelde it ayein at *one* yeres [ende]
B. 7.200	I sette youre patentes and youre pardon at *one* pies hele.
B. 8.97	Is hoked [at] þat *oon* ende to [holde men in good lif].
B. 9.114	Maidenes and martires out of *o* man come.
B. 9.148	The gospel is hera[g]ein in *o* degre, I fynde:
B.10.246	For al is but *oon* god and ech is god hymselue:
B.11.200	And breþeren as of *oo* blood, as wel beggeres as Erles.
B.11.202	And blody breþeren we bicome þere of *o* body ywonne,
B.12.176	As þow seest in þe Sauter in Salmes *oon* or tweyne
B.12.214	A[c] why þat *oon* þeef on þe cros creaunt hym yald
B.13.68	Ac *o* word þei ouerhuppen at ech tyme þat þei preche
B.13.124	For *oon* Piers þe Plowman haþ impugned vs alle,
B.13.210	Turne into þe trewe feiþ and intil *oon* bileue.'
B.14.1	'I haue but *oon* hool hater', quod haukyn, 'I am þe lasse to blame
B.15.316	And a mees þermyd of *o* maner kynde,
B.15.369	Neiþer þei konneþ ne knoweþ *oon* cours bifore anoþer.
B.15.394	For þei loue and bileue in *o* [lord] almyghty
B.15.395	And we lered and lewed [bileueþ in *oon* god;
B.15.396	Cristene and vncristene on *oon* god bileueþ.
B.15.397	A[c] *oon* Makometh, a man, in mysbileue
B.15.505	In [*o*] gre[et] god, and his grace asken,
B.15.606	Arn folk of *oon* feiþ; þe fader god þei honouren.
B.16.58	And to my mynde, as me þinkeþ, on *o* more þei growed;
B.16.59	And of *o* greetnesse and grene of greyn þei semen.'
B.16.92	That *oon* Iesus a Iustices sone moste Iouke in hir chambre
B.16.181	'Thre leodes in *oon* lyth, noon lenger þan ooþer,
B.16.182	Of *oon* muchel and myght in mesure and lengþe.
B.16.200	In menynge þat man moste on *o* god bileue,
B.16.208	And in heuene and here *oon* singuler name.
B.16.224	Which is þe holy goost of alle, and alle is but *o* god.
B.17.30	And alle þre but *o* god; þus Abraham me tauȝte;
B.17.37	To bileeue and louye in *o* lord almyghty
B.17.39	þe gome þat gooþ wiþ *o* staf, he semeþ in gretter heele
B.17.42	It is lighter to lewed men *o* lesson to knowe
B.17.130	And alle þre but *o* god? þus Abraham me tauȝte;
B.17.132	*O* god wiþ al my good, and alle gomes after
B.17.141	The fader was first as a fust wiþ *o* fynger foldynge
B.17.184	And alle [þre] but *o* god as is myn hand and my fyngres.
B.18.42	To fordoon it on *o* day, and in þre dayes after
B.18.234	That alle þe wise of þis world in *o* wit acor[de]den
B.19.27	That knyght, kyng, conquerour may be *o* persone.
B.19.86	That *o* kyng cam wiþ Reson couered vnder sense.
B.19.201	*Oon* Spiritus paraclitus to Piers and to hise felawes.
B.19.265	And Ioyned to hem *oon* Iohan, moost gentil of alle,
B.19.340	And his Spye Spille-loue, *oon* Spek-yuel-bihynde.
B.19.373	Saue sherewes *one* swiche as I spak of,
B.19.399	Boþe dregges and draf and drawe at *oon* hole
B.20.160	And wedded *oon* wanhope, a wenche of þe Stuwes.
B.20.162	*Oon* Tomme two-tonge, atteynt at ech [a q]ueste.
B.20.245	To vnitee and holy chirche; ac *o* þyng I yow preye:
B.20.315	*Oon* frere Flaterere is phisicien and surgien.'
C. 2.25	*Oon* fauel was he[re] fader þat hath a fykel tonge
C. 2.44	To *oon* fals faythlesse of þe fendes kynne.
C. 3.314	Hit is a permutacoun apertly, *on* peneworth for another.
C. 3.398	Sholde confourme hem to *o* kynde on holy kyrke to bileue
C. 3.442	And *o* cristene kyng kepe vs echone.
C. 3.474	Al shal be but [*o*] couert and o [buyrne] þe Iustice;
C. 3.474	Al shal be but [o] couert and *o* [buyrne] þe Iustice;
C. 4.27	*Ooen* wareyn wisman and wilyman his felawe
C. 5.185	That *o* wit and o wil al ȝoure wardes kepe.
C. 5.185	That o wit and *o* wil al ȝoure wardes kepe.
C. 6.38	Summe tyme in *o* sekte, summe tyme in another,
C. 6.181	Til bothe oure wil was *oen* and to þe werk we ȝeden,
C. 7.29	The barres aren of buxumnesse as bretherne of *o* wombe;
C.10.191	That alle landes loueden and in *on* lawe bileuede.
C.11.152	And alle thre bote *o* god, and herof he made
C.12.110	And blody bretherne we bycome there of *o* body ywonne,
C.13.34	And sholden wende *o* wey where bothe mosten reste
C.13.52	And ȝut thow they wende *o* way as to wynchestre fayre
C.14.116	As we seen in þe sauter in psalmes *oen* or tweyne
C.14.153	Ac why þat [*on*] theef vppon þe cros cryant hym ȝelde
C.15.275	'Meeknesse and mylde speche and men of *o* will;
C.16.181	And ayther is otheres hete and also of *o* will;
C.16.320	*Oen* aperis-tu-manum alle thynges hym fyndeth;
C.17.126	'[Lif in] loue and leutee in *o* byleue a[nd] lawe,
C.17.128	Alle kyne cristene cleuynge on *o* will,
C.17.134	And *o* god þat al bygan with gode herte they honoureth
C.17.135	And ayther loueth and byleueth in *o* [lord] almyhty.
C.18.20	Hit hadde schoriares to shuyuen hit vp, thre shides of *o* lenghe
C.18.21	And of *o* kyne colour & kynde, as me thoghte,
C.18.28	Of *o* will, of o wit; and he[r]with y kepe
C.18.28	Of o will, of *o* wit; and he[r]with y kepe
C.18.57	And askede efte tho where hit were all [of] *o* kynde.
C.18.59	Hit is al of *o* kynde, and þat shal y preuen,
C.18.62	Of *o* kynde apples aren nat iliche grete
C.18.63	Ne suynge smale ne of [*o*] swettenesse swete.
C.18.125	That *oen* Iesus, a Iustices sone, most iouken in here chaumbre
C.18.187	'Thre persones in *o* pensel,' quod he, 'departable fram oþere.
C.18.188	*O* speche and [o] spirit Springeth out of alle;
C.18.188	O speche and [*o*] spirit Springeth out of alle;
C.18.189	Of *o* wit and o will, [they] were neuere atwynne
C.18.189	Of o wit and *o* will, [they] were neuere atwynne
C.18.197	How *o* lord myhte lyue [in] thre; y leue hit nat,' y sayde.
C.18.210	*O* god almyhty þat man made and wrouhte
C.18.215	And *o* god almyhty, yf alle men ben of Adam.
C.18.217	And Abel of hem bothe and alle thre *o* kynde;
C.18.233	And as thre persones palpable is puy[r]lich bote *o* mankynde,
C.18.236	In matrimonie aren thre and of *o* man cam alle thre
C.18.237	And to godhede goth thre and *o* god is all thre.
C.18.239	'Hastow ysey this,' y seyde, 'alle thre and *o* god?'
C.19.31	And alle thre bote *o* god; thus abraham bereth witenesse
C.19.38	To godhede but *o* god and on god almyhty
C.19.38	To godhede but o god and *on* god almyhty
C.19.42	And for to louye and bileue in *o* lord almyhty
C.19.44	Ac for to bileue in *o* lord þat lyueth in thre persones
C.19.99	And alle thre bote *o* god? thus abraham me tauhte.
C.19.109	And as Abraham þe olde of *o* god the tauhte
C.19.150	And alle thre is bote *o* god as myn hoend and my fyngeres.
C.19.152	Al is bote *oen* hoend howso y turne hit.
C.20.243	That alle þe wyse of th[is] world in *o* wit acordede
C.21.27	That knyht, kyng, conquerour may be *o* persone.
C.21.86	That [*o*] kyng cam with reson ykyuered vnder ensense.
C.21.201	*Oen* spiritus paraclitus to Peres and to his felawes.
C.21.265	And ioyned til hem *oen* iohann, most gentill of all,
C.21.340	And his spye spille-loue, *oen* speke-euele-bihynde.
C.21.399	Bothe dregges and draf and drawe at *on* hole
C.22.160	And wedded *oen* wanhope, a wenche of þe stuyves.
C.22.162	*Oen* Tomme two-tonge, ateynt at vch [a q]ueste.
C.22.245	To vnite and holi churche; ac *o* thyng y ȝow praye:
C.22.315	*Oen* frere flaterrere is fiscicien and surgien.'

oon pron *on pron.* A 7 o (1) on (6); B 25 one (1) oon (24); C 30 oen
  (23) on (6) oon (1)
A. 1.23	Þat *on* is vesture fro chele þe to saue;
A. 3.219	Þat *on* god of his grace gyueþ in his blisse
A. 6.106	Þat *on* hattiþ abstinence, and [humylite] anoþer,
A. 9.91	þei han crounide *o* king to kepe hem alle,
A. 9.98	Corounid *on* to be kyng & be h[ere] counseil werchen,
A.12.62	'Al hayl,' quod *on* þo, and I answered, 'welcome, & with whom be ȝe?'
A.12.84	Þat *on* is called cotidian, a courrour of oure hous;
B. 1.23	That *oon* [is] vesture from [chele] þee to saue;
B. 3.232	That *oon* god of his grace [gyueþ]
B. 5.620	That *oon* hatte Abstinence, and humilite anoþer;
B. 8.108	Crouned *oon* to be kyng, [and by hir counseil werchen],
B.11.27	Thanne was þer *oon* þat hiȝte Elde, þat heuy was of chere;
B.11.118	That vnderfonged me atte font for *oon* of goddes chosene.
B.11.140	'Ye? baw for bokes!' quod *oon* was broken out of helle.
B.11.320	Ac muche moore in metynge þus wiþ me gan *oon* dispute,
B.11.410	And as I caste vp myne eiȝen *oon* loked on me.
B.12.162	That *oon* [kan] konnynge and kan swymmen and dyuen;

B.14.267   Muche is [þat maide] to loue of [a man] þat swich *oon* takeþ,
B.15.13   *Oon* wiþouten tonge and teeþ tolde me whider I sholde
B.15.50   'Thanne artow inparfit', quod he, 'and *oon* of prides knyȝtes.
B.15.375   [Ne] nauȝt *oon* among an hundred þat an Auctour kan construwe,
B.16.183   That *oon* dooþ alle dooþ and ech dooþ bi his one.
B.16.183   That oon dooþ alle dooþ and ech dooþ bi his *one*.
B.17.154   Thus are þei alle but *oon*, as it an hand weere,
B.17.155   And þre sondry sightes [shewynge in *oon*],
B.17.323   That *oon* is a wikkede wif þat wol noȝt be chastised;
B.18.10   *Oon* semblable to þe Samaritan and somdeel to Piers þe Plow[man]
B.18.65   'Lif and deeþ, in þis derknesse hir *oon* fordooþ hir ooþer.
B.19.263   That *oon* was Luk, a large beest and a lowe chered,
B.19.269   *Oon* highte Austyn and Ambrose anoþer,
B.20.158   *Oon* þat muche wo wroȝte, Sleuþe was his name.
B.20.343   I knew swich oon ones, noȝt eighte wynter [passed],
C. 1.108   He was an Archangel of heuene, *on* of goddes knyghtes;
C. 2.127   For treuthe plyhte here treuthe to wedde *on* of here douhteres,
C. 5.10   In hele and [unnit] *oen* me apposede;
C. 6.27   Semyng a souerayn *oen* whereso me byfull
C. 6.385   And there were othes an heep for *on* sholde haue þe worse.
C. 7.272   That *on* hatte a[b]stinence and vmbletee a[n]oþer,
C. 7.292   'ȝe! villam emi,' quod *oen*, 'and now y moste thedre
C. 7.299   Thenne was *oen* hihte actif; an hosbande he semede.
C. 9.212   Or *oen* of som ordre or elles a profete.
C.10.101   And crounede *oen* to be kyng to kull withoute synne
C.10.104   Crounede *oen* to be a kyng to kepen vs alle
C.10.125   Here is *oen* wolde ywyte yf wit couthe teche;
C.10.263   A bastard, a bond *oen*, a begeneldes douhter
C.11.186   Thenne was [there] *oen* þat hihte Elde þat heuy was of chere;
C.12.53   That vnderfeng me at þe fonte for *on* of godes chosene.
C.12.75   'ȝe? bawe for bokes!' quod *oen* was broken out of helle.
C.13.36   What *oen* hath, what [o]þer hath and what they hadde bothe,
C.13.55   For þat *on* bereth but a box, a breuet þerynne,
C.14.106   That *oen* hath connyng and can swymmen and dyuen;
C.16.107   Moche is [þat] mayde to louye of a man þat such *oen* taketh,
C.16.212   'Thenne artow inparfit', quod he, 'and *oen* of prudes knyhtes.
C.18.219   And abel here issue, aren bote *oen* in manhede.
C.19.129   Thus are they alle bote *oen* as hit an hand were,
C.19.303   That [*oon*] is a wikkede wyf þat wol nat be chasted;
C.20.8   *Oen* semblable to þe samaritaen and somdeel to Pers þe plouhman
C.20.67   'Lyf & deth, in this derkenesse here *oen* fordoth her oþer.
C.21.263   That *oen* was luc, a large beste and a lou chered,
C.21.269   *Oen* hihte Austyn and Ambros[e] anoþer,
C.22.158   *Oen* þat moche wo wrouhte, sleuthe was his name.
C.22.343   Y knewe such *oen* ones, nat eyhte wynter passed,

oone adv *on adv. (2)* A 2 one; B 14 one (8) oone (6); C 16 one

A. 1.146   Here miȝt þou sen ensaumplis in hymself *one*
A. 9.54   [And] as I wente be a wode, walkyng myn *one*,
B. 1.172   Here myȝtow sen ensample[s] in hymself *oone*
B. 8.63   And as I wente by a wode, walkyng myn [*one*],
B. 9.37   As who seiþ, "moore moot herto þan my word *oone*;
B.10.339   Helpeþ noȝt to heueneward [at] *oone* [y]eris ende,
B.11.299   That han neiþer konnynge ne kyn, but a crowne *one*
B.13.125   And set alle sciences at a sop saue loue *one*;
B.14.333   Ne neiþer sherte ne shoon, saue for shame *one*
B.15.53   That any creature sholde konne al except crist *oone*.
B.15.210   Neiþer þoruȝ wordes ne werkes, but þoruȝ wil *oone*,
B.19.122   He wroȝte þat by no wit but þoruȝ word *one*,
B.19.190   And assoille men of alle synnes saue of dette *one*.
B.19.299   Wiþ god, and nauȝt agast but of gile *one*.
B.19.368   Repenteden and [forsoke] synne, saue þei *one*,
B.20.151   And kille a[l] erþely creatur[e] saue conscience *oone*.
C. 1.168   Here myhtow se ensaumples in hymself *one*
C. 3.144   That alle [women, wantowen], shal [be] war [by] þe *one*
C. 5.52   Withoute bagge or botel but my wombe *one*.
C.10.61   I wente forth wydewhare walkynge myn *one*
C.11.198   'Go y to helle or to heuene y shal nat go myn *one*.
C.13.113   That [hath] noþer connyng ne kyn bote a croune *one*
C.16.215   That eny creature sholde conne al excepte crist *one*.
C.16.374   To begge or to borwe but of god *one*.
C.17.8   Withoute borwynge or beggynge bote of god *one*.
C.20.316   And entisedest Eue to eten bi here *one*–
C.21.122   He wrouhte þat by no wyt bote thorw word *one*,
C.21.190   And assoile men of alle synnes saue of dette *one*.
C.21.299   With god and nat agast bote of gyle *one*.
C.21.368   Repenteden and [forsoke] synne, saue thei *one*
C.21.373   [Saue shrewes *one* swiche as y spak of],
C.22.151   And culle all erthely creature saue Consience *one*.

oones > ones

oonly adj *onli adj. &> oonliche* B 1; C 1 only

B.19.117   And þanne was he [cleped and] called noȝt [*oonly*] crist but Iesu,

C.21.117   And tho was he cleped and calde not [*onl]y* Crist but iesu,

oonliche adv *onli adv.* B 4 oonly (1) oonliche (3); C 7 oenliche (1) onelich (1) onelyche (1) onliche (2) only (1) onlyche (1)

B. 9.144   Excepte *oonliche* of ech kynde a couple
B.11.145   But *oonliche* loue and leautee and my laweful domes.
B.20.61   And alle hise as wel as hym, saue *oonly* fooles;
B.20.267   A certein for a certein, saue *oonliche* of freres.
C.10.232   Excepte *onliche* of vch kynde a payre
C.12.29   To segge as they seen, saue *only* prestis;
C.12.80   Bote *onlyche* loue and leaute as in my lawes demynge.
C.16.155   A blessed lyf withoute bisinesse bote *onelyche* for þe soule:
C.17.32   Ac bestes brouhte hem no mete bute *onliche* þe foules
C.22.61   And alle hise as wel as hym, saue *onelich* foles;
C.22.267   A certeyne for a certeyne saue *oenliche* of freres.

oost(es > hoost

ooþer pron *other pron.* A 24 oþer (13) oþere (11); B 85 ooþer (49) ooþere (1) othere (1) oþer (5) oþere (27) oþeres (1) ouþer (1); C 80 other (16) othere (6) otheres (3) oþer (30) oþere (25)

A.Pr.53   Cloþide hem in copis to be knowen from *oþere*;
A. 1.24   Þat *oþer* is mete at meel for myseise of þiselue;
A. 1.86   For whoso is trewe of his tunge, telliþ non *oþer*,
A. 2.124   And alle be boun, beggeris & *oþere*,
A. 2.143   And makiþ of lyere a lang carte to leden al þis *oþere*,
A. 3.104   Before þe kyng & his counseil, clerkis & *oþere*.
A. 4.119   Ac I may shewe ensaumplis as I se [*oþer*],
A. 5.163   Dawe þe dykere & a dusȝeyn *oþere*,
A. 6.122   And þoruȝ þe helpe of hem [two], hope þou non *oþer*,
A. 7.76   To penaunce & to pilgrimage wile I passe with *oþere*;
A. 8.14   Loke on þat o lawe, & lere men þat *oþer*,
A. 8.85   Þat takiþ [þ]is meschief mekliche as myselis & *oþere*,
A. 8.99   And do euele & haue euele, & hope þou non *oþer*
A. 8.109   Be þat þe sauter vs seiþ, & so dede manye *oþere*.
A. 8.126   Þe prest & perkyn aposid eiþer *oþer*,
A. 9.108   Disputyng on dowel day aftir *oþer*,
A. 9.110   He was long & lene, lyk to non *oþer*,
A.10.179   And al for se[þ] & his sister children spouside eiþer *oþer*,
A.11.92   Þeiȝ dobest drawe on hym day aftir *oþer*.'
A.11.131   Aristotel & *oþere* mo to arguen I tauȝte;
A.11.191   Obedient as breþeren & sustren to *oþere*,
A.11.250   Þat is, iche cristene [creature] be kynde to *oþer*,
A.12.85   Tercian þat *oþer*; trewe drinkeres boþe.
A.12.108   By Iames and by Ierom, by Iop and by *oþere*,
B.Pr.56   Cloþed hem in copes to ben knowen from *oþere*;
B. 1.24   [That *oþer* is] mete at meel for mysese of þiselue;
B. 1.88   [For] who is trewe of his tonge, telleþ noon *ooþer*,
B. 2.160   And alle be bown, beggers and *oþere*,
B. 2.182   And makeþ of lyere a lang cart to leden alle þise *oþere*,
B. 3.115   Bifore þe kyng and his conseil, clerkes and *oþere*.
B. 4.136   Ac I may shewe ensamples as I se *ouþ[er]*.
B. 5.149   Thus þei speken of spiritualte þat eiþer despiseþ *ooþer*
B. 5.164   And eiþer hit[t]e *ooþer* vnder þe cheke.
B. 5.165   Hadde þei had knyues, by crist! eiþer hadde kild *ooþer*.
B. 5.294   What he lerned yow in lente, leue þow noon *ooþer*,
B. 5.313   Dawe þe dykere and a doȝeyne *oþere*,]
B. 5.402   I am ocupied eche day, halyday and *ooþer*,
B. 5.637   And þoruȝ þe help of hem two, hope þow noon *ooþer*,
B. 6.84   To penaunce and to pilgrimage I wol passe wiþ *oþere*;
B. 6.180   They hadde be [dede and] doluen, ne dene þow noon *ooþer*,
B. 7.40   Men of lawe leest pardon hadde, [leue þow noon *ooþer*],
B. 7.103   That taken þi[s] myschie[f] mekeliche as Mesels and *oþere*,
B. 7.117   And do yuel and haue yuel, [and] hope þow noon *ooþer*
B. 7.127   By þat þe Sauter [vs] seith, [and] so dide *othere* manye.
B. 7.144   The preest and Perkyn [a]pposeden eiþer *ooþer*,
B. 8.118   Disputyng [o]n dowel day after *ooþer*,
B. 8.120   He was long and lene, lik to noon *ooþer*;
B. 9.88   Eyþer of hem helpeþ *ooþer* of þat þat h[y]m nedeþ,
B. 9.155   And haue a Sauour after þe sire; selde sestow *ooþer*:
B.10.81   And yet þe wrecches of þis world is noon ywar by *ooþer*,
B.10.139   Theiȝ dobest drawe on hym day after *ooþer*.'
B.10.179   Aristotle and *oþere* mo to argue I tauȝte;
B.10.276   That ye were swiche as ye sey[d]e to salue wiþ *oþere*.
B.10.310   And gret loue and likyng for ech [loweþ hym to] *ooþer*.
B.10.362   And after alle cristene creatures, in commune ech man *ooþer*;
B.10.368   For euery cristene creature sholde be kynde til *ooþer*,
B.10.370   God hoteþ heiȝe and lowe þat no man hurte *ooþer*,
B.10.401   As Salomon dide and swiche *oþere*, þat shewed grete wittes
B.10.475   I se ensamples myself and so may manye *oþer*,
B.11.14   And Coueitise of eiȝes [þat *ooþer* was ycalled].
B.11.179   Loue hir eyþer *ooþer*, and lene hem as hemselue.
B.11.194   Youre festynge and youre faire ȝifte; ech frend quyteþ so *ooþer*.
B.11.209   Forþi loue we as leue [children shal], and ech man laughe of *ooþer*,

B.11.211   And euery man helpe *ooþer* for hennes shul we alle:
B.11.214   Forþi lakke no lif *ooþer* þou3 he moore latyn knowe,
B.11.241   That we sholde be lowe and loueliche, [and lele ech man to *oþer*],
B.11.337   And after cours of concepcion noon took kepe of *ooþer*,
B.11.391   Ech a lif wolde be laklees, leue þow noon *oþer*.
B.12.43   Aristotle and *oþere* mo, ypocras and virgile,
B.12.125   Lest cheste cha[fe] vs to choppe ech man *oþer*:
B.12.161   And boþe naked as a nedle, hir noon [sadder] þan *ooþer*.
B.12.163   That *ooþer* is lewed of þat labour, lerned neuere swymme.
B.12.258   And alle þe *oþere* þer it lith enuenymeþ þoru3 his attre.
B.13.117   [That trauailleþ to teche *oþere* I holde it for a dobet].
B.14.166   For alle my3testow haue maad noon mener þan *ooþer*
B.14.224   And eiþer hateþ *ooþer* in alle maner werkes.
B.14.240   And by þe nekke namely hir noon may hente *ooþer*;
B.15.33   And whan I loue leelly oure lord and alle *oþere*,
B.15.325   And ben founded and feffed ek to bidde for *oþere*.
B.15.355   That no lif loueþ *ooþer*, ne oure lord as it semeþ.
B.15.386   Lest þei ouerhuppen as *ooþere* doon in office and in houres.
B.15.498   And seide it in saluacion of Sar3ens and *oþere*;
B.16.57   For alle are þei aliche longe, noon lasse þan *ooþer*,
B.16.138   Eche day after *ooþer* hir tyme þei awaiteden
B.16.181   'Thre leodes in oon lyth, noon lenger þan *ooþer*,
B.16.207   And eiþer is *oþeres* ioye in þre sondry persones,
B.17.29   Thre persones in parcelles departable fro *ooþer*
B.17.165   Thus it is–nedeþ no man trowe noon *ooþer*–
B.17.234   Melteþ to mercy, to merciable and to [noon] *oþere*.
B.17.272   For þat ben vnkynde to hise, hope I noon *ooþer*
B.18.65   'Lif and deeþ, in þis derkenesse hir oon fordooþ hir *ooþer*,
B.18.122   Eiþer asked *ooþer* of þis grete wonder,
B.18.143   For Adam and Eue and Abraham wiþ *oþere*
B.18.169   Loue haþ coueited hire longe; leue I noon *ooþer*
B.18.178   Adam and Eue and *oþere* mo in helle.
B.18.417   Clippe we in couenaunt, and ech of vs [kisse] *ooþer*,
B.19.54   For he yaf Adam and Eue and *oþere* mo blisse
B.19.233   And by wit to wissen *oþere* as grace hem wolde teche.
B.19.250   And alle he lered to be lele, and ech a craft loue *ooþer*,
B.19.254   Lokeþ þat no[on] lakke *ooþer*, but loueþ as breþeren;
B.19.266   The pris neet of Piers plow, passynge alle *oþere*.
B.19.394   [Or] ech man for3yue *ooþer*, and þat wole þe Paternoster:
B.19.416   The comune clamat cotidie, ech a man til *ooþer*,
B.20.6   '[Coudes]tow no3t excuse þee as dide þe kyng and *oþer*;
B.20.208   'Lerne to loue', quod kynde, 'and leef alle *oþere*.'
B.20.262   Alle *oþere* in bataille ben yholde Brybours,
B.20.334   'He is sik', seide Pees, 'and so are manye *oþere*.
B.20.353   And acorde wiþ Consience and kisse hir eiþer *ooþer*.'
B.20.377   'He lyþ [adreynt] and dremeþ', seide Pees, 'and so do manye *oþere*.
C.Pr.54   Clothed hem in copis to be knowe fram *othere*
C.Pr.225   Bothe Bakeres and Breweres, Bochers and *other*,
C.1.109   He and *oþer* with hym helden nat with treuthe,
C.1.118   Then in þe north by many notes, no man leue *other*.
C.2.176   And bade hem alle bowen, beggares and *othere*,
C.2.195   And maketh of lyare a lang cart to lede al this *othere*,
C.3.152   Byfore þe kyng and his consayl, clerkes and *oþere*.
C.3.338   And ayther is *otheres* helpe; of hem cometh retribucoun
C.3.498   The whiche þat hatte, as y haue rad an[d] *oþer* þat can rede,
C.4.133   Ac y may s[hew]en ensaumples as y see *othere*.
C.5.111   Y saw þe felde ful of folk fram ende til *oþer*
C.5.189   Holde 3ow in vnite; and he þat *oþer* wolde
C.5.196   Of alle maner actions and eche man loue *other*.
C.6.20   Demed for here vuel vices and exitede *oþere*
C.6.22   And scornede hem and *oþere* yf y a skil founde,
C.6.42   And connyngest of my craft, Clerkysh *oþer* *other*,
C.6.122   Thus thei speke and dispute þat vchon dispiseth *oþer*.
C.6.127   That y ne mot folowe this folk: my fortune is non *oþer*.
C.6.149   Tyl ayþer clepede *oþer* "hore!" and o[f] with the clothes
C.6.188   Exited either *oþer* til oure olde synne;
C.6.298   3e! þe prest þat thy tythe t[a]k[eth], trowe y non *other*,
C.7.18   Y am occuepied vch day, haliday and *oþere*,
C.7.290   And thorw þe help[e] of hem two, hope þou non *oþer*,
C.8.93   To penaunc[e] and [to] pilgrim[age] y wol passe with *oþere*;
C.9.89   What *other* byhoueth þat hath many childrene
C.9.152   In idelnesse and in ese and by *otheres* trauayle.
C.9.174   Tho þat lyueth thus here lyf, leue 3e non *other*,
C.9.291   And do yuele and haue euele and hope thow non *oþere*
C.10.114   Disputyng vppon dowel lenge aftur *other*
C.10.116   He was long and lene, ylyk to noon *other*;
C.10.272   Ac they lyen le[i], here neyther lyketh *other*.
C.10.281   And [wedewares and wedewes] weddeth ayþer *oþer*;
C.11.61   And 3ut th[e]i wrechus of this world is noen ywar by *oþer*
C.11.119   Aristotel and *oþere* [mo] to Arguen y tauhte;
C.11.173   And coueytise-of-yes ycalde was þat *oþer*.
C.12.105   For vch frende fedeth *other* and fondeth hou beste to quite
C.12.106   Meles and manschipes, vch man *oþer*.

C.12.118   And euery man helpe *other* for hennes shal we alle
C.12.130   That we sholde be low and louelich and lele vch man til *oþer*
C.13.36   What oen hath, what [o]þer hath and what they hadde bothe,
C.13.145   Aftur cors of concepcion noon toek kepe of *oþer*,
C.13.209   Vch a lede wolde be lacles, leef thow non *other*.
C.14.68   Laste cheste chauf[e] vs to [c]hoppe vch man *oþer*.
C.14.105   And bothe naked as a nedle, here noen heuegore then *othere*.
C.14.107   That *oþer* is lewed of þat labour, lerned neuere swymme.
C.15.125   That trauayleth to teche *oþere* y halde hit for a dobet;
C.16.65   And ayther hateth *oþer* and may nat wone togyderes.
C.16.80   And by þe nekke namelyche here noen may henten *other*;
C.16.181   And ayther is *otheres* hete and also of o will;
C.16.195   And when y louye lelly oure lord and alle *oþere*
C.16.304   Lawhe þer men lawheth and loure þer *oþere* louren.
C.16.307   Ne þat eny gome wolde gyle [ne greue *oþere*]
C.17.12   Bothe Antony and arseny and *oþer* fol monye.
C.18.187   'Thre persones in o pensel,' quod he, 'departable fram *oþere*.
C.19.30   Thre persones parselmele depar[t]able fram *oþere*
C.19.98   In thre persones, a parceles departable fram *oþere*,
C.19.200   Melteth to mercy, to merciable and to non *oþere*.
C.19.253   For þat ben vn[k]ynde to hise, hope 3e noen *oþer*
C.20.67   'Lyf & deth, in this derkenesse here oen fordoth her *oþer*.
C.20.125   Ayþer asked *oþer* of this grete Wonder,
C.20.172   Loue hath coueyted here longe; leue y non *oþere*
C.20.175   Whenne pees in pacience yclothed aproched her ayþer *oþer*
C.20.181   Adam and Eue and *other* mo in helle.
C.20.217   Ne hadde god ysoffred of som *oþer* then hymsulue
C.20.338   To lere men for [be] lele and vch man to louye *oþer*;
C.20.351   Lucifer for his lesynges, leue y noen *oþer*
C.20.460   Cluppe we in couenaunt and vch of vs kusse *oþere*.'
C.21.54   For he 3af Adam and Eue and *oþere* mo blisse
C.21.233   And bi wit to wissen *oþere* as grace hem wolde teche.
C.21.250   And al he lered to be lele, and vch a craft loue *oþere*,
C.21.254   Loke þat noen lacke *oþere* bute loueth as bretherne
C.21.266   The pris neet of [Peres plouh], passynge alle *oþere*.
C.21.394   Or vch man for3eue *oþer*, and þat wol þe paternost[er]:
C.21.416   The comu[n]e clamat cotidie, vch a man to *oþer*.
C.22.6   'Couthest thow nat excuse the as dede the kyng and *oþere*:
C.22.208   'Lerne to loue,' quod kynde, 'and leef all *othere*.'
C.22.262   Alle *oþere* in bataile been yholde brybours,
C.22.334   'He is syke,' saide Pees, 'and so ar many *oþere*.
C.22.353   And acorde with Consience and kusse here ayther *oþer*.'
C.22.377   'He lyeth adreint [and dremeth],' saide pees, 'and so doth mony *oþere*.

ooþer adj *other adj.* A 11 *oþer* (5) *oþere* (6); B 39 ooþer (16) *oþer* (3) *oþere* (20); C 59 other (14) othere (5) othur (1) *oþer* (27) *oþere* (12)

A.Pr.101   Masonis, mynours, & manye *oþere* craftis,
A.1.9   Of *oþer* heuene þanne here holde þei no tale.'
A.3.79   Ryng[es] or *oþer* richesse, þ[ise] regratour[is] to meynteyne.
A.5.105   'I am sory,' quaþ enuye, 'I am but selde *oþere*,
A.6.16   In armonye, in alisaundre, in manye *oþere* places.
A.6.68   He is fre[þ]id in wiþ Floreynes & *oþere* [fees] manye.
A.7.101   *Oþere* werkmen þere were [þat] wrou3te ful faste,
A.8.79   Þanne of alle *oþer* maner men þat on þis molde wandriþ.
A.10.174   Boþe fisshis & foulis, forþ mi[d] *oþere* bestis,
A.11.146   In *oþer* science it seiþ, I sai3 it in catoun,
A.12.101   And wrou3the þat here is wryten and *oþer* werkes boþe
B.Pr.222   Masons, Mynours and many *oþere* craftes;
B.1.9   Of *ooþer* heuene þan here holde þei no tale.'
B.2.58   As of kny3tes and of clerkes and *ooþer* commune peple,
B.3.90   Rynges or *ooþer* richesse þ[ise] Regratiers to mayntene.
B.5.128   'I am sory', quod [enuye], 'I am but selde *ooþer*,
B.5.157   I was þe Prioresse potager and *oþere* pouere ladies,
B.5.436   Boþe flessh and fissh and manye *oþere* vitailles;
B.5.528   In Armonye, in Alisaundre, in manye *oþere* places.
B.5.581   He is fryþed In wiþ floryns and *oþere* fees manye;
B.6.109   *Oþere* werkmen þer were þat wro3ten ful [faste],
B.7.97   Than of alle [*oþere*] manere men þat on þis moolde [wandreþ].
B.9.143   And þe foweles þat fleen forþ wiþ *oþere* beestes.
B.10.96   Homliche at *oþere* mennes houses and hatien hir owene.
B.10.194   In *ooþer* Science it seiþ, I sei3 it in Catoun,
B.10.407   Was neuere wrighte saued þat wro3te þeron, ne *ooþer* werkman ellis,
B.11.246   Seint Iohan and *oþere* seintes were seyen in poore cloþyng,
B.11.343   Boþe hors and houndes and alle *oþere* beestes
B.11.351   Ac yet me merueilled moore how many *oþere* briddes
B.11.355   For fere of *oþere* foweles and for wilde beestes.
B.12.118   And manye mo *oþer* men, þat were no leuites,
B.12.197   As Seint Iohan and *oþere* Seintes þat deserued hadde bettre.
B.12.215   Raþer þan þat þei wolde, þou3 þow woldest appose.
B.13.54   And þanne a mees of *ooþer* mete of Miserere mei deus,_
B.13.108   Mortrews and *ooþer* mete, and we no morsel hadde.
B.13.366   And but I hadde by *ooþer* wey at þe laste I stale it,

B.14.150   And whan he haþ doon his deuoir wel men dooþ hym *ooþer*
                   bountee,
B.14.229   That mete or money of *oþere* men moot asken.
B.15.43   And *oþere* names an heep, Episcopus and Pastor.'
B.15.70   Freres and fele *oþere* maistres þat to [þe] lewed [folk] prechen,
B.15.77   As wel freres as *ooþer* folk, foliliche spenden
B.15.272   Antony and Egidie and *oþere* holy fadres
B.15.299   Neiþer bere ne boor ne *ooþer* beest wilde,
B.16.11   And to haue my fulle of þat fruyt forsake a[l] *ob[er]* saule[e].
B.16.251   That to patriarkes & prophetes and *ooþer* peple in derknesse
B.18.80   Bifore Pilat and *ooþer* peple in þe place he houed.
B.19.140   [Her]of Cayphas hadde enuye and *oþere* Iewes.
B.19.376   And *ob[er]* pryue penaunc[e], and somme þoru3 penyes delynge.
B.20.249   And *oþere* necessaries ynowe; yow shal no þyng [lakke]
B.20.289   And maken hym murie wiþ *ooþer* mennes goodes.
C.Pr.93   And summe aren as seneschalles and seruen *oþer* lordes
C. 1.9   Of *othere* heuene then here [halde thei] no tale.'
C. 2.13   And thereon rede rubies and *othere* riche stones.
C. 2.60   Of knyghtes, of clerkes [and] *other* comune peple,
C. 2.94   With vsurye and Auaryce and *other* fals sleythus
C. 3.24   Rynges with rubees and *othere* riche 3eftes.
C. 3.97   Morreyne or *other* meschaunc[e]: and mony tymes hit falleth.
C. 3.117   Or presentes without pans and *oþer* priue 3eftes.
C. 3.122   In amendement of mayres and *oþer* stywardes
C. 3.249   Loketh aftur lordschipe or *oþer* large mede
C. 3.316   3eue lond or lordschipe [or] *oþer* large 3eftes
C. 5.20   Or eny *other* kynes craft þat to þe comune nedeth,
C. 6.93   'I am sory,'sayde enuye, 'y am [but] selde *othur*;
C. 6.132   I was the Prioresse potager and *oþer* pore ladies
C. 6.160   Ac *other* while when wyn cometh and when y drynke late at euen
C. 6.265   And but y hadde by *other* wey at the laste y stale hit
C. 7.228   Is frithed in with floreynes and *othere* monye;
C. 8.116   *Oþer* werkemen þer were þat wrouhten fol 3erne,
C. 8.190   Prestes and *oþer* peple towarde [Peres] they drowe
C. 8.320   With craym and with croddes, with cresses and *oþere* erbes.
C. 9.84   And of monye *oþer* men þat moche wo soffren,
C. 9.105   A[nd] 3ut ar ther *oþere* beggares, in hele as hit semeth
C. 9.173   Then of many *oþere* men þat [o]n this molde walken.
C. 9.225   In frithes and in forestes for fox and *other* bestes
C. 9.235   Pouerte or *oþer* penaunc[e], as pilgrimages and trauayles.
C. 9.257   That soffreth suche sottes and *oþere* synnes regne.
C.10.161   So let lecherye and *other* luther synnes
C.10.167   Of gold and of *oþer* goed ac goddes grace hem fayleth.
C.10.231   And þe foules þat fl[e]eth forth with *oþer* bestes,
C.10.261   Bote he haue *oþer* goed haue wol here no ryche.
C.11.259   Withoute penaunce *oþer* passioun *oþer* eny *other* peyne
C.12.183   [And] *oþer* sedes also in þe same wyse
C.12.226   Erles and Erchedekenes and *oþere* riche clerkes
C.13.38   For þe parcel[s] of his pauper and *oþer* pryue dettes
C.13.61   Ac 3ut myhte þe marchaunt thorw moneye and *other* 3eftes
C.13.82   And *other* pryue penaunces þe which þe prest woet wel
C.13.162   And 3ut me merueylede more [how] mony [*other*] briddes
C.13.186   That thow ne reul[e]st rather renkes then *other* bestes.
C.13.190   They ouerdoen hit day and nyhte and so doth nat *oþer* bestes;
C.14.32   That wit wexeth therof and *oþer* w[y]rdes bothe:
C.14.136   A[s] seynt Ioh[a]n and *oþer* seyntes þat haen [de]serued bettere.
C.14.154   Rather then þat *oþer* [theef], thogh thow woldest apose,
C.14.162   And Adam and Eue and alle *othere* bestes
C.15.54   And to me þat was his mette tho, and *oþer* mete bothe.
C.16.164   And he soffrede me and saide, 'assay his *oþer* name.'
C.16.205   And *oþer* names an heep, Episcopus and pastor.'
C.16.236   As wel freres as *oþere* folk, foliliche spenden
C.16.317   [Rentes or *other* richesse to releue hym at his nede]?'
C.16.330   And when he hath visited thus fetured folk and *oþer* folke pore,
C.17.34   Fynde honest men and holy men and *oþer* rihtfole peple.
C.17.80   Is alayed with leccherye and *oþer* lustes of synne
C.17.95   Wedurwyse shipmen now and *oþer* witty peple
C.19.320   Been seeknesse[e] and *oþere* sorwes þat we soffren ouhte,
C.20.82   Bifore pilatus and *oþere* peple in þe place he houed
C.20.146   For Adam and Eue And abraham with *oþer*
C.21.140   Hereof hadde Cayphas enuye and *oþer* iewes
C.22.249   And *oþere* necessaries ynowe; 3ow shal no thyng lakke
C.22.289   And maken hym murye with *oþere* menne godes.

ooþer &> oþer,ooþerwise

ooþerwise adv *otherwise adv.* A 2 oþere_wise (1) oþerwise (1); B 5
       ooþerwise (2) ooþer_wise (1) oþerwise (2); C 8 otherwyse (3)
       oþerewise (1) oþerwyse (4)
A. 6.52   *Oþerwise* þanne þou woldist men wrou3te to þiselue;
A. 9.100   And *oþere wise* & ellis nou3t but as þei þre assent[e].'
B. 3.275   *Ooþerwise* þan he was warned of þe prophete,
B. 5.565   *Oþerwise* þan þow woldest [men] wrou3te to þiselue.

B. 8.110   And *ooþer wise* [and ellis no3t] but as þei þre assent[e].'
B.13.278   *Ooþerwise* þan he haþ wiþ herte or si3te shewynge hym;
B.17.177   *Oþerwise* þan þe wriþen fust or werkmanshipe of fyngres.
C. 3.428   *Otherwyse* then god wolde and warnede hym by þe prophete,
C. 5.81   And wol til hit be wered out [or] *oþerwyse* ychaunged.
C. 6.31   *Otherwyse* then y haue, withynne or withouten
C. 7.212   *Otherwyse* then 3e wolden they wrouhte 3ow alle tymes.
C.10.106   Bute *oþerewise* ne elles nat but as they thre assent[e].'
C.12.228   And haen þe world at he[re] wille *oþerwyse* to leuene.
C.16.277   Wolde neuere *oþerwyse* god but wikkede men hit hadde,
C.19.142   *Oþerwyse* then þe writhen f[u]ste or werkmanschupe of fyngres.

ope > up

opene v *openen v.* B 4 opene (2) opned (1) opnede (1); C 5 opene (3)
       opened (2)
B.Pr.106   And to *opene* it to hem and heuene blisse shewe.
B.18.249   Lo! helle my3te nat holde, but *opnede* þo god þolede,
B.18.322   For any wye or warde wide *opned* þe yates.
B.20.348   Hende speche heet pees, '*opene* þe yates.
C. 2.135   "God of thy grace heuene gates *opene*,
C. 7.249   To *opene* and vndo þe hye gate of heuene
C.20.258   Loo! helle myhte nat holde, bote *opened* tho god tholede,
C.20.365   For eny wey or warde wyde *open[ed]* þe 3ates.
C.22.348   Hende speche heet pees, '*opene* the 3ates.

or adv correl *or conj.* B 2; C 2
B.14.217   [*Or*] in þe maister [or] in þe man som mansion he haueþ.
B.14.217   [*Or*] in þe maister [or] in þe man som mansion he haueþ.
C.16.58   *Or* in þe maystre or in þe man som mansion he haueth.
C.16.58   *Or* in þe maystre or in þe man som mansion he haueth.

or conj *or conj.* cf. *oþer* A 74; B 295; C 316
       A.1.60, A.2.59, A.3.51, A.3.56, A.3.59, A.3.59, A.3.59, A.3.78, A.3.79, A.3.89,
       A.3.89, A.3.151, A.3.230, A.3.268, A.4.116, A.5.68, A.5.69, A.5.69, A.5.209, A.7.40,
       A.7.46, A.7.59, A.7.71, A.7.129, A.7.130, A.7.151, A.7.205, A.7.209, A.7.210,
       A.7.211, A.7.211, A.7.232, A.7.288, A.7.288, A.8.6, A.8.7, A.8.31, A.8.34, A.8.69,
       A.8.76, A.8.76, A.9.12, A.9.73, A.9.80, A.9.95, A.10.126, A.10.188, A.10.198, A.10.211,
       A.11.6, A.11.15, A.11.15, A.11.26, A.11.29, A.11.30, A.11.30, A.11.32, A.11.84,
       A.11.119, A.11.187, A.11.198, A.11.207, A.11.214, A.11.256, A.11.263, A.11.283,
       A.11.283, A.11.283, A.11.288, A.11.289, A.11.298, A.11.302, A.12.37

       B.Pr.154, B.Pr.168, B.Pr.171, B.Pr.171, B.1.53, B.1.62, B.2.77, B.2.77, B.2.194,
       B.2.194, B.3.71, B.3.89, B.3.90, B.3.100, B.3.162, B.3.236, B.3.251, B.3.293, B.3.303,
       B.3.305, B.3.306, B.3.308, B.3.308, B.3.309, B.3.310, B.3.313, B.3.319, B.4.38,
       B.4.39, B.4.115, B.4.132, B.4.132, B.4.133, B.4.133, B.5.85, B.5.151, B.5.154, B.5.212,
       B.5.230, B.5.282, B.5.286, B.5.381, B.5.386, B.5.406, B.5.407, B.5.417, B.5.418,
       B.5.424, B.5.429, B.5.505, B.5.589, B.6.49, B.6.51, B.6.65, B.6.79, B.6.135, B.6.136,
       B.6.136, B.6.141, B.6.141, B.6.142, B.6.142, B.6.166, B.6.182, B.6.219, B.6.223,
       B.6.224, B.6.231, B.6.248, B.6.248, B.6.248, B.6.304, B.6.304, B.7.6, B.7.7,
       B.7.29, B.7.32, B.7.67, B.7.94, B.7.94, B.8.12, B.8.82, B.8.89, B.8.105, B.8.130, B.9.24,
       B.9.59, B.9.100, B.9.167, B.9.197, B.10.6, B.10.15, B.10.15, B.10.34, B.10.37, B.10.38,
       B.10.38, B.10.95, B.10.101, B.10.131, B.10.167, B.10.208, B.10.292, B.10.301,
       B.10.306, B.10.351, B.10.367, B.10.375, B.10.378, B.10.382, B.10.424, B.10.424,
       B.10.424, B.10.429, B.10.430, B.10.440, B.11.51, B.11.83, B.11.117, B.11.136,
       B.11.172, B.11.196, B.11.216, B.11.219, B.11.263, B.11.277, B.11.293, B.11.295,
       B.11.302, B.11.305, B.11.308, B.11.308, B.11.377, B.11.396, B.11.431, B.12.9, B.12.9,
       B.12.14, B.12.28, B.12.41, B.12.41, B.12.74, B.12.115, B.12.115, B.12.158, B.12.166,
       B.12.176, B.12.183, B.12.200, B.12.207, B.12.239, B.12.242, B.12.270, B.12.291,
       B.13.10, B.13.18, B.13.184, B.13.184, B.13.227, B.13.229, B.13.278, B.13.292,
       B.13.292, B.13.293, B.13.293, B.13.296, B.13.307, B.13.308, B.13.328, B.13.328,
       B.13.335, B.13.339, B.13.346, B.13.363, B.13.367, B.13.368, B.13.368, B.13.371,
       B.13.373, B.13.376, B.13.377, B.13.380, B.13.388, B.13.392, B.13.414, B.13.416,
       B.13.447, B.13.459, B.14.8, B.14.13, B.14.14, B.14.14, B.14.14, B.14.40, B.14.40,
       B.14.52, B.14.52, B.14.59, B.14.59, B.14.120, B.14.144, B.14.210, B.14.227, B.14.229,
       B.14.258, B.14.289, B.14.311, B.14.331, B.14.331, B.15.6, B.15.6, B.15.31, B.15.31,
       B.15.107, B.15.113, B.15.124, B.15.138, B.15.150, B.15.168, B.15.176, B.15.176,
       B.15.289, B.15.320, B.15.321, B.15.376, B.15.403, B.15.433, B.15.453, B.15.491,
       B.15.532, B.15.604, B.16.96, B.16.129, B.16.143, B.16.232, B.16.268, B.17.75,
       B.17.102, B.17.116, B.17.124, B.17.138, B.17.139, B.17.172, B.17.177, B.17.183,
       B.17.185, B.17.191, B.17.191, B.17.192, B.17.206, B.17.217, B.17.220, B.17.223,
       B.17.249, B.17.278, B.17.282, B.17.289, B.17.328, B.17.330, B.17.332, B.18.27,
       B.18.30, B.18.30, B.18.70, B.18.83, B.18.84, B.18.84, B.18.188, B.18.298, B.18.322,
       B.18.387, B.19.11, B.19.25, B.19.77, B.19.138, B.19.307, B.19.307, B.19.348, B.19.350,
       B.19.389, B.19.394, B.19.412, B.19.423, B.19.433, B.19.452, B.19.461, B.20.21,
       B.20.68, B.20.228, B.20.241, B.20.287, B.20.319, B.20.319

       C.Pr.123, C.Pr.188, C.1.49, C.1.58, C.2.208, C.2.208, C.3.94, C.3.96, C.3.97,
       C.3.117, C.3.142, C.3.145, C.3.245, C.3.249, C.3.252, C.3.299, C.3.300, C.3.315, C.3.316,
       C.3.316, C.3.392, C.3.446, C.3.457, C.3.459, C.3.461, C.3.466, C.3.472, C.3.500, C.4.54,
       C.4.129, C.4.129, C.4.130, C.4.182, C.4.193, C.4.194, C.5.12, C.5.13, C.5.13, C.5.14,
       C.5.14, C.5.15, C.5.16, C.5.18, C.5.18, C.5.19, C.5.19, C.5.19, C.5.20, C.5.23,
       C.5.26, C.5.28, C.5.29, C.5.30, C.5.33, C.5.33, C.5.34, C.5.52, C.5.63, C.5.81,
       C.5.91, C.5.134, C.5.152, C.5.153, C.6.29, C.6.31, C.6.55, C.6.56, C.6.73,
       C.6.79, C.6.114, C.6.117, C.6.125, C.6.126, C.6.129, C.6.234, C.6.244, C.6.262, C.6.266,
       C.6.268, C.6.270, C.6.277, C.6.279, C.6.438, C.7.2, C.7.22, C.7.23, C.7.23, C.7.24,
       C.7.42, C.7.50, C.7.75, C.7.76, C.7.107, C.7.117, C.7.150, C.7.210, C.7.236, C.8.41,

C.8.46, C.8.46, C.8.49, C.8.66, C.8.81, C.8.142, C.8.143, C.8.143, C.8.163, C.8.232,
C.8.237, C.8.266, C.8.284, C.8.332, C.8.332, C.9.6, C.9.7, C.9.63, C.9.82, C.9.95,
C.9.99, C.9.99, C.9.118, C.9.130, C.9.143, C.9.148, C.9.149, C.9.170, C.9.170, C.9.182,
C.9.183, C.9.183, C.9.212, C.9.212, C.9.216, C.9.217, C.9.226, C.9.235, C.9.245,
C.9.246, C.9.249, C.9.273, C.9.279, C.10.150, C.10.195, C.10.253, C.10.265, C.10.269,
C.10.296, C.11.6, C.11.6, C.11.13, C.11.13, C.11.31, C.11.31, C.11.32, C.11.198,
C.11.206, C.11.263, C.11.266, C.11.271, C.11.297, C.12.52, C.12.94, C.12.149,
C.12.153, C.12.156, C.12.157, C.12.157, C.12.197, C.13.48, C.13.48, C.13.49, C.13.75,
C.13.75, C.13.86, C.13.107, C.13.109, C.13.119, C.13.122, C.13.122, C.13.195,
C.13.230, C.13.238, C.14.31, C.14.42, C.14.60, C.14.60, C.14.116, C.14.139, C.14.174,
C.14.180, C.14.182, C.14.184, C.14.191, C.14.193, C.14.193, C.14.213, C.15.12,
C.15.35, C.15.155, C.15.196, C.15.201, C.15.203, C.15.203, C.15.211, C.15.239,
C.15.239, C.15.251, C.15.251, C.15.258, C.15.296, C.15.305, C.16.34, C.16.34, C.16.51,
C.16.68, C.16.70, C.16.98, C.16.124, C.16.145, C.16.148, C.16.176, C.16.177, C.16.191,
C.16.191, C.16.193, C.16.193, C.16.268, C.16.301, C.16.314, C.16.316, C.16.317,
C.16.34, C.17.2, C.17.2, C.17.2, C.17.8, C.17.16, C.17.27, C.17.27, C.17.55, C.17.60,
C.17.61, C.17.61, C.17.61, C.17.110, C.17.145, C.17.147, C.17.282, C.17.287, C.18.54,
C.18.127, C.18.129, C.18.148, C.18.284, C.19.74, C.19.111, C.19.112, C.19.136,
C.19.142, C.19.149, C.19.151, C.19.151, C.19.157, C.19.157, C.19.158, C.19.172,
C.19.183, C.19.189, C.19.215, C.19.259, C.19.263, C.19.270, C.19.308, C.19.310,
C.19.312, C.20.26, C.20.29, C.20.29, C.20.72, C.20.85, C.20.86, C.20.86, C.20.193,
C.20.214, C.20.218, C.20.305, C.20.331, C.20.365, C.20.383, C.20.384, C.20.416,
C.20.429, C.21.11, C.21.25, C.21.77, C.21.138, C.21.307, C.21.307, C.21.348, C.21.350,
C.21.376, C.21.389, C.21.394, C.21.412, C.21.423, C.21.433, C.21.452, C.21.461,
C.22.21, C.22.68, C.22.228, C.22.241, C.22.287, C.22.319

or &> er

ordeyne v *ordeinen v.* A 1 ordeyned; B 5 ordeigne (1) ordeyne (1)
ordeyned (2) ordeyne (1); C 6 ordeyne (2) ordeyned (2) ordeynede
(2)

A.12.90   But lyue as þis lyf is *ordeyned* for the.
B.Pr.119   And for profit of al þe peple Plowmen *ordeyned*
B.10.220   Alle þise Sciences I myself sotilede and *ordeynede*,
B.10.250   And hymself *ordeyned* to sadde vs in bileue.
B.19.318   *Ordeigne* þee an hous, Piers, to herberwe Inne þi cornes.'
B.19.320   And *ordeyne* þat hous er ye hennes wende.'
C. 3.241   And as his wyrdus were *ordeyned* at þe wille of oure lorde.
C. 5.55   For by þe lawe of leuyticy þat oure lord *ordeynede*,
C.10.219   Þat lycame haen aȝen þe lawe þat oure lord *ordeynede*.
C.17.16   For he *ordeyned* þat ordre or elles þey gabben.
C.21.318   *Ordeyne* the an hous, [Peres], to herborwe in thy cornes.'
C.21.320   And *ordeyne* þat hous ar ȝe hennes wende.'

ordre n *ordre n.,* A 4 ordre (2) ordris (2); B 9 ordre (6) ordres (3); C 11
ordre (7) ordres (4)

A.Pr.55   I fond þere Freris, alle þe foure *ordris*,
A. 1.102   And whoso passiþ þat poynt is apostata in his *ordre*.
A. 7.151   'Or þou shalt abigge be þe lawe, be þe *ordre* þat I bere'.
A. 8.176   Þeiȝ þou be founde in þe fraternite among þe foure *ordris*,
B.Pr.58   I fond þere Freres, alle þe foure *ordres*,
B. 1.104   And whoso passe[þ] þat point [is] Apostata in [his] *ordre*.
B. 6.72   And frere faitour and folk of hi[s] *ordre*,
B. 6.166   'Or þow shalt abigge by þe lawe, by þe *ordre* þat I bere!'
B. 7.198   Theiȝ [þow] be founde in þe fraternite [among] þe foure *ordres*
B.11.290   And þe title þat ye take *ordres* by telleþ ye ben auaunced:
B.13.284   Yhabited as an heremyte, an *ordre* by hymselue.
B.15.289   Til he foundede freres of Austynes *ordre*, [or ellis freres lyen].
B.20.265   Hir *ordre* and hir reule wole to han a certein noumbre
C.Pr.56   I fonde þer Freris, alle þe foure *ordres*,
C. 1.97   Is þe professioun and puyr *ordre* that apendeth to knyghtes
C. 3.54   Solempneliche and softlyche as for a suster of oure *ordre*.'
C. 3.67   That euery seg shal se y am sustre of ȝoure *ordre*.'
C. 8.73   And frere faytour and folk of þat *ordre*,
C. 8.191   And freres of alle þe fyue *ordres*, alle for fere of hunger.
C. 9.212   Or oen or som *ordre* or elles a profete.
C. 9.344   Thow we be founden in the fraternite of alle fyue *ordres*
C.13.104   The tytle [þat] ȝe take *ordres* by telleth ȝe ben avaunsed
C.17.16   For he ordeyned þat *ordre* or elles þey gabben.
C.22.265   Here *ordre* and here reule wol to haue a certeyne nombre

organye n *orgnie n.* B 1; C 1 orgene
B.18.8   And how Osanna by *Organye* olde folk songen,
C.20.7   And how osanna by *orgene* oelde folke songe.

orientals n *oriental n.* B 1
B. 2.14   *Orientals* and Ewages enuenymes to destroye.

orysones n *orisoun n.* C 1
C.18.158   And saide, 'this is an hous of *orysones* and of holynesse

osay > oseye

osanna exclam *osanna interj.* B 1; C 1
B.18.8   And how *Osanna* by Organye olde folk songen,
C.20.7   And how *osanna* by orgene oelde folke songe.

oseye n prop *oseie n.* A 1 osay; B 1; C 1
A.Pr.107   'W[hit] wyn of *osay*, & wyn of gascoyne,
B.Pr.229   'Whit wyn of *Oseye* and wyn of Gascoigne,
C.Pr.233   'Whit wyn of *Oseye* and wyn of gascoyne,

ost(e > hoost

otes n *ote n.* A 2 hote (1) otis (1); B 2; C 2
A. 4.45   And takiþ me but a taile for ten quarteris *otis*,
A. 7.179   Hungir hem helide wiþ an *hot[e]* cake.
B. 4.58   And takeþ me but a taille for ten quarters *Otes*;
B. 6.282   A fewe cruddes and creme and [a cake of *otes*],
C. 4.61   And taketh me but a tayle for ten quarteres *otes*;
C. 8.304   A fewe croddes and craym and a cake of *otes*

oþer conj *other conj. &> ooþer,ouþerwhile cf. or* A 25; B 22 ooþer (2)
oþer (6) ouþer (14); C 56 other (9) othere (1) oþer (46)

A. 1.51   Et que sunt dei deo *oþer* ellis ȝe don ille."
A. 1.151   For þe same mesour ȝe mete, amys *oþer* ellis,
A. 2.155   Fals *oþer* fauel oþer any of his feris,
A. 2.155   Fals oþer fauel *oþer* any of his feris,
A. 3.62   *Oþer* to grede aftir godis men whan ȝe [g]iue dolis,
A. 4.106   And haten [to] here harlotrie *oþer* mouþe it;
A. 4.115   But it be marchaunt, *oþer* his man, oþer messang[er] with lettres,
A. 4.115   But it be marchaunt, oþer his man, *oþer* messang[er] with lettres,
A. 4.116   *Oþer* prouisour, or prest þat þe pope auauncip.
A. 5.117   Ferst I lernide to leiȝe a lef *oþer* tweiȝe;
A. 5.128   Til ten ȝardis *oþer* twelue tollide out þrittene.
A. 6.76   And boterasid wiþ beleue [so] *oþer* þou [be]st not sauid;
A. 7.12   But ȝif it be holy day *oþer* holy euen;
A. 7.215   'Ȝe, I hote þe,' quaþ hungir, '*oþer* ellis þe bible leiȝeþ.
A. 7.232   *Oþer* wiþ teching, oþer telling, or trauaillyng of hondis,
A. 7.232   Oþer wiþ teching, *oþer* telling, or trauaillyng of hondis,
A. 7.233   Actif lif *oþer* contemplatif; crist wolde it alse.
A. 7.294   But ȝif it be fressh flessh *oþer* fissh yfried,
A.10.24   Til kynde come *oþer* sende [and] kepe hire hymselue.'
A.10.65   For no werk þat þei werche, wykkide *oþer* wel.
A.10.75   For werche he wel *oþer* wrong, þe wyt is his owene.
A.10.108   Thrift *oþer* þedom with þo is selde yseiȝe:
A.10.113   Ȝif þou be man maried, monk, *oþer* chanoun,
A.10.117   Be paied wiþ þe porcioun, pore *oþer* riche.
A.11.260   For howso I werche in þis world, [wrong] *oþer* ellis,
B. 1.177   For þe same mesur[e] þat ye mete, amys *ouþer* ellis,
B. 3.306   Ax *ouþer* hachet or any wepene ellis,
B. 5.32   [He] bad Bette kutte a bouȝ *ouþer* tweye
B. 5.53   Moore þan gold *ouþer* giftes if ye wol god plese;
B. 5.201   First I lerned to lye a leef *ouþer* tweyne;
B. 6.310   But if it be fressh flessh *ouþer* fissh [y]fryed,
B. 9.108   Oure lord loueþ hem and lent, loude *ouþer* stille,
B.10.271   Which letteþ þee to loke, lasse *ouþer* moore?
B.12.224   How euere beest *ouþer* brid haþ so breme wittes.
B.13.48   And me þat was his [mette *oþer* mete boþe].
B.13.213   And confermen fauntekyns *ooþer* folk ylered
B.13.229   *Ouþer* mantel or moneie amonges lordes Mynstrals.
B.13.297   And most sotil of song *oþer* sleyest of hondes,
B.13.329   Auenge me fele tymes, *oþer* frete myselue wiþInne;
B.14.74   [*Oþer*] plentee makeþ pryde amonges poore and riche.
B.14.120   *Ouþer* here or elliswhere, kynde wolde it neuere.
B.14.330   That euere he hadde lond *ouþer* lordshipe lasse oþer moore.
B.14.330   That euere he hadde lond ouþer lordshipe lasse *oþer* moore.
B.15.432   [Ac] fressh flessh *ouþer* fissh, whan it salt failleþ,
B.16.133   And maken it as muche *ouþer* moore in alle manere poyntes
B.18.12   Wiþouten spores *oþer* spere; spakliche he lokede
B.18.382   There [a] feloun þole sholde deeþ *ooþer* Iuwise
C.Pr.185   A belle to byggen of bras *oþer* of] bryghte syluer
C.Pr.188   Wher he ri[t] *othere* reste or rometh to pleye;
C. 1.173   For þe same mesure þat ȝe meteth, amis *other* elles,
C. 2.50   That loueth here lordshipe, lasse *other* more.
C. 2.84   Then for holynesse *oþer* hendenesse oþer for hey kynde.
C. 2.84   Then for holynesse oþer hendenesse *oþer* for hey kynde.
C. 3.96   Feuer or foul[e] euel *other* fuyr on here houses,
C. 3.110   What maner muster *oþer* marchandise he vsed
C. 3.113   That vsurers *oþer* regraters for eny skynes ȝeftes
C. 3.200   Withoute presentes *oþer* pans he pleseth [wel] fewe.
C. 3.206   Withouten werre *oþer* wo oþer wickede lawe
C. 3.206   Withouten werre oþer wo *oþer* wickede lawe
C. 3.283   And glad for to grype here, gret lord *oþer* pore.'
C. 3.290   To ȝeue men mede, more *oþer* lasse.
C. 3.292   A desert for som doynge, derne *oþer* elles.
C. 3.323   That kyng *oþer* kayser hem gaf, Catel oþer rente.
C. 3.323   That kyng oþer kayser hem gaf, Catel *oþer* rente.
C. 3.458   For alle þat bereth baslard, br[ode] swerd *oþer* launce,
C. 3.459   Ax *oþer* hachet or eny kyne w[e]pne,
C. 3.461   Into sykel or [t]o sythe, to shar *oþer* to coltur:

C. 3.462 Vche man to pley with a plogh, a pikois *oþer* a spade,
C. 3.463 Spynne *oþer* speke of god and spille no tyme.
C. 4.38   For þey wolde do for a dyner *oþer* a d[o]seyne capones
C. 4.39   More then for oure lordes loue *oþer* oure lady, goddes moder.'
C. 4.110 And hatien alle harlotrie to heren *oþer* to mouthen hit;
C. 4.127 Nother ygraue ne vngraue, of gold *oþer* of suluer,
C. 4.130 Prouisour or preest *oþer* penaunt for his synnes.
C. 6.42   And connyngest of my craft, Clerkysh *oþer* other,
C. 6.74   Venged me vele tymes *other* vrete myself withynne
C. 6.209 Furste y lerned to lye a leef *oþer* tweye;
C. 6.220 Til ten ȝerde *other* twelue tolde out threttene.
C. 6.238 Thow wolt be hanged heye þerfore, here *oþer* in helle.
C. 7.37   Sixe sithe *oþer* seuene y forsake hit with othes
C. 9.108 And madden as þe mone sit, more *other* lasse;
C. 9.150 Loef *oþer* half loef other a lompe of chese
C. 9.150 Loef oþer half loef *other* a lompe of chese
C.10.12   Yf they knewe eny contre *oþer* costes aboute
C.10.282 And loke þat loue be more þe cause then lond *oþer* nobles.
C.11.109 Yf thow hit vse *þe* haunte, haue god my treuthe,
C.11.256 And ar Adam *oþer* ysaye oþer eny of the profetes
C.11.256 And ar Adam oþer ysaye *oþer* eny of the profetes
C.11.259 Withoute penaunce *oþer* passioun oþer eny other peyne
C.11.259 Withoute penaunce oþer passioun *oþer* eny other peyne
C.12.156 His fader or his frendes, fre[m]de *oþer* sybbe,
C.13.48   *Oþer* his hatt or his hoed or elles his gloues
C.14.123 And þat is aftur person *other* parsche preest, and parauntur bothe lewede
C.14.146 And as þe lawe lyketh to lyue *oþer* to dye:
C.14.171 And feblest foul of flyh[t is] þat fleeth *oþer* swym[m]eth.
C.15.20   For alle a wisseth and ȝeueth wit þat walketh *oþer* crepeth.
C.15.296 *Other* here or elliswher, elles hit were reuthe;
C.17.73   Me may now likene lettred men to a loscheborw *oþer* worse.
C.17.312 Moises *oþer* Macometh here maystres deuyneth
C.20.10   Withouten spores *oþer* spere; sp[a]keliche he lokede
C.20.384 Or eny manere membre maymeth *oþer* herteth,
C.20.424 Ther a thief tholie sholde deth *oþer* iewyse
C.22.319 Then person *oþer* parsche prest, penytauncer or bischope

oþere adv *other adv.* &> ooþer A 2; B 2; C 2 othere
A. 2.76   Munde þe myllere, & manye mo *oþere*.
A. 4.10   Of mede & of mo *oþere*, what man shal hire wedde,
B. 2.112 [Munde] þe Millere and many mo *oþere*:
B. 4.10   [Of Mede and of mo *oþere*, what man shal hire wedde],
C. 2.116 Munde þe mullere and monye mo *othere*:
C. 4.10   Of mede and of mo *othere* and what man shal here wedde

oþere &> oþergates; oþerewhiles > ouþerwhile; oþerewise > ooþerwise

oþergates adv *othergates adv.* A 1 oþere_gatis;B 1; C 1 oþergatus
A.10.209 Þat *oþere gatis* ben geten for gadelynges ben holden;
B. 9.195 [That] *oþergates* ben geten for gedelynges arn holden,
C.10.294 That *oþergatus* ben gete for gadelynges ben holden

oþerwhile(s > ouþerwhile adv; otherwyse > ooþerwise

oþes n *oth n.* A 5 oþes (3) oþis (2); B 10; C 8 othes
A. 2.64   Glotonye & grete *oþes* I gyue hem togidere;
A. 5.157 Þanne goþ [glotoun in], and grete *oþis* aftir.
A. 5.176 Þere were *oþes* an hep, [whoso it herde];
A. 8.40   Vsure, & auarice, & *oþes* I defende,
A.11.37   Glotonye & grete *oþis*, þise arn games nowadayes.
B. 2.70   That Gile wiþ hise grete *oþes* gaf hem togidere',
B. 2.93   Glotonye he [gyueþ] hem ek and grete *oþes* togidere,
B. 5.306 Thanne goþ Gloton In and grete *oþes* after.
B. 5.327 [There were *oþes* an heep, whoso it herde];
B. 5.424 Sixe siþes or seuene I forsake it wiþ *oþes*.
B.10.51   Glotonye and grete *oþes*, þis[e arn games nowadaies].
B.13.280 Forwhy he bosteþ and braggeþ wiþ manye bolde *oþes*;
B.13.382 That it coste me manye moore; swoor manye *oþes*.
B.13.399 [Yet glotoun wiþ grete *oþes* his [garnement] hadde soiled
B.20.225 And shotten ayein wiþ shot, many a sheef of *oþes*,
C.Pr.36   Wolleth neyther swynke ne swete bote sweren grete *othes*,
C. 2.100 Glotonye a gyueth hem and grete *othes* togederes,
C. 2.153 And thow Iustices enioynen hem thorw I[u]roures *othes*
C. 6.34   Bostyng and braggynge with many bolde *othes*,
C. 6.361 Thenne goth glotoun in and grete *othes* aftur.
C. 6.835 And there were *othes* an heep for on sholde haue þe worse.
C. 7.37   Sixe sithe oþer seuene y forsake hit with *othes*
C.22.225 And shoten aȝeyn[e with] shotte many a shef of *othes*

othur > ooþer; ouȝt > auȝt; oughtest ouȝte(st > owe

ouh exclam *ou interj.* C 1
C.12.18   'Ouh!' quod y tho and myn heued waggede,

ouht > auȝt; ouhte(n > owe; oune > owene; our(e > we; oures > houre

oureselue pron *oureselfe pron.* A 2 oureselue (1) oureseluen (1); B 1; C 2 ouresulue
A. 8.114   And shewiþ it vs be ensaumple *oureselue* to wisse.
A.11.248   And ȝiuen hem of oure good as good as *oureseluen*,
B.13.36   And seten bi *oureselue* at [a] side borde.
C.15.41   And seten by *ouresulue* at a syde table.
C.19.41   Alle manere men as moche as *ouresulue*.

out adv *oute adv.* &> out_of A 9; B 28 out (26) oute (2); C 28 out (25) oute (3)
A. 1.116   For pride þat he put *out* his peyne haþ non ende.
A. 1.170   ȝe ben acumbrid wiþ coueitise, ȝe [conne] not *out* crepe,
A. 1.176   Þat is þe lok of loue þat letiþ *out* my grace
A. 2.193   Ac he haþ leue to lepen *out* as ofte as him likiþ,
A. 4.149   'But I reule þus þi reaum rend *out* my ribbes.
A. 5.128   Til ten ȝardis oþer twelue tollide *out* þrittene.
A. 6.99   And so worst þou dryuen *out* as dew & þe dore closid,
A. 7.176   And doluen drit & dung to ditte *out* hunger.
A.11.190   And seken *out* þe seke & sende hem þat hem nediþ,
B. 1.117   Lopen *out* wiþ Lucifer in loþliche forme
B. 1.121   But fellen *out* in fendes liknesse [ful] nyne dayes togideres
B. 1.124   Whan þise wikkede wenten *out* wonderwise þei fellen,
B. 1.127   For pride þat he putte *out* his peyne hap noon ende.
B. 1.196   [Ye] ben acombred wiþ coueitise; [ye] konne noȝt [*out* crepe],
B. 1.202   [Th]at is þe lok of loue [þat] leteþ *out* my grace
B. 2.234   Ac he haþ leue to lepen *out* as ofte as hym likeþ,
B. 4.186   'But I rule þus youre Reaume rende *out* my guttes–
B. 5.163   Til "þow lixt!" and "þow lixt!" lopen *out* at ones
B. 5.212   Til ten yerdes or twelue tolled *out* þrittene.
B. 5.587   And alle þe walles ben of wit to holden wil *oute*;
B. 5.613   And [so] worstow dryuen *out* as dew and þe dore closed,
B. 6.190   And doluen [drit] and [dung] to [ditte *out*] hunger.
B.12.140   And loue shal lepen *out* after into þ[is] lowe erþe.
B.12.211   That oure lord ne hadde hym liȝtly *out*, so leue I [by] þe þef in heuene.
B.13.129   Whiche Infinites wiþ a feiþ fynden *out* dobest.
B.14.95   Ac satisfaccion sekeþ *out* þe roote, and boþe sleeþ and voideþ,
B.16.108   And souȝte *out* þe sike and [saluede blynde and crokede,
B.17.178   For [þe pawme] haþ power to putte *out* þe ioyntes
B.17.216   The blase þerof yblowe *out*, yet brenneþ þe weke–
B.18.148   For þat is ones in helle *out* comeþ [it] neuere.
B.18.250   And leet *out* Symondes sone[s] to seen hym hange on roode.
B.18.291   And so þow haddest hem *out* and hider at þe laste.'
B.18.313   For we leued þi lesynges [we lopen *out* alle;
B.19.161   Thus cam it *out* þat crist ouercoom, recouerede and lyuede:
B.19.345   Shulle come *out*, Conscience; and youre [caples two],
B.20.191   He buffetted me aboute þe mouþ [and bette *out* my wangteeþ];
B.20.346   As at þe laste þis lymytour, þo my lord was *oute*,
C.Pr.37   Fyndeth *out* foule fantasyes and foles hem maketh
C. 1.110   Lepen *out* in lothly forme for his [luþer] wille
C. 1.191   And ben acombred with coueytise: thei can nouȝt [*out* crepe]
C. 2.244   Ac he hath leue to lep *out* as ofte as hym liketh,
C. 3.345   Folowynge and fyndynge *out* þe fundement of a strenghe,
C. 5.81   And wol til hit be wered *out* [or] oþerwyse ychaunged.
C. 6.189   Sotiled songes and sente *out* olde baudes
C. 6.220   Til ten ȝerde other twelue tolde *out* threttene.
C. 6.222   [And] spak to þe spynnester[e] to spynnen [hit] *oute*.
C. 7.265   So worth thow dryuen *out* as de[w] and þe dore yclosed,
C. 9.147   And when he is rysen rometh *out* and riȝt wel aspyeth
C.14.85   And loue shal lepe *out* aftur into þis lowe erthe
C.14.150   That oure [lord] ne hauede [hym] lihtliche *out*, so leue y [by] þ[e] thef in heuene.
C.18.157   And drof hem *out*, alle þat þer bouhte and solde,
C.19.143   For þe paume hath power to pu[t]te *out* þe ioyntes
C.19.182   The blase be yblowen *out*, ȝut brenneth þe weke–
C.20.151   [For] þat ones is in helle *out* cometh hit neuere.
C.20.259   And lette *out* symondes sones to sen hym honge on rode:
C.20.287   Astarot, hoet *out* and haue out oure knaues,
C.20.287   Astarot, hoet out and haue *out* oure knaues,
C.20.289   Brumstoen boylaunt, brennyng *out* cast hit,
C.20.292   And sheteth *out* shot ynow his sheltrom to blende;
C.20.321   And so haddest hem *out* and hiddere at þe laste.'
C.20.383   And hoso hit *out* a mannes eye or elles his foreteth
C.21.161   Thus cam hit *out* þat Crist ouerkam, rekeuerede and lyuede:
C.21.345   Shal come *oute*, Consience; and ȝoure [caples two],
C.22.191   He boffeted me aboute þe mouthe and beet *out* my wangteeth
C.22.346   And at þe laste this lymytour, tho my lord was *oute*,

out_of prep *oute of prep.* A 9 out_of; B 42; C 57 out_of(44) oute_of (13)
A. 1.25   And drink whanne þe driȝeþ, ac do it nouȝt *out of* resoun
A. 1.113   *Out of* heuene into helle hobelide þei faste,
A. 2.20   *Out of* wrong heo wex to wroþerhele manye.
A. 5.145   And bidde þe rode of bromholm bringe me *out of* dette.'

A.10.124 *Out of* a raggit rote and a rou3 brere
A.10.126 Or as whete *out of* weed waxiþ, out of þe erþe,
A.10.126 Or as whete out of weed waxiþ, *out of* þe erþe,
A.10.127 So dobest *out of* dobet & dowel gynneþ springe
A.11.210 Þat *out of* couent & cloistre coueiten to libben".
B. 1.25 And drynke whan þ[ee] drie[þ], ac do [it] no3t *out of* reson
B. 2.65 Ac Fauel was þe firste þat fette hire *out of* boure
B. 2.85 Wiþ þe Chastilet of cheste and chaterynge *out of* reson,
B. 5.36 Ne for no poustee of pestilence plese hem no3t *out of* reson.
B. 5.229 And bidde þe Roode of Bromholm brynge me *out of* dette.'
B. 5.494 [Th]e li3t þat lepe *out of* þee, Lucifer [it] blent[e]
B. 5.624 Heo haþ holpe a þousand *out of* þe deueles punfolde.
B. 9.114 Maidenes and martires *out of* o man come.
B. 9.122 Wastours and wrecches *out of* wedlok, I trowe,
B.10.25 And þat þei ben lordes of ech a lond þat *out of* lawe libbeþ:
B.10.304 That *out of* couent and cloistre coueiten to libbe.
B.11.140 'Ye? baw for bokes!' quod oon was broken *out of* helle.
B.11.163 Pulte *out of* pyne a paynym of rome.
B.12.172 *Out of* synne and be saaf, þou3 he synne ofte,
B.13.349 And as [lef] in lente as *out of* lente, alle tymes yliche.
B.13.350 Swiche werkes with hem were neuere *out of* seson
B.14.5 It haþ be laued in lente and *out of* lente boþe
B.14.36 'No?' quod Pacience paciently, and *out of* his poke hente
B.14.65 And *out of* þe flynt sprong þe flood þat folk and beestes dronken.
B.14.108 And þat at þe rekenyng in Arrerage fel raþer þan *out of* dette.
B.14.135 And selden deyeþ he *out of* dette þat dyneþ er he deserue it,
B.15.63 [Adam and Eue putte *out of* Paradis]:
B.15.92 As holynesse and honeste *out of* holy chirche [spryngeþ]
B.15.94 Right so *out of* holi chirche alle yueles [spredeþ]
B.16.204 In tokenynge of þe Trinite, was [taken *out of* a man],
B.16.264 *Out of* þe poukes pondfold no maynprise may vs fecche–
B.16.266 That shal deliuere vs som day *out of* þe deueles power
B.17.208 And þanne a fir flawmynge forþ *out of* boþe.
B.18.62 Dede men for þat dene come *out of* depe graues
B.18.113 [Where] *out of* þe west coste a wenche as me þou3te
B.18.118 Euene *out of* þe Est and westward she lokede,
B.18.164 Ne haue hem *out of* helle; hold þi tonge, mercy!
B.18.164 *Out of* þe nyppe of þe North no3t ful fer hennes
B.18.254 [And to haue *out of* helle alle þat hym likeþ].
B.18.257 And conforte al his kyn and *out of* care brynge,
B.18.372 And haue *out of* helle alle mennes soules.
B.19.74 Aungeles *out of* heuene come knelynge and songe,
B.19.284 Ne [sholde] no scornere *out of* skile hym brynge;
B.19.378 Egreliche ernynge *out of* mennes eighen.
B.20.80 Kynde Conscience þo herde and cam *out of* þe planetes
B.20.201 And cryede to kynde: 'out of care me brynge!
B.20.269 It is wikked to wage yow; ye wexen *out of* noumbre.
C. 1.24 And drynke þat doth the good–a[c] drynke nat *out of* tyme.
C. 1.138 By what wey it wexeth and wheder *out of* my menynges.'
C. 2.67 Ac Fauel was þe furste þat fette here *out of* chambre
C. 2.92 With [þe] chastel of cheste and chaterynge *out of* resoun;
C. 2.250 Thy kynedom thorw Coueytise wol *out of* kynde wende,
C. 3.203 Religioun he al toreueth and *oute of* reule to lybbe.
C. 4.163 With mede þe mayde *out of* þe moethalle.
C. 5.151 That *out of* couent and Cloystre coueyteth to dwelle.
C. 5.157 Haen ryde *out of* aray, here reule euele yholde,
C. 6.183 As leef in lente as *out of* lente, alle tymes ylyche,
C. 6.184 Such werkes with vs were neuere *out of* sesoun
C. 6.435 *Out of* resoun among rybaudes here rybaudrye to here.
C. 7.134 The lihte þat lup *oute of* the, lucifer hit blente
C. 8.205 And bade hunger in haste hye hym *out of* contraye
C. 9.216 He þat lolleth is lame or his leg *out of* ioynte
C.10.42 Thow he thorw fondynges falle he falleth nat *out of* charite,
C.10.52 To repenten and arise and rowe *out of* synne
C.10.210 *Out of* matrimonye, nat moyloure, mowen nat haue þe grace
C.10.288 3e þat han wyues ben war and wo[r]cheth nat *out of* tyme
C.11.206 Or p[resci]t inparfit, pult *out of* grace,
C.12.75 '3e? bawe for bokes!' quod oen was broken *out of* helle.
C.12.209 And *out of* wo into wele 3oure wirdes shal chaunge."
C.13.6 And *out of* nombre tho men many mebles hadden.
C.13.154 For *out of* resoun they ryde and rechelesliche t[a]ken on
C.13.176 And how *out of* greeut and of gras gr[e]we so many hewes
C.13.188 In mete *out of* mesure and mony tymes in drynke,
C.13.227 The wisdom and the wit of god he was pot *out of* blisse.
C.14.112 *Out of* synne and be saef, thogh he synege ofte,
C.15.246 '3e!' quod pacience [paciently], and *oute of* his poke hente
C.15.264 And *oute of* þe flynt spronge þe floed þat folk and bestes dronke.
C.16.4 And selde deyeth [he] *oute of* dette [þat] dyne[th] ar he deserue hit,
C.16.225 Potte *out of* paradys Adam and Eue:
C.16.243 As holinesse and honestee *out of* holy churche
C.16.246 Riht [so] *oute of* holy churche al euel spredeth
C.17.158 And lyuen *oute of* lele byleue for they l[e]ue on a mene.
C.17.247 The whiche is þe hy holy gost þat *out of* heuene descendet[h]

C.18.188 O speche and [o] spirit Springeth *out of* alle;
C.18.216 Eue of Adam was and *out of* hym ydrawe
C.18.228 Wh[om] god wolde *oute of* þe wey [d]rawe.
C.18.231 So *oute of* þe syre and of þe sone he seynt spirit of hem bothe
C.18.282 That shal delyuere vs som day *out of* þe deueles power
C.19.302 *Out of* his oune house as holy writ sheweth.
C.20.64 And dede men for þat dene cam *oute of* depe graues
C.20.116 *Out of* þe west as hit were a wenche, as me thouhte,
C.20.121 Euene *oute of* þe eest and westward she thouhte,
C.20.149 Ne haue hem *out of* helle; holde thy tonge, mercy!
C.20.167 *Out of* þe nype of þe north nat ful fer hennes
C.20.263 And to haue *out [of* helle] alle þat hym liketh.
C.20.265 And comforte alle his kyn and *out of* care brynge
C.20.346 And *out of* heuene hidore thy pryde made vs falle.
C.20.414 And haue *out of* helle alle mennes soules.
C.21.74 Angele[s] *out of* heuene come knel[yng] and songe,
C.21.284 Ne sholde no scornare *out of* skille hym brynge
C.21.378 Egrelich ernynge *oute [of]* menne yes.
C.22.80 Kynde Consience tho herde and cam *oute of* the planetes
C.22.201 And cryede to kynde: '*out of* care me brynge!
C.22.269 Hit is wikked to wage 3ow; 3e wexeth *out of* nombre.

outcomen ptp *outcomen v.* B 1
B.17.116 And kennen *outcom[en]* men þat knowen no3t þe contree

oute adj *oute adj. &> out,out_of* B 2; C 2
B.12.144 Ne of lordes þat were lewed men, but of þe hyeste lettred *oute*:
B.12.269 Thus he likneþ in his logik þe leeste fowel *oute*.
C.14.190 Likneth in here logik þe leste foul *out[e]*.
C.20.420 Shal neuere in helle eft come be he ones *oute*:

ouþer > oþer,ooþer,ouþerwhile

ouþerwhile adv *otherwhile adv.* A 3 oþerwhile (2) oþer_while (1); B 9
ouþerwhile (5) ouþer_while (4); C 11 otherwhile (1) other_while (1)
oþerwhile (8) oþer_while (1)
A. 6.37 [I] haue myn here of hym [wel] & *oþerwhile* more;
A. 7.239 For summe of my seruauntis ben seke *oþer while*;
A. 9.21 He is *oþerwhile* elliswhere to wisse þe peple.'
B.Pr.164 And *ouþer while* þei arn elliswhere, as I here telle.
B. 5.178 Ac *ouþer while* whan wyn comeþ, [whan] I drynke at eue,
B. 5.403 Wiþ ydel tales at þe Ale and *ouþerwhile* [in] chirche[s];
B. 8.25 He is *ouþerwhile* elliswhere to wisse þe peple.'
B.12.23 And of holy men I her[e]', quod I, 'how þei *ouþerwhile*
B.15.159 That he ne wolde aske after his, and *ouþerwhile* coueite
B.15.182 And *ouþerwhile* he is woned to wenden on pilgrymages
B.19.103 And som tyme he fau3t faste and flei3 *ouþer while*,
B.19.300 For gile gooþ so pryuely þat good feiþ *ouþer while*
C. 5.50 To be welcome when y come *oþerwhile* in a monthe,
C. 6.160 Ac *other while* when wyn cometh and when y drynke late at euen
C. 7.19 With ydele tales at þe ale and *oþerwhile* in chirches;
C.10.29 He is *otherwhile* elleswher to wisse þe peple.'
C.10.163 A[s] somme hangeth hemsulue and *oþerwhile* adrencheth.
C.16.324 And *oþerwhile* his wone is to w[e]nde [o]n pilgrimages
C.17.3 And 3ut *oþerwhile* wroeth withouten eny synne.'
C.17.9 Excepte þat Egide a hynde *oþerwhile*
C.18.42 And þerwith y warde hit *oþerwhile* til hit waxe rype.
C.21.103 And som tyme he fauht faste and fley *oþerwhile*
C.21.300 For gyle goth so priuely þat goed fayth *oþer while*

ouþerwhiles adv *otherwhiles adv.* B 1; C 3 oþerewhiles (1) oþerwhiles
(2)
B. 5.550 I haue myn hire [of hym] wel and *ouþerwhiles* moore.
C. 7.194 Y haue myn huyre of hym wel and *oþerwhiles* more.
C.16.293 That he ne askede aftur his and *oþerewhiles* coueytede
C.16.367 Ac auaris *oþerwhiles* halt hym withoute þe gate.

outlawe n *outlaue n.* B 1
B.17.105 For [an] *Outlaw[e* is] in þe wode and vnder bank lotieþ,

outryderes n *outridere n.* C 1
C. 4.116 And religious *outryderes* be recluses in here Cloistres

outtake prep *outtaken prep.* A 1
A.10.175 *Outtake* þe ei3te soulis, & of iche beste a couple

outward adv *outwarde adv.* C 1
C. 9.85 Bothe afyngred and afurste, to turne þe fayre *outward*

outwit n *outwit n.* B 1
B.13.288 Wiþ Inwit and wiþ *outwit* ymagynen and studie

ouer adv *over adv.* A 1; B 6; C 5
A. 7.242 Þei han mangid *ouer* muche, þat makiþ hem grone ofte.
B. 5.184 And drynk nat *ouer* delically, ne to depe neiþer,
B. 5.374 *Ouer* delically on [feeste] dayes dronken and eten boþe,
B. 6.258 Ye han manged *ouer* muche; þat makeþ yow grone.

B.13.43   Ac hir sauce was *ouer* sour and vnsauourly grounde
B.13.133 'Thanne passe we *ouer* til Piers come and preue þis in dede.
B.20.27   And bete men *ouer* bittre, and so[m body] to litel,
C. 3.299   Y halde hym *ouer* hardy or elles nat trewe
C. 6.166   And drynke nat *ouer* delycatly n[e] to depe neyther
C. 8.270   3e han manged *ouer* moche; þat maketh 3ow to be syke.
C.15.48   Ac here sauce was *ouer*sour and vnsauerly ygrounde
C.22.27   And bete men *ouer* bitere and som body to litel

ouer prep *over prep. &> oueral* A 9; B 17; C 30
A. 1.106   And *ouer* his meyne made hem archaungelis;
A. 4.112   Bere no siluer *ouer* se þat signe of king shewi[þ],
A. 5.249   And lepe with hym *ouer* lond al his lif tyme,
A. 6.2   But blustrid forþ as bestis *ouer* [baches] & hilles
A. 6.120   'Mercy [is] a maiden [þere], haþ mi3t *ouer* [hem] alle;
A.10.63   *Ouer* suche maner of men mi3t in here soulis.
A.10.72   Is chief souereyn *ouer* hymself his soule to 3eme,
A.11.198 Prince *ouer* godis peple to prechen or to chaste.
A.11.203 Ne no leperis *ouer* lond ladies to shryue.
B. 1.108   And *ouer* his meynee made hem Archangeles;
B. 3.298   And *ouer* lordes lawes [ledeþ] þe Reaumes.
B. 4.129   Bere no siluer *ouer* see þat signe of kyng sheweþ,
B. 5.475   And lepe wiþ hym *ouer* lond al his lif tyme,
B. 5.514   But blustreden forþ as beestes *ouer* [baches] and hilles
B. 5.635   'Mercy is a maiden þere haþ my3t *ouer* [hem] alle;
B.13.391 And if I sente *ouer* see my seruaunt3 to Brugges,
B.14.331 Or maistrie *ouer* any man mo þan of hymselue.
B.19.139 Ne *ouer* Iewes Iustice, as Iesus was, hem þou3te.
B.19.222 Shullen come and be curatours *ouer* kynges and Erles;
B.19.443 And cleymeþ bifore þe kyng to be kepere *ouer* cristene,
B.20.64   And a fals fend Antecrist *ouer* alle folk regnede.
B.20.73   *Ouer* kynde cristene and Cardynale vertues.
B.20.183 And Elde after [hym]; and *ouer* myn heed yede
B.20.185 So harde he yede *ouer* myn heed it wole be sene euere.
B.20.187 Siþ whanne was þe wey *ouer* mennes heddes?
B.20.320 Saue Piers þe Plowman þat haþ power *ouer* alle
C. 3.257   'Ne be Marschal *ouer* my men there y moste fyhte.
C. 3.308   The huyre of his hewe *ouer* eue til amorwe:
C. 4.126   Bere no seluer *ouer* see þat sygne of kyng sheweth,
C. 4.155   That mekenesse worth maystre *ouer* mede at þe laste.'
C. 5.193   Amonges alle kyne kynges *ouer* cristene peple.
C. 6.138   Til "thow lixt!" and "thow lixt!" be lady *ouer* hem alle;
C. 6.278   And yf y sente *ouer* see my seruauntes to Bruges
C. 6.329   [And lepe wiþ hym *ouer* lond al his lif tyme]
C. 7.159   But blostrede forth as bestes *ouer* baches and hulles
C. 7.196   He withhalt non hewe his huyre *ouer* euen;
C. 7.271   And aren porteres *ouer* þe posternes þat to þ[e] place bilongen.
C. 7.288   'Mercy is a mayden there hath myhte *ouer* hem alle
C. 8.250   And ledares for here laboryng *ouer* al þe lordes godes;
C. 9.159   'Forthy lollares þat lyuen in sleuthe and *ouer* land strikares
C.11.94   And *ouer* skripture þe skilfole and screueynes were trewe
C.13.46   Ac if þe marchaunt make his way *ouer* menne corne
C.16.125 Ne to be mair *ouer* men ne mynistre vnder kynges;
C.17.148 And þat is charite, leue chield, to be cher *ouer* thy soule;
C.17.170 Be maistre *ouer* alle tho men and on this manere a wrouhte:
C.17.242 Bote thorw pacience and priue gyle he was prince *ouer* hem all.
C.19.39   The which alle men aren holde *ouer* al thyng to honoure
C.21.139 Ne *ouer* Iewes Iustice as iesus was, hem thouhte.
C.21.222 Shal come and be curatours *ouer* kynges and Erles;
C.21.443 And claymeth bifore þe kynge to be kepare *ouer* cristene
C.22.64   And a fals fende auntecrist *ouer* all folke regnede.
C.22.73   *Ouer* kynde cristene and cardinale vertues.
C.22.183 And Elde aftur hym; and *ouer* myn heued 3ede
C.22.185 So harde he 3ede *ouer* myn heued hit wol be sene euere.
C.22.187 Sennes whanne was þe way *ouer* menne heuedes?
C.22.320 Saue [Peres the Plouhman] þat haeth power *ouer* alle

oueral adv *overal adv.* A 2; B 3 ouer_al; C 1
A. 2.180   *Oueral* yhuntid & yhote trusse,
A.10.44   Þat is Anima, þat *oueral* in þe body wandriþ,
B. 2.221   *Ouer al* yhonted and yhote trusse,
B. 9.56   *Ouer al* in mannes body he[o] walkeþ and wandreþ,
B.13.290 And entremetten hym *ouer al* þer he haþ no3t to doone;
C. 2.231   *Oueral* yhonted and yhote trusse,

ouercam > ouercomen

ouercarke v *overcarken v.* B 1; C 1 ouerkarke
B. 3.316   *Ouer[carke]* þe commune ne to þe Court sompne,
C. 3.469   *Ouerkarke* þe commune ne to þe Court sompne

ouercomen v *overcomen v.* A 1 ouercome; B 6 ouercam (1) ouercom (1)
   ouercome (1) ouercomen (2) ouercoom (1); C 9 ouercam (1) ouercome
   (7) ouerkam (1)
A. 4.69   To *ouercome* þe king wiþ catel 3if þei mi3te.

B. 4.82   To *ouercomen* þe kyng wiþ catel if þei my3te.
B.10.455 And my3te no kyng *ouercomen* hym as by konnynge of speche.
B.13.11   And how þis Coueitise *ouercom* clerkes and preestes;
B.15.541 Than cristes cros þat *ouercam* deeþ and dedly synne.
B.19.161 Thus cam it out þat crist *ouercoom*, recouerede and lyuede:
B.20.122 *Ouercome* Conscience and Cardinale vertues;
C. 3.431   Thus was kyng sauel *ouercome* thorw coueytise of mede,
C. 4.78   To *ouercome* þe kyng [with] catel y[f] they myhte.
C.11.280 And myhte no kyng *ouercome* hym as in connynge of speche.
C.15.13   And how þis coueytyse *ouercome* al kyne sectes,
C.17.203 Thenne cristes cros þat *ouercome* deth and dedly synne.
C.17.289 To be culd and *ouercome* the comune to defende,
C.20.112 When Crist thorw croos *ouercam* 3oure kyndoem sholde tocleue:
C.21.161 Thus cam hit out þat Crist *ouerkam*, rekeuerede and lyuede:
C.22.122 *Ouercome* Consience and cardinal vertues

ouerdoen v *overdon v.* C 1
C.13.190 They *ouerdoen* hit day and nyhte and so doth nat oþer bestes;

ouergilte ptp *overgilden v.* B 1
B.15.124 A baselard or a ballokknyf wiþ botons *ouergilte*,

ouerhippe > ouerhuppen

ouerhoueþ v *overhoven v.* A 1 ouerhouiþ; B 2; C 1 ouerhoueth
A. 3.195   Þat is þe riccheste reaume þat re[yn] *ouer[houiþ]*.
B. 3.208   That is þe richeste Reaume þat reyn *ouerhoueþ*.
B.18.171 That *ouerhoueþ* helle þus; she vs shal telle.'
C.20.174 That *ouerhoueth* helle thus; he vs shal telle.'

ouerhuppen v *overhippen v.* B 3 ouerhuppe (1) ouerhuppen (2); C 1
   ouerhippe
B.13.68   Ac o word þei *ouerhuppen* at ech tyme þat þei preche
B.15.386 Lest þei *ouerhuppen* as ooþere doon in office and in houres.
B.15.387 [Ac] if þei *ouerhuppe*, as I hope no3t, oure bileue suffiseþ,
C.17.118 That they *ouerhippe* nat for hastite, as y hope they do nat,

ouerkam > ouercomen; ouerkarke > ouercarke; ouerleep > ouerlepe

ouerleyd ptp *overleien v.* C 1
C.12.231 Lo! lond *ouerleyd* with marl and with donge,

ouerlepe v *overlepen v.* B 2 ouerleep (1) ouerlepe (1); C 2 ouerleep (1)
   ouerlep (1)
B.Pr.150   And *ouerleep* hem li3tliche and lau3te hem at wille
B.Pr.200   Nere þe cat of þ[e] court þat kan yow *ouerlepe*;
C.Pr.171   And *ouerlep* hem lightliche and laghte hem at wille
C.20.357   (A litel y *ouerleep* for lesynges sake,

ouerlonge adj *overlonge adj.* B 2; C 2 ouerlong (1) ouerlonge (1)
B.11.222 For it is *ouerlonge* er logyk any lesson assoille,
B.20.362 'That is *ouerlonge*', quod þis Lymytour, 'I leue. I shal amende it!'
C.16.365 For *ouerlong* is here lawe but yf þay lacche suluer.
C.22.362 'That is *ouerlonge*,' quod this lymitour, 'y leue; y schal amenden
   hit!'

ouerlonge adv *overlonge adv.* B 2; C 1
B.15.240 For hir lawe dureþ *ouerlonge* but if þei lacchen siluer,
B.20.360 [And] lat hem ligge *ouerlonge* and looþ is to chaunge;
C.22.360 And lat hem lygge *ouerlonge* and loeth is to chaungen;

ouermaistreþ v *overmaistren v.* B 1
B. 4.176   Mede *ouermaistreþ* lawe and muche truþe letteþ.

ouermore adv *overmore adv.* C 1
C. 9.157   And *ouermore* to [a]n [ha]tur to hele with his bonis

ouerplente n *overplente n.* C 1
C.12.234 *Ouerplente* pruyde norischeth þer pouerte hit distrueth.

ouerreche v *overrechen v.* B 1; C 1
B.13.373 And if I r[o]þe *ouerreche*, or yaf hem reed þat ropen
C. 6.270   And [yf] y raap *ouerreche* or 3af hem red þat repe

ouersen v *oversen v.* A 1; B 3 ouerse (1) ouerseyen (1) ouersen (1); C 2
   ouerse (1) ouersey (1)
A. 7.105   To *ouersen* hem hymself; whoso best wrou3te
B. 5.371   And *ouerseyen* me at my soper and som tyme at Nones
B. 6.113   To *ouersen* hem hymself; whoso best wro3te
B.10.333 That þis worþ sooþ, seke ye þat ofte *ouerse* þe bible:
C. 8.120   [To] *ouersey* hem hymsulue; hoso beste wrouhte
C.11.113 Sey [to] hym thysulue *ouerse* m[y] bokes

ouerskipped ptp *overskippen v.* B 1; C 1
B.11.305 Or peynted parentrelynarie, parcelles *ouerskipped*.
C.13.119 Or peynted parentrelynarie, parseles *ouerskipped*.

ouerskipperis n *overskipper n* B 1; C 1 ouerskipperes
B.11.310 And also in þe Sauter seiþ Dauid to *ouerskipperis*,
C.13.123 [To] *ouerskipperes* also in þe sauter sayth dauid:

ouersopped v *oversopen v.* C 1
C. 6.429   And *ouersopped* at my soper and som tyme at nones

ouersour > ouer,sour

ouerspradde v *overspreden v.* B 1; C 1
B.19.206   Spiritus paraclitus *ouerspradde* hem alle.
C.21.206   Spiritus paraclitus *ouerspradde* hem alle.

ouertaken v *overtaken v.* B 2
B.12.244   For þe trailynge of his tail *ouertaken* is he soone.
B.17.85   To *ouertaken* hym and talke to hym er þei to towne coome.

ouerþrowe v *overthrouen v.* A 1; B 1; C 1 ouerthrowe
A. 9.31   Þe wynd wolde wiþ þe watir þe boot *ouerþrowe*.
B. 8.35   The wynd wolde wiþ þe water þe boot *ouerþrowe*.
C.18.159   And when þat my will is y wol hit *ouerthrowe*

ouertilte v *overtilten v.* B 2; C 2 ouertulde
B.20.54   Torned it [tid] vp so doun and *ouertilte* þe roote,
B.20.135   And *ouertilte* al his truþe wiþ 'tak þis vp amendement'.
C.22.54   Turned hit tyd vp so down and *ouertulde* þe rote
C.22.135   And *ouertulde* al his treuthe with 'taek this [vp] amendement.'

ouertorne v *overturnen v.* B 2 ouertorne (1) ouerturne (1); C 2 ouerturne
(1) ouerturnede (1)
B.15.547   Shul [*ouer]torne* as templers dide; þe tyme approcheþ faste.
B.16.131   'I shal *ouerturne* þis temple and adoun þrowe,
C.17.209   Sholle *ouerturne* as templers dede; þe tyme approcheth faste.
C.18.156   And *ouerturnede* in þe temple here tables and here stalles

ouertulde > ouertilte; ouerturne(de > ouertorne

ouerturnynge ger *overturninge ger.* C 1
C.18.162   Ac þe *ouerturnynge* of the temple bitokened his resureccioun.

ouerward adv *overward adv.* C 1
C. 4.128   Vp forfeture of þat fee, ho fyndeth h[y]m *ouerward*,

owe v *ouen v.* A 6 auȝte (3) auȝtest (1) owe (1) owyng (1); B 12 auȝte (1)
ouȝte (7) ouȝtest (1) owe (1) owen (1) owynge (1); C 12 oughtest (1)
ouhte (9) ouhten (1) owen (1)
A. 1.73   'Holy chirche I am,' quaþ heo, 'þou *auȝtest* me to knowe;
A. 2.21   I *auȝte* ben hiȝere þanne heo for I com of a betere.
A. 5.71   I miȝte not many day do as a man [*auȝte*,
A. 5.242   Ne neuere wen[e] to wynne wiþ craft þat [I *owe*],
A. 7.123   And I am his [h]olde hyne & *auȝte* hym to warne
A.10.69   Þanne is holichirche *owyng* to helpe hem & saue
B. 1.75   'Holi chirche I am', quod she; 'þow *ouȝtest* me to knowe.
B. 2.28   I *ouȝte* ben hyere þan she; I kam of a bettre.
B. 3.68   And þi cost and þi coueitise and who þe catel *ouȝte*.
B. 5.121   I myȝte noȝt ete many yeres as a man *ouȝte*
B. 6.131   And I am his [h]olde hyne and [*auȝte*] hym to warne
B. 9.69   [Holy chirche is *owynge* to helpe hem and saue,
B.11.158   Wel *ouȝte* ye lordes þat lawes kepe þis lesson haue in mynde
B.11.301   He [*ouȝte* no] bileue, as I leue, to lacche þoruȝ his croune
B.17.340   Ben siknesse and sorwes þat we suffren *o[uȝ]te*,
B.19.392   Al þat we *owen* any wight er we go to housel?'
B.20.276   That alle þynges vnder heuene *ouȝte* to ben in comune.
C. 1.72   'Holy churche y am,' quod she; 'þou *oughtest* me to knowe;
C. 2.30   Y *ouhte* ben herrore then he; y com of a bettere.
C. 3.72   Thi cost and here couetyse] and ho þe catel *ouhte*.
C. 3.108   Forthy mayres þat maketh fre men, me thynketh þat ȝe *ouhten*
C. 5.64   Redon and resceyuen þat resoun *ouhte* to spene\
C. 6.86   Y myhte nat ete many ȝer as a man *ouhte*
C. 7.98   Muche more, me thynketh, riche men *ouhte*
C. 9.230   To heren here euensong euery man *ouhte*.
C.12.90   Wel *ouhte* ȝe lordes þat lawes kepeth this lesson haue in mynde
C.19.320   Been seekness[e] and oþere sorwes þat we soffren *ouhte*,
C.21.392   Al þat we *owen* eny wyhte or we go to hosele?'
C.22.276   That alle thynges vnder heuene *ou[h]te* to be in comune.

owen > owe,owene

owene adj *ouen adj.* A 8 owene (7) owne (1); B 21; C 23 oune (8) owen
(1) owene (9) owne (5)
A. 3.26   And bidden hire be blyþe, 'for we ben þin *owene*
A. 5.132   Þanne [myn *owne*] aunsel dede, [whanne] I weiȝede treweþe.
A. 6.62   Loke þou breke no bowis þere but it be þin *owene*.
A. 7.75   'For [now] I am old & hor & haue of myn *owene*
A. 7.187   Hom into his *owene* er[d]e & holde him þere euere.
A. 9.74   Trusty of his tailende, takiþ but his *owene*,
A. 9.78   Whiles he haþ ouȝt of his *owene* he helpiþ þere nede is;
A.10.75   For werche he wel oþer wrong, þe wyt is his *owene*.
B.Pr.122   Shopen lawe and leaute, ech [lif] to knowe his *owene*.
B.Pr.208   Forþi ech a wis wiȝt I warne, wite wel his *owene*.'
B. 3.27   And beden hire be bliþe: 'for we beþ þyne *owene*

B. 5.216   Than myn *owene* Auncer [whan I] weyed truþe.
B. 5.575   Loke [þow] breke no bowes þere but if it be [þyn] *owene*.
B. 6.83   'For now I am old and hoor and haue of myn *owene*
B. 6.200   Hoom [in]to his *owene* [e]rd and holden hym þere [euere].
B. 8.83   Trusty of his tailende, takeþ but his *owene*,
B. 8.87   [Whiles he haþ ouȝt of his *owene* he helpeþ þer nede is];
B.10.96   Homliche at oþere mennes houses and hatien hir *owene*.
B.10.270   Siþen a beem [is] in þyn *owene* ablyndeþ þiselue–
B.10.371   And seiþ "slee noȝt þat semblable is to myn *owene* liknesse
B.10.416   That ben Carpenters holy kirk to make for cristes *owene* beestes:
B.11.169   God wrouȝte it and wroot it wiþ his [*owene*] fynger,
B.14.300   A collateral confort, cristes *owene* ȝifte:
B.15.534   How þei defouled hir flessh, forsoke hir *owene* wille,
B.16.192   Might and [a] mene [his *owene* myȝte to knowe],
B.17.275   The grace of þe holy goost, goddes *owene* kynde.
B.17.322   For to fleen his *owene* [hous] as holy writ sheweþ
B.20.20   So nede at gret nede may nymen as for his *owene*
B.20.92   'Alarme! alarme!' quod þat lord, 'ech lif kepe his *owene*!'
C.Pr.124   For ȝoure shrewed soffraunce and ȝoure *oune* synne.
C. 3.28   And beden here be blythe: 'for we beth thyn *owene*
C. 3.210   That no lond ne loueth the and ȝut leeste thyn *owene*.
C. 6.224   Then myn [*owene*] auncer when y wayed treuthe.
C. 7.222   Loke þou bere n[ouht] þere away but yf hit be thyn *owene*.
C. 8.92   'For now y am olde and hoer and haue of myn *owene*
C. 8.206   Hoem [in]to his *owene* [e]rd and halde hym þere euere.
C.10.80   And therto trewe of his tayl, [taketh but his *owne*]
C.10.176   For þat is goddes *oune* goed, his grace and his tresour,
C.12.98   And cristis *oune* clergie; he cam fro heuene to teche hit
C.14.175   And haue hem [in] haste at þyn *owen* wille
C.16.136   A collateral confort, cristes *oune* sonde:
C.17.82   And for þe synne of þe soule forsaketh his *oune* coyne.
C.17.195   How they deffoule[d] here flesche, forsoke here *owne* wille,
C.18.14   The whiche is Caritas ykald, Cristes *oune* fode,
C.18.76   Wedewes and wedewares þat here *own[e]* wil forsaken
C.18.165   Of Ieudas þe iew, iesus *oune* disciple.
C.18.201   Miȝte and a mene to se his *owne* myhte,
C.19.256   The grace of þe holy goest, godes *owne* kynde.
C.19.291   Thus hit fareth bi such folk þat folewen here *owene* will,
C.19.302   Out of his *oune* house as holy writ sheweth.
C.22.20   So nede at greet nede may nyme as for his *owne*
C.22.92   'Alarme! alarme!' quod þat lord, 'vch lyf kepe his *owene*!'

oxe n *oxe n.* B 3 oxe (1) oxen (2); C 2 oxen (1) oxes (1)
B.15.467   For as þe Cow þoruȝ kynde mylk þe calf norisseþ til an *Oxe*,
B.19.262   Grace gaf Piers a teeme, foure grete *Oxen*.
B.19.268   Al þat hise *oxen* eriede þei to harewen after.
C.21.262   Grace gaf [Peres] a teme, foure grete *oxen*.
C.21.268   All þat his *oxes* erede they t[o] harwe[n] aftur.

oȝias n prop *n.i.d.* B 2
B.15.574   Ac ysaie of yow spekeþ and *oȝias* boþe,
B.15.577   *Oȝias* seiþ for swiche þat sike ben and feble,

P

paas n *pase n.(1)* B 1; C 1 pase
B.14.304 The sixte is a path of pees; ye! þoruӡ þe *paas* of Aultoun
C.16.139 The sixte is a path of pees; ӡe! thorwe þe *pase* of Aultoun

paast n *paste .(1)* B 2
B.13.250 And þanne wolde I be prest to þe peple *paast* for to make,
B.14.29 'And I shal purueie þee *paast*', quod Pacience, 'þouӡ no plouӡ erye,

pacience n *pacience n.* A 2; B 52; C 47
A. 6.108 *Pacience* & pees mekil [peple] þei helpen,
A.11.230 Ac pore men in *pacience* & penaunce togidere
B. 5.622 *Pacience* and pees muche peple þei helpeþ;
B.10.346 And preiseden pouerte with *pacience*; þe Apostles bereþ witnesse
B.11.257 Preise[n] pouerte for best lif if *Pacience* it folw[e],
B.11.319 The which I preise, þer *pacience* is, moore parfit þan richesse.
B.12.61 *Pacience* and pouerte þe place [is] þer it groweþ,
B.13.29 A[c] *Pacience* in þe Paleis stood in pilgrymes cloþes
B.13.34 And þanne clergie and Conscience and *Pacience* cam after.
B.13.35 *Pacience* and I [prestly] were put to be [mettes],
B.13.47 Bifore *Pacience* breed to brynge, [bitynge apart],
B.13.52 'Here is propre seruice', quod *Pacience*, 'þer fareþ no Prince bettre.'
B.13.56 'Bryng *Pacience* som pitaunce pryueliche', quod Conscience,
B.13.57 And þanne hadde *Pacience* a pitaunce, Pro hac orabit ad te omnis
B.13.59 *Pacience* was proud of þat propre seruice
B.13.64 Thanne seide I to myself so *pacience* it herde,
B.13.86 *Pacience* parceyued what I þouӡte and [preynte] on me to be stille
B.13.99 And I sat stille as *Pacience* seide, and þus soone þis doctour,
B.13.113 And preynte vpon *pacience* to preie me be stille,
B.13.134 *Pacience* haþ be in many place, and paraunter [knoweþ]
B.13.136 'A[t] youre preiere', quod *Pacience* þo, 'so no man displese hym:
B.13.178 That *Pacience* þ[o] most passe, 'for pilgrymes konne wel lye'.
B.13.182 And be Pilgrym wiþ *pacience* til I haue preued moore.'
B.13.187 That *Pacience* þe pilgrym parfitly knew neuere.'
B.13.189 For al þat *Pacience* me profreþ proud am I litel.
B.13.201 Haue *pacience* parfitliche þan half þi pak of bokes.'
B.13.206 If *Pacience* be oure partyng felawe and pryue with vs boþe
B.13.214 Til *Pacience* haue preued þee and parfit þee maked.'
B.13.215 Conscience þo wiþ *Pacience* passed, pilgrymes as it were.
B.13.216 Thanne hadde *Pacience*, as pilgrymes han, in his poke vitailles:
B.13.222 *Pacience* apposed hym and preyde he sholde telle
B.13.354 Thanne *Pacience* parceyued of pointes [his] cote
B.14.10 To penaunce *pacience* and pouere men to fede,
B.14.29 'And I shal purueie þee *paast*', quod *Pacience*, 'þouӡ no plouӡ erye,
B.14.36 'No?' quod *Pacience* paciently, and out of his poke hente
B.14.48 [Th]at *pacience* so preisede, [and of his poke hente]
B.14.51 'Haue, haukyn', quod *Pacience*, 'and et þis whan þe hungreþ
B.14.100 'Ther parfit truþe and poore herte is, and *pacience* of tonge,
B.14.104 'Ye? quis est ille?' quod *Pacience*; 'quik, laudabimus eum!
B.14.193 And of pure *pacience* and parfit bileue.
B.14.215 For his pouerte and *pacience* a perpetuel blisse.
B.14.218 Ac in pouerte þer *pacience* is pride haþ no myӡte,
B.14.220 Ne haue power in pouerte, if *pacience* [it] folwe.
B.14.275 What is Pouerte, *pacience*', quod he, 'properly to mene?'
B.14.276 'Paupertas,' quod *Pacience*, 'est odibile bonum, Remocio curarum,
B.14.278 '[Al þis] in englissh', quod *Pacience*, 'it is wel hard to expounen,
B.14.317 For *pacience* is payn for pouerte hymselue,
B.15.598 And þoruӡ his *pacience* hir power to pure noӡt he brouӡte:
B.16.8 *Pacience* hatte þe pure tree and [pouere] symple of herte,
B.18.168 Where pees comeþ pleyinge in *pacience* ycloþed.
B.18.172 Whan Pees in *Pacience* ycloþed approched ner hem tweyne
B.18.415 And Pees þoruӡ *pacience* alle perils stoppeþ.'
B.19.249 In pouerte and in [*pacience*] to preie for alle cristene.
B.19.295 And pleieþ al wiþ *pacience* and Parce michi domine;
C. 2.204 And prykede forth on *pacience* and passed hem alle
C. 7.274 *Pacience* and pees muche peple þei helpe,
C.12.143 Preise[n] pouerte for beste [lif] if *pacience* hit folowe
C.12.196 And for here *pacience* be ypresed as for puyr martir
C.13.2 Among Pilours in pees yf *pacience* hym folowe.
C.13.21 Lo, how *pacience* and pouerte thise patriarkes releuede
C.14.16 That pees be and *pacience* and pore withoute defaute:
C.15.32 [*Pacience* as a pore thyng cam] and preeyede mete pur charite;
C.15.40 *Pacience* and y [prestly weren] pot to be mettes

C.15.53 And bringe breed for *pacience*, bytyng apartye,
C.15.58 'This is a semely seruyce,' saide *pacience*.
C.15.63 *Pacience* was wel apayed of this propre seruice
C.15.68 Thenne saide y to mysulue so *pacience* hit herde,
C.15.93 And why a lyueth nat as a lereth.' 'lat be,' quod *pacience*,
C.15.106 Y sae[t] stille as *pacience* wolde and thus sone this doctour,
C.15.120 And preynte vppon *pacience* to preie me be stille,
C.15.152 [And] *pacience* properliche spak, tho Peres was thus ypassed,
C.15.159 Tene þe eny tyme and þou take *pacience*
C.15.179 Haue *pacience* parfitlyche then half thy pak of bokes.
C.15.181 That they knoweth nat,' quod Concience, 'what is kynde *pacience*.
C.15.183 With *pacience* wol y passe parfitnesse to fynde.'
C.15.185 Thenne hadde *pacience*, as pilgrimes haen, in h[is] poke vitayles,
C.15.191 *Pacience* apposede hym and preyede a sholde telle
C.15.232 'Pees!' quod *pacience*, 'y preye ӡow, sire actyf,
C.15.246 'ӡe!' quod *pacience* [paciently], and oute of his poke hente
C.15.250 'Haue, Actyf,' quod *pacience*, 'and eet this when þe hungreth
C.15.272 'What is [properly] parfit *pacience*?' quod Actiua vita.
C.15.277 'Where pouerte and *pacience* plese more god almyhty
C.15.279 'ӡe? quis est ille?' quod *pacience*; 'quik, lauda[bi]mus eum!
C.16.56 For his pouerte and *pacience* perpetuel ioye,
C.16.59 Ac in pouerte þer *pacience* is pruyde hath no myhte,
C.16.61 Ne haue power in pouerte yf *pacience* h[it] folewe.
C.16.115 'What is pouerte, *pacience*?' quod he; 'y preye þat thow telle hit.'
C.16.116 'Paupertas,' quod *pacience*, 'est odibile bonum, Remocio curarum,
C.16.118 'Parfay!' quod *pacience*, 'propreliche to telle [this]
C.16.151 For *pacience* is his paniter and pouerte payn here fyndeth
C.16.154 That puyre pouerte and *pacience* was a louh lyuynge on erthe,
C.16.163 And preyde *pacience* þat y apose hym moste,
C.17.236 His preyeres with his *pacience* to pees sholde brynge
C.17.242 Bote thorw *pacience* and priue gyle he was prince ouer hem all.
C.17.306 And her power thorw his *pacience* to puyr nauht brouhte.
C.19.91 And ӡut [b]e plasterud with *pacience* when fondynges [priketh hym]–
C.20.171 Where cometh pees pleiynge in *pacience* yclothed.
C.20.175 Whenne pees in *pacience* yclothed aproched her ayþer oþer
C.20.458 And pees thorw *pacience* alle perelles stop[peth}.'
C.21.249 In pouerte and in *pacience* to preye for alle cristene;
C.21.295 And ple[ieþ] al with *pacience* and parce michi domine

pacient adj *paciente adj.* B 6 pacient (5) paciente (1); C 9
B.11.242 And [*pacient* as pilgrymes] for pilgrymes are we alle.
B.14.102 'Wheiþer *paciente* pouerte', quod Haukyn, 'be moore plesaunt to oure d[riӡte]
B.14.260 Forþi [al] poore þat *pacient* is [of pure riӡt] may cleymen,
B.14.272 And put hym to be *pacient* and pouerte weddeþ,
B.14.285 And loye to *pacient* pouere], pure spiritual helþe,
B.15.201 For þer are [pure] proude herted men, *pacient* of tonge
C. 9.179 And alle pore *pacient* apayed of goddes sonde,
C.12.131 And *pacient* as pilgrimes for pilgrimes are we alle.
C.12.177 Preueth *pacient* pouerte prince of alle vertues.
C.13.31 A[c] þe pore *pacient* purgatorye passeth
C.13.99 So pore and *pacient* parfitest lyf is of alle.
C.15.276 And þat is pore *pacient* alle perelles to soffre.'
C.15.283 Then eny pore *pacient*; and þat preue y be resoun.
C.16.100 Forthy alle pore þat *pacient* is of puyr rihte may claymen
C.16.112 And potte hym to be *pacient* and pouerte weddeth,

paciently adv *pacientli adv.* B 2; C 8 paciently (2) pacientliche (4) pacientlyche (2)
B.11.263 So after pouerte or penaunce *paciently* ytake:
B.14.36 'No?' quod Pacience *paciently*, and out of his poke hente
C. 6.14 '[I], pr[uyde], *pacientlyche* penaunce aske.
C.11.260 Passe[d] forth *paciently* to perpetuel blisse.
C.12.149 So aftur [pouerte or penaunce] *pacientliche* ytake:
C.12.201 So preueth this profetes þat *pacientliche* soffren.
C.15.246 'ӡe!' quod pacience [*paciently*], and oute of his poke hente
C.16.328 That pouerte and penaunce *pacientlyche* ytake
C.17.284 And *pacientliche* thorw his prouynce and to his peple hym shewe,
C.19.105 And moest inparfyt of alle persones; and *pacientliche* soffre

pay > paye,paien; paide > paien

504

paye n *paie n. &> paien* A 1 pay; B 3 paie (1) paye (2); C 7 pay (2)
  paie (1) paye (4)
A. 6.36   For, þeiȝ I sey it myself, I serue hym to *pay.*
B. 5.549   For þouȝ I seye it myself I serue hym to *paye;*
B.11.349   Ther nys wriȝte, as I wene, sholde werche hir nes[t] to *paye;*
B.14.254   And þouȝ Sleuþe suwe pouerte, and serue noȝt god to *paie,*
C. 3.300   That pre manibus is paied or his *pay* asketh.
C. 3.349   In his *pay* and in his pite and in his puyr treuthe,
C. 7.190   And yserued treuthe sothly, somdel to *paye.*
C. 7.193   And thow y sey hit mysulf y serue hym to *paye;*
C. 9.279   Purgatorie for thy *paie* O[r] perpetuel helle
C.13.160   Ther is no wriht, as y wene, sholde worch here neste to *paye;*
C.16.94   And thow sleuthe sewe pouerte and serue nat god to *paye*

paiement n *paiement n.* B 1; C 1 payement
B.20.364   Of 'a pryuee *paiement* and I shal praye for yow
C.22.364   Of 'a pryue *payement* and y shal preye for ȝow

paien v *paien v.* A 8 paye (2) paied (2) payed (1) payede (2) paieþ (1); B
  24 paide (2) paie (7) paye (1) paied (5) payed (2) paien (1) paieþ (4)
  ypaied (1) ypayed (1); C 33 pay (4) paied (1) paieth (3) payde (1)
  paye (6) payed (6) payede (4) payen (1) payeth (3) payth (1) ypaied (1)
  ypayd (1) ypayed (1)
A. 3.126   And letiþ passe prisoners & *paieþ* for hem ofte,
A. 4.61   For of hise penys he proffride handy dandy to *paye.*
A. 5.131   Þe pound þat heo [*payede*] by peisid a quarter more
A. 7.85   [I] *payede* hym prestly for peril of my soule;
A. 7.100   Þerewiþ was perkyn *payed,* and preisid hem ȝerne.
A. 7.293   May no penyale hem *paye,* ne no pece of bacoun,
A.10.117   Be *paied* wiþ þe porcioun, pore oþer riche.
A.10.130   Such wer[kis] to werche [þat] he is wiþ *paied.*
B. 3.62   Do peynten and portraye [who] *paie[d]* for þe makynge
B. 3.137   [And] leteþ passe prisoners and *paieþ* for hem ofte,
B. 4.75   To maken [his] pees wiþ his pens, handy dandy *payed.*
B. 5.215   [Th]e pound þat she *paied* by peised a quartron moore
B. 5.253   That *payed* neuere for his prentishode noȝt a peire gloues.'
B. 5.428   So wiþ wikked wil and wraþe my werkmen I *paye.*
B. 6.93   I *paide* [hym] prestly for peril of my soule;
B. 6.309   May no peny ale hem *paie,* ne no pece of bacoun,
B. 7.44   Princes and prelates sholde *paie* for hire trauaille
B.11.195   Ac for þe pouere I shal *paie,* and pure wel quyte hir trauaille
B.13.376   Wiþ presentes pryuely, or *paide* som certeyn;
B.13.380   But he profrede to *paie* þe a peny or tweyne
B.13.388   As whan I lened and leued it lost or longe er it were *paied.*
B.14.296   Ne borweþ of hise neighebores but þat he may wel *paie:*
B.15.155   And wollen lene þer þei leue lelly to ben *paied.*
B.17.240   In as muche as þei mowen amenden and *paien;*
B.17.320   His sorwe is satisfaccion for [swich] þat may noȝt *paie.*
B.19.186   In couenaunt þat þei come and knewelich[e] to *paie*
B.19.188   Thus haþ Piers power, b[e] his pardon *paied,*
B.19.194   *Paieþ* parfitly as pure truþe wolde.
B.19.195   And what persone *paieþ* it nouȝt punysshen he þenkeþ,
B.19.389   Or as ofte as þei hadde nede, þo þat hadde *ypaied*
B.19.414   And we clerkes, whan þei come, for hir comunes *paieþ,*
B.20.308   And þat Piers [pardon] were *ypayed,* redde quod debes.
C. 3.66   And [do] peynten and purtrayen ho *paye* for þe makyng
C. 3.175   He lat passe prisones [and] *paieth* for hem ofte
C. 3.300   That pre manibus is *paied* or his pay asketh.
C. 3.306   And but hit prestly be *ypayed* þe payere is to blame,
C. 3.350   To *pay* hym yf he parforme and haue pite yf he faileth
C. 3.390   Be the peccunie *ypaied,* thow parties chyde,
C. 4.55   ȝut is he bold for to borw Ac baddelyche he *payeth:*
C. 4.68   And for to haue here helpe handy dandy *payde.*
C. 6.223   The pound th[at] he *payede* by peysed a quarter more
C. 6.251   *Payed* neuere for his prentished nat a payre gloues.
C. 6.277   As whenne y lenede and leuede hit lost or longe or hit were *payed.*
C. 6.299   Shal parte with the in purgatorye and helpe *paye* thy dette
C. 7.41   So with wikkede will my werkemen y *paye.*
C. 7.277   For he *payeth* for prisones in places and in peynes.
C. 8.102   Y *payede* hit prestly for perel of my soule;
C. 8.115   Therwith was [Perkyn] apayed and *payede* wel here huyre.
C. 8.331   May no peny ale hem *pay* ne no pece of bacoun,
C. 9.45   But they pre manibus were *payed* for pledynge at þe barre;
C.12.107   Ac for þe pore may nat *paye* y wol pay mysulue;
C.12.107   Ac for þe pore may nat paye y wol *pay* mysulue;
C.16.31   And [operis satisfaccio] for soules *paieth* and alle synnes quyteth.
C.16.131   Ne boroweth of his neyhebore but þat he may wel *paye*
C.16.315   That neuere *payed* peny aȝeyn in places þer he borwede.'
C.16.325   There pore men and prisones ben and *paye* for here fode,
C.19.206   In as moche as they mowen amenden and *payen;*
C.19.300   As sorwe of herte is satisfaccioun for suche þat may nat *paye.*
C.21.186   In couenaunt þat they come and knolech[e] to *pay*
C.21.188   Thus hath Peres power, be his pardoun *payed,*
C.21.194   *Payeth* parfitly as puyr treuthe wolde.

C.21.195   And what persone *payth* hit nat punischen he thenketh
C.21.389   Or as ofte as they hadden nede, tho þat hadden *payed*
C.21.414   And we Clerkes, when they come, for here comunes *paieth,*
C.22.308   And þat Peres pardon were *ypayd,* redde quod debes.

paiere n *paiere n.* A 1 payere; B 1; C 2 payere
A. 6.38   He is þe presteste *payere* þat pore men knowen;
B. 5.551   He is þe presteste *paiere* þat pouere men knoweþ;
C. 3.306   And but hit prestly be ypayed þe *payere* is to blame,
C. 7.195   He is þe presteste *payere* þat eny pore man knoweth;

payn n *pain n.* A 1; B 8; C 8 payn (6) payne (2)
A. 8.108   Þe prophet his *p[a]yn* e[et] in penaunce & in wepyng
B. 6.150   Thei shul haue *payn* and potage and [a pitaunce biside],
B. 7.126   The prophete his *payn* eet in penaunce and in sorwe
B. 9.83   Ne faille *payn* ne potage and prelates dide as þei sholden.
B.13.243   I fynde *payn* for þe pope and prouendre for his palfrey,
B.13.259   Til pride be pureliche fordo, and [þat] þoruȝ *payn* defaute.
B.14.77   Weex þoruȝ plentee of *payn* and of pure sleuþe:
B.14.317   For pacience is *payn* for pouerte hymselue,
B.15.315   For hadde ye potage and *payn* ynogh and penyale to drynke,
C. 8.284   Part with men of thy *payne,* of potage or of sowl;
C. 9.92   There is *payne* and peny ale as for a pytaunce ytake
C.15.200   The pore and the ryche y plese and *payn* fynde
C.15.216   Y fynde *payn* for þe po[p]e and pre[y]en hym ych wolde
C.15.229   Til pruyde be puyreliche fordo and þat thorw *payn* defaute:
C.15.230   Plente of *payn* the peple of sodoume,
C.15.233   For þoȝ nere *payn* [of] plouh ne potage were
C.16.151   For pacience is his paniter and pouerte *payn* here fyndeth

payne > payn,peyne; paynede -eth > peynen; paynes > peyne

paynym n *painime n.* A 1; B 3 paynym (2) paynymes (1); C 2 paynyem
  (1) paynyme (1)
A. 6.4   Aparailid as a *paynym* in pilgrim[ys] wyse.
B. 5.516   Apparailled as a *paynym* in pilgrymes wise.
B.11.163   Pulte out of pyne a *paynym* of rome.
B.15.504   For alle *paynymes* preieþ and parfitly bileueþ
C. 7.161   [A]parayled as a *paynyem* in pilgrimes wyse.
C.17.255   For alle *paynyme* preyeth and parfitliche bileueth

paynted > peynten; payre > peire

pays n *OED pais n.* B 1; C 1
B.16.159   Suffreþ myne Apostles in [*pays*] and in [pees] gange.'
C.18.176   Soffreth my postles in *pays* and in pees gange.'

payth > paien

pak n *pake n.* B 2; C 2
B.13.201   Haue pacience parfitliche þan half þi *pak* of bokes.'
B.14.213   Ther þe poore preesseþ bifore wiþ a *pak* at his rugge:
B.15.179   Haue pacience parfitlyche then half thy *pak* of bokes.
C.16.54   There þe pore preseth byfore with a *pak* at his rugge,

pakke > paknedle

pakken v *pakken v.* B 1; C 1 pakketh
B.15.189   Pride wiþ al þe appurtenaunces, and *pakken* hem togideres,
C.16.332   Pruyde with alle [þe] purtinaunces and *pakketh* hem togyderes

paknedle n *pake n.* A 1 pakke_nedle; B 1
A. 5.126   Brochide hem wiþ a *pakke nedle,* & pleit hem togidere;
B. 5.210   [P]roche[d] hem wiþ a *paknedle* and playte hem togideres,

palays > paleis,paleys

pale adj *pale adj.* A 1; B 2; C 1
A. 5.60   He was as *pale* as a p[e]let, [in] þe palesie he semide;
B. 5.77   He was as *pale* as a pelet, in þe palsy he semed.
B.18.58   Pitousliche and *pale,* as a prison þat deieþ,
C.20.58   Pitousliche and *pale,* as [a] prisoun þat deyeth,

paleis n1 *palais n. &> paleys n2* A 1; B 2 paleis (1) paleises (1); C 2
  palays (1) paleis (1)
A. 2.18   In þe popis *paleis* heo is preuy as myselue;
B. 2.23   In þe popes *Paleis* she is pryuee as myselue,
B. 8.16   Boþe princes *paleises* and pouere mennes cotes,
C. 2.23   In þe popes *palays* he is pryue as myselue,
C.10.16   Bothe princes *paleis* and pore menne cotes

paleys n2 *palis n.* A 1 paleis; B 3 paleis (2) paleys (1); C 2 palays (1)
  paleys (1)
A.11.312   Percen wiþ a paternoster þe *paleis* of heuene
B.10.468   Percen wiþ a Paternoster þe *paleys* of heuene
B.13.29   A[c] Pacience in þe *Paleis* stood in pilgrymes cloþes.
B.18.335   For in my *paleis,* Paradis, in persone of an Addre
C.11.294   Persen with a paternoster [þe *paleys* of] heuene
C.20.378   For in my *palays,* paradys, in persone of an addere

palesie > palsy

palfrey n *palefrei n.* A 3 palfray (1) palfrey (1) palfreis (1); B 5 palfrey (3) palfreyes (2); C 3 palfrayes
A. 2.135   'And let apparaille þise prouisours in *palfreis* wise;
A. 2.151   But prikede forþ on his *palfray* & passide hem alle,
A.11.213   Poperiþ on a *palfrey* [fro] toune to toune;
B. 2.171   'And late apparaille þise prouisours in *palfreyes* wise;
B. 2.190   And priked [forþ on] his *palfrey* and passed hem alle
B.10.313   A prikere on a *palfrey* fro [place] to Manere.
B.13.243   I fynde payn for þe pope and prouendre for his *palfrey*,
B.19.415   For hir pelure and *palfreyes* mete and pilours þat hem folweþ.
C. 4.115   And here pelure and here *palfrayes* pore menne lyflode
C. 5.159   And pryked aboute on *palfrayes* fram places to maneres,
C.21.415   For here pelure and *palfrayes* mete and pelours þat hem folweth.

palle v *pallen v.(2)* B 2 palle (1) palleþ (1); C 1
B.16.30   Thanne with þe firste pil I *palle* hym doun, potencia de[i patris].
B.16.51   And *palleþ* adoun þe pouke pureliche þoruȝ grace
C.18.34   And with þe furste planke y *palle* hym down, potencia dei patris.

palmere n *palmere n.* A 3 palmere (1) palmeris (1) palmers (1); B 4 Palmere (1) palmeres (3); C 5 palmare (1) palmere (2) palmeres (1) palmers (1)
A.Pr.46   Pilgrimes & *palmeris* pliȝten hem togidere
A. 5.87   [For pilgrymes, for *palmers*, for all þe peple] aftir,
A. 6.23   'I sauȝ neuere *palmere* wiþ pik ne wiþ scrippe
B.Pr.46   Pilgrymes and *Palmeres* pliȝten hem togidere
B. 5.107   For Pilgrymes, for *Palmeres*, for al þe peple after,
B. 5.535   'I [ne] seiȝ neuere *Palmere* wiþ pyk ne wiþ scrippe
B. 6.64   To pilgrymage as *palmeres* doon pardon to haue.
C.Pr.47   Pilgrymes and *palmers* plighten hem togyderes
C. 7.180   'I [ne] saw neuere *palmere* with pyk ne with scrip[p]e
C. 8.63   To pilgrimag[e] as *palmeres* doen pardon to wynne.
C.15.33   Ilyk[e peres] the [ploghman], as he a *palmere* were,
C.15.130   For Peres loue þe *palmare* ȝent, þat inpugnede ones

palpable adj *palpable adj.* C 1
C.18.233   And as thre persones *palpable* is puy[r]lich bote o mankynde,

palsy n *palesie n.* A 1 palesie; B 2 palsy (1) palsie (1); C 1 palesye
A. 5.60   He was as pale as a p[e]let, [in] þe *palesie* he semide;
B. 5.77   He was as pale as a pelet, in þe *palsy* he semed.
B.20.176   A Phisicien wiþ a furred hood þat he fel in a *palsie*,
C.22.176   A fisician with a forred hoed that he ful in a *palesye*

paltok n *paltoke n.* B 2 paltok (1) paltokes (1); C 2 paltok (1) paltokes (1)
B.18.25   In Piers *paltok* þe Plowman þis prikiere shal ryde,
B.20.219   In *paltokes* and pyked shoes, [purses and] longe knyues,
C.20.24   In [Pers *paltok*] the [plouhman] this prikiare shal ryde
C.22.219   In *paltokes* and pikede shoes, [purses and] longe knyues.

pampilon n prop *n.i.d.* B 1; C 1
B.17.256   And purchace al þe pardon of *Pampilon* and Rome,
C.19.222   And purchase al the pardoun of *pampilon* and Rome

panel n *panel n.(1)* B 1; C 1 panele
B. 3.317   Ne putte hem in *panel* to doon hem pliȝte hir truþe;
C. 3.470   Ne potte [hem] in *panele* [to] do [hem] plihte here treuthe;

panelon n *n.i.d.* B 1; C 1
B. 3.296   Ne no pelure in his [*panelon*] for pledynge at þe barre;
C. 3.449   Ne no pelure in his *panelon* for pledyng at þe barre.

panes > peny

paniers n *paniere n.* B 1; C 1 paniars
B.15.290   Poul after his prechyng *paniers* he made
C.17.17   Paul aftur his prechyng *paniars* he made

panis > peny

paniter n *panetere n.* C 1
C.16.151   For pacience is his *paniter* and pouerte payn here fyndeth

panne n *panne n.(1)* A 1; B 1; C 1
A. 4.64   Pees putte forþ his heued & his *panne* blody:
B. 4.78   Pees putte forþ his heed, and his *panne* blody:
C. 4.74   Ȝut pees put forth his heued and his *panne* blody:

pans > massepens,peny

papelotes n *papelote n.* C 1
C. 9.75   Bothe in mylke and in mele to make with *papelotes*

paradis n *paradise n.* A 5 paradis (4) paradys (1); B 8 paradis (7) Paradys (1); C 5 paradis (1) paradys (4)
A. 7.109   'Be þe prince of *paradis*!' quaþ piers þo in wraþþe,
A. 8.12   Wiþ patriarkes in *paradis* to pleiȝe þereaftir.
A.11.12   Þanne al þe precious perrie þat in *paradis* wexiþ.

A.11.286   Wiþoute penaunce of purcatorie to haue *paradis* for euere.
A.12.95   Þat þi play be plentevous in *paradys* with aungelys.
B. 5.495   And blewe alle þi blessed into þe blisse of *Paradys*.
B. 7.12   Wiþ Patriarkes and prophetes in *paradis* to be felawe.
B.10.12   Than al þe precious perree þat in *paradis* wexeþ.
B.10.470   Into þe [parfit] blisse of *Paradis* for hir pure bileue,
B.11.417   Adam, whiles he spak noȝt, hadde *paradis* at wille,
B.15.63   [Adam and Eue putte out of *Paradis*]:
B.18.335   For in my paleis, *Paradis*, in persone of an Addre
B.19.61   Places in *Paradis* at hir partynge hennes
C. 9.12   With patriarkes and prophetes in *paradis* to sitton.
C.13.225   Adam, whiles he spak nat, hadde *paradys* at wille
C.16.225   Potte out of *paradys* Adam and Eue:
C.20.378   For in my palays, *paradys*, in persone of an addere
C.21.61   Places in *paradys* at here partyng hennes

parail n *appareil n.* C 3
C.10.117   Was no pruyde on his *parail* ne pouerte noythere;
C.12.125   For his pore *parail* and pilgrimes clothes
C.12.132   In þe *parail* of a pilgrime and in pore likenesse

paramours n *paramoure n.* C 2
C. 6.186   Of put[rie] and of *paramours* and proueden thorw speche
C.16.106   Here fader and alle here frendes and goth forth with here *paramours*:

parauenture adv *paraventure adv.* A 1; B 7 paraunter (2) parauenture (5); C 9 parauntur
A.12.8   Presumptuowsly, *parauenture*, apose so manye
B. 5.639   'Bi seint Poul!' quod a pardoner, '*parauenture* I be noȝt knowe þere;
B.11.11   And knowe þat þow coueitest and come þerto *paraunter*'.
B.11.423   Pryde now and presumpcion, *parauenture*, wol þee appele
B.12.183   And þat is after person or parissh preest, [and] *parauenture* vnkonnynge
B.13.134   Pacience haþ be in many place, and *paraunter* [knoweþ]
B.14.208   Ther þe poore is put bihynde, and *parauenture* kan moore
B.20.234   'And for þei are pouere, *parauenture*, for patrymoyne [hem] faille[þ],
C. 3.467   Shal lese þerfore his lyflode and his lyf *parauntur*.
C. 7.297   Forthy y pray ȝow, [Peres], *parauntur* ȝif ȝe m[e]ten
C. 8.43   Thogh he be here thyn vnderlynge in heuene *parauntur*
C. 9.181   As prisones and pilgrimes and *parauntur* men yrobbed
C.11.170   And knowe þat þou coueytest and come þerto *parauntur*.'
C.12.244   And he for his hard holdyng in helle *parauntur*:
C.14.123   And þat is aftur person other parsche preest, and *parauntur* bothe lewede
C.16.49   There þe pore is potte behynde and *parauntur* can more
C.22.234   'And for thei aren pore, *parauntur*, for patrimonye hem faileth,

parceyue v *perceiven v.* B 12 parceyue (1) parceyued (9) parceyueþ (2); C 5 parsceyued (1) parseued (1) perseyue (1) perseyued (2)
B.Pr.100   I *parceyued* of þe power þat Peter hadde to kepe,
B. 5.144   And now persons han *parceyued* þat freres parte wiþ hem
B.13.86   Pacience *parceyued* what I þouȝte and [preynte] on me to be stille
B.13.354   Thanne Pacience *parceyued* of pointes [his] cote
B.15.199   Ac Piers þe Plowman *parceyueþ* moore depper
B.16.23   Wiþ þre piles was it vnderpight; I *parceyued* it soone.
B.16.103   And Piers þe Plowman *parceyued* plener tyme
B.17.69   And *parceyued* bi his pous he was in peril to dye
B.17.153   Al þat þe pawme *parceyueþ* profitable to feele.
B.18.243   Peter þe Apostel *parceyued* his gate,
B.18.418   And leteþ no peple', quod pees, '*parceyue* þat we chidde;
B.19.163   Peter *parceyued* al þis and pursued after,
C.Pr.128   I *parsceyued* of þe power that Peter hadde to kepe,
C.19.68   And *parseued* by his poues he was in perel to deye
C.20.252   Peter þe Apostel *perseyued* his gate
C.20.461   'And lat no peple,' quod pees, '*perseyue* þat we chydde;
C.21.163   Peter *perseyued* al this and pursuede aftur,

parcel n *parcel* A 1; B 4 parcel (1) parcell (1) parcelles (2); C 5 parcel (1) parceles (1) parcels (1) parsel (1) parseles (1)
A.11.50   Þat þus partiþ wiþ þe poore a *parcel* whanne hym nediþ.
B.10.64   That þus parteþ wiþ þe pouere a *parcell* whan hym nedeþ.
B.11.305   Or peynted parentrelynarie, *parcelles* ouerskipped.
B.17.29   Thre persones in *parcelles* departable fro ooþer
B.20.292   A *parcel* to preye for hem and [pleye] wiþ þe remenaunt.
C.11.46   That so parteth with þe pore a *parsel* when hym nedeth.
C.13.38   For þe *parcel*[s] of his pauper and oþer pryue dettes
C.13.119   Or peynted parentrelynarie, *parseles* ouerskipped.
C.19.98   In thre persones, a *parceles* departable fram oþere,
C.22.292   A *parcel* to preye for hem and [pleye] with þe remenaunt

parcelmele adv *parcelmele adv.& n.* A 1 parcelmel; B 2; C 2 parselmele
A. 3.70   To þe pore peple þat *parcelmel* biggen,

B. 3.81   To þe pouere peple þat *parcelmele* buggen.
B.15.246 And cristes patrymonye to þe poore *parcelmele* dele;
C. 3.86   Thei han no pite on the peple þat *parcelmele* mot begge;
C.19.30   Thre persones *parselmele* depar[t]able fram oþere

parchemyn n *parchemin n.* B 3
B. 9.39   Right as a lord sholde make lettres; [if] hym lakked *parchemyn*,
B.14.192 Ac þe *parchemyn* of þis patente of pouerte be moste,
B.14.194 Of pompe and of pride þe *parchemyn* decourreþ,

pardon n *pardoun n.* A 17 pardon (1) pardoun (16); B 31 pardon (28) pardoun (3); C 30 pardon (15) pardoun (15)
A. 2.184 And ʒaf *pardoun* for panis poundmel aboute.
A. 8.3   And purchac[ide] hym a *pardoun* a pena & a culpa
A. 8.8   Part in þ[at] *pardoun* þe pope haþ hem grauntid.
A. 8.11   Han *pardoun* þoruʒ purcatorie to passe wel sone,
A. 8.18   Han *pardoun* wiþ þe apostlis whanne þei passe hennis,
A. 8.59   His *pardoun* in purcatorie wel [petit] is, I trowe,
A. 8.86   Han as pleyn *pardoun* as þe plouʒman hymselue;
A. 8.89   'Piers,' quaþ a prest [þo], 'þi *pardon* muste I rede,
A. 8.91   And peris at his preyour þe *pardoun* vnfoldiþ,
A. 8.97   'Petir,' quaþ þe prest þo, 'I can no *pardoun* fynde
A. 8.151 On peris þe plouʒman, whiche a *pardoun* he hauiþ,
A. 8.156 He passiþ al þe *pardoun* [of] seint petris chirche.
A. 8.157 Now haþ þe pope power *pardoun* to graunte
A. 8.161 Þat *pardoun*, & penaunce, & preyours do salue
A. 8.170 [To purchace *pardoun* and þe popes bulles],
A. 8.175 A pokeful of *pardoun* þere, ne þe prouincialis lettres,
A.11.78   And preye hym of *pardoun* & penaunce [in] þi lyue,
B. 2.225 And [gaf] *pardoun* for pens poundemele aboute.
B. 6.64   To pilgrymage as palmeres doon *pardon* to haue.
B. 7.3   And purchaced hym a *pardoun* a pena & a culpa
B. 7.8   *Pardon* wiþ Piers Plowman truþe haþ ygraunted.
B. 7.11   Han *pardon* þoruʒ purgatorie to passen ful liʒtly,
B. 7.16   Arn peres wiþ þe Apostles–þ[u]s *pardon* Piers sheweþ–
B. 7.40   Men of lawe leest *pardon* hadde, [leue þow noon ooþer],
B. 7.58   Hi[s] *pardon* is [wel] petit at hi[s] partyng hennes
B. 7.104 Han as pleyn *pardon* as þe Plowman hymselue;
B. 7.107 'Piers', quod a preest þoo, 'þi *pardon* moste I rede,
B. 7.109 And Piers at his preiere þe *pardon* vnfoldeþ,
B. 7.115 'Peter!' quod þe preest þoo, 'I kan no *pardon* fynde
B. 7.152 And which a *pardon* Piers hadde þe peple to conforte,
B. 7.174 And how þe preest preued no *pardon* to dowel
B. 7.178 [He] passeþ al þe *pardon* of Seint Petres cherche.
B. 7.179 Now haþ þe pope power *pardon* to graunte
B. 7.183 That *pardon* and penaunce and preieres doon saue
B. 7.192 To purchace *pardon* and þe popes bulles.
B. 7.197 A pokeful of *pardon* þere, ne prouincials lettres,
B. 7.200 I sette youre patentes and youre *pardon* at one pies hele.
B.10.125 And preie hym of *pardon* and penaunce in þi lyue,
B.11.57 To hir Priour prouincial a *pardon* for to haue,
B.13.246 Saue a *pardon* wiþ a peis of leed and two polles amyddes,
B.13.252 For hym and for alle hise, founde I þat his *pardoun*
B.15.183 Ther poore men and prisons liggeþ, hir *pardon* to haue;
B.17.256 And purchace al þe *pardon* of Pampilon and Rome,
B.19.183 And yaf Piers [*pardon*, and power] he grauntede hym,
B.19.187 To Piers *pardon* þe Plowman redde quod debes.
B.19.188 Thus haþ Piers power, b[e] his *pardon* paied,
B.19.390 To Piers *pardon* þe Plowman redde quod debes.'
B.20.308 And þat Piers [*pardon*] were ypayed, redde quod debes.
C. 2.235 And gaf *pardon* for pans poundmele aboute.
C. 8.63   To pilgrimag[e] as palmeres doen *pardon* to wynne.
C. 9.3   And purchasede hym a *pardoun* A pena & a culpa,
C. 9.8   *Pardoun* with [Peres] þe [Plouhman] perpetuelly he graunteth.
C. 9.11   Haen *pardon* thorw purgatorye to passe ful lyhtly,
C. 9.43   Alle þe peple hadde *pardon* ynow þat parfitliche lyuede.
C. 9.53   His *pardoun* is ful petyt at his partynge hennes
C. 9.60   *Pardoun* perpetuel riht as [Peres] þe [plouhman].
C. 9.175 Þai haue no part of *pardoun* ne of preyeres ne of penaunc[e].
C. 9.187 And *pardon* with the plouhman A pena & a culpa.
C. 9.280 For shal no *pardon* preye for ʒow there ne no princes lettres.
C. 9.281 '[Peres],' quod a prest tho, 'thy *pardon* moste y rede
C. 9.283 And [Peres] at his preeyre þe *pardon* vnfoldeth
C. 9.289 'Peter!' quod the prest tho, 'y kan no *pardoun* fynde
C. 9.293 The prest thus and perkyn of þe *pardon* iangelede
C. 9.301 And which a *pardoun* Peres hadde th[e] peple to glade
C. 9.319 And how þe prest preuede no *pardon* to do wel
C. 9.324 So dowel passeth *pardoun* and pilgrimages to Rome.
C. 9.325 Ʒut hath þe pope power *pardoun* to graunte
C. 9.339 That *pardoun* and penaunc[e] and preyere[s] don saue
C. 9.338 To pur[c]hace ʒow *pardoun* and the popes bulles.
C. 9.343 A pouhe ful of *pardon* there ne prouinciales lettres,
C. 9.346 Y sette nat by *pardon* a pese ne nat a pye hele.

C.12.9   To here priour prouincial [a] *pardon* to haue
C.19.222 And purchase al the *pardoun* of pampilon and Rome
C.21.183 And ʒaf [peres *pardoun*] and [power] he graunted [hym],
C.21.187 To Peres *pardoun* þe plouhman Redde quod debes.
C.21.188 Thus hath Peres power, be his *pardoun* payed,
C.21.390 To [Peres] *pardon* þe [plouhman] Redde quod debe[s].'
C.22.308 And þat Peres *pardon* were ypayd, redde quod debes.

pardoner n *pardoner n.* A 4 pardoner (3) pardoners (1); B 5 pardoner (4) Pardoners (1); C 5 Pardoner (3) Pardoners (2)
A.Pr.65   Þere prechide a *pardoner* as he a prest were;
A.Pr.78   Ac þe parissh prest & þe *pardoner* parte þe siluer
A. 2.73   And piers þe *pardoner*, poulynes doctor,
A. 2.181 Til *pardoners* hadde pite & pulden him to house,
B.Pr.68   Ther preched a *pardoner* as he a preest were;
B.Pr.81   [Ac] þe parisshe preest and þe *pardoner* parten þe siluer
B. 2.109 And Piers þe *Pardoner* of Paulynes doctrine,
B. 2.222 Til *Pardoners* hadde pite and pulled hym [to] house,
B. 5.639 'Bi seint Poul!' quod a *pardoner*, 'parauenture I be noʒt knowe þere;
C.Pr.66   Ther prechede a *Pardoner* as he a prest were,
C.Pr.79   For þe parsche prest and þe *Pardoner* parten þe seluer
C. 2.113 And Peres þe *Pardoner* of paulines queste,
C. 2.232 Tyl *Pardoners* hadde [pyte] and polleden hym [t]o house.
C.17.61   Or ar prestes or *pardoners* or eny peple elles.

pardoun > pardon

pare v *paren v.(1)* B 1; C 1
B. 5.240 To weye pens wiþ a peis and *pare* þe heuyeste
C. 6.242 To weye pans with a peyse and *par[e]* þe heuegeste

parentrelynarie adv *par prep.* B 1; C 1
B.11.305 Or peynted *parentrelynarie*, parcelles ouerskipped.
C.13.119 Or peynted *parentrelynarie*, parseles ouerskipped.

parfay exclam *par fei adv.& interj.* C 1
C.16.118 '*Parfay*!' quod pacience, 'propreliche to telle [this]

parfit adj *parfit adj.* A 1 perfite; B 20 parfit (18) parfite (1) parfiter (1); C 21 parfit (13) parfyt (5) parfite (1) parfyte (1) parfitest (1)
A. 1.120 And enden as I er seide, in *perfite* werkis,
B. 3.301 And swich pees among þe peple and a *parfit* truþe
B.10.470 Into þe [*parfit*] blisse of Paradis for hir pure bileue,
B.11.15   Pride of *parfit* lyuynge pursued hem boþe
B.11.33   And pride of *parfit* lyuynge to muche peril þee brynge.'
B.11.273 That *parfit* pouerte was no possession to haue,
B.11.276 Whoso wole be pure *parfit* moot possession forsake
B.11.319 The which I preise, þer pacience is, moore *parfit* þan richesse.
B.12.24   [In manye places pleyden þe *parfiter* to ben].
B.13.214 Til Pacience haue preued þee and *parfit* þee maked.'
B.14.100 'Ther *parfit* truþe and poore herte is, and pacience of tonge,
B.14.193 And of pure pacience and *parfit* bileue.
B.15.148 In preieres and in penaunces, and in *parfit* charite.'
B.15.418 Peeren to Apostles þoruʒ hire *parfit* lyuynge.
B.15.515 And þoruʒ penaunce and passion and *parfit* bile[ue].
B.15.568 If preesthode were *parfit* þe peple sholde amende
B.15.584 Dilige deum & proximum is *parfit* Iewen lawe;
B.15.588 [And] for a *parfit* prophete þat muche peple sauede
B.16.107 Til he was *parfit* praktisour if any peril fille.
B.18.149 Iob þe [*parfit*] patriark repreueþ þi sawes:
B.20.108 Leue pride pryuely and be *parfite* cristene.
C. 3.454 And such pees among þe peple and a *parfit* treuthe
C. 5.84   Preeyeres of a *parfit* man and penaunce d[iscret]e
C. 8.136 'ʒoure prayeres,' quod [Peres], 'and ʒe p[ar]fyt weren,
C.11.174 And pruyde-of-*parfit*-lyuynge pursuede me faste
C.11.192 And pruyde-of-*parfit*-lyuynge to moche perel þe brynge.'
C.11.295 And passen purgatorie penaunceles for here *parfit* bileue:
C.12.163 "Yf thow likest to lyue," quod god, "þe lyf þat is *parfit*,
C.13.99   So pore and pacient *parfitest* lyf is of alle.
C.13.100 Vch a *parfi[t]* prest to pouerte sholde drawe
C.13.230 [For] pruyde or presumpcioun of thy *parfit* lyuynge.
C.15.217 That pestilenc[e] to pees and *parfyt* loue turn[e].
C.15.272 'What is [properly] *parfit* pacience?' quod Actiua vita.
C.16.245 Thorw *parfit* preesthoed and prelates of holy churche,
C.17.51   Iop þe *parfite* patriarke this prouerbe wroet and tauhte
C.17.233 For were presthode more *parfyte*, that is, þe pope formost
C.17.250 Yf prestehode were *parfyt* and preyede thus the peple sholde amende
C.17.266 And thorw penaunce and passioun and *parfyt* bileue;
C.17.299 And for a *parfit* profete that moche peple sauede
C.18.102 Bothe *parfit* and inparfit.' Puyr fayn y wolde
C.20.152 Iop þe *parfit* patriarke repreueth thy sawes:
C.22.108 Leue pruyde priueyliche and be *parfyt* cristene.

parfitly adv *parfitli adv.* B 6 parfitly (4) parfitliche (2); C 8 parfitly (2) parfitliche (4) parfitlyche (2)

B. 5.394 I kan noȝt *parfitly* my Paternoster as þe preest it syngeþ,
B.13.187 That Pacience þe pilgrym *parfitly* knew neuere.'
B.13.201 Haue pacience *parfitliche* þan half þi pak of bokes.'
B.15.504 For alle paynymes preieþ and *parfitly* bileueþ
B.16.220 Thus in þre persones is *parfitliche* [pure] manhede,
B.19.194 Paieþ *parfitly* as pure truþe wolde.
C. 7.10 Y can nat *parfitly* my paternoster as þe prest hit syngeth;
C. 9.43 Alle þe peple hadde pardon ynow þat *parfitliche* lyuede.
C.15.179 Haue pacience *parfitlyche* then half thy pak of bokes.
C.16.340 'Peres the plouhman,' quod he, 'moste *parfitlyche* hym knoweth:
C.17.76 And ȝut is þe printe puyr trewe and *parfitliche* ygraue.
C.17.255 For alle paynyme preyeth and *parfitliche* bileueth
C.19.137 Portrey ne peynte *parfitliche*, y leue,
C.21.194 Payeth *parfitly* as puyr treuthe wolde.

parfitnesse n *parfitnesse n.* B 3; C 3

B.10.205 Poul preched þe peple, þat *parfitnesse* louede,
B.15.208 Than for penaunce and *parfitnesse*, þe pouerte þat swiche takeþ,
B.16.135 Of preieres and of *parfitnesse* þis place þat ye callen:
C. 5.90 Ac it semeth no sad *parfitnesse* in Citees to b[e]gge
C.15.183 With pacience wol y passe *parfitnesse* to fynde.'
C.18.41 The which is þe passioun & þe penaunce & þe *parfitnesse* of iesus

parfournen v *performen v.* A 1 perfourmde; B 10 parfourne (1) parfourned (1) parfournede (2) parfournen (2) parfourneþ (4); C 9 parforme (3) parformed (1) parformede (1) parformeth (2) parfourme (1) parfourmede (1)

A. 6.85 I *perfourmde* þe penaunce þe prest me enioynide,
B. 5.398 I *parfournede* neuere penaunce as þe preest me hiȝte,
B. 5.598 I *parfourned* þe penaunce þe preest me enioyned
B.13.79 Haþ no pite on vs pouere; he *parfourneþ* yuele
B.13.174 Kan noȝt [*parfournen*] a pees bitwene [þe pope] and hise enemys,
B.13.396 Ne neuere penaunce *parfournede* ne Paternoster seide
B.13.411 [Ac] penaunce þat þe preest enioyneþ *parfourneþ* yuele;
B.14.292 /Ergo pouerte and poore men *parfournen* þe comaundement
B.15.326 Who *parfourneþ* þis prophecie of þe peple þat now libbeþ,
B.15.328 If any peple *parfourne* þat text it are þise poore freres,
B.15.491 What pope or prelat now *parfourneþ* þat crist highte,
C. 3.350 To pay hym yf he *parforme* and haue pite yf he faileth
C. 6.283 Ne neuere penaunce *parformede* ne paternoster sayde
C. 7.14 Y *parfourmede* neuere penaunc[e] þat þe prest me hihte
C. 7.71 The penauns[e] þat þe prest enioyneth *parformeth* euele,
C. 7.247 And *parformed* þe penaunce þat þe prest me hihte."
C.13.93 So þe pore of puyr reuthe may *parforme* þe lawe
C.15.86 Hath no pyte on vs pore; he *parformeth* euele
C.15.172 Can nat *parfourme* a pees of the pope and his enemyes
C.16.127 Ergo pouerte and pore men *parforme* þe comandement

parissh n *parishe n.* A 4; B 11 parissh (3) parisshe (7) parisshes (1); C 10 parsch (1) parsche (8) parsches (1)

A.Pr.78 Ac þe *parissh* prest & þe pardoner parte þe siluer
A.Pr.79 Þat þe pore peple of þe *parissh* shulde haue ȝif þei ne were.
A.Pr.80 Personis & *parissh* prestis pleynide hem to here bisshop
A.Pr.81 Þat here *parissh* w[ere] pore siþþe þe pestilence tyme,
B.Pr.81 [Ac] þe *parisshe* preest and þe pardoner parten þe siluer
B.Pr.82 That þe [pouere peple] of þe *parisshe* sholde haue if þei ne were.
B.Pr.83 Persons and *parisshe* preestes pleyned hem to þe Bisshop
B.Pr.84 That hire *parissh[e]* wer[e] pouere siþ þe pestilence tyme,
B.10.273 As persons and *parissh* preestes, þat preche sholde and teche,
B.11.65 Be buried at hire hous but at my *parisshe* chirche,
B.12.183 And þat is after person or *parissh* preest, [and] parauenture vnkonnynge
B.20.263 Pylours and Pykeharneys, in ech a [*parisshe*] ycursed._
B.20.280 And yuele is þis yholde in *parisshes* of Engelonde,
B.20.281 For persons and *parissh* preestes þat sholde þe peple shryue
B.20.319 Than person or *parisshe* preest, penitauncer or bisshop,
C.Pr.79 For þe *parsche* prest and þe Pardoner parten þe seluer
C.Pr.80 That þe [pore] peple [of þe] *parsch[e]* sholde haue yf þei ne were.
C.Pr.81 Persones and *parsche* prestis pleyned [hem] to þe bischop
C.Pr.82 That here *parsch[e]* were pore sithe þ[e] pestelence tyme,
C.14.123 And þat is aftur person other *parsche* preest, and parauntur bothe lewede
C.15.210 Nere hit þat þe *parsche* [prest] preyeth for me on sonendayes,
C.22.263 Pilours and pikeharneys in vch a *parsch* acorsed.
C.22.280 And euele is this yholde in *parsches* of yngelond
C.22.281 For persones and *parsche* prestes þat sholde þe peple shryue
C.22.319 Then person oþer *parsche* prest, penytauncer or bischope,

parisshens n *parishen n.(1)* B 3; C 2 parschienes (1) parschiens (1)

B.Pr.89 And signe þat þei sholden shryuen hire *parisshens*,
B. 5.419 Construe clause[m]el[e] and kenne it to my *parisshens*.
B.20.283 Alle þat ben hir *parisshens* penaunce enioigne,
C. 6.120 And prelates pleyneth on hem for they here *parschiens* shryuen

C.22.283 Alle þat been here *parschienes* penauns[e] enioynen

parled ptp *parlen v.* B 1; C 1

B.18.271 Patriarkes and prophetes han *parled* herof longe
C.20.279 Patriarkes and prophetes haen *parled* herof longe

parlement n *parlemente n.* A 1; B 1; C 2

A. 4.34 Þanne com pes into þe *parlement* & putte vp a bille
B. 4.47 [Th]anne com pees into [þe] *parlement* and putte vp [vp] a bille
C. 4.45 Thenne cam p[ees] into [þe] *parlement* and putte vp a bille
C. 4.185 But be my cheef Chaunceller in Cheker and in *parlement*

parlour n *parlour n.* B 1

B.10.100 In a pryuee *parlour* for pouere mennes sake,

parroked ptp *parroken v.* B 1; C 2 yparroked (1) yparrokede (1)

B.15.286 Poul primus heremita hadde *parroked* hymselue
C. 6.144 *Yparroke[d]* in pues; the persone hit knoweth
C.17.13 Paul primus heremita hadde *yparrokede* hymsulue

parsceyued > parceyue; parsch(- parissh(- ; parsel(- > parcel(-; parseued > parceyue; parsilie > percile

part n *part n.* &> parteþ A 1; C 3

A. 8.8 *Part* in þ[at] pardoun þe pope haþ hem grauntid.
C. 3.246 May nat be sold sothliche, so many *part* asketh
C. 9.175 Þai haue no *part* of pardoun ne of preyeres ne of penaunc[e].
C.17.70 That pore peple by puyre riht here *part* myhte aske.

part(e > parteþ; parteyȝe > partie

parteþ v *parten v.* A 4 parte (2) parteþ (1) partiþ (1); B 5 parte (1) parten (1) parteþ (2) partyng (1); C 10 part (1) parte (5) parten (1) parteth (3)

A.Pr.78 Ac þe parissh prest & þe pardoner *parte* þe siluer
A. 1.156 Of such good as god sent goodlyche *parteþ*,
A. 3.57 A[c] so preuyliche *parte* it þat pride be not seiȝe,
A.11.50 Þat þus *partiþ* wiþ þe poore a parcel whanne hym nediþ.
B.Pr.81 [Ac] þe parisshe preest and þe pardoner *parten* þe siluer
B. 1.182 [Of] swich good as god sent goodliche *parteþ*,
B. 5.144 And now persons han parceyued þat freres *parte* wiþ hem
B.10.64 That þus *parteþ* wiþ þe pouere a parcell whan hym nedeþ.
B.13.206 If Pacience be oure *partyng* felawe and pryue with vs boþe
C.Pr.79 For þe parsche prest and þe Pardoner *parten* þe seluer
C. 1.178 Of such good as god sent goodliche *parte*,
C. 5.184 Lat no kyne consayl ne couetyse ȝow *parte*,
C. 6.299 Shal *parte* with the in purgatorye and helpe paye thy dette
C. 8.144 Such poore,' quod [Peres], 'shal *parte* with my godes,
C. 8.284 *Part* with hem of thy payne, of potage or of sowl,
C.11.46 That so *parteth* with þe pore a parsel when hym nedeth.
C.11.63 Ne *parteth* with þe pore as puyr charite wolde,
C.15.115 In þat ȝe *parteth* nat with vs pore, þat ȝe passeth dowel
C.16.258 *Parte* with þe pore and ȝoure pruyde leue

partie n *partie n.* A 1; B 4 party (1) partie (2) parties (1); C 10 parteyȝe (1) partie (2) parties (3) party (2) partye (2)

A. 1.7 Þe moste *partie* of þis peple þat passiþ on þis erþe,
B. 1.7 The mooste *partie* of þis peple þat passeþ on þis erþe,
B.14.269 As by assent of sondry *parties* and siluer to boote,
B.15.16 'I am cristes creature', quod he, 'and [of his kyn a *party*],
B.17.308 For þer þat *partie* pursueþ þe [peel] is so huge
C. 1.7 The moste *party* of this peple þat passeth on þis erthe,
C. 1.95 And for no lordene loue leue þe trewe *partie*.
C. 3.380 Bothe heued and here kyng, haldyng with no *parteyȝe*
C. 3.383 Ac þe moste *partie* of peple puyr indirect semeth
C. 3.390 Be the peccunie ypaied, thow *parties* chyde,
C.15.156 Y take wittenesse,' quod [þe wy], 'of holy writ a *partye*:
C.15.173 Profitable for bothe *parties*;' and potte þe boerd fro hym
C.16.109 As by assente of sondry p[arti]es and suluer to bote,
C.16.168 And in cristes court yknowe wel and of his kynne a *party*.
C.19.288 The[r] þat *partye* pursueth the apeel is so huge

partyng ger *partinge ger.* &> parteþ A 1; B 3 partyng (2) partynge (1); C 3 partyng (1) partynge (2)

A.11.313 Wiþoute penaunce at here *partyng*, into [þe] heiȝe blisse.
B. 7.58 Hi[s] pardon is [wel] petit at hi[s] *partyng* hennes
B.10.469 And passen Purgatorie penauncelees at hir hennes *partyng*
B.19.61 Places in Paradis at hir *partynge* hennes
C. 9.53 His pardoun is ful petyt at his *partynge* hennes
C.16.161 Shal be porest of power at his *partynge* hennes.'
C.21.61 Places in paradys at here *partyng* hennes

pasche > pask; paschte > passhed; pase > paas

pask n *paske n.* B 2 Pask (1) Pasqe (1); C 2 Pasche (1) paske (1)

B.11.234 Witnesse in þe *Pask* wyke, whan he yede to Emaus,
B.16.139 Til it bifel on a friday, a litel bifore *Pasqe*.
C.12.123 Witnesse in þe *paske* woke when he ȝede to Emaux:
C.18.166 This biful on a fryday, a litel bifore *Pasche*,

passen v *passen v.* A 14 passe (6) passeþ (1) passide (2) passiþ (5); B 31
 passe (10) passed (7) passede (1) passen (3) passeþ (5) passynge (3)
 ypassed (2); C 30 passe (8) passed (3) passede (2) passen (1) passeth
 (8) passyng (1) passynge (2) ypassed (4)

A. 1.7 Þe moste partie of þis peple þat *passiþ* on þis erþe,
A. 1.102 And whoso *passiþ* þat poynt is apostata in his ordre.
A. 2.151 But prikede forþ on his palfray & *passide* hem alle,
A. 3.126 And letiþ *passe* prisoners & paieþ for hem ofte,
A. 7.76 To penaunce & to pilgrimage wile I *passe* with oþere;
A. 7.188 'Ac ȝet I preye þe,' quaþ peris, 'er þou *passe* ferþere:
A. 8.11 Han pardoun þoruȝ purcatorie to *passe* wel sone,
A. 8.18 Han pardoun wiþ þe apostlis whanne þei *passe* hennis,
A. 8.153 And [dem]ide þat dowel indulgence *passiþ*,
A. 8.156 He *passiþ* al þe pardoun [of] seint petris chirche.
A. 8.158 Þe peple wiþoute penaunce [to *passe* to Ioye]?
A. 9.11 And preiȝede hem, pur charite, er þei *passide* ferþere.
A.10.73 And cheuissh[en] hym for any charge whan he childhod *passiþ*,
A.12.4 He *passeþ* þe apostolis lyf, and [peryth] to aungelys.
B.Pr.155 That vs loþeþ þe lif er he late vs *passe*.
B.Pr.193 For I herde my sire seyn, seuen yeer *ypassed*,
B. 1.7 The mooste partie of þis peple þat *passeþ* on þis erþe,
B. 1.104 And whoso *passe[þ]* þat point [is] Apostata in [his] ordre.
B. 2.190 And priked [forþ on] his palfrey and *passed* hem alle,
B. 3.137 [And] leteþ *passe* prisoners and paieþ for hem ofte,
B. 5.409 Vigilies and fastyng dayes, alle þise late I *passe*,
B. 5.415 I haue be preest and person *passynge* þritty wynter,
B. 6.84 To penaunce and to pilgrimage I wol *passe* wiþ oþere;
B. 6.202 Ac I preie þee, er þow *passe*, quod Piers to hunger,
B. 7.11 Han pardon þoruȝ purgatorie to *passen* ful liȝtly,
B. 7.175 And demed þat dowel Indulgences *passe[þ]*,
B. 7.178 [He] *passeþ* al þe pardon of Seint Petres cherche.
B. 7.180 [Th]e peple wiþouten penaunce to *passen* [to ioye]?
B. 8.11 And preide hem, p[u]r charite, er þei *passed* ferþer
B.10.469 And *passen* Purgatorie penauncelees at hir hennes partyng
B.13.20 And whan he hadde seid so, how sodeynliche he *passed*.
B.13.133 'Thanne *passe* we ouer til Piers come and preue þis in dede.
B.13.178 That Pacience þ[o] most *passe*, 'for pilgrymes konne wel lye'.
B.13.215 Conscience þo wiþ Pacience *passed*, pilgrymes as it were.
B.13.264 And louren whan þei lakken hem; it is noȝt longe *ypassed*
B.14.99 [Wye] þat wiþ hym spak, as wide as I haue *passed*.'
B.14.305 Pouerte myȝte *passe* wiþouten peril of robbyng.
B.14.306 For þer þat Pouerte *passeþ* pees folweþ after,
B.15.571 Thoruȝ his prouince to *passe* and to his peple shewe hym,
B.18.133 Siþ þis barn was ybore ben xxxti wynter *passed*
B.19.266 The pris neet of Piers plow, *passynge* alle oþere.
B.20.199 And as I seet in þis sorwe I sauȝ how kynde *passede*
B.20.218 Proude preestes coome with hym; [*passynge* an hundred]
B.20.338 'I praye þee', quod Pees þo, 'er þow *passe* ferþer,
B.20.343 I knew swich oon ones, noȝt eighte wynter [*passed*],
C.Pr.175 That vs loteth þe lyf ar he lette vs *passe*.
C.Pr.206 For y herde my syre sayn, seuene ȝer *ypassed*,
C. 1.7 The moste party of this peple þat *passeth* on þis erthe,
C. 1.98 And hoso *passeth* þat poynt is appostata of knyghthede.
C. 2.204 And prykede forth on pacience and *passed* hem alle,
C. 3.175 He lat *passe* prisones [and] paieth for hem ofte,
C. 7.30 I haue be prest and persoun *passynge* thritty wyntur
C. 8.93 To penaunc[e] and [to] pilgrim[age] y wol *passe* with oþere;
C. 9.11 Haen pardon thorw purgatorye to *passe* ful lyhtly,
C. 9.132 And ȝut more to suche men me doth ar they *passe*;
C. 9.320 And demede þat dowel indulgences *passeth*,
C. 9.324 So dowel *passeth* pardoun and pilgrimages to Rome.
C. 9.326 To peple wihtouten penaunce to *passe* into ioye,
C.10.11 And preyde hem, pur charite, ar they *passede* forthere
C.11.260 *Passe[d]* forth paciently to perpetuel blisse.
C.11.295 And *passen* purgatorie penaunceles for here parfit bileue:
C.13.31 A[c] þe pore pacient *passeth* parfyttest *passeth*
C.15.98 In þat ȝe parteth nat with vs pore, þat ȝe *passeth* dowel
C.15.152 [And] pacience properliche spak, tho Peres was thus *ypassed*,
C.15.183 With pacience wol y *passe* parfitnesse to fynde.'
C.16.140 Pouerte myhte *passe* wihtoute perel of robbynge.
C.16.141 For þer as pouerte *passeth* pes folleweth comunely
C.16.371 As y tolde þe with tonge a litel tyme *ypassed*,
C.17.5 'A *passeth* cheef charite yf holy churche be trewe:
C.20.136 Sethe this barn was ybore ben thritty wynter *ypassed*,
C.21.266 The pris neet of [Peres plouh], *passynge* alle oþere.
C.22.199 And as y saet in this sorwe y say how kynde *passede*
C.22.218 Proute prestes cam with hym; *passyng* an hundred
C.22.338 'Y preye the,' quod Pees tho, 'ar thow *passe* forþere,
C.22.343 Y knewe such oen ones, nat eyhte wynter *passed*,

passhed v *pashen v.* B 1; C 1 paschte
B.20.100 Deeþ cam dryuynge after and al to duste *passhed*
C.22.100 Deth cam dryuyng aftur and al to duste *paschte*

passion n *passioun n.* A 1 passioun; B 13; C 10 passion (1) passioun (9)
A.12.26 In þe *passioun*, whan pilat aposed god almyȝthi,
B. 5.404 Goddes peyne and his *passion* [pure] selde þenke I on.
B.13.91 And preuen it by hir Pocalips and *passion* of Seint Auereys
B.13.418 Penaunce [and] pouere men and þe *passion* of Seintes,
B.15.255 The mooste liflode he lyueþ by is loue in goddes *passion*;
B.15.270 What penaunce and pouerte and *passion* þei suffrede,
B.15.496 To be pastours and preche þe *passion* of Iesus,
B.15.515 And þoruȝ penaunce and *passion* and parfit bile[ue].
B.16.37 That is þe *passion* and þe power of oure prince Iesu,
B.16.38 Thoruȝ preieres and penaunces and goddes *passion* in mynde
B.17.98 And þanne plastred wiþ penaunce and *passion* of þat baby,
B.18.9 And of cristes *passion* and penaunce, þe peple þat ofrauȝte.
B.19.63 Ac þe cause þat he comeþ þus wiþ cros of his *passion*
B.19.326 And watlede it and walled it wiþ his[e] peyne[s] and his *passion*;
C. 7.20 Goddes payne and his *passioun* is puyre selde in my thouhte.
C. 7.78 Penaunse and pore men and the *passioun* of seyntes,
C.11.31 Or of þe *passioun* of Crist or of purgatorie þe peynes,
C.11.259 Withoute penaunce oþer *passioun* oþer eny other peyne
C.15.98 And prouen hit by here pocalips and þe *passioun* of seynt Aueroy
C.17.192 To be p[astor]s and preche the *passioun* of iesus
C.17.266 And thorw penaunce and *passioun* and parfyt bileue;
C.18.41 The which is þe *passioun* & þe penaunce & þe parfitnesse of iesus
C.21.63 Ac þe cause that he cometh thus with cros [of] his *passioun*
C.21.326 And wateled hit and walled hit with his paynes and his *passio[n]*

pastours n *pastour n.* A 1; B 3; C 3 pastors (1) pastours (2)
A.11.310 Þanne pore peple, as plouȝmen, and *pastours* of bestis,
B.10.466 Than Plowmen and *pastours* and [pouere] commune laborers,
B.12.148 To *pastours* and to poetes appered þe Aungel
B.15.496 To be *pastours* and preche þe passion of Iesus,
C.11.292 Then ploughmen an[d] *pastours* and pore comune peple.
C.14.92 To *pastours* and to poetes Appered þe Angel
C.17.192 To be p[astor]s and preche the passioun of iesus

patente n *patente n.(1)* A 1 patent; B 4 patente (3) patentes (1); C 2
A. 8.178 I ne wolde ȝiue for þi *patent* on pye hele.
B. 7.200 I sette youre *patentes* and youre pardon at one pies hele.
B.14.192 Ac þe parchemyn of þis *patente* of pouerte be moste,
B.17.11 [He plukkede] forþ a *patente*, a pece an hard roche
B.18.186 Lo! here þe *patente*', quod Pees, 'In pace in idipsum,
C.19.12 A pluhte forth a *patente*, a pece of an hard roche
C.20.191 Loo! here þe *patente*,' quod pees, 'In pace in idipsum,

paternoster n *paternoster n.* A 2; B 10; C 10
A. 5.189 He pisside a potel in a *paternoster* while,
A.11.312 Percen wiþ a *paternoster* þe paleis of heuene
B. 5.341 He pissed a potel in a *paternoster* while,
B. 5.394 I kan noȝt parfitly my *Paternoster* as þe preest it syngeþ,
B.10.468 Percen wiþ a *Paternoster* þe paleys of heuene
B.10.474 And principally hir *paternoster*; many a persone haþ wisshed.
B.13.236 Whan þe preest preieþ þe peple hir *Paternoster* to bidde
B.13.396 Ne neuere penaunce parfournede ne *Paternoster* seide
B.14.49 A pece of þe *Paternoster* [and profrede vs alle];
B.14.197 *Paternost[er]* and penaunce and Pilgrymag[e] to Rome,
B.15.181 He kan portreye wel þe *Paternoster* and peynte it with Aues
B.19.394 [Or] ech man forȝyue oþer, and þat wole þe *Paternoster*:
C. 5.46 Is *paternoster* and my primer,placebo and dirige,
C. 5.87 Nec in pane [nec] in pabulo; the *paternoster* wittenesseth
C. 5.107 S[yh]ing for my synnes, seggyng my *paternoster*,
C. 6.283 Ne neuere penaunce parformede ne *paternoster* sayde
C. 6.399 A pissede a potel in a *paternoster* whyle
C. 7.10 Y can nat parfitly my *paternoster* as þe prest hit syngeth;
C.11.294 Persen with a *paternoster* [þe paleys of] heuene
C.15.247 A pece of þe *paternoster* and profred vs all.
C.16.323 And purtraye wel þe *paternoster* and peynten hit with Auees.
C.21.394 Or vch man forȝeue oþer, and þat wol þe *paternost[er]*:

path n *path n.* B 1; C 1
B.14.304 The sixte is a *path* of pees; ye! þoruȝ þe paas of Aultoun
C.16.139 The sixte is a *path* of pees; ȝe! thorwe þe pase of Aultoun

patriark n *patriarke n.* A 1 patriarkes; B 15 patriark (3) patriarkes (12);
 C 16 patriarches (1) patriarke (3) Patriarkes (12)
A. 8.12 Wiþ *patriarkes* in paradis to pleiȝe þereaftir.
B. 7.12 Wiþ *Patriarkes* and prophetes in paradis to be felawe.
B.10.344 And *patriarkes* and prophetes and poetes boþe
B.12.115 But he were preest or preestes sone, *Patriark* or prophete.
B.12.136 *Patriarkes* and prophetes repreueden hir science
B.13.166 Pope ne *patriark*, þat pure reson ne shal [þee] make
B.13.427 *Patriarkes* and prophetes, prechours of goddes wordes,
B.16.198 *Patriarkes* and prophetes and Apostles were þe children,
B.16.251 That to *patriarkes* & prophetes and ooþer peple in derknesse
B.16.256 Amonges *patriarkes* and prophetes pleyinge togideres.
B.18.138 For *patriarkes* and prophetes han preched herof ofte

509

B.18.144   *Patriarkes* and prophetes þat in peyne liggen,
B.18.149   Iob þe [parfit] *patriark* repreueþ þi sawes:
B.18.271   *Patriarkes* and prophetes han parled herof longe
B.18.323   *Patriarkes* and prophetes, populus in tenebris,
B.19.16   *Patriarkes* and prophetes prophecied bifore
C. 7.87   *Patriarkes* and prophetes, precheours of goddes wordes,
C. 9.12   With *patriarkes* and prophetes in paradis to sitton.
C.10.206   Prophetus and *patriarkes*, popes and maydenes.
C.11.148   *Patriarkes* and prophetes, apostles and angelis;
C.13.21   Lo, how pacience and pouerte thise *patriarkes* releuede
C.14.60   Bote hit were pres[t] or prestis sone, *patriarke* or p[ro]phete.
C.14.81   *Patriarkes* and prophetus repreuede here science
C.17.51   Iop þe parfite *patriarke* this prouerbe wroet and tauhte
C.18.207   *Patriarches* and prophetes and apostles were the childerne.
C.18.272   With *patriarkes* and profetes pleynge togyderes.
C.20.141   For *patriarkes* and prophetes haen preched herof ofte
C.20.147   *Patriarkes* and prophetes þat in peyne liggen,
C.20.152   Iop þe parfit *patriarke* repreueth thy sawes:
C.20.279   *Patriarkes* and prophetes haen parled herof longe
C.20.366   *Patriarkes* and profetes, populus in tenebris,
C.21.16   *Patriarkes* & prophetes profecied bifore

patrymonye n *patrimoine n.*   B 2 patrymoyne (1) patrymonye (1); C 1 patrimonye
B.15.246   And cristes *patrymonye* to þe poore parcelmele dele;
B.20.234   'And for þei are pouere, parauenture, for *patrymoyne* [hem] faille[þ],
C.22.234   'And for thei aren pore, parauntur, for *patrimonye* hem faileth,

patron n *patroun n.*   B 1; C 1 patrones
B.12.227   He is þe pies *patron* and putteþ it in hir ere
C. 5.78   Popes and *patrones* pore gentel blood refused

paul(es > poul

paulynes n prop GLD *Paulines*   A 2 paulynes (1) poulynes (1); B 2; C 1 paulines
A. 2.73   And piers þe pardoner, *poulynes* doctor,
A. 2.139   *Paulynes* peple, for pleyntes in constorie,
B. 2.109   And Piers þe Pardoner of *Paulynes* doctrine,
B. 2.178   *Paulynes* pryuees for pleintes in Consistorie
C. 2.113   And Peres þe Pardoner of *paulines* queste,

paume > pawme

paunche n *paunche n.*   B 1; C 1
B.13.88   He shal haue a penaunce in his *paunche* and puffe at ech a worde,
C.15.95   He shal haue a penaunce in his *paunche* and poffe at vch a worde

pauper n *papire n.*   C 1
C.13.38   For þe parcel[s] of his *pauper* and oþer pryue dettes

pauyloun n *pavilioun n.*   A 1
A. 2.41   Was piȝt vp a *pauyloun* proud for þe nones,

pawme n *paume n.*   B 13 paume (1) pawme (12); C 12 paume
B.17.143   And profre[d] it forþ as with a *pawme* to what place it sholde.
B.17.144   The *pawme* is [þe piþ of] þe hand, and profreþ forþ þe fyngres
B.17.147   The holy goost of heuene: he is as þe *pawme*.
B.17.150   That touched and tastede at techynge of þe *pawme*
B.17.153   Al þat þe *pawme* parceyueþ profitable to feele.
B.17.156   The *paume* for [he] putteþ forþ fyngres and þe fust boþe.
B.17.160   Thoruȝ foure fyngres and a thombe forþ with þe *pawme*,
B.17.176   The *pawme* is pureliche þe hand, haþ power by hymselue
B.17.178   For [þe *pawme*] haþ power to putte out þe ioyntes
B.17.185   Vnfolden or folden, my fust and my *pawme*
B.17.190   For peyne of þe *pawme* power hem failleþ
B.17.201   For he prikeþ god as in þe *pawme* þat peccat in spiritu[m] sanct[um],
B.17.203   The holy goost of heuene [he] is as þe *pawme*.
C.19.117   And profered hit forth as with the *paume* to what place hit sholde.
C.19.118   The *paume* is the pethe of the hand and profereth [forth] the fyngeres
C.19.121   The holy goest of heuene: he is as þe *paume*.
C.19.124   Touchede and tastede at techyng of the *paume*
C.19.126   The fader is thenne as þe fuste with fynger and with *paume*
C.19.128   And þat the fynger gropeth he grypeth bote yf hit greue þe *paume*.
C.19.130   A fuste with a fynger and a fol *paume*.
C.19.141   The *paume* is puyrliche the hand and hath power by hymsulue
C.19.143   For þe *paume* hath power to pu[t]te out þe ioyntes
C.19.156   For peyne of þe *paume* power hem fayleth
C.19.167   For he priketh god as in [the] *paume* that peccat in spiritum sanctum.
C.19.169   The holy gost of heuene he is as þe *paume*.

peccunie n *pecunie n.*   C 1
C. 3.390   Be the *peccunie* ypaied, thow parties chyde,

pece n *pece n.*   A 3 pece (1) pecis (2); B 4 pece (3) pieces (1); C 4 pece (3) peces (1)
A. 3.21   Coupis of clene gold [and] *pecis* of siluer,
A. 3.78   Or presauntis wiþoute panis as *pecis* of siluer,
A. 7.293   May no penyale hem paye, ne no *pece* of bacoun,
B. 3.89   Or presentȝ wiþouten pens as *pieces* of siluer,
B. 6.309   May no peny ale hem paie, ne no *pece* of bacoun,
B.14.49   A *pece* of þe Paternoster [and profrede vs alle];
B.17.11   [He plukkede] forþ a patente, a *pece* of an hard roche
C. 8.331   May no peny ale hem pay ne no *pece* of bacoun
C.15.247   A *pece* of þe paternoster and profred vs all.
C.19.12   A pluhte forth a patente, a *pece* of an hard roche
C.20.61   The wal of the temple tocleyef euene [a] to *peces*;

pecok n *pocok n.*   B 7 pecock (1) pecok (5) pecokkes (1); C 6 pecok (2) pocok (4)
B.11.359   And some caukede; I took kepe how *pecokkes* bredden.
B.12.229   And kynde kenned þe *pecok* to cauken in swich a [wise.
B.12.240   And þat [is] þe *pecok* & þe Pehen [wiþ hir proude feþeres
B.12.242   For pursue a *pecok* or a pehen to cacche,
B.12.249   Riȝt as þe pennes of þe *pecok* peyneþ hym in his fliȝt,
B.12.262   Thus þe Poete preueþ þe *pecok* for hise feþeres;
B.12.265   And wel awey of wynge swifter þan þe *Pecock*,
C.13.170   And how þe *pocok* caukede [y toke kepe þerof],
C.14.161   He tauhte þe tortle to tre[d]e, the *pocok* to cauke
C.14.172   That is, þe *pocok* and þe popeiay with here proude fetheres
C.14.174   For pursue a *pocok* or a pohen to cacche
C.14.179   Ac for his peynted pennes þe *pocok* is honoured
C.14.183   Thus þe poete praiseth þe *pocok* for his fetheres

pedlere n *pedelere n.*   B 1
B. 5.255   'I haue as muche pite of pouere men as *pedlere* haþ of cattes,

peel n *appel n.*   B 1
B.17.308   For þer þat partie pursueþ þe [*peel*] is so huge

peere n *per n.*   A 2 pere; B 3 peere (1) peres (1) piere (1); C 5 pere (4) peres (1)
A. 3.192   Þe leste brol of his blood a barouns *pere*.
A.11.197   Forþi is dobest [a] bisshopis *pere*,
B. 3.205   The leeste brol of his blood a Barones *piere*.
B. 7.16   Arn *peres* wiþ þe Apostles–þ[u]s pardon Piers sheweþ–
B. 9.14   Dobest is aboue boþe, a Bisshopes *peere*;
C. 3.262   The leeste brolle of his blod a Barones *pere*.
C. 9.20   To be [*peres*] to þe apostles alle peple to reule
C. 9.307   Of Nabugodonasor þat no *pere* hadde
C.10.141   Dobest is aboue bothe, a bishopis *pere*,
C.18.89   For þat is euene with angelis and angeles *pere*.

peeren v1 *peren v.(1)*   B 1
B.Pr.173   And *peeren* in his presence þe while hym pleye likeþ,

peeren v2 *peren v.(2)*   A 1 peryth; B 1
A.12.4   He passeþ þe apostolis lyf, and [*peryth*] to aungelys.
B.15.418   *Peeren* to Apostles þoruȝ hire parfit lyuynge.

peeris n *pere n.(1)* cf. *pere_ionettes*   B 1
B.16.71   Maidenhode, Aungeles *peeris*, and [erst] wole be ripe

pees n *pes n.*   A 9 pees (5) pes (4); B 45; C 54 pees (53) pes (1)
A. 1.137   And ek þe plante of *pes*; preche it in þin harpe
A. 3.208   Þe king haþ [m]ede of his men to make *pes* in londis;
A. 4.34   Þanne com *pes* into þe parlement & putte vp a bille
A. 4.50   To make his *pes* with his panis & profride hym manye,
A. 4.52   Þeiȝ *pees* & his power pleynide hem euere'.
A. 4.64   *Pees* putte forþ his heued & his panne blody:
A. 4.82   And profride *pees* a presaunt al of purid gold;
A. 4.85   *Pees* þanne pitousliche preyede to þe king
A. 6.108   Pacience & *pees* mekil [peple] þei helpen,
B. 1.152   And [ek] þe pl[ante] of *pees*, moost precious of vertues.
B. 3.221   The kyng haþ mede of his men to make *pees* in londe;
B. 3.301   And swich *pees* among þe peple and a parfit truþe
B. 4.47   [Th]anne com *pees* into [þe] parlement and putte [vp] a bille
B. 4.64   To maken [his] *pees* with hise pens and profred hym manye,
B. 4.66   Theiȝ *pees* and his power pleyned h[e]m euere'.
B. 4.75   To maken [his] *pees* wiþ his pens, handy dandy payed.
B. 4.78   *Pees* putte forþ his heed, and his panne blody:
B. 4.95   And profrede *Pees* a present al of pure[d] golde.
B. 4.98   [*Pees* þanne pitously] preyde to þe kynge
B. 5.622   Pacience and *pees* muche peple þei helpeþ;
B.11.332   Pouerte and plentee, boþe *pees* and werre,
B.13.174   Kan noȝt [parfournen] a *pees* bitwene [þe pope] and hise enemys,
B.13.175   Ne bitwene two cristene kynges kan no wiȝt *pees* make
B.13.208   And conformen kynges to *pees*; and alle kynnes londes,
B.13.258   Ne mannes masse make *pees* among cristene peple
B.14.304   The sixte is a path of *pees*; ye! þoruȝ þe paas of Aultoun

B.14.306 For þer þat Pouerte passeþ *pees* folweþ after,
B.15.427 Hir preieres and hir penaunces to *pees* sholde brynge
B.15.538 And þo was plentee and *pees* amonges poore and riche,
B.15.563 That sholden preie for þe *pees*, possession hem letteþ;
B.16.159 Suffreþ myne Apostles in [pays] and in [*pees*] gange.'
B.18.168 Where *pees* comeþ pleyinge in pacience ycloþed.
B.18.172 Whan *Pees* in Pacience ycloþed approched ner hem tweyne
B.18.174 And preide *pees* to telle hire to what place she wolde,
B.18.184 And þat god haþ forgyuen and graunted me, *pees*, & mercy
B.18.186 Lo! here þe patente', quod *Pees*, 'In pace in idipsum,
B.18.203 'And I shal preue', quod *Pees*, 'hir peyne moot haue ende,
B.18.228 Woot no wight what werre is þer þat *pees* regneþ,
B.18.408 Thanne pipede *pees* of Poesie a note:
B.18.409 'After sharpe shoures', quod *pees*, 'moost shene is þe sonne;
B.18.412 Than after werre and wo whan loue and *pees* ben maistres.
B.18.415 And *Pees* þoruȝ pacience alle perils stoppeþ.'
B.18.418 And leteþ no peple', quod *pees*, 'parceyue þat we chidde;
B.18.421 *Pees*, and pees h[i]re, per secula seculorum:
B.18.421 Pees, and *pees* h[i]re, per secula seculorum:
B.19.154 The Iewes preide hem *pees*, and [preide] þe knyghtes
B.19.357 Praye we þat a *pees* weere in Piers berne þe Plowman.
B.20.298 And made *pees* porter to pynne þe yates
B.20.330 *Pees* vnpynned it, was Porter of vnitee,
B.20.334 'He is sik', seide *Pees*, 'and so are manye oþere.
B.20.338 'I praye þee', quod *Pees* þo, 'er þow passe ferþer,
B.20.341 'Ye? go þi gate!' quod *Pees*, 'by god! for al þi phisik,
B.20.348 Hende speche heet *pees*, 'opene þe yates.
B.20.377 'He lyþ [adreynt] and dremeþ', seide *Pees*, 'and so do manye oþere.
C. 1.148 Loue is [þe] plonte of *pees*, most precious of vertues,
C. 3.454 And such *pees* among þe peple and a parfit treuthe
C. 4.45 Thenne cam *p[ees]* into [þe] parlement and putte vp a bille
C. 4.50 Y dar nat for his felawschipe, in fayth,' *pees* sayde,
C. 4.70 Of *pees* and his power thow he pleyne euere.'
C. 4.74 Ȝut *pees* put forth his heued and his panne blody:
C. 4.91 And profrede *pees* a present al of puyre golde.
C. 4.94 Pitousliche *pees* tho preyede the kyng
C. 5.195 Enioyne hem *pees* for here penaunce and perpetuel forȝe[ue]nesse
C. 7.274 Pacience and *pees* muche peple þei helpe,
C.13.2 Among Pilours in *pees* yf pacience hym folowe.
C.13.76 And ȝut more, to maken *pees* and quyten menne dettes
C.13.140 Pouerte and plente, bothe *pees* and werre,
C.14.16 That *pees* be and pacience and pore withoute defaute:
C.15.138 Byfore perpetuel *pees* y shal proue þat y saide
C.15.172 Can nat parfourme a *pees* of the pope and his enemyes
C.15.217 That pestilenc[e] to *pees* and parfyt loue turn[e].
C.15.228 Ne mannes prayere maky *pees* amonges cristene peple
C.15.232 '*Pees*!' quod pacience, 'y preye ȝow, sire actyf,
C.16.139 The sixte is a path of *pees*; ȝe! thorwe þe pase of Aultoun
C.16.141 For þer as pouerte passeth *pes* folleweth comunely
C.17.87 May no preyere *pees* make in no place hit semeth.
C.17.94 Ther sholde be plente and *pees* perpetuel euere.
C.17.199 And tho was p[lente] and *p[ees]* amonges pore and ryche;
C.17.226 That sholde preye for þe *pees* possession hem letteth;
C.17.228 Yf the kynges coueyte in cristes pees to lyuene.
C.17.236 His preyeres with his pacience to *pees* sholde brynge
C.17.248 To make a perpetuel *pees* bitwene þe prince of heuene
C.18.176 Soffreth my postles in pays and in *pees* gange.'
C.20.171 Where cometh *pees* pleiynge in pacience yclothed.
C.20.175 Whenne *pees* in pacience yclothed aproched her ayþer oþer
C.20.176 Rihtwisnesse reuerenced *pees* in here rich clothyng
C.20.177 And preyede *pees* to tellen [here] to what place she [w]olde
C.20.179 'My wil is to wende,' quod *pees*, 'and welcomen hem alle
C.20.190 Into *pees* and pyte of his puyr grace.
C.20.191 Loo! here þe patente,' quod *pees*, 'In pace in idipsum,
C.20.208 'And y shal pre[u]e,' quod *pees*, 'here payne moet haue ende
C.20.237 For woet no wiht what werre is þer [þat] *pees* regneth
C.20.451 Thenne piped *pees* of poe[sie] a note:
C.20.455 'Aftur sharp[e] shoures,' quod *pees*, 'most shene is þe sonne;
C.20.455 Then aftur werre and wrake when loue and *pees* ben maistres.
C.20.458 And *pees* thorw pacience alle perelles stop[peth].'
C.20.461 'And lat no peple,' quod *pees*, 'perseyue þat we chydde;
C.20.464 *Pees*, and pees here, per secula seculorum:
C.20.464 Pees, and *pees* here, per secula seculorum:
C.21.154 The iewes preyed hem *pees* and preyede th[e] knyhtes
C.21.357 Preye we þat a *pees* were in [Peres] berne [þe Plouhman]
C.22.298 And made *pees* porter to pynne þe ȝates
C.22.330 *Pees* vnpynned hyt, was porter of vnite,
C.22.334 'He is syke,' saide *Pees*, 'and so ar many other.
C.22.338 'Y preye the,' quod *Pees* tho, 'ar thow passe forþere,
C.22.341 'Ȝe? go thy gate' quod *pees*, 'bi god! for al thi fisyk,
C.22.348 Hende speche heet *pees*, 'opene þe ȝates.
C.22.377 'He lyeth adreint [and dremeth],' saide *pees*, 'and so doth mony
    oþere.

pehen n *pohen n.* B 2; C 1 pohen
B.12.240 And þat [is] þe pecok & þe *Pehen* [wiþ hir proude feþeres
B.12.242 For pursue a pecok or a *pehen* to cacche
C.14.174 For pursue a pocok or a *pohen* to cacche

peyne n *peine n.* A 2; B 16 peyne (13) peynes (3); C 24 payne (12)
  paynes (1) peyne (7) peynes (4)
A. 1.116 For pride þat he put out his *peyne* haþ non ende.
A.10.30 Þe lord of lif & of li[ȝt], of lisse & of *peyne*.
B. 1.127 For pride þat he putte out his *peyne* haþ noon ende.
B. 1.169 And yet wolde he hem no wo þat wrouȝte hym þat *peyne*,
B. 2.106 Hire soules to Sathan to suffre with hym *peynes*,
B. 5.154 Hir [were] leuere swowe or swelte þan suffre any *peyne*.
B. 5.404 Goddes *peyne* and his passion [pure] selde þenke I on.
B. 9.29 Lord of lif and of li[ȝt], of lisse and of *peyne*.
B.11.153 Brouȝte me fro bitter *peyne* þer no biddyng myȝte.'
B.12.250 So is possession *peyne* of pens and of nobles
B.13.13 Thoruȝ vnkonnynge curatours to incurable *peynes*;
B.13.44 In a morter, Post mortem, of many bitter *peyne*
B.14.54 Prison ne *peyne*, for pacientes vincunt.
B.17.190 For *peyne* of þe pawme power hem failleþ
B.18.144 Patriarkes and prophetes past in *peyne* liggen,
B.18.200 That þat *peyne* be perpetuel and no preiere hem helpe.
B.18.203 'And I shal preue', quod Pees, 'hir *peyne* moot haue ende,
B.19.326 And watlede it and walled it wiþ his[e] *peyne*[s] and his passion;
C. 1.129 For pruyde th[at] hym pokede his *payne* hath non ende.
C. 1.165 And ȝut wolde he [he] hem no wo þat wrouhte hym þat [*p]e[y]ne*
C. 1.199 So loue is lecche of lyf and lysse of alle *payne*
C. 2.111 With alle þe [p]urtinaunc[e] of purgatorye and þe *peyne* of helle.'
C. 3.101 And haue here penaunce on puyre erthe and nat þe *peyne* of helle.
C. 6.129 Here were leuer swowe or swelte then soffre eny *payne*.
C. 7.20 Goddes *payne* and his passioun is puyre selde in my thouhte.
C. 7.117 To perpetuel *payne* or purgatorie a[s] wikke
C. 7.256 And solace thy soule and saue the fram *payne*
C. 7.277 For he payeth for prisones in places and in *peynes*.
C.10.155 Lord of lyf and of lyht, of lisse and of *payne*.
C.11.31 Or of þe passioun of Crist or of purgatorie þe *peynes*,
C.11.220 That for here werkes and wyt wonyeth now in *payne*,
C.11.259 Withoute penaunce oþer passioun oþer eny other *peyne*
C.15.16 Thorw vnkunynge curatours to incurable *peynes*;
C.15.49 In a morter, post mortem, of many bittere *peynes*
C.15.253 Prisoun ne *payne*, for [pacientes] vincunt.
C.19.156 For *peyne* of þe paume power hem fayleth
C.20.147 Patriarkes and prophetes þat in *peyne* liggen,
C.20.198 Sholde deye downriht and d[welle] in *payne* euere.
C.20.205 That her *peyne* [be] perpetuel [and] no preyer hem helpe.
C.20.208 'And y shal pre[u]e,' quod pees, 'here *payne* moet haue ende
C.20.416 And be at my biddyng, at blisse or at *payne*
C.21.326 And wateled hit and walled hit with his *paynes* and his passio[n]

peynen v *peinen v.* B 5 peyned (1) peynen (1) peyneþ (3); C 4 paynede
  (1) payneth (1) peyned (1) peyneth (1)
B. 1.171 To haue pite [on] þat peple þat *peyned* hym to deþe.
B. 7.43 Pledours sholde *peynen* hem to plede for swiche and helpe;
B.12.249 Riȝt as þe pennes of þe pecok *peyneþ* hym in his fliȝt,
B.19.434 Right so Piers þe Plowman *peyneþ* hym to tilye
B.19.437 [So blessed be Piers þe Plowman þat *peyneþ* hym to tilye],
C. 1.167 To haue pitee on þat peple þat *paynede* hym to dethe.
C.21.322 That Crist vpon Caluary for mankynde on *peyned*.
C.21.434 Rihte so [Peres] the [Plouhman] *payneth* hym to tulie
C.21.437 So yblessed be [Peres] the [plouhman] þat *payneth* hym to tulie

peynten v *peinten v.* B 8 peynte (1) peynted (4) peyntede (1) peynten (2);
  C 10 paynted (3) peynte (1) peynted (4) peynten (2)
B. 3.62 Do *peynten* and portraye [who] paie[d] for þe makynge
B. 3.66 An auenture pride be *peynted* þere and pomp of þe world;
B.11.305 Or *peynted* parentrelynarie, parcelles ouerskipped.
B.15.181 He kan portreye wel þe Paternoster and *peynte* it with Aues
B.17.172 The fyngres formen a ful hand to portreye or *peynten*;
B.19.6 That Piers þe Plowman was *peynted* al blody
B.19.11 Or it is Piers þe Plowman? who *peynted* hym so rede?'
B.20.115 And wiþ pryuee speche and *peyntede* wordes,
C. 3.66 And [do] *peynten* and purtrayen ho payede for þe makyng
C. 3.70 An Auntur pruyde be *paynted* there and pomp of the world,
C. 4.23 Lat peytrele [hym] and pole hym with *peynted* wittes.'
C.13.119 Or *peynted* parentrelynarie, parseles ouerskipped.
C.14.179 Ac for his *peynted* pennes þe pecok is honoured
C.16.323 And purtraye wel þe paternoster and *peynten* hit with Auees.
C.19.137 Portreye me *peynte* parfitliche, y leue,
C.21.6 That [Peres] þe [plouhman] was *peynted* al blody
C.21.11 Or hit is [Peres þe Plouhman? who *paynted* hym so rede?'
C.22.115 And with priue speche and *paynted* wordes

peire n *paire n.(1)* A 1; B 4; C 3 payre
A.10.191 Manye *peire* siþen þ[e] pestilence han p[l]iȝt hem togidere.

B. 5.253 That payed neuere for his prentishode no3t a *peire* gloues.'
B. 9.170 Many *peire* siþen þe pestilence han pli3t hem togideres.
B.12.19 And prechours to preuen what it is of many a *peire* freres.'
B.13.196 And þe poore widewe [purely] for a *peire* of mytes.
C. 6.251 Payed neuere for his prentished nat a *payre* gloues.
C.10.232 Excepte onliche of vch kynde a *payre*
C.10.271 Many a *payre* sethe th[e] pestelens[e] han plyhte treuthe to louye;

peis n *peis n.* B 2; C 1 peyse
B. 5.240 To weye pens wiþ a *peis* and pare þe heuyeste
B.13.246 Saue a pardon wiþ a *peis* of leed and two polles amyddes.
C. 6.242 To weye pans with a *peyse* and par[e] þe heuegeste

peised v *peisen v.* A 1 peisid; B 1; C 1 peysed
A. 5.131 Þe pound þat heo [payede] by *peisid* a quarter more
B. 5.215 [Th]e pound þat she paied by *peised* a quartron moore
C. 6.223 The pound th[at] he payede by *peysed* a quarter more

peisen v *pesen v.* A 1 peysen; B 1
A. 7.282 [Grene porret and pesen; to [*peysen*] him þei þou3te].
B. 6.298 Grene poret and pesen; to [*peisen*] hym þei þo3te.

peytrele v *peitrelen v.* C 1
C. 4.23 Lat *peytrele* [hym] and pole hym with peynted wittes.'

pelet n *pellet n.* A 1; B 1
A. 5.60 He was as pale as a *p[e]let*, [in] þe palesie he semide;
B. 5.77 He was as pale as a *pelet*, in þe palsy he semed.

pelour n *pelour n.* B 1; C 1
B.18.40 Tho putte hym forþ a *p[e]lour* bifore Pilat and seide,
C.20.39 Thenne potte hym forth a *pelour* bifore pilatus and saide,

pelours > pilour

pelure n *pelure n.* A 2; B 4; C 4
A. 2.9 Ipurfilid wiþ *pelure*, þe pureste [o]n erþe,
A. 3.271 Ne no ray robe [wiþ] riche *pelure*.
B. 2.9 Purfiled wiþ *Pelure*, þe [pureste on] erþe,
B. 3.296 Ne no *pelure* in his [panelon] for pledynge at þe barre;
B.15.7 As persons in *pelure* wiþ pendaunt3 of siluer;
B.19.415 For hir *pelure* and palfreyes mete and pilours þat hem folweþ.
C. 2.10 She was purfiled [with] *pelure*, non puyrere on erthe,
C. 3.449 Ne no *pelure* in his panelon for pledyng at þe barre.
C. 4.115 And here *pelure* and here palfrayes pore menne lyflode
C.21.415 For here *pelure* and palfrayes mete and pelours þat hem folweth.

penante > penaunt

penaunce n *penaunce n.* A 14; B 47 penaunce (43) penaunces (4); C 44
  penance (1) penaunce (37) penaunces (1) penaunse (5)
A.Pr.25 In preyours & *penaunce* putten hem manye,
A. 6.85 I perfourmde þe *penaunce* þe prest me enioynide,
A. 7.76 To *penaunce* & to pilgrimage wile I passe with oþere;
A. 8.88 Here *penaunce* & here purcatorie vpon þis pur erþe.
A. 8.106 Of preyours & of *penaunce* my plou3 shal ben hereaftir,
A. 8.108 Þe prophet his p[a]yn e[et] in *penaunce* & in wepyng
A. 8.158 Þe peple wiþoute *penaunce* [to passe to Ioye]?
A. 8.161 Þat pardoun, & *penaunce*, & preyours do salue
A. 9.95 And putten hem þere in *penaunce* wiþoute pite or grace,
A.11.26 Or prechen of þe *penaunce* þat pilat[u]s wrou3te
A.11.78 And preye hym of pardoun & *penaunce* [in] þi lyue,
A.11.230 Ac pore men in pacience & *penaunce* togidere
A.11.286 Wiþoute *penaunce* of purcatorie to haue paradis for euere.
A.11.313 Wiþoute *penaunce* at here partyng, into [þe] hei3e blisse.
B.Pr.25 In preieres and *penaunc[e]* putten hem manye,
B. 5.398 I parfournede neuere *penaunce* as þe preest me hi3te,
B. 5.593 Ech piler is of *penaunce*, of preieres-to-Seyntes;
B. 5.598 I parfourned þe *penaunce* þe preest me enioyned
B. 6.84 To *penaunce* and to pilgrimage I wol passe wiþ oþere;
B. 7.106 Hir *penaunce* and hir Purgatorie [vp]on þis [pure] erþe.
B. 7.124 Of preieres and of *penaunce* my plou3 shal ben herafter,
B. 7.126 The prophete his payn eet in *penaunce* and in sorwe
B. 7.180 [Th]e peple wiþouten *penaunce* to passen [to ioye]?
B. 7.183 That pardon and *penaunce* and preieres doon saue
B. 8.105 And putten hem þer in *penaunce* wiþoute pite or grace],
B. 9.79 Shul [purchace] *penaunce* in purgatorie but þei hem helpe.
B.10.34 Or prechen of þe *penaunce* þat Pilat wro3te
B.10.125 And preie hym of pardon and *penaunce* in þi lyue,
B.10.325 And puten [hem] to hir *penaunce*, Ad pristinum statum ire;
B.10.427 Wiþouten *penaunce* of purgatorie, to perpetuel blisse.
B.11.263 So after pouerte or *penaunce* paciently ytake:
B.11.281 To serue god goodliche, ne greueþ hym no *penaunce*:
B.12.9 Pouerte or *penaunce*, or preyeres bidde:
B.13.66 Preched of *penaunces* þat Poul þe Apostle suffrede
B.13.76 They prechen þat *penaunce* is profitable to þe soule,
B.13.85 [And appose hym] what *penaunce* is, of which he preched raþer.'

B.13.88 He shal haue a *penaunce* in his paunche and puffe at ech a worde,
B.13.98 Of dowel and dobet, and if do[best] be any *penaunce*.'
B.13.103 'What is dowel, sire doctour?' quod I; 'is [dobest] any *penaunce*?'
B.13.111 I wolde permute my *penaunce* with youre, for I am in point to dowel.'
B.13.396 Ne neuere *penaunce* parfournede ne Paternoster seide
B.13.411 [Ac] *penaunce* þat þe preest enioyneþ parfourneþ yuele;
B.13.418 *Penaunce* [and] pouere men and þe passion of Seintes,
B.14.10 To *penaunce* pacience and pouere men to fede,
B.14.197 Paternost[er] and *penaunce* and Pilgrymag[e] to Rome,
B.14.235 So for his glotonie and his greete sleuþe he haþ a greuous *penaunce*,
B.14.284 So pouerte propreliche *penaunce* [is to þe body,
B.15.148 In preieres and in *penaunces*, and in parfit charite.'
B.15.208 Than for *penaunce* and parfitnesse, þe pouerte þat swiche takeþ.
B.15.270 What *penaunce* and pouerte and passion þei suffrede,
B.15.427 Hir preieres and hir *penaunces* to pees sholde brynge
B.15.515 And þoru3 *penaunce* and passion and parfit bile[ue].
B.16.38 Thoru3 preieres and *penaunces* and goddes passion in mynde
B.17.98 And þanne plastred wiþ *penaunce* and passion of þat baby,
B.17.255 Delen and do *penaunce* day and nyght euere,
B.17.343 And ben inpacient in hir *penaunce*, pure reson knoweþ
B.18.9 And of cristes passion and *penaunce*, þe peple þat ofrau3te.
B.19.67 To *penaunce* and to pouerte he moste puten hymseluen,
B.19.376 And oþ[er] pryue *penaunc[e]*, and somme þoru3 penyes delynge.
B.20.283 Alle þat ben hir parisshens *penaunce* enioigne,
B.20.306 Shrift shoop sharp salue and made men do *penaunce*
C.Pr.27 In preiers and *penaunc[e]* potten hem mony,
C. 3.101 And haue here *penaunce* on puyre erthe and nat þe peyne of helle.
C. 3.400 To syke for here synnes and soffre harde *penaunc[e]*
C. 5.84 Preeyeres of a parfit man and *penaunce* d[iscret]e
C. 5.171 And potte 3ow to 3oure *penaunce*,ad pristinum statum ire,
C. 5.195 Enioyne hem pees for here *penaunce* and perpetuel for3e[ue]nesse
C. 6.14 '[I], pr[uyde], pacientlyche *penaunce* aske.
C. 6.110 Inpacient in alle *penaunc[e]* and pleyned, as hit were,
C. 6.283 Ne neuere *penaunce* parformede ne paternoster sayde
C. 6.304 And [what] *penaunce* the prest shal haue þat p[r]oud is of his tithes.
C. 7.14 Y parfourmede neuere *penaunc[e]* þat þe prest me hihte
C. 7.71 The *penauns[e]* þat þe prest enioyneth parformeth euele,
C. 7.78 *Penaunse* and pore men and the passioun of seyntes,
C. 7.241 Vche piler is of *penaunc[e]* and preyeres to seyntes;
C. 7.247 And parformed þe *penaunce* þat þe prest me hihte."
C. 8.93 To *penaunc[e]* and [to] pilgrim[age] y wol passe with oþere;
C. 9.175 Þai haue no part of pardoun ne of preyeres ne of *penaunc[e]*.
C. 9.186 Here *penaunce* and here purgatorie vppon this puyre erthe
C. 9.235 Pouerte or oþer *penaunc[e]*, as pilgrimages and trauayles.
C. 9.326 To peple withouten *penaunce* to passe into ioye,
C. 9.339 That pardoun and *penaunc[e]* and preyere[s] don saue
C.11.259 Withoute *penaunce* oþer passioun oþer eny other peyne
C.12.149 So aftur [pouerte or *penaunce*] pacientliche ytake
C.12.194 Riht so, sothly, þat soffry may *penaunc[e]*
C.12.206 Pouerte and *penaunce* and persecucoun of body.
C.13.82 And other pryue *penaunces* þe which þe prest woet wel
C.15.70 At poules byfore þe peple what *penaunce* they soffrede,
C.15.72 And how þat poul þe apostle *penaunce* tholede
C.15.82 They preche þat *penaunce* is profitable to þe soule
C.15.92 And apose hym what *penaunce* is and purgatorie on erthe
C.15.95 He shal haue a *penaunce* in his paunche and poffe at vch a worde
C.15.105 Of dowel and dobet and yf dobe[s]t [be] eny *penaunce*.'
C.15.110 'What is dowel, sire doctour?' quod y; 'is dobest eny *penaunce*?'
C.16.38 Oure preyeres and oure *penanc[e]* And pilgrimag[e] to Rome.
C.16.76 So for his glotonye and his grete synne he hath a greuous *penaunce*
C.16.328 That pouerte and *penaunce* pacientlyche ytake
C.17.266 And thorw *penaunce* and passioun and parfyt bileue;
C.18.41 The which is þe passioun & þe *penaunce* & þe parfitnesse of iesus
C.19.221 Dele and do *penaunce* day and nyht euere
C.19.323 And be inpacient in here *penaunc[e]*, puyr resoun knoweth
C.21.67 To *penaunce* and to pouerte he mot putte hymseluen
C.21.376 Or oþer priue *penauns[e]* and somme thorw pans delyng.
C.22.283 Alle þat been here parschienes *penauns[e]* enioynen
C.22.306 Shrift schupte scharp salue and made men do *penauns[e]*

penauncelees adj *penauncelees adj.* B 1; C 1 penaunceles
B.10.469 And passen Purgatorie *penauncelees* at hir hennes partyng
C.11.295 And passen purgatorie *penaunceles* for here parfit bileue:

penaunse > penaunce

penaunt n *penaunt n.* B 2; C 2 penante (1) penaunt (1)
B. 4.133 Prouysour or preest or *penaunt* for hise synnes.
B.13.93 Is neiþer fissh n[e] flessh, but fode for a *penaunt*.
C. 4.130 Prouisour or preest oþer *penaunt* for his synnes.
C.15.100 Is noþer fische ne flesche but fode for [a] *penant[e]*.

pencif adj *pensif adj.* A 1 pensif; B 1; C 1 pencyf
A. 8.132   And for peris loue þe plouȝman wel *pensif* in herte,
B. 7.151   And for Piers [loue] þe Plowman [wel] *pencif* in herte,
C. 9.300   And of [Peres] the [plouhman] fol *pencyf* in herte

pencioun n *pensioun* A 1
A. 8.47   Of princes & prelatis here *pencioun* shulde arise,

pendauntȝ n *pendaunt n.* B 1
B.15.7   As persons in pelure wiþ *pendauntȝ* of siluer;

peneworth(is > penyworþ

peny n *peni n. &> penyale* A 8 panis (4) peny (2) penis (1) penys (1); B 16 peny (6) penyes (2) pens (8); C 20 panes (3) pans (8) peny (8) penyes (1)
A.Pr.86   Pleten for *penis* & [poundide] þe lawe,
A. 1.45   Þo þe peple hym aposide with a *peny* in þe temple
A. 2.184   And ȝaf pardoun for *panis* poundmel aboute.
A. 3.78   Or presauntis wiþoute *panis* as pecis of siluer,
A. 3.151   Wiþoute presentis or *panis* he plesiþ [wel] fewe.
A. 4.50   To make his pes with his *panis* & profride hym manye,
A. 4.61   For of hise *penys* he proffride handy dandy to paye.
A. 7.264   'I haue no *peny*,' quaþ piers, 'pulettis to biggen,
B.Pr.213   Pleteden for *penyes* and pounde[d] þe lawe
B. 1.47   Tho þe poeple hym apposede wiþ a *peny* in þe temple
B. 2.225   And [gaf] pardoun for *pens* poundemele aboute.
B. 3.89   Or presentȝ wiþouten *pens* as pieces of siluer,
B. 3.162   Wiþouten presentȝ or *pens* [he] pleseþ wel fewe.
B. 4.64   To maken [his] pees with hise *pens* and profred hym manye,
B. 4.75   To maken [his] pees wiþ his *pens*, handy dandy payed.
B. 5.240   To weye *pens* wiþ a peis and pare þe heuyeste
B. 5.267   Ne haue a *peny* to my pitaunce, [for pyne of my soule],
B. 6.280   'I haue no *peny*', quod Piers, 'pulettes to bugge,
B. 6.309   May no *peny* ale hem paie, ne no pece of bacoun,
B.12.250   So is possession peyne of *pens* and of nobles
B.13.380   But he profrede to paie a *peny* or tweyne
B.15.166   As proud of a *peny* as of a pound of golde,
B.17.79   And he took hym two *pens* to liflode and seide,
B.19.376   And oþ[er] pryue penaunc[e], and somme þoruȝ *penyes* delynge.
C.Pr.163   Plededen for *penyes* and pounde[d] þe lawe
C. 1.45   Whenne þe peple aposed hym of a *peny* in þe temple
C. 2.235   And gaf pardon for *pans* poundmele aboute.
C. 3.32   'And purchace ȝow prouendres while ȝoure *panes* lasteth
C. 3.117   Or presentes without *pans* and oþer priue ȝeftes.
C. 3.200   Withoute presentes oþer *pans* he pleseth [wel] fewe.
C. 6.242   To weye *pans* with a peyse and par[e] þe heuegeste
C. 8.302   'Y haue no *peny*,' quod [Peres], 'polettes for to begge,
C. 8.331   May no *peny* ale hem pay ne no pece of bacoun
C. 9.91   And fele to fonge þerto and fewe *panes* taketh.
C. 9.92   There is payne and *peny* ale as for a pytaunce ytake
C.12.121   And pore peple fayle we nat while eny *peny* vs lasteth
C.12.165   Ȝef pore peple þe *panes*; þerof pors þou none
C.12.246   Lo, how *pans* purchaseth fayre places and d[r]ede,
C.16.299   As proud of a *peny* as of a pounde of golde,
C.16.315   That neuere payed *peny* aȝeyn in places þer he borwede.'
C.17.74   And to a badde *peny* with a gode printe:
C.18.164   And pursuede hym priueliche and for *pans* hym bouhte–
C.19.76   And toek two *pans* the hostiler to take kepe to hym;
C.21.376   Or oþer priue penauns[e] and somme thorw *pans* delyng.

penyale n *peniale n.* A 2; B 2 penyale (1) peny_ale (1); C 1 peny_ale
A. 5.134   *Penyale* & pilewhey heo pouride togidere.
A. 7.293   May no *penyale* hem paye, ne no pece of bacoun,
B. 5.218   *Peny ale* and puddyng ale she poured togideres;
B.15.315   For hadde ye potage and payn ynogh and *penyale* to drynke,
C. 6.226   *Peny ale* and poddyng ale [h]e poured togederes,

penyles adj *peniles adj.* C 1
C.12.26   And now y am pore and *penyles* at litel pris he sette[th] me.

penis > massepens,peny

penitauncer n *penitencer n.* B 1; C 2 penytaunce (1) pentauncers (1)
B.20.319   Than person or parisshe preest, *penitauncer* or bisshop,
C. 6.256   For þe pope with alle his *pentauncers* power hem fayleth
C.22.319   Then person oþer parsche prest, *penytauncer* or bischope

penyworþ n *peniworth n.* A 3 peneworthis (1) penyworþ (2); B 2 penyworþ (1) penyworþes (1); C 2 peneworth (1) penworthis (1)
A. 3.237   It is a permutacioun apertly, a *peny[worþ]* for anoþer.
A. 5.175   And preisiden þe *peneworthis* [aparte] be hemseluen.
A. 8.48   And of no pore peple no *peny[worþ]* to take.
B. 3.258   It is a permutacion apertly, a *penyworþ* for anoþer.
B. 5.326   And preised þ[e] *penyworþes* apart by hemselue.
C. 3.314   Hit is a permutacoun apertly, on *peneworth* for another.
C. 6.384   And preisede th[e] *penworthis* apart by hemsulue

penne n *penne n.* B 3 penne (2) pennes (1); C 2 penne (1) pennes (1)
B. 9.40   Thouȝ he [wiste to] write neuer so wel, [and] he hadde [a] *penne*,
B.12.249   Riȝt as þe *pennes* of þe pecok peyneþ hym in his fliȝt,
B.17.15   The glose was gloriously writen wiþ a gilt *penne*:
C.14.179   Ac for his peynted *pennes* þe pecok is honoured
C.19.16   The glose was gloriously writen with a gult *penne*:

pens > peny

pensel n *pencel n.(1)* C 1
C.18.187   'Thre persones in o *pensel*,' quod he, 'departable fram oþere.

pensif > pencif; pentauncers > penitauncer; penworthis > penyworþ

pepir n *peper n.* A 1; B 2; C 1 pepur
A. 5.155   I haue *pepir*, & p[ye]nye, & a pound of garlek,
B. 5.304   'I haue *pepir* and pion[e] and a pound of garleek,
B.15.203   And to poore peple han *pepir* in þe nose,
C. 6.359   'Y haue *pepur* and pyonie and a pound of garlek,

peple n *peple n.* A 33 peple (32) puple (1); B 93 peple (92) poeple (1); C 91
A.Pr.56   Prechinge þe *peple* for profit of þe wombe;
A.Pr.76   His sel sholde not be sent to disseyue þe *peple*.
A.Pr.79   Þat þe pore *peple* of þe parissh shulde haue ȝif þei ne were.
A.Pr.93   To preche þe *peple* & pore men to fede
A. 1.5   And seide 'sone, slepist þou? sest þou þis *peple*,
A. 1.7   Þe moste partie of þis *peple* þat passiþ on þis erþe,
A. 1.45   Þo þe *peple* hym aposide with a peny in þe temple
A. 1.145   To haue pite on þat *peple* þat pynede hym to deþe.
A. 2.38   Þer nas halle ne hous to herberwe þe *peple*,
A. 2.91   Ȝe & þe notories noye þe *peple*;
A. 2.139   Paulynes *peple*, for pleyntes in constorie,
A. 2.176   Aparailide hym as a prentice þe *peple* to serue.
A. 3.70   To þe pore *peple* þat parcelmel biggen,
A. 3.71   For þei poisone þe *peple* preuyly wel ofte,
A. 3.73   Of þat þe pore *peple* shulde putte in here wombe.
A. 3.210   Prestis þat preche þe *peple* to goode
A. 3.241   Þat agag of amaleg & [al] his *peple* aftir
A. 4.12   How þou lerist þe *peple*, þe lerid & þe lewid.'
A. 5.12   And preyede þe *peple* haue pite on hemselue,
A. 5.35   Þat þei preche þe *peple* proue it hemselue
A. 5.86   To preye for þe *peple* as þe prest techiþ,
A. 5.87   [For pilgrymes, for palmers, for all þe *peple*] aftir,
A. 6.108   Pacience & pees mekil [*peple*] þei helpen,
A. 7.276   Alle þe pore *peple* pesecoddis fetten;
A. 8.10   And r[iȝt]fulliche in reaum rewliþ þe *peple*
A. 8.48   And of no pore *peple* no peny[worþ] to take.
A. 8.158   Þe *peple* wiþoute penaunce [to passe to heuene]?
A. 9.21   He is oþerwhile elliswhere to wisse þe *peple*.'
A. 9.83   And prechiþ þe *peple* seint poulis wordis:
A.11.182   'It is a wel lel[e] lif,' quaþ she, 'among þe lewide *peple*;
A.11.198   Prince ouer godis *peple* to prechen or to chaste.
A.11.310   Þanne pore *peple*, as plouȝmen, and pastours of bestis,
A.12.102   Of peres þe plowman and mechel *puple* also.
B.Pr.59   Prechynge þe *peple* for profit of [þe wombe];
B.Pr.79   His seel sholde noȝt be sent to deceyue þe *peple*.
B.Pr.82   That þe [pouere *peple*] of þe parisshe sholde haue if þei ne were.
B.Pr.119   And for profit of al þe *peple* Plowmen ordeyned
B. 1.5   And seide, 'sone, slepestow? sestow þis *peple*,
B. 1.7   The mooste partie of þis *peple* þat passeþ on þis erþe,
B. 1.47   Tho þe *poeple* hym apposede wiþ a peny in þe temple
B. 1.171   To haue pite [on] þat *peple* þat peyned hym to deþe.
B. 2.58   As of knyȝtes and of clerkes and ooþer commune *peple*,
B. 2.127   The Notaries and ye noyen þe *peple*.
B. 2.217   Apparailed hym as [a p]rentice þe *peple* to serue.
B. 3.81   To þe pouere *peple* þat parcelmele buggen,
B. 3.82   For þei [p]oisone þe *peple* pryueliche [wel] ofte,
B. 3.84   [Of] þat þe pouere *peple* sholde putte in hire wombe.
B. 3.223   Preestes þat prechen þe *peple* to goode
B. 3.241   And enformeþ pouere [*peple*] and pursueþ truþe:
B. 3.262   That Agag of Amalec and al his *peple* after
B. 3.301   And swich pees among þe *peple* and a parfit truþe
B. 4.12   How þow lernest þe *peple*, þe lered and þe lewed.'
B. 4.159   And þe mooste *peple* in þe [moot] halle and manye of þe grete,
B. 5.23   How pertly afore þe *peple* [preche gan Reson].
B. 5.42   'That ye prechen þe *peple*, preue it yowselue,
B. 5.106   [To] preye for þe *peple* as þe preest techeþ,
B. 5.107   For Pilgrymes, for Palmeres, for al þe *peple* after,
B. 5.147   That whan þei preche þe *peple* in many places aboute.
B. 5.622   Pacience and pees muche *peple* þei helpeþ;
B. 6.163   Plentee among þe *peple* þe while my plowȝ liggeþ'.
B. 6.292   Al þe pouere *peple* pescoddes fetten;
B. 7.10   And riȝtfully in Rem[e] rulen þe *peple*
B. 7.30   Pouere *peple* [bedredene] and prisons [in stokkes]

B. 7.152 And which a pardon Piers hadde þe *peple* to conforte,
B. 7.180 [Th]e *peple* wiþouten penaunce to passen [to ioye]?
B. 8.25 He is ouþerwhile elliswhere to wisse þe *peple*.'
B. 8.92 And precheþ þe *peple* Seint Poules wordes,
B. 8.114 How dowel, dobet and dobest doon among þe *peple*.'
B. 9.197 Vngracious to gete good or loue of þe *peple*;
B.10.205 Poul preched þe *peple*, þat parfitnesse louede,
B.11.113 And whan þe *peple* was plener comen þe porter vnpynned þe yate
B.11.159 And on Troianus truþe to þenke, and do truþe to þe *peple*.
B.11.175 But al for loue of oure lord and þe bet to loue þe *peple*.
B.11.184 And [souereynly] pouere *peple*; hir preieres maye vs helpe
B.11.244 Many tyme god haþ ben met among nedy *peple*,
B.12.67 And of quod vidimus comeþ kynde wit, of siʒte of diuerse *peple*.
B.12.72 For Moyses witnesseþ þat god wroot for to wisse þe *peple*
B.12.110 To vnloken it at hir likyng, and to þe lewed *peple*
B.12.158 Than clerkes or kynde witted men of cristene *peple*.
B.13.8 And [*peple*] þat was pouere at litel pris þei sette,
B.13.69 That Poul in his Pistle to al þe *peple* tolde:
B.13.176 Profitable to eiþer *peple*;' and putte þe table fro hym,
B.13.236 Whan þe preest preieþ þe *peple* hir Paternoster to bidde
B.13.250 And þanne wolde I be prest to þe *peple* paast for to make,
B.13.258 Ne mannes masse make pees among cristene *peple*
B.13.277 As in apparaill and in porte proud amonges þe *peple*;
B.13.282 And so singuler by hymself [as to siʒte of þe *peple*
B.13.312 Which myʒte plese þe *peple* and preisen hymselue:
B.14.73 Ac vnkyndenesse caristiam makeþ amonges cristen *peple*,
B.14.174 Ac poore *peple*, þi prisoners, lord, in þe put of meschief,
B.14.183 [To hores, to harlotes, to alle maner *peple*];
B.14.195 And principalliche of al[l]e *peple* but þei be poore of herte.
B.14.291 Selde is any poore yput to punysshen any *peple*.
B.15.22 'What are ye called', quod I, 'in þat court among cristes *peple*?'
B.15.72 That [lome] þe lewed *peple* of hir bileue doute.
B.15.79 Moore for pompe þan for pure charite; þe *peple* woot þe soþe.
B.15.90 Ac of curatours of cristen *peple*, as clerkes bereþ witnesse,
B.15.100 [Is þe] roote of þe right feiþ to rule þe *peple*;
B.15.203 And to poore *peple* han paþir in þe nose,
B.15.326 Who parfourneþ þis prophecie of þe *peple* þat now libbeþ,
B.15.328 If any *peple* parfourne þat text it are þise poore freres,
B.15.389 That sola fides sufficit to saue wiþ lewed *peple*.
B.15.403 And if he among þe *peple* preched, or in places come,
B.15.568 If preesthode were parfit þe *peple* sholde amende
B.15.571 Thoruʒ his prouince to passe and to his *peple* shewe hym,
B.15.588 [And] for a parfit prophete þat muche *peple* sauede
B.15.591 Wiþ two fisshes and fyue loues fyue þousand *peple*,
B.16.251 That to patriarkes & prophetes and ooþer *peple* in derknesse
B.17.38 And siþþe riʒt as myself so louye alle *peple*.
B.17.341 As Poul þe Apostle to þe *peple* tauʒte:
B.18.9 And of cristes passion and penaunce, þe *peple* þat ofrauʒte.
B.18.36 Thanne cam Pilatus with muche *peple*, sedens pro tribunali,
B.18.80 Bifore Pilat and ooþer *peple* in þe place he houed.
B.18.418 And leteþ no *peple*', quod pees, 'parceyue þat we chidde;
B.19.7 And com in wiþ a cros bifore þe comune *peple*,
B.19.132 And þo was he called in contre of þe comune *peple*,
B.19.341 Thise two coome to Conscience and to cristen *peple*
B.19.361 And cryde and comaundede alle cristene *peple*
B.19.420 That no Cardynal coome among þe comune *peple*,
B.19.428 Inparfit is þat pope þat al [*peple*] sholde helpe
B.19.455 For Spiritus prudencie among þe *peple* is gyle,
B.20.86 Hadde ypriked and prayed polles of *peple*;
B.20.98 As pokkes and pestilences, and muche *peple* shente;
B.20.109 And kynde cessede [sone] to se þe *peple* amende.
B.20.125 Wiþ glosynges and gabbynges he giled þe *peple*.
B.20.281 For persons and parissh preestes þat sholde þe *peple* shryue
C.Pr.57 Prechyng þe *peple* for profyt of þe wombe;
C.Pr.77 His seel sholde nouʒt be ysent in deseyte of þe *peple*.
C.Pr.80 That þe [pore] *peple* [of þe] parsch[e] sholde haue yf þei ne were.
C.Pr.146 And for most profi[t to þe *peple*] a plogh gonne þei make,
C. 1.5 And sayde, 'Wille, slepestou? seestow þis *peple*,
C. 1.7 The moste party of this *peple* þat passeth on þis erthe,
C. 1.45 Whenne þe *peple* aposed hym of a peny in þe temple
C. 1.167 To haue pitee on þat *peple* þat paynede hym to dethe.
C. 1.194 And a luther ensau[m]ple, leef me, [to] þe lewed *peple*.
C. 2.60 Of knyghtes, of clerkes [and] other comune *peple*,
C. 2.201 Ac gyle was forgoere to gyen al th[e] *peple*,
C. 2.227 [A]paraylede hym [as a] prentys þe *peple* to serue.
C. 3.81 For thyse men don most harm to þe mene *peple*,
C. 3.83 With that þe pore *peple* sholde potte in here wombe.
C. 3.86 Thei han no pite on the *peple* þat parselmele mot begge;
C. 3.91 Bothe thorw fuyr and flood a[nd] thorw fals *peple*
C. 3.278 Prestes þat prechen and þe *peple* techen
C. 3.383 Ac þe moste partie of *peple* puyr indirect semeth
C. 3.386 Such inparfit *peple* repreueth alle resoun
C. 3.415 That agag of amalek and alle his leege *peple*

C. 3.454 And such pees among þe *peple* and a parfit treuthe
C. 4.12 How thow ledest my *peple*, lered and lewed.'
C. 5.141 'That ʒe prechen þe *peple*, p[ro]ue hit ʒowsulue;
C. 5.193 Amonges alle kyne kynges ouer cristene *peple*.
C. 6.30 Proud of aparayle in port amongus þe *peple*
C. 6.36 And ʒut so synguler be mysulue as to syhte of [þe] *peple*
C. 6.60 As to be preised amongus þe *peple* thow [y] pore seme:
C. 7.274 Pacience and pees muche *peple* þei helpe,
C. 8.190 Prestes and oþer *peple* towarde [Peres] they drowe
C. 8.204 Tho hadde [Peres] pitee vppon alle pore *peple*
C. 8.315 Alle þe pore *peple* tho pesecoddes fe[tt]e;
C. 8.347 Pruyde and pestilences shal moche *peple* feche;
C. 9.20 To be [peres] to þe apostles alle *peple* to reule
C. 9.34 Pore *peple* bedredene and prisones in stokkes
C. 9.43 Alle þe *peple* hadde pardon ynow þat parfitliche lyuede.
C. 9.114 To profecye of þe *peple*, pleinge as hit were
C. 9.118 Hit aren as his postles, suche *peple*, or as his priue disciples
C. 9.220 For holy churche hoteth alle manere *peple*
C. 9.301 And which a pardoun Peres hadde th[e] *peple* to glade
C. 9.326 To peple withouten penaunce to passe into ioye,
C.10.29 He is otherwhile elleswher to wisse þe *peple*.'
C.10.89 And precheth to þe *peple* seynt paules wordes:
C.10.296 Vngracious to gete goed or loue of [þe] *peple*,
C.11.6 To eny foel or to flaterere or to frentike *peple*,
C.11.19 He is reuerensed and yrobed þat can robbe þe *peple*
C.11.292 Then ploughmen an[d] pastours and pore comune *peple*.
C.11.293 Lewed lele laboreres and land tulyng *peple*
C.12.48 And whan þe *peple* was plenere ycome þe porter vnpynnede þe gate
C.12.100 And nameliche pore *peple*, here preeyeres may vs helpe
C.12.121 And pore *peple* fayle we nat while eny peny vs lasteth
C.12.165 ʒef pore *peple* be panes; þerof pors þou none
C.13.78 As Crist hymsulf comaundeth alle cristene *peple*:
C.15.10 And *peple* þat was pore at litel pris [þei] setten
C.15.70 At poules byfore þe *peple* what penaunce they soffrede,
C.15.75 A[s] poul þe apostle prechede to þe *peple* ofte:
C.15.194 Peres prentys þe plouhman, alle *peple* to conforte.'
C.15.212 Ac þe prest and [þe] *peple* preyeth for Peres þe Plouheman
C.15.228 Ne mannes prayere maky pees amonges cristene *peple*
C.15.230 Plente of payn the *peple* of sodoume,
C.16.126 Selde is eny pore ypot to p[u]nesche eny *peple*.
C.16.238 More for pompe and pruyde, as þe *peple* woet wel
C.16.244 Spryngeth and spredeth and enspireth þe *peple*
C.16.253 Is þe rote of [the] rihte fayth to reule þe *peple*;
C.17.34 Fynde honest men and holy men and oþer rihtfole *peple*.
C.17.61 Or ar prestes or pardoners or eny *peple* elles.
C.17.70 That pore *peple* by puyre riht here part myhte aske.
C.17.85 And worcheth nat as ʒe fyndeth ywryte and wisseth þe *peple*.
C.17.95 Wedurwyse shipmen now and oþer witty *peple*
C.17.121 That sola fides sufficit to saue with lewede *peple*.
C.17.174 And in what place he prechede and the *peple* tauhte
C.17.177 And when þe coluer ca[m] th[us] then knelede þe *peple*
C.17.180 Tolde hym and tauhte [hym] how to teche þe *peple*.
C.17.250 Yf prestehode were parfyt and preyede thus the *peple* sholde amende
C.17.284 And pacientliche thorw his prouynce and to his *peple* hym shewe,
C.17.299 And for a parfit profete that moche *peple* sauede
C.18.85 Matrimonye, a moist fruyt þat multiplieth þe *peple*;
C.20.35 Thenne cam Pilatus with moche *peple*, sedens pro tribunali,
C.20.82 Bifore pilatus and oþere *peple* in þe place he houed.
C.21.7 And cam in with a cros bifore þe comune *peple*
C.21.132 And tho was he cald in contreye of þe comune *peple*,
C.21.341 Thise two cam to Consience and to cristene *peple*
C.21.361 And cryede and comaundede alle cristene *peple*
C.21.420 That no cardinal come among þe comune *peple*
C.21.428 Inparfit is þat pope þat all *peple* sholde helpe
C.21.455 For spiritus prudencie among þe *peple* is gyle
C.22.86 Hadde ypriked and preyede polles of *peple*;
C.22.98 As pokkes and pestilences, and moche *peple* shente;
C.22.109 And kynde sesede [sone] to se þe *peple* amende.
C.22.125 With glosynges and gabbynges he gyled þe *peple*.
C.22.281 For persones and parsche prestes þat sholde þe *peple* shryue

pepur > pepir

percen v *percen v.* A 1; B 2 percen (1) yperissed (1); C 2 persen (1) ypersed (1)
A.11.312 *Percen* wiþ a paternoster þe paleis of heuene
B.10.468 *Percen* wiþ a Paternoster þe paleys of heuene
B.17.192 Were þe myddel of myn hand ymaymed or *yperissed*
C.11.294 *Persen* with a paternoster [þe paleys of] heuene
C.19.158 Were þe myddel of myn hand [ymaymed or *ypersed*]

percile n *perseli n.* A 1 persile; B 1; C 1 parsilie
A. 7.270   Ac I haue *persile* & poret, & many cole plantis,
B. 6.286   Ac I haue *percile* and pore[t] and manye [plaunte coles],
C. 8.308   Ac y haue poret-pl[o]ntes, *parsilie* and skalones,

pere > peere

pere_ionettes n *pere-jonette n.* C 1
C.12.221   As pesecoddes, *pere* ionettes, plommes and cheries;

perel(les > peril; peres > peere,piers; perfite > parfit; perfourmde > parfourned; perye > perree

peril n *peril n.* A 6 peril (5) periles (1); B 14 peril (12) perils (2); C 12 perel (9) perelles (3)
A. 4.123   Be vnpunisshit at my power for *peril* of my soule,
A. 6.44   'Nay, be þe *peril* of my soule!' quaþ piers & gan to swere:
A. 6.69   Loke þou plukke no plant[e] þere for *peril* of þi soule.
A. 7.85   [I] payede hym prestly for *peril* of my soule;
A. 7.156   'Now be þe *peril* of my soule!' quaþ peris, 'I shal appeire ȝow alle,'
A. 8.16   And prechen here personis þe *periles* of synne,
B. 4.140   Ben vnpunysshed [at] my power for *peril* of my soule,
B. 5.557   'Nay, by [þe *peril* of] my soul[e]!' quod Piers and gan to swere:
B. 5.582   Loke þow plukke no plaunte þere for *peril* of þi soule.
B. 6.93   I paide [hym] prestly for *peril* of my soule;
B. 6.117   'Now by þe *peril* of my soule!' quod Piers al in pure tene,
B. 6.171   'Now by þe *peril* of my soule!' quod Piers, 'I shal apeire yow alle',
B.11.33   And pride of parfit lyuynge to muche *peril* þee brynge.'
B.14.305   Pouerte myȝte passe wiþouten *peril* of robbyng.
B.15.509   And a *peril* to þe pope and prelates þat he makeþ
B.15.567   And purgen hem of poison er moore *peril* falle.
B.16.107   Til he was parfit praktisour if any *peril* fille.
B.17.69   And parceyued bi his pous he was in *peril* to dye
B.18.276   And where he wole is his wey; ac ware hym of þe *perils*:
B.18.415   And Pees þoruȝ pacience alle *perils* stoppeþ.'
C. 4.137   Be vnpunisched in my power for *perel* of [my] soule
C. 7.201   'Nay, bi þe *perel* of my soule!' Peres gan to swerie,
C. 7.229   Loke thow plokke no plonte þere for *perel* of thy soule.
C. 8.102   Y payede hit prestly for *perel* of my soule;
C.11.192   And pruyde-of-parfit-lyuynge to moche *perel* the brynge.'
C.15.276   And þat is pore pacient alle *perelles* to soffre.'
C.16.140   Pouerte myhte passe withoute *perel* of robbynge.
C.17.232   And purge hem of þe olde poysen Ar more *perel* falle.
C.17.260   And a *perel* for prelates þat þe pope maketh
C.19.68   And parseued by his poues he was in *perel* to deye
C.20.298   And where he wol is his way, ac waer hym of þe *perelles*:
C.20.458   And pees thorw pacience alle *perelles* stop[peth].'

perillousli adv *perilousli adv.* B 1; C 1 perilously
B.Pr.151   And pleide wiþ hem *perillousli* and possed aboute.
C.Pr.172   And playde with somme *perilously* and potte hem þer hym lykede.

perilous adj *perilous adj.* A 1; B 1
A. 7.43   In a wel *perilous* place þat purcatorie hattiþ;
B. 6.44   In a [wel] *perilous* place [þat] Purgatorie hatte.]

perimancie n *piromauance n.* A 1 perimansie; B 1
A.11.161   Nigromancie & *per[i]mansie* þe pouke to reisen;
B.10.218   Nigromancie and *perimancie* þe pouke to raise];]

peris > piers; peryth > peeren

perkyn n prop *OED Perkin n.1* A 8; B 8; C 6
A. 7.3   Quaþ *perkyn* þe plouȝman, 'be seint poule þe apostel,
A. 7.26   'Be seint poule,' quaþ *perkyn*, 'for þou profrist þe so lowe
A. 7.38   'Ȝa, & ȝet a poynt,' quaþ *perkyn*, 'I preye þe more:
A. 7.52   'And I shal apparaille me,' quaþ *perkyn*, 'in pilgrym[ys] wyse,
A. 7.100   Þerewiþ was *perkyn* payed, and preisid hem ȝerne.
A. 7.103   And summe to plese *perkyn* pykide vp þe wedis.
A. 8.118   'What!' quaþ þe prest to *perkyn*, 'peter, as me þinkeþ,
A. 8.126   Þe prest & *perkyn* aposid eiþer oþer,
B. 6.3   Quod *Perkyn* þe Plowman, 'by Seint Peter of Rome!
B. 6.24   'By Seint Poul!' quod *Perkyn*, '[for þow profrest þee so lowe]
B. 6.57   'And I shal apparaille me,' quod *Perkyn*, 'in pilgrymes wise
B. 6.105   Now is *Perkyn* and [þe] pilgrimes to þe plow faren.
B. 6.108   Therwiþ was *Perkyn* apayed and preised hem [yerne].
B. 6.111   And somme to plese *Perkyn* piked vp þe wedes.
B. 7.136   'What!' quod þe preest to *Perkyn*, 'Peter! as me þynkeþ
B. 7.144   The preest and *Perkyn* [a]pposeden eiþer ooþer,]
C. 8.1   Qvod [*perkyn*] þe [plouhman], 'be seynt petur of Rome!
C. 8.56   'And [y] shal [ap]parayle me,' quod *Perkyn*, 'in pilgrimes wyse
C. 8.112   Now is *perkyn* and þ[e] pilgrimes to þe plouh faren.
C. 8.115   Therwith was [*Perkyn*] apayed and payede wel here huyre.
C. 8.118   And somme to plese *Perkyn* [pykede vp þe] wedes.
C. 9.293   The prest thus and *perkyn* of þe pardon iangelede

perles n *perle n.(2)* A 1 perlis; B 1; C 1
A.11.9   And seide, 'Nolite mittere, Man, margerie *perlis*
B.10.9   And seide, 'noli[te] mittere, man, margery *perles*
C.11.7   And sayde, 'nolite mittere, ȝe men, Margerie *perles*

permutacion n *permutacioun n.* A 1 permutacioun; B 1; C 1 permutacoun
A. 3.237   It is a *permutacioun* apertly, a peny[worþ] for anoþer.
B. 3.258   It is a *permutacion* apertly, a penyworþ for anoþer.]
C. 3.314   Hit is a *permutacoun* apertly, on peneworth for another.

permute v *permuten v.* B 1; C 1 permuten
B.13.111   I wolde *permute* my penaunce with youre, for I am in point to dowel.']
C. 2.188   And notaries [vp]on persones þat *permuten* ofte

pernele n prop *Pernele n.* A 4 pernel (3) pernelis (1); B 6 Pernele (5) pernelles (1); C 6 purnele
A. 4.102   And *pernelis* purfile be put in hire hucche;
A. 5.26   And preyede *pernel* hire purfil to leue
A. 5.45   *Pernel* proud herte plat hire to þe erþe
A. 7.259   'Be seint *pernel*,' quaþ peris, 'þise arn profitable wordis.
B. 4.116   Til *pernelles* purfill be put in hire hucche,
B. 5.26   [And] preide *Pernele* hir purfil to le[u]e
B. 5.62   *Pernele* proud-herte platte hire to þe erþe
B. 5.160   And dame *Pernele* a preestes fyle; Prioresse worþ she neuere
B. 5.312   [Sire Piers of Pridie and *Pernele* of Flaundres,
B. 6.275   'By Seint [*Pernele*]', quod Piers, 'þise arn profitable wordes!]
C. 4.111   Tyl *purnele* porfiel be putte in here hucche,
C. 5.128   He p[ra]yde *p[ur]nele* here purfyel to leue
C. 6.3   *P[ur]nele* proude herte platte here to þe erthe
C. 6.135   And dame *purnele* a prestis fyle; Prioresse worth he neuere
C. 6.367   Syre [Peres] of prydie and *purnele* of Flaundres,
C.17.72   Prestes on aparayl and on *purnele* now spene.

perpetuel adj *perpetuelle adj.& adv.* B 4 perpetuel (3) perpetuele (1); C 11
B.10.427   Wiþouten penaunce of purgatorie, to *perpetuel* blisse.
B.14.215   For his pouerte and pacience a *perpetuel* blisse:
B.17.129   In þre persones departable þat *perpetuele* were euere,
B.18.200   That hir peyne be *perpetuel* and no preiere hem helpe.]
C. 5.195   Enioyne hem pees for here penaunce and *perpetuel* forȝe[ue]nesse
C. 7.117   To *perpetuel* payne or purgatorie a[s] wikke
C. 9.60   Pardoun *perpetuel* riht as [Peres] the [plouhman].
C. 9.279   Purgatorie for thy paie O[r] *perpetuel* helle
C.11.260   Passe[d] forth paciently to *perpetuel* blisse.
C.15.138   Byfore *perpetuel* pees y shal proue þat y saide
C.16.56   For his pouerte and pacience *perpetuel* ioye.
C.17.94   Ther sholde be plente and pees *perpetuel* euere.
C.17.248   To make a *perpetuel* pees bitwene þe prince of heuene
C.18.27   Thre persones indepartable, *perpetuel* were euere,
C.20.205   That her peyne [be] *perpetuel* [and] no preyer hem helpe.

perpetuelly adv *perpetuelli adv.* C 1
C. 9.8   Pardoun with [Peres] þe [Plouhman] *perpetuelly* he graunteth.

perree n *perrie n.* A 2 perreiȝe (1) perrie (1); B 1; C 1 perye
A. 2.12   Of þe pureste *perreiȝe* þat prince werde euere;
A.11.12   Þanne al þe precious *perrie* þat in paradis wexiþ.
B.10.12   Than al þe precious *perree* þat in paradis wexeþ.]
C.11.10   Then al þe preciouse *perye* þat eny prince weldeth.

pers > piers

persaunt adj *perceaunt adj.* B 1; C 1
B. 1.157   And portatif and *persaunt* as þe point of a nedle
C. 1.153   [And] portatif and *persaunt* as þe poynt of a nelde

persecucoun n *persecucioun n.* C 1
C.12.206   Pouerte and penaunce and *persecucoun* of body.

perseyue(d > parceyue; persen > percen; persile > percile

person n1 *persoune n.(2)* A 4 persones (1) personis (3); B 16 person (4) persones (1) persons (11); C 12 person (2) persone (1) persones (7) persoun (2)
A.Pr.80   *Personis* & parissh prestis pleynide hem to here bisshop
A. 3.139   Prouendrours, [*persones*], & [prestis] she maynteniþ
A. 3.231   Prestis & *personis* þat plesing desiriþ,
A. 8.16   And prechen here *personis* þe periles of synne,
B.Pr.83   *Persons* and parisshe preestes pleyned hem to þe Bisshop
B. 3.150   Prouendre[s], *persones* and preestes [she] maynteneþ
B. 3.252   Preestes and *persons* þat plesynge desireþ,
B. 3.311   Preestes and *persons* wiþ Placebo to hunte
B. 5.143   Shewen hire shriftes to hem þan shryue hem to hir *persons*,
B. 5.144   And now *persons* han parceyued þat freres parte wiþ hem
B. 5.415   I haue be preest and *person* passynge þritty wynter,

B.10.273 As *persons* and parissh preestes, þat preche sholde and teche,
B.10.319 In many places þer þei [*persons* ben, be þei purely] at ese,
B.11.98   Excepte *persons* and preestes and prelates of holy chirche
B.12.183 And þat is after *person* or parissh preest, [and] parauenture
               vnkonnynge
B.15.99   Right so *persons* and preestes and prechours of holi chirche
B.15.486 Ac who beþ þat excuseþ hem þat [arn] *persons* and preestes,
B.20.281 For *persons* and parissh preestes þat sholde þe peple shryue
B.20.319 Than *person* or parisshe preest, penitauncer or bisshop,
B.20.359 The plastres of þe *person* and poudres biten to soore;]
C.Pr.81   *Persones* and parsche prestis pleyned [hem] to þe bischop
C.2.188   And notaries [vp]on *persones* þat permuten ofte
C.3.188   He prouendreth *persones* and prestes he mayneteneth
C.3.464   Prestes and *persones* placebo and dirige,
C.5.165   In many places ther þei *persones* ben, be hemsulue at ese,
C.6.144   Yparroke[d] in pues; the *persone* hit knoweth
C.7.30   I haue be prest and *persoun* passynge thritty wyntur
C.14.123 And þat is aftur *person* other parsche preest, and parauntur bothe
               lewede
C.16.252 Riht so *persones* and prestes and prechours of holy churche
C.22.281 For *persones* and parsche prestes þat sholde þe peple shryue
C.22.319 Then *person* oþer parsche prest, penytauncer or bischope
C.22.359 The plasteres of the *persoun* and poudres b[it]en to sore;

personage n *personage n.(2)* B 1
B.13.245 Neiþer prouendre ne *personage* yet of [þe] popes ȝifte,]

persone n2 *persoune n.(1)* &> *person* A 1; B 18 persone (10) persones (7)
    persons (1); C 15 persone (5) persones (10)
A.3.166   Ne to depraue þi *persone* wiþ a proud herte.
B.3.179   Ne [to] depraue þi *persone* wiþ a proud herte.
B.9.116   And þus was wedlok ywroȝt wiþ a mene *persone*,
B.10.245 Thre [propre] *persones*, ac noȝt in plurel nombre,
B.10.474 And principally hir paternoster; many a *persone* haþ wisshed.
B.14.271 So it [preueþ] by ech a *persone* þat possession forsakeþ
B.15.7   As *persons* in pelure wiþ pendauntȝ of siluer;
B.15.196 'Wiþouten help of Piers Plowman', quod he, 'his *persone* sestow
               neuere.'
B.16.185 Pater is his propre name, a *persone* by hymselue.
B.16.188 The þridde highte þe holi goost, a *persone* by hymselue,
B.16.201 And þere hym likede and [he] louede, in þre *persones* hym
               shewede.
B.16.207 And eiþer is oþeres ioye in þre sondry *persones*,
B.16.220 Thus in þre *persones* is parfitliche [pure] manhede,
B.17.29   Thre *persones* in parcelles departable fro ooþer
B.17.46   It is lighter to leeue in þre louely *persones*
B.17.129 In þre *persones* departable þat perpetuele were euere,
B.18.335 For in my paleis, Paradis, in *persone* of an Addre
B.19.27   That knyght, kyng, conquerour may be o *persone*.
B.19.195 And what *persone* paieþ it nouȝt punysshen he þenkeþ,]
C.3.225   Ne to depraue thy *persone* with a pro[u]d herte.
C.16.111 So hit fareth by vch a *persone* þat possession forsaket
C.18.27   Thre *persones* indepartable, perpetuel were euere,
C.18.187 'Thre *persones* in o pensel,' quod he, 'departable fram oþere.
C.18.214 That he is thre *persones* departable y preue hit by mankynde,
C.18.233 And as thre *persones* palpable is puy[r]lich bote o mankynde,
C.18.235 So i[n] god [and] godes sone i[s] thre *persones*, the trinite.
C.19.30   Thre *persones* parselmele depar[t]able fram oþere
C.19.37   That of no trinite ne telleth ne taketh mo *persones*
C.19.44   Ac for to bileue in o lord þat lyueth in thre *persones*
C.19.98   In thre *persones*, a parceles departable fram oþere,
C.19.105 And moest inparfyt of alle *persones*; and pacientliche soffre
C.20.378 For in my palays, paradys, in *persone* of an addere
C.21.27   That knyht, kyng, conquerour may be o *persone*.
C.21.195 And what *persone* payth hit nat punischen he thenketh

persones persons > person,persone; persoun > person

pertliche adv *pertli adv.* B 2 pertly (1) pertliche (1); C 1
B.5.15   Was *pertliche* for pride and for no point ellis.]
B.5.23   How *pertly* afore þe peple [preche gan Reson].
C.5.117   Was *pertliche* for pruyde and for no poynt elles.

perus > piers; pes > pees,pese

pescoddes n *pesecod n.* A 1 pesecoddis; B 1; C 2 pesecoddes
A.7.276   Alle þe pore peple *pesecoddis* fetten;
B.6.292   Al þe pouere peple *pescoddes* fetten;]
C.8.315   Alle þe pore peple tho *pesecoddes* fe[tt]e;
C.12.221 As *pesecoddes*, pere ionettes, plommes and cheries;

pese n *pese n.* A 4 pese (2) pesen (1) pesis (1); B 5 pese (2) pesen (2)
    peses (1); C 4 pes (1) pese (2) peses (1)
A.7.154   And countide peris at a *pese* & his plouȝ boþe,
A.7.164   N[e] hadde peris [wiþ] a *pese* lof preyede hym beleue,
A.7.174   For a potel of pe[s]is þat peris hadde mad

A.7.282   [Grene porret and *pesen*; to [peysen] him þei þouȝte].
B.6.169   And sette Piers at a *pese* and his plowȝ boþe,
B.6.179   Ne hadde Piers wiþ a *pese* loof preyed [hym bileue]
B.6.186   For a pot[el] of *peses* þat Piers hadde ymaked
B.6.195   And ech a pouere man wel apaied to haue *pesen* for his hyre,
B.6.298   Grene poret and *pesen*; to [peisen] hym þei þoȝte.]
C.8.166   And sette [Peres] at a [*pes*], playne hym whare he wolde.
C.8.176   Ne hadde [Peres] with a *pese* loof preyede hym b[ile]ue.
C.8.305   And bred for my barnes of benes and of *peses*.
C.9.346   Y sette nat by pardon a *pese* ne nat a pye hele.

pesecoddes > pescoddes; pesen -es > pese

pestilence n *pestilence n.* A 4 pestilence (3) pestilences (1); B 9 pestilence
    (5) pestilences (4); C 8 pestelence (2) pestelences (1) pestelense (1)
    pestilence (1) pestilences (3)
A.Pr.81   þat here parissh w[ere] pore siþþe þe *pestilence* tyme,
A.5.13   And prouide þat þise *pestilences* wern for pur synne,
A.10.191 Manye peire siþen þ[e] *pestilence* han p[l]iȝt hem togidere.
A.11.59   To pleise wiþ proude men, siþen þe *pestilence* tyme,
B.Pr.84   That hire parissh[e] wer[e] pouere siþ þe *pestilence* tyme,
B.5.13   He preued þat þise *pestilences* were for pure synne,
B.5.36   Ne for no poustee of *pestilence* plese hem noȝt out of reson.
B.9.170   Many peire siþen þe *pestilence* han pliȝt hem togideres.
B.10.73   To pleise wiþ proude men syn þe *pestilence* tyme;
B.10.78   That preieres haue no power þ[ise] *pestilence*[s] to lette.
B.12.11   Wiþ poustees of *pestilences*, wiþ pouerte and with angres;
B.13.248 That he sente me vnder his seel a salue for þe *pestilence*,
B.20.98   As pokkes and *pestilences*, and muche peple shente;]
C.Pr.82   That here parsch[e] were pore sithe þ[e] *pestelence* tyme,
C.5.115   And preuede þat this *pesteleces* was for puyre synne
C.8.347   Pruyde and *pestilences* shal moche peple feche;
C.10.271 Many a payre sethe th[e] *pestelens[e]* han plyhte treuthe to louye;
C.11.53   To pleise with proude men senes th[e] *pestelenc[e* tyme]
C.11.58   That preyeres haen no power this *pestilences* to lette.
C.15.217 That *pestilenc[e]* to pees and parfyt loue turn[e].
C.22.98   As pokkes and *pestilences*, and moche peple shente;

peter n prop *Peter n.* A 5 peter (1) petir (3) petris (1); B 18 Peter (16)
    Petres (2); C 13 Peter (11) petres (1) petur (1)
A.6.25   '*Petir*,' quaþ a plouȝman and putte forþ his hed,
A.8.97   '*Petir*,' quaþ þe prest þo, 'I can no pardoun fynde
A.8.118   'What!' quaþ þe prest to perkyn, '*peter*, as me þinkeþ,
A.8.156   He passiþ al þe pardoun [of] seint *petris* chirche.
A.11.233 And prouen it be þe pistil þat *petir* is nempnid:
B.Pr.100 I parceyued of þe power þat *Peter* hadde to kepe,
B.Pr.109 To han [þe] power þat *Peter* hadde–impugnen I nelle–
B.5.537   '*Peter*!' quod a Plowman, and putte forþ his hed:
B.6.3   Quod Perkyn þe Plowman, 'by Seint *Peter* of Rome!
B.7.115   '*Peter*!' quod þe preest þoo, 'I kan no pardon fynde
B.7.136   'What!' quod þe preest to Perkyn, '*Peter*! as me þynkeþ
B.7.178   [He] passeþ al þe pardon of Seint *Petres* cherche.
B.10.350 And preuen it by [þe pistel þat *Peter* is nempned]:
B.10.450 For he seide to Seint *Peter* and to swiche as he louede,
B.11.87   'ȝis, by *Peter* and by Poul!' quod he and took hem boþe to
               witnesse:
B.13.254 For siþ he haþ þe power þat *Peter* hadde he haþ þe pot wiþ þe
               salue:
B.15.18   Is neiþer *Peter* þe Porter ne Poul wiþ [þe] fauchon
B.15.265 Ne han martired *Peter* ne Poul, ne in prison holden.
B.15.292 *Peter* fisshed for his foode and his felawe Andrew;
B.15.561 And þo þat han *Petres* power arn apoisoned alle."
B.18.243 *Peter* þe Apostle parceyued his gate,
B.19.163 *Peter* parceyued al þis and pursued after,
B.19.169 To *Peter* and to [h]ise Apostles and seide pax vobis;]
C.Pr.128 I parsceyued of þe power that *Peter* hadde to kepe,
C.Pr.136 To haue þe power þat *Peter* hadde inpugne y nelle
C.7.182   '[*Peter*]! quod a [plouhman], and potte forth his heued,
C.8.1   Qvod [perkyn] þe [plouhman], 'be seynt *petur* of Rome!
C.9.112   Riht as *Peter* dede and poul saue þat þey preche nat
C.9.289   '*Peter*!' quod the prest tho, 'y kan no pardoun fynde
C.15.224 For sethe he hath þe power þat *peter* hadde he hath þe pott with þe
               salue:
C.16.169 Is noþer *Peter* the porter ne poul with the fauchen
C.17.19   *Peter* fischede for his fode And his fere Androwe;
C.17.224 And [tho] þat haen *petres* power aren apo[y]sened alle."
C.20.252 *Peter* þe Apostel perseyued his gate
C.21.163 *Peter* perseyued al this and pursuede aftir,
C.21.169 To *peter* and to his apostlis and saide pax vobis;

pethe > piþ; pety > petit; petir > peter

petit adj *petit adj.* A 1; B 2; C 2 pety (1) petyt (1)
A.8.59   His pardoun in purcatorie wel [*petit*] is, I trowe,
B.7.58   Hi[s] pardon is [wel] *petit* at hi[s] partyng hennes

B.14.243 And Pouerte nys but a *petit* þyng, apereþ noȝt to his nauele,]
C. 9.53 His pardoun is ful *petyt* at his partynge hennes
C.16.83 And pouerte is bote a *pety* thyng, appereth nat to his nauele,

petres petur > peter

pharaoes n *Pharao n.* A 1 faraos; B 1; C 1 farao
A. 8.147 It befel as his fadir seide in *faraos* tyme
B. 7.170 It bifel as his fader seide in *Pharaoes* tyme
C. 9.314 Hit biful as his fadur saide in *farao* his tyme

pharisees n *pharise n.* B 1
B.15.605 Ac *pharisees* and Sarȝens, Scribes and [Grekes]]

philosofres n *philosophre n.* B 2 Philosofres (1) philosophres (1); C 4
 fylosofres (1) philosoferes (1) philosopheres (2)
B.19.244 As Astronomyens þoruȝ Astronomye, and *Philosofres* wise.
B.20.38 [*Philosophres*] forsoke wele for þei wolde be nedy
C.13.28 Worthiore as by holy writ and wyse *fylosofres*.
C.17.116 Bo[t]e they fayle in philosophie and *philosoferes* lyuede.
C.21.244 A[s] astro[nomy]ens thorw astronomye, & *philosopheres* wyse;
C.22.38 *Philosopheres* forsoke wel[e] for they wolde be nedy

philosophie n *philosophie n.* B 2; C 2 filosophye (1) philosophie (1)
B.15.384 Thei sholde faillen of hir *Philosophie* and in Phisik boþe.
B.20.295 And freres to *philosophie* he fond [hem] to scole,]
C.17.116 Bo[t]e they fayle in *philosophie* and philosoferes lyuede.
C.22.295 And freres to *filosophye* he foend hem to scole

philosophres > philosofres

phippe n *Phippe n.* B 1; C 1 fyppe
B.11.42 'Ye! farewel, *Phippe*', quod Faunteltee, and forþ gan me drawe
C.11.309 'Ȝe! farewel, *fyppe*,' quod fauntelete and forth gan me drawe

phisicien n *phisicien n.* A 1 fisician; B 2; C 3 fiscicien (1) fisciscyen (1)
 fisician (1)
A. 7.168 Ne hadde þ[e] *fisician* ferst defendite him watir
B.20.176 A *Phisicien* wiþ a furred hood þat he fel in a palsie,
B.20.315 Oon frere Flaterere is *phisicien* and surgien.']
C.18.140 Ne noon so faythfol *fisciscyen*, for all þat bysouhte hym
C.22.176 A *fisician* with a forred hoed that he ful in a palesye
C.22.315 Oen frere flaterrere is *fisicien* and surgien.'

phisik n *phisike n.* A 2 fesik (1) fisik (1); B 8 phisik (7) phisyk (1); C 8
 fisyk (4) fisik (2) fysyk (1) fysyke (1)
A. 7.253 Þat *fisik* shal his furrid hood for his foode selle,
A. 7.255 And be fayn be my feiþ his *fesik* to leten,
B. 6.269 That *Phisik* shal hi[s] furred ho[od] for his fode selle,
B. 6.271 And be fayn, by my feiþ, his *Phisik* to lete,
B.15.384 Thei sholde faillen of hir Philosophie and in *Phisik* boþe.
B.20.169 And lif fleiȝ for feere to *phisik* after helpe
B.20.178 'Now I se', seide lif, 'þat Surgerie ne *phisik*
B.20.314 And moore of *phisik* bi fer, and fairer he plastreþ;
B.20.341 'Ye? go þi gate!' quod Pees, 'by god! for al þi *phisik*,
B.20.378 The frere wiþ his *phisyk* þis folk haþ enchaunted,]
C. 8.266 Yf ȝe can or knowe eny kyne thyng[e] of *fisyk*
C. 8.290 That *fysik* shal his forred hod[e] for his fode sulle
C. 8.292 And be fayn, be my fayth, his *fysik* to leete
C.22.169 And lyf fley for fere to *fisyk* aftur helpe
C.22.178 'Now y see,' saide lyf, ' that surgerie ne *fysyke*
C.22.314 And more of *fysyk* bi fer, and fayror he plastereth;
C.22.341 'Ȝe? go thy gate!' quod pees, 'bi god! for al thi *fisyk*,
C.22.378 The frere with his *fisyk* this folk hath enchaunted

phisike v *phisiken v.* B 1; C 1 fisyk
B.20.323 That frere flaterere be fet and *phisike* yow sike.']
C.22.323 That frere flaterare be fet and *fisyk* ȝow seke.'

piche v *picchen v.* A 1 piȝt; C 2 piche (1) pyche (1)
A. 2.41 Was *piȝt* vp a pauyloun proud for þe nones,
C. 5.13 Or koke for my cokeres or to þe Cart *piche*,
C. 8.64 My plouhpote shal be my pykstaff and *pyche* ato þe rotes

pye n *pie n.(1) &> pies* B 3 pye (1) pies (2); C 1
B.11.347 I hadde wonder at whom and what þe *pye*
B.12.227 He is þe *pies* patron and putteþ it in hir ere
B.12.255 His ledene be in oure lordes ere lik a *pies* chiteryng;]
C.13.158 Y hadde wonder at wh[om] and where þe *pye*

pieces > pece

pyement n *piment n.* C 1
C.20.409 May no *pyement* ne pomade ne preciouse drynkes

pyenye > pione; piere > peere

piers n prop *n.i.d.* A 42 peres (1) peris (29) pieris (1) piers (11); B 112;
 C 112 Peres (104) Peris (1) Pers (4) Perus (3)
A. 2.73 And *piers* þe pardoner, poulynes doctor,

A. 6.43 'Ȝa, leue *piers*,' quaþ þe pilgrimes & profride hym hire.
A. 6.44 'Nay, be þe peril of my soule!' quaþ *piers* & gan to swere:
A. 6.119 'Ȝis,' quaþ *peris* þe plouȝman & pukide hym to goode:
A. 7.36 'Be my power, *piers*, I pliȝte þe my treuþe
A. 7.70 Dame werche whanne tyme is *piers* wyf hatte;
A. 7.97 Now is *peris* & þe pilgrimes to þe plouȝ faren;
A. 7.104 At heiȝ prime *peris* let þe plouȝ stande
A. 7.109 'Be þe prince of paradis!' quaþ *piers* þo in wraþþe,
A. 7.115 And pleynide hem to *peris* wiþ suche pitous wordis:
A. 7.117 Ac we preye for ȝow, *peris*, & for ȝoure plouȝ boþe,
A. 7.121 'Ȝef it be soþ,' quaþ *peris*, 'þat ȝe seyn, I shal it sone aspie.
A. 7.140 To *peris* þe plouȝman he profride his gloue.
A. 7.146 Þanne *peris* þe plouȝman pleynede hym to þe kniȝt
A. 7.154 And countide *peris* at a pese & his plouȝ boþe,
A. 7.156 'Now be þe peril of my soule!' quaþ *peris*, 'I shal appeire ȝow alle,'
A. 7.158 'Awreke me on wasto[urs],' quaþ *peris*, 'þat þis world [shend]iþ.'
A. 7.164 N[e] hadde *peris* [wiþ] a pese lof preyede hym beleue,
A. 7.174 For a potel of pe[s]is þat *peris* hadde mad
A. 7.181 And become knaues to kepe *peris* bestis,
A. 7.182 And preiȝede pur charite wiþ *peris* for to dwelle,
A. 7.184 And *pieris* was proud þerof, & putte hem in office,
A. 7.186 Þanne hadde *piers* pite & preiȝede hunger to wende
A. 7.188 'Ac ȝet I preye þe,' quaþ *peris*, 'er þou passe ferþere:
A. 7.213 'I wolde not greue god,' quaþ *peris*, 'for al þe gold on ground.
A. 7.214 Miȝte I synneles do as þou seist?' seide *peris* þanne.
A. 7.237 'Ȝet I preye þe,' quaþ *peris*, 'pur charite, ȝif þou kenne
A. 7.259 'Be seint pernel,' quaþ *peris*, 'þise arn profitable wordis.'
A. 7.264 'I haue no peny,' quaþ *piers*, 'pulettis to biggen,
A. 7.279 And profride *peris* [þis] present to plese þerewiþ hungir.
A. 8.1 Treuþe herde telle hereof, & to *peris* sente
A. 8.7 Or any maner mester þat myȝte *peris* helpen,
A. 8.66 Hadde þe same absolucioun þat sent was to *peris*.
A. 8.89 '*Piers*,' quaþ a prest [þo], 'þi pardon muste I rede,
A. 8.91 And *peris* at his preyour þe pardoun vnfoldiþ,
A. 8.101 And *piers* for [pure] tene pulde it assondir
A. 8.104 I shal cesse of my sowyng', quaþ *peris*, '& swynke not so harde,
A. 8.122 'Were þou a prest, *piers*,' quaþ he, 'þou miȝtest preche wh[an] þe
   liki[de];
A. 8.124 'Lewide lorel,' quaþ *peris*, 'litel lokest þou on þe bible;
A. 8.132 And for *peris* loue þe plouȝman wel pensif in herte,
A. 8.151 On *peris* þe plouȝman, whiche a pardoun he hauiþ,
A.12.102 Of *peres* þe plowman and mechel puple also.
B. 2.109 And *Piers* þe Pardoner of Paulynes doctrine,
B. 5.312 [Sire *Piers* of Pridie and Pernele of Flaundres,
B. 5.556 'Ye! leue *Piers*', quod þise pilgrimes and profred hym huyre.
B. 5.557 'Nay, by [þe peril of] my soul[e]!' quod *Piers* and gan to swere:
B. 5.634 'Ȝis!' quod *Piers* þe Plowman, and poked [hym] to goode,
B. 6.34 'By my power, *Piers*, I pliȝte þe my trouþe
B. 6.37 'Ye, and yet a point', quod *Piers*, 'I preye [þee] of moore:
B. 6.78 Dame werch-whan-tyme-is *Piers* wif hiȝte;
B. 6.112 At heiȝ prime *Piers* leet þe plowȝ stonde
B. 6.117 'Now by þe peril of my soule!' quod *Piers* al in pure tene,
B. 6.123 And made hir mone to *Piers* [how þei myȝte noȝt werche]:
B. 6.125 Ac we preie for yow, *Piers*, and for youre plowȝ boþe,
B. 6.129 'If it be sooþ', quod *Piers*, 'þat ye seyn, I shal it soone aspie.
B. 6.153 To *Piers* þe Plowman he profrede his gloue.
B. 6.154 A Bretoner, a braggere, [he b]osted *Piers* als
B. 6.159 Thanne *Piers* þe plowman pleyned hym to þe knyȝte
B. 6.169 And sette *Piers* at a pese and his plowȝ boþe,
B. 6.171 'Now by þe peril of my soule!' quod *Piers*, 'I shal apeire yow alle',
B. 6.179 Ne hadde *Piers* wiþ a pese loof preyed [hym bileue]
B. 6.186 For a pot[el] of peses þat *Piers* hadde ymaked
B. 6.196 And what *Piers* preide hem to do as prest as a Sperhauk.
B. 6.197 And [*Piers* was proud þerof] and putte hem [in office]
B. 6.199 Thanne hadde *Piers* pite and preide hunger to wende
B. 6.202 Ac I preie þee, er þow passe', quod *Piers* to hunger,
B. 6.229 'I wolde noȝt greue god', quod *Piers*, 'for al þe good on grounde!
B. 6.230 Miȝte I synnelees do as þow seist?' seide *Piers* þanne.
B. 6.253 'Yet I preie [þee]', quod *Piers*, 'p[u]r charite, and [þow] konne
B. 6.275 'By Seint [Pernele]', quod *Piers*, 'þise arn profitable wordes!
B. 6.280 'I haue no peny', quod *Piers*, 'pulettes to bugge,
B. 6.295 And profrede *Piers* þis present to plese wiþ hunger.
B. 7.1 TReuþe herde telle herof, and to *Piers* sente
B. 7.7 Or any [maner] mestier þat myȝte *Piers* [helpe],
B. 7.8 Pardon wiþ *Piers* Plowman truþe haþ ygraunted.
B. 7.16 Arn peres wiþ þe Apostles–þ[u]s pardon *Piers* sheweþ–
B. 7.39 And preiseden *Piers* þe Plowman þat purchaced þis bulle.
B. 7.64 Ha[dde] þe same absolucion þat sent was to *Piers*.
B. 7.107 '*Piers*', quod a preest þoo, 'þi pardon moste I rede,
B. 7.109 And *Piers* at his preiere þe pardon vnfoldeþ,
B. 7.119 And *Piers* for pure tene pulled it [asonder]
B. 7.122 I shal cessen of my sowyng', quod *Piers*, '& swynke noȝt so harde,

B. 7.140	'Were þow a preest, [*Piers*]', quod he, 'þow my3test preche [whan þee liked]
B. 7.142	'Lewed lorel!' quod *Piers*, 'litel lokestow on þe bible;
B. 7.151	And for *Piers* [loue] þe Plowman [wel] pencif in herte,
B. 7.152	And which a pardon *Piers* hadde þe peple to conforte,
B.13.124	For oon *Piers* þe Plowman haþ impugned vs alle,
B.13.130	Which shal saue mannes soule; þus seiþ *Piers* þe Plowman.'
B.13.131	'I kan no3t heron', quod Conscience, 'ac I knowe *Piers*.
B.13.133	'Thanne passe we ouer til *Piers* come and preue þis in dede.
B.13.237	For *Piers* þe Plowman and þat hym profit waiten.
B.15.196	'Wiþouten help of *Piers* Plowman', quod he, 'his persone sestow neuere.'
B.15.199	Ac *Piers* þe Plowman parceyueþ moore depper
B.15.212	But *Piers* þe Plowman, Petrus id est christus.
B.16.17	Vnder *Piers* þe Plowman to piken it and weden it.'
B.16.18	'*Piers* þe Plowman!' quod I þo, and al for pure Ioye
B.16.21	That *Piers* þe Plowman al þe place me shewed
B.16.24	'*Piers*', quod I, 'I preie þee, whi stonde þise piles here?'
B.16.53	'Now faire falle yow, *Piers*', quod I, 'so faire ye discryuen
B.16.60	'That is sooþ', [seide] *Piers*, 'so it may bifalle.
B.16.73	I preide *Piers* to pulle adoun an Appul and he wolde,
B.16.75	And *Piers* caste to þe crop and þanne comsed it to crye;
B.16.78	I hadde ruþe whan *Piers* rogged, it gradde so rufulliche;
B.16.86	And *Piers* for pure tene þat a pil he [l]au3te;
B.16.94	That *Piers* fruyt floured and felle to be rype.
B.16.103	And *Piers* þe Plowman parceyued plener tyme
B.16.168	And after *Piers* þe Plowman pried and stared.
B.16.171	After *Piers* þe Plowman; many a place I sou3te.
B.18.10	Oon semblable to þe Samaritan and somdeel to *Piers* þe Plow[man]
B.18.20	'And fecche þat þe fend claymeþ, *Piers* fruyt þe Plowman.'
B.18.21	'Is *Piers* in þis place?' quod I, and he preynte on me.
B.18.22	'This Iesus of his gentries wol Iuste in *Piers* armes,
B.18.25	In *Piers* paltok þe Plowman þis prikiere shal ryde,
B.18.33	And fecche fro þe fend *Piers* fruyt þe Plowman
B.19.6	That *Piers* þe Plowman was peynted al blody
B.19.11	Or it is *Piers* þe Plowman? who peynted hym so rede?'
B.19.12	Quod Conscience and kneled þo, 'þise arn *Piers* armes,
B.19.183	And yaf *Piers* [pardon, and power] he grauntede hym,
B.19.187	To *Piers* pardon þe Plowman redde quod debes.
B.19.188	Thus haþ *Piers* power, b[e] his pardon paied,
B.19.201	Oon Spiritus paraclitus to *Piers* and to hise felawes.
B.19.213	[Th]anne bigan grace to go wiþ *Piers* Plowman
B.19.258	For I make *Piers* þe Plowman my procuratour and my reue,
B.19.260	My prowor and my Plowman *Piers* shal ben on erþe,
B.19.262	Grace gaf *Piers* a teeme, foure grete Oxen.
B.19.266	The pris neet of *Piers* plow, passynge alle oþere.
B.19.267	And Grace gaf *Piers* of his goodnesse foure stottes,
B.19.271	Thise foure, þe feiþ to teche, folwe[de] *Piers* teme
B.19.274	And Grace gaf [*Piers*] greynes, Cardynal[es] vertues,
B.19.289	The þridde seed þat *Piers* sew was Spiritus fortitudinis,
B.19.297	The ferþe seed þat *Piers* sew was Spiritus Iusticie,
B.19.309	Thise foure sedes *Piers* sew, and siþþe he dide hem harewe
B.19.314	And so doon vices vertues'; [f]orþi', quod *Piers*,
B.19.318	Ordeigne þee an hous, *Piers*, to herberwe Inne þi cornes.'
B.19.319	'By god! Grace', quod *Piers*, 'ye moten gyue tymber,
B.19.330	A cart highte cristendom to carie [home] *Piers* sheues,
B.19.333	As wide as þe world is wiþ *Piers* to tilie truþe
B.19.335	Now is *Piers* to þe plow; pride it aspide
B.19.343	[Th]e sedes [þat sire] *Piers* [sew], þe Cardynale vertues.
B.19.344	'And *Piers* bern worþ ybroke; and þei þat ben in vnitee
B.19.357	Praye we þat a pees were in *Piers* berne þe Plowman.
B.19.386	Grace, þoru3 goddes word, [g]af *Piers* power,
B.19.390	To *Piers* pardon þe Plowman redde quod debes.'
B.19.406	The chief seed þat *Piers* sew, ysaued worstow neuere.
B.19.426	And [*Piers* þe Plowman] wiþ his newe plow and [þe] olde
B.19.430	A[c] wel worþe *Piers* þe plowman þat pursueþ god in doynge,
B.19.434	Right so *Piers* þe Plowman peyneþ hym to tilye
B.19.437	[So blessed be *Piers* þe Plowman þat peyneþ hym to tilye],
B.19.442	And [*Piers*] amende þe pope, þat pileþ holy kirke
B.20.77	Fooles fro þise fendes lymes, for *Piers* loue þe Plowman.
B.20.308	And þat *Piers* [pardon] were ypayed, redde quod debes.
B.20.320	Saue *Piers* þe Plowman þat haþ power ouer alle
B.20.382	To seken *Piers* þe Plowman, þat pryde [my3te] destruye,
B.20.385	And sende me hap and heele til I haue *Piers* þe Plowman.']
C. 2.113	And *Peres* þe Pardoner of paulines queste,
C. 6.367	Syre [*Peres*] of prydie and purnele of Flaundres,
C. 7.200	'3e! leue *Peres*,' quod thise pilgrimes and profrede Peres mede.
C. 7.200	'3e! leue Peres,' quod thise pilgrimes and profrede *Peres* mede.
C. 7.201	'Nay, bi þe perel of my soule!' *Peres* gan to swerie,
C. 7.287	'3us!' quod [*Perus*] þe [plouhman], and pokede hem alle to gode,
C. 7.293	To loke how me liketh hit,' and toek his leue at *Peres*.
C. 7.297	Forthy y pray 3ow, [*Peres*], paraunter 3if 3e m[e]ten

C. 7.303	Forthy, [*Peres*] the [plouhman], y preye the telle hit treuthe
C. 7.306	Famyne and defaute, folwen y wol *Peres*;
C. 8.7	'Y preye 3ow for 3oure profit,' quod *Peres* to þe ladyes,
C. 8.23	'Sikerliche, sire knyhte,' sayde [*Peris*] thenne,
C. 8.33	'By my power, [*Peres*], y plyhte the my treuthe
C. 8.35	'[Ye], and 3ut a poynt,' quod [*Peres*], 'y praye 3ow of more:
C. 8.80	Dame worch-when-tyme-is [*Peres*] wyf hehte;
C. 8.91	Ac aftur here doynge do thow nat, my dere sone,' quod *Peres*,
C. 8.119	At hey prime [*Peres*] leet þe plouh stande
C. 8.124	Quod [*Peres*] þe [plouhman] al in puyre tene:
C. 8.130	And maden here mone to [*Peres*] how þei m[yht] nat worche;
C. 8.131	'A[c] we praye for 3ow, [*peres*], and 3oure plouh bothe
C. 8.136	'3oure prayeres,' quod [*Peres*], 'and 3e p[ar]fyt weren,
C. 8.144	Such poore,' quod [*Peres*], 'shal parte with my godes,
C. 8.150	And to [*Peres*] þe [plouhman] profrede to fyhte
C. 8.152	A bretener cam braggyng, abostede [*Peres*] also:
C. 8.156	[*Peres*] the [plouhman] tho pleynede hym to þe knyhte
C. 8.160	For ther worth no plente,' quod [*Perus*], 'and þe plouh lygge.'
C. 8.166	And sette [*Peres*] at a [pes], playne hym whare he wolde.
C. 8.167	'Now, by Crist!' quod [*Peres*] the [plouhman], 'y shal apayre 3ow alle,'
C. 8.169	'Y preye the,' quod [*Perus*] tho, 'pur charite, sire hunger,
C. 8.176	Ne hadde [*Peres*] with a pese loof preyede hym b[ile]ue.
C. 8.177	'Haue mercy on hem, hunger,' quod [*Peres*], 'and lat me 3eue hem benes
C. 8.179	Tho were faytours afered and flowen into [*Peres*] bernes
C. 8.182	For a potte ful of potage þat [*Peres*] wyf made
C. 8.190	Prestes and oþer peple towarde [*Peres*] they drowe
C. 8.194	There was no ladde þat lyuede þat ne lowede hym to *Peres*
C. 8.197	Tho was [*Peres*] proud and potte hem alle a werke
C. 8.202	þat durste withsitte þat [*Peres*] sayde for fere of syre hunger
C. 8.204	Tho hadde [*Peres*] pitee vppon alle pore peple
C. 8.208	Ac y preye the,' quod [*Peres*], 'hunger, ar thow wende,
C. 8.214	But for fere of famyen, in fayth,' sayde [*Peres*].
C. 8.235	'Y wolde nat greue [god],' quod *Peres*, 'for al þe good on erthe!
C. 8.236	Myhte y synneles do as thow sayst?' sayde *Peres* þe plouhman.
C. 8.263	'By Crist!' quod [*Peres*] þe [plouhman] tho, 'this prouerbis [wol y] shewe
C. 8.265	Ac 3ut y praye 3ow,' quod [*Peres*], 'pur charite, syre hungur,
C. 8.282	And 3if thow [the pore be thy] pouer, [*Peres*], y þe rede;
C. 8.296	'By seynte Poul!' quod *Peres*, 'thow noynest neyh þe treuthe
C. 8.302	'Y haue no peny,' quod [*Peres*], 'polettes for to begge,
C. 8.317	And profrede [*Peres*] this present to plese with hongur.
C. 9.1	Treuthe herde telle herof and to [*Peres*] sente
C. 9.7	Or eny manere mester þat myhte [*Peres*] auayle
C. 9.8	Pardoun with [*Peres*] þe [Plouhman] perpetuelly he graunteth.
C. 9.42	And prey[se]de [*Peres*] the [plouhman] þat purchased þis bull[e].
C. 9.60	Pardoun perpetuel riht as [*Peres*] the [plouhman].
C. 9.160	Buth nat in this bulle,' quod [*Peres*], 'til they ben amended
C. 9.281	'[*Peres*],' quod a prest tho,' 'thy pardon moste y rede
C. 9.283	And [*Peres*] at his preeyre the pardon vnfoldeth
C. 9.300	And of [*Peres*] the [plouhman] fol pencyf in herte
C. 9.301	And which a pardoun *Peres* hadde th[e] peple to glade
C.15.33	Ilyk[e *peres*] the [ploghman], as he a palmere were,
C.15.130	For *Peres* loue þe palmare 3ent, þat inpugnede ones
C.15.137	Quod *Peres* the ploghman, 'Pacientes vinc[u]nt.
C.15.149	Where *Peres* the plogman bycam, so priueyliche he wente.
C.15.152	[And] pacience properliche spak, tho *Peres* was thus ypassed,
C.15.194	*Peres* prentys þe plouhman, alle peple to conforte.'
C.15.212	Ac þe prest and [þe] peple preyeth for *Peres* þe Plouheman
C.16.340	'*Peres* the plouhman,' quod he, 'moste parfitlyche hym knoweth:
C.20.8	Oen semblable to þe samaritaen and somdeel to *Peres* þe plouhman
C.20.18	'And feche þat þe fende claymeth, *pers* fruyt þe plouhman.'
C.20.19	'Is *Peres* in this place?' quod y, and he printe on me.
C.20.21	That this iesus of his gentrice shal iouste in *Pers* Armes,
C.20.24	In [*Pers* paltok] þe [plouhman] this prikiare shal ryde
C.20.32	And feche fro þe fende [*Peres*] fruyt þe [plouhman]
C.21.6	That [*Peres*] þe [plouhman] was peynted al blody
C.21.11	Or hit is [*Peres* þe Plouhman? who] paynted hym so rede?'
C.21.12	Quod Concience and knelede tho, 'this aren [*Peres*] Armes,
C.21.183	And 3af [*peres* pardoun] and [power] he graunted [hym],
C.21.187	To *Peres* pardoun þe plouhman Redde quod debes.
C.21.188	Thus hath *Peres* power, be his pardoun payed,
C.21.201	Oen spiritus paraclitus to *Peres* and to his felawes.
C.21.213	Thenne bigan grace to go with [*Peres*] Plouhman
C.21.258	For y make [*Peres* the plouhman] my proc[ur]atour and my reue
C.21.260	My prowour and my [plouhman *Peres*] shal ben on erthe
C.21.262	Grace gaf [*Peres*] a teme, foure grete oxen.
C.21.266	The pris neet of [*Peres* plouh], passynge alle oþere.
C.21.267	And grace [gaef *Peres* of his goednesse] foure stottes,
C.21.271	Thise foure, the fayth to teche, folewe[de *Peres*] teme
C.21.274	And grace gaf *Peres* graynes, cardinales vertues,
C.21.289	The thridde seed that [*Peres*] sewe was spiritus fortitudinis

C.21.297 The ferthe seed that [Peres] sewe was spiritus Iusticie
C.21.309 Thise foure sedes [Peres] sewe and sennes he dede hem harewe
C.21.314 And so doth vices vertues; forthy,' quod [Peres],
C.21.318 Ordeyne the an hous, [Peres], to herborwe in thy cornes.'
C.21.319 'By god! grace,' quod [Peres], 'ȝe moet gyue tymber
C.21.330 A Cart hihte Cristendoem to carie hoem Peres sheues
C.21.333 As wyde as the world is with Peres to tulye treuthe
C.21.335 Now is [Peres] to the [plouh]; Pryde hit aspiede
C.21.343 Þe sedes that sire [Peres] sewe, þe cardinale vertues.
C.21.344 'And Peres berne worth broke and þei þat ben in vnite
C.21.357 Preye we þat a pees were in [Peres] berne [þe Plouhman]
C.21.386 Grace thorw godes word gaf [Peres] power,
C.21.390 To [Peres] pardon þe [plouhman] Redde quod debe[s].'
C.21.406 The cheef seed þat [Peres] sewe, ysaued wo[r]st þou neuere.
C.21.426 And [Peres the Plowman] with his newe [plouh] and [þe] olde
C.21.430 Ac wel worth Peres the plouhman þat pursueth god in doyng[e],
C.21.434 Rihte so [Peres] the [Plouhman] payneth hym to tulie
C.21.437 So yblessed be [Peres] the [plouhman] þat peyneth hym to tulie
C.21.442 And [Peres] amende þe pope þat pileth holi churche
C.22.77 Foles fro this fendes lymes for [Peres] loue the [plouhman].
C.22.308 And þat Peres pardon were ypayd, redde quod debes.
C.22.320 Saue [Peres the Plouhman] þat haeth power ouer alle
C.22.382 To seke [Peres the Plouhman], þat pruyde myhte destruye,
C.22.385 And s[e]nde me hap and hele til y haue [Peres Plouhman]'.

pies n *pie n.(1)* &> *pye* A 2 pye (1) pyes (1); B 2; C 2 pye (1) pyes (1)
A.Pr.104 Cookis & here knaues crieþ 'hote *pyes*, hote!
A. 8.178 I ne wolde ȝiue for þi patent on *pye* hele.
B.Pr.226 Cokes and hire knaues cryden, 'hote *pies*, hote!
B. 7.200 I sette youre patentes and youre pardon at one *pies* hele.]
C.Pr.230 Cokes and here knaues cryede, 'hote *pyes*, hote!
C. 9.346 Y sette nat by pardon a pese ne nat a *pye* hele.

piȝt > piche

pik n *pike n.(1)* A 4 pik (3) pyk (1); B 4 pik (3) pyk (1); C 2 pyk
A. 5.248 Þat penitencia his *pik* he shulde pulsshe newe
A. 6.23 'I sauȝ neuere palmere wiþ *pik* ne wiþ scrippe
A. 7.95 My plouȝpote shal be my *pyk* & putte at þe rotis,
A. 9.88 A *pik* is in þat potent to pungen adoun þe wykkide,
B. 5.474 That penitencia his *pik* he sholde polshe newe
B. 5.535 'I [ne] seiȝ neuere Palmere wiþ *pyk* ne wiþ scrippe
B. 6.103 My plow[pote] shal be my *pi[k]* and [putte at] þe rotes,
B. 8.98 A *pik* is [in] þat potente to [punge] adown þe wikked
C. 7.180 'I [ne] saw neuere palmere with *pyk* ne with scrip[p]e
C.10.95 And with the *pyk* pulte adoun preuaricatores legis.

pykares n *pikere n.* C 1
C. 5.17 And kepe my corn in my croft f[or] *pykares* and theues

pyked adj *piked adj. &> piken* B 1; C 1 pikede
B.20.219 In paltokes and *pyked* shoes, [purses and] longe knyues,]
C.22.219 In paltokes and *pikede* shoes, [purses and] longe knyues

pikede > pyked,piken

pykeharneys n *pikeharneis n.* B 1; C 1 pikeharneys
B.20.263 Pylours and *Pykeharneys*, in ech a [parisshe] ycursed._]
C.22.263 Pilours and *pikeharneys* in vch a parsch acorsed.

piken v *piken v.* A 1 pykide; B 2 piked (1) piken (1); C 1 pykede
A. 7.103 And summe to plese perkyn *pykide* vp þe wedis.
B. 6.111 And somme to plese Perkyn *piked* vp þe wedes.
B.16.17 Vnder Piers þe Plowman to *piken* it and weden it.']
C. 8.118 And somme to plese Perkyn [*pykede* vp þe] wedes.

pikeporses n *piken v.* C 1
C. 6.370 Of portours and of *pikeporses* and of pilede tothdraweres,

pykoise n *pikeis n.* B 1; C 1 pikois
B. 3.309 Ech man to pleye with a plow, *Pykoise* or spade,]
C. 3.462 Vche man to pley with a plogh, a *pikois* oþer a spade,

pykstaff n *pike n.(1)* C 2
C. 6.328 That [penitencia] is *pykstaff* a wolde polesche newe
C. 8.64 My plouhpote shal be my *pykstaff* and pyche ato þe rotes

pil n1 *pile n.(3)* B 7 pil (3) piles (4)
B.16.23 Wiþ þre *piles* was it vnderpight; I parceyued it soone.
B.16.24 'Piers', quod I, 'I preie þee, whi stonde þise *piles* here?'
B.16.26 And in blowyng tyme abite þe floures but if þise *piles* helpe.
B.16.30 Thanne with þe firste *pil* I palle hym doun, potencia de[i] patris].
B.16.36 Thanne sette I to þe secounde *pil*, sapiencia dei patris,
B.16.55 Ac I haue þouȝtes a þreve of þise þre *piles*,
B.16.86 And Piers for pure tene þat a *pil* he [l]auȝte;]

pyl n2 *pile n.(4)* B 1; C 1 pyle
B.19.363 That holy chirche stode in [holynesse] as it a *Pyl* weere.]

C.21.363 That holi churche stoede in holinesse as hit [a *pyle* were].

pilat n prop *Pilate n.* A 2 pilat (1) pilatus (1); B 5 Pilat (3) Pilates (1) Pilatus (1); C 3 pilatus
A.11.26 Or prechen of þe penaunce þat *pilat[u]s* wrouȝte
A.12.26 In þe passioun, whan *pilat* aposed god almyȝthi,
B.10.34 Or prechen of þe penaunce þat *Pilat* wroȝte
B.18.36 Thanne cam *Pilatus* with muche peple, sedens pro tribunali,
B.18.40 Tho putte hym forþ a p[e]lour bifore *Pilat* and seide,
B.18.80 Bifore *Pilat* and ooþer peple in þe place he houed.
B.18.301 To warne *Pilates* wif what done man was Iesus,]
C.20.35 Thenne cam *Pilatus* with moche peple, sedens pro tribunali,
C.20.39 Thenne potte hym forth a pelour bifore *pilatus* and saide,
C.20.82 Bifore *pilatus* and oþere peple in þe place he houed.

pyle > pil; pilede > pileþ

piler n *pilere n.* B 1; C 1
B. 5.593 Ech *piler* is of penaunce, of preieres-to-Seyntes;]
C. 7.241 Vche *piler* is of penaunc[e] and preyeres to seyntes;

pileþ v *pilen v.(1)* A 1 pilide; B 1; C 3 pilede (1) pileth (1) pylie (1)
A. 7.142 And bad hym go pisse wiþ his plouȝ: 'pilide shrewe!
B.19.442 And [Piers] amende þe pope, þat *pileþ* holy kirke
C. 6.370 Of portours and of pikeporses and of *pilede* tothdraweres,
C. 9.81 [To] rybbe [and] to rele, rusches to *pylie*,
C.21.442 And [Peres] amende þe pope þat *pileth* holi churche

pilewhey n *pilewhei n.* A 1
A. 5.134 Penyale & *pilewhey* heo pouride togidere.

pilgrym n *pilgrim n.* A 7 pilgrym (1) pilgrimes (3) pilgrymes (1) pilgrimys (1) pilgrymys (1); B 19 pilgrym (4) pilgrimes (2) pilgrymes (13); C 13 pilgrime (2) pilgrimes (9) pilgrym (1) pilgrymes (1)
A.Pr.46 *Pilgrimes* & palmeris pliȝten hem togidere
A. 5.87 [For *pilgrymes*, for palmers, for all þe peple] aftir,
A. 6.4 Aparailid as a paynym in *pilgrim[ys]* wyse,
A. 6.43 'ȝa, leue piers,' quaþ þe *pilgrimes* & profride hym hire.
A. 7.52 'And I shal apparaille me,' quaþ perkyn, 'in *pilgrym[ys]* wyse,
A. 7.94 And ben his *pilgrym* at þe plouȝ for pore menis sake.
A. 7.97 Now is peris & þe *pilgrimes* to þe plouȝ faren;
B.Pr.46 *Pilgrimes* and Palmeres pliȝten hem togidere
B. 5.107 For *Pilgrymes*, for Palmeres, for al þe peple after,
B. 5.516 Apparailled as a paynym in *pilgrymes* wise.
B. 5.556 'Ye! leue Piers', quod þise *pilgrimes* and profred hym huyre.
B. 6.57 'And I shal apparaille me', quod Perkyn, 'in *pilgrymes* wise
B. 6.102 And ben his *pilgrym* atte plow for pouere mennes sake.
B. 6.105 Now is Perkyn and [þe] *pilgrimes* to þe plow faren.
B.11.236 For his pouere apparaill and *pilgrymes* wedes
B.11.242 And [pacient as *pilgrymes*] for pilgrymes are we alle.
B.11.242 And [pacient as pilgrymes] for *pilgrymes* are we alle.
B.11.243 And in þe apparaille of a pouere man and *pilgrymes* liknesse
B.11.247 And as pouere *pilgrymes* preyed mennes goodes.
B.13.29 A[c] Pacience in þe Paleis stood in *pilgrymes* cloþes
B.13.178 That Pacience þ[o] most passe, 'for *pilgrymes* konne wel lye'.
B.13.182 And be *Pilgrym* wiþ pacience til I haue preued moore.'
B.13.187 That Pacience þe *pilgrym* parfitly knew neuere.'
B.13.215 Conscience þo wiþ Pacience passed, *pilgrymes* as it were.
B.13.216 Thanne hadde Pacience, as *pilgrymes* han, in his poke vitailles:
B.20.380 'By crist!' quod Conscience þo, 'I wole bicome a *pilgrym*,]
C.Pr.47 *Pilgrymes* and palmers plighten hem togyderes
C. 7.161 [A]parayled as a paynym in *pilgrimes* wyse.
C. 7.200 'ȝe! leue Peres,' quod thise *pilgrimes* and profrede Peres mede.
C. 8.56 'And [y] shal [ap]parayle me,' quod Perkyn, 'in *pilgrimes* wyse
C. 8.111 And ben a *pilgrym* at þe plouh for profit to pore and ryche.'
C. 8.112 Now is perkyn and þ[e] *pilgrimes* to þe plouh faren.
C. 9.181 As prisones and *pilgrimes* and parauntur men yrobbed
C.12.125 For his pore parail and *pilgrimes* clothes
C.12.131 And pacient as *pilgrimes* for pilgrimes are we alle.
C.12.131 And pacient as pilgrimes for *pilgrimes* are we alle.
C.12.132 In þe parail of a *pilgrime* and in pore likenesse
C.15.185 Thenne hadde pacience, as *pilgrimes* haen, in h[is] poke vitayles,
C.22.380 'By Crist!' quod Consience tho, 'y wol bicome a *pilgrime*

pilgrymage n *pilgrimage n.* A 1 pilgrimage; B 5 pilgrimage (1) pilgrymage (3) pilgrymages (1); C 8 pilgrimage (4) pilgrimages (4)
A. 7.76 To penaunce & to *pilgrimage* wile I passe with oþere;
B. 6.64 To *pilgrymage* as palmeres doon pardon to haue.
B. 6.84 To penaunce and to *pilgrimage* I wol passe wiþ oþere;
B.14.197 Paternost[er] and penaunce and *Pilgrymag[e]* to Rome,
B.15.182 And ouþerwhile he is woned to wenden on *pilgrymages*
B.19.375 Some þoruȝ bedes biddynge and some [by] *pilgrymag[e]*]
C. 4.123 In prisones and in pore cotes be *pilgrimages* to Rome,
C. 8.63 To *pilgrimag[e]* as palmeres doen pardon to wynne.
C. 8.93 To penaunc[e] and [to] *pilgrim[age]* y wol passe with oþere;
C. 9.235 Pouerte or oþer penaunc[e], as *pilgrimages* and trauayles.

C. 9.324   So dowel passeth pardoun and *pilgrimages* to Rome.
C.16.38   Oure preyeres and oure penanc[e] And *pilgrimag[e]* to Rome.
C.16.324 And oþerwhile his wone is to w[e]nde [o]n *pilgrimages*
C.21.375 Somme thorw bedes biddynge and [somme] bi *pilgrimag[e]*

pilide pylie > pileþ

pillory n *pillorie n.* A 2 pillorie (1) pillories (1); B 2 Pillory (1) Pillories (1); C 2 pylorye (1) pilories (1)
A. 2.168   Er he be put on þe *pillorie*, for any preyour, I hote.'
A. 3.67   As to punisshen on *pillories* & on py[n]yng stolis
B. 2.207   Er he be put on þe *Pillory* for any preyere I hote.'_
B. 3.78   [As] to punysshe on *Pillories* and [on] pynynge stooles
C. 2.219   Ar he be put on þe *pylorye* for eny preyere ich hote.'
C. 3.79   To punischen [o]n *pilories* and [o]n pynyng stoles

pilour n *pilour n.(1)* A 1; B 3 Pilour (1) pilours (1) Pylours (1); C 3 pelours (1) Pilours (2)
A. 3.182 Wiþoute pite, *pilour*, pore men þou robb[ed]est,
B. 3.195 Wiþouten pite, *Pilour*, pouere men þow robbedest
B.19.415 For hir pelure and palfreyes mete and *pilours* þat hem folweþ.
B.20.263 *Pylours* and Pykeharneys, in ech a [parisshe] ycursed._]
C.13.2   Among *Pilours* in pees yf pacience hym folowe.
C.21.415 For here pelurre and palfrayes mete and *pelours* þat hem folweth.
C.22.263 *Pilours* and pikeharneys in vch a parsch acorsed.

pynched v *pinchen v.* B 1; C 1
B.13.370 If I yede to þe Plowȝ I *pynched* so narwe
C. 6.267   And yf y ȝede to þe plough y *pynched* on his half aker

pyne n *pine n.(1)* A 5; B 7; C 3
A. 1.143 And ȝet wolde he hem no woo þat wrouȝte him þat *pyne*,
A. 2.68   Wiþ alle þe purtenaunce of purcatorie into þe *pyne* of helle;
A. 2.70   Here soulis to sathanas to synken in *pyne*,
A. 5.29   And fecche [hom] felis fro wyuene *pyne*.
A.11.277 And for here werkis & here wyt wende to *pyne*,
B. 2.104 Wiþ alle þe [p]urtinaunces of Purgatorie into þe *pyne* of helle.
B. 5.29   And fecche Felice hom fro wyuen *pyne*.
B. 5.267 Ne haue a peny to my pitaunce, [for *pyne* of my soule],
B.10.393 That for hir werkes and wit now wonyeþ in *pyne*,
B.11.142 How [I] was ded and dampned to dwellen in *pyne*
B.11.163 Pulte out of *pyne* a paynym of rome.
B.18.193 Sholden deye downrighte and dwelle in *pyne* after
C. 5.131   And fette felyce hoem fram wyuene *pyne*.
C.11.271 Ho is worthy for wele or for wykkede [*pyne*]:
C.12.77   How y was ded and dampned to dwellen in [*pyne*]

pyned v *pinen v.* A 1 pynede; B 1
A. 1.145 To haue pite on þat peple þat *pynede* hym to deþe.
B.19.322 That crist vpon Caluarie for mankynde on *pyned*.]

pynynge ger *pininge ger.* A 1 pynyng; B 1; C 1 pynyng
A. 3.67   As to punisshen on pillories & on *py[n]yng* stolis
B. 3.78   [As] to punysshe on Pillories and [on] *pynynge* stooles
C. 3.79   To punischen [o]n pilories and [o]n *pynyng* stoles

pynne v *pinnen v.* A 1 pynnede; B 2 pynne (1) pynned (1); C 2 pynne (1) pynned (1)
A. 5.127 Putte hem in a pressour, & *pynnede* hem þereinne
B. 5.211 Putte hem in a press[our] and *pyn[ned]* hem þerInne
B.20.298 And made pees porter to *pynne* þe yates
C. 6.219 Potte hem in [a] pressou[r] and *pynne[d]* hem þerynne
C.22.298 And made pees porter to *pynne* þe ȝates

pynnes n *pin n.* C 1
C. 8.199 In threschynge, in thekynge, in thwytinge of *pynnes*,

pione n *pione n.* A 1 pyenye; B 1; C 1 pyonie
A. 5.155 I haue pepir, & p[ye]nye, & a pound of garlek,
B. 5.304 'I haue pepir and *pion[e]* and a pound of garleek,]
C. 6.359 'Y haue pepur and *pyonie* and a pound of garlek,

pipe v *pipen v.* B 3 pipe (2) pipede (1); C 3 pipe (1) pype (1) piped (1)
B.13.232 Iape ne Iogele ne gentilliche *pipe*,
B.18.408 Thanne *pipede* pees of Poesie a note:
B.20.93 [Th]anne mette þise men, er Mynstrals myȝte *pipe*,]
C.15.206 Iape ne i[o]gele ne genteliche *pipe*,
C.20.451 Thenne *piped* pees of poe[sie] a note:
C.22.93 Thenne mette thise men, ar muinstrals myhte *pype*

pyries n *pirie n.* A 1 piries; B 1; C 1 piries
A. 5.16   *Piries* & pl[umtr]es wern pu[ffid] to þe erþe
B. 5.16   *Pyries* and Plumtrees were puffed to þe erþe
C. 5.118 P[iri]es and plumtrees were po[ff]ed to þe erthe

pissen v *pissen v.* A 2 pisse (1) pisside (1); B 2 pissed (1) pissen (1); C 3 pisse (1) pissede (2)
A. 5.189 He *pisside* a potel in a paternoster while,

A. 7.142 And bad hym go *pisse* wiþ his plouȝ: 'pilide shrewe!
B. 5.341 He *pissed* a potel in a paternoster while,
B. 6.155 And bad hym go *pissen* with his plowȝ: [pyuysshe] sherewe!]
C. 6.67   Sholde no lyf lyue þat on his lond *pissede*.
C. 6.399 A *pissede* a potel in a paternoster whyle
C. 8.151 And bad hym go *pisse* with his plogh, pyuische shrewe.

pistle n *epistle n.* A 2 pistil; B 3 pistel (1) pistle (2); C 1 pistul
A.10.109 Poule þe apostel in his *pistil* wrot it
A.11.233 And prouen it be þe *pistil* þat petir is nempnid:
B.10.350 And preuen it by [þe *pistel*] þat Peter is nempned]:
B.12.29 'Poul in his *pistle*', quod he, 'preueþ what is dowel:
B.13.69 That Poul in his *Pistle* to al þe peple tolde:]
C.16.291 As poul in his *pistul* of hym bereth wittenesse:

pitaunce n *pitaunce n.* B 4; C 2 pytaunce
B. 5.267 Ne haue a peny to my *pitaunce*, [for pyne of my soule],
B. 6.150 Thei shul haue payn and potage and [a *pitaunce* biside],
B.13.56 'Bryng pacience som *pitaunce* pryueliche', quod Conscience,
B.13.57 And þanne hadde Pacience a *pitaunce*, Pro hac orabit ad te omnis
C. 9.92   There is payne and peny ale as for a *pytaunce* ytake
C.15.60 And brouhte forth a *pytaunce*, was pro h[a]c orabit [ad te] omnis

pite n *pite n.* A 7; B 14 pite (13) pitee (1); C 13 pite (7) pyte (4) pitee (2)
A. 1.145 To haue *pite* on þat peple þat pynede hym to deþe.
A. 2.181 Til pardoners hadde *pite* & pulden him to house,
A. 3.182 Wiþoute *pite*, pilour, pore men þou robb[ed]est,
A. 5.12   And preyede þe peple haue *pite* on hemselue,
A. 7.186 Þanne hadde piers *pite* & preiȝede hungir to wende
A. 9.95   And putten hem þere in penaunce wiþoute *pite* or grace,
A.11.289 Or poule þe apostil þat no *pite* hadde
B. 1.171 To haue *pite* [on] þat peple þat peyned hym to deþe.
B. 2.222 Til Pardoners hadde *pite* and pulled hym [to] house,
B. 3.195 Wiþouten *pite*, Pilour, pouere men þow robbedest
B. 5.50   And siþen he preide þe pope haue *pite* on holy chirche,
B. 5.254 'Hastow *pite* on pouere men þat [for pure nede] borwe?'
B. 5.255 'I haue as muche *pite* of pouere men as pedlere haþ of cattes,
B. 6.199 Thanne hadde Piers *pite* and preide hunger to wende
B. 8.105 And putten hem þer in penaunce wiþoute *pite* or grace],
B.10.320 Of þe pouere haue þei no *pite*, and þat is hir [pure chartre];
B.10.430 Or Poul þe Apostle þat no *pite* hadde
B.13.79 Haþ no *pite* on vs pouere; he parfourneþ yuele
B.17.87 And suwed þat Samaritan þat was so ful of *pite*,
B.17.298 Ne haue *pite* for any preiere þer þat he pleyneþ.'
B.19.92 And presented hym wiþ *pitee* apperynge by Mirre;]
C. 1.167 To haue *pitee* on þat peple þat paynede hym to dethe.
C. 2.232 Tyl Pardoners hadde [*pyte*] and polleden hym [t]o house.
C. 3.86   Thei han no *pite* on the peple þat parselmele mot begge;
C. 3.349 In his pay and in his *pite* and in his puyr treuthe,
C. 3.350 To pay hym yf he parforme and haue *pite* yf he faileth
C. 5.166 Of þe pore haueth thei no *pite* and þat is here puyre chartre.
C. 5.191 And sethe a preyede þe pope haue *pite* on holy chirche
C. 6.172 That he haue *pite* on me, p[u]tou[r], of his puyr mercy,
C. 8.204 Tho hadde [Peres] *pitee* vppon alle pore peple
C.11.266 [Or] Poul þe apostle [þat] no *pite* hadde
C.15.86 Hath no *pyte* on vs pore; he parformeth euele
C.20.190 Into pees and *pyte* of his puyr grace.
C.21.92 And presented hym with *pyte* apperynge bi Mirre

piþ n *pithe n.* B 1; C 1 pethe
B.17.144 The pawme is [þe *piþ* of] þe hand, and profreþ forþ þe fyngres
C.19.118 The paume is the *pethe* of the hand and profereth [forth] the fyngeres

pitous adj *pitous adj.* A 1
A. 7.115 And pleynide hem to peris wiþ suche *pitous* wordis:

pitously adv *pitousli adv.* A 2 pitously (1) pitousliche (1); B 3 pitously (2) pitousliche (1); C 3 pitously (1) pitousliche (2)
A. 1.78   Preiȝede hire *pitously* [to] preiȝe for my sennes,
A. 4.85   Pees þanne *pitousliche* preyede to þe king
B. 1.80   Preide hire *pitously* [to] preye for my synnes;
B. 4.98   [Pees þanne *pitously*] preyde to þe kynge
B.18.58 *Pitousliche* and pale, as a prison þat deieþ,]
C. 1.77   And preyede hire *pitously* to preye for me to amende
C. 4.94   *Pitousliche* pees tho preyede the kyng
C.20.58 *Pitousliche* and pale, as [a] prisoun þat deyeth,

pyuysshe adj *peivish adj.* B 1; C 1 pyuische
B. 6.155 And bad hym go pissen with his plowȝ: [*pyuysshe* sherewe!]
C. 8.151 And bad hym go pisse with his plogh, *pyuische* shrewe.

place n *place n.* A 6 place (5) places (1); B 35 place (24) places (11); C 33 place (21) places (11) plases (1)
A. 6.16   In armonye, in alisaundre, in manye oþere *places*.

A. 6.24 Axen aftir hym, er now in þis *place*.'
A. 6.27 Clene consience & wyt kende me to his *place*,
A. 6.42 I [wile] wisse ʒow wel riʒt to his *place*.'
A. 6.105 And ben porteris to þe posternis þat to þe *place* longiþ:
A. 7.43 In a wel perilous *place* þat purcatorie hattiþ;
B. 5.147 That whan þei preche þe peple in many *places* aboute
B. 5.528 In Armonye, in Alisaundre, in manye oþere *places*.
B. 5.536 Asken after hym er now in þis *place*.'
B. 5.539 Conscience and kynde wit kenned me to his *place*
B. 5.555 I [wol] wisse yow [wel riʒt] to his *place*.'
B. 5.619 And arn porters of þe Posternes þat to þe *place* longeþ.
B. 6.44 In a [wel] perilous *place* [þat] Purgatorie hatte.
B. 8.15 And knowen contrees and courtes and many kynnes *places*,
B.10.313 A prikere on a palfrey fro [*place*] to Manere,
B.10.319 In many *places* þer þei [persons ben, be þei purely] at ese,
B.12.24 [In manye *places* pleyden þe parfiter to ben].
B.12.61 Pacience and pouerte þe *place* [is] þer it groweþ,
B.12.147 But in a Burgeises *place*, of Bethlem þe beste:
B.13.134 Pacience haþ be in many *place*, and paraunter [knoweþ]
B.13.218 To conforte hym and Conscience if þei come in *place*
B.13.274 Ac it was moled in many *places* wiþ manye sondry plottes,
B.15.17 In cristes court yknowe wel and of [cristene in many a *place*].
B.15.161 Clerkes kenne me þat crist is in alle *places*
B.15.403 And if he among þe peple preched, or in *places* come,
B.16.21 That Piers þe Plowman al þe *place* me shewed
B.16.135 Of preieres and of parfitnesse þis *place* þat ye callen:
B.16.171 After Piers þe Plowman; many a *place* I souʒte.
B.17.143 And profre[d] it forþ as with a pawme to what *place* it sholde.
B.18.21 'Is Piers in þis *place*?' quod I, and he peynte on me.
B.18.80 Bifore Pilat and ooþer peple in þe *place* he houed.
B.18.155 May no medicyne [amende] þe *place* þer he styngeþ
B.18.174 And preide pees to telle hire to what *place* she wolde,
B.18.223 To [se] what he haþ suffred in þre sondry *places*,
B.18.264 "Prynces of þis *place*, vnpynneþ and vnloukeþ,
B.18.319 Dukes of þis dymme *place*, anoon vndo þise yates
B.18.350 Thow fettest myne in my *place* [maugree] alle resoun,
B.19.61 *Places* in Paradis at hir partynge hennes
B.20.3 I ne wiste wher to ete ne at what *place*,
B.20.42 So [he was nedy], as seiþ þe book in manye sondry *places*,
B.20.181 And rood [so to] reuel, a ryche *place* and a murye,]
C.Pr.96 And seide, 'ydolatrie ʒe soffren in sondrye *places* manye
C. 3.106 And thorw a candle clemynge in [a] cursed *place*
C. 5.159 And pryked aboute on palfrayes fram *places* to maneres,
C. 5.165 In many *places* ther thei persones ben, be hemsulue at ese,
C. 7.181 Axen aftur hym [er] now in þis *place*.'
C. 7.184 Consience and kynde wyt kenned me to his *place*
C. 7.199 Y wol wissen ʒow wel ryht to his *place*.'
C. 7.271 And aren porteres ouer þe posternes þat to þ[e] *place* bilongen.
C. 7.277 For he payeth for prisones in *places* and in peynes.
C. 9.226 That in wilde wodes been or in waste *places*,
C.10.15 And knowen contrees and Courtes and many kynne *plases*,
C.12.246 Lo, how pans purchaseth fayre *places* and d[r]ede,
C.13.51 Marchauntʒ for here marchaundyse in many *place* to tolle.
C.15.187 To conforte hym and Consience yf they come in *place*
C.15.274 The whiche wil loue lat to oure lordes *place*
C.16.122 Al þat may potte of pruyde in *place* þer he regneth;
C.16.167 'Y am cristes creature,' quod he, 'and cristene in mony a *place*
C.16.315 Ther neuere payed peny aʒeyn in *places* þer he borwede.'
C.17.87 May no preyere pees make in no *place* hit semeth.
C.17.173 Corn [þat þe] coluere eet when he come in *places*
C.17.174 And in what *place* he prechede and þe peple tauhte
C.19.117 And profered hit forth as with þe paume to what *place* hit sholde.
C.20.19 'Is Peres in this *place*?' quod y, and he printe on me.
C.20.82 Bifore pilatus and oþere peple in þe *place* he houed.
C.20.158 May no medecyne amende þe *place* there he styngeth
C.20.177 And preyede pees to tellen [here] to what *place* she [w]olde
C.20.232 To wyte what he hath soffred in thre sundry *places*,
C.20.272 'Princ[i]pes of this *place*, prest vndo this gates
C.20.362 Dukes of this demme *place*, anoen vndoth this ʒates
C.21.61 *Places* in paradys at here partyng hennes
C.22.3 Y ne wiste where to ete ne at what *place*
C.22.42 So he was nedy, as saith þe boek in mony sondry *places*,
C.22.181 And roed so to reuel, a ryche *place* and a murye:

placebo n *placebo n.* B 2; C 2
B. 3.311 Preestes and persons wiþ *Placebo* to hunte
B.15.125 Ac a Porthors þat sholde be his Plow, *Placebo* to sigge–]
C. 3.464 Prestes and persones *placebo* and dirige,
C. 5.46 Is paternoster and my primer,*placebo* and dirige,

play n *pleie n.* A 1
A.12.95 Þat þi *play* be plentevous in paradys with aungelys.

played > pleye; playere > pleyere; playne > pleyne

---

playte v *pleiten v.* A 1 pleit; B 1
A. 5.126 Brochide hem wiþ a pakke nedle, & *pleit* hem togidere;
B. 5.210 [P]roche[d] hem wiþ a paknedle and *playte* hem togideres,

planetes n *planete n.(1)* B 1; C 1
B.20.80 Kynde Conscience þo herde and cam out of þe *planetes*
C.22.80 Kynde Consience tho herde and cam oute of the *planetes*

planke n *planke n.* B 1; C 2
B.16.50 Thanne liberum arbitrium laccheþ þe [þridde] *plan[k]e*
C.18.34 And with þe furste *planke* y palle hym down, potencia dei patris.
C.18.40 Thenne sette y þe seconde *planke*, sapiencia dei patris,

plante -is > plaunte; plases > place

plastre n *plastre n.* B 3 plastre (1) plastres (2); C 3 plasteres (1) plastre (1) plastres (1)
B.20.359 The *plastres* of þe person and poudres biten to soore;
B.20.361 Fro lenten to lenten he lat hise *plastres* bite.'
B.20.363 And gooþ gropeþ Contricion and gaf hym a *plastre*
C.22.359 The *plasteres* of þe persoun and poudres b[it]en to sore;
C.22.361 Fro lente to lente he lat his *plastres* byte.'
C.22.363 And goeth gropeth contricion and gaf hym a *plastre*

plastre v *plastren v.* B 3 plastre (1) plastred (1) plastreþ (1); C 3 plastereth (1) plasterud (1) plastre (1)
B.17.98 And þanne *plastred* wiþ penaunce and passion of þat baby,
B.20.310 If any surgien were [in] þe seg[e] þat softer koude *plastre*.
B.20.314 And moore of phisik bi fer, and fairer he *plastreþ*;
C.19.91 And ʒut [b]e *plasterud* with pacience when fondynges [priketh hym]–
C.22.310 Yf eny surgien were in þe sege that softur couthe *plastre*.
C.22.314 And more of fysyk bi fer, and fayror he *plastereth*;

plat > platte

plato n prop *n.i.d.* A 1; B 3; C 5
A.11.130 *Plato* þe poete, I putte hym ferst to boke;
B.10.178 *Plato* þe poete, I putte [hym] first to boke;
B.11.37 'Homo proponit', quod a poete, and *Plato* he hiʒte,
B.20.275 And preche men of *Plato*, and preue it by Seneca
C.11.118 *Plato* þe poete y putte hym furste to boke;
C.11.303 'Homo pr[o]ponit,' quod a poete tho, and *plato* he hihte,
C.12.174 And poetes to preuen hit: Porfirie and *plato*,
C.14.189 Thus porfirie and *plato* and poetes monye
C.22.275 And preche men of *plato* and preuen hit by seneca

platte v *platten v.(2)* A 1 plat; B 1; C 1
A. 5.45 Pernel proud herte *plat* hire to þe erþe
B. 5.62 Pernele proud-herte *platte* hire to þe erþe
C. 6.3 P[ur]nele proude herte *platte* here to þe erthe

plaunte n *plaunte n.(1)* A 3 plante (2) plantis (1); B 2 plante (1) plaunte (1); C 5 plonte (4) plontes (1)
A. 1.137 And ek þe *plante* of pes; preche it in þin harpe
A. 6.69 Loke þou plukke no *plant[e]* þere for peril of þi soule.
A. 7.270 Ac I haue persile & poret, & many cole *plantis*,
B. 1.152 And [ek] þe *pl[ante]* of pees, moost precious of vertues.
B. 5.582 Loke þow plukke no *plaunte* þere for peril of þi soule.
C. 1.148 Loue is [þe] *plonte* of pees, most precious of vertues.
C. 7.229 Loke thow plokke no *plonte* þere for perel of thy soule.
C. 8.308 Ac y haue poret-*pl[o]ntes*, parsilie and skalones,
C.18.25 'Thise thre shorriares,' quod he,' that bereth vp this *plonte*
C.18.100 'This is a propre *plonte*,' quod y–'and priueliche hit bloweth

plaunte ptp *plaunten v.* B 1
B. 6.286 Ac I haue percile and pore[t] and manye [*plaunte* coles],

play- > pley-

pleden v *pleden v.* cf. plete B 6 plede (4) pleden (1) pleteden (1); C 4 plede (3) plededen (1)
B.Pr.213 *Pleteden* for penyes and pounde[d] þe lawe
B. 4.54 Ne no ferþyng þerfore for [n]ouʒt I koude *plede*.
B. 7.43 Pledours sholde peynen hem to *plede* for swiche and helpe;
B. 7.46 Than pro dei pietate [*pleden* at þe barre].
B.14.109 Ther þe poore dar *plede* and preue by pure reson
B.14.189 A[c] if þe [pouke] wolde *plede* herayein, and punysshe vs in conscience,
C.Pr.163 *Plededen* for penyes and pounde[d] þe lawe
C. 4.57 Ne [no] ferthyng therfore, for nouhte y couthe *plede*.
C. 9.44 Men of lawe hadde lest þat loth were to *plede*
C.15.285 There þe pore dar *plede* and preue by puyr resoun

pledynge ger *pledinge ger.* B 1; C 2 pledyng (1) pledynge (1)
B. 3.296 Ne no pelure in his [panelon] for *pledynge* at þe barre.
C. 3.449 Ne no pelure in his panelon for *pledyng* at þe barre.
C. 9.45 But they pre manibus were payed for *pledynge* at þe barre;

pledours n *pledour n.* B 1

B. 7.43   *Pledours* sholde peynen hem to plede for swiche and helpe;

pleid- > pleye

pleieþ v *pleien v.(2)* B 1; C 1

B.19.295   And *pleieþ* al wiþ pacience and Parce michi domine;
C.21.295   And *ple[ieþ]* al with pacience and parce michi domine

pleiȝ- pleyinge > pleye

pleyn adj *pleine adj.* A 1; B 1

A. 8.86   Han as *pleyn* pardoun as þe plouȝman hymselue;
B. 7.104   Han as *pleyn* pardon as þe Plowman hymselue;

pleyne v *pleinen v.* A 5 pleyne (1) pleynede (1) pleynide (3); B 7 pleyne (3) pleyned (3) pleyneþ (1); C 9 playne (2) pleyne (3) pleyned (2) pleynede (1) pleyneth (1)

A.Pr.80   Personis & parissh prestis *pleynide* hem to here bisshop
A. 3.155   For pouere men mowe haue no power to *pleyne* [þeiȝ] hem smerte,
A. 4.52   Þeiȝ pees & his power *pleynide* hem euere'.
A. 7.115   And *pleynide* hem to peris wiþ suche pitous wordis:
A. 7.146   Þanne peris þe plouȝman *pleynede* hym to þe kniȝt
B.Pr.83   Persons and parisshe preestes *pleyned* hem to þe Bisshop
B. 3.168   For pouere men may haue no power to *pleyne* þouȝ [hem] smerte,
B. 4.66   Theiȝ pees and his power *pleyned* h[e]m euere'.
B. 6.159   Thanne Piers þe plowman *pleyned* hym to þe knyȝte
B.13.110   But cheeste be þer charite sholde be, and yonge children dorste *pleyne.*
B.14.226   [For] if þei *pleyne* [þe feblere is þe poore];
B.17.298   Ne haue pite for any preiere þer þat he *pleyneþ.'*
C.Pr.81   Persones and parsche prestis *pleyned* [hem] to þe bischop
C. 3.214   For pore men dar nat *pleyne* ne no pleynt shewe,
C. 4.30   Byfore þe kyng an[d] Consience yf þe comune *playne*
C. 4.70   Of pees and his power thow he *pleyne* euere.'
C. 6.110   Inpacient in alle penaunc[e] and *pleyned*, as hit were,
C. 6.120   And prelates *pleyneth* on hem for they here parschiens shryuen
C. 8.156   [Peres] the [plouhman] tho *pleynede* hym to þe knyhte
C. 8.166   And sette [Peres] at a [pes], *playne* hym whare he wolde.
C.16.67   For yf they bothe *pleyne* the pore is bote feble;

pleynt n *pleinte n.* A 1 pleyntes; B 2 pleynt (1) pleintes (1); C 2 pleynt (1) pleynte (1)

A. 2.139   Paulynes peple, for *pleyntes* in constorie,
B. 2.178   Paulynes pryuees for *pleintes* in Consistorie
B.11.250   Martha on Marie Maudeleyne an huge *pleynt* made
C. 3.214   For pore men dar nat pleyne ne no *pleynt* shewe,
C.12.136   Marthe on marie maudelene an huge *pleynte* made

pleise > plese; pleit > playte; pleiȝ- pleiynge > pleye

plener adj *plenere adj.* B 1

B.16.103   And Piers þe Plowman parceyued *plener* tyme

plener adv *plenere adv.* B 1; C 1 plenere

B.11.113   And whan þe peple was *plener* comen þe porter vnpynned þe yate
C.12.48   And whan þe peple was *plenere* ycome þe porter vnpynnede þe gate

plentee n *plente n.* B 5; C 6 plente (5) plentee (1)

B. 6.163   *Plentee* among þe peple þe while my plowȝ liggeþ'.
B.11.332   Pouerte and *plentee*, boþe pees and werre,
B.14.74   [Oþer] *plentee* makeþ pryde amonges poore and riche.
B.14.77   Weex þoruȝ *plentee* of payn and of pure sleuþe:
B.15.538   And þo was *plentee* and pees amonges poore and riche,
C. 8.160   For ther worth no *plente*,' quod [Perus], 'and þe plouh lygge.'
C.12.204   Murthe for his mornyng, and þat muche *plentee.*
C.13.140   Pouerte and *plente*, bothe pees and werre,
C.15.230   *Plente* of payn the peple of sodoume,
C.17.94   Ther sholde be *plente* and pees perpetuel euere.
C.17.199   And tho was *p[lente]* and p[ees] amonges pore and ryche;

plenteuouse adj *plentevous adj.* A 1 plentevous; B 1

A.12.95   Þat þi play be *plentevous* in paradys with aungelys.
B.10.83   Ne beþ *plenteuouse* to þe pouere as pure charite wolde,

plesant > plesaunt

plesaunce n *plesaunce n.(1)* C 1

C. 8.14   For profit of the pore and *plesaunce* of ȝowsuluen.

plesaunt adj *plesaunte adj.* B 3; C 1 plesant

B.14.102   'Wheiþer paciente pouerte', quod Haukyn, 'be moore *plesaunt* to oure d[riȝte]
B.14.206   And þat is *plesaunt* to pride in poore and in riche.
B.15.156   Ac charite þat Poul preiseþ best, and moost *plesaunt* to oure [Saueour]–
C.16.47   And þat is *plesant* to pruyde in pore and in ryche.

plese v *plesen v.* A 7 pleise (1) plese (4) plesen (1) plesiþ (1); B 15 plese (12) plesed (1) plesen (1) pleseþ (1); C 13 plese (10) plesede (1) pleseth (2)

A.Pr.30   For no likerous liflode here likam to *plese.*
A. 3.11   Ac þere was merþe & mynstralcie mede to *plese;*
A. 3.151   Wiþoute presentis or panis he *plesiþ* [wel] fewe.
A. 7.103   And summe to *plese* perkyn pykide vp þe wedis.
A. 7.279   And profride peris [þis] present to *plese* þerewiþ hungir.
A.10.213   Aȝens dowel þei don euele, & þe deuil *plesen*,
A.11.59   To *pleise* wiþ proude men, siþen þe pestilence tyme,
B.Pr.30   For no likerous liflode hire likame to *plese.*
B. 3.11   A[c] þer was murþe & Mynstralcie Mede to *plese;*
B. 3.162   Wiþouten presentȝ or pens [he] *pleseþ* wel fewe.
B. 3.339   Was omnia probate, and þat *plesed* hire herte.
B. 5.36   Ne for no poustee of pestilence *plese* hem noȝt out of reson.
B. 5.53   Moore þan gold ouþer giftes if ye wol god *plese;*
B. 5.140   Til þei beere leues of lowe speche lordes to *plese*,
B. 6.111   And somme to *plese* Perkyn piked vp þe wedes.
B. 6.295   And profrede Piers þis present to *plese* wiþ hunger.
B. 9.199   Ayeins dowel þei doon yuel and þe deuel [*plese*],
B.10.73   To *plese* wiþ proude men syn þe pestilence tyme;
B.10.396   Thouȝ hir goost be vngracious god for to *plese.*
B.13.312   Which myȝte *plese* þe peple and preisen hymselue:
B.14.221   For þe poore is ay prest to *plese* þe riche
B.15.80   That I lye noȝt, loo! for lordes ye *plesen*
C.Pr.32   For no likerous liflode here lycame to *plese.*
C. 3.12   Ac there was myrthe and mynstracie mede to *plese;*
C. 3.200   Withoute presentes oþer pans he *pleseth* [wel] fewe.
C. 3.491   Was omnia probate; þat *plesede* here herte.
C. 5.85   Is the leuest labour þat oure lord *pleseth.*
C. 8.118   And somme to *plese* Perkyn [pykede vp þe] wedes.
C. 8.317   And profrede [Peres] this present to *plese* with hongur.
C.11.53   To *plese* with proude men senes th[e] pestelenc[e tyme]
C.11.227   Thogh here gost be vngracious god for to *plese.*
C.15.200   The pore and the ryche y *plese* and payn fynde
C.15.277   'Where pouerte and pacience *plese* more god almyhty
C.16.62   For þe pore is ay prest to *plese* þe ryche
C.16.239   That y lye nat; loo! for lordes ȝe *plese*

plesynge ger *plesinge ger.* A 1 plesing; B 1

A. 3.231   Prestis & personis þat *plesing* desiriþ,
B. 3.252   Preestes and persons þat *plesynge* desireþ,

plete v *pleten v. cf. pleden* A 2 plete (1) pleten (1)

A.Pr.86   *Pleten* for penis & [poundide] þe lawe,
A. 4.41   Ne no ferþing þerfore for nouȝt I couþe *plete.*

pleteden > pleden

pleye v *pleien v.* A 2 pleiȝe (1) pleiȝede (1); B 9 pleide (1) pleiden (1) pleyden (1) pleye (4) pleyinge (2); C 9 playde (2) pleiynge (1) pleinge (1) pley (1) pleye (3) pleynge (1)

A.Pr.20   Summe putte hem to plouȝ, *pleiȝede* ful selde,
A. 8.12   Wiþ patriarkes in paradis to *pleiȝe* þereaftir.
B.Pr.20   Some putten hem to plouȝ, *pleiden* ful selde,
B.Pr.151   And *pleide* wiþ hem perillousli and possed aboute.
B.Pr.171   Wher he ryt or rest or r[om]eþ to *pleye;*
B.Pr.173   And peeren in his presence þe while hym *pleye* likeþ,
B. 3.309   Ech man to *pleye* with a plow, Pykoise or spade,
B.12.24   [In manye places *pleyden* þe parfiter to ben].
B.16.256   Amonges patriarkes and prophetes *pleyinge* togideres.
B.18.168   Where pees comeþ *pleyinge* in pacience ycloþed.
B.20.292   A parcel to preye for hem and [*pleye*] wiþ þe remenaunt.
C.Pr.22   Somme potte hem to plogh, *playde* ful selde,
C.Pr.172   And *playde* with somme perilously and potte hem þer hym lykede.
C.Pr.188   Wher he ri[t] othere reste or rometh to *pleye;*
C.Pr.190   And apere in his presence þe while hym *pleye* lyketh
C. 3.462   Vche man to *pley* with a plogh, a pikois oþer a spade,
C. 9.114   To profecye of þe peple, *pleinge* as hit were
C.18.272   With patriarkes and profetes *pleynge* togyderes.
C.20.171   Where cometh pees *pleiynge* in pacience yclothed.
C.22.292   A parcel to preye for hem and [*pleye*] with þe remenaunt

pleyere n *pleiere n.* B 1; C 1 playere

B. 6.71   And danyel þe dees *pleyere* and Denote þe baude
C. 8.72   And danyel þe dees *playere* and denote þe baude

pliȝte v *plighten v.* A 4 pliȝt (1) pliȝte (1) pliȝten (1) ypliȝt (1); B 5 pliȝt (1) pliȝte (2) pliȝten (1) ypliȝt (1); C 6 plighten (1) plihte (1) plyhte (3) yplyht (1)

A.Pr.46   Pilgrimes & palmeris *pliȝten* hem togidere
A. 5.116   And was his prentis *ypliȝt* his profit to loke.
A. 7.36   'Be my power, piers, I *pliȝte* þe my treuþe
A.10.191   Manye peire siþen p[e] pestilence han *p[l]iȝt* hem togidere.
B.Pr.46   Pilgrymes and Palmeres *pliȝten* hem togidere

B. 3.317	Ne putte hem in panel to doon hem *pliȝte* hir truþe;
B. 5.200	And was his prentice *ypliȝt* his profit to [loke].
B. 6.34	'By my power, Piers, I *pliȝte* þee my trouþe
B. 9.710	Many peire siþen þe pestilence han *pliȝt* hem togideres.
C.Pr.47	Pilgrymes and palmers *plighten* hem togyderes
C. 2.127	For treuthe *plyhte* here treuthe to wedde on of here douhteres,
C. 3.470	Ne potte [hem] in panele [to] do [hem] *plihte* here treuthe;
C. 6.208	And was his prentis *yplyht* his profit to wayte
C. 8.33	'By my power, [Peres], y *plyhte* the my treuthe
C.10.271	Many a payre sethe th[e] pestelens[e] han *plyhte* treuthe to louye;

plihte v *plicchen v. &> pliȝte* C 2 plihte (1) pluhte (1)

C.12.49	And *plihte* in pauci preueiliche and lette þe remenaunt go rome.'
C.19.12	A *pluhte* forth a patente, a pece of an hard roche

plogh > plouȝ,plow; ploug(h)man > plowman; plokke > plukke

plommes n *ploume n.* C 1

C.12.221	As pesecoddes, pere ionettes, *plommes* and cheries;

plonte(s > plaunte

plot n *plot n.* B 4 plot (2) plottes (2)

B.13.274	Ac it was moled in many places wiþ manye sondry *plottes*,
B.13.275	Of pride here a *plot*, and þere a plot of vnbuxom speche,
B.13.275	Of pride here a plot, and þere a *plot* of vnbuxom speche,
B.13.317	Men sholde fynde manye frounces and manye foule *plottes*.'

plough > plouȝ; ploughman > plowman

plouȝ n *plough n.* A 7 plouȝ; B 15 plouȝ (2) plow (7) plowȝ (6); C 15 plogh (3) plough (2) plouh (10)

A. 7.94	And ben his pilgrym at þe *plouȝ* for pore menis sake.
A. 7.97	Now is peris & þe pilgrimes to þe *plouȝ* faren;
A. 7.104	At heiȝ prime peris let þe *plouȝ* stande
A. 7.117	Ac we preye for ȝow, peris, & for ȝoure *plouȝ* boþe,
A. 7.142	And bad hym go pissen wiþ his *plouȝ*: 'pilide shrewe!
A. 7.154	And countide peris at a pese & his *plouȝ* boþe.
A. 8.106	Of preyours & of penaunce my *plouȝ* shal ben hereaftir,
B. 3.309	Ech man to pleye with a *plow*, Pykoise or spade,
B. 6.102	And ben his pilgrym atte *plow* for pouere mennes sake.
B. 6.105	Now is Perkyn and [þe] pilgrimes to þe *plow* faren.
B. 6.112	At heiȝ prime Piers leet þe *plowȝ* stonde
B. 6.125	Ac we preie for yow, Piers, and for youre *plowȝ* boþe,
B. 6.155	And bad hym go pissen with his *plowȝ*: '[pyuysshe] sherewe!
B. 6.163	Plentee among þe peple þe while my *plowȝ* liggeþ'.
B. 6.169	And sette Piers at a pese and his *plowȝ* boþe.
B. 7.124	Of preieres and of penaunce my *plouȝ* shal ben herafter,
B.13.370	If I yede to þe *Plowȝ* I ne narwe
B.14.29	'And I shal purueie þee paast', quod Pacience, 'þou ȝus no *plouȝ* erye,
B.15.125	Ac a Porthors þat sholde be his *Plow*, Placebo to sigge–
B.19.266	The pris neet of Piers *plow*, passynge alle oþere.
B.19.335	Now is Piers to þe *plow*; pride it aspide
B.19.426	And Piers [þe Plowman] wiþ his newe *plow* and [þe] olde
C.Pr.146	And for most profi[t to þe peple] a *plogh* gonne þei make,
C. 3.462	Vche man to pley with a *plogh*, a pikois oþer a spade,
C. 6.267	And yf y ȝede to þe *plough* y pynched on his half aker
C. 7.192	Profitable as for þe *plouh* a potte me to lerne
C. 8.111	And ben a pilgrym at þe *plouh* for profit to pore and ryche.'
C. 8.112	Now is perkyn and þ[e] pilgrimes to þe *plouh* faren.
C. 8.119	At hey prime [Peres] leet þe *plouh* stande
C. 8.131	'A[c] we prayen for ȝow, [peres] and for ȝoure *plouh* bothe
C. 8.151	And bad hym go pisse with his *plogh*, pyuische shrewe.
C. 8.160	For ther worth no plente,' quod [Perus], 'and þe *plouh* lygge.'
C.15.233	For þoȝ nere payn [of] *plouh* ne potage were
C.15.234	Pruyde wolde potte hymsulf forth thogh no *plough* erye.
C.21.266	The pris neet of [Peres *plouh*], passynge alle oþere.
C.21.335	Now is [Peres to the *plouh*]; Pryde hit aspiede
C.21.426	And [Peres the Plowman] with his newe [*plouh*] and [þe] olde

plouȝ v *plouen v. &> plow* A 1; B 1; C 1 plogh

A.Pr.20	Summe putte hem to *plouȝ*, pleiȝede ful selde,
B.Pr.20	Some putten hem to *plouȝ*, pleiden ful selde,
C.Pr.22	Somme potte hem to *plogh*, playde ful selde,

plouȝman > plowman; plouȝpote > plowpote; plouh > plouȝ; plouh- > plow-; plow(ȝ > plouȝ

plowman n *ploughman n.* A 10 plouȝman (8) plouȝmen (1) plowman (1); B 43 plowman (41) plowmen (2); C 42 ploghman (2) plogman (1) ploughmen (1) plouheman (1) plouhman (36) Plowman (1)

A. 6.25	'Petir,' quaþ a *plouȝman* and putte forþ his hed,
A. 6.119	'ȝis,' quaþ [as Peres þe *plouȝman*] & pukide hym to goode;
A. 7.3	Quaþ perkyn þe *plouȝman*, 'be seint poule þe apostel,
A. 7.140	To peris þe *plouȝman* he profride his gloue.
A. 7.146	Þanne peris þe *plouȝman* pleynede hym to þe kniȝt
A. 8.86	Han as pleyn pardoun as þe *plouȝman* hymselue;

A. 8.132	And for peris loue þe *plouȝman* wel pensif in herte,
A. 8.151	On peris þe *plouȝman*, whiche a pardoun he hauiþ,
A.11.310	Þanne pore peple, as *plouȝmen*, and pastours of bestis,
A.12.102	Of peres þe *plouȝman* and mechel puple also.
B.Pr.119	And for profit of al þe peple *Plowmen* ordeyned
B. 5.537	'Peter!' quod a *Plowman*, and putte forþ his hed:
B. 5.634	'ȝis!' quod Piers þe *Plowman*, and poked [hym] to goode,
B. 6.3	Quod Perkyn þe *Plowman*, 'by Seint Peter of Rome!
B. 6.153	To Piers þe *Plowman* he profrede his gloue.
B. 6.159	Thanne Piers þe *plowman* pleyned hym to þe knyȝte
B. 7.8	Pardon wiþ Piers *Plowman* truþe haþ ygraunted.
B. 7.39	And preiseden Piers þe *Plowman* þat purchaced þis bulle.
B. 7.104	Han as pleyn pardon as þe *Plowman* hymselue;
B. 7.151	And for Piers [loue] þe *Plowman* [wel] pencif in herte,
B.10.466	Than *Plowmen* and pastours and [pouere] commune laborers,
B.13.124	For oon Piers þe *Plowman* haþ impugned vs alle,
B.13.130	Which þat saue mannes soule; þus seiþ Piers þe *Plowman*.'
B.13.237	For Piers þe *Plowman* and þat hym profit waiten.
B.15.196	'Wiþouten help of Piers *Plowman*', quod he, 'his persone sestow neuere.'
B.15.199	Ac Piers þe *Plowman* parceyueþ moore depper
B.15.212	But Piers þe *Plowman*, Petrus id est christus.
B.16.17	Vnder Piers þe *Plowman* to piken it and weden it.'
B.16.18	'Piers þe *Plowman*!' quod I þo, and al for pure Ioye
B.16.21	That Piers þe *Plowman* al þe place me shewed
B.16.103	And Piers þe *Plowman* parceyued plener tyme
B.16.168	And after Piers þe *Plowman* pried and stared.
B.16.171	After Piers þe *Plowman*; many a place I souȝte.
B.18.10	Oon semblable to þe Samaritan and somdeel to Piers þe *Plow[man]*
B.18.20	'And fecche þat þe fend claymeþ, Piers fruyt þe *Plowman*.'
B.18.25	In Piers paltok þe *Plowman* þis prikiere shal ryde,
B.18.33	And fecche fro þe fend Piers fruyt þe *Plowman*
B.19.6	That Piers þe *Plowman* was peynted al blody
B.19.11	Or it is Piers þe *Plowman*? who peynted hym so rede?'
B.19.187	To Piers pardon þe *Plowman* redde quod debes.
B.19.213	[Th]anne bigan grace to go wiþ Piers *Plowman*
B.19.258	For I make Piers þe *Plowman* my procuratour and my reue,
B.19.260	My prowor and my *Plowman* Piers shal ben on erþe,
B.19.357	Praye we þat a pees weere in Piers berne þe *Plowman*.
B.19.390	To Piers pardon þe *Plowman* redde quod debes.'
B.19.426	And Piers [þe *Plowman*] wiþ his newe plow and [þe] olde
B.19.430	A[c] wel worþe Piers þe *plowman* þat pursueþ god in doynge,
B.19.434	Right so Piers þe *Plowman* peyneþ hym to tilye
B.19.437	[So blessed be Piers þe *Plowman* þat peyneþ hym to tilye],
B.20.77	Fooles fro þise fendes lymes, for Piers loue þe *Plowman*.
B.20.320	Saue Piers þe *Plowman* þat haþ power ouer alle
B.20.382	To seken Piers þe *Plowman*, þat pryde [myȝte] destruye,
B.20.385	And sende me hap and heele til I haue Piers þe *Plowman*.'
C. 7.182	'[Peter]! quod a [*plouhman*], and potte forth his heued,
C. 7.287	'ȝus!' quod [Perus] þe [*plouhman*], and pokede hem alle to gode,
C. 7.303	Forthy, [Peres] the [*plouhman*], y preye the telle hit treuthe
C. 8.1	Qvod [perkyn] þe [*plouhman*], 'be seynt petur of Rome!
C. 8.124	Quod [Peres] þe [*plouhman*] al in puyre tene:
C. 8.150	And to [Peres] þe [*plouhman*] profrede to fyhte
C. 8.156	[Peres] the [*plouhman*] tho pleynede hym to þe knyhte
C. 8.167	'Now, by Crist!' quod [Peres] the [*plouhman*], 'y shal apayre ȝow alle,'
C. 8.236	Myhte y synneles do as thow sayst?' sayde Peres þe *plouhman*.
C. 8.263	'By Crist!' quod [Peres] þe [*plouhman*] tho, 'this prouerbis [wol y] shewe
C. 9.8	Pardoun with [Peres] þe [*Plouhman*] perpetuelly he graunteth.
C. 9.42	And prey[se]de [Peres] the [*plouhman*] þat purchased þis bull[e].
C. 9.60	Pardoun perpetuel riht as [Peres] the [*Plouhman*].
C. 9.187	And pardon with the *plouhman* A pena & a culpa.
C. 9.300	And of [Peres] the [*plouhman*] fol pencyf in herte
C.11.292	Then *ploughmen* an[d] pastours and pore comune peple.
C.15.33	Ilyk[e peres] the [*ploghman*], as he a palmere were,
C.15.137	Quod Peres the *ploghman*, 'Pacientes vinc[u]nt.
C.15.149	Where Peres the *plogman* bycam, so priueyliche he wente.
C.15.194	Peres prentys þe *plouhman*, alle peple to conforte.'
C.15.212	Ac þe prest and [þe] peple preyeth for Peres þe *Plouheman*
C.16.340	'Peres the *plouhman*,' quod he, 'moste parfitlyche hym knoweth:
C.20.8	Oen semblable to þe samaritaen and somdeel to Pers þe *plouhman*
C.20.18	'And feche þat þe fende claymeth, pers fruyt þe *plouhman*.'
C.20.24	In [Pers paltok] the [*plouhman*] this prikiare shal ryde
C.20.32	And feche fro þe fende [Peres] fruyt þe [*plouhman*]
C.21.6	That [Peres] þe [*plouhman*] was peynted al blody
C.21.11	Or hit is [Peres þe *Plouhman*? who] paynted hym so rede?'
C.21.187	To Peres pardoun þe *plouhman* Redde quod debes.
C.21.213	Thenne bigan grace to go with [Peres *Plouhman*]
C.21.258	For y make [Peres the *plouhman*] my proc[ur]atour and my reue
C.21.260	My prowour and my [*plouhman* Peres] shal ben on erthe

C.21.357 Preye we þat a pees were in [Peres] berne [þe *Plouhman*]
C.21.390 To [Peres] pardon þe [*plouhman*] Redde quod debe[s].'
C.21.426 And [Peres the *Plowman*] with his newe [plouh] and [þe] olde
C.21.430 Ac wel worth Peres the *plouhman* þat pursueth god in doyng[e],
C.21.434 Rihte so [Peres] the [*Plouhman*] payneth hym to tulie
C.21.437 So yblessed be [Peres] the [*plouhman*] þat peyneth hym to tulie
C.22.77   Foles fro this fendes lymes for [Peres] loue the [*plouhman*].
C.22.320 Saue [Peres the *Plowman*] þat haeth power ouer alle
C.22.382 To seke [Peres the *Plouhman*], þat pruyde myhte destruye,
C.22.385 And s[e]nde me hap and hele til y haue [Peres *Plouhman*]'.

plowpote n *plough n.* A 1 plouȝpote; B 1; C 1 plouhpote
A. 7.95   My *plouȝpote* shal be my pyk & putte at þe rotis,
B. 6.103 My *plow[pote]* shal be my pi[k] and [putte at] þe rotes,
C. 8.64   My *plouhpote* shal be my pykstaff and pyche ato þe rotes

pluhte > plihte

plukke v *plukken v.* A 1; B 4 plukke (1) plukked (2) plukkede (1); C 1 plokke
A. 6.69   Loke þou *plukke* no plant[e] þere for peril of þi soule.
B. 5.582 Loke þow *plukke* no plaunte þere for peril of þi soule.
B.11.114 And *plukked* in Pauci pryueliche and leet þe remenaunt go rome.'
B.12.251 To alle hem þat it holdeþ til hir tail be *plukked*.
B.17.11   [He *plukkede*] forþ a patente, a pece of an hard roche
C. 7.229 Loke thow *plokke* no plonte þere for perel of thy soule.

plumtrees n *ploumetre n.* A 1 plumtres; B 1; C 1
A. 5.16   Piries & *pl[umtr]es* wern pu[ffid] to þe erþe
B. 5.16   Pyries and *Plumtrees* were puffed to þe erþe
C. 5.118 P[iri]es and *plumtrees* were po[ff]ed to þe erthe

pluralites n *pluralite n.* A 1
A.11.200 And haþ possessions & *pluralites* for pore menis sake;

plurel adj *plurel adj.* B 1
B.10.245 Thre [propre] persones, ac noȝt in *plurel* nombre,

po n *po n.* B 1
B.12.259 By þe *po* feet is vnderstande, as I haue lerned in Auynet,

pocalips n *apocalipse n.* B 1; C 1
B.13.91   And preuen it by hir *Pocalips* and passion of Seint Auereys
C.15.98   And prouen hit by here *pocalips* and þe passioun of seynt Aueroy

pocok > pecok; poddyng(es > puddyng; poeple > peple

poesie n *poesie n.* B 1; C 1
B.18.408 Thanne pipede pees of *Poesie* a note:
C.20.451 Thenne piped pees of *poe[sie]* a note:

poete n *poete n.* A 1; B 6 poete (3) poetes (3); C 7 poete (3) poetes (4)
A.11.130 Plato þe *poete*, I putte hym ferst to boke;
B.10.178 Plato þe *poete*, I putte [hym] first to boke;
B.10.344 And patriarkes and prophetes and *poetes* boþe
B.11.37   'Homo proponit', quod a *poete*, and Plato he hiȝte,
B.12.148 To pastours and prophetes appered þe Aungel
B.12.237 Ensamples token and termes, as telleþ þ[ise] *poetes*,
B.12.262 Thus þe *Poete* preueþ þe pecok for hise feþeres;
C.11.118 Plato þe *poete* y putte hym furste to boke;
C.11.303 'Homo pr[o]ponit,' quod a *poete*, tho and plato he hihte,
C.12.174 And *poetes* to preuen hit: Porfirie and plato,
C.14.92   To pastours and to *poetes* Appered þe Angel
C.14.183 Thus þe *poete* praiseth þe pecok for his fetheres
C.14.189 Thus porfirie and plato and *poetes* monye
C.17.111 Ne [can] construe kyndelyche þat *poetes* made.

poffe(d > puffe; pohen > pehen

point n *pointe n.(1)* A 3 poynt; B 11 point (8) pointes (1) poyntes (2); C 7 poynt (5) poynte (1) poyntes (1)
A. 1.102 And whoso passiþ þat *poynt* is apostata in his ordre.
A. 5.15   Was apertly for pride & for no *poynt* ellis.
A. 7.38   'ȝa, & ȝet a *poynt*,' quaþ perkyn, 'I preye þe more:
B. 1.104 And whoso passe[þ] þat *point* [is] Apostata in [his] ordre.
B. 1.157 And portatif and persaunt as þe *point* of a nedle
B. 5.15   Was pertliche for pride and for no *point* ellis.
B. 6.37   'Ye, and yet a *point*', quod Piers, 'I preye [þee] of moore:
B.13.111 I wolde permute my penaunce with youre, for I am in *point* to dowel.'
B.13.186 And lere yow if yow like þe leeste *point* to knowe
B.13.354 Thanne Pacience parceyued of *pointes* [his] cote
B.14.280 Pouerte is þe firste *point* þat pride moost hateþ;
B.16.133 And maken it as muche ouþer moore in alle manere *poyntes*
B.18.44   And ȝit maken it as muche in alle manere *poyntes*,
B.20.31   And Spiritus prudencie in many a *point* shal faille
C. 1.98   And hoso passeth þat *poynt* is appostata of knyghthed.
C. 1.153 [And] portatif and persaunt as þe *poynt* of a nelde

C. 5.117 Was pertliche for pruyde and for no *poynt* elles.
C. 8.35   '[Ye], and ȝut a *poynt*,' quod [Peres], 'y praye ȝow of more:
C.16.120 Pouerte is þe furste *poynte* þat pruyde moest hateth;
C.20.43   And ȝut maken hit as moche in alle manere *poyntes*,
C.22.31   And spiritus Prudencie in many a *poynt* shal faile

poyntest v *pointen v.(1)* C 1
C. 8.296 'By seynte Poul!' quod Peres, 'thow *poyntest* neyh þe treuthe

poison n *poisoun n.* B 3; C 3 poysen
B.15.565 If possession be *poison* and inparfite hem make
B.15.567 And purgen hem of *poison* er moore peril falle.
B.18.52   And *poison* on a poole þei putte vp to hise lippes
C.17.229 For if possession be *poysen* and inparfit hem make,
C.17.232 And purge hem of þe olde *poysen* Ar more perel falle.
C.20.52   And with a pole *poysen* potten vp to his lippes

poisone v *poisonen v. &> poison* A 1; B 1
A. 3.71   For þei *poisone* þe peple preuyly wel ofte,
B. 3.82   For þei [*p]oisone* þe peple pryueliche [wel] ofte

poke n *poke n.* B 4 poke (3) pokes (1); C 4 poke (2) pokes (1) pouhe (1)
B.13.216 Thanne hadde Pacience, as pilgrymes han, in his *poke* vitailles:
B.14.36   'No?' quod Pacience paciently, and out of his *poke* hente
B.14.48   [Th]at pacience so preisede, [and of his *poke* hente]
B.14.246 For pouerte haþ but *pokes* to putten in hise goodes
C. 9.343 A *pouhe* ful of pardon there ne prouincials lettres,
C.15.185 Thenne hadde pacience, as pilgrimes haen, in h[is] *poke* vitayles,
C.15.246 'ȝe!' quod pacience [paciently], and oute of his *poke* hente
C.16.86   For pouerte hath bote *pokes* to potten in his godes

poked(e > pokeþ

pokeful n *pokeful n.* A 1; B 1
A. 8.175 A *pokeful* of pardoun þere, ne þe prouincialis lettres,
B. 7.197 A *pokeful* of pardon þere, ne þe prouincials lettres,

pokeþ v *poken v.(1)* A 2 pokiþ (1) pukide (1); B 2 poked (1) pokeþ (1); C 3 pokede (2) poketh (1)
A. 6.97   And *pokiþ* [forþ] pride to preise þiselue.
A. 6.119 'ȝis,' quaþ peris þe plouȝman & *pukide* hym to goode:
B. 5.611 And *pokeþ* forþ pride to preise þiseluen;
B. 5.634 'ȝis!' quod Piers þe Plowman, and *poked* [hym] to goode,
C. 1.129 For pruyde th[at] hym *pokede* his payne hath non ende.
C. 7.263 And *poketh* forth pruyde to preyse thysuluen,
C. 7.287 'ȝus!' quod [Perus] þe [*plouhman*], and *pokede* hem alle to gode,

pokkes n *pok n.* B 1; C 1
B.20.98   As *pokkes* and pestilences, and muche peple shente;
C.22.98   As *pokkes* and pestilences, and moche peple shente;

pol n *polle n.* B 4 pol (2) polles (2); C 3 pol (2) polles (1)
B.11.58   And preien for þee *pol* by pol if þow be pecuniosus.'
B.11.58   And preien for þee pol by *pol* if þow be pecuniosus.'
B.13.246 Saue a pardon wiþ a peis of leed and two *polles* amyddes
B.20.86   Hadde ypriked and prayed *polles* of peple;
C.12.10   And preeye for the *pol* by pol yf thow be peccuniosus.'
C.12.10   And preeye for the pol by *pol* yf thow be peccuniosus.'
C.22.86   Hadde ypriked and preyede *polles* of peple;

pole > poole,pulle; polesche > polshe; polettes > pulettes; polleden > pulle; polles > pol

polshe v *polishen v.* A 1 pulsshe; B 1; C 1 polesche
A. 5.248 Þat penitencia his pik he shulde *pulsshe* newe
B. 5.474 That penitencia his pik he sholde *polshe* newe
C. 6.328 That [penitencia] is pykstaff a wolde *polesche* newe

pomade n *pomade n.* C 1
C.20.409 May no pyement ne *pomade* ne preciouse drynkes

pomp n *pompe n.* B 3 pomp (1) pompe (2); C 2 pomp (1) pompe (1)
B. 3.66   An auenture pride be peynted þere and *pomp* of þe world;
B.14.194 Of *pompe* and of pride þe parchemyn decourreþ,
B.15.79   Moore for *pompe* þan for pure charite; þe peple woot þe soþe.
C. 3.70   An Auntur pruyde be paynted there and *pomp* of the world,
C.16.238 More for *pompe* and pruyde, as þe peple woet wel

pondfold n *pinfold n.* B 2 pondfold (1) punfolde (1); C 1 pondefold
B. 5.624 Heo haþ holpe a þousand out of þe deueles *punfolde*.
B.16.264 Out of þe poukes *pondfold* no maynprise may vs fecche–
C.18.280 Fro þe poukes *pondefold* no maynprise may vs feche–

poole n *pole n.(2)* B 1; C 1 pole
B.18.52   And poison on a *poole* þei putte vp to hise lippes
C.20.52   And with a *pole* poysen potten vp to his lippes

poore > pouere

pope n *pope n. &> pope holy* A 11 pope (8) popes (1) popis (2); B 30 pope (25) popes (5); C 32 pope (25) popes (7)

A. 2.18   In þe *popis* paleis heo is preuy as myselue;
A. 3.117   Apoisonide *popis*, apeiride holy chirche;
A. 3.136   She is preuy wiþ þe *pope*, prouisours it knowiþ;
A. 3.202   Þe *pope* wiþ his prelatis presentis vndirfongiþ,
A. 4.116   Oþer prouisour, or prest þat þe *pope* auaunciþ.
A. 6.87   Whanne I þenke þereon, þei3 I were a *pope*".
A. 8.8   Part in þ[at] pardoun þe *pope* haþ hem grauntid.
A. 8.21   But non a pena & a culpa þe *pope* wolde h[e]m graunte,
A. 8.157   Now haþ þe *pope* power pardoun to graunte
A. 8.170   [To purchace pardoun and þe *popes* bulles],
A.11.204   Gregory þe grete clerk, a good *pope* in his tyme,
B.Pr.108   And power presumed in hem a *pope* to make
B. 2.23   In þe *popes* Paleis she is pryuee as myselue,
B. 3.128   [A]poisoned *popes*, [a]peired holy chirche.
B. 3.147   She is pryuee wiþ þe *pope*, prouisours it knoweþ;
B. 3.215   The *Pope* [wiþ hise] prelates present3 vnderfonge[þ],
B. 5.50   And siþen he preide þe *pope* haue pite on holy chirche,
B. 5.166   Seint Gregory was a good *pope* and hadde a good forwit:
B. 5.600   Whan I þynke þeron, þei3 I were a *Pope*."
B. 7.19   Ac noon A pena & a culpa þe *pope* [w]olde hem graunte,
B. 7.179   Now haþ þe *pope* power pardon to graunte
B. 7.192   To purchace pardon and þe *popes* bulles.
B.10.298   Gregorie þe grete clerk and þe goode *pope*
B.11.141   '[I] Troianus, a trewe kny3t, [take] witnesse at a *pope*
B.11.156   Nou3t þoru3 preiere of a *pope* but for his pure truþe
B.13.166   *Pope* ne patriark, þat pure reson ne shal [þee] make
B.13.174   Kan no3t [parfournen] a pees bitwene [þe *pope*] and hise enemys,
B.13.243   I fynde payn for þe *pope* and prouendre for his palfrey,
B.13.245   Neiþer prouendre ne personage yet of [þe] *popes* 3ifte,
B.13.256   To haue þe grace of god, and no gilt of [þe] *pope*.
B.15.399   This Makometh was cristene [man], and for he moste no3t ben *pope*
B.15.441   Preestes and prechours and a *pope* aboue,
B.15.491   What *pope* or prelat now parfourneþ þat crist highte,
B.15.493   So manye prelates to preche as þe *Pope* makeþ,
B.15.509   And a peril to þe *pope* and prelates þat he makeþ
B.19.223   And Pride shal be *Pope*, Prynce of holy chirche,
B.19.413   I knew neuere Cardynal þat he ne cam fro þe *pope*.
B.19.428   Inparfit is þat *pope* þat al [peple] sholde helpe
B.19.442   And [Piers] amende þe *pope*, þat pileþ holy kirke
B.20.101   Kynges and knyghtes, kaysers and *popes*.
B.20.127   And [pressed on] þe [*pope*] and prelates þei maden
C.Pr.135   And power presumen in hemself a *pope* to make
C. 2.23   In þe *popes* palays he is pryue as mysulue,
C. 2.247   And putte hem thorw appeles in þe *popes* grace.
C. 3.165   He hath apoisend *popes*, he appeyreth holy churche.
C. 3.185   He is priue with þe *pope*, prouysours it knoweth,
C. 3.271   The *pope* and alle prelates presentes vnderfongen
C. 3.315   And thow the kyng of his cortesye, Cayser or *pope*,
C. 3.319   Bothe kyng and Cayser and þe crouned *pope*
C. 3.330   And ryhte so, sothly, may kyng and *pope*
C. 5.78   *Popes* and patrones pore gentel blood refused
C. 5.112   And resoun yreuestede ryht as a *pope*
C. 5.191   And sethe a preyede þe *pope* haue pite on holy chirche
C. 6.256   For þe *pope* with alle his pentauncers power hem fayleth
C. 9.325   3ut hath þe *pope* power pardoun to graunte
C. 9.338   To pur[c]hace 3ow pardoun and the *popes* bulles.
C.10.206   Prophetus and patriarkes, *popes* and maydenes.
C.12.76   'I troianes, a trewe knyht, take witnesse of a *pope*
C.15.215   Can nat peyurne a pees of þe *pope* and his enemyes
C.15.216   Y fynde payn for þe *po[p]e* and pre[y]en hym ych wolde
C.15.226   To haue þe grace of god and no gulte of þe *pope*.
C.17.167   And pursuede to haue be *pope*, prince of holy chirche;
C.17.188   So manye prelates to preche as þe *pope* maketh,
C.17.233   For were presthode more parfyte, that is, þe *pope* formost
C.17.238   The *pope* with alle prestes pax vobis sholde make
C.17.243   In such manere me thynketh moste þe *pope*,
C.17.260   And a perel for prelates þat þe *pope* maketh
C.21.223   And [pryde shal] prince of holy chirche,
C.21.413   Y knewe neuere cardinale þat he ne cam fro þe *pope*
C.21.428   Inparfit is þat *pope* þat all peple sholde helpe
C.21.442   And [Peres] amende þe *pope* þat pileth holi churche
C.22.101   Kynges and knyhtes, Caysers and *popes*.
C.22.127   And presed on þe *pope* and prelates thei made

pope_holy adj *popeholi adj.* B 1; C 1 popholy
B.13.283   Was noon swich as hymself], ne [noon] so *po[pe] holy*;
C. 6.37   Was non such as [my]sulue ne non so *popholy*;

popeiay n *papejaie n.* C 1
C.14.172   That is, þe pocok and þe *popeiay* with here proude fetheres

poperiþ v *poperen v.* A 1
A.11.213   *Poperiþ* on a palfrey [fro] toune to toune;

porche n *porche n.* B 1; C 1
B.16.225   Thus in a somer I hym sei3 as I sat in my *porche*;
C.18.240   'In a somur y hym seyh,' quod he, 'as y saet in my *porche*,

porcion n *porcioun n.* A 1 porcioun; B 1
A.10.117   Be paied wiþ þe *porcioun*, pore oþer riche.
B. 8.53   Wit and free wil, to euery wi3t a *porcion*,

pore(st > pouere

poret n *poret n.* A 2 poret (1) porret (1); B 2; C 1
A. 7.270   Ac I haue persile & *poret*, & many cole plantis,
A. 7.282   [Grene *porret* and pesen; to [peysen] him þei þou3te].
B. 6.286   Ac I haue percile and *pore[t]* and manye [plaunte coles],
B. 6.298   Grene *poret* and pesen; to [peisen] hym þei þo3te.
C. 8.308   Ac y haue *poret*-pl[o]ntes, parsilie and skalones,

porfiel > purfil

porfirie n prop *n.i.d.* C 2
C.12.174   And poetes to preuen hit: *Porfirie* and plato,
C.14.189   Thus *porfirie* and plato and poetes monye

porore > pouerer; porret > poret

pors v *pursen v. &> purs* C 1
C.12.165   3ef pore peple þe panes; þerof *pors* þou none

porse > purs; port > porte

portatif adj *portatif adj.* B 1; C 1
B. 1.157   And *portatif* and persaunt as þe point of a nedle
C. 1.153   [And] *portatif* and persaunt as þe poynt of a nelde

porte n *port n.(4)* B 1; C 1 port
B.13.277   As in apparaill and in *porte* proud amonges þe peple;
C. 6.30   Proud of aparayle in *port* amongus þe peple

porter n *porter n.* A 1 porteris; B 5 porter (4) porters (1); C 5 porter (4) porteres (1)
A. 6.105   And ben *porteris* to þe posternis þat to þe place longiþ:
B. 5.619   And arn *porters* of þe Posternes þat to þe place longeþ.
B.11.113   And whan þe peple was plener comen þe *porter* vnpynned þe yate
B.15.18   Is neiþer Peter þe *Porter* ne Poul wiþ [þe] fauchon
B.20.298   And made pees *porter* to pynne þe yates
B.20.330   Pees vnpynned it, was *Porter* of vnitee,
C. 7.271   And aren *porteres* ouer þe posternes þat to þ[e] place bilongen.
C.12.48   And whan þe peple was plenere ycome þe *porter* vnpynnede þe gate
C.16.169   Is noþer Peter the *porter* ne poul with the fauchen
C.22.298   And made pees *porter* to pynne þe 3ates
C.22.330   Pees vnpynned hyt, was *porter* of vnite,

porthors n *porthors n.* B 1
B.15.125   Ac a *Porthors* þat sholde be his Plow, Placebo to sigge–

portours n *portour n.* C 1
C. 6.370   Of *portours* and of pikeporses and of pilede tothdraweres,

portreye v *portraien v.* B 3 portraye (1) portreye (2); C 3 portrey (1) purtraye (1) purtrayen (1)
B. 3.62   Do peynten and *portraye* [who] paie[d] for þe makynge
B.15.181   He kan *portreye* wel þe Paternoster and peynte it with Aues.
B.17.172   The fyngres formen a ful hand to *portreye* or peynten;
C. 3.66   And [do] peynten and *purtrayen* ho payede for þe makyng
C.16.323   And *purtraye* wel þe paternoster and peynten hit with Auees.
C.19.137   *Portrey* ne peynte parfitliche, y leue,

pose v *posen v.* B 1; C 1
B.17.299   'I *pose* I hadde synned so and sholde [nouþe] deye,
C.19.279   'Y *pose* y hadde syneged so and sholde nouthe deye

possed v *pushen v.* B 1
B.Pr.151   And pleide wiþ hem perillousli and *possed* aboute.

possession n *possessioun n.* A 1 possessions; B 7; C 3
A.11.200   And haþ *possessions* & pluralites for pore menis sake;
B.11.273   That parfit pouerte was no *possession* to haue,
B.11.276   Whoso wole be pure parfit moot *possession* forsake
B.12.250   So is *possession* peyne of pens and of nobles
B.13.300   Pouere of *possession* in purs and in cofre;
B.14.217   So it [preueþ] by ech a persone þat *possession* forsakeþ
B.15.563   That sholden preie for þe pees, *possession* hem letteþ;
B.15.565   If *possession* be poison and inparfite hem make
C.16.111   So hit fareth by vch a persone þat *possession* forsaket
C.17.226   That sholde preye for þe pees *possession* hem letteth;
C.17.229   For if *possession* be poysen and inparfit hem make,

possessioners n *possessiouner n.* B 1
B. 5.145 Thise *possessioners* preche and depraue freres;

posternes n *posterne n.* A 1 posternis; B 1; C 1
A. 6.105 And ben porteris to þe *posternis* þat to þe place longiþ:
B. 5.619 And arn porters of þe *Posternes* þat to þe place longeþ.
C. 7.271 And aren porteres ouer þe *posternes* þat to þ[e] place bilongen.

postes n *post n.(1)* B 1
B.16.54 The power of þise *postes* and hire propre my3t[e].

postles n *apostle n.* B 1; C 2
B. 6.149 Ne *Postles*, but þei preche konne and haue power of þe bisshop:
C. 9.118 Hit aren as his *postles*, suche peple, or as his priue disciples
C.18.176 Soffreth my *postles* in pays and in pees gange.'

pot n *pote n.(1) &> putten, cf. potte_ful* B 1; C 1 pott
B.13.254 For siþ he haþ þe power þat Peter hadde he haþ þe *pot* wiþ þe salue:
C.15.224 For sethe he hath þe power þat peter hadde he hath þe *pott* with þe salue:

potage n *potage n.* B 4 potage (3) potages (1); C 4 potage (3) potages (1)
B. 6.150 Thei shul haue payn and *potage* and [a pitaunce biside],
B. 9.83 Ne faille payn ne *potage* and prelates dide as þei sholden.
B.13.41 Ac [he eet] mete of moore cost, mortrews and *potages*.
B.15.315 For hadde ye *potage* and payn ynogh and penyale to drynke,
C. 8.182 For a potte ful of *potage* þat [Peres] wyf made
C. 8.284 Part with hem of thy payne, of *potage* or of sowl;
C.15.46 Forthy eet he mete of more cost, mortrewes and *potages*.
C.15.233 For þo3 nere payn [of] plouh ne *potage* were

potager n *potagere n.* B 1; C 1
B. 5.157 I was þe Prioresse *potager* and oþere pouere ladies
C. 6.132 I was the Prioresse *potager* and oþer pore ladies

potel n *potelle n.* A 2; B 2; C 1
A. 5.189 He pisside a *potel* in a paternoster while,
A. 7.174 For a *potel* of pe[s]is þat peris hadde mad
B. 5.341 He pissed a *potel* in a paternoster while,
B. 6.186 For a *pot[el]* of peses þat Piers hadde ymaked
C. 6.399 A pissede a *potel* in a paternoster whyle

potente n *potente n.* A 1 potent; B 1
A. 9.88 A pik is in þat *potent* to pungen adoun þe wykkide,
B. 8.98 A pik is [in] þat *potente* to [punge] adown þe wikked

pott > pot

potte_ful n *OED potful &> putten, cf. pot* C 1
C. 8.182 For a *potte* ful of potage þat [Peres] wyf made

potten > putten

poudres n *poudre n.(1)* B 1; C 1
B.20.359 The plastres of þe person and *poudres* biten to soore;
C.22.359 The plasteres of the persoun and *poudres* b[it]en to sore;

pouer > power; poues > pous; pouhe > poke

pouke n *pouke n.* A 2 pouk (1) pouke (1); B 7 pouke (6) poukes (1); C 4 pouke (3) poukes (1)
A.10.62 Thanne haþ þe *pouk* power, sire princeps huius mundi,
A.11.161 Nigromancie & per[i]mansie þe *pouke* to reisen;
B.10.218 Nigromancie and perimancie þe *pouke* to raise];
B.13.161 Ne neiþer hete ne hayl ne noon helle *pouke*,
B.14.189 A[c] if þe [*pouke*] wolde plede herayein, and punysshe vs in conscience,
B.14.191 And putten of so þe *pouke*, and preuen vs vnder borwe.
B.16.51 And palleþ adoun þe *pouke* pureliche þoru3 grace
B.16.261 'It is a precious present', quod he, 'ac þe *pouke* it haþ attached,
B.16.264 Out of þe *poukes* pondfold no maynprise may vs fecche–
C.15.163 Ne n[oþ]ere hete ne hayl ne helle *pouke* hym greue,
C.18.50 And thenne [f]alle y adoune þe *pouke* with the thridde shoriere
C.18.277 'Hit is a preciouse present,' quod he, 'Ac the *pouke* hit hath attached,
C.18.280 Fro þe *poukes* pondefold no maynprise may vs feche–

poul n *prop Poule n.* A 9 Poul (2) poule (5) poulis (2); B 21 Poul (16) Poule (1) Poules (4); C 15 Paul (4) paules (1) poul (7) Poule (1) poules (2)
A.Pr.38 Þat *poule* prechiþ of hem I dar not proue it here:
A. 7.3 Quaþ perkyn þe plou3man, 'be seint *poule* þe apostel,
A. 7.26 'Be seint *poule*,' quaþ perkyn, 'for þou profrist þe so lowe
A. 9.83 And prechiþ þe peple seint *poulis* wordis:
A.10.109 *Poule* þe apostel in his pistil wrot it
A.11.33 Wolde neuere king, ne kni3t, ne canoun of seint *poulis*
A.11.229 *Poul* prouiþ it is vnpossible, riche men in heuene.
A.11.289 Or *poule* þe apostil þat no pite hadde
A.12.22 And *poul* precheþ hit often, prestes hit redyn:

B.Pr.38 That *Poul* precheþ of hem I [dar] nat preue it here;
B. 5.639 'Bi seint *Poul*!' quod a pardoner, 'parauenture I be no3t knowe þere;
B. 6.24 'By Seint *Poul*!' quod Perkyn, '[for þow profrest þee so lowe]
B. 8.92 And precheþ þe peple Seint *Poules* wordes;
B.10.47 [W]olde neuere kyng ne kny3t ne [c]anon of Seint *Poules*
B.10.74 And prechen at Seint *Poules*, for pure enuye of clerkes,
B.10.205 *Poul* preched þe peple, þat parfitnesse louede,
B.10.341 *Poule* preueþ it impossible, riche men [in] heuene;
B.10.430 Or *Poul* þe Apostle þat no pite hadde
B.11.87 '3is, by Peter and by *Poul*!' quod he and took hem boþe to witnesse:
B.12.29 '*Poul* in his pistle', quod he, 'preueþ what is dowel:
B.13.65 'It is no3t foure dayes þat þis freke, bifore þe deen of *Poules*,
B.13.66 Preched of penaunces þat *Poul* þe Apostle suffrede
B.13.69 That *Poul* in his Pistle to al þe peple tolde:
B.15.18 Is neiþer Peter þe Porter ne *Poul* wiþ [þe] fauchon
B.15.156 Ac charite þat *Poul* preiseþ best, and moost plesaunt to oure [Saueour]–
B.15.265 Ne han martired Peter ne *Poul*, ne in prison holden.
B.15.286 *Poul* primus heremita hadde parroked hymselue
B.15.290 *Poul* after his prechyng paniers he made
B.17.261 *Poul* þe Apostel preueþ wheiþer I lye:
B.17.341 As *Poul* þe Apostle to þe peple tau3te:
C.Pr.39 Tha[t] *Poule* preche[þ] of hem preue hit y myhte;
C. 8.296 'By seynte *Poul*!' quod Peres, 'thow poyntest neyh þe treuthe
C. 9.112 Riht as Peter dede and *poul* saue þat þey preche nat
C.10.89 And precheth to þe peple seynt *paules* wordes:
C.11.54 And prech[en] at seynt *poules*, [for] puyr enuye of clerkes,
C.11.266 [Or] *Poul* þe apostel [þat] no pite hadde
C.15.70 At *poules* byfore þe peple what penaunce they soffrede,
C.15.72 And how þat *poul* þe apostel penaunce tholede
C.15.75 A[s] *poul* þe apostle prechede to þe peple ofte:
C.16.169 Is noþer Peter the porter ne *poul* with the fauchen
C.16.291 As *poul* in his pistul of hym bereth wittenesse:
C.17.13 *Paul* primus heremita hadde yparrokede hymsulue
C.17.17 *Paul* aftur his prechyng paniars he made
C.19.227 *Paul* the apostel preueth where y lye:
C.19.321 As *Paul* þe apostel in his episteles techeth:

poulynes > paulynes

pound n *pounde n.(1)* A 2; B 4; C 3 pound (2) pounde (1)
A. 5.131 Þe *pound* þat heo [payede] by peisid a quarter more
A. 5.155 I haue pepir, & p[ye]nye, & a *pound* of garlek,
B. 5.215 [Th]e *pound* þat she paied by peised a quartron moore
B. 5.304 'I haue pepir and pion[e] and a *pound* of garleek,
B.10.295 And be prester at youre preiere þan for a *pound* of nobles,
B.15.166 As proud of a peny as of a *pound* of golde,
C. 6.223 The *pound* th[at] he payede by peysed a quarter more
C. 6.359 'Y haue pepur and pyonie and a *pound* of garlek,
C.16.299 As proud of a peny as of a *pounde* of golde

pounded v *OED pound v.2, MED pounden v.* A 1 poundide; B 1; C 1
A.Pr.86 Pleten for penis & [*poundide*] þe lawe,
B.Pr.213 Pleteden for penyes and *pounde[d]* þe lawe
C.Pr.163 Plededen for penyes and *pounde[d]* þe lawe

poundemele adv *poundmele adv.* A 1 poundmel; B 1; C 1 poundmele
A. 2.184 And 3af pardoun for panis *poundmel* aboute.
B. 2.225 And [gaf] pardoun for pens *poundemele* aboute.
C. 2.235 And gaf pardon for pans *poundmele* aboute.

poure > pouere

poured v *pouren v.(2)* A 1 pouride; B 1; C 1
A. 5.134 Penyale & pilewhey heo *pouride* togidere.
B. 5.218 Peny ale and puddyng ale she *poured* togideres;
C. 6.226 Peny ale and poddyng ale [h]e *poured* togederes,

pous n *pouse n.* B 1; C 1 poues
B.17.69 And parceyued bi his *pous* he was in peril to dye
C.19.68 And parseued by his *poues* he was in perel to deye

poustee n *pouste n.* B 2 poustee (1) poustees (1)
B. 5.36 Ne for no *poustee* of pestilence plese hem no3t out of reson.
B.12.11 Wiþ *poustees* of pestilences, wiþ pouerte and with angres;

pouere adj *povre adj.* A 26 poore (1) pore (23) pouere (2); B 88 poore (30) pouere (58); C 100 pouere (1) pore (97) porest (1) poure (1)
A.Pr.79 Þat þe *pore* peple of þe parissh shulde haue 3if þei ne were.
A.Pr.81 Þat here parissh w[ere] *pore* siþþe þe pestilence tyme,
A.Pr.93 To preche þe peple & *pore* men to fede
A. 1.119 Forþi I rede þe riche haue reuþe on þe *pore*;
A. 1.155 But 3if 3e loue lelly & lene þe *pore*,
A. 2.59 To be present in pride for *pouere* [or for] riche,
A. 3.70 To þe *pore* peple þat parcelmel biggen,
A. 3.73 Of þat þe *pore* peple shulde putte in here wombe.

A. 3.155 For *pouere* men mowe haue no power to pleyne [þei3] hem smerte,
A. 3.182 Wiþoute pite, pilour, *pore* men þou robb[ed]est,
A. 3.273 Þat lawe is lord waxen & leute is *pore*,
A. 6.38 He is þe presteste payere þat *pore* men knowen;
A. 7.40 And þei *pore* men profre þe presauntis or 3eftis
A. 7.94 And ben his pilgrym at þe plou3 for *pore* menis sake.
A. 7.276 Alle þe *pore* peple pesecoddis fetten;
A. 8.32 [*Pore*] wydewis þat wiln not be wyues aftir,
A. 8.48 And of no *pore* peple no peny[worþ] to take.
A. 8.49 Ac he þat spendiþ his speche & spekiþ for þe *pore*
A.10.68 And 3if þei ben *pore* & cateles, to kepe hem fro ille,
A.10.117 Be paied wiþ þe porcioun, *pore* oþer riche.
A.11.50 Þat þus partiþ wiþ þe *poore* a parcel whanne hym nediþ.
A.11.200 And haþ possessions & pluralites for *pore* menis sake;
A.11.230 Ac *pore* men in pacience & penaunce togidere
A.11.244 Oure enemys and alle men þat arn nedy & *pore*,
A.11.310 Þanne *pore* peple, as plou3men, and pastours of bestis,
A.12.50 Hy3t omnia probate, a *pore* þing withalle;
B.Pr.82 That þe [*pouere* peple] of þe parisshe sholde haue if þei ne were.
B.Pr.84 That hire parissh[e] wer[e] *pouere* siþ þe pestilence tyme,
B.Pr.90 Prechen and praye for hem, and þe *pouere* fede,
B. 1.175 Forþi I rede [þe] riche, haueþ ruþe [on] þe *pouere*;
B. 1.181 But if ye louen leelly and lene þe *pouere*,
B. 3.81 To þe *pouere* peple þat parcelmele buggen,
B. 3.84 [Of] þat þe *pouere* peple sholde putte in hire wombe.
B. 3.168 For *pouere* men may haue no power to pleyne þou3 [hem] smerte,
B. 3.195 Wiþouten pite, Pilour, *pouere* men þow robbedest
B. 3.241 And enforme[þe] [peple] and pursueþ truþe:
B. 4.119 Til clerkene coueitise be to cloþe þe *pouere* and fede,
B. 4.125 Hire haukes and hire houndes help to *pouere* Religious;
B. 5.157 I was þe Prioresse potager and oþere *pouere* ladies,
B. 5.254 'Hastow pite on *pouere* men þat [for pure nede] borwe?'
B. 5.255 'I haue as muche pite of *pouere* men as pedlere haþ of cattes,
B. 5.551 He is þe presteste paiere þat *pouere* men knoweþ;
B. 6.41 And þou3 *pouere* men profre [þee] presentes and 3iftes
B. 6.102 And ben his pilgrym atte plow for *pouere* mennes sake.
B. 6.195 And ech a *pouere* man wel apaied to haue pesen for his hyre,
B. 6.292 Al þe *pouere* peple pescoddes fetten;
B. 6.297 Thanne *pouere* folk for fere fedden hunger yerne
B. 7.30 *Pouere* peple [bedredene] and prisons [in stokkes]
B. 7.47 Ac he þat spendeþ his speche and spekeþ for þe *pouere*
B. 8.16 Boþe princes paleises and *pouere* mennes cotes,
B.10.64 That þus parteþ wiþ þe *pouere* a parcell whan hym nedeþ.
B.10.77 In Religion and in al þe Reme amonges riche and *pouere*
B.10.83 Ne beþ plenteuouse to þe *pouere* as puyr charite wolde,
B.10.100 In a pryuee parlour for *pouere* mennes sake,
B.10.320 Of þe *pouere* haue þei no pite, and þat is hir [pure chartre];
B.10.351 That is bapti3ed beþ saaf, be he riche or *pouere*.'
B.10.466 Than Plowmen and pastours and [*pouere*] commune laborers,
B.11.184 And [souereynly] *pouere* peple; hir preieres maye vs helpe.
B.11.186 In a *pouere* mannes apparaille pursue[þ] vs euere,
B.11.192 'Ac calleþ þe carefulle þerto, þe croked and þe *pouere*;
B.11.195 Ac for þe *pouere* I shal paie, and pure wel quyte hir trauaille
B.11.198 [Ac] for þe beste ben som riche and some beggeres and *pouere*.
B.11.208 And we hise breþeren þoru3 hym ybou3t, boþe riche and *pouere*.
B.11.232 Why I meue þis matere is moost for þe *pouere*;
B.11.236 For his *pouere* apparaill and pilgrymes wedes
B.11.243 And in þe apparaille of a *pouere* man and pilgrymes liknesse
B.11.246 Seint Iohan and oþere seintes were seyen in *poore* cloþyng,
B.11.247 And as *pouere* pilgrymes preyed mennes goodes.
B.11.249 Was a pure *pouere* maide and to a *pouere* man ywedded.
B.11.249 Was a pure *pouere* maide and to a *pouere* man ywedded.
B.11.267 And wel sikerer he slepeþ, þe [segge] þat is *pouere*,
B.11.372 No Reson hem [ruled, neiþer riche ne *pouere*].
B.12.74 That what womman were in auoutrye taken, whe[r] riche or *poore*,
B.13.8 And [peple] þat was *pouere* at litel pris þei sette,
B.13.30 And preyde mete 'p[u]r charite, for a *pouere* heremyte'.
B.13.79 Haþ no pite on vs *pouere*; he parfourneþ yuele
B.13.196 And þe *poore* widewe [purely] for a peire of mytes
B.13.299 And if he gyueþ ou3t to *pouere* gomes, telle what he deleþ;
B.13.300 *Pouere* of possession in purs and in cofre;
B.13.418 Penaunce [and] *pouere* men and þe passion of Seintes,
B.13.424 And 3yueþ hem mete and mede, and *pouere* men refuse,
B.13.443 The *pouere* for a fool sage sittyng at þ[i] table,
B.14.10 To penaunce pacience and *pouere* men to fede,
B.14.27 Ne no Mynstrall be moore worþ amonges *pouere* and riche
B.14.74 [Oþer] plentee makeþ pryde amonges *poore* and riche.
B.14.100 'Ther parfit truþe and *poore* herte is, and pacience of tonge,
B.14.109 Ther þe *poore* dar plede and preue by pure reson
B.14.145 Ac if ye riche haue ruþe and rewarde wel þe *poore*,
B.14.174 Ac *poore* peple, þi prisoners, lord, in þe put of meschief,
B.14.182 To robberis and to Reueris, to riche and to *poore*,
B.14.195 And principalliche of al[l]e peple but þei *poore* of herte.

B.14.206 And þat is plesaunt to pride in *poore* and in riche.
B.14.208 Ther þe *poore* is put bihynde, and parauenture kan moore
B.14.213 Ther þe *poore* preesseþ bifore wiþ a pak at his rugge:
B.14.221 For þe *poore* is ay prest to plese þe riche
B.14.225 If wraþe wrastle wiþ þe *poore* he haþ þe worse ende
B.14.226 [For] if þei pleyne [þe feblere is þe *poore*];
B.14.239 And if Coueitise cacche þe *poore* þei may no3t come togideres,
B.14.245 And þou3 Auarice wolde angre þe *poore* he haþ but litel my3te,
B.14.253 Hadde þei no[on haunt] but of *poore* men; hir houses stoode
  vntyled.
B.14.260 Forþi [al] *poore* þat pacient is [of pure ri3t] may cleymen,
B.14.285 And Ioye to pacient *pouere*], pure spiritual helþe,
B.14.289 [O]r as Iustice to Iugge men enioyned is no *poore*,
B.14.291 Selde is any *poore* yput to punysshen any peple.
B.14.292 /Ergo *pouere* and *poore* men parfournen þe comaundement
B.14.294 Selde is *poore* [ri3t] riche but of ri3tful heritage.
B.15.154 Men beþ merciable to mendinaunt3 and to *poore*,
B.15.183 Ther *poore* men and prisons liggeþ, hir pardon to haue;
B.15.203 And to *poore* peple han pepir in þe nose,
B.15.246 And cristes patrymonye to þe *poore* parcelmele dele;
B.15.328 If any peple parfourne þat text it are þise *poore* freres,
B.15.538 And þo was plentee and pees amonges *poore* and riche,
B.16.8 Pacience hatte þe pure tree and [*pouere*] symple of herte,
B.20.234 'And for þei are *pouere*, parauenture, for patrymoyne [hem]
  faille[þ],
C.Pr.80 That þe [*pore*] peple [of þe] parsch[e] sholde haue yf þei ne were.
C.Pr.82 That here parsch[e] were *pore* sithe þ[e] pestelence tyme,
C. 1.171 Forthy y rede 3ow riche, haueth reuthe [o]n þe *pore*;
C. 1.177 But yf 3e louye leeliche and lene þe *pore*,
C. 2.189 And on *pore* prouisores and appeles in þe Arches.
C. 3.83 With that þe *pore* peple sholde potte in here wombe.
C. 3.214 For *pore* men dar nat pleyne ne no pleynt shewe,
C. 3.283 And glad for to grype here, gret lord oþer *pore*.'
C. 4.26 Whiche a maistre mede was amonges *pore* and ryche.
C. 4.114 Til Clerkene Coueytise be cloth for þe *pore*
C. 4.115 And here pelure and here palfrayes *pore* menne lyflode
C. 4.122 And til saynt Iames be souhte there *pore* sykke lyggen,
C. 4.123 In prisones and in *pore* cotes be pilgrimages to Rome
C. 4.153 Resoun for his ryhtful speche; ryche and *pore* hym louede
C. 5.78 Popes and patrones *pore* gentel blood refused
C. 5.166 Of þe *pore* haueth thei no pite and þat is here puyre chartre.
C. 6.60 As to be preised amongus þe peple thow [y] *pore* seme:
C. 6.132 I was the Prioresse potager and oþer *pore* ladies
C. 7.78 Penaunse and *pore* men and the passiour of seyntes,
C. 7.84 And 3eueth [hem] mede & mete and *pore* men refuse,
C. 7.103 The *pore* for a f[o]l sage sittynge at thy table,
C. 7.195 He is þe presteste payere þat eny *pore* man knoweth;
C. 8.14 For profit of the *pore* and plesaunce of 3owsuluen.
C. 8.39 And thogh *pore* men profre 3ow presentes and 3yftes
C. 8.111 And ben a pilgrym at þe plouh for profit to *pore* and ryche.'
C. 8.144 Such *poore*,' quod [Peres], 'shal parte with my godes,
C. 8.147 And freres þat flateren nat and *pore* folke syke,
C. 8.204 Tho hadde [Peres] pitee vppon alle *pore* peple
C. 8.282 And 3if thow [the *pore* be thy] pouer, [Peres], y þe rede;
C. 8.315 Alle þe *pore* peple tho pesecoddes fe[tt]e;
C. 8.319 *Pore* folk for fere tho fedde honger 3erne
C. 9.34 *Pore* peple bedredene and prisones in stokkes
C. 9.46 Ac he [that] speneth his speche and speketh for þe *pore*
C. 9.72 As prisones in puttes and *pore* folk in cotes,
C. 9.179 And alle *pore* pacient apayed of goddes sonde,
C.10.16 Bothe princes paleis and *pore* menne cotes
C.11.26 Harlotes for here harlotrye aren holpe ar nedy *pore*;
C.11.46 That so parteth with þe *pore* a parsel when hym nedeth.
C.11.57 In religion and in al þe reume amongus riche and *pore*
C.11.63 Ne parteth with þe *pore* as puyr charite wolde,
C.11.65 And breketh nat here bred to þe *pore* as þe boke hoteth:
C.11.292 Then ploughmen an[d] pastours and *pore* comune peple.
C.12.26 And now y am *pore* and penyles at litel pris he sette[th] me.
C.12.100 And nameliche *pore* peple, here preeyeres may vs helpe
C.12.101 For god, as þe gospel saith, goth ay as þe *pore*
C.12.104 "Ac calleth the carefole þerto, the crokede and the *pore*;
C.12.107 Ac for þe *pore* may nat paye y wol pay mysulue;
C.12.121 And *pore* peple fayle we nat while eny peny vs lasteth
C.12.125 For his *pore* parail and pilgrimes clothes
C.12.132 In þe parail of a pilgrime and in *pore* likenesse
C.12.135 Was a puyre *pore* mayde and to a pore man ywedded.
C.12.135 Was a puyre *pore* mayde and to a pore man ywedded.
C.12.152 And wel sikorere he slepeth, þe segg þat is *pore*,
C.12.158 For loue of oure lord lo[w]eth hym to be *pore*,
C.12.165 3ef *pore* peple þe panes; þerof pors þou none
C.12.166 Ac 3ef hem forth to *pore* folk þat for my loue hit aske;
C.13.31 A[c] þe *pore* pacient purgatorye passeth
C.13.93 So þe *pore* of puyr reuthe may parforme þe lawe

527

C.13.99   So *pore* and pacient parfitest lyf is of alle.
C.13.182   Resoun re[ul]ede hem nat, noþer ryche ne *pore*.
C.14.16   That pees be and pacience and *pore* withoute defaute:
C.15.10   And peple þat was *pore* at litel pris [þei] setten
C.15.11   Ne no cors of *pore* comine in here kyrkeȝerde most lygge
C.15.32   [Pacience as a *pore* thyng cam] and preeyede mete pur charite;
C.15.35   A meles mete for a *pore* man or moneye yf they hadde.
C.15.86   Hath no pyte on vs *pore*; he parformeth euele
C.15.115   In þat ȝe parteth nat with vs *pore*, þat ȝe passeth dowel
C.15.200   The *pore* and the ryche y plese and payn fynde
C.15.276   And þat is *pore* pacient alle perelles to soffre.'
C.15.283   Then eny *pore* pacient; and þat preue y be resoun.
C.15.285   There þe *pore* dar plede and preue by puyr resoun
C.15.305   Then aren hit puyre *pore* thynges in purgatorie or in hell.
C.16.3   Hewen þat haen here huyre byfore aren eueremore *pore*
C.16.21   Ac for þe beste, as y hope, aren som *pore* and ryche.
C.16.24   Lowe and lele and louynge and of herte *pore*.
C.16.47   And þat is plesant to pruyde in *pore* and in ryche.
C.16.49   There þe *pore* is potte behynde and parauntur can more
C.16.54   There þe *pore* preseth byfore with a pak at his rugge,
C.16.62   For þe *pore* is ay prest to plese þe ryche
C.16.66   Yf wrathe wrastle with þe *pore* he hath þe worse ende
C.16.67   For yf they bothe pleyne þe *pore* is bote feble;
C.16.79   And thogh coueytyse [cacche] þe *pore* they may nat come togyderes
C.16.85   And thogh Auaryce wolde Angry [þe] *pou[r]e* he hath bote lytel myhte
C.16.90   Lecherye loueth no *pore* for he hath bote litel siluer
C.16.93   Hadde they noen haunt bote of *pore* [men; here houses stoed vntyled].
C.16.100   Forthy alle *pore* þat pacient is of puyr rihte may claymen
C.16.124   Or a[s] iustice to iuge men, me enioyneth þerto no *pore*,
C.16.126   Selde is eny *pore* ypot to p[u]nesche eny peple.
C.16.127   Ergo pouerte and *pore* men parforme þe comandement
C.16.129   Selde is *pore* rihte ryche but of rihtfole eritage.
C.16.132   And me leneth lyhtly fewe men and me wene hem *pore*:
C.16.161   Shal be *porest* of power at his partynge hennes.'
C.16.258   Parte with þe *pore* and ȝoure pruyde leue
C.16.325   There *pore* men and prisones ben and paye for here fode,
C.16.330   And when he hath visited thus fetured folk and oþer folke *pore*,
C.17.2   Or beggeth or biddeth, be he ryche or *pore*,
C.17.70   That *pore* peple by puyre riht here part myhte aske.
C.17.199   And tho was p[lente] and p[ees] amonges *pore* and ryche;
C.19.241   And for he was a nygard and a nythynge to the nedfol *pore*,
C.22.234   'And for thei aren *pore*, parauntur, for patrimonye hem faileth,

pouerer *adv cf. povre adj.* B 1; C 1 porore
B.20.50   Ne neuere noon so nedy ne *pouerer* deide.
C.22.50   Ne neuere noen so nedy ne *porore* deyede.'

pouerte *n poverte n.* A 1 pouert; B 41; C 44 pouert (1) pouerte (43)
A. 9.111   Was no pride on his apparail ne no *pouert* noþer,
B. 2.80   To be Princes in pride and *pouerte* to despise,
B. 8.121   Was no pride on his apparaill ne *pouerte* neiþer,
B.10.346   And preiseden *pouerte* with pacience; as Apostles bereþ witnesse
B.11.62   And *pouerte* pursued me and putte me lowe.
B.11.254   Ac *pouerte* god putte bifore and preised þe bettre:
B.11.257   Preise[n] *pouerte* for best lif if Pacience it folw[e],
B.11.263   So aftur *pouerte* or penaunce paciently ytake:
B.11.273   That parfit *pouerte* was no possession to haue,
B.11.318   This lokynge on lewed preestes haþ doon me lepe from *pouerte*
B.11.332   *Pouerte* and plentee, boþe pees and werre,
B.12.9   *Pouerte* or penaunce, or preyeres bidde:
B.12.11   Wiþ poustees of pestilences, wiþ *pouerte* and with angres;
B.12.61   Pacience and *pouerte* þe place [is] þer it groweþ,
B.13.158   For, by hym þat me made, myȝte neuere *pouerte*,
B.14.102   'Wheiþer paciente *pouerte*', quod Haukyn, 'be moore plesaunt to oure d[riȝte]
B.14.192   Ac þe parchemyn of þis patente of *pouerte* be moste,
B.14.215   For his *pouerte* and pacience a perpetuel blisse:
B.14.216   A[c] pride in richesse regneþ raþer þan in *pouerte*;
B.14.218   Ac in *pouerte* þer pacience is pride haþ no myȝte,
B.14.220   Ne haue power in *pouerte*, if pacience [it] folwe.
B.14.230   And if glotonie greue *pouerte* he gadereþ þe lasse
B.14.243   And *Pouerte* nys but a petit þyng, apereþ noȝt to his nauele,
B.14.246   For *pouerte* haþ but pokes to putten in hise goodes
B.14.254   And þouȝ Sleuþe suwe *pouerte*, and serue noȝt god to paie,
B.14.258   And wheiþer he be or be noȝt, he bereþ þe signe of *pouerte*
B.14.272   And put hym to be pacient and *pouerte* weddeþ,
B.14.273   The which is sib to god hymself, [so neiȝ is *pouerte*].'
B.14.274   'Haue god my trouþe', quod Haukyn '[I here yow] preise faste *pouerte*.
B.14.275   What is *Pouerte*, pacience', quod he, 'properly to mene?'
B.14.280   *Pouerte* is þe firste point þat pride moost hateþ;

B.14.284   So *pouerte* propreliche penaunce [is to þe body,
B.14.288   Selde sit *pouerte* þe soþe to declare,
B.14.292   /Ergo *pouerte* and poore men parfournen þe comaundement
B.14.305   *Pouerte* myȝte passe wiþouten peril of robbyng.
B.14.306   For þer þat *Pouerte* passeþ pees folweþ after,
B.14.317   For pacience is payn for *pouerte* hymselue,
B.14.322   That þ[u]s first wroot to wissen men what *Pouerte* was to mene.'
B.15.208   Than for penaunce and parfitnesse, þe *pouerte* þat swiche takeþ.
B.15.270   What penaunce and *pouerte* and passion þei suffrede,
B.19.67   To penaunce and to *pouerte* he moste puten hymseluen,
B.19.249   In *pouerte* and in [pacience] to preie for alle cristene.
C. 2.87   To ben pr[ince]s in pruyde and *pouert* to dispice,
C. 9.183   Or thorw fuyr or thorw floed yfalle into *pouerte*,
C. 9.235   *Pouerte* or oþer penaunc[e], as pilgrimages and trauayles.
C.10.117   Was no pruyde on his parail ne *pouerte* noythere;
C.12.14   And *pouerte* pursuede me and potte me to be lowe.
C.12.141   Ac *pouerte* god potte byfore and preuede for þe betere:
C.12.143   Preise[n] *pouerte* for beste [lif] if pacience hit folowe
C.12.149   So aftur [*pouerte* or penaunce] pacientliche ytake
C.12.177   Preueth pacient *pouerte* prince of alle vertues.
C.12.206   *Pouerte* and penaunce and persecucoun of body.
C.12.234   Ouerplente pruyde norischeth þer *pouerte* hit distrueth.
C.13.1   Ac wel worth *pouerte* for he may walke vnrobbed
C.13.3   Oure prince iesu *pouerte* chees and his apostles alle
C.13.8   For in greet *pouerte* he was put: a prince, as hit were,
C.13.21   Lo, how pacience and *pouerte* thise patriarkes releuede
C.13.27   Thogh y preeye *pouerte* thus and preue hit by ensau[m]ples
C.13.100   Vch a parfi[t] prest to *pouerte* sholde drawe
C.13.140   *Pouerte* and plente, bothe pees and werre,
C.15.157   For, by hym þat me made, myhte neuere *pouerte*,
C.15.277   'Where *pouerte* and pacience plese more god almyhty
C.16.18   That al here lyf leden in lownesse and in *pouerte*
C.16.32   Thise thre withoute doute tholieth alle *pouerte*
C.16.56   For his *pouerte* and pacience perpetuel ioye.
C.16.57   And pruyde in rychesse regneth rather then in *pouerte*;
C.16.59   Ac in *pouerte* þer pacience is pruyde hath no myhte
C.16.61   Ne haue power in *pouerte* yf pacience h[it] folewe.
C.16.71   And yf glotonye greue *pouerte* h[e] gadereth þe lasse
C.16.83   And *pouerte* is bote a pety thyng, appereth nat to his nauele,
C.16.86   For *pouerte* hath bote pokes to potten in his godes
C.16.94   And thow sleuthe sewe *pouerte* and serue nat god to paye
C.16.98   And where he be or be nat, a bereth þe signe of *pouerte*
C.16.112   And potte hym to be pacient and *pouerte* weddeth,
C.16.115   'What is *pouerte*, pacience?' quod he; 'y preye þat thow telle hit.'
C.16.120   *Pouerte* is the furste poynte þat pruyde moest hateth;
C.16.123   Selde syt *pouerte* þe soth to declare
C.16.127   Ergo *pouerte* and pore men parforme þe comandement
C.16.140   *Pouerte* myhte passe withoute perel of robbynge.
C.16.141   For þer as *pouerte* passeth pes folleweth comunely
C.16.151   For pacience is his paniter and *pouerte* payn here fyndeth
C.16.154   That puyre *pouerte* and pacience was a louh lyuynge on erthe,
C.16.157   That wroet thus to wisse men what *pouerte* was to mene.'
C.16.328   That *pouerte* and penaunce pacientlyche ytake
C.21.67   To penaunce and to *pouerte* he mot putte hymsuluen
C.21.249   In *pouerte* and in pacience to preye for alle cristene;

power *n pouere n.* A 7; B 31; C 28 pouer (1) power (27)
A. 3.155   For *pouere* men mowe haue no *power* to pleyne [þeiȝ] hem smerte,
A. 4.52   Þeiȝ pees & his *power* pleynide hem euere'.
A. 4.123   Be vnpunisshit at my *power* for peril of my soule,
A. 5.75   To apeire hym be my *power* I pursuide wel ofte,
A. 7.36   'Be my *power*, piers, I pliȝte þe my treuþe
A. 8.157   Now haþ þe pope *power* pardoun to graunte
A.10.62   Thanne haþ þe pouk *power*, sire princeps huius mundi,
B.Pr.100   I parceyued of þe *power* þat Peter hadde to kepe,
B.Pr.108   And *power* presumed in hem a pope to make
B.Pr.109   To han [þe] *power* þat Peter hadde–impugnen I nelle–
B. 2.49   And haue *power* to punysshe hem; þanne put forþ þi reson.
B. 3.168   For pouere men may haue no *power* to pleyne þouȝ [hem] smerte,
B. 3.282   For so is þis world went wiþ hem þat han *power*
B. 4.66   Theiȝ pees and his *power* pleyned h[e]m euere'.
B. 4.140   Ben vnpunysshed [at] my *power* for peril of my soule,
B. 5.95   To apeire hym bi my *power* pursued wel ofte,
B. 6.34   'By my *power*, Piers, I pliȝte þee my trouþe
B. 6.149   Ne Postles, but þei preche konne and haue *power* of þe bisshop:
B. 7.179   Now haþ þe pope *power* pardon to graunte
B.10.78   That preieres haue no *power* þ[ise] pestilence[s] to lette.
B.10.243   Fro þe dedly deeþ and [þe] deueles *power*
B.11.165   And saued þe sarsyn from sathanas *power*
B.13.105   'Do noon yuel to þyn euencristen, nouȝt by þi *power*.'
B.13.254   For siþ he haþ þe *power* þat Peter hadde he haþ þe pot wiþ þe salue:
B.14.220   Ne haue *power* in pouerte, if pacience [it] folwe.
B.15.61   Et verba vertit in opera fulliche to his *power*."

B.15.561 And þo þat han Petres *power* arn apoisoned alle."
B.15.598 And þoruȝ his pacience hir *power* to pure noȝt he brouȝte:
B.16.37 That is þe passion and þe *power* of oure prince Iesu.
B.16.54 The *power* of þise postes and hire propre myȝt[e].
B.16.266 That shal deliuere vs som day out of þe deueles *power*
B.17.176 The pawme is pureliche þe hand, haþ *power* by hymselue
B.17.178 For [þe pawme] haþ *power* to putte out þe ioyntes
B.17.190 For peyne of þe pawme *power* hem failleþ
B.19.183 And yaf Piers [pardon, and *power*] he grauntede hym,
B.19.188 Thus haþ Piers *power*, b[e] his pardon paied,
B.19.386 Grace, þoruȝ goddes word, [g]af Piers *power*,
B.20.320 Saue Piers þe Plowman þat haþ *power* ouer alle
C.Pr.128 I parsceyued of þe *power* that Peter hadde to kepe,
C.Pr.135 And *power* presumen in hemself a page
C.Pr.136 To haue þe *power* þat Peter hadde inpugne y nelle
C. 2.52 And haue *power* to p[uny]schen hem; thenne pot forth thy resoun.
C. 3.435 For so is the world went with hem þat han *power*
C. 4.70 Of pees and his *power* thow he pleyne euere.'
C. 4.137 Be vnpunisched in my *power* for perel of [my] soule
C. 6.256 For þe pope with alle his pentauncers *power* hem fayleth
C. 8.33 'By my *power*, [Peres], y plyhte the my treuthe
C. 8.282 And ȝif thow [the pore be thy] *pouer*, [Peres], y þe rede;
C. 9.17 Drede nat for no deth to distruye by here *power*
C. 9.325 ȝut hath þe pope *power* pardoun to graunte
C.11.58 That preyeres haen no *power* this pestilences to lette.
C.13.70 And haue reuthe and releue with his rychesse by his *power*
C.15.224 For sethe he hath þe *power* þat peter hadde he hath þe pott with þe salue:
C.16.61 Ne haue *power* in pouerte yf pacience h[it] folewe.
C.16.161 Shal be porest of *power* at his partynge hennes.'
C.16.223 Et verba vertit in opera emforth his *power*.'
C.17.224 And [tho] þat haen petres *power* aren apo[y]sened alle."
C.17.306 And her *power* thorw his pacience to puyr nauht brouhte.
C.18.282 That shal delyuere vs som day out of þe deueles *power*
C.19.141 The paume is puyrliche the hand and hath *power* by hymsulue
C.19.143 For þe paume hath *power* to pu[t]te out þe ioyntes
C.19.156 For peyne of þe paume *power* hem fayleth
C.21.183 And ȝaf [peres pardoun] and [*power*] he graunted [hym],
C.21.188 Thus hath Peres *power*, b[e] his pardoun payed,
C.21.386 Grace thorw godes word gaf [Peres] *power*,
C.22.320 Saue [Peres the Plouhman] þat haeth *power* ouer alle

pray(de > preien

praye n *preie n.(2) &> preien* B 1
B.18.311 For þi lesynges, Lucifer, lost is al oure *praye*.

prayed ptp *preien v.(2)* B 1; C 1 preyede
B.20.86 Hadde ypriked and *prayed* polles of peple;
B.22.86 Hadde ypriked and *preyede* polles of peple;

prayere(s > preiere; praiseth > preisen

praktisour n *practisoure n.* B 1
B.16.107 Til he was parfit *praktisour* if any peril fille.

prechares > prechours

prechen v *prechen v.* A 19 preche (7) prechen (3) precheþ (1) prechid (1)
    prechide (2) prechinge (1) prechiþ (4); B 39 preche (14) preched (8)
    prechen (9) precheþ (7) prechynge (1); C 32 preche (8) preched (1)
    prechede (7) prechen (8) precheth (5) precheþ (2) prechyng (1)
A.Pr.38 Þat poule *prechiþ* of hem I dar not proue it here:
A.Pr.56 *Prechinge* þe peple for profit of þe wombe:
A.Pr.65 Þere *prechide* a pardoner as he a prest were;
A.Pr.77 It is not be þe bisshop þat þe boy *prechiþ*,
A.Pr.93 To *preche* þe peple & pore men to fede
A. 1.137 And ek þe plante of pes; *preche* it in þin harpe
A. 3.64 For oure sauiour it seide & hymself *prechid*:
A. 3.210 Prestis þat *preche* þe peple to goode
A. 3.221 Þe prophet *prechiþ* it & putte it in þe sauter:
A. 5.11 And consience wiþ a cros com for to *preche*,
A. 5.23 How consience wiþ a cros cumside to *preche*.
A. 5.35 Þat þei *preche* þe peple proue it hemselue,
A. 8.16 And *prechen* here personis þe periles of synne,
A. 8.122 'Were þou a prest, piers,' quaþ he, 'þou miȝtest *preche* wh[an] þe liki[de];
A. 9.83 And *prechiþ* þe peple seint poulis wordis:
A.11.26 Or *prechen* of þe penaunce þat pilat[u]s wrouȝte
A.11.72 Ac austyn þe olde for alle suche *prechide*,
A.11.198 Prince ouer godis peple to *prechen* or to chaste.
A.12.22 And poul *precheþ* hit often, prestes hit redyn:
B.Pr.38 That Poul *precheþ* of hem I [dar] nat proue it here;
B.Pr.59 *Prechynge* þe peple for profit of [þe wombe];
B.Pr.68 Ther *preched* a pardoner as he a preest were;
B.Pr.80 It is noȝt by þe bisshop þat þe boy *precheþ*;

B.Pr.90 *Prechen* and praye for hem, and þe pouere fede,
B. 3.223 Preestes þat *prechen* þe peple to goode
B. 3.234 The prophete *precheþ* [it] and putte it in þe Sauter:
B. 5.11 And how Reson gan arayen hym al þe Reaume to *preche*;
B. 5.23 How pertly afore þe peple [*preche* gan Reson].
B. 5.42 'That ye *prechen* þe peple, preue it yowselue,
B. 5.145 Thise possessioners *preche* and depraue freres;
B. 5.147 That whan þei *preche* þe peple in many places aboute
B. 6.149 Ne Postles, but þei *preche* konne and haue power of þe bisshop:
B. 7.14 Legistres of boþe lawes þe lewed þerwiþ to *preche*,
B. 7.140 'Were þow a preest, [Piers]', quod he, 'þow myȝtest *preche* [whan þee liked]
B. 8.92 And *precheþ* þe peple Seint Poules wordes,
B.10.34 Or *prechen* of þe penaunce þat Pilat wroȝte
B.10.74 And *prechen* at Seint Poules, for pure enuye of clerkes,
B.10.205 Poul *prechede* þe peple, þat parfitnesse louede,
B.10.273 As persons and parissh preestes, þat *preche* sholde and teche,
B.10.389 Maistres þat of goddes mercy techen men and *prechen*,
B.10.394 Thanne wrouȝte I vnwisly, whatsoeuere ye *preche*.
B.11.107 'He seiþ sooþ', quod Scripture þo, and skipte an heiȝ and *preched*.
B.13.66 *Preched* of penaunces þat Poul þe Apostle suffrede
B.13.68 Ac o word þei ouerhuppen at ech tyme þat þei *preche*
B.13.76 They *prechen* þat penaunce is profitable to þe soule,
B.13.80 That he *precheþ* [and] preueþ noȝt [com]pacience', I tolde.
B.13.85 [And appose hym] what penaunce is, of which he *preched* raþer.'
B.13.118 And dobest doþ hymself so as he seiþ and *precheþ*:
B.15.70 Freres and fele oþere maistres þat to [þe] lewed [folk] *prechen*,
B.15.110 Than for to *prechen* and preuen it noȝt–ypocrisie it semeþ.
B.15.403 And if he among þe peple *preched*, or in places come,
B.15.444 Til Gregory garte clerkes to go here and *preche*.
B.15.493 So manye prelates to *preche* as þe Pope makeþ,
B.15.496 To be pastours and *preche* þe passion of Iesus,
B.18.138 For patriarkes and prophetes han *preched* herof ofte
B.18.296 Thise þritty wynter, as I wene, [he wente aboute] and *preched*.
B.20.275 And *preche* men of Plato, and preue it by Seneca
B.20.277 He lyeþ, as I leue, þat to þe lewed so *precheþ*,
C.Pr.39 Tha[t] Poule *preche[þ]* of hem preue hit y myhte;
C.Pr.57 *Prechyng* þe peple for profyt of þe wombe;
C.Pr.66 Ther *prechede* a Pardoner as he a prest were,
C.Pr.78 Ac it is nouȝt by þe bischop þat þe boy *precheþ*,
C. 3.278 Prestes þat *prechen* and þe peple techen
C. 5.114 Resoun reuerentliche tofore al þe reume *prechede*
C. 5.141 'That ȝe *prechen* þe peple, p[ro]ue hit ȝowsylue;
C. 9.112 Riht as Peter dede and Poul saue þat þey *preche* nat
C. 9.164 Hit nedeth nat nouthe anoon for to *preche*
C.10.89 And *precheth* to þe peple seynt paules wordes:
C.11.54 And *prech[en]* at seynt poules, [for] puyr enuye of clerkes,
C.11.205 Predestinaet thei *prechen*, prechours þat this sheweth,
C.11.215 Maistres þat [of goddis mercy techen men and *prechen*]
C.12.41 'A saith soth,' quod scripture tho, and skypte an heyh and *prechede*.
C.15.69 'Hit is nat thre daies doen this doctour þat he *prechede*
C.15.74 Ac me wondreth in my wit why þat they ne *prechen*
C.15.75 A[s] poul þe apostle *prechede* to þe peple ofte:
C.15.82 They *preche* þat penaunce is profitable to þe soule
C.15.87 That a *precheth* and preueth nat compacience,' ich tolde.
C.16.231 Freres fele tymes to þe folk þer they *prechen*
C.16.264 Then for to *prechen* and preue hit nat–ypocrisye hit semeth.
C.16.289 And fonde y neuere in faith, as freres hit *precheth*,
C.16.326 Clotheth hem and conforteth hem and of Crist *precheth* hem,
C.17.84 That fayre byfore folk *prechen* and techen
C.17.174 And in what place he *prechede* and the peple tauhte
C.17.188 So manye prelates to *preche* as þe pope maketh,
C.17.192 To be p[astor]s and *preche* the passioun of iesus
C.17.290 So is þe kynde of a curatour for criste[s] loue to *preche*
C.20.141 For patriarkes and prophetes haen *preched* herof ofte
C.20.329 This thritty wynter, as y wene, and wente aboute and *prechede*.
C.22.275 And *preche* men of plato and preuen hit by seneca
C.22.277 He lyeth, as y leue, þat to þe lewed so *precheth*,

precheours > prechours

prechyng ger *prechinge ger. &> prechen* A 2 preching (1) prechyng (1);
    B 5 prechyng (4) prechynge (1); C 2 prechyng (1) prechynge (1)
A. 4.107 Til prestis here *prechyng* preue it hemselue,
A. 6.118 Shulde I neuere ferþere a foote for no freris *preching*.'
B. 4.122 And til prechours *prechynge* be preued on hemselue,
B. 5.633 Sholde I neuere ferþere a foot for no freres *prechyng*.'
B.15.290 Poul after his *prechyng* paniers he made
B.15.406 And dide folk þanne falle on knees; for he swoor in his *prechyng*
B.15.449 Moore þoruȝ miracles þan þoruȝ muche *prechyng*;
C. 7.286 [Sh]olde y neuere forthere [a] foet for no frere *prechynge*.'
C.17.17 Paul aftur his *prechyng* paniars he made

prechynge > prechen,prechyng

prechours n *prechour n.* B 10; C 7 prechares (1) precheours (1) prechours (5)

B. 4.122 And til *prechours* prechynge be preued on hemselue;
B.12.19 And *prechours* to preuen what it is of many a peire freres.'
B.13.427 Patriarkes and prophetes, *prechours* of goddes wordes,
B.15.95 There inparfit preesthode is, *prechours* and techeris.
B.15.99 Right so persons and preestes and *prechours* of holi chirche
B.15.114 Right so [preestes, *prechours* and prelates manye],
B.15.131 The whiche arn preestes inparfite and *prechours* after siluer,
B.15.441 Preestes and *prechours* and a pope aboue,
B.15.499 For cristene and vncristene crist seide to *prechours*
B.19.231 As *prechours* and preestes and Prentices of lawe:
C. 7.87 Patriarkes and prophetes, *precheours* of goddes wordes,
C.11.205 Predestinae thei prechen, *prechours* þat this sheweth,
C.16.247 There inparfit preesthoed is, *prechares* and techares.
C.16.252 Riht so persones and prestes and *prechours* of holy churche
C.16.269 Riht so many prestes, *prechours* and prelates,
C.16.278 As inparfite prestes and *prechours* aftur suluer,
C.21.231 As *prechours* and prestes and prentises of lawe:

precious n *preciouse adj.* A 1; B 4 precious (3) preciouse (1); C 5 precious (1) preciouse (4)

A.11.12 Þanne al þe *precious* perrie þat in paradis wexiþ.
B. 1.152 And [ek] þe pl[ante] of pees, moost *precious* of vertues.
B.10.12 Than al þe *precious* perree þat in paradis wexeþ.
B.16.261 'It is a *precious* present', quod he, 'ac þe pouke it haþ attached,
B.19.96 Ac for alle þise *precious* present3 oure lord [prynce] Iesus
C. 1.148 Loue is [þe] plonte of pees, most *precious* of vertues,
C.11.10 Then al þe *preciouse* perye þat eny prince weldeth.
C.18.277 'Hit is a *preciouse* present,' quod he, 'Ac the pouke hit hath atached
C.20.409 May no pyement ne pomade ne *preciouse* drynkes
C.21.96 Ac for all this *preciouse* presentes oure lord prince iesu[s]

predestinae ptp *predestinaten v.* C 1

C.11.205 *Predestinaet* thei prechen, prechours þat this sheweth,

preey- > preie-

preesseþ v *pressen v.* B 2 preesseþ (1) pressed (1); C 2 presed (1) preseth (1)

B.14.213 Ther þe poore *preesseþ* bifore wiþ a pak at his rugge:
B.20.127 And [pressed on] þe [pope] and prelates þei maden
C.16.54 There þe pore *preseth* byfore with a pak at his rugge,
C.22.127 And *presed* on þe pope and prelates thei made

preest n *prest n.(3)* A 19 prest (11) prestes (1) prestis (7); B 54 preest (25) preestes (29); C 56 preest (2) prest (21) prestes (23) prestis (10)

A.Pr.65 Þere prechide a pardoner as he a *prest* were;
A.Pr.78 Ac þe parissh *prest* & þe pardoner parte þe siluer
A.Pr.80 Personis & parissh *prestis* pleynide hem to here bisshop
A. 3.139 Prouendrours, [persones], & [*prestis*] she mayntyniþ
A. 3.210 *Prestis* þat preche þe peple to goode
A. 3.231 *Prestis* & personis þat plesing desiriþ,
A. 4.107 Til *prestis* here prechyng preue it hemselue,
A. 4.116 Oþer prouisour, or *prest* þat be pope auaunciþ.
A. 5.34 He pre[yide] prelatis & *prestis* togidere,
A. 5.86 To preye for þe peple as þe *prest* techiþ,
A. 6.85 I perfourmde þe penaunce þe *prest* me enioynide,
A. 8.89 'Piers,' quaþ a *prest* [þo], 'þi pardon muste I rede,
A. 8.97 'Petir,' quaþ þe *prest* þo, 'I can no pardoun fynde
A. 8.118 'What!' quaþ þe *prest* to perkyn, 'peter, as me þinkeþ
A. 8.122 'Were þou a *prest*, piers,' quaþ he, 'þou mi3test preche wh[an] þe liki[de];
A. 8.126 Þe *prest* & perkyn aposid eiþer oþer,
A. 8.152 And how þe *prest* inpungid it al be [pu]re resoun,
A.11.298 'Wh[anne] 3e ben aposid of princes or of *prestis* of þe lawe
A.12.22 And poul precheþ hit often, *prestes* hir redyn:
B.Pr.68 Ther preched a pardoner as he a *preest* were;
B.Pr.81 [Ac] þe parisshe *preest* and þe pardoner parten þe siluer
B.Pr.83 Persons and parisshe *preestes* pleyned hem to þe Bisshop
B. 3.150 Prouendre[s], persones and *preestes* [she] maynteneþ
B. 3.223 *Preestes* þat prechen þe peple to goode
B. 3.252 *Preestes* and persons þat plesynge desireþ,
B. 3.311 *Preestes* and persons wiþ Placebo to hunte
B. 4.133 Prouysour or persoun or penaunt for hise synnes.
B. 5.41 And siþen he [preide] prelates and *preestes* togideres,
B. 5.106 [To] preye for þe peple as þe *preest* techeþ,
B. 5.160 And dame Pernele a *preestes* fyle; Prioresse worþ she neuere
B. 5.167 That no Prioresse were *preest*, for þat he [purueiede];
B. 5.394 I kan no3t parfitly my Paternoster as þe *preest* it syngeþ,
B. 5.398 I parfournede neuere penaunce as þe *preest* me hi3te,
B. 5.415 I haue be *preest* and person passynge þritty wynter,
B. 5.598 I parfourned þe penaunce þe *preest* me enioyned
B. 7.107 'Piers', quod a *preest* þoo, 'þi pardon moste I rede,
B. 7.115 'Peter!' quod þe *preest* þoo, 'I kan no pardon fynde

B. 7.136 'What!' quod þe *preest* to Perkyn, 'Peter! as me þynkeþ
B. 7.140 'Were þow a *preest*, [Piers]', quod he, 'þow my3test preche [whan þee liked]
B. 7.144 The *preest* and Perkyn [a]pposeden eiþer ooþer,
B. 7.153 And how þe *preest* inpugned it wiþ two propre wordes.
B. 7.174 And how þe *preest* preued no pardon to dowel
B.10.273 As persons and parissh *preestes*, þat preche sholde and teche,
B.10.284 In alle maner men þoru3 mansede *preestes*.
B.10.286 Bittre abou3te þe giltes of two badde *preestes*,
B.11.98 Excepte persons and *preestes* and prelates of holy chirche.
B.11.283 If *preestes* weren [wise] þei wolde no siluer take
B.11.287 Spera in deo spekeþ of *preestes* þat haue no spendyng siluer,
B.11.298 The same I segge for soþe by alle swiche *preestes*.
B.11.317 Non excusat episcopos nec ydiotes *preestes*'.
B.11.318 This lokynge on lewed *preestes* haþ doon me lepe from pouerte
B.12.115 But he were *preest* or preestes sone, Patriark or prophete.
B.12.115 But he were preest or *preestes* sone, Patriark or prophete.
B.12.183 And þat is after person or parissh *preest*, [and] parauenture vnkonnynge
B.13.11 And how þis Coueitise ouercom clerkes and *preestes*;
B.13.236 Whan þe *preest* preieþ þe peple hir Paternoster to bidde
B.13.411 [Ac] penaunce þat þe *preest* enioyneþ parfourneþ yuele;
B.14.9 And [siþþe] shryuen of þe *preest*, þat [for my synnes gaf me]
B.14.92 Per confessionem to a *preest* peccata occiduntur–
B.15.99 Right so persons and *preestes* and prechours of holi chirche
B.15.114 Right so [*preestes*, prechours and prelates manye],
B.15.117 Iohannes Crisostomus of clerkes [carpeþ] and *preestes*:
B.15.121 But if many *preest* [forbeere] hir baselardes and hir broches
B.15.128 Allas, ye lewed men, muche lese ye on *preestes*!
B.15.131 The whiche arn *preestes* inparfite and prechours after siluer,
B.15.441 *Preestes* and prechours and a pope aboue,
B.15.486 Ac who beþ þat excuseþ hem þat [arn] persons and *preestes*,
B.19.231 As prechours and *preestes* and Prentices of lawe:
B.20.218 Proude *preestes* coome with hym; [passynge an hundred]
B.20.221 'By [þe] Marie!' quod a mansed *preest*, [was] of þe March of [Irlonde]
B.20.229 Thoru3 inparfite *preestes* and prelates of holy chirche.'
B.20.281 For persons and parissh *preestes* þat sholde þe peple shryue
B.20.319 Than person or parisshe *preest*, penitauncer or bisshop,
C.Pr.66 Ther prechede a Pardoner as he a *prest* were,
C.Pr.79 For þe parsche *prest* and þe Pardoner parten þe seluer
C.Pr.81 Persones and parsche *prestis* pleyned [hem] to þe bischop
C.Pr.106 Ful on hem þat fre were thorwe two fals *prestis*!
C.Pr.116 And for þei were *prestis* and men of holy chirche
C.Pr.118 Forthy y sey 3[ow] *prestes* and men of holy churche
C.Pr.121 God shal take vengeaunce on alle suche *prestis*
C. 2.185 That *prestis* and prouisores sholden prelates serue
C. 3.188 He prouendreth persones and *prestes* he maynteneth
C. 3.278 *Prestes* þat prechen and þe peple techen
C. 3.311 The mede þat many *prest*[es] taken for masses þat thei syngen,
C. 3.464 *Prestes* and persones placebo and dirige,
C. 4.130 Prouisour or *preest* oþer penaunt for his synnes.
C. 5.140 And sethe a preide prelates and *prestes* togyderes,
C. 6.135 And dame purnele a *prestis* fyle; Prioresse worth he neuere
C. 6.298 3e! þe *prest* þat thy tythe t[a]k[eth], trowe y non other,
C. 6.304 And [what] penaunce the *prest* shal haue þat p[r]oud is of his tithes.
C. 7.10 Y can nat parfitly my paternoster as þe *prest* hit syngeth;
C. 7.14 Y parfourmede neuere penaunc[e] þat þe *prest* me hihte
C. 7.30 I haue be *prest* and persoun passynge thritty wyntur
C. 7.71 The penauns[e] þat þe *prest* enioyneth parformeth euele,
C. 7.247 And parformed þe penaunce þat þe *prest* me hihte."
C. 8.190 *Prestes* and oþer peple towarde [Peres] they drowe
C. 9.281 '[Peres],' quod a *prest* tho, 'thy pardon moste y rede,
C. 9.289 'Peter!' quod þe *prest* tho, 'y kan no pardoun fynde
C. 9.293 The *prest* thus and perkyn of þe pardon iangelede
C. 9.302 And how þe *prest* inpugnede hit thorw two propre wordes.
C. 9.319 And how þe *prest* preuede no pardon to do wel
C.10.197 Prelates and *prestes* and princes of holy churche
C.12.29 To segge as they seen, saue only *prestis*:
C.13.82 And other pryue penaunces þe which þe *prest* woet wel
C.13.100 Vch a parfi[t] *prest* to pouerte sholde drawe
C.13.101 For spera in deo speketh of *prestis* þat han no spendynge suluer
C.13.112 The same y segge for sothe by suche þat beth *prestes*
C.14.60 Bote hit were *pres*[t] or prestis sone, patriarke or p[ro]phete.
C.14.60 Bote hit were pres[t] or *prestis* sone, patriarke or p[ro]phete.
C.14.123 And þat is aftur person other parsche *preest*, and parauntur bothe lewede
C.15.210 Nere hit þat þe parsche [*prest*] preyeth for me on sonendayes,
C.15.212 Ac þe *prest* and [þe] peple preyeth for Peres þe Plouheman
C.16.252 Riht so persones and *prestes* and prechours of holy churche
C.16.269 Riht so many *prestes*, prechours and prelates,
C.16.272 Iohannes Crisostomus carpeth thus of clerkes [and *prestes*]:

C.16.278   As inparfite *prestes* and prechours aftur suluer,
C.17.61   Or ar *prestes* or pardoners or eny peple elles.
C.17.72   *Prestes* on aparayl and on purnele now spene.
C.17.117   Lord lete þat this *prestes* lelly seien here masse,
C.17.122   Ac ʒif *prestes* doen here deuer wel we shal do þe bettre
C.17.238   The pope with alle *prestes* pax vobis sholde make
C.17.244   Prelates and *prestis* preeye and biseche
C.17.317   Prelates and *prestes* sholde proue yf they myhte
C.21.231   As prechours and *prestes* and prentises of lawe:
C.22.218   Proute *prestes* cam with hym; passyng an hundred
C.22.221   'By þe Marie!' quod a mansed *prest*, was of þe march of Ireland,
C.22.229   Thorw inparfit *prestes* and prelates of holy chirche.'
C.22.281   For persones and parsche *prestes* þat sholde þe peple shryue
C.22.319   Then person oþer parsche *prest*, penytauncer or bischope

preesthod n *presthede* n. B 3 preesthod (1) preesthode (2); C 5 preesthoed (2) prestehode (1) presthode (1) presthoed (1)

B.15.95   There inparfit *preesthode* is, prechours and techeris.
B.15.568   If *preesthode* were parfit þe peple sholde amende
B.19.332   And made *preesthod* hayward þe while hymself wente
C.16.245   Thorw parfit *preesthoed* and prelates of holy churche,
C.16.247   There inparfit *preesthoed* is, prechares and techares.
C.17.233   For were *presthode* more parfyte, that is, þe pope formost
C.17.250   Yf *prestehode* were parfyt and preyede thus the peple sholde amende
C.21.332   And made *presthoed* hayward the while hymsulue wente

preyede > *prayed,preien*

preien v *preien* v.(1) A 16 preiʒe (1) preiʒede (4) preye (6) preyede (4) preyide (1); B 38 praye (5) preide (12) preyde (3) preie (8) preye (5) preyed (2) preien (1) preieþ (2); C 44 pray (1) prayde (1) praye (6) preeye (2) preeyede (1) preide (1) preie (1) preyde (2) preye (14) preyed (1) preyede (8) preyen (2) preyeth (4)

A.1.78   *Preiʒede* hire pitously [to] preiʒe for my sennes,
A.1.78   And preiʒede hire pitously [to] *preiʒe* for my sennes,
A.4.85   Pees þanne pitousliche *preyede* to þe king
A.5.12   And *preyede* þe peple haue pite on hemselue,
A.5.26   And *preyede* pernel hire purfil to leue
A.5.34   He *pre[yide]* prelatis & prestis togidere,
A.5.86   To *preye* for þe peple as þe prest techiþ,
A.7.38   'ʒa, & ʒet a poynt,' quaþ perkyn, 'I *preye* þe more:
A.7.117   Ac we *preye* for ʒow, peris, & for ʒoure plouʒ boþe,
A.7.164   N[e] hadde peris [wiþ] a pese lof *preyede* hym beleue,
A.7.182   And *preiʒede* pur charite wiþ peris for to dwelle,
A.7.186   Þanne hadde piers pite & *preiʒede* hungir to wende
A.7.188   'Ac ʒet I *preye* þe,' quaþ peris, 'er þou passe ferþere:
A.7.237   'ʒet I *preye* þe,' quaþ peris, 'pur charite, ʒif þou kenne
A.9.11   And *preiʒede* hem, pur charite, er þei passide ferþere,
A.11.78   And *preye* hym of pardoun & penaunce [in] þi lyue,
B.Pr.90   Prechen and *praye* for hem, and þe pouere fede,
B.1.80   *Preide* hire pitously [to] preye for my synnes,
B.1.80   Preide hire pitously [to] *preye* for my synnes;
B.2.71   And *preide* Cyuylle to see and Symonye to rede it.
B.4.98   [Pees þanne pitously] *preyde* to þe kynge
B.5.26   [And] *preide* Pernele hir purfil to le[u]e
B.5.41   And siþen he [*preide*] prelates and preestes togideres,
B.5.50   And siþen he *preide* þe pope haue pite on holy chirche,
B.5.106   [To] *preye* for þe peple as þe preest techeþ,
B.6.37   'Ye, and ʒet a point,' quod Piers, 'I *preye* [þee] of moore:
B.6.125   Ac we *preie* for yow, Piers, and for youre plowʒ boþe,
B.6.179   Ne hadde Piers wiþ a pese loof *preyed* [hym bileue]
B.6.196   And what Piers *preide* hem to do as prest as a Sperhauk.
B.6.199   Thanne hadde Piers pite and *preide* hunger to wende
B.6.202   Ac I *preie* þee, er þow passe,' quod Piers to hunger,
B.6.253   'Yet I *preie* [þee]', quod Piers, '[p]ur charite, and [þow] konne
B.8.11   And *preide* hem, p[u]r charite, er þei passed ferþer
B.10.125   And *preie* hym of pardon and penaunce in þi lyue,
B.11.58   And *preien* for þee pol by pol if þow be peccuniosus.'
B.11.247   And as pouere pilgrymes *preyed* mennes goodes.
B.13.30   And *preyde* mete 'p[u]r charite, for a pouere heremyte'.
B.13.113   And preynte vpon pacience to *preie* me be stille,
B.13.222   Pacience apposed hym and *preyde* he sholde telle
B.13.236   Whan þe preest *preieþ* þe peple hir Paternoster to bidde
B.15.504   For alle paynymes *preieþ* and parfitly bileueþ
B.15.563   That sholden *preie* for þe pees, possession hem letteþ;
B.16.24   'Piers', quod I, 'I *preie* þee, whi stonde þise piles here?'
B.16.73   I *preide* Piers to pulle adoun an Appul and he wolde,
B.18.174   And *preide* pees to telle hire to what place she wolde,
B.19.154   The Iewes *preide* hem pees, and [preide] þe knyghtes
B.19.154   The Iewes preide hem pees, and [*preide*] þe knyghtes
B.19.249   In pouerte and in [pacience] to *preie* for alle cristene.
B.19.357   *Praye* we þat a pees weere in Piers berne þe Plowman.
B.20.245   To vnitee and holy chirche; ac o þyng I yow *preye*:

B.20.292   A parcel to *preye* for hem and [pleye] wiþ þe remenaunt,
B.20.338   'I *praye* þee', quod Pees þo, 'er þow passe ferþer,
B.20.339   What hattestow, I *praye* þee? hele noʒt þi name.'
B.20.364   Of 'a pryuee paiement and I shal *praye* for yow
C.1.77   And *preyede* here pitously to preye for me to amende
C.1.77   And preyede here pitously to *preye* for me to amende
C.2.73   And *preyeth* syuile to se and s[y]monye to rede hit.
C.3.465   Here sauter and here seuene p[s]almes for alle synful *preyen*;
C.4.94   Pitousliche pees tho *preyede* the kyng
C.5.82   Forthy rebuke me ryhte nauhte, resoun, y ʒow *praye*,
C.5.128   He *p[ra]yde* p[ur]nele here purfyel to leue
C.5.140   And sethe a *preide* prelates and prestes togyderes,
C.5.191   And sethe a *preyede* þe pope haue pite on holy chirche
C.7.297   Forthy y *pray* ʒow, [Peres], paraunter ʒif ʒe m[e]ten
C.7.303   Forthy, [Peres] þe [plouhman], y *preye* the telle hit treuthe
C.8.7   'Y *preye* ʒow for ʒoure profit,' quod Peres to þe ladyes,
C.8.35   '[Ye], and ʒut a poynt,' quod [Peres], 'y *praye* ʒow of more:
C.8.131   'A[c] we *praye* for ʒow, [peres] and for ʒoure plouh bothe
C.8.169   'Y *preye* the,' quod [Perus] tho, 'pur charite, sire hunger,
C.8.176   Ne hadde [Peres] with a pese loof *preyede* hym b[ile]ue.
C.8.208   Ac y *preye* the,' quod [Peres], 'hunger, ar thow wende,
C.8.265   Ac ʒut y *praye* ʒow,' quod [Peres], 'pur charite, syre hungur,
C.9.280   For shal no pardon *preye* for ʒow there ne no princes lettres.
C.10.11   And *preyde* hem, pur charite, ar they passede forthere
C.12.10   And *preeye* for the pol by pol yf thow be peccuniosus.'
C.15.32   [Pacience as a pore thyng cam] and *preeyede* mete pur charite;
C.15.120   And preynte vppon pacience to *preie* me be stille,
C.15.191   Pacience apposede hym and *preyede* a sholde telle
C.15.210   Nere hit þat þe parsche [prest] *preyeth* for me on sonendayes,
C.15.212   Ac þe prest and [þe] peple *preyeth* for Peres þe Plouheman
C.15.216   Y fynde payn for þe po[p]le and *pre[y]en* hym ych wolde
C.15.232   'Pees!' quod pacience, 'y *preye* ʒow, sire actyf,
C.16.115   'What is pouerte, pacience?' quod he; 'y *preye* þat thow telle hit.'
C.16.163   And *preyde* pacience þat y apose hym moste.
C.17.226   That sholde *preye* for þe pees possession hem letteth;
C.17.244   Prelates and prestis *preeye* and biseche
C.17.250   Yf prestehode were parfyt and *preyede* thus the peple sholde amende
C.17.255   For alle paynyme *preyeth* and parfitliche bileueth
C.20.177   And *preyede* pees to tellen [here] to what place she [w]olde
C.21.154   The iewes *preyed* hem pees and preyede th[e] knyhtes
C.21.154   The iewes preyed hem pees and *preyede* th[e] knyhtes
C.21.249   In pouerte and in pacience to *preye* for alle cristene;
C.21.357   *Preye* we þat a pees were in [Peres] berne [þe Plouhman]
C.22.245   To vnite and holi chirche; ac o thyng y ʒow *praye*:
C.22.292   A parcel to *preye* for hem and [pleye] with þe remenaunt
C.22.338   'Y *preye* the,' quod Pees tho, 'ar thow passe forþere,
C.22.339   What hattest thow? y *praye* the, hele nat thy name.'
C.22.364   Of 'a pryue payement and y shal *preye* for ʒow

preiere n *preiere* n.(2) A 6 preyeres (1) preyour (2) preyours (3); B 20 preiere (7) preyere (1) preieres (11) preyeres (1); C 20 prayere (2) prayeres (1) preeyere (1) preeyeres (2) preeyre (1) preyer (1) preyere (3) preyeres (7) preiers (1)

A.Pr.25   In *preyours* & penaunce putten hem manye,
A.2.168   Er he be put on þe pillorie, for any *preyour*, I hote.'
A.8.91   And peris at his *preyour* þe pardoun vnfoldiþ,
A.8.106   Of *preyours* & of penaunce my plouʒ shal ben hereaftir,
A.8.161   Þat pardoun, & penaunce, & *preyours* do salue
A.12.98   And be prest to *preyeres* and profitable werkes.'
B.Pr.25   In *preieres* and penaunc[e] putten hem manye,
B.2.207   Er he be put on þe Pillory for any *preyere* I hote.'_
B.5.593   Ech piler is of penaunce, of *preieres*-to-Seyntes;
B.7.109   And Piers at his *preiere* þe pardon vnfoldeþ,
B.7.124   Of *preieres* and of penaunce my plouʒ shal ben herafter,
B.7.183   That pardon and penaunce and *preieres* doon saue
B.10.78   That *preieres* haue no power þ[ise] pestilence[s] to lette.
B.10.295   And be prester at youre *preiere* þan for a pound of nobles.
B.11.156   Nouʒt þoruʒ *preiere* of a pope but for his pure truþe
B.11.184   And [souereynly] pouere peple; hir *preieres* maye vs helpe.
B.12.9   Pouerte or penaunce, or *preyeres* bidde:
B.13.136   'A[t] youre *preiere*', quod Pacience þo, 'so no man displese hym:
B.15.148   In *preieres* and in penaunces, and in parfit charite.'
B.15.346   And many a prison fram purgatorie þoruʒ hise *preieres* delivereþ.
B.15.427   Hir *preieres* and hir penaunces to pees sholde brynge
B.16.38   Thoruʒ *preieres* and penaunces and goddes passion in mynde
B.16.153   Of *preieres* and of parfitnesse þis place þat we callen:
B.17.298   Ne haue pite for any *preiere* þer þat he pleyneþ.'
B.18.200   That hir peyne be perpetuel and no *preiere* hem helpe.
B.19.307   For present or for *preiere* or any Prynces lettres.
C.Pr.27   In *preiere* and penaunc[e] potten hem mony,
C.2.70   Thei assentede hit were so at sylueres *prayere*.
C.2.219   Ar he be put on þe pylorye for eny *preyere* ich hote.'
C.3.275   Bothe Beg[g]eres and bedemen crauen mede for here *preyeres*;

C. 5.84   *Preeyeres* of a parfit man and penaunce d[iscret]e
C. 7.210   Thenne eny dedly synne do for drede or for *preeyere*.
C. 7.231   In-none-manere-elles-nat-for-no-mannes-*preeyre*.
C. 7.241   Vche piler is of penaunc[e] and *preyeres* to seyntes;
C. 8.136   '3oure *prayeres*,' quod [Peres], 'and 3e p[ar]fyt weren,
C. 9.175   Þai haue no part of pardoun ne of *preyeres* ne of penaunc[e].
C. 9.283   And [Peres] at his *preeyre* the pardon vnfoldeth
C. 9.329   That pardoun and penaunc[e] and *preyere[s]* don saue
C.11.58   That *preyeres* haen no power this pestilences to lette.
C.12.100   And nameliche pore peple, here *preeyeres* may vs helpe
C.15.228   Ne mannes *prayere* maky pees amonges cristene peple
C.16.38   Oure *preyeres* and oure penanc[e] And pilgrimag[e] to Rome.
C.17.87   May no *preyere* pees make in no place hit semeth.
C.17.236   His *preyeres* with his pacience to pees sholde brynge
C.20.205   That her peyne [be] perpetuel [and] no *preyer* hem helpe.
C.21.307   For presente or for *preyere* or eny prinses lettres.

preynte v *prinken v.* B 3; C 2 preynte (1) printe (1)
B.13.86   Pacience parceyued what I þou3te and [*preynte*] on me to be stille
B.13.113   And *preynte* vpon pacience to preie me be stille,
B.18.21   'Is Piers in þis place?' quod I, and he *preynte* on me.
C.15.120   And *preynte* vppon pacience to preie me be stille
C.20.19   'Is Peres in this place?' quod y, and he *printe* on me.

preyour(s > preiere

preisen v *preisen v.* A 5 preise (2) preisid (1) preisiden (1) preisiþ (1); B 18 preise (6) preised (3) preisede (1) preiseden (2) preisen (2) preiseþ (4); C 17 praiseth (1) preyse (5) preised (1) preysed (2) preisede (1) preysede (1) preisen (1) preiseth (2) preyseth (1) ypresed (2)
A. 3.123   Sisours & sompnours, suche men hire *preisiþ*;
A. 5.172   Þere were chapmen chosen þat chaffare to *preise*:
A. 5.175   And *preisiden* þe peneworthis [aparte] be hemseluen.
A. 6.97   And pokiþ [forþ] pride to *preise* þiselue.
A. 7.100   Þerewiþ was perkyn payed, and *preisid* hem 3erne.
B. 3.134   Sisours and Somonours, swiche men hire *preiseþ*;
B. 5.323   Ther were chapmen ychose þis chaffare to *preise*
B. 5.326   And *preised* þ[e] penyworþes apart by hemselue.
B. 5.611   And pokeþ forþ pride to *preise* þiseluen;
B. 6.108   Therwiþ was Perkyn apayed and *preised* hem [yerne].
B. 7.39   And *preiseden* Piers þe Plowman þat purchaced þis bulle.
B.10.346   And *preiseden* pouerte with pacience; þe Apostles bereþ witnesse
B.11.254   Ac pouerte god putte bifore and *preised* þe bettre:
B.11.257   *Preise[n]* pouerte for best lif if Pacience it folw[e],
B.11.319   The which I *preise*, þer pacience is, moore parfit þan richesse.
B.11.388   And er þow lakke my lif loke [þyn] be to *preise*.
B.13.312   Which my3te plese þe peple and *preisen* hymselue:
B.14.48   [Th]at pacience so *preisede*, [and of his poke hente]
B.14.274   'Haue god my trouþe', quod Haukyn '[I here yow] *preise* faste pouerte.
B.15.156   Ac charite þat Poul *preiseþ* best, and moost plesaunt to oure [Saueour]–
B.15.252   Neiþer he blameþ ne banneþ, bosteþ ne *preiseþ*,
B.16.219   Ne matrimoyne withouten Mul[eri]e is no3t muche to *preise*:
B.20.149   And prike[d] forþ wiþ pride; *preiseþ* he no vertue,
C. 3.172   Sysores and somnours, suche men he[re] *preiseth*;
C. 5.31   The whiche is lollarne lyf þat lytel is *preysed*
C. 6.45   And likynge of such a lyf þat no lawe *preiseth*,
C. 6.60   As to be *preised* amongus þe peple thow [y] pore seme:
C. 6.380   There were chapmen ychose this chaffare to *preyse*;
C. 6.384   And *preisede* th[e] penworthis apart by hemsulue
C. 7.263   And poketh forth pruyde to *preyse* thysuluen
C. 9.42   And *prey[se]de* [Peres] the [plouhman] þat purchased þis bull[e].
C.10.307   The more he is worthy and worth, of wyse and goed *ypresed*.'
C.12.143   *Preise[n]* pouerte for beste [lif] if pacience hit folowe
C.12.196   And for here pacience is *ypresed* as for puyr martir
C.13.27   Thogh y *preyse* pouerte thus and preue hit by ensau[m]ples
C.13.206   And ar thow lacke eny lyf loke ho is to *preyse*.
C.14.183   Thus þe poete *praiseth* þe pecok for his fetheres
C.17.164   Ne kynde san3 cortesie in no contreye is *preysed*.
C.18.220   Matrimonye withoute moylere is nauht moche to *preyse*
C.22.149   And prike[d] forth with pruyde; *preyseth* he no vertue

prei3e(de preyide > preien

prelat n *prelate n.* A 3 prelatis; B 13 prelat (1) prelates (12); C 16 prelates
A. 3.202   Þe pope wiþ his *prelatis* presentis vndirfongiþ,
A. 5.34   He pre[yide] *prelatis* & prestis togidere,
A. 8.47   Of princes & *prelatis* here pencioun shulde arise,
B. 3.215   The Pope [wiþ hise] *prelates* present3 vnderfonge[þ],
B. 5.41   And siþen he [preide] *prelates* and preestes togideres,
B. 7.44   Princes and *prelates* sholde paie for hire trauaile:
B. 9.83   Ne faille payn ne potage and *prelates* dide as þei sholden.
B.11.98   Excepte persons and preestes and *prelates* of holy chirche.

B.15.114   Right so [preestes, prechours and *prelates* manye],
B.15.491   What pope or *prelat* now parfourneþ þat crist highte,
B.15.493   So manye *prelates* to preche as þe Pope makeþ,
B.15.509   And a peril to þe pope and *prelates* þat he makeþ
B.15.562   A medicyne moot þerto þat may amende *prelates*.
B.15.609   *Prelates* of cristene prouinces sholde preue if þei my3te
B.20.127   And [pressed on] þe [pope] and *prelates* þei maden
B.20.229   Thoru3 inparfite preestes and *prelates* of holy churche.'
C.Pr.101   A[c] for it profiteþ 3ow into pursward 3e *prelates* soffren
C. 2.185   That prestis and prouisores sholden *prelates* serue
C. 3.271   The pope and alle *prelates* presentes vnderfongen
C. 5.140   And sethe a preide *prelates* and prestes togyderes,
C. 6.119   And preuen inparfit *prelates* of holy churche;
C. 6.120   And *prelates* pleyneth on hem for they here parschiens shryuen
C.10.197   *Prelates* and prestes and princes of holy churche
C.16.245   Thorw parfit preesthood and *prelates* of holy churche.
C.16.269   Riht so many prestes, prechours and *prelates*,
C.17.188   So manye *prelates* to preche as þe pope maketh,
C.17.225   A medecyne moste þerto þat m[ay] amende *prelates*.
C.17.244   *Prelates* and prestis preeye and biseche
C.17.260   And a perel for *prelates* þat þe pope maketh
C.17.317   *Prelates* and prestes sholde proue yf they myhte
C.22.127   And presed on þe pope and *prelates* thei made
C.22.229   Thorw inparfit prestes and *prelates* of holy churche.'

prentice n *prentis n.* A 3 prentice (1) prentis (2); B 5 prentice (2) Prentices (2) Prentis (1); C 6 prenties (1) prentis (1) prentises (2) prentys (2)
A. 2.176   Aparailide hym as a *prentice* þe peple to serue.
A. 3.212   Alle kyn crafty men craue mede for here *prentis*;
A. 5.116   And was his *prentis* ypli3t his profit to loke.
B. 2.217   Apparailed hym as [a p]*rentice* þe peple to serue.
B. 3.225   Alle kynne craft[y] men crauen Mede for hir *Prentices*;
B. 5.200   And was his *prentice* ypli3t his profit to [loke].
B.13.392   Or into Prucelond my *Prentis* my profit to waiten,
B.19.231   As prechours and preestes and *Prentices* of lawe:
C. 2.227   [A]paraylede hym [as a] *prentys* the peple to serue.
C. 3.280   Alle kyn crafty men crauen mede for here *prentises*;
C. 6.208   And was his *prentis* yplyht his profit to wayte.
C. 6.279   Or in[to] pruyslond my *prenties* my profit to awayte,
C.15.194   Peres *prentys* þe plouhman, alle peple to conforte.'
C.21.231   As prechours and prestes and *prentises* of lawe:

prentishode n *prentished n.* B 1; C 1 prentished
B. 5.253   That payed neuere for his *prentishode* no3t a peire gloues.'
C. 6.251   Payed neuere for his *prentished* nat a payre gloues.

presaunt(is > present

prescit adj *prescite adj.* C 1
C.11.206   Or p[resci]t inparfit, pult out of grace,

presed > preeseþ

presence n *presence n.* B 1; C 1
B.Pr.173   And peeren in his *presence* þe while hym pleye likeþ,
C.Pr.190   And apere in his *presence* þe while hym pleye lyketh

present n *presente n.(2)* A 6 presaunt (1) presauntis (2) present (1) presentis (2); B 12 present (5) presentes (2) present3 (5); C 11 present (4) presente (1) presentes (6)
A. 3.78   Or *presauntis* wiþoute panis as pecis of siluer,
A. 3.151   Wiþoute *presentis* or panis he plesiþ [wel] fewe.
A. 3.202   Þe pope wiþ his prelatis *presentis* vndirfongiþ,
A. 4.82   And profride pees a *presaunt* al of purid gold;
A. 7.40   And þei pore men profre þe *presauntis* or 3eftis
A. 7.279   And profride peris [þis] *present* to plese þerewiþ hungir.
B. 3.89   Or *present3* wiþouten pens as pieces of siluer,
B. 3.162   Wiþouten *present3* or pens [he] pleseþ wel fewe.
B. 3.215   The Pope [wiþ hise] prelates *present3* vnderfonge[þ],
B. 4.95   And profrede Pees a *present* al of pure[d] golde.
B. 6.41   And þou3 pouere men profre [þee] *presentes* and 3iftes
B. 6.295   And profrede Piers þis *present* to plese wiþ hunger.
B.12.153   Clerkes knewen it wel and comen wiþ hir *present3*
B.13.376   Wiþ *presentes* pryuely, or paide som certeyn;
B.16.260   'This is a *present* of muche pris; what prynce shal it haue?'
B.16.261   'It is a precious *present*', quod he, 'ac þe pouke it haþ attached,
B.19.96   Ac for alle þise preciouse *present3* oure lord [prynce] Iesus
B.19.307   For *present* or for preiere or any Prynces lettres.
C. 3.117   Or *presentes* without pans and oþer priue 3eftes.
C. 3.200   Withoute *presentes* oþer pans he pleseth [wel] fewe.
C. 3.271   The pope and alle prelates *presentes* vnderfongen
C. 4.91   And profrede pees a *present* al of puyre golde.
C. 8.39   And thogh pore men profre 3ow *presentes* and 3yftes
C. 8.317   And profrede [Peres] this *present* to plese with hongur.
C.14.97   Clerkes kn[e]we [þe] comet and comen with here *presentes*

C.18.276 'This is a *present* of moche pris; what prince shal hit haue?'
C.18.277 'Hit is a preciouse *present*,' quod he, 'Ac the pouke hit hath atached
C.21.96 Ac for all this precioure *presentes* oure lord prince iesu[s]
C.21.307 For *presente* or for preyere or eny prinses lettres.

present adj *presente adj.* A 1
A. 2.59 To be *present* in pride for pouere [or for] riche,

presented v *presenten v.* B 1; C 1
B.19.92 And *presented* hym wiþ pitee apperynge by Mirre;
C.21.92 And *presented* hym with pyte apperynge bi Mirre

preseth > preeseþ; presoun > prison; pressed > preesseþ

pressour n *pressour n.* A 1; B 1; C 1
A. 5.127 Putte hem in a *pressour*, & pynnede hem þereinne
B. 5.211 Putte hem in a *press[our]* and pyn[ned] hem þerInne
C. 6.219 Potte hem in [a] *pressou[r]* and pynne[d] hem þerynne

prest adj *prest adj.* A 2 prest (1) presteste (1); B 5 prest (3) prester (1)
   presteste (1); C 2 prest (1) presteste (1)
A. 6.38 He is þe *presteste* payere þat pore men knowen;
A.12.98 And be *prest* to preyeres and profitable werkes.'
B. 5.551 He is þe *presteste* paiere þat pouere men knoweþ;
B. 6.196 And what Piers preide hem to do as *prest* as a Sperhauk.
B.10.256 And be *prest* at youre preiere þan for a pound of nobles,
B.13.250 And þanne wolde I be *prest* to þe peple paast for to make,
B.14.221 For þe poore is ay *prest* to plese þe riche
C. 7.195 He is þe *presteste* payere þat eny pore man knoweth;
C.16.62 For þe pore is ay *prest* to plese þe ryche

prest adv *prest adv.* C 1
C.20.272 'Princ[i]pes of this place, *prest* vndo this gates

prest &> preest; prestehode > preesthode; prestes -is > preest; presthode - hoed > preesthode

prestly adv *prestli adv.* A 1; B 2; C 3
A. 7.85 [I] payede hym *prestly* for peril of my soule;
B. 6.93 I paide [hym] *prestly* for peril of my soule;
B.13.35 Pacience and I [*prestly*] were put to be [mettes],
C. 3.306 And but hit *prestly* be ypayed þe payere is to blame,
C. 8.102 Y payede hit *prestly* for perel of my soule;
C.15.40 Pacience and y [*prestly* weren] pot to be mettes

presumen v *presumen v.* B 1 presumed; C 1
B.Pr.108 And power *presumed* in hem a pope to make
C.Pr.135 And power *presumen* in hemself a pope to make

presumpcion n *presumpcioun n.* A 1 presumpcioun; B 2; C 2
   presumpcioun
A.11.42 And putte forþ *presumpcioun* to proue þe soþe.
B.10.56 And puten forþ *presumpcion* to preue þe soþe.
B.11.423 Pryde now and *presumpcion*, parauenture, wol þee appele
C.11.37 And putten forth *presumpcioun* to preue þe sothe.
C.13.230 [For] pruyde or *presumpcioun* of thy parfit lyuynge,

presumptuowsly adv *presumptousli adv.* A 1
A.12.8 *Presumptuowsly*, parauenture, apose so manye

preueiliche > pryueliche

preuen v *preven v.* A 8 preue (1) proue (3) prouen (2) prouide (1) prouiþ
   (1); B 29 preue (8) preued (5) preuen (8) preueþ (7) ypreued (1); C
   30 preue (9) preuede (3) preuen (5) preueth (6) proue (3) proueden (1)
   prouen (2) ypreued (1)
A.Pr.38 Þat poule prechiþ of hem I dar not *proue* it here:
A. 4.107 Til prestis here prechyng *preue* it hemselue,
A. 5.13 And *prouide* þat þise pestilences wern for pur synne,
A. 5.35 Þat þei preche þe peple *preue* it hemselue,
A. 9.115 To putte forþ sum purpos [to] *prouen* hise wittes.
A.11.42 And putte forþ presumpcioun to *proue* þe soþe.
A.11.229 Poul *prouiþ* it is vnpossible, riche men in heuene.
A.11.233 And *prouen* it be þe pistil þat petir is nempnid:
B.Pr.38 That Poul precheþ of hem I [dar] nat *preue* it here;
B. 4.122 And til prechours prechynge be *preued* on hemselue;
B. 5.13 He *preued* þat þise pestilences were for pure synne,
B. 5.42 'That ye prechen þe peple, *preue* it yowselue,
B. 7.174 And how þe preest *preued* no pardon to dowel
B. 8.125 [To] pute forþ som purpos to *preuen* hise wittes,
B.10.56 And puten forþ presumpcion to *preue* þe soþe.
B.10.256 Ne man hadde no merite mi3te hit ben *ypreued*:
B.10.341 Poule *preueþ* it impossible, riche men [in] heuene.
B.10.350 And *preuen* it by [þe pistel þat Peter is nempned]:
B.11.89 'They wole aleggen also', quod I, 'and by þe gospel *preuen*:
B.12.19 And prechours to *preuen* what it is of many a peire freres.'
B.12.29 'Poul in his pistle', quod he, '*preueþ* what is dowel:
B.12.262 Thus þe Poete *preueþ* þe pecok for hise feþeres;

B.13.80 That he precheþ [and] *preueþ* no3t [com]pacience', I tolde.
B.13.91 And *preuen* it by hir Pocalips and passion of Seint Auereys
B.13.123 I am vnhardy', quod he, 'to any wi3t to *preuen* it.
B.13.133 'Thanne passe we ouer til Piers come and *preue* þis in dede.
B.13.182 And be Pilgrym wiþ pacience til I haue *preued* moore.'
B.13.214 Til Pacience haue *preued* þee and parfit þee maked.'
B.14.109 Ther þe poore dar plede and *preue* by pure reson
B.14.191 And putten of so þe pouke, and *preuen* vs vnder borwe.
B.14.271 So it [*preueþ*] by ech a persone þat possession forsakeþ
B.15.110 Than for to prechen and *preuen* it no3t–ypocrisie it semeþ.
B.15.609 Prelates of cristene prouinces sholde *preue* if þei my3te
B.17.158 How he þat is holy goost sire and sone *preueþ*.
B.17.261 Poul þe Apostel *preueþ* wheiþer I lye:
B.18.203 'And I shal *preue*', quod Pees, 'hir peyne moot haue ende,
B.20.275 And preche men of Plato, and *preue* it by Seneca
C.Pr.39 Tha[t] Poule preche[þ] of hem *preue* hit y myhte
C. 5.115 And *preuede* þat this pestelences was for puyre synne,
C. 5.141 'That 3e prechen þe peple, *p[ro]ue* hit 3owsylue;
C. 6.119 And *preuen* inparfit prelates of holy churche;
C. 6.186 Of put[rie] and of paramours and *proueden* thorw speche
C. 9.319 And how þe prest *preuede* no pardon to do wel
C.10.121 And potte forth som purpos to *prouen* his wittes,
C.11.37 And putten forth presumpcioun to *preue* þe sothe.
C.11.157 Ne man mouhte haue mery[t]e [thereof] mouhte hit be *ypreued*:
C.12.30 Thei wolle allegge also and by þe gospel *preuen*:
C.12.141 Ac pouerte god potte byfore and *preuede* for þe betere:
C.12.174 And poetes to *preuen* hit: Porfirie and plato,
C.12.177 *Preueth* pacient pouerte prince of alle vertues.
C.12.201 So *preueth* this profetes þat pacientliche soffren.
C.13.27 Thogh y preyse pouerte thus and *preue* hit by ensau[m]ples
C.15.87 That a precheth and *preueth* nat compacience,' ich tolde,
C.15.98 And *prouen* hit by here pocalips and þe passioun of seynt Aueroy
C.15.133 And no tixst ne taketh to *preue* this for trewe
C.15.135 And *preueth* by puyre skile inparfyt alle thynges–
C.15.138 Byfore perpetuel pees y shal *proue* þat y saide
C.15.283 Then eny pore pacient; and þat *preue* y be resoun.
C.15.285 There þe pore dar plede and *preue* by puyr resoun
C.16.264 Then for to prechen and *preue* hit nat–ypocrisye hit semeth.
C.17.4 'Ho is wroeth and wolde be awreke, holy writ *preueth*,' quod he,
C.17.317 Prelates and prestes sholde *proue* yf they myhte
C.18.59 Hit is al of o kynde, and þat shal y *preuen*,
C.18.214 That he is thre persones departable y *preue* hit by mankynde,
C.19.227 Paul the apostel *preueth* where y lye:
C.20.208 'And y shal *pre[u]e*,' quod pees, 'here payne moet haue ende
C.22.275 And preche men of plato and *preuen* hit by seneca

preuete n *privete n.* C 2 preuete (1) pryuatees (1)
C.13.229 And for thow woldest wyte why, resones *preue[t]e*,
C.18.5 Erber of alle *pryuatees* and of holynesse.

preuy(- > pryue(-

pride n *pride n.(2)* A 8; B 38 pride (31) pryde (6) prides (1); C 45 pryde
   (6) pruyde (38) pruydes (1)
A.Pr.23 And summe putte hem to *pride*, aparailde hem þereaftir,
A. 1.116 For *pride* þat he put out his peyne haþ non ende.
A. 2.59 To be present in *pride* for pouere [or for] riche,
A. 3.57 A[c] so preuyliche parte it þat *pride* be not sei3e,
A. 5.15 Was apertly for *pride* & for no poynt ellis.
A. 6.97 And pokiþ [forþ] *pride* to preise þiselue.
A. 9.111 Was no *pride* on his apparail ne no pouert noþer,
A.10.102 Þou mi3test lese þi lou3nesse for a litel *pride*.
B.Pr.23 And somme putten hem to *pride*, apparailed hem þerafter,
B. 1.127 For *pride* þat he putte out his peyne haþ noon ende.
B. 2.80 To be Princes in *pride* and pouerte to despise,
B. 3.36 An auenture *pride* be peynted þere and pomp of þe world;
B. 5.15 Was pertliche for *pride* and for no point ellis.
B. 5.611 And pokeþ forþ *pride* to preise þiseluen;
B. 8.121 Was no *pride* on his apparaill ne pouerte neiþer;
B.10.76 Ne sory for hire synnes; so is *pride* woxen
B.10.82 Ne for drede of þe deeþ wiþdrawe no3t hir *pride*,
B.11.15 *Pride* of parfit lyuynge pursued hem boþe
B.11.33 And *pride* of parfit lyuynge to muche peril þee brynge.'
B.11.423 Pryde now and presumpcion, parauenture, wol þee appele
B.13.259 Til *pride* be pureliche fordo, and [þat] þoru3 payn defaute.
B.13.275 Of *pride* here a plot, and þere a plot of vnbuxom speche,
B.14.74 [Oþer] plentee makeþ *pryde* amonges poore and riche.
B.14.194 Of pompe and of *pride* þe parchemyn decourreþ,
B.14.206 And þat is plesaunt to *pride* in poore and in riche.
B.14.216 A[c] *pride* in richesse regneþ raþer þan in pouerte;
B.14.218 Ac in pouerte þer pacience is *pride* haþ no my3te,
B.14.280 Pouerte is þe firste point þat *pride* moost hateþ;
B.14.281 Thanne is it good by good skile, al þat agasteþ *pride*.
B.15.50 'Thanne artow inparfit', quod he, 'and oon of *prides* kny3tes.

B.15.67   For in þe likynge liþ a *pride* and licames coueitise
B.15.189 *Pride* wiþ al þe appurtenaunces, and pakken hem togideres,
B.15.552 Shal þei demen dos ecclesie, and [depose yow for youre *pride*]:
B.19.223 And *Pride* shal be Pope, Prynce of holy chirche,
B.19.228 That ydelnesse encombre hym noȝt, enuye ne *pride*:
B.19.335 Now is Piers to þe plow; *pride* it aspide
B.19.351 Wiþ swiche colours and queyntise comeþ *pride* yarmed
B.19.354 Al þe world in a while þoruȝ oure wit,' quod *Pryde*.
B.19.359 To goon agayn *Pride* but Grace weere wiþ vs.'
B.19.381 'I care noȝt', quod Conscience, 'þouȝ *pride* come nouþe.
B.20.70   And *pride* [bar it bare] boldely aboute
B.20.108 Leue *pride* pryuely and be parfite cristene.
B.20.149 And prike[d] forþ wiþ *pride*; preiseþ he no vertue,
B.20.352 And be adrad of deeþ and wiþdrawe hym fram *pryde*
B.20.373 Sleuþe seigh þat and so dide *pryde*,
B.20.382 To seken Piers þe Plowman, þat *pryde* [myȝte] destruye,
C.Pr.25   And summe putte hem to *pruyde*, [a]parayled hem þeraftir
C. 1.129 For *pruyde* th[at] hym pokede his payne hath non ende.
C. 2.87   To ben pr[inces] in *pruyde* and pouert to dispice,
C. 3.70   An Auntur *pruyde* be paynted there and pomp of the world,
C. 5.117 Was pertliche for *pruyde* and for no poynt elles.
C. 6.13   And shryue the sharpeliche and shak of alle *pruyde*.'
C. 6.14   '[I], *pr[uyde*], pacientlyche penaunce aske.
C. 6.59   Al [y] wolde þat men wiste when it to *pruyde* souneth,
C. 7.263 And poketh forth *pruyde* to preyse thysuluen.
C. 8.347 *Pruyde* and pestilences shal moche peple feche;
C.10.117 Was no *pruyde* on his parail ne pouerte noythere;
C.11.56   Ne sory for here synnes; so [is] *pruyde* enhanced
C.11.62   Ne for drede of eny deth withdraweth h[e]m fro *pruyde*
C.11.174 And *pruyde*-of-parfit-lyuynge pursuede me faste
C.11.192 And *pruyde*-of-parfit-lyuynge to moche perel the brynge.'
C.12.234 Ouerplente *pruyde* norischeth þer pouerte hit distrueth.
C.13.230 [For] *pruyde* or presumpcioun of thy parfit lyuynge,
C.15.229 Til *pruyde* be puyreliche fordo and þat thorw payn defaute:
C.15.234 *Pruyde* wolde potte hymsulf forth thogh no plough erye.
C.16.47   And þat is plesant to *pruyde* in pore and in ryche.
C.16.57   And *pruyde* in rychesse regneth rather then in pouerte;
C.16.59   Ac in pouerte þer pacience is *pruyde* hath no myhte
C.16.120 Pouerte is the furste poynte þat *pruyde* moest hateth;
C.16.122 Al þat may potte of *pruyde* in place þer he regneth;
C.16.212 'Thenne artow inparfit,' quod he, 'and oen of *pruydes* knyhtes.
C.16.229 "Non plus sapere," saide þe wyse, [laste synne of *pruyde* wexe,]
C.16.238 More for pompe and *pruyde*, as þe peple woet wel
C.16.258 Parte with þe pore and ȝoure *pruyde* leue
C.16.265 Ypocrisye is a braunche of *pruyde* and most amonges clerkes
C.16.332 *Pruyde* with alle [þe] purtinaunces and pakketh hem togyderes
C.17.215 Shal dampne dos ecclesie and depose ȝow for ȝoure *pruyde*:
C.20.346 And out of heuene hidore thy *pryde* made vs falle.
C.21.223 And [*pryde* shal] be pope, prince of holy chirche,
C.21.228 That ydelnesse encombre h[y]m nat, enuye ne *pryde*:
C.21.335 Now is [Peres] to the [plouh]; *Pryde* hit aspiede
C.21.351 With such colours and queyntis[e] cometh *pruyde* yArmed
C.21.354 Alle the world in a while thorw oure wit,' quod *pruyde*.
C.21.359 To goen agayn *pruyde* bute grace were with vs.'
C.21.381 'Y care nat,' quod Consience, 'thow *pryde* come nouthe;
C.22.70   And *pryde* [baer] hit baer baldly aboute
C.22.108 Leue *pruyde* priueyliche and be parfyt cristene.
C.22.149 And prike[d] forth with *pruyde*; preyseth he no vertue
C.22.352 And be adrad of deth and withdrawe hym fro *pruyde*
C.22.373 Sle[u]th seyh þat and so dede *pruyde*
C.22.382 To seke [Peres the Plouhman], þat *pruyde* myhte destruye,

pridie adv *n.i.d., Latin pridie* B 1; C 1 prydie
B. 5.312 [Sire Piers of *Pridie* and Pernele of Flaundres,
C. 6.367 Syre [Peres] of *prydie* and purnele of Flaundres,

pried v *prien v.* B 1
B.16.168 And after Piers þe Plowman *pried* and stared.

pryke > prikeþ

prikere n *prikere n.* A 1; B 3 prikere (2) prikiere (1); C 2 prikeare (1) prikiare (1)
A.10.8   A proud *prikere* of Fraunce, Princeps huius mundi,
B. 9.8   A proud *prikere* of Fraunce, Princeps huius mundi,
B.10.313 A *prikere* on a palfrey fro [place] to Manere,
B.18.25   In Piers paltok þe Plowman þis *prikiere* shal ryde,
C.10.135 A proued *prikeare* of fraunce, princeps huius mundi,
C.20.24   In [Pers paltok] the [plouhman] this *prikiare* shal ryde

prikeþ v *priken v.* A 1 prikede; B 6 priked (2) prikede (1) prikeþ (1) prikye (1) ypriked (1); C 9 pryke (1) priked (1) pryked (1) prikede (1) prykede (1) priketh (2) prikye (1) ypriked (1)
A.2.151   But *prikede* forþ on his palfray & passide hem alle,
B. 2.190 And *priked* [forþ on] his palfrey and passed hem alle

B.17.201 For he *prikeþ* god as in þe pawme þat peccat in spiritu[m] sanct[um].
B.17.355 I may no lenger lette', quod he, and lyard he *prikede*
B.18.11   Barefoot on an Asse bak bootles cam *prikye*
B.20.86   Hadde *ypriked* and prayed polles of peple;
B.20.149 And *prike[d]* forþ wiþ pride; preiseþ he no vertue,
C. 2.204 And *prykede* forth on pacience and passed hem alle
C. 4.24   Thenne Consience on his capel comesed to *pryke*
C. 5.159 And *pryked* aboute on palfrayes fram places to maneres,
C.19.91   And ȝut [b]e plasterud with pacience when fondynges [*priketh* hym]–
C.19.167 For he *priketh* god as in [the] paume that peccat in spiritum sanctum.
C.19.335 Y may no lengore lette,' quod he, and lyard a *prikede*
C.20.9   Barfoet on an asse bake boetles cam *priky[e]*
C.22.86   Hadde *ypriked* and preyede polles of peple;
C.22.149 And *prike[d]* forth with pruyde; preyseth he no vertue

prikiare -iere > prikere

prime n *prime n.* A 2; B 1; C 1
A. 7.104 At heiȝ *prime* peris let þe plouȝ stande
A.12.60   As I ȝede thurgh ȝouþe, aȝen *prime* dayes,
B. 6.112 At heiȝ *prime* Piers leet þe plowȝ stonde
C. 8.119 At hey *prime* [Peres] leet þe plouh stande

primer n *primere n.* C 1
C. 5.46   Is paternoster and my *primer*,placebo and dirige,

prince n *prince n.* A 5 prince (3) princes (2); B 10 prince (2) prynce (3) Princes (3) Prynces (2); C 15 prince (10) princes (4) prinses (1)
A. 2.12   Of þe pureste perreiȝe þat *prince* werde euere;
A. 7.109 'Be þe *prince* of paradis!' quaþ piers þo in wraþþe,
A. 8.47   Of *princes* & prelatis here pencioun shulde arise,
A.11.198 *Prince* ouer godis peple to prechen or to chaste.
A.11.298 'Wh[anne] ȝe ben aposid of *princes* or of prestis of þe lawe
B. 2.80   To be *Princes* in pride and pouerte to despise,
B. 7.44   *Princes* and prelates sholde paie for hire trauaille:
B. 8.16   Boþe *princes* paleises and pouere mennes cotes,
B.13.52   'Here is propre seruice', quod Pacience, 'þer fareþ no *Prince* bettre.'
B.16.37   That is þe passion and þe power of oure *prince* Iesu.
B.16.260 'This is a present of muche pris; what *prynce* shal it haue?'
B.18.264 "*Prynces* of þis place, vnpynneþ and vnloukeþ,
B.19.96   Ac for alle þise preciouse present3 oure lord [*prynce*] Iesus
B.19.223 And Pride shal be Pope, *Prynce* of holy chirche,
B.19.307 For present or for preiere or any *Prynces* lettres.
C. 2.87   To ben pr[inces] in pruyde and pouert to dispice,
C. 9.280 For shal no pardon preye for ȝow there ne no *princes* lettres.
C.10.16   Bothe *princes* paleis and pore menne cotes
C.10.197 Prelates and prestes and *princes* of holy churche
C.11.10   Then al þe precious perye þat eny *prince* weldeth.
C.12.177 Preueth pacient pouerte *prince* of alle vertues.
C.13.3   Oure *prince* iesu peple chees and his apostles alle
C.13.8   For in greet pouerte he was put: a *prince*, as hit were,
C.17.167 And pursuede to haue be pope, *prince* of holy chirche;
C.17.242 Bote thorw pacience and priue gyle he was *prince* ouer hem all.
C.17.248 To make a perpetuel pees bitwene þe *prince* of heuene
C.18.276 'This is a present of moche pris; what *prince* shal hit haue?'
C.21.96   Ac for all this preciouse presentes oure lord *prince* iesu[s]
C.21.223 And [pryde shal] be pope, *prince* of holy chirche,
C.21.307 For presente or for preyere or eny *prinses* lettres.

principally adv *principallie adv.* B 2 principally (1) principalliche (1)
B.10.474 And *principally* hir paternoster; many a persone haþ wisshed.
B.14.195 And *principalliche* of al[l]e peple but þei be poore of herte.

prinses > prince

printe n *prente n. &> preynte* C 2
C.17.74   And to a badde peny with a gode *printe*:
C.17.76   And ȝut is þe *printe* puyr trewe and parfitliche ygraue.

printede v *prenten v.* C 1
C.17.81   That god coueyteth nat þe coyne þat crist hymsulue *printede*

prior > priour

prioresse n *prioresse n.* B 3; C 2
B. 5.157 I was þe *Prioresse* potager and oþere pouere ladies,
B. 5.160 And dame Pernele a preestes fyle; *Prioresse* worþ she neuere
B. 5.167 That no *Prioresse* were preest, for þat he [purueiede];
C. 6.132 I was the *Prioresse* potager and oþer pore ladies
C. 6.135 And dame purnele a prestis fyle; *Prioresse* worth he neuere

priour n *priour n.* B 2; C 3 prior (1) priour (2)
B. 5.171 Boþe *Priour* and Suppriour and oure Pater Abbas;
B.11.57   To hir *Priour* prouincial a pardon for to haue,
C. 5.91   But he be obediencer to *prior* or to mynistre.'

C. 6.153   That is *Priour* and supriour and oure pater Abbas.
C.12.9   To here *priour* prouincial [a] pardon to haue

pris n *pris n.(1)*   B 3;   C 3
B. 2.13   And Diamaundes of derrest *pris* and double manere Saphires,
B.13.8   And [peple] þat was pouere at litel *pris* þei sette,
B.16.260   'This is a present of muche *pris*; what prynce shal it haue?'
C.12.26   And now y am pore and penyles at litel *pris* he sette[th] me.
C.15.10   And peple þat was pore at litel *pris* [þei] setten
C.18.276   'This is a present of moche *pris*; what prince shal hit haue?'

pris adj *prise adj.*   B 1;   C 1
B.19.266   The *pris* neet of Piers plow, passynge alle oþere.
C.21.266   The *pris* neet of [Peres plouh], passynge alle oþere.

prison n *prisoun n.*   A 1 presoun;   B 9 prison (6) prisone (1) prisons (2);   C 11 prisone (1) prisones (7) prisoun (3)
A. 9.94   Þanne shulde þe kyng come & casten hem in *presoun*,
B. 7.30   Pouere peple [bedredene] and *prisons* [in stokkes]
B. 8.104   Thanne [sholde] þe kyng come and casten hem in [*prison*],
B.11.133   And putten hym after in *prison* in purgatorie to brenne;
B.14.54   *Prison* ne peyne, for pacientes vincunt.
B.15.183   Ther poore men and *prisons* liggeþ, hir pardon to haue;
B.15.265   Ne han martired Peter ne Poul, ne in *prison* holden.
B.15.346   And many a *prison* fram purgatorie þoruȝ hise preieres deliuereþ.
B.18.58   Pitousliche and pale, as a *prison* þat deieþ,
B.18.392   In my *prisone* Purgatorie til parce it hote.
C. 3.175   He lat passe *prisones* [and] paieth for hem ofte
C. 4.123   In *prisones* and in pore cotes be pilgrimages to Rome
C. 7.21   Y visitede neuere feble man ne fetered man in *prisone*.
C. 7.277   For he payeth for *prisones* in places and in peynes.
C. 9.34   Pore peple bedredene and *prisones* in stokkes
C. 9.72   As *prisones* in puttes and pore folk in cotes,
C. 9.181   As *prisones* and pilgrimes and paraunter men yrobbed
C.12.68   And potten hym aftur in *prisoun* in purgatorie to brenne
C.15.253   *Prisoun* ne payne, for [pacientes] vincunt.
C.16.325   There pore men and *prisones* ben and paye for here fode,
C.20.58   Pitousliche and pale, as [a] *prisoun* þat deyeth,

prisoners n *pisoner n.(2)*   A 1;   B 3
A. 3.126   And letiþ passe *prisoners* & paieþ for hem ofte,
B. 3.137   [And] leteþ passe *prisoners* and paieþ for hem ofte,
B.14.168   [And] haue ruþe on þise riche men þat rewarde noȝt þi *prisoners*;
B.14.174   Ac poore peple, þi *prisoners*, lord, in þe put of meschief,

pryuatees > preuete

pryue adj *prive adj.(1)*   A 2 preuy;   B 10 pryue (4) pryuee (6);   C 14 priue (7) pryue (6) priueoste (1)
A. 2.18   In þe popis paleis heo is *preuy* as myselue;
A. 3.136   She is *preuy* wiþ þe pope, prouisours it knowiþ;
B. 2.23   In þe popes Paleis she is *pryuee* as myselue,
B. 2.64   Were moost *pryuee* with Mede of any men me þouȝte.
B. 3.147   She is *pryuee* wiþ þe pope, prouisours it knoweþ;
B.10.100   In a *pryuee* parlour for pouere mennes sake,
B.11.105   [Th]yng þat is *pryue*, publice þow it neuere;
B.12.230   Kynde] kenned Adam to knowe hise *pryue* membres,
B.13.206   If Pacience be oure partyng felawe and *pryue* with vs boþe
B.19.376   And oþ[er] *pryue* penaunc[e], and somme þoruȝ penyes delynge.
B.20.115   And wiþ *pryuee* speche and peyntede wordes,
B.20.364   Of 'a *pryuee* paiement and I shal praye for yow
C. 2.23   In þe popes palays he is *pryue* as mysulue,
C. 2.66   Were most *pryue* with mede of eny men [me] thoghte.
C. 3.117   Or presentes without pans and oþer *priue* ȝeftes.
C. 3.185   He is *priue* with þe pope, prouysours it knoweth,
C. 4.189   And þat vnsittynge suffraunce ne sele ȝoure *priue* lettres
C. 9.118   Hit aren as his postles, suche peple, or as his *priue* disciples
C.12.39   Thyng þat wolde be *pryue* publische thow hit neuere;
C.13.38   For þe parcel[s] of his pauper and oþer *pryue* dettes
C.13.82   And other *pryue* penaunces þe which þe prest woet wel
C.17.242   Bote thorw pacience and *priue* gyle he may preue ouer hem all.
C.18.97   And in heuene is *priueoste* and next hym by resoun
C.21.376   Or oþer *priue* penauns[e] and somme thorw pans delyng.
C.22.115   And with *priue* speche and paynted wordes
C.22.364   Of 'a *pryue* payement and y shal preye for ȝow

pryuees n *GLD Prive*   B 1
B. 2.178   Paulynes *pryuees* for pleintes in Consistorie

pryueliche adv *privelie adv.*   A 2 preuyliche (1) preuyly (1);   B 7 pryuely (3) pryueliche (4);   C 8 preueiliche (1) priueyliche (2) priueyly (1) priueliche (4)
A. 3.57   A[c] so *preuyliche* parte it þat pride be not seiȝe,
A. 3.71   For þei poisone þe peple *preuyly* wel ofte,
B. 3.82   For þei [p]oisone þe peple *pryueliche* [wel] ofte
B.11.114   And plukked in Pauci *pryueliche* and leet þe remenaunt go rome.'

B.13.56   'Bryng pacience som pitaunce *pryueliche*', quod Conscience,
B.13.367   Or *pryueliche* his purs shook, vnpikede hise lokes.
B.13.376   Wiþ presentes *pryuely*, or paide som certeyn,
B.19.300   For gile gooþ so *pryuely* þat good feiþ ouþer while
B.20.108   Leue pride *pryuely* and be parfite cristene.
C. 6.266   Or *priueliche* his pors shoke, vnpiked his lokes.
C.12.49   And plihte in pauci preueiliche and lette þe remenaunt go rome.'
C.15.149   Where Peres the plogman bycam, so *priueyliche* he wente.
C.17.172   In ayþer of his eres *priueliche* he hadde
C.18.100   'This is a propre plonte,' quod y–'and *priueliche* hit bloweth
C.18.164   And pursuede hym *priueliche* and for pans hym bouhte–
C.21.300   For gyle goth so *priueyly* þat goed fayth oþer while
C.22.108   Leue pruyde *priueyliche* and be parfyt cristene.

priueoste > pryue

proched v *OED proche v., MED brochen v.*   B 1
B. 5.210   [P]roche[d] hem wiþ a paknedle and playte hem togideres,

procuratour n *procuratour n.*   B 1;   C 2 procuratour (1) procuratours (1)
B.19.258   For I make Piers þe Plowman my *procuratour* and my reue,
C. 7.89   Ryht so flateres and fooles aren þe fendes *procuratours*
C.21.258   For y make [Peres the plouhman] my *proc[ur]atour* and my reue

profecye(d > prophecied; profered -eth > profrest

profession n *professioun n.*   A 1 professioun;   B 1;   C 1 professioun
A. 1.98   Þat is þe *professioun* apertly þat apendiþ to kniȝtes,
B. 1.100   [That] is [þe] *profession* apertli þat apendeþ to knyȝtes,
C. 1.97   Is þe *professioun* and puyr ordre that apendeth to knyghtes

profete(s > prophete; proffride > profrest

profit n *profite n.(1)*   A 3;   B 11;   C 15 profit (11) profyt (4)
A.Pr.56   Prechinge þe peple for *profit* of þe wombe;
A. 5.116   And was his prentis ypliȝt his *profit* to loke.
A. 6.34   Wiþinne & wiþoute waytide his *profit*.
B.Pr.59   Prechynge þe peple for *profit* of [þe wombe];
B.Pr.119   And for *profit* of al þe peple Plowmen ordeyned
B.Pr.148   Comen to a counseil for þe commune *profit*.
B. 4.123   Til þe kynges counseil be þe commune *profit*;
B. 4.150   Al to construe þis clause for þe kynges *profit*,
B. 5.200   And was his prentice ypliȝt his *profit* to [loke].
B. 5.544   WiþInne and wiþouten waited his *profit*,
B.13.237   For Piers þe Plowman and þat hym *profit* waiten.
B.13.392   Or into Prucelond my Prentis my *profit* to waiten,
B.20.332   'In faiþ', quod þis frere, 'for *profit* and for helpe
C.Pr.57   Prechyng þe peple for *profyt* of þe wombe;
C.Pr.146   And for most *profi[t* to þe peple] a plogh gonne þei make,
C.Pr.169   Comen til a conseyl for [þe] comune *profyt*.
C.Pr.186   And knytten hit on a coler for oure comune *profyt*
C.Pr.204   Forthy y conseile for oure comune *profit* lat þe Cat yworthe
C. 4.119   And til þe kynges consayl be alle comune *profit*
C. 5.101   That alle tymes of my tyme to *profit* shal turne.'
C. 6.208   And was his prentis yplyht his *profit* to wayte,
C. 6.279   Or in[to] pruyslond my prenties my *profit* to awayte
C. 7.188   Withynne and withouten to wayten his *profit*.
C. 8.7   'Y preye ȝow for ȝoure *profit*,' quod Peres to þe ladyes,
C. 8.14   For *profit* of the pore and plesaunce of ȝowsuluen.
C. 8.111   And ben a pilgrym at þe plouh for *profit* to pore and ryche.'
C.13.200   Is no vertue so fair ne of valewe ne *profit*
C.22.332   'In fayth,' quod this frere, 'for *profyt* and for helthe

profitable adj *profitable adj.*   A 2;   B 5;   C 4
A. 7.259   'Be seint pernel,' quaþ peris, 'þise arn *profitable* wordis.
A.12.98   And be prest to preyeres and *profitable* werkes.
B. 6.275   'By Seint [Pernele]', quod Piers, 'þise arn *profitable* wordes!
B.13.76   They prechen þat penaunce is *profitable* to þe soule,
B.13.176   *Profitable* to eiþer peple;' and putte þe table fro hym,
B.13.364   Moore *profitable* þan myn, manye sleiȝtes I made.
B.17.153   Al þat þe pawme parceyueþ *profitable* to feele,
C. 6.263   More *profitable* then myn, y made many wentes.
C. 7.192   *Profitable* as for þe plouh a potte me to lerne.
C.15.82   They preche þat penaunce is *profitable* to þe soule
C.15.173   *Profitable* for bothe parties;' and potte þe boerd fro hym

profiteþ v *profiten v.*   C 1
C.Pr.101   A[c] for it *profiteþ* ȝow into pursward ȝe prelates soffren

profrest v *profren v.*   A 8 proffride (1) profre (1) profride (5) profrist (1);   B 12 profre (1) profred (3) profrede (5) profrest (1) profreþ (2);   C 9 profered (2) profereth (1) profre (1) profred (1) profrede (4)
A. 4.50   To make his pes with his panis & *profride* hym manye,
A. 4.61   For of hise penys he *proffride* handy dandy to paye.
A. 4.82   And *profride* pees a presaunt al of purid gold;
A. 6.43   'Ȝa, leue piers,' quaþ þe pilgrimes & *profride* hym hire.

A. 7.26   'Be seint poule,' quaþ perkyn, 'for þou *profrist* þe so lowe
A. 7.40   And þei pore men *profre* þe presauntis or ȝeftis
A. 7.140   To peris þe plouȝman he *profride* his gloue.
A. 7.279   And *profride* peris [þis] present to plese þerewiþ hungir.
B. 4.64   To maken [his] pees with hise pens and *profred* hym manye,
B. 4.95   And *profrede* Pees a present al of pure[d] golde.
B. 5.556   'Ye! leue Piers', quod þise pilgrimes and *profred* hym huyre.
B. 6.24   'By Seint Poul!' quod Perkyn, 'for þow *profrest* þee so lowe]
B. 6.41   And þouȝ pouere men *profre* [þee] presentes and ȝiftes
B. 6.153   To Piers þe Plowman he *profrede* his gloue.
B. 6.295   And *profrede* Piers þis present to plese wiþ hunger.
B.13.189   For al þat Pacience me *profreþ* proud am I litel.
B.13.380   But he *profrede* to paie a peny or tweyne
B.14.49   A pece of þe Paternoster [and *profrede* vs alle];
B.17.143   And *profre[d]* it forþ as with a pawme to what place it sholde.
B.17.144   The pawme is [þe piþ of] þe hand, and *profreþ* forþ þe fyngres
C. 4.67   On men of lawe wrong lokede and largelyche hem *profered*
C. 4.91   And *profrede* pees a present al of puyre golde.
C. 7.200   'ȝe! leue Peres,' quod thise pilgrimes and *profrede* Peres mede.
C. 8.39   And thogh pore men *profre* ȝow presentes and ȝyftes
C. 8.150   And to [Peres] þe [plouhman] *profrede* to fyhte
C. 8.317   And *profrede* [Peres] this present to plese with hongur.
C.15.247   A pece of þe paternoster and *profred* vs all.
C.19.117   And *profered* hit forth as with the paume to what place hit sholde.
C.19.118   The paume is the pethe of the hand and *profereth* [forth] the
           fyngeres

properly adv *proprelie adv.* B 2 properly (1) propreliche (1); C 3
   properly (1) properliche (1) propreliche (1)
B.14.275   What is Pouerte, pacience', quod he, '*properly* to mene?'
B.14.284   So pouerte *propreliche* penaunce [is to þe body,
C.15.152   [And] pacience *properliche* spak, tho Peres was thus ypassed,
C.15.272   'What is [*properly*] parfit pacience?' quod Actiua vita.
C.16.118   'Parfay!' quod pacience, '*propreliche* to telle [this]

prophecie n *prophecie n.* B 1
B.15.326   Who parfourneþ þis *prophecie* of þe peple þat now libbeþ,

prophecied v *prophecien v.* B 2; C 2 profecye (1) profecied (1)
B.18.108   Now youre goode dayes arn doon as daniel *prophecied*;
B.19.16   Patriarches and prophetes *prophecied* bifore
C. 9.114   To *profecye* of þe peple, pleinge as hit were
C.21.16   Patriarkes & prophetes *profecied* bifore

prophete n *prophete n.* A 3 prophet (2) prophetis (1); B 24 prophete (9)
   prophetes (15); C 23 profete (3) profetes (6) prophete (4) prophetes (8)
   Prophetus (2)
A. 3.221   Þe *prophet* prechiþ it & put it in þe sauter:
A. 8.108   Þe *prophet* his p[a]yn e[et] in penaunce & in wepyng
A.11.283   Or adam, or ysaye, or any of þe *prophetis*
B. 3.234   The *prophete* precheþ [it] and putte it in þe Sauter:
B. 3.261   God sente to Saul by Samuel þe *prophete*
B. 3.275   Ooþerwise þan he was warned of þe *prophete*,
B. 7.12   Wiþ Patriarkes and *prophetes* in paradis to be felawe.
B. 7.126   The *prophete* his payn eet in penaunce and in sorwe
B.10.344   And patriarkes and *prophetes* and poetes boþe
B.10.424   Or Adam or Ysaye or any of þe *prophetes*
B.11.94   And in þe Sauter also seiþ dauid þe *prophete*
B.12.115   But he were preest or preestes sone, Patriark or *prophete*.
B.12.136   Patriarkes and *prophetes* repreueden hir science
B.13.427   Patriarkes and *prophetes*, prechours of goddes wordes,
B.15.588   [And] for a parfit *prophete* þat muche peple sauede
B.16.81   Adam and Abraham and Ysaye þe *prophete*,
B.16.198   Patriarkes and *prophetes* and Apostles were þe children,
B.16.251   That to patriarkes & *prophetes* and ooþer peple in derknesse
B.16.256   Amonges patriarkes and *prophetes* pleyinge togideres.
B.18.138   For patriarkes and *prophetes* han preched herof ofte
B.18.144   Patriarkes and *prophetes* þat in peyne liggen,
B.18.271   Patriarkes and *prophetes* han parled herof longe
B.18.323   Patriarkes and *prophetes*, populus in tenebris,
B.19.16   Patriarkes and *prophetes* prophecied bifore
B.19.48   Tho was he Iesus of Iewes called, gentile *prophete*,
B.19.145   For no fren[d] sholde [it] fecche; for *prophetes* hem tolde
B.19.221   And false *prophetes* fele, flatereris and gloseris,
C. 3.414   How god sente to sauel be samuel þe *prophete*
C. 3.428   Otherwyse then god wolde and warnede hym by þe *prophete*,
C. 7.87   Patriarkes and *prophetes*, precheours of goddes wordes,
C. 9.12   With patriarkes and *prophetes* in paradis to sitton.
C. 9.212   Or oen of som ordre or elles a *profete*.
C.10.206   *Prophetus* and patriarkes, popes and maydenes.
C.11.148   Patriarkes and *prophetes*, apostles and angelis;
C.11.256   And ar Adam oþer ysaye oþer eny of the *profetes*
C.12.201   So preueth this *profetes* þat pacientliche soffren.
C.14.60   Bote hit were pres[t] or prestis sone, patriarke or p[ro]phete.
C.14.81   Patriarkes and *prophetus* repruede here science

C.17.299   And for a parfit *profete* that moche peple sauede
C.18.112   Adam and Abraham and ysaye þe *prophete*,
C.18.207   Patriarches and *prophetes* and apostles were the childrene.
C.18.272   With patriarkes and *profetes* pleynge togyderes.
C.20.141   For patriarkes and *prophetes* haen preched herof ofte
C.20.147   Patriarkes and *prophetes* þat in peyne liggen,
C.20.279   Patriarkes and *prophetes* haen parled herof longe
C.20.366   Patriarkes and *profetes*, populus in tenebris,
C.21.16   Patriarkes & *prophetes* profecied bifore
C.21.48   Tho was he iesu[s] of iewes [cald], gentel *profete*,
C.21.145   For no frende sholde hit fecche; for *profetes* hem tolde
C.21.221   And false *profetes* fele, flateres and glosares,

propre adj *propre adj.* B 6; C 3
B. 7.153   And how þe preest inpugned it wiþ two *propre* wordes.
B.10.245   Thre [*propre*] persones, ac noȝt in plurel nombre,
B.13.52   'Here is *propre* seruice', quod Pacience, 'þer fareþ no Prince bettre.'
B.13.59   Pacience was proud of þat *propre* seruice
B.16.54   The power of þise postes and hire *propre* myȝt[e].
B.16.185   Pater is his *propre* name, a persone by hymselue.
C. 9.302   And how þe prest inpugnede hit thorw two *propre* wordes.
C.15.63   Pacience was wel apayed of this *propre* seruice
C.18.100   'This is a *propre* plonte,' quod y–'and priueliche hit bloweth

propreliche > properly

proud adj *proud adj.* A 6 proud (5) proude (1); B 12 proud (8) proude
   (4); C 11 proud (5) proude (3) proued (1) prout (1) proute (1)
A. 2.41   Was piȝt vp a pauyloun *proud* for þe nones,
A. 3.166   Ne to depraue þi persone wiþ a *proud* herte.
A. 5.45   Pernel *proud* herte plat hire to þe erþe
A. 7.184   And pieris was *proud* þerof, & putte hem in office,
A.10.8   A *proud* prikere of Fraunce, Princeps huius mundi,
A.11.59   To pleise wiþ *proude* men, siþen þe pestilence tyme,
B. 3.179   Ne [to] depraue þi persone wiþ a *proud* herte.
B. 5.62   Pernele *proud*-herte platte hire to þe erþe
B. 6.197   And [Piers was *proud* þerof] and putte hem [in office]
B. 9.8   A *proud* prikere of Fraunce, Princeps huius mundi,
B.10.73   To plese wiþ *proude* men syn þe pestilence tyme;
B.12.240   And þat [is] þe pecok & þe Pehen [wiþ hir *proude* feþeres
B.13.59   Pacience was *proud* of þat propre seruice
B.13.189   For al þat Pacience me profreþ *proud* am I litel.
B.13.277   As in apparaill and in porte *proud* amonges þe peple;
B.15.166   As *proud* of a peny as of a pound of golde,
B.15.201   For þer are [pure] *proude* herted men, pacient of tonge
B.20.218   *Proude* preestes coome with hym; [passynge an hundred]
C. 3.225   Ne to depraue thy persone with a *pro[u]d* herte.
C. 6.3   P[ur]nele *proude* herte platte here to þe erthe
C. 6.30   *Proud* of aparayle in port amongus þe peple
C. 6.46   *Prout* of my fayre fetures and for y song shille;
C. 6.304   And [what] penaunce the prest shal haue þat p[r]oud is of his
           tithes.
C. 8.197   Tho was [Peres] *proud* and potte hem alle a werke
C.10.135   A *proued* prikeare of fraunce, princeps huius mundi,
C.11.53   To plese with *proude* men senes th[e] pestelenc[e tyme]
C.14.172   That is, þe pocok and þe popeiay with here *proude* fetheres
C.16.299   As *proud* of a peny as of a pounde of golde,
C.22.218   *Proute* prestes cam with hym; passyng an hundred

proue(den -n > preuen

prouendre n1 *provendre n.* B 1
B.13.243   I fynde payn for þe pope and *prouendre* for his palfrey,

prouendre n2 *provendrie n.* B 1; C 1 prouendres
B.13.245   Neiþer *prouendre* ne personage yet of [þe] popes ȝifte,
C. 3.32   'And purchace ȝow *prouendres* while ȝoure panes lasteth

prouendres n3 *provendrere n.* B 1; A 1 Prouendrours
A. 3.139   *Prouendrours*, [persones], & [prestis] she maynteniþ
B. 3.150   *Prouendre[s]*, persones and preestes [she] maynteneþ

prouendreth v *provendren v.* C 1
C. 3.188   He *prouendreth* persones and prestes he maynteneth

prouendrours > prouendres

prouerbe n *proverbe n.* C 3 prouerbe (1) prouerbes (1) prouerbis (1)
C. 8.263   'By Crist!' quod [Peres] þe [plouhman] tho, 'this *prouerbis* [wol y]
           shewe
C.12.172   Mo *prouerbes* y myhte haue of mony holy seyntes
C.17.51   Iop þe parfite patriarke this *prouerbe* wroet and tauhte

prouide > preuen

prouince n *province n.* B 2 prouince (1) prouinces (1); C 1 prouynce
B.15.571   Thoruȝ his *prouince* to passe and to his peple shewe hym,
B.15.609   Prelates of cristene *prouinces* sholde preue if þei myȝte

C.17.284   And pacientliche thorw his *prouynce* and to his peple hym shewe,

prouincial n *provincial n.(1)* A 1 prouincialis; B 2 prouincial (1)
   prouincials (1); C 2 prouincial (1) prouinciales (1)
A. 8.175   A pokeful of pardoun þere, ne þe *prouincialis* lettres,
B. 7.197   A pokeful of pardon þere, ne *prouincials* lettres,
B.11.57   To hir Priour *prouincial* a pardon for to haue,
C. 9.343   A pouhe ful of pardon there ne *prouinciales* lettres,
C.12.9   To here priour *prouincial* [a] pardon to haue

prouysour n *provisour n.* A 3 prouisour (1) prouisours (2); B 3 prouysour
   (1) prouisours (2); C 4 prouisores (2) prouisour (1) prouysours (1)
A. 2.135   'And let apparaille þise *prouisours* in palfreis wise;
A. 3.136   She is preuy wiþ þe pope, *prouisours* it knowiþ;
A. 4.116   Oþer *prouisour*, or prest þat þe pope auaunciþ.
B. 2.171   'And late apparaille þise *prouisours* in palfreyes wise;
B. 3.147   She is pryuee wiþ þe pope, *prouisours* it knoweþ;
B. 4.133   *Prouysour* or preest or penaunt for hise synnes.
C. 2.185   That prestis and *prouisores* sholden prelates serue
C. 2.189   And on pore *prouisores* and appeles in þe Arches.
C. 3.185   He is priue with þe pope, *prouysours* it knoweth,
C. 4.130   *Prouisour* or preest oþer penaunt for his synnes.

prouiþ > preuen

prowor n *purveiour n.* B 1; C 1 prowour
B.19.260   My *prowor* and my Plowman Piers shal ben on erþe,
C.21.260   My *prowour* and my [plouhman Peres] shal ben on erthe

prucelond n prop *Prusse n.* B 1; C 1 pruyslond
B.13.392   Or into *Prucelond* my Prentis my profit to waiten,
C. 6.279   Or in[to] *pruyslond* my prenties my profit to awayte,

pruyde(s > pride; pruyslond > prucelond

psalme n *Psalme n.* A 3 salme (2) salmis (1); B 4 psalme (1) psalmes (1)
   Salmes (2); C 4 psalmes
A. 3.227   And þerof sei[þ] þe sauter in a *salmis* ende
A. 7.234   The sauter seiþ in þe *salme* of Beati omnes:
A.10.86   And þerof seiþ þe sauter, þe *salme* þou miȝt rede:
B. 3.248   And þerof seiþ þe Sauter in a *Salmes* ende:
B. 6.250   The Sauter seiþ, in þe *psalme* of Beati omnes,
B.11.314   Synge ne *psalmes* rede ne seye a masse of þe day.
B.12.176   As þow seest in þe Sauter in *Salmes* oon or tweyne
C. 3.465   Here sauter and here seuene *p[s]almes* for alle synful preyen;
C. 5.47   And my sauter som tyme and my seuene *p[s]almes*.
C.13.126   Syng ne [*psalmes*] rede [ne sey a masse of the daye].
C.14.116   As we seen in þe sauter in *psalmes* oen or tweyne

publice *publishen v.* B 1; C 1 publische
B.11.105   [Th]yng þat is pryue, *publice* þow it neuere;
C.12.39   Thyng þat wolde be pryue *publische* thow hit neuere;

puddyng n *poding n.* B 3 puddyng (2) puddynges (1); C 2 poddyng (1)
   poddynges (1)
B. 5.218   Peny ale and *puddyng* ale she poured togideres;
B.13.62   He eet manye sondry metes, mortrews and *puddynges*,
B.13.107   For ye han harmed vs two in þat ye eten þe *puddyng*,
C. 6.226   Peny ale and *poddyng* ale [h]e poured togederes,
C.15.66   And ete manye sondry metes, mortrewes and *poddynges*,

pues n *peue n.(1)* C 1
C. 6.144   Yparroke[d] in *pues*; the persone hit knoweth

puffe v *puffen v.* A 1 puffid; B 2 puffe (1) puffed (1); C 2 poffe (1)
   poffed (1)
A. 5.16   Piries & pl[umtr]es wern *pu[ffid]* to þe erþe
B. 5.16   Pyries and Plumtrees were *puffed* to þe erþe
B.13.88   He shal haue a penaunce in his paunche and *puffe* at ech a worde,
C. 5.118   P[iri]es and plumtrees were *po[ff]ed* to þe erthe
C.15.95   He shal haue a penaunce in his paunche and *poffe* at vch a worde

puyr(- > pure(-; pukide > pokeþ; pulde(n > pulle

pulettes n *polet n.* A 1 pulettis; B 1; C 1 polettes
A. 7.264   'I haue no peny,' quaþ piers, '*pulettis* to biggen,
B. 6.280   'I haue no peny', quod Piers, '*pulettes* to bugge,
C. 8.302   'Y haue no peny,' quod [Peres], '*polettes* for to begge,

pulle v *pullen v.* A 2 pulde (1) pulden (1); B 4 pulle (1) pulled (2) pulte
   (1); C 2 pole (1) polleden (1)
A. 2.181   Til pardoners hadde pite & *pulden* him to house,
A. 8.101   And piers for [pure] tene *pulde* it assondir
B. 2.222   Til Pardoners hadde pite and *pulled* hym [to] house,
B. 7.119   And Piers for pure tene *pulled* it [asonder]
B.11.163   *Pulte* out of pyne a paynym of rome.
B.16.73   I preide Piers to *pulle* adoun an Appul and he wolde,
C. 2.232   Tyl Pardoners hadde [pyte] and *polleden* hym [t]o house.
C. 4.23   Lat peytrele [hym] and *pole* hym with peynted wittes.'

pulsshe > polshe

pult v *pilten v.* C 2 pult (1) pulte (1)
C.10.95   And with the pyk *pulte* adoun preuaricatores legis.
C.11.206   Or p[resci]t inparfit, *pult* out of grace,

pulte > pulle,pult; punesche > punysshen; punfolde > pondfond

punge v *pingen v.* A 1 pungen; B 1
A. 9.88   A pik is in þat potent to *pungen* adoun þe wykkide,
B. 8.98   A pik is [in] þat potente to [*punge*] adown þe wikked

punysshen v *punishen v.* A 2 punisshen; B 6 punysshe (4) punysshen (2);
   C 4 punesche (1) punischen (2) punyschen (1)
A. 3.67   As to *punisshen* on pilleries & on py[n]yng stolis
A.11.256   I shal *punisshen* in purcatory or in þe put of helle
B. 2.49   And haue power to *punysshe* hem; þanne put forþ þi reson.
B. 3.78   [As] to *punysshe* on Pillories and [on] pynynge stooles
B.10.375   "I shal *punysshe* in purgatorie or in þe put of helle
B.14.189   A[c] if þe [pouke] wolde plede herayein, and *punysshe* vs in
             conscience,
B.14.291   Selde is any poore yput to *punysshen* any peple.
B.19.195   And what persone paieþ it nouȝt *punysshen* he þenkeþ,
C. 2.52   And haue power to *p[uny]schen* hem; thenne put forth thy resoun.
C. 3.79   To *punischen* [o]n pilories and [o]n pynyng stoles
C.16.126   Selde is eny pore ypot to *p[u]nesche* eny peple.
C.21.195   And what persone payth hit nat *punischen* he thenketh

puple > peple; pur > pure; purcatory > purgatorie

purchace v *purchasen v.* A 2 purchace (1) purchacide (1); B 5 purchace
   (3) purchaced (2); C 8 purchace (2) purchase (1) purchased (1)
   purchasede (1) purchaseth (1) ypurchaced (1) ypurchased (1)
A. 8.3   And *purchac[ide]* hym a pardoun a pena & a culpa
A. 8.170   [To *purchace* pardoun and þe popes bulles],
B. 7.3   And *purchaced* hym a pardoun a pena & a culpa
B. 7.39   And preiseden Piers þe Plowman þat *purchaced* þis bulle.
B. 7.192   To *purchace* pardon and þe popes bulles.
B. 9.79   Shul [*purchace*] penaunce in purgatorie but þei hem helpe.
B.17.256   And *purchace* al þe pardon of Pampilon and Rome,
C. 3.32   'And *purchace* ȝow prouendres while ȝoure panes lasteth
C. 5.77   Imade here kyn knyhtes and knyhtes fees *ypurchased*,
C. 5.158   Ledares of l[ou]edays, and londes *ypurchased*
C. 9.3   And *purchasede* hym a pardoun A pena & A culpa,
C. 9.42   And prey[se]de [Peres] the [plouhman] þat *purchased* þis bull[e].
C. 9.338   To *pur[c]hace* ȝow pardoun and the popes bulles.
C.12.246   Lo, how pans *purchaseth* fayre places and d[r]ede,
C.19.222   And *purchase* al the pardoun of pampilon and Rome

pure adj *pure adj.* A 6 pur (2) pure (2) pureste (2); B 26 pure (25)
   pureste (1); C 23 puyr (13) puyre (9) puyrere (1)
A. 2.9   Ipurfilid wiþ pelure, þe *pureste* [o]n erþe,
A. 2.12   Of þe *pureste* perreiȝe þat prince werde euere;
A. 5.13   And prouide þat þise pestilences wern for *pur* synne.
A. 8.88   Here penaunce & here purcatorie vpon þis *pur* erþe.
A. 8.101   And piers for [*pure*] tene pulde it assondir
A. 8.152   And how þe prest inpugnid it al be [*pu]re* resoun,
B. 2.9   Purfiled wiþ Pelure, þe [*pureste* on] erþe,
B. 5.13   He preued þat þise pestilences were for *pure* synne,
B. 5.254   'Hastow pite on pouere men þat [for *pure* nede] borwe?'
B. 6.117   'Now by þe peril of my soule!' quod Piers al in *pure* tene,
B. 7.106   Hir penaunce and hir Purgatorie [vp]on þis [*pure*] erþe.
B. 7.119   And Piers for *pure* tene pulled it [asonder]
B.10.74   And prechen at Seint Poules, for *pure* enuye of clerkes,
B.10.83   Ne beþ plenteuouse to þe pouere as *pure* charite wolde,
B.10.320   Of þe pouere haue þei no pite, and þat is hir [*pure* chartre];
B.10.470   Into þe [parfit] blisse of Paradis for hir *pure* bileue,
B.11.156   Nouȝt þoruȝ preiere of a pope but for his *pure* truþe,
B.11.431   [To blame or] to bete hym þanne it were but *pure* synne.
B.13.166   Pope ne patriark, þat *pure* reson ne shal [þee] make
B.14.77   Weex þoruȝ plentee of payn and of *pure* sleuþe:
B.14.109   Ther þe poore dar plede and preue by *pure* reson
B.14.193   And of *pure* pacience and parfit bileue.
B.14.260   Forþi [al] poore þat pacient is [of *pure* riȝt] may cleymen,
B.14.285   And Ioye to pacient pouere, *pure* spiritual helþe,
B.15.79   Moore for pompe þan for *pure* charite; þe peple woot þe soþe.
B.15.598   And þoruȝ his pacience hir power to *pure* noȝt he brouȝte:
B.16.8   Pacience hatte þe *pure* tree and [pouere] symple of herte,
B.16.18   'Piers þe Plowman!' quod I þo, and al for *pure* Ioye
B.16.86   And Piers for *pure* tene þat a pil he [l]auȝte;
B.16.220   Thus in þre persones is parfitliche [*pure*] manhede,
B.17.343   And ben inpacient in hir penaunce, *pure* reson knoweþ
B.19.194   Paieþ parfitly as *pure* truþe wolde.
C. 1.97   Is þe professioun and *puyr* ordre that apendeth to knyghtes
C. 2.10   She was purfiled [with] pelure, non *puyrere* on erthe,
C. 3.101   And haue here penaunce on *puyre* erthe and nat þe peyne of helle.

C. 3.349   In his pay and in his pite and in his *puyr* treuthe,
C. 4.91   And profrede pees a present al of *puyre* golde.
C. 5.115   And preuede þat this pestelences was for *puyre* synne
C. 5.166   Of þe pore haueth thei no pite and þat is here *puyre* chartre.
C. 6.172   That he haue pite on me, p[u]tou[r], of his *puyr* mercy,
C. 8.124   Quod [Peres] þe [plouhman] al in *puyre* tene:
C. 9.186   Here penance and here purgatorie vppon this *puyre* erthe
C.11.54   And prech[en] at seynt poules, [for] *puyr* enuye of clerkes,
C.11.63   Ne parteth with þe pore as *puyr* charite wolde,
C.12.196   And for here pacience be ypresed as for *puyr* martir
C.13.93   So þe pore of *puyr* reuthe may parforme þe lawe
C.15.135   And preueth by *puyre* skile inparfyt alle thynges–
C.15.285   There þe pore dar plede and preue by *puyr* resoun
C.16.100   Forthy alle pore þat pacient is of *puyr* rihte may claymen
C.16.154   That *puyre* pouerte and pacience was a louh lyuynge on erthe,
C.17.70   That pore peple by *puyre* riht here part myhte aske.
C.17.306   And her power thorw his pacience to *puyr* nauht brouhte.
C.19.323   And be inpacient in here penaunc[e], *puyr* resoun knoweth
C.20.190   Into pees and pyte of his *puyr* grace.
C.21.194   Payeth parfitly as *puyr* treuthe wolde.

pure adv *pure adv.*   B 5; C 6   puyr (3)   puyre (3)
B. 5.404   Goddes peyne and his passion [*pure*] selde þenke I on.
B.11.195   Ac for þe pouere I shal paie, and *pure* wel quyte hir trauaille
B.11.249   Was a *pure* pouere maide and to a pouere man ywedded.
B.11.276   Whoso wole þe *pure* parfit moot possession forsake
B.15.201   For þer are [*pure*] proude herted men, pacient of tonge
C. 3.383   Ac þe moste partie of peple *puyr* indirect semeth
C. 7.20   Goddes payne and his passioun is *puyre* selde in my thouhte.
C.12.135   Was a *puyre* pore mayde and to a pore man ywedded.
C.15.305   Then aren hit *puyre* pore thynges in purgatorie or in hell.
C.17.76   And ȝut is þe printe *puyr* trewe and parfitliche ygraue.
C.18.102   Bothe parfit and inparfit.' *Puyr* fayn y wolde

pured ptp *puren v.*   A 1 purid; B 1
A. 4.82   And profride pees a presaunt al of *purid* gold;
B. 4.95   And profrede Pees a present al of *pure[d]* golde.

pureliche adv *pureli adv.*   B 5 purely (2) pureliche (3); C 3 puyrliche (1) puyrlich (1) puyrliche (1)
B.10.319   In many places þer þei [persons ben, þe þei *purely*] at ese,
B.13.196   And þe poore widewe [*purely*] for a peire of mytes
B.13.259   Til pride be *pureliche* fordo, and [þat] þoruȝ payn defaute.
B.16.51   And palleþ adoun þe pouke *pureliche* þoruȝ grace
B.17.176   The pawme is *pureliche* þe hand, haþ power by hymselue
C.15.229   Til pruyde be *puyreliche* fordo and þat thorw payn defaute:
C.18.233   And as thre persones palpable is *puy[r]lich* bote o mankynde,
C.19.141   The paume is *puyrliche* the hand and hath power by hymsulue

purfil n *purfile n.*   A 2 purfil (1) purfile (1); B 2 purfil (1) purfill (1); C 2 porfiel (1) purfyel (1)
A. 4.102   And pernelis *purfile* be put in hire hucche;
A. 5.26   And preyede pernel hire *purfil* to leue
B. 4.116   Til pernelles *purfill* be put in hire hucche,
B. 5.26   [And] preide Pernele hir *purfil* to le[u]e
C. 4.111   Tyl purnele *porfiel* be putte in here whicche
C. 5.128   He p[ra]yde p[ur]nele here *purfyel* to leue

purfiled ptp *purfiled ppl.*   A 1 ipurfilid; B 1; C 1
A. 2.9   *Ipurfilid* wiþ pelure, þe pureste [o]n erþe,
B. 2.9   *Purfiled* wiþ Pelure, þe [pureste on] erþe,
C. 2.10   She was *purfiled* [with] pelure, non puyrere on erthe,

purgatorie n *purgatorie n.*   A 7 purcatorie (6) purcatory (1); B 11; C 13 purgatorie (8) purgatory (1) purgatorye (4)
A. 2.68   Wiþ alle þe purtenaunce of *purcatorie* into þe pyne of helle;
A. 7.43   In a wel perilous place þat *purcatorie* hattiþ;
A. 8.11   Han pardoun þoruȝ *purcatorie* to passe wel sone,
A. 8.59   His pardoun in *purcatorie* wel [petit] is, I trowe,
A. 8.88   Here penaunce & here *purcatorie* vpon þis pur erþe.
A.11.256   I shal punisshen in *purcatory* or in þe put of helle
A.11.286   Wiþoute penaunce of *purcatorie* to haue paradis for euere.
B. 2.104   Wiþ alle þe [p]urtinaunces of *Purgatorie* into þe pyne of helle.
B. 6.44   In a [wel] perilous place [þat] *Purgatorie* hatte.
B. 7.11   Han pardon þoruȝ *purgatorie* to passen ful liȝtly,
B. 7.106   Hir penaunce and hir *Purgatorie* [vp]on þis [pure] erþe.
B. 9.79   Shul [purchace] penaunce in *purgatorie* but þei hem helpe.
B.10.375   "I shal punysshe in *purgatorie* or in þe put of helle
B.10.427   Wiþouten penaunce of *purgatorie*, to perpetuel blisse.
B.10.469   And passen *Purgatorie* penauncelees at hir hennes partyng
B.11.133   And putten hym after in prison in *purgatorie* to brenne;
B.15.346   And many a prison fram *purgatorie* þoruȝ hise preieres deliuereþ.
B.18.392   In my prisone *Purgatorie* til parce it hote.
C. 2.111   With alle þe [p]urtinaunc[e] of *purgatorye* and þe peyne of helle.'
C. 6.299   Shal parte with the in *purgatorye* and helpe paye thy dette

C. 7.117   To perpetuel payne or *purgatorie* a[s] wikke
C. 9.11   Haen pardon thorw *purgatorye* to passe ful lyhtly,
C. 9.186   Here penaunce and here *purgatorie* vppon this puyre erthe
C. 9.279   *Purgatorie* for thy paie O[r] perpetuel helle
C.11.31   Or of þe passioun of Crist or of *purgatorie* þe peynes,
C.11.295   And passen *purgatorie* penaunceles for here parfit bileue:
C.12.68   And potten hym aftur in prisoun in *purgatorie* to brenne
C.13.31   A[c] þe pore pacient *purgatorye* passeth
C.15.92   And apose hym what penaunce is and *purgatorie* on erthe
C.15.305   Then aren hit puyre pore thynges in *purgatorie* or in hell.
C.18.15   And solaceth alle soules sorwful in *purgatory*.'

purgen v *purgen v.(1)*   B 1; C 1   purge
B.15.567   And *purgen* hem of poison er moore peril falle.
C.17.232   And *purge* hem of þe olde poysen Ar more perel falle.

purid > pured; purnele > pernele

purpos n *purpos n.*   A 1; B 2; C 1
A. 9.115   To putte forþ sum *purpos* [to] prouen hise wittes.
B. 8.125   [To] pute forþ som *purpos* to preuen hise wittes,
B.10.119   Ymaginatif herafterward shal answere to [youre] *purpos*.
C.10.121   And potte forth som *purpos* to prouen his wittes,

purs n *purse n.*   A 1; B 4 purs (3) purses (1); C 4 pors (2) porse (1) purses (1)
A. 5.110   [And] as a l[e]þerene *purs* lollide his chekis.
B. 5.191   And [lik] a leþeren *purs* lolled hise chekes
B.13.300   Pouere of possession in *purs* and in cofre;
B.13.367   Or pryueliche his *purs* shook, vnpikede hise lokes.
B.20.219   In paltokes and pyked shoes, [*purses* and] longe knyues
C. 6.199   And as a letherne *pors* lollede his chekes
C. 6.266   Or priueliche his *pors* shoke, vnpiked his lokes.
C.13.49   The marchaunt mote forgo or moneye of his *porse*
C.22.219   In paltokes and pikede shoes, [*purses* and] longe knyues

pursueþ v *purseuen v.*   A 1 pursuide; B 9 pursue (1) pursued (4) pursueþ (4); C 8 pursue (1) pursuede (5) pursueth (2)
A. 5.75   To apeire hym be my power I *pursuide* wel ofte,
B. 3.241   And enformeþ pouere [peple] and *pursueþ* truþe:
B. 5.95   To apeire hym be my powe *pursued* wel ofte],
B.11.15   Pride of parfit lyuynge *pursued* hem boþe
B.11.62   And pouerte *pursued* me and putte me lowe.
B.11.186   In a pouere mannes apparaille *pursue[þ]* vs euere,
B.12.242   For *pursue* a pecok or a pehen to cacche,
B.17.308   For þer þat partie *pursueþ* þe [peel] is so huge
B.19.163   Peter parceyued al þis and *pursued* after,
B.19.430   A[c] wel worþe Piers þe plowman þat *pursueþ* god in doynge.
C.11.174   And pruyde-of-parfit-lyuynge *pursuede* me faste
C.12.14   And pouerte *pursuede* me and potte me to be lowe.
C.14.174   For *pursue* a pocok or a pohen to cacche
C.17.167   And *pursuede* to haue be pope, prince of holy chirche;
C.18.164   And *pursuede* hym priueliche and for pans hym bouhte–
C.19.288   The[r] þat partye *pursueth* the apeel is so huge
C.21.163   Peter perseyued al this and *pursuede* aftur,
C.21.430   Ac wel worth Peres the plouhman þat *pursueth* god in doyng[e],

pursward adv *purse n.*   C 1
C.Pr.101   A[c] for it profiteþ ȝow into *pursward* ȝe prelates soffren

purtinaunces n *purtenaunce n.sg.& pl.*   A 1 purtenaunce; B 1; C 2 purtinaunce (1) purtinaunces (1)
A. 2.68   Wiþ alle þe *purtenaunce* of purcatorie into þe pyne of helle;
B. 2.104   Wiþ alle þe [p]*urtinaunces* of Purgatorie into þe pyne of helle.
C. 2.111   With alle þe [p]*urtinaunc[e]* of purgatorye and þe peyne of helle.'
C.16.332   Pruyde with alle [þe] *purtinaunces* and pakketh hem togyderes

purtraye(n > portreye

purueie v *purveien v.*   B 2 purueie (1) purueiede (1)
B. 5.167   That no Prioresse were preest, for þat he [*purueiede*];
B.14.29   'And I shal *purueie* þee paast', quod Pacience, 'þouȝ no plouȝ erye,

put n *pit n. &> putten*   A 1; B 3 put (2) puttes (1); C 1 puttes
A.11.256   I shal punisshen in purcatory or in þe *put* of helle
B. 5.405   I visited neuere feble men ne fettred [men] in *puttes*.
B.10.375   "I shal punysshe in purgatorie or in þe *put* of helle
B.14.174   Ac poore peple, þi prisoners, lord, in þe *put* of meschief,
C. 9.72   As prisones in *puttes* and pore folk in cotes,

pute(n > putten

putour n *putour n.*   C 1
C. 6.172   That he haue pite on me, p[u]tou[r], of his puyr mercy,

putrie n *putrie n.*   C 1
C. 6.186   Of *put[rie]* and of paramours and proueden thorw speche

putten v *putten v.* A 19 put (4) putte (13) putten (2); B 39 put (7) pute (1)
puten (3) putte (18) putten (7) putteþ (2) yput (1) C 38 pot (3) potte
(19) potten (4) put (3) potte (7) putten (1) ypot (1)

A.Pr.20	Summe *putte* hem to plou3, plei3ede ful selde,
A.Pr.23	And summe *putte* hem to pride, aparailide hem þereaftir,
A.Pr.25	In preyours & penaunce *putten* hem manye,
A. 1.116	For pride þat he *put* out his peyne haþ non ende.
A. 2.168	Er he be *put* on þe pillorie, for any preyour, I hote.'
A. 3.73	Of þat þe pore peple shulde *putte* in here wombe.
A. 3.221	Þe prophet prechiþ it & *put* it in þe sauter:
A. 4.34	Þanne com pes into þe parlement & *putte* vp a bille
A. 4.64	Pees *putte* forþ his heued & his panne blody:
A. 4.102	And pernelis purfile be *put* in hire hucche;
A. 5.127	*Putte* hem in a pressour, & pynnede hem þereinne
A. 6.25	'Petir,' quaþ a plou3man and *putte* forþ his hed.
A. 7.95	My plou3pote shal be my pyk & *putte* at þe rotis,
A. 7.184	And pieris was proud þerof, & *putte* hem in office,
A. 9.95	And *putten* hem þere in penaunce wiþoute pite or grace,
A. 9.115	To *putte* forþ sum purpos [to] prouen hise wittes.
A.11.42	And *putte* forþ presumpcioun to proue þe soþe.
A.11.130	Plato þe poete, I *putte* hym ferst to boke;
A.12.112	To lyue as þat lord lykyþ þat lyf in hem *putte:*
B.Pr.20	Some *putten* hem to plou3, pleiden ful selde,
B.Pr.23	And somme *putten* hem to pride, apparailed hem þerafter,
B.Pr.25	In preieres and penaunc[e] *putten* hem manye,
B. 1.127	For pride þat he *putte* out his peyne haþ noon ende.
B. 2.49	And haue power to punysshe hem; þanne *put* forþ þi reson.
B. 2.207	Er he be *put* on þe Pillory for any preyere I hote.'_
B. 3.84	[Of] þat þe pouere peple sholde *putte* in hire wombe.
B. 3.234	The prophete precheþ [it] and *putte* it in þe Sauter:
B. 3.317	Ne *putte* hem in panel to doon hem pli3te hir truþe;
B. 4.47	[Th]anne com pees into [þe] parlement and *putte* [vp] a bille
B. 4.78	Pees *putte* forþ his heed, and his panne blody:
B. 4.116	Til pernelles purfill be *put* in hire hucche,
B. 5.211	*Putte* hem in a press[our] and pyn[ned] hem þerInne
B. 5.537	'Peter!' quod a Plowman, and *putte* forþ his hed:
B. 6.103	My plow[pote] shal be my pi[k] and [*putte* at] þe rotes,
B. 6.197	And [Piers was proud þerof] and *putte* hem [in office]
B. 8.105	And *putten* hem þer in penaunce wiþoute pite or grace],
B. 8.125	[To] *pute* forþ som purpos to preuen hise wittes,
B.10.56	And *puten* forþ presumpcion to preue þe soþe.
B.10.178	Plato þe poete, I *putte* [hym] first to boke;
B.10.325	And *puten* [hem] to hir penaunce, Ad pristinum statum ire;
B.11.62	And pouerte pursued me and *putte* me lowe.
B.11.133	And *putten* hym after in prison in purgatorie to brenne;
B.11.254	Ac pouerte god *putte* bifore and preised þe bettre:
B.11.419	The wisedom and þe wit of god, he was *put* fram blisse.
B.12.227	He is þe pies patron and *putteþ* it in hir ere
B.13.35	Pacience and I [prestly] were *put* to be [mettes],
B.13.176	Profitable to eiþer peple;' and *putte* þe table fro hym,
B.14.191	And *putten* of so þe pouke, and preuen vs vnder borwe.
B.14.208	Ther þe poore is *put* bihynde, and parauenture kan moore
B.14.246	For pouerte haþ but pokes to *putten* in hise goodes
B.14.272	And *put* hym to be pacient and pouerte weddeþ,
B.14.291	Selde is any poore *yput* to punysshen any peple.
B.15.63	[Adam and Eue *putte* out of Paradis]:
B.17.156	The paume for [he] *putteþ* forþ fyngres and þe fust boþe.
B.17.178	For [þe pawme] haþ power to *putte* out þe ioyntes
B.18.40	Tho *putte* hym forþ a p[e]lour bifore Pilat and seide,
B.18.52	And poison on a poole þei *putte* vp to hise lippes
B.19.67	To penaunce and to pouerte he moste *puten* hymseluen,
C.Pr.22	Somme *potte* hem to plogh, playde ful selde,
C.Pr.25	And summe *putte* hem to pruyde, [a]parayled hem þeraftir
C.Pr.27	In preiers and penaunc[e] *potten* hem mony,
C.Pr.172	And playde with somme perilously and *potte* hem þer hym lykede.
C. 2.52	And haue power to p[uny]schen hem; thenne *pot* forth thy resoun.
C. 2.219	Ar he be *put* on þe pylorye for eny preyere ich hote.'
C. 2.247	And *putte* hem thorw appeles in þe popes grace.
C. 3.83	With that þe pore peple sholde *potte* in here wombe.
C. 3.470	Ne *potte* [hem] in panele [to] do [hem] plihte here treuthe;
C. 4.45	Thenne cam p[ees] into [þe] parlement and *putte* vp a bille
C. 4.74	3ut pees *put* forth his heued and his panne blody:
C. 4.111	Tyl purnele porfiel be *putte* in here whicche
C. 5.171	And *potte* 3ow to 3oure penaunce, ad pristinum statum ire;
C. 6.219	*Potte* hem in [a] pressou[r] and pynne[d] hem þerynne
C. 7.182	'[Peter]! quod a [plouhman], and *potte* forth his heued,
C. 7.192	Profitable as for þe plouh a *potte* me to lerne
C. 8.197	Tho was [Peres] proud and *potte* hem alle a werke
C.10.121	And *potte* forth som purpos to prouen his wittes,
C.11.37	And *putten* forth presumpcioun to preue þe sothe.
C.11.118	Plato þe poete y *putte* hym furste to boke;
C.12.14	And pouerte pursuede me and *potte* me to be lowe.
C.12.68	And *potten* hym aftur in prisoun in purgatorie to brenne

C.12.141	Ac pouerte god *potte* byfore and preuede for þe betere:
C.13.8	For in greet pouerte he was *put*: a prince, as hit were,
C.13.227	The wisdom and the wit of god he was *pot* out of blisse.
C.15.40	Pacience and y [prestly weren] *pot* to be mettes
C.15.173	Profitable for bothe parties;' and *potte* þe boerd fro hym
C.15.234	Pruyde wolde *potte* hymsulf forth thogh no plough erye.
C.16.49	There þe pore is *potte* behynde and parauntur can more
C.16.86	For pouerte hath bote pokes to *potten* in his godes
C.16.112	And *potte* hym to be pacient and pouerte weddeth,
C.16.122	Al þat may *potte* of pruyde in place þer he regneth;
C.16.126	Selde is eny pore *ypot* to p[u]nesche eny peple.
C.16.225	*Potte* out of paradys Adam and Eue:
C.19.143	For þe paume hath power to *pu[t]te* out þe ioyntes
C.20.39	Thenne *potte* hym forth a pelour bifore pilatus and saide,
C.20.52	And with a pole poysen *potten* vp to his lippes
C.21.67	To penaunce and to pouerte he mot *putte* hymsuluen

puttes > put

Q

quake v *quaken v.* A 1; B 3 quake (2) quaked (1); C 4 quake (1) quaken (1) quakid (1) quoek (1)
A.11.46 Boþe for hungir & for þrest, & for chele *quak[e]*;
B.10.60 Boþe afyngred and afurst, and for chele *quake*;
B.18.248 *Quaked* as quyk þyng and al biquasshed þe roche.
B.20.200 And deeþ drogh neiȝ me; for drede gan I *quake*,
C.11.40 Ac þe carfole may crye and *quake* at þe ȝate,
C.20.63 The erthe toquasch[t]e and *quoek* as hit quyk were
C.20.257 *Quakid* as quyk thyng and a[l] toquasch[ed] þe roch[e].
C.22.200 And deth drow ney me; for drede gan y *quaken*

quantite n *quantite n.* B 1; C 1
B.19.374 That he ne halp a *quantite* holynesse to wexe,
C.21.374 That he ne halpe a *qua[n]tite* holinesse to wexe,

quarter n *quartere n.* A 2 quarter (1) quarteris (1); B 1 quarters; C 2 quarter (1) quarteres (1)
A. 4.45 And takiþ me but a taile for ten *quarteris* otis,
A. 5.131 Þe pound þat heo [payede] by peisid a *quarter* more
B. 4.58 And takeþ me but a taille for ten *quarters* Otes;
C. 4.61 And taketh me but a tayle for ten *quarteres* otes;
C. 6.223 The pound th[at] he payede by peysed a *quarter* more

quartron n *quartroun n.* B 1
B. 5.215 [Th]e pound þat she paied by peised a *quartron* moore

quaþ > quod

quaued v *quaven v.* B 1
B.18.61 The wal waggede and cleef and al þe world *quaued*.

queed n *quede n.(1)* B 1
B.14.190 [We] sholde take þe Acquitaunce as quyk and to þe *queed* shewen it:

queene n *quene n.(1)* C 1
C. 8.46 Or a knyhte [fram] a knaue or a quene fram a queene.

queynt > quenche

queynte adj *queinte adj. &> quenche* A 1 queyntere; C 2
A. 2.14 Þere nis no quen *queyntere* þat quyk is o lyue.
C. 4.161 For þe comune calde here *queynte* comune hore.
C.19.236 Ȝut wan he nat with wrong ne with *queynte* sleythes;

queyntely adv *queintlie adv.* B 1; C 1 queyntly
B.19.347 Shal be coloured so *queyntely* and couered vnder [oure] Sophistrie
C.21.347 Shal be coloured so *queyntly* and keuered vnder [o]ure sophistrie

queyntise n *queintise n.* B 2; C 2 queyntise (1) quentyse (1)
B.18.275 May no deeþ [þis lord] dere, ne no deueles *queyntise*,
B.19.351 Wiþ swiche colours and *queyntise* comeþ pride yarmed
C.20.297 May no deth this lord dere ne [n]o deueles *quentyse*
C.21.351 With such colours and *queyntis[e]* cometh pruyde yArmed

queyntly > queyntely

quelt ptp *quellen v.(1)* B 1
B.16.114 Quatriduanus *quelt* quyk dide hym walke.

quen > quene

quenche v *quenchen v.* B 5 queynt (1) quenche (1) quencheþ (3); C 5 queynte (1) quenche (1) quencheth (3)
B.17.205 God þat he grypeþ wiþ, and wolde his grace *quenche*.
B.17.259 For vnkyndenesse *quencheþ* hym þat he kan noȝt shyne
B.17.274 Thus is vnkyndenesse þe contrarie þat *quencheþ*, as it were,
B.17.348 That is coueitise and vnkyndenesse þat *quencheþ* goddes mercy;
B.18.346 And boþe quykne and quyte þat *queynt* was þoruȝ synne;
C.19.171 God þ[at] he gripeth [with] and wolde his grace *quenche*.
C.19.225 For vnkyndenesse *quencheth* hym þat he can nat shine
C.19.255 Thus is vnkyndenesse [the contrarie that] *quencheth*, as hit were,
C.19.328 That is coueytise and vnkyndenesse whiche *quencheth* godes mercy

C.20.391 And bothe quykie and quyte that *queynte* was thorw synne

quene n *quene n.(2)* A 1 quen; B 1; C 1
A. 2.14 Þere nis no *quen* queyntere þat quyk is o lyue.

B.13.169 Do kyng and *quene* and alle þe comune after
C. 8.46 Or a knyhte [fram] a knaue or a *quene* fram a queene.

quentyse > queyntise

queste n *queste n.* B 1; C 3 queste (2) questes (1)
B.20.162 Oon Tomme two-tonge, atteynt at ech [a q]ueste.
C. 2.113 And Peres þe Pardoner of paulines *queste*,
C.11.20 Thorw fallas and fals *questes* and thorw fikel speche.
C.22.162 Oen Tomme two-tonge, ateynt at vch [a q]ueste.

questions n *questioun n.* A 1 questiouns; B 1; C 1
A.11.58 Freris and faitours han founden vp suche *questiouns*
B.10.72 Freres and faitours han founde [vp] swiche *questions*
C.11.52 Freres and faytours haen founde vp suche *questions*

quiete n *quiete n.* B 1
B. 1.123 And [stable and stynte] and stonden in *quiete*.

quyk adj *quik adj.* A 1; B 5 quik (1) quyk (2) quyke (2); C 8 quyk (4) quyke (4)
A. 2.14 Þere nis no quen queyntere þat *quyk* is o lyue.
B.13.10 But *quik* he biqueþe [hem] auȝt [or sholde helpe] quyte hir dettes;
B.16.114 Quatriduanus quelt *quyk* dide hym walke.
B.18.248 Quaked as *quyk* þyng and al biquasshed þe roche.
B.19.53 And þo was he conquerour called of *quyke* and of dede,
B.19.196 And demen hem at domesday, boþe *quyke* and dede,
C. 9.21 And deme with hem at domesday bothe *quyke* and dede.
C.15.12 Bote *quyke* he byqu[e]th hem auht or wolde helpe quyte here dettes;
C.17.303 Quadriduanus coeld *quyk* dede hym walke.
C.18.144 Quadriduanus coeld, *quyk* dede hym rome.
C.20.63 The erthe toquasch[t]e and quoek as hit *quyk* were
C.20.257 Quakid as *quyk* thyng and a[l] toquasch[ed] þe roch[e].
C.21.53 And tho was he conquerour cald of *quyke* and of dede
C.21.196 And demen hem at domesday, bothe *quyke* and dede,

quik adv *quik adv.* B 2 quik (1) quyk (1); C 1
B.14.104 'Ye? quis est ille?' quod Pacience; '*quik*, laudabimus eum!
B.14.190 [We] sholde take þe Acquitaunce as *quyk* and to þe queed shewen it:
C.15.279 'Ȝe? quis est ille?' quod pacience; '*quik*, lauda[bi]mus eum!

quyke > quyk, quykne

quykne v *quiken v.* B 2; C 2 quyke (1) quykie (1)
B.15.23 'The whiles I *quykne* þe cors', quod he, 'called am I anima;
B.18.346 And boþe *quykne* and quyte þat queynt was þoruȝ synne;
C.16.183 And whiles y *quyke* þe cors ycald am y Anima;
C.20.391 And bothe *quykie* and quyte that queynte was thorw synne

quyte v *quiten v.* A 1 quyt; B 9 quyt (1) quyte (7) quyteþ (1); C 12 quyt (1) quite (1) quyte (7) quyten (1) quyteth (1) yquited (1)
A. 7.90 For þeiȝ I deiȝe today my dettis ben *quyt*;
B. 6.98 For þouȝ I deye today my dettes are *quyte*;
B.11.193 For youre frendes wol feden yow, and fonde yow to *quyte*
B.11.194 Youre festynge and youre faire ȝifte; ech frend *quyteþ* so ooþer.
B.11.195 Ac for þe pouere I shal paie, and pure wel *quyte* hir trauaille
B.13.10 But quik he biqueþe [hem] auȝt [or sholde helpe] *quyte* hir dettes;
B.16.262 And me þer[wiþ]', quod þat [wye]; 'may no wed vs *quyte*,
B.18.340 Ergo soule shal soule *quyte* and synne to synne wende,
B.18.346 And boþe quykne and *quyte* þat queynt was þoruȝ synne;
B.18.357 Graciousliche þi gile haue *quyt*: go gile ayein gile!
C. 4.98 So alle my claymes ben *quyt* by so þe kyng assente.'
C. 8.107 For thouh y dey today my dette[s ben] *yquited*;
C. 9.274 Thyn huyre, herde, as y hope, hath nat to *quyte* thy dette
C.12.105 For vch frende fedeth other and fondeth hou beste to *quite*
C.12.108 That louieth and leneth hem largeliche shal y *quyte*."
C.13.76 And ȝut more, to maken pees and *quyten* menne dettes
C.15.12 Bote quyke he byqu[e]th hem auht or wolde helpe *quyte* here dettes;
C.16.31 And [operis satisfaccio] for soules paieth and alle synnes *quyteth*.
C.18.278 And me þerwith', quod the weye; 'may no wed vs *quyte*
C.20.387 So þat lyf *quyte* lyf; þe olde lawe hit asketh.
C.20.388 Ergo soule shal soule *quyte* and synne to synne wende
C.20.391 And bothe quykie and *quyte* that queynte was thorw synne

quod v *quethen v.* A 105 quaþ (95) quod (10); B 302; C 302 quod (301) qvod (1)

A.1.12, A.1.41, A.1.44, A.1.50, A.1.73, A.1.127, A.1.129, A.2.15, A.2.154, A.3.50, A.3.80, A.3.101, A.3.109, A.3.162, A.3.215, A.3.217, A.4.3, A.4.4, A.4.6, A.4.16, A.4.74, A.4.83, A.4.91, A.4.100, A.4.117, A.4.148, A.4.151, A.4.155, A.4.157, A.5.103, A.5.105, A.5.114, A.5.150, A.5.152, A.5.153, A.5.154, A.6.20, A.6.25, A.6.43, A.6.44, A.6.115, A.6.116, A.6.117, A.6.119, A.7.3, A.7.7, A.7.23, A.7.25, A.7.26, A.7.38, A.7.52, A.7.109, A.7.121, A.7.152, A.7.156, A.7.158, A.7.188, A.7.198, A.7.213, A.7.215, A.7.237, A.7.241, A.7.243, A.7.259, A.7.262, A.7.264, A.8.89, A.8.97, A.8.104, A.8.118, A.8.122, A.8.124, A.8.145, A.9.14, A.9.16, A.9.24, A.9.33, A.9.48, A.9.63, A.9.64, A.9.65, A.9.67, A.9.69, A.9.105, A.10.1, A.10.25, A.10.27, A.11.5, A.11.13, A.11.104, A.11.114, A.11.165, A.11.182, A.11.225, A.11.232, A.11.235, A.12.1, A.12.23, A.12.28, A.12.30, A.12.51, A.12.62, A.12.69, A.12.81, A.12.89

B.Pr.160, B.Pr.167, B.Pr.202, B.1.12, B.1.43, B.1.46, B.1.52, B.1.75, B.1.138, B.1.140, B.2.19, B.2.50, B.2.193, B.3.51, B.3.59, B.3.91, B.3.112, B.3.120, B.3.175, B.3.228, B.3.230, B.3.332, B.3.337, B.4.3, B.4.4, B.4.6, B.4.16, B.4.87, B.4.96, B.4.104, B.4.113, B.4.134, B.4.156, B.4.169, B.4.182, B.4.185, B.4.192, B.4.194, B.5.90, B.5.126, B.5.128, B.5.137, B.5.182, B.5.198, B.5.230, B.5.231, B.5.233, B.5.237, B.5.258, B.5.260, B.5.271, B.5.300, B.5.302, B.5.303, B.5.367, B.5.378, B.5.392, B.5.441, B.5.532, B.5.537, B.5.556, B.5.557, B.5.630, B.5.631, B.5.632, B.5.634, B.5.639, B.5.641, B.6.3, B.6.7, B.6.21, B.6.23, B.6.24, B.6.37, B.6.57, B.6.117, B.6.129, B.6.167, B.6.171, B.6.173, B.6.202, B.6.212, B.6.229, B.6.231, B.6.253, B.6.257, B.6.259, B.6.275, B.6.278, B.6.280, B.7.107, B.7.115, B.7.122, B.7.136, B.7.140, B.7.142, B.7.168, B.8.18, B.8.20, B.8.28, B.8.37, B.8.57, B.8.59, B.8.72, B.8.73, B.8.74, B.8.76, B.8.78, B.8.115, B.9.1, B.9.25, B.9.26, B.10.5, B.10.13, B.10.152, B.10.162, B.10.238, B.10.336, B.10.337, B.10.349, B.10.352, B.10.377, B.11.25, B.11.28, B.11.34, B.11.37, B.11.38, B.11.42, B.11.44, B.11.53, B.11.71, B.11.85, B.11.86, B.11.87, B.11.89, B.11.91, B.11.107, B.11.123, B.11.140, B.11.171, B.11.380, B.11.383, B.11.387, B.11.411, B.11.435, B.11.438, B.11.439, B.12.1, B.12.23, B.12.29, B.12.170, B.12.277, B.12.280, B.12.282, B.12.295, B.13.51, B.13.52, B.13.56, B.13.78, B.13.103, B.13.104, B.13.106, B.13.116, B.13.119, B.13.123, B.13.131, B.13.136, B.13.137, B.13.140, B.13.172, B.13.183, B.13.188, B.13.224, B.13.313, B.13.315, B.14.1, B.14.16, B.14.29, B.14.36, B.14.51, B.14.98, B.14.102, B.14.104, B.14.274, B.14.275, B.14.276, B.14.277, B.14.278, B.14.323, B.14.325, B.14.326, B.14.332, B.14.334, B.15.16, B.15.22, B.15.23, B.15.40, B.15.50, B.15.52, B.15.149, B.15.152, B.15.165, B.15.195, B.15.196, B.15.197, B.15.198, B.16.1, B.16.4, B.16.10, B.16.12, B.16.13, B.16.18, B.16.24, B.16.25, B.16.53, B.16.67, B.16.151, B.16.176, B.16.180, B.16.257, B.16.258, B.16.259, B.16.261, B.16.262, B.17.1, B.17.10, B.17.17, B.17.26, B.17.48, B.17.77, B.17.81, B.17.93, B.17.134, B.17.355, B.18.21, B.18.27, B.18.28, B.18.46, B.18.47, B.18.50, B.18.57, B.18.127, B.18.142, B.18.151, B.18.176, B.18.186, B.18.188, B.18.203, B.18.232, B.18.237, B.18.273, B.18.293, B.18.295, B.18.309, B.18.317, B.18.400, B.18.409, B.18.416, B.18.418, B.19.10, B.19.12, B.19.26, B.19.207, B.19.209, B.19.225, B.19.252, B.19.314, B.19.317, B.19.319, B.19.354, B.19.355, B.19.381, B.19.383, B.19.391, B.19.393, B.19.396, B.19.403, B.19.409, B.19.419, B.19.451, B.19.477, B.20.74, B.20.92, B.20.140, B.20.153, B.20.186, B.20.188, B.20.189, B.20.207, B.20.208, B.20.221, B.20.268, B.20.316, B.20.318, B.20.332, B.20.338, B.20.341, B.20.356, B.20.357, B.20.358, B.20.362, B.20.380

C.Pr.138, C.Pr.184, C.Pr.210, C.1.12, C.1.41, C.1.44, C.1.72, C.1.116, C.1.137, C.1.139, C.1.203, C.2.18, C.2.53, C.2.207, C.3.63, C.3.119, C.3.149, C.3.157, C.3.221, C.3.256, C.3.284, C.3.286, C.3.341, C.3.344, C.3.417, C.3.485, C.3.489, C.4.3, C.4.4, C.4.6, C.4.13, C.4.16, C.4.33, C.4.83, C.4.92, C.4.99, C.4.108, C.4.131, C.4.134, C.4.176, C.4.179, C.4.183, C.4.190, C.5.26, C.5.89, C.5.102, C.5.104, C.5.182, C.6.12, C.6.62, C.6.91, C.6.105, C.6.164, C.6.173, C.6.206, C.6.234, C.6.235, C.6.237, C.6.253, C.6.286, C.6.331, C.6.339, C.6.355, C.6.358, C.7.8, C.7.55, C.7.177, C.7.182, C.7.200, C.7.283, C.7.284, C.7.285, C.7.287, C.7.292, C.7.305, C.8.1, C.8.5, C.8.7, C.8.19, C.8.21, C.8.35, C.8.56, C.8.91, C.8.124, C.8.136, C.8.144, C.8.160, C.8.164, C.8.167, C.8.169, C.8.177, C.8.208, C.8.222, C.8.235, C.8.237, C.8.261, C.8.263, C.8.265, C.8.269, C.8.296, C.8.300, C.8.302, C.9.160, C.9.281, C.9.289, C.9.312, C.10.20, C.10.32, C.10.41, C.10.56, C.10.58, C.10.70, C.10.71, C.10.72, C.10.74, C.10.76, C.10.111, C.10.128, C.10.151, C.10.152, C.11.5, C.11.11, C.11.78, C.11.90, C.11.103, C.11.104, C.11.111, C.11.139, C.11.184, C.11.187, C.11.193, C.11.303, C.11.304, C.11.309, C.12.1, C.12.18, C.12.19, C.12.24, C.12.32, C.12.41, C.12.58, C.12.75, C.12.163, C.13.197, C.13.205, C.13.219, C.13.241, C.13.245, C.14.1, C.14.110, C.14.199, C.14.202, C.14.204, C.15.57, C.15.84, C.15.93, C.15.110, C.15.111, C.15.123, C.15.127, C.15.128, C.15.137, C.15.153, C.15.156, C.15.170, C.15.177, C.15.181, C.15.182, C.15.193, C.15.195, C.15.232, C.15.245, C.15.246, C.15.250, C.15.272, C.15.279, C.16.114, C.16.115, C.16.116, C.16.117, C.16.118, C.16.160, C.16.165, C.16.167, C.16.174, C.16.179, C.16.179, C.16.202, C.16.212, C.16.214, C.16.286, C.16.316, C.16.337, C.16.339, C.16.340, C.17.4, C.17.39, C.17.40, C.17.125, C.18.1, C.18.9, C.18.25, C.18.100, C.18.151, C.18.155, C.18.168, C.18.183, C.18.184, C.18.186, C.18.187, C.18.191, C.18.196, C.18.198, C.18.238, C.18.240, C.18.273, C.18.274, C.18.275, C.18.277, C.18.278, C.19.1, C.19.4, C.19.11, C.19.18, C.19.26, C.19.27, C.19.46, C.19.78, C.19.83, C.19.108, C.19.335, C.20.19, C.20.26, C.20.27, C.20.46, C.20.47, C.20.50, C.20.57, C.20.90, C.20.130, C.20.145, C.20.154, C.20.179, C.20.191, C.20.193, C.20.208, C.20.241, C.20.246, C.20.295, C.20.323, C.20.325, C.20.328, C.20.343, C.20.360, C.20.370, C.20.443, C.20.452, C.20.459, C.20.461, C.21.10, C.21.12, C.21.26, C.21.207, C.21.209, C.21.225, C.21.252, C.21.314, C.21.317, C.21.319, C.21.354, C.21.355, C.21.381, C.21.383, C.21.391, C.21.393, C.21.396, C.21.403, C.21.409, C.21.419, C.21.451, C.21.477, C.22.74, C.22.92, C.22.140, C.22.153, C.22.186, C.22.188, C.22.189, C.22.207, C.22.208, C.22.221, C.22.268, C.22.316, C.22.318, C.22.332, C.22.338, C.22.341, C.22.356, C.22.357, C.22.358, C.22.362, C.22.380

quodlibet n *quodlibet n.* B 1; C 1

B.15.382 And answere to Argument3 and [assoile] a *Quodlibet*–

C.17.115 That sholde þe seuene ars conne and assoile a *quodlibet*

quoek > quake

quoer n *quer n.* C 1

C. 5.60 And in *quoer* and in kyrkes Cristes mynistres:

qvod > quod

R

raap > repe; rad(de- > reden

radegundes n *redgounde n.* B 1; C 1 Radegoundes
B.20.83   Rewmes and *Radegundes* and roynouse sca[ll]es,
C.22.83   Reumes and *Radegoundes* and roynouse sca[ll]es,

ragamoffyn n *ragamuffin n.* C 1
C.20.281   Ac [r]ise vp, *Ragamoffyn*, and [r]eche me alle þe barres

rage n *rage n.* C 1
C.13.129   Thus rechelesnesse in a *rage* aresenede clergie

rageman n *rageman n.* A 1; B 2; C 2 Rageman (1) ragman (1)
A.Pr.72   And rauȝte wiþ his *rageman* ryngis & brochis.
B.Pr.75   And rauȝte with his *Rageman* ryngges and broches.
B.16.89   To go robbe þat *Rageman* and reue þe fruyt fro hym.
C.Pr.73   And raughte with his *Rageman* Rynges and Broches.
C.18.121   To go ransake þat *ragman* and reue hym of his apples

raggede adj *raggede adj.* A 1 raggit; B 2; C 2 ragged (1) raggede (1)
A.10.124   Out of a *raggit* rote and a rouȝ brere
B.11.34   'Ye? recche þee neuere', quod Rechelesnesse, stood forþ in *raggede* cloþes;
B.15.226   Riden and rennen in *raggede* wedes
C.11.193   'Ȝe? reche þe neuere,' quod rechelesnesse, stod forth in *ragged* clothes;
C.16.351   Ryden and rennen in *raggede* clothes

ragman > rageman

ray adj *raie adj.* A 1
A. 3.271   Ne no *ray* robe [wiþ] riche pelure.

rayes n *raie n.(2)* A 1; B 1; C 1
A. 5.125   Among þe riche *rayes* I rendrit a lessoun;
B. 5.209   Among þe riche *Rayes* I rendred a lesson;
C. 6.217   Amongus the ryche *rayes* y rendrede a lessoun,

raik n *raike n.* B 1; C 1 reik
B.Pr.201   For hadde ye rattes youre [*raik*] ye kouþe noȝt rule yowselue.
C.Pr.219   For hadde ȝe ratones ȝoure [*reik*] ȝe couthe nat reule ȝowsuluen.'

raike v *raiken v.* A 1; B 1
A. 4.153   Ac redily, resoun, þou shalt not [*raike*] henne,
B. 4.190   Ac redily, Reson, þow shalt noȝt [*raike* henne];

rayme v *reimen v.* C 1
C.13.96   As al þat þe ryche may *rayme* and rihtfuly dele

raynald > reynald; rayne > reyn; rayneth > reyneþ

raise v *reisen v.(1)* A 1 reisen; B 1
A.11.161   Nigromancie & per[i]mansie þe pouke to *reisen*;
B.10.218   Nigromancie and perimancie þe pouke to *raise*];

rakiere n *rakere n.* A 1; B 1; C 1 rakeare
A. 5.164   A ribibour, a ratoner, & a *rakiere* of chepe;
B. 5.314   A Ribibour, a Ratoner, a *Rakiere* of Chepe,
C. 6.371   A rybibour, a ratoner, a *rakeare* and his knaue,

ran > rennen

randolf n prop *n.i.d.* A 1; B 1; C 1
A. 2.75   *Randolf* þe reue of rutelondis sokne,
B. 5.395   But I kan rymes of Robyn hood and *Randolf* Erl of Chestre,
C. 7.11   Y can rymes of robyn hode and of *randolf* Erle of Chestre

rang > rongen

ransake v *ransaken v.* C 1
C.18.121   To go *ransake* þat ragman and reue hym of his apples

rape n *rape n.(1)* &> rapiþ A 1; B 1; C 1
A. 5.174   Þo risen vp in *rape* & ro[wn]eden togideris,
B. 5.325   T[h]o risen vp in *Rape* and rouned togideres
C. 6.383   Tho rysen vp [in] *rape* and rounned togyderes

raped(e > rapiþ

---

rapeliche adv *rapeli adv.* B 2 rapely (1) rapeliche (1); C 2 raply (1) rappliche (1)
B.16.273   *Rapeliche* renne forþ þe riȝte wey [we] wente.
B.17.52   Ridynge ful *rapely* þe righte wey we yeden,
C.18.289   *Rappliche* renne þe riȝt way we wente.
C.19.50   Rydynge ful *raply* þe rihte way we ȝeden,

rapiþ v *rapen v.(1)* A 3 rape (2) rapiþ (1); B 4 rape (3) raped (1); C 5 rape (4) rapede (1)
A. 4.7   '*Rape* þe to riden, & resoun þat þou fecche.
A. 4.23   And resoun wiþ hym rit & *rapiþ* hym [swyþe].
A. 7.110   'But ȝe rise þe raþere, & *rape* ȝow to werche,
B. 4.7   '*Rape* þee to ryde and Reson [þat] þow fecche.
B. 5.392   'What! awake, renk!' quod Repentaunce, 'and *rape* þee to shryfte!'
B. 6.118   'But ye arise þe raþer and *rape* yow to werche
C. 4.7   '*Rape* the to ryde and resoun þat thow [f]lec[c]he.
C. 5.102   'Y rede the,' quod resoun tho, '*rape* þe to bigynne
C. 7.8   'What! awake, renke!' quod repentaunce, 'and *rape* [þe] to shryfte.'
C. 8.125   'But ȝe aryse þe rather and *rape* ȝow to worche
C.19.79   And *rapede* hym to ryde the rihte way to Ierusalem.

raply > rapeliche

rappen v *rappen v.(1)* A 1 rappe; B 1; C 1 rappe
A. 1.93   And riden & *rappe* doun in reaumes aboute,
B. 1.95   Riden and *rappen* doun in Reaumes aboute,
C. 1.91   Rydon and *rappe* adoun in reumes aboute

rappliche > rapeliche; rat > reden

raþe adv *rathe adv.* A 10 raþe (2) raþer (1) raþere (6) raþest (1); B 26 raþe (3) raþer (20) raþest (3); C 29 rathe (2) rather (20) rathest (5) raþer (2)
A. 3.55   Let not þi left hond, late ne *raþe*,
A. 4.4   'Nay be [Crist],' quaþ consience, 'cunge me *raþere*!
A. 4.5   But resoun rede me þerto [*raþer*] wole I deiȝe.'
A. 5.183   And whoso repentiþ *raþest* shulde rise aftir
A. 7.110   'But ȝe rise þe *raþere*, & rape ȝow to werche,
A. 9.30   For ȝif he ne arise þe *raþere* & [rauȝte þe stere],
A. 9.66   'I haue sewide þe seuen ȝer; seiȝe þou me no *raþere*?'
A.10.13   And seruiþ þis lady lelly boþe late & *raþe*.
A.11.285   A robbere hadde remission *raþere* þanne þei alle,
A.11.307   Arn none *raþere* yrauisshid fro þe riȝte beleue
B. 3.73   Lat noȝt þi left half, late ne *raþe*,
B. 4.4   'Nay, by crist!' quod Conscience; 'congeye me [*raþer*]!
B. 4.5   But Reson rede me þerto *raþer* wol I deye.'
B. 5.260   'Now [but þow repente þe *raþer*', quod Repentaunce,
B. 5.280   Ne hadde repentaunce þe *raþer* reconforted hym in þis manere:
B. 5.334   And whoso repente[þ] *raþest* sholde aryse after
B. 6.118   'But ye arise þe *raþer* and rape yow to werche
B. 8.34   For if he ne arise þe *raþer* and rauȝte þe steere
B. 8.75   'I haue sued þee seuen yeer; seye þow me no *raþer*?'
B. 9.13   To seruen þis lady leelly, boþe late and *raþe*.
B.10.149   As longe as I lyue, boþe late and *raþe*,
B.10.426   A Robbere was yraunsoned *raþer* þan þei alle,
B.10.463   Arn none *raþer* yrauysshed fro þe riȝte bileue
B.11.77   *Raþer* þan to baptiȝe barnes þat ben Catecumelynges.
B.12.215   *Raþer* þan þat ooþer þeef, þouȝ þow woldest appose,
B.12.234   *Raþer* þan his likame alogh; lewed asken þus clerkes.
B.13.24   And for Conscience of Clergie spak I com wel þe *raþer*.
B.13.85   [And appose hym] what penaunce is, of which he preched *raþer*.'
B.14.108   And þat at þe rekenyng in Arrerage fel *raþer* þan out of dette.
B.14.204   Ac wiþ richesse þ[o] Ribaud[es] *raþest* men bigileþ.
B.14.210   Than richesse or reautee, and *raþer* yherd in heuene.
B.14.216   A[c] pride in richesse regneþ *raþer* þan in pouerte;
B.15.81   And reuerencen þe riche *raþer* for hir siluer:
B.15.228   Ac in riche robes *raþest* he walkeþ.
B.15.342   Ac Religiouse þat riche ben sholde *raþer* feeste beggeris
B.17.70   And but he hadde recouerer þe ra[þ]er þat rise sholde he neuere.
C.Pr.117   God was wel þe wrother and took þe *raþer* vengeance.
C. 1.143   Dey *rather* þen do eny dedly synne:
C. 4.4   'Nay, by Crist!' quod Consience, 'congeie me [*rather*]!
C. 4.5   But resoun rede me þertyl *rather* wo[l] y dey.'

542

C. 6.290   Thow were such as thow sayst; y sholde *rather* s[t]erue:
C. 6.392   And hoso repente[th] *rathest* sholde aryse aftur
C. 7.209   That is to sey sothly ʒe sholde *rather* deye
C. 8.44   He worth *rather* reseyued and reuerentloker s[e]tte:
C. 8.125   'But ʒe aryse þe *rather* and rape ʒow to worche
C. 9.123   A reuerenseth hym ryht nauht, no *rather* then another:
C. 9.134   Ryht so, ʒe ryche, ʒut *rather* ʒe sholde
C. 9.148   Where he may *rathest* haue a repaest or a ronde of bacoun,
C.10.54   For *rather* haue we no reste til we restitue
C.10.73   'Y haue sued the seuen ʒer; saw thow me no *rather*?'
C.10.140   To serue þat lady leely bot[h] late and *rathe*.
C.11.27   And þat is no riht ne resoun for *rather* me sholde
C.11.87   As longe as y lyue, bothe late and *rathe*,
C.11.258   A robbare was yraunsomed *rather* then thei alle,
C.11.289   Aren noen *rather* yraueschid fro þe rihte bileue
C.12.223   And þat *rathest* rypeth rotieth most sonnest;
C.13.32   *Rather* then þe ryche thogh they renne at ones.
C.13.186   That thow ne reul[e]st *rather* renkes then other bestes.
C.14.154   *Rather* then þat oþer [theef], thogh thow woldest apose,
C.16.45   Ac with rychesse tho rybaudes *rathest* men bigileth.
C.16.51   Then rychesse or ryalte and *rather* yherde in heuene.
C.16.57   And pruyde in rychesse regneth *rather* then in pouerte;
C.16.240   And reuerence þe ryche þe *rather* for here suluer
C.16.353   Ac in riche robes *rathest* he walketh,
C.19.69   And bote he hadde recouerer the *raþer* þat ryse sholde he neuere

raton n *ratoun n. cf. rattes* B 8 Raton (3) Ratons (5); C 8 raton (2)
    ratones (5) ratoun (1)
B.Pr.146   Wiþ þat ran þer a route of *Ratons* at ones
B.Pr.158   A *Raton* of renoun, moost renable of tonge,
B.Pr.167   And riʒt so', quod þat *Raton*, 'Reson me sheweþ
B.Pr.175   Al þ[e] route of *Ratons* to þis reson assented.
B.Pr.177   Ther ne was *Raton* in þe route, for al þe Reaume of Fraunce,
B.Pr.184   And to þe route of *Ratons* reherced þise wordes:
B.Pr.197   For may no renk þer reste haue for *Ratons* by nyʒte,]
B.Pr.199   And also ye route of *Ratons* rende mennes cloþes
C.Pr.167   Than ran þer a route of *ratones* [at ones]
C.Pr.178   A *ratoun* of renown, moste resonable of tounge,
C.Pr.184   [Ryʒt so,'quod þe *raton*, 'reson me sheweth
C.Pr.192   Alle th[e] route of *ratones* to þis resoun assentide;
C.Pr.194   Ther ne was [raton in] þe route, for al þe reame of Fraunce,
C.Pr.201   And to þe route of *ratones* rehersede thise wordes:
C.Pr.217   And [ʒ]e route of *ratones* of reste men awake
C.Pr.219   For hadde ʒe *ratones* ʒoure [reik] ʒe couthe nat reule ʒowsuluen.'

ratoner n *ratonere n.* A 1; B 1; C 1
A. 5.164   A ribibour, a *ratoner*, & a rakiere of chepe,
B. 5.314   A Ribibour, a *Ratoner*, a Rakiere of Chepe,
C. 6.371   A rybibour, a *ratoner*, a rakeare and his knaue,

ratoun > raton

rattes n *rat n. cf. raton* B 1
B.Pr.201   For hadde ye *rattes* youre [raik] ye kouþe noʒt rule yowselue.

rau(ghte -ʒte -hte > rechen

raunsone v *raunsounen v.* B 3 raunsone (1) raunsoned (1) yraunsoned (1);
    C 3 raunsome (1) yraunsomed (2)
B.10.426   A Robbere was *yraunsoned* raþer þan þei alle,
B.17.307   Be *raunsoned* for his repentaunce þer alle reson hym dampneþ.
B.18.349   But by right and by reson *raunsone* here my liges:
C.11.258   A robbare was *yraunsomed* rather then thei alle,
C.19.287   Be *yraunsomed* for his repentaunce þer alle resoun hym dampneth.
C.20.395   Bote [by] riht and [by] resoun *raunsome* here my lege[s]:

raunsoun n *raunsoun n.* B 1
B.18.352   To recouere hem þoruʒ *raunsoun* and by no reson ellis,

raued v *raven v.(2)* B 1
B.15.10   That folk helden me a fool; and in þat folie I *raued*

raueners n *ravinour n.* C 2 raueners (1) rauenours (1)
C.17.43   And refuse reuerences and *raue[n]ers* offrynges.
C.17.47   Wolde religious refuse *rauenours* Almesses.

raueschede > rauysshed

rauest v *raven v.(1)* B 1 rauestow; C 1
B.18.188   'What, *rauestow*?' quod Rightwisnesse, 'or þow art right dronke?
C.20.193   'Rauest thow?' quod rihtwisnesse, 'or thow art riht dronke!

rauysshed v *ravishen v.* A 2 rauisshide (1) yrauisshid (1); B 5 rauysshed
    (3) rauysshede (1) yrauysshed (1); C 5 raueschede (3) rauysched (1)
    yraueschid (1)
A. 4.36   And how he *rauisshide* rose, reynaldis loue,
A.11.307   Arn none raþere *yrauisshid* fro þe riʒte beleue
B. 2.17   Hire array me *rauysshed*; swich richesse sauʒ I neuere.

B. 4.49   And how he *rauysshede* Rose, Reignaldes looue,
B.10.463   Arn none raþer *yrauysshed* fro þe riʒte bileue
B.11.7   [For] I was *rauysshed* riʒt þere; Fortune me fette
B.19.52   That he naroos and regnede and *rauysshed* helle.
C. 2.16   Here aray with here rychesse *rauesschede* my herte;
C. 4.47   And how he *rauesschede* Rose the ryche wydewe by nyhte
C.11.166   For y was *rauysched* rihte there; fortune me fette
C.11.289   Aren noen rather *yraueschid* fro þe rihte bileue
C.21.52   That he ne aroos and regnede and *rauesschede* helle.

raxed v *rasken v.* B 1
B. 5.391   *Raxed* and [remed] and rutte at þe laste.

raxlede v *raxlen v.* C 1
C. 7.7   R[a]xlede and r[e]mede and rotte at þe laste.

realte > reautee

reaume n *reaume n.* A 13 reaum (4) reaume (5) reaumes (2) reumes (1)
    rewme (1); B 20 Reames (1) Reaume (9) Reaumes (3) Reawme (1)
    Reme (3) reume (2) reumes (1); C 23 reame (1) reume (11) reumes (7)
    rewme (4)
A. 1.93   And riden & rappe doun in *reaumes* aboute,
A. 3.142   Þere she is wel wiþ þe king wo is þe *reaume*,
A. 3.195   Þat is þe riccheste *reaume* þat re[yn] ouer[houiþ].
A. 3.196   It becom[iþ] a king þat kepiþ a *reaume*
A. 3.261   Þat resoun shal regne & *reumes* gouerne,
A. 4.9   For he shal rewele my *reaume* & rede me þe beste
A. 4.121   Þat I were king wiþ croune to kepe a *reaume*,
A. 4.149   'But I reule þus þi *reaum* rend out my ribbes,
A. 8.10   And r[iʒt]fulliche in *reaum* rewliþ þe peple
A. 9.99   And rewele þe *reaum* be red of hem alle,
A.10.134   Þei be þe riccheste of *reaumes* & þe rote of dowel.
A.11.267   For to reule his *reaum* riʒt at his wille;
A.12.113   Furst to rekne Richard, kyng of þis *rewme*,
B.Pr.177   Ther ne was Raton in þe route, for al þe *Reaume* of Fraunce,
B. 1.95   Riden and rappen doun in *Reaumes* aboute,
B. 3.153   Ther she is wel wiþ þe kyng wo is þe *Reaume*,
B. 3.208   That is þe richeste *Reaume* þat reyn ouerhoueþ.
B. 3.209   It bicomeþ a kyng þat kepeþ a *Reaume*
B. 3.285   That Reson shal regne and *Reaumes* gouerne,
B. 3.298   And ouer lordes lawes [ledeþ] þe *Reaumes*.
B. 4.9   For he shal rule my *Reaume* and rede me þe beste
B. 4.138   That I were kyng with coroune to kepen a *Reaume*,
B. 4.186   'But I rule þus youre *Reaume* rende out my guttes–
B. 5.11   And how Reson gan arayen hym al þe *Reaume* to preche;
B. 7.10   And riʒtfully in *Rem[e]* rulen þe peple
B. 8.109   And rule þe *Reme* by [rede of hem alle],
B.10.77   In Religion and in al þe *Reme* amonges riche and pouere
B.10.386   [To rule þe *reume* and riche to make];
B.15.508   And þat is rouþe for riʒtful men þat in þe *Reawme* wonyen,
B.15.525   And for þe riʒt of al þis *reume* and alle reumes cristene.
B.15.525   And for þe riʒt of al þis reume and alle *reumes* cristene.
B.17.3   To rule alle *Reames* wiþ; I bere þe writ [riʒt] here.'
B.19.478   And rule þi *reaume* in reson [as right wol and] truþe
C.Pr.194   Ther ne was [raton in] þe route, for al þe *reame* of Fraunce,
C. 1.91   Rydon and rappe adoun in *reumes* aboute
C. 3.191   Ther she is wel with eny kyng wo is þ[e] *rewme*
C. 3.204   Ther ne is Cite vnder sonne ne noon so ryche *reume*
C. 3.255   A[t] Concience þat coueiteth to conquere a *reume*.
C. 3.265   Hit bycometh for a kyng þat shal kepe a *reume*
C. 3.294   And þat is nother resoun ne ryhte ne [i]n no *rewme* lawe
C. 3.438   That resoun shal regne and *reumes* gouerne
C. 4.9   For he shal reulen my *rewme* and rede me þe beste
C. 4.135   That y were kyng with c[r]oune to kepe [a] *reume*,
C. 4.180   'But [y] reule thus alle *reumes* reuet[h] me my syhte,
C. 4.182   Withouten mercement or manslauht amende alle *reumes*.'
C. 5.74   For the ryhte of this *reume* ryden aʒeyn oure enemyes
C. 5.114   Resoun reuerentliche tofore al þe *reume* prechede
C. 5.125   How resoun radde al the *reume* to heuene.
C. 5.190   Is cause of alle combraunc[e] to confounde a *reume*.'
C. 9.10   And ryhtfulliche in *reumes* ruylen þe comune
C.10.105   And reule alle *reumes* by here thre wittes
C.11.57   In religion and in al þe *reume* amongus riche and pore
C.11.212   To reule [þe] *reum[e]* and ryche to make
C.17.259   And þat is reuthe for rihtfole men þat in þ[e] *reume* wonyeth
C.19.3   To reule alle *reumes* þerwith in riʒhte and in resoun.
C.21.478   And rewle thy *rewme* in resoun [as] riht w[o]l and treuthe,

reautee n *realte n.(1)* A 1 realte; B 2; C 1 ryalte
A.11.228   Ne ricchesse, ne rentis, ne *realte* of lordis.
B.10.340   Ne richesse [ne rentes] ne *Reautee* of lordes.
B.14.210   Than richesse or *reautee*, and raþer yherd in heuene.
C.16.51   Then rychesse or *ryalte* and rather yherde in heuene.

reawme > reaume; rebaudes > ribaud

543

rebuken v *rebuken v.* B 7 rebuked (4) rebukede (1) rebuken (1) yrebuked (1); C 7 rebuke (2) rebuked (2) rebuken (2) rebuketh (1)
B. 5.364 And Repentaunce riȝt so *rebuked* hym þat tyme:
B.11.131 A[c] reson shal rekene wiþ hym [and *rebuken* hym at þe laste,
B.11.373 [Th]anne I *rebukede* Reson and riȝt til hym I seyde,
B.11.429 For þouȝ Reson *rebuked* hym þanne [reccheþ hym neuere;
B.11.438 Why ye wisse me þus', quod I, 'was for I *rebuked* Reson.'
B.14.162 Afurst soore and afyngred, and foule *yrebuked*
B.20.63 [Th]an to lyue lenger siþ [Leute] was so *rebuked*
C.Pr.110 And chastisid hem noght þerof and nolde noght *rebuken* hem
C. 5.82 Forthy *rebuke* me ryhte nauhte, resoun, y ȝow praye,
C.12.66 A[c] reson shal rekene with hym and *rebuken* hym at þe laste
C.13.236 For thogh resoun *rebuke* hym thenne recheth he neuere;
C.16.15 Afurste and afyngered and foule *rebuked*
C.20.352 Bote oure lord at þe laste lyares h[e] *rebuke[*th]
C.22.63 Then to lyue lengere sethe leautee was so *rebuked*

rebukynge ger *rebukinge ger.* B 1
B.12.218 And aresonedest Reson, a *rebukynge* as it were,

recche v *recchen v.(2)* A 2; B 10 recche (5) reccheþ (3) rekkeþ (1) rouȝte (1); C 13 reccheth (2) rech (1) reche (6) recheth (2) rekketh (1) rouhte (1)
A. 4.51 And seide, 'hadde I loue of my lord þe king, litel wolde I *recche*
A. 7.112 And þeiȝ ȝe deiȝe for doel þe deuil haue þat *recche*!'
B. 4.33 And bad Reson ryde faste and *recche* of hir neiþer.
B. 4.65 And seide, 'hadde I loue of my lord þe kyng litel wolde I *recche*
B. 6.120 And þouȝ ye deye for doel þe deuel haue þat *recch[e]*!'
B.11.34 'Ye? *recche* þee neuere', quod Rechelesnesse, stood forþ in raggede cloþes;
B.11.73 Riȝt so, by þe roode! *rouȝte* ye neuere
B.11.376 And Reson arated me and seide, '*recche* þee neuere
B.11.429 For þouȝ Reson rebuked hym þanne [*reccheþ* hym neuere;
B.15.177 'Of rentes n[e] of richesse *rekkeþ* he neuere,
B.18.2 As a recchelees renk þat [*reccheþ* of no wo],
B.19.448 He *reccheþ* riȝt noȝt of þe remenaunt.
C. 3.388 As rela[tifs] indirect *re[cc]heth* the[y] neuere
C. 4.34 Ryde forth, syre resoun, and *rech* nat of here tales
C. 4.69 'Hadde y loue of [my] lord lytel wolde y *reche*
C. 8.127 And thow ȝe deye for deul þe deuel haue þat *reche*!'
C. 9.101 *Reche* ȝe neuere, ȝe riche, Thouh suche lo[rell]es sterue.
C.11.193 'Ȝe? *reche* þe neuere,' quod rechelesnesse, stod forth in ragged cloþes;
C.12.4 'Rechelesnesse *reche* the neuere; By so thow riche were
C.12.21 Riht so, by þe rode, *rouhte* ȝe neuere
C.13.194 And resoun aresounede me and sayde, '*reche* þe neuere
C.13.236 For thogh resoun rebuke hym thenne *recheth* he neuere;
C.16.318 'Of rentes ne of rychesse *reccheth* he neuere;
C.20.2 As a recheles renk þat *recheth* nat of sorwe
C.21.448 He *rekketh* riht nauht of þe remenaunt.

recchelees adj *recheles adj.* A 2 reccheles; B 1; C 1 recheles
A.10.51 In rewele & in resoun, but *reccheles* it make.
A.10.106 Fro religioun to religioun, *reccheles* ben þei euere;
B.18.2 As a *recchelees* renk þat [reccheþ of no wo],
C.20.2 As a *recheles* renk þat recheth nat of sorwe

recchelesly adv *rechelesli adv.* B 1; C 2 rechelesliche
B.11.130 As a reneyed caytif *recchelesly* rennen aboute.
C.12.65 As a [reneyed] Caytyf [*rechelesliche* rennen aboute].
C.13.154 For out of resoun they ryde and *rechelesliche* t[a]ken on

receyue v *receiven v.* A 1 resceyueþ; B 5 receyue (4) receyued (1); C 11 receyue (2) receue (1) resceyue (1) resceyued (1) resceyuen (1) resceyueth (1) reseyued (1) reseyuen (1) reseue (1) resseyued (1)
A. 8.60 Þat any mede of mene men for motyng *resceyueþ*.
B.15.540 Is reuerenced er þe Roode, *receyued* for [þe] worþier
B.17.180 And *receyue* þat þe fyngres recheþ and refuse boþe
B.17.188 He may *receyue* riȝt noȝt; reson it sheweþ
B.17.193 I sholde *receyue* riȝt noȝt of þat I reche myghte;
B.19.259 And Registrer to *receyue* redde quod debes.
C. 3.500 Ac he þat resceyueth or rec[ett]eth here is rescetour of Gyle.'
C. 4.196 And *receyue* tho that resoun louede; and riht with þat y wakede.
C. 5.64 Redon and *resceyuen* þat resoun ouhte to spene\
C. 6.300 Yf he wiste thow were such when he *resseyued* thyn offrynge.
C. 8.44 He worth rather *reseyued* and reuerentloker s[e]tte:
C.17.42 Sholde *reseue* riht nauht but þat riht wolde
C.17.201 Is reuerenced byfore the rode and *resceyued* for the worthiore
C.19.145 And *receue* þat the fyngeres recheth and refuse, yf h[y]m liketh,
C.19.154 He may *resceyue* riht nauhte; resoun hit sheweth.
C.19.159 Y sholde *receyue* ryht nouht of þat y reche myhte;
C.21.259 And Registrer to *reseyuen* Redde quod debes.

recetteth v *recetten v.* C 1
C. 3.500 Ac he þat resceyueth or *rec[ett]eth* here is rescetour of Gyle.'

receue > receyue; rech > recche; reche > recche,rechen; recheles > recchelees; rechelesliche > recchelessly

rechelesnesse n *rechelenesse n.* B 1; C 8 rechelesnes (1) rechelesnesse (7)
B.11.34 'Ye? recche þee neuere', quod *Rechelesnesse*, stood forþ in raggede cloþes;
C.10.215 Withouten repentaunce of here *rechelesnesse* a rybaud þei engendrede.
C.11.193 'Ȝe? reche þe neuere,' quod *rechelesnesse*, stod forth in ragged clothes;
C.11.197 For *rechelesnesse* in his rybaud[i]e riht thus he saide:
C.11.272 Thus y, *rechelesnesse*, haue yrad registres and bokes
C.11.281 Sothly,' saide *rechelesnesse*, 'ȝe se by many euydences
C.12.4 '*Rechelesnesse* reche the neuere; By so thow riche were
C.12.69 And for his *rechelesnes* rewarde hym þere riht to þe day of dome
C.13.129 Thus *rechelesnesse* in a rage aresenede clergie

rechen v *rechen v.(1)* A 3 rauȝte; B 7 rauȝte (3) reche (2) rechen (1) recheþ (1); C 6 raughte (1) rauhte (1) reche (3) recheth (1)
A.Pr.72 And *rauȝte* wiþ his rageman ryngis & brochis.
A. 4.148 'Be hym þat [*rauȝte*] on þe rode,' quaþ resoun to þe king,
A. 9.30 For ȝif he ne arise þe raþere & [*rauȝte* þe stere],
B.Pr.75 And *rauȝte* with his Rageman rynges and broches.
B. 4.185 'By hym þat *rauȝte* on þe Rode!' quod Reson to þe kynge,
B. 8.34 For if he ne arise þe raþer and *rauȝte* þe steere
B.11.362 Ther neiþer burn ne beest may hir briddes *rechen*.
B.14.231 For his rentes ne wol nauȝt *reche* no riche metes to bigge;
B.17.180 And receyue þat þe fyngres *recheþ* and refuse boþe
B.17.193 I sholde receyue riȝt noȝt of þat I *reche* myghte;
C.Pr.73 And *raughte* with his Rageman Rynges and Broches.
C. 4.179 'By hym þat *rauhte* [on] þe rode,' quod resoun to the kyng,
C.16.72 For his rentes wol nat *reche* ryche metes to bugge;
C.19.145 And receue þat the fyngeres *recheth* and refuse, yf h[y]m liketh,
C.19.159 Y sholde receyue ryht nouht of þat y *reche* myhte;
C.20.281 Ac [r]ise vp, Ragamoffyn, and [r]*eche* me alle þe barres

recheth > recche,rechen

reclused ptp *reclusen v.* C 1
C. 4.116 And religious outryderes be *reclused* in here Cloistres

recomendeþ v *recommended v.* B 1; C 1 recomendeth
B.15.233 Riche men he *recomendeþ*, and of hir robes takeþ
C.16.358 Riche men a *recomendeth*, and of [here] robes taketh,

reconforted v *recomforten v.* B 1
B. 5.280 Ne hadde repentaunce þe raþer *reconforted* hym in þis manere:

record n *recorde n.* B 1; C 1
B.15.87 Ayein youre rule and Religion; I take *record* at Iesus
C. 3.344 'Relacioun rect,' quod Consience, 'is a *record* of treuthe–

recorden v *recorden v.* B 5 recorde (2) recordede (2) recorden (1); C 6 recorde (4) recordede (1) recorden (1)
B. 4.157 Alle riȝtfulle *recordede* þat Reson truþe tolde.
B. 4.172 And *recordede* þat Reson hadde riȝtfully shewed,
B.15.612 [*Recorden* it and rendren] it wiþ remissionem peccatorum
B.18.199 Ayeins Reson. [I], rightwisnesse, *recorde* þus wiþ truþe
B.18.330 [Al]þouȝ Reson *recorde*, and riȝt of myselue,
C. 3.471 But aftur þe dede þat is ydo the doom shal *recorde*.
C. 4.29 To take reed of resoun þat *recorde* sholde
C. 4.151 Ac al ryhtful *recordede* þat resoun treuthe sayde,
C.17.320 *Recorden* hit and re[n]d[r]en hit with remissionem peccatorum,
C.20.204 Aȝeynes resoun; y, rihtwysnesse, *recorde* [þus] with treuthe
C.20.373 Althouh resoun *record[e]*, and rihte of mysulue,

recouere v *recoveren v.(2)* B 3 recouere (2) recouerede (1); C 2 rekeuere (1) rekeuerede (1)
B.18.352 To *recouere* hem þoruȝ raunsoun and by no reson ellis,
B.19.161 Thus cam it out þat crist ouercoom, *recouerede* and lyuede:
B.19.245 And some to ryde and to *recouere* þat [vnriȝt]fully was wonne:
C.21.161 Thus cam hit out þat Crist ouerkam, *rekeuerede* and lyuede:
C.21.245 And somme to ryde & to *rekeuere* that vnrihtfulliche was wonne:

recouerer n *recoverer n.(1)* B 1; C 1
B.17.70 And but he hadde *recouerer* þe ra[þ]er þat rise sholde he neuere
C.19.69 And bote he hadde *recouerer* the raþer þat ryse sholde he neuere

recrayed ptp *recreien v.* A 1 recreiȝede; B 1
A. 3.238 Ac reddist þou neuere Regum, þou *recreiȝede* mede,
B. 3.259 Ac reddestow neuere Regum, þow *recrayed* Mede,

recreaunt adj *recreaunt adj.* B 1; C 1
B.18.100 Ȝilt hym *recreaunt* re[m]yng, riȝt at Iesus wille.
C.20.103 Ȝelde hym [re]creaunt remyng, riht at iesu[s] wille.

recreiȝed > recrayed

rect adj *rect adj.* C 7
C. 3.334   *Rect* and indirect, reninde bothe
C. 3.342   What is relacion *rect* and indirect aftur,
C. 3.344   'Relacioun *rect*,' quod Consience, 'is a record of treuthe–
C. 3.355   And man is relatif *rect* yf he be rihte trewe:
C. 3.361   This is relacion *rect*, ryht [as] adiectyf and sustantyf
C. 3.367   Þat is nat resonable ne *rect* to refuse my syre name,
C. 3.374   A[c] relacoun *rect* is a ryhtful custume,

red > reden,reed; redd(estow -ist > reden; rede > reden,reed

redels n *redels n.* B 2
B.13.167   Maister of alle þo men þoruʒ myʒt of þis *redels*,
B.13.184   After yeresʒeues or ʒiftes, or yernen to rede *redels*?

reden v *reden v.(1)* A 18 red (3) redde (3) reddist (1) rede (10) redyn (1);
   B 40 radde (4) redde (1) reddestow (1) rede (30) reden (3) reed (1); C
   46 rad (1) radde (4) radden (1) rat (4) redde (1) rede (29) reden (2)
   redon (1) ret (2) yrad (1)

A. 1.149   Forþi I *rede* þe riche haue reuþe on þe pore;
A. 2.32   And become a good man for any coueitise, I *rede*.'
A. 3.238   Ac *reddist* þou neuere Regum, þou recreiʒede mede,
A. 4.5   But resoun *rede* me þerto [raþer] wole I deiʒe.'
A. 4.9   For he shal rewele my reaume & *rede* me þe beste
A. 4.27   And riden faste for resoun shulde *rede* hem þe beste
A. 4.97   Summe *redde* resoun to haue reuþe on þat shrewe
A. 4.100   '*Rede* me not,' quaþ resoun, 'no reuþe to haue
A. 5.37   And siþþe he *redde* religioun here rewel[e] to holde
A. 5.103   'ʒis, redily,' quaþ repentaunce & *redde* hym to goode:
A. 5.178   Til robyn þe ropere was *red* to arisen,
A. 8.89   'Piers,' quaþ a prest [þo], 'þi pardon muste I *rede*,
A. 8.165   Forþi I *rede* ʒow renkes þat riche ben on erþe
A.10.86   And þerof seiþ þe sauter, þe salme þou miʒt *rede*:
A.11.221   For I haue seiʒe it myself, & siþþe *red* it aftir,
A.12.22   And poul precheþ hit often, prestes hit *redyn*:
A.12.30   Riʒt so I *rede*,' quod she, 'red þou no ferþe;
A.12.30   Riʒt so I rede,' quod she, '*red* þou no ferþe;
B.Pr.195   That witnesseþ holy writ, whoso wole it *rede*:
B. 1.175   Forþi I *rede* [þe] riche, haueþ ruþe [on] þe pouere;
B. 2.71   And preide Cyuylle to see and Symonye to *rede* it.
B. 3.259   Ac *reddestow* neuere Regum, þow recrayed Mede,
B. 3.338   Ac þow art lik a lady þat *radde* a lesson ones
B. 4.5   But Reson *rede* me þerto raþer wol I deye.'
B. 4.9   For he shal rule my Reaume and *rede* me þe beste
B. 4.30   And riden faste for Reson sholde *rede* hem þe beste
B. 4.110   Som[me] *radde* Reson to haue ruþe on þat shrewe;
B. 4.113   '*Reed* me noʒt', quod Reson, 'no ruþe to haue
B. 5.45   And siþen he *radde* Religion hir rule to holde
B. 5.126   'ʒis! redily', quod Repentaunce and *radde* hym to [goode]:
B. 5.235   'I wende riflynge were restitucion for I lerned neuere *rede* on boke,
B. 5.416   Yet kan I neyþer solue ne synge ne seintes lyues *rede*;
B. 5.421   Ac in Canoun nor in decretals I kan noʒt *rede* a lyne.
B. 5.427   Ruþe is to here rekenyng whan we shul *rede* acountes:
B. 5.477   [Th]anne hadde Repentaunce ruþe and *redde* hem alle to knele.
B. 7.107   'Piers', quod a preest þoo, 'þi pardon moste I *rede*,
B. 7.187   Forþi I *rede* yow renkes þat riche ben on erþe
B.10.272   I *rede* ech a blynd bosard do boote to hymselue,
B.10.308   But al is buxomnesse þere and boote, to *rede* and to lerne].
B.11.102   To *reden* it in Retorik to arate dedly synne?
B.11.314   Synge ne psalmes *rede* ne seye a masse of þe day.
B.11.387   Forþi I *rede*', quod reson, '[þow] rule þi tonge bettre,
B.12.49   Of manye swiche I may *rede*, of men and of wommen,
B.12.65   As þe book bereþ witnesse to burnes þat kan *rede*:
B.12.94   To oure lord, leue me; forþi loue hem, I *rede*.
B.13.73   And greue þerwiþ [þat goode ben]–ac gramariens shul *re[d]e*:
B.13.184   After yeresʒeues or ʒiftes, or yernen to rede *redels*?
B.13.441   Forþi I *rede* yow riche, reueles whan ye makeþ,
B.14.67   That no reyn ne roon; þus *rede* men in bokes,
B.14.105   Thouʒ men *rede* of richesse riʒt to þe worldes ende,
B.15.225   I haue yseyen charite also syngen and *reden*
B.15.376   Ne *rede* a lettre in any langage but in latyn or englissh.
B.15.388   As clerkes in Corpus Christi feeste syngen and *reden*
B.15.446   And þoruʒ miracles, as men mow *rede*, al þat marche he tornede
B.15.533   It is ruþe to *rede* how riʒtwise men lyuede,
B.15.539   And now is rouþe to *rede* how þe rede noble
B.17.270   Ech a riche, I *rede*, reward at hym take
B.18.309   I *rede* we fle', quod [þe fend], 'faste alle hennes,
C.Pr.208   Wyttenesse at holy wryt whoso kan *rede*:
C. 1.171   Forthy y *rede* ʒow riche, haueth reuthe [o]n þe pore,
C. 2.14   Here robynge was rychere þen y *rede* couthe;
C. 2.73   And preyeth syuile to se and s[y]monye to *rede* hit.
C. 3.407   Ac hoso *rat* of regum rede me may of mede,
C. 3.407   Ac hoso rat of regum *rede* me may of mede,
C. 3.413   As me *ret* in regum [of þe reuthe] of kynges,

C. 3.490   Thow art lyk a lady þat a lessoun *radde*
C. 3.498   The whiche þat hatte, as y haue *rad* an[d] oþer þat can rede,
C. 3.498   The whiche þat hatte, as y haue rad an[d] oþer þat can *rede*,
C. 4.5   But resoun *rede* me þertyl rather wo[l] y dey.'
C. 4.9   For he shal reulen my rewme and *rede* me the beste
C. 4.105   Summe *radden* resoun tho to haue reuthe vppon þat shrewe
C. 4.108   '*Rede* me nat,' quod resoun, 'no reuthe to haue
C. 5.64   *Redon* and resceyuen þat resoun ouhte to spene\
C. 5.102   'Y *rede* the,' quod resoun tho, 'rape the to bigynne
C. 5.125   How resoun *radde* al the reume to heuene.
C. 5.143   And sethe he *radde* religioun here reule to holde
C. 5.182   And also,' quod resoun, 'y *rede* ʒow ryche
C. 6.291   Y *rede* no faythful frere at thy feste to sytte.
C. 7.31   ʒut kan y nother solfe ne synge ne a seyntes lyf *rede*;
C. 7.34   Ac y can nat construe catoun ne clergialiche *reden*.
C. 7.40   Reuthe is to here rekenynge when we shal *rede* acountes,
C. 7.101   Forthy y *rede* ʒow ryche, reueles when ʒe maketh,
C. 7.119   Tho was repentaunce aredy and *redde* hem alle to knele:
C. 8.282   And ʒif thow [the pore be thy] pouer, [Peres], y þe *rede*;
C. 9.82   That reuthe is to *rede* or in ryme shewe
C. 9.281   '[Peres],' quod a prest tho, 'thy pardon moste y *rede*
C. 9.333   Forthy y *rede* ʒow renkes þat riche ben on this erthe
C.10.236   The gospel is hereagayn, as gomus may *rede*:
C.11.272   Thus y, rechelesnesse, haue *yrad* registres and bokes
C.12.210   Ac hoso *rat* of th[e] ryche the reuers may fynde,
C.13.5   ʒut *ret* me þat abraham and Iob weren wonder ryche
C.13.126   Syng ne [psalmes] *rede* [ne sey a masse of the daye].
C.13.205   Forthy,' quod Resoun, 'y *rede* thow reule thy tonge euere;
C.15.51   Thenne resoun *radde* anoon riht aftur
C.15.266   That no reyn ne roen; thus [*r*]*at* men [i]n bokes,
C.15.280   Thogh men *rede* of rychesse rihte to þe worldes ende
C.16.350   Ich haue yseye charite also syngen and *rede*,
C.17.120   As Clerkes in corpus cristi feste syngen and *reden*
C.17.194   Hit is reuthe to *rede* how riht holy men lyuede,
C.17.200   And now is reuthe to *rede* how þe rede noble
C.19.108   'A saide soeth,' quod the samaritaen, 'and so y *rede* the also.
C.19.237   Bute riʒtfulliche, as men [*r*]*at*, al his richesse cam hym
C.19.251   Vch a riche y *rede* reward herof take
C.20.343   Y *rede* we flee,' quod the fende, 'faste all hennes

redes > reedes

redy adj *redi adj.(3)* A 1; B 3; C 1
A. 4.155   'I am *redy*,' quaþ resoun, 'to reste wiþ ʒow euere;
B. 4.192   'I am *redy*', quod Reson, 'to reste wiþ yow euere;
B. 5.132   Whan he solde and I nouʒt þanne was I *redy*
B.16.79   For euere as þei dropped adoun þe deuel was *redy*
C.18.110   For euere as Elde hadde eny down, þe deuel was *redy*

redily adv *redili adv.(2)* A 2; B 3; C 4 redily (3) redyly (1)
A. 4.153   Ac *redily*, resoun, þou shalt not [raike] henne,
A. 5.103   'ʒis, *redily*,' quaþ repentaunce & redde hym to goode:
B. 4.190   Ac *redily*, Reson, þow shalt noʒt [raike henne];
B. 5.126   'ʒis! *redily*', quod Repentaunce and radde hym to [goode]:
B.17.157   Right so, *redily*, Reson it sheweth
C. 4.184   Forthy, resoun, *redyly* thow shalt nat ryden hennes
C. 6.91   'ʒus! *redily*,' quod repentaunce, 'and thow be ryht sory
C. 6.253   'Now *redily*,' quod repentaunce, 'and by þe rode, y leue,
C. 6.286   'Now *redily*,'quod repentaunce, 'y haue reuthe of thy lyuynge.'

redyn > reden

redyng ger *redinge ger.(1)* B 1
B. 7.88   Lat vsage be youre solas of seintes lyues *redyng*.

redyngkyng n *ridingking n., OED redingking* A 1 redyngking; B 1; C 2
   redyngkynge (1) redyngkynges (1)
A. 5.165   A ropere, a *redyngking*, & rose þe disshere;
B. 5.315   A Ropere, a *Redyngkyng* and Rose þe dyssher[e],
C. 2.115   Raynald þe reue and *redyngkynges* manye,
C. 6.372   A ropere, a *redyngkynge* and Rose þe disshere,

redon > reden

reed n *red n.(1)* A 1 red; B 2 rede (1) reed (1); C 2 red (1) reed (1)
A. 9.99   And rewele þe reaum be *red* of hem alle,
B. 8.109   And rule þe Reme by [*rede* of hem alle],
B.13.373   And if I r[o]þe ouerreche, or yaf hem *reed* þat ropen
C. 4.29   To take *reed* of resoun þat recorde sholde
C. 6.270   And [yf] y raap ouerreche or ʒaf hem *red* þat repe

reed adj *red adj.* A 2 red; B 6 rede (3) reed (3); C 4 rede (3) reed (1)
A. 2.13   In *red* scarlet robid & ribande wiþ gold.
A.10.123   Riʒt as a rose, [þat *red* is and] swet,
B. 2.12   And þeron [riche] Rubies as *rede* as any gleede,
B. 2.15   Hire Robe was ful riche, of *reed* scarlet engreyned,
B. 2.16   Wiþ Ribanes of *reed* gold and of riche stones.

B.15.539 And now is rouþe to rede how þe *rede* noble
B.19.11 Or it is Piers þe Plowman? who peynted hym so *rede*?'
B.19.88 Rightwisnesse vnder *reed* gold, Resones felawe;
C. 2.13 And thereon *rede* rubies and othere riche stones.
C.17.200 And now is reuthe to rede how þe *rede* noble
C.21.11 Or hit is [Peres þe Plouhman? who] paynted hym so *rede*?'
C.21.88 Rihtwisnesse vnder *reed* gold, resones felawe;

reed &> reden

reedes n *red n.(3)* B 1; C 1 redes
B.18.50 'Aue, raby', quod þat rybaud and þrew *reedes* at hym.
C.20.50 'Aue, raby,' quod þat ribaud, and *redes* shotte vp to his yes.

refte > reue

refuse v *refusen v.* B 4 refuse (3) refused (1); C 9 refuse (6) refused (1) refusede (2)
B.11.334 And how men token Mede and Mercy *refused*.
B.13.424 And ȝueþ hem mete and mede, and pouere men *refuse*,
B.15.31 And whan I chalange or chalange noȝt, chepe or *refuse*,
B.17.180 And receyue þat þe fyngres recheþ and *refuse* boþe
C. 3.367 Þat is nat resonable ne rect to *refuse* my syre name,
C. 5.78 Popes and patrones pore gentel blood *refused*
C. 7.84 And ȝeueth [hem] mede & mete and pore men *refuse*,
C.13.142 And how þat [men] mede toke and mercy *refusede*.
C.13.231 Resoun *refusede* the and wolde nat reste with the
C.16.191 And when y chalenge [or chalenge] nat, chepe or *refuse*
C.17.43 And *refuse* reuerences and raue[n]ers offrynges.
C.17.47 Wolde religious *refuse* rauenours Almesses.
C.19.145 And receue þat the fyngeres recheth and *refuse*, yf h[y]m liketh,

registre n *registre n.* B 2; C 2 registre (1) registres (1)
B. 5.272 And siþen þat Reson rolle it in þe *Registre* of heuene
B.20.271 Forþi I wolde witterly þat ye were in þe *Registre*
C.11.272 Thus y, rechelesnesse, haue yrad *registres* and bokes
C.22.271 Forthy y wolde witterly þat ȝe were in [þe] *registre*

registrer n *registrere n.* B 2 Registrer (1) Registrers (1); C 1
B. 2.174 Erchedekenes and Officials and alle youre *Registrers*,
B.19.259 And *Registrer* to receyue redde quod debes.
C.21.259 And *Registrer* to reseyuen Redde quod debes.

regne v *regnen v.* A 2 regne (1) regniþ (1); B 11 regne (3) regnede (2) regneþ (5) reigne (1); C 15 regne (4) regnede (2) regnest (1) regneth (7) regne (1)
A. 2.33 Alle þe riche retenaunce þat *regniþ* wiþ false
A. 3.261 Þat resoun shal *regne* & reumes gouerne,
B.Pr.113 Might of þe communes made hym to *regne*.
B. 2.54 That al þe riche retenaunce þat *regneþ* with [fals]
B. 3.285 That Reson shal *regne* and Reaumes gouerne,
B. 4.177 Ac Reson shal rekene wiþ yow if I *regne* any while,
B.12.241 Bitokneþ riȝt riche men þat *reigne* here on erþe.
B.14.205 For þer þat richesse *regneþ* reuerence[s] folweþ,
B.14.216 A[c] pride in richesse *regneþ* raþer þan in pouerte;
B.18.228 Woot no wight what werre is þer þat pees *regneþ*,
B.19.52 That he naroos and *regnede* and rauysshed helle.
B.19.418 And þer þei ligge and lenge moost lecherie þere *regneþ*".
B.20.64 And a fals fend Antecrist ouer alle folk *regnede*.
C.Pr.140 Myght of tho men made hym to *regne*.
C. 1.117 'Hit is sikerore bi southe þer þe sonne *regneth*
C. 3.438 That resoun shal *regne* and reumes gouerne
C. 4.171 Ac resoun shal rykene with ȝow yf y *regne* eny while
C. 9.257 That soffreth suche sottes and oþere synnes *regne*.
C.10.24 The rihtfulluste ren[k] þat *regneth* [o]n erthe.
C.13.185 Wherefore and why, as wyde as thow *regnes[t]*,
C.14.173 Bytokenen riht ryche men þat *reygne* here on erthe.
C.16.46 For [þer] þat rychess[e] *regneth* reuerences folleweth
C.16.57 And pruyde in rychesse *regneth* rather then in pouerte;
C.16.122 Al þat may potte of pruyde in place þer he *regneth*;
C.20.237 For woet no wiht what werre is þer [þat] pees *regneth*
C.21.52 That he ne aroos and *regnede* and raueschede helle.
C.21.418 And þer they lygge and lenge moest lecherye þer *regneth*".
C.22.64 And a fals fende auntecrist ouer all folke *regnede*.

regrater n *regrater n.* A 2 regratour (1) regratouris (1); B 2 Regrater (1) Regratiers (1); C 3 regrater (1) regraters (2)
A. 3.79 Ryng[es] or oþer richesse, þ[ise] *regratour[is* to meynteyne.
A. 5.140 Rose þe *regratour* was hire riȝte name;
B. 3.90 Rynges or oþer richesse þ[ise] *Regratiers* to mayntene.
B. 5.224 Rose þe *Regrater* was hir riȝte name;
C. 3.113 That vsurers oþer *regraters* for eny skynes ȝeftes
C. 3.118 'Haue reuthe on this *regraters* þat han riche handes,
C. 6.232 Rose þe *regrater* was here ryhte name;

regratrie n *regraterie n.* A 1; B 1; C 1 regraterye
A. 3.72 And ri[chen] þoruȝ *regrat[r]ie* & rentis hem biggen

B. 3.83 Thei richen þoruȝ *regratrie* and rentes hem biggen
C. 3.82 Rychen thorw *regraterye* and rentes hem beggeth

reherce v *rehersen v.* A 7 reherce (1) reherse (2) reherside (4); B 10 reherce (4) reherced (5) reherseþ (1); C 10 reherce (4) rehercen (1) reherse (2) rehersed (1) rehersede (2)
A. 1.22 And rekne hem in resoun; *reherse* þou hem aftir.
A. 4.134 Ac [whanne] resoun among þise renkis *reherside* þise wordis,
A. 4.145 And *reherside* þat resoun [hadde] riȝtfulliche shewide;
A. 5.43 Þanne [ran] repentaunce [and] *reherside* his teme
A. 8.174 What þou dedist day [by day] þe dom wile *reherce*.
A. 8.183 Þat, aftir oure deþ day, dowel *reherse*
A.11.205 Of religioun þe rewele he *reherside* in his morals,
B.Pr.184 And to þe route of Ratons *reherced* þise wordes:
B. 1.22 And rekene hem by reson: *reherce* þow hem after.
B. 5.60 Thanne ran Repentaunce and *reherced* his teme
B. 5.182 'Now repente', quod Repentaunce, 'and *reherce* neuere
B. 7.196 [What] þow didest day by day þe doom wole *reherce*.
B. 7.205 That, after oure deeþ day, dowel *reherce*
B.10.299 Of religion þe rule *reherseþ* in hise morales,
B.11.393 Of hire defautes foule bifore hem *reherced*].
B.11.415 For Reson wolde haue *reherced* þee riȝt as Clergie seid;
B.13.72 In englissh on auenture it sholde be *rehersed* to ofte,
C.Pr.201 And to þe route of ratones *rehersede* thise wordes:
C. 1.22 And rekene hem by rewe: *reherse* hem wher þe liketh.
C. 4.150 *Reherce* the[r] anon ryhte þat myhte resoun stoppe.
C. 6.1 With þat ran repentaunce and *rehersede* his teme
C. 6.164 'Now repente,' quod repentaunce, 'and *reherce* neuere
C. 9.342 And how we dede day be day the doem wol *reherce*.
C. 9.351 That aftur oure deth day dowel *reherce*
C.12.36 To *rehercen* hit by retoryk to arate dedly synne?
C.13.223 For resoun wolde haue *rehersed* þe riht as clergie seide;
C.17.25 Y can nat rykene hem riȝt now ne *reherse* here names

reignaldes > reynald; reigne > regne; reik > raik

reyn n *rein n.(1)* A 1; B 5 reyn (4) reyne (1); C 4 rayne (1) reyn (1) reyne (2)
A. 3.195 Þat is þe ricchheste reaume þat *re[yn]* ouer[houiþ].
B. 3.208 That is þe richeste Reaume þat *reyn* ouerhoueþ.
B.12.60 Ac grace ne groweþ noȝt [til good wil yeue *reyn*];
B.14.67 That no *reyn* ne roon; þus rede men in bokes,
B.17.325 And if his hous be vnhiled and *reyne* on his bedde
B.17.339 The *reyn* þat reyneþ þer we reste sholde
C.14.24 Ac grace ne groweth nat til gode wil gyue *reyne*
C.15.266 That no *reyn* ne roen; thus [r]at men [i]n bokes,
C.19.305 And if his hous be vnheled and *reyne* on his bedde
C.19.319 The *rayne* þat rayneth þere we reste sholde

reynald n prop *n.i.d.* A 1 reynaldis; B 2 Reynald (1) Reignaldes (1); C 1 Raynald
A. 4.36 And how he rauisshide rose, *reynaldis* loue,
B. 2.111 *Reynald* þe Reue of Rutland Sokene,
B. 4.49 And how he rauysshede Rose, *Reignaldes* looue,
C. 2.115 *Raynald* þe reue and redyngkynges manye,

reyne > reyn,ryne

reyneþ v *reinen v.(1) cf. ryne* B 2 reyne (1) reyneþ (1); C 1 rayneth
B.10.318 To Religiouse þat han no rouþe þouȝ it *reyne* on hir Auters.
B.17.339 The reyn þat *reyneþ* þer we reste sholde
C.19.319 The rayne þat *rayneth* þere we reste sholde

reisen > raise

reioisse v *rejoisen v.* B 1; C 1 reioysen
B.15.537 Ne no richesse but þe roode to *reioisse* hem Inne:
C.17.198 Ne no rychesse but þe rode to *reioysen* hem ynne:

rekene v *rekenen v.* A 1 rekne; B 7; C 9 rekene (3) rikene (1) rykene (5)
A. 1.22 And *rekne* hem in resoun; reherse þou hem aftir.
B. 1.22 And *rekene* hem by reson: reherce þow hem after.
B. 2.62 I kan noȝt *rekene* þe route þat ran aboute Mede.
B. 4.177 Ac Reson shal *rekene* wiþ yow if I regne any while,
B. 5.271 Til þow make restitucion', [quod Repentaunce], 'and *rekene* wiþ hem alle;
B.11.131 A[c] reson shal *rekene* wiþ hym [and rebuken hym at þe laste,
B.14.106 I wiste neuere renk þat riche was, þat whan he *rekene* sholde,
B.14.211 For þe riche haþ muche to *rekene*, and [riȝt softe] walkeþ;
C. 1.22 And *rekene* hem by rewe: reherse hem wher þe liketh.
C. 2.64 Y kan nouȝt *rykene* þe route þat ran aboute mede.
C. 4.171 Ac resoun shal *rykene* with ȝow yf y regne eny while
C.11.297 As doth the reue or Conturrollor þat *rykene* moet and acounten
C.12.66 A[c] reson shal *rekene* with hym and rebuken hym at þe laste
C.13.35 And *rikene* byfore resoun a resonable acounte
C.15.281 [Y wiste neuere renke þat ryche was þat whan he *rekene* sholde]
C.16.52 For þe ryche hath moche to *rykene* and riht softe walketh;

C.17.25   Y can nat *rykene* hem riȝt now ne reherse here names

rekenyng ger *rekeninge ger.* B 4; C 2 rekenynge (1) rykenynge (1)
B. 5.293   For þee and for many mo þat man shal yeue a *rekenyng*:
B. 5.420   I kan holde louedayes and here a Reues *rekenyng*,
B. 5.427   Ruþe is to here *rekenyng* whan we shul rede acountes:
B.14.108   And þat at þe *rekenyng* in Arrerage fel raþer þan out of dette.
C. 6.348   For the and for many mo þat man shal ȝeue a *rykenynge*
C. 7.40   Reuthe is to here *rekenynge* when we shal rede acountes,

rekeuere(de > recouere; rekkeþ > recche

rekne adj *reken adj. &> rekene* A 1
A.12.113   Furst to *rekne* Richard, kyng of þis rewme,

relacion n *relacioun n.* C 6 relacion (2) relacions (1) relacioun (1)
relacoun (2)
C. 3.333   Thus is mede and mercede as two maner *relacions*,
C. 3.342   What is *relacion* rect and indirect aftur,
C. 3.344   'Relacioun* rect,' quod Consience, 'is a record of treuthe–
C. 3.352   So of ho[l] herte cometh hope and hardy *relacoun*
C. 3.361   This is *relacion* rect, ryht [as] adiectyf and sustantyf
C. 3.374   A[c] *relacoun* rect is a ryhtful custume,

relatif n *relativ n.* C 2 relatif (1) relatifs (1)
C. 3.355   And man is *relatif* rect yf he be rihte trewe:
C. 3.388   As rela[tifs] indirect re[cc]heth the[y] neuere

rele v *relen v.(2)* C 1
C. 9.81   [To] rybbe [and] to *rele*, rusches to pylie,

relees n *reles n.(2)* A 1 reles; B 1; C 1
A. 7.82   To haue *reles* & remissioun, on þat rental I leue.
B. 6.90   To haue *relees* and remission, on þat rental I leue.
C. 8.99   To haue re[lees] and re[missioun]; on þat rental y leue.

relessed ptp *relesen v.(1)* B 1; C 1 relesed
B. 3.58   It is synne of þe seuene sonnest *relessed*.
C. 3.62   Hit is synne as of seuene noon sannour *relessed*.

releue v *releven v.* A 1; B 4; C 7 releue (6) releuede (1)
A. 8.35   *Releue* religioun & renten hem betere;
B. 7.33   *Releue* Religion and renten hem bettre.
B.15.603   And hopen þat he be to come þat shal hem *releue*;
B.18.141   And þat deeþ adown brouȝte, deeþ shal *releue*.'
B.18.345   And þat deeþ in hem fordide my deeþ shal *releue*
C. 9.36   *Releue* Religion and renten hem bettere.
C.13.21   Lo, how pacience and pouerte thise patriarkes *releuede*
C.13.70   And haue reuthe and *releue* with his rychesse by his power
C.16.317   [Rentes or other richesse to *releue* hym at his nede]?'
C.17.311   And hopen þat he be to come þat shal hem *releue*;
C.20.144   And þat deth down brouhte, deth shal *releue*.'
C.20.390   And þat deth fordede my deth to *releue*

relyede v *relien v.* B 1; C 1 relyed
B.20.148   Thus *relyede* lif for a litel fortune
C.22.148   Thus *relyed* lyf for a litel fo[rtune]

religion n *religioun n.* A 9 religioun; B 11; C 8 religion (2) religioun (6)
A. 5.37   And siþþe he redde *religioun* here rewel[e] to holde
A. 8.35   Releue *religioun* & renten hem betere;
A. 9.82   And is ronne to *religioun*, & haþ rendrit þe bible,
A.10.106   Fro *religioun* to religioun, reccheles ben þei euere;
A.10.106   Fro religioun to *religioun*, reccheles ben þei euere;
A.11.202   And þat is riȝtful *religioun*, none renneris aboute,
A.11.205   Of *religioun* þe rewele he reherside in his morals,
A.11.209   Riȝt so be *religioun*, it roileþ & steruiþ
A.11.211   Ac now is *religioun* a ridere & a rennere [be stretis],
B. 5.45   And siþen he radde *Religion* hir rule to holde
B. 6.151   For it is an vnresonable *Religion* þat haþ riȝt noȝt of certein.'
B. 7.33   Releue *Religion* and renten hem bettre.
B. 8.91   And is ronne to *Religion*, and haþ rendred þe bible,
B.10.77   In *Religion* and in al þe Reme amonges riche and pouere
B.10.299   Of *religion* þe rule reherseþ in hise morals,
B.10.303   Riȝt so [by] *religion*, [it] ro[i]leþ [and] sterueþ
B.10.311   Ac now is *Religion* a rydere, a [rennere by stretes],
B.13.285   *Religion* saunȝ rule [and] resonable obedience;
B.15.87   Ayein youre rule and *Religion*; I take record at Iesus
B.20.264   Monkes and Moniales and alle men of *Religion*,
C. 3.303   *Religioun* he al toreueth and oute of reule to lybbe.
C. 5.143   And sethe he radde *religioun* here reule to holde
C. 5.150   Ryht so *religioun* roteth and sterueth
C. 9.36   Releue *Religion* and renten hem bettere.
C. 9.222   Furste, Religious of *religioun* a reule to holde
C.10.88   And is ronne [t]o *religioun* and hath rendred þe bible
C.11.57   In *religion* and in al þe reume amongus riche and pore
C.22.264   Monkes and monyales and alle men of *religioun*,

religious n *religious n. &> religiouse* B 11 Religious (4) Religiouse (5)
Religiouses (2); C 7
B. 4.125   Hire haukes and hire houndes help to pouere *Religious*;
B.10.297   [Amonges riȝtful *religious* þis rule sholde be holde.
B.10.318   To *Religiouse* þat han no rouþe þouȝ it reyne on hir Auters.
B.10.322   Ac þer shal come a kyng and confesse yow *Religiouses*,
B.12.35   Riȝt so if þow be *Religious* ren þow neuere ferþer
B.15.307   [Riȝt so] *Religiouses* rightfulle men sholde [fynde],
B.15.317   Ye hadde riȝt ynoȝ, ye *Religiouse*, and so youre rule me tolde.
B.15.342   Ac *Religiouse* þat riche ben sholde raþer feeste beggeris
B.15.544   Boþe riche and *Religious*, þat roode þei honoure
B.15.550   Reson and rightful doom þ[o] *Religiouse* d[ampn]ede.
B.20.59   And *Religiouse* reuerenced hym and rongen hir belles,
C. 5.147   The reule of alle *religious* rihtful and obedient:
C. 5.164   To *religious* þat haen no reuthe thow it ryne on here auters.
C. 9.222   Furste, *Religious* of religioun a reule to holde
C.17.47   Wolde *religious* refuse rauenours Almesses.
C.17.206   Bothe riche and *religiou[s]* þat rode they honouren
C.17.213   Resoun and rihtfol doem tho *religious* dampnede.
C.22.59   And *religious* reuerensed hym and rongen here belles

religiouse adj *religious adj. &> religious* B 1; C 1 religious
B. 4.120   And *Religiouse* Romeris Recordare in hir cloistres
C. 4.116   And *religious* outryderes be reclused in here Cloistres

relyk n *relik n.* B 1 relikes; C 2 relikes (1) relyk (1)
B.19.423   Or in Rome as hir rule wole þe *relikes* to kepe;
C.20.472   And rihtfollokest A *relyk*, noon richore on erthe.
C.21.423   Or in Rome, as here reule wo[l], þe *relikes* to kepe;

reme > reaume

remed v *remen v.(1)* B 2 remed (1) remyng (1); C 2 remede (1) remyng
(1)
B. 5.391   Raxed and [*remed*] and rutte at þe laste.
B.18.100   ȝilt hym recreaunt re[m]yng, riȝt at Iesus wille.
C. 7.7   R[a]xlede and r[e]mede and rotte at þe laste.
C.20.103   ȝelde hym [re]creaunt *remyng*, riht at iesu[s] wille.

remembraunce n *remembraunce n.* C 1
C. 5.11   Romynge in *remembraunce* thus resoun me aratede:

remenaunt n *remenaunt n.* A 2; B 6; C 5 remenant (1) remenaunt (4)
A. 5.231   And wiþ þe residue & þe *remenaunt*, be þe roode of chestre,
A. 7.92   And wiþ þe residue & þe *remenaunt*, be þe rode of chestre,
B. 5.459   And wiþ þe residue and þe *remenaunt*, bi þe Rode of Chestre,
B. 6.100   And wiþ þe residue and þe *remenaunt*, by þe Rode of Lukes!
B.11.114   And plukked in Pauci pryueliche and leet þe *remenaunt* go rome.'
B.17.242   Mercy for his mekenesse wol maken good þe *remenaunt*.
B.19.448   He reccheþ riȝt noȝt of þe *remenaunt*.
B.20.292   A parcel to preye for hem and [pleye] wiþ þe *remenaunt*,
C. 8.109   And with þe res[i]due and þe *remenant*, by the rode of lukes!
C.12.49   And plihte in pauci preueiliche and lette þe *remenaunt* go rome.'
C.19.208   Mercy for his mekenesse wol maky good þe *remenaunt*.
C.21.448   He rekketh riht nauht of þe *remenaunt*.
C.22.292   A parcel to preye for hem and [pleye] with þe *remenaunt*

remyng > remed

remission n *remissioun n.* A 2 remission (1) remissioun (1); B 1; C 2
remissioun
A. 7.82   To haue reles & *remissioun*, on þat rental I leue.
A.11.285   A robbere hadde *remission* raþere þanne þei alle,
B. 6.90   To haue relees and *remission*, on þat rental I leue.
C. 3.358   In nombre, Rotye and aryse and *remissioun* to haue,
C. 8.99   To haue re[lees] and re[missioun]; on þat rental y leue.

ren > rennen

renable adj *renable adj.* B 1
B.Pr.158   A Raton of renoun, moost *renable* of tonge,

renaboute n *rennen v.(1), OED runaboute* B 1
B. 6.148   Ac Robert *Renaboute* shal [riȝt] noȝt haue of myne,

rende v *renden v.(2)* A 1 rend; B 2
A. 4.149   'But I reule þus þi reaum *rend* out my ribbes,
B.Pr.199   And also ye route of Ratons *rende* mennes cloþes
B. 4.186   'But I rule þus youre Reaume *rende* out my guttes–

rendren v *rendren v.* A 2 rendrit; B 3 rendred (2) rendren (1); C 3
rendred (1) rendrede (1) rendren (1)
A. 5.125   Among þe riche rayes I *rendrit* a lessoun;
A. 9.82   And is ronne to religioun, & haþ *rendrit* þe bible,
B. 5.209   Among þe riche Rayes I *rendred* a lesson;
B. 8.91   And is ronne to Religion, and haþ *rendred* þe bible,
B.15.612   [Recorden it and *rendren*] it wiþ remissionem peccatorum
C. 6.217   Amongus the ryche rayes y *rendrede* a lessoun,

C.10.88   And is ronne [t]o religioun and hath *rendred* þe bible
C.17.320   Recorden hit and *re[n]d[r]en* hit with remissionem peccatorum,

reneye v *reneien v.(1)* B 3 reneye (2) reneyed (1); C 3 reneyed (1) renoye (2)

B.11.125   For þou3 a cristen man coueited his cristendom to *reneye,*
B.11.126   Ri3tfully to *reneye* no reson it wolde.
B.11.130   As a *reneyed* caytif recchelesly rennen aboute.
C.12.60   For thogh a cristene man coueitede his cristendom to *renoye*
C.12.61   Rihtfolliche to *renoye* no resoun hit wolde.
C.12.65   As a [*reneyed*] Caytyf [rechelesliche rennen aboute].

reninde > rennen

renk n *rink n.* A 2 renkes (1) renkis (1); B 9 renk (5) renkes (4); C 10 renk (3) renke (2) renkes (5)

A. 4.134   Ac [whanne] resoun among þise *renkis* reherside þise wordis,
A. 8.165   Forþi I rede 3ow *renkes* þat riche ben on erþe.
B.Pr.197   For may no *renk* þer reste haue for Ratons by ny3te,]
B. 5.392   'What! awake, *renk!*' quod Repentaunce, 'and rape þee to shryfte!'
B. 7.187   Forþi I rede yow *renkes* þat riche ben on erþe.
B.12.51   And riche *renkes* ri3t so gaderen and sparen
B.12.170   'Right so', quod þe *renk*, 'Reson it sheweþ
B.14.106   I wiste neuere *renk* þat riche was, þat whan he rekene sholde,
B.14.124   Right so reson sheweþ þat [þo *renkes*] þat were [lordes]
B.18.2   As a recchelees *renk* þat [reccheþ of no wo],
B.18.278   For by right and by reson þe *renkes* þat ben here
C. 7.8   'What! awake, *renke!*' quod repentaunce, 'and rape [þe] to shryfte.'
C. 9.333   Forthy y rede 3ow *renkes* þat riche ben on this erthe.
C.10.24   The rihtfulluste *ren[k]* þat regneth [o]n erthe.
C.13.186   That thow ne reul[e]st rather *renkes* then other bestes.
C.13.191   They reule hem al by resoun Ac *renkes* ful fewe.
C.14.110   'Riht so,' quod þ[e] *renk*, 'resoun hit sheweth
C.15.281   [Y wiste neuere *renke* þat ryche was þat whan he rekene sholde]
C.16.22   Riht so haue reuthe on [thy *renkes*] alle
C.20.2   As a recheles *renk* þat recheth nat of sorwe
C.20.300   For bi riht and by resoun þ[e] *renkes* þat ben here

rennares > rennere

rennen v *rennen v.* A 6 3erne (1) ran (1) renne (1) rennen (1) renneþ (1) ronne (1); B 20 arne (1) ernynge (1) ran (3) ren (1) renne (3) rennen (2) renneþ (2) rennynge (2) ronne (1) yarn (2) yerne (2); C 19 ern (1) ernynge (1) 3erne (1) 3erneth (1) 3orn (1) ran (4) reninde (1) renne (3) rennen (3) renneth (1) rennynge (1) ronne (1)

A. 3.201   Þoru3 3eftis han 3onge men to [*3erne*] & to ride.
A. 4.14   And ri3t *renneþ* to resoun & rouniþ in his ere;
A. 5.43   Þanne [*ran*] repentaunce [and] reherside his teme
A. 9.82   And is *ronne* to religioun, & haþ rendrit þe bible,
A.10.105   And ri3t so be romberis þat *rennen* aboute
A.10.110   In ensaumple [þat] suche shulde not *renne* aboute,
B.Pr.146   Wiþ þat *ran* þer a route of Ratons at ones
B. 2.62   I kan no3t rekene þe route þat *ran* aboute Mede.
B. 3.214   [Thoru3] 3iftes han yonge men to [*yerne*] and to ride.
B. 4.14   And [ri3t *renneþ*] to Reson and rouneþ in his ere;
B. 5.60   Thanne *ran* Repentaunce and reherced his teme
B. 5.439   I [*yarn*] aboute in youþe and yaf me nau3t to lerne,
B. 8.91   And is *ronne* to Religion, and haþ rendred þe bible,
B.11.60   Til I for[yede] youþe and *yarn* into Elde.
B.11.129   Ac he may *renne* in arerage and rome fro home,
B.11.130   As a reneyed caytif recchelesly *rennen* aboute.
B.12.35   Ri3t so if þow be Religious *ren* þow neuere ferþer
B.15.188   And *yerne* into youþe and yepeliche [seche]
B.15.226   Riden and *rennen* in raggede wedes
B.15.461   Rude and vnresonable, *rennynge* wiþouten [keperes].
B.16.136   Enuye and yuel wil [*arne*] in þe Iewes.
B.16.273   Rapeliche *renne* forþ þe ri3te wey [we] wente.
B.17.86   And whan I sei3 þis I soiourned no3t but shoop me to *renne*
B.18.165   Rightwisnesse come *rennynge*; reste we þe while,
B.19.378   Egreliche *ernynge* out of mennes eighen.
B.20.381   And [wenden] as wyde as þe world [*renneþ*]
C.Pr.167   Than *ran* þer a route of ratones [at ones]
C. 2.64   Y kan nou3t rykene þe route þat *ran* aboute mede.
C. 2.196   As fobbes and faytours þat on here feet *rennen*.'
C. 3.270   Thorw 3eftes haen 3emen to *3erne* and to ryde;
C. 3.334   Rect and indirect, *reninde* bothe
C. 6.1   With þat *ran* repentaunce and rehersede his teme
C.10.88   And is *ronne* [t]o religioun and hath rendred þe bible
C.12.12   Til y for3et 3outhe and *3orn* into elde.
C.12.64   Ac he may *renne* in arerage and rome fro home
C.12.65   As a [reneyed] Caytyf [rechelesliche *rennen* aboute].
C.13.32   Rather then þe ryche thogh they *renne* at ones.
C.15.150   And resoun *ran* aftur and riht with hym 3ede,
C.16.331   Thenne *3erneth* he into 3outhe and 3eepliche he secheth
C.16.351   Ryden and *rennen* in raggede clothes

C.18.163   Enuye and euel wil *ern* in þe iewes
C.18.289   Rappliche *renne* þe ri3t way we wente.
C.20.168   Rihtwisnesse come *rennynge*; reste we the while
C.21.378   Egrelich *ernynge* oute [of] menne yes.
C.22.381   And wenden as wyde as þe world *re[n]neth*

rennere n *rennere n.* A 3 rennere (1) renneris (2); B 2 rennere (1) renneres (1); C 1 rennares

A. 4.111   And alle rome *renneris,* for robberis of be3onde,
A.11.202   And þat is ri3tful religioun, none *renneris* aboute,
A.11.211   Ac now is religioun a ridere & a *rennere* [þe stretis],
B. 4.128   And alle Rome *renneres,* for Robberes [of] biyonde,
B.10.311   Ac now is Religion a rydere, a [*rennere* by stretis],
C. 4.125   And alle Rome *rennares* for ruyflares in Fraunce

renoye > reneye

renoun n *renoun n.* B 1; C 1 renown
B.Pr.158   A Raton of *renoun,* moost renable of tonge,
C.Pr.178   A ratoun of *renown,* moste resonable of tounge,

rental n *rental n.* A 1; B 1; C 1
A. 7.82   To haue reles & remissioun, on þat *rental* I leue.
B. 6.90   To haue relees and remission, on þat *rental* I leue.
C. 8.99   To haue re[lees] and re[missioun]; on þat *rental* y leue.

rente n *rente n.* A 3 rentis; B 8 rentes; C 9 rente (2) rentes (7)
A. 3.72   And ri[chen] þoru3 regrat[r]ie & *rentis* hem biggen
A.11.15   Or ricchesse or *rentis,* & reste at here wille,
A.11.228   Ne ricchesse, ne *rentis,* ne realte of lordis.
B. 3.83   Thei richen þoru3 regratrie and *rentes* hem biggen
B.10.15   Or richesse or *rentes,* and reste at hir wille,
B.10.340   Ne richesse [ne *rentes*] ne Reautee of lordes.
B.14.231   For his *rentes* ne wol nau3t reche no riche metes to bigge;
B.15.176   'Haþ he anye *rentes* or richesse or any riche frendes?'
B.15.177   'Of *rentes* n[e] of richesse rekkeþ he neuere,
B.15.321   Er þei amortisede to monkes or [monyales] hir *rente[s].*
B.15.558   Wiþ londes and ledes, lordshipes and *rentes,*
C. 3.82   Rychen thorw regraterye and *rentes* hem beggeth
C. 3.323   That kyng oþer kayser hem gaf, Catel oþer *rente.*
C. 5.73   And ledes sones hem laboreres and leyde here *rentes* to wedde
C. 9.73   Charged with childrene and chief lordes *rente.*
C.14.184   And þe ryche for his *rentes* or for rychesse in his shopp[e].
C.16.72   For his *rentes* wol nat reche ryche metes to bugge;
C.16.317   [*Rentes* or other richesse to releue hym at his nede]?'
C.16.318   'Of *rentes* ne of rychesse reccheth he neuere;
C.17.221   With londes and ledes, lordschipes and *rentes,*

renten v *renten v.(1)* A 1; B 1; C 2 renten (1) yrented (1)
A. 8.35   Releue religioun & *renten* hem betere;
B. 7.33   Releue Religion and *renten* hem bettre.
C. 9.36   Releue Religion and *renten* hem bettere.
C.10.265   For riche or *yrented* wel, thouh he be reueled for elde

repaest n *repaste n.* C 1
C. 9.148   Where he may rathest haue a *repaest* or a ronde of bacoun,

repe v *repen v.(1)* B 2 rope (1) ropen (1); C 3 raap (1) repe (2)
B.13.373   And if I *r[o]pe* ouerreche, or yaf hem reed þat ropen
B.13.373   And if I r[o]pe ouerreche, or yaf hem reed þat *ropen*
C. 5.15   *Repe* or been a rypereue and aryse erly
C. 6.270   And [yf] y *raap* ouerreche or 3af hem red þat repe
C. 6.270   And [yf] y raap ouerreche or 3af hem red þat *repe*

repentaunce n *repentaunce n.* A 2; B 16; C 18
A. 5.43   Þanne [ran] *repentaunce* [and] reherside his teme
A. 5.103   '3is, redily,' quaþ *repentaunce* & redde hym to goode:
B. 5.60   Thanne ran *Repentaunce* and reherced his teme
B. 5.126   '3is! redily', quod *Repentaunce* and radde hym to [goode]:
B. 5.182   'Now repente', quod *Repentaunce,* 'and reherce neuere
B. 5.230   'Repentedestow euere', quod *Repentaunce,* 'or restitucion madest?'
B. 5.233   'That was no restitucion', quod *Repentaunce,* 'but a robberis þefte,
B. 5.237   'Vsedestow euere vsurie', quod *Repentaunce,* 'in al þi lif tyme?'
B. 5.260   'Now [but þow repente þe raþer', quod *Repentaunce,*
B. 5.271   Til þow make restitucion', [quod *Repentaunce*], 'and rekene wiþ hem alle;
B. 5.280   Ne hadde *repentaunce* þe raþer reconforted hym in þis manere:
B. 5.364   And *Repentaunce* ri3t so rebuked hym þat tyme:
B. 5.378   'This shewynge shrift', quod *Repentaunce,* 'shal be meryt to þe.'
B. 5.392   'What! awake, renk!' quod *Repentaunce,* 'and rape þee to shryfte!'
B. 5.441   'Repente[st]ow no3t?' quod *Repentaunce,* & ri3t wiþ þat he swowned
B. 5.477   [Th]anne hadde *Repentaunce* ruþe and redde hem alle to knele.
B.17.304   That rightwisnesse þoru3 *repentaunce* to ruþe my3te turne.
B.17.307   Be raunsoned for his *repentaunce* þer alle reson hym dampneþ.
C. 6.1   With þat ran *repentaunce* and rehersede his teme
C. 6.12   'Repente þe,'quod *repentaunce,* 'as resoun þe tauhte

C. 6.62   Quod *repentaunce* riht with þat; and thenne aroos enuye.
C. 6.91   'ȝus! redily,' quod *repentaunce*, 'and thow be ryht sory
C. 6.164 'Now repente,' quod *repentaunce*, 'and reherce neuere
C. 6.234 'Repentedest [thow e]uere,' quod *repentaunce*, '[or] Restitucioun
          madest?'
C. 6.237 'That was a ruful restitucioun,' quod *repentaunce*, 'for sothe;
C. 6.253 'Now redily,' quod *repentaunce*, 'and by þe rode, y leue,
C. 6.286 'Now redily,'quod *repentaunce*, 'y haue reuthe of thy lyuynge.'
C. 6.331 'Be þe rode,' quod *repentaunce*, 'thow romest toward heuene
C. 6.339 Repente þe anon,' quod *repentaunce* ryhte to the vsurer,
C. 6.423 To *repentaunce* ryht thus, 'haue reuthe on me,' he saide,
C. 7.8   'What! awake, renke!' quod *repentaunce*, 'and rape [þe] to shryfte.'
C. 7.55   'Repentest th[ow] nat?' quod *repentaunce*, and ryht with þat he
          swowened
C. 7.119 Tho was *repentaunce* aredy and redde hem alle to knele:
C.10.215 Withouten *repentaunce* of here rechelesnesse a rybaud þei
          engendrede.
C.19.284 That rihtwisnesse thorw *repentaunce* to reuthe myhte turne.
C.19.287 Be yraunsomed for his *repentaunce* þer alle resoun hym dampneth.

repente v *repenten v.* A 1 repentiþ; B 12 repente (5) repenteden (1) repentedestow (1) repenten (3) repentestow (1) repenteþ (1); C 13 repente (6) repenteden (1) repentedest (1) repenten (3) Repentest (1) repenteth (1)

A. 5.183 And whoso *repentiþ* raþest shulde rise aftir
B. 5.18   'Now *repente*', quod Repentaunce, 'and reherce neuere
B. 5.230 'Repentedestow euere', quod Repentaunce, 'or restitucion madest?'
B. 5.260 'Now [but þow *repente* þe raþer', quod Repentaunce,
B. 5.334 And whoso *repente[þ]* raþest sholde aryse after
B. 5.441 'Repente[st]ow noȝt?' quod Repentaunce, & riȝt wiþ þat he
          swowned
B. 5.504 And haue ruþe on þise Ribaudes þat *repenten* hem soore
B.12.83 So clergie is confort to creatures þat *repenten*,
B.12.252 And þouȝ þe riche *repente* þanne and birewe þe tyme
B.17.239 That rufully *repenten* and restitucion make,
B.17.303 'ȝis', seide þe Samaritan, 'so þow myght *repente*
B.19.368 *Repenteden* and [forsoke] synne, saue þei one,
B.19.441 And suffreþ þat synfulle be [til som tyme þat þei *repente*].
C. 6.12   'Repente þe,'quod *repentaunce*, 'as resoun þe tauhte
C. 6.164 'Now *repente*,' quod repentaunce, 'and reherce neuere
C. 6.234 'Repentedest [thow e]uere,' quod repentaunce, '[or] Restitucioun
          madest?'
C. 6.339 *Repente* þe anon,' quod repentaunce ryhte to the vsurer,
C. 6.392 And hoso *repente[th]* rathest sholde aryse aftur
C. 7.55   'Repentest th[ow] nat?' quod repentaunce, and ryht with þat he
          swowened
C. 7.149 Haue reuthe of alle these rybaudes þat *repenten* hem sore
C. 9.237 And hoso breketh this, be wel waer, but yf he *repente*,
C.10.52 To *repenten* and arise and rowe out of synne
C.19.205 That reufulliche *repenten* and restitucion make,
C.19.283 'ȝus,' saide þe samaritaen, 'so thow myhtest *repente*
C.21.368 *Repenteden* and [forsoke] synne, saue thei one,
C.21.441 And soffreth þat synnefole be til som tyme þat þei *repente*.

repreueþ v *repreven v.* B 3 repreueden (1) repreueþ (2); C 4 repreue (1) repreuede (1) repreueth (2)

B.10.267 God in þe gospel [grymly] *repreueþ*
B.12.136 Patriarkes and prophetes *repreueden* hir science
B.18.149 Iob þe [parfit] patriark *repreueþ* þi sawes:
C. 3.386 Such inparfit peple *repreueth* alle resoun
C. 5.172 And Barones and here barnes blame ȝow and *repreue*:
C.14.81 Patriarkes and prophetus *repreuede* here science
C.20.152 Iop þe parfit patriarke *repreueth* thy sawes:

rerages n *rerage n.* B 1

B. 5.243 I haue mo Manoirs þoruȝ *Rerages* þan þoruȝ Miseretur &
          com[m]odat.

resceyueþ(- > receyue

rescetour n *recettour n.* C 1

C. 3.500 Ac he þat resceyueth or rec[ett]eth here is *rescetour* of Gyle.'

reseyue- > receyue

resembleþ v *resemblen v.(1)* B 2 resembled (1) resembleþ (1); C 1 resembled

B.12.267 To lowe libbynge men þe larke is *resembled*.
B.16.214 The sone, if I dorste seye, *resembleþ* wel þe widewe:
C.14.187 To lowe lyuynge men þe larke is *resembled*

reseue > receyue

residue n *residue n.* A 2; B 2; C 2

A. 5.231 And wiþ þe *residue* & þe remenaunt, be þe roode of chestre,
A. 7.92   And wiþ þe *residue* & þe remenaunt, be þe rode of chestre,
B. 5.459 And wiþ þe *residue* and þe remenaunt, bi þe Rode of Chestre,

B. 6.100 And wiþ þe *residue* and þe remenaunt, by þe Rode of Lukes!
C. 8.109 And with þe *res[i]due* and þe remenant, by the rode of lukes!
C.12.216 An vnredy reue thy *residue* shal spene

reson n *resoun n.(2)* A 31 resonis (1) resoun (30); B 96 reson (93) Resones (1) resoun (2); C 116 resoen (1) reson (7) resones (2) resoun (106)

A. 1.22   And rekne hem in *resoun*; reherse þou hem aftir.
A. 1.25   And drink whanne þe driȝeþ, ac do it nouȝt out of *resoun*
A. 1.52   For riȝtfulliche *resoun* shulde rewele ȝow alle,
A. 1.92   Kinges & kniȝtes shulde kepe it be *resoun*,
A. 3.81   And suffre hem to selle sumdel aȝens *resoun*.'
A. 3.261 Þat *resoun* shal regne & reumes gouerne,
A. 4.5   But *resoun* rede me þerto [raþer] wole I deiȝe.'
A. 4.7   'Rape þe to riden, & *resoun* þat þou fecche.'
A. 4.14   And riȝt renneþ to *resoun* & rouniþ in his ere;
A. 4.16   'I shal araye me to ride,' quaþ *resoun*, 'reste þe a while,'
A. 4.23   And *resoun* wiþ hym rit & rapiþ hym [swyþe].
A. 4.27   And riden faste for *resoun* shulde rede hem þe beste
A. 4.30   And rombide forþ wiþ *resoun* riȝt to þe king.
A. 4.31   Curteisliche þe king þanne com in to *resoun*,
A. 4.95   But *resoun* haue reuþe on hym he shal reste in þe stokkis
A. 4.97   Summe redde *resoun* to haue reuþe on þat shrewe;
A. 4.99   Þat mede muste be meynpernour *resoun* þei besouȝte.
A. 4.100 'Rede me not,' quaþ *resoun*, 'no reuþe to haue
A. 4.117 And ȝet,' quaþ *resoun*, 'be þe rode, I shal no reuþe haue
A. 4.134 Ac [whanne] *resoun* among þise renkis reherside þise wordis,
A. 4.136 Þat he ne held *resoun* a maister & mede a muche wrecche.
A. 4.142 Couþe nouȝt warpen a word to wiþsigge *resoun*,
A. 4.144 Þe king acordite, be crist, to *resonis* sawis
A. 4.145 And reherside þat *resoun* [hadde] riȝtfulliche shewide;
A. 4.148 'Be hym þat [rauȝte] on þe rode,' quaþ *resoun* to þe king,
A. 4.153 Ac redily, *resoun*, þou shalt not [raike] henne,
A. 4.155 'I am redy,' quaþ *resoun*, 'to reste wiþ ȝow euere;
A. 8.152 And how þe prest inpugnid it al be [pu]re *resoun*,
A.10.51 In rewele & in *resoun*, but reccheles it make.
A.10.57 And ek wantoun & wilde, wiþoute any *resoun*.
A.11.41 And bringe forþ a ballid *resoun*, t[a]k[e] bernard to witnesse,
B.Pr.167 And riȝt so', quod þat Raton, 'Reson me sheweþ
B.Pr.175 Al þ[e] route of Ratons to þis *reson* assented.
B. 1.22   And rekene hem by *reson*: reherce þow hem after.
B. 1.25   And drynke whan þ[ee] drie[þ], ac do [it] noȝt out of *reson*
B. 1.54   For riȝtfully *reson* sholde rule yow alle,
B. 1.94   Kynges and knyȝtes sholde kepen it by *reson*,
B. 2.49   And haue power to punysshe hem; þanne put forþ þi *reson*.
B. 2.85   Wiþ þe Chastilet of cheste and chaterynge out of *reson*,
B. 3.92   And suffre hem to selle somdel ayeins *reson*.'
B. 3.239 And han ywroght werkes wiþ right and wiþ *reson*,
B. 3.285 That *Reson* shal regne and Reaumes gouerne,
B. 4.5   But *Reson* rede me þerto raþer wol I deye.'
B. 4.7   'Rape þee to ryde and *Reson* [þat] þow fecche.
B. 4.14   And [riȝt renneþ] to *Reson* and rouneþ in his ere;
B. 4.16   'I shal araye me to ryde', quod *Reson*, 'reste þee a while',
B. 4.25   And *Reson* wiþ hym ryt, rownynge togideres
B. 4.30   And riden faste for *Reson* sholde rede hem þe beste
B. 4.33   And bad *Reson* ryde faste and recche of hir neiþer.
B. 4.40   Forþi, *Reson*, lat hem ride þo riche by hemselue,
B. 4.42   And þanne *Reson* rood faste þe riȝte heiȝe gate
B. 4.44   Curteisly þe kyng þanne com [in to] *Reson*,
B. 4.108 But *Reson* haue ruþe on hym he shal reste in [þe] stokkes
B. 4.110 Som[me] radde *Reson* to haue ruþe on þat shrewe;
B. 4.112 That Mede moste be maynpernour *Reson* þei bisouȝte.
B. 4.113 'Reed me noȝt', quod *Reson*, 'no ruþe to haue
B. 4.134 And yet', quod *Reson*, 'by þe Rode! I shal no ruþe haue
B. 4.153 And þei lauȝynge lope to hire and lefte *Reson* manye.
B. 4.157 Alle riȝtfulle recordede þat *Reson* truþe tolde.
B. 4.171 The kyng callede Conscience and afterward *Reson*
B. 4.172 And recordede þat *Reson* hadde riȝtfully shewed,
B. 4.177 Ac *Reson* shal rekene wiþ yow if I regne any while,
B. 4.185 'By hym þat rauȝte on þe Rode!' quod *Reson* to þe kynge,
B. 4.190 Ac redily, *Reson*, þow shalt noȝt [raike henne];
B. 4.192 'I am redy', quod *Reson*, 'to reste wiþ yow euere;
B. 5.11   And how *Reson* gan arayen hym al þe Reaume to preche
B. 5.23   How pertly afore þe peple [preche gan *Reson*].
B. 5.36   Ne for no poustee of pestilence plese hem noȝt out of *reson*.
B. 5.59   That seweþ my sermon;' and þus seyde *Reson*.
B. 5.272 And siþen þat *Reson* rolle it in þe Registre of heuene
B. 6.316 He greueþ hym ageyn god and gruccheþ ageyn *Reson*,
B.10.55 And bryngen forþ a balled *reson*, taken Bernard to witnesse,
B.10.116 Roten and torende? *Reson* wolde it neuere!
B.11.126 Riȝtfully to reneye no *reson* it wolde.
B.11.131 A[c] *reson* shal rekene wiþ hym [and rebuken hym at þe laste,
B.11.269 Than he þat is riȝt riche; *Reson* bereþ witnesse:
B.11.335 *Reson* I seiȝ sooþly sewen alle beestes,

B.11.370	That *Reson* rewarded and ruled alle beestes
B.11.372	No *Reson* hem [ruled, neiþer riche ne pouere].
B.11.373	[Th]anne I rebukede *Reson* and riȝt til hym I seyde,
B.11.376	And *Reson* arated me and seide, 'recche þee neuere
B.11.387	Forþi I rede', quod *reson*, '[þow] rule þi tonge bettre,
B.11.414	Thow sholdest haue knowen þat clergie kan & [conceyued] moore þoruȝ *Res[on]*
B.11.415	For *Reson* wolde haue reherced þee riȝt as Clergie seid;
B.11.420	And riȝt so ferde *Reson* bi þee; þow wiþ rude speche
B.11.429	For þouȝ *Reson* rebuked hym þanne [reccheþ hym neuere;
B.11.438	Why ye wisse me þus', quod I, 'was for I rebuked *Reson*.'
B.12.104	Riȝt so [lereþ] lettrure lewed men to *Reson*.
B.12.170	'Right so', quod þe renk, '*Reson* it sheweþ
B.12.209	It were neiþer *reson* ne riȝt to rewarde boþe yliche.
B.12.218	And aresonedest *Reson*, a rebukynge as it were,
B.12.263	So is þe riche [reuerenced] by *reson* of hise goodes.
B.13.166	Pope ne patriark, þat pure *reson* ne shal [þee] make
B.14.109	Ther þe poore dar plede and preue by pure *reson*
B.14.124	Right so *reson* sheweþ þat [þo renkes] þat were [lordes]
B.14.207	[Ac] þe riche is reuerenced by *reson* of his richesse
B.14.311	[For] lordes alloweþ hym litel or listneþ to his *reson*;
B.15.11	Til *reson* hadde ruþe on me and rokked me aslepe,
B.15.28	Thanne is Racio my riȝte name, *reson* on englissh;
B.15.52	It were ayeins kynde', quod he, 'and alle kynnes *reson*
B.15.65	Right so þat þoruȝ *reson* wolde þe roote knowe
B.15.101	A[c] þer þe roote is roten, *reson* woot þe soþe,
B.15.476	Riȝt so rude men þat litel *reson* konneþ
B.15.513	In ensaumple þat men sholde se by sadde *reson*
B.15.550	*Reson* and rightful doom þ[o] Religiouse d[ampn]ede.
B.17.41	And riȝt so, bi þe roode, *Reson* me sheweþ
B.17.157	Right so, redily, *Reson* it sheweth
B.17.188	He may receyue riȝt noȝt; *reson* it sheweþ.
B.17.258	The holy goost hereþ þee noȝt ne helpe may þee by *reson*.
B.17.263	That riche ben and *reson* knoweþ ruleþ wel youre soule;
B.17.307	Be raunsoned for his repentaunce þer alle *reson* hym dampneþ.
B.17.343	And ben inpacient in hir penaunce, pure *reson* knoweþ
B.17.349	For vnkyndenesse is þe contrarie of alle kynnes *reson*.
B.18.199	Ayeins *Reson*. [I], rightwisnesse, recorde þus wiþ truþe
B.18.278	For by right and by *reson* þe renkes þat ben here
B.18.330	[Al]þouȝ *Reson* recorde, and riȝt of myselue,
B.18.334	Wiþ gile þow hem gete ageyn alle *reson*.
B.18.339	That gilours be bigiled and þat is good *reson*:
B.18.349	But by right and by *reson* raunsone here my liges:
B.18.350	Thow fettest myne in my place [maugree] alle *resoun*,
B.18.352	To recouere hem þoruȝ raunsoun and by no *reson* ellis,
B.19.26	'Thow knowest wel', quod Conscience, 'and þow konne *reson*,
B.19.83	*Reson* and Rightwisnesse and Ruþe þei offrede;
B.19.86	That o kyng cam wiþ *Reson* couered vnder sense.
B.19.88	Rightwisnesse vnder reed gold, *Resones* felawe;
B.19.460	'I holde it riȝt and *reson* of my Reue to take
B.19.478	And rule þi reaume in *reson* [as right wol and] truþe
C.Pr.184	[Ryȝt so,'quod þe raton', '*reson* me sheweth
C.Pr.192	Alle th[e] route of ratones to þis *resoun* assentide;
C. 1.50	For riȝtfulliche *resoun* sholde reule ȝow alle
C. 1.90	Kynges and knyghtes sholde kepen hit by *resoun*,
C. 2.52	And haue power to p[uny]schen hem; thenne pot forth thy *resoun*.
C. 2.92	With [þe] chastel of cheste and chaterynge out of *resoun*;
C. 3.146	And teche the to louye treuthe and take consail of *resoun*.
C. 3.294	And þat is nother *resoun* ne ryhte ne [i]n no rewme lawe
C. 3.309	And ther is *resoun* as a reue rewardynge treuthe
C. 3.325	Richesse and *resoun* the while he ryhte lyuede
C. 3.386	Such inparfit peple repreueth alle *resoun*
C. 3.438	That *resoun* shal regne and reumes gouerne
C. 3.446	And hoso taketh aȝeyn treuthe or transuerseth aȝeyns *resoun*
C. 4.5	But *resoun* rede me pertyl rather wo[l] y dey.'
C. 4.7	'Rape the to ryde and *resoun* þat thow [f]ec[c]he.
C. 4.14	And rood forth to *resoun* and rouned in his ere
C. 4.16	'Y shal aray me to ryde,' quod *resoun*, 'reste the [a] while,'
C. 4.25	And *resoun* with hym ry[t], rounynge togederes
C. 4.29	To take reed of *resoun* þat recorde sholde
C. 4.32	Ac Consience knewe hem wel and carped to *resoun*:
C. 4.34	Ryde forth, syre *resoun*, and rech nat of here tales
C. 4.40	Thenne *resoun* rood forth Ac took reward of no man
C. 4.42	Corteyslyche þe kyng thenne cam and grette *resoun*
C. 4.43	And bytwene hymsulue and his sone sette tho sire *resoun*
C. 4.103	Bute *resoun* haue reuth on hym he shal reste in [þe] stokkes
C. 4.105	Summe radden *resoun* tho to haue reuthe vppon þat shrewe
C. 4.107	That mede myhte be maynpernour [*resoun*] thei bysouhte.
C. 4.108	'Rede me nat,' quod *resoun*, 'no reuthe to haue
C. 4.131	And [ȝut],' quod *resoun*, 'by þe rode! y shal no reuthe haue
C. 4.134	Y sey it [by] mysulf,' quod *resoun*, 'and it so were
C. 4.150	Reherce the[r] anon ryhte þat myhte *resoun* stoppe.
C. 4.151	Ac al ryhtful recordede þat *resoun* treuthe sayde,

C. 4.153	*Resoun* for his ryhtful speche; ryche and pore hym louede
C. 4.154	And sayden, 'we seyn wel, syre *resoun*, be thi wordes
C. 4.166	The kyng to consayl tho toek Consience and *resoun*
C. 4.171	Ac *resoun* shal rykene with ȝow yf y regne eny while
C. 4.179	'By hym þat rauhte [on] þe rode,' quod *resoun* to the kyng,
C. 4.184	Forthy, *resoun*, redyly thow shalt nat ryden hennes
C. 4.187	'Y assente,' sayde *resoun*, 'by so ȝowsulue yhere
C. 4.190	Ne no supersedias sende but y assente,' quod *resoun*.
C. 4.196	And receyue tho that *resoun* louede; and riht with þat y wakede.
C. 5.5	For y made of tho men as *resoun* me tauhte.
C. 5.6	For as y cam by Consience with *resoun* y mette
C. 5.11	Romynge in remembraunce thus *resoun* me aratede:
C. 5.26	'Thenne hastow londes to lyue by,' quod *resoun*, 'or lynage ryche
C. 5.53	And also moreouer me [sem]eth, syre *resoun*,
C. 5.64	Redon and resceyuen þat *resoun* ouhte to spene\
C. 5.82	Forthy rebuke me ryhte nauhte, *resoun*, y ȝow praye,
C. 5.102	'Y rede the,' quod *resoun* tho, 'rape the to bigynne
C. 5.112	And *resoun* yreuestede ryht as a pope
C. 5.114	*Resoun* reuerentliche tofore al þe reume prechede
C. 5.125	How *resoun* radde al the reume to heuene.
C. 5.182	And also,' quod *resoun*, 'y rede ȝow ryche
C. 5.200	That sueth my sarmon;'[and] Thus [sayde] *resoun*.
C. 6.12	'Repente þe,'quod repentaunce, 'as *resoun* þe tauhte
C. 6.435	Out of *resoun* among rybaudes here rybaudrye to here.
C.11.27	And þat is no riht ne *resoun* for rather me sholde
C.11.36	And brynge forth [a] balle[d] *reso[n]*, taken bernard to witnesse
C.11.97	Of lore and of lettrure, of lawe and of *resoun*.
C.12.61	Rihtfolliche to renoye no *resoun* hit wolde.
C.12.66	A[c] *reson* shal rekene with hym and rebuken hym at þe laste
C.12.154	Then he þat is rihte ryche; *reson* bereth witnesse:
C.13.35	And rikene byfore *resoun* a resonable acounte
C.13.143	*Resoun* y sey sothly sewe alle bestes
C.13.154	For out of *resoun* they ryde and rechelesliche t[a]ken on
C.13.180	Was þat y seyh *resoun* sewen alle bestes
C.13.182	*Resoun* re[ul]ede hem nat, noþer ryche ne pore.
C.13.183	Thenne y [a]resonede *resoun* and ryht til hym y sayde,
C.13.191	They reule hem al by *resoun* Ac renkes ful fewe.
C.13.194	And *resoun* aresounede me and sayde, 'reche þe neuere
C.13.205	Forthy,' quod *Resoun*, 'y rede thow reule thy tonge euere
C.13.222	Thow sholdest haue yknowe þat clergie ca[n] & conseyued mor[e] [throw] *resoun*
C.13.223	For *resoun* wolde haue rehersed þe riht as clergie seide;
C.13.228	Rihte so ferde *Resoun* by the; for thy rude speche
C.13.229	And for thow woldest wyte why, *resones* preue[t]e,
C.13.231	*Resoun* refusede the and wolde nat reste with the
C.13.236	For thogh *resoun* rebuke hym thenne recheth he neuere;
C.13.244	Why ȝe worden to me thus was for y aresonede *Resoun*.'
C.14.49	Riht so lereth lettrure lewed men to *resoun*.
C.14.110	'Riht so,' quod þ[e] renk, '*resoun* hit sheweth
C.14.148	Hit were no *resoun* ne riht to rewarde bothe ylyche.
C.15.26	And beden me ryse and rome; with *reson* sholde y dyne.
C.15.27	And y aroos and romede forth and with *resoun* we mette.
C.15.28	We reuerensede *resoun* and romede forth softly
C.15.39	*Resoun* stoed and s[t]yhlede as for styward of halle.
C.15.51	Thenne *resoun* radde anoon riht aftur
C.15.150	And *resoun* ran aftur and riht with hym ȝede;
C.15.283	Then eny pore pacient; and þat preue y be *resoun*.
C.15.285	There þe pore dar plede and preue by puyr *resoun*
C.16.48	A[c] þe ryche is reuerenced by *resoun* of his rychesse
C.16.145	For lordes alloueth hym litel or leggeth ere to his *resoun*;
C.16.177	To do wel or wykke, a will with a *resoun*,
C.16.188	Thenne ys racio my rihte name, *reson* an englische;
C.16.214	Hit were aȝeyns kynde,' quod he, 'and alle kyne *resoun*
C.16.254	Ac þer þe rote is roton, *resoun* woet þe sothe,
C.17.213	*Resoun* and rihtfol doem tho religious dampnede.
C.17.264	In ensaumple þat men sholde se by sad *resoen*
C.18.97	And in heuene is priueoste and next hym by *resoun*
C.19.3	To reule alle reumes þerwith in riȝhte and in *resoun*.
C.19.154	He may resceyue riht nauhte; *resoun* hit sheweth.
C.19.229	That riche ben and *resoun* knoweth; reule wel ȝoure soul[e];
C.19.287	Be yraunsomed for his repentaunce þer alle *resoun* hym dampneth.
C.19.323	And be inpacient in here penaunc[e], puyr *resoun* knoweth
C.19.329	For vnkyndenesse is þe contrarie of alle kyne *resoun*.
C.20.204	Aȝeynes *resoun*; y, rihtwysnesse, recorde [þus] with treuthe
C.20.300	For bi riht and by *resoun* þ[e] renkes þat ben here
C.20.308	Reuen vs of oure riht sethe *resoun* hem dampnede.
C.20.373	Althouh *resoun* record[e], and rihte of mysulue,
C.20.377	With gyle thow hem gete agaynes all *resoun*.
C.20.395	Bote [by] riht and [by] *resoun* raunsome here my lege[s]:
C.21.26	'Thow knowest wel,' quod Concience, 'and þou kunne *resoun*,
C.21.83	*Resoun* and riht[wis]nesse and reuthe thei offrede;
C.21.86	That [o] kyng cam with *reson* ykyuered vnder ensense.
C.21.88	Rihtwisnesse vnder reed gold, *resones* felawe;

C.21.460 'Y halde hit riht and *resoun* of my reue to take
C.21.478 And rewle thy rewme in *resoun* [as] riht w[o]l and treuthe,

resonable adj *resonable adj.(2)* B 1; C 4
B.13.285 Religion saunȝ rule [and] *resonable* obedience;
C.Pr.178 A ratoun of renown, moste *resonable* of tounge,
C. 3.367 Þat is nat *resonable* ne rect to refuse my syre name,
C. 6.33 Ryche, and *resonable* and ryhtful of lyuynge;
C.13.35 And rikene byfore resoun a *resonable* acounte

resonably adv *resonabli adv.* B 1; C 2 resonableyche (1) resonably (1)
B.14.103 Than richesse riȝtfulliche wonne and *resonably* despended?'
C.12.17 To restitute *resonably* for al vnrihtfole wynnynge.
C.15.278 Then rihtfu[l] rychesse and *resonableyche* to spene?'

resoun > reson; resseyued > receyue; rest > reste,resten

reste n *reste n.(1) &> resten* A 3; B 12; C 10 rest (1) reste (9)
A. 2.138 For þei shuln bere þise bisshopis & bringe hem at *reste.*
A. 5.202 Þat he slepte satirday & sonneday til sonne ȝede to *reste.*
A.11.15 Or ricchesse or rentis, & *reste* at here wille,
B.Pr.197 For may no renk þer *reste* haue for Ratons by nyȝte,]
B. 5.360 That he sleep Saterday and Sonday til sonne yede to *reste.*
B. 7.80 For he þat yeueþ yeldeþ and yarkeþ hym to *reste,*
B. 9.57 A[c] in þe herte is hir hoom and hir mooste *reste.*
B.10.15 Or richesse or rentes, and *reste* at hir wille,
B.12.151 [Riche men rutte þo and in hir *reste* were
B.12.275 That god for his grace gyue hir soules *reste,*
B.14.156 That god rewarded double *reste* to any riche wye.
B.14.321 Now god þat alle good gyueþ graunte his soule *reste*
B.18.210 Sholde neuere riȝt riche man þat lyueþ in *reste* and ese
B.18.215 The which vnknytteþ alle care and comsynge is of *reste.*
B.20.45 And þe fissh haþ fyn to flete wiþ to *reste;*
C.Pr.217 And [ȝ]e route of ratones of *reste* men awake
C. 6.418 A sleep saturday and sonenday til sonne ȝede to *reste.*
C.10.54 For rather haue we no *reste* til we restitue
C.14.95 Ryche men rotte tho and in here *reste* were
C.14.197 That god for his grace gyue here soules *reste*
C.15.231 And *reste* and ryche metes, rebaudes hem made.'
C.16.156 Now god þat al [good] gyueth graunte his soule *reste*
C.20.219 For sholde neuere riȝt riche man þat lyueth in *rest* and hele
C.20.224 The which vnknytteth alle care and comsyng is of *reste.*
C.22.45 And þe fisch hath fyn to flete with to *reste;*

resten v *resten v.(1)* A 6 reste (5) resten (1); B 12 rest (2) reste (9) resten (1); C 11 reste
A.Pr.7 I was wery [for]wandrit & wente me to *reste*
A. 4.16 'I shal araye me to ride,' quaþ resoun, '*reste* þe a while,'
A. 4.95 But resoun haue reuþe on hym he shal *reste* in þe stokkis
A. 4.155 'I am redy,' quaþ resoun, 'to *reste* wiþ ȝow euere;
A.10.78 To routen ne to *resten* ne ro[t]en in þin herte.
A.11.116 And rid forþ be ricchesse, ac *reste* þou not þereinne,
B.Pr.7 I was wery forwandred and wente me to *reste*
B.Pr.171 Wher he ryt or *rest* or r[om]eþ to pleye.
B. 3.236 Or *resten* in þyne holy hilles: þis askeþ Dauid.
B. 4.16 'I shal arraye me to ryde', quod Reson, '*reste* þee a while',
B. 4.108 But Reson haue ruþe on hym he shal *reste* in [þe] stokkes
B. 4.192 'I am redy', quod Reson, 'to *reste* wiþ yow euere;
B. 5.151 Or ellis al riche and ryden; I, wraþe, *reste* neuere
B.10.164 And ryd forþ by richesse, ac *rest* þow noȝt þerInne,
B.11.338 As whan þei hadde ryde in Rotey tyme anoon [*reste* þei] after;
B.17.339 The reyn þat reyneþ þer we *reste* sholde
B.18.6 *Reste* me þere and rutte faste til Ramis palmarum.
B.18.165 Rightwisnesse come rennynge; *reste* we þe while,
C.Pr.188 Wher he ri[t] othere *reste* or rometh to pleye;
C. 4.16 'Y shal aray me to ryde,' quod resoun, '*reste* the [a] while,'
C. 4.103 Bute resoun haue reuth on hym he shal *reste* in [þe] stokkes
C. 6.126 Or alle riche and ryde, *reste* shal y nat, wrathe,
C. 9.144 *Reste* hym and roste [hym] and his rug turne,
C.11.106 And ryde forth by rychesse [ac] *reste* nat þerynne,
C.13.34 And sholden wende o wey where bothe mosten *reste*
C.13.146 As when þei hadde [ryde in] roteye[tyme] anon they *reste* aftur;
C.13.231 Resoun refusede the and wolde nat *reste* with me.
C.19.319 The rayne þat rayneth þere we *reste* sholde
C.20.168 Rihtwisnesse come rennynge; *reste* we the while

restitucion n *restitucioun n.* B 6; C 5 restitucion (2) restitucioun (3)
B. 5.230 'Repentedestow euere', quod Repentaunce, 'or *restitucion* madest?'
B. 5.233 'That was no *restitucion*', quod Repentaunce, 'but a robberis þefte;
B. 5.235 'I wende riflynge were *restitucion* for I lerned neuere rede on boke,
B. 5.271 Til þow make *restitucion*', [quod Repentaunce], 'and rekene wiþ hem alle;
B.17.239 That rufully repenten and *restitucion* make,
B.17.319 Ac er his rightwisnesse to ruþe torne som *restitucion* bihoueþ;
C. 6.234 'Repentedest [thow e]uere,' quod repentaunce, '[or] *Restiticioun* madest?'

C. 6.237 'That was a rufol *restitucioun*,' quod repentaunce, 'for sothe;
C. 6.295 Til thow haue ymad by thy myhte to alle men *restitucioun.*
C.19.205 That reufulliche repenten and *restitucion* make,
C.19.299 Ac ar [h]is rihtwisnesse to reuthe turne *rest[i]t[uci]on* hit maketh,

restitue v *restituen v.* B 2; C 4 restitue (3) restitute (1)
B. 5.275 [Is] holden at þe heiȝe doom to helpe þee to *restitue,*
B. 5.289 And if þow wite neuere to [whom] ne [where] to *restitue*
C. 6.297 [Ben] haldyng at the heye dome to helpe the *restitue.*
C. 6.344 And ȝif thow wyte neuere to whom ne where to *restitue*
C.10.54 For rather haue we no reste til we *restitue*
C.12.17 To *restitute* resonably for al vnrihtfole wynnynge.

restore v *restoren v.* B 1; C 1
B.11.262 Is a kernel of confort kynde to *restore.*
C.12.148 Is a cornel of confort kynde to *restore,*

resurexion n *resurreccioun n.* B 4 resurexcion (1) resurexion (3); C 5 resureccion (1) resureccioun (2) resureccoun (1) resurexioun (1)
B.11.207 And after his *resurexcion* Redemptor was his name,
B.18.259 And but þei reuer[en]sen his roode and his *Resurexion*
B.18.425 That men rongen to þe *resurexion*, and riȝt wiþ þat I wakede
B.18.427 '[Ariseþ] and reuerence[þ] goddes *resurexion*,
C.12.115 And aftur his *resureccoun* redemptor was his name
C.18.162 Ac þe ouerturnynge of the temple bitokened his *resureccioun.*
C.20.267 And bote they reuerense [h]is *resurexioun* and þe rode honure
C.20.468 That men rang to þe *resureccioun* and riht with þat y wakede
C.20.470 'Arise and go reuerense godes *resureccio[n]*'

ret > reden

retenaunce n *retenaunce n.* A 1; B 1; C 1
A. 2.33 Alle þe riche *retenaunce* þat regniþ wiþ false
B. 2.54 That al þe riche *retenaunce* þat regneþ with [fals]
C. 2.57 Al þe riche *retenaunce* þat ro[t]eth hem o fals lyuynge

retorik n *rethorike n.* B 1; C 1 retoryk
B.11.102 To reden it in *Retorik* to arate dedly synne?
C.12.36 To rehercen hit by *retoryk* to arate dedly synne?

retribucoun n *retribucioun n.* C 1
C. 3.338 And ayther is otheres helpe; of hem cometh *retribucoun*

reufulliche > rewfulliche

reule n *ruel n. &> rule,rulen* C 1
C. 9.79 To rise to þe *reule* to rokke þe cradel,

reule- > rulen; reume > reaume; reumes > reaume,rewmes; reuth(e > ruþe; reuares > reueris

reue n *reve n.* A 1; B 6 reue (3) reues (3); C 9 reue (7) reues (2)
A. 2.75 Randolf þe *reue* of rutelondis sokne,
B. 2.111 Reynald þe *Reue* of Rutland Sokene,
B. 5.420 I kan holde louedayes and here a *Reues* rekenyng,
B.10.477 But þo þat kepen þe lordes catel, clerkes and *Reues.*
B.19.258 For I make Piers þe Plowman my procuratour and my *reue,*
B.19.460 'I holde it riȝt and reson of my *Reue* to take
B.19.463 Wiþ Spiritus Intellectus þei [toke] þe *reues* rolles
C. 2.115 Raynald þe *reue* and redyngkynges manye,
C. 2.183 And ryde on hem and on *reue[s]* righte faste by mede.
C. 3.309 And ther is resoun as a *reue* rewardynge treuthe
C. 7.33 And holden a knyhtus Court and acounte with þe *reue*
C.11.297 As doth the *reue* or Conturrollor þat rykene moet and acounten
C.12.216 An vnredy *reue* thy residue shal spene
C.21.258 For y make [Peres the plouhman] my proc[ur]atour and my *reue*
C.21.460 'Y halde hit riht and resoun of my *reue* to take
C.21.463 With spiritus intellectus they [t]o[k]e þe *reues* rolles

reue v *reven v.* B 3; C 6 refte (1) reue (3) reuen (1) reueth (1)
B.14.132 Allas þat richesse shal *reue* and robbe mannes soule
B.16.89 To go robbe þat Rageman and *reue* þe fruyt fro hym.
B.18.277 If he *reu[e]* me my riȝt he robbeþ me by maistrie.
C. 3.327 A *refte* hym of his richesse and of his ryhte mynde
C. 4.180 'But [y] reule thus alle reumes *reuet[h]* me my syhte,
C.16.1 Allas þat rychesse shal *reue* and robbe mannes soule
C.18.121 To go ransake þat ragman and *reue* hym of his apples
C.20.299 Yf he *reue* me my rihte A robbeth me [by] maistrie
C.20.308 *Reuen* vs of oure riht sethe resoun hem dampnede.

reuel n *revel n.(1)* B 2 reuel (1) reueles (1) C 2 reuel (1) reueles (1)
B.13.441 Forþi I rede yow riche, *reueles* whan ye makeþ;
B.20.181 And rood [so to] *reuel*, a ryche place and a murye,
C. 7.101 Forthy y rede ȝow ryche, *reueles* when ȝe maketh,
C.22.181 And roed so to *reuel*, a ryche place and a murye:

reueled ptp *rivelen v.* C 1
C.10.265 For riche or yrented wel, thouh he be *reueled* for elde

reuerence n *reverence n. &> reuerencen* B 2 reuerence (1) reuerences (1); C 3 reuerences
B.12.119   That wiþ archa dei [wenten] in [worship and *reuerence*]
B.14.205   For þer þat richesse regneþ *reuerence[s]* folweþ,
C. 9.192   As rychesses and *reuerences* and ryche menne Almesse,
C.16.46   For [þer] þat rychess[e] regneth *reuerences* followeth
C.17.43   And refuse *reuerences* and raue[n]ers offrynges.

reuerencen v *reuerencen v.* B 14 reuerence (1) reuerenced (8) reuerencen (3) reuerenceþ (1) reuerensen (1); C 16 reuerence (1) reuerenced (3) reuerenceth (1) reuerense (3) reuerensed (5) reuerensede (1) reuerensen (1) reuerenseth (1)
B.11.440   And I aroos vp ri3t wiþ þat and [*reuerenced*] hym [faire,
B.12.263   So is þe riche [*reuerenced*] by reson of hise goodes.
B.14.207   [Ac] þe riche is *reuerenced* by reson of his richesse
B.15.5   And lete me for a lorel and looþ to *reuerencen*
B.15.81   And *reuerencen* þe riche þe raþer for hir siluer:
B.15.540   Is *reuerenced* er þe Roode, receyued for [þe] worþier
B.16.226   I roos vp and *reuerenced* hym and ri3t faire hym grette.
B.17.282   To a torche or a tapur to *reuerence* þe Trinite.
B.18.173   Rightwisnesse hire *reuerenced* by hir riche cloþyng
B.18.240   And tendeden [hire] as a torche to *reuerencen* his burþe;
B.18.259   And but þei *reuer[en]sen* his roode and his Resurexion
B.18.427   '[Ariseþ] and *reuerence[þ]* goddes resurexion,
B.19.73   *Reuerenced* hym [ri3t] faire wiþ richesses of erþe.
B.20.59   And Religiouse *reuerenced* hym and rongen hir belles,
C. 9.123   A *reuerenseth* hym ryht nauht, no rather then another:
C.11.19   He is *reuerensed* and yrobed þat can robbe þe peple
C.13.246   And [y] aroes vp riht with þat and *reuerensed* hym fayre
C.14.181   Riht so men *reuerence[th]* more þe ryche for h[is] mebles
C.15.28   We *reuerensede* resoun and romede forth softly
C.16.48   A[c] þe ryche is *reuerensed* by resoun of his rychesse
C.16.240   And *reuerence* þe ryche þe rather for here suluer
C.17.201   Is *reuerenced* byfore the rode and resceyued for the worthiore
C.18.242   Y roos vp and *reuerensed* god and ri3t fayre hym grette,
C.19.263   Or elles [to] a taper to *reuerense* with the trinite
C.20.176   Rihtwisnesse *reuerenced* pees in here rich clothyng
C.20.249   And tenden h[ere] as a torche to *reuerensen* his burthe;
C.20.267   And bote they *reuerense* [h]is resurexioun and þe rode honoure
C.20.470   'Arise and go *reuerense* godes resureccio[n]
C.21.73   *Reuerensed* hym riht fayre with richesses of erthe.
C.22.59   And religious *reuerensed* hym and rongen here belles

reuerentliche adv *reverentli adv.* B 1; C 3 reuerentlich (1) reuerentliche (1) reuerentloker (1)
B.18.420   'Thow seist sooþ', [seyde] Rightwisnesse, and *reuerentliche* hire kiste:
C. 5.114   Resoun *reuerentliche* tofore al þe reume prechede
C. 8.44   He worth rather reseyued and *reuerentloker* s[e]tte:
C.20.463   'Thowe saiste soeth,' saide rihtwisnesse, and *reuerentlich* here custe,

reueris n *revere n.* B 1; C 1 reuares
B.14.182   To robberis and to *Reueris*, to riche and to poore,
C.13.58   With robbares and *reuares* þat ryche men despoilen

reuers n *reverse n.* C 1
C.12.210   Ac hoso rat of th[e] ryche the *reuers* may fynde,

reward n *reward n.* B 1; C 2
B.17.270   Ech a riche, I rede, *reward* at hym take
C. 4.40   Thenne resoun rood forth Ac took *reward* of no man
C.19.251   Vch a riche y rede *reward* herof take

rewarden v *rewarden v.* B 10 rewarde (5) rewarded (3) rewarden (2); C 6 rewarde (3) rewardeth (1) rewardid (1) rewardynge (1)
B.Pr.127   And for þi ri3tful rulyng be *rewarded* in heuene'.
B. 3.318   But after þe dede þat is doon oon doom shal *rewarde*
B.11.134   For hise arerages *rewarden* hym þere [ri3t] to þe day of dome,
B.11.370   That Reson *rewarded* and ruled alle beestes
B.12.209   It were neiþer reson ne ri3t to *rewarde* boþe yliche.
B.14.145   Ac if ye riche haue ruþe and *rewarde* wel þe poore,
B.14.148   And *rewarden* alle double richesse þat rewful hertes habbeþ.
B.14.156   That god *rewarded* double reste to any riche wye.
B.14.168   [And] haue ruþe on þise riche men þat *rewarde* no3t þi prisoners;
B.19.193   And rewarde hym right wel þat reddit quod debet,
C.Pr.151   And for thy rightful ruylynge be *rewardid* in heuene.'
C. 3.309   And ther is resoun as a reue *rewardynge* treuthe
C. 5.32   There ryhtfulnesse *rewardeth* ryht as men deserueth–
C.12.69   And for his rechelesnesse *rewarde* hym þere riht to þe day of dome
C.14.148   Hit were no resoun ne riht to *rewarde* bothe ylyche.
C.21.193   And *rewarde* hym riht wel that redd[it] quod debet,

rewe n *reue n.(2)* C 2
C. 1.22   And rekene hem by *rewe*: reherse hem wher þe liketh.
C. 3.107   Ful adoun and forbrent forth alle þe *rewe*.

rewe v *reuen v.(1)* A 1; B 3; C 2
A. 5.241   So *rewe* on þis robert þat red[dere] ne hauiþ,
B. 5.467   So *rewe* on þis Robbere þat Reddere ne haue
B.16.142   'I am sold þoru3 [som] of yow; he shal þe tyme *rewe*
B.18.395   Ac blood may no3t se blood blede but hym *rewe*:
C. 6.321   So *rewe* on Robert þat reddere ne haue
C.20.438   Ac bloed may nat se bloed blede bote hym *rewe*:

rewele > rule,rulen

rewful adj *reuful adj.* B 1; C 1 rufol
B.14.148   And rewarden alle double richesse þat *rewful* hertes habbeþ.
C. 6.237   'That was a *rufol* restitucioun,' quod repentaunce, 'for sothe;

rewfulliche adv *reufulli adv.* B 4 reufulliche (1) rewfulliche (1) rufully (1) rufulliche (1); C 1 reufulliche
B.12.47   And Rosamounde ri3t so *reufulliche* [bisette]
B.14.152   Boþe to riche and to no3t riche þat *rewfulliche* libbeþ;
B.16.78   I hadde ruþe whan Piers rogged, it gradde so *rufulliche*;
B.17.239   That *rufully* repenten and restitucion make,
C.19.205   That *reufulliche* repenten and restitucion make,

rewle > rulen

rewlyche adj *reuli adj.(1)* A 1
A.12.78   [Lene & *rewlyche*, with leggys ful smale].

rewliþ > rulen; rewme > reaume

rewmes n *reume n.* B 1; C 1 reumes
B.20.83   *Rewmes* and Radegundes and roynouse sca[ll]es,
C.22.83   *Reumes* and Radegoundes and roynouse sca[ll]es,

ryalte > reaute

ryb n *ribbe n.(1)* A 1 ribbes; B 1
A. 4.149   'But I reule þus þi reaum rend out my *ribbes*,
B. 9.35   And Eue of his *ryb* bon wiþouten any mene.

ribande ptp *ribaned ppl.* A 1
A. 2.13   In red scarlet robid & *ribande* wiþ gold.

ribanes n *riban n.* B 1
B. 2.16   Wiþ *Ribanes* of reed gold and of riche stones.

ribaud n *ribaude n.* B 4 Ribaud (1) rybaud (1) Ribaudes (2); C 7 rebaudes (1) ribaud (1) rybaud (1) ribaude (1) rybaudes (3)
B. 5.504   And haue ruþe on þise *Ribaudes* þat repenten hem soore
B.14.204   Ac wiþ richesse þ[o] *Ribaud[es]* raþest men bigileþ.
B.16.151   'Aue, raby', quod þat *Ribaud*, and ri3t to hym he yede
B.18.50   'Aue, raby', quod þat *rybaud* and þrew reedes at hym.
C. 6.435   Out of resoun among *rybaudes* here rybaudrye to here.
C. 7.149   Haue reuthe of alle these *rybaudes* þat repenten hem sore
C.10.215   Withouten repentaunce of here rechelesnesse a *rybaud* þei engendrede.
C.15.231   And reste and ryche metes, *rebaudes* hem made.'
C.16.45   Ac with rychesse tho *rybaudes* rathest men bigileth.
C.18.168   'Aue raby,' quod th[at] *ribaud[e]*; and riht til hym [he] 3ede
C.20.50   'Aue, raby,' quod þat *ribaud*, and redes shotte vp to his yes.

rybauder > ribaudour

ribaudie n *ribaudie n.* A 1 ribaudrie; B 1; C 3 rybaudie (1) rybaudrye (2)
A.Pr.44   And risen vp wiþ *ribaudrie* as robertis knaues;
B.Pr.44   And risen [vp] wiþ *ribaudie* [as] Roberdes knaues;
C.Pr.45   And ryseþ with *rybaudrye*, þo robardus knaues;
C. 6.435   Out of resoun among rybaudes here *rybaudrye* to here.
C.11.197   For rechelesnesse in his *rybaud[i]e* riht thus he saide:

ribaudour n *ribaudoure n.* A 1; B 1; C 1 rybauder
A. 7.65   And robyn þe *ribaudour* for hise rusty woordis.
B. 6.73   And Robyn þe *Ribaudour* for hise rusty wordes.
C. 8.75   And Robyn þe *rybauder* for his rousty wordes.

ribaudrie > ribaudie

rybbe v *ribben v.* C 1
C. 9.81   [To] *rybbe* [and] to rele, rusches to pylie,

ribbes > ryb

ribibour n *ribibour n.* A 1; B 1; C 1 rybibour
A. 5.164   A *ribibour*, a ratoner, & a rakiere of chepe,
B. 5.314   A *Ribibour*, a Ratoner, a Rakiere of Chepe,
C. 6.371   A *rybibour*, a ratoner, a rakeare and his knaue,

ricch- > riche(-

richard n prop *n.i.d.* A 1
A.12.113   Furst to rekne *Richard*, kyng of þis rewme,

riche n *riche n.(1)* B 1
B.14.179 Conforte þi carefulle, crist, in þi *rich[e]*,

riche adj *riche adj.* A 16 riche (14) riccheste (2); B 86 riche (84) ryche
(1) richeste (1); C 93 rich (1) riche (29) ryche (61) rychere (1) richore
(1)
A.Pr.18 Of alle maner of men, þe mene & þe *riche*,
A. 1.149 Forþi I rede þe *riche* haue reuþe on þe pore;
A. 2.33 Alle þe *riche* retenaunce þat regniþ wiþ false
A. 2.59 To be present in pride for pouere [or for] *riche*,
A. 3.195 þat is þe *ricccheste* reaume þat re[yn] ouer[houiþ].
A. 3.271 Ne no ray robe [wiþ] *riche* pelure.
A. 3.272 Mede of mysdoeris makiþ hem so *riche*
A. 5.125 Among þe *riche* rayes I rendrit a lessoun;
A. 8.165 Forþi I rede ȝow renkes þat *riche* ben on erþe
A.10.117 Be paied wiþ þe porcioun, pore oþer *riche*.
A.10.134 þei be þe *ricccheste* of reaumes & þe rote of dowel.
A.10.198 For coueitise of catel or of kynrede *riche*,
A.11.51 Nere mercy in mene men more þan in *riche*
A.11.61 For now is iche boy bold, & he be *riche*,
A.11.229 Poul prouiþ it is vnpossible, *riche* men in heuene.
A.11.231 Hauen eritage in heuene, ac *riche* men non.'
B.Pr.18 Of alle manere of men, þe meene and þe *riche*,
B. 1.175 Forþi I rede [þe] *riche*, haueþ ruþe [on] þe pouere;
B. 2.12 And þeron [*riche*] Rubies as rede as any gleede,
B. 2.15 Hire Robe was ful *riche*, of reed scarlet engreyned,
B. 2.16 Wiþ Ribanes of reed gold and of *riche* stones.
B. 2.54 That al þe *riche* retenaunce þat regneþ with [fals]
B. 2.56 Of alle manere of men, þe meene and þe *riche*.
B. 2.78 Falsnesse is fayn of hire for he woot hire *riche*;
B. 3.208 That is þe *richeste* Reaume þat reyn ouerheoueþ.
B. 3.270 Bren it; bere it noȝt awey be it neuer so *riche*
B. 4.40 Forþi, Reson, lat hem ride þo *riche* by hemselue,
B. 5.151 Or ellis al *riche* and ryden; I, wraþe, reste neuere
B. 5.209 Among þe *riche* Rayes I rendred a lesson;
B. 7.187 Forþi I rede yow renkes þat *riche* ben on erþe
B. 9.177 For coueitise of catel ne of kynrede *riche*;
B.10.65 Ne were mercy in meene men moore þan in *riche*
B.10.77 In Religion and in al þe Reme amonges *riche* and pouere
B.10.88 Tobye [techeþ] noȝt so; takeþ hede ye *riche*
B.10.99 Now haþ ech *riche* a rule to eten by hymselue
B.10.341 Poule preueþ it impossible, *riche* men [in] heuene;
B.10.348 Ther *riche* men no riȝt may cleyme but of ruþe and grace.'
B.10.351 That is baptiȝed beþ saaf, be he *riche* or pouere.'
B.10.386 [To rule þe reume and *riche* to make];
B.11.191 We sholde noȝt clepe oure kyn þerto ne none kynnes *riche*:
B.11.197 [Alle myȝte god haue maad *riche* men if he wolde],
B.11.198 [Ac] for þe beste ben som *riche* and some beggeres and pouere.
B.11.199 For alle are we cristes creatures and of his cofres *riche*,
B.11.208 And we hise breþeren þoruȝ hym ybouȝt, boþe *riche* and pouere.
B.11.245 Ther neuere segge hym seiȝ in secte of þe *riche*.
B.11.269 Than he þat is riȝt *riche*; Reson bereþ witnesse:
B.11.297 That haþ no lond ne lynage *riche* ne good loos of hise handes.
B.11.372 No Reson hem [ruled, neiþer *riche* ne pouere].
B.12.51 And *riche* renkes riȝt so gaderen and sparen
B.12.74 That what womman were in auoutrye taken, whe[r *riche* or poore,
B.12.143 He spekeþ þere of *riche* men riȝt noȝt, ne of riȝt witty,
B.12.151 [*Riche* men rutte þo and in hir reste were
B.12.241 Bitokneþ riȝt *riche* men þat reigne here on erþe.
B.12.247 Right so þe *riche*, if he his richesse kepe
B.12.252 And þouȝ þe *riche* repente þanne and birewe þe tyme
B.12.263 So is þe *riche* [reuerenced] by reson of hise goodes.
B.13.7 And how þat freres folwede folk þat was *riche*
B.13.438 Muche moore, me þynkeþ, *riche* men sholde
B.13.441 Forþi I rede yow *riche*, reueles whan ye makeþ,
B.14.27 Ne no Mynstrall be moore worþ amonges pouere and *riche*
B.14.74 [Oþer] plentee makeþ pryde amonges poore and *riche*.
B.14.106 I wiste neuere renk þat *riche* was, þat whan he rekene sholde,
B.14.128 Riȝt so fareþ god by som *riche*; ruþe me it þynkeþ,
B.14.140 So I seye by yow *riche*, it semeþ noȝt þat ye shulle
B.14.144 It may noȝt be, ye *riche* men, or Mathew on god lyeþ:
B.14.145 Ac if ye *riche* haue ruþe and rewarde wel þe poore,
B.14.152 Boþe to *riche* and to noȝt riche þat rewfulliche libbeþ,
B.14.152 Boþe to riche and to noȝt *riche* þat rewfulliche libbeþ;
B.14.156 That god rewarded double reste to any *riche* wye.
B.14.157 For muche murþe is amonges *riche*, as in mete and cloþyng,
B.14.163 And arated of *riche* men þat ruþe is to here.
B.14.168 [And] haue ruþe on þise *riche* men þat rewarde noȝt þi prisoners;
B.14.182 To robberis and to Reueris, to *riche* and to poore,
B.14.201 Forþi cristene sholde be in commune *riche*, noon coueitous for
hymselue,
B.14.206 And þat is plesaunt to pride in poore and in *riche*.
B.14.207 [Ac] þe *riche* is reuerenced by reson of his richesse

B.14.211 For þe *riche* haþ muche to rekene, and [riȝt softe] walkeþ;
B.14.221 For þe poore is ay prest to plese þe *riche*
B.14.231 For his rentes ne wol nauȝt reche no *riche* metes to bigge;
B.14.294 Selde is poore [riȝt] *riche* but of riȝtful heritage.
B.15.81 And reuerencen þe *riche* þe raþer for hir siluer:
B.15.176 'Haþ he anye rentes or richesse or any *riche* frendes?'
B.15.228 Ac in *riche* robes raþest he walkeþ,
B.15.233 *Riche* men he recomendeþ, and of hir robes takeþ
B.15.324 And [bisette] to bidde for yow to swiche þat ben *riche*,
B.15.332 Ac clerkes and knyȝtes and communers þat ben *riche*,
B.15.336 Right so ye *riche*, ye robeþ þat ben riche
B.15.336 Right so ye riche, ye robeþ þat ben *riche*
B.15.340 Right so ye *riche*, ye robeþ and fedeþ
B.15.342 Ac Religiouse þat *riche* ben sholde raþer feeste beggeris
B.15.343 Than burgeises þat *riche* ben as þe book techeþ,
B.15.538 And þo was plentee and pees amonges poore and *riche*,
B.15.544 Boþe *riche* and Religious, þat roode þei honoure
B.17.263 That *riche* ben and reson knoweþ ruleþ wel youre soule;
B.17.265 For manye of yow *riche* men, by my soule, men telleþ,
B.17.267 [Mynne ye noȝt, *riche* men, to whiche a myschaunce
B.17.270 Ech a *riche*, I rede, reward at hym take
B.18.173 Rightwisnesse hire reuerenced by hir *riche* cloþyng
B.18.210 Sholde neuere riȝt *riche* man þat lyueþ in reste and ese
B.20.39 And woneden [wel elengely] and wolde noȝt be *riche*.
B.20.181 And rood [so to] reuel, a *ryche* place and a murye,
B.20.235 They wol flatere [to] fare wel folk þat ben *riche*.
C.Pr.20 Of alle manere [of] men, þe mene and þe [*riche*],
C.Pr.222 Ȝut mette me more of mene and of *riche*,
C. 1.171 Forthy y rede ȝow *riche*, haueth reuthe [o]n þe pore;
C. 2.13 And thereon rede rubies and othere *riche* stones.
C. 2.14 Here robynge was *rychere* þen y rede couthe;
C. 2.57 Al þe *riche* retenaunce þat ro[t]eth o fals lyuynge
C. 2.85 Falsnesse is fayn of here for he wot here *ryche*;
C. 2.187 Wol Ryde vppon Rectores and *ryche* men deuoutours,
C. 3.24 Rynges with rubees and othere *riche* ȝeftes,
C. 3.118 'Haue reuthe on this regraters þat han *riche* handes,
C. 3.204 Ther ne is Cite vnder sonne ne noon so *ryche* reume
C. 3.423 Bern hit; bere hit nat awey be hit neuer so *ryche*;
C. 4.26 Whiche a maistre mede was amonges pore and *ryche*.
C. 4.47 And how he rauesschede Rose the *ryche* wydewe by nyhte
C. 4.153 Resoun for his ryhtful speche; *ryche* and pore hym louede
C. 5.26 'Thenne hastow londes to lyue by,' quod resoun, 'or lynage *ryche*
C. 5.182 And also,' quod resoun, 'y rede ȝow *ryche*
C. 6.33 *Ryche*, and resonable and ryhtful of lyuynge;
C. 6.126 Or alle *riche* and ryde, reste shal y nat, wrathe,
C. 6.217 Amongus the *ryche* rayes y rendrede a lessoun,
C. 7.98 Muche more, me thynketh, *riche* men ouhte
C. 7.101 Forthy y rede ȝow *ryche*, reueles when ȝe maketh,
C. 8.111 And ben a pilgrym at þe plouh for profit to pore and *ryche*.'
C. 9.101 Reche ȝe neuere, ȝe *riche*, Thouh suche lo[rell]es sterue.
C. 9.129 To vnderfongen hem fayre byfalleth for þe *ryche*
C. 9.134 Ryht so, ȝe *ryche*, ȝut rather ȝe sholde
C. 9.192 As rychesses and reuerences and *ryche* menne Almesse,
C. 9.333 Forthy y rede ȝow renkes þat *riche* ben on this erthe
C.10.166 Such lyther lyuyng men lome been *ryche*
C.10.261 Bote he haue oþer goed haue wol here no *ryche*.
C.10.265 For *ryche* or yrented wel, thouh he be reueled for elde
C.11.23 The sauter saith þe same of alle suche *ryche*:
C.11.47 Ne were mercy in m[e]ne men more then in riht *riche*
C.11.57 In religion and in al þe reume amongus *riche* and pore
C.11.68 Tobie techeth nat so; taketh hede, ȝe *ryche*,
C.11.107 For yf thow coueytest to be *ryche* to clergie comest thow neuere.
C.11.212 To reule [þe] reum[e] and *ryche* to make
C.12.4 'Rechelesnesse reche the neuere; By so thow *riche* were
C.12.25 'For this frere flaterede me while he fond me *ryche*
C.12.103 We sholde nat clepie knyhtes þerto ne none kyne *ryche*:
C.12.133 Holy seyntes hym sey Ac neuere in secte of *riche*.
C.12.154 Then he þat is rihte *ryche*; reson bereth witnesse:
C.12.210 Ac hoso rat of th[e] *ryche* the reuers may fynde,
C.12.226 Erles and Erchedekenes and oþere *riche* clerkes
C.13.5 Ȝut ret me þat abraham and Iob weren wonder *ryche*
C.13.32 Rather then þe *ryche* thogh they renne at ones.
C.13.58 With robbares and reuares þat *ryche* men despoilen
C.13.66 The marchaunt is no more to mene but men þat ben *ryche*
C.13.80 Beth nat ybounde, as beth [þ]e *ryche*, to [bothe two] lawes,
C.13.96 As al þat þe *ryche* may rayme and rihtfuly dele
C.13.98 As þe *ryche* man for al his mone, and more as by þe gospell:
C.13.111 That hath n[o] lond ne lynage *ryche* ne good los of his handes.
C.13.182 Resoun re[ul]ede hem nat, noþer *ryche* ne pore.
C.14.87 Hit speketh þer of *ryche* men riht nouht ne of ryche lordes
C.14.87 Hit speketh þer of ryche men riht nouht ne of *ryche* lordes
C.14.95 *Ryche* men rotte tho and in here reste were
C.14.173 Bytokenen riht *ryche* men þat reygne here on erthe.

C.14.181 Riht so men reuerence[th] more þe *ryche* for h[is] mebles
C.14.184 And þe *ryche* for his rentes or for rychesse in his shopp[e].
C.15.9   And how þat freres folewede folk þat was *ryche*
C.15.200 The pore and the *ryche* y plese and payn fynde
C.15.231 And reste and *ryche* metes, rebaudes hem made.'
C.15.281 [Y wiste neuere renke þat *ryche* was þat whan he rekene sholde]
C.15.284 Hit are but fewe folk of this *ryche* that ne falleth in arrerage
C.15.304 Ac when deth awaketh hem of here we[le] þat were er so *ryche*
C.16.8   So y sey by ȝow *ryche*, hit semeth nat þat ȝe scholle
C.16.12   And moche murthe among *ryche* men is þat han meble ynow and hele
C.16.16   [And arated of] *ryche* men þat reuthe is to here.
C.16.21   Ac for þe beste, as y hope, aren som pore and *ryche*.
C.16.42   Forthy cristene sholde be in comune *ryche*, noon coueytous for hymsulue.
C.16.47   And þat is plesant to pruyde in pore and in *ryche*.
C.16.48   A[c] þe *ryche* is reuerenced by resoun of his rychesse
C.16.52   For þe *ryche* hath moche to rykene and riht softe walketh;
C.16.62   For þe pore is ay prest to plese þe *ryche*
C.16.72   For his rentes wol nat reche *ryche* metes to bugge;
C.16.129 Selde is pore rihte *ryche* but of rihtfole eritage.
C.16.240 And reuerence þe *ryche* þe rather for here suluer
C.16.353 Ac in *riche* robes rathest he walketh,
C.16.358 *Riche* men a recomendeth, and of [here] robes taketh,
C.17.2   Or beggeth or biddeth, be he *ryche* or pore,
C.17.199 And tho was p[lente] and p[ees] amonges pore and *ryche*;
C.17.206 Bothe *riche* and religiou[s] þat rode they honouren
C.19.229 That *riche* ben and resoun knoweth; reule wel ȝoure soul[e];
C.19.231 For mony of ȝow *riche* men, by my soule y lye nat,
C.19.233 Minne ȝe nat, *riche* men, to which a myschaunce
C.19.246 And is in helle for al þat, how wol *riche* nouthe
C.19.251 Vch a *riche* y rede reward herof take
C.20.176 Rihtwisnesse reuerenced pees in here *rich* clothyng
C.20.219 For sholde neuere riȝt *riche* man þat lyueth in rest and hele
C.20.472 And rihtfollokest A relyk, noon *richore* on erthe.
C.22.39   And woneden wel elyngly and wolden nat be *riche*.
C.22.181 And roed so to reuel, a *ryche* place and a murye.
C.22.235 Thei wol flatere to fare wel folk þat ben *riche*.

richeliche adv *richeli adv.* C 1

C. 2.12   On alle here fyue fyngeres ful *richeliche* yrynged,

richen v *richen v.(2)* A 1; B 1; C 1 rychen

A. 3.72   And ri[chen] þoruȝ regrat[r]ie & rentis hem biggen
B. 3.83   Thei *richen* þoruȝ regratrie and rentes hem biggen
C. 3.82   *Rychen* thorw regraterye and rentes hem beggeth

richesse n *richesse n.* A 6 ricchesse (5) richesse (1); B 27 richesse (25) richesses (2); C 29 richesse (8) rychesse (19) richesses (1) rychesses (1)

A. 3.22   Rynges wiþ rubies & *ricchesse* manye;
A. 3.79   Ryng[es] or oþer *richesse*, þ[ise] regratour[is] to meynteyne.
A.11.15   Or *ricchesse* or rentis, & reste at here wille,
A.11.116 And rid forþ be *ricchesse*, ac reste þou not þereinne,
A.11.228 Ne *ricchesse*, ne rentis, ne realte of lordis.
A.11.266 God ȝaf h[i]m grace & *ricchesse* togidere
B. 2.17   Hire array me rauysshed; swich *richesse* sauȝ I neuere.
B. 3.23   Rynges wiþ Rubies and *richesses* manye.
B. 3.90   Rynges or ooþer *richesse* þ[ise] Regratiers to mayntene.
B.10.15   Or *richesse* or rentes, and reste at hir wille,
B.10.86   And þe moore he wynneþ and welt welþes and *richesse*
B.10.164 And ryd forþ be *richesse*, ac rest þow noȝt þerInne,
B.10.340 Ne *richesse* [ne rentes] ne Reautee of lordes.
B.10.345 Writen to wissen vs to wilne no *richesse*,
B.11.258 And boþe bettre and blesseder by many fold þan *Richesse*.
B.11.319 The which I preise, þer pacience is, moore parfit þan *richesse*.
B.12.58   And *Richesse* riȝt so but if þe roote be trewe.
B.12.247 Right so þe riche, if he his *richesse* kepe
B.14.103 Than *richesse* riȝtfulliche wonne and resonably despended?'
B.14.105 Thouȝ men rede of *richesse* riȝt to þe worldes ende,
B.14.132 Allas þat *richesse* shal reue and robbe mannes soule
B.14.148 And rewarden alle double *richesse* þat rewful hertes habbeþ.
B.14.204 Ac wiþ *richesse* þ[o] Ribaud[es] raþest men bigileþ.
B.14.205 For þer þat *richesse* regneþ reuerence[s] folweþ,
B.14.207 [Ac] þe riche is reuerenced by reson of his *richesse*
B.14.210 Than *richesse* or reautee, and raþer yherd in heuene.
B.14.212 The heiȝe wey to heueneward [ofte] *Richesse* letteþ:
B.14.216 A[c] pride in *richesse* regneþ raþer þan in pouerte;
B.15.176 'Haþ he anye rentes or *richesse* or any riche frendes?'
B.15.177 'Of rentes n[e] of *richesse* rekkeþ he neuere,
B.15.537 Ne no *richesse* but þe roode to reioisse hem Inne:
B.19.73   Reuerenced hym [riȝt] faire wiþ *richesses* of erþe.
B.19.285 Ne wynnynge ne wele of worldliche *richesse*,
C. 2.16   Here aray with here *rychesse* raueschede my herte;

C. 2.83   That mede is maried more for here *richesse*
C. 3.325 *Richesse* and resoun the while he ryhte lyuede
C. 3.327 A refte hym of his *richesse* and of his ryhte mynde
C. 9.192 As *rychesses* and reuerences and ryche menne Almesse,
C.11.106 And ryde forth by *rychesse* [ac] reste nat þerynne,
C.12.144 And bothe bettere and blessedere by many fold then *richesse*.
C.12.230 So of *rychesse* ope rychesse ariste alle vices.
C.12.230 So of rychesse ope *rychesse* ariste alle vices.
C.12.247 That rote is of robbares, the *rychess[e]* withynne!
C.13.26   Ac leueth nat, lewede men, þat y lacke *rychesse*
C.13.70   And haue reuthe and releue with his *rychesse* by his power
C.14.19   Ac comunlyche connynge and vnkynde *ryche[sse]*,
C.14.184 And þe ryche for his rentes or for *rychesse* in his shopp[e].
C.15.278 Then rihtfu[l] *rychesse* and resonablelyche to spene?'
C.15.280 Thogh men rede of *rychesse* rihte to þe worldes ende
C.16.1   Allas þat *rychesse* shal reue and robbe mannes soule
C.16.45   Ac with *rychesse* tho rybaudes rathest men bigileth.
C.16.46   For [þer] þat *rychess[e]* regneth reuerences folleweth
C.16.48   A[c] þe ryche is reuerenced by resoun of his *rychesse*
C.16.51   Then *rychesse* or ryalte and rather yherde in heuene.
C.16.57   And pruyde in *rychesse* regneth rather then in pouerte;
C.16.317 [Rentes or other *richesse* to releue hym at his nede]?'
C.16.318 'Of rentes ne of *rychesse* reccheth he neuere;
C.17.198 Ne no *rychesse* but þe rode to reioysen hem ynne:
C.17.212 How tho corsede cristene catel and *richesse* worschipede;
C.19.237 Bute riȝtfulliche, as men [r]at, al his *richesse* cam hym
C.21.73   Reuerensed hym riht fayre with *richesses* of erthe.
C.21.285 Ne wynnynge ne wel[e] o[f] wordliche *richesse*,

richore > riche adj

riden v *riden v.* A 7 rid (1) ride (2) riden (3) rit (1); B 20 ryd (1) ride (1) ryde (8) riden (3) ryden (1) ridynge (1) ryt (2) rood (3); C 28 ryde (16) ryden (4) rydeth (1) rydynge (1) rydon (1) rit (1) ryt (1) roed (1) rood (2)

A. 1.93   And *riden* & rappe doun in reaumes aboute,
A. 3.201 Þoruȝ ȝeftis han ȝonge men to [ȝerne] & to *ride*.
A. 4.7   'Rape þe to *riden*, & resoun þat þou fecche.
A. 4.16   'I shal araye me to *ride*,' quaþ resoun, 'reste þe a while,'
A. 4.23   And resoun wiþ hym *rit* & rapiþ hym [swyþe].
A. 4.27   And *riden* faste for resoun shulde rede hem þe beste
A.11.116 And *rid* forþ be ricchesse, ac reste þou not þereinne,
B.Pr.171 Wher he *ryt* or rest or r[om]eþ to pleye;
B. 1.95   *Riden* and rappen doun in Reaumes aboute,
B. 3.214 [Thoruȝ] ȝiftes han yonge men to [yerne] and to *ryde*.
B. 4.7   'Rape þee to *ryde* and Reson [þat] þow fecche.
B. 4.16   'I shal arraye me to *ryde*,' quod Reson, 'reste þee a while',
B. 4.25   And Reson wiþ hym *ryt*, rownynge togideres
B. 4.30   And *riden* faste for Reson sholde rede hem þe beste
B. 4.33   And bad Reson *ryde* faste and recche of hir neiþer.
B. 4.40   Forþi, Reson, lat hem *ride* þo riche by hemselue,
B. 4.42   And þanne Reson *rood* faste þe riȝte heiȝe gate
B. 5.151 Or ellis al riche and *ryden*; I, wraþe, reste neuere
B.10.164 And *ryd* forþ by richesse, ac rest þow noȝt þerInne,
B.11.338 As whan þei hadde *ryde* in Rotey tyme anoon [reste þei] after;
B.15.226 *Riden* and rennen in raggede wedes
B.17.52   *Ridynge* ful rapely þe righte wey we yeden,
B.17.82   And raped hym to [*ryde* þe riȝte wey to Ierusalem].
B.17.102 That he ne was robbed or rifled, *rood* he þere or yede,
B.18.25   In Piers paltok þe Plowman þis prikiere shal *ryde*,
B.19.245 And some to *ryde* and to recouere þat [vnriȝt]fully was wonne:
B.20.181 And *rood* [so to] reuel, a ryche place and a murye,
C.Pr.188 Wher he *ri[t]* othere reste or rometh to pleye;
C. 1.91   *Rydon* and rappe adoun in reumes aboute
C. 2.183 And *ryde* on hem and on reue[s] righte faste by mede.
C. 2.187 Wol *Ryde* vppon Rectores and ryche men deuoutours,
C. 2.191 On hem þat loueth leccherye lyppeth vp and *rydeth*,
C. 2.197 Thenne fals and fauel *ryde* forth togederes
C. 3.270 Thorw ȝeftes haen ȝemen to ȝerne and to *ryde*;
C. 4.7   'Rape the to *ryde* and resoun þat thow [f]ec[c]he.
C. 4.14   And *rood* forth to resoun and rouned in his ere
C. 4.16   'Y shal aray me to *ryde*,' quod resoun, 'reste þe [a] while,'
C. 4.25   And resoun with hym *ry[t]*, rounynge togederes
C. 4.28   Fayn were to folowe hem and faste *ryden* aftur
C. 4.34   *Ryde* forth, syre resoun, and rech nat of here tales
C. 4.40   Thenne resoun *rood* forth Ac took reward of no man
C. 4.54   To robbe me or to ruyfle me yf y *ryde* softe.
C. 4.184 Forthy, resoun, redyly thow shalt nat *ryden* hennes
C. 5.74   For the ryhte of this reume *ryden* aȝeyn oure enemyes
C. 5.157 Haen *ryde* out of aray, here reule euele þolde,
C. 6.126 Or alle riche and *ryde*, reste shal y nat, wrathe,
C.11.106 And *ryde* forth by rychesse [ac] reste nat þerynne,
C.13.146 As when þei hadde [*ryde* in] roteye[tyme] anon they reste aftur;
C.13.154 For out of resoun they *ryde* and rechelesliche t[a]ken on

C.16.351 *Ryden* and rennen in raggede clothes
C.19.50 *Rydynge* ful raply þe rihte way we ȝeden,
C.19.79 And rapede hym to *ryde* the rihte way to Ierusalem.
C.20.24 In [Pers paltok] the [plouhman] this prikiare shal *ryde*
C.21.245 And somme to *ryde* & to rekeuere that vnrihtfulliche was wonne:
C.22.181 And *roed* so to reuel, a ryche place and a murye:

rydere n *ridere n.* A 1 ridere; B 1
A.11.211 Ac now is religioun a *ridere* & a rennere [be stretis],
B.10.311 Ac now is Religion a *rydere*, a [rennere by stretes],

rifled(e > ruyfle

riflynge ger *riflinge ger.(2)* B 1
B. 5.235 'I wende *riflynge* were restitucion for I lerned neuere rede on boke,

rygbones riggebones > ruggebones; right(e > riȝt; rightfole -ful(le > riȝtful

rightwisnesse n *rightwisnesse n.* B 11; C 12 rihtwisnesse (9) rihtwysnesse (3)
B.17.304 That *rightwisnesse* þoruȝ repentaunce to ruþe myȝte turne.
B.17.319 Ac er his *rightwisnesse* to ruþe torne som restitucion bihoueþ;
B.18.165 *Rightwisnesse* come rennynge; reste we þe while,
B.18.173 *Rightwisnesse* hire reuerenced by hir riche cloþyng,
B.18.188 'What, rauestow?' quod *Rightwisnesse*, 'or þow art right dronke?
B.18.199 Ayeins Reson. [I], *rightwisnesse*, recorde þus wiþ truþe
B.18.389 I [may] do mercy þoruȝ [my] *rightwisnesse* and alle my wordes trewe
B.18.396 Ac my *rightwisnesse* and right shul rulen al helle,
B.18.420 'Thow seist sooþ', [seyde] *Rightwisnesse*, and reuerentliche hire kiste.
B.19.83 Reson and *Rightwisnesse* and Ruþe þei offrede;
B.19.88 *Rightwisnesse* vnder reed gold, Resones felawe.
C.19.284 That *rihtwisnesse* thorw repentaunce to reuthe myhte turne.
C.19.299 Ac ar [h]is *rihtwisnesse* to reuthe turne rest[i]t[uci]on hit maketh,
C.20.168 *Rihtwisnesse* come rennynge; reste we the while
C.20.176 *Rihtwisnesse* reuerenced pees in here rich clothyng
C.20.189 And þat Crist hath conuerted the kynde of *rihtwisnesse*
C.20.193 'Rauest thow?' quod *rihtwisnesse*, 'or thow art riht dronke!
C.20.204 Aȝeynes resoun; y, *rihtwysnesse*, recorde [þus] with treuthe
C.20.431 [Y] may do mercy of my *rihtwysnesse* and alle myn wordes trewe
C.20.439 Ac my *rihtwysnesse* and rihte shal r[ul]en [al] helle
C.20.463 'Thowe saiste soeth,' saide *rihtwisnesse*, and reuerentlich here custe.
C.21.83 Resoun and *riht[wis]nesse* and reuthe thei offrede;
C.21.88 *Rihtwisnesse* vnder reed gold, resones felawe;

riȝt n *right n.* B 16 right (7) riȝt (8) riȝte (1); C 23 riȝhte (1) riht (13) rihte (5) ryhte (3) ryhtes (1)
B. 3.239 And han ywroght werkes wiþ *right* and wiþ reson,
B.10.347 That þei han Eritage in heuene, and by trewe *riȝte*,
B.10.348 Ther riche men no *riȝt* may cleyme but of ruþe and grace.'
B.12.209 It were neiþer reson ne *riȝt* to rewarde boþe yliche.
B.14.260 Forþi [al] poore þat pacient is [of pure *riȝt*] may cleymen,
B.15.525 And for þe *riȝt* of al þis reume and alle reumes cristene.
B.18.37 To se how doghtiliche deeþ sholde do and deme hir boþeres *right*.
B.18.277 If he reu[e] me my *riȝt* he robbeþ me by maistrie.
B.18.278 For by *right* and by reson þe renkes þat ben here
B.18.349 But by *right* and by reson raunsone here my liges;
B.18.396 Ac my rightwisnesse and *right* shul rulen al helle,
B.19.90 [For it shal turne tresoun to *riȝt* and to truþe].
B.19.350 Wheiþer he wynne wiþ *right*, wiþ wrong or wiþ vsure.'
B.19.460 'I holde it *riȝt* and reson of my Reue to take
B.19.478 And rule þi reaume in reson [as *right* wol and] truþe
B.20.96 And bar þe baner bifore deeþ; bi *riȝt* he it cleymede.
C. 3.294 And þat is nother resoun ne *ryhte* ne [i]n no rewme lawe
C. 3.368 Sethe y, his sone and his seruant, sewe for his *ryhte*.
C. 5.74 For the *ryhte* of this reume ryden aȝeyn oure enemyes
C. 8.53 Ne countreplede nat Consience ne holy kyrke *ryhtes*.'
C.11.25 Tho þat good most ȝeueth greueth most *riht* and treuthe:
C.11.27 And þat is no *riht* ne resoun for rather me sholde
C.14.148 Hit were no resoun ne *riht* to rewarde bothe ylyche.
C.16.100 Forthy alle pore þat pacient is of puyr *rihte* may claymen
C.17.42 Sholde resoun riht nauht but þat *riht* wolde
C.17.70 That pore peple by puyre *riht* here part myhte aske.
C.19.3 To reule alle reumes þerwith in *riȝhte* and in resoun.
C.20.36 To se how douhtyliche deth sholde do and demen [h]er beyre *rihte*.
C.20.299 Yf he reue me my *rihte* A robbeth me [by] maistrie
C.20.300 For bi *riht* and by resoun þ[e] renkes þat ben here
C.20.308 Reuen vs of oure *riht* sethe resoun hem dampnede.
C.20.371 For alle synfole soules, to saue oure bothe *rihte*.
C.20.395 Bote [by] *riht* and [by] resoun raunsome here my lege[s]:
C.20.439 Ac my rihtwysnesse and *rihte* shal r[ul]en [al] helle
C.21.90 [For it shal turne tresoun] to *riht* and to treuthe.
C.21.350 Where he wynne with *riht*, with wrong or with vsure.'
C.21.460 'Y halde hit *riht* and resoun of my reue to take

C.21.478 And rewle thy rewme in resoun [as] *riht* w[o]l and treuthe,
C.22.96 And baer þe baner bifore deth; bi *riht* he hit claymede.

riȝt adj *right adj.* A 3 riȝt (1) riȝte (2); B 9 right (1) righte (1) riȝt (1) riȝte (6); C 9 riȝt (1) rihte (5) ryhte (3)
A. 3.56 Be war what þi *riȝt* hond werchiþ or deliþ,
A. 5.140 Rose þe regratour was hire *riȝte* name;
A.11.307 Arn none raþere yrauisshid fro þe *riȝte* beleue
B. 3.74 Wite what þow werchest wiþ þi *riȝt* syde,
B. 4.42 And þanne Reson rood faste þe *riȝte* heiȝe gate
B. 5.224 Rose þe Regrater was hir *riȝte* name;
B.10.463 Arn none raþer yrauysshed fro þe *riȝte* bileue
B.15.28 Thanne is Racio my *riȝte* name, reson on englissh;
B.15.10 [Is þe] roote of þe *right* feiþ to rule þe peple;
B.16.273 Rapeliche renne forþ þe *riȝte* wey [we] wente.
B.17.52 Ridynge ful rapely þe *righte* wey we yeden,
B.17.82 And raped hym to [ryde þe *riȝte* wey to Ierusalem].
C. 3.76 Ywyte what thow delest with thi *ryhte* syde.
C. 3.327 A reste hym of his richesse and of his *ryhte* mynde
C. 6.232 Rose þe regrater was here *ryhte* name;
C.11.289 Aren noen rather yraueschid fro þe *rihte* bileue
C.16.188 Thenne ys racio my *rihte* name, reson an englische;
C.16.253 Is þe rote of [the] *rihte* fayth to reule þe peple;
C.18.289 Rappliche renne þe *riȝt* way we wente.
C.19.50 Rydynge ful raply þe *rihte* way we ȝeden,
C.19.79 And rapede hym to ryde the *rihte* way to Ierusalem.

riȝt adv *righte adv.* A 14; B 90 right (20) righte (1) riȝt (69); C 96 righte (1) riȝt (7) ryȝt (1) riht (54) ryht (16) rihte (11) ryhte (6)
A. 2.159 But *riȝt* as þe lawe lokis let falle on hem alle.'
A. 3.262 And *riȝt* as agag hadde happe shal somme:
A. 4.14 And *riȝt* renneþ to resoun & rouniþ in his ere;
A. 4.30 And rombide forþ wiþ resoun *riȝt* to þe king.
A. 6.42 I [wile] wisse ȝow wel *riȝt* to his place.'
A. 7.71 His douȝter hattiþ do *riȝt* [so] or þi damme shal þe bete.
A. 8.94 And was writen *riȝt* þus in witnesse of treuþe:
A. 9.33 *Riȝt* þus [it] fariþ,' quaþ þe Frere, 'be folk here on erþe.
A.10.105 And *riȝt* so be romberis þat rennen aboute
A.10.123 *Riȝt* as a rose, [þat red is and] swet,
A.10.200 Wydeweris & wydewis werchiþ *riȝt* also;
A.11.209 *Riȝt* so be religioun, it roileþ & steruiþ
A.11.267 For to reule his reaum *riȝt* at his wille;
A.12.30 *Riȝt* so I rede,' quod she, 'red þou no ferþer;
B.Pr.167 And *riȝt* so', quod þat Raton, 'Reson me sheweþ
B. 1.161 *Right* so is loue a ledere and þe lawe shapeþ;
B. 2.198 But *riȝt* as þe lawe [lokeþ] lat falle on hem alle.'
B. 3.286 And *riȝt* as Agag hadde happe shul somme.
B. 4.14 And [*riȝt* renneþ] to Reson and rouneþ in his ere;
B. 5.364 And Repentaunce *riȝt* so rebuked hym þat tyme:
B. 5.399 Ne *riȝt* sory for my synnes yet, [so þee I], was I neuere.
B. 5.441 'Repente[st]ow nouȝt?' quod Repentaunce, & *riȝt* wiþ þat he swowned
B. 5.555 I [wol] wisse yow [wel *riȝt*] to his place.'
B. 6.79 His douȝter hiȝte do-*riȝt*-so-or-þi-dame-shal-þee-bete;
B. 6.148 Ac Robert Renaboute shal [*riȝt*] noȝt haue of myne,
B. 6.151 For it is an vnresonable Religion þat haþ *riȝt* noȝt of certein.
B. 7.112 And was writen *riȝt* þus in witnesse of truþe:
B. 8.37 [*Riȝt*] þus it [fareþ]', quod þe frere, 'by folk here on erþe.
B. 9.39 *Right* as a lord sholde make lettres; [if] hym lakked parchemyn,
B. 9.179 [Wideweres and wodewes] wercheþ [*riȝt* also];
B.10.303 *Riȝt* so [by] religion, [it] ro[i]leþ [and] sterueþ
B.10.478 *Right* so lewed [laborers] and of litel knowyng
B.11.7 [For] I was rauysshed *riȝt* þere; Fortune me fette
B.11.73 *Riȝt* so, by þe roode! rouȝte ye neuere
B.11.134 For hise arerages rewarden hym þere [*riȝt*] to þe day of dome,
B.11.269 Than he þat is *riȝt* riche; Reson bereþ witnesse:
B.11.373 [Th]anne I rebukede Reson and *riȝt* til hym I seyde,
B.11.415 For Reson wolde haue reherced me *riȝt* as Clergie seid;
B.11.420 And *riȝt* so ferde Reson bi þee; þow wiþ rude speche
B.11.440 And I aroos vp *riȝt* wiþ þat and [reuerenced] hym [faire,
B.12.35 *Riȝt* so if þow be Religious ren þow neuere ferþer
B.12.47 And Rosamounde *riȝt* so reufulliche [bisette]
B.12.51 And riche renkes *riȝt* so gaderen and sparen
B.12.58 And Richesse *riȝt* so but if þe roote be trewe.
B.12.90 *Riȝt* so goddes body, breþeren, but it be worþili taken,
B.12.103 [And *riȝt* as siȝt serueþ a man to se þe heiȝe strete]
B.12.104 *Riȝt* so [lereþ] lettrure lewed men to Reson.
B.12.143 He spekeþ þere of riche men *riȝt* noȝt, ne of *riȝt* witty,
B.12.143 He spekeþ þere of riche men *riȝt* noȝt, ne of *riȝt* witty,
B.12.170 '*Right* so', quod he renk, 'Reson it sheweþ
B.12.198 *Riȝt* as som man yeue me mete and [sette me amydde þe floor];
B.12.210 And *riȝt* as Troianus þe trewe knyȝt [tilde] noȝt depe in helle
B.12.241 Bitokneþ *riȝt* riche men þat reigne here on erþe.
B.12.247 *Right* so þe riche, if he his richesse kepe

B.12.249 *Riȝt* as þe pennes of þe pecok peyneþ hym in his fliȝt,
B.12.297 And muche murþe and manhod;' and *riȝt* wiþ þat he vanysshed.
B.13.429 *Riȝt* so flatereris and fooles arn þe fendes disciples
B.14.105 Thouȝ men rede of richesse *riȝt* to þe worldes ende,
B.14.124 *Right* so reson sheweþ þat [þo renkes] þat were [lordes]
B.14.128 *Riȝt* so fareþ god by som riche; ruþe me it þynkeþ,
B.14.142 *Riȝt* as a seruaunt takeþ his salarie bifore, & siþþe wolde clayme
          moore
B.14.151 ȝyueþ hym a cote aboue his couenaunt, *riȝt* so crist ȝyueþ heuene
B.14.211 For þe riche haþ muche to rekene, and [*riȝt* softe] walkeþ;
B.14.282 *Riȝt* as contricion is confortable þyng, conscience woot wel,
B.14.294 Selde is poore [*riȝt*] riche but of riȝtful heritage.
B.15.64   And *riȝt* as hony is yuel to defie and engleymeþ þe mawe,
B.15.65   *Right* so þat þoruȝ reson wolde þe roote knowe
B.15.94   *Right* so out of holi chirche alle yueles [spredeþ]
B.15.99   *Right* so persons and preestes and prechours of holi chirche
B.15.114 *Right* so [preestes, prechours and prelates manye],
B.15.307 [*Riȝt* so] Religiouses rightfulle men sholde [fynde],
B.15.317 Ye hadde *riȝt* ynoȝ, ye Religiouse, and so youre rule me tolde.
B.15.336 *Right* so ye riche, ye robeþ þat ben riche
B.15.340 *Right* so ye riche, ye robeþ and fedeþ
B.15.470 *Right* as þe cow calf coueiteþ [swete melk];
B.15.474 *Riȝt* as capons in a court comeþ to mennes whistlyng,
B.15.476 *Riȝt* so rude men þat litel reson konneþ
B.15.551 *Right* so, ye clerkes, for youre coueitise er [come auȝt] longe
B.15.595 Dide hym rise and rome *riȝt* bifore þe Iewes.
B.16.35   And forbiteþ þe blosmes *riȝt* to þe bare leues.
B.16.151 'Aue, raby', quod þat Ribaud, and *riȝt* to hym he yede
B.16.226 I roos vp and reuerenced hym and *riȝt* faire hym grette.
B.17.3   To rule alle Reames wiþ; I bere þe writ [*riȝt*] here.'
B.17.38   And siþþe *riȝt* as myself so louye alle peple.
B.17.41   And *riȝt* so, bi þe roode, Reson me sheweþ
B.17.157 *Right* so, redily, Reson it sheweth
B.17.161 *Right* so þe fader and þe sone and Seint Spirit þe þridde
B.17.174 *Right* so is þe sone þe Science of þe fader
B.17.188 He may receyue *riȝt* noȝt; reson it sheweþ.
B.17.193 I sholde receyue *riȝt* noȝt of þat I reche myghte;
B.18.91   Haue on me ruþe, *riȝtful* Iesu;' and *riȝt* wiþ þat he wepte.
B.18.100 ȝilt hym recreaunt re[m]yng, *riȝt* at Iesus wille.
B.18.160 And *riȝt* as [þe gilour] þoruȝ gile [bigiled man formest]
B.18.188 'What, rauestow?' quod Rightwisnesse, 'or þow art *right* dronke?
B.18.210 Sholde neuere *riȝt* riche man þat lyueþ in reste and ese
B.18.330 [Al]þouȝ Reson recorde, and *riȝt* of myselue,
B.18.370 That I drynke *riȝt* ripe Must, Resureccio mortuorum.
B.18.425 That men rongen to þe resurexion, and *riȝt* wiþ þat I wakede
B.19.8   And *riȝt* lik in alle [lymes] to oure lord Ies[u].
B.19.73   Reuerenced hym [*riȝt*] faire wiþ richesses of erþe.
B.19.193 And rewarde hym *right* wel þat reddit quod debet,
B.19.434 *Right* so Piers þe Plowman peyneþ hym to tilye
B.19.448 He reccheþ *riȝt* noȝt of þe remenaunt.
B.20.17   Nede anoon *righte* nymeþ hym vnder maynprise.
C.Pr.184 [*Ryȝt* so,'quod þe raton, 'reson me sheweth
C.1.157   *Ryht* so is loue [a] ledare and þe lawe shapeth;
C.2.138   Hit semeth sothly *riȝt* so on erthe
C.2.183   And ryde on hem and on reue[s] *righte* faste by mede.
C.2.212   But *riht* as þe lawe loketh lat falle on hem alle.'
C.3.325   Richesse and resoun the while he *riht* lyuede
C.3.330   And *ryhte* so, sothly, may kyng and pope
C.3.355   And man is relatif rect yf he be *rihte* trewe:
C.3.361   This is relacion rect, *ryht* [as] adiectyf and sustantyf
C.3.439   And *riht* as agag hadde happe shal somme:
C.4.150   Reherce the[r] anon *ryhte* þat myhte resoun stoppe.
C.4.196   And receyue tho that resoun louede; and *riht* with þat y wakede
C.5.32   There ryhtfulnesse rewardeth *ryht* as men deserueth–
C.5.82   Forthy rebuke me *ryhte* nauhte, resoun, y ȝow praye,
C.5.112   And resoun yreuestede *ryht* as a pope
C.5.148   *Ryht* as fysches in floed whan hem fayleth water
C.5.150   *Ryht* so religioun roteth and sterueth
C.6.62   Quod repentaunce *riht* with þat; and thenne aroos enuye.
C.6.91   'ȝus! redily,' quod repentaunce, 'and thow be *ryht* sory
C.6.339   Repente þe anon,' quod repentaunce *ryhte* to the vsurer
C.6.423   To repentaunce *ryht* thus, 'haue reuthe on me,' he saide.
C.7.15   Ne *ryht* sory for my synnes–y seyh neuere þe tyme–
C.7.55   'Repentest th[ow] nat?' quod repentaunce, and *ryht* with þat he
          swowened
C.7.89   *Ryht* so flateres and fooles aren þe fendes procuratours
C.7.199   Y wol wissen ȝow wel *ryht* to his place.'
C.7.294   Anoþer anoen *riht* nede he sayde he hadde
C.8.81   His douhter hihte do-*rihte*-so-or-thy-dame-shal-þe-bete.
C.9.60   Pardoun perpetuel *riht* as [Peres] the [plouhman].
C.9.112   *Riht* as Peter dede and poul saue þat þey preche nat
C.9.123   A reuerenseth hym *ryht* nauht, no rather þen another:
C.9.134   *Ryht* so, ȝe ryche, ȝut rather ȝe sholde

C.9.147   And when he is rysen rometh out and *riȝt* wel aspyeth
C.9.218   *Rihte* so, sothly, such manere Ermytes
C.9.286   And was ywryte *ryhte* thus in witnesse of treuthe:
C.11.47   Ne were mercy in m[e]ne men more then in *riht* riche
C.11.166 For y was rauysched *rihte* there; fortune me fette
C.11.197 For rechelesnesse in his rybaud[i]e *riht* thus he saide:
C.12.21   *Riht* so, by þe rode, rouhte ȝe neuere
C.12.69   And for his rechelesnes rewarde hym þere *riht* to þe day of dome
C.12.140 And aytheres werkes and wille] *riht* wel alowede
C.12.154 Then he þat is *rihte* ryche; reson bereth witnesse:
C.12.194 *Riht* so, sothly, þat soffry may penaunc[e]
C.12.225 *Riht* so, sothly, suche þat ben bischopes,
C.12.229 *Riht* as wedes waxeth in wose and in donge
C.12.233 *Riht* so, sothly, for to segge treuthe,
C.13.183 Thenne y [a]resonede resoun and *ryht* til hym y sayde,
C.13.223 For resoun wolde haue rehersed þe *riht* as clergie seide;
C.13.228 *Rihte* so ferde Resoun by the; for thy rude speche
C.13.246 And [y] aroes vp *riht* with þat and reuerensed hym fayre
C.14.48   And *riht* as syht serueth a man to se [þe hye strete],
C.14.49   *Riht* so lereth lettrure lewed men to resoun.
C.14.87   Hit speketh þer of ryche men *riht* nouht ne of ryche lordes
C.14.110 '*Riht* so,' quod þ[e] renk, 'resoun hit sheweth
C.14.137 *Riht* As sum man ȝeueth me mete and sette me Amydde þe flore;
C.14.149 And *riht* as troianes þe trewe knyhte [telde] nat depe in helle
C.14.173 Bytokenen *riht* ryche men þat reygne here on erthe.
C.14.181 *Riht* so men reuerence[th] more þe ryche for h[is] mebles
C.15.51   Thenne resoun radde anoon *riht* aftur
C.15.150 And resoun ran aftur and *riht* with hym ȝede;
C.15.280 Thogh men rede of rychesse *rihte* to þe worldes ende
C.16.22   *Riht* so haue reuthe on [thy renkes] alle
C.16.52   For þe ryche hath moche to rykene and *riht* softe walketh;
C.16.129 Selde is pore *rihte* ryche but of rihtfole eritage.
C.16.226 And *riht* as hony is euel to defie,
C.16.227 *Riht* so sothly scienc[e] swelleth a mannes soule
C.16.246 *Riht* [so] oute of holy churche al euel spredeth
C.16.252 *Riht* so persones and prestes and prechours of holy churche
C.16.269 *Riht* so many prestes, prechours and prelates,
C.17.25   Y can nat rykene hem *riht* now ne reherse here names
C.17.42   Sholde reseue *riht* nauht but þat *riht* wolde
C.17.194 Hit is reuthe to rede how *riht* holy men lyuede,
C.17.214 *Riht* so, ȝe clerkes, ȝoure coueytise ar come auht longe
C.18.39   And al forb[i]t Caritas *rihte* to þe bare stalke.
C.18.71   As weddede men and wedewes and *riht* worthy maydones
C.18.168 'Aue raby,' quod th[at] ribaud[e]; and *riht* til hym [he] ȝede
C.18.241 Where god [*riȝt* be my gate cam gangynge a thre];
C.18.242 Y roos vp and reuerensed god and *riht* fayre hym grette,
C.19.89   And thouh he stande and steppe *riȝt* stronge worth he neuere
C.19.139 *Riht* so failed þe sone, the syre be ne myhte
C.19.154 He may resceyue *riht* nauhte; resoun hit sheweth.
C.19.159 Y sholde receyue *ryht* nouht of þat y reche myhte;
C.20.62   The hard roch al toroef and *riht* derk nyht hit semede;
C.20.94   Haue [on me reuthe], riȝtfol iesu;' and *riht* with þat a wepte.
C.20.103 ȝelde hym [re]creaunt remyng, *riht* at iesu[s] wille.
C.20.163 And *riht* as the gylour thorw gyle bigiled man formost
C.20.193 'Rauest thow?' quod rihtwisnesse, 'or thow art *riht* dronke!
C.20.219 For sholde neuere *riȝt* riche man þat lyueth in rest and hele
C.20.373 Althouh resoun record[e], and *rihte* of mysulue,
C.20.412 And [y] drynke *riht* rype m[o]st, resureccio mortuorum.
C.20.468 That men rang to þe resureccioun and *riht* with þat y wakede
C.21.8   And *riht* lyke in alle lymes to oure lord iesu.
C.21.73   Reuerensed hym *riht* fayre with richesses of erthe.
C.21.193 And rewarde hym *riht* wel that redd[it] quod debet,
C.21.434 *Rihte* so [Peres] the [Plouhman] payneth hym to tulie
C.21.448 He rekketh *riht* nauht of þe remenaunt.
C.22.17   Nede anoen *riht* nymeth hym vnder maynprise.

riȝtful adj *rightful adj.* A 2; B 13 rightful (1) rightfulle (2) riȝtful (6)
riȝtfulle (4); C 18 rightfole (1) rightful (1) riȝtfol (1) rihtfol (1) rihtfole
(4) rihtful (3) ryhtful (5) rihtfull (1) rihtfulluste (1)
A.9.17   Seue siþes, seiþ þe bok, [synneþ] þe *riȝtful*;
A.11.202 And þat is *riȝtful* religioun, none renneris aboute,
B.Pr.127 And for þi *riȝtful* rulyng be rewarded in heuene'.
B.3.242   And alle þat helpen þe Innocent and holden with þe *riȝtfulle*
B.4.157   Alle *riȝtfulle* recordede þat Reson truþe tolde.
B.8.21   Seuene siþes, seiþ þe book, synneþ þe *rightfulle*;
B.10.297 [Amonges *riȝtful* religious þis rule sholde be holde.
B.12.86   The which body is boþe boote to þe *riȝtfulle*
B.14.111 Ioye þat neuere ioye hadde of *riȝtful* Iugge he askeþ,
B.14.294 Selde is poore [*riȝt*] riche but of *riȝtful* heritage.
B.15.307 [*Riȝt* so] Religiouses *rightfulle* men sholde [fynde],
B.15.471 So [menen] *riȝtfulle* men [after] mercy and truþe.
B.15.508 And þat is rouþe for *riȝtful* men þat in þe Reawme wonyen,
B.15.550 Reson and *rightful* doom þ[o] Religiouse d[ampn]ede.
B.18.91   Haue on me ruþe, *riȝtful* Iesu;' and *riȝt* wiþ þat he wepte.

C.Pr.151   And for thy *rightful* ruylynge be rewardid in heuene.'
C. 3.374   A[c] relacoun rect is a *ryhtful* custume,
C. 4.151   Ac al *ryhtful* recordede þat resoun treuthe sayde,
C. 4.153   Resoun for his *ryhtful* speche; ryche and pore hym louede
C. 5.147   The reule of alle religious *rihtful* and obedient:
C. 6.33   Ryche, and resonable and *ryhtful* of lyuynge;
C.10.24   The *rihtfulluste* ren[k] þat regneth [o]n erthe.
C.10.38   A[c] 3ut is he saef and sound; and so hit fareth by þe *rihtfole*.
C.10.41   So hit fareth,' quod þe frere, 'by þe *ryhtful* mannus fallynge.
C.11.16   Ho can caste and contreue to disseyue þe *ri[gh]tfole*,
C.12.87   Loue withoute lele bileue a[nd] my lawe *riht[ful]*,
C.15.278   Then *rihtfu[l]* rychesse and resonablelyche to spene?'
C.15.287   Ioye þat neuere ioye hadde of *rihtfull* iuge he asketh
C.16.129   Selde is pore rihte ryche but of *rihtfole* eritage.
C.17.34   Fynde honest men and holy men and oþer *rihtfole* peple.
C.17.213   Resoun and *rihtfol* doem þo religious dampnede.
C.17.259   And þat is reuthe for *rihtfole* men þat in þ[e] reume wonyeth
C.20.94   Haue [on me reuthe], *ri3tfol* iesu;' and riht with þat a wepte.

ri3tfully adv *rightfulli adv.* A 3 ri3tfulliche; B 5 ri3tfully (4) ri3tfulliche (1); C 6 ri3tfulliche (2) rihtfolliche (1) rihtfollokest (1) rihtfuly (1) ryhtfulliche (1)

A. 1.52   For *ri3tfulliche* resoun shulde rewele 3ow alle,
A. 4.145   And reherside þat resoun [hadde] *ri3tfulliche* shewide;
A. 8.10   And *r[i3t]fulliche* in reaum rewliþ þe peple
B. 1.54   For *ri3tfully* reson sholde rule yow alle,
B. 4.172   And recordede þat Reson hadde *ri3tfully* shewed,
B. 7.10   And *ri3tfully* in Rem[e] rulen þe peple
B.11.126   *Ri3tfully* to reneye no reson it wolde.
B.14.103   Than richesse *ri3tfulliche* wonne and resonably despended?'
C. 1.50   For *ri3tfulliche* resoun sholde reule 3ow alle
C. 9.10   And *ryhtfulliche* in reumes ruylen þe comune
C.12.61   *Rihtfolliche* to renoye no resoun hit wolde.
C.13.96   As al þat þe ryche may rayme and *rihtfuly* dele
C.19.237   Bute *ri3tfulliche*, as men [r]at, al his richesse cam hym
C.20.472   And *rihtfollokest* A relyk, noon richore on erthe.

ri3twise adj *rightwise adj.* B 1
B.15.533   It is ruþe to rede how *ri3twise* men lyuede,

riht(e -es > ri3t; rihtfol(- rihtful(l rihtfuly -liche -luste > ri3tful(-

ryhtfulnesse n *rightfulness n.* C 1
C. 5.32   There *ryhtfulnesse* rewardeth ryht as men deserueth–

rihtwisnesse > rightwisnesse; rikene > rekene; rykenynge > rekenyng

ryme n *rime n.(2)* B 1 rymes; C 2 ryme (1) rymes (1)
B. 5.395   But I kan *rymes* of Robyn hood and Randolf Erl of Chestre,
C. 7.11   Y can *rymes* of robyn hode and of randolf Erle of Chestre
C. 9.82   That reuthe is to rede or in *ryme* shewe

ryn n prop *Rine n.(2)* A 1; B 1; C 1 ryne
A.Pr.108   Of þe *ryn* & of þe rochel, þe rost to defie!'
B.Pr.230   Of þe *Ryn* and of þe Rochel þe roost to defie!'
C.Pr.234   Of þe *r[yn]e* and of þe rochele the roost [to] defye!'

ryne v *rinen v.(2)* &> ryn; cf. reyneþ B 1 roon; C 3 ryne (2) roen (1)
B.14.67   That no reyn ne *roon*; þus rede men in bokes,
C. 5.164   To religious þat haen no reuthe thow it *ryne* on here auters.
C.15.266   That no reyn ne *roen*; thus [r]at men [i]n bokes,
C.17.100   Wisten w[hi]l[e] and tolde when hit sholde *ryne*.

rynges n *ring n.* A 4 rynges (3) ryngis (1); B 3; C 2
A.Pr.72   And rau3te wiþ his rageman *ryngis* & brochis.
A. 2.11   Alle here fyue fyngris were frettid wiþ *rynges*
A. 3.22   *Rynges* wiþ rubies & ricchesse manye;
A. 3.79   *Ryng[es]* or oþer richesse, þ[ise] regratour[is] to meynteyne;
B.Pr.75   And rau3te with his Rageman *rynges* and broches.
B. 3.23   *Rynges* wiþ Rubies and richesses manye,
B. 3.90   *Rynges* or ooþer richesse þ[ise] Regratiers to mayntene.
C.Pr.73   And raughte with his Rageman *Rynges* and Broches.
C. 3.24   *Rynges* with rubees and othere riche 3eftes,

ryngynge ger *ringinge ger.* B 1; C 1 ryngyng
B. 5.389   Sholde no *ryngynge* do me ryse er I were ripe to dyne.'
C. 7.5   Sholde no *ryngyng* do me ryse til y were rype to dyne.'

ripe adj *ripe adj.* &> ripen A 1; B 5 ripe (4) rype (1); C 6 rype
A. 7.278   Chibollis, & chiriuellis, & *ri[p]e* chiries manye,
B. 5.389   Sholde no ryngynge do me ryse er I were *ripe* to dyne.'
B. 6.294   Chibolles and Cheruelles and *ripe* chiries manye;
B.16.71   Maidenhode, Aungeles peeris, and [erst] wole be *ripe*
B.16.94   That Piers fruyt floured and felle to be *rype*.
B.18.370   That I drynke ri3t *ripe* Must, Resureccio mortuorum.
C. 7.5   Sholde no ryngyng do me ryse til y were *rype* to dyne.'
C.18.42   And þerwith y warde hit oþerwhile til hit waxe *rype*.
C.18.64   Tho that sitten in þe sonne syde sannore aren *rype*,

C.18.106   And shaken hit sharpeliche; the *rype* sholden falle.
C.18.127   That elde felde efte þe fruyt, or full to be *rype*.
C.20.412   And [y] drynke riht *rype* m[o]st, resureccio mortuorum.

ripen v *ripen v.(1)* B 2 ripe (1) ripen (1); C 3 rype (2) rypeth (1)
B.16.39   I saue it til I se it *ripen* and somdel yfruyted.
C.12.223   And þat rathest *rypeth* rotieth most sonnest;
C.12.232   Whete þat þeron wexeth worth lygge ar hit *rype*;
C.21.317   'A3eynes thy graynes,' quod grace, 'bigynneth for to *rype*,

rypereue n *ripereve n.* C 1
C. 5.15   Repe or been a *rypereue* and aryse erly

risen v *risen* A 4 rise (2) risen (2); B 10 rise (4) ryse (1) risen (3) roos (2); C 13 rise (2) ryse (6) rysep (1) ryseþ (1) roes (1) roos (1)
A.Pr.44   And *risen* vp wiþ ribaudrie as robertis knaues;
A. 5.174   Þo *risen* vp in rape & ro[wn]eden togideris,
A. 5.183   And whoso repentiþ raþest shulde *rise* aftir
A. 7.110   'But 3e *rise* þe raþere, & rape 3ow to werche,
B.Pr.44   And *risen* [vp] wiþ ribaudie [as] Roberdes knaues;
B. 5.232   I *roos* whan þei were areste and riflede hire males.'
B. 5.325   T[h]o *risen* vp in Rape and rouned togideres
B. 5.389   No ryngynge do me *ryse* er I were ripe to dyne.'
B. 7.193   At þe dredful dome, whan dede shulle *rise*
B.15.595   Dide hym *rise* and rome ri3t bifore þe Iewes.
B.16.226   I *roos* vp and reuerenced hym and ri3t faire hym grette.
B.17.70   And but he hadde recouerer þe ra[þ]er þat *rise* sholde he neuere
B.18.255   And I, book, wole be brent but Iesus rise to lyue
B.19.146   That þat blissede body of burieles [sholde *risen*]
C.Pr.45   And *ryseþ* with rybaudrye, þo robardus knaues;
C. 6.236   Y *roes* and ryflede here males when the[y] areste were.'
C. 6.383   Tho *rysen* vp [in] rape and rounned togyderes
C. 7.5   Sholde no ryngyng do me *ryse* til y were rype to dyne.'
C. 9.79   To *rise* to þe reule to rokke þe cradel,
C. 9.146   And whenne hym lyketh and luste, his leue is to *ryse*
C. 9.147   And whenne he is *rysen* rometh out and ri3t wel aspyeth
C. 9.339   At þe dredful dome, when dede shullen *ryse*
C.15.26   And beden me *ryse* and rome; with reson sholde y dyne.
C.18.242   Y *roos* vp and reuerensed god and ri3t fayre hym grette,
C.19.69   And bote he hadde recouerer the raþer þat *ryse* sholde he neuere
C.20.281   Ac [r]*ise* vp, Ragamoffyn, and [r]eche me alle þe barres
C.21.146   That þat blessed body of buyrielles sholde *ryse*

risyng ger *risinge ger.* B 1; C 1 rysynge
B.18.67   Er sonday aboute sonne *risyng*'; and sank wiþ þat til erþe.
C.20.69   Ar soneday aboute sonne *rysynge*'; and sank with þat til erthe.

risshe n *rishe n.* A 2; B 4; C 4 ruche (1) rusche (2) rusches (1)
A. 3.131   To be cursid in constorie heo countiþ not a *risshe*;
A.11.17   Wisdom and wyt now is not worþ a *risshe*
B. 3.142   To be corsed in Consistorie she counteþ no3t a [*risshe*]
B. 4.170   And yet yeue ye me neuere þe worþ of a *risshe.*'
B.10.17   Wisdom and wit now is no3t worþ a [*risshe*]
B.11.430   Of clergie ne of his counseil he counteþ no3t a *risshe*.
C. 3.180   To be cursed in constorie a counteth nat a *rusche*.
C. 9.81   [To] rybbe [and] to rele, *rusches* to pylie,
C.12.197   Or for a confessour ykud þat counteth nat a *ruche*
C.13.237   Of clergie ne of kynde wyt counteth he nat a *rusche*.

rit > riden; ryuet > ruwet

ryuer n *rivere n.* B 1
B.15.338   As whoso filled a tonne [ful] of a fressh *ryuer*

robardus > roberd; robbare(s > robbere

robbe v *robben v.* A 1 robbedest; B 9 robbe (2) robbed (3) robbedest (2) robbeþ (1) yrobbed (1); C 8 robbe (3) robbed (1) robbeth (1) yrobbed (3)
A. 3.182   Wiþoute pite, pilour, pore men þou *robb[ed]est*,
B. 3.195   Wiþouten pite, Pilour, pouere men þow *robbedest*
B.11.268   And lasse he dredeþ deeþ and in derke to ben *yrobbed*
B.14.132   Allas þat richesse shal reue and *robbe* mannes soule
B.16.89   To go *robbe* þat Rageman and reue þe fruyt fro hym.
B.17.92   For sighte of þ[e] sorweful [segge] þat *robbed* was with þeues.
B.17.102   That he ne was *robbed* or rifled, rood he þere or yede,
B.18.277   If he reu[e] me my ri3t he *robbeþ* me by maistrie.
B.18.338   Thefliche þow me *robbedest*; þe olde lawe graunteþ
B.19.444   And counteþ no3t þou3 cristene ben killed and *robbed*,
C. 4.54   To *robbe* me or to ruyfle me yf y ryde softe.
C. 9.181   As prisones and pilgrimes and parauntur men *yrobbed*
C.10.195   The[r]of was he *robbed* and ruyfled or he rode deyede
C.11.19   He is reuerensed and *yrobed* þat can *robbe* þe peple
C.12.153   And lasse drat [dethe] or in derke to ben *yrobbed*
C.16.1   Allas þat rychesse shal reue and *robbe* mannes soule
C.20.299   Yf he reue me my rihte A *robbeth* me [by] maistrie

557

C.21.444   And counteth nat thow cristene be culde and *yrobbed*

robbere n *robbere n.* A 3 robbere (1) robberis (1) robbour (1); B 6
      Robbere (3) Robberes (1) robberis (2); C 3 robbare (1) robbares (2)
A. 4.111   And alle rome renneris, for *robberis* of be3onde,
A. 5.233   Robert þe *robbour* on reddite lokide
A.11.285   A *robbere* hadde remission raþere þanne þei alle,
B. 4.128   And alle Rome renneres, for *Robberes* [of] biyonde,
B. 5.233   'That was no restitucion', quod Repentaunce, 'but a *robberis* þefte;
B. 5.461   Roberd þe *Robbere* on Reddite loked,
B. 5.467   So rewe on þis *Robbere* þat Reddere ne haue
B.10.426   A *Robbere* was yraunsoned raþer þan þei alle,
B.14.182   To *robberis* and to Reueris, to riche and to poore,
C.11.258   A *robbare* was yraunsomed rather then thei alle,
C.12.247   That rote is of *robbares*, the rychess[e] withynne!
C.13.58   With *robbares* and reuares þat ryche men despoilen

robbyng ger *robbinge ger.* B 1; C 1 robbynge
B.14.305   Pouerte my3te passe wiþouten peril of *robbyng*.
C.16.140   Pouerte myhte passe withoute perel of *robbynge*.

robbour > robbere

robe n *robe n.* A 1; B 4 Robe (1) robes (3); C 3 robes
A. 3.271   Ne no ray *robe* [wiþ] riche pelure.
B. 2.15   Hire *Robe* was ful riche, of reed scarlet engreyned,
B.13.227   [Ac] fewe *robes* I fonge or furrede gownes.
B.15.228   Ac in riche *robes* raþest he walkeþ,
B.15.233   Riche men he recomendeþ, and of hir *robes* takeþ,
C.15.201   And fewe *robes* y fonge or forrede gounes.
C.16.353   Ac in riche *robes* rathest he walketh,
C.16.358   Riche men a recomendeth, and of [here] *robes* taketh,

roberd n prop *Robert n.* A 3 robert (2) robertis (1); B 3 Roberd (1)
      Roberdes (1) Robert (1); C 3 robardus (1) Robert (2)
A.Pr.44   And risen vp wiþ ribaudrie as *robertis* knaues;
A. 5.233   *Robert* þe robbour on reddite lokide
A. 5.241   So rewe on þis *robert* þat red[dere] ne hauiþ,
B.Pr.44   And risen [vp] wiþ ribaudie [as] *Roberdes* knaues;
B. 5.461   *Roberd* þe Robbere on Reddite loked,
B. 6.148   Ac *Robert* Renaboute shal [ri3t] no3t haue of myne,
C.Pr.45   And ryseþ with rybaudrye, þo *robardus* knaues;
C. 6.315   *Robert* the ruyflare on reddite lokede
C. 6.321   So rewe on *Robert* þat reddere ne haue

robeþ v *roben v.* A 2 robid (1) yrobid (1); B 3 robeþ (2) yrobed (1); C 2
      yrobed
A. 2.13   In red scarlet *robid* & ribande wiþ gold.
A. 9.1   Thus, *yrobid* in rosset, I rombide aboute
B. 8.1   Thus, *yrobed* in russet, I romed aboute
B.15.336   Right so ye riche, ye *robeþ* þat ben riche
B.15.340   Right so ye riche, ye *robeþ* and fedeþ
C.10.1   Thus, *yrobed* in russet, y romede aboute
C.11.19   He is reuerensed and *yrobed* þat can robbe þe peple

robyn n prop *Robin n. &> robyn_hood* A 2; B 2; C 2
A. 5.178   Til *robyn* þe ropere was red to arisen,
A. 7.65   And *robyn* þe ribaudour for hise rusty woordis.
B. 5.329   Til *Robyn* þe Ropere [arise þei bisou3te],
B. 6.73   And *Robyn* þe Ribaudour for hise rusty wordes.
C. 6.387   Til *Robyn* þe Ropere aryse they bisouhte,
C. 8.75   And *Robyn* þe rybauder for his rousty wordes.

robyn_hood n prop *Robin n.* B 1; C 1 robyn_hode
B. 5.395   But I kan rymes of *Robyn hood* and Randolf Erl of Chestre,
C. 7.11   Y can rymes of *robyn hode* and of randolf Erle of Chestre

robynge ger *robinge ger.* C 1
C. 2.14   Here *robynge* was rychere þen y rede couthe;

roche n *roche n.(2)* B 2; C 3 roch (1) roche (2)
B.17.11   [He plukkede] forþ a patente, a pece of an hard *roche*
B.18.248   Quaked as quyk þyng and al biquasshed þe *roche*.
C.19.12   A pluhte forth a patente, a pece of an hard *roche*
C.20.62   The hard *roch* al toroef and riht derk nyht hit semede;
C.20.257   Quakid as quyk thyng and a[l] toquasch[ed] þe *roch[e]*.

rochel n prop *Rochelle n.* A 1; B 1; C 1 rochele
A.Pr.108   Of þe ryn & of þe *rochel*, þe rost to defie!'
B.Pr.230   Of þe Ryn and of þe *Rochel* þe roost to defie!'
C.Pr.234   Of þe r[yn]e and of þe *rochele* the roost [to] defye!'

rochemador n prop *n.i.d.* B 1
B.12.36   To Rome ne to *Rochemador*, but as þi rule techeþ,

rodded > ruddede; rode > roode

rody adj *rodi adj.* B 1; C 1
B.13.100   As *rody* as a Rose [ruddede] hise chekes,

C.15.107   As *rody* as a rose rodded his chekes,

roed > riden; roef > roof; roen > ryne

roep n *rop n.(2)* C 1
C.18.155   'Vnkynde and vnkunnynge!' quod Crist, and with a *roep* smoet
            hem

roes > risen

rogged v *ruggen v.* B 1
B.16.78   I hadde ruþe whan Piers *rogged*, it gradde so rufulliche;

roileþ v *roilen v.(1),(2)* A 1; B 1
A.11.209   Ri3t so be religioun, it *roileþ* & steruiþ
B.10.303   Ri3t so [by] religion, [it] *ro[i]leþ* [and] sterueþ

roynouse adj *roinouse adj.* B 1; C 1
B.20.83   Rewmes and Radegundes and *roynouse* sca[ll]es,
C.22.83   Reumes and Radegoundes and *roynouse* sca[ll]es,

rokke v *rokken v.* B 1 rokked; C 1
B.15.11   Til reson hadde ruþe on me and *rokked* me aslepe,
C. 9.79   To rise to þe reule to *rokke* þe cradel,

rolle v *rollen v.(1)* B 1
B. 5.272   And siþen þat Reson *rolle* it in þe Registre of heuene

rolles n *rolle n.* B 1; C 2
B.19.463   Wiþ Spiritus Intellectus þei [toke] þe reues *rolles*
C. 3.111   Ar he were vnderfonge fre and felawe in 3oure *rolles*.
C.21.463   With spiritus intellectus they [t]o[k]e þe reues *rolles*

romaynes n prop *Romain n.* B 1; C 1
B.15.531   Many man for cristes loue was martired [amonges] *Romayne[s]*
C.17.281   Many man for cristes loue was martired amonges *Romaynes*

romb- > rome(-

rome n prop *Rome n.* A 5; B 14; C 13
A.Pr.47   For to seke seint Iame & seintes at *rome*;
A. 4.111   And alle *rome* renneris, for robberis of be3onde,
A. 5.40   And 3e þat seke seint Iame & seintes at *rome*,
A. 5.232   I wile seke treuþe er I [se] *rome*.'
A. 6.10   And many crouch [o]n his cloke, & kei3es of *rome*,
B.Pr.47   For to seken Seint Iame and Seintes at *Rome*;
B. 4.128   And alle *Rome* renneres, for Robberes [of] biyonde,
B. 5.56   And ye þat seke Seynt Iames and Seyntes [at] *Rome*,
B. 5.248   And wiþ lumbardes lettres I ladde gold to *Rome*
B. 5.460   I shal seken treuþe er I se *Rome*.'
B. 5.522   And many crouch on his cloke and keyes of *Rome*,
B. 6.3   Quod Perkyn þe Plowman, 'by Seint Peter of *Rome*!
B.11.154   Lo! ye lordes, what leautee dide by an Emperour of *Rome*
B.11.163   Pulte out of pyne a paynym of *rome*.
B.12.36   To *Rome* ne to Rochemador, but as þi rule techeþ,
B.14.197   Paternost[er] and penaunce and Pilgrymag[e] to *Rome*,
B.15.559   An Aungel men herden an heigh at *Rome* crye,
B.17.256   And purchace al þe pardon of Pampilon and *Rome*,
B.19.423   Or in *Rome* as hir rule wole þe relikes to kepe;
C.Pr.48   To seke seynt Iame and seyntes [at] *Rome*;
C. 2.246   Symonye and syuile senten to *Rome*,
C. 4.123   In prisones and in pore cotes be pilgrimages to *Rome*
C. 4.125   And alle *Rome* rennares for ruyflares in Fraunce
C. 5.197   And 3e þat seketh seynt Iames and seyntes [at] *Rome*,
C. 6.246   And with lumbardus lettres le[d]e gold to *Rome*;
C. 7.167   And many crouch on his cloke [and] kayes of *Rome*
C. 8.1   Qvod [perkyn] þe [plouhman], 'be seynt petur of *Rome*!
C. 9.324   So dowel passeth pardoun and pilgrimages to *Rome*.
C.16.38   Oure preyeres and oure penanc[e] And pilgrimag[e] to *Rome*.
C.17.222   An angel men herde an hye at *rome* crye,
C.19.222   And purchase al the pardoun of pampilon and *Rome*
C.21.423   Or in *Rome*, as here reule wo[l], þe relikes to kepe;

rome v *romen v.* A 2 rombide; B 6 rome (4) romed (1) romeþ (1); C 12
      rome (5) romede (3) romest (1) rometh (2) romynge (1)
A. 4.30   And *rombide* forþ wiþ resoun ri3t to þe king.
A. 9.1   Thus, yrobid in rosset, I *rombide* aboute
B.Pr.171   Wher he ryt or rest or *r[om]eþ* to pleye;
B. 8.1   Thus, yrobed in russet, I *romed* aboute
B.11.114   And plukked in Pauci pryueliche and leet þe remenaunt go *rome*.'
B.11.129   Ac he may renne in arerage and *rome* fro home,
B.15.595   Dide hym rise and *rome* ri3t bifore þe Iewes.
B.20.212   And [I] by conseil of kynde comsed to *rome*
C.Pr.188   Wher he ri[t] othere reste or *rometh* to pleye;
C. 5.11   *Romynge* in remembrance thus resoun me aratede:
C. 6.331   'Be þe rode,' quod repentance, 'thow *romest* toward heuene
C. 9.147   And when he is rysen *rometh* out and ri3t wel aspyeth
C.10.1   Thus, yrobed in russet, y *romede* aboute

C.12.49 And plihte in pauci preueiliche and lette þe remenaunt go *rome*.'
C.12.64 Ac he may renne in arrerage and *rome* fro home
C.15.26 And beden me ryse and *rome*; with reson sholde y dyne.
C.15.27 And y aroos and *romede* forth and with resoun we mette.
C.15.28 We reuerensede resoun and *romede* forth softly
C.18.144 Quadriduanus coeld, quyk dede hym *rome*.
C.22.212 And y bi conseil of kynde comsed to *Rome*

romeris n *romere* n. A 1 romberis; B 1
A.10.105 And riȝt so be *romberis* þat rennen aboute
B. 4.120 And Religiouse *Romeris* Recordare in hir cloistres

ronde n *rand* n. C 1
C. 9.148 Where he may rathest haue a repaest or a *ronde* of bacoun,

rongen v *ringen* v. B 2; C 2 rang (1) rongen (1)
B.18.425 That men *rongen* to þe resurexion, and riȝt wiþ þat I wakede
B.20.59 And Religiouse reuerenced hym and *rongen* hir belles,
C.20.468 That men *rang* to þe resureccioun and riht with þat y wakede
C.22.59 And religious reuerensed hym and *rongen* here belles

ronges n *rung* n. B 1; C 1
B.16.44 And leiþ a laddre þerto, of lesynges are þe *ronges*,
C.18.44 And leyth a laddere þerto, of lesynges ben þe *ronges*,

ronne > rennen; rood > riden

roode n *rode* n.(5) A 10 rode (9) roode (1); B 21 Rode (5) roode (16); C
19 rode
A. 2.3 Þat bar þe blisside barn þat bouȝte vs on þe *rode*,
A. 2.133 Þanne swor cyuyle & seide be þe *rode*
A. 4.117 And ȝet', quaþ resoun, 'be þe *rode*, I shal no reuþe haue
A. 4.148 'Be hym þat [rauȝte] on þe *rode*,' quaþ resoun to þe king,
A. 5.85 Whanne I come to þe [k]ir[k]e & knel[e] to þe *rode*,
A. 5.145 And bidde þe *rode* of bromholm bringe me out of dette.'
A. 5.226 Til I haue euesong herd, I behote [to] þe *rode*.
A. 5.231 And wiþ þe residue & þe remenaunt, be þe *roode* of chestre,
A. 7.92 And wiþ þe residue & þe remenaunt, be þe *rode* of chestre,
A.12.117 Þat barn bryng vs to blys þat bled vpon þe *rode* amen.
B. 2.3 That bar þ[e] blis[sed] barn þat bouȝte vs on þe *Rode*,
B. 4.134 And yet', quod Reson, 'by þe *Rode*! I shal no ruþe haue
B. 4.185 'By hym þat rauȝte on þe *Rode*!' quod Reson to þe kynge,
B. 5.105 Whan I come to þe kirk and knele to *Roode*
B. 5.229 And bidde þe *Roode* of Bromholm brynge me out of dette.'
B. 5.454 Til I haue euensong herd: I bihote to þe *Roode*.
B. 5.459 And wiþ þe residue and þe remenaunt, bi þe *Rode* of Chestre,
B. 6.100 And wiþ þe residue and þe remenaunt, by þe *Rode* of Lukes!
B.11.73 Riȝt so, by þe *roode*! rouȝte ye neuere
B.15.264 Sholde neuere Iudas ne Iew haue Iesu doon on *roode*,
B.15.537 Ne no richesse but þe *roode* to reioisse hem Inne:
B.15.540 Is reuerenced er þe *Roode*, receyued for [þe] worþier
B.15.544 Boþe riche and Religious, þat *roode* þei honoure
B.17.41 And riȝt so, bi þe *roode*, Reson me sheweþ
B.18.51 Nailed hym with þre nailes naked on [a] *roode*;
B.18.55 If þow be crist and kynges sone com down of þe *roode*;
B.18.84 To touchen hym or to tasten hym or take doun of *roode*,
B.18.250 And leet out Symondes sone[s] to seen hym hange on *roode*.
B.18.259 And but þei reuer[en]sen his *roode* and his Resurexion
B.19.323 And of his baptisme and blood þat he bledde on *roode*
B.20.43 That he seide in his sorwe on þe selue *roode*:
C. 2.3 That bar þ[e] blessid bar[n] þat bouhte [vs] on þe *rode*,
C. 4.131 And [ȝut]',' quod resoun, 'by þe *rode*! y shal no reuthe haue
C. 4.179 'By hym þat rauhte [on] þe *rode*,' quod resoun to þe kyng,
C. 6.253 'Now redily,' quod repentaunce, 'and by þe *rode*, y leue,
C. 6.331 'Be þe *rode*,' quod repentaunce, 'thow romest toward heuene
C. 7.68 Til y haue euensong yherd: y bihote to þe *rode*.'
C. 8.109 And with þe res[i]due and þe remenant, by the *rode* of lukes!
C.10.195 The[r]of was he robbed and ruyfled or he on *rode* deyede
C.12.21 Riht so, by þe *rode*, ȝe neuere
C.17.198 Ne no rychesse but þe *rode* to reioysen hem ynne:
C.17.201 Is reuerenced byfore the *rode* and resceyued for the worthiore
C.17.206 Bothe riche and religiou[s] þat *rode* they honouren
C.20.51 [Thei] nayled hym with þre nayles naked vpon a *rode*
C.20.55 And 'yf thow be Crist and [kynges] sone come adoun of th[e] *rode*,
C.20.86 To touchen hym or to t[ast]en hym or taken down [of *rode*]
C.20.259 And lette out symondes sones to sen hym honge on *rode*:
C.20.267 And bote they reuerense [h]is resurexioun and þe *rode* honoure
C.21.323 And of his bapteme and bloed þat he bledde on *rode*
C.22.43 That he saide in his sorwe on þe sulue *rode*:

roof n *rof* n. B 1; C 1 roef
B.19.327 And of al holy writ he made a *roof* after;
C.21.327 And of all holy writ he made a *roef* aftur

roon > ryne; roos > risen

roost n *roste* n.(1) A 1 rost; B 1; C 1
A.Pr.108 Of þe ryn & of þe rochel, þe *rost* to defie!'
B.Pr.230 Of þe Ryn and of þe Rochel þe *roost* to defie!'
C.Pr.234 Of þe r[yn]e and of þe rochele the *roost* [to] defye!'

roote n *rote* n.(4) A 3 rote (2) rotis (1); B 12 roote (10) rootes (1) rotes
(1); C 8 rote (6) rotes (2)
A. 7.95 My plouȝpote shal be my pyk & putte at þe *rotis*,
A.10.124 Out of a raggit *rote* and a rouȝ brere
A.10.134 Þei be þe riccheste of reaumes & þe *rote* of dowel.
B. 6.103 My plow[pote] shal be my pi[k] and [putte at] þe *rotes*,
B.12.58 And Richesse riȝt so but if þe *roote* be trewe.
B.12.71 And namely Clergie for cristes loue, þat of Clergie is *roote*.
B.14.44 And bestes by gras and by greyn and by grene *rootes*,
B.14.95 Ac satisfaccion sekeþ out þe *roote*, and boþe sleeþ and voideþ,
B.15.65 Right so þat þoruȝ reson wolde þe *roote* knowe
B.15.100 [Is þe] *roote* of þe right feiþ to rule þe peple;
B.15.101 A[c] þer þe *roote* is roten, reson woot be soþe,
B.16.22 And bad me toten on þe tree, on top and on *roote*.
B.16.41 Wiþ alle þe wiles þat he kan, and waggeþ þe *roote*
B.18.292 'It is noȝt graiþly geten þer gile is þe *roote*,
B.20.54 Torned it [tid] vp so doun and ouertilte þe *roote*,
C. 8.64 My plouhpote shal be my pykstaff and pyche ato þe *rotes*
C.12.247 That *rote* is of robbares, the rychess[e] withynne!
C.15.242 Bestes by gra[s] by grayn and by grene *rotes*,
C.16.253 Is þe *rote* of [the] rihte fayth to reule þe peple;
C.16.254 Ac þer þe *rote* is roton, resoun woet þe sothe,
C.18.45 And with alle þe wyles þat he can waggeth þe *rote*
C.20.322 'Hit is nat graythly ygete ther gyle is þe *rote*
C.22.54 Turned hit tyd vp so down and ouertulde þe *rote*

rope(n > repe

ropere n *ropere* n. A 2; B 2; C 2
A. 5.165 A *ropere*, a redyngking, & rose þe disshere;
A. 5.178 Til robyn þe *ropere* was red to arisen,
B. 5.315 A *Ropere*, a Redyngkyng and Rose þe dyssher[e],
B. 5.329 Til Robyn þe *Ropere* [arise þei bisouȝte],
C. 6.372 A *ropere*, a redyngkynge and Rose þe disshere
C. 6.387 Til Robyn þe *Ropere* aryse they bisouhte

rosamounde n prop *n.i.d.* B 1
B.12.47 And *Rosamounde* riȝt so reufulliche [bisette]

rose n *rose* n.(1) A 4; B 4; C 4
A. 4.36 And how he rauisshide *rose*, reynaldis loue,
A. 5.140 *Rose* þe regratour was hire riȝte name;
A. 5.165 A ropere, a redyngking, & *rose* þe disshere;
A.10.123 Riȝt as a *rose*, [þat red is and] swet,
B. 4.49 And how he rauysshede *Rose*, Reignaldes looue,
B. 5.224 *Rose* þe Regrater was hir riȝte name;
B. 5.315 A Ropere, a Redyngkyng and *Rose* þe dyssher[e],
B.13.100 As rody as a *Rose* [ruddede] hise chekes,
C. 4.47 And how he raueschede *Rose* the ryche wydewe by nyhte
C. 6.232 *Rose* þe regrater was here ryhte name;
C. 6.372 A ropere, a redyngkynge and *Rose* þe disshere,
C.15.107 As rody as a *rose* rodded his chekes,

rosset > russet; rost > roost

roste v *rosten* v. C 1
C. 9.144 Reste hym and *roste* [hym] and his rug turne,

rote > roote; rotede > roten

rotey adj *rutei* n. B 1; C 1 roteye
B.11.338 As whan þei hadde ryde in *Rotey* tyme anoon [reste þei] after;
C.13.146 As when þei hadde [ryde in] *roteye*[tyme] anon they reste aftur;

roten adj *roten* adj. B 1; C 1 roton
B.15.101 A[c] þer þe roote is *roten*, reson woot þe soþe,
C.16.254 Ac þer þe rote is *roton*, resoun woet þe sothe,

roten v1 *roten* v.(1) B 1; C 5 rotede (1) roteth (1) rotye (2) rotieth (1)
B.10.116 *Roten* and torende? Reson wolde it neuere!
C. 3.358 In nombre, *Rotye* and aryse and remissioun to haue,
C. 5.150 Ryht so religioun *roteth* and sterueth
C.12.223 And þat rathest rypeth *rotieth* most sonnest;
C.13.22 And brouhte hem all aboue þat in bale *rotede*!
C.18.60 Ac somme ar swettore then somme and so[nner]e wollen *rotye*.

roten v2 *roten* v.(3) A 1; C 1 roteth
A.10.78 To routen ne to resten ne *ro[t]en* in þin herte;
C. 2.57 Al þe riche retenaunce þat *ro[t]eth* hem o fals lyuynge

rotes > roote; rotye roton > roten; rotte > rutte

rouȝ adj *roughe* adj. A 1
A.10.124 Out of a raggit rote and a *rouȝ* brere

rou3te rouhte > recche

roume v *roumen v.* B 1; C 1
B.Pr.166   Men my3te witen wher þei wente and [hire] wey r[oum]e.
C.Pr.183   Men Myghte ywete where þei wente and here [way roume].

rounde adj *rounde adj.* A 1; B 1; C 1 rownd
A. 5.190   And bleu3 þe *rounde* ryuet at þe riggebones ende
B. 5.342   And blew [þe] *rounde* ruwet at [þe] ruggebones ende
C. 6.400   A[nd] blew his *rownd* ruet at [þe] ry[g]bones ende

rouneþ v *rounen v.* A 2 rouniþ (1) rowneden (1); B 3 rouned (1) rouneþ (1) rownynge (1); C 3 rouned (1) rounynge (1) rounned (1)
A. 4.14   And ri3t renneþ to resoun & *rouniþ* in his ere;
A. 5.174   Þo risen vp in rape & *ro[wn]eden* togideris,
B. 4.14   And [ri3t renneþ] to Reson and *rouneþ* in his ere;
B. 4.25   And Reson wiþ hym ryt, *rownynge* togideres
B. 5.325   T[h]o risen vp in Rape and *rouned* togideres
C. 4.14   And rood forth to resoun and *rouned* in his ere
C. 4.25   And resoun with hym ry[t], *rounynge* togederes
C. 6.383   Tho rysen vp [in] rape and *rounned* togyderes

rousty > rusty

route n *route n.* B 8; C 7
B.Pr.146   Wiþ þat ran þer a *route* of Ratons at ones
B.Pr.175   Al þ[e] *route* of Ratons to þis reson assented.
B.Pr.177   Ther ne was Raton in þe *route*, for al þe Reaume of Fraunce,
B.Pr.184   And to þe *route* of Ratons reherced þise wordes:
B.Pr.199   And also ye *route* of Ratons rende mennes cloþes
B. 2.62   I kan no3t rekene þe *route* þat ran aboute Mede.
B. 4.168   And [also] a Sherreues clerk bisherewed al þe *route*:
B.18.404   Astroth and al þe *route* hidden hem in hernes;
C.Pr.167   Than ran þer a *route* of ratones [at ones]
C.Pr.192   Alle th[e] *route* of ratones to þis resoun assentide;
C.Pr.194   Ther ne was [raton in] þe *route*, for al þe reame of Fraunce,
C.Pr.201   And to þe *route* of ratones rehersede thise wordes:
C.Pr.217   And [3]e *route* of ratones of reste men awake
C. 2.64   Y kan nou3t rykene þe *route* þat ran aboute mede.
C.20.447   Astarot and alle [þe *route*] hidden hem in hernes;

routen v *routen v.(7)* A 1
A.10.78   To *routen* ne to resten ne ro[t]en in þin herte;

rouþe > ruþe

roued v *raven v.(2), OED rove v.1,II* C 1
C.20.126   Of the dene and the derkenesse and how þe day *roued*

rowe v1 *rouen v.(1)* C 1
C.10.52   To repenten and arise and *rowe* out of synne

roweth v2 *reuen v.(2)* B 1 rowed; C 1
B.18.123   Of þe dyn and þe derkenesse and how þe day *rowed*,
C. 1.114   Thenne sitten in þe sonne syde þere þe day *roweth*?'

rownd > rounde; rowneden rownynge > rouneþ

rubies n *rubie n.* A 1; B 2; C 2 rubees (1) rubies (1)
A. 3.22   Rynges wiþ *rubies* & ricchesse manye;
B. 2.12   And þeron [riche] *Rubies* as rede as any gleede,
B. 3.23   Rynges wiþ *Rubies* and richesses manye,
C. 2.13   And thereon rede *rubies* and othere riche stones.
C. 3.24   Rynges with *rubees* and othere riche 3eftes,

ruche > risshe

ruddede v *ruden v.* B 1; C 1 rodded
B.13.100   As rody as a Rose [*ruddede*] hise chekes,
C.15.107   As rody as a rose *rodded* his chekes,

rude adj *rude adj.* B 3; C 1
B.11.420   And ri3t so ferde Reson bi þee; þow wiþ *rude* speche
B.15.461   *Rude* and vnresonable, rennynge wiþouten [keperes].
B.15.476   Ri3t so *rude* men þat litel reson konneþ
C.13.228   Rihte so ferde Resoun by the; for thy *rude* speche

ruet > ruwet; rufol > rewful; rufully -iche > rewfulliche

rugge n *rigge n.* B 2; C 3 rug (1) rugge (2)
B.14.213   Ther þe poore preesseþ bifore wiþ a pak at his *rugge*:
B.19.287   Sholde no curious clooþ comen on his *rugge*,
C. 9.144   Reste hym and roste [hym] and his *rug* turne,
C.16.54   There þe pore preseth byfore with a pak at his *rugge*,
C.21.287   Sholde no curious cloth comen on his *rugge*

ruggebones n *riggebon n.* A 1 riggebones; B 1; C 1 rygbones
A. 5.190   And bleu3 þe rounde ryuet at þe *riggebones* ende
B. 5.342   And blew [þe] rounde ruwet at [þe] *ruggebones* ende
C. 6.400   A[nd] blew his rownd ruet at [þe] *ry[g]bones* ende

ruyflare n *riflere n.* C 2 ruyflare (1) ruyflares (1)
C. 4.125   And alle Rome rennares for *ruyflares* in Fraunce
C. 6.315   Robert the *ruyflare* on reddite lokede

ruyfle v *riflen v.* B 2 rifled (1) riflede (1); C 4 ryflede (1) ruyfle (1) ruyfled (1) yruyfled (1)
B. 5.232   I roos whan þei were areste and *riflede* hire males.'
B.17.102   That he ne was robbed or *rifled*, rood he þere or yede,
C. 4.54   To robbe me or to *ruyfle* me yf y ryde softe.
C. 6.236   Y roes and *ryflede* here males when the[y] areste were.'
C.10.195   The[r]of was he robbed and *ruyfled* or he on rode deyede
C.19.92   For wente neuere man this way þat he ne was here *yruyfled*

ruylen > rulen; ruylynge > rulyng

rule n *reule n. &> rulen* A 3 rewele; B 12 reule (2) rule (10); C 9 reule
A. 5.37   And siþþe he redde religioun here *rewel[e]* to holde
A.10.51   In *rewele* & in resoun, but reccheles it make.
A.11.205   Of religioun þe *rewele* he reherside in his morals,
B. 5.45   And siþen he radde Religion hir *rule* to holde
B.10.99   Now haþ ech riche a *rule* to eten by hymselue
B.10.297   [Amonges ri3tful religious þis *rule* sholde be holde.
B.10.299   Of religion þe *rule* reherseþ in hise morales,
B.10.323   And bete yow, as þe bible telleþ, for brekynge of youre *rule*,
B.12.36   To Rome ne to Rochemador, but as þi *rule* techeþ,
B.13.285   Religion saun3 *rule* [and] resonable obedience;
B.15.87   Ayein youre *rule* and Religion; I take record at Iesus
B.15.317   Ye hadde ri3t yno3, ye Religiouse, and so youre *rule* me tolde.
B.19.423   Or in Rome as hir *rule* wole þe relikes to kepe;
B.20.247   To lered ne to lewed, but lyueþ after youre *reule*.
B.20.265   Hir ordre and hir *reule* wole to han a certein noumbre
C. 3.203   Religioun he al toreueth and oute of *reule* to lybbe;
C. 5.143   And sethe he radde religioun here *reule* to holde
C. 5.147   The *reule* of alle religious rihtful and obedient:
C. 5.157   Haen ryde out of aray, here *reule* euele yholde,
C. 5.169   And bete 3ow, as þe bible telleth, for brekynge of 3oure *reule*
C. 9.222   Furste, Religious of religioun a *reule* to holde
C.21.423   Or in Rome, as here *reule* wo[l], þe relikes to kepe;
C.22.247   To lered ne to lewed, but lyueth aftur 3oure *reule*.
C.22.265   Here ordre and here *reule* wol to haue a certeyne nombre

rulen v *reulen v.* A 6 reule (2) rewele (3) rewliþ (1); B 17 rule (11) ruled (3) rulen (2) ruleþ (1); C 20 reule (13) reulede (1) reulen (1) reulest (1) rewle (1) ruylen (1) rulen (1) yruled (1)
A. 1.52   For ri3tfulliche resoun shulde *rewele* 3ow alle,
A. 4.9   For he shal *rewele* my reaume & rede me þe beste
A. 4.149   'But I *reule* þus þi reaum rend out my ribbes,
A. 8.10   And r[i3t]fulliche in reaum *rewliþ* þe peple
A. 9.99   And *rewele* þe reaum be red of hem alle,
A.11.267   For to *reule* his reaum ri3t at his wille;
B.Pr.201   For hadde ye rattes youre [raik] ye kouþe no3t *rule* yowselue.
B. 1.54   For ri3tfully reson sholde *rule* yow alle,
B. 4.9   For he shal *rule* my Reaume and rede me þe beste
B. 4.186   'But I *rule* þus youre Reaume rende out my guttes–
B. 7.10   And ri3tfully in Rem[e] *rulen* þe peple
B. 8.109   And *rule* þe Reme by [rede of hem alle],
B.10.386   [To *rule* þe reume and riche to make];
B.11.370   That Reson rewarded and *ruled* alle beestes
B.11.372   No Reson hem [*ruled*, neiþer riche ne pouere].
B.11.387   Forþi I rede', quod reson, '[þow] *rule* þi tonge bettre,
B.15.100   [Is þe] roote of þe right feiþ to *rule* þe peple;
B.17.3   To *rule* alle Reames wiþ; I bere þe writ [ri3t] here.'
B.17.263   That riche ben and reson knoweþ *ruleþ* wel youre soule;
B.18.396   Ac my rightwisnesse and right shul *rulen* al helle.
B.19.396   'Ye? baw!' quod a Brewere, 'I wol no3t be *ruled*,
B.19.466   'I am kyng wiþ croune þe comune to *rule*,
B.19.478   And *rule* þi reaume in reson [as right wol and] truþe.
C.Pr.219   For hadde 3e ratones 3oure [reik] 3e couthe nat *reule* 3owsuluen.'
C. 1.50   For ri3tfulliche resoun sholde *reule* 3ow alle
C. 4.9   For he shal *reulen* my rewme and rede me the beste
C. 4.180   'But [y] *reule* thus alle reumes reuet[h] me my syhte,
C. 9.10   And ryhtfulliche in reumes *ruylen* þe comune
C. 9.20   To be [peres] to þe apostles alle peple to *reule*
C.10.105   And *reule* alle reumes by here thre wittes
C.11.212   To *reule* [þe] reum[e] and ryche to make
C.13.182   Resoun *re[ul]ede* hem nat, noþer ryche ne pore.
C.13.186   That thow ne *reul[e]st* rather renkes then other bestes.
C.13.191   They *reule* hem al by resoun Ac renkes ful fewe.
C.13.205   Forthy,' quod Resoun, 'y rede thow *reule* thy tonge euere
C.14.36   Then eny connyng of kynde wit but clergi hit *reule*.
C.16.253   Is þe rote of [the] rihte fayth to *reule* þe peple;
C.19.3   To *reule* alle reumes þerwith in ri3hte and in resoun.
C.19.229   That riche ben and resoun knoweth; *reule* wel 3oure soul[e];
C.20.439   Ac my rihtwysnesse and rihte shal *r[ul]en* [al] helle
C.21.396   '3e? bawe!' quod a breware, 'y wol nat be *yruled*,

C.21.466   'Y am kyng with croune the comune to *reule*
C.21.478   And *rewle* thy rewme in resoun [as] riht w[o]l and treuthe,

rulyng ger *reulinge ger.* B 1; C 1 ruylynge
B.Pr.127   And for þi riȝtful *rulyng* be rewarded in heuene'.
C.Pr.151   And for thy rightful *ruylynge* be rewardid in heuene.'

rusche(s > risshe

russet n *russet n.* A 1 rosset; B 3; C 3
A. 9.1   Thus, yrobid in *rosset*, I rombide aboute
B. 8.1   Thus, yrobed in *russet*, I romed aboute
B.15.167   And is as glad of a gowne of a gray *russet*
B.15.220   For I haue seyen hym in silk and som tyme in *russet*,
C.10.1   Thus, yrobed in *russet*, y romede aboute
C.16.300   And as glad of a goune of a gray *russet*
C.16.345   Ych haue ysey hym mysulue som tyme in *russet*,

rusty adj *rusti adj.* A 1; B 1; C 1 rousty
A. 7.65   And robyn þe ribaudour for hise *rusty* woordis.
B. 6.73   And Robyn þe Ribaudour for hise *rusty* wordes.
C. 8.75   And Robyn þe rybauder for his *rousty* wordes.

rutelondis > rutland

ruþe n *reuthe n.* A 5 reuþe; B 25 rouþe (3) ruþe (22); C 26 reuth (1) reuthe (25)
A. 1.149   Forþi I rede þe riche haue *reuþe* on þe pore;
A. 4.95   But resoun haue *reuþe* on hym he shal reste in þe stokkis
A. 4.97   Summe redde resoun to haue *reuþe* on þat shrewe,
A. 4.100   'Rede me not,' quaþ resoun, 'no *reuþe* to haue
A. 4.117   And ȝet,' quaþ resoun, 'be þe rode, I shal no *reuþe* haue
B. 1.175   Forþi I rede [þe] riche, haueþ *ruþe* [on] þe pouere;
B. 4.108   But Reson haue *ruþe* on hym he shal reste in [þe] stokkes
B. 4.110   Som[me] radde Reson to haue *ruþe* on þat shrewe;
B. 4.113   'Reed me noȝt', quod Reson, 'no *ruþe* to haue
B. 4.134   And yet', quod Reson, 'by þe Rode! I shal no *ruþe* haue
B. 5.427   *Ruþe* is to here rekenyng whan we shul rede acountes:
B. 5.477   [Th]anne hadde Repentaunce *ruþe* and redde hem alle to knele.
B. 5.504   And haue *ruþe* on þise Ribaudes þat repenten hem soore
B.10.318   To Religiouse þat han no *rouþe* þouȝ it reyne on hir Auters.
B.10.348   Ther riche men no riȝt may cleyme but of *ruþe* and grace.'
B.14.128   Riȝt so fareþ god by som riche; *ruþe* me it þynkeþ,
B.14.145   Ac if ye riche haue *ruþe* and rewarde wel þe poore,
B.14.163   And arated of riche men þat *ruþe* is to here.
B.14.168   [And] haue *ruþe* on þise riche men þat rewarde noȝt þi prisoners;
B.15.11   Til reson hadde *ruþe* on me and rokked me aslepe,
B.15.508   And þat is *rouþe* for riȝtful men þat in þe Reawme wonyen,
B.15.533   It is *ruþe* to rede how riȝtwise men lyuede,
B.15.539   And now is *rouþe* to rede how þe rede noble
B.16.5   Mercy is þe more þerof; þe myddul stok is *ruþe*;
B.16.78   I hadde *ruþe* whan Piers rogged, it gradde so rufulliche;
B.17.304   That rightwisnesse þoruȝ repentaunce to *ruþe* myȝte turne.
B.17.319   Ac er his rightwisnesse to *ruþe* torne som restitucion bihoueþ;
B.18.91   Haue on me *ruþe*, riȝtful Iesu;' and riȝt wiþ þat he wepte.
B.19.83   Reson and Rightwisnesse and *Ruþe* þei offrede;
B.20.193   And of þe wo þat I was Inne my wif hadde *ruþe*
C. 1.171   Forthy y rede ȝow riche, haueth *reuthe* [o]n þe pore;
C. 3.118   'Haue *reuthe* on this regraters þat han riche handes,
C. 3.413   As me ret in regum [of þe *reuthe*] of kynges,
C. 4.103   Bute resoun haue *reuth* on hym he shal reste in [þe] stokkes
C. 4.105   Summe radden resoun tho to haue *reuthe* vppon þat shrewe
C. 4.108   'Rede me nat,' quod resoun, 'no *reuthe* to haue
C. 4.131   And [ȝut],' quod resoun, 'by þe rode! y shal no *reuthe* haue
C. 5.164   To religious þat haen no *reuthe* thow it ryne on here auters.
C. 6.286   'Now redily,' quod repentaunce, 'y haue *reuthe* of thy lyuynge.'
C. 6.423   To repentaunce ryht thus, 'haue *reuthe* on me,' he saide,
C. 7.40   *Reuthe* is to here rekenynge when we shal rede acountes.
C. 7.149   Haue *reuthe* of alle these rybaudes þat repenten hem sore
C. 9.82   That *reuthe* is to rede or in ryme shewe
C.13.70   And haue *reuthe* and releue with his rychesse by his power
C.13.93   So þe pore of puyr *reuthe* may parforme þe lawe
C.15.296   Other here or elliswher, elles hit were *reuthe*;
C.16.16   [And arated of] ryche men þat *reuthe* is to here.
C.16.22   Riht so haue *reuthe* on [thy renkes] alle
C.17.194   Hit is *reuthe* to rede how riht holy men lyuede,
C.17.200   And now is *reuthe* to rede how þe rede noble
C.17.259   And þat is *reuthe* for rihtfole men þat in þ[e] reume wonyeth
C.19.284   That rihtwisnesse thorw repentaunce to *reuthe* myhte turne.
C.19.299   Ac ar [h]is rihtwisnesse to *reuthe* turne rest[i]t[uci]on hit maketh,
C.20.94   Haue [on me *reuthe*], riȝtfol iesu;' and riht with þat a wepte.
C.21.83   Resoun and riht[wis]nesse and *reuthe* thei offrede;
C.22.193   And of þe wo þat y was ynne my wyf hadde *reuthe*

rutland n prop *n.i.d.* A 1 rutelondis; B 1
A. 2.75   Randolf þe reue of *rutelondis* sokne,

B. 2.111   Reynald þe Reue of *Rutland* Sokene,

rutte v *routen v.(2)* B 3 rutte; C 2 rotte
B. 5.391   Raxed and [remed] and *rutte* at þe laste.
B.12.151   [Riche men *rutte* þo and in hir reste were
B.18.6   Reste me þere and *rutte* faste til Ramis palmarum.
C. 7.7   R[a]xlede and r[e]mede and *rotte* at þe laste.
C.14.95   Ryche men *rotte* tho and in here reste were

ruwet n *ruet n.* A 1 ryuet; B 1; C 1 ruet
A. 5.190   And bleuȝ þe rounde *ryuet* at þe riggebones ende
B. 5.342   And blew [þe] rounde *ruwet* at [þe] ruggebones ende
C. 6.400   A[nd] blew his rownd *ruet* at [þe] ry[g]bones ende

S

saaf adj *sauf adj. &> sauf,saue* A 3 sauf; B 9; C 8 saef
A. 8.54 Þat he ne worþ *sauf* sykirly, & so seiþ þe sautir.
A. 9.29 And ȝet is he *sauf* & sound, & so hym behouiþ.
A. 9.44 Ay is þi soule *sauf* but þou þiself wilt
B. 7.52 That he ne worþ *saaf* [sikerly]; þe Sauter bereþ witnesse:
B. 8.33 Ac yet is he *saaf* and sound, and so hym bihoueþ,
B. 8.48 Ay is þi soule *saaf* but [þow þiselue wole
B.10.351 That is baptiȝed beþ *saaf*, be he riche or pouere.'
B.12.166 Or þe swymmere þat is *saaf* by so hymself like,
B.12.172 Out of synne and be *saaf*, þouȝ he synne ofte,
B.12.270 And wheiþer he be *saaf* or noȝt saaf, þe soþe woot no clergie,
B.12.270 And wheiþer he be saaf or noȝt *saaf*, þe soþe woot no clergie,
B.12.284 And he is *saaf*, seiþ þe book, and his soule in heuene.
C.10.38 A[c] ȝut is he *saef* and sound; and so hit fareth by þe rihtfole.
C.10.40 That ay is *saef* and sound þat sitte withynne þe borde.
C.14.112 Out of synne and be *saef*, thogh he synege ofte,
C.14.191 And wher he be *saef* or nat saef þe sothe woet no clergie
C.14.191 And wher he be saef or nat *saef* þe sothe woet no clergie
C.14.206 And he is *saef*, saith þe boek, and his soule in heuene.
C.17.313 And haen a suspeccioun to be *saef*, bothe sarresynes & iewes,
C.18.18 And sethen þat ȝe fouchen *saef* to sey me as hit hoteth.'

sacrefice > sacrifise

sacrificed v *sacrificen v.* B 1; C 1 sacreficede
B.12.116 [Saul for he *sacrificed* sorwe hym bitidde,
C.14.61 Saul for he *sacreficede* sorwe hym bytydde

sacrifise n *sacrifice n.* B 1; C 4 sacrefice (3) sacrefyce (1)
B.16.243 And siþþe he sente me to seye I sholde do *sacrifise*
C.Pr.98 To vndertake þe tol of vntrewe *sacrefice*.
C.Pr.119 That soffreth men do *sacrefyce* and worschipe maumettes
C.18.248 To make *sacrefice* of hym he heet me, hym to honoure.
C.18.263 And ma[k]e *sacrefice* so: somwhat hit bitokneth;

sad adj *sad adj.* A 4 sad (2) sadde (1) saddere (1); B 6 sad (1) sadde (3) sadder (2); C 7 sad (5) saddere (1) saddest (1)
A. 9.23 'How seue siþes þe *sadde* man synneþ on þe day;
A. 9.39 Synnes þe *sad* man seuene [siþes] in þe day.
A. 9.112 *Sad* of his semblaunt & of a softe speche.
A.11.309 Ne none sonnere ysauid, ne *saddere* of consience,
B. 8.27 'How seuen siþes þe *sadde* man [synneþ on þe day].
B. 8.43 Synneþ þe *sadde* man [seuen siþes a day].
B. 8.122 *Sad* of his semblaunt and of [a] softe [speche].
B.10.465 Ne none sonner saued, ne *sadder* of bileue.
B.12.161 And boþe naked as a nedle, hir noon [*sadder*] þan ooþer.
B.15.513 In ensaumple þat men sholde se by *sadde* reson
C. 3.335 On a *sad* and a siker semblable to hemsuluen.
C. 5.90 Ac it semeth no *sad* parfitnesse in Citees to b[e]gge
C.10.31 'How seuene sithes þe *sad* man synegeth on þe day.
C.10.49 Synegeth seue sithe þe *saddest* man on erthe
C.10.118 *Sad* of his semblant and with a softe speche.
C.11.142 Ne none sanere ysa[u]ed ne *saddere* in bileue
C.17.264 In ensaumple þat men sholde se by *sad* resoen

sadde v *saden v. &> sad* B 1
B.10.250 And hymself ordeyned to *sadde* vs in bileue.

sadder adv *sad adv. &> sad* A 1 saddere; B 1
A. 5.4 Þat I ne hadde yslepe *saddere* & yseyn more.
B. 5.4 That I ne hadde slept *sadder* and yseiȝen moore.

saddere > sad,sadder

sadel n *sadel n.* A 1 sadil; B 1; C 1
A. 4.18 'Sette my *sadil* vpon suffre til I se my tyme,
B. 4.20 'Set my *Sadel* vpon suffre-til-I-se-my-tyme
C. 4.20 Sette my *sadel* vpon soffre-tyl-y-se-my-tyme

sadle v *sadelen v.* A 1 sadelit; B 2 Sadeled (1) sadle (1)
A. 2.134 Þat somenours shulde be *sadelit* & serue hem ichone,
B. 2.170 That Somonours sholde be *Sadeled* and seruen hem echone,
B. 2.175 Lat *sadle* hem wiþ siluer oure synne to suffre,

sadnesse n *sadnesse n.* B 1
B. 7.156 To sette *sadnesse* in Songewarie for sompnia ne cures.

saef > fouchensaf,saaf; saet > sitten

safly adv *saufli adv.* C 1
C.13.64 And as *safly* as þe messager and a[s] sone at his hostiele.

sage n *sage n.* A 2; B 4 sage (3) sages (1); C 5 sage (4) sages (1)
A. 3.82 Salamon þe *sage* a sarmon he made
A.11.265 For salamon þe *sage*, þat sapience made,
B. 3.93 Salomon þe *sage* a sermon he made
B.10.384 For Salomon þe *sage* þat Sapience [made],
B.13.422 That fedeþ fooles *sages*, flatereris and lieris,
B.13.443 The pouere for a fool *sage* sittyng at þ[i] table,
C. 3.121 Salamon þe *sage* a sarmon he made
C. 7.82 That feden foel *sages*, flateres and lyares
C. 7.103 The pore for a f[o]l *sage* sittynge at thy table,
C. 8.242 And salomon þe *sage* with þe same acordeth:
C.11.209 For salomon þe *sage* þat sapience made,

say > seen,siggen; said(- saye(- > siggen; saiȝ sayh > seen

saille v *sailen v.(2)* B 1; C 1 sayle
B.13.233 Ne neiþer *saille* ne [sautrie] ne synge wiþ þe gyterne,
C.15.207 Ne noþer *sayle* ne sautrien ne syngen with þe geterne,

sayn > siggen; saynt(- > seint; sayst(e saith > siggen; saiȝ > seen

sak n *sak n.* A 1; B 1; C 1
A. 7.9 'Summe shal sewe þe *sak* for shedyng of þe whete;
B. 6.9 'Somme shul sowe þe *sak* for shedyng of þe Whete.
C. 8.8 'That somme sowe þe *sak* for shedynge of the whete,

sake n *sake n.* A 4; B 16; C 14
A. 3.176 In normandie was he nouȝt anoyed for my *sake*,
A. 5.238 And þou haddist mercy on þat man for memento *sake*,
A. 7.94 And ben his pilgrym at þe plouȝ for pore menis *sake*.
A.11.200 And haþ possessions & pluralites for pore menis *sake*;
B. 3.189 In Normandie was he noȝt noyed for my *sake*,
B. 5.466 And haddest mercy on þat man for Memento *sake*,
B. 5.488 On good fryday for mannes *sake* at ful tyme of þe daye;
B. 6.102 And ben his pilgrym atte plow for pouere mennes *sake*.
B. 9.92 Bisshopes shul be blamed for beggeres *sake*.
B.10.100 In a pryuee parlour for pouere mennes *sake*,
B.10.259 And þat is, man, bi þy myȝt, for mercies *sake*,
B.11.196 That ȝyueþ hem mete or moneie [and] loueþ hem for my *sake*.'
B.12.92 Forþi I counseille þee for cristes *sake* clergie þat þow louye;
B.14.324 I ne hadde be deed and doluen for dowelis *sake*!
B.15.91 I shal tellen it for truþes *sake*; take hede whoso likeþ.
B.15.244 [Amonges erchebisshopes and bisshopes, [for beggeres *sake*],
B.15.566 [Charite] were to deschargen hem for holy chirches *sake*,
B.16.162 That on þe friday folwynge for mankyndes *sake*
B.16.235 I circumscised my sone siþen for his *sake*,
B.18.367 I fauȝt so me þursteþ ȝit for mannes soule *sake*;
C.Pr.138 Contreplede hit noght,' quod Consience, 'for holi [k]ir[k]e *sake*.'
C. 2.200 Of many maner men for mede *sake* seude aftur.
C. 4.99 'Nay, by crist!' quod þe kyng, 'for Consiences *sake*
C. 6.320 And haddest mercy vppon þat man for memento *sake*,
C. 9.133 Me [g]yueth hem giftes and gold for grete lordes *sake*.
C.11.142 On þe maide Marie for mankynde *sake*
C.12.205 For crist saide [so] to seyntes þat for his *sake* tholeden
C.14.5 And conseyled the for cristes *sake* no creature to bygile,
C.16.366 With bisshopes a wolde be for beggares *sake*
C.17.231 Hit were charite to deschargen hem for holy churche *sake*,
C.18.251 Y circumsised my sone also for his *sake*,
C.19.40 And seth to louye and to lene for þat lordes *sake*
C.20.357 (A litel y ouerleep for lesynges *sake*,
C.20.357 Y fauht so me fursteth ȝut for mannes soule *sake*:

salamon(- > salomon

salarie n *salarie n.* B 2; C 1 salerie
B. 5.426 And my seruauntȝ som tyme: hir *salarie* is bihynde;
B.14.142 Riȝt as a seruaunt takeþ his *salarie* bifore, & siþþe wolde clayme
  moore

C. 7.39   And my seruauntes som tyme here *salerie* is bihynde;

salme(- > psalme

salomon n prop *Salomon n.* A 5 Salamon (4) salamonis (1); B 15
     Salomon (13) Salomons (2); C 9 salamon (6) salomon (3)
A. 3.82   *Salamon* þe sage a sarmon he made
A. 8.125   On *salamonis* sawis [seldom] þou beholdis:
A.10.81   *Salamon* it seide for a soþ tale:
A.11.16   Þanne alle þe soþe sawis þat *salamon* seide euere.
A.11.265   For *salamon* þe sage, þat sapience made,
B. 3.93   *Salomon* þe sage a sermon he made
B. 3.333   Se what *Salomon* seiþ in Sapience bokes!
B. 5.39   And *Salomon* seide þe same þat Sapience made,
B. 7.143   On *Salomons* sawes selden þow biholdest:
B. 9.96   [Ne] loueþ noȝt *Salomons* sawes þat Sapience tauȝte:
B.10.16   Than alle þe sooþ sawes þat *Salomon* seide euere.
B.10.342   *Salomon* seiþ also þat siluer is worst to louye;
B.10.384   For *Salomon* þe sage þat Sapience [made],
B.10.401   As *Salomon* dide and swiche oþere, þat shewed grete wittes
B.10.436   That *Salomon* seiþ I trowe be sooþ and certein of vs alle:
B.11.270   Alþouȝ *Salomon* seide, as folk seeþ in þe bible,
B.11.272   Wiser þan *Salomon* was bereþ witnesse and tauȝte
B.12.41   Or *Salomon* his sapience, or Sampson his strengþe?
B.12.271   Ne of Sortes ne of *Salomon* no scripture kan telle.
B.15.54   Ayein swiche *Salomon* spekeþ and despiseþ hir wittes
C. 3.121   *Salamon* þe sage a sarmon he made
C. 3.324   For god gaf *salomon* grace vpon erthe,
C. 3.485   'Loo what *salamon* sayth,' quod she, 'in sapiense in þe bible!
C. 8.242   And *salomon* þe sage with þe same acordeth:
C.11.209   For *salomon* þe sage þat sapience made,
C.11.270   By that þat *salomon* saith hit semeth þat no wyht woet
C.13.196   'Vch a segge for hymsulue, *salamon* vs techeth:
C.14.192   Ne of sortes ne of *salamon* n[o] scripture can telle
C.16.216   Aȝenes suche *salamon* speketh and despiseth here wittes

salt n *salt n.(1)* B 4
B.15.429   "*Salt* saueþ catel", siggen þise wyues:
B.15.431   Crist calleþ hem *salt* for cristene soules,
B.15.432   [Ac] fressh flessh ouþer fissh, whan it *salt* failleþ,
B.15.442   That goddes *salt* sholde be to saue mannes soule.

salt adj *salt adj.* A 1; B 2 salt (1) salte (1); C 2 salt (1) salte (1)
A. 7.268   And I seiȝe, be my soule, I haue no *salt* bacoun,
B. 6.284   And yet I seye, by my soule! I haue no *salt* bacon
B.13.45   But if þei synge for þo soules and wepe *salte* teris:
C. 8.306   And ȝut y say[e], be my soule! y haue no *sal[t]* bacoun
C.15.50   Bote yf they synge for tho soules and wepe *salte* teres.

saluacion -ioun > sauacion

salue n *salve n.(1) &> saluen* B 10 salue (9) salues (1); C 7 salue (6)
     salues (1)
B.Pr.159   Seide for a souereyn [*salue*] to [hem alle].
B.13.194   Hadde noȝt [Marie] Maudeleyne moore for a box of *salue*
B.13.248   That he sente me vnder his seel a *salue* for þe pestilence,
B.13.254   For siþ he haþ þe power þat Peter hadde he haþ þe pot wiþ þe
                salue:
B.17.78   And lo, here siluer', he seide, 'for *salue* to hise woundes.'
B.17.122   Til I haue *salue* for alle sike; and þanne shal I turne
B.20.170   And bisouȝte hym of socour and of his *salue* hadde;
B.20.306   Shrift shoop sharp *salue* and made men do penaunce
B.20.336   'I am a Surgien', seide þe [frere], 'and *salues* kan make.
B.20.372   That is þe souerayn[e] *salue* for alle [synnes of kynde].
C. 1.147   And most souerayne *salue* for soule and for body.
C. 9.264   Here *salue* is of supersedeas in sumnoures boxes;
C.15.224   For sethe he hath þe power þat peter hadde he hath þe pott with þe
                salue:
C.22.170   And bisouhte hym of socour and of h[is] *salue* hadde
C.22.306   Shrift schupte scharp *salue* and made men do penauns[e]
C.22.336   'Y am a surgien,' saide the frere, 'and *salues* can make.
C.22.372   That is the souereyne *salue* for alle [synnes of kynde].

saluen v *salven v.* A 1 salue; B 5 salue (2) saluede (2) saluen (1); C 2
     salue (1) salued (1)
A. 8.161   Þat pardoun, & penaunce, & preyours do *salue*
B.10.276   That ye were swiche as ye sey[d]e to *salue* wiþ oþere.
B.11.218   That Fides sua sholde sauen hire and *saluen* hire of synnes.
B.16.108   And souȝte out þe sike and [*saluede* blynde and crokede,
B.20.305   'Go *salue* þo þat sike ben and þoruȝ synne ywounded.'
B.20.347   He *saluede* so oure wommen til some were wiþ childe.'
C.22.305   'Go *salue* tho þat syke [ben] and thorw synne ywounded.'
C.22.347   He *salued* so oure wymmen til some were with childe.'

samaritan n prop *Samaritane n.* B 6; C 7 samaritaen
B.17.51   Thanne seiȝe we a *Samaritan* sittynge on a Mule,

B.17.66   Ac so soone so þe *Samaritan* hadde siȝte of þis leode
B.17.87   And suwed þat *Samaritan* þat was so ful of pite,
B.17.109   For he seigh me þat am *Samaritan* suwen Feiþ & his felawe
B.17.303   'ȝis', seide þe *Samaritan*, 'so þow myght repente
B.18.10   Oon semblable to þe *Samaritan* and somdeel to Piers þe
                Plow[man]
C.19.49   Thenne sey we a *samaritaen* cam sittynge on a muyle,
C.19.65   Ac so sone so the *samaritaen* hadde sihte of this carefole
C.19.81   Ac y sewede the *samaritaen* and saide how they bothe
C.19.83   'Haue hem excused,' quod [t]he *samaritaen*; 'here helpe may nat
                availe.
C.19.108   'A saide soeth,' quod the *samaritaen*, 'and so y rede the also.
C.19.283   'ȝus,' saide þe *samaritaen*, 'so thow myhtest repente
C.20.8   Oen semblable to þe *samaritaen* and somdeel to Pers þe plouhman

sambure n *samburi n.* C 1
C. 2.181   Softliche in *s[am]b[u]re* fram syse [to] syse,

same adj *same pron,same adj.* A 10; B 20; C 17
A.Pr.106   Tauerners to hem tolde þe *same*:
A. 1.151   For þe *same* mesour ȝe mete, amys oþer ellis,
A. 3.25   Wiþ þat come clerkis to conforten hire þe *same*,
A. 3.28   Hendely þanne heo behiȝte hem þe *same*,
A. 4.78   Wyt accordiþ þerewiþ & seide þe *same*:
A. 7.219   And sapience seiþ þe *same*, I saiȝ it in þe bible:
A. 8.66   Hadde þe *same* absolucioun þat sent was to peris.
A. 9.51   And þei seide, 'þe *same* saue þe fro myschaunce,
A.10.214   And aftir here deþ day shuln dwelle with þe *same*
A.11.69   And alle here seed for here synne þe *same* wo suffride?"
B.Pr.228   Tauerners [t]il hem tolden þe *same*:
B. 1.177   For þe *same* mesur[e] þat ye mete, amys ouþer ellis,
B. 3.26   Wiþ þat comen clerkes to conforten hire þe *same*
B. 3.29   Hendiliche heo þanne bihiȝte hem þe *same*,
B. 3.54   And lakkeþ noȝt ladies þat louen wel þe *same*.
B. 4.91   Wit acorde[þ] þerwiþ and [witnessede] þe *same*:
B. 5.39   And Salomon seide þe *same* þat Sapience made,
B. 6.235   And Sapience seiþ þe *same*–I seiȝ it in þe bible:
B. 7.64   Ha[dde] þe *same* absolucion þat sent was to Piers.
B. 8.60   And I seide 'þe *same* saue yow fro myschaunce,
B. 9.154   That bryngeþ forþ any barn but if he be þe *same*
B. 9.200   And after hir deeþ day shul dwelle wiþ þe *same*
B.10.26   The Sauter seiþ þe *same* by swiche þat doon ille:
B.10.111   And al hir seed for hir synne þe *same* deeþ suffrede?
B.10.197   Whoso gloseþ as gylours doon, go me to þe *same*,
B.11.22   The secounde seide þe *same*: 'I shal sewe þi wille;
B.11.298   The *same* I segge for soþe by alle swiche preestes
B.14.45   In menynge þat alle men myȝte be þe *same*
B.17.183   Than is þe sire [or] þe sone and in þe *same* myghte,
B.20.224   And so seiden sixty of þe *same* contree,
C.Pr.232   Tauerners til hem tolde þe *same*:
C. 1.173   For þe *same* mesure þat ȝe meteth, amis other elles,
C. 3.27   Thenne come clerkes to conforte here the *same*
C. 3.30   And Mede hendeliche behyhte hem þe *same*,
C. 3.58   And lacketh nat ladyes þat louyeth [wel] þe *same*.
C. 4.87   Witt acordede therwith and witnessede þe *same*:
C. 8.242   And salomon þe sage with þe *same* acordeth:
C. 9.188   And alle holy Eremytes haue shal þe *same*;
C.10.59   And y sayde, 'þe *same* saue ȝow fro meschaunce
C.11.23   The sauter saith þe *same* of alle suche ryche:
C.11.181   The seconde saide þe *same*: 'y [shal] sewe thy wille;
C.12.183   [And] oþer sedes also in þe *same* wyse
C.13.112   The *same* y segge for sothe by suche þat beth prestes
C.15.243   In menynge þat alle men myhte be þe *same*
C.19.149   Then is the syre or the sone and of þe *same* myhte,
C.20.385   The *same* sore shal he haue þat eny so smyteth;
C.22.224   And so sayde syxty of þe *same* contreye

samplarie n *saumplarie n.* B 1; C 1 saumplarie
B.12.102   And seint Spirit þe *Samplarie*, & seide what men sholde write.
C.14.47   And seynt spirit þe *saumplarie* and said what men sholde wryte.

sampson n prop *Sampsoun n.* B 2; C 1
B.12.41   Or Salomon his sapience, or *Sampson* his strengþe?
B.16.82   *Sampson* and Samuel and Seint Iohan þe Baptist,
C.18.113   *Sampson* and samuel and seynt Iohann þe Baptiste,

samrede adj *samred adj.* C 1
C. 8.309   Chibolles and chiruulles and cheries *samrede*

samuel n prop *n.i.d.* A 4 samuel (3) samuels (1); B 5; C 5
A. 3.240   God sente hym to segge þe *samuels* mouþ
A. 3.244   *Samuel* seide to saul, "god sendiþ þe & hotiþ
A. 3.254   God seide to *samuel* þat saul shulde deiȝe,
A. 3.263   *Samuel* shal slen hym, & saul shal be blamid,
B. 3.261   God sente to Saul by *Samuel* þe prophete

563

B. 3.264   "Forþi", seide *Samuel* to Saul, "god hymself hoteþ [þ]ee
B. 3.276   God seide to *Samuel* þat Saul sholde deye
B. 3.287   *Samuel* shal sleen hym and Saul shal be blamed
B.16.82   Sampson and *Samuel* and Seint Iohan þe Baptist,
C. 3.414   How god sente to sauel be *samuel* þe prophete
C. 3.417   "Sauel," quod *samuel*, "god hymsulue hoteth [the]
C. 3.429   God sayde to *samuel* þat sauel sholde deye
C. 3.440   *Samuel* shal sle hym and sauel shal be yblamed
C.18.113   Sampson and *samuel* and seynt Iohann þe Baptiste,

sand > sond

sandel n *cendal n.* A 1 sendel; B 1; C 1 sendel
A. 7.19   Þat han silk & *sendel*, sewiþ it whanne tyme is,
B. 6.11   That ye haue silk and *Sandel* to sowe whan tyme is
C. 8.10   That ȝe [han] selk and *sendel* to sowe whan tyme is

sanere > soone; sang > syngen; sank > synken; sannore -our > soone; sanȝ >
saunȝ

saphires *saphire n.* B 1
B. 2.13   And Diamaundes of derrest pris and double manere *Saphires*,

sapience n *sapience n.* A 4; B 10; C 4 sapience (3) sapiense (1)
A. 7.219   And *sapience* seiþ þe same, I saiȝ it in þe bible:
A. 8.46   For so seiþ þe sauter & *sapience* boþe:
A.11.127   And sette hire to *sapience* & to hire sauter yglosid.
A.11.265   For salamon þe sage, þat *sapience* made,
B. 3.333   Se what Salomon seiþ in *Sapience* bokes!
B. 3.345   Tho ye [souȝte] *Sapience* sittynge in youre studie.
B. 3.348   And if ye seche *Sapience* eft fynde shul ye þat folweþ,
B. 5.39   And Salomon seide þe same þat *Sapience* made,
B. 6.235   And *Sapience* seiþ þe same–I seiȝ it in þe bible:
B. 9.96   [Ne] loueþ noȝt Salomons sawes þat *Sapience* tauȝte:
B.10.175   And sette hire to *Sapience* and to þe Sauter glose[d].
B.10.384   For Salomon þe sage þat *Sapience* [made],
B.12.41   Or Salomon his *sapience*, or Sampson his strengþe?
B.12.57   *Sapience*, seiþ þe bok, swelleþ a mannes soule:
C. 3.485   'Loo what salamon sayth,' quod she, 'in *sapience* in þe bible!
C. 3.496   So hoso [s]echeth *sapience* fynde he shal [that] foloweth
C.11.115   And sette here to *sapience* and to þe sauter yglosed.
C.11.209   For salomon þe sage þat *sapience* made,

saresines sarisises > sarsen; sarmon(- sarmoun > sermon; sarrasin(-
sarresines > sarsen; sarrore > soore

sarsen n *Sarasine n.(1)* A 1 sarisises; B 15 Sarsen (1) Sarsens (2) Sarȝens
     (10) sarsyn (1) Sarȝynes (1); C 15 saresines (1) saresynes (1)
     sarrasines (2) sarrasyn (1) sarrasynes (3) sarrasyns (1) sarresines (1)
     sarresynes (5)
A.11.235   'Þat is in extremis,' quaþ scripture, 'as *sarisises* & Iewis
B. 3.328   And *Sarȝynes* for þat siȝte shul synge Gloria in excelsis &c,
B.10.352   'That is in extremis', quod Scripture, '[as] *Sarȝens* & Iewes
B.11.120   *Sarȝens* and scismatikes and so he dide þe Iewes:
B.11.157   Was þat *Sarsen* saued, as Seint Gregorie bereþ witnesse.
B.11.165   And saued þe *sarsyn* from sathanas power
B.12.278   Seyen in hir Sermons þat neiþer *Sarsen* ne Iewes
B.13.209   *Sarsens* and Surre, and so forþ alle þe Iewes,
B.15.390   And so may *Sarȝens* be saued, Scribes and [Grekes].
B.15.393   For *Sarȝens* han somwhat semynge to oure bileue,
B.15.398   Brouȝte *Sarȝens* of Surree, and see in what manere.
B.15.412   And siþþe oure Saueour suffred þe *Sarȝens* so bigiled
B.15.498   And seide it in saluacion of *Sarȝens* and oþere;
B.15.501   And siþ þat þise *Sarȝens*, Scribes and [Grekes]
B.15.605   Ac pharisees and *Sarȝens*, Scribes and [Grekes]
B.15.607   And siþen þat þe *Sarȝens* and also þe Iewes
C. 3.481   And *saresines* for þat syhte shal syng Credo in spiritum sanctum
C.12.55   *Sarrasynes* and sismatikes and so a ded þe iewes:
C.12.88   Saued me, *sarrasyn*, soule and body bothe.'
C.14.200   Segen [in] here sarmons þat noþer *saresynes* ne iewes
C.17.123   For *sarrasynes* may be saued so yf they so byleued
C.17.132   Iewes and gentel *sarresines* iugen hemsulue
C.17.150   'Where *sarresynes*,' y saide, 'yse nat what is charite?'
C.17.151   'Hit may be so þat *sarresynes* haen such a manere charite,
C.17.156   Ac many manere men þer ben, as *sarresynes* and iewes,
C.17.184   Disceue so the *sarrasyns*, sothlyche me thynketh
C.17.240   Hadde al surie as hymsulue wolde and *sarrasines* in equitee.
C.17.252   For sethe þat this *sarrasynes*, Scribȝ and this iewes
C.17.307   And ȝut they seyen sothly, and so doen þe *sarrasynes*,
C.17.313   And haen a suspectioun to be saef, bothe *sarresynes* & iewes,
C.17.315   And sethe þat th[e] *sarresynes* and also þe iewes

sat > sitten; satan > sathan

saterday n *Saterdai n.* A 3 satirday; B 4; C 3 saturday (2) saturdayes (1)
A. 5.14   And þe southwestryne wynd on *satirday* at eue
A. 5.56   Wiþ þat he [shulde] þe *satirday*, seue ȝer þeraftir,

A. 5.202   Þat he slepte *satirday* & sonneday til sonne ȝede to reste.
B. 5.14   And þe Southwestrene wynd on *Saterday* at euen
B. 5.73   Wiþ þat he sholde þe *Saterday*, seuen yer þerafter,
B. 5.360   That he sleep *Saterday* and Sonday til sonne yede to reste.
B.13.153   In a signe of þe *Saterday* þat sette first þe kalender,
C. 5.116   And the southweste wynde on *saturday* At euene
C. 6.173   With þat y said,' quod þat shrewe, '*saturdayes* for thy loue
C. 6.418   A sleep *saturday* and sonenday til sonne ȝede to reste.

sathan n prop *Satan n.,Satanas n.* A 3 sathan (2) sathanas (1); B 10
     Sathan (9) sathanas (1); C 5 satan (2) saton (1) satoun (2)
A. 2.70   Here soulis to *sathanas* to synken in pyne,
A.11.76   Suffre *sathan* his sed to bigile,
A.11.83   Suffren *sathan* his sed to bigile,
B. 2.106   Hire soules to *Sathan* to suffre with hym peynes,
B. 9.63   For þei seruen *Sathan* hir soules shal he haue;
B.10.123   Suffre *Sathan* his seed to bigile,
B.10.130   Suffre *Sathan* his seed to bigile,
B.11.165   And saued þe sarsyn from *sathanas* power
B.13.445   For to saue þi soule from *sathan* þyn enemy.
B.16.122   And *Sathan* youre Saueour; [youre]self now ye witnessen.
B.18.266   Thanne sikede *Sathan* and seide to he[l]le,
B.18.286   'That is sooþ', seide *Sathan*, 'but I me soore drede,
B.18.327   And seide to *Sathan*, 'lo! here my soule to amendes
C. 7.105   For to saue thy soule fram *satan* thyn enemye
C.18.151   'Thenne is *saton* ȝoure saueour,' quod iesus, '& hath ysaued ȝow
                 ofte.
C.20.274   Thenne syhed *satoun* and saide to helle,
C.20.312   'That is soeth,' saide *satoun*, 'bote y me sore doute
C.20.350   Sethe þat *satan* myssaide thus foule

satirday > saterday

satisfaccion n *satisfaccioun n.* B 3; C 2 satisfaccioun
B.14.21   And siþen sende þee to *Satisfaccion* for to [sonnen] it after:
B.14.95   Ac *satisfaccion* sekeþ out þe roote, and boþe sleeþ and voideþ,
B.17.320   His sorwe is *satisfaccion* for [swich] þat may noȝt paie.
C.16.27   And *satisfaccioun* þe whiche folfilleth þe fader will of heuene;
C.19.300   As sorwe of herte is *satisfaccioun* for suche þat may nat paye.

saton satoun > sathan; satourne > saturne; saturday(es > saterday

saturne n prop *Saturne n.* A 1 satourne; B 1; C 1
A. 7.307   And so seiþ *satourne* & sente ȝow to warne.
B. 6.326   And so sei[þ] *Saturne* and sente yow to warne.
C. 8.345   And so sayth *saturne* and sente [ȝow] to warne.

sauce n *sauce n.* A 1 saus; B 2; C 2
A. 7.246   And sende þe of his *saus* to sauoure þi lippes,
B. 6.262   And sende þee of his *Sauce* to sauore þi lippes,
B.13.43   Ac hir *sauce* was ouer sour and vnsauourly grounde
C. 8.272   And sende the of his *sauce* to sauery with thy lyppes
C.15.48   Ac here *sauce* was ouersour and vnsauerly ygrounde

sauel > saul

sauf adv *sauf adv. &> saaf* A 1
A. 8.38   Þat I ne shal sende [ȝour] soule *sauf* into heuene,

saufte n *savete n.* B 2
B. 7.37   And sende youre soules in *saufte* to my Seintes in Ioye.'
B.11.121   And bad hem souke for synne [*saufte*] at his breste

sauȝ > seen

sauȝtne v *saughten v.* A 1 sauȝte; B 1; C 1 sauhtene
A. 4.2   Ȝe shuln *sauȝte*, forsoþe, & serue me boþe.
B. 4.2   Ye shul *sauȝtne*, forsoþe, and serue me boþe.
C. 4.2   Ȝe shal *sauhtene*, forsothe, and serue me bothe.

sauhter > sauter

saul n prop *n.i.d.* A 4; B 7; C 9 sauel (6) saul (3)
A. 3.239   Why þe vengeaunce fel on *saul* & on his children?
A. 3.244   Samuel seide to *saul*, "god sendiþ þe & hotiþ
A. 3.254   God seide to samuel þat *saul* shulde deiȝe,
A. 3.263   Samuel shal slen hym, & *saul* shal be blamed,
B. 3.260   Whi þ[at] vengeaunce fel on *Saul* and on his children?
B. 3.261   God sente to *Saul* by Samuel þe prophete
B. 3.264   "Forþi", seide Samuel to *Saul*, "god hymself hoteþ [þ]ee
B. 3.276   God seide to Samuel þat *Saul* sholde deye
B. 3.287   Samuel shal sleen hym and *Saul* shal be blamed
B.12.116   [*Saul* for he sacrificed sorwe hym bitidde,
B.19.135   The burdes þo songe, *Saul* interfecit mille et dauid decem milia.
C. 3.409   And se[t]he, for *sauel* saued a kyng fo[r] mede
C. 3.411   That *saul* for þat synne and his sone deyede
C. 3.414   How god sente to *sauel* be samuel þe prophete
C. 3.417   "*Sauel*," quod samuel, "god hymsulue hoteth [the]
C. 3.429   God sayde to samuel þat *sauel* sholde deye

C. 3.431   Thus was kyng *sauel* ouercome thorw coueytise of mede,
C. 3.440   Samuel shal sle hym and *sauel* shal be yblamed
C.14.61   *Saul* for he sacreficede sorwe hym bytydde
C.21.135   The buyrdes tho songe, *Saul* interfecit mille & dauid decem milia.

saulee n *saule* n. B 1
B.16.11   And to haue my fulle of þat fruyt forsake a[l] oþ[er] *saule[e]*.

saumplarie > samplarie

saunȝ prep *sauns* prep. B 1; C 2 sanȝ
B.13.285   Religion *saunȝ* rule [and] resonable obedience;
C.17.163   Beaute *sanȝ* bounte blessed was [hit] neuere
C.17.164   Ne kynde *sanȝ* cortesie in no contreye is preysed.

saus > sauce

saut n *saut* n.(1) B 1; C 2 sawt
B.20.217   Sleuþe wiþ his slynge an hard [s]*aut* he made.
C.22.217   Sleuthe with his slynge a[n] hard *sawt* he made.
C.22.300   Ypocrisye and [h]y an hard *sawt* they ȝeuen.

sauter n *sauter* n. A 11 sauter (10) sautir (1); B 24; C 15 sauhter (1)
sauter (14)
A. 3.221   Þe prophet prechiþ it & put it in þe *sauter*:
A. 3.227   And þerof sei[þ] þe *sauter* in a salmis ende
A. 7.234   The *sauter* seiþ in þe salme of Beati omnes:
A. 8.46   For so seiþ þe *sauter* & sapience boþe:
A. 8.54   Þat he ne worþ sauf sykirly, & so seiþ þe *sautir*.
A. 8.109   Be þat þe *sauter* vs seiþ, & so dede manye oþere.
A.10.86   And þerof seiþ þe *sauter*, þe salme þou miȝt rede:
A.10.149   And so seiþ þe *sauter*, se it whanne þe likiþ:
A.11.55   And so seiþ þe *sauter*, se[ke] it in Memento:
A.11.127   And sette hire to sapience & to hire *sauter* yglosid.
A.11.192   Þ[i]s be[þ] dobet; so beriþ witnesse þe *sauter*:
B. 2.38   And how ye shul saue yourself? þe *Sauter* bereþ witnesse:
B. 3.234   The prophete precheþ [it] and putte it in þe *Sauter*:
B. 3.237   And Dauid assoileþ it hymself as þe *Sauter* telleþ:
B. 3.248   And þerof seiþ þe *Sauter* in a Salmes ende:
B. 5.276   And whoso leueþ [þat I liȝe] loke in þe *Sauter* glose,
B. 6.250   The *Sauter* seiþ, in þe psalme of Beati omnes,
B. 7.41   For þe *Sauter* saueþ hem noȝt, swiche as take ȝiftes,
B. 7.52   That he ne worþ saaf [sikerly]; þe *Sauter* bereþ witnesse:
B. 7.127   By þat þe *Sauter* [vs] seith, [and] so dide othere manye.
B. 9.125   Of swiche synfulle sherewes þe *Sauter* makeþ mynde.
B.10.26   The *Sauter* seiþ þe same by swiche þat doon ille:
B.10.69   And so seiþ þe *Sauter*; [seke it in memento]:
B.10.175   And sette hire to Sapience and to þe *Sauter* glose[d].
B.10.290   And þanne mowe ye [manly] seye, as Dauid made þe *Sauter*,
B.11.94   And in þe *Sauter* also seiþ dauid þe prophete
B.11.280   As Dauid seiþ in þe *Sauter*: to swiche þat ben in wille
B.11.286   And þei hir deuoir dide as Dauid seiþ in þe *Sauter*:
B.11.310   And also in þe *Sauter* seiþ Dauid to ouerskipperis,
B.12.13   And Dauid in þe *Sauter* seiþ, of swiche þat loueþ Iesus,
B.12.16   And þow medlest þee wiþ makynges and myȝtest go seye þi
sauter,
B.12.176   As þow seest in þe *Sauter* in Salmes oon or tweyne
B.13.432   What Dauid seiþ of swiche men as þe *Sauter* telleþ:
B.14.94   As Dauid seiþ in þe *Sauter*: et quorum tecta sunt peccata.
B.14.131   And whan he dyeþ ben disalowed, as Dauid seiþ in þe *Sauter*:
C. 3.288   As þe *sauhter* sayth by such þat ȝeueth mede:
C. 3.465   Here *sauter* and here seuene p[s]almes for alle synful preyen;
C. 5.47   And my *sauter* som tyme and my seuene p[s]almes.
C. 6.301   And what lede leueth þat y lye look in þe *sauter* glos[e],
C. 7.92   Wh[at] dauid sayth of such men as þe *sauter* telleth:
C. 8.258   Lo! what þe *sauter* sayth to swynkares with handes:
C.10.165   As þe *sauter* sayth by synnefole shrewes:
C.10.212   And þat my sawe is soth þe *sauter* bereth witnesse:
C.11.23   The *sauter* saith þe same of alle suche ryche:
C.11.49   And so saith þe *sauter*; y say hit [in] memento:
C.11.115   And sette here to sapience and to þe *sauter* yglosed.
C.12.28   The *sauter* sayth hit is no synne for suche men þat ben trewe
C.13.123   [To] ouerskipperes also in þe *sauter* sayth dauid:
C.14.116   As we seen in þe *sauter* in psalmes oen or tweyne
C.15.306   Dauid in þe *sauter* of suche maketh mynde and sayth: dormierunt

sautrie n *sautrie* n. B 1; C 1 sautrien
B.13.233   Ne neiþer saille ne [*sautrie*] ne synge wiþ þe gyterne,
C.15.207   Ne noþer sayle ne *sautrien* ne syngen with þe geterne,

sauacion n *savacioun* n. A 1 saluacioun; B 5 saluacion (1) sauacion (4);
C 5 sauacion (1) sauacioun (4)
A.11.282   Sonnere hadde he *saluacioun* þanne seint Ion þe baptist,
B. 5.127   'Sorwe [for] synn[e] is *sauacion* of soules.'
B.11.147   *Sauacion* for sooþnesse þat he seiȝ in my werkes.
B.15.498   And seide it in *saluacion* of Sarȝens and oþere;

B.15.523   In *sauacion* of [mannes soule] seint [Thomas] was ymartired;
B.17.34   Siþ þe firste suffiseþ to *sauacion* and to blisse?
C. 3.353   Seketh and seweth his sustantif *sauacioun*,
C. 5.198   Seketh seynt treuthe in *sauac[ioun]* of ȝoure soules
C.12.82   *Sauacion* for soethnesse [þat] a sey in my werkes.
C.17.119   Thogh hit suffice for oure *sauacioun* soethfaste byleue,
C.17.274   In *sauacioun* of mannes soule seynte Thomas of Canterbury

saue n *save* n.(1) C 1
C.12.56   And bad hem souke for synne *saue* at his breste

saue prep *sauf* prep. cf. *sauf* A 3; B 21; C 19
A. 2.196   *Saue* mede þe maiden no mo durste abide.
A. 7.64   *Saue* Iakke þe Iugelour & Ionete of þe stewis,
A.10.35   *Saue* man þat he made ymage to himselue.
B. 2.237   *Saue* Mede þe mayde na mo dorste abide.
B. 5.238   'Nay, soþly', he seide, '*saue* in my youþe.
B. 6.70   *Saue* Ia[kk]e þe Iogelour and Ionette of þe Stuwes
B. 9.34   [*Saue* man þat he made ymage] to hymself,
B.11.344   Medled noȝt wiþ hir makes, [*saue* man allone].
B.11.371   *Saue* man and his make; many tyme [me þouȝte]
B.13.125   And set alle sciences at a sop *saue* loue one;
B.13.235   For no breed þat I brynge forþ, *saue* a benyson on þe sonday
B.13.246   *Saue* a pardon wiþ a peis of leed and two polles amyddes.
B.14.333   Ne neiþer sherte ne shoon, *saue* for shame one
B.16.113   *Saue* þo he leched laȝar þat hadde yleye in graue;
B.17.103   *Saue* feiþ and [myselue and] Spes [his felawe].
B.19.190   And assoille men of alle synnes *saue* of dette one.
B.19.367   Thanne alle kynne cristene *saue* comune wommen
B.19.368   Repenteden and [forsoke] synne, *saue* þei one,
B.19.373   *Saue* sherewes one swiche as I spak of,
B.19.436   As for hymself and hise seruauntȝ, *saue* he is first yserued.
B.20.61   And alle hise as wel as hym, *saue* oonly fooles;
B.20.151   And kille a[l] erþely creatur[e] *saue* conscience oone.
B.20.267   A certein for a certein, *saue* oonliche of freres.
B.20.320   *Saue* Piers þe Plowman þat haþ power ouer alle
C. 2.253   *Saue* mede þe mayde no ma durste abyde.
C. 6.240   'Nay, sothly,' he saide, '*saue* in my ȝouthe.
C. 8.71   *Saue* Iacke þe iogelo‌ur and ionet of þe stuyues
C. 9.112   Riht as Peter dede and poul *saue* þat þey preche nat
C.12.29   To segge as they seen, *saue* only prestis:
C.13.153   *Saue* man and his make; and þerof me wondrede.
C.13.181   *Saue* man and mankynde; mony tymes me thouhte
C.15.132   *Saue* loue and leute and lowenesse of herte.
C.15.151   *Saue* Concience and clergie y couthe no mo aspye.
C.19.93   *Saue* mysulue soethly and such as y louede–
C.21.190   And assoile men of alle synnes *saue* of dette one.
C.21.367   Thenne alle kyne cristene *saue* commune wommen
C.21.368   Repenteden and [forsoke] synne, *saue* thei one,
C.21.373   [*Saue* shrewes one swiche as y spak of],
C.21.436   As for hymsulue and his seruauntes, *saue* he is furste yserued.
C.22.61   And alle hise as wel as hym, *saue* onelich foles;
C.22.151   And culle all erthely creature *saue* Consience one.
C.22.267   A certeyne for a certeyne *saue* oenliche of freres.
C.22.320   *Saue* [Peres the Plouhman] þat haeth power ouer alle

saue &> sauen

sauen v *saven* n. A 21 saue (12) sauen (2) sauid (3) sauiþ (2) ysauid (2);
B 87 saue (43) saued (32) sauede (1) sauen (3) saueþ (2) ysaued (6);
C 70 saue (32) saued (21) sauen (1) sauiþ (1) ysaued (15)
A. 1.23   Þat on is vesture fro chele þe to *saue*;
A. 1.82   How I may *sauen* my soule, þat seint art yho[ld]en.'
A. 3.184   Þere I lefte wiþ my lord his lif for to *saue*,
A. 4.28   For to *saue* hemself from shame & from harm.
A. 5.41   Sekiþ seint treuþe for he may *saue* ȝou alle
A. 5.104   'Sorewe for synne *sauiþ* wel manye.'
A. 6.75   Þe kirnelis ben of cristendom þat kynde to *saue*,
A. 6.76   And boterasid wiþ beleue [so] oþer ho[be]st not *sauid*;
A. 7.127   Boþe to setten & to sowen, & *sauen* his telþe,
A. 8.17   How þat shabbide shep shu[l] here wolle *saue*,
A. 8.27   And siþen selle it aȝen & *saue* þe wynnyng,
A. 9.51   And þei seide, 'þe same *saue* þe fro myschaunce,
A.10.22   Þise sixe ben yset to *saue* þe castel;
A.10.69   Þanne is holichirche owyng to helpe hem & *saue*
A.10.74   *Saue* hymself fro synne, for so hym behouiþ;
A.10.77   And *sauiþ* þe soule þat synne haþ no miȝt
A.10.176   Þat in þe [shynglid] ship shal ben *ysauid*;
A.11.236   Mowe be *sauid* so, & so is oure beleue.
A.11.279   A goode friday, I fynde, a feloun was *sauid*
A.11.309   Ne none sonnere *ysauid*, ne saddere of consience,
A.12.115   God *saue* hem sound by se and by land.
B.Pr.115   For to counseillen þe kyng and þe commune *saue*.
B. 1.23   That oon [is] vesture from [chele] þee to *saue*;
B. 1.84   How I may *saue* my soule þat Seint art yholden.'

B. 2.38	And how ye shul *saue* yourself? þe Sauter bereþ witnesse:
B. 3.197	Ther I lafte wiþ my lord his lif for to *saue*.
B. 3.292	Thise shul ben Maistres on moolde [trewe men] to *saue*.
B. 4.31	For to *saue* hem[seluen] from shame and from harmes.
B. 5.57	Sekeþ Seynt Truþe, for he may *saue* yow alle
B. 5.485	And bicam man of a maide mankynde to *saue*,
B. 5.588	[The] kernele[s ben of] cristendom [þat] kynde to *saue*,
B. 5.589	Botrased wiþ bileef-so-or-þow-beest-noзt-*saued*;
B. 7.25	And siþenes selle it ayein and *saue* þe wynnyng,
B. 7.41	For þe Sauter *saueþ* hem noзt, swiche as take зiftes,
B. 7.183	That pardon and penaunce and preieres doon *saue*
B. 8.60	And I seide 'þe same *saue* yow fro myschaunce,
B. 9.23	Thise [sixe] ben set to [*saue*] þis lady anima
B. 9.69	[Holy chirche is owynge to helpe hem and *saue*,
B. 9.145	That in [þe] shyngled ship shul ben *ysaued*."
B.10.242	And on þe sooþfast sone þat *saued* mankynde
B.10.353	Mowen be *saued* so, and [so] is oure bileue;
B.10.363	And þus bilongeþ to louye þat leueþ [to] be *saued*.
B.10.407	Was neuere wrighte *saued* þat wroзte þeron, ne ooþer werkman ellis,
B.10.410	Of w[r]ightes þat it wroзte was noon of hem *ysaued*.
B.10.412	Of holi chirche þat herberwe is, and goddes hous to *saue*
B.10.420	On good Friday, I fynde, a felon was *ysaued*
B.10.423	He was sonner *ysaued* þan seint Iohan Baptist
B.10.465	Ne none sonner *saued*, ne sadder of bileue,
B.10.481	The which is mannes soule to *saue*, as god seiþ in þe gospel:
B.11.82	Ac [a] barn wiþouten bapteme may noзt be *saued*:
B.11.148	And [for] he wepte and wilned [þat I] were [*saued*]
B.11.151	And I *saued* as ye [may] see, wiþouten syngynge of masses.
B.11.157	Was þat Sarsen *saued*, as Seint Gregorie bereþ witnesse.
B.11.165	And *saued* þe sarsyn from sathanas power
B.11.218	That Fides sua sholde *saue* hire and saluen hire of synnes,
B.11.227	That *saued* synful men as Seint Iohan bereþ witnesse:
B.12.31	And *sauen* men sondry tymes, ac noon so soone as Charite.
B.12.77	Ac crist of his curteisie þoruз clergie hir *saued*.
B.12.82	Holy kirke knoweþ þis þat cristes writyng *saued*;
B.12.89	The womman þat þe Iewes [iugged] þat Iesus þouзte to *saue*:
B.12.108	Come for al his kynde wit to cristendom and be *saued*;
B.12.133	Ac þoruз hir science sooþly was neuere soule *ysaued*
B.12.157	How þat lewed men liзtloker þan lettrede were *saued*,
B.12.188	That lyuynge after lettrure *saue[d]* hym lif and soule.
B.12.191	Ther lewed þeues ben lolled vp; loke how þei be *saued*!
B.12.202	So it fareþ by þat felon þat a good friday was *saued*;
B.12.273	To wissen vs [wyes] þerwiþ þat wiss[h]en to be *saued*–
B.12.279	Ne no creature of cristes liknesse withouten cristendom worþ *saued*.'
B.13.130	Which shal *saue* mannes soule; þus seiþ Piers þe Plowman.'
B.13.406	That into wanhope he [worþ] and wende nauзt to be *saued*.
B.13.428	*Sauen* þoruз hir sermo[n] mannes soule fro helle;
B.13.445	For to *saue* þi soule from sathan þyn enemy.
B.14.85	And þouз a man myзte noзt speke contricion myзte hym *saue*
B.14.259	And in þat secte oure saueour *saued* al mankynde.
B.15.126	Hadde he neuere [*saued*] siluer þerto [for spendyng at ale];
B.15.389	That sola fides sufficit to *saue* wiþ lewed peple.
B.15.390	And so may Sarзens be *saued*, Scribes and [Grekes].
B.15.429	"Salt *saueþ* catel", siggen þise wyues:
B.15.442	That goddes salt sholde be to *saue* mannes soule.
B.15.514	Men myзte noзt be *saued* but þoruз mercy and grace,
B.15.588	[And] for a parfit prophete þat muche peple *sauede*
B.16.39	I *saue* it til I se it ripen and somdel yfruyted.
B.16.104	And lered hym lechecraft his lif for to *saue*
B.16.123	For I haue *saued* yowself and youre sones after,
B.16.245	And called me foot of his feiþ, his folk for to *saue*
B.16.252	Seide þat he seiз here þat sholde *saue* vs alle:
B.17.20	For, þouз I seye it myself, I haue *saued* with þis charme
B.17.31	And haþ *saued* þat bileued so and sory for hir synnes,
B.17.125	For þe barn was born in Bethleem þat wiþ his blood shal *saue*
B.17.302	And myldeliche his mercy aske; myghte I noзt be *saued*?'
B.18.139	That man shal man *saue* þoruз a maydenes helpe,
B.18.151	'Thoruз experience', quod [heo], 'I hope þei shul be *saued*;
B.18.183	That mercy, my suster, and I mankynde sholde *saue*,
B.18.190	And *saue* mannes soule? suster, wene it neuere.
B.18.213	Bicam man of a mayde mankynde to *saue*
B.18.236	That mannes soule sholde *saue* and synne destroye.
B.18.306	To *saue* men from synne if hemself wolde.
B.18.328	For alle synfulle soules, to *saue* þo þat ben worþi.
B.19.22	And synfulle aren solaced and *saued* by þat name,
B.19.280	[That] caste for to ke[l]e a crokke to *saue* þe fatte aboue.
B.19.406	The chief seed þat Piers sew, *ysaued* worstow neuere.
B.19.429	And [soudeþ hem] þat sleeþ [swiche as] he sholde *saue*.
B.19.432	And sent þe sonne to *saue* a cursed mannes tilþe
B.19.449	And crist of his curteisie þe Cardinals *saue*
B.20.11	For þre þynges he takeþ his lif for to *saue*.
B.20.22	So þat he sewe and *saue* Spiritus temperancie.
B.20.128	To holden wiþ Antecrist, hir temporaltees to *saue*.
B.20.214	And þere was Conscience Constable, cristene to *saue*,
C.Pr.142	For to conseillen þe kyng and þe commune saue.
C. 1.80	How y may *saue* my soule, þat saynt art yholde.'
C. 3.234	Ac y haue *saued* myselue sixty thousend lyues,
C. 3.409	And se[t]he, for sauel *saued* a kyng fo[r] mede
C. 6.333	[T]rist in his mechel mercy and зut þou myhte be *saued*.
C. 7.88	*Sauen* thorw here sarmon mannes soule fram helle;
C. 7.105	For to *saue* thy soule fram satan thyn enemye
C. 7.235	The carneles ben of cristendom þat kynde to *saue*,
C. 7.236	Ibotrased with bileue-so-or-t[hou]-best-not-*ysaued*;
C. 9.29	And sethe sullen hit aзeyn and *saue* þe wynnyng[e],
C. 9.271	And of þe moneye thow haddest ther[myd] his mebles to [*s*]*aue*
C. 9.315	That Ioseph was Iustice Egipte to *saue*;
C. 9.329	That pardoun and penaunc[e] and preyere[s] don *saue*
C.10.59	And y sayde, 'þe same *saue* зow fro meschaunce
C.10.149	Thise fyue ben sette for to *saue* Anima
C.10.233	That in thi [s]hingled ship shal be with þe *ysaued*."
C.11.238	Was neuere wrihte þat þeron wrouhte ne werkman *ysaued*.
C.11.241	Of wryhtes þat hit wrouhte was noen of hem *ysaued*.
C.11.252	A gode friday, y fynde, a feloun was *ysaued*
C.11.255	He was sunnere *ysaued* then seynt Iohn þe baptiste
C.11.291	Ne none sanere *ysa[u]ed* ne saddere in bileue
C.11.301	As clerkes of holy [k]ir[k]e þat [kepe] sholde and *saue*
C.12.83	And for a wilnede wepynge þat y were *ysaued*
C.12.86	And y *saued*, as зe may se, withoute syngynge of masses.
C.12.88	*Saued* me, sarrasyn, soule and body bothe.'
C.14.12	Ac hit soffiseth to be *saued* [to] be such as y tauhte.
C.14.53	Come for al his kynde wit thorw cristendoem to be *saued*,
C.14.77	Ac thorw here science sothly was neuere soule *ysaued*
C.14.101	That is, how lewede men and luythere lyhtloker were *ysaued*
C.14.127	That lyuynge Aftur lettrure *saued* hy[m] lyf and soule.
C.14.130	There lewede theues ben lolled vp; loke how þei ben *saued*!
C.14.141	So hit f[areth] by þe feloun þat a goed fryday was *saued*:
C.14.163	A cantel of kynde wyt here kynde to *saue*.
C.14.195	To wissen vs weyes þerwith þat wenen to be *saued*–
C.14.201	Withoute bapteme, as by here bokes, beth nat *ysaued*.'
C.15.235	Hit am y þat fynde alle folke and fram hunger *saue*
C.16.99	And in þat secte oure saueour *saued* al mankynde.
C.17.121	That sola fides sufficit to *saue* with lewede peple.
C.17.123	For sarrasynes may be *saued* so yf they so byleued
C.17.265	That men myhte nat be *saued* but thorw mercy and grace,
C.17.299	And for a parfit profete that moche peple *sauede*
C.17.300	And of selcouthe sores *saued* men fol ofte.
C.18.134	And bycam man of þat maide mankynde to *saue*,
C.18.151	'Thenne is saton зoure saueour,' quod iesus, '& hath *ysaued* зow ofte.
C.18.152	Ac y *saued* зow sondry tymes and also y fe[d] зow
C.18.268	Saide þat a seyh here þat sholde *saue* vs alle:
C.19.21	For, thogh y sey hit mysulue, y haue *saued* with this charme
C.19.32	And hath *ysaued* þat bileued so and sory for here synnes;
C.19.35	Sethe þe furste sufficede to bileue and be *saued*?
C.19.86	Withoute þe bloed of a barn he beth nat *ysaued*,
C.19.282	And myldeliche his mercy aske; myhte y nat be *saued*?'
C.20.142	[That man shal man *saue* thorw a maydenes helpe
C.20.154	'Thorw experiense,' quod he, 'y hope they shal ben *saued*;
C.20.186	That mercy, my sustur, and y mankynde sh[olde] *saue*
C.20.195	And *saue* mannes soule? suster, wene hit neuere.
C.20.222	Bycam man of a mayde mankynde to *saue*
C.20.245	That mannes soule sholde *saue* and synne distruye.
C.20.288	Coltyng and al his kyn, the car to *saue*.
C.20.371	For alle synfole soules, to *saue* oure bothe rihte.
C.21.22	And synfole ben solaced and *saued* by þat name,
C.21.280	That caste for to kele a crok [to] *saue* þe fatte aboue.
C.21.406	The cheef seed þat [Peres] sewe, *ysaued* wo[r]st þou neuere.
C.21.429	And soudeth hem þat sleeth suche as he sholde *saue*.
C.21.432	And sente þe so[nn]e to *saue* a corsed mannes tulthe
C.21.449	And Crist of his cortesye þe cardinals *saue*
C.22.11	For thre thynges he taketh [h]is lyf for to *saue*.
C.22.22	So þat he sewe and *saue* spiritus temperancie.
C.22.128	To holde with auntecrist, here temperaltee[s] to *saue*.
C.22.214	And there was Consience Constable, cristene to *saue*,

saueour n *saveour* n. A 2 sauiour; B 9; C 6 saueour (3) sauiour (1) sauyour (2)

A. 3.64	For oure *sauiour* it seide & hymself prechid:
A.11.66	"Why wolde oure *sauiour* suffre such a worm in his blisse
B. 5.478	'I shal biseche for alle synfulle oure *Saueour* of grace
B. 9.130	Yet [seþ], ayein þe sonde of oure *Saueour* of heuene,
B.10.108	"Why wolde oure *Saueour* suffre swich a worm in his blisse
B.11.251	And to oure *Saueour* self seide þise wordes:
B.14.259	And in þat secte oure *saueour* saued al mankynde.

B.15.156   Ac charite þat Poul preiseþ best, and moost plesaunt to oure
           [*Saueour*]–
B.15.412   And siþþe oure *Saueour* suffred þe Sarȝens so bigiled
B.16.122   And Sathan youre *Saueour*; [youre]self now ye witnessen.
B.16.143   That euere he his *Saueour* solde for siluer or ellis.'
C. 7.120   'Y shal byseke for alle synnefole oure *sauiour* of grace
C. 7.144   And sethen oure *sauyour* and seydest with thy tonge
C.12.137   And to oure *sauyour* sulue saide þis wordes:
C.16.99   And in þat secte oure *sauour* saued al mankynde.
C.17.183   And seth oure *saueour* soffrede such a fals cristene
C.18.151   'Thenne is saton ȝoure *saueour*,' quod iesus, '& hath ysaued ȝow
           ofte.

sauereth sauery > sauore

saueriore adj *savourie adj.*   C 1
C.18.65   Swettore and *saueriore* and also more grettore

sauiour > saueour

sauore v *savouren v.*   A 2 sauore (1) sauouriþ (1); B 2 sauore (1) sauoreþ
  (1); C 2 sauereth (1) sauery (1)
A. 7.246   And sende þe of his saus to *sauoure* þi lippes,
A. 9.102   'Ac ȝet *sauouriþ* me nouȝt þi segging, so me god helpe!;
B. 6.262   And sende þee of his Sauce to *sauore* þi lippes,
B. 8.112   'Ac yet *sauoreþ* me noȝt þi seying, [so me god helpe!
C. 8.272   And sende the of his sauce [t]o *sauery* with thy lyppes
C.10.108   'Ac ȝut *sauereth* [me nat] thy sawes, so me Crist spede!

sauour n *savour n.*   B 3; C 2
B. 7.154   Ac I haue no *sauour* in songewarie for I se it ofte faille.
B. 9.155   And haue a *Sauour* after þe sire; selde sestow ooþer:
B.16.74   And suffre me to assaien what *sauour* it hadde.
C.14.186   And swettore of *sauour* and swyftore of weng[e].
C.18.103   Assay what *sauour* hit hadde and saide þat tyme,

sauoure -iþ > sauore; saw > seen

sawe n *saue n.(2)*   A 5 sawes (1) sawis (4); B 4 sawes; C 3 sawe (1)
  sawes (2)
A. 4.144   Þe king acordite, be crist, to resonis *sawis*
A. 8.125   On salamonis *sawis* [seldom] þou beholdis:
A.11.16   Þanne alle þe soþe *sawis* þat salamon seide euere.
A.11.274   Taken ensaumpl[e] of here *sawis* in sarmonis þat þei maken,
A.12.107   When he saw þes *sawes* busyly alegged
B. 7.154   On Salomons *sawes* selden þow biholdest:
B. 9.96   [Ne] loueþ noȝt Salomons *sawes* þat Sapience tauȝte:
B.10.16   Than alle þe sooþ *sawes* þat Salomon seide euere.
B.18.149   Iob þe [parfit] patriark repreueþ þi *sawes*:
C.10.108   'Ac ȝut sauereth [me nat] thy *sawes*, so me Crist spede!
C.10.212   And þat my *sawe* is soth þe sauter bereth witnesse:
C.20.152   Iop þe parfit patriarke repreueth thy *sawes*,

sawt > saut

scale n *scale n.(1)*   C 1
C.12.147   And aftur þat bittere barke, be þe *scale* aweye,

scalles n *scalle n.*   B 1; C 1
B.20.83   Rewmes and Radegundes and roynouse *sca[ll]es*,
C.22.83   Reumes and Radegoundes and roynouse *sca[ll]es*,

scape v *scapen v.(1)*   B 1
B. 3.57   Who may *scape* [þe] sclaundre, þe scaþe is soone amended;

scarlet n *scarlet n.*   A 1; B 3; C 1
A. 2.13   In red *scarlet* robid & ribande wiþ gold.
B. 2.15   Hire Robe was ful riche, of reed *scarlet* engreyned,
B.14.19   Dobet shal beten it and bouken it as bright as any *scarlet*
B.15.168   As of a tunycle of tarse or of trie *scarlet*.
C.16.301   As of a cote of ca[mm]aca or of clene *scarlet*.

scaþe n *scathe n.*   A 3 skaþe; B 4; C 3 scathe (2) skathe (1)
A. 4.65   'Wiþoute gilt, god wot, gat I þis *skaþe*.'
A. 4.83   'Haue þis of me, man,' quaþ heo, 'to amende þi *skaþe*,
A.12.17   Þat hit were boþe *skaþe* and sklaundre to holy cherche
B. 3.57   Who may scape [þe] sclaundre, þe *scaþe* is soone amended;
B. 4.79   'Wiþouten gilt, god woot, gat I þis *scaþe*.'
B. 4.96   'Haue þis [of me, man]', quod she, 'to amenden þi *scaþe*,
B.15.59   But he do þerafter, it doþ hym double *scaþe*.
C. 3.61   Ho may askape þe sclaundre, þe *skathe* myhte sone be mended;
C. 4.75   'Withouten gult, god wot, [gat y] this *s[c]athe*;
C. 4.92   'Haue this, man, of me,' quod she, 'to amende thy *scathe*

schaef > shef; schal > shal

schalkes n *shalke n.*   C 1
C.10.160   May nat shyne ne shewe on *schalkes* on erthe,

scharp > sharp; schew- > shew- ; schyreues > sherreue; scholde > shal;
schoriares > shoriare; schrewes > sherewe; schriuen > shryuen;
schupestares > shepsteres; schupte > shape

science n *science n.*   A 4 science (3) sciences (1); B 15 science (12)
  sciences (3); C 9 science (8) sciences (1)
A.11.140   It is no *science* forsoþe for to sotile þereinne.
A.11.146   In oþer *science* it seiþ, I saiȝ it in catoun,
A.11.158   For sorcerie is þe souerayn bok þat to þat *science* longiþ.
A.11.163   Alle þise *sciences*, sikir, I myself
B.10.188   It is no *Science* forsoþe for to sotile Inne,
B.10.194   In ooþer *Science* it seiþ, I seiȝ it in Catoun,
B.10.211   For is no *science* vnder sonne so souereyn for þe soule.
B.10.215   For sorcerie is þe Souereyn book þat to [þat] *Scienc[e]* [l]ongeþ.
B.10.220   Alle þise *Sciences* I myself sotilede and ordeynede,
B.11.167   Loue and lewtee is a leel *science*,
B.11.172   Or any *Science* vnder sonne, þe seuene artȝ and alle–
B.12.122   Ne sette short bi hir *science*, whatso þei don hemselue.
B.12.132   And helden it an heiȝ *science* hir wittes to knowe;
B.12.133   Ac þoruȝ hir *science* sooþly was neuere soule ysaued
B.12.136   Patriarkes and prophetes repreueden hir *science*
B.13.125   And set alle *sciences* at a sop saue loue one;
B.15.48   Alle þe *sciences* vnder sonne and alle þe sotile craftes
B.15.62   Coueitise to konne and to knowe *scienc[e]*
B.17.174   Right so is þe sone þe *Science* of þe fader
C.11.129   Hit is no *science* sothly bote a sothfaste bileue
C.12.94   Or eny *science* vnder sonne, the seuene ars and alle–
C.14.65   Ne sette shorte by here *science*, whatso þei doen hemsulue.
C.14.76   They helden hit an hey *science* here sotiltees to knowe,
C.14.77   Ac thorw here *science* sothly was neuere soule ysaued
C.14.81   Patriarkes and prophetus repreuede here *science*
C.16.210   Alle þe *sciences* vnder sonne and alle þe sotil craftes
C.16.224   Coueytyse to conne and to knowe *scienc[e]*
C.16.227   Riht so sothly *scienc[e]* swelleth a mannes soule

sciense n *sioun n., OED scion n.*   C 1
C.10.208   Thorw no sotil *sciense* on sour stok growe";

scismatikes n *scismatik n.*   B 1; C 1 sismatikes
B.11.120   Sarȝens and *scismatikes* and so he dide þe Iewes:
C.12.55   Sarrasynes and *sismatikes* and so a ded þe iewes:

sclaundre n *sclaundre n.*   A 1 sklaundre; B 3; C 2 sclaundre (1) sklaundre
  (1)
A.12.17   Þat hit were boþe skaþe and *sklaundre* to holy cherche
B. 2.82   To scorne and to scolde and *sclaundre* to make;
B. 3.57   Who may scape [þe] *sclaundre*, þe scaþe is soone amended;
B.12.46   Felice hir fairnesse fel hire al to *sclaundre*,
C. 2.89   To skorne and to skolde and *sklaundre* to make;
C. 3.61   Ho may askape þe *sclaundre*, þe skathe myhte sone be mended;

scleyre n *skleire n.*   A 1 scleire; B 1; C 1 slayre
A. 7.7   'Þis were a long lettyng,' quaþ a lady in a *scleire*;
B. 6.7   'This were a long lettyng', quod a lady in a *Scleyre*.
C. 8.5   'Th[is] were a long lettyng,' quod [a] lady in a *slayre*;

scoffyng ger *scoffing ger.*   B 1
B.13.276   Of scornyng and of *scoffyng* and of vnskilful berynge;

scolde v *scolden v. cf. skolde*   B 1; C 1 skolde
B. 2.82   To scorne and to *scolde* and sclaundre to make;
C. 2.89   To skorne and to *skolde* and sklaundre to make;

scole n *scole n.(2)*   A 4; B 8; C 9
A. 8.34   Sette scoleris to *scole* or [to] summe skynes craftis,
A.10.84   And alle kynde scoleris in *scole* to lerne.
A.11.125   Sey hym þis signe, I sette hym to *scole*,
A.11.145   For dobet & dobest ben drawen of louis *s[co]le*.
B. 7.32   Sette Scolers to *scole* or to som [kynnes] craftes,
B.10.173   Seye hym þis signe: I sette hym to *scole*,
B.10.193   For dobet and dobest ben [drawen] of loues [*scole*].
B.10.306   It is in cloistre or in *scole*, by manye skiles I fynde.
B.10.309   In *scole* þere is scorn but if a clerk wol lerne,
B.20.251   For loue lafte þei lordshipe, boþe lond and *scole*,
B.20.273   Enuye herde þis and heet freres go to *scole*
B.20.295   And freres to philosophie he fond [hem] to *scole*,
C. 5.36   My fader and my frendes foende me to *scole*
C. 5.153   Hit is in C[l]oystre or in *scole*, by many skilles y fynde.
C. 5.155   In *scole* is loue and louhnesse and lykyng to lerne.
C. 9.35   Fynde hem for godes loue and fauntkynes to *scole*,
C.13.169   'Where hadde thise wilde suche wit and at what *scole*?'
C.15.128   'Haue me excused,' quod Clergie, 'be crist, but in *scole*.
C.22.251   For loue lefte they lordshipe, bothe lond and *scole*,
C.22.273   Enuye herde this and heete freres go to *scole*
C.22.295   And freres to filosophye he foend hem to *scole*

scolers *n scolere n.* A 2 scoleris; B 1

A. 8.34 Sette *scoleris* to scole or [to] summe skynes craftis,
A.10.84 And alle kynde *scoleris* in scole to lerne.
B. 7.32 Sette *Scolers* to scole or to som [kynnes] craftes,

score *adj score n.* A 4; B 5; C 4

A. 1.99 And nouȝt to fasten a friday in fyue *score* wynter,
A. 3.112 She makiþ men mysdo manye *score* tymes,
A. 3.135 As ȝoure secre sel in seue *score* dayes.
A.11.137 Ac theologie haþ tenid me ten *score* tymes,
B. 1.101 And nauȝt to friday in fyue *score* wynter,
B. 3.123 [She] makeþ men mysdo many *score* tymes.
B. 3.146 As youre secret seel in sixe *score* dayes.
B.10.185 Ac Theologie haþ tened me ten *score* tymes;
B.17.21 Of men and of wommen many *score* þousand.'
C. 3.160 And maketh men mysdo manye *score* tymes.
C. 3.184 As ȝoure secrete seel in sixe *score* dayes.
C.11.126 Ac teologie hath tened me ten *score* tymes;
C.19.22 Of men and of wommen meny *score* thousand.'

scorn *n scorn n.* A 1 scorne; B 2 scorn (1) scorne (1); C 1 scorne

A. 4.137 Loue let of hire liȝt & louȝ hire to *scorne*,
B.10.309 In scole þere is *scorn* but if a clerk wol lerne,
B.15.172 Ne no likynge haþ to lye ne laughe men to *scorne*.
C.16.310 Hath he no lykynge to lawhe ne to likene men to *scorne*.

scornare > scornere

scorne *v scornen v. &> scorn* A 1; B 3 scorne (2) scorned (1); C 4
   scorned (1) scornede (2) skorne (1)

A.11.225 'I nile not *scorne*,' quaþ scripture, 'but scryueyns liȝe,
B. 2.82 To *scorne* and to scolde and sclaundre to make;
B.10.337 'I nel noȝt *scorne*', quod Scripture; 'but scryueynes lye,
B.11.1 Thanne Scripture *scorned* me and a skile tolde,
C. 2.89 To *skorne* and to skolde and sklaundre to make;
C. 6.22 And *scorned* hem and oþere yf y a skil founde,
C.11.160 Thenne scripture *scorned* me and mony skiles shewed
C.13.130 And scripture *scornede* þat many skilles shewede,

scornere *n scornere n.* B 1; C 2 scornare

B.19.284 Ne [sholde] no *scornere* out of skile hym brynge;
C. 6.25 *Scornare* and vnskilful to hem þat skil shewede,
C.21.284 Ne sholde no *scornare* out of skille hym brynge

scornyng *ger scorninge ger.* B 1

B.13.276 Of *scornyng* and of scoffyng and of vnskilful berynge;

scorpion *n scorpioun n.* B 1; C 1 scorpioun

B.18.154 For of alle venymes foulest is þe *scorpion*;
C.20.157 For of alle venymes [fou]lest is the *scorpioun*;

scourges *n scourge n.* B 1

B.13.67 In fame & frigore and flappes of *scourges*:

screueynes > scryueynes

scribes *n prop scribe n.* B 4 Scribes (3) Scrybes (1); C 2 scribȝ

B.15.390 And so may Sarȝens be saued, *Scribes* and [Grekes].
B.15.501 And siþ þat þise Sarȝens, *Scribes* and [Grekes]
B.15.605 Ac pharisees and Sarȝens, *Scribes* and [Grekes]
B.18.27 'Who shal Iuste wiþ Iesus', quod I, 'Iewes or *Scrybes*?'
C.17.252 For sethe þat this sarrasines, *Scribȝ* and this iewes
C.20.26 'Who shal iouste with iesus,' quod y, 'iewes or *scribȝ*?'

scrippe *n scrippe n.* A 2; B 2 scrippe (1) Scryppe (1); C 2 scrippe (1) scryppe (1)

A. 6.23 'I sauȝ neuere palmere wiþ pik ne wiþ *scrippe*
A. 7.56 And heng his hoper at his hals in stede of a *scrippe*:
B. 5.535 'I [ne] seiȝ neuere Palmere wiþ pyk ne wiþ *scrippe*
B. 6.61 And [heng his] hoper at [his] hals in stede of a *Scryppe*:
C. 7.180 'I [ne] saw neuere palmere with pyk ne with *scrip[p]e*
C. 8.60 And heng his hopur on his hal[s] in stede of a *scryppe*;

scripture *n scripture n.* A 6; B 13; C 13 scripture (12) skripture (1)

A.11.107 Is sib to þe seuene ars þat *scripture* is nempnid.
A.11.225 'I nile not scorne,' quaþ *scripture*, 'but scryueyns liȝe,
A.11.235 'Þat is in extremis,' quaþ *scripture*, 'as sarisines & Iewis
A.12.12 Skornfully þ[o] *scripture* she[t] vp h[ere] browes.
A.12.34 And when *scripture* þe skolde hadde þis [skele] ysheued
A.12.38 Þan held I vp myn handes to *scripture* þe wise
B.10.155 Is sib to [þe] seuen art3, [þat] *Scripture* is [nempned].
B.10.222 Tel Clergie þis[e] tokene[s], and [to] *Scripture* after,
B.10.252 And Crist cleped hymself so, þe [*scripture*] bereþ witnesse:
B.10.337 'I nel noȝt scorne', quod *Scripture*; 'but scryueynes lye,
B.10.352 'That is in extremis,' quod *Scripture*, '[as] Sarȝens & Iewes
B.11.1 Thanne *Scripture* scorned me and a skile tolde,
B.11.107 'He seiþ sooþ', quod *Scripture* þo, and skipte an heiȝ and preched.
B.11.137 'That is sooþ', seide *Scripture*; 'may no synne lette

B.12.271 Ne of Sortes ne of Salomon no *scripture* kan telle.
B.13.26 That lowe louted and loueliche to *scripture*.
B.13.37 Conscience called after mete and þanne cam *Scripture*
B.13.46 Conscience curteisly þo commaunded *scripture*
B.19.272 And harewede in an handwhile al holy *Scripture*
C.11.94 And ouer *skripture* þe skilfole and screueynes were trewe
C.11.98 So with þat clergie can and consail of *scripture*
C.11.160 Thenne *scripture* scorned me and mony skiles shewed
C.11.199 Were hit al soth þat ȝe seyn, thow *scripture* and thow clergie,
C.11.222 Ac y countresegge the nat, clergie, ne thy connyng, *scripture*;
C.12.41 'A saith soth,' quod *scripture* tho, and skypte an heyh and prechede.
C.12.72 'That is soth,' saide *scripture*; ' may no synne lette
C.13.130 And *scripture* scornede þat many skilles shewede,
C.14.192 Ne of sortes ne of salamon n[o] *scripture* can telle.
C.15.42 Clergie cald aftur mete and thenne cam *scripture*
C.15.52 That Consience comaunde sholde to do come *scripture*
C.15.61 Consience confortede vs, bothe clergie and *scripture*,
C.21.272 And harwed in an handwhile al holy *scripture*

scryueynes *n scrivein n.* A 1 scryueyns; B 1; C 1 screueynes

A.11.225 'I nile not scorne,' quaþ scripture, 'but *scryueyns* liȝe,
B.10.337 'I nel noȝt scorne', quod Scripture; 'but *scryueynes* lye,
C.11.94 And ouer skripture þe skilfole and *screueynes* were trewe

se > see,seen; seal > seel; secatours > seketoures; seche(- > seken

secounde *num second num.* B 5 seconde (2) secounde (3); C 7 seconde

B.11.22 The *secounde* seide þe same: 'I shal sewe þi wille;
B.16.36 Thanne sette I to þe *secounde* pil, sapiencia dei patris,
B.16.186 The *secounde* of þa[t] sire is Sothfastnesse filius,
B.19.87 The *seconde* kyng siþþe sooþliche offrede
B.19.281 The *seconde* seed highte Spiritus temperancie.
C. 1.23 The firste is fode and vesture þe *seconde*
C. 9.253 He sat at þe syde benche and at þe *seconde* table;
C.11.181 The *seconde* saide þe same: 'y [shal] sewe thy wille;
C.18.40 Thenne sette y þe *seconde* planke, sapiencia dei patris,
C.18.193 And þe *seconde* is a sone of þe sire, filius;
C.21.87 The *seconde* kyng seth soethliche offrede]
C.21.281 The *seconde* se[d]e hihte Spiritus temperancie.

secret *n secret n.* A 2 secre; B 2; C 3 secret (1) secrete (2)

A. 3.135 As ȝoure *secre* sel in seue score dayes.
A. 8.25 Ac vndir his *secre* sel treuþe sente h[e]m a lettre,
B. 3.146 As youre *secret* seel in sixe score dayes.
B. 7.23 Ac vnder his *secret* seel truþe sente hem a lettre,
C. 3.184 As ȝoure *secrete* seel in sixe score dayes.
C. 9.27 Ac vnder his *secrete* seal treuthe sente hem a lettre
C. 9.138 For vnder godes *secret* seal here synnes ben keuered.

secte *n secte n.* B 4; C 10 secte (4) sectes (1) sekte (4) sektes (1)

B. 5.490 But in oure *secte* be sorwe and þi sone it ladde:
B.11.245 Ther neuere segge hym seiȝ in *secte* of þe riche.
B.14.259 And in þat *secte* oure saueour saued al mankynde.
B.15.232 In þat *secte* siþþe to selde haþ he ben [knowe].
C. 6.38 Summe tyme in o *sekte*, summe tyme in another,
C. 7.129 And sethe in oure *secte*, as hit semed, deyedest,
C. 7.136 The thridde day þeraftur thow ȝedest i[n] oure *sekte*;
C. 7.140 Of thy douhtiokest dedes was don in oure *sekte*:
C.12.133 Holy seyntes hym sey Ac neuere in *secte* of riche.
C.15.13 And how þis coueytyse ouercome al kyne *sectes*,
C.15.78 Ac me thynketh loth, thogh y latyn knowe, to lacken eny *secte*
C.16.99 And in þat *secte* oure saueour saued al mankynde.
C.16.295 For thogh me souhte alle þe *sektes* of susturne and brethurne
C.16.357 In [þat] *sekte* sethe to selde hath he be [knowen].

seculer *adj seculere adj.* B 1; C 1

B. 9.182 And euery maner *seculer* [man] þat may noȝt continue
C.10.283 And euery maner *seculer* man þat may nat contynue

secutours > seketoures; sed sede(s > seed

seden *v seden v.* C 1

C.10.251 Soffre his seed *seden* with Caymus seed his brother.

sedes > seed

see *n se n.(1) &> seen* A 2 se; B 7; C 8 se (2) see (6)

A. 4.112 Bere no siluer ouer *se* þat signe of king shewi[þ],
A.12.115 God saue hym sound by *se* and by land.
B. 4.129 Bere no siluer ouer *see* þat signe of kyng sheweþ,
B. 5.283 Nis na moore to þe mercy of god þan [amyd] þe *see* a gleede:
B.11.327 I seiȝ þe sonne and þe *see* and þe sond after,
B.11.363 And siþen I loked on þe *see* and so forþ on þe sterres;
B.13.391 And if I sente ouer *see* my seruaunt3 to Brugges,
B.18.246 Whan she seiȝ hym suffre þat sonne and *see* made.
B.19.78 Boþe of [s]ond, sonne and *see*, and siþenes þei wente

C. 4.126 Bere no seluer ouer *see* þat sygne of kyng sheweth,
C. 6.278 And yf y sente ouer *see* my seruauntes to Bruges
C.13.135 And seyhe þe sonne and þe *see* and þe sond aftur
C.13.173 And sethe y lokede on þe *see* and so forth on [þe] sterres;
C.17.89 Noþer *see* ne s[o]nd ne þe seed ȝeldeth
C.17.92 And þe *se* and the seed, þe sonne and þe mone
C.20.255 When he sye hym soffre þat sonne and *se* made.
C.21.78 Bothe of sand, sonne and *see* and sennes þei wente

seed n *sed* n. A 7 sed (5) seed (2); B 17 sedes (2) seed (15); C 24 sede (3) sedes (5) seed (16)

A. 3.255 And al his *sed* for þat synne [shend]fully ende.
A. 5.156 And a [ferþingworþ] of [fenelsed] for fastyng dayes.'
A. 6.31 Boþe sowen his *seed*, & sewide hise bestis,
A.10.159 And siþen se[þ] & his suster [*sed*] wern spousid to kaymes;
A.11.69 And alle here *seed* for here synne þe same wo suffride?"
A.11.76 Suffre sathan his *sed* to bigile,
A.11.83 Suffren sathan his *sed* to bigile,
B. 3.277 And al his *seed* for þat synne shenfulliche ende.
B. 5.305 A ferþyngworþ of fenel *seed* for fastynge dayes.'
B. 5.543 Boþe ysowen his *seed* and suwed hise beestes,
B.10.111 And al hir *seed* for hir synne þe same deeþ suffrede?
B.10.123 Suffre Sathan his *seed* to bigile,
B.10.130 Suffre Sathan his *seed* to bigile,
B.15.365 By þe *seed* þat þei sewe what þei sel[l]e myȝte,
B.19.276 Spiritus prudencie þe firste *seed* highte,
B.19.281 The seconde *seed* highte Spiritus temperancie.
B.19.282 He þat ete of þat *seed* hadde swich a kynde:
B.19.289 The þridde *seed* þat Piers sew was Spiritus fortitudinis,
B.19.290 And who[so] ete [of] þat *seed* hardy was euere.
B.19.297 The ferþe *seed* þat Piers sew was Spiritus Iusticie,
B.19.298 And he þat ete of þat *seed* sholde be [euene] trewe
B.19.309 Thise foure *sedes* Piers sew, and siþþe he dide hem harewe
B.19.343 [Th]e *sedes* [þat sire] Piers [sew], þe Cardynale vertues.
B.19.406 The chief *seed* þat Piers sew, ysaued worstow neuere.
C. 3.430 And al [h]is [*sede*] for þat synne shentfolyche ende.
C. 6.360 A ferthyngworth [of] fenkel *sed[e]* for fastyng dayes.'
C. 7.187 And to sowen his *seed* [and] suewen his bestes,
C.10.221 And for þe synne of Caymes *seed* sayede god to Noe:
C.10.251 Soffre his *seed* seden with Caymus seed his brother.
C.10.251 Soffre his seed seden with Caymus *seed* his brother.
C.12.180 Bote if þe *seed* þat sowen is in the sloo sterue
C.12.183 [And] oþer *sedes* also in þe same wyse
C.12.187 A[c] *sedes* þat ben sowen and mowen soffre wyntres
C.12.189 Then *sedes* þat [in somer] sowe ben and mowen nat with forstes
C.17.89 Noþer see ne s[o]nd ne þe *seed* ȝeldeth
C.17.92 And þe se and the *seed*, þe sonne and þe mone
C.17.102 By the *seed* þat they sewe what þey sulle myhte,
C.18.225 Ne withoute a soware be suche *seed*; this we seen alle.
C.21.276 Spiritus prudencie the furste *seed* hihte
C.21.281 The seconde *se[d]e* hihte Spiritus temperancie.
C.21.282 He þat eet of that *seed* hadde such a kynde:
C.21.289 The thridde *seed* that [Peres] sewe was spiritus fortitudinis,
C.21.290 And hoso ete of þa[t] *seed* hardy was euere
C.21.297 The ferthe *seed* that [Peres] sewe was spiritus Iusticie
C.21.298 And he þat ete of þat *seed* sholde be euene trewe
C.21.309 Thise foure *sedes* [Peres] sewe and sennes he dede hem harewe
C.21.343 Þe *sedes* that sire [Peres] sewe, þe cardinale vertues.
C.21.406 The cheef *seed* þat [Peres] sewe, ysaued wo[r]st þou neuere.

seeknesse > siknesse

seel n *sele* n.(3) A 6 sel (3) selis (3); B 8 seel (5) seles (3); C 9 seal (2) seel (5) seeles (1) selys (1)

A.Pr.66 Brouȝte forþ a bulle wiþ bisshopis *selis*
A.Pr.76 His *sel* shulde not be sent to disseyue þe peple,
A. 2.107 Til he hadde siluer for his *selis* & signes.
A. 2.183 And senten hym on sundais wiþ *selis* to chirche,
A. 3.135 As ȝoure secre *sel* in seue score dayes.
A. 8.25 Ac vndir his secre *sel* treuþe sente h[e]m a lettre,
B.Pr.69 Brouȝte forþ a bulle wiþ Bisshopes *seles*,
B.Pr.79 His *seel* sholde noȝt be sent to deceyue þe peple.
B. 2.143 Til he hadde siluer for his [*seles*] and [signes of] Notaries.
B. 2.224 And senten hym [on Sondayes wiþ *seles*] to chirch[e],
B. 3.146 As youre secret *seel* in sixe score dayes.
B. 7.23 Ac vnder his secret *seel* truþe sente hem a lettre,
B.13.248 That he sente me vnder his *seel* a salue for þe pestilence,
B.17.5 'Nay', he seide, '[I] seke hym þat haþ þe *seel* to kepe,
C.Pr.67 Brouth forth a bulle with bischopis *selys*
C.Pr.77 His *seel* sholde nouȝt be ysent in deseyte of þe peple.
C. 2.159 Til he hadde seluer for the *seel* and signes of notaries.
C. 2.234 And senten hym on sonendayes with *seeles* to churche,
C. 3.184 As ȝoure secrete *seel* in six score dayes.
C. 9.27 Ac vnder his secrete *seal* treuthe sente hem a lettre

C. 9.138 For vnder godes secret *seal* here synnes ben keuered.
C.13.89 And sheweth be *seel* and seth by lettre with what lord he dwelleth,
C.19.7 'Nay,' he saide, 'y seke hym þat hath þe *seel* to kepe,

seem n *seme* n.(2) A 1 sem; B 1; C 1

A. 3.39 I shal assoile þe myself for a *sem* of whete,
B. 3.40 I shal assoille þee myself for a *seem* of whete,
C. 3.42 Y shal assoyle the mysulue for a *seem* [of] whete

seemely adj *semeli* adj. C 2 seemely (1) semely (1)

C. 3.112 Hit is nat *seemely*, forsothe, in Citee [ne] in borw toun
C.15.58 'This is a *semely* seruyce,' saide pacience.

seen v *sen* v.(1) A 44 saiȝ (6) sauȝ (7) saw (2) se (19) seiȝ (1) seiȝe (3) sen (3) sest (1) yseiȝe (1) yseyn (1); B 147 sauȝ (5) se (53) see (14) seen (5) seene (1) seest (4) seeþ (3) seye (1) seyen (3) seigh (3) seighe (1) seiȝ (34) seiȝe (1) seyȝe (1) seiȝen (4) sen (2) sene (1) sestow (3) yseien (1) yseyen (3) yseiȝe (1) ysey3e (1) yseiȝen (1); C 137 say (9) sayh (1) saw (4) se (56) see (7) seen (3) seest (1) seestow (1) seeth (1) sey (11) seye (1) seyen (2) seigh (1) seyh (18) seyhe (1) seyn (2) sen (2) sene (1) seste (1) seth (2) sye (2) sigh (1) syhe (1) ysaye (1) ysey (2) yseye (1) yseyen (1)

A.Pr.14 I *saiȝ* a tour on a toft triȝely Imakid;
A.Pr.90 I *sauȝ* bisshopis bolde & bacheleris of deuyn
A.Pr.97 I *sauȝ* in þat sem[b]le as ȝe shuln here aftir,
A.Pr.109 Al þis I *sauȝ* slepyng & seue siþes more.
A. 1.5 And seide 'sone, slepist þou? *sest* þou þis peple,
A. 1.49 "Cesar," þ[ei] seide, "we *se* wel ichone."
A. 1.146 Here miȝt þou *sen* ensaumplis in hymself one
A. 2.150 Soþnesse *seiȝ* hem wel & seide but litel,
A. 3.52 Þat iche segge shal *se* I am sistir of ȝour hous.'
A. 3.57 A[c] so preuyliche parte it þat pride be not *seiȝe*,
A. 3.204 Seruauntis for here seruyse, we *se* wel þe soþe,
A. 4.18 'Sette my sadil vpon suffre til I *se* my tyme,
A. 4.73 'He sh[al] not þis seue ȝer *se* hise feet ones!'
A. 4.119 Ac I may shewe ensaumplis as I *se* [oþer],
A. 5.4 Þat I ne hadde yslepe saddere & *yseyn* more.
A. 5.9 Þanne *sauȝ* I meke[l] more þan I before tolde,
A. 5.10 [For I *sauȝ*] þe feld ful of folk þat I before tolde],
A. 5.22 Ac I shal *seiȝe* as I *saiȝ*, so me god helpe,
A. 5.68 Wiþ werkis [or wiþ] wordis whanne he *saiȝ* his tyme.
A. 5.232 I wile seke treuþe er I [*se*] rome.'
A. 6.12 And *sen* be his signes whom he souȝt hadde.
A. 6.17 ȝe mowe *se* be my signes þat sitten on myn hat
A. 6.23 'I *sauȝ* neuere palmere wiþ pik ne wiþ scrippe
A. 6.57 So shalt þou *se* swere nouȝt but it be for nede,
A. 6.70 And þanne shalt þou [*se*] sey soþ, so it be to done;
A. 6.93 Þou shalt *se* treuþe himself wel sitte in þin herte
A. 7.219 And sapience *seiþ* þe same, I *saiȝ* it in þe bible:
A. 8.62 Siþen ȝe *sen* it is þus sewiþ to þe beste.
A. 8.128 And *sauȝ* þe sonne euene souþ sitte þat tyme,
A. 8.133 For þat I *saiȝ* slepyng ȝif it so be miȝte.
A. 9.66 'I haue sewide þe seuen ȝer; *seiȝe* þou me no raþere?'
A.10.19 Sire *se* wel, & sey wel, & here wel þe hende,
A.10.59 And ek in sottis þou miȝt *se*, þat sitten at þe nale.
A.10.108 Thrift oþer þedom with þo is selde *yseiȝe*:
A.10.119 For þoruȝ suffrance *se* þou miȝt how soueraynes ariseþ,
A.10.149 And so seyþ þe sauter, as it whanne þe likiþ:
A.10.182 For summe, as I *se* now, soþ for to telle,
A.11.122 Þanne shalt þou *se* sobirte, & simplite of speche,
A.11.146 In oþer science it seiþ, I *saiȝ* it in catoun,
A.11.181 And siþen aftirward to *se* sumwhat of dobest'.
A.11.221 For I haue *seiȝe* it myself, & siþþen red it aftir,
A.12.5 But I *se* now as I seye, as me soþ thinkyt3,
A.12.20 "I *saw* synful," he seyde, "þerfore I seyde no þing
A.12.107 When he *saw* þes sawes busyly alegged
B.Pr.14 I *seiȝ* a tour on a toft trieliche ymaked,
B.Pr.50 I *seiȝ* somme þat seiden þei hadde ysouȝt Seintes;
B.Pr.160 'I haue *yseyen* segges', quod he, 'in þe Cite of Londoun
B.Pr.202 I seye for me', quod þe Mous, 'I *se* so muchel after,
B.Pr.218 I *seiȝ* in þis assemblee, as ye shul here after.
B.Pr.231 [Al þis I *seiȝ* slepyng and seuene sythes more].
B. 1.5 And seide, 'sone, slepestow? *sestow* þis peple,
B. 1.51 "Cesar[i]s", þei seiden, "we *seen* wel echone."
B. 1.114 May no synne be on hym *seene* þat vseþ þat spice,
B. 1.172 Here myȝtow *sen* ensample[s] in hymself oone
B. 2.17 Hire array me rauysshed; swich richesse *sauȝ* I neuere.
B. 2.67 Whan Symonye and Cyuylle *seighe* hir boþer wille
B. 2.71 And preide Cyuylle to *see* and Symonye to rede it.
B. 2.189 Sothnesse *seiȝ* hem wel and seide but litel,
B. 3.63 That [ech] segge shal [*see*] I am suster of youre house.'
B. 3.217 Ser[u]aunt3 for hire seruyce, we *seeþ* wel þe soþe,
B. 3.333 *Se* what Salomon seiþ in Sapience bokes!
B. 4.20 'Set my Sadel vpon suffre-til-I-*se*-my-tyme

B. 4.86	'[He shal] no3t þise seuen yer *seen* his feet ones!'
B. 4.136	Ac I may shewe ensamples as I *se* ouþ[er].
B. 4.152	For I *sei3* Mede in þe moot halle on men of lawe wynke
B. 5.4	That I ne hadde slept sadder and *ysei3en* moore.
B. 5.10	For I *sei3* þe feld ful of folk þat I before [tolde],
B. 5.22	Ac I shal seye as I *sau3*, so me god helpe,
B. 5.85	With werkes or wiþ wordes whan he *sey3e* his tyme.
B. 5.460	I shal seken truþe er I *se* Rome.'
B. 5.497	A synful Marie þe *sei3* er seynte Marie þi dame,
B. 5.524	And *se* bi hise signes whom he sou3t hadde.
B. 5.529	Ye may *se* by my signes þat sitten on myn hatte
B. 5.535	'I [ne] *sei3* neuere Palmere wiþ pyk ne wiþ scrippe
B. 5.570	So shaltow *se* swere-no3t-but-it-be-for-nede-
B. 5.583	Thanne [shalt þow] *see* seye-sooþ-so-it-be-to-doone-
B. 5.606	Thow shalt *see* in þiselue truþe [sitte] in þyn herte
B. 6.235	And Sapience seiþ þe same–I *sei3* it in þe bible:
B. 6.327	Whan ye *se* þe [mone] amys and two monkes heddes,
B. 7.146	And *sei3* þe sonne [euene] South sitte þat tyme,
B. 7.150	Of þat I *sei3* slepynge, if it so be my3te,
B. 7.154	Ac I haue no sauour in songewarie for I *se* it ofte faille.
B. 8.75	'I haue sued þee seuen yeer; *seye* þow me no raþer?'
B. 9.20	Sire *Se*-wel, and Sey-wel, and here-wel þe hende,
B. 9.77	Godfad[er] and godmod[er] þat *seen* hire godchildren
B. 9.84	A Iew wolde no3t *se* a Iew go Ianglyng for defaute
B. 9.155	And haue a Sauour after þe sire; selde *sestow* ooþer:
B. 9.159	For some, as I *se* now, sooþ for to telle,
B. 10.170	Thanne shaltow *se* Sobretee and Sympletee-of-speche,
B. 10.194	In ooþer Science it seiþ, I *sei3* it in Catoun,
B. 10.265	Syþenes þow *seest* þiself as in soule clene;
B. 10.366	And oure bakkes þat moþeeten be and *seen* beggeris go naked,
B. 10.419	Wercheþ ye as ye *sen* ywrite, lest ye worþe no3t þerInne].
B. 10.460	Seide þus in a sermon–I *seigh* it writen ones–
B. 10.475	I *se* ensamples myself and so may manye oþer,
B. 11.10	[Siþen] she seide to me, 'here my3tow *se* wondres
B. 11.20	And in þis Mirour þow my3t *se* [myrþes] ful manye
B. 11.104	Thou3 þow *se* yuel seye it no3t first; be sory it nere amended.
B. 11.147	Sauacion for sooþnesse þat he *sei3* in my werkes.
B. 11.151	And I saued as ye [may] *see*, wiþouten syngynge of masses,
B. 11.245	Ther neuere segge hym *sei3* in secte of þe riche.
B. 11.246	Seint Iohan and oþere seintes were *seyen* in poore cloþyng,
B. 11.270	Alþou3 Salomon seide, as folk *seeþ* in þe bible,
B. 11.321	And slepynge I *sei3* al þis, and siþen cam kynde
B. 11.327	I *sei3* þe sonne and þe see and þe sond after,
B. 11.331	Man and his make I my3te [*se*] boþe.
B. 11.333	Blisse and bale boþe I *sei3* at ones,
B. 11.335	Reson I *sei3* sooþly sewen alle beestes,
B. 11.364	Manye selkouþes I *sei3* ben no3t to seye nouþe.
B. 11.365	I *sei3* floures in þe fryth and hir faire colours
B. 11.412	'To *se* muche and suffre moore, certes, is dowel.'
B. 11.435	'Ye siggen sooþ', quod I, 'ich haue *yseyen* it ofte.
B. 12.20	I *sei3* wel he seide me sooþ, and somwhat me to excuse
B. 12.53	And for þei suffren and *see* so manye nedy folkes
B. 12.99	For as a man may no3t *see* þat mysseþ hise ei3en,
B. 12.103	[And ri3t as si3t serueþ a man to *se* þe hei3e strete]
B. 12.131	[The] selkouþes þat þei *sei3en*, hir sones for to teche.
B. 12.159	And þow seidest sooþ of somme, ac *se* in what manere.
B. 12.176	As þow *seest* in þe Sauter in Salmes oon or tweyne
B. 13.87	And seide, 'þow shalt *see* þus soone, whan he may na moore,
B. 13.122	Til I *se* þo seuene and myself acorde
B. 13.203	But seide ful sobreliche, 'þow shalt *se* þe tyme
B. 13.211	'That is sooþ', [seide] Clergie, 'I *se* what þow menest.
B. 13.304	And segge þyng þat he neuere *sei3* and for soþe sweren it;
B. 13.309	What I suffrede and *sei3* and somtymes hadde,
B. 14.97	That it neuere eft is *sene* ne soor, but semeþ a wounde yheeled.'
B. 14.137	For whan a werkman haþ wro3t, þan may men *se* þe soþe,
B. 14.155	Ac it is but selde *yseien*, as by holy seintes bokes,
B. 15.12	Til I *sei3*, as it sorcerie were, a sotil þyng wiþ alle.
B. 15.44	'That is sooþ', seide he; 'now I *se* þi wille.
B. 15.96	[And] *se* it by ensaumple in somer tyme on trowes:
B. 15.158	I *sei3* neuere swich a man, so me god helpe,
B. 15.162	Ac I *sei3* hym neuere sooþly but as myself in a Mirour:
B. 15.196	'Wiþouten help of Piers Plowman', quod he, 'his persone *sestow* neuere.'
B. 15.220	For I haue *seyen* hym in silk and som tyme in russet,
B. 15.225	I haue *yseyen* charite also syngen and reden
B. 15.287	That no man my3te hym *se* for mosse and for leues.
B. 15.398	Brou3te Sar3ens of Surree, and *see* in what manere.
B. 15.434	So is mannes soule, sooþly, þat *seeþ* no goo[d] ensampl[e]
B. 15.513	In ensample þat men sholde *se* by sadde reson
B. 15.589	Of selkouþe sores; þei *sei3en* it ofte,
B. 15.592	And by þat mangerie [þei] my3te wel *se* þat Messie he semede;
B. 16.10	'I wolde trauaille', quod I, 'þis tree to *se* twenty hundred myle,
B. 16.39	I saue it til I *se* it ripen and somdel yfruyted.

B. 16.116	And wepte water with hise ei3en; þer *sei3en* it manye.
B. 16.117	Some þat þe sighte *sei3en* seiden þat tyme
B. 16.178	[I] seke after a segge þat I *sei3* ones,
B. 16.216	As widewe wiþouten wedlok was neuere 3it *ysey3e*,
B. 16.225	Thus in a somer I hym *sei3* as I sat in my porche;
B. 16.252	Seide þat he *sei3* here þat sholde saue vs alle:
B. 16.259	'Loo!' quod he and leet me *see*; 'lord, mercy!' I seide,
B. 16.272	I wepte for hise wordes; wiþ þat *sau3* I anoþer
B. 17.4	'Is it enseled?' I seide; 'may men *see* þ[e] lettres?'
B. 17.10	'Lat *se* þi lettres', quod I, 'we myghte þe lawe knowe.'
B. 17.25	Ye! and sixti þousand biside forþ þat ben no3t *seyen* here.'
B. 17.28	Abraham seiþ þat he *sei3* hoolly þe Trinite,
B. 17.51	Thanne *sei3e* we a Samaritan sittynge on a Mule,
B. 17.86	And whan I *sei3* þis I soiourned no3t but shoop me to renne
B. 17.106	And [may] ech man *see* and good mark take
B. 17.109	For he *seigh* me þat am Samaritan suwen Feiþ & his felawe
B. 17.198	By þis skile', [he seide], 'I *se* an euidence
B. 17.211	[That serueþ þise swynkeres to *se* by ani3tes],
B. 17.215	And as þow *seest* som tyme sodeynliche a torche,
B. 17.230	And melteþ hire my3t into mercy, as men may *se* in wyntre
B. 17.237	And solacen hem þat mowe [no3t] *se*, þat sitten in derknesse,
B. 17.305	Ac it is but selden *ysei3e*, þer sooþnesse bereþ witnesse,
B. 18.37	To *se* how doghtiliche deeþ sholde do and deme hir boþeres right.
B. 18.112	And þere I *sau3* sooþly, secundum scripturas,
B. 18.163	'Now suffre we', seide Truþe; 'I *se*, as me þynkeþ,
B. 18.167	'That is sooþ', seide Mercy, 'and I *se* here by Sowþe
B. 18.177	That many day my3te I no3t *se* for merknesse of synne,
B. 18.214	And suffrede to be sold to *se* þe sorwe of deying,
B. 18.223	To [*se*] what he haþ suffred in þre sondry places,
B. 18.246	Whan she *sei3* hym suffre þat sonne and see made.
B. 18.250	And leet out Symondes sone[s] to *seen* hym hange on roode.
B. 18.261	'Suffre we', seide truþe; 'I here and *see* boþe
B. 18.300	And whan I *sei3* it was so, [s]lepynge I wente
B. 18.307	And now I *se* wher a soule comeþ [silynge hiderward]
B. 18.395	Ac blood may no3t *se* blood blede but hym rewe:
B. 19.66	And *se* bi his sorwe þat whoso loueþ ioye
B. 19.180	That neuere shul *se* me in sighte as þow [seest] nowþe,
B. 19.180	That neuere shul *se* me in sighte as þow [*seest*] nowþe,
B. 19.242	And some to *se* and to seye what sholde bifalle,
B. 19.252	'Thou3 some be clenner þan some, ye *se* wel', quod Grace,
B. 20.107	To cesse and suffre, and *see* wher þei wolde
B. 20.109	And kynde cessede [sone] to *se* þe peple amende.
B. 20.178	'Now I *se*', seide lif, 'þat Surgerie ne phisik
B. 20.185	So harde he yede ouer myn heed it wole be *sene* euere.
B. 20.199	And as I seet in þis sorwe I *sau3* how kynde passede
B. 20.350	He may *se* and here [here, so] may bifalle,
B. 20.373	Sleuþe *seigh* þat and so dide pryde,
C. Pr.5	And *say* many selles and selkouthe thyngus.
C. Pr.11	Wynkyng as hit were, witterliche y *sigh* hit;
C. Pr.13	Al y *say* slepynge as y shal [3ow] telle.
C. Pr.15	And *say* a tour; as [y] trow[e], treuthe was thereynne.
C. Pr.17	And *seigh* a depe dale; deth, as y leue,
C. Pr.109	And for here syre *sey* hem synne and suffred hem do ille
C. Pr.179	Sayde, 'y haue *seyen* grete syres in Cytees and in townes
C. Pr.210	Y *seye* for me,' quod þe mous, 'y *se* so muche aftur,
C. Pr.224	Al y *say* slepynge, as 3e shal here [a]ftur,
C. Pr.235	[Al þis y *say* slepynge and seuene sythes more].
C. 1.5	And sayde, 'Wille, slepestou? *seestow* þis peple,
C. 1.39	And þat [*see*]th þ[i] soule and sayth hit the in herte
C. 1.44	'Go to þe gospel,' quod she, 'and *se* what god sayde
C. 1.55	'The dep dale and þe derk, so vnsemely to *se* to,
C. 1.168	Here myhtow *se* ensaumples in hymself one
C. 2.47	Soffre and thow shalt *see* suche as ben apayed
C. 2.56	And y *say* how mede was maried, metyng as it were.
C. 2.73	And preyeth syuile to *se* and s[y]monye to rede hit.
C. 2.203	Sothnesse *seyh* hem [wel] and sayde but lytel,
C. 3.67	That euery seg shal *se* y am sustre of 3oure ordre.'
C. 3.104	Al this haue we *seyn*, þat som tyme thorw a breware
C. 3.129	And sente to *se* here; y myhte nat *se* þat ladde here.
C. 3.129	And sente to *se* here; y myhte nat *se* þat ladde here.
C. 3.273	Seruantes for here seruyse, [we *see* wel þe sothe],
C. 3.326	And as sone as god *seyh* a sewed nat his wille
C. 4.20	Sette my sadel vpon soffre-tyl-y-*se*-my-tyme
C. 4.82	Ther he sholde nat in seuene 3er *see* his feet [ones].
C. 4.133	Ac y may s[hew]en ensaumples as y *see* othere.
C. 4.154	And sayden, 'we *seyn* wel, syre resoun, be thi wordes
C. 5.89	Quod Consience, 'by Crist, y can nat *se* this lyeth;
C. 5.111	Y *saw* þe felde ful of folk fram ende til oþer
C. 5.124	Ac y shal sey as y *sayh*, slepynge as hit were,
C. 6.51	Thyng þat neuere was thouhte and 3ut [y] swor [y] *seyh* hit
C. 6.57	What y soffrede and *seyh* and some tymes hadde
C. 7.15	Ne ryht sory for my synnes–y *seyh* neuere þe tyme–
C. 7.137	A synful marie þe *sey* ar seynte marye þy dame

C. 7.169   And *se* by [his] signes wham a souht hadde.
C. 7.174   ꝝe may *se* be [my] signes þat sitten on my cappe
C. 7.180   'I [ne] *saw* neuere palmere with pyk ne with scrip[p]e
C. 7.217   [So] shalt thow *se* swere-nat-but-it-be-for-nede-
C. 7.230   Thenne shaltow *se* say-soth-so-hit-be-to-done-
C. 7.255   Thow shalt *se* treuthe sitte in thy sulue herte
C. 8.280   And sethen y *say* hym sitte as he a syre were
C. 9.243   Where as we hem on sonendayes the seruise to here,
C. 9.245   Or sonendayes at euensong? *se* we wel fewe!
C. 9.295   And *seyh* the sonne in the sou[t]he sitte þat tyme,
C. 9.299   Of that y *seyh* slepynge, if hit so be myhte,
C. 9.303   Ac men setteth nat by sowngewarie for me *seth* hit often fayle;
C.10.73   'Y haue sued the seuen ꝝer; *saw* thow me no rather?'
C.10.146   Sire *se*-wel and sey-wel [and] here-wel þe [h]ende,
C.10.159   And as thow *seest* the sonne sum tyme for cloudes
C.11.49   And so saith þe sauter; y *say* hit [in] memento:
C.11.150   And he vs saide as he *sey*, and so y bileue,
C.11.151   That he *seyh* þe [syre] and þe sone and þe seynt spirit togederes
C.11.169   And senes he saide to me, 'here myhte thow *se* wondres
C.11.179   And in þis myrrour thow myhte *se* murthes fol monye
C.11.201   Sholde sitte in goddis sihte ne *se* god in his blisse:
C.11.202   For clergie saith þat he *seyh* in þe seynt euaungelie
C.11.234   Seldom ar they *seyen* so lyue as they lere;
C.11.281   Sothly,' saide rechelesnesse, 'ꝝe *se* by many euydences
C.11.284   For he þat most *se[y]h* and saide of the sothfaste trinite
C.12.29   To segge as they *seen*, saue only prestis:
C.12.38   Thouh tho[w] *se*, say nat sum tyme þat is treuthe.
C.12.82   Sauacion for soethnesse [þat] a *sey* in my werkes.
C.12.86   And y saued, as ꝝe may *se*, withoute syngynge of masses.
C.12.133   Holy seyntes hym *sey* Ac neuere in secte of riche.
C.13.135   And *seyhe* þe sonne and þe see and þe sond aftur
C.13.139   Man and his make y myhte *se* bothe;
C.13.141   Blisse and bale bothe y *sey* at ones
C.13.143   Resoun y *sey* sothly sewe alle bestes
C.13.174   Mony selcouthes y *seyh* aren nat to segge nouthe
C.13.180   Was þat y *seyh* resoun sewen alle bestes
C.13.187   Y *se* non so ofte forfeten sothly so mankynde;
C.13.220   'To *se* moche and soffre al, certes, is dowel.'
C.13.241   'ꝝe seggeth soth, be my soule,' quod y, 'I haue *sey* hit ofte.
C.14.41   "That *seth* hymsulue synnelees sese nat, y hote,
C.14.44   For as a man may nat *se* þat misseth his yes,
C.14.48   And riht as syht serueth a man to *se* [þe hye strete],
C.14.75   And of the selcouthes þat þei *sye* here sones þerof þei tauhten;
C.14.116   As we *seen* in þe sauter in psalmes oen or tweyne
C.14.165   *Sey* hit and soffred hit And saide hit be sholde:
C.15.94   And saide, 'Thow shalt *se* thus sone, when he may no more,
C.16.206   'That is soth,' he sayde; 'now y *se* thy wille.
C.16.248   And *s[e]* hit by ensample In somur tyme on trees
C.16.303   And sory when he *seth* men sory, as thow seest childerne
C.16.303   And sory when he seth men sory, as thow *seest* childerne
C.16.345   Ych haue *ysey* hym mysulue som tyme in russet,
C.16.350   Ich haue *yseye* charite also syngen and rede,
C.17.14   That no man myhte *se* hym for moes and for leues.
C.17.264   In ensaumple þat men sholde *se* by sad resoen
C.17.304   Iewes sayde þat hit *seye* with soercerye he wrouhte,
C.18.61   Me may *se* on an appul tree monye tyme and ofte
C.18.139   That suche a surgien sethen *ysaye* was þer neuere
C.18.147   Ac tho that *sey* that selcouth sayde þat tyme
C.18.190   And, sondry to *se* vpon, solus deus he hoteth.'
C.18.201   Miꝝte and a mene to *se* his owne myhte,
C.18.225   Ne withoute a soware be suche seed; this we *seen* alle.
C.18.239   'Hastow *ysey* this,' y seyde, 'alle thre and o god?'
C.18.240   'In a somur y hym *seyh*,' quod he, 'as y saet in my porche,
C.18.268   Saide þat a *seyh* here þat sholde saue vs alle:
C.18.275   'Loo!' quod he and lette me *see*: 'lord, mercy!' y saide,
C.18.288   [Y] wepte for his wordes; with þat *saw* y [a]nother
C.19.5   That that y *sey* is soeth of hoso liketh.
C.19.11   'Let *se* thy lettres,' quod y, 'we myhte þe lawe knowe.'
C.19.29   Abraham saith þat he *seyh* holly þe trinitee,
C.19.49   Thenne *sey* we a samaritaen cam sittynge on a muyle,
C.19.164   Bi this simile,' he saide, 'y *se* an euydence
C.19.177   That serueth this swynkares to [*see*] by a nyhtes,
C.19.181   And as thow *seest* som tyme sodeynliche of a torche
C.19.196   And melteth myhte into mercy, as we may *se* a wynter
C.19.203   And solacen [hem] þat mowen nat *se*, sittynge in derkeness[e]
C.19.285   Ac hit is bote selde *yseyen*, there sothnesse bereth witnesse,
C.20.36   To *se* how douhtyliche deth sholde do and demen [h]er beyre rihte.
C.20.115   And there y *seyh* sothly, secundum scripturas,
C.20.166   'Now *se* we,' saide Treuthe; 'as me thynketh,
C.20.170   'That is soth,' saide mercy, 'and y *se* here bi southe
C.20.180   That many day myhte y nat *se* for merkenesse of synne,
C.20.223   And soffred to be sold to *se* þe sorwe of deynge,
C.20.255   When he *sye* hym soffre þat sonne and se made.

C.20.259   And lette out symondes sones to *sen* hym honge on rode:
C.20.269   'Soffre we,' sayde treuthe; 'y here and *se* bothe
C.20.333   And when y *seyh* hit was so, y sotiled how y myhte
C.20.341   And now y *se* where his soule cometh sylinge hid[er]ward
C.20.358   That y ne sygge as y *syhe*, suynde my teme).
C.20.438   Ac bloed may nat *se* bloed blede bote hym rewe:
C.21.66   And *se* bi his sorwe þat hoso loueth ioye
C.21.180   Tha[t] neuere shal *se* me in sihte as thowe seste nowthe
C.21.180   Tha[t] neuere shal se me in sihte as thowe *seste* nowthe
C.21.242   And somme to *se* and to saye what sholde bifalle
C.21.252   'Thouh somme be clenner then somme, ꝝe *sen* wel,' quod grace,
C.22.107   To sese and soffre and *se* wher they wolde
C.22.109   And kynde sesede [sone] to *se* þe peple amende.
C.22.178   'Now y *see*,' saide lyf, ' that surgerie ne fysyke
C.22.185   So harde he ꝝede ouer myn heued hit wol be *sene* euere.
C.22.199   And as y saet in this sorwe y *say* how kynde passede
C.22.350   He may *se* and here here, so may bifalle,
C.22.373   Sle[u]th *seyh* þat and so dede pruyde

seet(e > sitten; seg > segge

sege n *sege n.(2)*   B 2; C 2
B.20.310   If any surgien were [in] þe *seg[e]* þat softer koude plastre.
B.20.313   'Ther is a Surgien in þ[e] *sege* þat softe kan handle,
C.22.310   Yf eny surgien were in þe *sege* that softur couthe plastre.
C.22.313   'Ther is a surgien in the *sege* that softe can handele

segen > siggen

segge n *segge n.(2)* &> *siggen* A 4 segge (2) segges (2); B 9 segge (6)
    segges (3); C 8 seg (1) segge (3) segges (2)
A. 2.123   And let somoune alle þe *segges* [in shires abouten],
A. 3.52   Þat iche *segge* shal se I am sistir of ꝝour hous.'
A. 5.17   In ensaumple, *se[gges]*, þat ꝝe shulde do þe betere;
A.12.54   Sey I sente hym þis *segge*, and þat he shewe hym dowel.'
B.Pr.160   'I haue yseyen *segges*', quod he, 'in þe Cite of Londoun
B. 2.159   And leten somone alle *segges* in shires aboute,
B. 3.63   That [ech] *segge* shal [see] I am suster of youre house.'
B. 5.17   In ensample, [*segges*, þat ye] sholden do þe bettre;
B.11.245   Ther neuere *segge* hym seiꝝ in secte of þe riche.
B.11.267   And wel sikerer he slepeþ, þe [*segge*] þat is pouere,
B.16.178   [I] seke after a *segge* þat I seiꝝ ones,
B.17.64   Ac whan he hadde sighte of þat *segge* aside he gan hym drawe
B.17.92   For sighte of þ[e] sorweful [*segge*] þat robbed was with þeues.
C. 2.175   And leten somne alle *seggus* in vche syde aboute,
C. 3.67   That euery *seg* shal se y am sustre of ꝝoure ordre.'
C. 5.119   In ensau[m]ple, *seggus*, þat we sholde do þe bettere;
C.12.152   And wel sikorere he slepeth, þe *segg* þat is pore,
C.12.162   What god saide hymsulue to a *segg* þat he louede:
C.13.196   'Vch a *segge* for hymsulue, salamon vs techeth:
C.15.123   'Y haue yseide,' quod þat *segg*, 'y can sey no bettre.
C.19.63   Ac when he hadde sihte of this *s[egg]e* asyde he gan hym drawe

seggen -eth > siggen; segging > seying,siggen; seggus > segge; sey >
seen,siggen; seid(- > siggen; seye > seen,siggen; seigh(- seiꝝ > seen; seyn >
seen,siggen

seyned v *signen v.(1)* A 1 seynide; B 1; C 1 seynede
A. 5.220   Þanne sat sleuþe vp & *seynide* hym faste,
B. 5.448   Thanne sat Sleuþe vp and *seyned* hym [faste]
C. 7.62   Thenne sat sleuthe vp and *seynede* hym ofte

seint n *seinte n.* A 3 seintes; B 23 seint (3) seintes (17) seyntes (3); C 21
    saynt (1) sayntes (2) seynt (1) seynte (1) seyntes (16)
A.Pr.47   For to seke seint Iame & *seintes* at rome;
A. 5.40   And ꝝe þat seke seint Iame & *seintes* at rome,
A. 6.19   And souꝝt goode *seintes* for my soule hele.'
B.Pr.47   For to seken Seint Iame and *Seintes* at Rome;
B.Pr.50   I seiꝝ somme þat seiden þei hadde ysouꝝt *Seintes*;
B. 3.235   Lord, who shal wonye in þi wones wiþ þyne holy *seintes*,
B. 4.39   Moore þan for] loue of oure lord or alle hise leeue *Seintes*.
B. 5.56   And ye þat seke Seynt Iames and *Seyntes* [at] Rome,
B. 5.416   Yet kan I neyþer solue ne synge ne *seintes* lyues rede;
B. 5.492   Aboute mydday, whan moost liꝝt is and meel tyme of *Seintes*,
B. 5.508   That alle *Seintes* [for synful] songen at ones
B. 5.531   And souꝝt goode *Seintes* for me soul[e] hel[e].'
B. 5.593   Ech piler is of penaunce, of preieres-to-*Seyntes*;
B. 7.37   And sende youre soules in saufte to my *Seintes* in Ioye.'
B. 7.88   Lat vsage be youre solas of *seintes* lyues redyng.
B.10.432   And now ben [swiche] as Souereyns wiþ *Seintes* in heuene,
B.11.246   Seint Iohan and oþere *seintes* were seyen in poore cloþyng,
B.12.39   Seke þow neuere *Seint* ferþer for no soule helpe.
B.12.197   As Seint Iohan and oþere *Seintes* þat deserued hadde bettre.
B.12.208   And for to seruen a *Seint* and swich a þef togideres,
B.13.418   Penaunce [and] pouere men and þe passion of *Seintes*,
B.13.453   In a welhope, [for he wrouꝝte so], amonges worþi *seyntes*],

B.14.155 Ac it is but selde yseien, as by holy *seintes* bokes,
B.15.224 And *seintes* yset; [stille] charite hem folwede.
B.15.269 [Lo]! in legenda sanctorum, þe lif of holy *Seintes*,
B.15.519 Many a *seint* syþen haþ suffred to deye
C.Pr.48 To seke seynt Iame and *seyntes* [at] Rome;
C. 1.80 How y may saue my soule, þat *saynt* art yholde.'
C. 3.98 That Innocence is herde in heuene amonge *seyntes*
C. 5.197 And ȝe þat seketh seynt Iames and *seyntes* [at] Rome,
C. 7.31 ȝut kan y nother solfe ne synge ne a *seyntes* lyf rede;
C. 7.78 Penaunse and pore men and the passioun of *seyntes*,
C. 7.113 In a welhope for a wrouhte so amongus worthy *seyntes*
C. 7.132 Aboute mydday, when most liht is and mel tyme of *sayntes*,
C. 7.153 That alle *seyntes* for synfol songen with dauid:
C. 7.176 [And] souht gode *seyntes* for my soule helthe.'\
C. 7.241 Vche piler is of penaunc[e] and preyeres to *seyntes*;
C.11.13 More then holynesse or hendenesse or al þat *seyntes* techeth.
C.11.268 And now beth this *seyntes*, by that men saith, and souereynes in heuene,
C.11.275 For Crist saide to *sayntes* and to suche as he louede,
C.12.133 Holy *seyntes* hym sey Ac neuere in secte of riche.
C.12.172 Mo prouerbes y myhte haue of mony holy *seyntes*
C.12.205 For crist saide [so] to *seyntes* þat for his sake tholeden
C.14.136 A[s] seynt Ioh[a]n and oþer *seyntes* þat haen [de]serued bettere.
C.14.147 And for to seruen a *seynt* and suche a thef togyderes,
C.16.348 Edmond and Edward, ayþer were *seyntes*,
C.17.270 Mony [a] *seynte* sethe soffrede deth also,

seint adj *seinte adj.* A 17 seint (15) seynt (1) seinte (1); B 45 seint (38) seynt (4) seinte (2) seynte (1); C 42 saynt (2) seynt (32) seynte (8)

A.Pr.47 For to seke *seint* Iame & seintes at rome;
A. 1.82 How I may sauen my soule, þat *seint* art yho[ld]en.'
A. 1.89 And ek lyk to oure lord be *seint* lukis wordis.
A. 4.109 Til *seint* Iame be souȝt þere I shal assigne.
A. 4.151 'And I assente,' quaþ þe king, 'be *seinte* marie my lady,
A. 5.40 And ȝe þat seke *seint* Iame & seintes at rome,
A. 5.41 Sekiþ *seint* treuþe for he may saue ȝou alle
A. 6.45 'I nolde fonge a ferþing for *seint* Thomas shryne,
A. 7.3 Quaþ perkyn þe plouȝman, 'be *seint* poule þe apostel,
A. 7.26 'Be *seint* poule,' quaþ perkyn, 'for þou profrist þe so lowe
A. 7.50 'I assente, be *seint* Iame,' seide þe kniȝt þanne,
A. 7.259 'Be *seint* pernel,' quaþ peris, 'þise arn profitable wordis.
A. 8.36 '[And] I shal sende myself *seynt* Michel myn aungel
A. 8.156 He passiþ al þe pardoun [of] *seint* petris chirche.
A. 9.83 And prechiþ þe peple *seint* poulis wordis:
A.11.33 Wolde neuere king, ne kniȝt, ne canoun of *seint* poulis
A.11.282 Sonnere hadde he saluacioun þanne *seint* Ion þe baptist,
B.Pr.47 For to seken *Seint* Iame and Seintes at Rome;
B. 1.84 How I may saue my soule þat *Seint* art yholde.'
B. 1.91 And [ek] ylik to oure lord by *Seint* Lukes wordes.
B. 4.121 As *Seynt* Beneyt hem bad, Bernard and Fraunceis;
B. 4.126 And til *Seint* Iames be souȝt þere I shal assigne,
B. 4.188 'And I assente', seiþ þe kyng, 'by *Seinte* Marie my lady,
B. 5.56 And ye þat seke *Seynt* Iames and Seyntes [at] Rome,
B. 5.57 Sekeþ *Seynt* Truþe, for he may saue yow alle
B. 5.166 *Seint* Gregory was a good pope and hadde a good forwit:
B. 5.497 A synful Marie þe seiȝ er *seynte* Marie þi dame.
B. 5.558 'I nolde fange a ferþyng for *Seint* Thomas Shryne;
B. 5.639 'Bi *seint* Poul!' quod a pardoner, 'parauenture I be noȝt knowe þere;
B. 6.3 Quod Perkyn þe Plowman, 'by *Seint* Peter of Rome!
B. 6.24 'By *Seint* Poul!' quod Perkyn, '[for þow profrest þee so lowe]
B. 6.55 'I assente, by *Seint* Iame,' seide þe knyȝt þanne,
B. 6.275 'By *Seint* [Pernele]', quod Piers, 'þise arn profitable wordes!
B. 7.34 'And I shal sende myselue *Seint* Michel myn [a]ngel
B. 7.178 [He] passeþ al þe pardon of *Seint* Petres cherche.
B. 8.92 And precheþ þe peple *Seint* Poules wordes,
B.10.47 [W]olde neuere kyng ne knyȝt ne [c]anon of *Seint* Poules
B.10.74 And prechen at *Seint* Poules, for pure enuye of clerkes,
B.10.423 He was sonner ysaued þan *seint* Iohan þe Baptist
B.10.450 For he seide to *Seint* Peter and to swiche as he louede,
B.11.157 Was þat Sarsen saued, as *Seint* Gregorie bereþ witnesse.
B.11.176 For *Seint* Iohan seide it, and soþe arn hise wordes:
B.11.227 That saued synful men as *Seint* Iohan bereþ witnesse:
B.11.230 And as *Seint* Gregorie seide, for mannes soule helþe
B.11.246 *Seint* Iohan and oþere seintes were seyen in poore cloþyng,
B.12.102 And *seint* Spirit þe Samplarie, & seide what men sholde write.
B.12.197 As *Seint* Iohan and oþere Seintes þat deserued hadde bettre.
B.12.203 He sit neiþer wiþ *Seint* Iohan, Symond ne Iude,
B.13.91 And preuen it by hir Pocalips and passion of *Seint* Auereys
B.13.440 As he seiþ hymself; *seynt* Iohan bereþ witnesse.
B.14.319 Thus lered me a lettred man for oure lordes loue, *Seint* Austyn:
B.15.60 "Beatus est", seiþ *Seint* Bernard, "qui scripturas legit
B.15.523 In sauacion of [mannes soule] *seint* [Thomas] was ymartired:
B.16.82 Sampson and Samuel and *Seint* Iohan þe Baptist,
B.17.151 *Seinte* Marie, a mayde, and mankynde lauȝte:

B.17.161 Right so þe fader and þe sone and *Seint* Spirit þe þridde
B.17.199 That whoso synneþ in þe *Seint* Spirit assoilled worþ he neuere,
B.17.204 So whoso synneþ in þe *Seint* Spirit, it semeþ þat he greueþ
B.17.224 Na moore dooþ sire ne sone ne *seint* spirit togidres
B.17.287 Synnen ayein þe *Seint* Spirit, assenten to destruye
B.17.300 And now am sory þat I so þe *Seint* Spirit agulte,
B.18.324 Songen *seint* Iohanes song, Ecce agnus dei.
C.Pr.48 To seke seynt Iame and seyntes [at] Rome;
C. 1.87 And also lyk [to] oure lord by *saynt* Lukes wordes.
C. 3.143 [And marre þe with myschef], be *seynte* mary my lady,
C. 4.51 'Bere sikerlyche eny seluer to *seynt* Gyles doune.
C. 4.122 And til *saynt* Iames be souhte there pore sykke lyggen,
C. 5.197 And ȝe þat seketh *seynt* Iames and seyntes [at] Rome,
C. 5.198 Seketh *seynt* treuthe in sauac[ioun] of ȝoure soules
C. 7.100 As he sayth hymsulf; *seynt* Ion bereth witnesse:
C. 7.137 A synful marie þe sey ar *seynte* marye þy dame
C. 7.202 'Y [nolde] fonge a ferthynge for *seynt* Thomas shryne;
C. 8.1 Qvod [perkyn] þe [plouhman], 'be *seynt* petur of Rome!
C. 8.54 'Y assente, by *seynt* Gyle,' sayde the knyht thenne,
C. 8.296 'By *seynte* Poul!' quod Peres, 'thow poyntest neyh þe treuthe
C. 9.37 'And y shal sende ȝow mysulue *seynt* Mihel myn Angel
C.10.89 And precheth to þe peple *seynt* paules wordes:
C.11.54 And prech[en] at *seynt* poules, [for] puyr enuye of clerkes,
C.11.151 That he seyh þe [syre] and þe sone and þe *seynt* spirit togederes
C.11.202 For clergie saith þat he seyh in þe *seynt* euaungelie
C.11.255 He was sunnere ysaued then *seynt* Iohn þe baptiste
C.12.99 And *seynt* Ion sethen saide hit of his techyng:
C.12.134 And *seynt* marie his moder, as Mathew bereth witnesse,
C.14.27 And sent forth the *seynt* espirit to do loue sprynge:
C.14.47 And *seynt* spirit þe saumplarie and said what men sholde wryte.
C.14.136 A[s] *seynt* Ioh[a]n and oþer seyntes þat haen [de]serued bettere.
C.14.142 A sit noþer with *seynte* Iohan, simond ne Iude,
C.15.98 And prouen hit by here pocalips and þe passioun of *seynt* Aueroy
C.16.153 Thus lered me a le[tte]red man for oure lordes loue, *seynt* Austyn:
C.16.222 "Beatus," saith *seynt* Bernard, "qui scripturas legit
C.17.235 Aȝen þe lore of oure lord as *seynt* luk witnesseth–
C.17.274 In sauacioun of mannes soule *seynte* Thomas of Canterbury
C.18.72 The whiche þe *seynt* spirit seweth, the sonne of al heuene,
C.18.113 Sampson and samuel and *seynt* Iohann þe Baptiste,
C.18.231 So oute of þe syre and of þe sone þe *seynt* spirit of hem bothe
C.18.267 Forthy y seke hym,' he saide, 'for *seynt* Iohann þe Baptiste
C.19.125 *Seynte* marie, a mayden, and mankynde lauhte:
C.19.165 That hoso synegeth in þe *seynt* spirit assoiled worth he neuere,
C.19.170 So hoso synegeth aȝeyn þe *seynt* spirit hit semeth þat he greueth
C.19.178 So doth þe sire and þe sone and *seynt* spirit togyderes
C.19.190 No more doth sire ne sone ne *seynt* spirit togyderes
C.19.268 Synegen aȝen þe *seynte* spirit, assente to destruye
C.19.280 And now am sory þat y so the *seynte* spirit agulte,
C.20.367 Songen *seynt* Iohann[es songe], ecce agnus dei.

seyntwarie n *seintuarie n.* C 1

C. 5.79 And taken Symondus sones *seyntwarie* to kepe,

seise v *seisen v.* A 1 sese; B 2 seise (1) seised (1); C 2 sese (1) sesed (1)

A. 2.66 In al þe signiure of slouþe I *se[se]* hem togidere;
B.13.374 To *seise* to me wiþ hir sikel þat I sewe neuere.
B.18.284 And siþen I [was] *seised* seuene [þousand] wynter
C. 6.271 To *sese* to me with here sikel þat y sewe neuere.
C.20.309 And sethen we haen ben *sesed* seuene thousand wynter

seist seiþ > siggen; *seiȝ* > seen; *seiȝe* > seen,siggen; *seiȝen* > seen; *sek* > seken; *seke* > seken,sik

seken v *sechen v.* A 16 sek (1) seke (7) seken (2) sekiþ (1) souȝt (3) souȝte (2); B 34 seche (3) seke (11) seken (3) sekest (1) sekeþ (5) souȝt (3) souȝte (7) ysouȝt (1); C 23 seche (6) secheth (2) seke (6) sekest (1) seketh (5) soughte (1) souht (2) souhte (5)

A.Pr.47 For to *seke* seint Iame & seintes at rome;
A. 3.119 Betwyn heuene & helle, & erþe þeiȝ men *souȝte*.
A. 4.49 Wrong was aferd þo & wisdom he *souȝte*
A. 4.109 Til seint Iame be *souȝt* þere I shal assigne.
A. 5.40 And ȝe þat *seke* seint Iame & seintes at rome,
A. 5.41 *Sekiþ* seint treuþe for he may saue ȝou alle
A. 5.232 I wile *seke* treuþe er I [se] rome.'
A. 5.254 To haue grace to *seke* treuþe; god leue þat hy moten!
A. 6.12 And sen be his signes whom he *souȝt* hadde.
A. 6.19 And *souȝt* goode seintes for my soule hele.'
A. 8.146 I myself & my sones, *seke* þe for nede.'
A. 9.2 Al a somer sesoun for to *seke* dowel.
A. 9.53 Þus I wente wydewhere dowel to *seken*,
A.10.99 But suffre & sit stille & *sek* þou no ferþere.
A.11.55 And so seiþ þe sauter, *se[ke]* it in Memento:
A.11.190 And *seken* out þe seke & sende hem þat hem nediþ,
B.Pr.47 For to *seken* Seint Iame and Seintes at Rome;
B.Pr.50 I seiȝ somme þat seiden þei hadde *ysouȝt* Seintes;

B. 3.130　Bitwene heuene and helle, [and] erþe þouȝ men *souȝte*.
B. 3.345　Tho ye [*souȝte*] Sapience sittynge in youre studie.
B. 3.348　And if ye *seche* Sapience eft fynde shul ye þat folweþ,
B. 4.63　Wrong was afered þ[o] and wisdom he *souȝte*
B. 4.126　And til Seint Iames be *souȝt* þere I shal assigne,
B. 5.56　And ye þat *seke* Seynt Iames and Seyntes [at] Rome,
B. 5.57　*Sekeþ* Seynt Truþe, for he may saue yow alle
B. 5.460　I shal *seken* truþe er I se Rome.'
B. 5.524　And se bi hise signes whom he *souȝt* hadde.
B. 5.531　And *souȝt* goode Seintes for me soul[e] hel[e].'
B. 7.169　I myself and my sones, *seche* þee for nede.'
B. 7.172　It bifel as his fader tolde, hise frendes þere hym *souȝte*.
B. 8.2　Al a somer seson for to *seke* dowel,
B. 8.62　[Th]us I wente widewher [dowel to *seke*,
B.10.69　And so seiþ þe Sauter; [*seke* it in memento]:
B.10.95　Nouȝt to fare as a fiþelere or a frere to *seke* festes,
B.10.333　That þis worþ sooþ, *seke* ye þat ofte ouerse þe bible.
B.12.39　*Seke* þow neuere Seint ferþer for no soule helþe.
B.12.217　And so I seye by þee þat *sekest* after þe whyes,
B.14.6　Wiþ þe sope of siknesse þat *sekeþ* wonder depe,
B.14.95　Ac satisfaccion *sekeþ* out þe roote, and boþe sleeþ and voideþ,
B.15.188　And yerne into youþe and yepeliche [*seche*]
B.15.400　Into Surrie he *souȝte*, and þoruȝ hise sotile wittes
B.16.108　And *souȝte* out þe sike and [saluede blynde and crokede,
B.16.171　After Piers þe Plowman; many a place I *souȝte*.
B.16.178　[I] *seke* after a segge þat I seiȝ ones,
B.16.249　And þus I *seke* hym', he seide, 'for I herde seyn late
B.17.5　'Nay', he seide, '[I] *seke* hym þat haþ þe seel to kepe,
B.17.326　He *sekeþ* and sekeþ til he slepe drye.
B.17.326　He *sekeþ* and *sekeþ* til he slepe drye.
B.19.164　Boþe Iames and Iohan, Iesu to *seke*,
B.20.382　To *seken* Piers þe Plowman, þat pryde [myȝte] destruye,
C.Pr.48　To *seke* seynt Iame and seyntes [at] Rome;
C. 3.167　Bytwene heuene and helle, and erthe thogh men *soughte*.
C. 3.353　*Seketh* and seweth his sustantif sauacioun,
C. 3.496　So hoso [*s*]*echeth* sapience fynde he shal [that] foloweth
C. 4.66　Tho was wrong afered and wisdom a *souhte*,
C. 4.122　And til saynt Iames be *souhte* there pore sykke lyggen,
C. 5.197　And ȝe þat *seketh* seynt Iames and seyntes [at] Rome,
C. 5.198　*Seketh* seynt treuthe in sauac[ioun] of ȝoure soules
C. 7.169　And se by [his] signes wham a *souht* hadde.
C. 7.176　[And] *souht* gode seyntes for my soule helthe.'\
C. 9.313　Y mysulue and my sones, *seche* the for nede.'
C. 9.316　His eleuene bretherne hym for nede *souhte*
C.10.2　Alle a somur seson for to *seke* dowel
C.14.156　And so y sey by þe þat *sekest* aftur þe whyes,
C.16.295　For thogh me *souhte* alle þe sektes of susturne and bretherne
C.16.331　Thenne ȝerneth he into ȝouthe and ȝeepliche he *secheth*
C.17.169　Forthy *souhte* [he] into surie and sotiled how he myhte
C.18.267　Forthy y *seke* hym,' he saide, 'for seynt Iohann þe Baptiste
C.19.7　'Nay,' he saide, 'y *seke* hym þat hath þe seel to kepe,
C.19.306　A *seketh* and seketh til he slepe druye.
C.19.306　A *seketh* and *seketh* til he slepe druye.
C.21.164　Bothe Iames and Iohann, iesu to *seke*,
C.22.382　To *seke* [Peres the Plouhman], þat pruyde myhte destruye,

sekenes(se > siknesse

seketoures n *secutour n. cf. executours* B 1; C 4 secatours (1) secutours (1) seketoures (1) secutors (1)
B.15.248　And for his *seketoures* & his seruauntȝ, & som for hir children].
C. 2.192　On *secatours* and such men cometh softly aftur.
C. 6.254　Shal neuere *seketoure[s]* wel bysette the syluer þat thow hem leuest
C.16.279　*Seketours* and sodenes, somnours and here lemmanes
C.22.291　As sisours and *secutours*; they shal ȝeue þe freres

seknesse > siknesse; sekte(s > secte; sel > seel; selcouth(- > selkouþ

selde adv *selde adv.* A 4; B 15; C 17
A.Pr.20　Summe putte hem to plouȝ, pleiȝede ful *selde*,
A. 5.105　'I am sory,' quaþ enuye, 'I am but *selde* oþere,
A.10.104　Þat *selde* m[os]eþ þe marbil þat men ofte [t]reden,
A.10.108　Thrift oþer þedom with þo is *selde* yseiȝe:
B.Pr.20　Some putten hem to plouȝ, pleiden ful *selde*,
B. 5.128　'I am sory', quod [enuye], 'I am but *selde* ooþer,
B. 5.404　Goddes peyne and his passion [pure] *selde* þenke I on.
B. 9.155　And haue a Sauour after þe sire; *selde* sestow ooþer:
B.10.404　As þei seyen hemself *selde* doon þerafter.
B.10.476　That seruauntȝ þat seruen lordes *selde* fallen in arerage,
B.14.2　Thouȝ it be soiled and *selde* clene: I slepe þerInne o nyȝtes;
B.14.155　Ac it is but *selde* yseien, as by holy seintes bokes,
B.14.178　And in somer tyme *selde* soupen on þe fulle.
B.14.288　*Selde* sit pouerte þe soþe to declare,
B.14.291　*Selde* is any poore yput to punysshen any peple.

B.14.294　*Selde* is poore [riȝt] riche but of riȝtful heritage.
B.15.232　In þat secte siþþe to *selde* haþ he ben [knowe].
B.15.237　In court amonges [þe commune] he comeþ but *selde*
B.15.275　In spekes and spelonkes; *selde* speken togideres.
C.Pr.22　Somme potte hem to plogh, playde ful *selde*,
C. 2.26　And *selde* soth sayth bote yf he souche gyle,
C. 2.130　For syuyle and thisylue *selde* fulfilleth
C. 6.93　'I am sory,'sayde enuye, 'y am [but] *selde* othur;
C. 6.252　That chaffared with my cheuesaunces cheued *selde* aftur.'
C. 7.20　Goddes payne and his passioun is puyre *selde* in my thouhte.
C.11.296　*Selde* falleth þe seruant so depe in arrerage
C.11.300　*Selde* falleth so foule and so depe in synne
C.16.4　And *selde* deyeth [he] oute of dette [þat] dyne[th] ar he deserue hit.
C.16.123　*Selde* syt pouerte þe soth to declare,
C.16.126　*Selde* is eny pore ypot to p[u]nesche eny peple.
C.16.129　*Selde* is pore rihte ryche but of rihtfole eritage.
C.16.357　In [þat] sekte sethe to *selde* hath he be [knowen].
C.16.362　Amongus þe comune in Court a cometh bote *selde*
C.17.10　To his selle *selde* cam and soffred be mylked.
C.18.66　Then tho that *selde* haen þe sonne and sitten in þe North half;
C.19.285　Ac hit is bote *selde* yseyen, there sothnesse bereth witnesse,

selden adv *selden adv.* A 1 seldom; B 5; C 1 seldom
A. 8.125　On salamonis sawis [*seldom*] þou beholdis:
B. 7.143　On Salomons sawes *selden* þow biholdest:
B.10.479　*Selden* falle so foule and so fer in synne
B.14.315　And *selden* deyeþ he out of dette þat dyneþ er he deserue it,
B.15.282　But *selden* and sondry tymes, as seiþ þe book and techeþ.
B.17.305　Ac it is but *selden* yseiȝe, þer sooþnesse bereþ witnesse,
C.11.234　*Seldom* ar they seyen so lyue as they lere;

seles > seel

seleþ v *selen v.* A 1 seliþ; B 1; C 3 sele (1) seled (1) seleth (1)
A. 3.137　Sire symonye & hireself *seliþ* þe bullis;
B. 3.148　Sire Symonie and hirselue *seleþ* [þe] bulles.
C. 3.88　And [t]how thei fillen nat ful þat for lawe is *seled*
C. 3.186　For symonye and heresulue *seleth* [þe] bulles.
C. 4.189　And þat vnsittynge suffraunce ne *sele* ȝoure priue lettres

self adj *self adj.,n.,& pron.* B 5 self (1) selue (4); C 8 sulue (7) suluen (1)
B. 1.204　Loue is leche of lif and next oure lord *selue*,
B. 5.487　And siþþe wiþ þi *selue* sone in oure s[u]te deidest
B. 7.132　And sheweþ vs by ensampl[e] vs *selue* to wisse.
B.11.251　And to oure Saueour *self* seide þise wordes:
B.20.43　That he seide in his sorwe on þe *selue* roode:
C. 7.207　Til ȝe come into Consience, yknowe of god *sulue*,
C. 7.255　Thow shalt se treuthe sitte in thy *sulue* herte
C.12.137　And to oure sauyour *sulue* saide þis wordes:
C.14.26　Ac Ar such a wil wexe worcheth go[d] *sulue*
C.17.179　And sothliche þat god *sulue* in suche a coluere lyknesse
C.18.95　Shollen serue for þe lord *sulue*, and so fareth god almyhty.
C.18.129　Who sholde fecche this fruyt, the fende or iesus *suluen*.
C.22.43　That he saide in his sorwe on þe *sulue* rode:

selis > seel; selk(e > silk

selkouþ adj *selcouth adj.* B 4 selkouþ (1) selkouþe (1) selkouþes (2); C 7 selcouth (3) selcouthe (3) selcouthe (2) selkouthe (1)
B.11.364　Manye *selkouþes* I seiȝ ben noȝt to seye nouþe.
B.11.367　And some soure and some swete; *selkouþ* me þouȝte.
B.12.131　[The] *selkouþes* þat þei seiȝen, hir sones for to teche.
B.15.589　Of *selkouþe* sores; þei seiȝen it ofte,
C.Pr.5　And say many selles and *selkouthe* thyngus.
C.12.46　He saide in here sarmon *selcouthe* wordes:
C.13.174　Mony *selcouthes* y seyh aren nat to segge nouthe
C.13.177　And some soure and some swete; *selcouthe* me thouhte.
C.14.75　And of the *selcouthes* þat þei sye here sones þerof þei tauhten;
C.17.300　And of *selcouthe* sores saued men fol ofte.
C.18.147　Ac tho that sey that *selcouth* sayde þat tyme

selle n *celle n.* A 2 cellis (1) sillis (1); B 1 selles; C 3 selle (1) selles (2)
A.Pr.28　As ancris & Ermytes þat holden hem in [here] *cellis*,
A. 7.133　Ankeris & heremytes þat holde hem in here *sillis*
B.Pr.28　As Ancres and heremites þat holden hem in hire *selles*,
C.Pr.30　As Ankeres and Eremites þat holdeth hem in here *selles*
C.17.7　Solitarie by hemsulue in here *selles* lyuede
C.17.10　To his *selle* selde cam and soffred be mylked.

selle v *sellen v.* A 8 selle (7) sellen (1); B 17 selle (12) sold (2) solde (3); C 19 selle (1) sold (2) solde (3) sull (1) sulle (10) sullen (2)
A. 3.81　And suffre hem to *selle* sumdel aȝens resoun.'
A. 3.183　And bar here bras on þi bak to caleis to *selle*,
A. 5.133　I bouȝte hire barly; heo breuȝ it to *selle*.
A. 5.169　And at þe newe feire nempnide it to *selle*.
A. 7.253　Þat fisik shal his furrid hood for his foode *selle*,

A. 7.290   But of þe beste & þe brunneste þat breusteris *sellen*.
A. 8.24   Aʒens clene consience here catel to *selle*.
A. 8.27   And siþen *selle* it aʒen & saue þe wynnyng,
B. 3.92   And suffre hem to *selle* somdel ayeins reson.'
B. 3.196   And bere hire bras at þi bak to Caleis to *selle*,
B. 5.132   Whan he *solde* and I nouʒt þanne was I redy
B. 5.217   I bouʒte hire barly; she brew it to *selle*.
B. 5.320   And at þe newe feire nempned it to *selle*.
B. 6.269   That Phisik shal hi[s] furred ho[od] for his fode *selle*,
B. 6.306   But of þe beste and þe brunneste þat [brewesteres] *selle*.
B. 7.22   Ayein clene Conscience hir catel to *selle*.
B. 7.25   And siþenes *selle* it ayein and saue þe wynnyng,
B.11.127   For may no cherl chartre make ne his c[h]atel *selle*
B.11.277   Or *selle* it, as seiþ þe book, and þe siluer dele
B.15.293   Som þei *solde* and som þei soden, and so þei lyued boþe.
B.15.365   By þe seed þat þei sewe what þei *sel[l]e* myʒte,
B.16.142   'I am *sold* þoruʒ [som] of yow; he shal þe tyme rewe
B.16.143   That euere he his Saueour *solde* for siluer or ellis.'
B.18.214   And suffrede to be *sold* to se þe sorwe of deying,
B.19.398   Ne after Conscience, by crist! while I kan *selle*
C. 3.120   'And soffre hem som tyme to *selle* aʒeyne þe lawe.'
C. 3.244   Vnconnynge is þat Consience a kyndom to *sulle*
C. 3.246   May nat be *sold* sothliche, so many part asketh
C. 6.97   When he *solde* and y nat thenne was y aredy
C. 6.225   Y bouhte here barly; [a] brew hit to *sulle*.
C. 6.377   And to þe newe fayre nempnede [hit] to *sull*;
C. 8.290   That fysik shal his forred hod[e] for his fode *sulle*
C. 8.328   Bote of þe beste and þe brouneste þat brewestares *sullen*.
C. 9.29   And sethe *sullen* hit aʒeyn and saue þe wynnyng[e],
C. 9.55   For hit is symonye to *sulle* þat sent is of grace,
C.12.62   For may no cherl chartre make ne his chatel *sulle*
C.12.164   Al þat thow has[t] here hastly go and *sulle* hit;
C.12.218   Vpholderes on þe hulle shal haue hit to *sulle*."
C.17.20   Som they *so[l]de* and som they s[o]de and so they lyuede bothe.
C.17.102   By the seed þat they sewe what þey *sulle* myhte
C.17.129   Withoute gyle and gabbyng gyue and *sulle* and lene.
C.18.157   And drof hem out, alle þat þer bouhte and *solde*,
C.20.223   And soffred to be *sold* to se þe sorwe of deynge,
C.21.398   Ne aftur Consience, bi Crist! [while] y c[an] *sulle*

selleris n *sellere n.* A 2; B 1; C 1 sullers
A. 2.44   For sisours, for somenours, for *selleris*, for beggeris,
A. 3.77   Of alle suche *selleris* siluer to take,
B. 3.88   Of alle swiche *Selleris* siluer to take,
C. 3.116   Of alle suche *sullers* seluer to take

selles n *selli n.* &> selle C 1
C.Pr.5   And say many *selles* and selkouthe thyngus.

sellynge ger *sellinge ger.* B 1; C 1 sullyng
B.19.235   [By] *sellynge* and buggynge hir bilyue to wynne.
C.21.235   [By] *sullyng* and buggynge here bileue to wynne.

selue > self; seluer > siluer

seluerles adj *silverles adj.* C 1
C. 9.119   For a sent hem forth *seluerles* in a somur garnement

sem > seem

semblable adj *semblable adj.* B 2; C 5
B.10.371   And seiþ "slee noʒt þat *semblable* is to myn owene liknesse
B.18.10   Oon *semblable* to þe Samaritan and somdeel to Piers þe Plow[man]
C. 3.335   On a sad and a siker *semblable* to hemsuluen.
C.10.158   And *semblable* in soule to god but if synne him make.
C.16.113   The whiche is syb to crist [hym]sulue and *semblable* bothe.'
C.18.211   *Semblable* to hymsulue ar eny synne were,
C.20.8   Oen *semblable* to þe samaritaen and somdeel to Pers þe plouhman

semblant > semblaunt

semblaunce n *semblaunce n.* B 1
B.18.288   And in *semblaunce* of a serpent sete vpon þe Appultree

semblaunt n *semblaunt* A 1; B 1; C 1 semblant
A. 9.112   Sad of his *semblaunt* & of a softe speche,
B. 8.122   Sad of his *semblaunt* and of [a] softe [speche].
C.10.118   Sad of his *semblant* and with a softe speche.

semble n *semble n.* A 1
A.Pr.97   I sauʒ in þat *sem[b]le* as ʒe shuln here aftir,

seme > semest

semed v *semen v.(3)* &> semest B 1; C 1 semede
B. 1.153   For heuene myʒte nat holden it, [so heuy it *semed*],
C. 1.149   For heuene holde hit ne myghte, so heuy hit *semede*,

semede > semed,semest; semely > seemely

semeliche adv *semeli adv.* C 1
C.19.249   To go *semeliche* ne sitte, seth holy writ techeth

semest v *semen v.(2)* A 5 semide (3) semiþ (2); B 29 semed (8) semede
(1) semen (2) semest (2) semeþ (14) semynge (2); C 39 seme (1)
semed (1) semede (11) semest (1) semeth (21) semeþ (1) semyng (3)
A.Pr.32   As it *semiþ* to oure siʒt þat suche men þriuen.
A.Pr.85   Seriauntis it *semide* þat seruide at þe barre;
A. 5.60   He was as pale as a p[e]llet, [in] þe palesie he *semide*;
A. 5.124   To drawe þe list along, þe lengere it *semide*;
A.11.138   For þe more I muse þeron þe mistlokere it *semiþ*,
B.Pr.32   As it *semeþ* to oure siʒt þat swiche men þryueþ.
B.Pr.52   Moore þan to seye soþ, it *semed* bi hire speche.
B.Pr.212   Sergeantʒ it [s]*emed* þat serueden at þe barre,
B. 5.77   He was as pale as a pelet, in þe palsy he *semed*.
B. 5.208   To drawe þe [list] along, þe lenger it *semed*;
B. 5.501   And by so muche [it] *semeþ* þe sikerer we mowe
B. 9.42   And so it *semeþ* by hym [þere he seide in þe bible
B.10.186   The moore I muse þerInne þe mystier it *semeþ*,
B.10.261   Swich as þow *semest* in siʒte be in assay yfounde:
B.10.263   But be swich in þi soule as þow *semest* wiþoute.
B.10.279   Ac it *semeþ* now sooþly, to [siʒte of þe worlde],
B.12.169   'That swymme kan noʒt', I seide, 'it *semeþ* to my wittes.'
B.13.319   It was fouler bi fele fold þan it first *semed*.
B.13.345   *Semynge* to synneward, and som he gan taste
B.14.97   That it neuere eft is sene ne soor, but *semeþ* a wounde yheeled.'
B.14.140   So I seye by yow riche, it *semeþ* noʒt þat ye shulle
B.15.110   Than for to prechen and preuen it noʒt–ypocrisie it *semeþ*.
B.15.206   Loken as lambren and *semen* [lif]holy,
B.15.355   That no lif loueþ ooþer, ne oure lord as it *semeþ*.
B.15.393   For Sarʒens han somwhat *semynge* to oure bileue,
B.15.592   And by þat mangerie [þei] myʒte wel se þat Messie he *semede*;
B.16.59   And of o greetnesse and grene of greyn þei *semen*.'
B.17.39   The gome þat gooþ wiþ o staf, he *semeþ* in gretter heele
B.17.58   Ne helpe hymself sooþly, for semyvif he *semed*,
B.17.204   So whoso synneþ in þe Seint Spirit, it *semeþ* þat he greueþ
B.17.293   That shente vs and shedde oure blood, forshapte vs as it [*semed*]:
B.18.117   Hir suster, as it *semed*, cam so[fte]ly walkynge
B.19.447   It *semeþ* bi so hymself hadde his wille
B.19.456   And alle þo faire vertues as vices þei *semeþ*.
C.Pr.34   As it *semeþ* to oure sighte þat suche men ythryueth.
C.Pr.162   Seriantʒ it *semede* that serue[d] at þe barre,
C. 2.138   Hit *semeth* sothly riʒt so on erthe
C. 3.383   Ac þe moste partie of peple puyr indirect *semeth*
C. 5.27   That fynde[th] the thy fode–for an ydel man þow *semest*,
C. 5.53   And also moreouer me [*sem]eth*, syre resoun,
C. 5.90   Ac it *semeth* no sad parfitnesse in Citees to b[e]gge
C. 6.27   *Semyng* a souerayn oen whereso me byfull
C. 6.60   As to be preised amongus þe peple thow [y] pore *seme*:
C. 6.179   *Semyng* to synneward and summe y gan taste
C. 6.216   To drawe the lyst along the lengur hit *semede*;
C. 7.129   And sethe in oure secte, as hit *semed*, deyedest,
C. 7.141   And by so muche hit *semeth* the sykerloker we mowe
C. 7.299   Thenne was oen hihte actif; an hosbande he *semede*.
C. 9.105   A[nd] ʒut ar ther oþere beggares, in hele as hit *semeth*
C. 9.115   And to oure syhte as hit *semeth*; seth god hath þe myhte
C. 9.117   And suffreth suche go so, it *semeth* to myn inwyt
C.11.2   That ful lene lokede and lyfholy *semede*.
C.11.43   Thenne *semeth* hit to my sihte to suche þat so biddeth
C.11.84   *Semyng* þat y sholde bysechen here of grace.
C.11.127   Þe more y muse þer[i]n the mystiloker hit *semeth*
C.11.161   And continaunce made on clergie, to congeie me hit *semede*,
C.11.270   By that þat salamon saith hit *semeth* þat no wyht woet
C.13.73   Tythen here goed tre[u]liche, a tol, as hit *semeth*,
C.14.109   'He þat can nat swymmen,' y sayde, 'hit *semeth* to alle wittes.'
C.15.114   'Sertes, sire,' thenne saide y, 'hit *semeth* nou[th]e here,
C.15.303   And slepeth, as hit *semeth*, and somur euere hem followeth.
C.16.8   So y sey by ʒow ryche, hit *semeth* nat þat ʒe sholle
C.16.264   Then for to prechen and preue hit nat–ypocrisye hit *semeth*.
C.17.87   May no preyere pees make in no place hit *semeth*.
C.17.301   By þe myracles þat he made messie he *semede*
C.19.57   Ne helpe hymsulue sothly for semyuief he *semede*
C.19.170   So hoso synegeth aʒeyn þe seynt spirit hit *semeth* þat he greueth
C.19.274   That shent vs and shedde oure bloed, forschupte vs as hit *semede*:
C.20.62   The hard roch al toroef and riht derk nyht hit *semede*;
C.20.120   Here suster, as hit *semede*, cam softly walkynge
C.20.404   And for þat drynke today y deyede as hit *semede*.
C.21.447   Hit *semeth* bi so hymsulue hadde his wille
C.21.456   And al tho fayre vertues as vises thei *semeth*.

semyvif adj *semivif adj.* B 1; C 1 semyuief
B.17.58   Ne helpe hymself sooþly, for *semyvif* he semed,
C.19.57   Ne helpe hymsulue sothly for *semyuief* he semede

sen > seen

senatours n *senatour n.* C 1
C. 8.87   Maystres, as mayres and grete menne, *senatours,*

sende v *senden v.(2)* A 23 sende (6) sendiþ (2) sent (3) sente (10) senten
(1) isent (1); B 40 sende (10) sendest (1) sent (7) sente (21) senten
(1); C 47 sende (12) sendest (1) sent (4) sente (25) senten (2) ysent
(2) ysente (1)
A.Pr.76   His sel shulde not be *sent* to disseyue þe peple.
A. 1.156   Of such good as god *sent* goodlyche parteþ,
A. 2.165   Symonye & cyuyle, I *sen[d]e* hem to warne
A. 2.183   And *senten* hym on sundais wiþ selis to chirche,
A. 2.185   Þanne louride lechis & lettris [hy] *sente*
A. 3.240   God *sente* hym to segge þe samuels mouþ
A. 3.244   Samuel seide to saul, "god *sendiþ* þe & hotiþ
A. 3.251   And for he kilde not þe king as crist [him] bode *sente*,
A. 4.15   Seide hym as þe king *sente* & siþþe tok his leue.
A. 7.246   And *sende* þe of his saus to sauoure þi lippes,
A. 7.307   And so seiþ satourne & *sente* 3ow to warne.
A. 8.1   Treuþe herde telle hereof, & to peris *sente*
A. 8.25   Ac vndir his secre sel treuþe *sente* h[e]m a lettre,
A. 8.36   '[And] I shal *sende* myself seynt Michel myn aungel
A. 8.38   Þat I ne shal *sende* [3our] soule sauf into heuene,
A. 8.66   Ha[dde] þe same absolucioun þat *sent* was to peris.
A.10.24   Til kynde come oþer *sende* [and] kepe hire hymselue.'
A.10.100   And be glad of þe grace þat god haþ *Isent* þe.
A.10.157   Forþi he *sente* to se[þ], & se[i]de hym be an aungel
A.10.201   And [þanne] glade 3e god þat al good *sendiþ*.
A.11.179   And I sei[d]e, 'soþliche, þei *sente* me hider
A.11.190   And seken out þe seke & *sende* hem þat hem nediþ,
A.12.54   Sey I *sente* him þis segge, and þat he shewe hym dowel.'
B.Pr.79   His seel sholde no3t be *sent* to deceyue þe peple.
B. 1.182   [Of] swich good as god *sent* goodliche parteþ,
B. 2.204   [Symonye and Cyuyle, I *sende* hem to warne
B. 2.224   And *senten* hym [on Sondayes wiþ seles] to chirch[e],
B. 2.226   Thanne lourede leches, and lettres þei *sente*
B. 3.261   God *sente* to Saul by Samuel þe prophete
B. 4.15   [Seide hym] as þe kyng [*sente*] and siþen took his leue.
B. 5.484   For þoru3 þat synne þi sone *sent* was to erþe
B. 6.262   And *sende* þee of his Sauce to sauore þi lippes,
B. 6.326   And so sei[þ] Saturne and *sente* yow to warne.
B. 7.1   TReuþe herde telle herof, and to Piers *sente*
B. 7.23   Ac vnder his secret seel truþe *sente* hem a lettre,
B. 7.34   'And I shal *sende* myselue Seint Michel myn [a]ngel
B. 7.37   And *sende* youre soules in saufte to my Seintes in Ioye.'
B. 7.64   Ha[dde] þe same absolucion þat *sent* was to Piers.
B. 9.24   Til kynde come or *sende* [and kepe] hire [hymselue].'
B. 9.127   [For] god *sente* to Se[þ] and seide by an Aungel,
B.10.236   I seide to h[y]m sooþly þat *sent* was I þider
B.10.372   But if I *sende* þee som tokene", and seiþ Non mecaberis,
B.13.248   That he *sente* me vnder his seel a salue for þe pestilence,
B.13.391   And if I *sente* ouer see my seruaunt3 to Brugges,
B.14.21   And siþen *sende* þee to Satisfaccion for to [sonnen] it after:
B.14.115   And after þow *sendest* hem somer þat is hir souereyn ioye
B.14.119   But god *sente* hem som tyme som manere Ioye
B.14.164   Now, lord, *sende* hem somer, and som maner ioye,
B.15.305   Ac god *sente* hem foode by foweles and by no fierse beestes
B.15.511   [Whan þe hye kyng of heuene *sente* his sone to erþe
B.16.195   *Sente* forþ his sone as for seruaunt þat tyme
B.16.243   And siþþe he *sente* me to seye I sholde do sacrifise
B.17.149   Bitoknen sooþly þe sone þat *sent* was til erþe,
B.18.170   But [loue] *sente* hire som lettre what þis light bymeneþ
B.18.182   Loue þat is my lemman swiche lettres me *sente*
B.19.291   To suffren al þat god *sente*, siknesse and Angres.
B.19.339   And *sente* forþ Surquidous, his sergeaunt of Armes,
B.19.432   And *sent* þe sonne to saue a cursed mannes tilþe
B.20.81   And *sente* forþ his forreyours, Feueres and Fluxes,
B.20.111   And bihighte hem long lif, and lecherie he *sente*
B.20.205   And hold þee þere euere til I *sende* for þee.
B.20.309   Some liked no3t þis leche and lettres þei *sente*
B.20.385   And *sende* me hap and heele til I haue Piers þe Plowman.'
C.Pr.77   His seel sholde nou3t be *ysent* in deseyte of þe peple.
C. 1.178   Of such good as god *sent* goodliche parte,
C. 2.234   And *senten* hym on sonendayes with seeles to churche,
C. 2.236   Thenne lourede leches and lettre[s] thei *sente*
C. 2.246   Symonye and syuile *senten* to Rome,
C. 3.95   That so bigileth hem of here goed, þat god on hem *sende*
C. 3.129   And *sente* to se here; y myhte nat se þat ladde here.
C. 3.414   How god *sente* to sauel be samuel þe prophete
C. 4.190   Ne no supersedias *sende* but y assente,' quod resoun.
C. 6.189   Sotiled songes and *sente* out olde baudes
C. 6.278   And yf y *sente* ouer see my seruauntes to Bruges

C. 7.126   For thorw þat synne thy sone *ysent* was til erthe
C. 8.272   And *sende* the of his sauce [t]o sauery with thy lyppes
C. 8.345   And so sayth saturne and *sente* [3ow] to warne.
C. 9.1   Treuthe herde telle herof and to [Peres] *sente*
C. 9.27   Ac vnder his secrete seal treuthe *sente* hem a lettre
C. 9.37   'And y shal *sende* 3ow mysulue seynt Mihel myn Angel
C. 9.39   And *sende* 3oure soules þer y mysulue dwelle
C. 9.55   For hit is symonye to sulle þat *sent* is of grace,
C. 9.119   For a *sent* hem forth seluerles in a somur garnement
C. 9.200   And somme hadde foreynes to frendes þat hem fode *sente*
C.10.150   Til kynde come o[r] *sende* and kepe here hymsulue.'
C.10.249   And god *sente* to seth so sone he was of age
C.11.264   Mouhte sleylokeste be slawe and *sente* hym to w[e]rre,
C.13.12   And for he soffrede and saide nauht oure lord *sente* tookene
C.14.27   And *sent* forth the seynt espirit to do loue sprynge:
C.15.236   Tho[r]w the helpe of hym þat me hyder *sente;*
C.15.291   [And] aftur thow *sendest* hem somer þat is here souereyne ioye
C.15.295   Bote god *sen[t]e* hem som tyme sum manere ioye
C.16.17   Now, lord, *sende* hem somur som tyme to solace and to ioye
C.16.25   And *sende* vs contricion [clereliche] to clanse with oure soules
C.17.155   To þat lord þat hym lyf lente lyflode hym *sende.*
C.17.246   And crie to Crist a wolde his coluer *sende*
C.17.262   For when þe hye kyng of heuene *sente* his so[n]e til erthe
C.18.204   *Sente* forth his sone As for seruaunt þat tyme
C.18.260   And sethe a *sente* me to seyn and saide that y sholde
C.19.123   Bitokneth soethly the sone þat *sente* was til erthe,
C.20.173   Bote loue haue *ysente* her som lettre what this liht bymeneth
C.20.185   Loue þat is my lemman such lettres me *sente*
C.21.291   To soffre al þat god *sente*, seeknesse and angeres.
C.21.339   And *sente* forth surquido[us], his seriaunt[e] of Armes,
C.21.432   And *sente* þe so[nn]e to saue a corsed mannes tulthe
C.22.81   And *sente* forth his forreours, feueres and fluxes,
C.22.111   And bihihte hem long lyf and lecherye he *sente*
C.22.205   And halde the there euere til y *sende* for the.
C.22.309   Somme liked nat this leche and letteres they *sente*
C.22.385   And *s[e]nde* me hap and hele til y haue [Peres Plouhman]'.

sendel > sandel; sene > seen

seneca n prop *n.i.d.* B 2; C 1
B.14.309   Forþi seiþ *Seneca* Paupertas est absque sollicitudine semita._
B.20.275   And preche men of Plato, and preue it by *Seneca*
C.22.275   And preche men of plato and preuen hit by *seneca*

senes > siþen

seneschalles n *seneshal n.* C 1
C.Pr.93   And summe aren as *seneschalles* and seruen oþer lordes

sengle adj *sengle adj.* A 2
A.10.206   As betwyn *sengle* & sengle, siþþe lawe haþ ygrauntid
A.10.206   As betwyn sengle & *sengle*, siþþe lawe haþ ygrauntid

senne > siþen; sennes > synne,siþen

sense n *cens n.* B 2; C 1
B.19.75   Kynges come after, knelede and offrede [*sense*],
B.19.86   That o kyng cam wiþ Reson couered vnder *sense.*
C.21.75   Kynges cam aftur, knelede and offrede [*sense*],

sent(- > senden

sepulcre n *sepulcre n.* A 1; B 1; C 1
A. 6.14   'Fro synay,' seide, '& fro þe *sepulcre.*
B. 5.526   'Fram Synay', he seide, 'and fram [þe *Sepulcre*].
C. 7.171   'Fro synoye,' he sayde, 'and fro þe *sepulcre.*

seraphyn n *seraphin n.* A 1; B 1; C 1 Ceraphyn
A. 1.104   Cherubyn & *seraphyn*, such seuene & anoþer;
B. 1.106   Cherubyn and *Seraphyn*, swiche seuene & [anoþer];
C. 1.106   Cherubyn and *Ceraphyn*, suche seuene and anoþer,

serelepes adj *serelepes adj.* B 1; C 1 suyrelepus
B.17.167   And aren *serel[e]pes* by hemself; asondry were þei neuere;
C.18.191   'Su[t]he they ben *suyrelepus*,' quod y, 'they haen sondry names?'

sergeaunt n *sergeaunt n.* A 3 seriaunt (1) seriauntis (2); B 6 sergeant (1)
sergeant3 (1) sergeaunt (1) sergeaunt3 (3); C 4 seriant3 (1) seriaunt (1)
seriaunte (1) seriauntes (1)
A.Pr.85   *Seriauntis* it semide þat seruide at þe barre;
A. 3.91   And ofsente hire as swiþe; *seriauntis* hire fe[tt]e
A. 3.270   Shal no *seriaunt* for þat seruyse were a silk houue,
B.Pr.212   *Sergeant3* it [s]emed þat serueden at þe barre,
B. 2.209   And how þe kyng comaunded Constables and *sergeaunt3*
B. 3.102   And ofsente hire as swiþe; [*sergeaunt3* hire fette
B. 3.295   Shal no *sergeant* for [þat] seruice were a silk howue,
B.15.8   To *sergeaunt3* ne to swiche seide no3t ones,
B.19.339   And sente forþ Surquidous, his *sergeaunt* of Armes,
C.Pr.162   *Seriant3* it semede that serue[d] at þe barre,

C. 3.78　Bothe Schyreues and *seriauntes* and suche as kepeth lawes,
C. 3.448　Shal no *ser[i]aunt* for [þat] seruic[e] werie a selk houe
C.21.339　And sente forth surquido[us], his *seriaunt[e]* of Armes,

serk n *serke* n. A 1 serke; B 1; C 2
A. 5.48　Heo shulde vnsewe hire *serke* & sette þere an heire
B. 5.65　She sholde vnsowen hir *serk* and sette þere an heyre
C. 1.99　For thei sholde nother faste ne forbere the *serk*
C. 6.6　A sholde vnsowen here *serk* and sette þe[r] an hayre

sermon n *sermoun* n. A 4 sarmon (1) sarmonis (1) sarmoun (1) sermoun
　　(1); B 5 sermon (4) Sermons (1); C 6 sarmon (5) sarmons (1)
A. 3.82　Salamon þe sage a *sarmon* he made
A.11.245　& suche [[shewiþ] þis *sermoun* þat [sewiþ] aftir]:
A.11.274　Taken ensampl[e] of here sawis in *sarmonis* þat þei maken,
A.11.304　Seide þis for a *sarmoun*, so me god helpe:
B. 3.93　Salomon þe sage a *sermon* he made
B. 5.59　That seweþ my *sermon*;' and þus seyde Resoun.
B.10.460　Seide þus in a *sermon*–I seigh it writen ones–
B.12.278　Seyen in hir *Sermons* þat neiþer Sarsens ne Iewes
B.13.428　Sauen þoru3 hir *sermo[n]* mannes soule fro helle;
C. 3.121　Salamon þe sage a *sarmon* he made
C. 5.200　That sueth my *sarmon*;'[and] Thus [sayde] resoun.
C. 7.88　Sauen thorw here *sarmon* mannes soule fram helle;
C.11.286　Saide thus in his *sarmon* for ensau[m]ple of grete clerkes,
C.12.46　He saide in here *sarmon* selcouthe wordes:
C.14.200　Segen [in] here *sarmons* þat noþer saresynes ne iewes

serpent n *serpent* n. B 1
B.18.288　And in semblaunce of a *serpent* sete vpon þe Appultree

serteyne > *certein*; *sertes -is* > *certes*

seruaunt n *servaunt* n. A 4 seruauntis (3) seruaunts (1); B 14 seruaunt (4)
　　seruaunt3 (10); C 11 seruant (5) seruantes (1) seruauntes (5)
A. 3.204　*Seruauntis* for here seruyse, we se wel þe soþe,
A. 6.61　Ne none of here *seruauntis*, þat noi3e hem mi3te;
A. 7.227　And siþen he seide, his *seruaunt[s]* it h[er]de:
A. 7.239　For summe of my *seruauntis* ben seke oþer while;
B.Pr.95　And somme seruen as *seruaunt3* lordes and ladies,
B. 3.217　*Ser[u]aunt3* for hire seruyce, we seeþ wel þe soþe,
B. 5.426　And my *seruaunt3* som tyme: hir salarie is bihynde;
B. 5.574　Ne-noon-of-hire-*seruaunt3*-þat-noyen-hem-my3te;
B. 6.243　And [siþen] he seide–[hise *seruaunt3*] it herde–
B. 6.255　For some of my *seruaunt3* and myself boþe
B.10.476　That *seruaunt3* þat seruen lordes selde fallen in arerage,
B.13.391　And if I sente ouer see my *seruaunt3* to Brugges,
B.14.142　Ri3t as a *seruaunt* takeþ his salarie bifore, & siþþe wolde clayme
　　　　moore
B.14.257　And he his *seruaunt*, as he seiþ, and of his sute boþe.
B.15.248　And for his seketoures & his *seruaunt3*, & som for hir children].
B.16.193　Of hym[self] and of his *seruaunt*, and what [suffreþ hem] boþe.
B.16.195　Sente forþ his sone as for *seruaunt* þat tyme
B.19.436　As for hymself and hise *seruaunt3*, saue he is first yserued.
C. 3.273　*Seruantes* for here seruyse, [we see wel þe sothe],
C. 3.368　Sethe y, his sone and his *seruant*, sewe for his ryhte.
C. 6.278　And yf y sente ouer see my *seruauntes* to Bruges
C. 7.39　And my *seruauntes* som tyme here salerie is bihynde;
C. 7.221　Ne-none-of-here-*seruauntes*-þat-nuye-hem-myhte;
C. 8.267　For somme of my *seruauntes* and mysulf bothe
C.11.296　Selde falleth þe *seruant* so depe in arerage,
C.16.97　And he [h]is *seruant*, a[s] he saith, and of his se[u]te bothe.
C.18.202　Of hymsulue and his *seruant*, and what soffreth hem bothe.
C.18.204　Sente forth his sone As for *seruant* þat tyme
C.21.436　As for hymsulue and his *seruauntes*, saue he is furste yserued.

serued v1 *serven* v.(2) &> *seruen* C 1
C.12.119　To haue as we haen *serued*, as holy chirche witnesseth:

seruen v2 *serven* v.(1) A 18 serue (10) seruen (3) seruid (1) seruide (2)
　　seruiþ (1) yseruid (1); B 34 serue (8) serued (4) serueden (1) seruen
　　(13) serueþ (5) yserued (3); C 33 serue (12) serued (4) seruen (7)
　　serueth (5) yserued (5)
A.Pr.85　Seriauntis it semide þat *seruide* at þe barre;
A.Pr.91　Become clerkis of acountis þe king for to *serue*;
A. 1.97　[Di]de hem swere on h[ere] swerd to *serue* treuþe euere.
A. 2.65　Wiþ alle þe delites of lust þe deuil for to *serue*,
A. 2.134　Þat somenours shulde be sadelid & *serue* hem ichone,
A. 2.140　Shuln *serue* myself þat cyuyle hatte;
A. 2.176　Aparailide hym as a prentice þe peple to *serue*.
A. 3.197　To 3iuen hise men mede þat mekly hym *seruen*,
A. 4.2　3e shuln sau3te, forsoþe, & *serue* me boþe.
A. 5.115　For sum tyme I *seruide* symme at þe nok
A. 5.182　And haue hikkes hood þe hostiller, & holde hym *yseruid*,
A. 6.28　And dede me sure hym [siþþe] to *serue* hym for euere;
A. 6.36　For, þei3 I sey it myself, I *serue* hym to pay.

A. 6.104　Ac þere arn seuene sistris þat [*seruen*] treuþe euere,
A.10.13　And *seruiþ* þis lady lelly boþe late & raþe.
A.11.22　And ben *seruid* as sires þat serue þe deuil
A.11.22　And ben *seruid* as sires þat *serue* þe deuil
A.11.300　For I shal graunte 30w grace of god þat 3e *seruen*,
B.Pr.92　Somme *seruen* þe kyng and his siluer tellen
B.Pr.95　And somme *seruen* as seruaunt3 lordes and ladies,
B.Pr.131　But suffren and *seruen*; forþi seide þe Aungel.
B.Pr.212　Sergeant3 it [s]emed þat *serueden* at þe barre,
B. 1.99　Dide hem sweren on hir swerd to *seruen* truþe euere.
B. 2.170　That Somonours sholde be Sadeled and *seruen* hem echone,
B. 2.179　Shul *seruen* myself þat Cyuyle is nempned.
B. 2.217　Apparailed hym as [a p]rentice þe peple to *serue*.
B. 3.210　To yeue [hise men mede] þat mekely hym *serueþ*,
B. 4.2　Ye shul sau3tne, forsoþe, and *serue* me boþe.
B. 5.155　I haue be cook in hir kichene and þe Couent *serued*
B. 5.199　For som tyme I *serued* Symme atte [Nok]
B. 5.333　And haue Hikkes hood [þe] hostiler and holden hym *yserued*,
B. 5.412　Come I to Ite missa est I holde me *yserued*.
B. 5.438　Forsleuþed in my seruice til it my3te *serue* no man.
B. 5.540　And diden me suren hym [siþþen] to *seruen* hym for euere;
B. 5.549　For þou3 I seye it myself I *serue* hym to paye;
B. 5.618　A[c] þer are seuen sustren þat *seruen* truþe euere
B. 9.13　To *seruen* þis lady leelly, boþe late and raþe.
B. 9.63　For þei *seruen* Sathan hir soules shal he haue;
B.10.476　That seruaunt3 þat *seruen* lordes selde fallen in arerage,
B.11.91　'And wherof *serueþ* law', quod lewtee, 'if no lif vndertoke it
B.11.279　For failed neuere man mete þat my3tful god *serueþ*;
B.11.281　To *serue* god goodliche, ne greueþ hym no penaunce:
B.12.103　[And ri3t as si3t *serueþ* a man to se þe hei3e strete]
B.12.205　But by hymself as a soleyn and *serued* on [þe] erþe.
B.12.208　And for to *seruen* a Seint and swich a þef togideres,
B.13.38　And *serued* hem þus soone of sondry metes manye,
B.13.120　'I haue seuene sones', he seide, *seruen* in a Castel
B.13.226　A wafrer, wol ye wite, and *serue* manye lordes,
B.14.254　And þou3 Sleuþe suwe pouerte, and *serue* no3t god to paie,
B.17.148　The fyngres þat fre ben to folde and to *serue*
B.17.211　[That *serueþ* þise swynkeres to se by ani3tes],
B.19.436　As for hymself and hise seruaunt3, saue he is first *yserued*.
C.Pr.90　Summe *seruen* þe kynge and his siluer tellen,
C.Pr.93　And summe aren as seneschalles and *seruen* oþer lordes
C.Pr.162　Seriant3 it semede that *serue[d]* at þe barre,
C. 1.103　Dede hem swere on here swerd to *serue* treuthe euere.
C. 2.185　That prestis and prouisores sholden prelates *serue*
C. 2.227　[A]paraylede hym [as a] prentys the peple to *serue*.
C. 3.266　To 3eue men mede þat meekliche hym *serueth*,
C. 3.310　That bothe the lord and the laborer be leely *yserued*.
C. 4.2　3e shal sauhtene, forsothe, and *serue* me bothe.
C. 4.33　'Here cometh,' quod Consience, 'þat Coueytise *seruen*.
C. 5.12　'Can thow *seruen*,' he sayde, 'or syngen in a churche
C. 5.61　Hit bycometh for clerkes Crist for to *serue*,
C. 5.69　Thyse bylongeth to labory and lordes kyn to *serue*.
C. 6.19　Inobedient to holy churche and to hem þat þer *serueth*,
C. 6.130　Y haue be coek in here kychene and the couent *serued*
C. 6.207　For som tyme y *serued* symme at þe style
C. 6.391　And haue hickes hood þe hostiler and holde hym *yserued*:
C. 7.185　And maden me sykere[n hym] sethen to *seruen* hym for euere,
C. 7.190　And *yserued* treuthe sothly, somdel to paye.
C. 7.193　And thow y sey hit mysulf y *serue* hym to paye;
C. 7.270　Ac ther ben seuene susteres þat *seruen* treuthe euere
C.10.140　To *serue* þat lady leely bot[h] late and rathe.
C.10.298　A3en dowel they do yuele and þe deuel *serue*
C.12.32　'And wherof *serueth* lawe,' quod leaute, ' and no lyf vndertoke
　　　　[hit],
C.14.48　And riht as syht *serueth* a man to se [þe hye strete],
C.14.144　Bote as a soleyn by hymsulue [and] *yserued* [o]n þe [erthe]
C.14.147　And for to *seruen* a seynt and suche a thef togyderes,
C.15.43　And *serued* hem thus sone of sondry metes monye,
C.16.94　And thow sleuthe sewe pouerte and *serue* nat god to paye
C.16.173　'Whareof *serue* 3e,' y saide, 'sir liberum arbitrium?'
C.18.95　Shollen *serue* for þe lord sulue, and so fareth god almyhty.
C.19.177　That *serueth* this swynkares to [see] by a nyhtes,
C.21.436　As for hymsulue and his seruauntes, saue he is furste *yserued*.

seruice n *servise* n. A 2 seruyse; B 6 seruice (5) seruyce (1); C 8 seruice
　　(4) seruise (2) seruyce (1) seruyse (1)
A. 3.204　Seruauntis for here *seruyse*, we se wel þe soþe,
A. 3.270　Shal no seriaunt for þat *seruyse* were a silk houue,
B. 3.217　Ser[u]aunt3 for hire *seruyce*, we seeþ wel þe soþe,
B. 3.295　Shal no sergeant for [þat] *seruice* were a silk howue,
B. 5.438　Forsleuþed in my *seruice* til it my3te serue no man.
B.13.52　'Here is propre *seruice*', quod Pacience, 'þer fareþ no Prince bettre.'
B.13.59　Pacience was proud of þat propre *seruice*
B.15.127　[He syngeþ *seruice* bokelees], seiþ it with ydel wille.

C. 3.273 Seruantes for here *seruyse*, [we see wel þe sothe],
C. 3.448 Shal no ser[i]aunt for [þat] *seruic[e]* werie a selk houe
C. 7.52 Forsleuthed in my *seruice* and set [hous] afuyre
C. 9.228 And vppon sonendayes to cese goddes *seruice* to here,
C. 9.232 Vcche halyday to here holly þe *seruise*,
C. 9.243 Where se we hem on sonendayes the *seruise* to here,
C.15.58 'This is a semely *seruyce*,' saide pacience.
C.15.63 Pacience was wel apayed of this propre *seruice*

sesares > cesar; sese > cessen,seise; sesed > seise; sesede > cessen

seson n *sesoun n.* A 2 sesoun; B 3; C 3 seson (1) sesoun (2)
A.Pr.1 IN a somer *sesoun* whanne softe was the sonne
A. 9.2 Al a somer *sesoun* for to seke dowel,
B.Pr.1 IN a somer *seson* whan softe was þe sonne
B. 8.2 Al a somer *seson* for to seke dowel,
B.13.350 Swiche werkes with hem were neuere out of *seson*
C.Pr.1 In a somur *sesoun* whan softe was þe sonne
C. 6.184 Such werkes with vs were neuere out of *sesoun*
C.10.2 Alle a somur *seson* for to seke dowel

sesse -iþ > cesse; sest(- > seen; set > sette; sete(n > sitten; seth > seen,seþ,siþen

seþ n prop *n.i.d.* A 4 seth (1) seþ (3); B 2; C 2 seth
A.10.153 [þat] of *seth* & his sistir siþþe forþ come
A.10.157 Forþi he sente to *se[þ]*, & se[i]de hym be an aungel
A.10.159 And siþen *se[þ]* & his suster [sed] wern spousid to kaymes;
A.10.179 And al for *se[þ]* & his sister children spouside eiþer oþer,
B. 9.127 [For] god sente to *Se[þ]* and seide by an Aungel,
B. 9.130 Yet [*seþ*], ayein þe sonde of oure Saueour of heuene,
C.10.248 *S[e]th*, adames sone, seth[en] was engendred.
C.10.249 And god sente to *seth* so sone he was of age

sethe(n > siþen

setis n *sete n.(2)* A 1
A. 8.39 And before þe face of my fadir fourme ȝoure *setis*.

sette v *setten v.* A 11 set (1) sette (8) setten (1) yset (1); B 30 set (5) sette (23) setten (1) yset (1); C 33 set (2) sette (25) setten (1) setteth (4) yset (1)
A. 1.39 [And þat] shend[iþ] þi soule; *set* it in þin herte;
A. 2.128 *Sette* mede on a shirreue shod al newe,
A. 4.18 '*Sette* my sadil vpon suffre til I se my tyme,
A. 4.32 And betwyn hymself & his sone *sette* hym a benche,
A. 5.48 Heo shulde vnsewe hire serke & *sette* þere an heire
A. 6.29 Boþe sowe [and *sette*] while I swynke miȝte,
A. 7.127 Boþe to *setten* & to sowen, & sauen his telþe,
A. 8.34 *Sette* scoleris to scole or [to] summe skynes craftis,
A.10.22 Þise sixe ben *yset* to saue þe castel;
A.11.125 Sey hym þis signe, I *sette* hym to scole,
A.11.127 And *sette* hire to sapience & to hire sauter yglosid.
B. 1.41 And that [shendeþ] þi soule; [*set*] it in þin herte.
B. 2.164 *Sette* Mede vpon a Sherreue shoed al newe,
B. 4.20 '*Set* my Sadel vpon suffre-til-I-se-my-tyme
B. 4.45 And bitwene hymself and his sone *sette* hym on benche,
B. 5.65 She sholde vnsowen hir serk and *sette* þere an heyre
B. 5.541 Boþe sowe and *sette* while I swynke myȝte,
B. 6.47 That he worþ worþier *set* and wiþ maunde blisse:
B. 6.169 And *sette* Piers at a pese and his plowȝ boþe,
B. 7.32 *Sette* Scolers to scole or to som [kynnes] craftes,
B. 7.156 To *sette* sadnesse in Songewarie for sompnia ne cures.
B. 7.200 I *sette* youre patentes and youre pardon at one pies hele.
B. 9.23 Thise [sixe] ben *set* to [saue] þis lady anima
B.10.173 Seye hym þis signe: I *sette* hym to Scole,
B.10.175 And *sette* hire to Sapience and to þe Sauter glose[d].
B.10.397 For many men on þis moolde moore *setten* hir hert[e]
B.11.2 And lakked me in latyn and liȝt by me *sette*,
B.12.122 Ne *sette* short bi hir science, whatso þei don hemselue.
B.12.187 Wel may þe barn blesse þat hym to book *sette*,
B.12.187 Riȝt as som man yeue me mete and [*sette* me amydde þe floor];
B.13.8 And [peple] þat was pouere at litel pris þei *sette*,
B.13.49 He *sette* a sour loof toforn vs and seide 'Agite penitenciam',
B.13.125 And *set* alle sciences at a sop saue loue one;
B.13.153 In a signe of þe Saterday þat *sette* first þe kalender,
B.15.224 And seintes *yset* [stille] charite hem folwede.
B.15.335 How I myȝte mo þerInne amonges hem *sette*.
B.16.36 Thanne *sette* I to þe secounde pil, sapiencia dei patris,
B.17.135 *Sette* [faste] þi feiþ and ferme bileue;
B.18.49 And *sette* it sore on his heed and seide in enuye:
B.18.219 *Sette* hym in solace and in souereyn murþe,
B.20.255 And *sette* [it] at a certain and [at] a siker nombre.
C.Pr.97 And boxes ben *yset* forth ybounde with yren
C. 1.119 For theder as þe fende fly his fote for to *sette*,
C. 4.20 *Sette* my sadel vpon soffre-tyl-y-se-my-tyme

C. 4.43 And bytwene hymsulue and his sone *sette* tho sire resoun
C. 5.97 And *sette* his los at a leef at the laste ende,
C. 6.6 A sholde vnsowen here serk and *sette* þe[r] an hayre
C. 7.52 Forsleuthed in my seruice and *set* [hous] afuyre
C. 7.186 Bothe to sowe and to *sette* þe while y swynke myhte
C. 7.262 For he hath enuye to hym þat in thyn herte *setteth*
C. 8.44 He worth rather reseyued and reuerentloker *s[e]tte*:
C. 8.166 And *sette* [Peres] at a [pes], playne hym whare he wolde.
C. 9.6 And alle þat holpe hym to erye, to *sette* or to sowe
C. 9.303 Ac men *setteth* nat by sowngewarie for me seth hit often fayle;
C. 9.346 Y *sette* nat by pardon a pese ne nat a pye hele.
C.10.149 Thise fyue ben *sette* for to saue Anima
C.11.115 And *sette* here to sapience and to þe sauter yglosed.
C.11.162 And lakkede [me in] latyn and lyhte by me *sette*
C.11.228 For mony men [o]n this molde more *sette* here herte
C.12.26 And now y am pore and penyles at litel pris he *sette[*th] me.
C.14.65 Ne *sette* shorte by here science, whatso þei doen hemsulue.
C.14.126 Wel may þe barne blesse þat hym to boek *sette*,
C.14.137 Riht As sum man ȝeueth me mete and *sette* me Amydde þe flore;
C.15.10 And peple þat was pore at litel pris [þei] *setten*
C.15.55 He *sette* a sour loef and saide, 'Agite penitenciam',
C.15.211 Y am sory þat y sowe or *sette* but for mysulue.
C.18.9 'The tree hatte trewe loue,' quod he, 'the trinite hit *sette*.
C.18.40 Thenne *sette* y þe seconde planke, sapiencia dei patris,
C.19.72 Enbaumed hym and boend his heued and on bayard hym *sette*
C.20.49 And *sette* hit sore on his heued and saide in Enuye:
C.20.228 *Sette* hym in solace and in souereyne merthe
C.20.291 *Setteth* bo[w]es of brake and brasene gonnes
C.20.293 *Set* Mahond at þe mang[n]el and mullestones throweth;
C.22.255 And *sette* hit at a serteyne and at a syker nombre

settynge ger *setting ger.* A 1 settyng; B 1; C 1
A.Pr.21 In *settyng* & sowyng swonke ful harde;
B.Pr.21 In *settynge* and sowynge swonken ful harde;
C.Pr.23 In *settynge* and sowynge swonken ful harde

seude > suwen; seute > sute

seuen num *seven num.* A 15 seue (9) seuen (1) seuene (5); B 29 seuen (12) seuene (17); C 31 seue (1) seuen (2) seuene (27) vii (1)
A.Pr.109 Al þis I sauȝ slepyng & *seue* siþes more.
A. 1.104 Cherubyn & seraphyn, such *seuene* & anoþer;
A. 3.135 As ȝoure secre sel in *seue* score dayes.
A. 4.73 'He sh[al] not þis *seue* ȝer se hise feet ones!'
A. 5.56 Wiþ þat he [shulde] þe satirday, *seue* ȝer þeraftir,
A. 5.122 It hadde be vnsold þis *seue* ȝer, so me god helpe.
A. 5.222 'Shal no sonneday be þis *seue* ȝer, but seknesse it make,
A. 6.104 Ac þere arn *seuene* sistris þat [seruen] treuþe euere,
A. 6.112 But ȝif ȝe be sibbe to summe of þis *seuene*
A. 8.162 Soulis þat han ysynned *seue* siþes dedly.
A. 9.17 *Seue* siþes, seiþ þe bok, [synneþ] þe riȝtful;
A. 9.23 'How *seue* siþes þe sadde man synneþ on þe day;
A. 9.39 Synnes þe sad man *seuene* [siþes] in þe day.
A. 9.66 'I haue sewide þe *seuene* ȝer; sei3e þou me no raþere?'
A.11.107 Is sib to þe *seuene* ars þat scripture is nempnid.
B.Pr.193 For I herde my sire seyn, *seuen* yeer ypassed,
B.Pr.231 [Al þis I sei3 slepyng and *seuene* sythes more].
B. 1.106 Cherubyn and Seraphyn, swiche *seuene* & [anoþer];
B. 3.58 It is synne of þe *seuene* sonnest relessed;
B. 4.86 '[He shal] noȝt þise *seuen* yer seen his feet ones!'
B. 5.73 Wiþ þat he sholde þe Saterday, *seuen* yer þerafter,
B. 5.206 It hadde ben vnsold þis *seuen* yer, so me god helpe.
B. 5.424 Sixe siþes or *seuene* I forsake it wiþ oþes.
B. 5.450 'Shal no Sonday be þis *seuen* yer, but siknesse it [make],
B. 5.618 A[c] þer are *seuen* sustren þat seruen truþe euere,
B. 5.627 But if ye be sibbe to some of þise *seuene*
B. 7.184 Soules þat haue synned *seuen* siþes dedly.
B. 8.21 *Seuene* siþes, seiþ þe book, synneþ þe rightfulle;
B. 8.27 'How *seuen* siþes þe sadde man [synneþ on þe day].
B. 8.43 Synneþ þe sadde man [*seuen* siþes a day].
B. 8.75 'I haue sued þee *seuen* yer; seye þow me no raþer?'
B.10.155 Is sib to [þe] *seuen* artȝ, [þat] Scripture is [nempned].
B.11.172 Or any Science vnder sonne, þe *seuene* artȝ and alle–
B.13.120 'I haue *seuene* sones', he seide, seruen in a Castel
B.13.122 Til I se þo *seuene* and myself acorde
B.14.69 *Seuene* slepe, as seiþ þe book, seuene hundred wynter
B.14.69 Seuene slepe, as seiþ þe book, *seuene* hundred wynter
B.14.202 For *seuene* synnes þer ben assaillen vs euere;
B.14.219 Ne none of þe *seuene* synnes sitten ne mowe þer longe,
B.15.74 And tellen men of þe ten comaundementȝ, and touchen þe *seuene* synnes,
B.15.296 I sholde noȝt þise *seuen* daies siggen hem alle
B.17.75 Wel sixe Mile or *seuene* biside þe newe Market;
B.18.284 And siþen I [was] seised *seuene* [þousand] wynter

B.20.215   And bisegede [sikerly] wiþ *seuene* grete geauntʒ
C.Pr.206   For y herde my syre sayn, *seuene* ʒer ypassed,
C.Pr.235   [Al þis y say slepynge and *seuene* sythes more].
C. 1.106   Cherubyn and Ceraphyn, suche *seuene* and anoþer,
C. 3.62   Hit is synne as of *seuene* noon sannour relesed.
C. 3.465   Here sauter and here *seuene* p[s]almes for alle synful preyen;
C. 4.82   Ther he sholde nat in *seuene* ʒer see his feet [ones].
C. 5.47   And my sauter som tyme and my *seuene* p[s]almes.
C. 6.108   Thow y sitte this *seuene* ʒer, y sholde nat wel telle
C. 6.214   Hit hadde be vnsold this *seuene* ʒer, so me god helpe.
C. 7.37   Sixe sithe oþer *seuene* y forsake hit with othes
C. 7.64   'Shal no sonday be this *seuene* ʒere, but seknesse hit make,
C. 7.270   Ac ther ben *seuene* susteres þat seruen treuthe euere
C. 7.278   And ho is sib to þis *seuene*, so me god helpe,
C. 7.280   Ho is nat syb to this *seuene*, sothly to telle,
C. 7.301   Were y *seuen* nyhte fro here syhte s[ynnen] he wolde
C. 8.348   Thre shypes and a schaef with [a *vii*] folwynge
C. 9.330   Soules þat haue syneged *seuene* sythes dedly.
C.10.23   *Seuene* sithe, sayth þe boek, synegeth day by day
C.10.31   'How *seuene* sithes þe sad man synegeth on þe day.
C.10.49   Synegeth *seue* sithe þe saddest man on erthe
C.10.73   'Y haue sued the *seuen* ʒer; saw thow me no rather?'
C.11.95   For he is sib to þe *seuene* ars–and also my suster
C.12.94   Or eny science vnder sonne, the *seuene* ars and alle–
C.15.268   *Seuene* slepen, as saith þe boek, more then syxty wynter
C.16.43   For *seuene* synnes þer ben þat ass[a]ilen vs euere;
C.16.60   Ne none of þe *seuene* synnes sitte ne may þer longe
C.17.99   Shipmen and sheepherdes by þe *seuene* sterres
C.17.115   That sholde þe *seuene* ars conne and assoile a quodlibet
C.19.74   Is syxe myle or *seuene* bisyde þe newe marcat,
C.20.309   And sethen we haen ben sesed *seuene* thousand wynter
C.22.215   And biseged s[iker]ly with *seuene* grete geauntes

seuenþe num *seuenthe num.* B 1; C 1 seuethe
B.14.310   The *seuenþe* is welle of wisedom and fewe wordes sheweþ
C.16.144   The *seuethe* is a welle of wysdoem and fewe wordes sheweth

sew > sowe; sewe > sowe,suwen; sewed(e sewen > suwen

seweris n *seuere n.(2)* A 1
A.11.311   Souteris & *seweris*; suche lewide iottis

sewest -þ sewide > suwen; sewiþ > sowe,suwen

seyen v *saien v. &> seen,siggen* B 1
B.14.279   Ac somdeel I shal *seyen* it, by so þow vnderstonde.

seying ger *seiinge ger.* A 1 segging; B 1
A. 9.102   'Ac ʒet sauouriþ me nouʒt þi *segging*, so me god helpe;
B. 8.112   'Ac yet sauoreþ me noʒt þi *seying*, [so me god helpe!

shaar n *share n.(1)* B 1; C 1 shar
B. 3.308   Into sikel or to siþe, to *Shaar* or to kultour:
C. 3.461   Into sykel or [t]o sythe, to *shar* oþer to coltur:

shabbide adj *shabbede adj.* A 1; C 1 shabbede
A. 8.17   How þat *shabbide* shep shu[l] here wolle saue,
C. 9.265   Thy shep ben ner al *shabbede*; the wolf shyt wolle:

shadde > shedde

shadweþ v *shadwen v.* B 1; C 1 shaddeweth
B.18.431   May no grisly goost glide þere it [*shadweþ*].'
C.20.475   May no grisly goest glyde þer hit *shaddeweth*.'

shaft n *shafte n.(1)* B 2 shaft (1) shafte (1)
B.11.397   The shap ne þe *shaft* þat god shoop hymselue,
B.13.296   Or feirest of feitures of forme and of *shafte*,

shaken v *shaken v.* B 1 shook; C 5 shak (1) shake (1) shaken (1) shaketh (1) shoke (1)
B.13.367   Or pryueliche his purs *shook*, vnpikede hise lokes.
C. 6.13   And shryue the sharpeliche and *shak* of alle pruyde.'
C. 6.266   Or priueliche his pors *shoke*, vnpiked his lokes.
C.18.47   And *shaketh* hit; ne were hit vndershored hit sholde nat stande.
C.18.104   'Leue liberum Arbitrium, lat some lyf hit *shake*.'
C.18.106   And *shaken* hit sharpeliche; the rype sholden falle.

shal v *shulen v.(1)* A 180 shal (91) shalt (19) sholde (1) shul (1) shulde (43) shuldist (3) shuln (22); B 490 shal (223) shalt (22) shaltow (10) sholde (153) sholden (8) sholdest (5) sholdestow (1) shul (56) shulde (1) shulle (6) shullen (5); C 463 schal (2) scholde (2) shal (251) shall (1) shalt (17) shaltow (6) shold (1) sholde (159) sholden (5) sholdest (3) sholle (6) shollen (4) shost (1) shulde (3) shullen (2)
A.Pr.76   His sel *shulde* not be sent to disseyue þe peple.
A.Pr.79   Þat þe pore peple of þe parissh *shulde* haue ʒif þei ne were.
A.Pr.97   I sauʒ in þat sem[b]le as ʒe *shuln* here aftir,
A. 1.2   And ek þe feld ful of folk I *shal* ʒow faire shewe.

A. 1.26   Þat þou worþe þe wers whanne þou werche *shuldist*.
A. 1.32   Dred delitable drynk & þou *shalt* do þe betere;
A. 1.40   And for þou *shuldist* be war I wisse þe þe beste.'
A. 1.46   ʒif þei [*shulde*] worsshipe þerwiþ cesar þe king.
A. 1.52   For riʒtfulliche resoun *shulde* rewele ʒow alle,
A. 1.90   Þe clerkis þat knowe it *shulde* kenne it aboute,
A. 1.92   Kinges & kniʒtes *shulde* kepe it be resoun,
A. 1.117   And alle þat werchen with wrong wenden þei *shuln*
A. 1.121   Mowe be sikur þat here soule *shal* wende into heuene,
A. 1.132   No dedly synne to do, diʒe þeiʒ þou *shuldist*.
A. 1.152   ʒe *shuln* be weiʒe þerwiþ whanne ʒe wende hennes.
A. 2.19   And so *shulde* [heo] not be for wrong was hire sire;
A. 2.50   In foreward þat falshed *shal* fynde hire for euere,
A. 2.92   ʒe *shuln* abigge boþe, be god þat me made.
A. 2.105   It *shal* besette ʒoure soulis wel sore at þe laste.'
A. 2.116   And seide, 'certis cesse *shuln* we neuere
A. 2.132   Þat symonye & cyuyle *shulde* on here fet gange.
A. 2.134   Þat somenours *shulde* be sadelit & serue hem ichone,
A. 2.136   Sire symonye hymself *shal* sitte on here bakkis;
A. 2.138   For þei *shuln* bere þise bisshopis & bringe hem at reste.
A. 2.140   *Shuln* serue myself þat cyuyle hatte;
A. 2.141   And let cartesadil þe Comissare, oure carte *shal* he drawe,
A. 2.158   *Shal* neuere man of þis molde meynprise þe [l]este,
A. 3.31   'Shal no lewidnesse hym lette, þe lede þat I louye,
A. 3.33   Þere cunnyng clerkis *shuln* clokke behynde.'
A. 3.39   I *shal* assoile þe myself for a sem of whete,
A. 3.49   Sikir *shulde* þi soule be heuene to haue'.
A. 3.51   Þat I ne *shulde* make or mende, & myn name writen
A. 3.52   Þat iche segge *shal* se I am sistir of ʒour hous.'
A. 3.73   Of þat þe pore peple *shulde* putte in here wombe.
A. 3.87   Þat fuyr *shal* falle & forbrenne at þe laste
A. 3.106   What þat his wille were & what he do *shulde*.
A. 3.190   He *shulde* haue be lord of þat lond in lengþe & in brede,
A. 3.230   *Shal* abiʒe it bitterly or þe bok liʒeþ.
A. 3.233   *Shal* haue mede on þis molde þat mattheu haþ grauntid:
A. 3.242   *Shulde* diʒe for a dede þat don hadde here eldren
A. 3.254   God seide to samuel þat saul *shulde* deiʒe,
A. 3.261   Þat resoun *shal* regne & reumes gouerne,
A. 3.262   And riʒt as agag hadde happe *shal* somme:
A. 3.263   Samuel *shal* slen hym, & saul shal be blamid,
A. 3.263   Samuel shal slen hym, & saul *shal* be blamid,
A. 3.264   And dauid *shal* be dyademid & daunten hem alle,
A. 3.266   *Shal* no more mede be maister on erþe,
A. 3.269   Leaute *shal* do hym lawe [and no] lif ellis.
A. 3.270   *Shal* no seriaunt for þat seruyse were a silk houue,
A. 3.275   Ac kynde wyt *shal* come ʒet, & consience togidere,
A. 3.276   And make of lawe a labourer, such loue *shal* arise.'
A. 4.2   ʒe *shuln* sauʒte, forsoþe, & serue me boþe.
A. 4.9   For he *shal* rewele my reaume & rede me þe beste
A. 4.10   Of mede & of mo oþere, what man *shal* hire wedde,
A. 4.16   'I *shal* araye me to ride,' quaþ resoun, 'reste þe a while,'
A. 4.27   And riden faste for resoun *shulde* rede hem þe beste
A. 4.57   I sey it be myself, þou *shalt* it sone fynde,
A. 4.71   [Þat wrong for his werkis *shulde* woo þole,
A. 4.73   'He *sh[al]* not þis seue ʒer se hise feet ones!'
A. 4.95   But resoun haue reuþe on hym he *shal* reste in þe stokkis
A. 4.109   Til seint Iame be souʒt þere I *shal* assigne,
A. 4.117   And ʒet,' quaþ resoun, 'be þe rode, I *shal* no reuþe haue
A. 4.122   *Shulde* neuere wrong in þis world þat I wyte miʒte
A. 4.130   Þat lawe *shal* ben a labourer & lede afeld donge,
A. 4.131   And loue *shal* lede þi land as þe lef likeþ.
A. 4.153   Ac redily, resoun, þou *shalt* not [raike] henne,
A. 5.17   In ensaumple, se[gges], þat ʒe *shulde* do þe betere;
A. 5.20   Þat dedly synne er domisday *shal* fordon hem alle.
A. 5.22   Ac I *shal* seiʒe as I saiʒ, so me god helpe,
A. 5.48   Heo *shulde* vnsewe hire serke & sette þere an heire
A. 5.50   'Shal neuere heiʒ herte me hente, but holde me lowe
A. 5.56   Wiþ þat he [*shulde*] þe satirday, seue ʒer þeraftir,
A. 5.102   ʒif shrift *shulde*, it shop[e] a gret wondir.
A. 5.113   He *shulde* wandre on þat walsshe, so was it þredbare.
A. 5.142   Ac I swere now, so þ[e I], þat synne *shal* I lete,
A. 5.173   Whoso hadde þe hood *shulde* haue amendis of þe cloke.
A. 5.181   In couenaunt þat clement [*shulde* þe cuppe felle],
A. 5.183   And whoso repentiþ raþest *shulde* rise aftir
A. 5.210   'Shal neuere fissh on þe Friday defie in my wombe,
A. 5.222   'Shal no sonneday be þis seue ʒer, but seknesse it make,
A. 5.223   Þat I ne *shal* do me er day to þe dere chirche
A. 5.225   *Shal* non ale aftir mete holde me þennis
A. 5.230   Þat iche man *shal* haue his er I hennis wende,
A. 5.248   Þat penitencia his pik he *shulde* pullshe newe
A. 6.11   And þe vernicle beforn for men *shulde* knowe
A. 6.56   And ʒe *shuln* lepe ʒe liʒtliere al ʒoure lif tyme;
A. 6.57   So *shalt* þou se swere nouʒt but it be for nede,

A. 6.59	Þanne *shalt* þou come be a croft, ac come þou nou3t þereinne;
A. 6.67	Þanne *shalt* þou blenche at a b[erw]e, bere no fals wytnesse;
A. 6.70	And þanne *shalt* þou [se] sey soþ, so it be to done;
A. 6.72	Þanne *shalt* þou come to a court, cler as þe sonne.
A. 6.86	And am sory for my synnes & so *shal* I euere
A. 6.93	Þou *shalt* se treuþe himself wel sitte in þin herte
A. 6.118	*Shulde* I neuere ferþere a foote for no freris preching.'
A. 7.8	'What *shulde* we wommen werche þe while?'
A. 7.9	'Summe *shal* sewe þe sak for shedyng of þe whete;
A. 7.16	For I *shal* lene hem lyflode, but 3if þe lond faile,
A. 7.27	I *shal* swynken & sweten & sowe for vs boþe,
A. 7.42	For þou *shalt* 3elde it a3en at one 3eris ende
A. 7.44	And mysbede nou3t þi bondemen, þe bet *shalt* þou spede;
A. 7.52	'And I *shal* apparaille me,' quaþ perkyn, 'in pilgrym[ys] wyse,
A. 7.60	*Shal* haue þe oure lord þe more here in heruist,
A. 7.63	I *shal* fynde hem foode þat feiþfulliche libbeþ,
A. 7.67	Deleantur de libro; I *shulde* not dele wiþ hem,
A. 7.71	His dou3ter hattiþ do ri3t [so] or þi damme *shal* þe bete;
A. 7.73	And deme hem nou3t for 3if þou dost þou *shalt* it dere abiggen,
A. 7.79	He *shal* haue my soule þat best haþ deseruid,
A. 7.83	Þe [k]ir[k]e *shal* haue my caroyn & kepe my bones,
A. 7.88	My wyf *shal* haue of þat I wan wiþ treuþe, & namore,
A. 7.95	My plou3pote *shal* be my pyk & putte at þe rotis,
A. 7.106	*Shulde* ben hirid þereaftir whan heruist tyme come.
A. 7.111	*Shal* no greyn þat here growiþ glade 3ow at nede;
A. 7.121	'3ef it be soþ,' quaþ peris, 'þat 3e seyn, I *shal* it sone aspie.
A. 7.125	3e eten þat [hy] *shulde* ete þat eren for vs alle.
A. 7.126	Ac treuþe *shal* teche 3ow his tem for to dryue,
A. 7.129	Or 3e *shuln* ete barly bred & of þe bro[k] drynke;
A. 7.131	Þei *shuln* ete as good as I, so me god helpe,
A. 7.134	*Shuln* haue of myn almesse al þe while I libbe,
A. 7.151	'Or þou *shalt* abigge be þe lawe, be þe ordre þat I bere'.
A. 7.156	'Now be þe peril of my soule!' quaþ peris, 'I *shal* appeire 3ow alle,'
A. 7.203	And he *shal* soupe swettere whanne he it haþ deseruid.
A. 7.217	In sudore & swynke þou *shalt* þi mete tilen
A. 7.221	He *shal* go [begge & bidde] & no man bete his hungir;
A. 7.228	"He þat haþ *shal* haue to helpe þere nede is,
A. 7.229	And he þat nou3t haþ *shal* nou3t haue ne no man him helpe,
A. 7.253	Þat fisik *shal* his furrid hood for his foode selle,
A. 7.304	He *shal* awake [þoru3] water wastours to chaste;
A. 7.305	Or fyue 3er be fulfild such famyn *shal* arise;
A. 7.306	Þoru3 flood [and] foule wederis fruytes *shuln* fa[i]lle,
A. 8.17	How þat shabbide shep *shu[l]* here wolle saue.
A. 8.36	'[And] I *shal* sende myself seynt Michel myn aungel
A. 8.37	Þat no deuil *shal* 3ow dere, di3e whan 3e di3e,
A. 8.38	Þat I ne *shal* sende [3our] soule sauf into heuene,
A. 8.47	Of princes & prelatis here pencioun *shulde* arise,
A. 8.53	*Shal* no deuil at his deþ day derie hym a myte
A. 8.81	Þat euere he was man wrou3t whanne he *shal* henne fare.
A. 8.90	For I *shal* construe iche clause & kenne it þe on englissh.'
A. 8.98	But do wel & haue wel, & god *shal* haue þi soule,
A. 8.100	Þat aftir þi deþ day to helle *shalt* þou wende.'
A. 8.104	I *shal* cesse of my sowyng,' quaþ peris, '& swynke not so harde,
A. 8.106	Of preyours & of penaunce my plou3 *shal* ben hereaftir,
A. 8.139	Þat [vncouþe] kni3t[is] *shal* come þi kingdom to cleyme;
A. 8.140	Among l[ower]e lordis þi londis *shuln* be departid'.
A. 8.145	'Beau fit3,' quaþ his fadir, 'for defaute we *shuln*,
A. 8.150	Manye tymes at mydni3t whan men *shulde* slepe,
A. 8.171	At þe dredful dom whanne dede *shal* arisen
A. 9.15	And euere haþ [as] I hope, & euere *shal* hereaftir.'
A. 9.22	'I *shal* sei3e þe, my sone,' seide þe Frere þanne,
A. 9.24	Be a forebisene,' quaþ þe Frere, 'I *shal* þe faire shewen:
A. 9.49	Ac 3if I may lyuen & loken I *shal* go lerne betere.
A. 9.94	Þanne *shulde* þe kyng come & casten hem in presoun,
A.10.37	Lif þat ay *shal* laste, & al his lynage aftir.
A.10.66	Ac þe fadir & þe Frendis for fauntis *shuln* be blamid
A.10.110	In ensaumple [þat] suche *shulde* not renne aboute,
A.10.171	"Bestis þat now ben *shuln* banne þe tyme
A.10.173	Alle *shuln* dei3e for his dedis be dounes & hilles,
A.10.176	Þat in þe [shynglid] ship *shal* ben ysauid;
A.10.177	Ellis *shal* alle di3en & to helle wenden."
A.10.189	Þat neuere *shal* bere [barne] but it be in armes.
A.10.203	*Shulde* no bedbourd be; but þei were boþe clene
A.10.205	Þat dede derne do no man ne *shulde*.
A.10.214	And aftir here deþ day *shuln* dwelle with þe same
A.11.99	In signe þat I *shulde* beseke hire of grace.
A.11.101	And seide, 'mercy madame, 3our man *shal* I worþe
A.11.105	I *shal* kenne þe to my cosyn þat clergie is hoten.
A.11.109	*Shuln* wisse þe to dowel, I dar wel vndirtake.
A.11.122	Þanne *shalt* þou se sobirte, & simplite of speche,
A.11.124	So *shalt* þou come to clergie þat can many wyttes.
A.11.206	And seide it in ensaumple þat þei *shulde* do þe betere:
A.11.217	Þis is þe lif of þis lordis þat lyuen *shulde* wiþ dobet,
A.11.243	Godis word witnessiþ we *shuln* 3iue & dele
A.11.256	I *shal* punisshen in purcatory or in þe put of helle
A.11.276	And 3if I *shal* werke be here werkis to wynne me heuene,
A.11.300	For I *shal* graunte 3ow grace of god þat 3e seruen,
A.12.14	That he shewe me hit ne *sholde* but 3if [I schriuen] were
A.12.46	I *shal* þe wisse [wynlyche] where þat he dwelleþ'.
A.12.51	'Þou *shalt* wende with wil,' quod she, 'whiles þat him lykyþ,
A.12.66	I *shal* felle þat freke in a fewe dayes.'
A.12.86	We han letteres of lyf, he *shal* his lyf ty[n]e.
A.12.96	Þou *shalt* be lau3th into ly3th with loking of an eye
B.Pr.79	His seel *sholde* no3t be sent to deceyue þe peple.
B.Pr.82	That þe [pouere peple] of þe parisshe *sholde* haue if þei ne were.
B.Pr.89	And signe þat þei *sholden* shryuen hire parisshens,
B.Pr.117	Casten þat þe commune *sholde* [hire communes] fynde.
B.Pr.130	Iangle ne lugge þat Iustifie hem *sholde*,
B.Pr.185	'Thou3 we [hadde] kille[d] þe cat yet *sholde* þer come anoþer
B.Pr.203	Þe neuere be cat ne þe kiton by my counseil be greued,
B.Pr.218	I sei3 in þis assemblee, as ye *shul* here after.
B. 1.2	And þe feld ful of folk I *shal* yow faire shewe.
B. 1.26	That þow worþe þe wers whan þow werche *sholdest*.
B. 1.34	Forþi dred delitable drynke and þow *shalt* do þe bettre;
B. 1.42	And for þow *sholdest* ben ywar I wisse þee þe beste.'
B. 1.48	[If] þei *sholde* [worshipe þerwiþ Cesar þe kyng].
B. 1.54	For ri3tfully reson *sholde* rule yow alle,
B. 1.92	The clerkes þat knowen [it] *sholde* kennen it aboute
B. 1.94	Kynges and kny3tes *sholde* kepen it by reson,
B. 1.128	And alle þat werchen with wrong wende þei *shulle*
B. 1.132	Mowe be siker þat hire soul[e] *sh[a]l* wende to heuene
B. 1.144	No dedly synne to do, deye þei3 þow *sholdest*,
B. 1.178	Ye *shulle* ben weyen þerwiþ whan ye wenden hennes:
B. 2.33	*Shal* be my lord and I his leef in þe hei3e heuene.
B. 2.35	That he *shal* lese for hire loue a l[i]ppe of Caritatis.
B. 2.38	And how ye *shul* saue yourself? þe Sauter bereþ witnesse:
B. 2.128	Ye *shul* abiggen boþe, by god þat me made!
B. 2.141	It *shal* bisitte youre soules [wel] soure at þe laste.'
B. 2.152	And seiden, 'certes, cessen *shul* we neuere
B. 2.168	For Symonye and Cyuylle *sholde* on hire feet gange.
B. 2.170	That Somonours *sholde* be Sadeled and seruen hem echone,
B. 2.172	Sire Symonye hymself *shal* sitte vpon hir bakkes.
B. 2.179	*Shul* seruen myself þat Cyuyle is nempned.
B. 2.180	And [lat] Cartsadle þe Commissarie; oure cart *shal* he [drawe]
B. 2.197	[Shal] manere man of þis molde meynprise þe leeste,
B. 3.32	'Shal no lewednesse [hym] lette, þe leode þat I louye,
B. 3.34	Ther konnynge clerkes *shul* clokke bihynde.'
B. 3.40	I *shal* assoille þee myself for a seem of whete,
B. 3.50	Syker *sholde* þi soule be heuene to haue'.
B. 3.60	And I *shal* couere youre kirk, youre cloistre do maken,
B. 3.63	That [ech] segge *shal* [see] I am suster of youre house.'
B. 3.84	[Of] þat þe pouere peple *sholde* putte in hire wombe.
B. 3.98	That fir *shal* falle & [forbrenne at þe laste]
B. 3.117	What his wille were and what he do [*sholde*].
B. 3.203	He *sholde* haue be lord of þat lond in lengþe and in brede,
B. 3.235	Lord, who *shal* wonye in þi wones wiþ þyne holy seintes,
B. 3.244	Swiche manere men, my leue, *shal* haue þis firste Mede
B. 3.251	*Shal* abien it bittre or þe book lieþ.
B. 3.254	[Shul] haue] Mede [on þis molde þat] Mathew [haþ] graunted]:
B. 3.263	*Sholden* deye for a dede þat doon hadde hire eldres.
B. 3.272	Spille it and spare it no3t, þow *shalt* spede þe bettre."
B. 3.276	God seide to Samuel þat Saul *sholde* deye
B. 3.285	That Reson *shal* regne and Reaumes gouerne,
B. 3.286	And ri3t as Agag hadde happe *shul* somme.
B. 3.287	Samuel *shal* sleen hym and Saul *shal* be blamed
B. 3.287	Samuel *shal* sleen hym and Saul *shal* be blamed
B. 3.288	And Dauid *shal* be diademed and daunten hem alle,
B. 3.290	*Shal* na moore Mede be maister [on erþe],
B. 3.292	Thise *shul* ben Maistres on moolde [trewe men] to saue.
B. 3.294	Leaute *shal* don hym lawe and no lif ellis.
B. 3.295	*Shal* no sergeant for [þat] seruice were a silk howue,
B. 3.299	Ac kynde loue *shal* come 3it and Conscience togideres
B. 3.300	And make of lawe a laborer; swich loue *shal* arise
B. 3.302	That Iewes *shul* wene in hire wit, and wexen glade,
B. 3.307	*Shal* be demed to þe deeþ but if he do it smyþye
B. 3.315	*Shal* neiþer kyng ne knyght, Constable ne Meire
B. 3.318	But after þe dede þat is doon oon doom *shal* rewarde
B. 3.321	Al *shal* be but oon court, and oon [burn] be Iustice,
B. 3.323	Batailles *shul* none be, ne no man wepene;
B. 3.325	And er þis fortune falle fynde men *shul* þe worste
B. 3.327	And þe myddel of a Moone *shal* make þe Iewes torne,
B. 3.328	And Sar3ynes for þat si3te *shul* synge Gloria in excelsis &c,
B. 3.329	For Makometh and Mede myshappe *shal* þat tyme;
B. 3.342	She *sholde* haue founden fel[l]e wordes folwynge þerafter:
B. 3.348	And if ye seche Sapience eft fynde *shul* ye þat folweþ,
B. 4.2	Ye *shul* sau3tne, forsoþe, and serue me boþe.

B. 4.9   For he *shal* rule my Reaume and rede me þe beste
B. 4.10   [Of Mede and of mo oþere, what man *shal* hire wedde],
B. 4.16   'I *shal* arraye me to ryde', quod Reson, 'reste þee a while',
B. 4.30   And riden faste for Reson *sholde* rede hem þe beste
B. 4.71   I seye it by myself, þow *shalt* it wel fynde,
B. 4.84   That wrong for hise werkes *sholde* wo þolie,
B. 4.86   '[He *shal*] noȝt þise seuen yer seen his feet ones!'
B. 4.108   But Reson haue ruþe on hym he lede afeld stokkes
B. 4.126   And til Seint Iames be souȝt þere I *shal* assigne,
B. 4.134   And yet', quod Reson, 'by þe Rode! I *shal* no ruþe haue
B. 4.139   *Sholde* neuere wrong in þis world þat I wite myȝte
B. 4.147   That lawe *shal* lede a laborer and lede afeld donge,
B. 4.148   And loue *shal* lede þi lond as þe leef likeþ.'
B. 4.177   Ac Reson *shal* rekene wiþ yow if I regne any while,
B. 4.179   Mede *shal* noȝt maynprise yow, by þe marie of heuene!
B. 4.181   And as moost folk witnesseþ wel wrong shal be demed.'
B. 4.190   Ac redily, Reson, þow *shalt* noȝt [raike henne];
B. 5.17   In ensample, [segges, þat ye] *sholden* do þe bettre;
B. 5.20   That dedly synne er domesday *shal* fordoon hem alle.
B. 5.22   Ac I *shal* seye as I sauȝ, so me god helpe,
B. 5.43   And dooþ it in dede, it *shal* drawe yow to goode.
B. 5.44   [Lyue] as ye leren vs; we *shul* leue yow þe bettre.'
B. 5.65   She *sholde* vnsowen hir serk and sette þere an heyre
B. 5.67   '*Shal* neuere heiȝ herte me hente, but holde me lowe
B. 5.73   Wiþ þat he *sholde* þe Saterday, seuen yer þerafter,
B. 5.197   She *sholde* noȝt [wandre] on þat wel[ch]e, so was it þredbare.
B. 5.292   For he *shal* answere for þee at þe heiȝe dome,
B. 5.293   For þee and for many mo þat man *shal* yeue a rekenyng:
B. 5.324   Whoso hadde þe hood *sholde* han amendes of þe cloke.
B. 5.332   In couenaunt þat Clement *sholde* þe cuppe fille,
B. 5.334   And whoso repente[þ] raþest *sholde* aryse after
B. 5.378   'This shewynge shrift', quod Repentaunce, '*shal* be meryt to þe.'
B. 5.382   '*Shal* neuere fyssh on [þe] Fryday defyen in my wombe
B. 5.386   'I moste sitte [to be shryuen] or ellis *sholde* I nappe,
B. 5.389   *Sholde* no ryngynge do me ryse er I were ripe to dyne.'
B. 5.393   'If I *sholde* deye bi þis day [I drede me sore].
B. 5.427   Ruþe is to here rekenyng whan we *shul* rede acountes:
B. 5.450   '*Shal* no Sonday be þis seuen yer, but siknesse it [make],
B. 5.451   That I ne *shal* do me er day to þe deere chirche
B. 5.453   *Shal* noon ale after mete holde me þennes
B. 5.458   That ech man *shal* haue his er I hennes wende;
B. 5.460   I *shal* seken truþe er I se Rome.'
B. 5.474   That penitencia his pik he *sholde* polshe newe
B. 5.478   'I *shal* biseche for alle synfulle oure Saueour of grace
B. 5.523   And þe vernycle bifore, for men *sholde* knowe
B. 5.569   And ye *shul* lepe þe liȝtloker al youre lif tyme.
B. 5.570   So *shaltow* se swere-noȝt-but-it-be-for-nede-
B. 5.572   Thanne *shaltow* come by a croft, [ac] come þow noȝt þerInne;
B. 5.580   Thanne *shaltow* blenche at a Bergh, bere-no-fals-witnesse;
B. 5.583   Thanne [*shalt* þow] see seye-sooþ-so-it-be-to-doone-
B. 5.585   Thanne *shaltow* come to a court, cler as þe sonne.
B. 5.599   And am sory for my synnes and so [*shal* I] euere
B. 5.606   Thow *shalt* see in þiselue truþe [sitte] in þyn herte
B. 5.633   *Sholde* I neuere ferþer a foot for no freres prechyng.'
B. 5.642   Thow *shalt* seye I am þi Suster.' I ne woot where þei bicome.
B. 6.8   'What *sholde* we wommen werche þe while?'
B. 6.9   'Somme *shul* sowe þe sak for shedyng of þe Whete.
B. 6.17   For I *shal* lenen hem liflode but if þe lond faille
B. 6.25   I *shal* swynke and swete and sowe for vs boþe,
B. 6.35   To fulfille þis forward þouȝ I fiȝte *sholde*.
B. 6.36   Als longe as I lyue I *shal* þee mayntene.'
B. 6.43   For þow *shalt* yelde it ayein at one yeres [ende]
B. 6.45   And mysbede noȝt þi bondem[a]n, þe bettre [*shalt*] þow spede;
B. 6.57   'And I *shal* apparaille me', quod Perkyn, 'in pilgrymes wise
B. 6.66   *Shal* haue leue, by oure lord, to lese here in heruest
B. 6.69   I *shal* fynden hem fode þat feiþfulliche libbeþ,
B. 6.75   Deleantur de libro viuencium; I *sholde* noȝt dele wiþ hem,
B. 6.79   His douȝter hiȝte do-riȝt-so-or-þi-dame-*shal*-þee-bete;
B. 6.81   Deme-hem-noȝt-for-if-þow-doost-þow-*shalt*-it-deere-abugge-
B. 6.87   He *shal* haue my soule þat best haþ deserued.
B. 6.91   The kirke *shal* haue my caroyne and kepe my bones
B. 6.96   My wif *shal* haue of þat I wan wiþ truþe and na moore,
B. 6.103   My plow[pote] *shal* be my pi[k] and [putte at] þe rotes,
B. 6.114   *Sholde* be hired þerafter whan heruest tyme come.
B. 6.119   *Shal* no greyn þat [here] groweþ glade yow at nede;
B. 6.129   'If it be sooþ', quod Piers, 'þat ye seyn, I *shal* it soone aspie.
B. 6.134   Ac truþe *shal* teche yow his teme to dryue,
B. 6.135   Or ye *shul* eten barly breed and of þe broke drynke;
B. 6.137   [Thei] *shal* ete [as good as I, so me god helpe],
B. 6.146   And na moore er morwe, myn almesse *shul* þei haue,
B. 6.148   Ac Robert Renaboute *shal* [riȝt] noȝt haue of myne,
B. 6.150   Thei *shul* haue payn and potage and [a pitaunce biside],
B. 6.166   'Or þow *shalt* abigge by þe lawe, by þe ordre þat I bere!'

B. 6.171   'Now by þe peril of my soule!' quod Piers, 'I *shal* apeire yow alle',
B. 6.217   And he *shal* soupe swetter whan he it haþ deserued.
B. 6.228   And biloue þee amonges [lowe] men: so *shaltow* lacche grace.'
B. 6.233   In sudore and swynk þow *shalt* þi mete tilie
B. 6.237   He *shal* [go] begge and bidde and no man bete his hunger.
B. 6.244   "He þat haþ *shal* haue and helpe þere [nede is]
B. 6.245   And he þat noȝt haþ *shal* noȝt haue and no man hym helpe,
B. 6.269   That Phisik *shal* hi[s] furred ho[od] for his fode selle,
B. 6.323   He *shal* awake [þoruȝ] water wastours to chaste;
B. 6.324   Er fyue [yer] be fulfilled swich famyn *shal* aryse.
B. 6.325   Thoruȝ flo[od] and foule wedres fruytes *shul* faille,
B. 6.329   Thanne *shal* deeþ wiþdrawe and derþe be Iustice,
B. 7.13   Bysshopes yblessed, if þei ben as þei *sholde*
B. 7.34   'And I *shal* sende myselue Seint Michel myn [a]ngel
B. 7.35   That no deuel *shal* yow dere ne [in youre deying fere yow],
B. 7.43   Pledours *sholde* peynen hem to plede for swiche and helpe;
B. 7.44   Princes and prelates *sholde* paie for hire trauaille.
B. 7.51   *Shal* no deuel at his deeþ day deren hym a myte
B. 7.56   That neuere *shul* wexe ne wanye wiþouten god hymselue.
B. 7.71   Anoþer that were moore nedy; so þe nedieste *sholde* be holpe.
B. 7.99   That euere [he was man] wroȝt whan [he] *shal* hennes fare.
B. 7.108   For I [*shal*] construe ech clause and kenne it þee on englissh.'
B. 7.116   But do wel and haue wel, and god *shal* haue þi soule,
B. 7.118   [That] after þi deeþ day þe deuel *shal* haue þi soule.'
B. 7.122   I *shal* cessen of my sowyng', quod Piers, '& swynke noȝt so harde,
B. 7.124   Of preieres and of penaunce my plouȝ *shal* ben herafter,
B. 7.125   And wepen whan I *sholde* [werche] þouȝ whete breed me faille.
B. 7.161   That vnkouþe knyȝtes *shul* come þi kyngdom to cleyme;
B. 7.162   Amonges lower lordes þi lond *shal* ben departed.'
B. 7.168   'Beau fitȝ', quod his fader, 'for defaute we *shullen*,
B. 7.193   At þe dredful dome, whan dede *shulle* rise
B. 8.19   And euere haþ as I hope, and euere *shal* herafter.'
B. 8.26   'I *shal* seye þee, my sone', seide þe frere þanne,
B. 8.28   By a forbisne', quod þe frere, 'I *shal* þee faire shewe.
B. 8.58   Ac if I may lyue and loke I *shal* go lerne bettre.'
B. 8.104   Thanne [*sholde*] þe kyng come and casten hem in [prison,
B. 9.39   Right as a lord *sholde* make lettres; [if] hym lakked parchemyn,
B. 9.49   Lif þat ay *shal* laste, [and] al his lynage after.
B. 9.63   For þei seruen Sathan hir soules *shal* he haue;
B. 9.66   Allas þat drynke *shal* fordo þat god deere bouȝte,
B. 9.79   *Shul* [purchace] penaunce in purgatorie but þei hem helpe.
B. 9.82   *Sholde* no cristene creature cryen at þe yate
B. 9.83   Ne faille payn ne potage and prelates dide as þei *sholden*.
B. 9.86   Allas þat a cristene creature *shal* be vnkynde til anoþer!
B. 9.90   [So] Iewes [*shul*] ben oure loresmen, shame to vs alle!
B. 9.91   The commune for hir vnkyndenesse, I drede me, *shul* abye;
B. 9.92   Bisshopes *shul* be blamed for beggeres sake.
B. 9.140   Beestes þat now ben *shul* banne þe tyme
B. 9.142   Alle *shul* deye for hise dedes by [dounes] and hulles,
B. 9.145   That in [þe] shyngled ship *shul* ben ysaued."
B. 9.151   That somdel þe sone *shal* haue þe sires tacches.
B. 9.163   [For] goode *sholde* wedde goode, þouȝ þei no good hadde;
B. 9.168   That neuere *shal* barn bere but it be in armes.
B. 9.190   *Sholde* no [bedbourde] be; but þei boþe were clene
B. 9.192   That [dede derne] do no man ne *sholde*.
B. 9.200   And after hir deeþ day *shul* dwelle wiþ þe same
B.10.92   For we haue no lettre of oure lif how longe it *shal* dure.
B.10.93   Swiche lessons lordes *sholde* louye to here,
B.10.103   And al to spare to [spille þat spende] *shal* anoþer.
B.10.115   Why *sholde* we þat now ben for þe werkes of Adam
B.10.119   Ymaginatif herafterward *shal* answere to [youre] purpos.
B.10.146   In signe þat I *sholde* bisechen hire of grace.
B.10.148   And seide, 'mercy, madame; youre man *shal* I worþe
B.10.153   I *shal* kenne þee to my Cosyn þat Clergie is hoten.
B.10.157   *Shullen* wissen þee to dowel, I dar [wel] vndertake.'
B.10.170   Thanne *shaltow* se Sobretee and Sympletee-of-speche,
B.10.172   [So] *shaltow* come to Clergie þat kan manye [wittes].
B.10.198   And so *shaltow* fals folk and feiþlees bigile:
B.10.273   As persons and parissh preestes, þat preche *sholde* and teche,
B.10.292   [Th]anne *shul* burel clerkes ben abassshed to blame yow or to
           greue,
B.10.297   [Amonges riȝtful religious þis rule *sholde* be holde]
B.10.300   And seiþ it in ensample [þat] þei *sholde* do þerafter:
B.10.315   And but if his knaue knele þat *shal* his coppe brynge
B.10.322   Ac þer *shal* come a kyng and confesse yow Religiouses,
B.10.328   And þanne Freres in hir fraytour *shul* fynden a keye
B.10.331   And þanne *shal* þe Abbot of Abyngdoun and al his issue for euere
B.10.334   Ac er þat kyng come Caym *shal* awake,
B.10.335   [Ac] dowel dyngen hym adoun and destruye his myȝte.'
B.10.360   He *sholde* louye and lene and þe lawe fulfille.
B.10.365   It *shal* bisitten vs ful soure þe siluer þat we kepen,
B.10.368   For euery cristene creature *sholde* be kynde til ooþer,
B.10.375   "I *shal* punysshe in purgatorie or in þe put of helle

B.10.392 And if I *sh[al]* werche by hir werkes to wynne me heuene,
B.10.400 Whan þei *shal* lif lete [a lippe of goddes grace]–
B.10.452 Beþ noȝt [afered of þat folk], for I *shal* [ȝyue yow tonge],
B.11.22 The secounde seide þe same: 'I *shal* sewe þi wille;
B.11.24 That I ne *shal* in felawship, if Fortune it like.'
B.11.25 'He *shal* fynde me his frend', quod Fortune þerafter;
B.11.29 Thow *shalt* fynde Fortune þee faille at þi mooste nede
B.11.31 Bittrely *shaltow* banne þanne, boþe dayes and nyȝtes,
B.11.36 A man may stoupe tyme ynoȝ whan he *shal* tyne þe crowne.'
B.11.41 Ne *shal* noȝt greue þee [graiþly], ne bigile [þee], but þow wolt.'
B.11.45 'That wit *shal* torne to wrecchednesse for wil to haue his likyng!'
B.11.67 [At kirke] þere a man were cristned by kynde he *sholde* be buryed.
B.11.101 þyng þat al þe world woot, wherfore *sholdestow* spare
B.11.131 A[c] reson *shal* rekene wiþ hym [and rebuken hym at þe laste,
B.11.191 We *sholde* noȝt clepe oure kyn þerto ne none kynnes riche:
B.11.195 Ac for þe pouere I *shal* paie, and pure wel quyte hir trauaille
B.11.209 Forþi loue we as leue [children *shal*], and ech man laughe of ooþer,
B.11.211 And euery man helpe ooþer for hennes *shul* we alle:
B.11.218 That Fides sua *sholde* sauen hire and saluen hire of synnes.
B.11.241 That we *sholde* be lowe and loueliche, [and lele ech man to oþer],
B.11.285 Ne neiþer kirtel ne cote, þeiȝ þei for cold *sholde* deye,
B.11.289 Hem *sholde* lakke no liflode, neyþer lynnen ne wollen.
B.11.292 For he þat took yow [a] title *sholde* take yow wages,
B.11.312 The bisshop *shal* be blamed bifore god, as I leue,
B.11.349 Ther nys wriȝte, as I wene, *sholde* werche hir nes[t] to paye;
B.11.353 [For men *sholde* hem noȝt fynde whan þei þerfro wente;
B.11.392 Ne þow *shalt* fynde but fewe fayne [wolde] heere
B.11.414 Thow *sholdest* haue knowen þat clergie kan & [conceyued] moore þoruȝ Res[on],
B.11.425 *Shal* neuere chalangynge ne chidynge chaste a man so soone
B.11.426 As *shal* shame, and shenden hym, and shape hym to amende.
B.12.75 Wiþ stones men *sholde* hir strike and stone hire to deþe.
B.12.102 And seint Spirit þe Samplarie, & seide what men *sholde* write.
B.12.119 For þe heiȝe holy goost heuene *shal* tocleue,
B.12.140 And loue *shal* lepen out after into þ[is] lowe erþe,
B.12.141 And clennesse *shal* cacchen it and clerkes shullen it fynde:
B.12.141 And clennesse shal cacchen it and clerkes *shullen* it fynde:
B.12.256 And whan his caroyne *shal* come in caue to be buryed
B.13.10 But quik he biqueþe [hem] auȝt [or *sholde* helpe] quyte hir dettes;
B.13.23 And bad me come to his court, wiþ clergie *sholde* I dyne.
B.13.32 'Welcome, wye, go and wassh; þow *shalt* sitte soone.'
B.13.72 In englissh on aventure it *sholde* be reherced ofte,
B.13.73 And greue þerwiþ [þat goode ben]–ac gramariens *shul* re[d]e:
B.13.84 'I *shal* Iangle to þis Iurdan wiþ his Iuste wombe,
B.13.87 And seide, 'þow *shalt* see þus soone, whan he may na moore,
B.13.88 He *shal* haue a penaunce in his paunche and puffe at ech a worde,
B.13.89 And þanne *shullen* hise guttes goþele and he shal galpen after.
B.13.89 And þanne shullen hise guttes goþele and he *shal* galpen after.
B.13.94 And þanne *shal* he testifie of [a] Trinite, and take his felawe to witnesse
B.13.110 But cheeste þe þer charite *sholde* be, and yonge children dorste pleyne,
B.13.130 Which *shal* saue mannes soule; þus seiþ Piers þe Plowman.'
B.13.166 Pope ne patriark, þat pure reson ne *shal* [þee] make
B.13.185 I *shal* brynge yow a bible, a book of þe olde lawe,
B.13.200 'Me were leuere, by oure lord, and I lyue *sholde*,
B.13.203 But seide ful sobreliche, 'þow *shalt* se þe tyme
B.13.207 Ther nys wo in þis world þat we ne *sholde* amende;
B.13.212 I *shal* dwelle as I do my deuoir to shewe,
B.13.222 Pacience apposed hym and preyde he *sholde* telle
B.13.228 Couþe I lye [and] do men lauȝe, þanne lacchen I *sholde*
B.13.253 Miȝte lechen a man as [me þynkeþ] it *sholde*.
B.13.317 Men *sholde* fynde manye frounces and manye foule plottes.'
B.13.431 Ac clerkes þat knowen holy writ *sholde* kenne lordes
B.13.433 *Sholde* noon harlot haue audience in halle n[e] in Chambre
B.13.438 Muche moore, me þynkeþ, riche men *sholde*
B.14.16 'And I *shal* kenne þee', quod Conscience, 'of Contricion to make
B.14.17 That shal clawe þi cote of alle kynnes filþe;
B.14.18 Dowel *shal* wasshen it and wryngen it þoruȝ a wis confessour:
B.14.19 Dobet *shal* beten it and bouken it as bright as any scarlet
B.14.22 Dobest [*shal* kepe it clene from vnkynde werkes].
B.14.23 *Shal* neuere [myx] bymolen it, ne moþe after biten it,
B.14.25 *Shal* noon heraud ne harpour haue a fairer garnement
B.14.29 'And I *shal* purueie þee paast', quod Pacience, 'þouȝ no plouȝ erye,
B.14.33 And þat ynogh; *shal* noon faille of þyng þat hem nedeþ:
B.14.50 And þanne was it fiat voluntas tua [*sholde* fynde vs alle].
B.14.53 *Shul* neuere gyues þee greue ne gret lordes wraþe,
B.14.71 And if men lyuede as mesure wolde *sholde* neuere moore be defaute
B.14.106 I wiste neuere renk þat riche was, þat whan he rekene *sholde*,
B.14.132 Allas þat richesse *shal* reue and robbe mannes soule
B.14.140 So I seye by yow riche, it semeþ noȝt þat ye *shulle*
B.14.147 Crist of his curteisie *shal* conforte yow at þe laste,

B.14.188 *Shulde* amenden vs as manye siþes as man wolde desire.
B.14.190 [We] *sholde* take þe Acquitaunce as quyk and to þe queed shewen it:
B.14.201 Forþi cristene *sholde* be in commune riche, noon coueitous for hymselue.
B.14.279 Ac somdeel I *shal* seyen it, by so þow vnderstonde.
B.15.13 Oon wiþouten tonge and teeþ tolde me whider I *sholde*
B.15.53 That any creature *sholde* konne al except crist oone.
B.15.91 I *shal* tellen it for truþes sake; take hede whoso likeþ.
B.15.102 *Shal* neuere flour ne fruyt [wexe] ne fair leef be grene.
B.15.125 Ac a Porthors þat *sholde* be his Plow, Placebo to sigge–
B.15.151 'Where *sholde* men fynde swich a frend wiþ so fre an herte?
B.15.209 Therfore by colour ne by clergie knowe *shaltow* [hym] neuere,
B.15.258 Amonges cristene men þis myldenesse *sholde* laste
B.15.261 In ensample we *sholde* do so, and take no vengeaunce
B.15.264 *Sholde* neuere Iudas ne Iew haue Iesu doon on roode,
B.15.266 Ac he suffrede in ensample þat we *sholde* suffren also,
B.15.296 I *sholde* noȝt þise seuen daies siggen hem alle
B.15.306 In menynge þat meke þyng mylde þyng *sholde* fede.
B.15.307 [Riȝt so] Religiouses rightfulle men *sholde* [fynde],
B.15.314 Til briddes brynge vs [wherby] we *sholde* lyue.
B.15.342 Ac Religiouse þat riche ben *sholde* raþer feeste beggeris
B.15.360 That whilom warned bifore what *sholde* falle after.
B.15.362 Wisten by þe walkne what *sholde* bitide;
B.15.381 That *sholde* konne and knowe alle kynnes clergie
B.15.384 Thei *sholde* faillen of hir Philosophie and in Phisik boþe.
B.15.419 Wolde neuere þe feiþful fader þat [þ]ise Ministres *sholde*
B.15.424 Grace *sholde* growe and be grene þoruȝ hir goode lyuynge,
B.15.425 And folkes *sholden* [fynde], þat ben in diuerse siknesse,
B.15.427 Hir preieres and hir penaunces to pees *sholde* brynge
B.15.435 Of hem of holi chirche þat þe heighe wey *sholde* teche
B.15.440 *Sholde* alle maner men; we han so manye maistres,
B.15.442 That goddes salt *sholde* be to saue mannes soule.
B.15.492 Allas, þat men so longe [*sholde* bileue on Makometh]!
B.15.503 Thei *sholde* turne, whoso trauail[e wolde] to teche hem of þe Trinite.
B.15.513 In ensaumple þat men *sholde* se by sadde reson
B.15.547 *Shul* [ouer]torne as templers dide; þe tyme approcheþ faste.
B.15.552 *Shal* þei demen dos ecclesie, and [depose yow for youre pride]:
B.15.555 The lordshipe of londes [lese ye *shul* for euere],
B.15.563 That *sholden* preie for þe pees, possession hem letteþ;
B.15.568 If preesthode were parfit þe peple *sholde* amende
B.15.575 That no man *sholde* be bisshop but if he hadde boþe
B.15.581 And han clerkes to kepen vs þerInne & hem þat *shul* come after.
B.15.583 In stoon for it stedefast was and stonde *sholde* euere.
B.15.603 And hopen þat he be to come þat *shal* hem releue;
B.15.609 Prelates of cristene prouinces *sholde* preue if þei myȝte
B.16.2 For Haukyns loue þe Actif man euere I *shal* yow louye.
B.16.61 I *shal* telle þee as tid what þis tree highte.
B.16.95 And þanne *sholde* Iesus Iuste þerfore bi Iuggement of armes
B.16.96 Wheiþer *sholde* fonge þe fruyt, þe fend or hymselue.
B.16.131 'I *shal* ouerturne þis temple and adoun þrowe,
B.16.142 'I am sold þoruȝ [som] of yow; he *shal* þe tyme rewe
B.16.156 Thow *shalt* be myrour to many men to deceyue,
B.16.157 Ac [to] þe [worldes ende] þi wikkednesse *shal* worþe vpon þiselue.
B.16.243 And siþþe he sente me to seye I *sholde* do sacrifise
B.16.252 Seide þat he seiȝ here þat *sholde* saue vs alle:
B.16.260 'This is a present of muche pris; what prynce *shal* it haue?'
B.16.266 That deliuere vs sen som day out of þe deueles power
B.16.270 'Allas!' I seide, 'þat synne so longe *shal* lette
B.17.8 That Luciferis lordshipe laste *shal* no lenger.
B.17.19 *Shal* neuere deuel hym dere ne deeþ in soule greue;
B.17.70 And but he hadde recouerer þe ra[þ]er þat rise *sholde* he neuere.
B.17.99 He *sholde* stonde and steppe; ac stalworþe worþ he neuere
B.17.115 And þanne *shal* Feiþ be forster here and in þis Fryth walke,
B.17.118 And Hope þe Hostile[r] *shal* be þer [an helyng þe man lith];
B.17.120 Hope *shal* lede hem forþ with loue as his lettre telleþ,
B.17.122 Til I haue salue for alle side; and þanne *shal* I turne
B.17.125 For þe barn was born in Bethleem þat with his blood *shal* saue
B.17.127 'A, swete sire', I seide þo, 'wher I *shal* bileue,
B.17.143 And profre[d] it forþ as with a pawme to what place it *sholde*.
B.17.189 For þe fyngres þat folde *sholde* and be fust make,
B.17.193 I *sholde* receyue riȝt noȝt of þat I reche myghte.
B.17.299 'I pose I hadde synned so and *sholde* [nouþe] deye,
B.17.315 Good hope, þat helpe *sholde*, to wanhope torneþ.
B.17.332 That *sholde* brynge in bettre wode or blowe it til it brende.
B.17.339 The reyn þat reyneþ þer we reste *sholde*
B.18.19 And who *sholde* Iuste in Ierusalem. 'Iesus', he seide,
B.18.25 In Piers paltok þe Plowman þis prikiere *shal* ryde,
B.18.26 For no dynt *shal* hym dere as in deitate patris.'
B.18.27 'Who *shal* Iuste wiþ Iesus', quod I, 'Iewes or Scrybes?'
B.18.29 Deeþ seiþ he *shal* fordo and adoun brynge
B.18.37 To se how doghtiliche deeþ *sholde* do and deme hir boþeres right.

B.18.56	Thanne *shul* we leue þat lif þee loueþ and wol noȝt lete þee deye.'	B.20.154	*Shal* do þee noȝt drede, neiþer deeþ ne elde,
B.18.66	*Shal* no wight wite witterly who shal haue þe maistrie	B.20.173	Lyf leeued þat lechecraft lette *sholde* Elde
B.18.66	Shal no wight wite witterly who *shal* haue þe maistrie	B.20.209	'How *shal* I come to catel so to cloþe me and to feede?'
B.18.102	And ye, lurdaynes, han ylost for lif *shal* haue þe maistrye;	B.20.210	'And þow loue lelly lakke *shal* þee neuere
B.18.104	And ye, cherles, and youre children cheue *shulle* [ye] neuere,	B.20.248	And I wol be youre boruȝ: ye *shal* haue breed and cloþes
B.18.109	Whan crist cam hir kyngdom þe crowne *sholde* [lese]:	B.20.249	And oþere necessaries ynowe; yow *shal* no þyng [lakke]
B.18.136	In menynge þat man *shal* fro merknesse be drawe	B.20.281	For persons and parissh preestes þat *sholde* þe peple shryue
B.18.137	The while þis light and þis leme *shal* Lucifer ablende.	B.20.291	As sisours and executours; þei [*shul*] ȝyue þe freres
B.18.139	That man *shal* man saue þoruȝ a maydenes helpe,	B.20.351	That lif þoruȝ his loore *shal* leue coueitise
B.18.140	And þat was tynt þoruȝ tree, tree *shal* it wynne,	B.20.362	'That is ouerlonge', quod þis Lymytour, 'I leue. I *shal* amende it!'
B.18.141	And þat deeþ adown brouȝte, deeþ *shal* releue.'	B.20.364	Of 'a pryuee paiement and I *shal* praye for yow
B.18.151	'Thoruȝ experience', quod [heo], 'I hope þei *shul* be saued;	C.Pr.13	Al y say slepynge as y *shal* [ȝow] telle.
B.18.153	That Adam and Eue haue *shul* bote].	C.Pr.77	His seel *sholde* nouȝt be ysent in deseyte of þe peple.
B.18.158	So *shal* þis deeþ fordo, I dar my lif legge,	C.Pr.80	That þe [pore] peple [of þe] parsch[e] *sholde* haue yf þei ne were.
B.18.161	So *shal* grace that bigan [al] make a good [ende	C.Pr.120	And ȝe *shulde* be here fadres and techen hem betre
B.18.171	That ouerhoueþ helle þus; she vs *shal* telle.'	C.Pr.121	God *shal* take vengeaunce on alle suche prestis
B.18.179	Moyses and many mo mer[ye] *shul* [synge];	C.Pr.144	Caste þat þe commun[e] *sholde* here comunes fynde.
B.18.180	[Thanne] I *shal* daunce þerto; do þow so suster.	C.Pr.202	'Thow we hadde ykuld þe Cat ȝut *shulde* ther come another
B.18.183	That mercy, my suster, and I mankynde *sholde* saue,	C.Pr.211	*Shal* neuer þe Cat ne [þe] kytoun be my conseil be greued
B.18.187	And þat þis dede *shal* dure dormiam & requiescam.'	C. 1.2	And þe feld ful of folk y *shal* ȝou fair shewe.
B.18.193	*Sholden* deye downrighte and dwelle in pyne after	C. 1.50	For riȝtfulliche resoun *sholde* reule ȝow alle
B.18.203	'And I *shal* preue', quod Pees, 'hir peyne moot haue ende,	C. 1.88	Clerkes þat knowen hit *sholde* kenne it aboute
B.18.209	*Sholde* wite witterly what day is to meene.	C. 1.90	Kynges and knyghtes *sholde* kepen hit by resoun,
B.18.210	*Sholde* neuere riȝt riche man þat lyueþ in reste and ese	C. 1.99	For thei *sholde* nother faste ne forbere the serk
B.18.226	So it *shal* fare by þis folk: hir folie and hir synne	C. 1.130	And alle þat worchen þat wikked is wenden thei *sholle*
B.18.227	*Shal* lere hem what langour is and lisse wiþouten ende.	C. 1.132	And alle þat han wel ywrouhte wende þey *sholle*
B.18.236	That mannes soule *sholde* saue and synne destroye.	C. 1.174	Ȝe *shal* be weye þerwith whenne ȝe wende hennes:
B.18.251	And now *shal* Lucifer leue it, þouȝ hym looþ þynke.	C. 2.28	For *shal* neuer breere bere berye as a vine,
B.18.272	That swich a lord and [a] light *sholde* lede hem alle hennes.'	C. 2.35	*Shal* haue grace to good ynow and a good ende,
B.18.281	If Adam ete þe Appul alle *sholde* deye	C. 2.37	He *shal* lese for here loue [a] lippe of trewe charite.
B.18.331	That if [þei] ete þe Appul alle *sholde* deye,	C. 2.47	Soffre and thow *shalt* see suche as ben apayed
B.18.340	Ergo soule *shal* soule quyte and synne to synne wende,	C. 2.48	That mede is thus ymaried; tomorwe þou *shalt* aspye.
B.18.345	And þat deeþ in hem fordide my deeþ *shal* releue	C. 2.144	Ȝe *shal* abyggen bothe but ȝe amende þe sonner.
B.18.359	Adam and alle þoruȝ a tree *shul* turne to lyue,	C. 2.157	Hit *shal* [bi]sitte ȝoure soules ful so[u]re at þe laste.'
B.18.371	And þanne *shal* I come as a kyng, crouned, wiþ Aungeles,	C. 2.168	And sayde softly, 'sese *shal* we neuere;
B.18.373	Fendes and f[e]ndekynes bifore me *shul* stande	C. 2.180	And shop þat a shereue *sholde* bere mede
B.18.378	*Shul* noȝt be dampned to þe deeþ þat [dureþ] wiþouten ende:	C. 2.185	That prestis and prouisores *sholden* prelates serue
B.18.382	There [a] feloun þole *sholde* deeþ ooþer Iuwise	C. 2.193	And lat cop[l]e þe commissarie; oure cart *shal* he drawe
B.18.384	And I þat am kyng of kynges *shal* come swich a tyme	C. 2.211	*Shal* neuere man on þis molde maynpryse þe leste,
B.18.391	They *shul* be clensed clerliche and [keuered] of hir synnes	C. 2.237	That lyare *sholde* wonye with hem watres to loke.
B.18.393	And my mercy *shal* be shewed to manye of my [halue]breþeren,	C. 3.5	'Y *shal* asaye here mysulue and sothliche appose
B.18.396	Ac my rightwisnesse and right *shul* rulen al helle.	C. 3.35	*Shal* no lewedenesse lette þe [lede] þat y louye
B.18.403	Thow *shalt* abyen it bittre!' and bond hym wiþ cheynes.	C. 3.37	There connynge clerkes *shal* clokke byhynde.'
B.19.17	That alle kynne creatures *sholden* knelen and bowen	C. 3.42	Y *shal* assoyle the mysulue for a seem [of] whete
B.19.28	To be called a knyght is fair for men *shul* knele to hym.	C. 3.53	In masse and in matynes for mede we *shal* synge
B.19.45	The lawe of lif þat laste *shal* euere,	C. 3.56	'Y *shal* be ȝoure frende, frere, and fayle ȝow neuere
B.19.89	Gold is likned to leautee þat laste *shal* euere	C. 3.64	And y *shal* cuuere ȝoure kyrke and ȝoure clo[i]stre make;
B.19.90	[For it *shal* turne tresoun to riȝt and to truþe].	C. 3.67	That euery seg *shal* se y am sustre of ȝoure ordre.'
B.19.120	That she first and formest ferme *sholde* bileue	C. 3.83	With that þe pore peple *sholde* potte in here wombe.
B.19.143	And siþen buriede his body, and beden þat men *sholde*	C. 3.126	That fuyr *shal* falle and forbrenne al to blew aysches
B.19.145	For no fren[d] *sholde* [it] fecche; for prophetes hem tolde	C. 3.136	Bothe to the and to thyne in hope thow *shost* amende;
B.19.146	That þat blissede body of burieles [*sholde* risen]	C. 3.141	In the Castel of Corf y *shal* do close the,
B.19.174	Deidest and deeþ þoledest and deme *shalt* vs alle,	C. 3.144	That alle [women, wantowen], *shal* [be] war [by] þe one
B.19.175	And now art lyuynge and lokynge and laste *shalt* euere."	C. 3.154	What his wille were and what he do sholde.
B.19.178	Blessed mote þow be, and be *shalt* for euere.	C. 3.205	Ther he is alowed and ylet by þat laste *shal* eny while
B.19.180	That neuere *shul* se me in sighte as þow [seest] nowþe,	C. 3.256	For *sholde* neuere Consience be my constable were y a kyng,' quod mede,
B.19.219	For Antecrist and hise al þe world *shul* greue	C. 3.260	He *sholde* haue [ben] lord of þat lond alenghe and abrede
B.19.222	*Shullen* come and be curatours ouer kynges and Erles;	C. 3.265	Hit bycometh for a kyng þat *shal* kepe a reume
B.19.223	And Pride *shal* be Pope, Prynce of holy chirche,	C. 3.398	*Sholde* confourme hem to o kynde on holy kyrke to bileue
B.19.242	And some to se and to seye what *sholde* bifalle,	C. 3.416	*Sholde* deye der[f]ly for dedes of here eldres.
B.19.260	My prowor and my Plowman Piers *shal* ben on erþe,	C. 3.425	Spille hit, spare hit nat and thow *shalt* spede th[e] bettere."
B.19.261	And for to tilie truþe a teeme *shal* he haue.'	C. 3.429	God sayde to samuel þat sauel *sholde* deye
B.19.277	And whoso ete þat ymagynen he *sholde*,	C. 3.438	That resoun *shal* regne and reumes gouerne
B.19.283	*Sholde* neuere mete ne [meschief] make hym to swelle;	C. 3.439	And riht as agag hadde happe *shal* somme:
B.19.284	Ne [*sholde*] no scornere out of skile hym brynge;	C. 3.440	Samuel *shal* sle hym and sauel *shal* be yblamed
B.19.287	*Sholde* no curious clooþ comen on his rugge,	C. 3.440	Samuel shal sle hym and sauel *shal* be yblamed
B.19.298	And he þat ete of þat seed *sholde* be [euene] trewe	C. 3.441	And dauid *shal* be ydyademed and [d]aunte alle oure enemyes
B.19.301	[*Shal*] nouȝt ben espied [þoruȝ] Spiritus Iusticie.	C. 3.443	*Shal* no mede be maistre neueremore aftur
B.19.342	And tolde hem tidynges, þat tyne þei *sholde*	C. 3.445	Tho *shal* be maistres on molde trewe men to helpe.
B.19.345	*Shulle* come out, Conscience; and youre [caples two],	C. 3.447	Lewete *shal* do hym lawe and no lyf elles.
B.19.347	*Shal* be coloured so queyntely and couered vnder [oure] Sophistrie	C. 3.448	*Shal* no ser[i]aunt for [þat] seruic[e] werie a selk houe
B.19.348	That Conscience *shal* noȝt knowe who is cristene or heþene,	C. 3.452	A[c] kynde loue *shal* come ȝut and Consience togyderes
B.19.382	The lord of lust *shal* be letted al þis lente, I hope.	C. 3.453	And maky of lawe [a] laborer; suche loue *shal* aryse
B.19.424	And þow Conscience in kynges court, and *sholdest* neuere come þennes;	C. 3.455	That iewes wene in he[re] wit, & wexen so glade,
B.19.428	Inparfit is þat pope þat al [peple] *sholde* helpe	C. 3.460	*Shal* be demed to þe deth but yf he do hit smythye
B.19.429	And [soudeþ hem] þat sleep [swiche as] he *sholde* saue.	C. 3.467	*Shal* lese þerfore his lyflode and his lyf parauntur.
B.20.10	And nede haþ no lawe ne neuere *shal* falle in dette	C. 3.468	*Shal* nother kyng ne knyght, Constable ne Mayre
B.20.26	He *shal* do moore þan mesure many tyme and ofte,	C. 3.471	But aftur þe dede þat is ydo the doom *shal* recorde
B.20.29	And Spiritus Iusticie *shal* Iuggen, wole he, nel he,	C. 3.474	Al *shal* be but [o] couert and o [buyrne] be Iustice.
B.20.31	And Spiritus prudencie in many a point *shal* faille	C. 3.476	Batailes *sholle* neuere eft be ne man bere eg toel
B.20.47	And suffre sorwes ful soure, þat *shal* to Ioye torne."	C. 3.478	Ac ar this fortune falle fynde me *shal* the worste
B.20.150	Ne careþ noȝt how Kynde slow and *shal* come at þe laste		

C. 3.480	And the [myddell] of [a] mone *shal* make þe iewes turne
C. 3.481	And saresines for þat syhte *shal* syng Credo in spiritum sanctum
C. 3.482	For Machameth and mede [*shal*] mishap þat tyme;
C. 3.494	A *sholde* haue yfonde [felle wordes folwynge] aftur:
C. 3.496	So hoso [s]echeth sapience fynde he *shal* [that] foloweth
C. 4.2	ȝe *shal* sauhtene, forsothe, and serue me bothe.
C. 4.9	For he *shal* reulen my rewme and rede me the beste
C. 4.10	Of mede and of mo othere and what man *shal* here wedde
C. 4.16	'Y *shal* aray me to ryde,' quod resoun, 'reste the [a] while,'
C. 4.29	To take reed of resoun þat recorde *sholde*
C. 4.80	That wrong for his werkes *sholde* w[oo] tholye
C. 4.82	Ther he *sholde* nat in seuene ȝer see his feet [ones].
C. 4.103	Bute resoun haue reuth on hym he *shal* reste in [þe] stokkes
C. 4.131	And [ȝut],' quod resoun, 'by þe rode! y *shal* no reuthe haue
C. 4.136	*Shulde* neuere wrong in this worlde þat y wyte myhte
C. 4.144	That lawe *shal* ben a laborer and lede afelde donge
C. 4.145	And loue *shal* leue thi land as the leef lyketh.'
C. 4.149	In signe þat thei *sholde* with som sotil speche
C. 4.171	Ac resoun *shal* rykene with ȝow yf y regne eny while
C. 4.173	Mede *shal* nat maynprise [ȝow], by marye of heuene!
C. 4.175	And by lele and lyfholy my lawe *shal* be demed.'
C. 4.184	Forthy, resoun, redyly thow *shalt* nat ryden hennes
C. 5.42	Yf y be labour *sholde* lyuen and lyflode deseruen,
C. 5.43	That laboure þat y lerned beste þerwith lyuen y *sholde*:
C. 5.54	Me *sholde* constrayne no Cler[k] to no knaues werkes,
C. 5.57	*Sholde* nother swynke ne swete ne swerien at enquestes
C. 5.66	For *sholde* no clerke be crouned but yf he come were
C. 5.76	And monkes and moniales þat mendenant[es] *sholde* fynde
C. 5.101	That alle tymes of my tyme to profit *shal* turne.'
C. 5.119	In ensau[m]ple, seggus, þat we *sholde* do þe bettere;
C. 5.122	That dedly synne ar domesday *shal* fordon hem alle.
C. 5.124	Ac y *shal* sey as y sayh, slepynge as hit were,
C. 5.142	Lyue as ȝe lereth vs; we *shall* leue ȝow þe bettere.'
C. 5.161	And but if his knaue knele þat *shal* his coppe holde
C. 5.168	Ac þer *shal* come a kyng and confesse ȝow alle
C. 5.173	Freres in here fraytour *shal* fynde þat tyme
C. 5.175	And constantyn *shal* be here cook and couerour of here churches,
C. 5.177	*Shal* haue a knok vppon here crounes and incurable þe wounde:
C. 5.179	Clerkes and holy [kyrke] *shal* be clothed newe.'
C. 6.6	A *sholde* vnsowen here serk and sette þe[r] an hayre
C. 6.8	'Shal* neuere heyh herte me hente, but holde me lowe
C. 6.23	Lauhyng al aloude for lewede men *sholde*
C. 6.67	*Sholde* no lyf lyue þat on his lond pissede
C. 6.108	Thow y sitte this seuene ȝer, y *sholde* nat wel telle
C. 6.126	Or alle riche and ryde, reste *shal* y nat, wrathe,
C. 6.173	With þat y *shal*,' quod shrewe, 'saturdayes for thy loue
C. 6.205	He *sholde* [nat] wandre [o]n þat walch, so was hit thredbare.
C. 6.254	*Shal* neuere seketoure[s] wel bysette þe syluer þat thow hem leuest
C. 6.290	Thow were such as thow sayst; y *sholde* rather s[t]erue:
C. 6.299	*Shal* parte with the in purgatorye and helpe paye thy dette
C. 6.303	There *shal* he wite witturly what vsure is to mene
C. 6.304	And [what] penaunce the prest *shal* haue þat pr[o]ud is of his tithes.
C. 6.307	And arste *shal* come to heuene, [by hym þat me made]!'
C. 6.312	That eche man *shal* haue his ar y hennes wende
C. 6.338	Confessen hem and cryen hym mercy; *shal* neuere come in helle:
C. 6.347	For he *shal* onswerie for the at the hey dome,
C. 6.348	For the and for many mo þat man *shal* ȝeue a rykenynge
C. 6.381	That hoso hadde the hood *sholde* nat haue þe cloke
C. 6.382	And that the bettere thyng, be arbitreres, bote *sholde* þe worse.
C. 6.385	And there were othes an heep for on *sholde* haue þe worse.
C. 6.390	In couenaunt þat clement *sholde* the coppe fulle
C. 6.392	And hoso repente[th] rathest *sholde* aryse aftur
C. 6.439	*Shal* neuere fysch [o]n þe fryday defyen in my wombe
C. 7.2	'Y moste sitte to be shryue or elles *sholde* y nappe;
C. 7.5	*Sholde* no ryngyng do me ryse til y were rype to dyne.'
C. 7.9	'Yf y *sholde* deye be þis day y drede me sore.
C. 7.40	Reuthe is to here rekenynge when we *shal* rede acountes
C. 7.64	'Shal* no sonday be this seuene ȝere, but seknesse hit make,
C. 7.65	That y ne *shal* do me ar day to þe dere chirche
C. 7.67	*Shal* non ale aftur m[e]te holde me thennes
C. 7.91	Clerkes þat knoweth this *sholde* kenne lordes
C. 7.93	*Sholde* non harlote haue audiense in halle ne in chaumbre
C. 7.120	'Y *shal* byseke for alle synnefole oure sauiour of grace
C. 7.146	For dedes that we han don ylle dampned *sholde* we ben neuere
C. 7.168	And þe vernicle bifore for men *sholde* yknowe
C. 7.209	That is to sey sothly ȝe *sholde* rather deye
C. 7.216	And ȝe *shal* lepe þe lihtloker al ȝoure lyf tyme:
C. 7.217	[So] *shalt* thow se swere-nat-but-it-be-for-nede-
C. 7.219	Thenne *shalt* thow come by a croft Ac come thow [nat] þerynne;
C. 7.227	Thenne *shaltow* blenche at a berw, bere-no-fals-witnesse-
C. 7.230	Thenne *shaltow* se say-soth-so-hit-be-to-done-
C. 7.232	And so *shaltow* come to a Court as cleer as þe sonne.

C. 7.234	And al þe wallyng is of wyt for wil ne *sholde* hit wynne;
C. 7.246	Y am sory [for] my synnes, and so [*shal* y] euere,
C. 7.255	Thow *shalt* se treuthe sitte in thy sulue herte
C. 7.286	[*Sh*]*olde* y neuere forthere [a] foet for no frere prechynge.'
C. 8.6	'What *sholde* we wommen wor[c]he þe whiles?'
C. 8.15	For y *shal* lene hem lyflode but [yf] þe lond faylle
C. 8.24	'Y *shal* swynke and swete and sowe for vs bothe
C. 8.34	To defende þe in fayth, fyhte thow y *sholde*.'
C. 8.41	For thow *shalt* ȝelden hit, so may be, or sumdel abuggen hit.
C. 8.56	'And [y] *shal* [ap]parayle me,' quod Perkyn, 'in pilgrimes wyse
C. 8.64	My plouhpote *shal* be my pykstaff and pyche ato þe rotes
C. 8.67	*Shal* haue leue, to [lese here in heruest]
C. 8.70	Y *shal* fynde hem fode þat fayfulleche libbeth,
C. 8.77	Del[e]antur de libro viuencium; y *sholde* nat dele with hem
C. 8.81	His douhter hihte do-rihte-so-or-thy-dame-*shal*-þe-bete;
C. 8.83	Deme-hem-nat-[for]-yf-thow-doest-thow-*shalt*-hit-dere-abygge.
C. 8.96	He *shal* haue my soule þat alle soules made
C. 8.100	The kyrke *shal* haue my caroyne and kepe my bones
C. 8.105	My wyf *shal* haue of þat y wan with treuthe and no more
C. 8.121	He *sholde* be huyred þeraftur when heruost tyme come.
C. 8.126	*Shal* no grayn þat here groweth gladyen ȝow at nede;
C. 8.141	Ac treuthe *shal* teche ȝow his teme to dryue
C. 8.142	Or ȝe *shal* ete barly breed and of þe broke drynke.
C. 8.144	Such poore,' quod [Peres], 'shal* parte with my godes,
C. 8.163	'Or y *shal* bete the by the lawe and brynge þe in stokkes.'
C. 8.167	'Now, by Crist!' quod [Peres] the [plouhman], 'y *shal* apayre ȝow alle,'
C. 8.227	And h[e] *shal* soupe swetture when [he] hit hath deserued.
C. 8.244	In somur for his sleuthe he *shal* haue defaute
C. 8.247	His suluer to thre maner men [in] menyng they *sholden*
C. 8.290	That fysik *shal* his forred hod[e] for his fode sulle
C. 8.343	He *shal* awake thorw water wastors to chaste;
C. 8.344	Ar fewe ȝeres be fulfeld famyne *shal* aryse.
C. 8.346	Thorw flodes and foule wederes fruyttes *shollen* fayle;
C. 8.347	Pruyde and pestilences *shal* moche peple feche;
C. 8.349	*Shal* brynge bane and batayle on bothe half þe mone;
C. 8.350	And thenne *shal* deth withdrawe and derthe be Iustice
C. 9.13	Bishopis yblessed, yf they ben as they *sholde*,
C. 9.37	'And y *shal* sende ȝow mysulue seynt Mihel myn Angel
C. 9.38	That no deuel *shal* ȝow dere ne despeyre in ȝoure d[e]ynge
C. 9.50	*Shal* haue grace of a good ende and greet ioye aftur.
C. 9.57	Thise foure *sholde* be fre to alle folk þat hit nede[th].
C. 9.125	We *sholde* [haue] hem to house and helpe hem when they come:
C. 9.134	Ryht so, ȝe ryche, ȝut rather ȝe *sholde*
C. 9.188	And alle holy Eremytes haue *shal* þe same;
C. 9.280	For *shal* no pardon preye for ȝow there ne no princes lettres.
C. 9.290	Bote do wel and haue wel, and [god] *shal* haue thy soule
C. 9.292	Bote he þat euele lyueth euele *shal* ende.'
C. 9.312	'Beau fitȝ,' quod the fadur, 'for defaute we *shal*,
C. 9.339	At þe dredful dome, when dede *shullen* ryse
C.10.30	'Y *shal* sey þe, my sone,' sayde þe frere thenne,
C.10.32	By a forbisene,' quod þe frere, 'y *shal* þe fayre shewe'
C.10.57	Ac yf y may lyue and loke y *shal* go lerne bettere.'
C.10.93	Dobest bere *sholde* þe bisshopes [c]rose
C.10.98	*Sholde* no bisshop be here biddynges to withsite.
C.10.99	Ac dobest *sholde* drede hem nat but do as god hihte:
C.10.184	Frendes *shal* fynde hem and fram folye kepe
C.10.185	And holy churche helpe to, so *sholde* no man begge
C.10.192	Bishope[s] *sholde* ben hereaboute and bryng this to hepe
C.10.196	And seth [he les] his lyf for lawe *sholde* loue wexe.
C.10.198	*Sholde* doute no deth ne no dere ȝeres
C.10.207	For god saith hymsulue, "shal* neuere goed appel
C.10.228	Bestes þat now beth *shal* banne þe tyme
C.10.230	Alle *sholle* deye for his dedes by dales and hulles
C.10.233	That in thi [s]hingled ship *shal* be with þe ysaued."
C.10.238	That þe sire by hymsulue doth þe sone *sholde* be þe worse.
C.10.241	The eritage þat þe eyer *sholde* haue is at þe kynges wille.
C.10.254	For goode *sholde* wedde goode thouh they no goode hadde
C.10.290	For *sholde* no bedbourde be bote yf they bothe were
C.10.292	For þat dede derne do no man *sholde*
C.10.299	And after her deth day dwellen *shollen* in helle
C.11.22	What *shal* worthen of suche when þei lyf leten:
C.11.27	And þat is no riht ne resoun for rather me *sholde*
C.11.84	Semyng þat y *sholde* bysechen here of grace.
C.11.86	And saide, 'mercy, madame; ȝoure man *shal* y worthen
C.11.91	Y *shal* kenne þe to clergie, my cosyn, þat knoweth
C.11.99	Thow *shalt* kunne and knowe kyndeliche dowel.'
C.11.110	To clergie *shaltow* neuere come ne knowe what is dowel
C.11.181	The seconde saide þe same: 'y [*shal*] sewe thy wille;
C.11.183	That y ne *shal* folowe thy felowschipe yf fortune [hit] lyke.'
C.11.184	'A *shal* fynde me his frende,' quod fortune þeraftur;

C.11.188 Thow *shalt* fynde fortune þe fayle At thy moste nede
C.11.190 Bitterliche *shaltow* banne thenne, bothe dayes and nyhtes,
C.11.195 A man may stoupe tyme ynowe when he *shal* tyne þe croune.'
C.11.198 'Go y to helle or to heuene y *shal* nat go myn one.
C.11.201 *Sholde* sitte in goddis sihte ne se god in his blisse:
C.11.219 And yf we *sholde* wurche aftur here werkes to wy[n]nen vs heuene
C.11.243 Of holy kirke þat *sholde* kepe alle cristene soules
C.11.277 Beth nat aferd of þat folk for y *shal* ʒeue ʒow tonge,
C.11.301 As clerkes of holy [k]ir[k]e þat [kepe] *sholde* and saue
C.11.308 Ne *shal* nat greue the gr[ayth]ly ne bigyle the, but thow wolle.'
C.12.2 'That wit *shal* turne to wrechednesse for wil hath al his wille!'
C.12.6 He *shal* asoile [the] thus sone how so euere thow wynne hit.
C.12.35 Thyng þat al þe world woet wherfore *sholdest* thow spare
C.12.66 A[c] reson *shal* rekene with hym and rebuken hym at þe laste
C.12.103 We *sholde* nat clepie knyhtes þerto ne none kyne ryche:
C.12.108 That louieth and leneth hem largeliche *shal* y quyte."
C.12.118 And euery man helpe other for hennes *shal* we alle
C.12.130 That we *sholde* be low and louelich and lele vch man til oþer
C.12.159 He *shal* haue an hundredfold of heueneryche blisse
C.12.181 *Shal* neuere spir sprynge vp ne spiek on straw kerne;
C.12.182 *Sholde* neuere wexe but whete furste deyede;
C.12.208 ʒoure sorwe into solace *shal* turne at þe laste
C.12.209 And out of wo into wele ʒoure wirdes *shal* chaunge."
C.12.212 And þat his gost *shal* go and [his] goed bileue
C.12.213 And asketh [hym after] ho *shal* hit haue,
C.12.215 "And art so loth to leue that lete *shal* thow nedes:
C.12.216 An vnredy reue thy residue *shal* spene
C.12.218 Vpholderes on þe hulle *shal* haue hit to sulle."
C.13.34 And *sholden* wende o wey where bothe mosten reste
C.13.100 Vch a parfi[t] prest to pouerte *sholde* drawe
C.13.103 Hem *sholde* neuere lacke lyflode, noþer lynnen ne wollene.
C.13.106 For he that toek ʒow a title *sholde* take ʒow wages
C.13.124 The bishop *shal* be blamed before god, as y leue,
C.13.160 Ther is no wriht, as y wene, *sholde* worch here neste to paye;
C.13.164 For no foul *sholde* hit fynde but his fere and hymsulue.
C.13.199 Ac he soffreth in ensaumple þat we *sholde* soffren alle.
C.13.222 Thow *sholdest* haue yknowe þat clergie ca[n] & conseyued mor[e] [thorw] resoun
C.13.233 For *shal* neuere, ar shame come, a shrewe wel [be] chaste[d].
C.14.47 And seynt spirit þe saumplarie and said what men *sholde* wryte.
C.14.84 For the hey holi gost heuene *shal* tocleue
C.14.85 And loue *shal* lepe out aftur into þis lowe erthe
C.14.86 And clennesse *shal* cach hit and clerkes shollen hit fynde:
C.14.86 And clennesse shal cach hit and clerkes *shollen* hit fynde:
C.14.125 Muchel wo was hym marked þat wade *shal* with þe lewede!
C.14.165 Sey hit and soffred hit And saide hit be *sholde*:
C.15.26 And beden me ryse and rome; with reson *sholde* y dyne.
C.15.52 That Consience comaunde *sholde* to do come scripture
C.15.91 'Y *schal* iangle to þis iurdan with his iuyste wombe
C.15.94 And saide, 'Thow *shalt* se thus sone, when he may no more,
C.15.95 He *shal* haue a penaunce in his paunche and poffe at vch a worde
C.15.96 And thenne *shal* [his gottes gothelen] and [he shal] galpe [after].
C.15.96 And thenne shal [his gottes gothelen] and [he *shal*] galpe [after].
C.15.101 And [thenne *shal* he testifie of] a trinite and take his felowe [t]o witnesse
C.15.129 *Shal* no such motyef be meued for me bote [þ]ere
C.15.138 Byfore perpetuel pees y *shal* proue þat y saide
C.15.162 *Shal* neuere buyren be abasched þat hath this abouten hym
C.15.178 Me were leuere, by oure lord, and y leue *sholde*,
C.15.191 Pacience apposede hym and preyede a *sholde* telle
C.15.202 [Cou]de y lye and do men lawhe thenne lacchen y *scholde*
C.15.249 And thenne was hit fiat voluntas tua þat *sholde* fynde vs alle.
C.15.252 *Shal* neuere gyues the greue ne grete lordes wrathe,
C.15.270 And yf men lyuede as mesure wolde *sholde* neuere[more] be defaute
C.15.281 [Y wiste neuere renke þat ryche was þat whan he rekene *sholde*]
C.16.1 Allas þat rychesse *shal* reue and robbe mannes soule
C.16.8 So y sey by ʒow ryche, hit semeth nat þat ʒe *sholle*
C.16.42 Forthy cristene *sholde* be in comune ryche, noon coueytous for hymsulue.
C.16.119 In engelysch is ful hard Ac sumdel y *shal* telle the.
C.16.161 *Shal* be porest of power at his partynge hennes.'
C.16.215 That eny creature *sholde* conne al excepte crist one.
C.16.221 The bittorere he *shal* abugge but yf he wel worche
C.16.255 *Shal* neuere flour ne fruyt wexe ne fayre leue be grene.
C.16.338 Thogh y my byliue *sholde* begge aboute at menne hacches.
C.16.341 By clothyng ne by carpynge knowe *shaltow* hym neuere
C.17.33 In tokenynge þat trewe man alle tymes *sholde*
C.17.42 *Sholde* reseue riht nauht but þat riht wolde
C.17.48 Thenne grace *sholde* growe ʒut and grene loue wexe
C.17.49 And charite þat chield is now *sholde* chaufen of hymsulue
C.17.66 That his mede and his manhede for eueremore *shal* laste:
C.17.94 Ther *sholde* be plente and pees perpetuel euere.

C.17.98 That whilum warnede byfore what *sholde* [f]alle aftur.
C.17.100 Wisten w[hi]l[e] and tolde when hit *sholde* ryne.
C.17.115 That *sholde* þe seuene ars conne and assoile a quodlibet
C.17.122 Ac ʒif prestes doen here deuer wel we *shal* do þe bettre
C.17.175 Thenne *sholde* þe coluere come to þe clerkes ere,
C.17.186 *Sholden* conuerte hem to Crist and cristendoem to take.
C.17.209 *Sholle* ouerturne as templers dede; þe tyme approcheth faste.
C.17.215 *Shal* dampne dos ecclesie and depose ʒow for ʒoure pruyde;
C.17.218 The lordschipe of londes lese ʒe *shal* for euer
C.17.226 That *sholde* preye for þe pees possession hem letteth;
C.17.236 His preyeres with his pacience to pees *sholde* brynge
C.17.238 The pope with alle prestes pax vobis *sholde* make
C.17.250 Yf prestehode were parfyt and preyede thus þe peple *sholde* amende
C.17.254 They *sholde* [turne], hoso trauayle wolde and of þe trinite teche hem.
C.17.264 In ensaumple þat men *sholde* se by sad resoen
C.17.283 Euery bisshope bi þe lawe *sholde* buxumliche walke
C.17.311 And hopen þat he be to come þat *shal* hem releue;
C.17.317 Prelates and prestes *sholde* proue yf they myhte
C.18.47 And shaketh hit; ne were hit vndershored hit *sholde* nat stande.
C.18.59 Hit is al of o kynde, and þat *shal* y preuen.
C.18.92 In menynge þat the fayrest thyng the furste thynge *shold* honoure
C.18.95 *Shollen* serue for þe lord sulue, and so fareth god almyhty.
C.18.106 And shaken hit sharpeliche; the rype *sholde* falle.
C.18.128 That iesus *sholde* iouste þerfore by iugement of Armes
C.18.129 Who *sholde* fecche this fruyt, the fende or iesus suluen.
C.18.173 Thow *shalt* be myrrour to monye men to disceue.
C.18.255 For hymsulue saide y *sholde* [haue], y and myn issue bothe,
C.18.260 And sethe a sente me to seyn and saide that y *sholde*
C.18.268 Saide þat a seyh here þat *sholde* saue vs alle:
C.18.276 'This is a present of moche pris; what prince *shal* hit haue?'
C.18.282 That *shal* delyuere vs som day out of þe deueles power
C.18.286 'Allas!' y saide, 'þat synne so longe *shal* lette
C.19.10 That luciferes lordschipe lowe *sholde* lygge.'
C.19.20 *Shal* neuere deuel hym dere ne deth in soule greue;
C.19.45 And lereth þat we louye *sholde* as wel lyares as lele.
C.19.69 And bote he hadde recouerer the raþer þat ryse *sholde* he neuere
C.19.95 That his lycame *shal* lechen at þe laste vs alle.'
C.19.96 'A, sire,' y saide, '*shal* nat we bileue,
C.19.107 Y *sholde* tholye and thonken hem þat me euel wolden.'
C.19.117 And profered it forth as with the paume to what place hit *sholde*.
C.19.138 *Sholde* n[o] wri[h]t worche were they awey.
C.19.155 For þe fyngeres þat folde *sholde* and þe fust make
C.19.159 Y *sholde* receyue ryht nouht of þat y reche myhte;
C.19.279 'Y pose y hadde syneged so and *sholde* nouthe deye
C.19.295 For goed hope, that helpe *scholde*, to wanhope turneth
C.19.312 That *sholde* brynge in bettere wode or blowen hit til hit brente.
C.19.319 The rayne þat rayneth þere we reste *sholde*
C.20.17 And ho *sholde* iouste in Ierusalem. 'Iesus,' he saide,
C.20.21 That this iesus of his gentrice *shal* iouste in Pers Armes,
C.20.24 In [Pers paltok] the [plouhman] this prikiare *shal* ryde
C.20.25 For no d[yn]t *shal* hym dere as in deitate patris.'
C.20.26 'Who *shal* iouste with iesus,' quod y, 'iewes or scrib3?'
C.20.36 To se how douhtyliche deth *sholde* do and demen [h]er beyre rihte.
C.20.56 Thenne *shal* we leue that lyf þe loueth and wol nat late the deye.'
C.20.68 Ac *shal* no wyht wyte witturlich ho shal haue þe maistry
C.20.68 Ac shal no wyht wyte witturlich ho *shal* haue þe maistry
C.20.105 And ʒe, lordeyne[s], haen lost for lyf *shal* haue [þe] maistrie,
C.20.107 And alle ʒoure childerne, cherles, cheue *shal* neuere
C.20.112 When Crist thorw croos ouercam ʒoure kyndoem *sholde* tocleue:
C.20.139 In menynge þat man shal fro me[r]kenesse be ydrawe
C.20.140 The while this lihte and this l[em]e *shal* lucifer ablende
C.20.142 [That man *shal* man saue thorw a maydenes helpe
C.20.143 And] that was tynt thorw tre, tre *shal* hit wynne.
C.20.144 þat deth down brouhte, deth *shal* releue.'
C.20.154 'Thorw experiense,' quod he, 'y hope they *shal* ben saued;
C.20.156 That Adam and Eue haue *shullen* bote.
C.20.161 And so *shal* this deth fordo, y dar my lyf legge,
C.20.164 So *shal* grace þat bigan al maken a goed ende
C.20.174 That ouerhoueth helle thus; he vs *shal* telle.'
C.20.182 Moises and many moo Mer[y] *shal* synge;
C.20.183 And y *shal* daunse þerto; do thow so sustur .
C.20.186 That mercy, my sustur, and y mankynde *sh[olde]* saue
C.20.192 And that this dede *shal* duyre, dormiam & requiescam.'
C.20.198 *Sholde* deye downriht and d[welle] in payne euere.
C.20.208 'And y *shal* pre[u]e,' quod pees, 'here payne moet haue ende
C.20.216 *Sholde* ywyte witterly what day is to mene.
C.20.219 For *sholde* neuere riʒt riche man þat lyueth in rest and hele
C.20.235 So hit *shal* fare bi this folk: here folye and here synne
C.20.236 *Shal* lere hem what l[angour] is and lisse withouten ende.
C.20.245 That mannes soule *sholde* saue and synne distruye.
C.20.260 And now *shal* lucife[r] leue [hit], thogh hym loeth thynk.

C.20.280   That such a lord and a lihte *sh[olde]* lede hem alle hennes.
C.20.283   And [y] *shal* lette this loerd and his liht stoppe.
C.20.304   [*Sh]olde* deye with doel and here dwelle euere
C.20.336   That if his soule hider cam hit *sholde* shende vs all.
C.20.340   Hit *shal* vndo vs deueles and down bryngen vs all.
C.20.374   That if they ete þe appul alle *sholde* deye,
C.20.385   The same sore *shal* he haue þat eny so smyteth:
C.20.386   So lyf *shal* lyf le[t]e ther lyf hath lyf an[y]en[t]ed
C.20.388   Ergo soule *shal* soule quyte and synne to synne wende
C.20.398   Adam and alle þorw a tre *shal* turne to lyue.
C.20.413   And thenne *shal* y come as [a] kynge, croune[d], with angeles
C.20.415   Fendes and fendekynes byfore me *shal* stande
C.20.420   *Shal* neuere in helle eft come be he ones oute:
C.20.424   Ther a thief tholie *sholde* deth oþer iewyse
C.20.426   And y þat am kynge o[f] kynges *shal* come such a tyme
C.20.435   A[c] ʒut my kynde [in] my kene ire *shal* constrayne my will–
C.20.439   Ac my rihtwysnesse and rihte *shal* r[ul]en [al] helle
C.20.446   Thow *shal[t]* abuye bittere!' and b[o]nde hym with chaynes.
C.21.17   T[hat] alle kyn creatures *sholde* knelen and bowen
C.21.28   To be cald a knyht is fayr for men *shal* knele to hym;
C.21.45   The lawe of lyf that laste *shal* euere
C.21.89   Gold is likened to lewetee that laste *shal* euere
C.21.90   [For it *shal* turne tresoun] to riht and to treuthe.
C.21.120   That [sh]e furste and formoste [ferme *sholde*] bileue
C.21.143   And sethen bur[ie]den his body and beden þat men *sholde*
C.21.145   For no frende *sholde* hit deyme; for profetes hem tolde
C.21.146   That þat blessed body of buyrielles *sholde* ryse
C.21.174   Deyedest and deth tholedest and deme *shalt* vs all
C.21.175   And now art lyuynge and lokynge and laste *shalt* euere."
C.21.178   Yblessed mote thow be and be *shalt* for euere.
C.21.180   Tha[t] neuere *shal* se me in sihte as thowe seste nowthe
C.21.219   For Auntecrist and hise al the world *shal* greue
C.21.222   *Shal* come and be curatours ouer kynges and Erles;
C.21.223   And [pryde *shal*] be pope, prince of holy chirche,
C.21.242   And somme to se and to saye what *sholde* bifalle
C.21.260   My prowour and my [plouhman Peres] *shal* ben on erthe
C.21.261   And for to tulye treuthe a teme *shal* he haue.'
C.21.277   [And] hoso ete þat ymageny he *sholde*,
C.21.283   *Sholde* neuere mete ne meschief maken hym to swelle
C.21.284   Ne *sholde* no scornare out of skille hym brynge
C.21.287   *Sholde* no curious cloth comen on his rugge
C.21.298   And he þat ete of þat seed *sholde* be euene trewe
C.21.301   [*Shal*] nat be aspyed thorw spiritus iusticie.
C.21.342   And toelde hem tydynges, þat tyne thei *sholde*
C.21.345   *Shal* come oute, Consience; and ʒoure [caples two],
C.21.347   *Shal* be coloured so queyntly and keuered vnder [o]ure sophistrie
C.21.348   That Consience *shal* nat knowe [ho is cristene or hethene]
C.21.382   The lord of lust *shal* be ylette al this lente, y hope.
C.21.424   And thow, Consience, in kynges Court and *sholdest* neuer come
           thennes;
C.21.428   Inparfit is þat pope þat all peple *sholde* helpe
C.21.429   And soudeth hem þat sleeth suche as he *sholde* saue.
C.22.10   And nede hath no lawe ne neuere *shal* falle in dette
C.22.26   He *shal* do more þe[n] mesure mony tymes and often
C.22.29   And spiritus iusticie *shal* iugen, wol he, nel he,
C.22.31   And spiritus Prudencie in many a poynt *shal* faile
C.22.47   And soffre sorwes ful soure þat *shal* to ioye torne."
C.22.150   Ne careth nat how kynde slowh and *shal* come at þe laste
C.22.154   *Shal* do the nat drede, noþer deth ne elde,
C.22.173   Lyf leuede þat lechecraft lette *sholde* Elde
C.22.209   'How *shal* y come to catel so to clothe me and to fede?'
C.22.210   'And thow loue lelly lacke *shal* the neuere
C.22.248   [And] y wol be ʒoure borwh: ʒe *shal* haue breed and clothes
C.22.249   And oþere necessaries neuere; ʒow *shal* no thyng lakke
C.22.281   For persones and parsche prestes þat *sholde* þe peple shryue
C.22.291   As sisours and secutours; they *shal* ʒeue þe freres
C.22.351   That lyf thorw his lore *shal* leue Couetyse
C.22.362   'That is ouerlonge,' quod this lymitour, 'y leue; y *schal* amenden
           hit!'
C.22.364   Of 'a pryue payement and y *shal* preye for ʒow

shame n *shame n.*   A 2; B 12; C 6
A. 4.28   For to saue hemself from *shame* & from harm.
A.12.16   And seyde so loude þat *shame* me thouʒthe,
B. 4.31   For to saue hem[seluen] from *shame* and from harmes.
B. 5.90   'I wolde ben yshryue', quod þis sherewe, 'and I for *shame* dorste.
B. 5.125   Ne neiþer shrifte ne *shame*, but whoso shrape my mawe?'
B. 9.90   [So] Iewes [shul] ben oure loresmen, *shame* to vs alle!
B.10.413   And shilden vs from *shame* þerinne, as Noes ship dide beestes.
B.11.426   As shal *shame*, and shenden hym, and shape hym to amende.
B.11.433   And *shame* shrapeþ hise cloþes and hise shynes wassheþ,
B.11.437   As *shame*: þere he sheweþ hym, [hym shonyeþ euery man].
B.12.80   Than þe womman þat þere was, and wenten awey for *shame*.
B.14.333   Ne neiþer sherte ne shoon, saue for *shame* one

B.15.383   I dar noʒt siggen it for *shame*–if swiche were apposed
B.20.284   And [be] ashamed in hir shrift; ac *shame* makeþ hem wende
C. 6.90   Ne noþer *shame* ne shryfte but hoso shrap[e] my mawe?'
C. 6.432   And spilde þat y aspele myhte; y kan nat speke for *shame*
C.13.233   For shal neuere, ar *shame* come, a shrewe wel [be] chaste[d].
C.13.243   As *shame*: ther he sheweth hym vch man shoneth his companye.
C.16.373   He halt hit for a vyce and a foule *shame*
C.22.284   And be aschamed in here shryft; ac *shame* maketh [hem] wende

shamedest v *shamen v.*   B 2   shamed (1)   shamedest (1)
B. 3.190   Ac þow þiself sooþly *shamedest* hym ofte;
B. 5.366   Shryue þee and be *shamed* þerof and shewe it with þi mouþe.'

shamelees adj *shameles adj.*   A 1 shameles; B 1; C 1 shameles
A. 3.43   And shrof hire of hire shrewidnesse *shameles* I trowe;
B. 3.44   And shrof hire of hire sherewednesse, *shamelees* I trowe;
C. 3.46   [And] shrofe here of here synne, *shameles* y [trowe];

shap n *shape n.* &> *shape*   A 1; B 2   shap (1)   shape (1)
A.10.32   Ac man is hym most lik of mark & of *shap*.
B. 9.31   Ac man is hym moost lik of marc and of [*shape*].
B.11.397   The *shap* ne þe shaft þat god shoop hymselue,

shape v *shapen v.* &> *shap*   A 6 shape (1) shapen (1) shapiþ (1) shop (1)
   shope (1) shopen (1); B 18 shape (3) shapen (2) shapeþ (2) shapte (2)
   shoop (7) shopen (2); C 16 schupte (1) shap (1) shape (2) shapen (1)
   shapeth (2) shoop (1) shop (2) shope (2) shopen (1) shupte (2) yschape
   (1)
A.Pr.2   I *shop* me into a shroud as I a shep were;
A.Pr.54   *Shopen* hem Ermytes here ese to haue.
A. 3.17   For we wile wisse þe king & þi wey [*shape*]
A. 5.102   ʒif shrift shulde, it *shop[e]* a gret wondir.'
A. 8.68   But ʒif þe suggestioun be soþ þat [*shapiþ* hem to] begge.
A.10.166   Swiþe to *shapen* a sship of shidis & bordis;
B.Pr.2   I *shoop* me into [a] shrou[d] as I a sheep weere.
B.Pr.57   *Shopen* hem heremytes hire ese to haue.
B.Pr.122   *Shopen* lawe and leaute, ech [lif] to knowe his owene.
B. 1.161   Right so is loue a ledere and þe lawe *shapeþ*;
B. 3.17   For we wol wisse þe kyng and þi wey *shape*
B. 7.66   But if þe suggestion be sooþ þat *shapeþ* hem to begge,
B. 9.67   And dooþ god forsaken hem þat he *shoop* to his liknesse:
B. 9.135   "Swiþe go *shape* a ship of shides and bordes;
B.10.406   Tho he *shoop* þat ship of shides and bordes.
B.11.397   The shap ne þe shaft þat god *shoop* hymselue,
B.11.426   As shal shame, and shenden hym, and *shape* hym to amende.
B.11.439   'Certes', quod he, 'þat is sooþ'; and *shoop* hym for to walken,
B.14.39   For lent neuere was lif but liflode were *shapen*,
B.14.121   For to wroþerhele was he wroʒt þat neuere was Ioye *shapen*.
B.17.86   And whan I seiʒ þis I soiourned noʒt but *shoop* me to renne
B.17.220   Lele loue or lif þat oure lord *shapte*.
B.20.139   Departen er deeþ cam and deuors *shapte*.
B.20.306   Shrift *shoop* sharp salue and made men do penaunce
C.Pr.2   Y *shope* me into [a] shroud[e] as y a shep were;
C.Pr.55   And [*shopen*] he[m] heremites here ese to haue.
C. 1.157   Ryht so is loue [a] ledare and þe lawe *shapeth*;
C. 2.180   And *shop* þat a shereue sholde bere mede
C. 3.18   For we w[o]l wisse the kyng and thy way *shape*
C. 5.18   Or *shap* shon or cloth or shep and kyne kepe,
C. 6.424   'Thow lord [þat] aloft art and alle lyues *shope*.
C. 9.62   Bote the sugestioun be soth þat *shapeth* h[e]m to begge
C.10.223   And bad go *shapen* a ship of shides and bordes.
C.11.237   Tho he *shoop* þe ship of shides and bordes:
C.13.245   'ʒe, certes,' quod he, 'þat is soth', and *shop* hym to walke;
C.15.238   For lente neuere was lyf but lyflode were *shape*,
C.15.297   For to wroþerhele was he wrouht þat neuere was ioye *yschape*.
C.19.186   Leel lycame and lyf þat oure lord *shupte*.
C.22.139   Departen ar dethe come and deuors *shupte*.
C.22.306   Shrift *schupte* scharp salue and made men do penauns[e]

shappere n *shapere n.*   B 1
B.17.170   So is þe fader a ful god, formour and *shappere*:

shar > shaar

sharp adj *sharp adj.*   B 2 sharp (1) sharpe (1); C 2 scharp (1) sharpe (1)
B.18.409   'After *sharpe* shoures', quod pees, 'moost shene is þe sonne;
B.20.306   Shrift shoop *sharp* salue and made men do penaunce
C.20.452   'Aftur *sharp[e]* shoures,' quod pees, 'most shene is þe sonne;
C.22.306   Shrift schupte *scharp* salue and made men do penauns[e]

sharpe adv *sharpe adv.* &> *sharp*   B 1; C 1
B.18.39   And al þe court on hym cryde 'crucifie!' *sharpe*.
C.20.38   And alle þe Court [on hym] cryede 'crucifige!' [*sharpe*].

sharpeliche adv *sharpli adv.*   C 2
C. 6.13   And shryue the *sharpeliche* and shak of alle pruyde.'
C.18.106   And shaken hit *sharpeliche*; the rype sholden falle.

sharre > shere

she pron *she pron.* A 29 she (28) sheo (1); B 87; C 46

A.2.97, A.3.111, A.3.112, A.3.120, A.3.125, A.3.134, A.3.136, A.3.138, A.3.139, A.3.142, A.3.143, A.3.144, A.3.145, A.3.148, A.3.158, A.5.141, A.6.121, A.11.3, A.11.5, A.11.13, A.11.104, A.11.165, A.11.168, A.11.182, A.12.30, A.12.40, A.12.49, A.12.51

B.1.10, B.1.12, B.1.46, B.1.73, B.1.74, B.1.75, B.1.140, B.2.18, B.2.18, B.2.23, B.2.24, B.2.28, B.2.50, B.2.133, B.2.133, B.2.155, B.2.238, B.2.239, B.3.7, B.3.87, B.3.119, B.3.122, B.3.123, B.3.124, B.3.127, B.3.131, B.3.135, B.3.136, B.3.140, B.3.142, B.3.143, B.3.144, B.3.145, B.3.147, B.3.149, B.3.150, B.3.153, B.3.154, B.3.155, B.3.158, B.3.163, B.3.165, B.3.171, B.3.332, B.3.341, B.3.342, B.4.96, B.5.33, B.5.63, B.5.65, B.5.160, B.5.161, B.5.197, B.5.215, B.5.217, B.5.218, B.5.225, B.5.302, B.5.636, B.9.7, B.10.3, B.10.5, B.10.13, B.10.152, B.10.162, B.11.8, B.11.9, B.11.10, B.11.53, B.11.108, B.11.248, B.11.348, B.12.48, B.13.140, B.15.402, B.18.114, B.18.118, B.18.119, B.18.120, B.18.171, B.18.174, B.18.175, B.18.176, B.18.246, B.19.120, B.19.160, B.20.195

C.1.10, C.1.12, C.1.44, C.1.70, C.1.71, C.1.72, C.1.139, C.1.204, C.2.10, C.2.24, C.2.53, C.2.255, C.3.7, C.3.131, C.3.156, C.3.159, C.3.164, C.3.164, C.3.168, C.3.191, C.3.192, C.3.193, C.3.485, C.3.493, C.4.92, C.6.146, C.6.147, C.6.147, C.7.289, C.10.134, C.11.3, C.11.5, C.11.11, C.11.78, C.11.90, C.11.167, C.11.168, C.12.42, C.20.117, C.20.121, C.20.122, C.20.123, C.20.177, C.20.178, C.21.120, C.22.195

shedde v *sheden v.* B 2 shadde (1) shedde (1); C 2
B.17.293   That shente vs and *shedde* oure blood, forshapte vs as it [semed]:
B.19.58   Who was hardiere þan he? his herte blood he *shadde*
C.19.274   That shent vs and *shedde* oure bloed, forschupte vs as hit semede:
C.21.58   Ho was hardior then he? his herte bloed he *she[d]de*

shedyng ger *shedinge ger.* A 1; B 2; C 3 shedyng (1) shedynge (2)
A. 7.9   'Summe shal sewe þe sak for *shedyng* of þe whete;
B. 6.9   'Somme shul sowe þe sak for *shedyng* of þe Whete.
B.12.285   [Ac] þer is fullynge of Font and fullynge in blood *shedyng*
C. 8.8   'That somme sowe þe sak for *shedynge* of the whete,
C.14.207   Ac þer is follyng of fonte and follyng in bloed [*s*]*hedyng*
C.15.155   Withoute brutteny[n]ge of buyren or eny bloed *shedynge*.

sheef > shef

sheep n *shep n.* A 2 shep; B 1; C 4 shep
A.Pr.2   I shop me into a shroud as I a *shep* were;
A. 8.17   How þat shabbide *shep* shu[l] here wolle saue,
B.Pr.2   I shoop me into [a] shrou[d] as I a *sheep* weere;
C.Pr.2   Y shope me into [a] shroud[e] as y a *shep* were;
C. 3.412   And ʒaf þe kyndom to his knaue þat kept *shep* and lambren;
C. 5.18   Or shap shon or cloth or *shep* and kyne kepe,
C. 9.265   Thy *shep* ben ner al shabbede; the wolf shyt wolle:

sheepherdes > shepherdes

shef n *shef n.* B 4 sheef (1) shef (1) sheues (2); C 5 schaef (1) shef (2) sheues (2)
B. 3.326   By sixe sonnes and a ship and half a *shef* of Arwes;
B. 6.141   Diken or deluen or dyngen vpon *sheues*
B.19.330   A cart highte cristendom to carie [home] Piers *sheues*,
B.20.225   And shotten ayein wiþ shot, many a *sheef* of oþes,
C. 3.479   Be sixe [s]onnes [and] a ship and half a *shef* of Arwes;
C. 5.14   Mowen or mywen or make bond to sheues,
C. 8.348   Thre shypes and a *schaef* with [a vii] folwynge
C.21.330   A Cart hihte Cristendoem to carie hoem Peres *sheues*
C.22.225   And shoten aʒeyn[e with] shotte many a *shef* of othes

shelle n *shelle n.* A 1 shilles; B 2 shelle (1) shelles (1); C 1 shelles
A. 6.9   Signes of synay, & *shilles* of galis,
B. 5.521   Signes of Synay and *shelles* of Galice,
B.11.261   And after þat bitter bark, be þe *shelle* aweye,
C. 7.166   Signes of syse and *shelles* of galys

sheltrom n *sheltroun n.* B 1; C 1
B.14.82   Forþi mesure we vs wel and make [we] feiþ oure *sheltrom*;
C.20.292   And sheteth out shot ynow his *sheltrom* to blende;

shenden v *shenden v.* A 8 shende (2) shenden (1) shendiþ (4) shent (1); B 10 shenden (2) shendeþ (4) shent (2) shente (2); C 6 shende (1) shenden (1) shendeth (1) shent (2) shente (1)
A.Pr.95   And ben clerkis of þe kinges bench þe cuntre to *shende*.
A. 1.39   [And þat] *shend[iþ]* þi soule; set it in þin herte.
A. 2.90   Symonye & þiself *shenden* holy chirche;
A. 3.124   Shirreues of shires were *shent* ʒif heo ne were.
A. 3.145   Be Iesu, wiþ hire Iuelx ʒoure Iustice she *shendiþ*,
A. 7.148   Fro wastours þat waite wynneres to *shende*.
A. 7.158   'Awreke me on wasto[urs],' quaþ peris, 'þat þis world [*shend*]*iþ*.'
A.10.218   And þat is wykkide wil þat many werk *shendiþ*.'
B. 1.41   And that [*shendeþ*] þi soule; [set] it in þin herte.
B. 2.126   Symonye and þiself *shenden* holi chirche;
B. 3.135   Sherreues of Shires were *shent* if she ne were.
B. 3.155   By Iesus! wiþ hire Ieweles youre Iustices she *shendeþ*

B. 4.174   And gan wexe wroþ with lawe for Mede almoost hadde *shent* it,
B. 6.173   'Awreke me of wastours', quod he, 'þat þis world *shendeþ*.'
B. 9.209   And þat is wikked wille þat many werk *shendeþ*,
B.11.426   As shal shame, and *shenden* hym, and shape hym to amende.
B.17.293   That *shente* vs and shedde oure blood, forshapte vs as it [semed]:
B.20.98   As pokkes and pestilences, and muche peple *shente*.
C. 3.173   Shyreues of shyres were *shent* yf he nere,
C. 3.193   By iesu! with here ieweles the Iustices she *shendeth*,
C.13.115   Euele beth thei ysoffred, suche þat [*shenden*] þe masse
C.19.274   That *shent* vs and shedde oure bloed, forschupte vs as hit semede:
C.20.336   That if his soule hider cam hit sholde *shende* vs all.
C.22.98   As pokkes and pestilences, and moche peple *shente*;

shendfully > shenfulliche

shene adj *shene adj.* B 1; C 1
B.18.409   'After sharpe shoures', quod pees, 'moost *shene* is þe sonne;
C.20.452   'Aftur sharp[e] shoures,' quod pees, 'most *shene* is þe sonne;

shenfulliche adv *shendfulli adv.* A 1 shendfully; B 1; C 1 shentfolyche
A. 3.255   And al his sed for þat synne [*shend*]*fully* ende.
B. 3.277   And al his seed for þat synne *shenfulliche* ende.
C. 3.430   And al [h]is [sede] for þat synne *shentfolyche* ende.

shent(e > shenden; shentfolyche > shenfulliche; sheo > she; shep > sheep

shepherdes n *shepherde n.* B 4; C 2 sheepherdes (1) shepherdes (1)
B.10.467   Souteres and *shepherdes*; [swiche] lewed Iuttes
B.12.152   Tho it shon to *shepherdes*, a shewer of blisse].
B.15.361   Shipmen and *shepherdes* þat wiþ [shipe] wenten
B.15.368   *Shepherdes* and shipmen, and so do þise tilieris.
C.14.96   Tho hit shoen to *shepherdes*, a sheware of blisse.
C.17.99   Shipmen and *sheepherdes* by þe seuene sterres

shepsteres n *shapster n.* B 1; C 1 schupestares
B.13.330   As a *shepsteres* shere ysherewed [myn euencristen]:
C. 6.75   Lyke a *schupestares* sharre and shrewed myn euencristene

shere n *shere n.(1)* B 1; C 1 sharre
B.13.330   As a shepsteres *shere* ysherewed [myn euencristen]:
C. 6.75   Lyke a schupestares *sharre* and shrewed myn euencristene

shereue > sherreue

sherewe n *shreue n.* A 8 shrewe (7) shrewis (1); B 18 sherewe (13) sherewes (4) shrewe (1); C 10 schrewes (1) shrewe (7) shrewes (2)
A. 1.118   Aftir here deþ day & dwelle wiþ þat *shrewe*.
A. 4.67   And wisten wel þat wrong was a *shrewe* euere.
A. 4.97   Summe redde resoun to haue reuþe on þat *shrewe*,
A. 5.206   Þanne was þat *shrewe* asshamide & shrapide hise eris,
A. 5.235   And ʒet þe synful *shrewe* seide to hymselue:
A. 6.95   Ac be war þanne of wraþþe, þat wykkide *shrewe*,
A. 7.142   And bad hym go pisse wiþ his plouʒ: 'pilide *shrewe*!
A. 7.147   To kepen hym as couenaunt was fro curside *shrewis*,
B.Pr.192   The maʒe among vs alle þeiʒ we mysse a *sherewe*,
B. 1.129   After hir deþ day and dwelle wiþ þat *sherewe*.
B. 2.40   And now worþ þis Mede ymaried [t]o a mansed *sherewe*,
B. 4.110   Som[me] radde Reson to haue ruþe on þat *shrewe*;
B. 4.160   And leten Mekenesse a maister and Mede a mansed *sherewe*.
B. 5.90   'I wolde ben yshryue', quod þis *sherewe*, 'and I for shame dorste.
B. 5.279   Thanne weex þ[e] *sherewe* in wanhope & wolde han hanged hym[self]
B. 5.463   Ac yet þe synfulle *sherewe* seide to hymselue:
B. 5.609   A[c] be war þanne of Wraþe, þat wikked *sherewe*,
B. 6.155   And bad hym go pissen with his plowʒ: '[pyuysshe] *sherewe*!
B. 6.160   To kepen hym as couenaunt was fro cursede *sherewes*,
B. 9.125   Of swiche synfulle *sherewes* þe Sauter makeþ mynde:
B. 9.150   Ac I fynde, if þe fader be fals and a *sherewe*,
B. 9.153   Muchel merueille me þynkeþ; and moore of a *sherewe*
B.10.27   "Lo!" seiþ holy lettrure, "whiche [lordes] beþ þise *sherewes*";
B.10.443   And who were a good man but if þer were som *sherewe*?
B.17.45   And wel awey worse ʒit for to loue a *sherewe*.
B.19.373   Saue *sherewes* one swiche as I spak of,
C. 4.105   Summe radden resoun tho to haue reuthe vppon þat *shrewe*
C. 6.173   With þat y shal,' quod þat *shrewe*, 'saturdayes for thy loue
C. 6.317   Ac ʒut þ[e] synful *shrewe* saide to heuene:
C. 6.422   A wax ashamed, þat *shrewe*, and shrofe hym a[s] swythe
C. 7.261   Ac be war thenne of wrath, þat wikkede *shrewe*,
C. 8.151   And bad hym go pisse with his plogh, pyuische *shrewe*.
C.10.165   As þe sauter sayth by synnefole *shrewes*:
C.11.24   "Lo!" saith holy letrure, "whiche lordes beth this *schrewes*";
C.13.233   For shal neuere, ar shame come, a *shrewe* wel [be] chaste[d].
C.21.373   [Saue *shrewes* one swiche as y spak of],

sherewednesse n *shreuednesse n.* A 1 shrewidnesse; B 1
A. 3.43   And shrof hire of hire *shrewidnesse* shameles I trowe;
B. 3.44   And shrof hire of hire *sherewednesse*, shamelees I trowe;

sherreue n *shirreve n.* A 2 shirreue (1) shirreues (1); B 4 Sherreue (1)
    Sherreues (3); C 5 Schyreues (1) shereue (1) shyreues (2) shyryues (1)

A. 2.128   Sette mede on a *shirreue* shod al newe,
A. 3.124   *Shirreues* of shires were shent ȝif heo ne were.
B. 2.59   As Sisours and Somonours, *Sherreues* and hire clerkes,
B. 2.164   Sette Mede vpon a *Sherreue* shoed al newe,
B. 3.135   *Sherreues* of Shires were shent if she ne were.
B. 4.168   And [also] a *Sherreues* clerk bisherewed al þe route:
C. 2.61   As sysores [and] sompnores, *shyryues* and here clerkes,
C. 2.180   And shop þat a *shereue* sholde bere mede
C. 3.78   Bothe *Schyreues* and seriauntes and suche as kepeth lawes,
C. 3.173   *Shyryues* of shyres were shent yf he nere,
C. 4.164   A *shyreues* Clerk cryede, 'a! capias mede

sherte n *shirte n.* B 1

B.14.333   Ne neiþer *sherte* ne shoon, saue for shame one

shet > sheteth

shete n *shete n.(2)* A 1; B 2 shete (1) shetes (1); C 1 shetes

A. 5.89   Þat bar awey my bolle & my broken *shete*.
B. 5.109   That [bar] awey my bolle and my broke *shete*.
B.14.234   For whan he streyneþ hym to strecche þe strawe is his *shetes*.
C.16.75   For when he streyneth hym to strecche the strawe is his *shetes*.

sheteth v *sheten v.* A 1 shet; B 1 shotten; C 3 sheteth (1) shoten (1)
    shotte (1)

A.12.12   Skornfully þ[o] scripture *she[t]* vp h[ere] browes,
B.20.225   And *shotten* ayein wiþ shot, many a sheef of oþes,
C.20.50   'Aue, raby,' quod þat ribaud, and redes *shotte* vp to his yes.
C.20.292   And *sheteth* out shot ynow his sheltrom to blende;
C.22.225   And *shoten* aȝeyn[e with] shotte many a shef of othes

shette v *shitten v.* A 1; B 2; C 1

A. 6.89   To weue [vp] þe wyket þat [þe wif] *shette*
B.Pr.105   There [crist is in] kyngdom, to close and to *shette*,
B. 5.602   To wayuen vp þe wiket þat þe womman *shette*
C. 7.250   That Adam and Eue aȝenes vs alle *shette*:

sheues > shef; sheware > shewer

shewen v *sheuen v.(1)* A 23 shewe (8) shewen (4) shewid (1) shewide (4)
    shewiþ (5) ysheued (1); B 56 shewe (20) shewed (11) shewede (1)
    shewen (4) sheweth (1) sheweþ (16) shewynge (3); C 43 schewe (1)
    shewe (20) shewed (2) shewede (4) shewen (2) sheweth (14)

A.Pr.89   Þanne gete a mom of here mouþ til mony be *shewid*.
A. 1.2   And ek þe feld ful of folk I shal ȝow faire *shewe*.
A. 1.70   Þat suche wise wordis of holy writ *shewide*,
A. 2.175   Besshette hym in here shoppis to *shewen* here ware;
A. 3.258   Þe culorum of þis [cas] kepe I not to *shewe*;
A. 4.112   Bere no siluer ouer se þat signe of king *shewi[þ]*,
A. 4.119   Ac I may *shewe* ensaumplis as I se [oþer],
A. 4.145   And reherside þat resoun [hadde] riȝtfulliche *shewide*,
A. 5.59   And carfulliche his cope [comsiþ] he to *shewe*.
A. 5.147   And ca[iriþ] hym to [k]ir[k]eward hise [coupe] to *shewe*.
A. 5.245   Ac what befel of þis feloun I can not faire *shewe*;
A. 8.15   And bere hem boþe on here bak as here baner *shewiþ*,
A. 8.52   Ac for oure lordis loue lawe for hym *shewiþ*,
A. 8.114   And *shewiþ* it vs be ensaumple oureselue to wisse.
A. 9.24   Be a forebisene,' quaþ þe Frere, 'I shal þe faire *shewen*:
A.10.185   As fel of þe folk [þat I] bifore *shewide*.
A.11.13   I say be þo,' quaþ she, 'þat *shewen* be here werkis
A.11.73   And for suche tale telleris suche a teme *shewide*:
A.11.123   Þat iche wiȝt be in wille his wyt þe to *shewen*;
A.11.245   & suche [[shewiþ] þis sermoun þat [sewiþ] aftir]:
A.12.14   That he *shewe* me hit ne sholde but ȝif [I schriuen] were
A.12.34   And when scripture þe skolde hadde þis [skele] *ysheued*
A.12.54   Sey I sente him þis segge, and þat he *shewe* hym dowel.'
B.Pr.106   And to opene it to hem and heuene blisse *shewe*.
B.Pr.167   And riȝt so!' quod Raton, 'Reson me *sheweþ*
B.Pr.188   And be we neuere [so] bolde þe belle hym to *shewe*.
B.Pr.216   Than gete a mom of hire mouþ til moneye be *shewed*.
B. 1.2   And þe feld ful of folk I shal yow faire *shewe*.
B. 1.72   That swiche wise wordes of holy writ *shewed*,
B. 2.216   And bishetten hym in hire shoppes to *shewen* hire ware;
B. 3.280   The culorum of þis cas kepe I noȝt to [*shewe*];
B. 3.351   And þat is þe tail of þe text of þat [teme ye] *shewed*,
B. 4.129   Bere no siluer ouer see þat signe of kyng *sheweþ*,
B. 4.136   Ac I may *shewe* ensamples as I se ouþ[er].
B. 4.172   And recordede þat Reson hadde riȝtfully *shewed*,
B. 5.76   And carefully [his coupe] he comse[þ] to *shewe*.
B. 5.89   [This was al his curteisie where þat euere he *shewed* hym].
B. 5.143   *Shewen* hire shriftes to hem þan shryue hem to hir persons.
B. 5.297   And [kaireþ] hym to kirkeward his coupe to *shewe*.
B. 5.366   Shryue þee and be shamed þerof and *shewe* it with þi mouþe.'
B. 5.378   'This *shewynge* shrift', quod Repentaunce, 'shal be meryt to þe.'

B. 5.471   What bifel of þis feloun I kan noȝt faire *shewe*.
B. 7.16   Arn peres wiþ þe Apostles–þ[u]s pardon Piers *sheweþ*–
B. 7.50   [Ac] for oure lordes loue [lawe for hym *sheweþ*],
B. 7.132   And *sheweþ* vs by ensampl[e] vs selue to wisse.
B. 8.28   By a forbisne', quod þe frere, 'I shal þee faire *shewe*.
B. 9.44   He moste werche wiþ his word and his wit *shewe*.
B. 9.162   As bifel of þe folk þat I bifore [*shewed*].
B.10.13   I seye by [þo]', quod she, 'þat *sheweþ* by hir werkes
B.10.171   That ech wight be in wille his wit þee to *shewe*.
B.10.260   Loke þow werche it in werk þat þi word *sheweþ*;
B.10.378   Where dowel is or dobet derkliche ye *shewen*.
B.10.401   As Salomon dide and swiche oþere, þat *shewed* grete wittes
B.11.54   Go confesse þee to som frere and *shewe* hym þi synnes.
B.11.437   As shame: þere he *sheweþ* hym, [hym shonyeþ euery man].
B.12.50   That wise wordes wolde *shewe* and werche þe contrarie:
B.12.88   As cristes caracte[s] confortede, and boþe coupable *shewed*
B.12.170   'Right so', quod þe renk, 'Reson it *sheweþ*
B.13.212   I shal dwelle as I do my deuoir to *shewe*,
B.13.278   Ooþerwise þan he haþ wiþ herte or siȝte *shewynge* hym;
B.13.448   To crie a largesse bifore oure lord, youre good loos to *shewe*.
B.14.124   Right so reson *sheweþ* þat [þo renkes] þat were [lordes]
B.14.126   Ac god is of [a] wonder wille, by þat kynde wit *sheweþ*,
B.14.190   [We] sholde take þe Acquitaunce as quyk and to þe queed *shewen*
           it:
B.14.310   The seuenþe is welle of wisedom and fewe wordes *sheweþ*
B.15.506   And make hir mone to Makometh hir message to *shewe*.
B.15.571   Thoruȝ his prouince to passe and to his peple *shewe* hym,
B.16.21   That Piers þe Plowman al þe place me *shewed*
B.16.201   And þere hym likede and [he] louede, in þre persones hym
           shewede.
B.16.202   And þat it may be so and sooþ [*sheweþ*] it manhode]:
B.17.41   And riȝt so, bi þe roode, Reson me *sheweþ*
B.17.139   Or Eretikes wiþ argumentȝ, þyn hond þow hem *shewe*.
B.17.155   And þre sondry sightes [*shewynge* in oon],
B.17.157   Right so, redily, Reson it *sheweth*
B.17.188   He may receyue riȝt noȝt; reson it *sheweþ*.
B.17.322   For to fleen his owene [hous] as holy writ *sheweþ*.
B.18.228   That he was god þat al wroȝte þe wolkne first *shewed*:
B.18.393   And my mercy shal be *shewed* to manye of my [halue]breþeren,
B.19.229   Some [wyes] he yaf wit with wordes to *shewe*,
C.Pr.166   Than gete a Mum of here mouth [til] moneye [be] *shewed*.
C.Pr.184   [Ryȝt so,'quod þe raton, 'reson me *shewe*
C.Pr.205   And be [we] neuere so bold the belle hym [to] *shewe*.
C. 1.2   And þe feld ful of folk y shal ȝou fair *shewe*.
C. 1.69   That suche wyse wordes of holy writ *shewede*,
C. 2.41   And dauid vndoth hymself as þe doumbe *sheweth*:
C. 2.110   In lordschip with lucifer, as this lettre *sheweth*,
C. 2.226   And byschytten hym in here shoppe[s] to *shewen* here ware;
C. 3.214   For pore men dar nat pleyne ne no pleynt *shewe*,
C. 3.433   The culorum of this kaes kepe y nat to *shewe*;
C. 4.126   Bere no seluer ouer see þat sygne of kyng *sheweth*,
C. 4.133   Ac y may *s[hew]en* ensamples as y see othere.
C. 6.21   Thorw my word and my witt here euel werkes to *shewe*;
C. 6.25   Scornare and vnskilful tom þat skil *shewede*,
C. 6.325   What byful of this feloun y can nat fayre *shewe*;
C. 6.351   And kayres hym to kyrkeward his coup[e] to *shewe*.
C. 7.108   To crye a largesse tofore oure lord ȝoure good loos to *shewe*.
C. 8.263   'By Crist!' quod [Peres] þe [plouhman] tho, 'this prouerbis [wol y]
           shewe
C. 9.82   That reuthe is to rede or in ryme *shewe*
C.10.32   By a forbisene,' quod þe frere, 'y shal the fayre *shewe*:
C.10.160   May nat shyne ne *shewe* on schalkes on erthe,
C.11.5   'Wel artow wyse,' quod she to wyt, 'suche wysdomes to *shewe*
C.11.11   Y syg hit by suche,' quod [she], 'þat *sheweth* by here werkes
C.11.78   Forthy, wit,' quod she, 'be waer holy writ to *shewe*
C.11.160   Thenne scripture scorned me and mony skiles *shewed*
C.11.205   Predestinaet thei prechen, prechours þat this *sheweth*,
C.11.207   Vnwriten for som wikkednesse, as holy writ *sheweth*:
C.12.173   To testifie for treuthe þe tale þat y *shewe*
C.13.41   His erende and his lettre *sheweth* and is anoon delyuered.
C.13.89   And *sheweth* be seel and seth by lettre with what lord he dwelleth,
C.13.130   And scripture scornede þat many skilles *shewede*,
C.13.232   Ne clergie of his connynge kepeth [t]he nat *shewe*.
C.13.243   As shame: ther he *sheweth* hym vch man shoneth his companye.
C.14.110   'Riht so,' quod þ[e] renk, 'resoun hit *shewede*
C.16.144   The seuethe is a welle of wysdoem and fewe wordes *sheweth*
C.17.257   And maken here mone to Macometh here message to *shewe*.
C.17.284   And pacientliche thorw his prouynce and to his peple hym *shewe*,
C.19.112   Or Eretikes with argumentes, thin hoend thow hem *shewe*.
C.19.133   As my fuste is furste ar y my fyngours *shewe*,
C.19.154   He may resceyue riht nauhte; resoun hit *sheweth*.
C.19.302   Out of his oune house as holy writ *sheweth*.
C.20.247   That he was god þat al wrouhte the welkene furste *shewede*:

C.21.229 Som [wyes] he ʒaf wyt with wordes to *schewe*,

shewer n *sheuere n.* B 1; C 1 sheware
B.12.152 Tho it shon to shepherdes, a *shewer* of blisse].
C.14.96   Tho hit shoen to shepherdes, a *sheware* of blisse.

shewyng ger *sheuinge ger.* B 2 shewyng (1) shewynge (1); C 1 schewynge
B.15.78   In housynge, in haterynge, [in] heigh clergie *shewynge*
B.16.1   'NOw faire falle yow', quod I þo, 'for youre faire *shewyng*!
C.16.237 In housynge, in helynge, in h[eyh] clergie *schewynge*

shewynge > *shewen,shewyng*

shides n *shide n.* A 1 shidis; B 2; C 3
A.10.166 Swiþe to shapen a sship of *shidis* & bordis;
B. 9.135 "Swiþe go shape a ship of *shides* and of bordes;
B.10.406 Tho he shoop þat ship of *shides* and bordes:
C.10.223 And bad go shapen a ship of *shides* and bordes.
C.11.237 Tho he shoop þe ship of *shides* and bordes:
C.18.20   Hit hadde schoriares to shuyuen hit vp, thre *shides* of o lenghe

shifte v *hiften v.* B 1; C 1
B.20.167 And Elde hente good hope and hastiliche *shifte* hym
C.22.167 And elde hente gode hope and hastiliche [he] *sh[ifte]* hym

shilden v *shelden v.* B 1
B.10.413 And *shilden* vs from shame þerinne, as Noes ship dide beestes;

shille adv *shille adv.* C 1
C. 6.46   Prout of my fayre fetures and for y song *shille*;

shilles > *shelle*

shillynges n *shilling n.* B 1; C 2
B.12.145 If any frere were founde þere I ʒyue þee fyue *shillynges*!
C. 3.392 Nyme he a noumbre of nobles or of *shillynges*,
C.14.89   Yf eny frere we[re] founde þere y ʒeue the fyue *shillynges*!

shyne v *shinen v.* B 2 shyne (1) shon (1); C 3 shine (1) shyne (1) shoen (1)
B.12.152 Tho it *shon* to shepherdes, a shewer of blisse].
B.17.259 For vnkyndenesse quencheþ hym þat he kan noʒt *shyne*
C.10.160 May nat *shyne* ne shewe on schalkes on erthe,
C.14.96   Tho hit *shoen* to shepherdes, a sheware of blisse.
C.19.225 For vnkyndenesse quencheth hym þat he can nat *shine*

shynes n *shine n.(1)* B 1
B.11.433 And shame shrapeþ hise cloþes and hise *shynes* wassheþ,

shyngled adj *shinglede adj.* A 1 shynglid; B 1; C 1 shingled
A.10.176 Þat in þe [*shynglid*] ship shal ben ysauid;
B. 9.145 That in [þe] *shyngled* ship shul ben ysaued."
C.10.233 That in thi [*s]hingled* ship shal be with þe ysaued."

ship n *ship n.* A 2 ship (1) sship (1); B 5; C 5 ship (4) shypes (1)
A.10.166 Swiþe to shapen a *sship* of shidis & bordis;
A.10.176 Þat in þe [shynglid] *ship* shal ben ysauid;
B. 3.326 By sixe sonnes and a *ship* and half a shef of Arwes;
B. 9.135 "Swiþe go shape a *ship* of shides and of bordes;
B. 9.145 That in [þe] shyngled *ship* shul ben ysaued."
B.10.406 Tho he shoop þat *ship* of shides and bordes:
B.10.413 And shilden vs from shame þerinne, as Noes *ship* dide beestes;
C. 3.479 Be sixe [s]onnes [and] a *ship* and half a shef of Arwes;
C. 8.348 Thre *shypes* and a schaef with [a vii] folwynge
C.10.223 And bad go shapen a *ship* of shides and bordes.
C.10.233 That in thi [s]hingled *ship* shal be with þe ysaued."
C.11.237 Tho he shoop þe *ship* of shides and bordes:

shipe n *shipe n.* B 1
B.15.361 Shipmen and shepherdes þat wiþ [*shipe*] wenten

shipmen n *ahipman n.* B 3; C 3
B.15.357 Wederwise *shipmen* and witty clerkes also
B.15.361 *Shipmen* and shepherdes þat wiþ [shipe] wenten
B.15.378 Shepherdes and *shipmen*, and so do þise tilieris.
C.17.95   Wedurwyse *shipmen* now and oþer witty peple
C.17.99   *Shipmen* and sheepherdes by þe seuene sterres
C.17.104 Now failleth this folk, bothe follwares and *shipmen*;

shire n *shire n. &> bokynghamshire* A 3 shire (1) shires (2); B 3 shire (1) shires (2); C 2 shyre (1) shyres (1)
A. 2.74   Bette þe bedel of bukyngham *shire*,
A. 2.123 And let somoune alle þe segges [in *shires* abouten],
A. 3.124 Shirreues of *shires* were shent ʒif heo ne were.
B. 2.159 And leten somone alle segges in *shires* aboute,
B. 3.135 Sherreues of *Shires* were shent if she ne were.
B. 5.355 Is noon so hungry hound in hertford *shire*
C. 3.173 Shyreues of *shyres* were shent yf he nere,

C. 6.413 Ys non so hungry hound in hertford *shyre*

shyreues -ryues -rreue(s > *sherreue*

shyt v *shiten v.* C 1
C. 9.265 Thy shep ben ner al shabbede; the wolf *shyt* wolle:

shoed ptp *shon v.* A 1 shod; B 1
A. 2.128 Sette mede on a shirreue *shod* al newe,
B. 2.164 Sette Mede vpon a Sherreue *shoed* al newe,

shoen > *shyne*; *shoes* > *shoon*; *shoke* > *shaken*; *shold(- sholle(n* > *shal; shon* > *shyne,shoon*

shonye v *shonen v.* B 3 shonye (2) shonyeþ (1); C 2 shoneth (1) shonye (1)
B.Pr.174 And if hym wraþeþ be war and his wey *shonye*.'
B. 5.169 Among Monkes I myʒte be ac many tyme I *shonye*
B.11.437 As shame: þere he sheweþ hym, [hym *shonye*þ euery man].
C.Pr.191 And yf hym wratheth ben war and his way [*shonye*].'
C.13.243 As shame: ther he sheweth hym vch man *shoneth* his companye.

shook > *shake*

shoon n *sho n.* B 2 shoes (1) shoon (1); C 2 shon (1) shoes (1)
B.14.333 Ne neiþer sherte ne *shoon*, saue for shame one
B.20.219 In paltokes and pyked *shoes*, [purses and] longe knyues,
C. 5.18   Or shap *shon* or cloth or shep and kyne kepe,
C.22.219 In paltokes and pikede *shoes*, [purses and] longe knyues

shoop shop(e -en > *shape*

shoppe n *shoppe n.* A 1 shoppis; B 1 shoppes; C 2 shoppe (1) shoppes (1)
A. 2.175 Besshette hym in here *shoppis* to shewen here ware;
B. 2.216 And bishetten hym in hire *shoppes* to shewen hire ware;
C. 2.226 And byschytten hym in here *shoppe[s]* to shewen here ware;
C.14.184 And þe ryche for his rentes or for rychesse in his *shopp[e]*.

shordych n prop *n.i.d.* B 1
B.13.339 To þe Soutere of Southwerk or of *Shordych* dame Emme;

shoriare n *shorer n.* C 4 schoriares (1) shoriare (1) shoriere (1) shorriares (1)
C.18.20   Hit hadde *schoriares* to shuyuen hit vp, thre shides of o lenghe
C.18.25   'Thise thre *shorriares*,' quod he,' that bereth vp this plonte
C.18.50   And thenne [f]alle y adoune the pouke with the thridde *shoriere*
C.18.118 That libera voluntas dei lauhte þe myddel *Shoriare*

short adj *short adj.* B 4 short (2) shorte (1) shorter (1); C 4 short (2) shorte (1) shortere (1)
B.12.122 Ne sette *short* bi hir science, whatso þei don hemselue.
B.14.60   For if þow lyue after his loore, þe *shorter* lif þe bettre:
B.14.244 And louely layk was it neuere bitwene þe longe and þe *shorte*.
B.18.298 Wheiþer he were god or goddes sone; he [g]af me *short* answere;
C.14.65   Ne sette *shorte* by here science, whatso þei doen hemsulue.
C.15.259 For if thow lyu[e] aftur his lore the *shortere* lyf þe betere:
C.16.84   And louely layk was hit neuere bytwene a longe and a *short*.
C.20.331 Where he were god or godes sone; he gaf me *short* answere.

shost > *shal*

shot n *shot n.* B 1; C 2 shot (1) shotte (1)
B.20.225 And shotten ayein wiþ *shot*, many a sheef of oþes,
C.20.292 And sheteth out *shot* ynow his sheltrom to blende;
C.22.225 And shoten aʒeyn[e with] *shotte* many a shef of othes

shoten > *sheteth*; *shotte* > *sheteth,shot*; *shotten* > *sheteth*

shoures n *shour n.* B 1; C 1
B.18.409 'After sharpe *shoures*', quod pees, 'moost shene is þe sonne;
C.20.452 'Aftur sharp[e] *shoures*,' quod pees, 'most shene is þe sonne;

shrapeþ v *shrapen v.* A 1 shrapide; B 2 shrape (1) shrapeþ (1); C 1 shrape
A. 5.206 Þanne was þat shrewe asshamide & *shrapide* hise eris,
B. 5.125 Ne neiþer shrifte ne shame, but whoso *shrape* my mawe?'
B.11.433 And shame *shrapeþ* hise cloþes and hise shynes wassheþ,
C. 6.90   Ne noþer shame ne shryfte but hoso *shrap[e]* my mawe?'

shrewe(s > *sherewe*

shrewed adj *shreued adj.* C 2
C.Pr.122 Wel hardere and grettere on suche *shrewed* faderes
C.Pr.124 For ʒoure *shrewed* soffraunce and ʒoure oune synne.

shrewed v *shreuen v.* C 1
C. 6.75   Lyke a schupestares sharre and *shrewed* myn euencristene

shrewidnesse > *sherewednesse*

shrift n *shrift n.* A 4 shrift (3) shrifte (1); B 15 shrift (7) shrifte (5) shryfte (1) shriftes (2); C 8 shrift (1) shrifte (3) shryft (1) shryfte (3)

A. 3.36	And seide [wel] softely, in *shrifte* as it were,
A. 5.58	Enuye wiþ heuy herte askide aftir *shrift*,
A. 5.102	ʒif *shrift* shulde, it shop[e] a gret wondir.'
A. 5.146	Now begynneþ glotoun for to [go to] *shrift*,
B. 3.37	And seide [wel] softely, in *shrift* as it were,
B. 5.75	Enuye wiþ heuy herte asked after *shrifte*,
B. 5.125	Ne neiþer *shrifte* ne shame, but whoso shrape my mawe?'
B. 5.141	And siþen þei blosmede abrood in boure to here *shriftes*.
B. 5.143	Shewen hire *shriftes* to hem þan shryue hem to hir persons.
B. 5.296	Now bigynneþ Gloton for to go *shrifte*
B. 5.378	'This shewynge *shrift*', quod Repentaunce, 'shal be meryt to þe.'
B. 5.392	'What! awake, renk!' quod Repentaunce, 'and rape þee to *shryfte*!'
B.12.181	And haþ no contricion er he come to *shrifte*; & þanne kan he litel telle
B.13.55	In a dissh of derne *shrifte*, Dixi & confitebor tibi.
B.14.89	And surgiens for dedly synnes whan *shrift* of mouþe failleþ.
B.14.90	Ac *shrift* of mouþ moore worþi is if man be y[n]liche contrit,
B.14.91	For *shrift* of mouþe sleeþ synne be it neuer so dedly–
B.20.284	And [be] ashamed in hir *shrift*; ac shame makeþ hem wende
B.20.306	*Shrift* shoop sharp salue and made men do penaunce
C. 6.63	Enuye with heuy herte asked aftur *shrifte*
C. 6.90	Ne noþer shame ne *shryfte* but hoso shrap[e] my mawe?'
C. 6.350	Now bygynneth glotoun for to go to *shryfte*
C. 7.8	'What! awake, renke!' quod repentaunce, 'and rape [þe] to *shryfte*.'
C.14.121	And hath no contricion ar he come to *shrifte*; and thenne can he lytel telle,
C.16.30	And oris confessio cometh of [knowlechyng and] *shrifte* of mouthe
C.22.284	And be aschamed in here *shryft*; ac shame maketh [hem] wende
C.22.306	*Shrift* schupte scharp salue and made men do penauns[e]

shryne n *shrine n.* A 1; B 1; C 1

A. 6.45	'I nolde fonge a ferþing for seint Thomas *shryne*,
B. 5.558	'I nolde fange a ferþyng for Seint Thomas *Shryne*;
C. 7.202	'Y [nolde] fonge a ferthynge for seynt Thomas *shryne*;

shryuars n *shriver n.* C 1

C.Pr.64	But holi chirche and charite choppe adoun suche *shryuars*

shryuen v *shriven v.* A 6 shryue (2) shriuen (1) schriuen (1) shrof (2); B 15 shryue (5) shryuen (5) shryueþ (2) yshryue (1); C 16 shryue (9) shryuen (2) shryueth (2) shrof (1) shrofe (2)

A.Pr.61	Siþen charite haþ ben chapman & chief to *shryue* lordis
A. 3.43	And *shrof* hire of hire shrewidnesse shameles I trowe;
A. 5.151	And siþen I wile be *shriuen* & synne no more.'
A.11.203	Ne no leperis ouer lond ladies to *shryue*.
A.11.281	And for he kneuʒ on þe crois & to crist *shr[o]f* hym,
A.12.14	That he shewe me hit ne sholde but ʒif [I *schriuen*] were
B.Pr.64	Siþ charite haþ ben chapman and chief to *shryue* lordes
B.Pr.89	And signe þat þei sholden *shryuen* hire parisshens,
B. 3.44	And *shrof* hire of hire sherewednesse, shamelees I trowe;
B. 5.90	'I wolde ben *yshryue*', quod þis sherewe, 'and I for shame dorste.
B. 5.143	Shewen hire shriftes to hem þan *shryue* hem to hir persons.
B. 5.301	And siþen I wole be *shryuen* and synne na moore.'
B. 5.366	*Shryue* þee and be shamed þerof and shewe it with þi mouþe.'
B. 5.386	'I moste sitte [to be *shryuen*] or ellis sholde I nappe;
B. 5.413	I [a]m noʒt *shryuen* som tyme but if siknesse it make
B.10.420	And for he bekne[w on] þe cros and to crist *shrof* hym
B.14.9	And [siþþe] *shryuen* of þe preest, þat [for my synnes gaf me]
B.20.281	For persons and parissh preestes þat sholde þe peple *shryue*
B.20.290	And so it fareþ with muche folk þat to freres *shryueþ*,
B.20.304	Conscience called a leche þat koude wel *shryue*:
B.20.368	Thus he gooþ and gadereþ and gloseþ þere he *shryueþ*
C.Pr.62	Ac sith charite hath be Chapman and [c]hief to *shryue* lordes
C. 3.46	[And] *shrofe* here of here synne, shameles y [trowe];
C. 5.194	'Comaunde þat alle confessours þat eny kyng *shryueth*
C. 6.13	And *shryue* the sharpeliche and shak of alle pruyde.'
C. 6.120	And prelates pleyneth on hem for they here parschiens *shryuen*
C. 6.175	Y, gulty in gost, to god y me *shryue*
C. 6.356	And sennes sitte and be *shryue* and synege no more.'
C. 6.422	A wax ashamed, þat shrewe, and *shrofe* hym a[s] swythe
C. 9.253	Amend[e] hym and mercy aske and mekeliche hym *shryue*,
C.11.254	And for he biknewe on þe croes and to crist *shrof* hym
C.22.281	For persones and parsche prestes þat sholde þe peple *shryue*
C.22.290	And so hit fareth with moche folke þat to freres *shryuen*,
C.22.304	Consience calde a leche þat couthe wel *shryue*:
C.22.368	Thus he goeth and gedereth and gloseth þer he *shryueth*

shroud n *shroud n.* A 1; B 1; C 1 shroude

A.Pr.2	I shop me into a *shroud* as I a shep were;
B.Pr.2	I shoop me into [a] *shrou[d]* as I a sheep weere;
C.Pr.2	Y shope me into [a] *shroud[e]* as y a shep were;

shuyuen v *shouven v.* C 1

C.18.20	Hit hadde schoriares to *shuyuen* hit vp, thre shides of o lenghe

shul(- > shal; shupte > shape

sib adj *sibbe adj.* A 4 sib (3) sibbe (1); B 5 sib (4) sibbe (1); C 7 sib (4) syb (2) sybbe (1)

A. 6.110	Ac whoso is *sib* to þis sistris, so me god helpe,
A. 6.112	But ʒif ʒe be *sibbe* to summe of þis seuene
A. 6.121	And she is *sib* to alle synful, & hire sone alse,
A.11.107	Is *sib* to þe seuene ars þat scripture is nempnid.
B. 5.625	A[c] who is *sib* to þise [sustren], so me god helpe,
B. 5.627	But if ye be *sibbe* to some of þise seuene
B. 5.636	And she is *sib* to alle synfulle and hire sone also,
B.10.155	Is *sib* to [þe] seuen artʒ, [þat] Scripture is [nempned].
B.14.273	The which is *sib* to god hymself, [so neiʒ is pouerte].'
C. 7.278	And ho is *sib* to þis seuene, so me god helpe,
C. 7.280	Ho is nat *syb* to this seuene, sothly to telle,
C. 7.289	And she is *sib* to alle synfole and here sone bothe,
C.11.95	For he is *sib* to þe seuene ars–and also my suster
C.11.196	Sir wanhope was *sib* to hym, as som men me tolde,
C.12.156	His fader or his frendes, fre[m]de oþer *sybbe*,
C.16.113	The whiche is *syb* to crist [hym]sulue and semblable bothe.'

sicurly > sikerly

sidder adj *side adj.* B 1; C 1 syddore

B. 5.192	Wel *sidder* þan his chyn; þei chyueled for elde;
C. 6.200	Wel *syddore* then his chyn, ycheueled for elde,

syde n *side n.* A 6 side (5) sides (1); B 11 side (1) syde (6) sides (2) sydes (2); C 11 syde (10) sides (1)

A.Pr.8	Vndir a brood bank be a bourn[e] *side*,
A. 2.34	Were beden to þe b[ri]dale on boþe two *sides*.
A. 5.62	A kertil & a courtepy, a knyf be his *side*,
A. 5.171	And bed bette þe bocher ben on his *side*.
A. 6.7	A bagge & a bolle he bar be his *side*;
A.11.214	A bidowe or a baselard he beriþ be his *side*;
B.Pr.8	Vnder a brood bank by a bourn[e] *syde*,
B. 2.55	Were boden to þe bridale on boþe two *sides*.
B. 2.99	Til Sleuþe and sleep sliken hise *sydes*;
B. 3.74	Wite what þow werchest wiþ þi riʒt *syde*,
B. 5.79	[A] kirtel and [a] Courtepy, a knyf by his *syde*,
B. 5.322	And bad Bette þe Bocher ben on his *syde*.
B. 5.369	Sworen goddes soule [and his *sydes*] and "so me god helpe"
B. 5.519	A bolle and a bagge he bar by his *syde*.
B.12.200	As þo þat seten at þe *syde* table or wiþ þe souereynes of þe halle,
B.13.36	And seten bi oureselue at [a] *side* borde.
B.13.316	What on bak, and what on body half, and by þe two *sides*
C. 1.114	Thenne sitten in þe sonne *syde* þere þe day roweth?'
C. 2.175	And leten somne alle seggus in vche *syde* aboute,
C. 3.76	Ywyte what thow delest with thi ryhte *syde*.
C. 6.379	And bade b[et]te þe bochere ben on his *syde*.
C. 6.427	Sworn godes soule and his *sides* and "so helpe [me] god almyhty"
C. 7.164	A bolle and a bagge a bar by his *syde*;
C. 9.253	He sat at þe *syde* benche and at þe seconde table;
C.10.62	By a wi[d]e wildernesse and by a wode *syde*.
C.14.139	As tho þat sitten at þe *syde* table or with þe souereyns [of þe] halle,
C.15.41	And seten by ouresulue at a *syde* table.
C.18.64	Tho that sitten in þe sonne *syde* sannore aren rype,

sye > seen

siggen v *seien v.(1)* A 99 say (1) sayde (1) segge (2) sey (8) seide (55) seyde (3) seye (2) seiʒe (7) seyn (2) seist (1) seiþ (16) seyþ (1); B 287 segge (3) seggen (1) sey (1) seid (2) seide (166) seyde (5) seiden (8) seidest (1) seie (1) seye (31) seyen (4) seist (2) seith (1) seiþ (52) sigge (1) siggen (6); C 290 said (2) saide (114) saiden (1) saidest (1) saiste (1) saith (18) say (1) sayde (69) sayden (2) saye (2) sayede (1) sayen (1) sayn (1) sayst (3) sayth (17) segen (1) segge (7) seggeth (2) seggyng (1) seid (1) seide (3) seien (2) sey (18) seyde (2) seyden (1) seydest (1) seye (3) seyen (2) seyn (3) seyth (2) syg (1) sygge (4) ysaide (1) yseide (1)

A.Pr.67	And *seide* þat hymself miʒte assoile hem alle
A. 1.5	And *seide* 'sone, slepist þou? sest þou þis peple,
A. 1.11	And *seide* 'mercy madame, what is þis to mene?'
A. 1.44	'Go to þe gospel,' quaþ heo, 'þat god *seide* himseluen,
A. 1.49	"Cesar," þ[ei] *seide*, "we se wel ichone."
A. 1.120	And enden as I er *seide*, in perfite werkis,
A. 1.123	Forþi I *seye* as I seide er, be siʒte of þise textis:
A. 1.123	Forþi I seye as I *seide* er, be siʒte of þise textis:
A. 1.134	Loke þou suffre hym to *seyn* & siþþe lere it aftir.
A. 1.180	Forþi I *seiʒe* as I seide er be siʒte of þise textes:
A. 1.180	Forþi I seiʒe as I *seide* er be siʒte of þise tixtes:
A. 2.2	And *seide*, 'mercy madame, for marie loue of heuene
A. 2.53	And as sire symonye wile *segge* to sewen his wille.

A. 2.80	And *seide* to cyuyle, 'now sorewe on þi bokes,
A. 2.116	And *seide*, 'certis cesse shuln we neuere
A. 2.133	Þanne swor cyuyle & *seide* be þe rode
A. 2.150	Soþnesse seiȝ hem wel & *seide* but litel,
A. 3.16	And *seide*, 'mourne nouȝt, mede, ne make þou no sorewe,
A. 3.36	And *seide* [wel] softely, in shrifte as it were,
A. 3.46	Þanne he assoilide hire sone, & siþen he *seide*,
A. 3.54	And *seiþ* Nesciat sinist[ra] quid faciat dexter[a].
A. 3.64	For oure sauiour it *seide* & hymself prechid:
A. 3.160	'Excuse þe ȝif þou canst; I can no more *seiȝe*,
A. 3.227	And þerof *sei[þ]* þe sauter in a salmis ende
A. 3.240	God sente hym to *segge* be samuels mouþ
A. 3.244	Samuel *seide* to saul, "god sendiþ þe & hotiþ
A. 3.254	God *seide* to samuel þat saul shulde deiȝe,
A. 4.1	'Sessiþ,' *seide* þe king, 'I suffre ȝow no lengere.
A. 4.13	'I am fayn of þat foreward,' *seide* þe frek þanne,
A. 4.15	*Seide* hym as þe king sente & siþþe tok his leue.
A. 4.48	[Þe king kneuȝ] he *seide* soþ for consience hym tolde.
A. 4.51	And *seide*, 'hadde I loue of my lord þe king, litel wolde I recche
A. 4.57	I *sey* it be myself, þou shalt it sone fynde,
A. 4.78	Wyt accordiþ þerewiþ & *seide* þe same.
A. 4.89	So [þat] ȝe assente I can *sey* no more,
A. 4.120	For I *seiȝe* it be myself, & it so were
A. 4.138	And *seide* it so loude þat soþnesse it herde:
A. 5.7	I sat softely [adoun] & *seide* my beleue,
A. 5.22	Ac I shal *seiȝe* as I saiȝ, so me god helpe,
A. 5.54	Lecchour *seide* 'allas!' & to oure lady criede
A. 5.216	And *seide*, 'war þe for wanhope wile þe betraye;
A. 5.217	"I am sory for my synne," *sey* to þiseluen,
A. 5.235	And ȝet þe synful shrewe *seide* to hymselue:
A. 6.14	'Fro synay,' he *seide*, '& fro þe sepulcre.
A. 6.22	'Nay, so [me god] helpe,' *seide* þe [gome] þanne.
A. 6.36	For, þeiȝ I *sey* it myself, I serue hym to pay.
A. 6.70	And þanne shalt þou [se] *sey* soþ, so it be to done;
A. 7.50	'I assente, be seint Iame,' *seide* þe kniȝt þanne,
A. 7.121	'Ȝef it be soþ,' quaþ peris, 'þat ȝe *seyn*, I shal it sone aspie,
A. 7.214	Miȝte I synneles do as þou seist?' seide peris þanne.
A. 7.214	Miȝte I synneles do as þou seist?' *seide* peris þanne.
A. 7.219	And sapience *seiþ* þe same, I saiȝ it in þe bible:
A. 7.227	And siþen he *seide*, his seruaunt[s] it h[er]de:
A. 7.234	The sauter *seiþ* in þe salme of Beati omnes:
A. 7.268	And I *seiȝe*, be my soule, I haue no salt bacoun,
A. 7.307	And so *seiþ* satourne & sente ȝow to warne.
A. 8.46	For so *seiþ* þe sauter & sapience boþe:
A. 8.54	Þat he ne worþ sauf sykirly, & so *seiþ* þe sautir.
A. 8.102	& *seide* 'Si ambulauero in medio umbre mortis
A. 8.109	Be þat þe sauter vs *seiþ*, & so dede manye oþere.
A. 8.113	Ne soliciti sitis he *seiþ* in his gospel,
A. 8.138	Daniel *seide*, 'sire king, þi sweuene is to mene
A. 8.147	It befel as his fadir *seide* in faraos tyme
A. 9.17	Seue siþes, *seiþ* þe bok, [synneþ] þe riȝtful;
A. 9.18	Ac whoso synneþ, I *seiȝe*, sertis, me þinkiþ
A. 9.22	'I shal *seiȝe* þe, my sone,' seide þe Frere þanne,
A. 9.22	'I shal seiȝe þe, my sone,' *seide* þe Frere þanne,
A. 9.51	And þei *seide*, 'þe same saue þe fro myschaunce,
A. 9.65	'Wot ich?' quaþ I; 'who art þou?' þouȝt,' *seide* he þanne.
A. 9.116	Þanne þouȝt, in þat tyme, *seide* þis wordis:
A.10.19	Sire se wel, & *sey* wel, & here wel þe hende,
A.10.81	Salamon it *seide* for a soþ tale.
A.10.86	And þerof *seiþ* þe sauter, þe salme þou miȝt rede:
A.10.149	And so *seiþ* þe sauter, se it shewiþ þe likiþ:
A.10.157	Forþi he sente to se[þ], & *se[i]de* hym be an aungel
A.10.161	Þat god was wroþ wiþ here werkis & [suche wordis *seide*]:
A.11.4	And sterneliche staringe dame studie *seide*:
A.11.9	And *seide*, 'Nolite mittere, Man, margerie perlis
A.11.13	I *say* be þo,' quaþ she, 'þat shewen be here werkis
A.11.16	Þanne alle þe soþe sawis þat salamon *seide* euere.
A.11.23	Iob þe ientile in his gestis *seide* it:
A.11.55	And so *seiþ* þe sauter, se[ke] it in Memento:
A.11.101	And *seide*, 'mercy madame, ȝour man shal I worþe
A.11.125	*Sey* hym þis signe, I sette hym to scole,
A.11.146	In oþer science it *seiþ*, I saiȝ it in catoun,
A.11.154	And *seide* it hymself in ensaumple for þe beste
A.11.166	I *seide* 'graunt mercy madame,' & mekly hire grette
A.11.179	And I *sei[d]e*, 'soþliche, þei sente me hider
A.11.206	And *seide* it in ensaumple þat þei shulde do þe betere:
A.11.253	For he *seiþ* it hymself in his ten hestis;
A.11.295	For he *seide* it hymself to summe of his disciplis:
A.11.304	*Seide* þis for a sarmoun, so me god helpe:
A.12.5	But I se now as I *seye*, as me soþ thinkytȝ,
A.12.16	And *seyde* so loude þat shame me thouȝthe,
A.12.20	"I saw synful," he *seyde*, "þerfore I seyde no þing,
A.12.20	"I saw synful," he seyde, "þerfore I *seyde* no þing

A.12.33	But as he *seyþ*, such I am, when he with me carpeþ.'
A.12.43	And *sayde*, 'my cosyn kynde wit knowen is wel wide,
A.12.54	*Sey* I sente him þis segge, and þat he shewe hym dowel.'
B.Pr.50	I seiȝ somme þat *seiden* þei hadde ysouȝt Seintes;
B.Pr.52	Moore þan to *seye* sooþ, it semed bi hire speche.
B.Pr.70	And *seide* þat hymself myȝte assoillen hem alle
B.Pr.124	And knelynge to þe kyng clergially he *seide*,
B.Pr.131	But suffren and seruen; forþi *seide* þe Aungel,
B.Pr.159	*Seide* for a souereyn [salue] to [hem alle]
B.Pr.193	For I herde my sire *seyn*, seuen yeer ypassed,
B.Pr.202	I *seye* for me', quod þe Mous, 'I se so muchel after,
B. 1.5	And *seide*, 'sone, slepestow? sestow þis peple,
B. 1.11	And *seide*, 'mercy, madame, what [may] þis [by]meene?'
B. 1.46	'Go to þe gospel', quod she, 'þat god *seide* hymseluen,
B. 1.51	"Cesar[i]s", þei *seiden*, "we seen wel echone."
B. 1.131	And enden, as I er *seide*, in truþe þat is þe beste,
B. 1.134	Forþi I *seye*, as I seyde er, by siȝte of þise textes:
B. 1.134	Forþi I seye, as I *seyde* er, by siȝte of þise textes:
B. 1.146	Loke þow suffre hym to *seye* and siþen lere it after.
B. 1.206	Forþi I *seye* as I seide er by [siȝte of þise] textes:
B. 1.206	Forþi I seye as I *seide* er by [siȝte of þise] textes:
B. 2.2	And *seide* 'mercy, madame, for Marie loue of heuene
B. 2.26	And neuere sooþ *seide* siþen he com to erþe,
B. 2.68	Thei assented for siluer to *seye* as boþe wolde.
B. 2.69	Thanne leep liere forþ and *seide*, 'lo! here a chartre
B. 2.116	And *seide* [to] Cyuyle, 'now sorwe [on þi bokes]
B. 2.152	And *seiden*, 'certes, cessen shul we neuere
B. 2.189	Sothnesse seiȝ hem wel and *seide* but litel,
B. 3.16	And *seiden*, 'mourne noȝt, Mede, ne make þow no sorwe,
B. 3.37	And *seide* [wel] softely, in shrift as it were,
B. 3.47	Thanne he assoiled hire soone and siþen he *seide*,
B. 3.173	'Excuse þee if þow kanst; I kan na moore *seggen*,
B. 3.248	And þerof *seiþ* þe Sauter in a Salmes ende:
B. 3.264	"Forþi", *seide* Samuel to Saul, "god hymself hoteþ [þ]ee
B. 3.276	God *seide* to Samuel þat Saul sholde deye
B. 3.283	That whoso *seiþ* hem soþe[s] is sonnest yblamed.
B. 3.333	Se what Salomon *seiþ* in Sapience bokes
B. 4.1	'CEsseþ', *sei[de]* þe kyng, 'I suffre yow no lenger.
B. 4.13	'I am fayn of þat foreward', *seide* þe freke þanne,
B. 4.15	[*Seide* hym] as þe kyng [sente] and siþen took his leue.
B. 4.61	The kyng knew he *seide* sooþ, for Conscience hym tolde
B. 4.65	And *seide*, 'hadde I loue of my lord þe kyng litel wolde I recche
B. 4.71	I *seye* it by myself, þow shalt it wel fynde,
B. 4.102	So þat [ye] assente I kan *seye* no [moore],
B. 4.137	I *seye* it by myself and it so were
B. 4.155	And *seide*, 'madame, I am youre man what so my mouþ Iangle.
B. 4.162	And *seid[e]* it so [loude] þat [soþnesse] it herde:
B. 4.175	And *seide*, 'þoruȝ [youre] lawe, as I leue, I lese manye eschetes;
B. 4.188	'And I assente', *seiþ* þe kyng, 'by Seinte Marie my lady,
B. 5.7	[I] sat softely adoun and *seide* my bileue,
B. 5.22	Ac I shal *seye* as I sauȝ, so me god helpe,
B. 5.37	My sire *seide* to me, and so dide my dame,
B. 5.39	And Salomon *seide* þe same þat Sapience made,
B. 5.59	That seweþ my sermon;' and þus *seyde* Resoun.
B. 5.71	Lechour *seide* 'allas!' and [to] oure lady cryde
B. 5.186	Esto sobrius!' he *seide* and assoiled me after,
B. 5.238	'Nay, soþly', he *seide*, 'saue in my youþe.
B. 5.444	And *seide*, 'ware þee, for wanhope wo[l] þee bitraye.
B. 5.445	"I am sory for my synn[e]", *seye* to þiselue,
B. 5.463	Ac yet þe synfulle sherewe *seide* to hymselue:
B. 5.526	'Fram Synay', he *seide*, 'and fram [þe Sepulcre].
B. 5.534	'Nay, so [god glade me]', *seide* þe gome þanne.
B. 5.549	For þouȝ I *seye* it myself I serue hym to paye;
B. 5.583	Thanne [shalt þow] see *seye-sooþ-so-it-be-to-doone-*
B. 5.608	To suffren hym and *segge* noȝt ayein þi sires wille.
B. 5.642	Thow shalt *seye* I am þi Suster.' I ne woot where þei bicome.
B. 6.55	'I assente, by Seint Iame', *seide* þe knyȝt þanne,
B. 6.129	'If it be sooþ', quod Piers, 'þat ye *seyn*, I shal it soone aspie.
B. 6.181	'[Lat] hem lyue', he *seide*, 'and lat hem ete wiþ hogges,
B. 6.230	Miȝte I synnelees do as þow seist?' seide Piers þanne.
B. 6.230	Miȝte I synnelees do as þow seist?' *seide* Piers þanne.
B. 6.235	And Sapience *seiþ* þe same–I seiȝ it in þe bible:
B. 6.243	And [siþen] he *seide*–[hise seruauntȝ] it herde–
B. 6.250	The Sauter *seiþ*, in þe psalme of Beati omnes,
B. 6.284	And yet I *seye*, by my soule! I haue no salt bacon
B. 6.326	And so *sei[þ]* Saturne and sente yow to warne.
B. 7.120	And *seide*, 'Si ambulauero in medio vmbre mortis
B. 7.127	By þat þe Sauter [vs] *seith*, [and] so dide othere manye.
B. 7.131	Ne soliciti sitis he *seiþ* in þe gospel,
B. 7.160	Daniel *seide*, 'sire kyng, þi [sweuene is to mene]
B. 7.170	It bifel as his fader *seide* in Pharaoes tyme
B. 8.21	Seuene siþes, *seiþ* þe book, synneþ þe rightfulle;
B. 8.22	A[c] whoso synneþ, I *sei[e*, certes], me þynkeþ

B. 8.26	'I shal *seye* þee, my sone', seide þe frere þanne,
B. 8.26	'I shal seye þee, my sone', *seide* þe frere þanne,
B. 8.60	And I *seide* 'þe same saue yow fro myschaunce,
B. 8.74	'Woot I?' [quod I; 'who art þow]?' 'þouȝt, *seide* he þanne.
B. 8.127	Thanne þoȝt in þat tyme *seide* þise wordes:
B. 9.20	Sire Se-wel, and *Sey*-wel, and here-wel þe hende,
B. 9.36	For he was synguler hymself and *seide* faciamus
B. 9.37	As who *seiþ*, 'moore moot herto þan my word oone;
B. 9.42	And so it semeþ by hym [þere he *seide* in þe bible
B. 9.127	[For] god sente to Se[þ] and *seide* by an Aungel,
B. 9.132	Til god wraþed [wiþ] hir werkes and swich a word *seide*,
B. 9.164	"I am via & veritas", *seiþ* crist, "I may auaunce alle."
B. 9.194	For he made wedlok first and [þus] hymself *seide*:
B.10.4	And al starynge dame Studie sterneliche [*seide*].
B.10.9	And *seide*, 'noli[te] mittere, man, margery perles
B.10.13	I *seye* by [þo], quod she, 'þat sheweþ by hir werkes
B.10.16	Than alle þe sooþ sawes þat Salomon *seide* euere.
B.10.26	The Sauter *seiþ* þe same by swiche þat doon ille:
B.10.27	"Lo!" *seiþ* holy lettrure, "whiche [lordes] beþ þise sherewes";
B.10.69	And so *seiþ* þe Sauter; [seke it in memento]:
B.10.148	And *seide*, 'mercy, madame; youre man shal I worþe
B.10.173	*Seye* hym þis signe: I sette hym to Scole,
B.10.194	In ooþer Science it *seiþ*, I seiȝ it in Catoun,
B.10.224	I *seide* 'grant mercy, madame', and mekely hir grette,
B.10.236	I *seide* to h[y]m sooþly þat sent was I þider
B.10.276	That ye were swiche as ye *sey*[d]e to salue wiþ oþere.
B.10.290	And þanne mowe ye [manly] *seye*, as Dauid made þe Sauter,
B.10.300	And *seiþ* it in ensample [þat] þei sholde do þerafter:
B.10.342	Salomon *seiþ* also þat siluer is worst to louye:
B.10.371	And *seiþ* "slee noȝt þat semblable is to myn owene liknesse
B.10.372	But if I sende þee som tokene", and *seiþ* Non mecaberis,
B.10.402	Ac hir werkes, as holy writ *seiþ*, [was] euere þe contrarie.
B.10.404	As þei *seyen* hemself selde doon þerafter:
B.10.436	That Salomon *seiþ* I trowe be sooþ and certein of vs alle:
B.10.447	For soþest word þat euer god *seide* was þo he seide Nemo bonus.
B.10.447	For soþest word þat euer god seide was þo he *seide* Nemo bonus.
B.10.450	For he *seide* to Seint Peter and to swiche as he louede,
B.10.460	*Seide* þus in a sermon–I seigh it writen ones–
B.10.481	The which is mannes soule to saue, as god *seiþ* in þe gospel:
B.11.3	And *seide* 'Multi multa sciunt et seipsos nesciunt'.
B.11.10	[Siþen] she *seide* to me, 'here myȝtow se wondres
B.11.18	And *seide*, 'þow art yong and yeep and hast yeres ynowe
B.11.22	The secounde *seide* þe same: 'I shal sewe þi wille,
B.11.64	Ayeins oure firste forward, for I *seide* I nolde
B.11.68	And for I *seide* þus to freres a fool þei me helden,
B.11.92	Falsnesse ne faiterie? for somwhat þe Apostle *seide*
B.11.94	And in þe Sauter also *seiþ* dauid þe prophete
B.11.104	Thouȝ þow se yuel *seye* it noȝt first; be sory it nere amended.
B.11.107	'He *seiþ* sooþ', quod Scripture þo, and skipte an heiȝ and prechede.
B.11.137	'That is sooþ', *seide* Scripture; 'may no synne lette
B.11.176	For Seint Iohan *seide* it, and soþe arn hise wordes,
B.11.217	Crist to a commune womman *seide*, in [comen] at a feste,
B.11.230	And as Seint Gregorie *seide*, for mannes soule helþe
B.11.251	And to oure Saueour self *seide* þise wordes:
B.11.270	Alþouȝ Salomon *seide*, as folk seeþ in þe bible,
B.11.277	Or selle it, as *seiþ* þe book, and þe siluer dele
B.11.280	As Dauid *seiþ* in þe Sauter: to swiche þat ben in wille
B.11.286	And þei hir deuoir dide as Dauid *seiþ* in þe Sauter:
B.11.298	The same I *segge* for soþe by alle swiche preestes
B.11.310	And also in þe Sauter *seiþ* Dauid to ouerskipperis,
B.11.314	Synge ne psalmes rede ne *seye* a masse of þe day.
B.11.364	Manye selkouþes I seiȝ ben noȝt to *seye* nouþe.
B.11.373	[Th]anne I rebukede Reson and riȝt til hym I *seyde*,
B.11.376	And Reson arated me and *seide*, 'recche þee neuere
B.11.408	[Th]anne *seide* I to myself, '[slepyng hadde I grace]
B.11.411	'[What is dowel?' quod þat wiȝt]; 'ywis, sire', I *seide*,
B.11.413	'Haddestow suffred', *seide* he, 'slepynge þo þow were,
B.11.415	For Reson wolde haue reherced þee riȝt as Clergie *seid*;
B.11.435	'Ye *siggen* sooþ', quod I, 'ich haue yseyen it ofte.
B.12.13	And Dauid in þe Sauter *seiþ*, of swiche þat loueþ Iesus,
B.12.16	And þow medlest þee wiþ makynges and myȝtest go *seye* þi sauter,
B.12.20	I seiȝ wel þe *seide* me sooþ, and somwhat me to excuse
B.12.21	*Seide*, 'Caton conforted his sone þat, clerk þouȝ he were,
B.12.57	Sapience, *seiþ* þe bok, swelleþ a mannes soule:
B.12.102	And seint Spirit þe Samplarie, & *seide* what men sholde write.
B.12.137	And *seiden* hir wordes [ne] hir wisdomes [w]as but a folye;
B.12.159	And þow *seidest* sooþ of somme, ac se in what manere.
B.12.169	'That swymme kan noȝt', I *seide*, 'it semeþ to my wittes.'
B.12.217	And so I *seye* by þat sekest after þe whyes
B.12.278	*Seyen* in hir Sermons þat neiþer Sarsens ne Iewes
B.12.281	And *seide*, 'Saluabitur vix Iustus in die Iudicij;
B.12.282	Ergo saluabitur', quod he and *seide* na moore latyn.
B.12.284	And he is saaf, *seiþ* þe book, and his soule in heuene.
B.13.19	And siþen how ymaginatif *seide* 'vix saluabitur [iustus]',
B.13.20	And whan he hadde *seid* so, how sodeynliche he passed.
B.13.31	Conscience called hym In and curteisliche *seide*
B.13.49	He sette a sour loof toforn vs and *seide* 'Agite penitenciam',
B.13.64	Thanne *seide* I to myself so pacience it herde,
B.13.87	And *seide*, 'þow shalt see þus soone, whan he may na moore,
B.13.99	And I sat stille as Pacience *seide*, and þus soone þis doctour,
B.13.114	And *seide* hymself, 'sire doctour, and it be youre wille,
B.13.118	And dobest doþ hymself so as he *seiþ* and precheþ.
B.13.120	'I haue seuene sones', he *seide*, seruen in a Castel
B.13.130	Which shal saue mannes soule; þus *seiþ* Piers þe Plowman.'
B.13.179	Ac Conscience carped loude and curteisliche *seide*,
B.13.195	Than ȝacheus for he *seide* "dimidium bonorum meorum do pauperibus",
B.13.199	And siþen softeliche he *seide* in clergies ere,
B.13.203	But *seide* ful sobreliche, 'þow shalt se þe tyme
B.13.205	'That is sooþ', [*seide*] Conscience, 'so me god helpe.
B.13.211	'That is sooþ', [*seide*] Clergie, 'I se what þow menest.
B.13.304	And *segge* þyng þat he neuere seiȝ and for soþe sweren it;
B.13.306	And of werkes þat he wel dide witnesse and *siggen*,
B.13.338	And *seye* þat no clerc ne kan, ne crist as I leue,
B.13.396	Ne neuere penaunce parfournede ne Paternoster *seide*
B.13.432	What Dauid *seiþ* of swiche men as þe Sauter telleþ:
B.13.440	As he *seiþ* hymself; seynt Iohan bereþ witnesse:
B.14.38	And *seide*, 'lo! here liflode ynogh, if youre bileue be trewe.
B.14.63	As holy writ witnesseþ whan men *seye* hir graces:
B.14.69	Seuene slepe, as *seiþ* þe book, seuene hundred wynter
B.14.94	As Dauid *seiþ* in þe Sauter: et quorum tecta sunt peccata.
B.14.112	And *seiþ*, "lo! briddes and beestes þat no blisse ne knoweþ
B.14.131	And whan he dyeþ ben disalowed, as Dauid *seiþ* in þe Sauter:
B.14.140	So I *seye* by yow riche, it semeþ noȝt þat ye shulle
B.14.181	Thus in genere of gentries Iesu crist *seide*
B.14.257	And he his seruaunt, as *seiþ* þe book, and of his sute boþe.
B.14.309	Forþi *seiþ* Seneca Paupertas est absque sollicitudine semita._
B.15.8	To sergeauntȝ ne to swiche *seide* noȝt ones,
B.15.44	'That is sooþ', *seide* he; 'now I se þi wille.
B.15.47	'Ye, sire!' I *seide*, 'by so no man were greued
B.15.55	And *seiþ*, Sicut qui mel comedit multum non est ei bonum, Sic qui
B.15.60	"Beatus est", *seiþ* Seint Bernard, "qui scripturas legit
B.15.88	That *seide* to hise disciples, "Ne sitis personarum acceptores".
B.15.125	Ac a Porthors þat schewe be his Plow, Placebo to *sigge*–
B.15.127	[He syngeþ] seruice bokelees], *seiþ* it with ydel wille.
B.15.149	'What is charite?' quod I þo; 'a childissh þyng', he *seide*,
B.15.173	Al þat men *seyn*, he leet it sooþ and in solace takeþ,
B.15.267	And *seide* to swiche þat suffre wolde,
B.15.282	But selden and sondry tymes, as *seiþ* þe book and techeþ.
B.15.296	I sholde noȝt þise seuen daies *siggen* hem alle
B.15.383	I dar noȝt *siggen* it for shame–if swiche were apposed
B.15.429	"Salt saueþ catel", *siggen* þise wyues:
B.15.462	Ye mynnen wel how Mathew *seiþ*, how a man made a feste.
B.15.497	And as hymself *seide* [so] to lyue and dye:
B.15.498	And *seide* it in saluacion of Sarȝens and oþere;
B.15.499	For cristene and vncristene crist *seide* to prechours,
B.15.577	Oȝias *seiþ* for swiche þat sike ben and feble,
B.15.596	Ac þei *seiden* and sworen wiþ sorcerie he wrouȝte,
B.15.599	Daniel of hire vndoynge deuyned and *seide*
B.16.60	'That is sooþ', [*seide*] Piers, 'so it may bifalle.
B.16.98	And *seide* hendeliche to hym, 'lo me his handmaiden
B.16.117	Some þat þe sighte seiȝen *seiden* þat tyme
B.16.120	And *seide* he wroȝte þoruȝ wichecraft & with þe deueles myȝte:
B.16.130	And *seide* it in sighte of hem alle so þat alle herden:
B.16.141	Sittynge at þe soper he *seide* þise wordes:
B.16.145	It was hymself sooþly and *seide* 'tu dicis'.
B.16.153	Thanne Iesus to Iudas and to þe Iewes *seide*,
B.16.214	The sone, if I dorste *seye*, resembleþ wel þe widewe:
B.16.243	And siþþe he sente me to *seye* I sholde do sacrifise
B.16.249	And þus I seke hym', he *seide*, 'for I herde seyn late
B.16.249	And þus I seke hym', he seide, 'for I herde *seyn* late
B.16.252	*Seide* þat he seiȝ here þat sholde saue vs alle:
B.16.259	'Loo!' quod he and leet me see; 'lord, mercy!' I *seide*,
B.16.270	'Allas!' I *seide*, 'þat synne so longe shal lette
B.17.4	'Is it enseled?' I *seide*; 'may men see þ[e] lettres?'
B.17.5	'Nay', he *seide*, '[I] seke hym þat haþ þe seel to kepe,
B.17.17	[Is] here alle þi lordes lawes?' quod I; 'ye, leue me', he *seide*.
B.17.20	For, þouȝ I *seye* it myself, I haue saued wiþ þis charme
B.17.22	'[He *seiþ*] sooþ', seide þis heraud; 'I haue [founded] it ofte.
B.17.22	'[He seiþ] sooþ', *seide* þis heraud; 'I haue [founded] it ofte.
B.17.28	Abraham *seiþ* þat he seiȝ hoolly þe Trinite,
B.17.32	He kan noȝt *siggen* þe somme, and some arn in his lappe.
B.17.78	And lo, here siluer', he *seide*, 'for salue to hise woundes.'
B.17.79	And he took hym two pens to liflode and *seide*,
B.17.88	And graunted hym to ben his [gome]; 'graunt mercy', he *seide*;
B.17.127	'A, swete sire', I *seide* þo, 'wher I shal bileue,

B.17.198	By þis skile', [he *seide*], 'I se an euidence
B.17.303	'ȝis', *seide* þe Samaritan, 'so þow myght repente
B.18.19	And who sholde Iuste in Ierusalem. 'Iesus', he *seide*,
B.18.29	Deeþ *seiþ* he shal fordo and adoun brynge
B.18.31	Lif *seiþ* þat he lieþ and leieþ his lif to wedde
B.18.40	Tho putte hym forþ a p[e]lour bifore Pilat and *seide*,
B.18.43	Edifie it eft newe–here he stant þat *seide* it–
B.18.49	And sette it sore on his heed and *seide* in enuye:
B.18.54	And [*seide*], 'if þat þow sotil be [þiselue] now [þow help].
B.18.64	'For a bitter bataille', þe dede body *seide*;
B.18.68	Some *seide* þat he was goddes sone þat so faire deide:
B.18.69	And some *seide* he was a wicche; 'good is þat we assaye
B.18.89	He sighed and *seide*, 'soore it me aþynkeþ!
B.18.125	'Ich haue ferly of þis fare, in feiþ', *seide* truþe,
B.18.163	'Now suffre we', *seide* Truþe; 'I se, as me þynkeþ,
B.18.167	'That is sooþ', *seide* Mercy, 'and I se here by Sowþe,
B.18.244	And as he wente on þe water wel hym knew and *seide*,
B.18.261	'Suffre we', *seide* truþe; 'I here and see boþe
B.18.266	Thanne sikede Sathan and *seide* to he[l]le,
B.18.280	For hymself *seide*, þat Sire is of heuene,
B.18.283	And [siþen] he þat Sooþnesse is *seide* þise wordes,
B.18.286	'That is sooþ', *seide* Sathan, 'but I me soore drede,
B.18.317	What lord artow?' quod Lucifer; þe light soone *seide*
B.18.327	And *seide* to Sathan, 'lo! here my soule to amendes
B.18.420	'Thow *seist* sooþ', [*seyde*] Rightwisnesse, and reuerentliche hire kiste:
B.18.420	'Thow *seist* sooþ', [*seyde*] Rightwisnesse, and reuerentliche hire kiste:
B.19.169	To Peter and to [h]ise Apostles and *seide* pax vobis;
B.19.172	Thomas touched it and wiþ his tonge *seide*:
B.19.176	Crist carpede þanne and curteisliche *seide*,
B.19.242	And some to se and to *seye* what sholde bifalle,
B.19.459	Thanne louȝ þer a loud and, 'by þis light!' *seide*,
B.19.465	And þanne cam þer a kyng and by his croune *seide*,
B.20.42	So [he was nedy], as *seiþ* þe book in manye sondry places,
B.20.43	That he *seide* in his sorwe on þe selue roode:
B.20.178	'Now I se', *seide* lif, 'þat Surgerie ne phisik
B.20.224	And so *seiden* sixty of þe same contree,
B.20.244	And *seide*, 'sires, sooþly welcome be ye alle
B.20.322	I may wel suffre', *seide* Conscience, 'syn ye desiren,
B.20.334	'He is sik', *seide* Pees, 'and so are manye oþere.
B.20.336	'I am a Surgien', *seide* þe [frere], 'and salues kan make.
B.20.340	'Certes', *seide* his felawe, 'sire Penetrans domos.'
B.20.377	'He lyþ [adreynt] and dremeþ', *seide* Pees, 'and so do manye oþere.
C.Pr.68	[And] *sayde* þat hymself myghte assoylen hem alle
C.Pr.96	And *seide*, 'ydolatrie ȝe soffren in sondrye places manye
C.Pr.118	Forthy y *sey* ȝ[ow] prestes and men of holy churche
C.Pr.148	Thenne kynde witt to þe kynge and to þe comune *saide*:
C.Pr.152	Consience to Clergie and to þe kynge *sayde*:
C.Pr.179	*Sayde*, 'y haue seyen grete syres in Cytees and in townes
C.Pr.206	For y herde my syre *sayn*, seuene ȝer ypassed,
C.Pr.210	Y *seye* for me,' quod þe mous, 'y se so muche aftur,
C.Pr.214	But soffre and *sey* nouȝt; and [so] is þe beste
C. 1.5	And *sayde*, 'Wille, slepestou? seestow þis peple,
C. 1.11	And *sayde*, 'mercy, madame, what may this [be]mene?'
C. 1.39	And þat [see]th þ[i] soule and *sayth* hit the in herte
C. 1.44	'Go to þe gospel,' quod she, 'and se what god *sayde*
C. 1.47	"Sesares," thei *sayde*, "sothliche we knoweth."
C. 1.48	"Reddite cesari," *sayde* god, "þat cesar[i] byfalleth
C. 1.145	Lok þow soffre hym to *seye* and so thow myht lerne.
C. 1.201	Forthi y may *seye*, as y *saide* eer, by s[ih]t of this tex[t]es:
C. 1.201	Forthi y may *seye*, as y *saide* eer, by s[ih]t of this tex[t]es:
C. 2.2	And *sayde* 'mercy, madame, for mary loue of heuene
C. 2.26	And selde soth *sayth* bote yf he souche gyle,
C. 2.71	Thenne lup lyare forth and *saide*, 'loo! here a Chartre
C. 2.76	Thenne *saide* symonye þat syuyle it herde:
C. 2.120	And *sayde* to Symonye, 'now sorwe mot thow haue
C. 2.134	Lokede vp to oure lord and alowed *sayde*:
C. 2.168	And *sayde* softly, 'sese shal we neuere;
C. 2.184	Symonye and syuyle *seyden* and sworen
C. 2.203	Sothnesse seyh hem [wel] and *sayde* but lytel,
C. 2.249	And *sayde*, 'syre kyng, by crist! but clerkes amende,
C. 3.17	And *sayden*, 'mourne nat, mede, ne make thow no sorwe
C. 3.39	To mede þe mayde myldeliche he *sayde*,
C. 3.50	And he assoilede here sone and sethen a *sayde*,
C. 3.55	Loueliche þat lady laghynge *sayde*,
C. 3.134	And *saide*, 'vnwittiliche, womman, wro[uh]t hastow ofte
C. 3.219	'Excuce the yf thow kanst; y can no more *segge*
C. 3.236	Ac thow thysolue sothly, ho[so] hit *segge* durste,
C. 3.288	As þe sauhter *sayth* by such þat ȝeueth mede:
C. 3.312	Amen Amen, Matheu *seyth*, Mercedem suam rec[e]p[er]unt.
C. 3.429	God *sayde* to samuel þat sauel sholde deye
C. 3.436	That he þat *sayth* men sothe[s] is sonnest yblamed.

C. 3.485	'Loo what salamon *sayth*,' quod she, 'in sapiense in þe bible!
C. 4.1	'[Cesseth],' *saide* þe kynge, 'y soffre ȝow no lengore.
C. 4.15	And *sayde* hym as þe kyng sayde and sennes took his leue.
C. 4.15	And sayde hym as þe kyng *sayde* and sennes took his leue.
C. 4.50	Y dar nat for his felawschipe, in fayth,' pees *sayde*,
C. 4.64	[The kyng knew he *sayde* soth for Conscience hym tolde]
C. 4.134	Y *sey* it [by] mysulf,' quod resoun, 'and it so were
C. 4.151	Ac al ryhtful recordede þat resoun treuthe *sayde*,
C. 4.154	And *sayden*, 'we seyn wel, syre resoun, be thi wordes
C. 4.168	And lourede vppon men of lawe and lyhtlych *sayde*:
C. 4.187	'Y assente,' *sayde* resoun, 'by so ȝowsulue yhere
C. 5.12	'Can thow seruen,' he *sayde*, 'or syngen in a church
C. 5.22	'Sertes,' y *sayde*, 'and so me god helpe,
C. 5.86	Non de solo,' y *sayde*, 'for sothe viuit homo,
C. 5.92	'That is soth,' y *saide*, 'and so y beknowe
C. 5.107	S[yh]ing for my synnes, *seggyng* my paternoster,
C. 5.124	Ac y shal *sey* as y sayh, slepynge as hit were,
C. 5.200	That sueth my sarmon;'[and] Thus [*sayde*] resoun.
C. 6.54	And *sygge* to suche þat sytte me byside:
C. 6.82	And *segge* þat no clerk ne can, ne Crist as y leue,
C. 6.93	'I am sory,'*sayde* enuye, 'y am [but] selde othur;
C. 6.168	Esto sobrius!' he *saide*, and assoiled hym aftur
C. 6.170	Thenne *seyde* lecherye 'alas!' and to oure lady cryede,
C. 6.240	'Nay, sothly,' he *saide*, 'saue in my ȝouthe.
C. 6.283	Ne neuere penaunce parformede ne paternoster *sayde*
C. 6.290	Thow were such as thow *sayst*; y sholde rather s[t]erue:
C. 6.317	Ac ȝut þ[e] synful shrewe *saide* to heuene.
C. 6.423	To repentaunce ryht thus, 'haue reuthe on me,' he *saide*,
C. 7.58	And *sayde*, 'war the for wanhope wo[l the] bytraye.
C. 7.59	"Y am sory for my synnes", *sey* to thysuluen
C. 7.92	Wh[at] dauid *sayth* of such men as þe sauter telleth:
C. 7.100	As he *sayth* hymsulf; seynt Ion bereth witnesse:
C. 7.144	And sethen oure sauyour and *seydest* with thy tonge
C. 7.171	'Fro synoye,' he *sayde*, 'and fro þe sepulcre.
C. 7.179	'Nay, so me god [h]elpe,' *sayde* þe gome thenne,
C. 7.193	And thow y *sey* hit mysulf y serue hym to paye;
C. 7.209	That is to soth ȝe sholde rather deye
C. 7.230	Thenne shaltow se *say*-soth-so-hit-be-to-done-
C. 7.294	Anoþer anoen riht nede he *sayde* he hadde
C. 7.302	And loure on me and lihtly chyde and *sygge* y louede another.
C. 8.23	'Sikerliche, sire knyhte,' *sayde* [Peris] thenne,
C. 8.54	'Y assente, by seynt Gyle,' *sayde* þe knyht thenne,
C. 8.202	Þat durste withsitte þat [Peres] *sayde* for fere of syre hunger
C. 8.214	But for fere of famyen, in fayth,' *sayde* [Peres].
C. 8.236	Myhte y synneles do as thow *sayst*?' sayde Peres þe plouhman.
C. 8.236	Myhte y synneles do as thow sayst?' *sayde* Peres þe plouhman.
C. 8.240	Þat *sayth*, "with swynke and with [swetande] face
C. 8.254	Þat leely hadde ylabored and thenne the lord *sayde*:
C. 8.258	Lo! what þe sauter *sayth* to swynkares with handes:
C. 8.297	And leelyche *sayst*, as y leue; lord hit be forȝeld!
C. 8.306	And ȝut y *say[e]*, be my soule! y haue no sal[t] bacoun
C. 8.345	And so *sayth* saturne and sente [ȝow] to warne.
C. 9.131	Men suffreth al þat suche *sayen* and in solace taketh
C. 9.258	Certes, hoso durste hit, Simon quasi dormit;
C. 9.308	And sethen aftur his sones, and *sayde* hem what they thouhte;
C. 9.314	Hit biful as his fadur *saide* in farao his tyme
C.10.18	'Sothly,' *saide* þe frere, 'a soiourneth with vs freres
C.10.21	And *saide*, 'sothly sepcies in die ca[d]it iust[us]ls,
C.10.23	Seuene sithe, *sayth* þe boek, synegeth day by day
C.10.25	And hoso synegeth, y *sayde*, 'certes he doth nat wel;
C.10.30	'Y shal *sey* þe, my sone,' sayde þe frere thenne,
C.10.30	'Y shal sey þe, my sone,' *sayde* þe frere thenne,
C.10.59	And y *sayde*, 'þe same saue ȝow fro meschaunce
C.10.72	'Woet y?' quod y; 'who art thow?' 'thouhte,' *sayde* he thenne.
C.10.123	Thenne thouht in þat tyme *sayde* this wordes:
C.10.146	Sire se-wel and *sey*-wel [and] here-wel þe [h]ende,
C.10.165	As þe sauter *sayth* by synnefole shrewes:
C.10.207	For god *saith* hymsulue, "shal neuere goed appel
C.10.221	And for þe synne of Caymes seed *sayede* god to Noe:
C.10.243	For god *seid* ensaumple of suche manere issue
C.10.252	And seth for he soffred hit god *sayde*, "me forthynketh
C.11.4	Al staryng dame studie sterneliche *sayde*.
C.11.7	And *sayde*, 'nolite mittere, ȝe men, Margerie perles
C.11.11	Y *syg* hit by suche,' quod [she], 'þat sheweth by here werkes
C.11.23	The sauter *saith* þe same of alle suche ryche:
C.11.24	"Lo!" *saith* holy letrure, "whiche lordes beth this schrewes";
C.11.49	And so *saith* þe sauter; y say hit [in] memento:
C.11.86	And *saide*, 'mercy, madame; ȝoure man shal y worthen
C.11.113	*Sey* [to] hym thysulue ouerse m[y] bokes
C.11.114	And *sey* y gre[t]e wel his wyf, for y wrot here a bible
C.11.135	And to clergie y cam as clerkes me *saide*.
C.11.150	And he vs *saide* as he sey, and so y bileue,
C.11.163	And *saide*, 'multi multa sciunt & seipsos nessiunt.'

C.11.169 And senes he *saide* to me, 'here myhte thow se wondres
C.11.177 And *saide*, 'þou art ʒong and ʒep and hast ʒeres ynowe
C.11.181 The seconde *saide* þe same: 'y [shal] sewe thy wille;
C.11.197 For rechelesnesse in his rybaud[i]e riht thus he *saide*:
C.11.199 Were hit al soth þat ʒe *seyn*, thow scripture and thow clergie,
C.11.202 For clergie *saith* þat he seyh in þe seynt euaungelie
C.11.268 And now beth this seyntes, by that men *saith*, and souereynes in heuene.
C.11.270 By that þat salamon *saith* hit semeth þat no wyht woet
C.11.275 For Crist *saide* to sayntes and to suche as he louede,
C.11.281 Sothly,' *saide* rechelesnesse, 'ʒe se by many euydences
C.11.284 For he þat most se[y]h and *saide* of the sothfaste trinite
C.11.286 *Saide* thus in his sarmon for ensau[m]ple of grete clerkes,
C.12.3 Couetyse-of-yes conforted me aftur and *saide*,
C.12.16 And *saide* he myhte [me nat] assoile but y suluer hadde
C.12.24 'Why lourest [thou]?' quod leaute; 'leue sire,' y *saide*,
C.12.27 Y wolde it were no synne,' y *saide*, 'to seien þat were treuthe.
C.12.27 Y wolde it were no synne,' y saide, 'to *seien* þat were treuthe.
C.12.28 The sauter *sayth* hit is no synne for suche men þat ben trewe
C.12.29 To *segge* as they seen, saue only prestis.
C.12.33 Falsnesse ne fayterye? for sumwhat þe apostel *saide*:
C.12.38 Thouh tho[w] se, *say* nat sum tyme þat is treuthe.
C.12.41 'A *saith* soth,' quod scripture tho, and skypte an heyh and prechede.
C.12.46 He *saide* in here sarmon selcouthe wordes:
C.12.72 'That is soth,' *saide* scripture; ' may no synne lette
C.12.99 And seynt Ion sethen *saide* hit of his techyng:
C.12.101 For god, as þe gospel *saith*, goth ay as þe pore
C.12.137 And to oure sauyour sulue aboute þis wordes:
C.12.162 What god *saide* hymsulue to a segg þat he louede:
C.12.205 For crist *saide* [so] to seyntes þat for his sake tholeden
C.12.233 Riht so, sothly, for to *segge* treuthe.
C.13.12 And for he soffrede and *saide* nauht oure lord sente tookene
C.13.112 The same y *segge* for sothe by suche þat beth prestes
C.13.123 [To] ouerskippers also in þe sauter *sayth* dauid:
C.13.126 Syng ne [psalmes] rede [ne *sey* a masse of the daye].
C.13.168 Dompynges dyuede; 'dere God,' y *sayde*,
C.13.174 Mony selcouthes y seyh aren nat to *segge* nouthe
C.13.183 Thenne y [a]resonede resoun and ryht til hym y *sayde*,
C.13.194 And resoun aresounede me and *sayde*, 'reche þe neuere
C.13.195 Why y soffre or nat soffre; certes,' he *sayde*,
C.13.216 And *saide* anoen to mysulue, 'slepynge hadde y grace
C.13.219 'What is dowel?' quod þat wyhte; 'ywis, sire,' y *saide*,
C.13.221 'Haddestow soffred,' he *sayde*, 'slepyng tho thow were,
C.13.223 For resoun wolde haue rehersed þe riht as clergie *seide*]
C.13.241 'ʒe *seggeth* soth, be my soule,' quod y, 'I haue sey hit ofte.
C.14.40 And in soend a signe wroet and *saide* to þe iewes,
C.14.47 And seynt spirit þe saumplarie and *said* what men sholde wryte.
C.14.82 And *saide* here wordes ne here wysdomes was but a folye;
C.14.103 And thow *saidest* sothe of somme, Ac [yse] in what manere.
C.14.109 'He þat can nat swymmen,' y *sayde*, 'hit semeth to alle wittes.'
C.14.156 And so y *sey* by þe þat sekest aftur þe whyes,
C.14.165 Sey hit and soffred hit And *saide* hit be sholde:
C.14.200 *Segen* [in] here sarmons nother saresynes ne iewes
C.14.203 And *saide*, 'Vix saluabitur iustus in die iudicij;
C.14.204 Ergo saluabitur,' quod he and *saide* no more latyn.
C.14.206 And he is saef, *saith* the boek, and his soule in heuene.
C.15.21 And y merueyle[d] in herte how ymaginatyf *saide*
C.15.23 And when he hadde *ysaide* so, how sodeynliche he vanschede.
C.15.55 He sette a sour loef and *saide*, 'Agite penitenciam',
C.15.58 'This is a semely seruyce,' *saide* pacience.
C.15.62 And *saide*, 'cor contritum & humiliatum, deus, non despicies.'
C.15.68 Thenne *saide* y to mysulue so pacience hit herde,
C.15.94 And *saide*, 'Thow shalt se thus sone, when he may no more,
C.15.114 'Sertes, sire,' thenne *saide* y, 'hit semeth nou[th]e here,
C.15.121 And *saide* hymsulue, 'sire doctour, [and] hit be ʒoure wille,
C.15.123 'Y haue *yseide*,' quod þat segg, 'y can sey no bettre.
C.15.123 'Y haue yseide,' quod þat segg, 'y can *sey* no bettre.
C.15.138 Byfore perpetuel pees y shal proue þat y *saide*
C.15.176 And sethe a *saide* to clergie so þat y hit herde:
C.15.192 What craft þat he couthe and cortey[s]liche he *saide*:
C.15.237 And *saide*, 'lo! here lyflode ynow yf oure beleue be trewe
C.15.262 As witnesseth holy writ when we *seggeth* oure graces:
C.15.268 Seuene slepen, as *saith* þe boek, more then syxty wynter
C.15.288 And *saith*, "loo! briddes and bestes þat no blisse ne knoweth
C.15.306 Dauid in þe sauter of suche maketh mynde and *sayth*: dormierunt
C.16.8 So y *sey* by ʒow ryche, hit semeth nat þat ʒe sholle
C.16.97 And he [h]is seruant, a[s] he *saith*, and of his se[u]te bothe.
C.16.164 And he soffrede me and *saide*, 'assay his oþer name.'
C.16.173 'Whareof serue ʒe,' y *saide*, 'sir liberum arbitrium?'
C.16.206 'That is soth,' he *sayde*; 'now y se thy wille.
C.16.209 'ʒe, sire!' y *sayde*, 'by so no man were ygreued,
C.16.217 And *sayth*, sicut qui mel comedit multum non est ei bonum; Sic
C.16.222 "Beatus," *saith* seynt Bernard, "qui scripturas legit

C.16.229 "Non plus sapere," *saide* þe wyse, [laste synne of pruyde wexe,]
C.17.1 'There is no such,' y *sayde*, 'þat som tyme ne borweth
C.17.37 As wittnesseth holy writ what tobie *saide*
C.17.117 Lord lete þat this prestes lelly *seien* here masse,
C.17.125 'What is holy churche, chere frende?' quod y; 'Charite,' he *saide*;
C.17.150 'Where sarresynes,' y *saide*, 'yse nat what is charite?'
C.17.193 And as hymsulue *saide* so to lyue and deye:
C.17.304 Iewes *sayde* þat hit seye with soercerye he wrouhte,
C.17.307 And ʒut they *seyen* sothly, and so doen þe sarrasynes,
C.18.16 'Now, certes,' y *sayde*, and siʒte for ioye,
C.18.18 And sethen þat ʒe fouchen saef to *sey* me as hit hoteth.'
C.18.58 'ʒe, sertes,' he *sayde*, 'and sothliche leue hit.
C.18.81 'ʒe, sire,' y *sayde*, 'and sethen þer aren but tweyne lyues
C.18.83 Why groweth this fruyt in thre degres?' 'A goed skil,' he *saide*.
C.18.103 Assay what sauour hit hadde and *saide* þat tyme,
C.18.131 And *saide* hendely to hym, 'lo me his hondmayden
C.18.147 Ac tho that sey that selcouth *sayde* þat tyme
C.18.149 And some iewes *saide* with sorserie he wrouhte,
C.18.158 And *saide*, 'this is an hous of orysones and of holynesse
C.18.161 The iewes tolde þe iustice how þat iesus *saide*;
C.18.170 Thenne iesus to Iudas and to þe iewes *sayde*,
C.18.192 'That is soth,' *saide* he thenne, 'the syre hatte pater
C.18.197 How o lord myhte lyue [in] thre; y leue hit nat,' y *sayde*.
C.18.239 'Hastow ysey this,' y *seyde*, 'alle thre and o god?'
C.18.255 For hymsulue *saide* y sholde [haue], y and myn issue bothe,
C.18.260 And sethe a sente me to *seyn* and saide that y sholde
C.18.260 And sethe a sente me to seyn and *saide* that y sholde
C.18.267 Forthy y seke hym,' he *saide*, 'for seynt Iohann þe Baptiste
C.18.268 *Saide* þat a seyh here þat sholde saue vs alle:
C.18.275 'Loo!' quod he and lette me see: 'lord, mercy!' y *saide*,
C.18.286 'Allas!' y *saide*, 'þat synne so longe shal lette
C.19.5 That that y *sey* is soeth se hoso liketh.'
C.19.6 'Is hit asseled?' y *saide*; 'may men yse th[e] lettres?'
C.19.7 'Nay,' he *saide*, 'y seke hym þat hath þe seel to kepe,
C.19.18 'Is here al thy lordes l[aw]es?' quod y; 'ʒe, leef me,' he *saide*,
C.19.21 For, thogh y *sey* hit mysulue, y haue saued with this charme
C.19.23 'He *seyth* soth,' saide fayth; 'y haue yfounde hit trewe.
C.19.23 'He seyth soth,' *saide* fayth; 'y haue yfounde hit trewe.
C.19.26 And six thousand mo,' quod fayth; 'y [can] nat *seyn* here names.'
C.19.29 Abraham *saith* þat he seyh holly þe trinitee,
C.19.81 Ac y sewede the samaritaen and *saide* how they bothe
C.19.96 'A, sire,' y *saide*, 'shal nat we bileue,
C.19.108 'A *saide* soeth,' quod the samaritaen, 'and so y rede the also.
C.19.164 Bi this simile,' he *saide*, 'y se an euydence
C.19.238 And hymsulue, *sayth* the boek, sotiled how he myhte
C.19.283 'ʒus,' *saide* þe samaritaen, 'so thow myhtest repente
C.20.17 And ho sholde iouste in Ierusalem. 'Iesus,' he *saide*,
C.20.28 Deth *saith* a wol fordo and adown brynge
C.20.30 Lyf *saith* þat a lyeth and [leyeth] his lyf to wedde,
C.20.39 Thenne potte hym forth a pelour bifore pilatus and *saide*,
C.20.42 Edefien hit eft newe–here he stant þat *saide* hit–
C.20.49 And sette hit sore on his heued and *saide* in Enuye;
C.20.54 And *saiden*, 'yf he sotil be hymsulue now he wol helpe;'
C.20.66 'For a bittur bataile,' þe ded body *saide*;
C.20.70 Somme *saide* he was godes sone þat so fayre deyede:
C.20.71 And somme *saide*, 'he can of soercerie; goed is þat we assaie
C.20.91 [He] syhed and *saide*, 'sore hit me forthenketh!
C.20.128 'Y haue ferly of this fare, in faith,' *seide* Treuthe,
C.20.166 'Now soffre we,' *saide* Treuthe; 'y se, as me thynketh,
C.20.170 'That is soth,' *saide* mercy, 'and y se here bi southe
C.20.253 And as he wente on þe watur wel hym knewe and *saide*,
C.20.269 'Soffre we,' *sayde* treuthe; 'y here and se bothe
C.20.271 A vois loude in þat liht to lucifer *saide*,
C.20.274 Thenne syhed satoun and *saide* to helle,
C.20.302 For hymsulue *said*, þat sire is of heuene,
C.20.312 'That is soeth,' *saide* satoun, 'bote y me sore doute
C.20.358 That y ne *sygge* as y syhe, suynde my teme).
C.20.360 'What lord artow?' quod lucifer; a voys aloude *saide*:
C.20.463 'Thowe *saiste* soeth,' saide rihtwisnesse, and reuerentlich here custe,
C.20.463 'Thowe saiste soeth,' *saide* rihtwisnesse, and reuerentlich here custe,
C.21.169 To peter and to his apostlis and *saide* pax vobis;
C.21.172 Thomas touched hit and and with his tonge *saide*:
C.21.176 Crist Carpede thenne and cortey[s]liche *saide*,
C.21.242 And somme to se and to *saye* what sholde bifalle
C.21.459 Thenne lowh ther a lord and 'bi this lihte!' *saide*,
C.21.465 And thenne cam þer a kyng and bi his corone *saide*,
C.22.42 So he was nedy, as *saith* the boek in mony sondry places,
C.22.43 That he *saide* in his sorwe on þe sulue rode:
C.22.178 'Now y see,' *saide* lyf, ' that surgerie ne fysyke
C.22.224 And so *sayde* syxty of þe same contreye
C.22.244 And *saide*, 'syres, soethly welcome be ʒe alle

C.22.322 Y may wel soffre,' *sayde* Consience, 'sennes ȝe desiren,
C.22.334 'He is syke,' *saide* Pees, 'and so ar many other.
C.22.336 'Y am a surgien,' *saide* the frere, 'and salues can make.
C.22.340 'Certes,' *saide* his felawe, 'sire penetrans domos.'
C.22.377 'He lyeth adreint [and dremeth],' *saide* pees, 'and so doth mony
                     oþere.

sigh > *seen*

sighed v *sighen v. cf. sike* B 1; C 4 siȝte (1) syhed (2) Syhing (1)

B.18.89   He *sighed* and seide, 'soore it me aþynkeþ!
C. 5.107 *S[yh]ing* for my synnes, seggyng my paternoster,
C.18.16   'Now, certes,' y sayde, and *siȝte* for ioye,
C.20.91   [He] *syhed* and saide, 'sore hit me forthenketh!
C.20.274 Thenne *syhed* satoun and saide to helle,

sight(- > *siȝt*

signe n *signe n.* A 8 signe (3) signes (5); B 12 signe (8) signes (4); C 10
    signe (4) sygne (2) signes (4)

A. 2.78   Be siȝte of sire symonye & *signes* of notaries.
A. 2.107   Til he hadde siluer for his selis & *signes*.
A. 4.112   Bere no siluer ouer se þat *signe* of king shewi[þ],
A. 6.9   *Signes* of synay, & shilles of galis,
A. 6.12   And sen be his *signes* whom he souȝt hadde.
A. 6.17   ȝe mowe se be my *signes* þat sitten on myn hat
A.11.99   In *signe* þat I shulde beseke hire of grace.
A.11.125 Sey hym þis *signe*, I sette hym to scole,
B.Pr.89   And *signe* þat þei sholden shryuen hire parisshens,
B. 2.143   Til he hadde siluer for his [seles] and [*signes* of] Notaries.
B. 4.129   Bere no siluer ouer see þat *signe* of kyng sheweþ,
B. 5.521   *Signes* of Synay and shelles of Galice,
B. 5.524   And se bi hise *signes* whom he souȝt hadde.
B. 5.529   Ye may se by my *signes* þat sitten on myn hatte
B.10.146 In *signe* þat I sholde bisechen hire of grace.
B.10.173 Seye hym þis *signe*: I sette hym to Scole,
B.13.153 In a *signe* of þe Saterday þat sette first þe kalender,
B.13.344 For ech a maide þat he mette he made hire a *signe*
B.14.258 And wheiþer he be or be noȝt, he bereþ þe *signe* of pouerte
B.20.272 And youre noumbre vnder Notaries *signe* and neiþer mo ne lasse.'
C. 2.159   Til he hadde seluer for the seel and *signes* of notaries.
C. 4.126   Bere no seluer ouer see þat *sygne* of kyng sheweth,
C. 4.149   In *signe* þat thei sholde with som sotil speche
C. 6.178   For eche mayde þat y mette y made here a *signe*
C. 7.166   *Signes* of syse and shelles of galys
C. 7.169   And se by [his] *signes* wham a souht hadde.
C. 7.174   ȝe may se be [my] *signes* þat sitten on my cappe
C.14.40   And in soend a *signe* wroet and saide to þe iewes,
C.16.98   And where he be or be nat, a bereth þe *signe* of pouerte
C.22.272 And ȝoure nombre vnde[r] notarie *sygne* and noþer mo ne lasse.'

siȝt n *sighte n.* A 9 siȝt (6) siȝte (3); B 38 sight (1) sighte (11) sightes (3)
    siȝt (3) siȝte (17) siȝtes (3); C 27 sighte (1) siht (3) syht (1) sihte (9)
    syhte (9) syhtes (1) sihtus (2) syhtus (1)

A.Pr.16   Wiþ depe dikes & derke & dredful of *siȝt*.
A.Pr.32   As it semiþ to oure *siȝt* þat suche men þriuen.
A. 1.57   'þe dungeon in þe dale þat dredful is of *siȝt*:
A. 1.110   And was þe louelokest [of *siȝt*] aftir oure lord
A. 1.123   Forþi I seye as I seide er, be *siȝte* of þise textis.
A. 1.180   Forþi I seiȝe as I seide er be *siȝte* of þise tixtes:
A. 2.78   Be *siȝte* of sire symonye & signes of notaries.
A. 3.58   Neiþer in *siȝt* ne in þi soule, for god hymself knowiþ
A.10.52   He eggiþ eiȝe *siȝt* & heryng to gode;
B.Pr.16   Wiþ depe diches and derke and dredfulle of *siȝte*.
B.Pr.32   As it semeþ to oure *siȝt* þat swiche men þryueþ.
B. 1.59   'Th[e] dongeon in þe dale þat dredful is of *siȝte*–
B. 1.134   Forþi I seye, as I seyde er, by *siȝte* of þise textis:
B. 1.206   Forþi I seye as I seide er by [*siȝt* of þise] textes:
B. 2.114   By *siȝte* of sire Symonie and Cyuyles leeue.'
B. 3.328   And Sarȝynes for þat *siȝte* shul synge Gloria in excelsis &c,
B. 5.491   The sonne for sorwe þerof lees [*s]iȝt* [for] a tyme.
B.10.261 Swich as þow semest in *siȝte* be in assay yfounde.
B.10.279 Ac it semeþ now sooþly, to [*siȝt* of þe worlde],
B.12.64   Clergie and kynde wit comeþ of *siȝte* and techyng
B.12.67   And of quod vidimus comeþ kynde wit, of *siȝte* of diuerse peple.
B.12.103 [And riȝt as *siȝt* serueþ a man to se þe heiȝe strete]
B.12.128 Ac kynde wit comeþ of alle kynnes *siȝtes*,
B.12.135 For alle hir kynde knowyn[g] co[m] but of diuerse *siȝtes*.
B.13.278 Ooþerwise þan he haþ wiþ herte or *siȝte* shewynge hym;
B.13.282 And so singuler by hymself [as to *siȝte* of þe peple
B.13.395 Neiþer masse ne matynes, ne none maner *siȝtes*;
B.14.13   That I ne soiled it wiþ *siȝte* or som ydel speche,
B.14.55   By so þat þow be sobre of *siȝte* and of tonge,
B.16.29   And forfreteþ neiȝ þe fruyt þoruȝ manye faire *sightes*.
B.16.33   That it norisseþ nyce *sightes* and [anoþer] tyme wordes

B.16.117 Some þat þe *sighte* seiȝen seiden þat tyme
B.16.130 And seide it in *sighte* of hem alle so þat alle herden:
B.16.227 Thre men, to my *siȝte*, I made wel at ese,
B.17.40   Than he þat gooþ wiþ two staues to *sighte* of vs alle;
B.17.60   Feiþ hadde first *siȝte* of hym, ac he fleiȝ aside
B.17.64   Ac whan he hadde *sighte* of þat segge aside he gan hym drawe
B.17.66   Ac so soone so þe Samaritan hadde *siȝte* of þis leode
B.17.92   For *sighte* of þ[e] sorweful [segge] þat robbed was with þeues.
B.17.155 And þre sondry *sightes* [shewynge in oon],
B.17.327 And whan smoke and smolder smyt in his *sighte*
B.18.79   Highte Longeus as þe lettre telleþ, and longe hadde lore his *sight*;
B.18.304 That his soule wolde suffre no synne in his *sighte*;
B.18.310 For vs were bettre noȝt be þan biden his *sighte*.
B.19.180 That neuere shul se me in *sighte* as þow [seest] nowþe,
B.19.234 And some he kennede craft and konnynge of *sighte*,
B.19.453 But [it soune], as by *sighte*, somwhat to wynnyng.
C.Pr.34   As it semeþ to oure *sighte* that suche men ythryueth.
C. 1.201   Forthi y may seye, as y saide eer, by *s[ih]t* of this tex[t]es:
C. 2.118   By *syhte* of sire Simonye and syuyles leue.'
C. 3.481   And saresines for þat *syhte* shal syng Credo in spiritum sanctum
C. 4.180   'But [y] reule thus alle reumes reuet[h] me my *syhte*,
C. 6.36   And ȝut so synguler be mysulue as to *syhte* of [þe] peple
C. 6.282   Nother matynes ne masse ne no maner *syhtus*;
C. 7.131   The sonne for sorwe þerof lees [*s]iht* for a tyme.
C. 7.301   Were y seuen nyhte fro here *syhte* s[ynnen] he wolde
C. 9.115   And to oure *syhte* as hit semeth; seth god hath þe myhte
C.11.43   Thenne semeth hit to my *sihte* to suche þat so biddeth
C.11.201 Sholde sitte in goddis *sihte* ne se god in his blisse:
C.14.30   Ac clergie cometh bote of *syhte* and kynde wit of sterres,
C.14.48   And riht as *syht* serueth a man to se [þe hye strete],
C.14.79   For al here kynde knowyng cam bote of diuerse *syhtes*,
C.15.254 By so þat þou be sobre of *syhte* and of tonge,
C.18.33   And forfret þat fruyt thorw many fayre *s[ih]tus*.
C.18.37   That hit norischeth nise *s[ih]tus* and som tyme wordes
C.19.59   Fayth [hadde furst *siht* of hym] Ac he fleyh asyde
C.19.63   Ac when he hadde *sihte* of this s[egg]e asyde he gan hym drawe
C.19.65   Ac so sone so the samaritaen hadde *sihte* of this carefole
C.19.307 Ac when smoke and smolder [smyt in his *sihte*
C.20.81   Hihte longies as þe lettre telleth, and longe hadde lore his *sihte*;
C.20.344 For vs were bettere nat be then abyde in his *sihte*.
C.21.180 Tha[t] neuere shal se me in *sihte* as thowe seste nowthe
C.21.234 And somme he kende craft and konnynge of *syhte*,
C.21.453 Bote hit sowne, as bi *sihte*, somwhat to wynnynge.

siȝte > *siȝt,sike; syhe* > *seen; syhed -ing* > *siked; siht(-* > *siȝt*

sik adj *sik adj.* A 2 seke; B 11 sik (2) sike (9); C 11 seke (1) sike (2)
    syke (7) sykke (1)

A. 7.239   For summe of my seruauntis ben *seke* oþer while;
A.11.190 And seken out þe *seke* & sende hem þat hem nediþ,
B.15.577 Oȝias seiþ for swiche þat *sike* ben and feble,
B.16.106 And dide hym assaie his surgenrie on hem þat *sike* were
B.16.108 And souȝte out þe *sike* and [saluede blynde and crokede,
B.16.110 And *sike* and synfulle boþe so] to goode turnede:
B.17.122 Til I haue salue for alle *sike*; and þanne shal I turne
B.17.123 And come ayein bi þis contree and conforten alle *sike*
B.17.350 For þer nys *sik* ne sory, ne noon so muche wrecche
B.20.305 'Go salue þo þat *sike* ben and þoruȝ synne ywounded.'
B.20.323 That frere flaterere be fet and phisike yow *sike*.'
B.20.334 'He is *sik*', seide Pees, 'and so are manye oþere.
B.20.356 'Thow art welcome', quod Conscience; 'kanstow heele *sike*?
C. 4.122   And til saynt Iames be souhte there pore *sykke* lyggen,
C. 8.147   And freres þat flateren nat and pore folke *syke*,
C. 8.270   ȝe han manged ouer moche; þat maketh ȝow to be *syke*.
C. 9.99   But they be blynde or tobroke or elles be *syke*,
C.15.117 And ȝe fare thus with ȝoure *syke* freres, ferly me thynketh
C.15.219 Lette this luythere [eir] and leche þe *sike*–
C.19.330 For þer ne is *sike* ne sory ne non so moche wrecche
C.22.305 'Go salue tho þat *syke* [ben] and thorw synne ywounded.'
C.22.323 That frere flaterare be fet and fisyk ȝow *seke*.'
C.22.334 'He is *syke*,' saide Pees, 'and so ar many other.
C.22.356 'Thow art welcome,' quod Consience; 'can[st] thow hele *syke*?

sike v *siken v.(2)* &> *sik cf. sighed* A 1; B 2 siked (1) sikede (1); C 1
    syke

A.11.193 *Sike* with þe sory, singe with þe glade,
B.14.329 Swouned and sobbed and *siked* ful ofte
B.18.266 Thanne *sikede* Sathan and seide to he[l]le,
C. 3.400   To *syke* for here synnes and soffre harde penaunc[e]

sikel n *sikel n.* B 2; C 3 sikel (1) sykel (2)

B. 3.308   Into *sikel* or to siþe, to Shaar or to kultour:
B.13.374 To seise to me wiþ hir *sikel* þat I sew neuere.
C. 3.461   Into *sykel* or [t]o sythe, to shar oþer to coltur:
C. 5.23   Y am to wayke to wurcche with *sykel* or with sythe

C. 6.271   To sese to me with here *sikel* þat y sewe neuere.

sykenesse > siknesse

siker adj *siker adj.* A 3 sikir (2) sikur (1); B 5 siker (4) syker (1); C 6
  siker (1) syker (3) sikerore (1) sykerost (1)
A. 1.121   Mowe be *sikur* þat here soule shal wende into heuene,
A. 3.49   *Sikir* shulde þi soule be heuene to haue'.
A. 8.164   It is not so *sikir* for þe soule, certis, as is do wel.
B. 1.132   Mowe be *siker* þat hire soul[e] sh[a]l wende to heuene
B. 3.50   *Syker* sholde þi soule be heuene to haue'.
B. 7.186   [It] is noȝt so *siker* for þe soule, certes, as is dowel.
B.16.234   I am ful *siker* in soule þerof, and my sone boþe.
B.20.255   And sette [it] at a certain and [at] a *siker* nombre.
C. 1.117   'Hit is *sikerore* bi southe þer þe sonne regneth
C. 3.335   On a sad and a *siker* semblable to hemsuluen.
C. 5.39   And *sykerost* for þe soule, by so y wol contenue.
C. 9.332   Hit is nat so *syker* for þe soule, certes, as [is] dowel.
C.14.29   May nat be, [be] þ[ow] *syker*, thogh we bidde euere.
C.22.255   And sette hit at a serteyne and at a *syker* nombre

siker adv *siker adv.* A 1 sikir; B 2 sikerer; C 1 sikorere
A.11.163   Alle þise sciences, *sikir*, I myself
B. 5.501   And by so muche [it] semeþ þe *sikerer* we mowe
B.11.267   And wel *sikerer* he slepeþ, þe [segge] þat is pouere
C.12.152   And wel *sikorere* he slepeth, þe segg þat is pore,

sykeren v *sikeren v.* C 1
C. 7.185   And maden me *sykere[n* hym] sethen to seruen hym for euere,

sikerly adv *sikerli adv.* A 1 sykirly; B 2; C 5 sicurly (1) sikerliche (1)
  sikerly (1) sikerlyche (1) sykerloker (1)
A. 8.54   Þat he ne worþ sauf *sykirly*, & so seiþ þe sautir.
B. 7.52   That he ne worþ saaf [*sikerly*]; þe Sauter bereþ witnesse:
B.20.215   And bisegede [*sikerly*] wiþ seuene grete geauntȝ
C. 4.51   'Bere *sikerlyche* eny seluer to seynt Gyles doune.
C. 7.141   And by so muche hit semeth the *sykerloker* we mowe
C. 8.23   '*Sikerliche*, sire knyhte,' sayde [Peris] thenne,
C.10.26   For hoso synegeth *sicurly* doth euele
C.22.215   And biseged *s[iker]ly* with seuene grete geauntes

sikerore -ost > siker; sikir(- > siker(-; sykke > sik

siknesse n *siknesse n.* A 3 seknesse; B 13; C 9 seeknesse (2) sekenes (1)
  sekenesse (1) seknesse (4) sykenesse (1)
A. 5.222   'Shal no sonneday be þis seue ȝer, but *seknesse* it make,
A. 7.120   For we mowe no[þer] swynke ne swete, such *seknesse* vs eileþ'.
A. 7.241   'I wot wel,' quaþ hunger, 'what *seknesse* hem eileþ.
B. 5.413   I [a]m noȝt shryuen som tyme but if *siknesse* it make
B. 5.450   'Shal no Sonday be þis seuen yer, but *siknesse* it [make],
B. 5.482   And siþen suffredest [hym] to synne, a *siknesse* to vs alle,
B. 6.128   For we may [neiþer] swynke ne swete, swich *siknesse* vs eyleþ.'
B. 6.257   'I woot wel', quod Hunger, 'what *siknesse* yow eyleþ.
B.12.2   Thouȝ I sitte by myself in *siknesse* n[e] in helþe.
B.13.404   'And kauȝte *siknesse* somtyme for my [surfetes] ofte
B.14.6   Wiþ þe sope of *siknesse* þat sekeþ wonder depe,
B.14.318   And sobretee swete drynke and good leche in *siknesse*.
B.15.425   And folkes sholden [fynde], þat ben in diuerse *siknesse*,
B.17.340   Ben *siknesse* and sorwes þat we suffren o[uȝ]te,
B.17.344   That þei han cause to contrarie by kynde of hir *siknesse*;
B.19.291   To suffren al þat god sente, *siknesse* and Angres.
C. 7.28   Y am nat shryue som tyme but yf *seknesse* hit make
C. 7.64   'Shal no sonday be this seuene ȝere, but *seknesse* hit make,
C. 7.124   And sethe soffredes[t] hym to synege, a *sykenesse* to vs alle,
C. 8.134   We may nother swynke ne swete, suche *sekenes* vs ayleth;
C. 8.269   'Y wot wel,' quod hungur, 'what *sekenesse* ȝow ayleth.
C.16.311   Alle *sekness[e]* and sorwes for solac[e] he hit taketh
C.19.320   Been *seekness[e]* and oþere sorwes þat we soffren ouhte,
C.19.324   That they haen cause to contrarien bi kynde of here *sekness[e]*;
C.21.291   To soffre al þat god sente, *seeknesse* and angeres.

sikorere sikur > siker

silynge prp *silen v.(3)* B 1; C 1 sylinge
B.18.307   And now I se wher a soule comeþ [*silynge* hiderward]
C.20.341   And now y se where his soule cometh *sylinge* hid[er]ward

silk n *silk n.* A 2; B 3 selk (1) silk (2); C 2 selk (1) selke (1)
A.Pr.84   Þere houide an hundrit in houuis of *silk*,
A. 7.19   Þat han *silk* & sendel, sewiþ it whanne tyme is,
B.Pr.211   Yet houed þer an hundred in howues of *selk*,
B. 6.11   That ye haue *silk* and Sandel to sowe whan tyme is
B.15.220   For I haue seyen hym in *silk* and som tyme in russet,
C.Pr.161   Where houed an hundrid in houes of *selke*,
C. 8.10   That ȝe [han] *selk* and sendel to sowe whan tyme is

silk adj *silke adj.* A 1; B 1; C 1 selk
A. 3.270   Shal no seriaunt for þat seruyse were a *silk* houue,

B. 3.295   Shal no sergeant for [þat] seruice were a *silk* howue,
C. 3.448   Shal no ser[i]aunt for [þat] seruic[e] werie a *selk* houe

siluer n *silver n.* A 10; B 40; C 33 seluer (8) siluer (3) syluer (4) sylueres
  (1) suluer (17)
A.Pr.78   Ac þe parissh prest & þe pardoner parte þe *siluer*
A.Pr.83   To synge for symonye for *siluer* is swete.
A. 1.65   Iudas he iapide wiþ Iewene *siluer*,
A. 2.107   Til he hadde *siluer* for his selis & signes.
A. 3.21   Coupis of clene gold [and] pecis of *siluer*,
A. 3.77   Of alle suche selleris *siluer* to take,
A. 3.78   Or presauntis wiþoute panis as pecis of *siluer*,
A. 3.194   To leuen his lordsshipe for a litel *siluer*,
A. 4.112   Bere no *siluer* ouer se þat signe of king shewi[þ],
A. 5.76   And belowen hym to lordis to don hym lese *siluer*,
B.Pr.81   [Ac] þe parisshe preest and þe pardoner parten þe *siluer*
B.Pr.86   [To] syngen for symonie for *siluer* is swete.
B.Pr.92   Somme seruen þe kyng and his *siluer* tellen
B.Pr.168   To bugge a belle of bras or of briȝt *siluer*
B. 1.67   Iudas he iaped wiþ Iewen *siluer*
B. 2.68   Thei assented for *siluer* to seye as boþe wolde.
B. 2.143   Til he hadde *siluer* for his [seles] and [signes of] Notaries.
B. 2.175   Lat sadle hem wiþ *siluer* oure synne to suffre,
B. 3.22   Coupes of clene gold and coppes of *siluer*,
B. 3.88   Of alle swiche Selleris *siluer* to take,
B. 3.89   Or presentȝ wiþouten pens as pieces of *siluer*,
B. 3.207   To leuen his lordship for a litel *siluer*,
B. 4.35   Theras wraþe and wranglynge is þer wynne þei *siluer*,
B. 4.129   Bere no *siluer* ouer see þat signe of kyng sheweþ,
B. 5.96   And [bilowen] hym to lordes to doon hym lese *siluer*,
B. 5.263   Ne þyne executours wel bisette þe *siluer* þat þow hem leuest;
B. 6.192   That seten to begge *siluer* soone were þei heeled,
B. 9.93   He is [lugged wiþ] Iudas þat ȝyueþ a Iaper *siluer*
B.10.342   Salomon seiþ also þat *siluer* is worst to louye'
B.10.365   It shal bisitten vs ful soure þe *siluer* þat we kepen,
B.11.74   Where my body were buryed by so ye hadde my *siluer*.
B.11.174   For no cause to cacche *siluer* þerby, ne to be called a maister,
B.11.223   And lawe is looþ to louye but if he lacche *siluer*.
B.11.277   Or selle it, as seiþ þe book, and þe *siluer* dele
B.11.283   If preestes weren [wise] þei wolde no *siluer* take
B.11.287   Spera in deo spekeþ of preestes þat haue no spendyng *siluer*,
B.11.291   Thanne nedeþ yow noȝt to [nyme] *siluer* for masses þat ye syngen,
B.14.250   Lecherie loueþ hym noȝt for he ȝyueþ but litel *siluer*
B.14.269   As by assent of sondry parties and *siluer* to boote,
B.15.7   As persons in pelure wiþ pendauntȝ of *siluer*;
B.15.81   And reuerencen þe riche þe raþer for hir *siluer*:
B.15.123   Sir Iohan and sire Geffrey haþ [of *siluer* a girdel]
B.15.126   Hadde he neuere [saued] *siluer* þerto [for spendyng at ale]
B.15.131   The whiche arn preestes inparfite and prechours after *siluer*,
B.15.240   For hir lawe dureþ ouerlonge but if þei lacchen *siluer*,
B.16.143   That euere he his Saueour solde for *siluer* or ellis.'
B.17.78   And lo, here *siluer*', he seide, 'for salue to hise woundes.'
B.19.371   And for *siluer* were forswore–sooþly þei wiste it.
B.20.222   'I counte na moore Conscience by so I cacche *siluer*
B.20.367   As frere[s] of oure Fraternytee, for a litel *siluer*'.
C.Pr.79   For þe parsche prest and þe Pardoner parten þe *seluer*
C.Pr.84   And synge þer for symonye [for] *seluer* is swete.
C.Pr.90   Summe seruen þe kynge and his *siluer* tellen,
C.Pr.185   A belle to byggen of bras oþer of] bryghte *syluer*
C. 1.63   Iudas he byiapede thorw iewene *seluer*
C. 1.101   And neuer leue for loue in hope to lacche *syluer*.
C. 2.70   Thei assentede hit were so at *sylueres* prayere.
C. 2.159   Til he hadde *seluer* for the seel and signes of notaries.
C. 3.23   Coupes of clene gold [and] coppes of *syluer*,
C. 3.109   For to spyre and to aspye, for eny speche of *suluer*,
C. 3.116   Of alle suche sullers *seluer* to take
C. 3.389   Of the cours of case so thei cache *suluer*.
C. 4.51   'Bere sikerlyche eny *seluer* to seynt Gyles doune.
C. 4.52   [A w]ayteth ful wel when y *seluer* take,
C. 4.126   Bere no *seluer* ouer see þat sygne of kyng sheweth,
C. 4.127   Nother ygraue ne vngraue, of gold oþer of *suluer*,
C. 4.191   'And y dar lege my lyf þat loue wol lene þe *seluer*
C. 5.72   And so[p]ares and here sones for *suluer* ben be knyhtes,
C. 6.254   Shal neuere seketoure[s] wel bysette the *syluer* þat thow hem
      leuest
C. 8.247   His *suluer* to thre maner men [in] menyng they sholden
C. 9.144   *Suluer* or sode mete and sum tyme bothe,
C.12.16   And saide he myhte [me nat] assoile but y *suluer* hadde
C.12.22   Wher my body were yber[i]ed by so ȝe hadde my [*suluer*].'
C.13.101   For spera in deo spekeþ of prestis þat han no spendynge *suluer*
C.13.105   And nedeth [ȝow] nat to nyme *siluer* for masses þat ȝe synge
C.16.90   Lecherye loueth no pore for he hath bote litel *siluer*
C.16.109   As by assente of sondry p[arti]es and *suluer* to bote,
C.16.240   And reuerence þe ryche þe rather for here *suluer*

C.16.278   As inparfite prestes and prechours aftur *suluer*,
C.16.365   For ouerlong is here lawe but yf þay lacche *suluer*.
C.21.371   And for *suluer* weren forswore–soth[ly] thei wisten hit.
C.22.222   'Y counte no more Consience bi so y cache *suluer*
C.22.367   [As] freres of oure fraternite for a litel *suluer*'.

simile n *simile n.*   C 2
C.18.227   Was þe sone in hymsulue, in a *simile* as Eue was,
C.19.164   Bi this *simile*,' he saide, 'y se an euydence

symme n prop *n.i.d.*   A 1; B 1; C 1
A. 5.115   For sum tyme I seruide *symme* at þe nok
B. 5.199   For som tyme I serued *Symme* atte [Nok]
C. 6.207   For som tyme y serued *symme* at þe style

symond n prop *Simon n.*   B 2 Symond (1) Symondes (1); C 4 Simon (1) simond (1) symondes (1) Symondus (1)
B.12.203   He sit neiþer wiþ Seint Iohan, *Symond* ne Iude,
B.18.250   And leet out *Symondes* sone[s] to seen hym hange on roode.
C. 5.79   And taken *Symondus* sones seyntwarie to kepe,
C. 9.258   Certes, hoso durste sygge hit, *Simon* quasi dormit;
C.14.142   A sit noþer with seynte Iohan, *simond* ne Iude,
C.20.259   And lette out *symondes* sones to sen hym honge on rode:

symonye n *simonie n.*   A 11; B 15 simonie (4) Symonye (11); C 16 simonye (4) symonye (12)
A.Pr.83   To synge for *symonye* for siluer is swete.
A. 2.35   Sire *symonye* is assent to asele þe chartres
A. 2.53   And as sire *symonye* wile segge to sewen his wille.
A. 2.54   *Symonye* & cyuyle stondiþ forþ boþe
A. 2.78   Be siȝte of sire *symonye* & signes of notories.
A. 2.90   *Symonye* & þiself shenden holy chirche;
A. 2.106   Hereto assentiþ Cyuyle, ac *symonye* ne wolde
A. 2.132   Þat *symonye* & cyuyle shulde on here fet gange.
A. 2.136   Sire *symonye* hymself shal sitte on here bakkis;
A. 2.165   *Symonye* & cyuyle, I sen[d]e hem to warne
A. 3.137   Sire *symonye* & hireself seliþ þe bullis;
B.Pr.86   [To] syngen for *symonie* for siluer is swete.
B. 2.63   Ac *Symonie* and Cyuylle and Sisours of courtes
B. 2.67   Whan *Symonye* and Cyuylle seighe hir boþer wille
B. 2.71   And preide Cyuylle to see and *Symonye* to rede it.
B. 2.72   *Symonye* and Cyuylle stonden forþ boþe
B. 2.114   By siȝte of sire *Symonie* and Cyuyles leeue.'
B. 2.126   *Symonye* and þiself shenden holi chirche:
B. 2.142   Herto assenteþ Cyuyle, ac *Symonye* ne wolde
B. 2.168   For *Symonye* and Cyuylle sholde on hire feet gange.
B. 2.169   Ac þanne swoor *Symonye* and Cyuylle boþe
B. 2.172   Sire *Symonye* hymself shal sitte vpon hir bakkes.
B. 2.204   [*Symonye* and Cyuyle, I sende hem to warne
B. 3.148   Sire *Symonie* and hirselue seleþ [þe] bulles.
B.20.126   *Symonye* hym [suede] to assaille Conscience,
B.20.137   And tornede Cyuyle into *Symonye*, and siþþe he took þe Official.
C.Pr.84   And synge þer for *symonye* [for] seluer is swete.
C. 2.65   Ac *simonye* and syuile and sysores of contrees
C. 2.69   When *simonye* and syuile ysey[e] þer bothe wille
C. 2.73   And preyeth syuile to se and *s[y]monye* to rede hit.
C. 2.74   Thenne *simonye* and syuyle standeth forth bothe
C. 2.76   Thenne saide *symonye* þat syuyle it herde:
C. 2.118   By syhte of sire *Simonye* and syuyles leue.'
C. 2.120   And sayde to *Symonye*, 'now sorwe mot thow haue
C. 2.158   Hereto assenteth syuyle, ac *symonye* ne wolde
C. 2.184   *Symonye* and syuyle seyden and sworen
C. 2.186   'And y mysulue, syuyle, and *symonye* my felawe
C. 2.246   *Symonye* and syuile senten to Rome,
C. 3.186   For *symonye* and heresulue seleth [þe] bulles.
C. 9.55   For hit is *symonye* to sulle þat sent is of grace,
C.22.126   *Symonye* hym suede to assaile Consience
C.22.137   And turnede syuyle into *symonye* and sethe he toek þe official.

symple adj *simple adj.*   B 2; C 1
B.13.217   Sobretee and *symple* speche and sooþfast bileue,
B.16.8   Pacience hatte þe pure tree and [pouere] *symple* of herte,
C.15.186   Sobrete [and] *symple* speche and sothfaste bileue,

sympletee n *simplete n.*   A 1 simplite; B 1
A.11.122   Þanne shalt þou se sobirte, & *simplite* of speche,
B.10.170   Thanne shaltow se Sobretee and *Sympletee*-of-speche,

syn > siþen

synay n prop *n.i.d.*   A 2; B 3; C 2 synay (1) synoye (1)
A. 6.9   Signes of *synay*, & shilles of galis,
A. 6.14   'Fro *synay*,' he seide, '& fro þe sepulcre.
B. 5.521   Signes of *Synay* and shelles of Galice,
B. 5.526   'Fram *Synay*', he seide, 'and fram [þe Sepulcre].
B.17.2   That took me a maundement vpon þe mount of *Synay*

C. 7.171   'Fro *synoye*,' he sayde, 'and fro þe sepulcre.
C.19.2   That toek me a maundement vpon þe mont of *synay*

synege(- > synnen

synful adj *sinful adj.*   A 4; B 16 synful (4) synfulle (12); C 15 synfol (1) synfole (6) synful (3) synnefole (5)
A. 5.235   And ȝet þe *synful* shrewe seide to hymselue:
A. 6.121   And she is sib to alle *synful*, & hire sone alse,
A.12.20   "I saw *synful*," he seyde, "þerfore I seyde no þing
A.12.24   Telle hit with tounge to *synful* wrecches."
B. 5.463   Ac yet þe *synfulle* sherewe seide to hymselue:
B. 5.478   'I shal biseche alle *synfulle* oure Saueour of grace,
B. 5.486   And madest þiself wiþ þi sone vs *synfulle* yliche:
B. 5.497   A *synful* Marie þe seiȝ er seynte Marie þi dame,
B. 5.498   And al to solace *synfulle* þow suffredest it so were:
B. 5.508   That alle Seintes [for *synful*] songen at ones
B. 5.636   And she is sib to alle *synfulle* and hire sone also,
B. 7.15   And in as muche as þei mowe amenden alle *synfulle*,
B. 9.64   That lyuen *synful* lif here hir soule is lich þe deuel.
B. 9.125   Of swiche *synfulle* sherewes þe Sauter makeþ mynde:
B.11.227   That saued *synful* men as Seint Iohan bereþ witnesse:
B.11.240   And al was ensample, [sooþliche], to vs *synfulle* here
B.16.110   And sike and *synfulle* boþe so] to goode turnede:
B.18.328   For alle *synfulle* soules, to saue þo þat ben worþi.
B.19.22   And *synfulle* aren solaced and saued by þat name,
B.19.441   And suffreþ þat *synfulle* be [til som tyme þat þei repente].
C. 3.465   Here sauter and here seuene p[s]almes for alle *synful* preyen;
C. 6.317   Ac ȝut þ[e] *synful* shrewe saide to heuene:
C. 7.120   'Y shal byseke for alle *synnefole* oure sauiour of grace,
C. 7.137   A *synful* marie þe sey ar seynte marye þy dame
C. 7.138   And a[l] to solace *synfole* thow soffredest it so were:
C. 7.145   That what tyme we *synnefole* men wolden be sory
C. 7.153   That alle seyntes for *synfol* songen with dauid:
C. 7.289   And she is sib to alle *synfole* and here sone bothe
C.10.162   That god [s]eweth nat *synnefole* men and soffreth hem mysfare,
C.10.165   As þe sauter sayth by *synnefole* shrewes:
C.12.129   And al was ensample, sothly, to vs *synfole* here
C.20.371   For alle *synfole* soules, to saue oure bothe rihte.
C.20.394   Here eny *synfole* soule souereynliche by maistrie,
C.21.22   And *synfole* ben solaced and saued by þat name.
C.21.441   And soffreth þat *synnefole* be til som tyme þat þei repente.

syngen v *singen* A 5 singe (1) synge (2) songe (1) sungen (1); B 28 synge (7) syngen (4) syngeþ (4) song (2) songe (3) songen (8); C 34 sang (1) syng (2) synge (9) syngen (5) syngeth (2) song (5) songe (3) songen (7)
A.Pr.83   To *synge* for symonye for siluer is swete.
A. 3.232   Þat take mede & money for massis þat þei *synge*,
A. 5.187   And seten so til euesong & *songe* [vmbe]while
A. 7.107   Þanne seten somme & *sungen* at þe ale,
A.11.193   Sike with þe sory, *singe* with þe glade,
B.Pr.86   [To] *syngen* for symonie for siluer is swete.
B. 3.253   That taken Mede and moneie for masses þat þei *syngeþ*,
B. 3.328   And Sarȝynes for þat siȝte shul *synge* Gloria in excelsis &c,
B. 5.338   And seten so til euensong and *songen* vmwhile
B. 5.394   I kan noȝt parfitly my Paternoster as þe preest it *syngeþ*,
B. 5.416   Yet kan I neyþer solue ne *synge* ne seintes lyues rede;
B. 5.508   That alle Seintes [for synful] *songen* at ones
B. 6.115   [Th]anne seten somme and *songen* atte Nale
B.11.291   Thanne nedeþ yow noȝt to [nyme] siluer for masses þat ye *syngen*,
B.11.314   *Synge* ne psalmes rede ne seye a masse of þe day.
B.12.150   And *songe* a song of solas, Gloria in excelsis deo.
B.13.45   But if þei *synge* for þo soules and wepe salte teris:
B.13.233   Ne neiþer saille ne [sautrie] ne *synge* wiþ þe gyterne,
B.15.127   [He *syngeþ* seruice bokelees], seiþ it with ydel wille.
B.15.193   [Th]anne he *syngeþ* whan he doþ so, and som tyme wepynge,
B.15.225   I haue yseyen charite also *syngen* and reden
B.15.388   As clerkes in Corpus Christi feeste *syngen* and reden
B.18.8   And how Osanna by Organye olde folk *songen*,
B.18.17   Olde Iewes of Ierusalem for ioye þei *songen*,
B.18.179   Moyses and many mo mer[ye] shul [*synge*];
B.18.324   *Songen* seint Iohanes song, Ecce agnus dei.
B.18.407   Manye hundred of Aungeles harpeden and *songen*,
B.18.422   Truþe trumpede þo and *song* Te deum laudamus,
B.19.74   Aungeles out of heuene come knelynge and *songe*,
B.19.135   The burdes þo *songe*, Saul interfecit mille et dauid decem milia.
B.19.151   Come knelynge to þe corps and *songen*
B.19.209   Knele now', quod Conscience, 'and if þow kanst *synge*
B.19.211   Thanne *song* I þat song; so dide manye hundred,
C.Pr.84   And *synge* þer for symonye [for] seluer is swete.
C. 3.53   In masse and in mataynes for mede we shal *synge*
C. 3.311   The mede þat many prest[es] taken for masses þat thei *syngen*,
C. 3.481   And saresines for þat syhte shal *syng* Credo in spiritum sanctum

C. 5.12 'Can thow seruen,' he sayde, 'or *syngen* in a churche
C. 5.48 Th[u]s y *s[yn]ge* for here soules of suche as me helpeth
C. 5.63 Somme to *synge* masses or sitten and wryten,
C. 6.46 Prout of my fayre fetures and for y *song* shille;
C. 6.396 And seten so til euenson[g] and *songen* vmbywhile
C. 7.10 Y can nat parfitly my paternoster as þe prest hit *syngeth*;
C. 7.31 ꝣut kan y nother solfe ne *synge* ne a seyntes lyf rede;
C. 7.153 That alle seyntes for synfol *songen* with dauid:
C. 8.122 Thenne seet somme and *songen* at the ale
C.13.17 And for a *song* in his sorwe, "si bona accepimus a domino &c,
C.13.105 And nedeth [ꝫow] nat to nyme siluer for masses þat ꝫe *synge*
C.13.126 *Syng* ne [psalmes] rede [ne sey a masse of the daye].
C.14.94 And *song* a song of solace, Gloria in excelcis deo.
C.14.94 And *song* a song of solace, Gloria in excelcis deo.
C.15.50 Bote yf they *synge* for tho soules and wepe salte teres:
C.15.207 Ne noþer sayle ne sautrien ne *syngen* with þe geterne.
C.16.336 Thenne *syngeth* he when he doth so and som tyme w[e]pynge:
C.16.350 Ich haue yseye charite also *syngen* and rede,
C.17.120 As Clerkes in corpus cristi feste *syngen* and reden
C.20.7 And how osanna by orgene oelde folke *songe*.
C.20.15 Olde iewes of Ierusalem for ioye they *songen*,
C.20.182 Moises and many moo Mer[y] shal *synge*;
C.20.367 *Songen* seynt Iohann[es songe], ecce agnus dei.
C.20.450 Many hundret of Angels harpeden and *songen*,
C.20.465 Treuth trompede tho and *song* te deum laudamus
C.21.74 Angele[s] out of heuene come knel[yng] and *songe*,
C.21.135 The buyrdes tho *songe*, Saul interfecit mille & dauid decem milia.
C.21.151 Comen knelyng to þ[e] Cors and *songen*
C.21.209 Knele now,' quod Consience, 'and yf thow canst *synge*,
C.21.211 [Thanne] *sang* [y] þat song; so dede many hundret

syngynge ger *singinge ger.* B 1; C 1
B.11.151 And I saued as ye [may] see, wiþouten *syngynge* of masses,
C.12.86 And y saued, as ꝫe may se, withoute *syngynge* of masses.

singuler adj *singulere adj.* B 3 singuler (2) synguler (1); C 1 synguler
B. 9.36 For he was *synguler* hymself and seide faciamus
B.13.282 And so *singuler* by hymself [as to siꝫte of þe peple
B.16.208 And in heuene and heuene oon *singuler* name.
C. 6.36 And ꝫut so *synguler* be mysulue as to syhte of [þe] peple

synken v *sinken v.* A 1; B 2 sank (1) sonken (1); C 1 sank
A. 2.70 Here soulis to sathanas to *synken* in pyne,
B.14.81 [So] thei *sonken* into helle, þe Citees echone.
B.18.67 Er sonday aboute sonne risyng'; and *sank* wiþ þat til erþe.
C.20.69 Ar soneday aboute sonne rysynge'; and *sank* with þat til erthe.

synne n *sinne n.* &> synnen A 19 sennes (1) synne (17) synnes (1); B 92 synne (67) synnes (25); C 94 synne (68) synnes (26)
A. 1.78 Preiꝫede hire pitously [to] preiꝫe for my *sennes*,
A. 1.132 No dedly *synne* to do, diꝫe þeiꝫ þou shuldist.
A. 1.177 To counforte þe carful acumbrid wiþ *synne*.
A. 3.255 And al his sed for þat *synne* [shend]fully ende.
A. 5.13 And prouide þat þise pestilences wern for pur *synne*,
A. 5.20 Þat dedly *synne* er domisday shal fordon hem alle.
A. 5.104 'Sorewe for *synne* sauiþ wel manye.'
A. 5.142 Ac I swere now, so þ[e I], þat *synne* shal I lete,
A. 5.205 His wyf [wit]ide hym þanne of wykkidnesse & *synne*.
A. 5.217 "I am sory for my *synne*," sey to þiseluen,
A. 6.86 And am sory for my *synnes* & so shal I euere
A. 8.16 And prechen here personis þe periles of *synne*,
A. 9.40 Ac dedly *synne* doþ he nouꝫt, for dowel hym helpiþ,
A. 9.41 Þat is charite þe champioun, chief helpe aꝫens *synne*.
A. 9.46 And don dedly *synne* & drenche þiseluen.
A.10.74 Saue hymself fro *synne*, for so hym behouiþ;
A.10.77 And sauiþ þe soule þat *synne* haþ no miꝫt
A.11.69 And alle here seed for here *synne* þe same wo suffride?"
A.12.21 Til þo wrecches ben in wil here *synne* to lete."
B. 1.80 Preide hire pitously [to] preye for my *synnes*;
B. 1.144 No dedly *synne* to do, deye þeiꝫ þow shuldest,
B. 1.149 May no *synne* be on hym seene þat vseþ þat spice,
B. 1.203 To conforten þe carefulle acombred wiþ *synne*.
B. 2.175 Lat sadle hem wiþ siluer oure *synne* to suffre,
B. 3.58 It is *synne* of þe seuene sonnest relessed.'
B. 3.277 And al his seed for þat *synne* shenfulliche ende.
B. 4.133 Prouysour or preest or penaunt for hise *synnes*.
B. 5.13 He preued þat þise pestilences were for pure *synne*,
B. 5.20 That dedly *synne* er domesday shal fordoon hem alle.
B. 5.127 'Sorwe [for] synn[e] is sauacion of soules.'
B. 5.226 Ac I swere now, so thee ik, þat *synne* wol I lete
B. 5.295 And what he lente yow of oure lordes good to lette yow fro *synne*.'
B. 5.363 His wif [edwyted] hym þo [of wikkednesse and *synne*],
B. 5.399 Ne riꝫt sory for my *synnes* yet, [so þee I], was I neuere.
B. 5.445 "I am sory for my *synn[e]*", seye to þiselue,
B. 5.484 For þoruꝫ þat *synne* þi sone sent was to erþe

B. 5.599 And am sory for my *synnes* and so [shal I] euere
B. 8.44 Ac dedly *synne* doþ he noꝫt for dowel hym [helpeþ],
B. 8.45 [Th]at is charite þe champioun, chief help ayein *synne*.
B. 8.50 And] do deedly *synne* and drenche þi[selue].
B. 9.183 Wisely go wedde and ware [þee] fro *synne*,
B. 9.210 And dryueþ awey dowel þoruꝫ dedliche *synnes*.'
B.10.76 Ne sory for hire *synnes*; so is pride woxen
B.10.111 And al hir seed for hir *synne* þe same deeþ suffrede?
B.10.479 Selden falle so foule and so fer in *synne*
B.11.54 Go confesse þee to som frere and shewe hym þi *synnes*.
B.11.100 Thouꝫ þi tale [were] trewe, and it touche[d] *synne*.
B.11.102 To reden it in Retorik to arate dedly *synne*?
B.11.121 And bad hem souke for *synne* [saufte] at his breste
B.11.137 'That is sooþ', seide Scripture; 'may no *synne* lette
B.11.204 No beggere ne boye amonges vs but if it *synne* made:
B.11.218 That Fides sua sholde sauen hire and saluen hire of *synnes*.
B.11.431 [To blame or] to bete hym þanne] it were but pure *synne*.
B.12.79 Giltier as afore god, and gretter in *synne*,
B.12.117 And his sones also for þat *synne* myscheued,
B.12.172 Out of *synne* and be saaf, þouꝫ he synne ofte,
B.12.174 For if þe clerk be konnynge he knoweþ what is *synne*,
B.12.177 How contricion is comended for it cacheþ awey *synne*:
B.13.191 Haþ meued my mood to moorne for my *synnes*.
B.13.387 As if I hadde dedly *synne* doon I dredde noꝫt þat so soore
B.13.405 And þanne I dradde to deye in dedlich *synne*',
B.13.412 Dooþ noon almes[dede]; dred hym of no *synne*,
B.13.430 To entice men þoruꝫ hir tales to *synne* and harlotrie.
B.14.9 And [siþþe] shryuen of þe preest, þat [for my *synnes* gaf me]
B.14.79 Diden dedly *synne* þat þe deuel liked,
B.14.80 Vengeaunce fil vpon hem for hir vile *synnes*;
B.14.84 Which dryueþ awey dedly *synne* and dooþ it to be venial.
B.14.89 And surgiens for dedly *synnes* whan shrift of mouþe failleþ.
B.14.91 For shrift of mouþe sleeþ *synne* be it neuer so dedly–
B.14.93 Ther contricion dooþ but dryueþ it doun into a venial *synne*
B.14.96 And as it neuere [n]adde ybe to noꝫte bryngeþ dedly *synne*
B.14.154 Here forꝫifnesse of hir *synnes*, and heuene blisse after.
B.14.185 And be clene þoruꝫ þat cristnyng of alle kynnes *synne*.
B.14.186 And if vs fille þoruꝫ folie to falle in *synne* after
B.14.202 For seuene *synnes* þer ben assaillen vs euere;
B.14.219 Ne none of þe seuene *synnes* sitten ne mowe þer longe,
B.14.237 And som tyme for his *synnes*; so he is neuere murie
B.14.249 Wiþ sobretee fram alle *synne* and also ꝫit moore;
B.14.325 So hard it is', quod haukyn, 'to lyue and to do *synne*.
B.14.326 *Synne* seweþ vs euere', quod he and sory gan wexe,
B.15.74 And tellen men of þe ten comaundementꝫ, and touchen þe seuene *synnes*,
B.15.353 Ac þe metal, þat is mannes soule, [myd] *synne* is foule alayed.
B.15.354 Boþe lettred and lewed beþ alayed now wiþ *synne*
B.15.541 Than cristes cros þat ouercam deeþ and dedly *synne*.
B.16.34 And wikkede werkes þerof, wormes of *synne*,
B.16.99 For to werchen his wille wiþouten any *synne*:
B.16.109 And commune wommen conuertede and clensed of *synne*,
B.16.270 'Allas!' I seide, 'þat *synne* so longe shal lette
B.17.31 And haþ saued þat bileued and sory for hir *synnes*,
B.17.214 That alle kynne cristene clenseþ of *synnes*.
B.17.225 Graunte no grace ne for[g]ifnesse of *synnes*
B.18.177 That many day myꝫte I noꝫt se for merknesse of *synne*,
B.18.226 So it shal fare by þis folk: hir folie and hir *synne*
B.18.236 That mannes soule sholde saue and *synne* destroye.
B.18.297 I haue assailled hym with *synne* and som tyme yasked
B.18.304 That his soule wolde suffre no *synne* in his sighte;
B.18.306 To saue men from *synne* if hemself wolde.
B.18.340 Ergo soule shal soule quyte and *synne* to synne wende
B.18.340 Ergo soule shal soule quyte and synne to *synne* wende,
B.18.346 And boþe quykne and quyte þat queynt was þoruꝫ *synne*;
B.18.388 Be it any þyng abouꝫt, þe boldnesse of hir *synnes*,
B.18.391 They shul be clensed clerliche and [keuered] of hir *synnes*
B.19.65 Therwith to fiꝫte and [f]enden vs fro fallynge in[to] *synne*,
B.19.184 [Myght [men] to assoille of alle manere *synne*[s],
B.19.190 And assoille men of alle *synnes* saue of dette one.
B.19.368 Repenteden and [forsoke] *synne*, saue þei one,
B.19.457 Ech man subtileþ a sleiꝫte *synne* to hide
B.20.155 And [so] forꝫyte sorwe and [of *synne* ꝫyue noꝫt].'
B.20.305 'Go salue þo þat sike ben and þoruꝫ *synne* ywounded.'
B.20.372 That is þe souerayn[e] salue for alle [*synnes* of kynde].
B.20.379 And [doþ men drynke dwale]; þei drede no *synne*.'
C.Pr.107 For Offines *s[yn]ne* and fines his brother
C.Pr.124 For ꝫoure shrewed soffraunce and ꝫoure oune *synne*.
C. 1.143 Dey rather þen do eny dedly *synne*:
C. 1.146 For treuthe telleth þat loue ys triacle [for] *synne*
C. 1.193 And þat is no treuthe of þe trinite but triccherye [and] *synne*
C. 1.198 That conforteth alle carefole acombred with *synne*.
C. 3.46 [And] shrofe here of here *synne*, shameles y [trowe];

C. 3.62	Hit is *synne* as of seuene noon sannour relesed.
C. 3.359	Of oure sory *synnes* to be assoiled and yclansed
C. 3.400	To syke for here *synnes* and soffre harde penaunc[e]
C. 3.411	That saul for þat *synne* and his sone deyede
C. 3.430	And al [h]is [sede] for þat *synne* shentfolyche ende.
C. 4.130	Prouisour or preest oþer penaunt for his *synnes*.
C. 5.107	S[yh]ing for my *synnes*, seggyng my paternoster,
C. 5.115	And preuede þat this pestelences was for puyre *synne*
C. 5.122	That dedly *synne* ar domesday shal fordon hem alle.
C. 6.92	For thy *synnes* souereynly and biseke god of mercy.'
C. 6.188	Exited either oþer til oure olde *synne*;
C. 6.257	To assoyle the of th[y] *synne* sine restitucion[e]:
C. 6.276	As thow y deddly *synne* dede y dradde [hit] nat so sore
C. 6.336	And deyede with a drop water; so doth alle *synnes*
C. 6.421	His wyf and his inwit Edwitede hym of his *synne*;
C. 7.15	Ne ryht sory for my *synnes*–y seyh neuere þe tyme–
C. 7.59	"Y am sory for my *synnes*", sey to thysuluen
C. 7.72	Doth non Almesdede, drat hym nat of *synne*,
C. 7.90	To entise men thorw here tales to *synne* and harlotrie.
C. 7.126	For thorw þat *synne* thy sone ysent was til erthe
C. 7.210	Thenne eny dedly *synne* do for drede or for preeyere.
C. 7.246	Y am sory [for] my *synnes*, and so [shal y] euere,
C. 8.52	For hit beeþ þe deueles dysors to drawe men to *synne*;
C. 9.138	For vnder godes secret seal here *synnes* ben keuered.
C. 9.239	Y drede me, and he dey, hit worth for dedly *synne*
C. 9.257	That soffreth suche sottes and oþere *synnes* regne.
C.10.43	So dedly *synne* doth he nat for dowel hym helpeth.
C.10.52	To repenten and arise and rowe out of *synne*
C.10.101	And crouned oen to be kyng to kull withoute *synne*
C.10.158	And semblable in soule to god but if *synne* hit make.
C.10.161	So let lecherye and other luther *synnes*
C.10.213	Caym þe corsede creature conseyued was in *synne*
C.10.221	And for þe *synne* of Caymes seed sayede god to Noe:
C.10.284	Wisely go wedde and war þe fro *synne*;
C.11.56	Ne sory for here *synnes*; so [is] pruyde enhanced
C.11.140	Kepe þe ten comaundementis and kepe þe fro *synne*
C.11.300	Selde falleth so foule and so depe in *synne*
C.12.27	Y wolde it were no *synne*,' y saide, 'to seien þat were treuthe.
C.12.28	The sauter sayth hit is no *synne* for suche men þat ben trewe
C.12.36	To rehercen hit by retoryk to arate dedly *synne*?
C.12.56	And bad hem souke for prute saue at his breste
C.12.72	'That is soth,' saide scripture; ' may no *synne* lette
C.12.112	No beggare ne boy among vs but [yf] hit *synne* ma[d]e:
C.13.238	To blame hym or to bete hym thenne y halde hit but *synne*.
C.14.62	And his sones for his *synnes* sorwe hem [becau3t]e
C.14.112	Out of *synne* and be saef, thogh he synege ofte,
C.14.114	For yf þe clerke be connynge [he] knoweth what is *synne*
C.14.117	How contricioun is comended for hit cacheth awey *synne*:
C.16.26	And confessioun to kulle alle kyne *synne*
C.16.31	And [operis satisfaccio] for soules paieth and alle *synnes* quyteth.
C.16.43	For seuene *synnes* þer ben þat ass[a]ilen vs euere;
C.16.60	Ne none of þe seuene *synnes* sitte ne may þer longe
C.16.76	So for his glotonye and his grete *synne* he hath a greuous penaunce
C.16.134	With sobrete fro alle *synnes* and also 3ut more;
C.16.229	"Non plus sapere," saide þe wyse, [laste *synne* of pruyde wexe,]
C.17.3	And 3ut oþerwhile wroeth withouten eny *synne*.'
C.17.80	Is alayed with leccherye and oþer lustes of *synne*
C.17.82	And for þe *synne* of þe soule forsaketh his oune coyne.
C.17.203	Thenne cristes cros þat ouercome deth and dedly *synne*.
C.17.245	Deuouteliche day and nyhte, withdrawe hem fro *synne*
C.17.285	Feden hem and follen hem and fere hem fro *synne*–
C.17.291	And deye for his dere childrene to de[struy]e dedly *synne*,
C.18.38	And manye wikkede werkes, wormes of *synne*,
C.18.132	For to worchen his wille withouten eny *synne*:
C.18.142	And comen wommen conuertede and clansed hem of *synne*
C.18.211	Semblable to hymsulue ar eny coyne were,
C.18.286	'Allas!' y saide, 'þat *synne* so longe shal lette
C.19.32	And hath ysaued þat bileued so and sory for here *synnes*;
C.19.180	That alle kyne cristene clanseth of *synne*[s].
C.19.191	Graunten [no] grace ne forgeuenesse of *synne*
C.20.180	That many day myhte y nat se for merkenesse of *synne*,
C.20.235	So hit shal fare bi this folk: here folye and here *synne*
C.20.245	That mannes soule sholde saue and *synne* distruye.
C.20.330	Y haue ass[a]yled hym with *synne* and som tyme ich askede
C.20.388	Ergo soule shal soule quyte and *synne* to synne wende
C.20.388	Ergo soule shal soule quyte and synne to *synne* wende
C.20.391	And bothe quykie and quyte that queynte was thorw *synne*
C.20.430	Be hit eny thyng aboute, þe boldenesse of here *synne*[s],
C.21.65	Therwith to fihte and fende vs fro fallyng into *synne*
C.21.184	/Myhte men to assoyle of alle manere *synnes*,
C.21.190	And assoile men of alle *synnes* saue of dette one.
C.21.368	Repenteden and [forsoke] *synne*, saue thei one
C.21.457	Vch man sotileth a sleythe *synne* to huyde

C.22.155	And [s]o for3ete [sorwe] and [of *synne* 3eue nouht].'
C.22.305	'Go salue tho þat syke [ben] and thorw *synne* ywounded.'
C.22.372	That is the souereyne salue for alle [*synnes* of kynde].
C.22.379	And doth men drynke dwale; [they] drat no *synne*.'

synnefole > *synful*

synnelees adj *sinneles adj.* A 1 synneles; B 1; C 2 synneslees (1) synneslees (1)

A. 7.214	Mi3te I *synneles* do as þou seist?' seide peris þanne.
B. 6.230	Mi3te I *synnelees* do as þow seist?' seide Piers þanne.
C. 8.236	Myhte y *synneles* do as thow sayst?' sayde Peres þe plouhman.
C.14.41	"That seth hymsulue *synnelees* sese nat, y hote,

synnen v *sinnen v.* A 7 synne (2) synnes (1) synneþ (3) ysynned (1); B 15 synne (5) synned (2) synnen (1) synneþ (7); C 20 synege (4) syneged (2) synegen (1) synegeth (8) synne (3) synnen (1) ysyneged (1)

A. 5.49	For to affaiten hire flessh þat fers was to *synne*:
A. 5.151	And siþen I wile be shriuen & *synne* no more.'
A. 8.162	Soulis þat han *ysynned* seue siþes dedly.
A. 9.17	Seue siþes, seiþ þe bok, [*synneþ*] þe ri3tful;
A. 9.18	Ac whoso *synneþ*, I sei3e, sertis, me þinkiþ
A. 9.23	'How seue siþes þe sadde man *synneþ* on þe day;
A. 9.39	*Synnes* þe sad man seuene [siþes] in þe day.
B. 5.66	To affaiten hire flessh þat fiers was to *synne*.
B. 5.301	And siþen I wole be shryuen and *synne* na moore.'
B. 5.482	And siþen suffredest [hym] to *synne*, a siknesse to vs alle,
B. 7.184	Soules þat haue *synned* seuen siþes dedly.
B. 8.21	Seuene siþes, seiþ þe book, *synneþ* þe rightfulle;
B. 8.22	A[c] whoso *synneþ*, I sei[e, certes], me þynkeþ
B. 8.27	'How seuen siþes þe sadde man [*synneþ* on þe day].
B. 8.43	*Synneþ* þe sadde man [seuen siþes a day].
B.12.172	Out of synne and be saaf, þou3 he *synne* ofte,
B.17.199	That whoso *synneþ* in þe Seint Spirit assoilled worþ he neuere,
B.17.204	So whoso *synneþ* in þe Seint Spirit, it semeþ þat he greueþ
B.17.287	*Synnen* ayein þe Seint Spirit, assenten to destruye
B.17.299	'I pose I hadde *synned* so and sholde [nouþe] deye,
B.18.220	And siþþe he suffred hym *synne* sorwe to feele,
B.20.15	He *synneþ* no3t, sooþliche, þat so wynneþ his foode.
C.Pr.109	And for here syre sey hem *synne* and suffred hem do ille
C. 6.7	To affayten here flesshe þat fers was to *synne*.
C. 6.356	And sennes sitte and be shryue and *synege* no more.'
C. 7.124	And sethe soffredes[t] hym to *synege*, a sykenesse to vs alle,
C. 7.301	Were y seuen nyhte fro here syhte *s[ynnen]* he wolde
C. 9.330	Soules þat haue *syneged* seuene sythes dedly.
C.10.23	Seuene sithe, sayth þe boek, *synegeth* day by day
C.10.25	And hoso *synegeth*,' y sayde, 'certes he doth nat wel;
C.10.26	For hoso *synegeth* sicurly doth euele
C.10.31	'How seuene sithes þe sad man *synegeth* on þe day.
C.10.49	*Synegeth* seue sithe þe saddest man on erthe
C.10.214	Aftur þat Adam and Eue hadden *ysyneged*;
C.12.240	To *synege* and to souche sotiltees of Gyle,
C.14.112	Out of synne and be saef, thogh he *synege* ofte,
C.19.165	That hoso *synegeth* in þe seynt spirit assoiled worth he neuere,
C.19.170	So hoso *synegeth* a3eyn þe seynt spirit hit semeth þat he greueth
C.19.268	*Synegen* a3en þe seynte spirit, assente to destruye
C.19.279	'Y pose y hadde *syneged* so and sholde nouthe deye
C.20.229	And sethe he soffrede hym *synne* sorwe to fele
C.22.15	He *synegeth* nat sothlich þat so wynneth his fode.

synnes > *synne,synnen*

synneward adv *OED sinward adv., MED sinne n.* B 1; C 1

B.13.345	Semynge to *synneward*, and som he gan taste
C. 6.179	Semyng to *synneward* and summe y gan taste

synoye > *synay*

sire n *sire n.* A 22 sire (21) sires (1); B 44 sir (1) sire (40) sires (3); C 59 sir (2) sire (33) syre (22) syres (2)

A. 2.19	And so shulde [heo] not be for wrong was hire *sire*;
A. 2.35	*Sire* symonye is assent to asele þe chartres
A. 2.53	And as syre symonye wile segge to sewen his wille.
A. 2.78	Be si3te of *sire* symonye & signes of notaries.
A. 2.136	*Sire* symonye hymself shal sitte on here bakkis;
A. 3.137	*Sire* symonye & hireself seliþ þe bullis;
A. 4.128	Let þi confessour, *sire* king, construe it þe on englissh,
A. 5.108	So hungirly & holewe *sire* heruy hym lokide.
A. 5.184	And grete *sire* glotoun wiþ a galoun ale.
A. 7.249	Let nou3t *sire* surfet sitten at þi bord;
A. 8.138	Daniel seide, '*sire* king, þi sweuene is to mene
A.10.1	'*Sire* dowel dwelliþ,' quaþ wyt, 'nou3t a day hennes,
A.10.11	And haþ don hire to *sire* dowel, duk of þise marchis
A.10.12	Dobet is hire damysele, *sire* dowelis [dou3ter],
A.10.17	Is a wys kni3t withalle, *sire* [inwit] he hatte,
A.10.19	*Sire* se wel, & sey wel, & here wel þe hende,

A.10.20   *Sire* werche wel wiþ þin hond, [a] wiȝt man of strengþe,
A.10.21   And *sire* godefrey go wel, grete lordis alle.
A.10.62   Thanne haþ þe pouk power, *sire* princeps huius mundi,
A.11.22   And ben seruid as *sires* þat serue þe deuil.
A.11.62   To tellen of þe trinite to be holden a *sire*,
A.11.195   *Sire* dobest haþ ben [in office], so is he best worþi
B.Pr.125   'Crist kepe þee, *sire* kyng, and þi kyngryche,
B.Pr.193   For I herde my *sire* seyn, seuen yeer ypassed,
B. 2.114   By siȝte of *sire* Symonie and Cyuyles leeue.'
B. 2.172   *Sire* Symonye hymself shal sitte vpon hir bakkes.
B. 3.148   *Sire* Symonie and hirselue seleþ [þe] bulles.
B. 4.67   Tho [wan] Wisdom and *sire* waryn þe witty
B. 4.145   Late [þi] Confessour, *sire* kyng, construe [it þee on englissh],
B. 5.37   My *sire* seide to me, and so dide my dame,
B. 5.159   And dame Clarice a knyȝtes douȝter ac a cokewold was hir *sire*,
B. 5.189   So hungrily and holwe *sire* heruy hym loked.
B. 5.312   [*Sire* Piers of Pridie and Pernele of Flaundres,
B. 5.335   And greten *sire* Gloton wiþ a Galon ale.
B. 5.608   To suffren hym and segge noȝt ayein þi *sires* wille.
B. 6.265   Lat noȝt *sire* Surfet sitten at þi borde,
B. 7.160   Daniel seide, '*sire* kyng, þi [sweuene is to mene]
B. 9.1   '*SIre* Dowel dwelleþ', quod Wit, 'noȝt a day hennes
B. 9.11   And [haþ] doo[n] hire wiþ *sire* dowel, duc of þise Marches.
B. 9.12   Dobet is hire damyselle, *sire* doweles douȝter,
B. 9.18   Is a wis knyȝt wiþalle, *sire* Inwit he hatte,
B. 9.20   *Sire* Se-wel, and Sey-wel, and here-wel þe hende,
B. 9.21   *Sire* werch-wel-wiþ-þyn-hand, a wiȝt man of strengþe,
B. 9.22   And *sire* Godefray Go-wel, grete lordes [alle].
B. 9.151   That somdel þe sone shal haue þe *sires* tacches.
B. 9.155   And haue a Sauour after þe *sire*; selde sestow ooþer:
B.11.411   '[What is dowel?' quod þat wiȝt]; 'ywis, *sire*', I seide,
B.13.103   'What is dowel, *sire* doctour?' quod I; 'is [dobest] any penaunce?'
B.13.106   'By þis day, *sire* doctour', quod I, 'þanne [in dowel be ye noȝt]!
B.13.114   And seide hymself, '*sire* doctour, and it be youre wille,
B.15.47   'Ye, *sire*!' I seide, 'by so no man were greued
B.15.123   *Sir* Iohan and *sire* Geffrey haþ [of siluer a girdel],
B.15.123   Sir Iohan and *sire* Geffrey haþ [of siluer a girdel],
B.16.186   The secounde of þa[t] *sire* is Sothfastnesse filius,
B.17.127   'A, swete *sire*', I seide þo, 'wher I shal bileue,
B.17.158   How he þat is holy goost *sire* and sone preueþ.
B.17.183   Than is þe *sire* [or] þe sone and in þe same myghte,
B.17.212   So dooþ þe *Sire* and þe sone and also spiritus sanctus
B.17.224   Na moore dooþ *sire* ne sone ne seint spirit togidres
B.18.280   For hymself seide, þat *Sire* is of heuene.
B.19.343   [Th]e sedes [þat *sire*] Piers [sew], þe Cardynale vertues.
B.20.161   Hir *sire* was a Sysour þat neuere swoor truþe,
B.20.186   '*Sire* yuele ytauȝt Elde!' quod I, 'vnhende go wiþ þe!
B.20.244   And seide, '*sires*, sooþly welcome be ye alle
B.20.311   *Sire* leef-to-lyue-in-lecherie lay þere and gronede;
B.20.340   'Certes', seide his felawe, '*sire* Penetrans domos.'
C.Pr.109   And for here *syre* sey hem synne and suffred hem do ille
C.Pr.149   'Crist kepe þe, [*sire*] kynge, and thy kyneriche,
C.Pr.179   Sayde, 'y haue seyen grete *syres* in Cytees and in townes
C.Pr.206   For y herde my *sire* sayn, seuene ȝer ypassed,
C. 2.118   By syhte of *sire* Simonye and syuyles leue.'
C. 2.146   That fals is faythles, the fende is his *syre*
C. 2.249   And sayde, '*syre* kyng, by crist! but clerkes amende,
C. 3.367   Þat is nat resonable ne rect to refuse my *syre* name,
C. 4.34   Ryde forth, *syre* resoun, and rech nat of here tales
C. 4.43   And bytwene hymsulue and his sone sette tho *sire* resoun
C. 4.142   Lat thy Confessour, *syre* kyng, construe this in englische
C. 4.154   And sayden, 'we seyn wel, *syre* resoun, be thi wordes
C. 5.53   And also moreouer me [sem]eth, *syre* resoun,
C. 6.134   And dame clarice a knyhtes douhter, a cokewolde was here *syre*,
C. 6.197   So hungrily and holow *sire* heruy hym lokede.
C. 6.367   *Syre* [Peres] of prydie and purnele of Flaundres,
C. 6.393   And grete *syre* glotoun with a galoun ale.
C. 8.23   'Sikerliche, *sire* knyhte,' sayde [Peris] thenne,
C. 8.169   'Y preye the,' quod [Perus] tho, 'pur charite, *sire* hunger,
C. 8.202   Þat durste withsitte þat [Peres] sayde for fere of *syre* hunger
C. 8.221   For here lyflode, lere me now, *sire* hunger.'
C. 8.265   Ac ȝut y praye ȝow,' quod [Peres], 'pur charite, *syre* hungur,
C. 8.275   Lat nat *sire* sorfeet sitt[en] at thy borde;
C. 8.280   And sethen y say hym sitte as he a *syre* were
C.10.127   And what þey drede and doute, dere *sire*, telleth.'
C.10.128   '*Sire* dowel dwelleth,' quod wit, 'nat a day hennes
C.10.138   And hath do here with *sire* dowel, duk of this marches.
C.10.139   Dobet is here damysele, *sire* dowelus douhtur,
C.10.144   Is a wise knyhte withalle, *sire* inwit he hatte,
C.10.146   *Sire* se-wel and sey-wel [and] here-wel þe [h]ende,
C.10.147   *Sire* worch-wel-with-thyn-hand, a wyht man of strenghe,
C.10.148   And *sire* go[dfray] go-wel, grete lordes alle.
C.10.238   That þe *sire* by hymsulue doth þe sone sholde be þe worse.

C.11.151   That he seyh þe [*syre*] and þe sone and þe seynt spirit togederes
C.11.196   *Sir* wanhope was sib to hym, as som men me tolde,
C.12.24   'Why lourest [thou]?' quod leaute; 'leue', y saide,
C.13.219   'What is dowel?' quod þat wyhte; 'ywis, *sire*', y saide,
C.15.110   'What is dowel, *sire* doctour?' quod y; 'is dobest eny penaunce?'
C.15.114   'Sertes, *sire*,' thenne saide y, 'hit semeth nou[th]e here,
C.15.121   And saide hymsulue, '*sire* doctour, [and] hit be ȝoure wille,
C.15.232   'Pees!' quod pacience, 'y preye ȝow, *sire* actyf,
C.16.173   'Whareof serue ȝe, y saide, '*sir* liberum arbitrium?'
C.16.209   'Ȝe, *sire*!' y sayde, 'by so no man were ygreued,
C.18.81   'Ȝe, *sire*,' y sayde, 'and sethen þer aren but tweyne lyues
C.18.192   'That is soth,' saide he thenne, 'the *syre* hatte pater
C.18.193   And þe seconde is a sone of þe *sire*, filius;
C.18.231   So oute of þe *syre* and of þe sone þe seynt spirit of hem bothe
C.19.96   'A, *sire*,' y saide, 'shal nat we bileue,
C.19.139   Riht so failed þe sone, the *syre* be ne myhte
C.19.149   Then is the *syre* or the sone and of þe same myhte,
C.19.178   So doth þe *sire* and þe sone and seynt spirit togyderes
C.19.190   No more doth *sire* ne sone ne seynt spirit togyderes
C.20.302   For hymsulue said, þat *sire* is of heuene,
C.21.343   Þe sedes that *sire* [Peres] sewe, þe cardinale vertues.
C.22.161   Here *syre* was a sysour þat neuere swoer treuthe,
C.22.186   '*Syre* euele yt[a]uȝte Elde,' quod y, 'vnhende go with the!
C.22.244   And saide, '*syres*, soethly welcome be ȝe alle
C.22.311   *Sire* l[ee]f-to-lyue-in-lecherye lay þer and groned;
C.22.340   'Certes,' saide his felawe, '*sire* penetrans domos.'

syse n *sise n.(1)* C 2
C. 2.181   Softliche in s[am]b[u]re fram *syse* [to] syse,
C. 2.181   Softliche in s[am]b[u]re fram syse [to] *syse*,

syse n prop *n.i.d.* C 1
C. 7.166   Signes of *syse* and shelles of galys

sismatikes > scismatikes

sisour n *sisour n.* A 3 sisour (1) sisours (2); B 8 sisour (3) Sysour (1)
   sisours (4); C 8 sysores (4) sisour (1) sysour (2) sisours (1)
A. 2.44   For *sisours*, for somenours, for selleris, for beggeris,
A. 2.129   And fals sat on a *sisour* þat softeliche trottide,
A. 3.123   *Sisours* & sompnours, suche men hire preisiþ;
B. 2.59   As *Sisours* and Somonours, Sherreues and hire clerkes,
B. 2.63   Ac Symonie and Cyuylle and *Sisours* of courtes
B. 2.165   And Fals sat on a *Sisour* þat softeli trotted,
B. 3.134   *Sisours* and Somonours, swiche men hire preiseþ;
B. 4.167   Ac a *Sisour* and a Somonour sued hire faste,
B.19.369   And [a *sisour* and a somonour] þat were forsworen ofte;
B.20.161   Hir sire was a *Sysour* þat neuere swoor truþe,
B.20.291   As *sisours* and executours; þei [shul] ȝyue þe freres
C. 2.61   As *sysores* [and] sompnores, shyryues and here clerkes,
C. 2.65   Ac simonye and syuile and *sysores* of contrees
C. 2.182   And fals and fauel fecche forth *sysores*
C. 3.172   *Sysores* and somnours, suche men he[re] preiseth;
C. 4.162   A *sysour* and a somnour tho softliche forth ȝede
C.21.369   And a *sisour* and [a] sompnour þat weren forsworen ofte;
C.22.161   Here syre was a *sysour* þat neuere swoer treuthe,
C.22.291   As *sisours* and secutours; they shal ȝeue þe freres

sister -ir > suster; sit(e > sitten; siþ > siþen; sithe > siþe,siþen,siþes

siþe n *sithe n.* B 1; C 2 sythe
B. 3.308   Into sikel or to *siþe*, to Shaar or to kultour:
C. 3.461   Into sykel or [t]o *sythe*, to shar oþer to coltur:
C. 5.23   Y am to wayke to wurcche with sykel or with *sythe*

siþen adv *sitthen adv.* A 16 siþen (9) siþþe (6) siþþen (1); B 51 siþen (26)
   syþen (1) siþenes (4) siþþe (18) siþþen (2); C 42 seth (4) sethe (21)
   sethen (10) senes (1) senne (1) sennes (5)
A. 1.66   And *siþen* on an Eldir hongide him aftir.
A. 1.134   Loke þou suffre hym to seyn & *siþþe* lere it aftir.
A. 3.46   Þanne he assoilide hire sone, & *siþen* he seide,
A. 4.15   Seide hym as þe king sente & *siþþe* tok his leue.
A. 5.37   And *siþþe* he redde religioun here rewel[e] to holde
A. 5.151   And *siþþen* I wile be shriuen & synne no more.'
A. 6.28   And dede me sure hym [*siþþe*] to serue hym for euere;
A. 7.58   For I wile sowe it myself, & *siþþe* wile I wende.
A. 7.227   And *siþen* he seide, his seruaunt[s] it h[er]de;
A. 8.27   And *siþen* selle it aȝen & saue þe wynnyng,
A.10.153   [Þat] of seth & his sistir *siþþe* forþ come
A.10.159   And *siþen* se[þ] & his suster [sed] wern spousid to kaymes;
A.10.167   Hymself & his sones þre, & *siþen* here wyues
A.11.181   And *siþen* aftirward to be sumwhat of dobest'.
A.11.221   For I haue seiȝe it myself, & *siþþen* red it aftir,
A.11.251   And *siþen* he[þen] to helpe in hope hem to amende
B. 1.146   Loke þow suffre hym to seye and *siþen* lere it after.
B. 3.47   Thanne he assoiled hire soone and *siþen* he seide,

B. 4.15   [Seide hym] as þe kyng [sente] and siþen took his leue.
B. 5.41   And siþen he [preide] prelates and preestes togideres,
B. 5.45   And siþen he radde Religion hir rule to holde
B. 5.48   And siþen he counseiled þe kyng his commune to louye,
B. 5.50   And siþen he preide þe pope haue pite on holy chirche,
B. 5.141   And siþen þei blosmede abrood in boure to here shriftes.
B. 5.272   And siþen þat Reson rolle it in þe Registre of heuene
B. 5.301   And siþen I wole be shryuen and synne na moore.'
B. 5.434   Sixty siþes I, Sleuþe, haue foryete it siþþe
B. 5.440   And euere siþþe be beggere [by cause of my] sleuþe:
B. 5.482   And siþen suffredest [hym] to synne, as semeþ to vs alle,
B. 5.487   And siþþe wiþ þi selue sone in oure s[u]te deidest
B. 5.540   And diden me suren hym [siþþen] to seruen hym for euere,
B. 6.63   For I wol sowe it myself, and siþenes wol I wende
B. 6.243   And [siþen] he seide–[hise seruaunt3] it herde–
B. 7.25   And siþenes selle it ayein and saue þe wynnyng.
B. 9.103   And siþþe to spille speche þat [spire] is of grace
B. 9.118   And siþenes by assent of hemself as þei two my3te acorde;
B. 9.136   Thyself and þi sones þre and siþen youre wyues,
B.10.369   And siþen heþen to helpe in hope of amendement.
B.11.10   [Siþen] she seide to me, 'here my3tow se wondres
B.11.321   And slepynge I sei3 al þis, and siþen cam kynde
B.11.363   And siþen I loked on þe see and so forþ on þe sterres;
B.12.272   Ac god is so good, I hope þat siþþe he gaf hem wittes
B.13.19   And siþen how ymaginatif seide 'vix saluabitur [iustus]',
B.13.50   And siþþe he [drou3] vs drynke, Di[u] perseuerans,
B.13.199   And siþen softeliche he seide in clergies ere,
B.14.9   And [siþþe] shryuen of þe preest, þat [for my synnes gaf me]
B.14.21   And siþen sende þee to Satisfaccion for to [sonnen] it after:
B.14.142   Ri3t as a seruaunt takeþ his salarie bifore, & siþþe wolde clayme
           moore
B.15.232   In þat secte siþþe to selde haþ he ben [knowe].
B.15.412   And siþþe oure Saueour suffred þe Sar3ens so bigiled
B.15.519   Many a seint syþen haþ suffred to deye
B.16.235   I circumscised my sone siþen for his sake,
B.16.243   And siþþe he sente me to seye I sholde do sacrifise
B.17.38   And siþþe ri3t as myself so louye alle peple.
B.17.90   And I þanked hym þo and siþþe [þus] I hym tolde
B.18.220   And siþþe he suffred hym synne sorwe to feele,
B.18.283   And [siþen] he þat Soothnesse is seide þise wordes,
B.19.78   Boþe of [s]ond, sonne and see, and siþenes þei wente
B.19.87   The seconde kyng siþþe sooþliche offrede
B.19.143   And siþen buriede his body, and beden þat men sholde
B.19.275   And sew [it] in mannes soule and siþen tolde hir names.
B.19.309   Thise foure sedes Piers sew, and siþþe he dide hem harewe
B.19.395   And so to ben assoilled and siþþen ben houseled.'
B.20.137   And tornede Cyuyle into Symonye, and siþþe he took þe Official.
B.20.236   And siþen þei chosen chele and cheitiftee
B.20.240   And siþen freres forsoke þe felicite of erþe
B.20.386   And siþþe he gradde after Grace til I gan awake.
C. 3.50   And he assoilede here sone and sethen a sayde,
C. 3.409   And se[t]he, for sauel saued a kyng fo[r] mede
C. 4.15   And sayde hym as þe kyng sayde and sennes took his leue.
C. 5.140   And sethe a preide prelates and prestes togyderes,
C. 5.143   And sethe he radde religioun here reule to holde
C. 5.180   And sethe a consailede þe kyng his comine to louie:
C. 5.191   And sethe a preyede þe pope haue pite on holy chirche
C. 6.356   And sennes sitte and be shryue and synege no more.'
C. 7.47   Sixty sythes y, sleuthe, haue for3eten hit sethe
C. 7.54   And sethe a beggare haue y be for my foule sleuthe:
C. 7.124   And sethe soffredes[t] hym to synege, a sykenesse to vs alle,
C. 7.129   And sethe in oure secte, as hit semed, deyedest,
C. 7.144   And sethen oure sauyour and seydest with thy tonge
C. 7.185   And maden me sykere[n hym] sethen to seruen hym for euere,
C. 8.62   'For y wol sowen hit mysulf and sethe wol y wende
C. 8.280   And sethen y say hym sitte as he a syre were
C. 9.29   And sethe sullen hit a3eyn and saue þe wynnyng[e],
C. 9.308   And sethen aftur his sones, and sayde hem what they thouhte;
C.10.224   "Thysulue and thy sones thre and sethen 3oure wyues,
C.10.248   S[e]th, adames sone, seth[en] was engendred,
C.10.252   And seth for he soffred hit god sayde, "me forthynketh
C.11.169   And senes he saide to me, 'here myhte thow se wondres
C.12.99   And seynt Ion sethen saide hit of his techyng:
C.13.89   And sheweth be seel and seth by lettre with what lord he dwelleth,
C.13.173   And sethe y lokede on þe see and so forth on [þe] sterres;
C.15.56   And sethe he drow vs drynke, di[u] p[er]seuerans,
C.15.176   And sethe a saide to clergie so þat y hit herde:
C.16.357   In [þat] sekte sethe to selde hath he be [knowen].
C.17.270   Mony [a] seynte sethe soffrede deth also,
C.18.139   That suche a surgien sethen ysaye was þer neuere
C.18.260   And sethe a sente me to seyn and saide that y sholde
C.19.40   And seth to louye and to lene for þat lordes sake
C.20.229   And sethe he soffrede hym synne sorwe to fele

C.21.78   Bothe of sand, sonne and see and sennes þei wente
C.21.87   The seconde kyng seth soethliche offrede]
C.21.143   And sethen bur[ie]den his body and beden þat men sholde
C.21.275   And sewe hit in mannes soule and sethe toelde here names.
C.21.309   Thise foure sedes [Peres] sewe and sennes he dede hem harewe
C.21.395   And so to ben assoiled and sennes be hoseled.'
C.22.137   And turnede syuyle into symonye and sethe he toek þe official.
C.22.240   And senne freres forsoke the felic[it]e of erthe
C.22.386   And sethe he gradde aftur grace tyl y gan awake.

siþen prep *sitthen prep.* A 3 siþen (2) siþþe (1); B 4 syn (1) siþ (2) siþen
    (1); C 3 sethe (1) senes (1) sennes (1)
A.Pr.81   Þat here parissh w[ere] pore siþþe þe pestilence tyme,
A.10.191   Manye peire siþen þ[e] pestilence han p[l]i3t hem togidere.
A.11.59   To pleise wiþ proude men, siþen þe pestilence tyme.
B.Pr.84   That hire parissh[e] wer[e] pouere siþ þe pestilence tyme,
B. 9.170   Many peire siþen þe pestilence han pli3t hem togideres.
B.10.73   To plese wiþ proude men syn þe pestilence tyme;
B.20.187   Siþ whanne was þe wey ouer mennes heddes?
C.10.271   Many a payre sethe th[e] pestelens[e] han plyhte treuthe to louye,
C.11.53   To plese with proude men senes th[e] pestelenc[e tyme]
C.22.187   Sennes whanne was þe way ouer menne heuedes?

siþen conj *sitthen conj.* A 8 sitthe (1) siþen (4) siþþe (3); B 24 syn (2) siþ
    (11) siþen (9) syþenes (1) siþþe (1); C 35 seth (6) sethe (18) sethen
    (4) sennes (2) sith (1) sithe (1) sythe (1) suthe (1)
A.Pr.61   Siþen charite haþ ben chapman & chief to shryue lordis
A. 5.228   Al þat I wykkidly wan siþen I wyt hadde,
A. 8.62   Siþen 3e sen it is þus sewiþ to þe beste.
A.10.200   As betwyn sengle & sengle, siþþe lawe haþ ygrauntid
A.11.89   Siþen he wilneþ to wyte which þei ben alle.
A.11.173   Was neuere [gome] vpon þis ground, siþþe god makid heuene,
A.11.273   For alle cunnyng clerkis siþþe crist 3ede on erþe
A.12.18   Sitthe theologie þe trewe to tellen hit defendeþ;
B.Pr.64   Siþ charite haþ ben chapman and chief to shryue lordes
B.Pr.128   And siþen in þe Eyr an hei3 an Aungel of heuene
B. 1.68   And siþen on an Eller hanged hym [after].
B. 2.26   And neuere sooþ seide siþen he com to erþe,
B. 5.456   Al þat I wikkedly wan siþen I wit hadde,
B. 9.87   Syn Iewes, þat we Iugge Iudas felawes,
B.10.136   Siþþe he wilneþ to wite whiche þei ben [alle].
B.10.230   Was neuere gome vpon þis ground, siþ god made [heuene],
B.10.265   Syþenes þow seest þiself as in soule clene;
B.10.270   Siþen a beem [is] in þyn owene ablyndeþ þiselue–
B.13.254   For siþ he haþ þe power þat Peter hadde he haþ þe pot wiþ þe
           salue:
B.15.495   That þei ne wente as crist wisseþ, siþen þei wille haue name,
B.15.501   And siþ þat þise Sar3ens, Scribes and [Grekes]
B.15.607   And siþen þat þe Sar3ens and also þe Iewes
B.17.34   Siþ þe firste suffiseþ to sauacion and to blisse?
B.17.295   And siþ holy chirche and charite chargeþ þis so soore
B.18.133   Siþ þis barn was ybore ben xxxti wynter passed,
B.18.284   And siþen I [was] seised seuene [þousand] wynter
B.19.15   'Why calle [ye] hym crist, siþen Iewes calle[d] hym Iesus?
B.19.60   And siþ [alle hise lele liges largely he yeueþ]
B.19.471   And siþ I am youre aller heed I am youre aller heele
B.20.49   Siþ he þat wro3te al þe world was wilfulliche nedy,
B.20.63   [Th]an to lyue lenger siþ [Leute] was so rebuked
B.20.322   I may wel suffre', seide Conscience, 'syn ye desiren,
C.Pr.62   Ac sith charite hath be Chapman and [c]hief to shryue lordes
C.Pr.82   That here parsch[e] were pore sithe þ[e] pestelence tyme,
C. 2.137   And se[t]he man may [o]n heye mede of god diserue
C. 3.368   Sethe y, his sone and his seruant, sewe for his ryhte.
C. 5.40   And foen[d y] nere, in fayth, seth my frendes deyede
C. 5.70   Ac sythe bondemen barnes haen be mad bisshopes
C. 6.310   Al-þat-y-wikkedly-wan-sithen-y-witte-hadde:
C. 9.115   And to oure syhte as hit semeth; seth god hath þe myhte
C.10.196   And seth [he les] his lyf for lawe sholde loue wexe.
C.14.194   Ac god is so gode, y hope þat seth he gaf hem wittes
C.15.224   For sethe he hath þe power þat peter hadde he hath þe pott with þe
           salue:
C.17.183   And seth oure saueour soffrede such a fals cristene
C.17.191   Ite in vniuersum mundum, sethe 3e wilne þe name
C.17.252   For sethe þat this sarrasines, Scrib3 and this iewes
C.17.315   And sethe þat th[e] sarresynes and also þe iewes
C.18.18   And sethen þat 3e fouchen saef to sey me as hit hoteth.'
C.18.81   '3e, sire,' y sayde, 'and sethen þer aren but tweyne lyues
C.18.175   Sethe y be tresoun am take and to 3oure will, iewes,
C.18.191   'Su[t]he they ben suyrelepus,' quod y, 'they haen sondry names?'
C.19.35   Sethe the furste sufficede to bileue and be saued?
C.19.244   Sethe he withoute wyles wan and wel myhte atymye
C.19.249   To go semeliche ne sitte, seth holy writ techeth
C.19.276   And sethe Charite þat holy churche is chargeth this so sore
C.20.136   Sethe this barn was ybore ben thritty wynter ypassed,

C.20.307 And *sethe* he is a lele lord y leue þat he wol nat
C.20.308 Reuen vs of oure riht *sethe* resoun hem dampnede.
C.20.309 And *sethen* we haen ben sesed seuene thousand wynter
C.20.350 *Sethe* þat satan myssaide thus foule
C.21.15 'Whi calle ȝe hym Crist *sennes* iewes callede hym iesus?
C.21.60 And *sethe* [all his lele leges largeliche he ȝeueth]
C.21.471 And *sethe* y am ȝoure alere heued y am ȝoure alere hele
C.22.49 *Sethe* [he] þat wrouhte al þe worlde was willefolliche nedy
C.22.63 Then to lyue lengere *sethe* leautee was so rebuked
C.22.236 And *sethen* thei chosen chele and Cheytyftee
C.22.322 Y may wel soffre,' sayde Consience, '*sennes* ȝe desiren,

siþes n *sith* n. A 6 siþes (5) syþes (1); B 8 sythes (1) siþes (7); C 10
sithe (4) sythe (2) sithes (1) sythes (3)

A.Pr.109 Al þis I sauȝ slepyng & seue *siþes* more.
A. 8.162 Soulis þat han ysynned seue *siþes* dedly.
A. 9.17 Seue *siþes*, seiþ þe bok, [synneþ] þe riȝtful;
A. 9.23 'How seue *siþes* þe sadde man synneþ on þe day;
A. 9.39 Synnes þe sad man seuene [*siþes*] in þe day.
A.12.48 And þanked hure a þousand *sypes* with þrobbant herte.
B.Pr.231 [Al þis I seiȝ slepyng and seuene *sythes* more].
B. 5.424 Six *siþes* or seuene I forsake it wiþ oþes.
B. 5.434 Sixty *siþes* I, Sleuþe, haue foryete it siþþe
B. 7.184 Soules þat haue synned seuen *siþes* dedly.
B. 8.21 Seuene *siþes*, seiþ þe book, synneþ þe rightfulle;
B. 8.27 'How seuen *siþes* þe sadde man [synneþ on þe day].
B. 8.43 Synneþ þe sadde man [seuen *siþes* a day].
B.14.188 Shulde amenden vs as manye *siþes* as man wolde desire.
C.Pr.235 [Al þis y say slepynge and seuene *sythes* more].
C. 6.428 There no nede ne was, many *sythe* falsly;
C. 7.37 Sixe *sithe* oþer seuene y forsake hit with othes
C. 7.47 Sixty *sythes* y, sleuthe, haue forȝeten hit sethe
C. 9.330 Soules þat haue syneged seuene *sythes* dedly.
C.10.23 Seuene *sithe*, sayth þe boek, synegeth day by day
C.10.31 'How seuene *sithes* þe sad man synegeth on þe day.
C.10.49 Synegeth seue *sithe* þe saddest man on erthe
C.16.234 To teche þe ten comaundementȝ ten *sythe* were bettere
C.18.17 'Y thonke ȝow a thousand *s[i]the* that ȝe me hider kende

siþþe(n > siþen

sitten v *sitten* v. A 18 sat (4) seten (3) sit (2) sitte (3) sitten (5) sitteþ (1);
B 41 sat (7) seet (1) sete (1) seten (6) sit (2) sitte (10) sitten (7) sitteþ
(3) sittyng (1) sittynge (3); C 53 saet (4) sat (3) seet (1) seete (1) sete
(2) seten (2) sit (2) syt (1) site (1) sitte (14) sytte (3) sitten (9) sytten
(1) sitteth (5) sittynge (3) sitton (1)

A. 2.129 And fals *sat* on a sisour þat softeliche trottide,
A. 2.136 Sire symonye hymself shal *sitte* on here bakkis;
A. 5.7 I *sat* softely [adoun] & seide my beleue,
A. 5.158 Cisse þe so[wes]tere *sat* on þe bench,
A. 5.187 And *seten* so til euesong & songe [vmbe]while
A. 5.220 Þanne *sat* sleuþe vp & seynide hym faste,
A. 6.8 An hundrit of ampollis on his hat *seten*,
A. 6.17 Ȝe mowe se be my signes þat *sitten* on myn hat
A. 6.93 Þou shalt se treuþe himself wel *sitte* in þin herte
A. 6.96 For he haþ enuye to hym þat in þin herte *sitteþ*
A. 7.107 Þanne *seten* somme & sungen at þe ale
A. 7.247 And kep sum [til] soper tyme, & *sit* nouȝt to longe;
A. 7.249 Let nouȝt sire surfet *sitten* at þi bord;
A. 8.19 At þe day of dom at here deis to *sitten*.
A. 8.128 And sauȝ þe sonne euene souþ *sitte* þat tyme,
A.10.59 And ek in sottis þou miȝt se, þat *sitten* at þe nale.
A.10.99 But suffre & *sit* stille & sek þou no ferþere,
A.11.60 Þat defouliþ oure f[eiþ] at fest[is] þere þei *sitten*.
B.Pr.96 And in stede of Stywardes *sitten* and demen.
B. 2.97 And þanne to *sitten* and soupen til sleep hem assaille,
B. 2.165 And Fals *sat* on a Sisour þat softeli trotted,
B. 2.172 Sire Symonye hymself shal *sitte* vpon hir bakkes.
B. 3.345 Tho ye [souȝte] Sapience *sittynge* in youre studie.
B. 5.7 [I] *sat* softely adoun and seide my bileue,
B. 5.307 Cesse þe [sowestere] *sat* on þe benche,
B. 5.338 And *seten* so til euensong and songen vmwhile
B. 5.375 And *sat* som tyme so longe þere þat I sleep and eet at ones.
B. 5.386 'I moste *sitte* [to be shryuen] or ellis sholde I nappe;
B. 5.448 Thanne *sat* Sleuþe vp and seyned hym [faste]
B. 5.520 An hundred of Ampulles on his hat *seten*,
B. 5.529 Ye may se by my signes þat *sitten* on myn hatte
B. 5.606 Thow shalt se in þiselue truþe [*sitte*] in þyn herte
B. 5.610 [For] he haþ enuye to hym þat in þyn herte *sitteþ*
B. 6.115 [Th]anne *seten* somme and songen atte Nale
B. 6.192 That *seten* to begge siluer soone were þei heeled,
B. 6.263 And keep som til soper tyme and *sitte* noȝt to longe;
B. 6.265 Lat noȝt sire Surfet *sitten* at þi borde;
B. 7.17 At þe day of dome at [hire] deys [to] *sitte*.

B. 7.146 And seiȝ þe sonne [euene] South *sitte* þat tyme,
B.10.98 Ther þe lord ne þe lady likeþ noȝt to *sitte*.
B.12.2 Thouȝ I *sitte* by myself in siknesse in[e] in helþe.
B.12.200 As þo þat *seten* at þe syde table or wiþ þe souereynes of þe halle,
B.12.203 He *sit* neiþer wiþ Seint Iohan, Symond ne Iude,
B.13.32 'Welcome, wye, go and wassh; þow shalt *sitte* soone.'
B.13.33 This maister was maad *sitte* as for þe mooste worþi;
B.13.36 And *seten* bi oureselue [a] side borde.
B.13.99 And I *sat* stille as Pacience seide, and þus soone þis doctour,
B.13.443 The pouere for a fool sage *sittyng* at þ[i] table,
B.14.219 Ne none of þe seuene synnes *sitten* ne mowe þer longe,
B.14.288 Selde *sit* pouerte þe soþe to declare,
B.15.217 And þe murieste of mouþ at mete where he *sitteþ*.
B.16.141 *Sittynge* at þe soper he seide þise wordes:
B.16.225 Thus in a somer I hym seiȝ as I *sat* in my porche;
B.17.51 Thanne seiȝe we a Samaritan *sittynge* on a Mule,
B.17.237 And solacen hem þat mowe [noȝt] se, þat *sitten* in derknesse,
B.17.244 For to murþen men [wiþ] þat in [m]erke *sitten*,
B.18.288 And in semblaunce of a serpent *sete* vpon þe Appultree
B.19.304 For counteþ he no kynges wraþe whan he in Court *sitteþ*;
B.20.199 And as I *seet* in þis sorwe I sauȝ how kynde passede
C.Pr.94 And ben in stede of stewardus and *sitten* and demen.
C.Pr.114 Fro his chayere þer he *sat* and brake his nekke atwene.
C. 1.114 Thenne *sitten* in þe sonne syde þe day roweth?'
C. 1.122 Euene þe contrarie *sitteth* Crist, Clerkes wyteth þe sothe:
C. 1.134 There treuthe is, þe tour that trinite ynne *sitteth*.
C. 3.11 Into Boure with blisse and by here gan *sitte*.
C. 5.63 Somme to synge masses or *sitten* and wryten,
C. 6.54 And sygge to suche þat *sytte* me byside.
C. 6.99 Here werkes and here wordes where þat y *seete*.
C. 6.108 Thow y *sitte* this seuene ȝer, y sholde nat wel telle
C. 6.137 Thus *sytte* they, sustres, sum tyme and disputen
C. 6.143 Amonges wyues and wydewes [y am woned] to *sitte*
C. 6.291 Y rede no faythful frere at thy feste to *sytte*
C. 6.356 And sennes *sitte* and be shryue and synege no more.'
C. 6.362 Sesse þe [sywestere] *saet* on þe benche,
C. 6.396 And *seten* so til euenson[g] and songen vmbywhile
C. 7.2 'Y moste *sitte* to be shryue or elles sholde y nappe;
C. 7.62 Thenne *sat* sleuthe vp and seynede hym ofte
C. 7.103 The pore for a f[o]l sage *sittynge* at thy table,
C. 7.165 An hundret of Aunpolles on his hat *se[t]e*,
C. 7.174 Ȝe may se be [my] signes þat *sitten* on my cappe
C. 7.255 Thow shalt se treuthe *sitte* in thy sulue herte
C. 8.122 Thenne *seet* somme and songen at the ale
C. 8.273 And kepe som til soper tyme and *site* nat to longe;
C. 8.275 Lat nat sire sorfeet *sitt[en]* at thy borde,
C. 8.280 And sethen y say hym *sitte* as he a syre were
C. 9.12 With patriarkes and prophetes in paradis to *sitton*.
C. 9.108 And madden as þe mone *sit*, more other lasse;
C. 9.142 In hope to *sitte* at euen by þe hote coles,
C. 9.251 Wascheth and wypeth and with þe furste *sitteth*.
C. 9.253 He *sat* at þe syde benche and at þe seconde table;
C. 9.295 And seyh the sonne in the sou[t]he *sitte* þat tyme,
C.10.40 That ay is saef and sound þat *sitte* withynne þe borde.
C.11.201 Sholde *sitte* in goddis sihte ne se god in his blisse:
C.14.2 Thogh y *sete* by mysulue, suche is my grace.
C.14.139 As þo þat *sitten* at þe syde table or with þe souereyns [of þe] halle
C.14.142 A *sit* noþer with seynte Iohan, simond ne Iude,
C.15.37 [They] woschen and wipeden and wenten to *sytten*.
C.15.38 The maistre was maed *sitte* As for þe moste worthy;
C.15.41 And *seten* by ouresulue at a syde table.
C.15.106 Y *sae[t]* stille as pacience wolde and thus sone this doctour,
C.16.60 Ne none of þe seuene synnes *sitte* ne may þer longe
C.16.123 Selde *syt* pouerte þe soth to declare,
C.16.343 He is þe murieste of mouthe at mete þer he *sitteth*
C.18.64 Tho that *sitten* in þe sonne syde sannore aren rype,
C.18.66 Then tho that selde haen þe sonne and *sitten* in þe North half;
C.18.240 'In a somur y hym seyh,' quod he, 'as y *saet* in my porche,
C.19.49 Thenne sey we a samaritaen cam *sittynge* on a muyle,
C.19.203 And solacen [hem] þat mowen nat se, *sittynge* in derkeness[e],
C.19.210 For to murthe men with þat in merke *sitten*,
C.19.249 To go semeliche ne *sitte*, seth holy writ techeth
C.21.304 For counteth he no kynges wreth when he in Court *sitteth*;
C.22.199 And as y *saet* in this sorwe y say how kynde passede

sitthe > siþen; syuyle(s > cyuylle; sywestere > sowestere

sixe num *six* num. A 2; B 7; C 5 six (1) sixe (3) syxe (1)

A.10.22 Þise *sixe* ben yset to saue þe castel;
A.11.106 He haþ weddit a wif wiþinne þise woukes *sixe*,
B. 3.146 As youre secret seel in *sixe* score dayes.
B. 3.326 By *sixe* sonnes and a ship and half a shef of Arwes;
B. 5.424 *Sixe* siþes or seuene I forsake it wiþ oþes.
B. 9.23 Thise [*sixe*] ben set to [saue] þis lady anima

B.10.154 He haþ wedded a wif wiþInne þise [woukes *sixe*],
B.15.320 And auisen hem bifore a fyue dayes or *sixe*
B.17.75 Wel *sixe* Mile or seuene biside þe newe Market;
C. 3.184 As ȝoure secrete seel in *sixe* score dayes.
C. 3.479 Be *sixe* [s]onnes [and] a ship and half a shef of Arwes;
C. 7.37 *Sixe* sithe oþer seuene y forsake hit with othes
C.19.26 And *six* thousand mo,' quod fayth; 'y [can] nat seyn here names.'
C.19.74 Is *syxe* myle or seuene bisyde þe newe marcat,

sixte *num* *sixte num.* B 1; C 1
B.14.304 The *sixte* is a path of pees; ye! þoruȝ þe paas of Aultoun
C.16.139 The *sixte* is a path of pees; ȝe! thorwe þe pase of Aultoun

sixty *num* *sixti num.* B 3 sixti (1) sixty (2); C 4 sixty (2) syxty (2)
B. 5.434 *Sixty* siþes I, Sleuþe, haue foryete it siþþe
B.17.25 Ye! and *sixti* þousand biside forþ þat ben noȝt seyen here.'
B.20.224 And so seiden *sixty* of þe same contree,
C. 3.234 Ac y haue saued myselue *sixty* thousend lyues,
C. 7.47 *Sixty* sythes y, sleuthe, haue forȝeten hit sethe
C.15.268 Seuene slepen, as saith þe boek, more then *syxty* wynter
C.22.224 And so sayde *syxty* of þe same contreye

skalones n *scaloun n.* C 1
C. 8.308 Ac y haue poret-pl[o]ntes, parsilie and *skalones*,

skaþe > scaþe; skele > skile; skenis > kyn

skile n *skil n.* A 1 skele; B 7 skile (5) skiles (2); C 11 skil (3) skile (1) skyle (1) skiles (2) skill (1) skile (1) skilles (2)
A.12.34 And when scripture þe skolde hadde þis [*skele*] ysheued
B.10.306 It is in cloistre or in scole, by manye *skiles* I fynde.
B.11.1 Thanne Scripture scorned me and a *skile* tolde,
B.12.216 Alle þe clerkes vnder crist ne kouþe þe *skile* assoille:
B.14.281 Thanne is it good by good *skile*, al þat agasteþ pride.
B.17.198 By þis *skile*', [he seide], 'I se an euidence
B.17.336 And þouȝ it falle it fynt *skiles* þat "frelete it made",
B.19.284 Ne [sholde] no scornere out of *skile* hym brynge;
C. 5.153 Hit is in C[l]oystre or in scole, by many *skiles* y fynde.
C. 6.22 And scornede hem and oþere yf y a *skil* founde.
C. 6.25 Scornare and vnskilful to hem þat *skil* shewede,
C.11.160 Thenne scripture scorned me and mony *skiles* shewed
C.13.130 And scripture scornede þat many *skilles* shewede,
C.14.155 Alle þe Clerkes vnder Crist ne couthe [þe *skyle*] assoille:
C.15.135 And preueth by puyre *skile* inparfyt alle thynges–
C.16.121 Thenne is [hit] goed by goed *skill*, thouh hit greue a litel,
C.18.83 Why groweth this fruyt in thre degres?' 'A goed *skil*,' he saide.
C.19.316 And thogh he falle he fynte *skiles* þat "freletee hit made"
C.21.284 Ne sholde no scornare out of *skille* hym brynge

skilfole adj *skilful adj.* C 1
C.11.94 And ouer skripture þe *skilfole* and screueynes were trewe

skill(- > skile; skynes > kyn

skynnes n *skin n.(1)* B 1
B. 5.256 That wolde kille hem if he cacche hem myȝte for coueitise of hir *skynnes*

skipte v *skippen v.* B 1; C 1 skypte
B.11.107 'He seiþ sooþ', quod Scripture þo, and *skipte* an heiȝ and preched.
C.12.41 'A saith soth,' quod scripture tho, and *skypte* an heyh and prechede.

sklaundre > sclaundre

skolde n *scolde n. &> scolde* A 1
A.12.34 And when scripture þe *skolde* hadde þis [skele] ysheued

skorne > scorne

skornfully adv *scornfulli adv.* A 1
A.12.12 *Skornfully* þ[o] scripture she[t] vp h[ere] browes,

skripture > scripture; slayre > scleyre

slake v *slaken v.(1)* B 2; C 1 slokke
B.15.281 And day bi day hadde he hire noȝt his hunger for to *slake*,
B.18.368 May no drynke me moiste, ne my þurst *slake*,
C.20.410 Moiste me to þe fulle ne my furste *slokke*

sleen v *slen v.* A 5 sle (2) slen (2) slowe (1); B 12 sle (2) slee (2) sleen (1) sleeþ (4) slen (1) slow (1) slowe (1); C 11 slawe (3) sle (4) sleeth (1) sleth (1) slowe (1) slowh (1)
A. 3.263 Samuel shal *slen* hym, & saul shal be blamid,
A. 6.64 Þei hote stele nouȝt, ne *sle* nouȝt; strik forþ be boþe.
A.11.40 Þanne telle þei of þe trinite how two *slowe* þe þridde,
A.11.252 To harme hem ne *slen* hem god hiȝte vs neuere,
A.11.254 Ne mecaberis, ne *sle* nouȝt, is þe kynde englissh;
B.Pr.206 But suffren as hymself wolde ne [*slen* þat] hym likeþ,
B. 3.266 Weend to Amalec with þyn oost & what þow fyndest þere *sle* it,
B. 3.287 Samuel shal *sleen* hym and Saul shal be blamed

B. 5.577 Thei hiȝte Stele-noȝt-[ne]-*Sle*-noȝt; strik forþ by boþe;
B.10.54 Than telleþ þei of þe Trinite [how two *slowe* þe þridde],
B.10.371 And seiþ "*slee* noȝt þat semblable is to myn owene liknesse
B.10.373 Is *slee* noȝt but suffre and [so] for þe beste,
B.14.91 For shrift of mouþe *sleeþ* synne be it neuer so dedly–
B.14.95 Ac satisfaccion sekeþ out þe roote, and boþe *sleeþ* and voideþ,
B.17.278 *Sleeþ* a man for hise moebles wiþ mouþ or with handes.
B.19.429 And [soudeþ hem] þat *sleeþ* [swiche as] he sholde saue.
B.20.150 Ne careþ noȝt how Kynde *slow* and shal come at þe laste
C.Pr.113 And his sones *slawe* anon he ful for sorwe
C. 3.420 And alle þat leueth on þat lond oure [lord] wol þat thow *sle* hit;
C. 3.440 Samuel shal *sle* hym and sauel shal be yblamed
C. 6.107 To *sle* hym sleyliche sleythes y bythenke.
C. 7.224 Thei hatte stele-nat and *sle*-nat; stryk forth by bothe
C.11.35 And tellen of þe trinite how t[w]o *slowe* þe thridde
C.11.264 Mouhte sleylokeste be *slawe* and sente hym to w[e]rre,
C.17.275 Amonges v[n]kynde cristene in holy [kirke] was *slawe*
C.19.259 *Sleth* a man for his mebles with mouthe or with handes.
C.21.429 And soudeth hem þat *sleeth* suche as he sholde saue.
C.22.150 Ne careth nat how kynde *slowh* and shal come at þe laste

sleep n *slep n. &> slepe* A 2 slep (1) slepe (1); B 3; C 1 slep
A.Pr.45 *Slep* & sleuþe sewiþ hem euere.
A. 9.58 Blisse of þ[e] briddis brouȝte me a *slepe*;
B.Pr.45 *Sleep* and sleuþe seweþ hem euere.
B. 2.97 And þanne to sitten and soupen til *sleep* hem assaille,
B. 2.99 Til Sleuþe and *sleep* sliken hise sydes;
C.Pr.46 *Slep* and slewthe sueth [hem] euer.

sleighte n *sleight n.* B 8 sleighte (3) sleightes (2) sleiȝte (1) sleiȝtes (2); C 10 sleithe (1) slethe (3) sleythes (5) sleythus (1)
B.13.364 Moore profitable þan myn, manye *sleiȝtes* I made.
B.13.407 The whiche is sleuþe so slow þat may no *sleiȝtes* helpe it,
B.15.129 Ac þing þat wikkedly is wonne, and wiþ false *sleightes*,
B.18.162 And bigile þe gilour, and þat is good] *sleighte*:
B.19.98 In þe manere of a man and þat by muchel *sleighte*,
B.19.99 As it bicomeþ a conquerour to konne manye *sleightes*,
B.19.457 Ech man subtileþ a *sleiȝte* synne to hide
B.20.14 And he [cacche] in þat caas and come þerto by *sleighte*
C. 2.94 With vsurye and Auaryce and other fals *sleythus*
C. 6.73 'Or thorw myhte of mouthe or thorw mannes *sleythes*
C. 6.107 To sle hym sleyliche *sleythes* y bythenke.
C.16.276 Ac thyng þat wykkedliche is wonne and with fals *sleythes*
C.19.236 Ȝut wan he nat with wrong ne with queynte *sleythes*;
C.20.165 And bigile þe gilour, and þat is goed *sleythe*:
C.21.98 In þe manere of a man and þat by moche *sleythe*,
C.21.99 As hit bicometh a conquerour to conne mony *sleythes*
C.21.457 Vch man sotileth a *sleythe* synne to huyde
C.22.14 And he cacche in þat caes and come therto by *sleithe*

sleiȝ adj *sleigh adj.* B 2 sleyest (1) sleiȝ (1); C 1 sley
B.13.297 And most sotil of song oþer *sleyest* of hondes,
B.20.163 This Sleuþe [wex *sleiȝ*] of werre and a slynge made,
C.22.163 This sleuthe wa[x] *sley* of werre and a slynge made

sleiȝte(s sleithe(s -us > sleighte; slen > sleen; slep > sleep

slepe v *slepen v. &> sleep* A 8 slepe (3) slepist (1) slepyng (2) slepte (1) yslepe (1); B 22 sleep (2) slepe (9) slepestow (1) slepeþ (1) slepyng (2) slepynge (4) slept (1) slepte (2); C 24 sleep (1) slepe (9) slepen (1) slepestou (1) slepeth (2) slepyng (1) slepynge (6) slepte (3)
A.Pr.109 Al þis I sauȝ *slepyng* & seue siþes more.
A. 1.5 And seide 'sone, *slepist* þou? sest þou þis peple,
A. 5.4 Þat I ne hadde *yslepe* saddere & yseyn more.
A. 5.202 Þat he *slepte* satirday & sonneday til sonne ȝede to reste.
A. 6.91 For he haþ þe keiȝes & þe cliket þeiȝ þe king *slepe*.
A. 7.285 Wiþ good ale & glotonye h[y] gart hym to *slepe*.
A. 8.133 For þat I saiȝ *slepyng* ȝif it so be miȝte.
A. 8.150 Many tymes at mydniȝt whan men shulde *slepe*,
B.Pr.231 [Al þis I seiȝ *slepyng* and seuene sythes more].
B. 1.5 And seide, 'sone, *slepestow*? sestow þis peple,
B. 5.4 That I ne hadde *slept* sadder and yseiȝen moore.
B. 5.350 That he *sleep* Saterday and Sonday til sonne yede to reste.
B. 5.375 And sat som tyme so longe þere þat I *sleep* and eet at ones.
B. 5.604 For he haþ þe keye and þe cliket þouȝ þe kyng *slepe*.
B. 6.301 Wiþ good Ale as Gloton taȝte [þei] garte [hym to] *slepe*.
B. 7.150 Of þat I seiȝ *slepynge*, if it so be myȝte,
B. 8.67 Murþe of hire mouþes made me to *slep[e]*;
B.11.267 And wel sikerer he *slepeþ*, þe [segge] þat is pouere,
B.11.321 And *slepynge* I seiȝ al þis, and siþen cam kynde
B.11.408 [Th]anne seide I to myself, '[*slepyng* hadde I grace]
B.11.413 'Haddestow suffred', he seide, '*slepynge* þo þow were,
B.12.28 And þere bidde my bedes but whan ich ete or *slepe*.
B.13.21 I lay doun longe in þis þoȝt and at þe laste I *slepte*,
B.14.2 Thouȝ it be soiled and selde clene: I *slepe* þerInne o nyȝtes;

B.14.69   Seuene *slepe*, as seiþ þe book, seuene hundred wynter
B.17.326   He sekeþ and sekeþ til he *slepe* drye.
B.17.328   It dooþ hym worse þan his wif or wete to *slepe*;
B.18.4   Til I weex wery of þe world and wilned eft to *slepe*
B.18.5   And lened me to a lenten, and longe tyme I *slepte*;
B.18.300   And whan I sei3 it was so, [*s*]*lepynge* I wente
C.Pr.7   Me biful for to *slepe*, for werynesse ofwalked,
C.Pr.8   And in a launde as y lay lened y and *slepte*
C.Pr.13   Al y say *slepynge* as y shal [3ow] telle.
C.Pr.224   Al y say *slepynge*, as 3e shal here [a]ftur,
C.Pr.235   [Al þis y say *slepynge* and seuene sythes more].
C. 1.5   And sayde, 'Wille, *slepestou*? seestow þis peple,
C. 5.9   And no dede to do but drynke and *slepe*.
C. 5.124   Ac y shal sey as y sayh, *slepynge* as hit were,
C. 6.418   A *sleep* saturday and sonenday til sonne 3ede to reste.
C. 7.252   And he hath þe keye and þe clycat thow þe kyng *slepe*
C. 8.323   And thenne gloton with gode ale garte hunger *slepe*.
C. 9.299   Of that y seyh *slepynge*, if hit so be myhte,
C.10.66   Murthe of here mouthes made me to *slepe*
C.12.152   And wel sikorere he *slepeth*, þe segg þat is pore,
C.13.215   That y ne hadde met more, so murye as y *slepte*,
C.13.216   And saide anoen to mysulue, '*slepynge* hadde y grace
C.13.217   'Haddestow soffred,' he sayde, '*slepyng* tho thow were,
C.15.24   And so y musede vppon þis matere þat me lust to *slepe*.
C.15.268   Seuene *slepen*, as saith þe boek, more then syxty wynter
C.15.303   And *slepeth*, as hit semeth, and somur euere hem folleweth.
C.19.306   A seketh and seketh til he *slepe* druye.
C.19.308   Hit doth hym worse then his wyf or wete to *slepe*;
C.20.4   Til y waxe wery of the world and wilnede eefte to *slepe*
C.20.5   And lened me to lenten: and long tyme y *slepte*.

slepyng ger *slepinge ger. &> slepe* A 2; B 2 slepyng (1) slepynge (1)
A.Pr.10   I *slomeride* into a *slepyng*, it swi3ede so merye.
A. 5.6   Þat I ne mi3te ferþere a fote for defaute of *slepyng*.
B.Pr.10   I *slombred* into a slepyng, it sweyed so murye.
B. 5.6   That I ne my3te ferþer a foot for defaute of *slepynge*.

slepynge > sleep,slepyng; sleth > sleen

sleuþe n *sleuthe n.* A 5 sleuþe (3) slouþe (2); B 20; C 18 sleuth (1) sleuthe (14) slewthe (3)
A.Pr.45   Slep & *sleuþe* sewiþ hem euere.
A. 2.66   In al þe signiure of *slouþe* I se[se] hem togidere;
A. 5.213   *Sleuþe* for sorewe fil doun a swowe
A. 5.220   Þanne sat *sleuþe* vp & seynide hym faste,
A. 5.221   And made auowe tofore god for his foule *slouþe*:
B.Pr.45   Sleep and *sleuþe* seweþ hem euere.
B. 2.99   Til *Sleuþe* and sleep sliken hise sydes;
B. 3.310   Spynne or sprede donge or spille hymself with *sleuþe*.
B. 5.385   Thanne cam *Sleuþe* al bislabered wiþ two slymy ei3en.
B. 5.434   Sixty siþes I, *Sleuþe*, haue foryete it siþþe
B. 5.440   And euere siþþe be beggere [by cause of my] *sleuþe*:
B. 5.448   Thanne sat *Sleuþe* vp and seyned hym [faste]
B. 5.449   And made auow tofore god for his foule *sleuþe*:
B. 6.143   In lecherie and in losengerie ye lyuen, and in *Sleuþe*,
B. 8.51   God wole suffre wel þi *sleuþe* if þiself likeþ,
B.13.407   The whiche is *sleuþe* so slow þat may no slei3tes helpe it,
B.13.409   [Ac] whiche ben þe braunches þat bryngen a man to *sleuþe*?
B.14.77   Weex þoru3 plentee of payn and of pure *sleuþe*:
B.14.235   So for his glotonie and his greete *sleuþe* he haþ a greuous
            penaunce,
B.14.254   And þou3 *Sleuþe* suwe pouerte, and serue no3t god to paie,
B.20.158   Oon þat muche we wro3te, *Sleuþe* was his name.
B.20.159   *Sleuþe* wax wonder yerne and soone was of age
B.20.163   This *Sleuþe* [wex slei3] of werre and a slynge made,
B.20.217   *Sleuþe* wiþ his slynge an hard [s]aut he made.
B.20.373   *Sleuþe* seigh þat and dide pryde,
C.Pr.46   Slep and *slewthe* sueth [hem] euer.
C. 2.106   And sue forth suche felawschipe til they ben falle in *Slewthe*
C. 7.1   Thenne cam *sleuthe* al byslobered with two slim[y] yes.
C. 7.47   Sixty sythes y, *sleuthe*, haue for3eten hit sethe
C. 7.54   And sethe a beggare haue y be for my foule *sleuthe*:
C. 7.62   Thenne sat *sleuthe* vp and seynede hym ofte
C. 7.63   And made [a]uowe tofore god for his foule *sleuthe*:
C. 7.69   Ac wheche been þe braunches þat bryngeth men to *sleuthe*?
C. 8.244   In somur for his *sleuthe* he shal haue defaute
C. 8.252   The lord for his lachesse and his luther *sleuthe*
C. 9.159   'Forthy lollares þat lyuen in *sleuthe* and ouer land strikares
C.11.108   Bothe wymmen and wyn, wr[a]the, [enuy] and *slewthe*
C.16.94   And thow *sleuthe* sewe pouerte and serue nat god to paye
C.22.158   Oen þat moche wo wrouhte, *sleuthe* was his name.
C.22.159   *Sleuthe* wax wonder 3erne and sone was of age
C.22.163   This *sleuthe* wa[x] sley of werre and a slynge made
C.22.217   *Sleuthe* with his slynge a[n] hard sawt he made.

C.22.373   *Sle[u]th* seyh þat and so dede pruyde

sley sleyest > slei3

sleyliche adv *sleighli adv.* C 2 sleyliche (1) sleylokeste (1)
C. 6.107   To sle hym *sleyliche* sleythes y bythenke.
C.11.264   Mouhte *sleylokeste* be slawe and sente hym to w[e]rre,

sliken v *sliken v.(1)* B 1
B. 2.99   Til Sleuþe and sleep *sliken* hise sydes;

slymy adj *slimie adj.* B 1; C 1 slimy
B. 5.385   Thanne cam Sleuþe al bislabered wiþ two *slymy* ei3en.
C. 7.1   Thenne cam sleuthe al byslobered with two *slim[y]* yes.

slynge n *slinge n.* B 2; C 2
B.20.163   This Sleuþe [wex slei3] of werre and a *slynge* made,
B.20.217   Sleuþe wiþ his *slynge* an hard [s]aut he made.
C.22.163   This sleuthe wa[x] sley of werre and a *slynge* made
C.22.217   Sleuthe with his *slynge* a[n] hard sawt he made.

slokke > slake

slombred v *slomberen v.* A 1 slomeride; B 1
A.Pr.10   I *slomeride* into a slepyng, it swi3ede so merye.
B.Pr.10   I *slombred* into a slepyng, it sweyed so murye.

sloo n *slough n.(1)* C 1
C.12.180   Bote if þe seed þat sowen is in the *sloo* sterue

slouþe > sleuþe

slow adj *slou adj. &> sleen* B 1; C 1 slowe
B.13.407   The whiche is sleuþe so *slow* þat may no slei3tes helpe it,
C. 8.243   "The *slowe* Caytif for colde wolde no corn tylye;

slowe > sleen,slow; slowh > sleen

smale adj *smal adj.* A 1; B 2; C 3
A.12.78   [Lene & rewlyche, with leggys ful *smale*].
B.Pr.147   And *smale* mees myd hem; mo þan a þousand
B.16.80   And gadrede hem alle togideres, boþe grete and *smale*,
C.Pr.168   And *smale* muys [mid] hem; mo then a thousend
C.18.63   Ne suynge *smale* ne of [o] swettenesse swete.
C.18.111   And gadered hem alle togyderes, bothe grete & *smale*,

smau3te v *smacchen v.* B 1; C 1 smauhte
B. 5.356   Dorste lape of þat leuynges, so vnlouely [it] *smau3te*.
C. 6.414   Durste lape of þat lyuynge, so vnlouely hit *smauhte*.

smelleþ > smylle

smerte adv *smerte adv. &> smerteþ* B 1; C 1
B.11.436   Ther smyt no þyng so *smerte*, ne smelleþ so [foule]
C.13.242   Ther smyt no thyng so *smerte* ne smelleth so foule

smerteþ v *smerten v.* A 1 smerte; B 2 smerte (1) smerteþ (1); C 1 smerteth
A. 3.155   For pouere men mowe haue no power to pleyne [þei3] hem *smerte*,
B. 3.168   For pouere men may haue no power to pleyne þou3 [hem] *smerte*,
B.17.329   For smoke and smolder [*smerteþ*] hise eighen
C.19.309   For smoke & smolder] *smerteth* his [yes]

smethe > smyþye

smylle v *smellen v.* B 1 smelleþ; C 2 smelleth (1) smylle (1)
B.11.436   Ther smyt no þyng so smerte, ne *smelleþ* so [foule]
C. 7.50   Til eche lyf hit lothed to loke þeron or *smylle* hit;
C.13.242   Ther smyt no thyng so smerte ne *smelleth* so foule

smyte v *smiten v.* B 4 smyt (3) smyte (1); C 7 smyt (3) smyte (2) smyteth (1) smoet (1)
B. 3.324   And what smyth þat any smyþeþ be *smyte* þerwiþ to deþe:
B.11.436   Ther *smyt* no þyng so smerte, ne smelleþ so [foule]
B.17.327   And whan smoke and smolder *smyt* in his sighte
B.17.347   Ac þe smoke and þe smolder þat *smyt* in oure eighen,
C. 3.477   And yf eny smyth smeth[e] hit be *smyte* þerwith to dethe:
C. 6.105   'I am wr[a]the,' quod weye, 'wol gladliche *smyte*
C.13.242   Ther *smyt* no thyng so smerte ne smelleth so foule
C.18.155   'Vnkynde and vnkunnynge!' quod Crist, and with a roep *smoet* hem
C.19.307   Ac when smoke and smolder [*smyt* in his sihte
C.19.327   Ac þe smoke and þe smolder þat *smyt* in oure yes,
C.20.385   The same sore shal he haue þat eny so *smyteth*:

smyth n *smith n.* B 1; C 1
B. 3.324   And what *smyth* þat any smyþeþ be smyte þerwiþ to deþe:
C. 3.477   And yf eny *smyth* smeth[e] hit be smyte þerwith to dethe:

smyþye v *smither v.* B 2 smyþeþ (1) smyþye (1); C 2 smethe (1) smythye (1)
B. 3.307   Shal be demed to þe deeþ but if he do it *smyþye*
B. 3.324   And what smyth þat any *smyþeþ* be smyte þerwiþ to deþe:

C. 3.460   Shal be demed to þe deth but yf he do hit *smythye*
C. 3.477   And yf eny smyth *smeth[e]* hit be smyte þerwith to dethe:

smoet > smyt

smoke n *smoke n.* B 3; C 3
B.17.327   And whan *smoke* and smolder smyt in his sighte
B.17.329   For *smoke* and smolder [smerteþ] hise eighen
B.17.347   Ac þe *smoke* and þe smolder þat smyt in oure eighen,
C.19.307   Ac when *smoke* and smolder [smyt in his sihte
C.19.309   For *smoke* & smolder] smerteth his [yes]
C.19.327   Ac þe *smoke* and þe smolder þat smyt in oure yes,

smolder n *smolder n.* B 3; C 3
B.17.327   And whan smoke and *smolder* smyt in his sighte
B.17.329   For smoke and *smolder* [smerteþ] hise eighen
B.17.347   Ac þe smoke and þe *smolder* þat smyt in oure eighen,
C.19.307   Ac when smoke and *smolder* [smyt in his sihte
C.19.309   For smoke & *smolder*] smerteth his [yes]
C.19.327   Ac þe smoke and þe *smolder* þat smyt in oure yes,

snakes n *snake n.* B 1; C 1
B.15.112   That were bisnewed wiþ snow and *snakes* wiþInne
C.16.267   That were bysnewed al with snowe and *snakes* withynne

snow n *snou n.* B 1; C 1 snowe
B.15.112   That were bisnewed wiþ *snow* and snakes wiþInne,
C.16.267   That were bysnewed al with *snowe* and snakes withynne

so adv *so adv. &> by_so,vp_so_doun,whatso* A 110; B 356; C 331
    A.Pr.10, A.1.42, A.1.72, A.1.171, A.2.19, A.2.24, A.2.86, A.2.156, A.3.8, A.3.57, A.3.74, A.3.98, A.3.147, A.3.150, A.3.229, A.3.272, A.4.11, A.4.53, A.4.54, A.4.84, A.4.89, A.4.91, A.4.92, A.4.93, A.4.120, A.4.124, A.4.138, A.4.156, A.5.8, A.5.22, A.5.51, A.5.65, A.5.106, A.5.108, A.5.113, A.5.122, A.5.142, A.5.187, A.5.219, A.5.227, A.5.241, A.5.244, A.6.1, A.6.22, A.6.53, A.6.57, A.6.70, A.6.76, A.6.86, A.6.99, A.6.110, A.6.123, A.7.15, A.7.26, A.7.71, A.7.74, A.7.131, A.7.160, A.7.163, A.7.191, A.7.207, A.7.212, A.7.218, A.7.236, A.7.240, A.7.301, A.7.307, A.8.23, A.8.46, A.8.54, A.8.104, A.8.105, A.8.109, A.8.133, A.8.160, A.8.164, A.9.28, A.9.29, A.9.47, A.9.85, A.9.101, A.9.102, A.10.61, A.10.74, A.10.94, A.10.105, A.10.120, A.10.127, A.10.149, A.10.217, A.11.3, A.11.55, A.11.94, A.11.124, A.11.149, A.11.175, A.11.192, A.11.195, A.11.209, A.11.236, A.11.240, A.11.304, A.12.8, A.12.16, A.12.30, A.12.88, A.12.97, A.12.106
    B.Pr.10, B.Pr.126, B.Pr.167, B.Pr.188, B.Pr.202, B.1.44, B.1.74, B.1.120, B.1.153, B.1.161, B.1.197, B.2.19, B.2.24, B.2.100, B.2.122, B.2.195, B.3.8, B.3.85, B.3.109, B.3.157, B.3.161, B.3.250, B.3.270, B.3.282, B.3.304, B.3.344, B.3.353, B.4.11, B.4.68, B.4.97, B.4.102, B.4.104, B.4.105, B.4.106, B.4.137, B.4.141, B.4.162, B.4.193, B.5.8, B.5.22, B.5.37, B.5.68, B.5.82, B.5.129, B.5.168, B.5.189, B.5.197, B.5.206, B.5.226, B.5.338, B.5.355, B.5.356, B.5.364, B.5.369, B.5.375, B.5.399, B.5.428, B.5.447, B.5.455, B.5.467, B.5.470, B.5.498, B.5.501, B.5.513, B.5.534, B.5.566, B.5.570, B.5.583, B.5.589, B.5.599, B.5.613, B.5.625, B.5.638, B.6.14, B.6.16, B.6.24, B.6.79, B.6.82, B.6.88, B.6.137, B.6.175, B.6.178, B.6.205, B.6.221, B.6.228, B.6.234, B.6.256, B.6.320, B.6.326, B.7.21, B.7.71, B.7.122, B.7.123, B.7.127, B.7.150, B.7.182, B.7.186, B.8.32, B.8.33, B.8.95, B.8.111, B.8.112, B.9.40, B.9.42, B.9.90, B.9.158, B.9.208, B.10.3, B.10.69, B.10.76, B.10.88, B.10.90, B.10.141, B.10.172, B.10.198, B.10.200, B.10.211, B.10.232, B.10.252, B.10.257, B.10.303, B.10.321, B.10.353, B.10.353, B.10.373, B.10.411, B.10.441, B.10.475, B.10.478, B.10.479, B.10.479, B.11.59, B.11.70, B.11.73, B.11.75, B.11.120, B.11.164, B.11.194, B.11.238, B.11.239, B.11.263, B.11.306, B.11.307, B.11.361, B.11.363, B.11.366, B.11.382, B.11.420, B.11.425, B.11.436, B.11.436, B.12.5, B.12.22, B.12.31, B.12.35, B.12.47, B.12.51, B.12.53, B.12.55, B.12.58, B.12.83, B.12.90, B.12.104, B.12.170, B.12.199, B.12.202, B.12.211, B.12.217, B.12.222, B.12.222, B.12.224, B.12.235, B.12.247, B.12.250, B.12.253, B.12.253, B.12.263, B.12.272, B.13.20, B.13.61, B.13.64, B.13.90, B.13.109, B.13.118, B.13.136, B.13.142, B.13.205, B.13.209, B.13.262, B.13.282, B.13.283, B.13.295, B.13.370, B.13.377, B.13.387, B.13.389, B.13.407, B.13.408, B.13.429, B.13.453, B.14.48, B.14.75, B.14.81, B.14.86, B.14.91, B.14.124, B.14.128, B.14.140, B.14.151, B.14.159, B.14.191, B.14.235, B.14.237, B.14.271, B.14.273, B.14.284, B.14.325, B.15.3, B.15.19, B.15.20, B.15.65, B.15.94, B.15.99, B.15.114, B.15.134, B.15.151, B.15.158, B.15.163, B.15.193, B.15.261, B.15.293, B.15.307, B.15.317, B.15.336, B.15.340, B.15.351, B.15.366, B.15.368, B.15.390, B.15.407, B.15.412, B.15.434, B.15.440, B.15.456, B.15.468, B.15.471, B.15.476, B.15.480, B.15.492, B.15.493, B.15.497, B.15.551, B.16.9, B.16.32, B.16.53, B.16.60, B.16.66, B.16.78, B.16.110, B.16.130, B.16.180, B.16.191, B.16.194, B.16.202, B.16.218, B.16.223, B.16.270, B.17.31, B.17.38, B.17.41, B.17.48, B.17.62, B.17.66, B.17.66, B.17.74, B.17.87, B.17.95, B.17.157, B.17.161, B.17.170, B.17.174, B.17.182, B.17.204, B.17.212, B.17.218, B.17.227, B.17.233, B.17.238, B.17.245, B.17.252, B.17.295, B.17.299, B.17.300, B.17.303, B.17.308, B.17.346, B.17.350, B.18.63, B.18.68, B.18.72, B.18.75, B.18.77, B.18.88, B.18.158, B.18.161, B.18.180, B.18.212, B.18.226, B.18.291, B.18.300, B.18.312, B.18.325, B.18.348, B.18.353, B.18.367, B.18.413, B.19.11, B.19.13, B.19.20, B.19.44, B.19.101, B.19.106, B.19.115, B.19.137, B.19.211, B.19.300, B.19.314, B.19.347, B.19.395, B.19.425, B.19.434, B.19.437, B.19.475, B.20.15, B.20.16, B.20.20, B.20.22, B.20.42, B.20.50, B.20.63, B.20.99, B.20.141, B.20.155, B.20.181, B.20.185, B.20.198, B.20.209, B.20.224, B.20.260, B.20.277, B.20.290, B.20.334, B.20.347, B.20.350, B.20.373, B.20.377
    C.Pr.150, C.Pr.184, C.Pr.205, C.Pr.210, C.Pr.214, C.1.42, C.1.55, C.1.71, C.1.145, C.1.149, C.1.157, C.1.192, C.1.199, C.2.24, C.2.70, C.2.128, C.2.128, C.2.138, C.3.8, C.3.84, C.3.95, C.3.195, C.3.199, C.3.204, C.3.233, C.3.246, C.3.264, C.3.297,

C.3.329, C.3.330, C.3.352, C.3.371, C.3.378, C.3.389, C.3.423, C.3.435, C.3.455, C.3.457, C.3.496, C.4.11, C.4.93, C.4.98, C.4.100, C.4.101, C.4.124, C.4.134, C.5.22, C.5.33, C.5.44, C.5.92, C.5.99, C.5.139, C.5.150, C.5.167, C.6.9, C.6.18, C.6.36, C.6.37, C.6.49, C.6.94, C.6.100, C.6.197, C.6.205, C.6.214, C.6.247, C.6.276, C.6.309, C.6.321, C.6.324, C.6.336, C.6.396, C.6.413, C.6.414, C.6.427, C.6.431, C.7.41, C.7.49, C.7.61, C.7.89, C.7.113, C.7.138, C.7.141, C.7.158, C.7.179, C.7.213, C.7.217, C.7.230, C.7.232, C.7.236, C.7.246, C.7.265, C.7.278, C.7.291, C.7.304, C.8.41, C.8.81, C.8.97, C.8.172, C.8.175, C.8.201, C.8.211, C.8.229, C.8.230, C.8.268, C.8.340, C.8.345, C.9.25, C.9.95, C.9.117, C.9.134, C.9.218, C.9.242, C.9.299, C.9.324, C.9.328, C.9.332, C.10.36, C.10.37, C.10.38, C.10.41, C.10.43, C.10.107, C.10.108, C.10.161, C.10.185, C.10.218, C.10.218, C.10.249, C.11.3, C.11.42, C.11.43, C.11.46, C.11.49, C.11.56, C.11.68, C.11.98, C.11.150, C.11.211, C.11.234, C.11.242, C.11.296, C.11.300, C.11.300, C.12.6, C.12.11, C.12.21, C.12.55, C.12.97, C.12.127, C.12.128, C.12.149, C.12.167, C.12.192, C.12.192, C.12.194, C.12.201, C.12.205, C.12.214, C.12.215, C.12.225, C.12.230, C.12.233, C.12.242, C.12.245, C.12.18, C.13.24, C.13.53, C.13.54, C.13.93, C.13.99, C.13.120, C.13.121, C.13.173, C.13.176, C.13.184, C.13.187, C.13.187, C.13.190, C.13.200, C.13.201, C.13.201, C.13.202, C.13.215, C.13.228, C.13.242, C.13.242, C.14.28, C.14.33, C.14.49, C.14.110, C.14.138, C.14.141, C.14.150, C.14.156, C.14.181, C.14.194, C.15.6, C.15.23, C.15.24, C.15.65, C.15.68, C.15.97, C.15.149, C.15.176, C.15.304, C.16.8, C.16.11, C.16.22, C.16.76, C.16.78, C.16.78, C.16.111, C.16.170, C.16.171, C.16.182, C.16.227, C.16.246, C.16.252, C.16.269, C.16.297, C.16.308, C.16.336, C.17.20, C.17.77, C.17.88, C.17.93, C.17.103, C.17.123, C.17.123, C.17.151, C.17.184, C.17.187, C.17.188, C.17.193, C.17.214, C.17.290, C.17.307, C.18.36, C.18.48, C.18.67, C.18.95, C.18.140, C.18.231, C.18.235, C.18.263, C.18.286, C.19.32, C.19.46, C.19.61, C.19.65, C.19.65, C.19.85, C.19.108, C.19.132, C.19.139, C.19.170, C.19.178, C.19.184, C.19.193, C.19.199, C.19.204, C.19.211, C.19.218, C.19.276, C.19.279, C.19.280, C.19.283, C.19.288, C.19.326, C.19.330, C.20.65, C.20.70, C.20.74, C.20.77, C.20.161, C.20.164, C.20.183, C.20.221, C.20.235, C.20.321, C.20.327, C.20.333, C.20.368, C.20.385, C.20.386, C.20.387, C.20.393, C.20.396, C.20.408, C.20.429, C.20.434, C.21.11, C.21.13, C.21.20, C.21.44, C.21.101, C.21.106, C.21.115, C.21.137, C.21.211, C.21.300, C.21.314, C.21.347, C.21.395, C.21.425, C.21.434, C.21.437, C.21.475, C.22.15, C.22.16, C.22.20, C.22.22, C.22.42, C.22.50, C.22.63, C.22.99, C.22.141, C.22.155, C.22.181, C.22.185, C.22.198, C.22.209, C.22.224, C.22.260, C.22.277, C.22.290, C.22.334, C.22.347, C.22.350, C.22.373, C.22.377

sobbed v *sobben v.* B 1
B.14.329   Swouned and *sobbed* and siked ful ofte

sobirte > sobretee

sobre adj *sobre adj.* B 1; C 1
B.14.55   By so þat þow be *sobre* of siȝte and of tonge,
C.15.254   By so þat þou be *sobre* of syhte and of tonge,

sobreliche adv *sobreli adv.* B 1
B.13.203   But seide ful *sobreliche*, 'þow shalt se þe tyme

sobretee n *sobrete n.* A 1 sobirte; B 4; C 3 sobrete
A.11.122   Þanne shalt þou se *sobirte*, & simplite of speche,
B.10.170   Thanne shaltow se *Sobretee* and Sympletee-of-speche,
B.13.217   *Sobretee* and symple speche and sooþfast bileue,
B.14.298   Wiþ *sobretee* fram alle synne and also ȝit moore;
B.14.318   And *sobretee* swete drynke and good leche in siknesse.
C.15.186   *Sobrete* [and] symple speche and sothfaste bileue
C.16.134   With *sobrete* fro alle synnes and also ȝut more;
C.16.152   And *sobrete* ȝeueth here swete drynke and solaceth here in all angrys.

socour n *socour n.* B 1; C 1
B.20.170   And bisouȝte hym of *socour* and of his salue hadde;
C.22.170   And bisouhte hym of *socour* and of h[is] salue hadde

sode > soden

sodeynliche adv *sodeinli adv.* B 3 sodeynly (1) sodeynliche (2); C 3
B.13.20   And whan he hadde seid so, how *sodeynliche* he passed.
B.17.215   And as þow seest som tyme *sodeynliche* a torche,
B.19.5   I fel eftsoones aslepe, and *sodeynly* me mette
C.15.23   And when he hadde ysaide so, how *sodeynliche* he vanschede.
C.19.181   And as thow seest som tyme *sodeynliche* of a torche
C.21.5   Y ful eftesones aslepe and *sodeynliche* me mette

soden v *sethen v.(1)* B 2 soden (1) ysoden (1); C 2 sode
B.15.293   Som þei solde and som þei *soden*, and so þei lyued boþe.
B.15.433   It is vnsauory, forsoþe, *ysoden* or ybake,
C. 9.149   Suluer or *sode* mete and sum tyme bothe,
C.17.20   Som they so[l]de and som they *s[o]de* and so they lyuede bothe.

sodenes n *souden n.* A 1 southdenis; B 2 Sodenes (1) Southdenes (1); C 2
A. 2.137   And alle þe denis & *southdenis*, as destreris hem diȝte,
B. 2.173   Denes and *Southdenes*, drawe yow togideres;
B.15.132   Executours and *Sodenes*, Somonours and hir lemmannes.
C. 2.190   Sommnours and *sod[e]nes* [þat] supersedias taketh
C.16.279   Seketours and *sodenes*, somnours and here lemmanes

sodome n prop *OED Sodom* B 1; C 1 sodoume
B.14.76   For þe meschief and þe meschaunce amonges men of *Sodome*
C.15.230   Plente of payn the peple of *sodoume*,

soend > sond; soercerie > sorcerie; soeth(- > sooþ(-; soff- > suff-

sofistre n *sophistre n.* C 1
C.17.309   And a *sofistre* of soercerie and seudopropheta

softe adj *softe adj.* A 2; B 2; C 2
A.Pr.1   IN a somer sesoun whanne *softe* was the sonne
A. 9.112   Sad of his semblaunt & of a *softe* speche,
B.Pr.1   IN a somer seson whan *softe* was þe sonne
B. 8.122   Sad of his semblaunt and of [a] *softe* [speche].
C.Pr.1   In a somur sesoun whan *softe* was þe sonne
C.10.118   Sad of his semblant and with a *softe* speche.

softe adv *softe adv.* A 1; B 4 softe (3) softer (1); C 4 softe (3) softur (1)
A. 5.130   And spak to þe spynstere to spynnen it *softe*.
B. 5.214   [And] spak to [þe] Spynnester[e] to spynnen it [*softe*].
B.14.211   For þe riche haþ muche to rekene, and [riȝt *softe*] walkeþ;
B.20.310   If any surgien were [in] þe seg[e] þat *softer* koude plastre.
B.20.313   'Ther is a Surgien in þ[e] sege þat *softe* kan handle,
C. 4.54   To robbe me or to ruyfle me yf y ryde *softe*.
C.16.52   For þe ryche hath moche to rykene and riht *softe* walketh;
C.22.310   Yf eny surgien were in þe sege that *softur* couthe plastre.
C.22.313   'Ther is a surgien in þe sege that *softe* can handele

softely adv *softli adv.* A 3 softely (2) softeliche (1); B 5 softeli (1) softely (3) softeliche (1); C 7 softly (4) softliche (2) softlyche (1)
A.2.129   And fals sat on a sisour þat *softeliche* trottide,
A. 3.36   And seide [wel] *softely*, in shrifte as it were,
A. 5.7   I sat *softely* [adoun] & seide my beleue,
B. 2.165   And Fals sat on a Sisour þat *softeli* trotted,
B. 3.37   And seide [wel] *softely*, in shrift as it were,
B. 5.7   [I] sat *softely* adoun and seide my bileue,
B.13.199   And siþen *softeliche* he seide in clergies ere,
B.18.117   Hir suster, as it semed, cam so[fte]ly walkynge
C. 2.168   And sayde *softly*, 'sese shal we neuere;
C. 2.181   *Softliche* in s[am]b[u]re fram syse [to] syse,
C. 2.192   On secatours and such men cometh *softly* aftur.
C. 3.54   Solempneliche and *softlyche* as for a suster of oure ordre.'
C. 4.162   A sysour and a somnour tho *softliche* forth ȝede
C.15.28   We reuerensede resoun and romede forth *softly*
C.20.120   Here suster, as hit semede, cam *softly* walkynge

soiled v *soilen v.(1)* B 5 soiled (3) soilled (1) ysoiled (1)
B.13.342   I waitede wisloker and þanne was it *soilled*
B.13.399   [Yet glotoun wiþ grete oþes his [garnement] hadde *soiled*
B.13.457   Thus haukyn þe Actif man hadde *ysoiled* his cote
B.14.2   Thouȝ it be *soiled* and selde clene: I slepe þerInne o nyȝtes;
B.14.13   That I ne *soiled* it wiþ siȝte or som ydel speche,

soiourned v *sojournen v.* B 1; C 1 soiourneth
B.17.86   And whan I seiȝ þis I *soiourned* noȝt but shoop me to renne
C.10.18   'Sothly,' saide þe frere, 'a *soiourneth* with vs freres

sokene n *soke n.(1)* A 1 sokne; B 1; C 1
A. 2.75   Randolf þe reue of rutelondis *sokne*,
B. 2.111   Reynald þe Reue of Rutland *Sokene*,
C. 2.114   Butte þe Bedel of Bannebury *sokene*,

solace n *solas n.* &> solacen B 6 solace (4) solas (2); C 9
B. 7.88   Lat vsage be youre *solas* of seintes lyues redyng.
B.12.150   And songe a song of *solas*, Gloria in excelsis deo.
B.14.159   And so forþ while somer lasteþ hir *solace* dureþ.
B.14.283   And a sorwe of hymself and *solace* to þe soule,
B.15.173   Al þat men seyn, he leet it sooþ and in *solace* takeþ,
B.18.219   Sette hym in *solace* and in souereyn murþe,
C. 8.22   Y wolde [assaye] som tyme, for *solace* as hit were.'
C. 9.131   Men suffreth al þat suche sayen and in *solace* taketh
C.12.208   Ȝoure sorwe into *solace* shal turne at þe laste
C.13.19   Alle his sorwe to *solace* thorw that song turnede
C.14.94   And song a song of *solace*, Gloria in excelcis deo.
C.16.11   And so forth whiles somur laste[th] here *solace* duyreth
C.16.17   Now, lord, sende hem somur som tyme to *solace* and to ioye
C.16.311   Alle sekness[e] and sorwes for *solac[e]* he hit taketh
C.20.228   Sette hym in *solace* and in souereyne merthe

solacen v *solasen v.* B 6 solace (2) solaced (1) solacen (2) solaceþ (1); C 8 solace (3) solaced (1) solacen (1) solaceth (2) solaseth (1)
B. 5.498   And al to *solace* synfulle þow suffredest it so were:
B.12.22   To *solacen* hym som tyme; [so] I do whan I make:
B.13.442   For to *solace* youre soules swiche minstrales to haue:
B.13.452   Thise *solaceþ* þe soule til hymself be falle
B.17.237   And *solacen* hem þat mowe [noȝt] se, þat sitten in derknesse,
B.19.22   And synfulle aren *solaced* and saued by þat name,
C. 7.102   For to *solace* ȝoure soules suche munstrals to haue:
C. 7.112   Thise *solaseth* þe soule til hymsulue be yfalle
C. 7.138   And a[l] to *solace* synfole thow soffredest it so were:
C. 7.256   And *solace* thy soule and saue the fram payne

C.16.152   And sobrete ȝeueth here swete drynke and *solaceth* here in all angrys.
C.18.15   And *solaceth* alle soules sorwful in purgatory.'
C.19.203   And *solacen* [hem] þat mowen nat se, sittynge in derkeness[e],
C.21.22   And synfole ben *solaced* and saued by þat name.

solas(- > solace(-; sold(e > sellen

soleyn n *soleine adj.* B 1; C 1
B.12.205   But by hymself as a *soleyn* and serued on [þe] erþe.
C.14.144   Bote as a *soleyn* by hymsulue [and] yserued [o]n þe [erthe].

solempneliche adv *solempneli adv.* C 1
C. 3.54   *Solempneliche* and softlyche as for a suster of oure ordre.'

solfe > solue

solitarie adj *solitaire adj.* C 1
C.17.7   *Solitarie* by hemsulue in here selles lyuede

solue v *solfen v.* B 1; C 1 solfe
B. 5.416   Yet kan I neyþer *solue* ne synge ne seintes lyues rede;
C. 7.31   Ȝut kan y nother *solfe* ne synge ne a seyntes lyf rede;

som pron *som pron.* A 18 somme (5) sum (1) summe (12); B 58 som (8) some (31) somme (19); C 58 som (7) some (3) somme (35) summe (13)
A.Pr.20   *Summe* putte hem to plouȝ, pleiȝede ful selde,
A.Pr.23   And *summe* putte hem to pride, aparailde hem þereaftir,
A.Pr.31   And *summe* chosen [hem] to chaffare, þei cheuide þe betere
A.Pr.33   And *summe* merþis to make as mynstrales conne,
A. 1.114   *Summe* in eir, summe in erþe, summe in helle depe.
A. 1.114   Summe in eir, *summe* in erþe, summe in helle depe.
A. 1.114   Summe in eir, summe in erþe, *summe* in helle depe.
A. 3.262   And riȝt as agag hadde happe shal *somme*:
A. 4.97   *Summe* redde resoun to haue reuþe on þat shrewe,
A. 6.112   But ȝif ȝe be sibbe to *summe* of þis seuene
A. 7.9   'Summe shal sewe þe sak for shedyng of þe whete;
A. 7.103   And *summe* to plese perkyn pykide vp þe wedis.
A. 7.107   Þanne seten *somme* & sungen at þe ale,
A. 7.114   *Summe* leide here leg alery as suche lorellis cunne,
A. 7.239   For *summe* of my seruauntis ben seke oþer while;
A. 7.247   And kep *sum* [til] soper tyme, & sit nouȝt to longe;
A.10.182   For *summe*, as I se now, soþ for to telle,
A.11.295   For he seide it hymself to *summe* of his disciplis:
B.Pr.20   *Some* putten hem to plouȝ, pleiden ful selde,
B.Pr.23   And *somme* putten hem to pride, apparailed hem þerafter,
B.Pr.31   And *somme* chosen [hem to] chaffare; þei cheueden þe bettre,
B.Pr.33   And *somme* murþes to make as Mynstralles konne,
B.Pr.50   I seiȝ *somme* þat seiden þei hadde ysouȝt Seintes;
B.Pr.92   *Somme* seruen þe kyng and his siluer tellen
B.Pr.95   And *somme* seruen as seruauntȝ lordes and ladies,
B.Pr.162   And *somme* colers of crafty werk; vncoupled þei wen[d]en
B.Pr.223   Of alle kynne lybbynge laborers lopen forþ *somme*,
B. 1.125   *Somme* in Eyr, somme in erþe, somme in helle depe.
B. 1.125   Somme in Eyr, *somme* in erþe, somme in helle depe.
B. 1.125   Somme in Eyr, somme in erþe, *somme* in helle depe.
B. 3.286   And riȝt as Agag hadde happe shul *somme*.
B. 4.110   *Som[me]* radde Reson to haue ruþe on þat shrewe,
B. 5.627   But if ye be sibbe to *some* of þise seuene
B. 6.9   'Somme shul sowe þe sak for shedyng of þe Whete.
B. 6.111   And *somme* to plese Perkyn piked vp þe wedes.
B. 6.115   [Th]anne seten *somme* and songen atte Nale,
B. 6.122   *Somme* leide hir le[g] aliry as swiche lo[r]els konneþ,
B. 6.255   For *some* of my seruauntȝ and myself boþe
B. 6.263   And keep *som* til soper tyme and sitte noȝt to longe;
B. 9.159   For *some*, as I se now, soþ for to telle,
B.11.198   [Ac] for þe beste ben *som* riche and some beggeres and pouere.
B.11.198   [Ac] for þe beste ben som riche and *some* beggeres and pouere.
B.11.356   And *some* troden, [I took kepe], and on trees bredden,
B.11.359   And *some* caukede; I took kepe how pecokkes bredden.
B.11.367   And *some* soure and some swete; selkouþ me þouȝte.
B.11.367   And some soure and *some* swete; selkouþ me þouȝte.
B.12.159   And þow seidest sooþ of somme, ac se in what manere.
B.12.220   Why *some* be alouȝ & some aloft, þi lykyng it were;
B.12.220   Why some be alouȝ & *some* aloft, þi lykyng it were;
B.13.345   Semynge to synneward, and *som* he gan taste
B.15.4   And *some* lakkede my lif–allowed it fewe;
B.15.97   Ther some bowes ben leued and *some* bereþ none
B.15.248   And for his seketoures & his seruauntȝ, & *som* for hir children].
B.15.293   *Som* þei solde and som þei soden, and so þei lyued boþe.
B.15.293   Som þei solde and *som* þei soden, and so þei lyued boþe.
B.15.330   And on hemself *som*, and swiche as ben hir laborers;
B.16.117   *Some* þat þe sighte seiȝen seiden þat tyme
B.16.142   'I am sold þoruȝ [*som*] of yow; he shal þe tyme rewe
B.17.32   He kan noȝt siggen þe somme, and *some* arn in his lappe.

B.18.68	*Some* seide þat he was goddes sone þat so faire deide:
B.18.69	And *some* seide he was a wicche; 'good is þat we assaye
B.19.234	And *some* he kennede craft and konnynge of sighte,
B.19.236	And *some* he lered to laboure [on lond and on watre
B.19.238	And *some* he tauʒte to tilie, to [coke] and to thecche,
B.19.240	And *some* to deuyne and diuide, [figures] to kenne;
B.19.241	And *some* to [kerue and compace], and colours to make;
B.19.242	And *some* to se and to seye what sholde bifalle,
B.19.245	And *some* to ryde and to recouere þat [vnriʒt]fully was wonne:
B.19.248	And *some* he lered to lyue in longynge to ben hennes,
B.19.252	'Thouʒ *some* be clenner þan some, ye se wel', quod Grace,
B.19.252	'Thouʒ some be clenner þan *some*, ye se wel', quod Grace,
B.19.375	*Some* þoruʒ bedes biddynge and some [by] pilgrymag[e]
B.19.375	Some þoruʒ bedes biddynge and *some* [by] pilgrymag[e]
B.19.376	And oþ[er] pryue penaunc[e], and *somme* þoruʒ penyes delynge.
B.20.309	*Some* liked noʒt þis leche and lettres þei sente
B.20.347	He saluede so oure wommen til *some* were wiþ childe.'
C.Pr.22	*Somme* potte hem to plogh, playde ful selde,
C.Pr.25	And *somme* putte hem to pruyde, [a]parayled hem þeraftir
C.Pr.33	And *summe* chesen chaffare; þei cheue[den] þe bettre
C.Pr.35	And *summe* murthes to make, as mynstrels conneth,
C.Pr.59	For coueytise of copis contraryed *somme* doctours.
C.Pr.90	*Summe* seruen þe kynge and his siluer tellen,
C.Pr.93	And *summe* aren as seneschalles and seruen oþer lordes
C.Pr.172	And playde with *somme* perilously and potte hem þer hym lykede.
C. 1.127	*Summe* in erthe, summe in ayr, summe in helle depe.
C. 1.127	Summe in erthe, *summe* in ayr, summe in helle depe.
C. 1.127	Summe in erthe, summe in ayr, *summe* in helle depe.
C. 3.439	And riht as agag hadde happe shal *somme*:
C. 4.105	*Summe* radden resoun tho to haue reuthe vppon þat shrewe
C. 5.63	*Somme* to synge masses or sitten and wryten,
C. 6.179	Semyng to synneward and *summe* y gan taste
C. 8.8	'That *somme* sowe þe sak for shedynge of the whete,
C. 8.118	And *somme* to plese Perkyn [pykede vp þe] wedes.
C. 8.122	Thenne seet *somme* and songen at the ale
C. 8.129	[*Somme*] leyde here legges alery as suche lorelles conneth
C. 8.267	For *somme* of my seruauntes and mysulf bothe
C. 8.273	And kepe *som* til soper tyme and site nat to longe;
C. 8.285	Lene hem *som* of thy loef thouh thow þe lasse chewe
C. 9.198	*Summe* hadde lyflode of h[ere] lynage and of no lyf elles
C. 9.199	And *summe* lyuede by here letterure and labour of here handes
C. 9.200	And *somme* hadde foreynes to frendes þat hem fode sente
C. 9.201	And briddes brouhte *somme* bred þat they by lyuede.
C.10.163	A[s] *somme* hangeth hemsulue and oþerwhile adrencheth.
C.13.165	And *som* treden, y toke kepe, and on trees bredde
C.13.177	And *some* soure and some swete; selcouthe me thouhte.
C.13.177	And some soure and *some* swete; selcouthe me thouhte.
C.14.103	And thow saidest sothe of *somme*, Ac [yse] in what manere.
C.16.249	Þere *som* bowes bereth leues and som bereth none:
C.17.20	*Som* they so[l]de and som they s[o]de and so they lyuede bothe.
C.17.20	Som they so[l]de and *som* they s[o]de and so they lyuede bothe.
C.18.60	Ac *somme* ar swettore then somme and so[nner]e wollen rotye.
C.18.60	Ac somme ar swettore then *somme* and so[nner]e wollen rotye.
C.18.69	*Somme* of vs soethfaste and somme variable,
C.18.69	Somme of vs soethfaste and *somme* variable,
C.18.70	*Summe* litel, somme large, ylik apples of kynde,
C.18.70	Summe litel, *somme* large, ylik apples of kynde,
C.19.33	He can no certeyn somme telle and *somme* aren in his lappe.
C.20.70	*Somme* saide he was godes sone þat so fayre deyede:
C.20.71	And *somme* saide, 'he can of soercerie; goed is þat we assaie
C.21.234	And *somme* he kende craft and konnynge of syhte,
C.21.236	And *som* he lered to laboure a londe and a watre
C.21.238	And *somme* he tauhte to tulye, to [coke] and to [thecche,
C.21.240	And *somme* to deuyne and deuyde, [figu]res to kenne;
C.21.241	[And *somme* to kerue a]nd compace and coloures to make;
C.21.242	And *somme* to se and to saye what sholde bifalle
C.21.245	And *somme* to ryde & to rekeuere that vnrihtfulliche was wonne:
C.21.248	And *somme* he [l]ered to lyue in longyng to be hennes,
C.21.252	'Thouh *somme* be clenner then somme, ʒe sen wel,' quod grace,
C.21.252	'Thouh somme be clenner then *somme*, ʒe sen wel,' quod grace,
C.21.375	*Somme* thorw bedes biddynge and [somme] bi pilgrimag[e]
C.21.375	Somme thorw bedes biddynge and [*somme*] bi pilgrimag[e]
C.21.376	Or oþer priue penauns[e] and *somme* thorw pans delyng.
C.22.309	*Somme* liked nat this leche and letteres þey sente
C.22.347	He salued so oure wymmen til *some* were with childe.'

som adj *som adj. &> som_tyme* A 5 sum (4) summe (1); B 28 som (24) some (4); C 29 som (24) some (2) sum (3)

A. 2.4	Kenne me be *sum* craft to k[now]e þe false'.
A. 5.25	And wynne þat he wastide wiþ *sum* maner craft,
A. 8.34	Sette scoleris to scole or [to] *summe* skynes craftis,
A. 9.115	To putte forþ *sum* purpos [to] prouen his wittes.
A.11.113	'And tel me *sum* tokne to hym, for tyme is þat I wende'.
B. 2.4	Kenne me by *som* craft to knowe þe false'.

B. 5.25	And wynnen his wastyng wiþ *som* maner crafte.
B. 5.373	And yspilt þat myʒte be spared and spended on *som* hungry;
B. 7.32	Sette Scolers to scole or to *som* [kynnes] craftes,
B. 8.125	[To] pute forþ *som* purpos to preuen hise wittes,
B.10.161	'And tel me *som* tokene [to hym], for tyme is þat I wende'.
B.10.372	But if I sende þee *som* tokene", and seiþ Non mecaberis,
B.10.443	And who were a good man but if þer were *som* sherewe?
B.11.54	Go confesse þee to *som* frere and shewe hym þi synnes
B.11.226	For *some* wordes I fynde writen, were of Feiþes techyng,
B.11.358	And *some* briddes at þe bile þoruʒ breþyng conceyued,
B.11.382	Ac he suffreþ for *som* mannes goode, and so is oure bettre.
B.12.198	Riʒt as *som* man yeue me mete and [sette me amydde þe floor]
B.13.56	'Bryng pacience *som* pitaunce pryueliche', quod Conscience,
B.13.376	Wiþ presentes pryuely, or paide *som* certeyn;
B.14.13	That I ne soiled it wiþ siʒte and *som* ydel speche,
B.14.119	But god sente hem *som* tyme *som* manere Ioye
B.14.128	Riʒt so fareþ god by *som* riche; ruþe me it þynkeþ,
B.14.164	Now, lord, sende hem somer, and *som* maner ioye,
B.14.217	[Or] in þe maister [or] in þe man *som* mansion he haueþ.
B.15.97	Ther *some* bowes ben leued and some bereþ none
B.15.351	And so it fareþ by *som* folk now; þei han a fair speche,
B.16.266	That shal deliuere vs *som* day out of þe deueles power
B.17.319	Ac er his rightwisnesse to ruþe torne *som* restitucion bihoueþ;
B.18.170	But [loue] sente hire *som* lettre what þis light bymeneþ
B.19.229	*Some* [wyes] he yaf wit with wordes to shewe,
B.20.27	And bete men ouer bittre, and *so[m* body] to litel,
B.20.206	And loke þow konne *som* craft er þow come þennes.'
C. 2.4	Kenne me by *sum* craft to knowe þe false'.
C. 2.131	That god wolde were ydo withoute *som* deseyte.
C. 3.292	A desert for *som* doynge, derne oþer elles.
C. 4.149	In signe þat thei sholde with *som* sotil speche
C. 5.34	Or ymaymed thorw *som* myshap whereby thow myhte be excused?'
C. 5.127	Thorw *som* trewe trauail and no tyme spille.
C. 7.75	But harlotrie and horedom or elles of *som* wynnynge;
C. 9.33	Amende in *som* manere wyse and ma[y]dones helpe;
C. 9.170	Or þe bak or *som* bon þey breke of he[re] children
C. 9.212	Or oen of *som* ordre or elles a profete.
C. 9.217	Or ymaymed in *som* membre, for to meschief hit souneth,
C.10.121	And potte forth *som* purpos to prouen his wittes,
C.11.103	'And telle me *som* tokene,' quod y, 'for tyme is þat y wende.'
C.11.196	Sir wanhope was sib to hym, as *som* men me tolde,
C.11.207	Vnwriten for *som* wikkednesse, as holy writ sheweth:
C.12.5	[Haue no consience how þou come to good]; confesse the to *som* frere.
C.14.137	Riht As *sum* man ʒeueth me mete and sette me Amydde þe flore;
C.15.295	Bote god sen[t]e hem som tyme *sum* manere ioye
C.16.21	Ac for þe beste, as y hope, aren *som* pore and ryche.
C.16.58	Or in þe maystre or in þe man *som* mansion he haueth.
C.16.249	Þere *som* bowes bereth leues and som bereth none:
C.18.104	'Leue liberum Arbitrium, lat *some* lyf hit shake.'
C.18.149	And *some* iewes saide with sorserie he wrouhte
C.18.282	That shal delyuere vs *som* day out of þe deueles power
C.20.173	Bote loue haue ysente her *som* lettre what this liht bymeneth
C.20.217	Ne hadde god ysoffred of *som* oþer then hymsulue
C.21.229	*Som* [wyes] he ʒaf wyt with wordes to schewe,
C.22.27	And bete men ouer bitere and *som* body to litel
C.22.206	And loke thow conne *som* craft ar thow come thennes.'

somdel adv *somdel adv.* A 1 sumdel; B 6 somdeel (2) somdel (4); C 5 somdeel (1) somdel (1) sumdel (3)

A. 3.81	And suffre hem to selle *sumdel* aʒens resoun.'
B. 3.92	And suffre hem to selle *somdel* ayeins reson.'
B. 5.431	For I haue and haue had *somdel* haukes maneres;
B. 9.151	That *somdel* þe sone shal haue þe sires tacches.
B.14.279	Ac *somdeel* I shal seyen it, by so þow vnderstonde.
B.16.39	I saue it til I se it ripen and *somdel* yfruyted.
B.18.10	Oon semblable to þe Samaritan and *somdeel* to Piers þe Plow[man]
C. 7.44	For y haue and haue yhad *sumdel* haukes maners;
C. 7.190	And yserued treuthe sothly, *somdel* to paye.
C. 8.41	For thow shalt ʒelden hit, so may be, or *sumdel* abuggen hit.
C.16.119	In engelysch is ful hard Ac *sumdel* y shal telle the.
C.20.8	Oen semblable to þe samaritaen and *somdeel* to Pers þe plouhman

some > som; somenours > somonour

somer n *somer n.* A 2; B 10; C 13 somer (2) somur (11)

A.Pr.1	IN a *somer* sesoun whanne softe was the sonne
A. 9.2	Al a *somer* sesoun for to seke dowel,
B.Pr.1	IN a *somer* seson whan softe was þe sonne
B. 5.406	I haue leuere here an harlotrye or a *Somer* game of Souters,
B. 8.2	Al a *somer* seson for to seke dowel,
B.14.115	And after þow sendest hem *somer* þat is hir souereyn ioye
B.14.159	And so forþ while *somer* lasteþ hir solace dureþ.

B.14.164   Now, lord, sende hem *somer*, and som maner Ioye,
B.14.178   And in *somer* tyme selde soupen in þe fulle.
B.14.314   Than he may [soþly] deserue, in *somer* or in wynter;
B.15.96   [And] se it by ensaumple in *somer* tyme on trowes:
B.16.225   Thus in a *somer* I hym seiȝ as I sat in my porche;
C.Pr.1   In a *somur* sesoun whan softe was þe sonne
C. 6.112   As som tyme in *somur* and also in heruest,
C. 8.244   In *somur* for his sleuthe he shal haue defaute
C. 9.119   For a sent hem forth seluerles in a *somur* garnement
C.10.2   Alle a *somur* seson for to seke dowel
C.12.189   Then sedes þat [in *somer*] sowe ben and mowen nat with forstes
C.15.291   [And] aftur thow sendest hem *somer* þat is here souereyne ioye
C.15.303   And slepeth, as hit semeth, and *somur* euere hem folleweth.
C.16.11   And so forth whiles *somur* laste[th] here solace duyreth
C.16.17   Now, lord, sende hem *somur* som tyme to solace and to ioye
C.16.148   Then he may sothly deserue in *Somur* or in wynter;
C.16.248   And s[e] hit by ensample In *somur* tyme on trees
C.18.240   'In a *somur* y hym seyh,' quod he, 'as y saet in my porche,

somme n *somme n.(2)* B 1; C 1
B.17.32   He kan noȝt siggen þe *somme*, and some arn in his lappe.
C.19.33   He can no certeyn *somme* telle and somme aren in his lappe.

somme adv *same adv.* A 1; B 1; C 1
A. 3.13   Ientily wiþ ioye þe Iustices so[mm]e
B. 3.13   Gentilliche wiþ ioye þe Iustices *somme*
C. 3.14   Genteliche with ioye the Iustices *somme*

somme &> som; sommnours > somonour; somne somone > sompne

somonour n *somnour n.* A 3 somenours (2) sompnours (1); B 6 somonour
      (2) Somonours (4); C 7 sommnours (1) somnour (1) somnours (2)
      sompnores (1) sompnour (1) sumnoures (1)
A. 2.44   For sisours, for *somenours*, for selleris, for beggeris,
A. 2.134   Þat *somenours* shulde be sadelit & serue hem ichone,
A. 3.123   Sisours & *sompnours*, suche men hire preisiþ;
B. 2.59   As Sisours and *Somonours*, Sherreues and hire clerkes,
B. 2.170   That *Somonours* sholde be Sadeled and seruen hem echone,
B. 3.134   Sisours and *Somonours*, swiche men hire preiseþ;
B. 4.167   Ac a Sisour and a *Somonour* sued hire faste,
B.15.132   Executours and Sodenes, *Somonours* and hir lemmannes.
B.19.369   And [a sisour and a *somonour*] þat were forsworen ofte;
C. 2.61   As sysores [and] *sompnores*, shyryues and here clerkes,
C. 2.190   *Sommnours* and sod[e]nes [þat] supersedias taketh
C. 3.172   Sysores and *somnours*, suche men he[re] preiseth;
C. 4.162   A sysour and a *somnour* tho softliche forth ȝede
C. 9.264   Here salue is of supersedeas in *sumnoures* boxes;
C.16.279   Seketours and sodenes, *sentnours* and here lemmanes
C.21.369   And a sisour and [a] *sompnour* þat weren forsworen ofte;

sompne v *somnen v.* A 1 somoune; B 4 somone (1) sompne (2) sompned
      (1); C 4 somne (1) sompne (2) sompned (1)
A. 2.123   And let *somoune* alle þe segges [in shires abouten],
B. 2.159   And leten *somone* alle segges in shires aboute,
B. 3.316   Ouer[carke] þe commune ne to þe Court *sompne*,
B.11.112   'Multi to a mangerie and to þe mete were *sompned*,
B.19.214   And counseillede hym and Conscience þe comune to *sompne*:
C. 2.175   And leten *somne* alle seggus in vche syde aboute,
C. 3.469   Ouerkarke þe comune ne to þe Court *sompne*
C.12.47   'Multi to a mangerye and to þe mete were *sompned*
C.21.214   And conseilede hym and Consience the comune to *sompne*:

sompnores sompnour(s > somonour

som_tyme adv *somtime adv.* A 3 sum_tyme; B 34 som_tyme (33)
      somtyme (1); C 41 som_tyme (28) some_tyme (1) sum_tyme (9)
      sume_tyme (1) summe_tyme (2)
A. 5.115   For *sum tyme* I seruide symme at þe nok
A. 5.195   *Sum tyme* asid, & sum tyme arere,
A. 5.195   Sum tyme asid, & *sum tyme* arere,
B. 5.137   'I am wraþe', quod he, 'I was *som tyme* a frere,
B. 5.199   For *som tyme* I serued Symme atte [Nok]
B. 5.347   *Som tyme* aside and som tyme arere,
B. 5.347   Som tyme aside and *som tyme* arere,
B. 5.371   And ouerseyen me at my soper and *som tyme* at Nones
B. 5.375   And sat *som tyme* so longe þere þat I sleep and eet at ones.
B. 5.413   I [a]m noȝt shryuen some tyme but if siknesse it make
B. 5.426   And my seruauntȝ *som tyme*: hir salarie is bihynde,
B. 5.546   *Som tyme* I sowe and som tyme I þresshe,
B. 5.546   Som tyme I sowe and *som tyme* I þresshe,
B.11.403   That *som tyme* hym bitit to folewen his kynde;
B.12.22   To solacen hym *som tyme*; [so] I do whan I make:
B.12.295   And wit and wisdom', quod þat wye, 'was *som tyme* tresor
B.13.334   That I cacche þe crampe, þe Cardiacle *som tyme*,
B.13.335   Or an Ague in swich an Angre and *som tyme* a Feuere
B.13.404   'And kauȝte siknesse *somtyme* for my [surfetes] ofte

B.14.119   But god sente hem *som tyme* som manere Ioye
B.14.122   Aungeles þat in helle now ben hadden ioye *som tyme*,
B.14.237   And *som tyme* for his synnes; so he is neuere murie
B.15.186   And whan he is wery of þat werk þan wole he *som tyme*
B.15.193   [Th]anne he syngeþ whan he doþ so, and *som tyme* wepynge,
B.15.220   For I haue seyen hym in silk and *som tyme* in russet,
B.15.245   For to wonye wiþ hem his wone was *som tyme*,
B.15.443   Al was hethynesse *som tyme* Engelond and Walis
B.16.45   And feccheþ awey my floures *som tyme* afore boþe myne eighen.
B.16.46   Ac liberum arbitrium letteþ hym *som tyme*,
B.17.215   And as þow seest *som tyme* sodeynliche a torche,
B.18.297   I haue assailled hym with synne and *som tyme* yasked
B.19.102   *Som tyme* he suffrede, and som tyme he hidde hym,
B.19.102   Som tyme he suffrede, and *som tyme* he hidde hym,
B.19.103   And *som tyme* he fauȝt faste and fleiȝ ouþer while,
B.19.104   And *som tyme* he gaf good and graunted heele boþe.
B.19.441   And suffreþ þat synfulle be [til *som tyme* þat þei repente].
B.20.182   The compaignye of confort men cleped it *som tyme*
C. 3.104   Al this haue we seyn, þat *som tyme* thorw a breware
C. 3.120   'And soffre hem *som tyme* to selle aȝeyne þe lawe.'
C. 5.47   And my sauter *som tyme* and my seuene p[s]almes.
C. 6.38   *Summe tyme* in o sekte, summe tyme in another,
C. 6.38   Summe tyme in o sekte, *summe tyme* in another,
C. 6.78   That y cache þe crompe, the cardiacle *sume tyme*
C. 6.79   Or an ague in suche [an] angre and *som tyme* a feuere
C. 6.112   As *som tyme* in somur and also in heruest,
C. 6.115   Amonges alle manere men my dwellyng is *som tyme*,
C. 6.137   Thus sytte they, sustres, *sum tyme* and disputen
C. 6.191   By sorserie *sum tyme* and sum tyme by maistrie.
C. 6.191   By sorserie sum tyme and *sum tyme* by maistrie.
C. 6.207   For *som tyme* y serued symme at þe style
C. 6.405   *Sum tyme* asyde and sum tyme arere,
C. 6.405   Sum tyme asyde and *sum tyme* arere,
C. 6.429   And ouersopped at my soper and *som tyme* at nones
C. 7.28   Y am nat shryue *som tyme* but yf seknesse hit make
C. 7.39   And my seruauntes *som tyme* here salerie is bihynde;
C. 8.22   Y wolde [assaye] *som tyme*, for solace as hit were.'
C. 9.149   Suluer or sode mete and *sum tyme* bothe,
C.10.159   And as thow seest the sonne *sum tyme* for cloudes
C.12.38   Thouh tho[w] se, say nat *sum tyme* þat is treuthe.
C.13.211   That *some tyme* hym bitit to folewen his kynde;
C.15.295   Bote god sen[t]e hem *som tyme* sum manere ioye
C.15.298   Angeles þat in helle now ben hadden *som tyme* ioye
C.16.17   Now, lord, sende hem somur *som tyme* to solace and to ioye
C.16.175   And *som tyme* to soffre bothe [sorwe] and [tene],
C.16.336   Thenne syngeth he when he doth so and *som tyme* w[e]pynge:
C.16.345   Ych haue ysey hym mysulue *som tyme* in russet,
C.16.368   Kynge[s] and Cardynals kn[o]wen hym *sum tyme*
C.17.1   'There is no such,' y sayde, 'þat *som tyme* ne borweth
C.18.37   That hit norischeth nise s[ih]tus and *som tyme* wordes
C.18.49   And feccheth away þe fruyt *som tyme* byfore bothe myn yes.
C.19.181   And as thow seest *som tyme* sodeynliche of a torche
C.20.330   Y haue ass[a]yled hym with synne and *som tyme* ich askede
C.21.102   *Som tyme* he soffrede and som tyme he hudde hym
C.21.102   Som tyme he soffrede and *som tyme* he hudde hym
C.21.103   And *som tyme* he fauht faste and fley oþerwhile
C.21.104   And *som tyme* he gaf good and graunted hele bothe;
C.21.441   And soffreth þat synnefole be til *som tyme* þat þei repente.
C.22.182   The company of comfort men clepede hit *som tyme*.

somtymes adv *somtimes adv.* B 1; C 1 some_tymes
B.13.309   What I suffrede and seiȝ and *somtymes* hadde,
C. 6.57   What y soffrede and seyh and *some tymes* hadde

somur > somer

somwhat pron *somwhat pron.* A 2 sumwhat; B 3; C 3 somwhat (1)
      sumwhat (2)
A. 7.244   Þat þou drynke no day er þou dyne *sumwhat*,
A.11.181   And siþen aftirward to se *sumwhat* of dobest'.
B. 6.260   That þow drynke no day er þow dyne *somwhat*.
B.11.92   Falsnesse ne faiterie? for *somwhat* þe Apostle seide
B.15.393   For Sarȝens han *somwhat* semynge to oure bileue,
C. 8.276   And loke þou drynke no day ar thow dyne *sumwhat*.
C.12.33   Falsnesse ne fayterye? for *sumwhat* þe apostel saide:
C.18.263   And ma[k]e sacrefice so: *somwhat* hit bitokneth;

somwhat adv *somwhat adv.* B 2; C 1
B.12.20   I seiȝ wel he seide me sooþ, and *somwhat* me to excuse
B.19.453   But [it soune], as by sighte, *somwhat* to wynnyng.
C.21.453   Bote hit sowne, as bi sihte, *somwhat* to wynnynge.

sond n *sand n.* B 2; C 4 sand (1) soend (1) sond (2)
B.11.327   I seiȝ þe sonne and þe see and þe *sond* after,
B.19.78   Boþe of [s]ond, sonne and see, and siþenes þei wente

C.13.135   And seyhe þe sonne and þe see and þe *sond* aftur
C.14.40   And in *soend* a signe wroet and saide to þe iewes,
C.17.89   Noþer see ne *s[o]nd* ne þe seed ȝeldeth
C.21.78   Bothe of *sand*, sonne and see and sennes þei wente

sonday n *sondai* n. A 3 sonneday (2) sundais (1); B 6 sonday (5)
　　Sondayes (1); C 9 sonday (1) soneday (1) sonenday (2) sonendayes (5)

A. 2.183   And senten hym on *sundais* wiþ selis to chirche,
A. 5.202   Þat he slepte satirday & *sonneday* til sonne ȝede to reste.
A. 5.222   'Shal no *sonneday* be þis seue ȝer, but seknesse it make,
B. 2.224   And senten hym [on *Sondayes*] wiþ seles] to chirch[e],
B. 5.360   That he sleep Saterday and *Sonday* til sonne yede to reste.
B. 5.450   'Shal no *Sonday* be þis seuen yer, but siknesse it [make],
B.13.235   For no breed þat I brynge forþ, saue a benyson on þe *sonday*
B.16.172   And þanne mette I wiþ a man, a mydlenten *sonday*,
B.18.67   Er *sonday* aboute sonne risyng'; and sank wiþ þat til erþe.
C. 2.234   And senten hym on *sonendayes* with seeles to churche,
C. 6.418   A sleep saturday and *sonenday* til sonne ȝede to reste.
C. 9.228   And vppon *sonendayes* to cese goddes seruice to here,
C. 9.243   Where se we hem on *sonendayes* the seruise to here,
C. 9.245   Or *sonendayes* at euensong? se we wel fewe!
C.15.210   Nere hit þat þe parsche [prest] preyeth for me on *sonendayes*,
C.18.181   And thenne mette y with a man a *myddelento[n] sonenday*,
C.20.69   Ar *soneday* aboute sonne rysynge'; and sank with þat til erthe.

sonde n *sonde* n. B 1; C 3

B. 9.130   Yet [seþ], ayein þe *sonde* of oure Saueour of heuene,
C. 6.111   On god when me greued auht and grocheed of his *sonde*:
C. 9.179   And alle pore pacient apayed of goddes *sonde*,
C.16.136   A collateral confort, cristes oune *sonde*:

sondry adj *sondri* adj. B 10; C 10 sondry (8) sondrye (1) sundry (1)

B.12.31   And sauen men *sondry* tymes, ac noon so soone as Charite.
B.13.38   And serued hem þus soone of *sondry* metes manye,
B.13.62   He eet manye *sondry* metes, mortrews and puddynges,
B.13.274   Ac it was moled in many places wiþ manye *sondry* plottes,
B.14.269   As by assent of *sondry* parties and siluer to boote,
B.15.282   But selden and *sondry* tymes, as seiþ þe book and techeþ.
B.16.207   And eiþer is oþeres ioye in þre *sondry* persones,
B.17.155   And þre *sondry* sightes [shewynge in oon],
B.18.223   To [se] what he haþ suffred in þre *sondry* places,
B.20.42   So [he was nedy], as seiþ þe book in manye *sondry* places,
C.Pr.96   And seide, 'ydolatrie ȝe soffren in *sondrye* places manye
C. 3.90   Many *sondry* sorwes in Citees falleth ofte
C.15.43   And serued hem thus sone of *sondry* metes monye,
C.15.66   And ete manye *sondry* metes, mortrewes and poddynges,
C.16.109   As by assente of *sondry* p[arti]es and suluer to bote,
C.18.125   Ac y saued ȝow and also y fe[d] ȝow
C.18.190   And, *sondry* to se vpon, solus deus he hoteth.
C.18.191   'Su[t]he they ben suyrelepus,' quod y, 'they haen *sondry* names?'
C.20.232   To wyte what he hath soffred in thre *sundry* places,
C.22.42   So he was nedy, as saith the boek in mony *sondry* places,

sone n *sone* n. &> *soone* A 9 sone (6) sones (3); B 46 sone (36) sones
(10); C 53 sone (39) sones (14)

A. 1.5   And seide '*sone*, slepist þou? sest þou þis peple,
A. 1.141   Lokide on vs wiþ loue, & let his *sone* deiȝe
A. 4.32   And betwyn hymself & his *sone* sette hym a benche,
A. 6.121   And she is sib to alle synful, & hire *sone* alse,
A. 7.72   His *sone* hattiþ suffre þi souereynes to hauen here wille
A. 8.146   I myself & my *sones*, seke þe for nede.'
A. 9.22   'I shal seiȝe þe, my *sone*,' seide þe Frere þanne,
A.10.18   And haþ fyue faire *sones* be his furste wyf:
A.10.167   Hymself & his *sones* þre, & siþen here wyues
B. 1.5   And seide, '*sone*, slepestow? sestow þis peple,
B. 1.167   Loked on vs wiþ loue and leet his *sone* dye
B. 4.45   And bitwene hymself and his *sone* sette hym on benche,
B. 5.484   For þoruȝ þat synne þi *sone* sent was to erþe
B. 5.486   And madest þiself wiþ þi *sone* vs synfulle yliche:
B. 5.487   And siþþe wiþ þi selue *sone* in oure s[u]te deidest
B. 5.489   Ther þiself ne þi *sone* no sorwe in deeþ feledest,
B. 5.490   But in oure secte was þe sorwe and þi *sone* it ladde:
B. 5.636   And she is sib to alle synfulle and hire *sone* also,
B. 6.80   His *sone* hiȝte Suffre-þi-Souereyns-to-hauen-hir-wille-
B. 7.169   I myself and my *sones*, seche þee for nede.'
B. 8.26   'I shal seye þee, my *sone*,' seide þe frere þanne,
B. 9.19   And haþ fyue faire *sones* bi his firste wyue:
B. 9.136   Thyself and þi *sones* þre and siþen youre wyues,
B. 9.151   That somdel þe *sone* shal haue þe sires tacches.
B.10.224   And on þe sooþfast *sone* þat saued mankynde
B.10.247   God þe fader, god þe *sone*, god holy goost of boþe,
B.10.409   And his wif wiþ hise *sones* and also hire wyues;
B.11.205   In þe olde lawe, as [þe] lettre telleþ, mennes *sones* men calle[d] vs
B.12.21   Seide, 'Caton conforted his *sone* þat, clerk þouȝ he were,

B.12.115   But he were preest or preestes *sone*, Patriark or prophete.
B.12.117   And his *sones* also for þat synne myscheued,
B.12.131   [The] selkouþes þat þei seiȝen, hir *sones* for to teche.
B.13.120   'I haue seuene *sones*', he seide, seruen in a Castel
B.15.511   [Whan þe hye kyng of heuene sente his *sone* to erþe
B.16.92   That oon Iesus a Iustices *sone* moste Iouke in hir chambre
B.16.123   For I haue saued yowself and youre *sones* after,
B.16.195   Sente forþ his *sone* as for seruaunt þat tyme
B.16.214   The *sone*, if I dorste seye, resembleþ wel þe widewe:
B.16.223   So is þe fader forþ with þe *sone* and fre wille of boþe,
B.16.234   I am ful siker in soule þerof, and my *sone* boþe.
B.16.235   I circumscised my *sone* siþen for his sake,
B.17.149   Bitoknen sooþly þe *sone* þat sent was til erþe,
B.17.158   How he þat is holy goost sire and *sone* preueþ.
B.17.161   Right so þe fader and þe *sone* and Seint Spirit þe þridde
B.17.174   Right so is þe *sone* Science of þe fader
B.17.183   Than is þe sire [or] þe *sone* and in þe same myghte,
B.17.202   For god þe fader is as a fust; þe *sone* is as a fynger;
B.17.212   So dooþ þe Sire and þe *sone* and also spiritus sanctus
B.17.224   Na moore dooþ sire ne *sone* ne seint spirit togidres
B.18.55   If þow be crist and kynges *sone* com down of þe roode;
B.18.68   Some seide þat he was goddes *sone* þat so faire deide:
B.18.76   For he was knyȝt and kynges *sone* kynde foryaf þat [þrowe]
B.18.250   And leet out Symondes sone[s] to teen hym hange on roode
B.18.298   Wheiþer he were god or goddes *sone*; he [g]af me short answere;
B.18.320   That crist may come In, þe kynges *sone* of heuene!'
C.Pr.113   And his *sones* slawe anon he ful for sorwe
C. 1.163   Lokede on vs with loue [and] let his *sone* deye
C. 3.368   Sethe y, his *sone* and his seruant, sewe for his ryhte.
C. 3.411   That saul for þat synne and his *sone* deyede
C. 4.43   And bytwene hymsulue and his *sone* sette tho sire resoun
C. 5.72   And so[p]ares and here *sones* for suluer han be knyhtes,
C. 5.73   And lordes *sones* here laboreres and leyde here rentes to wedde
C. 5.79   And taken Symondus *sones* seyntwarie to kepe,
C. 6.171   'Lady, to thy leue *sone* loute for me nouthe
C. 7.126   For thorw þat synne thy *sone* ysent was til erthe
C. 7.128   And madest thysulue with thy *sone* oure soule & body ilych:
C. 7.289   And she is sib to alle synfole and here *sone* bothe
C. 8.82   His *sone* hihte soffre-thy-souereynes-haue-her-wille-
C. 8.91   Ac aftur here doynge do thow nat, my dere *sone*,' quod Peres,
C. 9.308   And sethen aftur his *sones*, and sayde hem what they thouhte;
C. 9.313   Y mysulue and my *sones*, seche the for nede.'
C.10.30   'Y shal sey þe, my *sone*,' sayde þe frere thenne,
C.10.145   And hath fyue fayre *sones* by his furste wyue:
C.10.224   "Thysulue and thy *sones* thre and sethen ȝoure wyues,
C.10.238   That þe sire by hymsulue doth þe *sone* sholde be þe worse.
C.10.248   S[e]th, adames *sone*, seth[en] was engendred.
C.11.69   How he tolde in a tyme and tauhte his *sone* dele:
C.11.72   And yf thow haue litel, leue *sone*, loke by þy lyue
C.11.151   That he seyh þe [syre] and þe *sone* and þe seynt spirit togederes
C.11.240   And his wyf with his *sones* and his sones wyues;
C.11.240   And his wyf with his sones and his *sones* wyues;
C.12.113   In þe olde lawe, as þe lettre telleth, mennes *sones* me calde vs
C.14.60   Bote hit were pres[t] or prestis *sone*, patriarke or p[ro]phete.
C.14.62   And his *sones* for his synnes sorwe hem [becauȝte]
C.14.75   And of the selcouthes þat þei sye here *sones* þerof þei tauhten;
C.17.262   For when þe hye kyng of heuene sente his *so[n]e* til erthe
C.18.67   And so hit fareth sothly, *sone*, by oure kynde.
C.18.125   That oen Iesus, a Iustices *sone*, most iouken in here chaumbre
C.18.148   That he was god or godes *sone* for þat grete wonder;
C.18.193   And þe seconde is a *sone* of þe sire, filius;
C.18.204   Sente forth his *sone* As for seruaunt þat tyme
C.18.227   Was þe *sone* in hymsulue, in a simile as Eue was,
C.18.231   So oute of þe syre and of þe *sone* þe seynt spirit of hem bothe
C.18.235   So i[n] god [and] godes *sone* i[s] thre persones, the trinite.
C.18.247   How he fondede me furste; my fayre *sone* ysaak
C.18.251   Y circumsised my *sone* also for his sake,
C.19.123   Bitokneth soethly the *sone* þat sente was til erthe,
C.19.139   Riht so failed þe *sone*, the syre be ne myhte
C.19.149   Then is þe syre or the *sone* and of þe same myhte
C.19.168   For [g]o[d] the fader is as þe fust; þe *sone* is as þe fynger;
C.19.178   So doth þe sire and þe *sone* and seynt spirit togyderes
C.19.190   No more doth sire ne *sone* ne seynt spirit togyderes
C.20.55   And 'yf thow be Crist and [kynges] *sone* come adoun of th[e] rode;
C.20.70   Somme saide he was godes *sone* þat so fayre deyede:
C.20.78   For he was knyht and kynges *sone* kynde forȝaf þat [þrowe]
C.20.259   And lette out symondes *sones* to sen hym honge on rode:
C.20.331   Where he were god or godes *sone*; he gaf me short answere.
C.20.363   That Crist may come in, the kynges *sone* of h[e]uene!'

soneday sonenday(es > *sonday; sonest* > *soone*

song n *song* n. &> *syngen* B 4; C 5 song (2) songe (1) songes (2)

B.12.150   And songe a *song* of solas, Gloria in excelsis deo.

B.13.297   And most sotil of *song* oþer sleyest of hondes,
B.18.324   Songen seint Iohanes *song*, Ecce agnus dei.
B.19.211   Thanne song I þat *song*; so dide manye hundred,
C. 6.189   Sotiled *songes* and sente out olde baudes
C.13.19   Alle his sorwe to solace thorw that *song* turnede
C.13.59   Ther þe messager is ay merye and his mouth ful of *songes*
C.20.367   Songen seynt Iohann[es *songe*], ecce agnus dei.
C.21.211   [Thanne] sang [y] þat *song*; so dede many hundret

songe > syngen,song; songen > syngen

songewarie n *songewarie n.* B 2; C 1 sowngewarie
B. 7.154   Ac I haue no sauour in *songewarie* for I se it ofte faille.
B. 7.156   To sette sadnesse in *Songewarie* for sompnia ne cures.
C. 9.303   Ac men setteth nat by *sowngewarie* for me seth hit often fayle;

sonken > sank

sonne n *sonne n.* A 8; B 22 sonne (21) sonnes (1); C 30 sonne (29) sonnes (1)
A.Pr.1   IN a somer sesoun whanne softe was the *sonne*
A.Pr.13   Ac as I beheld into þe Est an heiȝ to þe *sonne*
A. 5.64   As a lek þat hadde leyn longe in þe *sonne*,
A. 5.202   Þat he slepte satirday & sonneday til *sonne* ȝede to reste.
A. 6.72   Þanne shalt þou come to a court, cler as þe *sonne*.
A. 6.79   Þe tour þere treuþe is hymself is vp to þe *sonne*;
A. 8.128   And sauȝ þe *sonne* euene souþ sitte þat tyme,
A. 8.143   And Iosep mette merueillously how þe mone & þe *sonne*
B.Pr.1   IN a somer seson whan softe was þe *sonne*
B.Pr.13   [Ac] as I biheeld into þe Eest, an heiȝ to þe *sonne*,
B. 3.326   By sixe *sonnes* and a ship and half a shef of Arwes;
B. 5.81   As a leek þat hadde yleye longe in þe *sonne*,
B. 5.360   That he sleep Saterday and Sonday til *sonne* yede to reste.
B. 5.491   The *sonne* for sorwe þerof lees [s]iȝt [for] a tyme.
B. 5.585   Thanne shaltow come to a court, cler as þe *sonne*.
B. 7.146   And seiȝ þe *sonne* [euene] South sitte þat tyme,
B. 7.165   And Ioseph mette merueillously how þe moone and þe *sonne*
B.10.211   For is no science vnder *sonne* so souereyn for þe soule.
B.11.172   Or any Science vnder *sonne*, þe seuene artȝ and alle–
B.11.327   I seiȝ þe *sonne* and þe see and þe sond after,
B.15.48   Alle þe sciences vnder *sonne* and alle þe sotile craftes
B.17.231   Ysekeles in euesynges þoruȝ hete of þe *sonne*
B.18.60   The day for drede wiþdrouȝ and derk bicam þe *sonne*;
B.18.67   Er sonday aboute *sonne* risyng'; and sank wiþ þat til erþe.
B.18.135   Of þat is cause of þis clips þat closeþ now þe *sonne*,
B.18.245   And lo! how þe *sonne* gan louke hire light in hirselue
B.18.246   Whan she seiȝ hym suffre þat *sonne* and see made.
B.18.409   'After sharpe shoures', quod pees, 'moost shene is þe *sonne*;
B.19.78   Boþe of [s]ond, *sonne* and see, and siþenes þei wente
B.19.432   And sent þe *sonne* to saue a cursed mannes tilþe
C.Pr.1   In a somur sesoun whan softe was þe *sonne*
C.Pr.14   Estward y beheld aftir þe *sonne*
C. 1.114   Thenne sitten in þe *sonne* syde þere þe day roweth?'
C. 1.117   'Hit is sikerore bi southe þer þe *sonne* regneth
C. 3.204   Ther ne is Cite vnder *sonne* ne noon so ryche reume
C. 3.479   Be sixe [s]onnes [and] a ship and half a shef of Arwes;
C. 6.418   A sleep saturday and sonenday til *sonne* ȝede to reste.
C. 7.131   The *sonne* for sorwe þerof lees [s]iht for a tyme.
C. 7.232   And so shaltow come to a Court as cleer as þe *sonne*.
C. 9.295   And seyh þe *sonne* in the sou[t]he sitte þat tyme,
C. 9.309   And Ioseph mette merueilously how þe mone and þe *sonne*
C.10.50   And lyf[holie]st of lyf þat lyueth vnder *sonne*.
C.10.159   And as thow seest þe *sonne* sum tyme for cloudes
C.12.94   Or eny science vnder *sonne*, the seuene ars and alle–
C.13.135   And seyhe þe *sonne* and þe see and þe sond aftur
C.16.210   Alle þe sciences vnder *sonne* and alle þe sotil craftes
C.17.92   And þe se and the seed, þe *sonne* and þe mone
C.18.64   Tho that sitten in þe *sonne* syde sannore aren rype,
C.18.66   Then tho that selde haen þe *sonne* and sitten in þe North half;
C.18.72   The whiche þe seynt spirit seweth, þe sonne of al heuene,
C.18.75   These haen þe [hete] of þe holi goest as þe crop of tre [the] *sonne*.
C.19.197   Isekeles in euesynges thorwe hete of the *sonne*
C.20.60   The daye for drede withdrouh and derke bicam þe *sonne*;
C.20.69   Ar soneday aboute *sonne* rysynge'; and sank with þat til erthe.
C.20.138   And þat is cause of this clips þat [c]loseth now þe *sonne*,
C.20.254   And lo! how þe *sonne* gan louke here lihte in heresulue
C.20.255   When he sye hym soffre þat *sonne* and se made.
C.20.452   'Aftur sharp[e] shoures', quod pees, 'most shene is þe *sonne*;
C.21.78   Bothe of sand, *sonne* and see and sennes þei wente
C.21.432   And sente þe so[nn]e to saue a corsed mannes tulthe

sonneday > sonday

sonnen v *sonnen v.* B 1
B.14.21   And siþen sende þee to Satisfaccion for to [sonnen] it after:

soone adv *sone adv.* A 10 sone (7) sonnere (2) sonnest (1); B 27 sone (1) sonner (3) sonnest (3) soone (20); C 28 sanere (1) sannore (1) sannour (1) sone (18) sonest (1) sonner (1) sonnere (1) sonnest (2) sonnore (1) sunnere (1)
A. 1.68   Þat tresten on his tresour betraid arn *sonnest*.'
A. 3.46   Þanne he assoilide hire *sone*, & siþen he seide,
A. 3.133   Heo is assoilid [as] *sone* as hireself likiþ.
A. 4.57   I sey it be myself, þou shalt it *sone* fynde,
A. 7.121   'ȝef it be soþ,' quaþ peris, 'þat ȝe seyn, I shal it *sone* aspie.
A. 8.11   Han pardoun þoruȝ purcatorie to passe wel *sone*,
A.11.175   I myself soþly so *sone* [as] heo it wiste
A.11.282   *Sonnere* hadde he saluacioun þanne seint Ion þe baptist,
A.11.309   Ne none *sonnere* ysauid, ne saddere of consience,
A.12.47   And þanne I kneled on my knes and kyste her [fete] *sone*,
B. 1.70   That trusten on his tresour bitraye[d are] *sonnest*.'
B. 3.47   Thanne he assoiled hire *soone* and siþen he seide,
B. 3.57   Who may scape [þe] sclaundre, þe scaþe is *soone* amended;
B. 3.58   It is synne of þe seuene *sonnest* relessed.
B. 3.144   She is assoiled as *soone* as hireself likeþ.
B. 3.283   That whoso seiþ hem soþe[s] is *sonnest* yblamed.
B. 6.129   'If it be sooþ', quod Piers, 'þat ye seyn, I shal it *soone* aspie.
B. 6.192   That seten to begge siluer *soone* were þei heeled,
B.10.232   Than myself sooþly *soone* so he wiste
B.10.423   He was *sonner* ysaued þan seint Iohan þe Baptist
B.10.465   Ne none *sonner* saued, ne sadder of bileue;
B.11.425   Shal neuere chalangynge ne chidynge chaste a man so *soone*
B.12.31   And sauen men sondry tymes, ac noon so *soone* as Charite.
B.12.171   That he þat knoweþ clergie kan *sonner* arise
B.12.244   For þe trailynge of his tail ouertaken is he *soone*.
B.13.32   'Welcome, wye, go and wassh; þow shalt sitte *soone*.'
B.13.38   And serued hem þus *soone* of sondry metes manye,
B.13.87   And seide, 'þow shalt see þus *soone*, whan he may na moore,
B.13.90   For now he haþ dronken so depe he wole deuyne *soone*
B.13.99   And I sat stille as Pacience seide, and þus *soone* þis doctour,
B.16.23   Wiþ þre piles was it vnderpight; I parceyued it *soone*.
B.17.66   Ac so *soone* so þe Samaritan hadde siȝte of þis leode
B.18.317   What lord artow?' quod Lucifer; þe light *soone* seide
B.20.69   Antecrist hadde þus *soone* hundredes at his baner,
B.20.87   Largeliche a legion loste [þe] lif *soone*.
B.20.109   And kynde cessede [sone] to se þe peple amende.
B.20.159   Sleuþe wax wonder ȝerne and *soone* was of age
C. 1.66   That tristeth in tresor of erthe he bytrayeth *sonest*.
C. 2.144   ȝe shal abyggen bothe but ȝe amende þe *sonner*.
C. 3.50   And he assoilede here *sone* and sethen a sayde,
C. 3.61   Ho may askape þe sclaundre, þe skathe myhte *sone* be mended;
C. 3.62   Hit is synne as of seuene noon *sannour* relesed.
C. 3.182   He is assoiled [as] *sone* as heresulue lyketh.
C. 3.326   And as *sone* as god seyh a sewed nat his wille
C. 3.436   That he þat sayth men sothe[s] is *sonnest* yblamed.
C.10.249   And god sente to seth so *sone* he was of age
C.11.255   He was *sunnere* ysaued then seynt Iohn þe baptiste
C.11.291   Ne none *sanere* ysa[u]ed ne saddere in bileue
C.12.6   He shal asoile [the] thus *sone* how so euere thow wynne hit.
C.12.223   And þat rathest rypeth rotieth most *sonnest*;
C.13.64   And as safly as þe messager and a[s] *sone* at his hostiele.
C.15.43   And serued hem thus *sone* of sondry metes manye,
C.15.94   And saide, 'Thow shalt se thus *sone*, when he may no more,
C.15.97   [For] now he hath dronke so depe a wol deuyne *sone*
C.15.106   Y sae[t] stille as pacience wolde and thus *sone* this doctour,
C.15.175   Ac Concience, y toek kepe, coniey[e]d *sone* this doctour
C.18.8   Thenne gan y aske what hit hihte and he me *sone* tolde:
C.18.60   Ac somme ar swettore then somme and so[nner]e wollen rotye.
C.18.64   Tho that sitten in þe sonne syde *sannore* aren rype,
C.19.65   Ac so *sone* so þe samaritaen hadde sihte of this carefole
C.22.69   Auntecrist hadde thus *sone* hondredes at his baner
C.22.87   Largeliche a legioun lees the lyf *sone*.
C.22.109   And kynde sesede [sone] to se þe peple amende.
C.22.159   Sleuthe wax wonder ȝerne and *sone* was of age

soor adj *sore adj.(2)* B 1
B.14.97   That it neuere eft is sene ne *soor*, but semeþ a wounde yheeled.'

soore adv *sore adv.* A 3 sore; B 18 soore (15) sore (3); C 14 sarrore (1) sore (13)
A. 2.105   It shal besette ȝoure soulis wel *sore* at þe laste.'
A. 5.78   His grace & hise gode happis greuide me wel *sore*.
A. 5.234   Ac for þere was nouȝt wherewith he wepte swiþe *sore*.
B. 5.98   His grace and his goode happes greuen me [wel] *soore*.
B. 5.393   'If I sholde deye now bi þis day [I drede me *sore*].
B. 5.462   And for þer was noȝt wher[wiþ] he wepte swiþe *soore*.
B. 5.504   And haue ruþe on þise Ribaudes þat repenten hem *soore*
B.11.225   I conseille alle cristne clyue noȝt þeron to *soore*,
B.13.387   As if I hadde dedly synne doon I dredde noȝt þat so *soore*

B.13.425   In youre deeþ deyinge I drede me *soore*
B.14.107   Whan he drogh to his deeþ day þat he ne dredde hym *soore*,
B.14.162   Afurst *soore* and afyngred, and foule yrebuked
B.17.295   And siþ holy chirche and charite chargeþ þis so *soore*
B.18.49   And sette it *sore* on his heed and seide in enuye;
B.18.88   'Ayein my wille it was, lord, to wownde yow so *soore*.'
B.18.89   He sighed and seide, '*soore* it me aþynkeþ!
B.18.286   'That is *soþ*', seide Sathan, 'but I me *soore* drede,
B.19.127   *Sore* afyngred folk, mo þan fyue þousand.
B.19.438   And trauailleþ and tilieþ for a tretour also *soore*
B.20.260   /Wol no [tresorer take] hem [wages], trauaille þei neuer so *soore*,
B.20.359   The plastres of þe person and poudres biten to *soore*;
C. 6.276   As thow y deddly synne dede y dradde [hit] nat so *sore*
C. 6.316   And for þer was nat wherwith a wep swythe *sore*.
C. 7.9   'Yf y sholde deye be þis day y drede me *sore*.
C. 7.85   In ȝoure deth deynge y drede me *sore*
C. 7.149   Haue reuthe of alle these rybaudes þat repenten hem *sore*
C.15.282   When he drow to þe deth that he ne dradd hym *sarrore*
C.19.276   And sethe Charite þat holy churche is chargeth this so *sore*
C.20.49   And sette hit *sore* on his heued and saide in Enuye;
C.20.91   [He] syhed and saide, '*sore* hit me forthenketh!
C.20.312   'That is *soeth*,' saide satoun, 'bote y me *sore* doute
C.21.127   *Sore* afyngred folk, mo then fyue thousend.
C.21.438   And trauaileth and tulieth for a tretour also *sore*
C.22.260   Wol no tresorer taken hem wages, trauayle they neuere so *sore*,
C.22.359   The plasteres of the persoun and poudres b[it]en to *sore*;

soores > sore

sooþ n *soth n.* A 15 soþ (3) soþe (12); B 41 sooþ (12) sooþe (1) soþe (27)
soþes (1); C 36 soeth (3) sooth (1) soth (7) sothe (24) sothes (1)
A. 1.84   I do it on Deus caritas to deme þe *sothe*.
A. 2.86   Þe text[e] tell[iþ] not so, treuþe wot þe *sobe*:
A. 3.204   Seruauntis for here seruyse, we se wel þe *soþe*,
A. 4.48   [Þe king kneuȝ] he seide *soþ* for consience hym tolde.
A. 4.66   Consience & þe king kneuȝ wel þe *soþe*,
A. 6.49   Til ȝe come into consience þat crist wyte þe *soþe*,
A. 6.70   And þanne shalt þou [se] sey *soþ*, so it be to done;
A. 6.84   Tel hym þis tokne, "treuþe wot þe *soþe*:
A. 7.122   Ȝe ben wastours, I wot wel, & treuþe wot þe *soþe*;
A. 8.56   Ne wolde neuere holy writ, god wot þe *soþe*,
A.10.182   For summe, as I se now, *soþ* for to telle,
A.11.30   Or daun[cel]id or drawe forþ; þise disours wyte þe *soþe*.
A.11.42   And putte forþ presumpcioun to proue þe *soþe*.
A.11.194   [Dredles] þis is dobet; [dobest wot þe *soþe*].
A.12.99   Wille þurgh inwit [wiste] wel þe *soþe*,
B.Pr.52   Moore þan to seye *soþ*, it semed bi hire speche.
B. 1.86   I do it on Deus caritas to deme þe *sothe*.
B. 2.26   And neuere *soþ* seide siþen he com to erþe,
B. 2.122   [The] text telleþ þee noȝt so, Truþe woot þe *soþe*,
B. 3.217   Ser[u]auntȝ for hire seruyce, we seeþ wel þe *soþe*,
B. 3.283   That whoso seiþ hem *soþe[s]* is sonnest yblamed.
B. 3.332   'I kan no latyn?' quod she, 'clerkes wite þe *soþe*!
B. 4.37   Thei ne [gy]ueþ noȝt of [good feiþ, woot god þe *soobe*]:
B. 4.61   The kyng knew he seide *sooþ*, for Conscience hym tolde
B. 4.80   Conscience and þe commune kn[e]wen [wel] þe *soþe*,
B. 5.562   Til ye come into Conscience þat crist wite þe *sobe*,
B. 5.583   Thanne [shalt þow] see seye-*soþ*-so-it-be-to-doone-
B. 5.595   Grace hatte þe gateward, a good man for *soþe*-
B. 5.597   Telleþ hym þis tokene: "[truþe woot] þe *soþe*;
B. 6.130   Ye ben wastours, I woot wel, and truþe woot þe *soþe*;
B. 9.101   [Tynynge] of tyme, truþe woot þe *soþe*,
B. 9.159   For some, as I se now, *sooþ* for to telle,
B.10.56   And puten forþ presumpcion to preue þe *soþe*.
B.10.438   In þe hondes of almyȝty god, and he woot þe *soþe*
B.11.96   It is licitum for lewed men to [legge] þe *sobe*
B.11.107   'He seiþ *sooþ*', quod Scripture þo, and skipte an heiȝ and prechd.
B.11.143   For an vncristene creature; clerkes wite þe *soþe*
B.11.180   Whoso leneþ noȝt he loueþ noȝt, [lord] woot þe *sobe*
B.11.298   The same I segge for *soþe* by alle swiche preestes
B.11.435   'Ye siggen *sooþ*', quod I, 'ich haue yseyen it ofte.
B.12.20   I seiȝ wel he seide me *sooþ*, and somwhat me to excuse
B.12.159   And þow seidest *sooþ* of somme, ac se in what manere.
B.12.270   And wheiþer he be saaf or noȝt saaf, þe *soþe* woot no clergie,
B.13.304   And segge þyng þat he neuere seiȝ and for *soþe* sweren it;
B.14.137   For whan a werkman haþ wroȝt, þan may men se þe *soþe*,
B.14.288   Selde sit pouerte þe *soþe* to declare,
B.15.79   Moore for pompe þan for pure charite; þe peple woot þe *sobe*.
B.15.101   A[c] þer þe roote is roten, reson woot þe *sobe*,
B.15.549   Moore tresor þan trouþe? I dar noȝt telle þe *soþe*;
B.17.7   And whan it is enseled [þerwiþ] I woot wel þe *soþe*
B.17.22   '[He seiþ] *sooþ*', seide þis heraud; 'I haue [founded] it ofte.
B.18.147   It is trufle þat þow tellest; I, truþe, woot þe *soþe*,

B.18.416   'Trewes', quod Truþe, 'þow tellest vs *sooþ*, by Iesus!
B.18.420   'Thow seist *sooþ*', [seyde] Rightwisnesse, and reuerentliche hire
kiste:
B.19.9   And þanne called I Conscience to kenne me þe *sope*:
C. 1.82   I do it [o]n deus caritas to deme þe *sothe*.
C. 1.122   Euene þe contrarie sitteth Crist, Clerkes wyteth þe *sothe*:
C. 2.26   And selde *soth* sayth bote yf he souche gyle,
C. 3.273   Seruantes for here seruyse, [we see wel þe *sothe*],
C. 3.286   'Nay,' quod Consience to þe kyng, 'clerkes witeth þe *sothe*,
C. 3.436   That he þat sayth men *sothe[s]* is sonnest yblamed.
C. 4.37   They gyue n[ouh]t of good fayth, woe[t] god þe *sothe*,
C. 4.64   [The kyng knew he sayde *soth* for Conscience hym tolde]
C. 5.3   And lytel ylet by, leueth me for *sothe*,
C. 5.86   Non de solo,' y sayde, 'for *sothe* viuit homo,
C. 6.237   'That was a rufol restitucioun,' quod repentaunce, 'for *sothe*.
C. 7.230   Thenne shaltow se say-*soth*-so-hit-be-to-done-
C. 7.243   Grace hatte þe gateward, a goed man for *sothe*;
C. 7.245   Tel hym this tokene: "treuthe woet þe *sothe*;
C. 7.285   'Wyte god,' quod a wafre[re], 'wiste y this for *sothe*
C. 9.128   And alle manere munstrals, me woet wel þe *sothe*,
C.10.22   Fallyng fro ioye, iesu woet þe *sothe*!
C.11.37   And putten forth presumpcioun to preue þe *sothe*.
C.12.41   'A saith *soth*,' quod scripture tho, and skypte an heyh and prechede.
C.12.78   For an vncristene creature; [clerkes] woet þe *sothe*
C.12.161   Crist acordeth efte herwith; clerkes wyteth þe *sothe*,
C.13.112   The same y segge for *sothe* by suche þat beth prestes
C.13.241   'Ȝe seggeth *soth*, be my soule,' quod y, 'I haue sey hit ofte.
C.14.103   And thow saidest *sothe* of somme, Ac [yse] in what manere.
C.14.191   And wher he be saef or nat saef þe *sothe* woet no clergie
C.16.123   Selde syt pouerte þe *soth* to declare
C.16.254   Ac þer he rote is roton, resoun woet þe *sothe*,
C.16.305   And when a man swereth "forsoth" for *sooth* he hit troweth;
C.17.211   More tresor then treuthe? Y dar nat telle þe *sothe*
C.19.9   Were hit þerwith aseled y woet wel þe *sothe*
C.19.23   'He seyth *soth*,' saide fayth; 'y haue yfounde hit trewe.
C.19.108   'A saide *soeth*,' quod the samaritan, 'and so y rede the also.
C.20.150   Hit is truyfle þat thow tellest; y, treuthe, woet þe *sothe*,
C.20.459   'Trewes,' quod treuthe; 'thow tellest vs *soeth*, by iesus!
C.20.463   'Thowe saiste *soeth*,' saide rihtwisnesse, and reuerentlich here
custe,
C.21.9   And thenne calde y Consience to kenne me þe *sothe*:

sooþ adj *soth adj.* A 5 soþ (4) soþe (1); B 17 sooþ (15) soþe (1) soþest
(1); C 11 soeth (2) soth (9)
A. 7.121   'Ȝef it be *soþ*,' quaþ peris, 'þat ȝe seyn, I shal it sone aspie.
A. 8.68   But ȝif þe suggestioun be *soþ* þat [shapiþ hem to] begge.
A.10.81   Salamon it seide for a *soþ* tale:
A.11.16   Þanne alle þe *soþe* sawis þat salamon seide euere.
A.12.5   But I se now as I seye, as me *soþ* thinkytȝ,
B. 6.129   'If it be *sooþ*', quod Piers, 'þat ye seyn, I shal it soone aspie.
B. 7.66   But if þe suggestion be *sooþ* þat shapeþ hem to begge,
B.10.16   Than alle þe *sooþ* sawes þat Salomon seide euere.
B.10.333   That þis worþ *sooþ*, seke ye þat ofte ouerse þe bible:
B.10.436   That Salomon seiþ I trowe be *sooþ* and certein of vs alle:
B.10.447   For *soþest* word þat euer god seide was þo he seide Nemo bonus.
B.11.137   'That is *sooþ*', seide Scripture; 'may no synne lette
B.11.176   For Seint Iohan seide it, and *soþe* arn hise wordes:
B.11.439   'Certes', quod he, 'þat is *sooþ*'; and shoop hym for to walken,
B.13.205   'That is *sooþ*', [seide] Conscience, 'so me god helpe.
B.13.211   'That is *sooþ*', [seide] Clergie, 'I se what þow menest.
B.15.44   'That is *sooþ*', seide he; 'now I se þi wille.
B.15.173   Al þat men seyn, he leet it *sooþ* and in solace takeþ,
B.16.60   'That is *sooþ*', [seide] Piers, 'so it may bifalle.
B.16.202   And þat it may be so and *sooþ* [sheweþ it manhode]:
B.18.167   'That is *sooþ*', seide Mercy, 'and I se here by Sowþe
B.18.286   'That is *sooþ*', seide Sathan, 'but I me soore drede,
C. 5.92   'That is *soth*,' y saide, 'and so y beknowe
C. 9.62   Bote the sugestioun be *soth* þat shapeth h[e]m to begge
C.10.212   And þat my sawe is *soth* þe sauter bereth witnesse:
C.11.199   Were hit al *soth* þat ȝe seyn, thow scripture and thow clergie,
C.12.72   'That is *soth*,' saide scripture; ' may no synne lette
C.13.245   'Ȝe, certes,' quod he, 'þat is *soth*', and shop hym to walke;
C.16.206   'That is *soth*,' he sayde; 'now y se thy wille.
C.18.192   'That is *soth*,' saide he thenne, 'the syre hatte pater
C.19.5   That that y sey is *soeth* se hoso liketh.'
C.20.170   'That is *soth*,' saide mercy, 'and y se here bi southe
C.20.312   'That is *soeth*,' saide satoun, 'bote y me sore doute

sooþfast adj *sothfast adj.* B 2; C 6 soethfaste (2) sothfaste (4)
B.10.242   And on þe *sooþfast* sone þat saued mankynde
B.13.217   Sobretee and symple speche and *sooþfast* bileue,
C.11.129   Hit is no science sothly bote a *sothfaste* bileue
C.11.284   For he þat most se[y]h and saide of the *sothfaste* trinite
C.15.186   Sobrete [and] symple speche and *sothfaste* bileue

C.17.119 Thogh hit suffice for oure sauacioun *soethfaste* byleue,
C.18.51   The whiche is spiritus sanctus and *sothfaste* bileue
C.18.69   Somme of vs *soethfaste* and somme variable.

sooþly adv *sothli adv.* A 4 soþliche (1) soþly (3); B 21 sooþly (15)
sooþliche (4) soþly (2); C 39 soethliche (1) soethly (3) sothly (28)
sothlich (1) sothliche (5) sothlyche (1)
A. 3.5   'I wile assaie hire myself, and *soþly* apose
A. 3.177   Ac þou þiself, *soþly*, asshamidest hym ofte;
A.11.175   Þanne myself *soþly* so sone [as] heo it wiste
A.11.179   And I sei[d]e, '*soþliche*, þei sente me hider
B. 3.5   'I [wol] assayen hire myself and *sooþliche* appose
B. 3.190   Ac þow þiself *sooþly* shamedest hym ofte;
B. 5.238   'Nay, *soþly*', he seide, 'saue in my youþe.
B.10.232   Than myself *sooþly* soone so he wiste
B.10.236   I seide to h[y]m *sooþly* þat sent was I þider
B.10.279   Ac it semeþ now *sooþly*, to [si3te of þe worlde],
B.11.240   And al was ensample, [*sooþliche*], to vs synfulle here
B.11.335   Reson I sei3 *sooþly* sewen alle beestes,
B.12.133   Ac þoru3 hir science *sooþly* was neuere soule ysaued
B.12.173   If hym likeþ and lest, þan any lewed [*sooþly*].
B.14.314   Than he may [*soþly*] deserue, in somer or in wynter;
B.15.162   Ac I sei3 hym neuere *sooþly* but as myself in a Mirour:
B.15.434   So is mannes soule, *sooþly*, þat seeþ no goo[d] ensampl[e]
B.16.145   It was hymself *sooþly* and seide 'tu dicis'.
B.17.58   Ne helpe hymself *sooþly*, for semyvif he semed,
B.17.149   Bitoknen *sooþly* þe sone þat sent was til erþe,
B.18.112   And þere I sau3 *sooþly*, secundum scripturas,
B.19.87   The seconde kyng siþþe *sooþliche* offrede
B.19.371   And for siluer were forswore–*sooþly* þei wiste it.
B.20.15   He synneþ no3t, *sooþliche*, þat so wynneþ his foode.
B.20.244   And seide, 'sires, *sooþly* welcome be ye alle
C. 1.47   "Sesares," thei sayde, "*sothliche* we knoweth."
C. 1.116   Ac y wol lacky no lyf,' quod þat lady *sothly*;
C. 2.138   Hit semeth *sothly* ri3t so on erthe
C. 3.5   'Y shal asaye here mysulue and *sothliche* appose
C. 3.236   Ac thow thysulue *sothly*, ho[so] hit segge durste,
C. 3.246   May nat be sold *sothliche*, so many part asketh
C. 3.330   And ryhte so, *sothly*, may kyng and pope
C. 6.240   'Nay, *sothly*,' he saide, 'saue in my 3outhe.
C. 7.190   And yserued treuthe *sothly*, somdel to paye.
C. 7.209   That is to sey *sothly* 3e sholde rather deye
C. 7.280   Ho is nat syb to this seuene, *sothly* to telle,
C. 9.218   Rihte so, *sothly*, such manere Ermytes
C.10.18   '*Sothly*,' saide þe frere, 'a soiourneth with vs freres
C.10.21   And saide, '*sothly* sepcies in die ca[d]it iust[u]s,
C.11.129   Hit is no science *sothly* bote a sothfaste bileue
C.11.281   *Sothly*,' saide rechelesnesse, '3e se by many euydences
C.12.129   And al was ensample, *sothly*, to vs synfole here
C.12.194   Riht so, *sothly*, þat soffry may penaunc[e]
C.12.225   Riht so, *sothly*, suche þat ben bischopes,
C.12.233   Riht so, *sothly*, for to segge treuthe,
C.13.143   Resoun y sey *sothly* sewe alle bestes
C.13.187   Y se non so ofte forfeten *sothly* so mankynde;
C.14.77   Ac thorw here science *sothly* was neuere soule ysaued
C.14.113   Yf hym liketh and luste, then eny lewede *sothly*.
C.16.148   Then he may *sothly* deserue in Somur or in wynter;
C.16.227   Riht so *sothly* scienc[e] swelleth a mannes soule
C.17.179   And *sothliche* þat god sulue in suche a coluere lyknesse
C.17.184   Disceue so the sarrasyns, *sothlyche* me thynketh
C.17.307   And 3ut they seyen *sothly*, and so doen þe sarrasynes.
C.18.58   '3e, sertes,' he sayde, 'and *sothliche* leue hit.
C.18.67   And so hit fareth *sothly*, sone, by oure kynde.
C.19.57   Ne helpe hymsulue *sothly* for semyuief he semede
C.19.93   Saue mysulue *soethly* and such as y louede–
C.19.123   Bitokneth *soethly* the sone þat sente was til erthe,
C.20.115   And there y seyh *sothly*, secundum scripturas,
C.21.87   The seconde kyng seth *soethliche* offrede
C.21.371   And for suluer weren forswore–*soth[ly]* thei wisten hit.
C.22.15   He synegeth nat *sothlich* þat so wynneth his fode.
C.22.244   And saide, 'syres, *soethly* welcome be 3e alle

sooþness n *sothnesse n.* A 2 soþnesse; B 6 sooþnesse (4) sothnesse (1)
soþnesse (1); C 4 soethnesse (1) sothnesse (3)
A. 2.150   *Soþnesse* sei3 hem wel & seide but litel,
A. 4.138   And seide it so loude þat *soþnesse* it herde;
B. 2.24   But *sooþnesse* wolde no3t so for she is a Bastard.
B. 2.189   *Sothnesse* sei3 hem wel and seide but litel,
B. 4.162   And seid[e] it so [loude] þat [*soþnesse*] it herde;
B.11.147   Sauacion for *sooþnesse* þat he sei3 in my werkes.
B.17.305   Ac it is but selden yseie3e, þer *sooþnesse* bereþ witnesse,
B.18.283   And [siþen] he þat *Sooþnesse* is seide þise wordes,
C. 2.24   Ac *sothnesse* wolde nat so for she is a bastard.
C. 2.203   *Sothnesse* seyh hem [wel] and sayde but lytel,

C.12.82   Sauacion for *soethnesse* [þat] a sey in my werkes.
C.19.285   Ac hit is bote selde yseyen, there *sothnesse* bereth witnesse,

sop n *soppe n.(1)* B 2
B.13.125   And set alle sciences at a *sop* saue loue one;
B.15.180   And if he soupeþ eteþ but a *sop* of Spera in deo.

sopares n *sopere n.(2)* C 1
C. 5.72   And *so[p]ares* and here sones for suluer han be knyhtes,

sope n *sope n.(2)* B 1
B.14.6   Wiþ þe *sope* of siknesse þat sekeþ wonder depe,

soper n *sopere n.(1)* A 1; B 3; C 3 soper (2) sopere (1)
A. 7.247   And kep sum [til] *soper* tyme, & sit no3t to longe;
B. 5.371   And ouerseyen me at my *soper* and som tyme at Nones
B. 6.263   And keep som til *soper* tyme and sitte no3t to longe;
B.16.141   Sittynge at þe *soper* he seide þise wordes:
C. 6.429   And ouersopped at my *soper* and som tyme at nones
C. 8.273   And kepe som til *soper* tyme and site nat to longe;
C. 8.274   At noon ne at no tyme and nameliche at *sopere*

sophistrie n *sophistrie n.* B 1; C 1
B.19.347   Shal be coloured so queyntely and couered vnder [oure] *Sophistrie*
C.21.347   Shal be coloured so queyntly and keuered vnder [o]ure *sophistrie*

sorcerie n *sorcerie n.* A 1; B 3; C 5 soercerie (2) soercerye (1) sorserie (2)
A.11.158   For *sorcerie* is þe souerayn bok þat to þat science longiþ.
B.10.215   For *sorcerie* is þe Souereyn book þat to [þat] Scienc[e] [l]ongeþ.
B.15.12   Til I sei3, as it *sorcerie* were, a sotil þyng wiþ alle.
B.15.596   Ac þei seiden and sworen wiþ *sorcerie* he wrou3te,
C. 6.191   By *sorserie* sum tyme and sum tyme by maistrie
C.17.304   Iewes sayde þat hit seye with *soercerye* he wrouhte,
C.17.309   And a sofistre of *soercerie* and seudopropheta
C.18.149   And some iewes saide with *sorserie* he wrouhte
C.20.71   And somme saide, 'he can of *soercerie*; goed is þat we assaie

sore n *sore n.(1)* &> *soore* B 3 soores (2) sores (1); C 4 sore (1) sores (3)
B.15.589   Of selkouþe *sores*; þei sei3en it ofte,
B.20.97   Kynde cam after wiþ many kene *soores*
B.20.358   Conforte hym', quod Conscience, 'and tak kepe to hise *soores*.
C.17.300   And of selcouthe *sores* saued men fol ofte.
C.20.385   The same *sore* shal he haue þat eny so smyteth:
C.22.97   Kynde cam aftur with many k[e]ne *sores*,
C.22.358   Conforte hym,' quod Consience, 'and taek kepe to his *sores*.

sorewe > sorwe; sorfeet > surfet

sory adj *sori adj.* A 4; B 10; C 15
A. 5.105   'I am *sory*,' quaþ enuye, 'I am but selde oþere,
A. 5.217   "I am *sory* for my synne," sey to þiseluen,
A. 6.86   And am *sory* for my synnes & so shal I euere
A.11.193   Sike with þe *sory*, singe with þe glade,
B. 5.128   'I am *sory*', quod [enuye], 'I am but selde ooþer,
B. 5.399   Ne ri3t *sory* for my synnes yet, [so þee I], was I neuere.
B. 5.445   "I am *sory* for my synn[e]", seye to þiselue,
B. 5.559   And am *sory* for my synnes and so [shal I] euere
B.10.76   Ne *sory* for hire synnes; so is pride woxen
B.11.104   Thou3 þow se yuel seye it no3t first; be *sory* it nere amended.
B.14.326   Synne seweþ vs euere', quod he and *sory* gan wexe,
B.17.31   And haþ saued þat bileued so and *sory* for hir synnes,
B.17.300   And now am *sory* þat I so þe Seint Spirit agulte,
B.17.350   For þer nys sik ne *sory*, ne noon so muche wrecche
C. 3.359   Of oure *sory* synnes to be assoiled and yclansed
C. 6.91   '3us! redily,' quod repentaunce, 'and thow be ryht *sory*
C. 6.93   'I am *sory*,'sayde enuye, 'y am [but] selde othur,
C. 6.308   Thenne was there a walschman was wonderly *sory*,
C. 7.15   Ne ryht *sory* for my synnes–y seyh neuere þe tyme–
C. 7.59   "Y am *sory* for my synnes", sey to thysuluen
C. 7.145   That what tyme we synnefole men wolden be *sory*
C. 7.246   Y am *sory* [for] my synnes, and so [shal y] euere,
C.11.56   Ne *sory* for here synnes; so [is] pruyde enhanced
C.15.211   Y am *sory* þat y sowe or sette but for mysulue,
C.16.303   And *sory* when he seth men sory, as thow seest childerne
C.16.303   And sory when he seth men *sory*, as thow seest childerne
C.19.32   And hath ysaued þat bileued so and *sory* for here synnes;
C.19.280   And now am *sory* þat y so the seynte spirit agulte,
C.19.330   For þer ne is sike ne *sory* ne non so moche wrecche

sorserie > sorcerie

sortes n prop *n.i.d.* B 1; C 1
B.12.271   Ne of *Sortes* ne of Salomon no scripture kan telle.
C.14.192   Ne of *sortes* ne of salomon n[o] scripture can telle.

sorwe n *sorew n.* A 8 sorewe; B 30 sorwe (28) sorwes (2); C 33 sorwe (29) sorwes (4)

A. 2.80   And seide to cyuyle, 'now *sorewe* on þi bokes,
A. 2.85   And þou hast gyuen hire to a gilour, now god ȝiue þe *sorewe*!
A. 3.16   And seide, 'mourne nouȝt, mede, ne make þou no *sorewe*,
A. 3.144   Barouns & burgeis she bringeþ in *sorewe*;
A. 3.153   Þis is þe lif of þat lady, now lord ȝif hire *sorewe*!
A. 5.88   Þanne I criȝe on my knes þat crist gyue hym *sorewe*
A. 5.104   'Sorewe for synne sauiþ wel manye.'
A. 5.213   Sleuþe for *sorewe* fil doun a swowe
B.Pr.191   For bettre is a litel los þan a long *sorwe*.
B. 2.116   And seide [to] Cyuyle, 'now *sorwe* [on þi bokes]
B. 2.121   And þow hast gyuen hire to a gilour, now god gyue þee *sorwe*!
B. 3.16   And seiden, 'mourne noȝt, Mede, ne make þow no *sorwe*,
B. 3.163   Barons and Burgeises she bryngeþ in *sorwe*,
B. 3.166   This is þe lif of þat lady, now lord ȝyue hire *sorwe*,
B. 4.62   That wrong was a wikked luft and wroȝte muche *sorwe*.
B. 5.108   Thanne I crye on my knees þat crist ȝyue h[y]m *sorwe*
B. 5.127   'Sorwe [for] synn[e] is sauacion of soules.'
B. 5.489   Ther þiself ne þi sone no *sorwe* in deeþ feledest,
B. 5.490   But in oure secte was þe *sorwe* and þi sone it ladde:
B. 5.491   The sonne for *sorwe* þerof lees [s]iȝt [for] a tyme.
B. 7.126   The prophete his payn eet in penaunce and in *sorwe*
B.12.116   [Saul for he sacrificed *sorwe* hym bitidde,
B.12.248   And deleþ it noȝt til his deeþ day, þe tail[le is al of] *sorwe*.
B.13.410   [Is whan men] moorneþ noȝt for hise mysdedes, ne makeþ no *sorwe*,
B.13.426   Lest þo þre maner men to muche *sorwe* yow brynge:
B.13.456   Wiþ turpiloquio, a l[a]y of *sorwe*, and luciferis fiþele.
B.14.283   And a *sorwe* of hymself and solace to þe soule,
B.17.320   His *sorwe* is satisfaccion for [swich] þat may noȝt paie.
B.17.331   Cogheþ and curseþ þat crist gyue h[y]m *sorwe*
B.17.340   Ben siknesse and *sorwes* þat we suffren o[uȝ]te,
B.18.214   And suffrede to be sold to se þe *sorwe* of deying,
B.18.220   And siþþe he suffred hym synne sorwe to feele,
B.19.66   And se bi his *sorwe* þat whoso loueþ ioye
B.20.43   That he seide in his *sorwe* on þe selue roode:
B.20.47   And suffre *sorwes* ful soure, þat shal to Ioye torne."
B.20.105   Swowned and swelted for *sorwe* of [depes] dyntes.
B.20.155   And [so] forȝyte *sorwe* and [of synne noȝt].
B.20.199   And as I seet in þis *sorwe* I sauȝ how kynde passede
C.Pr.113   And his sones slawe anon he ful for *sorwe*
C. 2.120   And sayde to Symonye, 'now *sorwe* mot thow haue
C. 2.129   And thow has[t] gyue hire as gyle tauhte, now god ȝeue þe *sorwe*!
C. 3.17   And sayden, 'mourne nat, mede, ne make thow no *sorwe*
C. 3.90   Many sondry *sorwes* in Citees falleth ofte
C. 3.213   Thus lereth this lady thi lond, now lord ȝeue here *sorwe*!
C. 7.86   Laste tho manere men to muche *sorwe* ȝow brynge:
C. 7.116   With turpiloquio, a lay of *sorwe* and luciferes fythele,
C. 7.130   On a friday in fourme of man feledest oure *sorwe*:
C. 7.131   The sonne for *sorwe* þerof lees [s]iht for a tyme.
C.12.208   Ȝoure *sorwe* into solace shal turne at þe laste
C.13.17   And for a song in his *sorwe*, "si bona accepimus a domino &c,
C.13.19   Alle his *sorwe* to solace thorw that song turnede
C.14.61   Saul for he sacrificede *sorwe* hym bytydde,
C.14.62   And his sones for his synnes *sorwe* hem [becauȝte]
C.14.80   Of briddes and of bestes, of blisse and of *sorwe*.
C.16.29   Cordis contricio cometh of sor[w]e of herte
C.16.175   And som tyme to soffre bothe [*sorwe*] and [tene],
C.16.331   Alle sekenes[e] and *sorwes* for solac[e] he hit taketh
C.16.327   What *sorwe* he soffrede in ensaumple of vs alle
C.17.145   Thenne seweth the [thy] soule to *sorwe* or to ioye
C.19.300   As *sorwe* of herte is satisfaccioun for suche þat may nat paye.
C.19.311   Coueth and corseth þat Crist ȝeue hym *sorwe*
C.19.320   Been seekness[e] and oþere *sorwes* þat we soffren ouhte,
C.20.2   As a recheles renk þat recheth nat of *sorwe*
C.20.223   And soffred to be sold to se þe *sorwe* of deynge,
C.20.229   And sethe he soffrede hym synne *sorwe* to fele
C.21.66   And se bi his *sorwe* þat hoso loueth ioye
C.22.43   That he saide in his *sorwe* on þe sulue rode:
C.22.47   And soffre *sorwes* ful soure þat shal to ioye torne."
C.22.105   Swowened and swel[t]e for *sorwe* of dethus duntes.
C.22.155   And [s]o forȝete [*sorwe*] and [of synne ȝeue nouht].'
C.22.199   And as y saet in this *sorwe* y say how kynde passede

sorweful adj *sorewful adj.* B 1; C 1 sorwful

B.17.92   For sighte of þ[e] *sorweful* [segge] þat robbed was with þeues.
C.18.15   And solaceth alle soules *sorwful* in purgatory.'

soth(e,soþ(e > sooþ; sothfaste > soþfast

sothfastnesse n *sothfastnesse n.* B 1

B.16.186   The secounde of þa[t] sire is *Sothfastnesse* filius.

sothli(- > sooþly; sothnesse > sooþness

sotil adj *sotil adj.* B 5 sotil (3) sotile (2); C 4

B.13.297   And most *sotil* of song oþer sleyest of hondes,
B.15.12   Til I seiȝ, as it sorcerie were, a *sotil* þyng wiþ alle.
B.15.48   Alle þe sciences vnder sonne and alle þe *sotile* craftes
B.15.400   Into Surrie he souȝte, and þoruȝ hise *sotile* wittes
B.18.54   And [seide], 'if þat þow *sotil* be [þiselue] now [þow help].
C. 4.149   In signe þat thei sholde with som *sotil* speche
C.10.208   Thorw no *sotil* sciense on sour stok growe";
C.16.210   Alle þe sciences vnder sonne and alle þe *sotil* craftes
C.20.54   And saiden, 'yf he *sotil* be hymsulue now he wol helpe;'

sotile v *sotilen v. &> sotil* A 1; B 3 sotile (1) sotilede (1) subtileþ (1); C 5 sotiled (4) sotileth (1)

A.11.140   It is no science forsoþe for to *sotile* þereinne.
B.10.188   It is no Science forsoþe for to *sotile* Inne;
B.10.220   Alle þise Sciences I myself *sotilede* and ordeynede,
B.19.457   Ech man *subtileþ* a sleiȝte synne to hide
C. 6.189   *Sotiled* songes and sente out olde baudes
C.17.169   Forthy souhte [he] into surie and *sotiled* how he myhte
C.19.238   And hymsulue, sayth the boek, *sotiled* how he myhte
C.20.333   And when y seyh hit was so, y *sotiled* how y myhte
C.21.457   Vch man *sotileth* a sleythe synne to huyde

sotiltees n *sotilte n.* C 2

C.12.240   To synege and to souche *sotiltees* of Gyle,
C.14.76   They helden hit an hey science here *sotiltees* to knowe,

sottes n *sot n.(1)* A 1 sottis; B 1; C 1

A.10.59   And ek in *sottis* þou miȝt se, þat sitten at þe nale.
B.10.8   'Wiþ swiche wise wordes to wissen any *sottes*!'
C. 9.257   That soffreth suche *sottes* and oþere synnes regne.

souche v *souchen v.* C 2

C. 2.26   And selde soth sayth bote yf he *souche* gyle,
C.12.240   To synege and to *souche* sotiltees of Gyle,

soude n *soude n.(2)* B 1

B. 3.353   The soule þat þe *soude* takeþ by so muche is bounde.'

soudeþ v *souden v.(2)* B 1; C 1 soudeth

B.19.429   And [*soudeþ* hem] þat sleeþ [swiche as] he sholde saue.
C.21.429   And *soudeth* hem þat sleeth suche as he sholde saue.

soughte souȝt(e souht(e > seken

souke v *souken v.* B 1; C 1

B.11.121   And bad hem *souke* for synne [saufte] at his breste
C.12.56   And bad hem *souke* for synne saue at his breste

soule n1 *soule n.* A 32 soule (27) soulis (5); B 107 soule (91) soules (16); C 93 soule (73) soules (20)

A. 1.35   Ne liflode to þe lykam þat lef is to þe *soule*.
A. 1.39   [And þat] shend[iþ] þi *soule*; set it in þin herte;
A. 1.60   May banne þat he born was to body or to *soule*.
A. 1.82   How I may sauen my *soule*, þat seint art yho[ld]en.'
A. 1.121   Mowe be sikur þat here *soule* shal wende into heuene.
A. 2.70   Here *soulis* to sathanas to synken in pyne,
A. 2.105   It shal besette ȝoure *soulis* wel sore at þe laste.'
A. 3.49   Sikir shulde þi *soule* be heuene to haue'.
A. 3.58   Neiþer in siȝt ne in þi *soule*, for god hymself knowiþ
A. 4.123   Be vnpunisshit at my power for peril of my *soule*,
A. 6.19   And souȝt goode seintes for my *soule* hele.'
A. 6.44   'Nay, be þe peril of my *soule*!' quaþ piers & gan to swere:
A. 6.69   Loke þou plukke no plant[e] þere for peril of þi *soule*.
A. 7.79   He shal haue my *soule* þat best haþ deseruid,
A. 7.85   [I] payede hym prestly for peril of my *soule*;
A. 7.136   Lest his flessh & þe fend foulide his *soule*.
A. 7.156   'Now be þe peril of my *soule*!' quaþ peris, 'I shal appeire ȝow alle,'
A. 7.268   And I seiȝe, be my *soule*, I haue no salt bacoun,
A. 8.23   And for þei swere be here *soule*, & so god muste hem helpe,
A. 8.38   Þat I ne shal sende [ȝour] *soule* sauf into heuene,
A. 8.98   But do wel & haue wel, & god shal haue þi *soule*,
A. 8.162   *Soulis* þat han ysynned seue siþes dedly.
A. 8.164   It is not so sikir for þe *soule*, certis, as is do wel.
A. 9.42   For he strengþeþ þe to stonde & steriþ þi *soule*
A. 9.44   Ay is þi *soule* sauf but þou þiself wilt
A.10.39   As muche to mene [as] man with his *soule*,
A.10.49   Inwyt in þe heuid is, & an help to þe *soule*,
A.10.63   Ouer suche maner of men miȝt in here *soulis*.
A.10.72   Is chief souereyn ouer hymself his *soule* to ȝeme,
A.10.77   And sauiþ þe *soule* þat synne haþ no miȝt
A.10.175   Outtake þe eiȝte *soulis*, & of iche beste a couple
A.12.105   And is closed vnder clom, crist haue his *soule*.
B. 1.37   Ne liflode to þ[e] likame [þat leef is to þ[e] *soule*.
B. 1.41   And that [shendeþ] þi *soule*; [set] it in þin herte.
B. 1.62   May banne þat he born was to bodi or to *soule*.
B. 1.84   How I may saue my *soule* þat Seint art yholden.'

B. 1.132	Mowe be siker þat hire *soul[e]* sh[a]l wende to heuene
B. 2.106	Hire *soules* to Sathan to suffre with hym peynes,
B. 2.141	It shal bisitte youre *soules* [wel] soure at þe laste.'
B. 3.50	Syker sholde þi *soule* be heuene to haue'.
B. 3.353	The *soule* þat þe soude takeþ by so muche is bounde.'
B. 4.140	Ben vnpunysshed [at] my power for peril of my *soule*,
B. 4.151	Ac noȝt for confort of þe commune ne for þe kynges *soule*.
B. 5.127	'Sorwe [for] synn[e] is sauacion of *soules*.'
B. 5.267	Ne haue a peny to my pitaunce, [for pyne of my *soule*],
B. 5.291	Bisette it hymself as best [be] for þi *soule*.
B. 5.369	Sworen goddes *soule* [and his sydes] and "so me god helpe"
B. 5.531	And souȝt goode Seintes for me *soul[e]* hel[e].'
B. 5.557	'Nay, by [þe peril of] my *soul[e]*!' quod Piers and gan to swere:
B. 5.582	Loke þow plukke no plaunte þere for peril of þi *soule*.
B. 6.87	He shal haue my *soule* þat best haþ deserued,
B. 6.93	I paide [hym] prestly for peril of my *soule*,
B. 6.117	'Now by þe peril of my *soule*!' quod Piers al in pure tene,
B. 6.171	'Now by þe peril of my *soule*!' quod Piers, 'I shal apeire yow alle',
B. 6.252	He is blessed by þe book in body and in *soule*:
B. 6.284	And yet I seye, by my *soule*! I haue no salt bacon
B. 7.21	And for þei swere by hir *soule* and so god moste hem helpe
B. 7.37	And sende youre *soules* in saufte to my Seintes Ioye.'
B. 7.116	But do wel and haue wel, and god shal haue þi *soule*,
B. 7.118	[That] after þi deeþ day þe deuel shal haue þi *soule*.'
B. 7.184	*Soules* þat haue synned seuen siþes dedly.
B. 7.186	[It] is noȝt so siker for þe *soule*, certes, as is dowel.
B. 8.46	For he strengþeþ [þee] to stonde and steereþ [þi] *soule*
B. 8.48	Ay is þi *soule* saaf but [þow þiselue wole
B. 9.51	As muche to mene as man wiþ a *Soule*.
B. 9.63	For þei seruen Sathan hir *soules* shal he haue;
B. 9.64	That lyuen synful lif here hir *soule* is lich þe deuel.
B.10.211	For is no science vnder sonne so souereyn for þe *soule*.
B.10.257	[So] is dobet to suffre for þ[i] *soules* helþe
B.10.263	But be swich in þi *soule* as þow semest wiþoute.
B.10.265	Syþenes þow seest þiself as in *soule* clene;
B.10.305	For if heuene be on þis erþe, and ese to any *soule*,
B.10.435	Of wit and of wisedom wiþ dampned *soules* wonye.
B.10.481	The which is mannes *soule* to saue, as god seiþ in þe gospel:
B.11.146	Gregorie wiste þis wel, and wilned to my *soule*
B.11.230	And as Seint Gregorie seide, for mannes *soule* helþe.
B.11.266	Of which crist is a kernell to conforte þe *soule*.
B.12.15	It is but murþe as for me to amende my *soule*.
B.12.39	Seke þow neuere Seint ferþer for no *soule* helþe.
B.12.54	And loue hem noȝt as oure lord bit, lesen hir *soules*:
B.12.57	Sapience, seiþ þe bok, swelleþ a mannes *soule*
B.12.133	Ac þoruȝ hir science sooþly was neuere *soule* ysaued
B.12.175	And how contricion wiþoute confession conforteþ þe *soule*,
B.12.188	That lyuynge after lettrure saue[d] hym lif and *soule*.
B.12.275	That god for his grace gyue hir *soules* reste,
B.12.284	And he is saaf, seiþ þe book, and his *soule* in heuene.
B.13.45	But if þei synge for þo *soules* and wepe salte teris:
B.13.76	They prechen þat penaunce is profitable to þe *soule*,
B.13.130	Which shal saue mannes *soule*; þus seiþ Piers þe Plowman.'
B.13.141	Thow loue leelly þi *soule* al þi lif tyme.
B.13.164	[And ek, haue god my *soule*, and þow wilt it craue
B.13.287	In likynge of lele lif and a liere in *soule*;
B.13.416	Whan men carpen of crist or clennesse of *soul[e]*
B.13.428	Sauen þoruȝ hir sermo[n] mannes *soule* fro helle;
B.13.442	For to solace youre *soules* swiche minstrales to haue:
B.13.445	For to saue þi *soule* from sathan þyn enemy.
B.13.452	Thise solaceþ þe *soule* til hymself be falle
B.14.30	And flour to fede folk wiþ as best be for þe *soule*;
B.14.86	And brynge his *soule* to blisse, so þat feiþ bere witnesse
B.14.132	Allas þat richesse shal reue and robbe mannes *soule*
B.14.283	And a sorwe of hymself and solace to þe *soule*:
B.14.297	The ferþe is a fortune þat florissheþ þe *soule*
B.14.316	The nynþe is swete to þe *soule*, no sugre swetter,
B.14.320	A blessed lif wiþouten bisynesse for body and *soule*:
B.14.321	Now god þat alle good gyueþ graunte his *soule* reste
B.15.141	To frend ne to fremmed: "þe fend haue his *soule*!
B.15.345	For charite wiþouten chalangynge vnchargeþ þe *soule*,
B.15.353	Ac þe metal, þat is mannes *soule*, [myd] synne is foule alayed.
B.15.413	Thoruȝ a cristene clerk acorsed in his *soule*–
B.15.426	The bettre for hir biddynges in body and in *soule*.
B.15.431	Crist calleþ hem salt for cristene *soules*,
B.15.434	So is mannes *soule*, sooþly, þat seeþ no goo[d] ensampl[e]
B.15.442	That goddes salt sholde be to saue mannes *soule*.
B.15.458	It is heþene as to heueneward and helplees to þe *soule*.
B.15.523	In sauacion of [mannes *soule*] seint [Thomas] was ymartired;
B.16.234	I am ful siker in *soule* þerof, and my sone boþe.
B.17.19	Shal neuere deuel hym dere ne deeþ in *soule* greue;
B.17.27	And lelest to leue [on] for lif and for *soule*?
B.17.263	That riche ben and reson knoweþ ruleþ wel youre *soule*;

B.17.265	For manye of yow riche men, by my *soule*, men telleþ,
B.17.335	For kynde clyueþ on hym euere to contrarie þe *soule*;
B.18.190	And saue mannes *soule*? suster, wene it neuere.
B.18.236	That mannes *soule* sholde saue and synne destroye.
B.18.260	And bileue on a newe lawe be lost, lif and *soule*.'
B.18.279	Body and *soule* beþ myne, boþe goode and ille.
B.18.304	That his *soule* wolde suffre no synne in his sighte;
B.18.307	And now I se wher a *soule* comeþ [silynge hiderward]
B.18.327	And seide to Sathan, 'lo! here my *soule* to amendes
B.18.328	For alle synfulle *soules*, to saue þo þat ben worþi.
B.18.340	Ergo *soule* shal *soule* quyte and synne to synne wende,
B.18.340	Ergo *soule* shal *soule* quyte and synne to synne wende,
B.18.367	I fauȝt so me þursteþ ȝit for mannes *soule* sake;
B.18.372	And haue out of helle alle mennes *soules*.
B.19.179	And blessed mote þei be, in body and in *soule*,
B.19.275	And sew [it] in mannes *soule* and siþen tolde hir names.
B.19.293	Maken hym, for any mournynge, þat he nas murie in *soule*,
B.19.408	Leue it wel [þow art] lost, boþe lif and *soule*.'
B.19.450	And torne hir wit to wisdom and to welþe of *soules*.
B.20.233	That þei come for coueitise, to haue cure of *soules*.
C. 1.35	Ne liflode to þe lycame þat lef is [to] þe *soule*.
C. 1.39	And þat [see]th þ[i] *soule* and sayth hit the in herte
C. 1.58	May banne þat he born was [to] body [or to] *soule*.
C. 1.80	How y may saue my *soule*, þat saynt art yholde.'
C. 1.147	And most souerayne salue for *soule* and for body.
C. 2.157	Hit shal [bi]sitte ȝoure *soules* ful so[u]re at þe laste.'
C. 4.137	Be vnpunisched in my power for perel of [my] *soule*
C. 5.39	And sykerost for þe *soule*, by so y wol contenue.
C. 5.48	Th[u]s y s[yn]ge for here *soules* of suche as me helpeth
C. 5.103	The l[y]f þat is louable and leele to thy *soule*.'
C. 5.152	For yf heuene be on this erthe or ese to [eny] *soule*
C. 5.198	Seketh seynt treuthe in sauac[ioun] of ȝoure *soules*
C. 6.314	Then in lysse to lyue and lese lyf and *soule*.'
C. 6.346	To bysetten hit hymsulue as beste be for thy *soule*.
C. 6.427	Sworn godes *soule* and his sides and "so helpe [me] god almyhty"
C. 7.76	When me carpeth of Crist or clannesse of *soule*
C. 7.88	Sauen thorw here sarmon mannes *soule* fram helle;
C. 7.102	For to solace ȝoure *soules* suche munstrals to haue:
C. 7.105	For to saue thy *soule* fram satan thyn enemye
C. 7.112	Thise solaseth þe *soule* til hymsulue be yfalle
C. 7.128	And madest thysulue with thy sone oure *soule* & body ilych:
C. 7.176	[And] souht gode seyntes for my *soule* helthe.'\
C. 7.201	'Nay, bi þe perel of my *soule*!' Peres gan to swerie,
C. 7.229	Loke thow plokke no plonte þere for perel of thy *soule*.
C. 7.256	And solace thy *soule* and saue the fram payne
C. 7.259	And fynde alle manere folk fode to here *soules*
C. 8.96	He shal haue my *soule* þat alle soules made
C. 8.96	He shal haue my soule þat alle *soules* made
C. 8.102	Y payede hit prestly for perel of my *soule*;
C. 8.306	And ȝut y say[e], be my *soule*! y haue no sal[t] bacoun
C. 9.25	And for they sw[e]re by here *soule* and [so] god mote hem helpe
C. 9.39	And sende ȝoure *soules* þer y mysulue dwelle
C. 9.40	And abyde þer in my blisse body and *soule* for euere.'
C. 9.290	Bote do wel and haue wel, and [god] shal haue thy *soule*
C. 9.330	*Soules* þat haue syneged seuene sythes dedly.
C. 9.332	Hit is nat so syker for þe *soule*, certes, as [is] dowel.
C.10.158	And semblable in *soule* to god but if synne hit make.
C.10.291	Clene of lyf and in loue of *soule* and in lele wedlok.
C.11.243	Of holy kirke þat sholde kepe alle cristene *soules*
C.12.81	Gregori wiste this wel and wilned to my *soule*
C.12.88	Saued me, sarrasyn, and body bothe.'
C.12.151	The which is þe cornel of confort for alle cristene *soules*.
C.13.241	'ȝe seggeth soth, be my *soule*,' quod y, 'I haue sey hit ofte.
C.14.77	Ac thorw here science sothly was neuere *soule* ysaued
C.14.115	And how contricion withoute confessioun conforteth þe *soule*,
C.14.127	That lyuynge Aftur lettrure saued hy[m] lyf and *soule*.
C.14.197	That god for his grace gyue here *soules* reste
C.14.206	And he is saef, saith þe boek, and his *soule* in heuene.
C.15.50	Bote yf they synge for tho *soules* and wepe salte teres:
C.15.82	They preche þat penaunce is profitable to þe *soule*
C.16.1	Allas þat rychesse shal reue and robbe mannes *soule*
C.16.25	And sende vs contricion [clereliche] to clanse with oure *soules*
C.16.31	And [operis satisfaccio] for *soules* paieth and alle synnes quyteth.
C.16.133	The furthe is a fortune þat florischeth þe *soule*
C.16.150	The nythe is swete to [þe] *soul[e]*, no sucre swettore,
C.16.155	A blessed lyf withoute bisinesse bote onelyche for þe *soule*:
C.16.156	Now god þat al [good] gyueth graunte his *soule* reste
C.16.227	Riht so sothly scienc[e] swelleth a mannes *soule*
C.16.275	Vnk[ynd]e curatours to be kepares of ȝoure *soules*.
C.17.22	Loue and lele byleue held lyf and *soule* togyderes.
C.17.79	Ac þe metal þat is mannes *soule* of [many of] this techares
C.17.82	And for þe synne of þe *soule* forsaketh his oune coyne.
C.17.140	The whiche is þe heued of charite and hele of mannes *soule*:

C.17.143 Loue thy frende þat folleweth thy wille, that is thy fayre *soule*.
C.17.145 Thenne seweth the [thy] *soule* to sorwe or to ioye
C.17.148 And þat is charite, leue chield, to be cher ouer thy *soule*;
C.17.274 In sauacioun of mannes *soule* seynte Thomas of Canterbury
C.18.15 And solaceth alle *soules* sorwful in purgatory.'
C.19.20 Shal neuere deuel hym dere ne deth in *soule* greue;
C.19.28 And lele to bileue on for [lif and] for *soule*?
C.19.229 That riche ben and resoun knoweth; reule wel ȝoure *soul[e]*;
C.19.231 For mony of ȝow riche men, by my *soule* y lye nat,
C.19.315 For kynde cleueth on hym euere to contrarie þe *soule*;
C.20.195 And saue mannes *soule*? suster, wene hit neuere.
C.20.245 That mannes *soule* sholde saue and synne distruye.
C.20.268 And bile[u]e on a newe lawe be ylost, lyf and *soule*.'
C.20.301 Body and *soule* beth myne, bothe gode and ille.
C.20.336 That if his *soule* hider cam hit sholde shende vs all.
C.20.341 And now y se where his *soule* cometh sylinge hid[er]ward
C.20.370 'Lo! me here, ' quod oure lord, 'lyf and *soule* bothe,
C.20.371 For alle synfole *soules*, to saue oure bothe rihte.
C.20.388 Ergo *soule* shal soule quyte and synne to synne wende
C.20.388 Ergo soule shal *soule* quyte and synne to synne wende
C.20.394 Here eny synfole *soule* souereynliche by maistrie,
C.20.406 Bote of comune coppes, alle cristene *soules*;
C.20.408 Y fauht so me fursteth ȝut for mannes *soule* sake:
C.20.414 And haue out of helle alle mennes *soules*.
C.21.179 And yblessed mote they be, in body and in *soule*,
C.21.275 And sewe hit in mannes *soule* and sethe toelde here names.
C.21.293 Makyn hym, for eny mornynge, þat he ne was murye in *soule*
C.21.408 Leue hit [wel thou] be[st] lost, bothe lyf and *soule*.'
C.21.450 And turne here wi[t] to wisdoem and to wel[th]e [of] *soule*.
C.22.233 That they cam for Couetyse, to haue cure of *soules*.

soule *n2 souel n.(2)* C 2 soule (1) sowl (1)

C. 8.284 Part with hem of thy payne, of potage or of *sowl*;
C.17.24 Bote thre litle loues and loue was here *soule*.

sound *adj sounde adj.* A 2; B 1; C 2

A. 9.29 And ȝet is he sauf & *sound*, & so hym behouiþ.
A.12.115 God saue hem *sound* by se and by land.
B. 8.33 Ac yet is he saaf and *sound*, and so hym bihoueþ,
C.10.38 A[c] ȝut is he saef and *sound*; and so hit fareth by þe rihtfole.
C.10.40 That ay is saef and *sound* þat sitte withynne þe borde.

souneth *v sounen v.* B 1 soune; C 4 soune (1) souneth (2) sowne (1)

B.19.453 But [it soune], as by sighte, somwhat to wynnyng.
C. 6.59 Al [y] wolde þat men wiste when it to purude *souneth*,
C. 9.217 Or ymaymed in som membre, for to meschief hit *souneth*,
C.11.77 For is no wit worth now but hit of wynnynge *soune*.
C.21.453 Bote hit *sowne*, as bi sihte, somwhat to wynnynge.

soupen *v soupen v.(2)* A 1 soupe; B 5 soupe (2) soupen (2) soupeþ (1); C 2 soupe

A. 7.203 And he shal *soupe* swettere whanne he it haþ deseruid.
B. 2.97 And þanne to sitten and *soupen* til sleep hem assaille,
B. 6.217 And he shal *soupe* swetter whan he it haþ deserued.
B.14.160 Ac beggeris aboute Midsomer bredlees þei [*soupe*],
B.14.178 And in somer tyme selde *soupen* to þe fulle.
B.15.180 And if he *soupeþ* eteþ but a sop of Spera in deo.
C. 8.227 And h[e] shal *soupe* swetture when [he] hit hath deserued.
C.16.13 Ac beggares aboute myssomur bredles they *soupe*

sour *adj sour adj.* B 6 sour (4) soure (2); C 8 sour (6) soure (2)

B.11.259 [Al]þouȝ it be *sour* to suffre, þe[r] comeþ swete [after].
B.11.367 And some *soure* and some swete; selkouþ me þouȝte.
B.13.43 Ac hir sauce was ouer *sour* and vnsauourly grounde
B.13.49 He sette a *sour* loof toforn vs and seide 'Agite penitenciam',
B.16.72 And swete wiþouten swellyng; *sour* worþ it neuere.'
B.20.47 And suffre sorwes ful *soure*, þat shal to Ioye torne."
C.10.208 Thorw no sotil sciense on sour stok growe";
C.12.145 Althouh h[it] be *sour* to soffre þer cometh a swete aftur.
C.13.177 And some *soure* and some swete; selcouthe me thouhte.
C.15.48 Ac here sauce was ouer*sour* and vnsauerly ygrounde
C.15.55 He sette a *sour* loef and saide, 'Agite penitenciam',
C.18.99 And swete withoute swellynge; *sour* worth hit neuere'–
C.20.218 He hadde nat wist witterly where deth were *sour* or swete.
C.22.47 And soffre sorwes ful *soure* þat shal to ioye torne."

soure *adv soure adv. &> sour* B 2; C 1

B. 2.141 It shal bisitte youre soules [wel] *soure* at þe laste.'
B.10.365 It shal bisitten vs ful *soure* þe siluer þat we kepen,
C. 2.157 Hit shal [bi]sitte ȝoure soules ful *so[u]re* at þe laste.'

soutere *n soutere n.* A 2 souteris; B 3 Soutere (1) souteres (1) Souters (1); C 1

A.11.184 Trewe tilieris on erþe, taillours & *souteris*
A.11.311 *Souteris* & seweris; suche lewide iottis
B. 5.406 I haue leuere here an harlotrye or a Somer game of *Souters*,

B.10.467 *Souteres* and shepherdes; [swiche] lewed Iuttes
B.13.339 To þe *Soutere* of Southwerk or of Shordych dame Emme;
C. 6.83 To the *soutere* of southewerk, suche is his grace.

south *adv south adv. cf. sowþe* A 1 souþ; B 1

A. 8.128 And sauȝ þe sonne euene *souþ* sitte þat tyme,
B. 7.146 And seiȝ þe sonne [euene] *South* sitte þat tyme,

southdenes > sodenes; southe > sowþe

southwerk *n prop n.i.d.* B 1; C 1 southewerk

B.13.339 To þe Soutere of *Southwerk* or of Shordych dame Emme;
C. 6.83 To the soutere of *southewerk*, suche is his grace.

southwestrene *adj southwesterne adj.* A 1 southwestryne; B 1; C 1 southweste

A. 5.14 And þe *southwestryne* wynd on satirday at eue
B. 5.14 And þe *Southwestrene* wynd on Saterday at euen
C. 5.116 And the *southweste* wynde on saturday At euene

souereyn *n soverain n.* A 4 soueraynes (1) souereyn (1) souereynes (2); B 4 souereyn (1) souereynes (1) Souereyns (2); C 4 souereyn (1) souereynes (2) souereyns (1)

A. 7.72 His sone hattiþ suffre þi *souereynes* to hauen here wille
A.10.72 Is chief *souereyn* ouer hymself his soule to ȝeme,
A.10.119 For þoruȝ suffrraunce se þou miȝt how *soueraynes* ariseþ,
A.11.291 And arn no[ne], forsoþe, *souereynes* in heuene
B. 6.80 His sone hiȝte Suffre-þi-*Souereyns*-to-hauen-hir-wille-
B.10.432 And now bén [swiche] as *Souereyns* wiþ Seintes in heuene,
B.12.200 As þo þat seten at þe syde table or wiþ þe *souereynes* of þe halle,
B.19.77 Or any kynnes catel; but knowelich[ede] hym *souereyn*
C. 8.82 His sone hihte soffre-thy-*souereynes*-haue-her-wille-
C.11.268 And now beth this seyntes, by that men saith, and *souereynes* in heuene,
C.14.139 As tho þat sitten at þe syde table or with þe *souereyns* [of þe] halle
C.21.77 Or eny kyne catel; bote knoweleched hym *souereyn*

souereyn *adj soverain adj.* A 1 souerayn; B 7 souerayn (1) souerayne (1) souereyn (5); C 5 souerayn (1) souerayne (1) souereyne (3)

A.11.158 For sorcerie is þe *souerayn* bok þat to þat science longiþ.
B.Pr.159 Seide for a *souereyn* [salue] to [hem alle].
B.10.211 For is no science vnder sonne so *souereyn* for þe soule.
B.10.215 For sorcerie is þe *Souereyn* book þat to [þat] Scienc[e] [l]ongeþ.
B.11.379 Suffraunce is a *souerayn* vertue, and a swift vengeaunce.
B.14.115 And after þow sendest hem somer þat is hir *souereyn* ioye
B.18.219 Sette hym in solace and in *souereyn* murþe,
B.20.372 That is þe *souerayn[e* salue for alle [synnes of kynde].
C. 1.147 And most *souerayne* salue for soule and for body.
C. 6.27 Semyng a *souerayn* oen whereso me byfull
C.15.291 [And] aftur thow sendest hem somer þat is here *souereyne* ioye
C.20.228 Sette hym in solace and in *souereyne* merthe
C.22.372 That is the *souereyne* salue for alle [synnes of kynde].

souereynly *adv soverainli adv.* A 1 souereynliche; B 3 souereynly (2) souereynliche (1); C 4 souereynly (1) souereynliche (3)

A.11.249 And *souereynliche* to suche þat sewen oure beleue:
B.10.207 And [*souereynly*] to swiche [þat] suwen oure beleue,
B.11.184 And [*souereynly*] pouere peple; hir preieres maye vs helpe.
B.15.528 And *souereynliche* to swiche þat of surrye bereþ þe name],
C. 6.92 For thy synnes *souereynly* and biseke god of mercy.'
C.13.201 So is soffrance *souereynliche*, so hit be for godes loue.
C.17.278 And *souereynliche* [to] suche þat of surie bereth þe name
C.20.394 Here eny synfole soule *souereynliche* by maistrie,

soware *n souere n.* C 1

C.18.225 Ne withoute a *soware* be suche seed; this we seen alle.

sowe *n soue n.(2)* B 2 sowe (1) sowes (1); C 2 sowe (1) sowes (1)

B. 5.340 Hise guttes bigonne to goþelen as two gredy *sowes*;
B.11.342 That wolde [bere] after bol[e], ne boor after *sowe*;
C. 6.398 His gottes gan to gothly as t[w]o g[re]dy *sowes*,
C.13.150 That wolde bere aftur bole ne boer aftur *sowe*;

sowe *v1 souen v.(1)* A 6 sowe (3) sowen (3); B 15 sew (7) sewe (1) sowe (5) sowen (1) ysowen (1); C 19 sewe (8) sowe (6) sowen (4) ysowed (1)

A. 6.29 Boþe *sowe* [and sette] while I swynke miȝte.
A. 6.31 Boþe *sowen* his seed, & sewide hise bestis,
A. 7.27 I shal swynken & sweten & *sowe* for vs boþe,
A. 7.58 For I wile *sowe* it myself, & siþþe wile I wende.
A. 7.127 Boþe to setten & to *sowen*, & sauen his telþe,
A. 8.6 And [alle] þat holpen to erien or to *sowen*,
B. 5.541 Boþe *sowe* and sette while I swynke miȝte,
B. 5.543 Boþe *ysowen* his seed and suwed hise beestes,
B. 5.546 Som tyme I *sowe* and som tyme I þresshe,
B. 6.5 Hadde I eryed þis half acre and *sowen* it after
B. 6.25 I shal swynke and swete and *sowe* for vs boþe,

B. 6.63	For I wol *sowe* it myself, and siþenes wol I wende
B. 7.6	And alle þat holpen to erye or to *sowe*,
B.13.374	To seise to me wiþ hir sikel þat I *sew* neuere.
B.15.365	By þe seed þat þei *sewe* what þei sel[l]e my3te,
B.19.275	And *sew* [it] in mannes soule and siþen tolde hir names.
B.19.289	The þridde seed þat Piers *sew* was Spiritus fortitudinis,
B.19.297	The ferþe seed þat Piers *sew* was Spiritus Iusticie.
B.19.309	Thise foure sedes Piers *sew*, and siþþe he dide hem harewe
B.19.343	[Th]e sedes [þat sire] Piers [*sew*], þe Cardynale vertues.
B.19.406	The chief seed þat Piers *sew*, ysaued worstow neuere.
C. 6.271	To sese to me wiþ here sikel þat y *sewe* neuere.
C. 7.186	Bothe to *sowe* and to sette þe while y swynke myhte.
C. 7.187	And to *sowen* his seed [and] suewen his bestes,
C. 8.3	Haued ich yered þis half aker and *ysowed* hit aftur
C. 8.24	'Y shal swynke and swete and *sowe* for vs bothe
C. 8.62	'For y wol *sowen* hit mysulf and sethe wol y wende
C. 9.6	And alle þat holpe hym to erye, to sette or to *sowe*
C.10.216	As an hewe þat erieth nat aun[t]reth hym to *sowe*
C.12.180	Bote if þe seed þat *sowen* is in the sloo sterue
C.12.187	A[c] sedes þat ben *sowen* and mowen soffre wyntres
C.12.189	Then sedes þat [in somer] *sowe* ben and mowen nat with forstes
C.15.211	Y am sory þat y *sowe* or sette but for mysulue.
C.17.102	By the seed þat they *sewe* what þey sulle myhte
C.21.275	And *sewe* hit in mannes soule and sethe toelde here names.
C.21.289	The thridde seed that [Peres] *sewe* was spiritus fortitudinis,
C.21.297	The ferthe seed that [Peres] *sewe* was spiritus Iusticie
C.21.309	Thise foure sedes [Peres] *sewe* and sennes he dede hem harewe
C.21.343	Þe sedes þat sire [Peres] *sewe*, þe cardinale vertues.
C.21.406	The cheef seed þat [Peres] *sewe*, ysaued wo[r]st þou neuere.

sowe v2 *seuen v.(2)* A 2 sewe (1) sewiþ (1); B 2; C 2

A. 7.9	'Summe shal *sewe* þe sak for shedyng of þe whete;
A. 7.19	Þat han silk & sendel, *sewiþ* it whanne tyme is,
B. 6.9	'Somme shul *sowe* þe sak for shedyng of þe Whete.
B. 6.11	That ye haue silk and Sandel to *sowe* whan tyme is
C. 8.8	'That somme *sowe* þe sak for shedynge of the whete,
C. 8.10	That 3e [han] selk and sendel to *sowe* whan tyme is

sowestere n *seuestre n.* A 1; B 1; C 1 sywestere

A. 5.158	Cisse þe so[wes]tere sat on þe bench,
B. 5.307	Cesse þe [*sowestere*] sat on þe benche,
C. 6.362	Sesse þe [*sywestere*] saet on þe benche,

sowyng ger *souinge ger.* A 2; B 2 sowyng (1) sowynge (1); C 1 sowynge

A.Pr.21	In settyng & *sowyng* swonken ful harde;
A. 8.104	I shal cesse of my *sowyng*,' quaþ peris, '& swynke not so harde,
B.Pr.21	In settynge and *sowynge* swonken ful harde;
B. 7.122	I shal cessen of my *sowyng*', quod Piers, '& swynke no3t so harde,
C.Pr.23	In settynge and *sowynge* swonken ful harde

sowl > soule; sowne > souneth; sowngewarie > songewarie

sowþe n *south n.(2) cf. south* B 1; C 3 southe

B.18.167	'That is sooþ', seide Mercy, 'and I se here by *Sowþe*
C. 1.117	'Hit is sikerore bi *southe* þer þe sonne regneth
C. 9.295	And seyh the sonne in the *sou[t]he* sitte þat tyme,
C.20.170	'That is soth,' saide mercy, 'and y se here bi *southe*

space n *space n.* A 1; B 2; C 1

A. 3.158	To haue *space* to speke, spede 3if she mi3te.
B. 3.171	To haue *space* to speke, spede if she my3te.
B. 9.100	To spille any speche or any *space* of tyme:
C. 3.217	To haue *space* to speke, spede yf a myhte.

spade n *spade n.* A 1 spadis; B 2 spade (1) spades (1); C 2 spade (1) spades (1)

A. 7.175	[A]n he[p] of heremites henten hem *spadis*,
B. 3.309	Ech man to pleye with a plow, Pykoise or *spade*,
B. 6.187	An heep of heremytes henten hem *spades*
C. 3.462	Vche man to pley with a plogh, a pikois oþer a *spade*,
C. 8.183	An heep of Eremytes henten hem *spades*,

spayne n prop *Spaine n.* B 1; C 1

B.15.521	In ynde, in alisaundre, in ermonye and *spayne*,
C.17.272	In ynde, in alisandre, in Armonye [and] *spayne*

spak(e > speken

spakliche adv *spakli adv.* B 2; C 1 spakeliche

B.17.84	And Spes *spakliche* hym spedde, spede if he my3te,
B.18.12	Wiþouten spores oþer spere; *spakliche* he lokede
C.20.10	Withouten spores oþer spere; *sp[a]keliche* he lokede

spare v *sparen v.* A 1 spariþ; B 11 spare (4) spared (4) sparen (1) spareþ (2); C 9 spare (6) sparede (1) spareth (2)

A. 7.11	Spynneþ it spedily, *spariþ* not 3oure fyngris
B. 3.51	'Wiste I þat', quod þ[e] womman 'I wolde no3t *spare*
B. 3.272	Spille it and *spare* it no3t, þow shalt spede þe bettre."

B. 3.273	And for he coueited hir catel and þe kyng *spared*,
B. 5.40	Whoso *spareþ* þe spryng spilleþ hise children.'
B. 5.373	And yspilt þat my3te be *spared* and spended on som hungry;
B.10.103	And al to *spare* to [spille þat spende] shal anoþer.
B.11.101	Þyng þat al þe world woot, wherfore sholdestow *spare*
B.12.51	And riche renkes ri3t so gaderen and *sparen*
B.15.143	And þat he *spared* and bisperede [s]pende we in murþe."
B.16.64	And egreliche he loked on me and þerfore I *spared*
B.19.302	Spiritus Iusticie *spareþ* no3t to spille [þe] gilty,
C. 3.425	Spille hit, *spare* hit nat and thow shalt spede th[e] bettere."
C. 3.426	And for a coueytede here catel and the kyng *sparede*,
C. 5.138	For hoso *spareth* the spry[n]g spilleth h[is] children;
C. 6.151	Amonges monkes y myhte be Ac mony tyme y *spare*
C. 9.74	Þat they with spynnyng may *spare* spenen hit [i]n hous huyre,
C.10.84	And helpeth alle men of þat he may *spare*.
C.12.35	Thyng þat al þe world woet wherfore sholdest thow *spare*
C.13.77	And spele and *spare* to spene vppon þe nedfole
C.21.302	Spiritus iusticie *spareth* nat to spille [the] gulty

sparynge ger *sparinge ger.* B 1; C 1 sparyng

B. 5.435	In speche and in *sparynge* of speche; yspilt many a tyme
C. 7.48	In speche and in *sparyng* of speche; yspilde many a tyme

speche n *speche n.* A 22; B 55; C 45

A.Pr.69	Lewide men leuide [hym] wel & likide his *speche*;
A. 2.23	Fauel wiþ fair *speche* haþ forgid hem togidere;
A. 2.118	For we haue mede amaistried wiþ oure mery *speche*
A. 2.130	And fauel vpon fair *speche*, fe[int]liche atirid.
A. 2.191	Freris wiþ fair *speche* fetten hym þennes;
A. 3.111	She is freel of hire feiþ, fikel of hire *speche*;
A. 4.17	And calde catoun his knaue, curteis of *speche*:
A. 6.40	He is as lou3 as a lomb & loueliche of *speche*.
A. 6.53	And so bo[wiþ] forþ be a [brok], be buxum of *speche*,
A. 8.49	Ac he þat spendiþ his *speche* & spekiþ for þe pore
A. 9.71	Whoso is mek of his mouþ, mylde of his *speche*,
A. 9.77	He is as lou3 as a lomb, louelich of *speche*,
A. 9.112	Sad of his semblaunt & of a softe *speche*,
A.10.34	And al at his wil was wrou3t wiþ a *speche*,
A.10.53	Of good *speche* & [going] he is þe begynnere;
A.10.83	Þat he makiþ men meke & mylde of here *speche*,
A.11.104	'For þi meknesse, man,' quaþ she, 'and for þi mylde *speche*
A.11.121	F[ro] lesinges & li[þer] *speche* & likerous drinkes.
A.11.122	Þanne shalt þou se sobirte, & simplite of *speche*;
A.11.156	Geometrie & geomesie is gynful of *speche*;
A.11.241	For cristene han a degre & is þe comun *speche*:
A.12.100	Þat þis *speche* was spedelich, and sped him wel faste,
B.Pr.52	Moore þan to seye sooþ, it semed bi hire *speche*.
B.Pr.72	Lewed men leued [hym] wel and liked hi[s *speche*];
B. 2.42	Fauel þoru3 his faire *speche* haþ þis folk enchaunted,
B. 2.79	And Fauel wiþ his fikel *speche* feffeþ by þis chartre
B. 2.154	For we haue Mede amaistried wiþ oure murie *speche*
B. 2.166	And Fauel on [Fair *Speche*] fe[ynt]ly atired.
B. 2.232	Freres wiþ fair *speche* fetten hym þennes;
B. 3.122	She is frele of hire feiþ, fikel of hire *speche*;
B. 4.17	And called Caton his knaue, curteis of *speche*,
B. 4.156	I falle in floryns', quod þat freke, 'and faile *speche* ofte.'
B. 5.100	That boþe lif and lyme is lost þoru3 my *speche*.
B. 5.140	Til þei beere leues of lowe *speche* lordes to plese,
B. 5.183	Counseil þat þow knowest by contenaunce ne by [*speche*],
B. 5.435	In speche and in sparynge of *speche*; yspilt many a tyme
B. 5.435	In *speche* and in sparynge of speche; yspilt many a tyme
B. 5.553	He is as lowe as a lomb and louelich of *speche*.
B. 5.566	And so boweþ forþ by a brook, beþ-buxom-of-*speche*,
B. 7.47	Ac he þat spendeþ his *speche* and spekeþ for þe pouere
B. 8.80	Whoso is [meke of his mouþ, milde of his *speche*],
B. 8.86	He is as lowe as a lomb, louelich of *speche*;
B. 8.112	Sad of his semblaunt and of [a] softe [*speche*].
B. 9.33	[And al at his wil was wrou3t wiþ a *speche*],
B. 9.38	My my3t moot helpe forþ wiþ my *speche*".
B. 9.100	To spille any *speche* or any space of tyme:
B. 9.103	And siþþe to spille *speche* þat [spire] is of grace
B.10.152	'For þi mekenesse, man', quod she, 'and for þi mylde *speche*
B.10.169	Fro-lesynges-and-liþer-*speche*-and-likerouse-drynkes.
B.10.170	Thanne shaltow se Sobretee and Sympletee-of-*speche*,
B.10.213	Geometrie and Geomesie [is] gynful of *speche*;
B.10.455	And my3te no kyng ouercomen hym as by konnynge of *speche*.
B.11.4	Tho wepte I for wo and wraþe of hir *speche*
B.11.69	And loued me þe lasse for my lele *speche*.
B.11.420	And ri3t so ferde Reson bi þee; þow wiþ rude *speche*
B.13.144	Cast coles on his heed of alle kynde *speche*;
B.13.150	Kynde loue coueiteþ no3t no catel but *speche*.
B.13.217	Sobretee and symple *speche* and sooþfast bileue;
B.13.275	Of pride here a plot, and þere a plot of vnbuxom *speche*,
B.13.301	And as a lyoun on to loke and lordlich of *speche*;

B.13.321 Wiþ enuye and yuel *speche* entisynge to fighte,
B.13.400 And foule beflobered it, as wiþ fals *speche*,
B.14.13   That I ne soiled it wiþ siȝte or som ydel *speche*.
B.14.228 [For lowliche he lokeþ, and louelich is his *speche*
B.15.46   And of [myne] if þow myȝtest, me þynkeþ by þi *speche*.'
B.15.218 The loue þat liþ in his herte makeþ hym liȝt of *speche*,
B.15.351 And so it fareþ by som folk now; þei han a fair *speche*,
B.16.7   The blosmes beþ buxom *speche* and benigne lokynge.
B.16.154 'Falsnesse I fynde in þi faire *speche*
B.18.116 A ful benigne burde and Buxom of *speche*.
B.18.129 Of any kynnes creature, conceyued þoruȝ *speche*
B.18.231 Book highte þat beaupeere, a bold man of *speche*.
B.19.93   For Mirre is mercy to mene and mylde *speche* of tonge.
B.19.286 Waste word of ydelnesse ne wikked *speche* moeue;
B.20.115 And wiþ pryuee *speche* and peyntede wordes,
B.20.348 Hende *speche* heet pees, 'opene þe yates.
B.20.354 Thus þoruȝ hende *speche* [þe frere entred]
C.2.45   Fauel thorw his flaterynge *speche* hath mede foule enchaunted,
C.2.86   And fauel þat hath a fals *speche* Feffeth hem by þis lettre
C.2.104   With spiserye, speke ydelnesse in vayne *spe[ch]e* and spene
C.2.170   For we haue mede amaystred [with] oure mery [*speche*]
C.2.242   Freres [with] fayre *speche* fetten hym thennes,
C.3.109   For to spyre and to aspye, for eny *speche* of suluer,
C.3.159   For she [is] frele of here fayth, fikel of here *speche*
C.4.17   And kalde Catoun his knaue, Corteys of *speche*,
C.4.138   Ne gete my grace thorw eny gyfte ne glosynge *spe[ch]e*
C.4.149   In signe þat thei sholde with som sotil *speche*
C.4.153   Resoun for his ryhtful *speche*; ryche and pore hym louede
C.6.165   Consayl þat thow knowest by continaunce ne by *speche*.
C.6.186   Of put[rie] and of paramours and proueden thorw *speche*
C.7.48   In *speche* and in sparyng of speche; yspilde many a tyme
C.7.48   In speche and in sparyng of *speche*; yspilde many a tyme
C.7.213   And so [boweth] forth by [a] brok, [beth-buxum-of-*speche*],
C.7.238   With no leed but with loue and with lele *speche*;
C.8.215   'Ther is no fi[al] loue with this folk for al here fayre *speche*
C.9.46   Ac he [that] speneth his *speche* and speketh for þe pore
C.10.56   'Y haue no kynde kno[w]yng,' [quod y], 'to conseyue al this *speche*
C.10.83   He is [as] logh as a lomb and loueliche of *speche*
C.10.118 Sad of his semblant and with a softe *speche*.
C.10.186 Ne spille *speche* ne tyme ne myspende noyther
C.11.20   Thorw fallas and fals questes and thorw fikel *speche*.
C.11.90   'For thy mekenesse, [man],' quod she, 'and for thy mylde *speche*
C.11.280 And myhte no kyng ouercome hym as in connynge of *speche*.
C.13.228 Rihte so ferde Resoun by the; for thy rude *speche*
C.14.7   Ne to spille *speche*, As to speke an ydel,
C.15.142 Caste coles on his heued of alle kyn[de] *speche*,
C.15.145 Conforte hym with thy catel and with thy kynde *speche*;
C.15.186 Sobrete [and] symple *speche* and sothfaste bileue
C.15.273 'Meeknesse and mylde *speche* and men of o will,
C.16.69   For lo[w]lyche he loketh and lo[uelych]e is his *speche*
C.16.208 And of myn yf thow myhtes[t], me thynketh by thy *speche*.'
C.18.11   The whiche blosmes buirnes benigne *speche* hit calleth.
C.18.171 'Falsnesse y fynde in thy fayre *speche*
C.18.188 O *speche* and [o] spirit Springeth out of alle;
C.20.119 A fol benyngne buyrde and buxum of *speche*.
C.20.132 Of eny kyn[nes] creature, conceyued thorw *speche*
C.20.240 Boek hihte þat beaupere, a bolde man of *speche*.
C.21.93   For Mirre is mercy to mene and mylde *speche* of tonge.
C.21.286 Wast[e] word of ydelnesse ne wikede *speche* meue;
C.22.115 And with priue *speche* and paynted wordes
C.22.348 Hende *speche* heet pees, 'opene þe ȝates.
C.22.354 Thus thorw hende *speche* [the frere entred]

specheles adj *specheles adj.* B 1; C 1
B.15.36   Thanne am I spirit *specheles*; Spiritus þanne ich hatte.
C.16.198 Thenne am [y] spirit *specheles*; spiritus then y hote.

special adj *speciale adj.* B 1; C 1
B.19.30   Ac to be conquerour called, þat comeþ of *special* grace,
C.21.30   Ac to be conquerour cald, þat cometh of *special* grace

spede v *speden v.* A 3 sped (1) spede (2); B 7 spedde (1) spede (6); C 7 spedde (1) spede (6)
A.3.158   To haue space to speke, *spede* ȝif she miȝte.
A.7.44   And mysbede nouȝt þi bondemen, þe bet shalt þou *spede*;
A.12.100 Þat þis speche was spedelich, and *sped* him wel faste,
B.3.171   To haue space to speke, *spede* if she myȝte.
B.3.272   Spille it and spare it noȝt, þow shalt *spede* þe bettre."
B.5.592   The brugg[e] is of bidde-wel-þe-bet-may-þow-*spede*;
B.6.45   And mysbede noȝt þi bondem[a]n, þe bettre [shalt] þow *spede*.
B.17.84   And Spes spakliche hym *spedde*, spede if he myȝte,
B.17.84   And Spes spakliche hym spedde, *spede* if he myȝte,
B.20.55   And [made] fals sprynge and sprede and *spede* mennes nedes.
C.3.217   To haue space to speke, *spede* yf a myhte.

C.3.425   Spille hit, spare hit nat and thow shalt *spede* th[e] bettere."
C.7.240   The Brygge hatte b[id]-wel-þe-bet-may-th[ow]-*spede*;
C.8.42   Misbede nat thy bondeman, the bette may th[ow] *spede*;
C.10.108 'Ac ȝut sauereth [me nat] thy sawes, so me Crist *spede*!
C.13.24   Spryngeth and spredeth, so spedde þe fader Abraham
C.22.55   And made fals sprynge and sprede and *spe[d]e* menne nedes.

spedelich adj *spedeli adj.* A 1
A.12.100 Þat þis speche was *spedelich*, and sped him wel faste,

spedily adv *spedili adv.* A 1
A.7.11   Spynneþ it *spedily*, spariþ not ȝoure fyngris

speken v *speken v.* A 6 spak (3) speke (2) spekiþ (1); B 34 spak (10) spek (11) speke (11) spoken (4) spekest (1) spekeþ (7); C 30 spak (7) spake (2) speke (13) spoken (1) spekest (1) speketh (6)
A.1.47   And he askide of hem of whom *spak* þe lettre,
A.2.187   Spiceris *speke* wiþ h[i]m to aspie here ware,
A.3.158   To haue space to *speke*, spede ȝif she miȝte.
A.5.130   And *spak* to þe spynstere to spynnen it softe.
A.5.204   Þe ferste woord þat he *spak* was 'where is þe bolle?'
A.8.49   Ac he þat spendiþ his speche & *spekiþ* for þe pore
B.Pr.111 Forþi I kan & kan nauȝt of court *speke* moore.
B.Pr.129 Lowed to *speke* in latyn, for lewed men ne koude
B.1.49   And [he] asked of h[e]m of whom *spak* þe lettre,
B.2.228   Spycers *speken* with hym to spien hire ware
B.3.171   To haue space to *speke*, spede if she myȝte.
B.5.149   Thus þei *spoken* of spiritualte þat eiþer despiseþ ooþer
B.5.214   [And] *spak* to [þe] Spynnester[e] to spynnen it [softe].
B.5.362   The firste word þat he [*spak*] was 'where is þe bolle?'
B.7.47   Ac he þat spendeþ his speche and *spekeþ* for þe pouere
B.10.41   Spitten and spuen and *speke* foule wordes,
B.10.454 Dauid makeþ mencion, he *spak* amonges kynges,
B.11.287 Spera in deo *spekeþ* of preestes þat haue no spendyng siluer,
B.11.417 Adam, whiles he *spak* noȝt, hadde paradis at wille,
B.12.143 He *spekeþ* þere of riche men riȝt noȝt, ne of riȝt witty,
B.12.192 The þef þat hadde grace of god on good fryday, as þow *spek[e]*,
B.13.24   And for Conscience of Clergie *spak* I com wel þe raþer.
B.13.132 He wol noȝt ayein holy writ *speken*, I dar vndertake.'
B.13.180 'Frendes, fareþ wel', and faire *spak* to clergie,
B.14.85   And þou a man myȝte noȝt *speke* contricion myȝte hym saue
B.14.99   [Wye] þat wiþ hym *spak*, as wide as I haue passed.'
B.15.54   Ayein swiche Salomon *spekeþ* and despiseþ hir wittes
B.15.56   To englisshe men þis is to mene, þat mowen *speke* and here,
B.15.275 In spekes and spelonkes; selde *spoken* togideres.
B.15.574 Ac ysaie of yow *spekeþ* and oȝias boþe,
B.15.611 Til þei kouþe *speke* and spelle et in Spiritum sanctum,
B.16.90   And þanne *spak* spiritus sanctus in Gabrielis mouþe
B.17.35   And now com[s]eþ Spes and *spekeþ*, þat [haþ] aspied þe lawe,
B.18.262 A spirit *spekeþ* to helle and biddeþ vnspere þe yates:
B.19.70   Faithly for to *speke*, his firste name was Iesus.
B.19.80   And þere was þat word fulfilled þe which þow of *speke*,
B.19.130 For deue þoruȝ hise doynges and dombe [and herde],
B.19.340 And his Spye Spille-loue, oon *Spek*-yuel-bihynde.
B.19.373 Saue sherewes one swiche as I *spak* of,
B.19.402 Of Spiritus Iusticie þow *spekest* muche on ydel.'
C.2.104   With spiserye, *speke* ydelnesse in vayne spe[ch]e and spene
C.2.238   Spysours *spoken* to hym to aspye he[re] ware
C.3.217   To haue space to *speke*, spede yf a myhte.
C.3.463   Spynne oþer *speke* of god and spille no tyme.
C.4.44   And *speke* wyse wordes a longe while togederes.
C.6.122   Thus thei *speke* and dispute þat vchon dispiseth oþer.
C.6.222   [And] *spak* to þe spynnester[e] to spynnen [hit] oute.
C.6.420   The furste [word] þat he *spake* was '[wh]o halt þe bolle?'
C.6.432   And spilde þat y aspele myhte; y kan nat *speke* for shame
C.9.46   Ac he [that] speneth his speche and *speketh* for þe pore
C.11.279 Dauid maketh mensioun he *spake* among kynges
C.13.101 For spera in deo *speketh* of prestis þat han no spendynge suluer
C.13.225 Adam, whiles he *spak* nat, hadde paradys at wille
C.14.7   Ne to spille speche, Ne to *speke* an ydel,
C.14.87   Hit *speketh* þer of ryche men riht nouht ne of ryche lordes
C.15.152 [And] pacience properliche *spak*, tho Peres was thus ypassed,
C.16.36   And bote these thre þat y *spak* of at domesday vs defende
C.16.216 Aȝenes suche salamon *speketh* and despiseth here wittes
C.16.218 To engelische men this is to mene, þat mowen *speke* and here,
C.17.319 Til they couthe *speke* and spele et in spiritum sanctum,
C.18.123 And thenne *spak* spiritus sanctus in gabrieles mouthe
C.18.230 Sprang forth and *spak*, a spyer of hem tweyne,
C.19.36   And now cometh this sp[es and *speketh*] that hath aspyed þe lawe,
C.20.270 A spirit *speketh* to helle and bit vnspere þe ȝates:
C.21.70   Faythly for to *speke* his furste name was iesus.
C.21.80   And þer was þat word fulfuld þe which þou of *speke*,
C.21.130 For deue thorw his doynges and dombe *speke* [&] herde
C.21.340 And his spye spille-loue, oen *speke*-euele-bihynde.

C.21.373 [Saue shrewes one swiche as y *spak* of],
C.21.402 Of spiritus Iusticie thow *spekest* moche an ydel.'

spekes n *speke n.(1)* B 1
B.15.275 In *spekes* and spelonkes; selde speken togideres.

spele v *spelen v. &> spelle* C 1
C.13.77 And *spele* and spare to spene vppon þe nedfole

spelle v *pellen v.(1)* B 1; C 1 spele
B.15.611 Til þei kouþe speke and *spelle* et in Spiritum sanctum,
C.17.319 Til they couthe speke and *spele* et in spiritum sanctum,

spelonkes n *spelunke n.* B 1
B.15.275 In spekes and *spelonkes*; selde speken togideres.

spences n *spense n.(1)* B 1; C 1 spensis
B.14.198 But oure *spences* and spendynge sprynge of a trewe w[e]lle;
C.16.39 Bote oure *spensis* and spendyng sprynge of a trewe welle

spende v *spenden v.* A 2 spende (1) spendiþ (1); B 12 spende (7) spended (2) spenden (2) spendeþ (2); C 13 spenden (1) spene (9) spenen (1) speneth (1) yspened (1)
A. 7.209 Þat nedy ben or nakid, & nouȝt han to *spende*,
A. 8.49 Ac he þat *spendiþ* his speche & spekiþ for þe pore
B. 5.373 And yspilt þat myȝte be spared and *spended* on som hungry;
B. 6.223 That nedy ben [or naked, and nouȝt han to *spende*,
B. 7.47 Ac he þat *spendeþ* his speche and spekeþ for þe pouere
B.10.90 Whoso haþ muche *spende* manliche, so [meneþ] Tobye,
B.10.103 And al to spare to [spille þat *spende*] shal anoþer.
B.11.294 For made neuere kyng no knyȝt but he hadde catel to *spende*
B.15.77 As wel freres as ooþer folk, foliliche *spenden*
B.15.133 [This] þat wiþ gile was geten vngraciousliche is [*s]pended*.
B.15.143 And þe spared and bisperede [*s]pende* we in murþe."
B.15.144 By lered, by lewed, þat looþ is to [*s]pende*
B.15.329 For þat þei beggen aboute in buyldynge þei *spende*,
B.17.80 'What he *spendeþ* moore [for medicyne] I make þee good herafter,
C. 2.104 With spiserye, speke ydelnesse in vayne spe[ch]e and *spene*
C. 5.28 A spendour þat *spene* mot or a spilletyme–
C. 5.64 Redon and resceyuen þat resoun ouhte to *spene*
C. 9.46 Ac he [that] *speneth* his speche and speketh for þe pore
C. 9.74 Þat they with spynnyng may spare *spenen* hit [i]n hous huyre,
C.11.75 Bote lythen how þey myhte lerne leest go[e]d *spene*.
C.12.216 An vnredy reue thy residue shal *spene*
C.13.77 And spele and spare to *spene* vppon þe nedfole
C.13.108 For made neuere kyng no knyhte but he hadde catel to *spene*
C.15.278 Then rihtfu[l] rychesse and bisperede resonablelyche to *spene*?'
C.16.236 As wel freres as oþere folk, foliliche *spenden*
C.16.280 And þat with gyle was gete vngraciousliche be *yspened*.
C.17.72 Prestes on aparayl and on purnele now *spene*.

spendyng ger *spendinge ger.* B 3 spendyng (2) spendynge (1); C 2 spendyng (1) spendynge (1)
B.11.287 Spera in deo spekeþ of preestes þat haue no *spendyng* siluer,
B.14.198 But oure spences and *spendynge* sprynge of a trewe w[e]lle;
B.15.126 Hadde he neuere [saued] siluer þerto [for *spendyng* at ale];
C.13.101 For spera in deo speketh of prestis þat han no *spendynge* suluer
C.16.39 Bote oure spensis and *spendyng* sprynge of a trewe welle

spendour n *spendere n.* C 1
C. 5.28 A *spendour* þat spene mot or a spilletyme–

spene(- > spende; spensis > spences

spere n *spere n.(1) &> spire* B 3; C 3
B.18.12 Wiþouten spores oþer *spere*; spakliche he lokede
B.18.78 Ac þer cam forþ a knyȝt wiþ a kene *spere* ygrounde,
B.18.86 The blood sprong doun by þe *spere* and vnspered [his] eiȝen.
C.20.10 Withouten spores oþer *spere*; sp[a]keliche he lokede
C.20.80 Ac þer cam forth a knyhte with a kene *spere* ygrounde,
C.20.88 The bleed sprang down by the *spere* and vnspered [his] yes.

sperhauk n *sparhauk n.* B 1
B. 6.196 And what Piers preide hem to do as prest as a *Sperhauk*.

spice n *spice n.(1)* A 1 spices; B 2 spice (1) spices (1); C 1 spyces
A. 5.153 'Hast þou,' quaþ he, 'any hote *spices*?'
B. 1.149 May no synne be on hym seene þat vseþ þat *spice*,
B. 5.303 'Hastow', quod he, 'any hote *spices*?'
C. 6.358 'Hastow,' quod he, 'eny hote *spyces*?'

spicede ptp *spicen v.* B 1; C 1 spyced
B.19.288 Ne no mete in his mouþ þat maister Iohan *Spicede*.
C.21.288 Ne no mete in his mouth þat maistre iohann *spyced*.

spycers n *spicer n.* A 2 spiceris; B 1; C 1 spysours
A. 2.187 *Spiceris* speke wiþ h[i]m to aspie here ware,
A.10.125 Springeþ & sprediþ, þat *spiceris* desiriþ,
B. 2.228 *Spycers* speken with hym to spien hire ware

C. 2.238 *Spysours* speken to hym to aspye he[re] ware

spie n *spie n.* B 2 spie (1) Spye (1); C 2 spie (1) spye (1)
B.17.1 'I am Spes, [a *spie*', quod he], 'and spire after a Knyght
B.19.340 And his *Spye* Spille-loue, oon Spek-yuel-bihynde.
C.19.1 'I am spes, a *spie*,' quod he, 'and spere aftur a knyȝte
C.21.340 And his *spye* spille-loue, oen speke-euele-bihynde.

spiek n *spike n.(2)* C 1
C.12.181 Shal neuere spir sprynge vp ne *spiek* on straw kerne;

spien v *spien v.(1)* B 1
B. 2.228 Spycers speken with hym to *spien* hire ware

spyer n *spire n.(2) cf. spire* C 1
C.18.230 Sprang forth and spak, a *spyer* of hem tweyne,

spille v *spillen v.* B 12 spille (8) spillen (1) spilleþ (1) yspilt (2); C 12 spilde (1) spille (9) spilleth (1) yspilde (1)
B. 3.272 *Spille* it and spare it noȝt, þow shalt spede þe bettre."
B. 3.310 Spynne or sprede donge or *spille* hymself with sleuþe.
B. 5.40 Whoso spareþ þe spryng *spilleþ* hise children.'
B. 5.373 And *yspilt* þat myȝte be spared and spended on som hungry;
B. 5.435 In speche and in sparynge of speche; *yspilt* many a tyme
B. 9.100 To *spille* any speche or any space of tyme:
B. 9.103 And siþþe to *spille* speche þat [spire] is of grace
B.10.103 And al to spare to [*spille* þat spende] shal anoþer.
B.15.135 A[c] goddes folk for defaute þerof forfaren and *spillen*.
B.19.302 Spiritus Iusticie spareþ noȝt to *spille* [þe] gilty.
B.19.340 And his Spye *Spille*-loue, oon Spek-yuel-bihynde.
B.19.445 And fynt folk to fiȝte and cristen blood to *spille*
C. 3.425 *Spille* hit, spare hit nat and thow shalt spede th[e] bettre."
C. 3.463 Spynne oþer speke of god and *spille* no tyme.
C. 5.127 Thorw som trewe trauail and no tyme *spille*.
C. 5.138 For hoso spareth the spry[n]g *spilleth* h[is] children;
C. 6.432 And *spilde* þat y aspele myhte; y kan nat speke for shame
C. 7.48 In speche and in sparyng of speche; *yspilde* many a tyme
C.10.186 Ne *spille* speche ne tyme ne myspende noyther
C.11.41 Bothe afyngred and afurst, and for defaute *spille*;
C.14.7 Ne to *spille* speche, As to speke an ydel,
C.21.302 Spiritus iusticie spareth nat to *spille* [the] gulty
C.21.340 And his spye *spille*-loue, oen speke-euele-bihynde.
C.21.445 And fynde[th] folke to fihte and cristene bloed to *spille*

spilletyme n *spillen v.* C 1
C. 5.28 A spendour þat spene mot or a *spilletyme*–

spynnen v *spinnen v.* A 2 spynnen (1) spynneþ (1); B 3 spynne (1) spynnen (1) spynneþ (1); C 3 spynne (1) spynnen (1) spynneth (1)
A. 5.130 And spak to þe spynstere to *spynnen* it softe.
A. 7.11 *Spynneþ* it spedily, spariþ not ȝoure fyngris
B. 3.310 *Spynne* or sprede donge or spille hymself with sleuþe.
B. 5.214 [And] spak to [þe] Spynnester[e] to *spynnen* it [softe].
B. 6.13 Wyues and widewes wolle and flex *spynneþ*;
C. 3.463 *Spynne* oþer speke of god and spille no tyme.
C. 6.222 [And] spak to þe spynnester[e] to *spynnen* [hit] oute.
C. 8.12 Wyue[s] and wyddewes wolle an[d] flex *spynneth*;

spynnestere n *spinnestre n.* A 1 spynstere; B 1; C 1
A. 5.130 And spak to þe *spynstere* to spynnen it softe.
B. 5.214 [And] spak to [þe] *Spynnester[e]* to spynnen it [softe].
C. 6.222 [And] spak to þe *spynnester[e]* to spynnen [hit] oute.

spynnyng ger *spinninge ger.* C 1
C. 9.74 Þat they with *spynnyng* may spare spenen hit [i]n hous huyre,

spynstere > spynnestere

spire n *spire n.(1)* B 1; C 1 spir
B. 9.103 And siþþe to spille speche þat [*spire*] is of grace
C.12.181 Shal neuere *spir* sprynge vp ne spiek on straw kerne;

spire v *spiren v.(1)* B 1; C 2 spere (1) spyre (1)
B.17.1 'I am Spes, [a spie', quod he], 'and *spire* after a Knyght
C. 3.109 For to *spyre* and to aspye, for eny speche of suluer,
C.19.1 'I am spes, a spie,' quod he, 'and *spere* aftur a knyȝte

spirit n *spirit n.* B 9; C 13
B.12.102 And seint *Spirit* þe Samplarie, & seide what men sholde write.
B.15.36 Thanne am I *spirit* spechelees; Spiritus þanne ich hatte.
B.17.161 Right so þe fader and þe sone and Seint *Spirit* þe þridde
B.17.199 That whoso synneþ in þe Seint *Spirit* assoilled worþ he neuere,
B.17.204 So whoso synneþ in þe Seint *Spirit*, it semeþ þat he greueþ
B.17.224 Na moore dooþ sire ne sone ne seint *spirit* togidres
B.17.287 Synnen ayein þe Seint *Spirit*, assenten to destruye
B.17.300 And now am sory þat I so þe Seint *Spirit* agulte,
B.18.262 A *spirit* spekeþ to helle and biddeþ vnspere þe yates:
C.11.151 That he seyh þe [syre] and þe sone and þe seynt *spirit* togederes

spirit

C.14.47　And seynt *spirit* þe saumplarie and said what men sholde wryte.
C.16.198　Thenne am [y] *spirit* spechelees; spiritus then y hote.
C.18.72　The whiche þe seynt *spirit* seweth, the sonne of al heuene,
C.18.188　O speche and [o] *spirit* Springeth out of alle;
C.18.231　So oute of þe syre and of þe sone þe seynt *spirit* of hem bothe
C.19.165　That hoso synegeth in þe seynt *spirit* assoiled worth he neuere,
C.19.170　So hoso synegeth aзeyn þe seynt *spirit* hit semeth þat he greueth
C.19.178　So doth þe sire and sone and seynt *spirit* togyderes
C.19.190　No more doth sire ne sone ne seynt *spirit* togydere
C.19.268　Synegen aзen þe seynte *spirit*, assente to destruye
C.19.280　And now am sory þat y so the seynte *spirit* agulte,
C.20.270　A *spirit* speketh to helle and bit vnspere þe зates:

spiritual adj *spiritual adj.*　B 1

B.14.285　And Ioye to pacient pouere], pure *spiritual* helþe,

spiritualte n *spiritualite*　B 2; C 1

B. 5.149　Thus þei speken of *spiritualte* þat eiþer despiseþ ooþer
B. 5.150　Til þei be boþe beggers and by my *spiritualte* libben,
C. 6.125　Or til they bothe be beggares and by [my] *spiritual[t]e* libbe

spiserye n *spicerie n.*　C 1

C. 2.104　With *spiserye*, speke ydelnesse in vayne spe[ch]e and spene

spysours > spycers

spitteden v *spitten v.(2)*　C 1

C. 8.184　*Sp[it]teden* and spradden donge in dispit of hunger.

spitten v *spitten v.(1)*　B 1

B.10.41　*Spitten* and spuen and speke foule wordes,

spores n *spore n.(2)*　B 2; C 2

B.18.12　Wiþouten *spores* oþer spere; spakliche he lokede
B.18.14　To geten hym gilte *spores* [and] galoches ycouped.
C.20.10　Withouten *spores* oþer spere; sp[a]keliche he lokede
C.20.12　To geten h[ym] gult *spores* and galoches ycouped.

spottes n *spot n.(1)*　B 1

B.13.314　Haþ manye moles and *spottes*; it moste ben ywasshe.'

spouse n *spouse n.*　C 1

C.13.11　Ne for brihtnesse of here beaute here *spouse* to be byknowe.

spousid v *spousen v.*　A 2 spousid (1) spouside (1)

A.10.159　And siþen se[þ] & his suster [sed] wern *spousid* to kaymes;
A.10.179　And al for se[þ] & his sister children *spouside* eiþer oþer,

spradden > sprede; sprang > sprynge

sprede v *spreden v.*　A 1 sprediþ; B 3 sprede (2) spredeþ (1); C 5 spradden (1) sprede (1) spredeth (3)

A.10.125　Springeþ & *sprediþ*, þat spiceris desiriþ,
B. 3.310　Spynne or *sprede* donge or spille hymself with sleuþe.
B.15.94　Right so out of holi chirche alle yueles [*spredeþ*]
B.20.55　And [made] fals sprynge and *sprede* and spede mennes nedes.
C. 8.184　Sp[it]teden and *spradden* donge in dispit of hunger.
C.13.24　Spryngeth and *spredeth*, so spedde þe fader Abraham
C.16.244　Spryngeth and *spredeth* and enspireth þe peple
C.16.246　Riht [so] oute of holy churche al euel *spredeth*
C.22.55　And made fals sprynge and *sprede* and spe[d]e menne nedes.

spryng n *spring n.*　B 1; C 1

B. 5.40　Whoso spareþ þe *spryng* spilleþ hise children.'
C. 5.138　For hoso spareth the *spry[n]g* spilleth h[is] children;

sprynge v *springen v.*　A 2 springe (1) springeþ (1); B 10 sprynge (3) spryngeþ (2) sprong (2) spronge (2) yspronge (1); C 15 sprang (2) sprynge (5) Springeth (1) Spryngeth (2) sponge (4) ysronge (1)

A.10.125　*Springeþ* & spredeþ, þat spiceris desiriþ,
A.10.127　So dobest out of dobet & dowel gynneþ *springe*
B.11.201　For [at] Caluarie of cristes blood cristendom gan *sprynge*,
B.12.68　Ac grace is a gifte of god and of greet loue *spryngeþ*;
B.14.65　And out of þe flynt *sprong* þe flood þat folk and beestes dronken.
B.14.198　But oure spences and spendynge *sprynge* of a trewe w[e]lle
B.15.92　As holynesse and honeste out of holy chirche [*spryngeþ*]
B.16.196　To ocupie hym here til issue were *spronge*,
B.16.209　And þus is mankynde and manhede of matrimoyne *yspronge*
B.18.86　The blood *sprong* doun by þe spere and vnspered [his] eiзen.
B.19.150　That Aungeles and Archaungeles, er þe day *spronge*,
B.20.55　And [made] fals *sprynge* and sprede and spede mennes nedes.
C.10.227　Clene awey þe corsed bloed þat of Caym *spronge*.
C.10.260　A mayde and wel yma[ner]ed and of gode men *yspronge*,
C.12.109　A[t] Caluarie of cristis bloed cristendoem gan *sprynge*
C.12.181　Shal neuere spir *sprynge* vp ne spiek on straw kerne;
C.13.24　*Spryngeth* and spredeth, so spedde þe fader Abraham
C.14.27　And sent forth the seynt espirit to do loue *sprynge*:
C.15.264　And oute of þe flynt *spronge* þe floed þat folk and bestes dronke.
C.16.39　Bote oure spensis and spendyng *sprynge* of a trewe welle

spryngeth and spredeth and enspireth þe peple

C.16.244　*Spryngeth* and spredeth and enspireth þe peple
C.18.188　O speche and [o] spirit *Springeth* out of alle;
C.18.205　To ocupien hym here til issue were *sprong*e
C.18.230　*Sprang* forth and spak, a spyer of hem tweyne,
C.20.88　The bloed *sprang* down by the spere and vnspered [his] yes.
C.21.150　That Angeles and Archangeles, ar the day *spronge*,
C.22.55　And made fals *sprynge* and sprede and spe[d]e menne nedes.

spuen v *speuen v.*　B 1

B.10.41　Spitten and *spuen* and speke foule wordes,

squier n1 *squire n.*　C 2 squier (1) squieres (1)

C.Pr.181　And colers of crafty werk, bothe knyghte[s] and *squieres*.
C.10.266　Ther ne is *squier* ne knyhte in contreye aboute

squire n2 *square n.*　C 1

C.11.124　And caste [mette] by *squire* bothe lyne and leuele.

sship > ship

stable adj *stable adj.*　A 1

A.10.114　Hold þe *stable* & stedefast & strengþe þiseluen

stable v *stablen v.(1)*　B 1

B. 1.123　And [*stable* and stynte] and stonden in quiete.

staf n *staf n.*　A 3 staf (1) staues (2); B 6 staf (3) staues (3); C 5 staf (3) staues (2)

A.Pr.50　Ermytes on an hep, wiþ hokide *staues*,
A. 5.28　Thomas he tauзte to take two *staues*
A. 5.193　He hadde no strengþe to stonde er he his *staf* hadde,
B.Pr.53　Heremytes on an heep with hoked *staues*
B. 5.28　Tomme Stowue he tauзte to take two *staues*
B. 5.345　He [hadde no strengþe to] stonde er he his *staf* hadde,
B.12.14　Alþouз þow strike me wiþ þi *staf*, wiþ stikke or wiþ yerde,
B.17.39　The gome þat gooþ wiþ o *staf*, he semeþ in gretter heele
B.17.40　Than he þat gooþ wiþ two *staues* to sighte of vs alle;
C.Pr.51　Eremites on an hep with hokede *staues*
C. 5.130　Tomme stoue he tauhte to take t[w]o *staues*
C. 6.106　Bothe with stoon and with *staf* and stele vppon myn enemye;
C. 6.403　He myhte noþer steppe ne stande til he a *staf* hadde
C.14.42　To strike with stoen or with *staf* this strompet to dethe."

stake n *stake n.*　C 1

C. 3.381　Bote standynge as a *stake* þat stikede in a mere

stale > stele

stalke n *stalke n.*　C 1

C.18.39　And al forb[i]t Caritas rihte to þe bare *stalke*.

stalles n *stalle n.*　B 1; C 1

B.16.128　And knokked on hem wiþ a corde, and caste adoun hir *stalles*
C.18.156　And ouerturnede in þe temple here tables and here *stalles*

stalworþe adj *stalworth adj.*　B 1

B.17.99　He sholde stonde and steppe; ac *stalworþe* worþ he neuere

stand(- > stonden

stank v *stinken v.*　B 1

B.15.594　And vnder stoon deed and *stank*; wiþ stif vois hym callede:

stant > stonden

stared v *staren v.*　A 3 stared (1) stariden (1) staringe (1); B 2 stared (1) starynge (1); C 1 staryng

A. 4.143　But *stari[den* for] stodyenge [and] stoden as bestis.
A.11.4　And sterneliche *staringe* dame studie seide:
A.12.61　I stode stille in a stodie and *stared* abowte.
B.10.4　And al *starynge* dame Studie sterneliche [seide].
B.16.168　And after Piers þe Plowman pried and *stared*.
C.11.4　Al *staryng* dame studie sterneliche sayde.

statut n *statute n.*　A 1; B 1; C 1 statuyt

A. 7.301　Ne stryue aзen þe *statut*, so sternely he lokide.
B. 6.320　Ne stryuen ayeins [þe] *statut*, so sterneliche he loked.
C. 8.340　Ne stryue aзeynes [þe] *statuyt*, [so sturnliche a lokede].

staues > staf

stede n1 *stede n.(1)*　A 2; B 3; C 3 stede (2) stedes (1)

A. 5.39　And be steward of зoure *stede* til зe be stewid betere.
A. 7.56　And heng his hoper at his hals in *stede* of a scrippe:
B.Pr.96　And in *stede* of Stywardes sitten and demen.
B. 5.47　And be Stywar[d] of youre *sted[e]* til ye be [stewed] bettre'.
B. 6.61　And [heng his] hoper at [his] hals in *stede* of a Scryppe:
C.Pr.94　And ben in *stede* of stewardus and sitten and demen.
C. 5.145　And be stewar[d] of зoure *stedes* til зe be stewed bettere.'
C. 8.60　And heng his hopur on his hal[s] in *stede* of a scryppe;

stede n2 *stede n.(2)* B 1; C 1
B.13.293 Or strengest on *stede*, or styuest vnder girdel,
C. 6.43 And strengest vppon *stede* and styuest vnder gyrdel

stedefast adj *stedfast adj.* A 1; B 1
A.10.114 Hold þe stable & *stedefast* & strengþe þiseluen
B.15.583 In stoon for it *stedefast* was and stonde sholde euere.

steere n *stere n.(2)* A 1 stere; B 1
A. 9.30 For ȝif he ne arise þe raþere & [rauȝte þe *stere*],
B. 8.34 For if he ne arise þe raþer and rauȝte þe *steere*

steereþ v *steren v.(1)* A 1 steriþ; B 1
A. 9.42 For he strengþeþ þe to stonde & *steriþ* þi soule
B. 8.46 For he strengþeþ [þee] to stonde and *steereþ* [þi] soule

stekie v *steken v.* B 1
B. 1.122 Til god of his goodnesse [ȝarte þe heuene to *stekie*]

stele n1 *stele n.(1)* B 1; C 1 stale
B.19.279 And lerned men a ladel bugge wiþ a long *stele*
C.21.279 And lered men a ladel bugge with a longe *stale*

stele n2 *stele .(3)* C 1
C. 6.106 Bothe with stoon and with staf and *stele* vppon myn enemye;

stele v *stelen v.* A 1; B 3 stale (1) stele (1) stolen (1); C 4 stale (1) stele (1) stelen (1) stole (1)
A. 6.64 þei hote *stele* nouȝt, ne sle nouȝt; strik forþ be boþe.
B. 5.577 Thei hiȝte *Stele*-noȝt-[ne]-Sle-noȝt; strik forþ by boþe;
B.13.366 And but I hadde by ooþer wey at þe laste I *stale* it,
B.19.156 And biwicched hem as þei woke and awey *stolen* it.
C. 6.265 And but y hadde by other wey at the laste y *stale* hit
C. 7.224 Thei hatte *stele*-nat and sle-nat; stryk forth by bothe
C.17.40 Lord leue," quod þat lede, " no *stole* thynge be herynne!'
C.21.156 And bywiched [hem] as they woke and away *stelen* hit.

steppe v *steppen v.* B 2; C 3 stepe (1) steppe (2)
B.17.57 He myȝte neiþer *steppe* ne stande ne stere foot ne handes
B.17.99 He sholde stonde and *steppe*; ac stalworþe worþ he neuere
C. 6.403 He myhte noþer *steppe* ne stande til he a staf hadde
C.19.56 For he ne myhte *stepe* ne stande ne stere foet ne handes
C.19.89 And thouh he stande and *steppe* riȝt stronge worth he neuere

stere v *stiren v. &> steere* B 2 stere (1) stired (1); C 2 stere (1) stured (1)
B.17.57 He myȝte neiþer steppe ne stande ne *stere* foot ne handes
B.20.103 That he hitte euene, þat euere *stired* after.
C.19.56 For he ne myhte stepe ne stande ne *stere* foet ne handes
C.22.103 That he hi[t]te euene, þat euere *stured* aftur.

steryng ger *steringe ger.* C 1
C.10.36 For stonde he neuere so stifliche, thorw *steryng* of þe bote

steriþ > steere

sterlyng n *sterling n.* B 1; C 1 sterlynges
B.15.349 As in lussheburwes is a luþer alay, and yet lokeþ he lik a *sterlyng*;
C.17.83 Thus ar ȝe luyþer yliknd to losssheborw[e] *sterlynges*

sterne adv *sterne adv.* B 1
B.15.253 Lakkeþ ne loseþ ne lokeþ vp *sterne*,

sterneliche adv *sternli adv.* A 2 sterneliche (1) sternely (1); B 3 sternely (1) sterneliche (2); C 3 sterneliche (1) sturnely (1) sturnliche (1)
A. 7.301 Ne stryue aȝen þe statut, so *sternely* he lokide.
A.11.4 And *sterneliche* staringe dame studie seide:
B.Pr.183 Strook forþ *sternely* and stood bifore hem alle
B. 6.320 Ne stryuen ayeins [þe] statut, so *sterneliche* he loked.
B.10.4 And al starynge dame Studie *sterneliche* [seide].
C.Pr.200 Strok forth *sturnely* and stod byfore hem alle
C. 8.340 Ne stryue aȝeynes [þe] statuyt, [so *sturnliche* a lokede].
C.11.4 Al staryng dame studie *sterneliche* sayde.

sterre n *sterre n.* A 2 sterre (1) sterris (1); B 5 sterre (1) sterres (4); C 6 sterre (1) sterres (5)
A. 6.80 He may do wiþ þe day *sterre* what hym dere likiþ;
A. 8.144 And þe enleuene *sterris* ha[i]lsiden hym alle.
B. 7.166 And þe elleuene *sterres* hailsed hym alle;
B.11.363 And siþen I loked on þe see and so forþ on þe *sterres*;
B.12.223 And of þe stones and of þe *sterres*; þow studiest, as I leue,
B.18.233 That þo þis barn was ybore þer blased a *sterre*
B.20.256 And nempnede [hem names], and noumbrede þe *sterres*:
C. 9.310 And the eleuene *s[t]erres* haylsede hym alle;
C.13.173 And sethe y lokede on þe see and so forth on [þe] *sterres*;
C.14.30 Ac clergie cometh bote of syhte and kynde wit of *sterres*,
C.17.99 Shipmen and sheepherdes by þe seuene *sterres*
C.20.242 [That tho] this barn was ybore þ[er] blased a *sterre*
C.22.256 And nempned hem names and nombred þe *sterres*:

sterte v *sterten v.* C 1
C.19.301 Thre thynges ther ben þat doth a man to *sterte*

sterue v *sterven v.* A 1 steruiþ; B 2 sterue (1) sterueþ (1); C 5 sterue (4) sterueth (1)
A.11.209 Riȝt so be religioun, it roileþ & *steruiþ*
B.10.303 Riȝt so [by] religion, [it] ro[i]leþ [and] *sterueþ*
B.11.432 Ac whan nede nymeþ hym vp for [nede] lest he *sterue*,
C. 5.150 Ryht so religioun roteth and *sterueth*
C. 6.290 Thow were such as thow sayst; y sholde rather *s[t]erue*:
C. 9.101 Reche ȝe neuere, ȝe riche, Thouh suche lo[rell]es *sterue*.
C.10.201 For hoso loueth, leueth h[it] wel, god wol nat laton hym *sterue*
C.12.180 Bote if þe seed þat sowen is in the sloo *sterue*

steward(- > styward

stewed ptp *steuen v.(1)* A 1 stewid; B 1; C 1
A. 5.39 And be steward of ȝoure stede til ȝe be *stewid* betere.
B. 5.47 And be Stywar[d] of youre sted[e] til ye be [*stewed*] bettre'.
C. 5.145 And be stewar[d] of ȝoure stedes til ȝe be *stewed* bettere.'

stewes > stuwes

stif adj *stif adj.* B 2 stif (1) styuest (1); C 1 styuest
B.13.293 Or strengest on stede, or *styuest* vnder girdel,
B.15.594 And vnder stoon deed and stank; wiþ *stif* vois hym callede:
C. 6.43 And strengest vppon stede and *styuest* vnder gyrdel

stif adv *stif adv.* A 1; B 1
A. 9.28 For stande he neuere so *stif* he stumbliþ in þe waggyng,
B. 8.32 For stonde he neuer so *stif*, he stumbleþ [in þe waggyng],

styfliche adv *stifli adv.* C 2 styfliche (1) stifliche (1)
C. 3.346 And *styfliche* stande forth to strenghe þe fundement,
C.10.36 For stonde he neuere so *stifliche*, thorw steryng of þe bote

styhlede v *stightelen v.* C 1
C.15.39 Resoun stoed and *s[t]yhlede* as for styward of halle.

stikede v *stiken v.* C 1
C. 3.381 Bote standynge as a stake þat *stikede* in a mere

stikke n *stikke n.* B 2 stikke (1) stikkes (1); C 1 stikkes
B.11.348 Lerned to legge þe *stikkes* in whiche she leyeþ and bredeþ.
B.12.14 Alþouȝ þow strike me wiþ þi staf, wiþ *stikke* or wiþ yerde,
C.13.159 Lernede to [l]egge *stikkes* þat ley on here neste.

style n *stile n.(1)* C 2
C. 6.145 How lytel y louye letyse at þe *style*.
C. 6.207 For som tyme y serued symme at þe *style*

stille adj *stille adj.* A 3; B 4; C 2
A.11.7 And blamide hym [and bannide hym] & bad hym be *stille*–
A.11.39 At mete [in here] merþe, whanne mynstralis ben *stille*,
A.12.75 Þer bad me hunger haue gode day but I helde me *stille*;
B.10.7 And blamed hym and banned hym and bad hym be *stille*–
B.10.53 At mete in hir murþe whan Mynstrals beþ *stille*,
B.13.86 Pacience parceyued what I þouȝte and [preynte] on me to be *stille*
B.13.113 And preynte vpon pacience to preie me be *stille*,
C.11.33 Nowe is þe manere at mete when munstrals ben *stille*
C.15.120 And preynte vppon pacience to preie me be *stille*

stille adv *stille adv.* A 2; B 5; C 3
A.10.99 But suffre & sit *stille* & sek þou no ferþere,
A.12.61 I stode *stille* in a stodie and stared abowte.
B. 9.108 Oure lord loueþ hem and lent, loude ouþer *stille*,
B.12.180 Ther þe lewed liþ *stille* and lokeþ after lente,
B.13.19 And I sat *stille* as Pacience seide, and þus soone þis doctour,
B.15.224 And seintes yset; [*stille*] charite hem folwede.
B.19.421 But in hir holynesse helden hem *stille*
C.14.120 There þe lewede lyth *stille* and loketh aftur lente
C.15.150 Y sae[t] *stille* as pacience wolde and thus sone this doctour,
C.21.421 Bote in here holinesse h[e]lden hem *stille*

styngeþ v *stingen v.* B 1; C 1 styngeth
B.18.155 May no medicyne [amende] þe place þer he *styngeþ*
C.20.158 May no medecyne amende the place there he *styngeth*

stynte v *stinten v.* A 2; B 3; C 2 stynte (1) stunte (1)
A. 6.63 Two stokkis þere stonde, but *stynte* þou not þere;
A.11.169 And er I com to clergie coude I neuere *stynte*.
B. 1.123 And [stable and *stynte*] and stonden in quiete.
B. 5.576 Two stokkes þer stonde, ac *stynte* [þow] noȝt þere;
B.10.226 And [er] I com to clergie [koude I] neuere *stynte*.
C. 2.169 Til mede be thy wedded wyf wolle we nat *stunte*,
C. 7.223 T[w]o stokkes þere stondeth ac *stynte* thow nat þere;

stired > stere; styuest > stif

styward n *steuard n.* A 1 steward; B 4 Stiward (1) Styward (2) Stywardes (1); C 6 steward (1) stewardus (1) styward (3) stywardes (1)
A. 5.39   And be *steward* of ʒoure stede til ʒe be stewid betere.
B.Pr.96   And in stede of *Stywardes* sitten and demen.
B. 5.47   And be *Stywar[d]* of youre sted[e] til ye be [stewed] bettre'.
B.19.256   And crouneþ Conscience kyng and makeþ craft youre *Stiward*,
B.19.461   Al þat myn Auditour or ellis my *Styward*
C.Pr.94   And ben in stede of *stewardus* and sitten and demen.
C. 3.122   In amendement of mayres and oþer *stywardes*
C. 5.145   And be *stewar[d]* of ʒoure stedes til ʒe be stewed bettere.'
C.15.39   Resoun stoed and s[t]yhlede as for *styward* of halle.
C.21.256   And crouneth Consience kyng and maketh craft ʒoure *styward*
C.21.461   Al þat myn Auditour or elles my *styward*

stod(e -en > stonden; stodie > studie

stodyenge ger *studiinge ger.* A 1
A. 4.143   But stari[den for] *stodyenge* [and] stoden as bestis.

stoed(e > stonden; stoel > stool; stoen > stoon

stok n *stok n.(1)* A 2 stokkis; B 7 stok (1) stokke (1) stokkes (5); C 7 stok (2) stokkes (5)
A. 4.95   But resoun haue reuþe on hym he shal reste in þe *stokkis*
A. 6.63   Two *stokkis* þere stonde, but stynte þou not þere;
B. 4.108   But Reson haue ruþe on hym he shal reste in [þe] *stokkes*
B. 5.576   Two *stokkes* þer stondeþ, ac stynte [þow] noʒt þere;
B. 7.30   Pouere peple [bedredene] and prisons [in *stokkes*]
B.15.98   Ther is a meschief in þe more of swiche manere [*stokkes*].
B.15.453   Til it be fulled vnder foot or in fullyng *stokkes*,
B.16.5   Mercy is þe more þerof; þe myddul *stok* is ruþe;
B.16.14   Amyddes mannes body; þe more is of þat *stokke*.
C. 4.103   Bute resoun haue reuth on hym he shal reste in [þe] *stokkes*
C. 7.223   T[w]o *stokkes* þere stondeth ac stynte thow nat þere;
C. 8.163   'Or y shal bete the by the lawe and brynge þe in *stokkes*.'
C. 9.34   Pore peple bedredene and prisones in *stokkes*
C.10.208   Thorw no sotil sciense on sour *stok* growe";
C.16.251   There is a meschief in þe more of suche manere *stokkes*.
C.18.30   [And fro fallynge the *stok*; hit fayle nat of his myhte].

stole(n > stele; stoles > stool

stomble v *stomblen v.* A 1 stumbliþ; B 1 stumbleþ; C 1
A. 9.28   For stande he neuere so stif he *stumbliþ* in þe waggyng,
B. 8.32   For stonde he neuer so stif, he *stumbleþ* [in þe waggyng],
C.10.35   Maketh þe man many tyme to *stomble* yf he stande.

stonden v *stonden v.(1)* A 15 stande (4) standis (2) stant (1) stode (1) stoden (1) stonde (4) stondiþ (1) stood (1); B 30 stande (3) stant (2) stode (2) stonde (11) stonden (3) stondeþ (3) stood (4) stoode (2); C 28 stand (1) stande (13) standeth (2) standynge (1) stant (1) stod (3) stode (1) stoed (3) stoede (1) stonde (1) stondeth (1)
A. 1.48   And þe [Image ilike], þat þereinne *standis*.
A. 2.5   'Loke on þi left half, & lo where he *standis*,
A. 2.54   Symonye & cyuyle *stondiþ* forþ boþe
A. 2.169   Dreed at þe dore *stood* & þat doom herde,
A. 3.47   'We haue a wyndowe [in] werching wile *stonde* vs wel heiʒe;
A. 4.143   But stari[den for] stodyenge [and] *stoden* as bestis.
A. 5.193   He hadde no strengþe to *stonde* er he his staf hadde,
A. 6.63   Two stokkis þere *stonde*, but stynte þou not þere;
A. 7.37   To fulfille þe foreward whiles I may *stande*'.
A. 7.104   At heiʒ prime peris let þe plouʒ *stande*
A. 9.27   Makeþ man many tymes to falle & to *stande*.
A. 9.28   For *stande* he neuere so stif he stumbliþ in þe waggyng,
A. 9.42   For he strengþeþ þe to *stonde* & steriþ þi soule
A.10.133   Þat þoruʒ wedlak þe world *stant*, whoso wile it knowen.
A.12.61   I *stode* stille in a stodie and stared abowte.
B.Pr.183   Strook forþ sternely and *stood* bifore hem alle
B. 1.50   And þe ymage [y]lik[e] þat þerInne *stondeþ*.
B. 1.123   And [stable and stynte] and *stonden* in quiete.
B. 2.5   'Loke [o]n þi left half, and lo where he *stondeþ*,
B. 2.72   Symonye and Cyuylle *stonden* forþ boþe
B. 2.208   Drede at þe dore *stood* and þe doom herde,
B. 3.48   'We haue a wyndow in werchynge wole [*stonden*] vs [wel] hye;
B. 5.345   He [hadde no strengþe to] *stonde* er he his staf hadde,
B. 5.387   I may noʒt *stonde* ne stoupe ne wiþoute stool knele.
B. 5.576   Two stokkes þer *stondeþ*, ac stynte [þow] noʒt þere;
B. 6.112   At heiʒ prime Piers leet þe plowʒ *stonde*
B. 8.31   Makeþ þe man many tyme to falle and to *stonde*.
B. 8.32   For *stonde* he neuer so stif, he stumbleþ [in þe waggyng],
B. 8.46   For he strengþeþ [þee] to *stonde* and steereþ [þi] soule
B.11.34   'Ye? recche þee neuere', quod Rechelesnesse, *stood* forþ in raggede cloþes;
B.13.29   A[c] Pacience in þe Paleis *stood* in pilgrymes cloþes,
B.14.252   A straw for þe stuwes! [it] *stoode* noʒt, I trowe,

B.14.253   Hadde þei no[on haunt] but of poore men; hir houses *stoode* vntyled.
B.15.543   For coueitise after cros; þe croune *stant* in golde.
B.15.583   In stoon for it stedefast was and *stonde* sholde euere.
B.16.24   'Piers', quod I, 'I preie þee, whi *stonde* þise piles here?'
B.16.218   So widewe withouten wedlok may noʒt wel *stande*,
B.17.57   He myʒte neiþer steppe ne *stande* ne stere foot ne handes
B.17.99   He sholde *stonde* and steppe; ac stalworþe worþ he neuere
B.18.43   Edifie it eft newe–here he *stant* þat seide it–
B.18.83   For alle þei were vnhardy þat houed [þer] or *stode*
B.18.373   Fendes and f[e]ndekynes bifore me shul *stande*
B.19.363   That holy chirche *stode* in [holynesse] as it a Pyl weere.
B.19.380   Made vnitee holy chirche in holynesse *stonde*.
B.20.102   Lered [ne] lewed he leet no man *stonde*,
C.Pr.200   Strok forth sturnely and *stod* byfore hem alle
C. 2.5   'Loke [o]n thy left half, and loo where he *standeth*,
C. 2.74   Thenne simonye and syuyle *standeth* forth bothe
C. 2.220   Drede *stod* at þe dore and [þe] d[om]e herde,
C. 3.51   'We han a wyndowe awurchynge wol *stande* vs [wel] heye;
C. 3.346   And styfliche *stande* forth to strenghe þe fundement,
C. 3.381   Bote *standynge* as a stake þat stikede in a mere
C. 5.113   And Consience his crocer byfore þe kyng *stande*.
C. 6.403   He myhte noþer steppe ne *stande* til he a staf hadde
C. 7.3   Y may nat *stande* ne stoupe ne withouten stoel knele.
C. 7.223   T[w]o stokkes þere *stondeth* ac stynte thow nat þere;
C. 8.119   At hey prime [Peres] leet þe plouh *stande*
C.10.35   Maketh þe man many tyme to stomble yf he *stande*.
C.10.36   For *stonde* he neuere so stifliche, thorw steryng of þe bote
C.11.193   'ʒe? reche þe neuere,' quod rechelesnesse, *stod* forth in ragged clothes;
C.15.39   Resoun *stoed* and s[t]yhlede as for styward of halle.
C.16.92   A straw for the stuyues! hit *stoed* nat, [y trowe],
C.16.93   Hadde they noen haunt bote of pore [men; here houses *stoed* vntyled.
C.17.205   For couetyse aftur cros; the corone *stand* in golde.
C.18.47   And shaketh hit; ne were hit vndershored hit sholde nat *stande*.
C.19.56   For he ne myhte stepe ne *stande* ne stere foet ne handes
C.19.89   And thouh he *stande* and steppe riʒt stronge worth he neuere
C.20.42   Edefien hit eft newe–here he *stant* þat saide hit–
C.20.85   For alle [they were] vnhardy þat houed þer or *stode*
C.20.415   Fendes and fendekynes byfore me shal *stande*
C.21.363   That holi churche *stoede* in holinesse as hit [a pyle were].
C.21.380   Made vnite holi churche in holinesse *stande*.
C.22.102   Lered ne lewed he lefte no man *stande*,

stone v *stonen v.(1)* B 1
B.12.75   Wiþ stones men sholde hir strike and *stone* hire to deþe.

stones > stoon; stood(e > stonden

stool n *stol n.* A 1 stolis; B 2 stool (1) stooles (1); C 2 stoel (1) stoles (1)
A. 3.67   As to punisshen on pillories & on py[n]yng *stolis*
B. 3.78   [As] to punysshe on Pillories and [on] pynynge *stooles*
B. 5.387   I may noʒt stonde ne stoupe ne wiþoute *stool* knele.
C. 3.79   To punischen [o]n pilories and [o]n pynyng *stoles*
C. 7.3   Y may nat stande ne stoupe ne withouten *stoel* knele.

stoon n *ston n.* B 5 stones (3) stoon (2); C 4 stoen (2) stones (1) stoon (1)
B. 2.16   Wiþ Ribanes of reed gold and of riche *stones*.
B.12.75   Wiþ *stones* men sholde hir strike and stone hire to deþe.
B.12.223   And of þe *stones* and of þe sterres; þow studiest, as I leue,
B.15.583   In *stoon* for it stedefast was and stonde sholde euere.
B.15.594   And vnder *stoon* deed and stank; wiþ stif vois hym callede:
C. 2.13   And thereon rede rubies and othere riche *stones*.
C. 6.106   Bothe with *stoon* and with staf and stele vppon myn enemye;
C.14.37   For moyses witnesseth þat god wroet [in *stoen* with his fynger;
C.14.42   To strike with *stoen* or with staf this strompet to dethe."

stoppe v *stoppen v.* B 1 stoppeþ; C 4 stoppe (3) stoppeth (1)
B.18.415   And Pees þoruʒ pacience alle perils *stoppeþ*.'
C. 4.150   Reherce the[r] anon ryhte þat myhte resoun *stoppe*.
C.20.283   And [y] shal lette this loerd and his lint *stoppe*.
C.20.285   Cheke and cheyne we and vch a [c]hine *stoppe*
C.20.458   And pees thorw pacience alle perelles *stop[peth]*.'

stories n *storie n.(1)* B 2
B. 7.72   Caton kenneþ me þus and þe clerc of *stories*.
B. 7.74   And in þe *stories* he techeþ to bistowe þyn almesse:

stottes n *stot n.* B 1; C 1
B.19.267   And Grace gaf Piers of his goodnesse foure *stottes*,
C.21.267   And grace [gaef Peres of his goednesse] foure *stottes*,

stoue > stowue

stounde n *stounde n.* A 1; B 1; C 1
A. 9.56   And vndir a lynde vpon a launde lenide I me a *stounde*

B. 8.65   And vnder a lynde vpon a launde lened I a *stounde*
C.10.64   And vnder lynde vpon a launde lened y a *stounde*

stoupe v *stoupen v.* B 2; C 3
B. 5.387   I may no3t stonde ne *stoupe* ne wiþoute stool knele.
B.11.36   A man may *stoupe* tyme yno3 whan he shal tyne þe crowne.'
C. 5.24   And to long, lef me, lowe to *stoupe*,
C. 7.3   Y may nat stande ne *stoupe* ne withouten stoel knele.
C.11.195   A man may *stoupe* tyme ynowe when he shal tyne þe croune.'

stowue n prop *n.i.d.* B 1; C 1 stoue
B. 5.28   Tomme *Stowue* he tau3te to take two staues
C. 5.130   Tomme *stoue* he tauhte to take t[w]o staues

strayues > streyues

stratford n prop *n.i.d.* B 1
B.13.266   Wiþ [bake] breed fro *Stratford*; þo gonnen beggeris wepe

straunge adj *straunge adj.* C 1
C.16.70   That mete or moneye of *straunge* men moet begge.

straw n *strau n.* B 2 straw (1) strawe (1); C 3 straw (2) strawe (1)
B.14.234   For whan he streyneþ hym to strecche þe *strawe* is his shetes.
B.14.252   A *straw* for þe stuwes! [it] stoode no3t, I trowe,
C.12.181   Shal neuere spir sprynge vp ne spiek on *straw* kerne;
C.16.75   For when he streyneth hym to strecche the *strawe* is his shetes.
C.16.92   A *straw* for the stuyues! hit stoed nat, [y trowe],

strecche v *strecchen v.* B 1; C 1
B.14.234   For whan he streyneþ hym to *strecche* þe strawe is his shetes.
C.16.75   For when he streyneth hym to *strecche* the strawe is his shetes.

streyneþ v *streinen v.(1)* B 1; C 1 streyneth
B.14.234   For whan he *streyneþ* hym to strecche þe strawe is his shetes.
C.16.75   For when he *streyneth* hym to strecche the strawe is his shetes.

streyte adv *streite adv.* A 1 streite; B 1; C 1
A.Pr.26   Al for loue of oure lord lyuede wel *streite*
B.Pr.26   Al for loue of oure lord lyueden [wel] *streyte*
C.Pr.28   Al for loue of oure lord lyueden [ful] *streyte*

streyves n *straif n.* B 1; C 1 strayues
B.Pr.94   Of wardes and of wardemotes, weyues and *streyves*.
C.Pr.92   Of wardus and of wardemotis, wayues and *strayues*.

strenede v *strenen v.* C 1
C.13.171   How vncortey[s]liche þat cok his kynde for[th] *strenede*

strengest > stronge

strenghe n *strenge n. cf. strengþe* C 6
C. 3.345   Folowynge and fyndynge out þe fundement of a *strenghe*,
C.10.147   Sire worch-wel-with-thyn-hand, a wyht man of *strenghe*,
C.15.171   Al th[e] wit of this world and wyhte menne *strenghe*
C.17.241   Naught thorw manslaght and mannes *strenghe* Macometh hadde þe maistrie
C.21.358   For witterly, y woet wel, we be nat of *strenghe*
C.21.365   And make a moche moet þat myhte be a *strenghe*

strenghe v *strengen v.(1) cf. strengþeþ* C 1
C. 3.346   And styfliche stande forth to *strenghe* þe fundement,

strengþe n *strengthe n. &> strengþeþ, cf. strenghe* A 3; B 10; C 2 strenghtes (1) strenthe (1)
A. 5.193   He hadde no *strengþe* to stonde er he his staf hadde,
A. 8.82   Ac olde men & hore þat helpeles ben of *strengþe*,
A.10.20   Sire werche wel wiþ þin hond, [a] wi3t man of *strengþe*,
B. 5.345   He [hadde no *strengþe* to] stonde er he his staf hadde,
B. 7.100   Ac olde men and hore þat helplees ben of *strengþe*,
B. 9.21   Sire werch-wel-wiþ-þyn-hand, a wi3t man of *strengþe*.
B.11.295   As bifel for a kny3t, or foond hym for his *strengþe*.
B.12.41   Or Salomon his sapience, or Sampson his *strengþe*?
B.13.173   Al þe wit of þis world and wi3t mennes *strengþe*
B.13.328   'Or wiþ my3t [of] mouþ or þoru3 m[a]nnes *strengþe*
B.17.321   Thre þynges þer ben þat doon a man by *strengþe*
B.19.358   For witterly, I woot wel, we beþ no3t of *strengþe*
B.19.365   And make a muche moot þat myghte ben a *strengþe*
C. 3.238   To berne and to bruttene, to bete adoun *strenghtes.*
C.13.109   As byful for a knyht or fond hym for his *strenthe.*

strengþeþ v *strengthen v. cf. strenghe* A 2 strengþe (1) strengþeþ (1); B 1
A. 9.42   For he *strengþeþ* þe to stonde & steriþ þi soule
A.10.114   Hold þe stable & stedefast & *strengþe* þiseluen
B. 8.46   For he *strengþeþ* [þee] to stonde and steereþ [þi] soule

strenthe > strengþe

strete n *strete n.(2)* A 1 stretis; B 2 strete (1) stretes (1); C 3 strete (2) stretes (1)
A.11.211   Ac now is religioun a ridere & a rennere [be *stretis*],
B.10.311   Ac now is Religion a rydere, a [rennere by *stretes*],
B.12.103   [And ri3t as si3t serueþ a man to se þe hei3e *strete*]
C. 6.50   Tales to telle in tauernes and in *stretes*,
C. 9.122   And thauh a mete with the mayre ameddes þe *strete*
C.14.48   And riht as syht serueth a man to se [þe hye *strete*],

stryk > strike

strikares n *strikere n.* C 1
C. 9.159   'Forthy lollares þat lyuen in sleuthe and ouer land *strikares*

strike v *striken v.* A 1 strik; B 4 strik (1) strike (2) strook (1); C 3 strike (1) stryk (1) strok (1)
A. 6.64   Þei hote stele nou3t, ne sle nou3t; *strik* forþ be boþe.
B.Pr.183   *Strook* forþ sternely and stood bifore hem alle
B. 5.577   Thei hi3te Stele-no3t-[ne]-Sle-no3t; *strik* forþ by boþe;
B.12.14   Alþou3 þow *strike* me wiþ þi staf, wiþ stikke or wiþ yerde,
B.12.75   Wiþ stones men sholde hir *strike* and stone hire to deþe.
C.Pr.200   *Strok* forth sturnely and stod byfore hem alle
C. 7.224   Thei hatte stele-nat and sle-nat; *stryk* forth by bothe
C.14.42   To *strike* with stoen or with staf this strompet to dethe."

stryuen v *striven v.* A 1 stryue; B 1; C 1 stryue
A. 7.301   Ne *stryue* a3en þe statut, so sternely he lokide.
B. 6.320   Ne *stryuen* ayeins [þe] statut, so sterneliche he loked.
C. 8.340   Ne *stryue* a3eynes [þe] statuyt, [so sturnliche a lokede].

strok > strike

strompet n *strumpet n.* C 1
C.14.42   To strike with stoen or with staf this *strompet* to dethe."

stronge adj *strong adj.* B 3 strengest (1) stronge (2); C 4 strengest (1) stronge (3)
B.12.160   Tak two *stronge* men and in Themese cast hem,
B.12.190   That haþ take fro Tybourne twenty *stronge* þeues,
B.13.293   Or *strengest* on stede, or styuest vnder girdel,
C. 6.43   And *strengest* vppon stede and styuest vnder gyrdel
C.14.104   Take two *stronge* men and in temese cast hem,
C.14.129   Hit hath take fro tybourne twenty *stronge* theues
C.19.89   And thouh he stande and steppe ri3t *stronge* worth he neuere

strook > strike

struyen v *stroien v.* B 2 struyden (1) struyen (1); C 3 struyden (1) struye (1) struyen (1)
B. 8.27   Fro wastores and wikked men þat þis world *struyen*
B.15.597   And studieden to *struyen* hym and struyden hemselue,
B.15.597   And studieden to struyen hym and *struyden* hemselue,
C.17.305   And studeden to *struye* hym and struyden hemsulue
C.17.305   And studeden to struye hym and *struyden* hemsulue

studeden > studie v

studie n *studie n.* A 6 stodie (2) studie (4); B 7; C 6 study (1) studie (5)
A.11.1   Þanne hadde wyt a wyf þat hatte dame *studie*,
A.11.4   And sterneliche staringe dame *studie* seide:
A.11.98   But al lau3inge he loutide & lokide vpon *studie*
A.11.176   Þat I was of wyttis hous & wiþ his wyf dame *stodie*.
A.11.178   And axide how wyt ferde & his wif *studie*,
A.12.61   I stode stille in a *stodie* and stared abowte.
B.Pr.181   And leten hire labour lost and al hire longe *studie*.
B. 3.345   Tho ye [sou3te] Sapience sittynge in youre *studie*.
B.10.1   Thanne hadde wit a wif was hote dame *Studie*,
B.10.4   And al starynge dame *Studie* sterneliche [seide].
B.10.145   But al lau3ynge he louted and loked vpon *Studie*
B.10.233   That I was of wittes hous and wiþ his wif dame *Studie*.
B.10.235   And askede how wit ferde and his wif *studie*].
C.Pr.198   And leten here labour ylost and al here longe *study*.
C.11.1   Thenne hadde wit a wyf was hote dame *studie*
C.11.4   Al staryng dame *studie* sterneliche sayde.
C.11.81   And when wit was ywar what *studie* menede
C.11.83   But al lauhynge he louted and loked vppon *stud[i]e*,
C.15.180   Lettrure and longe *studie* letteth fol monye

studie v *studien v.* A 2 stodie; B 4 studie (2) studieden (1) studiest (1); C 3 studeden (1) studie (2)
A. 8.131   Manye tyme þis metelis han mad me to *stodie*,
A.12.6   Þe were lef to lerne but loþ for to *stodie*;
B. 7.149   Many tyme þis metels haþ maked me to *studie*
B.12.223   And of þe stones and of þe sterres; þow *studiest*, as I leue,
B.13.288   Wiþ Inwit and wiþ outwit ymagynen and *studie*
B.15.597   And *studieden* to struyen hym and struyden hemselue,
C. 9.298   Mony tyme this meteles hath maked me to *studie*
C. 9.318   Al this maketh me on meteles to *studie*

C.17.305   And *studeden* to struye hym and struyden hemsulue

stuyues > stuwes; stumbleþ > stomble; stunte > stynte; stured > stere;
sturnely -liche > sterneliche

stuwes n *steue n.(2)* A 1 stewis; B 4 stewes (1) stuwes (3); C 5 stuyues
   (3) stuyves (2)
A. 7.64   Saue Iakke þe Iugelour & Ionete of þe *stewis*,
B. 6.70   Saue Ia[kk]e þe Iogelour and Ionette of þe *Stuwes*
B.14.252   A straw for þe *stuwes!* [it] stoode noȝt, I trowe,
B.19.435   As wel for a wastour and wenches of þe *stewes*
B.20.160   And wedded oen wanhope, a wenche of þe *Stuwes*.
C. 8.71   Saue Iacke þe iogelour and ionet of þe *stuyues*
C.13.75   Withoute wyles or wronges or wymmen at þe *stuyues*;
C.16.92   A straw for the *stuyues!* hit stoed nat, [y trowe],
C.21.435   As wel for a wastour [and] wenche[s] of the *stuyves*
C.22.160   And wedded oen wanhope, a wenche of þe *stuyves*.

subtileþ > sotile; such(e > swich; sucre > sugre; sue(- > suwen

suffiseþ v *suffisen v.* B 3 suffise (1) suffiseþ (2); C 4 soffiseth (1) suffice
   (2) sufficede (1)
B.15.387   [Ac] if þei ouerhuppe, as I hope noȝt, oure bileue *suffiseþ*,
B.17.34   Siþ þe firste *suffiseþ* to sauacion and to blisse?
B.17.241   And if it *suffise* noȝt for asseȝ, þat in swich a wille deyeþ,
C.14.12   Ac hit *soffiseth* to be saued [to] be such as y tauhte.
C.17.119   Thogh hit *suffice* for oure sauacioun soethfaste byleue,
C.19.35   Sethe the furste *sufficede* to bileue and be saued?
C.19.207   And yf hit *suffic[e]* nat for ase[t]h þat in suche a will deyeth

suffraunce n *sufferaunce n.* A 1; B 2; C 4 soffrance (1) soffraunce (2)
   suffraunce (1)
A.10.119   For þoruȝ *suffraunce* se þou miȝt how soueraynes ariseþ,
B. 6.144   And al is þoruȝ *suffraunce* þat vengeaunce yow ne takeþ,
B.11.379   *Suffraunce* is a souerayn vertue, and a swift vengeaunce.
C.Pr.124   For ȝoure shrewed *soffraunce* and ȝoure oune synne.
C. 3.208   Vnsittyng *soffraunce*, here suster, and heresulue
C. 4.189   And þat vnsittynge *suffraunce* ne sele ȝoure priue lettres
C.13.201   So is *soffrance* souereynliche, so hit be for godes loue.

suffren v *sufferen v.* A 16 suffre (13) suffren (1) suffride (1) suffriþ (1); B
   72 suffre (37) suffred (6) suffrede (10) suffredest (2) suffren (9)
   suffreþ (8); C 81 soffre (35) soffred (6) soffrede (12) soffredest (2)
   soffren (9) soffreth (8) soffry (1) suffre (1) suffred (1) suffrede (1)
   suffreth (2) ysoffred (3)
A. 1.134   Loke þou *suffre* hym to seyn & siþþe lere it aftir.
A. 3.81   And *suffre* hem to selle sumdel aȝens resoun.'
A. 4.1   'Sessiþ,' seide þe king, 'I *suffre* ȝow no lengere.
A. 4.18   'Sette my sadil vpon *suffre* til I se my tyme,
A. 5.51   And *suffre* to be misseid, & so dide I neuere.
A. 7.72   His sone hattiþ *suffre* þi souereynes to hauen here wille
A. 9.47   God wile *suffre* þe to deiȝe so for þiself hast þe maistrie.'
A. 9.84   [Ȝ]e wise *suffriþ* þe vnwise with ȝow to libbe,
A.10.99   But *suffre* & sit stille & sek þou no ferþere,
A.10.118   Þus in dred liþ dowel, [and] dobet to *suffre*,
A.10.216   Þanne is dowel to dreden, & dobet to *suffre*,
A.11.66   "Why wolde oure sauiour *suffre* such a worm in his blisse
A.11.69   And alle here seed for here synne þe same wo *suffride*?"
A.11.76   *Suffre* sathan his sed to bigile,
A.11.83   *Suffren* sathan his sed to bigile,
A.11.114   'Axe þe heiȝe wey,' quaþ heo, 'from henis to *suffre*
B.Pr.131   But *suffren* and seruen; forþi seide þe Aungel,
B.Pr.206   But *suffren* as hymself wolde to [slen þat] hym likeþ,
B. 1.146   Loke þow *suffre* hym to seye and siþen lere it after.
B. 2.106   Hire soules to Sathan to *suffre* with hym peynes,
B. 2.175   Lat sadle hem wiþ siluer oure synne to *suffre*,
B. 3.92   And *suffre* hem to selle somdel ayeins reson.'
B. 4.1   'CEsseþ', sei[de] þe kyng, 'I *suffre* yow no lenger.
B. 4.20   'Set my Sadel vpon *suffre*-til-I-se-my-tyme
B. 5.68   And *suffre* to be mysseyd, and so dide I neuere.
B. 5.154   Hir [were] leuere swowe or swelte þan *suffre* any peyne.
B. 5.482   And siþen *suffredest* [hym] to synne, a siknesse to vs alle,
B. 5.498   And al to solace synfulle þow *suffredest* it so were:
B. 5.608   To *suffren* hym and segge noȝt ayein þi sires wille.
B. 6.80   His sone hiȝte *Suffre*-þi-Souereyns-to-hauen-hir-wille-
B. 8.51   God wole *suffre* wel þi sleuþe if þiself likeþ,
B. 8.94   [Ye wise] *suffreþ* þe vnwise wiþ yow to libbe,
B. 9.207   [Thanne is dowel] to drede, and dobet to *suffre*,
B.10.108   "Why wolde oure Saueour *suffre* swich a worm in his blisse
B.10.111   And al hir seed for hir synne þe same deeþ *suffrede*?
B.10.123   *Suffre* Sathan his seed to bigile,
B.10.130   *Suffre* Sathan his seed to bigile,
B.10.162   'Aske þe heighe wey', quod she, 'hennes to *Suffre*-
B.10.257   [So] is dobet to *suffre* for þ[i] soules helþe
B.10.373   Is slee noȝt but *suffre* and [so] for þe beste,
B.11.259   [Al]þouȝ it be sour to *suffre*, þe[r] comeþ swete [after].

B.11.377   Why I *suffre* or noȝt suffre; þiself hast noȝt to doone.
B.11.377   Why I suffre or noȝt *suffre*; þiself hast noȝt to doone.
B.11.380   Who *suffre[þ]* moore þan god?' quod he; 'no gome, as I leeue
B.11.382   Ac he *suffreþ* for som mannes goode, and so is oure bettre.
B.11.383   [Holy writ', quod þat wye, 'wisseþ men to *suffre*:
B.11.412   'To se muche and *suffre* moore, certes, is dowel.'
B.11.413   'Haddestow *suffred*', he seide, 'slepynge þo þow were,
B.12.8   In þyn olde elde, þat yuele kan *suffre*
B.12.53   And for þei *suffren* and see so manye nedy folkes
B.13.66   Preched of penaunces þat Poul þe Apostle *suffrede*
B.13.309   What I *suffrede* and seiȝ and somtymes hadde.
B.13.444   And a lered man to lere þee what our lord *suffred*
B.14.175   Conforte þo creatures þat muche care *suffren*
B.15.174   And alle manere meschiefs in myldenesse he *suffreþ*.
B.15.200   What is þe wille and wherfore þat many wight *suffreþ*:
B.15.260   That þeiȝ þei *suffrede* al þis, god suffrede for vs moore
B.15.260   That þeiȝ þei suffrede al þis, god *suffrede* for vs moore
B.15.266   Ac he *suffrede* in ensample þat we sholde suffren also,
B.15.266   Ac he suffrede in ensample þat we sholde *suffren* also,
B.15.267   And seide to swiche þat *suffre* wolde,
B.15.270   What penaunce and pouerte and passion þei *suffrede*,
B.15.412   And siþþe oure Saueour *suffred* þe Sarȝens so bigiled
B.15.519   Many a seint syþen haþ *suffred* to deye
B.16.74   And *suffre* me to assaien what sauour it hadde.
B.16.159   *Suffreþ* myne Apostles in [pays] and in [pees] gange.'
B.16.193   Of hym[self] and of his seruaunt, and what [*suffreþ* hem] boþe.
B.17.340   Ben siknesse and sorwes þat we *suffren* o[uȝ]te,
B.17.346   Haþ mercy on swiche men þat so yuele may *suffre*.
B.18.163   'Now *suffre* we', seide Truþe; 'I se, as me þynkeþ,
B.18.206   For no wight woot what wele is þat neuere wo *suffrede*,
B.18.214   And *suffrede* to be sold to se þe sorwe of deying,
B.18.220   And siþþe he *suffred* hym synne sorwe to feele,
B.18.223   To [se] what he haþ *suffred* in þre sondry places,
B.18.246   Whan she seiȝ hym *suffre* þat sonne and see made.
B.18.247   The Erþe for heuynesse þat he wolde *suffre*
B.18.261   '*Suffre* we', seide truþe; 'I here and see boþe
B.18.304   That his soule wolde *suffre* no synne in his sighte;
B.18.394   For blood may *suffre* blood boþe hungry and acale
B.19.68   And muche wo in þis world willen and *suffren*.
B.19.102   Som tyme he *suffrede*, and som tyme he hidde hym,
B.19.291   To *suffren* al þat god sente, siknesse and Angres.
B.19.294   And bold and abidynge bismares to *suffre*;
B.19.441   And *suffreþ* þat synfulle be [til som tyme þat þei repente].
B.20.47   And *suffre* sorwes ful soure, þat shal to Ioye torne."
B.20.107   To cesse and *suffre*, and see wher þei wolde
B.20.293   And *suffre* þe dede in dette to þe day of doome.
B.20.322   I may wel *suffre*', seide Conscience, 'syn ye desiren,
C.Pr.96   And seide, 'ydolatrie ȝe *soffren* in sondrye places manye
C.Pr.101   A[c] for it profiteþ ȝow into pursward ȝe prelates *soffren*
C.Pr.109   And for here syre sey hem synne and *suffred* hem do ille
C.Pr.119   That *soffreth* men do sacrefyce and worschipe maumettes
C.Pr.214   But *soffre* and sey nouȝt; and [so] is þe beste
C. 1.145   Lok þow *soffre* hym to seye and so thow myht lerne.
C. 2.47   *Soffre* and thow shalt see suche as ben apayed
C. 3.120   'And *soffre* hem som tyme to selle aȝeyne þe lawe.'
C. 3.328   And [*soffrede*] hym lyue in mysbileue; y leue he be in helle.
C. 3.400   To syke for here synnes and *soffre* harde penaunc[e]
C. 3.450   Muchel [euel] is thorw mede mony tymes *ysoffred*
C. 4.1   '[Cesseth],' saide þe kynge, 'y *soffre* ȝow no lengere.
C. 4.20   Sette my sadel vpon *soffre*-tyl-y-se-my-tyme
C. 6.9   And *soffre* to be mysseyde, and so dyde y neuere.
C. 6.57   What y *soffrede* and seyh and some tymes hadde
C. 6.129   Here were leuer swowe or swelte then *soffre* eny payne.
C. 7.104   With a lered man to lere the what oure lord *soffrede*
C. 7.124   And sethe *soffredes[t]* hym to synege, a sykenesse to vs alle,
C. 7.138   And a[l] to solace synfole thow *soffredest* it so were:
C. 7.305   [Quod contemplacion, 'by Crist, thow y care *soffre*],
C. 8.82   His sone hihte *soffre*-thy-souereynes-haue-her-wille-
C. 8.89   Al þat they hoten, y hote; heiliche thow *soffre* hem
C. 9.77   And hemsulue also *soffre* muche hungur
C. 9.84   And of monye oþer men þat moche wo *soffren*,
C. 9.117   And *suffreth* suche go so, it semeth to myn inwyt
C. 9.131   Men *suffreth* al þat suche sayen and in solace taketh
C. 9.257   That *soffreth* suche sottes and oþere synnes regne.
C.10.91   "ȝe wordliche wyse, vnwyse þat ȝe *soffre*,
C.10.162   That god [s]eweth nat synnefole men and *soffreth* hem mysfare,
C.10.251   *Soffre* his seed seden with Caymus seed his brother.
C.10.252   And seth for he *soffred* hit god sayde, "me forthynketh
C.10.253   þat y man made or matrimonye *soffrede*
C.11.104   'Aske þe hey wey,' [quod he], 'hennes to *soffre*-
C.12.145   Althouh h[it] be sour to *soffre* þer cometh a swete aftur.
C.12.179   Mesc[h]iefes on molde mekeliche to *soffren*:
C.12.187   A[c] sedes þat ben sowen and mowen *soffre* wyntres

C.12.194   Riht so, sothly, þat *soffry* may penaunc[e]
C.12.201   So preueth this profetes þat pacientliche *soffren*.
C.13.12   And for he *soffrede* and saide nauht oure lord sente tookene
C.13.115   Euele beth thei *ysoffred*, suche þat [shenden] þe masse
C.13.195   Why y *soffre* or nat soffre; certes,' he sayde,
C.13.195   Why y soffre or nat *soffre*; certes,' he sayde,
C.13.197   Ho *soffreth* more then god?' quod he; 'no gome, as y leue.
C.13.199   Ac he *soffreth* in ensaumple þat we sholde soffren alle.
C.13.199   Ac he soffreth in ensaumple þat we sholde *soffren* alle.
C.13.220   'To se moche and *soffre* al, certes, is dowel.'
C.13.221   'Haddestow *soffred*,' he sayde, 'slepyng tho thow were,
C.14.165   Sey hit and *soffred* hit And saide hit be sholde:
C.15.70   At poules byfore þe peple what penaunce they *soffrede*,
C.15.276   And þat is pore pacient alle perelles to *soffre*.'
C.16.164   And he *soffrede* me and saide, 'assay his oþer name.'
C.16.175   And som tyme to *soffre* bothe [sorwe] and [tene],
C.16.327   What sorwe he *soffrede* in ensaumple of vs alle
C.16.329   Worth moche meryte to þat man þat hit may *soffre*.
C.17.10   To his selle selde cam and *soffred* be mylked.
C.17.183   And seth oure saueour *soffrede* such a fals cristene
C.17.270   Mony [a] seynte sethe *soffrede* deth also,
C.18.176   *Soffreth* my postles in pays and in pees gange.'
C.18.202   Of hymsulue and his seruant, and what *soffreth* hem bothe.
C.19.105   And moest inparfyt of alle persones; and pacientliche *soffre*
C.19.320   Been seekness[e] and oþere sorwes þat we *soffren* ouhte,
C.19.326   Haeth mercy on suche men þat [so] euele may *soffre*.
C.20.146   'Now *soffre* we,' saide Treuthe; 'y se, as me thynketh,
C.20.211   For no wiht woet what wele is þat neuere wo *soffrede*
C.20.217   Ne hadde god *ysoffred* of som oþer then hymsulue
C.20.223   And *soffred* to be sold to se þe sorwe of deynge,
C.20.229   And sethe he *soffred* hym synne sorwe to fele
C.20.232   To wyte what he hath *soffred* in thre sundry places,
C.20.255   When he sye hym *soffre* þat sonne and se made.
C.20.256   Þe erthe for heuynesse þat he wolde *soffre*
C.20.269   'Soffre we,' sayde treuthe; 'y here and se bothe
C.20.437   For bloed may *s[uffr]e* bloed bothe afurst and acale
C.21.68   And moche wo in this world wilnen and *soffren*.
C.21.102   Som tyme he *soffrede* and som tyme he hudde hym
C.21.291   To *soffre* al þat god sente, seeknesse and angeres.
C.21.294   And bold and abidynge busmares to *soffre*
C.21.441   And *soffreth* þat synnefole be til som tyme þat þei repente.
C.22.47   And *soffre* sorwes ful soure þat shal to ioye torne."
C.22.107   To sese and *soffre* and se wher they wolde
C.22.293   And *soffren* þe dede in dette to þe day of dome.
C.22.322   Y may wel *soffre*,' sayde Consience, 'sennes 3e desiren,

suggestion n *suggestioun n.* A 1 suggestioun; B 1; C 1 sugestioun
A. 8.68   But 3if þe *suggestioun* be soþ þat [shapiþ hem to] begge.
B. 7.66   But if þe *suggestion* be sooþ þat shapeþ hem to begge,
C. 9.62   Bote the *sugestioun* be soth þat shapeth h[e]m to begge

sugre n *sugre n.* A 1; B 2; C 2 sucre (1) sugre (1)
A. 5.100   May no *sugre* ne swet þing swage it an vnche,
B. 5.123   May no *sugre* ne swete þyng aswage my swellyng,
B.14.316   The nynþe is swete to þe soule, no *sugre* swetter,
C. 6.88   May no *sugre* ne swete thyng aswage my swellynge
C.16.150   The nythe is swete to [þe] soul[e], no *sucre* swettore,

suyn- > suwen; suyrelepus > serelepes; sull(- > sell-; sulue(n > self; suluer > siluer; sum > som; sumdel > somdel; summe > som; sumnoures > somonour; sumwhat > somwhat; sundais > sonday; sundry > sondry; sungen > syngen; sunnere > soone

supersedias n *supersedeas n.* C 3 supersedeas (1) supersedias (2)
C. 2.190   Sommnours and sod[e]nes [þat] *supersedias* taketh
C. 4.190   Ne no *supersedias* sende but y assente,' quod resoun.
C. 9.264   Here salue is of *supersedeas* in sumnoures boxes;

suppriour n *subprior n.* B 1; C 1 supriour
B. 5.171   Boþe Priour and *Suppriour* and oure Pater Abbas;
C. 6.153   That is Priour and *supriour* and oure pater Abbas.

suren v *seuren v.* A 1 sure; B 1
A. 6.28   And dede me *sure* hym [sib]þe] to serue hym for euere;
B. 5.540   And diden me *suren* hym [sibþen] to seruen hym for euere,

surfet n *surfet n.* A 2; B 2 Surfet (1) surfetes (1); C 1 sorfeet
A. 5.201   And aftir al þis *surfet* an axesse he hadde
A. 7.249   Let nou3t sire *surfet* sitten at þi bord;
B. 6.265   Lat no3t sire *Surfet* sitten at þi borde;
B.13.404   'And kau3te siknesse somtyme for my [*surfetes*] ofte
C. 8.275   Lat nat sire *sorfeet* sitt[en] at thy borde,

surgenrie n *surgeonri n.* B 1
B.16.106   And dide hym assaie his *surgenrie* on hem þat sike were

surgerie n *ciurgie n.* B 1; C 1
B.20.178   'Now I se', seide lif, 'þat *Surgerie* ne phisik
C.22.178   'Now y see,' saide lyf, ' that *surgerie* ne fysyke

surgien n *cirugien n.* B 5 surgien (4) surgiens (1); C 5
B.14.89   And *surgiens* for dedly synnes whan shrift of mouþe failleþ.
B.20.310   If any *surgien* were [in] þe seg[e] þat softer koude plastre.
B.20.313   'Ther is a *Surgien* in þ[e] sege þat softe kan handle,
B.20.315   Oon frere Flaterere is phisicien and *surgien*.'
B.20.336   'I am a *Surgien*', seide þe [frere], 'and salues kan make.
C.18.139   That suche a *surgien* sethen ysaye was þer neuere
C.22.310   Yf eny *surgien* were in þe sege that softur couthe plastre.
C.22.313   'Ther is a *surgien* in the sege that softe can handele
C.22.315   Oen frere flaterrere is fiscician and *surgien*.'
C.22.336   'Y am a *surgien*,' saide the frere, 'and salues can make.

surie > surrie

surquidous adj *surquidous adj.* B 1; C 1
B.19.339   And sente forþ *Surquidous*, his sergeaunt of Armes,
C.21.339   And sente forth *surquido[us]*, his seriaunt[e] of Armes,

surrie n prop *Sirie n.* B 4 Surre (1) Surree (1) Surrie (1) surrye (1); C 3 surie
B.13.209   Sarsens and *Surre*, and so forþ alle þe Iewes,
B.15.398   Brou3te Sar3ens of *Surree*, and see in what manere.
B.15.400   Into *Surrie* he sou3te, and þoru3 hise sotile wittes
B.15.528   And souereynliche to swiche þat of *surrye* bereþ þe name],
C.17.169   Forthy souhte [he] into *surie* and sotiled how he myhte
C.17.240   Hadde al *surie* as hymsulue wolde and sarrasines in equitee.
C.17.278   And souereynliche [to] suche þat of *surie* bereth þe name

suspectioun n *suspecioun n.* C 1
C.17.313   And haen a *suspectioun* to be saef, bothe sarresynes & iewes,

sustantyf n *substantif n.* C 6 sustantif (2) sustantyf (4)
C. 3.336   Ac adiectif and *sustantif* vnite asken,
C. 3.343   Thenne adiectyf an[d] *sustantyf*, for englisch was it neuere.'
C. 3.353   Seketh and seweth his *sustantif* sauacioun,
C. 3.361   This is relacion rect, ryht [as] adiectyf and *sustantyf*
C. 3.394   Ac adiectyf and *sustantyf* is as y [e]r tolde,
C. 3.404   Thus is man and mankynde in maner of [a] *sustantyf*,

susteyne- > sustene

sustenaunce n *sustenaunce n.* B 1; C 2 sustinaunce
B.20.7   That þow toke to þi bilyue, to cloþes and to *sustenaunce*,
C. 5.126   He bad wastoures [g]o wurche and wynne here *sustinaunce*
C.22.7   That thow toke to [thy bylyue], to clothes and to *sustinaunce*

sustene v *sustenen v.* B 3 sustene (1) sustened (1) susteneþ (1); C 2 susteyned (1) susteyneth (1)
B. 9.111   For þei mote werche and wynne and þe world *sustene*;
B.15.280   And þoru3 þe mylk of þat mylde beest þe man was *sustened*;
B.15.468   So loue and leaute lele men *susteneþ*.
C. 8.17   And alle manere men þat by þe molde is *susteyned*
C.10.204   As this wedded men þat this world *susteyneth*,

suster n *suster n.* A 7 sister (1) sistir (2) sistris (2) suster (1) sustren (1); B 9 suster (6) sustren (2) sustres (1); C 14 suster (6) susteres (1) sustre (1) sustres (2) sustur (3) susturne (1)
A. 3.52   Þat iche segge shal se I am *sistir* of 3our hous.'
A. 6.104   Ac þere arn seuene *sistris* þat [seruen] treuþe euere,
A. 6.110   Ac whoso is sib to þis *sistris*, so me god helpe,
A.10.153   [Þat] of seth & his *sistir* sibþe forþ come
A.10.159   And siþen se[þ] & his *suster* [sed] wern spousid to kaymes;
A.10.179   And al for se[þ] & his *sister* children spouside eiþer oþer,
A.11.191   Obedient as breþeren & *sustren* to oþere,
B. 3.63   That [ech] segge shal [see] I am *suster* of youre house.'
B. 5.618   A[c] þer are seuen *sustren* þat seruen truþe euere,
B. 5.625   A[c] who is sib to þise [*sustren*], so me god helpe,
B. 5.642   Thow shalt seye I am þi *Suster*.' I ne woot where þei bicome.
B.18.117   Hir *suster*, as it semed, cam so[fte]ly walkynge
B.18.180   [Thanne] I shal daunce þerto; do þow so *suster*.
B.18.183   That mercy, my *suster*, and I mankynde sholde saue,
B.18.190   And saue mannes soule? *suster*, wene it neuere.
B.18.201   Forþi lat hem chewe as þei chosen and chide we no3t, *sustres*,
C. 3.54   Solempneliche and softlyche as for a *suster* of oure ordre.'
C. 3.67   That euery seg shal se y am *sustre* of 3oure ordre.'
C. 3.208   Vnsittyng soffraunce, here *suster*, and heresulue
C. 6.137   Thus sytte they, *sustres*, sum tyme and disputen
C. 7.270   Ac ther ben seuene *susteres* þat seruen treuthe euere,
C.11.95   For he is sib to þe seuene ars–and also my *suster*
C.12.170   He moet forsaken hymsulue his *suster* and his broþer
C.16.295   For thogh me souhte alle þe sektes of *susturne* and brethurne
C.20.120   Here *suster*, as hit semede, cam softly walkynge
C.20.183   And y shal daunse þerto; do thow so *sustur* .

C.20.186   That mercy, my *sustur*, and y mankynde sh[olde] saue
C.20.188   Mercy, [my *sustur*], and me to maynprisen hem alle
C.20.195   And saue mannes soule? *suster*, wene hit neuere.
C.20.206   Forthy [let] hem che[w]e as they chose and chyde we nat, *sustres*,

sustinaunce > sustenaunce; sustre(s sustur(ne > suster

sute n *sute n.* B 3; C 1 seute
B. 5.487   And siþþe wiþ þi selue sone in oure *s[u]te* deidest
B. 5.496   The þridde day [þer]after þow yedest in oure *sute*;
B.14.257   And he his seruaunt, as he seiþ, and of his *sute* boþe.
C.16.97   And he [h]is seruant, a[s] he saith, and of his *se[u]te* bothe.

suthe > siþen

suwen v *seuen v.(1)* A 7 sewen (2) sewide (2) sewiþ (3); B 18 sewe (2)
    sewen (1) sewest (1) seweþ (3) sued (2) suede (1) suwe (2) suwed (2)
    suwede (1) suwen (3); C 22 seude (1) sewe (5) sewed (1) sewede (1)
    sewen (1) seweth (4) sue (2) sued (1) suede (1) sueth (2) suewen (1)
    suynde (1) suynge (1)
A.Pr.45   Slep & sleuþe *sewiþ* hem euere.
A. 2.53   And as sire symonye wile segge to *sewen* his wille.
A. 6.31   Boþe sowen his seed, & *sewide* hise bestis,
A. 8.62   Siþen ȝe sen it is þus *sewiþ* to þe beste.
A. 9.66   'I haue *sewide* þe seuen ȝer; seiȝe þow me no raþere?'
A.11.245   & suche [[shewiþ] þis sermoun þat [*sewiþ*] aftir]:
A.11.249   And souereynliche to suche þat *sewen* oure beleue:
B.Pr.45   Sleep and sleuþe *seweþ* hem euere.
B. 4.167   Ac a Sisour and a Somonour *sued* hire faste,
B. 5.59   That *seweþ* my sermon;' and þus seyde Resoun.
B. 5.543   Boþe ysowen his seed and *suwed* hise beestes,
B. 8.75   'I haue *sued* þee seuen yeer; seye þow me no raþer?'
B.10.207   And [souereynly] to swiche [þat] *suwen* oure bileue;
B.11.22   The secounde seide þe same: 'I shal *sewe* þi wille;
B.11.335   Reson I seiȝ sooþly *sewen* alle beestes,
B.11.375   Why þow ne *sewest* man and his make þat no mysfeet hem folwe.'
B.11.442   That Clergie þi compaignye kepeþ noȝt to *suwe*.
B.14.254   And þouȝ Sleuþe *suwe* pouerte, and serue noȝt god to paie,
B.14.326   Synne *seweþ* vs euere', quod he and sory gan wexe,
B.17.87   And *suwed* þat Samaritan þat was so ful of pite,
B.17.104   And þiself now and swiche as *suwen* oure werkes.
B.17.109   For he seigh me þat am Samaritan *suwen* Feiþ & his felawe
B.18.192   That Adam and Eue and alle þat hem *suwede*
B.20.22   So þat he *sewe* and saue Spiritus temperancie.
B.20.126   Symonye hym [*suede*] to assaille Conscience,
C.Pr.46   Slep and slewthe *sueth* [hem] euer.
C. 2.106   And *sue* forth suche felawschipe til they ben falle in Slewthe
C. 2.200   Of many maner men for mede sake *seude* aftur.
C. 3.326   And as sone as god seyh a *sewed* nat his wille
C. 3.353   Seketh and *seweth* his sustantif sauacioun,
C. 3.368   Sethe y, his sone and his seruant, *sewe* for his ryhte.
C. 5.200   That *sueth* my sarmon;'[and] Thus [sayde] resoun.
C. 7.187   And to sowen his seed [and] *suewen* his bestes,
C.10.73   'Y haue *sued* the seuen ȝer; saw thow me no rather?'
C.10.162   That god [*s]eweth* nat synnefole men and soffreth hem mysfare,
C.11.181   The seconde saide þe same: 'y [shal] *sewe* thy wille;
C.12.167   Forsaek al and *sue* me and so is th[e] beste:"
C.13.143   Resoun y sey sothly *sewe* alle bestes
C.13.180   Was þat y seyh resoun *sewen* alle bestes
C.16.94   And thow sleuthe *sewe* pouerte and serue nat god to paye
C.17.145   Thenne *seweth* the [thy] soule to sorwe or to ioye
C.18.63   Ne *suynge* smale ne of [o] swettenesse wexe.
C.18.72   The whiche þe seynt spirit *seweth*, the sonne of al heuene.
C.19.81   Ac y *sewede* the samaritaen and saide how they bothe
C.20.358   That y ne sygge as y syhe, *suynde* my teme).
C.22.22   So þat he *sewe* and saue spiritus temperancie.
C.22.126   Symonye hym *suede* to assaile Consience

swaer > sweren

swage v *swagen v.(2)* A 1
A. 5.100   May no sugre ne swet þing *swage* it an vnche,

swanwhit adj *swan n.* C 1
C.20.214   Yf all þe world were whit or *swanwhit* all thynges?

swelle v *swellen v.* A 1 swellyd; B 2 swelle (1) swelleþ (1); C 2 swelle
(1) swelleth (1)
A.12.74   [But ete as hunger me hete til my belly *swellyd*.
B.12.57   Sapience, seiþ þe bok, *swelleþ* a mannes soule:
B.19.283   Sholde neuere mete ne [meschief] make hym to *swelle*;
C.16.227   Riht so sothly scienc[e] *swelleth* a mannes soule
C.21.283   Sholde neuere mete ne meschief maken hym to *swelle*

swellyng ger *swelinge ger.* B 2; C 2 swellynge
B. 5.123   May no sugre ne swete þyng aswage my *swellyng*,
B.16.72   And swete wiþouten *swellyng*; sour worþ it neuere.'

C. 6.88   May no sugre ne swete thyng aswage my *swellynge*
C.18.99   And swete withoute *swellynge*; sour worth hit neuere'–

swelte v *swelten v.* B 2 swelte (1) swelted (1); C 2
B. 5.154   Hir [were] leuere swowe or *swelte* þan suffre any peyne.
B.20.105   Swowned and *swelted* for sorwe of [deþes] dyntes.
C. 6.129   Here were leuer swowe or *swelte* then soffre eny payne.
C.22.105   Swowened and *swel[t]e* for sorwe of dethus duntes.

swerd n *sword n.* A 1; B 2; C 2
A. 1.97   [Di]de hem swere on h[ere] *swerd* to serue treuþe euere.
A. 1.99   Dide hem sweren on hir *swerd* to seruen truþe euere.
B. 3.305   Alle þat beren baselard, brood *swerd* or launce,
C. 1.103   Dede hem swere on here *swerd* to serue treuthe euere.
C. 3.458   For alle þat bereth baslard, br[ode] *swerd* oþer launce,

sweren v *sweren v.* A 7 swere (5) swor (2); B 16 swere (5) sweren (2)
    swerye (1) swoor (5) swor (1) sworen (2); C 14 swaer (1) swere (3)
    swerien (1) swereth (1) swerie (2) swerien (1) swoer (1) swor (2)
    sworen (1) sworn (1)
A. 1.97   [Di]de hem *swere* on h[ere] swerd to serue treuþe euere.
A. 2.133   Þanne *swor* cyuyle & seide be þe rode
A. 4.70   Þe king *swor* be crist & be his croune boþe
A. 5.142   Ac I *swere* now, so þ[e I], þat synne shal I lete,
A. 6.44   'Nay, be þe peril of my soule!' quaþ piers & gan to *swere*:
A. 6.57   So shalt þou se *swere* nouȝt but it be for nede,
A. 8.23   And for þei *swere* be here soule, & so god muste hem helpe,
B. 1.99   Dide hem *sweren* on hir swerd to seruen truþe euere.
B. 2.169   Ac þanne *swoor* Symonye and Cyuylle boþe
B. 4.83   The kyng *swor* by crist and by his crowne boþe
B. 5.226   Ac I *swere* now, so thee ik, þat synne wol I lete
B. 5.369   *Sworen* goddes soule [and his sydes] and "so me god helpe"
B. 5.557   'Nay, by [þe peril of] my soul[e]!' quod Piers and gan to *swere*:
B. 5.570   So shaltow se *swere*-noȝt-but-it-be-for-nede-
B. 7.21   And for þei *swere* by hir soule and so god moste hem helpe
B.13.304   And segge þyng þat he neuere seiȝ and for soþe *sweren* it;
B.13.381   Moore þan it was worþ, and yet wolde I *swere*
B.13.382   That it coste me muche moore; *swoor* manye oþes.
B.13.402   *Swoor* þerby swiþe ofte and al biswatte his cote;
B.14.34   Thanne laughed haukyn a litel and lightly gan *swerye*;
B.15.406   And dide folk þanne falle on knees; for he *swoor* in his prechyng
B.15.596   Ac þei seiden and *sworen* wiþ sorcerie he wrouȝte,
B.20.161   Hir sire was a Sysour þat neuere *swoor* truþe,
C.Pr.36   Wolleth neyther swynke ne swete bote *sweren* grete othes,
C. 1.103   Dede hem *swere* on here swerd to serue treuthe euere.
C. 2.184   Symonye and syuyle seyden and *sworen*
C. 4.79   The kyng [*s]wor* by Crist and by his croune bothe
C. 5.57   Sholde nother swynke ne swete ne *swerien* at enquestes
C. 6.51   Thyng þat neuere was thouhte and ȝut [y] *swor* [y] seyh hit
C. 6.427   *Sworn* godes soule and his sides and "so helpe [me] god almyhty"
C. 7.201   'Nay, bi þe perel of my soule!' Peres gan to *swerie*,
C. 7.217   [So] shalt thow se *swere*-nat-but-it-be-for-nede-
C. 9.25   And for they *sw[e]re* by here soule and [so] god mote hem helpe
C.16.305   And when a man *swereth* "forsoth" for sooth he hit troweth;
C.16.306   Weneth he þat no wyhte wolde lye and *swerie*
C.17.178   For Macometh to men *swaer* hit was a messager of heuene
C.22.161   Here syre was a sysour þat neuere *swoer* truthe,

swete adj *swete adj.* A 3 swet (2) swete (1); B 14 swete (11) swetter (3);
    C 15 swete (11) swettore (4)
A.Pr.83   To synge for symonye for siluer is *swete*.
A. 5.100   May no sugre ne *swet* þing swage it an vnche,
A.10.123   Riȝt as a rose, [þat red is and] *swet*,
B.Pr.86   [To] syngen for symonie for siluer is *swete*.
B. 5.123   May no sugre ne *swete* þyng aswage my swellyng,
B. 9.152   Impe on an Ellere, and if þyn appul be *swete*
B.11.59   By wissynge of þis wenche I [dide], hir wordes were so *swete*,
B.11.259   [Al]þouȝ it be sour to suffre, þe[r] comeþ *swete* [after].
B.11.367   And some soure and some *swete*; selkouþ me þouȝte.
B.12.266   And of flessh by fele fold fatter and *swetter*.
B.14.316   The nynþe is *swete* to þe soule, no sugre swetter,
B.14.316   The nynþe is swete to þe soule, no sugre *swetter*,
B.14.318   And sobretee *swete* drynke and good leche in siknesse.
B.15.184   Thouȝ he bere hem no breed he bereþ hem *swetter* liflode;
B.15.470   Right as þe cow calf coueiteþ [*swete* melk];
B.16.72   And *swete* wiþouten swellyng; sour worþ it neuere.'
B.17.127   'A, *swete* sire', I seide þo, 'wher I shal bileue,
C.Pr.84   And synge þer for symonye [for] seluer is *swete*.
C. 6.88   May no sugre ne *swete* thyng aswage my swellynge
C.12.111   By wissyng of this wenche y dede, here wordes were so *swete*,
C.12.145   Althouh h[it] be sour to soffre þer cometh a *swete* aftur.
C.12.220   Hit lasteth nat longe þat is lycour-*swete*,
C.13.177   And some soure and some *swete*; selcouthe me thouhte.
C.14.186   And *swettore* of sauour and swyftore of weng[e].
C.16.150   The nythe is *swete* to [þe] soul[e], no sucre *swettore*,

C.16.150 The nythe is swete to [þe] soul[e], no sucre *swettore*,
C.16.152 And sobrete ʒeueth here *swete* drynke and solaceth here in all angrys.
C.18.60 Ac somme ar *swettore* then somme and so[nner]e wollen rotye.
C.18.63 Ne suynge smale ne of [o] swettenesse *swete*.
C.18.65 *Swettore* and saueriore and also more grettore
C.18.99 And *swete* withoute swellynge; sour worth hit neuere.'
C.20.218 He hadde nat wist witterly where deth were sour or *swete*.

swete v *sweten v.(1)* A 2 swete (1) sweten (1); B 3; C 5 swete (4) swetande (1)

A. 7.27 I shal swynken & *sweten* & sowe for vs boþe,
A. 7.120 For we mowe no[þer] swynke ne *swete*, such seknesse vs eileþ'.
B. 6.25 I shal swynke and *swete* and sowe for vs boþe,
B. 6.128 For we may [neiþer] swynke ne *swete*, swich siknesse vs eyleþ.'
B.13.260 For er I haue breed of mele ofte moot I *swete*,
C.Pr.36 Wolleth neyther swynke ne *swete* bote sweren grete othes,
C. 5.57 Sholde nother swynke ne *swete* ne swerien at enquestes
C. 8.24 'Y shal swynke and *swete* and sowe for vs bothe
C. 8.134 We may nother swynke ne *swete*, suche sekenes vs ayleth;
C. 8.240 Þat sayth, "with swynke and with [*swetande*] face

swettenesse n *swetenesse n.* C 1

C.18.63 Ne suynge smale ne of [o] *swettenesse* swete.

swetter adv *swete adv. &> swete* A 1 swettere; B 1; C 1 swetture

A. 7.203 And he shal soupe *swettere* whanne he it haþ deseruid.
B. 6.217 And he shal soupe *swetter* whan he it haþ deserued.
C. 8.227 And h[e] shal soupe *swetture* when [he] hit hath deserued.

swettore > swete; swetture > swetter

sweuene n *sweven n.* A 2; B 3; C 1

A.Pr.11 Þanne gan I mete a merueillous *sweuene*,
A. 8.138 Daniel seide, 'sire king, þi *sweuene* is to mene
B.Pr.11 Thanne gan I meten a merueillous *sweuene*,
B. 7.160 Daniel seide, 'sire kyng, þi [*sweuene*] is to mene]
B. 7.167 Thanne Iacob iugged Iosephes *sweuene*:
C. 9.311 Thenne Iacob iuged Iosepes *sweuene*:

sweyed v *sweien v.(1)* A 1 swiʒede; B 1

A.Pr.10 I slomeride into a slepyng, it *swiʒede* so merye.
B.Pr.10 I slombred into a slepyng, it *sweyed* so murye.

swich pron *swich pron.* A 5 suche; B 25 swich (1) swiche (24); C 30 such (4) suche (25) swiche (1)

A. 7.205 Wiþ fuyr or wiþ false men, fond *suche* [to] knowen;
A. 8.33 Fynde *suche* here foode for oure lordis loue of heuene,
A.10.110 In ensaumple [þat] *suche* shulde not neuere aboute,
A.11.245 & *suche* [[shewiþ] þis sermoun þat [sewiþ] aftir]:
A.11.249 And souereynliche to *suche* þat sewen oure beleue:
B. 6.219 [Wiþ fir or wiþ] false men, fonde *swiche* to knowe.
B. 7.31 Fynden [*swiche*] hir foode [for oure lordes loue of heuene],
B. 7.41 For þe Sauter saueþ hem noʒt, *swiche* as take ʒiftes,
B. 7.43 Pledours sholde peynen hem to plede for *swiche* and helpe;
B.10.26 The Sauter seiþ þe same by *swiche* þat doon ille:
B.10.207 And [souereynly] to *suche* [þat] suwen oure bileue;
B.10.432 And now ben [*swiche*] as Souereyns wiþ Seintes in heuene,
B.10.450 For he seide to Seint Peter and to *swiche* as he louede,
B.11.280 As Dauid seiþ in þe Sauter: to *swiche* þat ben in wille
B.12.13 And Dauid in þe Sauter seiþ, of *swiche* þat loueþ Iesus,
B.12.49 Of manye *swiche* I may rede, of men and of wommen,
B.15.8 To sergeauntʒ ne to *swiche* seide noʒt ones,
B.15.54 Ayein *swiche* Salomon spekeþ and despiseþ hir wittes
B.15.208 Than for penaunce and parfitnesse, þe pouerte þat *swiche* takeþ.
B.15.214 Ne at Ancres þere a box hangeþ; alle *swiche* þei faiten.
B.15.267 And seide to *swiche* þat suffre wolde,
B.15.324 And [bisette] to bidde for yow to *swiche* þat ben riche,
B.15.330 And on hemself som, and *swiche* as ben hir laborers;
B.15.383 I dar noʒt siggen it for shame–if *swiche* were apposed
B.15.528 And souereynliche to *swiche* þat of surrye bereþ þe name],
B.15.577 Oʒias seiþ for *swiche* þat sike ben and feble,
B.16.112 Ofte [he] heeled *swiche*; he held it for no maistrie
B.17.104 And þiself now and *swiche* as suwen oure werkes.
B.17.320 His sorwe is satisfaccion for [*swich*] þat may noʒt paie.
B.19.429 And [soudeþ hem] þat sleeþ [*swiche* as] he sholde saue.
C. 2.47 Soffre and thow shalt see *suche* as ben apayed
C. 3.78 Bothe Schyreues and seriauntes and *suche* as kepeth lawes,
C. 3.288 As þe sauhter sayth by *such* þat ʒeueth mede:
C. 5.48 Th[u]s y s[yn]ge for here soules of *suche* as me helpeth
C. 6.54 And sygge to *suche* þat sytte me byside:
C. 9.19 And *suche* liue as þei lereth men oure lord treuthe hem graunteth
C. 9.48 That conforteth *suche* in eny caes and coueyteth nat he[re] ʒiftes
C. 9.117 And suffreth *suche* go so, it semeth to myn inwyt
C. 9.131 Men suffreth al þat *suche* sayen and in solace taketh
C. 9.214 Kyndeliche, by Crist, ben *suche* ycald lollares.

C.11.11 Y syg hit by *suche*,' quod [she], 'þat sheweth by here werkes
C.11.12 What shal worthen of *suche* when þei lyf leten;
C.11.43 Thenne semeth hit to my sihte to *suche* þat so biddeth
C.11.275 For Crist saide to sayntes and to *suche* as he louede,
C.12.225 Riht so, sothly, *suche* þat ben bischopes,
C.13.63 Wolde noon *suche* assailen hym for such as hym foloweth
C.13.63 Wolde noon suche assailen hym for *such* as hym foloweth
C.13.112 The same y segge for sothe by *suche* þat beth prestes
C.13.115 Euele beth thei ysoffred, *suche* þat [shenden] þe masse
C.13.125 That crouneth *suche* goddes knyhtes þat conne [nat] sapienter
C.14.15 And þat is dobet, yf eny *suche* be, a blessed man þat helpeth
C.15.306 Dauid in þe sauter of *suche* maketh mynde and sayth: dormierunt
C.16.216 Aʒenes *suche* salamon speketh and despiseth here wittes
C.17.1 'There is no *such*,' y sayde, 'þat som tyme ne borweth
C.17.57 To feffe *suche* and fede þat founded ben to þe fulle
C.17.278 And souereynliche [to] *suche* þat of surie bereth þe name
C.19.93 Saue mysulue soethly and *such* as y louede–
C.19.300 As sorwe of herte is satisfaccioun for *suche* þat may nat paye.
C.21.373 [Saue shrewes one *swiche* as y spak of],
C.21.429 And soudeth hem þat sleeth *suche* as he sholde saue.

swich adj *swich adj.* A 43 such (19) suche (22) swyche (2); B 83 swich (49) swiche (34); C 98 such (42) suche (56)

A.Pr.32 As it semiþ to oure siʒt þat *suche* men þriuen.
A. 1.70 Þat *suche* wise wordis of holy writ shewide,
A. 1.104 Cherubyn & seraphyn, *such* seuene & anoþer;
A. 1.156 Of *such* good as god sent goodlyche parteþ,
A. 1.168 *Such* chastite wiþoute charite worþ cheynid in helle.
A. 2.81 *Such* weddyng to werche to wraþþe wiþ treuþe;
A. 3.53 Ac god alle good folk *such* grauyng defendiþ
A. 3.60 Forþi I lere ʒow lordis, leuiþ *such* wrytyng,
A. 3.77 Of alle *suche* selleris siluer to take,
A. 3.110 Er I wedde *such* a wif wo me betide!
A. 3.123 Sisours & sompnours, *suche* men hire preisiþ;
A. 3.156 *Such* a maister is mede among men of goode.'
A. 3.256 *Such* a meschef mede made þe kyng [to] haue
A. 3.276 And make of lawe a labourer, *such* loue shal arise.'
A. 4.55 And warnide wrong þo wiþ *suche* a wys tale:
A. 5.72 *Such* wynd in my wombe wexiþ er I dyne.
A. 7.48 And nameliche at mete *suche* men eschew[e],
A. 7.114 Somme leide here leg alery as *suche* lorellis cunne,
A. 7.115 And pleynide hem to peris wiþ *suche* pitous wordis:
A. 7.120 For we mowe no[þer] swynke ne *swete*, such seknesse vs eileþ'.
A. 7.124 *Suche* wastours in þis world his werkmen distroyeþ;
A. 7.299 *Suche* lawis to loke laboureris to chast[e].
A. 7.305 Or fyue ʒer be fulfild *such* famyn shal arise;
A. 8.182 *Suche* werkis to werche, whiles we ben here.
A.10.63 Ouer *suche* maner of men miʒt in here soulis.
A.10.82 For doute men doþ þe bet; dred is *such* a maister
A.10.130 *Such* wer[kis] to werche [þat] he is wiþ paied.
A.10.161 Þat god was wroþ wiþ here werkis & [*such* wordis seide]:
A.10.184 A carful concepcioun comiþ of *such* weddyng
A.11.8 Wiþ *suche* wise wordis to wisse any foolis!
A.11.21 Þat *suche* craftis conne [to counseil ben yclepid],
A.11.29 Litel is he louid or lete by þat *suche* a lessoun techiþ,
A.11.58 Freris and faitours han founden vp *suche* questiouns
A.11.66 "Why wolde oure sauiour suffre *such* a worm in his blisse
A.11.70 *Suche* motifs þei meuen, þise maistris in here glorie,
A.11.72 Ac austyn þe olde for alle *suche* prechide,
A.11.73 And for *suche* tale telleris suche a teme shewide,
A.11.73 And for suche tale telleris *suche* a teme shewide:
A.11.311 Souteris & seweris; *suche* lewide iottis
A.12.33 But as he seyþ, *such* I am, when he with me carpeþ.'
A.12.68 Me folweþ *such* a fentyse, I may no ferþer walke.'
A.12.87 Fro deþ þat is oure duk *swyche* dedis we brynge.'
A.12.111 God for his goudnesse gif hem *swyche* happes
B.Pr.32 As it semeþ to oure siʒt þat *swiche* men þryueþ.
B. 1.72 That *swiche* wise wordes of holy writ shewed,
B. 1.106 Cherubyn and Seraphyn, *swiche* seuene & [anoþer];
B. 1.182 [Of] *swich* good as god sent goodliche parteþ,
B. 1.194 *Swich* chastite wiþouten charite worþ cheyned in helle.
B. 2.17 Hire array me rauysshed; *swich* richesse sauʒ I neuere.
B. 2.117 *Swic[h]* weddyng[e] to werche to wraþe wiþ truþe;
B. 3.64 Ac god alle good folk *swich* grauynge defendeþ,
B. 3.69 Forþi I lere yow lordes, leueþ *swic[h]* writynge,
B. 3.88 Of alle *swiche* Selleris siluer to take,
B. 3.121 Er I wedde *swich* a wif wo me bitide!
B. 3.134 Sisours and Somonours, *swiche* men hire preiseþ;
B. 3.169 *Swich* a maister is Mede among men of goode.'
B. 3.244 *Swiche* manere men, my lord, shul haue þis firste Mede
B. 3.278 *Swich* a meschief Mede made þe kyng to haue
B. 3.300 And make of lawe a laborer; *swich* loue shal arise
B. 3.301 And *swich* pees among þe peple and a parfit truþe
B. 4.69 And warnede wrong þo with *swich* a wis tale:

B. 5.152 [That] I ne moste folwe this folk, for *swich* is my grace.
B. 5.242 *Swiche* dedes I dide write if he his day breke;
B. 5.246 Eschaunges and cheuysaunces, wiþ *swich* chaffare I dele,
B. 5.259 Amonges my neȝebores namely *swich* a name ich haue.'
B. 5.269 And I wiste witterly þow were *swich* as þow tellest.
B. 6.53 And namely at mete *swiche* men eschuwe,
B. 6.122 Somme leide hir le[g] aliry as *swiche* lo[r]els konneþ
B. 6.128 For we may [neiþer] swynke ne swete, *swich* siknesse vs eyleþ.'
B. 6.318 *Swiche* lawes to loke laborers to [chaste].
B. 6.324 Er fyue [yer] be fulfilled *swich* famyn shal aryse.
B. 7.204 *Swiche* werkes to werche, while we ben here,
B. 9.125 Of *swiche* synfulle sherewes þe Sauter makeþ mynde:
B. 9.132 Til god wraþed [wiþ] hir werkes and *swich* a word seide,
B. 9.161 [A] careful concepcion comeþ of [*swich* weddynge]
B.10.8 'Wiþ *swiche* wise wordes to wissen any sottes!'
B.10.21 [That] *swiche* craftes k[onne] to counseil [are] cleped;
B.10.37 Litel is he loued [or lete by] þat *swich* a lesson [techeþ],
B.10.72 Freres and faitours han founde [vp] *swiche* questions
B.10.93 *Swiche* lessons lordes sholde louye to here,
B.10.108 "Why wolde oure Saueour suffre *swich* a worm in his blisse
B.10.117 *Swiche* motyues þei meue, þise maistres in hir glorie,
B.10.120 Austyn to *swiche* Argueres [he] telleþ þis teme:
B.10.261 *Swich* an þow semest in siȝte be in assay yfounde:
B.10.263 But be *swich* in þi soule as þow semest wiþoute.
B.10.276 That ye were *swiche* as ye sey[d]e to salue wiþ oþere.
B.10.281 But in *swich* manere as Marc meneþ in þe gospel:
B.10.401 As Salomon dide and *swiche* oþere, þat shewed grete wittes
B.10.467 Souteres and shepherdes; [*swiche*] lewed Iuttes
B.11.298 The same I segge for soþe by alle *swiche* preestes
B.11.313 That crouneþ *swiche* goddes knyȝtes, þat konneþ noȝt sapienter
B.11.402 For man was maad of *swich* a matere he may noȝt wel asterte
B.12.208 And for to seruen a Seint and *swich* a þef togideres,
B.12.229 And kynde kenned þe pecok to cauken in *swich* a [wise.
B.12.268 [*Swiche* tales telleþ Aristotle þe grete clerk]:
B.12.289 And if þer were he wolde amende, and in *swich* wille deieþ–
B.13.283 Was noon *swich* as hymself], ne [noon] so po[pe] holy;
B.13.335 Or an Ague in *swich* an Angre and som tyme a Feuere
B.13.350 *Swiche* werkes with hem were neuere out of seson
B.13.432 What Dauid seiþ of *swiche* men as þe Sauter telleþ
B.13.442 For to solace youre soules *swiche* minstrales to haue:
B.14.165 Heuene after hir hennes goyng þat here han *swich* defaute.
B.14.267 Muche is [þat maide] to loue of [a man] þat *swich* oon takeþ,
B.15.51 For *swich* a lust and likyng Lucifer fel from heuene.
B.15.73 Bettre it were [by] manye doctours to [bi]leuen *swich* techyng
B.15.98 Ther is a meschief in þe more of *swiche* manere [stokkes].
B.15.134 So harlotes and hores arn holpe wiþ *swiche* goodes
B.15.151 'Where sholde men fynde *swich* a frend wiþ so fre an herte?
B.15.158 I seiȝ neuere *swich* a man, so me god helpe,
B.15.207 Ac it is moore to haue hir mete [on] *swich* an esy manere
B.15.251 For whoso myȝte meete [wiþ] hym *swiche* maneres hym eileþ:
B.16.269 Lollynge in my lappe til *swich* a lord vs fecche.'
B.17.241 And if it suffise noȝt for assetȝ, þat in *swich* a wille deyeþ,
B.17.311 Thus it fareþ by *swich* folk þat [folwen] al hire [wille],
B.17.346 Haþ mercy on *swiche* men þat so yuele may suffre.
B.18.182 Loue þat is my lemman *swiche* lettres me sente
B.18.235 That *swich* a barn was ybore in Bethleem þe Citee
B.18.267 'Swich a light, ayeins oure leue laȝar [i]t fette.
B.18.272 That *swich* a lord and [a] light sholde lede hem alle hennes.'
B.18.384 And I þat am kyng of kynges shal come *swich* a tyme
B.18.399 And nameliche at *swich* a nede þer nedes help bihoueþ:
B.18.430 And it afereþ þe fend, for *swich* is þe myȝte
B.19.282 He þat ete of þat seed hadde *swich* a kynde:
B.19.351 Wiþ *swiche* colours and queyntise comeþ pride yarmed
B.19.373 Saue sherewes one *swiche* as I spak of,
B.20.343 I knew *swich* oon ones, noȝt eighte wynter [passed],
C.Pr.34 As it semeþ to oure sighte that *suche* men ythryueth.
C.Pr.64 But holi chirche and charite choppe adoun *suche* shryuars
C.Pr.121 God shal take vengeaunce on alle *suche* prestis
C.Pr.122 Wel hardere and grettere on *suche* shrewed faderes
C.Pr.134 Ac of þe Cardinales at Court þat caught han *such* a name
C. 1.69 That *suche* wyse wordes of holy writ shewede
C. 1.106 Cherubyn and Ceraphyn, *suche* seuene and anoþer,
C. 1.178 Of *such* good as god sent goodliche parte,
C. 2.80 Mede and *suche* men þat aftur mede wayten.
C. 2.106 And sue forth *suche* felawschipe til they ben falle in Slewthe
C. 2.121 *Suche* a weddyng to wurche þat wrathe myhte treuthe;
C. 2.140 And thow hast feffed here with fals; fy on *suche* lawe.
C. 2.192 On secatours and *such* men cometh softly aftur.
C. 3.68 Ac god to alle good folk *suche* grauynge defendeth,
C. 3.73 Forthy, l[e]ue lordes, leueth *suche* writynges;
C. 3.74 God in þe gospel *suche* grauynge nouȝt alloueth:
C. 3.116 Of alle *suche* sullers seluer to take
C. 3.158 Ar y wedde *suche* a wyf wo me bytyde!

C. 3.172 Sysores and somnours, *suche* men he[re] preiseth;
C. 3.215 *Such* a maistre is mede among men of gode.'
C. 3.386 *Such* inparfit peple repreueth alle resoun
C. 3.410 Agaynes godes comandement, god tok *such* a vengeaunce
C. 3.453 And maky of lawe [a] laborer; *suche* loue shal aryse
C. 3.454 And *such* pees among þe peple and a parfit treuthe
C. 5.96 A boute *suche* a bargayn he was þe bet euere
C. 5.98 *Suche* a wynnyng hym warth thorw w[y]rdes of grace:
C. 6.37 Was non *such* as [my]sulue ne non so popholy;
C. 6.45 And likynge of *such* a lyf þat no lawe preiseth,
C. 6.79 Or an ague in *suche* [an] angre and som tyme a feuere
C. 6.83 To the soutere of southewerk, *suche* is his grace.
C. 6.141 Byte and bete and brynge forth *suche* thewes
C. 6.184 *Such* werkes with vs were neuere out of sesoun
C. 6.290 Thow were *such* as thow sayst; y sholde rather s[t]erue:
C. 6.300 Yf he wiste thow were *such* when he resseyued thyn offrynge.
C. 7.92 Wh[at] dauid sayth of *such* men as þe sauter telleth:
C. 7.102 For to solace ȝoure soules *suche* munstrals to haue:
C. 8.51 Ac [manliche] at mete *suche* men eschewe
C. 8.129 [Somme] leyde here legges alery as *suche* lorelles conneth
C. 8.134 We may nother swynke ne swete, *suche* sekenes vs ayleth;
C. 8.144 *Such* poore,' quod [Peres], 'shal parte with my godes,
C. 8.187 Al for drede of here deth, *such* duntus ȝaf hunger.
C. 8.338 *Suche* lawes to lerne laboreres to greue:
C. 9.95 Were a feste with *suche* folk or so fele cockes.
C. 9.96 These are Almusse to helpe þat han *suche* charges
C. 9.97 And to conforte *suche* coterelles and crokede men and blynde.
C. 9.101 Reche ȝe neuere, ȝe riche, Thouh *suche* lo[rell]es sterue.
C. 9.118 Hit aren as his postles, *suche* peple, or as his priue disciples
C. 9.124 *Suche* manere men, Matheu vs techeth,
C. 9.132 And ȝut more to *suche* men me doth ar they passe;
C. 9.172 Ther aren mo mysshape amonges *suche* beggares
C. 9.218 Rihte so, sothly, *such* manere Ermytes
C. 9.257 That soffreth *suche* sottes and oþere synnes regne.
C. 9.350 *Suche* werkes to worche the while we ben here
C.10.97 For here mok and here mebles *suche* men thenketh
C.10.166 *Such* lyther lyuyng men lome been ryche
C.10.243 For god seid ensaumple of *suche* manere issue
C.11.5 'Wel artow wyse,' quod she to wyt, '*suche* wysdomes to shewe
C.11.23 The sauter saith þe same of alle *suche* ryche;
C.11.52 Freres and faytours haen founde vp *suche* questions
C.12.28 The sauter sayth hit is no synne for *suche* men þat ben trewe
C.13.83 That þe lawe ȝeueth leue *such* low folk to be excused;
C.13.169 'Where hadde thise wilde *suche* wit and at what scole?'
C.13.210 Man was made of *such* [a] matere he may nat wel asterte
C.14.2 Thogh y sete by mysulue, *suche* is my grace.
C.14.12 Ac hit soffiseth to be saued [to] be *such* as y tauhte.
C.14.26 Ac Ar *such* a wil wexe worcheth go[d] sulue
C.14.31 As to be bore or bygete in *such* a constillacioun;
C.14.147 And for to seruen a seynt and *suche* a thef togyderes,
C.14.221 And yf þer were a wolde [amende], and in *suche* a wille deyeth–
C.15.129 Shal no *such* motyef be meued for me bote [þ]eise
C.15.245 'Hastow,' quod actyf, 'ay *such* mete with the?'
C.16.107 Moche is [þat] mayde to louye of a man þat *such* oen taketh,
C.16.213 For *such* a lust and lykynge lucifer ful fram heuene.
C.16.251 There is a meschief in þe more of *suche* manere stokkes.
C.16.370 And hoso coueyteth to knowe [hym] *such* a kynde hym foloweth
C.17.6 Holy writ witnesseth þer were *suche* eremytes,
C.17.151 'Hit may be so þat sarresynes haen *such* a manere charite,
C.17.179 And sothliche þat god sulue in *suche* a coluere lyknesse
C.17.183 And seth oure saueour soffrede *such* a fals cristene
C.17.243 In *such* manere me thynketh moste þe pope,
C.18.139 That *suche* a surgien sethen ysaye was þer neuere
C.18.225 Ne withoute a soware be *suche* seed; this we seen alle.
C.18.285 Lollyng in my lappe til *suche* a lord vs feche.'
C.19.207 And yf hit suffic[e] nat for ase[t]h þat in *suche* a will deyeth
C.19.291 Thus hit fareth bi *such* folk þat folewen here owene will,
C.19.326 Haeth mercy on *suche* men þat [so] euele may soffre.
C.20.185 Loue þat is my lemman *such* lettres me sente
C.20.244 That *such* a barn was ybore in Bethleem þe Citee
C.20.275 '*Such* a lyht aȝenes oure leue laȝar hit fette;
C.20.280 That *such* a lord and a lihte sh[olde] lede hem alle hennes.
C.20.306 Thus this lord of liht *such* a lawe made
C.20.426 And y þat am kynge o[f] kynges shal come *such* a tyme
C.20.442 And namliche at *such* a nede þat nedes helpe asketh:
C.20.474 And hit afereth th[e] fende, for *such* is þe myhte
C.21.282 He þat eet of that seed hadde *such* a kynde:
C.21.351 With *such* colours and queyntis[e] cometh pruyde yArmed
C.22.343 Y knewe *such* oen ones, nat eyhte wynter passed,

swift adj *swifte adj.* B 2 swift (1) swifter (1); C 1 swyftore
B.11.379 Suffraunce is a souerayn vertue, and a *swift* vengeaunce.
B.12.265 And wel awey of wynge *swifter* þan þe Pecock,

C.14.186   And swettore of sauour and *swyftore* of weng[e].

swymmen v *swimmen v.* B 5 swymme (3) swymmen (1) swymmeþ (1); C
    4 swymme (1) swymmen (2) swymmeth (1)
B.12.162   That oon [kan] konnynge and kan *swymmen* and dyuen;
B.12.163   That ooþer is lewed of þat labour, lerned neuere *swymme.*
B.12.168   And is in drede to drenche, þat neuere dide *swymme?'*
B.12.169   'That *swymme* kan noȝt', I seide, 'it semeþ to my wittes.'
B.12.239   And feblest fowel of fliȝt is þat fleeþ or *swymmeþ·*
C.14.106   That oen hath connyng and can *swymmen* and dyuen;
C.14.107   That oþer is lewed of þat labour, lerned neuere *swymme.*
C.14.109   'He þat can nat *swymmen*,' y sayde, 'hit semeth to alle wittes.'
C.14.171   And feblest foul of flyh[t is] þat fleeth oþer *swym[m]eth*:

swymmere n *swimmere n.* B 1
B.12.166   Or þe *swymmere* þat is saaf by so hymself like,

swymmyng ger *swimminge ger.* B 1
B.12.165   He þat neuere ne dyued ne noȝt kan of *swymmyng,*

swyn n *swine n.* B 1; C 1
B. 2.98   And breden as Burgh *swyn*, and bedden hem esily
C. 5.19   Heggen or harwen or *swyn* or gees dryue

swynk n *swink n.* A 1 swynke; B 1; C 1 swynke
A. 7.217   In sudore & *swynke* þou shalt þi mete tilen
B. 6.233   In sudore and *swynk* þow shalt þi mete tilie
C. 8.240   Þat sayth, "with *swynke* and with [swetande] face

swynkares > swynkeres

swynke v *swinken v. &> swynk* A 8 swynke (6) swynken (1) swonke (1);
    B 9 swynke (8) swonken (1); C 9 swynke (8) swonken (1)
A.Pr.21   In settyng & sowyng *swonke* ful harde;
A.Pr.52   Grete lobies & longe þat loþ were to *swynke*
A. 6.29   Boþe sowe [and sette] while I *swynke* miȝte.
A. 7.27   I shal *swynken* & sweten & sowe for vs boþe,
A. 7.59   And whoso helpiþ me to eren, or any þing *swynke,*
A. 7.120   For we mowe no[þer] *swynke* ne swete, such seknesse vs eileþ'.
A. 7.202   And ȝif þe [g]omes grucche bidde hem gon & *swynke,*
A. 8.104   I shal cesse of my sowyng,' quaþ peris, '& *swynke* not so harde,
B.Pr.21   In settynge and sowynge *swonken* ful harde;
B.Pr.55   Grete lobies and longe þat loþe were to *swynke*
B. 5.541   Boþe sowe and sette while I *swynke* myȝte.
B. 6.25   I shal *swynke* and swete and sowe for vs boþe,
B. 6.65   And whoso helpeþ me to erie [or any þyng *swynke]*
B. 6.128   For we may [neiþer] *swynke* ne swete, swich siknesse vs eyleþ.'
B. 6.194   And many a beggere for benes buxum was to *swynke,*
B. 6.216   And if þe gomes grucche bidde hem go [and] *swynke*
B. 7.122   I shal cessen of my sowyng', quod Piers, '& *swynke* noȝt so harde,
C.Pr.23   In settynge and sowynge *swonken* ful harde
C.Pr.36   Wolleth neyther *swynke* ne swete bote sweren grete othes,
C.Pr.53   Grete lobies and longe þat loth were to *swynke*
C. 5.57   Sholde nother *swynke* ne swete ne swerien at enquestes
C. 7.186   Bothe to sowe and to sette þe while y *swynke* myhte
C. 8.24   'Y shal *swynke* and swete and sowe for vs bothe
C. 8.134   We may nother *swynke* ne swete, suche sekenes vs ayleth;
C. 8.226   And yf þe [g]omes gruche bid[d]e hem go and *swynke*
C. 8.261   This aren euidences,' quod hunger, 'for hem þat wolle nat *swynke*

swynkeres n *swinkere n.* B 1; C 2 swynkares
B.17.211   [That serueþ þise *swynkeres* to se by aniȝtes],
C. 8.258   Lo! what þe sauter sayth to *swynkares* with handes:
C.19.177   That serueth this *swynkares* to [see] by a nyhtes,

swiþe adv *swithe adv.* A 4 swiþe (3) swyþe (1); B 4; C 3 swythe
A. 3.91   And ofsente hire as *swiþe*; seriauntis hire fe[tt]e
A. 4.23   And resoun wiþ hym rit & rapiþ hym [*swyþe*].
A. 5.234   Ac for þere was nouȝt wherewith he wepte *swiþe* sore.
A.10.166   *Swiþe* to shapen a sship of shidis & bordis;
B. 3.102   And ofsente hire as *swiþe*; [sergeauntȝ hire fette]
B. 5.462   And for þer was noȝt wher[wiþ] he wepte *swiþe* soore.
B. 9.135   "*Swiþe* go shape a ship of shides and of bordes;
B.13.402   Swoor þerby *swiþe* ofte and al biswatte his cote;
C. 6.316   And for þer was nat wherwith a wep *swythe* sore.
C. 6.422   A wax ashamed, þat shrewe, and shrofe hym a[s] *swythe*
C.13.53   The marchaunt with his marchauntdyse may nat go so *swythe*

swiȝede > sweyed; swoene > swoune; swoer > sweren; swonk(en > swynke;
swoor swor(- > swere

swoune v *swounen v.* B 5 swoune (1) swouned (1) swowned (3); C 3
    swoene (1) swowened (2)
B. 5.441   'Repente[st]ow noȝt?' quod Repentaunce, & riȝt wiþ þat he
            swowned
B.14.329   *Swouned* and sobbed and siked ful ofte
B.16.19   That I herde nempne his name anoon I *swowned* after,
B.18.57   'Consummatum est', quod crist and comsede for to *swoune.*

B.20.105   *Swowned* and swelted for sorwe of [deþes] dyntes.
C. 7.55   'Repentest th[ow] nat?' quod repentaunce, and ryht with þat he
            swowened
C.20.57   'Consummatum est,' quod Crist and comsed for to *swoene.*
C.22.105   *Swowened* and swel[t]e for sorwe of dethus duntes.

swowe n *swoue n.* A 1
A. 5.213   Sleuþe for sorewe fil doun a *swowe*

swowe v *swouen v.(2)* B 1; C 1
B. 5.154   Hir [were] leuere *swowe* or swelte þan suffre any peyne.
C. 6.129   Here were leuer *swowe* or swelte then soffre eny payne.

swowened swowned > swoune

T

tabard n *tabarde n.(1)* A 1 tabbard; B 1; C 1
A. 5.111   In a torn *tabbard* of twelue wynter age,
B. 5.195   In a [torn] *tabard* of twelf wynter age,
C. 6.203   In a tore *tabard* of twelue wynter age;

table n *table n.* B 4; C 5 table (4) tables (1)
B.10.104   I haue yherd heiȝe men etynge at þe *table*
B.12.200   As þo þat seten at þe syde *table* or wiþ þe souereyns of þe halle,
B.13.176   Profitable to eiþer peple;' and putte þe *table* fro hym,
B.13.443   The pouere for a fool sage sittyng at þ[i] *table*,
C. 7.103   The pore for a f[o]l sage sittynge at thy *table*,
C. 9.253   He sat at þe syde benche and at þe seconde *table*;
C.14.139   As tho þat sitten at þe syde *table* or with þe souereyns [of þe] halle
C.15.41   And seten by ouresulue at a syde *table*.
C.18.156   And ouerturnede in þe temple here *tables* and here stalles

taboure v *tabouren v.* B 1; C 1 tabre
B.13.230   Ac for I kan neiþer *taboure* ne trompe ne telle no gestes,
C.15.204   [Ac for] y can nat *tabre* ne trompy ne telle [no] gestes,

tacches n *tache n.(3)* B 1
B. 9.151   That somdel þe sone shal haue þe sires *tacches*.

taddee > thaddee; taek > taken; taȝte > techen

tail n *tail n.* A 3; B 8 tail (7) tailles (1); C 6 tayl (5) tayles (1)
A. 2.147   I haue no tom to telle þe *tail* þat hem folewiþ
A. 3.120   She is tykil of hire *tail*, talewys of hire tunge,
A. 5.19   And turnide vpward here *tail* in toknyng of drede
B. 2.186   I haue no tome to telle þe *tail* þat [hem] folwe[þ]
B. 3.131   She is tikel of hire *tail*, talewis of tonge,
B. 3.351   And þat is þe *tail* of þe text of þat [teme ye] shewed,
B. 5.19   [And] turned vpward hire *tai[l]* in tokenynge of drede
B.12.244   For þe trailynge of his *tail* ouertaken is he soone.
B.12.251   To alle hem þat it holdeþ til hir *tail* be plukked.
B.15.105   Trewe of youre tonge and of youre *tail* boþe,
B.15.300   That ne fil to hir feet and reuied wiþ þe *tailles*;
C. 2.199   Y haue no tome to telle the *tayl* whan he folewe[th]
C. 3.168   For she is tikel of here *tayl*, talewys of tonge,
C. 5.121   And turned vpward here *tayl* in tokenynge of drede
C.10.80   And therto trewe of his *tayl*, [taketh but his owne]
C.16.259   And þerto trewe of ȝoure tonge and of ȝoure *tayl* also
C.17.31   And faire byfore tho men faunede with þe *tayles*.

taile > taille

tailende n *tailende n.* A 1; B 2; C 2 taylende
A. 9.74   Trusty of his *tailende*, takiþ but his owene,
B. 5.388   Were I brouȝt abedde, but if my *tailende* it made,
B. 8.83   Trusty of his *tailende*, takeþ but his owene,
C. 3.370   I wolde feffe hym with here fayre and [with] here foule *taylende*.
C. 7.4   Were y brouhte [o]n bed, but yf my *taylende* hit made,

taylers > taillours

taillage n *taillage n.* B 1; C 1 talage
B.19.37   But vnder tribut and *taillage* as tikes and cherles.
C.21.37   Bote vnder tribuyt and *talage* as tykes and cherles.

taille n *taille n.* A 1 taile; B 2; C 1 tayle
A. 4.45   And takiþ me but a *taile* for ten quarteris otis,
B. 4.58   And takeþ me but a *taille* for ten quarters Otes;
B.12.248   And deleþ it noȝt til his deeþ day, þe *tail[le* is al of]* sorwe.
C. 4.61   And taketh me but a *tayle* for ten quarteres otes;

tailles > tail

taillours n *taillour n.* A 2; B 3; C 3 taylers (1) taylours (2)
A.Pr.100   *Taillours*, t[okk]eris & to[ll]eris boþe,
A.11.184   Trewe tilieris on erþe, *taillours* & souteris
B.Pr.221   *Taillours*, Tynkers and Tollers in Markettes,
B. 5.547   In *taillours* craft and tynkeris craft, what truþe kan deuyse,
B.15.455   Ytouked and yteynted and vnder *taillours* hande.
C.Pr.227   As *taylers* and tanners and tulyers [of] þe erthe,
C. 4.120   And til byschopes ben bakeres, Breweres and *taylours*
C. 9.205   Whilen were werkmen, webbes and *taylours*

taken v *taken v.* A 33 tak (2) take (10) taken (5) takiþ (9) tok (6) toke (1); B 128 tak (3) take (37) taken (23) takeþ (22) toke (6) token (4) took (31) Itake (1) ytake (1); C 129 taek (2) take (43) taken (13) taketh (25) toek (22) tok (2) toke (11) token (2) took (5) ytake (4)
A. 1.54   And tutour of ȝour tresour, & *take* it ȝow at nede;
A. 1.94   And *taken* trespassours & teiȝen hem faste
A. 2.49   Þanne fauel fettiþ hire forþ & to fals *takiþ*
A. 3.4   To *take* mede þe maide & make hire at ese.
A. 3.10   *Tok* mede be þe myddel & brouȝte hire to chaumbre.
A. 3.44   Tolde hym a tale, & *tok* hym a noble
A. 3.74   For *tok* h[y] on trewely h[y] tymbride not so heiȝe,
A. 3.77   Of alle suche selleris siluer to *take*,
A. 3.84   And *tok* hym þis teeme þat I telle þenke:
A. 3.96   Ac wers wrouȝtest þou neuere þan þo þou fals *toke*.
A. 3.129   He[o] *takiþ* þe trewe be þe top, teiȝeþ hym faste,
A. 3.205   *Takiþ* mede of here maistris as þei mowe accorde;
A. 3.222   *Tak* no mede, my lord, of [men] þat ben trewe;
A. 3.226   To mayntene mysdoeris mede þei *taken*,
A. 3.232   Þat *take* mede & money for massis þat þei synge,
A. 3.234   Þat laboureris & louȝ folk *taken* of here maistris
A. 3.268   And whoso trespassiþ [to treuþe, or] *takiþ* [aȝeyn his wille],
A. 4.15   Seide hym as þe king sente & siþþe *tok* his leue.
A. 4.35   How wrong aȝen his wil hadde his wyf *take*,
A. 4.45   And *takiþ* me but a taile for ten quarteris otis,
A. 4.63   And *tok* mede wiþ hem mercy to wynne.
A. 5.28   Thomas he tauȝte to *take* two staues
A. 7.245   And ete nouȝt, I hote þe, er hunger þe *take*
A. 8.2   To *take* his tem & [tilien þe erþe],
A. 8.48   And of no pore peple no peny[worþ] to *take*.
A. 8.64   Þat trewely *taken*, & trewely wynnen,
A. 8.78   Þere ben mo mysshapen amonges hem, whoso *takiþ* hede,
A. 8.85   Þat *takiþ* [þ]is meschief mekliche as myselis & oþere,
A. 9.74   Trusty of his tailende, *takiþ* but his owene,
A.10.97   Catoun counseilliþ—*tak* kep of his teching—
A.11.41   And bringe forþ a ballid resoun, *t[a]k[e]* bernard to witnesse,
A.11.149   Ac theologie techiþ not so, who[so] *takiþ* heed;
A.11.274   *Taken* ensaumpl[e] of here sawis in sarmonis þat þei maken,
B. 1.56   And tutour of youre tresor, and *take* it yow at nede;
B. 1.96   And *taken* transgressores and tyen hem faste
B. 1.155   And whan it hadde of þis fold flessh and blood *taken*
B. 2.34   And what man *takeþ* Mede, myn heed dar I legge,
B. 3.4   To *take* Mede þe maide and maken hire at ese.
B. 3.10   *Took* Mede bi þe myddel and broȝte hire into chambre.
B. 3.45   Tolde hym a tale and *took* hym a noble
B. 3.85   For *toke* þei on trewely þei tymbred nouȝt so heiȝe,
B. 3.88   Of alle swiche Selleris siluer to *take*,
B. 3.95   And [*took* hym] þis teme þat I telle þynke:
B. 3.107   Ac worse wroȝtest [þ]ow neuere þan þo þow Fals *toke*.
B. 3.140   [She] *takeþ* þe trewe bi þe top, tieþ h[y]m faste,
B. 3.218   *Taken* Mede of hir maistres as þei mowe acorde;
B. 3.247   To mayntene mysdoers Mede þei *take*;
B. 3.253   That *taken* Mede and moneie for masses þat þei syngeþ,
B. 3.255   That laborers and lowe [lewede] folk *taken* of here maistres
B. 3.293   And whoso trespaseþ [to] truþe or *takeþ* ayein his wille,
B. 3.334   That ȝyuen ȝiftes, [*takeþ* yeme], þe victorie wynneþ
B. 3.349   A ful teneful text to hem þat *takeþ* Mede:
B. 3.353   The soule þat þe soude *takeþ* by so muche is bounde.'
B. 4.15   [Seide hym] as þe kyng [sente] and siþen *took* his leue.
B. 4.48   How wrong ayeins his wille hadde his wif *taken*,
B. 4.58   And *takeþ* me but a taille for ten quarters Otes;
B. 4.77   And *token* Mede myd hem mercy to wynne.
B. 5.28   Tomme Stowue he tauȝte to *take* two staues
B. 5.172   And if I telle any tales þei *taken* hem togideres,
B. 5.249   And *took* it by tale here and tolde hem þere lasse.'
B. 6.139   Ac ye myȝte trauaille as truþe wolde and *take* mete and hyre
B. 6.144   And al is þoruȝ suffraunce þat vengeaunce yow ne *takeþ*.
B. 6.225   Loue hem and lakke hem noȝt; lat god *take* þe vengeaunce;
B. 6.261   Ete noȝt, I hote þee, er hunger þee *take*
B. 7.2   To [*t]aken* his teme and tilien þe erþe,
B. 7.41   For þe Sauter saueþ hem noȝt, swiche as *take* ȝiftes,
B. 7.59   That any Mede of mene men for motyng *takeþ*.

628

B. 7.62	That treweliche *taken* and treweliche wynnen
B. 7.79	In hym þat *takeþ* is þe trecherie if any treson walke,
B. 7.103	That *taken* þi[s] myschie[f] mekeliche as Mesels and oþere,
B. 8.83	Trusty of his tailende, *takeþ* but his owene,
B.10.55	And bryngen forþ a balled reson, *taken* Bernard to witnesse,
B.10.88	Tobye [techeþ] noȝt so; *takeþ* hede ye riche
B.10.200	Ac Theologie techeþ noȝt so, whoso *takeþ* yeme;
B.11.87	'ȝis, by Peter and by Poul!' quod he and *took* hem boþe to witnesse:
B.11.111	This was hir teme and hir text–I *took* ful good hede–
B.11.141	'[I] Troianus, a trewe knyȝt, [*take*] witnesse at a pope
B.11.170	And *took* it moises vpon þe mount alle men to lere].
B.11.263	So after pouerte or penaunce paciently *ytake*:
B.11.283	If preestes weren [wise] þei wolde no siluer *take*
B.11.290	And þe title þat ye *take* ordres by telleþ ye ben auaunced:
B.11.292	For he þat *took* yow [a] title sholde take yow wages,
B.11.292	For he þat took yow [a] title sholde *take* yow wages,
B.11.323	And þoruȝ þe wondres of þis world wit for to *take*.
B.11.334	And how men *token* Mede and Mercy refused.
B.11.337	And after cours of concepcion noon *took* kepe of ooþer,
B.11.356	And some troden, [I *toke* kepe], and on trees bredden,
B.11.359	And some caukede; I *took* kepe how pecokkes bredden.
B.12.74	That what womman were in auoutrye *taken*, whe[r] riche or poore,
B.12.90	Riȝt so goddes body, breþeren, but it be worþili *taken*,
B.12.123	*Take* we hir wordes at worþ, for hir witnesse be trewe,
B.12.155	Why I haue told [þee] al þis, I *took* ful good hede
B.12.160	*Tak* two stronge men and in Themese cast hem,
B.12.190	That haþ *take* fro Tybourne twenty stronge þeues,
B.12.237	Ensamples *token* and termes, as telleþ þ[ise] poetes,
B.12.283	"Troianus was a trewe knyght and *took* neuere cristendom
B.13.75	*Taken* it for his teme and telle it wiþouten glosyng.
B.13.94	And þanne shal he testifie of [a] Trinite, and *take* his felawe to witnesse
B.13.97	And þanne is tyme to *take* and to appose þis doctour
B.13.126	And no text ne *takeþ* to mayntene his cause
B.13.163	Tene þee any tyme, and þow *take* it wiþ þe:
B.13.177	And *took* Clergie and Conscience to conseil as it were
B.13.202	Clergie of Conscience no congie wolde *take*,
B.13.271	I *took* [greet] kepe, by crist! and Conscience boþe,
B.13.315	'Ye, whoso *toke* hede', quod haukyn, 'bihynde and bifore,
B.13.318	And he torned hym as tyd and þanne *took* I hede;
B.13.333	And whan I may noȝt haue þe maistrie [wiþ] malencolie I *take*,
B.13.336	That *takeþ* me al a tweluemonþe, til þat I despise
B.14.142	Riȝt as a seruaunt *takeþ* his salarie bifore, & siþþe wolde clayme moore
B.14.184	Thou tauȝtest hem in þe Trinite to *taken* bapteme
B.14.190	[We] sholde *take* þe Acquitaunce as quyk and to þe queed shewen it:
B.14.267	Muche is [þat maide] to loue of [a man] þat swich oon *takeþ*,
B.14.313	The eighteþe is a lele labour and loþ to *take* moore
B.15.87	Ayein youre rule and Religion; I *take* record at Iesus
B.15.91	I shal tellen it for truþes sake; *take* hede whoso likeþ.
B.15.173	Al þat men seyn, he leet it sooþ and in solace *takeþ*,
B.15.208	Than for penaunce and parfitnesse, þe pouerte þat swiche *takeþ*,
B.15.233	Riche men he recomendeþ, and of hir robes *takeþ*
B.15.261	In ensample we sholde do so, and *take* no vengeaunce
B.15.277	Of leons ne of leopardes no liflode ne *toke*,
B.15.310	And to *taken* of hir tenauntȝ moore þan trouþe wolde,
B.15.331	And of hem þat habbeþ þei *taken* and ȝyueþ hem þat [ne] habbeþ,
B.15.420	Of tirauntȝ þat teneþ trewe men *taken* any almesse,
B.15.489	They wol be wrooþ for I write þus, ac to witnesse I *take*
B.15.564	*Takeþ* hire landes, ye lordes, and leteþ hem lyue by dymes.
B.15.585	And *took* it Moyses to teche men til Messie coome,
B.16.158	Thouȝ I bi treson be *take* [to] youre [iewene] wille
B.16.160	On a þursday in þesternesse þus was he *taken*;
B.16.164	On cros vpon Caluarie crist *took* þe bataille
B.16.204	In tokenynge of þe Trinite, was [*taken* out of a man],
B.17.2	That *took* me a maundement vpon þe mount of Synay
B.17.14	This was the tixte, trewely; I *took* ful good yeme.
B.17.36	And telleþ noȝt of þe Trinite þat *took* hym hise lettres,
B.17.56	Where a man was wounded and wiþ þeues *taken*.
B.17.79	And he *took* hym two pens to liflode and seide,
B.17.106	And [may] ech man see and good mark *take*
B.17.110	On my Capul þat highte caro–of mankynde I *took* it–
B.17.249	But þow haue tow to *take* it wiþ, tonder or broches,
B.17.270	Ech a riche, I rede, reward at hym *take*
B.18.47	'Tolle, tolle!' quod anoþer, and *took* of kene þornes
B.18.70	Wher he be deed or noȝt deed doun er he be *taken*.'
B.18.84	To touchen hym or to tasten hym or *taken* doun of roode,
B.18.132	And þat my tale be trewe I *take* god to witnesse.
B.18.222	And after god Auntrede hymself and *took* Adames kynd[e]
B.18.239	[The oostes] in heuene *token* stella com[a]ta
B.19.39	Aren frankeleyns, free men þoruȝ fullynge þat þei *toke*
B.19.56	[And *took* [Lucifer þe loþely] þat lord was of helle
B.19.72	And cam to *take* mankynde kynges and Aungeles
B.19.170	And *took* Thomas by þe hand and tauȝte hym to grope
B.19.460	'I holde þi riȝt and reson of my Reue to *take*
B.19.468	And if me lakkeþ to lyue by þe lawe wole I *take* it
B.19.473	And what I *take* of yow two, I take it at þe techynge
B.19.473	And what I take of yow two, I *take* it at þe techynge
B.19.480	The viker hadde fer hoom and faire *took* his leeue
B.20.7	That þow *toke* to þi bilyue, to cloþes and to sustenaunce,
B.20.11	For þre þynges he *takeþ* his lif for to saue.
B.20.41	And cam and *took* mankynde and bicam nedy.
B.20.135	And ouertilte at his truþe wiþ 'tak þis vp amendement'.
B.20.137	And tornede Cyuyle into Symonye, and siþþe he *took* þe Official.
B.20.260	/Wol no [tresorer *take*] hem [wages], trauaille þei neuer so soore,
B.20.358	Conforte hym', quod Conscience, 'and *tak* kepe to hise soores.
C.Pr.117	God was wel þe wrother and *took* þe raþer vengeaunce.
C.Pr.121	God shal *take* vengeaunce on alle suche prestis
C. 1.52	And tutor of ȝoure tresor and *take* it ȝow at nede;
C. 1.92	And *take* transgressores and teyen hem faste
C. 1.96	Treweliche to *take* and treweliche to fyghte
C. 1.151	/A[nd] when hit hadde of þe folde flesch and blode *taken*
C. 2.190	Sommnours and sod[e]nes [þat] supersedias *taketh*
C. 3.4	To *take* mede þe mayde and maken here at ese.
C. 3.10	*Took* mede by þe myddel and myldeliche here brouhte
C. 3.47	Tolde hym a tale and *toke* hym a noble
C. 3.84	For *tok* thei [o]n trewely they tymbred nat so heye
C. 3.87	Thow thei *take* hem vntidy thyng no tresoun þei ne halden hit;
C. 3.116	Of alle suche sullers seluer to *take*
C. 3.123	And wittenesseth what worth of hem þat wolleth *take* mede:
C. 3.127	The houses and þe homes of hem þat *taketh* ȝeftes.
C. 3.138	For wors wrouhtest [thow] neuere then tho thow fals *toke*.
C. 3.146	And teche the to louye treuthe and *take* consail of resoun.
C. 3.178	And *taketh* [þe] tre[we] by þe top and te[i]eth hym f[aste]
C. 3.274	*Taken* mede of here maistres as þei mowen acorde;
C. 3.295	That eny man Mede *toke* but he hi[t] myhte deserue,
C. 3.311	The mede þat many prest[es] *taken* for masses þat thei syngen,
C. 3.351	And *take* hym for his trauaile al þat treuthe wolde,
C. 3.410	Agaynes godes comandement, god *tok* such a vengeaunce
C. 3.446	And hoso *taketh* aȝeyn treuthe or transuerseth aȝeyns resoun
C. 3.486	That ȝeueth ȝeftes, *taketh* ȝeme, the victorie a wynneth
C. 3.497	A ful teneful tyxst to hem þat *taketh* mede,
C. 4.15	And sayde hym as þe kyng sayde and sennes *took* his leue.
C. 4.29	To *take* reed of resoun þat recorde sholde
C. 4.40	Thenne resoun rood forth Ac *took* reward of no man
C. 4.49	'Bothe my gees and my grys and my g[r]as he *taketh*.
C. 4.52	[A w]ayteth ful wel when y seluer *take*,
C. 4.61	And *taketh* me but a tayle for ten quarteres otes;
C. 4.73	And *token* mede [myd] hem mercy to wynne.
C. 4.166	The kyng to consayl tho *toek* Consience and resoun
C. 5.79	And *taken* Symondus sones seyntwarie to kepe,
C. 5.130	Tomme stoue he tauhte to *take* t[w]o staues
C. 6.53	Of werkes þat y wel dede witnesses *take*
C. 6.77	And when y may nat haue þe maystrie [with] malecolie *ytake*,
C. 6.80	That *taketh* me al [a] twelmonthe til þat y despise
C. 6.154	And yf y telle eny tales they *taken* hem togyderes
C. 6.289	Ne *take* a meles mete of thyn and myn herte hit wiste
C. 6.298	ȝe! þe prest þat thy tythe *t[a]k[eth]*, trowe y non other,
C. 7.203	Were hit itolde treuthe þat y *toke* mede
C. 7.293	To loke how me liketh hit,' and *toek* his leue at Peres.
C. 8.271	Ac ete nat, y hote, Ar hungur the *take*
C. 9.2	To *taken* his teme and tilion þe erthe
C. 9.54	That mede of mene men for here motynge *taken*.
C. 9.65	And also gileth hym þat gyueth and *taketh* agayne his wille.
C. 9.91	And fele to fonge þerto and fewe panes *taketh*.
C. 9.92	There is payne and peny ale as for a pytaunce *ytake*
C. 9.131	Men suffreth al þat suche sayen and in solace *ytake*
C. 9.184	That *taketh* thise meschiefes mekeliche and myldeliche at herte
C. 9.276	But 'haue this for þat tho þat thow *toke*
C.10.80	And therto trewe of his tayl, [*taketh* but his owne]
C.11.36	And brynge forth [a] balle[d] reso[n], *taken* bernard to witnesse
C.11.68	Tobie techeth nat so; *taketh* hede, ȝe ryche,
C.12.45	Of here teme and here tales y *took* ful good hede;
C.12.76	'I troianes, a trewe knyht, *take* witnesse of a pope
C.12.149	So aftur [pouerte or penaunce] pacientliche *ytake*
C.12.219	Lo! lordes, lo! and ladyes, *taketh* hede;
C.13.44	Wol no wys man be wroth ne his wed *take*–
C.13.45	Ne non haiward is hote his wed for to *taken*.
C.13.104	The tytle [þat] ȝe *take* ordres by telleth ȝe ben avaunsed
C.13.106	For he that *toek* ȝow a title sholde take ȝow wages
C.13.106	For he that toek ȝow a title sholde *take* ȝow wages
C.13.142	And how þat [men] mede *toke* and mercy refusede.
C.13.145	Aftur cors of concepcion noon *toek* kepe of oþer,
C.13.154	For out of resoun they ryde and rechelesliche *t[a]ken* on
C.13.165	And som treden, y *toke* kepe, and on trees bredde

C.13.170	And how þe pocok caukede [y *toke* kepe þerof],
C.14.66	*Take* we here wordes at worthe, for here witteness[e] b[e] trewe,
C.14.99	Why y haue tolde [the] al þis, y *toek* ful gode hede
C.14.104	*Take* two stronge men and in temese cast hem,
C.14.129	Hit hath *take* fro tybourne twenty stronge theues
C.14.205	'Troianes was a trewe knyhte and *toek* neuere cristendoem
C.15.81	Þat *toek* this for his tene and tolde hit withoute glose.
C.15.101	And [thenne shal he testifie of] a trinite and *take* his felowe [t]o witnesse
C.15.104	And thenne is tyme to *take* and to appose this doctour
C.15.133	And no tixst ne *taketh* to preue this for trewe
C.15.156	Y *take* wittenesse,' quod [þe wy] 'of holy writ a partye:
C.15.159	Tene þe eny tyme and þou *take* pacience
C.15.174	And *toek* Clergie and Consience to conseyle as hit were.
C.15.175	Ac Concience, y *toek* kepe, coniey[e]d sone this doctour
C.16.107	Moche is [þat] mayde to louye of a man þat such oen *taketh*,
C.16.147	The ey3te is a lel labour and loeth to *take* more
C.16.311	Alle sekness[e] and sorwes for solac[e] he hit *taketh*
C.16.328	That pouerte and penaunce pacientlyche *ytake*
C.16.358	Riche men a recomendeth, and of [here] robes *taketh*,
C.17.36	*Toke* lyflode of luyther wynnynges in all here lyf tyme.
C.17.45	And to *take* of here tenauntes more then treuthe wolde
C.17.186	Sholden conuerte hem to Crist and cristendoem to *take*.
C.17.227	*Taketh* here londe[s], 3e lordes, and lat hem lyue by dymes
C.17.239	And *take* hede [how] Macometh thorw a mylde dowue
C.17.287	For as þe kynde is of a knyhte or [of] a kynge to be *take*
C.18.19	And he thonkede me tho; bote thenne y *hede*
C.18.53	I toted vpon þ[e] tree tho and thenne *toek* y hede
C.18.175	Sethe y be tresoun am *take* and to 3oure will, iewes,
C.19.2	That *toek* me a maundement vpon þe mont of synay
C.19.15	This was the tyxt trewly; y *toek* ful good gome.
C.19.37	That of no trinite ne telleth ne *taketh* mo persones
C.19.76	And *toek* two pans the hostiler to take kepe to hym;
C.19.76	And toek two pans the hostiler to *take* kepe to hym;
C.19.215	Bote thow haue tasch to *take* hit with, tender [or] broches,
C.19.251	Vch a riche y rede reward herof *take*
C.20.47	'Tolle, tolle!' quod another, and *toek* of kene thornes
C.20.72	Wher he be ded or nat ded down or he be *taken*.'
C.20.86	To touchen hym or to t[ast]en hym or *taken* down [of rode]
C.20.93	Bothe my lond and my licame at 3oure likynge *taketh* hit.
C.20.135	And þat my tale [be] trewe y *take* god to witnesse.
C.20.231	And aftur god auntred hymsulue and *toek* Adames kynde
C.20.248	Tho þat weren in heuene *token* stella comata
C.20.305	Yf they touched a tre or *toek* þerof an appul.
C.20.434	And so of alle wykkede y wol here *take* veniaunce.
C.21.39	Aren frankeleynes, fre men Thorw follyng þat they *toke*
C.21.56	And *toek* lucifer the loethliche þat lord was of helle
C.21.72	And cam to *take* mankynde kynges and angeles
C.21.170	And *toek* Thomas by the hoende and tauhte hym to grope
C.21.460	'Y halde hit riht and resoun of my reue to *take*
C.21.468	And yf me lakketh to lyue by þe lawe wol y *take* hit
C.21.473	And what y *take* of 3ow two y take hit at þe techynge
C.21.473	And what y take of 3ow two y *take* hit at þe techynge
C.21.480	The vicory hadde fer hoem and [fayre] *toek* his leue
C.22.7	That thow *toke* to [thy bylyue], to clothes and to sustinaunce
C.22.11	For thre thynges he *taketh* [h]is lyf for to saue.
C.22.41	And cam and *toek* mankynde and bicam nedy.
C.22.135	And ouertulde al his treuthe with '*taek* this [vp] amendement.'
C.22.137	And turnede syuyle into symonye and sethe he *toek* þe official.
C.22.260	Wol no tresorer *taken* hem wages, trauayle they neuere so sore,
C.22.358	Conforte hym,' quod Consience, 'and *taek* kepe to his sores.

talage > taillage

tale n *tale n. &> taletelleris* A 11 tale (6) talis (5); B 32 tale (14) tales (18); C 27 tale (12) tales (15)

A.Pr.48	Wenten forþ in here wey wiþ many wise *talis*,
A.1.9	Of oþer heuene þanne here holde þei no *tale*.'
A.2.79	Þanne tenide hym theologie whan he þis *tale* herde.
A.2.179	He was nowhere welcome for his many *talis*,
A.3.44	Tolde hym a *tale*, & tok hym a noble
A.4.55	And warnide wrong þo wiþ suche a wys *tale*:
A.7.45	And þat þou be trewe of [þi] tunge, & *talis* þou hate,
A.7.47	Holde wiþ none harlotis ne here nou3t here *talis*,
A.10.81	Salamon it seide for a soþ *tale*:
A.11.36	Leccherie & losengerie & loselis *talis*;
A.11.222	How crist counseilliþ þe comune & kenneþ hem þis *tale*:
B.Pr.48	Wenten forþ in hire wey wiþ many wise *tales*,
B.Pr.51	To ech a *tale* þat þei tolde hire tonge was tempred to lye
B.1.9	Of ooþer heuene þan here holde þei no *tale*'
B.2.115	Thanne tened hym Theologie whan he þis *tale* herde,
B.2.220	He was nowher welcome for his manye *tales*,
B.3.45	Tolde hym a *tale* and took hym a noble
B.4.18	And also Tomme trewe-tonge-tel-me-no-*tales*-

B.4.69	And warnede wrong þo with swich a wis *tale*:
B.5.172	And if I telle any *tales* þei taken hem togideres,
B.5.249	And took it by *tale* here and tolde hem þere lasse.'
B.5.376	For loue of *tales* in Tauernes [to] drynke þe moore I [hyed;
B.5.403	Wiþ ydel *tales* at þe Ale and oþerwhile [in] chirche[s];
B.6.50	And þat þow be trewe of þi tonge and *tales* þow hatie
B.6.52	Hold wiþ none harlotes ne here no3t hir *tales*,
B.9.74	Of þis matere I my3te make a long *tale*
B.10.50	Lecherie, losengerye and losels *tales*;
B.10.379	Manye *tales* ye tellen þat Theologie lerneþ,
B.11.99	It falleþ no3t for þat folk no *tales* to telle
B.11.100	Thou3 þe *tale* [were] trewe, and it touche[d] synne.
B.11.300	And a title, a *tale* of no3t, to his liflode at meschief.
B.12.268	[Swiche *tales* telleþ Aristotle þe grete clerk]:
B.13.58	And Conscience conforted vs and carped vs murye *tales*:
B.13.172	'It is but a dido', quod þis doctour, 'a disours *tale*.
B.13.303	In towne and in Tauernes *tales* to telle
B.13.332	For *tales* þat I telle no man trusteþ to me.
B.13.351	Til þei my3te na moore; and þanne [hadde] murye *tales*,
B.13.430	To entice men þoru3 *tales* to synne and harlotrie.
B.18.132	And þat my *tale* be trewe I take god to witnesse.
B.18.142	'That þow tellest', quod Truþe, 'is but a *tale* of waltrot!
B.18.290	And toldest hire a *tale*, of treson were þe wordes;
B.19.454	Of gile ne of gabbyng gyue þei neuere *tale*,
B.20.119	Wiþ vntidy *tales* he tened ful ofte
C.Pr.49	Wenten forth [i]n here way with many wyse *tales*
C.1.9	Of othere heuene then here [halde thei] no *tale*.'
C.2.119	Thenne tened hym teologie when he this *tal[e]* herde
C.2.230	He was nawher welcome for his many *tales*,
C.3.47	Tolde hym a *tale* and toke hym a noble
C.3.391	He þat mede may lacche maketh lytel *tale*;
C.4.18	And also th[omm]e trewe-tonge-telle-me-no-*tales*-
C.4.34	Ryde forth, syre resoun, and rech nat of here *tales*
C.6.28	To telle eny *tale*; y trowed me wysor
C.6.50	*Tales* to telle in tauernes and in stretes,
C.6.154	And yf y telle eny *tales* they taken hem togyderes
C.6.185	Til we myhte no more; thenne hadde we mery *tales*
C.6.194	Y hadde likyng to lythe of lecherye *tales*.
C.7.19	With ydele *tales* at þe ale and oþerwhile in chirches;
C.7.90	To entise men thorw here *tales* to synne and harlotrie.
C.8.48	Treuwe of thy tonge and *tales* loth to here
C.8.50	Hoold with non harlotes ne here nat here *tales*
C.12.45	Of here teme and here *tales* y took ful good hede;
C.12.173	To testifie for treuthe þe *tale* þat y shewe
C.13.88	Telleth þe lord a *tale* as a trewe messager
C.13.114	And a title, a *tale* of nauht, to his lyflode as hit were.
C.15.170	'This is a dido,' quod this doctour, 'a dysores *tale*!
C.18.3	Thenne louh liberum Arbitrium and ladde me forth with *tales*
C.20.135	And þat my *tale* [be] trewe y take god to witnesse.
C.20.145	'That thow tellest,' quod treuthe, 'is bote a *tale* of walterot!
C.21.454	Of gyle ne of gabbyng[e] gyueth they neuer *tale*
C.22.119	With vntidy *tales* he tened ful ofte

taletelleris n *taletellere n.* A 1 tale_telleris; B 1; C 1 taletellares

A.11.73	And for suche *tale telleris* suche a teme shewide:
B.20.299	Of alle *taletelleris* and titeleris in ydel
C.22.299	Of all *taletellares* and titerares an ydel.

talewis adj *talewise adj.* A 1 talewys; B 1; C 1 talewys

A.3.120	She is tykil of hire tail, *talewys* of hire tunge,
B.3.131	She is tikel of hire tail, *talewis* of tonge,
C.3.168	For she is tikel of here tayl, *talewys* of tonge,

talke v *talken v.* B 1

B.17.85	To ouertaken hym and *talke* to hym er þei to towne coome.

tame adj *tame adj.* B 1; C 1

B.14.116	And blisse to alle þat ben, boþe wilde and *tame*."
C.15.292	And blisse to all þat been, bothe wilde and *tame*."

tanners n *tannere n.* C 1

C.Pr.227	As taylers and *tanners* and tulyers [of] þe erthe,

tapur n *taper n.* B 2; C 2 taper

B.17.206	[For] to a torche or a *tapur* þe Trinite is likned,
B.17.282	To a torche or a *tapur* to reuerence þe Trinite,
C.19.172	For to a torche or a *taper* þe trinite is likned,
C.19.263	Or elles [to] a *taper* to reuerense with the trinite

tarre n *ter n.* C 1

C.9.263	The *tarre* is vntydy þat to þe [tripe] bylongeth;

tarse n *Tarse n.* B 1

B.15.168	As of a tunycle of *tarse* or of trie scarlet.

tasch n *tache n.(2)* C 1

C.19.215	Bote thow haue *tasch* to take hit with, tender [or] broches,

taseles n *tesel n.* B 1
B.15.454 Wasshen wel wiþ water and wiþ *taseles* cracched,

tasten v *tasten v.* B 3 taste (1) tastede (1) tasten (1); C 3 taste (1) tastede (1) tasten (1)
B.13.345 Semynge to synneward, and som he gan *taste*
B.17.150 That touched and *tastede* at techynge of þe pawme
B.18.84 To touchen hym or to *tasten* hym or taken doun of roode,
C.6.179 Semyng to synneward and summe y gan *taste*
C.19.124 Touchede and *tastede* at techyng of the paume
C.20.86 To touchen hym or to *t[ast]en* hym or taken down [of rode]

tastes n *taste n.(1)* B 1
B.12.129 Of briddes and of beestes, [by] *tastes* of truþe.

tauȝt(- tauhte(n > techen

tauerners n *tavernere n.* A 1; B 1; C 1
A.Pr.106 *Tauerners* to hem tolde þe same:
B.Pr.228 *Tauerners* [t]il hem tolden þe same:
C.Pr.232 *Tauerners* til hem tolde þe same:

tauernes n *taverne n.* B 4; C 2
B.2.94 And al day to drynken at diuerse *Tauernes*,
B.5.376 For loue of tales in *Tauernes* [to] drynke þe moore I [hyed;
B.9.106 Ne his gleman a gedelyng, a goere to *tauernes*.
B.13.303 In towne and in *Tauernes* tales to telle
C.2.101 Al day to drynke at diuerse *tauernes*,
C.6.50 Tales to telle in *tauernes* and in stretes,

taxeþ v *taxen v.* B 1; C 1 taxeth
B.1.162 Vpon man for hise mysdedes þe mercyment he *taxeþ*.
C.1.158 Vp man for his mysdedes the mercement he *taxeth*.

taxour n *taxoure n.* B 1; C 1
B.6.39 And þouȝ [þow] mowe amercy hem lat mercy be *taxour*
C.8.37 And whan ȝe mersyen eny man late mercy be *taxour*,

techen v *techen v.* A 36 tauȝt (1) tauȝte (12) teche (6) techeþ (1) techiþ (15) ytauȝt (1); B 89 taȝte (1) tauȝt (2) tauȝte (31) tauȝtest (1) teche (18) techen (5) techeþ (30) ytauȝt (1); C 97 tauhte (35) tauhten (1) tecche (1) teche (19) techen (5) techest (2) techeth (31) ytauȝte (1) ytauhte (2)
A.1.13 And wolde þat ȝe wrouȝten as his word *techiþ*.
A.1.36 Leue not þi lycam for a li[ȝ]er hym *techiþ*.
A.1.74 I vndirfang þe ferst and þi feiþ [þe] *tauȝte*.
A.1.107 *Tauȝte* hem þoruȝ þe trinite þe trouþe to knowe:
A.1.119 Ac þo þat werchen þe word þat holy writ *techiþ*.
A.1.133 Þis I trowe be treuþe; who can *teche* þe betere,
A.2.7 I lokide on [my] left half as þat lady me *tauȝte*,
A.3.114 Wyues & wydewis wantonnesse *techiþ*,
A.3.260 [I] consience knowe þis, for kynde [w]it me *tauȝte*,
A.4.87 'For he haþ wagid me wel as wysdom hym *tauȝte*
A.5.28 Thomas he *tauȝte* to take two staues
A.5.86 To preye for þe peple as þe prest *techiþ*,
A.7.24 Ac on þe tem trewely *tauȝt* was I neuere.
A.7.74 Let god worþe wiþal for so his woord *techiþ*.
A.7.81 Til I come to his acountes as my crede me *techiþ*–
A.7.126 Ac treuþe shal *teche* ȝow his tem for to dryue,
A.7.194 Treuþe *tauȝte* me ones to loue hem ichone
A.7.212 Make þe Frendis þermi[d] for so matheu vs *techiþ*:
A.8.22 For þei h[o]lde nouȝt here haly dayes as holy chirche *techiþ*,
A.8.120 'Abstinence þe abbesse myn a b c me *tauȝte*,
A.8.159 Þis is [a] l[e]f of oure beleue, as lettrid men vs [tech]iþ:
A.9.101 I þankide þouȝt þo þat he me so *tauȝte*.
A.9.118 Here is wil wolde wyte ȝif wit couþe hym *teche*.'
A.11.3 She was wondirliche wroþ þat wyt so *tauȝte*,
A.11.28 On crois vpon caluarie, as clerkis vs *techiþ*:
A.11.29 Litel is he louid or lete by þat suche a lessoun *techiþ*,
A.11.131 Aristotel & oþere mo to arguen I *tauȝte*;
A.11.149 Ac theologie *techiþ* not so, who[so] takiþ heed;
A.11.165 I bekenne þe crist,' quaþ she, 'I can *teche* þe no betere.'
A.11.170 I grette þe goode man as þe gode wyf me *tauȝte*,
A.11.172 And tolde hire þe toknes þat me *ytauȝt* were.
A.11.196 Be þat god in þe gospel grauntiþ & *techiþ*,
A.11.268 De[m]lide he not wel & wisly, as holy [writ] *techiþ*,
A.12.2 I haue do my deuer þe dowel to *teche*,
A.12.97 So þat þou werke þe word þat holy wryt *techeþ*,
B.1.13 And wolde þat ye wrouȝte as his word *techeþ*.
B.1.38 Lef nauȝt þi licame] for a liere hym *techeþ*,
B.1.76 I vnderfeng þee first and þ[i] feiþ [þee] *tauȝte*.
B.1.83 'Teche me to no tresor, but tel me þis ilke,
B.1.109 *Tauȝte* hem [þoruȝ] þe Trinitee [þe] treuþe to knowe:
B.1.145 This I trowe be truþe; who kan *teche* þee bettre,
B.2.7 I loked on my left half as þe lady me *tauȝte*

B.3.125 Wyues and widewes wantoun[nesse] *techeþ*,
B.3.284 I, Conscience, knowe þis for kynde wit me *tauȝte*
B.4.100 'For he haþ waged me wel as wisdom hym *tauȝte*
B.5.12 And wiþ a cros afore þe kyng comsede þus to *techen*.
B.5.28 Tomme Stowue he *tauȝte* to take two staues
B.5.106 [To] preye for þe peple as þe preest *techeþ*,
B.6.6 I wolde wende wiþ yow and þe wey *teche*.'
B.6.22 Ac on þe teme trewely *tauȝt* was I neuere.
B.6.82 Lat-god-yworþe-wiþ-al-for-so-his-word-*techeþ*.
B.6.89 Til I come to hise acountes as my [crede] me [techeþ]–
B.6.134 Ac truþe shal *teche* yow his teme to dryue,
B.6.208 Truþe *tauȝte* me ones to louen hem ech one,
B.6.227 And if þow wilt be gracious to god do as þe gospel *techeþ*
B.6.301 Wiþ good Ale as Gloton *taȝte* [þei] garte [hym to] slepe.
B.7.20 For þei holde noȝt hir halidayes as holy chirche *techeþ*,
B.7.74 And in þe stories he *techeþ* to bistowe þyn almesse:
B.7.138 'Abstynence þe Abbesse myn a b c me *tauȝte*,
B.7.181 This is [a leef of] oure bileue, as lettred men vs *techeþ*:
B.8.56 But if he werche wel þerwiþ as dowel hym *techeþ*.'
B.8.111 I þonked þoȝt þo þat he me [so] *tauȝte*.
B.8.129 Here is wil wolde wite if wit koude [hym *teche*];
B.9.96 [Ne] loueþ noȝt Salomons sawes þat Sapience *tauȝte*:
B.9.202 Dowel, my [deere], is to doon as lawe *techeþ*.
B.10.3 She was wonderly wroþ þat wit [so] *tauȝte*,
B.10.36 [On cros vpon caluarye as clerkes vs *techeþ*],
B.10.37 Litel is he loued [or lete by] þat swich a lesson [*techeþ*],
B.10.85 And brekeþ noȝt to þe beggere as þe book *techeþ*:
B.10.88 Tobye [*techeþ*] noȝt so; takeþ hede ye riche
B.10.179 Aristotle and oþere mo to argue I *tauȝte*;
B.10.200 Ac Theologie *techeþ* noȝt so, whoso takeþ yeme;
B.10.208 And alle þat lakkeþ vs or lyeþ oure lord *techeþ* vs to louye,
B.10.227 [I] grette þe goode man as [þe goode wif] me *tauȝte*,
B.10.229 And tolde [hire] þe tokenes þat me *tauȝt* were.
B.10.273 As persons and parissh preestes, þat preche sholde and *teche*,
B.10.275 This text was told yow to ben ywar er ye *tauȝte*
B.10.343 And Caton kenneþ vs to coueiten it nauȝt but as nede *techeþ*:
B.10.389 Maistres þat of goddes mercy *techen* men and prechen,
B.10.411 God lene it fare noȝt so bi folk þat þe feiþ *techeþ*
B.11.110 [The bileue [of oure] lord þat lettred men *techeþ*].
B.11.229 Forþi lerne we þe lawe of loue as oure lord *tauȝte*
B.11.272 Wiser þan Salomon was bereþ witnesse and *tauȝte*
B.11.361 And who *tauȝte* hem on trees to tymbre so heiȝe
B.12.32 For he dooþ wel, wiþouten doute, þat dooþ as lewte *techeþ*.
B.12.36 To Rome ne to Rochemador, but as þi rule *techeþ*,
B.12.107 Na moore kan a kynde witted man, but clerkes hym *teche*,
B.12.131 [The] selkouþes þat þei seiȝen, hir sones for to *teche*.
B.12.231 And *tauȝte* hym and Eue to helien hem wiþ leues.
B.12.288 But lyueþ as his lawe *techeþ* and leueþ þer be no bettre,
B.13.116 'Dowel,' quod þis doctour, 'do as clerkes *techeþ*,
B.13.117 [That trauailleþ to *teche* oþere I holde it for a dobet].
B.14.146 And lyuen as lawe *techeþ*, doon leaute to hem alle,
B.14.184 Thou *tauȝtest* hem in þe Trinite to taken bapteme
B.15.27 And whan I deme domes and do as truþe *techeþ*
B.15.93 Thoruȝ lele libbynge men þat goddes lawe *techen*,
B.15.282 But selden and sondry tymes, as seiþ þe book and *techeþ*.
B.15.343 Than burgeises þat riche ben as þe book *techeþ*,
B.15.408 As messager to Makometh, men for to *teche*.
B.15.422 [Boþe] Beneit and Bernard, þe whiche hem first *tauȝte*
B.15.435 Of hem of holi chirche þat þe heighe wey sholde *teche*
B.15.448 And follede folk faste, and þe feiþ *tauȝte*
B.15.503 Thei sholde turne, whoso trauail[e wolde] to *teche* hem of þe Trinite.
B.15.556 And lyuen as Leuitici as oure lord [yow] *techeþ*:
B.15.572 Tellen hem and *techen* hem on þe Trinite to bileue,
B.15.585 And took it Moyses to *teche* men til Messie coome,
B.15.587 And ȝit knewe þei crist þat cristendom *tauȝte*,
B.17.30 And alle þre but o god; þus Abraham me *tauȝte*;
B.17.43 Than for to *techen* hem two, and to hard to lerne þe leeste!
B.17.119 And alle þat feble and feynte be, þat Feiþ may noȝt *teche*,
B.17.130 And alle þre but o god? þus Abraham me *tauȝte*.
B.17.341 As Poul þe Apostle to þe peple *tauȝte*:
B.18.198 And folwede þat þe fend *tauȝte* and his [flesshes] wille
B.18.229 Ne what is witterly wele til weylawey hym *teche*.'
B.18.351 Falsliche and felonliche; good feiþ me it *tauȝte*
B.19.44 And so dide Iesus þe Iewes; he Iustified and *tauȝte* hem
B.19.170 And took Thomas by þe hand and *tauȝte* hym to grope
B.19.233 And by wit to wissen oþere as grace hem wolde *teche*.
B.19.238 And some he *tauȝte* to tilie, to [coke] and to thecche,
B.19.271 Thise foure, þe feiþ to *teche*, folwe[de] Piers teme
B.19.360 And þanne kam Kynde wit Conscience to *teche*,
B.20.9 And þow nome na moore þan nede þee *tauȝte*?
B.20.186 'Sire yuele *ytauȝt* Elde!' quod I, 'vnhende go wiþ þe!
B.20.278 For god made to men a lawe and Moyses it *tauȝte*:

C.Pr.120　And ȝe shulde be here fadres and *techen* hem betre
C. 1.13　And wolde þat ȝe wroghtoun as his word *techeth*.
C. 1.36　Leef nat thy lycame for a lyare hym *techeth*
C. 1.79　'*Teche* me to [no] tresor but telle me this ilke,
C. 1.144　And this y trowe be treuth; [ho] kan *tecche* þe bettre
C. 2.8　Y lokede [o]n my luft half as þe lady me *techeth*
C. 2.129　And thow has[t] gyue here as gyle *tauhte*, now god ȝeue þe sorwe!
C. 3.75　Lat nat thy lyft ha[lf], oure lord *techeth*,
C. 3.146　And *teche* the to louye treuthe and take consail of resoun.
C. 3.162　Wyues and wedewes wantounesse *techeth*
C. 3.278　Prestes þat prechen and þe peple *techen*
C. 3.437　[I], Consience,knowe this for kynde wit me *tauhte*
C. 4.96　'For he [hath] waged me wel as wysdom hym *tauhte*
C. 4.118　Til þat lerede men lyue as thei lere and *teche*
C. 5.5　For y made of tho men as resoun me *tauhte*.
C. 5.130　Tomme stoue he *tauhte* to take t[w]o staues
C. 6.12　'Repente þe,'quod repentaunce, 'as resoun þe *tauhte*
C. 8.4　Y wol[de] wende with ȝow and þe way *teche*.'
C. 8.20　Ac [on þe] t[ee]me treuely *ytauhte* was y neuere.
C. 8.59　His cokeres and his coffes, as kynde wit hym *tauhte*,
C. 8.86　Lat god yworthe with al, as holy wryt *techeth*:
C. 8.141　Ac treuthe shal *teche* ȝow his teme to dryue
C. 8.217　Treuthe *tauhte* me ones to louye hem vchone
C. 8.299　For thow hast wel awroke me and also wel *ytauhte* me.'
C. 9.24　For they holde nat here haliday[es] as holi chirch [*tech*]eth
C. 9.88　This [y] woet witturly, as þe world *techeth*,
C. 9.124　Suche manere men, Matheu vs *techeth*,
C. 9.352　At þe day of dome we dede as he *tauhte*.
C.10.102　That wolde nat do as dobest de[m]ede and *tauhte*.
C.10.107　Y thonkede thoght tho þat he me so *tauhte*;
C.10.125　Here is oen wolde ywyte yf wit couthe *teche*;
C.10.200　To tulie þe erthe with tonge and *teche* men to louye.
C.10.293　Bote wyues and wedded men, as holy writ *techeth*:
C.10.301　And thus is dowel, my frende, to do as lawe *techeth*:
C.11.3　She was wonderly wroth þat wit me so *tauhte*
C.11.13　More then holynesse or hendenesse or al þat seyntes *techeth*.
C.11.68　Tobie *techeth* nat so; taketh hede, ȝe ryche,
C.11.69　How he tolde in a tyme and *tauhte* his sone dele:
C.11.119　Aristotel and oþere [mo] to Arguen y *tauhte*;
C.11.147　Ho was his Autor And hym of god *tauhte*?
C.11.214　Aristotel and he, ho *tauhte* men bettere?
C.11.215　Maistres þat [of goddis mercy *techen* men and prechen]
C.11.242　God lene hit fare nat so by folk þat þe faith *techen*
C.11.250　Worcheth, ȝe wrihtus of holy churche, as holy writ *techeth*,
C.12.44　The bileue of oure lord þat lettred men *techeth*.
C.12.59　By þ[e] bloed [that] he bouhte vs with and bapteme, as he *tauhte*:
C.12.98　And cristis oune clergie; he cam fro heuene to *teche* hit
C.12.120　Forthy lerne we t[he] lawe of loue as oure lord *tauhte*
C.12.178　And by þe grayn þat groweth god vs all *techeth*
C.13.87　For if he loueth and byleueth as the lawe *techeth*–
C.13.193　Why he ne loueth thy lore and leueth as þou *techest*.'
C.13.196　'Vch a segge for hymsulue, salamon vs *techeth*
C.14.12　Ac hit soffiseth to be saued [to] be such as y *tauhte*.
C.14.52　No more can a kynde witted man, but clerkes hym *teche*,
C.14.69　And do we as dauid *techeth* for doute of godes veniance:
C.14.75　And of the selcouthes þat þei sye here sones þerof þei *tauhten*;
C.14.161　He *tauhte* þe tortle to tre[d]e, the pocok to cauke
C.14.210　Bote lyue[th] as his lawe *t[echeth]* and leueth þer be no bettere,
C.15.124　Bote do as doctours *techeth*, for dowel y hit holde;
C.15.125　That trauayleth to *teche* oþere y halde hit for a dobet,
C.15.126　And he þat doth as he *techeth* y halde hit for þe beste:
C.15.169　As for here lord and here ledare and l[y]ue as thow *techest*.'
C.16.187　And when y deme domus and do as treuthe *techeth*
C.16.234　To *teche* þe ten comaundementȝ ten sythe were betere
C.16.308　For drede of god þat so goed is and thusgates vs *techeth*:
C.16.344　And compenable in companye a[s] Crist hymsulue *techeth*:
C.17.51　Iop þe parfite patriarke this prouerbe wroet and *tauhte*
C.17.59　For god bad his blessed as þe boek *techeth*–
C.17.84　That fayre byfore folk prechen and *techen*
C.17.139　And lele men lyue as lawe *techeth* and loue þerof aryseth
C.17.174　And in what place he prechede and the peple *tauhte*
C.17.180　Tolde hym and *tauhte* [hym] how to teche þe peple.
C.17.180　Tolde hym and tauhte [hym] how to *teche* þe peple.
C.17.219　And lyuen as leuitici, as oure lord ȝow *techeth*:
C.17.254　They sholde [turne], hoso trauayle wolde and of þe trinite *teche* hem.
C.17.294　Bischope[s] and bokes the bileue to *teche*.
C.17.295　Iewes lyuen in þe lawe þat oure lord *tauhte*
C.17.298　And ȝut knewe they crist þat cristendoem *tauhte*
C.18.2　Thow couthest telle me and *teche* me [in] charite [to] leue.'
C.18.82　That oure lord alloweth, as lered men vs *teche*
C.18.137　Ac liberum Arbitrium lechecraeft hym *tauhte*
C.19.99　And alle thre bote o god? thus abraham me *tauhte*.

C.19.109　And as Abraham þe olde of o god the *tauhte*
C.19.249　To go semeliche ne sitte, seth holy writ *techeth*
C.19.321　As Paul þe apostel in his episteles *techeth*:
C.20.203　And folewede þat þe fend *tauhte* and his flesch[es] will
C.20.238　Ne what is witterliche wele til welaway hym *teche*.'
C.20.381　Aȝeyne my loue and my leue: þe olde lawe *techeth*
C.21.44　And so dede iesus þe iewes; he iustified and *tauhte* hem
C.21.170　And toek Thomas by the hoende and *tauhte* hym to grope
C.21.233　And bi wit to wissen oþere as grace hem wolde *teche*.
C.21.238　And somme he *tauhte* to tulye, to [coke] and to [thecche,
C.21.271　Thise foure, the fayth to *teche*, folewe[þ Peres] teme
C.21.360　And thenne cam kynde wit Consience to *teche*
C.22.9　And thow nome no more then nede the *tauhte*?
C.22.186　'Syre euele yt[a]uȝte Elde,' quod y, 'vnhende go with the!
C.22.278　For god made to men a lawe and Moyses hit *tauhte*:

techere n *techere n.* B 3 techere (1) techeris (2); C 6 techare (1) techares (5)

B.15.95　There inparfit preesthode is, prechours and *techeris*.
B.20.120　Conscience and his compaignye, of holy [kirke] þe *techeris*.
B.20.302　And woundede wel wikkedly many a wys *techere*
C.14.20　As loreles to be lordes and lewede men *techares*,
C.16.242　Lo, what holy writ wittnesseth of wikkede *techares*:
C.16.247　There inparfit preesthoed is, prechares and *techares*.
C.17.79　Ac þe metal þat is mannes soule of [many of] this *techares*
C.22.120　Consience and his companye, of holy [kirke] þe *techares*.
C.22.302　And wounded wel wykkedly many a wys *techare*

techyng ger *techinge ger.* A 3 teching; B 16 techyng (8) techynge (8); C 10 techyng (4) techynge (6)

A. 7.232　Oþer wiþ *teching*, oþer telling, or trauaillyng of hondis,
A.10.97　Catoun counseilliþ–tak kep of his *teching*–
A.11.293　And ȝet [haue] I forget[e ferþer] of fyue wyttis *teching*
B. 6.248　Or [wiþ *tech*]ynge or [tell]ynge or trauaillynge [of hondes],
B. 7.73　Cui des videto is Catons *techyng*,
B.10.258　Al þat þe book bit bi holi cherches *techyng*;
B.10.326　And Barons wiþ Erles beten hem þoruȝ Beatus virres *techyng*;
B.10.448　[And yet haue I forgete ferþer of fyue wittes *techyng*,
B.11.226　For some wordes I fynde writen, were of Feiþes *techyng*,
B.12.64　Clergie and kynde wit comeþ of siȝte and *techyng*
B.14.26　Than Haukyn þe Actif man, and þow do by my *techyng*,
B.15.68　Ayein cristes counseil and alle clerkes *techyng*,
B.15.73　Bettre it were [by] manye doctours to [bi]leuen swich *techyng*
B.17.126　Alle þat lyuen in Feiþ and folwen his felawes *techynge*.'
B.17.150　That touched and tastede at *techynge* of þe pawme
B.19.239　To wynne wiþ hir liflode bi loore of his *techynge*;
B.19.316　And tilieþ [to] hir *techynge* þe Cardynale vertues.'
B.19.473　And what I take of yow two, I take it at þe *techynge*
B.20.8　[Was] by *techynge* and by tellynge of Spiritus temperancie,
C. 2.22　In kynges court, in comune court contra[r]ieth my *techynge*.
C. 9.215　As by þe engelisch of oure eldres of olde mennes *techynge*
C.11.221　Thenne wrouhte [we] vnwysly for alle ȝoure wyse *techynge*.
C.12.99　And seynt Ion sethen saide hit of his *techyng*:
C.14.34　And clergie a connynge of kynde wittes *techyng*.
C.19.124　Touchede and tastede at *techyng* of the paume
C.21.239　To wynne with here lyflode bi lore of his *techynge*];
C.21.316　And tulieth [to] here *techynge* the cardinal vertues.'
C.21.473　And what y take of ȝow two y take hit at þe *techynge*
C.22.8　Was bi *techyng* and by tellyng of spiritus temperancie

teeme > teme

teeþ n *toth n.* B 2; C 1 teth

B.15.13　Oon wiþouten tonge and *teeþ* tolde me whider I sholde
B.18.81　Maugree his manye *teeþ* he was maad þat tyme
C.20.83　Maugre his mony *teth* he was mad þat tyme

teye- teiȝe- > tyen; tel > tellen; teld- > tilde

tellen v *tellen v.* A 38 tel (5) telle (16) tellen (2) telleþ (1) telliþ (4) told (1) tolde (9); B 138 tel (5) telle (45) tellen (10) tellest (4) telleþ (36) told (5) tolde (30) tolden (2) toldest (1); C 135 tel (1) tell (1) telle (45) tellen (4) tellest (3) telleth (41) toelde (4) told (1) tolde (31) tolden (1) toldest (1) itolde (1) ytolde (1)

A.Pr.106　Tauerners to hem *tolde* þe same:
A. 1.43　*Tel* me to whom þat tresour apendiþ.'
A. 1.81　'Teche me to no tresour but *tel* þis ilke,
A. 1.86　For whoso is trewe of his tunge, *telliþ* non oþer,
A. 1.182　Now haue I *told* þe what treuþe is, þat no tresour is betere,
A. 2.26　Tomorewe worþ þe mariage ymad as I þe *telle*;
A. 2.86　þe text[e] *tell[iþ]* not so, treuþe wot þe soþe:
A. 2.147　I haue no tom to *telle* þe tail þat hem folewiþ
A. 2.152　And come to þe kinges court & consience *tolde*,
A. 2.197　Ac trewely to *telle* heo tremblide for fere,
A. 3.44　*Tolde* hym a tale, & tok hym a noble
A. 3.84　And tok hym þis teeme þat I *telle* þenke:

A. 3.93	[Curteisly] þe king compsiþ to *telle*;
A. 3.253	But brouȝte wiþ hym þe bestis as þe bible [*telliþ*],
A. 4.48	[þe king kneuȝ] he seide soþ for consience hym *tolde*.
A. 5.9	Þanne sauȝ I meke[l] more þan I before *tolde*,
A. 5.10	[For I [sauȝ] þe feld ful of folk þat I before *tolde*],
A. 6.84	*Tel* hym þis tokne, "treuþe wot þe soþe:
A. 7.66	Treuþe *tolde* me ones & bad me telle it forþ:
A. 7.66	Treuþe *tolde* me ones & bad me *telle* it forþ:
A. 8.1	Treuþe herde *telle* hereof, & to peris sente
A. 9.67	'Art þou þouȝt, þo?' quaþ I; 'þou couþest me *telle*
A.10.26	[And what [kenis] þing is kynde, conne ȝe me *telle*]?'
A.10.107	Ne men þat conne manye craftis, clergie [it *telliþ*],
A.10.182	For summe, as I se now, soþ for to *telle*,
A.11.5	'Wel art þou wys, wyt,' quaþ she, 'any wisdomis to *telle*
A.11.25	And can *telle* of tobie & of þe twelue apostlis,
A.11.40	Þanne *telle* þei of þe trinite how two slowe þe þridde,
A.11.62	To *tellen* of þe trinite to be holden a sire,
A.11.86	And al worþ as þou wilt, whatso we *telle*–
A.11.93	And whanne þat wyt was war how his wif *tolde*
A.11.113	'And *tel* me sum tokne to hym, for tyme is þat I wende'.
A.11.172	And *tolde* hire þe toknes þat me ytauȝt were.
A.11.218	And welawey wers and I [wo]lde al *telle*.'
A.12.3	And whoso coueyteþ don betere þan þe boke *telleþ*,
A.12.18	Sitthe theologie þe trewe to *tellen* hit defendeþ;
A.12.24	*Telle* hit with tounge to synful wrecches."
A.12.28	"Quid est ueritas?" quod he; "verilyche *tel* vs."
B.Pr.51	To ech a tale þat þei *tolde* hire tonge was tempred to lye
B.Pr.92	Somme seruen þe kyng and his siluer *tellen*
B.Pr.101	To bynden and vnbynden as þe book *telleþ*,
B.Pr.164	And ouþer while þei arn elliswhere, as I here *telle*.
B.Pr.228	Tauerners [t]il hem *tolden* þe same:
B. 1.45	*Tel* me to whom þat tresour appendeþ.'
B. 1.83	'Teche me to no tresor, but *tel* me þis ilke,
B. 1.88	[For] who is trewe of his tonge, *telleþ* noon ooþer,
B. 1.130	[Ac] þo þat werche wel as holy writ *telleþ*,
B. 1.148	For truþe *telleþ* þat loue is triacle of heuene.
B. 1.208	Now haue I *told* þee what truþe is, þat no tresor is bettre,
B. 2.122	[The] text *telleþ* þee noȝt so, Truþe woot þe soþe,
B. 2.186	I haue no tome to *telle* þe tail þat [hem] folwe[þ]
B. 2.191	And com to þe kynges court and Conscience *tolde*,
B. 2.238	Ac trewely to *telle* she trembled for [fere],
B. 3.45	*Tolde* hym a tale and took hym a noble
B. 3.95	And [took hym] þis teme þat I *telle* þynke:
B. 3.104	Curteisly þe kyng comse[þ] to *telle*;
B. 3.237	And Dauid assoileþ it hymself as þe Sauter *telleþ*:
B. 3.335	And [muche] worshipe ha[þ] þerwiþ as holy writ *telleþ*:
B. 3.346	This text þat ye han *told* were [trewe] for lordes,
B. 4.18	And also Tomme trewe-tonge-*tel*-me-no-tales–
B. 4.61	The kyng knew he seide sooþ, for Conscience hym *tolde*
B. 4.157	Alle riȝtfulle recordede þat Reson truþe *tolde*.
B. 5.9	[Th]anne [mette me] muche moore þan I bifore *tolde*,
B. 5.10	For I seiȝ þe feld ful of folk þat I before [*tolde*],
B. 5.54	For whoso contrarieþ truþe, he *telleþ* in þe gospel,
B. 5.172	And if I *telle* any tales þei taken hem togideres,
B. 5.249	And took it by tale here and *tolde* hem þere lasse.'
B. 5.269	And I wiste witterly þow were swich as þow *tellest*.
B. 5.368	That I haue trespased with my tonge, I kan noȝt *telle* how ofte;
B. 5.401	That I *telle* wiþ my tonge is two myle fro myn herte.
B. 5.414	Nouȝt twyes in two yer, and þanne [*telle* I vp gesse].
B. 5.483	And for þe beste as I bileue whateuere þe book *telleþ*,
B. 5.597	*Telleþ* hym þis tokene: "[truþe woot] þe soþe;
B. 6.74	Truþe *tolde* me ones and bad me telle it [forþ]:
B. 6.74	Truþe tolde me ones and bad me *telle* it [forþ]:
B. 7.1	TReuþe herde *telle* herof, and to Piers sente
B. 7.172	It bifel as his fader *tolde*, hise frendes þere hym souȝte.
B. 8.76	'Artow þouȝt?' quod I þoo; 'þow koudest me [*telle*]
B. 9.25	'What kynnes þyng is kynde?' quod I; 'kanstow me *telle*?'
B. 9.159	For some, as I se now, sooþ for to *telle*,
B.10.5	'Wel artow wis, [wit], quod she, 'any wisdomes to *telle*
B.10.33	And kan *telle* of Tobye and of [þe] twelue Apostles
B.10.54	Than *telleþ* þei of þe Trinite [how two slowe þe þridde]:
B.10.120	Austyn to swiche Argueres [he] *telleþ* þis teme:
B.10.140	And whan þat wit was ywar [how his wif] *tolde*
B.10.161	'And *tel* me sum tokene [to hym], for tyme is þat I wende'.
B.10.222	*Tel* Clergie þis[e] tokene[s], and [to] Scripture after,
B.10.229	And *tolde* [hire] þe tokenes þat me tauȝt were.
B.10.275	This text was *told* yow to ben ywar er ye tauȝte
B.10.323	And bete yow, as þe bible *telleþ*, for brekynge of youre rule,
B.10.379	Manye tales ye *tellen* þat Theologie lerneþ,
B.10.387	He demed wel and wisely as holy writ *telleþ*;
B.11.1	Thanne Scripture scorned me and a skile *tolde*,
B.11.66	For I herde ones how Conscience it *tolde*,
B.11.80	For a baptiȝed man may, as maistres *telleþ*,
B.11.99	It falleþ noȝt for þat folk no tales to *telle*
B.11.139	For þei beþ, as oure bokes *telleþ*, aboue goddes werkes:
B.11.161	The legend[a] sanctorum yow lereþ more largere þan I yow *telle*.
B.11.205	In þe olde lawe, as [þe] lettre *telleþ*, mennes sones men calle[d] vs
B.11.290	And þe title þat ye take ordres by *telleþ* ye ben auaunced:
B.11.441	And if his wille were he wolde his name *telle*].
B.12.18	To *telle* men what dowel is, dobet and dobest boþe,
B.12.25	Ac if þer were any wight þat wolde me *telle*
B.12.63	And þoruȝ þe gifte of þe holy goost as þe gospel *telleþ*:
B.12.73	In þe olde lawe as þe lettre *telleþ*, þat was þe lawe of Iewes,
B.12.155	Why I haue *told* [þee] al þis, I took ful good hede
B.12.181	And haþ no contricion he come to shrifte; & þanne kan he litel *telle*
B.12.237	Ensamples token and termes, as *telleþ* þ[ise] poetes,
B.12.268	[Swiche tales *telleþ* Aristotle þe grete clerk]:
B.12.271	Ne of Sortes ne of Salomon no scripture kan *telle*.
B.13.14	And how þat Ymaginatif in dremels me *tolde*
B.13.69	That Poul in his Pistle to al þe peple *tolde*:
B.13.75	Taken it for his teme and *telle* it wiþouten glosyng.
B.13.80	That he precheþ [and] preueþ noȝt [com]pacience', I *tolde*.
B.13.102	And *tolde* hym of a Trinite, and toward vs he loked.
B.13.222	Pacience apposed hym and preyde he sholde *telle*
B.13.230	Ac for I kan neiþer taboure ne trompe ne *telle* no gestes,
B.13.299	And if he gyueþ ouȝt to pouere gomes, *telle* what he deleþ;
B.13.303	In towne and in Tauernes tales to *telle*
B.13.308	Askeþ at hym or at hym and he yow kan *telle*
B.13.323	Al þat he wiste wikked by any wight *tellen* it,
B.13.325	And þat he wiste by wille [to watte *tellen* it],
B.13.332	For tales þat I *telle* no man trusteþ to me.
B.13.353	And of hir harlotrye and horedom in hir elde *tellen*.
B.13.419	He hateþ to here þerof and alle þat it *telleþ*.
B.13.432	What Dauid seiþ of swiche men as þe Sauter *telleþ*:
B.15.13	Oon wiþouten tonge and teeþ *tolde* me whider I sholde
B.15.15	If he were cristes creature [for cristes loue] me to *tellen*.
B.15.29	And whan I feele þat folk *telleþ* my firste name is sensus,
B.15.71	Ye moeuen materes vnmesurable to *tellen* of þe Trinite
B.15.74	And *tellen* men of þe ten comaundementȝ, and touchen þe seuene synnes,
B.15.91	I shal *tellen* it for truþes sake; take hede whoso likeþ.
B.15.163	And so I trowe trewely, by þat men *telleþ* of [it,
B.15.317	Ye hadde riȝt ynoȝ, ye Religiouse, and so youre rule me *tolde*.
B.15.364	Tilieris þat tiled þe erþe *tolden* hir maistres
B.15.414	[Ac] for drede of þe deeþ I dar noȝt *telle* truþe,
B.15.549	Moore tresor þan trouþe? I dar noȝt *telle* þe soþe.
B.15.572	*Tellen* hem and techen hem on þe Trinite to bileue,
B.16.4	'It is a ful trie tree', quod he, 'trewely to *telle*.
B.16.61	I shal *telle* þee as tid what þis tree highte.
B.16.63	And I haue *told* þee what hiȝte þe tree; þe Trinite it meneþ.'
B.16.144	Iudas iangled þerayein, ac Iesus hym *tolde*
B.16.147	And *tolde* hem a tokne to knowe wiþ Iesus;
B.16.212	And bitokneþ trewely, *telle* if I dorste,
B.16.230	Ful trewe toknes bitwene vs is to *telle* whan me likeþ.
B.16.275	What he highte & whider he wolde, and wightly he *tolde*.
B.17.36	And *telleþ* noȝt of þe Trinite þat took hym hise lettres,
B.17.90	And I þanked hym þo and siþþe [þus] I hym *tolde*
B.17.120	Hope shal lede hem forþ with loue as his lettre *telleþ*,
B.17.146	And bitokneþ trewely, *telle* whoso likeþ,
B.17.200	Neiþer here ne ellisswhere, as I herde *telle*:
B.17.265	For manye of yow riche men, by my soule, men *telleþ*,
B.17.310	And eyþer haue equyte, as holy writ *telleþ*:
B.17.318	Than alle oure wikkede werkes as holy writ *telleþ*–
B.17.333	Thise þre þat I *telle* of ben þus to vnderstonde:
B.18.63	And *tolde* why þat tempeste so longe tyme durede:
B.18.79	Highte Longeus as þe lettre *telleþ*, and longe hadde lore his sight;
B.18.142	'That þow *tellest*', quod Truþe, 'is but a tale of waltrot!
B.18.147	It is trufle þat þow *tellest*; I, truþe, woot þe soþe,
B.18.171	That ouerhoueþ helle þus; she vs shal *telle*.'
B.18.174	And preide pees to *telle* hire to what place she wolde,
B.18.290	And *toldest* hire a tale, of treson were þe wordes;
B.18.416	'Trewes', quod Truþe, 'þow *tellest* vs sooþ, by Iesus!
B.19.23	And ye callen hym crist; for what cause, *telleþ* me.
B.19.71	Tho he was born in Bethleem, as þe book *telleþ*,
B.19.101	And so dide Iesu in hise dayes, whoso [dorste] *telle* it.
B.19.109	Water into wyn turnede, as holy writ *telleþ*,
B.19.115	So at þat feeste first as I bifore *tolde*
B.19.145	For no fren[d] sholde [it] fecche; for prophetes hem *tolde*
B.19.155	*Telle* þe comune þat þer cam a compaignie of hise Apostles
B.19.275	And sew [it] in mannes soule and siþen *tolde* hir names.
B.19.342	And *tolde* hem tidynges, þat tyne þei sholde
B.19.411	Man to me þat me kouþe *telle* of Cardinale vertues,
B.20.232	Nede neghede þo neer and Conscience he *tolde*
B.20.253	And if ye coueite cure, kynde wol yow [*telle*]
B.20.268	Forþi', quod Conscience, 'by crist! kynde wit me *telleþ*

C.Pr.9   And merueylousliche me mette, as y may [ʒow] *telle*.
C.Pr.13   Al y say slepynge as y shal [ʒow] *telle*.
C.Pr.90   Summe seruen þe kynge and his siluer *tellen*,
C.Pr.104   That al þe world be [þe] wors, as holy writ *telleth*.
C.Pr.111   Anon as it was *tolde* hym that þe children of Irael
C.Pr.129   To bynde and vnbynde as þe boke *telleth*,
C.Pr.232   Tauernes til hem *tolde* þe same:
C. 1.28   And lay by hem bothe as þe boke *telleth*;
C. 1.43   *Telleth* me to wham þat tresour bylongeth.'
C. 1.79   'Teche me to [no] tresor but *telle* me this ilke,
C. 1.115   'Nere hit for northerne men anon y wolde ʒow *telle*
C. 1.126   Wonderwyse, holy wryt *telleth*, how þei fullen,
C. 1.146   For treuthe *telleth* þat loue ys triacle [for] synne
C. 2.15   For to *telle* of here atyer no tyme haue y nouthe.
C. 2.145   For wel ʒe wyte, wernardus, as holy writ *telleth*,
C. 2.199   Y haue no tome to *telle* the tayl þat hem folewe[th]
C. 2.205   And kam to þe kynges Court and Consience *tolde*,
C. 2.254   Ac treuliche to *telle* a tremblede for fere
C. 3.47   *Tolde* hym a tale and toke men a noble
C. 3.133   Til treuthe hadde *ytolde* here a tokene fram hymsulue.
C. 3.394   Ac adiectyf and sustantyf is as y [e]r *tolde*,
C. 3.487   And muche worschipe therwith, as holy writ *telleth*:
C. 4.18   And also th[omm]e trewe-tonge-*telle*-me-no-tales-
C. 4.64   [The kyng knew he sayde soth for Conscience hym *tolde*]
C. 5.38   And what is beste for the body, as the boek *telleth*,
C. 5.109   Thenne mette me muche more then y byfore *tolde*
C. 5.156   Ac mony day, men *telleth*, bothe monkes and chanons
C. 5.169   And bete ʒow, as þe bible *telleth*, for brekynge of ʒoure reule
C. 5.178   Ac ar þat kyng come, as cronicles me *tolde*,
C. 6.28   To *telle* eny tale; y trowed me wysor
C. 6.47   And what y gaf for godes loue to gossipus y *tolde*,
C. 6.50   Tales to *telle* in tauernes and in stretes,
C. 6.56   Ascuth at hym or at h[ym] and he ʒow can *telle*
C. 6.70   And þat a wiste by wille to watekyn he *tolde* hit
C. 6.71   And þat he wiste by watte *tolde* hit wille aftur
C. 6.108   Thow y sitte this seuene ʒer, y sholde nat wel *telle*
C. 6.154   And yf y *telle* eny tales they taken hem togyderes
C. 6.426   Of þat y haue trespased with tonge, y can nat *telle* how ofte;
C. 7.17   That y *telle* with my tonge is t[wo] myle fro myn herte.
C. 7.29   Nat twies in ten ʒer and thenne *telle* y nat þe haluendele.
C. 7.92   Wh[at] dauid sayth of such men as þe sauter *telleth*:
C. 7.125   And for [þe] beste, as y beleue, what[euere] þe boek *telle*:
C. 7.203   Were hit *itolde* treuthe þat y toke mede
C. 7.245   *Tel* hym this tokene: "treuthe woet þe sothe;
C. 7.280   Ho is nat syb to this seuene, sothly to *telle*,
C. 7.298   Treuth *telleth* [this to hym], þat y be excused.'
C. 7.303   Forthy, [Peres] the [plouhman], y preye the *telle* hit treuthe
C. 8.76   Treuthe t[o]lde me ones and bad me telle hit fort[h]:
C. 8.76   Treuthe t[o]lde me ones and bad me *telle* hit fort[h]:
C. 8.98   Til y come til his acountes as my crede *telleth*,
C. 9.1   Treuthe herde *telle* herof and to [Peres] sente
C. 9.120   Withoute bagge and bred as þe book *telleth*:
C. 9.127   And godes boys, bourdyors as the book *telleth*:
C.10.13   Wher þat dowel dwelleth; 'dere frendes, *telleth* me,
C.10.127   And what þey drede and doute, dere sire, *telleth*.'
C.10.151   'What kynne thyng is kynde?' quod y; 'canst thow me *telle*?'
C.10.245   Ac why þe world was adreynt, holy writ *telleth*,
C.10.289   As Adam dede and Eue, as y whil er *tolde*.
C.11.30   And can *telle* of treuthe and of þe twelue aposteles
C.11.35   And *tellen* of þe trinite how t[w]o slowe þe thridde
C.11.69   How he *tolde* in a tyme and tauhte his sone dele:
C.11.103   'And *telle* me som tokene,' quod y, 'for tyme is þat y wende.'
C.11.136   Y grette hym goodly and graythly y hym *tolde*
C.11.196   Sir wanhope was sib to hym, as som men me *tolde*,
C.11.211   Neuere to man so moche þat man can of *telle*
C.11.273   And fonde y neuere in faith, for to *telle* treuthe,
C.12.74   They b[e]t[h], as oure bokes *telleth*, [aboue] godes werkes:
C.12.113   In þe olde lawe, as þe lettre *telleth*, mennes sones me calde vs
C.12.176   Tulius, tolomeus–ye can nat *tell* here names–
C.12.211   How god, as þe gospelle *telleth*, gyueth [hym] foel to name,
C.13.16   How bittere he hit abouhte, as þe book *telleth*!
C.13.40   Ther þe messager doth no more but with his mouth *telleth*
C.13.88   *Telleth* þe lord a tale as a trewe messager
C.13.104   The tytle [þat] ʒe take ordres by *telleth* ʒe ben avaunsed
C.13.247   And yf his wille were A wolde his name *telle*.
C.14.99   Why y haue *tolde* [the] al þis, y toek ful gode hede
C.14.121   And hath no contricion ar he come to shrifte; and thenne can he
           lytel *telle*,
C.14.131   The thef þat hadde grace of god a gode fryday, As thow *toldest*,
C.14.169   To briddes and to bestes, As here bokes *telleth*
C.14.192   Ne of sortes ne of salamon n[o] scripture can *telle*
C.15.17   And how þat ymaginatyf in dremeles me *tolde*
C.15.73   For oure lordes loue, as holy lettre *telleth*:

C.15.81   Þat toek this for his teme and *tolde* hit withoute glose.
C.15.87   That a precheth and preueth nat compacience,' ich *tolde*,
C.15.109   And *tolde* hym of a trinite, and toward me he lokede.
C.15.191   Pacience apposede hym and preyede a sholde *telle*
C.15.204   [Ac for] y can nat tabre ne trompy ne *telle* [no] gestes,
C.16.115   'What is pouerte, pacience?' quod he; 'y preye þat thow *telle* hit.'
C.16.118   'Parfay!' quod pacience, 'propreliche to *telle* [this]
C.16.119   In engelysch is ful hard Ac sumdel y shal *telle* the.
C.16.166   And yf thow be cristes creature, for cristes loue *telle* me.'
C.16.189   And when y fele þat folke *telleth* my furste name is sensus
C.16.194   Thenne am y liberum Arbitrium, as le[tt]red men *telleth*;
C.16.297   And so y trowe truly, by þat me *telleth* of charite.'
C.16.371   As y *tolde* þe with tonge a litel tyme ypassed;
C.17.65   Lo laurence for his largenesse, as holy lore *telleth*
C.17.100   Wisten w[hi]l[e] and *tolde* when hit sholde ryne.
C.17.101   Tilyares þat tilede þe erthe *tolden* here maystres
C.17.180   *Tolde* hym and tauhte [hym] how to teche þe peple.
C.17.211   More tresor then treuthe? Y dar nat *telle* þe sothe
C.18.2   Thow couthest *telle* me and teche me [in] charite [to] leue.'
C.18.8   Thenne gan y aske what hit hihte and he me sone *tolde*:
C.18.161   The iewes *tolde* þe iustice how þat iesus saide.
C.18.244   And what y thouhte and my wyf he vs wel *tolde*.
C.18.291   What he hihte and whoder he wolde & whithliche he *tolde*.
C.19.33   He can no certeyn somme *telle* and somme aren in his lappe.
C.19.37   That of no trinite ne *telleth* ne taketh mo persones
C.19.100   And hope afturward of god more me *toelde*
C.19.120   And bitokeneth trewly, *telle* hoso liketh,
C.19.127   To huyde and to holde as holy writ *telleth*–
C.19.166   Noþer here ne elleswhere, as y herde *telle*:
C.19.242   For godes tretor he is [to]ld for al his trewe catel
C.19.298   Thenne al oure wikkede werkes as holy writ *telleth*:
C.19.313   Thise thre that y *telle* of thus ben [to] vnderstande:
C.20.65   And *tolde* why þ[at] tempest so longe tyme durede:
C.20.81   Hihte longies as þe lettre *telleth*, and longe hadde lore his sihte;
C.20.111   Now ben ʒoure gode dayes ydoen, as daniel of ʒow *telleth*;
C.20.145   'That thow *tellest*,' quod treuthe, 'is bote a tale of walterot!
C.20.150   Hit is truyfle þat thow *tellest*; y, treuthe, woet þe sothe,
C.20.174   That ouerhoueth helle thus; he vs shal *telle*.'
C.20.177   And preyede pees to *tellen* [here] to what place she [w]olde
C.20.459   'Trewes,' quod treuthe; 'thow *tellest* vs soeth, by iesus!
C.21.23   And ʒe callen hym Crist; for what cause, *telleth* me.
C.21.71   Tho he was bore in Bedlehem, as þe boek *telleth*,
C.21.101   And so dede iesu in his dayes, whoso durste *tellen* hit.
C.21.109   [Watur into wyn turned], As holy writ *telleth*.
C.21.115   So at þat feste furste as y before *tolde*
C.21.145   For no frende sholde hit fecche; for profetes hem *tolde*
C.21.155   *Telle* þe comune þat þer cam a companie of his apostles
C.21.275   And sewe hit in mannes soule and sethe *toelde* here names.
C.21.342   And *toelde* hem tydynges, þat tyne thei sholde
C.21.411   Man to me þat me couthe *telle* of cardinal[e] vertues
C.22.232   Nede neyhede tho ner and Consience he *toelde*
C.22.253   And yf ʒe coueiteth cure kynde wol ʒow *telle*
C.22.268   For[thy],' quod Consience, 'bi Crist! kynde wit me *telleth*

telleris > taletelleris

tellynge ger1 *tillinge ger.(1)* A 1 telling; B 2 tellynge (1) tulying (1)
A. 7.232   Oþer wiþ teching, oþer *telling*, or trauaillyng of hondis,
B. 6.248   Or [wiþ tech]ynge or [*tell*]ynge or trauaillynge [of hondes],
B.14.64   It is founden þat fourty wynter folk lyuede withouten *tulying*,

tellynge ger2 *tillinge ger.* B 1; C 1 tellyng
B.20.8   [Was] by techynge and by *tellynge* of Spiritus temperancie,
C.22.8   Was bi techyng and by *tellyng* of spiritus temperancie

telþe > tilþe; tem > teme n1,n2

teme n1 *teme n.(1)* A 2 tem; B 5 teeme (2) teme (3); C 5
A. 7.126   Ac treuþe shal teche ʒow his *tem* for to dryue,
A. 8.2   To take his *tem* & [tilien þe erþe],
B. 6.134   Ac truþe shal teche yow his *teme* to dryue,
B. 7.2   To [t]aken his *teme* and tilien þe erþe,
B.19.261   And for to tilie truþe a *teeme* shal he haue.'
B.19.262   Grace gaf Piers a *teeme*, foure grete Oxen.
B.19.271   Thise foure, þe feiþ to teche, folwe[de] Piers *teme*
C. 8.141   Ac treuthe shal teche ʒow his *teme* to dryue
C. 9.2   To taken his *teme* and tilion þe erthe
C.21.261   And for to tulye treuthe a *teme* shal he haue.'
C.21.262   Grace gaf [Peres] a *teme*, foure grete oxen.
C.21.271   Thise foure, the fayth to teche, folewe[de Peres] *teme*

teme n2 *teme n.(2)* A 5 teeme (1) tem (1) teme (3); B 8; C 5 teeme (1)
           teme (4)
A. 3.84   And tok hym þis *teeme* þat I telle þenke:
A. 5.43   Þanne [ran] repentaunce [and] reherside his *teme*
A. 7.24   Ac on þe *tem* trewely tauʒt was I neuere.

A. 8.123   Quoniam literaturam non cognoui, þat miȝte be þi *teme*.'
A.11.73   And for suche tale telleris suche a *teme* shewide:
B. 3.95   And [took hym] þis *teme* þat I telle þynke:
B. 3.351   And þat is þe tail of þe text of þat [*teme* ye] shewed,
B. 5.60   Thanne ran Repentaunce and rehercd his *teme*
B. 6.22   Ac on þe *teme* trewely tauȝt was I neuere.
B. 7.141   As diuinour in diuinite, wiþ Dixit inspiens to þi *teme*.'
B.10.120   Austyn to swiche Argueres [he] telleþ þis *teme*:
B.11.111   This was hir *teme* and hir text–I took ful good hede–
B.13.75   Taken it for his *teme* and telle it wiþouten glosyng.
C. 6.1   With þat ran rehercde his *teme*
C. 8.20   Ac [on þe] *t[ee]me* treuely ytauhte was y neuere.
C.12.45   Of here *teme* and here tales y took ful good hede;
C.15.81   Þat toek this for his *teme* and tolde hit withoute glose.
C.20.358   That y ne sygge as y syhe, suynde my *teme*).

temese > themese; temperaltees > temporaltees

tempeste n *tempest n.* B 1; C 1 tempest
B.18.63   And tolde why þat *tempeste* so longe tyme durede:
C.20.65   And tolde why þ[at] *tempest* so longe tyme durede:

temple n *temple n.(1)* A 1; B 3; C 5
A. 1.45   Þo þe peple hym aposide with a peny in þe *temple*
B. 1.47   Tho þe poeple hym apposede wiþ a peny in þe *temple*
B.16.131   'I shal ouerturne þis *temple* and adoun þrowe,
B.18.41   'This Iesus of oure Iewes *temple* Iaped and despised,
C. 1.45   Whenne þe peple aposed hym of a peny in þe *temple*
C.18.156   And ouerturnede in þe *temple* here tables and here stalles
C.18.162   Ac þe ouerturnynge of the *temple* bitokened his resureccioun.
C.20.40   'This iesus of oure iewene *temple* iaped and despised,
C.20.61   The wal of the *temple* tocleyef euene [a] to peces;

templers n *templer n.(1)* B 1; C 1
B.15.547   Shul [ouer]torne as *templers* dide; þe tyme approcheþ faste.
C.17.209   Sholle ouerturne as *templers* dede; þe tyme approcheth faste.

temporaltees n *temporalite n.* B 1; C 1 temperaltees
B.20.128   To holden wiþ Antecrist, hir *temporaltees* to saue.
C.22.128   To holde with auntecrist, here *temperaltee[s]* to saue.

tempreþ v *tempren v.* B 2 tempred (1) tempreþ (1); C 1 tempreth
B.Pr.51   To ech a tale þat þei tolde hire tonge was *tempred* to lye
B.14.312   He *tempreþ* þe tonge to truþeward [þat] no tresor coueiteþ:
C.16.146   A *tempreth* þe tonge to treuthward þat no tresor coueyteth:

tempted ptp *tempten v.* B 1; C 1 ytempted
B.19.64   Is to wissen vs þerwiþ, þat whan we ben *tempted*,
C.21.64   Is to wissen vs þerwith, þat when we ben *ytempted*

ten num *ten num.* A 8 tene (1) ten (7); B 11 ten (10) x (1); C 13 ten (12) tene (1)
A. 1.103   And crist, king[ene] kin[g], kniȝtide *tene*,
A. 2.42   And *ten* þousand of tentis teldit beside
A. 4.45   And takiþ me but a taile for *ten* quarteris otis,
A. 5.128   Til *ten* ȝardis oþer twelue tollide out þrittene.
A. 7.226   And ȝaf [it] hym in haste þat hadde *ten* before,
A. 8.167   Be þou neuere þe baldere to breke þe *ten* hestis;
A.11.137   Ac theologie haþ tenid me *ten* score tymes,
A.11.253   For he seiþ it hymself in his *ten* hestis;
B. 1.105   [And] crist, kyngene kyng, knyȝted *ten*,
B. 2.83   Vnbuxome and bolde to breke þe *ten* hestes;
B. 4.58   And takeþ me but a taille for *ten* quarters Otes;
B. 5.212   Til *ten* yerdes or twelue tolled out þrittene.
B. 5.425   And þus tene I trewe men *ten* hundred tymes,
B. 6.242   And yaf [it hym in haste þat hadde *ten* bifore];
B. 7.189   Be [þow] neuer þe bolder to breke þe *x* hestes,
B.10.185   Ac Theologie haþ tened me *ten* score tymes;
B.13.269   A thousand and þre hundred, twies [þritty] and *ten*,
B.15.74   And tellen men of þe *ten* comaundementȝ, and touchen þe seuene synnes,
B.19.165   Thaddee and *ten* mo wiþ Thomas of Inde.
C. 1.105   Made knyghtes in his Couert creatures *tene*,
C. 2.90   Vnbuxom and bold to breke þe *ten* hestes,
C. 4.61   And taketh me but a tayle for *ten* quarteres otes;
C. 6.220   Til *ten* ȝerde other twelue tolde out threttene.
C. 7.29   Nat twies in *ten* ȝer and thenne telle y nat þe haluendele.
C. 7.38   And thus haue y tened trewe men *ten* hundrit tymes.
C. 9.335   Be ȝe neuere þe baldere to breke þe *ten* hestes
C.11.126   Ac teologie hath tened me *ten* score tymes;
C.11.140   Kepe þe *ten* comaundementis and kepe þe fro synne
C.13.68   That holde mote þe hey way, euene the *ten* hestes,
C.16.234   To teche þe *ten* comaundementȝ ten sythe were bettere
C.16.234   To teche þe ten comaundementȝ *ten* sythe were bettere
C.21.165   Taddee and *ten* mo with Thomas of ynde.

tenaunt n *tenaunt n.* A 1; B 2 tenaunt (1) tenauntȝ (1); C 2 tenaunt (1) tenauntes (1)
A. 7.39   Loke þou tene no *tenaunt* but treuþe wile assent,
B. 6.38   Loke [þow] tene no *tenaunt* but truþe wole assente,
B.15.310   And to taken of hir *tenauntȝ* moore þan trouþe wolde,
C. 8.36   Loke ȝe tene no *tenaunt* but treuthe wol assente
C.17.45   And to take of here *tenauntes* more then treuthe wolde

tendeden v *tenden v.(3)* B 1; C 1 tenden
B.18.240   And *tendeden* [hire] as a torche to reuerencen his burþe;
C.20.249   And *tenden* h[ere] as a torche to reuerensen his burthe;

tender > tonder

tene n *tene n.(2)* A 3; B 5; C 4
A. 8.101   And piers for [pure] *tene* pulde it assondir
A.10.145   In *tene* & trauaille to here lyues ende;
A.12.9   That myȝthe turne m[e] to *tene* & theologie boþe.
B. 6.117   'Now by þe peril of my soule!' quod Piers al in pure *tene*,
B. 6.133   Ye wasten þat men wynnen wiþ trauaille and *tene*.
B. 7.119   And Piers for pure *tene* pulled it [asonder]
B.11.115   Al for *tene* of hir text trembled myn herte,
B.16.86   And Piers for pure *tene* þat a pil he [l]auȝte;
C. 8.124   Quod [Peres] þe [plouhman] al in puyre *tene*:
C.12.50   Al for *tene* of here tyxst tremblede myn herte,
C.13.7   Abraham for his [auȝte] hadde moche *tene*
C.16.175   And som tyme to soffre bothe [sorwe] and [*tene*],

tene v *tenen v.* A 5 tene (1) tenen (1) tenid (1) tenide (1) teniþ (1); B 10 tene (4) tened (4) teneþ (2); C 10 tene (4) tene (5) teneth (1)
A. 2.79   Þanne *tenide* hym theologie whan he þis tale herde,
A. 3.113   In trist of hire tresour she *teniþ* [wel] manye,
A. 7.39   Loke þou *tene* no tenaunt but treuþe wile assent,
A. 9.89   Þat waiten any wikkidnesse dowel to *tenen*.
A.11.137   Ac theologie haþ ten score tymes,
B. 2.115   Thanne *tened* hym Theologie whan he þis tale herde,
B. 3.124   [In] trust of hire tresor [she *teneþ*] wel] manye.
B. 3.322   Tha[t] worþ Trewe-tonge, a tidy man þat *tened* me neuere.
B. 5.425   And þus *tene* I trewe men ten hundred tymes,
B. 6.38   Loke [þow] *tene* no tenaunt but truþe wole assente,
B. 8.99   That waiten any wikkednesse dowel to *tene*.
B.10.185   Ac Theologie haþ *tened* me ten score tymes;
B.13.163   *Tene* þee any tyme, and þow take it wiþ [þ]e.
B.15.420   Of tirauntȝ þat *teneþ* trewe men taken any almesse,
B.20.119   Wiþ vntidy tales he *tened* ful ofte
C. 2.119   Thenne *tened* hym teologie when he this tal[e] herde,
C. 3.140   Thow *tene* me and treuthe: and thow mowe ate ake
C. 3.161   In trist of here tresor he *teneth* fol monye,
C. 3.475   Þat worth trewe-tonge, a tydy man þat *tened* me neuere.
C. 7.38   And thus haue y *tened* trewe men ten hundrit tymes.
C. 8.36   Loke ȝe *tene* no tenaunt but treuthe wol assente
C.11.126   Ac teologie hath *tened* me ten score tymes;
C.14.8   Ne no tyme to tyne ne trewe thyng *tene*,
C.15.159   *Tene* þe eny tyme and þou take pacience
C.22.119   With vntidy tales he *tened* ful ofte

tene &> ten

teneful adj *teneful adj.* B 1; C 1
B. 3.349   A ful *teneful* text to hem þat takeþ Mede:
C. 3.497   A ful *teneful* tyxst to hem þat taketh mede,

tentis n *tente n.* A 1
A. 2.42   And ten þousand of *tentis* teldit beside

teologie > theologie

tercian n *tercian n.* A 1
A.12.85   *Tercian* þat oþer; trewe drinkeres boþe.

teris n *tere n.* B 1; C 1 teres
B.13.45   But if þei synge for þo soules and wepe salte *teris*:
C.15.50   Bote yf they synge for tho soules and wepe salte *teres*:

termes n *terme n.* B 1
B.12.237   Ensamples token and *termes*, as telleþ þ[ise] poetes,

termined > ytermyned

termisonus n *termison n.* C 1
C. 3.406   Of thre trewe *termisonus*, trinitas vnus deus:

testifie v *testifien v.* B 1; C 3 testifie (2) testifieth (1)
B.13.94   And þanne shal he *testifie* of [a] Trinite, and take his felawe to witnesse
C.11.305   All þat treuth attacheth and *testifieth* for gode
C.12.173   To *testifie* for treuthe þe tale þat y shewe
C.15.101   And [þenne shal he *testifie* of] a trinite and take his felowe [t]o witnesse

teth > teeþ

text n *texte n.* A 3 texte (1) textis (1) tixtes (1); B 13 text (10) textes (2)
    tixte (1); C 7 textes (1) tixst (2) tyxst (2) tixt (1) tyxt (1)

A. 1.123   Forþi I seye as I seide er, be siȝte of þise *textis*:
A. 1.180   Forþi I seiȝe as I seide er be siȝte of þise *tixtes*:
A. 2.86   Þe *text[e]* tell[iþ] not so, treuþe wot þe soþe:
B. 1.134   Forþi I seye, as I seyde er, by siȝte of þise *textes*:
B. 1.206   Forþi I seye er by [siȝte] of þise] *textes*:
B. 2.122   [The] *text* telleþ þee noȝt so, Truþe woot þe soþe,
B. 3.343   Quod bonum est tenete; truþe þat *text* made.
B. 3.346   This *text* þat ye han told were [trewe] for lordes,
B. 3.349   A ful teneful *text* to hem þat takeþ Mede:
B. 3.351   And þat is þe tail of þe *text* of þat [teme ye] shewed,
B. 10.275   This *text* was told yow to ben ywar er ye tauȝte,
B. 11.111   This was hir teme and hir *text*–I took ful good hede–
B. 11.115   Al for tene of hir *text* trembled myn herte,
B. 13.126   And no *text* ne takeþ to mayntene his cause
B. 15.328   If any peple parfourne þat *text* it are þise poore freres,
B. 17.14   This was the *tixte*, trewely; I took ful good yeme.
C. 1.201   Forthi y may seye, as y saide eer, by sihte of this *tex[t]es*:
C. 2.132   Y, Theo[lo]gie, þe *tixt* knowe yf trewe doom wittenesseth,
C. 3.495   Quod bonum est tenete, a *tixst* of treuthe [m]akynge.
C. 3.497   A ful teneful *tyxst* to hem þat taketh mede,
C. 12.50   Al for tene of here *tyxst* tremblede myn herte,
C. 15.133   And no *tixst* ne taketh to preue this for trewe
C. 19.15   This was the *tyxt* trewly; y toek ful good gome.

thaddee n prop *n.i.d.* B 1; C 1 Taddee
B. 19.165   *Thaddee* and ten mo wiþ Thomas of Inde.
C. 21.165   *Taddee* and ten mo with Thomas of ynde.

þai thay > þei; than > þan,thanne

þan conj *than conj.* &> *thanne* A 34 þan (10) þanne (24); B 127 than
    (44) þan (83); C 115 than (3) þan (1) then (101) þen (5) thenne (5)

    A.Pr.89, A.1.9, A.1.131, A.1.158, A.1.160, A.1.165, A.2.21, A.3.96, A.3.172,
A.4.80, A.5.9, A.5.83, A.5.97, A.5.132, A.6.50, A.6.52, A.7.257, A.8.79, A.10.56,
A.11.12, A.11.16, A.11.32, A.11.51, A.11.111, A.11.175, A.11.216, A.11.282, A.11.285,
A.11.287, A.11.288, A.11.308, A.11.310, A.12.3, A.12.92

    B.Pr.52, B.Pr.147, B.Pr.191, B.Pr.216, B.1.9, B.1.116, B.1.143, B.1.184, B.1.186,
B.1.191, B.2.28, B.2.77, B.3.107, B.3.185, B.3.275, B.4.39, B.4.93, B.5.9, B.5.53,
B.5.92, B.5.103, B.5.118, B.5.143, B.5.154, B.5.192, B.5.216, B.5.243, B.5.283, B.5.408,
B.5.418, B.5.565, B.6.273, B.7.46, B.7.97, B.9.37, B.9.81, B.10.12, B.10.16, B.10.45,
B.10.65, B.10.159, B.10.232, B.10.295, B.10.398, B.10.423, B.10.426, B.10.428,
B.10.429, B.10.464, B.10.466, B.10.473, B.11.51, B.11.77, B.11.161, B.11.258,
B.11.269, B.11.272, B.11.302, B.11.319, B.11.380, B.12.80, B.12.157, B.12.158,
B.12.161, B.12.173, B.12.199, B.12.215, B.12.234, B.12.265, B.13.195, B.13.197,
B.13.201, B.13.278, B.13.319, B.13.356, B.13.364, B.13.381, B.13.386, B.13.398,
B.13.403, B.14.26, B.14.28, B.14.103, B.14.108, B.14.166, B.14.210, B.14.216,
B.14.249, B.14.268, B.14.270, B.14.314, B.14.331, B.15.79, B.15.110, B.15.208,
B.15.310, B.15.343, B.15.449, B.15.541, B.15.549, B.16.57, B.16.181, B.16.267,
B.17.40, B.17.43, B.17.47, B.17.108, B.17.177, B.17.183, B.17.318, B.17.328, B.18.166,
B.18.310, B.18.380, B.18.410, B.18.412, B.19.25, B.19.58, B.19.127, B.19.252, B.20.9,
B.20.26, B.20.28, B.20.63, B.20.223, B.20.239, B.20.319

    C.Pr.123, C.Pr.166, C.Pr.168, C.1.9, C.1.114, C.1.118, C.1.136, C.1.143,
C.1.180, C.1.182, C.1.187, C.2.14, C.2.30, C.2.84, C.3.138, C.3.231, C.3.428, C.4.39,
C.4.89, C.4.193, C.5.109, C.5.188, C.6.24, C.6.29, C.6.31, C.6.129, C.6.159, C.6.200,
C.6.224, C.6.244, C.6.263, C.6.275, C.6.285, C.6.293, C.6.306, C.6.314, C.6.430, C.7.24,
C.7.210, C.7.212, C.9.123, C.9.173, C.10.169, C.10.282, C.11.10, C.11.13, C.11.28,
C.11.47, C.11.101, C.11.225, C.11.229, C.11.255, C.11.258, C.11.261, C.11.290,
C.11.292, C.12.144, C.12.154, C.12.189, C.13.32, C.13.37, C.13.186, C.13.197, C.14.3,
C.14.36, C.14.102, C.14.105, C.14.113, C.14.138, C.14.154, C.14.180, C.14.182,
C.14.216, C.15.119, C.15.268, C.15.278, C.15.283, C.16.51, C.16.57, C.16.89, C.16.108,
C.16.110, C.16.148, C.16.179, C.16.264, C.17.45, C.17.203, C.17.211, C.18.60, C.18.66,
C.18.78, C.18.87, C.18.283, C.19.104, C.19.142, C.19.149, C.19.298, C.19.308,
C.20.169, C.20.217, C.20.344, C.20.422, C.20.453, C.20.455, C.21.25, C.21.58,
C.21.127, C.21.252, C.22.9, C.22.26, C.22.28, C.22.63, C.22.223, C.22.239, C.22.319

þanked > þonked

thankes n *thank n.* C 1
C. 9.66   For he þat gyueth for goddes loue wolde nat gyue, his *thankes*,

thanne adv1 *thanne adv.* A 91 than (1) þan (3) thanne (1) þanne (86); B
    213 than (2) þan (2) thanne (114) þanne (95); C 193 than (2) thanne
    (4) then (5) thenne (182)

    A.Pr.11, A.Pr.42, A.1.56, A.1.69, A.1.77, A.1.112, A.2.49, A.2.79, A.2.108,
A.2.122, A.2.126, A.2.127, A.2.133, A.2.172, A.2.185, A.3.9, A.3.19, A.3.24, A.3.28,
A.3.34, A.3.42, A.3.46, A.3.103, A.3.157, A.4.6, A.4.13, A.4.22, A.4.31, A.4.34, A.4.60,
A.4.62, A.4.81, A.4.85, A.5.3, A.5.9, A.5.43, A.5.88, A.5.92, A.5.107, A.5.123, A.5.157,
A.5.180, A.5.194, A.5.197, A.5.203, A.5.205, A.5.206, A.5.220, A.6.22, A.6.51, A.6.59,
A.6.67, A.6.70, A.6.72, A.6.95, A.6.98, A.7.50, A.7.107, A.7.113, A.7.139, A.7.146,
A.7.149, A.7.159, A.7.186, A.7.214, A.7.275, A.7.281, A.7.284, A.7.298, A.8.42, A.9.22,
A.9.59, A.9.65, A.9.94, A.9.116, A.10.56, A.10.62, A.10.69, A.10.76, A.10.85, A.10.201,

    A.10.216, A.11.1, A.11.40, A.11.110, A.11.122, A.11.278, A.12.38, A.12.42, A.12.47,
A.12.72

    B.Pr.11, B.Pr.42, B.Pr.112, B.Pr.114, B.Pr.123, B.Pr.139, B.Pr.143, B.Pr.170,
B.Pr.172, B.1.58, B.1.71, B.1.79, B.2.49, B.2.69, B.2.97, B.2.100, B.2.115, B.2.144,
B.2.158, B.2.162, B.2.163, B.2.169, B.2.211, B.2.213, B.2.226, B.3.9, B.3.20, B.3.25,
B.3.29, B.3.35, B.3.43, B.3.47, B.3.114, B.3.170, B.4.6, B.4.13, B.4.24, B.4.42, B.4.44,
B.4.47, B.4.74, B.4.76, B.4.94, B.4.98, B.5.3, B.5.9, B.5.60, B.5.108, B.5.112, B.5.132,
B.5.168, B.5.188, B.5.207, B.5.279, B.5.306, B.5.331, B.5.346, B.5.349, B.5.361,
B.5.379, B.5.385, B.5.411, B.5.414, B.5.448, B.5.477, B.5.506, B.5.534, B.5.564,
B.5.572, B.5.580, B.5.583, B.5.585, B.5.609, B.5.612, B.6.55, B.6.115, B.6.152, B.6.159,
B.6.164, B.6.199, B.6.230, B.6.291, B.6.297, B.6.300, B.6.317, B.6.329, B.7.38, B.7.167,
B.8.26, B.8.68, B.8.74, B.8.104, B.8.127, B.9.181, B.9.207, B.10.1, B.10.54, B.10.158,
B.10.170, B.10.264, B.10.290, B.10.292, B.10.328, B.10.331, B.10.336, B.10.394,
B.11.1, B.11.6, B.11.12, B.11.27, B.11.31, B.11.61, B.11.123, B.11.219, B.11.291,
B.11.373, B.11.406, B.11.408, B.11.429, B.11.431, B.11.434, B.12.181, B.13.22,
B.12.254, B.13.34, B.13.37, B.13.54, B.13.57, B.13.64, B.13.89, B.13.94, B.13.97,
B.13.106, B.13.112, B.13.133, B.13.216, B.13.228, B.13.250, B.13.318, B.13.342,
B.13.351, B.13.354, B.13.405, B.14.34, B.14.137, B.15.28, B.15.32, B.15.34, B.15.36,
B.15.36, B.15.50, B.15.138, B.15.186, B.15.193, B.15.309, B.15.391, B.15.406,
B.15.406, B.16.30, B.16.36, B.16.40, B.16.50, B.16.69, B.16.70, B.16.75, B.16.90,
B.16.95, B.16.121, B.16.146, B.16.153, B.16.172, B.17.51, B.17.98, B.17.115, B.17.122,
B.17.152, B.17.208, B.17.229, B.17.313, B.17.314, B.18.15, B.18.18, B.18.36, B.18.56,
B.18.87, B.18.92, B.18.150, B.18.180, B.18.230, B.18.266, B.18.371, B.18.375,
B.18.408, B.18.423, B.19.9, B.19.117, B.19.176, B.19.200, B.19.211, B.19.213,
B.19.360, B.19.367, B.19.377, B.19.409, B.19.459, B.19.465, B.20.1, B.20.53, B.20.93,
B.20.110, B.20.121, B.20.143, B.20.286

    C.Pr.139, C.Pr.141, C.Pr.148, C.Pr.167, C.Pr.187, C.Pr.189, C.1.54, C.1.68,
C.1.76, C.2.1, C.2.52, C.2.71, C.2.74, C.2.76, C.2.119, C.2.174, C.2.179, C.2.197,
C.2.236, C.3.9, C.3.21, C.3.27, C.3.38, C.3.45, C.3.102, C.3.151, C.3.216, C.3.343,
C.4.6, C.4.24, C.4.40, C.4.42, C.4.45, C.4.90, C.5.26, C.5.109, C.6.62, C.6.97, C.6.103,
C.6.139, C.6.140, C.6.170, C.6.185, C.6.196, C.6.215, C.6.308, C.6.361, C.6.404,
C.6.407, C.6.419, C.7.1, C.7.27, C.7.29, C.7.62, C.7.179, C.7.211, C.7.217, C.7.219,
C.7.227, C.7.230, C.7.261, C.7.264, C.7.299, C.8.23, C.8.32, C.8.54, C.8.122, C.8.149,
C.8.161, C.8.254, C.8.314, C.8.322, C.8.323, C.8.337, C.8.350, C.9.145, C.9.272,
C.9.311, C.10.30, C.10.72, C.10.123, C.10.188, C.11.1, C.11.43, C.11.100, C.11.160,
C.11.171, C.11.186, C.11.190, C.11.121, C.12.13, C.12.23, C.12.58, C.13.183, C.13.214,
C.13.218, C.13.236, C.13.238, C.13.240, C.14.10, C.14.121, C.15.25, C.15.42, C.15.51,
C.15.59, C.15.68, C.15.96, C.15.101, C.15.104, C.15.113, C.15.114, C.15.119, C.15.185,
C.15.202, C.15.222, C.15.305, C.16.6, C.16.158, C.16.162, C.16.179, C.16.180,
C.16.188, C.16.192, C.16.194, C.16.196, C.16.198, C.16.198, C.16.212, C.16.331,
C.16.336, C.17.44, C.17.48, C.17.145, C.17.162, C.17.175, C.17.177, C.18.3, C.18.8,
C.18.19, C.18.35, C.18.40, C.18.43, C.18.50, C.18.53, C.18.86, C.18.88, C.18.107,
C.18.117, C.18.123, C.18.151, C.18.170, C.18.181, C.18.192, C.18.269, C.19.34,
C.19.49, C.19.126, C.19.174, C.19.195, C.19.293, C.19.294, C.20.13, C.20.16, C.20.35,
C.20.39, C.20.56, C.20.95, C.20.153, C.20.239, C.20.274, C.20.311, C.20.413, C.20.417,
C.20.451, C.20.466, C.21.9, C.21.176, C.21.200, C.21.211, C.21.213, C.21.360,
C.21.367, C.21.377, C.21.409, C.21.459, C.21.465, C.22.1, C.22.53, C.22.93, C.22.110,
C.22.121, C.22.143, C.22.286

þanne adv2 *thenne adv.* &> *thanne adv1, þan conj, cf. þenne* A 1 þenne; B
    4 thanne (2) þanne (2); C 5 thenne

A. 11.48   But hunsen hym as an hound & hoten hym go *þenne*.
B. 2.218   Liȝtliche Lyere leep awey *þanne*,
B. 14.50   And *þanne* was it fiat voluntas tua [sholde fynde vs alle].
B. 14.117   *Thanne* may beggeris, as beestes, after boote waiten
B. 14.281   *Thanne* is it good by good skile, al þat agasteþ pride.
C. 2.228   Lyhtliche lyare lep awey *thenne*,
C. 3.263   Vnconnyngliche [þow], Consience, conseiledest hym *thenne*
C. 15.249   And *thenne* was hit fiat voluntas tua þat sholde fynde vs alle.
C. 15.293   *Thenne* may beggares, as bestes, aftur blisse aske
C. 16.121   *Thenne* is [hit] goed by goed skill, thouh hit greue a litel,

thare > þer

þat pron dem *that pron.* A 32; B 100 that (38) þat (62); C 94 that (28)
    þat (66)

A. 1.37   Þat is þe wrecchide world [wolde] þe betraye.
A. 1.39   [And *þat*] shend[iþ] þi soule; set it in þin herte;
A. 1.59   'Þ[at] is þe castel of care; who[so] comiþ þereinne
A. 1.98   *Þat* is þe professioun apertly þat apendiþ to kniȝtes,
A. 1.140   And *þat* falliþ to þe fadir þat fourmide vs alle,
A. 1.172   *Þ[at]* is no treuþe of trinite but treccherie of helle,
A. 1.176   *Þat* is þe lok of loue þat letiþ out my grace
A. 2.16   '*Þat* is mede þe maide, haþ noiȝede me ful ofte,
A. 3.25   Wiþ *þat* come clerkis to conforten hire þe same,
A. 3.50   'Wiste I *þat*,' quaþ þe womman, 'þere nis wyndowe ne auter
A. 4.74   'God wot,' quaþ wysdom, '*þat* were not þe beste.
A. 5.97   And whoso haþ more þanne I, *þat* angriþ myn herte.
A. 5.106   And *þat* makiþ me so ma[t] for I ne may me venge.'
A. 5.135   For laboureris & louȝ folk *þat* lay be h[y]mselue;
A. 6.117   'Wyte god,' quaþ a waffrer, 'wiste I *þat* forsoþe,
A. 7.242   Þei han mangid ouer muche, *þat* makiþ hem grone ofte.
A. 7.274   Be *þat* I hope to haue heruest in my croft,
A. 7.283   Be *þat* it neiȝide ner heruest [þat] newe corn com to chepyng.

A. 8.123 Quoniam literaturam non cognoui, þat miȝte be þi teme.'
A. 9.41   Þat is charite þe champioun, chief helpe aȝens synne.
A. 9.64   'Þat þou wost wel,' quaþ he, '& no wiȝt betere.'
A.10.29   And þat is þe grete god þat gynnyng had neuere,
A.10.38   Þat is þe castel þat kynde made, caro it hatte,
A.10.44   Þat is Anima, þat oueral in þe body wandriþ,
A.10.79   And þat is dred of god, dowel it makiþ.
A.10.210 And þat ben fals folk, & fals eires also, foundlynges & [leiȝeris],
A.10.218 And þat is wykkide wil þat many werk shendiþ.'
A.11.202 And þat is riȝtful religioun, none renneris aboute,
A.11.235 'Þat is in extremis,' quaþ scripture, 'as sarisines & Iewis
A.11.250 Þat is, iche cristene [creature] be kynde to oþer,
A.11.303 Þat [was] austyn þe olde, & hiȝeste of þe foure,
A.12.77   With þat cam a knaue with a confessoures face,
B.Pr.146 Wiþ þat ran þer a route of Ratons at ones
B.Pr.195 That witnesseþ holy writ, whoso wole it rede:
B. 1.39   That is þe wrecched world wolde þee bitraye.
B. 1.41   And that [shendeþ] þi soule; [set] it in þin herte.
B. 1.61   'That is þe castel of care; whoso comþ þerInne
B. 1.100 [That] is [þe] profession apertli þat apendeþ to knyȝtes,
B. 1.166 And þat falleþ to be fader þat formed vs alle,
B. 1.198 [Th]is is no truþe of þe Trinite but tricherie of helle,
B. 1.202 [Th]at is þe lok of loue [þat] leteþ out my grace
B. 2.20   'That is Mede þe mayde, haþ noyed me ful ofte.
B. 2.87   That is vsure and Auarice; al I hem graunte
B. 3.26   Wiþ þat comen clerkes to conforten hire þe same
B. 3.51   'Wiste I þat', quod þ[e] womman 'I wolde noȝt spare
B. 3.322 Tha[t] worþ Trewe-tonge, a tidy man þat tened me neuere.
B. 3.339 Was omnia probate, and þat plesed hire herte
B. 3.351 And þat is þe tail of þe text of þat [teme ye] shewed,
B. 4.87   'God woot', quod wisdom, 'þat were noȝt þe beste.
B. 5.118 [And] whoso haþ moore þan I, þat angreþ [myn herte].
B. 5.129 And þat makeþ me [so mat], for I ne may me venge.
B. 5.219 For laborers and lowe folk þat lay by hymselue.
B. 5.233 'That was no restitucion', quod Repentaunce, 'but a robberis þefte;
B. 5.441 'Repente[st]ow noȝt?' quod Repentaunce, & riȝt wiþ þat he
          swowned
B. 6.258 Ye han manged ouer muche; þat makeþ yow grone.
B. 6.290 By þat I hope to haue heruest in my crofte;
B. 6.299 By þat it neȝed neer heruest newe corn cam to chepyng.
B. 6.311 And þat chaud and plus chaud for chillynge of hir mawe.
B. 8.45   [Th]at is charite þe champion, chief help ayein synne.
B. 8.73   'That þow woost wel', quod he, 'and no wiȝt bettre.'
B. 9.28   And þat is þe grete god þat gynnyng hadde neuere,
B. 9.50   [Th]at is þe Castel þat kynde made; caro it hatte,
B. 9.52   [Th]at he wroȝte wiþ werk and wiþ word boþe;
B. 9.62   And þat ben glotons, glubberes; hir god is hire wombe:
B. 9.88   Eyþer of hem helpeþ ooþer of þat h[y]m nedeþ,
B. 9.204 Ac to loue and to lene], leue me, þat is dobet:
B. 9.209 And þat is wikked wille þat many werk shendeþ,
B.10.209 And noȝt to greuen hem þat greueþ vs; god [þat forbedeþ]:
B.10.240 And þat is to bileue lelly, boþe lered and lewed,
B.10.259 And þat is, man, bi þy myȝt, for mercies sake,
B.10.277 For goddes word wolde noȝt be lost, for þat wercheþ euere;
B.10.320 Of þe pouere haue þei no pite, and þat is hir [pure chartre];
B.10.349 'Contra!' quod I, 'by crist! þat kan I [wiþseye].
B.10.352 In extremis,' quod Scripture, '[as] Sarȝens & Iewes
B.10.361 That is, loue þi lord god leuest abouen alle,
B.11.137 'That is sooþ', seide Scripture; 'may no synne lette
B.11.168 For þat is þe book blissed of blisse and of ioye;
B.11.187 And lokeþ on vs in hir liknesse and þat wiþ louely chere
B.11.316 For hir eiþer is endited, and that [of] 'Ignorancia
B.11.439 'Certes', quod he, 'þat is sooþ'; and shoop hym for to walken,
B.11.440 And I aroos vp riȝt wiþ þat and [reuerenced] hym [faire,
B.12.33   That is, if þow be man maryed þi make þow louye
B.12.183 And þat is after person or parissh preest, [and] parauenture
          vnkonnynge
B.12.240 And þat [is] þe pecok & þe Pehen [wiþ hir proude feþeres
B.12.286 And þoruȝ fir is fullyng, and þat is ferme bileue.
B.12.297 And muche murþe and manhod;' and riȝt wiþ þat he vanysshed.
B.13.205 'That is sooþ', [seide] Conscience, 'so me god helpe.
B.13.211 'That is sooþ', [seide] Clergie, 'I se what þow menest.
B.13.238 And þat am I, Actif, þat ydelnesse hatie,
B.13.259 Til pride be pureliche fordo, and [þat] þoruȝ payn defaute.
B.13.387 As if I hadde dedly synne doon I dredde noȝt þat so soore
B.14.33   And þat ynogh; shal noon faille of þyng þat hem nedeþ:
B.14.206 And þat is plesaunt to pride in poore and in riche.
B.14.236 That is welawo whan he wakeþ and wepeþ for colde,
B.15.30   And þat is wit and wisdom, þe welle of alle craftes;
B.15.44   'That is sooþ', seide he; 'now I se þi wille.
B.15.69   That is Non plus sapere quam oportet sapere.
B.15.211 And þat knoweþ no clerk ne creature on erþe
B.15.262 Of oure foes þat dooþ vs falsnesse; þat is oure fadres wille.

B.15.508 And þat is rouþe for riȝtful men þat in þe Reawme wonyen,
B.15.570 Euery bisshop þat bereþ cros, by þat he is holden
B.16.37   That is þe passion and þe power of oure prince Iesu.
B.16.60   'That is sooþ', [seide] Piers, 'so it may bifalle.
B.16.149 That is kissynge and fair contenaunce and vnkynde wille.
B.16.197 That is children of charite, and holi chirche þe moder.
B.16.215 That is, creatour weex creature to knowe what was boþe.
B.16.221 That is man and his make and mulliere children;
B.16.268 That is lif for lif; or ligge þus euere
B.16.272 I wepte for hise wordes; wiþ þat sauȝ I anoþer
B.17.6   And þat is cros and cristendom and crist þeron to honge;
B.17.266 Ye brenne but ye blase noȝt; þat is a blynd bekene:
B.17.337 And "þat is lightly forȝyuen and forȝeten boþe
B.17.348 That is coueitise and vnkyndenesse þat quencheþ goddes mercy;
B.18.67   Er sonday aboute sonne risyng'; and sank wiþ þat til erþe.
B.18.91   Haue on me ruþe, riȝtful Iesu;' and riȝt wiþ þat he wepte.
B.18.135 And þat is cause of þis clips þat closeþ now þe sonne,
B.18.162 And bigile þe gilour, and þat is good] sleighte:
B.18.167 'That is sooþ', seide Mercy, 'and I se here by Sowþe
B.18.286 'That is sooþ', seide Sathan, 'but I me soore drede,
B.18.339 That gilours be bigiled and þat is good reson:
B.18.425 That men rongen to þe resurexion, and riȝt wiþ þat I wakede
B.19.30   Ac to be conquerour called, þat comeþ of special grace,
B.19.62   He may [be wel] called conquerour, and þat is crist to mene
B.19.122 He wroȝte þat by no wit but þoruȝ word one,
B.19.204 I wondred what þat was and waggede Conscience,
B.19.277 And whoso ete þat ymagynen he sholde,
B.19.393 'That is my conseil', quod Conscience, 'and Cardinale vertues;
B.19.394 [Or] ech man forȝyue ooþer, and þat wole þe Paternoster:
B.19.400 Thikke ale and þynne ale; þat is my kynde,
B.20.12   That is mete whan men hym werneþ and he no moneye weldeþ;
B.20.362 'That is ouerlonge', quod þis Lymytour, 'I leue. I shal amende it!'
B.20.373 Sleuþe seigh þat and so dide pryde,
C. 1.39   And þat [see]th þ[i] soule and sayth hit the in herte
C. 1.57   'That is þe Castel of care; whoso cometh þerynne
C. 1.67   To combre men with coueytise, þat is his kynde and his lore.'
C. 1.162 And þat falleth to þe fader þat formede vs alle,
C. 1.193 And þat is no treuthe of þe trinite but triccherye [and] synne
C. 1.197 Þat is þe lok of loue [þat] vnloseth grace
C. 2.19   'That is mede þe mayde, hath niyed me ful ofte
C. 3.251 And þat is þe kynde of a kyng þat conquereth on his enemys,
C. 3.294 And þat is nother resoun ne ryhte ne [i]n no rewme lawe
C. 3.305 And þat is no mede but a mercede, a manere dewe dette,
C. 3.354 That is god, the ground of al, a graciouse antecedent.
C. 3.367 Þat is nat resonable ne rect to refuse my syre name,
C. 3.395 That is vnite, acordaun[c]e in case, in gendre and in noumbre,
C. 3.475 Þat worth trewe-tonge, a tydy man þat tened me neuere.
C. 3.491 Was omnia probate; þat plesede here herte.
C. 4.83   'God woot,' quod [wysdom], 'þat were nat þe beste.
C. 4.196 And receyue tho that resoun louede; and riht with þat y wakede.
C. 5.92   'That is soth,' y saide, 'and so y beknowe
C. 5.166 Of þe pore haueth thei no pite and þat is here puyre chartre;
C. 6.1   With þat ran repentaunce and rehersede his teme
C. 6.62   Quod repentaunce riht with þat; and thenne aroos enuye.
C. 6.94   And þat maketh me so megre for y ne may me venge.
C. 6.153 That is Priour and subpriour and oure pater Abbas.
C. 6.237 'That was a rufol restitucioun,' quod repentaunce, 'for sothe;
C. 7.55   'Repentest th[ow] nat?' quod repentaunce, and ryht with þat he
          swowoned
C. 7.209 That is to sey sothly ȝe sholde rather deye
C. 8.270 Ȝe han manged ouer moche; þat maketh ȝow to be syke.
C. 8.313 And by [t]hat y hope to haue heruost in my croft[e];
C. 8.321 By that hit nyhed neyh heruost and newe corn cam to chepyng.
C. 8.333 And þat chaut and pluchaut for chillyng of h[ere] mawe.
C. 9.56   Þat is wit and watur and wynde and fuyre the ferthe;
C. 9.276 But 'haue this for þat tho þat thow toke
C.10.71   'That þou [wost] w[el],' quod he, 'and no wyht betere.'
C.10.176 For þat is goddes oune goed, his grace and his tresour,
C.10.303 Ac to louye and to l[e]ne, leef me, þat is dobet;
C.11.27   And þat is no riht ne resoun for rather me sholde
C.11.76   And þat loueth lordes now and leten hit a dowel
C.11.270 By that þat salamon saith hit semeth þat no wyht woet
C.12.72   'That is soth,' saide scripture; ' may no synne lette
C.12.204 Murthe for his mornyng, and þat muche plentee.
C.13.245 'Ȝe, certes,' quod he, 'þat is soth', and shop hym to walke;
C.13.246 And [y] aroes vp riht with þat and reuerensed hym fayre
C.14.15   And þat is dobet, yf eny suche be, a blessed man þat helpeth
C.14.101 That is, how lewede men and luythere lyhtloker were ysaued
C.14.118 And þat conforteth vch a clerk and keuereth fro wanhope,
C.14.123 And þat is aftur person other parsche preest, and parauntur bothe
          lewede
C.14.172 That is, þe pocok and þe popeiay with here proude fetheres
C.14.208 And thorw fuyr is fullyng; and [þat] is ferme bileue:

C.14.215 And *þat* is loue and large huyre, yf þe lord be trewe,
C.15.229 Til pruyde be puyreliche fordo and *þat* thorw payn defaute:
C.15.275 And *þat* is charite, chaumpion chief of all vertues,
C.15.276 And *þat* is pore pacient alle perelles to soffre.'
C.15.283 Then eny pore pacient; and *þat* preue y be resoun.
C.16.47 And *þat* is plesant to pruyde in pore and in ryche.
C.16.190 And *þat* is wit and wysdoem, the welle of alle craftes;
C.16.206 '*That* is soth,' he sayde; 'now y se thy wille.
C.16.286 'Charite,' quod y tho, '*þat* is a thyng forsothe
C.17.64 And þer helpe yf thow has[t]; and *þat* halde y charite.
C.17.71 Of *þat* þat holy churche of þe olde lawe claymeth
C.17.143 Loue thy frende þat folleweth thy wille, *that* is thy fayre soule.
C.17.148 And *þat* is charite, leue chield, to be cher ouer thy soule;
C.17.233 For were presthode more parfyte, *that* is, þe pope formost
C.17.237 Alle londes into loue And *þat* in lytel tyme;
C.17.259 And *þat* is reuthe for rihtfole men þat in þ[e] reume wonyeth
C.18.52 And *that* is grace of þe holy gost; and thus gete y the maystrye.'
C.18.59 Hit is al of o kynde, and *þat* shal y preuen,
C.18.89 For *þat* is euene with angelis and angeles pere.
C.18.192 '*That* is soth,' saide he thenne, 'the syre hatte pater
C.18.284 And *þat* is lyf for lyf or ligge thus euere
C.18.288 [Y] wepte for his wordes; with *þat* saw y [a]nother
C.19.232 ȝe brenneth ac ȝe blaseth nat; and *þat* is a blynde bekne:
C.19.246 And is in helle for al *þat*, how wol riche nouthe
C.19.250 [*That* that wickedliche is wonne to wasten hit and make frendes?]
C.19.317 And "*þat* is lihtliche forȝeue and forȝete bothe
C.19.328 *That* is coueytise and vnkyndenesse whiche quencheth godes mercy
C.20.69 Ar soneday aboute sonne rysynge'; and sank with *þat* til erthe.
C.20.94 Haue [on me reuthe], riȝtfol iesu;' and riht with *þat* a wepte.
C.20.138 And *þat* is cause of this clips þat [c]loseth now þe sonne,
C.20.165 And bigile þe gilour, and *þat* is goed sleythe:
C.20.170 '*That* is soth,' saide mercy, 'and y se here bi southe
C.20.312 '*That* is soeth,' saide satoun, 'bote y me sore doute
C.20.468 That men rang to þe resurreccioun and riht with *þat* y wakede
C.21.30 Ac to be conquerour cald, *þat* cometh of special grace
C.21.62 He may be wel called conquerour and *that* is Crist to mene.
C.21.98 In þe manere of a man and *þat* by moche sleythe,
C.21.122 He wrouhte *þat* by no wyt bote thorw word one,
C.21.204 Y wondred what *þat* was and wagged Consience
C.21.277 [And] hoso ete *þat* ymageny he sholde,
C.21.393 '*That* is my conseil,' quod Consience, 'and cardinale vertues,
C.21.394 Or vch man forȝeue oþer, and *þat* wol þe paternost[er]:
C.21.400 Thikke ale [&] thynne ale; *þat* is my kynde
C.22.12 *That* is mete when men hym werneth [and] he no money weldeth
C.22.362 '*That* is ouerlonge,' quod this lymitour, 'y leue; y schal amenden hit!'
C.22.373 Sle[u]th seyh *þat* and so dede pruyde

þat pron rel *that rel.pron.* A 329; B 1039 that (149) þat (890); C 1053 that (222) þat (831)

A.Pr.22, A.Pr.28, A.Pr.38, A.Pr.52, A.Pr.74, A.Pr.79, A.Pr.85, A.Pr.92, A.Pr.102, A.1.7, A.1.28, A.1.34, A.1.35, A.1.42, A.1.44, A.1.48, A.1.50, A.1.56, A.1.57, A.1.61, A.1.68, A.1.70, A.1.72, A.1.80, A.1.82, A.1.90, A.1.98, A.1.100, A.1.116, A.1.117, A.1.119, A.1.119, A.1.130, A.1.136, A.1.140, A.1.143, A.1.145, A.1.148, A.1.154, A.1.158, A.1.163, A.1.169, A.1.176, A.1.178, A.1.179, A.2.3, A.2.3, A.2.12, A.2.14, A.2.28, A.2.33, A.2.36, A.2.55, A.2.57, A.2.92, A.2.129, A.2.140, A.2.144, A.2.147, A.2.148, A.2.156, A.2.157, A.2.160, A.3.6, A.3.12, A.3.31, A.3.51, A.3.65, A.3.69, A.3.70, A.3.73, A.3.83, A.3.84, A.3.88, A.3.115, A.3.118, A.3.130, A.3.154, A.3.195, A.3.195, A.3.196, A.3.197, A.3.209, A.3.210, A.3.220, A.3.222, A.3.225, A.3.229, A.3.231, A.3.232, A.3.232, A.3.233, A.3.234, A.3.242, A.4.86, A.4.112, A.4.116, A.4.122, A.4.132, A.4.145, A.4.148, A.5.10, A.5.25, A.5.35, A.5.40, A.5.47, A.5.49, A.5.53, A.5.64, A.5.81, A.5.89, A.5.131, A.5.191, A.5.204, A.5.208, A.5.228, A.5.236, A.5.241, A.5.242, A.6.1, A.6.17, A.6.20, A.6.35, A.6.38, A.6.47, A.6.61, A.6.81, A.6.89, A.6.96, A.6.104, A.6.105, A.6.116, A.7.2, A.7.10, A.7.19, A.7.21, A.7.22, A.7.30, A.7.32, A.7.43, A.7.62, A.7.63, A.7.79, A.7.88, A.7.91, A.7.101, A.7.111, A.7.119, A.7.121, A.7.125, A.7.125, A.7.133, A.7.137, A.7.138, A.7.148, A.7.151, A.7.157, A.7.158, A.7.174, A.7.178, A.7.195, A.7.199, A.7.204, A.7.208, A.7.209, A.7.226, A.7.228, A.7.229, A.7.230, A.7.235, A.7.236, A.7.287, A.7.290, A.7.291, A.8.6, A.8.7, A.8.9, A.8.13, A.8.30, A.8.32, A.8.49, A.8.50, A.8.60, A.8.63, A.8.64, A.8.66, A.8.68, A.8.69, A.8.73, A.8.75, A.8.79, A.8.80, A.8.82, A.8.83, A.8.85, A.8.107, A.8.109, A.8.110, A.8.112, A.8.133, A.8.137, A.8.162, A.8.165, A.8.169, A.9.3, A.9.6, A.9.34, A.9.36, A.9.37, A.9.50, A.9.57, A.9.60, A.9.63, A.9.80, A.9.89, A.9.106, A.10.2, A.10.6, A.10.16, A.10.25, A.10.29, A.10.33, A.10.35, A.10.37, A.10.38, A.10.40, A.10.43, A.10.44, A.10.47, A.10.59, A.10.65, A.10.71, A.10.76, A.10.100, A.10.104, A.10.105, A.10.107, A.10.120, A.10.123, A.10.125, A.10.128, A.10.130, A.10.131, A.10.135, A.10.142, A.10.147, A.10.151, A.10.153, A.10.155, A.10.156, A.10.170, A.10.171, A.10.176, A.10.185, A.10.189, A.10.192, A.10.201, A.10.209, A.10.218, A.11.1, A.11.2, A.11.6, A.11.10, A.11.12, A.11.13, A.11.16, A.11.19, A.11.21, A.11.22, A.11.24, A.11.26, A.11.27, A.11.29, A.11.49, A.11.50, A.11.60, A.11.64, A.11.71, A.11.80, A.11.82, A.11.90, A.11.105, A.11.107, A.11.111, A.11.118, A.11.124, A.11.141, A.11.152, A.11.157, A.11.158, A.11.172, A.11.185, A.11.189, A.11.190, A.11.196, A.11.210, A.11.217, A.11.232, A.11.233, A.11.237, A.11.244, A.11.245, A.11.246, A.11.249, A.11.265, A.11.274, A.11.278, A.11.280, A.11.284, A.11.288, A.11.289, A.11.292, A.11.297, A.11.300, A.11.308, A.12.7, A.12.11, A.12.23, A.12.31, A.12.44, A.12.49, A.12.53, A.12.87, A.12.97, A.12.101, A.12.110, A.12.112, A.12.114, A.12.117

B.Pr.22, B.Pr.28, B.Pr.38, B.Pr.50, B.Pr.51, B.Pr.55, B.Pr.77, B.Pr.82, B.Pr.88, B.Pr.100, B.Pr.104, B.Pr.107, B.Pr.109, B.Pr.130, B.Pr.178, B.Pr.182, B.Pr.200, B.Pr.204, B.Pr.206, B.Pr.209, B.Pr.212, B.Pr.224, B.1.7, B.1.28, B.1.33, B.1.36, B.1.37, B.1.44, B.1.46, B.1.50, B.1.52, B.1.58, B.1.59, B.1.63, B.1.70, B.1.72, B.1.74, B.1.82, B.1.84, B.1.92, B.1.100, B.1.102, B.1.118, B.1.120, B.1.127, B.1.128, B.1.130, B.1.131, B.1.142, B.1.149, B.1.166, B.1.169, B.1.171, B.1.174, B.1.177, B.1.180, B.1.184, B.1.189, B.1.195, B.1.202, B.1.205, B.2.3, B.2.3, B.2.21, B.2.22, B.2.25, B.2.36, B.2.37, B.2.46, B.2.54, B.2.62, B.2.65, B.2.70, B.2.73, B.2.75, B.2.128, B.2.165, B.2.179, B.2.183, B.2.186, B.2.187, B.2.195, B.2.196, B.2.199, B.3.6, B.3.12, B.3.32, B.3.53, B.3.54, B.3.59, B.3.76, B.3.80, B.3.81, B.3.84, B.3.94, B.3.95, B.3.99, B.3.126, B.3.129, B.3.141, B.3.159, B.3.164, B.3.167, B.3.208, B.3.208, B.3.209, B.3.210, B.3.222, B.3.223, B.3.233, B.3.238, B.3.240, B.3.242, B.3.246, B.3.250, B.3.252, B.3.253, B.3.253, B.3.254, B.3.255, B.3.263, B.3.282, B.3.305, B.3.318, B.3.322, B.3.324, B.3.334, B.3.338, B.3.346, B.3.347, B.3.348, B.3.349, B.3.353, B.4.99, B.4.129, B.4.139, B.4.149, B.4.185, B.5.10, B.5.39, B.5.42, B.5.52, B.5.56, B.5.59, B.5.64, B.5.66, B.5.70, B.5.81, B.5.86, B.5.101, B.5.109, B.5.167, B.5.180, B.5.183, B.5.215, B.5.247, B.5.253, B.5.254, B.5.256, B.5.262, B.5.263, B.5.264, B.5.274, B.5.282, B.5.287, B.5.343, B.5.362, B.5.373, B.5.380, B.5.396, B.5.401, B.5.408, B.5.433, B.5.456, B.5.464, B.5.467, B.5.468, B.5.480, B.5.494, B.5.499, B.5.503, B.5.504, B.5.529, B.5.532, B.5.545, B.5.551, B.5.560, B.5.594, B.5.602, B.5.610, B.5.618, B.5.619, B.5.631, B.6.2, B.6.19, B.6.20, B.6.28, B.6.30, B.6.44, B.6.68, B.6.69, B.6.87, B.6.96, B.6.99, B.6.109, B.6.119, B.6.120, B.6.127, B.6.129, B.6.133, B.6.145, B.6.147, B.6.151, B.6.161, B.6.166, B.6.172, B.6.173, B.6.186, B.6.192, B.6.193, B.6.209, B.6.213, B.6.218, B.6.222, B.6.223, B.6.242, B.6.244, B.6.245, B.6.246, B.6.251, B.6.303, B.6.306, B.6.307, B.7.6, B.7.7, B.7.9, B.7.28, B.7.39, B.7.42, B.7.47, B.7.48, B.7.56, B.7.59, B.7.61, B.7.62, B.7.64, B.7.66, B.7.67, B.7.71, B.7.77, B.7.77, B.7.79, B.7.80, B.7.81, B.7.83, B.7.86, B.7.91, B.7.93, B.7.97, B.7.98, B.7.100, B.7.101, B.7.103, B.7.127, B.7.128, B.7.130, B.7.150, B.7.159, B.7.184, B.7.187, B.7.191, B.8.3, B.8.6, B.8.14, B.8.38, B.8.40, B.8.41, B.8.59, B.8.66, B.8.69, B.8.72, B.8.89, B.8.99, B.8.116, B.9.2, B.9.6, B.9.15, B.9.17, B.9.28, B.9.32, B.9.34, B.9.49, B.9.50, B.9.55, B.9.61, B.9.64, B.9.65, B.9.66, B.9.67, B.9.68, B.9.70, B.9.71, B.9.72, B.9.76, B.9.77, B.9.87, B.9.88, B.9.93, B.9.95, B.9.96, B.9.97, B.9.97, B.9.99, B.9.102, B.9.103, B.9.107, B.9.112, B.9.126, B.9.139, B.9.140, B.9.143, B.9.145, B.9.154, B.9.158, B.9.162, B.9.168, B.9.171, B.9.182, B.9.195, B.9.209, B.10.2, B.10.6, B.10.10, B.10.12, B.10.13, B.10.16, B.10.19, B.10.21, B.10.25, B.10.26, B.10.28, B.10.29, B.10.32, B.10.34, B.10.35, B.10.37, B.10.39, B.10.43, B.10.63, B.10.64, B.10.102, B.10.103, B.10.106, B.10.109, B.10.113, B.10.115, B.10.118, B.10.127, B.10.129, B.10.134, B.10.137, B.10.153, B.10.155, B.10.159, B.10.166, B.10.172, B.10.189, B.10.199, B.10.203, B.10.205, B.10.206, B.10.207, B.10.208, B.10.209, B.10.214, B.10.215, B.10.229, B.10.239, B.10.241, B.10.242, B.10.254, B.10.258, B.10.260, B.10.268, B.10.273, B.10.300, B.10.304, B.10.315, B.10.318, B.10.327, B.10.330, B.10.333, B.10.350, B.10.351, B.10.354, B.10.363, B.10.365, B.10.366, B.10.371, B.10.379, B.10.384, B.10.389, B.10.393, B.10.401, B.10.407, B.10.410, B.10.411, B.10.412, B.10.414, B.10.416, B.10.421, B.10.425, B.10.429, B.10.430, B.10.433, B.10.434, B.10.436, B.10.446, B.10.447, B.10.464, B.10.471, B.10.472, B.10.476, B.10.477, B.10.480, B.11.9, B.11.11, B.11.21, B.11.26, B.11.27, B.11.27, B.11.35, B.11.70, B.11.72, B.11.77, B.11.101, B.11.105, B.11.108, B.11.110, B.11.118, B.11.124, B.11.147, B.11.155, B.11.158, B.11.164, B.11.183, B.11.196, B.11.210, B.11.224, B.11.227, B.11.237, B.11.256, B.11.267, B.11.269, B.11.275, B.11.278, B.11.279, B.11.280, B.11.287, B.11.290, B.11.291, B.11.292, B.11.293, B.11.297, B.11.299, B.11.306, B.11.307, B.11.313, B.11.313, B.11.324, B.11.341, B.11.342, B.11.345, B.11.369, B.11.374, B.11.381, B.11.397, B.11.398, B.11.400, B.11.414, B.11.421, B.12.8, B.12.13, B.12.17, B.12.25, B.12.32, B.12.37, B.12.44, B.12.50, B.12.52, B.12.56, B.12.65, B.12.71, B.12.73, B.12.78, B.12.80, B.12.83, B.12.87, B.12.89, B.12.89, B.12.99, B.12.118, B.12.119, B.12.131, B.12.144, B.12.154, B.12.165, B.12.166, B.12.168, B.12.169, B.12.171, B.12.186, B.12.187, B.12.188, B.12.190, B.12.192, B.12.194, B.12.195, B.12.197, B.12.200, B.12.202, B.12.206, B.12.217, B.12.233, B.12.239, B.12.241, B.12.251, B.12.260, B.12.261, B.12.264, B.12.273, B.12.277, B.12.287, B.13.2, B.13.7, B.13.8, B.13.18, B.13.26, B.13.42, B.13.48, B.13.66, B.13.69, B.13.73, B.13.74, B.13.117, B.13.135, B.13.149, B.13.153, B.13.158, B.13.170, B.13.187, B.13.189, B.13.197, B.13.207, B.13.235, B.13.237, B.13.238, B.13.247, B.13.254, B.13.279, B.13.302, B.13.304, B.13.305, B.13.306, B.13.323, B.13.325, B.13.326, B.13.331, B.13.332, B.13.336, B.13.338, B.13.344, B.13.369, B.13.373, B.13.374, B.13.378, B.13.408, B.13.409, B.13.411, B.13.419, B.13.420, B.13.422, B.13.431, B.13.451, B.13.455, B.14.4, B.14.6, B.14.8, B.14.9, B.14.17, B.14.32, B.14.33, B.14.48, B.14.65, B.14.79, B.14.99, B.14.106, B.14.106, B.14.108, B.14.111, B.14.112, B.14.115, B.14.116, B.14.118, B.14.121, B.14.122, B.14.124, B.14.126, B.14.134, B.14.135, B.14.143, B.14.148, B.14.149, B.14.152, B.14.153, B.14.165, B.14.168, B.14.169, B.14.173, B.14.175, B.14.196, B.14.209, B.14.229, B.14.260, B.14.262, B.14.267, B.14.268, B.14.271, B.14.280, B.14.281, B.14.296, B.14.297, B.14.307, B.14.312, B.14.321, B.14.322, B.14.328, B.15.19, B.15.29, B.15.56, B.15.57, B.15.65, B.15.70, B.15.75, B.15.86, B.15.88, B.15.93, B.15.112, B.15.113, B.15.125, B.15.129, B.15.133, B.15.136, B.15.137, B.15.140, B.15.143, B.15.144, B.15.156, B.15.160, B.15.163, B.15.170, B.15.173, B.15.178, B.15.197, B.15.208, B.15.218, B.15.222, B.15.234, B.15.242, B.15.262, B.15.267, B.15.278, B.15.284, B.15.284, B.15.291, B.15.297, B.15.298, B.15.300, B.15.303, B.15.323, B.15.324, B.15.326, B.15.329, B.15.331, B.15.331, B.15.332, B.15.334, B.15.336, B.15.337, B.15.341, B.15.342, B.15.343, B.15.347, B.15.353, B.15.360, B.15.361, B.15.364, B.15.365, B.15.371, B.15.374, B.15.375, B.15.381, B.15.402, B.15.407, B.15.415, B.15.420, B.15.425, B.15.428, B.15.434, B.15.435, B.15.437, B.15.442, B.15.452, B.15.456, B.15.464, B.15.465, B.15.466, B.15.473, B.15.475, B.15.476, B.15.481, B.15.482, B.15.486, B.15.486, B.15.487,

B.15.487, B.15.488, B.15.491, B.15.508, B.15.509, B.15.510, B.15.518, B.15.528, B.15.541, B.15.545, B.15.561, B.15.562, B.15.563, B.15.569, B.15.570, B.15.577, B.15.579, B.15.581, B.15.587, B.15.588, B.15.593, B.15.603, B.16.13, B.16.15, B.16.27, B.16.41, B.16.47, B.16.66, B.16.91, B.16.106, B.16.113, B.16.117, B.16.119, B.16.129, B.16.150, B.16.162, B.16.178, B.16.183, B.16.187, B.16.189, B.16.191, B.16.194, B.16.206, B.16.211, B.16.213, B.16.236, B.16.246, B.16.248, B.16.250, B.16.251, B.16.252, B.16.254, B.16.265, B.16.266, B.16.271, B.17.2, B.17.5, B.17.23, B.17.25, B.17.31, B.17.35, B.17.36, B.17.39, B.17.40, B.17.49, B.17.53, B.17.62, B.17.87, B.17.92, B.17.108, B.17.109, B.17.110, B.17.114, B.17.116, B.17.117, B.17.119, B.17.119, B.17.124, B.17.125, B.17.126, B.17.129, B.17.145, B.17.148, B.17.149, B.17.150, B.17.153, B.17.158, B.17.164, B.17.180, B.17.189, B.17.193, B.17.201, B.17.205, B.17.211, B.17.214, B.17.219, B.17.220, B.17.222, B.17.223, B.17.237, B.17.237, B.17.239, B.17.241, B.17.244, B.17.254, B.17.262, B.17.263, B.17.269, B.17.271, B.17.272, B.17.274, B.17.276, B.17.279, B.17.284, B.17.286, B.17.288, B.17.290, B.17.293, B.17.297, B.17.301, B.17.311, B.17.315, B.17.317, B.17.320, B.17.321, B.17.323, B.17.332, B.17.333, B.17.334, B.17.338, B.17.339, B.17.340, B.17.346, B.17.347, B.17.348, B.18.2, B.18.9, B.18.13, B.18.20, B.18.30, B.18.32, B.18.43, B.18.58, B.18.68, B.18.83, B.18.90, B.18.103, B.18.107, B.18.120, B.18.128, B.18.135, B.18.140, B.18.141, B.18.142, B.18.144, B.18.147, B.18.148, B.18.159, B.18.161, B.18.171, B.18.177, B.18.182, B.18.192, B.18.198, B.18.202, B.18.206, B.18.207, B.18.210, B.18.212, B.18.225, B.18.236, B.18.238, B.18.246, B.18.247, B.18.253, B.18.254, B.18.265, B.18.278, B.18.280, B.18.283, B.18.326, B.18.328, B.18.333, B.18.336, B.18.341, B.18.345, B.18.346, B.18.353, B.18.355, B.18.356, B.18.363, B.18.364, B.18.364, B.18.365, B.18.377, B.18.378, B.18.384, B.18.390, B.18.401, B.18.402, B.18.414, B.18.419, B.19.10, B.19.13, B.19.25, B.19.32, B.19.33, B.19.34, B.19.38, B.19.39, B.19.45, B.19.47, B.19.55, B.19.56, B.19.59, B.19.89, B.19.98, B.19.100, B.19.107, B.19.123, B.19.131, B.19.133, B.19.149, B.19.162, B.19.180, B.19.193, B.19.216, B.19.218, B.19.230, B.19.245, B.19.255, B.19.268, B.19.273, B.19.280, B.19.282, B.19.288, B.19.289, B.19.291, B.19.297, B.19.298, B.19.315, B.19.322, B.19.323, B.19.343, B.19.344, B.19.349, B.19.352, B.19.365, B.19.366, B.19.369, B.19.372, B.19.384, B.19.389, B.19.392, B.19.406, B.19.411, B.19.412, B.19.415, B.19.417, B.19.425, B.19.428, B.19.429, B.19.430, B.19.437, B.19.440, B.19.441, B.19.442, B.19.461, B.20.5, B.20.15, B.20.32, B.20.36, B.20.47, B.20.49, B.20.65, B.20.65, B.20.66, B.20.67, B.20.71, B.20.72, B.20.72, B.20.89, B.20.90, B.20.103, B.20.103, B.20.110, B.20.141, B.20.158, B.20.161, B.20.171, B.20.177, B.20.193, B.20.195, B.20.216, B.20.235, B.20.238, B.20.239, B.20.257, B.20.261, B.20.277, B.20.281, B.20.283, B.20.286, B.20.290, B.20.303, B.20.304, B.20.305, B.20.307, B.20.310, B.20.313, B.20.320, B.20.365, B.20.372, B.20.382, B.20.383

C.Pr.24, C.Pr.30, C.Pr.39, C.Pr.53, C.Pr.75, C.Pr.80, C.Pr.86, C.Pr.88, C.Pr.106, C.Pr.119, C.Pr.128, C.Pr.132, C.Pr.134, C.Pr.136, C.Pr.162, C.Pr.195, C.Pr.199, C.Pr.212, C.Pr.215, C.Pr.220, C.Pr.228, C.1.7, C.1.24, C.1.29, C.1.34, C.1.35, C.1.37, C.1.42, C.1.48, C.1.54, C.1.59, C.1.66, C.1.69, C.1.71, C.1.80, C.1.88, C.1.94, C.1.97, C.1.111, C.1.111, C.1.129, C.1.130, C.1.130, C.1.132, C.1.134, C.1.141, C.1.162, C.1.165, C.1.167, C.1.170, C.1.173, C.1.176, C.1.180, C.1.185, C.1.197, C.1.198, C.2.3, C.2.3, C.2.20, C.2.21, C.2.25, C.2.31, C.2.32, C.2.34, C.2.38, C.2.50, C.2.57, C.2.59, C.2.64, C.2.67, C.2.72, C.2.75, C.2.77, C.2.79, C.2.80, C.2.82, C.2.86, C.2.105, C.2.121, C.2.131, C.2.133, C.2.142, C.2.166, C.2.188, C.2.190, C.2.191, C.2.196, C.2.199, C.2.210, C.2.213, C.3.6, C.3.13, C.3.35, C.3.57, C.3.58, C.3.63, C.3.83, C.3.86, C.3.88, C.3.92, C.3.95, C.3.95, C.3.99, C.3.108, C.3.118, C.3.123, C.3.127, C.3.129, C.3.145, C.3.163, C.3.166, C.3.179, C.3.197, C.3.205, C.3.237, C.3.245, C.3.247, C.3.248, C.3.251, C.3.253, C.3.255, C.3.265, C.3.266, C.3.277, C.3.278, C.3.282, C.3.282, C.3.288, C.3.289, C.3.300, C.3.307, C.3.311, C.3.311, C.3.320, C.3.323, C.3.332, C.3.339, C.3.339, C.3.351, C.3.381, C.3.391, C.3.401, C.3.412, C.3.420, C.3.424, C.3.435, C.3.436, C.3.458, C.3.471, C.3.475, C.3.486, C.3.490, C.3.497, C.3.498, C.3.498, C.3.499, C.3.500, C.4.29, C.4.33, C.4.86, C.4.95, C.4.121, C.4.126, C.4.136, C.4.146, C.4.150, C.4.179, C.4.192, C.4.194, C.4.196, C.5.20, C.5.21, C.5.27, C.5.28, C.5.31, C.5.41, C.5.43, C.5.45, C.5.49, C.5.55, C.5.59, C.5.64, C.5.76, C.5.85, C.5.94, C.5.99, C.5.101, C.5.103, C.5.110, C.5.141, C.5.151, C.5.161, C.5.164, C.5.188, C.5.189, C.5.194, C.5.197, C.5.200, C.6.5, C.6.7, C.6.11, C.6.19, C.6.25, C.6.32, C.6.45, C.6.51, C.6.53, C.6.54, C.6.67, C.6.70, C.6.71, C.6.80, C.6.82, C.6.109, C.6.114, C.6.116, C.6.142, C.6.162, C.6.165, C.6.178, C.6.223, C.6.227, C.6.244, C.6.245, C.6.249, C.6.252, C.6.254, C.6.255, C.6.259, C.6.270, C.6.271, C.6.296, C.6.298, C.6.304, C.6.307, C.6.310, C.6.318, C.6.321, C.6.322, C.6.335, C.6.337, C.6.342, C.6.353, C.6.401, C.6.420, C.6.424, C.6.426, C.6.431, C.6.432, C.7.12, C.7.14, C.7.17, C.7.24, C.7.46, C.7.69, C.7.71, C.7.79, C.7.80, C.7.82, C.7.91, C.7.111, C.7.115, C.7.118, C.7.122, C.7.134, C.7.139, C.7.143, C.7.146, C.7.149, C.7.158, C.7.174, C.7.177, C.7.191, C.7.195, C.7.242, C.7.247, C.7.250, C.7.253, C.7.262, C.7.270, C.7.271, C.7.284, C.7.308, C.8.17, C.8.18, C.8.27, C.8.29, C.8.57, C.8.66, C.8.69, C.8.70, C.8.74, C.8.85, C.8.89, C.8.96, C.8.105, C.8.108, C.8.116, C.8.126, C.8.133, C.8.138, C.8.140, C.8.146, C.8.147, C.8.158, C.8.168, C.8.178, C.8.182, C.8.192, C.8.194, C.8.194, C.8.200, C.8.202, C.8.202, C.8.223, C.8.228, C.8.231, C.8.240, C.8.246, C.8.249, C.8.251, C.8.253, C.8.254, C.8.255, C.8.256, C.8.257, C.8.259, C.8.261, C.8.264, C.8.278, C.8.283, C.8.325, C.8.328, C.8.329, C.9.6, C.9.7, C.9.9, C.9.42, C.9.43, C.9.44, C.9.46, C.9.47, C.9.48, C.9.54, C.9.55, C.9.57, C.9.58, C.9.62, C.9.63, C.9.65, C.9.66, C.9.68, C.9.71, C.9.74, C.9.76, C.9.83, C.9.84, C.9.89, C.9.96, C.9.100, C.9.102, C.9.130, C.9.131, C.9.159, C.9.161, C.9.168, C.9.173, C.9.174, C.9.176, C.9.177, C.9.184, C.9.189, C.9.191, C.9.197, C.9.200, C.9.201, C.9.204, C.9.209, C.9.216, C.9.226, C.9.227, C.9.242, C.9.250, C.9.257, C.9.261, C.9.263, C.9.267, C.9.292, C.9.299, C.9.307, C.9.330, C.9.333, C.9.337, C.10.3, C.10.6, C.10.14, C.10.24, C.10.40, C.10.40, C.10.44, C.10.46, C.10.47, C.10.48, C.10.50, C.10.58, C.10.70, C.10.84, C.10.86, C.10.96, C.10.102, C.10.112, C.10.129, C.10.133, C.10.143, C.10.153, C.10.154, C.10.169, C.10.170, C.10.175, C.10.177, C.10.181, C.10.183, C.10.194, C.10.204, C.10.209, C.10.211, C.10.216, C.10.219, C.10.219, C.10.220, C.10.227, C.10.228, C.10.231, C.10.233, C.10.238, C.10.241, C.10.246, C.10.264, C.10.273, C.10.283, C.10.288, C.10.294, C.10.297, C.11.2, C.11.8, C.11.10, C.11.11, C.11.13, C.11.18, C.11.19, C.11.25, C.11.28, C.11.28, C.11.29, C.11.43, C.11.45, C.11.46, C.11.71, C.11.79, C.11.91, C.11.98, C.11.101, C.11.103, C.11.144, C.11.155, C.11.159, C.11.168, C.11.170, C.11.180, C.11.185, C.11.186, C.11.186, C.11.194, C.11.199, C.11.200, C.11.205, C.11.209, C.11.211, C.11.215, C.11.220, C.11.225, C.11.235, C.11.238, C.11.241, C.11.242, C.11.243, C.11.245, C.11.247, C.11.251, C.11.253, C.11.257, C.11.263, C.11.266, C.11.268, C.11.269, C.11.270, C.11.284, C.11.285, C.11.288, C.11.297, C.11.298, C.11.298, C.11.301, C.11.305, C.11.306, C.12.15, C.12.20, C.12.27, C.12.28, C.12.35, C.12.38, C.12.39, C.12.42, C.12.44, C.12.53, C.12.59, C.12.82, C.12.90, C.12.96, C.12.108, C.12.117, C.12.142, C.12.152, C.12.154, C.12.162, C.12.163, C.12.164, C.12.166, C.12.171, C.12.173, C.12.178, C.12.180, C.12.184, C.12.187, C.12.189, C.12.194, C.12.197, C.12.201, C.12.205, C.12.214, C.12.215, C.12.217, C.12.220, C.12.222, C.12.223, C.12.225, C.12.227, C.12.232, C.12.236, C.12.241, C.12.243, C.12.247, C.13.22, C.13.23, C.13.26, C.13.30, C.13.58, C.13.66, C.13.68, C.13.74, C.13.74, C.13.79, C.13.96, C.13.101, C.13.104, C.13.105, C.13.106, C.13.107, C.13.111, C.13.112, C.13.113, C.13.115, C.13.120, C.13.121, C.13.125, C.13.125, C.13.130, C.13.149, C.13.150, C.13.151, C.13.152, C.13.156, C.13.159, C.13.179, C.13.198, C.13.207, C.13.222, C.14.6, C.14.11, C.14.15, C.14.18, C.14.41, C.14.44, C.14.63, C.14.75, C.14.98, C.14.109, C.14.111, C.14.125, C.14.126, C.14.127, C.14.131, C.14.133, C.14.136, C.14.139, C.14.141, C.14.145, C.14.156, C.14.159, C.14.160, C.14.167, C.14.171, C.14.173, C.14.177, C.14.185, C.14.188, C.14.195, C.14.199, C.14.209, C.14.214, C.15.2, C.15.9, C.15.10, C.15.20, C.15.47, C.15.54, C.15.59, C.15.71, C.15.80, C.15.81, C.15.125, C.15.126, C.15.130, C.15.136, C.15.138, C.15.153, C.15.157, C.15.162, C.15.165, C.15.192, C.15.209, C.15.213, C.15.223, C.15.224, C.15.235, C.15.236, C.15.249, C.15.264, C.15.281, C.15.281, C.15.284, C.15.287, C.15.288, C.15.291, C.15.292, C.15.294, C.15.297, C.15.298, C.15.302, C.15.304, C.16.3, C.16.4, C.16.12, C.16.18, C.16.36, C.16.43, C.16.50, C.16.70, C.16.77, C.16.100, C.16.102, C.16.107, C.16.108, C.16.111, C.16.120, C.16.122, C.16.131, C.16.133, C.16.143, C.16.146, C.16.156, C.16.157, C.16.158, C.16.160, C.16.170, C.16.172, C.16.182, C.16.189, C.16.218, C.16.219, C.16.228, C.16.250, C.16.267, C.16.270, C.16.274, C.16.276, C.16.280, C.16.281, C.16.282, C.16.285, C.16.287, C.16.290, C.16.294, C.16.297, C.16.302, C.16.308, C.16.315, C.16.319, C.16.319, C.16.329, C.16.339, C.16.347, C.16.359, C.17.1, C.17.18, C.17.26, C.17.42, C.17.49, C.17.52, C.17.57, C.17.58, C.17.68, C.17.69, C.17.71, C.17.79, C.17.81, C.17.84, C.17.98, C.17.101, C.17.102, C.17.107, C.17.110, C.17.111, C.17.115, C.17.134, C.17.143, C.17.154, C.17.154, C.17.155, C.17.159, C.17.173, C.17.203, C.17.207, C.17.224, C.17.225, C.17.226, C.17.230, C.17.234, C.17.247, C.17.249, C.17.251, C.17.259, C.17.260, C.17.261, C.17.269, C.17.278, C.17.295, C.17.298, C.17.299, C.17.301, C.17.302, C.17.304, C.17.311, C.17.314, C.18.7, C.18.13, C.18.25, C.18.31, C.18.45, C.18.64, C.18.66, C.18.73, C.18.76, C.18.79, C.18.82, C.18.85, C.18.90, C.18.122, C.18.124, C.18.140, C.18.143, C.18.147, C.18.157, C.18.174, C.18.194, C.18.200, C.18.203, C.18.210, C.18.213, C.18.218, C.18.222, C.18.222, C.18.252, C.18.266, C.18.268, C.18.270, C.18.281, C.18.282, C.18.287, C.19.2, C.19.5, C.19.7, C.19.24, C.19.32, C.19.36, C.19.37, C.19.44, C.19.47, C.19.51, C.19.61, C.19.77, C.19.107, C.19.113, C.19.119, C.19.122, C.19.123, C.19.128, C.19.140, C.19.145, C.19.146, C.19.155, C.19.159, C.19.167, C.19.171, C.19.177, C.19.180, C.19.185, C.19.186, C.19.188, C.19.189, C.19.203, C.19.205, C.19.207, C.19.210, C.19.220, C.19.228, C.19.229, C.19.235, C.19.247, C.19.250, C.19.252, C.19.253, C.19.255, C.19.257, C.19.260, C.19.265, C.19.267, C.19.269, C.19.271, C.19.274, C.19.276, C.19.278, C.19.281, C.19.291, C.19.292, C.19.295, C.19.297, C.19.300, C.19.301, C.19.303, C.19.312, C.19.313, C.19.314, C.19.316, C.19.318, C.19.319, C.19.320, C.19.326, C.19.327, C.20.2, C.20.11, C.20.18, C.20.29, C.20.31, C.20.42, C.20.58, C.20.70, C.20.85, C.20.87, C.20.92, C.20.106, C.20.110, C.20.123, C.20.131, C.20.138, C.20.143, C.20.144, C.20.145, C.20.147, C.20.150, C.20.151, C.20.162, C.20.164, C.20.174, C.20.180, C.20.185, C.20.203, C.20.207, C.20.211, C.20.212, C.20.219, C.20.221, C.20.234, C.20.245, C.20.247, C.20.248, C.20.255, C.20.256, C.20.262, C.20.263, C.20.282, C.20.290, C.20.300, C.20.302, C.20.311, C.20.334, C.20.348, C.20.353, C.20.361, C.20.369, C.20.376, C.20.379, C.20.385, C.20.389, C.20.390, C.20.391, C.20.396, C.20.401, C.20.402, C.20.402, C.20.403, C.20.419, C.20.426, C.20.432, C.20.442, C.20.444, C.20.445, C.20.457, C.20.462, C.21.10, C.21.13, C.21.25, C.21.32, C.21.33, C.21.34, C.21.38, C.21.39, C.21.45, C.21.47, C.21.55, C.21.56, C.21.59, C.21.89, C.21.100, C.21.107, C.21.123, C.21.131, C.21.133, C.21.149, C.21.162, C.21.180, C.21.193, C.21.216, C.21.218, C.21.230, C.21.245, C.21.255, C.21.268, C.21.273, C.21.280, C.21.282, C.21.288, C.21.289, C.21.291, C.21.297, C.21.298, C.21.315, C.21.322, C.21.323, C.21.343, C.21.344, C.21.349, C.21.352, C.21.365, C.21.366, C.21.369, C.21.372, C.21.384, C.21.389, C.21.392, C.21.406, C.21.411, C.21.412, C.21.413, C.21.415, C.21.417, C.21.425, C.21.428, C.21.429, C.21.430, C.21.437, C.21.440, C.21.441, C.21.442, C.21.461, C.22.5, C.22.7, C.22.15, C.22.32, C.22.36, C.22.47, C.22.49, C.22.65, C.22.65, C.22.66, C.22.67, C.22.71, C.22.72, C.22.72, C.22.89, C.22.90, C.22.103, C.22.103, C.22.110, C.22.141, C.22.158, C.22.161, C.22.171, C.22.193, C.22.195, C.22.216, C.22.235, C.22.238, C.22.239, C.22.257, C.22.261, C.22.277, C.22.281, C.22.283, C.22.286, C.22.290, C.22.303, C.22.304, C.22.305, C.22.307, C.22.310, C.22.313, C.22.320, C.22.365, C.22.372, C.22.382, C.22.383

þat adj dem *that def.art.& adj.* A 74; B 184 that (11) þat (173); C 172 that (28) þat (144)

A.Pr.97 I sauȝ in *þat* sem[b]le as ȝe shuln here aftir,
A. 1.4 Com doun fro *þat* [clyf] & callide me faire,
A. 1.23 *Þat* on is vesture fro chele þe to saue;
A. 1.24 *Þat* oþer is mete at meel for myseise of þiselue;
A. 1.31 And al he wytide it wyn *þ[at]* wykkide dede.

A. 1.43	Tel me to whom þat tresour apendiþ.'
A. 1.102	And whoso passiþ þat poynt is apostata in his ordre.
A. 1.118	Aftir here deþ day & dwelle wiþ þat shrewe.
A. 1.143	And ʒet wolde he hem no woo þat wrouʒte him þat pyne,
A. 1.145	To haue pite on þat peple þat pynede hym to deþe.
A. 2.7	I lokide on [my] left half as þat lady me tauʒte,
A. 2.28	Þat longiþ to þ[at] lordsshipe, þe lasse & þe more.
A. 3.42	Þanne mede for hire mysdedis to þat man knelide,
A. 3.80	'For my loue,' quaþ þat lady, 'loue hem ichone,
A. 3.101	'ʒa lord,' quaþ þat lady, 'lord forbede ellis;
A. 3.153	Þis is þe lif of þat lady, now lord ʒif hire sorewe!
A. 3.162	'Nay lord,' quod þat lady, 'leu[iþ] him þe wers
A. 3.190	He shulde haue be lord of þat lond in lengþe & in brede,
A. 3.191	And ek king of þat kiþ his kyn for to helpe,
A. 3.219	Þat on god of his grace gyueþ in his blisse
A. 3.255	And al his sed for þat synne [shend]fully ende.
A. 3.270	Shal no seriaunt for þat seruyse were a silk houue,
A. 4.13	'I am fayn of þat foreward,' seiþ þe frek þanne,
A. 4.77	Amende þat mysdede, & eueremore þe betere.'
A. 4.86	To haue mercy on þat man þat mysdede hym ofte:
A. 4.88	I forgyue hym þ[at] gilt wiþ a good wille;
A. 4.97	Somme redde resoun to haue reuþe on þat shrewe,
A. 4.114	Vpe forfaiture of þat fe, who fynt hym [at douere],
A. 5.113	He shulde wandre on þat walsshe, so was it þredbare.
A. 5.114	'I haue [ben] coueit[ous],' quaþ [þat caitif], 'I [bi]knowe [hit] h[e]re,
A. 5.139	Whanne it com in cuppemel; þat craft my wyf vside.
A. 5.172	Þere were chapmen chosen þat chaffare to preise;
A. 5.191	[Þat] alle þat herden þat horn held here nose aftir
A. 5.206	Þanne was þat shrewe asshamide & shrapide hise eris,
A. 5.238	And þou haddist mercy on þat man for memento sake,
A. 6.21	Canst þou wisse vs þe wey where þat wy dwelliþ?'
A. 6.41	And ʒif ʒe wilneþ wyte where þat wy dwelliþ
A. 6.55	Wadiþ in þat watir & wasshiþ ʒow wel þere,
A. 6.75	Þe kirnelis ben of cristendom þat kynde to saue,
A. 6.95	Ac be war þanne of wraþþe, þat wykkide shrewe,
A. 6.106	Þat on hattiþ abstinence, and [humylite] anoþer,
A. 7.5	Hadde y [erid] þat half akir
A. 7.82	To haue reles & remissioun, on þat rental I leue.
A. 7.112	And þeiʒ ʒe deiʒe for doel þe deuil haue þat recche!'
A. 7.180	And lame menis lymes wern li[þ]id þat tyme,
A. 8.8	Part in þ[at] pardoun þe pope haþ hem grauntid.
A. 8.14	Loke on þat o lawe, & lere men þat oþer,
A. 8.14	Loke on þat o lawe, & lere men þat oþer,
A. 8.51	Counfortiþ hym in þat cas, coueitiþ nouʒt his goodis,
A. 8.128	And sauʒ þe sonne euene souþ sitte þat tyme,
A. 9.87	Is hokid at þat on ende to holde men in good lif.
A. 9.88	A pik is in þat potent to pungen adoun þe wykkide,
A. 9.116	Þanne þouʒt, in þat tyme, seide þis wordis:
A.10.25	'What calle ʒe þat castel,' quaþ I, 'þat kynde haþ ymakid?
A.10.43	For loue of þat lady þat lif is ynempnid.
A.10.146	In þat curside constellacioun þei knewe togideris,
A.10.151	Alle þat comen of þat caym crist hatid aftir,
A.10.155	For alle þat comen of þat caym acursid þei were,
A.10.156	And alle þat couplide hem with þat kyn crist hatide [dedliche].
A.10.168	Busk[en hem] to þat boot & biden þereInne
A.10.196	But ʒif þei boþe be forsworn þat bacoun þei tyne.
A.10.205	Þat dede derne do no man ne shulde.
A.11.49	Litel louiþ he þat lord þat leniþ hym al þat blisse,
A.11.49	Litel louiþ he þat lord þat leniþ hym al þat blisse,
A.11.158	For sorcerie is þe souerayn bok þat to þat science longiþ.
A.11.237	Þat arn vncristene in þat cas may cristene an heþene,
A.12.42	Þat lady þan low and lauʒte me in here armes
A.12.66	I shal felle þat freke in a fewe dayes.'
A.12.84	Þat on is called cotidian, a courrour of oure hous;
A.12.85	Tercian þat oþer; trewe drinkeres boþe.
A.12.89	'Nay, wil,' quod þat wyʒth, 'wend þou no ferther,
A.12.112	To lyue as þat lord lykyþ þat lyf in hem putte:
A.12.117	Þat barn bryng vs to blys þat bled vpon þe rode amen.
B.Pr.107	Ac of þe Cardinals at court þat kauʒte of þat name,
B.Pr.167	And riʒt so', quod þat Raton, 'Reson me sheweþ
B. 1.23	That oon [is] vesture from [chele] þee to saue;
B. 1.24	[That oþer is] mete at meel for mysese of þiselue.
B. 1.31	And al he witte it wyn þat wikked dede:
B. 1.45	Tel me to whom þat tresour appendeþ.'
B. 1.104	And whoso passe[þ] þat point [is] Apostata in [his] ordre.
B. 1.114	And fel fro þat felawshipe in a fendes liknesse
B. 1.129	After hir deþ day and dwelle with þat sherewe.
B. 1.149	May no synne be on hym seene þat vseþ þat spice,
B. 1.161	And ʒet wolde he hem no wo þat wrouʒte hym þat peyne,
B. 1.171	To haue pite [on] þat peple þat peyned hym to deþe.
B. 2.43	And al is lieres ledynge þat [lady] is þus ywedded.

B. 2.46	That longen to þat lordshipe, þe lasse and þe moore.
B. 2.52	Thus lefte me þat lady liggynge aslepe,
B. 3.43	Thanne Mede for hire mysdedes to þat man kneled
B. 3.91	'For my loue', quod þat lady, 'loue hem echone,
B. 3.112	'Ye, lord', quod þat lady, 'lord forbede ellis!
B. 3.166	This is þe lif of þat lady, now lord ʒyue hire sorwe,
B. 3.175	'Nay lord', quod þat lady, 'leueþ hym þe werse
B. 3.203	He sholde haue be lord of þat lond in lengþe and in brede,
B. 3.204	And [ek] kyng of þat kiþ his kyn for to helpe,
B. 3.232	That oon god of his grace [gyueþ] in his blisse
B. 3.277	And al his seed for þat synne shenfulliche ende.
B. 3.295	Shal no sergeant for [þat] seruice were a silk howue,
B. 3.328	And Sarʒynes for þat siʒte shul synge Gloria in excelsis &c,
B. 3.329	For Makometh and Mede myshappe shul þat tyme;
B. 3.340	For þat lyne was no lenger at þe leues ende.
B. 3.341	Hadde she loked þat [left] half and þe leef torned
B. 3.343	Quod bonum est tenete; truþe þat text made.
B. 3.351	And þat is þe tail of þe text of þat [teme ye] shewed,
B. 4.13	'I am fayn of þat foreward', seide þe freke þanne,
B. 4.90	Amenden þat [mysdede] and eueremoore þe bettre.'
B. 4.99	To haue mercy on þat man þat mysdide hym ofte:
B. 4.101	I forgyue hym þat gilt wiþ a good wille
B. 4.110	Som[me] radde Reson to haue ruþe on þat shrewe;
B. 4.131	V[p] forfeiture of þat fee, wh[o] fynt [hym] at Douere,
B. 4.156	I falle in floryns', quod þat freke, 'and faile speche ofte.'
B. 4.166	For þe mooste commune of þat court called hire an hore.
B. 5.197	She sholde noʒt [wandre] on þat wel[ch]e, so was it þredbare.
B. 5.265	For were I frere of þat hous þer good feiþ and charite
B. 5.293	For þee and for many mo þat man shal yeue a rekenyng:
B. 5.343	That alle þat herde þat horn helde hir nos[e] after
B. 5.356	Dorste lape of þat leuynges, so vnlouely [it] smauʒte.
B. 5.364	And Repentaunce riʒt so rebuked hym þat tyme:
B. 5.466	And haddest mercy on þat man for Memento sake,
B. 5.484	For þoruʒ þat synne þi sone sent was to erþe.
B. 5.533	[Kanstow] wissen vs þe wey wher þat wye dwelleþ?'
B. 5.554	And if ye wilneþ wite where þat [wye] dwelleþ
B. 5.568	Wadeþ in þat water and wasshe yow wel þer,
B. 5.588	[The] kernele[s ben of] cristendom [þat] kynde to saue,
B. 5.609	A[c] be war þanne of Wraþe, þat wikked sherewe,
B. 5.620	That oon hatte Abstinence, and humilite anoþer,
B. 6.90	To haue relees and remission, on þat rental I leue.
B. 7.49	Conforteþ hym in þat caas, [coueiteþ noʒt hise] ʒiftes,
B. 7.146	And seiʒ þe sonne [euene] South sitte þat tyme,
B. 8.97	Is hoked [at] þat oon ende to [holde men in good lif].
B. 8.98	A pik is [in] þat potente to [punge] adown þe wikked
B. 8.127	Thanne þoʒt in þat tyme seide þise wordes:
B. 9.16	[By his leryng is lad þat lady Anima].
B. 9.61	Muche wo worþ þat man þat mysruleþ his Inwit,
B. 9.126	And alle þat come of þat Caym come to yuel ende,
B. 9.137	Buskeþ yow to þat boot and bideþ þerInne
B. 9.175	But þei boþe be forswore þat bacon þei tyne.
B. 9.192	That [dede derne] do no man ne sholde.
B.10.63	Litel loueþ he þat lord þat lent hym al þat blisse
B.10.63	Litel loueþ he þat lord þat lent hym al þat blisse
B.10.75	That folk is noʒt fermed in þe feiþ ne free of hire goodes
B.10.215	For sorcerie is þe Souereyn book þat to [þat] Scienc[e] [l]ongeþ.
B.10.334	Ac er þat kyng come Caym shal awake,
B.10.354	That [arn] vncristene in þat caas may cristen an heþen,
B.10.406	Tho he shoop þat ship of shides and bordes:
B.10.452	Beþ noʒt [afered of þat folk], for I shal [ʒyue yow tonge],
B.11.14	And Coueitise of eiʒes [þat ooþer was ycalled].
B.11.99	It falleþ noʒt for þat folk no tales to telle
B.11.157	Was þat Sarsen saued, as Seint Gregorie bereþ witnesse.
B.11.261	And after þat bitter bark, be þe shelle aweye,
B.11.304	If fals latyn be in þat lettre þe lawe it impugneþ,
B.11.383	[Holy writ', quod þat wye, 'wisseþ men to suffre:
B.11.411	'[What is dowel?' quod þat wiʒt]; 'ywis, sire', I seide,
B.12.76	A womman, as [we] fynde[n], was gilty of þat dede,
B.12.114	Hadde neuere lewed man leue to leggen hond on þat cheste
B.12.117	And his sones also for þat synne myscheued,
B.12.146	Ne in none [beggers] cote [n]as þat barn born,
B.12.162	That oon [kan] konnynge and kan swymmen and dyuen;
B.12.163	That ooþer is lewed of þat labour, lerned neuere swymme.
B.12.163	That ooþer is lewed of þat labour, lerned neuere swymme.
B.12.196	Ac þouʒ þat þeef hadde heuene he hadde noon heiʒ blisse,
B.12.202	So it fareþ by þat felon þat a good friday was saued;
B.12.214	A[c] why þat oon þeef on þe cros creaunt hym yald
B.12.215	Raþer þan þat ooþer þeef, þouʒ þow woldest appose.
B.12.294	The glose graunteþ vpon þat vers a greet mede to truþe.
B.12.295	And wit and wisdom', quod þat wye, 'was som tyme tresor
B.13.22	And as crist wolde þer com Conscience to conforte me þat tyme
B.13.59	Pacience was proud of þat propre seruice
B.13.224	'I am a Mynstrall', quod þat man, 'my name is Actiua vita.

B.14.185   And be clene þoru3 *þat* cristnyng of alle kynnes synne.
B.14.259   And in *þat* secte oure saueour saued al mankynde.
B.14.267   Muche is [*þat* maide] to loue of [a man] *þat* swich oon takeþ,
B.15.10   That folk helden me a fool; and in *þat* folie I raued
B.15.22   'What are ye called', quod I, 'in *þat* court among cristes peple?'
B.15.40   'Ye ben as a bisshop', quod I, al bourdynge *þat* tyme,
B.15.186   And whan he is wery of *þat* werk þan wole he som tyme
B.15.232   In *þat* secte siþþe to selde haþ he ben [knowe].
B.15.276   Ac neiþer Antony ne Egidie ne heremyte *þat* tyme
B.15.280   And þoru3 þe mylk of *þat* mylde beest þe man was sustened;
B.15.302   Thei wolde haue yfed *þat* folk bifore wilde foweles;
B.15.303   [For al þe curteisie þat beestes konne þei kidde *þat* folk ofte,
B.15.328   If any peple parfourne *þat* text it are þise poore freres,
B.15.339   And wente forþ wiþ *þat* water to woke wiþ Temese.
B.15.350   The merk of *þat* monee is good ac þe metal is feble;
B.15.446   And þoru3 miracles, as men mow rede, al *þat* marche he tornede
B.15.507   Thus in a feiþ leue *þat* folk, and in a fals mene,
B.15.544   Boþe riche and Religious, þat roode þei honoure
B.15.546   For coueitise of *þat* cros [clerkes] of holy kirke
B.15.586   And on *þat* lawe þei l[e]ue and leten it þe beste.
B.15.592   And by *þat* mangerie [þei] my3te wel se þat Messie he semede;
B.16.11   And to haue my fulle of *þat* fruyt forsake a[l] oþ[er] saule[e].
B.16.14   Amyddes mannes body; þe more is of *þat* stokke.
B.16.28   Coueitise comþ of *þat* wynd and crepeþ among þe leues
B.16.86   And Piers for pure tene *þat* a pil he [l]au3te;
B.16.89   To go robbe *þat* Rageman and reue þe fruyt fro hym.
B.16.100   And in þe wombe of *þat* wenche was he fourty woukes
B.16.117   Some *þat* þe sighte sei3en seiden *þat* tyme
B.16.146   Thanne wente forþ *þat* wikked man and wiþ þe Iewes mette
B.16.151   'Aue, raby', quod *þat* Ribaud, and ri3t to hym he yede
B.16.176   'I am feiþ', quod *þat* freke, 'and i3t falleþ no3t to lye,
B.16.180   'What berþ *þat* buyrn', quod I þo, 'so blisse þee bitide?'
B.16.186   The secounde of *þa[t]* sire is Sothfastnesse filius,
B.16.195   Sente forþ his sone as for seruaunt *þat* tyme,
B.16.237   Bledden blood for *þat* lordes loue and hope to blisse þe tyme.
B.16.262   And me þer[wiþ]', quod *þat* [wye]; 'may no wed vs quyte,
B.17.23   Lo! here in my lappe *þat* leeued on *þat* charme,
B.17.64   Ac whan he hadde sighte of *þat* segge aside he gan hym drawe
B.17.81   For I may no3t lette', quod *þat* Leode and lyard he bistrideþ
B.17.87   And suwed *þat* Samaritan þat was so ful of pite.
B.17.97   And [he be] baþed in *þat* blood, baptised as it were,
B.17.98   And þanne plastred wiþ penaunce and passion of *þat* baby,
B.17.101   For wente neuere wye in þis world þoru3 *þat* wildernesse
B.17.111   He was vnhardy, *þat* harlot, and hidde hym in Inferno.
B.17.113   That he worþ fettred, *þat* feloun, faste wiþ Cheynes,
B.17.134   'After Abraham', quod he, '*þat* heraud of armes,
B.17.271   And gyueþ youre good to *þat* god þat grace of ariseþ.
B.17.297   Wol loue [*þat* lif] þat [lakkeþ charite],
B.17.308   For þer *þat* partie pursueþ þe [peel] is so huge
B.17.323   *That* oon is a wikkede wif þat wol no3t be chastised;
B.18.18   Thanne I frayned at Feiþ what al *þat* fare bymente,
B.18.50   'Aue, raby', quod *þat* rybaud and þrew reedes at hym.
B.18.62   Dede men for *þat* dene come out of depe graues
B.18.63   And tolde why *þat* tempeste so longe tyme durede:
B.18.71   Two þeues [*þat* tyme] þoled deeþ [also]
B.18.76   For he was kny3t and kynges sone kynde foryaf *þat* [þrowe]
B.18.81   Maugree his manye teeþ he was maad *þat* tyme
B.18.111   I drow me in *þat* derknesse to descendit ad inferna
B.18.115   Mercy highte *þat* mayde, a meke þyng wiþ alle,
B.18.196   Freet of fayre fruyt and forsook, as it weere,
B.18.231   Book highte *þat* beaupeere, a bold man of speche.
B.18.263   A vois loude in *þat* light to lucifer crieþ,
B.18.285   I leeue *þat* lawe nyl no3t lete hym þe leeste.'
B.18.321   And wiþ *þat* breeþ helle brak wiþ Belialles barres;
B.18.343   And lif for lif also, and by *þat* lawe I clayme
B.18.366   And for *þat* drynke today I deide vpon erþe.
B.18.381   And if þe kyng of *þat* kyngdom come in *þat* tyme
B.18.381   And if þe kyng of *þat* kyngdom come in *þat* tyme
B.19.22   And synfulle aren solaced and saued by *þat* name,
B.19.69   Ac to carpe moore of crist and how he com to *þat* name,
B.19.80   And þere was *þat* word fulfilled þe which þow of speke,
B.19.84   Wherfore and why wise men *þat* tyme,
B.19.86   *That* o kyng cam wiþ Reson couered vnder sense.
B.19.115   So at *þat* feeste first as I bifore tolde
B.19.119   For bifore his moder Marie made he *þat* wonder
B.19.146   That *þat* blissede body of burieles [sholde risen]
B.19.211   Thanne song I *þat* song; so dide manye hundred,
B.19.237   And lyue, by *þat* labour, a lele lif and a trewe.
B.19.263   *That* oon was Luk, a large beest and a lowe chered,
B.19.282   He *þat* ete of *þat* seed hadde swich a kynde:
B.19.290   And who[so] ete [of] *þat* seed hardy was euere
B.19.298   And he *þat* ete of *þat* seed sholde be [euene] trewe
B.19.320   And ordeyne *þat* hous er ye hennes wende.'

B.19.328   And called *þat* hous vnitee, holy chirche on englissh.
B.19.428   Inparfit is *þat* pope þat al [peple] sholde helpe
B.20.14   And he [cacche] in *þat* caas and come þerto by sleighte
B.20.58   Freres folwede *þat* fend for he gaf hem copes,
B.20.92   'Alarme! alarme!' quod *þat* lord, 'ech lif kepe his owene!'
C. 1.30   And al he witte [it] wyn [*þat*] wikkede dede:
C. 1.43   Telleth me to wham *þat* tresour bylongeth.'
C. 1.98   And hoso passeth *þat* poynt is appostata of knyghthed.
C. 1.104   And god whan he bigan heuene in *þat* grete blisse
C. 1.112   'Lord! why wolde he tho, *þat* wykkede lucifer,
C. 1.116   Ac y wol lacky no lyf,' quod *þat* lady sothly;
C. 1.165   And 3ut wolde [he] hem no wo *þat* wrouhte hym *þat* [p]e[y]ne
C. 1.167   To haue pitee on *þat* peple þat paynede hym to dethe;
C. 1.203   Loue hit,' quod *þat* lady; 'lette may y no lengore
C. 2.46   And al is lyares ledynge *th[at]* lady is thus ywedded.
C. 2.55   Thus le[f]te me *that* lady lyggynge as aslepe,
C. 3.45   Thenne mede for here mysdedes to *th[at]* man knelede
C. 3.55   Loueliche *þat* lady laghynge sayde,
C. 3.149   '3e, lord,' quod *that* lady, 'lord hit me forbede
C. 3.221   'Nay, lord,' quod *þat* lady, 'leueth hym þe worse
C. 3.244   Vnconnynge is *þat* Consience a kyndom to sulle
C. 3.260   He sholde haue [ben] lord of *þat* lond alenghe and abrede
C. 3.261   And also kyng of *þat* kuth his kyn for to helpe,
C. 3.401   For *þat* lordes loue that for oure loue deyede
C. 3.411   That saul for *þat* synne and his sone deyede
C. 3.420   And alle þat leueth on *þat* lond oure [lord] wol þat thow sle hit;
C. 3.430   And al [h]is [sede] for *þat* synne shentfolyche ende.
C. 3.448   Shal no ser[i]aunt for [*þat*] seruic[e] werie a selk houe
C. 3.481   And saresines for *þat* syhte shal syng Credo in spiritum sanctum
C. 3.482   For Machameth and mede [shal] mishap *þat* tyme;
C. 3.489   'I leue the, lady,' quod Consience, 'for *þat* latyn is trewe.
C. 3.492   *That* l[yne] was no lengur and at þe leues ende
C. 4.13   'Y am fayn of *that* foroward, in fayth,' tho quod Consience,
C. 4.95   To haue mercy on *þat* man that many tymes hym greuede:
C. 4.105   Summe radden resoun tho to haue reuthe vppon *þat* shrewe
C. 4.128   Vp forfeture of *þat* fee, ho fyndeth h[y]m ouerward,
C. 5.43   *That* laboure þat y lerned beste þerwith lyuen y sholde:
C. 5.173   Freres in here fraytour shal fynde *þat* tyme
C. 5.178   Ac ar *þat* kyng come, as cronicles me tolde,
C. 6.40   Be holden for holy and honoured by *þat* enchesoun;
C. 6.105   'I am wr[a]the,' quod *þat* weye, 'wol gladliche smyte
C. 6.173   With *þat* y shal,' quod *þat* shrewe, 'saturdayes for thy loue
C. 6.193   When y was olde and hoor and hadde ylore *þat* kynde
C. 6.205   He sholde [nat] wandre [o]n *þat* walch, so was hit thredbare.
C. 6.320   And haddest mercy vppon *þat* man for memento sake,
C. 6.348   For the and for many mo *þat* man shal 3eue a rykenynge
C. 6.401   That alle þat herde þ[*at*] hor[n] helde here nose aftur
C. 6.414   Durste lape of *þat* lyuynge, so vnlouely hit smauthe.
C. 6.422   A wax ashamed, *þat* shrewe, and shrofe hym a[s] swythe
C. 7.126   For thorw *þat* synne thy sone ysent was til erthe
C. 7.148   And for [that] muchel mercy and marie loue thi moder
C. 7.215   Wadeth in *þat* water and wascheth 3ow wel there
C. 7.235   The carneles ben of cristendom *þat* kynde to saue,
C. 7.261   Ac be war thenne of wrath, *þat* wikkede shrewe,
C. 7.272   *That* on hatte a[b]stinence and vmbletee a[n]oþer,
C. 8.73   And frere faytour and folk of *þat* ordre,
C. 8.99   To haue re[lees] and re[missioun]; on *þat* rental y leue.
C. 8.127   And thow 3e deye for deul þe deuel haue *þat* reche!'
C. 9.295   And seyh the sonne in the sou[t]he sitte *þat* tyme,
C. 9.323   Worth fayre vnderfonge byfore god *þat* tyme
C.10.67   And merueilousliche me mette amyddes al *þat* blisse.
C.10.123   Thenne thouht in *þat* tyme sayde this wordes:
C.10.140   To serue *þat* lady leely bot[h] late and rathe.
C.10.142   And by his lyrynge is lad *þat* lady Anima.
C.10.225   Boske 3ow to *þat* boet and abideth þerynne
C.10.246   Was for mariages ma[ugre kynd]e þat men made *þat* tyme.
C.10.267   That he ne wol bowe to *þat* bonde to beden here an hosebonde
C.10.277   Bote they bothe be forswore *þat* bacon þei tyne.
C.10.285   *That* lecherye is a lykyng thynge, a lym3erd of helle.
C.10.292   For *þat* dede derne do no man sholde
C.11.44   God is nat in *þat* hoem ne his helpe nother.
C.11.45   Lytel loueth he *þat* lord þat lente hym al *þat* blisse
C.11.45   Lytel loueth he *þat* lord þat lente hym al *þat* blisse
C.11.85   And when y was war of his wille to *þat* womman gan y louten
C.11.143   And bycam man of *þat* maide withoute mankynde;
C.11.173   And coueytise-of-yes ycalde was *þat* oþer.
C.11.277   Beth nat aferd of *þat* folk for y shal 3eue 3ow tonge,
C.12.147   And aftur *þat* bittere barke, be þe scale aweye,
C.13.19   Alle his sorwe to solace thorw *that* song turnede
C.13.55   For *þat* on bereth but a box, a breuet þerynne,
C.13.118   Yf fals latyn be in *þat* lettre þe lawe hit enpugneth,
C.13.171   How vncortey[s]liche *þat* cok his kynde for[th] strenede
C.13.219   'What is dowel?' quod *þat* wyhte; 'ywis, sire,' y saide,

C.14.32   *That* wit wexeth therof and oþer w[y]rdes bothe:
C.14.59   Hadde neuere lewede [man] leue to legge hand on *þat* cheste
C.14.106   *That* oen hath connyng and can swymmen and dyuen;
C.14.107   *That* oþer is lewed of *þat* labour, lerned neuere swymme.
C.14.107   That oþer is lewed of *þat* labour, lerned neuere swymme.
C.14.135   Ac thogh *th[at]* theef hadde heuene he hadde noen hey blisse
C.14.153   Ac why *þat* [on] theef vppon þe cros cryant hym ȝelde
C.14.154   Rather then *þat* oþer [theef], thogh thow woldest apose,
C.14.166   Ac why a wolde *þat* wykke were, y wene and y leue
C.15.45   Ac of this mete *þat* maystre myhte nat we[l c]hewe;
C.15.89   Þat in þ[e] mawe of *þat* maystre alle þo metes were,
C.15.123   'Y haue yseide,' quod *þat* segg, 'y can sey no bettre.
C.16.99   And in *þat* secte oure saueour saued al mankynde.
C.16.107   Moche as [*þat*] mayde to louye of a man þat such oen taketh,
C.16.108   More then *þat* mayde is þat is maried by brocage,
C.16.162   Thenne hadde y wonder what he was, *þat* l[i]berum Arbitrium,
C.16.179   'Thenne is *þat* body bettere þen þou?' quod y. 'Nay,' quod he, 'no bettere,
C.16.202   'Ȝe beth as a bischop,' quod y, al bourdynge *þat* tyme,
C.16.314   Ne mysliked thogh he lore or lened *þat* ilke
C.16.329   Worth moche meryte to *þat* man þat hit may soffre.
C.16.357   In [*þat*] sekte sethe to selde hath he be [knowen].
C.17.16   For he ordeyned *þat* ordre or elles þey gabben.
C.17.40   Lord leue," quod *þat* lede, " no stole thynge be herynne!"
C.17.155   To *þat* lord þat hym lyf lente lyflode hym sende.
C.17.157   Louyeth nat *þat* lord aryht as by þe legende sanctorum
C.17.206   Bothe riche and religiou[s] *þat* rode they honouren
C.17.208   For coueytse of *th[at]* croes clerkes of holi churche
C.17.258   Thus in a fayth l[e]ueth *þat* folk and in a fals mene,
C.17.276   And alle holy kirke honoured thorw *that* deyng.
C.17.297   And on *þat* lawe they leue and leten hit for þe beste.
C.18.32   Couetyse cometh of *þat* wynde and Caritas hit abiteth
C.18.33   And forfret *þat* fruyt thorw many fayre s[ih]tus.
C.18.80   *That* [lyf Actiua] lettred men in here langage calleth.'
C.18.103   Assay what sauour hit hadde and saide *þat* tyme,
C.18.121   To go ransake *þat* ragman and reue hym of his apples
C.18.128   *That* iesus sholde iouste þerfore by iugement of Armes
C.18.133   And in þe wombe of *þat* wenche was he fourty wokes
C.18.134   And bycam man of *þat* mayde mankynde to saue,
C.18.145   Ac ar he made *þat* miracle mestus cepit esse
C.18.147   Ac tho that sey *that* selcouth sayde *þat* tyme
C.18.147   Ac tho that sey that selcouth sayde *þat* tyme
C.18.148   That he was god or godes sone for *þat* grete wonder;
C.18.168   'Aue raby,' quod *th[at]* ribaud[e]; and riht til hym [he] ȝede
C.18.178   With moche noyse *þat* nyhte nere frentyk y wakede;
C.18.184   'I am with fayth,' quod *þat* freke, 'hit falleth nat me to lye,
C.18.204   Sente forth his sone As for seruant *þat* tyme
C.18.253   Bledden bloed for *þat* lordes loue [and] hope to blisse þ[e] tyme.
C.19.24   Lo! here in my lappe *þat* leuede vpon *þat* lettre,
C.19.40   And seth to louye and to lene for *þat* lordes sake
C.19.78   For y may nat lette,' quod *that* lede; and lyard he bystrideth
C.19.88   And with þe bloed of *þat* barn enbaumed and ybaptised.
C.19.94   And ȝut bote they l[e]ue lelly vpon *þat* litel baby,
C.19.116   Til hym likede and luste to vnlose *that* fynger
C.19.252   And gyueth ȝoure goed to *þat* god þat grace of aryseth.
C.19.278   Wol louye *þat* lyf þat loue and Charite destruyeth.'
C.19.288   The[r] *þat* partye pursueth the apeel is so huge
C.19.303   *That* [oon] is a wikkede wyf þat wol nat be chasted;
C.20.16   Thenne y [f]raynede at fayth what al *þat* fare bymente
C.20.50   'Aue, raby,' quod *þat* ribaud, and redes shotte vp to his yes.
C.20.64   And dede men for *þat* dene cam oute of depe graues
C.20.65   And tolde why þ[at] tempest so longe tyme durede:
C.20.73   T[w]o theues tho tholed deth *þat* tyme
C.20.78   For he was knyht and kynges sone kynde forȝaf *þat* [þrowe]
C.20.83   Maugre his mony teth he was mad *þat* tyme
C.20.114   Y [d]row [me] in *þat* derkenesse to descendit ad inferna
C.20.118   Mercy hihte *þat* mayde, a mylde thynge with alle,
C.20.201   Freet of *th[at]* fruyt and forsoke, as hit were,
C.20.240   Boek hihte *þat* beaupere, a bolde man of speche.
C.20.271   A vois louder in *þat* liht to louder saide,
C.20.359   For efte *þat* lihte bade vnlouke [and lucifer answerede].
C.20.364   And with *þat* breth helle braek with belialles barres;
C.20.369   And tho that oure lord louede forth with *þat* liht flowen.
C.20.404   And for *þat* drynke today y deyede as hit semede.
C.21.22   And synfole ben solaced and saued by *þat* name.
C.21.69   Ac to carpe more of Crist and how he cam to *þat* name;
C.21.80   And þer was *þat* word fulfuld þe which þou of speke,
C.21.84   [Wherefore & why wyse men of *þat* tyme,
C.21.86   *That* [o] kyng cam with reson ykyuered vnder ensense.
C.21.115   So at *þat* feste furste as y before tolde
C.21.119   For bifore his moder Marie made he *þat* wonder
C.21.146   That *þat* blessed body of buyrielles sholde ryse
C.21.211   [Thanne] sang [y] *þat* song; so dede many hundret

C.21.237   And lyue by *þat* laboure a leele lyf and a trewe.
C.21.263   *That* oen was luc, a large beste and a lou chered,
C.21.282   He *þat* eet of *that* seed hadde such a kynde:
C.21.290   And hoso ete of *þa[t]* seed hardy was euere
C.21.298   And he *þat* ete of *þat* seed sholde be euene trewe
C.21.320   And ordeyne *þat* hous ar ȝe hennes wende.'
C.21.328   And calde *þat* hous vnite, holy chirche an englisch.
C.21.428   Inparfit is *þat* pope þat all peple sholde helpe
C.22.14   And he cacche in *þat* caes and come therto by sleithe
C.22.58   Freres folewed *þat* fende for he ȝaf hem copes
C.22.92   'Alarme! alarme!' quod *þat* lord, 'vch lyf kepe his owene!'
C.22.177   And þere deyede *þat* doctour ar thre dayes aftur.

þat conj *that conj., that particle* A 162 that (3) þat (159); B 436 that (208) þat (228); C 430 that (213) þat (217)

    A.Pr.12, A.Pr.32, A.Pr.67, A.Pr.77, A.Pr.81, A.1.13, A.1.26, A.1.60, A.1.80, A.1.121, A.1.126, A.1.136, A.1.147, A.1.160, A.1.182, A.2.25, A.2.39, A.2.47, A.2.50, A.2.58, A.2.94, A.2.110, A.2.119, A.2.120, A.2.132, A.2.134, A.2.166, A.3.32, A.3.52, A.3.57, A.3.87, A.3.106, A.3.147, A.3.164, A.3.179, A.3.241, A.3.254, A.3.257, A.3.261, A.3.273, A.4.7, A.4.8, A.4.54, A.4.67, A.4.71, A.4.79, A.4.89, A.4.99, A.4.110, A.4.121, A.4.130, A.4.136, A.4.138, A.4.150, A.5.4, A.5.6, A.5.13, A.5.17, A.5.20, A.5.31, A.5.56, A.5.66, A.5.88, A.5.96, A.5.99, A.5.142, A.5.179, A.5.181, A.5.191, A.5.199, A.5.202, A.5.219, A.5.223, A.5.230, A.5.240, A.5.244, A.5.248, A.5.254, A.6.3, A.6.13, A.6.18, A.6.39, A.6.49, A.6.50, A.6.71, A.7.29, A.7.45, A.7.118, A.7.160, A.7.162, A.7.173, A.7.231, A.7.244, A.7.253, A.7.261, A.7.283, A.7.297, A.8.17, A.8.37, A.8.38, A.8.41, A.8.54, A.8.58, A.8.81, A.8.100, A.8.139, A.8.148, A.8.153, A.8.161, A.8.181, A.8.183, A.8.184, A.9.13, A.9.19, A.9.38, A.9.43, A.9.92, A.9.101, A.9.117, A.10.77, A.10.83, A.10.88, A.10.104, A.10.110, A.10.133, A.10.141, A.10.161, A.10.164, A.10.169, A.10.172, A.10.207, A.11.3, A.11.14, A.11.67, A.11.75, A.11.82, A.11.93, A.11.99, A.11.113, A.11.115, A.11.123, A.11.126, A.11.143, A.11.176, A.11.206, A.11.219, A.11.224, A.11.294, A.12.9, A.12.14, A.12.16, A.12.17, A.12.27, A.12.40, A.12.46, A.12.51, A.12.54, A.12.80, A.12.80, A.12.95, A.12.97, A.12.100

    B.Pr.12, B.Pr.32, B.Pr.70, B.Pr.80, B.Pr.84, B.Pr.89, B.Pr.117, B.Pr.155, B.1.13, B.1.26, B.1.62, B.1.82, B.1.132, B.1.137, B.1.148, B.1.158, B.1.173, B.1.186, B.1.208, B.2.35, B.2.54, B.2.76, B.2.130, B.2.146, B.2.155, B.2.156, B.2.170, B.2.205, B.3.33, B.3.63, B.3.98, B.3.157, B.3.177, B.3.192, B.3.260, B.3.262, B.3.276, B.3.279, B.3.283, B.3.285, B.3.302, B.3.303, B.3.304, B.3.337, B.3.352, B.4.7, B.4.8, B.4.62, B.4.68, B.4.84, B.4.92, B.4.102, B.4.112, B.4.127, B.4.138, B.4.147, B.4.157, B.4.162, B.4.172, B.5.4, B.5.6, B.5.13, B.5.17, B.5.20, B.5.31, B.5.58, B.5.73, B.5.83, B.5.89, B.5.91, B.5.100, B.5.108, B.5.117, B.5.120, B.5.142, B.5.144, B.5.147, B.5.149, B.5.152, B.5.158, B.5.167, B.5.181, B.5.185, B.5.226, B.5.272, B.5.273, B.5.276, B.5.330, B.5.332, B.5.343, B.5.360, B.5.368, B.5.372, B.5.375, B.5.447, B.5.451, B.5.458, B.5.470, B.5.474, B.5.505, B.5.508, B.5.512, B.5.515, B.5.530, B.5.552, B.5.562, B.5.563, B.5.574, B.6.11, B.6.27, B.6.47, B.6.50, B.6.126, B.6.144, B.6.175, B.6.177, B.6.185, B.6.247, B.6.260, B.6.269, B.6.277, B.6.313, B.7.35, B.7.52, B.7.99, B.7.118, B.7.161, B.7.171, B.7.175, B.7.183, B.7.203, B.7.205, B.8.13, B.8.23, B.8.42, B.8.47, B.8.102, B.8.111, B.9.66, B.9.76, B.9.86, B.9.124, B.9.128, B.9.133, B.9.138, B.9.141, B.9.151, B.10.3, B.10.14, B.10.24, B.10.25, B.10.78, B.10.80, B.10.122, B.10.129, B.10.138, B.10.140, B.10.146, B.10.161, B.10.163, B.10.171, B.10.174, B.10.191, B.10.233, B.10.236, B.10.276, B.10.280, B.10.282, B.10.285, B.10.333, B.10.342, B.10.347, B.10.358, B.10.359, B.10.370, B.10.380, B.10.449, B.10.473, B.10.476, B.11.24, B.11.32, B.11.45, B.11.48, B.11.144, B.11.148, B.11.178, B.11.190, B.11.218, B.11.235, B.11.238, B.11.241, B.11.273, B.11.288, B.11.328, B.11.370, B.11.375, B.11.403, B.11.407, B.11.424, B.12.21, B.12.72, B.12.74, B.12.82, B.12.92, B.12.157, B.12.171, B.12.211, B.12.228, B.12.253, B.12.272, B.12.275, B.13.6, B.13.7, B.13.12, B.13.14, B.13.65, B.13.68, B.13.76, B.13.80, B.13.82, B.13.92, B.13.107, B.13.128, B.13.166, B.13.178, B.13.248, B.13.249, B.13.252, B.13.279, B.13.291, B.13.307, B.13.311, B.13.334, B.13.336, B.13.352, B.13.371, B.13.382, B.13.385, B.13.397, B.13.406, B.13.407, B.14.13, B.14.15, B.14.45, B.14.55, B.14.64, B.14.67, B.14.68, B.14.86, B.14.87, B.14.97, B.14.107, B.14.124, B.14.132, B.14.140, B.14.156, B.14.163, B.14.205, B.14.241, B.14.256, B.14.306, B.14.323, B.14.328, B.14.330, B.15.10, B.15.21, B.15.25, B.15.53, B.15.58, B.15.72, B.15.76, B.15.80, B.15.109, B.15.159, B.15.161, B.15.200, B.15.260, B.15.266, B.15.279, B.15.287, B.15.306, B.15.311, B.15.355, B.15.389, B.15.392, B.15.407, B.15.411, B.15.416, B.15.419, B.15.484, B.15.492, B.15.495, B.15.501, B.15.513, B.15.575, B.15.592, B.15.601, B.15.602, B.15.603, B.15.607, B.16.19, B.16.21, B.16.33, B.16.56, B.16.92, B.16.94, B.16.105, B.16.118, B.16.130, B.16.135, B.16.143, B.16.175, B.16.200, B.16.202, B.16.252, B.16.270, B.17.8, B.17.28, B.17.70, B.17.91, B.17.102, B.17.113, B.17.136, B.17.166, B.17.199, B.17.204, B.17.227, B.17.228, B.17.259, B.17.268, B.17.296, B.17.298, B.17.300, B.17.304, B.17.309, B.17.314, B.17.316, B.17.331, B.17.336, B.17.342, B.17.344, B.17.351, B.18.24, B.18.31, B.18.32, B.18.54, B.18.56, B.18.68, B.18.69, B.18.77, B.18.132, B.18.136, B.18.139, B.18.145, B.18.153, B.18.183, B.18.184, B.18.187, B.18.189, B.18.192, B.18.194, B.18.200, B.18.228, B.18.233, B.18.234, B.18.235, B.18.238, B.18.242, B.18.272, B.18.304, B.18.320, B.18.331, B.18.339, B.18.347, B.18.370, B.18.387, B.18.390, B.18.418, B.18.425, B.19.6, B.19.17, B.19.27, B.19.52, B.19.63, B.19.64, B.19.66, B.19.120, B.19.121, B.19.129, B.19.143, B.19.146, B.19.150, B.19.155, B.19.161, B.19.186, B.19.228, B.19.253, B.19.254, B.19.293, B.19.300, B.19.306, B.19.310, B.19.342, B.19.348, B.19.357, B.19.363, B.19.374, B.19.413, B.19.420, B.19.427, B.19.441, B.19.477, B.20.7, B.20.19, B.20.22, B.20.43, B.20.46, B.20.52, B.20.76, B.20.78, B.20.141, B.20.173, B.20.176, B.20.178, B.20.194, B.20.233, B.20.250, B.20.254, B.20.271, B.20.276, B.20.308, B.20.323, B.20.351, B.20.383

    C.Pr.34, C.Pr.68, C.Pr.78, C.Pr.82, C.Pr.102, C.Pr.104, C.Pr.111, C.Pr.144, C.Pr.175, C.Pr.215, C.1.13, C.1.58, C.1.146, C.1.154, C.1.169, C.1.182, C.2.48, C.2.76,

C.2.83, C.2.99, C.2.133, C.2.139, C.2.146, C.2.162, C.2.171, C.2.180, C.2.185, C.2.237, C.3.36, C.3.67, C.3.93, C.3.98, C.3.104, C.3.108, C.3.113, C.3.126, C.3.131, C.3.144, C.3.195, C.3.210, C.3.212, C.3.223, C.3.240, C.3.287, C.3.295, C.3.310, C.3.329, C.3.377, C.3.393, C.3.397, C.3.411, C.3.415, C.3.420, C.3.429, C.3.432, C.3.436, C.3.438, C.3.455, C.3.456, C.3.457, C.3.496, C.4.7, C.4.8, C.4.80, C.4.88, C.4.107, C.4.118, C.4.124, C.4.135, C.4.144, C.4.149, C.4.151, C.4.155, C.4.189, C.4.191, C.5.93, C.5.115, C.5.119, C.5.122, C.5.133, C.5.185, C.5.187, C.5.194, C.5.199, C.6.41, C.6.48, C.6.55, C.6.59, C.6.78, C.6.80, C.6.99, C.6.100, C.6.122, C.6.127, C.6.142, C.6.163, C.6.167, C.6.172, C.6.173, C.6.268, C.6.274, C.6.284, C.6.301, C.6.312, C.6.324, C.6.328, C.6.381, C.6.382, C.6.388, C.6.390, C.6.401, C.7.61, C.7.65, C.7.145, C.7.150, C.7.153, C.7.157, C.7.160, C.7.198, C.7.203, C.7.208, C.7.221, C.7.298, C.8.8, C.8.10, C.8.26, C.8.132, C.8.138, C.8.172, C.8.174, C.8.181, C.8.262, C.8.277, C.8.290, C.8.300, C.8.335, C.9.38, C.9.82, C.9.112, C.9.276, C.9.315, C.9.320, C.9.329, C.9.349, C.9.351, C.10.13, C.10.75, C.10.91, C.10.107, C.10.162, C.10.191, C.10.212, C.10.214, C.10.229, C.10.237, C.10.244, C.10.247, C.10.250, C.10.253, C.10.267, C.10.269, C.10.282, C.10.306, C.11.3, C.11.12, C.11.55, C.11.58, C.11.84, C.11.89, C.11.111, C.11.137, C.11.151, C.11.183, C.11.191, C.11.200, C.11.202, C.11.203, C.11.216, C.11.223, C.11.270, C.11.274, C.11.282, C.12.2, C.12.79, C.12.83, C.12.124, C.12.127, C.12.130, C.12.212, C.12.238, C.13.5, C.13.13, C.13.60, C.13.83, C.13.94, C.13.102, C.13.131, C.13.136, C.13.142, C.13.180, C.13.186, C.13.199, C.13.211, C.13.215, C.14.16, C.14.37, C.14.111, C.14.150, C.14.170, C.14.194, C.14.197, C.14.200, C.15.7, C.15.9, C.15.15, C.15.17, C.15.22, C.15.24, C.15.52, C.15.69, C.15.72, C.15.74, C.15.77, C.15.82, C.15.87, C.15.89, C.15.99, C.15.115, C.15.115, C.15.140, C.15.176, C.15.181, C.15.210, C.15.211, C.15.217, C.15.218, C.15.220, C.15.243, C.15.254, C.15.263, C.15.266, C.15.267, C.15.282, C.16.1, C.16.8, C.16.16, C.16.46, C.16.81, C.16.96, C.16.115, C.16.142, C.16.154, C.16.163, C.16.172, C.16.185, C.16.215, C.16.220, C.16.233, C.16.235, C.16.239, C.16.284, C.16.293, C.16.306, C.16.307, C.16.328, C.17.9, C.17.14, C.17.33, C.17.35, C.17.66, C.17.70, C.17.81, C.17.91, C.17.117, C.17.118, C.17.121, C.17.133, C.17.151, C.17.165, C.17.179, C.17.187, C.17.190, C.17.252, C.17.264, C.17.265, C.17.292, C.17.308, C.17.310, C.17.311, C.17.315, C.18.17, C.18.18, C.18.37, C.18.48, C.18.92, C.18.118, C.18.125, C.18.127, C.18.139, C.18.148, C.18.159, C.18.161, C.18.167, C.18.214, C.18.246, C.18.260, C.18.264, C.18.268, C.18.286, C.19.5, C.19.10, C.19.29, C.19.45, C.19.69, C.19.92, C.19.95, C.19.103, C.19.165, C.19.170, C.19.193, C.19.194, C.19.225, C.19.234, C.19.277, C.19.280, C.19.284, C.19.289, C.19.290, C.19.294, C.19.296, C.19.311, C.19.322, C.19.324, C.19.331, C.20.21, C.20.23, C.20.30, C.20.31, C.20.56, C.20.71, C.20.79, C.20.90, C.20.135, C.20.139, C.20.142, C.20.148, C.20.156, C.20.186, C.20.187, C.20.189, C.20.192, C.20.194, C.20.197, C.20.199, C.20.205, C.20.237, C.20.242, C.20.243, C.20.244, C.20.247, C.20.251, C.20.280, C.20.286, C.20.303, C.20.307, C.20.336, C.20.350, C.20.355, C.20.358, C.20.363, C.20.374, C.20.382, C.20.387, C.20.427, C.20.432, C.20.461, C.20.468, C.21.6, C.21.17, C.21.27, C.21.52, C.21.63, C.21.64, C.21.66, C.21.120, C.21.121, C.21.129, C.21.143, C.21.146, C.21.150, C.21.155, C.21.161, C.21.186, C.21.228, C.21.253, C.21.254, C.21.293, C.21.300, C.21.306, C.21.310, C.21.342, C.21.348, C.21.357, C.21.363, C.21.374, C.21.420, C.21.427, C.21.441, C.21.477, C.22.19, C.22.22, C.22.43, C.22.46, C.22.52, C.22.76, C.22.78, C.22.141, C.22.173, C.22.176, C.22.178, C.22.194, C.22.233, C.22.250, C.22.254, C.22.271, C.22.276, C.22.308, C.22.323, C.22.351, C.22.383

thauh > þouȝ

þe art def *the def.art.* *&> thee,þow* A 798 the (4) þe (794); B 2147 the (187) þe (1960); C 2079 the (658) þe (1421)

A.Pr.1, A.Pr.9, A.Pr.13, A.Pr.13, A.Pr.18, A.Pr.18, A.Pr.19, A.Pr.31, A.Pr.42, A.Pr.55, A.Pr.56, A.Pr.57, A.Pr.64, A.Pr.75, A.Pr.76, A.Pr.77, A.Pr.77, A.Pr.78, A.Pr.78, A.Pr.78, A.Pr.79, A.Pr.79, A.Pr.81, A.Pr.85, A.Pr.86, A.Pr.91, A.Pr.93, A.Pr.95, A.Pr.95, A.Pr.103, A.Pr.106, A.Pr.108, A.Pr.108, A.Pr.108, A.1.1, A.1.1, A.1.2, A.1.6, A.1.7, A.1.12, A.1.12, A.1.17, A.1.26, A.1.28, A.1.29, A.1.32, A.1.34, A.1.34, A.1.35, A.1.35, A.1.37, A.1.38, A.1.40, A.1.42, A.1.44, A.1.45, A.1.45, A.1.46, A.1.47, A.1.48, A.1.57, A.1.57, A.1.59, A.1.71, A.1.83, A.1.84, A.1.87, A.1.88, A.1.90, A.1.95, A.1.98, A.1.100, A.1.105, A.1.107, A.1.107, A.1.110, A.1.119, A.1.124, A.1.126, A.1.136, A.1.137, A.1.140, A.1.149, A.1.149, A.1.151, A.1.155, A.1.159, A.1.161, A.1.173, A.1.174, A.1.174, A.1.176, A.1.177, A.1.178, A.1.179, A.1.181, A.2.3, A.2.3, A.2.4, A.2.9, A.2.10, A.2.12, A.2.16, A.2.18, A.2.22, A.2.26, A.2.28, A.2.28, A.2.33, A.2.34, A.2.35, A.2.38, A.2.41, A.2.46, A.2.48, A.2.55, A.2.56, A.2.60, A.2.61, A.2.62, A.2.63, A.2.63, A.2.65, A.2.65, A.2.66, A.2.68, A.2.68, A.2.72, A.2.73, A.2.74, A.2.75, A.2.76, A.2.77, A.2.77, A.2.77, A.2.86, A.2.86, A.2.87, A.2.91, A.2.91, A.2.97, A.2.101, A.2.102, A.2.105, A.2.110, A.2.113, A.2.115, A.2.123, A.2.127, A.2.133, A.2.137, A.2.141, A.2.146, A.2.147, A.2.152, A.2.153, A.2.154, A.2.157, A.2.158, A.2.159, A.2.160, A.2.168, A.2.169, A.2.170, A.2.172, A.2.176, A.2.196, A.3.1, A.3.2, A.3.3, A.3.4, A.3.8, A.3.9, A.3.9, A.3.10, A.3.13, A.3.14, A.3.14, A.3.17, A.3.23, A.3.25, A.3.28, A.3.31, A.3.35, A.3.48, A.3.50, A.3.66, A.3.66, A.3.66, A.3.70, A.3.71, A.3.73, A.3.76, A.3.76, A.3.82, A.3.83, A.3.87, A.3.88, A.3.88, A.3.90, A.3.93, A.3.94, A.3.97, A.3.104, A.3.105, A.3.109, A.3.121, A.3.127, A.3.128, A.3.129, A.3.129, A.3.132, A.3.136, A.3.137, A.3.142, A.3.142, A.3.146, A.3.146, A.3.149, A.3.153, A.3.157, A.3.159, A.3.162, A.3.163, A.3.173, A.3.175, A.3.186, A.3.192, A.3.195, A.3.202, A.3.204, A.3.208, A.3.210, A.3.215, A.3.216, A.3.217, A.3.217, A.3.221, A.3.221, A.3.227, A.3.230, A.3.239, A.3.248, A.3.251, A.3.253, A.3.253, A.3.256, A.3.258, A.4.1, A.4.3, A.4.6, A.4.9, A.4.12, A.4.12, A.4.12, A.4.13, A.4.15, A.4.20, A.4.27, A.4.30, A.4.31, A.4.34, A.4.48, A.4.51, A.4.66, A.4.66, A.4.69, A.4.70, A.4.74, A.4.77, A.4.78, A.4.80, A.4.85, A.4.91, A.4.94, A.4.95, A.4.98, A.4.116, A.4.117, A.4.118, A.4.126, A.4.135, A.4.144, A.4.148, A.4.148, A.4.151, A.4.157, A.5.1, A.5.1, A.5.2, A.5.10, A.5.12, A.5.14, A.5.16, A.5.17, A.5.18, A.5.35, A.5.36, A.5.38, A.5.45, A.5.56, A.5.57, A.5.60, A.5.63, A.5.64, A.5.85, A.5.85, A.5.86, A.5.86, A.5.87, A.5.90, A.5.92, A.5.94, A.5.115, A.5.119, A.5.121, A.5.124, A.5.124, A.5.125, A.5.130, A.5.131, A.5.136, A.5.136, A.5.140, A.5.145, A.5.148, A.5.158, A.5.158, A.5.159, A.5.160, A.5.161, A.5.161, A.5.162, A.5.162, A.5.163, A.5.165, A.5.166, A.5.168, A.5.169, A.5.170, A.5.171, A.5.173, A.5.173, A.5.175, A.5.178, A.5.180, A.5.180, A.5.181, A.5.182, A.5.185, A.5.190, A.5.190, A.5.197, A.5.198, A.5.198, A.5.199, A.5.199, A.5.204, A.5.204, A.5.210, A.5.214, A.5.218, A.5.223, A.5.226, A.5.231, A.5.231, A.5.231, A.5.233, A.5.235, A.5.236, A.6.1, A.6.11, A.6.14, A.6.21, A.6.22, A.6.38, A.6.43, A.6.44, A.6.46, A.6.47, A.6.49, A.6.50, A.6.56, A.6.58, A.6.60, A.6.72, A.6.73, A.6.73, A.6.74, A.6.75, A.6.77, A.6.79, A.6.79, A.6.80, A.6.82, A.6.84, A.6.85, A.6.85, A.6.89, A.6.89, A.6.91, A.6.91, A.6.91, A.6.98, A.6.99, A.6.105, A.6.105, A.6.109, A.6.114, A.6.119, A.6.122, A.7.3, A.7.3, A.7.4, A.7.8, A.7.9, A.7.9, A.7.14, A.7.14, A.7.16, A.7.17, A.7.21, A.7.23, A.7.24, A.7.25, A.7.33, A.7.35, A.7.37, A.7.44, A.7.49, A.7.50, A.7.53, A.7.60, A.7.61, A.7.64, A.7.64, A.7.65, A.7.80, A.7.83, A.7.84, A.7.92, A.7.92, A.7.92, A.7.94, A.7.95, A.7.96, A.7.97, A.7.97, A.7.99, A.7.103, A.7.104, A.7.107, A.7.108, A.7.109, A.7.110, A.7.112, A.7.122, A.7.129, A.7.134, A.7.135, A.7.136, A.7.138, A.7.140, A.7.146, A.7.146, A.7.149, A.7.151, A.7.151, A.7.153, A.7.153, A.7.156, A.7.157, A.7.159, A.7.160, A.7.161, A.7.161, A.7.167, A.7.168, A.7.169, A.7.169, A.7.178, A.7.196, A.7.202, A.7.207, A.7.210, A.7.211, A.7.213, A.7.215, A.7.216, A.7.219, A.7.219, A.7.222, A.7.234, A.7.234, A.7.240, A.7.254, A.7.272, A.7.276, A.7.284, A.7.290, A.7.290, A.7.297, A.7.298, A.7.298, A.7.301, A.8.2, A.8.8, A.8.10, A.8.16, A.8.18, A.8.19, A.8.20, A.8.21, A.8.27, A.8.39, A.8.41, A.8.46, A.8.49, A.8.54, A.8.55, A.8.56, A.8.62, A.8.66, A.8.67, A.8.68, A.8.70, A.8.70, A.8.71, A.8.80, A.8.86, A.8.91, A.8.92, A.8.97, A.8.108, A.8.109, A.8.110, A.8.112, A.8.115, A.8.115, A.8.116, A.8.118, A.8.120, A.8.124, A.8.126, A.8.128, A.8.132, A.8.135, A.8.136, A.8.142, A.8.143, A.8.143, A.8.144, A.8.151, A.8.152, A.8.155, A.8.156, A.8.157, A.8.158, A.8.164, A.8.167, A.8.167, A.8.169, A.8.170, A.8.171, A.8.174, A.8.175, A.8.176, A.8.176, A.8.184, A.9.9, A.9.14, A.9.17, A.9.17, A.9.21, A.9.22, A.9.23, A.9.23, A.9.24, A.9.26, A.9.26, A.9.26, A.9.26, A.9.27, A.9.28, A.9.30, A.9.30, A.9.31, A.9.31, A.9.31, A.9.32, A.9.33, A.9.34, A.9.34, A.9.35, A.9.35, A.9.37, A.9.37, A.9.38, A.9.38, A.9.38, A.9.39, A.9.39, A.9.41, A.9.43, A.9.45, A.9.47, A.9.50, A.9.51, A.9.55, A.9.57, A.9.58, A.9.59, A.9.69, A.9.79, A.9.79, A.9.80, A.9.82, A.9.83, A.9.84, A.9.88, A.9.94, A.9.97, A.9.99, A.10.10, A.10.14, A.10.16, A.10.16, A.10.19, A.10.22, A.10.28, A.10.29, A.10.30, A.10.33, A.10.38, A.10.41, A.10.44, A.10.45, A.10.47, A.10.48, A.10.48, A.10.49, A.10.49, A.10.53, A.10.59, A.10.62, A.10.64, A.10.66, A.10.66, A.10.75, A.10.77, A.10.82, A.10.85, A.10.86, A.10.86, A.10.95, A.10.100, A.10.104, A.10.109, A.10.117, A.10.122, A.10.122, A.10.126, A.10.133, A.10.134, A.10.134, A.10.141, A.10.142, A.10.149, A.10.170, A.10.171, A.10.175, A.10.176, A.10.180, A.10.185, A.10.191, A.10.192, A.10.194, A.10.195, A.10.213, A.10.214, A.11.12, A.11.16, A.11.20, A.11.22, A.11.23, A.11.25, A.11.26, A.11.27, A.11.30, A.11.34, A.11.40, A.11.40, A.11.42, A.11.43, A.11.44, A.11.45, A.11.45, A.11.50, A.11.53, A.11.55, A.11.59, A.11.62, A.11.64, A.11.67, A.11.67, A.11.69, A.11.72, A.11.77, A.11.80, A.11.84, A.11.90, A.11.96, A.11.107, A.11.111, A.11.112, A.11.114, A.11.118, A.11.126, A.11.128, A.11.129, A.11.130, A.11.138, A.11.138, A.11.139, A.11.139, A.11.141, A.11.142, A.11.150, A.11.154, A.11.158, A.11.161, A.11.170, A.11.170, A.11.172, A.11.182, A.11.189, A.11.190, A.11.192, A.11.193, A.11.193, A.11.194, A.11.196, A.11.204, A.11.205, A.11.206, A.11.207, A.11.207, A.11.208, A.11.216, A.11.217, A.11.222, A.11.233, A.11.241, A.11.254, A.11.256, A.11.258, A.11.262, A.11.263, A.11.265, A.11.278, A.11.281, A.11.282, A.11.283, A.11.287, A.11.289, A.11.298, A.11.301, A.11.301, A.11.302, A.11.302, A.11.303, A.11.303, A.11.307, A.11.312, A.11.313, A.12.3, A.12.4, A.12.15, A.12.18, A.12.25, A.12.26, A.12.34, A.12.36, A.12.38, A.12.40, A.12.52, A.12.57, A.12.59, A.12.69, A.12.72, A.12.73, A.12.82, A.12.97, A.12.99, A.12.102, A.12.104, A.12.117

B.Pr.1, B.Pr.9, B.Pr.13, B.Pr.13, B.Pr.18, B.Pr.18, B.Pr.19, B.Pr.31, B.Pr.42, B.Pr.58, B.Pr.59, B.Pr.59, B.Pr.60, B.Pr.67, B.Pr.78, B.Pr.79, B.Pr.80, B.Pr.80, B.Pr.81, B.Pr.81, B.Pr.81, B.Pr.82, B.Pr.82, B.Pr.83, B.Pr.84, B.Pr.90, B.Pr.92, B.Pr.98, B.Pr.100, B.Pr.101, B.Pr.107, B.Pr.109, B.Pr.110, B.Pr.113, B.Pr.115, B.Pr.115, B.Pr.116, B.Pr.117, B.Pr.118, B.Pr.119, B.Pr.121, B.Pr.121, B.Pr.121, B.Pr.124, B.Pr.128, B.Pr.131, B.Pr.140, B.Pr.143, B.Pr.144, B.Pr.148, B.Pr.155, B.Pr.160, B.Pr.170, B.Pr.173, B.Pr.175, B.Pr.176, B.Pr.176, B.Pr.177, B.Pr.177, B.Pr.178, B.Pr.178, B.Pr.184, B.Pr.185, B.Pr.187, B.Pr.187, B.Pr.188, B.Pr.189, B.Pr.192, B.Pr.194, B.Pr.194, B.Pr.200, B.Pr.200, B.Pr.202, B.Pr.203, B.Pr.203, B.Pr.212, B.Pr.213, B.Pr.225, B.Pr.228, B.Pr.230, B.Pr.230, B.Pr.230, B.1.1, B.1.1, B.1.2, B.1.4, B.1.6, B.1.7, B.1.12, B.1.12, B.1.17, B.1.26, B.1.28, B.1.29, B.1.34, B.1.36, B.1.36, B.1.37, B.1.37, B.1.39, B.1.40, B.1.42, B.1.44, B.1.46, B.1.47, B.1.47, B.1.48, B.1.49, B.1.50, B.1.59, B.1.59, B.1.61, B.1.73, B.1.85, B.1.86, B.1.89, B.1.90, B.1.92, B.1.97, B.1.100, B.1.102, B.1.107, B.1.109, B.1.109, B.1.112, B.1.122, B.1.131, B.1.135, B.1.137, B.1.151, B.1.152, B.1.154, B.1.157, B.1.159, B.1.160, B.1.160, B.1.160, B.1.161, B.1.162, B.1.164, B.1.164, B.1.164, B.1.166, B.1.175, B.1.175, B.1.177, B.1.181, B.1.185, B.1.187, B.1.198, B.1.199, B.1.200, B.1.202, B.1.203, B.1.205, B.1.207, B.2.3, B.2.3, B.2.4, B.2.7, B.2.9, B.2.10, B.2.20, B.2.23, B.2.29, B.2.33, B.2.36, B.2.38, B.2.44, B.2.46, B.2.46, B.2.54, B.2.55, B.2.56, B.2.56, B.2.61, B.2.62, B.2.65, B.2.73, B.2.74, B.2.83, B.2.84, B.2.85, B.2.86, B.2.86, B.2.88, B.2.89, B.2.103, B.2.104, B.2.104, B.2.108, B.2.109, B.2.110, B.2.111, B.2.112, B.2.113, B.2.113, B.2.113, B.2.122, B.2.122, B.2.127, B.2.127, B.2.133, B.2.137, B.2.138, B.2.141, B.2.146, B.2.149, B.2.151, B.2.163, B.2.180, B.2.185, B.2.186, B.2.191, B.2.192, B.2.193, B.2.196, B.2.197, B.2.198, B.2.199, B.2.207, B.2.208, B.2.209, B.2.211, B.2.213, B.2.217, B.2.237, B.3.1, B.3.2, B.3.3, B.3.4, B.3.8, B.3.9, B.3.9, B.3.10, B.3.13, B.3.14, B.3.14, B.3.17, B.3.24, B.3.26, B.3.29, B.3.32, B.3.36, B.3.49, B.3.51, B.3.54, B.3.57, B.3.57, B.3.58, B.3.62, B.3.66, B.3.68, B.3.75, B.3.77, B.3.77, B.3.77, B.3.81, B.3.82, B.3.84, B.3.87, B.3.87, B.3.93, B.3.94, B.3.98, B.3.99, B.3.99, B.3.101, B.3.104, B.3.105, B.3.108, B.3.115, B.3.116, B.3.120, B.3.132, B.3.138, B.3.139, B.3.140, B.3.140, B.3.143, B.3.147, B.3.148, B.3.153, B.3.153, B.3.156, B.3.156, B.3.160, B.3.164, B.3.166, B.3.170, B.3.172, B.3.175, B.3.176, B.3.186, B.3.188, B.3.199, B.3.205, B.3.208, B.3.215, B.3.217, B.3.221, B.3.223, B.3.228, B.3.229, B.3.230,

B.3.230, B.3.234, B.3.234, B.3.237, B.3.240, B.3.242, B.3.242, B.3.243, B.3.248, B.3.251, B.3.261, B.3.272, B.3.273, B.3.274, B.3.275, B.3.278, B.3.280, B.3.296, B.3.298, B.3.301, B.3.307, B.3.316, B.3.316, B.3.318, B.3.325, B.3.327, B.3.327, B.3.331, B.3.332, B.3.334, B.3.340, B.3.341, B.3.347, B.3.351, B.3.351, B.3.353, B.3.353, B.4.1, B.4.3, B.4.6, B.4.9, B.4.12, B.4.12, B.4.12, B.4.13, B.4.15, B.4.22, B.4.30, B.4.37, B.4.42, B.4.43, B.4.44, B.4.47, B.4.61, B.4.65, B.4.67, B.4.80, B.4.80, B.4.82, B.4.83, B.4.87, B.4.90, B.4.91, B.4.93, B.4.98, B.4.104, B.4.107, B.4.108, B.4.111, B.4.119, B.4.123, B.4.123, B.4.134, B.4.135, B.4.143, B.4.150, B.4.151, B.4.151, B.4.152, B.4.159, B.4.159, B.4.159, B.4.166, B.4.168, B.4.169, B.4.170, B.4.171, B.4.173, B.4.179, B.4.182, B.4.182, B.4.185, B.4.185, B.4.188, B.4.194, B.5.1, B.5.1, B.5.2, B.5.10, B.5.11, B.5.12, B.5.14, B.5.16, B.5.17, B.5.18, B.5.23, B.5.38, B.5.38, B.5.39, B.5.40, B.5.42, B.5.44, B.5.46, B.5.48, B.5.50, B.5.54, B.5.62, B.5.73, B.5.74, B.5.77, B.5.80, B.5.81, B.5.105, B.5.105, B.5.106, B.5.106, B.5.107, B.5.110, B.5.112, B.5.114, B.5.136, B.5.138, B.5.147, B.5.155, B.5.157, B.5.164, B.5.174, B.5.175, B.5.180, B.5.181, B.5.203, B.5.205, B.5.208, B.5.208, B.5.209, B.5.214, B.5.215, B.5.220, B.5.220, B.5.224, B.5.229, B.5.236, B.5.240, B.5.241, B.5.260, B.5.263, B.5.268, B.5.268, B.5.272, B.5.275, B.5.276, B.5.279, B.5.280, B.5.282, B.5.283, B.5.283, B.5.287, B.5.290, B.5.292, B.5.298, B.5.307, B.5.307, B.5.308, B.5.309, B.5.310, B.5.310, B.5.311, B.5.311, B.5.313, B.5.315, B.5.316, B.5.317, B.5.319, B.5.320, B.5.321, B.5.322, B.5.324, B.5.324, B.5.326, B.5.329, B.5.331, B.5.331, B.5.332, B.5.333, B.5.336, B.5.342, B.5.342, B.5.349, B.5.350, B.5.350, B.5.351, B.5.351, B.5.353, B.5.357, B.5.357, B.5.362, B.5.362, B.5.367, B.5.376, B.5.382, B.5.391, B.5.394, B.5.396, B.5.397, B.5.398, B.5.403, B.5.411, B.5.432, B.5.433, B.5.442, B.5.446, B.5.451, B.5.454, B.5.459, B.5.459, B.5.459, B.5.461, B.5.463, B.5.464, B.5.480, B.5.483, B.5.483, B.5.488, B.5.490, B.5.491, B.5.494, B.5.495, B.5.496, B.5.501, B.5.513, B.5.523, B.5.526, B.5.533, B.5.534, B.5.551, B.5.557, B.5.559, B.5.560, B.5.562, B.5.569, B.5.571, B.5.573, B.5.585, B.5.586, B.5.586, B.5.587, B.5.588, B.5.590, B.5.592, B.5.592, B.5.594, B.5.594, B.5.595, B.5.597, B.5.598, B.5.598, B.5.602, B.5.602, B.5.604, B.5.604, B.5.604, B.5.612, B.5.613, B.5.619, B.5.619, B.5.623, B.5.624, B.5.629, B.5.634, B.5.637, B.6.3, B.6.4, B.6.6, B.6.8, B.6.9, B.6.9, B.6.15, B.6.15, B.6.17, B.6.18, B.6.19, B.6.21, B.6.22, B.6.23, B.6.33, B.6.45, B.6.54, B.6.55, B.6.58, B.6.70, B.6.70, B.6.71, B.6.71, B.6.73, B.6.88, B.6.91, B.6.92, B.6.100, B.6.100, B.6.100, B.6.103, B.6.104, B.6.105, B.6.105, B.6.107, B.6.111, B.6.112, B.6.116, B.6.117, B.6.118, B.6.120, B.6.130, B.6.135, B.6.140, B.6.140, B.6.140, B.6.149, B.6.153, B.6.159, B.6.159, B.6.161, B.6.163, B.6.163, B.6.164, B.6.166, B.6.166, B.6.168, B.6.168, B.6.171, B.6.172, B.6.174, B.6.175, B.6.176, B.6.176, B.6.210, B.6.216, B.6.221, B.6.224, B.6.225, B.6.227, B.6.229, B.6.231, B.6.232, B.6.235, B.6.235, B.6.250, B.6.250, B.6.251, B.6.252, B.6.270, B.6.288, B.6.292, B.6.300, B.6.306, B.6.306, B.6.313, B.6.317, B.6.317, B.6.320, B.6.327, B.6.328, B.6.330, B.7.2, B.7.10, B.7.14, B.7.16, B.7.17, B.7.18, B.7.19, B.7.25, B.7.39, B.7.41, B.7.46, B.7.47, B.7.52, B.7.53, B.7.54, B.7.57, B.7.64, B.7.65, B.7.66, B.7.68, B.7.68, B.7.69, B.7.71, B.7.72, B.7.74, B.7.79, B.7.85, B.7.89, B.7.98, B.7.104, B.7.109, B.7.110, B.7.115, B.7.118, B.7.126, B.7.127, B.7.130, B.7.131, B.7.133, B.7.133, B.7.134, B.7.136, B.7.138, B.7.142, B.7.144, B.7.146, B.7.151, B.7.152, B.7.153, B.7.157, B.7.158, B.7.164, B.7.165, B.7.165, B.7.166, B.7.174, B.7.177, B.7.178, B.7.179, B.7.180, B.7.186, B.7.189, B.7.189, B.7.191, B.7.192, B.7.193, B.7.196, B.7.198, B.7.198, B.7.206, B.8.9, B.8.18, B.8.21, B.8.21, B.8.25, B.8.26, B.8.27, B.8.27, B.8.28, B.8.30, B.8.30, B.8.30, B.8.30, B.8.31, B.8.32, B.8.34, B.8.34, B.8.35, B.8.35, B.8.35, B.8.36, B.8.37, B.8.38, B.8.38, B.8.39, B.8.39, B.8.41, B.8.41, B.8.42, B.8.42, B.8.42, B.8.43, B.8.45, B.8.47, B.8.49, B.8.59, B.8.60, B.8.64, B.8.66, B.8.68, B.8.78, B.8.88, B.8.88, B.8.89, B.8.91, B.8.92, B.8.94, B.8.98, B.8.104, B.8.107, B.8.109, B.8.114, B.9.10, B.9.17, B.9.17, B.9.20, B.9.27, B.9.28, B.9.32, B.9.41, B.9.41, B.9.42, B.9.47, B.9.50, B.9.53, B.9.55, B.9.57, B.9.58, B.9.58, B.9.60, B.9.60, B.9.64, B.9.75, B.9.80, B.9.80, B.9.81, B.9.82, B.9.85, B.9.91, B.9.94, B.9.98, B.9.101, B.9.105, B.9.111, B.9.115, B.9.115, B.9.117, B.9.117, B.9.120, B.9.120, B.9.124, B.9.125, B.9.130, B.9.139, B.9.140, B.9.143, B.9.145, B.9.146, B.9.146, B.9.147, B.9.148, B.9.150, B.9.151, B.9.151, B.9.154, B.9.155, B.9.157, B.9.162, B.9.170, B.9.171, B.9.173, B.9.174, B.9.197, B.9.199, B.9.200, B.10.12, B.10.16, B.10.20, B.10.23, B.10.24, B.10.26, B.10.26, B.10.29, B.10.33, B.10.34, B.10.35, B.10.40, B.10.45, B.10.48, B.10.54, B.10.54, B.10.56, B.10.57, B.10.58, B.10.59, B.10.59, B.10.64, B.10.67, B.10.69, B.10.73, B.10.75, B.10.77, B.10.81, B.10.82, B.10.83, B.10.85, B.10.85, B.10.86, B.10.87, B.10.89, B.10.97, B.10.97, B.10.98, B.10.98, B.10.101, B.10.104, B.10.106, B.10.109, B.10.109, B.10.111, B.10.113, B.10.115, B.10.124, B.10.127, B.10.131, B.10.137, B.10.143, B.10.155, B.10.159, B.10.160, B.10.162, B.10.166, B.10.174, B.10.175, B.10.176, B.10.177, B.10.178, B.10.186, B.10.186, B.10.187, B.10.187, B.10.189, B.10.190, B.10.197, B.10.201, B.10.205, B.10.211, B.10.215, B.10.218, B.10.227, B.10.227, B.10.229, B.10.239, B.10.239, B.10.241, B.10.242, B.10.243, B.10.243, B.10.244, B.10.244, B.10.244, B.10.247, B.10.247, B.10.249, B.10.251, B.10.252, B.10.253, B.10.255, B.10.258, B.10.264, B.10.267, B.10.278, B.10.279, B.10.281, B.10.282, B.10.283, B.10.285, B.10.285, B.10.286, B.10.290, B.10.298, B.10.298, B.10.299, B.10.301, B.10.301, B.10.320, B.10.323, B.10.329, B.10.331, B.10.332, B.10.333, B.10.346, B.10.350, B.10.355, B.10.358, B.10.360, B.10.364, B.10.365, B.10.373, B.10.375, B.10.377, B.10.381, B.10.384, B.10.386, B.10.399, B.10.402, B.10.408, B.10.411, B.10.414, B.10.415, B.10.417, B.10.418, B.10.423, B.10.424, B.10.430, B.10.438, B.10.438, B.10.441, B.10.451, B.10.456, B.10.457, B.10.458, B.10.458, B.10.459, B.10.459, B.10.463, B.10.468, B.10.470, B.10.472, B.10.477, B.10.481, B.10.481, B.11.8, B.11.13, B.11.17, B.11.22, B.11.22, B.11.26, B.11.36, B.11.49, B.11.63, B.11.69, B.11.73, B.11.81, B.11.84, B.11.89, B.11.92, B.11.94, B.11.94, B.11.96, B.11.100, B.11.101, B.11.103, B.11.103, B.11.108, B.11.109, B.11.110, B.11.112, B.11.113, B.11.113, B.11.113, B.11.114, B.11.120, B.11.124, B.11.131, B.11.134, B.11.143, B.11.144, B.11.159, B.11.161, B.11.165, B.11.168, B.11.170, B.11.172, B.11.173, B.11.175, B.11.175, B.11.180, B.11.189, B.11.189, B.11.190, B.11.192, B.11.192, B.11.192, B.11.195,

B.11.198, B.11.205, B.11.205, B.11.229, B.11.232, B.11.234, B.11.237, B.11.243, B.11.245, B.11.254, B.11.256, B.11.261, B.11.266, B.11.267, B.11.270, B.11.277, B.11.277, B.11.280, B.11.286, B.11.290, B.11.293, B.11.298, B.11.304, B.11.306, B.11.310, B.11.312, B.11.314, B.11.315, B.11.315, B.11.319, B.11.323, B.11.327, B.11.327, B.11.327, B.11.346, B.11.347, B.11.348, B.11.357, B.11.358, B.11.363, B.11.363, B.11.365, B.11.366, B.11.394, B.11.394, B.11.394, B.11.397, B.11.397, B.11.401, B.11.401, B.11.419, B.11.419, B.11.434, B.12.13, B.12.24, B.12.26, B.12.40, B.12.42, B.12.48, B.12.50, B.12.52, B.12.57, B.12.58, B.12.61, B.12.63, B.12.63, B.12.63, B.12.65, B.12.69, B.12.72, B.12.73, B.12.73, B.12.73, B.12.78, B.12.80, B.12.81, B.12.86, B.12.86, B.12.89, B.12.89, B.12.91, B.12.91, B.12.91, B.12.101, B.12.102, B.12.103, B.12.109, B.12.109, B.12.110, B.12.113, B.12.131, B.12.138, B.12.139, B.12.144, B.12.147, B.12.148, B.12.166, B.12.167, B.12.170, B.12.174, B.12.175, B.12.176, B.12.179, B.12.180, B.12.186, B.12.187, B.12.192, B.12.198, B.12.200, B.12.200, B.12.200, B.12.201, B.12.205, B.12.210, B.12.211, B.12.212, B.12.213, B.12.214, B.12.216, B.12.216, B.12.217, B.12.221, B.12.221, B.12.223, B.12.223, B.12.225, B.12.226, B.12.227, B.12.228, B.12.229, B.12.233, B.12.238, B.12.240, B.12.240, B.12.244, B.12.247, B.12.248, B.12.249, B.12.249, B.12.252, B.12.252, B.12.257, B.12.258, B.12.259, B.12.262, B.12.262, B.12.263, B.12.264, B.12.265, B.12.267, B.12.268, B.12.269, B.12.270, B.12.274, B.12.284, B.12.291, B.12.294, B.13.21, B.13.24, B.13.28, B.13.29, B.13.33, B.13.39, B.13.61, B.13.65, B.13.66, B.13.69, B.13.76, B.13.96, B.13.107, B.13.121, B.13.124, B.13.130, B.13.142, B.13.153, B.13.153, B.13.154, B.13.154, B.13.154, B.13.155, B.13.155, B.13.155, B.13.169, B.13.173, B.13.174, B.13.176, B.13.185, B.13.186, B.13.187, B.13.190, B.13.190, B.13.190, B.13.192, B.13.192, B.13.196, B.13.198, B.13.203, B.13.209, B.13.210, B.13.220, B.13.233, B.13.235, B.13.236, B.13.236, B.13.237, B.13.239, B.13.243, B.13.245, B.13.248, B.13.250, B.13.254, B.13.254, B.13.254, B.13.256, B.13.256, B.13.261, B.13.268, B.13.272, B.13.277, B.13.282, B.13.291, B.13.292, B.13.312, B.13.316, B.13.333, B.13.334, B.13.334, B.13.339, B.13.346, B.13.347, B.13.356, B.13.359, B.13.362, B.13.366, B.13.369, B.13.370, B.13.375, B.13.394, B.13.398, B.13.407, B.13.408, B.13.409, B.13.411, B.13.413, B.13.418, B.13.420, B.13.429, B.13.432, B.13.439, B.13.443, B.13.446, B.13.452, B.13.457, B.14.1, B.14.6, B.14.7, B.14.9, B.14.26, B.14.28, B.14.30, B.14.41, B.14.42, B.14.42, B.14.42, B.14.43, B.14.43, B.14.45, B.14.49, B.14.60, B.14.60, B.14.65, B.14.65, B.14.69, B.14.70, B.14.76, B.14.76, B.14.79, B.14.81, B.14.87, B.14.94, B.14.95, B.14.101, B.14.105, B.14.108, B.14.109, B.14.110, B.14.131, B.14.133, B.14.137, B.14.143, B.14.145, B.14.147, B.14.169, B.14.174, B.14.178, B.14.184, B.14.189, B.14.190, B.14.190, B.14.191, B.14.192, B.14.194, B.14.200, B.14.200, B.14.203, B.14.207, B.14.208, B.14.211, B.14.212, B.14.213, B.14.217, B.14.217, B.14.219, B.14.221, B.14.221, B.14.225, B.14.225, B.14.226, B.14.226, B.14.227, B.14.230, B.14.234, B.14.239, B.14.240, B.14.244, B.14.244, B.14.245, B.14.252, B.14.258, B.14.273, B.14.280, B.14.283, B.14.284, B.14.288, B.14.292, B.14.297, B.14.297, B.14.299, B.14.301, B.14.303, B.14.304, B.14.304, B.14.307, B.14.307, B.14.310, B.14.312, B.14.313, B.14.316, B.14.316, B.14.323, B.14.327, B.15.14, B.15.18, B.15.18, B.15.19, B.15.23, B.15.23, B.15.30, B.15.35, B.15.35, B.15.45, B.15.48, B.15.48, B.15.57, B.15.58, B.15.64, B.15.65, B.15.67, B.15.70, B.15.71, B.15.72, B.15.74, B.15.74, B.15.75, B.15.79, B.15.79, B.15.81, B.15.81, B.15.82, B.15.82, B.15.98, B.15.100, B.15.100, B.15.100, B.15.101, B.15.101, B.15.103, B.15.130, B.15.131, B.15.138, B.15.141, B.15.145, B.15.181, B.15.187, B.15.189, B.15.199, B.15.200, B.15.203, B.15.208, B.15.212, B.15.217, B.15.218, B.15.235, B.15.236, B.15.237, B.15.239, B.15.239, B.15.246, B.15.247, B.15.255, B.15.269, B.15.280, B.15.280, B.15.282, B.15.285, B.15.300, B.15.303, B.15.326, B.15.343, B.15.345, B.15.347, B.15.347, B.15.348, B.15.350, B.15.350, B.15.352, B.15.353, B.15.358, B.15.358, B.15.362, B.15.364, B.15.365, B.15.366, B.15.367, B.15.367, B.15.371, B.15.371, B.15.372, B.15.392, B.15.402, B.15.403, B.15.404, B.15.404, B.15.407, B.15.412, B.15.414, B.15.419, B.15.422, B.15.426, B.15.430, B.15.435, B.15.438, B.15.439, B.15.445, B.15.448, B.15.452, B.15.457, B.15.458, B.15.465, B.15.466, B.15.467, B.15.467, B.15.470, B.15.472, B.15.481, B.15.481, B.15.481, B.15.488, B.15.493, B.15.496, B.15.502, B.15.503, B.15.508, B.15.509, B.15.511, B.15.517, B.15.520, B.15.525, B.15.528, B.15.530, B.15.537, B.15.539, B.15.540, B.15.540, B.15.543, B.15.547, B.15.549, B.15.553, B.15.555, B.15.563, B.15.568, B.15.572, B.15.579, B.15.580, B.15.586, B.15.595, B.15.606, B.15.607, B.15.607, B.15.608, B.16.2, B.16.5, B.16.5, B.16.6, B.16.6, B.16.7, B.16.8, B.16.9, B.16.14, B.16.15, B.16.16, B.16.17, B.16.18, B.16.20, B.16.21, B.16.21, B.16.22, B.16.26, B.16.27, B.16.28, B.16.29, B.16.30, B.16.31, B.16.35, B.16.35, B.16.36, B.16.36, B.16.37, B.16.37, B.16.40, B.16.41, B.16.41, B.16.42, B.16.44, B.16.48, B.16.48, B.16.48, B.16.50, B.16.51, B.16.52, B.16.52, B.16.54, B.16.62, B.16.63, B.16.63, B.16.66, B.16.69, B.16.70, B.16.75, B.16.79, B.16.81, B.16.82, B.16.85, B.16.88, B.16.89, B.16.96, B.16.96, B.16.97, B.16.97, B.16.100, B.16.102, B.16.103, B.16.108, B.16.111, B.16.115, B.16.117, B.16.120, B.16.127, B.16.136, B.16.140, B.16.141, B.16.142, B.16.146, B.16.152, B.16.153, B.16.157, B.16.162, B.16.164, B.16.165, B.16.168, B.16.171, B.16.184, B.16.186, B.16.188, B.16.188, B.16.189, B.16.197, B.16.198, B.16.204, B.16.206, B.16.210, B.16.211, B.16.213, B.16.214, B.16.214, B.16.223, B.16.223, B.16.224, B.16.232, B.16.237, B.16.246, B.16.261, B.16.264, B.16.266, B.16.271, B.16.273, B.17.2, B.17.3, B.17.4, B.17.5, B.17.7, B.17.10, B.17.14, B.17.15, B.17.28, B.17.32, B.17.34, B.17.35, B.17.36, B.17.39, B.17.41, B.17.43, B.17.50, B.17.52, B.17.55, B.17.65, B.17.66, B.17.68, B.17.70, B.17.75, B.17.76, B.17.77, B.17.82, B.17.92, B.17.94, B.17.96, B.17.100, B.17.105, B.17.116, B.17.117, B.17.118, B.17.118, B.17.125, B.17.141, B.17.144, B.17.144, B.17.144, B.17.144, B.17.147, B.17.147, B.17.148, B.17.149, B.17.150, B.17.152, B.17.153, B.17.156, B.17.156, B.17.159, B.17.160, B.17.161, B.17.161, B.17.161, B.17.162, B.17.163, B.17.170, B.17.171, B.17.172, B.17.173, B.17.174, B.17.174, B.17.174, B.17.175, B.17.176, B.17.176, B.17.177, B.17.178, B.17.178, B.17.179, B.17.180, B.17.181, B.17.181, B.17.182, B.17.183, B.17.183, B.17.183, B.17.187, B.17.187, B.17.189, B.17.189, B.17.190, B.17.192, B.17.195,

B.17.199, B.17.201, B.17.202, B.17.202, B.17.203, B.17.203, B.17.204, B.17.206, B.17.212, B.17.212, B.17.216, B.17.216, B.17.217, B.17.218, B.17.226, B.17.227, B.17.231, B.17.233, B.17.233, B.17.233, B.17.238, B.17.242, B.17.243, B.17.247, B.17.252, B.17.256, B.17.258, B.17.261, B.17.262, B.17.274, B.17.275, B.17.275, B.17.279, B.17.280, B.17.280, B.17.282, B.17.284, B.17.285, B.17.286, B.17.287, B.17.296, B.17.300, B.17.303, B.17.308, B.17.309, B.17.316, B.17.330, B.17.330, B.17.334, B.17.335, B.17.339, B.17.341, B.17.341, B.17.347, B.17.347, B.17.349, B.18.4, B.18.9, B.18.10, B.18.10, B.18.13, B.18.20, B.18.20, B.18.25, B.18.28, B.18.33, B.18.33, B.18.38, B.18.38, B.18.39, B.18.55, B.18.59, B.18.60, B.18.60, B.18.61, B.18.61, B.18.64, B.18.66, B.18.72, B.18.79, B.18.80, B.18.85, B.18.86, B.18.86, B.18.87, B.18.90, B.18.92, B.18.95, B.18.95, B.18.98, B.18.102, B.18.109, B.18.110, B.18.113, B.18.114, B.18.118, B.18.120, B.18.123, B.18.123, B.18.123, B.18.130, B.18.135, B.18.137, B.18.147, B.18.149, B.18.154, B.18.155, B.18.156, B.18.157, B.18.159, B.18.160, B.18.162, B.18.164, B.18.164, B.18.165, B.18.186, B.18.191, B.18.191, B.18.194, B.18.197, B.18.198, B.18.202, B.18.204, B.18.211, B.18.214, B.18.215, B.18.218, B.18.234, B.18.235, B.18.237, B.18.237, B.18.238, B.18.239, B.18.241, B.18.241, B.18.241, B.18.242, B.18.243, B.18.244, B.18.245, B.18.247, B.18.248, B.18.258, B.18.262, B.18.276, B.18.278, B.18.281, B.18.285, B.18.288, B.18.290, B.18.291, B.18.292, B.18.295, B.18.305, B.18.309, B.18.312, B.18.316, B.18.317, B.18.318, B.18.320, B.18.322, B.18.329, B.18.331, B.18.333, B.18.338, B.18.342, B.18.348, B.18.363, B.18.369, B.18.369, B.18.378, B.18.381, B.18.385, B.18.388, B.18.404, B.18.405, B.18.409, B.18.424, B.18.425, B.18.428, B.18.430, B.18.430, B.19.3, B.19.4, B.19.6, B.19.7, B.19.9, B.19.10, B.19.11, B.19.18, B.19.19, B.19.34, B.19.36, B.19.38, B.19.44, B.19.45, B.19.56, B.19.63, B.19.71, B.19.80, B.19.81, B.19.82, B.19.82, B.19.87, B.19.91, B.19.98, B.19.123, B.19.129, B.19.132, B.19.133, B.19.135, B.19.136, B.19.138, B.19.149, B.19.150, B.19.151, B.19.154, B.19.154, B.19.155, B.19.157, B.19.170, B.19.187, B.19.192, B.19.197, B.19.199, B.19.205, B.19.208, B.19.214, B.19.219, B.19.230, B.19.258, B.19.264, B.19.266, B.19.270, B.19.270, B.19.271, B.19.276, B.19.278, B.19.280, B.19.281, B.19.289, B.19.296, B.19.297, B.19.302, B.19.303, B.19.303, B.19.311, B.19.313, B.19.313, B.19.316, B.19.321, B.19.321, B.19.332, B.19.333, B.19.334, B.19.334, B.19.335, B.19.338, B.19.343, B.19.343, B.19.346, B.19.352, B.19.352, B.19.354, B.19.357, B.19.370, B.19.379, B.19.382, B.19.390, B.19.391, B.19.394, B.19.406, B.19.413, B.19.416, B.19.417, B.19.417, B.19.420, B.19.423, B.19.426, B.19.426, B.19.427, B.19.430, B.19.432, B.19.433, B.19.433, B.19.434, B.19.435, B.19.437, B.19.442, B.19.443, B.19.446, B.19.448, B.19.449, B.19.451, B.19.452, B.19.455, B.19.463, B.19.466, B.19.468, B.19.472, B.19.473, B.19.477, B.19.480, B.20.1, B.20.4, B.20.6, B.20.18, B.20.30, B.20.30, B.20.42, B.20.43, B.20.45, B.20.49, B.20.53, B.20.54, B.20.60, B.20.77, B.20.78, B.20.80, B.20.87, B.20.90, B.20.95, B.20.95, B.20.96, B.20.109, B.20.120, B.20.125, B.20.127, B.20.129, B.20.133, B.20.136, B.20.137, B.20.150, B.20.157, B.20.160, B.20.175, B.20.182, B.20.184, B.20.187, B.20.190, B.20.191, B.20.193, B.20.195, B.20.202, B.20.221, B.20.221, B.20.224, B.20.240, B.20.256, B.20.261, B.20.266, B.20.271, B.20.277, B.20.281, B.20.285, B.20.291, B.20.292, B.20.293, B.20.293, B.20.296, B.20.298, B.20.301, B.20.310, B.20.313, B.20.320, B.20.324, B.20.327, B.20.329, B.20.336, B.20.346, B.20.348, B.20.349, B.20.354, B.20.359, B.20.359, B.20.372, B.20.376, B.20.378, B.20.381, B.20.382, B.20.385

C.Pr.1, C.Pr.4, C.Pr.10, C.Pr.10, C.Pr.10, C.Pr.14, C.Pr.20, C.Pr.20, C.Pr.21, C.Pr.33, C.Pr.43, C.Pr.56, C.Pr.57, C.Pr.57, C.Pr.58, C.Pr.65, C.Pr.76, C.Pr.77, C.Pr.78, C.Pr.78, C.Pr.79, C.Pr.79, C.Pr.79, C.Pr.80, C.Pr.80, C.Pr.81, C.Pr.82, C.Pr.90, C.Pr.95, C.Pr.98, C.Pr.100, C.Pr.104, C.Pr.104, C.Pr.105, C.Pr.111, C.Pr.117, C.Pr.117, C.Pr.126, C.Pr.128, C.Pr.129, C.Pr.134, C.Pr.136, C.Pr.137, C.Pr.142, C.Pr.142, C.Pr.144, C.Pr.145, C.Pr.146, C.Pr.148, C.Pr.148, C.Pr.152, C.Pr.160, C.Pr.162, C.Pr.163, C.Pr.169, C.Pr.175, C.Pr.184, C.Pr.187, C.Pr.190, C.Pr.192, C.Pr.193, C.Pr.193, C.Pr.194, C.Pr.194, C.Pr.195, C.Pr.195, C.Pr.201, C.Pr.202, C.Pr.204, C.Pr.205, C.Pr.207, C.Pr.207, C.Pr.210, C.Pr.211, C.Pr.211, C.Pr.214, C.Pr.218, C.Pr.218, C.Pr.227, C.Pr.229, C.Pr.232, C.Pr.234, C.Pr.234, C.Pr.234, C.1.1, C.1.1, C.1.2, C.1.4, C.1.6, C.1.7, C.1.12, C.1.12, C.1.16, C.1.17, C.1.23, C.1.23, C.1.28, C.1.34, C.1.34, C.1.35, C.1.35, C.1.37, C.1.38, C.1.42, C.1.44, C.1.45, C.1.45, C.1.46, C.1.55, C.1.55, C.1.57, C.1.70, C.1.81, C.1.82, C.1.85, C.1.86, C.1.93, C.1.95, C.1.97, C.1.99, C.1.114, C.1.114, C.1.117, C.1.118, C.1.119, C.1.122, C.1.122, C.1.124, C.1.134, C.1.148, C.1.151, C.1.153, C.1.155, C.1.156, C.1.156, C.1.156, C.1.157, C.1.158, C.1.160, C.1.160, C.1.160, C.1.162, C.1.171, C.1.173, C.1.177, C.1.181, C.1.183, C.1.193, C.1.194, C.1.195, C.1.197, C.1.200, C.1.202, C.2.3, C.2.3, C.2.4, C.2.8, C.2.11, C.2.19, C.2.23, C.2.31, C.2.39, C.2.41, C.2.44, C.2.57, C.2.58, C.2.58, C.2.63, C.2.64, C.2.67, C.2.75, C.2.90, C.2.91, C.2.92, C.2.93, C.2.95, C.2.96, C.2.111, C.2.111, C.2.112, C.2.113, C.2.114, C.2.115, C.2.116, C.2.117, C.2.117, C.2.117, C.2.132, C.2.133, C.2.133, C.2.144, C.2.146, C.2.149, C.2.154, C.2.156, C.2.157, C.2.159, C.2.162, C.2.165, C.2.167, C.2.177, C.2.189, C.2.193, C.2.198, C.2.199, C.2.201, C.2.202, C.2.205, C.2.206, C.2.207, C.2.210, C.2.211, C.2.212, C.2.213, C.2.219, C.2.220, C.2.220, C.2.221, C.2.223, C.2.227, C.2.247, C.2.248, C.2.253, C.3.1, C.3.2, C.3.3, C.3.4, C.3.9, C.3.9, C.3.10, C.3.14, C.3.15, C.3.16, C.3.18, C.3.25, C.3.27, C.3.29, C.3.30, C.3.35, C.3.39, C.3.44, C.3.52, C.3.57, C.3.58, C.3.61, C.3.61, C.3.66, C.3.70, C.3.72, C.3.74, C.3.77, C.3.81, C.3.83, C.3.86, C.3.89, C.3.93, C.3.101, C.3.107, C.3.115, C.3.115, C.3.120, C.3.121, C.3.127, C.3.127, C.3.128, C.3.130, C.3.137, C.3.137, C.3.141, C.3.152, C.3.153, C.3.157, C.3.169, C.3.176, C.3.177, C.3.178, C.3.178, C.3.181, C.3.185, C.3.186, C.3.191, C.3.192, C.3.193, C.3.194, C.3.194, C.3.196, C.3.198, C.3.202, C.3.207, C.3.212, C.3.212, C.3.216, C.3.218, C.3.221, C.3.222, C.3.232, C.3.239, C.3.241, C.3.242, C.3.247, C.3.248, C.3.248, C.3.251, C.3.262, C.3.271, C.3.273, C.3.278, C.3.284, C.3.285, C.3.286, C.3.286, C.3.288, C.3.293, C.3.303, C.3.304, C.3.304, C.3.306, C.3.307, C.3.308, C.3.310, C.3.310, C.3.311, C.3.315, C.3.317, C.3.318, C.3.319, C.3.325, C.3.329, C.3.339, C.3.341, C.3.345, C.3.346, C.3.354, C.3.375, C.3.377, C.3.383, C.3.385, C.3.385, C.3.385, C.3.389, C.3.390, C.3.399, C.3.412, C.3.413, C.3.414, C.3.419, C.3.425, C.3.426, C.3.427, C.3.428, C.3.433, C.3.435, C.3.449, C.3.451, C.3.454, C.3.456, C.3.460, C.3.469, C.3.469, C.3.471, C.3.471, C.3.478, C.3.480, C.3.480, C.3.484, C.3.485, C.3.486, C.3.492, C.3.493, C.3.493, C.3.498, C.4.1, C.4.3, C.4.6, C.4.9, C.4.15, C.4.22, C.4.30, C.4.30, C.4.37, C.4.41, C.4.42, C.4.45, C.4.47, C.4.64, C.4.76, C.4.78, C.4.79, C.4.83, C.4.86, C.4.87, C.4.89, C.4.94, C.4.98, C.4.99, C.4.102, C.4.103, C.4.106, C.4.114, C.4.119, C.4.131, C.4.132, C.4.132, C.4.140, C.4.148, C.4.155, C.4.157, C.4.161, C.4.163, C.4.163, C.4.166, C.4.176, C.4.176, C.4.179, C.4.179, C.4.183, C.4.195, C.5.13, C.5.20, C.5.31, C.5.38, C.5.38, C.5.39, C.5.45, C.5.55, C.5.74, C.5.75, C.5.75, C.5.85, C.5.87, C.5.95, C.5.96, C.5.97, C.5.103, C.5.104, C.5.105, C.5.106, C.5.110, C.5.111, C.5.113, C.5.114, C.5.116, C.5.118, C.5.119, C.5.120, C.5.125, C.5.138, C.5.139, C.5.141, C.5.142, C.5.144, C.5.146, C.5.147, C.5.166, C.5.169, C.5.176, C.5.176, C.5.177, C.5.180, C.5.181, C.5.181, C.5.187, C.5.191, C.6.3, C.6.30, C.6.36, C.6.41, C.6.60, C.6.76, C.6.77, C.6.78, C.6.78, C.6.83, C.6.109, C.6.113, C.6.130, C.6.132, C.6.136, C.6.136, C.6.144, C.6.145, C.6.149, C.6.157, C.6.163, C.6.174, C.6.180, C.6.181, C.6.192, C.6.207, C.6.211, C.6.213, C.6.216, C.6.216, C.6.217, C.6.222, C.6.223, C.6.228, C.6.232, C.6.242, C.6.243, C.6.243, C.6.244, C.6.247, C.6.253, C.6.254, C.6.256, C.6.261, C.6.265, C.6.267, C.6.281, C.6.285, C.6.287, C.6.297, C.6.298, C.6.301, C.6.304, C.6.315, C.6.317, C.6.318, C.6.331, C.6.334, C.6.339, C.6.342, C.6.345, C.6.347, C.6.353, C.6.354, C.6.362, C.6.362, C.6.363, C.6.364, C.6.365, C.6.365, C.6.366, C.6.366, C.6.368, C.6.369, C.6.372, C.6.373, C.6.373, C.6.374, C.6.376, C.6.377, C.6.378, C.6.379, C.6.381, C.6.381, C.6.382, C.6.382, C.6.384, C.6.385, C.6.387, C.6.389, C.6.389, C.6.390, C.6.391, C.6.394, C.6.400, C.6.407, C.6.408, C.6.408, C.6.409, C.6.409, C.6.411, C.6.415, C.6.415, C.6.420, C.6.420, C.6.433, C.6.439, C.7.7, C.7.10, C.7.12, C.7.14, C.7.15, C.7.19, C.7.27, C.7.29, C.7.33, C.7.45, C.7.46, C.7.56, C.7.60, C.7.65, C.7.68, C.7.69, C.7.71, C.7.71, C.7.73, C.7.78, C.7.80, C.7.89, C.7.92, C.7.99, C.7.103, C.7.106, C.7.112, C.7.122, C.7.125, C.7.125, C.7.131, C.7.134, C.7.135, C.7.136, C.7.141, C.7.158, C.7.168, C.7.171, C.7.178, C.7.179, C.7.186, C.7.192, C.7.195, C.7.201, C.7.204, C.7.205, C.7.216, C.7.218, C.7.220, C.7.232, C.7.233, C.7.233, C.7.233, C.7.234, C.7.235, C.7.237, C.7.239, C.7.240, C.7.240, C.7.242, C.7.242, C.7.243, C.7.245, C.7.247, C.7.247, C.7.249, C.7.252, C.7.252, C.7.252, C.7.264, C.7.265, C.7.271, C.7.271, C.7.275, C.7.282, C.7.287, C.7.290, C.7.303, C.7.307, C.8.1, C.8.2, C.8.4, C.8.6, C.8.7, C.8.8, C.8.8, C.8.14, C.8.15, C.8.16, C.8.17, C.8.19, C.8.20, C.8.21, C.8.32, C.8.42, C.8.45, C.8.52, C.8.54, C.8.64, C.8.65, C.8.71, C.8.71, C.8.72, C.8.72, C.8.75, C.8.84, C.8.84, C.8.88, C.8.97, C.8.100, C.8.101, C.8.109, C.8.109, C.8.109, C.8.111, C.8.112, C.8.112, C.8.114, C.8.118, C.8.119, C.8.122, C.8.124, C.8.125, C.8.127, C.8.142, C.8.150, C.8.156, C.8.156, C.8.160, C.8.161, C.8.163, C.8.165, C.8.165, C.8.167, C.8.168, C.8.170, C.8.171, C.8.172, C.8.173, C.8.173, C.8.191, C.8.219, C.8.226, C.8.235, C.8.236, C.8.237, C.8.238, C.8.242, C.8.242, C.8.243, C.8.250, C.8.252, C.8.254, C.8.258, C.8.263, C.8.277, C.8.278, C.8.282, C.8.285, C.8.287, C.8.296, C.8.311, C.8.311, C.8.315, C.8.328, C.8.328, C.8.335, C.8.337, C.8.337, C.8.340, C.8.349, C.8.351, C.9.2, C.9.8, C.9.10, C.9.15, C.9.20, C.9.22, C.9.29, C.9.32, C.9.42, C.9.43, C.9.45, C.9.46, C.9.49, C.9.51, C.9.52, C.9.56, C.9.60, C.9.61, C.9.62, C.9.64, C.9.79, C.9.79, C.9.83, C.9.85, C.9.88, C.9.98, C.9.104, C.9.107, C.9.108, C.9.110, C.9.114, C.9.115, C.9.120, C.9.122, C.9.122, C.9.127, C.9.128, C.9.129, C.9.130, C.9.130, C.9.137, C.9.140, C.9.142, C.9.162, C.9.170, C.9.187, C.9.188, C.9.189, C.9.194, C.9.195, C.9.204, C.9.208, C.9.213, C.9.215, C.9.219, C.9.221, C.9.232, C.9.234, C.9.243, C.9.244, C.9.246, C.9.250, C.9.251, C.9.252, C.9.253, C.9.253, C.9.254, C.9.256, C.9.262, C.9.263, C.9.263, C.9.265, C.9.267, C.9.267, C.9.271, C.9.272, C.9.283, C.9.284, C.9.289, C.9.293, C.9.293, C.9.295, C.9.295, C.9.300, C.9.301, C.9.302, C.9.305, C.9.306, C.9.309, C.9.309, C.9.310, C.9.312, C.9.319, C.9.322, C.9.325, C.9.332, C.9.335, C.9.335, C.9.337, C.9.338, C.9.339, C.9.342, C.9.344, C.9.350, C.9.352, C.10.9, C.10.18, C.10.22, C.10.23, C.10.24, C.10.29, C.10.30, C.10.31, C.10.31, C.10.32, C.10.34, C.10.34, C.10.34, C.10.34, C.10.35, C.10.36, C.10.37, C.10.38, C.10.40, C.10.41, C.10.41, C.10.44, C.10.44, C.10.45, C.10.45, C.10.47, C.10.48, C.10.48, C.10.48, C.10.49, C.10.58, C.10.59, C.10.63, C.10.76, C.10.85, C.10.85, C.10.86, C.10.88, C.10.89, C.10.93, C.10.94, C.10.95, C.10.103, C.10.137, C.10.143, C.10.143, C.10.146, C.10.154, C.10.159, C.10.165, C.10.170, C.10.174, C.10.178, C.10.179, C.10.180, C.10.194, C.10.199, C.10.200, C.10.210, C.10.211, C.10.212, C.10.213, C.10.219, C.10.221, C.10.227, C.10.228, C.10.231, C.10.234, C.10.234, C.10.235, C.10.236, C.10.238, C.10.238, C.10.238, C.10.239, C.10.240, C.10.241, C.10.241, C.10.241, C.10.242, C.10.242, C.10.245, C.10.247, C.10.268, C.10.271, C.10.273, C.10.275, C.10.276, C.10.282, C.10.296, C.10.298, C.10.306, C.10.307, C.11.10, C.11.16, C.11.19, C.11.21, C.11.23, C.11.23, C.11.30, C.11.31, C.11.31, C.11.33, C.11.34, C.11.34, C.11.34, C.11.35, C.11.35, C.11.37, C.11.38, C.11.38, C.11.40, C.11.40, C.11.46, C.11.49, C.11.53, C.11.55, C.11.57, C.11.61, C.11.63, C.11.65, C.11.65, C.11.66, C.11.66, C.11.67, C.11.80, C.11.80, C.11.80, C.11.94, C.11.95, C.11.101, C.11.102, C.11.104, C.11.115, C.11.116, C.11.117, C.11.118, C.11.123, C.11.127, C.11.127, C.11.128, C.11.128, C.11.130, C.11.140, C.11.142, C.11.146, C.11.149, C.11.151, C.11.151, C.11.151, C.11.154, C.11.156, C.11.158, C.11.167, C.11.172, C.11.181, C.11.181, C.11.185, C.11.195, C.11.202, C.11.204, C.11.209, C.11.212, C.11.225, C.11.230, C.11.232, C.11.237, C.11.239, C.11.242, C.11.246, C.11.251, C.11.254, C.11.255, C.11.256, C.11.263, C.11.266, C.11.276, C.11.282, C.11.283, C.11.284, C.11.285, C.11.289, C.11.294, C.11.296, C.11.297, C.12.15, C.12.19, C.12.20, C.12.21, C.12.23, C.12.28, C.12.30, C.12.33, C.12.35, C.12.37, C.12.37, C.12.42, C.12.43, C.12.44, C.12.47, C.12.48, C.12.48, C.12.48, C.12.49, C.12.53, C.12.55, C.12.59, C.12.66, C.12.69, C.12.78, C.12.79, C.12.94, C.12.95, C.12.101, C.12.101, C.12.102, C.12.104, C.12.104, C.12.104, C.12.107, C.12.113, C.12.113, C.12.120, C.12.123, C.12.132, C.12.141, C.12.142, C.12.147, C.12.151, C.12.151, C.12.152, C.12.158, C.12.161, C.12.163, C.12.165, C.12.167, C.12.171, C.12.173, C.12.178, C.12.180, C.12.180, C.12.183, C.12.185, C.12.186, C.12.193, C.12.193, C.12.200, C.12.208, C.12.210, C.12.210,

C.12.211, C.12.214, C.12.218, C.12.228, C.12.243, C.12.247, C.13.4, C.13.4, C.13.13, C.13.14, C.13.15, C.13.16, C.13.23, C.13.24, C.13.25, C.13.31, C.13.32, C.13.37, C.13.37, C.13.38, C.13.39, C.13.40, C.13.42, C.13.43, C.13.43, C.13.46, C.13.47, C.13.49, C.13.50, C.13.53, C.13.54, C.13.56, C.13.59, C.13.61, C.13.64, C.13.66, C.13.67, C.13.68, C.13.68, C.13.72, C.13.75, C.13.77, C.13.79, C.13.79, C.13.80, C.13.82, C.13.82, C.13.83, C.13.84, C.13.87, C.13.88, C.13.91, C.13.93, C.13.93, C.13.95, C.13.96, C.13.98, C.13.98, C.13.104, C.13.107, C.13.112, C.13.115, C.13.118, C.13.120, C.13.123, C.13.124, C.13.126, C.13.127, C.13.127, C.13.132, C.13.135, C.13.135, C.13.135, C.13.152, C.13.157, C.13.158, C.13.166, C.13.170, C.13.173, C.13.173, C.13.202, C.13.227, C.13.227, C.14.9, C.14.27, C.14.40, C.14.47, C.14.48, C.14.54, C.14.54, C.14.55, C.14.58, C.14.75, C.14.83, C.14.84, C.14.91, C.14.91, C.14.92, C.14.97, C.14.110, C.14.114, C.14.115, C.14.116, C.14.119, C.14.120, C.14.125, C.14.126, C.14.131, C.14.137, C.14.139, C.14.139, C.14.139, C.14.140, C.14.141, C.14.144, C.14.146, C.14.149, C.14.150, C.14.151, C.14.152, C.14.153, C.14.155, C.14.155, C.14.156, C.14.158, C.14.158, C.14.159, C.14.161, C.14.161, C.14.164, C.14.170, C.14.172, C.14.172, C.14.179, C.14.181, C.14.183, C.14.183, C.14.184, C.14.185, C.14.187, C.14.190, C.14.191, C.14.193, C.14.196, C.14.206, C.14.213, C.14.215, C.15.14, C.15.31, C.15.33, C.15.38, C.15.38, C.15.44, C.15.65, C.15.70, C.15.72, C.15.75, C.15.75, C.15.80, C.15.82, C.15.89, C.15.90, C.15.98, C.15.103, C.15.126, C.15.130, C.15.137, C.15.149, C.15.156, C.15.161, C.15.168, C.15.168, C.15.171, C.15.172, C.15.173, C.15.189, C.15.194, C.15.199, C.15.199, C.15.200, C.15.200, C.15.207, C.15.210, C.15.212, C.15.212, C.15.212, C.15.216, C.15.219, C.15.220, C.15.224, C.15.224, C.15.224, C.15.226, C.15.226, C.15.230, C.15.236, C.15.240, C.15.241, C.15.241, C.15.241, C.15.243, C.15.247, C.15.259, C.15.259, C.15.264, C.15.264, C.15.268, C.15.269, C.15.274, C.15.280, C.15.282, C.15.285, C.15.286, C.15.306, C.16.2, C.16.21, C.16.27, C.16.27, C.16.41, C.16.41, C.16.44, C.16.48, C.16.49, C.16.52, C.16.53, C.16.54, C.16.58, C.16.58, C.16.60, C.16.62, C.16.62, C.16.66, C.16.66, C.16.67, C.16.68, C.16.71, C.16.75, C.16.79, C.16.80, C.16.85, C.16.92, C.16.98, C.16.110, C.16.113, C.16.120, C.16.123, C.16.127, C.16.133, C.16.133, C.16.135, C.16.137, C.16.139, C.16.139, C.16.142, C.16.142, C.16.144, C.16.146, C.16.147, C.16.150, C.16.150, C.16.155, C.16.160, C.16.169, C.16.169, C.16.170, C.16.183, C.16.190, C.16.197, C.16.197, C.16.207, C.16.210, C.16.210, C.16.219, C.16.220, C.16.221, C.16.229, C.16.231, C.16.234, C.16.238, C.16.240, C.16.240, C.16.241, C.16.244, C.16.251, C.16.253, C.16.253, C.16.253, C.16.254, C.16.254, C.16.256, C.16.258, C.16.260, C.16.284, C.16.285, C.16.295, C.16.323, C.16.332, C.16.333, C.16.340, C.16.343, C.16.362, C.16.364, C.16.367, C.17.27, C.17.31, C.17.32, C.17.51, C.17.57, C.17.59, C.17.71, C.17.75, C.17.76, C.17.78, C.17.79, C.17.81, C.17.82, C.17.82, C.17.85, C.17.89, C.17.91, C.17.92, C.17.92, C.17.92, C.17.92, C.17.96, C.17.96, C.17.99, C.17.101, C.17.102, C.17.103, C.17.107, C.17.107, C.17.108, C.17.115, C.17.122, C.17.124, C.17.136, C.17.137, C.17.137, C.17.138, C.17.140, C.17.140, C.17.146, C.17.157, C.17.173, C.17.174, C.17.175, C.17.175, C.17.177, C.17.177, C.17.180, C.17.184, C.17.185, C.17.188, C.17.190, C.17.191, C.17.192, C.17.198, C.17.200, C.17.201, C.17.201, C.17.205, C.17.209, C.17.211, C.17.216, C.17.218, C.17.226, C.17.228, C.17.230, C.17.232, C.17.233, C.17.235, C.17.238, C.17.241, C.17.243, C.17.247, C.17.247, C.17.248, C.17.250, C.17.253, C.17.254, C.17.256, C.17.259, C.17.260, C.17.262, C.17.268, C.17.271, C.17.278, C.17.280, C.17.283, C.17.287, C.17.289, C.17.290, C.17.293, C.17.294, C.17.295, C.17.297, C.17.301, C.17.307, C.17.308, C.17.315, C.17.315, C.17.316, C.18.6, C.18.9, C.18.9, C.18.11, C.18.12, C.18.14, C.18.26, C.18.29, C.18.30, C.18.31, C.18.34, C.18.35, C.18.39, C.18.40, C.18.41, C.18.41, C.18.41, C.18.41, C.18.43, C.18.44, C.18.45, C.18.45, C.18.48, C.18.49, C.18.50, C.18.50, C.18.51, C.18.52, C.18.52, C.18.53, C.18.54, C.18.55, C.18.64, C.18.66, C.18.66, C.18.72, C.18.72, C.18.72, C.18.75, C.18.75, C.18.75, C.18.75, C.18.79, C.18.85, C.18.90, C.18.90, C.18.92, C.18.92, C.18.93, C.18.94, C.18.95, C.18.98, C.18.106, C.18.107, C.18.110, C.18.112, C.18.113, C.18.116, C.18.118, C.18.119, C.18.120, C.18.127, C.18.129, C.18.130, C.18.130, C.18.133, C.18.136, C.18.146, C.18.150, C.18.156, C.18.161, C.18.161, C.18.162, C.18.162, C.18.163, C.18.165, C.18.169, C.18.170, C.18.174, C.18.177, C.18.192, C.18.193, C.18.193, C.18.194, C.18.206, C.18.206, C.18.207, C.18.209, C.18.213, C.18.221, C.18.221, C.18.227, C.18.228, C.18.231, C.18.231, C.18.234, C.18.235, C.18.253, C.18.262, C.18.267, C.18.277, C.18.278, C.18.280, C.18.282, C.18.287, C.18.289, C.19.2, C.19.4, C.19.6, C.19.7, C.19.8, C.19.9, C.19.11, C.19.15, C.19.16, C.19.29, C.19.35, C.19.36, C.19.39, C.19.48, C.19.50, C.19.65, C.19.67, C.19.69, C.19.74, C.19.76, C.19.79, C.19.81, C.19.82, C.19.83, C.19.84, C.19.86, C.19.87, C.19.88, C.19.90, C.19.95, C.19.104, C.19.108, C.19.109, C.19.113, C.19.117, C.19.118, C.19.118, C.19.118, C.19.118, C.19.121, C.19.121, C.19.122, C.19.123, C.19.124, C.19.126, C.19.126, C.19.128, C.19.128, C.19.131, C.19.132, C.19.132, C.19.134, C.19.135, C.19.136, C.19.139, C.19.139, C.19.141, C.19.141, C.19.142, C.19.143, C.19.143, C.19.144, C.19.145, C.19.146, C.19.146, C.19.147, C.19.148, C.19.149, C.19.149, C.19.149, C.19.153, C.19.153, C.19.155, C.19.155, C.19.156, C.19.158, C.19.161, C.19.165, C.19.167, C.19.168, C.19.168, C.19.168, C.19.168, C.19.169, C.19.169, C.19.170, C.19.172, C.19.178, C.19.178, C.19.182, C.19.183, C.19.184, C.19.192, C.19.193, C.19.197, C.19.199, C.19.199, C.19.199, C.19.204, C.19.208, C.19.209, C.19.213, C.19.218, C.19.222, C.19.224, C.19.227, C.19.228, C.19.238, C.19.241, C.19.243, C.19.255, C.19.256, C.19.256, C.19.260, C.19.261, C.19.261, C.19.263, C.19.265, C.19.266, C.19.267, C.19.268, C.19.277, C.19.280, C.19.283, C.19.288, C.19.296, C.19.310, C.19.310, C.19.314, C.19.315, C.19.319, C.19.321, C.19.327, C.19.327, C.19.329, C.20.4, C.20.8, C.20.8, C.20.11, C.20.18, C.20.18, C.20.24, C.20.27, C.20.32, C.20.32, C.20.37, C.20.37, C.20.38, C.20.55, C.20.59, C.20.60, C.20.60, C.20.61, C.20.61, C.20.62, C.20.63, C.20.66, C.20.68, C.20.74, C.20.81, C.20.82, C.20.87, C.20.88, C.20.88, C.20.89, C.20.92, C.20.95, C.20.98, C.20.98, C.20.101, C.20.105, C.20.110, C.20.113, C.20.116, C.20.117, C.20.121, C.20.123, C.20.126, C.20.126, C.20.126, C.20.133, C.20.138, C.20.140, C.20.150, C.20.152, C.20.157, C.20.158, C.20.159, C.20.160, C.20.162, C.20.163, C.20.165, C.20.167, C.20.167, C.20.168, C.20.189, C.20.191, C.20.196, C.20.196, C.20.199, C.20.202, C.20.203, C.20.207, C.20.209, C.20.214, C.20.220, C.20.223, C.20.224, C.20.227, C.20.243, C.20.244, C.20.246, C.20.246, C.20.247, C.20.250, C.20.250, C.20.250, C.20.251, C.20.252, C.20.253, C.20.254, C.20.256, C.20.257, C.20.266, C.20.267, C.20.270, C.20.273, C.20.281, C.20.284, C.20.288, C.20.290, C.20.293, C.20.298, C.20.300, C.20.321, C.20.322, C.20.325, C.20.337, C.20.339, C.20.343, C.20.352, C.20.353, C.20.355, C.20.361, C.20.363, C.20.365, C.20.372, C.20.374, C.20.376, C.20.381, C.20.385, C.20.387, C.20.392, C.20.393, C.20.401, C.20.410, C.20.411, C.20.411, C.20.423, C.20.423, C.20.423, C.20.427, C.20.430, C.20.445, C.20.447, C.20.448, C.20.452, C.20.467, C.20.468, C.20.471, C.20.474, C.20.474, C.21.3, C.21.4, C.21.6, C.21.7, C.21.9, C.21.10, C.21.11, C.21.18, C.21.19, C.21.34, C.21.36, C.21.38, C.21.44, C.21.45, C.21.56, C.21.63, C.21.71, C.21.80, C.21.81, C.21.82, C.21.82, C.21.87, C.21.91, C.21.98, C.21.123, C.21.129, C.21.132, C.21.133, C.21.135, C.21.136, C.21.138, C.21.149, C.21.150, C.21.151, C.21.154, C.21.154, C.21.155, C.21.157, C.21.170, C.21.187, C.21.192, C.21.197, C.21.199, C.21.205, C.21.208, C.21.214, C.21.219, C.21.230, C.21.258, C.21.264, C.21.266, C.21.270, C.21.270, C.21.271, C.21.276, C.21.278, C.21.280, C.21.281, C.21.289, C.21.296, C.21.297, C.21.302, C.21.303, C.21.303, C.21.311, C.21.313, C.21.313, C.21.316, C.21.321, C.21.321, C.21.332, C.21.333, C.21.334, C.21.334, C.21.335, C.21.338, C.21.343, C.21.343, C.21.346, C.21.352, C.21.352, C.21.354, C.21.357, C.21.370, C.21.379, C.21.382, C.21.390, C.21.391, C.21.394, C.21.406, C.21.413, C.21.416, C.21.417, C.21.417, C.21.420, C.21.423, C.21.426, C.21.426, C.21.427, C.21.430, C.21.432, C.21.433, C.21.433, C.21.434, C.21.435, C.21.437, C.21.442, C.21.443, C.21.446, C.21.448, C.21.449, C.21.451, C.21.452, C.21.455, C.21.463, C.21.466, C.21.468, C.21.472, C.21.473, C.21.477, C.21.480, C.22.1, C.22.4, C.22.6, C.22.18, C.22.30, C.22.30, C.22.42, C.22.43, C.22.45, C.22.49, C.22.53, C.22.54, C.22.60, C.22.77, C.22.78, C.22.80, C.22.87, C.22.90, C.22.95, C.22.95, C.22.96, C.22.109, C.22.120, C.22.125, C.22.127, C.22.129, C.22.133, C.22.136, C.22.137, C.22.150, C.22.157, C.22.160, C.22.175, C.22.182, C.22.184, C.22.187, C.22.190, C.22.191, C.22.193, C.22.195, C.22.202, C.22.221, C.22.221, C.22.224, C.22.224, C.22.240, C.22.256, C.22.261, C.22.266, C.22.271, C.22.277, C.22.281, C.22.285, C.22.291, C.22.292, C.22.293, C.22.293, C.22.296, C.22.298, C.22.301, C.22.310, C.22.313, C.22.320, C.22.324, C.22.327, C.22.329, C.22.336, C.22.346, C.22.348, C.22.349, C.22.354, C.22.359, C.22.359, C.22.372, C.22.376, C.22.378, C.22.381, C.22.382

thecche v *thacchen v.* B 1; C 1

B.19.238 And some he tauȝte to tilie, to [coke] and to *thecche*,
C.21.238 And somme he tauhte to tulye, to [coke] and to [*thecche*,

theddere theder > þider

þedom n *thedom n.* A 1; C 1 thedom

A.10.108 Thrift oþer *þedom* with þo is selde yseiȝe:
C. 7.53 And ȝede aboute in my ȝouthe and ȝaf me to no *thedom*

thedre > þider

thee v *then v. &> þow* A 1 þe; B 2 thee (1) þee (1)

A. 5.142 Ac I swere now, so *þ[e* I], þat synne shal I lete,
B. 5.226 Ac I swere now, so *thee* ik, þat synne wol I lete
B. 5.399 Ne riȝt sory for my synnes yet, [so *þee* I], was I neuere.

þef n *thef n.(2)* A 1 þeuis; B 17 þeef (3) þef (4) þeues (10); C 17 theef (3) thef (4) theues (9) thief (1)

A.10.139 Ac fals folk & feiþles, *þeuis* & leiȝeris,
B. 9.121 Ac fals folk, feiþlees, *þeues* and lyeres,
B.12.190 That haþ take fro Tybourne twenty stronge *þeues*,
B.12.191 Ther lewed *þeues* ben lolled vp; loke how þei be saued!
B.12.192 The *þef* þat hadde grace of god on good fryday, as þow spek[e],
B.12.196 Ac þouȝ þat *þeef* hadde heuene he hadde noon heiȝ blisse,
B.12.206 For he þat is ones a *þef* is eueremoore in daunger,
B.12.208 And for to seruen a Seint and swich a *þef* togideres,
B.12.211 That oure lord ne hadde hym liȝtly out, so leue I [by] þe *þef* in heuene.
B.12.214 A[c] why þat oon *þeef* on þe cros creaunt hym yald
B.12.215 Raþer þan þat ooþer *þeef*, þouȝ þow woldest appose,
B.13.160 Coold ne care ne compaignye of *þeues*,
B.14.308 And an hardy man of herte among an heep of *þeues*;
B.17.56 Where a man was wounded and wiþ *þeues* taken.
B.17.92 For sighte of þ[e] sorweful [segge] þat robbed was with *þeues*.
B.17.276 For þat kynde dooþ vnkynde fordooþ, as þise corsede *þeues*,
B.18.71 Two *þeues* [þat tyme] þoled deeþ [also]
B.18.74 And [hir] armes after of eiþer of þo *þeues*.
C. 5.17 And kepe my corn in my croft f[or] pykares and *theues*
C.13.62 Haue hors and hardy men; thogh he mette *theues*
C.14.129 Hit hath take fro tybourne twenty stronge *theues*
C.14.130 There lewede *theues* ben lolled vp; loke how þei ben saued!
C.14.131 The *thef* þat hadde grace of god a gode fryday, As thow toldest,
C.14.135 Ac thogh th[at] *theef* hadde heuene he hadde noen hey blisse
C.14.145 For he þat is ones a *thef* is eueremore in daunger
C.14.147 And for to seruen a seynt and suche a *thef* togyderes,
C.14.150 That oure [lord] ne hauede [hym] lihtliche out, so leue y [by] þ[e] *thef* in heuene.
C.14.153 Ac why þat [on] *theef* vppon þe cros cryant hym ȝelde
C.14.154 Rather then þat oþer [*theef*], thogh thow woldest apose,

C.17.138 And *theues* louyen and leute hatien and at þe laste ben hanged
C.19.54   In a wi[d]e wildernesse where *theues* hadde ybounde
C.19.257 For þat kynde doth vnkynde fordoth, as this corsede *theues*,
C.20.73   T[w]o *theues* tho tholed deth þat tyme
C.20.76   And here arme[s] aftur of e[ither] of tho *theues*.
C.20.424 Ther a *thief* tholie sholde deth oþer iewyse

thefliche adv *thefli adv.* B 1
B.18.338 *Thefliche* þow me robbedest; þe olde lawe graunteþ

þefte n *thefte n.* A 1; B 3; C 2 thefte
A.11.280 Þat hadde lyued al his lyf wiþ lesinges & *þeft[e]*,
B. 2.88   In bargaynes and brocages wiþ þe Burgh of *þefte*,
B. 5.233 'That was no restitucion', quod Repentaunce, 'but a robberis *þefte*;
B.10.421 That hadde lyued al his lif wiþ lesynges and *þefte*,
C. 2.95   In bargaynes and Brocages with the borw of *thefte*,
C. 6.349 What a lered ȝow to lyue with and to lette ȝow fram *thefte*.'

þei pron *thei pron.* &> þeiȝ, cf. hij A 94; B 351 thei (21) they (14) þei
(316); C 332 thay (1) þai (1) þay (1) thei (68) they (204) þei (37) þey
(18) ther (1) þer (1)

thay C 3 thay (1) þai (1) þay (1)
C.9.175, C.16.365, C.20.210

þei A 94 &> þeiȝ
A.Pr.31, A.Pr.43, A.Pr.58, A.Pr.79, A.1.6, A.1.8, A.1.8, A.1.9, A.1.46, A.1.49,
A.1.113, A.1.117, A.2.27, A.2.67, A.2.100, A.2.131, A.2.138, A.3.71, A.3.138, A.3.205,
A.3.207, A.3.220, A.3.226, A.3.232, A.4.69, A.4.99, A.5.8, A.5.33, A.5.35, A.5.177,
A.6.20, A.6.64, A.6.108, A.7.14, A.7.69, A.7.131, A.7.170, A.7.185, A.7.242, A.7.258,
A.7.282, A.8.18, A.8.22, A.8.23, A.8.44, A.8.45, A.8.72, A.8.73, A.8.76, A.8.117,
A.9.11, A.9.12, A.9.51, A.9.91, A.9.100, A.10.60, A.10.65, A.10.67, A.10.67, A.10.68,
A.10.70, A.10.106, A.10.134, A.10.135, A.10.146, A.10.148, A.10.154, A.10.155,
A.10.158, A.10.192, A.10.193, A.10.194, A.10.195, A.10.196, A.10.196, A.10.203,
A.10.212, A.11.11, A.11.38, A.11.40, A.11.43, A.11.60, A.11.68, A.11.70, A.11.89,
A.11.108, A.11.133, A.11.179, A.11.206, A.11.208, A.11.208, A.11.274, A.11.285,
A.11.292

þei B 351 thei (21) þei (316) they (14)
B.Pr.31, B.Pr.43, B.Pr.50, B.Pr.51, B.Pr.61, B.Pr.82, B.Pr.89, B.Pr.162, B.Pr.164,
B.Pr.166, B.Pr.207, B.1.6, B.1.8, B.1.8, B.1.9, B.1.48, B.1.51, B.1.118, B.1.124, B.1.128,
B.1.191, B.2.45, B.2.68, B.2.102, B.2.136, B.2.162, B.2.167, B.2.226, B.3.25, B.3.82,
B.3.83, B.3.85, B.3.85, B.3.149, B.3.218, B.3.220, B.3.233, B.3.245, B.3.247, B.3.253,
B.4.28, B.4.32, B.4.34, B.4.35, B.4.37, B.4.38, B.4.41, B.4.43, B.4.82, B.4.112, B.4.153,
B.5.8, B.5.35, B.5.140, B.5.141, B.5.147, B.5.149, B.5.150, B.5.165, B.5.168, B.5.168,
B.5.172, B.5.192, B.5.232, B.5.328, B.5.329, B.5.505, B.5.512, B.5.515, B.5.532,
B.5.577, B.5.622, B.5.642, B.6.15, B.6.77, B.6.123, B.6.132, B.6.137, B.6.146, B.6.149,
B.6.150, B.6.162, B.6.170, B.6.180, B.6.192, B.6.198, B.6.204, B.6.205, B.6.226,
B.6.274, B.6.293, B.6.298, B.6.301, B.7.13, B.7.13, B.7.15, B.7.20, B.7.21, B.7.57,
B.7.90, B.7.91, B.7.91, B.7.94, B.7.135, B.8.11, B.8.12, B.8.17, B.8.101, B.8.110,
B.8.131, B.9.63, B.9.79, B.9.83, B.9.112, B.9.118, B.9.128, B.9.157, B.9.158,
B.9.163, B.9.171, B.9.172, B.9.173, B.9.174, B.9.175, B.9.175, B.9.190, B.9.193,
B.9.198, B.9.199, B.10.11, B.10.22, B.10.24, B.10.25, B.10.28, B.10.44, B.10.52,
B.10.54, B.10.57, B.10.105, B.10.110, B.10.117, B.10.136, B.10.156, B.10.181,
B.10.293, B.10.300, B.10.302, B.10.302, B.10.319, B.10.319, B.10.320, B.10.321,
B.10.347, B.10.390, B.10.400, B.10.404, B.10.426, B.10.433, B.10.473, B.11.68,
B.11.89, B.11.109, B.11.139, B.11.173, B.11.237, B.11.238, B.11.239, B.11.283,
B.11.285, B.11.286, B.11.288, B.11.328, B.11.338, B.11.338, B.11.353, B.11.360,
B.12.23, B.12.52, B.12.53, B.12.122, B.12.131, B.12.191, B.12.222, B.12.232, B.12.243,
B.12.261, B.13.8, B.13.28, B.13.42, B.13.45, B.13.68, B.13.68, B.13.76, B.13.170,
B.13.171, B.13.218, B.13.220, B.13.220, B.13.221, B.13.264, B.13.351, B.13.450,
B.14.70, B.14.81, B.14.129, B.14.160, B.14.161, B.14.172, B.14.173, B.14.195,
B.14.226, B.14.239, B.14.253, B.15.108, B.15.109, B.15.137, B.15.155, B.15.185,
B.15.214, B.15.240, B.15.243, B.15.260, B.15.270, B.15.293, B.15.293, B.15.293,
B.15.301, B.15.302, B.15.303, B.15.304, B.15.311, B.15.319, B.15.319, B.15.321,
B.15.329, B.15.329, B.15.331, B.15.351, B.15.363, B.15.365, B.15.365, B.15.369,
B.15.371, B.15.384, B.15.386, B.15.387, B.15.391, B.15.394, B.15.430, B.15.480,
B.15.489, B.15.495, B.15.495, B.15.503, B.15.534, B.15.544, B.15.552, B.15.586,
B.15.587, B.15.589, B.15.592, B.15.596, B.15.606, B.15.609, B.15.611, B.16.56,
B.16.56, B.16.57, B.16.58, B.16.59, B.16.79, B.16.137, B.16.137, B.16.138, B.16.206,
B.16.228, B.17.85, B.17.154, B.17.167, B.17.236, B.17.240, B.17.273, B.17.344,
B.18.17, B.18.38, B.18.52, B.18.83, B.18.151, B.18.194, B.18.201, B.18.202, B.18.205,
B.18.205, B.18.259, B.18.294, B.18.329, B.18.331, B.18.333, B.18.387, B.18.387,
B.18.391, B.18.405, B.19.34, B.19.35, B.19.39, B.19.78, B.19.83, B.19.141, B.19.156,
B.19.179, B.19.186, B.19.232, B.19.268, B.19.273, B.19.313, B.19.342, B.19.344,
B.19.368, B.19.371, B.19.389, B.19.414, B.19.418, B.19.441, B.19.454, B.19.456,
B.19.463, B.20.38, B.20.68, B.20.78, B.20.107, B.20.127, B.20.172, B.20.220, B.20.231,
B.20.233, B.20.234, B.20.235, B.20.236, B.20.237, B.20.251, B.20.259, B.20.259,
B.20.260, B.20.261, B.20.291, B.20.300, B.20.307, B.20.309, B.20.335, B.20.379

they C 326 thei (68) they (204) þei (37) þey (18)
C.Pr.33, C.Pr.38, C.Pr.44, C.Pr.80, C.Pr.108, C.Pr.116, C.Pr.146, C.Pr.183, C.1.6,
C.1.8, C.1.8, C.1.9, C.1.47, C.1.99, C.1.125, C.1.125, C.1.126, C.1.130, C.1.132,
C.1.188, C.1.191, C.2.70, C.2.106, C.2.178, C.2.233, C.2.236, C.3.16, C.3.26, C.3.84,
C.3.84, C.3.86, C.3.87, C.3.87, C.3.88, C.3.187, C.3.274, C.3.276, C.3.302, C.3.302,
C.3.311, C.3.320, C.3.322, C.3.333, C.3.388, C.3.389, C.3.594, C.4.35, C.4.37, C.4.38,
C.4.78, C.4.106, C.4.107, C.4.118, C.4.149, C.5.137, C.5.149, C.5.165, C.5.166, C.6.48,
C.6.120, C.6.122, C.6.125, C.6.137, C.6.154, C.6.236, C.6.386, C.6.387, C.7.110,
C.7.150, C.7.157, C.7.160, C.7.177, C.7.212, C.7.224, C.7.274, C.8.31, C.8.49, C.8.79,
C.8.88, C.8.89, C.8.130, C.8.159, C.8.185, C.8.190, C.8.203, C.8.210, C.8.211, C.8.213,
C.8.224, C.8.247, C.8.295, C.8.316, C.9.13, C.9.13, C.9.16, C.9.19, C.9.24, C.9.25,
C.9.45, C.9.74, C.9.99, C.9.109, C.9.110, C.9.112, C.9.121, C.9.125, C.9.130, C.9.132,
C.9.139, C.9.160, C.9.161, C.9.167, C.9.168, C.9.170, C.9.194, C.9.201, C.9.202,
C.9.208, C.9.210, C.9.308, C.10.11, C.10.12, C.10.17, C.10.106, C.10.126, C.10.126,
C.10.127, C.10.168, C.10.205, C.10.215, C.10.254, C.10.256, C.10.272, C.10.273,
C.10.274, C.10.275, C.10.276, C.10.277, C.10.277, C.10.290, C.10.297, C.10.298,
C.11.9, C.11.12, C.11.22, C.11.38, C.11.75, C.11.121, C.11.205, C.11.234, C.11.234,
C.11.258, C.11.269, C.11.298, C.11.306, C.12.29, C.12.30, C.12.43, C.12.74, C.12.127,
C.12.128, C.12.227, C.13.4, C.13.4, C.13.32, C.13.36, C.13.42, C.13.52, C.13.102,
C.13.115, C.13.136, C.13.146, C.13.146, C.13.154, C.13.190, C.13.191, C.14.11,
C.14.65, C.14.73, C.14.75, C.14.75, C.14.76, C.14.83, C.14.130, C.14.176, C.14.193,
C.15.10, C.15.31, C.15.35, C.15.37, C.15.47, C.15.50, C.15.70, C.15.74, C.15.82,
C.15.181, C.15.187, C.15.189, C.15.189, C.15.190, C.15.199, C.15.302, C.16.13,
C.16.14, C.16.67, C.16.79, C.16.93, C.16.231, C.16.262, C.16.271, C.16.282, C.16.335,
C.17.11, C.17.16, C.17.20, C.17.20, C.17.20, C.17.30, C.17.54, C.17.55, C.17.90,
C.17.102, C.17.102, C.17.105, C.17.107, C.17.116, C.17.118, C.17.118, C.17.123,
C.17.133, C.17.134, C.17.158, C.17.159, C.17.160, C.17.182, C.17.190, C.17.195,
C.17.206, C.17.254, C.17.297, C.17.298, C.17.307, C.17.317, C.17.319, C.18.23,
C.18.24, C.18.167, C.18.177, C.18.189, C.18.191, C.18.191, C.18.243, C.19.55, C.19.81,
C.19.94, C.19.129, C.19.136, C.19.138, C.19.202, C.19.206, C.19.254, C.19.324,
C.20.15, C.20.37, C.20.51, C.20.85, C.20.154, C.20.199, C.20.206, C.20.207, C.20.210,
C.20.267, C.20.305, C.20.334, C.20.372, C.20.374, C.20.376, C.20.429, C.20.429,
C.20.448, C.21.34, C.21.35, C.21.39, C.21.78, C.21.83, C.21.141, C.21.156, C.21.179,
C.21.186, C.21.232, C.21.268, C.21.273, C.21.313, C.21.342, C.21.344, C.21.368,
C.21.371, C.21.389, C.21.414, C.21.418, C.21.441, C.21.454, C.21.456, C.21.463,
C.22.38, C.22.68, C.22.78, C.22.107, C.22.127, C.22.172, C.22.220, C.22.231, C.22.233,
C.22.234, C.22.235, C.22.236, C.22.237, C.22.251, C.22.259, C.22.259, C.22.260,
C.22.291, C.22.300, C.22.307, C.22.309, C.22.335, C.22.379

ther C 2 ther (1) þer (1)
C.2.69, C.12.8

þeiȝ conj *though conj.* cf. þouȝ A 27 þei (2) þeiȝ (25); B 14 theiȝ (5) þeiȝ
(9)
A. 1.10   I was aferd of hire face þeiȝ heo fair were,
A. 1.33   Mesure is medicine þeiȝ þou muche ȝerne.
A. 1.132 No dedly synne to do, diȝe þeiȝ þou shuldist.
A. 1.150 Þeiȝ ȝe ben miȝty to mote beþ mek of ȝour werkis;
A. 1.153 For þ[ei ȝe] be trewe of ȝoure tunge & treweliche wynne,
A. 3.37   'Þeiȝ lerid & lewide hadde leie be þe reuone,
A. 3.38   And þeiȝ falshed hadde folewid þe þis fiftene wynter,
A. 3.119 Betwyn heuene & helle, & erþe þeiȝ men souȝte.
A. 3.149 Þe mase for a mene man þeiȝ he mote euere.
A. 3.155 For pouere men mowe haue no power to pleyne [þeiȝ] hem smerte,
A. 4.52   Þeiȝ pees & his power pleynide hem euere'.
A. 5.229 [And] þeiȝ my liflode lakke leten I nille
A. 6.36   For, þeiȝ I sey it myself, I serue hym to pay.
A. 6.87   Whanne I þenke þereon, þeiȝ I were a pope".
A. 6.91   For he haþ þe keiȝes & þe cliket þeiȝ þe king slepe.
A. 7.40   And þei pore men profre þe presauntis or ȝeftis
A. 7.90   For þeiȝ I deiȝe today my dettis ben quyt.
A. 7.112 And þeiȝ ȝe deiȝe for doel þe deuil haue þat recche!'
A. 8.107 And beloure þat I [be]lou[ȝ] er þeiȝ liflode me faile.
A. 8.176 Þeiȝ þou be founde in þe fraternite among þe foure ordris,
A. 9.43   þat, þeiȝ þi body bowe as bot doþ in þe watir,
A.10.115 To be blissid for þi beryng, [ȝ]e, b[e]ggere þeiȝ þou were.
A.10.116 Loke þou grucche nouȝt on god þeiȝ he gyue þe litel;
A.10.194 Þeiȝ þei don hem to dunmowe, but ȝif þe deuil helpe
A.11.92   Þeiȝ dobest drawe on hym day aftir oþer.'
A.11.136 And lernide h[e]m lyuel & lyne þeiȝ I loke dymme.
A.12.65   [To kyllyn him ȝif I can, þei kynde wit helpe]
B.Pr.192 The maȝe among vs alle þeiȝ we mysse a sherewe.
B. 1.10   I was afered of hire face þeiȝ she fair weere
B. 1.144 No dedly synne to do, deye þeiȝ þow sholdest,
B. 3.38   'Theiȝ [lered and lewed] hadde leyen by þee [echone],
B. 3.39   And [þeiȝ] Fals[hede] hadde yfolwed þee alle þise fift[ene] wynter,
B. 3.352 That þeiȝ we wynne worship and with Mede haue victorie,
B. 4.66   Theiȝ pees and his power pleyned h[e]m euere'.
B. 5.268 For þe beste book in oure hous, þeiȝ brent gold were þe leues,
B. 5.600 Whan I þynke þeron, þeiȝ I were a Pope."
B. 6.226 Theiȝ þei doon yuele lat [þow] god yworþe:
B. 7.198 Theiȝ [þow] be founde in þe fraternite [among] þe foure ordres
B.10.139 Theiȝ þei dobest drawe on hym day after ooþer.'
B.11.285 Ne neiþer kirtel ne cote, þeiȝ þei for cold sholde deye,
B.15.260 That þeiȝ þei suffrede al þis, god suffrede for vs moore

thekynge ger *thacchinge ger.* C 1
C. 8.199 In threschynge, in *thekynge*, in thwytinge of pynnes,

themese n prop *Temese n.* B 3 Temese (1) Themese (2); C 3 Temese
B.12.160 Tak two stronge men and in *Themese* cast hem,
B.12.164 Which trowestow of þo two [in *Themese*] is in moost drede,
B.15.339 And wente forþ wiþ þat water to woke wiþ *Temese*.

C. 6.335	Fareth as flo[nke] of fuyr þat ful amydde *Temese*
C.14.104	Take two stronge men and in *temese* cast hem,
C.14.108	Which trowest [þou] of tho two in *temese* [is] in moste drede?'

þen > þan; then > þanne,þan; þenk(- > þynke; thenne > þan,thanne
adv1,þanne adv2

þennes adv *thennes adv. cf. þanne* A 5 þennes (3) þennis (2); B 7; C 6
thennes

A. 1.71	And h[a]lside hire on þe heiȝe name, er heo þennis ȝede,
A. 2.177	Liȝtliche liȝere lep awey *þennes,*
A. 2.191	Freris wiþ fair speche fetten hym *þennes;*
A. 3.193	[Cowardly þou consience conceiledest him *þennes*]
A. 5.225	Shal non ale aftir mete holde me *þennis*
B. 1.73	And [halsede] hire on þe heiȝe name, er she *þennes* yede,
B. 2.232	Freres wiþ fair speche fetten hym *þennes;*
B. 3.206	Cowardly þow, Conscience, conseiledest hym *þennes*
B. 5.453	Shal noon ale after mete holde me *þennes*
B.10.62	But [hunsen] hym as an hound and hoten hym go *þennes.*
B.19.424	And þow Conscience in kynges court, and sholdest neuere come *þennes;*
B.20.206	And loke þow konne som craft er þow come *þennes.'*
C. 1.70	And ha[ls]ede here on þe hey name or she *thennes* [ȝede]
C. 2.242	Freres [with] fayre speche fetten hym *thennes,*
C. 7.67	Shal non ale aftur m[e]te holde me *thennes*
C. 7.135	And brouhte thyne yblessed fro *thennes* into þe blisse of heuene.
C.21.424	And thow, Consience, in kynges Court and sholdest neuer come *thennes;*
C.22.206	And loke thow conne som craft ar thow come *thennes.'*

theologie n *theologie n.* A 5; B 4; C 3 teologie (2) theologie (1)

A. 2.79	Þanne tenide hym *theologie* whan he þis tale herde,
A.11.137	Ac *theologie* haþ tened me ten score tymes,
A.11.149	Ac *theologie* techiþ not so, who[so] takiþ heed;
A.12.9	That myȝthe turne m[e] to tene & *theologie* boþe.
A.12.18	Sitthe *theologie* þe trewe to tellen hit defendeþ;
B. 2.115	Thanne tened hym *Theologie* whan he þis tale herde,
B.10.185	Ac *Theologie* haþ tened me ten score tymes,
B.10.200	Ac *Theologie* techeþ noȝt so, whoso takeþ yeme;
B.10.379	Manye tales ye tellen þat *Theologie* lerneþ,
C. 2.119	Thenne tened hym *teologie* when he this tal[e] herde,
C. 2.132	Y, *Theo[lo]gie,* þe tixt knowe yf trewe doom wittenesseth,
C.11.126	Ac *teologie* hath tened me ten score tymes;

þer adv *ther adv. &> þei,theras* A 49 þer (3) þere (46); B 144 ther (21)
þer (55) there (8) þere (60); C 137 ther (37) þer (46) there (38) þere
(16)

A.Pr.17	A fair feld ful of folk fand I *þere* betwene
A.Pr.55	I fond *þere* Freris, alle þe foure ordris,
A.Pr.65	*Þere* prechide a pardoner as he a prest were,
A.Pr.84	*Þere* houide an hundrit in houuis of silk,
A. 1.139	For in kynde knowyng in herte *þer* comsiþ a miȝt,
A.2.14	*Þere* nis no quen queyntere þat quyk is o lyue.
A.2.27	*Þere* miȝte þou wyte ȝif þou wilt whiche þei ben alle
A.2.29	Knowe hem *þere* ȝif þou canst and kep þe from hem alle
A.2.38	*Þer* nas halle ne hous to herberwe þe peple,
A.2.71	*Þere* to wone wiþ wrong while god is in heuene.'
A.3.11	Ac *þere* was merþe & mynstralcie mede to plese;
A.3.34	Þanne com *þere* a confessour ycopid as a frere;
A.3.48	Woldist þou glase þe gable, & graue *þere* þin name,
A.3.50	'Wiste I þat,' quaþ þe womman, '*þere* nis wyndowe ne auter
A.3.218	*Þere* arn to maner of medis, my lord, be ȝoure leue.
A.3.225	*Þere* is a mede mesurles þat maistris desiriþ;
A.4.21	And ȝet wile [h]e make many wehe er we come *þere.'*
A.4.135	*Þere* nas man in þe mothalle, more ne lesse,
A.5.48	Heo shulde vnsewe hire serke & sette *þere* an heire
A.5.172	*Þere* were chapmen chosen þat chaffare to preise;
A.5.176	*Þere* were oþes an hep, [whoso it herde];
A.5.185	*Þere* was lauȝing & louryng & 'lete go þe cuppe!'
A.5.234	Ac for *þere* was nouȝt wherewith he wepte swiþe sore.
A.6.1	Ac *þere* w[ere] fewe men so wys þat þe [wey] þider couþe,
A.6.35	*Þere* is no labourer in his lordsshipe þat he louiþ beter
A.6.55	Wadiþ in þat watir & wasshiþ ȝow wel *þere,*
A.6.62	Loke þou breke no bowis *þere* but it be þin owene.
A.6.63	Two stokkis *þere* stonde, but stynte þou not *þere;*
A.6.63	Two stokkis *þere* stonde, but stynte þou not *þere;*
A.6.69	Loke þou plukke no plant[e] *þere* for peril of þi soule.
A.6.104	Ac *þere* arn seuene sistris þat [seruen] treuþe euere,
A.6.115	'Be crist,' quaþ a cuttepurs, 'I haue no kyn *þere.'*
A.6.120	'Mercy [is] a maiden [*þere*], haþ miȝt ouer [hem] alle;
A.6.123	Þou miȝt gete grace [*þere*] so þou go be tyme.'
A.7.2	Þat miȝte folewe vs iche fote [forto] we were *þere.'*
A.7.6	I wolde wende wiþ ȝow til ȝe were *þere'.*
A.7.101	Oþere werkmen *þere* were [þat] wrouȝte ful faste,
A.7.187	Hom into his owene er[d]e & holde him *þere* euere.

A.7.257	*Þere* arn mo liȝeris þan lechis, lord hem amende.
A.7.300	Ac while hunger was here maister wolde *þere* non chide,
A.8.78	*Þere* ben mo mysshapen amonges hem, whoso takiþ hede,
A.8.175	A pokeful of pardoun *þere,* ne þe prouincialis lettres,
A.9.32	*Þere* were þe manis lif lost for lacchesse of hymselue.
A.9.95	And putten hem *þere* in penaunce wiþoute pite or grace,
A.9.96	But dobest bede for hem abide *þere* for euere.
A.10.55	*Þere* is his bour bremest but ȝif blod it make;
A.11.159	Ȝet arn *þere* febicchis of Forellis of many manis wittes,
A.11.272	And was *þere* neuere in þis world to wysere of werkis,
A.12.75	*Þer* bad me hunger haue gode day but I helde me stille;
B.Pr.17	A fair feeld ful of folk fond I *þer* bitwene
B.Pr.58	I fond *þere* Freres, alle þe foure ordres,
B.Pr.68	*Ther* preched a pardoner as he a preest were;
B.Pr.112	Thanne kam *þer* a kyng; knyȝthod hym ladde;
B.Pr.146	Wiþ þat ran *þer* a route of Ratons at ones
B.Pr.165	Were *þer* a belle on hire beiȝe, by Iesu, as me þynkeþ,
B.Pr.177	*Ther* ne was Raton in þe route, for al þe Reaume of Fraunce,
B.Pr.185	'Thouȝ we [hadde] kille[d] þe cat yet sholde *þer* come anoþer
B.Pr.197	For may no renk þar reste haue for Ratons by nyȝte,]
B.Pr.211	Yet houed *þer* an hundred in howues of selk,
B.1.32	Thoruȝ wyn and þoruȝ wommen *þer* was loth acombred,
B.1.33	And *þere* gat in glotonie gerles þat were cherles.
B.1.115	Into a deep derk helle to dwelle *þere* for euere;
B.1.164	And in þe herte *þere* is þe heed and þe heiȝe welle.
B.1.165	For in kynde knowynge in herte *þer* [comseþ a myȝt],
B.2.45	[*There*] myȝtow witen if þow wilt whiche þei ben alle
B.2.47	Knowe hem *þere* if þow kanst and kepe [þee from hem alle],
B.2.95	And *þere* to Iangle and Iape and Iugge hir euencristen,
B.3.11	A[c] *þer* was murþe & Mynstralcie Mede to plese;
B.3.35	Thanne cam *þer* a Confessour coped as a frere;
B.3.49	Woldestow glaȝe þ[e] gable & graue [*þere*] þy name
B.3.66	An auenture pride be peynted *þere* and pomp of þe world;
B.3.231	'*Ther* are two manere of Medes, my lord, [bi] youre leue.
B.3.246	*Ther* is [a] Mede mesurelees þat maistres desireþ;
B.3.266	Weend to Amalec with þyn oost & what þow fyndest *þere* sle it.
B.4.23	For he wol make wehee twies er [we] be *þere.*
B.4.34	'*Ther* are wiles in hire wordes, and with Mede þei dwelleþ,
B.4.35	Theras wraþe and wranglynge is *þer* wynne þei siluer,
B.4.36	Ac [þ]ere is loue and leautee [hem likeþ] noȝt come *þere:*
B.5.65	She sholde vnsowen hir serk and sette *þere* an heyre
B.5.170	For *þere* ben manye felle frekes my feeris to aspie,
B.5.177	I ete *þere* vnþende fissh and feble ale drynke.
B.5.249	And took it by tale here and tolde hem *þere* lasse.'
B.5.323	*Ther* were chapmen ychose þis chaffare to preise:
B.5.327	[*There* were oþes an heep, whoso it herde];
B.5.336	*There* was lauȝynge and lourynge and 'lat go þe cuppe!'
B.5.432	I am noȝt lured wiþ loue but *þer* ligge auȝt vnder þe þombe.
B.5.462	And for *þer* was noȝt wher[wiþ] he wepte swiþe soore.
B.5.489	*Ther* þiself ne þi sone no sorwe in deeþ feledest,
B.5.513	Ac *þere* was [wye] noon so wys þe wey þider couþe,
B.5.568	Wadeþ in þat water and wasshe yow wel *þer*
B.5.575	Loke [þow] breke no bowes *þere* but if it be [þyn] owene.
B.5.576	Two stokkes *þer* stondeþ, ac stynte [þow] noȝt þere;
B.5.576	Two stokkes *þer* stondeþ, ac stynte [þow] noȝt *þere;*
B.5.582	Loke þow plukke no plaunte *þere* for peril of þi soule.
B.5.618	A[c] *þer* are seuen sustren þat seruen truþe euere
B.5.630	'By Crist!' quod a kuttepurs, 'I haue no kyn *þere.'*
B.5.635	'Mercy is a maiden *þere* haþ myȝt ouer [hem] alle;
B.5.638	Thow myȝt gete grace *þere* so þow go bityme.'
B.5.639	'Bi seint Poul!' quod a pardoner, 'parauenture I be noȝt knowe *þere;*
B.6.109	Oþere werkmen *þer* were þat wroȝten ful [faste],
B.6.200	Hoom [in]to his owene [e]rd and holden hym *þere* [euere].
B.6.273	[*Ther* are mo lieres þan] leches; lord hem amende!
B.6.319	Ac whiles hunger was hir maister *þer* wolde noon chide
B.7.96	*Ther* is moore mysshapen amonges þise beggeres.
B.7.172	It bifel as his fader tolde, hise frendes *þere* hym souȝte.
B.7.197	A pokeful of pardon *þere,* ne prouincials lettres,
B.8.36	[*There*] were [þe mannes] lif lost [for] lachesse of hymselue.
B.8.105	And putten hem *þer* in penaunce wiþoute pite or grace],
B.8.106	But dobest bede for hem [abide] *þer* for euere.
B.10.216	Yet ar *þer* fibicches in [forelles] of fele mennes [wittes],
B.10.308	But al is buxomnesse *þere* and bokes, to rede and to lerne].
B.10.309	In scole *þere* is scorn but if a clerk wol lerne,
B.10.322	Ac *þer* shal come a kyng and confesse yow Religiouses,
B.10.437	*Ther* are witty and wel libbynge ac hire werkes ben yhudde,
B.10.439	Wher fo[r loue] a man worþ allowed *þere* and hise lele werkes,
B.10.443	And who were a good man but if *þer* were som sherewe?
B.11.7	[For] I was rauȝsshed riȝt *þere;* Fortune me fette
B.11.27	Thanne was *þer* oon þat hiȝte Elde, þat heuy was of chere;
B.11.123	'Thanne may alle cristene come', quod I, 'and cleyme *þere* entree
B.11.134	For hise arerages rewarden hym *þere* [riȝt] to þe day of dome,
B.11.171	'Lawe wiþouten loue', quod Troianus, 'ley *þer* a bene!'

B.11.202 And blody breþeren we bicome þere of o body ywonne,
B.11.259 [Al]þou3 it be sour to suffre, þe[r] comeþ swete [after].
B.11.341 Ther ne was cow ne cowkynde þat conceyued hadde
B.11.349 Ther nys wri3te, as I wene, sholde werche hir nes[t] to paye;
B.11.436 Ther smyt no þyng so smerte, ne smelleþ so [foule]
B.12.17 And bidde for hem þat 3yueþ þee breed, for þer are bokes y[n]owe
B.12.125 Ac if þer were any wight þat wolde me telle
B.12.28 And þere bidde my bedes but whan ich ete or slepe.
B.12.80 Than þe womman þat þere was, and wenten awey for shame.
B.12.81 [Thus Clergie þere] conforted þe womman.
B.12.127 Was þer neuere [kyng ne] kny3t but clergie hem made.
B.12.143 He spekeþ þere of riche men ri3t no3t, ne of ri3t witty,
B.12.145 If any frere were founde þere I 3yue þee fyue shillynges!
B.12.180 Ther þe lewed liþ stille and lokeþ after lente,
B.12.213 And wel lose[l]þ he lolleþ þere by þe lawe of holy chirche:
B.12.285 [Ac] þer is fullynge of Font and fullynge in blood shedyng
B.12.288 But lyueþ as his lawe techeþ and leueþ þer be no bettre,
B.12.289 And if þer were he wolde amende, and in swich wille deieþ–
B.13.22 And as crist wolde þer com Conscience to conforte me þat tyme
B.13.25 And as I [mette] a maister, what man he was I nyste,
B.13.52 'Here is propre seruice', quod Pacience, 'þer fareþ no Prince bettre.'
B.13.152 I bere þer, [in a bouste] faste ybounde, dowel,
B.13.165 There nys neiþer emperour ne emperesse, erl ne baroun,
B.13.193 For þer [is] no tresour [þerto] to a trewe wille.
B.13.207 Ther nys wo in þis world þat we ne sholde amende;
B.13.265 There was a careful commune whan no cart com to towne
B.13.275 Of pride here a plot, and þere a plot of vnbuxom speche,
B.13.331 Ther is no lif þat me loueþ lastynge any while.
B.13.401 As þere no nede was goddes name an Idel;
B.14.101 There is Charite þe chief, chaumbrere for god hymselue.'
B.14.109 Ther þe poore dar plede and preue by pure reson
B.14.202 For seuene synnes þer ben assaillen vs euere;
B.14.219 Ne none of þe seuene synnes sitten ne mowe þer longe,
B.15.98 Ther is a meschief in þe more of swiche manere [stokkes].
B.15.201 For þer are [pure] proude herted men, pacient of tonge
B.15.205 For þer are beggeris and bidderis, bedemen as it were,
B.15.298 Ac þer ne was leoun ne leopard þat on laundes wenten–
B.15.347 Ac þer is a defaute in þe folk þat þe feiþ kepeþ,
B.15.411 That [lered] þere and [lewed] 3it leeuen on hise lawes.
B.16.116 And wepte water with hise ei3en; þer sei3en it manye.
B.17.102 That he ne was robbed or rifled, rood he þer or yede,
B.17.321 Thre þynges þer ben þat doon a man by strengþe
B.17.350 For þer nys sik ne sory, ne noon so muche wrecche
B.18.6 Reste me þere and rutte faste til Ramis palmarum.
B.18.78 Ac þer cam forþ a kny3t wiþ a kene spere ygrounde,
B.18.83 For alle þei were vnhardy þat houed [þer] or stode
B.18.112 And þere I sau3 sooþly, secundum scripturas,
B.18.152 For venym fordooþ venym, [þer fecche I euydence
B.18.230 Thanne was þer a wight wiþ two brode ei3en;
B.18.233 That þo þis barn was ybore þer blased a sterre
B.19.36 As wide as þe world is [wonyeþ þer noon]
B.19.80 And þere was þat word fulfilled þe which þow of speke,
B.19.110 And þere bigan god of his grace to do wel:
B.19.123 After þe kynde þat he cam of; þere comsede he do wel.
B.19.155 Telle þe comune þat þer cam a compaignie of hise Apostles
B.19.192 He wente, and wonyeþ þere, and wol come at þe laste
B.19.356 Hastiliche into vnitee and holde we vs þere.
B.19.372 Ther nas no cristene creature þat kynde wit hadde
B.19.418 And þer þei ligge and lenge moost lecherie þere regneþ".
B.19.459 Thanne lou3 þer a lord and, 'by þis light!' seide,
B.19.465 And þanne cam þer a kyng and by his croune seide,
B.19.469 Ther I may hastilokest it haue, for I am heed of lawe;
B.20.57 And gerte gile growe þere as he a god weere.
B.20.75 Into vnite holy chirche and holde we vs þere
B.20.79 And þere abide and bikere ayeins Beliales children.'
B.20.88 There was 'harrow!' and 'help! here comeþ kynde
B.20.177 And þere dyed þat doctour er þre dayes after.
B.20.205 And hold þee þere euere til I sende for þee.
B.20.214 And þere was Conscience Conestable, cristene to saue,
B.20.311 Sire leef-to-lyue-in-lecherie lay þere and gronede;
B.20.313 'Ther is a Surgien in þ[e] sege þat softe kan handle,
C.Pr.19 A fair feld ful of folk fond y þer bytwene
C.Pr.56 I fonde þer Freris, alle þe foure ordres,
C.Pr.66 Ther prechede a Pardoner as he a prest were,
C.Pr.84 And synge þer for symonye [for] seluer is swete.
C.Pr.99 In menynge of myracles muche wex hangeth there;
C.Pr.139 Thenne cam the[r] a kyng; knygh[t]hede hym la[dd]e;
C.Pr.167 Than ran þer a route of ratones [at ones]
C.Pr.182 Wer þer a belle on here beygh, by iesu, as me thynketh,
C.Pr.194 Ther ne was [raton in] þe route, for al þe reame of Fraunce,
C.Pr.202 'Thow we hadde ykuld þe Cat 3ut shulde ther come anoþer;
C.1.31 Thorw wyn and thorw wom[e]n there was loot acombred;

C.1.120 Ther he faylede and ful and his felawes alle;
C.1.121 And helle is þer he is and [he] þere ybounde.
C.1.161 For [in] kynde knowynge [in] herte þer comseth a myhte
C.2.102 And there to iangele and iape and iuge here Emcristene,
C.3.12 Ac there was myrthe and mynstracie mede to plese;
C.3.38 Thenne come þer a confessour ycoped as a frere;
C.3.52 Wolde 3e glase þ[e] gable and graue ther 3oure name
C.3.70 An Auntur pruyde be paynted there and pomp of the world,
C.3.102 And thenne falleth ther fuyr on fals men houses
C.3.142 Or in a wel wors, wo[en ther as an ancre,
C.3.191 Ther she is wel with eny kyng wo is þ[e] rewme
C.3.204 Ther ne is Cite vnder sonne ne noon so ryche reume
C.3.291 Ac ther is mede and mercede and bothe men demen
C.3.309 And ther is resoun as a reue rewardynge treuthe
C.4.35 For there is wrath and wranglynge there wol they abyde;
C.4.71 Thorw wrong and his werkes there was mede yknowe
C.4.150 Reherce the[r] anon ryhte þat myhte resoun stoppe.
C.5.168 Ac þer shal come a kyng and confesse 3ow alle
C.6.6 A sholde vnsowen here serk and sette þe[r] an hayre
C.6.19 Inobedient to holy churche and to hem þat þer serueth;
C.6.152 For there aren many felle frekes myn aferes to aspye,
C.6.159 For y ete more fysch then flesche there and feble ale drynke.
C.6.303 There shal he wite witturly what vsure is to mene
C.6.308 Thenne was there a walschman was wonderly sory,
C.6.316 And for þer was nat wherwith a wep swythe sore.
C.6.380 There were chapmen ychose this chaffare to preyse;
C.6.385 And there were othes an heep for on sholde haue þe worse.
C.6.394 There was leyhing and louryng and 'lat go the coppe!'
C.7.45 Y am nat luyred with loue but þer lygge ouht vnder þe t[h]umbe.
C.7.158 Ac þer was wye non so wys þat the way thider couthe
C.7.215 Wadeth in þat water and wascheth 3ow wel there
C.7.222 Loke þou bere n[ouht] þere away but yf hit be thyn owene.
C.7.223 T[w]o stokkes þere stondeth ac stynte thow nat þere;
C.7.223 T[w]o stokkes þere stondeth ac stynte thow nat þere;
C.7.229 Loke thow plokke no plonte þere for perel of thy soule.
C.7.270 Ac þer ben seuene sustres þat seruen treuthe euere
C.7.283 'By Crist!' quod a cottepors, 'y haue no kyn there.'
C.7.288 'Mercy is a mayden there hath myhte ouer hem alle
C.7.291 Thow myhte gete grace there so thow go bytymes.'
C.8.116 Oþer werkemen þer were þat wrouhten fol 3erne,
C.8.160 For ther worth no plente,' quod [Perus], 'and þe plouh lygge.'
C.8.194 There was no ladde þat lyuede þat ne lowede hym to Peres
C.8.206 Hoem [in]to his owene [e]rd and halde hym þere euere.
C.8.215 'Ther is no fi[al] loue with this folk for al here fayre speche
C.8.294 Ther ar many luther leches Ac lele leches fewe;
C.8.339 Ac whiles hungur was here maistre ther wolde non chyde
C.9.40 And abyde þer in my blisse body and soule for euere.'
C.9.92 There is payne and peny ale as for a pytaunce ytake
C.9.105 A[nd] 3ut ar ther oþere beggares, in hele as hit semeth
C.9.172 Ther aren mo mysshape amonges suche beggares
C.9.280 For shal no pardon preye for 3ow there ne no princes lettres.
C.9.343 A pouhe ful of pardon there ne prouinciales lettres,
C.10.242 Ac þe gospel is glose ther and huydeth þe grayth treuthe;
C.10.266 Ther ne is squier ne knyhte in contreye aboute
C.11.166 For y was rauysched rihte there; fortune me fette
C.11.186 Thenne was [there] oen þat hihte Elde þat heuy was of chere;
C.12.58 'Thenne may alle cristene come,' [quod y], 'and clayme þer entre
C.12.69 And for his rechelesnes rewarde hym þere riht to þe day of dome
C.12.93 For lawe withouten leutee, ley þer a bene!
C.12.110 And blody bretherne we bycome there of o body ywonne,
C.12.145 Althouh h[it] be sour to soffre þer cometh a swete aftur.
C.13.91 Ther is no lawe, as y leue, wol lette hym þe gate
C.13.97 And as moche mede for a myte þer he offreth
C.13.149 Ther ne [was] cow ne cowkynde þat conseyued hadde
C.13.151 Ther ne was no kyne kynde þat conseyued hadde
C.13.160 Ther is no wriht, as y wene, sholde worch here neste to paye;
C.13.218 And thenne was ther a wyhte, what he was y neste.
C.13.242 Ther smyt no thyng so smerte ne smelleth so foule
C.14.87 Hit speketh þer of ryche men riht nouht ne of ryche lordes
C.14.89 Yf eny frere we[re] founde þere y 3eue þe fyue shillynges!
C.14.120 There þe lewede lyth stille and loketh aftur lente
C.14.152 And wel lo[s]liche he lolleth þere by þe lawe of holy churche:
C.14.207 Ac þer is follyng of fonte and follyng in bloed [s]hedyng
C.14.210 Bote lyue[th] as his lawe t[echeth] and leueth þer be no bettre,
C.14.211 And yf þer were a wolde [amende], and in suche a wille deyeth–
C.15.129 Shal no such motyef be meued for me bote [þ]ere
C.15.165 Þer [n]is wyht in this world þat wolde the lette
C.16.43 For seuene synnes þer ben þat ass[a]ilen vs euere;
C.16.60 Ne none of þe seuene synnes sitte ne may þer longe
C.16.142 And euere þe lasse þat [eny] lede þe lihtere his herte is there,
C.16.251 There is a meschief in þe more of suche manere stokkes.
C.17.1 'There is no such,' y sayde, 'þat som tyme ne borweth
C.17.6 Holy writ witnesseth þer were suche eremytes,

C.17.62	Helpe thy kyn, Crist bid, for *þer* [coms]eth charite
C.17.64	And *þer* helpe yf thow has[t]; and þat halde y charite.
C.17.94	*Ther* sholde be plente and pees perpetuel euere.
C.17.154	For *þer* is no man þat mynde hath þat ne meketh [hym] and bysecheth
C.17.156	Ac many manere men *þer* ben, as sarresynes and iewes,
C.17.282	Or cristendoem were knowe *þere* or eny croos honoured.
C.18.81	'Ʒe, sire,' y sayde, 'and sethen *þer* aren but tweyne lyues
C.18.139	That suche a surgien sethen ysaye was *þer* neuere
C.18.157	And drof hem out, alle þat *þer* bouhte and solde,
C.18.266	And conforted many a carfol *þere* þat aftur his comyng loke[n].
C.19.75	And lefte hym *þere* a lechyng to lyue yf he myhte
C.19.103	Noþer lacke ne alose ne leue þat *þer* were
C.19.288	The[r] þat partye pursueth the apeel is so huge
C.19.301	Thre thynges *ther* ben þat doth a man to sterte
C.19.330	For *þer* ne is sike ne sory ne non so moche wrecche
C.20.80	Ac *þer* cam forth a knyhte with a kene spere ygrounde,
C.20.85	For alle [they were] vnhardy þat houed *þer* or stode
C.20.115	And *there* y seyh sothly, secundum scripturas,
C.20.155	For venym fordoth venym, *þer* feche y euydence
C.20.239	Thenne wa[s] *ther* a wihte with two brode yes;
C.20.242	[That tho] this barn was ybore *þ[er]* blased a sterre
C.20.347	For we leued on thy lesynges [*there* losten we blisse;
C.20.379	Falsliche [thow] fettest *there* þat me biful to loke,
C.21.36	As wyd[e] as þe worlde is wonyeth *þer* none
C.21.80	And *þer* was þat word fulfuld þe which þou of speke,
C.21.110	And *þer* bigan god of his grace to do wel:
C.21.123	Aftur þe kynde þat he cam of; *þer* comsede he do wel.
C.21.155	Telle þe comune þat *þer* cam a companie of his apostles
C.21.192	He wente and woneth *there* and wol come at þe laste
C.21.356	Hastiliche [in]to vnite and holde we vs *there*.
C.21.372	*Ther* ne was cristene creature that kynde wit hadde
C.21.418	And þer they lygge and lenge moest lecherye *þer* regneth".
C.21.459	Thenne lowh *ther* a lord and 'bi this lihte!' saide,
C.21.465	And thenne cam *þer* a kyng and bi his corone saide,
C.22.57	And garte gyle [growe] *þere* as he a god were.
C.22.75	Into vnite holi churche and halde we vs *there*.
C.22.79	And *þere* abyde and bikere aʒeyn beliales childrene.'
C.22.88	*There* was 'harow!' and 'helpe! here cometh kynde
C.22.177	And *þere* deyede þat doctour ar thre dayes aftur.
C.22.205	And halde the *there* euere til y sende for the.
C.22.214	And *there* was Consience Constable, cristene to saue,
C.22.311	Sire l[ee]f-to-lyue-in-lecherye lay *þer* and groned;
C.22.313	'*Ther* is a surgien in the sege that softe can handele

þer conj *ther adv.* A 15 þer (1) þere (14); B 93 ther (24) þer (40) there (7) þere (22); C 86 thare (1) ther (21) þer (34) there (26) þere (4)

A. 1.122	*Þere* treuþe is in trinite & tron[iþ] h[e]m alle.
A. 1.138	[*Þer*] þou art m[er]y at mete, ʒif men bidde þe ʒedde.
A. 2.99	Lediþ hire to lundoun *þere* lawe is yhandlit
A. 3.14	Buski[de] hem to þe bour *þere* þe burde dwelliþ,
A. 3.33	*Þere* cunnyng clerkis shuln clokke behynde.'
A. 3.142	*Þere* she is wel wiþ þe king wo is þe reaume.
A. 3.164	*Þere* þat meschief is gret mede may helpe.
A. 3.184	*Þere* I lefte wiþ my lord his lif for to saue,
A. 4.109	Til seint Iame be souʒt *þere* I shal assigne,
A. 5.95	I deme men *þere* [hy] don ille, & ʒet I do wers;
A. 6.79	Þe tour *þere* treuþe is hymself is vp to þe sonne;
A. 7.228	"He þat haþ shal haue to helpe *þere* nede is,
A. 9.78	Whiles he haþ ouʒt of his owene he helpiþ *þere* nede is;
A.11.60	Þat defouliþ oure f[eiþ] at fest[is] *þere* þei sitten.
A.11.143	For *þere* þat loue is lord lakkiþ neuere grace.
B.Pr.105	*There* [crist is in] kyngdom, to close and to shette,
B.Pr.194	*Ther* þe cat is a kitoun þe court is ful elenge;
B. 1.133	*Ther* Treuþe is in Trinitee and troneþ hem alle.
B. 2.135	Ledeþ hire to Londoun *þere* [lawe] is [yhandled],
B. 3.14	Busked hem to þe bour *þer* þe burde dwelle[þ],
B. 3.34	*Ther* konnynge clerkes shul clokke bihynde.'
B. 3.153	*Ther* she is wel wiþ þe kyng wo is þe Reaume.
B. 3.177	*Ther* þat meschief is [most] Mede may helpe.
B. 3.197	*Ther* I lafte wiþ my lord his lif for to saue.
B. 4.36	Ac [þ]ere is loue and leautee [hem likeþ] noʒt come þere:
B. 4.126	And til Seint Iames be souʒt *þere* I shal assigne,
B. 5.115	[I] deme [men *þere* hij] doon ille, [and yet] I do werse;
B. 5.265	For were I frere of þat hous *þer* good feiþ and charite is
B. 5.370	*There* no nede was nyne hundred tymes;
B. 5.375	And sat som tyme so longe *þere* þat I sleep and eet at ones.
B. 6.244	"He þat haþ shal haue and helpe *þere* [nede is]
B. 8.87	[Whiles he haþ ouʒt of his owene he helpeþ *þer* nede is];
B. 9.42	And so it semeþ by hym [*þere* he seide in þe bible
B.10.98	*Ther* þe lord ne lady likeþ noʒt to sitte.
B.10.191	For *þere* þat loue is ledere lakke[þ] neuere grace.
B.10.319	In many places *þer* þei [persons ben, be þei purely] at ese,
B.10.329	Of Costantyns cofres [*þer* þe catel is Inne]
B.10.348	*Ther* riche men no riʒt may cleyme but of ruþe and grace.'
B.11.67	[At kirke] *þere* a man were cristned by kynde he sholde be buryed.
B.11.153	Brouʒte me fro bitter peyne *þer* no biddyng myʒte.'
B.11.166	*Ther* no clergie ne kouþe, ne konnyng of lawes.
B.11.210	And of þat ech man may forbere amende *þere* it nedeþ,
B.11.245	*Ther* neuere segge hym seiʒ in secte of þe riche.
B.11.319	The which I preise, *þer* pacience is, moore parfit þan richesse.
B.11.362	*Ther* neiþer burn ne beest may hir briddes rechen.
B.11.437	As shame: *þere* he sheweþ hym, [hym shonyeþ euery man].
B.12.61	Pacience and pouerte þe place [is] *þer* it groweþ,
B.12.167	*Ther* his felawe fleteþ forþ as þe flood likeþ
B.12.191	*Ther* lewed þeues ben lolled vp; loke how þei be saued!
B.12.228	[That *þ]ere* þe þorn is þikkest to buylden and brede;
B.12.258	And alle þe oþere *þer* it lith enuenymeþ þoruʒ his attre.
B.13.110	But cheeste be *þer* charite sholde be, and yonge children dorste pleyne.
B.13.121	*Ther* þe lord of lif wonyeþ, to leren [hem] what is dowel.
B.13.156	And herwith am I welcome *þer* I haue it wiþ me.
B.13.219	*There* vnkyndenesse and coueitise is, hungry contrees boþe.
B.13.290	And entremetten hym ouer al *þer* he haþ noʒt to doone;
B.13.434	*Ther* wise men were, witnesseþ goddes wordes,
B.13.454	[*There*] flateres and fooles þoruʒ hir foule wordes
B.14.93	*Ther* contricion dooþ but dryueþ it doun into a venial synne
B.14.100	'*Ther* parfit truþe and poore herte is, and pacience of tonge,
B.14.205	For *þer* þat richesse regneþ reuerence[s] folweþ,
B.14.208	*Ther* þe poore is put bihynde, and parauenture kan moore
B.14.213	*Ther* þe poore preesseþ bifore wiþ a pak at his rugge:
B.14.218	Ac in pouerte *þer* pacience is pride haþ no myʒte,
B.14.247	*Ther* Auarice haþ Almaries and yren bounden cofres.
B.14.306	For *þer* þat Pouerte passeþ pees folweþ after,
B.15.95	*There* inparfit preesthode is, prechours and techeris.
B.15.97	*Ther* some bowes ben leued and some bereþ none
B.15.101	A[c] *þer* þe roote is roten, reson woot þe soþe,
B.15.155	And wollen lene *þer* þei leue lelly to ben paied;
B.15.183	*Ther* poore men and prisons liggeþ, hir pardon to haue;
B.15.204	And as a lyoun he lokeþ *þer* men lakken hise werkes.
B.15.214	Ne at Ancres *þere* a box hangeþ; alle swiche þei faiten.
B.15.235	In kynges court he comeþ ofte *þer* þe counseil is trewe,
B.15.304	In likkyng and in lowynge, *þer* þei on laundes yede].
B.15.312	And bidden hem bere it *þere* it [yborwed was].
B.15.337	And helpeþ hem þat helpeþ yow and ʒyueþ *þer* no nede is,
B.15.576	Bodily foode and goostly foode to] gyue *þere* it nedeþ:
B.16.62	The ground *þere* it groweþ, goodnesse it hatte;
B.16.85	*There* is derknesse and drede and þe deuel maister.
B.16.140	The þursday bifore, *þere* he made his [cene],
B.16.201	And *þere* hym likede and [he] louede, in þre persones hym shewede.
B.17.118	And Hope þe Hostile[r] shal be *þer* [an helyng þe man lith];
B.17.273	But þei dwelle *þer* Diues is dayes wiþouten ende.
B.17.298	Ne haue pite for any preiere *þer* þat he pleyneþ.
B.17.305	Ac it is but selden yseiʒe, *þer* sooþnesse bereþ witnesse,
B.17.307	Be raunsoned for his repentaunce *þer* alle reson hym dampneþ.
B.17.308	For *þer* þat partie pursueþ þe [peel] is so huge
B.17.339	The reyn þat reyneþ *þer* we reste sholde
B.18.34	And legge it *þer* hym likeþ, and Lucifer bynde,
B.18.155	May no medicyne [amende] þe place *þer* he styngeþ
B.18.228	Woot no wight what werre is *þer* þat pees regneþ,
B.18.270	And lede it *þer* [laʒar is] and lightliche me bynde.
B.18.292	'It is noʒt graiþly geten *þer* gile is þe roote,
B.18.382	*There* [a] feloun þole sholde deeþ ooþer Iuwise
B.18.385	*Ther* doom to þe deeþ dampneþ alle wikked,
B.18.399	And nameliche at swich a nede *þer* nedes help bihoueþ:
B.18.431	May no grisly goost glide *þere* it [shadweþ].'
B.19.136	Forþi þe contree *þer* Iesu cam called hym fili dauid,
B.19.160	In ech a compaignie *þer* she cam, Christus resurgens.
B.19.313	Foulen þe fruyt in þe feld *þer* þei growen togideres,
B.19.418	And *þer* þei ligge and lenge moost lecherie þere regneþ".
B.20.46	*Ther* nede haþ ynome me þat I moot nede abide
B.20.56	In ech a contree *þer* he cam he kutte awey truþe
B.20.328	In contrees *þer* he coome confessions to here;
B.20.329	And cam *þere* Conscience was and knokked at þe yate.
B.20.344	Coom in þus ycoped at a Court *þere* I dwelde,
B.20.368	Thus he gooþ and gadereþ and gloseþ *þere* he shryueþ
C.Pr.114	Fro his chayere *þer* he sat and brake his nekke atwene.
C.Pr.133	*Thare* Crist is in kynedom to close with heuene.
C.Pr.172	And playde with somme perilously and potte hem *þer* hym lykede.
C.Pr.207	*Ther* þe Cat [is] a kytoun þe Court is ful elynge.
C. 1.114	Thenne sitten in þe sonne syde *þere* þe day roweth?'
C. 1.117	'Hit is sikerore bi southe *þer* þe sonne regneth
C. 1.121	And helle is *þer* he is and [he] *þere* ybounde.
C. 1.131	Aftur here deth day and dwelle *ther* wrong is;
C. 1.134	*There* treuthe is, þe tour that trinite ynne sitteth.
C. 1.160	And in þe herte *þer* is þe hed and þe heye welle.

C. 2.99   *There* þat wille wolde and wer[k]manschip faileth.
C. 2.151   And ledeth here to londone *there* lawe may declare
C. 3.15   Boskede hem to þe bour *ther* th[e] buyrde dwel[leth],
C. 3.37   *There* connynge clerkes shal clokke byhynde.'
C. 3.205   *Ther* he is alowed and ylet by þat laste shal eny while
C. 3.223   *Ther* þat meschief is greet mede may helpe;
C. 3.239   In contrees *there* the kyng cam, consience hym lette
C. 3.257   'Ne be Marschal ouer my men *there* y moste fyhte.
C. 3.331   Bothe gyue and graunte *there* his grace lyketh
C. 4.35   For *there* is wrath and wranglynge there wol they abyde;
C. 4.36   Ac *there* is loue and leutee hit lyketh nat here hertes:
C. 4.82   *Ther* he sholde nat in seuene 3er see his feet [ones].
C. 4.122   And til saynt Iames be souhte *there* pore sykke lyggen,
C. 4.132   Whiles mede hath the maistrie *þer* motyng is at [þe] Barr[e].
C. 5.32   *There* ryhtfulnesse rewardeth ryht as men deserueth–
C. 5.165   In many places *ther* his persones ben, he hemsulue at ese,
C. 6.428   *There* no nede ne was, many sythe falsly;
C. 7.94   *There* wyse men were, wittnesseth goddes wordes,
C. 7.114   *There* flaterers and foles with here foule wordes
C. 7.205   Ac hoso wol wende *þer* treuthe is, this is þe way thede[r]:
C. 8.255   "He þat hath shal haue and helpe *þer* hym liketh
C. 9.39   And sende 3oure soules *þer* y mysulue dwelle
C. 9.67   Bote *ther* he wiste were wel grete nede
C.11.42   Is non so hende to haue hym [in] but hote hym go *þer* god is.
C.12.234 Ouerplente pruyde norischeth *þer* pouerte hit distrueth.
C.13.40   *Ther* þe messager doth no more but with his mouth telleth
C.13.56   *Ther* þe marchaunt l[et] a male with many kyne thynges
C.13.59   *Ther* þe messager is ay merye and his mouth ful of songes
C.13.92   *Ther* god is gateward hymsulf and vch a gome knoweth.
C.13.243 As shame: *ther* he sheweth hym vch man shoneth his companye.
C.14.130 *There* lewede theues ben lolled vp; loke how þei ben saued!
C.15.188 *There* vnkyndenesse and coueytise [is], hungry contreys bothe.
C.15.285 *There* þe pore dar plede and preue by puyr resoun
C.16.46   For [þer] þat rychess[e] regneth reuerences followeth
C.16.49   *There* þe pore is potte behynde and parauntur can more
C.16.54   *There* þe pore preseth byfore with a pak at his rugge,
C.16.59   Ac in pouerte *þer* pacience is pruyde hath no myhte
C.16.87   *There* Auaryce hath almaries and yrebounden coffres.
C.16.122 Al þat may potte of pruyde in place *þer* he regneth;
C.16.231 Freres fele tymes to þe folk *þer* they prechen
C.16.247 *There* inparfit preesthoed is, prechares and techares.
C.16.249 *Þere* som bowes bereth leues and som bereth none:
C.16.254 Ac *þer* þe rote is roton, resoun woet þe sothe,
C.16.304 Lawhe *þer* men lawheth and loure þer oþere louren.
C.16.304 Lawhe þer men lawheth and loure *þer* oþere louren.
C.16.315 That neuere payed peny a3eyn in places *þer* he borwede.'
C.16.325 *There* pore men and prisones ben and paye for here fode,
C.16.343 He is þe murieste of mouthe at mete *þer* he sitteth
C.17.11   Elles foules fedde hem in frythes *þer* they wonede,
C.17.292 And nameliche *þer* þat lewede lyuen and no lawe knoweth.
C.18.116 *There* is derkenesse and drede and þe deuel maister.
C.18.212 A thre he is *þer* he is and hereof bereth wittnesse
C.19.254 Bote thay dwelle *there* diues is dayes withouten ende.
C.19.285 Ac hit is bote selde yseyen, *there* sothnesse bereth witnesse,
C.19.287 Be yraunsomed for his repentaunce *þer* alle resoun hym dampneth.
C.19.319 The rayne þat rayneth *þere* we reste sholde
C.20.33   And legge hit *þere* hym liketh and lucifer bynde
C.20.158 May no medecyne amende the place *there* he styngeth
C.20.237 For woet no wiht what werre is *þer* [þat] pees regneth
C.20.278 And lede hit *þer* la3ar is and lihtliche me bynde.
C.20.352 'Hit is nat graythly ygete *þer* gyle is þe rote
C.20.386 So lyf shal lyf le[t]e *ther* lyf hath lyf an[y]en[t]ed
C.20.424 *Ther* a thief tholie sholde deth oþer iewyse
C.20.427 *Ther* þat doem to þe deth dampneth alle wikkede
C.20.475 May no grisly goest glyde *þer* hit shaddeweth.'
C.21.136 Forthy þe contre *þer* iesu cam calde hym fili dauid
C.21.160 In vch a companye *þer* he cam, christus resurgens.
C.21.313 Fouleth the fruyt in the feld *ther* thei growe togyderes
C.21.418 And *þer* they lygge and lenge moest lecherye þer regneth".
C.21.469 *Ther* y may hastilokest hit haue, for y am heed of lawe;
C.22.46   *Ther* nede hath ynome me þat y moet nede abyde
C.22.56   In vch a Contrey *ther* he cam [he] kutte awey treuthe
C.22.328 In contreys *þer* he cam confessiones to here;
C.22.329 And cam *þer* Consience was and knokked at þe 3ate.
C.22.344 Kam ynne thus ycoped at a Court *þer* y dwelte
C.22.368 Thus he goeth and gedereth and gloseth *þer* he shryueth

ther > *þei,theras*

þerafter adv *therafter adv.* A 10 þerafter (1) þeraftir (3) þereaftir (6); B 17; C 11 theraftur (1) þeraftir (1) þeraftur (9)

A.Pr.23 And summe putte hem to pride, aparailide hem *þereaftir*,
A. 1.135 For þus [wytnessiþ] his woord, werche þou *þeraftir*,
A. 3.174 For kilde I neuere no king ne counseilide *þeraftir*,

A. 5.56   Wiþ þat he [shulde] þe satirday, seue 3er *þeraftir*,
A. 5.137 And whoso bummide þerof, bou3te it *þereaftir*,
A. 6.65   Leue hym on þi left half, & loke nou3t *þereaftir*,
A. 7.106 Shulde ben hirid *þereaftir* whan heruist tyme come.
A. 8.12   Wiþ patriarkes in paradis to plei3e *þereaftir*.
A.11.180 To lere at 3ow dowel & dobet *þereaftir*,
A.12.10 3if I wiste witterly þou woldest don *þerafter*,
B.Pr.23 And somme putten hem to pride, apparailed hem *þerafter*.
B. 1.147 [For þus witnesseþ his word; werche þow *þerafter*].
B. 1.156 Was neuere leef vpon lynde lighter *þerafter*,
B. 3.187 For killed I neuere no kyng, ne counseiled *þerafter*,
B. 3.342 She sholde haue founden fel[l]e wordes folwynge *þerafter*:
B. 5.73   Wiþ þat he sholde þe Saterday, seuen yer *þerafter*,
B. 5.221 And whoso bummed þerof bou3te it *þerafter*,
B. 5.496 The þridde day [þer]after þow yedest in oure sute;
B. 5.578 Leue hem on þi lift half and loke no3t *þerafter*.
B. 6.114 Sholde be hired *þerafter* whan heruest tyme come.
B.10.91 And whoso litel weldeþ [wisse] hym *þerafter*,
B.10.300 And seiþ it in ensample [þat] þei sholde do *þerafter*:
B.10.404 As þei seyen hemself selde doon *þerafter*:
B.11.25 'He shal fynde me his frend', quod Fortune *þerafter*;
B.14.141 Haue heuene in youre her[berw]yng and heuene *þerafter*
B.15.59 But he do *þerafter*, it dooþ hym double scaþe.
B.17.124 That craueþ it [or] coueiteþ it [and] crieþ *þerafter*
C.Pr.25 And summe putte hem to pruyde, [a]parayled hem *þeraftir*
C. 1.152 Was neuer lef vppon lynde lyhtere *theraftur*
C. 3.484 As wroth as [þe] wynd wax mede *þeraftur*:
C. 6.229 And hoso boumode therof bouhte hit *þeraftur*:
C. 7.136 The thridde day *þeraftur* thow 3edest i[n] oure sekte;
C. 7.225 And leu[e] hem [o]n þ[y] luft ha[lf] and loke [nat] *þeraftur*
C. 8.90   And aftur here warnynge and wor[d]ynge worche þou *þeraftur*:
C. 8.121 He sholde be huyred *þeraftur* when heruost tyme come.
C.11.145 Leue hit lelly and loke þou do *þeraftur*.
C.11.184 'A shal fynde me his frende,' quod fortune *þeraftur*;
C.16.220 The witt[i]ore þat eny wihte is, but yf he worche *þeraftur*,

theras conj *theras adv.& conj.* B 2 theras (1) there_as (1); C 2 ther_as (1) þer_as (1)

B. 2.92   *There as* wil wolde and werkmanshipe fayleþ.'
B. 4.35   *Theras* wraþe and wranglynge is þer wynne þei siluer.
C. 9.275 *Ther as* mede ne mercy may nat a myte availle
C.16.141 For *þer as* pouerte passeth pes followeth comunely

þerayein adv *therayen adv.* B 3; C 1 þera3eyne

B.16.119 Iewes iangled *þerayein* [þat] Iuggede lawes,
B.16.144 Iudas iangled *þerayein*, ac Iesus hym tolde
B.17.138 And if Conscience carpe *þerayein*, or kynde wit eyþer,
C.20.310 And neuere [n]as *þera3eyne* and now wolde bigynne,

þerby adv *therbi adv.* B 4; C 2

B.11.174 For no cause to cacche siluer *þerby*, ne to be called a maister,
B.13.298 And large to lene, [loos] *þerby* to cacche].
B.13.402 Swoor *þerby* swiþe ofte and al biswatte his cote;
B.16.152 And kiste hym to be caught *þerby* and kulled of þe Iewes.
C.10.172 By loue and by leute, *þerby* lyueth anima
C.18.169 And kuste iesus to be knowe *þerby* and cauht of þe iewes.

there(- > þer(-

þerf adj *therf adj.* B 1

B. 5.173 And doon me faste frydayes to [þerf] breed and to watre;

þerfor adv *therfore adv.* A 4 þerfore; B 9 þerfor (1) therfore (1) þerfore (7); C 14 therfore (2) þerfore (12)

A. 1.17   And *þerfore* he hi3te þe erþe to helpe 3ow ichone
A. 4.41   Ne no ferþing *þerfore* for nou3t I couþe plete.
A.12.20 "I saw synful," he seyde, "*þerfore* I seyde no þing
A.12.94 And *þerfore* do after dowel whil þi dayes duren.
B. 1.17   And *þerfore* he hi3te þe erþe to helpe yow echone
B. 4.54   Ne no ferþyng *þerfore* for [n]ou3t I koude plede.
B. 5.234 Thow haddest be bettre worþi ben hanged *þerfore*.'
B. 9.98   And [dredeþ hym] no3t for drede of vengeaunce dooþ *þerfore* þe bettre;
B.12.59 Ac grace is a gras *þer[for]* þo greuaunces to abate.
B.15.209 *Therfore* by colour ne by clergie knowe shaltow [hym] neuere,
B.16.64 And egreliche he loked on me and *þerfore* I spared
B.16.95 And þanne sholde Iesus Iuste *þerfore* bi Iuggement of armes
B.20.333 Carpe I wolde wiþ contricion, and *þerfore* cam I hider.'
C. 3.89   A grypeth *þerfore* a[s] gret as for þe grayeth treuthe.
C. 3.247 Of folk þat fauht *þerfore* and folwede þe kynges wille.
C. 3.277 Maistres þat kenneth clerkes craueth *therfore* mede;
C. 3.467 Shal lese *þerfore* his lyflode and his lyf parauntur.
C. 4.57   Ne [no] ferthyng *þerfore*, for nouhte y couthe plede.
C. 6.238 Thow wolt be hanged heye *þerfore*, here oþer in helle.
C. 7.147 Yf we knowlechede and cryde Crist *þerfore* mercy:
C.10.193 For to lese *þerfore* her lond and her lyf aftur.

C.12.243   And tho that dede þe dede ydampned *þerfore* aftur
C.13.57   And dredeth to be ded *þerfore* and he in derke mette
C.13.192   And *þerfore* merueileth me, for man is moste yliche the,
C.14.23   Ac grace is a graes *þerfore* to don hem [growe efte];
C.18.128   That iesus sholde iouste *þerfore* by iugement of Armes
C.22.333   Karpe y wolde with Contricioun and *þerfore* [cam y] heddere.'

þerfro adv *therfrom adv.* B 1; C 1
B.11.353   [For men sholde hem no3t fynde whan þei *þerfro* wente;
C.12.237   For if he be fer *þerfro* fol ofte hath he drede

þerinne adv *therinne adv.* A 15 þerein (1) þereinne (12) þerinne (2); B 25 therInne (1) þerInne (24); C 17 thereynne (1) þerin (1) therynne (2) þerynne (13)
A.Pr.15   A dep dale beneþe, a dungeoun *þereinne*
A. 1.12   'Þe tour [on] þe toft,' quaþ heo, 'treuþe is *þereinne,*
A. 1.48   And þe [Image ilike], þat *þereinne* standis.
A. 1.59   'Þ[at] is þe castel of care; who[so] comiþ *þereinne*
A. 1.61   *Þereinne* woniþ a wy þat wrong is yhoten;
A. 5.127   Putte hem in a pressour, & pynnede hem *þereinne*
A. 5.200   Bere hym to his bed & brou3te hym *þerinne.*
A. 6.59   Þanne shalt þou come be a croft, ac come þou nou3t *þereinne;*
A. 7.57   'A busshel of breed corn br[yng m]e *þereinne,*
A.10.5   Kynde haþ closid *þereinne,* craftili wiþalle,
A.10.42   Inwit & alle wyttes enclosid ben *þerinne,*
A.10.168   Busk[en hem] to þat boot & biden *þereInne*
A.11.116   And rid forþ be ricchesse, ac reste þou not *þereinne.*
A.11.140   It is no science forsoþe for to sotile *þereinne.*
A.11.141   Ne were þe loue þat liþ *þerein* a wel lewid þing it were.
B.Pr.15   A deep dale byneþe, a dongeon *þerInne*
B. 1.12   'The tour on þe toft', quod she, 'treuþe is *þerInne,*
B. 1.50   And þe ymage [y]lik[e] þat *þerInne* stondeþ.
B. 1.61   'That is þe castel of care; whoso comþ *þerInne*
B. 1.63   *TherInne* wonyeþ a [wye] þat wrong is yhote;
B. 5.211   Putte hem in a press[our] and pyn[ned] hem *þerInne*
B. 5.358   Baren hym to his bed and brou3te hym *þerInne,*
B. 6.62   'A busshel of bredcorn brynge me *þerInne,*
B. 9.5   Kynde haþ closed *þerInne,* craftili wiþalle,
B. 9.54   Inwit and alle wittes [en]closed ben *þerInne*
B. 9.137   Buskeþ yow to þat boot and bideþ *þerInne*
B.10.164   And ryd forþ by richesse, ac rest þow no3t *þerInne,*
B.10.186   The moore I muse *þerInne* þe mystier it semeþ,
B.10.189   [Ne were þe loue þat liþ *þerinne* a wel lewed þyng it were].
B.10.413   And shilden vs from shame *þerinne,* as Noes ship dide beestes;
B.10.419   Wercheþ ye as ye sen ywrite, lest ye worþe no3t *þerInne].*
B.12.292   And an hope hangynge *þerInne* to haue a mede for his truþe;
B.13.157   Vndo it; lat þis doctour deme if dowel be *þerInne.*
B.14.2   Thou3 it be soiled and selde clene: I slepe *þerInne* o ny3tes;
B.15.236   Ac if coueitise be of þe counseil he wol no3t come *þerInne.*
B.15.335   How I my3te mo *þerInne* amonges hem sette.
B.15.581   And han clerkes to kepen vs *þerInne* & hem þat shul come after.
B.16.255   And I loked in his lappe; a la3ar lay *þerInne*
B.17.164   Heuene and helle and al þat is *þerInne.*
C.Pr.15   And say a tour; as [y] trow[e], treuthe was *thereynne.*
C. 1.12   'The tour vppon þe tofte,' quod she, 'treuthe is *þerynne*
C. 1.57   'That is þe Castel of care; whoso cometh *þerynne*
C. 1.59   *Therynne* wonyeth a wyghte þat wrong is [ihote];
C. 3.105   Many burgages ybrent and bodies *þerynne*
C. 6.219   Potte hem in [a] pressou[r] and pynne[d] hem *þerynne,*
C. 6.416   Beren hym to his bed and brouhten hym *þerynne*
C. 7.219   Thenne shalt thow come by a croft Ac come thow [nat] *þerynne;*
C. 8.61   A busshel of breedcorn brouht was *þerynne.*
C.10.132   Kynde hath closed *therynne,* craftili withalle,
C.10.171   Inwit and alle wittes closed been *þerynne:*
C.10.225   Boske 3ow to þat boet and abideth *þerynne*
C.11.106   And ryde forth by rychesse [ac] reste nat *þerynne,*
C.11.127   Þe more y muse *þer[i]n* the mystiloker hit semeth
C.13.55   For þat on bereth but a box, a breuet *þerynne,*
C.16.361   Ac yf couetyse be of his consaile a wol nat come *þerynne.*
C.18.271   And y lokede in his lappe; a la3ar lay *þerynne*

þermyd adv *thermid adv.* A 2 þermid (1) þermyd (1); B 2; C 3 thermid (1) thermyd (1) þermyd (1)
A. 2.37   And feffe mede *þer[myd]* in mariage for euere.
A. 7.212   Make þe Frendis *þermi[d]* for so matheu vs techiþ:
B. 6.67   And make h[y]m murie *þermyd,* maugree whoso bigruccheþ it.
B.15.316   And a mees *þermyd* of o maner kynde,
C. 3.253   Al þat his men may wynne, do *ther[mid]* here beste.
C. 8.68   And m[a]ken hym merye *þermy[d],* maugrey ho[so] bigruchen hit;
C. 9.271   And of þe moneye thow haddest *ther[myd]* his mebles to [s]aue

þerof adv *therof adv.* A 5; B 16; C 17 thereof (2) therof (3) þerof (12)
A. 3.63   An aunter 3e haue 3oure hire *þerof* h[e]re;
A. 3.227   And *þerof* sei[þ] þe sauter in a salmis ende

A. 5.137   And whoso bummide *þerof,* bou3te it þereaftir,
A. 7.184   And pieris was proud *þerof,* & putte hem in office,
A.10.86   And *þerof* seiþ þe sauter, þe salme þou mi3t rede:
B. 3.248   And *þerof* seiþ þe Sauter in a Salmes ende:
B. 5.142   And now is fallen *þerof* a fruyt þat folk han wel leuere
B. 5.221   And whoso bummed *þerof* bou3te it þerafter,
B. 5.366   Shryue þee and be shamed *þerof* and shewe it with þi mouþe.'
B. 5.491   The sonne for sorwe *þerof* lees [s]i3t [for] a tyme.
B. 6.197   And [Piers was proud *þerof*] and putte hem [in office]
B. 8.55   Ac man haþ moost *þerof* and moost is to blame
B.12.253   That euere he gadered so grete and gaf *þerof* so litel,
B.13.419   He hateþ to here *þerof* and alle þat it telleþ.
B.13.458   Til conscience acouped hym *þerof* in a curteis manere.
B.15.135   A[c] goddes folk for defaute *þerof* forfaren and spillen.
B.16.5   Mercy is þe more *þerof;* þe myddul stok is ruþe;
B.16.34   And wikkede werkes *þerof,* wormes of synne,
B.16.65   To asken hym any moore *þerof,* and bad hym ful faire
B.16.234   I am ful siker in soule *þerof,* and my sone boþe.
B.17.216   The blase *þerof* yblowe out, yet brenneþ þe weke–
C.Pr.110   And chastisid hem noght *þerof* and nolde noght rebuken hem
C. 6.229   And hoso boumode *therof* bouhte hit þeraftur,
C. 7.79   He hateth to here *thereof* and alle þat þerof carpeth.
C. 7.79   He hateth to here thereof and alle þat *þerof* carpeth.
C. 7.131   The sonne for sorwe *þerof* lees [s]iht for a tyme.
C.10.195   *The[r]of* was he robbed and ruyfled or he on rode deyede
C.11.71   Be large *þerof* whil hit lasteth to ledes þat ben nedy
C.11.157   Ne man mouhte haue mery[t]e [*thereof*] mouhte hit be ypreued:
C.12.165   3ef pore peple þe panes; *þerof* pors þou non
C.13.153   Saue man and his make; and *þerof* me wondrede.
C.13.170   And how þe pocok caukede [y toke kepe *þerof*],
C.14.32   That wit wexeth *therof* and oþer w[y]rdes bothe:
C.14.75   And of þe selcouthes þat þei sye here sones *þerof* þei tauhten;
C.17.139   And lele men lyue as lawe techeth and loue *þerof* aryseth
C.17.296   Moises to be maister *þerof* til messie come
C.18.12   And *þerof* cometh a goed fruyt þe wiche men calleth werkes
C.20.305   Yf they touched a tre or toek *þerof* an appul.

þeron adv *theron adv.* A 5 þereon (1) þeron (4); B 7; C 12 thereon (1) theron (1) þeron (10)
A. 6.87   Whanne I þenke *þereon,* þei3 I were a pope".
A. 7.13   Lokiþ forþ 3oure lynen & laboureþ *þeron* faste.
A.11.11   Þei do but drauele *þeron;* draf were hem leuere
A.11.138   For þe more I muse *þeron* þe mistlokere it semiþ,
A.11.144   Leue lelly *þeron* 3if þou nedist do wel,
B. 2.12   And *þeron* [riche] Rubies as rede as any gleede,
B. 5.600   Whan I þynke *þeron,* þei3 I were a Pope."
B.10.11   Thei doon but dr[a]uele *þeron;* draf were hem leuere
B.10.407   Was neuere wrighte saued þat wro3te *þeron,* ne ooþer werkman ellis.
B.11.225   I conseille alle cristne clyue no3t *þeron* to soore,
B.12.120   And leiden hand *þeron* to liften it vp loren here lif after.
B.17.6   And þat is cros and cristendom and crist *þeron* to honge;
C. 2.13   And *thereon* rede rubies and othere riche stones.
C. 7.50   Til eche lyf hit lothed to loke *þeron* or smylle hit;
C.11.9   They do bote dr[a]uele *þeron;* draf were hem leuere
C.11.130   Ac for hit lereth men to louie y beleue *þeron* þ[e] bettere
C.11.238   Was neuere wrihte þat *þeron* wrouhte ne werkman ysaued
C.12.96   Of hym þat trauaileth [*t]heron* bote treuthe be his lyuynge.
C.12.232   Whete þat *þeron* wexeth worth lygge ar hit rype;
C.14.63   And all lewede þat leide hand *þeron* loren lyf aftir.
C.14.74   And markede hit in here manere and mused *þeron* to knowe.
C.14.214   And hope hangeth ay *þeron* to haue þat treuthe deserueth:
C.18.198   'Muse nat to moche *þeron,*' quod faith, 'til thow more knowe
C.19.8   The which is Cr[oes] and cristendoem and cr[ist] *þer[o]n* [to] hang[e];

þeroute adv *theroute adv.* A 2; C 1
A. 6.74   And alle þe wallis ben of wyt to holde wil *þeroute;*
A. 6.100   Ike3id & ycliket to kepe þe *þeroute*
C. 5.16   Or haue an horn and be hayward and lygge *þeroute* [a]nyhtes

þertyl adv *thertil adv.* C 1
C. 4.5   But resoun rede me *þertyl* rather wo[l] y dey.'

þerto adv *therto adv.* A 2; B 14; C 15 therto (2) þerto (13)
A. 4.5   But resoun rede me *þerto* [raþer] wole I dei3e.'
A. 4.46   And 3et he betiþ me *þerto* & liþ be my maiden
B. 4.5   But Reson rede me *þerto* raþer wol I deye.'
B. 4.59   And yet he beteþ me *þerto* and lyþ by my mayde.
B.11.11   And knowe þat þow coueitest and come *þerto* paraunter'.
B.11.191   We sholde no3t clepe oure kyn *þerto* ne none kynnes riche:
B.11.192   'Ac calleþ þe carefulle *þerto,* þe croked and þe pouere;
B.11.350   If any Mason made a molde *þerto* muche wonder it were.
B.13.193   For þer [is] no tresour [*þerto*] to a trewe wille.
B.15.126   Hadde he neuere [saued] siluer *þerto* [for spendyng at ale];

B.15.562 A medicyne moot *þerto* þat may amende prelates.
B.16.44 And leiþ a laddre *þerto*, of lesynges are þe ronges,
B.18.156 Til he be deed and do *þerto*; þe yuel he destruyeþ,
B.18.180 [Thanne] I shal daunce *þerto*; do þow so suster.
B.19.200 And counseiled me to knele *þerto*; and þanne cam, me þouȝte,
B.20.14 And he [cacche] in þat caas and come *þerto* by sleighte
C. 9.91 And fele to fonge *þerto* and fewe panes taketh.
C.10.80 And *therto* trewe of his tayl, [taketh but his owne]
C.11.170 And knowe þat þou coueytest and come *þerto* parauntur.'
C.12.103 We sholde nat clepie knyhtes *þerto* ne none kyne ryche:
C.12.104 "Ac calleth the carefole *þerto*, the crokede and the pore;
C.13.161 Yf eny mason made a molde *þerto* moche wonder me thynketh.
C.16.124 Or a[s] iustice to iuge men, me enioyneth *þerto* no pore,
C.16.259 And *þerto* trewe of ȝoure tonge and of ȝoure tayl also
C.17.225 A medecyne moste *þerto* þat m[ay] amende prelates.
C.18.44 And leyth a laddere *þerto*, of lesynges ben þe ronges,
C.18.48 So this lordeynes lithereth *þerto* þat alle þe leues falleth
C.20.159 Til he [be] ded [and] ydo *þerto*; [þe yuel] he destruyeth,
C.20.183 And y shal daunse *þerto*; do þow so sustur .
C.21.200 And conseyled me to knele *þerto*; and thenne cam, me thouhte,
C.22.14 And he cacche in þat caes and come *therto* by sleithe

þervnder adv *therunder adv.* B 2; C 1
B.15.116 Ac youre werkes and wordes *þervnder* aren ful [wol]ueliche.
B.19.385 Here is breed yblessed, and goddes body *þervnder*.
C.21.385 Here is bred yblessed and godes body *þervnder*.

þerwiþ adv *therwith adv.* A 13 þerewith (1) þerewiþ (6) þerwiþ (6); B 32
therwith (1) therwiþ (1) þerwith (2) þerwiþ (28); C 32 therwith (7)
þerwith (25)
A. 1.16 For to worsshipe hym *þerewiþ* whiles ȝe ben here.
A. 1.46 ȝif þei [shulde] worsshipe *þerewiþ* cesar þe king.
A. 1.87 Doþ þe werkis *þerwiþ* & wilneþ no man ille,
A. 1.152 ȝe shuln be weiȝe *þerewiþ* whanne ȝe wende hennes.
A. 3.224 Godis mede & his mercy *þerewiþ* miȝte þou wynne.
A. 4.78 Wyt accordiþ *þerewiþ* & seide þe same:
A. 7.93 I wile worsshipe *þerewiþ* treuþe in my lyue,
A. 7.100 *Þerewiþ* was perkyn payed, and preisid hem ȝerne.
A. 7.145 And make vs merye *þerewiþ* maugre þi chekis'.
A. 7.166 And hitte hunger *þerewiþ* amydde hise lippes,
A. 7.279 And profride peris [þis] present to plese *þerewiþ* hungir.
A. 8.28 And make mesonis deux *þerewiþ* myseis[e] to helpe,
A.11.162 ȝif þou þenke do wel deile *þerewith* neuere.
B. 1.16 For to worshipe hym *þerwiþ* while ye ben here.
B. 1.48 [If] þei sholde [worshipe *þerwiþ* Cesar þe kyng].
B. 1.89 Dooþ þe werkes *þerwiþ* and wilneþ no man ille,
B. 1.178 Ye shulle ben weyen *þerwiþ* whan ye wenden hennes.
B. 3.324 And what smyth þat any smyþeþ be smyte *þerwiþ* to deþe:
B. 3.335 And [muche] worshipe ha[þ] *þerwiþ* as holy writ telleþ:
B. 4.91 Wit acorde[þ] *þerwiþ* and [witnessede] þe same:
B. 4.158 [Kynde] wit acorded *þerwiþ* and comendede hise wordes,
B. 5.33 And bete Beton *þerwith* but if she wolde werche.
B. 5.288 And as longe as þow lyuest *þerwith* þow yeldest noȝt but borwest;
B. 6.101 I wol worshipe *þerwiþ* truþe by my lyue,
B. 6.108 *Therwiþ* was Perkyn apayed and preised hem [yerne].
B. 6.158 And maken vs murye *þer[wiþ]* maugree þi chekes.'
B. 7.14 Legistres of boþe lawes þe lewed *þerwiþ* to preche,
B. 7.26 And [make] Mesondieux *þer[wiþ]* myseise [to] helpe,
B. 8.56 But if he werche wel *þerwiþ* as dowel hym techeþ.'
B.10.219 If þow þynke to dowel deel *þerwiþ* neuere.
B.11.404 Caton acordeþ *þerwiþ*: Nemo sine crimine viuit.'
B.11.406 And awaked *þerwiþ*; wo was me þanne
B.12.273 To wissen vs [wyes] *þerwiþ* þat wiss[h]en to be saued–
B.13.1 And I awaked *þerwiþ*, witlees nerhande,
B.13.73 And greue *þerwiþ* [þat goode ben]–ac gramariens shul re[d]e:
B.14.335 And wepte and wailede, and *þerwiþ* I awakede.
B.15.139 And makeþ murþe *þer[wiþ]* and hise me[yne] boþe;
B.16.167 And I awaked *þerwiþ* and wiped myne eiȝen
B.16.262 And me *þer[wiþ]*', quod þat [wye] 'may no wed vs quyte
B.17.7 And whan it is enseled [*þerwiþ*] I woot wel þe soþe
B.17.356 And wente awey as wynd and *þerwiþ* I awakede.
B.19.64 Is to wissen vs *þerwiþ*, þat whan we ben tempted,
B.19.65 *Therwiþ* to fiȝte and [f]enden vs fro fallynge in[to] synne,
B.19.325 And *þerwiþ* Grace bigan to make a good foundement,
B.19.481 And I awakned *þerwiþ* and wroot as me mette.
C. 1.16 For to worschipe hym *þerwith* þe whiles ȝe lyuen here.
C. 1.85 And doth þe werkes *þerwith* and wilneth no man ylle,
C. 1.174 ȝe shal be weye *þerwith* whenne ȝe wende hennes:
C. 3.320 May desa[u]owe that thei dede and do[uwe] *þerwith* another
C. 3.477 And yf eny smyth smeth[e] hit be smyte *þerwith* to dethe:
C. 3.487 And muche worschipe *therwith*, as holy writ telleth.
C. 4.87 Witt acordede *therwith* and witnessede þe same:
C. 5.43 That laboure þat y lerned beste *þerwith* lyuen y sholde:
C. 5.135 And bete Betene *þerwith* but yf a wolde worche.

C. 6.343 And as longe as thow lyuest *therwith* þou ȝeldest nat bote borwest;
C. 8.110 Y wol worschipe *þerwith* treuthe al my lyue
C. 8.115 *Therwith* was [Perkyn] apayed and payede wel here huyre.
C. 8.155 And maken vs murye *þer[with]* maugreye h[o] begrucheth.'
C. 8.248 Chaffare and cheue *þerwith* in chele and in hete.
C. 9.30 Amende mesondewes *þerwith* and myseyse men fynde
C. 9.69 Catoun acordeth *therwith*: cui des video.
C.10.287 Awrek the *þerwith* on wyfyng, for godes werk y holde hit:
C.11.73 Get þe loue *þerwith* thogh thow worse fare".
C.13.212 Caton acordeth *therwith*: nemo sine crimine viuit.'
C.13.214 And awakede *þerwith*; wo was me thenne
C.14.195 To wissen vs weyes *þerwith* þat wenen to be saued–
C.14.217 For al worth as god wol;' and *þerwith* he vanschede.
C.15.1 And y awakede *þerwith*, witteles nerhande,
C.18.42 And *þerwith* y warde hit oþerwhile til hit waxe rype.
C.18.278 And me *þerwith*', quod the weye; 'may no wed vs quyte
C.19.3 To reule alle reumes *þerwith* in riȝte and in resoun.
C.19.9 Were hit *þerwith* aseled y woet wel þe sothe
C.19.336 And wente away as wynd and *þerwith* y awakede.
C.21.64 Is to wissen vs *þerwith*, þat when we ben ytempted
C.21.65 *Therwith* to fihte and fende vs fro fallyng into synne.
C.21.325 And *þerwith* grace bigan to make a goode fo[un]dement,
C.21.481 And y [a]wakned *þerwith* and wroet as [me] mette.

þes > þis adj dem; these > þis pron dem, þis adj dem

þesternesse n *thesternesse n.* B 1
B.16.160 On a þursday in *þesternesse* þus was he taken;

theues > þef

thewes n *theu n.(1`)* C 1
C. 6.141 Byte and bete and brynge forth suche *thewes*

thi > þow

þider adv *thider adv.* A 4 þider (3) þidir (1); B 5; C 5 theddere (1)
theder (2) thedre (1) thider (1)
A. 2.126 Þanne car[i]de hy fo[r] capelis to carien hem *þider*;
A. 3.246 Wende *þidir* with þin ost wommen to kille;
A. 6.1 Ac þere w[ere] fewe men so wys þat þe [wey] *þider* couþe,
A. 6.47 Ac ȝe þat wilneþ to wende, þis is þe weye *þider*:
B. 2.162 Ac þanne cared þei for caples to carien hem *þider*;
B. 5.513 Ac þere was [wye] noon so wys þe wey *þider* kouþe,
B. 5.560 Ac [ye þat] wilneþ to wende, þis is þe wey *þider*.
B.10.236 I seide to h[y]m sooþly þat sent was I *þider*
B.20.286 That borweþ and bereþ it *þider* and þanne biddeþ frendes
C. 1.119 For *theder* as þe fende fly his fote for to sette,
C. 7.158 Ac þer was wye non so wys þat the way *thider* couthe
C. 7.205 Ac hoso wol wende þer treuthe is, this is þe way *thede[r]*:
C. 7.292 'ȝe! villam emi,' quod oen, 'and now y moste *thedre*
C.22.286 That borweth and bereth hit *theddere* and thenne biddeth frendes

thief > þef; thien > þow

thikke adj *thikke adj. &> þikke adv* B 2 thikke (1) þikkest (1); C 1
B.12.228 [That þ]ere þe þorn is *þikkest* to buylden and brede;
B.19.400 *Thikke* ale and þynne ale; þat is my kynde,
C.21.400 *Thikke* ale [&] thynne ale; þat is my kynde

þikke adv *thikke adv.* A 1; B 1; C 1 thykke
A. 3.147 Þat feiþ may not haue his forþ, hire floreynes go so *þikke*.
B. 3.157 That feiþ may noȝt haue his forþ, hire floryns go so *þikke*.
C. 3.195 That fayth may nat haue his forth, here floreynes goth so *thykke*,

thilke pron *thilke pron.* B 1
B.10.28 *Thilke* þat god [moost gyueþ] leest good þei deleþ,

thyn(e > þow

þyng n *thing n.* A 18 þing (15) þinges (3); B 51 thyng (2) þing (1) þyng
(35) þynges (13); C 61 thyng (33) thynges (20) thyngus (1)
A. 1.20 And comaundite of his curteisie in comoun þre *þinges*;
A. 1.136 Þat loue is þe leuest *þing* þat oure lord askiþ,
A. 1.178 Loue is þe leueste *þing* þat oure lord askiþ,
A. 2.69 ȝeldinge for þis *þing* at o ȝeris ende
A. 2.72 In witnesse of whiche *þing* wrong was þe furste,
A. 4.26 In cheker & in chauncerie, to be dischargid of *þinges*,
A. 5.100 May no sugre ne swet *þing* swage it an vnche,
A. 6.81 Deþ dar not do þat *þing* þat he defendiþ.
A. 7.59 And whoso helpiþ me to eren, or any *þing* swynke,
A. 7.195 And helpe hem of alle *þing* [aftir] þat hem nedi[þ].
A.10.2 In a castel þat kynde made of foure skenis *þinges*.
A.10.26 [And what [kenis] *þing* is kynde, conne ȝe me telle]?'
A.10.28 Fadir & fourmour, þe ferste of alle *þing*.
A.10.31 Aungelis & alle *þing* arn at his wille,
A.11.141 Ne were þe loue þat liþ þerein a wel lewid *þing* it were.
A.11.155 Astronomye is hard *þing* & euil for to knowe;

A.12.20　"I saw synful," he seyde, "þerfore I seyde no *þing*
A.12.50　Hy3t omnia probate, a pore *þing* withalle;
B.Pr.123　Thanne loked vp a lunatik, a leene *þyng* wiþalle,
B. 1.20　And comaunded of his curteisie in commune þree *þynges*;
B. 1.151　And lered it Moyses for þe leueste *þyng* and moost lik to heuene,
B. 2.105　Yeldynge for þis *þyng* at one [yeres ende]
B. 2.108　In witnesse of which *þyng* wrong was þe firste,
B. 4.29　In [c]heker and in Chauncerye, to ben descharged of *þynges*.
B. 5.123　May no sugre ne swete *þyng* aswage my swellyng,
B. 5.563　That ye louen oure lord god leuest of alle *þynges*.
B. 6.65　And whoso helpeþ me to erie [or any *þyng* swynke]
B. 6.209　And helpen hem of alle *þyng* [after þat] hem nedeþ.
B. 9.2　In a Castel þat kynde made of foure kynnes *þynges*.
B. 9.25　'What kynnes *þyng* is kynde?' quod I; 'kanstow me telle?'
B. 9.27　Fader and formour, [þe first of alle *þynges*].
B. 9.30　Aungeles and alle *þyng* arn at his wille
B.10.189　[Ne were þe loue þat liþ þerinne a wel lewed *þyng* it were].
B.10.212　Ac Astronomye is hard *þyng* and yuel for to knowe;
B.10.442　And wherby wiste men which [is] whit if alle *þyng* blak were,
B.11.101　*Þyng* þat al þe world woot, wherfore sholdestow spare
B.11.105　[*Th*]*yng* þat is pryue, publice þow it neuere;
B.11.421　Lakkedest and losedest *þyng* þat longed no3t to doone;
B.11.436　Ther smyt no *þyng* so smerte, ne smelleþ so [foule]
B.13.304　And segge *þyng* þat he neuere sei3 and for sobe sweren it;
B.14.33　And þat ynogh; shal noon faille of *þyng* þat hem nedeþ,
B.14.243　And Pouerte nys but a petit *þyng*, apereþ no3t to his nauele,
B.14.282　Ri3t as contricion is confortable *þyng*, conscience woot wel,
B.15.12　Til I sei3, as it sorcerie were, a sotil *þyng* wiþ alle.
B.15.107　Tiþes [of vn]trewe *þyng* ytilied or chaffared,
B.15.129　Ac *þing* þat wikkedly is wonne, and wiþ false sleightes,
B.15.149　'What is charite?' quod I þo; 'a childissh *þyng*', he seide:
B.15.160　*Thyng* þat neded hym no3t and nyme it if he my3te.
B.15.306　In menynge þat meke *þyng* mylde þyng sholde fede.
B.15.306　In menynge þat meke þyng mylde *þyng* sholde fede.
B.16.91　To a maide þat hi3te Marie, a meke *þyng* wiþalle,
B.16.184　The firste haþ my3t and maiestee, makere of alle *þynges*;
B.16.254　For in his bosom he bar a *þyng* þat he blissed euere.
B.17.159　And as þe hand halt harde and alle *þyng* faste,
B.17.166　That þre *þynges* bilongeþ in oure [fader] of heuene
B.17.171　Al þe my3t myd hym is in makynge of *þynges*.
B.17.288　For coueitise of any kynnes *þyng* þat crist deere bou3te.
B.17.321　Thre *þynges* þer ben þat doon a man by strengþe
B.18.115　Mercy highte þat mayde, a meke *þyng* wiþ alle,
B.18.248　Quaked as quyk *þyng* and al biquasshed þe roche.
B.18.336　Falsliche þow fettest *þyng* þat I louede.
B.18.388　Be it any *þyng* abou3t, þe boldnesse of hir synnes,
B.18.419　For inpossible is no *þyng* to hym þat is almyghty.'
B.19.94　[Er]þeliche] honeste *þynges* w[as] offred þus at ones
B.20.11　For þre *þynges* he takeþ his lif for to saue.
B.20.245　To vnitee and holy chirche; ac o *þyng* I yow preye:
B.20.249　And oþere necessaries ynowe; yow shal no *þyng* [lakke]
B.20.254　That in mesure god made alle manere *þynges*,
B.20.276　That alle *þynges* vnder heuene ou3te to ben in comune.
C.Pr.5　And say many selles and selkouthe *thyngus*.
C. 1.20　And comaundede of his cortesye in commune thre *thynges*.
C. 2.112　In wittenesse of [which] *thyng* wrong was the furste,
C. 3.87　Thow thei take hem vntidy *thyng* no tresoun þei ne halden hit;
C. 3.363　Indirect *thyng* is as hoso coueytede
C. 3.378　So comune claymeth of a kyng thre kyne *thynges*,
C. 3.422　Mebles and vnmebles, man and alle [*thynges*],
C. 5.88　Fiat voluntas dei fynt vs alle *thynges*.'
C. 6.51　*Thyng* þat neuere was thouhte and 3ut [y] swor [y] seyh hit
C. 6.88　May no sugre ne swete *thyng* aswage my swellynge
C. 6.382　And that the bettere *thyng*, be arbitreres, bote sholde þe worse.
C. 8.218　And helpe hem of alle *thyng* ay as hem nedeth.
C. 8.266　Yf 3e can or knowe eny kyne *thyng[e]* of fisyk
C.10.129　In a Castel þat kynde made of foure kyne *thynges*.
C.10.151　'What kynne *thyng* is kynde?' quod y; 'canst thow me telle?'
C.10.152　'Kynde is creatour,' quod wit, 'of [alle] kyne *thynges*,
C.10.156　Angeles and alle *thyng* aren at his wille;
C.10.169　On catel more then on kynde that alle kyne *thynges* wrouhte,
C.10.285　That lecherye is a lykyng *thynge*, a lym3erd of helle.
C.11.131　For loue is a lykyng *thing* and loth for to greue.
C.12.35　*Thyng* þat al þe world woet wherfore sholdest thow spare
C.12.39　*Thyng* þat wolde be pryue publische thow hit neuere;
C.12.236　Worldly wele y[s] wykked *thyng* to hem þat hit kepeth.
C.13.56　Ther þe marchaunt l[et] a male with many kyne *thynges*
C.13.242　Ther smyt no *thyng* so smerte ne smelleth so foule
C.14.8　Ne no tyme to tyne ne trewe *thyng* tene,
C.14.73　Of cloudes and of costumes they contreuede mony *thynges*
C.15.32　[Pacience as a pore *thyng* cam] and preeyede mete pur charite;
C.15.135　And preueth by puyre skile inparfyt alle *thynges*–
C.15.153　'That loueth lely,' quod he, 'bote litel *thyng* coueyteth.

C.15.305　Then aren hit puyre pore *thynges* in purgatorie or in hell.
C.16.83　And pouerte is bote a pety *thyng*, appereth nat to his nauele,
C.16.276　Ac *thyng* þat wykkedliche is wonne and with fals sleythes
C.16.286　'Charite,' quod y tho, 'þat is a *thyng* forsothe
C.16.294　*Thyng* that nedede hym nauhte and nyme hit yf a myhte.
C.16.298　'Charite is a childische *thyng*, as holy churche witnesseth:
C.16.320　Oen aperis-tu-manum alle *thynges* hym fyndeth;
C.17.40　Lord leue," quod þat lede, " no stole *thynge* be herynne!"
C.17.153　Hit is kyndly *thyng* creature his creatour to honoure,
C.18.92　In menynge þat the fayrest *thyng* the furste thynge shold honoure
C.18.92　In menynge þat the fayrest thyng the furste *thynge* shold honoure
C.18.124　To a mayde þat nedede hym marie, a meke *thyng* withalle,
C.18.194　The thridde is þat halt al, a *thyng* by hymsulue:
C.18.196　'This is myrke *thyng* for me,' quod y, 'and for many anoþer,
C.18.270　For in his bosome a baer [a] *thyng* þat [a] blessede [euere].
C.19.39　The which alle men aren holde ouer al *thyng* to honoure
C.19.134　And he fader and for[m]eour, þe furste of alle *thynges*–
C.19.269　For coueytise of eny kyne *thynge* þat Crist dere bouhte.
C.19.301　Thre *thynges* ther ben þat doth a man to sterte
C.20.118　Mercy hihte þat mayde, a mylde *thynge* with alle,
C.20.214　Yf all þe world were whit or swanwhit all *thynges*?
C.20.257　Quakid as quyk *thyng* and a[l] toquasch[ed] þe roch[e].
C.20.361　'The lord of myhte and of mayne þat made alle *thynges*.
C.20.430　Be hit eny *thyng* abouhte, þe boldenesse of here synne[s],
C.20.462　For inposible is no *thynge* to hym þat is almyhty.'
C.21.94　Ertheliche honeste *thynges* was offred thus at ones
C.22.11　For thre *thynges* he taketh [h]is lyf for to saue.
C.22.245　To vnite and holi churche; ac o *thyng* y 3ow praye:
C.22.249　And oþere necessaries ynowe; 3ow shal no *thyng* lakke
C.22.254　That in mesure god made alle [manere] *thynges*
C.22.276　That alle *thynges* vnder heuene ou[h]te to be in comune.

þynke v1 *thinken v.(2) &> þynkeþ v2* A 9 þenke (5) þinke (1) þinkeþ (1) þou3te (2); B 24 þenke (2) þenkeþ (3) þynke (7) þynkeþ (2) þo3te (1) þou3t (1) þou3te (8); C 17 thenk (1) thenke (3) thenketh (6) thouhte (7)
A. 1.21　Arn none nedful but þo & nempne hem I *þenke*,
A. 3.84　And tok hym þis teeme þat I telle *þenke*:
A. 5.67　And wroþliche he wroþ his fest, to wreke hym he *þou3te*,
A. 6.87　Whanne I *þenke* þereon, þei3 I were a pope"
A. 7.282　[Grene porret and pesen; to [peysen] him þei *þou3te*].
A. 8.149　Al þis makiþ me on metelis to *þinke*
A.11.144　Leue lelly þeron 3if þou *þenke* do wel,
A.11.157　Þat *þinkeþ* werche wiþ þo þre þriueþ wel late,
A.11.162　3if þou *þenke* do wel deile þerewith neuere.
B. 1.21　Are none nedfulle but þo; and nempne hem I *þynke*
B. 3.95　And [took hym] þis teme þat I telle *þynke*:
B. 5.84　And [wroþliche he wroþ his] fust, to wreke hym he *þou3te*
B. 5.282　And al þe wikkednesse in þis world þat man my3te werche or *þynke*
B. 5.404　Goddes peyne and his passion [pure] selde *þenke* I on.
B. 5.600　Whan I *þynke* þereon, þei3 I were a Pope."
B. 6.298　Grene poret and pesen; to [peisen] hem þei *þo3te*.
B. 7.173　Al þis makeþ me on metels to *þynke*,
B.10.214　[That] *þynkeþ* werche with þo [þre] þryueþ [wel] late,
B.10.219　If þow *þynke* to dowel deel þerwiþ neuere.
B.11.117　Wheiþer I were chosen or no3t chosen; on holi chirche I *þou3te*
B.11.159　And on Troianus truþe to *þenke*, and do truþe to þe peple.
B.12.89　The womman þat þe Iewes [iugged] þat Iesus *þou3te* to saue:
B.13.86　Pacience parceyued what I *þou3te* and [preynte] on me to be stille
B.13.267　And werkmen were agast a lite; þis wole be *þou3t* longe:
B.14.255　Meschief is [ay a mene] and makeþ hem to *þynke*
B.16.175　And of whennes he were and whider þat he [*þ*]*ou3te*.
B.16.229　Calues flessh and Cakebreed; and knewe what I *þou3te*.
B.17.338　To man þat mercy askeþ and amende *þenkeþ*";
B.18.175　And in hire gaye garnement3 whom she grete *þou3te*.
B.18.224　Boþe in heuene and in erþe, and now til helle he *þenkeþ*
B.19.182　And whan þis dede was doon do best he [*þou3te*],
B.19.195　And what persone rapide it nou3t punysshen he *þenkeþ*,
B.19.336　And gadered hym a greet Oost; greuen he *þynkeþ*
C. 1.21　Aren non [ni]defole but tho and nemne hem y *thenke*
C. 6.51　Thyng þat neuere was *thouhte* and 3ut [y] swor [y] seyh hit
C. 8.277　*Thenk* þat [diues] for his delicat lyf to þe deuel wente
C. 9.308　And sethen aftur his sones, and sayde hem what they *thouhte*
C.10.97　For here mok and here mebles suche men *thenketh*
C.12.52　Where y were chose [or nat chose]; on holy churche y *thouhte*
C.12.91　And on Troianus treuthe to *thenke* alle tyme[s] in 3oure lyue
C.16.95　Meschief is ay a mene and maketh hym to *þenke*
C.18.244　And what y *thouhte* and my wyf he vs wel tolde.
C.18.264　I leue þat ilke lord *thenketh* a newe lawe to make:
C.19.318　To man þat mercy asketh and amende *thenketh*."
C.20.121　Euene oute of þe eest and westward she *thouhte*,
C.20.178　And [in] here gay garnementes wham she gladie *thouhte*.
C.20.233　Bothe in heuene and in erthe, and now to helle he *thenketh*

C.21.182   And when this dede was doen do best he *thouhte*
C.21.195   And what persone payth hit nat punischen he *thenketh*
C.21.336   And gadered hym a grete oeste; greue he *thenketh*

þynkeþ v2 *thinken v.(1) &> þynke v1*   A 12 þinkeþ (3) þinkiþ (3) thinkytȝ
(1) þouȝte (4) thouȝthe (1); B 41 þynke (1) þinkeþ (3) þynkeþ (20)
þoȝte (1) þouȝte (16); C 34 thynk (1) thynketh (19) thoghte (3)
thoughte (1) thouhte (10)

A.Pr.6   Me befel a ferly, of fairie me *þouȝte*:
A. 1.105   Ȝaf hem miȝt in his mageste, þe meyere hem *þouȝte*,
A. 3.170   Why þou wraþþest þe now wondir me *þinkiþ*.
A. 3.215   Quaþ þe king to consience, 'be crist, as me *þinkiþ*,
A. 8.118   'What!' quaþ þe prest to perkyn, 'peter, as me *þinkeþ*,
A. 8.163   A[c] to triste on þis trionalis, trewely, me *þinkeþ*,
A. 9.18   Ac whoso synneþ, I seiȝe, sertis, me *þinkiþ*
A. 9.61   A muchel man, me *þouȝte*, lik to myselue,
A.10.186   It is an vncomely copil, be crist, as [me *þinkeþ*],
A.11.139   And þe deppere I deuynide þe derkere me *þouȝte*;
A.12.5   But I se now as I seye, as me soþ *thinkytȝ*,
A.12.16   And seyde so loude þat shame me *thouȝthe*,
B.Pr.6   Me bifel a ferly, of Fairye me *þoȝte*.
B.Pr.165   Were þer a belle on hire beiȝe, by Iesu, as me *þynkeþ*,
B.Pr.182   A Mous þat muche good kouþe, as me [þo] *þouȝte*,
B. 1.107   Yaf hem myȝt in his maiestee, þe murier hem *þouȝte*,
B. 2.53   And how Mede was ymaried in Metels me *þouȝte*;
B. 2.64   Were moost pryuee with Mede of any men me *þouȝte*.
B. 3.183   Whi þow wraþest þe now wonder me me *þynkeþ*.
B. 3.228   Quod þe kyng to Conscience, 'by crist, as me *þynkeþ*,
B. 3.229   Mede is worþi, [me *þynkeþ*], þe maistrie to haue'.
B. 7.136   'What!' quod þe preest to Perkyn, 'Peter! as me *þynkeþ*
B. 7.185   Ac to truste [on] þise triennals, trewely, me *þynkeþ*
B. 8.22   A[c] whoso synneþ, I sei[e, certes], me *þynkeþ*
B. 8.70   A muche man me *þouȝte*, lik to myselue,
B. 9.153   Muchel merueille me *þynkeþ*; and moore of a sherewe
B. 9.165   It is an vncomely couple, by crist! as me *þynkeþ*,
B.10.187   And þe depper I deuyne[d] þe derker me [*þouȝte*].
B.11.48   That of dowel ne dobet no deyntee me *þouȝte*;
B.11.79   Ac muche moore meritorie, me *þynkeþ*, is to baptiȝe,
B.11.324   And on a mountaigne þat myddelerþe hiȝte, as me [þo] *þouȝte*,
B.11.367   And some soure and some swete; selkouþ me *þouȝte*.
B.11.371   Saue man and his make; many tyme [me *þouȝte*]
B.13.109   And if ye fare so in youre Fermerye, ferly me *þynkeþ*
B.13.221   Thei mette wiþ a Mynstral, as me þo *þouȝte*.
B.13.253   Miȝte lechen a man as [me *þynkeþ*] it sholde.
B.13.438   Muche moore, me *þynkeþ*, riche men sholde
B.14.128   Riȝt so fareþ god by som riche; ruþe me it *þynkeþ*,
B.15.46   And of [myne] if þow myȝtest, me *þynkeþ* by þi speche.'
B.15.84   For as [me *þynkeþ*] ye forsakeþ no mannes almesse,
B.15.120   And who was myn Auctour, muche wonder me *þinkeþ*
B.15.379   Flaterere his felawe, ferly me *þynkeþ*].
B.15.439   Into lele bileue; þe lightloker me *þinkeþ*
B.15.502   Han a lippe of oure bileue, þe lightlier me *þynkeþ*
B.16.20   And lay longe in a louedreem; and at þe laste me *þouȝte*
B.16.58   And to my mynde, as me *þinkeþ*, on o more þei growed;
B.16.194   So god, þat gynnyng hadde neuere but þo hym good *þouȝte*,
B.17.283   And who[so] morþereþ a good man, me *þynkeþ*, bi myn Inwit,
B.18.113   [Where] out of þe west coste a wenche as me *þouȝte*
B.18.163   'Now suffre we', seide Truþe; 'I se, as me *þynkeþ*,
B.18.251   And now shal Lucifer leue it, þouȝ hym looþ *þynke*.
B.19.139   Ne ouer Iewes Iustice, as Iesus was, hem *þouȝte*.
B.19.200   And counseiled me to knele þerto; and þanne cam, me *þouȝte*,
C.Pr.182   Wer ther a belle on here beygh, by iesu, as me *thynketh*,
C.Pr.199   A mous þat moche good couthe, as me tho *thoughte*,
C. 2.66   Were most pryue with mede of eny men [me] *thoghte*.
C. 3.108   Forthy mayres þat maketh fre men, me *thynketh* þat ȝe ouhten
C. 3.229   Why thow wrathest þe now wonder me *thynketh*!
C. 3.284   Quod þe kyng to Consience, 'by crist, as me *thynketh*,
C. 3.285   Mede is worthy, me *thynketh*, þe maistrye to haue.'
C. 7.98   Muche more, me *thynketh*, riche men ouhte
C. 9.331   Ac to triste vp this trionales, treuly, me *thynketh*
C.10.68   A muche man, me *thoghte*, ylike to mysulue,
C.11.128   And þe deppore y deuine þe derkore me *thynketh* hit.
C.11.311   Of dowel ne of dobet no deynte me *thouhte*;
C.13.161   Yf eny mason made a molde þerto moche wonder me *thynketh*.
C.13.177   And some soure and some swete; selcouthe me *thouhte*.
C.13.181   Saue man and mankynde; mony tymes me *thouhte*
C.15.78   Ac me *thynketh* loth, thogh y latyn knowe, to lacken eny secte
C.15.117   And ȝe fare thus with ȝoure syke freres, ferly me *thynketh*
C.15.190   They mette with a mynstral, as me tho *thouhte*.
C.16.208   And of myn yf thow myhtes[t], me *thynketh* by thy speche.'
C.16.296   And fynde hym, but f[i]guratyfly, a ferly me *thynketh*:
C.17.113   And flaterrere for his vscher, ferly me *thynketh*.
C.17.184   Disceue so the sarrasyns, sothlyche me *thynketh*
C.17.243   In such manere me *thynketh* moste þe pope,

C.17.253   Haen a lyppe of oure bileue, the lihtlokour me *thynketh*
C.18.21   And of o kyne colour & kynde, as me *thoghte*,
C.18.56   A[c] in thre degrees hit grewe; grete ferly me *thouhte*,
C.18.203   God [that] bigynnyng hadde neuere bote tho hym goed *thouhte*
C.19.55   A man, as me tho *thouhte*, to moche care they brouhte
C.19.264   And hoso morthereth a goed man, me *thynketh* bi myn inwit,
C.20.116   Out of þe west as hit were a wenche, as me *thouhte*,
C.20.166   'Now soffre we,' saide Treuthe; 'y se, as me *thynketh*,
C.20.260   And now shal lucife[r] leue [hit], thogh hym loeth *thynk*.
C.21.139   Ne ouer Iewes Iustice as iesus was, hem *thouhte*.
C.21.200   And conseyled me to knele þerto; and thenne cam, me *thouhte*,

þynne adj *thinne adj.*   B 1; C 1 thynne
B.19.400   Thikke ale and *þynne* ale; þat is my kynde,
C.21.400   Thikke ale [&] *thynne* ale; þat is my kynde

þirled v *thirlen v.*   A 1 þirlide; B 1; C 1 thorlede
A. 1.148   To hem þat hongide him [heiȝe] & his herte *þirlide*.
B. 1.174   To hem þat hengen hym heiȝ and his herte *þirlede*.
C. 1.170   To hem þat hengen [hym] hye and [his] herte *thorlede*.

þis pron dem *this pron.*   A 24 þis (18) þise (6); B 68 this (15) þis (41)
thise (4) þise (8); C 66 these (3) this (59) þis (2) thise (1) thyse (1)
A.Pr.109   Al *þis* I sauȝ slepyng & seue siþes more.
A. 1.11   And seide 'mercy madame, what is *þis* to mene?'
A. 1.133   *Þis* I trowe be treuþe; who can teche þe betere,
A. 1.174   For *þise* arn þe wordis writen in þe Euaungelie:
A. 3.69   For *þise* arn men of þise molde þat most harm werchiþ
A. 3.153   *Þis* is þe lif of þat lady, now lord ȝif hire sorewe!
A. 3.260   [I] consience knowe *þis*, for kynde [w]it me tauȝte,
A. 4.83   'Haue *þis* of me, man,' quaþ heo, 'to amende þi skaþe,
A. 6.47   Ac ȝe þat wilneþ to wende, *þis* is þe weye þider.
A. 7.1   '*Þis* were a wikkide weye, but whoso hadde a gide
A. 7.7   '*Þis* were a long lettyng,' quaþ a lady in a scleire;
A. 7.34   For *þise* comiþ to my croft & croppiþ my whete.'
A. 7.259   'Be seint pernel,' quaþ peris, '*þise* arn profitable wordis.
A. 7.260   *Þis* is a louely lessoun, lord it þe forȝelde.
A. 7.280   Hungir [eet] *þis* in haste & askide aftir more.
A. 8.14   Al *þis* makiþ me on metelis to þinke
A. 8.159   *Þis* is [a] l[e]f of oure beleue, as lettrid men vs [tech]iþ:
A.10.10   Ac kynde knowiþ [*þis*] wel and kepiþ hire þe betere.
A.11.37   Glotonye & grete oþis, *þise* arn games nowadayes.
A.11.192   *Þ[i]s* be[þ] dobet; so beriþ witnesse þe sauter:
A.11.194   [Dredles] *þis* is dobet; [dobest wot þe soþe].
A.11.217   *Þis* is þe lif of þis lordis þat lyuen shulde wiþ dobet,
A.11.292   As *þise* þat wrouȝte wykkidly in world whanne þei were.
A.11.304   Seide *þis* for a sarmoun, so me god helpe:
B.Pr.231   [Al *þis* I seiȝ slepyng and seuene sythes more].
B. 1.11   And seide, 'mercy, madame, what [may] *þis* [by]meene?'
B. 1.145   *This* I trowe be truþe; who kan teche þee bettre,
B. 1.200   Fo[r] *þise* [ben wordes] writen in þe [euaungelie]:
B. 2.101   For he leueþ be lost, [þis is] *þis* laste ende.
B. 3.80   For *þise* are men on þis molde þat moost harm wercheþ
B. 3.166   *This* is þe lif of þat lady, now lord ȝyue hire sorwe,
B. 3.236   Or resten in þyne holy hilles: *þis* askeþ Dauid.
B. 3.284   I, Conscience, knowe *þis* for kynde wit me tauȝte
B. 3.292   *Thise* shul ben Maistres on moolde [trewe men] to saue.
B. 4.96   'Haue *þis* [of me, man]', quod she, 'to amenden þi scaþe,
B. 5.89   [*This* was al his curteisie where þat euere he shewed hym].
B. 5.134   I wole amende *þis* if I may þoruȝ myȝt of god almyȝty.'
B. 5.278   Cum sancto sanctus eris: construwe me *þis* on englissh.'
B. 5.409   Vigilies and fastyng dayes, alle *þise* late I passe,
B. 5.560   Ac [ye þat] wilneþ to wende, *þis* is þe wey þider.
B. 5.632   'Wite god', quod a waf[erer], 'wiste I *þis* for soþe
B. 6.1   '*This* were a wikkede wey but whoso hadde a gyde
B. 6.7   '*This* were a long lettyng', quod a lady in a Scleyre.
B. 6.32   For [*þise*] comeþ to my croft and croppeþ my whete.'
B. 6.49   Or a knyȝt from a knaue; knowe *þis* in þyn herte.
B. 6.275   'By Seint [Pernele]', quod Piers, '*þise* arn profitable wordes.
B. 6.276   /[Th]is is a louely lesson; lord it þee foryelde.
B. 6.296   [Hunger eet *þis*] in haste and axed after moore.
B. 7.55   *Thise* ben truþes tresores trewe folk to helpe,
B. 7.173   Al *þis* makeþ me on metels to þynke,
B. 7.181   *This* is [a leef of] oure bileue, as lettred men vs techeþ:
B. 8.131   And werchen as þei þre wolde; th[i]s is his entente.'
B. 9.10   Ac kynde knoweþ *þis* wel and kepeþ hire þe bettre,
B. 9.73   Alle *þise* lakken Inwit and loore [hem] bihoueþ.
B.10.51   Glotonye and grete oþes, *þis[e* arn games nowadaies].
B.10.199   *This* is Catons kennyng to clerkes þat he lereþ.
B.10.253   Alle þe clerkes vnder crist ne koude *þis* assoille,
B.10.296   And al for youre holynesse; haue ye *þis* in herte.
B.10.333   That *þis* worþ sooþ, seke ye þat ofte ouerse þe bible:
B.10.377   '*This* is a long lesson', quod I, 'and litel am I þe wiser;
B.11.111   *This* was hir teme and hir text–I took ful good hede–

B.11.146 Gregorie wiste *þis* wel, and wilned to my soule
B.11.321 And slepynge I seiȝ al *þis*, and siþen cam kynde
B.12.82 Holy kirke knoweþ *þis* þat cristes writyng saued;
B.12.155 Why I haue told [þee] al *þis*, I took ful good hede
B.12.178 And *þis* conforteþ ech a clerk and couereþ fro wanhope,
B.13.133 'Thanne passe we ouer til Piers come and preue *þis* in dede.
B.13.267 And werkmen were agast a lite; *þis* wole be þouȝt longe:
B.13.420 *Thise* ben þe braunches, beþ war, þat bryngen a man to wanhope.
B.13.452 *Thise* solaceþ þe soule til hymself be falle
B.14.51 'Haue, haukyn', quod Pacience, 'and et *þis* whan þe hungreþ
B.14.277 'I kan noȝt construe', quod haukyn; 'ye moste kenne me *þis* on englissh.
B.14.278 '[Al *þis*] in englissh', quod Pacience, 'it is wel hard to expounen,
B.15.56 To englisshe men *þis* is to mene, þat mowen speke and here,
B.15.133 [*This*] þat wiþ gile was geten vngraciousliche is [s]pended.
B.15.259 In alle manere angres, haue *þis* at herte
B.15.260 That þeiȝ þei suffrede al *þis*, god suffrede for vs moore
B.16.260 '*This* is a present of muche pris; what prynce shal it haue?'
B.17.14 *This* was the tixte, trewely; I took ful good yeme.
B.17.86 And whan I seiȝ *þis* I soiourned noȝt but shoop me to renne
B.17.286 Ac *þis* is þe worste wise þat any wight myghte
B.17.295 And siþ holy chirche and charite chargeþ *þis* so soore
B.19.10 'Is *þis* Iesus þe Iustere', quod I, 'þat Iewes dide to deþe?
B.19.12 Quod Conscience and knelede þo, '*þise* arn Piers armes,
B.19.163 Peter parceyued al *þis* and pursued after,
B.19.177 "Thomas, for þow trowest *þis* and treweliche bileuest it
B.19.181 And lelliche bileue al *þis*; I loue hem and blesse hem:
B.19.207 Quod Conscience and knelede, '*þis* is cristes messager
B.20.135 And ouertilte al his truþe wiþ 'tak *þis* vp amendement'.
B.20.156 *This* likede lif and his lemman fortune
B.20.273 Enuye herde *þis* and heet freres go to scole
B.20.280 And yuele is *þis* yholde in parisshes of Engelonde,
C.Pr.235 [Al *þis* y say slepynge and seuene sythes more]
C. 1.11 And sayde, 'mercy, madame, what may *this* [be]mene?'
C. 1.144 And *this* y trowe be treuth; [ho] kan tecche þe bettre
C. 1.195 For *this* aren wordes ywryten in þe ewangelie:
C. 2.78 Leueth hit le[l]ly *this* worth here laste mede
C. 3.104 Al *this* haue we seyn, þat som tyme thorw a breware
C. 3.361 *This* is relacion rect, ryht [as] adiectyf and sustantyf
C. 3.437 [I], Consience,knowe *this* for kynde wit me tauhte
C. 4.92 'Haue *this*, man, of me,' quod she, 'to amende thy scathe
C. 4.142 Lat thy Confessour, syre kyng, construe *this* in englische
C. 5.69 *Thyse* bylongeth to labory and lordes kyn to serue.
C. 5.89 Quod Consience, 'by Crist, y can nat se *this* lyeth;
C. 7.80 *This* beth þe branches, beth ywar, þat bryngeth a man to wanhope.
C. 7.91 Clerkes þat knoweth *this* sholde kenne lered
C. 7.112 *Thise* solaseth þe soule til hymsulue be yfalle
C. 7.205 Ac hoso wol wende þer treuthe is, *this* is þe way thede[r]:
C. 7.285 'Wyte god,' quod a wafre[re], 'wiste y *this* for sothe
C. 7.298 Treuth telleth [*this* to hym], þat y be excused.'
C. 8.5 '*Th[is*] were a long lettyng,' quod [a] lady in a slayre;
C. 8.261 *This* aren euidences,' quod hunger, 'for hem þat wolle nat swynke
C. 9.88 *This* [y] woet witturly, as þe world techeth,
C. 9.96 *These* are Almusse to helpe þat han suche charges
C. 9.237 And hoso breketh *this*, be wel waer, but yf he repente,
C. 9.276 But 'haue *this* for þat tho þat thow toke
C. 9.318 Al *this* maketh me on meteles to studie
C.10.82 Dobet doth al *this* Ac ȝut he doth more.
C.10.137 A[c] kynde knoweth *this* wel and kepeth here þe betere
C.10.192 Bishope[s] sholde ben hereaboute and bryng *this* to hepe
C.10.256 Ac fewe folke now folweth *this* for thei ȝeue her childurne
C.11.154 Alle þe Clerkes vnder Crist ne couthe *this* assoile
C.11.205 Predestinaet thei prechen, prechours þat *this* sheweth,
C.12.81 Gregori wiste *this* wel and wilned to my soule
C.13.65 Ȝe wyte, ȝe wyse men, what *this* is to mene:
C.14.99 Why y haue tolde [the] al *þis*, y toek ful gode hede
C.15.58 '*This* is a semely seruyce,' saide pacience.
C.15.81 Þat toek *this* for his teme and tolde hit withoute glose.
C.15.133 And no tixst ne taketh to preue *this* for trewe
C.15.162 Shal neuere buyren be abasched þat hath *this* abouten hym
C.15.170 '*This* is a dido,' quod this doctour, 'a dysores tale!
C.15.250 'Haue, Actyf,' quod pacience, 'and eet *this* when þe hungreth
C.16.28 And *these* ben dowel and dobet and dobest of alle.
C.16.117 'Y can nat construe al *this*,' quod Actiua vita.
C.16.118 'Parfay!' quod pacience, 'propreliche to telle [*this*]
C.16.218 To engelische men *this* is to mene, þat mowen speke and here,
C.17.41 *This* is no more to mene bote men of holy churche
C.18.75 *These* haen þe [hete] of þe holi goest as þe crop of tre [the] sonne.
C.18.100 ('*This* is a propre plonte,' quod y); 'and priueliche hit bloweth
C.18.158 And saide, '*this* is an hous of orysones and of holynesse
C.18.166 *This* biful on a fryday, a litel bifore Pasche.
C.18.196 '*This* is myrke thyng for me,' quod y, 'and for many anoþer,
C.18.225 Ne withoute a soware be suche seed; *this* we seen alle.

C.18.239 'Hastow ysey *this*,' y seyde, 'alle thre and o god?'
C.18.276 '*This* is a present of moche pris; what prince shal hit haue?'
C.19.15 *This* was the tyxt trewly; y toek ful good gome.
C.19.267 Ac *this* is the worste wyse þat eny wiht myhte
C.19.276 And sethe Charite þat holy churche is chargeth *this* so sore
C.20.45 And as wyde as hit euere was; *this* we witnesseth alle.'
C.21.12 Quod Conciense and knelede tho, '*this* aren [Peres] Armes,
C.21.163 Peter perseyued al *this* and pursuede aftur,
C.21.177 "Thomas, for thow trowest *this* and treweliche bileuest hit
C.21.181 And leelliche bileuen al *this*; y loue hem and blesse hem:
C.21.207 Quod Consience and knelede, '*this* is Cristes messager
C.22.135 And ouertulde al his treuthe with 'taek *this* [vp] amendement.'
C.22.156 *This* likede lyf and his lemman fortune
C.22.273 Enuye herde *this* and heete freres go to scole
C.22.280 And euele is *this* yholde in parsches of yngelond

þis adj dem *this adj.* A 118 þes (1) þis (85) þise (32); B 305 this (13) þis (207) thise (9) þise (76); C 268 thes (1) these (2) this (209) þis (30) thise (24) þise (1) thyse (1)

A.Pr.4, A.Pr.22, A.Pr.59, A.1.5, A.1.7, A.1.7, A.1.8, A.1.42, A.1.81, A.1.123, A.1.180, A.2.15, A.2.69, A.2.79, A.2.82, A.2.113, A.2.125, A.2.135, A.2.138, A.2.143, A.2.146, A.2.148, A.2.156, A.2.158, A.2.161, A.3.6, A.3.24, A.3.38, A.3.69, A.3.79, A.3.84, A.3.86, A.3.85, A.3.94, A.3.107, A.3.138, A.3.233, A.3.258, A.4.45, A.4.63, A.4.118, A.4.122, A.4.133, A.4.134, A.4.134, A.5.13, A.5.21, A.5.122, A.5.201, A.5.222, A.5.241, A.5.245, A.6.13, A.6.24, A.6.30, A.6.84, A.6.92, A.6.110, A.6.112, A.7.35, A.7.98, A.7.124, A.7.158, A.7.170, A.7.222, A.7.263, A.7.273, A.7.279, A.7.281, A.8.57, A.8.79, A.8.85, A.8.88, A.8.131, A.8.137, A.8.163, A.8.169, A.9.7, A.9.35, A.9.52, A.9.104, A.9.116, A.10.11, A.10.13, A.10.15, A.10.15, A.10.22, A.10.23, A.10.23, A.10.71, A.10.89, A.10.128, A.10.144, A.10.172, A.11.30, A.11.38, A.11.38, A.11.53, A.11.70, A.11.106, A.11.125, A.11.163, A.11.173, A.11.217, A.11.222, A.11.245, A.11.260, A.11.272, A.11.308, A.12.34, A.12.54, A.12.90, A.12.100, A.12.103, A.12.107, A.12.109, A.12.113

B.Pr.4, B.Pr.22, B.Pr.62, B.Pr.175, B.Pr.184, B.Pr.204, B.Pr.209, B.Pr.218, B.1.5, B.1.7, B.1.7, B.1.8, B.1.44, B.1.83, B.1.118, B.1.124, B.1.134, B.1.155, B.1.206, B.2.19, B.2.37, B.2.40, B.2.42, B.2.57, B.2.79, B.2.105, B.2.115, B.2.118, B.2.149, B.2.161, B.2.171, B.2.182, B.2.185, B.2.187, B.2.197, B.3.6, B.3.25, B.3.39, B.3.80, B.3.90, B.3.95, B.3.97, B.3.97, B.3.105, B.3.118, B.3.149, B.3.244, B.3.254, B.3.280, B.3.282, B.3.325, B.3.346, B.4.26, B.4.79, B.4.86, B.4.135, B.4.139, B.4.150, B.4.178, B.5.13, B.5.21, B.5.90, B.5.92, B.5.145, B.5.152, B.5.198, B.5.206, B.5.223, B.5.280, B.5.282, B.5.323, B.5.359, B.5.378, B.5.393, B.5.450, B.5.467, B.5.471, B.5.504, B.5.505, B.5.525, B.5.536, B.5.542, B.5.556, B.5.597, B.5.605, B.5.625, B.5.627, B.6.2, B.6.5, B.6.33, B.6.35, B.6.106, B.6.132, B.6.161, B.6.173, B.6.206, B.6.238, B.6.279, B.6.289, B.6.295, B.7.39, B.7.54, B.7.54, B.7.89, B.7.96, B.7.97, B.7.103, B.7.106, B.7.148, B.7.149, B.7.159, B.7.185, B.7.191, B.8.7, B.8.14, B.8.39, B.8.61, B.8.127, B.8.130, B.9.11, B.9.13, B.9.23, B.9.23, B.9.45, B.9.74, B.9.85, B.9.110, B.9.141, B.10.24, B.10.27, B.10.52, B.10.52, B.10.67, B.10.78, B.10.81, B.10.112, B.10.117, B.10.120, B.10.134, B.10.154, B.10.173, B.10.220, B.10.222, B.10.230, B.10.275, B.10.297, B.10.305, B.10.397, B.10.415, B.10.464, B.11.20, B.11.59, B.11.71, B.11.86, B.11.158, B.11.160, B.11.232, B.11.251, B.11.275, B.11.318, B.11.323, B.12.3, B.12.12, B.12.140, B.12.237, B.12.277, B.13.4, B.13.11, B.13.21, B.13.33, B.13.40, B.13.40, B.13.61, B.13.65, B.13.78, B.13.82, B.13.84, B.13.97, B.13.99, B.13.104, B.13.106, B.13.116, B.13.147, B.13.157, B.13.167, B.13.172, B.13.173, B.13.181, B.13.207, B.13.234, B.13.449, B.14.168, B.14.192, B.15.86, B.15.89, B.15.119, B.15.258, B.15.296, B.15.319, B.15.326, B.15.328, B.15.368, B.15.373, B.15.399, B.15.419, B.15.429, B.15.501, B.15.525, B.15.560, B.16.10, B.16.24, B.16.26, B.16.54, B.16.55, B.16.61, B.16.131, B.16.135, B.16.141, B.16.148, B.16.163, B.17.12, B.17.18, B.17.20, B.17.22, B.17.65, B.17.66, B.17.77, B.17.101, B.17.112, B.17.114, B.17.115, B.17.123, B.17.198, B.17.211, B.17.221, B.17.276, B.17.333, B.18.21, B.18.22, B.18.25, B.18.41, B.18.65, B.18.82, B.18.85, B.18.94, B.18.101, B.18.110, B.18.121, B.18.122, B.18.125, B.18.126, B.18.131, B.18.133, B.18.134, B.18.135, B.18.137, B.18.137, B.18.150, B.18.158, B.18.170, B.18.187, B.18.226, B.18.232, B.18.233, B.18.234, B.18.264, B.18.269, B.18.273, B.18.274, B.18.274, B.18.275, B.18.282, B.18.283, B.18.296, B.18.299, B.18.319, B.18.319, B.18.413, B.18.424, B.19.68, B.19.96, B.19.108, B.19.166, B.19.182, B.19.271, B.19.309, B.19.315, B.19.329, B.19.341, B.19.382, B.19.384, B.19.419, B.19.451, B.19.459, B.20.77, B.20.93, B.20.114, B.20.163, B.20.199, B.20.242, B.20.309, B.20.332, B.20.346, B.20.362, B.20.378

C.Pr.24, C.Pr.60, C.Pr.192, C.Pr.201, C.Pr.212, C.Pr.220, C.1.5, C.1.7, C.1.7, C.1.8, C.1.42, C.1.79, C.1.123, C.1.201, C.2.86, C.2.105, C.2.110, C.2.119, C.2.122, C.2.165, C.2.195, C.2.198, C.2.211, C.3.6, C.3.26, C.3.41, C.3.81, C.3.94, C.3.118, C.3.119, C.3.125, C.3.125, C.3.139, C.3.155, C.3.187, C.3.213, C.3.433, C.3.478, C.4.75, C.4.136, C.4.147, C.4.172, C.5.41, C.5.51, C.5.74, C.5.115, C.5.123, C.5.152, C.6.108, C.6.127, C.6.206, C.6.214, C.6.231, C.6.233, C.6.313, C.6.325, C.6.334, C.6.380, C.6.417, C.7.9, C.7.64, C.7.109, C.7.149, C.7.170, C.7.181, C.7.189, C.7.200, C.7.245, C.7.254, C.7.278, C.7.280, C.8.3, C.8.27, C.8.32, C.8.113, C.8.123, C.8.158, C.8.158, C.8.170, C.8.212, C.8.215, C.8.263, C.8.301, C.8.312, C.8.317, C.9.42, C.9.57, C.9.83, C.9.153, C.9.160, C.9.162, C.9.165, C.9.165, C.9.173, C.9.184, C.9.186, C.9.193, C.9.204, C.9.210, C.9.236, C.9.241, C.9.242, C.9.256, C.9.298, C.9.331, C.9.333, C.9.337, C.10.7, C.10.14, C.10.45, C.10.56, C.10.60, C.10.92, C.10.123, C.10.138, C.10.149, C.10.204, C.10.204, C.10.229, C.11.24, C.11.58, C.11.61, C.11.176, C.11.179, C.11.228, C.11.246, C.11.268, C.12.11, C.12.25, C.12.90, C.12.137, C.12.157, C.12.201, C.12.207, C.13.21, C.13.169, C.14.42, C.14.85, C.14.199, C.15.4, C.15.13, C.15.24, C.15.45, C.15.63, C.15.65, C.15.69, C.15.84, C.15.91, C.15.104, C.15.106, C.15.111, C.15.147, C.15.165, C.15.170, C.15.171, C.15.175, C.15.193, C.15.208, C.15.219, C.15.284, C.16.32, C.16.36, C.17.51, C.17.54, C.17.79, C.17.104, C.17.117,

C.17.170, C.17.223, C.17.249, C.17.252, C.17.252, C.18.25, C.18.25, C.18.29, C.18.48,
C.18.83, C.18.129, C.18.177, C.18.213, C.18.218, C.18.250, C.18.254, C.19.13, C.19.19,
C.19.21, C.19.36, C.19.48, C.19.63, C.19.65, C.19.92, C.19.164, C.19.177, C.19.187,
C.19.257, C.19.313, C.20.19, C.20.21, C.20.24, C.20.40, C.20.67, C.20.84, C.20.87,
C.20.97, C.20.104, C.20.113, C.20.124, C.20.125, C.20.128, C.20.129, C.20.134,
C.20.136, C.20.137, C.20.138, C.20.140, C.20.140, C.20.153, C.20.161, C.20.173,
C.20.192, C.20.235, C.20.241, C.20.242, C.20.243, C.20.272, C.20.272, C.20.277,
C.20.283, C.20.295, C.20.296, C.20.296, C.20.297, C.20.306, C.20.329, C.20.332,
C.20.355, C.20.362, C.20.362, C.20.456, C.20.467, C.21.10, C.21.68, C.21.96, C.21.108,
C.21.166, C.21.182, C.21.271, C.21.309, C.21.315, C.21.329, C.21.341, C.21.382,
C.21.384, C.21.419, C.21.451, C.21.459, C.22.77, C.22.93, C.22.114, C.22.163,
C.22.199, C.22.242, C.22.309, C.22.332, C.22.346, C.22.362, C.22.378

thise > þis pron, þis adj

þiself pron *thiself pron.* A 15 þiself (6) þiselue (5) þiseluen (4); B 28
thyself (1) þiself (9) þiselue (17) þiseluen (1); C 14 thisylue (1)
thysulue (11) thysuluen (2)
A. 1.24   Þat oþer is mete at meel for myseise of *þiselue*;
A. 1.131   For to loue þi lord leuere þanne *þiselue*;
A. 2.90   Symonye & *þiself* shenden holy chirche;
A. 3.177   Ac þou *þiself*, soþly, asshamidest hym ofte;
A. 5.217   "I am sory for my synne," sey to *þiseluen*,
A. 5.218   And beet *þiself* on þe brest & bidde hym of grace,
A. 6.52   Oþerwise þanne þou woldist men wrou3te to *þiselue*;
A. 6.97   And pokiþ [forþ] pride to preise *þiselue*.
A. 6.102   Þus mi3t þou lese his loue, to lete wel be *þiselue*,
A. 9.44   Ay is þi soule sauf but þou *þiself* wilt
A. 9.46   And don dedly synne & drenche *þiseluen*.
A. 9.47   God wile suffre þe to dei3e so for *þiself* hast þe maistrie.'
A.10.88   Ac 3if clene consience acorde þat *þiself* dost wel
A.10.93   For 3if þou comist a3en consience þou combrist *þiseluen*,
A.10.114   Hold þe stable & stedefast & strengþe *þiseluen*
B. 1.24   [That oþer is] mete at meel for mysese of *þiselue*;
B. 1.143   For to louen þi lord leuere þan *þiselue*.
B. 2.126   Symonye and *þiself* shenden holi chirche;
B. 3.190   Ac þow *þiself* sooþly shamedest hym ofte;
B. 5.445   "I am sory for my synn[e]", seye to *þiselue*,
B. 5.446   And beet *þiself* on þe brest and bidde hym of grace,
B. 5.481   And of nau3t madest au3t and man moost lik to *þiselue*.
B. 5.486   And madest *þiself* wiþ þi sone vs synfulle yliche:
B. 5.489   Ther *þiself* ne þi sone no sorwe in deeþ feledest,
B. 5.565   Oþerwise þan þow woldest [men] wrou3te to *þiselue*.
B. 5.606   Thow shalt see in *þiselue* truþe [sitte] in þyn herte
B. 5.611   And pokeþ forþ pride to preise *þiseluen*;
B. 5.616   Thus my3testow lesen his loue, to lete wel by *þiselue*,
B. 8.48   Ay is þi soule saaf but [þow *þiselue* wole
B. 8.50   And] do deedly synne and drenche *þi[selue]*.
B. 8.51   God wole suffre wel þi sleuþe if *þiself* likeþ,
B. 8.52   For he yaf þee [to] yeres3yue to yeme wel *þiselue*
B. 9.136   *Thyself* and þi sones þre and siþen youre wyues,
B.10.265   Syþenes þow seest *þiself* as in soule clene;
B.10.270   Siþen a beem [is] in þyn owene ablyndeþ *þiselue*–
B.11.377   Why I suffre or no3t suffre; *þiself* hast no3t to doone.
B.13.143   Thyn enemy in alle wise eueneforþ wiþ *þiselue*.
B.13.168   Nou3t þoru3 wicchecraft but þoru3; and þow wilt *þiselue*
B.16.157   Ac [to] þe [worldes ende] þi wikkednesse shal worþe vpon *þiselue*:
B.17.104   And *þiself* now and swiche as suwen oure werkes.
B.17.137   Thyn euenecristene eueremoore eueneforþ with *þiselue*.
B.18.54   And [seide], 'if þat þow sotil be [*þiselue*] now [þow help].
B.18.363   [Þe bitternesse þat þow hast browe, now brouke it *þiselue*];
C. 2.130   For syuyle and *thisylue* selde fulfulleth
C. 3.236   Ac thow *thysulue* sothly, ho[so] hit segge durste,
C. 6.101   Lord, ar y lyf lete, for loue of *thysulue*
C. 7.59   "Y am sory for my synnes", sey to *thysuluen*
C. 7.60   And bete *thysulue* [o]n þe breste and bidde hym of grace
C. 7.123   And [of nauhte madest] auhte and man liche *thysulue*
C. 7.128   And madest *thysulue* with thy sone oure soule & body ilych:
C. 7.263   And poketh forth pruyde to preyse *thysuluen*.
C. 7.268   Thus myhte thow lesen his loue, to lete wel by *thysulue*,
C.10.224   "*Thysulue* and thy sones thre and sethen 3oure wyues,
C.11.113   Sey [to] hym *thysulue* ouerse m[y] bokes
C.15.112   'Do thy neyhebore non harm ne *thysulue* nother
C.18.172   And kene care in thy kissyng and combraunce to *thysulue*.
C.20.401   The bitternesse þat thow hast browe, now brouk hit *thysulue*;

þo pron dem *tho pron.* A 6; B 22 tho (5) þo (16) þoo (1); C 28 tho
A. 1.21   Arn none nedful but *þo* & nempne hem I þenke,
A. 1.119   Ac *þo* þat werchen þe word þat holy writ techiþ,
A. 5.174   *Þo* risen vp in rape & ro[wn]eden togideris,
A. 8.80   *Þo* þat lyuen þus here lif mowe loþe þe tyme
A.10.108   Thrift oþer þedom with *þo* is selde ysei3e:
A.11.13   I say be *þo*,' quaþ she, 'þat shewen be here werkis
B. 1.21   Are none nedfulle but *þo*; and nempne hem I þynke

þo adj dem *tho def. art.& adj.* A 5; B 27 tho (1) þo (26); C 27 tho (23)
þo (4)
A. 9.105   'But wyt can wisse þe,' quaþ þou3t, 'where *þo* þre dwellen,
A.11.157   Þat þinkeþ werche wiþ *þo* þre þriueþ wel late,
A.11.201   For mendynaunt3 at meschief *þ[o]* men were dewid,
A.11.224   Forþi I wende þat *þo* wyes wern dobest of alle.'
A.12.21   Til *þo* wrecches ben in wil here synne to lete."
B. 2.195   I wolde be wroken of *þo* wrecches þat wercheþ so ille,
B. 2.200   To attachen *þo* Tyraunt3 'for any [tresor], I hote;
B. 4.40   Forþi, Reson, lat hem ride *þo* riche by hemselue,
B. 5.176   Forþi haue I no likyng, [leue me], wiþ *þo* leodes to wonye;
B. 8.115   'But wit konne wisse þee', quod þo3t, 'where *þo* þre dwelle
B.10.214   [That] þynkeþ werche with *þo* [þre] þryueþ [wel] late,
B.12.52   And *þo* men þat þei moost haten mynistren it at þe laste;
B.12.59   Ac grace is a gras þer[for] *þo* greuances to abate,
B.12.164   Which trowestow of *þo* two [in Themese] is in moost drede,
B.13.45   But if þei synge for *þo* soules and wepe salte teris:
B.13.122   Til I se *þo* seuene and myself acorde
B.13.167   Maister of alle *þo* men þoru3 my3t of þis redels,
B.13.426   Lest *þo* þre maner men to muche sorwe yow brynge:
B.14.124   Right so reson sheweþ þat [*þo* renkes] þat were [lordes]
B.14.175   Conforte *þo* creatures þat muche care suffren
B.14.204   Ac wiþ richesse *þ[o]* Ribaud[es] raþest men bigileþ.
B.15.243   Thei vndoon it vn[digne]ly, *þo* doctours of lawe.
B.15.479   And as *þo* foules to fynde fode after whistlyng
B.15.548   [Mynne] ye no3t, wise men, how *þo* men honoured
B.15.550   Reson and rightful doom *þ[o]* Religiouse d[ampn]ede,
B.15.601   And [3it] wenen *þo* wrecches þat he were pseudopropheta
B.17.279   For þat þe holy goost haþ to kepe *þ[o]* harlotes destruyeþ,
B.18.74   And [hir] armes after of eiþer of *þo* þeues.
B.18.401   *Tho* [ledes] þat [I] lou[e], and leued in my comynge:
B.19.82   And al þe wit of þe world was in *þo* þre kynges.
B.19.456   And alle *þo* faire vertues as vices þei semeþ.
B.20.110   Fortune gan flatere þanne *þo* fewe þat were alyue

B. 1.130   [Ac] *þo* þat werche wel as holy writ telleþ,
B. 3.238   *Tho* þat entren of o colour and of one wille
B. 5.325   T[h]o risen vp in Rape and rouned togideres
B. 7.98   [*Tho*] þat lyue þus hir lif mowe loþe þe tyme
B.10.13   I seye by [*þo*]', quod she, 'þat sheweþ by hir werkes
B.10.39   But *þoo* þat feynen hem foolis, and wiþ faityng libbeþ
B.10.134   And *þo* þat vseþ þise hauylons [for] to blende mennes wittes,
B.10.433   *Tho* þat wrou3te wikkedlokest in world þo þei were;
B.10.434   And *þo* þat wisely wordeden and writen manye bokes
B.10.477   But *þo* þat kepen þe lordes catel, clerkes and Reues.
B.12.200   As *þo* þat seten at þe syde table or wiþ þe souereynes of þe halle,
B.13.197   Than alle *þo* þat offrede into Ga3ophilacium?'
B.13.455   Leden *þo* þat [liþeþ] hem to Luciferis feste
B.15.561   And *þo* þat han Petres power arn apoisoned alle."
B.17.49   *Tho* þat lernen þi lawe wol litel while vsen it.'
B.18.326   And *þo* þat oure lord louede into his light he laughte,
B.18.328   For alle synfulle soules, to saue *þo* þat ben worþi.
B.18.355   Getest bi gile *þo* þat god louede;
B.19.38   And *þo* þat bicome cristene bi counseil of þe baptis[t]e
B.19.389   Or as ofte as þei hadde nede, *þo* þat hadde ypaied
B.20.305   'Go salue *þo* þat sike ben and þoru3 synne ywounded.'
C. 1.21   Aren non [ni]defole but *tho* and nemne hem y thenke
C. 3.445   *Tho* shal be maistres on molde trewe men to helpe.
C. 4.196   And receyue *tho* that resoun louede; and riht with þat y wakede.
C. 5.49   And *tho* þa[t] fynden me my fode fouchensaf, y trowe,
C. 6.383   *Tho* rysen vp [in] rape and rounned togyderes
C. 7.115   Leden *tho* that lythed hem to luciferes feste
C. 8.25   And labory for *tho* thow louest al my lyf tyme.
C. 8.57   And wende with alle *tho* þat wolden lyue in treuthe.'
C. 8.259   "Yblessed be al *tho* that here bylyue biswynketh
C. 9.174   *Tho* þat lyueth thus here lyf, leue 3e non other,
C.11.25   *Tho* þat god most goed 3eueth greueth most riht and treuthe:
C.11.28   Helpe hym þat hath nauhte then *tho* that haen no nede.
C.11.269   *Tho* that worste wrouhten while thei here were.
C.12.243   And *tho* that dede þe dede ydampned þerfore aftur
C.14.139   As *þo* þat sitten at þe syde table or wiþ þe souereyns [of þe] halle
C.16.359   Of *tho* that lelelyche lyuen and louen and byleuen:
C.17.224   And [*tho*] þat haen petres power aren apo[y]sened alle."
C.17.230   The heuedes of holy churche and *tho* that ben vnder hem,
C.18.64   *Tho* that sitten in þe sonne syde sannore aren rype,
C.18.66   Then *tho* that selde haen þe sonne and sitten in þe North half;
C.18.147   Ac *tho* that sey that selcouth sayde þat tyme
C.18.174   Wo to *tho* þat thy wyles vysen to þe wo[r]ldes ende:
C.19.47   *Tho* þat lerneth thy lawe wollen litel while hit vse.'
C.20.248   *Tho* þat weren in heuene token stella comata
C.20.369   And *tho* that oure lord louede forth with þat liht flowen.
C.21.38   And *tho* þat bycome cristene bi consail of þe baptist
C.21.389   Or as ofte as they hadden nede, *þo* þat hadden payed
C.22.305   'Go salue *tho* þat syke [ben] and thorw synne ywounded.'

C.Pr.18   Woned in *tho* wones and wikkede spiritus.
C.Pr.44   In glotonye *þ[o]* gomus goth þei to bedde
C.Pr.45   And ryseþ with rybaudrye, *þo* robardus knaues;
C.Pr.140   Myght of *tho* men made hym to regne.
C. 2.209   Y wolde be awreke [o]n *tho* wreches and on here werkes alle,
C. 2.214   [T]o atache *tho* tyrauntes, 'for eny tresor, y hote;
C. 5.5   For y made of *tho* men as resoun me tauhte.
C. 7.86   Laste *tho* manere men to muche sorwe 30w brynge:
C.10.111   'Bote wit wol the wisse,' quod thouhte, 'where *tho* thre dwelleth,
C.13.6   And out of nombre *tho* men many mebles hadden.
C.13.42   And thogh they wen[d]e by the wey, *tho* two togederes,
C.14.108   Which trowest [þou] of *tho* two in temese [is] in moste drede?'
C.15.50   Bote yf they synge for *tho* soules and wepe salte teres:
C.15.89   Þat in þ[e] mawe of þat maystre alle *þo* metes were,
C.16.45   Ac with rychesse *tho* rybaudes rathest men bigileth.
C.16.250   *Tho* bowes þat bereth nat and beth nat grene yleued,
C.17.31   And faire byfore *tho* men faunede with þe tayles.
C.17.170   Be maistre ouer alle *tho* men and on this manere a wrouhte:
C.17.210   Minne 3e [nat], lettred men, how *tho* men honourede
C.17.212   How *tho* corsede cristene catel and richesse worschipede;
C.17.213   Resoun and rihtful doem *tho* religious dampnede.
C.19.260   For that the holy goest hath to kepe *tho* harlotes distruyeth,
C.20.76   And here arme[s] aftur of e[ither] of *tho* theues.
C.20.444   *Tho* [ledes] þat y louye and leued in my comynge,
C.21.82   And al þe wit of the world was in [*þo*] thre kynges.
C.21.456   And al *tho* fayre vertues as vises thei semeth.
C.22.110   Fortune gan flateren thenne *t[h]o* fewe þat were alyue

þo adv *tho adv.* A 17; B 70 tho (9) þo (54) þoo (7); C 84 tho (82) þo (2)

A. 2.131   *Þ[o]* hadde notories none; anoyed þei were
A. 4.49   Wrong was aferd *þo* & wisdom he sou3te
A. 4.53   Wysdom wan *þo* & so dede wyt also
A. 4.55   And warnide wrong *þo* wiþ suche a wys tale:
A. 4.141   War[yn] wisdom *þo*, ne [witty] his fere,
A. 5.251   [A] þousand of men *[þ]rong[en]* togideris,
A. 7.23   'Be crist,' quaþ a kni3t *þo*, 'þou [kenn]ist vs þe beste;
A. 7.109   'Be þe prince of paradis!' quaþ piers *þo* in wraþþe,
A. 7.286   And *þo* nolde wastour not werche, but wandrite aboute,
A. 8.89   'Piers,' quaþ a prest *[þo]*, 'þi pardon muste I rede,
A. 8.97   'Petir,' quaþ þe prest *þo*, 'I can no pardoun fynde
A. 9.63   'What art þou,' quaþ I *þo*, 'þat my name knowist?'
A. 9.67   'Art þou þou3t, *þo*?' quaþ I; 'þou couþest me telle
A. 9.101   I þankide þou3t *þo* þat he me so tau3te,
A. 9.114   But as I bad þou3t *þo* be mene betwene,
A.12.12   Skornfully *þ[o]* scripture she[t] vp h[ere] browes,
A.12.62   'Al hayl,' quod on *þo*, and I answered, 'welcome, & with whom be 3e?'
B.Pr.182   A Mous þat muche good kouþe, as me [*þo*] þou3te,
B. 2.167   *Tho* hadde Notaries none; anoyed þei were
B. 4.63   Wrong was afered *þ[o]* and wisdom he sou3te
B. 4.67   *Tho* [wan] Wisdom and sire waryn þe witty
B. 4.69   And warnede wrong *þo* with swich a wis tale:
B. 4.165   Mede mornede *þo* and made heuy chere
B. 5.363   His wif [edwyted] hym *þo* [of wikkednesse and synne],
B. 5.510   A þousand of men *þo* þrungen togideres,
B. 6.21   'By crist!' quod a kny3t *þoo*, '[þow] kenne[st] vs þe beste;
B. 6.121   *Tho* were faitours afered and feyned hem blynde;
B. 6.162   For [þei] wasten and wynnen no3t and [*þo*] worþ neuere
B. 6.174   Hunger in haste *þoo* hente wastour by þe [mawe]
B. 6.302   And *þo* [n]olde Wastour no3t werche, but wandre[d] aboute,
B. 7.107   'Piers', quod a preest *þoo*, 'þi pardon moste I rede,
B. 7.115   'Peter!' quod þe preest *þoo*, 'I kan no pardon fynde
B. 8.72   'What art [þ]ow', quod I *þo*, 'þat my name knowest?'
B. 8.76   'Artow þou3t?' quod I *þoo*; 'þow koudest me [telle]
B. 8.111   I þonked þo3t *þo* þat he me [so] tau3te,
B. 8.124   But as I bad þo3t *þoo* be mene bitwene,
B.11.4   *Tho* wepte I for wo and wraþe of hir speche
B.11.63   And *þo* fond I þe frere afered and flittynge boþe
B.11.107   'He seiþ sooþ', quod Scripture *þo*, and skipte an hei3 and preched.
B.11.324   And on a mountaigne þat myddelerþe hi3te, as me [*þo*] þou3te,
B.11.405   *Tho* cau3te I colour anoon and comsed to ben ashamed
B.11.422   *Tho* hadde he [litel] likyng for to lere þe moore.
B.12.151   [Riche men rutte *þo* and in hir reste were
B.12.277   'Alle þise clerkes', quod I *þo*, "þat [o]n crist leuen
B.12.280   'Contra!' quod Ymaginatif *þoo* and comsed to loure,
B.13.46   Conscience curteisly *þo* commaunded Scripture
B.13.136   'A[t] youre preiere', quod Pacience *þo*, 'so no man displese hym:
B.13.178   That Pacience *þ[o]* most passe, 'for pilgrymes konne wel lye'.
B.13.215   Conscience *þo* wiþ Pacience passed, pilgrymes as it were.
B.13.221   Thei mette wiþ a Mynstral, as me [*þo*] þou3te.
B.13.266   Wiþ [bake] breed fro Stratford; *þo* gonnen beggeris wepe
B.13.313   'By crist!' quod Conscience *þo*, 'þi beste cote, Haukyn,
B.14.323   'Allas', quod Haukyn þe Actif man *þo*, 'þat after my cristendom
B.15.149   'What is charite?' quod I *þo*; 'a childissh þyng', he seide:

B.15.538   And *þo* was plentee and pees amonges poore and riche,
B.16.1   'NOw faire falle yow', quod I *þo*, 'for youre faire shewyng!
B.16.18   'Piers þe Plowman!' quod I *þo*, and al for pure Ioye
B.16.67   'Heer now byneþe', quod he *þo*, 'if I nede hadde,
B.16.97   The maide myldeliche *þo* þe messager graunted
B.16.150   And [þus] was wiþ Iudas *þo* þat Iesus bitrayed:
B.16.161   'What berþ þat buyrn', quod I *þo*, 'so blisse þee bitide?'
B.16.258   'I wolde wite', quod I *þo*, 'what is in youre lappe.'
B.17.90   And I þanked hym *þo* and siþþe [þus] I hym tolde
B.17.127   'A, swete sire', I seide *þo*, 'wher I shal bileue,
B.18.40   *Tho* putte hym forþ a p[e]lour bifore Pilat and seide,
B.18.59   The lord of lif and of light *þo* leide hise eighen togideres.
B.18.422   Truþe trumpede *þo* and song Te deum laudamus,
B.19.12   Quod Conscience and kneled *þo*, 'þise arn Piers armes,
B.19.48   *Tho* was he Iesus of Iewes called, gentile prophete,
B.19.50   And *þo* conquered he on cros as conquerour noble,
B.19.53   And *þo* was he conquerour called of quyke and of dede,
B.19.71   *Tho* he was born in Bethleem, as þe book telleþ,
B.19.91   The þridde kyng *þo* kam knelynge to Iesu
B.19.112   And lawe lakkede *þo* for men louede no3t hir enemys,
B.19.132   And *þo* was he called in contre of þe comune peple,
B.19.135   The burdes *þo* songe, Saul interfecit mille et dauid decem milia.
B.19.355   Quod Conscience to alle cristene *þo*, 'my counseil is to wende
B.19.364   Conscience comaundede *þo* alle cristene to delue,
B.20.74   'I conseille', quod Conscience *þo*, 'comeþ wiþ me, ye fooles
B.20.80   Kynde Conscience *þo* herde and cam out of þe planetes
B.20.90   The lord þat lyued after lust *þo* aloud cryde
B.20.106   Conscience of his curteisie [kal] kynde he bisou3te
B.20.165   For care Conscience *þo* cryde vpon Elde
B.20.232   Nede neghede *þo* neer and Conscience he tolde
B.20.242   Conscience of þis counseil *þo* comsede for to laughe,
B.20.338   'I praye þee', quod Pees *þo*, 'er þow passe ferþer,
B.20.380   'By crist!' quod Conscience *þo*, 'I wole bicome a pilgrym,
C.Pr.199   A mous þat moche good couthe, as me *tho* thoughte,
C. 1.107   Lucifer, louelokest *tho*, ac litel while it duyred.
C. 1.112   'Lord! why wolde he *tho*, þat wykkede lucifer,
C. 2.18   'Leue lady,' quod y *tho*,'layn nought yf 3e knowen.'
C. 2.160   *T[h]o* fette fauel forth floreynes ynowe
C. 2.223   Falsnesse for fere *tho* fleyh to þe freres;
C. 4.13   'Y am fayn of that foroward, in fayth,' *tho* quod Consience,
C. 4.43   And bytwene hymsulue and his sone sette *tho* sire resoun
C. 4.66   *Tho* was wrong afered and wisdom a souhte;
C. 4.72   For wysdom and wyt *tho* wenton togyderes
C. 4.94   Pitousliche pees *tho* preyede the kyng
C. 4.105   Summe radden resoun *tho* to haue reuthe vppon þat shrewe
C. 4.148   Mede in the mothalle *tho* on men of lawe gan wynke
C. 4.160   Mede mornede *tho* and made heuy chere
C. 4.162   A sysour and a somnour *tho* softliche forth 3ede
C. 4.166   The kyng to consayl *tho* toek Consience and resoun
C. 4.195   The kyng comaundede Consience *tho* to congeye alle his offeceres
C. 5.102   'Y rede the,' quod resoun *tho*, 'rape the to bygynne
C. 7.119   *Tho* was repentaunce aredy and redde hem alle to knele:
C. 7.133   Feddest *tho* with thy [fresshe] blood oure forfadres in helle:
C. 7.155   A thousend of men *tho* throngen togyderes,
C. 8.19   'By Crist!' quod a knyhte *tho*, 'a kenneth vs þe beste
C. 8.128   *Tho* were faytours aferd and fayned hem blynde;
C. 8.156   [Peres] the [plouhman] *tho* pleynede hym to þe knyhte
C. 8.169   'Y preye the,' quod [Perus] *tho*, 'pur charite, sire hunger,
C. 8.171   Hunger in haste *tho* hente wastour by þe mawe
C. 8.179   *Tho* were faytours afered and flowen into [Peres] bernes
C. 8.197   *Tho* was [Peres] proud and potte hem alle a werke
C. 8.204   *Tho* hadde [Peres] pitee vppon alle pore peple
C. 8.263   'By Crist!' quod [Peres] þe [plouhman] *tho*, 'this prouerbis [wol y] shewe
C. 8.315   Alle þe pore peple *tho* pesecoddes fe[tt]e;
C. 8.319   Pore folk for fere *tho* fedde honger 3erne
C. 8.324   And *tho* wolde wastor nat worche bote wandre[d] aboute
C. 9.41   *Tho* were Marchauntes mury; many wopen for ioye
C. 9.281   '[Peres],' quod a prest *tho*, 'thy pardon moste y rede
C. 9.289   'Peter!' quod the prest *tho*, 'y kan no pardoun fynde
C.10.70   'What art thow,' quod y [*þo*], 'þat my name knowest?'
C.10.74   'Art thow thouht?' quod y *tho*; 'thow couthest me wisse
C.10.107   Y thonkede thoght *tho* þat he me so tauhte.
C.10.120   Bote as y bad thouht *tho* be mene betwene
C.11.134   *Tho* wente y my way withouten more lettynge
C.11.164   *Tho* wepte y for wo and wrathe of here wordes
C.11.303   'Homo pr[o]ponit,' quod a poete *tho*, and plato he hihte,
C.12.18   'Ouh!' quod y *tho* and myn heued waggede,
C.12.41   'A saith soth,' quod scripture *tho*, and skypte an heyh and prechede.
C.13.213   *Tho* cauhte y colour anoen and comesede to ben ashamed
C.14.95   Ryche men rotte *tho* and in here reste were
C.14.199   'Alle thise clerkes,' quod y *tho*, 'þat [o]n crist leuen
C.14.202   'Contra!' quod ymagynatif *tho* and comesed to loure

C.15.54   And to me þat was his mette *tho*, and oþer mete bothe.
C.15.190   They mette with a mynstral, as me *tho* thouhte.
C.16.114   Quod Actyf *tho* al angryliche and Arguinge as hit were:
C.16.286   'Charite,' quod y *tho*, 'þat is a thyng forsothe
C.17.199   And *tho* was p[lente] and p[ees] amonges pore and ryche;
C.18.19   And he thonkede me *tho*; bote thenne toek y hede
C.18.53   I toted vpon þ[e] tree *tho* and thenne toek y hede
C.18.57   And askede efte *tho* where hit were all [of] o kynde.
C.18.130   The mayde myldeliche [*tho*] the messager grauntede
C.18.274   'I wolde ywyte,' quod y *tho*, 'what is in thy lappe.'
C.19.55   A man, as me *tho* thouhte, to moche care they brouhte
C.20.59   The lord of lyf and of liht *tho* leyde his eyes togederes.
C.20.73   T[w]o theues *tho* tholed deth þat tyme
C.20.89   *Tho* ful the knyhte vppon knees and criede iesu mercy:
C.20.465   Treuth trompede *tho* and song te deum laudamus
C.21.12   Quod Conciense and knelede *tho*, 'this aren [Peres] Armes,
C.21.48   *Tho* was he iesu[s] of iewes [cald], gentel profete,
C.21.50   And *tho* conquerede he on cros as conquerour noble;
C.21.53   And *tho* was he conquerour cald of quyke and of dede
C.21.91   The thridde kyng cam [þo] knel[ynge] to iesu
C.21.112   And lawe lakked *tho* for men loued nat her enemyes
C.21.117   And *tho* was he cleped and calde not [onl]y Crist but iesu,
C.21.132   And *tho* was he cald in contreye of þe comune peple,
C.21.135   The buyrdes *tho* songe, Saul interfecit mille & dauid decem milia.
C.21.355   Quod Consience to alle cristene *tho*, 'my consayl is [to] wende
C.21.364   Consience comaundede t[h]o alle cristene to delue
C.22.74   'Y consail,' quod Consi[e]nce *tho*, 'cometh with me, ȝe foles,
C.22.80   Kynde Consience *tho* herde and cam oute of the planetes
C.22.90   The lord þat lyuede aftur lust *tho* aloud cryede
C.22.106   Concience of his cortesye *tho* kynde he bisouhte
C.22.165   For care Consience *tho* cryede vpon elde
C.22.232   Nede neyhede *tho* ner and Consience he toelde
C.22.242   Con[s]ience of this con[s]ail *tho* comesed for to lawhe
C.22.338   'Y preye the,' quod Pees *tho*, 'ar thow passe forþere,
C.22.380   'By Crist!' quod Consience *tho*, 'y wol bicome a pilgrime

þo conj *tho adv.* A 5; B 18 tho (7) þo (11); C 18 tho
A. 1.45   *Þo* þe peple hym aposide with a peny in þe temple
A. 2.113   *Þo* þis gold was gyue gret was þe þonking
A. 3.96   Ac wers wrouȝtest þou neuere þan *þo* þou fals toke.
A. 5.237   *Þo* dismas my broþer besouȝte þe of grace,
A. 6.90   *Þo* Adam & Eue eten here bane,
B.Pr.176   Ac *þo* þe belle was ybrouȝt and on þe beiȝe hanged
B. 1.47   *Tho* þe poeple hym apposede wiþ a peny in þe temple
B. 2.149   *Tho* þis gold was ygyue gret was þe þonkyng
B. 3.107   Ac worse wrouȝtest [þ]ow neuere þan *þo* þow Fals toke.
B. 3.345   *Tho* ye [souȝte] Sapience sittynge in youre studie.
B. 5.465   *Tho* Dysmas my broþer bisouȝte [þee] of grace
B. 5.603   *Tho* Adam and Eue eten apples vnrosted:
B.10.406   *Tho* he shoop þat ship of shides and bordes:
B.10.433   Tho þat wrouȝte wikkedlokest in world *þo* þei were;
B.10.447   For soþest word þat euer god seide was *þo* he seide Nemo bonus.
B.11.413   'Haddestow suffred', he seide, 'slepynge *þo* þow were,
B.12.152   *Tho* it shon to shepherdes, a shewer of blisse].
B.16.113   Saue *þo* he leched laȝar þat hadde yleye in graue;
B.16.194   So god, þat gynnyng hadde neuere but *þo* hym good þouȝte,
B.18.233   That *þo* þis barn was ybore þer blased a sterre
B.18.249   Lo! helle myȝte nat holde, but opnede *þo* god þolede,
B.19.4   In myddes of þe masse *þo* men yede to offrynge
B.20.346   And at þe laste þis lymytour, *þo* my lord was oute,
C.Pr.193   Ac *tho* þe belle was ybroughte and on þe beygh hangid
C. 2.165   *Tho* this gold was ygyue grete was the thonkynge
C. 3.138   For wors wrouhtest [thow] neuere then *tho* thow fals toke.
C. 3.240   That he ne felde nat his foes *tho* fortune hit wolde
C. 6.319   *Tho* dysmas my brother bisouhte [þe]
C. 8.238   Go to oure bygynnynge *tho* god the world made,
C. 9.276   But 'haue this for þat *tho* þat thow toke
C.11.237   *Tho* he shoop þe ship of shides and bordes:
C.13.221   'Haddestow soffred,' he sayde, 'slepyng *tho* thow were,
C.14.96   *Tho* hit shoen to shepherdes, a sheware of blisse.
C.15.152   [And] pacience properliche spak, *tho* Peres was thus ypassed,
C.17.302   *Tho* he luft vp lasar þat layde was in graue;
C.18.203   God [that] bigynnyng hadde neuere bote *tho* hym goed thouhte
C.20.242   [That *tho*] this barn was ybore þ[er] blased a sterre
C.20.258   Loo! helle myhte nat holde, bote opened *tho* god tholede
C.21.4   In myddes of þe masse *tho* men ȝede to offrynge
C.21.71   *Tho* he was bore in Bedlehem, as þe boek telleth,
C.22.346   And at þe laste this lymytour, *tho* my lord was oute,

*thogh > þouȝ; thoght > þouȝt; thoghte > þynkeþ; þoȝ > þouȝ; þoȝt > þouȝt;
þoȝte > þynke,þynkeþ*

þole v *tholen v.* A 1; B 9 þole (1) þoled (2) þolede (2) þoledest (1) þolie
  (2) þolye (1); C 11 tholed (1) tholede (4) tholeden (1) tholedest (1)
  tholie (1) tholye (1) tholieth (1)
A. 4.71   [Þat wrong for his werkis shulde woo *þole*,
B. 4.84   That wrong for hise werkes sholde wo *þolie*,
B.11.400   Al to murþe wiþ man þat moste wo *þolie*,
B.13.77   And what meschief and maleese crist for man *þolede*,
B.13.262   So er my wafres be ywroȝt muche wo I *þolye*.
B.18.71   Two þeues [þat tyme] *þoled* deeþ [also]
B.18.134   Which deide and deeþ *þoled* þis day aboute mydday,
B.18.249   Lo! helle myȝte nat holde, but opnede þo god *þolede*,
B.18.382   There [a] feloun *þole* sholde deeþ ooþer Iuwise
B.19.174   Deidest and deeþ *þoledest* and deme shalt vs alle,
C. 4.80   That wrong for his werkes sholde w[oo] *tholye*
C.12.205   For crist saide [so] to seyntes þat for his sake *tholeden*
C.15.72   And how þat poul þe apostel penaunce *tholede*
C.15.83   And what meschief and maleese crist for man *tholede*.
C.16.32   Thise thre withoute doute *tholieth* alle pouerte
C.19.107   Y sholde *tholye* and thonken hem þat me euel wolden.'
C.20.73   T[w]o theues tho *tholed* deth þat tyme
C.20.137   [Which] deyede and deth *tholede* this day aboute mydday
C.20.258   Loo! helle myhte nat holde, bote opened tho god *tholede*
C.21.174   Deyedest and deth *tholedest* and deme shalt vs all

thomas n prop *n.i.d.* A 2; B 6; C 6
A. 5.28   *Thomas* he tauȝte to take two staues
A. 6.45   'I nolde fonge a ferþing for seint *Thomas* shryne,
B. 5.558   'I nolde fange a ferþyng for Seint *Thomas* Shryne;
B.15.523   In sauacion of [mannes soule] seint [*Thomas*] was ymartired;
B.19.165   Thaddee and ten mo wiþ *Thomas* of Inde.
B.19.170   And took *Thomas* by þe hand and tauȝte hym to grope
B.19.172   *Thomas* touched it and wiþ his tonge seide:
B.19.177   "*Thomas*, for þow trowest þis and treweliche bileuest it
C. 7.202   'Y [nolde] fonge a ferthynge for seynt *Thomas* shryne;
C.17.274   In sauacioun of mannes soule seynte *Thomas* of Canterbury
C.21.165   Taddee and ten mo with *Thomas* of ynde.
C.21.170   And toek *Thomas* by the hoende and tauhte hym to grope
C.21.172   *Thomas* touched hit and and with his tonge saide:
C.21.177   "*Thomas*, for thow trowest this and treweliche bileuest hit

þombe n *thoume n.* B 3 thombe (1) þombe (2); C 3 thombe (2) thumbe
  (1)
B. 5.432   I am noȝt lured wiþ loue but þer ligge auȝt vnder þe *þombe*.
B.17.160   Thoruȝ foure fyngres and a *thombe* forþ with þe pawme,
B.17.194   Ac þouȝ my *þombe* and my fyngres boþe were toshullen
C. 7.45   Y am nat luyred with loue but þer lygge ouht vnder þe t[h]umbe.
C.19.136   The fyngeres is a fol hand for failed they or *thombe*
C.19.160   Ac thouh my *thombe* and my fyngeres bothe were toshullen

thomme > tomme

þonken v *thanken v.* A 2 þanked (1) þankide (1); B 2 þanked (1) þonked
  (1); C 6 thonke (1) thonkede (3) thonken (1) thonketh (1)
A. 9.101   I *þankide* þouȝt þo þat he me so tauȝte.
A.12.48   And *þanked* hure a þousand syþes with þrobbant herte.
B. 8.111   I *þonked* þoȝt þo þat he me [so] tauȝte.
B.17.90   And I *þanked* hym þo and siþþe [þus] I hym tolde
C. 4.152   And kynde [wit] and Consience corteysliche *thonkede*
C. 8.135   [We haue] none lymes to labory with, lord god we *thonketh*.'
C.10.107   Y *thonkede* thoght tho þat he me so tauhte.
C.18.17   'Y *thonke* ȝow a thousand s[i]the that ȝe me hider kende
C.18.19   And he *thonkede* me tho; bote thenne toek y hede
C.19.107   Y sholde tholye and *thonken* hem þat me euel wolden.'

þonkyng ger *thankinge ger.* A 1 þonking; B 1; C 1 thonkynge
A. 2.113   Þo þis gold was gyue gret was þe *þonking*
B. 2.149   Tho þis gold was ygyue gret was þe *þonkyng*
C. 2.165   Tho this gold was ygyue grete was the *thonkynge*

þoo > þo; thorgh þorȝ > þoruȝ; þorled > þirled

þorn n *thorn n.* B 5 þorn (2) þornes (3); C 5 thorn (2) thornes (3)
B.12.228   [That þ]ere þe *þorn* is þikkest to buylden and brede;
B.18.47   'Tolle, tolle!' quod anoþer, and took of kene *þornes*
B.18.48   And bigan of [grene] *þorn* a garland to make,
B.19.4   And kyng of hir kyngdom and croune bar of *þornes*.
B.19.321   And Grace gaf hym þe cros, wiþ þe [garland] of *þornes*,
C. 2.29   Ne on a croked kene *thorn* kynde fyge wexe:
C.20.47   'Tolle, tolle!' quod another, and toek of kene *thornes*
C.20.48   And bigan of grene *thorn* a garlond to make
C.21.49   And kyng of here kyngdoem and croune baer of *thornes*.
C.21.321   And grace gaf hym þe cros with [the garlond] of *thornes*

thorpus > þropis

þoruȝ prep *thurgh prep.* A 30 þoruȝ (28) thurgh (1) þurgh (1); B 164
thorgh (1) þorȝ (1) thorugh (1) thoruȝ (21) þoruȝ (140); C 148 thorw
(144) thorwe (4)

A. 1.107 Tauȝte hem *þoruȝ* þe trinite þe trouþe to knowe:
A. 1.111 Til he brak buxumnesse *þoruȝ* bost of hymseluen.
A. 2.117 Til mede be þi weddit wyf *þoruȝ* wyt of vs alle,
A. 2.178 Lurkyng *þoruȝ* lanes, toluggid of manye.
A. 3.72 And ri[chen] *þoruȝ* regrat[r]ie & rentis hem biggen
A. 3.116 ȝoure fadir he[o] fellide *þoruȝ* false behest,
A. 3.201 *Þoruȝ* ȝeftis han ȝonge men to [ȝerne] & to ride.
A. 4.124 Ne gete my grace *þoruȝ* giftes, so me god helpe!
A. 5.77 And don hise frendis ben hise fon *þoruȝ* my false tunge.
A. 5.80 Boþe his lyme & his lif was lost *þoruȝ* my tunge.
A. 6.48 ȝe mote go *þoruȝ* meknesse, boþe men & wyues,
A. 6.103 And geten it aȝen *þoruȝ* grace & *þoruȝ* no gift ellis.
A. 6.103 And geten it aȝen *þoruȝ* grace & *þoruȝ* no gift ellis.
A. 6.122 And *þoruȝ* þe helpe of hem [two], hope þou non oþer,
A. 7.258 Þei do men diȝe *þoruȝ* here drynkes er destenye it wolde.'
A. 7.304 He shal awake [*þoruȝ*] water wastours to chaste;
A. 7.306 *Þoruȝ* flood [and] foule wederis fruytes shuln fa[i]lle,
A. 8.11 Han pardoun *þoruȝ* purcatorie to passe wel sone,
A. 8.127 And *þoruȝ* here wordis I wok & waitide aboute,
A. 9.38 Þat *þoruȝ* þe fend, & þe flessh, & þe false world,
A. 9.73 And *þoruȝ* his labour or his lond his liflode wynneþ,
A. 10.33 For *þoruȝ* þe woord þat he warp wexe forþ bestis,
A. 10.41 *Þoruȝ* miȝt of þe maieste man was ymakid:
A. 10.50 For *þoruȝ* his connyng is kept caro & anima
A. 10.119 For *þoruȝ* suffraunce se þou miȝt how soueraynes ariseþ,
A. 10.133 Þat *þoruȝ* wedlak þe world stant, whoso wile it knowen.
A. 10.178 [Þus] *þoruȝ* curside caym cam care vpon alle,
A. 11.68 *Þoruȝ* whiche a werk & wille þei wenten to helle,
A. 12.60 As I ȝede *thurgh* ȝouþe, aȝen prime dayes,
A. 12.99 Wille *þurgh* inwit [wiste] wel þe soþe,
B. 1.32 *Thoruȝ* wyn and *þoruȝ* wommen þer was loth acombred,
B. 1.32 *Thoruȝ* wyn and *þoruȝ* wommen þer was loth acombred,
B. 1.109 Tauȝte hem [*þoruȝ*] þe Trinitee [þe] treuþe to knowe:
B. 2.42 Fauel *þoruȝ* his faire speche haþ þis folk enchaunted,
B. 2.153 Til Mede be þi wedded wif *þoruȝ* wi[t] of vs alle,
B. 2.219 Lurkynge *þoruȝ* lanes, tolugged of manye.
B. 3.83 Thei richen *þoruȝ* regratrie and rentes hem biggen
B. 3.127 Youre fader she felled *þoruȝ* false biheste,
B. 3.159 And doþ men lese *þoruȝ* hire loue þat lawe myȝte wynne
B. 3.214 [*Thoruȝ*] ȝiftes han yonge men to [yerne] and to ryde.
B. 4.141 Ne gete my grace [*þoruȝ*] giftes, so me god [helpe]!
B. 4.175 And seide, *þoruȝ* [youre] lawe, as I leue, I lese manye eschetes;
B. 5.97 And [doon] his frendes be his foon *þoruȝ* my false tonge.
B. 5.100 That boþe lif and lyme is lost *þoruȝ* my speche.
B. 5.134 I wole amende þis if I may *þoruȝ* myȝt of god almyȝty.'
B. 5.243 I haue mo Manoirs *þoruȝ* Rerages þan *þoruȝ* Miseretur &
com[m]odat.
B. 5.243 I haue mo Manoirs *þoruȝ* Rerages þan *þoruȝ* Miseretur &
com[m]odat.
B. 5.484 For *þoruȝ* þat synne þi sone sent was to erþe
B. 5.561 Ye moten go *þoruȝ* mekenesse, boþe men and wyues,
B. 5.617 And [gete it ayein *þoruȝ*] grace [ac *þoruȝ* no gifte ellis].
B. 5.617 And [gete it ayein *þoruȝ*] grace [ac *þoruȝ* no gifte ellis].
B. 5.637 And *þoruȝ* þe help of hem two, hope þow non ooþer,
B. 6.144 And al is *þoruȝ* suffraunce þat vengeaunce yow ne takeþ.
B. 6.201 'I am wel awroke of wastours *þoruȝ* þy myȝte.
B. 6.274 They do men deye *þoruȝ* hir drynkes er destynee it wolde.'
B. 6.323 He shal awake [*þoruȝ*] water wastours to chaste;
B. 6.325 *Thoruȝ* flo[od] and foule wedres fruytes shul faille,
B. 7.11 Han pardon *þoruȝ* purgatorie to passen ful liȝtly,
B. 7.145 And [*þoruȝ* hir wordes I wook] and waited aboute,
B. 8.42 That *þoruȝ* þe fend and þe flessh and þe [false] worlde
B. 8.82 And *þoruȝ* his labour or his land his liflode wynneþ,
B. 9.32 For *þoruȝ* þe word þat he [warp] woxen forþ beestes,
B. 9.45 And in þis manere was man maad *þoruȝ* myȝt of god almyȝty,
B. 9.53 *Thorgh* myȝt of þe mageste man was ymaked.
B. 9.156 And þus *þoruȝ* cursed Caym cam care vpon erþe,
B. 9.210 And dryueþ awey dowel *þoruȝ* dedliche synnes.'
B. 10.110 *Thoruȝ* whic[h] werk and wil] þei wente to helle,
B. 10.244 *Thoruȝ* þe help of þe holy goost þe which is of boþe;
B. 10.284 In alle maner men *þoruȝ* mansede preestes.
B. 10.326 And Barons wiþ Erles beten hem *þoruȝ* Beatus virres techyng;
B. 11.81 *Thoruȝ* contricion [clene] come to þe heiȝe heuene–
B. 11.124 By þe blood þat he bouȝte vs wiþ, and *þoruȝ* bapteme after:
B. 11.149 Graunted [me worþ] grace [*þorȝ*] his grete wille).
B. 11.156 Nouȝt *þoruȝ* preiere of a pope but for his pure truþe
B. 11.208 And we hise breþeren *þoruȝ* hym ybouȝt, boþe riche and pouere.
B. 11.301 He [ouȝte no] bileue, as I leue, to lacche *þoruȝ* his croune
B. 11.323 And *þoruȝ* þe wondres of þis world wit for to take.
B. 11.326 *Thorough* ech a creature kynde my creatour to louye,

B. 11.358 And some briddes at þe bile *þoruȝ* breþyng conceyued,
B. 11.414 Thow sholdest haue knowen þat clergie kan & [conceyued] moore
þoruȝ Res[on],
B. 12.63 And *þoruȝ* þe gifte of þe holy goost as þe gospel telleþ:
B. 12.77 Ac crist of his curteisie *þoruȝ* clergie hir saued.
B. 12.78 [For] *þoruȝ* caractes þat crist wroot þe Iewes knewe hemselue
B. 12.100 Na moore kan no Clerk but if he cauȝte it first *þoruȝ* bokes.
B. 12.133 Ac *þoruȝ* hir science sooþly was neuere soule ysaued
B. 12.258 And alle þe oþere þer it lith enuenymeþ *þoruȝ* his attre.
B. 12.286 And *þoruȝ* fir is fullyng, and þat is ferme bileue:
B. 13.13 *Thoruȝ* vnkonnynge curatours to incurable peynes;
B. 13.167 Maister of alle þo men *þoruȝ* myȝt of þis redels,
B. 13.168 Nouȝt *þoruȝ* wicchecraft but *þoruȝ* wit; and þow wilt þiselue
B. 13.168 Nouȝt *þoruȝ* wicchecraft but *þoruȝ* wit; and þow wilt þiselue
B. 13.259 Til pride be pureliche fordo, and [þat] *þoruȝ* payn defaute.
B. 13.327 And made of frendes foes *þoruȝ* a fals tonge.
B. 13.328 'Or wiþ myȝt [of] mouþ or *þoruȝ* m[a]nnes strengþe
B. 13.341 But *þoruȝ* a charme hadde I chaunce and my chief heele.'
B. 13.355 [Was] colomy *þoruȝ* coueitise and vnkynde desiryng.
B. 13.358 [*Thoruȝ*] false mesures and met, and wiþ fals witnesse;
B. 13.360 And awaited *þoruȝ* [wittes wyes] to bigile;
B. 13.369 *Thoruȝ* gile to gaderen þe good þat ich haue.
B. 13.428 Sauen *þoruȝ* hir sermo[n] mannes soule fro helle;
B. 13.430 To entice men *þoruȝ* hir tales to synne and harlotrie.
B. 13.454 [There] flateres and fooles *þoruȝ* hir foule wordes
B. 14.14 Or *þoruȝ* werk or *þoruȝ* word or wille of myn herte
B. 14.14 Or *þoruȝ* werk or *þoruȝ* word or wille of myn herte
B. 14.18 Dowel shal wasshen it and wryngen it *þoruȝ* a wis confessour:
B. 14.46 Lyue *þoruȝ* leel bileue, [as oure lord] witnesseþ:
B. 14.59 Or *þoruȝ* hunger or *þoruȝ* hete, at his wille be it;
B. 14.59 Or *þoruȝ* hunger or *þoruȝ* hete, at his wille be it;
B. 14.61 For *þoruȝ* his breeþ beestes woxen and abrood yeden:
B. 14.62 Ergo *þoruȝ* his breeþ [boþe] men and beestes lyuen,
B. 14.77 Weex *þoruȝ* plentee of payn and of pure sleuþe.
B. 14.83 And *þoruȝ* feiþ comeþ contricion, conscience woot wel,
B. 14.113 And wilde wormes in wodes, *þoruȝ* wyntres þow hem greuest
B. 14.176 *Thoruȝ* derþe, *þoruȝ* droghte, alle hir dayes here,
B. 14.176 *Thoruȝ* derþe, *þoruȝ* droghte, alle hir dayes here,
B. 14.185 And be clene *þoruȝ* þat cristnyng of alle kynnes synne.
B. 14.186 And if vs fille *þoruȝ* folie to falle in synne after
B. 14.268 [Moore] þan [a maiden is] þat is maried *þoruȝ* brocage
B. 14.304 The sixte is a path of pees; ye! *þoruȝ* þe paas of Aultoun
B. 15.65 Right so þat *þoruȝ* reson wolde þe roote knowe
B. 15.93 *Thoruȝ* lele libbynge men þat goddes lawe techen,
B. 15.210 Neiþer *þoruȝ* wordes ne werkes, but *þoruȝ* wil oone,
B. 15.210 Neiþer *þoruȝ* wordes ne werkes, but *þoruȝ* wil oone,
B. 15.280 And *þoruȝ* þe mylk of þat mylde beest þe man was sustened;
B. 15.295 Ac moost *þoruȝ* [meditacion] and mynde of god almyghty.
B. 15.346 And many a prison fram purgatorie *þoruȝ* hise preieres deliuereþ;
B. 15.356 For *þoruȝ* werre and wikkede werkes and wederes vn[s]esonable
B. 15.400 Into Surrie he souȝte, and *þoruȝ* hise sotile wittes
B. 15.409 And þus *þoruȝ* wiles of his wit and a whit Dowue
B. 15.413 *Thoruȝ* a cristene clerk acorsed in his soule–
B. 15.418 Peeren to Apostles *þoruȝ* hire parfit lyuynge.
B. 15.424 Grace sholde growe and be grene *þoruȝ* hir goode lyuynge,
B. 15.446 And *þoruȝ* miracles, as men mow rede, al þat marche he tornede
B. 15.449 Moore *þoruȝ* miracles þan *þoruȝ* muche prechyng;
B. 15.449 Moore *þoruȝ* miracles þan *þoruȝ* muche prechyng;
B. 15.450 As wel *þoruȝ* hise werkes as wiþ hise holy wordes
B. 15.467 For as þe Cow *þoruȝ* kynde mylk þe calf norisseþ til an Oxe,
B. 15.480 So hope þei to haue heuene *þoruȝ* hir whistlyng.
B. 15.514 Men myȝte noȝt be saued but *þoruȝ* mercy and grace,
B. 15.515 And *þoruȝ* penaunce and passion and parfit bile[ue].
B. 15.526 Holy chirche is honoured heiȝliche *þoruȝ* his deying;
B. 15.571 *Thoruȝ* his prouince to passe and to his peple shewe hym,
B. 15.598 And *þoruȝ* his pacience hir power to pure noȝt he brouȝte;
B. 16.9 And so *þoruȝ* god and goode men groweþ þe fruyt Charite.'
B. 16.29 And forfreteþ neiȝ þe fruyt *þoruȝ* manye faire sightes.
B. 16.32 *Thoruȝ* likynge and lustes so loude he gynneþ blowe
B. 16.38 *Thoruȝ* preieres and penaunces and goddes passion in mynde
B. 16.51 And palleþ adoun þe pouke pureliche *þoruȝ* grace
B. 16.101 Til he weex a faunt *þoruȝ* hir flessh and of fightyng kouþe
B. 16.120 And seide he wroȝte *þoruȝ* wichecraft & with þe deueles myȝt:
B. 16.142 'I am sold *þoruȝ* [som] of yow; he shal þe tyme rewe
B. 16.161 *Thoruȝ* Iudas and Iewes Iesus was [ynome]
B. 17.101 For wente neuere wye in þis world *þoruȝ* þat wildernesse
B. 17.121 And hostele hem and heele *þoruȝ* holy chirche bileue
B. 17.160 *Thoruȝ* foure fyngres and a thombe forþ with þe pawme,
B. 17.231 Ysekeles in euesynges *þoruȝ* hete of þe sonne
B. 17.304 That rightwisnesse *þoruȝ* repentaunce to ruþe myȝte turne.
B. 18.85 But þis blynde bacheler baar hym *þoruȝ* þe herte.
B. 18.129 Of any kynnes creature, conceyued *þoruȝ* speche
B. 18.139 That man shal man saue *þoruȝ* a maydenes helpe,

B.18.140 And þat was tynt *þoruȝ* tree, tree shal it wynne.
B.18.151 'Thoruȝ experience', quod [heo], 'I hope þei shul be saued;
B.18.157 The first venymouste, *þoruȝ* [vertu] of hymselue.
B.18.159 Al þat deeþ [d]ide first *þoruȝ* þe deueles entisyng,
B.18.160 And riȝt as [þe gilour] *þoruȝ* gile [bigiled man formest]
B.18.294 We haue no trewe title to hem, for *þoruȝ* treson were þei dampned.'
B.18.312 First *þoruȝ* þe we fellen fro heuene so heiȝe:
B.18.346 And boþe quykne and quyte þat queynt was *þoruȝ* synne;
B.18.352 To recouere hem *þoruȝ* raunsoun and by no reson ellis,
B.18.353 So þat *þoruȝ* gile þow gete *þoruȝ* grace it is ywonne.
B.18.353 So þat *þoruȝ* gile þow gete *þoruȝ* grace it is ywonne.
B.18.358 And as Adam and alle *þoruȝ* a tree deyden,
B.18.359 Adam and alle *þoruȝ* a tree shul turne to lyue,
B.18.389 I [may] do mercy *þoruȝ* [my] rightwisnesse and alle my wordes trewe;
B.18.415 And Pees *þoruȝ* pacience alle perils stoppeþ.'
B.19.39 Aren frankeleyns, free men *þoruȝ* fullynge þat þei toke
B.19.95 *Thoruȝ* þre kynne kynges knelynge to Iesu.
B.19.121 That he *þoruȝ* grace was gete and of no gome ellis.
B.19.122 He wroȝte þat by no wit but *þoruȝ* word one,
B.19.130 For deue *þoruȝ* hise doynges and dombe speke [and herde],
B.19.244 As Astronomyens *þoruȝ* Astronomye, and Philosofres wise.
B.19.246 He wissed hem wynne it ayein *þoruȝ* wightnesse of handes
B.19.301 [Shal] nouȝt ben espied [*þoruȝ*] Spiritus Iusticie.
B.19.354 Al þe world in a while *þoruȝ* oure wit', quod Pryde.
B.19.375 Some *þoruȝ* bedes biddynge and some [by] pilgrymag[e]
B.19.376 And op[er] pryue penaunc[e], and somme *þoruȝ* penyes delynge.
B.19.386 Grace, *þoruȝ* goddes word, [g]af Piers power,
B.20.99 So kynde *þoruȝ* corrupcions kilde ful manye.
B.20.213 *Thoruȝ* Contricion and Confession til I cam to vnitee.
B.20.229 *Thoruȝ* inparfite preestes and prelates of holy chirche.'
B.20.305 'Go salue þo þat sike ben and *þoruȝ* synne ywounded.'
B.20.317 For here is many a man hurt *þoruȝ* ypocrisye.'
B.20.351 That lif *þoruȝ* his loore shal leue coueitise
B.20.354 Thus *þoruȝ* hende speche [þe frere entred]
C.Pr.106 Ful on hem þat fre were *thorwe* two fals prestis!
C. 1.25 Loot in his lyue *thorw* likerous drynke
C. 1.31 *Thorw* wyn and thorw wom[e]n there was loot acombred;
C. 1.31 Thorw wyn and *thorw* wom[e]n there was loot acombred;
C. 1.63 Iudas he byiapede *thorw* iewene suluer
C. 2.45 Fauel *thorw* his flaterynge speche hath mede foule enchaunted,
C. 2.153 And thow Iustices enioynen hem *thorw* I[u]roures othes
C. 2.229 Lorkyng *thorw* lanes, tologged of moneye.
C. 2.247 And putte hem *thorw* appeles in þe popes grace.
C. 2.250 Thy kynedom thorw Coueytise wol out of kynde wende,
C. 2.251 And holy churche *thorw* hem worth harmed for euere.'
C. 3.82 Rychen *thorw* regraterye and rentes hem beggeth
C. 3.91 Bothe *thorw* fuyr and flood a[nd] thorw fals peple
C. 3.91 Bothe thorw fuyr and flood a[nd] *thorw* fals peple
C. 3.104 Al this haue we seyn, þat som tyme *thorw* a breware
C. 3.106 And *thorw* a candle clemynge in [a] cursed place
C. 3.197 *Thorw* which loueday is loste þat leute myhte wynne;
C. 3.245 For þat [is] conquere[d] *thorw* a comune helpe, a kyndom or ducherie.
C. 3.270 *Thorw* ȝeftes haen ȝemen to ȝerne and to ryde;
C. 3.377 That here loue to his lawe *Thorw* al þe lond acorde.
C. 3.431 Thus was kyng sauel ouercome *thorw* coueytise of mede,
C. 3.450 Muchel [euel] is *thorw* mede mony tymes ysoffred
C. 3.451 And letteth the lawe *thorw* here large ȝeftes.
C. 4.71 *Thorw* wrong and his werkes there was mede yknowe
C. 4.138 Ne gete my grace *thorw* eny gyfte ne glosynge spe[ch]e
C. 4.139 Ne *thorw* mede mercy, by marie of heuene!
C. 4.169 'Thorw ȝoure lawe, as y leue, y lese many chetes;
C. 5.34 Or ymaymed *thorw* som myshap whereby thow myhte be excused?'
C. 5.98 Suche a wynnyng hym warth *thorw* w[y]rdes of grace:
C. 5.127 *Thorw* som trewe trauail and no tyme spille.
C. 6.21 *Thorw* my word and my witt here euel werkes to shewe;
C. 6.72 And made of frendes foes *thorw* fikel and fals tonge.
C. 6.73 'Or *thorw* myhte of mouthe or thorw mannes sleythes
C. 6.73 'Or thorw myhte of mouthe or *thorw* mannes sleythes
C. 6.85 But *thorw* a charme hadde y chaunce and my chef hele.
C. 6.186 Of put[rie] and of paramours and proueden *thorw* speche
C. 6.187 And handlyng and halsyng and also *thorw* kyssyng,
C. 7.88 Sauen *thorw* here sarmon mannes soule fram helle,
C. 7.90 To entise men *thorw* here tales to synne and harlotrie.
C. 7.126 For *thorw* þat synne thy sone ysent was til erthe
C. 7.206 Ȝe mote go *thorw* mekenesse, alle men and wommen,
C. 7.269 And geten hit agayne *thorw* grace Ac thorw no gifte elles.
C. 7.269 And geten hit agayne thorw grace Ac *thorw* no gifte elles.
C. 7.290 And *thorw* þe help[e] of hem two, hope þou non oþer,
C. 8.207 'Y am wel awroke of wastours *thorw* thy myhte
C. 8.260 *Thorw* eny lele labour as thorw lymes and handes:

C. 8.260 Thorw eny lele labour as *thorw* lymes and handes:
C. 8.295 They don men deye *thorw* here drynkes Ar destyne hit wolde.'
C. 8.343 He shal awake *thorw* water wastors to chaste;
C. 8.346 *Thorw* flodes and foule wederes fruyttes shollen fayle;
C. 9.11 Haen pardon *thorw* purgatorye to passe ful lyhtly,
C. 9.156 *Thorw* which craft a couthe come to bred and to ale
C. 9.182 Or bylowe *thorw* luther men and lost here catel aftur
C. 9.183 Or *thorw* fuyr or thorw floed yfalle into pouerte,
C. 9.183 Or thorw fuyr or *thorw* floed yfalle into pouerte,
C. 9.254 Cam no wyn in his wombe *thorw* þe woke longe
C. 9.294 And *thorw* here wordes [y] awoke and waytede aboute
C. 9.302 And how þe prest inpugnede hit *thorw* two propre wordes.
C.10.36 For stonde he neuere so stifliche, *thorw* steryng of þe bote
C.10.42 Thow he *thorw* fondynges falle he falleth nat out of charite;
C.10.48 That *thorw* the fend and [the] flesch and th[e] freel worlde
C.10.79 And *thorw* lele labour lyueth and loueth his emcristene
C.10.177 That many lede leseth *thorw* lykerous drynke,
C.10.208 *Thorw* no sotil sciense on sour stok growe";
C.11.20 *Thorw* fallas and fals questes and thorw fikel speche.
C.11.20 Thorw fallas and fals questes and *thorw* fikel speche.
C.11.125 Thus *thorw* my lore ben men ylered thogh y loke demme.
C.12.185 And *thorw* þe grace of god and grayn dede [i]n erthe
C.13.19 Alle his sorwe to solace *thorw* that song turnede
C.13.23 As grayn þat lith in greut and *thorw* grace at the laste
C.13.61 Ac ȝut myhte þe marchaunt *thorw* moneye and other ȝeftes
C.13.116 *Thorw* here luyther lyuynge and lewede vnderstondynge.
C.13.222 Thow sholdest haue yknowe þat clergie ca[n] & conseyued mor[e] [*thorw*] resoun
C.14.25 And w[o]lky *thorw* gode werkes wikkede hertes.
C.14.53 Come for al his kynde wit *thorw* cristendoem to be saued,
C.14.77 Ac *thorw* here science sothly was neuere soule ysaued
C.14.208 And *thorw* fuyr is fullyng; and [þat] is ferme bileue:
C.15.16 *Thorw* vnkunynge curatours to incurable peynes;
C.15.77 That no fals frere *thorw* flaterynge hem bygyle;
C.15.229 Til pruyde be puyreliche fordo and þat *thorw* payn defaute:
C.15.236 Tho[r]w the helpe of hym þat me hyder sente;
C.15.244 Leue *thorw* lele bileue, As oure lord wittenesseth:
C.15.258 Wheþer *thorw* hunger or [thorw] hete, at his wille be hit;
C.15.258 Wheþer thorw hunger or [*thorw*] hete, at his wille be hit;
C.15.260 [For] *thorw* his breth bestes wexe and abroed ȝeden,
C.15.261 Ergo *thorw* his breth bestes lyueth, bothe men and fisches,
C.15.289 And wilde wormes in wodes, *thorw* wyntres thow hem greuest
C.16.139 The sixte is a path of pees; ȝe! *thorwe* þe pase of Aultoun
C.16.245 *Thorw* parfit preesthoed and prelates of holy churche,
C.16.342 Ac *thorw* werkes thow myhte wyte wher forth he walketh:
C.16.369 Ac *thorw* Coueytyse and his consaile ycongeyed is he ofte.
C.17.86 For what *thorw* werre and wrake and wikkede hefdes
C.17.185 Holy men, as y hope, *thorw* helpe of the holy goste
C.17.239 And take hede [how] Macometh *thorw* a mylde dowue
C.17.241 Naught *thorw* manslaght and mannes strenghe Macometh hadde þe maistrie
C.17.242 Bote *thorw* pacience and priue gyle he was prince ouer hem all.
C.17.265 That men myhte nat be saued but *thorw* mercy and grace
C.17.266 And *thorw* penaunce and passioun and parfyt bileue;
C.17.276 And alle holy kirke honoured *thorw* that deyng.
C.17.284 And pacientliche *thorw* his prouynce and to his peple hym shewe,
C.17.306 And her power *thorw* his pacience to puyr nauht brouhte.
C.17.314 *Thorw* Moises and Macometh and myhte of god þat made al.
C.18.10 *Thorw* louely lokyng[e] hit lyueth and launseth vp blosmes,
C.18.33 And forfret þat fruyt *thorw* many fayre s[ih]tus.
C.18.36 *Thorw* lecherie and lustes so loude he gynneth blowe
C.18.46 *Thorw* bagbitares and braule[r]s and thorw bolde chidares
C.18.46 Thorw bagbitares and braule[r]s and *thorw* bolde chidares
C.18.122 That *thorw* fals biheste and fruyt furste man disseyued.
C.18.150 And *thorw* the myhte of Mahond and thorw misbileue.
C.18.150 And thorw the myhte of Mahond and *thorw* misbileue.
C.19.197 Isekeles in euesynges *thorwe* hete of the sonne
C.19.284 That rihtwisnesse *thorw* repentaunce to reuthe myhte turne.
C.20.87 Bote this blynde bacheler that bar hym *thorw* the herte.
C.20.101 When Crist *thorw* croos ouercam ȝoure kyndoem sholde tocleue:
C.20.132 Of eny kyn[nes] creature, conceyued *thorw* speche
C.20.142 [That man shal man saue *thorw* a maydenes helpe
C.20.143 And] that was tynt *thorw* tre, tre shal hit wynne.
C.20.154 'Thorw experiense', quod he, 'y hope they shal ben saued;
C.20.160 The [f]erste venemouste, *thorw* vertu of hymsulue.
C.20.163 And riht as the gylour *thorw* gyle bigiled man formost
C.20.284 Ar we *thorw* brihtnesse be b[l]ente go barre þe ȝates;
C.20.320 And dust hem breke here buxumnesse *thorw* fals bihestes
C.20.391 And bothe quykie and quyte that queynte was *thorw* synne
C.20.392 And gyle [be] bigyled *thorw* grace at þe laste:
C.20.396 So þat [*thorw*] gyle was gete thorw grace is now ywonne
C.20.396 So þat [thorw] gyle was gete *thorw* grace is now ywonne
C.20.397 And as Adam and alle *thorwe* a tre deyede,

C.20.398 Adam and alle *thorw* a tre shal turne to lyue.
C.20.458 And pees *thorw* pacience alle perelles stop[peth].'
C.21.39 Aren frankeleynes, fre men *Thorw* follyng þat they toke
C.21.95 *Thorw* thre kyne kynges knelyng to iesu.
C.21.121 That he *thorw* grace was gete and of no gome elles.
C.21.122 He wrouhte þat by no wyt bote *thorw* word one,
C.21.130 For deue *thorw* his doynges and dombe speke [&] herde
C.21.244 A[s] astro[nomy]ens *thorw* astronomye, & philosopheres wyse;
C.21.246 He wissede [h]e[m] wynne hit aȝeyn *thorw* whitnesse of handes
C.21.301 [Shal] nat be aspyed *thorw* spiritus iusticie.
C.21.354 Alle the world in a while *thorw* oure wit,' quod pruyde.
C.21.375 Somme *thorw* bedes biddynge and [somme] bi pilgrimag[e]
C.21.376 Or oþer priue penauns[e] and somme *thorw* pans delyng.
C.21.386 Grace *thorw* godes word gaf [Peres] power,
C.22.99 So kynde *thorw* corupcions kulde fol mony.
C.22.213 *Thorw* contricion and confessioun til y cam to vnite.
C.22.229 *Thorw* inparfit prestes and prelates of holy churche.'
C.22.305 'Go salue tho þat syke [ben] and *thorw* synne ywounded.'
C.22.317 For here is many [a] man hert *thorw* ypocrisye.'
C.22.351 That lyf *thorw* his lore shal leue Coueytise.
C.22.354 Thus *thorw* hende speche [the frere entred]

thou > þow; thoughte > þynkeþ

þouȝ *conj* *though conj. cf. þeiȝ* B 68 thouȝ (18) þouȝ (50); C 96 thauh (1) thogh (44) þoȝ (1) thouh (12) thow (38)

B.Pr.185 'Thouȝ we [hadde] kille[d] þe cat yet sholde þer come anoþer
B.Pr.186 To c[r]acchen vs & al oure kynde *þouȝ* we cropen vnder benches;
B.Pr.205 And *þouȝ* it costned me catel biknowen it I nolde
B. 1.35 Mesure is medicine *þouȝ* þow muchel yerne.
B. 1.176 *Thouȝ* ye be myȝt[y] to mote beeþ meke [of] youre werkes,
B. 1.179 For *þouȝ* ye be trewe of youre tonge and treweliche wynne,
B. 3.130 Bitwene heuene and helle, [and] erþe þouȝ men souȝte.
B. 3.160 The maȝe for a mene man *þouȝ* he mote euere!
B. 3.168 For pouere men may haue no power to pleyne *þouȝ* [hem] smerte,
B. 5.92 Than *þouȝ* I hadde þis wouke ywonne a weye of Essex chese.
B. 5.457 And *þouȝ* my liflode lakke leten I nelle
B. 5.549 For *þouȝ* I seye it myself I serue hym to paye;
B. 5.604 For he haþ þe keye and þe cliket *þouȝ* þe kyng slepe.
B. 6.35 To fulfille þis forward *þouȝ* I fiȝte sholde.
B. 6.39 And *þouȝ* [þow] mowe amercy hem lat mercy be taxour
B. 6.41 And *þouȝ* pouere men profre [þee] presentes and ȝiftes
B. 6.46 *Thouȝ* he be þyn vnderlyng here wel may happe in heuene
B. 6.98 For *þouȝ* I deye today my dettes are quyte;
B. 6.120 And *þouȝ* ye deye for doel þe deuel haue þat recch[e]!'
B. 7.86 He haþ ynouȝ þat haþ breed ynouȝ, *þouȝ* he haue noȝt ellis:
B. 7.125 And wepen whan I sholde [werche] *þouȝ* whete breed me faille.
B. 8.47 [That], *þouȝ* þ[i] body bowe as boot dooþ in þe watre,
B. 9.40 *Thouȝ* he [wiste to] write neuer so wel, [and] he hadde [a] penne,
B. 9.163 [For] goode sholde wedde goode, *þouȝ* þei no good hadde;
B. 9.173 [Th]ouȝ þei do hem to Dunmowe, but if þe deuel helpe
B.10.184 And lerned hem leuel and lyne *þouȝ* I loke dymme.
B.10.278 [Thouȝ] it auailled noȝt þe commune it myȝte auaille yowselue.
B.10.318 To Religiouse þat han no rouþe *þouȝ* it reyne on hir Auters.
B.10.396 *Thouȝ* hir goost be vngracious god for to plese.
B.10.451 *Thouȝ* ye come bifore kynges and clerkes of þe lawe
B.11.100 *Thouȝ* þe tale [were] trewe, and it touche[d] synne.
B.11.104 *Thouȝ* þow se yuel seye it noȝt first; be sory it nere amended.
B.11.125 For *þouȝ* a cristen man coueited his cristendom to reneye,
B.11.214 Forþi lakke no lif ooþer *þouȝ* he moore latyn knowe,
B.11.248 Iesu crist on a Iewes doȝter liȝte, gentil womman *þouȝ* she were,
B.11.429 For *þouȝ* Reson rebuked hym [þanne [recche]þ hym neuere;
B.12.2 *Thouȝ* I sitte by myself in siknesse n[e] in helpe.
B.12.21 Seide, 'Caton conforted his sone þat, clerk *þouȝ* he were,
B.12.172 Out of synne and be saaf, *þouȝ* he synne ofte,
B.12.196 Ac *þouȝ* þat þeef hadde heuene he hadde noon heiȝ blisse,
B.12.215 Raþer þan þat ooþer þeef, *þouȝ* þow woldest appose,
B.12.252 And *þouȝ* þe riche repente þanne and birewe þe tyme
B.12.254 *Thouȝ* he crye to crist þanne wiþ kene wil, I leue
B.14.2 *Thouȝ* it be soiled and selde clene: I slepe þerInne o nyȝtes;
B.14.29 'And I shal purueie þee paast', quod Pacience, '*þouȝ* no plouȝ erye,
B.14.31 *Thouȝ* neuere greyn growed, ne grape vpon vyne,
B.14.85 And *þouȝ* a man myȝte noȝt speke contricion myȝte hym saue
B.14.105 *Thouȝ* men rede of richesse riȝt to þe worldes ende,
B.14.232 And *þouȝ* his glotonye be to good ale he goþ to cold beddyng
B.14.245 And *þouȝ* Auarice wolde angre þe poore he haþ but litel myȝte,
B.14.254 And *þouȝ* Sleuþe suwe pouerte, and serue noȝt god to paie,
B.14.315 And [þouȝ] he chaffareþ he chargeþ no losse, mowe he charite wynne:
B.15.184 *Thouȝ* he bere hem no breed he bereþ hem swetter liflode;
B.15.285 And *þouȝ* þe gome hadde a gest god fond hem boþe.
B.16.105 That, *þouȝ* he were wounded with his enemy, to warisshen hymselue.
B.16.158 *Thouȝ* I bi treson be take [to] youre [iewene] wille

B.17.20 For, *þouȝ* I seye it myself, I haue saued with þis charme
B.17.194 Ac *þouȝ* my þombe and my fyngres boþe were toshullen
B.17.197 Boþe meue and amende, *þouȝ* alle my fyngres oke.
B.17.336 And *þouȝ* it falle it fynt skiles þat "frelete it made",
B.17.342 And *þouȝ* þat men make muche doel in hir angre
B.18.251 And now shal Lucifer leue it, *þouȝ* hym looþ þynke.
B.18.380 Ofter þan ones *þouȝ* he were a tretour.
B.18.390 And *þouȝ* holy writ wole þat I be wroke of hem þat diden ille–
B.19.252 'Thouȝ some be clenner þan some, ye se wel', quod Grace,
B.19.381 'I care noȝt', quod Conscience, '*þouȝ* pride come nouþe.
B.19.444 And counteþ noȝt *þouȝ* cristene ben killed and robbed,
B.20.16 And *þouȝ* he come so to a clooþ and kan no bettre cheuyssaunce
C.Pr.202 'Thow we hadde ykuld þe Cat ȝut shulde ther come another
C.Pr.203 To crache vs and alle oure kynde *thogh* we crope vnder benches;
C.Pr.213 And *thow* hit costed m[e] catel byknowen [hit] y ne wolde
C. 1.10 Y was afeerd of here face *thow* she fayre were
C. 1.19 And, in mesure *thow* muche were, to make ȝow attese
C. 1.33 Mesure is medecyne *thogh* þow muche ȝerne;
C. 1.125 Ac thei caren nat *thow* hit be cold, knaues, when þe[i] worche.
C. 1.172 *Thow* ȝe be myhty to mote beth meke in ȝoure werkes,
C. 1.175 For *thow* ȝe ben trewe of ȝoure tong[e] and treweliche wynne,
C. 2.153 And *thow* Iustices enioynen hem thorw I[u]roures othes
C. 3.40 'Thow le[r]red men and le[w]ed haued layn by the bothe
C. 3.87 *Thow* thei take hem vntidy thyng no tresoun þei ne halden hit;
C. 3.88 And [t]how thei fillen nat ful þat for lawe is seled
C. 3.167 Bytwene heuene and helle, and erthe *thogh* men soughte.
C. 3.187 He blesseth this bischopes *thow* thei ben lewede;
C. 3.198 The mase for a mene man *thow* he mote euere!
C. 3.315 And *thow* the kyng of his cortesye, Cayser or pope,
C. 3.385 *Thow* the kyng and þe comune al the coest hadde.
C. 3.390 Be the peccunie ypaied, *thow* parties chyde,
C. 4.70 Of pees and his power *thow* he pleyne euere.'
C. 5.164 To religious þat haen no reuthe *thow* it ryne on here auters.
C. 6.60 As to be preised amongus þe peple *thow* [y] pore seme:
C. 6.108 *Thow* y sitte this seuene ȝer, y sholde nat wel telle
C. 6.276 As *thow* y deddly synne dede y dradde [hit] nat so sore
C. 6.311 'And *thow* m[y] lyflode lakke leten y nelle
C. 7.193 And *thow* y sey hit mysulf y serue hym to paye;
C. 7.252 And he hath þe keye and þe clycat *thow* þe kyng slepe
C. 7.305 [Quod contemplacion, 'by Crist, *thow* y care soffre],
C. 8.34 To defende þe in fayth, fyhte *thow* y sholde.'
C. 8.39 And *thogh* pore men profre ȝow presentes and ȝyftes
C. 8.43 *Thogh* he be here thyn vnderlynge in heuene parauntur
C. 8.107 For *thouh* y dey today my dette[s ben] yquited;
C. 8.127 And *thow* ȝe deye for deul þe deuel haue þat reche!'
C. 8.195 To be his holde hewe *thow* he hadde no more
C. 8.285 Lene hem som of thy loef *thouh* thow þe lasse chewe.
C. 8.286 And *thouh* lyares and l[a]chdraweres and lollares knocke
C. 9.100 *Thouh* he falle for defaute þat fayteth for his lyflode
C. 9.101 Reche ȝe neuere, ȝe riche, *Thouh* suche lo[rell]es sterue.
C. 9.122 And *thauh* a mete with the mayre ameddes þe strete
C. 9.344 *Thow* we be founden in the fraternite of alle fyue ordres
C.10.39 *Thow* he falle he falleth nat bot [as] hoso ful in a boet
C.10.42 *Thow* he thorw fondynges falle he falleth nat out of charite
C.10.240 For *thogh* þe fader be a frankeleyn and for a felon be hanged
C.10.254 For goode sholde wedde goode *thouh* they no goode hadde
C.10.259 And *thogh* he be louelich to loke[n] on and lossum abedde,
C.10.265 For riche or yrented wel, *thouh* he be reueled for elde
C.10.275 *Thogh* they [do] hem to donemowe, bote þe deuel helpe
C.11.73 Get þe loue þerwith *thogh* thow worse fare".
C.11.125 Thus thorw my lore ben men ylered *thogh* y loke demme.
C.11.227 *Thogh* here goost be vngracious god for to plese.
C.11.276 *Thogh* ȝe come bifore kynges and clerkes of þe law[e]
C.11.306 *Thow* thei folowe þat fortune wole [no] folye ich it holde.
C.12.38 *Thouh* tho[w] se, say nat sum tyme þat is treuthe.
C.12.60 For *thogh* a cristene man coueitede his cristendom to renoye
C.13.27 *Thogh* y preyse pouerte thus and preue hit by ensau[m]ples
C.13.32 Rather then þe ryche *thogh* they renne at ones.
C.13.42 And *thogh* they wen[d]e by the wey, tho two togederes,
C.13.43 *Thogh* the messager make his way amyddde the fayre whete
C.13.52 And ȝut *thow* they wende o way as to wynchestre fayre
C.13.62 Haue hors and hardy men; *thogh* he mette theues
C.13.85 Ne in none enquestes to come ne cont[u]max *thogh* he worche
C.13.236 For *thogh* resoun rebuke hym thenne recheth he neuere;
C.14.2 *Thogh* y sete by mysulue, suche is my grace.
C.14.29 May nat be, [be] þ[ow] syker, *thogh* we bidde euere.
C.14.112 Out of synne and be saef, *thogh* he synege ofte,
C.14.135 Ac thaw th[at] theef hadde heuene he hadde noen hey blisse
C.14.154 Rather then þat oþer [theef], *thogh* thow woldest apose,
C.15.78 Ac me thynketh loth, *thogh* y latyn knowe, to lacken eny secte
C.15.79 For alle be we brethrene *thogh* we be diuerse yclothed.
C.15.233 For *þoȝ* nere payn [of] plouh ne potage were
C.15.234 Pruyde wolde potte hymsulf forth *thogh* no plough erye.

C.15.280   *Thogh* men rede of rychesse rihte to þe worldes ende
C.16.73   And *thogh* his glotonye be of gode ale he goth to a colde beddynge
C.16.79   And *thogh* coueytyse [cacche] þe pore they may nat come togyderes
C.16.85   And *thogh* Auaryce wolde Angry [þe] pou[r]e he hath bote lytel myhte
C.16.94   And þow sleuthe sewe pouerte and serue nat god to paye
C.16.121   Thenne is [hit] goed by goed skill, *thouh* hit greue a litel,
C.16.149   And *thogh* he chaffare he chargeth no loes may he charite wynne:
C.16.290   Charite þat chargeth nauht ne chyt *thow* me greue hym,
C.16.295   For *thogh* me souhte alle þe sektes of susturne and brethurne
C.16.314   Ne mysliked *thogh* he lore or lened þat ilke
C.16.338   *Thogh* y my byliue sholde begge aboute at menne hacches.
C.17.119   *Thogh* hit suffice for oure sauacioun soethfaste byleue,
C.19.21   For, *thogh* y sey hit mysulue, y haue saued with this charme
C.19.89   And *thouh* he stande and steppe ri3t stronge worth he neuere
C.19.106   Alle manere men and *thogh* y myhte venge
C.19.160   Ac *thouh* my thombe and my fyngeres bothe were toshullen
C.19.163   Bothe meue and amende, *thogh* alle my fyngeres oke.
C.19.316   And *thogh* he falle he fynte skiles þat "freelete hit made"
C.19.322   And *thogh* that men make moche deul in here anger
C.20.260   And now shal lucife[r] leue [hit], *thogh* hym loeth thynk.
C.20.422   Oftur then ones *thogh* [he] were [a] tretou[r].
C.21.252   'Thouh somme be clenner then somme, 3e sen wel,' quod grace,
C.21.381   'Y care nat,' quod Consience, '*thow* pryde come nouthe'
C.21.444   And counteth nat *thow* cristene be culde and yrobbed
C.22.16   And *thow* he come so to a cloth and can no bettere cheuesaunce

þou3t *n* thought *n*. &> þynke   A 7; B 12 Tho3t (1) þo3t (5) þou3t (4) þou3tes (2); C 12 thoght (1) thouht (4) thouhte (5) thouhtes (2)
A. 9.65   'Wot ich?' quaþ I; 'who art þou?' '*þou3t*,' seide he þanne.
A. 9.67   'Art þou *þou3t*, þo?' quaþ I; 'þou couþest me telle
A. 9.101   I þankide *þou3t* þo þat he me so tau3te.
A. 9.105   'But wyt can wisse þe,' quaþ *þou3t*, 'where þo þre dwellen,
A. 9.107   *Þou3t* & I þus þre dayes we 3eden,
A. 9.114   But as I bad *þou3t* þo be mene betwene,
A. 9.116   Þanne *þou3t* in þat tyme, seide þis wordis:
B. 2.91   And in we[n]es and in wisshynges and wiþ ydel *þou3tes*
B. 5.505   That euere þei wraþed þee in þis world in word, *þou3t* or dedes.'
B. 8.74   'Woot I?' [quod I; 'who art *þow*]?' '*þou3t*', seide he þanne.
B. 8.76   'Artow *þou3t*?' quod I þo; 'þow koudest me [telle]
B. 8.111   I þonked *þo3t* þo þat he me [so] tau3te.
B. 8.115   'But wit konne wisse þee', quod *þo3t*, 'where þo þre dwelle
B. 8.117   *Tho3t* and I þus þre daies we yeden,
B. 8.124   But as I bad *þo3t* þo be mene bitwene,
B. 8.127   Thanne *þo3t* in þat tyme seide þise wordes:
B.13.4   And of þis metyng many tyme muche *þou3t* I hadde,
B.13.21   I lay doun longe in þis *þo3t* and at þe laste I slepte,
B.16.55   Ac I haue *þou3tes* a þreve of þise þre piles,
C. 2.98   In we[e]des and in weschynges and with ydel *thouhtes*
C. 6.100   Now hit athynketh me in my *thouhte* þat euere y so wrouhte.
C. 7.20   Goddes payne and his passioun is puyre selde in my *thouhte*.
C.10.72   'Woet y?' quod y; 'who art þow?' '*thouhte*,' sayde he thenne.
C.10.74   'Art thow *thouht*?' quod y tho; 'thow couthest me wisse
C.10.107   Y thonkede *thoght* tho þat he me so tauhte.
C.10.111   'Bote wit wol the wisse,' quod *thouhte*, 'where tho thre dwelleth,
C.10.113   *Thouht* and y thus thre dayes we 3eden
C.10.120   Bote as y bad *thouht* tho be mene betwene
C.10.123   Thenne *thouht* in þat tyme sayde this wordes:
C.15.4   And many tym[e] of this meteles moche *thouhte* y hadde:
C.19.111   And yf kynde wit carpe herea3en or eny kyne *thouhtes*

þou3te > *þynke,þynkeþ*; *thou3the* > *þynkeþ*; *thouh* > *þou3*; *thouhte* > *þynke,þynkeþ,þou3t*

þousand *num* thousand *num*. A 4; B 11 thousand (1) þousand (9) þousandes (1); C 10 thousand (2) thousend (8)
A. 2.42   And ten *þousand* of tentis teldit beside
A. 5.251   [A] *þousand* of men þ[o þ]rong[en] togideris,
A. 7.177   Blynde & bedrede were botind a *þousand*
A.12.48   And þanked hure a *þousand* syþes with þrobbant herte.
B.Pr.147   And smale mees myd hem; mo þan a *þousand*
B. 1.116   And mo *þousandes* myd hym þan man kouþe nombre
B. 5.510   A *þousand* of men þo þrungen togideres,
B. 5.624   Heo haþ holpe a *þousand* out of þe deueles punfolde.
B. 6.191   Blynde and bedreden were bootned a *þousand*;
B.13.269   A *thousand* and þre hundred, twies [þritty] and ten,
B.15.591   Wiþ two fisshes and fyue loues fyue *þousand* peple,
B.17.21   Of men and of wommen many score *þousand*.'
B.17.25   Ye! and sixti *þousand* biside forþ þat ben no3t seyen here.'
B.18.284   And siþen I [was] seised seuene [þousand] wynter
B.19.127   Sore afyngred folk, mo þan fyue *þousand*.
C.Pr.168   And smale muys [mid] hem; mo then a *thousend*
C. 3.234   Ac y haue saued myselue sixty *thousend* lyues,

C. 7.155   A *thousend* of men tho throngen togyderes,
C. 8.188   Blynde and Brokelegged were botened a *thousand*
C.18.17   'Y thonke 3ow a *thousand* s[i]the that 3e me hider kende
C.18.153   With [two] fisches and [fyue] loues, fyue *thousen[d]* at ones,
C.19.22   Of men and of wommen meny score *thousend*.'
C.19.26   And six *thousand* mo,' quod fayth; 'y [can] nat seyn here names.'
C.20.309   And sethen we haen ben sesed seuene *thousand* wynter
C.21.127   Sore afyngered folk, mo then fyue *thousand*.

þow *pron* thou *pron*. &> *þou3*   A 353 the (1) þe (94) þi (82) þin (14) þine (1) thou (1) þou (160); B 688 þe (14) þee (165) þi (194) þy (5) thyn (3) þin (1) þyn (26) þyne (7) thou (1) thow (22) þow (250); C 663 the (127) þe (52) thi (12) thy (161) þi (1) þy (6) thien (1) thyn (23) þin (1) þyn (1) thyne (4) thow (3) þou (40) thow (221) þow (7) thowe (3)

þe **A 95 the (1) þe (94)**
A.1.23, A.1.25, A.1.37, A.1.40, A.1.58, A.1.74, A.1.74, A.1.133, A.1.138, A.1.182, A.1.183, A.2.26, A.2.29, A.2.31, A.2.82, A.2.85, A.3.37, A.3.38, A.3.39, A.3.97, A.3.97, A.3.100, A.3.160, A.3.161, A.3.161, A.3.169, A.3.170, A.3.171, A.3.181, A.3.244, A.4.6, A.4.7, A.4.11, A.4.16, A.4.128, A.4.131, A.4.154, A.5.216, A.5.216, A.5.237, A.6.92, A.6.94, A.6.98, A.6.100, A.7.26, A.7.33, A.7.36, A.7.38, A.7.40, A.7.49, A.7.71, A.7.188, A.7.212, A.7.215, A.7.237, A.7.243, A.7.245, A.7.245, A.7.246, A.7.252, A.7.260, A.7.275, A.8.90, A.8.119, A.8.122, A.8.146, A.8.177, A.9.22, A.9.24, A.9.42, A.9.47, A.9.51, A.9.52, A.9.66, A.9.105, A.10.95, A.10.96, A.10.96, A.10.100, A.10.114, A.10.116, A.10.149, A.11.105, A.11.109, A.11.117, A.11.165, A.11.165, A.11.232, A.12.1, A.12.2, A.12.6, A.12.46, A.12.67, A.12.90

þe **B 14 &> þe**
B.4.148, B.5.378, B.5.497, B.6.54, B.11.28, B.11.56, B.11.422, B.12.7, B.13.142, B.13.146, B.13.163, B.14.20, B.14.51, B.20.186

the **C 179 the (127) þe (52) &> þe**
C.Pr.149, C.Pr.150, C.Pr.150, C.1.22, C.1.24, C.1.37, C.1.39, C.1.40, C.1.40, C.1.56, C.1.73, C.1.73, C.1.144, C.1.204, C.2.49, C.2.53, C.2.129, C.3.19, C.3.40, C.3.41, C.3.42, C.3.135, C.3.136, C.3.137, C.3.137, C.3.139, C.3.141, C.3.143, C.3.144, C.3.145, C.3.146, C.3.148, C.3.209, C.3.210, C.3.219, C.3.220, C.3.220, C.3.228, C.3.229, C.3.230, C.3.417, C.3.419, C.3.489, C.4.6, C.4.7, C.4.11, C.4.16, C.4.21, C.4.145, C.4.191, C.5.27, C.5.102, C.5.102, C.6.12, C.6.12, C.6.13, C.6.61, C.6.257, C.6.294, C.6.297, C.6.299, C.6.319, C.6.339, C.6.341, C.6.347, C.6.348, C.6.425, C.7.8, C.7.58, C.7.104, C.7.106, C.7.134, C.7.137, C.7.142, C.7.150, C.7.254, C.7.256, C.7.264, C.7.266, C.7.303, C.8.33, C.8.34, C.8.47, C.8.81, C.8.163, C.8.163, C.8.169, C.8.208, C.8.237, C.8.271, C.8.272, C.8.282, C.8.289, C.8.297, C.8.300, C.9.272, C.9.278, C.9.282, C.9.313, C.10.30, C.10.32, C.10.58, C.10.73, C.10.111, C.10.233, C.10.284, C.10.287, C.10.302, C.11.73, C.11.91, C.11.132, C.11.140, C.11.144, C.11.180, C.11.182, C.11.187, C.11.188, C.11.189, C.11.192, C.11.193, C.11.222, C.13.192, C.13.194, C.13.223, C.13.228, C.13.231, C.13.231, C.13.232, C.14.3, C.14.4, C.14.5, C.14.9, C.14.89, C.14.99, C.14.156, C.15.146, C.15.155, C.15.165, C.15.166, C.15.168, C.15.182, C.15.245, C.15.250, C.15.252, C.15.256, C.16.119, C.16.371, C.17.145, C.19.77, C.19.108, C.19.109, C.19.224, C.19.224, C.20.56, C.20.56, C.20.399, C.21.220, C.21.220, C.21.318, C.21.404, C.22.6, C.22.9, C.22.154, C.22.186, C.22.205, C.22.205, C.22.210, C.22.338, C.22.339

þee **B 165 &> thee**
B.Pr.125, B.Pr.126, B.Pr.126, B.1.23, B.1.25, B.1.39, B.1.42, B.1.60, B.1.76, B.1.76, B.1.145, B.1.208, B.1.209, B.2.47, B.2.50, B.2.51, B.2.118, B.2.121, B.2.122, B.3.18, B.3.38, B.3.39, B.3.40, B.3.108, B.3.108, B.3.111, B.3.173, B.3.174, B.3.182, B.3.183, B.3.184, B.3.194, B.3.264, B.4.6, B.4.7, B.4.11, B.4.16, B.4.145, B.4.191, B.5.261, B.5.262, B.5.270, B.5.273, B.5.275, B.5.285, B.5.292, B.5.293, B.5.366, B.5.392, B.5.444, B.5.444, B.5.465, B.5.494, B.5.505, B.5.605, B.5.612, B.5.614, B.6.24, B.6.31, B.6.34, B.6.36, B.6.37, B.6.41, B.6.79, B.6.202, B.6.228, B.6.231, B.6.253, B.6.259, B.6.261, B.6.261, B.6.262, B.6.268, B.6.276, B.6.291, B.7.108, B.7.137, B.7.140, B.7.169, B.7.199, B.8.26, B.8.28, B.8.46, B.8.52, B.8.59, B.8.75, B.8.115, B.9.76, B.9.183, B.9.186, B.9.203, B.10.153, B.10.157, B.10.165, B.10.171, B.10.192, B.10.223, B.10.271, B.10.372, B.11.21, B.11.23, B.11.29, B.11.30, B.11.33, B.11.34, B.11.41, B.11.41, B.11.54, B.11.55, B.11.56, B.11.58, B.11.376, B.11.415, B.11.420, B.11.423, B.12.3, B.12.4, B.12.10, B.12.16, B.12.17, B.12.37, B.12.92, B.12.98, B.12.145, B.12.155, B.12.217, B.13.149, B.13.163, B.13.166, B.13.170, B.13.170, B.13.188, B.13.214, B.13.214, B.13.444, B.13.446, B.14.16, B.14.21, B.14.29, B.14.53, B.14.167, B.16.24, B.16.61, B.16.63, B.16.180, B.17.80, B.17.136, B.17.258, B.17.258, B.18.56, B.18.56, B.18.361, B.19.220, B.19.220, B.19.318, B.19.404, B.20.6, B.20.9, B.20.154, B.20.205, B.20.210, B.20.338, B.20.339

þi **A 82**
A.1.36, A.1.38, A.1.39, A.1.74, A.1.76, A.1.131, A.2.5, A.2.80, A.2.88, A.2.117, A.3.17, A.3.27, A.3.27, A.3.40, A.3.49, A.3.55, A.3.56, A.3.58, A.3.98, A.3.108, A.3.108, A.3.166, A.3.172, A.3.178, A.3.181, A.3.183, A.4.58, A.4.59, A.4.59, A.4.83, A.4.128, A.4.131, A.4.149, A.5.239, A.5.243, A.6.65, A.6.69, A.6.98, A.7.28, A.7.44, A.7.45, A.7.46, A.7.51, A.7.51, A.7.72, A.7.144, A.7.144, A.7.206, A.7.217, A.7.218, A.7.246, A.7.249, A.7.261, A.7.275, A.8.89, A.8.98, A.8.100, A.8.123, A.8.138, A.8.139, A.8.140, A.8.173, A.8.178, A.9.42, A.9.43, A.9.44, A.9.45, A.9.48, A.9.102, A.10.92, A.10.92, A.10.102, A.10.115, A.11.78, A.11.104, A.11.104, A.11.119, A.11.120, A.12.70, A.12.94, A.12.95

þi **B 199 þi (194) þy (5)**
B.Pr.125, B.Pr.126, B.Pr.127, B.1.38, B.1.40, B.1.41, B.1.76, B.1.78, B.1.140, B.1.141, B.1.143, B.2.5, B.2.49, B.2.116, B.2.124, B.2.153, B.3.17, B.3.18, B.3.28, B.3.28, B.3.41, B.3.49, B.3.50, B.3.67, B.3.67, B.3.68, B.3.68, B.3.73, B.3.74, B.3.109,

B.3.119, B.3.119, B.3.179, B.3.185, B.3.191, B.3.194, B.3.196, B.3.235, B.3.337, B.4.72, B.4.73, B.4.73, B.4.96, B.4.145, B.4.148, B.5.49, B.5.49, B.5.185, B.5.185, B.5.237, B.5.257, B.5.257, B.5.261, B.5.266, B.5.274, B.5.281, B.5.281, B.5.284, B.5.286, B.5.286, B.5.291, B.5.365, B.5.366, B.5.469, B.5.480, B.5.484, B.5.486, B.5.487, B.5.489, B.5.490, B.5.493, B.5.495, B.5.497, B.5.502, B.5.578, B.5.582, B.5.608, B.5.612, B.5.641, B.5.642, B.6.26, B.6.40, B.6.45, B.6.50, B.6.51, B.6.56, B.6.79, B.6.80, B.6.157, B.6.157, B.6.158, B.6.201, B.6.220, B.6.233, B.6.234, B.6.26, B.6.265, B.6.277, B.6.291, B.7.107, B.7.116, B.7.118, B.7.118, B.7.141, B.7.160, B.7.161, B.7.162, B.7.195, B.8.46, B.8.47, B.8.48, B.8.49, B.8.51, B.8.57, B.8.112, B.9.129, B.9.136, B.9.185, B.10.125, B.10.152, B.10.152, B.10.167, B.10.168, B.10.257, B.10.259, B.10.260, B.10.262, B.10.263, B.10.269, B.10.269, B.10.361, B.11.21, B.11.22, B.11.24, B.11.29, B.11.54, B.11.55, B.11.387, B.11.424, B.12.6, B.12.7, B.12.14, B.12.16, B.12.33, B.12.36, B.12.220, B.13.105, B.13.141, B.13.141, B.13.148, B.13.201, B.13.313, B.13.443, B.13.445, B.14.17, B.14.24, B.14.56, B.14.168, B.14.170, B.14.174, B.14.179, B.14.179, B.14.187, B.15.44, B.15.46, B.16.154, B.16.155, B.16.155, B.16.157, B.17.10, B.17.17, B.17.48, B.17.49, B.17.89, B.17.89, B.17.135, B.17.250, B.17.250, B.17.257, B.18.146, B.18.149, B.18.311, B.18.313, B.18.314, B.18.333, B.18.357, B.18.361, B.18.402, B.19.317, B.19.318, B.19.401, B.19.407, B.19.478, B.19.479, B.20.7, B.20.211, B.20.339, B.20.341, B.20.341

thy *C 180* thi (12) thy (161) þi (1) þy (6)
C.Pr.149, C.Pr.150, C.Pr.151, C.1.36, C.1.38, C.1.39, C.1.75, C.1.139, C.1.140, C.1.142, C.2.5, C.2.52, C.2.54, C.2.135, C.2.136, C.2.169, C.2.250, C.3.18, C.3.19, C.3.29, C.3.43, C.3.71, C.3.71, C.3.72, C.3.75, C.3.76, C.3.145, C.3.156, C.3.156, C.3.213, C.3.225, C.3.231, C.4.92, C.4.142, C.4.145, C.4.154, C.4.193, C.4.193, C.5.27, C.5.29, C.5.103, C.6.92, C.6.167, C.6.167, C.6.171, C.6.173, C.6.195, C.6.239, C.6.257, C.6.286, C.6.288, C.6.291, C.6.295, C.6.296, C.6.298, C.6.299, C.6.323, C.6.332, C.6.340, C.6.346, C.7.103, C.7.105, C.7.122, C.7.126, C.7.128, C.7.133, C.7.137, C.7.140, C.7.142, C.7.144, C.7.148, C.7.225, C.7.229, C.7.255, C.7.256, C.7.264, C.8.30, C.8.38, C.8.42, C.8.48, C.8.55, C.8.81, C.8.82, C.8.154, C.8.207, C.8.229, C.8.233, C.8.272, C.8.275, C.8.282, C.8.283, C.8.284, C.8.285, C.8.314, C.9.260, C.9.261, C.9.261, C.9.265, C.9.268, C.9.270, C.9.274, C.9.278, C.9.279, C.9.281, C.9.290, C.10.108, C.10.224, C.10.233, C.10.286, C.11.72, C.11.90, C.11.90, C.11.180, C.11.181, C.11.183, C.11.188, C.11.222, C.12.7, C.12.216, C.13.193, C.13.205, C.13.228, C.13.230, C.15.112, C.15.141, C.15.145, C.15.145, C.15.160, C.15.166, C.15.179, C.15.196, C.15.255, C.16.22, C.16.23, C.16.206, C.16.208, C.17.60, C.17.62, C.17.143, C.17.143, C.17.143, C.17.145, C.17.148, C.18.171, C.18.172, C.18.174, C.18.199, C.18.274, C.19.11, C.19.18, C.19.46, C.19.47, C.19.110, C.19.216, C.19.216, C.19.223, C.20.149, C.20.152, C.20.282, C.20.282, C.20.324, C.20.345, C.20.346, C.20.347, C.20.376, C.20.399, C.20.407, C.20.407, C.21.317, C.21.318, C.21.401, C.21.407, C.21.478, C.21.479, C.22.7, C.22.211, C.22.339, C.22.341, C.22.341

thien *C 1*
C.19.112

þin *A 14*
A.1.39, A.1.130, A.1.137, A.3.26, A.3.40, A.3.48, A.3.246, A.6.62, A.6.66, A.6.93, A.6.96, A.7.243, A.10.20, A.10.78

þyn *B 30* thyn (3) þin (1) þyn (26)
B.1.41, B.1.142, B.3.41, B.3.266, B.5.575, B.5.579, B.5.606, B.5.610, B.6.46, B.6.49, B.6.259, B.7.74, B.9.21, B.9.128, B.9.128, B.9.152, B.10.270, B.11.388, B.11.416, B.12.4, B.12.8, B.13.105, B.13.140, B.13.143, B.13.162, B.13.445, B.17.137, B.17.139, B.17.254, B.19.479

thyn *C 25* thyn (23) þin (1) þyn (1)
C.1.141, C.3.28, C.3.150, C.3.210, C.3.419, C.4.192, C.6.255, C.6.289, C.6.300, C.6.332, C.7.105, C.7.222, C.7.226, C.7.262, C.8.43, C.9.266, C.9.266, C.9.274, C.10.147, C.13.224, C.14.175, C.15.140, C.17.142, C.19.220, C.21.479

þine *A 1*
A.1.129

þyne *B 7*
B.3.27, B.3.235, B.3.236, B.5.262, B.5.263, B.5.500, B.13.149

thyne *C 4*
C.3.136, C.7.135, C.7.258, C.8.288

þou *A 161* thou (1) þou (160)
A.Pr.88, A.1.5, A.1.5, A.1.22, A.1.26, A.1.26, A.1.32, A.1.33, A.1.40, A.1.73, A.1.75, A.1.129, A.1.132, A.1.134, A.1.135, A.1.138, A.1.146, A.2.27, A.2.27, A.2.29, A.2.30, A.2.85, A.2.88, A.2.89, A.3.16, A.3.48, A.3.95, A.3.96, A.3.96, A.3.98, A.3.100, A.3.107, A.3.160, A.3.165, A.3.167, A.3.167, A.3.168, A.3.170, A.3.172, A.3.173, A.3.175, A.3.177, A.3.182, A.3.193, A.3.224, A.3.238, A.3.238, A.3.248, A.4.7, A.4.12, A.4.57, A.4.129, A.4.153, A.5.152, A.5.153, A.5.238, A.6.20, A.6.21, A.6.52, A.6.57, A.6.59, A.6.59, A.6.62, A.6.63, A.6.67, A.6.69, A.6.70, A.6.71, A.6.72, A.6.76, A.6.93, A.6.99, A.6.101, A.6.102, A.6.123, A.6.123, A.7.23, A.7.26, A.7.29, A.7.39, A.7.41, A.7.42, A.7.44, A.7.45, A.7.45, A.7.73, A.7.73, A.7.143, A.7.143, A.7.151, A.7.188, A.7.190, A.7.196, A.7.204, A.7.208, A.7.211, A.7.214, A.7.217, A.7.237, A.7.243, A.7.244, A.7.244, A.7.252, A.7.261, A.8.99, A.8.100, A.8.119, A.8.122, A.8.122, A.8.124, A.8.125, A.8.167, A.8.173, A.8.174, A.8.176, A.9.44, A.9.63, A.9.64, A.9.65, A.9.66, A.9.67, A.9.67, A.10.59, A.10.86, A.10.89, A.10.92, A.10.93, A.10.93, A.10.95, A.10.99, A.10.101, A.10.102, A.10.113, A.10.115, A.10.116, A.10.119, A.11.5, A.11.85, A.11.86, A.11.115, A.11.116, A.11.117, A.11.117, A.11.120, A.11.122, A.11.124, A.11.144, A.11.162, A.12.7, A.12.10, A.12.11, A.12.30, A.12.45, A.12.51, A.12.89, A.12.91, A.12.91, A.12.96, A.12.97, A.12.116

þow *B 273* thou (1) thow (22) þow (250)
B.Pr.215, B.1.22, B.1.26, B.1.26, B.1.34, B.1.35, B.1.42, B.1.75, B.1.77, B.1.140, B.1.141, B.1.144, B.1.146, B.1.147, B.2.45, B.2.47, B.2.121, B.2.124, B.2.125, B.3.16, B.3.74, B.3.107, B.3.107, B.3.109, B.3.173, B.3.178, B.3.180, B.3.180, B.3.181, B.3.183,

B.3.185, B.3.186, B.3.188, B.3.190, B.3.195, B.3.206, B.3.259, B.3.266, B.3.269, B.3.271, B.3.272, B.3.338, B.4.7, B.4.12, B.4.71, B.4.146, B.4.190, B.5.163, B.5.163, B.5.183, B.5.234, B.5.260, B.5.262, B.5.263, B.5.269, B.5.269, B.5.270, B.5.271, B.5.273, B.5.285, B.5.287, B.5.288, B.5.288, B.5.289, B.5.294, B.5.365, B.5.496, B.5.498, B.5.565, B.5.572, B.5.575, B.5.576, B.5.582, B.5.583, B.5.589, B.5.592, B.5.606, B.5.607, B.5.615, B.5.637, B.5.638, B.5.638, B.5.642, B.6.21, B.6.24, B.6.27, B.6.38, B.6.39, B.6.42, B.6.43, B.6.45, B.6.50, B.6.50, B.6.81, B.6.81, B.6.166, B.6.180, B.6.202, B.6.204, B.6.210, B.6.218, B.6.222, B.6.226, B.6.230, B.6.233, B.6.253, B.6.259, B.6.260, B.6.260, B.6.268, B.6.277, B.7.40, B.7.117, B.7.137, B.7.140, B.7.140, B.7.143, B.7.189, B.7.195, B.7.196, B.7.198, B.8.48, B.8.72, B.8.73, B.8.74, B.8.75, B.8.76, B.9.185, B.9.186, B.10.132, B.10.133, B.10.163, B.10.164, B.10.165, B.10.165, B.10.168, B.10.192, B.10.210, B.10.210, B.10.219, B.10.260, B.10.263, B.10.265, B.10.266, B.10.266, B.11.11, B.11.18, B.11.20, B.11.23, B.11.29, B.11.32, B.11.35, B.11.41, B.11.53, B.11.58, B.11.103, B.11.104, B.11.105, B.11.375, B.11.378, B.11.378, B.11.387, B.11.388, B.11.391, B.11.392, B.11.413, B.11.414, B.11.420, B.12.6, B.12.10, B.12.10, B.12.12, B.12.16, B.12.33, B.12.33, B.12.35, B.12.38, B.12.39, B.12.92, B.12.97, B.12.156, B.12.159, B.12.176, B.12.192, B.12.215, B.12.223, B.13.32, B.13.87, B.13.119, B.13.141, B.13.142, B.13.163, B.13.164, B.13.168, B.13.171, B.13.203, B.13.204, B.13.211, B.14.26, B.14.52, B.14.55, B.14.60, B.14.113, B.14.115, B.14.169, B.14.180, B.14.184, B.14.279, B.15.38, B.15.39, B.15.39, B.15.45, B.15.46, B.16.156, B.17.89, B.17.136, B.17.139, B.17.215, B.17.249, B.17.254, B.17.303, B.18.54, B.18.54, B.18.55, B.18.142, B.18.145, B.18.147, B.18.180, B.18.188, B.18.287, B.18.291, B.18.334, B.18.336, B.18.338, B.18.350, B.18.353, B.18.354, B.18.363, B.18.364, B.18.402, B.18.403, B.18.416, B.18.420, B.19.26, B.19.26, B.19.80, B.19.173, B.19.177, B.19.178, B.19.180, B.19.209, B.19.391, B.19.402, B.19.405, B.19.408, B.19.424, B.19.425, B.19.477, B.19.479, B.20.7, B.20.9, B.20.188, B.20.204, B.20.206, B.20.206, B.20.210, B.20.338, B.20.342, B.20.342, B.20.356

þou *C 271* thou (3) thow (221) þou (40) þow (7) &> þou₃
C.Pr.165, C.1.33, C.1.72, C.1.74, C.1.139, C.1.140, C.1.145, C.1.145, C.2.47, C.2.48, C.2.49, C.2.120, C.2.129, C.2.140, C.3.17, C.3.29, C.3.76, C.3.136, C.3.138, C.3.138, C.3.140, C.3.140, C.3.148, C.3.219, C.3.224, C.3.226, C.3.226, C.3.227, C.3.229, C.3.231, C.3.232, C.3.236, C.3.242, C.3.263, C.3.420, C.3.424, C.3.425, C.3.490, C.4.7, C.4.12, C.4.184, C.4.192, C.5.12, C.5.27, C.5.33, C.5.34, C.6.91, C.6.138, C.6.138, C.6.165, C.6.234, C.6.238, C.6.239, C.6.248, C.6.254, C.6.255, C.6.290, C.6.290, C.6.294, C.6.295, C.6.300, C.6.331, C.6.333, C.6.341, C.6.342, C.6.343, C.6.343, C.6.344, C.6.424, C.7.55, C.7.136, C.7.138, C.7.177, C.7.178, C.7.217, C.7.219, C.7.219, C.7.222, C.7.223, C.7.236, C.7.240, C.7.255, C.7.265, C.7.267, C.7.268, C.7.290, C.7.291, C.7.291, C.8.25, C.8.26, C.8.40, C.8.41, C.8.42, C.8.83, C.8.83, C.8.89, C.8.90, C.8.91, C.8.153, C.8.153, C.8.208, C.8.210, C.8.219, C.8.228, C.8.231, C.8.232, C.8.234, C.8.236, C.8.276, C.8.276, C.8.282, C.8.285, C.8.289, C.8.296, C.8.298, C.8.298, C.8.299, C.9.259, C.9.268, C.9.271, C.9.276, C.8.289, C.9.291, C.10.70, C.10.71, C.10.72, C.10.73, C.10.74, C.10.74, C.10.151, C.10.159, C.10.286, C.11.72, C.11.73, C.11.99, C.11.105, C.11.107, C.11.107, C.11.109, C.11.111, C.11.111, C.11.139, C.11.145, C.11.169, C.11.170, C.11.177, C.11.179, C.11.182, C.11.188, C.11.191, C.11.194, C.11.199, C.11.199, C.11.199, C.11.308, C.12.4, C.12.5, C.12.6, C.12.10, C.12.24, C.12.35, C.12.37, C.12.38, C.12.39, C.12.163, C.12.164, C.12.165, C.12.215, C.13.184, C.13.185, C.13.186, C.13.193, C.13.205, C.13.206, C.13.209, C.13.221, C.13.222, C.13.229, C.14.10, C.14.29, C.14.100, C.14.103, C.14.108, C.14.131, C.14.154, C.15.94, C.15.113, C.15.127, C.15.141, C.15.159, C.15.160, C.15.169, C.15.251, C.15.254, C.15.259, C.15.289, C.15.291, C.16.19, C.16.115, C.16.166, C.16.179, C.16.200, C.16.201, C.16.201, C.16.207, C.16.208, C.16.303, C.16.342, C.17.64, C.17.149, C.18.2, C.18.173, C.18.198, C.18.273, C.18.273, C.19.110, C.19.112, C.19.181, C.19.215, C.19.220, C.19.224, C.19.283, C.20.55, C.20.145, C.20.148, C.20.150, C.20.183, C.20.193, C.20.193, C.20.194, C.20.313, C.20.319, C.20.348, C.20.377, C.20.379, C.20.401, C.20.402, C.20.445, C.20.446, C.20.459, C.21.26, C.21.26, C.21.80, C.21.173, C.21.177, C.21.178, C.21.209, C.21.391, C.21.402, C.21.404, C.21.405, C.21.406, C.21.408, C.21.424, C.21.425, C.21.477, C.21.479, C.22.6, C.22.7, C.22.9, C.22.188, C.22.188, C.22.204, C.22.206, C.22.206, C.22.210, C.22.338, C.22.339, C.22.342, C.22.342, C.22.356, C.22.356

thowe *C 3*
C.20.326, C.20.463, C.21.180

þraldom *n* *thraldom n.* B 1; C 1 thraldoem
B.18.103   And youre fraunchise þat fre was fallen is in þraldom;
C.20.106   And ȝoure franchise þat fre was yfallen is i[n] thraldoem;

þralles *n* *thral n.(1)* A 1 þrallis; B 1; C 1 thralles
A. 8.57   Þise þre for þrallis ben þrowe among vs alle
B.19.33   And fre men foule þralles þat folwen noȝt hise lawes.
C.21.33   And fre men foule thralles þat followeth nat his lawes.

þre *num* *thre num.* A 8; B 41 thre (5) þre (35) þree (1); C 57 thre
A. 1.20   And comaundite of his curteisie in comoun þre þinges;
A. 8.57   Þise þre for þrallis ben þrowe among vs alle
A. 9.70   Arn þre faire vertues, & ben not f[e]r to fynde.
A. 9.100   And oþere wise & ellis nouȝt but as þei þre assent[e].'
A. 9.105   'But wyt can wisse þe,' quaþ þouȝt, 'where þo þre dwellen'
A. 9.107   Þouȝt & I þus þre dayes we ȝeden,
A.10.167   Hymself & his sones þre, & siþen here wyues
A.11.157   Þat þinkeþ werche wiþ þo þre þriueþ wel late,
B. 1.20   And comaundede of his curteisie in commune þree þynges;
B. 8.79   Arn þre faire vertues, and ben noȝt fer to fynde.
B. 8.110   And ooþer wise [and ellis noȝt] but as þei þre assent[e].'

B. 8.115   'But wit konne wisse þee', quod þoʒt, 'where þo *þre* dwelle
B. 8.117   Thoʒt and I þus *þre* daies we yeden,
B. 8.131   And werchen as þei þus *þre* wolde; th[i]s is his entente.'
B. 9.136   Thyself and þi sones *þre* and siþen youre wyues,
B.10.214   [That] þynkeþ werche with þo [*þre*] þryueþ [wel] late,
B.10.245   *Thre* [propre] persones, ac noʒt in plurel nombre,
B.13.269   A thousand and *þre* hundred, twies [þritty] and ten,
B.13.426   Lest þo *þre* maner men to muche sorwe yow brynge:
B.13.449   Thise *þre* maner minstrales makeþ a man to lauʒe,
B.16.23   Wiþ *þre* piles was it vnderpight; I parceyued it soone.
B.16.55   Ac I haue þouʒtes a þreve of þise *þre* piles,
B.16.132   And in *þre* daies after edifie it newe,
B.16.181   '*Thre* leodes in oon lyth, noon lenger þan ooþer,
B.16.191   So *þre* bilongeþ for a lord þat lordshipe cleymeþ:
B.16.201   And þere hym likede and [he] louede, in *þre* persones hym shewede.
B.16.207   And eiþer is oþeres ioye in *þre* sondry persones,
B.16.220   Thus in *þre* persones is parfitliche [pure] manhede,
B.16.227   *Thre* men, to my siʒte, I made wel at ese,
B.17.29   *Thre* persones in parcelles departable fro ooþer
B.17.30   And alle *þre* but o god; þus Abraham me tauʒte;
B.17.46   It is lighter to leeue in *þre* louely persones,
B.17.112   Ac er þis day *þre* daies I dar vndertaken
B.17.129   In *þre* persones departable þat perpetuele were euere,
B.17.130   And alle *þre* but o god? þus Abraham me tauʒte;
B.17.155   And *þre* sondry sightes [shewynge in oon],
B.17.162   [Halt] al þe wide world wiþInne hem *þre*,
B.17.166   That *þre* þynges bilongeþ in oure [fader] of heuene
B.17.184   And alle [*þre*] but o god as is myn hand and my fyngeres.
B.17.321   *Thre* þynges þer ben þat doon a man by strengþe
B.17.333   Thise *þre* þat I telle of ben þus to vnderstonde:
B.18.32   That, for al þat deeþ kan do, wiþInne *þre* daies to walke
B.18.42   To fordoon it on o day, and in *þre* dayes after
B.18.51   Nailed hym with *þre* nailes naked on [a] roode
B.18.223   To [se] what he haþ suffred in *þre* sondry places,
B.19.82   And al þe wit of þe world was in þo *þre* kynges.
B.19.95   Thoruʒ *þre* kynne kynges knelynge to Iesu.
B.20.11   For *þre* þynges he takeþ his lif for to saue.
B.20.177   And þere dyed þat doctour er *þre* dayes after.
C. 1.20   And comaundede of his cortesye in comune *thre* thynges.
C. 3.378   So comune claymeth a kyng *thre* kyne thynges,
C. 3.406   Of *thre* trewe termisonus, trinitas vnus deus:
C. 7.109   Thise *thre* manere munstrals maketh a man to lauhe
C. 8.247   His suluer to *thre* maner men [in] menyng they sholden
C. 8.348   *Thre* shypes and a schaef with [a vii] folwynge
C.10.77   Aren *thre* fayre vertues and ben nat fer to fynde.
C.10.105   And reule alle reumes by here *thre* wittes
C.10.106   Bute oþerewise ne elles nat but as they *thre* assent[e].'
C.10.111   'Bote wit wol the wisse,' quod thouhte, 'where tho *thre* dwelleth,
C.10.113   Thouht and y thus *thre* dayes we ʒeden
C.10.194   The catel that Crist hadde, *thre* clothes hit were;
C.10.224   "Thysulue and thy sones *thre* and sethen ʒoure wyues,
C.11.152   And alle *thre* bote o god, and herof he made
C.15.69   'Hit is nat *þre* daies doen this doctour þat he prechede
C.16.32   Thise *thre* withoute doute tholieth alle pouerte
C.16.36   And bote these *thre* þat y spak of at domesday vs defende
C.17.24   Bote *thre* litle loues and loue was here soule.
C.18.20   Hit hadde schoriares to shuyuen hit vp, *thre* shides of o lenghe
C.18.22   Alle *thre* yliche long and yliche large.
C.18.25   'Thise *thre* shorriares,' quod he,' that bereth vp this plonte
C.18.27   *Thre* persones indepartable, perpetuel were euere,
C.18.29   The fruyt of this fayre tre fro *thre* wikkede wyndes
C.18.56   A[c] in *thre* degrees hit grewe; grete ferly me thouhte,
C.18.83   Why groweth this fruyt in *thre* degres?' 'A goed skil,' he saide.
C.18.160   And ar *thre* dayes aftur edefye hit newe.'
C.18.187   '*Thre* persones in o pensel,' quod he, 'departable fram oþere.
C.18.197   How o lord myhte lyue [in] *thre*; y leue hit nat,' y sayde.
C.18.200   *Thre* bilongeth to a lord þat leiaunce claymeth,
C.18.212   A *thre* he is þer he is and hereof bereth wittnesse
C.18.214   That he is *thre* persones departable y preue hit by mankynde,
C.18.217   And Abel of hem bothe and alle *thre* o kynde;
C.18.218   And thise *thre* þat y Carp of, Adam and Eue
C.18.233   And as *thre* persones palpable is puy[r]lich bote o mankynde,
C.18.235   So i[n] god [and] godes sone i[s] *thre* persones, the trinite.
C.18.236   In matrimonie aren *thre* and of o man cam alle thre
C.18.236   In matrimonie aren thre and of o man cam alle *thre*
C.18.237   And to godhede goth *thre* and o god is all thre.
C.18.237   And to godhede goth thre and o god is all *thre*.
C.18.239   'Hastow ysey this,' y seyde, 'alle *thre* and o god?'
C.18.241   Where god [riʒt be my gate cam gangynge a *thre*];
C.19.30   *Thre* persones parselmele depar[t]able fram oþere
C.19.31   And alle *thre* bote o god; thus abraham bereth witenesse
C.19.44   Ac for to bileue in o lord þat lyueth in *thre* persones

C.19.98   In *thre* persones, a parceles departable fram oþere,
C.19.99   And alle *thre* bote o god? thus abraham me tauhte.
C.19.150   And alle *thre* is bote o god as myn hoend and my fyngeres.
C.19.301   *Thre* thynges ther ben þat doth a man to sterte
C.19.313   Thise *thre* that y telle of thus ben [to] vnderstande:
C.20.31   That for al þat deth can do, withynne *thre* dayes to walke
C.20.41   To fordoen hit on a day, and in *thre* dayes aftur
C.20.51   [Thei] nayled hym with *thre* nayles naked vpon a rode
C.20.232   To wyte what he hath soffred in *thre* sundry places,
C.21.82   And al þe wit of the world was in [þo] *thre* kynges.
C.21.95   Thorw *thre* kyne kynges knelyng to iesu.
C.22.11   For *thre* thynges he taketh [h]is lyf for to saue.
C.22.177   And þere deyede þat doctour ar *thre* dayes aftur.

þredbare adj *thredbare adj.*   A 1; B 1; C 1   thredbare
A. 5.113   He shulde wandre on þat walsshe, so was it *predbare*.
B. 5.197   She sholde noʒt [wandre] on þat wel[ch]e, so was it *predbare*.
C. 6.205   He sholde [nat] wandre [o]n þat walch, so was hit *thredbare*.

þree > þre

threschynge ger *threshinge ger.*   C 1
C. 8.199   In *threschynge*, in thekynge, in thwytinge of pynnes,

thresfold > þresshfold

þresshe v *threshen v.*   B 1
B. 5.546   Som tyme I sowe and som tyme I *þresshe*,

þresshfold n *threshwolde n.*   A 1 þresshewold; B 1; C 1 thresfold
A. 5.198   He [þr]umblide on þe *presshewold* & [þrew] to þe erþe
B. 5.350   He [þr]umbled on þe *presshfold* and þrew to þe erþe.
C. 6.408   [A] thromblede at the *thresfold* and threw þe erthe.

þrest > þurst

þretynge ger *threting ger.*   B 1
B.18.282   And dwelle wiþ vs deueles; þis *þretynge* [driʒten] made.

threttene > þrittene

þreve n *threve n.*   B 1
B.16.55   Ac I haue þouʒtes a *þreve* of þise þre piles,

threw > þrowe

þridde num *thrid num.*   A 5; B 11; C 10   thridde
A. 8.55   Ac to bigge watir ne wynd, ne wyt is þe *þridde*,
A. 9.69   'Dowel,' quaþ he, '& dobet, & dobest þe *þridde*,
A. 9.97   Þus dowel, & dobet, & dobest þe *þridde*,
A.10.14   Þus dowel, & dobet, & dobest þe *þridde*,
A.11.40   Þanne telle þei of þe trinite how two slowe þe *þridde*,
B.Pr.121   The kyng and þe commune and kynde wit þe *þridde*
B. 5.496   The *þridde* day [þer]after þow yedest in oure sute;
B. 8.78   'Dowel,' [quod he], 'and dobet and dobest þe *þridde*
B. 8.107   Thus dowel and dobet and dobest þe *þridde*
B.10.54   Than telleþ þei of þe Trinite [how two slowe þe *þridde*],
B.16.50   Thanne liberum arbitrium laccheþ þe [*þridde*] plan[k]e
B.16.188   The *þridde* highte þe holi goost, a persone by hymselue,
B.17.161   Right so þe fader and þe sone and Seint Spirit þe *þridde*
B.19.91   The *þridde* kyng þo kam knelynge to Iesu
B.19.264   And Mark, and Mathew þe *þridde*, myghty beestes boþe;
B.19.289   The *þridde* seed þat Piers sew was Spiritus fortitudinis,
C. 7.136   The *thridde* day þeraftur thow ʒedest i[n] oure sekte;
C.10.76   'Dowel and dobet,' quod he, ' and dobest the *thridde*
C.10.103   Thus dowel and dobet and dobest the *thridde*
C.11.35   And tellen of þe trinite how t[w]o slowe þe *thridde*
C.11.158   Thus bileue and le[ute], and loue is the *thridde*
C.18.50   And thenne [f]alle y adoune the pouke with the *thridde* shoriere
C.18.194   The *thridde* is þat halt al, a thyng by hymsulue;
C.21.91   The *thridde* kyng cam [þo] knel[ynge] to iesu
C.21.264   And Marc and Mathewe the *thridde*, myhty bestes bothe;
C.21.289   The *thridde* seed that [Peres] sewe was spiritus fortitudinis

thrift n *thrift n.*   A 1
A.10.108   *Thrift* oþer þedom with þo is selde yseiʒe:

þrist > þurst

þrittene num *thritene num.*   A 1; B 1; C 1   threttene
A. 5.128   Til ten ʒardis oþer twelue tollide out *þrittene*.
B. 5.212   Til ten yerdes or twelue tolled out *þrittene*.
C. 6.220   Til ten ʒerde other twelue tolde out *threttene*.

þritty num *thriti num.*   B 5 þritty (4) xxxti (1); C 5 thritty
B. 5.415   I haue be preest and person passynge *þritty* wynter,
B.13.269   A thousand and þre hundred, twies [*þritty*] and ten,
B.18.133   Siþ þis barn was ybore ben *xxxti* wynter passed
B.18.296   Thise *þritty* wynter, as I wene, [he wente aboute] and preched.

B.18.299   And þus haþ he trolled forþ [lik a tidy man] þise two and *þritty*
                wynter.
C. 7.30   I haue be prest and persoun passynge *thritty* wyntur
C.17.23   Marie Egipciaca eet in *thritty* wynter
C.20.136   Sethe this barn was ybore ben *thritty* wynter ypassed,
C.20.329   This *thritty* wynter, as y wene, and wente aboute and prechede.
C.20.332   Thus hath he trolled forth lyke a tydy man this two & *thritty*
                wynter.

þryueþ v *thriven v.* A 2 þriuen (1) þriueþ (1); B 2
A.Pr.32   As it semiþ to oure siȝt þat suche men *þriuen*.
A.11.157   Þat þinkeþ werche wiþ þo þre *þriueþ* wel late,
B.Pr.32   As it semeþ to oure siȝt þat swiche men *þryueþ*.
B.10.214   [That] þynkeþ werche with þo [þre] *þryueþ* [wel] late,

þrobbant prp *throbben v.* A 1
A.12.48   And þanked hure a þousand syþes with *þrobbant* herte.

thromblede > þrumbled; þrongen > þrungen

þropis n *thorp n.* A 1; C 1 thorpus
A. 2.45   For lerid, for lewid, for laboureris of *þropis*,
C.Pr.223   As Barones and Burgeys and bondemen of *thorpus*.

þrote n *throte n.* B 1; C 1 throte
B.17.330   Til he be blereighed or blynd and [þe borre] in þe *þrote*;
C.19.310   Til he be blereyede or blynde and þe borre in [the] *throte*,

þrowe n *throu n.(1)* B 1; C 1
B.18.76   For he was knyȝt and kynges sone kynde foryaf þat [*þrowe*]
C.20.78   For he was knyht and kynges sone kynde forȝaf þat [*þrowe*]

þrowe v *throuen v.(1)* A 2 þrew (1) þrowe (1); B 4 threw (1) þrew (2)
                þrowe (1); C 3 threw (2) throweth (1)
A. 5.198   He [þr]umblide on þe þresshewold & [*þrew*] to þe erþe
A. 8.57   Þise þre for þrallis ben *þrowe* among vs alle
B. 5.350   He [þr]umbled on þe þresshfold and *þrew* to þe erþe.
B.16.131   'I shal ouerturne þis temple and adoun *þrowe*,
B.18.50   'Aue, raby', quod þat rybaud and *þrew* reedes at hym.
B.20.164   And *threw* drede of dispair a doȝeyne myle aboute.
C. 6.408   [A] thromblede at the thresfold and *threw* to þe erthe.
C.20.293   Set Mahond at þe mang[n]el and mullestones *throweth*;
C.22.164   And th[re]w drede of dispayr a doysayne myle aboute.

þrumbled v *thrumblen v.* A 1 þrumblide; B 1; C 1 thromblede
A. 5.198   He [þr]umblide on þe þresshewold & [þrew] to þe erþe
B. 5.350   He [þr]umbled on þe þresshfold and þrew to þe erþe.
C. 6.408   [A] *thromblede* at the thresfold and threw to þe erthe.

þrungen v *thringen v.* A 1 þrongen; B 1; C 1 throngen
A. 5.251   [A] þousand of men þ[o þ]rong[en] togideris,
B. 5.510   A þousand of men þo *þrungen* togideres,
C. 7.155   A thousand of men tho *throngen* togyderes,

thumbe > þombe; þurgh > þoruȝ

þursday n *Thuresdai n.* B 2
B.16.140   The *þursday* bifore, þere he made his [cene],
B.16.160   On a *þursday* in þesternesse þus was he taken;

þurst n *thirst n.* A 2 þrest (1) þrist (1); B 3 þurst (2) þurste (1); C 3
                furste
A. 5.209   And auowide to faste, for hungir or *þrist*:
A.11.46   Boþe for hungir & for *þrest*, & for chele quak[e];
B. 5.381   And auowed to faste for hunger or *þurste*:
B.18.368   May no drynke me moiste, ne my *þurst* slake,
B.20.19   That he dronke at ech dych er he [deye for *þurst*].
C. 6.438   For y vowe to verray god, for hungur or *furste*,
C.20.410   Moiste me to þe fulle ne my *furste* slokke
C.22.19   That he dronke at vch a dy[c]h ar he deye for *furste*.

þursteþ v *thirsten v.* B 1; C 1 fursteth
B.18.367   I fauȝt so me *þursteþ* ȝit for mannes soule sake;
C.20.408   Y fauht so me *fursteth* ȝut for mannes soule sake:

þus adv *thus adv.* A 28 thus (1) þus (27); B 114 thus (39) þus (75); C
                103 thus (101) þus (2)
        A.Pr.73, A.1.125, A.1.135, A.2.15, A.2.56, A.4.147, A.4.149, A.5.98, A.6.102,
        A.7.192, A.7.252, A.8.44, A.8.62, A.8.80, A.8.94, A.9.1, A.9.33, A.9.53, A.9.76, A.9.97,
        A.9.107, A.10.14, A.10.118, A.10.121, A.10.178, A.11.43, A.11.50, A.12.55
        B.Pr.76, B.1.136, B.1.147, B.2.43, B.2.52, B.2.74, B.3.75, B.4.184, B.4.186,
        B.5.12, B.5.59, B.5.119, B.5.149, B.5.425, B.5.616, B.6.2, B.6.268, B.7.16, B.7.36,
        B.7.72, B.7.98, B.7.112, B.8.1, B.8.37, B.8.62, B.8.85, B.8.107, B.8.117, B.9.47, B.9.95,
        B.9.116, B.9.119, B.9.156, B.9.193, B.9.194, B.10.57, B.10.64, B.10.254, B.10.282,
        B.10.363, B.10.364, B.10.460, B.11.68, B.11.162, B.11.320, B.11.384, B.11.438,
        B.11.438, B.12.81, B.12.234, B.12.262, B.12.269, B.13.38, B.13.87, B.13.99, B.13.130,
        B.13.139, B.13.146, B.13.148, B.13.198, B.13.457, B.14.67, B.14.181, B.14.319,
        B.14.322, B.15.38, B.15.145, B.15.278, B.15.297, B.15.405, B.15.409, B.15.489,
        B.15.507, B.16.52, B.16.150, B.16.160, B.16.209, B.16.220, B.16.225, B.16.247,

B.16.249, B.16.268, B.17.9, B.17.30, B.17.50, B.17.90, B.17.130, B.17.154, B.17.165,
B.17.274, B.17.294, B.17.311, B.17.333, B.18.171, B.18.199, B.18.299, B.18.337,
B.18.400, B.19.1, B.19.63, B.19.94, B.19.113, B.19.128, B.19.148, B.19.161, B.19.188,
B.19.199, B.20.1, B.20.51, B.20.69, B.20.148, B.20.344, B.20.354, B.20.368
        C.Pr.74, C.1.135, C.2.46, C.2.48, C.2.55, C.3.213, C.3.333, C.3.404, C.3.431,
C.4.178, C.4.180, C.5.1, C.5.11, C.5.48, C.5.200, C.6.122, C.6.123, C.6.137, C.6.423,
C.7.38, C.7.268, C.8.213, C.8.289, C.9.174, C.9.204, C.9.231, C.9.286, C.9.293, C.10.1,
C.10.100, C.10.103, C.10.113, C.10.301, C.11.18, C.11.38, C.11.125, C.11.155,
C.11.158, C.11.197, C.11.272, C.11.286, C.12.6, C.13.27, C.13.129, C.13.244, C.14.183,
C.14.189, C.15.43, C.15.94, C.15.106, C.15.117, C.15.146, C.15.148, C.15.152,
C.15.266, C.16.153, C.16.157, C.16.200, C.16.272, C.16.284, C.16.330, C.17.26,
C.17.83, C.17.176, C.17.177, C.17.181, C.17.250, C.17.258, C.18.52, C.18.265,
C.18.284, C.19.31, C.19.48, C.19.99, C.19.129, C.19.148, C.19.255, C.19.275, C.19.291,
C.19.313, C.20.174, C.20.204, C.20.306, C.20.319, C.20.332, C.20.350, C.20.443,
C.21.1, C.21.63, C.21.94, C.21.113, C.21.128, C.21.148, C.21.161, C.21.188, C.21.199,
C.22.1, C.22.51, C.22.69, C.22.148, C.22.344, C.22.354, C.22.368

thusgates adv *thusgates adv.* C 1
C.16.308   For drede of god þat so goed is and *thusgates* vs techeth:

thwytinge ger *thwitinge ger.* C 1
C. 8.199   In threschynge, in thekynge, in *thwytinge* of pynnes,

tybourne n prop *Tiburne n.* B 1; C 2
B.12.190   That haþ take fro *Tybourne* twenty stronge þeues,
C. 6.368   An hayward, an heremyte, the hangeman of *tybourne*,
C.14.129   Hit hath take fro *tybourne* twenty stronge theues

tid adv *tite adv.* B 3 tid (2) tyd (1); C 1 tyd
B.13.318   And he torned hym as *tyd* and þanne took I hede;
B.16.61   I shal telle þee as *tid* what þis tree highte.
B.20.54   Torned it [*tid*] vp so doun and ouertilte þe roote,
C.22.54   Turned hit *tyd* vp so down and ouertulde þe rote

tide n *tide n.* A 1
A. 2.40   In myddis a mounteyne at mydmorewe *tide*

tidy adj *tidi adj.* B 4; C 4 tydy (3) tidiore (1)
B. 3.322   Tha[t] worþ Trewe-tonge, a *tidy* man þat tened me neuere.
B. 9.107   To alle trewe *tidy* men þat trauaille desiren,
B.18.299   And þus haþ he trolled forþ [lik a *tidy* man] þise two and þritty
                wynter.
B.19.439   As for a trewe *tidy* man alle tymes ylike.
C. 3.475   Þat worth trewe-tonge, a *tydy* man þat tened me neuere.
C.12.188   Aren *tidiore* and touore to mannes byhofte
C.20.332   Thus hath he trolled forth lyke a *tydy* man this two & thritty
                wynter.
C.21.439   As for a trewe *tydy* man alle tymes ylyke.

tidynges n *tidinge n.* B 1; C 1 tydynges
B.19.342   And tolde hem *tidynges*, þat tyne þei sholde
C.21.342   And toelde hem *tydynges*, þat tyne thei sholde

tidiore > tidy

tyen v *teien v.* A 2 teiȝen (1) teiȝeþ (1); B 2 tyen (1) tieþ (1); C 2 teyen
                (1) teieth (1)
A. 1.94   And taken trespassours & *teiȝen* hem faste
A. 3.129   He[o] takiþ þe trewe be þe top, *teiȝeþ* hym faste,
B. 1.96   And taken transgressores and *tyen* hem faste
B. 3.140   [She] takeþ þe trewe bi þe top, *tieþ* h[y]m faste,
C. 1.92   And take transgressores and *teyen* hem faste
C. 3.178   And taketh [þe] tre[we] by the top and *te[i]eth* hym f[aste]

tikel adj *tikel adj.* A 1 tykil; B 1; C 1
A. 3.120   She is *tykil* of hire tail, talewys of hire tunge,
B. 3.131   She is *tikel* of hire tail, talewis of tonge,
C. 3.168   For she is *tikel* of here tayl, talewys of tonge,

tikes n *tike n.(3)* B 1; C 1 tykes
B.19.37   But vnder tribut and taillage as *tikes* and cherles.
C.21.37   Bote vnder tribuyt and talage as *tykes* and cherles.

til prep *til prep.* A 7; B 24; C 25
A. 5.187   And seten so *til* euesong & songe [vmbe]while
A. 6.3   *Til* late & longe þat hy a lede mette,
A. 6.66   And hold wel þin haliday heiȝ *til* euen.
A. 7.135   Inouȝ iche day at non, ac no more *til* on þe morewe
A. 7.172   And fla[ppid]e on wiþ flailes fro morewe *til* eue,
A. 7.247   And kep sum [*til*] soper tyme, & sit nouȝt to longe;
A. 7.273   Be þis liflode I mote lyue *til* lammasse tyme;
B.Pr.228   Tauerners [t]*il* hem tolden þe same;
B. 3.312   And dyngen vpon Dauid eche day *til* eue;
B. 5.338   And seten so *til* euensong and songen vmwhile
B. 5.515   *Til* late and longe, þat þei a leode mette
B. 5.579   And hold wel þyn haliday heighe *til* euen.
B. 5.601   Biddeþ amende-yow meke hym *til* his maister ones
B. 6.184   And flapten on wiþ flailes fro morwe *til* euen

B. 6.263 And keep som *til* soper tyme and sitte no3t to longe;
B. 6.289 By þis liflode [I moot] lyue *til* lammesse tyme,
B. 9.86 Allas þat a cristene creature shal be vnkynde *til* anoþer!
B.10.368 For euery cristene creature sholde be kynde *til* ooþer,
B.11.35 'Folwe forþ þat Fortune wole; þow hast wel fer *til* Elde.
B.11.373 [Th]anne I rebukede Reson and ri3t *til* hym I seyde,
B.12.248 And deleþ it no3t *til* his deeþ day, þe tail[le is al of] sorwe.
B.14.15 That I ne flobre it foule fro morwe *til* euen.'
B.15.169 He is glad wiþ alle glade and good *til* alle wikkede
B.15.467 For as þe Cow þoru3 kynde mylk þe calf norisseþ *til* an Oxe,
B.17.149 Bitoknen sooþly þe sone þat sent was *til* erþe,
B.18.6 Reste me þere and rutte faste *til* Ramis palmarum.
B.18.67 Er sonday aboute sonne risyng'; and sank wiþ þat *til* erþe.
B.18.224 Boþe in heuene and in erþe, and now *til* helle he þenkeþ
B.18.402 And for þi lesynge, lucifer, þat þow leighe *til* Eue
B.19.416 The comune clamat cotidie, ech a man *til* ooþer,
B.19.441 And suffreþ þat synfulle be [*til* som tyme þat þei repente].
C.Pr.169 Comen *til* a conseyl for [þe] comune profyt.
C.Pr.232 Tauerners *til* hem tolde þe same:
C. 1.133 Estward *til* heuene, euere to abyde
C. 3.308 The huyre of his hewe ouer eue *til* amorwe.
C. 5.111 Y saw þe felde ful of folk fram ende *til* oþer
C. 6.188 Exited either oþer *til* oure olde synne.
C. 6.396 And seten so *til* euenson[g] and songen vmbywhile
C. 7.126 For thorw þat synne thy sone ysent was *til* erthe
C. 7.226 And hold wel þ[in] haliday heye *til* euen.
C. 8.98 Til y come *til* his acountes as my crede telleth,
C. 8.180 And flapton on with f[lay]les fro morwen *til* euen
C. 8.273 And kepe som *til* soper tyme and site nat to longe;
C. 8.312 By this lyflode we mote lyue *til* l[a]masse tyme
C.10.53 To contricion, to confessioun, til he come *til* his ende.
C.11.310 Til Concupiscencia Carnis acorded *til* al my werkes.
C.12.130 That we sholde be low and louelich and lele vch man *til* oþer
C.13.183 Thenne y [a]resonede resoun and ryht *til* hym y sayde,
C.17.262 For when þe hye kyng of heuene sente his so[n]e *til* erthe
C.18.168 'Aue raby,' quod th[at] ribaud[e]; and riht *til* hym [he] 3ede
C.19.123 Bitokneth soethly þe sone þat sente was *til* erthe,
C.20.69 Ar soneday aboute sonne rysynge'; and sank with þat *til* erthe.
C.20.348 And now for a later lesynge] þat thow lowe *til* Eue
C.20.445 Ac for þe lesynge þat thow low, lucifer, *til* eue
C.21.265 And ioyned *til* a man oen iohann, most gentill of all,
C.22.134 He iogged *til* a iustice and iustede in his ere

til conj *til conj.* A 34; B 109; C 104 til (98) tyl (6)

A.Pr.41 *Til* here bely & here bagge were bratful ycrammid;
A.Pr.89 Þanne gete a mom of here mouþ *til* mony be shewid.
A. 1.95 *Til* treuþe hadde termined here trespas to þe ende.
A. 1.111 *Til* he brak buxumnesse þoru3 bost of hymseluen.
A. 2.107 *Til* he hadde siluer for his selis & signes.
A. 2.117 *Til* mede be þi weddit wyf þoru3 wyt of vs alle,
A. 2.181 *Til* pardoners hadde pite & pulden him to house,
A. 4.18 'Sette my sadil vpon suffre *til* I se my tyme,
A. 4.101 *Til* lordis & ladies louen alle treuþe,
A. 4.103 *Til* childris cherisshing be chastisid with 3erdis;
A. 4.105 *Til* clerkis & kni3tes be curteis of here mouþes,
A. 4.107 *Til* prestis here prechyng preue it hemselue,
A. 4.109 *Til* seint Iame be sou3t þere I shal assigne.
A. 5.39 And be steward of 3oure stede *til* 3e be stewid betere.
A. 5.128 *Til* ten 3ardis oþer twelue tollide out þrittene.
A. 5.178 *Til* robyn þe ropere reste to arisen,
A. 5.188 *Til* glotoun hadde ygulpid a galoun & a gille.
A. 5.202 Þat he slepte satirday & sonneday *til* sonne 3ede to reste.
A. 5.214 *Til* Vigilate [þe veil] fet watir [at] his ei3en,
A. 5.226 *Til* I haue euesong herd, I behote [to] þe rode.
A. 6.49 *Til* 3e come into consience þat crist wyte þe soþe,
A. 7.6 I wolde wende wiþ 3ow *til* 3e were þere'.
A. 7.53 And wende wiþ 3ow þe wey *til* we fynde treuþe.'
A. 7.81 *Til* I come to his acountes as my crede me techiþ—
A. 7.132 *Til* god of his grace gare h[e]m to arise.
A. 9.8 *Til* it befel on a Friday two Freris I mette,
A.10.24 *Til* kynde come oþer sende [and] kepe hire hymselue.'
A.10.60 Þei helde ale in here hed *til* Inwyt be drenchit,
A.10.70 Fro folies, & fynde hem *til* þei ben wise.
A.10.169 *Til* fourty dayes be fulfild, þat flood haue ywasshe
A.11.120 *Til* þou come to a court, kepe wel þi tunge
A.12.21 *Til* þo wrecches ben in wil here synne to lete."
A.12.52 *Til* 3e come to þe burg[h] quod bonum est faste.
A.12.74 [But ete as hunger me hete *til* my belly swellyd.
B.Pr.41 [*Til*] hire bel[y] and hire bagg[e were bret]ful ycrammed;
B.Pr.216 Than gete a mom of hire mouþ *til* moneie be shewed.
B. 1.97 *Til* treuþe hadde ytermyned hire trespas to þe ende.
B. 1.113 *Til]* he brak buxomnesse; his blisse gan he tyne
B. 1.122 *Til* god of his goodnesse [garte þe heuene to stekie]
B. 1.154 *Til* it hadde of þe erþe [y]eten [hitselue].

B. 2.48 And lakke hem no3t but lat hem worþe *til* leaute be Iustice
B. 2.97 And þanne to sitten and soupen *til* sleep hem assaille,
B. 2.99 *Til* Sleuþe and sleep sliken hise sydes;
B. 2.143 *Til* he hadde siluer for his [seles] and [signes of] Notaries.
B. 2.153 *Til* Mede be þi wedded wif þoru3 wi[t] of vs alle,
B. 2.222 *Til* Pardoners hadde pite and pulled hym [to] house,
B. 4.20 'Set my Sadel vpon suffre-*til*-I-se-my-tyme'
B. 4.43 As Conscience hym kenned *til* þei come to þe kynge.
B. 4.114 *Til* lordes and ladies louen alle truþe
B. 4.116 *Til* pernelles purfill be put in hire hucche.
B. 4.119 *Til* clerkene coueitise be to cloþe þe pouere and fede,
B. 4.122 And *til* prechours prechynge be preued on hemselue;
B. 4.123 *Til* þe kynges counseil þe commune profit;
B. 4.124 *Til* Bisshopes Bayardes ben beggeris Chaumbres,
B. 4.126 And *til* Seint Iames be sou3t þere I shal assigne.
B. 5.47 And be Stywar[d] of youre sted[e] *til* ye be [stewed] bettre'.
B. 5.140 *Til* þei beere leues of lowe speche lordes to plese,
B. 5.150 *Til* þei be boþe beggers and by my spiritualte libben,
B. 5.163 *Til* "þow lixt!" and "þow lixt!" lopen out at ones
B. 5.212 *Til* ten yerdes or twelue tolled out þrittene.
B. 5.271 *Til* þow make restitucion', [quod Repentaunce], 'and rekene wiþ hem alle;
B. 5.329 *Til* Robyn þe Ropere [arise þei bisou3te],
B. 5.339 *Til* Gloton hadde yglubbed a galon and a gille.
B. 5.360 That he sleep Saterday and Sonday *til* sonne yede to reste.
B. 5.383 *Til* Abstinence myn Aunte haue 3yue me leeue,
B. 5.411 *Til* matyns and masse be do, and þanne [moste] to þe freres;
B. 5.438 Forsleuþed in my seruice *til* it my3te serue no man.
B. 5.442 *Til* vigilate þe veille fette water at hise ei3en,
B. 5.454 *Til* I haue euensong herd: I bihote to þe Roode.
B. 5.562 *Til* ye come into Conscience þat crist wite þe soþe,
B. 6.58 And wende wiþ yow [þe wey] *til* we fynde truþe.'
B. 6.89 *Til* I come to hise acountes as my [crede] me [techeþ]—
B. 6.138 *Til* god of his [grace gare hem to arise].
B. 8.8 *Til* it bifel on a Friday two freres I mette,
B. 9.24 *Til* kynde come or sende [and kepe] hire [hymselue].'
B. 9.132 *Til* god wraþed [wiþ] hir werkes and swich a word seide,
B. 9.138 *Til* fourty daies be fulfild, þat flood haue ywasshen
B.10.168 *Til* þow come to a court, kepe-wel-þi-tunge-
B.11.5 And in a wynkynge [worþ *til* I weex] aslepe.
B.11.23 þow be a lord and haue lond leten [þe] I nelle
B.11.43 *Til* Concupiscencia carnis acorded alle my werkes.
B.11.60 *Til* I for[yede] youþe and yarn into Elde.
B.11.206 Of Adames issue and Eue ay *til* god man deide;
B.11.237 *Til* he blessede and brak þe breed þat þei eten.
B.11.428 Lat hym ligge, loke no3t on hym *til* hym list aryse.
B.12.60 Ac grace ne groweþ no3t [*til* good wil yeue reyn];
B.12.251 To alle hem þat it holdeþ *til* hir tail be plukked.
B.13.122 *Til* I se þo seuene and myself acorde
B.13.133 'Thanne passe we ouer *til* Piers come and preue þis in dede.
B.13.146 And leye on hym þus with loue *til* he lau3e on þe.
B.13.182 And be Pilgrym wiþ pacience *til* I haue preued moore.'
B.13.214 *Til* Pacience haue preued þee and parfit þee maked.'
B.13.259 *Til* pride be pureliche fordo, and [þat] þoru3 payn defaute.
B.13.336 That takeþ me al a tweluemonþe, *til* þat I despise
B.13.347 *Til* eiþeres wille wexeþ kene and to þe werke yeden,
B.13.351 *Til* þei my3te na moore; and þanne [hadde] murye tales,
B.13.452 Thise solaceþ þe soule *til* hymself be falle
B.13.458 *Til* conscience acouped hym þerof in a curteis manere.
B.14.136 And *til* he haue doon his deuoir and his dayes iournee.
B.15.3 And so my wit weex and wanyed *til* I a fool weere.
B.15.11 *Til* reson hadde ruþe on me and rokked me aslepe,
B.15.12 *Til* I sei3, as it sorcerie were, a sotil þyng wiþ alle.
B.15.289 *Til* he foundede freres of Austynes ordre, [or ellis freres lyen].
B.15.314 *Til* briddes brynge vs [wherby] we sholde lyue.
B.15.444 *Til* Gregory garte clerkes to go here and preche
B.15.453 *Til* it be fulled vnder foot or in fullyng stokkes.
B.15.457 *Til* it be cristned in cristes name and confermed of þe bisshop
B.15.585 And took it Moyses to teche men *til* Messie coome,
B.15.611 *Til* þei kouþe speke and spelle et in Spiritum sanctum,
B.16.39 I saue it *til* I se it ripen and somdel yfruyted.
B.16.93 *Til* plenitudo temporis [tyme] comen were
B.16.101 *Til* he weex a faunt þoru3 hir flessh of fightyng kouþe
B.16.107 *Til* he was parfit praktisour if any peril fille.
B.16.139 *Til* it bifel on a friday, a litel bifore Pasqe.
B.16.196 To ocupie hym here *til* issue were spronge,
B.16.265 *Til* he come þat I carpe of; crist is his name
B.16.269 Lollynge in my lappe *til* swich a lord vs fecche.'
B.17.77 'Haue, kepe þis man', [quod he], '*til* I come fro þe Iustes.
B.17.100 *Til* he haue eten al þe barn and his blood ydronke.
B.17.122 *Til* I haue salue for alle sike; and þanne shal I turne
B.17.142 *Til* hym [likede] and liste to vnlosen his fynger,
B.17.226 *Til* þe holy goost gynne to glowe and to blase,

B.17.228	*Til* þat lele loue ligge on hym and blowe.
B.17.309	That þe kyng may do no mercy *til* boþe men acorde
B.17.312	Yuele lyuen and leten noȝt *til* lif hem forsake.
B.17.326	He sekeþ and sekeþ *til* he slepe drye.
B.17.330	*Til* he be blereighed or blynd and [þe borre] in þe þrote;
B.17.332	That sholde brynge in bettre wode or blowe it *til* it brende.
B.18.4	*Til* I weex wery of þe world and wilned eft to slepe
B.18.156	*Til* he be deed and do þerto; þe yuel he destruyeþ,
B.18.216	For *til* modicum mete with vs, I may it wel auowe,
B.18.229	Ne what is witterly wele *til* weylawey hym teche.'
B.18.369	*Til* þe vendage falle in þe vale of Iosaphat,
B.18.392	In my prisone Purgatorie *til* parce it hote.
B.18.424	*Til* þe day dawed þise damyseles [carolden]
B.19.97	Was neiþer kyng ne conquerour *til* he [comsed] wexe
B.19.107	*Til* he hadde alle hem þat he for bledde.
B.20.205	And hold þee þere euere *til* I sende for þee.
B.20.213	Thoruȝ Contricion and Confession *til* I cam to vnitee.
B.20.347	He saluede so oure wommen *til* some were wiþ childe.'
B.20.369	*Til* Contricion hadde clene foryeten to crye and to wepe
B.20.385	And sende me hap and heele *til* I haue Piers þe Plowman.'
B.20.386	And siþþe he gradde after Grace *til* I gan awake.
C.Pr.42	*Til* here [bely] and here [bagge] w[ere] bretful ycrammed,
C.Pr.166	Than gete a Mum of here mouth [*til*] moneye [be] shewed.
C.Pr.215	*Til* þat meschief amende hem þat many man chasteth,
C. 1.93	*Til* treuthe hadde termyned here trespas to þe ende
C. 1.150	*Til* hit hadde of erthe yȝoten hitsilue.
C. 2.51	Lacke hem nat but lat hem worthe *til* leutee be Iustice
C. 2.106	And sue forth suche felawschipe *til* they ben falle in Slewthe
C. 2.159	*Til* he hadde seluer for the seel and signes of notaries.
C. 2.169	*Til* mede be thy wedded wyf wolle we nat stunte,
C. 2.232	*Tyl* Pardoners hadde [pyte] and polleden hym [t]o house.
C. 3.133	*Til* treuthe hadde ytolde here a tokene fram hymsulue.
C. 4.20	Sette my sadel vpon soffre-*tyl-y-se-my-tyme*
C. 4.41	Bute dede as Consience hym kennede *til* he þe kyng mette.
C. 4.109	*Til* lordes and ladies louen alle treuthe
C. 4.111	*Tyl* purnele porfiel be putte in here whicche
C. 4.114	*Til* Clerkene Coueytise be cloth for þe pore
C. 4.118	*Til* þat lerede men lyue as thei lere and teche
C. 4.119	And *til* þe kynges consayl be alle comune profit
C. 4.120	And *til* byschopes ben bakeres, Breweres and taylours
C. 4.122	And *til* saynt Iames be souhte there pore sykke lyggen,
C. 5.37	*Tyl* y wyste witterly what holy writ menede
C. 5.81	And wol *til* hit be wered out [or] oþerwyse ychaunged.
C. 5.108	Wepyng and waylyng *til* y was aslepe.
C. 5.145	And be stewar[d] of ȝoure stedes *til* ȝe be stewed bettere.'
C. 5.187	*Til* lucifer þe lyare leued þat hymsulue
C. 5.192	And no grace [to] graunte *til* good loue were
C. 6.80	That taketh me al [a] twelmonthe *til* þat y despise
C. 6.124	*Til* y, wrathe, wexe an hey and walke with hem bothe;
C. 6.125	Or *til* they bothe be beggares and by [my] spiritual[t]e libbe
C. 6.138	*Til* "thow lixt!" and "thow lixt!" be lady ouer hem alle;
C. 6.149	*Tyl* ayþer clepede oþer "hore!" and o[f] with the clothes
C. 6.150	*Til* bothe here hedes were bar and blody here chekes.
C. 6.181	*Til* bothe oure wil was oen and to þe werk we ȝeden
C. 6.185	*Til* we myhte no more; thenne hadde we mery tales
C. 6.220	*Til* ten ȝerde other twelue tolde out threttene.
C. 6.295	*Til* thow haue ymad by thy myhte to alle men restitucioun,
C. 6.387	*Til* Robyn þe Ropere aryse they bisouhte
C. 6.397	*Til* glotoun hadde yglobbed a galoun and a gylle.
C. 6.403	He myhte noþer steppe ne stande *til* he a staf hadde
C. 6.418	A sleep saturday and sonenday *til* sonne ȝede to reste.
C. 6.440	*Til* abstinence myn aunte haue ȝeue me leue;
C. 7.5	Sholde no ryngyng do me ryse *til* y were rype to dyne.'
C. 7.27	*Til* matynes and masse be ydo; thenne haue y a memorie at þe freres.
C. 7.50	*Til* eche lyf hit lothed to loke þeron or smylle hit;
C. 7.56	*Til* vigilate the veile fette water at his eyus
C. 7.68	*Til* y haue euensong yherd: y bihote to þe rode.'
C. 7.112	Thise solaseth þe soule *til* hymsulue be yfalle
C. 7.160	*Til* late was and longe þat thei a lede mette
C. 7.207	*Til* ȝe come into Consience, yknowe of god sulue,
C. 8.98	*Til* y come til his acountes as my crede telleth,
C. 8.287	Lat hem abyde *til* the bord be drawe; Ac bere hem none crommes
C. 8.288	*Til* alle thyne nedy neyhbores haue noen ymaked.
C. 9.160	Buth nat in this bulle,' quod [Peres], '*til* they ben amended
C. 9.244	As matynes by þe morwe *til* masse bygynne,
C.10.8	*Til* hit biful [o]n [a] fryday two freres y mette,
C.10.53	To contricion, to confessioun, *til* he come til his ende
C.10.54	For rather haue we no reste *til* we restitue
C.10.150	*Til* kynde come o[r] sende and kepe here hymsulue.'
C.10.226	*Til* fourty [dayes] be fulfild and floed haue ywasche
C.11.182	*Til* thow be a lord and haue lond leten y nelle
C.11.310	*Til* Concupiscencia Carnis acorded til al my werkes.

C.12.12	*Til* y forȝet ȝouthe and ȝorn into elde.
C.12.114	Of Adames issue and Eue ay *til* god man deyede;
C.12.126	*Til* he blessed here bred and brake hit hem bitwene.
C.13.131	*Til* þat kynde cam clergie to helpe
C.13.235	Lat hym lygge, lok nat on hym *til* hym luste [a]ryse.
C.14.24	Ac grace ne groweth nat *til* gode wil gyue reyne
C.15.146	And ley on hym thus with loue *til* he lauhe on þe.
C.15.229	*Til* pruyde be puyreliche fordo and þat thorw payn defaute:
C.16.335	And with warm water of his yes woketh h[em] *til* [t]he[y] white:
C.17.296	Moises to be maister þerof *til* messie come
C.17.319	*Til* they couthe speke and spele et in spiritum sanctum,
C.18.4	*Til* we cam into a contre, cor hominis hit heihte,
C.18.42	And þerwith y warde hit oþerwhile *til* hit waxe rype.
C.18.126	*Til* plenitudo temporis tyme ycome were
C.18.138	*Til* plenitudo temporis [h]y tyme aprochede,
C.18.198	'Muse nat to moche þeron,' quod faith, '*til* thow more knowe
C.18.205	To ocupien hym here *til* issue were spronge
C.18.281	*Til* he come þat y carpe of; Crist is his name
C.18.285	Lollyng in my lappe *til* suche a lord vs feche.'
C.19.90	*Til* he haue eten al þ[e] barn and his bloed dronken
C.19.116	*Til* hym likede and luste to vnlose that fynger
C.19.192	*Til* the holy goest gynne to glowe and [to] blase,
C.19.194	*Til* þat loue and bileue leliche to hym blowe.
C.19.289	That may no kynge mercy graunte *til* bothe men acorde
C.19.292	That euele lyuen and leten nat *t[il* lif] hem forsake.
C.19.306	A seketh and seketh *til* he slepe druye.
C.19.310	*Til* he be blereyede or blynde and þe borre in [the] throte,
C.19.312	That sholde brynge in bettere wode or blowen hit *til* hit brente.
C.20.4	*Til* y waxe wery of the world and wilnede eefte to slepe
C.20.159	*Til* he [be] ded [and] ydo þerto; [þe yuel] he destruyeth,
C.20.225	For *til* [modicum] mete with vs, y may hit wel avowe,
C.20.238	Ne what is witterliche wele *til* welaway hym teche.'
C.20.411	*Til* þe ventage valle in þe vale of Iosophat
C.20.467	*Til* þe day dawed thes damoyseles caroled
C.21.97	Was noþer kyng ne conquerour *til* he comsed wexe
C.21.107	*Til* he hadde all hem þat he fore bledde.
C.21.441	And soffreth þat synnefole be *til* som tyme þat þei repente.
C.22.205	And halde the there euere *til* y sende for the.
C.22.213	Thorw contricion and confessioun *til* y cam to vnite.
C.22.347	He salued so oure wymmen *til* some were with childe.'
C.22.369	*Til* Contricioun hadde clene forȝete to crye and to wepe
C.22.385	And s[e]nde me hap and hele *til* y haue [Peres Plouhman]'.
C.22.386	And sethe he gradde aftur grace *tyl* y gan awake.

tilde v *telden v. &> tilien* A 1 teldit; B 1; C 1 telde
A. 2.42	And ten þousand of tentis *teldit* beside
B.12.210	And riȝt as Troianus þe trewe knyȝt [*tilde*] noȝt depe in helle
C.14.149	And riht as troianes þe trewe knyhte [*telde*] nat depe in helle

tiled(e tilen > tilien; tilyares > tilieris

tilien v *tillen v.(1)* A 3 tilen (1) tilie (1) tilien (1); B 15 tiled (1) tilie (6) tilye (3) tilien (1) tilieþ (2) tulieden (1) ytilied (1); C 17 tylde (1) tilede (1) tylede (1) tylie (1) tylye (1) tilynge (1) tilion (1) tulie (3) tulieth (2) tulye (4) tulyng (1)
A. 7.217	In sudore & swynke þou shalt þi mete *tilen*
A. 7.220	Piger propter frigus no feld wolde *tilie*;
A. 8.2	To take his tem & [*tilien* þe erþe],
B.Pr.120	To *tilie* and to trauaille as trewe lif askeþ.
B. 6.233	In sudore and swynk þow shalt þi mete *tilie*
B. 6.236	Piger [propter frigus] no feeld [w]olde *tilie*;
B. 7.2	To [t]aken his teme and *tilien* þe erþe,
B.14.68	That manye wyntres men lyueden and no mete ne *tulieden*.
B.15.107	Tiþes [of vn]trewe þyng *ytilied* or chaffared,
B.15.364	Tilieris þat *tiled* þe erþe tolden hir maistres
B.18.105	[Ne] haue lordshipe in londe ne no lond *tilye*,
B.19.238	And some he tauȝte to *tilie*, to [coke] and to thecche,
B.19.261	And for to *tilie* truþe a teeme shal he haue.'
B.19.316	And *tilieþ* [to] hir techynge þe Cardynale vertues.'
B.19.333	As wide as þe world is wiþ Piers to *tilie* truþe
B.19.434	Right so Piers þe Plowman peyneþ hym to *tilye*
B.19.437	[So blessed be Piers þe Plowman þat peyneþ hym to *tilye*],
B.19.438	And trauailleþ and *tilieþ* for a tretour also soore
C.Pr.87	Ben charged with holy chirche charite to *tylie*,
C. 8.140	That lele land *tilynge* men leely byswynken.
C. 8.243	"The slowe Caytif for colde wolde no corn *tylye*;
C. 9.2	To taken his teme and *tilion* þe erthe
C.10.200	To *tulie* þe erthe with tonge and teche men to louye
C.11.293	Lewed lele laboreres and land *tulyng* peple
C.15.263	Hit is founde þat fourty wynter folke lyuede and *tylde* nat
C.15.267	That manye wynter men lyuede and no mete ne *tylede*.
C.17.101	Tilyares þat *tilede* þe erthe tolden here maystres
C.20.108	Ne haue lordshipe in londe ne no londe *tulye*
C.21.238	And somme he tauhte to *tulye*, to [coke] and to [thecche,

C.21.261	And for to *tulye* treuthe a teme shal he haue.'
C.21.316	And *tulieth* [to] here techynge the cardinal vertues.'
C.21.333	As wyde as the world is with Peres to *tulye* treuthe
C.21.434	Rihte so [Peres] the [Plouhman] payneth hym to *tulie*
C.21.437	So yblessed be [Peres] the [plouhman] þat peyneth hym to *tulie*
C.21.438	And trauaileth and *tulieth* for a tretour also sore

tilieris n *tillere* n.   A 1;   B 3 tilieris (2) tiliers (1);   C 2 tilyares (1) tulyers (1)

A.11.184	Trewe *tilieris* on erþe, taillours & souteris
B.13.239	For alle trewe trauaillours and *tiliers* of þe erþe
B.15.364	*Tilieris* þat tiled þe erþe tolden hir maistres
B.15.368	Shepherdes and shipmen, and so do þise *tilieris*.
C.Pr.227	As taylers and tanners and *tulyers* [of] þe erthe,
C.17.101	*Tilyares* þat tilede þe erthe tolden here maystres

tilion > *tilien*

tilþe n *tilth* n.   A 1 telþe;   B 1;   C 1 tulthe

A. 7.127	Boþe to setten & to sowen, & sauen his *telþe*,
B.19.432	And sent þe sonne to saue a cursed mannes *tilþe*
C.21.432	And sente þe so[nn]e to saue a corsed mannes *tulthe*

tymber n *timber* n.   B 1;   C 1

B.19.319	'By god! Grace', quod Piers, 'ye moten gyue *tymber*,
C.21.319	'By god! grace,' quod [Peres], 'ȝe moet gyue *tymber*

tymbre v *timbren* v.(1)   A 1 tymbride;   B 2 tymbre (1) tymbred (1);   C 1 tymbred

A. 3.74	For tok h[y] on trewely h[y] *tymbride* not so heiȝe,
B. 3.85	For toke þei on trewely þei *tymbred* nouȝt so heiȝe,
B.11.361	And who tauȝte hem on trees to *tymbre* so heiȝe
C. 3.84	For tok thei [o]n trewely they *tymbred* nat so heye

tyme n *time* n.(2) &> *lif_tyme, som_tyme, som_tymes* A 30 tyme (25) tymes (5); B 97 tyme (84) tymes (13); C 113 tyme (86) tymes (27)

A.Pr.81	Þat here parissh w[ere] pore siþþe þe pestilence *tyme*,
A. 3.112	She makiþ men mysdo manye score *tymes*;
A. 3.168	Þou hast hongid on myn half enleuene *tymes*,
A. 4.18	'Sette my sadil vpon suffre til I se my *tyme*,
A. 5.68	Wiþ werkis [or wiþ] wordis whanne he saiȝ his *tyme*.
A. 5.94	Ac of his wynnyng I wepe and weile þe *tyme*.
A. 6.46	For treuþe wolde loue me þe wers a long *tyme* aftir.
A. 6.123	Þou miȝt gete grace [þere] so þou go be *tyme*.'
A. 7.19	Þat han silk & sendel, sewiþ it whanne *tyme* is,
A. 7.70	Dame werche whanne *tyme* is piers wyf hatte;
A. 7.106	Shulde ben hirid þereaftir whan heruist *tyme* come.
A. 7.180	And lame menis lymes wern li[þ]id þat *tyme*,
A. 7.247	And kep sum [til] soper *tyme*, & sit nouȝt to longe;
A. 7.273	Be þis liflode I mote lyue til lammasse *tyme*;
A. 7.297	Þat he was werkman ywrouȝt warie þe *tyme*,
A. 8.80	Þo þat lyuen þus here lif mowe loþe þe *tyme*
A. 8.128	And sauȝ þe sonne euene souþ sitte þat *tyme*,
A. 8.131	Manye *tyme* þis metelis han mad me to stodie,
A. 8.147	It befel as his fadir seide in faraos *tyme*
A. 8.150	Manye *tymes* at mydniȝt whan men shulde slepe,
A. 9.27	Makeþ þe man many *tymes* to falle & to stonde.
A. 9.116	Þanne þouȝt, in þat *tyme*, seide þis wordis:
A.10.140	Ben conseyuid in cursid *tyme* as kaym was on Eue
A.10.148	Caym þei hym callide, in cursid *tyme* engendrit.
A.10.171	"Bestis þat now ben shuln banne þe *tyme*
A.11.59	To pleise wiþ proude men, siþen þe pestilence *tyme*,
A.11.113	'And tel me sum tokne to hym, for *tyme* is þat I wende'.
A.11.137	Ac theologie haþ tenid me ten score *tymes*,
A.11.204	Gregory þe grete clerk, a good pope in his *tyme*,
A.11.269	Boþe in werk & in woord, in world in his *tyme*?
B.Pr.84	That hire parissh[e] wer[e] pouere siþ þe pestilence *tyme*,
B. 2.96	And in fastynge dayes to frete er ful *tyme* were.
B. 3.123	[She] makeþ men mysdo many score *tymes*.
B. 3.181	Thow hast hanged on myn half elleuene *tymes*,
B. 3.329	For Makometh and Mede myshappe shul þat *tyme*;
B. 4.20	'Set my Sadel vpon suffre-til-I-se-my-*tyme*
B. 5.85	With werkes or wiþ wordes whan he seyȝe his *tyme*.
B. 5.114	[Ac of his] wynnynge I wepe and waille þe *tyme*.
B. 5.169	Among Monkes I myȝte be ac many *tyme* I shonye
B. 5.364	And Repentaunce riȝt so rebuked hym þat *tyme*:
B. 5.370	There no nede was nyne hundred *tymes*;
B. 5.425	And þus tene I trewe men ten hundred *tymes*,
B. 5.435	In speche and in sparynge of speche; yspilt many a *tyme*
B. 5.488	On good fryday for mannes sake at ful *tyme* of þe daye;
B. 5.491	The sonne for sorwe þerof lees [s]iȝt [for] a *tyme*.
B. 5.492	Aboute mydday, whan moost liȝt is and meel *tyme* of Seintes,
B. 5.559	Truþe wolde loue me þe lasse a long *tyme* after.
B. 6.11	That ye haue silk and Sandel to sowe whan *tyme* is
B. 6.78	Dame werch-whan-*tyme*-is Piers wif hiȝte;
B. 6.114	Sholde be hired þerafter whan heruest *tyme* come.

B. 6.263	And keep som til soper *tyme* and sitte noȝt to longe;
B. 6.289	By þis liflode [I moot] lyue til lammesse *tyme*,
B. 6.313	[That] he was werkman wroȝt [warie] þe *tyme*.
B. 7.98	[Tho] þat lyue þus hir lif mowe loþe þe *tyme*
B. 7.146	And seiȝ þe sonne [euene] South sitte þat *tyme*,
B. 7.149	Many *tyme* þis metels haþ maked me to studie
B. 7.170	It bifel as his fader seide in Pharaoes *tyme*
B. 8.31	Makeþ þe man many *tyme* to falle and to stonde.
B. 8.127	Thanne þoȝt in þat *tyme* seide þise wordes:
B. 9.100	To spille any speche or any space of *tyme*:
B. 9.101	[Tynynge] of *tyme*, truþe woot þe soþe,
B. 9.123	Conceyued ben in [cursed] *tyme* as Caym was on Eue
B. 9.140	Beestes þat now ben shul banne þe *tyme*
B. 9.187	Whan ye han wyued beþ war and wercheþ in *tyme*,
B.10.73	To plese wiþ proude men syn þe pestilence *tyme*;
B.10.161	'And tel me som tokene [to hym], for *tyme* is þat I wende'.
B.10.185	Ac Theologie haþ tened me ten score *tymes*;
B.10.390	Of hir wordes þei wissen vs for wisest as in hir *tyme*,
B.10.405	Ac I wene it worþ of manye as was in Noes *tyme*
B.10.472	Ye, men knowe clerkes þat han corsed þe *tyme*
B.11.36	A man may stoupe *tyme* ynoȝ whan he shal tyne þe crowne.'
B.11.173	But þei ben lerned for oure lordes loue, lost is al þe *tyme*,
B.11.244	Many *tyme* god haþ ben met among nedy peple,
B.11.313	As whan þei hadde ryde in Rotey *tyme* anoon [reste þei] after;
B.11.371	Saue man and his make; many *tyme* [me þouȝte].
B.11.378	Amende þow, if þow myȝt, for my *tyme* is to abide.
B.12.4	And manye *tymes* haue meued þee to [mynne] on þyn ende,
B.12.31	And sauen men sondry *tymes*, ac noon so soone as Charite.
B.12.232	Lewed men many *tymes* maistres þei apposen
B.12.236	Ac of briddes and of beestes men by olde *tyme*
B.12.252	And þouȝ þe riche repente þanne and birewe þe *tyme*
B.13.4	And of þis metyng many *tyme* muche þouȝt I hadde,
B.13.22	And as crist wolde þer com Conscience to conforte me þat *tyme*
B.13.68	Ac o word þei ouerhuppen at ech *tyme* þat þei preche
B.13.97	And þanne is *tyme* to take and to appose þis doctour
B.13.163	Tene þee any *tyme*, and þow take it wiþ þe:
B.13.203	But seide ful sobreliche, 'þow shalt se þe *tyme*
B.13.329	Auenge me fele *tymes*, oþer frete myselue wiþInne;
B.13.349	And as [lef] in lente as out of lente, alle *tymes* yliche.
B.13.375	And [what body] borwed of me abouȝte þe *tyme*
B.13.394	Miȝte neuere me conforte in þe mene [tyme]
B.14.4	That wollen bymolen it many *tyme* maugree my chekes.
B.14.66	And in Elyes *tyme* heuene was yclosed
B.14.177	Wo in wynter *tymes* for wantynge of cloþes,
B.14.178	And in somer *tyme* selde soupen to þe fulle.
B.14.327	And wepte water wiþ hise eighen and weyled þe *tyme*
B.15.40	'Ye ben as a bisshop', quod I, al bourdynge þat *tyme*,
B.15.96	[And] se it by ensaumple in somer *tyme* on trowes:
B.15.231	Ac it is fern [and fele yeer in] Fraunceis *tyme*
B.15.276	Ac neiþer Antony ne Egidie ne heremyte þat *tyme*
B.15.282	But selden and sondry *tymes*, as seiþ þe book and techeþ.
B.15.283	Antony adayes aboute noon *tyme*
B.15.547	Shul [ouer]torne as templers dide; þe *tyme* approcheþ faste.
B.16.26	And in blowyng *tyme* abite þe floures but if þise piles helpe.
B.16.31	The flessh is a fel wynd, and in flouryng *tyme*,
B.16.33	That it norisseþ nyce sightes and [anoþer] *tyme* wordes
B.16.93	Til plenitudo temporis [*tyme*] comen were
B.16.102	To haue yfouȝte wiþ þe fend er ful *tyme* come.
B.16.103	And Piers þe Plowman parceyued plener *tyme*
B.16.117	Some þat þe sighte seiȝen seiden þat *tyme*
B.16.138	Eche day after ooþer hir *tyme* þei awaiteden
B.16.142	'I am sold þoruȝ [som] of yow; he shal þe *tyme* rewe
B.16.195	Sente forþ his sone as for seruaunt þat *tyme*
B.16.237	Bledden blood for þat lordes loue and hope to blisse þe *tyme*.
B.16.242	Mercy for oure mysdedes as many *tyme* as we asken:
B.18.5	And lened me to a lenten, and longe *tyme* I slepte;
B.18.63	And tolde why þat tempeste so longe *tyme* durede.
B.18.71	Two þeues [þat *tyme*] þoled deeþ [also]
B.18.81	Maugree his manye teeþ he was maad þat *tyme*
B.18.381	And if þe kyng of þat kyngdom come in þat *tyme*
B.18.384	And I þat am kyng of kynges shal come swich a *tyme*
B.19.84	Wherfore and why wise men þat *tyme*,
B.19.134	For dauid was doghtiest of dedes in his *tyme*;
B.19.384	That han laboured al þis lenten *tyme*.
B.19.410	'I am a Curatour of holy kirke, and cam neuere in my *tyme*
B.19.439	As for a trewe tidy man alle *tymes* ylike.
B.20.26	He shal do moore þan mesure many *tyme* and ofte,
C.Pr.82	That here parsch[e] were pore sithe þ[e] pestelence *tyme*,
C. 1.17	Wherfore he hette þe elementis to helpe ȝow alle *tymes*
C. 1.24	And drynke þat doth the good–a[c] drynke nat out of *tyme*.
C. 1.65	He is lettere of loue and lyeth alle *tymes*;
C. 2.15	For to telle of here atyer no *tyme* haue y nouthe.
C. 3.97	Morreyne or other meschaunc[e]: and mony *tymes* hit falleth

C. 3.160　And maketh men mysdo manye score *tymes*.
C. 3.227　Thow hast hanged on my half enleuene *tymes*
C. 3.293　Mede many *tymes* men ȝeueth bifore þe doynge
C. 3.450　Muchel [euel] is thorw mede mony *tymes* ysoffred
C. 3.463　Spynne oþer speke of god and spille no *tyme*.
C. 3.482　For Machameth and mede [shal] mishap þat *tyme*;
C. 4.20　Sette my sadel vpon soffre-tyl-y-se-my-*tyme*
C. 4.95　To haue mercy on þat man that many *tymes* hym greuede:
C. 4.167　And modiliche vppon mede many *tym[e]* lokede
C. 5.93　That y haue ytynt *tyme* and tyme myspened;
C. 5.93　That y haue ytynt tyme and *tyme* myspened;
C. 5.100　A gobet of his grace and bigynne a *tyme*
C. 5.101　That alle *tymes* of my tyme to profit shal turne.'
C. 5.101　That alle tymes of my *tyme* to profit shal turne.'
C. 5.127　Thorw som trewe trauail and *tyme* spille.
C. 5.173　Freres in here fraytour shal fynde þat *tyme*
C. 6.74　Venged me vele *tymes* other vrete myself withynne
C. 6.96　Amongus marchauntes many *tymes* and nameliche in londone.
C. 6.118　Freres folewen my [f]ore fele *tyme* and ofte
C. 6.151　Amonges monkes y myhte be Ac mony *tyme* y spare
C. 6.183　As leef in lente as out of lente, alle *tymes* ylyche,
C. 6.247　So what buyrn of me borewede abouhte the *tyme*.'
C. 6.281　Myhte neuere me comforte in the mene *tyme*
C. 7.15　Ne ryht sory for my synnes–y seyh neuere þe *tyme*–
C. 7.38　And thus haue y tened trewe men ten hundrit *tymes*.
C. 7.48　In speche and in sparyng of speche; yspilde many a *tyme*
C. 7.131　The sonne for sorwe þerof lees [s]iht for a *tyme*.
C. 7.132　Aboute mydday, when most liht is and mel *tyme* of sayntes,
C. 7.145　That what *tyme* we synnefole men wolden be sory
C. 7.204　A wolde loue me þe lasse a long *tyme* aftur.
C. 7.212　Otherwyse then ȝe wolden they wrouhte ȝow alle *tymes*.
C. 8.10　That ȝe [han] selk and sendel to sowe whan *tyme* is
C. 8.80　Dame worch-when-*tyme*-is [Peres] wyf hehte;
C. 8.121　He sholde be huyred þeraftur when heruost *tyme* come.
C. 8.273　And kepe som til soper *tyme* and site nat to longe;
C. 8.274　At noon ne at no *tyme* and nameliche at sopere
C. 8.312　By this lyflode we mote lyue til l[a]masse *tyme*
C. 8.335　Þat he was werkeman ywrouhte warien þe *tyme*.
C. 9.78　And wo in wynter *tym[e]* and wakynge on nyhtes
C. 9.113　Ne none muracles maken; Ac many *tymes* hem happeth
C. 9.247　Ac aboute mydday at mele *tyme* y mette with hem ofte,
C. 9.295　And seyh the sonne in the sou[t]he sitte þat *tyme*,
C. 9.298　Mony *tyme* this meteles hath maked me to studie
C. 9.314　Hit biful as his fadur saide in farao his *tyme*
C. 9.323　Worth fayre vnderfonge byfore god þat *tyme*
C.10.35　Maketh þe man many *tyme* to stomble yf he stande.
C.10.123　Thenne thouht in þat *tyme* sayde this wordes:
C.10.186　Ne spille speche ne *tyme* ne myspende noyther
C.10.228　Bestes þat now beth shal banne þe *tyme*
C.10.246　Was for mariages ma[ugre kynd]e þat men made þat *tyme*.
C.10.288　ȝe þat han wyues ben war and wo[r]cheth nat out of *tyme*
C.11.48　Mony *tym[e]* mendenauntes myhte goen afyngred.
C.11.53　To plese with proude men senes th[e] pestelenc[e *tyme*]
C.11.69　How he tolde in a *tyme* and tauhte his sone dele:
C.11.103　'And telle me som tokene,' quod y, 'for *tyme* is þat y wende.'
C.11.126　Ac teologie hath tened me ten score *tymes*;
C.11.195　A man may stoupe *tyme* ynowe when he shal tyne þe croune.'
C.11.217　Were wonder goed and wisest in here *tyme*
C.11.236　Ac y wene hit worth of monye as was in noes *tyme*
C.12.91　And on Troianus treuthe to thenke alle *tyme[s]* in ȝoure lyue
C.12.95　Bote loue and leute hem lede ylost is al þe *tyme*
C.12.190　Ne wynde ne wederes as in wynter *tym[e]*,
C.12.203　Bitokeneth treuly in *tyme* comyng aftur
C.12.239　And ȝut more hit maketh men mony *tymes* & ofte
C.13.146　As when þei hadde [ryde in] roteye[*tyme*] anon they reste aftur;
C.13.181　Saue man and mankynde; mony *tymes* me thouhte
C.13.188　In mete out of mesure and mony *tymes* in drynke,
C.14.8　Ne no *tyme* to tyne ne trewe thyng tene,
C.15.4　And many *tym[e]* of this meteles moche thouhte y hadde:
C.15.104　And thenne is *tyme* to take and to appose this doctour
C.15.159　Tene þe eny *tyme* and þou take pacience
C.15.265　And in Elies *tyme* heuene was yclosed
C.16.143　As he þat woet neuere with wham on nyhtes *tyme* to mete:
C.16.174　'Of [fele] *tyme* to fihte,' quod he, 'falsnesse to destruye
C.16.202　'Ȝe beth as a bischop,' quod y, al bourdynge þat *tyme*,
C.16.231　Freres fele *tymes* to þe folk þer they prechen
C.16.232　Mouen motyues, mony *tymes* insolibles and falaes,
C.16.248　And s[e] hit by ensample In somur *tyme* on trees
C.16.356　Ac hit is fer and fele ȝer in franceys *tyme*;
C.16.371　As y tolde þe with tonge a litel *tyme* ypassed;
C.17.33　In tokenynge þat trewe man alle *tymes* sholde
C.17.209　Sholle ouerturne as templers dede; þe *tyme* approcheth faste.
C.17.237　Alle londes into loue And þat in lytel *tyme*;

C.18.35　Thenne is þe flesch a fel wynde and in flouryng *tyme*
C.18.61　Me may se on an appul tree monye *tyme* and ofte
C.18.103　Assay what sauour hit hadde and saide þat *tyme*,
C.18.126　Til plenitudo temporis *tyme* ycome were
C.18.136　To haue yfouhte with þe fende Ar fol *tyme* come.
C.18.138　Til plenitudo temporis [h]y *tyme* aprochede,
C.18.147　Ac tho that sey that selcouth sayde þat *tyme*
C.18.152　Ac y saued ȝow sondry *tymes* and also y fe[d] ȝow
C.18.204　Sente forth his sone As for seruaunt þat *tyme*
C.18.246　Fol trewe tokenes bitwene vs is wh[at] *tyme* þat y met[t]e hym,
C.18.253　Bledden bloed for þat lordes loue [and] hope to blisse þ[e] *tyme*.
C.18.258　Mercy for oure mysdedes as many *tymes*
C.20.5　And lened me to lenten: and long *tyme* y slepte.
C.20.65　And tolde why þ[at] tempest so longe *tyme* durede:
C.20.73　T[w]o theues tho tholed deth þat *tyme*
C.20.83　Maugre his mony teth he was mad þat *tyme*
C.20.423　And yf þe kynge of þe kyngdoem come in þe *tyme*
C.20.426　And y þat am kynge o[f] kynges shal come such a *tyme*
C.21.84　[Wherefore & why wyse men þat *tyme*,
C.21.134　For dauid was douhtiest of dedes in his *tyme*
C.21.384　That haen labored lelly al this lenten *tyme*.
C.21.410　'Ich am a Curatour of holi [kirke] and cam neuer in my *tyme*
C.21.439　As for a trewe tydy man alle *tymes* ylyke.
C.22.26　He shal do more þe[n] mesure mony *tymes* and often

tymme n prop *n.i.d.* A 1; B 1; C 1
A. 5.160　[T]*ymme* þe tynkere & tweyne of his knaues,
B. 5.309　*Tymme* þe Tynkere and tweyne of his [knaues],
C. 6.364　*Tymme* þe Tynekare and tweyne of his knaues,

tyne v *tinen v.(2)* A 3 tyne (2) tyneþ (1); B 6 tyne (4) tyneþ (1) tynt (1);
　　C 6 tyne (4) tynt (1) ytynt (1)
A.10.196　But ȝif þei boþe be forsworn þat bacoun þei *tyne*.
A.11.238　And for his lele beleue, whanne he his lif *tyneþ*,
A.12.86　We han letteres of lyf, he shal his lyf *ty[n]e*.
B. 1.113　Til he brak buxomnesse; his blisse gan he *tyne*
B. 9.175　But þei boþe be forswore þat bacon þei *tyne*.
B.10.355　And for his lele bileue, whan he þe lif *tyneþ*,
B.11.36　A man may stoupe tyme ynoȝ whan he shal *tyne* þe crowne.'
B.18.140　And þat was *tynt* þoruȝ tree, tree shal it wynne.
B.19.342　And tolde hem tidynges, þat *tyne* þei sholde
C. 5.93　That y haue *ytynt* tyme and tyme myspened;
C.10.277　Bote they bothe be forswore þat bacon þei *tyne*.
C.11.195　A man may stoupe tyme ynowe when he shal *tyne* þe croune.'
C.14.8　Ne no tyme to *tyne* ne trewe thyng tene,
C.20.143　And] that was *tynt* thorw tre, tre shal hit wynne.
C.21.342　And toelde hem tydynges, þat *tyne* thei sholde

tynekare > tynkere

tynynge ger *tininge g.(2)* B 1
B. 9.101　[*Tynynge*] of tyme, truþe woot þe soþe,

tynkere n *tinkere n.* A 1; B 3 Tynkere (1) tynkeris (1) Tynkers (1); C 1
　　Tynekare
A. 5.160　[T]*ymme* þe *tynkere* & tweyne of his knaues,
B.Pr.221　Taillours, *Tynkers* and Tollers in Markettes,
B. 5.309　Tymme þe *Tynkere* and tweyne of his [knaues],
B. 5.547　In taillours craft and *tynkeris* craft, what truþe kan deuyse,
C. 6.364　Tymme þe *Tynekare* and tweyne of his knaues,

tynt > tyne

tyraunt n *tiraunt n.* A 1 tirauntis; B 3 tyraunt (1) Tyrauntȝ (1) tirauntȝ
　　(1); C 2 tyraunt (1) tyrauntes (1)
A. 2.161　To atache þis *tiraunt[is]* 'for any tresor, I hote;
B. 2.200　To attachen þo *Tyrauntȝ* 'for any [tresor], I hote;
B.15.420　Of *tirauntȝ* þat teneþ trewe men taken any almesse,
B.20.60　And al þe Couent cam to welcome [a] *tyraunt*
C. 2.214　[T]o atache tho *tyrauntes*, 'for eny tresor, y hote;
C.22.60　And al þe couent cam to welcome a *tyraunt*

titeleris n *titiller n.* B 1; C 1 titerares
B.20.299　Of alle taletelleris and *titeleris* in ydel.
C.22.299　Of all taletellares and *titerares* an ydel.

tiþe n *tithe n.(2)* A 2 tiþe (1) tiþes (1); B 3 tiþe (2) tiþes (1); C 6 tithes
　　(1) tythe (3) tythes (2)
A. 7.68　For holy chirche is holden of hem no *tiþes* to asken,
A. 7.84　For of my corn & my catel [he] crauide þe *tiþ[e]*;
B. 6.76　For holy chirche is [holde] of hem no *tiþe* to [aske],
B. 6.92　For of my corn and [my] catel [h]e craued þe *tiþe*;
B.15.107　*Tiþes* [of vn]trewe þyng ytilied or chaffared,
C. 6.298　Ȝe! þe prest þat thy *tythe* t[a]k[eth], trowe y non other,
C. 6.304　And [what] penaunce the prest shal haue þat p[r]oud is of his
　　　　tithes.
C. 8.78　For holy chirche is ho[ld]e of hem no *tythe* to aske,

C. 8.101   For of my corn and my catel he craued [þe] *tythe*.
C.13.84   As none *tythes* to tythe ne to clothe the nakede
C.16.260   And hatien harlotrie and to vnderfonge þe *tythes*

tiþe num *tithe num.*   B 1
B.15.488   Wiþouten trauaille þe *tiþe* deel þat trewe men biswynken?

tythe v *tithen v.(2)   &> tiþe*   C 3   tythe (2) tythen (1)
C. 6.305   For an hore of here ers wynnynge may hardiloker *tythe*
C.13.73   *Tythen* here goed tre[u]liche, a tol, as hit semeth,
C.13.84   As none tythes to *tythe* ne to clothe the nakede

title n *title n.*   B 4;   C 4   title (3)   tytle (1)
B.11.290   And þe *title* þat ye take ordres by telleþ ye ben auaunced:
B.11.292   For he þat took yow [a] *title* sholde take yow wages,
B.11.300   And a *title*, a tale of no3t, to his liflode at meschief.
B.18.294   We haue no trewe *title* to hem, for þoru3 treson were þei dampned.'
C.13.104   The *tytle* [þat] 3e take ordres by telleth 3e ben avaunsed
C.13.106   For he that toek 3ow a *title* sholde take 3ow wages
C.13.114   And a *title*, a tale of nauht, to his lyflode as hit were.
C.20.324   We haen no trewe *title* to hem for thy tresoun hit maketh.'

tixst tixt(- > text

to adv1 *to adv.(1)*   B 1;   C 2
B. 7.135   Haue þei no gerner to go *to* but god fynt hem alle.'
C. 1.55   'The dep dale and þe derk, so vnsemely to se *to*,
C. 3.365   And withoute ca[s]e to cache [*to*] and come to bothe nombres,

to adv2 *to adv.(2)*   A 2;   B 12;   C 11
A. 7.138   He abideþ wel þe betere þat bummiþ nou3t *to* ofte.'
A. 7.247   And kep sum [til] soper tyme, & sit nou3t *to* longe;
B. 1.141   *To* litel latyn þow lernedest, leode, in þi youþe:
B. 5.184   And drynk nat ouer delically, ne *to* depe neiþer,
B. 6.263   And keep som til soper tyme and sitte no3t *to* longe;
B.11.225   I conseille alle cristne clyue no3t þeron *to* soore,
B.11.368   Of hir kynde and hir colour to carpe it were *to* longe.
B.13.72   In englissh on auenture it sholde be reherced *to* ofte,
B.14.75   [Ac] mesure is [so] muche worþ it may no3t be *to* deere.
B.15.232   In þat secte siþþe *to* selde haþ he ben [knowe].
B.16.148   And which tokne to þis day *to* muche is yvsed,
B.17.43   Than for to techen hem two, and *to* hard to lerne þe leeste!
B.20.27   And bete men ouer bittre, and so[m body] *to* litel,
B.20.359   The plastres of þe person and poudres biten *to* soore;
C. 1.140   *To* lyte [Latyn þow] lernedest, leode, in thy 3owthe:
C. 5.23   Y am *to* wayke to wurcche with sykel or with sythe
C. 5.24   And *to* long, lef me, lowe to stoupe,
C. 6.166   And drynke nat ouer delycatly n[e] *to* depe neyther
C. 8.273   And kepe som til soper tyme and site nat *to* longe;
C.10.185   And holy churche helpe *to*, so sholde no man begge
C.13.178   Of here kynde and here colour to carpe hit were *to* longe.
C.16.357   In [þat] sekte sethe *to* selde hath he be [knowen].
C.18.198   'Muse nat *to* moche þeron,' quod faith, 'til thow more knowe
C.22.27   And bete men ouer bitere and som body *to* litel
C.22.359   The plasteres of þe persoun and poudres b[it]en *to* sore;

to prtcl *to verbal particle   &> for_to*   A 397;   B 1052;   C 1043
A.Pr.4   Wente wyde in þis world wondris *to* here.
A.Pr.7   I was wery [for]wandrit & wente me *to* reste
A.Pr.20   Summe putte hem to plou3, plei3ede ful selde,
A.Pr.29   Coueite not in cuntre *to* cairen aboute
A.Pr.30   For no likerous liflode here likam *to* plese.
A.Pr.33   And somme merþis *to* make as mynstralis conne,
A.Pr.37   And haue wyt at wille *to* wirche 3if hym list.
A.Pr.49   And hadde leue to lei3e al here lif aftir.
A.Pr.52   Grete lobies & longe þat loþ were *to* swynke,
A.Pr.53   Cloþide hem in copis *to* be knowen from oþere;
A.Pr.54   Shopen hem Ermytes here ese *to* haue.
A.Pr.61   Siþen charite haþ ben chapman & chief *to* shryue lordis
A.Pr.70   Comen vp knelynge *to* kissen his bulle.
A.Pr.73   Þus [3e gyuen 3oure] gold glotonis *to* helpe
A.Pr.76   His sel shulde not be sent *to* disseyue þe peple.
A.Pr.82   *To* haue a licence & leue at lundoun *to* dwelle,
A.Pr.82   *To* haue a licence & leue at lundoun *to* dwelle,
A.Pr.83   *To* synge for symonye for siluer is swete.
A.Pr.93   *To* preche þe peple & pore men to fede
A.Pr.93   *To* preche þe peple & pore men *to* fede
A.Pr.95   And ben clerkis of þe kinges bench þe cuntre *to* shende.
A.Pr.108   Of þe ryn & of þe rochel, þe rost *to* defie!'
A. 1.11   And seide 'mercy madame, what is þis *to* mene?'
A. 1.17   And þerfore me hi3te þe erþe *to* helpe 3ow ichone
A. 1.19   In mesurable maner *to* make 3ow at ese;
A. 1.23   Þat on is vesture fro chele þe *to* saue;
A. 1.53   And kynde wyt be wardeyn 3oure welþe *to* kepe,
A. 1.64   Counseilid kaym *to* kiln his broþer,
A. 1.73   'Holy chirche I am,' quaþ heo, 'þou au3test me *to* knowe;

A. 1.75   Þou brou3test me borewis my biddyng *to* werche,
A. 1.76   *To* loue me lelly whiles þi lif duriþ.'
A. 1.78   Prei3ede hire pitously [*to*] prei3e for my sennes,
A. 1.79   And ek kenne me kyndely on crist *to* beleue,
A. 1.84   I do it on Deus caritas *to* deme þe soþe.
A. 1.97   [Di]de hem swere on h[ere] swerd *to* serue treuþe euere.
A. 1.99   And nou3t *to* fasten a friday in fyue score wynter,
A. 1.107   Tau3te hem þoru3 þe trinite þe troube *to* knowe:
A. 1.108   *To* be buxum at his bidding; he bad hem nou3t ellis.
A. 1.132   No dedly synne *to* do, di3e þei3 þou shuldist.
A. 1.134   Loke þou suffre hym *to* seyn & siþþe lere it aftir.
A. 1.142   Mekliche for oure misdedis *to* amende vs alle.
A. 1.145   *To* haue pite on þat peple þat pynede hym to deþe.
A. 1.150   Þei3 3e ben mi3ty *to* mote beþ mek of 3our werkis;
A. 1.173   And a lering to lewide men þe lattere *to* dele.
A. 1.177   *To* counforte þe carful acumbrid wiþ synne.
A. 2.4   Kenne me be sum craft *to* k[now]e þe false'.
A. 2.30   3if þou wilnest *to* wone wiþ treuþe in his blisse.
A. 2.35   Sire symonye is assent *to* asele þe chartres
A. 2.38   Þer nas halle ne hous *to* herberwe þe peple,
A. 2.46   Alle *to* wytnesse wel what þe writ wolde.
A. 2.48   *To* be fastnid wiþ fals þe fyn is arerid.
A. 2.51   And he[o] be bou[n] at his bode his bidding *to* fulfille,
A. 2.53   And as sire symonye wile segge *to* sewen his wille.
A. 2.59   *To* be present in pride for pouere [or for] riche,
A. 2.60   Wiþ þe Erldom of enuye for euere *to* laste,
A. 2.67   Þei *to* haue & *to* holde & here eires aftir
A. 2.67   Þei *to* haue & *to* holde & here eires aftir
A. 2.70   Here soulis to sathanas *to* synken in pyne,
A. 2.71   Þere *to* wone wiþ wrong while god is in heuene.'
A. 2.81   Such weddyng *to* werche *to* wraþþe wiþ treuþe;
A. 2.81   Such weddyng *to* werche *to* wraþþe wiþ treuþe;
A. 2.84   God grauntide *to* gyue mede to treuþe.
A. 2.87   Worþi is þe werkman his mede *to* haue,
A. 2.101   And 3if þe iustice iugge hire *to* be ioyned with fals,
A. 2.115   And comen to counforte fro care þe false,
A. 2.119   Þat he[o] grauntiþ *to* gon wiþ a good wille
A. 2.120   *To* lundoun *to* loke 3if þat lawe wolde
A. 2.125   *To* wende wiþ hem to westmynstre to wytnesse þ[is] dede.
A. 2.125   *To* wende wiþ hem to westmynstre to wytnesse þ[is] dede.
A. 2.126   Þanne car[i]de hy fo[r] capelis *to* carien hem þider;
A. 2.143   And makiþ of lyere a lang carte *to* leden al þis oþere,
A. 2.147   I haue no tom *to* telle þe tail þat hem folewiþ
A. 2.161   *To* atache þis tiraunt[is] 'for any tresour, I hote;
A. 2.165   Symonye & cyuyle, I sen[d]e hem *to* warne
A. 2.170   And wi3tliche wente *to* warne þe false,
A. 2.173   And gile doþ him *to* go agast for *to* dei3e.
A. 2.175   Besshette hym in here shoppis *to* shewen here ware;
A. 2.176   Aparailide hym as a prentice þe peple *to* serue
A. 2.186   For to wone wiþ hem, watris *to* loke.
A. 2.187   Spiceris speke wiþ h[i]m *to* aspie here ware,
A. 2.193   Ac he haþ leue *to* lepen out as ofte as him likiþ,
A. 2.197   Ac trewely *to* telle heo tremblide for fere,
A. 3.4   *To* take mede þe maide & make hire at ese.
A. 3.11   Ac þere was merþe & mynstralcie mede *to* plese;
A. 3.25   Wiþ þat come clerkis *to* conforten hire þe same,
A. 3.29   *To* loue hem lelly & lordis hem make,
A. 3.41   Among clerkis & kni3tes consience *to* felle'.
A. 3.49   Sikir shulde þi soule be heuene *to* haue'.
A. 3.61   *To* writen in wyndowis of 3oure wel dedis,
A. 3.62   Oþer *to* grede aftir godis men whan 3e [g]iue dolis,
A. 3.66   Betwyn þe king & þe comunes, to kepe þe lawis,
A. 3.67   As *to* punisshen on pillories & on py[n]yng stolis
A. 3.77   Of alle suche selleris siluer *to* take,
A. 3.79   Ryng[es] or oþer richesse, þ[ise] regratour[is] *to* meynteyne.
A. 3.81   And suffre þe selle sumdel a3ens resoun.'
A. 3.89   *To* haue 3eftis [or 3eris3iuys] in 3ouþe or in elde.
A. 3.93   [Curteisly] þe king compsiþ *to* telle;
A. 3.103   Þanne was consience callid *to* comen & aperen
A. 3.128   *To* vnfetere þe fals, fle where hym lykiþ.
A. 3.131   *To* be cursid in constorie heo countiþ not a risshe;
A. 3.140   *To* holde lemmanis & lotebies alle here lif dayes,
A. 3.150   Lawe is so lordlich & loþ *to* make ende,
A. 3.155   For pouere men mowe haue no power *to* pleyne [þei3] hem smerte,
A. 3.158   *To* haue space *to* speke, spede 3if she mi3te.
A. 3.158   *To* haue space *to* speke, spede 3if she mi3te.
A. 3.161   For consience acusiþ þe *to* cunge [þe] for euere.'
A. 3.165   And þou knowist, consience, I ca[m] nou3t *to* chide,
A. 3.166   Ne *to* depraue þi persone wiþ a proud herte.
A. 3.180   And dreddist *to* be ded for a dym cloud,
A. 3.183   And bar here bras on þi bak to caleis *to* selle,
A. 3.185   And made hym merþe mournyng *to* leue,
A. 3.187   Dede hym hoppe for hope *to* haue me at wille.

A. 3.194	*To* leuen his lordsshipe for a litel siluer,
A. 3.197	*To* ʒiuen hise men mede þat mekly hym seruen;
A. 3.198	To alienes, to alle men, *to* honoure hem with ʒeftis.
A. 3.201	Þoruʒ ʒeftis han ʒonge men *to* [ʒerne] & to ride.
A. 3.201	Þoruʒ ʒeftis han ʒonge men to [ʒerne] & *to* ride.
A. 3.203	And mediþ men hymself *to* mayntene here lawis;
A. 3.208	Þe king haþ [m]ede of his men *to* make pes in londis;
A. 3.216	Mede is worþi þe maistrie *to* haue'.
A. 3.226	*To* mayntene mysdoeris mede þei taken,
A. 3.240	God sente hym *to* segge be samuels mouþ
A. 3.245	*To* be buxum & boun his bidding to fulfille.
A. 3.245	To be buxum & boun his bidding *to* fulfille.
A. 3.246	Wende þidir with þin ost wommen *to* kille;
A. 3.256	Such a meschef mede made þe kyng [*to*] haue
A. 3.258	Þe culorum of þis [cas] kepe I not fo shewe;
A. 4.7	'Rape þe *to* riden, & resoun þat þou fecche.
A. 4.8	Comaunde hym þat he come my counseil *to* here,
A. 4.16	'I shal araye me *to* ride,' quaþ resoun, 'reste þe a while,'
A. 4.20	Hange on hym þe heuy bridel *to* holde his hed lowe,
A. 4.25	Folewide hem faste for hy hadden *to* done
A. 4.26	In cheker & in chauncerie, *to* be dischargid of þinges,
A. 4.42	He mayntenib his men *to* murþre myne hynen,
A. 4.47	I am not hardy [for hym vnneþe] *to* loke.'
A. 4.50	*To* make his pes with his panis & profride hym manye,
A. 4.60	Wrong þanne on wysdom wepi[de] hym *to* helpe,
A. 4.61	For of hise penys he proffride handy dandy *to* paye.
A. 4.63	And tok mede wiþ mercy *to* wynne.
A. 4.69	*To* ouercome þe king wiþ catel ʒif þei miʒte.
A. 4.72	& comaundid a cunstable *to* caste hym in yrens]:
A. 4.81	Þanne gan mede *to* meke hire, & mercy besouʒte,
A. 4.83	'Haue þis of me, man,' quaþ heo, '*to* amende þi skaþe,
A. 4.86	*To* haue mercy on þat man þat mysdede hym ofte:
A. 4.94	And ofte þe boldere be *to* bete myn hynen.
A. 4.97	Summe redde resoun *to* haue reuþe on þat shrewe,
A. 4.98	And *to* counseile þe king & consience boþe;
A. 4.100	'Rede me not,' quaþ resoun, 'no reuþe *to* haue
A. 4.106	And haten [*to*] here harlotrie oþer mouþe it;
A. 4.108	And do it in dede *to* drawe vs to goode;
A. 4.118	Whil mede haþ þe maistrie *to* mo[te] in þis halle.
A. 4.121	Þat I were king wiþ croune *to* kepe a reaume,
A. 4.142	Couþe nouʒt warpen a word *to* wiþsigge resoun,
A. 4.146	'Ac it is wel hard, be myn hed, herto *to* bringe it.
A. 4.147	And alle my lige ledis *to* lede þus euene.'
A. 4.155	'I am redy,' quaþ resoun, '*to* reste wiþ ʒow euere;
A. 5.2	*To* here matynes & masse, and to þe mete aftir.
A. 5.23	How consience wiþ a cros cumside *to* preche.
A. 5.26	And preyede pernel hire purfil *to* leue
A. 5.28	Thomas he tauʒte *to* take two staues
A. 5.30	He warnide watte his wyf was *to* blame
A. 5.32	He chargide chapmen *to* chastice here children:
A. 5.37	And siþþe he redde religioun here rewel[e] *to* holde
A. 5.44	And made wil *to* wepe watir wiþ his eiʒen.
A. 5.49	For to affaiten hire flessh þat fers was *to* synne:
A. 5.51	And suffre *to* be misseid, & so dide I neuere.
A. 5.55	*To* make mercy for his mysdede betwyn god & hym
A. 5.59	And carfulliche his cope [comsiþ] he *to* shewe.
A. 5.67	And wroþliche he wroþ his fest, *to* wreke hym he þouʒte,
A. 5.74	And blamide hym behynde his bak *to* bringe hym in fame;
A. 5.75	*To* apeire hym be my power I pursuide wel ofte,
A. 5.76	And belowen hym to lordis *to* don hym lese siluer,
A. 5.86	*To* preye for þe peple as þe prest techiþ,
A. 5.116	And was his prentis ypliʒt his profit *to* loke.
A. 5.117	Ferst I lernide *to* leiʒe a lef oþer tweiʒe;
A. 5.118	Wykkidly *to* weiʒe was my ferste lessoun.
A. 5.123	Þanne drouʒ I me among drapers my donet *to* lere,
A. 5.124	*To* drawe þe list along, þe lengere it semide;
A. 5.130	And spak to þe spynstere *to* spynnen it softe.
A. 5.133	I bouʒte hire barly; heo breuʒ it *to* selle.
A. 5.147	And ca[iriþ] hym to [k]ir[k]eward hise [coupe] *to* shewe.
A. 5.169	And at þe newe feire nempnide it *to* selle.
A. 5.172	Þere were chapmen chosen þat chaffare *to* preise;
A. 5.178	Til robyn þe ropere was red *to* arisen,
A. 5.193	He hadde no strengþe or stonde er he his staf hadde,
A. 5.194	And þanne gan he *to* go [lik a glemans bicche],
A. 5.196	As whoso leide lynes *to* lacche wiþ [foules].
A. 5.209	And auowide *to* faste, for hungir or þrist:
A. 5.240	*To* waxen helle for euere ʒif þat hope nere.
A. 5.242	Ne neuere wen[e] *to* wynne wiþ craft þat [I owe],
A. 5.254	*To* haue grace to seke treuþe; god leue þat hy moten!
A. 5.254	To haue grace *to* seke treuþe; god leue þat hy moten!
A. 6.28	And sede me sure hym [siþþe] *to* serue hym for euere;
A. 6.36	For, þeiʒ I sey it myself, I serue hym *to* pay.
A. 6.44	'Nay, be þe peril of my soule!' quaþ piers & gan *to* swere:

A. 6.47	Ac ʒe þat wilneþ *to* wende, þis is þe weye þider:
A. 6.70	And þanne shalt þou [se] sey soþ, so it be *to* done;
A. 6.74	And alle þe wallis ben of wyt *to* holde wil þeroute;
A. 6.75	Þe kirnelis ben of cristendom þat kynde *to* saue,
A. 6.89	*To* weue [vp] þe wyket þat [þe wif] shette
A. 6.92	And ʒif grace graunte þe *to* gon in [on] þis wise,
A. 6.97	And pokiþ [forþ] pride *to* preise þiselue.
A. 6.100	Ikeiʒid & ycliket *to* kepe þe þeroute
A. 6.102	Þus miʒt þou lese his loue, *to* lete wel be þiselue,
A. 6.114	*To* gete ingang at any gate but grace be þe more.'
A. 7.4	I haue an half akir *to* er[e]n be þe heiʒe weiʒe;
A. 7.20	Chesiblis for chapellis chirches *to* honoure.
A. 7.33	And fecche þe hom fauconis þe foulis *to* kille,
A. 7.37	*To* fulfille þe foreward whiles I may stande'.
A. 7.46	But it be of wysdom or of wyt þi werkmen *to* chaste;
A. 7.49	For it arn þe deuelis disours I do þe *to* vndirstonde.
A. 7.59	And whoso helpiþ me *to* eren, or any þing swynke,
A. 7.68	For holy chirche is holden of hem no tiþes *to* asken;
A. 7.72	His sone hattiþ suffre þi souereynes *to* hauen here wille
A. 7.82	*To* haue reles & remissioun, on þat rental I leue.
A. 7.86	He is holden, I hope, *to* haue me in mynde,
A. 7.96	And helpe my cultir *to* kerue & close þe forewis.'
A. 7.98	*To* erien þis half akir helpen hym manye;
A. 7.102	Eche man on his maner made hymself *to* done,
A. 7.103	And summe *to* plese perkyn pykide vp þe wedis.
A. 7.105	*To* ouersen hem hymself; whoso best wrouʒte
A. 7.108	And holpen [*to*] ere þe half akir wiþ 'hey trolly lolly'.
A. 7.110	'But ʒe rise þe raþere, & rape ʒow *to* werche,
A. 7.116	'We haue none [lymes] *to* laboure wiþ, lord, ygracid be ʒe;
A. 7.123	And I am his [h]olde hyne & auʒte hym *to* warne.
A. 7.127	Boþe *to* setten & to sowen, & sauen his telþe,
A. 7.127	Boþe to setten & *to* sowen, & sauen his telþe,
A. 7.132	Til god of his grace gare h[e]m *to* arise.
A. 7.147	*To* kepen hym as couenaunt was fro curside shrewis,
A. 7.148	Fro wastours þat waite wynneres *to* shende.
A. 7.152	'I was not wonid *to* werche,' quaþ wastour, 'now wile I not begynne,'
A. 7.169	*To* abate þe barly bred & þe benis ygrounde,
A. 7.176	And doluen drit & dung *to* ditte out hunger.
A. 7.181	And become knaues *to* kepe peris bestis,
A. 7.183	Al for coueitise of his corn *to* [cacche] awey hungir;
A. 7.186	Þanne hadde piers pite & preiʒede hungir *to* wende
A. 7.189	Of beggeris & bidderis what best is *to* done.
A. 7.194	Treuþe tauʒte me ones *to* loue hem ichone
A. 7.197	And how I miʒte amaistrie hem & make hem *to* werche.'
A. 7.205	Wiþ fuyr or wiþ false men, fond suche [*to*] knowen;
A. 7.209	Þat nedy ben or nakid, & nouʒt han *to* spende,
A. 7.228	"He þat haþ shal haue *to* helpe þere nede is,
A. 7.230	And þat he weniþ wel *to* haue I wile it be hym bereuid".
A. 7.246	And sende þe of his saus *to* sauoure þi lippes,
A. 7.255	And be fayn be my feiþ his fesik *to* leten,
A. 7.256	And lerne *to* laboure wiþ lond lest liflode hym faile.
A. 7.264	'I haue no peny,' quaþ piers, 'pulettis *to* biggen,
A. 7.269	Ne no cokenay, be crist, colopis *to* maken.
A. 7.272	*To* drawe on feld my dong while þe drouʒt lastiþ.
A. 7.274	Be þat I hope *to* haue heruest in my croft,
A. 7.279	And profride peris [þis] present *to* plese þerewiþ hungir.
A. 7.282	[Grene porret and pesen; *to* [peysen] him þei þouʒte].
A. 7.285	Wiþ good ale & glotonye h[y] gart hym *to* slepe.
A. 7.291	Laboureris þat haue no land [*to*] lyue on [but] here handis
A. 7.292	Deyneþ nouʒt *to* dyne a day niʒt olde wortis.
A. 7.299	Suche lawis *to* loke laboureris to chast[e].
A. 7.299	Suche lawis to loke laboureris *to* chast[e].
A. 7.304	He shal awake [þoruʒ] water wastours *to* chaste;
A. 7.307	And so seiþ satourne & sente ʒow *to* warne.
A. 8.2	*To* take his tem & [tilien þe erþe],
A. 8.6	And [alle] þat holpen *to* erien or to sowen,
A. 8.6	And [alle] þat holpen to erien or *to* sowen,
A. 8.11	Han pardoun þoruʒ purcatorie *to* passe wel sone,
A. 8.12	Wiþ patriarkes in paradis *to* pleiʒe þereaftir.
A. 8.19	At þe day of dom at here deis *to* sitten.
A. 8.24	Aʒens clene consience here catel *to* selle.
A. 8.28	And make mesonis deux þerewiþ myseis[e] *to* helpe,
A. 8.29	Wykkide weyes wiʒtly *to* amende,
A. 8.48	And of no pore peple no peny[worþ] *to* take.
A. 8.55	Ac *to* bigge watir ne wynd, ne wyt is þe þridde,
A. 8.58	*To* waxen & wanyen where þat god likiþ.
A. 8.68	But ʒif þe suggestioun be soþ þat [shapiþ hem *to*] begge.
A. 8.114	And shewiþ it vs be ensaumple oureselue *to* wisse.
A. 8.117	Haue þei no garner [*to* go] to, but god fynt hem alle.'
A. 8.131	Manye tyme þis metelis han mad me *to* stodie,
A. 8.138	Daniel seide, 'sire king, þi sweuene is *to* mene
A. 8.139	Þat [vncouþe] kniʒt[is] shal come þi kingdom *to* cleyme;

A. 8.148	Þat Iosep was Iustice Egipt *to* kepe–
A. 8.149	Al þis makiþ me on metelis *to* þinke
A. 8.157	Now haþ þe pope power pardoun *to* graunte
A. 8.158	Þe peple wiþoute penaunce [*to* passe to Ioye]?
A. 8.163	A[c] *to* triste on þis trionalis, trewely, me þinkeþ,
A. 8.166	Vpon trist of 3our tresour trienalis *to* haue
A. 8.167	Be þou neuere þe baldere *to* breke þe ten hestis;
A. 8.170	[*To* purchace pardoun and þe popes bulles],
A. 8.172	And come [alle] before crist acountes *to* 3elden,
A. 8.179	Forþi I counseil alle cristene [*to*] cri3e god mercy,
A. 8.180	And marie his modir *to* be mene betwene,
A. 8.182	Suche werkis *to* werche, whiles we ben here,
A. 9.13	'Where þat dowel dwelli[þ], do me *to* wisse'.
A. 9.16	'Contra,' quaþ I as a clerk & comside *to* dispute:
A. 9.21	He is oþerwhile elliswhere *to* wisse þe peple.'
A. 9.27	Makeþ þe man many tymes *to* falle & to stande.
A. 9.27	Makeþ þe man many tymes to falle & *to* stande.
A. 9.42	For he strengþeþ þe *to* stonde & steriþ þi soule
A. 9.47	God wile suffre þe *to* dei3e so for þiself hast þe maistrie.'
A. 9.48	'I haue no kynde knowyng,' quaþ I, '*to* conseyue þi wordis,
A. 9.52	And [g]iue þe grace on þis erþe in good lif *to* ende'.
A. 9.53	Þus I wente wydewhere dowel *to* seken,
A. 9.57	*To* lerne þe laies þat louely [foulis] maden.
A. 9.68	Where dowel dwelliþ, & do me *to* wisse.'
A. 9.70	Arn þre faire vertues, & ben not f[e]r *to* fynde
A. 9.84	[3]e wise suffriþ þe vnwise with 3ow *to* libbe,
A. 9.87	Is hokid at þat on ende *to* holde men in good lif.
A. 9.88	A pik is in þat potent *to* pungen adoun þe wykkide,
A. 9.89	Þat waiten any wikkidnesse dowel *to* tenen.
A. 9.90	And as dowel & dobet dede hem *to* vndirstonde,
A. 9.91	Þei han crounide o king *to* kepe hem alle,
A. 9.93	And were vnbuxum at his bidding, and bold *to* don ille,
A. 9.98	Corounid on *to* be kyng & be h[ere] counseil werchen,
A. 9.103	More kynde knowyng I coueyte *to* lere,
A. 9.113	I durste meue no mater *to* make hym to iangle,
A. 9.113	I durste meue no mater to make hym *to* iangle,
A. 9.115	*To* putte forþ sum purpos [to] prouen hise wittes.
A. 9.115	To putte forþ sum purpos [*to*] prouen hise wittes.
A.10.15	Beþ maistris of þis maner þis maide *to* kepe.
A.10.22	Þise sixe ben yset *to* saue þe castel;
A.10.23	*To* kepe þise womman þise wise men ben chargid,
A.10.39	As muche *to* mene [as] man with his soule,
A.10.54	In manis brayn is he most & mi3tiest *to* knowe.
A.10.68	And 3if þei ben pore & cateles, *to* kepe hem fro ille,
A.10.69	Þanne is holichirche owyng *to* helpe hem & saue
A.10.72	Is chief souereyn ouer hymself his soule *to* 3eme,
A.10.78	*To* routen ne to resten ne ro[t]en in þin herte;
A.10.78	To routen ne *to* resten ne ro[t]en in þin herte;
A.10.84	And alle kynde scoleris in scole *to* lerne.
A.10.85	Þanne is dobet *to* ben ywar for betyng of þe 3arde,
A.10.101	For 3if þou comsist *to* clymbe, & coueitest herre,
A.10.115	*To* be blissid for þi beryng, [3]e, b[e]ggere þei3 þou were.
A.10.118	Þus in dred liþ dowel, [and] dobet *to* suffre,
A.10.130	Such wer[kis] *to* werche [þat] he is wiþ paied.
A.10.143	An aungel in angir hi3te h[e]m *to* wende
A.10.144	Into þis wrecchide world *to* wonen & to libben
A.10.144	Into þis wrecchide world to wonen & *to* libben
A.10.158	*To* kepe his kynrede fro kaymes, þei couplide nou3t togideris;
A.10.163	And is as muche *to* mene, among vs alle,
A.10.166	Swiþe *to* shapen a sship of shidis & bordis;
A.10.187	*To* 3iuen a 3ong wenche to an old feble,
A.10.195	*To* folewe aftir þe flicche, fecche þei it neuere;
A.10.211	Vngracious *to* gete loue or any good ellis,
A.10.215	But 3if god [g]iue h[e]m grace here *to* amende.
A.10.216	Þanne is dowel *to* dreden, & dobet to suffre,
A.10.216	Þanne is dowel to dreden, & dobet *to* suffre,
A.11.5	'Wel art þou wys, wyt,' quaþ she, 'any wisdomis *to* telle
A.11.8	Wiþ suche wise wordis *to* wisse any foolis!
A.11.20	And lede forþ a loueday *to* lette þe treuþe,
A.11.41	And bringe forþ a ballid resoun, t[a]k[e] bernard *to* witnesse,
A.11.42	And putte forþ presumpcioun *to* proue þe soþe.
A.11.43	Þus þei dryuelen at here deis þe deite *to* knowe,
A.11.47	Is non *to* nymen hym In ne his [noye] amende.
A.11.59	*To* pleise wiþ proude men, siþen þe pestilence tyme,
A.11.62	*To* tellen of þe trinite to be holden a sire,
A.11.62	To tellen of þe trinite *to* be holden a sire,
A.11.63	And fyndiþ forþ fantasies oure feiþ *to* apeire,
A.11.71	And make men *to* mysbeleue þat musen on here wordis.
A.11.75	Wilneþ neuere *to* wyte why that god wolde
A.11.76	Suffre sathan his sed *to* bigile,
A.11.79	And for his muchel mercy *to* amende vs here.
A.11.80	For alle þat wilneþ *to* wyte þe [whyes] of god almi3t,
A.11.82	Þat euere eft wilneþ *to* wyte why [þat] god wolde
A.11.83	Suffren sathan his sed *to* bigile,
A.11.89	Siþen he wilneþ *to* wyte which þei ben alle.
A.11.103	[*To*] kenne me kyndely to knowe what is dowel'.
A.11.103	[*To*] kenne me kyndely to knowe what is dowel'.
A.11.114	'Axe þe hei3e wey,' quaþ heo, 'from henis *to* suffre
A.11.123	Þat iche wi3t in wille his wyt þe *to* shewen;
A.11.129	And alle þe musons of musik I made hire [*to*] knowe.
A.11.131	Aristotel & oþere mo *to* arguen I tau3te;
A.11.161	Nigromancie & per[i]mansie þe pouke *to* reisen;
A.11.164	Foundit hem formest folk *to* desceyue.
A.11.180	*To* lere at 3ow dowel & dobet þereaftir,
A.11.181	And siþen aftirward *to* se sumwhat of dobest'.
A.11.188	*To* breke beggeris bred & bakken hem with cloþis,
A.11.198	Prince ouer godis peple *to* prechen or to chaste.
A.11.198	Prince ouer godis peple to prechen or *to* chaste.
A.11.203	Ne no leperis ouer lond ladies *to* shryue.
A.11.210	Þat out of couent & cloistre coueiten *to* libben".
A.11.247	We be holde hei3ly *to* herie & honoure,
A.11.251	And siþen he[þen] *to* helpe in hope hem to amende.
A.11.251	And siþen he[þen] to helpe in hope hem *to* amende.
A.11.252	*To* harme hem ne slen hem god hi3te vs neuere,
A.11.259	*To* wyte what is dowel witterly in herte,
A.11.276	And 3if I shal werke be here werkis *to* wynne me heuene,
A.11.286	Wiþoute penaunce of purcatorie *to* haue paradis for euere.
A.11.290	Cristene kynde *to* kille to deþe?
A.11.297	And is as muche *to* mene, to men þat ben lewid,
A.11.301	Þe help of þe holy gost *to* answere hem [alle]'.
A.11.306	And is *to* mene in oure mouþ, more ne lesse,
A.12.2	I haue do my deuer þe dowel *to* teche,
A.12.6	Þe were lef *to* lerne but loþ for to stodie;
A.12.18	Sitthe theologie þe trewe *to* tellen hit defendeþ;
A.12.21	Til þo wrecches ben in wil here synne *to* lete."
A.12.32	For he cam not by cause *to* lerne to dowel
A.12.32	For he cam not by cause to lerne *to* dowel
A.12.39	*To* be hure man 3if I most for eueremore after,
A.12.65	[*To* kyllyn him 3if I can, þei kynde wit helpe].
A.12.112	*To* lyue as þat lord lykyþ þat lyf in hem putte:
B.Pr.4	Wente wide in þis world wondres *to* here.
B.Pr.7	I was wery forwandred and wente me *to* reste
B.Pr.20	Some putten hem *to* plou3, pleiden ful selde,
B.Pr.29	Coueiten no3t in contree *to* [cairen] aboute
B.Pr.30	For no likerous liflode hire likame *to* plese.
B.Pr.33	And somme murþes *to* make as Mynstralles konne,
B.Pr.37	And han wit at wille *to* werken if [hem liste].
B.Pr.49	And hadden leue *to* lyen al hire lif after.
B.Pr.51	To ech a tale þat þei tolde hire tonge was tempred *to* lye
B.Pr.52	Moore þan *to* seye sooþ, it semed bi hire speche.
B.Pr.55	Grete lobies and longe þat loþe were *to* swynke
B.Pr.56	Cloþed hem in copes *to* ben knowen from oþere;
B.Pr.57	Shopen hem heremytes hire ese *to* haue.
B.Pr.64	Siþ charite haþ ben chapman and chief *to* shryue lordes
B.Pr.73	Comen vp knelynge *to* kissen hi[s] bull[e].
B.Pr.76	Thus [ye] gyuen [youre] gold glotons *to* [helpe]
B.Pr.79	His seel sholde no3t be sent *to* deceyue þe peple.
B.Pr.85	*To* haue a licence and leue at London to dwelle,
B.Pr.85	To haue a licence and leue at London *to* dwelle,
B.Pr.86	[*To*] syngen for symonie for siluer is swete.
B.Pr.100	I parceyued of þe power þat Peter hadde *to* kepe,
B.Pr.101	*To* bynden and vnbynden as þe book telleþ,
B.Pr.105	There [crist is in] kyngdom, *to* close and to shette.
B.Pr.105	There [crist is in] kyngdom, to close and *to* shette.
B.Pr.106	And *to* opene it to hem and heuene blisse shewe.
B.Pr.108	And power presumed in hem a pope *to* make
B.Pr.109	*To* han [þe] power þat Peter hadde–impugnen I nelle–
B.Pr.113	Might of þe communes made hym *to* regne.
B.Pr.120	*To* tilie and to trauaille as trewe lif askeþ.
B.Pr.120	To tilie and *to* trauaille as trewe lif askeþ.
B.Pr.122	Shopen lawe and leaute, ech [lif] *to* knowe his owene.
B.Pr.129	Lowed *to* speke in latyn, for lewed men ne koude
B.Pr.168	*To* bugge a belle of bras or of bri3t siluer
B.Pr.171	Wher he ryt or rest or r[om]eþ *to* pleye;
B.Pr.186	*To* c[r]acchen vs & al oure kynde þou3 we cropen vnder benches;
B.Pr.187	Forþi I counseille al þe commune *to* late þe cat worþe,
B.Pr.188	And be we neuere [so] bolde þe belle hym *to* shewe.
B.Pr.206	But suffren as hymself wolde *to* [slen þat] hym likeþ,
B.Pr.207	Coupled and vncoupled *to* cacche what þei mowe.
B.Pr.230	Of þe Ryn and of þe Rochel þe roost *to* defie!'
B. 1.17	And þerfore he hi3te þe erþe *to* helpe yow echone
B. 1.19	In mesurable manere *to* make yow at ese;
B. 1.23	That oon [is] vesture from [chele] þee *to* saue;
B. 1.55	And kynde wit be wardeyn youre welþe *to* kepe
B. 1.66	Counseilled Kaym *to* killen his broþer,
B. 1.75	'Holi chirche I am', quod she; 'þow ou3test me *to* knowe.

B. 1.77   [Thow] brouȝtest me borwes my biddyng *to* [werche],
B. 1.78   *To* louen me leelly while þi lif dureþ.'
B. 1.80   Preide hire pitously [*to*] preye for my synnes;
B. 1.81   And [ek] kenne me kyndely on crist *to* bileue,
B. 1.86   I do it on Deus caritas *to* deme þe soþe.
B. 1.99   Dide hem sweren on hir swerd *to* seruen truþe euere.
B. 1.101   And nauȝt *to* fasten o friday in fyue score wynter,
B. 1.109   Tauȝte hem [þoruȝ] þe Trinitee [þe] treuþe *to* knowe:
B. 1.110   *To* be buxom at his biddyng, he bad hem nouȝt ellis.
B. 1.115   Into a deep derk helle *to* dwelle þere for euere;
B. 1.122   Til god of his goodnesse [garte þe heuene *to* stekie]
B. 1.144   No dedly synne *to* do, deye þeiȝ þow sholdest.
B. 1.146   Loke þow suffre hym *to* seye and siþen lere it after.
B. 1.168   Mekely for oure mysdedes *to* amenden vs alle.
B. 1.171   *To* haue pite [on] þat peple þat peyned hym to deþe.
B. 1.176   Thouȝ ye be myȝt[y] *to* mote beeþ meke [of] youre werkes,
B. 1.199   And lernynge to lewed men þe latter *to* deele.
B. 1.203   *To* conforten þe carefulle acombred wiþ synne.
B. 2.4   Kenne me by som craft *to* knowe þe false.
B. 2.14   Orientals and Ewages enuenymes *to* destroye.
B. 2.22   And bilowen h[ym] to lordes þat lawes han *to* kepe.
B. 2.31   And haþ yeuen me mercy *to* marie wiþ myselue,
B. 2.49   And haue power *to* punysshe hem; þanne put forþ þi reson.
B. 2.57   *To* marien þis mayde [was] many m[a]n assembled,
B. 2.66   And as a Brocour brouȝte hire *to* be wiþ fals enioyned.
B. 2.68   Thei assented for siluer *to* seye as boþe wolde.
B. 2.71   And preide Cyuylle *to* see and Symonye to rede it.
B. 2.71   And preide Cyuylle to see and Symonye *to* rede it.
B. 2.80   *To* be Princes in pride and pouerte to despise,
B. 2.80   To be Princes in pride and pouerte *to* despise,
B. 2.81   *To* bakbite and to bosten and bere fals witnesse,
B. 2.81   To bakbite and *to* bosten and bere fals witnesse,
B. 2.82   *To* scorne and to scolde and sclaundre to make;
B. 2.82   To scorne and *to* scolde and sclaundre to make;
B. 2.82   To scorne and to scolde and sclaundre *to* make;
B. 2.83   Vnbuxome and bolde *to* breke þe ten hestes;
B. 2.94   And al day *to* drynken at diuerse Tauernes,
B. 2.95   And þere *to* Iangle and Iape and Iugge hir euencristen,
B. 2.96   And in fastynge dayes *to* frete er ful tyme were.
B. 2.97   And þanne *to* sitten and soupen til sleep hem assaille,
B. 2.100   And þanne wanhope *to* awaken h[y]m so wiþ no wil to amende
B. 2.100   And þanne wanhope to awaken h[y]m so wiþ no wil *to* amende
B. 2.102   'And þei *to* haue and to holde, and hire heires after,
B. 2.102   'And þei to haue and *to* holde, and hire heires after,
B. 2.106   Hire soules to Sathan *to* suffre with hym peynes,
B. 2.107   And with hym *to* wonye [in] wo while god is in heuene.'
B. 2.117   Swic[h] weddyng[e] *to* werche to wraþe wiþ truþe;
B. 2.117   Swic[h] weddyng[e] to werche *to* wraþe wiþ truþe;
B. 2.120   God graunte[d] *to* gyue Mede to truþe,
B. 2.123   For Dignus est operarius his hire *to* haue,
B. 2.137   And [if þe] Iustic[e] Iugg[e] hire *to* be Ioyned [wiþ] Fals
B. 2.151   And comen *to* conforten from care þe false
B. 2.155   That she graunteþ *to* goon wiþ a good wille
B. 2.156   To london *to* loken if [þat] lawe wolde
B. 2.161   *To* wenden wiþ hem to westmynstre to witnesse þis dede.
B. 2.161   To wenden wiþ hem to westmynstre *to* witnesse þis dede.
B. 2.162   Ac þanne cared þei for caples *to* carien hem þider;
B. 2.175   Lat sadle hem wiþ siluer oure synne *to* suffre,
B. 2.177   *To* bere Bisshopes aboute abrood in visitynge.
B. 2.182   And makeþ of lyere a lang cart *to* leden alle þise oþere,
B. 2.186   I haue no tome *to* telle þe tail þat [hem] folwe[þ]
B. 2.200   *To* attachen þo Tyrauntȝ 'for any [tresor], I hote;
B. 2.204   [Symonye and Cyuylle, I sende hem *to* warne
B. 2.210   Falsnesse and his felawship *to* fettren and to bynden.
B. 2.210   Falsnesse and his felawship to fettren and *to* bynden.
B. 2.214   And Gyle dooþ hym *to* go agast for to dye.
B. 2.216   And bishetten hym in hire shoppes *to* shewen hire ware;
B. 2.217   Apparailed hym as [a p]rentice þe peple *to* serue.
B. 2.227   [For to] wonye wiþ hem watres to ese.
B. 2.228   Spycers speken with hym *to* spien hire ware
B. 2.234   Ac he haþ leue *to* lepen out as ofte as hym likeþ,
B. 2.238   Ac trewely *to* telle she trembled for [fere],
B. 3.4   *To* take Mede þe maide and maken hire at ese.
B. 3.11   A[c] þer was murþe & Mynstralcie Mede *to* plese;
B. 3.18   *To* be wedded at þi wille and wher þee leef likeþ
B. 3.26   Wiþ þat comen clerkes *to* conforten hire þe same
B. 3.30   To louen hem lelly and lordes [hem] make
B. 3.42   Amonges [clerkes] and [knyȝtes] Conscience *to* [felle]'.
B. 3.50   Syker sholde þi soule be heuene *to* haue'.
B. 3.65   *To* writen in wyndowes of hir wel dedes,
B. 3.70   *To* writen in wyndowes of youre wel dedes
B. 3.71   Or *to* greden after goddes men whan ye [gyue] doles
B. 3.77   The kyng and þe comune *to* kepe þe lawes,

B. 3.78   [As] *to* punysshe on Pillories and [on] pynynge stooles
B. 3.88   Of alle swiche Selleris siluer *to* take,
B. 3.90   Rynges or ooþer richesse þ[ise] Regratiers *to* mayntene.
B. 3.92   And suffre hem *to* selle somdel ayeins reson.'
B. 3.104   Curteisly þe kyng comse[þ] *to* telle;
B. 3.114   [Th]anne was Conscience called *to* come and appere
B. 3.139   *To* vnfettre þe fals, fle where hym likeþ.
B. 3.142   *To* be corsed in Consistorie she counteþ noȝt a [risshe];
B. 3.151   *To* [holde] lemmans and lotebies alle hire lifdaies,
B. 3.161   Lawe is so lordlich and looþ *to* maken ende;
B. 3.168   For pouere men may haue no power *to* pleyne þouȝ [hem] smerte,
B. 3.171   *To* haue space to speke, spede if she myȝte.
B. 3.171   To haue space *to* speke, spede if she myȝte.
B. 3.174   For Conscience accuseþ þee *to* congeien þee for euere.'
B. 3.178   And þow knowest, Conscience, I kam noȝt *to* chide,
B. 3.179   Ne [*to*] depraue þi persone wiþ a proud herte.
B. 3.193   And dreddest *to* be ded for a dym cloude,
B. 3.196   And bere hire bras at þi bak to Caleis *to* selle,
B. 3.200   And dide hem hoppe for hope *to* haue me at wille.
B. 3.207   *To* leuen his lordshipe for a litel siluer,
B. 3.210   *To* yeue [hise men mede] þat mekely hym serueþ,
B. 3.214   [Thoruȝ] ȝiftes han yonge men *to* [yerne] and to ryde.
B. 3.214   [Thoruȝ] ȝiftes han yonge men to [yerne] and *to* ryde.
B. 3.216   And medeþ men h[y]mseluen *to* mayntene hir lawes.
B. 3.221   The kyng haþ mede of his men *to* make pees in londe;
B. 3.229   Mede is worþi, [me þynkeþ], þe maistrie *to* haue'.
B. 3.247   *To* mayntene mysdoers Mede þei take;
B. 3.265   Be buxom at his biddynge his wil *to* fulfille.
B. 3.278   Swich a meschief Mede made þe kyng *to* haue
B. 3.280   The culorum of þis cas kepe I noȝt *to* [shewe];
B. 3.292   Thise shul ben Maistres on moolde [trewe men] *to* saue.
B. 3.309   Ech man *to* pleye with a plow, Pykoise or spade,
B. 3.311   Preestes and persons wiþ Placebo *to* hunte
B. 3.317   Ne putte hem in panel *to* doon hem pliȝte hir truþe;
B. 4.7   'Rape þee *to* ryde and Reson [þat] þow fecche.
B. 4.8   Comaunde hym þat he come my counseil *to* here,
B. 4.16   'I shal arraye me *to* ryde', quod Reson, 'reste þee a while',
B. 4.19   Ne-lesynge-*to*-lauȝen-of-for-I-loued-hem-neuere.
B. 4.22   Hange on hym þe heuy brydel *to* holde his heed lowe,
B. 4.28   Folwed h[e]m faste for þei hadde *to* doone
B. 4.29   In [c]heker and in Chauncerye, *to* ben descharged of þynges.
B. 4.55   He maynteneþ hise men *to* murþere myne hewen,
B. 4.60   I am noȝt hardy for hym vnneþe *to* loke.'
B. 4.64   *To* maken [his] pees with hise pens and profred hym manye,
B. 4.75   *To* maken [his] pees wiþ his pens, handy dandy payed.
B. 4.77   And token Mede myd hem mercy *to* wynne.
B. 4.82   *To* ouercomen þe kyng wiþ catel if þei myȝte.
B. 4.85   And comaunded a Constable *to* casten hym in Irens;
B. 4.94   [Th]anne gan Mede *to* me[k]en hire, and mercy bisouȝte,
B. 4.96   'Haue þis [of me, man]', quod she, '*to* amenden þi scaþe,
B. 4.99   *To* haue mercy on þat man þat mysdide hym ofte:
B. 4.107   And [ofte] þe boldere be *to* bete myne hewen.
B. 4.110   Som[me] radde Reson *to* haue ruþe on þat shrewe;
B. 4.111   And *to* counseille þe kyng and Conscience [boþe]
B. 4.113   'Reed me noȝt', quod Reson, 'no ruþe *to* haue
B. 4.115   And haten alle harlotrie *to* heren or to mouþen it;
B. 4.115   And haten alle harlotrie to heren or *to* mouþen it;
B. 4.119   Til clerkene coueitise be *to* cloþe þe pouere and fede,
B. 4.135   While Mede haþ þe maistrie [*to* mote in þis] halle.
B. 4.138   That I were kyng with coroune *to* kepen a Reaume,
B. 4.150   Al *to* construe þis clause for þe kynges profit,
B. 4.183   It is [wel] hard, by myn heed, hert[o] *to* brynge it,
B. 4.184   [And] alle youre lige leodes *to* lede þus euene'.
B. 4.192   'I am redy', quod Reson, '*to* reste wiþ yow euere;
B. 5.2   *To* here matyns [and masse and to þe mete] after.
B. 5.11   And how Reson gan arayen hym al þe Reaume *to* preche;
B. 5.12   And wiþ a cros afore þe kyng comsede þus *to* techen.
B. 5.26   [And] preide Pernele hir purfil *to* le[u]e
B. 5.28   Tomme Stowue hir tauȝte *to* take two staues
B. 5.30   He warnede watte his wif was *to* blame
B. 5.34   He chargede Chapmen *to* chastiȝen hir children:
B. 5.45   And siþen he radde Religion hir rule *to* holde
B. 5.48   And siþen he counseiled þe kyng his commune *to* louye:
B. 5.52   'And ye þat han lawes *to* [loke], lat truþe be youre coueitise
B. 5.61   And [made] wille *to* wepe water wiþ hise eiȝen.
B. 5.66   *To* affaiten hire flessh þat fiers was to synne.
B. 5.66   To affaiten hire flessh þat fiers was *to* synne.
B. 5.68   And suffre he be mysseyd, and so dide I neuere.
B. 5.72   *To* maken mercy for hi[s] mysded[e] bitwene god and [hym]
B. 5.76   And carefully [his coupe] he comse[þ] *to* shewe.
B. 5.84   And [wroþliche he wroþ his] fust, *to* wreke hym he þouȝte
B. 5.94   [And blamed hym bihynde his bak *to* brynge hym in fame;
B. 5.95   *To* apeire hym bi my power pursued wel ofte],

B. 5.96 And [bilowen] hym to lordes *to* doon hym lese siluer,
B. 5.106 [*To*] preye for þe peple as þe preest techeþ,
B. 5.122 For enuye and yuel wil is yuel *to* defie.
B. 5.131 And gart bakbityng be a brocour *to* blame mennes ware.
B. 5.133 *To* lye and to loure on my neȝebore and to lakke his chaffare.
B. 5.133 To lye and *to* loure on my neȝebore and to lakke his chaffare.
B. 5.133 To lye and to loure on my neȝebore and *to* lakke his chaffare.
B. 5.140 Til þei beere leues of lowe speche lordes *to* plese,
B. 5.141 And siþen þei blosmede abrood in boure *to* here shriftes.
B. 5.170 For þere ben manye felle frekes my feeris *to* aspie,
B. 5.176 Forþi haue I no likyng, [leue me], wiþ þo leodes *to* wonye;
B. 5.187 And bad me wilne *to* wepe my wikkednesse to amende.
B. 5.187 And bad me wilne to wepe my wikkednesse *to* amende.
B. 5.200 And was his prentice ypliȝt his profit *to* [loke].
B. 5.201 First I lerned *to* lye a leef ouþer tweyne;
B. 5.202 Wikkedly *to* weye was my firste lesson.
B. 5.207 Thanne drouȝ I me among drapiers my donet *to* lerne,
B. 5.208 *To* drawe þe [list] along, þe lenger it semed;
B. 5.214 [And] spak to [þe] Spynnester[e] *to* spynnen it [softe].
B. 5.217 I bouȝte hire barly; she brew it *to* selle.
B. 5.240 *To* weye pens wiþ a peis and pare þe heuyeste
B. 5.241 And lene it for loue of þe cros, *to* legge a wed and lese it.
B. 5.261 'God lene þee neuere grace] þi good wel *to* bisette,
B. 5.275 [Is] holden at þe heiȝe doom *to* helpe þee to restitue,
B. 5.275 [Is] holden at þe heiȝe doom to helpe þee *to* restitue,
B. 5.285 For þow hast no good ground *to* gete þee wiþ a wastel
B. 5.289 And if þow wite neuere to [whom] ne [where] *to* restitue.'
B. 5.295 And what he lente yow of oure lordes good *to* lette yow fro synne.'
B. 5.297 And [kaireþ] hym to kirkeward his coupe *to* shewe.
B. 5.320 And at þe newe feire nempned it *to* selle.
B. 5.323 Ther were chapmen ychose þis chaffare *to* preise:
B. 5.337 [Bargaynes and beuerages bigonne *to* arise],
B. 5.340 Hise guttes bigonne *to* goþelen as two gredy sowes;
B. 5.345 He [hadde no strengþe *to*] stonde er he his staf hadde,
B. 5.346 And þanne gan he *to* go lik a glemannes bicche
B. 5.348 As whoso leiþ lynes *to* lacche [wiþ] foweles.
B. 5.376 For loue of tales in Tauernes [*to*] drynke þe moore I [hyed;
B. 5.379 And þanne gan Gloton greete and gret doel *to* make
B. 5.381 And auowed *to* faste for hunger or þurste:
B. 5.386 'I moste sitte [*to* be shryuen] or ellis sholde I nappe;
B. 5.389 Sholde no ryngynge do me ryse er I were ripe *to* dyne.'
B. 5.407 Or lesynge[s] *to* lauȝen [of] and bilye my neȝebores,
B. 5.427 Ruþe is *to* here rekenyng whan we shul rede acountes:
B. 5.439 I [ȝarn] aboute in youþe and yaf me nauȝt *to* lerne,
B. 5.468 Ne neuere wene *to* wynne wiþ craft þat I owe;
B. 5.477 [Th]anne hadde Repentaunce ruþe and redde hem alle *to* knele.
B. 5.479 *To* amenden vs of oure mysdedes: do mercy to vs alle,
B. 5.482 And siþen suffredest [hym] *to* synne, a siknesse to vs alle,
B. 5.485 And bicam man of a maide mankynde *to* saue,
B. 5.498 And al *to* solace synfulle þow suffredest it so were:
B. 5.512 *To* haue grace to go [to] truþe, [God leue þat þei moten].
B. 5.512 To haue grace *to* go [to] truþe, [God leue þat þei moten].
B. 5.540 And diden me suren hym [siþþen] *to* seruen hym for euere,
B. 5.549 For þouȝ I seye it myself I serue hym *to* paye;
B. 5.557 'Nay, by [þe peril of] my soul[e]!' quod Piers and gan *to* swere:
B. 5.560 Ac [ye þat] wilneþ *to* wende, þis is þe wey þider.
B. 5.583 Thanne [shalt þow] see seye-sooþ-so-it-be-or-doone-
B. 5.587 And alle þe walles ben of wit *to* holden wil oute:
B. 5.588 [The] kernele[s ben of] cristendom [þat] kynde *to* saue,
B. 5.602 *To* wayuen vp þe wiket þat þe womman shette
B. 5.605 And if grace graunte þee *to* go in [in] þis wise
B. 5.608 *To* suffren hym and segge noȝt ayein þi sires wille.
B. 5.611 And pokeþ forþ pride *to* preise þiseluen;
B. 5.614 Keyed and cliketted *to* kepe þee wiþouten
B. 5.616 Thus myȝtestow lesen his loue, *to* lete wel by þiselue;
B. 5.629 *To* geten ing[o]ng at any gate but grace be þe moore.'
B. 6.4 I haue an half acre *to* erie by þe heiȝe weye;
B. 6.11 That ye haue silk and Sandel *to* sowe whan tyme is
B. 6.12 Chesibles for Chapeleyns chirches *to* honoure.
B. 6.31 And [fette þee hoom] faucons foweles *to* kille
B. 6.35 *To* fulfille þis forward þouȝ I fiȝte sholde.
B. 6.48 For in Charnel at chirche cherles ben yuel *to* knowe,
B. 6.51 But if [it be] of wisdom or of wit þi werkmen *to* chaste;
B. 6.54 For it ben þe deueles disours, I do þe *to* vnderstonde.'
B. 6.64 To pilgrymage as palmeres doon pardon *to* haue.
B. 6.65 And whoso helpeþ me *to* erie [or any þyng swynke]
B. 6.66 Shal haue leue, by oure lord, *to* lese here in heruest
B. 6.76 For holy chirche is [holde] if hem no tiþe *to* [aske],
B. 6.80 His sone hiȝte Suffre-þi-Souereyns-*to*-hauen-hir-wille-
B. 6.90 *To* haue relees and remission, on þat rental I leue.
B. 6.94 [He is] holden, I hope, *to* haue me in [mynde]
B. 6.104 And helpe my cultour *to* kerue and [close] þe furwes.'
B. 6.106 *To* erie þis half acre holpen hym manye;

B. 6.110 Ech man in his manere made hymself *to* doone,
B. 6.111 And somme to plese Perkyn piked vp þe wedes.
B. 6.113 *To* ouersen hem hymself; whoso best wroȝte
B. 6.118 'But ye arise þe raþer and rape yow *to* werche
B. 6.124 'We haue no lymes *to* laboure with; lord, ygraced be [y]e!
B. 6.131 And I am his [h]olde hyne and [auȝte] hym *to* warne
B. 6.134 Ac truþe shal teche yow his teme *to* dryue,
B. 6.138 Til god of his [grace gare hem *to* arise].
B. 6.140 *To* kepe kyen in þe feld, þe corn fro þe beestes,
B. 6.147 And catel *to* [cope] hem wiþ þat han Cloistres and chirches.
B. 6.152 [Th]anne gan wastour *to* wraþen hym and wolde haue yfouȝte;
B. 6.160 *To* kepen hym as couenaunt was fro cursede sherewes,
B. 6.167 'I was noȝt wont *to* werche', quod Wastour, 'now wol I noȝt bigynne!'
B. 6.190 And doluen [drit] and [dung] *to* [ditte out] hunger.
B. 6.192 That seten *to* begge siluer soone were þei heeled,
B. 6.194 And many a beggere for benes buxum was *to* swynke,
B. 6.195 And ech a pouere man wel apaied *to* haue pesen for his hyre,
B. 6.196 And what Piers preide hem *to* do as prest as a Sperhauk.
B. 6.199 Thanne hadde Piers pite and preide hunger *to* wende
B. 6.203 'Of beggeris and bidderis what best be *to* doone,
B. 6.208 Truþe tauȝte me ones *to* louen hem ech one,
B. 6.211 And how I myȝte amaistren hem and make hem *to* werche.'
B. 6.219 [Wiþ fir or wiþ] false men, fonde swiche *to* knowe.
B. 6.223 That nedy ben [or naked, and nouȝt han *to* spende,
B. 6.246 And þat he weneþ wel *to* haue I wole it hym bireue".
B. 6.262 And sende þee of his Sauce *to* sauore þi lippes,
B. 6.271 And be fayn, by my feiþ, his Phisik *to* lete,
B. 6.272 And lerne *to* laboure wiþ lond [lest] liflode [hym faille].
B. 6.280 'I haue no peny', quod Piers, 'pulettes *to* bugge,
B. 6.285 Ne no cokeney, by crist! coloppes *to* maken.
B. 6.288 *To* drawe afeld my dong⸗ while þe droȝte lasteþ.
B. 6.290 By þat I hope *to* haue heruest in my crofte;
B. 6.295 And profrede Piers þis present *to* plese wiþ hunger.
B. 6.298 Grene poret and pesen; *to* [peisen] hym þei þoȝte.
B. 6.301 Wiþ good Ale as Gloton taȝte [þei] garte [hym *to*] slepe.
B. 6.307 Laborers þat haue no land *to* lyue on but hire handes
B. 6.308 Deyne[þ] noȝt *to* dyne a day nyȝt olde wortes.
B. 6.314 Ayeins Catons counseil comseþ he *to* Iangle:
B. 6.318 Swiche lawes *to* loke laborers to [chaste].
B. 6.318 Swiche lawes to loke laborers *to* [chaste].
B. 6.323 He shal awake [þoruȝ] water wastours *to* chaste;
B. 6.326 And so sei[þ] Saturne and sente yow *to* warne.
B. 7.2 *To* [t]aken his teme and tilien þe erþe,
B. 7.6 And alle þat holpen to erye or *to* sowe,
B. 7.6 And alle þat holpen *to* erye or to sowe,
B. 7.11 Han pardon þoruȝ purgatorie *to* passen ful liȝtly,
B. 7.12 Wiþ Patriarkes and prophetes in paradis *to* be felawe.
B. 7.14 Legistres of boþe lawes þe lewed þerwiþ *to* preche,
B. 7.17 At þe day of dome at [hire] deys [*to*] sitte.
B. 7.22 Ayein clene Conscience hir catel *to* selle.
B. 7.26 And [make] Mesondieux þer[wiþ] myseise [*to*] helpe,
B. 7.43 Pledours sholde peynen hem *to* plede for swiche and helpe,
B. 7.53 Ac *to* bugge water ne wynd ne wit ne fir þe ferþe,
B. 7.55 Thise ben truþes tresores trewe folk *to* helpe,
B. 7.66 But if þe suggestion be sooþ þat shapeþ hem *to* begge,
B. 7.74 And in þe stories he techeþ *to* bistowe þyn almesse.
B. 7.83 *To* yelden hem þat yeueþ hem and yet vsure moore:
B. 7.85 For whoso haþ *to* buggen hym breed, þe book bereþ witnesse,
B. 7.132 And sheweþ vs by ensampl[e] vs selue to synne.
B. 7.135 Haue þei no gerner to go but god fynt hem alle.'
B. 7.149 Many tyme þis metels haþ maked me *to* studie,
B. 7.152 And which a pardon Piers hadde þe peple *to* conforte,
B. 7.155 Caton and Canonistres counseillen vs *to* leue
B. 7.156 *To* sette sadnesse in Songewarie for sompnia ne cures.
B. 7.160 Daniel seide, 'sire kyng, þi [sweuene is *to* mene]
B. 7.161 That vnkouþe knyȝtes shul come þi kyngdom *to* cleyme;
B. 7.171 That Ioseph was Iustice Egipte *to* loke;
B. 7.173 Al þis makeþ noȝt on metels *to* þynke,
B. 7.179 Now haþ þe pope power pardon *to* graunte
B. 7.180 [Th]e peple wiþouten penaunce *to* passen [to ioye]?
B. 7.185 Ac *to* truste [on] þise triennals, trewely, me þynkeþ
B. 7.188 Vpon trust of youre tresor triennals *to* haue,
B. 7.189 Be [þow] neuer þe bolder *to* breke þe x hestes,
B. 7.192 *To* purchace pardon and þe popes bulles.
B. 7.194 And comen alle [bi]fore crist acountes *to* yelde,
B. 7.201 Forþi I counseille alle cristene *to* crie god mercy,
B. 7.204 Swiche werkes *to* werche, while we ben here,
B. 8.13 'Where þat dowel dwelleþ, dooþ me *to* witene.'
B. 8.20 'Contra!' quod I as a clerc and comsed *to* disputen:
B. 8.25 He is ouþerwhile elliswhere *to* wisse þe peple.'
B. 8.31 Makeþ þe man many tyme *to* falle and to stonde.
B. 8.31 Makeþ þe man many tyme to falle and *to* stonde.

B. 8.46	For he strengþeþ [þee] to stonde and steereþ [þi] soule
B. 8.52	For he yaf þee [to] yeresȝyue to yeme wel þiselue
B. 8.55	Ac man haþ moost þerof and moost is to blame
B. 8.57	'I haue no kynde knowyng', quod I, 'to conceyuen [þi] wordes
B. 8.61	And ȝyue yow grace on þis grounde goode men to worþe'.
B. 8.62	[Th]us I wente widewher [dowel to seke,
B. 8.66	To [lerne] þe layes [þat] louely foweles made.
B. 8.67	Murþe of hire mouþes made me to slep[e];
B. 8.77	Where dowel dwelleþ, and do me [to wisse].'
B. 8.79	Arn þre faire vertues, and ben noȝt fer to fynde.
B. 8.94	[Ye wise] suffreþ þe vnwise wiþ yow to libbe,
B. 8.97	Is hoked [at] þat oon ende to [holde men in good lif].
B. 8.98	A pik is [in] þat potente to [punge] adown þe wikked
B. 8.99	That waiten any wikkednesse dowel to tene.
B. 8.100	And [as] dowel and dobet [dide] hem [to vnderstonde],
B. 8.101	[Thei han] crowne[d a] kyng to [kepen] hem [alle],
B. 8.103	[And were vnbuxum at his biddyng, and bold to don ille],
B. 8.108	Crouned oon to be kyng, [and by hir counseil werchen],
B. 8.113	More kynde knowynge I coueite to lerne,
B. 8.123	I dorste meue no matere to maken hym to Iangle,
B. 8.123	I dorste meue no matere to maken hym to Iangle,
B. 8.125	[To] pute forþ som purpos to preuen hise wittes,
B. 8.125	[To] pute forþ som purpos to preuen hise wittes,
B. 9.13	To seruen þis lady leelly, boþe late and raþe.
B. 9.23	Thise [sixe] ben set to [saue] þis lady anima
B. 9.40	Thouȝ he [wiste to] write neuer so wel, [and] he hadde [a] penne,
B. 9.46	Wiþ his word and werkmanship and wiþ lif to laste.
B. 9.51	As muche to mene as man wiþ a Soule.
B. 9.69	[Holy chirche is owynge to helpe hem and saue,
B. 9.71	And widewes þat han noȝt wherwith to wynnen hem hir foode,
B. 9.100	To spille any speche or any space of tyme:
B. 9.103	And siþþe to spille speche þat [spire] is of grace
B. 9.109	Grace to go to hem and ofgon hir liflode:
B. 9.166	To yeuen a yong wenche to [a yolde] feble,
B. 9.174	To folwen after þe flicche, fecche þei it neuere;
B. 9.181	And þanne gete ye grace of god and good ynouȝ to lyue wiþ.
B. 9.197	Vngracious to gete good or loue of þe peple;
B. 9.201	But god gyue hem grace here to amende.
B. 9.202	Dowel, my [deere], is to doon as lawe techeþ:
B. 9.203	To loue [and to lowe þee and no lif to greue;
B. 9.203	To loue [and to lowe þee and no lif to greue;
B. 9.203	To loue [and to lowe þee and no lif to greue;
B. 9.204	Ac to loue and to lene], leue me, þat is dobet;
B. 9.204	Ac to loue and to lene], leue me, þat is dobet;
B. 9.205	To ȝyuen and to yemen boþe yonge and olde,
B. 9.205	To ȝyuen and to yemen boþe yonge and olde,
B. 9.206	To helen and to helpen, is dobest of alle.
B. 9.206	To helen and to helpen, is dobest of alle.
B. 9.207	[Thanne is dowel] to drede, and dobet to suffre,
B. 9.207	[Thanne is dowel] to drede, and dobet to suffre,
B.10.5	'Wel artow wis, [wit', quod she], 'any wisdomes to telle
B.10.8	'Wiþ swiche wise wordes to wissen any sottes!'
B.10.20	And lede forþ a loueday to lette [þe] truþe,
B.10.44	Thei konne na moore mynstralcie ne Musik men to glade
B.10.56	And puten forþ presumpcion to preue þe soþe.
B.10.57	Thus þei dryuele at hir deys þe deitee to knowe,
B.10.61	Is noon to nyme hym [in, ne] his [n]oy amende.
B.10.73	To plese wiþ proude men syn þe pestilence tyme;
B.10.78	That preieres haue no power þ[ise] pestilence[s] to lette.
B.10.79	[For god is def nowadayes and deyneþ [noȝt vs to here],
B.10.93	Swiche lessons lordes sholde louye to here,
B.10.95	Nouȝt to fare as a fiþelere or a frere to seke festes,
B.10.95	Nouȝt to fare as a fiþelere or a frere to seke festes,
B.10.98	Ther þe lord ne þe lady likeþ noȝt to telle
B.10.99	Now haþ ech riche a rule to eten by hymselue
B.10.102	That was maad for meles men to eten Inne,
B.10.103	And al to spare to [spille þat spende] shal anoþer.
B.10.103	And al to spare to [spille þat spende] shal anoþer.
B.10.122	Wilneþ neuere to wite why þat god wolde
B.10.123	Suffre Sathan his seed to bigile,
B.10.126	And for his muche mercy to amende [vs] here.
B.10.127	For alle þat wilneþ to wite þe [whyes] of god almyȝty,
B.10.129	That euere [eft] wilneþ to wite why þat god wolde
B.10.130	Suffre Sathan his seed to bigile,
B.10.136	Siþþe he wilneþ to wite whiche þei ben [alle].
B.10.151	[To] kenne me kyndely to knowe what is dowel.'
B.10.151	[To] kenne me kyndely to knowe what is dowel.'
B.10.171	That ech wight be in wille his wit þee to shewe.
B.10.177	And alle [þe] Musons in Musik I made hire to knowe.
B.10.179	Aristotle and oþere mo to argue I tauȝte;
B.10.206	To do good for goddes loue and gyuen men þat asked.
B.10.208	And alle þat lakkeþ vs or lyeþ oure lord techeþ vs to louye,
B.10.209	And noȝt to greuen hem þat greueþ vs; god [þat forbedeþ]:

B.10.218	Nigromancie and perimancie þe pouke to raise];
B.10.219	If þow þynke to dowel deel þerwiþ neuere.
B.10.221	Founded hem formest folk to deceyue;
B.10.223	To counseille þee kyndely to knowe what is dowel.'
B.10.223	To counseille þee kyndely to knowe what is dowel.'
B.10.237	Dowel and dobet and dobest to lerne.
B.10.238	'It is a commune lyf', quod Clergie, 'on holy chirche to bileue
B.10.239	Wiþ alle þe articles of þe feiþ þat falleþ to be knowe.
B.10.240	And þat is to bileue lelly, boþe lered and lewed,
B.10.250	And hymself ordeyned to sadde vs in bileue.
B.10.254	But þus it bilongeþ to bileue to lewed þat willen dowel.
B.10.255	For hadde neuere freke fyn wit þe feiþ to dispute,
B.10.257	[So] is dobet to suffre for þ[i] soules helþe
B.10.264	Thanne is dobest to be boold to blame þe gilty,
B.10.264	Thanne is dobest to be boold to blame þe gilty,
B.10.271	Which letteþ þee to loke, lasse ouþer moore?
B.10.274	Alle maner men to amenden bi hire myȝtes;
B.10.275	This text was told yow to ben ywar er ye tauȝte
B.10.276	That ye were swiche as ye sey[d]e to salue wiþ oþere.
B.10.292	[Th]anne shul burel clerkes ben abasshed to blame yow or to greue,
B.10.292	[Th]anne shul burel clerkes ben abasshed to blame yow or to greue,
B.10.294	And drede to wraþe yow in any word youre werkmanship to lette,
B.10.294	And drede to wraþe yow in any word youre werkmanship to lette,
B.10.304	That out of couent and cloistre coueiten to libbe.
B.10.307	For in cloistre comeþ [no] man to [carpe] ne to fiȝte
B.10.307	For in cloistre comeþ [no] man to [carpe] ne to fiȝte
B.10.308	But al is buxomnesse þere and bokes, to rede and to lerne].
B.10.308	But al is buxomnesse þere and bokes, to rede and to lerne].
B.10.317	Litel hadde lordes to doon to ȝyue lond from hire heires
B.10.317	Litel hadde lordes to doon to ȝyue lond from hire heires
B.10.342	Salomon seiþ also þat siluer is worst to louye:
B.10.343	And Caton kenneþ vs to coueiten it nauȝt but as nede techeþ:
B.10.345	Writen to wissen vs to wilne no richesse,
B.10.345	Writen to wissen vs to wilne no richesse,
B.10.359	That whoso wolde and wilneþ wiþ crist to arise,
B.10.363	And þus bilongeþ to louye þat leueþ [to] be saued.
B.10.363	And þus bilongeþ to louye þat leueþ [to] be saued.
B.10.369	And siþen heþen to helpe in hope of amendement.
B.10.386	[To rule þe reume and riche to make];
B.10.386	[To rule þe reume and riche to make];
B.10.392	And if I sh[al] werche by hir werkes to wynne me heuene,
B.10.412	Of holi chirche þat herberwe is, and goddes hous to saue
B.10.415	The culorum of þis clause curatours is to mene,
B.10.416	That ben Carpenters holy kirk to make for cristes owene beestes:
B.10.431	Cristene kynde to kille to deþe?
B.10.453	Konnyng [and clergie] to conclude hem alle".
B.10.462	And is to mene to [Englissh] men, moore ne lesse,
B.10.481	The which is mannes soule to saue, as god seiþ in þe gospel:
B.11.19	For to lyue longe and ladies to louye,
B.11.39	If truþe wol witnesse it be wel do Fortune to folwe
B.11.45	'That wit shal torne to wrecchednesse for wil to haue his likyng!'
B.11.49	I hadde no likyng, leue me, [þe leste] of hem to knowe.
B.11.76	Whi youre Couent coueiteþ to confesse and to burye
B.11.76	Whi youre Couent coueiteþ to confesse and to burye
B.11.77	Raþer þan to baptiȝe barnes þat ben Catecumelynges.
B.11.79	Ac muche moore meritorie, me þynkeþ, is to baptiȝe,
B.11.87	'ȝis, by Peter and by Poul!' quod he and took hem boþe to witnesse:
B.11.96	It is licitum for lewed men to [legge] þe soþe
B.11.99	It falleþ noȝt for þat folk no tales to telle
B.11.102	To reden it in Retorik to arate dedly synne?
B.11.102	To reden it in Retorik to arate dedly synne?
B.11.113	Ac be [þow] neueremoore þe firste [þe] defaute to blame;
B.11.116	And in a weer gan I wexe, and wiþ myself to dispute
B.11.125	For þouȝ a cristen man coueited his cristendom to reneye,
B.11.126	Riȝtfully to reneye no reson it wolde.
B.11.133	And putten hym after in prison in purgatorie to brenne;
B.11.138	Mercy al to amende and Mekenesse hir folwe;
B.11.142	How [I] was ded and dampned to dwellen in pyne
B.11.159	And on Troianus truþe to þenke, and do truþe to þe peple.
B.11.170	And took it moises vpon þe mount alle men to lere].
B.11.174	For no cause to cacche siluer þerby, ne to be called a maister,
B.11.174	For no cause to cacche siluer þerby, ne to be called a maister,
B.11.175	But al for loue of oure lord and þe bet to loue þe peple.
B.11.181	[And] comaundeþ ech creature to conformen hym to louye
B.11.181	[And] comaundeþ ech creature to conformen hym to louye
B.11.183	For hem þat haten vs is oure merite to louye,
B.11.188	To knowen vs by oure kynde herte and castynge of oure eiȝen,
B.11.193	For youre frendes wol feden yow, and fonde yow to quyte
B.11.213	For woot no man how neiȝ it is to ben ynome fro boþe.
B.11.223	And lawe is looþ to louye but if he lacche siluer.
B.11.224	Boþe logyk and lawe, þat loueþ noȝt to lye,

B.11.259 [Al]þouȝ it be sour *to* suffre, þe[r] comeþ swete [after].
B.11.262 Is a kernel of confort kynde *to* restore.
B.11.264 Makeþ a man *to* haue mynde in god and a gret wille
B.11.265 *To* wepe and to wel bidde, wherof wexeþ Mercy
B.11.265 To wepe and *to* wel bidde, wherof wexeþ Mercy
B.11.266 Of which crist is a kernell *to* conforte þe soule.
B.11.268 And lasse he dredeþ deeþ and in derke *to* ben yrobbed
B.11.273 That parfit pouerte was no possession *to* haue,
B.11.275 And is *to* mene to men þat on þis moolde lyuen,
B.11.281 *To* serue god goodliche, ne greueþ hym no penaunce:
B.11.291 Thanne nedeþ yow noȝt *to* [nyme] siluer for masses þat ye syngen,
B.11.294 For made neuere kyng no knyȝt but he hadde catel *to* spende
B.11.301 He [ouȝte no] bileue, as I leue, *to* lacche þoruȝ his croune
B.11.325 I was fet forþ by [forbisenes] *to* knowe
B.11.326 Thorugh ech a creature kynde my creatour *to* louye.
B.11.346 Hadde neuere wye wit *to* werche þe leeste.
B.11.348 Lerned *to* legge þe stikkes in whiche she leyeþ and bredeþ.
B.11.361 And who tauȝte hem on trees *to* tymbre so heiȝe
B.11.364 Manye selkouþes I seiȝ ben noȝt *to* seye nouþe.
B.11.368 Of hir kynde and hir colour *to* carpe it were to longe.
B.11.377 Why I suffre or noȝt suffre; þiself hast noȝt *to* doone.
B.11.378 Amende þow, if þow myȝt, for my tyme is *to* abide.
B.11.383 [Holy writ', quod þat wye, 'wisseþ men *to* suffre:
B.11.388 And er þow lakke my lif loke [þyn] *to* preise.
B.11.396 For be a man fair or foul it falleþ noȝt *to* lakke.
B.11.400 Al *to* murþe wiþ man þat moste wo þolie,
B.11.403 That som tyme hym bitit *to* folwen his kynde;
B.11.405 Tho cauȝte I colour anoon and comsed *to* ben ashamed
B.11.409 [*To* wite] what dowel is, [ac wakyng neuere]'.
B.11.412 '*To* se muche and suffre moore, certes, is dowel.'
B.11.418 Ac whan he mamelede about mete, and entremetede *to* knowe
B.11.421 Lakkedest and losedest kynge þat longed noȝt *to* doone;
B.11.424 That Clergie þi compaignye kepeþ noȝt *to* suwe.
B.11.426 As shal shame, and shenden hym, and shape hym *to* amende.
B.11.431 [*To* blame or] to bete hym þanne] it were but pure synne.
B.11.431 [To blame or] *to* bete hym þanne] it were but pure synne.
B.11.434 Thanne woot þe dronken [wye] wherfore he is *to* blame.'
B.12.4   And manye tymes haue meued þee *to* [mynne] on þyn ende,
B.12.5   And how fele fernyeres are faren and so fewe *to* come;
B.12.7   *To* amende it in þi myddel age, lest myȝt þe faill[e]
B.12.15   It is but murþe as for me *to* amende my soule.
B.12.18   *To* telle men what dowel is, dobet and dobest boþe,
B.12.19   And prechours *to* preuen what it is of many a peire freres.'
B.12.20   I seiȝ wel he seide me sooþ, and somwhat me *to* excuse
B.12.22   *To* solacen hym som tyme; [so] I do whan I make:
B.12.24   [In manye places pleyden þe parfiter *to* ben].
B.12.38   And if þow be maiden *to* marye and myȝt wel continue,
B.12.40   [Lo! what made lucifer *to* lese þe heiȝe heuene,
B.12.59   Ac grace is a gras þer[for] þo greuaunces to abate.
B.12.70   Ac yet is Clergie *to* comende and kynde wit boþe,
B.12.89   The womman þat þe Iewes [iugged] þat Iesus þouȝte *to* saue:
B.12.95   For boþe ben as Mirours *to* amenden [by] defautes
B.12.103 [And riȝt as siȝt serueþ a man *to* se þe heiȝe strete]
B.12.105 And as a blynd man in bataille bereþ wepne *to* fiȝte
B.12.106 And haþ noon hap wiþ his ax his enemy *to* hitte,
B.12.110 *To* vnloken it at hir likyng, and to þe lewed peple
B.12.114 Hadde neuere lewed man leue *to* leggen hond on þat cheste
B.12.120 And leiden hand þeron *to* liften it vp loren here lif after.
B.12.121 Forþi I conseille alle creatures no clergie *to* dispise
B.12.124 And medle noȝt muche wiþ hem *to* meuen any wraþe
B.12.125 Lest cheste cha[fe] vs *to* choppe ech man oþer:
B.12.132 And helden it an heiȝ science hir wittes *to* knowe;
B.12.149 And bad hem go to Beþlem goddes burþe *to* honoure
B.12.168 And is in drede *to* drenche, þat neuere dide swymme?'
B.12.184 *To* lere lewed men as luc bereþ witnesse:
B.12.195 [Th]at buxomliche biddeþ it and ben in wille *to* amenden hem.
B.12.207 And as lawe likeþ *to* lyue or to deye:
B.12.207 And as lawe likeþ to lyue or *to* deye:
B.12.209 It were neiþer reson ne riȝt *to* rewarde boþe yliche.
B.12.228 [That þ]ere þe þorn is þikkest *to* buylden and brede;
B.12.229 And kynde kenned þe pecok *to* cauken in swich a [wise.
B.12.230 Kynde] kenned Adam *to* knowe hise pryue membres,
B.12.231 And tauȝte hym and Eue *to* helien hem wiþ leues.
B.12.242 For pursue a pecok or a pehen *to* cacche,
B.12.256 And whan his caroyne shal come in caue *to* be buryed
B.12.261 That was writen, and þei witnesse *to* werche as it wolde.
B.12.273 *To* wissen vs [wyes] þerwiþ þat wiss[h]en to be saued–
B.12.273 To wissen vs [wyes] þerwiþ þat wiss[h]en *to* be saued–
B.12.274 And þe bettre for hir bokes *to* bidden we ben holden–
B.12.280 'Contra!' quod Ymaginatif þoo and comsed *to* loure,
B.12.292 And an hope hangynge þerInne *to* haue a mede for his truþe
B.12.296 *To* kepe wiþ a commune; no catel was holde bettre,
B.13.22   And as crist wolde þer com Conscience *to* conforte me þat tyme

B.13.35   Pacience and I [prestly] were put *to* be [mettes],
B.13.47   Bifore Pacience breed *to* brynge, [bitynge apart],
B.13.86   Pacience parceyued what I þouȝte and [preynte] on me *to* be stille
B.13.97   And þanne is tyme *to* take and to appose þis doctour
B.13.97   And þanne is tyme to take and *to* appose þis doctour
B.13.111 I wolde permute my penaunce with youre, for I am in point *to* dowel.'
B.13.113 And preynte vpon pacience *to* preie me be stille,
B.13.117 [That trauailleþ *to* teche oþere I holde it for a dobet].
B.13.121 Ther þe lord of lif wonyeþ, *to* leren [hem] what is dowel.
B.13.123 I am vnhardy', quod he, 'to any wiȝt *to* preuen it.
B.13.126 And no text ne takeþ *to* mayntene his cause
B.13.142 And so þow lere þe *to* louye, for [þe] lordes loue of heuene,
B.13.145 Boþe wiþ wer[k] and with wor[d] fonde his loue *to* wynne;
B.13.184 After yeresȝeues or ȝiftes, or yernen *to* rede redels?
B.13.186 And lere yow if yow like þe leeste point *to* knowe
B.13.191 Haþ meued my mood *to* moorne for my synnes.
B.13.212 I shal dwelle as I do my deuoir *to* shewe,
B.13.218 *To* conforte hym and Conscience if þei come in place
B.13.236 Whan þe preest preieþ þe peple þat Paternoster *to* bidde
B.13.256 *To* haue þe grace of god, and no gilt of [þe] pope.
B.13.281 And inobedient *to* ben vndernome of any lif lyuynge;
B.13.289 As best for his body be *to* haue a [bold] name;
B.13.290 And entremetten hym ouer al þer he haþ noȝt *to* doone,
B.13.294 And louelokest *to* loken on and lelest of werkes,
B.13.298 And large *to* lene, [loos] þerby to cacche].
B.13.298 And large to lene, [loos] þerby *to* cacche].
B.13.301 And as a lyoun on loke and lordlich of speche,
B.13.303 In towne and in Tauernes tales *to* telle
B.13.321 Wiþ enuye and yuel speche entisynge *to* fiȝte,
B.13.322 Lyinge and la[kk]ynge and leue tonge *to* chide;
B.13.346 Aboute þe mouþ, or byneþe bigynneþ *to* grope,
B.13.359 Lened for loue of þe wed and looþ *to* do truþe;
B.13.360 And awaited þoruȝ [wittes wyes] *to* bigile,
B.13.369 Thoruȝ gile *to* gaderen þe good þat ich haue.
B.13.374 *To* seise to me wiþ hir sikel þat I sew neuere.
B.13.380 But he profrede *to* paie a peny or tweyne
B.13.384 Hadde I neuere wille, woot god, witterly *to* biseche
B.13.389 So if I kidde any kyndenesse myn euencristen *to* helpe
B.13.392 Or into Prucelond my Prentis my profit *to* waiten,
B.13.405 And þanne I dradde to deye in dedlich synne',
B.13.406 That into wanhope he [worþ] and wende nauȝt *to* be saued.
B.13.419 He hateþ *to* here þerof and alle þat it telleþ.
B.13.423 And han likynge *to* liþen hem [in hope] to do yow lauȝe–
B.13.423 And han likynge to liþen hem [in hope] *to* do yow lauȝe–
B.13.430 *To* entice men þoruȝ hir tales to synne and harlotrie.
B.13.442 For to solace youre soules swiche minstrales *to* haue:
B.13.444 And a lered man *to* lere þee what our lord suffred
B.13.448 *To* crie a largesse bifore oure lord, youre good loos to shewe.
B.13.448 To crie a largesse bifore oure lord, youre good loos *to* shewe.
B.13.449 Thise þre maner minstrales makeþ a man *to* lauȝe,
B.13.451 That bi his lyue liþed hem and loued hem *to* here.
B.14.1   'I haue but oon hool hater', quod haukyn, 'I am þe lasse *to* blame
B.14.8   *To* agulte god or good man by aught þat I wiste,
B.14.10   To penaunce pacience and pouere men *to* fede,
B.14.11   Al for coueitise of my cristendom in clennesse *to* kepen it.
B.14.16   'And I shal kenne þee', quod Conscience, 'of Contricion *to* make
B.14.20   And engreynen it wiþ good wille and goddes grace *to* amende þe,
B.14.30   And flour *to* fede folk wiþ as best be for þe soule;
B.14.40   Wherof or wherfore or wherby *to* libbe'
B.14.42   Fissh *to* lyue in þe flood and in þe fir þe Criket,
B.14.84   Which dryueþ awey dedly synne and dooþ it *to* be venial.
B.14.110 *To* haue allowaunce of his lord; by þe lawe he it cleymeþ.
B.14.127 *To* ȝyue many m[e]n his [mercymonye] er he it haue deserued.
B.14.130 And greet likynge *to* lyue wiþouten labour of bodye,
B.14.139 And noȝt *to* fonge bifore for drede of disalowyng.
B.14.163 And arated of riche men þat ruþe is *to* here.
B.14.170 Ac god, of þi goodnesse gyue hem grace *to* amende.
B.14.184 Thou tauȝtest hem in þe Trinite *to* taken bapteme
B.14.186 And if vs fille þoruȝ folie *to* falle in synne after
B.14.203 The fend folweþ hem alle and fondeþ hem *to* helpe,
B.14.211 For þe riche haþ muche *to* rekene, and [riȝt softe] walkeþ;
B.14.221 For þe poore is ay prest *to* plese þe riche
B.14.231 For his rentes ne wol nauȝt reche no riche metes *to* bigge;
B.14.234 For whan he streyneþ hym *to* strecche þe strawe is his shetes.
B.14.246 For pouerte haþ but pokes *to* putten in hise goodes
B.14.248 And wheiþer be liȝter *to* breke? lasse boost [it] makeþ
B.14.255 Meschief is [ay a mene] and makeþ hem *to* þynke
B.14.267 Muche is [þat maide] *to* loue of [a man] þat swich oon takeþ,
B.14.272 And put hym *to* be pacient and pouerte weddeþ,
B.14.275 What is Pouerte, pacience', quod he, 'properly *to* mene?'
B.14.278 '[Al þis] in englissh', quod Pacience, 'it is wel hard *to* expounen,
B.14.288 Selde sit pouerte þe soþe *to* declare,

B.14.289 [O]r as Iustice *to* Iugge men enioyned is no poore,
B.14.290 Ne *to* be Mair aboue men ne Mynystre vnder kynges;
B.14.291 Selde is any poore yput *to* punysshen any peple.
B.14.313 The eighteþe is a lele labour and looþ *to* take moore
B.14.322 That þ[u]s first wroot *to* wissen men what Pouerte was to mene.'
B.14.322 That þ[u]s first wroot to wissen men what Pouerte was *to* mene.'
B.14.325 So hard it is', quod haukyn, '*to* lyue and to do synne.
B.14.325 So hard it is', quod haukyn, 'to lyue and *to* do synne.
B.14.332 'I were noȝt worþi, woot god', quod haukyn, '*to* werien any cloþes,
B.14.334 *To* couere my careyne', quod he, and cride mercy faste
B.15.5 And lete me for a lorel and looþ *to* reuerencen
B.15.15 If he were cristes creature [for cristes loue] me *to* tellen.
B.15.39 How þow coueitest *to* calle me, now þow knowest [alle] my
names.
B.15.56 To englisshe men þis is *to* mene, þat mowen speke and here,
B.15.62 Coueitise *to* konne and to knowe scienc[e]
B.15.62 Coueitise to konne and *to* knowe scienc[e]
B.15.64 And riȝt as hony is yuel *to* defie and engleymeþ þe mawe,
B.15.71 Ye moeuen materes vnmesurable *to* tellen of þe Trinite
B.15.73 Bettre it were [by] manye doctours *to* [bi]leuen swich techyng
B.15.100 [Is þe] roote of þe right feiþ *to* rule þe peple;
B.15.106 And hatien *to* here harlotrie, and [au]ȝt to vnderfonge
B.15.106 And hatien to here harlotrie, and [au]ȝt *to* vnderfonge
B.15.125 Ac a Porthors þat sholde be his Plow, Placebo *to* sigge–
B.15.144 By lered, by lewed, þat looþ is *to* [s]pende
B.15.155 And wollen lene þer þei leue lelly *to* ben paied.
B.15.172 Ne no likynge haþ *to* lye ne laughe men to scorne.
B.15.172 Ne no likynge haþ to lye ne laughe men *to* scorne.
B.15.182 And ouþerwhile he is woned *to* wenden on pilgrymages
B.15.183 Ther poore men and prisons liggeþ, hir pardon *to* haue;
B.15.207 Ac it is moore *to* haue hir mete [on] swich an esy manere
B.15.250 And gyue vs grace, goode god, charite *to* folwe.
B.15.256 Neiþer he biddeþ ne beggeþ ne borweþ *to* yelde.
B.15.309 And þanne wolde lordes and ladies be looþ *to* agulte
B.15.310 And *to* taken of hir tenauntȝ moore þan trouþe wolde,
B.15.315 For hadde ye potage and payn ynogh and penyale *to* drynke,
B.15.323 *To* ȝyue from youre heires þat youre Aiels yow lefte,
B.15.324 And [bisette] *to* bidde for yow to swiche þat ben riche,
B.15.325 And ben founded and feffed ek *to* bidde for oþere.
B.15.339 And wente forþ wiþ þat water *to* woke wiþ Temese.
B.15.344 Forþi I counseille alle cristene *to* conformen hem to charite,
B.15.366 And what *to* leue and to lyue by; þe lond was so trewe.
B.15.366 And what to leue and *to* lyue by; þe lond was so trewe.
B.15.378 [And as vsher vnder hym *to* fourmen vs alle
B.15.389 That sola fides sufficit *to* saue wiþ lewed peple.
B.15.423 *To* lyue by litel and in lowe houses by lele mennes almesse.
B.15.442 That goddes salt sholde be *to* saue mannes soule.
B.15.444 Til Gregory garte clerkes *to* go here and preche.
B.15.447 To crist and to cristendom and cros *to* honoure,
B.15.451 [Enformed] hem what fullynge and feiþ was *to* mene.'
B.15.452 Clooþ þat comeþ fro þe weuyng is noȝt comly *to* were
B.15.459 Heþen is *to* mene after heeþ and vntiled erþe,
B.15.473 That loþ ben *to* louye wiþouten lernyng of ensaumples.
B.15.479 And as þo foules *to* fynde fode after whistlyng
B.15.480 So hope þei *to* haue heuene þoruȝ hir whistlyng.
B.15.484 Where þat his wille is *to* worshipen vs alle,
B.15.493 So manye prelates *to* preche as þe Pope makeþ,
B.15.496 *To* be pastours and preche þe passion of Iesus,
B.15.497 And as hymself seide [so] *to* lyue and dye:
B.15.503 Thei sholde turne, whoso trauail[e wolde] *to* teche hem of þe
Trinite.
B.15.506 And make hir mone to Makometh hir message *to* shewe.
B.15.519 Many a seint syþen haþ suffred *to* deye
B.15.529 [And nauȝt to] huppe aboute in Engelond to halwe mennes Auteres
B.15.533 It is ruþe *to* rede how riȝtwise men lyuede,
B.15.537 Ne no richesse but þe roode *to* reioisse hem Inne:
B.15.539 And now is rouþe *to* rede how þe rede noble
B.15.566 [Charite] were *to* deschargen hem for holy chirches sake,
B.15.571 Thoruȝ his prouince *to* passe and to his peple shewe hym,
B.15.572 Tellen hem and techen hem on þe Trinite *to* bileue,
B.15.573 And feden hem wiþ goostly foode and [nedy folk *to* fynden]
B.15.576 Bodily foode and goostly foode *to*] gyue þere it nedeþ:
B.15.581 And han clerkes *to* kepen vs þerInne & hem þat shul come after.
B.15.585 And took it Moyses *to* teche men til Messie coome,
B.15.597 And studieden *to* struyen hym and struyden hemselue,
B.15.603 And hopen þat he be *to* come þat shal hem releue;
B.16.3 Ac ȝit I am in a weer what charite is *to* mene.'
B.16.4 'It is a ful trie tree', quod he, 'trewely *to* telle.
B.16.10 'I wolde trauaille', quod I, 'þis tree *to* se twenty hundred myle,
B.16.11 And *to* haue my fulle of þat fruyt forsake a[l] oþ[er] saule[e].
B.16.16 And liberum arbitrium haþ þe lond [*to*] ferme,
B.16.17 Vnder Piers þe Plowman *to* piken it and weden it.'
B.16.25 'For wyndes, wiltow wite', quod he, '*to* witen it fro fallyng:

B.16.40 And þanne fondeþ þe fend my fruyt *to* destruye
B.16.47 That is lieutenaunt *to* loken it wel bi leue of myselue:
B.16.65 *To* asken hym any moore þerof, and bad hym ful faire
B.16.66 '*To* [dyuyse] þe fruyt þat so faire hangeþ'.
B.16.73 I preide Piers *to* pulle adoun an Appul and he wolde,
B.16.74 And suffre me *to* assaien what sauour it hadde.
B.16.75 And Piers caste *to* þe crop and þanne comsed it *to* crye;
B.16.89 *To* go robbe þat Rageman and reue þe fruyt fro hym.
B.16.94 That Piers fruyt floured and felle *to* be rype.
B.16.102 *To* haue yfouȝte wiþ þe fend er ful tyme come.
B.16.105 That, þouȝ he were wounded with his enemy, *to* warisshen
hymselue:
B.16.127 And mysseide þe Iewes manliche and manaced hem *to* bete
B.16.137 Thei casten and contreueden *to* kulle hym whan þei myȝte;
B.16.147 And tolde hem a tokne *to* knowe wiþ Iesus;
B.16.152 And kiste hym *to* be caught þerby and kulled of þe Iewes.
B.16.156 Thow shalt be myrour to many men *to* deceyue,
B.16.170 And yede forþ as an ydiot in contree *to* aspie
B.16.176 'I am feiþ', quod þat freke, 'it falleþ noȝt *to* lye,
B.16.192 Might and [a] mene [his owene myȝte *to* knowe],
B.16.196 *To* ocupie hym here til issue were spronge,
B.16.215 That is, creatour weex creature *to* knowe what was boþe.
B.16.219 Ne matrimoyne withouten Mul[eri]e is noȝt muche *to* preise:
B.16.230 Ful trewe toknes bitwene vs is *to* telle whan me likeþ.
B.16.237 Bledden blood for þat lordes loue and hope *to* blisse þe tyme.
B.16.243 And siþþe he sente me *to* seye I sholde do sacrifise
B.17.3 *To* rule alle Reames wiþ; I bere þe writ [riȝt] here.'
B.17.5 'Nay', he seide, '[I] seke hym þat haþ þe seel *to* kepe,
B.17.6 And þat is cros and cristendom and crist þeron *to* honge;
B.17.27 And lelest *to* leue [on] for lif and for soule?
B.17.33 What neded it [now] a newe lawe *to* [brynge]
B.17.37 *To* bileeue and louye in o lord almyghty
B.17.42 It is lighter to lewed men o lesson *to* knowe
B.17.43 Than for to techen hem two, and to hard *to* lerne þe leeste!
B.17.46 It is lighter *to* leeue in þre louely persones
B.17.68 And *to* þe wye he wente hise woundes to biholde,
B.17.68 And to þe wye he wente hise woundes *to* biholde,
B.17.69 And parceyued bi his pous he was in peril *to* dye
B.17.82 And raped hym *to* [ryde þe riȝte wey to Ierusalem].
B.17.83 Feiþ folwede after faste and fondede *to* mete hym,
B.17.85 *To* ouertaken hym and liste to hym er þei to towne coome.
B.17.86 And whan I seiȝ þis I soiourned noȝt but shoop me *to* renne
B.17.88 And graunted hym *to* ben his [gome]; 'graunt mercy', he seide;
B.17.131 And Hope afterward he bad me *to* louye
B.17.142 Til hym [likede] and liste *to* vnlosen his fynger,
B.17.145 *To* ministren and to make þat myȝt of hand knoweþ;
B.17.145 To ministren and *to* make þat myȝt of hand knoweþ;
B.17.148 The fyngres þat fre ben *to* folde and to serue
B.17.148 The fyngres þat fre ben to folde and *to* serue
B.17.152 The fader is [þanne] as a fust wiþ fynger *to* touche–
B.17.153 Al þat þe pawme parceyueþ profitable *to* feele.
B.17.172 The fyngres formen a ful hand *to* portreye or peynten;
B.17.178 For [þe pawme] haþ power *to* putte out þe ioyntes
B.17.179 And *to* vnfolde þe fust, [for hym it bilongeþ].
B.17.191 *To* clucche or to clawe, to clippe or to holde.
B.17.191 To clucche or *to* clawe, to clippe or to holde.
B.17.191 To clucche or to clawe, *to* clippe or to holde.
B.17.191 To clucche or to clawe, to clippe or *to* holde.
B.17.211 [That serueþ þise swynkeres *to* se by aniȝtes],
B.17.219 To alle vnkynde creatures þat coueite *to* destruye
B.17.226 Til þe holy goost gynne *to* glowe and to blase,
B.17.226 Til þe holy goost gynne to glowe and *to* blase,
B.17.247 [Fro] þe fader of heuene forȝifnesse *to* haue.
B.17.249 But þow haue tow *to* take it wiþ, tonder or broches,
B.17.279 For þat þe holy goost haþ *to* kepe þ[o] harlotes destruyeþ,
B.17.282 To a torche or a tapur *to* reuerence þe Trinite,
B.17.287 Synnen ayein þe Seint Spirit, assenten *to* destruye
B.17.317 *To* amende al þat amys is, and his mercy gretter
B.17.328 It dooþ hym worse þan his wif or wete *to* slepe;
B.17.333 Thise þre þat I telle of ben þus *to* vnderstonde:
B.17.335 For kynde clyueþ on hym euere *to* contrarie þe soule,
B.17.344 That þei han cause *to* contrarie by kynde of hir siknesse;
B.18.4 Til I weex wery of þe world and wilned eft *to* slepe
B.18.13 As is þe kynde of a knyght þat comeþ *to* be dubbed,
B.18.14 *To* geten hym gilte spores [and] galoches ycouped
B.18.28 'Nay', quod [feiþ, 'but] þe fend and fals doom [*to* deye].
B.18.32 That, for al þat deeþ kan do, wiþInne þre daies *to* walke
B.18.37 *To* se how doghtiliche deeþ sholde do and deme hir boþeres right.
B.18.42 *To* fordoon it on o day, and in þre dayes after
B.18.48 And bigan of [grene] þorn a garland *to* make,
B.18.53 And beden hym drynken his deeþ [*to* lette and] hise daies [lengþe],
B.18.75 Ac was no bo[y] so boold goddes body *to* touche;
B.18.77 That noon harlot were so hardy *to* leyen hond vpon hym.

B.18.82   *To* [Iusten wiþ Iesus, þis blynde Iew Longeus].
B.18.84   *To* touchen hym or to tasten hym or taken doun of roode,
B.18.84   To touchen hym or *to* tasten hym or taken doun of roode,
B.18.88   'Ayein my wille it was, lord, *to* wownde yow so soore.'
B.18.95   *To* do þe blynde bete [þe dede], it was a boyes counseille.
B.18.97   *To* [bete a body ybounde wiþ any briȝt wepene].
B.18.126   'And am wendynge *to* wite what þis wonder meneþ.'
B.18.174   And preide pees *to* telle hire to what place she wolde,
B.18.176   'My wil is *to* wende', quod she, 'and welcome hem alle
B.18.185   *To* be mannes meynpernour for eueremoore after.
B.18.209   Sholde wite witterly what day is *to* meene.
B.18.213   Bicam man of a mayde mankynde *to* saue
B.18.214   And suffrede *to* be sold to se þe sorwe of deying,
B.18.214   And suffrede to be sold *to* se þe sorwe of deying,
B.18.217   Woot no wight, as I wene, what [is ynogh] *to* mene.
B.18.220   And siþþe he suffred hym synne sorwe *to* feele,
B.18.221   *To* wite what wele was, kyndeliche [to] knowe it.
B.18.221   To wite what wele was, kyndeliche [*to*] knowe it.
B.18.223   *To* [se] what he haþ suffred in þre sondry places,
B.18.225   *To* wite what alle wo is [þat woot of] alle ioye.
B.18.240   And tendeden [hire] as a torche *to* reuerencen his burþe;
B.18.250   And leet out Symondes sone[s] *to* seen hym hange on roode.
B.18.253   *To* breke and to bete adoun [alle] þat ben ayeins [hym],
B.18.253   To breke and *to* bete adoun [alle] þat ben ayeins [hym],
B.18.254   [And to haue out of helle alle þat hym likeþ].
B.18.289   And eggedest hem *to* ete, Eue by hirselue,
B.18.301   *To* warne Pilates wif what done man was Iesus,
B.18.306   *To* saue men from synne if hemself wolde.
B.18.328   For alle synfulle soules, *to* saue þo þat ben worþi.
B.18.352   *To* recouere hem þoruȝ raunsoun and by no reson ellis,
B.18.361   Now bigynneþ þi gile ageyn þee *to* turne
B.18.362   And my grace *to* growe ay gretter and widder.
B.18.375   A[c] *to* be merciable to man þanne my kynde [it] askeþ
B.18.379   It is noȝt vsed in erþe to hangen a feloun
B.19.3   *To* here holly þe masse and to be housled after.
B.19.3   To here holly þe masse and *to* be housled after..
B.19.9   And þanne called I Conscience *to* kenne me þe soþe:
B.19.20   Ne noon so nedeful *to* nempne by nyȝte ne by daye.
B.19.21   For alle derke deueles arn adrad *to* heren it,
B.19.28   *To* be called a knyght is fair for men shul knele to hym.
B.19.29   *To* be called a kyng is fairrer for he may knyghtes make.
B.19.30   Ac *to* be conqueror called, þat comeþ of special grace,
B.19.32   *To* make lordes of laddes of lond þat he wynneþ
B.19.42   It bicomeþ to a kyng *to* kepe and to defende,
B.19.42   It bicomeþ to a kyng to kepe and *to* defende,
B.19.59   *To* maken alle folk free þat folwen his lawe].
B.19.62   He may [be wel] called conquerour, and þat is crist *to* mene.
B.19.64   Is *to* wissen vs þerwiþ, þat whan we ben tempted,
B.19.65   Therwith *to* fiȝte and [f]enden vs fro fallynge in[to] synne,
B.19.69   Ac *to* carpe moore of crist and how he com to þat name,
B.19.72   And cam *to* take mankynde kynges and Aungeles
B.19.93   For Mirre is mercy *to* mene and mylde speche of tonge.
B.19.99   As it bicomeþ a conquerour *to* konne manye sleightes,
B.19.110   And þere bigan god of his grace *to* do wel:
B.19.114   [Boþe] to lered and to lewede, *to* louyen oure enemys.
B.19.116   Bigan god of his grace and goodnesse *to* dowel,
B.19.125   He made lame *to* lepe and yaf light to blynde
B.19.138   *To* be kaiser or kyng of þe kyngdom of Iuda,
B.19.164   Boþe Iames and Iohan, Iesu *to* seke,
B.19.170   And took Thomas by þe hand and tauȝte hym *to* grope
B.19.184   [Myght [men] *to* assoille of alle manere synne[s],
B.19.186   In couenaunt þat þei come and knewelich[e] *to* paie
B.19.189   *To* bynde and vnbynde boþe here and elli[s],
B.19.198   And wikkede *to* wonye in wo wiþouten ende.'
B.19.200   And counseiled me *to* knele þerto; and þanne cam, me þouȝte,
B.19.213   [Th]anne bigan grace *to* go wiþ Piers Plowman
B.19.214   And counseillede hym and Conscience þe comune *to* sompne:
B.19.217   Tresour *to* lyue by to hir lyues ende,
B.19.218   And wepne *to* fighte wiþ þat wole neuere faille.
B.19.224   Coueitise and vnkyndenesse Cardinals hym *to* lede.
B.19.226   And wepne *to* fighte wiþ whan Antecrist yow assailleþ.'
B.19.227   And gaf ech man a grace *to* gide wiþ hymseluen
B.19.229   Some [wyes] he yaf wit with wordes *to* shewe,
B.19.230   [To wynne wiþ truþe þat] þe world askeþ,
B.19.232   They lelly *to* lyue by labour of tonge,
B.19.233   And by wit *to* wissen oþere as grace hem wolde teche,
B.19.235   [By] sellynge and buggynge hir bilyue *to* wynne.
B.19.236   And some he lered *to* laboure [on lond and on watre
B.19.238   And some he tauȝte *to* tilie, to [coke] and to thecche,
B.19.238   And some he tauȝte to tilie, *to* [coke] and to thecche,
B.19.238   And some he tauȝte to tilie, to [coke] and *to* thecche,
B.19.239   *To* wynne wiþ hir liflode bi loore of his techynge;
B.19.240   And some *to* deuyne and diuide, [figures] to kenne;

B.19.240   And some to deuyne and diuide, [figures] *to* kenne;
B.19.241   And some *to* [kerue and compace], and colours to make;
B.19.241   And some to [kerue and compace], and colours *to* make;
B.19.242   And some *to* se and to seye what sholde bifalle,
B.19.242   And some to se and *to* seye what sholde bifalle,
B.19.245   And some *to* ryde and to recouere þat [vnriȝt]fully was wonne:
B.19.245   And some to ryde and *to* recouere þat [vnriȝt]fully was wonne:
B.19.248   And some he lered *to* lyue in longynge to ben hennes,
B.19.248   And some he lered to lyue in longynge *to* ben hennes,
B.19.249   In pouerte and in [pacience] *to* preie for alle cristene.
B.19.250   And alle he lered *to* be lele, and ech a craft loue ooþer,
B.19.259   And Registrer *to* receyue redde quod debes.
B.19.268   Al þat hise oxen eriede þei *to* harewen after.
B.19.271   Thise foure, þe feiþ *to* teche, folwe[de] Piers teme
B.19.280   [That] caste for to ke[l]e a crokke *to* saue þe fatte aboue.
B.19.283   Sholde neuere mete ne [meschief] make hym *to* swelle;
B.19.291   *To* suffren al þat god sente, siknesse and Angres,
B.19.294   And bold and abidynge bismares *to* suffre;
B.19.302   Spiritus Iusticie spareþ noȝt *to* spille [þe] gilty,
B.19.303   And *to* correcte [þ]e kyng if [þe kyng] falle in gilt.
B.19.305   *To* demen as a domesman adrad was he neuere
B.19.318   Ordeigne þee an hous, Piers, *to* herberwe Inne þi cornes.'
B.19.325   And þerwiþ Grace bigan *to* make a good foundement,
B.19.330   A cart highte cristendom *to* carie [home] Piers sheues,
B.19.333   As wide as þe world is wiþ Piers *to* tilie truþe
B.19.353   '*To* wasten on welfare and in wikked [kepyng]
B.19.355   Quod Conscience to alle cristene þo, 'my counseil is *to* wende
B.19.359   *To* goon agayn Pride but Grace weere wiþ vs.'
B.19.360   And þanne kam Kynde wit Conscience *to* teche,
B.19.362   *To* deluen a dych depe aboute vnitee
B.19.364   Conscience comaundede þo alle cristene *to* delue,
B.19.366   *To* helpe holy chirche and hem þat it kepeþ.
B.19.374   That he ne halp a quantite holynesse *to* wexe,
B.19.387   [Myȝt] *to* maken it and men to ete it after
B.19.387   [Myȝt] to maken it and men *to* ete it after
B.19.391   'How?' quod al þe comune; 'þow conseillest vs *to* yelde
B.19.395   And so for þe comune; 'þow conseillest vs *to* ... [?]
B.19.423   Or in Rome as hir rule wole þe relikes *to* kepe;
B.19.432   And sent þe sonne *to* saue a cursed mannes tilþe
B.19.437   [So blessed be Piers þe Plowman þat peyneþ hym *to* tilye],
B.19.443   And cleymeþ bifore þe kyng *to* be kepere ouer cristene,
B.19.445   And fynt folk *to* fiȝte and cristen blood to spille
B.19.445   And fynt folk to fiȝte and cristen blood *to* spille
B.19.457   Ech man subtileþ a sleiȝte synne *to* hide
B.19.460   'I holde it riȝt and reson of my Reue *to* take
B.19.466   'I am kyng wiþ croune þe comune *to* rule,
B.19.467   And holy kirke and clergie fro cursed men *to* [de]fende.
B.19.468   And if me lakkeþ *to* lyue by þe lawe wole I take it
B.20.3   I ne wiste wher *to* ete ne at what place,
B.20.13   Ne wight noon wol ben his boruȝ, ne wed haþ noon *to* legge;
B.20.45   And þe fissh haþ fyn *to* flete wiþ to reste;
B.20.48   Forþi be noȝt abasshed *to* bide and to be nedy
B.20.48   Forþi be noȝt abasshed to bide and *to* be nedy
B.20.60   And al þe Couent cam *to* welcome [a] tyraunt
B.20.62   Whiche foolis were wel [gladdere] *to* deye
B.20.63   [Th]an *to* lyue lenger siþ [Leute] was so rebuked
B.20.89   Wiþ deeþ þat is dredful *to* vndo vs alle!'
B.20.91   After Confort a knyght *to* come and bere his baner:
B.20.107   *To* cesse and suffre, and see wher þei wolde
B.20.109   And kynde cessede [sone] *to* se þe peple amende.
B.20.124   His wepne was al wiles, *to* wynnen and to hiden;
B.20.124   His wepne was al wiles, to wynnen and *to* hiden;
B.20.126   Symonye hym [suede] *to* assaille Conscience,
B.20.128   *To* holden wiþ Antecrist, hir temporaltees to saue.
B.20.128   To holden wiþ Antecrist, hir temporaltees *to* saue.
B.20.131   And garte good feiþ flee and fals *to* abide,
B.20.141   That Coueitise were cristene þat is so kene [*to* fighte],
B.20.166   And bad hym fonde *to* fighte and afere wanhope.
B.20.179   May noȝt a myte auaille *to* med[l]e ayein Elde.'
B.20.195   For þe lyme þat she loued me fore and leef was *to* feele
B.20.207   'Counseille me, kynde', quod I, 'what craft is best *to* lerne?'
B.20.208   'Lerne *to* loue', quod kynde, 'and leef alle oþere.'
B.20.209   'How shal I come to catel so *to* cloþe me and to feede?'
B.20.209   'How shal I come to catel so to cloþe me and *to* feede?'
B.20.212   And [I] by conseil of kynde comsed *to* rome
B.20.214   And þere was Conscience Conestable, cristene *to* saue,
B.20.223   Than I do *to* drynke a drauȝte of good ale.'
B.20.230   Freres herden hym crye and comen hym *to* helpe,
B.20.233   That þei come for coueitise, *to* haue cure of soules.
B.20.235   They wol flatere [to] fare wel folk þat ben riche.
B.20.252   Frere Frounceys and Domynyk, for loue *to* be holye.
B.20.265   Hir ordre and hir reule wole *to* han a certein noumbre
B.20.269   It is wikked *to* wage yow; ye wexen out of noumbre.

B.20.276	That alle þynges vnder heuene ouȝte *to* ben in comune.
B.20.282	Ben Curatours called *to* knowe and to hele,
B.20.282	Ben Curatours called to knowe and *to* hele,
B.20.292	A parcel *to* preye for hem and [pleye] wiþ þe remenaunt,
B.20.298	And made pees porter *to* pynne þe yates
B.20.311	Sire leef-*to*-lyue-in-lecherie lay þere and gronede;
B.20.325	To a lord for a lettre leue *to* haue
B.20.326	*To* curen as a Curatour; and cam with hi[s] lettr[e]
B.20.328	In contrees þer he coome confessions *to* here;
B.20.360	[And] lat hem ligge ouerlonge and looþ is *to* chaunge;
B.20.369	Til Contricion hadde clene foryeten *to* crye and to wepe
B.20.369	Til Contricion hadde clene foryeten to crye and *to* wepe
B.20.370	And wake for hise wikked werkes as he was wont *to* doone.
B.20.374	And comen wiþ a kene wille Conscience *to* assaille.
B.20.375	Conscience cryed eft [Clergie *to* helpe],
B.20.376	And [bad] Contricion [come] *to* kepe þe yate.
B.20.382	*To* seken Piers þe Plowman, þat pryde [myȝte] destruye,
C.Pr.4	Wente forth in þe world wondres *to* here
C.Pr.22	Somme potte hem *to* plogh, playde ful selde,
C.Pr.29	In hope *to* haue a good ende and heuenriche blisse,
C.Pr.31	Coueyten noȝt in contre[y] *to* cayren aboute
C.Pr.32	For no likerous liflode here lycame *to* plese.
C.Pr.35	And summe murthes *to* make, as mynstrels conneth,
C.Pr.38	And [han] wytt at wille *to* worche yf þei wolde.
C.Pr.48	*To* seke seynt Iame and seyntes [at] Rome;
C.Pr.50	And hadde leue *to* lye [al here lyf aftir].
C.Pr.53	Grete lobies and longe þat loth were *to* swynke
C.Pr.54	Clothed hem in copis *to* be knowe fram othere
C.Pr.55	And [shopen] he[m] heremites here ese *to* haue.
C.Pr.62	Ac sith charite hath be Chapman and [c]hief *to* shryue lordes
C.Pr.71	Comen [vp] knel[yng] *to* kyssen his bull[e].
C.Pr.74	Thus ȝe gyue ȝoure gold glotons *to* helpe
C.Pr.83	*To* haue a licence and leue [at] Londoun to dwelle
C.Pr.83	To haue a licence and leue [at] Londoun *to* dwelle
C.Pr.87	Ben charged with holy chirche charite *to* tylie,
C.Pr.98	*To* vndertake þe tol of vntrewe sacrefice.
C.Pr.128	I parsceyued of þe power that Peter hadde *to* kepe,
C.Pr.129	*To* bynde and vnbynde as þe boke telleth,
C.Pr.133	Thare Crist is in kynedom *to* close with heuene.
C.Pr.135	And power presumen in hemself a pope *to* make
C.Pr.136	*To* haue þe power þat Peter hadde inpugne y nelle
C.Pr.140	Myght of tho men made hym *to* regne.
C.Pr.147	With lele labour *to* lyue while lif on londe lasteth.
C.Pr.185	A belle *to* byggen of bras oþer of] bryghte syluer
C.Pr.188	Wher he ri[t] othere reste or rometh *to* pleye;
C.Pr.196	Ne hanged it aboute his hals al yngelond *to* wynne;
C.Pr.203	*To* crache vs and alle oure kynde thogh we crope vnder benches;
C.Pr.205	And be [we] neuere so bold the belle hym [*to*] shewe.
C.Pr.234	Of þe r[yn]e and of þe rochele the roost [*to*] defye!'
C.1.15	*To* be fayful to hym [he] ȝaf ȝow fyue wittes
C.1.17	Wherfore he hette þe elementis *to* helpe ȝow alle tymes
C.1.19	And, in mesure thow muche were, *to* make ȝow attese
C.1.40	And wysseth þe *to* ywar what wolde þe desseyue.'
C.1.51	And kynde witte be wardeyn ȝoure welthe *to* kepe
C.1.55	'The dep dale and þe derk, so vnsemely *to* se to,
C.1.62	Conseylede Caym *to* cullen his brother,
C.1.67	*To* combre men with coueytise, þat is his kynde and his lore.'
C.1.72	'Holy churche y am,' quod she; 'þou oughtest me *to* knowe;
C.1.74	Thow broughtest me borewes my biddyng *to* fulfille,
C.1.75	[*To*] leue on me and loue me al thy lyf tyme.'
C.1.77	And preyede here pitously *to* preye for me to amende
C.1.77	And preyede here pitously to preye for me *to* amende
C.1.78	And also kenne me kyndly on crist *to* bileue.
C.1.82	I do it [o]n deus caritas *to* deme þe sothe.
C.1.96	Treweliche *to* take and treweliche to fyghte
C.1.96	Treweliche to take and treweliche *to* fyghte
C.1.101	And neuer leue for loue in hope *to* lacche syluer.
C.1.103	Dede hem swere on here swerd *to* serue treuthe euere.
C.1.111	That hadde [lu]st *to* be lyk his lord þat was almyghty:
C.1.133	Estward til heuene, euere *to* abyde
C.1.145	Lok þow soffre hym *to* seye and so thow myht lerne.
C.1.164	Mekeliche for oure mysdedes *to* amende vs alle.
C.1.167	*To* haue pitee on þat peple þat paynede hym to dethe.
C.1.172	Thow ȝe be myhty to mote beth meke in ȝoure werkes,
C.1.204	*To* lere the what loue is;' and leue at me she lauhte.
C.2.4	Kenne me by sum craft *to* knowe þe false.'
C.2.21	And [ylow on] hym to lordes þat lawes han *to* kepe;
C.2.52	And haue power *to* p[uny]schen hem; thenne pot forth thy resoun.
C.2.68	And [as] a brokor brouhte here *to* be [with fals enioyned].
C.2.73	And preyeth syuile *to* se and s[y]monye to rede hit.
C.2.73	And preyeth syuile to se and s[y]monye *to* rede hit.
C.2.87	*To* ben pr[inces] in pruyde and pouert to dispice,
C.2.87	To ben pr[inces] in pruyde and pouert *to* dispice,
C.2.88	*To* bacbite and to boste and bere fals witnesse,
C.2.88	To bacbite and *to* boste and bere fals witnesse,
C.2.89	*To* skorne and to skolde and sklaundre to make;
C.2.89	To skorne and *to* skolde and sklaundre to make;
C.2.89	To skorne and to skolde and sklaundre *to* make;
C.2.90	Vnbuxum and bold *to* breke þe ten hestes;
C.2.101	Al day to drynke at diuerse tauernes,
C.2.102	And there *to* iangele and iape and iuge here Emcristene,
C.2.103	And fastyng dayes *to* frete byfore noone and drynke
C.2.105	/This lyf *to* folowe falsnesse and folk þat on hym leueth,
C.2.107	And awake with wanhope and no wille *to* amende,
C.2.121	Suche a weddyng *to* wurche þat wrathe myhte treuthe;
C.2.167	And comen ful courteysly *to* conforte the false
C.2.171	That he grauntep *to* go with a goode wille
C.2.172	To londone *to* loke yf lawe wille iugge;
C.2.173	*To* be maried for mone med[e] hath assented.'
C.2.177	*To* wende with h[e]m to westminstre [the] weddyng to honoure.
C.2.177	To wende with h[e]m to westminstre [the] weddyng *to* honoure.
C.2.195	And maketh of lyare a lang cart *to* lede al this othere,
C.2.199	Y haue no tome *to* telle the tayl þat hem folewe[th]
C.2.201	Ac gyle was forgoere *to* gyen al th[e] peple,
C.2.214	[T]o atache tho tyrauntes, 'for eny tresor, y hote;
C.2.222	And bad falsnesse *to* fle and his feres alle.
C.2.224	And gyle doth hym *to* gone agaste for to deye.
C.2.226	And byschytten hym in here shoppe[s] *to* shewen here ware;
C.2.227	[A]paraylede hym [as a] prentys the peple *to* serue.
C.2.237	That lyare sholde wonye with hem watres *to* loke.
C.2.238	Spysours speken to hym *to* aspye he[re] ware
C.2.244	Ac he hath leue *to* lep out as ofte as hym liketh.
C.2.254	Ac treuliche *to* telle a tremblede for fere
C.3.4	*To* take mede þe mayde and maken here at ese.
C.3.12	Ac there was myrthe and mynstracie mede *to* plese;
C.3.27	Thenne come clerkes *to* conforte here the same
C.3.31	*To* louye hem leeliche and lordes [hem] make,
C.3.33	And bygge ȝow benefices, [here bonchef] *to* haue,
C.3.49	Among knyhtes and clerkes consience *to* turne.
C.3.69	*To* writen [i]n wyndowes of eny wel dedes,
C.3.79	*To* punischen [o]n pilories and [o]n pynyng stoles
C.3.100	Graunte gylours on erthe grace *to* amende
C.3.109	For to spyre and *to* aspye, for eny speche of suluer;
C.3.116	Of alle suche sullers seluer *to* take
C.3.120	'And soffre hem som tyme *to* selle aȝeyne þe lawe.'
C.3.125	Amonge thise lettred lordes this latyn is *to* mene
C.3.129	And sente *to* se here; y myhte nat se þat ladde here.
C.3.132	And wilned to be wedded withouten his leue,
C.3.146	And teche the *to* louye treuthe and take consail of resoun.
C.3.151	Thenne was Consience ykald *to* come and apere
C.3.177	*To* vnfetere the fals, fle wher hym liketh,
C.3.180	*To* be cursed in constorie a counteth nat a rusche;
C.3.189	*To* holde lemmanes and lotebyes al here lyfdayes
C.3.199	Lawe is so lordliche and loth *to* make ende;
C.3.203	Religioun he al toreueth and oute of reule *to* lybbe.
C.3.207	And custumes of coueytise þe comune *to* destruye.
C.3.217	*To* haue space to speke, spede yf a myhte.
C.3.217	To haue space *to* speke, spede yf a myhte.
C.3.220	For Consience acuseth the *to* congeye the foreuere.'
C.3.224	And þ[ou] knowe[st], Consience, y cam nat *to* chyde
C.3.225	Ne *to* depraue thy persone with a pro[u]d herte.
C.3.233	For kulde y neuere no kyng ne conseilede so *to* done;
C.3.237	Hast arwed many hardy man þat hadde wille *to* fyhte,
C.3.238	*To* berne and to bruttene, to bete adoun strenghtes.
C.3.238	To berne and *to* bruttene, to bete adoun strenghtes.
C.3.238	To berne and to bruttene, *to* bete adoun strenghtes.
C.3.244	Vnconnynge is þat Consience a kyndom *to* sulle
C.3.252	*To* helpe heyliche alle his oste or elles graunte
C.3.255	A[t] Concience þat coueiteth to conquere a reume.
C.3.264	*To* lete so his lordschipe for a litel mone.
C.3.266	*To* ȝeue men mede þat meekliche hym serueth,
C.3.267	To aliens, to alle men, *to* honoure hem with ȝeftes;
C.3.270	Thorw ȝeftes haen ȝemen *to* ȝerne and to ryde;
C.3.270	Thorw ȝeftes haen ȝemen to ȝerne and *to* ryde;
C.3.272	And ȝeuen mede to men *to* meyntene here lawes;
C.3.285	Mede is worthy, me thynketh, þe maistrye *to* haue.'
C.3.290	*To* ȝeue men mede, more oþer lasse.
C.3.296	And for to vndertake [*to*] trauaile for another
C.3.298	Ne haue hap to his hele mede *to* deserue.
C.3.306	And but hit prestly be ypayed þe payere is *to* blame,
C.3.322	Noyther [thei ne] here ayres hardy *to* claymen
C.3.346	And styfliche stande forth *to* strenghe þe fundement,
C.3.350	*To* pay hym yf he parforme and haue pite yf he faileth
C.3.357	In case, credere in ecclesia, in holy kyrke *to* bileue;
C.3.358	In nombre, Rotye and aryse and remissioun *to* haue,
C.3.359	Of oure sory synnes *to* be assoiled and yclansed

C. 3.364   Alle kyn kynde *to* knowe and to folowe
C. 3.364   Alle kyn kynde to knowe and *to* folowe
C. 3.365   And withoute ca[s]e *to* cache [*to*] and come to bothe nombres,
C. 3.367   Þat is nat resonable ne rect *to* refuse my syre name,
C. 3.371   So indirect is inlyche *to* coueyte
C. 3.372   *To* acorde in alle kynde and in alle kyn nombre,
C. 3.375   As a kyng *to* clayme the comune at his wille
C. 3.376   *To* folowe and to fynde hym and [f]eche at hem his consayl
C. 3.376   To folowe and *to* fynde hym and [f]eche at hem his consayl
C. 3.396   And is *to* [mene] in oure mouth more n[e] mynne
C. 3.398   Sholde confourme hem to o kynde on holy kyrke *to* bileue
C. 3.400   *To* syke for here synnes and soffre harde penaunc[e]
C. 3.418   *To* be buxum at my byddyng his [b]o[n]e to fulfille.
C. 3.418   To be buxum at my byddyng his [b]o[n]e *to* fulfille.
C. 3.433   The culorum of this kaes kepe y nat *to* shewe;
C. 3.445   Tho shal be maistres on molde trewe men *to* helpe.
C. 3.462   Vche man *to* pley with a plogh, a pikois oþer a spade,
C. 3.470   Ne potte [hem] in panele [*to*] do [hem] plihte here treuthe;
C. 4.7   'Rape the *to* ryde and resoun þat thow [f]ec[c]he.
C. 4.8   Comaunde hym þat he come my consayle *to* here
C. 4.16   'Y shal aray me *to* ryde,' quod resoun, 'reste the [a] while,'
C. 4.19   Ne-lesynges-*to*-lauhe-of-for-y-louede-hit-neuere.
C. 4.22   For hit is þe wone of wil *to* wynse and to kyke
C. 4.22   For hit is þe wone of wil to wynse and *to* kyke
C. 4.24   Thenne Consience on his capel comesed *to* pryke
C. 4.28   Fayn were *to* folowe hem and faste ryden aftur
C. 4.29   *To* take reed of resoun þat recorde sholde
C. 4.54   *To* robbe me or to ruyfle me yf y ryde softe.
C. 4.54   To robbe me or *to* ruyfle me yf y ryde softe.
C. 4.58   A meynteyneth his men *to* morthere myn hewes,
C. 4.63   Y am nat hardy for hym vnnethe *to* loke.'
C. 4.73   And token mede [myd] hem mercy *to* wynne.
C. 4.78   *To* ouercome þe kyng [with] catel y[f] they myhte.
C. 4.81   And comaundede a Constable *to* caste [hym] in yrones
C. 4.90   Then gan mede *to* m[e]ken here and mercy bisouhte
C. 4.92   'Haue this, man, of me,' quod she, '*to* amende thy scathe
C. 4.95   *To* haue mercy of þat man þat many tymes hym greuede:
C. 4.102   And efte the baldore be *to* bete myn hewes.
C. 4.105   Summe radden resoun tho *to* haue reuthe vppon þat shrewe
C. 4.108   'Rede me nat,' quod resoun, 'no reuthe *to* haue
C. 4.110   And hatien alle harlotrie *to* heren oþer to mouthen hit;
C. 4.110   And hatien alle harlotrie to heren oþer *to* mouthen hit;
C. 4.135   That y were kyng with c[r]oune *to* kepe [a] reume,
C. 4.147   *To* construe this c[l]ause, kyndeliche what it meneth.
C. 4.177   Hit is ful hard, by myn heued, herto *to* bryngen hit
C. 4.178   And alle ȝoure lege l[e]des *to* lede thus euene.'
C. 4.181   And brynge alle men *to* bowe withouten bittere wounde,
C. 4.192   *To* wage thyn and helpe wynne þat thow wilnest aftur
C. 4.195   The kyng comaundede Consience tho *to* congeye alle his offeceres
C. 5.8   And lymes *to* labory with and louede wel fare
C. 5.9   And no dede *to* do but drynke and slepe.
C. 5.21   [Hem þat bedreden be] byleue t[*o*] fynden?'
C. 5.23   Y am to wayke *to* wurcche with sykel or with sythe
C. 5.24   And to long, lef me, lowe *to* stoupe,
C. 5.25   *To* wurche as a werkeman eny while to duyren.'
C. 5.25   To wurche as a werkeman eny while *to* duyren.'
C. 5.26   'Thenne hastow londes *to* lyue by,' quod resoun, 'or lynage ryche
C. 5.50   *To* be welcome when y come oþerwhile in a monthe,
C. 5.63   Somme *to* synge masses or sitten and wryten,
C. 5.64   Redon and resceyuen þat resoun ouhte *to* spene\
C. 5.65   And knaue[s] vncrounede *to* carte and to worche.
C. 5.65   And knaue[s] vncrounede to carte and *to* worche.
C. 5.69   Thyse bylongeth *to* labory and lordes kyn to serue.
C. 5.69   Thyse bylongeth to labory and lordes kyn *to* serue.
C. 5.79   And taken Symondus sones seyntwarie *to* kepe,
C. 5.90   Ac it semeth no sad parfitnesse in Citees *to* b[e]gge
C. 5.99   So hope y *to* haue of hym þat is almyghty
C. 5.102   'Y rede the,' quod resoun tho, 'rape the *to* bigynne
C. 5.105   And to þe kyrke y gan go god *to* honoure;
C. 5.128   He p[ra]yde p[ur]nele here purfyel *to* leue
C. 5.130   Tomme stoue he tauhte *to* take t[w]o staues
C. 5.132   He warnede watte his wyf was *to* blame
C. 5.136   He chargede Chapmen *to* chasten here children:
C. 5.139   And so wrot the wyse *to* wyssen vs alle:
C. 5.143   And sethe he radde religioun here reule *to* holde
C. 5.151   That out of couent and Cloystre coueyteth *to* dwelle.
C. 5.154   For in C[l]oystre cometh no man *to* chyde ne to fyhte;
C. 5.154   For in C[l]oystre cometh no man to chyde ne *to* fyhte;
C. 5.155   In scole is loue and louhnesse and lykyng *to* lerne.
C. 5.163   Lytel hadde lordes ado *to* ȝeue lond fro [here] heyres
C. 5.174   Bred withouten beggynge *to* lyue by euere aftur
C. 5.180   And sethe a consailede þe kyng his comine *to* louie:
C. 5.183   And comuners [*to*] acorde in alle kyn treuthe.

C. 5.190   Is cause of alle combraunc[e] *to* confounde a reume.'
C. 5.192   And no grace [*to*] graunte til good loue were
C. 6.2   And made will *to* wepe water with his eyes
C. 6.7   *To* affayten here flesshe þat fers was to synne.
C. 6.7   To affayten here flesshe þat fers was *to* synne.
C. 6.9   And soffre *to* be mysseyde, and so dyde y neuere.
C. 6.17   And [bold haue] y be, nat abaschet *to* agulte
C. 6.21   Thorw my word and my witt here euel werkes *to* shewe;
C. 6.26   In alle [manere] maneres my name *to* be knowe;
C. 6.28   *To* telle eny tale; y trowed me wysor
C. 6.29   *To* carpe and to consayle then eny Clerk or lewed;
C. 6.29   To carpe and *to* consayle then eny Clerk or lewed;
C. 6.44   And louelokest *to* loke vppon a[nd] lykyngest abedde
C. 6.48   They *to* wene þat y were wel holy and almesfull
C. 6.49   And non so bolde a beggare *to* bidde and to craue,
C. 6.49   And non so bolde a beggare to bidde and *to* craue,
C. 6.50   Tales *to* telle in tauernes and in stretes,
C. 6.60   As *to* be preised amongus þe peple thow [y] pore seme:
C. 6.61   'Now god for his goodnesse gyue the grace *to* amende,'
C. 6.87   For enuye and euyl wil is euel *to* defye.
C. 6.95   Ȝut am y brokour of bakbytynge *to* blame menne w[a]re
C. 6.98   *To* lye and to loure and to lakke myn neyhebores,
C. 6.98   To lye and *to* loure and to lakke myn neyhebores,
C. 6.98   To lye and to loure and *to* lakke myn neyhebores,
C. 6.107   *To* sle hym sleyliche sleythes y bythenke.
C. 6.116   With lewed and lered þat leef ben *to* here
C. 6.143   Amonges wyues and wydewes [y am woned] *to* sitte
C. 6.152   For there aren many felle frekes myn aferes *to* aspye,
C. 6.158   Y haue no luste, lef me, *to* longe amonges monkes
C. 6.169   And bad hym bid to god be his helpe *to* amende
C. 6.180   Aboute þe mouthe and bynethe bygan y *to* grope
C. 6.190   *To* wynne to my wille wymmen with gyle,
C. 6.194   Y hadde likyng *to* lythe of lecherye tales.
C. 6.208   And was his prentis yplyht his profit *to* wayte
C. 6.209   Furste y lerned *to* lye a leef oþer tweye;
C. 6.210   Wykkedliche *to* waye was my furste lessoun.
C. 6.215   Thenne drow y me amonge drapers my donet *to* lere,
C. 6.216   *To* drawe the lyst along the lengur hit semede;
C. 6.218   *To* brochen hem with a batnelde and bande hem togyderes,
C. 6.222   [And] spak to þe spynnester[e] *to* spynnen [hit] oute.
C. 6.225   Y bouhte here barly; [a] brew hit *to* sulle.
C. 6.242   *To* weye pans with a peyse and par[e] þe heuegeste
C. 6.257   *To* assoyle the of th[y] synne sine restitucion[e]:
C. 6.271   *To* sese to me with here sikel þat y sewe neuere.
C. 6.273   Hadde y neuere will, [woot god], witterly *to* byseche
C. 6.279   Or in[to] pruyslond my prenties my profit *to* awayte,
C. 6.280   *To* marchaunde with my moneye and maken here eschaunges,
C. 6.291   Y rede no faythful frere at thy feste *to* sytte.
C. 6.297   [Ben] haldyng at the heye dome *to* helpe the restitue.
C. 6.303   There shal he wite witturly what vsure is *to* mene
C. 6.314   Then in lysse *to* lyue and lese lyf and soule.'
C. 6.322   Ne neuere wene *to* wynne with craft þat y knowe;
C. 6.341   For thow hast no good, by good fayth, *to* gete the with a wastel.
C. 6.344   And ȝif thow wyte neuere to whom ne where *to* restitue
C. 6.346   *To* bysetten hit hymsulue as beste be for thy soule.
C. 6.349   What a lered ȝow *to* lyue with and to lette ȝow fram thefte.'
C. 6.349   What a lered ȝow to lyue with and *to* lette ȝow fram thefte.'
C. 6.351   And kayres hym to kyrkeward his coup[e] *to* shewe.
C. 6.377   And to þe newe fayre nempnede [hit] *to* sull;
C. 6.380   There were chapmen ychose this chaffare *to* preyse;
C. 6.395   Bargaynes and Beuereges bygan *to* a[rys]e
C. 6.398   His gottes gan *to* gothly as t[w]o g[re]dy sowes,
C. 6.431   And as an hound þat eet gras so gan y *to* brake
C. 6.435   Out of resoun among rybaudes here rybaudrye *to* here.
C. 7.2   'Y moste sitte *to* be shryue or elles sholde y nappe;
C. 7.5   Sholde no ryngyng do me ryse til y were rype *to* dyne.'
C. 7.22   Y hadde leuere here an harlotrye or a lesyng *to* lauhen of
C. 7.40   Reuthe is *to* here rekenynge when we shal rede acountes,
C. 7.50   Til eche lyf hit lothed *to* loke þeron or smylle hit;
C. 7.74   And hath no likynge *to* lerne ne of oure lord to here
C. 7.74   And hath no likynge to lerne ne of oure lord *to* here
C. 7.79   He hateth *to* here thereof and alle þat þerof carpeth.
C. 7.83   And han lykyng *to* lythen hem in hope to do ȝow lawhe–
C. 7.83   And han lykyng to lythen hem in hope *to* do ȝow lawhe–
C. 7.90   *To* entise men thorw here tales to synne and harlotrie.
C. 7.102   For to solace ȝoure soules suche munstrals *to* haue:
C. 7.104   With a lered man *to* lere the what oure lord suffrede
C. 7.108   *To* crye a largesse tofore oure lord ȝoure good loos to shewe.
C. 7.108   To crye a largesse tofore oure lord ȝoure good loos *to* shewe.
C. 7.109   Thise thre manere munstrals maketh a man *to* lauhe
C. 7.111   That by his lyue l[yth]ed hem and louede hem *to* here.
C. 7.119   Tho was repentaunce aredy and redde hem alle *to* knele:
C. 7.121   *To* Amende vs of oure mysdedes, do mercy to vs alle.

C. 7.124	And sethe soffredes[t] hym *to* synege, a sykenesse to vs alle,
C. 7.127	And bicam man of a mayde mankynde *to* amende
C. 7.138	And a[l] *to* solace synfole thow soffredest it so were:
C. 7.157	*To* haue grace to go to treuthe; god leue þat they mote.
C. 7.157	To haue grace *to* go to treuthe; god leue þat they mote.
C. 7.185	And maden me sykere[n hym] sethen *to* seruen hym for euere,
C. 7.186	Bothe *to* sowe and to sette þe while y swynke myhte
C. 7.186	Bothe to sowe and *to* sette þe while y swynke myhte
C. 7.187	And *to* sowen his seed [and] suewen his bestes,
C. 7.188	Withynne and withouten *to* wayten his profit.
C. 7.192	Profitable as for þe plouh a potte me *to* lerne
C. 7.198	And hoso wilneth *to* wyte where þat treuthe woneth
C. 7.201	'Nay, bi þe perel of my soule!' Peres gan *to* swerie,
C. 7.209	That is *to* sey sothly ȝe sholde rather deye
C. 7.230	Thenne shaltow se say-soth-so-hit-be-*to*-done-
C. 7.235	The carneles ben of cristendom þat kynde *to* saue,
C. 7.249	*To* opene and vndo þe hye gate of heuene
C. 7.254	And yf grace graunte the *to* go in [in] this wyse
C. 7.257	And charge charite a churche *to* make
C. 7.258	In thyne hole herte *to* herborwe alle trewe
C. 7.263	And poketh forth pruyde *to* preyse thysuluen.
C. 7.266	Ykeyed and yclyketed *to* [kepe] the withouten,
C. 7.268	Thus myhte thow lesen his loue, *to* lete wel by thysulue,
C. 7.280	Ho is nat syb to this seuene, sothly *to* telle,
C. 7.282	*To* geten ingang at eny ȝate bote grace be þe more.'
C. 7.293	*To* loke how me liketh hit,' and toek his leue at Peres.
C. 7.295	*To* falewe with fiue ȝo[k]es; 'forthy me bihoueth
C. 7.296	*To* goo with a good wil and graytheliche hem dryue.
C. 8.2	Ich haue an half aker *to* erye by þe hele [way];
C. 8.10	That ȝe [han] selk and sendel *to* sowe whan tyme is
C. 8.11	Chesibles for chapeleynes churches *to* honoure.
C. 8.30	And afayte thy faucones [wylde foules *to* culle]
C. 8.31	For þey cometh to my croft my corn *to* diffoule.
C. 8.34	*To* defende þe in fayth, fyhte thow y sholde.'
C. 8.45	At churche in the Charnel cherles Aren euele *to* knowe
C. 8.47	Hit bicometh to the, knyhte, *to* be corteys and hende,
C. 8.48	Treuwe of thy tonge and tales loth *to* here
C. 8.52	For hit beeþ þe deueles dysors *to* drawe men to synne;
C. 8.63	To pilgrimag[e] as palmeres doen pardon *to* wynne.
C. 8.65	And helpe my Coltur *to* kerue and cl[o]se þe forwes;
C. 8.66	And alle þat helpen me [*to*] erye or elles to wedy
C. 8.66	And alle þat helpen me [to] erye or elles *to* wedy
C. 8.67	Shal haue leue, by oure lord, *to* [lese here in heruest]
C. 8.78	For holy chirche is ho[ld]e of hem no tythe *to* aske,
C. 8.84	'Consayle nat þe comune þe kyng *to* desplese
C. 8.85	Ne hem þat han lawes *to* lede lacke hem nat, y hote;
C. 8.99	*To* haue re[lees] and re[missioun]; on þat rental y leue.
C. 8.103	He is holdyng, y hope, *to* haue me in his masse
C. 8.113	*To* erien this half ak[er] holpen hym monye;
C. 8.117	Vch man in his manere made hymsulue *to* done
C. 8.118	And somme *to* plese Perkyn [pykede vp þe] wedes.
C. 8.120	[*To*] ouersey hem hymsulue; hoso beste wrouhte
C. 8.125	'But ȝe aryse þe rather and rape ȝow *to* worche
C. 8.135	[We haue] none lymes *to* labory with, lord god we thonketh.'
C. 8.141	Ac treuthe shal teche ȝow his teme *to* dryue
C. 8.145	Bothe of my corn and of my cloth *to* kepe hem fram defaute.
C. 8.149	Thenne gan wastor *to* wrath hym and wolde haue yfouhte
C. 8.150	And to [Peres] þe [plouhman] profrede *to* fyhte
C. 8.157	*To* kepe hym and his catel as couenant was bitwene hem:
C. 8.164	'I was nat woned *to* worche,' quod wastour, 'now wol y nat bygynne!'
C. 8.195	*To* be his holde hewe thow he hadde no more
C. 8.209	Of beggares and biddares what beste be *to* done.
C. 8.217	Treuthe tauhte me ones *to* louye hem vchone
C. 8.220	How y myhte amaystre hem *to* louye and labory
C. 8.257	And þat he weneth wel *to* haue y wol hit hym bireue".
C. 8.264	To beggares and to boys þat loth ben *to* worche.
C. 8.270	Ȝe han manged ouer moche; þat maketh ȝow *to* be syke.
C. 8.272	And sende the of his sauce [t]*o* sauery with thy lyppes
C. 8.292	And be fayn, be my fayth, his fysik *to* leete
C. 8.293	And lerne *to* labory with lode lest lyflode h[y]m fayle.
C. 8.307	Ne no cokeney, be Crist! colloppes *to* make.
C. 8.311	*To* drawe afeld my donge þe while þe drouthe lasteth.
C. 8.313	And by [t]hat y hope *to* haue heruost in my croft[e];
C. 8.317	And profrede [Peres] this present *to* ete with hongur.
C. 8.329	Laborers þat han no lond *to* lyue on but here handes
C. 8.330	Deyne[th noght] *to* dyne a day nyhte olde wortes;
C. 8.336	Aȝenes Catones consayle comseth he *to* gruche:
C. 8.338	Suche lawes *to* lerne laboreres to greue.
C. 8.338	Suche lawes to lerne laboreres *to* greue.
C. 8.343	He shal awake thorw water wastors *to* chaste;
C. 8.345	And so sayth saturne and sente [ȝow] *to* warne.
C. 9.2	*To* taken his teme and tilion þe erthe

C. 9.4	For hym and [for] his ayres for euere *to* ben assoiled.
C. 9.6	And alle þat holpe hym *to* erye, to sette or to sowe
C. 9.6	And alle þat holpe hym to erye, *to* sette or to sowe
C. 9.6	And alle þat holpe hym to erye, to sette or *to* sowe
C. 9.11	Haen pardon thorw purgatorye *to* passe ful lyhtly,
C. 9.12	With patriarkes and prophetes in paradis *to* sitton.
C. 9.17	Drede nat for no deth *to* distruye by here power
C. 9.20	*To* be [peres] to þe apostles alle peple to reule
C. 9.20	To be [peres] to þe apostles alle peple *to* reule
C. 9.44	Men of lawe hadde lest þat loth were *to* plede
C. 9.55	For hit is symonye *to* sulle þat sent is of grace,
C. 9.62	Bote the sugestioun be soth þat shapeth h[e]m *to* begge
C. 9.70	Woet no man, as y wene, who is worthy *to* haue
C. 9.75	Bothe in mylke and in mele *to* make with papelotes
C. 9.76	*To* aglotye with here gurles that greden aftur fode.
C. 9.79	*To* rise to þe reule to rokke þe cradel,
C. 9.79	To rise to þe reule *to* rokke þe cradel,
C. 9.80	Bothe *to* carde and to kembe, to cloute and to wasche,
C. 9.80	Bothe to carde and *to* kembe, to cloute and to wasche,
C. 9.80	Bothe to carde and to kembe, *to* cloute and to wasche,
C. 9.80	Bothe to carde and to kembe, to cloute and *to* wasche,
C. 9.81	[*To*] rybbe [and] to rele, rusches to pylie,
C. 9.81	[To] rybbe [and] *to* rele, rusches to pylie,
C. 9.81	[To] rybbe [and] to rele, rusches *to* pylie,
C. 9.82	That reuthe is *to* rede or in ryme shewe
C. 9.85	Bothe afyngred and afurste, *to* turne þe fayre outward
C. 9.90	And hath no catel but his craft *to* clothe h[e]m and to fede
C. 9.90	And hath no catel but his craft to clothe h[e]m and *to* fede
C. 9.91	And fele *to* fonge þerto and fewe panes taketh.
C. 9.96	These are Almusse *to* helpe þat han suche charges
C. 9.97	And *to* conforte suche coterelles and crokede men and blynde.
C. 9.103	And lymes *to* labory with and lollares lyf vsen
C. 9.114	*To* profecye of þe peple, pleinge as hit were
C. 9.116	*To* ȝeue vch a wyht wyt, welthe and his hele
C. 9.129	*To* vnderfongen hem fayre byfalleth for þe ryche
C. 9.141	Loken louhliche *to* lache men Almesse,
C. 9.142	In hope *to* sitte at euen by þe hote coles,
C. 9.146	And whenne hym lyketh and luste, his leue is *to* ryse
C. 9.151	And ca[ry]eth hit hoem to his cote and cast hym *to* lyuene
C. 9.157	And ouermore to [a]n [ha]tur *to* hele with his bonis
C. 9.221	Vnder obedience *to* be and buxum to þe lawe:
C. 9.222	Furste, Religious of religioun a reule *to* holde
C. 9.224	Lewede men *to* labory; lordes to honte
C. 9.224	Lewede men to labory; lordes *to* honte
C. 9.228	And vppon sonendayes *to* cese goddes seruice to here,
C. 9.228	And vppon sonendayes to cese goddes seruice *to* here,
C. 9.230	*To* heren here euensong euery man ouhte.
C. 9.232	Vcche halyday *to* here holly þe seruise,
C. 9.233	Vigilies and fastyngdays forthermore *to* knowe
C. 9.243	Where se we hem on sonendayes the seruise *to* here,
C. 9.270	When thy lord loketh *to* haue allouaunce of his bestes
C. 9.271	And of þe moneye thow haddest ther[myd] his mebles *to* [s]aue
C. 9.274	Thyn huyre, herde, as y hope, hath nat *to* quyte thy dette
C. 9.298	Mony tyme this meteles hath maked me *to* studie
C. 9.301	And which a pardoun Peres hadde th[e] peple *to* glade
C. 9.315	That Ioseph was Iustice Egipte *to* saue;
C. 9.318	Al this maketh me on meteles *to* studie
C. 9.325	Ȝut hath þe pope power pardoun *to* graunte
C. 9.326	To pele withouten penaunce *to* passe into ioye,
C. 9.331	Ac *to* triste vp this trionales, truely, me thynketh
C. 9.334	Vp truste of ȝoure tresor trionales *to* haue,
C. 9.335	Be ȝe neuere þe baldere *to* breke þe ten hestes
C. 9.338	*To* pur[c]hace ȝow pardoun and the popes bulles
C. 9.340	And comen alle bifore Crist acountes *to* ȝelde,
C. 9.347	Forthy y consayle alle cristene *to* crye god mercy.
C. 9.350	Suche werkes *to* worche the while we ben here
C.10.20	'Contra!' quod y as a Clerk and comsed *to* despute
C.10.29	He is otherwhile elleswher *to* wisse the peple.'
C.10.35	Maketh þe man many tyme *to* stomble yf he stande.
C.10.52	*To* repenten and arise and rowe out of synne
C.10.56	'Y haue no kynde kno[w]yng,' [quod y], '*to* conseyue al this speche
C.10.60	And gyue me grace on þis grounde with good ende *to* deye.'
C.10.65	*To* lythen here layes and here louely notes.
C.10.66	Murthe of here mouthes made me *to* slepe
C.10.75	Where þat dowel dwelleth And do me *to* knowe.'
C.10.77	Aren thre fayre vertues and ben nat fer *to* fynde.
C.10.92	Lene hem and loue hem", this latyn is *to* mene.
C.10.98	Sholde no bisshop be here biddynges *to* withsite.
C.10.101	And crounede oen *to* be kyng to kull withoute synne
C.10.101	And crounede oen to be kyng *to* kull withoute synne
C.10.104	Crounede oen *to* be a kyng to kepen vs alle
C.10.104	Crounede oen to be a kyng *to* kepen vs alle
C.10.109	More kynd[e] knowynge coueyte y *to* here

C.10.119 Y durste meue no matere *to* maken hym to iangle
C.10.119 Y durste meue no matere to maken hym *to* iangle
C.10.121 And potte forth som purpos *to* prouen his wittes,
C.10.140 *To* serue þat lady leely bot[h] late and rathe.
C.10.182 Hath tresor ynow of treuthe *to* fynden hymsulue.
C.10.188 Ac thenne dede we alle wel, and wel bet ȝut, *to* louye
C.10.190 And ȝut were best *to* ben aboute and brynge hit to hepe
C.10.199 *To* wende as wyde as þe worlde were
C.10.200 *To* tulie þe erthe with tonge and teche men to louye.
C.10.200 To tulie þe erthe with tonge and teche men *to* louye.
C.10.209 And is no more *to* mene but men þat ben bygeten
C.10.216 As an hewe þat erieth nat aun[t]reth hym *to* sowe
C.10.259 And thogh he be louelich *to* loke[n] on and lossum abedde,
C.10.267 That he ne wol bowe to þat bonde *to* beden here an hosebonde
C.10.271 Many a payre sethe th[e] pestelens[e] han plyhte treuthe *to* louye;
C.10.276 *To* folwe for þe flicche, feccheth they hit neuere;
C.10.296 Vngracious *to* gete goed or loue of [þe] peple,
C.10.300 Bote god ȝeue hem grace her [g]oynge here *to* amende.
C.10.301 And thus is dowel, my frende, *to* do as lawe techeth:
C.10.302 *To* louye and to loue the and no lyf to greue;
C.10.302 To louye and *to* loue the and no lyf to greue;
C.10.302 To louye and to loue the and no lyf *to* greue;
C.10.303 Ac *to* louye and to l[e]ne, leef me, þat is dobet;
C.10.303 Ac to louye and *to* l[e]ne, leef me, þat is dobet;
C.10.304 *To* ȝeue and to ȝeme bothe ȝonge and olde,
C.10.304 To ȝeue and *to* ȝeme bothe ȝonge and olde,
C.11.5 'Wel artow wyse,' quod she to wyt, 'suche wysdomes *to* shewe
C.11.16 Ho can caste and contreue to disseyue þe ri[gh]tfole,
C.11.34 The lewed aȝen þe lered þe holy lore *to* disp[u]te
C.11.37 And putten forth presumpcioun *to* preue þe sothe.
C.11.38 Thus they dreuele a[t] the deyes the deite *to* knowe
C.11.42 Is non so hende or haue hym [in] nat holy *to* here þer god is.
C.11.53 *To* plese with proude men senes th[e] pestelenc[e tyme]
C.11.58 That preyeres haen no power this pestilences *to* lette.
C.11.59 For god is deef nowadayes and deyneth [nat vs] *to* here
C.11.70 And is *to* mene no more þen "who[so] muche goed weldeth
C.11.74 Ac lust no lord now ne lettred man of suche lore *to* here
C.11.78 Forthy, wit,' quod she, 'be waer holy writ *to* shewe
C.11.89 With þat ȝe kenne me kyndeliche *to* knowe what is dowel.'
C.11.104 'Aske þe hey wey,' [quod he], 'hennes *to* soffre-
C.11.107 For yf thow coueytest *to* ryche to clergie comest thow neuere.
C.11.117 And alle þe musons in musyk y made here *to* knowe.
C.11.119 Aristotel and oþere [mo] *to* Arguen y tauhte;
C.11.130 Ac for hit lereth men *to* louie y beleue þeron þ[e] bettere
C.11.138 *To* kenne and to knowe kyndeliche dowel.
C.11.138 To kenne and *to* knowe kyndeliche dowel.
C.11.155 Bote thus hit bilongeth *to* bileue alle þat liketh dowel.
C.11.156 For hadde neuere frek fyn wi[t] the faith *to* dispute
C.11.161 And continaunce made on clergie, *to* congeie me hit semede,
C.11.168 And in a myrrour þat hihte myddelerd she made me *to* loke.
C.11.178 For to lyue longe and ladyes *to* louye
C.11.185 'The man þat me liketh *to* helpe myhte nat myshappe.'
C.11.212 *To* reule [þe] reum[e] and ryche to make
C.11.212 To reule [þe] reum[e] and ryche *to* make
C.11.219 And yf we sholde wurche aftur here werkes *to* wy[n]nen vs heuene
C.11.244 For Archa Noe, nymeth hede, ys no more *to* mene
C.11.246 The culorum of this clause curatores is *to* mene
C.11.247 That [ben] carpentares vnder Crist holy kirke *to* make
C.11.267 Cristene [kynde] *to* culle to dethe?
C.11.278 Connyng and clergie *to* conclude [hem] alle".
C.11.288 And is *to* mene no more to men þat beth lewed:
C.12.9 To here priour prouincial [a] pardon *to* haue
C.12.14 And pouerte pursuede me and potte me *to* be lowe.
C.12.17 *To* restitute resonably for al vnrihtfole wynnynge.
C.12.27 Y wolde it were no synne,' y saide, 'to seien þat were treuthe.
C.12.29 *To* segge as they seen, saue only prestis:
C.12.36 *To* rehercen hit by retoryk to arate dedly synne?
C.12.36 To rehercen hit by retoryk *to* arate dedly synne?
C.12.37 Ac be [thow] neueremore þe furste the defaute *to* blame;
C.12.51 And in a wer gan y wex and with mysulue *to* despute
C.12.60 For thogh a cristene man coueitede his cristendom *to* renoye
C.12.61 Rihtfolliche *to* renoye no resoun hit wolde.
C.12.68 And potten hym aftur in prisoun in purgatorie *to* brenne
C.12.73 Mercy al [*to*] amende and mekenesse her folowe;
C.12.77 How y was ded and dampned *to* dwellen in [pyne]
C.12.91 And on Troianus treuthe *to* thenke alle tyme[s] in ȝoure lyue
C.12.98 And cristis oune clergie; he cam fro heuene *to* teche hit
C.12.105 For vch frende cheaff[e] and ryche *to* quite
C.12.119 *To* haue as we haen serued, as holy chirche witnesseth:
C.12.145 Althouh h[it] be sour *to* soffre þer cometh a swete aftur.
C.12.148 Is a cornel of confort kynde *to* restore,
C.12.150 Maketh man *to* haue mynde in god and his mercy to craue,
C.12.150 Maketh man to haue mynde in god and his mercy *to* craue,

C.12.153 And lasse drat [dethe] or in derke *to* ben yrobbed
C.12.158 For þe loue of oure lord lo[w]eth hym *to* be pore,
C.12.163 "Yf thow likest *to* lyue," quod god, "þe lyf þat is parfit,
C.12.169 "Hoso coueiteth *to* come to my kyneriche
C.12.173 *To* testifie for treuthe þe tale þat y shewe
C.12.174 And poetes *to* preuen hit: Porfirie and plato,
C.12.179 Mesc[h]iefes on molde mekeliche *to* soffren:
C.12.200 Yf god gyueth hym þe lyf, *to* haue a goed heruost,
C.12.211 How god, as þe gospelle telleth, gyueth [hym] foel *to* name,
C.12.215 "And art so loth *to* leue that lete shal thow nedes:
C.12.218 Vpholderes on þe hulle shal haue hit *to* sulle."
C.12.228 And haen þe world at he[re] wille oþerwyse *to* leuene.
C.12.240 *To* synege and to souche sotiltees of Gyle,
C.12.241 For coueytyse of catel *to* culle hym þat hit kepeth.
C.13.10 And Abraham not hardy ones *to* letten hym
C.13.11 Ne for brihtnesse of here beaute here spouse *to* be byknowe.
C.13.51 Marchauntȝ for here marchaundyse in many place *to* tolle.
C.13.57 And dredeth *to* be ded þerfore and he in derke mette
C.13.65 ȝe wyte, ȝe wyse men, what this is *to* mene:
C.13.66 The marchaunt is no more *to* mene but men þat ben ryche
C.13.76 And ȝut more, *to* maken pees and quyten menne dettes
C.13.77 And spele and spare *to* spene vppon þe nedfole
C.13.81 *To* lene ne to lerne ne lentones to faste
C.13.81 To lene ne *to* lerne ne lentones to faste
C.13.81 To lene ne to lerne ne lentones *to* faste
C.13.83 That þe lawe ȝeueth leue such low folk *to* be excused,
C.13.84 As none tythes *to* tythe ne to clothe the nakede
C.13.84 As none tythes to tythe ne *to* clothe the nakede
C.13.85 Ne in none enquestes *to* come ne cont[u]max thogh he worche
C.13.86 Halyday or holy euene his mete *to* discerue.
C.13.105 And nedeth [ȝow] nat *to* nyme siluer for masses þat ȝe synge
C.13.108 For made neuere kyng no knyhte but he hadde catel *to* spene
C.13.131 Til þat kynde cam clergie *to* helpe
C.13.132 And in þe myrrour of mydelerthe made him efte *to* loke,
C.13.133 *To* knowe by vch a creature kynde to louye.
C.13.133 To knowe by vch a creature kynde *to* louye.
C.13.157 Hadde neuere weye wyt *to* worche þe leste.
C.13.159 Lernede *to* [l]egge stikkes þat ley on here neste.
C.13.174 Mony selcouthes y seyh aren nat *to* segge nouthe
C.13.178 Of here kynde and here colour *to* carpe hit were to longe.
C.13.206 And ar thow lacke eny lyf loke ho is *to* preyse.
C.13.211 That some tyme hym bitit *to* folewen his kynde;
C.13.213 Tho cauhte y colour anoen and comesede *to* ben aschamed
C.13.217 *To* wyte what dowel is Ac wakynge neuere.'
C.13.220 'To se moche and soffre al, certes, is dowel.'
C.13.226 Ac when he mamelede aboute mete and musede *to* knowe
C.13.238 *To* blame hym or to bete hym thenne y halde hit but synne.
C.13.238 To blame hym or *to* bete hym thenne y halde hit but synne.
C.13.240 And thenne woet he wherfore and why he is *to* blame.'
C.13.245 'ȝe, certes,' quod he, 'þat is soth', and shop hym *to* walke:
C.14.4 And wissed the [wel] ofte what dowel was *to* mene
C.14.5 And conseyled the for cristes sake no creature *to* bygile,
C.14.6 Noþer to lye ne to lacke ne lere þat is defended
C.14.6 Noþer to lye ne *to* lacke ne lere þat is defended
C.14.7 Ne *to* spille speche, As to speke an ydel,
C.14.7 Ne to spille speche, As *to* speke an ydel,
C.14.8 Ne no tyme *to* tyne ne trewe thyng tene,
C.14.12 Ac hit soffiseth *to* be saued [to] be such as y tauhte.
C.14.12 Ac hit soffiseth to be saued [*to*] be such as y tauhte.
C.14.13 Ac *to* louye and lene and lyue wel and byleue
C.14.20 As loreles to be lordes and lewede men techares,
C.14.23 Ac grace is a graes þerfore *to* don hem [growe efte];
C.14.27 And sent forth the seynt espirit *to* do loue sprynge:
C.14.31 As *to* be bore or bygete in such a constillacioun;
C.14.35 And ȝut is clergie *to* comende for cristes loue more
C.14.42 *To* strike with stoen or with staf this strompet to dethe."
C.14.43 Forthy y conseile vch a creature clergie *to* honoure
C.14.48 And riht as syht serueth a man *to* se [þe hye strete],
C.14.50 And as a blynde man in bataile bereth wepene *to* fyhte
C.14.51 And hath non hap with his ax his enemye *to* hutte,
C.14.53 Come for al his kynde wit thorw cristendoem *to* be saued,
C.14.55 *To* v[n]louken hit at here lykynge the lewed to helpe,
C.14.55 To v[n]louken hit at here lykynge the lewed *to* helpe,
C.14.56 *To* ȝeue mercy for mysde[de]s ȝif men hit wol aske
C.14.59 Hadde neuere lewede [man] leue *to* legge hand on þat cheste
C.14.64 Forthy y conseyle all creatures no cler[gie] *to* despice
C.14.67 And medle we nat moche with hem *to* meuen eny wrathe
C.14.68 Laste cheste chauff[e] vs to [c]hoppe vch man oþer.
C.14.70 For clergy is cristes vycary *to* conforte and to cure;
C.14.70 For clergy is cristes vycary to conforte and *to* cure;
C.14.74 And markede hit in here manere and mused þeron *to* knowe.
C.14.76 They helden hit an hey science here sotiltees *to* knowe,
C.14.93 And bad hem go to Bedlem goddes berthe *to* honoure

C.14.124 *To* lere lewede men As luk bereth witnesse:
C.14.146 And as þe lawe lyketh *to* lyue oþer to dye:
C.14.146 And as þe lawe lyketh to lyue oþer *to* dye:
C.14.148 Hit were no resoun ne riht *to* rewarde bothe ylyche.
C.14.161 He tauhte þe tortle *to* tre[d]e, the pocok to cauke
C.14.161 He tauhte þe tortle to tre[d]e, the pocok *to* cauke
C.14.163 A cantel of kynde wyt here kynde *to* saue.
C.14.174 For pursue a pocok or a pohen *to* cacche
C.14.177 For here fetheres þat fayre beth *to* fle fer hem letteth.
C.14.195 *To* wissen vs weyes þerwith þat wenen to be saued–
C.14.195 To wissen vs weyes þerwith þat wenen *to* be saued–
C.14.196 And be bettere for here bokes *to* bidden we ben yholde–
C.14.202 'Contra!' quod ymagynatif tho and comesed *to* loure
C.14.214 And hope hangeth ay þeron *to* haue þat treuthe deserueth:
C.15.24   And so y musede vppon þis matere þat me lust *to* slepe.
C.15.37   [They] woschen and wipeden and wenten *to* sytten.
C.15.40   Pacience and y [prestly weren] pot *to* be mettes
C.15.52   That Consience comaunde sholde *to* do come scripture
C.15.71   Alle þat coueyte[d] *to* come to eny kyne ioye,
C.15.78   Ac me thynketh loth, thogh y latyn knowe, *to* lacken eny secte
C.15.104 And thenne is tyme *to* take and to appose this doctour
C.15.104 And thenne is tyme to take and *to* appose this doctour
C.15.120 And preynte vppon pacience *to* preie me be stille
C.15.125 That trauayleth *to* teche oþere y halde hit for a dobet;
C.15.133 And no tixst ne taketh *to* preue this for trewe
C.15.136 Bote lele loue and treuthe that loth is *to* be founde.'
C.15.143 Fond [with] wit & word his loue *to* wynne,
C.15.166 *To* haue alle londes at thy likyng and the here lord make
C.15.174 And toek Clergie and Consience *to* conseyle as hit were.
C.15.183 With pacience wol y passe parfitnesse *to* fynde.'
C.15.187 *To* conforte hym and Consience yf they come in place
C.15.194 Peres prentys þe plouhman, alle peple *to* conforte.'
C.15.209 For no breed þat y betrauaile *to* [brynge] byfore lordes.
C.15.222 Thenne wolde y be bysy and buxum *to* helpe
C.15.226 *To* haue þe grace of god and no gulte of þe pope.
C.15.239 Wherof or wherfore [or] wherwith *to* lyuene?
C.15.276 And þat is pore pacient alle perelles *to* soffre.'
C.15.278 Then rihtfu[l] rychesse and resonablelyche *to* spene?'
C.15.286 *To* haue allouaunce of his lord; by [þe] lawe he [hit] claymeth.
C.16.7   A[nd] nat *to* fonge byfore for drede [of] dessallouwynge.
C.16.16   [And arated of] ryche men þat reuthe is *to* here.
C.16.25   And sende vs contricion [clereliche] *to* clanse with oure soules
C.16.26   And confessioun *to* kulle alle kyne synnes
C.16.33   And lereth lewed and lered, hey and lowe *to* knowe
C.16.44   The fend followeth hem alle and fondeth hem *to* helpe
C.16.52   For þe ryche hath moche *to* rykene and riht softe walketh;
C.16.62   For þe pore is ay prest *to* plese þe ryche
C.16.72   For his rentes wol nat reche ryche metes *to* bugge;
C.16.75   For when he streyneth hym *to* strecche the strawe is his shetes.
C.16.86   For pouerte hath bote pokes *to* potten in his godes
C.16.88   And where be [lyh]tere *to* breke? lasse boest hit maketh
C.16.95   Meschief is ay a mene and maketh hym *to* thenke
C.16.107 Moche is [þat] mayde *to* louye of a man þat such oen taketh,
C.16.112 And potte hym *to* be pacient and pouerte weddeth,
C.16.118 'Parfay!' quod pacience, 'propreliche *to* telle [this]
C.16.123 Selde syt pouerte þe soth *to* declare
C.16.124 Or a[s] iustice *to* iuge men, me enioyneth þerto no pore,
C.16.125 Ne *to* be mair ouer men ne mynistre vnder kynges;
C.16.126 Selde is eny pore ypot *to* p[u]nesche eny peple.
C.16.143 As he þat woet neuere with wham on nyhtes tyme *to* mete:
C.16.147 The ey3te is a lel labour and loeth *to* take more
C.16.157 That wroet thus *to* wisse men what pouerte was to mene.'
C.16.157 That wroet thus to wisse men what pouerte was *to* mene.'
C.16.174 'Of [fele] tyme *to* fihte,' quod he, 'falsnesse to destruye
C.16.174 'Of [fele] tyme to fihte,' quod he, 'falsnesse *to* destruye
C.16.175 And som tyme *to* soffre bothe [sorwe] and [tene],
C.16.177 *To* do wel or wykke, a will with a resoun,
C.16.178 And may nat be withoute a body *to* bere me where hym liketh.'
C.16.201 How þou coueytest *to* calle me, now þou knowest al my namus.
C.16.218 To engelische mene this is *to* mene, þat mowen speke and here,
C.16.224 Coueytyse *to* conne and to knowe scienc[e]
C.16.224 Coueytyse to conne and *to* knowe scienc[e]
C.16.226 And riht as hony is euel *to* defie,
C.16.228 And doth hym *to* be deynous and deme þat beth nat lered.
C.16.234 *To* teche þe ten comaundement3 ten sythe were bettere
C.16.253 Is þe rote of [the] rihte fayth *to* reule þe peple;
C.16.260 And hatien harlotrie and *to* vnderfonge þe tythes
C.16.275 Vnk[ynd]e curatours *to* lawe kepares of 3oure soules.
C.16.310 Hath he no lykynge *to* lawhe ne to likene men to scorne.
C.16.310 Hath he no lykynge to lawhe ne *to* likene men to scorne.
C.16.317 [Rentes or other richesse *to* releue hym at his nede]?'
C.16.324 And oþerwhile his wone is *to* w[e]nde [o]n pilgrimages
C.16.370 And hoso coueyteth *to* knowe [hym] such a kynde hym foloweth

C.16.372 For noþer he beggeth ne biddeth ne borweth *to* 3elde.
C.16.374 *To* begge or to borwe but of god one:
C.16.374 To begge or *to* borwe but of god one:
C.17.41   This is no more *to* mene bote men of holy churche
C.17.44   Thenne wolde lordes and ladyes be loth *to* agulte
C.17.45   And *to* take of here tenauntes more then treuthe wolde
C.17.52   *To* make men louye mesure þat monkes ben and freres:
C.17.57   *To* feffe suche and fede þat founded ben *to* þe fulle
C.17.60   *To* helpe thy fader formost byfore freres or monkes
C.17.121 That sola fides sufficit *to* saue with lewede peple.
C.17.124 In þe lettynge of here lyf *to* leue on holy churche.'
C.17.131 God lereth no lyf *to* l[eu]e withouten lele cause.
C.17.142 Loue thyn enemye entierely goddes heste *to* fulfille;
C.17.146 And ay hopeth eft *to* be with here body at þe laste
C.17.147 In murthe or in mournynge and neuere[more] *to* departe.
C.17.148 And þat is charite, leue chield, *to* be cher ouer thy soule;
C.17.153 Hit is kyndly thyng creature his creatour *to* honoure,
C.17.167 And pursuede *to* haue be pope, prince of holy chirche;
C.17.180 Tolde hym and tauhte [hym] how *to* teche þe peple.
C.17.186 Sholden conuerte hem to Crist and cristendoem *to* take.
C.17.188 So manye prelates *to* preche as þe pope maketh
C.17.192 *To* be p[astor]s and preche the passioun of iesus
C.17.193 And as hymsulue saide so *to* lyue and deye:
C.17.194 Hit is reuthe *to* rede how riht holy men lyuede,
C.17.198 Ne no rychesse but þe rode *to* reioysen hem ynne:
C.17.200 And now is reuthe *to* rede how þe rede noble
C.17.202 *To* amende and to make, as with men of holy churche,
C.17.202 To amende and *to* make, as with men of holy churche,
C.17.228 Yf the kynges coueyte in cristes pees *to* lyuene,
C.17.231 Hit were charite *to* deschargen hem for holy churche sake,
C.17.234 That with moneye maynteyneth men [t]o werre vppon cristene
C.17.248 *To* make a perpetuel pees bitwene þe prince of heuene
C.17.257 And maken here mone to Macometh here message *to* shewe.
C.17.279 And nat in Ingelond *to* huppe aboute and halewe men auters
C.17.286 And enchaunten hem to charite on holy churche *to* bileue.
C.17.287 For as þe kynde is of a knyhte or [of] a kynge *to* be take
C.17.289 *To* be culd and ouercome the comune to defende,
C.17.289 To be culd and ouercome the comune *to* defende,
C.17.290 So is þe kynde of a curatour for criste[s] loue *to* preche
C.17.291 And deye for his dere childrene *to* de[struy]e dedly synne,
C.17.294 Bischope[s] and bokes the belaue *to* teche.
C.17.296 Moises *to* be maister þerof til messie come
C.17.305 And studeden *to* struye hym and struyden hemsulue
C.17.311 And hopen þat he be *to* come þat shal hem releue;
C.17.313 And haen a suspectioun *to* be saef, bothe sarresynes & iewes,
C.18.2   Thow couthest telle me and teche me [in] charite [*to*] leue.'
C.18.18   And sethen þat 3e fouchen saef *to* sey me as hit hoteth.'
C.18.20   Hit hadde schoriares *to* shuyuen hit vp, thre shides of o lenghe
C.18.43   And thenne fondeth the fende my fruyte *to* destruye
C.18.107 And Elde clemp to þe c[r]opward; thenne comsed hit *to* crye.
C.18.121 *To* go ransake þat ragman and reue hym of his apples
C.18.127 That elde felde efte þe fruyt, or full *to* be rype.
C.18.134 And bycam man of þat maide mankynde *to* saue,
C.18.136 *To* haue yfouthte with þe fende Ar fol tyme come.
C.18.169 And kuste iesus *to* be knowe þerby and cauht of þe iewes.
C.18.173 Thow shalt be myrrour to monye men *to* disceue.
C.18.184 'I am with fayth,' quod þat freke, 'hit falleth nat me *to* lye,
C.18.190 And, sondry to se vpon, solus deus he hoteth.'
C.18.201 Mi3te and a mene *to* se his owne myhte,
C.18.205 *To* ocupien hym here til issue were spronge
C.18.220 Matrimonye withoute moylere is nauht moche *to* preyse
C.18.248 *To* make sacrefice of hym he heet me, hym to honoure.
C.18.248 To make sacrefice of hym he heet me, hym *to* honoure.
C.18.253 Bledden bloed for þat lordes loue [and] hope *to* blisse þ[e] tyme.
C.18.260 And sethe a sente me *to* seyn and saide that y sholde
C.18.264 I leue þat ilke lord thenketh a newe lawe *to* make:
C.19.3   *To* reule alle reumes þerwith in ri3te and in resoun.
C.19.7   'Nay,' he saide, 'y seke hym þat hath þe seel *to* kepe,
C.19.8   The which is Cr[oes] and cristendoem and cr[ist] þer[o]n [*to*] hang[e];
C.19.28   And lele *to* bileue on for [lif and] for soule?
C.19.34   What nedede hit thanne a newe lawe *to* brynge
C.19.35   Sethe the furste sufficede *to* bileue and be saued?
C.19.39   The which alle men aren holde ouer al thyng *to* honoure
C.19.40   And seth *to* louye and to lene for þat lordes sake
C.19.40   And seth to louye and *to* lene for þat lordes sake
C.19.52   *To* ioust in Ierusalem he Iaced awey faste.
C.19.67   And to th[e] wey a wente his woundes *to* byholde
C.19.68   And parseued by his poues he was in perel *to* deye
C.19.75   And lefte hym þere a lechyng *to* lyue yf he myhte
C.19.76   And toek two pans the hostiler *to* take kepe to hym;
C.19.79   And rapede hym *to* ryde the rihte way to Ierusalem.
C.19.101 And lered me for his loue *to* louye al mankynde

C.19.116	Til hym likede and luste *to* vnlose that fynger
C.19.119	*To* ministre and to make þat myhte of hand knoweth
C.19.119	To ministre and *to* make þat myhte of hand knoweth
C.19.122	The fyngres þat fre ben *to* folde and [to] blase,
C.19.122	The fyngres þat fre ben to folde and *to* cluche
C.19.127	*To* huyde and to holde as holy writ telleth–
C.19.127	To huyde and *to* holde as holy writ telleth–
C.19.143	For þe paume hath power *to* pu[t]te out þe ioyntes
C.19.144	And *to* vnfolde þe fust, for hym hit bilongeth,
C.19.157	*To* cluche or to clawe, to clippe or to holde.
C.19.157	To cluche or *to* clawe, to clippe or to holde.
C.19.157	To cluche or to clawe, to clippe or *to* holde.
C.19.157	To cluche or to clawe, *to* clippe or to holde.
C.19.177	That serueth this swynkares *to* [see] by a nyhtes,
C.19.185	To alle vnkynde creatures þat coueyten *to* destruye
C.19.192	Til þe holy goest gynne *to* glowe and [to] blase,
C.19.192	Til þe holy goest gynne to glowe and [*to*] blase,
C.19.213	To þe fader of heuene forȝe[ue]nesse *to* haue.
C.19.215	Bote thow haue tasch *to* take hit with, tender [or] broches,
C.19.249	*To* go semeliche ne sitte, seth holy writ techeth
C.19.250	[That that wickedliche is wonne *to* wasten hit and make frendes?]
C.19.260	For that the holy goest hath *to* kepe tho harlotes distruyeth,
C.19.263	Or elles [to] a taper *to* reuerense with the trinite
C.19.265	A fordoth the lihte þat oure lord loketh *to* haue worschipe of.
C.19.268	Synegen aȝen þe seynte spirit, assente *to* destruye
C.19.297	*To* amende al þat amys is and his mercy grettore.
C.19.301	Thre thynges ther ben þat doth a man *to* sterte
C.19.308	Hit doth hym worse then his wyf or wete *to* slepe;
C.19.313	Thise thre that y telle of thus ben [*to*] vnderstande:
C.19.315	For kynde cleueth on hym euere *to* contrarie þe soule;
C.19.324	That they haen cause *to* contrarien bi kynde of here sekness[e];
C.20.4	Til y waxe wery of the world and wilnede eefte *to* slepe
C.20.11	As is þe kynde of a knyhte þat cometh to be dobbet,
C.20.12	*To* geten h[ym] gult spores and galoches ycouped
C.20.14	As doth an heraud of Armes when Auntres cometh *to* ioustes.
C.20.27	'Nay,' quod faith, 'bote the fende and fals doem *to* deye.
C.20.31	That for al þat deth can do, withynne thre dayes *to* walke
C.20.36	*To* se how douhtyliche deth sholde do and demen [h]er beyre rihte.
C.20.41	*To* fordoen hit on a day, and in thre dayes aftur
C.20.48	And bigan of grene thorn a garlond *to* make
C.20.53	And beden hym drynke his deth *to* lette and his dayes lenghe
C.20.77	Ac was no boie so bold godes body *to* touche;
C.20.79	That hadde no boie hardynesse hym *to* touche in deynge.
C.20.84	[*To*] iouste with iesus, this blynde iewe longies.
C.20.86	*To* touchen hym or to t[ast]en hym or taken down [of rode]
C.20.86	To touchen hym or to t[ast]en hym or taken down [of rode]
C.20.98	[*To* do] þe blynde bete the dede, [hit] was a boyes [conseille].
C.20.100	*To* bete a body ybounde with eny briht wypene.
C.20.129	'And am wendynge *to* wyte what þis wonder meneth.'
C.20.177	And preyede pees *to* tellen [here] to what place she [w]olde
C.20.179	'My wil is *to* wende,' quod pees, 'and welcomen hem alle
C.20.188	Mercy, [my sustur], and me *to* maynprisen hem alle
C.20.216	Sholde ywyte witterly what day is *to* mene.
C.20.222	Bycam man of a mayde mankynde *to* saue
C.20.223	And soffred *to* be sold to se þe sorwe of deynge,
C.20.223	And soffred to be sold *to* se þe sorwe of deynge,
C.20.226	Ne woet no wyht, as y wene, what is ynow *to* mene.
C.20.229	And sethe he soffrede hym synne sorwe *to* fele
C.20.230	*To* wyte what wele [was], kyndeliche to knowe [hit].
C.20.230	To wyte what wele [was], kyndeliche *to* knowe [hit].
C.20.232	*To* wyte what he hath soffred in thre sundry places,
C.20.234	*To* wyte what a wo is þat woet of alle ioye:
C.20.249	And tenden h[ere] as a torche *to* reuerensen his burthe.
C.20.259	And lette out symondes sones *to* sen hym honge on rode:
C.20.262	*To* breke and to bete adoun all þat ben agaynes hym
C.20.262	To breke and *to* bete adoun all þat ben agaynes hym
C.20.263	And *to* haue out [of helle] alle þat hym liketh.
C.20.288	Coltyng and al his kyn, the car *to* saue.
C.20.292	And sheteth out shot ynow his sheltrom *to* blende;
C.20.316	And entisedest Eue *to* eten bi here one–
C.20.317	And byhihtest here and hym aftur *to* knowe
C.20.338	*To* lere men to [be] lele and vch man to louye oþer;
C.20.338	To lere men *to* [be] lele and vch man to louye oþer;
C.20.338	To lere men to [be] lele and vch man *to* louye oþer;
C.20.371	For alle synfole soules, *to* saue oure bothe rihte.
C.20.379	Falsliche [thow] fettest there þat me biful *to* loke,
C.20.389	And al þat m[a]n mysdede, y man *to* amenden hit
C.20.390	And þat deth fordede my deth *to* releue
C.20.399	And now bygynneth thy gyle agayne the *to* turne
C.20.400	And my grace *to* growe ay [gretter] and wyddore.
C.20.417	Ac *to* be merciable to man thenne my kynde [hit] asketh
C.20.421	Hit is nat vsed [i]n erthe *to* hangen [a] felo[n]
C.20.436	*To* be merciable to monye of my haluebretherne.
C.21.3	*To* here holly þe masse and to [be] hoseled aftur.
C.21.3	To here holly þe masse and *to* [be] hoseled aftur.
C.21.9	And thenne calde y Consience *to* kenne me þe sothe:
C.21.20	Ne noen so niedfol to nemnie by nyhte ne by day
C.21.21	For alle derke deueles aren drad *to* heren hit
C.21.28	*To* be cald a knyht is fayr for men shal knele to hym;
C.21.29	*To* be cald a kyng is fairor for he may knyhtes make;
C.21.30	Ac *to* be conquerour cald, þat cometh of special grace
C.21.32	*To* make lordes of laddes of lond þat he wynneth
C.21.42	Hit bicometh [to] a kyng *to* kepe and to defende
C.21.42	Hit bicometh [to] a kyng to kepe and *to* defende
C.21.59	*To* make alle folk fre þat folweth his lawe.
C.21.62	He may be wel called conquerour and that is Crist *to* mene.
C.21.64	Is *to* wissen vs þerwith, þat when we ben ytempted
C.21.65	Therwith *to* fihte and fende vs fro fallyng into synne
C.21.69	Ac *to* carpe more of Crist and how he cam to þat name;
C.21.72	And cam *to* take mankynde kynges and angeles
C.21.93	For Mirre is mercy *to* mene and mylde speche of tonge.
C.21.99	As hit bicometh a conquerour *to* conne mony sleythes
C.21.110	And þer bigan god of his grace *to* do wel:
C.21.114	Bothe to lered and to lewed, *to* louye oure enemyes.
C.21.116	Bigan god of his grace and goodnesse *to* do wel
C.21.125	He made lame *to* lepe and ȝaf liht to blynde
C.21.138	*To* be Cayser or kyng of the kyngdoem of Iuda
C.21.164	Bothe Iames and Iohann, iesu to seke,
C.21.170	And toek Thomas by the hoende and tauhte hym *to* grope
C.21.184	/Myhte men *to* assoyle of alle manere synnes,
C.21.186	In couenaunt þat they come and knolech[e] *to* pay
C.21.189	*To* bynde and vnbynde bothe here and elles
C.21.198	And wikked *to* wonye in wo withouten ende.'
C.21.200	And conseyled me *to* knele þerto; and thenne cam, me thouhte,
C.21.213	Thenne bigan grace *to* go with [Peres Plouhman]
C.21.214	And conseilede hym and Consience the comune *to* sompne:
C.21.217	Tresor *to* lyue by to here lyues ende
C.21.218	And wepne *to* fihte with þat wol neuere fayle.
C.21.224	Coueytise and vnkyndenesse Cardynales hym [*to*] lede.
C.21.226	And wepne *to* fihte with when Auntecrist ȝow assaileth.'
C.21.227	And gaf vch man a grace *to* gye with hymsuluen
C.21.229	Som [wyes] he ȝaf wyt with wordes *to* schewe,
C.21.230	*To* wynne with treuthe þat the world asketh,
C.21.232	They leely *to* lyue bi labour of tonge
C.21.233	And bi wit *to* wissen oþere as grace hem wolde teche
C.21.235	[By] sullyng and buggynge here bileue *to* wynne.
C.21.236	And som he lered *to* laboure a londe and a watre
C.21.238	And somme he tauhte to tulye, to [coke] and *to* [thecche,
C.21.238	And somme he tauhte to tulye, *to* [coke] and to [thecche,
C.21.238	And somme he tauhte *to* tulye, to [coke] and to [thecche,
C.21.239	*To* wynne with here lyflode bi lore of his techynge];
C.21.240	And somme *to* deuyne and deuyde, [figu]res to kenne;
C.21.240	And somme to deuyne and deuyde, [figu]res *to* kenne;
C.21.241	[And somme *to* kerue a]nd compace and coloures to make;
C.21.241	[And somme to kerue a]nd compace and coloures *to* make;
C.21.242	And somme *to* se and to saye what sholde bifalle
C.21.242	And somme to se and *to* saye what sholde bifalle
C.21.245	And somme *to* ryde & to rekeuere that vnrihtfulliche was wonne:
C.21.245	And somme to ryde & *to* rekeuere that vnrihtfulliche was wonne:
C.21.248	And somme he [l]ered *to* lyue in longyng to be hennes,
C.21.248	And somme he [l]ered to lyue in longyng *to* be hennes,
C.21.249	In pouerte and in pacience *to* preye for alle cristene
C.21.250	And al he lered *to* be lele, and vch a craft loue oþere,
C.21.259	And Registrer *to* reseyuen Redde quod debes.
C.21.268	All þat his oxes erede they *t[o]* harwe[n] aftur.
C.21.271	Thise foure, the fayth *to* teche, folewe[de Peres] teme
C.21.280	That caste for to kele a crok [*to*] saue þe fatte aboue.
C.21.283	Sholde neuere mete ne meschief maken hym *to* swelle
C.21.291	*To* soffre al þat god sente, seeknesse and angeres.
C.21.294	And bold and abidynge busmares *to* soffre
C.21.302	Spiritus iusticie spareth nat *to* spille [the] gulty
C.21.303	And *to* corecte the kyng and the kyng falle in [g]ulte.
C.21.305	*To* demen as a domesman adrad was he neuere
C.21.318	Ordeyne the an hous, [Peres], *to* herborwe in thy cornes.'
C.21.325	And þerwith grace bigan *to* make a goode fo[un]dement
C.21.330	A Cart hihte Cristendoem *to* carie hoem Peres sheues
C.21.333	As wyde as the world is with Peres *to* tulye treuthe
C.21.353	'*To* waston on welfare and in wikked kepynge
C.21.355	Quod Consience to alle cristene tho, 'my consayl is [*to*] wende
C.21.359	*To* goen agayn pruyde bute grace were with vs.'
C.21.360	And thenne cam kynde wit Consience *to* teche
C.21.362	*To* deluen dich depe aboute vnite
C.21.364	Consience comaundede t[h]o alle cristene *to* delue
C.21.366	*To* helpe holi churche and hem þat hit kepeth.
C.21.374	That he ne halpe a qua[n]tite holinesse *to* wexe,
C.21.387	Myhte *to* make hit and men to eten hit [aftur]

C.21.387   Myhte to make hit and men *to* eten hit [aftur]
C.21.391   'How?' quod alle þe comune; 'thow conseylest vs *to* ȝelde
C.21.395   And so *to* ben assoiled and sennes be hoseled.'
C.21.423   Or in Rome, as here reule wo[l], þe relikes *to* kepe;
C.21.432   And sente þe so[nn]e *to* saue a corsed mannes tulthe
C.21.434   Rihte so [Peres] the [Plouhman] payneth hym *to* tulie
C.21.437   So yblessed be [Peres] the [plouhman] þat peyneth hym *to* tulie
C.21.443   And claymeth bifore þe kynge *to* be kepare ouer cristene
C.21.445   And fynde[th] folke *to* fihte and cristene bloed to spille
C.21.445   And fynde[th] folke to fihte and cristene bloed *to* spille
C.21.457   Vch man sotileth a sleythe synne *to* huyde
C.21.460   'Y halde hit riht and resoun of my reue *to* take
C.21.466   'Y am kyng with croune the comune *to* reule
C.21.467   And holy kyrke and clerge fro cursed men *to* defende.
C.21.468   And yf me lakketh *to* lyue by þe lawe wol y take hit
C.22.3   Y ne wiste where *to* ete ne at what place
C.22.13   Ne wyht no[n] wol be his borwe ne wed hath [non] *to* legge;
C.22.45   And þe fisch hath fyn *to* flete with to reste;
C.22.48   Forthy be nat abasched *to* byde and to be nedy
C.22.48   Forthy be nat abasched to byde and *to* be nedy
C.22.60   And al þe couent cam *to* welcome a tyraunt
C.22.62   [Whiche foles] were wel gladere *to* deye
C.22.63   Then *to* lyue lengere sethe leautee was so rebuked
C.22.89   With deth þat is dredful *to* vndoen vs alle!'
C.22.91   Aftur conforte, a knyhte, [*to*] come and beer his baner:
C.22.107   *To* sese and soffre and se wher they wolde
C.22.109   And kynde sesede [sone] *to* se þe peple amende.
C.22.124   His wepne was al wyles, *to* wynnen and to hyden;
C.22.124   His wepne was al wyles, to wynnen and *to* hyden;
C.22.126   Symonye hym suede *to* assaile Consience
C.22.128   *To* holde with auntecrist, here temperaltee[s] to saue.
C.22.128   To holde with auntecrist, here temperaltee[s] *to* saue.
C.22.131   And gert goed faith fle and fals *to* abyde
C.22.141   That couetyse were cristene þat is so kene *to* fihte
C.22.166   And baed hym fonde *to* fihte and afere wanhope.
C.22.179   May nat a myte avayle to medlen aȝen Elde.
C.22.195   For þe lyme þat she loued me fore and leef was *to* fele
C.22.207   'Consaileth me, kynde,' quod y, 'what craft be beste *to* lere?'
C.22.208   'Lerne *to* loue,' quod kynde, 'and leef all othere.'
C.22.209   'How shal y come to catel so *to* clothe me and to fede?'
C.22.209   'How shal y come to catel so to clothe me and *to* fede?'
C.22.214   And there was Consience Constable, cristene *to* saue.
C.22.223   Then y do *to* drynke a drauht of goed ale.'
C.22.230   Freres herde hym crye and comen hym *to* helpe
C.22.233   That they cam for Couetyse, to haue cure of soules.
C.22.235   Thei wol flatere *to* fare wel folk þat ben riche.
C.22.252   Frere fraunceys and domynyk, for loue *to* be holy.
C.22.265   Here ordre and here reule wol *to* haue a certeyne nombre
C.22.269   Hit is wikked *to* wage ȝow; ȝe wexeth out of nombre.
C.22.276   That alle thynges vnder heuene ou[h]te *to* be in comune.
C.22.282   Ben curatours cald *to* knowe and to hele,
C.22.282   Ben curatours cald to knowe and *to* hele,
C.22.292   A parcel to preye for hem and [pleye] with þe remenaunt
C.22.298   And made pees porter *to* pynne þe ȝates
C.22.311   Sire l[ee]f-*to*-lyue-in-lecherye lay þer and groned;
C.22.325   To a lord for a lettre leue *to* haue
C.22.326   *To* curen a curatour; and kam with his lettre
C.22.328   In contreys þer he cam confessiones *to* here;
C.22.360   And lat hem lygge ouerlonge and loeth is *to* chaungen;
C.22.369   Til Contricioun hadde clene forȝete *to* crye and to wepe
C.22.369   Til Contricioun hadde clene forȝete to crye and *to* wepe
C.22.370   And wake for his wikkede werkes as he was woned [*to* do].
C.22.374   And comen with a kene wil Consience *to* assaile.
C.22.375   Consience cryede efte clergie [*to*] helpe
C.22.376   And baed contricioun come *to* kepe þe ȝate.
C.22.382   *To* seke [Peres the Plouhman], þat pruyde myhte destruye,

to prep *to prep.* A 234; B 669; C 626
A.Pr.13   Ac as I beheld into þe Est an heiȝ *to* þe sonne
A.Pr.23   And summe putte hem *to* pride, aparailide hem þereaftir,
A.Pr.31   And somme chosen [hem] *to* chaffare, þei cheuide þe betere
A.Pr.32   As it semiþ *to* oure siȝt þat suche men þriuen.
A.Pr.43   In glotonye, god wot, go þei *to* bedde,
A.Pr.51   Wenten *to* walsyngham, & here wenchis aftir;
A.Pr.80   Personis & parissh prestis pleynide hem *to* here bisshop
A.Pr.94   Ben ylope *to* lundoun be leue of hire bisshop,
A.Pr.106   Tauerners *to* hem tolde þe same:
A.1.34   Al is not good *to* þe gost þat þe gut [ask]iþ,
A.1.35   Ne liflode *to* þe lykam þat lef is to þe soule.
A.1.35   Ne liflode to þe lykam þat lef is *to* þe soule.
A.1.43   Tel me *to* whom þat tresour apendiþ.'
A.1.44   'Go *to* þe gospel,' quaþ heo, 'þat god seide himseluen,
A.1.60   May banne þat he born was *to* body or to soule.
A.1.60   May banne þat he born was to body or *to* soule.

A.1.63   Adam & Eue he eggide *to* ille,
A.1.80   Þat I miȝte werchen his wil þat wrouȝte me *to* man:
A.1.81   'Teche me *to* no tresour but tel me þis ilke,
A.1.89   And ek lyk *to* oure lord be seint lukis wordis.
A.1.95   Til treuþe hadde termined here trespas *to* þe ende.
A.1.98   Þat is þe professioun apertly þat apendiþ *to* kniȝtes,
A.1.140   And þat falliþ *to* þe fadir þat fourmide vs alle,
A.1.145   To haue pite on þat peple þat pynede hym *to* deþe.
A.1.148   *To* hem þat hongide him [heiȝe] & his herte þirlide.
A.1.166   Vnkynde *to* here kyn & ek to alle cristene,
A.1.166   Vnkynde to here kyn & ek *to* alle cristene,
A.1.173   And a lering *to* lewide men þe lattere to dele.
A.2.17   And lakkide my lore *to* lordis aboute.
A.2.20   Out of wrong heo wex *to* wroþerhele manye.
A.2.28   Þat longiþ *to* þ[at] lordsshipe, þe lasse & þe more.
A.2.34   Were beden *to* þe b[ri]dale on boþe two sides.
A.2.49   Þanne fauel fettiþ hire forþ & *to* fals takiþ
A.2.58   Þat I, fauel, feffe falsnesse *to* mede,
A.2.70   Here soulis *to* sathanas to synken in pyne,
A.2.80   And seide *to* cyuyle, 'now sorewe on þi bokes,
A.2.84   God grauntide *to* gyue mede to treuþe,
A.2.85   And þou hast gyuen hire *to* a gilour, now god ȝiue þe sorewe!
A.2.99   Lediþ hire *to* lundoun þere lawe is yhandlit
A.2.110   'And nameliche *to* þe notories, þat hem non fail[e];
A.2.114   *To* false & to fauel for here faire ȝeftis,
A.2.114   To false & *to* fauel for here faire ȝeftis,
A.2.120   *To* lundoun to loke ȝif þat lawe wolde
A.2.125   To wende wiþ hem *to* westmynstre to wytnesse þ[is] dede.
A.2.152   And come *to* þe kinges court & consience tolde,
A.2.153   And consience *to* þe king carpide it aftir.
A.2.164   And bringeþ mede *to* me maugre hem alle.
A.2.172   Þanne fal[s]nesse for feer fleiȝ *to* þe Freris,
A.2.181   Til pardoners hadde pite & pulden him *to* house,
A.2.183   And senten hym on sundais wiþ selis *to* chirche,
A.3.2   Wiþ bedelis & baillifs ybrouȝt *to* þe king.
A.3.10   Tok mede be þe myddel & brouȝte hire *to* chaumbre.
A.3.14   Buski[de] hem *to* bour þere þe burde dwelliþ,
A.3.35   *To* mede þe maiden mekeliche he loutide,
A.3.42   Þanne mede for hire mysdedis *to* þat man knelide,
A.3.70   *To* þe pore peple þat parcelmel biggen,
A.3.92   And brouȝte hire *to* bo[ure] wiþ blisse & wiþ ioye.
A.3.94   *To* mede þe maide melis þise wordis:
A.3.98   Henis *to* þi deþ day do þou so no more.
A.3.100   Ȝif he wilneþ þe *to* wyue wilt þou hym haue?'
A.3.105   Knelynge, consience *to* þe kyng loutide,
A.3.109   Quaþ consience *to* þe kyng, 'crist it [me] forbede!
A.3.121   As comoun as þe cartewey *to* knaue & to [alle],
A.3.121   As comoun as þe cartewey to knaue & *to* [alle],
A.3.122   *To* [monkis], to [mynstrelis], to myselis in heggis.
A.3.122   To [monkis], *to* [mynstrelis], to myselis in heggis.
A.3.122   To [monkis], to [mynstrelis], *to* myselis in heggis.
A.3.143   For she is fauourable *to* fals & fouliþ treuþe ofte;
A.3.157   Þanne mournide mede & menide hire *to* þe king
A.3.183   And bar here bras on þi bak *to* caleis to selle.
A.3.198   *To* alienes, to alle men, to honoure hem with ȝeftis.
A.3.198   To alienes, *to* alle men, to honoure hem with ȝeftis.
A.3.210   Prestis þat preche þe peple *to* goode
A.3.215   Quaþ þe king *to* consience, 'be crist, as me þinkiþ,
A.3.217   'Nay,' quaþ consience *to* þe king & knelide to þe erþe,
A.3.217   'Nay,' quaþ consience to þe king & knelide *to* þe erþe,
A.3.220   To hem þat werchen wel whiles þei ben here.
A.3.244   Samuel seide to saul, "god sendiþ þe & hotiþ
A.3.247   Children & cherlis, choppe hem *to* deþe.
A.3.250   Barnes and bestis brenne hem *to* deþe."
A.3.254   God seide *to* samuel þat saul shulde deiȝe,
A.3.268   And whoso trespassiþ [*to* treuþe, or] takiþ [aȝeyn his wille,
A.4.6   'And I comaunde þe,' quaþ þe king *to* consience þanne,
A.4.14   And riȝt renneþ *to* resoun & rouniþ in his ere;
A.4.29   Ac consience com arst *to* court be a myle wey
A.4.30   And rombide forþ wiþ resoun riȝt *to* þe king.
A.4.31   Curteisliche þe king þanne com in *to* resoun,
A.4.85   Pees þanne pitousliche preyede *to* þe king
A.4.108   And do it in dede to drawe vs *to* goode;
A.4.110   Þat no man go *to* galis but ȝif he go for euere;
A.4.137   Loue let of hire liȝt & louȝ hire *to* scorne,
A.4.139   'Whoso wilneþ hire *to* wyue for welþe of hire godis,
A.4.144   Þe king acordite, be crist, *to* resonis sawis.
A.4.148   'Be hym þat [rauȝte] on þe rode,' quaþ resoun *to* þe king,
A.5.1   Þe king & [his] kniȝtes *to* þe [k]ir[k]e wente
A.5.2   To here matynes & masse, and *to* þe mete aftir.
A.5.16   Piries & pl[umtr]es wern pu[ffid] *to* þe erþe
A.5.18   Bechis & broode okis wern blowen *to* [þe] grounde,
A.5.45   Pernel proud herte plat hire *to* þe erþe

A. 5.47	And behiȝte *to* hym þat vs alle made
A. 5.54	Lecchour seide 'allas!' & *to* oure lady criede
A. 5.76	And belowen hym *to* lordis to don hym lese siluer,
A. 5.85	Whanne I come *to* þe [k]ir[k]e & knel[e] to þe rode,
A. 5.85	Whanne I come to þe [k]ir[k]e & knel[e] *to* þe rode,
A. 5.103	'ȝis, redily,' quaþ repentaunce & redde hym *to* goode:
A. 5.119	*To* wynchestre & to wy I [wente] to þe feire
A. 5.119	To wynchestre & *to* wy I [wente] to þe feire
A. 5.119	To wynchestre & to wy I [wente] *to* þe feire
A. 5.130	And spak *to* þe spynstere to spynnen it softe.
A. 5.144	But wende *to* walsyngham, & my wyf alse,
A. 5.146	Now begynneþ glotoun for to [go *to*] shrift,
A. 5.147	And ca[riþ] hym *to* [k]ir[k]eward hise [coupe] to shewe.
A. 5.150	'*To* holy chirche,' quaþ he, 'for to here masse,
A. 5.167	ȝeue glotoun wiþ glad chiere good ale to hansele.
A. 5.197	Whanne he drouȝ *to* þe dore þanne dymmede hise eiȝen;
A. 5.198	He [þr]umblide on þe þresshewold & [þrew] *to* þe erþe
A. 5.200	Bere hym *to* his bed & brouȝte hym þerinne.
A. 5.202	Þat he slepte satirday & sonneday til sonne ȝede *to* reste.
A. 5.217	"I am sory for my synne," sey *to* þiseluen;
A. 5.223	Þat I ne shal do me er day *to* þe dere chirche
A. 5.226	Til I haue euesong herd, I behote [*to*] þe rode.
A. 5.235	And ȝet þe synful shrewe seide *to* hymselue:
A. 5.247	And knowelechide his [coupe] *to* crist ȝet eftsones,
A. 5.253	Criede vpward *to* crist & to his [clene] modir
A. 5.253	Criede vpward to crist & *to* his [clene] modir
A. 6.27	Clene consience & wyt kende me *to* his place,
A. 6.32	And kepide his corn, & cariede it *to* house,
A. 6.42	I [wile] wisse ȝow wel riȝt *to* his place.'
A. 6.52	Oþerwise þanne þou woldist men wrouȝte *to* þiselue;
A. 6.72	Þanne shalt þou come *to* a court, cler as þe sonne.
A. 6.79	Þe tour þere treuþe is hymself is vp *to* þe sonne;
A. 6.88	Biddiþ amende ȝow meke hym *to* his maister ones
A. 6.96	For he haþ enuye *to* hym þat in þin herte sitteþ
A. 6.105	And ben porteris *to* þe posternis þat to þe place longiþ:
A. 6.105	And ben porteris to þe posternis þat *to* þe place longiþ:
A. 6.110	Ac whoso is sib *to* þis sistris, so me god helpe,
A. 6.112	But ȝif ȝe be sibbe *to* summe of þis seuene
A. 6.119	'ȝis,' quaþ peris þe plouȝman & pukide hym *to* goode:
A. 6.121	And she is sib *to* alle synful, & hire sone alse,
A. 7.31	And go hunte hardily [*to*] har[is] & [to] fox[is],
A. 7.31	And go hunte hardily [to] har[is] & [*to*] fox[is],
A. 7.32	And [*to*] boris & [to] bukkes þat breken myn heggis,
A. 7.32	And [to] boris & [*to*] bukkes þat breken myn heggis,
A. 7.34	For þise comiþ *to* my croft & croppiþ my whete.
A. 7.76	*To* penaunce & to pilgrimage wile I passe with oþere;
A. 7.76	To penaunce & *to* pilgrimage wile I passe with oþere;
A. 7.81	Til I come *to* his acountes as my crede me techiþ–
A. 7.91	I bar hom þat I borewide er I *to* bedde ȝede.
A. 7.97	Now is peris & þe pilgrimes *to* þe plouȝ faren;
A. 7.115	And pleynide hem *to* peris wiþ suche pitous wordis:
A. 7.140	*To* peris þe plouȝman he profride his gloue.
A. 7.146	Þanne peris þe plouȝman pleynede hym *to* þe kniȝt
A. 7.216	Go *to* genesis þe geaunt, engendrour of vs alle:
A. 7.283	Be þat it neiȝide ner heruest [þat] newe corn com *to* chepyng.
A. 8.1	Treuþe herde telle hereof, & *to* peris sente
A. 8.34	Sette scoleris to scole or [*to*] summe skynes craftis,
A. 8.34	Sette scoleris *to* scole or [to] summe skynes craftis,
A. 8.62	Siþen ȝe sen it is þus sewiþ *to* þe beste.
A. 8.66	Hadde þe same absolucioun þat sent was *to* peris.
A. 8.100	Þat aftir þi deþ day *to* helle shalt þou wende.'
A. 8.117	Haue þei no garner [to go] *to*, but god fynt hem alle.'
A. 8.118	'What!' quaþ þe prest *to* perkyn, 'peter, as me þinkeþ,
A. 8.158	Þe peple wiþoute penaunce [to passe *to* Ioye]?
A. 9.34	Þe watir is liknid *to* þe world þat waniþ & waxiþ,
A. 9.37	Þe boot is lik[nid] *to* þe body þat britel is of kynde,
A. 9.61	A muchel man, me þouȝte, lik *to* myselue,
A. 9.82	And is ronne *to* religioun, & haþ rendrit þe bible,
A. 9.110	He was long & lene, lyk *to* non oþer,
A. 10.6	A lemman þat he louiþ lik *to* hymselue.
A. 10.7	Anima he[o] ha[tte]; *to* hire [haþ] enuye
A. 10.11	And haþ don hire *to* sire dowel, duk of þise marchis.
A. 10.35	Saue man þat he made ymage *to* himselue,
A. 10.49	Inwyt in þe heuid is, & an help *to* þe soule,
A. 10.52	He eggiþ eiȝe siȝt & heryng *to* gode;
A. 10.106	Fro religioun *to* religioun, reccheles ben þei euere;
A. 10.131	Formest & ferst *to* folk þat ben weddit
A. 10.145	In tene & trauaille *to* here lyues ende;
A. 10.157	Forþi he sente *to* se[þ], & se[i]de hym be an aungel
A. 10.159	And siþen se[þ] & his suster [sed] wern spousid *to* kaymes;
A. 10.165	And com *to* noe anon, and bad hym nouȝt lette
A. 10.168	Busk[en hem] *to* þat boot & biden þereInne.
A. 10.177	Ellis shal alle diȝen & *to* helle wenden."
A. 10.187	*To* ȝiuen a ȝong wenche to an old feble,
A. 10.194	Þeiȝ þei don hem *to* dunmowe, but ȝif þe deuil helpe
A. 11.6	*To* flatereris or to folis þat frentyk ben of wittis,'
A. 11.6	To flatereris or *to* folis þat frentyk ben of wittis,'
A. 11.21	Þat suche craftis conne [*to* counseil ben yclepid],
A. 11.27	*To* iesu þe gentil þat Iewis todrowe
A. 11.34	ȝiue hem *to* here ȝerisȝiue þe value of a grote.
A. 11.52	[Mendynauntȝ] meteles miȝte go *to* bedde.
A. 11.68	Þoruȝ whiche a werk & wille þei wenten *to* helle,
A. 11.90	But he lyue in þe leste degre þat longiþ *to* dowel
A. 11.96	Ac for no carping I couþe, ne knelyng *to* þe ground,
A. 11.100	And whanne I was war of his wil *to* his wif gan I knele,
A. 11.105	I shal kenne þe *to* my cosyn þat clergie is hoten.
A. 11.107	Is sib *to* þe seuene ars þat scripture is nempnid.
A. 11.109	Shuln wisse þe *to* dowel, I dar wel vndirtake.'
A. 11.111	Gladdere þanne þe gleman þat gold haþ *to* ȝifte,
A. 11.113	'And tel me sum tokne *to* hym, for tyme is þat I wende'.
A. 11.117	For ȝif þou coupl[e] þe with hym *to* clergie comist þou neuere;
A. 11.120	Til þou come *to* a court, kepe wel þi tunge
A. 11.124	So shalt þou come *to* clergie þat can many wyttes.
A. 11.125	Sey hym þis signe, I sette hym *to* scole,
A. 11.127	And sette hire *to* sapience & to hire sauter yglosid.
A. 11.127	And sette hire to sapience & *to* hire sauter yglosid.
A. 11.130	Plato þe poete, I putte hym ferst *to* boke;
A. 11.158	For sorcerie is þe souerayn bok þat *to* þat science longiþ.
A. 11.169	And er I com *to* clergie coude I neuere stynte.
A. 11.191	Obedient as breþeren & sustren *to* oþere,
A. 11.213	Poperiþ on a palfrey [fro] toune *to* toune.'
A. 11.227	Helpiþ nouȝt *to* heuene[ward] at one ȝeris ende,
A. 11.240	Ac cristene men, god wot, comiþ not so *to* heuene,
A. 11.246	Alle kynne creatures þat *to* crist be[n] l[yche]
A. 11.249	And souereynliche *to* suche þat sewen oure beleue:
A. 11.250	Þat is, iche cristene [creature] be kynde to oþer,
A. 11.275	And be here werkis & here wordis wissen vs *to* dowel,
A. 11.277	And for here werkis & here wyt wende *to* pyne,
A. 11.281	And for he kneuȝ on þe crois & *to* crist shr[o]f hym,
A. 11.290	Cristene kynde to kille *to* deþe?
A. 11.295	For he seide it hymself *to* summe of his disciplis:
A. 11.297	And is as muche to mene, *to* men þat ben lewid,
A. 12.4	He passeþ þe apostolis lyf, and [peryth] *to* aungelys.
A. 12.9	That myȝthe turne m[e] *to* tene & theologie boþe.
A. 12.17	Þat hit were boþe skaþe and sklaundre *to* holy cherche
A. 12.24	Telle hit with tounge *to* synful wrecches."
A. 12.38	Þan held I vp myn handes *to* scripture þe wise
A. 12.52	Til ȝe come *to* þe burg[h] quod bonum est tenete.
A. 12.53	Ken him *to* my cosenes hous þat kinde wit hyȝth.
A. 12.57	And ere I cam *to* þe court quod bonum est tenete
A. 12.64	*To* lyf in his lordshepe longyt my weye
A. 12.98	And be prest *to* preyeres and profitable werkes.'
A. 12.104	Deþ delt him a dent and drof him *to* þe erþe
A. 12.113	Furst *to* rekne Richard, kyng of þis rewme,
A. 12.117	Þat barn bryng vs *to* blys þat bled vpon þe rode amen.
B.Pr.13	[Ac] as I biheeld into þe Eest, an heiȝ *to* þe sonne,
B.Pr.23	And somme putten hem *to* pride, apparailed hem þerafter,
B.Pr.31	And somme chosen [hem *to*] chaffare; þei cheueden þe bettre,
B.Pr.32	As it semeþ *to* oure siȝt þat swiche men þryueþ.
B.Pr.43	In glotonye, god woot, go þei *to* bedde,
B.Pr.51	*To* ech a tale þat þei tolde hire tonge was tempred to lye
B.Pr.54	Wenten *to* walsyngham, and hire wenches after;
B.Pr.83	Persons and parisshe preestes pleyned hem *to* þe Bisshop
B.Pr.106	And to opene it *to* hem and heuene blisse shewe.
B.Pr.124	And knelynge *to* þe kyng clergially he seide,
B.Pr.140	And *to* þe Aungel an heiȝ answerde after:
B.Pr.144	*To* þe kynges counseil, construe whoso wolde,
B.Pr.148	Comen to a counseil for þe commune profit.
B.Pr.159	Seide for a souereyn [salue] *to* [hem alle].
B.Pr.175	Al þ[e] route of Ratons *to* þis reson assented.
B.Pr.179	Ne hangen it aboute [his] hals al Engelond *to* wynne;
B.Pr.—	And *to* þe route of Ratons reherced þise wordes.
B. 1.36	[Al is nouȝt] good *to* þe goost þat þe gut askeþ,
B. 1.37	Ne liflode þ[e] likame [þat leef is to þ[e] soule.
B. 1.37	Ne liflode þ[e] likame [þat leef is *to* þ[e] soule.
B. 1.45	Tel me *to* whom þat tresour appendeþ.'
B. 1.46	'Go *to* þe gospel', quod she, 'þat god seide hymseluen,
B. 1.62	May banne þat he born was *to* bodi or to soule.
B. 1.62	May banne þat he born was to bodi or *to* soule.
B. 1.65	Adam and Eue he egged *to* ille,
B. 1.82	That I myȝte werchen his wille þat wroȝte me *to* man.
B. 1.83	'Teche me *to* no tresor, but tel me þis ilke,
B. 1.91	And [ek] ylik *to* oure lord by Seint Lukes wordes.
B. 1.97	Til treuþe hadde ytermyned hire trespas *to* þe ende.
B. 1.100	[That] is [þe] profession apertli þat apendeþ *to* knyȝtes,
B. 1.132	Mowe be siker þat hire soul[e] sh[a]l wende *to* heuene

B. 1.151 And lered it Moyses for þe leueste þyng and moost lik *to* heuene,
B. 1.166 And þat falleþ *to* þe fader þat formed vs alle,
B. 1.171 To haue pite [on] þat peple þat peyned hym *to* deþe.
B. 1.174 *To* hem þat hengen hym heiȝ and his herte þirled.
B. 1.192 Vnkynde *to* hire kyn and to alle cristene,
B. 1.192 Vnkynde to hire kyn and *to* alle cristene,
B. 1.199 And lernynge *to* lewed men þe latter to deele.
B. 2.22 And bilowen h[ym] *to* lordes þat lawes han to kepe.
B. 2.26 And neuere sooþ seide siþen he com *to* erþe,
B. 2.40 And now worþ þis Mede ymaried [t]*o* a mansed sherewe,
B. 2.41 *To* oon fals fikel-tonge, a fendes biyete.
B. 2.46 That longen *to* þat lordshipe, þe lasse and þe moore.
B. 2.55 Were boden *to* þe bridale on boþe two sides,
B. 2.106 Hire soules *to* Sathan to suffre with hym peynes,
B. 2.116 And seide [*to*] Cyuyle, 'now sorwe [on þi bokes]
B. 2.120 God graunte[d] to gyue Mede *to* truþe,
B. 2.121 And þow hast gyuen hire *to* a gilour, now god gyue þee sorwe!
B. 2.135 Ledeþ hire *to* Londoun þere [lawe] is [yhandled],
B. 2.146 And namely *to* þe Notaries þat hem noon faille.
B. 2.150 *To* Fals and to Fauel for hire faire ȝiftes,
B. 2.150 To Fals and *to* Fauel for hire faire ȝiftes,
B. 2.156 *To* london to loken if [þat] lawe wolde
B. 2.161 To wenden wiþ hem *to* westmynstre to witnesse þis dede.
B. 2.191 And com *to* þe kynges court and Conscience tolde,
B. 2.192 And Conscience *to* þe kyng carped it after.
B. 2.203 /And bryngeþ Mede *to* me maugree hem alle.
B. 2.213 [Thanne] Falsnesse for fere fleiȝ *to* þe Freres;
B. 2.222 Til Pardoners hadde pite and pulled hym [*to*] house,
B. 2.224 And senten hym [on Sondayes wiþ seles] *to* chirch[e],
B. 3.2 Wiþ Bedeles and baillies brouȝt [*to*] þe kyng.
B. 3.14 Busked hem *to* þe bour þer þe burde dwelle[þ],
B. 3.36 *To* Mede þe mayde [mekeliche he loutede]
B. 3.43 Thanne Mede for hire mysdedes *to* þat man kneled
B. 3.81 *To* þe pouere peple þat parcelmele buggen.
B. 3.103 And brouȝte hire *to* boure wiþ blisse and wiþ ioye.
B. 3.105 *To* Mede þe mayde [melleþ] þise wordes:
B. 3.109 Hennes *to* þi deeþ day do [þow] so na moore.
B. 3.111 If he wilneþ þee *to* wif wiltow hym haue?'
B. 3.116 Knelynge, Conscience *to* þe kyng louted,
B. 3.120 Quod Conscience *to* þe kyng, 'crist it me forbede!
B. 3.132 As commune as [þe] Cartwey *to* [knaue and to alle],
B. 3.132 As commune as [þe] Cartwey to [knaue and *to* alle],
B. 3.133 *To* Monkes, to Mynstrales, to Meseles in hegges.
B. 3.133 To Monkes, *to* Mynstrales, to Meseles in hegges.
B. 3.133 To Monkes, to Mynstrales, *to* Meseles in hegges.
B. 3.154 For she is fauourable *to* fals and [f]ouleþ truþe ofte.
B. 3.170 Thanne mournede Mede and mened hire *to* þe kynge
B. 3.196 And bere hire bras at þi bak *to* Caleis to selle.
B. 3.211 *To* aliens, to alle men, to honouren hem with ȝiftes;
B. 3.211 To aliens, *to* alle men, to honouren hem with ȝiftes;
B. 3.211 To aliens, to alle men, *to* honouren hem with ȝiftes;
B. 3.223 Preestes þat prechen þe peple *to* goode
B. 3.228 Quod þe kyng *to* Conscience, 'by crist, as me þynkeþ,
B. 3.230 'Nay', quod Conscience *to* þe kyng and kneled to þe erþe,
B. 3.230 'Nay', quod Conscience to þe kyng and kneled *to* þe erþe.
B. 3.233 *To* [hem] þat [werchen wel] while þat ben here.
B. 3.261 God sente *to* Saul by Samuel þe prophete
B. 3.264 "Forþi", seide Samuel *to* Saul, "god hymself hoteþ [þ]ee
B. 3.266 Weend *to* Amalec with þyn oost & what þow fyndest þere sle it.
B. 3.267 Burnes and beestes, bren hem *to* deþe;
B. 3.276 God seide *to* Samuel þat Saul sholde deye
B. 3.293 And whoso trespaseþ [*to*] truþe or takeþ ayein his wille,
B. 3.307 Shal be demed *to* þe deeþ but if he do it smyþye
B. 3.308 Into sikel or *to* siþe, to Shaar or to kultour:
B. 3.308 Into sikel or to siþe, *to* Shaar or to kultour:
B. 3.308 Into sikel or to siþe, to Shaar or *to* kultour:
B. 3.316 Ouer[carke] þe commune ne *to* þe Court sompne,
B. 3.324 And what smyth þat any smyþeþ be smyte þerwiþ *to* deþe:
B. 3.349 A ful teneful text *to* hem þat takeþ Mede:
B. 4.6 'And I comaunde þee', quod þe kyng *to* Conscience þanne,
B. 4.14 And [riȝt renneþ] *to* Reson and rouneþ in his ere;
B. 4.43 As Conscience hym kenned til þei come *to* þe kynge.
B. 4.44 Curteisly þe kyng þanne com [in *to*] Reson,
B. 4.98 [Pees þanne pitously] preyde *to* þe kynge
B. 4.125 Hire haukes and hire houndes help *to* pouere Religious;
B. 4.127 That no man go *to* Galis but if he go for euere.
B. 4.153 And þei lauȝynge lope *to* hire and lefte Reson manye.
B. 4.163 'Whoso wilneþ hire *to* wif for welþe of hire goodes,
B. 4.182 Quod Conscience *to* þe kyng, 'but þe commune wole assente
B. 4.185 'By hym þat rauȝte on þe Rode!' quod Reson *to* þe kynge,
B. 5.1 The kyng and hise knyȝtes *to* þe kirke wente
B. 5.2 To here matyns [and masse and *to* þe mete] after.
B. 5.16 Pyries and Plumtrees were puffed *to* þe erþe,

B. 5.18 Beches and brode okes were blowen *to* þe grounde
B. 5.37 My sire seide *to* me, and so dide my dame,
B. 5.43 And dooþ it in dede, it shal drawe yow *to* goode.
B. 5.62 Pernele proud-herte platte hire *to* þe erþe
B. 5.64 And bihiȝte *to* hym þat vs alle made
B. 5.71 Lechour seide 'allas!' and [*to*] oure lady cryde
B. 5.96 And [bilowen] hym *to* lordes to doon hym lese siluer,
B. 5.105 Whan I come *to* þe kirk and knele to þe Roode
B. 5.105 Whan I come to þe kirk and knele *to* þe Roode
B. 5.126 'ȝis! redily', quod Repentaunce and radde hym *to* [goode]:
B. 5.143 Shewen hire shriftes *to* hem þan shryue hem to hir persons.
B. 5.143 Shewen hire shriftes to hem þan shryue hem *to* hir persons.
B. 5.153 I haue an Aunte *to* Nonne and an Abbesse boþe;
B. 5.173 And doon me faste frydayes *to* [þerf] breed and to watre;
B. 5.173 And doon me faste frydayes to [þerf] breed and *to* watre;
B. 5.185 That þi wille [ne þi wit] *to* wraþe myȝte turne:
B. 5.203 *To* Wy and to Wynchestre I wente to þe Feyre
B. 5.203 To Wy and *to* Wynchestre I wente to þe Feyre
B. 5.203 To Wy and to Wynchestre I wente *to* þe Feyre
B. 5.214 [And] spak *to* [þe] Spynnester[e] to spynnen it [softe].
B. 5.228 But wenden *to* walsyngham, and my wif als,
B. 5.248 And wiþ lumbardes lettres I ladde gold *to* Rome
B. 5.267 Ne haue a peny *to* my pitaunce, [for pyne of my soule],
B. 5.283 Nis na moore *to* þe mercy of god þan [amyd] þe see a gleede:
B. 5.289 And if þow wite neuere *to* [whom] ne [where] to restitue
B. 5.290 Ber it *to* þe Bisshop, and bid hym of his grace
B. 5.296 Now bigynneþ Gloton for to go *to* shrifte
B. 5.297 And [kaireþ] hym *to* kirkeward his coupe to shewe.
B. 5.300 'To holy chirche', quod he, 'for to here masse,
B. 5.318 Geue Gloton wiþ glad chere good ale *to* hanselle.
B. 5.349 A[c] whan he drouȝ *to* þe dore þanne dymmed hise eiȝen;
B. 5.350 He [þr]umbled on þe þresshfold and þrew *to* þe erþe.
B. 5.358 Baren hym *to* his bed and brouȝte hym þerInne,
B. 5.360 That he sleep Saterday and Sonday til sonne yede *to* reste.
B. 5.378 'This shewynge shrift', quod Repentaunce, 'shal be meryt *to* þe.'
B. 5.392 'What! awake, renk!' quod Repentaunce, 'and rape þee *to* shryfte!'
B. 5.411 Til matyns and masse be do, and þanne [moste] *to* þe freres;
B. 5.412 Come I *to* Ite missa est I holde me yserued.
B. 5.419 Construe clause[m]el[e] and kenne it *to* my parisshens.
B. 5.445 "I am sory for my synn[e]", seye *to* þiselue,
B. 5.451 That I ne shal do me er day *to* þe deere chirche
B. 5.454 Til I haue euensong herd: I bihote *to* þe Roode.
B. 5.463 Ac yet þe synfulle sherewe seide *to* hymselue:
B. 5.473 And knoweliched his [coupe] *to* crist yet eftsoones,
B. 5.479 To amenden vs of oure mysdedes: do mercy *to* vs alle,
B. 5.481 And of nauȝt madest auȝt and man moost lik *to* þiselue,
B. 5.482 And siþen suffredest [hym] to synne, a siknesse *to* vs alle,
B. 5.484 For þoruȝ þat synne þi sone sent was *to* erþe
B. 5.503 That art oure fader and oure broþer, be merciable *to* vs,
B. 5.511 Cride vpward *to* Crist and to his clene moder
B. 5.511 Cride vpward to Crist and *to* his clene moder
B. 5.512 To haue grace to go [*to*] truþe, [God leue þat þei moten].
B. 5.539 Conscience and kynde wit kenned me *to* his place
B. 5.555 I [wol] wisse yow [wel riȝt] *to* his place.'
B. 5.565 Oþerwise þan þow woldest [men] wrouȝte *to* þiselue.
B. 5.585 Thanne shaltow come *to* a court, cler as þe sonne.
B. 5.593 Ech piler is of penaunce, of preieres-*to*-Seyntes;
B. 5.610 [For] he haþ enuye *to* hym þat in þyn herte sitteþ
B. 5.619 And arn porters of þe Posternes þat *to* þe place longeþ.
B. 5.625 A[c] who is sib *to* þise [sustren], so me god helpe,
B. 5.627 But if ye be sibbe *to* some of þise seuene
B. 5.634 'ȝis!' quod Piers þe Plowman, and poked [hym] *to* goode,
B. 5.636 And she is sib *to* alle synfulle and hire sone also,
B. 6.29 And go hunte hardiliche *to* hares and to foxes,
B. 6.29 And go hunte hardiliche to hares and *to* foxes,
B. 6.30 *To* bores and to [bukkes] þat breken myne hegges,
B. 6.30 To bores and *to* [bukkes] þat breken myne hegges,
B. 6.32 For [þise] comeþ *to* my croft and croppeþ my whete.'
B. 6.64 *To* pilgrymage as palmeres doon pardon to haue.
B. 6.84 *To* penaunce and to pilgrimage I wol passe wiþ oþere,
B. 6.84 To penaunce and *to* pilgrimage I wol passe wiþ oþere;
B. 6.89 Til I come *to* hise acountes as my [crede] me [techeþ]—
B. 6.99 I bar hom þat I borwed er I *to* bedde yede.
B. 6.105 Now is Perkyn and [þe] pilgrimes *to* þe plow faren.
B. 6.123 And made hir mone *to* Piers [how þei myȝte noȝt werche]:
B. 6.153 *To* Piers þe Plowman he profrede his gloue.
B. 6.159 Thanne Piers þe plowman pleyned hym *to* þe knyȝte
B. 6.189 And wente as werkmen [*to* wedynge] and [mowynge]
B. 6.202 Ac I preie þee, er þow passe', quod Piers *to* hunger.
B. 6.227 And if þow wilt be gracious *to* god do as þe gospel techeþ
B. 6.232 Go *to* Genesis þe geaunt, engendrour of vs alle:
B. 6.299 By þat it neȝed neer heruest newe corn cam *to* chepyng.
B. 7.1 TReuþe herde telle herof, and *to* Piers sente

B. 7.32	Sette Scolers *to* scole or to som [kynnes] craftes,
B. 7.32	Sette Scolers to scole or *to* som [kynnes] craftes,
B. 7.37	And sende youre soules in saufte *to* my Seintes in Ioye.'
B. 7.54	Thise foure þe fader of heuene made *to* þis foold in commune;
B. 7.57	Whan þei drawen on *to* [þe deþ] and Indulgences wolde haue,
B. 7.64	Ha[dde] þe same absolucion þat sent was *to* Piers.
B. 7.80	For he þat yeueþ yeldeþ and yarkeþ hym *to* reste,
B. 7.136	'What!' quod þe preest *to* Perkyn, 'Peter! as me þynkeþ
B. 7.141	As diuinour in diuinite, wiþ Dixit inspiens *to* þi teme.'
B. 7.174	And how þe preest preued no pardon *to* dowel
B. 7.180	[Th]e peple wiþouten penaunce to passen [*to* ioye]?
B. 8.38	The water is likned *to* þe world þat wanyeþ and wexeþ,
B. 8.41	The boot is likned *to* [þe] body þat brotel is of kynde,
B. 8.52	For he yaf þee [*to*] yeresȝyue to yeme wel þiselue
B. 8.53	Wit and free wil, to euery wiȝt a porcion,
B. 8.54	*To* fleynge foweles, to fisshes and to beestes.
B. 8.54	To fleynge foweles, *to* fisshes and to beestes.
B. 8.54	To fleynge foweles, to fisshes and *to* beestes.
B. 8.70	A muche man me þouȝte, lik *to* myselue.
B. 8.91	And is ronne *to* Religion, and haþ rendred þe bible,
B. 8.120	He was long and lene, lik *to* noon ooþer;
B. 9.6	A lemman þat he loueþ lik *to* hymselue.
B. 9.7	Anima she hatte; [*to* hir haþ enuye]
B. 9.34	[Saue man þat he made ymage] *to* hymself,
B. 9.58	Ac Inwit is in þe heed and *to* þe herte he lokeþ
B. 9.65	And alle þat lyuen good lif are lik *to* god almyȝty:
B. 9.67	And dooþ god forsaken hem þat he shoop *to* his liknesse:
B. 9.80	For moore bilongeþ *to* þe litel barn er he be lawe knowe
B. 9.90	[So] Iewes [shul] ben oure loresmen, shame *to* vs alle!
B. 9.106	Ne his gleman a gedelyng, a goere *to* tauernes.
B. 9.107	*To* alle trewe tidy men þat trauaille desiren,
B. 9.109	Grace to go *to* hem and ofgon hir liflode:
B. 9.126	And alle þat come of þat Caym come *to* yuel ende,
B. 9.127	[For] god sente *to* Se[þ] and seide by an Aungel,
B. 9.134	And com *to* Noe anon and bad hym noȝt lette:
B. 9.137	Buskeþ yow to þat boot and bideþ þerInne
B. 9.166	To yeuen a yong wenche *to* [a yolde] feble,
B. 9.173	[Th]ouȝ þei do hem *to* Dunmowe, but if þe deuel helpe
B.10.6	*To* flatereres or to fooles þat frenetike ben of wittes',
B.10.6	To flatereres or *to* fooles þat frenetike ben of wittes',
B.10.21	[That] swiche craftes k[onne] *to* counseil [are] cleped;
B.10.29	And moost vnkynde *to* þe commune þat moost catel weldeþ:
B.10.35	*To* Iesu þe gentile þat Iewes todrowe
B.10.48	ȝyue hem *to* hir yeresȝyue þe [value] of a grote.
B.10.55	And bryngen forþ a balled reson, taken Bernard *to* witnesse,
B.10.66	Mendinauntȝ metelees myȝte go *to* bedde.
B.10.83	Ne beþ plenteuouse *to* þe pouere as pure charite wolde,
B.10.85	And brekeþ noȝt *to* þe beggere as þe book techeþ:
B.10.110	Thoruȝ whic[h werk and wil] þei wente to helle,
B.10.119	Ymaginatif herafterward shal answere *to* [youre] purpos.
B.10.120	Austyn *to* swiche Argueres [he] telleþ þis teme:
B.10.137	But he lyue in þe [leeste degre] þat longeþ *to* dowel
B.10.143	A[c] for no carpyng I kouþe, ne knelyng *to* þe grounde,
B.10.147	And whan I was war of his wille *to* his wif gan I [knele]
B.10.153	I shal kenne þee *to* my Cosyn þat Clergie is hoten.
B.10.155	Is sib *to* [þe] seuen artȝ, [þat] Scripture is [nempned].
B.10.157	Shullen wissen þee *to* dowel, I dar [wel] vndertake.'
B.10.159	Gladder þan þe gleman þat gold haþ *to* ȝifte.
B.10.161	'And tel me som tokene [*to* hym], for tyme is þat I wende'.
B.10.162	'Aske þe heighe wey', quod she, 'hennes *to* Suffre-
B.10.165	For if þow coupl[e] þee [wiþ] Clergie comest [þow] neuere;
B.10.168	Til þow come *to* a court, kepe-wel-þi-tunge-
B.10.172	[So] shaltow come *to* Clergie þat kan manye [wittes].
B.10.173	Seye hym þis signe: I sette hym *to* Scole,
B.10.175	And sette hire *to* Sapience and to þe Sauter glose[d].
B.10.175	And sette hire to Sapience and *to* þe Sauter glose[d].
B.10.178	Plato þe poete, I putte [hym] first *to* boke;
B.10.197	Whoso gloseþ as gylours doon, go me *to* þe same,
B.10.199	This is Catons kennyng *to* clerkes þat he lereþ.
B.10.207	And [souereynly] *to* swiche [þat] suwen oure bileue;
B.10.215	For sorcerie is þe Souereyn book þat *to* [þat] Scienc[e] [l]ongeþ.
B.10.222	Tel Clergie þis[e] tokene[s], and [*to*] Scripture after,
B.10.226	And [er] I com *to* clergie [koude I] neuere stynte.
B.10.236	I seide to h[y]m sooþly þat sent was I þider
B.10.254	But þus it bilongeþ to bileue *to* lewed þat willen dowel
B.10.272	I rede ech a blynd bosard do boote *to* hymselue,
B.10.279	Ac it semeþ now sooþly, to [siȝte of þe worlde],
B.10.305	For if heuene be on þis erþe, and ese *to* any soule,
B.10.310	And gret loue and likyng for ech [loweþ hym *to*] ooþer.
B.10.313	A prikere on a palfrey fro [place] *to* Manere,
B.10.318	*To* Religiouse þat han no rouþe þouȝ it reyne on hir Auters.
B.10.325	And puten [hem] *to* hir penaunce, Ad pristinum statum ire;
B.10.339	Helpeþ noȝt *to* heueneward [at] oone [y]eris ende,
B.10.357	Ac cristene men wiþoute moore maye noȝt come *to* heuene,
B.10.371	And seiþ "slee noȝt þat semblable is *to* myn owene liknesse
B.10.422	And for he bekne[w on] þe cros and *to* crist shrof hym
B.10.427	Wiþouten penaunce of purgatorie, *to* perpetuel blisse.
B.10.431	Cristene kynde to kille *to* deþe?
B.10.450	For he seide *to* Seint Peter and to swiche as he louede,
B.10.450	For he seide to Seint Peter and *to* swiche as he louede,
B.10.462	And is to mene *to* [Englissh] men, moore ne lesse,
B.11.10	[Siþen] she seide *to* me, 'here myȝtow se wondres
B.11.21	That leden þee wole *to* likynge al þi lif tyme'.
B.11.33	And pride of parfit lyuynge *to* muche peril þee brynge.'
B.11.45	'That wit shal torne *to* wrecchednesse for wil to haue his likyng!'
B.11.53	'Haue no conscience', [quod she],'how þow come *to* goode;
B.11.54	Go confesse þee *to* som frere and shewe hym þi synnes.
B.11.57	*To* hir Priour prouincial a pardon for to haue,
B.11.68	And for I seide þus *to* freres a fool þei me helden,
B.11.81	Thoruȝ contricion [clene] come *to* þe heiȝe heuene–
B.11.112	'Multi *to* a mangerie and to þe mete were sompned,
B.11.112	'Multi to a mangerie and *to* þe mete were sompned,
B.11.134	For hise arerages rewarden hym þere [riȝt] *to* þe day of dome,
B.11.146	Gregorie wiste þis wel, and wilned *to* my soule
B.11.159	And on Troianus truþe to þenke, and do truþe *to* þe peple.
B.11.217	Crist *to* a commune womman seide, in [comen] at a feste,
B.11.234	Witnesse in þe Pask wyke, whan he yede *to* Emaus;
B.11.240	And al was ensample, [sooþliche], *to* vs synfulle here
B.11.241	That we sholde be lowe and loueliche, [and lele ech man *to* oþer],
B.11.249	Was a pure pouere maide and *to* a pouere man ywedded.
B.11.251	And *to* oure Saueour self seide þise wordes:
B.11.274	And lif moost likynge *to* god as luc bereþ witnesse.
B.11.275	And is to mene *to* men þat on þis moolde lyuen,
B.11.278	*To* beggeris þat begge and bidden for goddes loue.
B.11.280	As Dauid seiþ in þe Sauter: *to* swiche þat ben in wille
B.11.300	And a title, a tale of noȝt, *to* his liflode at meschief.
B.11.310	And also in þe Sauter seiþ Dauid *to* ouerskipperis,
B.11.339	Males drowen hem *to* males [al mornyng] by hemselue,
B.11.340	And [femeles *to* femeles ferded and drowe].
B.11.349	Ther nys wriȝte, as I wene, sholde werche hir nes[t] *to* paye;
B.11.408	[Th]anne seide I *to* myself, '[slepyng hadde I grace]
B.12.27	Wolde I neuere do werk, but wende *to* holi chirche
B.12.36	*To* Rome ne to Rochemador, but as þi rule techeþ,
B.12.36	To Rome ne *to* Rochemador, but as þi rule techeþ,
B.12.37	And hold þee vnder obedience þat heigh wey is *to* heuene.
B.12.45	Catel and kynde wit was combraunce *to* hem alle.
B.12.46	Felice hir fairnesse fel hire al *to* sclaundre,
B.12.65	As þe book bereþ witnesse *to* burnes þat kan rede.
B.12.75	Wiþ stones men sholde hir strike and stone hire *to* deþe.
B.12.83	So clergie is confort *to* creatures þat repenten,
B.12.84	And *to* mansede men meschief at hire ende.
B.12.86	The which body is boþe boote *to* þe riȝtfulle
B.12.87	And deeþ and dampnacion *to* hem þat deyeþ yuele,
B.12.94	*To* oure lord, leue me; forþi loue hem, I rede.
B.12.104	Riȝt so [lereþ] lettrure lewed men *to* Reson.
B.12.108	Come for al his kynde wit *to* cristendom and be saued;
B.12.110	To vnloken it at hir likyng, and *to* þe lewed peple
B.12.134	Ne broȝt by hir bokes *to* blisse ne ioye,
B.12.134	Ne broȝt by hir bokes to blisse ne ioye,
B.12.138	A[s] to þe clergie of crist counted it but a trufle:
B.12.148	*To* pastours and to poetes appered þe Aungel
B.12.148	To pastours and *to* poetes appered þe Aungel
B.12.149	And bad hem go *to* Bethlem goddes burþe to honoure
B.12.152	Tho it shon to shepherdes, a shewer of blisse].
B.12.154	And diden [hir] homage honurably *to* hym þat was almyȝty.
B.12.169	'That swymme kan noȝt', I seide, 'it semeþ *to* my wittes.'
B.12.181	And haþ no contricion er he come *to* shrifte; & þanne kan he litel telle
B.12.187	Wel may þe barn blesse þat hym *to* book sette,
B.12.193	Was for he yald hym creaunt *to* crist & knewliched hym gilty,
B.12.251	*To* alle hem þat it holdeþ ti! hir tail be plukked.
B.12.254	Thouȝ he crye *to* crist þanne wiþ kene wil, I leue
B.12.267	*To* lowe libbynge men þe larke is resembled.
B.12.294	The glose graunteþ vpon þat vers a greet mede *to* truþe.
B.13.13	Thoruȝ vnkonnynge curatours *to* incurable peynes;
B.13.15	Of kynde and of his konnynge, and how curteis he is *to* bestes,
B.13.16	And how louynge he is *to* [ech lif] on londe and on watre–
B.13.23	And bad me come *to* his court, wiþ clergie sholde I dyne,
B.13.26	That lowe louted and loueliche *to* scripture.
B.13.28	Thei wesshen and wipeden and wenten *to* þe dyner.
B.13.64	Thanne seide I *to* myself so pacience it herde,
B.13.69	That Poul in his Pistle *to* al þe peple tolde:
B.13.76	They prechen þat penaunce is profitable *to* þe soule,
B.13.84	'I shal Iangle *to* þis Iurdan wiþ his Iuste wombe
B.13.94	And þanne shal he testifie of [a] Trinite, and take his felawe *to* witnesse

B.13.105 'Do noon yuel *to* þyn euencristen, nou3t by þi power.'
B.13.123 I am vnhardy', quod he, '*to* any wi3t to preuen it.
B.13.176 Profitable *to* eiþer peple;' and putte þe table fro hym,
B.13.177 And took Clergie and Conscience *to* conseil as it were
B.13.180 'Frendes, fareþ wel', and faire spak *to* clergie,
B.13.183 'What!' quod Clergie *to* Conscience, 'ar ye coueitous nouþe
B.13.188 'Nay, by crist!' quod Conscience *to* Clergie, 'god þee foryelde;
B.13.192 The goode wil of a wight was neuere bou3t *to* þe fulle.
B.13.193 For þer [is] no tresour [þerto] *to* a trewe wille.
B.13.204 Whan þow art wery [for]walked; wille me *to* counseille'.
B.13.208 And conformen kynges *to* pees; and alle kynnes londes,
B.13.223 *To* Conscience what craft he kouþe, and to what contree he wolde.
B.13.223 To Conscience what craft he kouþe, and *to* what contree he wolde.
B.13.240 Fro Mighelmesse *to* Mighelmesse I fynde hem wiþ wafres.
B.13.250 And þanne wolde I be prest *to* þe peple paast for to make,
B.13.265 There was a careful commune whan no cart com *to* towne
B.13.282 And so singuler by hymself [as *to* si3te of þe peple
B.13.299 And if he gyueþ ou3t *to* pouere gomes, telle what he deleþ;
B.13.325 And þat he wiste by wille [*to* watte tellen it],
B.13.332 For tales þat I telle no man trusteþ *to* me.
B.13.339 *To* þe Soutere of Southwerk or of Shordych dame Emme;
B.13.345 Semynge *to* synneward, and som he gan taste
B.13.347 Til eiþeres wille wexeþ kene and *to* þe werke yeden,
B.13.356 Moore *to* good þan to god þe gome his loue caste,
B.13.356 Moore to good þan *to* god þe gome his loue caste,
B.13.370 If I yede *to* þe Plow3 I pynched so narwe
B.13.374 To seise *to* me wiþ hir sikel þat I sew neuere.
B.13.378 And boþe *to* kiþ and to kyn vnkynde of þat ich hadde;
B.13.378 And boþe to kiþ and *to* kyn vnkynde of þat ich hadde;
B.13.391 And if I sente ouer see my seruaunt3 *to* Brugges,
B.13.393 *To* marchaunden wiþ [my] moneie and maken [here] eschaunges,
B.13.409 [Ac] whiche ben þe braunches þat bryngen a man *to* sleuþe?
B.13.420 Thise ben þe braunches, beþ war, þat bryngen a man *to* wanhope.
B.13.426 Lest þo þre maner men *to* muche sorwe yow brynge:
B.13.430 To entice men þoru3 hir tales *to* synne and harlotrie.
B.13.455 Leden þo þat [liþed] hem *to* Luciferis feste
B.14.10 *To* penaunce pacience and pouere men to fede,
B.14.21 And siþen sende þee *to* Satisfaccion for to [sonnen] it after:
B.14.86 And brynge his soule *to* blisse, so þat feiþ bere witnesse
B.14.92 Per confessionem *to* a preest peccata occiduntur–
B.14.96 And as it neuere [n]adde ybe *to* no3t bryngeþ dedly synne
B.14.102 'Wheiþer paciente pouerte', quod Haukyn, 'be moore plesaunt *to* oure d[ri3te]
B.14.105 Thou3 men rede of richesse ri3t *to* þe worldes ende,
B.14.107 Whan he drogh *to* his deeþ day þat he ne dredde hym soore,
B.14.116 And blisse *to* alle þat ben, boþe wilde and tame."
B.14.121 For *to* wroþerhele was he wro3t þat neuere was Ioye shapen.
B.14.146 And lyuen as lawe techeþ, doon leaute *to* hem alle,
B.14.152 Boþe *to* riche and to no3t riche þat rewfulliche libbeþ;
B.14.152 Boþe to riche and *to* no3t riche þat rewfulliche libbeþ;
B.14.156 That god rewarded double reste *to* any riche wye.
B.14.178 And in somer tyme selde soupen *to* þe fulle.
B.14.182 *To* robberis and to Reueris, to riche and to poore,
B.14.182 To robberis and *to* Reueris, to riche and to poore,
B.14.182 To robberis and to Reueris, *to* riche and to poore,
B.14.182 To robberis and to Reueris, to riche and *to* poore,
B.14.183 [*To* hores, to harlotes, to alle maner peple]
B.14.183 [To hores, *to* harlotes, to alle maner peple].
B.14.183 [To hores, to harlotes, *to* alle maner peple].
B.14.190 [We] sholde take þe Acquitaunce as quyk and *to* þe queed shewen it:
B.14.197 Paternost[er] and penaunce and Pilgrymag[e] *to* Rome,
B.14.206 And þat is plesaunt *to* pride in poore and in riche.
B.14.212 The hei3e wey *to* heueneward [ofte] Richesse letteþ:
B.14.232 And þou3 his glotonye be *to* good ale he goþ to cold beddyng
B.14.232 And þou3 his glotonye be to good ale he goþ *to* cold beddyng
B.14.238 Wiþoute mournynge amonge, and meschief *to* bote].
B.14.243 And Pouerte nys but a petit þyng, apereþ no3t *to* his nauele,
B.14.254 And þou3 Sleuþe suwe pouerte, and serue no3t god *to* paie,
B.14.269 As by assent of sondry parties and siluer *to* boote,
B.14.273 The which is sib *to* god hymself, [so nei3 is pouerte].'
B.14.283 And a sorwe of hymself and solace *to* þe soule,
B.14.284 So pouerte propreliche penaunce [is *to* þe body,
B.14.285 And Ioye *to* pacient pouere], pure spiritual helþe,
B.14.311 [For] lordes alloweþ hym litel or listneþ *to* his reson;
B.14.312 He trempreþ þe tonge *to* truþeward [þat] no tresor coueiteþ:
B.14.316 The nynþe is swete *to* þe soule, no sugre swetter,
B.15.8 *To* sergeaunt3 ne to swiche seide no3t ones,
B.15.8 To sergeaunt3 ne *to* swiche seide no3t ones,
B.15.26 And whan I make mone *to* god memoria is my name;
B.15.38 Nempnede me þus *to* name; now þow my3t chese
B.15.56 *To* englisshe men þis is to mene, þat mowen speke and here,
B.15.61 Et verba vertit in opera fulliche *to* his power."

B.15.70 Freres and fele oþere maistres þat *to* [þe] lewed [folk] prechen,
B.15.75 And of þe braunches þat burioneþ of hem and bryngen men *to* helle,
B.15.82 Gooþ *to* þe glose of þ[e] vers, ye grete clerkes;
B.15.83 If I lye on yow *to* my lewed wit, ledeþ me to brennyng!
B.15.83 If I lye on yow to my lewed wit, ledeþ me *to* brennyng!
B.15.86 And louten *to* þise lordes þat mowen lene yow nobles
B.15.88 That seide to hise disciples, "Ne sitis personarum acceptores".
B.15.111 [For ypocrisie] in latyn is likned *to* a [loþly] dongehill
B.15.113 Or *to* a wal þat were whitlymed and were foul wiþInne;
B.15.141 *To* frend ne to fremmed: "þe fend haue his soule!
B.15.141 To frend ne *to* fremmed: "þe fend haue his soule!
B.15.154 Men beþ merciable *to* mendinaunt3 and to poore,
B.15.154 Men beþ merciable to mendinaunt3 and *to* poore,
B.15.156 Ac charite þat Poul preiseþ best, and moost plesaunt *to* oure [Saueour]–
B.15.202 And buxome as of berynge *to* burgeises and to lordes,
B.15.202 And buxome as of berynge to burgeises and *to* lordes,
B.15.203 And *to* poore peple han pepir in þe nose,
B.15.222 And as gladliche he it gaf *to* gomes þat it neded.
B.15.246 And cristes patrymonye *to* þe poore parcelmele dele;
B.15.267 And seide *to* swiche þat suffre wolde,
B.15.300 That ne fil *to* hir feet and fawned wiþ þe tailles;
B.15.308 And lawefulle men *to* lifholy men lifloode brynge;
B.15.321 Er þei amortisede *to* monkes or [monyales] hir rente[s].
B.15.324 And [bisette] to bidde for yow *to* swiche þat ben riche,
B.15.344 Forþi I counseille alle cristene to conformen hem *to* charite,
B.15.358 Han no bileue *to* þe lifte ne to þe [lodesterre].
B.15.358 Han no bileue to þe lifte ne *to* þe [lodesterre].
B.15.377 Go now *to* any degree, and but if gile be maister,
B.15.382 And answere *to* Argument3 and [assoile] a Quodlibet–
B.15.393 For Sar3ens han somwhat semynge *to* oure bileue,
B.15.404 Thanne wolde þe coluere come *to* þe clerkes ere
B.15.408 As messager *to* Makometh, men for to teche.
B.15.418 Peeren *to* Apostles þoru3 hire parfit lyuynge.
B.15.427 Hir preieres and hir penaunces *to* pees sholde brynge
B.15.447 *To* crist and to cristendom and cros to honoure,
B.15.447 To crist and *to* cristendom and cros to honoure,
B.15.458 It is heþene as *to* heueneward and helplees to þe soule.
B.15.458 It is heþene as to heueneward and helplees *to* þe soule.
B.15.474 Ri3t as capons in a court comeþ *to* mennes whistlyng,
B.15.489 They wol be wrooþ for I write þus, ac *to* witnesse I take
B.15.499 For cristene and vncristene crist seide *to* prechours
B.15.506 And make hir mone *to* Makometh hir message to shewe.
B.15.509 And a peril *to* þe pope and prelates þat he makeþ
B.15.511 [Whan þe hye kyng of heuene sente his sone *to* erþe
B.15.527 He is a forbisene *to* alle bisshopes and a bri3t myrour,
B.15.528 And souereynliche *to* swiche þat of surrye bereþ þe name],
B.15.529 [And nau3t to] huppe aboute in Engelond *to* halwe mennes Auteres
B.15.571 Thoru3 his prouince to passe and *to* his peple shewe hym,
B.15.598 And þoru3 his pacience hir power *to* pure no3t he brou3te:
B.16.27 The world is a wikked wynd *to* hem þat willen truþe.
B.16.35 And forbiteþ þe blosmes ri3t *to* þe bare leues.
B.16.36 Thanne sette I *to* þe secounde pil, sapiencia dei patris,
B.16.42 And casteþ vp *to* þe crop vnkynde Neighebores,
B.16.58 And *to* my mynde, as me þinkeþ, on o more þei growed;
B.16.75 And Piers caste *to* þe crop and þanne comsed it to crye;
B.16.91 *To* a maide þat hi3te Marie, a meke þyng wiþalle,
B.16.98 And seide hendeliche *to* hym, 'lo me his handmaiden
B.16.110 And sike and synfulle boþe so] *to* goode turnede:
B.16.148 And which tokne *to* þis day to muche is yvsed,
B.16.151 'Aue, raby', quod þat Ribaud, and ri3t *to* hym he yede
B.16.153 Thanne Iesus *to* Iudas and to þe Iewes seide,
B.16.153 Thanne Iesus to Iudas and *to* þe Iewes seide,
B.16.156 Thow shalt be myrour *to* many men to deceyue,
B.16.157 Ac [*to*] þe [worldes ende] þi wikkednesse shal worþe vpon þiselue:
B.16.158 Thou3 I bi treson be take [*to*] youre [iewene] wille
B.16.163 Iusted in Iherusalem, a ioye *to* vs alle.
B.16.227 Thre men, *to* my si3te, I made wel at ese,
B.16.239 For hymself bihi3te *to* me and to myn issue boþe
B.16.239 For hymself bihi3te to me and *to* myn issue boþe
B.16.241 *To* me and to myn issue moore yet he [me] grauntede,
B.16.241 To me and *to* myn issue moore yet he [me] grauntede,
B.16.251 That to patriarkes & prophetes and ooþer peple in derknesse
B.17.34 Siþ þe firste suffiseþ *to* sauacion and to blisse?
B.17.34 Siþ þe firste suffiseþ to sauacion and *to* blisse?
B.17.40 Than he þat gooþ wiþ two staues *to* sighte of vs alle;
B.17.42 It is lighter *to* lewed men o lesson to knowe
B.17.48 Go þi gate!' quod I *to* Spes, 'so me god helpe,
B.17.54 *To* a Iustes in Ierusalem he [I]aced awey faste.
B.17.71 [And breide *to* hise boteles and boþe he atamede];
B.17.74 And ladde hym so forþ on Lyard *to* lex Christi, a graunge
B.17.78 And lo, here siluer', he seide, 'for salue *to* hise woundes.'

B.17.79   And he took hym two pens *to* liflode and seide,
B.17.82   And raped hym to [ryde þe riȝte wey *to* Ierusalem].
B.17.85   To ouertaken hym and talke *to* hym er þei to towne coome.
B.17.85   To ouertaken hym and talke to hym er þei *to* towne coome.
B.17.94   May no medicyne [vnder mone] þe man *to* heele bringe,
B.17.117 Which is þe wey þat I wente and wher forþ *to* Ierusalem;
B.17.143 And profre[d] it forþ as with a pawme *to* what place it sholde.
B.17.206 [For] *to* a torche or a tapur þe Trinite is likned,
B.17.219 *To* alle vnkynde creatures þat coueite to destruye
B.17.232 Melte in a Mynut while *to* myst and to watre.
B.17.232 Melte in a Mynut while to myst and *to* watre.
B.17.234 Melteþ *to* mercy, to merciable and to [noon] oþere.
B.17.234 Melteþ to mercy, *to* merciable and to [noon] oþere.
B.17.234 Melteþ to mercy, to merciable and *to* [noon] oþere.
B.17.253 *To* alle vnkynde creatures; crist hymself witnesseþ:
B.17.254 Be vnkynde to þyn euenecristene and al þat þow kanst bidde,
B.17.257 And Indulgences ynowe, and be ingratus *to* þi kynde,
B.17.264 Beþ noȝt vnkynde, I conseille yow, *to* youre euenecristene.
B.17.267 [Mynne ye noȝt, riche men, *to* whiche a myschaunce
B.17.269 Of his mete and moneie to men þat it nedede?
B.17.271 And gyueþ youre good *to* þat god þat grace of ariseþ.
B.17.272 For þat ben vnkynde *to* hise, hope I noon ooþer
B.17.282 *To* a torche or a tapur to reuerence þe Trinite,
B.17.304 That rightwisnesse þoruȝ repentaunce *to* ruþe myȝte turne.
B.17.315 Good hope, þat helpe sholde, *to* wanhope torneþ
B.17.319 Ac er his rightwisnesse *to* ruþe torne som restitucion bihoueþ;
B.17.338 *To* man þat mercy askeþ and amende þenkeþ".
B.17.341 As Poul þe Apostle *to* þe peple tauȝte:
B.18.5   And lened me *to* a lenten, and longe tyme I slepte;
B.18.10   Oon semblable *to* þe Samaritan and somdeel to Piers þe Plow[man]
B.18.10   Oon semblable to þe Samaritan and somdeel *to* Piers þe Plow[man]
B.18.16   As dooþ an heraud of armes whan Auentrous comeþ *to* Iustes.
B.18.31   Lif seiþ þat he lieþ and leieþ his lif *to* wedde
B.18.52   And poison on a poole þei putte vp *to* hise lippes
B.18.94   'For þis foule vileynye vengeaunce *to* yow falle!
B.18.111 I drow me in þat derknesse *to* descendit ad inferna
B.18.114 Cam walkynge in þe wey; *to* helleward she loked.
B.18.132 And þat my tale be trewe I take god *to* witnesse.
B.18.174 And preide pees to telle hire *to* what place she wolde,
B.18.255 And I, book, wole be brent but Iesus rise *to* lyue
B.18.262 A spirit spekeþ *to* helle and biddeþ vnspere þe yates:
B.18.263 A vois loude in þat light *to* lucifer crieþ,
B.18.266 Thanne sikede Sathan and seide *to* he[l]le,
B.18.268 Care and [c]ombraunce is comen *to* vs alle.
B.18.294 We haue no trewe title *to* hem, for þoruȝ treson were þei dampned.'
B.18.302 For Iewes hateden hym and han doon hym *to* deþe.
B.18.327 And seide *to* Sathan, 'lo! here my soule to amendes
B.18.327 And seide to Sathan, 'lo! here my soule *to* amendes
B.18.340 Ergo soule shal soule quyte and synne *to* synne wende,
B.18.359 Adam and alle þoruȝ a tree shul turne *to* lyue,
B.18.375 A[c] to be merciable *to* man þanne my kynde [it] askeþ
B.18.378 Shul noȝt be dampned *to* þe deeþ þat [dureþ] wiþouten ende:
B.18.385 Ther doom *to* þe deeþ dampneþ alle wikked,
B.18.393 And my mercy shal be shewed *to* manye of my [halue]breþeren,
B.18.414 That loue, and hym liste, *to* laughynge ne brouȝte;
B.18.419 For inpossible is no þyng *to* hym þat is almyghty.'
B.18.425 That men rongen *to* þe resurexion, and riȝt wiþ þat I wakede
B.18.428 And crepe[þ] *to* þe cros on knees and kisse[þ] it for a Iuwel
B.19.2   And dighte me derely and dide me *to* chirche
B.19.4   In myddes of þe masse þo men yede *to* offryng
B.19.10   'Is þis Iesus þe Iustere', quod I, 'þat Iewes dide *to* deþe?
B.19.19   Ergo is no name *to* þe name of Iesus.
B.19.28   To be called a knyght is fair for men shul knele *to* hym.
B.19.42   It bicomeþ *to* a kyng to kepe and to defende,
B.19.67   *To* penaunce and to pouerte he moste puten hymseluen,
B.19.67   To penaunce and *to* pouerte he moste puten hymseluen,
B.19.69   Ac to carpe moore of crist and how he com *to* þat name,
B.19.89   Gold is likned *to* leautee þat laste shal euere
B.19.90   [For it shal turne tresoun *to* riȝt and to truþe].
B.19.90   [For it shal turne tresoun to riȝt and *to* truþe].
B.19.91   The þridde kyng þo kam knelynge *to* Iesu
B.19.95   Thoruȝ þre kynne kynges knelynge *to* Iesu.
B.19.111 For wyn is likned *to* lawe and lifholynesse,
B.19.114 [Boþe] *to* lered and to lewede, to louyen oure enemys.
B.19.114 [Boþe] to lered and *to* lewede, to louyen oure enemys.
B.19.125 He made lame to lepe and yaf light *to* blynde
B.19.141 And for to doon hym *to* deþe day and nyȝt þei casten.
B.19.151 Come knelynge *to* þe corps and songen
B.19.169 *To* Peter and to [h]ise Apostles and seide pax vobis;
B.19.169 To Peter and *to* [h]ise Apostles and seide pax vobis;
B.19.185 *To* alle maner men mercy and forȝifnesse]
B.19.187 *To* Piers pardon þe Plowman redde quod debes.

B.19.197 The goode *to* godhede and to greet Ioye,
B.19.197 The goode to godhede and *to* greet Ioye,
B.19.201 Oon Spiritus paraclitus *to* Piers and to hise felawes.
B.19.201 Oon Spiritus paraclitus to Piers and *to* hise felawes.
B.19.216 *To* alle kynne creatures þat [k]an hi[se] fyue wittes,
B.19.217 Tresour to lyue by *to* hir lyues ende,
B.19.265 And Ioyned *to* hem oon Iohan, moost gentil of alle,
B.19.308 He dide equyte *to* alle eueneforþ his [knowynge].
B.19.316 And tilieþ [*to*] hir techynge þe Cardynale vertues.'
B.19.331 And gaf hym caples *to* his carte, contricion and confession;
B.19.335 Now is Piers *to* þe plow; pride it aspide
B.19.341 Thise two coome *to* Conscience and to cristen peple
B.19.341 Thise two coome to Conscience and *to* cristen peple
B.19.355 Quod Conscience *to* alle cristene þo, 'my counseil is to wende
B.19.390 *To* Piers pardon þe Plowman redde quod debes.'
B.19.392 Al þat we owen any wight er we go *to* housel?'
B.19.411 Man *to* me þat me couþe telle of Cardinale vertues,
B.19.433 As brighte as *to* þe beste man or to þe beste womman.
B.19.433 As brighte as to þe beste man or *to* þe beste womman.
B.19.434 Right so Piers þe Plowman peyneþ hym *to* tilye
B.19.450 And torne hir wit *to* wisdom and to welþe of soule.
B.19.450 And torne hir wit to wisdom and *to* welþe of soule.
B.19.453 But [it soune], as by sighte, somwhat *to* wynnyng.
B.20.7   That þow toke *to* þi bilyue, to cloþes and to sustenaunce,
B.20.7   That þow toke to þi bilyue, *to* cloþes and to sustenaunce,
B.20.7   That þow toke to þi bilyue, to cloþes and *to* sustenaunce,
B.20.16   And þouȝ he come so *to* a clooþ and kan no bettre cheuyssaunce
B.20.23   For is no vertue bi fer *to* Spiritus temperancie.
B.20.44   "Boþe fox and fowel may fle *to* hole and crepe
B.20.45   And þe fissh haþ fyn to flete wiþ *to* reste;
B.20.47   And suffre sorwes ful soure, þat shal *to* Ioye torne."
B.20.76   And crye we *to* kynde þat he come and defende vs
B.20.78   And crye we [on] al þe comune þat þei come *to* vnitee
B.20.100 Deeþ cam dryuynge after and al *to* duste passhed
B.20.129 And cam *to* þe kynges counseille as a kene baroun
B.20.134 He logged *to* a Iustice and Iusted in his reve
B.20.136 An[d] *to* þe Arches in haste he yede anoon after
B.20.169 And lif fleiȝ for feere *to* phisik after helpe
B.20.181 And rood [so *to*] reuel, a ryche place and a murye,
B.20.201 And cryde *to* kynde: 'out of care me brynge!
B.20.209 'How shal I come *to* catel so to cloþe me and to feede?'
B.20.213 Thoruȝ Contricion and Confession til I cam *to* vnitee.
B.20.245 *To* vnitee and holy chirche; ac o þyng I yow preye:
B.20.247 *To* lered ne to lewed, but lyueþ after youre reule.
B.20.247 To lered ne *to* lewed, but lyueþ after youre reule.
B.20.259 And if þei wage men *to* werre þei write hem in noumbre;
B.20.273 Enuye herde þis and heet freres go *to* scole
B.20.277 He lyeþ, as I leue, þat *to* þe lewed so precheþ,
B.20.278 For god made *to* men a lawe and Moyses it tauȝte:
B.20.285 And fleen *to* þe freres, as fals folk to westmynstre
B.20.285 And fleen to þe freres, as fals folk *to* westmynstre
B.20.290 And so it fareþ with muche folk þat *to* freres shryueþ,
B.20.293 And suffre þe dede in dette *to* þe day of doome.
B.20.295 And freres *to* philosophie he fond [hem] to scole,
B.20.295 And freres to philosophie he fond [hem] *to* scole,
B.20.316 Quod Contricion *to* Conscience, 'do hym come to vnitee,
B.20.316 Quod Contricion to Conscience, 'do hym come *to* vnitee,
B.20.325 *To* a lord for a lettre leue to haue
B.20.327 Boldely *to* þe bisshop and his brief hadde
B.20.355 And cam *to* Conscience and curteisly hym grette.
B.20.358 Conforte hym', quod Conscience, 'and tak kepe *to* hise soores.
B.20.361 Fro lenten *to* lenten he lat hise plastres bite.'
B.20.365 [And] for [hem] þat ye ben holden *to* al my lif tyme,
C.Pr.25   And summe putte hem *to* pruyde, [a]parayled hem þeraftir
C.Pr.34   As it semeþ *to* oure sighte that suche men ythryueth,
C.Pr.44   In glotonye þ[o] gomus goth þei *to* bedde
C.Pr.52   Wenten *to* Walsyngham and here wenches aftir;
C.Pr.81   Persones and parsche prestis pleyned [hem] *to* þe bischop
C.Pr.105 What cheste and meschaunce *to* þe children of Irael
C.Pr.146 And for most profi[t *to* þe peple] a plogh gonne þei make,
C.Pr.148 Thenne kynde witt *to* þe kynge and to þe comune saide:
C.Pr.148 Thenne kynde witt to þe kynge and *to* þe comune saide:
C.Pr.152 Consience *to* Clergie and to þe kynge sayde:
C.Pr.152 Consience to Clergie and *to* þe kynge sayde:
C.Pr.174 *To* his clees clawe vs and [in] his cloches halde
C.Pr.192 Alle th[e] route of ratones *to* þis resoun assentide;
C.Pr.201 And *to* þe route of ratones rehersede thise wordes:
C. 1.15   To be fayful *to* hym [he] ȝaf ȝow fyue wittes
C. 1.34   Al is nat good *to* þe gost þat þe gott ascuth
C. 1.35   Ne liflode *to* þe lycame þat lef is [to] þe soule.
C. 1.35   Ne liflode to þe lycame þat lef is [*to*] þe soule.
C. 1.43   Telleth me *to* wham þat tresour bylongeth.'
C. 1.44   'Go *to* þe gospel,' quod she, 'and se what god sayde

C. 1.58	May banne þat he born was [*to*] body [or *to*] soule.		C. 3.429	God sayde *to* samuel þat sauel sholde deye
C. 1.58	May banne þat he born was [*to*] body [or *to*] soule.		C. 3.460	Shal be demed *to* þe deth but yf he do hit smythye
C. 1.61	Adam and Eue he eggede *to* ylle,		C. 3.461	Into sykel or [*t*]*o* sythe, to shar oþer to coltur:
C. 1.79	'Teche me *to* [no] tresor but telle me this ilke,		C. 3.461	Into sykel or [t]*o* sythe, to shar oþer to coltur:
C. 1.87	And also lyk [*to*] oure lord by saynt Lukes wordes.		C. 3.461	Into sykel or [t]o sythe, to shar oþer *to* coltur:
C. 1.93	Til treuthe hadde termyned here trespas *to* þe ende		C. 3.469	Ouerkarke þe comune ne *to* þe Court sompne
C. 1.97	Is þe professioun and puyr ordre that apendeth *to* knyghtes		C. 3.477	And yf eny smyth smeth[e] hit be smyte þerwith *to* dethe:
C. 1.162	And þat falleth *to* þe fader þat formede vs alle,		C. 3.497	A ful teneful tyxst *to* hem þat taketh mede,
C. 1.167	To haue pitee on þat peple þat paynede hym *to* dethe.		C. 4.6	'And y comaunde [the],'quod the kyng *to* Consience thenne,
C. 1.170	To hem þat hengen [hym] hye and [his] herte thorlede.		C. 4.14	And rood forth *to* resoun and rouned in his ere
C. 1.189	Vnkynde *to* here kyn and to alle cristene,		C. 4.32	Ac Consience knewe hem wel and carped *to* resoun:
C. 1.189	Vnkynde to here kyn and *to* alle cristene,		C. 4.51	'Bere sikerlyche eny seluer *to* seynt Gyles doune.
C. 1.194	And a luther ensau[m]ple, leef me, [*to*] þe lewed peple.		C. 4.123	In prisones and in pore cotes be pilgrimages *to* Rome
C. 1.200	And þe graffe of grace and gray[th]est way *to* heuene.		C. 4.124	So þat noon go *to* galys but yf he go for euere;
C. 2.21	And [ylow on] hym *to* lordes þat lawes han to kepe;		C. 4.157	And cryede *to* Consience, the kyng myhte hit here:
C. 2.35	Shal haue grace *to* good ynow and a good ende,		C. 4.158	'Hoso wilneth here *to* wy[u]e for welthe of here goodes
C. 2.38	That helpeth man moste *to* heuene mede most letteth.		C. 4.166	The kyng *to* consayl tho toek Consience and resoun
C. 2.43	Tomorwe worth mede ymaried *to* a mansed wrecche,		C. 4.176	Quod Consience *to* þe kyng, 'withoute þe comune helpe
C. 2.44	To oon fals faythlesse of þe fendes kynne.		C. 4.179	'By hym þat rauhte [on] þe rode,' quod resoun *to* the kyng,
C. 2.58	Were beden *to* þe Bridale a bothe half þe contre,		C. 5.13	Or koke for my cokeres or *to* þe Cart piche,
C. 2.72	That Gyle hath gyue *to* falsnesse and grauntid also mede,'		C. 5.14	Mowen or mywen or make bond *to* sheues,
C. 2.93	Th[e] count[e] of coueytise [he] consenteth *to* hem bothe,		C. 5.20	Or eny other kynes craft þat *to* þe comune nedeth,
C. 2.120	And sayde *to* Symonye, 'now sorwe mot thow haue		C. 5.36	My fader and my frendes foende me *to* scole
C. 2.122	And ar this weddyng he wrouhte wo *to* al ȝoure consayle!		C. 5.54	Me sholde constrayne no Cler[k] *to* no knaues werkes,
C. 2.127	For treuthe plyhte here treuthe *to* wedde on of here douhteres,		C. 5.73	And lordes sones here laboreres and leyde here rentes *to* wedde
C. 2.134	Lokede vp *to* oure lord and alowed sayde:		C. 5.91	But he be obediencer *to* prior or to mynistre.'
C. 2.139	That mede may be wedded *to* no man bot treuthe,		C. 5.91	But he be obediencer to prior or *to* mynistre.'
C. 2.142	That ȝe nymeth [and] notaries *to* nauhte gynneth brynge		C. 5.101	That alle tymes of my tyme *to* profit shal turne.'
C. 2.151	And ledeth here *to* londone there lawe may declare		C. 5.103	The l[y]f þat is louable and leele *to* thy soule.'
C. 2.162	And [name]liche [*to*] the notaries þat [hem noon] fayle.		C. 5.104	'Ȝe! and contynue,' quod Consience, 'and *to* þe kyrke ywen[d]e.'
C. 2.172	*To* londone to loke yf lawe wille iugge;		C. 5.105	And *to* þe kyrke y gan go god to honoure;
C. 2.177	To wende with h[e]m *to* westminstre [the] weddyng to honoure.		C. 5.118	P[iri]es and plumtrees were po[ff]ed *to* þe erthe
C. 2.178	Ac hakeneys hadde thei none bote hakeneys *to* huyre;		C. 5.120	Beches and brode okes were blowe *to* þe grounde
C. 2.181	Softliche in s[am]b[u]re fram syse [*to*] syse,		C. 5.125	How resoun radde al the reume *to* heuene.
C. 2.205	And kam *to* þe kynges Court and Consience tolde,		C. 5.152	For yf heuene be on this erthe or ese *to* [eny] soule
C. 2.206	And consience *to* þe kyng carpede hit aftur.		C. 5.159	And pryked aboute on palfrayes fram places *to* maneres,
C. 2.217	And bryngeth mede *to* me maugrey hem alle.		C. 5.164	*To* religious þat haen no reuthe thow it ryne on here auters.
C. 2.223	Falsnesse for fere tho fleyh *to* þe freres;		C. 5.171	And potte ȝow *to* ȝoure penaunce,ad pristinum statum ire,
C. 2.232	Tyl Pardoners hadde [pyte] and polleden hym [*t*]*o* house.		C. 6.3	P[ur]nele proude herte platte here *to* þe erthe
C. 2.234	And senten hym on sonendayes with seeles *to* churche,		C. 6.5	And bihyhte *to* hym þat vs alle made
C. 2.238	Spysours speken *to* hym to aspye he[re] ware		C. 6.15	For y, formost and furste, *to* fader and moder
C. 2.246	Symonye and syuile senten *to* Rome,		C. 6.19	Inobedient *to* holy churche and to hem þat þer serueth;
C. 2.248	Ac Consience *to* þe kyng accused hem bothe		C. 6.19	Inobedient to holy churche and *to* hem þat þer serueth;
C. 3.13	That wendeth *to* Westmynstre worschipe[th] here monye.		C. 6.25	Scornare and vnskilful *to* hem þat skil shewede,
C. 3.15	Boskede hem *to* þe bour ther th[e] buyrde dwel[leth],		C. 6.36	And ȝut so synguler as *to* syhte of [þe] peple
C. 3.39	*To* mede þe mayde myldeliche he sayde,		C. 6.47	And what y gaf for godes loue *to* gossipus y tolde,
C. 3.45	Thenne mede for here mysdedes *to* th[at] man knelede		C. 6.54	And sygge *to* suche þat sytte me byside:
C. 3.68	Ac god *to* alle good folk suche grauynge defendeth,		C. 6.59	Al [y] wolde þat men wiste when it *to* pruyde souneth,
C. 3.81	For thyse men don most harm *to* þe mene peple,		C. 6.70	And þat a wiste by wille *to* watekyn he tolde nat
C. 3.99	That louten for hem *to* oure lord and to oure lady bothe		C. 6.83	*To* the soutere of southewerk, suche is his grace.
C. 3.99	That louten for hem to oure lord and *to* oure lady bothe		C. 6.128	Y haue an Aunte *to* nonne and an abbesse;
C. 3.126	That fuyr shal falle and forbrenne al *to* blew ayesches		C. 6.155	And doen me faste fridayes *to* bred and to water;
C. 3.136	Bothe *to* the and to thyne in hope thow shost amende;		C. 6.155	And doen me faste fridayes to bred and *to* water;
C. 3.136	Bothe to the and *to* thyne in hope thow shost amende;		C. 6.167	That thy wil ne thy wit to wr[at]he myhte turne.
C. 3.148	Yf he wilneth the *to* wyue wolt thow hym haue?'		C. 6.169	And bad hym bid *to* god be his helpe to amende.
C. 3.153	Knelyng, consience *to* þe kyng loutede,		C. 6.170	Thenne seyde lecherye 'alas!' and *to* oure lady cryede,
C. 3.157	Quod Consience *to* the kyng, 'Crist hit me forbede!		C. 6.171	'Lady, *to* thy leue sone loute for me nouthe
C. 3.169	As comyn as þe cartway *to* knaues and to alle,		C. 6.175	Y, gulty in gost, *to* god y me shryue
C. 3.169	As comyn as þe cartway to knaues and *to* alle,		C. 6.179	Semyng *to* synneward and summe y gan taste
C. 3.170	*To* Monekes, to [mynstrals, to] musels in hegge[s];		C. 6.181	Til bothe oure wil was oen and *to* þe werk we ȝeden,
C. 3.170	To Monekes, *to* [mynstrals, to] musels in hegge[s];		C. 6.190	To wynne *to* my wille wymmen with gyle,
C. 3.170	To Monekes, to [mynstrals, *to*] musels in hegge[s];		C. 6.211	*To* wy and to wynchestre y wente to þe fayre
C. 3.192	For she is fauerable *to* fals the whiche defouleth treuthe.		C. 6.211	To wy and *to* wynchestre y wente to þe fayre
C. 3.201	Trewe Burgeys and bonde he bryngeth *to* nauhte ofte		C. 6.211	To wy and to wynchestre y wente *to* þe fayre
C. 3.216	Thenne mournede mede and menede here *to* þe kyng		C. 6.222	[And] spak *to* þe spynnester[e] to spynnen [hit] oute.
C. 3.267	*To* aliens, to alle men, to honoure hem with ȝeftes		C. 6.246	And with lumbardus lettres le[d]e gold *to* Rome;
C. 3.267	To aliens, *to* alle men, to honoure hem with ȝeftes;		C. 6.267	And yf y ȝede *to* þe plough y pynched on his half aker
C. 3.272	And ȝeuen mede *to* men to meyntene here lawes;		C. 6.271	To sese *to* me with here sikel þat y sewe neuere.
C. 3.284	Quod þe kyng *to* Consience, 'by crist, as me thynketh,		C. 6.278	And yf y sente ouer see my seruauntes *to* Bruges
C. 3.286	'Nay,' quod Consience *to* þe kyng, 'clerkes witeth þe sothe,		C. 6.295	Til thow haue ymad þy myhte *to* alle men restitucioun,
C. 3.298	Ne haue hap *to* his hele mede to deserue.		C. 6.307	And arste shal come *to* heuene, [by hym þat me made]!'
C. 3.317	*To* here [lele] and lege, loue [is] the cause;		C. 6.317	Ac ȝut þ[e] synful shrewe saide *to* heuene:
C. 3.335	On a sad and a siker semblable *to* hemsuluen.		C. 6.327	And knolechede [his coupe *to* Crist] ȝut eftsones,
C. 3.339	That [is] þe gyft þat god gyueth *to* alle lele lyuynge,		C. 6.339	Repente þe anon,' quod repentaunce ryhte *to* the vsurer,
C. 3.341	Quod the kyng *to* Consience, 'knowen y wolde		C. 6.344	And ȝif thow wyte neuere *to* whom ne where to restitue
C. 3.365	And withoute ca[s]se to cache [*to*] and come to bothe nombres,		C. 6.345	Bere hit *to* th[e] bischop and bide hym of his grace
C. 3.369	For hoso wolde *to* wyue haue my worliche douhter		C. 6.350	Now bygynneth glotoun for to go *to* shryfte
C. 3.377	That here loue *to* his lawe Thorw al þe lond acorde.		C. 6.351	And kayres hym *to* kyrkeward his coup[e] to shewe.
C. 3.398	Sholde confourme hem *to* o kynde on holy kyrke to bileue		C. 6.355	'*To* holy churche,' quod he, 'for to here masse
C. 3.408	How he absoloun *to* hangynge brouhte;		C. 6.375	Geuen glotoun with glad chere good ale *to* hansull
C. 3.412	And ȝaf the kyndom *to* his knaue þat kept shep and lambren;		C. 6.377	And *to* þe newe fayre nempnede [hit] to sull;
C. 3.414	How god sente *to* sauel be samuel þe prophete		C. 6.407	And when he drow *to* the dore thenne dymmede his yes;
C. 3.419	Haste the with al thyn oste *to* þe lond of Amalek		C. 6.408	[A] thromblede at the thresfold and threw *to* þe erthe.

C. 6.416	Beren hym *to* his bed and brouhten hym þerynne
C. 6.418	A sleep saturday and sonenday til sonne ȝede *to* reste.
C. 6.423	*To* repentaunce ryht thus, 'haue reuthe on me,' he saide,
C. 6.445	*To* the, god, y glotoun, gulty me ȝelde
C. 6.438	For y vowe *to* verray god, for hungur or furste,
C. 7.8	'What! awake, renke!' quod repentaunce, 'and rape [þe] *to* shryfte.'
C. 7.53	And ȝede aboute in my ȝouthe and ȝaf me *to* no thedom
C. 7.59	"Y am sory for my synnes", sey *to* thysuluen
C. 7.65	That y ne shal do me ar day *to* þe dere chirche
C. 7.68	Til y haue euensong yherd: y bihote *to* þe rode.'
C. 7.69	Ac wheche been þe braunches þat bryngeth men *to* sleuthe?
C. 7.80	This beth þe branches, beth ywar, þat bryngeth a man *to* wanhope.
C. 7.86	Laste tho manere men *to* muche sorwe ȝow brynge:
C. 7.90	*To* entise men thorw here tales *to* synne and harlotrie.
C. 7.115	Leden tho that lythed hem *to* luciferes feste
C. 7.117	*To* perpetuel payne or purgatorie a[s] wikke
C. 7.121	To Amende vs of oure mysdedes, do mercy *to* vs alle,
C. 7.124	And sethe soffredes[t] hym to synege, a sykenesse *to* vs alle,
C. 7.156	Criede vpward *to* Crist and to his clene moder
C. 7.156	Criede vpward to Crist and *to* his clene moder
C. 7.157	To haue grace to go *to* treuthe; god leue þat they mote.
C. 7.184	Consience and kynde wyt kenned me *to* his place
C. 7.190	And yserued treuthe sothly, somdel *to* paye.
C. 7.193	And thow y sey hit mysulf y serue hym *to* paye;
C. 7.199	Y wol wissen ȝow wel ryht *to* his place.'
C. 7.232	And so shaltow come *to* a Court as cleer as þe sonne.
C. 7.241	Vche piler is of penaunc[e] and preyeres *to* seyntes;
C. 7.248	Biddeth amende-ȝow meke [hym] *to* his maistre grace
C. 7.259	And fynde alle manere folk fode *to* here soules
C. 7.262	For he hath enuye *to* hym þat in thyn herte setteth
C. 7.271	And aren porteres ouer þe posternes þat *to* þ[e] place bilongen.
C. 7.278	And ho is sib *to* þis seuene, so me god helpe,
C. 7.280	Ho is nat syb *to* þis seuene, sothly to telle,
C. 7.287	'Ȝus!' quod [Perus] þe [plouhman], and pokede hem alle *to* gode,
C. 7.289	And she is sib *to* alle synfole and here sone bothe
C. 7.298	Treuth telleth [this *to* hym], þat y be excused.'
C. 8.7	'Y preye ȝow for ȝoure profit,' quod Peres *to* þe ladyes,
C. 8.28	And go hunte hardelyche *to* hares and to foxes,
C. 8.28	And go hunte hardelyche to hares and *to* foxes,
C. 8.29	*To* bores and to bokkes þat breketh adoun myn hegges
C. 8.29	To bores and *to* bokkes þat breketh adoun myn hegges
C. 8.31	For þey cometh *to* my croft my corn to diffoule.'
C. 8.47	Hit bicometh *to* the, knyhte, to be corteys and hende,
C. 8.52	For hit beeþ þe deueles dysors to drawe men *to* synne;
C. 8.63	*To* pilgrimag[e] as palmeres doen pardon to wynne.
C. 8.93	*To* penaunc[e] and [to] pilgrim[age] y wol passe with oþere;
C. 8.93	To penaunc[e] and [*to*] pilgrim[age] y wol passe with oþere;
C. 8.108	I bar hoem þat y borwed ar y *to* bedde ȝede.
C. 8.111	And ben a pilgrym at þe plouh for profit *to* pore and ryche.'
C. 8.112	Now is perkyn and þ[e] pilgrimes *to* þe plouh faren.
C. 8.130	And maden here mone *to* [Peres] how þei m[yht] nat worche;
C. 8.150	And *to* [Peres] þe [plouhman] profrede to fyhte
C. 8.156	[Peres] the [plouhman] tho pleynede hym *to* þe knyhte
C. 8.186	And wenten as werkemen *to* wedynge and mowynge
C. 8.194	There was no ladde þat lyuede þat ne lowede hym *to* Peres
C. 8.238	Go *to* oure bygynnynge tho god the world made,
C. 8.247	His suluer *to* thre maner men [in] menyng they sholden
C. 8.253	Byno[m] hym al þat he hadde and ȝaf hit *to* his felawe
C. 8.258	Lo! what þe sauter sayth *to* swynkares with handes:
C. 8.264	*To* beggares and to boys þat loth ben to worche.
C. 8.264	To beggares and *to* boys þat loth ben to worche.
C. 8.277	Thenk þat [diues] for his delicat lyf *to* þe deuel wente
C. 8.321	By that hit nyhed neyh heruost and newe corn cam *to* chepyng.
C. 9.1	Treuthe herde telle herof and *to* [Peres] sente
C. 9.15	Merciable *to* meke and mylde to þe gode
C. 9.15	Merciable to meke and mylde *to* þe gode
C. 9.20	To be [peres] *to* þe apostles alle peple to reule
C. 9.35	Fynde hem for godes loue and fauntkynes *to* scole,
C. 9.52	For whenne ȝe drawe *to* þe deth and indulgences wolde haue
C. 9.57	Thise foure sholde be fre *to* alle folk þat hit nede[th].
C. 9.68	And moste merytorie to men þat he ȝeueth fore.
C. 9.79	To rise *to* þe reule to rokke þe cradel,
C. 9.115	And *to* oure syhte as hit semeth; seth god hath þe myhte
C. 9.117	And suffreth suche go so, it semeth *to* myn inwyt
C. 9.125	We sholde [haue] hem *to* house and helpe hem when they come:
C. 9.132	And ȝut more *to* suche men me doth ar they passe;
C. 9.145	Drynke druie and depe and drawe hym thenne *to* bedde;
C. 9.151	And ca[ry]eth hit hoem *to* his cote and cast hym to lyuene
C. 9.156	Thorw which craft a couthe come *to* bred and to ale
C. 9.156	Thorw which craft a couthe come to bred and *to* ale
C. 9.157	And ouermore to [a]n [ha]tur to hele with his bonis
C. 9.200	And somme hadde foreynes *to* frendes þat hem fode sente
C. 9.217	Or ymaymed in som membre, for *to* meschief hit souneth,
C. 9.221	Vnder obedience to be and buxum *to* þe lawe:
C. 9.263	The tarre is vntydy þat *to* þe [tripe] bylongeth;
C. 9.319	And how þe prest preuede no pardon *to* do wel
C. 9.324	So dowel passeth pardoun and pilgrimages *to* Rome.
C. 9.326	*To* peple withouten penaunce to passe into ioye,
C. 9.348	And marie his moder be oure mene *to* hym
C.10.44	The water is likned *to* þe wor[l]d þat wanyeth and waxeth;
C.10.47	The boet is liknet to oure body þat bretil is of kynde,
C.10.53	*To* contricion, to confessioun, til he come til his ende.
C.10.53	To contricion, *to* confessioun, til he come til his ende.
C.10.55	Oure lyf *to* oure lord god for oure lycames gultes.'
C.10.68	A muche man, me thoghte, ylike *to* mysulue,
C.10.88	And is ronne [*t*]o religioun and hath rendred þe bible
C.10.89	And precheth *to* þe peple seynt paules wordes:
C.10.94	And halie with þe hoked ende [i]lle men *to* gode
C.10.116	He was long and lene, ylyk *to* noon other;
C.10.133	A lemman þat he louyeth ylyke *to* hymsulue.
C.10.134	Anima she hatte; *to* here hath enuye
C.10.158	And semblable in soule *to* god but if synne hit make.
C.10.190	And ȝut were best to ben aboute and brynge hit *to* hepe
C.10.192	Bishope[s] sholde ben hereaboute and bryng this *to* hepe
C.10.221	And for þe synne of Caymes seed sayede god *to* Noe:
C.10.225	Boske ȝow *to* þat boet and abideth þerynne
C.10.249	And god sente *to* seth so sone he was of age
C.10.267	That he ne wol bowe *to* þat bonde to beden here an hosebonde
C.10.275	Thogh they [do] hem *to* donemowe, bote þe deuel helpe
C.11.5	'Wel artow wyse,' quod she *to* wyt, 'suche wysdomes to shewe
C.11.6	*To* eny foel or to flaterere or to frentike peple,'
C.11.6	To eny foel or *to* flaterere or to frentike peple,'
C.11.6	To eny foel or to flaterere or *to* frentike peple,'
C.11.36	And brynge forth [a] balle[d] reso[n], taken bernard *to* witnesse
C.11.43	Thenne semeth hit *to* my sihte to suche þat so biddeth
C.11.43	Thenne semeth hit to my sihte *to* suche þat so biddeth
C.11.60	And gode men for oure gultes he al togrynt *to* deth.
C.11.65	And breketh nat here bred *to* þe pore as þe boke hoteth:
C.11.71	Be large þerof whil hit lasteth *to* ledes þat ben nedy
C.11.85	And when y was war of his wille *to* þat womman gan y louten
C.11.91	Y shal kenne þe *to* clergie, my cosyn, þat knoweth
C.11.95	For he is sib *to* þe seuene ars–and also my suster
C.11.101	Gladdere then [þe] gleman þat gold hath *to* ȝefte
C.11.107	For yf thow coueytest to be ryche *to* clergie comest thow neuere.
C.11.110	*To* clergie shaltow neuere come ne knowe what is dowel.
C.11.113	Sey [*to*] hym thysulue ouerse m[y] bokes
C.11.115	And sette here *to* sapience and to þe sauter yglosed.
C.11.115	And sette here to sapience and *to* þe sauter yglosed.
C.11.118	Plato þe poete y putte hym furste *to* boke;
C.11.135	And *to* clergie y cam as clerkes me saide.
C.11.137	How þat wit and his wyf wissede me *to* hym
C.11.149	And þe trewe trinite *to* Austyn apperede
C.11.169	And senes he saide *to* me, 'here myhte thow se wondres
C.11.180	That lede þe wol *to* lykynge Al thy lyf tyme.'
C.11.192	And pruyde-of-parfit-lyuynge *to* moche perel the brynge.'
C.11.194	'Folowe forth þat fortune wole; þou hast [wel] fer *to* elde.
C.11.196	Sir wanhope was sib *to* hym, as som men me tolde,
C.11.198	'Go y *to* helle or to heuene y shal nat go myn one.
C.11.198	'Go y to helle or *to* heuene y shal nat go myn one.
C.11.211	Neuere to man so moche *to* þat man can of telle,
C.11.245	Bote holy churche, herborw *to* alle þat ben yblessed.
C.11.254	And for he biknewe on þe croes and *to* crist shrof hym
C.11.260	Passe[d] forth paciently *to* perpetuel blisse.
C.11.264	Mouhte sleylokeste be slawe and sente hym *to* w[e]rre,
C.11.267	Cristene [kynde] to culle *to* dethe?
C.11.275	For Crist saide *to* sayntes and to suche as he louede,
C.11.275	For Crist saide to sayntes and *to* suche as he louede,
C.11.288	And is to mene no more *to* men þat beth lewed:
C.12.2	'That wit shal turne *to* wrechednesse for wil hath al his wille!'
C.12.5	[Haue no consience how þou come *to* good]; confesse the to som frere.
C.12.5	[Haue no consience how þou come to good]; confesse the *to* som frere.
C.12.9	*To* here prior prouincial [a] pardon to haue
C.12.47	'Multi *to* a mangerye and to þe mete were sompned
C.12.47	'Multi to a mangerye and *to* þe mete were sompned
C.12.69	And for his rechelesnes rewarde hym þere riht *to* þe day of dome
C.12.81	Gregori wiste this wel and wilned *to* my soule
C.12.123	Witnesse in þe paske woke when he ȝede *to* Emaux:
C.12.129	And al was ensample, sothly, *to* vs synfole here
C.12.135	Was a puyre pore mayde and *to* a pore man ywedded.
C.12.137	And *to* oure sauyour sulue saide þis wordes:
C.12.162	What god saide hymsulue *to* a segg þat he louede:
C.12.166	Ac ȝef hem forth *to* pore folk þat for my loue hit aske;
C.12.169	"Hoso coueiteth to come *to* my kyneriche
C.12.188	Aren tidiore and touore *to* mannes byhofte

C.12.205   For crist saide [so] *to* seyntes þat for his sake tholeden
C.12.236   Worldly wele y[s] wykked thyng *to* hem þat hit kepeth.
C.12.240   To synege and *to* souche sotiltees of Gyle,
C.12.245   So coueytise of catel was combraunce *to* hem alle.
C.13.19   Alle his sorwe *to* solace thorw that song turnede
C.13.30   And lyues þat oure lord loueth and large weyes *to* heuene;
C.13.52   And ȝut thow they wende o way as *to* wynchestre fayre
C.13.67   Aren alle acountable *to* crist and to þe kyng of heuene,
C.13.67   Aren alle acountable to crist and *to* þe kyng of heuene,
C.13.80   Beth nat ybounde, as beth [þ]e ryche, *to* [bothe two] lawes,
C.13.100   Vch a parfi[t] prest *to* pouerte sholde drawe
C.13.114   And a title, a tale of nauht, *to* his lyflode as hit were.
C.13.123   [*To*] ouerskippere also in þe sauter sayth dauid:
C.13.147   Males drow hem *to* males a[l mour]nynge by hemsulue
C.13.148   And femeles *to* femeles ferddede and drowe.
C.13.160   Ther is no wriht, as y wene, sholde worch here neste *to* paye;
C.13.216   And saide anoen *to* mysulue, 'slepynge hadde y grace
C.13.244   Why ȝe worden *to* me thus was for y aresonede Resoun.'
C.14.40   And in soend a signe wroet and saide *to* þe iewes,
C.14.42   To strike with stoen or with staf this strompet *to* dethe."
C.14.49   Riht so lereth lettrure lewed men *to* resoun.
C.14.78   Ne brouhte by here bokes *to* blisse ne to ioye,
C.14.78   Ne brouhte by here bokes to blisse ne *to* ioye,
C.14.83   As *to* þe clergie of crist thei counted hit but a tryfle:
C.14.92   *To* pastours and to poetes Appered þe Angel
C.14.92   To pastours and *to* poetes Appered þe Angel
C.14.93   And bad hem go *to* Bedlem goddes berthe to honoure
C.14.96   Tho hit shoen *to* shepherdes, a sheware of blisse.
C.14.98   And deden here homage honerably *to* hym þat was almyhty.
C.14.109   'He þat can nat swymmen,' y sayde, 'hit semeth *to* alle wittes.'
C.14.121   And hath no contricion ar he come *to* shrifte; and thenne can he
           lytel telle,
C.14.126   Wel may þe barne blesse þat hym *to* boek sette,
C.14.132   Was for A ȝeld hym creaunt *to* crist and his grace askede.
C.14.133   And god is ay gracious *to* alle þat gredeth to hym
C.14.133   And god is ay gracious to alle þat gredeth *to* hym
C.14.157   How creatures han kynde wit and how clerkes come *to* bokes
C.14.158   And how þe floures in þe fryth cometh *to* fayre hewes:
C.14.169   *To* briddes and to bestes, As here bokes telleth
C.14.169   To briddes and *to* bestes, As here bokes telleth
C.14.187   *To* lowe lyuynge men þe larke is resembled
C.14.188   And *to* lele and lyfholy þat louyeth alle treuthe.
C.15.16   Thorw vnkunynge curatours *to* incurable peynes;
C.15.19   And how louyng he is *to* vch lyf a londe and o watere
C.15.31   They woschen and wypeden and wenten *to* þe dyner.
C.15.54   And *to* me þat was his mette tho, and oþer mete bothe.
C.15.68   Thenne saide y *to* mysulue so pacience hit herde,
C.15.71   Alle þat coueyte[d] to come *to* eny kyne ioye,
C.15.75   A[s] poul þe apostle prechede *to* þe peple ofte:
C.15.82   They preche þat penaunce is profitable *to* þe soule
C.15.91   'Y schal iangle *to* þis iurdan with his iuyste wombe
C.15.101   And [thenne shal he testifie of] a trinite and take his felowe [t]*o*
           witnesse
C.15.168   The kyng and alle þe comune and clergie *to* þe loute
C.15.176   And sethe a saide *to* clergie so þat y hit herde:
C.15.215   Fro Mihelmasse *to* Mihelmasse y fynde mete and drynke.
C.15.217   That pestilenc[e] *to* pees and parfyt loue turn[e].
C.15.274   The whiche wil loue lat *to* oure lordes place
C.15.280   Thogh men rede of rychesse rihte *to* þe worldes ende
C.15.282   When he drow *to* þe deth that he ne dradd hym sarrore
C.15.292   And blisse *to* all þat been, bothe wilde and tame."
C.15.297   For *to* wroþerhele was he wrouht þat neuere was ioye yschape.
C.16.17   Now, lord, sende hem somur som tyme *to* solace and to ioye
C.16.17   Now, lord, sende hem somur som tyme to solace and *to* ioye
C.16.38   Oure preyeres and oure penanc[e] And pilgrimag[e] *to* Rome.
C.16.47   And þat is plesant *to* pruyde in pore and in ryche.
C.16.53   The hey way *to* heueneward he halt hit nat fol euene.
C.16.73   And thogh his glotonye be of gode ale he goth *to* a colde beddynge
C.16.83   And pouerte is bote a pety thyng, appereth nat *to* his nauele,
C.16.94   And thow sleuthe sewe pouerte and serue nat god *to* paye
C.16.109   As by assente of sondry p[arti]es and suluer *to* bote,
C.16.113   The whiche is syb *to* crist [hym]sulue and semblable bothe.'
C.16.145   For lordes alloueth hym litel or leggeth ere *to* his resoun;
C.16.146   A tempreth þe tonge *to* treuthward þat no tresor coueyteth:
C.16.150   The nythe is swete *to* [þe] soul[e], no sucre swettore,
C.16.186   And when y make mone *to* god Memoria y hatte;
C.16.200   Nempned me thus *to* name; now þou myhte chese
C.16.218   *To* engelische men this is to mene, þat mowen speke and here,
C.16.231   Freres fele tymes *to* þe folk þer they prechen
C.16.266   And is ylikned in latyn *to* a lothly donghep
C.16.268   Or *to* a wal ywhitlymed and were blak withynne;
C.16.310   Hath he no lykynge to lawhe ne to likene men *to* scorne.
C.16.329   Worth moche meryte *to* þat man þat hit may soffre.

C.16.347   And also gladliche he hit gaf *to* gomes þat hit nedede.
C.17.10   *To* his selle selde cam and soffred be mylked.
C.17.38   *To* his wyf; when he was blynde he herde a la[m]be blete:
C.17.57   To feffe suche and fede þat founded ben *to* þe fulle
C.17.73   Me may now likene lettred men *to* a loscheborw oþer worse
C.17.74   And *to* a badde peny with a gode prynte:
C.17.83   Thus ar ȝe luyþer ylikned *to* lossheborw[e] sterlynges
C.17.96   Haen no byleue *to* þe lyft ne to þe lodesterr[e].
C.17.96   Haen no byleue to þe lyft ne *to* þe lodesterr[e].
C.17.112   Go now *to* eny degre and bote gyle be holde a maistre
C.17.145   Thenne seweth the [thy] soule *to* sorwe or to ioye
C.17.145   Thenne seweth the [thy] soule to sorwe or *to* ioye
C.17.149   Contrarie her nat as in Consience yf thow wol[t] come *to* heuene.'
C.17.155   *To* þat lord þat hym lyf lente lyflode hym sende.
C.17.175   Thenne sholde þe coluere come *to* þe clerkes ere,
C.17.178   For Macometh *to* men swaer hit was a messager of heuene
C.17.186   Sholden conuerte hem *to* Crist and cristendoem to take.
C.17.236   His preyeres with his pacience *to* pees sholde brynge
C.17.246   And crie *to* Crist a wolde his coluer sende
C.17.257   And maken here mone *to* Macometh here message to shewe.
C.17.277   He is a forbisene *to* alle bisshopis and a briht myrrour
C.17.278   And souereynliche [*to*] suche þat of surie bereth þe name
C.17.284   And pacientliche thorw his prouynce and *to* his peple hym shewe,
C.17.286   And enchaunten hem *to* charite on holy churche to bileue.
C.17.306   And her power thorw his pacience *to* puyr nauht brouhte.
C.18.31   The world is a wikkede wynd *to* hem þat wo[l] treuthe;
C.18.39   And al forb[i]t Caritas rihte *to* þe bare stalke.
C.18.78   And more lykynde *to* oure lord then lyue as kynde asketh
C.18.107   And Elde clemp *to* þe c[r]opward; thenne comsed hit to crye.
C.18.124   *To* a mayde þat hihte marie, a meke thyng withalle,
C.18.131   And saide hendely *to* hym, 'lo me his hondmayden
C.18.170   Thenne iesus *to* Iudas and to þe iewes sayde,
C.18.170   Thenne iesus to Iudas and *to* þe iewes sayde,
C.18.172   And kene care in thy kissyng and combraunce *to* thysulue.
C.18.173   Thow shalt be myrrour *to* monye men to disceue.
C.18.174   Wo *to* tho þat thy wyles vysen to þe wo[r]ldes ende:
C.18.174   Wo to tho þat thy wyles vysen *to* þe wo[r]ldes ende:
C.18.175   Sethe y be tresoun am take and *to* ȝoure will, iewes,
C.18.177   This iewes *to* þe iustices iesus they ladde.
C.18.200   Thre bilongeth *to* a lord þat leiaunce claymeth,
C.18.211   Semblable *to* hymsulue ar eny synne were,
C.18.226   Now go we *to* godhede: in god, fader of heuene,
C.18.237   And *to* godhede goth thre and o god is all thre.
C.18.257   *To* me and [to] myn issue more he me bihihte,
C.18.257   To me and [*to*] myn issue more he me bihihte,
C.19.38   *To* godhede but o god and on god almyhty
C.19.46   Go thy gate!' quod y *to* spes; 'so me god helpe,
C.19.55   A man, as me tho thouhte, *to* moche care they brouhte
C.19.67   And *to* th[e] wey a wente his woundes to byholde
C.19.73   And ladde hym forth *to* lauacrum lex dei, a grang[e]
C.19.76   And toek two pans the hostiler to take kepe *to* hym;
C.19.79   And rapede hym to ryde the rihte way *to* Ierusalem.
C.19.84   Ne no medicyne vnder molde the man *to* hele brynge,
C.19.117   And profered hit forth as with the paume *to* what place hit sholde.
C.19.172   For *to* a torche or a taper þe trinite is likned,
C.19.185   *To* alle vnkynde creatures þat coueyten to destruye
C.19.194   Til þat loue and bileue leliche *to* hym blowe.
C.19.198   Melteth in a myntwhile *to* myst and to water.
C.19.198   Melteth in a myntwhile to myst and *to* water.
C.19.200   Melteth *to* mercy, to merciable and to non oþere.
C.19.200   Melteth to mercy, *to* merciable and to non oþere.
C.19.200   Melteth to mercy, to merciable and *to* non oþere.
C.19.213   *To* þe fader of heuene forȝe[ue]nesse to haue.
C.19.219   *To* alle vnkynde creatures, as Crist hymsulue witnesseth:
C.19.220   Be vnkynde *to* thyn emcristene and al þat thow canst bidde,
C.19.223   And indulgences ynowe and be ingrat[u]s to thy kynde,
C.19.230   Beth nat vnkynde, y conseyle ȝow, *to* ȝoure emcristene.
C.19.233   Minne ȝe nat, riche men, *to* which a myschaunce
C.19.235   Of his mete and mone *to* men þat hit nedede?
C.19.241   And for he was a nygard and a nythynge *to* the nedfol pore,
C.19.252   And gyueth ȝoure goed *to* þat god þat grace of aryseth.
C.19.253   For þat ben vn[k]ynde *to* hise, hope ȝe noen oþer
C.19.262   For euery manere goed man may be likned *to* a torche
C.19.263   Or elles [*to*] a taper to reuerense with the trinite
C.19.284   That rihtwisnesse thorw repentaunce *to* reuthe myhte turne.
C.19.295   For goed hope, that helpe scholde, *to* wanhope turneth
C.19.299   Ac ar [h]is rihtwisnesse *to* reuthe turne rest[i]t[uci]on hit maketh,
C.19.318   *To* man þat mercy asketh and amende thenketh."
C.20.5   And lened me *to* lenten: and long tyme y slepte.
C.20.8   Oen semblable *to* þe samaritaen and somdeel to Pers þe plouhman
C.20.8   Oen semblable to þe samaritaen and somdeel *to* Pers þe plouhman
C.20.30   Lyf saith þat a lyeth and [leyeth] his lyf *to* wedde,
C.20.50   'Aue, raby,' quod þat ribaud, and redes shotte vp *to* his yes.

C.20.52   And with a pole poysen potten vp *to* his lippes
C.20.97   'For þis [fou]l vilanye vengeaunce [*to*] ȝow [f]all[e]!
C.20.114   Y [d]row [me] in þat derkenesse *to* descendit ad inferna
C.20.117   Cam walkynge in þe way; *to* hellward she lokede.
C.20.135   And þat my tale [be] trewe y take god *to* witnesse.
C.20.162   All þat deth and þe deuel dede formost *to* Eue
C.20.177   And preyede pees to tellen [here] *to* what place she [w]olde
C.20.187   And þat god hath forgyue and graunted *to* mankynde
C.20.233   Bothe in heuene and in erthe, and now *to* helle he thenketh
C.20.264   And y, boek, wol be brente bote he aryse *to* lyue
C.20.270   A spirit speketh *to* helle and bit vnspere þe ȝates:
C.20.271   A vois loude in þat liht *to* lucifer saide,
C.20.274   Thenne syhed satoun and saide *to* helle,
C.20.276   Care and combraunce is come *to* vs all.
C.20.324   We haen no trewe title *to* hem for thy tresoun hit maketh.'
C.20.388   Ergo soule shal soule quyte and synne *to* synne wende
C.20.398   Adam and alle thorw a tre shal turne *to* lyue.
C.20.410   Moiste me *to* þe fulle ne my furste slokke
C.20.417   Ac to be merciable *to* man thenne my kynde [hit] asketh
C.20.427   Ther þat doem *to* þe deth dampneth alle wikkede
C.20.436   To be merciable *to* monye of my haluebretherne.
C.20.457   That loue, and hym luste, *to* l[a]u[h]ynge [ne] brouhte;
C.20.462   For inposible is no thynge *to* hym þat is almyhty.'
C.20.468   That men rang *to* þe resureccioun and riht with þat y wakede
C.20.471   And crepe *to* þe croes on knees and kusse hit for a iewel
C.21.2   And dihte me derely and dede me *to* kyrke
C.21.4   In myddes þe masse tho men ȝede *to* offrynge
C.21.8   And riht lyke in alle lymes *to* oure lord iesu.
C.21.10   'Is this iesus the ioustare,' quod y, 'þat iewes dede *to* dethe?
C.21.19   Ergo is no name *to* þe name of iesus
C.21.28   To be cald a knyht is fayr for men shal knele *to* hym;
C.21.42   Hit bicometh [*to*] a kyng to kepe and to defende
C.21.67   *To* penaunce and to pouerte he mot putte hymsuluen
C.21.67   To penaunce and *to* pouerte he mot putte hymsuluen
C.21.69   Ac to carpe more of Crist and how he cam *to* þat name;
C.21.89   Gold is likened *to* lewetee that laste shal euere
C.21.90   [For it shal turne tresoun] *to* riht and to treuthe.
C.21.90   [For it shal turne tresoun] to riht and *to* treuthe.
C.21.91   The thridde kyng cam [þo] knel[ynge] *to* iesu
C.21.95   Thorw thre kyne kynges knelyng *to* iesu.
C.21.111   For wyn is likned *to* lawe and lyfholinesse
C.21.114   Bothe *to* lered and to lewed, to louye oure enemyes.
C.21.114   Bothe to lered and *to* lewed, to louye oure enemyes.
C.21.125   He made lame to lepe and ȝaf liht *to* blynde
C.21.141   And for to do hym *to* dethe day and nyhte they casten,
C.21.151   Comen knelyng *to* þ[e] Cors and songen
C.21.169   *To* peter and to his apostlis and saide pax vobis;
C.21.169   To peter and *to* his apostlis and saide pax vobis;
C.21.185   *To* alle manere men mercy and forȝeuenesse\
C.21.187   *To* Peres pardoun þe plouhman Redde quod debes.
C.21.197   The gode *to* godhede and to grete ioye
C.21.197   The gode to godhede and *to* grete ioye
C.21.201   Oen spiritus paraclitus *to* Peres and to his felawes.
C.21.201   Oen spiritus paraclitus to Peres and *to* his felawes.
C.21.216   *To* alle kyne creatures þat can his fyue wittes,
C.21.217   Tresor to lyue by *to* here lyues ende
C.21.308   He dede equite *to* alle eueneforth his knowyng.
C.21.316   And tulieth [*to*] here techynge þe cardinal vertues.'
C.21.331   And gaf hym caples *to* his Carte, Contrissioun & confessioun;
C.21.335   Now is [Peres] *to* the [plouh]; Pryde hit aspiede
C.21.341   Thise two cam *to* Consience and to cristene peple
C.21.341   Thise two cam to Consience and *to* cristene peple
C.21.355   Quod Consience *to* alle cristene tho, 'my consayl is [to] wende
C.21.390   *To* [Peres] pardon þe [plouhman] Redde quod debe[s].'
C.21.392   Al þat we owen eny wyhte or we go *to* hosele?'
C.21.411   Man *to* me þat me couthe telle of cardinal[e] vertues
C.21.416   The comu[n]e clamat cotidie, vch a man *to* oþer,
C.21.433   As brihte as *to* þe beste man or to þe beste womman.
C.21.433   As brihte as to þe beste man or *to* þe beste womman.
C.21.450   And turne here wi[t] *to* wisdoem and to wel[th]e [of] soule.
C.21.450   And turne here wi[t] to wisdoem and *to* wel[th]e [of] soule.
C.21.453   Bote hit sowne, as bi sihte, somwhat *to* wynnynge.
C.22.7   That thow toke *to* [thy bylyue], to clothes and to sustinaunce
C.22.7   That thow toke to [thy bylyue], *to* clothes and to sustinaunce
C.22.7   That thow toke to [thy bylyue], to clothes and *to* sustinaunce
C.22.16   And thow he come so *to* a cloth and can no bettere cheuesaunce
C.22.23   [For is no vertue by fer *to* spiritus temperancie],
C.22.44   "Bothe fox and foule may fle *to* hole and crepe
C.22.45   And þe fisch hath fyn to flete with *to* reste;
C.22.47   And soffre sorwes ful soure þat shal *to* ioye torne."
C.22.76   And crye we *to* kynde þat he come and defende vs
C.22.78   And crye we on al þe comune þat thei come *to* vnite

C.22.100   Deth cam dryuyng aftur and al *to* duste paschte
C.22.129   And cam *to* þe kynges consail as a kene Baroun
C.22.136   And [*t*]*o* þe Arches in haste he ȝede anoen aftur
C.22.169   And lyf fley for fere *to* fisyk aftur helpe
C.22.181   And roed so *to* reuel, a ryche place and a murye:
C.22.201   And cryede *to* kynde: 'out of care me brynge!
C.22.209   'How shal y come *to* catel so to clothe me and to fede?'
C.22.212   And y bi conseil of kynde comsed *to* Rome
C.22.213   Thorw contricion and confessioun til y cam *to* vnite.
C.22.245   *To* vnite and holi churche; ac o thyng y ȝow praye:
C.22.247   *To* lered ne to lewed, but lyueth aftur ȝoure reule.
C.22.247   To lered ne *to* lewed, but lyueth aftur ȝoure reule.
C.22.259   And yf thei wage men *to* werre thei writen hem in nombre;
C.22.273   Enuye herde this and heete freres go *to* scole
C.22.277   He lyeth, as y leue, þat *to* þe lewed so precheth,
C.22.278   For god made *to* men a lawe and Moyses hit tauhte:
C.22.285   And fle *to* þe freres, as fals folk to Westmynstre
C.22.285   And fle to þe freres, as fals folk *to* Westmynstre
C.22.290   And so hit fareth with moche folke þat *to* freres shryuen,
C.22.293   And soffren þe dede in dette *to* þe day of dome.
C.22.295   And freres *to* filosophye he foend hem to scole
C.22.295   And freres to filosophye he foend hem *to* scole
C.22.316   Quod contricion *to* Consience, 'do hym come to vnite
C.22.316   Quod contricion to Consience, 'do hym come *to* vnite
C.22.325   *To* a lord for a lettre leue to haue
C.22.327   Baldly *to* þe bishope and his breef hadde
C.22.355   And cam *to* Consience and cortey[s]liche hym grette.
C.22.358   Conforte hym,' quod Consience, 'and taek kepe *to* his sores.
C.22.361   Fro lente *to* lente he lat his plastres byte.'
C.22.365   And for hem þat ȝe aren holde *to* al my lyf tyme

to &> two,for_to,forto

tobye n prop *n.i.d.* A 1 tobie; B 3; C 2 tobie
A.11.25   And can telle of *tobie* & of þe twelue apostlis,
B.10.33   And kan telle of *Tobye* and of [þe] twelue Apostles
B.10.88   *Tobye* [techeþ] noȝt so; takeþ hede ye riche
B.10.90   Whoso haþ muche spende manliche, so [meneþ] *Tobye*,
C.11.68   *Tobie* techeth nat so; taketh hede, ȝe ryche,
C.17.37   As wittnesseth holy writ what *tobie* saide

tobroke ptp *tobreken v.* A 1; B 1; C 2 tobroke (1) tobrokene (1)
A. 8.30   And bynde brugges aboute þat *tobroke* were,
B. 7.28   And [bynde] brugges [aboute] þat *tobroke* were,
C. 9.32   And brugges *tobrokene* by the heye wayes
C. 9.99   But they be blynde or *tobroke* or elles be syke,

tocleue v *tocleven v.* B 1; C 3 tocleyef (1) tocleue (2)
B.12.139   For þe heiȝe holy goost heuene shal *tocleue*,
C.14.84   For the hey holi gost heuene shal *tocleue*
C.20.61   The wal of the temple *tocleyef* euene [a] to peces;
C.20.112   When Crist thorw croos ouercam ȝoure kyndoem sholde *tocleue*:

today adv *todai adv.* A 1; B 3; C 3
A. 7.90   For þeiȝ I deiȝe *today* my dettis ben quyt;
B. 6.98   For þouȝ I deye *today* my dettes are quyte;
B.18.366   And for þat drynke *today* I deide vpon erþe.
B.19.215   'For I wole dele *today* and [dyuyde] grace
C. 8.107   For thouh y dey *today* my dette[s ben] yquited;
C.20.404   And for þat drynke *today* y deyede as hit semede.
C.21.215   'For y wol dele *today* and deuyde grace

todrowe v *todrauen v.* A 1; B 1
A.11.27   To iesu þe gentil þat Iewis *todrowe*
B.10.35   To Iesu þe gentile þat Iewes *todrowe*

toek > taken; toel > tooles; toelde > tellen; toethaches > tooþaches

toforn prep *toforen prep.* A 1 tofore; B 3 tofore (1) toforn (2); C 3 tofore
A. 5.221   And made auowe *tofore* god for his foule slouþe:
B. 5.449   And made auow *tofore* god for his foule sleuþe:
B.12.130   [Dyuyneris] *toforn* vs [viseden and markeden]
B.13.49   He sette a sour loof *tofor* vs and seide 'Agite penitenciam',
C. 5.114   Resoun reuerentliche *tofore* al þe reume preschede
C. 7.63   And made [a]uowe *tofore* god for his foule sleuthe:
C. 7.108   To crye a largesse *tofore* oure lord ȝoure good loos to shewe.

toft n *toft n.* A 2; B 2; C 1 tofte
A.Pr.14   I saiȝ a tour on a *toft* triȝely Imakid;
A. 1.12   'þe tour [on] þe *toft*,' quaþ heo, 'treuþe is þereinne,
B.Pr.14   I seiȝ a tour on a *toft* trieliche ymaked,
B. 1.12   'The tour on þe *toft*', quod she, 'truþe is þerInne,
C. 1.12   'The tour vppon þe *tofte*,' quod she, 'treuthe is þerynne

695

togideres adv *togederes adv.* A 38 togedere (1) togidere (24) togideris
(13); B 51 togidere (4) togideres (41) togidres (6); C 48 togederes
(17) togedres (1) togyderes (30)

A.Pr.46	Pilgrimes & palmeris pli3ten hem *togidere*
A.Pr.60	For here mony & here marchaundise meten *togidere.*
A.Pr.63	But holy chirche & [hy] holden bet *togidere*
A. 1.38	For þe fend & þi flessh folewiþ *togidere,*
A. 1.55	For husbondrie & he holden *togideris.'*
A. 1.171	So [harde] haþ auarice haspide 3ow *togideris.*
A. 2.23	Fauel wiþ fair speche haþ forgid hem *togidere;*
A. 2.25	And al is li3eris ledyng þat hy li3en *togidere.*
A. 2.62	Wiþ þe kingdom of coueitise I croune hem *togidere;*
A. 2.64	Glotonye & grete oþes I gyue hem *togidere;*
A. 2.66	In al þe signiure of slouþe I se[se] hem *togidere;*
A. 2.100	3if any Leaute wile loke þei ligge *togidere.*
A. 2.145	Fals & fauel fariþ forþ *togidere,*
A. 3.127	And [g]iueþ þe gaileris gold & grotis *togidere*
A. 3.152	Clergie and coueitise he[o] coupliþ *togidere.*
A. 3.213	Mede & marchaundise mote nede go *togidere;*
A. 3.267	But loue & lou3nesse & leaute *togideris;*
A. 3.275	Ac kynde wyt shal come 3et, & consience *togidere,*
A. 4.33	And wordiden a gret while wel wisly *togidere.*
A. 4.62	Þanne wisdom & wyt wente *togidere*
A. 4.132	Clerkis þat wern confessours couplide hem *togideris,*
A. 4.158	As longe as I lyue libbe we *togideris.'*
A. 5.34	He pre[3yde] prelatis & prestis *togidere,*
A. 5.126	Brochide hem wiþ a pakke nedle, & pleit hem *togidere;*
A. 5.134	Penyale & pilewhey heo pouride *togidere.*
A. 5.174	Þo risen vp in rape & ro[wn]eden *togideris,*
A. 5.177	Þei couþe [not] be here consience acorden *togidere*
A. 5.251	[A] þousand of men þ[o þ]rong[en] *togideris,*
A. 8.74	But as wilde bestis wiþ wehe, & worþ vp *togideris*
A. 9.19	[Þat] dowel & do euele mowe not dwelle *togidere.*
A.10.3	Of erþe & eir it is mad, medlit *togideris;*
A.10.146	In þat curside constellacioun þei knewe *togideris,*
A.10.158	To kepe his kynrede fro kaymes, þei couplide nou3t *togideris;*
A.10.180	A3en þe lawe of oure lord le[i3en] *togideris,*
A.10.191	Manye peire siþen þ[e] pestilence han p[l]i3t hem *togidere.*
A.11.230	Ac pore men in pacience & penaunce *togidere*
A.11.266	God 3af h[i]m grace & ricchesse *togidere*
A.12.93	Whil his lyf and his lykhame lesten *togedere.*
B.Pr.46	Pilgrymes and Palmeres pli3ten hem *togidere*
B.Pr.63	For hire moneie and hire marchaundi3e marchen *togideres.*
B.Pr.66	But holy chirche and hij holde bettre *togidres*
B. 1.40	For þe fend and þi flessh folwen *togidere,*
B. 1.57	For housbondrie and h[e] holden *togidres.'*
B. 1.121	But fellen out in fendes liknesse [ful] nyne dayes *togideres*
B. 1.197	So harde haþ Auarice yhasped [yow] *togideres,*
B. 2.70	That Gile wiþ hise grete oþes gaf hem *togidere',*
B. 2.84	And þe Erldom of Enuye and [Ire] *togideres,*
B. 2.93	Glotonye he [gyueþ] hem ek and grete oþes *togidere,*
B. 2.136	If any [lewte] wol loke þei ligge *togideres.*
B. 2.173	Denes and Southdenes, drawe yow *togideres;*
B. 2.184	Fals and Fauel fareþ forþ *togideres*
B. 3.138	And gyueþ þe Gailers gold and grotes *togidres*
B. 3.165	Clergie and coueitise she coupleþ *togidres.*
B. 3.226	[Mede and Marchaundi3e] mote nede go *togideres,*
B. 3.291	Ac loue and lowenesse and leautee *togideres;*
B. 3.299	Ac kynde loue shal come 3it and Conscience *togidere*
B. 4.25	And Reson wiþ hym ryt, rownynge *togideres*
B. 4.46	And wordeden [a gret while wel wisely] *togideres.*
B. 4.76	[Thanne Wisdom and wit] wenten *togidres*
B. 4.149	Clerkes þat were Confessours coupled hem *togidere*
B. 4.195	Als longe as [I lyue] lyue we *togideres.'*
B. 5.41	And siþen he [preide] prelates and preestes *togideres,*
B. 5.172	And if I telle any tales þei taken hem *togideres,*
B. 5.210	[P]roche[d] hem wiþ a paknedle and playte hem *togideres,*
B. 5.218	Peny ale and puddyng ale she poured *togideres;*
B. 5.325	T[h]o risen vp in Rape and rouned *togideres*
B. 5.328	Thei couþe no3t, by hir Conscience, acorden [*togideres*]
B. 5.510	A þousand of men þo þrungen *togideres,*
B. 6.182	Or ellis benes [and] bren ybaken *togideres.'*
B. 8.23	[That] dowel and do yuele mowe no3t dwelle *togideres.*
B. 9.3	Of erþe and Eyr [it is] maad, medled *togidere,*
B. 9.131	Caymes kynde and his kynde coupled *togideres,*
B. 9.170	Many peire siþen þe pestilence han pli3t hem *togideres.*
B.12.208	And for to seruen a Seint and swich a þef *togideres,*
B.14.239	And if Coueitise cacche þe poore þei may no3t come *togideres,*
B.15.189	Pride wiþ al þe appurtenaunces, and pakken hem *togideres,*
B.15.275	In spekes and spelonkes; selde speken *togideres.*
B.15.554	*Togideres* loue leelly, leueþ it wel, ye bisshopes,
B.16.80	And gadrede hem alle *togideres,* boþe grete and smale,
B.16.256	Amonges patriarkes and prophetes pleyinge *togideres*

B.17.50	And as we wenten þus in þe wey wordynge *togideres*
B.17.169	And as my fust is ful hand y[f]olden *togideres*
B.17.207	As wex and a weke were twyned *togideres,*
B.17.209	And as wex and weke and [warm] fir *togideres*
B.17.224	Na moore dooþ sire ne sone ne seint spirit *togidres*
B.17.236	Wol brennen and blasen, be þei *togideres,*
B.18.59	The lord of lif and of light þo leide hise eighen *togideres,*
B.19.166	And as alle þise wise weyes weren *togideres*
B.19.313	Foulen þe fruyt in þe feld þer þei growen *togideres,*
C.Pr.47	Pilgrymes and palmers plighten hem *togyderes*
C.Pr.61	Here moneye and [here] marchandise ma[rch]en *togyderes.*
C.Pr.143	Conscience & kynde wit] and knyghthed *togedres*
C. 1.38	For the fend and thy flesch folewen *togederes*
C. 1.53	For hosbondrye and he holdeth *togederes.'*
C. 1.192	So harde haþ auaryce yhapsed hem *togyderes.*
C. 2.100	Glotonye a gyueth hem and grete othes *togyderes,*
C. 2.197	Thenne fals and fauel ryde forth *togederes*
C. 3.164	3oure fader she [f]elde, fals and she *togederes;*
C. 3.176	And gyueth the gaylers gold and grotes *togederes*
C. 3.211	For clerkes and coueitise mede hath knet *togederes*
C. 3.281	Marchaundise and mede mot nede [go] *togederes.*
C. 3.444	Ac loue and lownesse and lewete *togyderes;*
C. 3.452	A[c] kynde loue shal come 3ut and Consience *togyderes*
C. 4.25	And resoun with hym ry[t], rounynge *togederes*
C. 4.44	And speke wyse wordes a longe while *togederes.*
C. 4.72	For wysdom and wyt tho wenten *togyderes*
C. 4.146	Clerkes [þat were confessours] co[u]plede hem *togederes*
C. 5.140	And sethe a preide prelates and prestes *togyderes,*
C. 6.154	And yf y telle eny tales they taken hem *togyderes*
C. 6.218	To brochen hem with a batnelde and bande hem *togyderes,*
C. 6.226	Peny ale and poddyng ale [h]e poured *togederes,*
C. 6.383	Tho rysen vp [in] rape and rounned *togyderes*
C. 7.155	A thousend of men tho thronge *togyderes,*
C.10.27	And dowel and do euele may nat dwelle *togyderes.*
C.10.130	Of erthe and ayer [hit is] maed, ymedled *togyderes,*
C.10.280	Bote maydones and maydones marie 3ow *togyderes.*
C.11.151	That he seyh þe [syre] and þe sone and þe seynt spirit *togederes*
C.13.33	For yf a marchant and [a] mesager metten *togyderes*
C.13.42	And thogh they wen[d]e by the wey, tho two *togederes,*
C.14.147	And for to seruen a seynt and suche a thef *togyderes,*
C.16.65	And ayther hateth oþer and may nat wone *togyderes.*
C.16.79	And thogh coueytyse [cacche] þe pore they may nat come *togyderes*
C.16.332	Pruyde with alle [þe] purtinaunces and pakketh hem *togyderes*
C.17.22	Loue and lele byleue held lyf and soule *togyderes.*
C.17.217	*Togederes* louyen lelelyche, l[e]ueth hit [wel], bisshopes,
C.18.111	And gadered hem alle *togyderes,* bothe grete & smale,
C.18.272	With patriarkes and profetes pleynge *togyderes.*
C.19.115	As a fuste wit[h] a fynger yfolde *togyderes*
C.19.131	And as þe fuste is a ful hand yfolde *togyderes,*
C.19.173	As wexe and a weke were twyned *togyderes*
C.19.175	And as wex and weke and warm fuyr *togyderes*
C.19.178	So doth þe sire and þe sone and seynt spirit *togyderes*
C.19.190	No more doth sire ne sone ne seynt spirit *togyderes*
C.19.202	Wol brennen and blasen, be they *togyderes,*
C.20.59	The lord of lyf and of liht tho leyde his eyes *togederes*
C.21.166	And as al thise wyse weyes weren *togyderes*
C.21.313	Fouleth the fruyt in the feld ther thei growe *togyderes*

togrynt v *togrinden v.* C 1

C.11.60	And gode men for oure gultes he al *togrynt* to deth.

toille v *toilen v.* A 1

A.11.186	Wiþ any trewe trauaille *toille* for here foode,

tok > taken

toke v *tuken v. &> taken* B 2 toke (1) ytouked (1); C 1

B.15.455	*Ytouked* and yteynted and vnder taillours hande.
B.19.463	Wiþ Spiritus Intellectus þei [*toke*] þe reues rolles
C.21.463	With spiritus intellectus they [*t]o[k]e* þe reues rolles

token > taken

tokene n *token n.* A 3 tokne (2) toknes (1); B 9 tokene (4) tokenes (2)
tokne (2) toknes (1); C 6 tokene (4) tokenes (1) tookene (1)

A. 6.84	Tel hym þis *tokne,* "treuþe wot þe soþe:
A.11.113	'And tel me sum *tokne* to hym, for tyme is þat I wende'.
A.11.172	And tolde hire þe *toknes* þat me ytau3t were.
B.Pr.88	That han cure vnder crist, and crownynge in *tokene*
B. 5.597	Telleþ hym þis *tokene:* "[truþe woot] þe soþe;
B.10.161	'And tel me som *tokne* [to hym], for tyme is þat I wende'
B.10.222	Tel Clergie þis[e] *tokene[s],* and [to] Scripture after,
B.10.229	And tolde [hire] þe *tokenes* þat me tau3t were.
B.10.372	But if I sende þee som *tokene",* and seiþ Non mecaberis,
B.16.147	And tolde hem a *tokne* to knowe wiþ Iesus;

B.16.148   And which *tokne* to þis day to muche is yvsed,
B.16.230   Ful trewe *toknes* bitwene vs is to telle whan me likeþ.
C.Pr.86   That han cure vnder crist and crownyng in *tokene*
C. 3.133   Til treuthe hadde ytolde here a *tokene* fram hymsulue.
C. 7.245   Tel hym this *tokene*: "treuthe woet þe sothe;
C.11.103   'And telle me som *tokene*,' quod y, 'for tyme is þat y wende.'
C.13.12   And for he soffrede and saide nauht oure lord sente *tookene*
C.18.246   Fol trewe *tokenes* bitwene vs is wh[at] tyme þat y met[t]e hym,

tokenynge ger *tokninge ger.* A 1 toknyng; B 2; C 2
A. 5.19   And turnide vpward here tail in *toknyng* of drede
B. 5.19   [And] turned vpward hire tai[l] in *tokenynge* of drede
B.16.204   In *tokenynge* of þe Trinite, was [taken out of a man],
C. 5.121   And turned vpward here tayl in *tokenynge* of drede
C.17.33   In *tokenynge* þat trewe man alle tymes sholde

tokkeris n *tukere n.* A 1
A.Pr.100   Taillours, *t[okk]eris* & to[ll]eris boþe,

tokn- > token-

tol n *tol n.(1)* C 2
C.Pr.98   To vndertake þe *tol* of vntrewe sacrefice.
C.13.73   Tythen here goed tre[u]liche, a *tol*, as hit semeth,

told > tellen; tolde > tellen,tolled; tolden -est > tellen; toles > tooles

tolle v *tollen v.(2)* C 1
C.13.51   Marchauntȝ for here marchaundyse in many place to *tolle*.

tolled v *tollen v.(1)* A 1 tollide; B 1; C 1 tolde
A. 5.128   Til ȝardis oþer twelue *tollide* out þrittene.
B. 5.212   Til ten yerdes or twelue *tolled* out þrittene.
C. 6.220   Til ten ȝerde other twelue *tolde* out threttene.

tollers n *toller n.(1)* A 1 tolleris; B 1
A.Pr.100   Taillours, t[okk]eris & *to[ll]eris* boþe,
B.Pr.221   Taillours, Tynkers and *Tollers* in Markettes,

tollide > tolled; tologged > tolugged

tolomeus n prop *n.i.d.* C 1
C.12.176   Tulius, *tolomeus*-y can nat tell here names–

tolugged ptp *toluggen v.* A 1 toluggid; B 1; C 1 tologged
A. 2.178   Lurkyng þoruȝ lanes, *toluggid* of manye.
B. 2.219   Lurkynge þoruȝ lanes, *tolugged* of manye.
C. 2.229   Lorkyng thorw lanes, *tologged* of moneye.

tom > tome

tombe n *tombe n.* C 1
C.18.143   And luft vp laȝar þat lay in his *tombe*;

tomblest v *tumblen v.* A 1
A.12.91   Þ[ou] *tomblest* wiþ a trepget ȝif þou my tras folwe,

tome n *tome n.* A 1 tom; B 1; C 1
A. 2.147   I haue no *tom* to telle þe tail þat hem folewiþ
B. 2.186   I haue no *tome* to telle þe tail þat [hem] folwe[þ]
C. 2.199   Y haue no *tome* to telle the tayl þat hem folewe[th]

tomme n prop *Tomme n.* B 3; C 3 thomme (1) Tomme (2)
B. 4.18   And also *Tomme* trewe-tonge-tel-me-no-tales-
B. 5.28   *Tomme* Stowue he tauȝte to take two staues
B.20.162   Oon *Tomme* two-tonge, atteynt at ech [a q]ueste.
C. 4.18   And also th[omm]e trewe-tonge-telle-me-no-tales-
C. 5.130   *Tomme* stoue he tauhte to take t[w]o staues
C.22.162   Oen *Tomme* two-tonge, ateynt at vch [a q]ueste.

tomorwe adv *tomorwe adv.* A 2 tomorewe; B 1; C 2
A. 2.22   *Tomorewe* worþ þe mariage mad of mede & of fals;
A. 2.26   *Tomorewe* worþ ymad as I þe telle;
B. 2.44   *Tomorwe* worþ ymaked þe maydenes bridale.
C. 2.43   *Tomorwe* worth mede ymaried to a mansed wrecche,
C. 2.48   That mede is thus ymaried; *tomorwe* þou shalt aspye.

tonder n *tinder n.* B 1; C 1 tender
B.17.249   But þow haue tow to take it wiþ, *tonder* or broches,
C.19.215   Bote thow haue tasch to take hit with, *tender* [or] broches,

tonge n *tonge n.(2)* A 11 tounge (2) tunge (9); B 37 tonge (34) tunge (3);
          C 35 tonge (33) tonges (1) tunge (1)
A. 1.86   For whoso is trewe of his *tunge*, telliþ non oþer,
A. 1.153   For þ[ei3 3e] be trewe of 3oure *tunge* & treweliche wynne,
A. 3.120   She is tykil of hire tail, talewys of hire *tunge*,
A. 5.77   And don hise frendis ben hise fon þoruȝ my false *tunge*.
A. 5.80   Boþe his lyme & his lif was lost þoruȝ my *tunge*.
A. 7.45   And þat þou be trewe of [þi] *tunge*, & talis þou hate,
A. 7.250   L[o]ue hym nouȝt, for he is a lecchour & likerous of *tunge*,
A. 9.72   Trewe of his *tunge* & of his two handis,

A.11.120   Til þou come to a court, kepe wel þi *tunge*
A.12.24   Telle hit with *tounge* to synful wrecches."
A.12.29   God gaf him non answere but gan his *tounge* holde.
B.Pr.51   To ech a tale þat þei tolde hire *tonge* was tempred to lye
B.Pr.158   A Raton of renoun, moost renable of *tonge*,
B. 1.88   [For] who is trewe of his *tonge*, telleþ noon ooþer,
B. 1.179   For þou3 ye be trewe of youre *tonge* and treweliche wynne,
B. 2.25   For Fals was hire fader þat haþ a fikel *tonge*
B. 2.41   To oon fals fikel-*tonge*, a fendes biyete.
B. 3.131   She is tikel of hire tail, talewis of *tonge*,
B. 3.322   Tha[t] worþ Trewe-*tonge*, a tidy man þat tened me neuere.
B. 4.18   And also Tomme trewe-*tonge*-tel-me-no-tales-
B. 5.86   Ech a word þat he warp was of a Neddres *tonge*;
B. 5.97   And [doon] his frendes be his foon þoru3 my false *tonge*.
B. 5.286   But if it were wiþ þi *tonge* or ellis wiþ þi hondes.
B. 5.368   That I haue trespased with my *tonge*, I kan no3t telle how ofte;
B. 5.401   That I telle wiþ my *tonge* is two myle fro myn herte.
B. 6.50   And þat þow be trewe of þi *tonge* and tales þow hatie
B. 6.266   L[o]ue hym no3t for he is [a] lech[our] and likerous of *tunge*,
B. 8.81   Trewe of his *tunge* and of his two handes,
B.10.168   Til þow come to a court, kepe-wel-þi-*tunge*-
B.10.452   Beþ no3t [afered of þat folk], for I shal [3yue yow *tonge*],
B.11.387   Forþi I rede', quod reson, '[þow] rule þi *tonge* bettre,
B.13.159   Misese ne meschief ne man wiþ þi *tonge*,
B.13.322   Lyinge and la[kk]ynge and leue *tonge* to chide;
B.13.327   And made of frendes foes þoru3 a fals *tonge*.
B.13.415   And if he au3t wole here it is an harlotes *tonge*.
B.14.55   By so þat þow be sobre of si3te and of *tonge*,
B.14.100   'Ther parfit truþe and poore herte is, and pacience of *tonge*,
B.14.312   He tempreþ þe *tonge* to truþeward [þat] no tresor coueiteþ:
B.15.13   Oon wiþouten *tonge* and teeþ tolde me whider I sholde
B.15.105   Trewe of youre *tonge* and of youre tail boþe,
B.15.201   For þer are [pure] proude herted men, pacient of *tonge*,
B.17.324   Hir feere fleeþ hire for feere of hir *tonge*.
B.18.146   Ne haue hem out of helle; hold þi *tonge*, mercy!
B.19.93   For Mirre is mercy to mene and mylde speche of *tonge*.
B.19.172   Thomas touched it and wiþ his *tonge* seide:
B.19.232   They lelly to lyue by labour of *tonge*,
B.19.401   And no3t hakke after holynesse; hold þi *tonge*, Conscience!
B.20.162   Oon Tomme two-*tonge*, atteynt at ech [a q]ueste.
C.Pr.178   A ratoun of renown, moste resonable of *tounge*,
C. 1.84   For who is trewe of his *tonge* and of his two handes
C. 1.175   For thow 3e ben trewe of 3oure *tong[e]* and treweliche wynne,
C. 2.6   [Boþe] fals and fauel and fikel *tonge* lyare
C. 2.25   Oon fauel was he[re] fader þat hath a fykel *tonge*
C. 2.124   Althow fals were here fader and fikel *tonge* her belsyre
C. 3.168   For she is tikel of here tayl, talewys of *tonge*,
C. 3.475   Þat worth trewe-*tonge*, a tydy man þat tened me neuere.
C. 4.18   And also th[omm]e trewe-*tonge*-telle-me-no-tales-
C. 6.72   And made of frendes foes thorw fikel and fals *tonge*.
C. 6.109   The harm þat y haue do with hand and with *tonge*.
C. 6.332   By so hit be in thyn herte as y here thy *tonge*.
C. 6.426   Of þat y haue trespased with *tonge*, y can nat telle how ofte;
C. 7.17   That y telle with my *tonge* is t[wo] myle fro myn herte.
C. 7.144   And sethen oure sauyour and seydest with thy *tonge*
C. 7.197   He is as louh as a lombe and leel of his *tonge*.
C. 8.48   Treuwe of thy *tonge* and tales loth to here
C.10.78   Ho[so] is trewe of his *tonge* and of his two handes
C.10.200   To tulie þe erthe with *tonge* and teche men to louye.
C.11.277   Beth nat aferd of þat folk for y shal 3eue 3ow *tonge*,
C.12.198   Fere ne famyne ne fals mennes *tonges*.
C.13.205   Forthy,' quod Resoun, 'y rede thow reule thy *tonge* euere
C.15.158   Meseyse ne meschief ne man with his *tonge*
C.15.254   By so þat þou be sobre of syhte and of *tonge*,
C.16.141   A tempreth þe *tonge* to treuthward þat no tresor coueyteth:
C.16.259   And þerto trewe of 3oure *tonge* and of 3oure tayl also
C.16.371   As y tolde þe with *tonge* a litel tyme ypassed;
C.17.293   Ac we cristene conneth þe [crede] and haen of oure *tonge*
C.19.304   Here f[e]re fleeth here for fere of here *tonge*.
C.20.149   Ne haue hem out of helle; holde thy *tonge*, mercy!
C.21.93   For Mirre is mercy to mene and mylde speche of *tonge*.
C.21.172   Thomas touched hit and and with his *tonge* saide:
C.21.232   They leely to lyue bi labour of *tonge*
C.21.401   And nat hacky aftur holinesse; hold thy *tonge*, consience!
C.22.162   Oen Tomme two-*tonge*, ateynt at vch [a q]ueste.

tonne n *tonne n.* B 1
B.15.338   As whoso filled a *tonne* [ful] of a fressh ryuer

took > taken; tookene >tokene

tooles n *tol n.(3)* A 1 tolis; B 1; C 2 toel (1) toles (1)
A.11.134   [Of] alle kynne craftis I contreuide *tolis*,
B.10.182   Of alle kynne craftes I contreued *tooles*,

C. 3.476   Batailes sholle neuere eft be ne man bere eg *toel*
C.11.122   Of alle kyne craftes y contreuede *toles*,

tooþaches n *toth n.(1)* B 1; C 1 toethaches
B.20.82   Coughes and Cardiacles, Crampes and *tooþaches*,
C.22.82   Cowhes and cardiacles, crampes and *toethaches*,

top n *top n.(1)* A 1; B 2; C 1
A. 3.129   He[o] takiþ þe trewe be þe *top*, tei3eþ hym faste,
B. 3.140   [She] takeþ þe trewe bi þe *top*, tieþ h[y]m faste,
B.16.22   And bad me toten on þe tree, on *top* and on roote.
C. 3.178   And taketh [þe] tre[we] by the *top* and te[i]eth hym f[aste]

toquasched v *toquashen v.* C 2 toquasched (1) toquaschte (1)
C.20.63   The erthe *toquasch[t]e* and quoek as hit quyk were
C.20.257   Quakid as quyk thyng and a[l] *toquasch[ed]* þe roch[e].

torche n *torche n.* B 4; C 4
B.17.206   [For] to a *torche* or a tapur þe Trinite is likned,
B.17.215   And as þow seest som tyme sodeynliche a *torche*,
B.17.282   To a *torche* or a tapur to reuerence þe Trinite,
B.18.240   And tendeden [hire] as a *torche* to reuerencen his burþe,
C.19.172   For to a *torche* or a taper þe trinite is likned,
C.19.181   And as thow seest som tyme sodeynliche of a *torche*
C.19.262   For euery manere goed man may be likned to a *torche*
C.20.249   And tenden h[ere] as a *torche* to reuerensen his burthe;

tore > torn

torende ptp *torenden v.* B 1
B.10.116   Roten and *torende*? Reson wolde it neuere!

toreueth v *toreven v.* C 1
C. 3.203   Religioun he al *toreueth* and oute of reule to lybbe.

torn ptp *teren v.(2)* A 1; B 1; C 1 tore
A. 5.111   In a *torn* tabbard of twelue wynter age,
B. 5.195   In a [*torn*] tabard of twelf wynter age;
C. 6.203   In a *tore* tabard of twelue wynter age;

torne(- > turne

toroef v *toriven v.* C 1
C.20.62   The hard roch al *toroef* and riht derk nyht hit semede;

tortle n *turtel n.* C 1
C.14.161   He tauhte þe *tortle* to tre[d]e, the pocok to cauke

toshullen ptp *?toshellen v.* B 1; C 1
B.17.194   Ac þou3 my þombe and my fyngres boþe were *toshullen*
C.19.160   Ac thouh my thombe and my fyngeres bothe were *toshullen*

toten v *toten v.(1)* B 1; C 1 toted
B.16.22   And bad me *toten* on þe tree, on top and on roote.
C.18.53   I *toted* vpon þ[e] tree tho and thenne toek y hede

tothdraweres n *toth n.(1)* C 1
C. 6.370   Of portours and of pikeporses and of pilede *tothdraweres*,

touchen v *touchen v.* B 8 touche (2) touched (3) touchede (1) touchen (2); C 8 touche (2) touched (3) touchede (1) touchen (1) toucheth (1)
B.11.100   Thou3 þe tale [were] trewe, and it *touche[d]* synne.
B.15.74   And tellen men of þe ten comaundement3, and *touchen* þe seuene synnes,
B.17.150   That *touched* and tastede at techynge of þe pawme
B.17.152   The fader is [þanne] as a fust wiþ fynger to *touche*–
B.18.75   Ac was no bo[y] so boold goddes body to *touche*;
B.18.84   To *touchen* hym or to tasten hym or taken doun of roode,
B.18.194   If þat þei *touchede* a tree and þe [trees] fruyt eten.
B.19.172   Thomas *touched* it and wiþ his tonge seide:
C.19.124   *Touchede* and tastede at techyng of þe paume
C.19.146   Alle þat þe fyngeres and þe fust feleth and *toucheth*.
C.20.77   Ac was no boie so bold godes body to *touche*;
C.20.79   That hadde no boie hardynesse hym to *touche* in deynge.
C.20.86   To *touchen* hym or to t[ast]en hym or taken down [of rode]
C.20.199   Yf that thei *touche[d a]* tre and of þe [trees] fruyt eten.
C.20.305   Yf they *touched* a tre or toek þerof an appul.
C.21.172   Thomas *touched* hit and and with his tonge saide:

toun(e > towne; tounge > tonge

tour n *tour n.(1)* A 3; B 2; C 3
A.Pr.14   I sai3 a *tour* on a toft tri3ely Imakid;
A. 1.12   'Þe *tour* [on] þe toft,' quaþ heo, 'treuþe is þereinne,
A. 6.79   Þe *tour* þere treuþe is hymself is vp to þe sonne;
B.Pr.14   I sei3 a *tour* on a toft trieliche ymaked,
B. 1.12   'The *tour* on þe toft', quod she, 'truþe is þerInne,
C.Pr.15   And say a *tour*; as [y] trow[e], treuthe was thereynne.
C. 1.12   'The *tour* vppon þe tofte,' quod she, 'treuthe is þerynne
C. 1.134   There treuthe is, þe *tour* that trinite ynne sitteth.

touore adj *tough adj.* C 1
C.12.188   Aren tidiore and *touore* to mannes byhofte

tow n *tou n.(1)* B 1
B.17.249   But þow haue *tow* to take it wiþ, tonder or broches,

toward adj *toward adj.* C 1
C.Pr.218   Ne were þe Cat of þe Court and 3onge kitones *toward*;

toward prep *toward prep.* B 2; C 4 toward (3) towarde (1)
B.13.102   And tolde hym of a Trinite, and *toward* vs he loked.
B.19.158   Goynge *toward* Galilei in godhede and manhede
C. 6.331   'Be þe rode,' quod repentaunce, 'thow romest *toward* heuene
C. 8.190   Prestes and oþer peple *towarde* [Peres] they drowe
C.15.109   And tolde hym of a trinite, and *toward* me he lokede.
C.21.158   Goynge *toward* galilee in godhede and manhede

towne n *toun n.* A 4 toun (1) toune (2) tounes (1); B 3; C 3 toun (1) toune (1) townes (1)
A.10.138   Barouns & burgeis, & bondemen of *tounes*.
A.11.213   Poperiþ on a palfrey [fro] *toune* to toune;
A.11.213   Poperiþ on a palfrey [fro] toune to *toune*;
A.12.40   With þat she wolde me wisse wher þe *toun* were
B.13.265   There was a careful commune whan no cart com to *towne*
B.13.303   In *towne* and in Tauernes tales to telle
B.17.85   To ouertaken hym and talke to hym er þei to *towne* coome.
C.Pr.179   Sayde, 'y haue seyen grete syres in Cytees and in *townes*
C. 3.112   Hit is nat seemely, forsothe, in Citee [ne] in borw *toun*
C.14.91   Bote in a burgeises hous], the beste of þe *toune*.

trailynge ger *trailinge ger.(1)* B 1
B.12.244   For þe *trailynge* of his tail ouertaken is he soone.

transuerseth v *transversen v.* C 1
C. 3.446   And hoso taketh a3eyn treuthe or *transuerseth* a3eyns resoun

tras n *trace n.(1)* A 1
A.12.91   Þ[ou] tomblest wiþ a trepget 3if þou my *tras* folwe,

trauaile > trauaille n, trauaille v

trauaille n *travail n.* A 3 trauaile (1) trauaille (2); B 6; C 6 trauail (1) trauaile (2) trauayle (2) trauayles (1)
A. 7.235   He þat get his fode here wiþ *trauaile* of his hondis,
A.10.145   In tene & *trauaille* to here lyues ende;
A.11.186   Wiþ any trewe *trauaille* toille for here foode,
B. 6.133   Ye wasten þat men wynnen wiþ *trauaille* and tene.
B. 7.44   Princes and prelates sholde paie for hire *trauaille*:
B.11.195   Ac for þe pouere I shal paie, and pure wel quyte hir *trauaille*
B.14.153   And alle þat doon hir deuoir wel han double hire for hir *trauaille*,
B.15.488   Wiþouten *trauaille* þe tiþe deel þat trewe men biswynken?
B.17.250   Al þi labour is lost and al þi long *trauaille*,
C. 3.351   And take hym for his *trauaile* al þat treuthe wolde,
C. 3.373   Withouten coest and care and alle kyn *trauayle*.
C. 5.127   Thorw som trewe *trauail* and no tyme spille.
C. 9.152   In idelnesse and in ese and by otheres *trauayle*.
C. 9.235   Pouerte or oþer penaunc[e], as pilgrimages and *trauayles*.
C.19.216   Al thy labor is loste and al thy longe *trauaile*;

trauaille v *travaillen v.* B 9 trauaile (1) trauaille (6) trauailleþ (2); C 8 trauaile (3) trauayle (2) trauaileth (2) trauayleth (1)
B.Pr.120   To tilie and to *trauaille* as trewe lif askeþ.
B. 6.139   Ac ye my3te *trauaille* as truþe wolde and take mete and hyre
B. 9.107   To alle trewe tidy men þat *trauaille* desiren,
B.11.288   That if þei *trauaille* truweliche, and truste in god almy3ty,
B.13.117   [That *trauailleþ* to teche oþere I holde it for a dobet].
B.15.503   Thei sholde turne, whoso *trauail[e* wolde] to teche hem of þe Trinite.
B.16.10   'I wolde *trauaille*', quod I, 'þis tree to se twenty hundred myle,
B.19.438   And *trauailleþ* and tilieþ for a tretour also soore
B.20.260   /Wol no [tresorer take] hem [wages], *trauaille* þei neuer so soore,
C. 3.296   And for to vndertake [to] *trauaile* for another
C. 8.251   Ac he þat was a wreche and wolde nat *trauaile*
C.12.96   Of hym þat *trauaileth* [t]heron bote treuthe be his lyuynge.
C.13.102   That yf th[ey] *trauaile* treulyche and trist in god almyhty
C.15.125   That *trauayleth* to teche oþere y halde hit for a dobet.
C.17.254   They sholde [turne], hoso *trauayle* wolde and of þe trinite teche hem.
C.21.438   And *trauaileth* and tulieth for a tretour also sore
C.22.260   Wol no tresorer taken hem wages, *trauayle* they neuere so sore,

trauaillynge ger *travailinge ger.* A 1 trauaillyng; B 1
A. 7.232   Oþer wiþ teching, oþer telling, or *trauaillyng* of hondis,
B. 6.248   Or [wiþ tech]ynge or [tell]ynge or *trauaillynge* [of hondes],

trauaillours n *travailour n.* B 1
B.13.239   For alle trewe *trauaillours* and tiliers of þe erþe

trauersed v *traversen v.* B 1; C 1 trauersede
B.12.287 Ac truþe þat trespased neuere ne *trauersed* ayeins his lawe,
C.14.209 Ac treuth þat trespassed neuere ne *trauersede* aȝens his lawe

tre > tree

trecherie n *trecherie n.* A 1 treccherie; B 2 trecherie (1) tricherie (1); C 3 triccherye (1) tricherie (1) tricherye (1)
A. 1.172 Þ[at] is no treuþe of trinite but *treccherie* of helle,
B. 1.198 [Th]at is no truþe of þe Trinite but *tricherie* of helle,
B. 7.79 In hym þat takeþ is þe *trecherie* if any treson walke,
C.Pr.12 Of treuthe and *tricherye*, tresounn and gyle
C. 1.193 And þat is no treuthe of þe trinite but *triccherye* [and] synne
C.20.319 Thus with treson and *tricherie* thow troyledest hem bothe

trede v *treden v.* A 1 treden; B 1 troden; C 2 trede (1) treden (1)
A.10.104 Þat selde m[os]eþ þe marbil þat men ofte [t]*reden,*
B.11.356 And some *troden,* [I took kepe], and on trees bredden,
C.13.165 And som *treden,* y toke kepe, and on trees bredde
C.14.161 He tauhte þe tortle to *tre[d]e,* the pocok to cauke

tree n *tre n.* B 16 tree (11) trees (4) trowes (1); C 15 tre (9) tree (3) trees (3)
B.11.356 And some troden, [I took kepe], and on *trees* bredden,
B.11.361 And who tauȝte hem on *trees* to tymbre so heiȝe
B.15.96 [And] se it by ensample in somer tyme on *trowes:*
B.15.334 That were ful of faire *trees,* and I fondede and caste
B.16.4 'It is a ful trie *tree',* quod he, 'trewely to telle.
B.16.8 Pacience hatte þe pure *tree* and [pouere] symple of herte,
B.16.10 'I wolde trauaille', quod I, 'þis *tree* to se twenty hundred myle,
B.16.22 And bad me toten on þe *tree,* on top and on roote.
B.16.61 I shal telle þee as tid what þis *tree* highte.
B.16.63 And I haue told þee what hiȝte þe *tree';* þe Trinite it meneþ.'
B.18.140 And þat was tynt þoruȝ *tree,* tree shal it wynne.
B.18.140 And þat was tynt þoruȝ tree, *tree* shal it wynne.
B.18.194 If þat þei touchede a *tree* and þe [trees] fruyt eten.
B.18.194 If þat þei touchede a tree and þe [*trees*] fruyt eten.
B.18.358 And as Adam and alle þoruȝ a *tree* deyden,
B.18.359 Adam and alle þoruȝ a *tree* shul turne to lyue,
C.13.165 And som treden, y toke kepe, and on *trees* bredde
C.16.248 And s[e] hit by ensample In somur tyme on *trees*
C.18.9 'The *tree* hatte trewe loue,' quod he, 'the trinite hit sette.
C.18.29 The fruyt of this fayre *tre* fro thre wikkede wyndes
C.18.53 I toted vpon þ[e] *tre* tho and thenne toek y hede
C.18.61 Me may se on an appul *tree* monye tyme and ofte
C.18.68 Adam was as *tre* and we aren as his apples,
C.18.75 These haen þe [hete] of þe holi goest as þe crop of *tre* [the] sonne.
C.20.143 And] that was tynt thorw *tre,* tre shal hit wynne.
C.20.143 And] that was tynt thorw tre, *tre* shal hit wynne.
C.20.199 Yf that thei touche[d a] *tre* and of þe [trees] fruyt eten.
C.20.199 Yf that thei touche[d a] tre and of þe [*trees*] fruyt eten.
C.20.305 Yf they touched a *tre* or toek þerof an appul.
C.20.397 And as Adam and alle thorwe a *tre* deyede,
C.20.398 Adam and alle thorw a *tre* shal turne to lyue.

treys n *trei n.(3)* C 2
C.18.238 Lo! *treys* encountre treys,' quod he, 'in godhede and in manhede.'
C.18.238 Lo! treys encountre *treys',* quod he, 'in godhede and in manhede.'

trembled v *tremblen v.* A 1 tremblide; B 2; C 2 tremblede
A. 2.197 Ac trewely to telle heo *tremblide* for fere,
B. 2.238 Ac trewely to telle she *trembled* for [fere],
B.11.115 Al for tene of hir text *trembled* myn herte,
C. 2.254 Ac treuliche to telle a *tremblede* for fere
C.12.50 Al for tene of here tyxst *tremblede* myn herte,

trepget n *trepeget n.* A 1
A.12.91 Þ[ou] tomblest wiþ a *trepget* ȝif þou my tras folwe,

treson n *treisoun n.* B 6 treson (5) tresoun (1); C 6 treson (1) tresoun (4) tresounn (1)
B. 5.49 'It is þi [tresor if *treson* ne were], and tryacle at þy nede.'
B. 7.79 In hym þat takeþ is þe trecherie if any *treson* walke,
B.16.158 Thouȝ I bi *treson* be take [to] youre [iewene] wille
B.18.290 And toldest hire a tale, of *treson* were þe wordes;
B.18.294 We haue no trewe title to hem, for þoruȝ *treson* were þei dampned.'
B.19.90 [For it shal turne *tresoun* to riȝt and to truþe].
C.Pr.12 Of treuthe and tricherye, *tresounn* and gyle
C. 3.87 Thow thei take hem vntidy thyng no *tresoun* þei ne halden hit;
C.18.175 Sethe y be *tresoun* am take and to ȝoure will, iewes,
C.20.319 Thus with *treson* and tricherie thow troyledest hem bothe
C.20.324 We haen no trewe title to hem for thy *tresoun* hit maketh.'
C.21.90 [For it shal turne *tresoun*] to riht and to treuthe.

tresor n *tresour n.* A 12 tresouris (1) tresours (2) tresour (9); B 22 tresor (14) tresores (1) tresors (3) tresour (4); C 19 tresor (15) tresores (2) tresour (2)
A. 1.43 Tel me to whom þat *tresour* apendiþ.'
A. 1.54 And tutour of ȝour *tresour,* & take it ȝow at nede;
A. 1.68 Þat tresten on his *tresour* betraid arn sonnest.'
A. 1.81 'Teche me to no *tresour* but tel me þis ilke,
A. 1.83 'Whanne alle *tresours* arn triȝed treuþe is þe beste;
A. 1.124 Whanne alle *tresours* arn triȝed treuþe is þe beste.
A. 1.126 Þat treuþe is þe *tresour* triȝest on erþe.'
A. 1.181 Whan alle *tresouris* arn triȝede treuþe is þe beste.
A. 1.182 Now haue I told þe what treuþe is, þat no *tresour* is betere,
A. 2.161 To atache þis tiraunt[is] 'for any *tresour,* I hote;
A. 3.113 In trist of hire *tresour* she teniþ [wel] manye,
A. 8.166 Vpon trist of ȝour *tresour* trienalis to haue.
B. 1.45 Tel me to whom þat *tresour* appendeþ.'
B. 1.56 And tutour of youre *tresor,* and take it yow at nede;
B. 1.70 That trusten on his *tresour* bitraye[d are] sonnest.'
B. 1.83 'Teche me to no *tresor,* but tel me þis ilke,
B. 1.85 'Whan alle *tresors* arn tried treuþe is þe beste.
B. 1.135 Whan alle *tresors* arn tried truþe is þe beste.
B. 1.137 That Treuþe is *tresor* þe trieste on erþe.'
B. 1.207 Whan alle *tresors* arn tried treuþe is þe beste.
B. 1.208 Now haue I told þee what truþe is, þat no *tresor* is bettre,
B. 2.200 To attachen þo Tyrauntȝ 'for any [*tresor*], I hote;
B. 3.124 [In] trust of hire *tresor* [she teneþ wel] manye.
B. 5.49 'It is þi [*tresor* if treson ne were], and tryacle at þy nede.'
B. 7.55 Thise ben truþes *tresores* trewe folk to helpe,
B. 7.188 Vpon trust of youre *tresor* triennals to haue,
B.10.480 As clerkes of holy [k]ir[k]e þat kepen cristes *tresor,*
B.12.109 Which is þe cofre of cristes *tresor,* and clerkes kepe þe keyes
B.12.295 And wit and wisdom', quod þat wye, 'was som tyme *tresor*
B.13.193 For þer [is] no *tresour* [þerto] to a trewe wille.
B.14.312 He tempreþ þe tonge to truþeward [þat] no *tresor* coueiteþ:
B.15.549 Moore *tresor* þan trouþe? I dar noȝt telle þe soþe;
B.19.217 *Tresour* to lyue by to hir lyues ende.
B.19.225 Forþi', quod grace, 'er I go I wol gyue yow *tresor*
C. 1.43 Telleth me to wham þat *tresour* bylongeth.'
C. 1.52 And tutor of ȝoure *tresor* and take it ȝow at nede;
C. 1.66 That tristeth in *tresor* of erthe he bytrayeth sonest.'
C. 1.79 'Teche me to [no] *tresor* but telle me this ilke,
C. 1.81 'When alle *tresores* ben tried treuthe is þe beste;
C. 1.136 Tha[n] treuthe and trewe loue is no *tresor* bettre.'
C. 1.202 "Whenne alle *tresores* ben tried treuthe is þe beste."
C. 2.214 [T]o atache tho tyrauntes, 'for eny *tresor,* y hote;
C. 3.161 In trist of here *tresor* he teneth fol monye,
C. 5.181 'For þe comune is the kynges *tresor,* Consience woet wel.
C. 9.334 Vp truste of ȝoure *tresor* trionales to haue,
C.10.176 For þat is goddes oune goed, his grace and his *tresour,*
C.10.182 Hath *tresor* ynow of treuthe to fynden hymsulue.
C.14.54 Whiche [is the] coffre of cristis *tresor,* and clerkes kepeth þe keyes
C.16.146 A tempreth þe tonge to treuthward þat no *tresor* coueyteth:
C.17.69 Y dar nat carpe of clerkes now þat cristes [*tresor*] kepe
C.17.211 More *tresor* then treuthe? Y dar nat telle þe sothe
C.21.217 *Tresor* to lyue by to here lyues ende
C.21.225 Forthy,' quod grace, 'or y go y wol gyue ȝow *tresor*

tresorer n *tresourer n.* B 1; C 1
B.20.260 /Wol no [*tresorer* take] hem [wages], trauaille þei neuer so soore,
C.22.260 Wol no *tresorer* taken hem wages, trauayle they neuere so sore,

tresoun(n > treson; tresour(is > tresor

trespas n *trespas n.* A 1; B 1; C 1
A. 1.95 Til treuþe hadde termined here *trespas* to þe ende.
B. 1.97 Til treuþe hadde ytermyned hire *trespas* to þe ende.
C. 1.93 Til treuthe hadde termyned here *trespas* to þe ende

trespaseþ v *trespassen v.* A 1 trespassiþ; B 3 trespased (2) trespaseþ (1); C 2 trespased (1) trespassed (1)
A. 3.268 And whoso *trespassiþ* [to treuþe, or] takiþ [aȝeyn his wille],
B. 3.293 And whoso *trespaseþ* [to] truþe or takeþ aȝein his wille,
B. 5.368 That I haue *trespased* with my tonge, I kan noȝt telle how ofte;
B.12.287 Ac truþe þat *trespased* neuere ne trauersed ayeins his lawe,
C. 6.426 Of þat y haue *trespased* with tonge, y can nat telle how ofte;
C.14.209 Ac treuth þat *trespassed* neuere ne trauersede aȝens his lawe

trespassours n *trespassour n.* A 1
A. 1.94 And taken *trespassours* & teiȝen hem faste

tresten > truste

tretour n *traitour n.* B 2; C 3 tretor (1) tretour (2)
B.18.380 Ofter þan ones þouȝ he were a *tretour.*
B.19.438 And trauailleþ and tilieþ for a *tretour* also soore,
C.19.242 For godes *tretor* he is [to]ld for al his trewe catel

C.20.422   Oftur then ones thogh [he] were [a] *tretou[r]*.
C.21.438   And trauaileth and tulieth for a *tretour* also sore

treuely treuly(che > trewely; treuth(- > truþe(-

trewe n *treue n.(1)*   B 2 trewe (1) trewes (1);   C 2 trewe (1) trewes (1)
B. 6.331   But [if] god of his goodnesse graunte vs a *trewe*.
B.18.416   'Trewes', quod Truþe, 'þow tellest vs sooþ, by Iesus!
C. 8.352   But yf [god] of his goodnesse graunte vs a *trewe*.
C.20.459   'Trewes,' quod treuthe; 'thow tellest vs soeth, by iesus!

trewe adj *treue adj.*   A 10;   B 47 trewe (46) trewest (1);   C 68 treuwe (1) trewe (67)
A. 1.86   For whoso is *trewe* of his tunge, telliþ non oþer,
A. 1.153   For þ[eiȝ ȝe] be *trewe* of ȝoure tunge & treweliche wynne,
A. 3.129   He[o] takiþ þe *trewe* be þe top, teiȝeþ hym faste,
A. 3.222   Tak no mede, my lord, of [men] þat ben *trewe*;
A. 7.45   And þat þou be *trewe* of [þi] tunge, & talis þou hate,
A. 9.72   *Trewe* of his tunge & of his two handis,
A.11.184   *Trewe* tilieris on erþe, taillours & souteris
A.11.186   Wiþ any *trewe* trauaille toille for here foode,
A.12.18   Sitthe theologie þe *trewe* to tellen hit defendeþ;
A.12.85   Tercian þat oþer; *trewe* drinkeres bęþe.
B.Pr.120   To tilie and to trauaille as *trewe* lif askeþ.
B. 1.88   [For] who is *trewe* of his tonge, telleþ noon ooþer,
B. 1.179   For þouȝ ye be *trewe* of youre tonge and treweliche wynne,
B. 3.140   [She] takeþ þe *trewe* bi þe top, tieþ h[y]m faste,
B. 3.292   Thise shul ben Maistres on moolde [*trewe* men] to saue.
B. 3.304   And haue wonder in hire hertes þat men beþ so *trewe*.
B. 3.322   Tha[t] worþ *Trewe*-tonge, a tidy man þat tened me neuere.
B. 3.337   'I leue wel, lady,' quod Conscience, 'þat þi latyn be *trewe*.
B. 3.346   This text þat ye han told were [*trewe*] for lordes.
B. 4.18   And also Tomme *trewe*-tonge-tel-me-no-tales-
B. 5.425   And þus tene I *trewe* men ten hundred tymes,
B. 6.50   And þat þow be *trewe* of þi tonge and tales þow hatie
B. 7.55   Thise ben truþes tresores *trewe* folk to helpe,
B. 8.81   *Trewe* of his tunge and of his two handes,
B. 9.107   To alle *trewe* tidy men þat trauaille desiren,
B. 9.110   [Dowel in þis world is *trewe* wedded libbynge folk],
B.10.347   That þei han Eritage in heuene, and þe *trewe* riȝte,
B.11.100   Thouȝ þe tale [were] *trewe*, and it touche[d] synne.
B.11.141   '[I] Troianus, a *trewe* knyȝt, [take] witnesse at a pope
B.12.58   And Richesse riȝt so but if þe roote be *trewe*.
B.12.123   Take we hir wordes at worþ, for hir witnesse be *trewe*,
B.12.210   And riȝt as Troianus þe *trewe* knyȝt [tilde] noȝt depe in helle
B.12.212   For he is in þe loweste of heuene, if oure bileue be *trewe*,
B.12.283   "Troianus was a *trewe* knyght and took neuere cristendom
B.12.290   Ne wolde neuere *trewe* god but [*trewe*] truþe were allowed.
B.12.290   Ne wolde neuere trewe god but [*trewe*] truþe were allowed.
B.13.193   For þer [is] no tresour [þerto] to a *trewe* wille.
B.13.210   Turne into þe *trewe* feiþ and intil oon bileue.'
B.13.239   For alle *trewe* trauaillours and tiliers of þe erþe
B.14.38   And seide, 'lo! here liflode ynogh, if oure bileue be *trewe*.
B.14.72   Amonges cristene creatures, if cristes wordes ben *trewe*.
B.14.198   But oure spences and spendynge sprynge of a *trewe* w[e]lle;
B.15.105   *Trewe* of youre tonge and of youre tail boþe,
B.15.235   In kynges court he comeþ ofte þer þe counseil is *trewe*,
B.15.366   And what to leue and to lyue by; þe lond was so *trewe*.
B.15.420   Of tirauntȝ þat teneþ *trewe* men taken any almesse,
B.15.428   Alle þat ben at debaat and bedemen were *trewe*:
B.15.488   Wiþouten trauaille þe tiþe deel þat *trewe* men biswynken?
B.16.210   And bitokneþ þe Trinite and *trewe* bileue.
B.16.230   Ful *trewe* toknes bitwene vs is to telle whan me likeþ.
B.17.26   'Youre wordes arn wonderfulle', quod I, 'which of yow is *trewest*
B.18.132   And þat my tale be *trewe* I take god to witnesse.
B.18.294   We haue no *trewe* title to hem, for þoruȝ treson were þei dampned.'
B.18.389   I [may] do mercy þoruȝ [my] rightwisnesse and alle my wordes *trewe*;
B.19.237   And lyue, by þat labour], a lele lif and a *trewe*.
B.19.298   And he þat ete of þat seed sholde be [euene] *trewe*
B.19.439   As for a *trewe* tidy man alle tymes ylike.
C.Pr.100   Al þe world wot wel hit myghte nouȝt be *trewe*
C. 1.84   For who is *trewe* of his tonge and of his two handes
C. 1.94   And halden with h[y]m and [with] here þat han *trewe* action
C. 1.95   And for no lordene loue leue þe *trewe* partie
C. 1.136   Tha[n] treuthe and *trewe* loue is no tresor bettre.'
C. 1.175   For thow ȝe ben *trewe* of ȝoure tong[e] and treweliche wynne
C. 2.37   He shal lese for here loue [a] lippe of *trewe* charite;
C. 2.125   Amendes was here moder by *trewe* menne lokynge,
C. 2.132   Y, Theo[lo]gie, þe tixt knowe yf *trewe* doom wittenesseth,
C. 3.178   And taketh [þe] *tre[we]* by the top and te[i]eth hym f[aste]
C. 3.201   *Trewe* Burgeys and bonde he bryngeth to nauhte ofte
C. 3.299   Y halde hym ouer hardy or elles nat *trewe*
C. 3.355   And man is relatif rect yf he be rihte *trewe*:

C. 3.382   Bytwene two lo[n]des for a *trewe* marke.
C. 3.406   Of thre *trewe* termisonus, trinitas vnus deus:
C. 3.445   Tho shal be maistres on molde *trewe* men to helpe.
C. 3.457   Moises or messie, þat men ben so *trewe*.
C. 3.472   Mercy or no mercy as most *trewe* acorden.
C. 3.475   Þat worth *trewe*-tonge, a tydy man þat tened me neuere.
C. 3.489   'I leue the, lady,' quod Consience, 'for þat latyn is *trewe*.
C. 4.18   And also th[omm]e *trewe*-tonge-telle-me-no-tales-
C. 4.76   Consience knoweth hit wel and al þe Comune *trewe*.'
C. 5.127   Thorw som *trewe* trauail and no tyme spille.
C. 7.38   And thus haue y tened *trewe* men ten hundrit tymes.
C. 7.258   In thyne hole herte to herborwe alle *trewe*
C. 7.260   Ȝef loue and leute and oure lawe [be] *trewe*:
C. 8.48   *Treuwe* of thy tonge and tales loth to here
C. 8.200   In alle kyne *trewe* craft þat man couthe deuyse.
C. 9.213   Aȝen þe lawe he lyueth yf latyn be *trewe*:
C.10.78   Ho[so] is *trewe* of his tonge and of his two handes
C.10.80   And therto *trewe* of his tayl, [taketh but his owne]
C.11.94   And ouer skripture þe skilfole and screueynes were *trewe*
C.11.149   And þe *trewe* trinite to Austyn apperede
C.12.28   The sauter sayth hit is no synne for suche men þat ben *trewe*
C.12.76   'I troianes, a *trewe* knyht, take witnesse of a pope
C.13.88   Telleth þe lord a tale as a *trewe* messager
C.14.8   Ne no tyme to tyne ne *trewe* thyng tene,
C.14.66   Take we here wordes at worthe, for here witteness[e] b[e] *trewe*,
C.14.149   And riht as troianes þe *trewe* knyhte [telde] nat depe in helle
C.14.151   For he is in þe loweste of heuene, yf oure byleue be *trewe*,
C.14.205   'Troianes was a *trewe* knyhte and toek neuere cristendoem
C.14.212   Ne wolde neuere *trewe* god bote trewe treuthe were alloued.
C.14.212   Ne wolde neuere trewe god bote *trewe* treuthe were alloued.
C.14.215   And þat is loue and large huyre, yf þe lord be *trewe*,
C.15.133   And no tixst ne taketh to preue this for *trewe*
C.15.237   And saide, 'lo! here lyflode ynow yf oure beleue be *trewe*
C.15.271   Amonges cristene creatures, yf cristes wordes be *trewe*:
C.16.39   Bote oure spensis and spendyng sprynge of a *trewe* welle
C.16.259   And þerto *trewe* of ȝoure tonge and of ȝoure tayl also
C.16.360   In kynges Court a cometh yf his consaile be *trewe*
C.17.5   'A passeth cheef charite yf holy churche be *trewe*:
C.17.15   Foules hym fedde yf frere Austynes be *trewe*
C.17.33   In tokenynge þat *trewe* man alle tymes sholde
C.17.76   And ȝut is þe printe puyr *trewe* and parfitliche ygraue.
C.17.77   And so hit fareth by false cristene: here follynge is *trewe*,
C.17.103   And what lyue by and leue, the londe was so *trewe*.
C.18.9   'The tree hatte *trewe* loue,' quod he, 'the trinite hit sette.
C.18.209   Bitokeneth þe trinite and *trewe* bileue.
C.18.246   Fol *trewe* tokenes bitwene vs is wh[at] tyme þat y met[t]e hym,
C.19.23   'He seyth soth,' saide fayth; 'y haue yfounde hit *trewe*.
C.19.27   'Ȝoure wordes aren wonderfol,' quod y; 'where eny of [hem] be *trewe*
C.19.242   For godes tretor he is [to]ld for al his *trewe* catel
C.20.135   And þat my tale [be] *trewe* y take god to witnesse.
C.20.324   We haen no *trewe* title to hem for thy tresoun hit maketh.'
C.20.431   [Y] may do mercy of my rihtwysnesse and alle myn wordes *trewe*
C.21.237   And lyue by þat laboure a leele lyf and a *trewe*.
C.21.298   And he þat ete of þat seed sholde be euene *trewe*
C.21.439   As for a *trewe* tydy man alle tymes ylyke.

trewely adv *treuli adv.*   A 8 treweliche (2) trewely (6);   B 15 trewely (10) treweliche (4) truweliche (1);   C 16 treuely (1) treuly (3) treuliche (2) treulyche (1) trewely (3) treweliche (4) trewly (2)
A. 1.153   For þ[eiȝ ȝe] be trewe of ȝoure tunge & *treweliche* wynne,
A. 2.197   Ac *trewely* to telle heo tremblide for fere,
A. 3.74   For tok h[y] on *trewely* h[y] tymbride not so heiȝe,
A. 7.24   Ac on þe tem *trewely* tauȝt was I neuere.
A. 8.64   Þat *trewely* taken, & trewely wynnen,
A. 8.64   Þat trewely taken, & *trewely* wynnen,
A. 8.163   A[c] to triste on þis trionalis, *trewely*, me þinkeþ,
A.10.202   For in [vn]tyme, *treweliche*, betwyn m[a]n & womm[a]n
B. 1.179   For þouȝ ye be trewe of youre tonge and *treweliche* wynne,
B. 2.238   Ac *trewely* to telle she trembled for [fere],
B. 3.85   For toke þei on *trewely* þei tymbred nouȝt so heiȝe,
B. 6.22   Ac on þe teme *trewely* tauȝt was I neuere.
B. 7.62   That *treweliche* taken and treweliche wynnen
B. 7.62   That treweliche taken and *treweliche* wynnen
B. 7.185   Ac to truste [on] þise triennals, *trewely*, me þynkeþ
B. 9.189   For in vntyme, *trewely*, bitwene man and womman
B.11.288   That if þei trauaille *truweliche*, and truste in god almyȝty,
B.15.163   And so I trowe *trewely*, by þat men telleþ of [it,
B.16.4   'It is a ful triste tree', quod he, '*trewely* to telle.
B.16.212   And bitokneþ *trewely*, telle if I dorste.
B.17.14   This was the tixte, *trewely*; I took ful good yeme.
B.17.146   And bitokneþ *trewely*, telle whoso likeþ,
B.19.177   "Thomas, for þow trowest þis and *treweliche* bileuest it
C. 1.96   *Treweliche* to take and treweliche to fyghte

C. 1.96   Treweliche to take and *treweliche* to fyghte
C. 1.175   For thow ȝe ben trewe of ȝoure tong[e] and *treweliche* wynne
C. 2.254   Ac *treuliche* to telle a tremblede for fere
C. 3.84   For tok thei [o]n *trewely* they tymbred nat so heye
C. 8.20   Ac [on þe] t[ee]me *treuely* ytauhte was y neuere.
C. 8.241   Bytu[lye] and bytrauayle *trewely* [ȝ]oure lyflode:
C. 9.331   Ac to triste vp this trionales, *treuly*, me thynketh
C.12.203   Bitokeneth *treuly* in tyme comyng aftur
C.13.73   Tythen here goed *tre[u]liche*, a tol, as hit semeth,
C.13.102   That yf th[ey] trauaile *treulyche* and trist in god almyhty
C.16.297   And so y trowe *treuly*, by þat me telleth of charite.'
C.18.26   Bytokeneth *trewely* the trinite of heuene,
C.19.15   This was the tyxt *trewly*; y toek ful good gome.
C.19.120   And bitokeneth *trewly*, telle hoso liketh,
C.21.177   "Thomas, for thow trowest this and *treweliche* bileuest hit

treweþe > truþe

triacle n *triacle n.*   B 2 triacle (1) tryacle (1); C 1
B. 1.148   For truþe telleþ þat loue is *triacle* of heuene:
B. 5.49   'It is þi [tresor if treson ne were], and *tryacle* at þy nede.'
C. 1.146   For treuthe telleth þat loue ys *triacle* [for] synne

tribuyt > tribut

tribulacions n *tribulacioun n.*   C 1
C.12.202   Mescheues and myshappes and many *tribulac[ion]s*

tribut n *tribute n.*   B 1; C 1 tribuyt
B.19.37   But vnder *tribut* and taillage as tikes and cherles.
C.21.37   Bote vnder *tribuyt* and talage as tykes and cherles.

triccherye tricherie > trecherie

trie adj *trie adj.*   A 1 triȝest; B 3 trie (2) trieste (1)
A. 1.126   þat treuþe is þe tresour *triȝest* on erþe.'
B. 1.137   That Treuþe is tresor þe *trieste* on erþe.'
B.15.168   As of a tunycle of tarse or of *trie* scarlet.
B.16.4   'It is a ful *trie* tree', quod he, 'trewely to telle.

tried ptp *trien v.*   A 3 triȝed (2) triȝede (1); B 3; C 2
A. 1.83   'Whanne alle tresours arn *triȝed* treuþe is þe beste;
A. 1.124   Whanne alle tresours arn *triȝed* treuþe is þe beste.
A. 1.181   Whan alle tresouris arn *triȝede* treuþe is þe beste.
B. 1.85   'Whan alle tresors arn *tried* treuþe is þe beste;
B. 1.135   Whan alle tresors arn *tried* truþe is þe beste.
B. 1.207   Whan alle tresors ben *tried* treuþe is þe beste.
C. 1.81   'When alle tresores ben *tried* treuthe is þe beste;
C. 1.202   "Whenne alle tresores ben *tried* treuthe is þe beste."

trieliche adv *trieli adv.*   A 1 triȝely; B 1
A.Pr.14   I saiȝ a tour on a toft *triȝely* Imakid;
B.Pr.14   I seiȝ a tour on a toft *trieliche* ymaked,

triennals n *triennale n.*   A 3 trienalis (2) trionalis (1); B 3; C 3 trionales
A. 8.154   Bienalis & *trienalis* & bisshopis lettres.
A. 8.163   A[c] to triste on þis *trionalis*, trewely, me þinkeþ,
A. 8.166   Vpon trist of ȝour tresour *trienalis* to haue.
B. 7.176   Biennals and *triennals* and Bisshopes lettres.
B. 7.185   Ac to truste [on] þise *triennals*, trewely, me þynkeþ,
B. 7.188   Vpon trust of youre tresor *triennals* to haue.
C. 9.321   Bionales and *trionales* and bisshopes lettres.
C. 9.331   Ac to triste vp this *trionales*, treuly, me thynketh
C. 9.334   Vp truste of ȝoure tresor *trionales* to haue,

tryfle > trufle

trinite n *trinite n.*   A 6; B 19 Trinite (16) Trinitee (3); C 18 trinite (17) trinitee (1)
A. 1.107   Tauȝte hem þoruȝ þe *trinite* þe trouþe to knowe:
A. 1.122   Þere treuþe is in *trinite* & tron[iþ] h[e]m alle.
A. 1.172   Þ[at] is no treuþe of *trinite* but treccherie of helle,
A.11.40   Þanne telle þei of þe *trinite* how two slowe þe þridde,
A.11.62   To tellen of þe *trinite* to be holden a sire,
A.11.302   Þe douȝtiest doctour or dyuynour of þe *trinite*,
B. 1.109   Tauȝte hem [þoruȝ] þe *Trinitee* [þe] treuþe to knowe:
B. 1.133   Ther Treuþe is in *Trinitee* and troneþ hem alle.
B. 1.198   [Th]at is no truþe of þe *Trinite* but tricherie of helle,
B.10.54   Than telleþ þei of þe *Trinite* [how two slowe þe þridde],
B.10.458   The douȝtieste doctour and deuinour of þe *trinitee*
B.13.94   And þanne shal he testifie of [a] *Trinite*, and take his felawe to witnesse
B.13.102   And tolde hym of a *Trinite*, and toward vs he loked.
B.14.184   Thou tauȝtest hem in þe *Trinite* to taken bapteme
B.15.71   Ye moeuen materes vnmesurable to tellen of þe *Trinite*
B.15.503   Thei sholde turne, whoso trauail[e wolde] to teche hem of þe *Trinite*.
B.15.572   Tellen hem and techen hem on þe *Trinite* to bileue,

B.16.63   And I haue told þee what hiȝte þe tree; þe *Trinite* it meneþ.'
B.16.204   In tokenynge of þe *Trinite*, was [taken out of a man],
B.16.210   And bitokneþ þe *Trinite* and trewe bileue.
B.17.28   Abraham seiþ þat he seiȝ hoolly þe *Trinite*,
B.17.36   And telleþ noȝt of þe *Trinite* þat took hym hise lettres,
B.17.206   [For] to a torche or a tapur þe *Trinite* is likned,
B.17.233   So grace of þe holy goost þe grete myȝt of þe *Trinite*
B.17.282   To a torche or a tapur to reuerence þe *Trinite*,
C. 1.134   There treuthe is, þe tour that *trinite* ynne sitteth.
C. 1.193   And þat is no treuthe of þe *trinite* but triccherye [and] synne
C.11.35   And tellen of þe *trinite* how t[w]o slowe þe thridde
C.11.149   And þe trewe *trinite* to Austyn apperede
C.11.284   For he þat most se[y]h and saide of the sothfaste *trinite*
C.15.101   And [thenne shal he testifie of] a *trinite* and take his felowe [t]o witnesse
C.15.109   And tolde hym of a *trinite*, and toward me he lokede.
C.17.254   They sholde [turne], hoso trauayle wolde and of þe *trinite* teche hem.
C.18.9   'The tree hatte trewe loue,' quod he, 'the *trinite* hit sette.
C.18.26   Bytokeneth þe *trinite* and trewe bileue.
C.18.209   Bitokeneth þe *trinite* and trewe bileue.
C.18.235   So i[n] god [and] godes sone i[s] thre persones, the *trinite*.
C.18.262   At ones on an auter in worschipe of th[e] *trinite*
C.19.29   Abraham saith þat he seyh holly þe *trinitee*,
C.19.37   That of no *trinite* ne telleth ne taketh mo persones
C.19.172   For to a torche or a taper þe *trinite* is likned,
C.19.199   So grace of þe holi gost þe grete myhte of þe *trinite*
C.19.263   Or elles [to] a taper to reuerense with the *trinite*

trionales > triennals

tripe n *trippe n.(2)*   C 1
C. 9.263   The tarre is vntydy þat to þe [*tripe*] bylongeth;

trist > trust,truste; triste(- > truste; triȝed(e > tried; triȝely > trieliche; triȝest > trie; troden > trede

troianus n prop *n.i.d.*   B 5; C 4 troianes (3) Troianus (1)
B.11.141   '[I] *Troianus*, a trewe knyȝt, [take] witnesse at a pope
B.11.159   And on *Troianus* truþe to þenke, and do truþe to þe peple.
B.11.171   'Lawe wiþouten loue', quod *Troianus*, 'ley þer a bene!'
B.12.210   And riȝt as *Troianus* þe trewe knyȝt [tilde] noȝt depe in helle
B.12.283   "*Troianus* was a trewe knyght and took neuere cristendom
C.12.76   'I *troianes*, a trewe knyht, take witnesse of a pope
C.12.91   And on *Troianus* treuthe to thenke alle tyme[s] in ȝoure lyue
C.14.149   And riht as *troianes* þe trewe knyhte [telde] nat depe in helle
C.14.205   '*Troianes* was a trewe knyhte and toek neuere cristendoem

troyledest v *troilen v.*   C 1
C.20.319   Thus with treson and tricherie thow *troyledest* hem bothe

trolled ptp *trollen v.*   B 1; C 1
B.18.299   And þus haþ he *trolled* forþ [lik a tidy man] þise two and þritty wynter.
C.20.332   Thus hath he *trolled* forth lyke a tydy man this two & thritty wynter.

trolly trollilolly > how_trolly_lolly

trompe v *trompen v.*   B 2 trompe (1) trumpede (1); C 2 trompede (1) trompy (1)
B.13.230   Ac for I kan neiþer taboure ne *trompe* ne telle no gestes,
B.18.422   Truþe *trumpede* þo and song Te deum laudamus,
C.15.204   [Ac for] y can nat tabre ne *trompy* ne telle [no] gestes,
C.20.465   Treuth *trompede* tho and song te deum laudamus

troneþ v *tronen v.*   A 1 troniþ; B 1
A. 1.122   Þere treuþe is in trinite & *troniþ* h[e]m alle.
B. 1.133   Ther Treuþe is in Trinitee and *troneþ* hem alle.

trotted v *trotten v.*   A 1 trottide; B 1
A. 2.129   And fals sat on a sisour þat softeliche *trottide*,
B. 2.165   And Fals sat on a Sisour þat softeli *trotted*,

trouþe > truþe

trowe v *trouen v.*   A 6; B 16 trowe (12) trowen (1) trowest (1) trowestow (1) troweþ (1); C 14 trowe (9) trowed (1) trowest (2) troweth (2)
A.Pr.34   And gete gold wiþ here gle giltes, I *trowe*.
A. 1.133   Þis I *trowe* be treuþe; who can teche þe betere,
A. 3.18   For al consiences cast a[nd] craft as I *trowe*'.
A. 3.43   And shrof hire of hire shrewidnesse shameles I *trowe*;
A. 5.69   'Venym, [or] verious, or vynegre I *trowe*,
A. 8.59   His pardoun in purcatorie wel [petit] is, I *trowe*,
B. 1.145   This I *trowe* be truþe; who kan teche þee bettre,
B. 3.19   For al Consciences cast [and] craft, as I *trowe*'.
B. 3.44   And shrof hire of hire sherewednesse, shamelees I *trowe*;
B. 4.41   For Conscience know[e þei] noȝt, ne crist, as I *trowe*.'

B. 5.196   But if a lous couþe [lepe, I leue and I *trowe*],
B. 9.122   Wastours and wrecches out of wedlok, I *trowe*,
B.10.436   That Salomon seiþ I *trowe* be sooþ and certein of vs alle:
B.12.164   Which *trowestow* of þo two [in Themese] is in moost drede,
B.12.182   But as his loresman lereþ hym bileueþ and *troweþ*,
B.14.252   A straw for þe stuwes! [it] stoode no3t, I *trowe*,
B.15.163   And so I *trowe* trewely, by þat men telleþ of [it,
B.15.164   Charite] is no3t chaumpions fight ne chaffare as I *trowe*.'
B.15.301   And if þei couþe han ycarped, by crist! as I *trowe*,
B.15.478   And by hire wordes and werkes wenen and *trowen*;
B.17.165   Thus it is–nedeþ no man *trowe* noon ooþer–
B.19.177   "Thomas, for þow *trowest* þis and treweliche bileuest it
C.Pr.15   And say a tour; as [y] *trow[e]*, treuthe was thereynne.
C. 1.144   And this y *trowe* be treuth; [ho] kan tecche þe bettre
C. 3.20   For al Consiences cast and craft, as y *trowe*.'
C. 3.46   [And] shrofe here of here synne, shameles y [*trowe*];
C. 5.49   And tho þa[t] fynden me my fode fouchensaf, y *trowe*,
C. 6.28   To telle eny tale; y *trowed* me wysor
C. 6.204   But yf a lous couthe lepe, y leue [and] y *trowe*,
C. 6.298   3e! þe prest þat thy tythe t[a]k[eth], *trowe* y non other,
C.14.108   Which *trowest* [þou] of tho two in temese [is] in moste drede?'
C.14.122   But as his loresman [lereth hym] byleueth and *troweth*,
C.16.92   A straw for the stuyues! hit stoed nat, [y *trowe*],
C.16.297   And so y *trowe* treuly, by þat me telleth of charite.'
C.16.305   And when a man swereth "forsoth" for sooth he hit *troweth*;
C.21.177   "Thomas, for thow *trowest* this and treweliche bileuest hit

trowes > tree

trufle n *trufle n.*   B 2; C 2 tryfle (1) truyfle (1)
B.12.138   A[s] to þe clergie of crist counted it but a *trufle*:
B.18.147   It is *trufle* þat þow tellest; I, truþe, woot þe soþe,
C.14.83   As to þe clergie of crist thei counted hit but a *tryfle*:
C.20.150   Hit is *truyfle* þat thow tellest; y, treuthe, woet þe sothe,

trumpede > trompe

trusse v *trussen v.*   A 1; B 1; C 1
A. 2.180   Oueral yhuntid & yhote *trusse*,
B. 2.221   Ouer al yhonted and yhote *trusse*,
C. 2.231   Oueral yhonted and yhote *trusse*,

trust n *trust n.*   A 2 trist; B 2; C 2 trist (1) truste (1)
A. 3.113   In *trist* of hire tresour she teniþ [wel] manye;
A. 8.166   Vpon *trist* of 3our tresour trienalis to haue
B. 3.124   [In] *trust* of hire tresor [she teneþ wel] manye.
B. 7.188   Vpon *trust* of youre tresor triennals to haue,
C. 3.161   In *trist* of here tresor he teneth fol monye,
C. 9.334   Vp *truste* of 3oure tresor trionales to haue,

truste v *&> trust*   A 2 tresten (1) triste (1); B 4 truste (2) trusten (1) trusteþ (1); C 4 trist (2) triste (1) tristeth (1)
A. 1.68   Þat *tresten* on his tresour betraid arn sonnest.'
A. 8.163   A[c] to *triste* on þis trionalis, trewely, me þinkeþ,
B. 1.70   That *trusten* on his tresour bitraye[d are] sonnest.'
B. 7.185   Ac to *truste* [on] þise triennals, trewely, me þynkeþ
B.11.288   That if þei trauaille truweliche, and *truste* in god almy3ty,
B.13.332   For tales þat I telle no man *trusteþ* to me.
C. 1.66   That *tristeth* in tresor of erthe he bytrayeth sonest.
C. 6.333   [T]*rist* in his mechel mercy and 3ut þou myhte be saued.
C. 9.331   Ac to *triste* vp this trionales, treuly, me thynketh
C.13.102   That yf th[ey] trauaile treulyche and *trist* in god almyhty

trusty adj *trusti adj.*   A 1; B 1
A. 9.74   *Trusty* of his tailende, takiþ but his owene,
B. 8.83   *Trusty* of his tailende, takeþ but his owene,

truþe n *treuth n.*   A 49 treuþe (46) treweþe (1) trouþe (2); B 115 treuþe (7) trouþe (8) Truthe (1) truþe (97) truþes (2); C 123 treuth (6) treuthe (117)
A. 1.12   'Þe tour [on] þe toft,' quaþ heo, '*treuþe* is þereinne,
A. 1.83   'Whanne alle tresours arn tri3ed *treuþe* is þe beste;
A. 1.95   Til *treuþe* hadde termined here trespas to þe ende.
A. 1.97   [Di]de hem swere on h[ere] swerd to serue *treuþe* euere.
A. 1.100   But holde wiþ hym & wiþ hire þat aske þe *treuþe*,
A. 1.107   Tau3te hem þoru3 þe trinite þe *trouþe* to knowe:
A. 1.122   Þere *treuþe* is in trinite & tron[iþ] h[e]m alle.
A. 1.124   Whanne alle tresours arn tri3ed *treuþe* is þe beste.
A. 1.126   Þat *treuþe* is þe tresour tri3est on erþe.'
A. 1.133   Þis I trowe be *treuþe*; who can teche þe betere,
A. 1.172   Þ[at] is no *treuþe* of trinite but treccherie of helle,
A. 1.181   Whan alle tresouris arn tri3ede *treuþe* is þe beste.
A. 1.182   Now haue I told þe what *treuþe* is, þat no tresour is betere,
A. 2.30   3if þou wilnest to wone wiþ *treuþe* in his blisse.
A. 2.81   Such weddyng to werche to wraþþe wiþ *treuþe*;
A. 2.84   God grauntide to gyue mede to *treuþe*,

A. 2.86   Þe text[e] tell[iþ] not so, *treuþe* wot þe soþe:
A. 2.102   3et be war of þe weddyng for witty is *treuþe*.
A. 3.143   For she is fauourable to fals & fouliþ *treuþe* ofte;
A. 3.146   And leiþ a3en þe lawe & lettiþ þe *treuþe*
A. 3.268   And whoso trespassiþ [to *treuþe*, or] takiþ [a3eyn his wille],
A. 4.101   Til lordis & ladies louen alle *treuþe*,
A. 5.41   Sekiþ seint *treuþe* for he may saue 3ou alle
A. 5.132   Þanne [myn owne] aunsel dede, [whanne] I wei3ede *treweþe*.
A. 5.232   I wile seke *treuþe* er I [se] rome.'
A. 5.254   To haue grace to seke *treuþe*; god leue þat hy moten!
A. 6.20   'Knowist þou ou3t a corseint,' quaþ þei, 'þat men callen *treuþe*?
A. 6.46   For *treuþe* wolde loue me þe wers a long tyme aftir.
A. 6.79   Þe tour þere *treuþe* is hymself is vp to þe sonne;
A. 6.84   Tel hym þis tokne, "*treuþe* wot þe soþe,"
A. 6.93   Þou shalt se *treuþe* himself wel sitte in þin herte
A. 6.104   Ac þere arn seuene sistris þat [seruen] *treuþe* euere.
A. 7.15   Caste hem cloþis for cold for so wile *treuþe*.
A. 7.36   'Be my power, piers, I pli3te þe my *treuþe*
A. 7.39   Loke þou tene no tenaunt but *treuþe* wile assent,
A. 7.53   And wende wiþ 3ow þe wey til we fynde *treuþe*.'
A. 7.62   And alle kyne crafty men þat conne lyue in *treuþe*,
A. 7.66   *Treuþe* tolde me ones & bad me telle it forþ:
A. 7.88   My wyf shal haue of þat I wan wiþ *treuþe*, & namore,
A. 7.93   I wile worsshipe þerewiþ *treuþe* in my lyue,
A. 7.122   3e ben wastours, I wot wel, & *treuþe* wot þe soþe,
A. 7.126   Ac *treuþe* shal teche 3ow his tem for to dryue,
A. 7.194   *Treuþe* tau3te me ones to loue hem ichone
A. 8.1   *Treuþe* herde telle hereof, & to peris sente
A. 8.25   Ac vndir his secre sel *treuþe* sente h[e]m a lettre,
A. 8.41   Þat no gile go wiþ 3ow but þe graiþ *treuþe*.'
A. 8.94   And was writen ri3t þus in witnesse of *treuþe*:
A.11.20   And lede forþ a loueday to lette þe *treuþe*,
A.11.31   For 3if harlotrie ne halp[e] hem betere, haue god my *trouþe*,
B. 1.12   'The tour on þe toft', quod she, '*truþe* is þerInne,
B. 1.85   'Whan alle tresors arn tried *treuþe* is þe beste:
B. 1.97   Til *treuþe* hadde ytermyned hire trespas to þe ende.
B. 1.99   Dide hem sweren on hir swerd to seruen *truþe* euere.
B. 1.102   But holden wiþ hym and with here þat [asken þe] *truþe*,
B. 1.109   Tau3te hem [þoru3] þe Trinitee [þe] *treuþe* to knowe:
B. 1.131   And enden, as I er seide, in *truþe* þat is þe beste.
B. 1.133   Ther *Treuþe* is in Trinitee and troneþ hem alle.
B. 1.135   Whan alle tresors arn tried *truþe* is þe beste.
B. 1.137   That *Treuþe* is þe trieste on erþe.'
B. 1.145   This I trowe be *truþe*; who kan teche þee bettre,
B. 1.148   For *truþe* telleþ þat loue is triacle of heuene:
B. 1.198   [Th]at is no *truþe* of þe Trinite but tricherie of helle,
B. 1.207   Whan alle tresors ben tried *treuþe* is þe beste.
B. 1.208   Now haue I told þee what *truþe* is, þat no tresor is bettre,
B. 2.37   And men of þis moolde þat maynteneþ *truþe*,
B. 2.117   Swic[h] weddyng[e] to werche to wraþe wiþ *truþe*;
B. 2.120   God graunte[d] to gyue Mede to *truþe*,
B. 2.122   [The] text telleþ þee no3t so, *Truþe* woot þe soþe,
B. 2.138   Yet be war of [þe] weddynge; for witty is *truþe*,
B. 3.154   For she is fauourable to fals and [f]ouleþ *truþe* ofte.
B. 3.164   And al þe comune in care þat coueiten lyue in *truþe*.
B. 3.241   And enformeþ pouere [peple] and pursueþ *truþe*.
B. 3.243   Wiþouten Mede doþ hem good and þe *truþe* helpeþ,
B. 3.293   And whoso trespaseþ [to] *truþe* or takeþ ayein his wille,
B. 3.301   And swich pees among þe peple and a parfit *truþe*.
B. 3.317   Ne putte hem in panel to doon hem pli3te hir *truþe*;
B. 3.319   Mercy or no mercy as *Truthe* [may] acorde.
B. 3.343   Quod bonum est tenete; *truþe* þat text made.
B. 4.114   Til lordes and ladies louen alle *truþe*
B. 4.157   Alle ri3tfulle recordede þat Reson *truþe* tolde.
B. 4.176   Mede ouermaistreþ lawe and muche *truþe* letteþ.
B. 5.52   'And ye þat han lawes to [loke], lat *truþe* be youre coueitise
B. 5.54   For whoso contrarieþ *truþe*, he telleþ in þe gospel,
B. 5.57   Sekeþ Seynt *Truþe*, for he may saue yow alle
B. 5.216   Than myn owene Auncer [whan I] weyed *truþe*.
B. 5.274   For a[l] þat ha[þ] of þi good, haue god my *truþe*,
B. 5.277   In Miserere mei deus, wher I mene *truþe*:
B. 5.460   I shal seken *truþe* er I se Rome.'
B. 5.512   To haue grace to go [to] *truþe*, [God leue þat þei moten].
B. 5.532   'Knowestow au3t a corseint', [quod þei], 'þat men calle *truþe*?
B. 5.547   In taillours craft and tynkeris craft, what *truþe* kan deuyse,
B. 5.548   I weue and I wynde and do what *truþe* hoteþ.
B. 5.559   *Truþe* wolde loue me þe lasse a long tyme after.
B. 5.597   Telleþ hym þis tokene: "[*truþe* woot] þe soþe;
B. 5.606   Thow shalt see in þiselue *truþe* [sitte] in þyn herte
B. 5.618   A[c] þer are seuen sustren þat seruen *truþe* euere
B. 6.16   Casteþ hem cloþes [for cold] for so [wol] *truþe*.
B. 6.34   'By my power, Piers, I pli3te þee my *trouþe*
B. 6.38   Loke [þow] tene no tenaunt but *truþe* wole assente,

B. 6.58	And wende wiþ yow [þe wey] til we fynde *truþe*.'
B. 6.68	And alle kynne crafty men þat konne lyuen in *truþe*,
B. 6.74	*Truþe* tolde me ones and bad me telle it [forþ]:
B. 6.96	My wif shal haue of þat I wan wiþ *truþe* and na moore,
B. 6.101	I wol worshipe þerwiþ *truþe* by my lyue,
B. 6.130	Ye ben wastours, I woot wel, and *truþe* woot þe soþe;
B. 6.134	Ac *truþe* shal teche yow his teme to dryue,
B. 6.139	Ac ye myȝte trauaille as *truþe* wolde and take mete and hyre
B. 6.208	*Truþe* tauȝte me ones to louen hem ech one,
B. 7.1	T*Reuþe* herde telle herof, and to Piers sente
B. 7.8	Pardon wiþ Piers Plowman *truþe* haþ ygraunted.
B. 7.23	Ac vnder his secret seel *truþe* sente hem a lettre,
B. 7.55	Thise ben *truþes* tresores trewe folk to helpe,
B. 7.112	And was writen riȝt þus in witnesse of *truþe*:
B. 9.101	[Tynynge] of tyme, *truþe* woot þe soþe,
B.10.20	And lede forþ a loueday to lette [þe] *truþe*,
B.10.22	Thei lede lordes wiþ lesynges and bilieþ *truþe*.
B.10.46	Ne [holpe hir] harlotrye, haue god my *trouþe*,
B.11.39	If *truþe* wol witnesse it be wel do Fortune to folwe
B.11.152	By loue and by lernyng of my lyuynge in *truþe*;
B.11.156	Nouȝt þoruȝ preiere of a pope but for his pure *truþe*
B.11.159	And on Troianus *truþe* to þenke, and do *truþe* to þe peple.
B.11.159	And on Troianus *truþe* to þenke, and do *truþe* to þe peple.
B.11.162	Ac þus leel loue and lyuyng in *truþe*
B.11.164	Yblissed be *truþe* þat so brak helle yates
B.12.129	Of briddes and of beestes, [by] tastes of *truþe*.
B.12.287	Ac *truþe* þat trespased neuere ne trauersed ayeins his lawe,
B.12.290	Ne wolde neuere trewe god but [trewe] *truþe* were allowed.
B.12.291	And wheiþer it worþ [of *truþe*] or noȝt, [þe] worþ [of] bileue is gret,
B.12.292	And an hope hangynge þerInne to haue a mede for his *truþe*;
B.12.294	The glose graunteþ vpon þat vers a greet mede to *truþe*.
B.13.244	And I hadde neuere of hym, haue god my *trouþe*,
B.13.359	Lened for loue of þe wed and looþ to do *truþe*;
B.14.100	Ther parfit *truþe* and poore herte is, and pacience of tonge,
B.14.274	'Haue god my *trouþe*', quod Haukyn '[I here yow] preise faste pouerte.
B.15.27	And whan I deme domes and do as *truþe* techeþ
B.15.91	I shal tellen it for *truþes* sake; take hede whoso likeþ.
B.15.310	And to taken of hir tenauntȝ moore þan *trouþe* wolde,
B.15.414	[Ac] for drede of þe deeþ I dar noȝt telle *truþe*,
B.15.416	And ben manered after Makometh þat no man vseþ *trouþe*.
B.15.471	So [menen] riȝtfulle men [after] mercy and *truþe*.
B.15.549	Moore tresor þan *trouþe*? I dar noȝt telle þe soþe.
B.16.27	The world is a wikked wynd to hem þat willen *truþe*.
B.18.119	A comely creature [and a clene]; *truþe* she highte.
B.18.121	Whan þise maydenes mette, mercy and *truþe*,
B.18.125	'Ich haue ferly of þis fare, in feiþ', seide *truþe*,
B.18.142	'That þow tellest', quod *Truþe*, 'is but a tale of waltrot!
B.18.147	It is trufle þat þow tellest; I, *truþe*, woot þe soþe,
B.18.163	'Now suffre we', seide *Truþe*; 'I se, as me þynkeþ,
B.18.189	Ayeins Reson. [I], rightwisnesse, recorde þus wiþ *truþe*
B.18.261	'Suffre we', seide *truþe*; 'I here and see boþe
B.18.295	'Certes I drede me', quod þe deuel, 'lest *truþe* [do] hem fecche.
B.18.416	'Trewes', quod *Truþe*, 'þow tellest vs sooþ, by Iesus!
B.18.422	*Truþe* trumpede þo and song Te deum laudamus,
B.19.90	[For it shal turne tresoun to riȝt and to *truþe*].
B.19.194	Paieþ parfitly as pure *truþe* wolde.
B.19.230	[To wynne wiþ *truþe* þat] þe world askeþ,
B.19.261	And for to tilie *truþe* a teeme shal he haue.'
B.19.333	As wide as þe world is wiþ Piers to tilie *truþe*
B.19.478	And rule þi reaume in reson [as right wol and] *truþe*
B.20.53	Antecrist cam þanne, and al þe crop of *truþe*
B.20.56	In ech a contree þer he cam he kutte awey *truþe*
B.20.118	Weren feþered wiþ fair biheste and many a fals *truþe*.
B.20.135	And ouertilte al his *truþe* wiþ 'tak þis vp amendement'.
B.20.161	Hir sire was a Sysour þat neuere swoor *truþe*,
C.Pr.12	Of *treuthe* and tricherye, tresoun and gyle
C.Pr.15	And say a tour; as [y] trow[e], *treuthe* was thereynne.
C. 1.12	'The tour vppon þe tofte,' quod she, '*treuthe* is þerynne
C. 1.81	'When alle tresores ben tried *treuthe* is þe beste;
C. 1.93	Til *treuthe* hadde termyned here trespas to þe ende
C. 1.100	But [feithfullich] fyghte and fende *treuthe*
C. 1.103	Dede hem swere on here swerd to serue *treuthe* euere.
C. 1.109	He and oþer with hym helden nat with *treuthe*,
C. 1.134	There *treuthe* is, þe tour that trinite ynne sitteth.
C. 1.136	Tha[n] *treuthe* and trewe loue is no tresor bettre.'
C. 1.144	And this y trowe be *treuth*; [ho] kan tecche þe bettre
C. 1.146	For *treuthe* telleth þat loue ys triacle [for] synne
C. 1.193	And þat is no *treuthe* of þe trinite but triccherye [and] synne
C. 1.202	"Whenne alle tresores ben tried *treuthe* is þe beste."
C. 2.121	Suche a weddyng to wurche þat wrathe myhte *treuthe*;
C. 2.127	For *treuthe* plyhte here treuthe to wedde on of here douhteres,
C. 2.127	For treuthe plyhte here *treuthe* to wedde on of here douhteres,
C. 2.139	That mede may be wedded to no man bot *treuthe*,
C. 2.154	ȝut beth ywar of þe weddynge; for witty is *treuthe*
C. 3.89	A grypeth þerfore a[s] gret as for þe grayeth *treuthe*.
C. 3.133	Til *treuthe* hadde ytolde here a tokene fram hymsulue.
C. 3.137	And ay the lengur y late [the] go the lasse *treuthe* is with the,
C. 3.140	Thow tene me and *treuthe*: and thow mowe be atake
C. 3.146	And teche the to louye *treuthe* and take consail of resoun.
C. 3.192	For she is fauerable to fals the whiche defouleth *treuthe*.
C. 3.309	And ther is resoun as a reue rewardynge *treuthe*
C. 3.344	'Relacioun rect,' quod Consience, 'is a record of *treuthe*–
C. 3.349	In his pay and in his pite and in his puyr *treuthe*,
C. 3.351	And take hym for his trauaile al þat *treuthe* wolde,
C. 3.446	And hoso taketh aȝeyn *treuthe* or transuerseth aȝeyns resoun
C. 3.454	And such pees among þe peple and a parfit *treuthe*
C. 3.470	Ne potte [hem] in panele [to] do [hem] plihte here *treuthe*;
C. 3.495	Quod bonum est tenete, a tixst of *treuthe* [m]akynge.
C. 4.109	Til lordes and ladies louen alle *treuthe*
C. 4.151	Ac al ryhtful recordede þat resoun *treuthe* sayde,
C. 4.170	Mede and men of ȝoure craft muche *treuthe* letteth.
C. 5.183	And comuners [to] acorde in alle kyn *treuthe*.
C. 5.198	Seketh seynt *treuthe* in sauac[ioun] of ȝoure soules
C. 6.224	Then myn [owene] auncer when y wayed *treuthe*.
C. 6.296	For alle that hauen of thy good, haue god my *treuthe*,
C. 6.306	Then an errant vsurer, haue god my *treuthe*,
C. 6.386	They couthe nat by here Consience acorden for *treuthe*
C. 7.157	To haue grace to go to *treuthe*; god leue þat they mote.
C. 7.177	'Knowest thow auht a corsent,' quod they, 'þat men calleth *treuthe*?
C. 7.178	[Can]st [thow] wissen vs [þe w]ay whoderout *treuth* woneth?'
C. 7.190	And yserued *treuthe* sothly, somdel to paye.
C. 7.198	And hoso wilneth to wyte where þat *treuthe* woneth
C. 7.203	Were hit itolde *treuthe* þat y toke mede
C. 7.205	Ac hoso wol wende þer *treuthe* is, this is þe way thede[r]:
C. 7.245	Tel hym this tokene: "*treuthe* woet þe sothe;
C. 7.255	Thow shalt se *treuthe* sitte in thy sulue herte
C. 7.270	Ac ther ben seuene susteres þat seruen *treuthe* euere
C. 7.298	*Treuth* telleth [this to hym], þat y be excused.'
C. 7.303	Forthy, [Peres] the [plouhman], y preye the telle hit *treuthe*
C. 8.33	'By my power, [Peres], y plyhte the my *treuthe*
C. 8.36	Loke ȝe tene no tenaunt but *treuthe* wol assente
C. 8.49	Bute they be of bounte, of batayles or of *treuthe*.
C. 8.57	And wende with alle tho þat wolden lyue in *treuthe*.'
C. 8.69	And alle kyne craftes men þat conne lyue in *treuthe*,
C. 8.76	*Treuthe* t[o]lde me ones and bad me telle hit fort[h]:
C. 8.105	My wyf shal haue of þat y wan with *treuthe* and no more,
C. 8.110	Y wol worschipe þerwith *treuthe* al my lyue
C. 8.137	Myhte helpe, as y hope; Ac hey *treuthe* wolde
C. 8.141	Ac *treuthe* shal teche ȝow his teme to dryue
C. 8.217	*Treuthe* tauhte me ones to louye hem vchone
C. 8.229	Conforte hem with thy catel, for so comaundeth *treuthe*;
C. 8.296	'By seynte Poul!' quod Peres, 'thow poyntest neyh þe *treuthe*
C. 9.1	*Treuthe* herde telle herof and to [Peres] sente
C. 9.19	And suche liue as þei lereth men oure lord *treuthe* hem graunteth
C. 9.23	Ac no [a] pena & a culpa *treuthe* wolde hem graunte
C. 9.27	Ac vnder his secrete seal *treuthe* sente hem a lettre
C. 9.59	Lellyche and lauhfollyche, oure lord *treuthe* hem graunteth
C. 9.252	Ac while a wrouhte in þe world and wan his mete with *treuthe*
C. 9.286	And was ywryte ryhte thus in witnesse of *treuthe*:
C.10.182	Hath tresor ynow of *treuthe* to fynden hymsulue.
C.10.242	Ac þe gospel is a glose ther and huydeth þe grayth *treuthe*,
C.10.271	Many a payre sethe th[e] pestelens[e] han plyhte *treuthe* to louye;
C.11.17	And lette with a loueday [lewed] *treuthe* and bigile
C.11.25	Tho þat god most goed ȝeueth greueth most riht and *treuthe*:
C.11.30	And can telle of *treuthe* and of þe twelue aposteles
C.11.109	Yf thow hit vse oþer haunte, haue god my *treuthe*,
C.11.273	And fonde y neuere in faith, for to telle *treuthe*,
C.11.305	All þat *treuth* attacheth and testifieth for gode
C.12.27	Y wolde it were no synne,' y saide, 'to seien þat were *treuthe*.
C.12.38	Thouh tho[w] se, say nat sum tyme þat is *treuthe*.
C.12.91	And on Troianus *treuthe* to thenke alle tyme[s] in ȝoure lyue
C.12.96	Of hym þat trauaileth [t]heron bote *treuthe* be his lyuynge.
C.12.173	To testifie for *treuthe* þe tale þat y shewe
C.12.233	Riht so, sothly, for to segge *treuthe*,
C.14.188	And to lele and lyfholy þat louyeth alle *treuthe*.
C.14.209	Ac *treuth* þat trespassed neuere ne trauersede aȝens his lawe
C.14.212	Ne wolde neuere trewe god bote trewe *treuthe* were alloued.
C.14.213	And wher hit worth or worth nat, the bileue is gret of *treuthe*
C.14.214	And hope hangeth ay þeron to haue þat *treuthe* deserueth:
C.15.136	Bote lele loue and *treuthe* that loth is to be founde.'
C.16.187	And when y deme domus and do as *treuthe* techeth
C.17.45	And to take of here tenauntes more then *treuthe* wolde
C.17.141	Loue god for he is goed and grounde of alle *treuthe*;
C.17.211	More tresor then *treuthe*? Y dar nat telle þe sothe

C.18.31 The world is a wikkede wynd to hem þat wo[l] *treuthe*;
C.20.122 A comely creature and a clene; *Treuthe* she hihte.
C.20.124 When this maydones metten, Mercy and *treuthe*,
C.20.128 'Y haue ferly of this fare, in faith,' seide *Treuthe*,
C.20.145 'That thow tellest,' quod *treuthe*, 'is bote a tale of walterot!
C.20.150 Hit is truyfle þat thow tellest; y, *treuthe*, woet þe sothe,
C.20.166 'Now soffre we,' saide *Treuthe*; 'y se, as me thynketh,
C.20.204 Aȝeynes resoun; y, rihtwysnesse, recorde [þus] with *treuthe*
C.20.269 'Soffre we,' sayde *treuthe*; 'y here and se bothe
C.20.311 Thenne were he vnwrast of his word þat witnesse is of *treuthe*.'
C.20.325 'Forthy y drede me,' quod þe deuel, 'laste *treuthe* wol hem fecche.
C.20.459 'Trewes,' quod *treuthe*; 'thow tellest vs soeth, by iesus!
C.20.465 *Treuth* trompede tho and song te deum laudamus
C.21.90 [For it shal turne tresoun] to riht and to *treuthe*.
C.21.194 Payeth parfitly as puyr *treuthe* wolde.
C.21.230 To wynne with *treuthe* þat the world asketh,
C.21.261 And for to tulye *treuthe* a teme shal he haue.'
C.21.333 As wyde as the world is with Peres to tulye *treuthe*
C.21.478 And rewle thy rewme in resoun [as] riht w[o]ll and *treuthe*.
C.22.53 Auntecrist cam thenne and al the crop of *treuthe*
C.22.56 In vch a Contrey ther he cam [he] kutte awey *treuthe*
C.22.118 Weren fythered with fayre biheste and many a fals *treuthe*.
C.22.135 And ouertulde al his *treuthe* with 'taek this [vp] amendement.'
C.22.161 Here syre was a sysour þat neuere swoer *treuthe*,

truþeward n *treuth* n. B 1; C 1 treuthward
B.14.312 He tempreþ þe tonge to *truþeward* [þat] no tresor coueiteþ:
C.16.146 A tempreth the tonge to *treuthward* þat no tresor coueyteth:

truweliche > trewely; tulie(den > tilien; tulyers > tilieris; tulieth tulyng > tilien; tulying > tellynge

tulius n prop *n.i.d.* C 1
C.12.176 *Tulius*, tolomeus–y can nat tell here names–

tulthe > tilþe; tunge > tonge

tunycle n *tunicle* n. B 1
B.15.168 As of a *tunycle* of tarse or of trie scarlet.

turne v *turnen* v. A 3 turne (2) turnide (1); B 27 torne (5) torned (4) tornede (3) torneþ (1) turne (11) turned (1) turnede (2); C 27 torne (2) turne (17) turned (4) turnede (3) turneth (1)
A. 5.19 And *turnide* vpward here tail in tokynyng of drede
A. 5.90 [Awey] fro þe auter myn eiȝe I *turne*
A.12.9 That myȝthe *turne* m[e] to tene & theologie boþe.
B. 3.327 And þe myddel of a Moone shal make þe Iewes *torne*,
B. 3.341 Hadde she loked þat [left] half and be leef *torned*
B. 3.347 Ac yow failed a konnynge clerk þat kouþe þe leef han *torned*.
B. 5.19 [And] *turned* vpward hire tai[l] in tokenynge of drede
B. 5.110 Awey fro þe Auter *turne* I myne eiȝen
B. 5.185 That þi wille [ne þi wit] to wraþe myȝte *turne*:
B.11.45 'That wit shal *torne* to wrecchednesse for wil to haue his likyng!'
B.13.210 *Turne* into þe trewe feiþ and intil oon bileue.'
B.13.318 And he *torned* hym as tyd and þanne took I hede;
B.15.438 Elleuene holy men al þe world *tornede*
B.15.446 And þoruȝ miracles, as men mow rede, al þat marche he *tornede*
B.15.503 Thei sholde *turne*, whoso trauail[e wolde] to teche hem of þe Trinite.
B.15.512 Many myracles he wrouȝte m[e]n for to *turne*,
B.16.110 And sike and synfulle boþe so] to goode *turnede*:
B.17.122 Til I haue salue for alle sike; and þanne shal I *turne*
B.17.186 Al is but an hand, [howso I *turne* it.
B.17.304 That rightwisnesse þoruȝ repentaunce to ruþe myȝte *turne*.
B.17.315 Good hope, þat helpe sholde, to wanhope *torneþ*
B.17.319 Ac er his rightwisnesse to ruþe *torne* som restitucion bihoueþ;
B.18.359 Adam and alle þoruȝ a tree shul *turne* to lyue,
B.18.361 Now bigynneþ þi gile ageyn þee to *turne*
B.19.90 [For it shal *turne* tresoun to riȝt and to truþe].
B.19.109 Water into wyn *turnede*, as holy writ telleþ.
B.19.450 And *torne* hir wit to wisdom and to welþe of soule.
B.20.47 And suffre sorwes ful soure, þat shal to Ioye *torne*."
B.20.54 *Torned* it [tid] vp so doun and ouertilte þe roote.
B.20.137 And *tornede* Cyuyle into Symonye, and siþþe he took þe Official.
C. 3.49 Among knyhtes and clerkes consience to *turne*.
C. 3.480 And the [myddell] of [a] mone shal make þe iewes *turne*
C. 3.493 Ac hadde she loked in þe luft half and þe lef *turned*
C. 5.101 That alle tymes of my tyme to profit shal *turne*.'
C. 5.121 And *turned* vpward here tayl in tokenynge of drede
C. 6.167 That thy wil ne thy wit to wr[at]he myhte *turne*.
C. 9.85 Bothe afyngred and afurste, to laste þe fayre outward
C. 9.144 Reste hym and roste [hym] and his rug *turne*,
C.12.2 'That wit shal *turne* to wrechednesse for wil hath al his wille!'
C.12.208 Ȝoure sorwe into solace shal *turne* at þe laste
C.13.19 Alle his sorwe to solace thorw that song *turnede*
C.15.217 That pestilenc[e] to pees and parfyt loue turn[e].

C.17.254 They sholde [*turne*], hoso trauayle wolde and of þe trinite teche hem.
C.17.263 Mony myracles a wrouhte men for to *torne*,
C.17.273 And fro mysbileue mony men *turnede*.
C.19.152 Al is bote oen hoend howso y *turne* hit.
C.19.284 That rihtwisnesse thorw repentaunce to reuthe myhte *turne*.
C.19.295 For goed hope, that helpe scholde, to wanhope *turneth*
C.19.299 Ac ar [h]is rihtwisnesse to reuthe *turne* rest[i]t[uci]on hit maketh,
C.20.398 Adam and alle thorw a tre shal *turne* to lyue,
C.20.399 And now bygynneth thy gyle agayne the to *turne*
C.21.90 [For it shal *turne* tresoun] to riht and to treuthe.
C.21.109 [Watur into wyn *turned*], As holy writ telleth.
C.21.450 And *turne* here wi[t] to wisdoem and to wel[th]e [of] soule.
C.22.47 And soffre sorwes ful soure þat shal to ioye *torne*."
C.22.54 *Turned* hit tyd vp so down and ouertulde þe rote
C.22.137 And *turnede* syuyle into symonye and sethe he toek þe official.

tutour n *tutour* n. A 1; B 1; C 1 tutor
A. 1.54 And *tutour* of ȝour tresour, & take it ȝow at nede;
B. 1.56 And *tutour* of youre tresor, and take it yow at nede;
C. 1.52 And *tutor* of ȝoure tresor and take it ȝow at nede;

tweyne num *twein* num. cf. two A 3 tweiȝe (1) tweyne (2); B 6 tweye (1) tweyne (5); C 6 tweye (1) tweyne (4) twene (1)
A. 5.117 Ferst I lernide to leiȝe a lef oþer *tweiȝe*;
A. 5.160 [T]ymme þe tynkere & *tweyne* of his knaues,
A.12.83 I am masager of deþ; men haue I *tweyne*:
B. 5.32 [He] bad Bette kutte a bouȝ ouþer *tweye*
B. 5.201 First I lerned to lye a leef ouþer *tweyne*;
B. 5.309 Tymme þe Tynkere and *tweyne* of his [knaues],
B.12.176 As þow seest in þe Sauter in Salmes oon or *tweyne*
B.13.380 But he profrede to paie a peny or *tweyne*
B.18.172 Whan Pees in Pacience ycloþed approched ner hem *tweyne*
C. 5.134 He bad b[e]tte kutte a bo[u]he or *twene*
C. 6.209 Furste y lerned to lye a leef oþer *tweye*;
C. 6.364 Tymme þe Tynekare and *tweyne* of his knaues,
C.14.116 As we seen in þe sauter in psalmes oon or *tweyne*
C.18.81 'Ȝe, sire,' y sayde, 'and sethen þer aren but *tweyne* lyues
C.18.230 Sprang forth and spak, a spyer of hem *tweyne*,

twelf num *twelve* num. A 3 twelue; B 3 twelf (1) twelue (2); C 3 twelue
A. 5.111 In a torn tabbard of *twelue* wynter age,
A. 5.128 Til ten ȝardis oþer *twelue* tollide out þrittene.
A.11.25 And can telle of tobie & of þe *twelue* apostlis,
B. 5.195 In a [torn] tabard of *twelf* wynter age,
B. 5.212 Til ten yerdes or *twelue* tolled out þrittene.
B.10.33 And kan telle of Tobye and of [þe] *twelue* Apostles
C. 6.203 In a tore tabard of *twelue* wynter age,
C. 6.220 Til ten ȝerde other *twelue* tolde out threttene.
C.11.30 And can telle of treuthe and of þe *twelue* aposteles

tweluemonþe n *twelvemonth* n. B 1; C 1 twelmonthe
B.13.336 That takeþ me al a *tweluemonþe*, til þat I despise
C. 6.80 That taketh me al [a] *twelmonthe* til þat y despise

twene > tweyne

twenty num *twenti* num. B 2; C 1
B.12.190 That haþ take fro Tybourne *twenty* stronge þeues,
B.16.10 'I wolde trauaille', quod I, 'þis tree to se *twenty* hundred myle,
C.14.129 Hit hath take fro tybourne *twenty* stronge theues

twies adv *twies* adv. B 3 twies (2) twyes (1); C 1
B. 4.23 For he wol make wehee *twies* er [we] be þere.'
B. 5.414 Nouȝt *twyes* in two yer, and þanne [telle I vp gesse].
B.13.269 A thousand and þre hundred, *twies* [þritty] and ten,
C. 7.29 Nat *twies* in ten ȝer and thenne telle y nat þe haluendele.

twyned ptp *twinen* v. B 1; C 1
B.17.207 As wex and a weke were *twyned* togideres,
C.19.173 As wexe and a weke were *twyned* togyderes

two num *two* num. cf. tweyne A 13 to (2) two (11); B 44; C 41 to (1) two (40)
A. 2.34 Were beden to þe b[ri]dale on boþe *two* sides.
A. 3.218 'Þere arn *to* maner of medis, my lord, be ȝour leue.
A. 5.28 Thomas he tauȝte to take *two* staues
A. 5.109 He was [betil]browid & babirlippid wiþ *two* bleride eiȝen,
A. 6.63 *Two* stokkis þere stonde, but stynte þou not þere;
A. 6.122 And þoruȝ þe helpe of hem [*two*], hope þou non oþer,
A. 7.265 Noþer gees ne gris, but *two* grene chesis,
A. 8.93 In *two* lynes it lay & nouȝt to lettre more,
A. 9.8 Til it befel on a Friday *two* Freris I mette.
A. 9.72 Trewe of his tunge & of his *two* handis,
A.11.40 Þanne telle þei of þe trinite how *two* slowe þe þridde,
A.11.108 Þei *two*, [as] I hope, aftir my besekyng,
A.11.272 And was þere neuere in þis world *to* wysere of werkis,

B. 2.55   Were boden to þe bridale on boþe *two* sides,
B. 3.231 'Ther are *two* manere of Medes, my lord, [bi] youre leue.
B. 5.28   Tomme Stowue he tauȝte to take *two* staues
B. 5.135 Now awakeþ Wraþe wiþ *two* white eiȝen,
B. 5.190 He was bitelbrowed and baberlipped wiþ *two* blered eiȝen;
B. 5.340 Hise guttes bigonne to goþelen as *two* gredy sowes;
B. 5.385 Thanne cam Sleuþe al bislabered wiþ *two* slymy eiȝen.
B. 5.401 That I telle wiþ my tonge is *two* myle fro myn herte.
B. 5.414 Nouȝt twyes in *two* yer, and þanne [telle I vp gesse].
B. 5.576 *Two* stokkes þer stondeþ, ac stynte [þow] noȝt þere;
B. 5.637 And þoruȝ þe help of hem *two*, hope þow noon ooþer,
B. 6.281 Neiþer gees ne grys, but *two* grene cheses,
B. 6.327 Whan ye se þe [mone] amys and *two* monkes heddes,
B. 7.111 In *two* lynes it lay and noȝt a [lettre] moore,
B. 7.153 And how þe preest inpugned it wiþ *two* propre wordes.
B. 8.8   Til it bifel on a Friday *two* freres I mette,
B. 8.81 Trewe of his tunge and of his *two* handes,
B. 9.118 And siþenes by assent of hemself as þei *two* myȝte acorde;
B.10.54 Than telleþ þei of þe Trinite [how *two* slowe þe þridde],
B.10.156 They *two*, as I hope, after my [bis]echyng
B.10.286 Bittre abouȝte þe giltes of *two* badde preestes,
B.11.12 Thanne hadde Fortune folwynge hire *two* fair damyseles:
B.12.160 Tak *two* stronge men and in Themese cast hem,
B.12.164 Which trowestow of þo *two* [in Themese] is in moost drede,
B.13.107 For ye han harmed vs *two* in þat ye eten þe puddyng,
B.13.128 And [demeþ] þat dowel and dobet arn *two* Infinites,
B.13.175 Ne bitwene *two* cristene kynges kan no wiȝt pees make
B.13.246 Saue a pardon wiþ a peis of leed and *two* polles amyddes.
B.13.316 What on bak, and what on body half, and by þe *two* sides
B.15.591 Wiþ *two* fisshes and fyue loues fyue þousand peple,
B.16.125 And fed yow wiþ *two* fisshes and wiþ fyue loues,
B.17.12 Wheron [was] writen *two* wordes on þis wise yglosed.
B.17.40 Than he þat gooþ wiþ *two* staues to sighte of vs alle;
B.17.43 Than for to techen hem *two*, and to hard to lerne þe leeste!
B.17.79 And he took hym *two* pens to liflode and seide,
B.18.71 *Two* þeues [þat tyme] þoled deeþ [also]
B.18.230 Thanne was þer a wight wiþ *two* brode eiȝen;
B.18.299 And þus haþ he trolled forþ [lik a tidy man] þise *two* and þritty
             wynter.
B.19.126 And fedde wiþ *two* fisshes and with fyue loues
B.19.273 Wiþ *two* [aiþes] þat þei hadde, an oold and a newe:
B.19.341 Thise *two* coome to Conscience and to cristen peple
B.19.345 Shulle come out, Conscience; and youre [caples *two*],
B.19.473 And what I take of yow *two*, I take it at þe techynge
B.20.162 Oon Tomme *two*-tonge, atteynt at ech [a q]ueste.
C.Pr.106 Ful on hem þat fre were thorwe *two* fals prestis!
C. 1.84 For who is trewe of his tonge and of his *two* handes
C. 3.333 Thus is mede and mercede as *two* maner relacions,
C. 3.382 Bytwene *two* lo[n]des for a trewe marke.
C. 5.130 Tomme stoue he tauhte to take t[w]o staues
C. 6.103 Thenne awakede wrathe with *two* w[hy]te eyes
C. 6.198 He was bitelbrowed and baburlippid with *two* blered eyes
C. 6.398 His gottes gan to gothly as t[w]o g[re]dy sowes,
C. 7.1   Thenne cam sleuthe al byslobered with *two* slim[y] yes.
C. 7.17 That y telle with my tonge is t[wo] myle fro myn herte.
C. 7.223 T[w]o stokkes þere stondeth ac stynte thow nat þere;
C. 7.290 And thorw þe help[e] of hem *two*, hope þou non oþer,
C. 8.303 Noþer goos ne gries but *two* grene cheses,
C. 9.285 In *two* lynes hit lay and nat a lettre more
C. 9.302 And how þe prest inpugnede hit thorw *two* propre wordes.
C.10.8   Til hit biful [o]n [a] fryday *two* freres y mette,
C.10.78 Ho[so] is trewe of his tonge and of his *two* handes
C.11.35 And tellen of þe trinite how t[w]o slowe þe thridde
C.11.171 Thenne hadde fortune folwyng here *two* fayre maydenes:
C.13.29 Bothe t[w]o ben gode, be ȝe ful certeyn,
C.13.42 And thogh they wen[d]e by the wey, tho *two* togederes,
C.13.80 Beth nat ybounde, as beth [þ]e ryche, to [bothe *two*] lawes,
C.14.104 Take *two* stronge men and in temese cast hem,
C.14.108 Which trowest [þou] of tho *two* in temese [is] in moste drede?'
C.15.85 And also a gnedy glotoun with *two* grete chekes,
C.16.9 Haue *two* heuenes for ȝoure her[berw]ynge.
C.18.86 And thenne aboue is bettere fruyt, ac bothe *two* ben gode,
C.18.153 With [*two*] fisches and [fyue] loues, fyue thousen[d] at ones,
C.19.13 Whereon was writen *two* wordes on this wyse yglosed:
C.19.76 And toek *two* pans the hostiler to take kepe to hym;
C.20.61 The wal of the temple tocleyef euene [a] *to* peces;
C.20.73 T[w]o theues tho tholed deth þat tyme
C.20.239 Thenne wa[s] ther a wihte with *two* brode yes;
C.20.318 As *two* godes, with god, bothe goed and ille.
C.20.332 Thus hath he trolled forth lyke a tydy man this *two* & thritty
             wynter.
C.21.126 And fedde with *two* fisshes and with fyue loues
C.21.273 With *two* aythes þat they hadde, an oelde and a newe:

C.21.341 Thise *two* cam to Consience and to cristene peple
C.21.345 Shal come oute, Consience; and ȝoure [caples *two*],
C.21.473 And what y take of ȝow *two* y take hit at þe techynge
C.22.162 Oen Tomme *two*-tonge, ateynt at vch [a q]ueste.

U

vcche vch(e > ech; vchon(e > echone; vysen > vsen; vmbewhile > vmwhile;
vmbletee > humilite

vmwhile adv *umwhile adv.* A 1 vmbewhile; B 1; C 1 vmbywhile
A. 5.187   And seten so til euesong & songe [*vmbe*]while
B. 5.338   And seten so til euensong and songen *vmwhile*
C. 6.396   And seten so til euenson[g] and songen *vmbywhile*

vnbynden v *unbinden v.* B 2 vnbynde (1) vnbynden (1); C 2 vnbynde
B.Pr.101   To bynden and *vnbynden* as þe book telleþ,
B.19.189   To bynde and *vnbynde* boþe here and elli[s],
C.Pr.129   To bynde and *vnbynde* as þe boke telleth,
C.21.189   To bynde and *vnbynde* bothe here and elles

vnblessed ptp *unblessed ppl.* B 1; C 1
B.19.404   *Vnblessed* artow, Brewere, but if þee god helpe.
C.21.404   *Vnblessed* art thow, breware, but yf the god helpe.

vnbokelede v *unbokelen v.* C 1
C.19.70   And *vnbokelede* his boteles and bothe he atamede.

vnbuxom adj *unbuxom adj.* A 1 vnbuxum; B 3 vnbuxom (1) vnbuxome
   (1) vnbuxum (1); C 2 vnbuxum
A. 9.93   And were *vnbuxum* at his bidding, and bold to don ille,
B. 2.83   *Vnbuxome* and bolde to breke þe ten hestes;
B. 8.103   [And were *vnbuxum* at his biddyng, and bold to don ille],
B.13.275   Of pride here a plot, and þere a plot of *vnbuxom* speche,
C. 2.90   *Vnbuxum* and bold to breke þe ten hestes;
C. 6.16   Haue be *vnbuxum*, y byseche god of mercy;

vnchargeþ v *unchargen v.* B 1
B.15.345   For charite wiþouten chalangynge *vnchargeþ* þe soule,

vnche n *inche n.* A 1
A. 5.100   May no sugre ne swet þing swage it an *vnche*,

vncomly adj *uncomli adj.* A 1 vncomely; B 1
A.10.186   It is an *vncomely* copil, be crist, as [me þinkeþ],
B. 9.165   It is an *vncomly* couple, by crist! as me þynkeþ,

vnconnynge > vnkonnynge

vnconnyngliche adv *unconningli adv.* C 1
C. 3.263   *Vnconnyngliche* [þow], Consience, conseiledest hym thenne

vncorteysliche adv *uncourtesli adv.* C 1
C.13.171   How *vncortey[s]liche* þat cok his kynde for[th] strenede

vncoupled ptp *uncouplen v.* B 2
B.Pr.162   And somme colers of crafty werk; *vncoupled* þei wen[d]en
B.Pr.207   Coupled and *vncoupled* to cacche what þei mowe.

vncouþe > vnkouþe

vncristen adj *uncristene adj.* A 2 vncristene; B 6 vncristen (1) vncristene
   (5); C 2 vncristene
A. 1.91   For cristene & *vncristene* cleymeþ it ichone,
A.11.237   Þat arn *vncristene* in þat cas may cristene an heþene,
B. 1.93   For cristen and *vncristen* cleymeþ it echone.
B.10.354   That [arn] *vncristene* in þat caas may cristen an heþen,
B.11.143   For an *vncristene* creature; clerkes wite þe soþe
B.11.155   That was an *vncristene* creature, as clerkes fyndeþ in bokes:
B.15.396   Cristene and *vncristene* on oon god bileueþ,
B.15.499   For cristene and *vncristene* crist seide to prechours
C. 1.89   For cristene and *vncristene* claymeth it echone.
C.12.78   For an *vncristene* creature; [clerkes] woet þe sothe

vncrounede ptp *uncorounen v.* C 1
C. 5.65   And knaue[s] *vncrounede* to carte and to worche.

vndede > vndo

vnder prep *under prep.* A 4 vnder (1) vndir (3); B 39; C 36
A.Pr.8   *Vndir* a brood bank be a bourn[e] side,
A. 8.25   Ac *vndir* his secre sel treuþe sente h[e]m a lettre,
A. 9.56   And *vndir* a lynde vpon a launde lenide I me a stounde
A.12.105   And is closed *vnder* clom, crist haue his soule.
B.Pr.8   *Vnder* a brood bank by a bourn[e] syde,

B.Pr.88   That han cure *vnder* crist, and crownynge in tokene
B.Pr.186   To c[r]acchen vs & al oure kynde þouȝ we cropen *vnder* benches;
B. 5.164   And hit[t]e *vnder* þe cheke.
B. 5.432   I am noȝt lured wiþ loue but þer ligge auȝt *vnder* þe þombe.
B. 7.23   Ac *vnder* his secret seel truþe sente hem a lettre,
B. 8.65   And *vnder* a lynde vpon a launde lened I a stounde
B.10.211   For is no science *vnder* sonne so souereyn for þe soule.
B.10.253   Alle þe clerkes *vnder* crist ne koude þis assoille,
B.11.144   That al þe clergie *vnder* crist ne myȝte me cracche fro helle,
B.11.172   Or any Science *vnder* sonne, þe seuene artȝ and alle–
B.11.389   For is no creature *vnder* crist can formen hymseluen,
B.12.37   And hold þee *vnder* obedience þat heigh wey is to heuene.
B.12.126   For Clergie is kepere *vnder* crist of heuene;
B.12.216   Alle þe clerkes *vnder* crist ne kouþe þe skile assoille:
B.13.248   That he sente me *vnder* his seel a salue for þe pestilence,
B.13.293   Or strengest on stede, or styuest *vnder* girdel,
B.14.41   First þe wilde worm *vnder* weet erþe,
B.14.191   And putten of so þe pouke, and preuen vs *vnder* borwe.
B.14.290   Ne to be Mair aboue men ne Mynystre *vnder* kynges;
B.15.48   Alle þe sciences *vnder* sonne and alle þe sotile craftes
B.15.122   [And beere] bedes in hir hand and a book *vnder* hir arme.
B.15.378   [And as vsher *vnder* hym to fourmen vs alle
B.15.453   Til it be fulled *vnder* foot or in fullyng stokkes,
B.15.455   Ytouked and yteynted and *vnder* taillours hande.
B.15.594   And *vnder* stoon deed and stank; wiþ stif vois hym callede:
B.16.17   *Vnder* Piers þe Plowman to piken it and weden it.'
B.17.94   May no medicyne [*vnder* mone] þe man to heele bringe,
B.17.105   For [an] Outlaw[e is] in þe wode and *vnder* bank lotieþ,
B.19.37   But *vnder* tribut and taillage as tikes and cherles.
B.19.86   That o kyng cam wiþ Reson couered *vnder* sense.
B.19.88   Rightwisnesse *vnder* reed gold, Resones felawe;
B.19.296   And couered hym *vnder* conseille of Caton þe wise:
B.19.347   Shal be coloured so queyntely and couered *vnder* [oure] Sophistrie
B.20.17   Nede anoon righte nymeþ hym *vnder* maynprise.
B.20.190   And hitte me *vnder* þe ere; vnneþe [may] ich here.
B.20.258   Han Officers *vnder* hem, and ech of hem a certein.
B.20.272   And youre noumbre *vnder* Notaries signe and neiþer mo ne lasse.'
B.20.276   That alle þynges *vnder* heuene ouȝte to ben in comune.
C.Pr.86   That han cure *vnder* crist and crownyng in tokene
C.Pr.203   To crache vs and alle oure kynde thogh we crope *vnder* benches;
C. 3.204   Ther ne is Cite *vnder* sonne ne noon so ryche reume
C. 6.43   And strengest vppon stede and styuest *vnder* gyrdel
C. 7.45   Y am nat luyred with loue but þer lygge ouht *vnder* þe t[h]umbe.
C. 9.27   Ac *vnder* his secrete seal treuthe sente hem a lettre
C. 9.138   For *vnder* godes secret seal here synnes ben keuered.
C. 9.139   For they bereth none bagges ne boteles *vnder* clokes,
C. 9.221   *Vnder* obedience to be and buxum to þe lawe:
C. 9.223   And *vnder* obedience be by dayes and by nyhtes;
C. 9.236   *Vnder* this obedience ar we vchone
C.10.50   And lyf[holie]st of lyf þat lyueth *vnder* sonne.
C.10.64   And *vnder* lynde vpon a launde lened y a stounde
C.11.154   Alle þe Clerkes *vnder* Crist ne couthe this assoile
C.11.247   That [ben] carpentares *vnder* Crist holy kirke to make
C.11.251   Laste ȝe be loste as þe laboreres were þat lab[o]red *vnder* Noe.
C.12.79   That al þe cristendoem *vnde[r]* Crist ne myhte me crache fro
              [helle]
C.12.94   Or eny science *vnder* sonne, the seuene ars and alle–
C.13.207   For is no creature *vnder* Crist þat can hymsulue make
C.14.155   Alle þe Clerkes *vnder* Crist ne couthe [þe skyle] assoile:
C.14.159   Was neuere creature *vnder* crist þat knewe wel þe bygynnyng
C.15.240   Þe worm and wonte *vnder* erthe and in water fisches,
C.16.125   Ne to be maire ouer men ne mynistre *vnder* kynges;
C.16.210   Alle þe sciences *vnder* sonne and alle þe sotil craftes
C.17.230   The heuedes of holy churche and tho that ben *vnder* hem,
C.19.84   Ne no medicyne *vnder* molde the man to hele brynge,
C.21.37   Bote *vnder* tribuyt and talage as tykes and cherles.
C.21.86   That [o] kyng cam with reson ykyuered *vnder* ensense.
C.21.88   Rihtwisnesse *vnder* reed gold, resones felawe;
C.21.296   And keuered hym *vnder* consayl of Caton the wyse:
C.21.347   Shal be coloured so queyntly and keuered *vnder* [o]ure sophistrie
C.22.17   Nede anoen riht nymeth hym *vnder* maynprise.
C.22.190   And hitte me *vnder* þe ere; vnnethe may ich here.

C.22.258 Haen officerys *vnder* hem and vch of hem a certeyne.
C.22.272 And ȝoure nombre *vnde[r]* notarie sygne and noþer mo ne lasse.'
C.22.276 That alle thynges *vnder* heuene ou[h]te to be in comune.

vnderfonge v *underfon v.* A 5 vndirfang (1) vndirfonge (2) vndirfongen (1)
 vndirfongiþ (1); B 8 vnderfeng (1) vnderfonge (1) vnderfonged (1)
 vnderfongen (4) vnderfongeþ (1); C 9 vnderfeng (1) vnderfonge (5)
 vnderfongen (2) vndirfenge (1)
A. 1.74   I *vndirfang* þe ferst and þi feiþ [þe] tauȝte.
A. 3.202 Þe pope wiþ his prelatis presentis *vndirfongiþ*,
A. 6.111 He is wondirliche welcome & faire *vndirfonge*.
A. 8.155 Dowel at þe day of dome is digneliche *vndirfongen*;
A.11.174 Fairere *vndirfonge* ne frendliere mad at ese
B. 1.76   I *vnderfeng* þee first and þ[i] feiþ [þee] tauȝte.
B. 3.215 The Pope [wiþ hise] prelates presentȝ *vnderfonge[þ]*,
B. 5.626 He is wonderly welcome and faire *vnderfongen*.
B. 7.177 Dowel at þe day of dome is digneliche *vnderfongen*;
B.10.231 Fairer *vnderfongen* ne frendlier at ese
B.11.118 That *vnderfonged* me atte font for oon of goddes chosene.
B.11.150 Wiþouten bede biddyng his boone was *vnderfongen*
B.15.106 And hatien to here harlotrie, and [au]ȝt to *vnderfonge*
C. 1.73   Y *vndirfenge* þe formeste and fre man the made.
C. 3.111 Ar he were *vnderfonge* fre and felawe in ȝoure rolles.
C. 3.271 The pope and alle prelates presentes *vnderfongen*
C. 7.279 Is wonderliche welcome and fayre *vnderfonge*;
C. 9.129 To *vnderfongen* hem fayre byfalleth for þe ryche
C. 9.323 Worth fayre *vnderfonge* byfore god þat tyme
C.12.53   That *vnderfeng* me at þe fonte for on of godes chosene.
C.12.85   Withouten bed[e] biddyng his bone was *vnderfonge*
C.16.260 And hatien harlotrie and to *vnderfonge* þe tythes

vnderlyng n *underling n.* B 1; C 1 vnderlynge
B. 6.46   Thouȝ he be þyn *vnderlyng* here wel may happe in heuene
C. 8.43   Thogh he be here thyn *vnderlynge* in heuene parauntur

vndernymeþ v *undernimen v.* B 4 vndernyme (1) vndernymeþ (1)
 vndernome (2); C 1 vndernome
B. 5.116 Whoso *vndernymeþ* me herof, I hate hym dedly after.
B.11.215 Ne *vndernyme* noȝt foule, for is noon wiþoute defaute.
B.13.281 And inobedient to ben *vndernome* of any lif lyuynge;
B.20.51   Whan nede ha[dde] *vndernome* me þus anoon I fil aslepe
C.22.51   Whenne nede hadde *vndernome* [me] thus anoen y ful aslepe

vndernymynge ger *underniminge ger.* C 1
C. 6.35   Vantyng vp my vaynglorie for eny *vndernymynge*;

vndernome > vndernymeþ

vnderpight ptp *underpicchen v.* B 1
B.16.23   Wiþ þre piles was it *vnderpight*; I parceyued it soone.

vndershored ptp *undershoren v.* C 1
C.18.47   And shaketh hit; ne were hit *vndershored* hit sholde nat stande.

vnderstand- > vnderstond-

vnderstonden v *understonden v.* A 2 vndirstonde; B 7 vnderstande (1)
 vnderstonde (5) vnderstonden (1); C 3 vnderstande
A. 7.49   For it arn þe deuelis disours I do þe to *vndirstonde*.
A. 9.90   And as dowel & dobet dede hem to *vndirstonde*.
B. 5.430 I am vnkynde ayeins [his] curteisie and kan nouȝt *vnderstonden* it,
B. 6.54   For it ben þe deueles disours, I do þe to *vnderstonde*.'
B. 8.100 And [as] dowel and dobet [dide] hem [to *vnderstonde*],
B.12.259 By þe po feet is *vnderstande*, as I haue lerned in Auynet,
B.14.279 Ac somdeel I shal seyen it, by so þow *vnderstonde*
B.15.472 [And by þe hond fedde foules [i]s folk *vnderstonde*
B.17.333 Thise þre þat I telle of ben þus to *vnderstonde*:
C. 3.399 And coueyte þe case, when thei couthe *vnderstande*,
C. 7.43   Y am vnkynde aȝen his cortesie [and] can nat *vnderstande* hit
C.19.313 Thise thre that y telle of thus ben [to] *vnderstande*:

vnderstondyng ger *understondinge ger.* A 1 vndirstonding; C 5
 vnderstandyng (1) vnderstondyng (1) vnderstondynge (3)
A.10.71   A[c] iche wiȝt in þis world þat haþ wys *vndirstonding*
C. 5.56   Clerkes ycrouned, of kynde *vnderstondynge*,
C.11.112 And hast *vnderstandyng* what a wolde mene
C.11.299 Ac lewede laborers of litel *vnderstondyng*
C.13.116 Thorw here luyther lyuynge and lewede *vnderstondynge*.
C.14.102 The[n] connynge clerkes of kynde *vnderstondynge*.

vndertaken v *undertaken v.* A 1 vndirtake; B 5 vndertake (2) vndertaken
 (2) vndertoke (1); C 5 vndertake (3) vndertaken (1) vndertoke (1)
A.11.109 Shuln wisse þe to dowel, I dar wel *vndirtake*.'
B.10.157 Shullen wissen þee to dowel, I dar [wel] *vndertake*.'
B.11.91   'And wherof serueþ law', quod lewtee, 'if no lif *vndertoke* it
B.13.132 He wol noȝt ayein holy writ speken, I dar *vndertake*.'
B.17.18   'Whoso wercheþ after þis writ, I wol *vndertaken*,
B.17.112 Ac er þis day þre daies I dar *vndertaken*

C.Pr.98   To *vndertake* þe tol of vntrewe sacrefice.
C. 3.296 And for to *vndertake* [to] trauaile for another
C.12.32   'And wherof serueth lawe,' quod leaute, ' and no lyf *vndertoke* [hit],
C.19.19   'And ho[so] worcheth aftur this writ, y wol *vndertaken*,
C.20.20   'Liberum dei Arbitrium for loue hath *vndertake*

vndeuoutliche adv *undevoutli adv.* B 1; C 1 vndeueouteliche
B.Pr.98   Arn doon *vndeuoutliche*; drede is at þe laste
C.Pr.126 Ar don *vndeueouteliche*; drede is at þe laste

vndignely adv *undigneli adv.* B 1
B.15.243 Thei vndoon it *vn[digne]ly*, þo doctours of lawe.

vndir > vnder; vndirfang -fenge > vnderfonge; vndir- > vnder-

vndo v *undon v.* B 4 vndo (3) vndoon (1); C 7 vndede (1) vndo (3)
 vndoen (1) vndoth (2)
B.13.157 *Vndo* it; lat þis doctour deme if dowel be þerInne.
B.15.243 Thei *vndoon* it vn[digne]ly, þo doctours of lawe.
B.18.319 Dukes of þis dymme place, anoon *vndo* þise yates
B.20.89   Wiþ deeþ þat is dredful to *vndo* vs alle!'
C. 2.41   And dauid *vndoth* hymself as þe doumbe sheweth:
C. 7.249 To opene and *vndo* be hye gate of heuene
C. 9.306 How danyel deuynede and *vndede* þe dremes of kynges,
C.20.272 'Princ[i]pes of this place, prest *vndo* this gates
C.20.340 Hit shal *vndo* vs deueles and down bryngen vs all.'
C.20.362 Dukes of this demme place, anoen *vndoth* this ȝates
C.22.89   With deth þat is dredful to *vndoen* vs alle!'

vndoynge ger *undoinge ger.* B 1
B.15.599 Daniel of hire *vndoynge* deuyned and seide

vndoon > vndo

vnesiliche adv *unesili adv.* B 1; C 1 vnesylyche
B.14.233 And his heued vnheled, *vnesiliche* ywrye
C.16.74   And his heued vnheled, *vnesylyche* ywrye

vnfettre v *unfeteren v.* A 1 vnfetere; B 1; C 1 vnfetere
A. 3.128 To *vnfetere* þe fals, fle where hym lykiþ.
B. 3.139 To *vnfettre* þe fals, fle where hym likeþ.
C. 3.177 To *vnfetere* the fals, fle wher hym liketh,

vnfolde v *unfolden v.(2)* A 2 vnfolde (1) vnfoldiþ (1); B 4 vnfolde (1)
 vnfolden (1) vnfoldeþ (2); C 4 vnfolde (1) vnfolden (1) vnfoldeth (2)
A. 2.55   And *vnfolde* þe feffement þat fals haþ ymakid;
A. 8.91   And peris at his preyour þe pardoun *vnfoldiþ*,
B. 2.73   And *vnfoldeþ* þe feffement that Fals hath ymaked.
B. 7.109 And Piers at his preiere þe pardon *vnfoldeþ*,
B.17.179 And to *vnfolde* þe fust, [for hym it bilongeþ,
B.17.185 *Vnfolden* or folden, my fust and my pawme
C. 2.75   And *vnfoldeth* the feffament þat fals hath ymaked.
C. 9.283 And [Peres] at his preeyre the pardon *vnfoldeth*
C.19.144 And to *vnfolde* þe fust, for hym hit bilongeth,
C.19.151 *Vnfolden* or folden, a fuste wyse or elles,

vnglade adj *unglad adj.* B 1
B.17.227 So þat þe holy goost gloweþ but as a [glede *vn]glade*

vngodly adv *ungodli adv.* B 1
B.10.330 That Gregories godchildren [*vngodly*] despended.

vngracious adj *ungracious adj.* A 1; B 2; C 2
A.10.211 *Vngracious* to gete loue or any good ellis,
B. 9.197 *Vngracious* to gete good or loue of þe peple;
B.10.396 Thouȝ hir goost be *vngracious* god for to plese.
C.10.296 *Vngracious* to gete good or loue of [þe] peple,
C.11.227 Thogh here gost be *vngracious* god for to plese.

vngraciousliche adv *ungraciousli adv.* B 1; C 1
B.15.133 [This] þat wiþ gile was geten *vngraciousliche* is [s]pended.
C.16.280 And þat with gyle was gete *vngraciousliche* be yspened.

vngraue ptp *ungraven ppl.* C 1
C. 4.127 Nother ygraue ne *vngraue*, of gold oþer of suluer,

vnhardy adj *unhardi adj.* B 4; C 2
B.Pr.180 [Ac] helden hem *vnhardy* and hir counseil feble,
B.13.123 I am *vnhardy*', quod he, 'to any wiȝt to preuen it.
B.17.111 He was *vnhardy*, that harlot, and hidde hym in Inferno.
B.18.83   For alle þei were *vnhardy* þat houed [þer] or stode
C.Pr.197 [Ac helden hem *vnhardy* and here conseil feble]
C.20.85   For alle [they were] *vnhardy* þat houed þer or stode

vnheled ptp *unhelen v.* B 2 vnheled (1) vnhiled (1); C 2
B.14.233 And his heued *vnheled*, vnesiliche ywrye
B.17.325 And if his hous be *vnhiled* and reyne on his bedde
C.16.74   And his heued *vnheled*, vnesylyche ywrye
C.19.305 And if his hous be *vnheled* and reyne on his bedde

vnhende adj *unhende adj.* B 1; C 1
B.20.186   'Sire yuele ytau3t Elde!' quod I, 'vnhende go wiþ þe!
C.22.186   'Syre euele yt[a]u3te Elde,' quod y, 'vnhende go with the!

vnhiled > vnheled

vnholy adj *unholi adj.* A 1; B 1; C 1
A.Pr.3   In abite as an Ermyte, vnholy of werkis,
B.Pr.3   In habite as an heremite, vnholy of werkes,
C.Pr.3   In abite as an heremite, vnholy of werkes,

vnitee n *unite n.* B 15 vnite (1) vnitee (14); C 18 vnite
B.19.328   And called þat hous vnitee, holy chirche on englissh.
B.19.344   'And Piers bern worþ ybroke; and þei þat ben in vnitee
B.19.356   Hastiliche into vnitee and holde we vs þere.
B.19.362   To deluen a dych depe aboute vnitee
B.19.380   Made vnitee holy chirche in holynesse stonde.
B.20.75   Into vnite holy chirche and holde we vs þere.
B.20.78   And crye we [on] al þe comune þat þei come to vnitee
B.20.204   'If þow wolt be wroken wend into vnitee
B.20.213   Thoru3 Contricion and Confession til I cam to vnitee.
B.20.227   And hadden almoost vnitee and holynesse adown.
B.20.245   To vnitee and holy chirche; ac o þyng I yow preye:
B.20.246   Holdeþ yow in vnitee, and haueþ noon enuye
B.20.297   In vnitee holy chirche Conscience held hym
B.20.316   Quod Contricion to Conscience, 'do hym come to vnitee,
B.20.330   Pees vnpynned it, was Porter of vnitee,
C. 3.336   Ac adiectif and sustantif vnite asken,
C. 3.395   That is vnite, acordaun[c]e in case, in gendre and in noumbre,
C. 5.189   Holde 3ow in vnite; and he þat oþer wolde
C.21.328   And calde þat hous vnite, holy chirche an englisch.
C.21.344   'And Peres berne worth broke and þei þat ben in vnite
C.21.356   Hastiliche [in]to vnite and holde we vs there.
C.21.362   To deluen a dich depe aboute vnite
C.21.380   Made vnite holi churche in holinesse stande.
C.22.75   Into vnite holi churche and halde we vs there.
C.22.78   And crye we on al þe comune þat thei come to vnite
C.22.204   'Yf thow wol[t] be wreke wende into vnite
C.22.213   Thorw contricion and confessioun til y cam to vnite.
C.22.227   And hadden almost vnite and holynesse adowne.
C.22.245   To vnite and holi churche; ac o thyng y 3ow praye:
C.22.246   Holdeth 3ow in vnite and haueth noen enuye
C.22.297   In vnite holi church Consience heeld hym
C.22.316   Quod contricion to Consience, 'do hym come to vnite
C.22.330   Pees vnpynned hyt, was porter of vnite,

vnioynen v *unjoinen v.* B 1; C 1
B.18.258   And al þe Iewene Ioye vnioynen and vnlouken;
C.20.266   And alle þe iewene ioye vnioynen and vnlouken;

vnkynde adj *unkinde adj.* A 1; B 20; C 16
A. 1.166   Vnkynde to here kyn & ek to alle cristene,
B. 1.192   Vnkynde to hire kyn and to alle cristene,
B. 5.270   Thow art an vnkynde creature; I kan þee no3t assoille
B. 5.430   I am vnkynde ayeins [his] curteisie and kan nou3t vnderstonden it,
B. 9.86   Allas þat a cristene creature shal be vnkynde til anoþer!
B.10.29   And moost vnkynde to þe commune þat moost catel weldeþ;
B.11.212   And be we no3t vnkynde of oure catel, ne of oure konnyng neiþer,
B.13.355   [Was] colomy þoru3 coueitise and vnkynde desiryng.
B.13.378   And boþe to kiþ and to kyn vnkynde of þat ich hadde;
B.14.22   Dobest [shal kepe it clene from vnkynde werkes].
B.15.524   Amonges vnkynde cristene for cristes loue he deyede,
B.16.42   And casteþ vp to þe crop vnkynde Neighebores,
B.16.149   That is kissynge and fair contenaunce and vnkynde wille.
B.17.219   To alle vnkynde creatures þat coueite to destruye
B.17.253   To alle vnkynde creatures; crist hymself witnesseþ:
B.17.254   Be vnkynde to þyn euenecristene and al þat þow kanst bidde,
B.17.264   Beþ no3t vnkynde, I conseille yow, to youre euenecristene.
B.17.272   For þat ben vnkynde to hise, hope I noon ooþer
B.17.276   For þat kynde dooþ vnkynde fordooþ, as þise corsede þeues,
B.17.277   Vnkynde cristene men, for coueitise and enuye
B.18.398   For I were an vnkynde kyng but I my kynde helpe,
C. 1.189   Vnkynde to here kyn and to alle cristene,
C. 6.294   Thow art an vnkynde creature; y can nat assoile
C. 7.43   Y am vnkynde a3en his cortesie [and] can nat vnderstande hit
C.14.19   Ac comunlyche connynge and vnkynde ryche[sse],
C.16.275   Vnk[ynd]e curatours to be kepares of 3oure soules.
C.17.275   Amonges v[n]kynde cristene in holy [kirke] was slawe
C.18.155   'Vnkynde and vnkunnynge!' quod Crist, and with a roep smoet hem
C.19.185   To alle vnkynde creatures þat coueyten to destruye
C.19.219   To alle vnkynde creatures, as Crist hymsulue witnesseth:
C.19.220   Be vnkynde to thyn emcristene and al þat thow canst bidde,
C.19.230   Beth nat vnkynde, y conseyle 3ow, to 3oure emcristene.
C.19.247   Excuse hem þat ben vnkynde and 3ut here [catel] ywonne
C.19.253   For þat ben vn[k]ynde to hise, hope 3e noen oþer

C.19.257   For þat kynde doth vnkynde fordoth, as this corsede theues,
C.19.258   Vnkynde cristene men, for coueytise and enuye
C.20.441   For y were an vnkynde kyng bote y my kyn helpe

vnkyndely adv *unkindeli adv.* A 1; B 1
A.10.183   For coueitise of catel vnkyndely be maried.
B. 9.160   For coueitise of catel vnkyndely ben [maried].

vnkyndenesse n *unkindenesse n.* A 1; B 11; C 9
A. 3.274   Vnkyndenesse is comaundour, & kyndenesse is banisshit.
B. 9.91   The commune for hir vnkyndenesse, I drede me, shul abye;
B.13.219   There vnkyndenesse and coueitise is, hungry contrees boþe.
B.14.73   Ac vnkyndenesse caristiam makeþ amonges cristen peple,
B.17.259   For vnkyndenesse quencheþ hym þat he kan no3t shyne
B.17.260   Ne brenne ne blase clere, fo[r] blowynge of vnkyndenesse.
B.17.268   That] Diues deyde, dampned for his vnkyndenesse
B.17.274   Thus is vnkyndenesse þe contrarie þat quencheþ, as it were,
B.17.348   That is coueitise and vnkyndenesse þat quencheþ goddes mercy;
B.17.349   For vnkyndenesse is þe contrarie of alle kynnes reson.
B.19.224   Coueitise and vnkyndenesse Cardinals hym to lede.
B.20.296   The while coueitise and vnkyndenesse Conscience assaillede.
C.15.188   There vnkyndenesse and coueytise [is], hungry contreys bothe.
C.19.225   For vnkyndenesse quencheth hym þat he can nat shine
C.19.226   Ne brenne ne blase clere for blowynge of vnkyndenesse.
C.19.234   That diues deyede, dampned for his vnkyndenesse
C.19.255   Thus is vnkyndenesse [the contrarie that] quencheth, as hit were,
C.19.328   That is coueitise and vnkyndenesse whiche quencheth godes mercy
C.19.329   For vnkyndenesse is þe contrarie of alle kyne resoun.
C.21.224   Coueytise and vnkyndenesse Cardynales hym [to] lede.
C.22.296   The while Couetyse and vnkyndenesse Consience assailede.

vnknytteþ v *unknitten v.* B 1; C 1 vnknytteth
B.18.215   The which vnknytteþ alle care and comsynge is of reste.
C.20.224   The which vnknytteth alle care and comsyng is of reste.

vnknowe ptp *unknowen v.* C 1
C.17.162   Thenne is lawe ylefte and leute vnknowe.

vnkonnynge prp *unconninge ppl.* B 2; C 3 vnconnynge (1) vnkunynge (1) vnkunnynge (1)
B.12.183   And þat is after person or parissh preest, [and] parauenture vnkonnynge
B.13.13   Thoru3 vnkonnynge curatours to incurable peynes;
C. 3.244   Vnconnynge is þat Consience a kyndom to sulle
C.15.16   Thorw vnkunynge curatours to incurable peynes;
C.18.155   'Vnkynde and vnkunnynge!' quod Crist, and with a roep smoet hem

vnkouþe adj *uncouth adj.* A 1 vncouþe; B 1
A. 8.139   Þat [vncouþe] kni3t[is] shal come þi kingdom to cleyme;
B. 7.161   That vnkouþe kny3tes shul come þi kyngdom to cleyme;

vnkun(n)ynge > vnkonnynge

vnlawefulliche adv *unlaufulli adv.* C 2 vnlaufulliche (1) vnlawefulliche (1)
C. 3.289   Tha[t] vnlaufulliche lyuen hauen large handes
C.11.253   That vnlawefulliche hadde ylyued al his lyf tyme

vnlek > vnlouken

vnlele adj *unlele adj.* C 1
C.13.69   Bothe louye and lene le[l]e and vnlele

vnlikyng prp *unliken v.* C 1
C. 7.23   Or lacke men or likene hem in vnlikyng manere

vnlofsum adj *unlofsom adj.* C 1
C.10.262   Ac lat he[r] be vnlouely and vnlofsum abedde,

vnloken > vnlouken

vnlosen v *unlosen v.* A 1 vnlose; B 2 vnlose (1) vnlosen (1); C 3 vnlose (2) vnloseth (1)
A.Pr.87   A[c] nou3t for loue of oure lord vnlose here lippes ones.
B.Pr.214   [Ac] no3t for loue of oure lord vnlose hire lippes ones.
B.17.142   Til hym [likede] and liste to vnlosen his fynger,
C.Pr.164   And nat for loue of oure lord vnlose here lyppes ones.
C. 1.197   Þat is þe lok of loue [þat] vnloseth grace
C.19.116   Til hym likede and luste to vnlose that fynger

vnlouken *unlouken v.* B 5 vnloken (1) vnlouke (2) vnlouken (1) vnloukeþ (1); C 6 vnlek (1) vnlouke (3) vnlouken (2)
B.12.110   To vnloken it at hir likyng, and to þe lewed peple
B.18.189   Leuestow þat yond light vnlouke my3te helle
B.18.258   And al þe Iewene Ioye vnioynen and vnlouken;
B.18.264   "Prynces of þis place, vnpynneþ and vnloukeþ,
B.18.316   Eft þe light bad vnlouke and Lucifer answerde
C. 7.251   A ful leel lady vnlek hit of grace
C. 9.143   Vnlouke his legges abrood or ligge at his ese,
C.14.55   To v[n]louken hit at here lykynge the lewed to helpe,

C.20.194   Leuest thow þat ȝone lihte *vnlouke* myhte helle
C.20.266   And alle þe iewene ioye vnioynen and *vnlouken*;
C.20.359   For efte þat lihte bade *vnlouke* [and lucifer answerede].

vnlouely adv *unloveli adv. &> vnlouelich* B 1; C 1
B. 5.356   Dorste lape of þat leuynges, so *vnlouely* [it] smauȝte.
C. 6.414   Durste lape of þat lyuynge, so *vnlouely* hit smauhte.

vnlouelich adj *unloveli adj.* B 1; C 2 vnlouely (1) vnloueliche (1)
B.12.246   And *vnlouelich* of ledene and looþ for to here.
C.10.262   Ac lat he[r] be *vnlouely* and vnlofsum abedde,
C.14.178   His le[d]ene is *vnloueliche* and lothliche his careyne

vnmaken v *unmaken v.* B 1
B.15.241   And matrimoyne for moneie maken and *vnmaken*,

vnmeble(s > vnmoebles

vnmesurable adj *unmesurable adj.* B 1
B.15.71   Ye moeuen materes *vnmesurable* to tellen of þe Trinite

vnmoebles adj *unmevable adj.* B 1; C 2 vnmeble (1) vnmebles (1)
B. 3.269   Moebles and *vnmoebles*, and al þow myȝt fynde,
C. 3.422   Mebles and *vnmebles*, man and alle [thynges],
C.10.187   Meble ne *vnmeble*, mete noþer drynke.

vnneþe adv *unethe adv.* A 1; B 2; C 2 vnnethe
A. 4.47   I am not hardy [for hym *vnneþe*] to loke.'
B. 4.60   I am noȝt hardy for hym *vnneþe* to loke.'
B.20.190   And hitte me vnder þe ere; *vnneþe* [may] ich here.
C. 4.63   Y am nat hardy for hym *vnnethe* to loke.'
C.22.190   And hitte me vnder þe ere; *vnnethe* may ich here.

unnit adj *unnit adj.* C 1
C. 5.10   In hele and [*unnit*] oen me apposede;

vnpikede v *unpiken v.* B 1; C 1 vnpiked
B.13.367   Or pryueliche his purs shook, *vnpikede* hise lokes.
C. 6.266   Or priueliche his pors shoke, *vnpiked* his lokes.

vnpynneþ v *unpinnen v.* B 3 vnpynned (2) vnpynneþ (1); C 2 vnpynned (1) vnpynnede (1)
B.11.113   And whan þe peple was plener comen þe porter *vnpynned* þe yate
B.18.264   "Prynces of þis place, *vnpynneþ* and vnloukeþ,
B.20.330   Pees *vnpynned* it, was Porter of vnitee,
C.12.48   And whan þe peple was plenere ycome þe porter *vnpynnede* þe gate
C.22.330   Pees *vnpynned* hyt, was porter of vnite,

vnpossible adj *unpossible adj.* A 1
A.11.229   Poul prouiþ it is *vnpossible*, riche men in heuene.

vnpunysshed ptp *unpunished ppl.* A 1 vnpunisshit; B 1; C 1 vnpunisched
A. 4.123   Be *vnpunisshit* at my power for peril of my soule,
B. 4.140   Ben *vnpunysshed* [at] my power for peril of my soule,
C. 4.137   Be *vnpunisched* in my power for perel of [my] soule

vnredy adj *unredi adj.(1)* C 1
C.12.216   An *vnredy* reue thy residue shal spene

vnresonable adj *unresonable adj.* B 2
B. 6.151   For it is an *vnresonable* Religion þat haþ riȝt noȝt of certein.'
B.15.461   Rude and *vnresonable*, rennynge wiþouten [keperes].

vnriȝtfully adv *unrightfulli adv.* B 1; C 1 vnrihtfulliche
B.19.245   And some to ryde and to recouere þat [*vnriȝt]fully* was wonne:
C.21.245   And somme to ryde & to rekeuere that *vnrihtfulliche* was wonne:

vnrihtfole adj *unrightful adj.* C 1
C.12.17   To restitute resonably for al *vnrihtfole* wynnynge.

vnrihtfulliche > vnriȝtfully

vnrobbed ptp *unrobbede ppl.* C 1
C.13.1   Ac wel worth pouerte for he may walke *vnrobbed*

vnrosted ptp *unrosted ppl.* B 1
B. 5.603   Tho Adam and Eue eten apples *vnrosted*:

vnsauerly > vnsauourly

vnsauory adj *unsavouri adj.* B 1
B.15.433   It is *vnsauory*, forsoþe, ysoden or ybake;

vnsauourly adv *unsavourili adv.* B 1; C 1 vnsauerly
B.13.43   Ac hir sauce was ouer sour and *vnsauourly* grounde
C.15.48   Ac here sauce was ouersour and *vnsauerly* ygrounde

vnseled ptp *unselen v.* B 1; C 1 vnselede
B.14.295   Wynneþ he noȝt wiþ wiȝtes false ne wiþ *vnseled* mesures,
C.16.130   Wynneth he nat with w[ih]tus false ne with *vnselede* mesures

vnsemely adj *unsemeli adj.* C 1
C. 1.55   'The dep dale and þe derk, so *vnsemely* to se to,

vnsesonable adj *unsesonable adj.* B 1
B.15.356   For þoruȝ werre and wikkede werkes and wederes *vn[s]esonable*

vnsewe > vnsowen

vnsittyng prp *unsittinge ppl.* C 2 vnsittyng (1) vnsittynge (1)
C. 3.208   *Vnsittyng* soffraunce, here suster, and hereslue
C. 4.189   And þat *vnsittynge* suffraunce ne sele ȝoure priue lettres

vnskilful adj *unskilful adj.* B 1; C 1
B.13.276   Of scornyng and of scoffyng and of *vnskilful* berynge;
C. 6.25   Scornare and *vnskilful* to hem þat skil shewede,

vnsold ptp *unsolde ppl.* A 1; B 1; C 1
A. 5.122   It hadde be *vnsold* þis seue ȝer, so me god helpe.
B. 5.206   It hadde ben *vnsold* þis seuen yer, so me god helpe.
C. 6.214   Hit hadde be *vnsold* this seuene ȝer, so me god helpe.

vnsowen v *unseuen v.* A 1 vnsewe; B 1; C 1
A. 5.48   Heo shulde *vnsewe* hire serke & sette þere an heire
B. 5.65   She sholde *vnsowen* hir serk and sette þere an heyre
C. 6.6   A sholde *vnsowen* here serk and sette þe[r] an hayre

vnspere v *unsperen v.* B 2 vnspere (1) vnspered (1); C 2 vnspere (1) vnspered (1)
B.18.86   The blood sprong doun by þe spere and *vnspered* [his] eiȝen.
B.18.262   A spirit spekeþ to helle and biddeþ *vnspere* þe yates:
C.20.88   The bloed sprang down by the spere and *vnspered* [his] yes.
C.20.270   A spirit speketh to helle and bit *vnspere* þe ȝates:

vnstable adj *unstable adj.* C 1
C.10.37   [A] bendeth and boweth, the body is so *vnstable*,

vnstedefast adj *unstedfast adj.* C 1
C. 3.387   And halt hem *vnstedefast* for hem lakketh case.

vntempred ptp *untempred ppl.* B 1
B. 9.105   Wolde neuere þe feiþful fader [h]is fiþele were *vntempred*

unþende adj *unthen v., OED unthende a.* B 1
B. 5.177   I ete þere *unþende* fissh and feble ale drynke.

vntidy adj *untidi adj.* B 1; C 3 vntidy (2) vntydy (1)
B.20.119   Wiþ *vntidy* tales he tened ful ofte
C. 3.87   Thow thei take hem *vntidy* thyng no tresoun þei ne halden hit;
C. 9.263   The tarre is *vntydy* þat to þe [tripe] bylongeth;
C.22.119   With *vntidy* tales he tened ful ofte

vntiled ptp1 *untilled ppl.* B 1
B.15.459   Heþen is to mene after heeþ and *vntiled* erþe,

vntyled ptp2 *untilen v.* B 1; C 1
B.14.253   Hadde þei no[on haunt] but of poore men; hir houses stoode *vntyled*.
C.16.93   Hadde they noen haunt bote of pore [men; here houses stoed *vntyled*].

vntyme n *untime n.* A 1; B 1
A.10.202   For in [*vn]tyme*, treweliche, betwyn m[a]n & womm[a]n
B. 9.189   For in *vntyme*, trewely, bitwene man and womman

vntrewe adj *untreue adj.* B 1; C 2
B.15.107   Tiþes [of *vn]trewe* þyng ytilied or chaffared,
C.Pr.98   To vndertake þe tol of *vntrewe* sacrefice.
C.11.235   Wittnesseth godes word þat was neuere *vntrewe*:

vnwedded ptp *unweddede ppl.* B 1; C 1
B.20.112   Amonges alle manere men, wedded and *vnwedded*,
C.22.112   Amonges alle manere men, wedded and *vnwedded*,

vnwise adj *unwise adj.* A 1; B 1; C 1 vnwyse
A. 9.84   [Ȝ]e wise suffriþ þe *vnwise* with ȝow to libbe,
B. 8.94   [Ye wise] suffreþ þe *vnwise* wiþ yow to libbe,
C.10.91   "Ȝe wordliche wyse, *vnwyse* þat ȝe suffre,

vnwisly adv *unwiseli adv.* A 1; B 1; C 1 vnwysly
A.11.278   Þanne wrouȝte I *vnwisly* wiþ alle þe wyt þat I lere,
B.10.394   Thanne wrouȝt I *vnwisly*, whatsoeuere ye preche.
C.11.221   Thenne wrouhte [we] *vnwysly* for alle ȝoure wyse techynge.

vnwittily adv *unwittili adv.* A 1; B 1; C 1 vnwittiliche
A. 3.95   '*Vnwittily*, [wy], wrouȝt hast þou ofte;
B. 3.106   '*Vnwittily*, [wye], wroȝt hastow ofte,
C. 3.134   And saide, '*vnwittiliche*, womman, wro[uh]t hastow ofte

vnwrast adj *unwreste adj.* C 1
C.20.311   Thenne were he *vnwrast* of his word þat witnesse is of treuthe.'

vnwriten ptp *unwriten ppl.* A 1; B 1; C 1
A.11.263   Or ellis [*vn*]writen for wykkid as witnessiþ þe gospel:
B.10.382   Or ellis *vnwriten* for wikkednesse as holy writ witnesseþ:
C.11.207   *Vnwriten* for som wikkednesse, as holy writ sheweth:

vp adv *up adv.* A 20 vp (19) vppe (1); B 30 vp (28) vppe (2); C 31
A.Pr.44   And risen *vp* wiþ ribaudrie as robertis knaues;
A.Pr.64   Þe moste meschief on molde is mountyng *vp* faste.
A.Pr.70   Comen *vp* knelynge to kissen his bulle.
A. 2.41   Was piȝt *vp* a pauyloun proud for þe nones,
A. 4.34   Þanne com pes into þe parlement & putte *vp* a bille
A. 4.44   Brekiþ *vp* my berne doris, beriþ awey my whete,
A. 4.58   But ȝif mede it make [þi] meschief is *vppe*,
A. 5.174   Þo risen *vp* in rape & ro[wn]eden togideris,
A. 5.220   Þanne sat sleuþe *vp* & seynide hym faste,
A. 6.79   Þe tour þere treuþe is hymself is *vp* to þe sonne.
A. 6.89   To weue [*vp*] þe wyket þat [þe wif] shette
A. 7.99   Dikeris & delueres dy[gg]eþ *vp* þe balkis.
A. 7.103   And summe to plese perkyn pykide *vp* þe wedis.
A. 7.200   Wiþ houndis bred & hors bred holde *vp* here hertis,
A. 7.248   Aris *vp* er ap[e]ti[t] ha[ue] eten his fille;
A. 8.74   But as wilde bestis wiþ wehe, & worþ *vp* togideris
A.11.58   Freris and faitours han founden *vp* suche questiouns
A.12.12   Skornfully þ[o] scripture she[t] *vp* h[ere] browes,
A.12.38   Þan held I *vp* myn handes to scripture þe wise
A.12.72   Than maunged I wit[h him] *vp* at þe fulle;
B.Pr.44   And risen [*vp*] wiþ ribaudie [as] Roberdes knaues;
B.Pr.67   The mooste meschief on Molde is mountyng [*vp*] faste.
B.Pr.73   Comen *vp* knelynge to kissen hi[s] bull[e].
B.Pr.123   Thanne loked *vp* a lunatik, a leene þyng wiþalle,
B. 4.47   [Th]anne com pees into [þe] parlement and putte [*vp*] a bille
B. 4.57   Brekeþ *vp* my bern[e] dore[s], bereþ awey my whete,
B. 4.72   But if Mede it make þi meschief is *vppe*,
B. 5.181   I cou[ȝ]e it [*vp*] in oure Cloistre þat al [þe] Couent woot it.'
B. 5.325   T[h]o risen *vp* in Rape and rouned togideres
B. 5.354   And kouȝed *vp* a cawdel in Clementes lappe.
B. 5.372   That I, Gloton, girte it *vp* er I hadde gon a myle,
B. 5.448   Thanne sat Sleuþe *vp* and seyned hym [faste]
B. 5.602   To wayuen *vp* þe wiket þat þe womman shette
B. 6.107   Dikeres and Delueres digged *vp* þe balkes;
B. 6.111   And somme to plese Perkyn piked *vp* þe wedes.
B. 6.214   Wiþ houndes breed and horse breed hoold *vp* hir hertes,
B. 6.264   [A]rys *vp* er Appetit haue eten his fille.
B. 7.92   But as wilde bestes with wehee worþen *vppe* and werchen,
B.10.72   Freres and faitours han founde [*vp*] swiche questions
B.11.410   And as I caste *vp* myne eiȝen oon loked on me.
B.11.432   Ac whan nede nymeþ hym *vp* for [nede] lest he sterue,
B.11.440   And I aroos *vp* riȝt wiþ þat and [reuerenced] hym [faire,
B.12.120   And leiden hand þeron to liften it *vp* loren here lif after.
B.12.191   Ther lewed þeues ben lolled *vp*; loke how þei be saued!
B.15.253   Lakkeþ ne loseþ ne lokeþ *vp* sterne,
B.15.593   And whan he lifte *vp* Laȝar þat leid was in graue
B.16.42   And casteþ *vp* to þe crop vnkynde Neighebores,
B.16.226   I roos *vp* and reuerenced hym and riȝt faire hym grette.
B.18.52   And poison on a poole þei putte *vp* to hise lippes
B.19.191   Anoon after an heigh *vp* into heuene
C.Pr.65   The moste meschief on molde mounteth *vp* faste.
C.Pr.71   Comen [*vp*] knel[yng] to kyssen his bull[e].
C. 2.134   Lokede *vp* to oure lord and alowed sayde:
C. 2.191   On hem þat loueth leccherye lyppeth *vp* and rydeth,
C. 4.45   Thenne cam p[ees] into [þe] parlement and putte *vp* a bille
C. 4.60   And breketh *vp* my bern[e] dores and [b]ereth awey my whete
C. 6.35   Vantyng *vp* my vaynglorie for eny vndernymynge;
C. 6.163   Y cou[ȝ]e hit *vp* in oure Cloystre þat al þe couent woet hit.'
C. 6.383   Tho rysen *vp* [in] rape and rounned togyderes
C. 6.412   And cowed *vp* a caudel in Clementis lappe.
C. 7.62   Thenne sat sleuthe *vp* and seynede hym ofte
C. 8.114   Dikares and deluares digged *vp* þe balkes;
C. 8.118   And somme to plese Perkyn [pykede *vp* þe] wedes.
C.11.52   Freres and faytours haen founde *vp* suche questions
C.12.181   Shal neuere spir sprynge *vp* ne spiek on straw kerne;
C.12.186   At the laste launceth *vp* whereby we lyuen all.
C.12.222   That lihtlich launseth *vp* litel while dureth
C.13.239   Ac when nede nymeth hym *vp* anoen he is aschamed
C.13.246   And [y] aroes *vp* riht with þat and reuerensed hym fayre
C.14.22   Druy[e]th *vp* dowel and distruyeth dobest.
C.14.130   There lewede theues ben lolled *vp*; loke how þei ben saued!
C.17.302   Tho he luft *vp* lasar þat layde was in graue
C.18.10   Thorw louely lokyng[e] hit lyueth and launseth *vp* blosmes.
C.18.20   Hit hadde schoriares to shuyuen hit *vp*, thre shides of o lenghe
C.18.25   'Thise thre shorriares,' quod he,' that bereth *vp* this plonte
C.18.143   And luft *vp* laȝar þat lay in his tombe;
C.18.242   Y roos *vp* and reuerensed god and riȝt fayre hym grette,

C.20.50   'Aue, raby,' quod þat ribaud, and redes shotte *vp* to his yes.
C.20.52   And with a pole poysen potten *vp* to his lippes
C.20.281   Ac [r]ise *vp*, Ragamoffyn, and [r]eche me alle þe barres
C.21.191   Anoon aftur an heyh *vp* into heuene

vp prep *up prep.* A 1 vpe; B 3; C 8 ope (1) vp (7)
A. 4.114   *Vpe* forfaiture of þat fe, who fynt hym [at douere],
B. 4.131   *V[p]* forfeture of þat fee, wh[o] fynt [hym] at Douere,
B. 5.414   Nouȝt twyes in two yer, and þanne [telle I *vp* gesse].
B.20.135   And ouertilte al his truþe wiþ 'tak þis *vp* amendement'.
C. 1.158   *Vp* man for his mysdedes the mercement he taxeth.
C. 2.77   'Al þat loueth and byleueth *vp* lykyng of mede,
C. 4.128   *Vp* forfeture of þat fee, ho fyndeth h[y]m ouerward,
C. 5.44   And so y leue in london and [*vp*] lond[on] bothe.
C. 9.331   Ac to triste *vp* this trionales, treuly, me thynketh
C. 9.334   *Vp* truste of ȝoure tresor trionales to haue,
C.12.230   So of rychesse *ope* rychesse ariste alle vices.
C.22.135   And ouertulde al his treuthe with 'taek this [*vp*] amendement.'

vp &> vp_so_doun

vp_so_doun adv *up-so-doun adv. phr.* B 1; C 1 vp_so_down
B.20.54   Torned it [tid] *vp so doun* and ouertilte þe roote,
C.22.54   Turned hit tyd *vp so down* and ouertulde þe rote

vpe > vp prep

vpholderes n *upholdere n.* A 1 vpholderis; B 1; C 2 vphalderes (1) vpholderes (1)
A. 5.166   Of *vpholderis* an hep, erliche be þe morewe,
B. 5.317   [Of] *vpholderes* an heep, erly by þe morwe,
C. 6.374   And of *vphalderes* an heep, [e]rly by þe morwe,
C.12.218   *Vpholderes* on þe hulle shal haue hit to sulle."

vpon adv *upon adv.* C 2 vpon (1) vppon (1)
C. 6.44   And louelokest to loke *vppon* a[nd] lykyngest abedde
C.18.190   And, sondry to se *vpon*, solus deus he hoteth.'

vpon prep *upon prep.* A 13; B 39; C 40 vpon (13) vppon (27)
A. 2.57   'Wyten & wytnessen þat wonen *vpon* erþe,
A. 2.130   And fauel *vpon* fair speche, fe[int]liche atirid.
A. 4.18   'Sette my sadil *vpon* suffre til I se my tyme,
A. 5.236   'Crist, þat on caluarie *vpon* þe [cros] diȝedist,
A. 5.239   Þi wil w[or]þe *vpon* me, as I haue wel deseruid
A. 8.88   Here penaunce & here purcatorie *vpon* þis pur erþe.
A. 8.166   *Vpon* trist of ȝour tresour trienalis to haue
A. 9.56   And vndir a lynde *vpon* a launde lenide I me a stounde
A.10.178   [Þus] þoruȝ curside caym cam care *vpon* alle,
A.11.28   On crois *vpon* caluarie, as clerkis vs techiþ,
A.11.98   But al lauȝinge he loutide & lokide *vpon* studie
A.11.173   Was neuere [gome] *vpon* þis ground, siþþe god makid heuene,
A.12.117   Þat barn bryng vs to blys þat bled *vpon* þe rode amen.
B.Pr.170   [And hangen it *vpon* þe cattes hals; þanne here we mowen]
B. 1.118   For þei leueden *vpon* [Lucifer] þat lyed in þis manere:
B. 1.156   Was neuere leef *vpon* lynde lighter þerafter,
B. 1.162   *Vpon* man for his mysdedes þe mercyment he taxeþ.
B. 2.75   Witeþ and witnesseþ þat wonieþ *vpon* erþe
B. 2.164   Sette Mede *vpon* a Sherreue shoed al newe,
B. 2.172   Sire Symonye hymself shal sitte *vpon* hir bakkes.
B. 3.312   And dyngen *vpon* Dauid eche day til eue;
B. 4.20   'Set my Sadel *vpon* suffre-til-I-se-my-tyme
B. 4.154   Waryn wisdom wynked *vpon* Mede
B. 4.173   And modiliche *vpon* Mede wiþ myȝt þe kyng loked,
B. 5.464   'Crist, þat on Caluarie *vpon* þe cros deidest,
B. 6.141   Diken or deluen or dyngen *vpon* sheues
B. 7.106   Hir penaunce and hir Purgatorie [*vp*]on þis [pure] erþe.
B. 7.188   *Vpon* trust of youre tresor triennals to haue,
B. 8.65   And vnder a lynde *vpon* a launde lened I a stounde
B. 9.102   Is moost yhated *vpon* erþe of hem þat ben in heuene;
B. 9.156   And þus þoruȝ cursed Caym cam care *vpon* erþe,
B.10.36   [On cros *vpon* caluarye as clerkes vs techeþ],
B.10.106   And leyden fautes *vpon* þe fader þat formede vs alle,
B.10.145   But al lauȝynge he louted and loked *vpon* Studie
B.10.230   Was neuere gome *vpon* þis ground, siþ god made [heuene],
B.11.170   And took it moises *vpon* þe mount alle men to lere].
B.12.294   The glose graunteþ *vpon* þat vers a greet mede to truþe.
B.13.113   And preynte *vpon* pacience to preie me be stille,
B.13.390   *Vpon* a cruwel coueitise m[y conscience] gan hange:
B.14.31   Thouȝ neuere greyn growed, ne grape *vpon* vyne,
B.14.80   Vengeaunce fil *vpon* hem for hir vile synnes;
B.16.157   Ac [to] þe [worldes ende] þi wikkednesse shal worþe *vpon* þiselue:
B.16.164   On cros *vpon* Caluarie crist took þe bataille
B.17.2   That took me a maundement *vpon* þe mount of Synay
B.18.72   *Vpon* a croos bisides crist; so was þe comune lawe.
B.18.77   That noon harlot were so hardy to leyen hond *vpon* hym.
B.18.87   Thanne fil þe knyȝt *vpon* knees and cryde [Iesu] mercy:

B.18.288 And in semblaunce of a serpent sete *vpon* þe Appultree
B.18.366 And for þat drynke today I deide *vpon* erþe.
B.19.41 And *vpon* Caluarie on cros ycrouned kyng of Iewes.
B.19.322 That crist *vpon* Caluarie for mankynde on pyned.
B.20.165 For care Conscience þo cryde *vpon* Elde
C. 1.12 'The tour *vppon* þe tofte,' quod she, 'treuthe is þerynne
C. 1.64 And afterward anhengede hym hey *vppon* an hellerne.
C. 1.152 Was neuer lef *vppon* lynde lyhtere theraftur\
C. 2.39 Y do hit *vppon* dauyd; the doumbe wil noȝt lyen:
C. 2.187 Wol Ryde *vppon* Rectores and ryche men deuoutours,
C. 2.188 And notaries [*vp*]on persones þat permuten ofte
C. 3.324 For god gaf salomon grace *vpon* erthe,
C. 4.20 Sette my sadel *vpon* soffre-tyl-y-se-my-tyme
C. 4.105 Summe radden resoun tho to haue reuthe *vppon* þat shrewe
C. 4.167 And modiliche *vppon* mede many tym[e] lokede
C. 4.168 And lourede *vppon* men of lawe and lyhtlych sayde:
C. 5.30 Or faytest *vppon* frydayes or festeday[es] in churches,
C. 5.177 Shal haue a knok *vppon* here crounes and incurable þe wounde:
C. 6.43 And strengest *vppon* stede and styuest vnder gyrdel
C. 6.66 A wroth his f[u]ste wrath; hadde [he] wesches at wille
C. 6.106 Bothe with stoon and with staf and stele *vppon* myn enemye;
C. 6.320 And haddest mercy *vppon* þat man for memento sake,
C. 8.204 Tho hadde [Peres] pitee *vppon* alle pore peple
C. 9.186 Here penaunce and here purgatorie *vppon* this puyre erthe
C. 9.228 And *vppon* sonendayes to cese goddes seruice to here,
C.10.64 And vnder lynde *vpon* a launde lened y a stounde
C.10.114 Disputyng *vppon* dowel day aftur other
C.11.83 But al lauhynge he louted and loked *vppon* stud[i]e,
C.13.77 And spele and spare to spene *vppon* þe nedfole
C.14.153 Ac why þat [on] theef *vppon* þe cros cryant hym ȝelde
C.14.167 Was neuere man *vppon* molde þat myhte hit aspie.
C.15.24 And so y musede *vppon* þis matere þat me lust to slepe.
C.15.120 And preynte *vppon* pacience to preie me be stille
C.17.234 That with moneye maynteyneth men [t]o werre *vppon* cristene
C.18.53 I toted *vpon* þ[e] tree tho and thenne toek y hede
C.19.2 That toek me a maundement *vpon* þe mont of synay
C.19.24 Lo! here in my lappe þat leuede *vpon* þat lettre,
C.19.94 And ȝut bote they l[e]ue lelly *vpon* þat litel baby,
C.19.201 And as wex withouten more *vpo[n]* a warm glede
C.20.51 [Thei] nayled hym with thre nayles naked *vpon* a rode
C.20.74 *Vppon* cros bisyde Crist; so was þe comune lawe.
C.20.89 Tho ful the knyhte *vppon* knees and criede iesu mercy:
C.21.41 And *vpon* Caluarie on cros ycrouned kyng of iewes.
C.21.322 That Crist *vpon* Caluary for mankynde on peyned.
C.22.165 For care Consience tho cryede *vpon* elde

vppe > vp adv; vppon > vpon

vpward adv *upward adv.* A 2; B 2; C 2
A. 5.19 And turnide *vpward* here tail in tokynyng of drede
A. 5.253 Criede *vpward* to crist & to his [clene] modir
B. 5.19 [And] turned *vpward* hire tai[l] in tokenynge of drede
B. 5.511 Cride *vpward* to Crist and to his clene moder
C. 5.121 And turned *vpward* here tayl in tokenynge of drede
C. 7.156 Criede *vpward* to Crist and to his clene moder

vrie n prop *n.i.d.* A 1; B 1 vries; C 1 vrye
A.11.288 Or who dede wers þanne dauid þat *vrie* destroyede,
B.10.429 Or who [dide] worse þan Dauid þat *vries* deeþ conspired,
C.11.263 Or dauid þe douhty þat de[uyn]ed how *vrye*

vs > we

vsage n *usage n.* B 1
B. 7.88 Lat *vsage* be youre solas of seintes lyues redyng.

vscher> vsher

vsen v *usen v.* A 4 vsen (2) vside (1) vsiþ (1); B 13 vse (3) vsed (2)
  vsede (1) vsedestow (1) vsen (1) vseþ (4) yvsed (1); C 15 vysen (1)
  vse (4) vsed (3) vsede (2) vsedest (1) vsen (2) yvysed (1) yvsed (1)
A. 5.139 Whanne it com in cuppemel; þat craft my wyf *vside*.
A. 7.137 Ones at noon is ynouȝ þat no werk *vsiþ*;
A. 7.223 Seruus nequam had a nam, & for he nolde it *vsen*,
A.11.183 Actif it is hoten; [husbondis] it *vsen*,
B. 1.149 May no synne be on hym seene þat *vseþ* þat spice,
B. 3.240 And he þat *vseþ* noȝt þe lyf of vsurie,
B. 3.313 Huntynge or haukynge if any of hem *vse*
B. 5.223 [Whan] it cam In cuppemele, þis craft my wif *vsed*.
B. 5.227 And neuere wikkedly weye ne wikke chaffare *vse*,
B. 5.237 '*Vsedestow* euere vsurie', quod Repentaunce, 'in al þi lif tyme?'
B. 6.239 Seruus nequam hadde a Mnam and for he [n]olde [it *vse*]
B.10.134 And þo þat *vseþ* þise hauylons [for] to blende mennes wittes,
B.15.416 And ben manered after Makometh þat no man *vseþ* trouþe.
B.16.148 And which tokne to þis day to muche is *yvsed*,
B.17.49 Tho þat lernen þi lawe wol litel while *vsen* it.'

B.18.379 It is noȝt *vsed* in erþe to hangen a feloun
B.20.66 Defyed alle falsnesse and folk þat it *vsede*;
C. 3.110 What maner muster oþer marchandise he *vsed*
C. 3.466 Haukyng or huntyng yf eny of hem hit *vse*
C. 6.231 When hit cam in coppemele; this crafte my wyf *vsede*.
C. 6.239 *Vsedest* [thow] euere vsurye in al thy lyf tyme?'
C. 9.103 And lymes to labory with and lollares lyf *vsen*
C. 9.155 And can eny craft in caes he wolde hit *vse*,
C.10.126 And what lyues they lyue and what lawe þei *vsen*
C.11.109 Yf thow hit *vse* oþer haunte, haue god my treuthe,
C.12.89 'Lo! lordes, what leute dede and leele dome *yvsed*.
C.15.196 'Hastow *vsed* or haunted al thy lyf tyme?'
C.18.174 Wo to tho þat thy wyles *vysen* to þe wo[r]ldes ende:
C.19.47 Tho þat lerneth thy lawe wollen litel while hit *vse*.'
C.20.339 The which lyf and lawe, be hit longe *yvysed*,
C.20.421 Hit is nat *vsed* [i]n erthe to hangen [a] felo[n]
C.22.66 Defyede alle falsnesse and folke þat hit *vsede*

vsererus > vsurer

vsher n *usher n.* B 1; C 1 vscher
B.15.378 [And as *vsher* vnder hym to fourmen vs alle
C.17.113 And flaterrere for his *vscher*, ferly me thynketh.

vsure > vsurie

vsurer n *usurere n.* B 2 vsureres (1) vsurers (1); C 4 vsererus (1) vsurer
  (2) vsurers (1)
B.11.284 For masses ne for matyns, noȝt hir mete of *vsureres*,
B.15.85 Of *vsurers*, of hoores, of Auarouse chapmen,
C. 3.110 That *vsurers* oþer regraters for eny skynes ȝeftes
C. 6.306 Then an errant *vsurer*, haue god my treuthe,
C. 6.339 Repente þe anon,' quod repentaunce ryhte to the *vsurer*,
C.16.261 Of *vsererus*, of hores, of alle euel wynnynges,

vsurie n *usurie n.* A 2 vsure (1) vsurie (1); B 7 vsure (3) vsurie (4); C 5
  vsure (3) vsurye (2)
A. 2.63 And al þe Ile of *vsurie*, & auarice þe faste,
A. 8.40 *Vsure*, & auarice, & oþes I defende,
B. 2.87 That is *vsure* and Auarice; al I hem graunte
B. 2.176 As [de]uoutrye and diuorses and derne *vsurie*,
B. 3.240 And he þat vseþ noȝt þe lyf of *vsurie*,
B. 5.237 '*Vsedestow* euere *vsurie*', quod Repentaunce, 'in al þi lif tyme?'
B. 7.83 To yelden hem þat yeueþ hem and yet *vsure* moore:
B.18.106 But [as] barayne be and [by] *vsurie* [libben],
B.19.350 Wheiþer he wynne wiþ right, wiþ wrong or wiþ *vsure*.'
C. 2.94 With *vsurye* and Auaryce and other fals sleythus
C. 6.239 Vsedest [thow] euere *vsurye* in al thy lyf tyme?'
C. 6.303 There shal he wite witturly what *vsure* is to mene
C.20.109 [But] as bareyne be and by *vsure* libbe,
C.21.350 Where he wynne with riht, with wrong or with *vsure*.'

vuel > yuel

V

vayne adj *vein adj.* C 1
C. 2.104   With spiserye, speke ydelnesse in *vayne* spe[ch]e and spene

vaynglorie n *veinglorie n.* C 1
C. 6.35   Vantyng vp my *vaynglorie* for eny vndernymynge;

vayre > fair

vale n *vale n.* B 1; C 1
B.18.369   Til þe vendage falle in þe *vale* of Iosaphat,
C.20.411   Til þe ventage valle in þe *vale* of Iosophat

valewe > value; valle > falle

value n *value n.* A 1; B 1; C 1 valewe
A.11.34   Ȝiue hem to here ȝerisȝiue þe *value* of a grote.
B.10.48   ȝyue hem to hir yeresȝyue þe [*value*] of a grote.
C.13.200   Is no vertue so fair ne of *valewe* ne profit

vanysshed v *vanishen v.* B 1; C 3 vansche (1) vanschede (2)
B.12.297   And muche murþe and manhod;' and riȝt wiþ þat he *vanysshed.*
C.14.217   For al worth as god wol;' and þerwith he *vanschede.*
C.15.8   And *vansche* alle my vertues and my fayre lotus;
C.15.23   And when he hadde ysaide so, how sodeynliche he *vanschede.*

vantyng ger *vaunting ger.* C 1
C. 6.35   *Vantyng* vp my vaynglorie for eny vndernymynge;

variable adj *variable adj.* C 1
C.18.69   Somme of vs soethfaste and somme *variable,*

vaunsed ptp *vauncen v.* C 1
C. 3.36   That he ne worth furste *vaunsed,* for y am byknowe

vauntwarde n *vauntwarde n.* B 1; C 2 faumewarde (1) Vawwarde (1)
B.20.95   Elde þe hoore; [he] was in þe *vauntwarde*
C. 5.58   Ne fyhte in no *faumewarde* ne his foe greue:
C.22.95   Elde þe hore; he was in þe *Vawwarde*

veille n *veil n.(2)* A 1 veil; B 1; C 1 veile
A. 5.214   Til Vigilate [þe *veil*] fet watir [at] his eiȝen,
B. 5.442   Til vigilate þe *veille* fette water at hise eiȝen
C. 7.56   Til vigilate the *veile* fette water at his eyus

vele > fele; velynge > felyng

vendage n *vendage n.* B 1; C 1 ventage
B.18.369   Til þe *vendage* falle in þe vale of Iosaphat,
C.20.411   Til þe *ventage* valle in þe vale of Iosophat

venemouste > venymouste

venge v *vengen v.* A 1; B 1; C 3 venge (2) venged (1)
A. 5.106   And þat makiþ me so ma[t] for I ne may me *venge.'*
B. 5.129   And þat makeþ me [so mat], for I ne may me *venge.*
C. 6.74   *Venged* me vele tymes other vrete myself withynne
C. 6.94   And þat maketh me so megre for y ne may me *venge.*
C.19.106   Alle manere men and thogh y myhte *venge*

vengeaunce n *vengeaunce n.* A 1; B 12; C 11 vengeance (2) vengeaunce (3) veniance (1) veniaunce (5)
A. 3.239   Why þe *vengeaunce* fel on saul & on his children?
B. 3.260   Whi þ[at] *vengeaunce* fel on Saul and on his children?
B. 6.144   And al is þoruȝ suffraunce þat *vengeaunce* yow ne takeþ.
B. 6.225   Loue hem and lakke hem noȝt; lat god take þe *vengeaunce;*
B. 9.98   And [dredeþ hym] noȝt for drede of *vengeaunce* dooþ þerfore þe bettre;
B.11.379   Suffraunce is a souerayn vertue, and a swift *vengeaunce.*
B.14.80   *Vengeaunce* fil vpon hem for hir vile synnes;
B.15.261   In ensample we sholde do so, and take no *vengeaunce*
B.17.292   "*Vengeaunce,* vengeaunce! forȝyue be it neuere
B.17.292   "Vengeaunce, *vengeaunce!* forȝyue be it neuere
B.17.294   Thus "*vengeaunce,* vengeaunce!" verrey charite askeþ.
B.17.294   Thus "vengeaunce, *vengeaunce!*" verrey charite askeþ.
B.18.94   'For þis foule vileynye *vengeaunce* to yow falle!
C.Pr.115   And al was for *vengeance* he bet noght his children
C.Pr.117   God was wel þe wrother and took þe raþer *vengeance.*

C.Pr.121   God shal take *vengeaunce* on alle suche prestis
C. 3.410   Agaynes godes comandement, god tok such a *vengeaunce*
C.14.69   And do we as dauid techeth for doute of godes *veniance:*
C.19.273   "*Veniaunce,* veniaunce! forȝeue be hit neuere
C.19.273   "Veniaunce, *veniaunce!* forȝeue be hit neuere
C.19.275   Thus "*veniaunce,* veniaunce!" verray charite asketh
C.19.275   Thus "veniaunce, *veniaunce!*" verray charite asketh.
C.20.97   'For þis [fou]l vilanye *vengeaunce* [to] ȝow [f]all[e]!
C.20.434   And so of alle wykkede y wol here take *veniaunce.*

venial adj *venial adj.* B 2
B.14.84   Which dryueþ awey dedly synne and dooþ it to be *venial.*
B.14.93   Ther contricion dooþ but dryueþ it doun into a *venial* synne

venia(u)nce > vengeaunce

venym n *venim n.* A 1; B 4 venym (3) venymes (1); C 4 venym (3) venymes (1)
A. 5.69   '*Venym,* [or] verious, or vynegre I trowe,
B.15.560   "Dos ecclesie þis day haþ ydronke *venym*
B.18.152   For *venym* fordooþ venym, [þer fecche I euydence
B.18.152   For venym fordooþ *venym,* [þer fecche I euydence
B.18.154   For of alle *venymes* foulest is þe scorpion;
C.17.223   "Dos ecclesie this day hath ydronke *venym*
C.20.155   For *venym* fordoth venym, þer feche y euydence
C.20.155   For venym fordoth *venym,* þer feche y euydence
C.20.157   For of alle *venymes* [fou]lest is the scorpioun;

venymouste n *venimouste n.* B 1; C 1 venemouste
B.18.157   The first *venymouste,* þoruȝ [vertu] of hymselue.
C.20.160   The [f]erste *venemouste,* thorw vertu of hymsulue.

venyson n *venesoun n.* B 2; C 1 venisoun
B.Pr.190   But fedeþ hym al wiþ *venyson,* defame we hym neuere;
B.15.463   He fedde hem wiþ no *venyson* ne fesauntȝ ybake
C. 9.93   And colde flesche and fische as *venisoun* were bake;

ventage > vendage

verilyche adv *verreili adv.* A 1
A.12.28   "Quid est ueritas?" quod he; "*verilyche* tel vs."

verious n *verjous n.* A 1
A. 5.69   'Venym, [or] *verious,* or vynegre I trowe,

vernycle n *vernicle n.* A 1 vernicle; B 1; C 1 vernicle
A. 6.11   And þe *vernicle* beforn for men shulde knowe
B. 5.523   And þe *vernycle* bifore, for men sholde knowe
C. 7.168   And þe *vernicle* bifore for men sholde yknowe

verray adj *verrei adj.* B 3 verray (2) verrey (1); C 4
B.17.294   Thus "vengeaunce, vengeaunce!" *verrey* charite askeþ.
B.19.153   *Verray* m[a]n bifore hem alle and forþ wiþ hem yede.
B.19.419   Forþi', quod þis vicory, 'by *verray* god I wolde
C. 6.438   For y vowe to *verray* god, for hungur or furste,
C.19.275   Thus "veniaunce, veniaunce!" *verray* charite asketh.
C.21.153   *Verray* man bifore [hem] alle, and forth with hem ȝede.
C.21.419   Forthy,' quod this vicory, 'bi *verray* god y wolde

verred v *OED ver v.2* B 1
B.15.268   Pacientes Vincunt verbi gracia, and [*verred*] ensamples manye.

verrey > verray

vers n *verse n.* B 3
B.Pr.143   Thanne [comsed] al þe commune crye in *vers* of latyn
B.12.294   The glose graunteþ vpon þat *vers* a greet mede to truþe.
B.15.82   Gooþ to þe glose of þ[e] *vers,* ye grete clerkes;

verset n *verset n.* B 1; C 1
B.12.189   Dominus pars hereditatis mee is a murye *verset*
C.14.128   Dominus pars hereditatis [mee] is A merye *verset;*

versifie v *versifien v.* B 1; C 1 versifye
B.15.374   [That kan *versifie* faire ne formaliche enditen],
C.17.110   þat can *versifye* vayre or formallych endite

vertue n *vertu n.* A 1 vertues; B 27 vertu (1) vertue (5) vertues (21); C 28 vertu (1) vertue (4) vertues (23)

A. 9.70   Arn þre faire *vertues*, & ben not f[e]r to fynde.
B.Pr.103 Amonges foure *vertues*, [most vertuous of alle],
B. 1.152 And [ek] þe pl[ante] of pees, moost precious of *vertues*.
B. 2.77 Than for any *vertue* or fairnesse or any free kynde.
B. 8.79 Arn þre faire *vertues*, and ben noȝt fer to fynde.
B.11.379 Suffraunce is a souerayn *vertue*, and a swift vengeaunce.
B.14.37 Vitailles of grete *vertues* for alle manere beestes
B.18.120 For þe *vertue* þat hire folwede afered was she neuere.
B.18.157 The first venymouste, þoruȝ [*vertu*] of hymselue.
B.18.318 [The] lord of myght and of ma[y]n and alle manere *vertues*,
B.19.274 And Grace gaf [Piers] greynes, Cardynal[es] *vertues*,
B.19.311 Among þ[e] foure *vertues* and vices destruye.
B.19.314 And so doon vices *vertues*; [f]orþi', quod Piers,
B.19.316 And tilieþ [to] hir techynge þe Cardynale *vertues*.'
B.19.337 Conscience and alle cristene and Cardinale *vertues*,
B.19.343 [Th]e sedes [þat sire] Piers [sew], þe Cardynale *vertues*.
B.19.393 'That is my conseil', quod Conscience, 'and Cardinale *vertues*;
B.19.407 But Conscience [be þi] comune[s] and Cardinale *vertues*
B.19.411 Man to me þat me kouþe telle of Cardynale *vertues*,
B.19.452 The counseil of Conscience or Cardinale *vertues*
B.19.456 And alle þo faire *vertues* as vices þei semeþ.
B.20.21 Wiþouten conseil of Conscience or Cardynale *vertues*,
B.20.23 For is no *vertue* bi fer to Spiritus temperancie,
B.20.34 [God] gouerneþ alle goode *vertues*.
B.20.73 Ouer kynde cristene and Cardynale *vertues*.
B.20.122 Ouercome Conscience and Cardinale *vertues*;
B.20.149 And prike[d] forþ wiþ pride; preiseþ he no *vertue*,
B.20.303 That wiþ Conscience acordede and Cardynale *vertues*.
C.Pr.131 Amonge foure *vertues*, most vertuous of vertues,
C.Pr.131 Amonge foure vertues, most vertuous of *vertues*,
C. 1.148 Loue is [þe] plonte of pees, most precious of *vertues*,
C.10.77 Aren thre fayre *vertues* and ben nat fer to fynde.
C.12.177 Preueth pacient pouerte prince of alle *vertues*.
C.13.200 Is no *vertue* so fair ne of valewe ne profit
C.15.8 And vansche alle my *vertues* and my fayre lotus;
C.15.275 And þat is charite, chaumpion chief of all *vertues*,
C.20.123 For þe *vertue* þat her folewede afered was she neuere.
C.20.160 The [f]erste venemouste, thorw *vertu* of hymsulue.
C.21.274 And grace gaf Peres graynes, cardinales *vertues*,
C.21.311 Among th[e] foure *vertues* and vices distruye.
C.21.314 And so doth vices *vertues*; forthy,' quod [Peres],
C.21.316 And tulieth [to] here techynge the cardinal *vertues*.'
C.21.337 Consience and alle cristene and cardinale *vertues*,
C.21.343 Þe sedes that sire [Peres] sewe, þe cardinale *vertues*.
C.21.393 'That is my conseil,' quod Consience, 'and cardinale *vertues*,
C.21.407 Bote Consience [be] thy comune[s] and cardinale *vertues*
C.21.411 Man to me þat me couthe telle of cardinal[e] *vertues*
C.21.452 The conseyl of Consience or cardinal[e] *vertues*
C.21.456 And al tho fayre *vertues* as vises thei semeth.
C.22.21 Withouten consail of Consience or cardinale *vertues*
C.22.23 [For is no *vertue* by fer to spiritus temperancie],
C.22.34 God gouerneth all gode *vertues*.
C.22.73 Ouer kynde cristene and cardinale *vertues*.
C.22.122 Ouercome Consience and cardinal *vertues*
C.22.149 And prike[d] forth with pruyde; preyseth he no *vertue*
C.22.303 That with Consience acordede and cardinal *vertues*.

vertuous adj *vertuous adj.* B 1; C 2
B.Pr.103 Amonges foure vertues, [most *vertuous* of alle],
C.Pr.131 Amonge foure vertues, most *vertuous* of vertues,
C.18.88 Thenne is virginite, more *vertuous* and fayrest, as in heuene,

vesture n *vesture n.* A 1; B 1; C 1
A. 1.23 Þat on is *vesture* fro chele þe to saue;
B. 1.23 That oon [is] *vesture* from [chele] þee to saue;
C. 1.23 The firste is fode and *vesture* þe seconde

vicary > vicory

vyce n *vice n.* A 1 vices; B 3 vices; C 6 vyce (1) vices (4) vises (1)
A.10.76 Þanne is dowel a duc þat destroyeþ *vices*,
B.19.311 Among þ[e] foure vertues and *vices* destruye.
B.19.314 And so doon *vices* vertues; [f]orþi, quod Piers,
B.19.456 And alle þo faire vertues as *vices* þei semeþ.
C. 6.20 Demed for here vuel *vices* and exitede oþere
C.12.230 So of rychesse ope rychesse ariste alle *vices*.
C.16.373 He halt hit for a *vyce* and a foule shame
C.21.311 Among th[e] foure vertues and *vices* distruye.
C.21.314 And so doth *vices* vertues; forthy,' quod [Peres],
C.21.456 And al tho fayre vertues as *vises* thei semeth.

vicory n *vicarie n.(1)* B 2; C 4 vycary (1) vicory (3)
B.19.409 'Thanne is many a [lif] lost', quod a lewed *vicory*.

B.19.419 Forþi', quod þis *vicory*, 'by verray god I wolde
C.14.70 For clergy is cristes *vycary* to conforte and to cure;
C.21.409 'Thenne is many [a lyf] ylost,' quod a lewed *vicory*.
C.21.419 Forthy,' quod this *vicory*, 'bi verray god y wolde
C.21.480 The *vicory* hadde fer hoem and [fayre] toek his leue

victorie n *victorie n.(1)* B 2; C 1
B. 3.334 That ȝyuen ȝiftes, [takeþ yeme], þe *victorie* wynneþ
B. 3.352 That þeiȝ we wynne worship and with Mede haue *victorie*,
C. 3.486 That ȝeueth ȝeftes, taketh ȝeme, the *victorie* a wynneth

vigilies n *vigilie n.* B 1; C 2
B. 5.409 *Vigilies* and fastyng dayes, alle þise late I passe,
C. 7.25 *Vigilies* and fastyngdayes y can forȝeten hem alle
C. 9.233 *Vigilies* and fastyngdays forthermore to knowe

vii > seuen

viker n *vicare n.* B 1
B.19.480 The *viker* hadde fer hoom and faire took his leeue

vilanye > vilenye

vile adj *vile adj.* B 1
B.14.80 Vengeaunce fil vpon hem for hir *vile* synnes;

vileynye n *vileinie n.* B 1; C 2 vilanye (1) vilony (1)
B.18.94 'For þis foule *vileynye* vengeaunce to yow falle!
C. 6.433 The *vilony* of my foule mouthe and of my foule mawe:
C.20.97 'For þis [fou]l *vilanye* vengeaunce [to] ȝow [f]all[e]!

vyne n *vine n.(1)* B 1; C 1 vine
B.14.31 Thouȝ neuere greyn growed, ne grape vpon *vyne*,
C. 2.28 For shal neuer breere bere berye as a *vine*,

vynegre n *vinegre n.* A 1
A. 5.69 'Venym, [or] verious, or *vynegre* I trowe,

virgile n prop *n.i.d.* B 1
B.12.43 Aristotle and oþere mo, ypocras and *virgile*,

virginite n *virginite n.* B 1; C 1
B.16.203 Wedlok and widwehode wiþ *virginite* ynempned,
C.18.88 Thenne is *virginite*, more vertuous and fayrest, as in heuene,

virres n *Lat. vir + ME gen.* B 2
B.10.326 And Barons wiþ Erles beten hem þoruȝ Beatus *virres* techyng;
B.13.53 /And he brouȝte vs of Beati quorum of Beatus *virres* makyng,

visage n *visage n.* B 1
B.18.337 Thus ylik a Lusard wiþ a lady *visage*

viseden v *visen v.* B 1
B.12.130 [Dyuyneris] toforn vs [*viseden* and markeden]

vises > vyce

visited v *visiten v.* B 1; C 2 visited (1) visitede (1)
B. 5.405 I *visited* neuere feble men ne fettred [men] in puttes.
C. 7.21 Y *visitede* neuere feble man ne fetered man in prisone.
C.16.330 And when he hath *visited* thus fetured folk and oþer folke pore,

visitynge ger *visitinge ger.* B 1
B. 2.177 To bere Bisshopes aboute abrood in *visitynge*.

vitailes > vitailles

vitaillers n *vitailer n.* B 1; C 1 vitalers
B. 2.61 Forgoers and *vitaillers* and [v]okettes of þe Arches;
C. 2.63 Vorgoers and *vitalers* and voketes of the Arches;

vitailles n *vitaile n.* A 1 vitailes; B 4; C 3 vitailes (2) vitayles (1)
A. 2.142 And fetten oure *vitailes* [of] fornicatouris,
B. 2.181 And fecchen [oure] *vitailles* at Fornicatores.
B. 5.436 Boþe flessh and fissh and manye oþere *vitailles*;
B.13.216 Thanne hadde Pacience, as pilgrymes han, in his poke *vitailles*:
B.14.37 *Vitailles* of grete vertues for alle manere beestes
C. 2.194 And fecchen oure *vitailes* a[t] fornicatores,
C. 7.49 Bothe flesch and fysch and *vitailes* kepte so longe
C.15.185 Thenne hadde pacience, as pilgrimes haen, in h[is] poke *vitayles*,

vitalers > vitaillers

voideþ v *voiden v.* B 1
B.14.95 Ac satisfaccion sekeþ out þe roote, and boþe sleeþ and *voideþ*,

vois n *voice n.* B 3; C 3 vois (2) voys (1)
B.15.20 At mydnyght, at mydday, my *vois* so is knowe
B.15.594 And vnder stoon deed and stank; wiþ stif *vois* hym callede:
B.18.263 A *vois* loude in þat light to lucifer crieþ,
C.16.171 At mydnyhte, at mydday, my *vois* is so yknowe
C.20.271 A *vois* loude in þat liht to lucifer saide,

C.20.360   'What lord artow?' quod lucifer; a *voys* aloude saide:

vokettes n *vocat n.* B 1; C 1 voketes
B. 2.61   Forgoers and vitaillers and [*v*]*okettes* of þe Arches;
C. 2.63   Vorgoers and vitalers and *voketes* of the Arches;

vorgoers > forgoer; voues > vowes

vowe v *vouen v.(2)* C 1
C. 6.438   For y *vowe* to verray god, for hungur or furste,

vowes n *voue n.(1)* C 2 voues (1) vowes (1)
C.Pr.69   Of falsness[e of] fastyng[e and] of *vowes* ybrokene.
C. 7.13   Y haue [made] *voues* fourty and forȝeten hem amorwen.

vrete > frete

W

waast n *waste n.(1)* B 1
B.Pr.163 Boþe in wareyne and in *waast* where hem [leue] like[þ];

wade v *waden v.* A 1 wadiþ; B 2 wade (1) wadeþ (1); C 2 wade (1) wadeth (1)
A. 6.55 *Wadiþ* in þat watir & wasshiþ ȝow wel þere,
B. 5.568 *Wadeþ* in þat water and wasshe yow wel þer
B.12.186 Wo was hym marked þat *wade* moot wiþ þe lewed!
C. 7.215 *Wadeth* in þat water and wascheth ȝow wel there
C.14.125 Muchel wo was hym marked þat *wade* shal with þe lewede!

waer > war,ware

wafrer n *waferer n.* A 2 waffrer; B 3 waferer (1) wafrer (2); C 2 waferer (1) wafrere (1)
A. 5.159 Watte þe *waffrer* & his wyf boþe,
A. 6.117 'Wyte god,' quaþ a *waffrer*, 'wiste I þat forsoþe,
B. 5.632 'Wite god', quod a *waf[e]rer*], 'wiste I þis for soþe
B.13.226 A *wafrer*, wol ye wite, and serue manye lordes,
B.14.28 Than Hauky[n] wi[l] þe *wafrer*, [which is] Actiua vita.'
C. 7.285 'Wyte god,' quod a *wafre[re]*, 'wiste y this for sothe
C.15.198 As a *waf[e]rer* with wafres, a[nd] welcome godes gestes.

wafres n *wafer n.* B 4; C 1
B.13.240 Fro Mighelmesse to Mighelmesse I fynde hem wiþ *wafres,*
B.13.262 So er my *wafres* be ywroȝt muche wo I þolye.
B.13.263 Al londoun, I leue, likeþ wel my *wafres,*
B.13.270 My *wafres* were gesene whan Chichestre was Maire.'
C.15.198 As a *waf[e]rer* with wafres, a[nd] welcome godes gestes.

wage v *wagen v.* A 2 wage (1) wagid (1); B 6 wage (4) waged (1) ywaged (1); C 7 wage (4) waged (1) wagen (1) ywaged (1)
A. 4.84 For I wile *wage* for wrong, he [wile] do so no more.'
A. 4.87 'For he haþ *wagid* me wel as wysdom hym tauȝte
B. 4.97 For I wol *wage* for wrong, he wol do so na moore.'
B. 4.100 'For he haþ *waged* me wel as wisdom hym tauȝte
B.16.267 And bettre wed for us [*wage*] þan we ben alle worþi,
B.20.259 And if þei *wage* men to werre þei write hem in noumbre;
B.20.261 [But þei ben nempned in þe noumbre of hem þat ben *ywaged*].
B.20.269 It is wikked to *wage* yow; ye wexen out of noumbre.
C. 4.93 For y wol *wage* for wrong; he wol do so no mare.'
C. 4.96 'For he [hath] *waged* me wel as wysdom hym tauhte
C. 4.192 To *wage* thyn and helpe wynne þat thow wilnest aftur
C.18.283 And bettere wed for vs *wagen* then we ben alle worthy;
C.22.259 And yf thei *wage* men to werre thei writen hem in nombre;
C.22.261 Bote hy ben nempned in þe nombre of hem þat been *ywaged.*
C.22.269 Hit is wikked to *wage* ȝow; ȝe wexeth out of nombre.

wages n *wage n.* B 2; C 2
B.11.292 For he þat took yow [a] title sholde take yow *wages,*
B.20.260 /Wol no [tresorer take] hem [*wages*], trauaille þei neuer so soore,
C.13.106 For he that toek ȝow a title sholde take ȝow *wages*
C.22.260 Wol no tresorer taken hem *wages*, trauayle they neuere so sore,

waggeþ v *waggen v.* B 4 waggede (3) waggeþ (1); C 4 wagged (1) waggede (2) waggeth (1)
B.16.41 Wiþ alle þe wiles þat he kan, and *waggeþ* þe roote
B.16.76 And *waggede* widwehode and it wepte after;
B.18.61 The wal *waggede* and cleef and al þe world quaued.
B.19.204 I wondred what þat was and *waggede* Conscience,
C.12.18 'Ouh!' quod y tho and myn heued *waggede,*
C.18.45 And with alle þe wyles þat he can *waggeth* þe rote
C.18.108 A *waggede* wedewhed and hit wepte aftur;
C.21.204 Y wondred what þat was and *wagged* Consience

waggyng ger *wagginge ger.* A 2; B 2; C 1
A. 9.26 Þe wynd, & þe watir, & þe *waggyng* of þe boot,
A. 9.28 For stande he neuere so stif he stumbliþ in þe *waggyng,*
B. 8.30 The wynd and þe water and þe [*waggyng* of þe boot]
B. 8.32 For stonde he neuer so stif, he stumbleþ [in þe *waggyng*],
C.10.34 The wynde and þe water and [þe] *wag[g]yng* of the bote

wagid > wage; way(e- > wey

wayke adj *weik adj.* C 1
C. 5.23 Y am to *wayke* to wurcche with sykel or with sythe

waille v *weilen v.* A 2 weile (1) weylyng (1); B 3 wailede (1) waille (1) weyled (1); C 1 waylyng
A. 5.94 Ac of his wynnyng I wepe and *weile* þe tyme.
A. 5.252 Wepynge & *weylyng* for here wykkide dedis;
B. 5.114 [Ac of his] wynnynge I wepe and *waille* þe tyme.
B.14.327 And wepte water wiþ hise eighen and *weyled* þe tyme
B.14.335 And wepte and *wailede*, and þerwiþ I awakede.
C. 5.108 Wepyng and *waylyng* til y was aslepe.

waiten v1 *waiten v.* A 3 waite (1) waitide (1) waytide (1); B 7 waited (3) waitede (1) waiten (3); C 8 wayte (1) waytede (3) wayten (3) wayteth (1)
A. 6.34 Wiþinne & wiþoute *waytide* his profit.
A. 7.148 Fro wastours þat *waite* wynneres to shende.
A. 8.127 And þoruȝ here wordis I wok & *waitide* aboute,
B. 5.544 WiþInne and wiþouten *waited* his profit,
B. 7.145 And [þoruȝ hir wordes I wook] and *waited* aboute,
B.13.342 I *waitede* wisloker and þanne was it soilled
B.13.392 Or into Prucelond my profit to *waiten,*
B.14.117 Thanne may beggeris, as beestes, after boote *waiten*
B.16.169 Estward and westward I *waited* after faste
B.16.248 And conforted many a careful þat after his comynge *waite[n]*,
C.Pr.16 Westward y *waytede* in a while aftir
C. 1.124 Hewes in þe haliday after hete *wayten*
C. 2.80 Mede and suche men þat aftur mede *wayten.*
C. 4.52 [A w]*ayteth* ful wel when y seluer take,
C. 6.208 And was his prentis yplyht his profit to *wayte.*
C. 7.188 Withynne and withouten to *wayten* his profit.
C. 9.294 And thorw here wordes [y] awoke and *waytede* aboute
C.18.180 Y *waytede* witterly; Ac whoder he wende y ne wiste.

waiten v2 *weiten v.* A 1; B 2
A. 9.89 Þat *waiten* any wikkidnesse dowel to tenen.
B. 8.99 That *waiten* any wikkednesse dowel to tene.
B.13.237 For Piers þe Plowman and þat hym profit *waiten.*

waityng ger *waitinge ger.* B 1; C 2 waytynge
B. 2.90 As in werkes and in wordes and *waityn[g]* with eiȝes
C. 2.97 As in werkes and in wordes and *waytyng[e]* of yes,
C. 6.177 In word, in wedes, in *waytynge* of eyes.

wayuen v *weiven v.(2)* A 1 weue; B 2 wayued (1) wayuen (1); C 1 wayued
A. 6.89 To *weue* [vp] þe wyket þat [þe wif] shette
B. 5.602 To *wayuen* vp þe wiket þat þe womman shette
B.20.168 And *wayued* awey wanhope and wiþ lif he fighteþ.
C.22.168 And *wayued* away wanhope and with lyf he fihteth.

wayues > weyues

wake v *waken v.(1)* A 3 wakide (2) wok (1); B 10 wake (1) waked (2) wakede (1) waken (1) wakeþ (1) wakyng (1) woke (1) woken (1) wook (1); C 11 wake (1) wakede (5) waken (1) waketh (1) wakynge (2) woke (1)
A. 5.3 Þanne *wakide* I of my wynkyng, & wo was wiþalle
A. 5.203 Þanne *wakide* he of his wynkyng & wypide his eiȝen;
A. 8.127 And þoruȝ here wordis I *wok* & waitide aboute,
B. 5.3 Thanne *waked* I of my wynkyng and wo was withalle
B. 5.361 Thanne *waked* he of his wynkyng and wiped hise eiȝen;
B. 7.145 And [þoruȝ hir wordes I *wook*] and waited aboute,
B.11.409 [To wite] what dowel is, [ac *wakyng* neuere]'.
B.14.70 And lyueden wiþouten liflode and at þe laste þei *woken.*
B.14.236 That is welawo whan he *wakeþ* and wepeþ for colde,
B.17.222 That werchen and *waken* in wyntres nyȝtes
B.18.425 That men rongen to þe resurexion, and riȝt wiþ þat I *wakede*
B.19.156 And biwicched hem as þei *woke* and awey stolen it.
B.20.370 And *wake* for hise wikked werkes as he was wont to doone.
C. 4.196 And receyue tho that resoun louede; and riht with þat y *wakede.*
C. 6.419 Then [*wakede* he] wel wanne and wolde haue ydronke;
C. 9.78 And wo in wynter tym[e] and *wakynge* on nyhtes
C.13.217 To wyte what dowel is Ac *wakynge* neuere.'

C.16.77   Þat is welowo when he [w]aketh and wepeth for colde;
C.18.178 With moche noyse þat nyhte nere frentyk y wakede;
C.19.188 That worchen and waken in wynteres nyhtes
C.20.468 That men rang to þe resureccioun and riht with þat y wakede
C.21.1   Thus y wakede and wrot what y hadde ydremed
C.21.156 And bywiched [hem] as they woke and away stelen hit.
C.22.370 And wake for his wikkede werkes as he was woned [to do].

wakere adj *waker adj.* C 1
C. 9.260 For many wakere wolues ar wr[iþ]en into thy foldes;

wakynge ger *wakinge ger. &> wake* B 1
B.15.1   AC after my wakynge it was wonder longe

wal n *wal n.(1)* A 1 wallis; B 5 wal (2) walle (1) walles (2); C 4 wal (2) walles (2)
A. 6.74   And alle þe wallis ben of wyt to holde wil þeroute;
B. 1.158 That myȝte noon Armure it lette ne none heiȝe walles.
B. 5.220 The beste [in my bedchambre] lay [by þe walle],
B. 5.587 And alle þe walles ben of wit to holden wil oute;
B.15.113 Or to a wal þat were whitlymed and were foul wiþInne;
B.18.61   The wal waggede and cleef and al þe world quaued.
C. 1.154 [That myȝte] non Armure hit lette ne none heye walles.
C.16.268 Or to a wal ywhitlymed and were blak withynne;
C.20.61   The wal of the temple tocleyef euene [a] to peces;
C.20.290 Al hoet on here hedes þat entrith ney þe walles;

walch > welche

walet n *walet n.* C 1
C.10.269 That his wyf were wexe or a walet ful of nobles.

walewiþ v *walwen v.* A 2 walwen (1) walewiþ (1)
A. 5.70   Walewiþ in my wombe & waxiþ as I wene.
A. 9.36   Þat as wyndis & watris wa[l]wen aboute;

walis n prop *Wales n.* B 1
B.15.443 Al was hethynesse som tyme Engelond and Walis

walken v *walken v.(1)* A 4 walke (1) walkid (2) walkyng (1); B 17 walke (6) walked (1) walken (3) walkeþ (4) walkyng (1) walkynge (2); C 20 walke (8) walken (3) walketh (5) walkynge (3) ywalked (1)
A. 6.18   Þat I haue walkid wel wide in wet & in driȝe,
A. 9.54   [And] as I wente be a wode, walkyng myn one,
A.11.258 –ȝet am I neuere þe ner for nouȝt I haue walkid
A.12.68   Me folweþ such a fentyse, I may no ferþer walke.'
B. 5.148 I, wraþe, walke wiþ hem and wisse hem of my bokes.
B. 5.530 That I haue walked [wel] wide in weet and in drye
B. 7.79   In hym þat takeþ is þe trecherie if any treson walke,
B. 8.14   For [ye] be men of þis moolde þat moost wide walken,
B. 8.40   That as wyndes and [watres] walkeþ aboute;
B. 8.63   And as I wente by a wode, walkyng myn one],
B. 9.56   Ouer al in mannes body he[o] walkeþ and wandreþ,
B.11.439 'Certes', quod he, 'þat is sooþ'; and shoop hym for to walken,
B.13.2   And as a freke þat [fey] were forþ gan I walke
B.13.18   [For alle] creatures þat crepen [or walken] of kynde ben engendred;
B.14.211 For þe riche haþ muche to rekene, and [riȝt softe] walkeþ;
B.15.228 Ac in riche robes raþest he walkeþ,
B.16.114 Quatriduanus quelt quyk dide hym walke.
B.17.115 And þanne shal Feiþ be forster here and in þis Fryth walke,
B.18.32   That, for al þat deeþ kan do, wiþInne þre daies to walke
B.18.114 Cam walkynge in þe wey; to helleward she loked.
B.18.117 Hir suster, as it semed, cam so[fte]ly walkynge
C. 6.124 Til y, wrathe, wexe an hey and walke with hem bothe;
C. 7.175 /[Y haue] ywalked ful wyde in wete and in drye
C. 9.110 And aren meuynge aftur þe mone; moneyeles þey walke
C. 9.173 Then of many oþere men þat [o]n this molde walken.
C.10.14   For ȝe ar men of this molde þat moste wyde walken
C.10.46   That as wyndes and wederes wal[k]eth aboute;
C.10.61   I wente forth wydewhare walkynge myn one
C.13.1   Ac wel worth pouerte for he may walke vnrobbed
C.13.245 'Ȝe, certes,' quod he, 'þat is soth', and shop hym to walke;
C.15.2   And as a freke þ[at] fay were forth can y walken
C.15.20   For alle a wisseth and ȝeueth wit þat walketh oþer crepeth.
C.16.52   For þe ryche hath moche to rykene and riht softe walketh;
C.16.342 Ac thorw werkes thow myhte wyte wher forth he walketh:
C.16.353 Ac in riche robes rathest he walketh,
C.17.283 Euery bisshope bi þe lawe sholde buxumliche walke
C.17.303 Quadriduanus coeld quyk dede hym walke.
C.18.250 Where y walke in this worlde a wol hit me allowe;
C.20.31   That for al þat deth can do, withynne thre dayes to walke
C.20.117 Cam walkynge in þe wey; to hellward she lokede.
C.20.120 Here suster, as hit semede, cam softly walkynge

walkeres n *walkere n.(2)* C 1
C.Pr.226 Webbesteres and walkeres and wynners with handes,

walkne > wolkne; walle(s) > wal

walled v *wallen v.(2) &> wellede* B 1; C 1
B.19.326 And watlede it and walled it wiþ his[e] peyne[s] and his passion;
C.21.326 And wateled hit and walled hit with his paynes and his passio[n]

wallyng ger *wallinge ger.* C 1
C. 7.234 And al þe wallyng is of wyt for wil ne sholde hit wynne;

walnote n *walnote n.* B 1; C 1
B.11.260 As on a walnote wiþoute is a bitter barke,
C.12.146 As on a walnote withoute is a bittere barke

walschman n *Welshman n.* C 1
C. 6.308 Thenne was there a walschman was wonderly sory,

walshe > welche

walsyngham n prop *Walsingham n.* A 2; B 2; C 1
A.Pr.51   Wenten to walsyngham, & here wenchis aftir;
A. 5.144 But wende to walsyngham, & my wyf alse,
B.Pr.54   Wenten to walsyngham, and hire wenches after;
B. 5.228 But wenden to walsyngham, and my wif als,
C.Pr.52   Wenten to Walsyngham and here wenches aftir;

walsshe > welche

waltrot n *waltrot n.* B 1; C 1 walterot
B.18.142 'That þow tellest', quod Truþe, 'is but a tale of waltrot!
C.20.145 'That thow tellest,' quod treuthe, 'is bote a tale of walterot!

walwen > walewiþ; wan > wynnen

wandre v *wandren v.* A 6 wandre (1) wandringe (1) wandrite (1) wandriþ (3); B 6 wandre (1) wandred (1) wandren (1) wandreþ (2) wandrynge (1); C 3 wandre (1) wandred (1) wondryng (1)
A.Pr.19   Worching & wandringe as þe world askiþ.
A. 5.113 He shulde wandre on þat walsshe, so was it þredbare.
A. 7.286 And þo nolde wastour not werche, but wandrite aboute,
A. 8.79   Þanne of alle oþer maner men þat on þis molde wandriþ
A.10.44   Þat is Anima, þat oueral in þe body wandriþ,
A.10.212 But wandriþ [as wolues] & wastiþ [ȝif] þei mowe;
B.Pr.19   Werchynge and wandrynge as þe world askeþ.
B. 5.197 She sholde noȝt [wandre] on þat wel[ch]e, so was it þredbare.
B. 6.302 And þo [n]olde Wastour noȝt werche, and wandre[d] aboute,
B. 7.97   Than of alle [oþere] manere men þat on þis moolde [wandreþ].
B. 9.56   Ouer al in mannes body he[o] walkeþ and wandreþ,
B. 9.198   Wandren [as wolues] and wasten [if þei] mowe;
C.Pr.21   Worchyng and wondryng as þ[e] world ascuth.
C. 6.205   He sholde [nat] wandre [o]n þat walch, so was hit thredbare.
C. 8.324   And tho wolde wastor nat worche bote wandre[d] aboute

wangteeþ n *wongtoth n.* B 1; C 1 wangteeth
B.20.191 He buffetted me aboute þe mouþ [and bette out my wangteeþ];
C.22.191 He boffeted me aboute þe mouthe and beet out my wangteeth

wanhope n *wanhope n.* A 1; B 11; C 9
A. 5.216 And seide, 'war þe for wanhope wile þe betraye;
B. 2.100 And þanne wanhope to awaken h[y]m so wiþ no wil to amende
B. 5.279 Thanne weex þ[e] sherewe in wanhope & wolde han hanged hym[self]
B. 5.444 And seide, 'ware þee, for wanhope wo[l] þee bitraye.
B. 7.36   And witen yow fro wanhope, if ye wol þus werche,
B.12.178 And þis conforteþ ech a clerk and couereþ fro wanhope,
B.13.406 That into wanhope he [worþ] and wende nauȝt to be saued.
B.13.420 Thise ben þe braunches, beþ war, þat bryngen a man to wanhope.
B.17.315 Good hope, þat helpe sholde, to wanhope torneþ.
B.20.160 And wedded oon wanhope, a wenche of þe Stuwes.
B.20.166 And bad hym fonde to fighte and afere wanhope.
B.20.168 And wayued awey wanhope and wiþ lif he fighteþ.
C. 2.107 And awake with wanhope and no wille to amende,
C. 7.58   And sayde, 'war the for wanhope wo[l] the] bytraye.
C. 7.80   This beth þe branches, beth ywar, þat bryngeth a man to wanhope.
C.11.196 Sir wanhope was sib to hym, as som men me tolde,
C.14.118 And þat conforteth vch a clerk and keuereth fro wanhope,
C.19.295 For goed hope, that helpe scholde, to wanhope turneth
C.22.160 And wedded oen wanhope, a wenche of þe stuyves.
C.22.166 And baed hym fonde to fihte and afere wanhope.
C.22.168 And wayued away wanhope and with lyf he fihteth.

wanye v *wanen v.* A 2 waniþ (1) wanyen (1); B 3 wanye (1) wanyed (1) wanyeþ (1); C 1 wanyeth
A. 8.58   To waxen & wanyen where þat god likiþ.
A. 9.34   Þe watir is liknid to þe world þat waniþ & waxiþ;
B. 7.56   That neuere shul wexe ne wanye wiþouten god hymselue.
B. 8.38   The water is likned to þe world þat wanyeþ and wexeþ;
B.15.3   And so my wit weex and wanyed til I a fool weere.
C.10.44   The water is likned to þe wor[l]d þat wanyeth and waxeth;

wanne adj *wan adj.* C 1
C. 6.419   Then [wakede he] wel *wanne* and wolde haue ydronke;

wanteþ v *wanten v.* B 1; C 1 wanteth
B.14.173   Of þat þei wilne and wolde *wanteþ* hem noȝt here.
C. 9.106   Ac hem *wanteth* wyt, men and women bothe,

wantynge ger *wantinge ger.* B 1
B.14.177   Wo in wynter tymes for *wantynge* of cloþes,

wantonnesse > wantounnesse

wantoun *wantoun adj.* A 1; C 2 wantowen
A.10.57   And ek *wantoun* & wilde, wiþoute any resoun.
C. 3.144   That alle [women, *wantowen*], shal [be] war [by] þe one
C. 7.300   'Y haue wedded a wyf wel *wantowen* of maneres;

wantounnesse n *wantounnesse n.* A 2 wantonnesse (1) wauntounesse (1);
        B 2 wantounnesse (1) wantownesse (1); C 1 wantounesse
A. 3.114   Wyues & wydewis *wantonnesse* techiþ,
A.10.67   But þei witen hem fro *wauntounesse* whiles þei ben ȝon[g]e.
B. 3.125   Wyues and widewes *wantoun[nesse]* techeþ,
B.12.6   And of þi wilde *wantownesse* [whiles] þow yong were
C. 3.162   Wyues and wedewes *wantounesse* techeth

wantowen > wantoun

war adj *ware adj. &> ware v* A 7; B 11 war (10) ware (1); C 10 waer
        (3) war (7)
A. 1.40   And for þou shuldist be *war* I wisse þe þe beste.'
A. 2.8   And was *war* of a womman wondirliche cloþide,
A. 2.102   ȝet be *war* of þe weddyng for witty is treuþe.
A. 3.56   Be *war* what þi riȝt hond werchiþ or deliþ,
A. 6.95   Ac be *war* þanne of wraþþe, þat wykkide shrewe,
A.11.93   And whanne þat wyt was *war* how his wif tolde
A.11.100   And whanne I was *war* of his wil to his wif gan I knele,
B.Pr.174   And if hym wraþeþ be *war* and his wey shonye.'
B. 2.8   And was *war* of a womman [wonder]liche ycloþed,
B. 2.138   ȝet be *war* of [þe] weddynge; for witty is truþe,
B. 5.609   A[c] be *war* þanne of Wraþe, þat wikked sherewe,
B. 8.119   A[c] er we [*war* were] wiþ wit gonne we mete.
B. 9.187   Whan ye han wyued beþ *war* and wercheþ in tyme,
B.10.147   And whan I was *war* of his wille to his wif gan I [knele]
B.13.71   Holi writ bit men be *war*–I wol noȝt write it here
B.13.420   Thise ben þe braunches, beþ *war*, þat bryngen a man to wanhope.
B.17.262   Forþi beþ *war*, ye wise men þat wiþ þe world deleþ;
B.19.243   Boþe of wele and of wo [and be *ware* bifore],
C.Pr.191   And yf hym wratheth ben *war* and his way [shonye].'
C. 2.9   And [was *war* of] a womman wonderly yclothed,
C. 3.144   That alle [women, wantowen], shal [be] *war* [by] þe one
C. 6.148   And y, wrath, was *war* and w[o]rthe on hem bothe
C. 7.261   Ac be *war* thenne of wrath, þat wikkede shrewe,
C. 9.237   And hoso breketh this, be wel *waer*, but yf he repente,
C.10.288   ȝe þat han wyues ben *war* and wo[r]cheth nat out of tyme
C.11.78   Forthy, wit,' quod she, 'be *waer* holy writ to shewe
C.11.85   And when y was *war* of his wille to þat womman gan y louten
C.15.76   Holy writ byt men be *waer* and wysly hem kepe

warde n *warde n.* B 2 warde (1) wardes (1); C 3 warde (1) wardes (1)
        wardus (1)
B.Pr.94   Of *wardes* and of wardemotes, weyues and streyves.
B.18.322   For any wye or *warde* wide opned þe yates.
C.Pr.92   Of *wardus* and of wardemotis, wayues and strayues.
C. 5.185   That o wit and o wil al ȝoure *wardes* kepe.
C.20.365   Or eny wey or *warde* wyde open[ed] þe ȝates.

warde v *warden v.(1)* C 1
C.18.42   And þerwith y *warde* hit oþerwhile til hit waxe rype.

wardeyn n *wardein n.* A 1; B 2; C 1
A. 1.53   And kynde wyt be *wardeyn* ȝoure welþe to kepe
B. 1.55   And kynde wit be *wardeyn* youre welþe to kepe
B.16.187   *Wardeyn* of þat wit haþ; was euere wiþouten gynnyng.
C. 1.51   And kynde witte be *wardeyn* ȝoure welthe to kepe

wardemotes n *warde n.* B 1; C 1 wardemotis
B.Pr.94   Of wardes and of *wardemotes*, weyues and streyves.
C.Pr.92   Of wardus and of *wardemotis*, wayues and strayues.

wardus > warde n

ware n *ware n.(2)* A 3; B 4; C 4
A. 2.175   Besshette hym in here shoppis to shewen here *ware*;
A. 2.187   Spiceris speke wiþ h[i]m to aspie here *ware*,
A. 5.121   Ne hadde [þe] grace of gile gon among my *ware*
B. 2.216   And bishetten hym in hire shoppes to shewen hire *ware*;
B. 2.228   Spycers speken with hym to spien hire *ware*
B. 5.131   And gart bakbityng be a brocour to blame mennes *ware*.

B. 5.205   Ne hadde þe grace of gyle ygo amonges my [*ware*]
C. 2.226   And byschytten hym in here shoppe[s] to shewen here *ware*;
C. 2.238   Spysours speken to hym to aspye he[re] *ware*
C. 6.95   ȝut am y brokour of bakbytynge to blame menne *w[a]re*
C. 6.213   Ne hadde þe grace of Gyle go among my *ware*

ware v *waren v.(1)* A 1 war; B 3; C 3 waer (1) war (2)
A. 5.216   And seide, '*war* þe for wanhope wile þe betraye;
B. 5.444   And seide, '*ware* þee, for wanhope wo[l] þee bitraye.
B. 9.183   Wisely go wedde and *ware* [þee] fro synne,
B.18.276   And where he wole is his wey; ac *ware* hym of þe perils:
C. 7.58   And sayde, '*war* the for wanhope wo[l the] bytraye.
C.10.284   Wisely go wedde and *war* þe fro synne,
C.20.298   And where he wol is his way, ac *waer* hym of þe perelles:

ware &> war; wareyn > waryn

wareyne n *warein n. &> waryn* B 1
B.Pr.163   Boþe in *wareyne* and in waast where hem [leue] like[þ];

warie v *warien v.* A 1; B 1; C 1 warien
A. 7.297   Þat he was werkman ywrouȝt *warie* þe tyme,
B. 6.313   [That] he was werkman wroȝt [*warie*] þe tyme.
C. 8.335   Þat he was werkeman ywrouhte *warien* þe tyme.

waryn n prop *n.i.d.* A 2; B 3; C 2 wareyn (1) wareyne (1)
A. 4.24   Ac [o]n *wary[n]* wisdom, and witty his fere
A. 4.141   *War[yn]* wisdom þo, ne [witty] his fere,
B. 4.27   Oon *waryn* wisdom and witty his feere
B. 4.67   Tho [wan] Wisdom and sire *waryn* þe witty
B. 4.154   *Waryn* wisdom wynked vpon Mede
C. 4.27   Ooen *wareyn* wisman and wilyman his felawe
C. 4.31   [O]n wilyman and wittyman and *wareyne* wrynglawe.

warisshen v *warishen v.* B 1
B.16.105   That, þouȝ he were wounded with his enemy, to *warisshen*
        hymselue;

warm adj *warm adj.* A 1; B 5 warm (4) warmer (1); C 5 warm (4)
        warmore (1)
A. 7.170   Þei hadde be ded be þis day & doluen al *warm*.
B.15.192   And wiþ *warm* water at hise eiȝen wasshen hem after.
B.17.209   And as wex and weke and [*warm*] fir togideres
B.17.235   And as wex wiþouten moore on a *warm* glede
B.17.243   And as þe weke and fir wol maken a *warm* flaumbe
B.18.410   Is no weder *warmer* þan after watry cloudes;
C.16.335   And with *warm* water of his yes woketh h[em] til [t]he[y] white:
C.19.175   And as wex and weke and *warm* fuyr togyderes
C.19.201   And as wex withouten more vpo[n] a *warm* glede
C.19.209   And as þe wyke and [fuyr wol make a *warm*] flaume
C.20.453   Is no wedore *warmore* then aftur watri cloudes;

warnare > warner

warne v *warnen v.* A 9 warne (6) warnide (3); B 15 warne (6) warned (5)
        warnede (3) warneþ (1); C 6 warne (2) warnede (4)
A. 2.165   Symonye & cyuyle, I sen[d]e hem to *warne*
A. 2.170   And wiȝtliche wente to *warne* þe false,
A. 4.55   And *warnide* wrong þo wiþ suche a wys tale:
A. 5.30   He *warnide* watte his wyf was to blame
A. 7.123   And I am his [h]olde hyne & auȝte hym to *warne*.
A. 7.150   *Warnide* wastour & wisside hym betere,
A. 7.302   I *warne* ȝow werkmen, wynneþ while ȝe mowe,
A. 7.307   And so seiþ satourne & sente ȝow to *warne*.
A.10.95   Ac ȝif þou werchist be godis word I *warne* þe þe beste,
B.Pr.208   Forþi ech a wis wiȝt I *warne*, wite wel his owene.'
B. 2.204   [Symonye and Cyuyle, I sende hem to *warne*
B. 2.211   Thanne Drede wente wyȝtliche and *warned* þe False
B. 3.275   Ooþerwise þan he was *warned* of þe prophete,
B. 4.69   And *warnede* wrong þo with swich a wis tale:
B. 5.30   He *warnede* watte his wif was to blame
B. 6.131   And I am his [h]olde hyne and [auȝte] hym to *warne*
B. 6.165   *Warnede* wastour and wissed hym bettre:
B. 6.321   Ac I *warne* yow werkmen, wynneþ whil ye mowe
B. 6.326   And so sei[þ] Saturne and sente yow to *warne*.
B.12.10   Amende þee while þow myȝt; þow hast ben *warned* ofte
B.15.360   That whilom *warned* bifore what sholde falle after.
B.15.363   As of wedres and wyndes þei *warned* men ofte.
B.15.483   Wiþ wederes and wiþ wondres he *warneþ* vs wiþ a whistlere
B.18.301   To *warne* Pilates wif what done man was Iesus,
C. 3.428   Otherwyse then god wolde and *warnede* hym by þe prophete,
C. 5.132   He *warnede* watte his wyf was to blame
C. 8.162   *Warnede* wastour and wissede hym betere:
C. 8.341   Ac y *warne* ȝow werkmen, wynneth whiles ȝe mowe
C. 8.345   And so sayth saturne and sente [ȝow] to *warne*.
C.17.98   That whilum *warnede* byfore what sholde [f]alle aftur.

warner n *wareiner n.* B 1; C 1 warnare
B. 5.308   Watte þe *warner* and his wif boþe,
C. 6.363   Watte þe *w[a]rnare* and his wyf dronke,

warnynge ger *warninge ger.* C 1
C. 8.90   And aftur here *warnynge* and wor[d]ynge worche þou þeraftur:

warpen v *werpen v.* A 2 warp (1) warpen (1); B 2 warp
A. 4.142   Couþe nouȝt *warpen* a word to wiþsigge resoun,
A.10.33   For þoruȝ þe woord þat he *warp* wexe forþ bestis,
B. 5.86   Ech a word þat he *warp* was of a Neddres tonge;
B. 9.32   For þoruȝ þe word þat he [*warp*] woxen forþ beestes,

warroke v *warroken v.* A 1; B 1; C 1 warrokye
A. 4.19   And let *warroke* hym wel wiþ [wy]tful gerþis.
B. 4.21   And lat *warroke* hym wel wiþ wit[ful] gerþes.
C. 4.21   And lat *warrokye* [hym] w[e]l with auys[e]-þe-byfore;

warth > worþe; was > ben

wasshen v *washen v.* A 3 wasshiþ (1) wysshen (1) ywasshe (1); B 13 wassh (1) wasshe (1) wasshed (1) wasshen (4) wassheþ (1) wessh (1) wesshen (2) ywasshe (1) ywasshen (1); C 9 wasche (1) wascheth (2) wosch (1) woschen (3) ywasche (2)
A. 2.182   *Wysshen* hym & wypide him & wounde hym in cloþis,
A. 6.55   Wadiþ in þat watir & *wasshiþ* ȝow wel þere,
A.10.169   Til fourty dayes be fulfild, þat flood haue *ywasshe*
B. 2.223   *Wesshen* hym & wiped hym & wounden hym in cloutes,
B. 5.568   Wadeþ in þat water and *wasshe* yow wel þere,
B. 9.138   Til fourty daies be fulfild, þat flood haue *ywasshen*
B.11.433   And shame shrapeþ hise cloþes and hise shynes *wassheþ*,
B.13.28   Thei *wesshen* and wipeden and wenten to þe dyner.
B.13.32   'Welcome, wye, go and *wassh*; þow shalt sitte soone.'
B.13.314   Haþ manye moles and spottes; it moste ben *ywasshe*.'
B.13.459   Why he ne hadde [*w]asshen* it or wiped it wiþ a brusshe.
B.14.18   Dowel shal *wasshen* it and wryngen it þoruȝ a wis confessour:
B.15.192   And wiþ warm water at hise eiȝen *wasshen* hem after.
B.15.454   *Wasshen* wel wiþ water and wiþ taseles cracched,
B.16.228   *Wessh* hir feet and wiped hem, and afterward þei eten
B.17.72   Wiþ wyn and with oille hise woundes he *wasshed*,
C. 2.233   Thei *woschen* hym and wypeden hym and wonden hym in cloutes,
C. 7.215   Wadeth in þat water and *wascheth* ȝow wel there
C. 9.80   Bothe to carde and to kembe, to cloute and to *wasche*,
C. 9.251   *Wascheth* and wypeth and with þe furste sitteth.
C. 9.269   And many a fayre flees falsliche is *ywasche*!
C.10.226   Til fourty [dayes] be fulfild and floed haue *ywasche*
C.15.31   They *woschen* and wypeden and wenten to þe dyner.
C.15.37   [They] *woschen* and wipeden and wenten to sytten.
C.18.243   *Wosch* he[re] feet and wypede hem and afturward they eten,

waste adj *waste adj. &> wasten* B 1; C 2
B.19.286   *Waste* word of ydelnesse ne wikked speche moeue;
C. 9.226   That in wilde wodes been or in *waste* places,
C.21.286   *Wast[e]* word of ydelnesse ne wikede speche meue;

wastel n *wastel n.* B 1; C 1
B. 5.285   For þow hast no good ground to gete þee wiþ a *wastel*
C. 6.341   For thow hast no good, by good fayth, to gete the with a *wastel*.

wasten v *wasten v.* A 2 wastide (1) wastiþ (1); B 4; C 4 waste (1) wasten (2) waston (1)
A. 5.25   And wynne þat he *wastide* wiþ sum maner craft,
A.10.212   But wandriþ [as wolues] & *wastiþ* [ȝif] þei mowe;
B. 6.133   Ye *wasten* þat men wynnen wiþ trauaille and tene.
B. 6.162   For [þei] *wasten* and wynnen noȝt and [þo] worþ neuere
B. 9.198   Wandren [as wolues] and *wasten* [if þei] mowe;
B.19.353   'To *wasten* on welfare and in wikked [kepyng]
C. 8.139   Ȝe been wastours, y woet wel, and *waste* and deuouren
C.10.297   Awayten and *wasten* alle þat they cacche mowe;
C.19.250   [That that wickedliche is wonne to *wasten* hit and make frendes?]
C.21.353   'To *waston* on welfare and in wikked kepynge

wastyng ger *wastinge ger.* B 1
B. 5.25   And wynnen his *wastyng* wiþ som maner crafte.

wastour n *wastour n.* A 13 wastour (6) wastours (7); B 16 wastour (8) wastours (8); C 15 wastor (2) wastores (1) wastors (4) wastour (5) wastoures (1) wastours (2)
A.Pr.22   [Wonne] þat þise *wastours* wiþ glotonye destroiȝeþ.
A. 5.24   He bad *wastour* go werche what he best couþe
A. 7.30   Fro *wastours* [and wikkide men] þat wolde me destroye,
A. 7.122   Ȝe ben *wastours*, I wot wel, & treuþe wot þe soþe;
A. 7.124   Suche *wastours* in þis world his werkmen distroyeþ;
A. 7.139   Þanne gan *wastour* arise & wolde haue yfouȝte
A. 7.148   Fro *wastours* þat waite wynneres to shende.
A. 7.150   Warnide *wastour* & wisside hym betere,

A. 7.152   'I was not wonid to werche,' quaþ *wastour*, 'now wile I not begynne,'
A. 7.158   'Awreke me on *wasto[urs]*,' quaþ peris, '[þat þis world [shend]iþ.'
A. 7.159   Hungir in haste þanne hente *wastour* be þe mawe,
A. 7.286   And þo nolde *wastour* not werche, but wandrite aboute,
A. 7.304   He shal awake [þoruȝ] water *wastours* to chaste;
B.Pr.22   Wonnen þat [þise] *wastours* with glotonye destruyeþ.
B. 5.24   He bad *wastour* go werche what he best couþe
B. 6.28   Fro *wastours* and wikked men þat [wolde me destruye],
B. 6.130   Ye ben *wastours*, I woot wel, and truþe woot þe soþe;
B. 6.152   [Th]anne gan *wastour* to wraþen hym and wolde haue yfouȝte
B. 6.161   'And fro þise *wastours* wolueskynnes þat makeþ þe world deere,
B. 6.165   Warnede *wastour* and wissed hym bettre:
B. 6.167   'I was noȝt wont to werche', quod *Wastour*, 'now wol I noȝt bigynne!'
B. 6.173   'Awreke me of *wastours*', quod he, 'þat þis world shendeþ.'
B. 6.174   Hunger in haste þoo hente *wastour* by þe [mawe]
B. 6.201   'I am wel awroke of *wastours* þoruȝ þy myȝte.
B. 6.302   And þo [n]olde *Wastour* noȝt werche, but wandre[d] aboute,
B. 6.323   He shal awake [þoruȝ] water *wastours* to chaste;
B. 9.122   *Wastours* and wrecches out of wedlok, I trowe,
B.19.435   As wel for a *wastour* and wenches of þe stewes
B.20.145   And heeld holynesse a Iape and hendenesse a *wastour*,
C.Pr.24   And wonne þat þis *wastors* with glotony destrueth.
C. 5.126   He bad *wastoures* [g]o wurche and wynne here sustinaunce
C. 8.27   Fro *wastores* and wikked men þat þis world struyen
C. 8.139   Ȝe been *wastours*, y woet wel, and waste and deuouren
C. 8.149   Thenne gan *wastor* to wrath hym and wolde haue yfouhte
C. 8.158   'Awreke me of this *wastors* þat maketh this world dere–
C. 8.162   Warnede *wastour* and wissede hym betere:
C. 8.164   'I was nat woned to worche,' quod *wastour*, 'now wol y nat bygynne!'
C. 8.170   Awreke [me] of this *wastors* for þe knyhte wil nat.'
C. 8.171   Hunger in haste tho hente *wastour* by þe mawe
C. 8.207   'Y am wel awroke of *wastours* thorw thy myhte
C. 8.324   And tho wolde *wastor* nat worche bote wandre[d] aboute
C. 8.343   He shal awake thorw water *wastors* to chaste;
C.21.435   As wel for a *wastour* [and] wenche[s] of the stuyves
C.22.145   And helde holinesse a iape and hendenesse a *wastour*

watekyn > watte; wateled > watlede

water n *water n.* A 17 water (1) watir (13) watris (3); B 32 water (21) watre (8) watres (3); C 26 water (16) watere (1) watre (2) watres (2) watur (5)
A.Pr.9   And as I lay & lenide & lokide on þe *watris*
A. 2.186   For to wone wiþ hem, *watris* to loke.
A. 5.44   And made wil to wepe *watir* wiþ his eiȝen.
A. 5.214   Til Vigilate [þe veil] fet *watir* [at] his eiȝen,
A. 5.246   Wel I woot he wep faste *watir* wiþ his eiȝen,
A. 6.55   Wadiþ in þat *watir* & wasshiþ ȝow wel þere,
A. 7.168   Ne hadde þ[e] fisician ferst defendite him *watir*
A. 7.304   He shal awake [þoruȝ] *water* wastours to chaste;
A. 8.55   Ac to bigge *watir* ne wynd, ne wyt is þe þridde,
A. 9.25   Let bringe a man in a bot amydde a brood watir;
A. 9.26   Þe wynd, & þe *watir*, & þe waggyng of þe boot,
A. 9.31   Þe wynd wolde wiþ þe *watir* þe boot ouerþrowe.
A. 9.34   Þe *watir* is liknid to þe world þat waniþ & waxiþ;
A. 9.36   Þat as wyndis & *watris* wa[l]wen aboute;
A. 9.43   Þat, þeiȝ þi body bowe as bot doþ in þe *watir*,
A.10.4   Wiþ wynd & wiþ *watir* wi[tti]liche enioynede.
A.11.207   "Whanne fisshes faile þe flood or þe fresshe *watir*
B.Pr.9   And as I lay and lenede and loked on þe *watres*
B. 2.227   [For to] wonye with hem *watres* to loke.
B. 5.61   And [made] wille to wepe *water* wiþ hise eiȝen.
B. 5.173   And doon me faste frydayes to [þerf] breed and to *watre*;
B. 5.442   Til vigilate þe veille fette *water* at hise eiȝen
B. 5.472   Wel I woot he wepte faste *water* wiþ hise eiȝen,
B. 5.568   Wadeþ in þat *water* and wasshe yow wel þer
B. 6.323   He shal awake [þoruȝ] *water* wastours to chaste;
B. 7.53   Ac to bugge *water* ne wynd ne wit ne fir þe ferþe,
B. 8.29   Lat brynge a man in a boot amydde a bro[od] *watre*;
B. 8.30   The wynd and þe *water* and þe [waggyng of þe boot]
B. 8.35   The wynd wolde wiþ þe *water* þe boot ouerþrowe.
B. 8.38   The *water* is likned to þe world þat wanyeþ and wexeþ;
B. 8.40   That as wyndes and [*watres*] walkeþ aboute;
B. 8.47   [That], þouȝ þ[i] body bowe as boot dooþ in þe *watre*,
B. 9.4   Wiþ wynd and wiþ *water* witt[i]ly enioyned.
B.10.301   Whan fisshes faillen þe flood or þe fresshe *water*
B.13.16   And how louynge he is to [ech lif] on londe and on *watre*–
B.14.327   And wepte *water* wiþ hise eighen and weyled þe tyme
B.15.192   And wiþ warm *water* at hise eiȝen wasshen hem after.
B.15.339   And wente forþ wiþ þat *water* to woke wiþ Temese.
B.15.454   Wasshen wel wiþ *water* and wiþ taseles cracched,

B.16.116 And wepte *water* with hise ei3en; þer sei3en it manye.
B.16.189 The light of al þat lif haþ a londe and a *watre*,
B.17.163 Boþe wolkne and þe wynd, *water* and erþe,
B.17.232 Melte in a Mynut while to myst and to *watre*.
B.18.30 Al þat lyueþ [or] lokeþ in londe [or] in *watre*.
B.18.242 The *water* witnesse[þ] þat he was god for he wente on it;
B.18.244 And as he wente on þe *water* wel hym knew and seide,
B.19.109 *Water* into wyn turnede, as holy writ telleþ.
B.19.236 And some he lered to laboure [on lond and on *watre*
B.19.377 And þanne wellede *water* for wikkede werkes
C. 2.237 That lyare sholde wonye with hem *watres* to loke.
C. 5.148 Ryht as fysches in floed whan hem fayleth *water*
C. 6.2 And made will to wepe *water* with his eyes
C. 6.155 And doen me faste fridayes to bred and to *water*;
C. 6.326 Wel y woet a wepte faste *water* with his yes
C. 6.336 And deyede with a drop *water*; so doth alle synnes
C. 7.56 Til vigilate the veile fette *water* at his eyus
C. 7.215 Wadeth in þat *water* and wascheth 3ow wel there
C. 8.343 He shal awake thorw *water* wastors to chaste;
C. 9.56 Þat is wit and *watur* and wynde and fuyre the ferthe;
C.10.33 Lat bryng a man in a boet amydde a brood *water*;
C.10.34 The wynde and þe *water* and [þe] wag[g]yng of the bote
C.10.44 The *water* is likned to þe wor[l]d þat wanyeth and waxeth;
C.10.131 With wynd and with *water* wittyly enioyned.
C.13.167 In mareys and in mores, in myres and in *watres*,
C.15.19 And how louyng he is to vch lyf a londe and o *watere*
C.15.240 Þe worm and wonte vnder erthe and in *water* fisches,
C.16.335 And with warm *water* of his yes woketh h[em] til [t]he[y] white:
C.18.146 And wepte *watur* with [his] yes; the why weten fewe.
C.19.198 Melteth in a myntwhile to myst and to *water*.
C.20.29 Alle þat lyueth or loketh a londe or a *watre*.
C.20.251 The *water* witnesseth þat he was god for a wente on h[it];
C.20.253 And as he wente on þe *watur* wel hym knewe and saide,
C.21.109 [*Watur* into wyn turned], As holy writ telleth.
C.21.236 And som he lered to laboure a londe and a *watre*
C.21.377 And thenne walled *watur* for wikked werkes

watlede v *watelen* v. B 1; C 1 wateled
B.19.326 And *watlede* it and walled it wiþ his[e] peyne[s] and his passion;
C.21.326 And *wateled* hit and walled hit with his paynes and his passio[n]

watre(s > water

watrede v *watren* v. A 1 watride; B 1; C 1
A. 7.160 And wrong hym so be þe wombe þat al *watride* his ei3en,
B. 6.175 And wrong hym so by þe wombe þat [al *watrede* his ei3en].
C. 8.172 And wronge hym so by þe wombe þat al *watrede* his yes;

watry adj *wateri* adj. B 1; C 1 watri
B.18.410 Is no weder warmer þan after *watry* cloudes;
C.20.453 Is no wedore warmore then aftur *watri* cloudes;

watshoed > weetshoe

watte n prop *n.i.d.* A 2; B 4; C 4 watekyn (1) watte (3)
A. 5.30 He warnide *watte* his wyf was to blame
A. 5.159 *Watte* þe waffrer & his wyf boþe,
B. 5.30 He warnede *watte* his wif was to blame
B. 5.308 *Watte* þe warner and his wif boþe,
B.13.325 And þat he wiste by wille [to *watte* tellen it],
B.13.326 And þat [by] *watte* [he] wiste wille wiste it after,
C. 5.132 He warnede *watte* his wyf was to blame
C. 6.70 And þat a wiste by wille to *watekyn* he tolde hit
C. 6.71 And þat he wiste by *watte* tolde hit wille aftur
C. 6.363 *Watte* þe w[a]rnare and his wyf dronke,

watur > water; wauntounesse > wantounnesse

wawes n *waue* n. A 1; B 1; C 1
A. 9.35 Þe goodis of þis ground be lik þe grete *wawes*,
B. 8.39 The goodes of þis grounde arn like þe grete *wawes*,
C.10.45 The godes of this grounde ar like þe grete *wawes*

wax- > wexen; waye(d > weye

we pron *we* pron. A 112 oure (38) vs (41) we (33); B 409 our (1) oure (147) us (1) vs (140) we (120); C 416 oure (167) vs (107) we (142)

our B 1
B.13.444

oure A 38
A.Pr.26, A.Pr.32, A.Pr.87, A.1.89, A.1.110, A.1.136, A.1.142, A.1.178, A.1.183, A.2.118, A.2.141, A.2.142, A.3.64, A.3.223, A.5.54, A.7.60, A.7.143, A.7.218, A.8.33, A.8.52, A.8.87, A.8.159, A.8.183, A.10.129, A.10.180, A.11.60, A.11.63, A.11.66, A.11.151, A.11.236, A.11.244, A.11.248, A.11.249, A.11.264, A.11.306, A.12.55, A.12.84, A.12.87

oure B 147
B.Pr.26, B.Pr.32, B.Pr.102, B.Pr.157, B.Pr.169, B.Pr.186, B.Pr.189, B.Pr.214, B.1.91, B.1.112, B.1.168, B.1.204, B.1.209, B.2.154, B.2.175, B.2.180, B.2.181, B.4.39, B.5.71, B.5.161, B.5.171, B.5.180, B.5.181, B.5.266, B.5.268, B.5.295, B.5.396, B.5.396, B.5.478, B.5.479, B.5.487, B.5.490, B.5.493, B.5.496, B.5.500, B.5.503, B.5.503, B.5.563, B.6.66, B.6.156, B.6.234, B.6.256, B.7.31, B.7.50, B.7.105, B.7.181, B.7.205, B.9.90, B.9.108, B.9.130, B.10.40, B.10.80, B.10.92, B.10.108, B.10.202, B.10.207, B.10.208, B.10.353, B.10.366, B.10.383, B.11.64, B.11.110, B.11.139, B.11.173, B.11.175, B.11.183, B.11.185, B.11.185, B.11.188, B.11.188, B.11.191, B.11.212, B.11.212, B.11.229, B.11.233, B.11.251, B.11.382, B.12.54, B.12.94, B.12.211, B.12.212, B.12.255, B.13.12, B.13.200, B.13.206, B.13.268, B.13.337, B.13.448, B.14.35, B.14.38, B.14.46, B.14.82, B.14.102, B.14.133, B.14.198, B.14.199, B.14.259, B.14.319, B.15.33, B.15.156, B.15.170, B.15.185, B.15.262, B.15.262, B.15.297, B.15.355, B.15.387, B.15.391, B.15.393, B.15.412, B.15.502, B.15.556, B.15.582, B.15.608, B.16.37, B.16.205, B.16.242, B.16.263, B.17.104, B.17.133, B.17.166, B.17.220, B.17.284, B.17.293, B.17.296, B.17.318, B.17.334, B.17.345, B.17.347, B.18.41, B.18.107, B.18.197, B.18.267, B.18.311, B.18.315, B.18.326, B.18.400, B.18.405, B.18.429, B.19.8, B.19.25, B.19.96, B.19.114, B.19.347, B.19.354, B.20.347, B.20.367

oure C 167
C.Pr.28, C.Pr.34, C.Pr.103, C.Pr.130, C.Pr.164, C.Pr.186, C.Pr.203, C.Pr.204, C.1.87, C.1.164, C.2.134, C.2.170, C.2.193, C.2.194, C.3.54, C.3.75, C.3.99, C.3.99, C.3.241, C.3.359, C.3.360, C.3.396, C.3.401, C.3.402, C.3.402, C.3.403, C.3.420, C.3.441, C.4.39, C.4.39, C.5.55, C.5.74, C.5.85, C.6.81, C.6.153, C.6.156, C.6.162, C.6.163, C.6.170, C.6.181, C.6.188, C.6.288, C.6.292, C.7.12, C.7.12, C.7.74, C.7.104, C.7.108, C.7.120, C.7.121, C.7.128, C.7.129, C.7.130, C.7.133, C.7.136, C.7.140, C.7.143, C.7.143, C.7.144, C.7.260, C.8.67, C.8.153, C.8.238, C.8.268, C.9.19, C.9.49, C.9.59, C.9.71, C.9.115, C.9.185, C.9.215, C.9.341, C.9.348, C.9.351, C.10.47, C.10.55, C.10.55, C.10.55, C.10.189, C.10.219, C.11.60, C.11.208, C.11.224, C.12.44, C.12.74, C.12.92, C.12.97, C.12.120, C.12.122, C.12.137, C.12.158, C.12.160, C.12.195, C.13.3, C.13.12, C.13.30, C.13.74, C.14.38, C.14.150, C.14.151, C.15.15, C.15.73, C.15.116, C.15.178, C.15.237, C.15.244, C.15.262, C.15.274, C.16.2, C.16.25, C.16.37, C.16.38, C.16.38, C.16.39, C.16.40, C.16.99, C.16.153, C.16.195, C.17.26, C.17.119, C.17.136, C.17.152, C.17.168, C.17.183, C.17.219, C.17.235, C.17.253, C.17.293, C.17.295, C.17.316, C.18.67, C.18.78, C.18.82, C.18.245, C.18.258, C.18.279, C.19.186, C.19.265, C.19.274, C.19.277, C.19.298, C.19.314, C.19.325, C.19.327, C.20.40, C.20.110, C.20.202, C.20.275, C.20.287, C.20.308, C.20.345, C.20.349, C.20.352, C.20.369, C.20.370, C.20.371, C.21.8, C.21.25, C.21.96, C.21.114, C.21.347, C.21.354, C.22.347, C.22.367

vs A 41
A.1.140, A.1.141, A.1.142, A.2.3, A.2.117, A.3.47, A.3.265, A.4.108, A.5.36, A.5.47, A.6.21, A.7.2, A.7.23, A.7.27, A.7.119, A.7.120, A.7.125, A.7.144, A.7.145, A.7.193, A.7.212, A.7.216, A.8.57, A.8.69, A.8.111, A.8.114, A.8.159, A.8.181, A.9.14, A.10.120, A.10.163, A.11.28, A.11.64, A.11.79, A.11.150, A.11.151, A.11.152, A.11.252, A.11.275, A.12.28, A.12.117

vs B 141 *us* (1) *vs* (140)
B.Pr.153, B.Pr.154, B.Pr.155, B.Pr.155, B.Pr.186, B.Pr.192, B.1.166, B.1.167, B.1.168, B.2.3, B.2.153, B.3.48, B.3.289, B.5.44, B.5.64, B.5.266, B.5.479, B.5.479, B.5.482, B.5.486, B.5.503, B.5.533, B.6.2, B.6.21, B.6.25, B.6.127, B.6.128, B.6.157, B.6.158, B.6.207, B.6.232, B.6.331, B.7.76, B.7.77, B.7.127, B.7.129, B.7.132, B.7.132, B.7.155, B.7.181, B.7.203, B.8.18, B.9.90, B.10.36, B.10.79, B.10.106, B.10.113, B.10.126, B.10.201, B.10.202, B.10.203, B.10.208, B.10.208, B.10.209, B.10.250, B.10.343, B.10.345, B.10.365, B.10.390, B.10.413, B.10.436, B.10.446, B.11.119, B.11.124, B.11.183, B.11.184, B.11.186, B.11.187, B.11.188, B.11.190, B.11.204, B.11.205, B.11.240, B.12.91, B.12.125, B.12.130, B.12.273, B.13.49, B.13.50, B.13.53, B.13.58, B.13.58, B.13.79, B.13.102, B.13.107, B.13.124, B.13.206, B.13.257, B.14.49, B.14.50, B.14.82, B.14.186, B.14.188, B.14.189, B.14.191, B.14.202, B.14.326, B.15.249, B.15.250, B.15.260, B.15.262, B.15.314, B.15.378, B.15.391, B.15.483, B.15.484, B.15.485, B.15.485, B.15.581, B.16.163, B.16.230, B.16.252, B.16.262, B.16.263, B.16.264, B.16.266, B.16.267, B.16.269, B.17.40, B.17.246, B.17.293, B.17.293, B.18.171, B.18.216, B.18.268, B.18.282, B.18.310, B.18.416, B.18.417, B.19.64, B.19.65, B.19.174, B.19.212, B.19.356, B.19.359, B.19.391, B.20.75, B.20.76, B.20.89

vs C 107
C.Pr.173, C.Pr.174, C.Pr.175, C.Pr.175, C.Pr.177, C.Pr.203, C.1.162, C.1.163, C.1.164, C.2.3, C.3.51, C.3.360, C.3.442, C.5.88, C.5.139, C.5.142, C.6.5, C.6.184, C.7.121, C.7.121, C.7.124, C.7.178, C.7.250, C.7.308, C.8.19, C.8.24, C.8.133, C.8.134, C.8.154, C.8.155, C.8.216, C.8.352, C.9.124, C.9.327, C.9.345, C.9.349, C.10.18, C.10.104, C.11.59, C.11.150, C.11.219, C.12.54, C.12.59, C.12.100, C.12.112, C.12.113, C.12.121, C.12.129, C.12.168, C.12.178, C.13.196, C.14.68, C.14.195, C.15.56, C.15.61, C.15.86, C.15.115, C.15.221, C.15.227, C.15.247, C.15.249, C.16.23, C.16.23, C.16.25, C.16.36, C.16.43, C.16.308, C.16.327, C.18.69, C.18.82, C.18.244, C.18.245, C.18.246, C.18.268, C.18.278, C.18.279, C.18.280, C.18.282, C.18.283, C.18.285, C.18.287, C.19.95, C.19.212, C.19.274, C.19.274, C.20.174, C.20.225, C.20.276, C.20.308, C.20.327, C.20.336, C.20.340, C.20.340, C.20.344, C.20.346, C.20.459, C.20.460, C.21.64, C.21.65, C.21.174, C.21.212, C.21.356, C.21.359, C.21.391, C.22.75, C.22.76, C.22.89

we A 33
A.Pr.105, A.Pr.105, A.1.49, A.2.116, A.2.118, A.3.17, A.3.26, A.3.47, A.3.204, A.4.21, A.4.158, A.5.36, A.7.2, A.7.8, A.7.53, A.7.116, A.7.117, A.7.120, A.7.143, A.8.145, A.8.181, A.8.182, A.8.184, A.9.107, A.9.109, A.9.109, A.11.86, A.11.243, A.11.247, A.12.55, A.12.69, A.12.86, A.12.87

we B 120

B.Pr.152, B.Pr.153, B.Pr.156, B.Pr.157, B.Pr.170, B.Pr.172, B.Pr.185, B.Pr.186,
B.Pr.188, B.Pr.190, B.Pr.192, B.Pr.198, B.Pr.227, B.Pr.227, B.1.51, B.2.152, B.2.154,
B.3.17, B.3.27, B.3.48, B.3.56, B.3.217, B.3.352, B.4.23, B.4.195, B.5.44, B.5.427,
B.5.501, B.6.8, B.6.58, B.6.124, B.6.125, B.6.128, B.6.156, B.7.168, B.7.203, B.7.204,
B.7.206, B.8.117, B.8.119, B.8.119, B.9.87, B.9.89, B.10.92, B.10.115, B.10.133,
B.10.364, B.10.365, B.10.444, B.11.119, B.11.189, B.11.190, B.11.191, B.11.199,
B.11.202, B.11.208, B.11.211, B.11.212, B.11.229, B.11.241, B.11.242, B.11.242,
B.12.76, B.12.123, B.12.274, B.13.6, B.13.108, B.13.133, B.13.207, B.13.257, B.14.82,
B.14.82, B.14.190, B.14.196, B.15.143, B.15.261, B.15.266, B.15.313, B.15.314,
B.15.395, B.15.440, B.15.579, B.16.242, B.16.267, B.16.273, B.17.10, B.17.50, B.17.51,
B.17.52, B.17.339, B.17.340, B.18.56, B.18.69, B.18.163, B.18.165, B.18.166, B.18.166,
B.18.201, B.18.261, B.18.294, B.18.309, B.18.312, B.18.313, B.18.313, B.18.314,
B.18.376, B.18.417, B.18.418, B.19.64, B.19.356, B.19.357, B.19.358, B.19.392,
B.19.392, B.19.414, B.20.75, B.20.76, B.20.78, B.20.196, B.20.318

we C 142

C.Pr.173, C.Pr.176, C.Pr.177, C.Pr.187, C.Pr.189, C.Pr.202, C.Pr.203, C.Pr.205,
C.Pr.216, C.Pr.231, C.Pr.231, C.1.47, C.2.168, C.2.169, C.2.170, C.3.18, C.3.28, C.3.51,
C.3.53, C.3.60, C.3.104, C.3.273, C.4.154, C.5.119, C.5.142, C.6.181, C.6.185, C.6.185,
C.7.40, C.7.141, C.7.145, C.7.146, C.7.146, C.7.147, C.8.6, C.8.131, C.8.134, C.8.135,
C.8.135, C.8.153, C.8.312, C.9.71, C.9.125, C.9.236, C.9.240, C.9.245, C.9.312, C.9.341,
C.9.342, C.9.344, C.9.349, C.9.350, C.9.352, C.10.54, C.10.54, C.10.113, C.10.115,
C.10.115, C.10.188, C.11.219, C.11.221, C.12.54, C.12.102, C.12.103, C.12.110,
C.12.116, C.12.117, C.12.118, C.12.119, C.12.120, C.12.121, C.12.130, C.12.131,
C.12.186, C.13.18, C.13.199, C.14.29, C.14.66, C.14.67, C.14.69, C.14.116, C.14.196,
C.15.27, C.15.28, C.15.79, C.15.79, C.15.227, C.15.262, C.17.39, C.17.93, C.17.122,
C.17.293, C.18.4, C.18.68, C.18.225, C.18.226, C.18.259, C.18.283, C.18.289, C.19.11,
C.19.45, C.19.48, C.19.49, C.19.50, C.19.96, C.19.196, C.19.319, C.19.320, C.20.45,
C.20.56, C.20.71, C.20.166, C.20.168, C.20.169, C.20.169, C.20.206, C.20.269,
C.20.284, C.20.285, C.20.294, C.20.309, C.20.324, C.20.343, C.20.345, C.20.347,
C.20.347, C.20.349, C.20.418, C.20.460, C.20.461, C.21.64, C.21.356, C.21.357,
C.21.358, C.21.392, C.21.392, C.21.414, C.22.75, C.22.76, C.22.78, C.22.196, C.22.318

web n *web n.* A 1 webbe; B 1

A. 5.92   [Þanne] I wysshe it were myn [and al þe *webbe* aftir].
B. 5.112   [Thanne I wisshe] it were myn and al þe *web* after.

webbe n *webbe n. &> web* C 2 webbe (1) webbes (1)

C. 6.221   My wyf was a *webbe* and wollone cloth made
C. 9.205   Whilen were werkmen, *webbes* and taylours

webbesters n *webbestere n.* A 1 websteris; B 1; C 1 webbesteres

A.Pr.99   Wollene *websteris* and weueris of lynen,
B.Pr.220   Wollen *webbesters* and weueres of lynnen,
C.Pr.226   *Webbesteres* and walkeres and wynners with handes,

wed n *wed n.* A 1; B 7 wed (5) wedde (2); C 9 wed (6) wedde (3)

A. 3.189   I durste han leid my lif & no lesse *wed*
B. 3.202   I dorste haue leyd my lif and no lasse *wedde*
B. 5.241   And lene it for loue of þe cros, to legge a *wed* and lese it.
B.13.359   Lened for loue of þe *wed* and looþ to do truþe;
B.16.262   And me þer[wiþ]', quod þat [wye]; 'may no *wed* vs quyte,
B.16.267   And bettre *wed* for us [wage] þan we ben alle worþi,
B.18.31   Lif seiþ þat he lieþ and leieþ his lif to *wedde*
B.20.13   Ne wight noon wol ben his boru3, ne *wed* haþ noon to legge;
C. 3.259   Y durste haue yleyd my lyf and no lasse *wedde*
C. 5.73   And lordes sones here laboreres and leyde here rentes to *wedde*
C. 6.243   And len[e] for loue of þe *wed* the whych y lette bettere
C.13.44   Wol no wys man be wroth ne his *wed* take–
C.13.45   Ne non haiward is hote his *wed* for to taken.
C.18.278   And me þerwith', quod the weye; 'may no *wed* vs quyte
C.18.283   And bettere *wed* for vs wagen then we ben alle worthy;
C.20.30   Lyf saith þat a lyeth and [leyeth] his lyf to *wedde*,
C.22.13   Ne wyht no[n] wol be his borwe ne *wed* hath [non] to legge;

wedde > wed,wedden

wedden v *wedden v.* A 10 wedde (6) weddit (4); B 21 wedde (8) wedded
(9) wedden (1) weddeþ (1) ywedded (2); C 28 wedde (9) wedded (11)
weddede (1) wedden (1) weddeth (3) ywedded (3)

A. 2.117   Til mede be þi *weddit* wyf þoru3 wyt of vs alle,
A. 3.107   'Wilt þou *wedde* þis womman 3if I wile assente?
A. 3.110   Er I *wedde* such a wif wo me betide!
A. 4.10   Of mede & of mo oþere, what man shal hire *wedde*,
A. 4.129   And 3if þou werche [it in] werk I *wedde* myne eris
A. 8.73   Þei wolden no womman þat hy wiþ delen
A.10.131   Formest & ferst to folk þat ben *weddit*
A.10.188   Or *wedde* any wydewe for any wele of godis,
A.10.197   Forþi I counseile alle cristene coueite to be *weddit*
A.11.106   He haþ *weddit* a wif wiþinne þise woukes sixe,
B. 2.43   And al is lieres ledynge þat [lady] is þus *ywedded*
B. 2.153   Til Mede be þi *wedded* wif þoru3 wi[t] of vs alle,
B. 3.18   To be *wedded* at þi wille and wher þee leef likeþ
B. 3.118   'Woltow *wedde* þis womman if I wole assente?
B. 3.121   Er I *wedde* swich a wif wo me bitide!
B. 4.10   [Of Mede and of mo oþere, what man shal hire *wedde*],
B. 4.146   And if [þow] werch[e] it in werk I *wedde* myne eris
B. 7.91   [Thei] *wedde* [no] womman þat [þei] wiþ deele
B. 9.110   [Dowel in þis world is trewe *wedded* libbynge folk],
B. 9.128   "Thyn issue in þyn issue, I wol þat þei be *wedded*,
B. 9.163   [For] goode sholde *wedde* goode, þou3 þei no good hadde;
B. 9.167   Or *wedden* any wodewe for [wele] of hir goodes
B. 9.176   Forþi I counseille alle cristene coueite no3t be *wedded*
B. 9.180   For no londes, but for loue, loke ye be *wedded*
B. 9.183   Wisely go *wedde* and ware [þee] fro synne,
B.10.154   He haþ *wedded* a wif wiþInne þise [woukes sixe],
B.11.72   That *wedde* none widwes but for to welden hir goodes.
B.11.249   Was a pure pouere maide and to a pouere man *ywedded*.
B.14.272   And put hym to be pacient and pouerte *weddeþ*,
B.20.112   Amonges alle manere men, *wedded* and vnwedded,
B.20.160   And *wedded* oon wanhope, a wenche of þe Stuwes.
C. 2.36   And what [man] mede loueth, my lyf [dar y] *wedde*,
C. 2.46   And al is lyares ledynge th[at] lady is thus *ywedded*.
C. 2.126   And wihouten here moder amendes mede may [nat] be *wedded*.
C. 2.127   For treuthe plyhte here treuthe to wedde on of here douhteres,
C. 2.139   That mede may be *wedded* to no man bot treuthe,
C. 2.169   Til mede be thy *wedded* wyf wolle we nat stunte,
C. 3.19   For to *wedde* at thy wille [and] where the leef li[k]eth
C. 3.132   And wilned to be *wedded* withouten his leue,
C. 3.155   'Woltow *wedde* this m[ai]de yf y wol assente?
C. 3.158   Ar y *wedde* suche a wyf wo me bytyde!
C. 4.10   Of mede and of mo othere and what man shal here *wedde*
C. 4.143   And yf 3e wor[c]he it in werke y *wedde* bothe myn handes
C. 5.67   Of frankeleynes and fremen and of folke *ywedded*.
C. 7.300   'Y haue *wedded* a wyf wel wantowen of maneres;
C. 9.168   Ne *weddeth* none wymmen þat they with deleth,
C.10.204   As this *wedded* men þat this world susteyneth,
C.10.254   For goode sholde *wedde* goode thouh they no goode hadde
C.10.268   And *wedden* here for here welthe and weschen on þe morwe
C.10.278   Forthy y conseyle alle cristene coueyte neuere be *wedded*
C.10.281   And [wedewares and wedewes] *weddeth* ayþer oþer;
C.10.284   Wisely go *wedde* and war þe fro synne,
C.10.293   Bote wyues and *wedded* men, as holy writ techeth:
C.11.96   And clergi[es] *wedded* wyf, as wyse as hymsulue
C.12.135   Was a puyre pore mayde and to a pore man *ywedded*.
C.16.112   And potte hym to be pacient and pouerte *weddeth*,
C.18.71   As *weddede* men and wedewes and riht worthy maydones
C.22.112   Amonges alle manere men, *wedded* and vnwedded,
C.22.160   And *wedded* oen wanhope, a wenche of þe stuyves.

weddewes > widewe

weddynge ger *weddinge ger.* A 4 weddyng; B 4; C 4 weddyng (3)
weddynge (1)

A. 2.81   Such *weddyng* to werche to wraþþe wiþ treuþe;
A. 2.82   [And] er þis *weddyng* be wrou3t wo þe betide!
A. 2.102   3et be war of þe *weddyng* for witty is treuþe.
A.10.184   A carful concepcioun comiþ of such *weddyng*
B. 2.117   Swic[h] *weddyng[e]* to werche to wraþe wiþ truþe;
B. 2.118   And er þis *weddynge* be wro3t wo þee bitide!
B. 2.138   Yet be war of [þe] *weddynge*; for witty is truþe,
B. 9.161   [A] careful concepcion comeþ of [swich *weddynge*]
C. 2.121   Suche a *weddyng* to wurche þat wrathe myhte treuthe;
C. 2.122   And ar this *weddyng* be wrouhte wo to al 3oure consayle!
C. 2.154   3ut beth ywar of þe *weddynge*; for witty is treuthe
C. 2.177   To wende with h[e]m to westminstre [the] *weddyng* to honoure.

wede > weede

weden v *weden v.(1)* B 1; C 1 wedy

B.16.17   Vnder Piers þe Plowman to piken it and *weden* it.'
C. 8.66   And alle þat helpen me [to] erye or elles to *wedy*

weder n *weder n.* A 1 wederis; B 5 weder (1) wederes (2) wedres (2); C
5 weder (1) wederes (3) wedore (1)

A. 7.306   Þoru3 flood [and] foule *wederis* fruytes shuln fa[i]lle,
B. 6.325   Thoru3 flo[od] and foule *wedres* fruytes shul faille,
B.15.356   For þoru3 werre and wikkede werkes and *wederes* vn[s]esonable
B.15.363   As of *wedres* and wyndes þei warned men ofte.
B.15.483   Wiþ *wederes* and wiþ wondres he warneþ vs wiþ a whistlere
B.18.410   Is no *weder* warmer þan after watry cloudes;
C. 6.113   But y hadde *weder* at my wille y witte god þe cause
C. 8.346   Thorw flodes and foule *wederes* fruyttes shollen fayle;
C.10.46   That as wyndes and *wederes* wal[k]eth aboute;
C.12.190   Ne wynde ne *wederes* as in wynter tym[e],
C.20.453   Is no *wedore* warmore then aftur watri cloudes;

wederwise adj *OED weatherwise a.* B 1; C 1 wedurwyse

B.15.357   *Wederwise* shipmen and witty clerkes also
C.17.95   *Wedurwyse* shipmen now and oþer witty peple

wedes > weed,weede; wedewares > wideweres; wedewe(s > widewe;
wedwhed > widwehode; wedy > weden

wedynge ger *wedinge ger.* B 1; C 1
B. 6.189   And wente as werkmen [to *wedynge*] and [mowynge]
C. 8.186   And wenten as werkemen to *wedynge* and mowynge

wedis > weed

wedlok n *wedlok n.* A 2 wedlak; B 8 wedlok (7) wedlokes (1); C 2
A.10.133   Þat þoruȝ *wedlak* þe world stant, whoso wile it knowen.
A.10.207   Þat iche man haue a make in [mariage] of *wedlak*
B. 9.116   And þus was *wedlok* ywroȝt wiþ a mene persone,
B. 9.119   And þus was *wedlok* ywroȝt and god hymself it made.
B. 9.122   Wastours and wrecches out of *wedlok*, I trowe,
B. 9.157   And al for þei wroȝte *wedlokes* ayein [þe wille of god].
B. 9.194   For he made *wedlok* first and [þus] hymself seide:
B.16.203   *Wedlok* and widwehode wiþ virginite ynempned,
B.16.216   As widewe wiþouten *wedlok* was neuere ȝit yseyȝe,
B.16.218   So widewe withouten *wedlok* may noȝt wel stande,
C.10.291   Clene of lyf and in loue of soule and in lele *wedlok*.
C.18.87   Wydewhode, more worthiore then *wedlok*, as in heuene;

wedore wedres > weder; wedurwyse > wederwise

weed n *wede n.(1)* A 2 wedis (1) weed (1); B 2 wedes; C 4 wedes
A. 7.103   And summe to plese perkyn pykide vp þe *wedis*.
A.10.126   Or as whete out of *weed* waxiþ, out of þe erþe,
B. 6.111   And somme to plese Perkyn piked vp þe *wedes*.
B.19.312   'For comunliche in contrees cammokes and *wedes*
C. 8.118   And somme to plese Perkyn [pykede vp þe] *wedes*.
C.12.224   On fat lond ful of donge foulest *wedes* groweth.
C.12.229   Riht as *wedes* waxeth in wose and in donge
C.21.312   'For cominliche in Contrayes cammokes and *wedes*

weede n *wede n.(2)* B 3 weede (1) wedes (2); C 4 wede (1) wedes (3)
B.11.236   For his pouere apparaill and pilgrymes *wedes*
B.15.226   Riden and rennen in raggede *wedes*
B.20.211   [*Weede*] ne worldly [mete] while þi lif lasteþ.'
C. 2.98   In w[e]des and in weschynges and with ydel thouhtes
C. 6.177   In word, in *wedes*, in waytynge of eyes.
C.13.189   In wommen, in *wedes* and in wordes bothe
C.22.211   *Wede* ne worldly mete while thy lif lasteth.'

weend > wenden

weer n *were n.(5)* B 2; C 1 wer
B.11.116   And in a *weer* gan I wexe, and wiþ myself to dispute
B.16.3   Ac ȝit I am in a *weer* what charite is to mene.'
C.12.51   And in a *wer* gan y wex and with mysulue to despute

weere > ben

weet n *wet n.* A 1 wet; B 2; C 1 wete
A. 6.18   Þat I haue walkid wel wide in *wet* & in driȝe,
B. 5.530   That I haue walked [wel] wide in *weet* and in drye
B.14.171   For may no derþe hem deere, droghte ne *weet*,
C. 7.175   /[Y haue] ywalked ful wyde in *wete* and in drye

weet adj *wet adj.* B 2 weet (1) wete (1); C 1 wete
B.14.41   First þe wilde worm vnder *weet* erþe,
B.17.328   It dooþ hym worse þan his wif or *wete* to slepe;
C.19.308   Hit doth hym worse then his wyf or *wete* to slepe;

weetshoed adj *wetshod adj.* B 2; C 2 watschoed (1) weetshoed (1)
B.14.161   And yet is wynter for hem worse, for *weetshoed* þei [gange],
B.18.1   Wolleward and *weetshoed* wente I forþ after
C.16.14   And ȝut is wynter for hem worse for *weetshoed* þey g[ang]e,
C.20.1   Wollewaerd and *watschoed* wente y forth aftur

weex > wexen

wehee n *wehe n.* A 2 wehe; B 2
A. 4.21   And ȝet wile [h]e make many *wehe* er we come þere.'
A. 8.74   But as wilde bestis wiþ *wehe*, & worþ vp togideris
B. 4.23   For he wol make *wehee* twies er [we] be þere.'
B. 7.92   But as wilde bestes with *wehee* worþen vppe and werchen,

wey n *wei n.(1)* &> wye A 17 way (1) waye (1) wey (10) weye (3) weiȝe
  (1) weyes (1); B 32 wey (27) weye (3) weyes (2); C 46 way (32)
  wayes (2) wey (7) weye (4) weyes (1)
A.Pr.48   Wenten forþ in here *wey* wiþ many wise talis,
A. 3.17   For we wile wisse þe king & þi *wey* [shape]
A. 4.29   Ac consience com arst to court be a myle *wey*
A. 6.1   Ac þere w[ere] fewe men so wys þat þe [*wey*] þider couþe,
A. 6.21   Canst þou wisse vs þe *wey* where þat wy dwelliþ?'
A. 6.47   Ac ȝe þat wilneþ to wende, þis is þe *weye* þider:
A. 7.1   'Þis were a wikkide *weye*, but whoso hadde a gide
A. 7.4   I haue an half akir to er[e]n be þe heiȝe *weiȝe*;

A. 7.53   And wende wiþ ȝow þe *wey* til we fynde treuþe.'
A. 7.178   [Þat leyȝe [blereyed] and brokelegged by þe hye *waye*];
A. 8.29   Wykkide *weyes* wiȝtly to amende,
A. 8.130   Musyng on þis metelis a myle *wey* I ȝede;
A.11.112   And axide hire þe heiȝe *wey* where clergie [dwell]ide,
A.11.114   'Axe þe heiȝe *wey*,' quaþ heo, 'from henis to suffre
A.11.167   And wente wiȝtly my *wey* wiþoute more lettyng,
A.12.56   And wente forþ on my *way* with omnia probate,
A.12.64   To lyf in his lordshepe longyt my *weye*
B.Pr.48   Wenten forþ in hire *wey* wiþ many wise tales,
B.Pr.166   Men myȝte witen wher þei wente and [hire] *wey* r[oum]e.
B.Pr.174   And if hym wrapeþ be war and his *wey* shonye.'
B. 3.17   For we wol wisse þe kyng and þi *wey* shape
B. 5.513   Ac þere was [wye] noon so wys þe *wey* þider kouþe,
B. 5.533   [Kanstow] wissen vs þe *wey* wher þat wye dwelleþ?'
B. 5.560   Ac [ye þat] wilneþ to wende, þis is þe *wey* þider.
B. 6.1   'This were a wikkede *wey* but whoso hadde a gyde
B. 6.4   I haue an half acre to erie by þe heiȝe *weye*;
B. 6.6   I wolde wende wiþ yow and þe *wey* teche.'
B. 6.58   And wende wiþ yow [þe *wey*] til we fynde truþe.'
B. 7.27   Wikkede *weyes* wightly amende
B. 7.148   Musynge on þis metels [a myle] *wey* ich yede.
B.10.160   And asked hire þe heighe *wey* where Clergie dwelte,
B.10.162   'Aske þe heighe *wey*', quod she, 'hennes to Suffre-
B.10.225   And wente wightly [my w]ey wiþoute moore lettyng,
B.12.37   And hold þee vnder obedience þat heigh *wey* is to heuene.
B.12.69   Knew neuere clerk how it comeþ forþ, ne kynde wit þe *weyes*:
B.13.220   And as þe[i] wente by þe *weye*–of dowel þei carped–
B.13.366   And but I hadde by ooþer *wey* at þe laste I stale it,
B.14.212   The heiȝe *wey* to heueneward [ofte] Richesse letteþ:
B.15.435   Of hem of holi chirche þat þe heighe *wey* sholde teche
B.16.273   Rapeliche renne forþ þe riȝte *wey* [we] wente.
B.17.50   And as we wenten þus in þe *wey* wordynge togideres
B.17.52   Ridynge ful rapely þe righte *wey* we yeden,
B.17.82   And raped hym to [ryde þe riȝte *wey* to Ierusalem].
B.17.117   Which is þe *wey* þat I wente and wher forþ to Ierusalem;
B.18.114   Cam walkynge in þe *wey*; to helleward she loked.
B.18.276   And where he wole is his *wey*; ac ware hym of þe perils;
B.19.157   Ac Marie Maudeleyne mette hym by þe *weye*
B.20.1   Thanne as I wente by þe *wey*, whan I was thus awaked,
B.20.187   Siþ whanne was þe *wey* ouer mennes heddes?'
C.Pr.49   Wenten forth [i]n here *way* with many wyse tales,
C.Pr.183   Men Myghte ywete where þei wente and here [*way* roume].
C.Pr.191   And yf hym wratheth ben war and his *way* [shonye].'
C. 1.138   By what *wey* it wexeth and wheder out of my menynges.'
C. 1.174   Ȝe shal be *weye* þerwith whenne ȝe wende hennes:
C. 1.200   And þe graffe of grace and gray[th]est *way* to heuene.
C. 2.202   For to wisse hem þe *way* and with mede abyde.
C. 3.18   For we w[o]l wisse the kyng and thy *way* shape
C. 4.53   What *wey* y wende wel ȝerne he aspyeth
C. 6.265   And but y hadde by other *wey* at the laste y stale hit
C. 7.158   Ac þer was wye non so wys þat the *way* thider couthe
C. 7.178   [Can]st [thow] wissen vs [þe w]*ay* whoderout treuth woneth?'
C. 7.205   Ac hoso wol wende þer treuthe is, this is þe *way* thede[r]:
C. 7.307   Ac þe *way* is ful wikked but hoso hadde a gyde
C. 8.2   Ich haue an half aker to erye by þe heye [*way*];
C. 8.4   Y wol[de] wende with ȝow and þe *way* teche.'
C. 9.31   And wyckede *wayes* with here goed amende
C. 9.32   And brugges tobrokene by the heye *wayes*
C. 9.189   Ac Ermytes þat inhabiten by the heye *weye*
C. 9.204   Ac thise Ermytes þat edifien thus by the heye *weye*
C. 9.297   Musyng on this meteles A myle *way* y ȝede.
C.11.102   And askede here þe hey *way* whare clergie dwelte;
C.11.104   'Aske þe hey *wey*,' [quod he], 'hennes to soffre-
C.11.134   Tho wente y my *way* withouten more lettynge
C.13.30   And lyues þat oure lord loueth and large *weyes* to heuene.
C.13.34   And sholden wende o *wey* where bothe mosten reste
C.13.42   And thogh they wen[d]e by the *wey*, tho two togederes,
C.13.43   Thogh the messager make his *way* amydde the fayre whete
C.13.46   Ac if þe marchaunt make his *way* ouer menne corne
C.13.52   And ȝut thow they wende o *way* as to wynchestre fayre
C.13.68   That holde mote þe hey *way*, euene the ten hestes,
C.15.184   And wenten forth here *way*; with grete wille y folowede.
C.15.189   And as they wente by the *way*–of dowel can they carpe–
C.16.50   Of wit and of wisdoem þat fer *way* is bettere
C.16.53   The hey *way* to heueneward he halt hit nat fol euene
C.17.190   That they ne wente [þe *wey*] as holy writ byd:
C.18.289   Rappliche renne þe riȝt *way* we wente.
C.19.48   And as we wenten in þe *way* thus wordyng of this matere
C.19.50   Rydynge ful raply þe rihte *way* we ȝeden,
C.19.79   And rapede hym to ryde the rihte *way* to Ierusalem.
C.19.92   For wente neuere man this *way* þat he ne was here yruyfled
C.20.117   Cam walkynge in þe *way*; to hellward she lokede.

C.20.298   And where he wol is his *way*, ac waer hym of þe perelles:
C.21.157   Ac Marie Maudeleyne mette hym by þe *weye*
C.22.1   [Thenne] as y wente by the *way*, when y was thus awaked,
C.22.187   Sennes whanne was þe *way* ouer menne heuedes?

weye > *wey,wye,weye,weyen; weyes* > *wey,wye; weylawey* > *welawo; weile(d
-yng* > *waille*

weyues n *weif n.* B 1; C 1 wayues

B.Pr.94   Of wardes and of wardemotes, *weyues* and streyves.
C.Pr.92   Of wardus and of wardemotis, *wayues* and strayues.

weiȝe > *wey, weye v; weiȝede* > *weye v*

weke n *weke n.(1)* B 4; C 4 weke (3) wyke (1)

B.17.207   As wex and a *weke* were twyned togideres,
B.17.209   And as wex and *weke* and [warm] fir togideres
B.17.216   The blase þerof yblowe out, yet brenneþ þe *weke*–
B.17.243   And as þe *weke* and fir wol maken a warm flaumbe
C.19.173   As wexe and a *weke* were twyned togyderes,
C.19.175   And as wex and *weke* and warm fuyr togyderes
C.19.182   The blase be yblowen out, ȝut brenneth þe *weke*–
C.19.209   And as þe *wyke* and [fuyr wol make a warm] flaume

wel adj *wel adj.* A 3; B 4; C 5

A. 3.61   To writen in wyndowis of ȝoure *wel* dedis,
A. 3.142   Þere she is *wel* wiþ þe king wo is þe reaume,
A. 7.261   Wende now whanne þi wille is, þat *wel* be þou euere.'
B. 3.65   To writen in wyndowes of hir *wel* dedes,
B. 3.70   To writen in wyndowes of youre *wel* dedes
B. 3.153   Ther she is *wel* wiþ þe kyng wo is þe Reaume,
B. 6.277   Wend now whan [þi wil is], þat *wel* be þow euere.'\
C. 3.69   To writen [i]n wyndowes of eny *wel* dedes,
C. 3.191   Ther she is *wel* with eny kyng wo is þ[e] rewme
C. 4.183   'Y wolde hit were,' quod the kynge, '*wel* al aboute.
C. 8.298   Wende nouthe when thow wol[t] and *wel* [be thow] euere
C.15.301   Many man hath his ioye here for al here *wel* dedes

wel adv *wel adv.* A 80; B 172; C 159

A.Pr.26   Al for loue of oure lord lyuede *wel* streite
A.Pr.69   Lewide men leuide [hym] *wel* & likide his speche;
A. 1.41   'A madame mercy,' quaþ I, 'me likiþ *wel* ȝoure wordis.
A. 1.49   "Cesar," þ[ei] seide, "we se *wel* ichone."
A. 2.46   Alle to wytnesse *wel* what þe writ wolde:
A. 2.56   Þus begynne þe gomes & gredde *wel* heiȝe:
A. 2.93   *Wel* ȝe wyte, wernardis, but ȝif ȝoure wyt faile,
A. 2.105   It shal besette ȝoure soulis *wel* sore at þe laste.'
A. 2.150   Soþnesse seiȝ hem *wel* & seide but litel,
A. 3.36   And seide [*wel*] softely, in shrifte as it were,
A. 3.40   And ek be þi baudekyn, & bere *wel* þin arnede
A. 3.47   'We haue a wyndowe [in] werching wile stonde vs *wel* heiȝe;
A. 3.71   For þei poisone þe peple preuyly *wel* ofte,
A. 3.75   Ne bouȝte none burgages, be ȝe *wel* certayn.
A. 3.113   In trist of hire tresour she teniþ [*wel*] manye;
A. 3.151   Wiþoute presentis or panis he plesiþ [*wel*] fewe.
A. 3.167   *Wel* þou wost, consience, but ȝif þou wilt leiȝe,
A. 3.204   Seruauntis for here seruyse, we se *wel* þe soþe,
A. 3.220   To hem þat werchen *wel* whiles þei ben here.
A. 3.236   In marchaundie is no mede, I may it *wel* auowe;
A. 4.19   And let warroke hym *wel* wiþ [wy]tful gerþis.
A. 4.33   And wordiden a gret while *wel* wisly togidere.
A. 4.66   Consience & þe king kneuȝ *wel* þe soþe,
A. 4.67   And wisten *wel* þat wrong was a shrewe euere.
A. 4.87   'For he haþ wagid me *wel* as wysdom hym tauȝte
A. 4.146   'Ac it is *wel* hard, be myn hed, herto to bringe it.
A. 5.21   Of þis mater I miȝte mamele *wel* longe,
A. 5.75   To apeire hym be my power I pursuide *wel* ofte,
A. 5.78   His grace & hise gode happis greuide me *wel* sore.
A. 5.104   'Sorewe for synne sauiþ *wel* manye.'
A. 5.154   'Ȝa, glotoun gossib,' quaþ heo, 'god wot, *wel* hote:
A. 5.239   Þi wil w[orþ]e vpon me, as I haue *wel* deseruid
A. 5.246   *Wel* I woot he wep faste watir wiþ his eiȝen,
A. 6.18   Þat I haue walkid *wel* wide in wet & in driȝe,
A. 6.37   [I] haue myn here of hym [*wel*] & oþerwhile more;
A. 6.42   I [wile] wisse ȝow *wel* riȝt to his place.'
A. 6.55   Wadiþ in þat watir & wasshiþ ȝow *wel* þere,
A. 6.66   And hold *wel* þin haliday heiȝ til euen.
A. 6.93   Þou shalt se treuþe himself *wel* sitte in þin herte
A. 6.102   Þus miȝt þou lese his loue, to lete *wel* be þiselue,
A. 6.109   Largenesse þe lady let in *wel* manye.
A. 6.113   It is *wel* hard, be myn hed, any of ȝow alle,
A. 7.43   In a *wel* perilous place þat purcatorie hattiþ;
A. 7.122   Ȝe ben wastours, I wot *wel*, & treuþe wot þe soþe;
A. 7.138   He abideþ *wel* þe betere þat bummiþ nouȝt to ofte.'
A. 7.190   For I wot *wel*, be þou ywent, hy wile werche ille;
A. 7.230   And þat he weniþ *wel* to haue I wile it be hym bereuid".

A. 7.241   'I wot *wel*,' quaþ hunger, 'what seknesse hem eileþ.
A. 8.11   Han pardoun þoruȝ purcatorie to passe *wel* sone,
A. 8.59   His pardoun in purcatorie *wel* [petit] is, I trowe,
A. 8.98   But do *wel* & haue wel, & god shal haue þi soule,
A. 8.98   But do wel & haue *wel*, & god shal haue þi soule,
A. 8.132   And for peris loue þe plouȝman *wel* pensif in herte,
A. 8.164   It is not so sikir for þe soule, certis, as is do *wel*.
A. 9.64   'þat þou wost *wel*,' quaþ he, '& no wiȝt betere.'
A.10.10   Ac kynde knowiþ [þis] *wel* and kepiþ hire þe betere,
A.10.19   Sire se *wel*, & sey wel, & here wel þe hende,
A.10.19   Sire se wel, & sey *wel*, & here wel þe hende,
A.10.19   Sire se wel, & sey wel, & here *wel* þe hende,
A.10.20   Sire werche *wel* wiþ þin hond, [a] wiȝt man of strengþe,
A.10.21   And sire godefrey go *wel*, grete lordis alle.
A.10.75   For werche he *wel* oþer wrong, þe wyt is his owene.
A.10.88   Ac ȝif clene consience acorde þat þiself dost *wel*
A.11.5   '*Wel* art þou wys, wyt,' quaþ she, 'any wisdomis to telle
A.11.109   Shuln wisse þe to dowel, I dar *wel* vndirtake.'
A.11.120   Til þou come to a court, kepe *wel* þi tunge
A.11.126   And þat [I] grete wel his wyf for I wrot hire þe bible,
A.11.141   Ne were þe loue þat liþ þerein a *wel* lewid þing it were.
A.11.144   Leue lelly þeron ȝif þou þenke do *wel*,
A.11.157   Þat þinkeþ werche wiþ þo þre þriueþ *wel* late,
A.11.162   Ȝif þou þenke do *wel* deile þerewith neuere.
A.11.182   'It is a *wel* lel[e] lif,' quaþ she, 'among þe lewide peple;
A.11.199   Dobet doþ ful *wel*, & dewid he is also,
A.11.218   And *wel*awey wers and I [wo]lde al telle.'
A.11.268   De[m]de he not *wel* & wisly, as holy [writ] techiþ,
A.12.36   And drow þe dore after him and bad me go do *wel*
A.12.43   And sayde, 'my cosyn kynde wit knowen is *wel* wide,
A.12.99   Wille þurgh inwit [wiste] *wel* þe soþe,
A.12.100   Þat þis speche was spedelich, and sped him *wel* faste,
A.12.106   And so bad Iohan bat busily *wel* ofte
B.Pr.26   Al for loue of oure lord lyueden [*wel*] streyte
B.Pr.72   Lewed men leued [hym] *wel* and liked hi[s speche];
B.Pr.152   'For doute of diuerse d[e]des we dar noȝt *wel* loke,
B.Pr.208   Forþi ech a wis wiȝt I warne, wite *wel* his owene.
B. 1.43   '[A] madame, mercy', quod I, 'me likeþ *wel* youre wordes.
B. 1.51   "Cesar[i]s", þei seiden, "we seen *wel* echone."
B. 1.130   [Ac] þo þat werche *wel* as holy writ telleþ,
B. 2.74   [Th]us bigynnen þ[e] gomes [and] greden [*wel*] heiȝe:
B. 2.129   *Wel* ye witen, wernardes, but if youre wit faille,
B. 2.141   It shal bisitte youre soules [*wel*] soure at þe laste.'
B. 2.189   Sothnesse seiȝ hem *wel* and seide but litel,
B. 3.37   And seide [*wel*] softely, in shrift as it were,
B. 3.41   And [ek] be þi [baudekyn] and bere *wel* þ[yn erende]
B. 3.48   'We haue a wyndow in werchynge wole [stonden] vs *wel* hye;
B. 3.54   And lakkeþ noȝt ladies þat louen *wel* þe same.
B. 3.82   For þei [p]oisone þe peple pryueliche [*wel*] ofte
B. 3.86   Ne bouȝte none burgages, be ye [*wel*] certeyne.
B. 3.124   [In] trust of hire tresor [she teneþ *wel*] manye.
B. 3.162   Wiþouten presentȝ or pens [he] pleseþ *wel* fewe.
B. 3.180   *Wel* þow woost, [Conscience], but if þow wolt [lie],
B. 3.217   Ser[u]auntȝ for here seruyce, we se[þ] *wel* þe soþe,
B. 3.233   To [hem] þat [werchen *wel*] while þei ben here.
B. 3.257   In marchaundise is no Mede, I may it *wel* auowe;
B. 3.337   'I leue *wel*, lady', quod Conscience, 'þat þi latyn be trewe.
B. 4.21   And lat warroke hym *wel* wiþ wit[ful] gerþes.
B. 4.32   A[c] Conscience knew hem *wel*, þei loued coueitise,
B. 4.46   And wordeden [a gret while *wel* wisely] togideres.
B. 4.71   I seye it by myself, þow shalt it *wel* fynde.
B. 4.80   Conscience and þe commune kn[e]wen [*wel*] þe soþe,
B. 4.100   'For he haþ waged me *wel* as wisdom hym tauȝte
B. 4.181   And as moost folk witnesseþ *wel* wrong shal be demed.'
B. 4.183   It is [*wel*] hard, by myn heed, hert[o] to brynge it,
B. 5.21   Of þis matere I myȝte mamelen [*wel*] longe,
B. 5.95   To apeire hym bi my power pursued *wel* ofte],
B. 5.98   His grace and his goode happes greuen me [*wel*] soore.
B. 5.142   And now is fallen þerof a fruyt þat folk han *wel* leuere
B. 5.179   [I] haue a flux of a foul mouþ *wel* fyue dayes after;
B. 5.192   *Wel* sidder þan his chyn; þei chyueled for elde;
B. 5.261   'God lene þee neuere grace] þi good *wel* to bisette,
B. 5.263   Ne þyne executours *wel* bisette þe siluer þat þow hem leuest;
B. 5.472   *Wel* I woot he wepte faste water wiþ hise eiȝen,
B. 5.530   That I haue walked [*wel*] wide in weet and in drye
B. 5.550   I haue myn hire [of hym] *wel* and ouþerwhiles moore.
B. 5.555   I [wol] wisse yow [*wel* riȝt] to his place.'
B. 5.568   Wadeþ in þat water and wasshe yow *wel* þer
B. 5.579   And hold *wel* þyn haliday heighe til euen.
B. 5.592   The brugg[e] is of bidde-wel-þe-bet-may-þow-spede;
B. 5.616   Thus myȝtestow lesen his loue, to lete *wel* by þiselue,
B. 5.623   Largenesse þe lady let in [*wel*] manye;
B. 5.628   It is [*wel*] hard, by myn heed, any of yow alle

B. 6.44	In a [*wel*] perilous place [þat] Purgatorie hatte.
B. 6.46	Thouȝ he be þyn vnderlyng here *wel* may happe in heuene
B. 6.130	Ye ben wastours, I woot *wel*, and truþe woot þe soþe;
B. 6.195	And ech a pouere man *wel* apaied to haue pesen for his hyre,
B. 6.201	'I am *wel* awroke of wastours þoruȝ þy myȝte.
B. 6.204	For I woot *wel*, be þow went þei wol werche ille;
B. 6.246	And þat he weneþ *wel* to haue I wole it hym bireue".
B. 6.257	'I woot *wel*', quod hunger, 'what siknesse yow eyleþ.
B. 7.58	Hi[s] pardon is [*wel*] petit at hi[s] partyng hennes
B. 7.116	But do *wel* and haue wel, and god shal haue þi soule,
B. 7.116	But do wel and haue *wel*, and god shal haue þi soule,
B. 7.151	And for Piers [loue] þe Plowman [*wel*] pencif in herte,
B. 8.51	God wole suffre *wel* þi sleuþe if þiself likeþ,
B. 8.52	For he yaf þee [to] yeresȝyue to yeme *wel* þiselue
B. 8.56	But if he werche *wel* þerwiþ as dowel hym techeþ.'
B. 8.73	'That þow woost *wel*', quod he, 'and no wiȝt bettre.'
B. 9.10	Ac kynde knoweþ þis *wel* and kepeþ hire þe bettre.
B. 9.20	Sire Se-*wel*, and Sey-wel, and here-wel þe hende,
B. 9.20	Sire Se-wel, and Sey-*wel*, and here-wel þe hende,
B. 9.20	Sire Se-wel, and Sey-wel, and here-*wel* þe hende,
B. 9.21	Sire werch-*wel*-wiþ-þyn-hand, a wiȝt man of strengþe,
B. 9.22	And sire Godefray Go-*wel*, grete lordes [alle].
B. 9.40	Thouȝ he [wiste to] write neuer so *wel*, [and] he hadde [a] penne,
B. 9.95	He dooþ noȝt *wel* þat dooþ þus, ne drat noȝt god almyȝty,
B. 9.97	That dredeþ god, he dooþ *wel*; þat dredeþ hym for loue
B.10.5	'Wel artow wis, [wit], quod she], 'any wisdomes to telle
B.10.157	Shullen wissen þee to dowel, I dar [*wel*] vndertake.'
B.10.168	Til þow come to a court, kepe-*wel*-þi-tunge-
B.10.174	And þat I grete *wel* his wif, for I wroot hire [þe bible],
B.10.189	[Ne were þe loue þat liþ þerinne a *wel* lewed þyng it were].
B.10.214	[That] þynkeþ werche with þo [þre] þryue[þ *wel*] late,
B.10.219	If þow þynke to dowel *wel* berwiþ neuere.
B.10.383	I leue it *wel* by oure lord and on no lettrure bettre.
B.10.387	He demed *wel* and wisely as holy writ telleþ;
B.10.403	Forþi wise witted men and *wel* ylettrede clerkes
B.10.437	Ther are witty and *wel* libbynge ac hire werkes ben yhudde
B.11.35	'Folwe forþ þat Fortune wole; þow hast *wel* fer til Elde.
B.11.39	If truþe wol witnesse it be *wel* do Fortune to folwe
B.11.42	'Ye! fare*wel*, Phippe', quod Faunteltee, and forþ gan me drawe
B.11.146	Gregorie wiste þis *wel*, and wilned to my soule
B.11.158	*Wel* ouȝte ye lordes þat lawes kepe þis lesson haue in mynde
B.11.195	Ac for þe pouere I shal paie, and pure *wel* quyte hir trauaille
B.11.200	And breþeren as of oo blood, as *wel* beggeres as Erles.
B.11.265	To wepe and to *wel* bidde, wherof wexeþ Mercy
B.11.267	And *wel* sikerer he slepeþ, þe [segge] þat is pouere,
B.11.398	For al þat he [wrouȝt] was *wel* ydo, as holy writ witnesseþ:
B.11.402	For man was maad of swich a matere he may noȝt *wel* asterte
B.12.20	I seiȝ *wel* he seide me sooþ, and somwhat me to excuse
B.12.32	For he dooþ *wel*, wiþouten doute, þat dooþ as lewte techeþ.
B.12.38	And if þow be maiden to marye and myȝt *wel* continue,
B.12.56	Wo is hym þat hem weldeþ but he hem [*wel*] despende:
B.12.153	Clerkes knewen it *wel* and comen wiþ hir presentȝ
B.12.187	*Wel* may þe barn blesse þat hym to book sette,
B.12.213	And *wel* lose[l]ly he lolleþ þere by þe lawe of holy chirche:
B.12.265	And *wel* awey of wynge swifter þan þe Pecock,
B.13.24	And for Conscience of Clergie spak I com *wel* þe raþer.
B.13.27	Conscience knew hym *wel* and welcomed hym faire.
B.13.42	Of þat men myswonne þei made hem *wel* at ese,
B.13.111	I wolde permute my penaunce with youre, for I am in point to do*wel*.'
B.13.178	That Pacience þ[o] most passe, 'for pilgrymes konne *wel* lye'.
B.13.180	'Frendes, fareþ *wel*', and faire spak to clergie,
B.13.263	Al londoun, I leue, likeþ *wel* my wafres,
B.13.306	And of werkes þat he *wel* dide witnesse and siggen,
B.13.348	As *wel* fastyng dayes [as] Fridaies [and] forboden nyȝtes,
B.14.82	Forþi mesure we vs *wel* and make [we] feiþ oure sheltrom;
B.14.83	And þoruȝ feiþ comeþ contricion, conscience woot *wel*,
B.14.114	And makest hem *wel* neiȝ meke and mylde for defaute,
B.14.145	Ac if ye riche haue ruþe and rewarde *wel* þe poore,
B.14.150	And whan he haþ doon his deuoir *wel* men dooþ hym ooþer bountee,
B.14.153	And alle þat doon hir deuoir *wel* han double hire for hir trauaille,
B.14.167	And yliche witty and wise, if þee *wel* hadde liked.
B.14.241	For men knowen *wel* þat Coueitise is of [a] kene wille
B.14.278	'[Al þis] in englissh', quod Pacience, 'it is *wel* hard to expounen
B.14.282	Riȝt as contricion is confortable þyng, conscience woot *wel*,
B.14.296	Ne borweþ of hise neighebores but þat he may *wel* paie:
B.15.17	In cristes court yknowe *wel* and of [cristene in many a place].
B.15.77	As *wel* freres as ooþer folk, foliliche spenden
B.15.181	He kan portreye *wel* þe Paternoster and peynte it with Aues
B.15.187	Labouren in [a] lauendrye *wel* þe lengþe of a Mile,
B.15.234	That wiþouten wiles ledeþ [*wel*] hir lyues:
B.15.263	For *wel* may euery man wite, if god hadde wold hymselue,
B.15.450	As *wel* þoruȝ hise werkes as wiþ hise holy wordes
B.15.454	Wasshen *wel* wiþ water and wiþ taseles cracched,
B.15.462	Ye mynnen *wel* how Mathew seiþ, how a man made a feste.
B.15.554	Togideres loue leelly, leueþ it *wel*, ye bisshopes,
B.15.592	And by þat mangerie [þei] myȝte *wel* se þat Messie he semede;
B.16.47	That is lieutenaunt to loken it *wel* bi leue of myselue:
B.16.214	The sone, if I dorste seye, resembleþ *wel* þe widewe:
B.16.218	So widewe withouten wedlok may noȝt *wel* stande,
B.16.227	Thre men, to my siȝte, I made *wel* at ese,
B.17.7	And whan it is enseled [þerwiþ] I woot *wel* þe soþe
B.17.45	And wel awey worse ȝit for to loue a sherewe.
B.17.47	Than for to louye and lene as *wel* lorels as lele.
B.17.75	*Wel* sixe Mile or seuene biside þe newe Market;
B.17.263	That riche ben and reson knoweþ ruleþ *wel* youre soule;
B.18.181	For Iesus Iustede *wel* ioye bigynneþ dawe:
B.18.216	For til modicum mete with vs, I may it *wel* auowe,
B.18.244	And as he wente on þe water *wel* hym knew and seide,
B.18.308	Wiþ glorie and with gret light; god it is, I woot *wel*.
B.19.26	'Thow knewest *wel*', quod Conscience, 'and þow konne reson,
B.19.62	He may [be *wel*] called conquerour, and þat is crist to mene.
B.19.110	And þere bigan god of his grace to do *wel*:
B.19.116	Bigan god of his grace and goodnesse to do*wel*,
B.19.123	After þe kynde þat he cam of; þere comsede he do *wel*.
B.19.162	For þat womm[a]n witeþ may noȝt *wel* be counseille.
B.19.193	And rewarde hym right *wel* þat reddit quod debet,
B.19.252	'Thouȝ some be clenner þan some, ye se *wel*', quod Grace,
B.19.278	Er he [dide] any [dede] deuyse *wel* þe ende;
B.19.358	For witterly, I woot *wel*, we beþ noȝt of strengþe
B.19.408	Leue it *wel* [þow art] lost, boþe lif and soule.'
B.19.430	A[c] *wel* worþe Piers þe plowman þat pursueþ god in doynge,
B.19.435	As *wel* for a wastour and wenches of þe stewes
B.20.25	For Spiritus fortitudinis forfeteþ [*wel*] ofte;
B.20.39	And woneden [*wel*] elengely] and wolde noȝt be riche.
B.20.61	And alle hise as *wel* as hym, saue oonly fooles;
B.20.62	Whiche foolis were *wel* [gladdere] to deye
B.20.231	Ac for þei kouþe noȝt *wel* hir craft Conscience forsook hem.
B.20.235	They wol flatere [to] fare *wel* folk þat ben riche.
B.20.302	And woundede *wel* wikkedly many a wys techere
B.20.304	Conscience called a leche þat koude *wel* shryue:
B.20.322	I may *wel* suffre', seide Conscience, 'syn ȝe desiren,
B.20.337	Conscience knoweþ me *wel* and what I kan boþe.
C.Pr.70	Lewed men leued hym *wel* and lykede his wordes;
C.Pr.100	Al þe world wot *wel* hit myghte nouȝt be trewe
C.Pr.117	God was *wel* þe wrother and took þe raþer vengeance.
C.Pr.122	*Wel* hardere and grettere on suche shrewed faderes
C. 1.41	'A madame, mercy,' [quod I], 'me lyketh *wel* ȝoure wordes.
C. 1.132	And alle þat han *wel* ywrouhte wende þey sholle
C. 2.49	Knowe hem *wel* yf þou kanst and kepe the fro hem alle
C. 2.145	For *wel* ȝe wyte, wernardus, as holy writ telleth,
C. 2.203	Sothnesse seyh hem [*wel*] and sayde but lytel,
C. 3.48	For to ben here bedman and bere *wel* here ernde
C. 3.51	'We han a wyndowe awurchynge wol stande vs [*wel*] heye;
C. 3.58	And laketh na ladyes þat louyeth [*wel*] þe same.
C. 3.142	Or in a *wel* wors, wo[ne ther as an ancre,
C. 3.200	Withoute presentes oþer pans he pleseth [*wel*] fewe.
C. 3.226	*Wel* thow wost, weye, but yf thow wille gabbe,
C. 3.273	Seruantes for here seruyse, [we see *wel*] þe sothe],
C. 3.313	In Marchandise is no mede, y may hit *wel* avowe;
C. 4.21	And lat warrokye [hym] w[e]l with auys[e]-þe-byfore;
C. 4.32	Ac Consience knewe hem *wel* and carped to resoun:
C. 4.52	[A w]ayteth ful *wel* when y seluer take,
C. 4.53	What wey y wende *wel* ȝerne he aspyeth
C. 4.76	Consience knoweth hit *wel* and al þe Comune trewe.'
C. 4.96	'For he [hath] waged me *wel* as wysdom hym tauhte
C. 4.154	And sayden, 'we seyn *wel*, syre resoun, be thi wordes
C. 5.8	And lymes to labory with and louede *wel* fare
C. 5.123	Of this mater y myhte mamele [*wel*] longe
C. 5.181	'For þe comune is the kynges tresor, Consience woet *wel*.
C. 6.48	They to wene þat y were *wel* holy and almesfull
C. 6.53	Of werkes þat y *wel* dede witnesse take
C. 6.108	Thow y sitte this seuene ȝer, y sholde nat *wel* telle
C. 6.161	Y haue a flux of a foul mouth *wel* fyue daies aftur;
C. 6.182	As *wel* fastyng dayes and frydayes and heye fest[e] euenes.
C. 6.200	*Wel* syddore then his chyn, ycheueled for elde,
C. 6.254	Shal neuere seketoure[s] *wel* bysette the syluer þat thow hem leuest
C. 6.326	*Wel* y woet a wepte faste water with his yes
C. 6.419	Then [wakede he] *wel* wanne and wolde haue ydronke;
C. 7.194	Y haue myn huyre of hym *wel* and oþerwhiles more.
C. 7.199	Y wol wissen ȝow *wel* ryht to his place.'
C. 7.215	Wadeth in þat water and wascheth ȝow *wel* there
C. 7.226	And hold *wel* þ[in] haliday heye til euen.
C. 7.240	The Brygge hatte b[id]-*wel*-the-bet-may-th[ow]-spede;
C. 7.268	Thus myhte thow lesen his loue, to lete *wel* by thysulue,

C. 7.300   'Y haue wedded a wyf *wel* wantowen of maneres;
C. 8.115   Therwith was [Perkyn] apayed and payede *wel* here huyre.
C. 8.139   3e been wastours, y woet *wel*, and waste and deuouren
C. 8.207   'Y am *wel* awroke of wastours thorw thy myhte
C. 8.210   For y woet *wel*, be [thow] went, worche þei wol ful ille;
C. 8.257   And þat he weneth *wel* to haue y wol hit hym bireue".
C. 8.269   'Y wot *wel*,' quod hungur, 'what sekenesse 3ow ayleth.
C. 8.299   For thow hast *wel* awroke me and also wel ytauhte me.'
C. 8.299   For thow hast wel awroke me and also *wel* ytauhte me.'
C. 9.67   Bote ther he wiste were *wel* grete nede
C. 9.128   And alle manere munstrals, me woet *wel* þe sothe,
C. 9.147   And when he is rysen rometh out and ri3t *wel* aspyeth
C. 9.237   And hoso breketh this, be *wel* waer, but yf he repente,
C. 9.245   Or sonendayes at euensong? se we *wel* fewe!
C. 9.290   Bote do *wel* and haue wel, and [god] shal haue thy soule
C. 9.290   Bote do wel and haue *wel*, and [god] shal haue thy soule
C. 9.319   And how þe prest preuede no pardon to do *wel*:
C. 9.322   For hoso doth *wel* here at þe day of dome
C.10.25   And hoso synegeth,' y sayde, 'certes he doth nat *wel*;
C.10.71   'That þou [wost] w[el],' quod he, 'and no wyht bettere.'
C.10.137   A[c] kynde knoweth this *wel* and kepeth here þe betere
C.10.146   Sire se-*wel* and sey-wel [and] here-wel þe [h]ende,
C.10.146   Sire se-wel and sey-*wel* [and] here-wel þe [h]ende,
C.10.146   Sire se-wel and sey-wel [and] here-*wel* þe [h]ende,
C.10.147   Sire worch-*wel*-with-thyn-hand, a wyht man of strenghe,
C.10.148   And sire go[dfray] go-*wel*, grete lordes alle.
C.10.188   Ac thenne dede we alle *wel*, and wel bet 3ut, to louye
C.10.188   Ac thenne dede we alle wel, and *wel* bet 3ut, to louye
C.10.201   For hoso loueth, leueth h[it] *wel*, god wol nat laton hym sterue
C.10.203   Hoso lyueth in lawe and in loue doth *wel*
C.10.239   Ac Westm[in]stre lawe, y woet *wel*, worcheth þe contra[r]ye;
C.10.260   A mayde and *wel* yma[ner]ed and of gode men yspronge,
C.10.265   For riche or yrented *wel*, thouh he be reueled for elde
C.11.5   '*Wel* artow wyse,' quod she to wyt, 'suche wysdomes to shewe
C.11.114   And sey y gre[t]e *wel* his wyf, for y wrot here a bible
C.11.194   'Folowe forth þat fortune wole; þou hast [*wel*] fer to elde.
C.11.208   Y leue hit *wel* by oure lord and on no lettrure bettere.
C.11.213   And demede *wel* and wysly; wymmen bereth wittenesse:
C.11.223   That hoso doth by 3oure doctrine doth *wel*, y leue,
C.11.233   *Wel* ywitted men and wel ylettred clerkes,
C.11.233   Wel ywitted men and *wel* ylettred clerkes,
C.11.309   '3e! fare*wel*, fyppe,' quod fauntelete and forth gan me drawe
C.12.81   Gregori wiste this *wel* and wilned to my soule
C.12.90   *Wel* ouhte 3e lordes þat lawes kepeth this lesson haue in mynde
C.12.116   And we his blody bretherne, as *wel* beggares as lordes.
C.12.140   And aytheres werkes and wille] riht *wel* alowede
C.12.152   And *wel* sikorere he slepeth, þe segg þat is pore,
C.12.192   Aren not so worthy as whete ne so *wel* mowe
C.12.235   For, how [euere hit] be ywonne, but hit [be] *wel* despene[d]
C.13.1   Ac *wel* worth pouerte for he may walke vnrobbed
C.13.82   And other pryue penaunces þe which þe prest woet *wel*
C.13.210   Man was made of such [a] matere he may nat *wel* asterte
C.13.233   For shal neuere, ar shame come, a shrewe *wel* [be] chaste[d].
C.14.4   And wissed the [*wel*] ofte what dowel was to mene
C.14.10   And thenne dost thow *wel*, withoute drede; ho can do bet no force.
C.14.13   Ac to louye and lene and lyue *wel* and byleue
C.14.18   Wo is hym þat hem weldeth but he hem *wel* despene:
C.14.126   *Wel* may þe barne blesse þat hym to boek sette,
C.14.152   And *wel* lo[s]liche he lolleth þere by þe lawe of holy churche:
C.14.159   Was neuere creature vnder crist þat knewe *wel* þe bygynnyng
C.15.14   As *wel* lered as lewede and lorde as þe [b]oende,
C.15.30   Concience knewe hym [*wel* and] welcomede hym fayre.
C.15.36   Concience knewe h[y]m *wel* and welcomede hem all;
C.15.45   Ac of this mete þat maystre myhte nat we[l c]hewe;
C.15.47   Of þat men myswonne they made hem *wel* at ese
C.15.63   Pacience was *wel* apayed of this propre seruice
C.15.113   And thenne dost thow *wel* and wysly, y dar hit wel avowe.'
C.15.113   And thenne dost thow wel and wysly, y dar hit *wel* avowe.'
C.15.290   And makest hem *wel* neyh meke and mylde for defaute
C.16.34   Ho doth *wel* or bet or beste aboue alle;
C.16.81   For men knowen *wel* þat coueytise is of a kene will
C.16.131   Ne boreweth of his neyhebore but þat he may *wel* paye
C.16.159   A knewe Consience ful *wel* and clergie bothe.
C.16.168   And in cristes court yknowe *wel* and of his kynne a party.
C.16.177   To do *wel* or wykke, a will with a resoun,
C.16.221   The bittorere he shal abugge but yf he *wel* worche
C.16.236   As *wel* freres as oþere folk, fotiliche spenden
C.16.238   More for pompe and pruyde, as þe peple woet *wel*
C.16.283   Leueth hit *wel*, lordes, both lewed and lered,
C.16.323   And purtraye *wel* þe paternoster and peynten hit with Auees.
C.17.122   Ac 3if prestes doen here deuer *wel* we shal do þe bettre
C.17.182   And on his lore thei l[e]uen 3ut, as *wel* lered as lewed.
C.17.217   Togederes louyen lelelyche, l[e]ueth hit [*wel*], bisshopes,

C.18.223   And man withoute a make myhte nat *wel* of kynde
C.18.244   And what y thouhte and my wyf he vs *wel* tolde.
C.19.9   Were hit þerwith aseled y woet *wel* þe sothe
C.19.45   And lereth þat we louye sholde as *wel* lyares as lele.
C.19.229   That riche ben and resoun knoweth; reule *wel* 3oure soul[e];
C.19.244   Sethe he withoute wyles wan and *wel* myhte atymye
C.20.184   For iesus ioustede *wel* ioy bigynneth dawe:
C.20.225   For til [modicum] mete with vs, y may hit *wel* avowe;
C.20.253   And as he wente on þe watur *wel* hym knewe and saide,
C.20.342   With glorie and with [grete] lihte; god hit is ich woet *wel*.
C.21.26   'Thow knowest *wel*,' quod Concience, 'and þou kunne resoun,
C.21.62   He may be *wel* called conquerour and that is Crist to mene.
C.21.110   And þer bigan god of his grace to do *wel*:
C.21.116   Bigan god of his grace and goodnesse to do *wel*
C.21.123   Aftur þe kynde þat he cam of; þer comsede he do *wel*.
C.21.162   For þat womman witeth [may] nat [*wel* be] conseyl.
C.21.193   And rewarde hym riht *wel* that redd[it] quod debet,
C.21.252   'Thouh somme be clenner then somme, 3e sen *wel*,' quod grace,
C.21.278   Ar he dede eny dede deuyse *wel* þe ende;
C.21.358   For witterly, y woet *wel*, we be nat of strenghe
C.21.408   Leue hit [*wel* thou] be[st] lost, bothe lyf and soule.'
C.21.430   Ac *wel* worth Peres the plouhman þat pursueth god in doyng[e],
C.21.435   As *wel* for a wastour [and] wenche[s] of the stuyves
C.22.25   For spiritus fortitudinis forfeteth *wel* ofte;
C.22.39   And woneden *wel* elyngly and wolden nat be riche.
C.22.61   And alle hise as *wel* as hym, saue onelich foles;
C.22.62   [Whiche foles] were *wel* gladere to deye
C.22.194   And wesched *wel* witterly þat y were in heuene.
C.22.231   A[c] for they couthe nat *wel* here crafte Consience forsoek hem.
C.22.235   Thei wol flatere to fare *wel* folk þat ben riche.
C.22.302   And wounded *wel* wykkedly many a wys techare
C.22.304   Consience calde a leche þat couthe *wel* shryue:
C.22.322   Y may *wel* soffre,' sayde Consience, 'sennes 3e desiren,
C.22.337   Consience knoweth me *wel* and what y can bothe.'

wel &> dowel; welaway > welawo; welawey > wel,awey

welawo n *weilawei n.* B 2 weylawey (1) welawo (1); C 2 welaway (1)
   welowo (1)
B.14.236   That is *welawo* whan he wakeþ and wepeþ for colde,
B.18.229   Ne what is witterly wele til *weylawey* hym teche.'
C.16.77   Þat is *welowo* when he [w]aketh and wepeth for colde;
C.20.238   Ne what is witterliche wele til *welaway* hym teche.'

welche adj *Welsh adj.* A 1 walsshe; B 2 walshe (1) welche (1); C 2
   walch (1) walshe (1)
A. 5.113   He shulde wandre on þat *walsshe*, so was it þredbare.
B. 5.197   She sholde no3t [wandre] on þat *wel[ch]e*, so was it þredbare.
B. 5.316   Godefray of Garlekhiþe and Griffyn þe *walshe*;
C. 6.205   He sholde [nat] wandre [o]n þat *walch*, so was hit thredbare.
C. 6.373   Godefray þe garlekmonger and Gryffyth þe *walshe*

welcome adj *welcome adj.* A 4; B 7; C 6
A. 2.179   He was nowhere *welcome* for his many talis,
A. 2.194   And is *welcome* whanne he wile & woniþ wiþ hem ofte.
A. 6.111   He is wondirliche *welcome* & faire vndirfonge.
A.12.62   'Al hayl,' quod on þo, and I answered, '*welcome*, & with whom be
          3e?'
B. 2.220   He was nowher *welcome* for his manye tales,
B. 2.235   And is *welcome* whan he wile and woneþ with hem ofte.
B. 5.626   He is wonderly *welcome* and faire vnderfongen.
B.13.32   '*Welcome*, wye, go and wassh; þow shalt sitte soone.'
B.13.156   And herwith am I *welcome* þer I haue it wiþ me.
B.20.244   And seide, 'sires, sooþly *welcome* be ye alle
B.20.356   'Thow art *welcome*', quod Conscience; 'kanstow heele sike?
C. 2.230   He was nawher *welcome* for his many tales,
C. 2.245   And is *welcome* when he cometh and woneth with hem ofte.
C. 5.50   To be *welcome* when y come oþerwhile in a monthe,
C. 7.279   Is wonderliche *welcome* and fayre vnderfonge;
C.22.244   And saide, 'syres, soethly *welcome* be 3e alle
C.22.356   'Thow art *welcome*,' quod Consience; 'can[st] thow hele syke?

welcome v *welcomen v. (1)* B 6 welcome (3) welcomed (1) welcomeþ (2);
   C 9 welcome (3) welcomede (2) welcomen (2) welcometh (2)
B.13.27   Conscience knew hym wel and *welcomed* hym faire.
B.13.436   [Clerkes and kni3tes *welcome*þ kynges minstrales,
B.15.21   That ech a creature of his court *welcome*þ me faire.'
B.18.176   'My wil is to wende', quod she, 'and *welcome* hem alle
B.19.210   *Welcome* hym and worshipe hym wiþ Veni creator Spiritus.'
B.20.60   And al þe Couent cam to *welcome* [a] tyraunt
C. 7.96   Clerkes and knyhtes *welcometh* kynges munstrals
C. 9.135   *Welcomen* and worschipen and with 3oure goed helpen
C.15.30   Concience knewe hym [wel and] *welcomede* hym fayre.
C.15.36   Concience knewe h[y]m wel and *welcomede* hem all;
C.15.198   As a waf[e]rer with wafres, a[nd] *welcome* godes gestes.

C.16.172 That vch a creature þat loueth crist *welcometh* me faire.'
C.20.179 'My wil is to wende,' quod pees, 'and *welcomen* hem alle
C.21.210 *Welcome* hym and worschipe hym with veni creator spiritus.'
C.22.60 And al þe couent cam to *welcome* a tyraunt

welden v *welden v.* B 7 welden (2) weldeþ (4) welt (1); C 5 welde (1)
  weldeth (4)
B.10.24 That wikked men þei *welden* þe welþe of þis worlde,
B.10.29 And moost vnkynde to þe commune þat moost catel *weldeþ*:
B.10.86 And þe moore he wynneþ and *welt* welþes and richesse
B.10.91 And whoso litel *weldeþ* [wisse] hym þerafter,
B.11.72 That wedde none widwes but for to *welden* hir goodes.
B.12.56 Wo is hym þat hem *weldeþ* but he hem [wel] despende:
B.20.12 That is mete whan men hym werneþ and he no moneye *weldeþ*,
C.11.10 Then al þe precious perye þat eny prince *weldeth*.
C.11.70 And is to mene no more bote "who[so] muche goed *weldeth*
C.12.20 That wilneth nat þe wedewe bote for to *welde* here godes.
C.14.18 Wo is hym þat hem *weldeth* but he hem wel despene:
C.22.12 That is mete when men hym werneth [and] he no money *weldeth*

wele n *wele n.(1)* A 2; B 10; C 13
A.10.188 Or wedde any wydewe for any *wele* of godis,
A.11.115 Boþe *wele* & wo ȝif þat þou wile lerne,
B.9.167 Or wedden any wodewe for [*wele*] of hir goodes,
B.10.163 Boþe-*wele*-and-wo if þat þow wolt lerne;
B.18.204 And wo into *wele* mowe wenden at þe laste.
B.18.205 For hadde þei wist of no wo, *wele* hadde þei noȝt knowen;
B.18.206 For no wight woot what *wele* is þat neuere wo suffrede,
B.18.221 To wite what *wele* was, kyndeliche [to] knowe it.
B.18.229 Ne what is witterly *wele* til weylawey hym teche.'
B.19.243 Boþe of *wele* and of wo [and be ware bifore],
B.19.285 Ne wynnynge ne *wele* of worldliche richesse,
B.20.38 [Philosphres] forsoke *wele* for þei wolde be nedy
C.11.105 Bothe-*wele*-and-wo yf þou wilt lerne;
C.11.271 Ho is worthy for *wele* or for wykkede [pyne]:
C.12.209 And out of wo into *wele* ȝoure wirdes shal chaunge."
C.12.236 Worldly *wele* y[s] wykked thyng to hem þat hit kepeth.
C.15.304 Ac when deth awaketh hem of here *we[le]* þat were er so ryche
C.20.209 And wo into *wele* moet wende at þe laste.
C.20.210 For hadde they wist of no wo, *wele* hadde thay nat knowen;
C.20.211 For no wiht woet what *wele* is þat neuere wo soffrede
C.20.230 To wyte what *wele* [was], kyndeliche to knowe [hit].
C.20.238 Ne what is witterliche *wele* til welaway hym teche.'
C.21.243 Bothe of *wele* and of wo and be ywaer bifore,
C.21.285 Ne wynnynge ne *wel[e]* o[f] wordliche richesse,
C.22.38 Philosoperes forsoke *wel[e]* for they wolde be nedy

welfare n *welfare n.* B 1; C 1
B.19.353 'To wasten on *welfare* and in wikked [kepyng]
C.21.353 'To waston on *welfare* and in wikked kepynge

welhope n *n.i.d.* B 1; C 1
B.13.453 In a *welhope*, [for he wrouȝte so], amonges worþi seyntes],
C.7.113 In a *welhope* for a wrouhte so amongus worthy seyntes

welkene > *wolkne*

welle n *welle n.* B 4; C 4
B.1.164 And in þe herte þere is þe heed and þe heiȝe *welle*.
B.14.198 But oure spences and spendynge sprynge of a trewe *w[e]lle*;
B.14.310 The seuenþe is *welle* of wisedom and fewe wordes sheweþ
B.15.30 And þat is wit and wisdom, þe *welle* of alle craftes;
C.1.160 And in þe herte þer is þe hed and þe heye *welle*.
C.16.39 Bote oure spensis and spendyng sprynge of a trewe *welle*
C.16.144 The seuethe is a *welle* of wysdoem and fewe wordes sheweth
C.16.190 And þat is wit and wysdoem, the *welle* of alle craftes;

wellecresses n *wellecresse n.* C 1
C.6.292 Ȝut were me leuer, by oure lord, lyue al by *wellecresses*

wellede v *wellen v.* B 1; C 1 walled
B.19.377 And þanne *wellede* water for wikkede werkes
C.21.377 And thenne *walled* watur for wikked werkes

welowo > *welawo*; *welt* > *welden*

welþe n *welthe n.* A 3; B 6 welþe (5) welþes (1); C 10 welthe
A.1.53 And kynde wyt be wardeyn ȝoure *welþe* to kepe,
A.4.139 'Whoso wilneþ hire to wyue for *welþe* of hire godis,
A.8.169 þat han þe [*welþe* of þis] world, & wise men ben holden,
B.1.55 And kynde wit be wardeyn youre *welþe* to kepe
B.4.163 'Whoso wilneþ hire to wif for *welþe* of hire goodes,
B.7.191 That haue þe *welþe* of þis world and wise men ben holden
B.10.24 That wikked men þei welden þe *welþe* of þis worlde,
B.10.86 And þe moore he wynneþ and welt *welþes* and richesse
B.19.450 And torne hir wit to wisdom and to *welþe* of soule.
C.Pr.10 Al þe *welthe* of the world and þe wo bothe,

C.1.51 And kynde witte be wardeyn ȝoure *welthe* to kepe
C.4.158 'Hoso wilneth here to wy[u]e for *welthe* of here goodes
C.9.116 To ȝeue vch a wyht wyt, *welthe* and his hele
C.9.337 That haen the *welthe* of this world and wise men ben holde
C.10.268 And wedden here for here *welthe* and weschen on þe morwe
C.12.157 Or eny *welthe* in this world, his wyf or his childrene,
C.13.14 And delyuerede the weye his wyf with moche *welthe* aftur.
C.16.19 For al myhtest þou haue ymad men of grete *welthe*
C.21.450 And turne here wi[t] to wisdoem and to *wel[th]e* [of] soule.

wem n *wem n.* B 1; C 1
B.18.131 Wiþouten [wommene] *wem* into þis world broȝte hym.
C.20.134 Withouten wommane *wem* into this world brouhte hym.

wenche n *wenche n.* A 3 wenche (2) wenchis (1); B 8 wenche (6)
  wenches (2); C 7 wenche (5) wenches (2)
A.Pr.51 Wenten to walsyngham, & here *wenchis* aftir;
A.5.199 Þat wiþ al þe wo of þe world his wyf & his *wenche*
A.10.187 To ȝiuen a ȝong *wenche* to an old feble,
B.Pr.54 Wenten to walsyngham, and hire *wenches* after;
B.5.357 Wiþ al þe wo of þ[e] world his wif and his *wenche*
B.9.166 To yeuen a yong *wenche* to [a yolde] feble,
B.11.59 By wissynge of þis *wenche* I [dide], hir wordes were so swete,
B.16.100 And in þe wombe of þat *wenche* was he fourty woukes
B.18.113 [Where] out of þe west coste a *wenche* as me þouȝte
B.19.435 As wel for a wastour and *wenches* of þe stewes
B.20.160 And wedded oon wanhope, a *wenche* of þe Stuwes.
C.Pr.52 Wenten to Walsyngham and here *wenches* aftir;
C.6.415 With alle þe wo of th[e] world his wyf and his *wenche*
C.12.11 By wissyng of this *wenche* y dede, here wordes were so swete,
C.18.133 And in þe wombe of þat *wenche* was he fourty wokes
C.20.116 Out of þe west as hit were a *wenche*, as me thouhte,
C.21.435 As wel for a wastour [and] *wenche[s]* of the stuyves
C.22.160 And wedded oen wanhope, a *wenche* of þe stuyves.

wende > *wenden,wene*

wenden v *wenden v.* A 39 wend (1) wende (20) wenden (2) wendiþ (1)
  wente (11) wenten (3) ywent (1); B 74 weend (1) wend (2) wende (17)
  wenden (7) wendest (1) wendeþ (1) wendynge (1) went (2) wente (32)
  wenten (10); C 70 wende (29) wenden (2) wendest (2) wendeth (1)
  wendynge (1) went (2) wente (25) wenten (7) wenton (1)
A.Pr.4 *Wente* wyde in þis world wondris to here.
A.Pr.7 I was wery [for]wandrit & *wente* me to reste
A.Pr.48 *Wenten* forþ in here wey wiþ many wise talis,
A.Pr.51 *Wenten* to walsyngham, & here wenchis aftir;
A.1.117 And alle þat werchen with wrong *wenden* þei shuln
A.1.121 Mowe be sikur þat here soule shal *wende* into heuene,
A.1.152 Ȝe shuln be weiȝe þerwiþ whanne ȝe *wende* hennes.
A.2.125 To *wende* wiþ hem to westmynstre to wytnesse þ[is] dede.
A.2.170 And wiȝtliche *wente* to warne þe false,
A.3.246 *Wende* þidir with þin ost wommen to kille;
A.4.62 Þanne wisdom & wyt *wente* togidere
A.4.92 Wrong *wendiþ* not so awey er I wyte more.
A.5.1 Þe king & [his] kniȝtes to þe [k]ir[k]e *wente*
A.5.119 To wynchestre & to wy I [*wente*] to þe feire
A.5.144 But *wende* to walsyngham, & my wyf alse,
A.5.230 Þat iche man shal haue his er I hennis *wende*,
A.6.47 Ac ȝe þat wilneþ to *wende*, þis is þe weye þider:
A.7.6 I wolde *wende* wiþ ȝow til ȝe were þere'.
A.7.53 And *wende* wiþ ȝow þe wey til we fynde treuþe.'
A.7.58 For I wile sowe it myself, & siþþe wile I *wende*.
A.7.77 Forþi I wile er I *wende* do w[r]yte my bequest.
A.7.186 Þanne hadde piers pite & preiȝede hungir to *wende*
A.7.190 For I wot wel, be þou *ywent*, hy wile werche elles;
A.7.261 *Wende* now whanne þi wille is, þat wel be þou euere.'
A.7.262 'I behote god,' quaþ hunger, 'henis nile I *wende*
A.8.100 Þat aftir þi deþ day to helle shalt þou *wende*.'
A.9.6 Was neuere wiȝt as I *wen[t]e* þat me wisse couþe
A.9.53 Þus I *wente* wydewhere dowel to seken,
A.9.54 [And] as I *wente* be a wode, walkyng myn one,
A.10.143 An aungel in angir hiȝte h[e]m to *wende*
A.10.177 Ellis shal alle diȝen & to helle *wenden*."
A.11.68 Þoruȝ whiche a werk & wille þei *wenten* to helle,
A.11.113 'And tel me sum tokne to hym, for tyme is þat I *wende*'.
A.11.167 And *wente* wiȝtly my wey wiþoute more lettyng,
A.11.168 And fond as she foretolde & forþ gan I *wende*,
A.11.267 For here werkis & here wit to *wende* to pyne,
A.12.51 'Þou shalt *wende* with wil,' quod she, 'whiles þat him lykyþ,
A.12.56 And *wente* forþ on my way with omnia probate,
A.12.89 'Nay, wil,' quod þat wyȝth, '*wend* þou no ferther,
B.Pr.4 *Wente* wide in þis world wondres to here.
B.Pr.7 I was wery forwandred and *wente* me to reste
B.Pr.48 *Wenten* forþ in hire wey wiþ many wise tales,
B.Pr.54 *Wenten* to walsyngham, and hire wenches after;

B.Pr.162 And somme colers of crafty werk; vncoupled þei *wen[d]en*
B.Pr.166 Men my3te witen wher þei *wente* and [hire] wey r[oum]e.
B. 1.124 Whan þise wikkede *wenten* out wonderwise þei fellen,
B. 1.128 And alle þat werchen with wrong *wende* þei shulle
B. 1.132 Mowe be siker þat hire soul[e] sh[a]l *wende* to heuene
B. 1.178 Ye shulle ben weyen þerwiþ whan ye *wenden* hennes:
B. 2.161 To *wenden* wiþ hem to westmynstre to witnesse þis dede.
B. 2.211 Thanne Drede *wente* wy3tliche and warned þe False
B. 3.192 *Wendest* þat wynter wolde han ylasted euere;
B. 3.266 *Weend* to Amalec with þyn oost & what þow fyndest þere sle it.
B. 3.282 For so is þis world *went* wiþ hem þat han power
B. 4.76 [Thanne Wisdom and wit] *wenten* togidres
B. 4.105 Wrong *wendeþ* no3t so awey [er] I wite moore.
B. 5.1 The kyng and hise kny3tes to þe kirke *wente*
B. 5.203 To Wy and to Wynchestre I *wente* to þe Feyre
B. 5.228 But *wenden* to walsyngham, and my wif als,
B. 5.458 That ech man shal haue his er I hennes *wende*;
B. 5.560 Ac [ye þat] wilneþ to *wende*, þis is þe wey þider.
B. 6.6 I wolde *wende* wiþ yow and þe wey teche.'
B. 6.58 And *wende* wiþ yow [þe wey] til we fynde truþe.'
B. 6.63 For I wol sowe it myself, and siþenes wol I *wende*
B. 6.85 Forþi I wole er I *wende* do write my biqueste.
B. 6.189 And *wente* as werkmen [to wedynge] and [mowynge]
B. 6.199 Thanne hadde Piers pite and preide hunger to *wende*
B. 6.204 For I woot wel, be þow *went* þei wol werche ille;
B. 6.277 *Wend* now whan [þi wil is], þat wel be þow euere.'\
B. 6.278 '[I] bihote god', quod hunger, 'hennes [nil] I *wende*
B. 8.6 Was neuere wi3t as I *wente* þat me wisse kouþe
B. 8.62 [Th]us I *wente* widewher [dowel to seke,
B. 8.63 And as I *wente* by a wode, walkyng myn one],
B.10.110 Thoru3 whic[h werk and wil] þei *wente* to helle,
B.10.161 'And tel me som tokene [to hym], for tyme is þat I *wende*'.
B.10.225 And *wente* wightly [my w]ey wiþoute moore lettyng,
B.11.353 [For men sholde hem no3t fynde whan þei þerfro *wente*;
B.12.27 Wolde I neuere do werk, but *wende* to holi chirche
B.12.80 Than þe womman þat þere was, and *wenten* away for shame.
B.12.119 That wiþ archa dei [*wenten*] in [worship and reuerence]
B.13.28 Thei wesshen and wipeden and *wenten* to þe dyner.
B.13.220 And as þe[i] *wente* by þe weye–of dowel þei carped–
B.15.182 And ouþerwhile he is woned to *wenden* on pilgrymages
B.15.298 Ac þer ne was leoun ne leopard þat on laundes *wenten*,
B.15.339 And *wente* forþ wiþ þat water to woke wiþ Temese.
B.15.361 Shipmen and shepherdes þat wiþ [shipe] *wenten*
B.15.495 That þei ne *wente* as crist wisseþ, siþen þei wille haue name,
B.16.146 Thanne *wente* forþ þat wikked man and wiþ þe Iewes mette
B.16.273 Rapeliche renne forþ þe ri3te wey [we] *wente*.
B.17.50 And as we *wenten* þus in þe wey wordynge togideres
B.17.68 And to þe wye he *wente* hise woundes to biholde,
B.17.101 For *wente* neuere wye in þis world þoru3 þat wildernesse
B.17.117 Which is þe wey þat I *wente* and wher forþ to Ierusalem;
B.17.356 And *wente* awey as wynd and þerwiþ I awakede.
B.18.1 Wolleward and weetshoed *wente* I forþ after
B.18.126 'And am *wendynge* to wite what þis wonder meneþ.'
B.18.176 'My wil is to *wende*', quod she, 'and welcome hem alle
B.18.204 And wo into wele mowe *wenden* at þe laste.
B.18.242 The water witnesse[þ] þat he was god for he *wente* on it;
B.18.244 And as he *wente* on þe water wel hym knewe and seide,
B.18.296 Thise þritty wynter, as I *wene*, [he *wente* aboute] and preched.
B.18.300 And whan I sei3 it was so, [s]lepynge I *wente*
B.18.340 Ergo soule shal soule quyte and synne to synne *wende*,
B.19.78 Boþe of [s]ond, sonne and see, and siþenes þei *wente*
B.19.129 The which was dobet, where þat he *wente*.
B.19.192 He *wente*, and wonyeþ þere, and wol come at þe laste
B.19.320 And ordeyne þat hous er ye hennes *wende*.'
B.19.332 And made preesthod hayward þe while hymself *wente*
B.19.355 Quod Conscience to alle cristene þo, 'my counseil is to *wende*
B.20.1 Thanne as I *wente* by þe wey, whan I was thus awaked,
B.20.204 'If þow wolt be wroken *wend* into vnitee
B.20.284 And [be] ashamed in hir shrift; ac shame makeþ hem *wende*
B.20.381 And [*wenden*] as wyde as þe world [renneþ]
C.Pr.4 *Wente* forth in þe world wondres to here
C.Pr.49 *Wenten* forth [i]n here way with many wyse tales
C.Pr.52 *Wenten* to Walsyngham and here wenches aftir;
C.Pr.160 Consience and þe kynge into Court *wente*
C.Pr.183 Men Myghte ywete where þei *wente* and here [way roume].
C. 1.130 And alle þat worchen þat wikked is *wenden* thei sholle
C. 1.132 And alle þat han wel ywrouhte *wende* þey sholle
C. 1.174 3e shal be weye þerwith whenne 3e *wende* hennes:
C. 2.177 To *wende* with h[e]m to westminstre [the] weddyng to honoure.
C. 2.221 What was þe kynges wille and wyghtliche *wente*
C. 2.250 Thy kynedom thorw Coueytise wol out of kynde *wende*,
C. 3.13 That *wendeth* to Westmynstre worschipe[th] here monye
C. 3.435 For so is the world *went* with hem þat han power

C. 4.53 What wey y *wende* wel 3erne he aspyeth
C. 4.72 For wysdom and wyt tho *wenton* togyderes
C. 6.211 To wy and to wynchestre y *wente* to þe fayre
C. 6.312 That eche man shal haue his ar y hennes *wende*
C. 6.352 Fastyng on a friday forth gan he *wende*
C. 7.205 Ac hoso wol *wende* þer treuthe is, this is þe way thede[r]:
C. 8.4 Y wol[de] *wende* with 3ow and þe way teche.'
C. 8.57 And *wende* with alle tho þat wolden lyue in treuthe.
C. 8.62 'For y wol sowen hit mysulf and sethe wol y *wende*
C. 8.94 Forthy y wol ar y *wende* do wryte my biqueste.
C. 8.186 And *wenten* as werkemen to wedynge and mowynge
C. 8.208 Ac y preye the,' quod [Peres], 'hunger, ar thow *wende*,
C. 8.210 For y woet wel, be [thow] *went*, worche þei wol ful ille;
C. 8.219 Now wolde y wyte, ar thow *wendest*, what were þe beste;
C. 8.277 Thenk þat [dives] for his delicat lyf to þe deuel *wente*
C. 8.298 *Wende* nouthe when thow wol[t] and wel [be thow] euere
C. 8.300 'Y behote the,' quod hunger, 'þat hennes ne wol y *wende*
C.10.6 Was neuere wihte [as y *wente*] þat me wisse couthe
C.10.61 I *wente* forth wydewhare walkynge myn one
C.10.199 To *wende* as wyde as þe worlde were
C.11.103 'And telle me som tokene,' quod y, 'for tyme is þat y *wende*.'
C.11.134 Tho *wente* y my way withouten more lettynge
C.13.34 And sholden *wende* o wey where bothe mosten reste
C.13.42 And thogh they *wen[d]e* by the wey, tho two togederes,
C.13.52 And 3ut thow they *wende* o way as to wynchestre fayre
C.15.31 They woschen and wypeden and *wenten* to þe dyner.
C.15.37 [They] woschen and wipeden and *wenten* to sytten.
C.15.149 Where Peres the plogman bycam, so priueyliche he *wente*.
C.15.160 And bere hit in thy bosom aboute where þou *wendest*
C.15.184 And *wenten* forth here way; with grete wille y folowede.
C.15.189 And as they *wente* by the way–of dowel can they carpe–
C.16.324 And oþerwhile his wone is to *w[e]nde* [o]n pilgrimages
C.17.190 That they ne *wente* [þe wey] as holy writ byd:
C.18.180 Y waytede witterly; Ac whoder he *wende* y ne wiste.
C.18.289 Rappliche renne þe ri3t way we *wente*.
C.19.48 And as we *wenten* in þe way thus wordyng of this matere
C.19.67 And to th[e] wey a *wente* his woundes to byholde
C.19.92 For *wente* neuere man this way þat he ne was here yruyfled
C.19.336 And *wente* away as wynd and þerwith y awakede.
C.20.1 Wollewaerd and watschoed *wente* y forth aftur
C.20.129 'And am *wendynge* to wyte what þis wonder meneth.'
C.20.179 'My wil is to *wende*,' quod pees, 'and welcomen hem alle
C.20.209 And wo into wele moet *wende* at þe laste.
C.20.251 The water witnesseth þat he was god for a *wente* on h[it];
C.20.253 And as he *wente* on þe watur wel hym knewe and saide,
C.20.329 This thritty wynter, as y *wene*, and *wente* aboute and prechede.
C.20.388 Ergo soule shal soule quyte and synne to synne *wende*
C.21.78 Bothe of sand, sonne and see and sennes þei *wente*
C.21.129 The which was dobet, where þat he *wente*.
C.21.192 He *wente* and woneth there and wol come at þe laste
C.21.320 And ordeyne þat hous ar 3e hennes *wende*.'
C.21.332 And made presthoed hayward the while hymsulue *wente*
C.21.355 Quod Consience to alle cristene tho, 'my consayl is [to] *wende*
C.22.1 [Thenne] as y *wente* by the way, when y was thus awaked,
C.22.204 'Yf thow wol[t] be wreke *wende* into vnite
C.22.284 And be aschamed in here shryft; ac shame maketh [hem] *wende*
C.22.381 And *wenden* as wyde as þe world re[n]neth

wendist > *wene*

wene v *wenen v.(2)* A 8 *wende* (2) *wendist* (1) *wene* (4) *weniþ* (1); B 18
  wende (4) *wene* (9) *wenen* (3) *weneþ* (2); C 19 *wende* (1) *wene* (12)
  wenen (2) *weneth* (3) *wente* (1)
A. 3.179 *Wendist* þat wynter wolde han last euere;
A. 3.214 No wi3t as I *wene* wiþoute mede mi3te libbe.'
A. 5.70 Walewiþ in my wombe & waxiþ as I *wene*.
A. 5.242 Ne neuere *wen[e]* to wynne wiþ craft þat [I owe]
A. 7.230 And þat he *weniþ* wel to haue I wile it hym bereuid".
A. 9.60 Þat euere dremide dri3t in doute, as I *wene*.
A.11.219 'I *wende* þat kinghed, & kni3thed, & caiseris wiþ Erlis
A.11.224 Forþi I *wende* þat po wyes wern dobest of alle.'
B. 3.227 No wi3t, as I *wene*, wiþouten Mede may libbe.'
B. 3.302 That Iewes shul *wene* in hire wit, and wexen glade,
B. 5.235 'I *wende* riflynge were restitucion for I lerned neuere rede on boke,
B. 5.468 Ne neuere *wene* to wynne wiþ craft þat I owe;
B. 6.246 And þat he *weneþ* wel to haue I wole it hym bireue".
B. 8.69 That euer dremed [dri3t] in [doute], as I *wene*.
B.10.405 Ac I *wene* it worþ of manye as was in Noes tyme
B.11.349 Ther nys wri3te, as I *wene*, sholde werche hir nes[t] to paye;
B.13.279 Willyng þat alle men *wende* he were þat he is no3t,
B.13.291 Willynge þat men *wende* his wit were þe beste,
B.13.307 'Lo! if ye leue me no3t, or þat I lye *wenen*,
B.13.406 That into wanhope he [worþ] and *wende* nau3t to be saued.
B.15.478 And by hire wordes and werkes *wenen* and trowen;

B.15.601 And [ʒit] *wenen* þo wrecches þat he were pseudopropheta
B.18.190 And saue mannes soule? suster, *wene* it neuere.
B.18.217 Woot no wight, as I *wene*, what [is ynogh] to mene.
B.18.296 Thise þritty wynter, as I *wene*, [he wente aboute] and preched.
B.20.32 Of þat he *weneþ* wolde falle if his wit ne weere;
C. 3.455 That iewes shal *wene* in he[re] wit, & wexen so glade,
C. 6.24 *Wene* y were witty and wiser then another;
C. 6.32 Me wilnynge þat men *wen[t]e* y were as in auer
C. 6.41 Wilnynge þat men *wen[d]e* myne werkes weren þe beste
C. 6.48 They to *wene* þat y were wel holy and almesfull
C. 6.55 "Lo! yf ʒe leue me nat or þat y lye *wenen*
C. 6.322 Ne neuere *wene* to wynne with craft þat y knowe;
C. 8.257 And þat he *weneth* wel to haue y wol hit hym bireue".
C. 9.70 Woet no man, as y *wene*, who is worthy to haue
C.11.236 Ac y *wene* hit worth of monye as was in noes tyme
C.13.160 Ther is no wriht, as y *wene*, sholde worch here neste to paye;
C.14.166 Ac why a wolde þat wykke were, y *wene* and y leue
C.14.195 To wissen ·s weyes þerwith þat *wenen* to be saued–
C.16.132 And me leneth lyhtly fewe men and me *wene* hem pore:
C.16.306 *Weneth* he þat no wyhte wolde lye and swerie
C.20.195 And saue mannes soule? suster, *wene* hit neuere.
C.20.226 Ne woet no wyht, as y *wene*, what is ynow to mene.
C.20.329 This thritty wynter, as y *wene*, and wente aboute and prechede.
C.22.32 Of þat he *weneth* wolde falle yf his wit ne were;

wenes n *wene* n. B 1
B. 2.91 And in *we[n]es* and in wisshynges and wiþ ydel þouʒtes

wenge > wynge

wenynge ger *weneninge ger.(2)* B 1; C 1 wenyng
B.20.33 *Wenynge* is no wysdom, ne wys ymaginacion:
C.22.33 *Wenyng* is no wisdoem ne wyse ymaginacioun:

went(en) > wenden; wente > wene,wenden

wentes n *wente* n. C 1
C. 6.263 More profitable then myn, y made many *wentes*.

wenton > wenden

wepen v *wepen* v. A 9 wep (2) wepe (3) wepide (1) wepynge (1) wepiþ (1) wepte (1); B 23 wepe (7) wepen (1) wepeþ (2) wepynge (1) wepte (11) wepten (1); C 16 wep (1) wepe (3) wepeth (1) wepyng (1) wepynge (2) wepte (7) wopen (1)
A. 1.154 And ek as chast as a child þat in chirche *wepiþ*,
A. 2.198 And ek *wep* & wrang whan heo was atachid.
A. 4.60 Wrong þanne on wysdom *wepi[de]* hym to helpe,
A. 5.44 And made wil to *wepe* watir wiþ his eiʒen.
A. 5.94 Ac of his wynnyng I *wepe* and weile þe tyme.
A. 5.234 Ac for þere was nouʒt wherewith he *wepte* swiþe sore.
A. 5.246 Wel I woot he *wep* faste watir wiþ his eiʒen,
A. 5.252 *Wepynge* & weylyng for here wykkide dedis;
A. 8.42 þanne were marchauntis merye; many *wepe* for ioye,
B. 1.180 And as chaste as a child þat in chirche *wepeþ*,
B. 2.239 And ek *wepte* and wrong whan she was attached.
B. 5.61 And [made] wille to *wepe* water wiþ hise eiʒen.
B. 5.114 [Ac of his] wynnynge I *wepe* and waile þe tyme.
B. 5.187 And bad me wilne to *wepe* my wikkednesse to amende.
B. 5.462 And for þer was noʒt wher[wiþ] he *wepte* swiþe soore.
B. 5.472 Wel I woot he *wepte* faste water wiþ hise eiʒen,
B. 7.38 Thanne were Marchauntʒ murie; manye *wepten* for ioye
B. 7.125 And *wepen* whan I sholde [werche] þouʒ whete breed me faille.
B.11.4 Tho *wepte* I for wo and wraþe of hir speche
B.11.148 And [for] he *wepte* and wilned [þat I] were [saued]
B.11.265 To *wepe* and to wel bidde, wherof wexeþ Mercy
B.13.45 But if þei synge for þo soules and *wepe* salte teris:
B.13.266 Wiþ [bake] breed fro Stratford; þo gonnen beggeris *wepe*
B.14.236 That is welawo when he wakeþ and *wepeþ* for colde,
B.14.327 And *wepte* water wiþ hise eighen and weyled þe tyme
B.14.335 And *wepte* and wailede, and þerwiþ I awakede.
B.15.193 [Th]anne he syngeþ whan he doþ so, and som tyme *wepynge*,
B.16.76 And waggede widwehode and it *wepte* after;
B.16.116 And *wepte* water with hise eiʒen; þer seiʒen it manye.
B.16.272 I *wepte* for hise wordes; wiþ þat sauʒ I anoþer
B.18.91 Haue on me ruþe, riʒtful Iesu;' and riʒt wiþ þat he *wepte*.
B.20.369 Til Contricion hadde clene foryeten to crye and to *wepe*
C. 2.255 And bothe *wepte* and wrang when she was attached.
C. 5.108 *Wepyng* and waylyng til y was aslepe.
C. 6.2 And made will to *wepe* water with his eyes
C. 6.316 And for þer was nat wherwith a *wep* swythe sore.
C. 6.326 Wel y woet a *wepte* faste water with his yes
C. 9.41 Tho were Marchauntes mury; many *wopen* for ioye
C.11.164 Tho *wepte* y for wo and wrathe of here wordes
C.12.83 And for a wilnede *wepynge* þat y were ysaued
C.15.50 Bote yf they synge for tho soules and *wepe* salte teres:

C.16.77 þat is welowo when he [w]aketh and *wepeth* for colde;
C.16.336 Thenne syngeth he when he doth so and som tyme *w[e]pynge*:
C.18.108 A waggede wedewhed and hit *wepte* aftur;
C.18.146 And *wepte* watur with [his] yes; the why weten fewe.
C.18.288 [Y] *wepte* for his wordes; with þat saw y [a]nother
C.20.94 Haue [on me reuthe], riʒtfol iesu;' and riht with þat a *wepte*.
C.22.369 Til Contricioun hadde clene forʒete to crye and to *wepe*

wepene n *wepne* n. B 8 wepene (4) wepne (4); C 7 wepene (2) wepne (4) wypene (1)
B. 3.306 Ax ouþer hachet or any *wepene* ellis,
B. 3.323 Batailles shul none be, ne no man bere *wepene*,
B. 9.185 Whiles þow art yong [and yeep] and þi *wepene* [yet] kene
B.12.105 And as a blynd man in bataille bereþ *wepne* to fiʒte
B.18.97 To [bete a body ybounde wiþ any briʒt *wepene*].
B.19.218 And *wepne* to fighte wiþ þat wole neuere faille.
B.19.226 And *wepne* to fighte wiþ whan Antecrist yow assailleþ.'
B.20.124 His *wepne* was al wiles, to wynnen and to hiden;
C. 3.459 Ax oþer hachet or eny kyne *w[e]pne*,
C.10.286 And whil þou art ʒong an[d] ʒep and thy *wepene* kene
C.14.50 And as a blynde man in bataile bereth *wepene* to fyhte
C.20.100 To bete a body ybounde with eny briht *wypene*.
C.21.218 And *wepne* to fihte with þat wol neuere fayle.
C.21.226 And *wepne* to fihte with when Auntecrist ʒow assaileth.'
C.22.124 His *wepne* was al wyles, to wynnen and to hyden;

wepyng ger *wepinge ger.* &> *wepen* A 1
A. 8.108 þe prophet his p[a]yn e[et] in penaunce & in *wepyng*

wepne > wepene; weps > wispe; wepte(n > wepen; wer > ben,weer

werchen v *werken v.(1)* A 69 werche (28) werchen (6) werchist (1) werchiþ (7) werke (2) werkiþ (1) wirche (1) worching (1) wrouʒt (6) wrouʒte (12) wrouʒten (1) wrouʒtest (1) wrouʒthe (1) ywrouʒt (1); B 104 werch (2) werche (38) werchen (8) werchest (1) wercheþ (10) werken (1) wroʒt (8) wroʒte (16) wroʒten (1) wroʒtest (1) wrouʒt (2) wrouʒte (10) ywroght (1) ywroʒt (4) werchynge (1); C 84 worch (3) worche (26) worchen (3) worcheth (8) worchyng (1) wroghte (1) wroghtoun (1) wrouht (4) wrouhte (27) wrouhten (2) wrouhtest (1) wurcche (1) wurche (4) ywrouhte (2)
A.Pr.19 *Worching* & wandringe as þe world askiþ.
A.Pr.37 And haue wyt at wille to *wirche* ʒif hem list.
A. 1.13 And wolde þat ʒe *wrouʒten* as his word techiþ.
A. 1.26 þat þou worþe þe wers whanne þou *werche* shuldist.
A. 1.75 þou brouʒtest me borewis my biddyng to *werche*,
A. 1.80 þat I miʒte *werchen* his wil þat wrouʒte me to man:
A. 1.80 þat I miʒte werchen his wil þat *wrouʒte* me to man:
A. 1.117 And alle þat *werchen* with wrong wenden þei shuln
A. 1.119 Ac þo þat *werchen* þe word þat holy writ techiþ,
A. 1.135 For þus [wytnessiþ] his woord, *werche* þou þeraftir,
A. 1.143 And ʒet wolde he hem no woo þat *wrouʒte* him þat pyne,
A. 2.81 Such weddyng to *werche* to wraþþe wiþ treuþe:
A. 2.82 [And] er þis weddyng be *wrouʒt* wo be betide!
A. 2.98 *Werchiþ* be wysdom & be wyt aftir;
A. 2.156 I wolde be wroken of þise wrecchis þat *werchen* so ille,
A. 3.7 And ʒif heo *werche* be wyt & my wil folewe
A. 3.27 For to *werche* þi wil while þi lif lastiþ.'
A. 3.56 Be war what þi riʒt hond *werchiþ* or deliþ,
A. 3.69 For þise arn men of þise molde þat most harm *werchiþ*
A. 3.95 'Vnwittily, [wy], *wrouʒt* hast þou ofte;
A. 3.96 Ac wers *wrouʒtest* þou neuere þan þo þou fals toke.
A. 3.220 To hem þat *werchen* wel whiles þei ben here.
A. 4.54 For þat wrong hadde *wrouʒt* so wykkide a dede,
A. 4.56 'Whoso *werchiþ* be wil wraþþe makiþ ofte.
A. 4.129 And ʒif þou *werche* [it in] werk I wedde myne eris
A. 5.24 He bad wastour go *werche* what he best couþe
A. 6.52 Oþerwise þanne þou woldist men *wrouʒte* to þiselue;
A. 7.8 'What shulde we wommen *werche* þe while?'
A. 7.10 And wyues þat han woll[e] *werchiþ* it faste,
A. 7.22 Helpiþ hem *werche* wiʒtly þat wynne ʒoure foode.'
A. 7.51 'For to *werche* be þi woord while my lif duriþ.'
A. 7.70 Dame *werche* whanne tyme is piers wyf hatte;
A. 7.101 Oþere werkmen þere were [þat] *wrouʒte* ful faste,
A. 7.105 To ouersen hem hymself; whoso best *wrouʒte*
A. 7.110 'But ʒe rise þe raþere, & rape ʒow to *werche*,
A. 7.152 'I was not wonid to *werche*,' quaþ wastour, 'now wile I not begynne,'
A. 7.190 For I wot wel, be þou ywent, hy wile *werche* ille,
A. 7.192 And for defaute of foode þus faste hy *werchiþ*,
A. 7.197 And how I miʒte amaistrie hem & make hem to *werche*.'
A. 7.225 And benom hym his nam for he nolde *werche*,
A. 7.240 Of alle þe wyke [hy] *werkiþ* nouʒt, so here wombe akiþ.'
A. 7.286 And þo nolde wastour not *werche*, but wandrite aboute,
A. 7.297 þat he was werkman *ywrouʒt* warie þe tyme,

A. 8.81	Þat euere he was man *wrouȝt* whanne he shal henne fare.
A. 8.83	And wommen wiþ childe þat *werche* ne mowe,
A. 8.182	Suche werkis to *werche*, whiles we ben here,
A. 9.98	Corounid on to be kyng & be h[ere] counseil *werchen*
A.10.20	Sire *werche* wel wiþ þin hond, [a] wiȝt man of strengþe,
A.10.34	And al at his wil was *wrouȝt* wiþ a speche,
A.10.40	Þat he *wrouȝte* wiþ werkis & with wordis boþe.
A.10.65	For no werk þat þei *werche*, wykkide oþer ellis.
A.10.75	For *werche* he wel oþer wrong, þe wyt is his owene.
A.10.95	Ac ȝif þou *werchist* be godis word I warne þe þe beste,
A.10.130	Such wer[kis] to *werche* [þat] he is wiþ paied.
A.10.147	And brouȝt forþ a barn þat muche bale *wrouȝte*;
A.10.200	Wydeweris & wydewis *werchiþ* riȝt also;
A.10.208	And [*werche*] on his wyf & on no womman ellis,
A.11.26	Or prechen of þe penaunce þat pilat[u]s *wrouȝte*
A.11.102	For to *werche* ȝour wil [while] my lif duriþ,
A.11.157	Þat þinkeþ *werche* wiþ þo þre þriueþ wel late,
A.11.260	For howso I *werche* in þis world, [wrong] oþer ellis,
A.11.270	Aristotle & he, who *wrouȝte* betere?
A.11.276	And ȝif I shal *werke* be here werkis to wynne me heuene,
A.11.278	Þanne *wrouȝte* I vnwisly wiþ alle þe wyt þat I lere.
A.11.292	As þise þat *wrouȝte* wykkidly in world whanne þei were.
A.12.97	So þat þou *werke* þe word þat holy wryt techeþ,
A.12.101	And *wrouȝthe* þat here is wryten and oþer werkes boþe
A.12.103	And whan þis werk was *wrouȝt*, ere wille myȝte aspie,
B.Pr.19	*Werchynge* and wandrynge as þe world askeþ.
B.Pr.37	And han wit at wille to *werken* if [hem liste].
B. 1.13	And wolde þat ȝe *wrouȝte* as his word techeþ,
B. 1.26	That þow worþe þe wers whan þow *werche* sholdest.
B. 1.77	[Thow] brouȝtest me borwes my biddyng to [*werche*],
B. 1.82	That I myȝte *werchen* his wille þat *wroȝte* me to man.
B. 1.82	That I myȝte *werchen* his wille þat *werche* me to man.
B. 1.128	And alle þat *werchen* with wrong wende þei shulle
B. 1.130	[Ac] þo þat *werche* wel as holy writ telleþ,
B. 1.147	[For þus witnesseþ his word; *werche* þow þerafter].
B. 1.150	And alle hise werkes he *wrouȝte* with loue as hym liste;
B. 1.169	And yet wolde he hem no wo þat *wrouȝte* hym þat peyne.
B. 2.117	Swic[h] weddyng[e] to *werche* to wraþe wiþ truþe;
B. 2.118	And er þis weddynge be *wroȝt* wo þee bitide!
B. 2.134	*Wercheþ* by wisdom and by wit [after];
B. 2.195	I wolde be wroken of þo wrecches þat *wercheþ* so ille;
B. 3.7	And if she *werche* bi wit and my wil folwe
B. 3.28	For to *werche* þi wille [while þi lif lasteþ].'
B. 3.74	Wite what þow *werchest* wiþ þi riȝt syde,
B. 3.80	For þise are men on þis molde þat moost harm *wercheþ*
B. 3.106	'Vnwittily, [wye], *wroȝt* hastow ofte,
B. 3.107	Ac worse *wroȝtest* [þ]ow neuere þan þo þow Fals toke.
B. 3.233	To [hem] þat [*werchen* wel] while þei ben here.
B. 3.239	And han *ywroȝt* werkes wiþ right and wiþ reson,
B. 4.62	That wrong was a wikked luft and *wroȝte* muche sorwe.
B. 4.68	For þat wrong hadde *ywroȝt* so wikked a dede,
B. 4.70	'Whoso *wercheþ* by wille wraþe makeþ ofte.
B. 4.146	And if [þow] werch[e] it in werk I wedde myne eris
B. 5.24	He bad wastour go *werche* what he best kouþe
B. 5.33	And bete Beton þerwith but if she wolde *werche*.
B. 5.282	And al þe wikkednesse in þis world þat man myȝte *werche* or þynke
B. 5.365	'As þow wiþ wordes & werkes hast *wroȝt* yuele in þi lyue
B. 5.565	Oþerwise þan þow woldest [men] *wrouȝte* to þiselue.
B. 6.8	'What sholde we wommen *werche* þe while?'
B. 6.20	Helpeþ hym *werche* wiȝtliche þat wynneþ youre foode.'
B. 6.56	'For to *werche* by þi wor[d] while my lif dureþ.'
B. 6.78	Dame *werch*-whan-tyme-is Piers wif hiȝte;
B. 6.109	Oþere werkmen þer were þat *wroȝten* ful [faste],
B. 6.113	To ouersen hem hymself; whoso best *wroȝte*
B. 6.118	'But ye arise þe raþer and rape yow to *werche*
B. 6.123	And made hir mone to Piers [how þei myȝte noȝt *werche*]:
B. 6.167	'I was noȝt wont to *werche*', quod Wastour, 'now wol I noȝt bigynne!'
B. 6.204	For I woot wel, be þow went þei wol *werche* ille;
B. 6.211	And how I myȝte amaistren hem and make hem to *werche*.'
B. 6.241	And bynam hym his Mnam for he [n]olde *werche*
B. 6.247	Kynde wit wolde þat ech wiȝt *wroȝte*,
B. 6.256	Of al a wike *werche* noȝt, so oure wombe akeþ.'
B. 6.302	And þo [n]olde Wastour noȝt *werche*, but wandre[d] aboute,
B. 6.313	[That] he was werkman *wroȝt* [warie] þe tyme.
B. 7.36	And witen yow fro wanhope, if ye wol þus *werche*,
B. 7.92	But as wilde bestes wiþ wehee worþen vppe and *werchen*,
B. 7.99	That euere [he was man] *wroȝt* whan [he] shal hennes fare.
B. 7.101	And wommen wiþ childe þat *werche* ne mowe,
B. 7.125	And wepen whan I sholde [*werche*] þouȝ whete breed me faille.
B. 7.204	Swiche werkes to *werche*, while we ben here,
B. 8.56	But if he *werche* wel þerwiþ as dowel hym techeþ.

B. 8.108	Crouned oon to be kyng, [and by hir counseil *werchen*],
B. 8.131	And *werchen* as þei þre wolde; th[i]s is his entente.'
B. 9.21	Sire *werch*-wel-wiþ-þyn-hand, a wiȝt man of strengþe,
B. 9.33	[And al at his wil was *wrouȝt* wiþ a speche]
B. 9.44	He moste *werche* wiþ his word and his wit shewe.
B. 9.52	[Th]at he *wroȝte* wiþ werk and wiþ word boþe;
B. 9.111	For þei mote *werche* and wynne and þe world sustene;
B. 9.115	The wif was maad þe w[y]e for to helpe *werche*,
B. 9.116	And þus was wedlok *ywroȝt* wiþ a mene persone,
B. 9.119	And þus was wedlok *ywroȝt* and god hymself it made.
B. 9.157	And al for þei *wroȝte* wedlokes ayein [þe wille of god].
B. 9.179	[Wideweres and wodewes] *wercheþ* [riȝt also].
B. 9.187	Whan ye han wyued beþ war and *wercheþ* in tyme,
B.10.34	Or prechen of þe penaunce þat Pilat *wroȝte*
B.10.150	For to *werche* youre wille while my lif dureþ.
B.10.214	[That] þynkeþ *werche* with þo [þre] þrueþ [wel] late,
B.10.260	Loke þow *werche* it in werk þat þi word sheweþ;
B.10.277	For goddes word wolde noȝt be lost, for þat *wercheþ* euere;
B.10.280	That goddes word *wercheþ* noȝt on [wis] ne on lewed
B.10.392	And if I sh[al] *werche* by hir werkes to wynne me heuene,
B.10.394	Thanne *wrouȝte* I vnwisly, whatsoeuere ye preche.
B.10.407	Was neuere wrighte saued þat *wroȝte* þeron, ne ooþer werkman ellis,
B.10.410	Of w[r]ightes þat it *wroȝte* was noon of hem ysaued.
B.10.419	*Wercheþ* ye as ye sen ywrite, lest ye worþe noȝt þerInne].
B.10.433	Tho þat *wroȝte* wikkedlokest in world þo þei were.
B.11.169	God *wrouȝte* it and wroot it wiþ his [owene] fynger,
B.11.346	Hadde neuere wye wit to *werche* þe leeste.
B.11.349	Ther nys wriȝte, as I wene, sholde *werche* hir nes[t] to paye;
B.11.398	For al þat he [*wrouȝt*] was wel ydo, as holy writ witnesseþ:
B.12.50	That wise wordes wolde shewe and *werche* þe contrarie:
B.12.261	That was writen, and þei witnesse to *werche* as it wolde.
B.13.262	So er my wafres be *ywroȝt* muche wo I þolye.
B.13.453	In a welhope, [for he *wrouȝte* so], amonges worþi seyntes],
B.14.121	For to wroþerhele was he *wroȝt* þat neuere was Ioye shapen.
B.14.137	For whan a werkman haþ *wroȝt*, þan may men se þe soþe,
B.15.512	Many myracles he *wrouȝte* m[e]n for to turne,
B.15.596	Ac þei seiden and sworen wiþ sorcerie he *wrouȝte*,
B.16.99	For to *werchen* his wille wiþouten any synne:
B.16.120	And seide he *wroȝte* þoruȝ wichecraft & with þe deueles myȝte:
B.17.18	'Whoso *wercheþ* after þis writ, I wol vndertaken,
B.17.222	That *werchen* and waken in wyntres nyȝtes
B.18.238	That he was god þat al *wroȝte* þe wolkne first shewed:
B.19.105	Lif and lyme as hym liste he *wroȝte*.
B.19.122	He *wroȝte* þat by no wit but þoruȝ word one,
B.19.440	And worshiped be he þat *wroȝte* al, boþe good and wikke.
B.20.49	Siþ he þat *wroȝte* al þe world was wilfulliche nedy,
B.20.158	Oon þat muche wo *wroȝte*, Sleuþe was his name.
B.20.307	For hir mys[fetes] þat þei *wroȝt* hadde,
C.Pr.21	*Worchyng* and wondryng as þ[e] world ascuth.
C.Pr.38	And [han] wytt at wille to *worche* yf þei wolde.
C. 1.13	And wolde þat ȝe *wroghtoun* as his word techeth.
C. 1.26	Wykked[ly] *wroghte* and wrathed god almyhty.
C. 1.125	Ac thei caren nat thow hit be cold, knaues, when þe[i] *worche*
C. 1.130	And alle þat *worchen* þat wikked is wenden thei sholle
C. 1.132	And alle þat han wel *ywrouhte* wende þey sholle
C. 1.165	And ȝut wolde [he] hem no wo þat *wrouhte* hym þat [p]e[y]ne
C. 2.121	Suche a weddyng to *wurche* þat wrathe myhte treuthe.
C. 2.122	And ar this weddyng be *wrouhte* wo to al ȝoure consayle!
C. 2.150	Forthy *worcheth* by wisdom and by witt also,
C. 3.7	And yf she *werche* wysely and by wys men consayl
C. 3.29	For to *worche* thy wille the while þou myhte dure.
C. 3.134	And saide, 'vnwittiliche, womman, *wro[uh]t* hastow ofte
C. 3.138	For wors *wrouhtest* [thow] neuere then tho thow fals toke.
C. 4.65	How wrong was a wykked man and muche wo *wrouhte*.
C. 4.143	And yf ȝe *wor[c]he* it in werke y wedde bothe myn handes
C. 5.23	Y am to wayke to *wurcche* with sykel or with sythe,
C. 5.25	To *wurche* as a werkeman eny while to duyren.'
C. 5.65	And knaue[s] vncrounede to carte and to *worche*,
C. 5.83	For in my Consience y knowe what Crist w[o]lde y *wrouhte*.
C. 5.126	He bad wastoures [g]o *wurche* and wynne here sustinaunce
C. 5.135	And bete Betene þerwith but yf a wolde *worche*.
C. 6.100	Now hit athynketh me in my thouhte þat euere y so *wrouhte*.
C. 7.113	In a welhope for a *wrouhte* so amongus worthy seyntes
C. 7.212	Otherwyse then ȝe wolden they *wrouhte* ȝow alle tymes.
C. 8.6	'What sholde we wommen *wor[c]he* þe whiles?'
C. 8.18	Helpeth hym *worche* wi[ȝt]liche þat wynneth ȝoure fode.'
C. 8.55	'For to *worche* by thy wit and my wyf bothe.'
C. 8.80	Dame *worch*-when-tyme-is [Peres] wyf hehte;
C. 8.90	And aftur here warnynge and wor[d]ynge *worche* þou þeraftur:
C. 8.116	Oþer werkemen þer were þat *wrouhten* fol ȝerne,
C. 8.120	[To] ouersey hem hymsulue; hoso beste *wrouhte*
C. 8.125	'But ȝe aryse þe rather and rape ȝow to *worche*

C. 8.130	And maden here mone to [Peres] how þei m[yht] nat *worche*;
C. 8.164	'I was nat woned to *worche*,' quod wastour, 'now wol y nat bygynne!'
C. 8.210	For y woet wel, be [thow] went, *worche* þei wol ful ille;
C. 8.264	To beggares and to boys þat loth ben to *worche*.
C. 8.268	Of al a woke *worche* nat, so oure wombe greueth.'
C. 8.324	And tho wolde wastor nat *worche* bote wandre[d] aboute
C. 8.335	Þat he was werkeman ywrouhte warien þe tyme.
C. 9.177	And wymmen with childe þat *worche* ne mowe,
C. 9.252	Ac while a *wrouhte* in þe world and wan his mete with treuthe
C. 9.350	Suche werkes to *worche* þe while we ben here
C.10.147	Sire *worch*-wel-with-thyn-hand, a wyht man of strenghe,
C.10.169	On catel more then on kynde that alle kyne thynges *wrouhte*,
C.10.239	Ac Westm[in]stre lawe, y woet wel, *worcheth* þe contra[r]ye;
C.10.288	3e þat han wyues ben war and *wo[r]cheth* nat out of tyme
C.11.88	For to *worche* 3oure wille while my lyf duyreth
C.11.219	And yf we sholde *wurche* aftur here werkes to wy[n]nen vs heuene
C.11.221	Thenne *wrouhte* [we] vnwysly for alle 3oure wyse techynge.
C.11.238	Was neuere wrihte þat þeron *wrouhte* ne werkman ysaued
C.11.241	Of wryhtes þat hit *wrouhte* was noen of hem ysaued.
C.11.250	*Worcheth*, 3e wrihtus of holy churche, as holy writ techeth,
C.11.269	Tho that worste *wrouhten* while thei here were.
C.13.85	Ne in none enquestes to come ne cont[u]max thogh he *worche*
C.13.157	Hadde neuere weye wyt to *worche* þe leste.
C.13.160	Ther is no wriht, as y wene, sholde *worch* here neste to paye;
C.14.26	Ac Ar such a wil wexe *worcheth* go[d] sulue
C.14.38	Lawe of loue oure lord *wrouht*] long ar crist were.
C.15.297	For to wroþerhele was he *wrouht* þat neuere was ioye yschape.
C.16.180	Bote as wode were afuyre thenne *worcheth* bothe
C.16.220	The witt[i]ore þat eny wihte is, but yf he *worche* þeraftur,
C.16.221	The bittorere he shal abugge but yf he wel *worche*.
C.17.85	And *worcheth* nat as 3e fyndeth ywryte and wisseth þe peple.
C.17.170	Be maistre ouer alle tho men and on this manere a *wrouhte*:
C.17.263	Mony myracles a *wrouhte* men for to torne,
C.17.304	Iewes sayde þat hit seye with soercerye he *wrouhte*,
C.18.132	For to *worchen* his wille withouten eny synne:
C.18.149	And some iewes saide with sorserie he *wrouhte*
C.18.210	O god almyhty þat man made and *wrouhte*
C.18.213	The werkes þat hymsulue *wr[o]uhte* and this world bothe:
C.19.19	'And ho[so] *worcheth* aftur this writ, y wol vndertaken,
C.19.138	Sholde n[o] wri[h]t *worche* were they awey.
C.19.188	That *worchen* and waken in wynteres nyhtes
C.20.247	That he was god þat al *wrouhte* the welkene furste shewede:
C.20.353	And wyte[th] hem al þe wrechednesse þat *wrouhte* is on erthe.
C.20.432	For holy writ wol þat y be wreke of hem þat *wrouhte* ille–
C.21.105	Lyf and lyme as hym luste he *wrouhte*.
C.21.122	He *wrouhte* þat by no wyt bote thorw word one,
C.21.440	And worschiped be he þat *wrouhte* all, bothe gode and wicke,
C.22.49	Sethe [he] þat *wrouhte* al þe worlde was willefolliche nedy
C.22.158	Oen þat moche wo *wrouhte*, sleuthe was his name.
C.22.307	For here mys[fetes] that thei *wrouht* hadde

werchynge ger *werkinge ger.(1)* &> werchen A 1 werching; B 1

A. 3.47	'We haue a wyndowe [in] *werching* wile stonde vs wel hei3e;
B. 3.48	'We haue a wyndow in *werchynge* wole [stonden] vs [wel] hye;

were v *weren v.(2)* &> ben A 2 werde (1) were (1); B 3 were (2) werien (1); C 3 wered (1) werie (2)

A. 2.12	Of þe pureste perrei3e þat prince *werde* euere;
A. 3.270	Shal no seriaunt for þat seruyse *were* a silk houue,
B. 3.295	Shal no sergeant for [þat] seruice *were* a silk howue,
B.14.332	'I were no3t worþi, woot god', quod haukyn, 'to *werien* any cloþes,
B.15.452	Clooþ þat comeþ fro þe weuyng is no3t comly to *were*
C. 3.448	Shal no ser[i]aunt for [þat] seruic[e] *werie* a selk houe
C. 5.81	And wol til hit be *wered* out [or] oþerwyse ychaunged.
C.19.239	Moste lordliche lyue and 3ut [on] his lycame *werie*

weren > ben

wery adj *weri adj.* A 1; B 4; C 1

A.Pr.7	I was *wery* [for]wandrit & wente me to reste
B.Pr.7	I was *wery* forwandred and wente me to reste
B.13.204	Whan þow art *wery* [for]walked; wille me to counseille'.
B.15.186	And whan he is *wery* of þat werk þan wole he som tyme
B.18.4	Til I weex *wery* of þe world and wilned eft to slepe
C.20.4	Til y waxe *wery* of the world and wilnede eefte to slepe

werie(n > were

werynesse n *werinesse n.* C 1

C.Pr.7	Me biful for to slepe, for *werynesse* ofwalked,

werk n *werk n.(1)* A 29 werk (8) werkes (2) werkis (19); B 56 werk (11) werke (1) werkes (44); C 38 werk (3) werke (2) werkes (33)

A.Pr.3	In abite as an Ermyte, vnholy of *werkis*,
A. 1.87	Doþ þe *werkis* þerwiþ & wilneþ no man ille,

A. 1.120	And enden as I er seide, in perfite *werkis*,
A. 1.150	Þei3 3e ben mi3ty to mote beþ mek of 3our *werkis*;
A. 2.89	For al þe lesinges þou lyuest, & leccherous *werkis*,
A. 2.94	Þat fals is a faitour [and] feyntles of *werkis*,
A. 4.71	[Þat wrong for his *werkis* shulde woo þole,
A. 4.129	And 3if þou werche [it in] *werk* I wedde myne eris
A. 5.68	Wiþ *werkis* [or wiþ] wordis whanne he sai3 his tyme.
A. 7.137	Ones at noon is ynou3 þat no *werk* vsiþ;
A. 7.211	[Or with *werk* or with word þe while þou art here].
A. 8.182	Suche *werkis* to werche, whiles we ben here,
A.10.40	Þat he wrou3te wiþ *werkis* & with wordis boþe.
A.10.65	For no *werk* þat þei werche, wykkide oþer ellis.
A.10.92	Loke þou wisse þi wyt & þi *werkis* aftir;
A.10.130	Such *wer[kis]* to werche [þat] he is wiþ paied.
A.10.161	Þat god was wroþ wiþ here & [suche wordis seide],
A.10.218	And þat is wykkide wil þat many *werk* shendiþ.'
A.11.13	I say be þo,' quaþ she, 'þat shewen be here *werkis*
A.11.54	Ac among [mene] men hise mercy & his *werkis*,
A.11.168	Þoru3 whiche a *werk* & wille þei wenten to helle.
A.11.269	Boþe in *werk* & in woord, in world in his tyme?
A.11.272	And was þere neuere in þis world to wysere of *werkis*,
A.11.275	And be here *werkis* & here wordis wissen vs to dowel,
A.11.276	And 3if I shal werke be here *werkis* to wynne me heuene,
A.11.277	And for here *werkis* & here wyt wende to pyne,
A.12.98	And be prest to preyeres and profitable *werkes*.'
A.12.101	And wrou3the þat here is wryten and oþer *werkes* boþe
A.12.103	And whan þis *werk* was wrou3t, ere wiche my3te aspie,
B.Pr.3	In habite as an heremite, vnholy of *werkes*,
B.Pr.162	And somme colers of crafty *werk*; vncoupled þei wen[d]en
B. 1.89	Dooþ þe *werkes* þerwiþ and wilneþ no man ille,
B. 1.150	And alle hise *werkes* he wrou3te with loue as hym liste;
B. 1.176	Thou3 ye be my3t[y] to mote beeþ meke [of] youre *werkes*,
B. 2.90	As in *werkes* and in wordes and waityn[g] with ei3es
B. 2.125	For al bi lesynges þow lyuest and lecherouse *werkes*;
B. 2.130	That Fals is fe[ynt]lees and fikel in hise *werkes*,
B. 3.239	And han ywroght *werkes* wiþ right and wiþ reson,
B. 4.84	That wrong for hise *werkes* sholde wo þolie,
B. 4.146	And if [þow] werch[e] it in *werk* I wedde myne eris.
B. 5.85	With *werkes* or wiþ wordes whan he sey3e his tyme.
B. 5.365	'As þow wiþ wordes & *werkes* hast wro3t yuele in þi lyue
B. 7.204	Swiche *werkes* to werche, while we ben here,
B. 9.52	[Th]at he wro3te wiþ *werk* and wiþ word boþe;
B. 9.132	Til god wraþed [wiþ] hir *werkes* and swich a word seide,
B. 9.209	And þat is wikked wille þat many *werk* shendeþ,
B.10.13	I seye by [þo]', quod she, 'þat sheweþ by hir *werkes*
B.10.68	Ac amonges meene men his mercy and hise *werkes*.
B.10.110	Thoru3 whic[h *werk* and wil] þei wente to helle,
B.10.115	Why sholde we þat now ben for þe dede-werkes of Adam
B.10.260	Loke þow werche it in *werk* þat þi word sheweþ;
B.10.392	And if I sh[al] werche by hir *werkes* to wynne me heuene,
B.10.393	That for hir *werkes* and wit now wonyeþ in pyne,
B.10.402	Ac hir *werkes*, as holy writ seiþ, [was] euere þe contrarie.
B.10.437	Ther are witty and wel libbynge ac hire *werkes* ben yhudde
B.10.439	Wher fo[r loue] a man worþ allowed þere and hise lele *werkes*,
B.11.43	Til Concupiscencia carnis acorded alle my *werkes*.
B.11.139	For þei beþ, as oure bokes telleþ, aboue goddes *werkes*:
B.11.147	Sauacion for sooþnesse þat he sei3 in my *werkes*.
B.11.238	So bi hise *werkes* þei wisten þat he was Iesus,
B.12.27	Wolde I neuere do *werk*, but wende to holi chirche
B.13.140	"Wiþ wordes and *werkes*", quod she, "and wil of þyn herte
B.13.145	Boþe wiþ *wer[k]* and wiþ wor[d] fonde his loue to wynne",
B.13.294	And louelokest to loken on and lelest of *werkes*,
B.13.306	And of *werkes* þat he wel dide witnesse and siggen,
B.13.311	Al he wolde þat men wiste of *werkes* and wordes
B.13.347	Til eiþeres wille wexeþ kene and to þe *werke* yeden,
B.13.350	Swiche *werkes* with hem were neuere out of seson
B.14.14	Or þoru3 *werk* or þoru3 word or wille of myn herte
B.14.22	Dobest [shal kepe it clene from vnkynde *werkes*].
B.14.138	What he were worþi for his *werk* and what he haþ deserued,
B.14.224	And eiþer hateþ ooþer in alle maner *werkes*.
B.15.116	Ac youre *werkes* and wordes þervnder aren ful [wol]ueliche.
B.15.186	And whan he is wery of þat *werk* þan wole he som tyme
B.15.198	'Clerkes haue no knowyng', quod he, 'but by *werkes* and wordes.
B.15.210	And as a lyoun he lokeþ þer men lakken hise *werkes*.
B.15.210	Neiþer þoru3 wordes ne *werkes*, but þoru3 wil oone,
B.15.356	For þoru3 werre and wikkede *werkes* and wederes vn[s]esonable
B.15.450	As wel þoru3 hise *werkes* as wiþ hise holy wordes
B.15.478	And by hire wordes and *werkes* wenen and trowen;
B.16.34	And wikkede *werkes* þerof, wormes of synne,
B.17.104	And þiself now and swiche as suwen oure *werkes*.
B.17.318	Than alle oure wikkede *werkes* as holy writ telleþ–
B.19.377	And þanne wellede water for wikkede *werkes*
B.20.370	And wake for hise wikked *werkes* as he was wont to doone.

C.Pr.3	In abite as an heremite, vnholy of *werkes*,
C.Pr.181	And colers of crafty *werk*, bothe knyghte[s] and squieres.
C. 1.85	And doth þe *werkes* þerwith and wilneth no man ylle,
C. 1.172	Thow ȝe be myhty to mote beth meke in ȝoure *werkes*,
C. 2.97	As in *werkes* and in wordes and waytyng[e] of yes,
C. 2.209	Y wolde be awreke [o]n tho wreches and on here *werkes* alle,
C. 4.71	Thorw wrong and his *werkes* there was mede yknowe
C. 4.80	That wrong for his *werkes* sholde w[oo] tholye
C. 4.104	As longe as y lyue for his luther *werkes*.'
C. 4.143	And yf ȝe wor[c]he it in *werke* y wedde bothe myn handes
C. 5.54	Me sholde constrayne no Cler[k] to no knaues *werkes*,
C. 6.21	Thorw my word and my witt here euel *werkes* to shewe;
C. 6.41	Wilnynge þat men wen[d]e myne *werkes* weren þe beste
C. 6.53	Of *werkes* þat y wel dede witnesses take
C. 6.99	Here *werkes* and here wordes where þat y seete.
C. 6.181	Til bothe oure wil was oen and to þe *werk* we ȝeden,
C. 6.184	Such *werkes* with vs were neuere out of sesoun
C. 8.197	Tho was [Peres] proud and potte hem alle a *werke*
C. 9.350	Suche *werkes* to worche the while we ben here
C.10.287	Awrek þe þerwith on wyfyng, for godes *werk* y holde hit:
C.11.11	Y syg hit by suche,' quod [she], 'þat sheweth by here *werkes*
C.11.216	Wittenesseth þat here wordes and here *werkes* bothe
C.11.219	And yf we sholde wurche aftur here werke[s] to wy[n]nen vs heuene
C.11.220	That for here *werkes* and wyt wonyeth now in payne,
C.11.310	Til Concupiscencia Carnis acorded til al my *werkes*.
C.12.74	They b[e]t[h], as oure bokes telleth, [aboue] godes *werkes*:
C.12.82	Sauacion for soethnesse [þat] a sey in my *werkes*.
C.12.127	So by [h]is *werkes* thei wisten þat he was iesu
C.12.140	And aytheres *werkes* and wille] riht wel alowede
C.14.25	And w[o]ky thorw gode *werkes* wikkede hertes.
C.14.28	So grace withouten grace of god and also gode *werkes*
C.16.342	Ac thorw *werkes* thow myhte wyte wher forth he walketh:
C.18.12	And þerof cometh a goed fruyt þe wiche men calleth *werkes*
C.18.38	And manye wikkede *werkes*, wormes of synne,
C.18.213	The *werkes* þat hymsulue wr[o]uhte and this world bothe:
C.19.298	Thenne al oure wikkede *werkes* as holy writ telleth:
C.21.377	And thenne walled watur for wikked *werkes*
C.22.370	And wake for his wikkede *werkes* as he was woned [to do].

werke > werchen,werk; werkeman > werkman; werken -iþ > werchen

werkman n *werkman n.* A 6 werkman (2) werkmen (4); B 11 werkman (3) werkmen (8); C 9 werkeman (2) werkemen (3) werkman (1) werkmen (3)

A. 2.87	Worþi is þe *werkman* his mede to haue,
A. 7.46	But it be of wysdom or of wyt þi *werkmen* to chaste;
A. 7.101	Oþere *werkmen* þere were [þat] wrouȝte ful faste,
A. 7.124	Suche wastours in þis world his *werkmen* distroyeþ;
A. 7.297	Þat he was *werkman* ywrouȝt warie þe tyme,
A. 7.302	I warne ȝow *werkmen*, wynneþ while ȝe mowe,
B. 5.428	So wiþ wikked wil and wraþe my *werkmen* I paye.
B. 6.51	But if [it be] of wisdom or of wit þi *werkmen* to chaste;
B. 6.109	Oþere *werkmen* þer were þat wroȝten ful [faste],
B. 6.132	Whiche þei were in þis world hise *werkmen* apeired.
B. 6.189	And wente as *werkmen* [to wedynge] and [mowynge]
B. 6.313	[That] he was *werkman* wroȝt [warie] þe tyme.
B. 6.321	Ac I warne yow *werkmen*, wynneþ whil ye mowe
B.10.407	Was neuere wrighte saued þat wroȝte þeron, ne ooþer *werkman* ellis,
B.13.267	And *werkmen* were agast a lite; þis wole be þouȝt longe:
B.14.137	For whan a *werkman* haþ wroȝt, þan may men se þe soþe,
B.17.221	And as glowynge gledes gladeþ noȝt þise *werkmen*
C. 5.25	To wurche as a *werkeman* eny while to duyren.'
C. 7.41	So with wikkede will my *werkemen* y paye.
C. 8.116	Oþer *werkemen* þer were þat wrouhten fol ȝerne,
C. 8.186	And wenten as *werkemen* to wedynge and mowynge
C. 8.335	Þat he was *werkman* ywrouhte warien þe tyme.
C. 8.341	Ac y warne ȝow *werkmen*, wynneth whiles ȝe mowe,
C. 9.205	Whilen were *werkmen*, webbes and taylours
C.11.238	Was neuere wrihte þat þeron wrouhte ne *werkman* ysaued
C.19.187	And as glowyng gledes gladeth nat this *werkmen*

werkmanship n *werkmanshipe n.* B 4 werkmanship (1) werkmanshipe (3); C 2 werkmanschip (1) werkmanschupe (1)

B. 2.92	There as wil wolde and *werkmanshipe* fayleþ.'
B. 9.46	Wiþ his word and *werkmanshipe* and wiþ lif to laste.
B.10.294	And drede to wraþe yow in any word youre *werkmanship* to lette,
B.17.177	Oþerwise þan þe wriþen fust or *werkmanshipe* of fyngres.
C. 2.99	There þat wille wolde and *wer[k]manschip* faileth.
C.19.142	Oþerwyse then þe writhen f[u]ste or *werkmanschupe* of fyngres.

wern > ben

wernardes n *wernard n.* A 1 wernardis; B 1; C 1 wernardus

A. 2.93	Wel ȝe wyte, *wernardis*, but ȝif ȝoure wyt faile,

B. 2.129	Wel ye witen, *wernardes*, but if youre wit faille,
C. 2.145	For wel ȝe wyte, *wernardus*, as holy writ telleth,

werneþ v *wernen v.(1)* B 1; C 1 werneth

B.20.12	That is mete whan men hym *werneþ* and he no moneye weldeþ,
C.22.12	That is mete when men hym *werneth* [and] he no money weldeth

werre n *werre n.* B 9; C 11

B.11.332	Pouerte and plentee, boþe pees and *werre*,
B.14.223	And buxomnesse and boost [ben] eueremoore at *werre*,
B.15.356	For þoruȝ *werre* and wikkede werkes and wederes vn[s]esonable
B.15.542	And now is *werre* and wo, and whoso why askeþ:
B.18.228	Woot no wight what *werre* is þer þat pees regneþ,
B.18.412	Than after *werre* and wo whan loue and pees ben maistres.
B.18.413	Was neuere *werre* in þis world ne wikkednesse so kene
B.20.163	This Sleuþe [wex sleiȝ] of *werre* and a slynge made,
B.20.259	And if þei wage men to *werre* þei write hem in noumbre;
C. 3.206	Withouten *werre* oþer wo oþer wickede lawe
C.11.264	Mouhte sleylokeste be slawe and sente hym to w[e]*rre*,
C.13.140	Pouerte and plente, bothe pees and *werre*,
C.16.64	And buxomnesse and b[o]est [b]en eueremore at *werre*
C.17.86	For what thorw *werre* and wrake and wikkede hefdes
C.17.204	And now is *werre* and wo and whoso why asketh:
C.20.237	For woet no wiht what *werre* is þer [þat] pees regneth,
C.20.455	Then aftur *werre* and wake when loue and pees ben maistres.
C.20.456	Was neuere *werre* in this world ne wikkedere enuye
C.22.163	This sleuthe wa[x] sley of *werre* and a slynge made
C.22.259	And yf thei wage men to *werre* thei writen hem in nombre;

werre v *werren v.(1)* C 1

C.17.234	That with moneye maynteyneth men [t]o *werre* vppon cristene

wers(e > worse; wesched -en > wisshen

wesches n *wish n.(1)* C 1

C. 6.66	A wroth his f[u]ste vppon wrath; hadde [he] *wesches* at wille

weschynges > wisshynges; wessh(en > wasshen

west n *west n.* B 1; C 1

B.18.113	[Where] out of þe *west* coste a wenche as me þouȝte
C.20.116	Out of þe *west* as hit were a wenche, as me thouhte,

westmynstre n prop *Westminster n.* A 2 westmenstre (1) westmynstre (1); B 5; C 6 westminstre (2) Westmynstre (3) Westmunstre (1)

A. 2.125	To wende wiþ hem to *westmynstre* to wytnesse þ[is] dede.
A. 3.12	Þat woniþ at *westmenstre* worsshipeþ hire alle;
B. 2.161	To wenden wiþ hem to *westmynstre* to witnesse þis dede.
B. 3.12	[That] wonyeþ [at] *westmynstre* worshipeþ hire alle.
B.20.133	Muche of þe wit and wisdom of *westmynstre* halle.
B.20.285	And fleen to þe freres, as fals folk to *westmynstre*
B.20.288	Ac while he is in *westmynstre* he wol be bifore
C. 2.177	To wende with h[e]m to *westminstre* [the] weddyng to honoure.
C. 3.13	That wendeth to *Westmynstre* worschipe[th] here monye.
C.10.239	Ac *Westm[in]stre* lawe, y woet wel, worcheth be contra[r]ye,
C.22.133	Moche of þe Wyt and Wisdoem of *Westmunstre* halle.
C.22.285	And fle to þe freres, as fals folk to *Westmynstre*
C.22.288	Ac while he is in *Westmynstre* he wol be bifore

westward adv *westward adv.* B 2; C 2

B.16.169	Estward and *westward* I waited after faste
B.18.118	Euene out of þe Est and *westward* she lokede,
C.Pr.16	*Westward* y waytede in a while aftir
C.20.121	Euene oute of þe eest and *westward* she thouhte,

wet > weet; wete > weet n, weet adj, witen; weten > witen

wetheres n *wether n.* C 1

C. 9.268	Y leue, for thy lacchesse, thow lesest many *wetheres*

wethewynde(s > wiþwyndes

weue v *weven v.(1)* &> *wayuen* B 1

B. 5.548	I *weue* and I wynde and do what truþe hoteþ.

weueres n *wevere n.* A 1 weueris; B 1

A.Pr.99	Wollene websteris and *weueris* of lynen,
B.Pr.220	Wollen webbesters and *weueres* of lynnen,

weuyng ger *wevinge ger.(1)* B 1

B.15.452	Clooþ þat comeþ fro þe *weuyng* is noȝt comly to were

wex n *wax n.(1)* &> *wexen* B 3; C 5 wex (3) wexe (2)

B.17.207	As *wex* and a weke were twyned togideres,
B.17.209	And as *wex* and weke and [warm] fir togideres
B.17.235	And as *wex* wiþouten moore on a warm glede
C.Pr.99	In menynge of myracles muche *wex* hangeth there;
C.10.269	That his wyf were *wexe* or a walet ful of nobles.
C.19.173	As *wexe* and a weke were twyned togyderes
C.19.175	And as *wex* and weke and warm fuyr togyderes

C.19.201   And as *wex* withouten more vpo[n] a warm glede

wexe > wex,wexen

wexed v *waxen v.(2)* A 1 wexid; B 1; C 1
A. 5.192   And wisshide it hadde be *wexid* wiþ a wysp of firsen.
B. 5.344   And wisshed it hadde ben *wexed* wiþ a wispe of firses.
C. 6.402   And wesched hit hadde [be *wexed*] with a weps of breres.

wexen v *waxen v.(1)* A 10 waxen (2) waxiþ (3) wex (1) wexe (1) wexiþ
(3); B 32 wax (1) weex (9) wexe (8) wexen (2) wexeþ (6)
woxen (5); C 30 wax (5) waxe (3) waxeth (2) wex (1) wexe (12)
wexen (2) wexeth (5) woxe (1)
A. 2.20   Out of wrong heo *wex* to wroþerhele manye.
A. 3.273   Þat lawe is lord *waxen* & leute is pore,
A. 5.70   Walewiþ in my wombe & *waxiþ* as I wene.
A. 5.72   Such wynd in my wombe *wexiþ* er I dyne.
A. 8.58   To *waxen* & wanyen where þat god likiþ.
A. 9.34   Þe watir is liknid to þe world þat waniþ & *waxiþ*;
A.10.33   For þoruȝ þe woord þat he warp *wexe* forþ bestis,
A.10.61   And ben braynwood as bestis, so here blood *wexiþ*.
A.10.126   Or as whete out of weed *waxiþ*, out of þe erþe,
A.11.12   Þanne al þe precious perrie þat in paradis *wexiþ*.
B. 3.302   That Iewes shul wene in hire wit, and *wexen* glade,
B. 3.331   Also wroþ as þe wynd *weex* Mede in a while.
B. 4.174   And gan *wexe* wroþ with lawe for Mede almoost hadde shent it,
B. 5.279   Thanne *weex* þ[e] sherewe in wanhope & wolde han hanged
             hym[self]
B. 7.56   That neuere shul *wexe* ne wanye wiþouten god hymselue.
B. 8.38   The water is likned to þe world þat wanyeþ and *wexeþ*;
B. 9.32   For þoruȝ þe word þat he [warp] *woxen* forþ beestes,
B.10.12   Than al þe precious perree þat in paradis *wexeþ*.
B.10.76   Ne sory for hire synnes; so is pride *woxen*.
B.11.5   And in a wynkynge [worþ til I *weex*] aslepe.
B.11.116   And in a weer gan I *wexe*, and wiþ myself to dispute
B.11.265   To wepe and to wel bidde, wherof *wexeþ* Mercy
B.13.347   Til eiþeres wille *wexeþ* kene and to þe werke yeden:
B.13.417   He *wexeþ* wroþ, and wol noȝt here but wordes of murþe;
B.14.61   For þoruȝ his breeþ beestes *woxen* and abrood yeden:
B.14.77   *Weex* þoruȝ plentee of payn and of pure sleuþe:
B.14.326   Synne seweþ vs euere', quod he and sory gan *wexe*,
B.15.3   And so my wit *weex* and wanyed til I a fool weere.
B.15.102   Shal neuere flour ne fruyt [*wexe*] ne fair leef be grene.
B.15.460   As in wildernesse *wexeþ* wilde beestes
B.16.56   In what wode þei *woxen* and where þat þei growed,
B.16.101   Til he *weex* a faunt þoruȝ hir flessh and of fightyng kouþe,
B.16.215   That is, creatour *weex* creature to knowe what was boþe.
B.18.4   Til I *weex* wery of þe world and wilned eft to slepe
B.18.130   And grace of þe holy goost; *weex* greet wiþ childe,
B.19.97   Was neiþer kyng ne conquerour til he [comsed] *wexe*
B.19.124   And whan he [was *woxen*] moore, in his moder absence,
B.19.310   Wiþ olde lawe and newe lawe þat loue myȝte *wexe*
B.19.374   That he ne halp a quantite holynesse to *wexe*,
B.20.159   Sleuþe *wax* wonder yerne and soone was of age
B.20.163   This Sleuþe [*wex* sleiȝ] of werre and a slynge made,
B.20.269   It is wikked to wage yow; ye *wexen* out of noumbre.
C. 1.138   By what wey it *wexeth* and wheder out of my menynges.'
C. 2.29   Ne on a croked kene thorn kynde fyge *wexe*:
C. 3.212   That al þe witt of the world is *woxe* into Gyle.
C. 3.455   That iewes shal wene in he[re] wit, & *wexen* so glade,
C. 3.484   As wroth as [þe] wynd *wax* mede þeraftur:
C. 6.124   Til y, wrathe, *wexe* an hey and walke with hem bothe;
C. 6.422   A *wax* ashamed, þat shrewe, and shrofe hym a[s] swythe
C. 7.77   A *wexeth* wroth and wol not here but wordes of murthe.
C.10.44   The water is likned to þe wor[l]d þat wanyeth and *waxeth*;
C.10.196   And seth [he les] his lyf for lawe sholde loue *wexe*.
C.12.51   And in a wer gan y *wex* and with mysulue to despute
C.12.182   Sholde neuere whete *wexe* but whete furste deyede;
C.12.229   Riht as wedes *waxeth* in wose and in donge
C.12.232   Whete þat þeron *wexeth* worth lygge ar hit rype.
C.14.26   Ac Ar such a wil *wexe* worcheth go[d] sulue
C.14.32   That wit *wexeth* therof and oþer w[y]rdes bothe:
C.15.260   [For] thorw his breth bestes *wexe* and abrood ȝeden.
C.16.229   "Non plus sapere," saide þe wyse, [laste synne of pruyde *wexe*,]
C.16.255   Shal neuere flour ne fruyt *wexe* ne fayre leue be grene.
C.17.48   Thenne grace sholde growe ȝut and grene loue *wexe*
C.18.42   And þerwith y warde hit oþerwhile til hit *waxe* rype.
C.20.4   Til y *waxe* wery of the world and wilnede eefte to slepe
C.20.133   And grace of the holy gost; *wax* grete with childe,
C.21.97   Was noþer kyng ne conquerour til he comsed *wexe*
C.21.124   And when he was *wexen* more, in his moder absence,
C.21.310   With olde lawe and newe [lawe] þat loue myhte *wexe*
C.21.374   That he ne halpe a qua[n]tite holinesse to *wexe*,
C.22.159   Sleuthe *wax* wonder ȝerne and sone was of age

C.22.163   This sleuthe *wa[x]* sley of werre and a slynge made
C.22.269   Hit is wikked to wage ȝow; ȝe *wexeth* out of nombre.

wexid > wexed

weye n *wei n.(2)* B 1
B. 5.92   Than þouȝ I hadde þis wouke ywonne a *weye* of Essex chese.

weye v *weien v.(1)* A 4 weiȝe (3) weiȝede (1); B 5 weye (3) weyed (1)
weyen (1); C 4 waye (1) wayed (1) weye (2)
A. 1.152   Ȝe shuln be *weiȝe* þerwiþ whanne ȝe wende hennes.
A. 5.118   Wykkidly to *weiȝe* was my ferste lessoun.
A. 5.132   Þanne [myn owne] aunsel dede, [whanne] I *weiȝede* treweþe.
A. 5.143   Ne neuere wykkidly *weiȝe* ne wykkide chaffare make,
B. 1.178   Ye shulle ben *weyen* þerwiþ whan ye wenden hennes:
B. 5.202   Wikkedly to *weye* was my firste lesson.
B. 5.216   Than myn owene Auncer [whan I] *weyed* truþe.
B. 5.227   And neuere wikkedly *weye* ne wikke chaffare vse,
B. 5.240   To *weye* pens wiþ a peis and pare þe heuyeste
C. 6.210   Wykkedliche to *waye* was my furste lessoun.
C. 6.224   Then myn [owene] auncer when y *wayed* treuthe.
C. 6.242   To *weye* pans with a peyse and par[e] þe heuegeste
C. 9.272   And þe wolle worth *weye*, wo is the thenne!

wham > who

whan conj *whanne adv. & conj.* A 53 whan (13) whanne (37) when (3); B
135 whan (132) whanne (3); C 129 whan (10) whanne (1) when (106)
whenne (12)
A.Pr.1   IN a somer sesoun *whanne* softe was the sonne
A. 1.25   And drink *whanne* þe driȝeþ, ac do it nouȝt out of resoun
A. 1.26   Þat þou worþe þe wers *whanne* þou werche shuldist.
A. 1.83   'Whanne alle tresours arn triȝed treuþe is þe beste;
A. 1.124   *Whanne* alle tresours arn triȝed treuþe is þe beste.
A. 1.152   Ȝe shuln be weiȝe þerwiþ *whanne* ȝe wende hennes.
A. 1.165   Arn none hardere þan [hy] *whanne* [hy] ben auauncid,
A. 1.181   *Whan* alle tresouris arn triȝede treuþe is þe beste.
A. 2.79   Þanne tenide hym theologie *whan* he þis tale herde,
A. 2.194   And is welcome *whanne* he wile & woniþ wiþ hem ofte.
A. 2.198   And ek wep & wrang *whan* heo was atachid.
A. 3.62   Oþer to grede aftir godis men *whan* ȝe [g]iue dolis,
A. 3.163   *Whanne* ȝe wyte wytterly where þe wrong liggeþ;
A. 4.134   Ac [*whanne*] resoun among þise renkis reherside þise wordis,
A. 5.68   Wiþ werkis [or wiþ] wordis *whanne* he saiȝ his tyme.
A. 5.81   *Whanne* I mette hym in market þat I most hatide
A. 5.85   *Whanne* I come to þe [k]ir[k]e & knel[e] to þe rode,
A. 5.132   Þanne [myn owne] aunsel dede, [*whanne*] I weiȝede treweþe.
A. 5.139   *Whanne* it com in cuppemel; þat craft my wyf vside.
A. 5.197   *Whanne* he drouȝ to þe dore þanne dymmede hise eiȝen;
A. 6.87   *Whanne* I þenke þereon, þeiȝ I were a pope".
A. 7.19   Þat han silk & sendel, sewiþ it *whanne* tyme is,
A. 7.70   Dame werche *whanne* tyme is piers wyf hatte;
A. 7.106   Shulde ben hirid þereaftir *whan* heruist tyme come.
A. 7.144   Of þ[i] flour, and þi flessh fecche *whanne* vs likeþ,
A. 7.155   And manacide hym & his men *whanne* h[y] next metten.
A. 7.203   And he shal soupe swettere *whanne* he it haþ deseruid.
A. 7.261   Wende now *whanne* þi wille is, þat wel be þou euere.'
A. 8.18   Han pardoun wiþ þe apostlis *whanne* þei passe hennis,
A. 8.37   Þat no deuil shal ȝow dere, diȝe *whan* ȝe diȝe,
A. 8.81   Þat euere he was man wrouȝt *whanne* he shal henne fare.
A. 8.116   *Whan* þe frost fresiþ foode hem behouiþ;
A. 8.122   'Were þou a prest, piers,' quaþ he, 'þou miȝtest preche *wh[an]* þe
             liki[de];
A. 8.150   Manye tymes at mydniȝt *whan* men shulde slepe,
A. 8.171   At þe dredful dom *whanne* dede shal arisen
A.10.56   For *whan* blood is bremere þanne brayn, þan is Inwit bounde,
A.10.73   And cheuissh[en] hym for any charge *whan* he childhod passiþ,
A.10.149   And so seiþ þe sauter, se it *whanne* þe likiþ:
A.11.39   At mete [in here] merþe, *whanne* mynstralis ben stille,
A.11.44   And gnawen god in [þe gorge] *whanne* here guttis fullen.
A.11.50   Þat þus partiþ wiþ þe poore a parcel *whanne* hym nediþ.
A.11.93   And *whanne* þat wyt was war how his wif tolde
A.11.100   And *whanne* I was war of his wil to his wif gan I knele,
A.11.207   "*Whanne* fisshes faille þe flood or þe fresshe watir
A.11.208   Þei diȝe for þe drouȝte, *whanne* þei dreiȝe lengen;
A.11.238   And for his lele beleue, *whanne* he his lif tyneþ,
A.11.292   As þise þat wrouȝte wykkidly in world *whanne* þei were.
A.11.298   'Wh[anne] ȝe ben aposid of princes or of prestis of þe lawe
A.12.26   In þe passioun, *whan* pilat aposed god almyȝthi,
A.12.33   But as he seyþ, such I am, *when* he with me carpeþ.'
A.12.34   And *when* scripture þe skolde hadde þis [skele] ysheued
A.12.103   And *whan* þis werk was wrouȝt, ere wille myȝte aspie,
A.12.107   *When* he saw þes sawes busyly alegged
B.Pr.1   IN a somer seson *whan* softe was þe sonne
B.Pr.149   For a cat of a [court] cam *whan* hym liked

B. 1.25	And drynke *whan* þ[ee] drie[þ], ac do [it] noȝt out of reson
B. 1.26	That þow worþe þe wers *whan* þow werche sholdest.
B. 1.85	'Whan alle tresors arn tried treuþe is þe beste;
B. 1.124	*Whan* þise wikkede wenten out wonderwise þei fellen,
B. 1.135	*Whan* alle tresors arn tried truþe is þe beste.
B. 1.155	And *whan* it hadde of þis fold flessh and blood taken
B. 1.178	Ye shulle ben weyen þerwiþ *whan* ye wenden hennes:
B. 1.191	Are [none hardere] þan hij *whan* þei ben auaunced,
B. 1.207	*Whan* alle tresors ben tried treuþe is þe beste.
B. 2.67	*Whan* Symonye and Cyuylle seighe hir boþer wille
B. 2.115	Thanne tened hym Theologie *whan* he þis tale herde,
B. 2.235	And is welcome *whan* he wile and woneþ with hem ofte.
B. 2.239	And ek wepte and wrong *whan* she was attached.
B. 3.71	Or to greden after goddes men *whan* [e [gyue] doles
B. 3.176	*Whan* ye witen witterly wher þe wrong liggeþ.
B. 3.245	Of god at a gret nede *whan* þei gon hennes.
B. 5.85	With werkes or wiþ wordes *whan* he seyȝe his tyme.
B. 5.101	*Whan* I met[t]e hym in Market þat I moost hate[de]
B. 5.105	*Whan* I come to þe kirk and knele to þe Roode
B. 5.132	*Whan* he solde and I nouȝt þanne was I redy
B. 5.147	That *whan* þei preche þe peple in many places aboute
B. 5.178	Ac ouþer while *whan* wyn comeþ, [whan] I drynke at eue,
B. 5.178	Ac ouþer while whan wyn comeþ, [*whan*] I drynke at eue,
B. 5.216	Than myn owene Auncer [*whan* I] weyed truþe.
B. 5.223	[*Whan*] it cam In cuppemele, þis craft my wif vsed.
B. 5.232	I roos *whan* þei were areste and riflede hire males.'
B. 5.349	A[c] *whan* he drouȝ to þe dore þanne dymmed hise eiȝen;
B. 5.377	Fedde me bifore] noon *whan* fastyng dayes were.'
B. 5.427	Ruþe is to here rekenyng *whan* we shul rede acountes:
B. 5.492	Aboute mydday, *whan* moost liȝt is and meel tyme of Seintes,
B. 5.600	*Whan* I þynke þeron, þeiȝ I were a Pope."
B. 6.11	That ye haue silk and Sandel to sowe *whan* tyme is
B. 6.78	Dame werch-*whan*-tyme-is Piers wif hiȝte;
B. 6.114	Sholde be hired þerafter *whan* heruest tyme come.
B. 6.157	Of þi flour and þi flessh, fecche *whanne* vs likeþ,
B. 6.217	And he shal soupe swetter *whan* he it haþ deserued.
B. 6.277	Wend now *whan* [þi wil is], þat wel be þow euere.'\
B. 6.327	*Whan* ye se þe [mone] amys and two monkes heddes,
B. 7.57	*Whan* þei drawen on to [þe deþ] and Indulgences wolde haue.
B. 7.99	That euere [he was man] wroȝt *whan* [he] shal hennes fare.
B. 7.125	And wepen *whan* I sholde [werche] þouȝ whete breed me faille.
B. 7.134	[*Whan* þe frost freseþ fode hem bihoueþ];
B. 7.140	'Were þow a preest, [Piers]', quod he, 'þow myȝtest preche [*whan* þee liked]
B. 7.193	At þe dredful dome, *whan* dede shulle rise
B. 9.187	*Whan* ye han wyued beþ war and wercheþ in tyme,
B. 9.188	Noȝt as Adam and Eue *whan* Caym was engendred;
B.10.53	At mete in hir murþe *whan* Mynstrals beþ stille,
B.10.58	And gnawen god [in] þe gorge *whanne* hir guttes fullen.
B.10.64	That þus parteþ wiþ þe pouere a parcell *whan* hym nedeþ.
B.10.140	And þat wit was ywar [how his wif] tolde
B.10.147	And *whan* I was war of his wille to his wif gan I [knele]
B.10.301	*Whan* fisshes faillen þe flood or þe fresshe water
B.10.302	Thei deyen for drouȝte, *whan* þei drie [lenge];
B.10.355	And for his lele bileue, *whan* þe lif tyneþ,
B.10.400	*Whan* þei shal lif lete [a lippe of goddes grace]–
B.10.457	*Whan* man was at meschief wiþoute þe moore grace.
B.11.36	A man may stoupe tyme ynoȝ *whan* he shal tyne þe crowne.'
B.11.113	And *whan* þe peple come þ þe porter vnpynned þe yate
B.11.190	And exciteþ vs by þe Euaungelie þat, *whan* we maken festes,
B.11.234	Witnesse in þe Pask wyke, *whan* he yede to Emaus,
B.11.338	As *whan* þei hadde ryde in Rotey tyme anoon [reste þei] after;
B.11.353	[For men sholde hem noȝt fynde *whan* þei þerfro wente;
B.11.418	Ac man he mamelede about mete, and entremetede to knowe
B.11.432	Ac *whan* nede nymeþ hym vp for [nede] lest he sterue,
B.12.22	To solacen hym som tyme; [so] I do *whan* I make:
B.12.28	And þere bidde my bedes but *whan* ich ete or slepe.
B.12.256	And *whan* his caroyne shal come in caue to be buryed
B.13.20	And *whan* he hadde seid so, how sodeynliche he passed.
B.13.87	And seide, 'þow shalt see þus soone, *whan* he may na moore,
B.13.204	*Whan* þow art wery [for]walked; wille me to counseille'.
B.13.236	*Whan* þe preest preieþ þe peple hir Paternoster to bidde
B.13.264	And louren *whan* þei lakken hem; it is noȝt longe ypassed
B.13.265	There was a careful commune *whan* no cart com to towne
B.13.270	My wafres were gesene *whan* Chichestre was Maire.'
B.13.333	And *whan* I may noȝt haue þe maistrie [wiþ] malencolie Itake,
B.13.383	[I]n haly daies at holy chirche *whan* ich herde masse
B.13.388	As *whan* I lened and leued it lost or longe er it were paied.
B.13.410	[Is *whan* men] moorneþ noȝt for hise mysdedes, ne makeþ no sorwe,
B.13.416	*Whan* men carpen of crist or clennesse of soul[e]
B.13.441	Forþi I rede yow riche, reueles *whan* ye makeþ,
B.14.51	'Haue, haukyn', quod Pacience, 'and et þis *whan* þe hungreþ
B.14.52	Or *whan* þow clomsest for cold or clyngest for drye.
B.14.63	As holy writ witnesseþ *whan* men seye hir graces:
B.14.89	And surgiens for dedly synnes *whan* shrift of mouþe failleþ.
B.14.106	I wiste neuere renk þat riche was, þat *whan* he rekene sholde,
B.14.107	*Whan* he drogh to his deeþ day þat he ne dredde hym soore,
B.14.131	And *whan* he dyeþ ben disalowed, as Dauid seiþ in þe Sauter:
B.14.137	For *whan* a werkman haþ wroȝt, þan may men se þe soþe,
B.14.150	And *whan* he haþ doon his deuoir wel men dooþ hym ooþer bountee,
B.14.234	For *whan* he streyneþ hym to strecche þe strawe is his shetes.
B.14.236	That is welawo *whan* he wakeþ and wepeþ for colde,
B.15.24	And *whan* I wilne and wolde animus ich hatte;
B.15.26	And *whan* I make mone to god memoria is my name;
B.15.27	And *whan* I deme domes and do as truþe techeþ
B.15.29	And *whan* I feele þat folk telleþ my firste name is sensus,
B.15.31	And *whan* I chalange or chalange noȝt, chepe or refuse,
B.15.33	And *whan* I loue leelly oure lord and alle oþere,
B.15.35	And *whan* I flee fro þe flessh and forsake þe careyne
B.15.186	And *whan* he is wery of þat werk þan wole he som tyme
B.15.193	[Th]anne he syngeþ *whan* he doþ so, and som tyme wepynge,
B.15.432	[Ac] fressh flessh ouþer fissh, *whan* it salt failleþ,
B.15.511	[*Whan* þe hye kyng of heuene sente his sone to erþe
B.15.557	*Whan* Costantyn of curteisie holy kirke dowed
B.15.593	And *whan* he lifte vp Laȝar þat leid was in graue
B.16.48	Ac *whan* þe fend and þe flessh forþ wiþ þe world
B.16.77	And *whan* [he] meued matrimoyne it made a foul noise.
B.16.78	I hadde ruþe *whan* Piers rogged, it gradde so rufulliche.
B.16.137	Thei casten and contreueden to kulle hym *whan* þei myȝte.
B.16.230	Ful trewe toknes bitwene vs is to telle *whan* me likeþ.
B.17.7	And *whan* it is enseled [þerwiþ] I woot wel þe soþe
B.17.64	Ac *whan* he hadde sighte of þat segge aside he gan hym drawe
B.17.86	And *whan* I seiȝ þis I soiourned noȝt but shoop me to renne
B.17.181	*Whan* he feleþ þe fust and] þe fyngres wille;
B.17.327	And *whan* smoke and smolder smyt in his sighte
B.18.16	As dooþ an heraud of armes *whan* Auentrous comeþ to Iustes.
B.18.109	*Whan* crist cam hir kyngdom þe crowne sholde [lese]:
B.18.121	*Whan* þise maydenes mette, mercy and truþe,
B.18.172	*Whan* Pees in Pacience ycloþed approched ner hem tweyne
B.18.246	*Whan* she seiȝ hym suffre þat sonne and see made.
B.18.300	And *whan* I seiȝ it was so, [s]lepynge I wente
B.18.412	Than after werre and wo *whan* loue and pees ben maistres.
B.19.64	Is to wissen vs þerwiþ, þat *whan* we ben tempted,
B.19.124	And *whan* he [was woxen] moore, in his moder absence,
B.19.182	And *whan* þis dede was doon do best he [þouȝte],
B.19.226	And wepne to fighte wiþ *whan* Antecrist yow assailleþ.'
B.19.304	For counteþ he no kynges wraþe *whan* he in Court sitteþ;
B.19.329	And *whan* þis dede was doon Grace deuysede
B.19.414	And we clerkes, *whan* þei come, for hir comunes paieþ,
B.20.1	Thanne as I wente by þe wey, *whan* I was thus awaked,
B.20.12	That is mete *whan* men hym werneþ and he no moneye weldeþ,
B.20.51	*Whan* nede ha[dde] vndernome me þus anoon I fil aslepe
B.20.187	Siþ *whanne* was þe wey ouer mennes heddes?
B.20.196	On nyghtes namely, *whan* we naked weere,
C.Pr.1	In a somur sesoun *whan* softe was þe sonne
C.Pr.170	For a Cat of a Court cam *whan* hym likede
C. 1.45	*Whenne* þe peple was aposed hym of a peny in þe temple
C. 1.81	'When alle tresores ben tried treuthe is þe beste;
C. 1.104	And god *whan* he bigan heuene in þat grete blisse
C. 1.125	Ac thei caren nat thow hit be cold, knaues, *when* þe[i] worche.
C. 1.151	/A[nd] *when* hit hadde of þe folde flesch and blode taken
C. 1.174	Ȝe shal be weye þerwith *whenne* ȝe wende hennes:
C. 1.188	Auerous and euel willed *when* þei ben avaunsed,
C. 1.202	"Whenne alle tresores ben tried treuthe is þe beste."
C. 2.69	*When* simonye and syuile ysey[e] þer bothe wille
C. 2.108	For a leuethe be lost *when* he his lyf leteth,\
C. 2.119	Thenne tened hym teologie *when* he this tal[e] herde,
C. 2.245	And is welcome *when* he cometh and woneth with hem ofte.
C. 2.255	And bothe wepte and wrang *when* she was attached.
C. 3.26	[W]henne they hadde lauhte here leue at this lady mede
C. 3.171	Lyggeth by here, *when* hem lust, lered and lewed.
C. 3.222	*When* ȝe [wyten] witterly [where] þe wrong liggeth.
C. 3.304	*When* þe dede is ydo and þe day endit.
C. 3.399	And coueyte þe case, *when* thei couthe vnderstande.
C. 4.52	[A w]ayteth ful wel *when* y seluer take,
C. 5.1	Thus y awakede, woet god, *whan* y wonede in Cornehull,
C. 5.7	In an hot heruest *whenne* y hadde myn hele
C. 5.35	'When y [ȝut] ȝong was, many ȝer hennes,
C. 5.50	To be welcome *when* y come oþerwhile in a monthe,
C. 5.148	Ryht as fysches in floed *whan* hem fayleth water
C. 5.149	Dyen for drouthe *whenne* they drye lygge,
C. 6.59	Al [y] wolde þat men wiste *when* it to pruyde souneth,
C. 6.77	And *when* y may nat haue þe maystrie [with] malencolie ytake,
C. 6.97	*When* he solde and y nat thenne was y aredy

C. 6.111	On god *when* me greued auht and grochede of his sonde:
C. 6.160	Ac other while *when* wyn cometh and when y drynke late at euen
C. 6.160	Ac other while when wyn cometh and *when* y drynke late at euen
C. 6.193	*When* y was olde and hoor and hadde ylore þat kynde
C. 6.224	Then myn [owene] auncer *when* y wayed treuthe
C. 6.231	*When* hit cam in coppemele; this crafte my wyf vsede.
C. 6.236	Y roes and ryflede here males *when* the[y] areste were.'
C. 6.272	In halydayes at holy churche *when* y herde masse
C. 6.277	As *whenne* y lenede and leuede hit lost or longe or hit were payed.
C. 6.300	Yf he wiste thow were such *when* he resseyued thyn offrynge.
C. 6.407	And *when* he drow to þe dore thenne dymmede his yes;
C. 7.40	Reuthe is to here rekenynge *when* we shal rede acountes,
C. 7.70	Is *when* men mourneth not for his mysdedes,
C. 7.76	*When* me carpeth of Crist or clannesse of soule
C. 7.101	Forthy y rede ȝow ryche, reueles *when* ȝe maketh,
C. 7.132	Aboute mydday, *when* most liht is and mel tyme of sayntes,
C. 8.10	That ȝe [han] selk and sendel to sowe *whan* tyme is
C. 8.37	And *when* ȝe mersyen eny man late mercy be taxour,
C. 8.80	Dame worch-when-tyme-is [Peres] wyf hehte.
C. 8.121	He sholde be huyred þeraftur *when* heruost tyme come.
C. 8.224	With houndes bred and hors breed hele hem *when* þei hungren
C. 8.227	And h[e] shal soupe swetture *when* [he] hit hath deserued.
C. 8.298	Wende nouthe *when* thow wol[t] and wel [be thow] euere.
C. 9.52	For *whenne* ȝe drawe to þe deth and indulgences wolde haue
C. 9.125	We sholde [haue] hem to house and helpe hem *when* they come:
C. 9.146	And *whenne* hym lyketh and luste, his leue is to ryse
C. 9.147	And *when* he is rysen rometh out and riȝt wel aspyeth
C. 9.270	*When* thy lord loketh to haue allouaunce of his bestes
C. 9.339	At þe dredful dome, *when* dede shullen ryse
C.11.22	What shal worthen of suche *when* þei lyf leten:
C.11.33	Nowe is þe manere at mete *when* munstrals ben stille
C.11.39	And gnawen god with gorge *when* here gottes f[u]llen.
C.11.46	That so parteth with þe pore a parsel *when* hym nedeth.
C.11.81	And *when* wit was ywar what studie menede
C.11.85	And *when* y was war of his wille to þat womman gan y louten
C.11.195	A man may stoupe tyme ynowe *when* he shal tyne þe croune.'
C.12.48	And *whan* þe peple was plenere ycome þe porter vnpynnede þe gate
C.12.102	And, as þe euauengelie witnesseth, *when* we maken festes
C.12.123	Witnesse in þe paske woke *when* he ȝede to Emaux:
C.13.146	As *when* þei hadde [ryde in] roteye[tyme] anon they reste aftur;
C.13.226	Ac *when* he mamelede aboute mete and musede to knowe
C.13.239	Ac *when* nede nymeth hym vp anoen he is aschamed
C.15.23	And *when* he hadde ysaide so, how sodeynliche he vanschede.
C.15.94	And saide, 'Thow shalt se thus sone, *when* he may no more,
C.15.148	And *whan* he hadde yworded thus wiste no man aftur
C.15.250	'Haue, Actyf,' quod pacience, 'and eet this *when* þe hungreth
C.15.251	Or *when* thow cl[o]msest fo[r] colde or clingest for drouthe.
C.15.262	As witnesseth holy writ *when* we seggeth oure graces:
C.15.281	[Y wiste neuere renke þat ryche was þat *whan* he rekene sholde]
C.15.282	*When* he drow to þe deth that he ne dradd hym sarrore
C.15.304	Ac *when* deth awaketh hem of here we[le] þat were er so ryche
C.16.5	*When* his d[eu]er is doen and his dayes iourne
C.16.75	For *when* he streyneth hym to strecche the strawe is his shetes.
C.16.77	Þat is welowo *when* he [w]aketh and wepeth for colde;
C.16.184	And *when* y wilne and wolde Animus y hatte;
C.16.186	And *when* y make mone to god Memoria y hatte;
C.16.187	And *when* y deme domus and do as treuthe techeth
C.16.189	And *when* y fele þat fecche telleth my furste name is sensus
C.16.191	And *when* y chalenge [or chalenge] nat, chepe or refuse
C.16.193	And *when* y wol do or [nat do] gode dedes or ille
C.16.195	And *when* y louye lelly oure lord and alle oþere
C.16.197	And *when* y fle fro þe [flessh] and feye leue þe caroyne
C.16.303	And sory *when* he seth men sory, as thow seest childerne
C.16.305	And *when* a man swereth "forsoth" for sooth he hit troweth;
C.16.330	And *when* he hath visited thus fetured folk and oþer folke pore,
C.16.336	Thenne syngeth he *when* he doth so and sum tyme w[e]pynge:
C.17.30	Bote myldelyche *when* þey metten maden lowe [c]here
C.17.38	To his wyf; *when* he was blynde he herde a la[m]be blete:
C.17.100	Wisten w[hi]l[e] and tolde *when* hit sholde ryne.
C.17.144	For *when* alle frendes faylen and fleen away in deynge
C.17.161	And *when* kynde hath his cours and no contrarie fyndeth
C.17.173	Corn [þat þe] coluere eet *when* he come in places
C.17.177	And *when* þe coluer ca[m] th[us] then knelede þe peple
C.17.220	*Whan* Constantyn of cortesye holy kirke dowede
C.17.262	For *when* þe hye kyng of heuene sente his so[n]e til erthe
C.18.159	And *when* þat my will is y wol hit ouerthrowe
C.19.63	Ac *when* he hadde sihte of this s[egg]e asyde he gan hym drawe
C.19.91	And ȝut [b]e plasterud with pacience *when* fondynges [priketh hym]–
C.19.307	Ac *when* smoke and smolder [smyt in his sihte
C.20.14	As doth an heraud of Armes *when* Auntres cometh to ioustes.
C.20.112	*When* Crist thorw croos ouercam ȝoure kyndoem sholde tocleue:
C.20.124	*When* this maydones metten, Mercy and treuthe,
C.20.175	*Whenne* pees in pacience yclothed aproched her ayþer oþer
C.20.255	*When* he sye hym soffre þat sonne and se made.
C.20.333	And *when* y seyh hit was so, y sotiled how y myhte
C.20.455	Then aftur werre and wrake *when* loue and pees ben maistres.
C.21.64	Is to wissen vs þerwith, þat *when* we ben ytempted
C.21.124	And *when* he was wexen more, in his moder absence,
C.21.182	And *when* this dede was doen do best he thouhte
C.21.226	And wepne to fihte with *when* Auntecrist ȝow assaileth.'
C.21.304	For counteth he no kynges wreth *when* he in Court sitteth;
C.21.329	And *when* this dede was doen grace deuysed
C.21.414	And we Clerkes, *when* they come, for here comunes paieth,
C.22.1	[Thenne] as y wente by þe way, *when* y was thus awaked,
C.22.12	That is mete *when* men hym werneth [and] he no money weldeth
C.22.51	*Whenne* nede hadde vndernome [me] thus anoen y ful aslepe
C.22.187	Sennes *whanne* was þe way ouer menne heuedes?
C.22.196	Anyhtes nameliche, *when* we naked were,

whar- > *wher-*

what pron *what pron.* A 24; B 105; C 110

A. 1.1	*What* þe mounteyne [be]meniþ, & ek þe [m]erke dale,
A. 1.11	And seide 'mercy madame, *what* is þis to mene?'
A. 1.58	*What* may it [be]mene, madame I þe bseche?'
A. 1.72	*What* he[o] were witterly þat wisside me so faire.
A. 1.182	Now haue I told þe *what* treuþe is, þat no tresour is betere,
A. 2.15	'*What* is þis womman,' quaþ I, 'þus worþily atirid?'
A. 2.46	Alle to wytnesse wel *what* þe writ wolde.
A. 3.56	Be war *what* þi riȝt hond werchiþ or deliþ,
A. 3.106	*What* þat his wille were & what he do shulde.
A. 3.106	What þat his wille were & *what* he do shulde.
A. 5.24	He bad wastour go werche *what* he best couþe
A. 5.245	Ac *what* befel of þis feloun I can not faire shewe;
A. 6.33	Dyke[d] & d[o]luen & do *what* he hiȝte,
A. 6.80	He may do wiþ þe day sterre *what* hym dere likiþ;
A. 7.8	'*What* shulde we wommen werche þe while?'
A. 7.189	Of beggeris & bidderis *what* best is to done.
A. 7.196	[Now wolde I] wite, ȝif þou wistest, *what* were þe beste,
A. 8.26	And bad h[e]m begge boldely *what* [hem best] likeþ,
A. 8.174	*What* þou dedist day [by day] þe dom wile reherce.
A. 9.63	'*What* art þou,' quaþ I þo, 'þat my name knowist?'
A.10.25	'*What* calle ȝe þat castel,' quaþ I, 'þat kynde haþ ymakid?
A.11.88	*What* is dowel fro dobet; now def mote he worþe,
A.11.103	[To] kenne me kyndely to knowe *what* is dowel'.
A.11.259	To wyte *what* is dowel witterly in herte.
B.Pr.207	Coupled and vncoupled to cacche *what* þei mowe.
B.Pr.209	*What* þis metels bymeneþ, ye men þat ben murye,
B. 1.1	*What* þ[e] Mountaigne bymeneþ and þe merke dale
B. 1.11	And seide, 'mercy, madame, *what* [may] þis [by]meene?'
B. 1.60	*What* may it [by]meene, madame, I [þee] bseche?'
B. 1.74	*What* she were witterly þat wissed me so faire.
B. 1.208	Now haue I told þe *what* truþe is, þat no tresor is bettre,
B. 2.18	I hadde wonder *what* she was and whos wif she were.
B. 2.19	'*What* is þis womman', quod I, 'so worþili atired?'
B. 3.74	Wite *what* þow werchest wiþ þi riȝt syde,
B. 3.117	*What* his wille were and what he do [sholde].
B. 3.117	What his wille were and *what* he do [sholde].
B. 3.266	Weend to Amalec with þyn oost & *what* þow fyndest þere sle it.
B. 3.333	Se *what* Salomon seiþ in Sapience bokes!
B. 5.24	He bad wastour go werche *what* he best kouþe
B. 5.294	*What* he lerned yow in lente, leue þow noon ooþer,
B. 5.295	And *what* he lente yow of oure lordes good to lette yow fro synne.'
B. 5.471	*What* bifel of þis feloun I kan noȝt faire shewe.
B. 5.547	In taillours craft and tynkeris craft, *what* truþe kan deuyse,
B. 5.548	I weue and I wynde and do *what* truþe hoteþ.
B. 6.8	'*What* sholde we wommen werche þe while?'
B. 6.196	And *what* Piers preide hem to do as prest as a Sperhauk.
B. 6.203	'Of beggeris and bidderis *what* best be to doone.
B. 6.210	Now wolde I wite, [if þow wistest], *what* were þe beste,
B. 7.24	[And bad hem] buggen boldely [*what*] hem best liked
B. 7.196	[*What*] þow didest day by day þe doom wole reherce.
B. 8.72	'*What* art [þ]ow', quod I þo, 'þat my name knowest?'
B. 8.126	*What* was Dowel fro dobet and dobest from boþe.
B. 9.59	*What* anima is leef or looþ; he l[e]t hire at his wille,
B.10.135	*What* is dowel fro dobet, [now] deef mote he worþe,
B.10.151	[To] kenne me kyndely to knowe *what* is dowel.'
B.10.223	To counseille þee kyndely to knowe *what* is dowel.'
B.11.154	Lo! ye lordes, *what* leautee dide by an Emperour of Rome
B.11.409	[To wite] *what* dowel is, [ac wakyng neuere]'.
B.11.411	'[*What* is dowel?' quod þat wiȝt]; 'ywis, sire', I seide,
B.12.18	To telle men *what* dowel is, dobet and dobest boþe,
B.12.19	And prechours to preuen *what* it is of many a peire freres.'
B.12.26	*What* were dowel and dobet and dobest at þe laste,

B.12.29	'Poul in his pistle', quod he, 'preueþ *what* is dowel:
B.12.40	[Lo]! *what* made lucifer to lese þe heiȝe heuene,
B.12.102	And seint Spirit þe Samplarie, & seide *what* men sholde write.
B.12.174	For if þe clerk be konnynge he knoweþ *what* is synne,
B.13.85	[And appose hym] *what* penaunce is, of which he preched raþer.'
B.13.86	Pacience parceyued *what* I þouȝte and [preynte] on me to be stille
B.13.95	*What* he fond in a [forel of] a freres lyuyng,
B.13.103	'*What* is dowel, sire doctour?' quod I; 'is [dobest] any penaunce?'
B.13.115	*What* is dowel and dobet? ye dyuynours knoweþ.'
B.13.119	'Now þow, Clergie', quod Conscience, 'carp[e] *what* is dowel.'
B.13.121	Ther þe lord of lif wonyeþ, to leren [hem] *what* is dobest.
B.13.211	'That is sooþ', [seide] Clergie, 'I se *what* þow menest.'
B.13.299	And if he gyueþ ouȝt to pouere gomes, telle *what* he deleþ;
B.13.309	*What* I suffrede and seiȝ and somtymes hadde,
B.13.310	And *what* I kouþe and knew and what kyn I com of'.
B.13.121	Ther þe lord of lif wonyeþ, to leren [hem] *what* is dobest.
B.13.432	*What* Dauid seiþ of swiche men as þe Sauter telleþ:
B.13.444	And a lered man to lere þee *what* our lord suffred
B.14.138	*What* he were worþi for his werk and what he haþ deserued,
B.14.138	What he were worþi for his werk and what he haþ deserued,
B.14.275	*What* is Pouerte, pacience', quod he, 'properly to mene?'
B.14.322	That þ[u]s first wroot to wissen men *what* Pouerte was to mene.'
B.15.2	Er I koude kyndely knowe *what* was dowel,
B.15.22	'*What* are ye called', quod I, 'in þat court among cristes peple?'
B.15.119	If lewed [ledes] wiste *what* þis latyn meneþ,
B.15.149	'*What* is charite?' quod I þo; 'a childissh þyng', he seide:
B.15.200	*What* is þe wille and wherfore þat many wight suffreþ:
B.15.270	*What* penaunce and pouerte and passion þei suffrede,
B.15.360	That whilom warned bifore *what* sholde falle after.
B.15.362	Wisten by þe walkne *what* sholde bitide;
B.15.365	By þe seed þat þei sewe *what* þei sel[l]e myȝte,
B.15.356	And *what* to leue and to lyue by; þe lond was so trewe
B.15.451	[Enformed] hem *what* fullynge and feiþ was to mene.
B.16.3	Ac ȝit I am in a weer *what* charite is to mene.'
B.16.61	I shal telle þee as tid *what* þis tree highte.
B.16.63	And I haue told þee *what* hiȝte þe tree; þe Trinite it meneþ.'
B.16.180	'*What* berþ þat buyrn', quod I þo, 'so blisse þee bitide?'
B.16.193	Of hym[self] and of his seruaunt, and *what* [suffreþ hem] boþe.
B.16.215	That is, creatour weex creature to knowe *what* was boþe.
B.16.229	Calues flessh and Cakebreed; and knewe *what* I þouȝte.
B.16.257	'*What* awaitestow?' quod he, 'and what woldestow haue?'
B.16.257	'What awaitestow?' quod he, 'and *what* woldestow haue?'
B.16.258	'I wolde wite', quod I þo, '*what* is in youre lappe.'
B.16.275	*What* he highte & whider he wolde, and wightly he tolde.
B.17.80	'*What* he spendeþ moore [for medicyne] I make þee good herafter,
B.18.18	Thanne I frayned at Feiþ *what* al þat fare bymente,
B.18.126	'And am wendynge to wite *what* þis wonder meneþ.'
B.18.170	But [loue] sente hire som lettre *what* þis light bymeneþ
B.18.206	For no wight woot *what* wele is þat neuere wo suffrede,
B.18.207	Ne *what* is hoot hunger þat hadde neuere defaute.
B.18.209	Sholde wite witterly *what* day is to meene.
B.18.211	Wite *what* wo is, ne were þe deeþ of kynde.
B.18.217	Woot no wight, as I wene, *what* [is ynogh] to mene.
B.18.221	To wite *what* wele was, kyndeliche [to] knowe it.
B.18.223	To [se] *what* he haþ suffred in þre sondry places,
B.18.225	To wite *what* alle wo is [þat woot of] alle ioye.
B.18.227	Shal lere hem *what* langour is and lisse wiþouten ende.
B.18.228	Woot no wight *what* werre is þer þat pees regneþ,
B.18.229	Ne *what* is witterly wele til weylawey hym teche.'
B.18.406	But leten hym lede forþ [*what*] hym liked and lete [what] hym liste.
B.18.406	But leten hym lede forþ [what] hym liked and lete [*what*] hym liste.
B.19.1	Thus I awaked and wroot *what* I hadde ydremed,
B.19.204	I wondred *what* þat was and waggede Conscience,
B.19.242	And some to seye *what* sholde bifalle,
B.19.473	And *what* I take of yow two, I take it at þe techynge
B.20.331	And in haste askede *what* his wille were.
B.20.337	Conscience knoweþ me wel and *what* I kan boþe.'
B.20.339	*What* hattestow, I praye þee? hele noȝt þi name.'
C.Pr.220	*What* þis meteles bymeneth, ȝe men þat ben merye,
C.1.1	*What* the montaigne bymeneth and þe merke dale
C.1.11	And sayde, 'mercy, madame, *what* may this [be]mene?'
C.1.40	And wysseth þe to ben ywar *what* wolde þe desseyue.'
C.1.44	'Go to þe gospel', quod she, 'and se *what* god sayde
C.1.56	*What* may hit bymene, madame, y [þe] byseche?'
C.1.68	Thenne hadde y wonder in my wit *what* woman he were
C.1.71	*What* she were wytterly þat wissede me so [faire].
C.1.204	To lere the *what* loue is;' and leue at me she lauhte.
C.2.17	[Wh]os wyf a were and *what* was here name,
C.2.221	*What* was þe kynges wille and wyghtliche wente
C.3.76	Ywyte *what* thow delest with thi ryhte syde.
C.3.123	And wittenesseth *what* worth of hem þat wolleth take mede:
C.3.154	*What* his wille were and what he do sholde.
C.3.154	What his wille were and *what* he do sholde.
C.3.342	*What* is relacion rect and indirect aftur,
C.3.485	'Loo *what* salamon sayth', quod she, 'in sapiense in þe bible!
C.4.147	To construe this c[l]ause, kyndeliche *what* it meneth.
C.5.37	Tyl y wyste witterly *what* holy writ menede
C.5.38	And *what* is beste for the body, as the boek telleth.
C.5.83	For in my Consience y knowe *what* Crist w[o]lde y wrouhte.
C.6.47	And *what* y gaf for godes loue to gossipus y tolde,
C.6.57	*What* y soffrede and seyh and some tymes hadde
C.6.58	And *what* y couthe and knewe and what kyn y cam of."
C.6.303	There shal he wite witturly *what* vsure is to mene
C.6.325	*What* byful of this feloun y can nat fayre shewe:
C.6.349	*What* a lered ȝow to lyue with and to lette ȝow fram thefte.'
C.7.92	Wh[at] dauid sayth of such men as þe sauter telleth:
C.7.104	With a lered man to lere the *what* oure lord suffrede
C.8.6	'*What* sholde we wommen wor[c]he þe whiles?'
C.8.88	*What* þei comaunde as by þe kyng countreplede hit neuere;
C.8.148	What! y and myn wolle fynde hem *what* hem nedeth.'
C.8.209	Of beggares and biddares *what* beste be to done.
C.8.219	Now wolde y wyte, ar thow wendest, *what* were þe beste;
C.8.258	Lo! *what* þe sauter sayth to swynkares with handes:
C.9.28	[And] bad hem bugge boldly *what* hem best likede
C.9.87	*What* h[e]m nede[th] at here neyhebores at noon and at eue.
C.9.165	And lere this lewede men *what* þis latyn meneth
C.9.278	Loke now, for thy lacchesse, *what* lawe wol the graunte:
C.9.308	And sethen aftur his sones, and sayde hem *what* they thouhte;
C.10.70	'*What* art thow', quod y [þo], 'þat my name knowest?'
C.10.122	*What* was dowel fro dobet and dobest fro hem bothe,
C.10.127	And *what* þey drede and doute, dere sire, telleth.'
C.11.22	*What* shal worthen of suche when þei lyf leten:
C.11.81	And when wit was ywar *what* studie menede
C.11.89	With þat ȝe kenne me kyndeliche to knowe *what* is dowel.'
C.11.110	To clergie shaltow neuere come ne knowe *what* is dowel.
C.11.112	And hast vnderstandyng *what* a wolde mene
C.12.89	'Lo! lordes, *what* leute dede and leele dome yvsed.
C.12.162	*What* god saide hymsulue to a segg þat he louede:
C.13.36	*What* oen hath, what [o]þer hath and what they hadde bothe,
C.13.36	What oen hath, *what* [o]þer hath and what they hadde bothe,
C.13.36	What oen hath, what [o]þer hath and *what* they hadde bothe,
C.13.65	3e wyte, ȝe wyse men, *what* this is to mene:
C.13.175	Ne *what* o[f] floures on felde and of here fayre coloures
C.13.217	To wyte *what* dowel is Ac wakynge neuere.'
C.13.218	And thenne was ther a wyhte, *what* he was y neste.
C.13.219	'*What* is dowel?' quod þat wyhte; 'ywis, sire,' y saide,
C.14.4	And wissed the [wel] ofte *what* dowel was to mene
C.14.47	And seynt spirit þe saumplarie and said *what* men sholde wryte.
C.14.114	For yf þe clerke be connynge [he] knoweth *what* is synne
C.15.92	And apose hym *what* penaunce is and purgatorie on erthe
C.15.102	*What* a fond in a forel of a frere[s] lyuynge,
C.15.110	'*What* is dowel, sire doctour?' quod y; 'is dobest eny penaunce?'
C.15.122	*What* is dowel and dobet? ȝe deuynours knoweth.'
C.15.127	'Now þou, Clergie', quod Consience, 'carpe *what* is dowel.'
C.15.181	That they knoweth nat', quod Concience, '*what* is kynde pacience
C.15.272	'*What* is [properly] parfit pacience?' quod Actiua vita.
C.16.6	Thenne may men wyte *what* he is worth and what he hath deserued
C.16.6	Thenne may men wyte what he is worth and *what* he hath deserued
C.16.115	'*What* is pouerte, pacience?' quod he; 'y preye þat thow telle hit.'
C.16.157	That wroet thus to wisse men *what* pouerte was to mene.'
C.16.162	Thenne hadde y wonder *what* he was, þat l[i]berum Arbitrium,
C.16.242	Lo, *what* holy writ wittnesseth of wikkede techares:
C.17.37	As wittnesseth holy writ *what* tobie saide
C.17.39	"Wyf! be ywar," quod he; "*what* haue we herynne?
C.17.98	That whilum warnede byfore *what* sholde [f]alle aftur.
C.17.102	By the seed þat they sewe *what* þey sulle myhte
C.17.103	And *what* lyue by and leue, the londe was so trewe.
C.17.125	'*What* is holy churche, chere frende?' quod y; 'Charite,' he saide;
C.17.150	'Where sarresynes', y saide, 'yse nat *what* is charite?'
C.18.8	Thenne gan y aske *what* hit hihte and he me sone tolde:
C.18.186	'*What* is his [conn]esaunc[e]', quod y, 'in his cote Armure?'
C.18.202	Of hymsulue and his seruant, and *what* soffreth hem bothe.
C.18.244	And *what* y thouhte and my wyf he vs wel tolde.
C.18.273	'*What* [a]waytest thow', quod fayth, 'and what wost thow haue?'
C.18.273	'What [a]waytest thow', quod fayth, 'and *what* wost thow haue?'
C.18.274	'I wolde ywyte', quod y tho, '*what* is in thy lappe.'
C.18.291	*What* he hihte and whoder he wolde & whithliche he tolde.
C.20.16	Thenne y [f]raynede at fayth *what* al þat fare bymente
C.20.129	'And am wendynge to wyte *what* þis wonder meneth.'
C.20.173	Bote loue haue ysente her som lettre *what* this liht bymeneth
C.20.212	Ne *what* is hoet hunger þat hadde neuere defaute.
C.20.216	Sholde ywyte witterly *what* day is to mene.
C.20.220	Ywyte *what* wo is ne were we þe deth of kynde.
C.20.226	Ne woet no wyht, as y wene, *what* is ynow to mene.
C.20.230	To wyte *what* wele [was], kyndeliche to knowe [hit].

C.20.232   To wyte *what* he hath soffred in thre sundry places,
C.20.234   To wyte *what* al wo is þat woet of alle ioye:
C.20.236   Shal lere hem *what* l[angour] is and lisse withouten ende.
C.20.237   For woet no wiht *what* werre is þer [þat] pees regneth
C.20.238   Ne *what* is witterliche wele til welaway hym teche.'
C.20.356   Witnesseth in his writyng[e] *what* is lyares mede:
C.21.1   Thus y wakede and wrot *what* y hadde ydremed
C.21.204   Y wondred *what* þat was and wagged Consience
C.21.242   And somme to se and to saye *what* sholde bifalle
C.21.473   And y take of ȝow two y take hit at þe techynge
C.22.331   And in haste eschete *what* his wille were.
C.22.337   Consience knoweth me wel and *what* y can bothe.'
C.22.339   *What* hattest thow? y praye the, hele nat thy name.'

what adj *what adj.(1)*   A 8; B 35; C 48
A. 1.69   Þanne hadde I wondir in my wyt *what* womman it were
A. 1.128   Be *what* craft in my cors it compsiþ, & where.'
A. 2.47   In *what* maner þat mede in mariage was feffid;
A. 3.6   *What* man of þis world þat hire were leuist;
A. 4.10   Of mede & of mo oþere, *what* man shal hire wedde,
A. 7.241   'I wot wel,' quaþ hunger, '*what* seknesse man eileþ.
A. 9.5   And *what* man he miȝte be of many man I askide.
A.10.26   [And *what* [kenis] þing is kynde, conne ȝe me telle]?'
B. 1.71   Thanne hadde I wonder in my wit *what* womman it weere
B. 1.139   By *what* craft in my cors it comseþ, and where.'
B. 2.32   And *what* man be merciful and leelly me loue
B. 2.34   And *what* man takeþ Mede, myn heed dar I legge,
B. 3.6   *What* man of þis [world] þat hire were leuest.
B. 3.324   And *what* smyth þat any smyþeþ be smyte þerwiþ to deþe:
B. 4.10   [Of Mede and of mo oþere, *what* man shal hire wedde],
B. 6.257   'I woot wel', quod hunger, '*what* siknesse yow eyleþ.
B. 8.5   And *what* man he myȝte be of many man I asked.
B. 9.25   '*What* kynnes þyng is kynde?' quod I; 'kanstow me telle?'
B.11.360   Muche merueilled me *what* maister [þei hadde],
B.12.74   That *what* womman were in auoutrye taken, whe[r] riche or poore,
B.12.159   And þow seidest sooþ of somme, ac se in *what* manere.
B.13.25   And þere I [mette] a maister, *what* man he was I nyste,
B.13.77   And *what* meschief and maleese crist for man þolede,
B.13.223   To Conscience *what* craft he kouþe, and to what contree he wolde.
B.13.223   To Conscience what craft he kouþe, and to *what* contree he wolde.
B.13.310   And what I kouþe and knew and *what* kyn I com of'.
B.13.375   And [*what* body] borwed of me abouȝte þe tyme
B.14.47   But I [listnede and] lokede *what* liflode it was
B.15.14   And wherof I cam & of *what* kynde. I coniured hym at þe laste
B.15.398   Brouȝte Sarȝens of Surree, and see in *what* manere.
B.15.491   *What* pope or prelat now parfourneþ þat crist highte,
B.16.56   In *what* wode þei woxen and where þat þei growed,
B.16.74   And suffre me to assaien *what* sauour it hadde.
B.16.260   'This is a present of muche pris; *what* prynce shal it haue?'
B.17.143   And profre[d] it forþ as with a pawme to *what* place it sholde.
B.18.174   And preide pees to telle hire to *what* place she wolde.
B.18.301   To warne Pilates wif *what* done man was Iesus,
B.18.317   *What* lord artow?' quod Lucifer; þe light soone seide
B.19.23   And ye callen hym crist; for *what* cause, telleþ me.
B.19.195   And *what* persone paieþ it nouȝt punysshen he þenkeþ,
B.20.3   I ne wiste wher to ete ne at *what* place,
B.20.67   And *what* kyng þat hem conforted, knowynge [hir gile],
B.20.207   'Counseille me, kynde', quod I, '*what* craft is best to lerne?'
C.Pr.105   *What* cheste and meschaunce to þe children of Irael
C. 1.138   By *what* wey it wexeth and wheder out of my menynges.'
C. 2.34   [W]hat man [that] me louyeth and my wille foleweth
C. 2.36   And *what* [man] mede loueth, my lyf [dar y] wedde,
C. 3.6   *What* man of this world þat here [were leuest].
C. 3.110   *What* maner muster oþer marchandise he vsed
C. 4.10   Of mede and of mo othere and *what* man shal here wedde
C. 4.53   *What* wey y wende wel ȝerne he aspyeth
C. 6.58   And what y couthe and knewe and *what* kyn y cam of."
C. 6.247   So *what* buyrn of me borewede abouhte the tyme.'
C. 6.301   And *what* lede leueth þat y lye look in þe sauter glos[e],
C. 6.304   And [*what*] penaunce the prest shal haue þat p[r]oud is of his tithes.
C. 7.145   That *what* tyme we synnefole men wolden be sory
C. 8.269   'Y wot wel,' quod hungur, '*what* sekenesse ȝow ayleth.
C. 9.89   *What* other byhoueth þat hath many childrene
C. 9.153   And *what* freke on this folde fiscuth aboute
C.10.5   And *what* man a myhte be of mony m[a]n y askede.
C.10.126   And *what* lyues they lyue and what lawe þei vsen
C.10.126   And what lyues they lyue and *what* lawe þei vsen
C.10.151   '*What* kynne thyng is kynde?' quod y; 'canst thow me telle?'
C.13.15   Iob þe gentele, *what* ioye hadde he on erthe?
C.13.89   And sheweth be seel and seth by lettre with *what* lord he dwelleth,
C.13.169   'Where hadde thise wilde suche wit and at *what* scole?'
C.14.103   And thow saidest sothe of somme, Ac [yse] in *what* manere.
C.15.18   Of kynde and [of] his connynge and *what* connynge he ȝaf bestes

C.15.70   At poules byfore þe peple *what* penaunce they soffrede,
C.15.83   And *what* meschief and maleese crist for man tholede.
C.15.192   *What* craft þat he couthe and cortey[s]liche he saide:
C.15.195   '*What* manere munstracye, my dere frende,' quod Concience,
C.15.248   And y lystnede and lokede *what* lyflode hit were
C.16.165   'Leue liberum arbitrium,' quod y, 'of *what* lond ar ȝe?
C.16.316   'H[o] fynt hym his fode,' quod y, 'or *what* frendes hath he,
C.16.327   *What* sorwe he soffrede in ensaumple of vs alle
C.17.174   And in *what* place he prechede and the peple tauhte
C.18.23   Moche merueyled me on *what* more thei growede
C.18.24   And askede [e]fte of hym of *what* wode they were.
C.18.103   Assay *what* sauour hit hadde and saide þat tyme,
C.18.246   Fol trewe tokenes bitwene vs is wh[at] tyme þat y met[t]e hym,
C.18.276   'This is a present of moche pris; *what* prince shal hit haue?'
C.19.117   And profered hit forth as with the paume to *what* place hit sholde.
C.20.177   And preyede pees to tellen [here] to *what* place she [w]olde
C.20.211   For no wiht woet *what* wele is þat neuere wo soffrede
C.20.360   '*What* lord artow?' quod lucifer; a voys aloude saide:
C.21.23   And ȝe callen hym Crist; for *what* cause, telleth me.
C.21.195   And *what* persone payth hit nat punischen he thenketh
C.22.3   Y ne wiste where to ete ne at *what* place
C.22.67   And *what* kyng þat hem conforted, knowynge here gyle,
C.22.207   'Consaileth me, kynde,' quod y, '*what* craft be beste to lere?'

what adv *what adv.*   B 5; C 3
B.13.316   *What* on bak, and what on body half, and by þe two sides
B.13.316   What on bak, and *what* on body half, and by þe two sides
B.17.33   *What* neded it [now] a newe lawe to [brynge]
B.18.110   *What* for feere of þis ferly and of þe false Iewes
B.18.188   '*What*, rauestow?' quod Rightwisnesse, 'or þow art right dronke?
C.17.86   For *what* thorw werre and wrake and wikkede hefdes
C.19.34   *What* nedede hit thanne a newe lawe to brynge
C.20.113   *What* for fere of this ferly and of þe false iewes

what exclam *what interj.*   A 1; B 3; C 2
A. 8.118   '*What*!' quaþ þe prest to perkyn, 'peter, as me þinkeþ,
B. 5.392   '*What*! awake, renk!' quod Repentaunce, 'and rape þee to shryfte!'
B. 7.136   '*What*!' quod þe preest to Perkyn, 'Peter! as me þynkeþ
B.13.183   '*What*!' quod Clergie to Conscience, 'ar ye coueitous nouþe
C. 7.8   '*What*! awake, renke!' quod repentaunce, 'and rape [þe] to shryfte.'
C. 8.148   *What*! y and myn wolle fynde hem what hem nedeth.'

what &> whatso

whateuere adj *whatever adj.*   B 2; C 1
B. 5.483   And for þe beste as I bileue *whateuere* þe book telleþ:
B.11.216   For *whateuere* clerkes carpe of cristendom or ellis,
C. 7.125   And for [þe] beste, as y beleue, *what[euere]* þe boek telle:

whatso pron *whatso pron.*   A 2; B 3 whatso (2) what_so (1); C 2 whatso (1) what_so (1)
A.10.96   *Whatso* men worden of þe wraþþe þe neuere;
A.11.86   And al worþ as þou wilt, *whatso* we telle–
B. 4.155   And seide, 'madame, I am youre man *what so* my mouþ Iangle,
B.10.133   And al worþ as þow wolt *whatso* we dispute–
B.12.122   Ne sette short bi hir science, *whatso* þei don hemselue.
C.14.65   Ne sette shorte by here science, *whatso* þei doen hemsulue.
C.14.216   And a cortesye more þen couenant was, *what so* clerkes carpe,

whatsoeuere pron *whatsoever pron.*   B 1
B.10.394   Thanne wrouȝte I vnwisly, *whatsoeuere* ye preche.

wheche > which; wheder > wheiþer,whider

wheiþer pron *whether pron.*   A 1 wheþer; B 2; C 1 where
A.12.37   Or wycke ȝif I wolde, *wheþer* me lyked.
B.14.248   And *wheiþer* be liȝter to breke? lasse boost [it] makeþ
B.16.96   *Wheiþer* sholde fonge þe fruyt, þe fend or hymselue.
C.16.88   And *where* be [lyh]tere to breke? lasse boest hit maketh

wheiþer conj *whether adv. & conj.*   B 20 wher (7) wheiþer (13); C 25 wheder (1) wher (6) where (17) wheþer (1)
B.Pr.171   *Wher* he ryt or rest or r[om]eþ to pleye;
B. 5.277   In Miserere mei deus, *wher* I mene truþe:
B. 8.130   And *wheiþer* he be man or [no man] þis man wolde aspie
B.10.439   *Wher* fo[r loue] a man worþ allowed þere and hise lele werkes,
B.11.83   Loke, ye lettred men, *wheiþer* I lye or noȝt.'
B.11.117   *Wheiþer* I were chosen or noȝt chosen; on holi chirche I þouȝte
B.11.189   *Wheiþer* we loue þe lordes here bifore þe lord of blisse;
B.12.74   That what womman were in auoutrye taken, *whe[r]* riche or poore,
B.12.270   And *wheiþer* he be saaf or noȝt saaf, þe soþe woot no clergie,
B.12.291   And *wheiþer* it worþ [of truþe] or noȝt, [þe] worþ [of] bileue is gret,
B.14.102   '*Wheiþer* paciente pouerte', quod Haukyn, 'be moore plesaunt to oure d[riȝte]
B.14.258   And *wheiþer* he be or be noȝt, he bereþ þe signe of pouerte
B.15.197   '*Wheiþer* clerkes knowen hym', quod I, 'þat kepen holi kirke?'

B.17.127   'A, swete sire', I seide þo, '*wher* I shal bileue,
B.17.261   Poul þe Apostel preueþ *wheiþer* I lye:
B.18.70   *Wher* he be deed or noȝt deed doun er he be taken.'
B.18.298   *Wheiþer* he were god or goddes sone; he [g]af me short answere;
B.18.387   *Wheiþer* þei deye or deye noȝt for þat þei diden ille.
B.19.350   *Wheiþer* he wynne wiþ right, wiþ wrong or wiþ vsure.'
B.20.107   To cesse and suffre, and see *wher* þei wolde
C.Pr.188   *Wher* he ri[t] othere reste or rometh to pleye;
C. 1.138   By what wey it wexeth and *wheder* out of my menynges.'
C. 2.152   *Where* matrymonye may be of mede and of falshede.
C. 3.297   And wot neuere witterly *where* he lyue so longe
C. 9.241   Loke now *where* this lollares and lewede Ermites
C.12.52   *Where* y were chose [or nat chose]; on holy churche y thouhte
C.13.169   '*Where* hadde thise wilde suche wit and at what scole?'
C.14.191   And *wher* he be saef or nat saef þe sothe woet no clergie
C.14.193   *Wher* þey ben in hell or in heuene or Aristotel þe wyse.
C.14.213   And *wher* hit worth or worth nat, the bileue is gret of treuthe
C.15.258   *Wheþer* thorw hunger or [thorw] hete, at his wille be hit;
C.15.277   '*Where* pouerte and pacience plese more god almyhty
C.16.98   And *where* he be or be nat, a bereth þe signe of pouerte
C.16.339   *Where* clerkes knowe hym nat,' quod y, 'þat kepen holy churche?'
C.17.150   '*Where* sarresynes,' y saide, 'yse nat what is charite?'
C.18.54   *Where* þe fruyt were fayre or foul for to loke on.
C.18.57   And askede efte tho *where* hit were all [of] o kynde.
C.19.27   'Ȝoure wordes aren wonderfol,' quod y; '*where* eny of [hem] be trewe
C.19.227   Paul the apostel preueth *where* y lye:
C.20.72   *Wher* he be ded or nat ded down or he be taken.'
C.20.218   He hadde nat wist witterly *where* deth were sour or swete.
C.20.331   *Where* he were god or godes sone; he gaf me short answere.
C.20.429   *Where* they deye or dey nat, dede they neuere so ille.
C.21.350   *Where* he wynne with riht, with wrong or with vsure.'
C.22.107   To sese and soffre and se *wher* they wolde

when *adv* *whenne adv. & conj. &> whan, cf. whennes* A 1
A.12.80   Of *when* þat he were, and wheder þat he wolde.

whenis > whennes; whenne > whan

whennes *adv* *whennes adv. & conj.* A 1 whenis; B 4; C 3
A. 6.13   Þis folk fraynide hym faire [fro] *whenis* þat he come.
B. 5.525   This folk frayned hym [faire] fro *whennes* he come.
B.16.174   I frayned hym first fram *whennes* he come
B.16.175   And of *whennes* he were and whider þat he [þ]ouȝte.
B.16.274   I affrayned hym first fram *whennes* he come,
C. 7.170   This folk frayned hym furste fro *whennes* he come.
C.18.183   'Of *whennes* artow?' quod y, and hendeliche hym grette.
C.18.290   And y fraynede hym furst fro *whennes* he come,

wher > wheiþer, where

wherby *adv* *wherbi adv. & conj.* B 3; C 3 wherby (1) whereby (2)
B.10.442   And *wherby* wiste men which [is] whit if alle þyng blak were,
B.14.40   Wherof or wherfore or *wherby* to libbe:
B.15.314   Til briddes brynge vs [*wherby*] we sholde lyue.
C. 3.250   *Wherby* he may as a man for eueremore lyue aftur.
C. 5.34   Or ymaymed thorw som myshap *whereby* thow myhte be excused?'
C.12.186   At the laste launceth vp *whereby* we lyuen all.

where *adv* *when adv. & conj.* A 2; B 4; C 3
A.Pr.12   Þat I was in a wildernesse, wiste I neuere *where*;
A. 5.204   Þe ferste woord þat he spak was '*where* is þe bolle?'
B.Pr.12   That I was in a wildernesse, wiste I neuere *where*.
B. 5.362   The firste word þat he [spak] was '*where* is þe bolle?'
B.14.98   '*Where* wonyeþ Charite?' quod Haukyn; 'I wiste neuere in my lyue
B.15.151   '*Where* sholde men fynde swich a frend wiþ so fre an herte?'
C. 9.243   *Where* se we hem on sonendayes the seruise to here,
C. 9.266   How, herde! *where* is thyn ho[u]nd[e] and thyn hardy herte
C.16.287   That maistres commenden moche. *Where* may hit be yfounde?

where *conj* *wher adv. & conj.* A 17 wher (1) where (16); B 36 wher (11) where (25); C 37 whare (3) wher (5) where (29)
A. 1.128   Be what craft in my cors it compsiþ, & *where*.'
A. 2.5   'Loke on þi left half, & lo *where* he standis,
A. 3.128   To vnfetere þe fals, fle *where* hym lykiþ.
A. 3.163   Whanne ȝe wyte wytterly *where* þe wrong liggeþ;
A. 3.169   And ek grepe my gold & gyue it *where* þe likiþ.
A. 6.21   Canst þou wisse vs þe wey *where* þat wy dwelliþ?'
A. 6.41   And ȝif ȝe wilneþ wyte *where* þat wy dwelliþ
A. 8.58   To waxen & wanyen *where* þat god likiþ.
A. 9.4   Ȝif any wiȝt wiste *where* dowel was at Inne;
A. 9.7   *Where* þis lede lengide, lesse ne more,
A. 9.13   '*Where* þat dowel dwelli[þ], do me to wisse'.
A. 9.68   *Where* dowel dwelliþ, & do me to wisse.'
A. 9.105   'But wyt can wisse þe,' quaþ þouȝt, '*where* þo þre dwellen,

A. 9.117   '*Where* þat dowel, & dobet, & dobest beþ in londe,
A.11.112   And axide hire þe heiȝe wey *where* clergie [dwell]ide,
A.12.40   With þat she wolde me wisse *wher* þe toun were
A.12.46   I shal þe wisse [wynlyche] *where* þat he dwelleþ'.
B.Pr.163   Boþe in wareyne and in waast *where* hem [leue] like[þ];
B.Pr.166   Men myȝte witen *wher* þei wente and [hire] wey r[oum]e.
B. 1.139   By what craft in my cors it comseþ, and *where*.'
B. 2.5   'Loke [o]n þi left half, and lo *where* he stondeþ,
B. 3.18   To be wedded at þi wille and *wher* þee leef likeþ.
B. 3.139   To vnfettre þe fals, fle *where* hym likeþ.
B. 3.176   Whan ye witen witterly *wher* þe wrong liggeþ.
B. 3.182   And [ek] griped my gold [and] gyue it *where* þee liked.
B. 5.89   [This was al his curteisie *where* þat euere he shewed hym].
B. 5.289   And if þow wite neuere to [whom] ne [*where*] to restitue
B. 5.533   [Kanstow] wissen vs þe wey *wher* þat wye dwelleþ?'
B. 5.554   And if ye wilneþ wite *where* þat [wye] dwelleþ
B. 5.642   Thow shalt seye I am þi Suster.' I ne woot *where* þei bicome.
B. 8.4   If any wiȝt wiste *wher* dowel was at Inne;
B. 8.7   *Where* þis leode lenged, lasse ne moore,
B. 8.13   '*Where* þat dowel dwelleþ, dooþ me to witene.
B. 8.17   And dowel and do yuele, *wher* þei dwelle boþe.'
B. 8.77   *Where* dowel dwelleþ, and do me [to wisse].'
B. 8.115   'But wit konne wisse þee', quod boȝt, '*where* þo þre dwelle
B. 8.128   '*Wher* dowel [and] dobet and dobest ben in londe
B.10.160   And asked hire þe heighe wey *where* Clergie dwelte,
B.10.378   *Where* dowel is or dobet derkliche ye shewen.
B.11.74   *Where* my body were buryed by so ye hadde my siluer.
B.11.328   And *where* þat briddes and beestes by hir mak[e þei] yeden,
B.11.347   I hadde wonder at whom and *wher* þe pye
B.15.217   And þe murieste of mouþ at mete *where* he sitteþ.
B.15.484   *Where* þat his wille is to worshipen vs alle,
B.16.56   In what wode þei woxen and *where* þat þei growed,
B.17.56   *Where* a man was wounded and wiþ þeues taken.
B.17.117   Which is þe wey þat I wente and *wher* forþ to Ierusalem;
B.18.113   [*Where*] out of þe west coste a wenche as me þouȝte
B.18.168   *Where* pees comeþ pleyinge in pacience ycloþed.
B.18.276   And *where* he wole is his wey; ac ware hym of þe perils:
B.18.307   And now I se *wher* a soule comeþ [silynge hiderward]
B.19.129   The which was dobet, *where* þat he wente.
B.20.3   I ne wiste *wher* to ete ne at what place,
C.Pr.161   *Where* houed an hundrid in houes of selke,
C.Pr.183   Men Myghte ywete *where* þei wente and here [way roume].
C. 1.22   And rekene hem by rewe: reherse hem *wher* þe liketh.
C. 2.5   'Loke [o]n thy left half, and loo *where* he standeth,
C. 3.19   For to wedde at thy wille [and] *where* the leef li[k]eth
C. 3.177   To vnfetere the fals, fle *wher* hym liketh,
C. 3.222   When ȝe [wyten] witterly [*where*] þe wrong liggeth.
C. 3.228   And also gryp[en] my gold and gyue hit *where* þe liked.
C. 6.99   Here werkes and here wordes *where* þat y seete.
C. 6.344   And ȝif thow wyte neuere to whom ne *where* to restitue
C. 7.198   And hoso wilneth to wyte *where* þat treuthe woneth
C. 8.166   And sette [Peres] at a [pes], playne hym *whare* he wolde.
C. 9.148   *Where* he may rathest haue a repaest or a ronde of bacoun,
C.10.4   Yf eny wiht wiste *where* dowel was at ynne;
C.10.7   *Where* this [lede] l[e]nged, lasse ne more,
C.10.13   *Wher* þat dowel dwelleth; 'dere frendes, telleth me,
C.10.17   And dowel and do euele, *where* þei dwellen bothe.'
C.10.75   *Where* þat dowel dwelleth And do me to knowe.'
C.10.111   'Bote wit wol the wisse,' quod thouhte, '*where* tho thre dwelleth,
C.10.124   '*Whare* dowel and dobet And dobest ben in londe
C.11.102   And askede here þe hey way *whare* clergie dwelte;
C.12.22   *Wher* my body were yber[i]ed by so ȝe hadde my [suluer].'
C.13.34   And sholden wende o wey *where* bothe mosten reste
C.13.136   And *where* þat briddes and bestis by here make þei ȝeden,
C.13.158   Y hadde wonder at wh[om] and *where* þe pye
C.15.149   *Where* Peres the plogman bycam, so priueyliche he wente.
C.15.160   And bere hit in thy bosom aboute *where* þou wendest
C.16.178   And may nat be withoute a body to bere me *where* hym liketh.'
C.16.342   Ac thorw werkes thow myhte wyte *wher* forth he walketh:
C.18.241   *Where* god [riȝt be my gate cam gangynge a thre];
C.18.250   *Where* y walke in this worlde a wol hit me allowe.
C.20.171   *Where* cometh pees pleiynge in pacience yclothed.
C.20.298   And *where* he wol is his way, ac waer hym of þe perelles:
C.20.341   And now y se *where* his soule cometh sylinge hid[er]ward
C.21.129   The which was dobet, *where* þat he wente.
C.22.3   Y ne wiste *where* to ete ne at what place

where &> wheiþer; where- > wher-

wherfore *adv* *wherfore adv. & conj.* B 9; C 6 wherefore (2) wherfore (4)
B.11.85   '*Wherfore* lourestow?' quod lewtee, and loked on me harde.
B.11.101   Þyng þat al þe world woot, *wherfore* sholdestow spare
B.11.434   Thanne woot þe dronken [wye] *wherfore* he is to blame.'

B.14.40   Wherof or *wherfore* or wherby to libbe:
B.15.200 What is þe wille and *wherfore* þat many wight suffreþ:
B.15.348 *Wherfore* folk is þe febler and noȝt ferm of bileue.
B.15.385 *Wherfore* I am afered of folk of holy kirke,
B.16.134 As euere it was and as wid; *wherfore* I hote yow
B.19.84   *Wherfore* and why wise men þat tyme,
C. 1.17   *Wherfore* he hette þe elementis to helpe ȝow alle tymes,
C.12.35 Thyng þat al þe world woet *wherfore* sholdest thow spare
C.13.185 *Wherefore* and why, as wyde as thow regnes[t],
C.13.240 And thenne woet he *wherfore* and why he is to blame.'
C.15.239 Wherof or *wherfore* [or] wherwith to lyuene:
C.21.84   [*Wherefore* & why wyse men þat tyme,

wherof adv *wherof adv. & conj.* B 6; C 4 whareof (1) wherof (3)
B. 3.56   And a cours of kynde *wherof* we comen alle;
B.11.91 'And *wherof* serueþ law', quod lewtee, 'if no lif vndertoke it
B.11.265 To wepe and to wel bidde, *wherof* wexeþ Mercy
B.12.222 *Wherof* þei cacche hir colours so clere and so briȝte,
B.14.40 And *wherof* or wherfore or wherby to libbe:
B.15.14 And *wherof* I cam & of what kynde. I coniured hym at þe laste
C. 3.60   And [a] cours of kynde *wherof* we comen alle.
C.12.32 'And *wherof* serueth lawe,' quod leaute, ' and no lyf vndertoke [hit],
C.15.239 *Wherof* or wherfore [or] wherwith to lyuene:
C.16.173 '*Whareof* serue ȝe,' y saide, 'sir liberum arbitrium?'

wheron conj *wheron adv. & conj.* B 1; C 1 whereon
B.17.12   *Wheron* [was] writen two wordes on þis wise yglosed.
C.19.13 *Whereon* was writen two wordes on this wyse yglosed:

wherso adv *wherso adv. & conj.* B 1; C 1 whereso
B.18.374 And be at my biddyng *wherso* [best] me likeþ.
C. 6.27   Semyng a souerayn oen *whereso* me byfull

wherwiþ adv *wherwith adv. & conj.* A 1 wherewith; B 2 wherwith (1)
    wherwiþ (1); C 2 wherwith
A. 5.234 Ac for þere was nouȝt *wherewith* he wepte swiþe sore.
B. 5.462 And for þer was noȝt *wher[wiþ]* he wepte swiþe soore.
B. 9.71 And widewes þat han noȝt *wherwith* to wynnen hem hir foode,
C. 6.316 And for þer was nat *wherwith* a wep swythe sore.
C.15.239 Wherof or wherfore [or] *wherwith* to lyuene:

whete n *shete n.* A 6; B 6; C 9
A. 3.39   I shal assoile þe myself for a sem of *whete*,
A. 4.44 Brekiþ vp my berne doris, beriþ awey my *whete*,
A. 7.9   'Summe shal sewe þe sak for shedyng of þe *whete*;
A. 7.34 For þise comiþ to my croft & croppiþ my *whete*.'
A. 7.288 But coket, or clermatyn, or of clene *whete*,
A.10.126 Or as *whete* out of weed waxiþ, out of þe erþe,
B. 3.40   I shal assoille þee myself for a seem of *whete*,
B. 4.57 Brekeþ vp my bern[e] dore[s], beryþ awey my *whete*,
B. 6.9   'Somme shul sowe þe sak for shedyng of þe *Whete*.
B. 6.32 For [þise] comeþ to my croft and croppeþ my *whete*.'
B. 6.304 But Coket [or] clermatyn or of clene *whete*,
B. 7.125 And wepen whan I sholde [werche] þou ȝa *whete* breed me faille.
C. 3.42   Y shal assoyle the mysulue for a seem [of] *whete*
C. 4.60 And breketh vp my bern[e] dores and [b]ereth awey my *whete*
C. 8.8   'That somme sowe þe sak for shedynge of the *whete*,
C. 8.326 Bote clermatyn and coket and of clene *whete*
C.12.182 Sholde neuere *whete* wexe but whete furste deyede;
C.12.182 Sholde neuere whete wexe but *whete* furste deyede;
C.12.192 Aren not so worthy as *whete* ne so wel mowe
C.12.232 *Whete* þat þeron wexeth worth lygge ar hit rype;
C.13.43 Thogh the messager make his way amydde the fayre *whete*

wheþer > wheiþer

why n *whi n.* A 1 whyes; B 2 whyes; C 2 why (1) whyes (1)
A.11.80 For alle þat wilneþ to wyte þe [*whyes*] of god almiȝt,
B.10.127 For alle þat wilneþ to wite þe [*whyes*] of god almyȝty,
B.12.217 And so I seye by þee þat sekest after þe *whyes*
C.14.156 And so y sey by þe þat sekest aftur þe *whyes*,
C.18.146 And wepte watur with [his] yes; the *why* weten fewe.

why adv *whi adv. & conj.* A 5; B 24 whi (6) why (18); C 20 whi (1) why
    (19)
A. 3.170 *Why* þou wraþþest þe now wondir me þinkiþ.
A. 3.239 *Why* þe vengeaunce fel on saul & on his children?
A.11.66 "*Why* wolde oure sauiour suffre such a worm in his blisse
A.11.75 Wilneþ neuere to wyte *why* that god wolde
A.11.82 Þat euere eft wilneþ to wyte *why* [þat] god wolde
B. 3.183 *Whi* þow wraþþest þe now þynkeþ.
B. 3.260 *Whi* þ[at] vengeaunce fel on Saul and on his children?
B. 9.89 *Whi* [ne wol] we cristene of cristes good be as kynde?
B.10.108 "*Why* wolde oure Saueour suffre swich a worm in his blisse
B.10.115 *Why* sholde we þat now ben for þe werkes of Adam
B.10.122 Wilneþ neuere to wite *why* þat god wolde

B.10.129 That euere [eft] wilneþ to wite *why* þat god wolde
B.10.269 *Why* meuestow þi mood for a mote in þi broþeres eiȝe,
B.11.76 *Whi* youre Couent coueiteþ to confesse and to burye
B.11.232 *Why* I meue þis matere is moost for þe pouere;
B.11.375 *Why* þow ne sewest man and his make þat no mysfeet hem folwe.'
B.11.377 *Why* I suffre or noȝt suffre; þiself hast noȝt to doone.
B.11.438 *Why* ye wisse me þus', quod I, 'was for I rebuked Reson.'
B.12.155 *Why* I haue told [þee] al þis, I took ful good hede
B.12.214 A[c] *why* þat oon þeef on þe cros creaunt hym yald
B.12.220 *Why* some be alouȝ & some aloft, þi likyng it were;
B.12.233 *Why* Adam hiled noȝt first his mouþ þat eet þe Appul
B.12.235 Kynde knoweþ *whi* he dide so, ac no clerk ellis.
B.13.459 *Why* he ne hadde [w]asshen it or wiped it wiþ a brusshe.
B.15.542 And now is werre and wo, and whoso *why* asketh:
B.16.24 'Piers', quod I, 'I preie þee, *whi* stonde þise piles here?'
B.18.63 And tolde *why* þat tempeste so longe tyme durede:
B.19.15 '*Why* calle [ye] hym crist, siþen Iewes calle[d] hym Iesus?
B.19.84 Wherfore and *why* wise men þat tyme,
C. 1.112 'Lord! *why* wolde he tho, þat wykkede lucifer,
C. 3.229 *Why* thow wrathest þe now wonder me thynketh!
C.10.245 Ac *why* þe world was adreynt, holy writ telleth,
C.12.24 '*Why* lourest [thou]?' quod leaute; 'leue sire,' y saide,
C.13.185 Wherefore and *why*, as wyde as thow regnes[t],
C.13.193 *Why* he ne loueth thy lore and leueth as þou techest.'
C.13.195 *Why* y soffre or nat soffre; certes,' he sayde,
C.13.229 And for thow woldest wyte *why*, resones preue[t]e,
C.13.240 And thenne woet he wherfore and *why* he is to blame.'
C.13.244 *Why* ȝe worden to me thus was for y aresonede Resoun.'
C.14.99 *Why* y haue tolde [the] al þis, y toek ful gode hede
C.14.153 Ac *why* þat [on] theef vppon þe cros cryant hym ȝelde
C.14.166 Ac *why* a wolde þat wykke were, y wene and y leue
C.15.74 Ac me wondreth in my wit *why* þat they ne preche
C.15.93 And *why* a lyueth nat as a lereth.' 'lat be,' quod pacience,
C.17.204 And now is werre and wo and whoso *why* asketh:
C.18.83 *Why* groweth this fruyt in thre degres?' 'A goed skil,' he saide,
C.20.65 And tolde *why* þ[at] tempest so longe tyme durede:
C.21.15 '*Whi* calle ȝe hym Crist sennes iewes callede hym iesus?
C.21.84 [Wherefore & *why* wyse men þat tyme,

whicche > hucche

which pron *which pron.* A 3 which (2) whiche (1); B 33 which (24)
    whiche (9); C 41 wheche (1) which (18) whych (1) whiche (20) wiche
    (1)
A. 2.27   Þere miȝte þou wyte ȝif þou wilt *whiche* þei ben alle
A.10.122 *Which* is þe flour & þe fruyt fostrid of boþe.
A.11.89 Siþen he wilneþ to wyte *which* þei ben alle.
B. 2.45   [There] myȝtow witen if þow wilt *whiche* þei ben alle
B. 6.132 *Whiche* þei were in þis world hise werkmen apeired.
B.10.136 Siþþe he wilneþ to wite *whiche* þei ben [alle].
B.10.244 Thoruȝ þe help of þe holy goost þe *which* is of boþe;
B.10.271 *Which* letteþ þee to loke, lasse ouþer moore?
B.10.442 And wherby wiste men *which* [is] whit if alle þyng blak were,
B.10.481 The *which* is mannes soule to saue, as god seiþ in þe gospel:
B.11.266 Of *which* crist is a kernell to conforte þe soule.
B.11.319 The *which* I preise, þer pacience is, moore parfit þan richesse.
B.11.348 Lerned to legge þe stikkes in *whiche* she leyeþ and bredeþ.
B.12.109 *Which* is þe cofre of cristes tresor, and clerkes kepe þe keyes
B.12.164 *Which* trowestow of þo two [in Themese] is in moost drede,
B.13.85 [And appose hym] what penaunce is, of *which* he preched raþer.'
B.13.130 *Which* shal saue mannes soule; þus seiþ Piers þe Plowman.'
B.13.312 *Which* myȝte plese þe peple and preisen hymselue:
B.13.407 The *whiche* is sleuþe so slow þat may no sleiȝtes helpe it,
B.13.409 [Ac] *whiche* ben þe braunches þat bryngen a man to sleuþe?
B.13.439 Haue beggeres bifore hem þe *whiche* ben goddes minstrales
B.14.28 Than Hauky[n] wi[l] þe wafrer, [*which* is] Actiua vita.'
B.14.84 *Which* dryueþ awey dedly synne and dooþ it to be venial.
B.14.273 The *which* is sib to god hymself, [so neiȝ is pouerte].'
B.15.131 The *whiche* arn preestes inparfite and prechours after siluer,
B.15.422 [Boþe] Beneit and Bernard, þe *whiche* hem first tauȝte
B.16.224 *Which* is þe holy goost of alle, and alle is but o god.
B.16.232 Hym or Ysaak myn heir, þe *which* he hiȝte me kulle.
B.17.26 'Youre wordes arn wonderfulle', quod I, '*which* of yow is trewest
B.17.117 *Which* is þe wey þat I wente and wher forþ to Ierusalem;
B.17.280 The *which* is lif and loue, þe leye of mannes body.
B.18.107 *Which* is lif þat oure lord in alle lawes acurseþ.
B.18.134 *Which* deide and deeþ þoled þis day aboute mydday,
B.18.215 The *which* vnknytteþ alle care and comsynge is of reste.
B.19.80 And þere was þat word fulfilled þe *which* þow of speke,
B.19.129 The *which* was dobet, where þat he wente.
C. 3.93   The *whiche* crien on here knees þat crist hem auenge,
C. 3.192 For she is fauerable to fals the *whiche* defouleth treuthe.
C. 3.366 In *whiche* ben gode and nat gode, and graunte here n[eyther] will.
C. 3.498 The *whiche* þat hatte, as y haue rad an[d] oþer þat can rede,

C. 5.31 | The *whiche* is lollarne lyf þat lytel is preysed
C. 6.243 | And len[e] for loue of þe wed the *whych* y lette bettere
C. 7.69 | Ac *wheche* been þe braunches þat bryngeth men to sleuthe?
C. 7.99 | Haue beggares byfore hem þe *whiche* ben goddes mu[n]strals
C. 9.98 | Ac beggares with bagges þe *whiche* brewhous[es] ben here churches.
C. 9.107 | The *whiche* aren lunatyk lollares and lepares aboute
C. 9.137 | The *whiche* [arn] lunatyk loreles and lepares aboute
C. 9.140 | The *whiche* is lollarne lyf and lewede Ermytes;
C.10.154 | The *which* is god grettest [þat gynnynge] hadde neuere,
C.10.170 | The *which* is loue and lyf þat last withouten ende.
C.11.80 | The *which* is a lykyng and luste, þe loue of þe world.'
C.12.151 | The *which* is þe cornel of confort for alle cristene soules.
C.13.82 | And other pryue penaunces þe *which* þe prest woet wel
C.14.54 | *Whiche* [is the] coffre of cristis tresor, and clerkes kepeth þe keyes
C.14.108 | *Which* trowest [þou] of tho two in temese [is] in moste drede?'
C.16.27 | And satisfaccioun þe *whiche* folfilleth þe fader will of heuene;
C.16.113 | The *whiche* is syb to crist [hym]sulue and semblable bothe.'
C.17.140 | The *whiche* is þe heued of charite and hele of mannes soule:
C.17.247 | The *whiche* is þe hy holy gost þat out of heuene descendet[h]
C.18.12 | And þerof cometh a goed fruyt þe *wiche* men calleth werkes
C.18.14 | The *whiche* is Caritas ykald, Cristes oune fode,
C.18.41 | The *which* is þe passioun & þe penaunce & þe parfitnesse of iesus
C.18.51 | The *whiche* is spiritus sanctus and sothfaste bileue
C.18.72 | The *whiche* þe seynt spirit seweth, the sonne of al heuene,
C.18.206 | The *whiche* aren childrene of charite and holy church [the] moder.
C.18.234 | The *which* is man and his make and moilere here issue,
C.19.8 | The *which* is Cr[oes] and cristendoem and cr[ist] þer[o]n [to] hang[e];
C.19.39 | The *which* alle men aren holde ouer al thyng to honoure
C.19.261 | The *which* is lyf and loue, the leye of mannes body.
C.19.328 | That is coueytise and vnkyndenesse *whiche* quencheth godes mercy
C.20.110 | The *which* is lif þat oure lord in all lawes defendeth.
C.20.137 | [*Which*] deyede and deth tholede this day aboute mydday
C.20.224 | The *which* vnknytteth alle care and comsyng is of reste.
C.20.449 | Bote leten hym lede forth *which* hym luste and leue which hym likede.
C.20.449 | Bote leten hym lede forth which hym luste and leue *which* hym likede.
C.21.80 | And þer was þat word fulfuld þe *which* þou of speke,
C.21.129 | The *which* was dobet, where þat he wente.

which adj *which adj.* A 3 whiche; B 12 which (7) whiche (5); C 14 which (7) whiche (7)

A. 2.72 | In witnesse of *whiche* þing wrong was þe furste,
A. 8.151 | On peris þe plou3man, *whiche* a pardoun he hauiþ,
A.11.68 | Þoru3 *whiche* a werk & wille þei wenten to helle,
B. 2.108 | In witnesse of *which* þyng wrong was þe firste,
B. 4.26 | *Whiche* maistries Mede makeþ on þis erþe.
B. 7.152 | And *which* a pardon Piers hadde þe peple to conforte,
B.10.27 | "Lo!" seiþ holy lettrure, "*whiche* [lordes] beþ þise sherewes";
B.10.110 | Thoru3 *whic[h* werk and wil] þei wente to helle,
B.12.86 | The *which* body is boþe boote to þe ri3tfulle
B.12.179 | In *which* flood þe fend fondeþ a man hardest.
B.13.129 | *Whiche* Infinites wiþ a feiþ fynden out dobest,
B.16.148 | And *which* tokne to þis day to muche is yvsed,
B.17.267 | [Mynne ye no3t, riche men, to *whiche* a myschaunce
B.18.124 | And *which* a light and a leme lay bifore helle.
B.20.62 | *Whiche* foolis were wel [gladdere] to deye
C. 2.112 | In wittenesse of [*which*] thyng wrong was the furste,
C. 3.197 | Thorw *which* loueday is loste þat leute myhte wynne;
C. 4.26 | *Whiche* a maistre mede was amonges pore and ryche.
C. 9.156 | Thorw *which* craft a couthe come to bred and to ale
C. 9.301 | And *which* a pardoun Peres hadde th[e] peple to glade
C.11.24 | "Lo!" saith holy letrure, "*whiche* lordes beth this schrewes";
C.14.119 | In *whiche* floed þe fende fondeth [a] man hardest.
C.15.274 | The *whiche* wol loue lat to oure lordes place
C.18.11 | The *whiche* blosmes buirnes benigne speche hit calleth
C.19.87 | The *whiche* barn mote nedes be born of a mayde,
C.19.233 | Minne 3e nat, riche men, to *which* a myschaunce
C.20.127 | And *which* a lihte and a leem lay bifore helle.
C.20.339 | The *which* lyf and lawe, be hit longe yvysed,
C.22.62 | [*Whiche* foles] were wel gladere to deye

whider adv *whider adv. & conj.* A 1 wheder; B 3; C 2 whoder

A.12.80 | Of when þat he were, and *wheder* þat he wolde.
B.15.13 | Oon wiþouten tonge and teeþ tolde me *whider* I sholde
B.16.175 | And of whennes he were and *whider* þat he [þ]ou3te,
B.16.275 | What he highte & *whider* he wolde, and wightly he tolde.
C.18.180 | Y waytede witterly; Ac *whoder* he wende y ne wiste.
C.18.291 | What he hihte and *whoder* he wolde & whithliche he tolde.

whiderout adv *whideroute adv. & conj.* B 1; C 1 whoderout

B.16.12 | Lord!' quod I, 'if any wight wite *whiderout* it groweþ?'
C. 7.178 | [Can]st [thow] wissen vs [þe w]ay *whoderout* treuth woneth?'

whiderward adv *whiderward adv. & conj.* A 1 whidirward; B 1; C 1 whoderward

A. 5.149 | And heo askide of hym *whidirward* he wolde.
B. 5.299 | And [heo] asked [of hym] *whiderward* he wolde.
C. 6.354 | And *whode[r]ward* he wolde the breuhwyf hym askede.

whyes > why

while n *while n. &> ouþerwhile* A 5; B 12; C 12 whil (1) while (10) whyle (1)

A. 4.16 | 'I shal araye me to ride,' quaþ resoun, 'reste þe a *while*,'
A. 4.33 | And wordiden a gret *while* wel wisly togidere.
A. 5.189 | He pisside a potel in a paternoster *while*,
A. 7.8 | 'What shulde we wommen werche þe *while*?'
A. 7.134 | Shuln haue of myn almesse al þe *while* I libbe,
B. 3.331 | Also wroþ as þe wynd weex Mede in a *while*.
B. 4.16 | 'I shal arraye me to ryde', quod Reson, 'reste þee a *while*',
B. 4.46 | And wordeden [a gret *while* wel wisely] togideres.
B. 4.177 | Ac Reson shal rekene wiþ yow if I regne any *while*,
B. 5.341 | He pissed a potel in a paternoster *while*,
B. 6.8 | 'What sholde we wommen werche þe *while*?'
B.11.381 | He my3te amende in a Minute *while* al þat mysstandeþ,
B.13.331 | Ther is no lif þat me loueþ lastynge any *while*.
B.17.49 | Tho þat lernen þi lawe wol litel *while* vsen it.'
B.17.232 | Melte in a Mynut *while* to myst and to watre.
B.18.165 | Rightwisnesse come rennynge; reste we þe *while*,
B.19.354 | Al þe world in a *while* þoru3 oure wit', quod Pryde.
C.Pr.16 | Westward y waytede in a *while* aftir
C. 1.107 | Lucifer, louelokest tho, ac litel *while* it duyred.
C. 3.205 | Ther he is alowed and ylet by þat laste shal eny *while*
C. 4.16 | 'Y shal aray me to ryde,' quod resoun, 'reste the [a] *while*,'
C. 4.44 | And speke wyse wordes a longe *while* togederes.
C. 4.171 | Ac resoun shal rykene with 3ow yf y regne eny *while*
C. 5.25 | To wurche as a werkeman eny *while* to duyren.'
C. 6.399 | A pissede a potel in a paternoster *whyle*
C.12.222 | That lihtlich launseth vp litel *while* dureth
C.19.47 | Tho þat lerneth thy lawe wollen litel *while* hit vse.'
C.20.168 | Rihtwisnesse come rennynge; reste we the *while*
C.21.354 | Alle the world in a *while* thorw oure wit,' quod pruyde.

while adv *while adv.* C 2

C.10.289 | As Adam dede and Eue, as y *whil* er tolde.
C.17.100 | Wisten w[hi]l[e] and tolde when hit sholde ryne.

while conj *while conj.* A 12 whil (3) while (9); B 28 whil (1) while (27); C 24 whil (2) while (22)

A. 2.71 | Þere to wone wiþ wrong *while* god is in heuene.'
A. 3.27 | For to werche þi wil *while* þi lif lastiþ.'
A. 4.118 | *Whil* mede haþ þe maistrie to mo[te] in þis halle.
A. 6.29 | Boþe sowe [and sette] *while* I swynke mi3te.
A. 7.51 | 'For to werche be þi woord *while* my lif duriþ.'
A. 7.211 | [Or with werk or with word þe *while* þou art here].
A. 7.272 | To drawe on feld my dong *while* þe drou3t lastiþ.
A. 7.300 | Ac *while* hunger was here maister wolde þere non chide,
A. 7.302 | I warne 3ow werkmen, wynneþ *while* 3e mowe,
A.11.102 | For to werche 3our wil [*while*] my lif duriþ,
A.12.93 | *Whil* his lyf and his lykhame lesten togedere.
A.12.94 | And þerfore do after dowel *whil* þi dayes duren,
B.Pr.173 | And peeren in his presence þe *while* hym pleye likeþ,
B.Pr.189 | [The *while* he caccheþ conynges he coueiteþ no3t [o]ure caroyne
B. 1.16 | For to worshipe hym þerwiþ *while* ye ben here.
B. 1.78 | To louen me leelly *while* þi lif dureþ.'
B. 2.107 | And with hym to wonye [in] wo *while* god is in heuene.'
B. 3.28 | For to werche þi wille [*while* þi lif lasteþ].'
B. 3.53 | *While* ye loue lordes þat lecherie haunten
B. 3.233 | To [hem] þat [werchen wel] *while* þei ben here.
B. 4.135 | *While* Mede haþ þe maistrie [to mote in þis] halle.
B. 5.35 | 'Late no wynnyng [forwanye hem] *while* þei be yonge,
B. 5.541 | Boþe sowe and sette *while* I swynke my3te.
B. 6.56 | 'For to werche by þi wor[d] *while* my lif dureþ.'
B. 6.163 | Plentee among þe peple þe *while* my plow3 liggeþ'.
B. 6.288 | To drawe afeld my donge *while* þe dro3te lasteþ.
B. 6.321 | Ac I warne yow werkmen, wynneþ *whil* ye mowe
B. 7.204 | Swiche werkes to werche, *while* we ben here,
B.10.150 | For to werche youre wille *while* my lif dureþ,
B.12.10 | Amende þee *while* þow my3t; þow hast ben warned ofte
B.12.34 | And lyue forþ as lawe wole *while* ye lyuen boþe.
B.14.159 | And so forþ *while* somer lasteþ hir solace dureþ.
B.18.137 | The *while* þis light and þis leme shal Lucifer ablende.
B.18.305 | For þe body, *while* it on bones yede, aboute was euere
B.19.332 | And made preesthod hayward þe *while* hymself wente

B.19.398	Ne after Conscience, by crist! *while* I kan selle
B.20.142	And boold and bidynge *while* his bagge lasteþ.'
B.20.211	[Weede] ne worldly [mete] *while* þi lif lasteþ.'
B.20.288	Ac *while* he is in westmynstre he wol be bifore
B.20.296	The *while* coueitise and vnkyndenesse Conscience assaillede.
C.Pr.147	With lele labour to lyue *while* lif on londe lasteth
C.Pr.190	And apere in his presence þe *while* hym pleye lyketh
C. 3.29	For to worche thy wille the *while* þou myhte dure.'
C. 3.32	'And purchace ȝow prouendres *while* ȝoure panes lasteth
C. 3.325	Richesse and resoun the ryhte lyuede
C. 5.137	'Late no wynnynge forwanyen hem *while* thei ben ȝonge
C. 7.186	Bothe to sowe and to sette þe *while* y swynke myhte
C. 8.311	To drawe afeld my donge þe *while* þe drouthe lasteth.
C. 9.252	Ac *while* a wrouhte in þe world and wan his mete with treuthe
C. 9.350	Suche werkes to worche the *while* we ben here
C.10.286	And *whil* þou art ȝong an[d] ȝep and thy wepene kene
C.11.71	Be large þerof *whil* hit lasteth to ledes þat ben nedy
C.11.88	For to worche ȝoure wille *while* my lyf duyreth
C.11.269	Tho that worste wrouhten *while* thei here were.
C.12.7	For *while* fortune is thy frende freres wol the louye
C.12.25	'For this frere flaterede me *while* he fond me ryche
C.12.121	And pore peple fayle we nat *while* eny peny vs lasteth
C.20.140	The *while* this lihte and this l[em]e shal lucifer ablende.
C.21.332	And made presthoed hayward the *while* hymsulue wente
C.21.398	Ne aftur Consience, bi Crist! [*while*] y c[an] sulle
C.22.142	And bolde and [b]ydynge *while* his bagge lasteth.'
C.22.211	Wede ne worldly mete *while* thy lif lasteth.'
C.22.288	Ac *while* he is in Westmynstre he wol be bifore
C.22.296	The *while* Couetyse and vnkyndenesse Consience assailede,

while &> ouþerwhile; whilen > whilom

whiles adv *whiles n.* C 1
C. 8.6	'What sholde we wommen wor[c]he þe *whiles*?'

whiles conj *whiles conj.* A 9; B 8; C 9
A. 1.16	For to worsshipe hym þerewiþ *whiles* ȝe ben here.
A. 1.76	To loue me lelly *whiles* þi lif duriþ.'
A. 3.220	To hem þat werchen wel *whiles* þei ben here.
A. 5.53	'Let no wynnyng forwanye hem *whiles* þei ben ȝonge'.
A. 7.37	To fulfille þe foreward *whiles* I may stande'.
A. 8.182	Suche werkis to werche, *whiles* we ben here,
A. 9.78	*Whiles* he haþ ouȝt of his owene he helpiþ þere nede is;
A.10.67	But þei witen hem fro wauntounesse *whiles* þei ben ȝon[g]e.
A.12.51	'þou shalt wende with wil,' quod she, '*whiles* þat him lykyþ,
B. 6.319	Ac *whiles* hunger was hir maister þer wolde noon chide
B. 8.87	[*Whiles* he haþ ouȝt of his owene he helpeþ þer nede is];
B. 9.185	*Whiles* þow art yong [and yeep] and þi wepene [yet] kene
B.11.55	For *whiles* Fortune is þi frend freres wol þee louye,
B.12.6	And of þi wilde wantownesse [*whiles*] þow yong were
B.14.87	That *whiles* he lyuede he bileuede in þe loore of holy chirche.
B.15.23	'The *whiles* I quykne þe cors', quod he, 'called am I anima;
C. 1.16	For to worschipe hym þerwith þe *whiles* ȝe lyuen here.
C. 3.57	The *whiles* ȝe louyen lordes that lecherye haunteth
C. 4.132	*Whiles* mede hath the maistrie þer motyng is at [þe] Barr[e].
C. 8.339	Ac *whiles* hungur was here maistre ther wolde non chyde
C. 8.341	Ac y warne ȝow werkmen, wynneth *whiles* ȝe mowe
C.13.225	Adam, *whiles* he spak nat, hadde paradys at wille
C.16.11	And so forth *whiles* somur laste[th] here solace duyreth
C.16.183	And *whiles* y quyke þe cors ycald am y Anima;
C.20.337	For þe body, *whiles* hit on bones ȝede, aboute was hit euere

whilom adv *whilom adv.* *** END W 4 *** B 1; C 3 whilen (1) whilom (1) whilum (1)
B.15.360	That *whilom* warned bifore what sholde falle after.
C. 9.197	That wonede *whilom* in wodes with beres and lyons.
C. 9.205	*Whilen* were werkmen, webbes and taylours
C.17.98	That *whilum* warnede byfore what sholde [f]alle aftur.

whistlen v *whistlen v.* B 1
B.15.475	In menyng after mete folweþ men þat *whistlen*;

whistlere n *whistlere n.* B 1
B.15.483	Wiþ wederes and wiþ wondres he warneþ vs wiþ a *whistlere*

whistlyng ger *whistlinge ger.* B 4
B.15.464	But wiþ foweles þat fram hym nolde but folwede his *whistlyng*:
B.15.474	Riȝt as capons in a court comeþ to mennes *whistlyng*,
B.15.479	And as þo foules to fynde fode after *whistlyng*
B.15.480	So hope þei to haue heuene þoruȝ hir *whistlyng*.

whit adj *whit adj.* A 1; B 4 whit (3) white (1); C 5 whit (3) whyte (2)
A.Pr.107	'*W[hit]* wyn of osay, & wyn of gascoyne,
B.Pr.229	'*Whit* wyn of Oseye and wyn of Gascoigne,
B. 5.135	Now awakeþ Wraþe wiþ two *white* eiȝen,

B.10.442	And wherby wiste men which [is] *whit* if alle þyng blak were,
B.15.409	And þus þoruȝ wiles of his wit and a *whit* Dowue
C.Pr.233	'*Whit* wyn of Oseye and wyn of gascoyne,
C. 6.103	Thenne awakede wrathe with two *w[hy]te* eyes
C. 9.255	Ne no blanke[t] on his bed ne *whyte* bred byfore hym.
C.20.213	Ho couthe kyndeliche *whit* colour descreue
C.20.214	Yf all þe world were *whit* or swanwhit all thynges?

white > whit,whiten

whiten v *whiten v.* B 1; C 1 white
B. 3.61	Wowes do *whiten* and wyndowes glaȝen,
C.16.335	And with warm water of his yes woketh h[em] til [t]he[y] *white*:

whithliche > wightly

whitlymed ptp *whitlimen v.* B 1; C 1 ywhitlymed
B.15.113	Or to a wal þat were *whitlymed* and were foul wiþInne;
C.16.268	Or to a wal *ywhitlymed* and were blak withynne;

whitnesse > wightnesse; whitus > wit

who pron *who pron.* A 13 who (9) whom (4); B 44 who (36) whom (7) whos (1); C 47 ho (29) hoes (1) wham (5) who (8) whom (3) whos (1)
A. 1.43	Tel me to *whom* þat tresour apendiþ.'
A. 1.47	And he askide of hem of *whom* spak þe lettre,
A. 1.133	þis I trowe be treuþe; *who* can teche þe betere,
A. 3.59	*Who* is curteis or kynde or coueitous, or ellis.
A. 4.114	Vpe forfaiture of þat fe, *who* fynt hym [at douere],
A. 6.12	And sen be his signes *whom* he souȝt hadde.
A. 8.115	þe foulis in þe firmament, *who* fynt hem a wynter?
A. 8.119	þou art le[ttr]id a litel; *who* lernide þe on boke?'
A. 9.65	'Wot ich?' quaþ I; '*who* art þou?' 'þouȝt', seide he þanne.
A.11.270	Aristotle & he, *who* wrouȝte betere?
A.11.287	þanne marie þe maudeleyn *who* miȝte do wers?
A.11.288	Or *who* dede wers þanne dauid þat vrie destroyede,
A.12.62	'Al hayl,' quod on þo, and I answered, 'welcome, & with *whom* be ȝe?
B. 1.45	Tel me to *whom* þat tresour appendeþ.'
B. 1.49	And [he] asked of h[e]m of *whom* spak þe lettre,
B. 1.88	[For] *who* is trewe of his tonge, telleþ noon ooþer,
B. 1.145	This I trowe be truþe; *who* kan teche þee betere,
B. 2.18	I hadde wonder what she was and *whos* wif she were.
B. 3.57	*Who* may scape [þe] sclaundre, þe scaþe is soone amended;
B. 3.62	Do peynten and portraye [*who*] paie[d] for þe makynge
B. 3.68	And þi cost and þi coueitise and *who* þe catel ouȝte.
B. 3.235	Lord, *who* shal wonye in þi wones wiþ þyne holy seintes,
B. 4.131	V[p] forfeiture of þat fee, *wh[o]* fynt [hym] at Douere,
B. 5.289	And if þow wite neuere to [*whom*] ne [where] to restitue
B. 5.524	And se bi hise signes *whom* he souȝt hadde.
B. 5.625	A[c] *who* is sib to þise [sustren], so me god helpe,
B. 7.78	For wite ye neuere *who* is worþi, ac god woot who haþ nede.
B. 7.78	For wite ye neuere who is worþi, ac god woot *who* haþ nede.
B. 7.133	The foweles in þe [firmament], *who* fynt hem at wynter?
B. 7.137	Thow art lettred a litel; *who* lerned þee on boke?'
B. 8.74	'Woot I?' [quod I; '*who* art þow]?' 'þouȝt', seide he þanne.
B. 9.37	As *who* seiþ, "moore moot herto þan my word oone;
B.10.251	*Who* was his Auctour? alle þe foure Euaungelistes.
B.10.316	Who loureþ on hym and [lakkeþ] hym: *who* [lered] hym curteisie?
B.10.388	Aristotle and he, *who* wissed men bettre?
B.10.428	Than Marie Maudeleyne [*who* myȝte do] werse?
B.10.429	Or *who* [dide] worse þan Dauid þat vries deeþ conspired,
B.10.443	And *who* were a good man but if þer were som sherewe?
B.11.347	I hadde wonder at *whom* and wher þe pye
B.11.361	And *who* tauȝte hem on trees to tymbre so heiȝe
B.11.380	*Who* suffre[þ] moore þan god?' quod he; 'no gome, as I leeue.
B.15.120	And *who* was myn Auctour, muche wonder me þinkeþ
B.15.319	If lewed men knewe þis latyn þei wolde loke *whom* þei yeue,
B.15.326	*Who* parfourneþ þis prophecie of þe peple þat now libbeþ,
B.15.486	Ac *who* beþ þat excuseþ hem þat [arn] persons and preestes,
B.17.107	*Who* is bihynde and who bifore and who ben on horse;
B.17.107	Who is bihynde and *who* bifore and who ben on horse;
B.17.107	Who is bihynde and who bifore and *who* ben on horse;
B.17.187	Ac *who* is hurte in þe hand], euene in þe myddes,
B.18.19	And *who* sholde Iuste in Ierusalem. 'Iesus', he seide,
B.18.27	'*Who* shal Iuste wiþ Iesus', quod I, 'Iewes or Scrybes?'
B.18.66	Shal no wight wite witterly *who* shal haue þe maistrie
B.18.175	And in hire gaye garnementȝ *whom* she grete þouȝte.
B.19.11	Or it is Piers þe Plowman? *who* peynted hym so rede?'
B.19.58	*Who* was hardiere þan he? his herte blood he shadde
B.19.255	And *who* þat moost maistries kan be myldest of berynge
B.19.348	That Conscience shal noȝt knowe *who* is cristene or heþene,
C. 1.43	Telleth me to *wham* þat tresour bylongeth.'
C. 1.46	And god askede at hem *hoes* was þe koyne.
C. 1.84	For *who* is trewe of his tonge and of his two handes

C. 1.144	And this y trowe be treuth; [ho] kan tecche þe bettre
C. 2.17	[Wh]os wyf a were and what was here name,
C. 3.61	Ho may askape þe sclaundre, þe skathe myhte sone be mended;
C. 3.66	And [do] peynten and purtrayen ho payede for þe makyng
C. 3.72	Thi cost and here couetyse] and ho þe catel ouhte.
C. 4.128	Vp forfeture of þat fee, ho fyndeth h[y]m ouerward,
C. 6.344	And ʒif thow wyte neuere to whom ne where to restitue
C. 6.420	The furste [word] þat he spake was '[wh]o halt þe bolle?'
C. 7.169	And se by [his] signes wham a souht hadde.
C.7.278	And ho is sib to þis seuene, so me god helpe,
C. 7.280	Ho is nat syb to this seuene, sothly to telle,
C. 8.155	And maken vs murye þer[with] maugreye h[o] begrucheth.'
C. 9.70	Woet no man, as y wene, who is worthy to haue
C.10.72	'Woet y?' quod y; 'who art thow?' 'thouhte,' sayde he thenne.
C.10.110	Of dowel and dobet and ho doth best of alle.'
C.11.16	Ho can caste and contreue to disseyue þe ri[gh]tfole,
C.11.147	Ho was his Autor And hym of god tauhte?
C.11.153	[Bisily] bokes; ho beth his witnesses.
C.11.214	Aristotel and he, ho tauhte men bettere?
C.11.261	Then marie maudelene who myhte do worse?
C.11.271	Ho is worthy for wele or for wykkede [pyne]:
C.12.213	And asketh [hym after] ho shal hit haue,
C.13.158	Y hadde wonder at wh[om] and where þe pye
C.13.197	Ho soffreth more then god?' quod he; 'no gome, as y leue.
C.13.206	And ar thow lacke eny lyf loke ho is to preyse.
C.14.10	And thenne dost thow wel, withoute drede; ho can do bet no force.
C.16.34	Ho doth wel or bet or beste aboue alle;
C.16.143	As he þat woet neuere with wham on nyhtes tyme to mete:
C.16.316	'H[o] fynt hym his fode,' quod y, 'or what frendes hath he,
C.17.4	'Ho is wroeth and wolde be awreke, holy writ preueth,' quod he,
C.17.63	And afturward awayte ho hath moest nede
C.17.90	As they ywoned were; in wham is defaute?
C.18.129	Who sholde fecche this fruyt, the fende or iesus suluen.
C.18.228	Wh[om] god wolde oute of þe wey [d]rawe.
C.19.153	Ac ho is herte in the hand euene in þe myddes
C.20.17	And ho sholde iouste in Ierusalem. 'Iesus,' he saide,
C.20.26	'Who shal iouste with iesus,' quod y, 'iewes or scrib ʒ?'
C.20.68	Ac thow no wyht wyte witturlich ho shal haue þe maistry
C.20.178	And [in] here gay garnementes wham she gladie thouhte.
C.20.213	Ho couthe kyndeliche whit colour descreue
C.21.11	Or hit is [Peres þe Plouhman? who] paynted hym so rede?'
C.21.58	Ho was hardior then he? his herte bloed he she[d]de
C.21.255	And [ho] þat moest maistries can be myldest of berynge.
C.21.348	That Consience shal nat knowe [ho is cristene or hethene]

whoder(- > whider(-; whom whos > who

whoso pron *whoso pron.* A 23; B 54; C 52 hoso (47) whoso (5)

A. 1.59	'Þ[at] is þe castel of care; who[so] comiþ þereinne
A. 1.86	For whoso is trewe of his tunge, telliþ non oþer,
A. 1.102	And whoso passiþ þat poynt is apostata in his ordre.
A. 3.268	And whoso trespassiþ [to treuþe, or] takiþ [aʒeyn his wille],
A. 4.56	'Whoso werchiþ be wil wraþþe makiþ ofte.
A. 4.139	'Whoso wilneþ hire to wyue for welþe of hire godis,
A. 5.97	And whoso haþ more þanne I, þat angriþ myn herte.
A. 5.137	And whoso bummide þerof, bouʒte it þereaftir,
A. 5.173	Whoso hadde þe hood shulde haue amendis of þe cloke.
A. 5.176	Þere were oþes an hep, [whoso it herde];
A. 5.183	And whoso repentiþ raþest shulde rise aftir
A. 5.196	As whoso leide lynes to lacche wiþ [foules].
A. 6.110	Ac whoso is sib to þis sistris, so me god helpe,
A. 7.1	'Þis were a wikkide weye, but whoso hadde a gide
A. 7.59	And whoso helpiþ me to eren, or any þing swynke,
A. 7.61	And make hym mery wiþ þe corn whoso it begrucchiþ.
A. 7.105	To ouersein hem hymself; whoso best wrouʒte
A. 8.78	Þere ben mo mysshapen amonges hem, whoso takiþ hede,
A. 9.18	Ac whoso synneþ, I seiʒe, sertis, me þinkiþ
A. 9.71	Whoso is mek of his mouþ, mylde of his speche,
A.10.133	Þat þoruʒ wedlak þe world stant, whoso wile it knowen.
A.11.149	Ac theologie techiþ not so, who[so] takiþ heed;
A.12.3	And whoso coueyteþ don betere þan þe boke telleþ,
B.Pr.144	To þe kynges counseil, construe whoso wolde,
B.Pr.195	That witnesseþ holy writ, whoso wole it rede:
B. 1.61	'That is þe castel of care; whoso comþ þerInne
B. 1.104	And whoso passe[þ] þat point [is] Apostata in [his] ordre.
B. 3.283	That whoso seiþ hem soþe[s] is sonnest yblamed.
B. 3.293	And whoso trespaseþ [to] truþe or takeþ ayein his wille,
B. 4.70	'Whoso wercheþ by wille wraþe makeþ ofte.
B. 4.163	'Whoso wilneþ hire to wif for welþe of hire goodes,
B. 5.40	Whoso spareþ þe spryng spilleþ hise children.'
B. 5.54	For whoso contrarieþ truþe, he telleþ in þe gospel,
B. 5.116	Whoso vndernymeþ me herof, I hate hym dedly after.
B. 5.118	[And] whoso haþ moore þan I, þat angreþ [myn herte].
B. 5.125	Ne neiþer shrifte ne shame, but whoso shrape my mawe?'

B. 5.221	And whoso bummed þerof bouʒte it þerafter,
B. 5.276	And whoso leueþ [þat I liʒe] loke in þe Sauter glose,
B. 5.324	Whoso hadde þe hood sholde han amendes of þe cloke.
B. 5.327	[There were oþes an heep, whoso it herde];
B. 5.334	And whoso repente[þ] raþest sholde aryse after
B. 5.348	As whoso leiþ lynes to lacche [wiþ] foweles.
B. 6.1	'This were a wikkede wey but whoso hadde a gyde
B. 6.65	And whoso helpeþ me to erie [or any þyng swynke]
B. 6.67	And make h[y]m murie þermyd, maugree whoso bigruccheþ it.
B. 6.113	To ouersen hem hymself; whoso best wroʒte
B. 7.85	For whoso haþ to buggen hym breed, þe book bereþ witnesse,
B. 8.22	A[c] whoso synneþ, I sei[e, certes], me þynkeþ
B. 8.80	Whoso is [meke of his mouþ, milde of his speche],
B.10.90	Whoso haþ muche spende manliche, so [meneþ] Tobye,
B.10.91	And whoso litel weldeþ [wisse] hym þerafter,
B.10.197	Whoso gloseþ as gylours doon, go me to þe same,
B.10.200	Ac Theologie techeþ noʒt so, whoso takeþ yeme;
B.10.359	That whoso wolde and wilneþ wiþ crist to arise,
B.11.122	And drynke boote for bale, brouke it whoso myʒte.
B.11.177	Whoso loueþ noʒt, leue me, he lyueþ in deeþ deyinge.
B.11.180	Whoso leneþ noʒt he loueþ noʒt, [lord] woot þe soþe,
B.11.276	Whoso wole be pure parfit moot possession forsake
B.13.315	'Ye, whoso toke hede', quod haukyn, 'bihynde and bifore,
B.13.379	And whoso cheped my chaffare, chiden I wolde
B.14.35	'Whoso leueþ yow, by oure lord! I leue noʒt he be blessed.'
B.15.91	I shal tellen it for truþes sake; take hede whoso likeþ.
B.15.251	For whoso myʒte meete [wiþ] hym swiche maneres hym eileþ;
B.15.338	As whoso filled a tonne [ful] of a fressh ryuer
B.15.373	For is noon of þise newe clerkes, whoso nymeþ hede,
B.15.503	Thei sholde turne, whoso trauail[e wolde] to teche hem of þe Trinite.
B.16.126	And lefte baskettes ful of broke mete, bere awey whoso wolde.'
B.17.18	'Whoso wercheþ after þis writ, I wol vndertaken,
B.17.146	And bitokneþ trewely, telle whoso likeþ.
B.17.199	That whoso synneþ in þe Seint Spirit assoilled worþ he neuere.
B.17.204	So whoso synneþ in þe Seint Spirit, it semeþ þat he greueþ
B.17.283	And who[so] morþereþ a good man, me þynkeþ, by myn Inwit,
B.19.66	And se bi his sorwe þat whoso loueþ ioye
B.19.101	And so dide Iesu in hise dayes, whoso [dorste] telle it.
B.19.277	And whoso ete þat ymagynen he sholde,
B.19.290	And who[so] ete [of] þat seed hardy was euere
C.Pr.122	Wyttenesse at holy wryt whoso kan rede:
C. 1.57	'That is þe Castel of care; whoso cometh þerynne
C. 1.98	And hoso passeth þat poynt is appostata of knyghthed.
C. 3.236	Ac thow thysulue sothly, ho[so] hit segge durste,
C. 3.363	Indirect thyng is as hoso coueytede
C. 3.369	For hoso wolde to wyue haue my worliche douhter
C. 3.407	Ac hoso rat of regum rede me may of mede,
C. 3.446	And hoso taketh aʒeyn treuthe or transuerseth aʒeyns resoun
C. 3.496	So hoso [s]lecheth sapience fynde he shal [that] foloweth
C. 4.158	'Hoso wilneth here to wy[u]e for welthe of here goodes
C. 5.138	For hoso spareth þe spry[n]g spilleth h[is] children;
C. 6.90	Ne noþer shame ne shryfte but hoso shrap[e] my mawe?'
C. 6.229	And hosomode therof bouhte hit þeraftur,
C. 6.381	That hoso hadde the hode sholde nat haue þe cloke
C. 6.392	And hoso repente[th] rathest sholde aryse aftur
C. 6.406	As hoso layth lynes for to lacche foules.
C. 7.198	And hoso wilneth to wyte where þat treuthe woneth
C. 7.205	Ac hoso wol wende þer treuthe is, this is þe way thede[r]:
C. 7.307	Ac þe way is ful wikked but hoso hadde a gyde
C. 8.68	And m[a]ken hym merye þermy[d], maugrey ho[so] bigruchen hit;
C. 8.120	[To] ouersey hem hymsulue; hoso beste wrouhte
C. 9.237	And hoso breketh this, be wel waer, but yf he repente,
C. 9.258	Certes, hoso durste sygge hit, Simon quasi dormit;
C. 9.322	For hoso doth wel here at þe day of dome
C.10.25	And hoso synegeth,' y sayde, 'certes he doth nat wel;
C.10.26	For hoso synegeth sicurly doth euele
C.10.39	Thow he falle he falleth nat but [as] hoso ful in a boet
C.10.78	Ho[so] is trewe of his tonge and of his two handes
C.10.201	For hoso loueth, leueth h[it] wel, god wol nat laton hym sterue
C.10.203	Hoso lyueth in lawe and in loue doth wel
C.11.70	And is to mene no more bote "who[so] muche goed weldeth
C.11.223	That hoso doth by ʒoure doctrine doth wel, y leue,
C.12.57	And drynke bote for bale, brouke hit hoso myhte.\
C.12.155	Holy [writ] witnesseth hoso forsaketh
C.12.169	"Hoso coueiteth to come to my kyneriche
C.12.210	Ac hoso rat of th[e] ryche the reuers may fynde,
C.16.370	And hoso coueyteth to knowe [hym] such a kynde hym foloweth
C.17.109	For is [now] noon, hoso nymeth hede,
C.17.204	And now is werre and wo and whoso why asketh:
C.17.254	They sholde [turne], hoso trauayle wolde and of þe trinite teche hem.

C.18.154   And lefte basketes ful of Broke mete, bere awey *hoso* wolde.
C.19.5   That that y sey is soeth se *hoso* liketh.'
C.19.19   'And *ho[so]* worcheth aftur this writ, y wol vndertaken,
C.19.120   And bitokeneth trewly, telle *hoso* liketh,
C.19.165   That *hoso* synegeth in þe seynt spirit assoiled worth he neuere,
C.19.170   So *hoso* synegeth aȝeyn þe seynt spirit hit semeth þat he greueth
C.19.264   And *hoso* morthereth a goed man, me thynketh bi myn inwit,
C.20.383   And *hoso* hit out a mannes eye or elles his foreteth
C.21.66   And se bi his sorwe þat *hoso* loueth ioye
C.21.101   And so dede iesu in his dayes, *whoso* durste tellen hit.
C.21.277   [And] *hoso* ete þat ymageny he sholde,
C.21.290   And *hoso* ete of þa[t] seed hardy was euere

wy n prop *n.i.d.* &> *wye* A 1; B 1; C 1
A. 5.119   To wynchestre & to *wy* I [wente] to þe feire
B. 5.203   To *Wy* and to Wynchestre I wente to þe Feyre
C. 6.211   To *wy* and to wynchestre y wente to þe fayre

wicche n *wicche n.(2)* B 2; C 1 wycche
B.13.337 Lechecraft of oure lord and leue on a *wicche*,
B.18.69   And some seide he was a *wicche*; 'good is þat we assaye
C. 6.81   Lechecraft of oure lord and leue on a *wycche*

wicchecraft n *wicchecraft n.* B 3 wicchecraft (2) wichecraft (1); C 1
   wycchecrafte
B.13.168 Nouȝt þoruȝ *wicchecraft* but þoruȝ wit; and þow wilt þiselue
B.16.120 And seide he wroȝte þoruȝ *wichecraft* & with þe deueles myȝte:
B.18.46   'Crucifige!' quod a Cachepol, '[he kan of *wicchecraft*]!'
C.20.46   'Crucifige!' q[uo]d a cachepol, 'he can of *wycchecrafte*!'

wiche > which; wicke(- > wikke(-

wid adj *wid adj.* B 4 wid (1) widder (1) wide (2); C 6 wyddore (1) wide
   (2) wyde (3)
B.16.134 As euere it was and as *wid*; wherfore I hote yow
B.16.253 I hadde wonder of hise wordes and of hise *wide* cloþes
B.17.162 [Halt] al þe *wide* world wiþInne hem þre,
B.18.362 And my grace to growe ay gretter and *widder*.
C. 9.111   With a good will, witteles, mony *wyde* contreyes
C.10.62   By a *wi[d]e* wildernesse and by a wode syde.
C.18.269 Thenne hadde y wonder of his wordes and of [his] *wyde* clothes
C.19.54   In a *wi[d]e* wildernesse where theues hadde ybounde
C.20.45   And as *wyde* as hit euere was; this we witnesseth alle.'
C.20.400 And my grace to growe ay [gretter] and *wyddore*.

wyddewes > widewe; wyddore > wid,wide

wide adv *wide adv.* &> *wid* A 3 wide (2) wyde (1); B 8; C 9 wyddore
   (1) wyde (8)
A.Pr.4   Wente *wyde* in þis world wondris to here.
A. 6.18   Þat I haue walkid wel *wide* in wet & in driȝe,
A.12.43   And sayde, 'my cosyn kynde wit knowen is wel *wide*,
B.Pr.4   Wente *wide* in þis world wondres to here.
B. 5.530 That I haue walked [wel] *wide* in weet and in drye
B. 8.14   For [ye] be men of þis moolde þat moost *wide* walken,
B.14.99   [Wye] þat wiþ hym spak, as *wide* as I haue passed.'
B.18.322 For any wye or warde *wide* opned þe yates.
B.19.36   As *wide* as þe world is [wonyeþ þer noon]
B.19.333 As *wide* as þe world is wiþ Piers to tilie truþe,
B.20.381 And [wenden] as *wide* as þe world [renneþ]
C. 2.216   And gurdeth of gyles heed; lat hym goo no *wyddore*
C. 7.175   /[Y haue] ywalked ful *wyde* in wete and in drye
C.10.14   For ȝe ar men of this molde þat moste *wyde* walken
C.10.199 To wende as *wyde* as þe worlde were
C.13.185 Wherefore and why, as *wyde* as thow regnes[t],
C.20.365 For eny wey or warde *wyde* open[ed] þe ȝates.
C.21.36   As *wyd[e]* as þe worlde is wonyeth þer none
C.21.333 As *wyde* as the world is with Peres to tulye treuthe,
C.22.381 And wenden as *wyde* as þe world re[n]neth

widewe n *widwe n.* A 4 wydewe (1) wydewis (3); B 12 widewe (4)
   widewes (3) wydewes (1) widwes (2) wodewe (1) wodewes (1); C 10
   weddewes (1) wedewe (2) wedewes (4) wyddewes (1) wydewe (1)
   wydewes (1)
A. 3.114   Wyues & *wydewis* wantonnesse techiþ,
A. 8.32   [Pore] *wydewis* þat wiln not be wyues aftir,
A.10.188 Or wedde any *wydewe* for any wele of godis,
A.10.200 *Wydeweris* & *wydewis* werchiþ riȝt also;
B. 3.125   Wyues and *widewes* wantoun[nesse] techeþ,
B. 3.268 *Widwes* and wyues, wommen and children,
B. 6.13   Wyues and *widewes* wolle and flex spynneþ;
B. 9.71   And *widewes* þat han noȝt wherwith to wynnen hem hir foode,
B. 9.167 Or wedden any *wodewe* for [wele] of hir goodes
B. 9.179 [Wideweres and *wodewes*] wercheþ [riȝt also];
B.11.72   That wedde none *widwes* but for to welden hir goodes.
B.12.204 Ne wiþ maydenes ne with martires [ne wiþ mylde] *wydewes*,

B.13.196 And þe poore *widewe* [purely] for a peire of mytes
B.16.214 The sone, if I dorste seye, resembleþ wel þe *widewe*:
B.16.216 As *widewe* wiþouten wedlok was neuere ȝit yseyȝe,
B.16.218 So *widewe* withouten wedlok may noȝt wel stande,
C. 3.162   Wyues and *wedewes* wantounesse techeth
C. 3.421   Man, womman and wyf, childe, *wedewe* and bestes,
C. 4.47   And how he raueschede Rose the ryche *wydewe* by nyhte
C. 6.143   Amonges wyues and *wydewes* [y am woned] to sitte
C. 8.12   Wyue[s] and *wyddewes* wolle an[d] flex spynneth;
C.10.281 And [wedewares and *wedewes*] weddeth ayþer oþer;
C.12.20   That wilneth nat þe *wedewe* bote for to welde here godes.
C.14.143 Ne with maydenes ne with martires ne with mylde *weddewes*,
C.18.71   As weddede men and *wedewes* and riht worthy maydones
C.18.76   *Wedewes* and wedewares þat here own[e] wil forsaken

wideweres n *widwer n.* A 1 wydeweris; B 1; C 2 wedewares
A.10.200 *Wydeweris* & *wydewis* werchiþ riȝt also;
B. 9.179 [*Wideweres* and wodewes] wercheþ [riȝt also];
C.10.281 And [*wedewares* and wedewes] weddeth ayþer oþer;
C.18.76   Wedewes and *wedewares* þat here own[e] wil forsaken

widewher adv *widewher adv.* A 1 wydewhere; B 1; C 2 wydewhare
A. 9.53   Þus I wente *wydewhere* dowel to seken,
B. 8.62   [Th]us I wente *widewher* [dowel to seke,
C.10.61   I wente forth *wydewhare* walkynge myn one
C.17.271 For to enf[ou]rme þe fayth ful *wydewhare* deyede,

widwehode n *widwehod n.* B 2; C 2 wedewhed (1) wydewhode (1)
B.16.76   And waggede *widwehode* and it wepte after;
B.16.203 Wedlok and *widwehode* wiþ virginite ynempned,
C.18.87   *Wydewhode*, more worthiore then wedlok, as in heuene;
C.18.108 A waggede *wedewhed* and hit wepte aftur;

widwes > widewe

wye n *wie n.* A 7 wy (6) wyes (1); B 23 wye (19) wyes (4); C 14 wey
   (3) weye (6) weyes (2) wy (1) wye (1) wyes (1)
A. 1.61   Þereinne woniþ a *wy* þat wrong is yhoten;
A. 3.95   'Vnwittily, [*wy*], wrouȝt hast þou ofte;
A. 6.21   Canst þou wisse vs þe wey where þat *wy* dwelliþ?'
A. 6.41   And ȝif ȝe wilneþ wyte where þat *wy* dwelliþ
A.10.89   Wilne þou neuere in þis world, [*wy*], for to do betere,
A.11.67   Þat he gilide þe womman & þe *wy* aftir,
A.11.224 Forþi I wende þat þo *wyes* wern dobest of alle.'
B. 1.63   TherInne wonyeþ a [*wye*] þat wrong is yhote;
B. 3.106   'Vnwittily, [*wye*], wroȝt hastow ofte,
B. 5.513   Ac þere was [*wye*] noon so wys þe wey þider kouþe,
B. 5.533   [Kanstow] wissen vs þe wey wher þat *wye* dwelleþ?'
B. 5.554   And if ye wilneþ wite where þat [*wye*] dwelleþ
B. 9.115   The wif was maad þe w[y]e for to helpe werche,
B.10.109 That bi[w]iled þe womman and þe [*wye*] after,
B.11.346 Hadde neuere *wye* wit to werche þe leeste.
B.11.383 [Holy writ', quod þat *wye*, 'wisseþ men to suffre:
B.11.434 Thanne woot þe dronken [*wye*] wherfore he is to blame.'
B.12.273 To wissen vs [*wyes*] þerwiþ þat wiss[h]en to be saued—
B.12.295 And wit and wisdom', quod þat *wye*, 'was som tyme tresor
B.13.32   'Welcome, *wye*, go and wassh; þow shalt sitte soone.'
B.13.190 Ac þe wil of þe *wye* and þe wil of folk here
B.13.360 And awaited þoruȝ [wittes *wyes*] to bigile;
B.14.99   [*Wye*] þat wiþ hym spak, as wide as I haue passed.'
B.14.156 That god rewarded double reste to any riche *wye*.
B.16.262 And me þer[wiþ]', quod þat [*wye*]; 'may no wed vs quyte,
B.17.68   And to þe *wye* he wente hise woundes to biholde,
B.17.101 For wente neuere *wye* in þis world þoruȝ þat wildernesse
B.18.322 For any *wye* or warde wide opned þe yates.
B.19.166 And as alle þise wise *wyes* weren togideres
B.19.229 Some [*wyes*] he yaf wit with wordes to shewe,
C. 3.226   Wel thow wost, *weye*, but yf thow wille gabbe,
C. 6.105   'I am wr[a]the,' quod þat *weye*, 'wol gladliche smyte
C. 7.158   Ac þer was *wye* non so wys þat the way thider couthe
C.13.14   And delyuerede the *weye* his wyf with moche welthe aftur.
C.13.157 Hadde neuere *weye* wyt to worche þe leste.
C.14.195 To wissen vs *weyes* þerwith þat wenen to be saued—
C.15.155 Y take wittenesse', quod [þe *wy*], 'of holy writ a partye';
C.18.228 Wh[om] god wolde oute of þe *wey* [d]rawe.
C.18.278 And me þerwith', quod the *weye*; 'may no wed vs quyte
C.19.67   And to th[e] *wey* a wente his woundes to byholde
C.20.327 So hath god bigiled vs alle in goynge of a *weye*.'
C.20.365 For eny *wey* or warde wyde open[ed] þe ȝates.
C.21.166 And as al thise wyse *weyes* weren togyderes
C.21.229 Som [*wyes*] he ȝaf wyt with wordes to schewe,

wif n *wif n.* A 33 wif (6) wyf (18) wyue (2) wyuene (1) wyues (6); B 42
   wif (32) wyue (1) wyuen (1) wyues (8); C 46 wyf (33) wyue (4)
   wyuene (1) wyues (8)
A. 2.117   Til mede be þi weddit *wyf* þoruȝ wyt of vs alle,

A. 3.100	ʒif he wilneþ þe to *wyue* wilt þou hym haue?'
A. 3.110	Er I wedde such a *wif* wo me betide!
A. 3.114	*Wyues* & wydewis wantonnesse techiþ,
A. 4.35	How wrong aʒen his wil hadde his *wyf* take,
A. 4.139	'Whoso wilneþ hire to *wyue* for welþe of hire godis,
A. 5.29	And fecche [hom] felis fro *wyuene* pyne.
A. 5.30	He warnide watte his *wyf* was to blame
A. 5.129	My *wyf* was a wynstere & wollene cloþ made,
A. 5.139	Whanne it com in cuppemel; þat craft my *wyf* vside.
A. 5.144	But wende to walsyngham, & my *wyf* alse,
A. 5.159	Watte þe waffrer & his *wyf* boþe,
A. 5.199	Þat wiþ al þe wo of þe world his *wyf* & his wenche
A. 5.205	His *wyf* [wit]ide hym þanne of wykkidnesse & synne.
A. 6.48	ʒe mote go þoruʒ meknesse, boþe men & *wyues*,
A. 6.60	Þ[e] croft hattiþ coueite nouʒt menis catel ne here *wyues*,
A. 6.89	To weue [vp] þe wyket þat [þe *wif*] shette
A. 7.10	And *wyues* þat han woll[e] werchiþ it faste,
A. 7.70	Dame werche whanne tyme is piers *wyf* hatte;
A. 7.88	My *wyf* shal haue of þat I wan wiþ treuþe, & namore,
A. 8.32	[Pore] wydewis þat wiln not be *wyues* aftir,
A.10.18	And haþ fyue faire sones be his furste *wyf*:
A.10.167	Hymself & his sones þre, & siþen here *wyues*
A.10.208	And [werche] on his *wyf* & on no womman ellis,
A.11.1	Þanne hadde wyt a *wyf* þat hatte dame studie,
A.11.93	And whanne þat wyt was war how his *wif* tolde
A.11.100	And whanne I was war of his wil to his *wif* gan I knele,
A.11.106	He haþ weddit a *wif* wiþinne þise woukes sixe,
A.11.126	And þat [I] grete wel his *wyf* for I wrot hire þe bible,
A.11.170	I grette þe goode man as þe gode *wyf* me tauʒte,
A.11.171	And aftirward his *wyf* I worsshipide boþe,
A.11.176	Þat I was of wyttis hous & wiþ his *wyf* dame stodie.
A.11.178	And axide how wyt ferde & his *wif* studie.
B. 2.18	I hadde wonder what she was and whos *wif* she were.
B. 2.153	Til Mede be þi wedded *wif* þoruʒ wi[t] of vs alle,
B. 3.111	If he wilneþ þee to *wif* wiltow hym haue?'
B. 3.121	Er I wedde swich a *wif* wo me bitide!
B. 3.125	*Wyues* and widewes wantoun[nesse] techeþ,
B. 3.268	Widwes and *wyues*, wommen and children,
B. 4.48	How wrong ayeins his wille hadde his *wif* taken,
B. 4.163	'Whoso wilneþ hire to *wif* for welþe of hire goodes,
B. 5.29	And fecche Felice hom fro *wyuen* pyne.
B. 5.30	He warnede watte his *wif* was to blame
B. 5.213	My *wif* was a [wynnestere] and wollen cloþ made,
B. 5.223	[Whan] it cam In cuppemele, þis craft my *wif* vsed.
B. 5.228	But wenden to walsyngham, and my *wif* als,
B. 5.308	Watte þe warner and his *wif* boþe,
B. 5.357	Wiþ al þe wo of þ[e] world his *wif* and his wenche
B. 5.363	His *wif* [edwyted] hym þo [of wikkednesse and synne],
B. 5.561	Ye moten go þoruʒ mekenesse, boþe men and *wyues*,
B. 5.573	Th[e] croft hatte Coueite-noʒt-mennes-catel-ne-hire-*wyues*-
B. 6.13	*Wyues* and widewes wolle and flex spynneþ;
B. 6.78	Dame werch-whan-tyme-is Piers *wif* hiʒte;
B. 6.96	My *wif* shal haue of þat I wan wiþ truþe and na moore,
B. 9.19	And haþ fyue faire sones bi his firste *wyue*:
B. 9.115	The *wif* was maad þe w[y]e for to helpe werche,
B. 9.136	Thyself and þi sones þre and siþen youre *wyues*,
B.10.1	Thanne hadde wit a *wif* was hote dame Studie.
B.10.140	And whan þat wit was ywar [how his *wif*] tolde
B.10.147	And whan I was war of his wille to his *wif* gan I [knele]
B.10.154	He haþ wedded a *wif* wiþInne þise [woukes sixe],
B.10.174	And þat I grete wel his *wif*, for I wroot hire [þe bible],
B.10.227	[I] grette þe goode man as [þe goode *wif*] me tauʒte,
B.10.228	And afterwardes [his] *wif* [I] worshiped boþe,
B.10.233	That I was of wittes hous and wiþ his *wif* dame Studie.
B.10.235	And askede how wit ferde and his *wif* studie]
B.10.409	And his *wif* wiþ hise sones and also hire wyues;
B.10.409	And his wif wiþ hise sones and also hire *wyues*;
B.15.429	"Salt saueþ catel", siggen þise *wyues*:
B.17.323	That oon is a wikkede *wif* þat wol noʒt be chastised;
B.17.328	It dooþ hym worse þan his *wif* or wete to slepe;
B.17.334	The *wif* is oure wikked flessh þat wol noʒt be chastised
B.18.301	To warne Pilates *wif* what done man was Iesus,
B.18.426	And callede kytte my *wif* and Calote my doghter:
B.20.193	And of þe wo þat I was Inne my *wif* hadde ruþe
C. 2.17	[Wh]os *wyf* a were and what was here name,
C. 2.169	Til mede be thy wedded *wyf* wolle we nat stunte,
C. 3.148	Yf he wilneth þe to *wyue* wolt thow hym haue?'
C. 3.158	Ar y wedde suche a *wyf* wo me bytyde!
C. 3.162	*Wyues* and wedewes wantounesse techeth
C. 3.369	For hoso wolde to *wyue* haue my worliche douhter
C. 3.421	Man, womman and *wyf*, childe, wedewe and bestes,
C. 4.46	How wrong wilfully hadde his *wyf* forleyn
C. 4.158	'Hoso wilneth here to *wy[u]e* for welthe of here goodes

C. 5.131	And fette felyce hoem fram *wyuene* pyne.
C. 5.132	He warnede watte his *wyf* was to blame
C. 6.143	Amonges *wyues* and wydewes [y am woned] to sitte
C. 6.221	My *wyf* was a webbe and wollone cloth made
C. 6.231	When hit cam in coppemele; this crafte my *wyf* vsede.
C. 6.363	Watte þe w[a]rnare and his *wyf* dronke,
C. 6.415	With alle þe wo of th[e] world his *wyf* and his wenche
C. 6.421	His *wyf* and his inwit Edwitede hym of his synne;
C. 7.220	The croft hatte coueyte-nat-menne-catel-ne-here-*wyues*-
C. 7.300	'Y haue wedded a *wyf* wel wantowen of maneres;
C. 8.12	*Wyue[s*] and wyddewes wolle an[d] flex spynneth;
C. 8.55	'For to worche by thy wit and my *wyf* bothe.'
C. 8.80	Dame worch-when-tyme-is [Peres] *wyf* hehte;
C. 8.105	My *wyf* shal haue of þat y wan with treuthe and no more
C. 8.182	For a potte ful of potage þat [Peres] *wyf* made
C.10.145	And hath fyue fayre sones by his furste *wyue*:
C.10.224	"Thysulue and thy sones thre and sethen ʒoure *wyues*,
C.10.269	That his *wyf* were wexe or a walet ful of nobles.
C.10.288	ʒe þat han *wyues* ben war and wo[r]cheth nat out of tyme
C.10.293	Bote *wyues* and wedded men, as holy writ techeth:
C.11.1	Thenne hadde wit a *wyf* was hote dame studie
C.11.96	And clergi[es] wedded *wyf*, as wyse as hymsulue
C.11.114	And sey y gre[t]e wel his *wyf*, for y wrot here a bible
C.11.137	How þat wit and his *wyf* wissede me to hym
C.11.240	And his *wyf* with his sones and his sones wyues;
C.11.240	And his wyf with his sones and his sones *wyues*;
C.12.157	Or eny welthe in this world, his *wyf* or his childrene,
C.13.14	And delyuerede the weye his *wyf* with moche welthe aftur.
C.17.38	To his *wyf*; when he was blynde he herde a la[m]be blete:
C.17.39	"*Wyf*! be ywar," quod he; "what haue we herynne?
C.18.229	And as abel of Adam and of his *wyf* Eue
C.18.244	And what y thouhte and my *wyf* he vs wel tolde.
C.19.303	That [oon] is a wikkede *wyf* þat wol nat be chasted;
C.19.308	Hit doth hym worse then his *wyf* or wete to slepe;
C.19.314	The *wyf* is oure wikkede flesche [þat] wol nat be chasted
C.20.469	And calde kitte my *wyf* and Calote my douhter:
C.22.193	And of þe wo þat y was ynne my *wyf* hadde reuthe

wyfyng > *wyuyng*

wight n *wight n.* A 9 wiʒt (8) wyʒth (1); B 25 wight (15) wiʒt (10); C 21
wyghte (1) wiht (5) wyht (8) wihte (3) wyhte (4)

A. 3.214	No *wiʒt* as I wene wiþoute mede miʒte libbe.'
A. 5.96	I wolde þat iche *wiʒt* were my knaue;
A. 7.231	Kynde wyt wolde þat iche *wiʒt* wrouʒte
A. 9.4	ʒif any *wiʒt* wiste where dowel was at Inne
A. 9.6	Was neuere *wiʒt* as I wen[t]e þat me wisse couþe
A. 9.64	'Þat þou wost wel,' quaþ he, '& no *wiʒt* betere.'
A.10.71	A[c] iche *wiʒt* in þis world þat haþ wys vndirstonding
A.11.123	Þat iche *wiʒt* be in wille his wyt þe to shewen;
A.12.89	'Nay, wil,' quod þat *wyʒth*, 'wend þou no ferther,
B.Pr.208	Forþi ech a wis *wiʒt* I warne, wite wel his owene.'
B. 3.227	No *wiʒt*, as I wene, wiþouten Mede may libbe.'
B. 5.117	I wolde þat ech *wight* were my knaue.
B. 6.247	Kynde wit wolde þat ech *wiʒt* wroʒte,
B. 8.4	If any *wiʒt* wiste wher dowel was at Inne;
B. 8.6	Was neuere *wiʒt* as I wente þat me wisse kouþe
B. 8.53	Wit and free wil, to euery *wiʒt* a porcion,
B. 8.73	'That þow woost wel', quod he, 'and no *wiʒt* bettre.'
B.10.171	That ech *wight* be in wille his wit þee to shewe.
B.11.411	'[What is dowel?' quod þat *wiʒt*]; 'ywis, sire', I seide,
B.12.25	Ac if þer were any *wight* þat wolde me telle
B.13.123	I am vnhardy, quod he, 'to any *wiʒt* to preuen it.
B.13.175	Ne bitwene two cristene kynges kan no *wiʒt* pees make
B.13.192	The goode wil of a *wight* was neuere bouʒt to þe fulle,
B.13.323	Al þat he wiste wikked by any *wight* tellen it,
B.15.200	What is þe wille and wherfore þat many *wight* suffreþ:
B.16.12	Lord!' quod I, 'if any *wight* wite whiderout it groweþ?'
B.17.286	Ac þis is þe worste wise þat any *wight* myghte
B.18.66	Shal no *wight* wite witterly who shal haue þe maistrie
B.18.206	For no *wight* woot what wele is þat neuere wo suffrede,
B.18.217	Woot no *wight*, as I wene, what [is ynogh] to mene.
B.18.228	Woot no *wight* what werre is þer þat pees regneþ,
B.18.230	Thanne was þer a *wight* wiþ two brode eiʒen,
B.19.392	Al þat we owen any *wight* er we go to housel?'
B.20.13	Ne *wight* noon wol ben his boruʒ, ne wed haþ noon to legge;
C. 1.59	Therynne wonyeth a *wyghte* þat wrong is [ihote];
C. 3.131	Lacked here a litel w[iht] for þat she louede gyle
C. 9.116	To ʒeue vch a *wyht* wyt, welthe and his hele
C.10.4	Yf eny *wiht* wiste where dowel was at ynne
C.10.6	Was neuere *wihte* [as y wente] þat me wisse couthe
C.10.71	'That þou [wost] w[el],' quod he, 'and no *wyht* bettere.'
C.11.270	By that þat salamon saith hit semeth þat no *wyht* woet
C.13.94	In þat a wilneth and wolde vch *wyht* as hymsulue.

C.13.218 And thenne was ther a *wyhte*, what he was y neste.
C.13.219 'What is dowel?' quod *þat wyhte*; 'ywis, sire,' y saide,
C.15.165 Þer [n]is *wyht* in this world þat wolde the lette
C.16.220 The witt[i]ore þat eny *wihte* is, but yf he worche þeraftur,
C.16.306 Weneth he þat no *wyhte* wolde lye and swerie
C.19.267 Ac this is the worste wyse þat *eny* myhte
C.20.68 Ac shal no *wyht* wyte witturlich ho shal haue þe maistry
C.20.211 For no *wiht* woet what wele is þat neuere wo soffrede
C.20.226 Ne woet no *wyht*, as y wene, what is ynow to mene.
C.20.237 For woet no *wiht* what werre is þer [þat] pees regneth
C.20.239 Thenne wa[s] ther a *wihte* with two brode yes;
C.21.392 Al þat we owen eny *wyhte* or we go to hosele?'
C.22.13 Ne *wyht* no[n] wol be his borwe ne wed hath [non] to legge;

wightly adv *wightli adv.* A 4 wi3tliche (1) wi3tly (3); B 5 wightly (3)
wi3tliche (1) wi3tly (1) wy3tliche (1); C 3 whithliche (1) wyghtliche (1) wi3tliche (1)

A. 2.170 And *wi3tliche* wente to warne þe false,
A. 7.22 Helpiþ hem werche *wi3tly* þat wynne 3oure foode.'
A. 8.29 Wykkide weyes *wi3tly* to amende,
A.11.167 And wente *wi3tly* my wey wiþoute more lettyng,
B. 2.211 Thanne Drede wente *wy3tliche* and warned þe False
B. 6.20 Helpeþ hym werche *wi3tliche* þat wynneþ youre foode.'
B. 7.27 Wikkede weyes *wightly* amende
B.10.225 And wente *wightly* [my w]ey wiþoute moore lettyng,
B.16.275 What he highte & whider he wolde, and *wightly* he tolde.
C. 2.221 What was þe kynges wille and *wyghtliche* wente
C. 8.18 Helpeth hym worche *wi[3t]liche* þat wynneth 3oure fode.'
C.18.291 What he hihte and whoder he wolde & *whithliche* he tolde.

wightnesse n *wightnesse n.* B 1; C 1 whitnesse
B.19.246 He wissed hem wynne it ayein þoru3 *wightnesse* of handes
C.21.246 He wissede [h]e[m] wynne hit a3eyn thorw *whitnesse* of handes

wi3t adj *wight adj. &> wight* A 1; B 2; C 2 wyht (1) wyhte (1)
A.10.20 Sire werche wel wiþ þin hond, [a] *wi3t* man of strengþe,
B. 9.21 Sire werch-wel-wiþ-þyn-hand, a *wi3t* man of strengþe,
B.13.173 Al þe wit of þis world and *wi3t* mennes strengþe
C.10.147 Sire worch-wel-with-thyn-hand, a *wyht* man of strenghe,
C.15.171 Al th[e] wit of this world and *wyhte* menne strenghe

wi3tes n *weght n.(1)* B 1; C 1 wihtus
B.14.295 Wynneþ he no3t wiþ *wi3tes* false ne wiþ vnseled mesures,
C.16.130 Wynneth he nat with *w[ih]tus* false ne with vnselede mesures

wy3th > wight; wi3tly -liche > wightly; wyht(e > wight,wi3t; wihttus > wi3tes; wyke > weke,wouke; wikede > wikked

wiket n *wiket n.* A 1 wyket; B 1
A. 6.89 To weue [vp] þe *wyket* þat [þe wif] shette
B. 5.602 To wayuen vp þe *wiket* þat þe womman shette

wikke adj *wikke adj.* A 1 wycke; B 2; C 5 wicke (1) wikke (1) wykke (3)
A.12.37 Or *wycke* 3if I wolde, wheþer me lyked.
B. 5.227 And neuere wikkedly weye ne *wikke* chaffare vse,
B.19.440 And worshiped be he þat wro3te al, boþe good and *wikke*,
C. 7.117 To perpetuel payne or purgatorie a[s] *wikke*
C.14.164 Of goed and of *wykke* kynde was þe furste:
C.14.166 Ac why a wolde þat *wykke* were, y wene and y leue
C.16.177 To do wel or *wykke*, a will with a resoun,
C.21.440 And worschiped be he þat wrouhte all, bothe gode and *wicke*,

wikked adj *wikked adj.* A 12 wykkid (1) wikkide (2) wykkide (9); B 32
wikked (19) wikkede (13); C 37 wickede (1) wyckede (1) wikede (1)
wikked (3) wykked (3) wikkede (19) wykkede (3) wikkedere (2)
A. 1.31 And al he wytide it wyn þ[at] *wykkide* dede.
A. 4.54 For þat wrong hadde wrou3t so *wykkide* a dede,
A. 5.143 Ne neuere wykkidly wei3e ne *wykkide* chaffare make,
A. 5.252 Wepynge & weylyng for here *wykkide* dedis;
A. 6.95 Ac be war þanne of wraþþe, þat *wykkide* shrewe,
A. 7.1 'Þis were a *wikkide* weye, but whoso hadde a gide
A. 7.30 Fro wastours [and *wikkide* men] þat wolde me destroye,
A. 8.29 Wykkide weyes *wi3tly* to amende,
A. 9.88 A pik is in þat potent to pungen adoun þe *wykkide*,
A.10.65 For no werk þat þei werche, *wykkide* oþer ellis.
A.10.218 And þat is *wykkide* wil þat many werk shendiþ.'
A.11.263 Or ellis [vn]writen for *wykkid* as witnessiþ þe gospel:
B. 1.31 And al he witte it wyn þat *wikked* dede:
B. 1.124 Whan þise *wikkede* wenten out wonderwise þei fellen,
B. 4.62 That wrong was a *wikked* luft and wro3te muche sorwe.
B. 4.68 For þat wrong hadde ywro3t so *wikked* a dede,
B. 5.162 Of *wikkede* wordes I, wraþe, hire wortes made
B. 5.264 And þat was wonne wiþ wrong wiþ *wikked* men be despended.
B. 5.428 So wiþ *wikked* wil and wraþe my werkmen I paye.
B. 5.609 A[c] be war þanne of Wraþe, þat *wikked* sherewe,

B. 6.1 'This were a *wikkede* wey but whoso hadde a gyde
B. 6.28 Fro wastours and *wikked* men þat [wolde me destruye],
B. 7.27 *Wikkede* weyes wightly amende
B. 8.98 A pik is [in] þat potente to [punge] adown þe *wikked*
B. 9.209 And þat is *wikked* wille þat many werk shendeþ,
B.10.24 That *wikked* men þei welden þe welþe of þis worlde,
B.13.320 It was bidropped wiþ wraþe and *wikkede* wille,
B.13.323 Al þat he wiste *wikked* by any wight tellen it,
B.15.130 Wolde neuere þe wit of witty god but *wikkede* men it hadde,
B.15.169 He is glad wiþ alle glade and good til alle *wikkede*
B.15.356 For þoru3 werre and *wikkede* werkes and wederes vn[s]esonable
B.16.27 The world is a *wikked* wynd to hem þat willen truþe.
B.16.34 And *wikkede* werkes þerof, wormes of synne,
B.16.146 Thanne wente forþ þat *wikked* man and wiþ þe Iewes mette
B.17.318 Than alle oure *wikkede* werkes as holy writ telleþ–
B.17.323 That oon is a *wikked* wif þat wol no3t be chastised;
B.17.334 The wif is oure *wikked* flessh þat wol no3t be chastised
B.18.385 Ther doom to þe deþ dampneþ alle *wikked*,
B.19.198 And *wikkede* to wonye in wo wiþouten ende.'
B.19.286 Waste word of ydelnesse ne *wikked* speche moeue;
B.19.353 'To wasten on welfare and in *wikked* [kepyng]
B.19.377 And þanne wellede water for *wikkede* werkes
B.20.269 It is *wikked* to wage yow; ye wexen out of noumbre.
B.20.370 And wake for hise *wikked* werkes as he was wont to doone.
C.Pr.18 Woned in tho wones and *wikkede* spiritus.
C. 1.30 And al he witte [it] wyn [þat] *wikkede* dede:
C. 1.112 'Lord! why wolde he tho, þat *wykkede* lucifer,
C. 1.130 And alle þat worchen þat *wikked* is wenden thei sholle
C. 3.206 Withouten werre oþer wo oþer *wickede* lawe
C. 4.65 How wrong was a *wykked* man and muche wo wrouhte.
C. 6.162 Al þat y wiste *wykked* by eny of oure couent
C. 6.334 For al the wrecchednesse of this world and *wikkede* dedes
C. 7.41 So with *wikkede* will my werkemen y paye.
C. 7.261 Ac be war thenne of wrath, þat *wikkede* shrewe,
C. 7.307 Ac þe way is ful *wikked* but hoso hadde a gyde
C. 8.27 Fro wastores and *wikked* men þat þis world struyen
C. 9.31 And *wyckede* wayes with here goed amende
C.10.237 Holy writ witnesseth þat for no *wikkede* dede
C.11.271 Ho is worthy for wele or for *wykkede* [pyne]:
C.12.236 Worldly wele y[s] *wykked* thyng to hem þat hit kepeth.
C.14.25 And w[o]ky thorw gode werkes *wikkede* hertes.
C.14.134 And wol no *wikkede* man [be] lost bote if he wol hymsulue:
C.16.242 Lo, what holy writ witnesseth of *wikkede* techares:
C.16.277 Wolde neuere oþerwyse god but *wikkede* men hit hadde,
C.17.86 For what thorw werre and wrake and *wikkede* hefdes
C.18.29 The fruyt of this fayre tre fro thre *wikkede* wyndes
C.18.31 The world is a *wikkede* wynd to hem þat wo[l] treuthe;
C.18.38 And manye *wikkede* werkes, wormes of synne,
C.19.104 Eny *wikkedere* in þe worlde then y were mysulue
C.19.298 Thenne al oure *wikkede* werkes as holy writ telleth:
C.19.303 That [oon] is a *wikkede* wyf þat wol nat be chasted;
C.19.314 The wyf is oure *wikkede* flesche [þat] wol nat be chasted
C.20.427 Ther þat doem to þe deth dampneth alle *wikkede*
C.20.434 And so of alle *wykkede* y wol here take veniaunce.
C.20.456 Was neuere werre in this world ne *wikkedere* enuye
C.21.198 And *wikkede* to wonye in wo wiþouten ende.'
C.21.286 Wast[e] word of ydelnesse ne *wikede* speche meue;
C.21.353 'To waston on welfare and in *wikked* kepynge
C.21.377 And thenne walled watur for *wikked* werkes
C.22.269 Hit is *wikked* to wage 3ow; 3e wexeth out of nombre.
C.22.370 And wake for his *wikkede* werkes as he was woned [to do].

wikkedly adv *wikkedli adv.* A 4 wykkidly; B 7 wikkedly (5) wikkedliche
(1) wikkedlokest (1); C 8 wickedliche (1) wikkedly (1) wykkedly (2)
wikkedliche (2) wykkedliche (2)
A. 5.118 *Wykkidly* to wei3e was my ferste lessoun.
A. 5.143 Ne neuere wykkidly wei3e ne wykkide chaffare make,
A. 5.228 Al þat I *wykkidly* wan siþen I wyt hadde,
A.11.292 As þise þat wrou3te *wykkidly* in world whanne þei were.
B. 5.202 *Wikkedly* to weye was my firste lesson.
B. 5.227 And neuere *wikkedly* weye ne wikke chaffare vse,
B. 5.456 Al þat I *wikkedly* wan siþen I wit hadde,
B.10.433 Tho þat wrou3te *wikkedlokest* in world þo þei were;
B.15.129 Ac þing þat *wikkedly* is wonne, and wiþ false sleightes,
B.17.290 That *wikkedliche* and wilfulliche wolde mercy aniente?
B.20.302 And woundede wel *wikkedly* many a wys techere
C. 1.26 *Wykked[ly]* wroghte and wrathed god almyhty.
C. 6.210 *Wykkedliche* to waye was my furste lessoun.
C. 6.310 Al-þat-y-*wikkedly*-wan-sithen-y-witte-hadde:
C. 8.234 Yf thow hast wonne auht *wikkedliche*, wiseliche despene hit:
C.16.276 Ac thyng þat *wykkedliche* is wonne and with fals sleythes
C.19.250 [That that *wickedliche* is wonne to wasten hit and make frendes?]
C.19.271 That *wikkedliche* and wilfulliche wolde mercy anyente?
C.22.302 And wounded wel *wykkedly* many a wys techare

wikkednesse n *wikkednesse n.* A 2 wikkidnesse (1) wykkidnesse (1); B 8; C 1

A. 5.205	His wyf [wit]ide hym þanne of *wykkidnesse* & synne.
A. 9.89	Þat waiten any *wikkidnesse* dowel to tenen.
B. 5.180	Al þe *wikkednesse* þat I woot by any of oure breþeren,
B. 5.187	And bad me wilne to wepe my *wikkednesse* to amende.
B. 5.282	And al þe *wikkednesse* in þis world þat man myȝte werche or þynke
B. 5.363	His wif [edwyted] hym þo [of *wikkednesse* and synne],
B. 8.99	That waiten any *wikkednesse* dowel to tene.
B.10.382	Or ellis vnwriten for *wikkednesse* as holy writ witnesseþ:
B.16.157	Ac [to] þe [worldes ende] þi *wikkednesse* shal worþe vpon þiselue:
B.18.413	Was neuere werre in þis world ne *wikkednesse* so kene
C.11.207	Vnwriten for som *wikkednesse*, as holy writ sheweth:

wil > wille,willen

wilde adj *wilde adj.* A 2; B 13; C 8 wilde (7) wylde (1)

A. 8.74	But as *wilde* bestis wiþ wehe, & worþ vp togideris
A.10.57	And ek wantoun & *wilde*, wiþoute any resoun.
B. 7.92	But as *wilde* bestes with wehee worþen vppe and werchen,
B.11.329	*Wilde* wormes in wodes, and wonderful foweles
B.11.355	For fere of oþere foweles and for *wilde* beestes.
B.12.6	And of þi *wilde* wantownesse [whiles] þow yong were
B.13.63	Wombe cloutes and *wilde* brawen and egges yfryed wiþ grece.
B.14.41	First þe *wilde* worm vnder weet erþe,
B.14.113	And *wilde* wormes in wodes, þoruȝ wyntres þow hem greuest
B.14.116	And blisse to alle þat ben, boþe *wilde* and tame."
B.14.158	And muche murþe in May is amonges *wilde* beestes;
B.15.273	Woneden in wildernesse among *wilde* beestes.
B.15.299	Neiþer bere ne boor ne ooþer beest *wilde*,
B.15.302	Thei wolde haue yfed þat folk bifore *wilde* foweles;
B.15.460	As in wildernesse wexeþ *wilde* beestes
C. 8.30	And afayte thy faucones [*wylde* foules to culle]
C. 9.226	That in *wilde* wodes been or in waste places,
C.13.137	*Wilde* wormes in wodes and wondurfol foules
C.13.169	'Where hadde thise *wilde* suche wit and at what scole?'
C.15.289	And *wilde* wormes in wodes, thorw wyntres thow hem greuest
C.15.292	And blisse to all þat been, bothe *wilde* and tame."
C.16.10	Muche murthe is in may amonge *wilde* bestes
C.17.28	And woneden in wildernesses amonges *wilde* bestes.

wildefowel n *wilde foul(e phr. & n.* B 1

B.10.367	Or delit in wyn and *wildefowel* and wite any in defaute.

wildernesse n *wildernesse n.* A 1; B 4; C 3 wildernesse (2) wildernesses (1)

A.Pr.12	þat I was in a *wildernesse*, wiste I neuere where;
B.Pr.12	That I was in a *wildernesse*, wiste I neuere where.
B.15.273	Woneden in *wildernesse* among wilde beestes,
B.15.460	As in *wildernesse* wexeþ wilde beestes
B.17.101	For wente neuere wye in þis world þoruȝ þat *wildernesse*
C.10.62	By a wi[d]e *wildernesse* and by a wode syde.
C.17.28	And woneden in *wildernesses* amonges wilde bestes.
C.19.54	In a wi[d]e *wildernesse* where theues hadde ybounde

wile > willen

wiles n *wile n.* A 1 wyles; B 7; C 9 wyles

A.10.9	And wolde wynne hire awey with *wyles* ȝif he miȝte.
B. 4.34	'Ther are *wiles* in hire wordes, and with Mede þei dwelleþ;
B. 9.9	And wolde wynne hire awey wiþ *wiles* [if] he myȝte.
B.15.234	That wiþouten *wiles* ledeþ [wel] hir lyues:
B.15.409	And þus þoruȝ *wiles* of his wit and a whit Dowue
B.16.41	Wiþ alle þe *wiles* þat he kan, and waggeþ þe roote
B.19.100	And manye *wiles* and wit þat wole ben a ledere.
B.20.124	His wepne was al *wiles*, to wynnen and to hiden;
C. 4.77	Ac *wyles* and wyt were aboute faste
C.10.136	And wol[d]e wynne here awaye with *wyles* [ȝif] he myhte.
C.13.75	Withoute *wyles* or wronges or wymmen at þe stuyues;
C.18.45	And with alle þe *wyles* þat he can waggeth þe rote
C.18.174	Wo to tho þat thy *wyles* vysen to þe wo[r]ldes ende:
C.19.244	Sethe he withoute *wyles* wan and wel myhte atymye
C.19.248	With *wyles* and with luyther whitus and ȝut wollen nat atymye
C.21.100	And many *wyles* and wyt þat wol be a ledare.
C.22.124	His wepne was al *wyles*, to wynnen and to hyden;

wilfulliche adv *wilfulli adv.* B 3 wilfully (1) wilfulliche (2); C 4 wilfully (2) wilfulliche (1) willefolliche (1)

B.17.290	That wikkedliche and *wilfulliche* wolde mercy aniente?
B.19.370	Wytynge and *wilfully* wiþ þe false helden,
B.20.49	Siþ þat wroȝte al þe world was *wilfulliche* nedy,
C. 4.46	How wrong *wilfully* hadde his wyf forleyn
C.19.271	That wikkedliche and *wilfulliche* wolde mercy anyente?
C.21.370	Wytyng and *wilfully* with the false helden
C.22.49	Sethe [he] þat wrouthe al þe worlde was *willefolliche* nedy

wilyman n *wili adj.* C 2

C. 4.27	Ooen wareyn wisman and *wilyman* his felawe
C. 4.31	[O]n *wilyman* and wittyman and wareyne wrynglawe.

will > wille n, wille n prop

wille n *wille n.* A 34 wil (15) wille (19); B 110 wil (21) wille (89); C 103 wil (17) wille (23) will (63)

A.Pr.37	And haue wyt at *wille* to wirche ȝif hem list.
A. 1.80	Þat I miȝte werchen his *wil* þat wrouȝte me to man:
A. 2.24	Gile haþ begon hire so heo grauntiþ alle his *wille*;
A. 2.53	And as sire symonye wile segge to sewen his *wille*.
A. 2.112	For he may mede amaistrien and maken at my *wille*'.
A. 2.119	Þat he[o] grauntiþ to gon wiþ a good *wille*
A. 3.7	And ȝif heo werche be wyt & my *wil* folewe
A. 3.27	For to werche þi *wil* while þi lif lastiþ.'
A. 3.106	What þat his *wille* were & what he do shulde.
A. 3.159	Þe king grauntide hire grace wiþ a good *wille*:
A. 3.187	Dede hym hoppe for hope to haue me at *wille*.
A. 3.268	And whoso trespassiþ [to treuþe, or] takiþ [aȝeyn his *wille*],
A. 4.35	How wrong aȝen his *wil* hadde his wyf take,
A. 4.56	'Whoso werchiþ be *wil* wraþþe makiþ ofte.
A. 4.88	I forgyue hym þ[at] gilt wiþ a good *wille*;
A. 5.239	Þi *wil* w[orþ]e vpon me, as I haue wel deseruid
A. 6.74	And alle þe wallis ben of wyt to holde wil þeroute;
A. 7.72	His sone hattiþ suffre þi souereynes to hauen here *wille*
A. 7.143	Wilt þou, nilt þou, we wile haue oure *wil*
A. 7.261	Wende now whanne þi *wille* is, þat wel be þou euere.'
A. 8.71	And [ek] giliþ þe gyuere ageyns his *wille*.
A. 9.45	Folewe þi flesshis *wil* & þe fendis aftir,
A. 9.85	And wiþ glad *wil* doþ hem good for so god [hiȝte].
A.10.31	Aungelis & alle þing arn at his *wille*,
A.10.34	And al at his *wil* was wrouȝt wiþ a speche,
A.10.218	And þat is wykkide *wil* þat many werk shendiþ.'
A.11.10	Among hogges þat hauen hawen at *wille*.
A.11.15	Or ricchesse or rentis, & reste at here *wille*,
A.11.68	Þoruȝ whiche a werk & *wille* þei wenten to helle,
A.11.100	And whanne I was war of his *wil* to his wif gan I knele,
A.11.102	For to werche ȝour *wil* [while] my lif duriþ,
A.11.123	Þat iche wiȝt be in *wille* his wyt þe to shewen;
A.11.267	For to reule his reaum riȝt at his *wille*;
A.12.21	Til þo wrecches ben in *wil* here synne to lete."
B.Pr.37	And han wit at *wille* to werken if [hem liste].
B.Pr.150	And ouerleep hem liȝtliche and lauȝte hem at *wille*
B.Pr.156	Miȝte we wiþ any wit his *wille* wiþstonde
B. 1.82	That I myȝte werchen his *wille* þat wroȝte me to man.
B. 2.67	Whan Symonye and Cyuylle seighe hir boþer *wille*
B. 2.92	There as *wil* wolde and werkmanshipe fayleþ.'
B. 2.100	And þanne wanhope to awaken h[y]m so wiþ no *wil* to amende
B. 2.148	For [he] may Mede amaistrye and maken at my *wille*'.
B. 2.155	That she graunteþ to goon wiþ a good *wille*
B. 3.7	And if she werche bi wit and my *wil* folwe
B. 3.18	To be wedded at þi *wille* and wher þee leef likeþ
B. 3.28	For to werche þi *wille* [while þi lif lasteþ].'
B. 3.67	For [god] knoweþ þi conscience and þi kynde *wille*
B. 3.117	What his *wille* were and what he do [sholde].
B. 3.172	The kyng graunted hire grace wiþ a good *wille*.
B. 3.200	And dide hem hoppe for hope to haue me at *wille*.
B. 3.238	Tho þat entren of o colour and of one *wille*
B. 3.265	Be buxom at his biddynge his *wil* to fulfille.
B. 3.293	And whoso trespaseþ [to] truþe or takeþ ayein his *wille*,
B. 4.48	How wrong ayeins his *wille* hadde his wif taken,
B. 4.70	'Whoso wercheþ by *wille* wraþe makeþ ofte.
B. 4.101	I forgyue hym þat gilt wiþ a good *wille*
B. 5.122	For enuye and yuel *wil* is yuel to defie.
B. 5.185	That þi *wille* [ne þi wit] to wraþe myȝte turne:
B. 5.428	So wiþ wikked *wil* and wraþe my werkmen I paye.
B. 5.502	Bidde and biseche, if it be þi *wille*,
B. 5.587	And alle þe walles ben of wit to holden *wil* oute;
B. 5.608	To suffren hym and segge noȝt ayein þi sires *wille*.
B. 6.80	His sone hiȝte Suffre-þi-Souereyns-to-hauen-hir-*wille*-
B. 6.156	Wiltow, neltow, we wol haue oure *wille*.
B. 6.206	And for defaute of foode þis folk is at my *wille*.
B. 6.277	Wend now whan [þi *wil* is], þat wel be þow euere.'\
B. 7.69	And [ek g]ileþ þe gyuere ageynes his *wille*.
B. 8.49	Folwe þi flesshes *wille* and þe fendes after,
B. 8.53	Wit and free *wil*, to euery wiȝt a porcion,
B. 8.95	And wiþ glad *wille* dooþ hem good for so god hoteþ.
B. 9.30	Aungeles and alle þyng arn at his *wille*
B. 9.33	[And al at his *wil* was wrouȝt wiþ a speche],
B. 9.59	What anima is leef or looþ; he l[e]t hire at his *wille*,
B. 9.117	First by þe fadres *wille* and þe frendes conseille,
B. 9.157	And al for þei wroȝte wedlokes ayein [þe *wille* of god].
B. 9.209	And þat is wikked *wille* þat many werk shendeþ,

B.10.10   Among hogges þat han hawes at *wille*.
B.10.15   Or richesse or rentes, and reste at hir *wille*,
B.10.110   Thoruȝ whic[h werk and *wil*] þei wente to helle,
B.10.147   And whan I was war of his *wille* to his wif gan I [knele]
B.10.150   For to werche youre *wille* while my lif dureþ,
B.10.171   That ech wight be in *wille* his wit þee to shewe.
B.10.440   Or ellis for his yuel *wille* and enuye of herte,
B.11.22   The secounde seide þe same: 'I shal sewe þi *wille*;
B.11.26   'The freke þat folwede my *wille* failled neuere blisse.'
B.11.38   'And Deus disponit', quod he; 'lat god doon his *wille*.
B.11.149   Graunted [me worþ] grace [þorȝ his grete *wille*].
B.11.252   And hastily god answerde, and eiþeres wille [lowed],
B.11.264   Makeþ a man to haue mynde in god and a gret *wille*
B.11.280   As Dauid seiþ in þe Sauter: to swiche þat ben in *wille*
B.11.417   Adam, whiles he spak noȝt, hadde paradis at *wille*,
B.11.441   And if his *wille* were he wolde his name telle].
B.12.60   Ac grace ne groweþ noȝt [til good *wil* yeue reyn];
B.12.195   [Th]at buxomliche biddeþ it and ben in *wille* to amenden hem.
B.12.254   Thouȝ he crye to crist þanne wiþ kene *wil*, I leue
B.12.260   Executours, false frendes, þat fulfille noȝt his *wille*
B.12.289   And if þer were he wolde amende, and in swich *wille* deieþ–
B.13.81   And wisshed witterly, wiþ *wille* ful egre,
B.13.114   And seide hymself, 'sire doctour, and it be youre *wille*,
B.13.140   "Wiþ wordes and werkes", quod she, "and *wil* of þyn herte
B.13.190   Ac þe *wil* of þe wye and þe wil of folk here
B.13.190   Ac þe wil of þe wye and þe *wil* of folk here
B.13.192   The goode *wil* of a wight was neuere bouȝt to þe fulle,
B.13.193   For þer [is] no tresour [þerto] to a trewe *wille*.
B.13.320   It was bidropped wiþ wraþe and wikkede *wille*,
B.13.347   Til eiþeres *wille* wexeþ kene and to þe werke yeden,
B.13.384   Hadde I neuere *wille*, woot god, witterly to biseche
B.14.14   Or þoruȝ werk or þoruȝ word or *wille* of myn herte
B.14.20   And engreynen it wiþ good *wille* and goddes grace to amende þe,
B.14.59   Or þoruȝ hunger or þoruȝ hete, at his *wille* be it;
B.14.126   Ac god is of [a] wonder *wille*, by þat kynde wit sheweþ,
B.14.241   For men knowen wel þat Coueitise is of [a] kene *wille*
B.14.262   Muche hardier may he asken þat kene myȝte haue his *wille*
B.15.44   'That is sooþ', seide he; 'now I se þi *wille*.
B.15.127   [He syngeþ seruice bokelees], seiþ it with ydel *wille*.
B.15.150   Wiþouten fauntelte or folie a fre liberal *wille*.'
B.15.200   What is þe *wille* and wherfore þat many wight suffreþ:
B.15.210   Neiþer þoruȝ wordes ne werkes, but þoruȝ *wil* oone,
B.15.262   Of oure foes þat dooþ vs falsnesse; þat is oure fadres *wille*.
B.15.484   Where þat his *wille* is to worshipen vs alle,
B.15.487   That heuedes of holy chirche ben, þat han hir *wil* here,
B.15.534   How þei defouled hir flessh, forsoke hir owene *wille*,
B.16.88   Filius by þe fader *wille* and frenesse of spiritus sancti
B.16.99   For to werchen his *wille* wiþouten any synne:
B.16.136   Enuye and yuel *wil* [arne] in þe Iewes.
B.16.149   That is kissynge and fair contenaunce and vnkynde *wille*.
B.16.158   Thouȝ I bi treson be take [to] youre [iewene] *wille*
B.16.223   So is þe fader forþ with þe sone and fre *wille* of boþe,
B.16.233   He wiste my *wille* bi hym; he wol me it allowe.
B.17.181   Whan he feleþ þe fust and þe fyngres *wille*;
B.17.241   And if it suffise noȝt for assetȝ, þat in swich a *wille* deyeþ,
B.17.311   Thus it fareþ by swich folk þat [folwen] al hire [*wille*],
B.17.352   Good *wille*, good word [boþe], wisshen and willen
B.18.88   'Ayein my *wille* it was, lord, to wownde yow so soore.'
B.18.100   ȝilt hym recreaunt re[m]yng, riȝt at Iesus *wille*.
B.18.176   'My *wil* is to wende', quod she, 'and welcome hem alle
B.18.198   And folwede þat þe fend tauȝte and his [flesshes] *wille*
B.18.212   So god þat bigan al of his goode *wille*
B.18.344   Adam and al his issue at my *wille* herafter;
B.19.447   It semeþ bi so hymself hadde his *wille*
B.20.197   I ne myghte in no manere maken it at hir *wille*,
B.20.203   Awreke me if youre *wille* be for I wolde ben hennes.'
B.20.331   And in haste askede what his *wille* were.
B.20.374   And comen wiþ a kene *wille* Conscience to assaille.
C.Pr.38   And [han] wytt at *wille* to worche yf þei wolde.
C.Pr.171   And ouerlep hem lightliche and laghte hem at *wille*
C.Pr.176   Myghte [we] with eny wyt his *wille* w[i]thsytte
C.1.110   Lepen out in lothly forme for his [luþer] *wille*
C.2.34   [W]hat man [that] me louyeth and my *wille* foleweth
C.2.69   When simonye and syuile ysey[e] þer boþe *wille*
C.2.99   There þat *wille* wolde and wer[k]manschip faileth
C.2.107   And awake with wanhope and no *wille* to amende,
C.2.164   For he may mede amaystrye [and maken at my *wille*].'
C.2.171   That he graunteþ to go with a goode *wille*
C.2.221   What was þe kynges *wille* and wyghtliche wente
C.3.19   For to wedde at thy *wille* [and] where the leef li[k]eth
C.3.29   For to worche thy *wille* the while þou myhte dure.'
C.3.71   For god knoweth thi consience [and þy kynde *wille*,
C.3.154   What his *wille* were and what he do sholde.

C.3.218   The kyng grauntede here grace with a goode *wille*:
C.3.237   Hast arwed many hardy man þat hadde *wille* to fyhte,
C.3.241   And as his wyrdus were ordeyned at þe *wille* of oure lorde.
C.3.247   Of folk þat fauht þerfore and folwede þe kynges *wille*.
C.3.326   And as sone as god seyh a sewed nat his *wille*
C.3.366   In whiche ben gode and nat gode, and graunte here n[eyther] *will*.
C.4.22   For hit is þe wone of wit to wynse and to kyke
C.5.185   That o wit and o *wil* al ȝoure wardes kepe.
C.6.66   A wroth his f[u]ste vppon wrath; hadde [he] wesches at *wille*
C.6.87   For enuye and euyl *wil* is euel to defye.
C.6.113   But y hadde weder at my *wille* y witte god þe cause
C.6.167   That thy *wil* ne thy wit to wr[at]he myhte turne.
C.6.181   Til bothe oure *wil* was oen and to þe werk we ȝeden,
C.6.190   To wynne to my *wille* wymmen with gyle,
C.6.273   Hadde y neuere *will*, [woot god], witterly to byseche
C.6.337   Of alle manere men þat [mid] goode *wille*
C.7.41   So with wikkede *will* my werkemen y paye.
C.7.142   Bidde and biseche the, yf hit be thy *wille*,
C.7.234   And al þe wallyng is of wyt for *wil* ne sholde hit wynne;
C.7.296   To goo with a good *wil* and graytheliche hem dryue.
C.8.82   His sone hihte soffre-thy-souereynes-haue-her-*wille*-
C.8.153   'Wolle thow, nulle thow, we wol haue oure *wille*
C.9.65   And also gileth hym þat gyueth and taketh agayne his *wille*.
C.9.111   With a good *will*, witteles, mony wyde contreyes
C.10.51   Ac fre *wil* and fre wit foleweth man euere
C.10.156   Angeles and alle thyng aren at his *wille*;
C.10.217   On a leye land aȝeynes his lordes *wille*,
C.10.241   The eritage þat þe eyer sholde haue is at þe kynges *wille*.
C.11.8   Among hoggus þat han hawes at *wille*.
C.11.66   Ac þe more a wynneth and hath þe world at his *wille*
C.11.79   Amonges hem þat haen hawes at *wille*,
C.11.85   And when y was war of his *wille* to þat womman gan y louten
C.11.88   For to worche ȝoure *wille* while my lyf duyreth
C.11.181   The seconde saide þe same: 'y [shal] sewe thy *wille*;
C.11.304   'Et deus disponit,' quod he; 'la[t] god do his *wille*.
C.12.2   'That wit shal turne to wrechednesse for wil hath al his *wille*!'
C.12.84   God of his goodnesse ysey his grete *will*.
C.12.139   And here aytheres *wille* [hasteliche god assoilede
C.12.140   And aytheres werkes and *wille*] riht wel alowede
C.12.171   And al þat þe world wolde and my *will* foleweth
C.12.228   And haen þe world at he[re] *wille* oþerwyse to leuene;
C.13.95   For þe *wil* is as moche worthe of a wrecche beggare
C.13.225   Adam, whiles he spak nat, hadde paradys at *wille*
C.13.247   And yf his *wille* were A wolde his name telle.
C.14.24   Ac grace ne groweth nat til gode *wil* gyue reyne
C.14.26   Ac Ar such a *wil* wexe worcheth go[d] sulue
C.14.160   Bote kynde þat contreuede hit furst of his corteyse *wille*.
C.14.175   And haue hem [in] haste at þyn owen *wille*
C.14.211   And yf þer were a wolde [amende], and in suche a *wille* deyeth–
C.15.88   And wisched witterly with *will* ful egre,
C.15.121   And saide hymsulue, 'sire doctour, [and] hit be ȝoure *wille*,
C.15.154   Y wolde, and y *will* hadde, wynnen all fraunce
C.15.184   And wenten forth here way; with grete *wille* y folowede.
C.15.258   Wheþer thorw hunger or [thorw] hete, at his *wille* be hit;
C.15.273   'Meeknesse and mylde speche and men of o *will*,
C.15.274   The whiche *wil* loue lat to oure lordes place
C.16.27   And satisfaccioun þe whiche folfilleth þe fader *will* of heuene;
C.16.81   For men knowen wel þat coueytise is of a kene *will*
C.16.102   Moche hardyore may he aske þat here myhte haue his *wille*
C.16.177   To do wel or wykke, a *will* with a resoun,
C.16.181   And ayther is otheres hete and also of o *will*;
C.16.206   'That is soth,' he sayde; 'now y se thy *wille*.
C.17.128   Alle kyne cristene cleuynge on o *will*,
C.17.143   Loue thy frende þat folleweth thy *wille*, that is thy fayre soule.
C.17.195   How they deffoule[d] here flesche, forsoke here owne *wille*,
C.18.28   Of o *will*, of o wit; and he[r]with y kepe
C.18.76   Wedewes and wedewares þat here own[e] *wil* forsaken
C.18.120   Filius by þe fadres *wille* fley with spiritus sanctus
C.18.132   For to worchen his *wille* withouten eny synne:
C.18.159   And when þat my *will* is y wol hit ouerthrowe
C.18.163   Enuye and euel *wil* ern in þe iewes
C.18.175   Sethe y be tresoun am take and to ȝoure *will*, iewes,
C.18.189   Of o wit and o *will*, [they] were neuere atwynne
C.19.207   And yf hit suffic[e] nat for ase[t]h þat in suche a *will* deyeth
C.19.291   Thus hit fareth bi such folk þat folewen here owene *will*,
C.19.332   Goed *wil*, goed word bothe, wischen and wilnen
C.20.90   'Aȝeyn my *will* hit was,' quod he, 'þat y ȝow wounde made.'
C.20.103   ȝelde hym [re]creaunt remyng, riht at iesu[s] *will*.
C.20.179   'My *wil* is to wende,' quod pees, 'and welcomen hem alle
C.20.203   And folewede þat þe fend tauhte and his flesch[es] *will*
C.20.221   So god þat bigan al of his gode *wille*
C.20.435   A[c] ȝut my kynde [in] my kene ire shal constrayne my *will*–

C.21.447　Hit semeth bi so hymsulue hadde his *wille*
C.22.197　Y ne myhte in none manere maken hit at here *wille*
C.22.203　Awreke me ʒif ʒoure *wille* be for y wolde be hennes.'
C.22.331　And in haste eschete what his *wille* were.
C.22.374　And comen with a kene *wil* Consience to assaile.

wille n prop *OED Will n.3*　A 7 wil (4) wille (3); B 6 wil (2) wille (4); C
　5 wil (1) will (1) wille (3)

A. 5.44　And made *wil* to wepe watir wiþ his eiʒen.
A. 8.43　And ʒaf *wille* for his wrytyng wollene cloþis;
A. 9.118　Here is *wil* wolde wyte ʒif wit couþe hym teche.'
A.12.51　'Þou shalt wende with *wil*,' quod she, 'whiles þat him lykyþ,
A.12.89　'Nay, *wil*,' quod þat wyʒth, 'wend þou no ferther,
A.12.99　*Wille* þurgh inwit [wiste] wel þe soþe,
A.12.103　And whan þis werk was wrouʒt, ere *wille* myʒte aspie,
B. 5.61　And [made] *wille* to wepe water wiþ hise eiʒen.
B. 8.129　Here is *wil* wolde wite if wit koude [hym teche];
B.11.45　'That wit shal torne to wrecchednesse for *wil* to haue his likyng!'
B.13.325　And þat he wiste by *wille* [to watte tellen it],
B.13.326　And þat [by] watte [he] wiste *wille* wiste it after,
B.15.152　I haue lyued in londe', quod [I], 'my name is longe *wille*,
C. 1.5　And sayde, '*Wille*, slepestou? seestow þis peple,
C. 6.2　And made *will* to wepe water with his eyes
C. 6.70　And þat a wiste by *wille* to watekyn he tolde hit
C. 6.71　And þat he wiste by watte tolde hit *wille* aftur
C.12.2　'That wit shal turne to wrechednesse for *wil* hath al his wille!'

wille &> willen

willed adj *willed adj.*　C 1

C. 1.188　Auerous and euel *willed* when þei ben avaunsed,

willefolliche > wilfulliche

willen v *willen v.*　A 112 nile (3) nille (1) nilt (1) nolde (4) wile (38) wiln
　(1) wilt (8) wolde (51) woldest (2) woldist (2) wole (1); B 319 nel (3)
　nelle (4) neltow (1) nil (1) nyl (1) nolde (9) wil (2) wile (2) wille (2)
　willen (4) willest (1) willyng (1) willynge (1) wilt (4) wiltow (3) wol
　(67) wold (1) wolde (145) woldest (4) woldestow (2) wole (51) wollen
　(2) wolt (6) woltow (2); C 308 nel (1) nelle (4) nolde (3) null (1)
　nulle (1) wil (2) wille (2) wilt (1) wol (117) wolde (139) wolden (7)
　woldest (3) wole (5) wolle (7) wollen (4) wolleth (2) wolt (5) woltow
　(2) wost (2)

A.Pr.58　For coueitise of copis construide it as þei *wolde*.
A. 1.13　And *wolde* þat ʒe wrouʒten as his word techiþ.
A. 1.29　[Delyted hym in drynke as the deuyl *wolde*],
A. 1.37　Þat is þe wrecchide world [*wolde*] þe betraye.
A. 1.143　And ʒet *wolde* he hem no woo þat wrouʒte him þat pyne,
A. 2.27　Þere miʒte þou wyte ʒif þou *wilt* whiche þei ben alle
A. 2.46　Alle to wytnesse wel what þe writ *wolde*,
A. 2.53　And as sire symonye *wile* segge to sewen his wille.
A. 2.97　She miʒte kisse þe king for cosyn ʒif he[o] *wolde*.
A. 2.100　ʒif any Leaute *wile* loke þei ligge togidere.
A. 2.106　Hereto assentiþ Cyuyle, ac symonye ne *wolde*
A. 2.120　To lundoun to loke ʒif þat lawe *wolde*
A. 2.156　I *wolde* be wroken of þise wrecchis þat werchen so ille,
A. 2.194　And is welcome whanne he *wile* & woniþ wiþ hem ofte.
A. 3.5　'I *wile* assaie hire myself, and soþly apose
A. 3.8　I *wile* forgyue hire þe gilt, so me god helpe.'
A. 3.17　For we *wile* wisse þe king & þi wey [shape]
A. 3.47　'We haue a wyndowe [in] werching *wile* stonde vs wel heiʒe;
A. 3.48　*Woldist* þou glase þe gable, & graue þere þin name,
A. 3.100　ʒif he wilneþ þe to wyue *wilt* þou hym haue?'
A. 3.107　'*Wilt* þou wedde þis womman ʒif I *wile* assente?
A. 3.107　'*Wilt* þou wedde þis womman ʒif I *wile* assente?
A. 3.167　Wel þou wost, consience, but ʒif þou *wilt* leiʒe,
A. 3.179　Wendist þat wynter *wolde* han last euere;
A. 3.259　An aunter it [noiʒide me non] ende *wile* I make.
A. 4.5　But resoun rede me þerto [raþer] *wole* I deiʒe.'
A. 4.21　And ʒet *wile* [h]e make many wehe er we come þere.'
A. 4.51　And seide, 'hadde I loue of my lord þe king, litel *wolde* I recche
A. 4.84　For I *wile* wage for wrong, he [wile] do so no more.'
A. 4.84　For I wile wage for wrong, he [*wile*] do so no more.'
A. 4.93　Le[pe] he so liʒtly awey, lauʒen he *wolde*,
A. 4.154　For as longe as I lyue l[et]e þe I [n]ile.'
A. 5.36　'And libbe as ʒe lere vs, we *wile* leue ʒow þe betere'.
A. 5.52　But now *wile* I meke me & mercy beseke
A. 5.84　Ac hadde I maistrie & miʒt I *wolde* murdre hym for euere.
A. 5.96　I *wolde* þat iche wiʒt were my knaue;
A. 5.149　And heo askide of hym whidirward he *wolde*.
A. 5.151　And siþen I *wile* be shriuen & synne no more.'
A. 5.152　'I haue good ale, gossib,' quaþ heo; 'glotoun, *wilt* þou assaie?'
A. 5.216　And seide, 'war þe for wanhope *wile* þe betraye.
A. 5.227　And ʒet *wile* I ʒelde aʒen, ʒif I so muchel haue,
A. 5.229　[And] þeiʒ my liflode lakke leten I *nille*

A. 5.232　I *wile* seke treuþe er I [se] rome.'
A. 6.42　I [*wile*] wisse ʒow wel riʒt to his place.'
A. 6.45　'I *nolde* fonge a ferþing for seint Thomas shryne,
A. 6.46　For treuþe *wolde* loue me þe wers a long tyme aftir.
A. 6.52　Oþerwise þanne þou *woldist* men wrouʒte to þiselue;
A. 7.6　I *wolde* wende wiþ ʒow til ʒe were þere'.
A. 7.15　Caste hem cloþis for cold for so *wile* treuþe.
A. 7.25　Ac kenne me,' quaþ þe kniʒt, '& I *wile* [conne] eren.'
A. 7.30　Fro wastours [and wikkide men] þat *wolde* me destroye,
A. 7.39　Loke þou tene no tenaunt but treuþe *wile* assent,
A. 7.58　For I *wile* sowe it myself, & siþþe wile I wende.
A. 7.58　For I wile sowe it myself, & siþþe *wile* I wende.
A. 7.76　To penaunce & to pilgrimage *wile* I passe with oþere;
A. 7.77　Forþi I *wile* er I wende do w[r]yte my bequest.
A. 7.93　I *wile* worsshipe þerewiþ treuþe in my lyue,
A. 7.139　Þanne gan wastour arise & *wolde* haue yfouʒte;
A. 7.143　*Wilt* þou, nilt þou, we wile haue oure wil
A. 7.143　Wilt þou, nilt þou, we *wile* haue oure wil
A. 7.143　Wilt þou, nilt þou, we *wile* haue oure wil
A. 7.149　Curteisliche þe kniʒt þanne as his kynde *wolde*
A. 7.152　'I was not wonid to werche,' quaþ wastour, 'now *wile* I not
　　　begynne,'
A. 7.190　For I wot wel, be þou ywent, hy *wile* werche ille;
A. 7.196　[Now *wolde* I] wite, ʒif þou wistest, what were þe beste,
A. 7.207　Loue hem & lene hem & so þe lawe of kynde *wolde*.
A. 7.213　'I *wolde* not greue god,' quaþ peris, 'for al þe gold on ground.
A. 7.220　Piger propter frigus no feld *wolde* tilie;
A. 7.223　Seruus nequam had a nam, & for he *nolde* it vsen,
A. 7.225　And benom hym his nam for he *nolde* werche,
A. 7.230　And þat he weniþ wel to haue I *wile* it be hym bereuid".
A. 7.231　Kynde wyt *wolde* þat iche wiʒt wrouʒte
A. 7.233　Actif lif oþer contemplatif; crist *wolde* it alse.
A. 7.258　Þei do men diʒe þoruʒ here drynkes er destenye it *wolde*.'
A. 7.262　'I behote god,' quaþ hunger, 'henis *nile* I wende
A. 7.286　And þo *nolde* wastour not werche, but wandrite aboute,
A. 7.296　But he be heiʒliche hirid ellis *wile* he chide,
A. 7.300　Ac while hunger was here maister *wolde* þere non chide,
A. 8.21　But non a pena & a culpa þe pope h[e]m graunte,
A. 8.32　[Pore] wydewis þat *wiln* not be wyues aftir,
A. 8.56　Ne *wolde* neuere holy writ, god wot þe soþe.
A. 8.174　What þou dedist day [by day] þe dom *wile* reherce.
A. 8.178　I ne *wolde* ʒiue for þi patent on pye hele.
A. 9.31　Þe wynd *wolde* wiþ þe watir þe boot ouerþrowe.
A. 9.44　Ay is þi soule sauf but þou þiself *wilt*
A. 9.47　God *wile* suffre þe to deiʒe so for þiself hast þe maistrie.'
A. 9.118　Here is *wil* wolde wyte ʒif wit couþe hym teche.'
A.10.9　And *wolde* wynne hire awey with wyles ʒif he miʒte.
A.10.132　And lyuen as here law[e] *wil[e]*; it likeþ god almiʒty
A.10.133　Þat þoruʒ wedlak þe world stant, whoso *wile* it knowen.
A.11.33　*Wolde* neuere king, ne kniʒt, ne canoun of seint poulis
A.11.66　"Why *wolde* oure sauiour suffre such a worm in his blisse
A.11.75　Wilneþ neuere to wyte why that god *wolde*
A.11.81　I *wolde* his eiʒen wern in his ars & his hele aftir
A.11.82　Þat euere eft wilneþ to wyte why [þat] god *wolde*
A.11.85　–Al was as he *wolde*; lord yworsshipid be þou,
A.11.86　And al worþ as þou *wilt*, whatso we telle–
A.11.87　And now comiþ a conyon & *wolde* cacche of my wittes
A.11.91　I dar be his bolde boruʒ do bet *wile* he neuere,
A.11.115　Boþe wele & wo ʒif þat þou *wile* lerne,
A.11.133　And bet hem wiþ a baleis but ʒif þei *wolde* lerne.
A.11.218　And welawey wers and I [*wo]lde* al telle.'
A.11.225　'I *nile* not scorne,' quaþ scripture, 'but scryueyns liʒe,
A.12.7　Þou *woldest* konne þat I can and carpen hit after;
A.12.10　ʒif I wiste witterly þou *woldest* don þerafter.
A.12.11　Al þat þou askest asoylen I *wolde*.'
A.12.31　Of þat he *wolde* wite wis him no betere;
A.12.37　Or wycke ʒif I *wolde*, wheþer me lyked.
A.12.40　With þat she *wolde* me wisse wher þe toun were
A.12.67　'I *wolde* folwe þe fayn, but fentesye me hendeþ;
A.12.80　Of when þat he were, and wheder þat he *wolde*.
A.12.88　'Myʒth I so, god wot, ʒoure gates *wolde* I holden.'
B.Pr.61　For coueitise of copes construwed it as þei *wolde*.
B.Pr.109　To han [þe] power þat Peter hadde–impugnen I *nelle*–
B.Pr.144　To þe kynges counseil, construe whoso *wolde*,
B.Pr.153　And if we grucche of his gamen he *wol* greuen vs alle,
B.Pr.195　That witnesseþ holy writ, whoso *wole* it rede:
B.Pr.198　[And] many m[a]nnes malt we mees *wolde* destruye,
B.Pr.205　And þouʒ it costned me catel biknowen it I *nolde*
B.Pr.206　But suffren as hymself *wolde* to [slen þat] hym likeþ.
B. 1.13　And *wolde* þat ye wrouʒte as his word techeþ.
B. 1.29　Delited hym in drynke as þe deuel *wolde*,
B. 1.39　That is þe wrecched world *wolde* þee bitraye.
B. 1.169　And yet *wolde* he hem no wo þat wrouʒte hym þat peyne,

B. 2.24	But soopnesse *wolde* no3t so for she is a Bastard.
B. 2.45	[There] my3tow witen if þow *wilt* whiche þei ben alle
B. 2.68	Thei assented for siluer to seye as boþe *wolde*.
B. 2.92	There as wil *wolde* and werkmanshipe fayleþ.'
B. 2.133	[She] my3te kisse þe kyng for cosyn and she *wolde*.
B. 2.136	If any [lewte] *wol* loke þei ligge togideres.
B. 2.142	Herto assenteþ Cyuyle, ac Symonye ne *wolde*
B. 2.156	To london to loken if [þat] lawe *wolde*
B. 2.195	I *wolde* be wroken of þo wrecches þat wercheþ so ille.
B. 2.235	And is welcome whan he *wile* and woneþ with hem ofte.
B. 3.5	'I [*wol*] assayen hire myself and sooþliche appose
B. 3.8	I *wol* forgyuen hire þ[e] gilt, so me god helpe.'
B. 3.17	For we *wol* wisse þe kyng and þi wey shape
B. 3.48	'We haue a wyndow in werchynge *wole* [stonden] vs [wel] hye;
B. 3.49	*Woldestow* gla3e þ[e] gable & graue [þere] þy name
B. 3.51	'Wiste I þat', quod þ[e] womman 'I *wolde* no3t spare
B. 3.111	If he wilneþ þee to wif *wiltow* hym haue?'
B. 3.118	'*Woltow* wedde þis womman if I *wole* assente?
B. 3.118	'*Woltow* wedde þis womman if I *wole* assente?
B. 3.180	Wel þow woost, [Conscience], but if þow *wolt* [lie],
B. 3.192	Wendest þat wynter *wolde* han ylasted euere;
B. 3.281	On auenture it noyed m[e] noon ende *wol* I make,
B. 4.5	But Reson rede me þerto raþer *wol* I deye.'
B. 4.23	For he *wol* make wehee twies er [we] be þere.'
B. 4.38	For [þei *wolde* do for a dyner or a do3eyne capons
B. 4.65	And seide, 'hadde I loue of my lord þe kyng litel *wolde* I recche
B. 4.97	For I *wol* wage for wrong, he *wol* do so na moore.'
B. 4.97	For I *wol* wage for wrong, he *wol* do so na moore.'
B. 4.106	Lope his lawe li3tly [awey], lau3en he *wolde*,
B. 4.180	I *wole* haue leaute in lawe, and lete be al youre ianglyng;
B. 4.182	Quod Conscience to þe kyng, 'but þe commune *wole* assente
B. 4.191	For as longe as I lyue lete þee I *nelle*.'
B. 5.33	And bete Beton þerwith but if she *wolde* werche.
B. 5.53	Moore þan gold ouþer giftes if ye *wol* god plese;
B. 5.69	But now [*wole* I] meke me and mercy biseche
B. 5.90	'I *wolde* ben yshryue', quod þis sherewe, 'and I for shame dorste.
B. 5.91	I *wolde* be gladder, by god! þat Gybbe hadde meschaunce
B. 5.104	Ac hadde I maistrie and my3t [I *wolde* murþere hym for euere].
B. 5.117	I *wolde* þat ech wight were my knaue.
B. 5.134	I *wole* amende þis if I may þoru3 my3t of god almy3ty.'
B. 5.226	Ac I swere now, so thee ik, þat synne *wol* I lete
B. 5.247	And lene folk þat lese *wole* a lippe at euery noble.
B. 5.256	That *wolde* kille hem if he cacche hem my3te for coueitise of hir skynnes
B. 5.266	I *nolde* cope vs wiþ þi catel ne oure kirk amende
B. 5.279	Thanne weex þ[e] sherewe in wanhope & *wolde* han hanged hym[self]
B. 5.299	And [heo] asked [of hym] whiderward he *wolde*.
B. 5.301	And siþen I *wole* be shryuen and synne na moore.'
B. 5.302	'I haue good Ale, gossib', quod she, 'Gloton, *woltow* assaye?'
B. 5.444	And seide, 'ware þee, for wanhope *wo[l]* þee bitraye.
B. 5.455	And yet *wole* I yelde ayein, if I so muche haue,
B. 5.457	And þou3 my liflode lakke leten I *nelle*
B. 5.555	I [*wol*] wisse yow [wel ri3t] to his place.'
B. 5.558	'I *nolde* fange a ferþyng for Seint Thomas Shryne,
B. 5.559	Truþe *wolde* loue me þe lasse a long tyme after.
B. 5.565	Oþerwise þan þow *woldest* [men] wrou3te to þiselue.
B. 5.640	I *wol* go fecche my box wiþ my breuettes & a bulle with bisshopes lettres
B. 5.641	'By crist!' quod a comune womman, 'þi compaignie *wol* I folwe.
B. 6.6	I *wolde* wende wiþ yow and þe wey teche.'
B. 6.16	Casteþ hem cloþes [for cold] for so [*wol*] truþe.
B. 6.23	[Ac] kenne me', quod þe kny3t, 'and [I *wole* konne erie].'
B. 6.28	Fro wastours and wikked men þat [*wolde* me destruye],
B. 6.38	Loke [þow] tene no tenaunt but truþe *wole* assente,
B. 6.63	For I *wol* sowe it myself, and siþenes *wol* I wende
B. 6.63	For I *wol* sowe it myself, and siþenes *wol* I wende
B. 6.84	To penaunce and to pilgrimage I *wol* passe wiþ oþere;
B. 6.85	Forþi I *wole* er I wende do write my biqueste.
B. 6.101	I *wol* worshipe þerwiþ truþe by my lyue,
B. 6.139	Ac ye my3te trauaille as truþe *wolde* and take mete and hyre
B. 6.152	[Th]anne gan wastour to wraþen hym and *wolde* haue yfou3te;
B. 6.156	*Wiltow*, neltow, we wol haue oure wille
B. 6.156	Wiltow, *neltow*, we wol haue oure wille
B. 6.156	Wiltow, neltow, we *wol* haue oure wille
B. 6.164	Curteisly þe kny3t þanne, as his kynde *wolde*,
B. 6.167	'I was no3t wont to werche', quod Wastour, 'now *wol* I no3t bigynne!'
B. 6.204	For I woot wel, be þow went þei *wol* werche ille;
B. 6.210	Now *wolde* I wite, [if þow wistest], what were þe beste,
B. 6.221	Loue hem and lene hem [and] so [þe] lawe of [kynde *wolde*]:
B. 6.227	And if þow *wilt* be gracious to god do as þe gospel techeþ
B. 6.229	'I *wolde* no3t greue god', quod Piers, 'for al þe good on grounde!

B. 6.236	Piger [propter frigus] no feeld [*w*]olde tilie;
B. 6.239	Seruus nequam hadde a Mnam and for he [*n*]olde [it vse]
B. 6.241	And bynam hym his Mnam for he [*n*]olde werche
B. 6.246	And þat he weneþ wel to haue I *wole* it hym bireue".
B. 6.247	Kynde wit *wolde* þat ech wi3t wro3te,
B. 6.249	Contemplatif lif or Actif lif; crist *wolde* [it als].
B. 6.274	They do men deye þoru3 hir drynkes er destynee it *wolde*.'
B. 6.278	'[I] bihote god', quod hunger, 'hennes [*nil*] I wende
B. 6.302	And þo [*n*]olde Wastour no3t werche, but wandre[d] aboute,
B. 6.312	But he be hei3liche hyred ellis *wole* he chide;
B. 6.319	Ac whiles hunger was hir maister þer *wolde* noon chide
B. 7.19	Ac noon A pena & a culpa þe pope [*w*]olde hem graunte
B. 7.36	And witen yow fro wanhope, if ye *wol* þus werche,
B. 7.45	Ac many a Iustice and Iurour *wolde* for Iohan do moore
B. 7.57	Whan þei drawen on to [þe deþ] and Indulgences *wolde* haue,
B. 7.70	For if he wiste he were no3t nedy he *wolde* [it 3yue]
B. 7.196	[What] þow didest day by day þe doom *wole* reherce.
B. 8.35	The wynd *wolde* wiþ þe water þe boot ouerþrowe.
B. 8.48	Ay is þi soule saaf but [þow þiselue *wole*
B. 8.51	God *wole* suffre wel þi sleuþe if þiself likeþ,
B. 8.129	Here is wil *wolde* wite if wit koude [hym teche];
B. 8.130	And wheiþer he be man or [no man] þis man *wolde* aspie,
B. 8.131	And werchen as þei þre *wolde*; th[i]s is his entente.'
B. 9.9	And wolde wynne hire awey wiþ wiles [if] he my3te.
B. 9.84	A Iew *wolde* no3t se a Iew go Ianglyng for defaute
B. 9.89	Whi [ne *wol*] we cristene of cristes good be as kynde?
B. 9.105	*Wolde* neuere þe feiþful fader [h]is fiþele were vntempred
B. 9.128	"Thyn issue in þyn issue, I *wol* þat þei be wedded,
B. 9.186	Wreke þee wiþ wyuyng if þow *wolt* ben excused:
B.10.47	[*W*]olde neuere kyng ne kny3t ne [c]anon of Seint Poules
B.10.83	Ne beþ plenteuouse to þe pouere as pure charite *wolde*,
B.10.108	"Why *wolde* oure Saueour suffre swich a worm in his blisse
B.10.116	Roten and torende? Reson seide it neuere!
B.10.122	Wilneþ neuere to wite why þat god *wolde*
B.10.128	I *wolde* his ei3e were in his ers and his [hele] after,
B.10.129	That euere [eft] wilneþ to wite why þat god *wolde*
B.10.132	Al was as [he] wold[e]–lord, yworshiped be þ[ow],
B.10.133	And al worþ as þow *wolt* whatso we dispute–
B.10.138	I dar ben his bolde borgh þat dobet *wole* he neuere,
B.10.163	Boþe-wele-and-wo if þat þow *wolt* lerne;
B.10.181	And bette hem wiþ a baleys but if þei *wolde* lerne.
B.10.254	But þus it bilongeþ to bileue to lewed þat *willen* dowel.
B.10.277	For goddes word *wolde* no3t be lost, for þat wercheþ euere;
B.10.309	In scole þere is scorn but if a clerk *wol* lerne,
B.10.337	'I *nel* no3t scorne', quod Scripture; 'but scryueynes lye,
B.10.359	That whoso *wolde* and wilneþ wiþ crist to arise,
B.11.21	That leden þee *wole* to likynge al þi lif tyme'.
B.11.23	Til þow be a lord and haue lond leten þee I *nelle*
B.11.35	'Folwe forþ þat Fortune *wole*; þow hast wel fer til Elde.
B.11.39	If truþe *wol* witnesse it be wel do Fortune to folwe
B.11.41	Ne shal no3t greue þee [graiþly], ne bigile [þee], but þow *wolt*.'
B.11.55	For whiles Fortune is þi frend freres *wol* þee louye,
B.11.64	Ayeins oure firste forward, for I seide I *nolde*
B.11.89	'They *wole* aleggen also', quod I, 'and by þe gospel preuen:
B.11.109	Þe lasse, as I leue, louyen þei *wolde*
B.11.119	For crist cleped vs alle, come if we *wolde*,
B.11.126	Ri3tfully to reneye no reson it *wolde*.
B.11.128	Wiþouten leue of his lord; no lawe *wol* it graunte
B.11.135	But if Contricion *wol* come and crye by his lyue
B.11.193	For youre frendes *wol* feden yow, and fonde yow to quyte
B.11.197	[Alle my3te god haue maad riche men if he *wolde*],
B.11.276	Whoso *wole* be pure parfit moot possession forsake
B.11.283	If preestes weren [wise] þei *wolde* no siluer take
B.11.342	That *wolde* [bere] after bol[e], ne boor after sowe,
B.11.391	Ech a lif *wolde* be laklees, leue þow noon oþer.
B.11.392	Ne þow shalt fynde but fewe fayne [*wolde*] heere
B.11.415	For Reson *wolde* haue reherced þee ri3t as Clergie seid;
B.11.423	Pryde now and presumpcion, parauenture, *wol* þee appele
B.11.441	And if his wille were he *wolde* his name telle
B.12.25	Ac if þer were any wight þat *wolde* me telle
B.12.27	*Wolde* I neuere do werk, but wende to holi chirche
B.12.34	And lyue forþ as lawe *wole* while ye lyuen boþe.
B.12.50	That wise wordes *wolde* shewe and werche þe contrarie:
B.12.111	3yue mercy for hire mysdedes, if men it *wole* aske
B.12.215	Raþer þan þat ooþer þeef, þou3 þow *woldest* appose,
B.12.219	/And *willest* of briddes & beestes and of hir bredyng knowe,
B.12.261	That was writen, and þei witnesse to werche as it *wolde*.
B.12.289	And if þer were he *wolde* amende, and in swich wille deieþ–
B.12.290	Ne *wolde* neuere trewe god but [trewe] truþe were allowed.
B.13.22	And as crist *wolde* þer com Conscience to conforte me þat tyme
B.13.71	Holi writ bit men be war–I *wol* no3t write it here
B.13.90	For now he haþ dronken so depe he *wole* deuyne soone

B.13.111 I *wolde* permute my penaunce with youre, for I am in point to
          dowel.'
B.13.132 He *wol* no3t ayein holy writ speken, I dar vndertake.'
B.13.164 [And ek, haue god my soule, and þow *wilt* it craue
B.13.168 Nou3t þoru3 wicchecraft but þoru3 wit; and þow *wilt* þiselue
B.13.171 And as þow demest *wil* þei do alle hir dayes after:
B.13.181 'For I *wol* go wiþ þis gome, if god *wol* yeue me grace,
B.13.181 'For I *wol* go wiþ þis gome, if god *wol* yeue me grace,
B.13.202 Clergie of Conscience no congie *wolde* take,
B.13.204 .Whan þow art wery [for]walked; *wille* me to counseille'.
B.13.223 To Conscience what craft he kouþe, and to what contree he *wolde*.
B.13.226 A wafrer, *wol* ye wite, and serue manye lordes,
B.13.247 Hadde ich a clerc þat couþe write I *wolde* caste hym a bille
B.13.250 And þanne *wolde* I be prest to þe peple paast for to make,
B.13.257 For may no blessynge doon vs boote but if we *wile* amende,
B.13.267 And werkmen were agast a lite; þis *wole* be þou3t longe:
B.13.279 *Willyng* þat alle men wende he were þat he is no3t,
B.13.291 *Willynge* þat men wende his wit were þe beste,
B.13.311 Al he *wolde* þat men wiste of werkes and wordes
B.13.371 That a foot lond or a forow fecchen I *wolde*
B.13.377 So, [wolde he] or no3t wolde, wynnen I wolde.
B.13.377 So, [wolde he] or no3t *wolde*, wynnen I wolde.
B.13.377 So, [wolde he] or no3t wolde, wynnen I *wolde*.
B.13.379 And whoso cheped my chaffare, chiden I *wolde*
B.13.381 Moore þan it was worþ, and yet *wolde* I swere
B.13.415 And if he au3t *wole* here it is an harlotes tonge.
B.13.417 He wexeþ wroþ, and *wol* no3t here but wordes of murþe;
B.14.4 That *wollen* bymolen in many tyme maugree my chekes.
B.14.28 Than Hauky[n] *wi[l]* þe wafrer, [which is] Actiua vita.'
B.14.32 All þat lyueþ and lokeþ liflode *wolde* I fynde
B.14.71 And if men lyuede as mesure *wolde* sholde neuere moore be
          defaute
B.14.120 Ouþer here or elliswhere, kynde *wolde* it neuere;
B.14.142 Ri3t as a seruaunt takeþ his salarie bifore, & siþþe *wolde* clayme
          moore
B.14.173 Of þat þei wilne and *wolde* wanteþ hem no3t here.
B.14.188 Shulde amenden vs as manye siþes as man *wolde* desire.
B.14.189 A[c] if þe [pouke] *wolde* plede herayein, and punysshe vs in
          conscience,
B.14.231 For his rentes ne *wol* nau3t reche no riche metes to bigge;
B.14.245 And þou3 Auarice *wolde* angre þe poore he haþ but litel my3te,
B.15.19 That *wole* defende me þe dore, dynge I neuer so late.
B.15.24 And whan I wilne and *wolde* animus ich hatte;
B.15.45 Thow *woldest* knowe and konne þe cause of alle [hire] names,
B.15.49 I *wolde* I knewe and kouþe kyndely in myn herte.'
B.15.65 Right so þat þoru3 reson *wolde* þe roote knowe
B.15.103 Forþi *wolde* ye lettrede leue þe lecherie of cloþyng,
B.15.130 *Wolde* neuere þe wit of witty god but wikkede men it hadde,
B.15.155 And *wollen* lene þer þei leue lelly to ben paied.
B.15.159 That he ne *wolde* aske after his, and ouþerwhile coueite
B.15.186 And whan he is wery of þat werk þan *wole* he som tyme
B.15.195 'By crist! I *wolde* I knewe hym', quod I, 'no creature leuere.'
B.15.236 Ac if coueitise be of þe counseil he *wol* no3t come þerInne.
B.15.263 For wel may euery man wite, if god hadde *wold* hymselue,
B.15.267 And seide to swiche þat suffre *wolde*,
B.15.302 Thei *wolde* haue yfed þat folk bifore wilde foweles;
B.15.309 And þanne *wolde* lordes and ladies be looþ to agulte,
B.15.310 And to taken of hir tenaunt3 moore þan trouþe *wolde*,
B.15.311 Founde þei þat freres *wolde* forsake hir almesses
B.15.319 If lewed men knewe þis latyn þei *wolde* loke whom þei yeue,
B.15.404 Thanne *wolde* þe coluere come to þe clerkes ere
B.15.419 *Wolde* neuere þe feiþful fader þat [þ]ise Ministres sholde
B.15.464 But wiþ foweles þat fram hym *nolde* but folwede his whistlyng:
B.15.489 They *wol* be wrooþ for I write þus, ac to witnesse I take
B.15.495 That þei ne wente as crist wisseþ, siþen þei *wille* haue name,
B.15.503 Thei sholde turne, whoso trauail[e *wolde*] to teche hem of þe
          Trinite.
B.15.518 Alle þat wilned and *wolde* wiþ Inwit bileue it.
B.16.10 'I *wolde* trauaille', quod I, 'þis tree to se twenty hundred myle,
B.16.25 'For wyndes, *wiltow* wite', quod he, 'to witen it fro fallyng:
B.16.27 The world is a wikked wynd to hem þat *willen* truþe.
B.16.71 Maidenhode, Aungeles peeris, and [erst] *wole* be ripe.
B.16.73 I preide Piers to pulle adoun an Appul and he *wolde*,
B.16.126 And lefte baskettes ful of broke mete, bere awey whoso *wolde*.'
B.16.233 He wiste my wille bi hym; he *wol* me it allowe.
B.16.257 'What awaitestow?' quod he, 'and what *woldestow* haue?'
B.16.258 'I *wolde* wite', quod I þo, 'what is in youre lappe.'
B.16.275 What he highte & whider he *wolde*, and wightly he tolde.
B.17.18 'Whoso wercheþ after þis writ, I *wol* vndertaken,
B.17.49 Tho þat lernen þi lawe *wol* litel while vsen it.'
B.17.61 And *nolde* no3t neghen hym by nyne londes lengþe.
B.17.205 God þat he grypeþ wiþ, and *wolde* his grace quenche.
B.17.236 *Wol* brennen and blasen, be þei togideres,

B.17.238 So *wol* þe fader for3yue folk of mylde hertes
B.17.242 Mercy for his mekenesse *wol* maken good þe remenaunt.
B.17.243 And as þe weke and fir *wol* maken a warm flaumbe
B.17.245 So *wole* crist of his curteisie, and men crye hym mercy,
B.17.290 That wikkedliche and wilfulliche *wolde* mercy aniente?
B.17.297 *Wol* loue [þat lif] þat [lakkeþ] charite],
B.17.323 That oon is a wikkede wif þat *wol* no3t be chastised;
B.17.334 The wif is oure wikked flessh þat *wol* no3t be chastised
B.17.352 Good wille, good word [boþe], wisshen and *willen*.
B.18.22 'This Iesus of his gentries *wol* Iuste in Piers armes,
B.18.56 Thanne shul we leue þat lif þee loueþ and *wol* no3t lete þee deye.'
B.18.174 And preide pees to telle hire to what place she *wolde*,
B.18.232 'By goddes body', quod þis book, 'I *wol* bere witnesse
B.18.247 The Erþe for heuynesse þat he *wolde* suffre
B.18.255 And I, book, *wole* be brent but Iesus rise to lyue
B.18.269 If þis kyng come In mankynde *wole* he fecche
B.18.285 And where he *wole* is his wey; ac ware hym of þe perils:
B.18.293 For god *wol* no3t be bigiled', quod Gobelyn, 'ne byiaped.
B.18.303 I *wolde* haue lengþed his lif for I leued if he deide
B.18.304 That his soule *wolde* suffre no synne in his sighte;
B.18.306 To saue men from synne if hemself *wolde*.
B.18.341 And al þat man haþ mysdo I man *wole* amende.
B.18.383 Lawe *wolde* he yeue hym lif if he loked on hym.
B.18.386 And if lawe *wole* loke on hem it liþ in my grace
B.18.390 And þou3 holy writ *wole* þat I be wroke of hem þat diden ille–
B.18.400 Thus by lawe', quod oure lord, 'lede I *wole* fro hennes
B.19.68 And muche wo in þis world *willen* and suffren.
B.19.100 And manye wiles and wit þat *wole* ben a bonde,
B.19.192 He wente, and wonye3 þere, and *wol* come at þe laste
B.19.194 Paieþ parfitly as pure truþe *wolde*.
B.19.215 'For I *wole* dele today and [dyuyde] grace
B.19.218 And wepne to fighte wiþ þat *wole* neuere faille.
B.19.225 Forþi', quod grace, 'er I go I *wol* gyue yow tresor
B.19.233 And by wit to wissen oþere as grace hem *wolde* teche.
B.19.394 [Or] ech man for3yue ooþer, and þat *wole* þe Paternoster:
B.19.396 'Ye? baw!' quod a Brewere, 'I *wol* no3t be ruled,
B.19.419 Forþi', quod þis vicory, 'by verray god I *wolde*
B.19.423 Or in Rome as hir rule *wole* þe relikes to kepe;
B.19.464 And wiþ Spiritus fortitudinis fecche it, [wole he, nel he].'
B.19.464 And wiþ Spiritus fortitudinis fecche it, [*wole* he, *nel* he].'
B.19.468 And if me lakkeþ to lyue by þe lawe *wole* I take it
B.19.478 And rule þi reaume in reson [as right *wol* and] truþe
B.20.13 Ne wight noon *wol* ben his boru3, ne wed haþ noon to legge;
B.20.18 And if hym list for to lape þe lawe of kynde *wolde*
B.20.28 And greue men gretter þan good feiþ it wolde.
B.20.29 And Spiritus Iusticie shal Iuggen, wole he, nel he,
B.20.29 And Spiritus Iusticie shal Iuggen, *wole* he, *nel* he,
B.20.32 Of þat he weneþ *wolde* falle if his wit ne weere;
B.20.38 [Philosophres] forsoke wele for þei *wolde* be nedy
B.20.39 And woneden [wel elengely] and *wolde* no3t be riche.
B.20.107 To cesse and suffre, and see wher þei *wolde*
B.20.140 'Allas!' quod Conscience and cryde, '*wolde* crist of his grace
B.20.185 So harde he yede ouer myn heed it *wole* be neuere euere.
B.20.188 Haddestow be hende', quod I, 'þow *woldest* haue asked leeue.'
B.20.203 Awreke me if youre wille be for I *wolde* ben hennes.'
B.20.204 'If þow *wolt* be wroken wend into vnitee
B.20.235 They *wol* flatere [to] fare wel folk þat ben riche.
B.20.248 And I *wol* be youre boru3: ye shal haue breed and cloþes
B.20.253 And if ye coueite cure, kynde *wol* yow [telle]
B.20.260 /*Wol* no [tresorer take] hem [wages], trauaille þei neuer so soore,
B.20.265 Hir ordre and hir reule *wole* to han a certein noumbre
B.20.266 Of lewed and of lered; þe lawe *wole* and askeþ
B.20.271 Forþi I *wolde* witterly þat ye were in þe Registre
B.20.288 Ac while he is in westmynstre he *wol* be bifore
B.20.312 For fastynge of a fryday he ferde as he *wolde* deye.
B.20.333 Carpe I *wolde* wiþ contricion, and þerfore cam I hider.'
B.20.380 'By crist!' quod Conscience þo, 'I *wole* bicome a pilgrym,
C.Pr.36 *Wolleth* neyther swynke ne swete bote sweren grete othes,
C.Pr.38 And [han] wytt at wille to worche yf þei *wolde*.
C.Pr.110 And chastisid hem nogth þerof and *nolde* nogth rebuken hem
C.Pr.130 Hou he it lefte with loue as oure lord *wolde*
C.Pr.136 To haue þe power þat Peter hadde inpugne y *nelle*
C.Pr.173 'And yf we groche of his game a *wol* greue vs [alle],
C.Pr.213 And thow hit costed m[e] catel byknowen [hit] y ne *wolde*
C.Pr.216 For many mannys malt we muys *wolde* distruye
C. 1.13 And *wolde* þat 3e wroghtoun as his word techeth.
C. 1.37 [That] is þe wrecchede world *wolde* þe bigyle.
C. 1.40 And wysseth þe to ben ywar what *wolde* þe desseyue.'
C. 1.112 'Lord! why *wolde* he tho, þat wykkede lucifer,
C. 1.115 'Nere hit for northerne men anon y *wolde* 3ow telle
C. 1.116 Ac y *wol* lacky no lyf,' quod þat lady sothly;
C. 1.123 Ac of þis matere no more [meu]en y *nelle*.

748

C. 1.165	And ȝut *wolde* [he] hem no wo þat wrouhte hym þat [p]e[y]ne
C. 2.24	Ac sothnesse *wolde* nat so for she is a bastard.
C. 2.39	Y do hit vppon dauyd; the doumbe *wil* noȝt lyen:
C. 2.99	There þat wille *wolde* and wer[k]manschip faileth.
C. 2.131	That god *wolde* were ydo withoute som deseyte.
C. 2.158	Hereto assenteth syuyle, ac symonye ne *wolde*
C. 2.169	Til mede be thy wedded wyf *wolle* we nat stunte,
C. 2.172	To londone to loke yf lawe *wille* iugge;
C. 2.187	*Wol* Ryde vppon Rectores and ryche men deuoutours,
C. 2.209	Y *wolde* be awreke [o]n tho wreches and on here werkes alle,
C. 2.250	Thy kynedom thorw Coueytise *wol* out of kynde wende,
C. 3.8	Y *wol* forgyue here alle gultes, so me god helpe.'
C. 3.18	For we w[o]l wisse the kyng and thy way shape
C. 3.51	'We han a wyndowe awurchynge *wol* stande vs [wel] heye;
C. 3.52	*Wolde* ȝe glase þ[e] gable and graue ther ȝoure name
C. 3.65	Bothe wyndowes and wowes y *wol* amende and glase
C. 3.123	And wittenesseth what worth of hem þat *wolleth* take mede:
C. 3.130	Corteisliche þe kynge, as his kynde *wolde*,
C. 3.148	Yf he wilneth the to wyue *wolt* thow hym haue?'
C. 3.155	'*Woltow* wedde this m[ai]de yf y wol assente?
C. 3.155	'*Woltow* wedde this m[ai]de yf y *wol* assente?
C. 3.226	Wel thow wost, weye, but yf thow *wille* gabbe,
C. 3.240	That he ne felde nat his foes tho fortune hit *wolde*
C. 3.341	Quod the kyng to Consience, 'knowen y *wolde*
C. 3.351	And take hym for his trauaile al þat treuthe *wolde*,
C. 3.369	For hoso *wolde* to wyue haue my worliche douhter
C. 3.370	I *wolde* feffe hym with here fayre and [with] here foule taylende.
C. 3.384	For they wilnen and *wolden* as beste were for hemsulue
C. 3.420	And alle þat leueth on þat lond oure [lord] *wol* þat thow sle hit;
C. 3.428	Otherwyse then god *wolde* and warnede hym by þe prophete,
C. 3.434	An Auntur hit nuyede me noen ende *wol* y make,
C. 3.499	Worschipe a wynneth þat *wol* ȝeue mede
C. 4.5	But resoun rede me þertyl rather wo[l] y dey.'
C. 4.35	For there is wrath and wranglynge there *wol* they abyde;
C. 4.38	For þey *wolde* do for a dyner oþer a d[o]seyne capones
C. 4.69	'Hadde y loue of [my] lord lytel *wolde* y reche.'
C. 4.93	For y *wol* wage for wrong; he wol do so no mare.'
C. 4.93	For y wol wage for wrong; he *wol* do so no mare.'
C. 4.101	Lope he so lihtliche [awey], lawen he *wolde*
C. 4.174	Y *wol* haue leutee for my lawe and late be al ȝoure iangl[ing]
C. 4.183	'Y *wolde* hit were,' quod the kynge, 'wel al aboute
C. 4.191	'And y dar lege my lyf þat loue *wol* lene þe seluer
C. 5.39	And sykerost for þe soule, by so y *wol* contenue.
C. 5.81	And *wol* til hit be wered out [or] oþerwyse ychaunged.
C. 5.83	For in my Consience y knowe what Crist w[o]lde y wrouhte.
C. 5.135	And bete Betene þerwith but yf a *wolde* worche.
C. 5.189	Holde ȝow in vnite; and he þat oþer *wolde*
C. 6.10	But now *wol* y meke me and mercy byseche
C. 6.59	Al [y] *wolde* þat men wiste when it to pruyde souneth,
C. 6.105	'I am wr[a]the,' quod þat weye, '*wol* gladliche smyte
C. 6.139	And thenne awake y, wrathe, and *wolde* be avenged.
C. 6.238	Thow *wolt* be hanged heye þerfore, here oþer in helle.
C. 6.245	Y lene folk þat lese *wole* a lyppe [at] vch a noble
C. 6.268	That a foet lond or a fore fecchen y *wolde*
C. 6.288	Y ne *wolde* cope me with thy catel ne oure kyrke mende
C. 6.311	'And thow m[y] lyflode lakke leten y *nelle*
C. 6.328	That [penitencia] is pykstaff a *wolde* polesche newe
C. 6.354	And whode[r]ward he *wolde* the breuhwyf hym askede.
C. 6.357	'Y haue good ale, gossip Glotoun, *woltow* assaye?'
C. 6.419	Then [wakede he] wel wanne and *wolde* haue ydronke;
C. 7.58	And sayde, 'war the for wanhope wo[l the] bytraye.
C. 7.77	A wexeth wroth and *wol* nat here but wordes of murthe;
C. 7.145	That what tyme we synnefole men *wolden* be sory
C. 7.199	Y *wol* wissen ȝow wel ryht to his place.'
C. 7.202	'Y [*nolde*] fonge a ferthynge for seynt Thomas shryne;
C. 7.204	A *wolde* loue me þat loue no tyme aftur.
C. 7.205	Ac hoso *wol* wende þer treuthe is, this is þe way thede[r]:
C. 7.212	Otherwyse then ȝe *wolden* they wrouhte ȝow alle tymes.
C. 7.301	Were y seuen nyhte fro here syhte s[ynnen] he *wolde*
C. 7.306	Famyne and defaute, folwen y *wol* Peres.
C. 8.4	Y wol[de] wende with ȝow and þe way teche.'
C. 8.21	Y *wolde* y couthe,' quod the knyhte, 'by Crist and his moder!
C. 8.22	Y *wolde* [assaye] som tyme, for solace as hit were.'
C. 8.36	Loke ȝe tene no tenaunt but treuthe *wol* assente
C. 8.57	And wende with alle tho þat *wolden* lyue in treuthe.'
C. 8.62	'For y *wol* sowen hit mysulf and sethe wol y wende
C. 8.62	'For y wol sowen hit mysulf and sethe *wol* y wende
C. 8.93	To penaunc[e] and [to] pilgrim[age] y *wol* passe with oþere;
C. 8.94	Forthy y *wol* ar y wende do wryte my biqueste.
C. 8.110	Y *wol* worschipe þerwith treuthe al my lyue
C. 8.137	Myhte helpe, as y hope; Ac hey treuthe *wolde*
C. 8.148	What! y and myn *wolle* fynde hem what hem nedeth.'
C. 8.149	Thenne gan wastor to wrath hym and *wolde* haue yfouhte
C. 8.153	'*Wolle* thow, nulle thow, we wol haue oure wille
C. 8.153	'Wolle thow, *nulle* thow, we wol haue oure wille
C. 8.153	'Wolle thow, nulle thow, we *wol* haue oure wille
C. 8.161	Courteisliche the knyhte thenne, as his kynde *wolde*,
C. 8.164	'I was nat woned to worche,' quod wastour, 'now *wol* y nat bygynne!'
C. 8.166	And sette [Peres] at a [pes], playne hym whare he *wolde*.
C. 8.170	Awreke [me] of this wastors for þe knyhte *wil* nat.'
C. 8.210	For y woet wel, be [thow] went, worche þei *wol* ful ille;
C. 8.219	Now *wolde* y wyte, ar thow wendest, what were þe beste;
C. 8.230	Loue hem and lene hem and so lawe of kynde *wolde*:
C. 8.235	'Y *wolde* nat greue [god],' quod Peres, 'for al þe good on erthe!
C. 8.243	"The slowe Caytif for colde *wolde* no corn tylye;
C. 8.251	Ac he þat was a wreche and *wolde* nat trauaile
C. 8.257	And þat he weneth wel to haue y *wol* hit hym bireue".
C. 8.261	This aren euidences,' quod hunger, 'for hem þat *wolle* nat swynke
C. 8.263	'By Crist!' quod [Peres] þe [plouhman] tho, 'this prouerbis [*wol* y] shewe
C. 8.295	They don men deye thorw here drynkes Ar destyne hit *wolde*.'
C. 8.298	Wende nouthe when thow wol[t] and wel [be thow] euere
C. 8.300	'Y behote the,' quod hunger, 'þat hennes ne *wol* y wende
C. 8.324	And tho *wolde* wastor nat worche bote wandre[d] aboute
C. 8.334	But he be heyliche yhuyred elles *wol* he chy[d]e;
C. 8.339	Ac whiles hungur was here maistre ther *wolde* non chyde
C. 9.16	And bitynge in badde men but yf they *wol* amende,
C. 9.23	Ac no [a] pena & a culpa treuthe *wolde* hem graunte
C. 9.47	That innocent and nedy is and no man harm *wolde*,
C. 9.52	For whenne ȝe drawe to þe deth and indulgences *wolde* haue
C. 9.66	For he þat gyueth for goddes loue *wolde* nat gyue, his thankes,
C. 9.86	And ben abasched for to begge and *wollen* nat be aknowe
C. 9.155	And can eny craft in caes he *wolde* hit vse,
C. 9.246	Or labory for here lyflode as þe lawe *wolde*?
C. 9.278	Loke now, for thy lacchesse, what lawe *wol* the graunte;
C. 9.342	And how we dede day be day the doem *wol* reherce.
C. 10.19	And euere hath, as y hope, and euere *wol* hereaftur.'
C. 10.102	That *wolde* nat do as dobest de[m]ede and tauhte.
C. 10.111	'Bote wit *wol* the wisse,' quod thouhte, 'where tho thre dwelleth,
C. 10.125	Here is oen *wolde* ywyte yf wit couthe teche;
C. 10.136	And wol[d]e wynne here away with wyles [ȝif] he myhte.
C. 10.164	God *wol* nat of hem wyte bute lat hem yworthe,
C. 10.201	For hoso loueth, leueth h[it] wel, god *wol* nat laton hym sterue
C. 10.261	Bote he haue oþer goed haue *wol* here no ryche.
C. 10.267	That he ne *wol* bowe to þat bonde to beden here an hosebonde
C. 11.63	Ne parteth with þe pore as puyr charite *wolde*,
C. 11.105	Bothe-wele-and-wo yf þou *wilt* lerne.
C. 11.112	And hast vnderstandyng what a *wolde* mene
C. 11.121	And be[t] hem with a baleyse bute yf þei *wolde* lerne.
C. 11.180	That legde þe *wol* to lykynge Al thy lyf tyme.'
C. 11.182	Til thow be a lord and haue lond leten y the *nelle*
C. 11.194	'Folowe forth þat fortune *wole*; þou hast [wel] fer to elde.
C. 11.306	Thow thei folowe þat fortune *wole* [no] folye ich it holde.
C. 11.308	Ne shal nat greue the gr[ayth]ly ne bigyle the, but thow *wolle*.'
C. 12.7	For while fortune is thy frende freres *wol* the louye
C. 12.27	Y *wolde* it were no synne,' y saide, 'to seien þat were treuthe.
C. 12.30	Thei *wolle* allegge also and by þe gospel preuen:
C. 12.39	Thyng þat *wolde* be pryue publische thow hit neuere;
C. 12.43	The lasse, as y leue, louyon þey *wolde*
C. 12.54	For crist clepede vs alle, come yf we *wolde*,
C. 12.61	Rihtfolliche to renoye no resoun hit *wolde*.
C. 12.63	Withouten leue of [his] lord; no lawe *wol* hit graunte.
C. 12.107	Ac for þe pore may nat paye y *wol* pay mysulue;
C. 12.171	And al þat þe world *wolde* and my will folowe:
C. 13.39	*Wol* lette hym, as y leue, the lenghe of a myle
C. 13.44	*Wol* no wys man be wroth ne his wed take—
C. 13.60	And leueth for his lettres þat no [lede] *wole* hym greue.
C. 13.63	*Wolde* noon suche assailen hym for such as hym foloweth
C. 13.91	Ther is no lawe, as y leue, *wol* lette hym þe gate
C. 13.94	In þat a wilneth and *wolde* vch wyht as hymsulue.
C. 13.150	That *wolde* bere aftur bole ne boer aftur sowe;
C. 13.209	Vch a lede *wolde* be lacles, leef thow non other.
C. 13.223	For resoun *wolde* haue rehersed þe riht as clergie seide;
C. 13.229	And for thow *woldest* wyte why, resones preue[t]e,
C. 13.231	Resoun refusede the and *wolde* nat reste with the
C. 13.247	And yf his wille were A *wolde* his name telle.
C. 14.56	To ȝeue mercy for mysde[de]s ȝif men hit *wol* aske
C. 14.134	And *wol* no wikkede man [be] lost bote if he wol hymsulue:
C. 14.134	And wol no wikkede man [be] lost bote if he *wol* hymsulue:
C. 14.154	Rather then þat oþer [theef], thogh thow *woldest* apose.
C. 14.166	Ac why a *wolde* þat wykke were, y wene and y leue
C. 14.211	And yf þer were a *wolde* [amende], and in suche a wille deyeth—
C. 14.212	Ne *wolde* neuere trewe god bote trewe treuthe were alloued.
C. 14.217	For al worth as god *wol*;' and þerwith he vanschede.

C.15.12   Bote quyke he byqu[e]th hem auht or *wolde* helpe quyte here
           dettes;
C.15.97   [For] now he hath dronke so depe a *wol* deuyne sone
C.15.106   Y sae[t] stille as pacience *wolde* and thus sone this doctour,
C.15.116   Ne l[yu]eth as ȝe lereth, as oure lord *wolde*:
C.15.154   Y *wolde*, and y will hadde, wynnen all fraunce
C.15.165   Þer [n]is wyht in this world þat *wolde* the lette
C.15.177   'By Crist!' quod Consience, 'clergie, y *wol* nat lye;
C.15.183   With pacience *wol* y passe parfitnesse to fynde.'
C.15.216   Y fynde payn for þe po[p]le and pre[y]en hym ych *wolde*
C.15.222   And thenne *wolde* y be bysy and buxum to helpe
C.15.227   For may no blessynge doen vs bote but yf we *wol* amende
C.15.234   Pruyde *wolde* potte hymsulf forth thogh no plough erye.
C.15.270   And yf men lyuede as mesure *wolde* sholde neuere[more] be
           defaute
C.16.72   For his rentes *wol* nat reche ryche metes to bugge;
C.16.85   And thogh Auaryce *wolde* Angry [þe] pou[r]e he hath bote lytel
           myhte
C.16.170   That *wol* defende me [þe] dore, dynge y neuere so late.
C.16.184   And when y wilne and *wolde* Animus y hatte;
C.16.193   And when y *wol* do or [nat do] gode dedes or ille
C.16.207   Thow *woldest* knowe and conne þe cause of all here names
C.16.211   Y *wolde* y knewe and couthe kyndeliche in myn herte.'
C.16.256   For *wolde* ȝe lettered leue þ[e] lecherye of clothyng
C.16.277   *Wolde* neuere oþerwyse god but wikkede men hit hadde,
C.16.306   Weneth he þat no wyhte *wolde* lye and swerie
C.16.307   Ne þat eny gome *wolde* gyle [ne greue oþere]
C.16.337   'Were y with hym by Cr[i]st,' quod y, 'y *wolde* neuere fro hym
C.16.361   Ac yf couetyse be of his consaile a *wol* nat come þerynne.
C.16.366   With bisshopes a *wolde* be for beggares sake
C.17.4   'Ho is wroeth and *wolde* be awreke, holy writ preueth,' quod he,
C.17.35   For *wolde* neuere faythfull god þat freres and monkes
C.17.42   Sholde reseue riht nauht but þat riht *wolde*
C.17.44   Thenne *wolde* lordes and ladyes be loth to agulte
C.17.45   And to take of here tenauntes more then treuthe *wolde*
C.17.46   And marchauntȝ merciable *wolde* be and men of lawe bothe
C.17.47   *Wolde* religious refuse rauenours Almesses.
C.17.50   And conforte alle cristene *wolde* holy [kirke] amende.
C.17.54   Yf lewede men knewe this latyn a litel they *wolden* auysen hem
C.17.149   Contrarie her nat as in Consience yf thow *wol[t]* come to heuene.'
C.17.240   Hadde al surie as hymsulue *wolde* and sarrasines in equitee.
C.17.246   And crie to Crist a *wolde* his coluer sende
C.17.254   They sholde [turne], hoso trauayle *wolde* and of þe trinite teche
           hem.
C.17.269   Alle þat wilnede and *wolde* with inwit bileue hit.
C.18.31   The world is a wikkede wynd to hem þat wo[n/l] treuthe;
C.18.60   Ac somme ar swettore then somme and so[nner]e *wollen* rotye.
C.18.79   And folewe þat the flesche *wole* and fruyt forth brynge.
C.18.102   Bothe parfit and inparfit.' Puyr fayn y *wolde*
C.18.154   And lefte basketes ful of Broke mete, bere awey hoso *wolde*.
C.18.159   And when þat my will is y *wol* hit ouerthrowe
C.18.228   Wh[om] god *wolde* oute of þe wey [d]rawe.
C.18.250   Where y walke in this worlde a *wol* hit me allowe.
C.18.259   As we wilnede and *wolde* with mou[th]e and herte aske.
C.18.273   'What [a]waytest thow,' quod fayth, 'and what *wost* thow haue?'
C.18.274   'I *wolde* ywyte,' quod y tho, 'what is in thy lappe.'
C.18.291   What he hihte and whoder he *wolde* & whithliche he tolde.
C.19.19   'And ho[so] worcheth aftur this writ, y *wol* vndertaken,
C.19.47   Tho þat lerneth thy lawe *wollen* litel while hit vse.'
C.19.60   And [n]olde nat neyhele hym by nyne londes lenghe.
C.19.107   Y sholde tholye and thonken hem þat me euel *wolden*.'
C.19.171   God þ[at] he gripeth [with] and *wolde* his grace quenche.
C.19.202   *Wol* brennen and blasen, be they togyderes,
C.19.204   So *wol* þe fader forȝeue folke of mylde hertes
C.19.208   Mercy for his mekenesse *wol* maky good þe remenaunt.
C.19.209   And as þe wyke and [fuyr *wol* make a warm] flaume
C.19.211   So *wol* Crist of his cortesye, and men crien hym mercy,
C.19.246   And is in helle for al þat, how *wol* riche nouthe
C.19.248   With wyles and with luyther whitus and ȝut *wollen* nat atymye
C.19.271   That wikkedliche and wilfulliche *wolde* mercy anyente?
C.19.278   *Wol* louye þat lyf þat loue and Charite destruyeth.'
C.19.303   That [oon] is a wikkede wyf þat *wol* nat be chasted;
C.19.314   The wyf is oure wikkede flesche [þat] *wol* nat be chasted
C.20.28   Deth saith a *wol* fordo and adown brynge
C.20.54   And saiden, 'yf he sotil be hymsulue now he *wol* helpe;'
C.20.56   Thenne shal we leue that lyf þe loueth and *wol* nat late the deye.'
C.20.177   And preyede pees to tellen [here] to what place she [w]olde
C.20.241   'By godes body,' quod this boek, 'y *wol* [b]ere witnesse
C.20.256   Þe erthe for heuynesse þat he *wolde* soffre
C.20.264   And y, boek, *wol* be brente bote he aryse to lyue
C.20.277   Yf this kyng come in mankynde *wol* he fecche
C.20.298   And where he *wol* is his way, ac waer hym of þe perelles:
C.20.307   And sethe he is a lele lord y leue þat he *wol* nat

C.20.310   And neuere [n]as þeraȝeyne and now *wolde* bigynne,
C.20.323   [For] god *wol* nat be [bi]gyled,' quod gobelyne, 'n[e] byiaped.
C.20.325   'Forthy y drede me,' quod þe deuel, 'laste treuthe *wol* hem fecche.
C.20.334   Lette hem þat louede hym nat laste they *wolde* hym martre.
C.20.335   Y *wolde* haue lenghed his lyf for y leued, yf he deyede,
C.20.405   Ac y *wol* drynke of no dische ne of deep clergyse
C.20.425   Lawe *wolde* he ȝoue hym lyf and he loked on hym.
C.20.428   And if lawe *wol* y loke on hem hit lith in my grace
C.20.432   For holy writ *wol* þat y be wreke of hem þat wrouhte ille–
C.20.434   And so of alle wykkede y *wol* here take veniaunce.
C.20.443   Thus by lawe,' quod oure lord, 'lede y *wol* fro hennes
C.21.100   And many wyles and wyt þat *wol* be a ledare.
C.21.192   He wente and woneth there and *wol* come at þe laste
C.21.194   Payeth parfitly as puyr treuthe *wolde*.
C.21.215   'For y *wol* dele today and deuyde grace
C.21.218   And wepne to fihte with þat *wol* neuere fayle.
C.21.225   Forthy,' quod grace, 'or y go y *wol* gyue ȝow tresor
C.21.233   And bi wit to wissen oþere as grace hem *wolde* teche.
C.21.394   Or vch man forȝeue oþer, and þat *wol* þe paternost[er]:
C.21.396   'Ȝe? bawe!' quod a breware, 'y *wol* nat ȝelde,
C.21.419   Forthy,' quod this vicory, 'bi verray god y *wolde*
C.21.423   Or in Rome, as here reule wo[l], þe relikes to kepe;
C.21.464   And with spiritus fortitudinis fecche hit, *wolle* he, null he.'
C.21.464   And with spiritus fortitudinis fecche hit, *null* he.'
C.21.468   And yf me lakketh to lyue by þe lawe *wol* y take hit
C.21.478   And rewle thy rewme in resoun [as] riht w[o]l and treuthe,
C.22.13   Ne wyht no[n] *wol* be his borwe ne wed hath [non] to legge;
C.22.18   And yf [hym] lust for to lape the lawe of kynde *wolde*
C.22.28   And greue men grettore then goed faith hit w[o]lde.
C.22.29   And spiritus iusticie shal iugen, *wol* he, nel he,
C.22.29   And spiritus iusticie shal iugen, wol he, *nel* he,
C.22.32   Of þat he weneth *wolde* falle yf his wit ne were;
C.22.38   Philosopheres forsoke wel[e] for they *wolde* be nedy
C.22.39   And woneden wel elyngly and *wolden* nat be riche.
C.22.107   To sese and soffre and se wher they *wolde*
C.22.140   'Allas!' quod Consience and cryede, '*wolde* crist of his grace
C.22.185   So harde he ȝede ouer myn heued hit *wol* be sene euere.
C.22.188   Haddest thow be hende,' quod y, 'thow *wost* haue asked leue.'
C.22.203   Awreke me ȝif ȝoure wille be for y *wolde* be hennes.'
C.22.204   'Yf thow wol[t] be wreke wende into vnite
C.22.235   Thei *wol* flatere to fare wel folk þat ben riche.
C.22.248   [And] y *wol* be ȝoure borwh: ȝe shal haue breed and clothes
C.22.253   And yf ȝe coueiteth cure kynde *wol* ȝow telle
C.22.260   *Wol* no tresorer taken hem wages, trauayle they neuere so sore,
C.22.265   Here ordre and here reule *wol* to haue a certeyne nombre
C.22.266   Of lewed and of lered; the lawe *wol* and asketh
C.22.271   Forthy y *wolde* witterly þat ȝe were in [þe] registre
C.22.288   Ac while he is in Westmynstre he *wol* be bifore
C.22.312   For fastyng of a fryday a feerde as he *wolde* deye.
C.22.333   Karpe y *wolde* with Contricioun and þerfore [cam y] heddere.'
C.22.380   'By Crist!' quod Consience tho, 'y *wol* bicome a pilgrime

wilne v *wilnen v.* A 12 wilne (1) wilnest (2) wilneþ (9); B 19 wilne (4)
   wilned (4) wilnest (1) wilneþ (10); C 21 wilne (2) wilned (2) wilnede
   (4) wilnen (3) wilnest (1) wilneth (7) wilnynge (2)

A. 1.87   Doþ þe werkis þerwiþ & *wilneþ* no man ille,
A. 2.30   Ȝif þou *wilnest* to wone wiþ treuþe in his blisse.
A. 3.100   Ȝif he *wilneþ* þe to wyue wilt þou hym haue?'
A. 4.139   'Whoso *wilneþ* hire to wyue for welþe of hire godis,
A. 6.41   And ȝif ȝe *wilneþ* wyte where þat wy dwelliþ
A. 6.47   Ac ȝe þat *wilneþ* to wende, þis is þe weye þider:
A. 7.243   Ac I hote þe,' quaþ hunger, 'as þou þin hele *wilnest*,
A.10.89   *Wilne* þou neuere in þis world, [wy], for to do betere,
A.11.75   *Wilneþ* neuere to wyte why that god wolde
A.11.80   For alle þat *wilneþ* to wyte þe [whyes] of god almiȝt,
A.11.82   Þat euere eft *wilneþ* to wyte why [þat] god wolde
A.11.89   Siþen he *wilneþ* to wyte which þei ben alle.
B. 1.89   Dooþ þe werkes þerwiþ and *wilneþ* no man ille,
B. 3.111   If he *wilneþ* þee to wif wiltow hym haue?'
B. 4.163   'Whoso *wilneþ* hire to wif for welþe of hire goodes,
B. 5.187   And bad me *wilne* to wepe my wikkednesse to amende.
B. 5.554   And if ye *wilneþ* wite where þat [wye] dwelleþ
B. 5.560   Ac [ye þat] *wilneþ* to wende, þis is þe weye þider.
B. 6.259   Ac I hote þee', quod hunger, 'as þow þyn hele *wilnest*,
B.10.122   *Wilneþ* neuere to wite why þat god wolde
B.10.127   For alle þat *wilneþ* to wite þe [whyes] of god almyȝty,
B.10.129   That euere [eft] *wilneþ* to wite why þat god wolde
B.10.136   Siþþe he *wilneþ* to wite whiche þei ben [alle].
B.10.345   Writen to wissen vs to *wilne* no richesse,
B.10.359   That whoso wolde and *wilneþ* wiþ crist to arise,
B.11.146   Gregorie wiste þis wel, and *wilned* in my soule
B.11.148   And [for] he wepte and *wilned* [þat I] were [saued]
B.14.173   Of þat þei *wilne* and wolde wanteþ hem noȝt here.
B.15.24   And whan I *wilne* and wolde animus ich hatte;

B.15.518 Alle þat *wilned* and wolde wiþ Inwit bileue it.
B.18.4 Til I weex wery of þe world and *wilned* eft to slepe
C. 1.8 Ha[u]e thei worship in this world thei *wilneth* no bettere;
C. 1.85 And doth þe werkes þerwith and *wilneth* no man ylle,
C. 3.132 And *wilned* to be wedded withouten his leue,
C. 3.148 Yf he *wilneth* the to wyue wolt thow hym haue?'
C. 3.384 For they *wilnen* and wolden as beste were for hemsulue
C. 4.158 'Hoso *wilneth* here to wy[u]e for welthe of here goodes
C. 4.192 To wage thyn and helpe wynne þat thow *wilnest* aftur
C. 6.32 Me *wilnynge* þat men wen[t]e y were as in auer
C. 6.41 *Wilnynge* þat men wen[d]e myne werkes weren þe beste
C. 7.198 And hoso *wilneth* to wyte where þat treuthe woneth
C.12.20 That *wilneth* nat þe wedewe bote for to welde here godes.
C.12.81 Gregori wiste this wel and *wilned* to my soule
C.12.83 And for a *wilnede* wepynge þat y were ysaued
C.13.94 In þat a *wilneth* and wolde vch wyht as hymsulue.
C.16.184 And when y *wilne* and wolde Animus y hatte;
C.17.191 Ite in vniuersum mundum, sethe ʒe *wilne* þe name
C.17.269 Alle þat *wilnede* and wolde with inwit bileue hit.
C.18.259 As we *wilnede* and wolde with mou[th]e and herte aske.
C.19.332 Goed wil, goed word bothe, wischen and *wilnen*
C.20.4 Til y waxe wery of the world and *wilnede* eefte to slepe
C.21.68 And moche wo in this world *wilnen* and soffren.

wilt(ow > willen; wymmen > womman

wyn *n win n.* A 3; B 12; C 13 wyn (12) wyne (1)
A.Pr.107 'W[hit] *wyn* of osay, & wyn of gascoyne,
A.Pr.107 'W[hit] wyn of osay, & *wyn* of gascoyne,
A. 1.31 And al he wytide it *wyn* þ[at] wykkide dede.
B.Pr.229 'Whit *wyn* of Oseye and wyn of Gascoigne,
B.Pr.229 'Whit wyn of Oseye and *wyn* of Gascoigne,
B. 1.31 And al he witte it *wyn* þat wikked dede:
B. 1.32 Thoruʒ *wyn* and þoruʒ wommen þer was loth acombred,
B. 5.178 Ac ouþer while whan *wyn* comeþ, [whan] I drynke at eue,
B.10.367 Or delit in *wyn* and wildefowel and wite any in defaute.
B.13.61 For þis doctour on þe heiʒe dees drank *wyn* so faste;
B.14.251 Ne dooþ hym noʒt dyne delicatly ne drynke *wyn* ofte.
B.16.244 And doon hym worship with breed and wiþ *wyn* boþe,
B.17.72 Wiþ *wyn* and with oille hise woundes he wasshed,
B.19.109 Water into *wyn* turnede, as holy writ telleþ.
B.19.111 For *wyn* is likned to lawe and lifholynesse,
C.Pr.233 'Whit *wyn* of Oseye and wyn of gascoyne,
C.Pr.233 'Whit wyn of Oseye and *wyn* of gascoyne,
C. 1.30 And al he witte [it] *wyn* [þat] wikked dede:
C. 1.31 Thorw *wyn* and thorw wom[e]n there was loot acombred;
C. 6.160 Ac other while when *wyn* cometh and when y drynke late at euen
C. 9.254 Cam no *wyn* in his wombe thorw þe woke longe
C.11.108 Bothe wymmen and *wyn*, wr[a]the, [enuy] and slewthe
C.15.65 For [this] doctour at þe hey deys dranke *wyn* [so] faste–
C.16.91 Ne doth men dyne delicatlyche ne drynke *wyne* ofte.
C.18.261 Worschipe hym with *wyn* and with breed bothe
C.19.71 With *wyn* and with oyle his woundes he gan li[th]e,
C.21.109 [Watur into *wyn* turned], As holy writ telleth.
C.21.111 For *wyn* is likned to lawe and lyfholinesse

wynchestre *n prop Winchestre n.* A 1; B 1; C 2
A. 5.119 To *wynchestre* & to wy I [wente] to þe feire
B. 5.203 To Wy and to *Wynchestre* I wente to þe Feyre
C. 6.211 To wy and to *wynchestre* y wente to þe fayre
C.13.52 And ʒut thow they wende o way as to *wynchestre* fayre

wynd *n wind n.(1)* A 7 wynd (6) wyndis (1); B 14 wynd (11) wyndes (3); C 13 wynd (9) wyndes (2)
A. 5.14 And þe southwestryne *wynd* on satirday at eue
A. 5.72 Such *wynd* in my wombe wexiþ er I dyne.
A. 8.55 Ac to bigge watir ne *wynd*, ne wyt is þe þridde,
A. 9.26 Þe *wynd*, & þe watir, & þe waggyng of þe boot,
A. 9.31 Þe wylnd wolde wiþ þe watir þe boot ouerþrowe.
A. 9.36 Þat as *wyndis* & watris wa[l]wen aboute;
A.10.4 Wiþ *wynd* & wiþ watir wi[tti]liche enioynede.
B. 3.331 Also wroþ as þe *wynd* weex Mede in a while.
B. 5.14 And þe Southwestrene *wynd* on Saterday at euen
B. 7.53 Ac to bugge water ne *wynd* ne wit ne fir þe ferþe,
B. 8.30 The *wynd* and þe water and þe [waggyng of þe boot]
B. 8.35 The *wynd* wolde wiþ þe water þe boot ouerþrowe.
B. 8.40 That as *wyndes* and [watres] walkeþ aboute;
B. 9.4 Wiþ *wynd* and wiþ water witt[i]ly enioynede.
B.15.363 As of wedres and *wyndes* þei warned men ofte.
B.16.25 'For *wyndes*, wiltow wite', quod he, 'to witen it fro fallyng:
B.16.27 The world is a wikked *wynd* to hem þat willen truþe.
B.16.28 Coueitise comþ of þat *wynd* and crepeþ among þe leues
B.16.31 The flessh is a fel *wynd*, and in flouryng tyme,
B.17.163 Boþe wolkne and þe *wynd*, water and erþe,
B.17.356 And wente awey as *wynd* and þerwiþ I awakede.

C. 3.484 As wroth as [þe] *wynd* wax mede þeraftur:
C. 5.116 And the southweste *wynde* on saturday At euene
C. 9.56 Þat is wit and watur and *wynde* and fuyre the ferthe;
C.10.34 The *wynde* and þe water and [þe] wag[g]yng of the bote
C.10.46 That as *wyndes* and wederes wal[k]eth aboute;
C.10.131 With *wynd* and with water wittyly enioyned.
C.12.190 Ne *wynde* ne wederes as in wynter tym[e],
C.15.241 The Cryket by kynde of þe fuyr and corleu by þe *wynde*,
C.18.29 The fruyt of this fayre tre fro thre wikkede *wyndes*
C.18.31 The world is a wikkede *wynd* to hem þat wo[l] treuthe;
C.18.32 Couetyse cometh of þat *wynde* and Caritas hit abiteth
C.18.35 Thenne is þe flesch a fel *wynde* and in flouryng tyme
C.19.336 And wente away as *wynd* and þerwith y awakede.

wynde *v winden v.(2)* &> *wynd* B 1
B. 5.548 I weue and I *wynde* and do what truþe hoteþ.

wyndow *n windoue n.* A 3 wyndowe (2) wyndowis (1); B 4 wyndow (1) wyndowes (3); C 3 wyndowe (1) wyndowes (2)
A. 3.47 'We haue a *wyndowe* [in] werching wile stonde vs wel heiʒe;
A. 3.50 'Wiste I þat,' quaþ þe womman, 'þere nis *wyndowe* ne auter
A. 3.61 To writen in *wyndowis* of ʒoure wel dedis,
B. 3.48 'We haue a *wyndow* in werchynge wole [stonden] vs [wel] hye;
B. 3.61 Wowes do whiten and *wyndowes* glaʒen,
B. 3.65 To writen in *wyndowes* of hir wel dedis,
B. 3.70 To writen in *wyndowes* of youre wel dedes,
C. 3.51 'We han a *wyndowe* awurchynge wol stande vs [wel] heye;
C. 3.65 Bothe *wyndowes* and wowes y wol amende and glase
C. 3.69 To writen [i]n *wyndowes* of eny wel dedes,

wyne > wyn

wynge *n wing n.* B 1; C 1 wenge
B.12.265 And wel awey of *wynge* swifter þan þe Pecock,
C.14.186 And swettore of sauour and swyftore of *weng[e]*.

wynke *v winken v.* B 2 wynke (1) wynked (1); C 2 wynke (1) wynkyng (1)
B. 4.152 For I seiʒ Mede in þe moot halle on men of lawe *wynke*
B. 4.154 Waryn wisdom *wynked* vpon Mede
C.Pr.11 *Wynkyng* as hit were, witterliche y sigh hit;
C. 4.148 Mede in the mothalle tho on men of lawe gan *wynke*

wynkyng *ger winkinge ger.* &> *wynke* A 2; B 3 wynkyng (2) wynkynge (1); C 1 wynkynge
A. 5.3 Þanne wakide I of my *wynkyng*, & wo was wiþalle
A. 5.203 Þanne wakide he of his *wynkyng* & wypide his eiʒen;
B. 5.3 Thanne waked I of my *wynkyng* and wo was withalle
B. 5.361 Thanne waked he of his *wynkyng* and wiped hise eiʒen;
C.11.165 And in a *wynkynge* y warth and wonderliche me mette

wynlyche *adv winli adv.* A 1
A.12.46 I shal þe wisse [*wynlyche*] where þat he dwelleþ'.

wynnen *v winnen v.* A 17 wan (3) wynne (9) wynnen (1) wynneþ (3) wonne (1); B 48 wan (6) wynne (18) wynnen (7) wynnest (1) wynneþ (8) wonne (4) wonnen (1) ywonne (3); C 52 wan (7) wynne (22) wynnen (3) wynneth (9) wonne (6) ywonne (5)
A.Pr.22 [*Wonne*] þat þise wastours wiþ glotonye destroiʒeþ.
A. 1.153 For þ[eiʒ ʒe] be trewe of ʒoure tunge & treweliche *wynne*,
A. 3.224 Godis mede & his mercy þerwith miʒte þou *wynne*.
A. 4.53 Wysdom *wan* þo & so dede wyt also
A. 4.63 And tok mede wiþ hem mercy to *wynne*.
A. 5.25 And *wynne* þat he wastide wiþ sum maner craft,
A. 5.228 Al þat I wykkidly *wan* siþen I wyt hadde,
A. 5.242 Ne neuere wen[e] to *wynne* wiþ craft þat [I owe],
A. 7.22 Helpiþ hem werche wiʒtly þat *wynne* ʒoure foode.'
A. 7.88 My wyf shal haue of þat I *wan* wiþ treuþe, & namore,
A. 7.236 God ʒiueþ [hem] his blissing þat here liflode so *wynneþ.*'
A. 7.302 I warne ʒow werkmen, *wynneþ* while ʒe mowe,
A. 8.64 Þat trewely taken, & trewely *wynnen*,
A. 9.73 And þoruʒ his labour or his lond his liflode *wynneþ*,
A.10.9 And wolde *wynne* hire awey with wyles ʒif he miʒte.
A.11.185 And alle kyne crafty men þat cunne here foode *wynne*,
A.11.276 And ʒif I shal werke be here werkis to *wynne* me heuene,
B.Pr.22 *Wonnen* þat [þise] wastours with glotonye destruyeþ;
B.Pr.179 Ne hangen it aboute [his] hals al Engelond to *wynne*;
B. 1.179 For þouʒ ye be trewe of youre tonge and treweliche *wynne*,
B. 3.159 And doþ men lese þoruʒ hire loue þat lawe myʒte *wynne*;
B. 3.334 That ʒyuen ʒiftes, [takeþ] yeme], þe victorie *wynneþ*
B. 3.352 That þeiʒ we worship and with Mede haue victorie,
B. 4.35 Theras wraþe and wranglynge is þer *wynne* þei siluer,
B. 4.67 Tho [*wan*] Wisdom and sire waryn þe witty
B. 4.77 And token Mede myd hem mercy to *wynne*.
B. 5.25 And *wynnen* his wastyng wiþ som maner crafte.

B. 5.92   Than þou3 I hadde þis wouke *ywonne* a weye of Essex chese.
B. 5.262   Ne þyne heires after þee haue ioie of þat þow *wynnest*,
B. 5.264   And þat was *wonne* wiþ wrong wiþ wikked men be despended.
B. 5.456   Al þat I wikkedly *wan* siþen I wit hadde,
B. 5.468   Ne neuere wene to *wynne* wiþ craft þat I owe;
B. 6.20   Helpeþ hym werche wi3tliche þat *wynneþ* youre foode.'
B. 6.96   My wif shal haue of þat I *wan* wiþ truþe and na moore,
B. 6.133   Ye wasten þat men *wynnen* wiþ trauaille and tene.
B. 6.162   For [þei] wasten and *wynnen* no3t and [þo] worþ neuere
B. 6.321   Ac I warne yow werkmen, *wynneþ* whil ye mowe
B. 7.62   That treweliche taken and treweliche *wynnen*
B. 8.82   And þoru3 his labour or his land his liflode *wynneþ*,
B. 9.9   And wolde *wynne* hire awey wiþ wiles [if] he my3te.
B. 9.71   And widewes þat han no3t wherwith to *wynne* hem hir foode,
B. 9.111   For þei mote werche and *wynne* and þe world sustene;
B.10.86   And þe moore he *wynneþ* and welt welþes and richesse,
B.10.392   And if I sh[al] werche by hir werkes to *wynne* me heuene,
B.10.456   But wit [ne] wisedom *wan* neuere þe maistrie
B.11.202   And blody breþeren we bicome þere of o body *ywonne*,
B.12.44   Alisaundre þat al *wan*, elengliche ended.
B.13.145   Boþe wiþ wer[k] and with wor[d] fonde his loue to *wynne*;
B.13.377   So, [wolde he] or no3t wolde, *wynnen* I wolde.
B.14.103   Than richesse ri3tfulliche *wonne* and resonably despended?'
B.14.295   *Wynneþ* he no3t wiþ wi3tes false ne wiþ vnseled mesures,
B.14.315   And [þou3] he chaffareþ he chargeþ no losse, mowe he charite
           wynne:
B.15.129   Ac þing þat wikkedly is *wonne*, and wiþ false sleightes,
B.15.291   And *wan* wiþ hise hondes þat his wombe neded.
B.18.140   And þat was tynt þoru3 tree, tree shal it *wynne*.
B.18.353   So þat þoru3 gile þow gete þoru3 grace it is *ywonne*.
B.19.32   To make lordes of laddes of lond þat he *wynneþ*
B.19.230   [To *wynne* wiþ truþe þat] þe world asketh;
B.19.235   [By] sellynge and buggynge hir bilyue to *wynne*.
B.19.239   To *wynne* wiþ hir liflode bi loore of his techynge;
B.19.245   And some to ryde and to recouere þat [vnri3t]fully was *wonne*:
B.19.246   He wissed hem *wynne* it ayein þoru3 wightnesse of handes
B.19.350   Wheiþer he *wynne* wiþ right, wiþ wrong or wiþ vsure.'
B.20.15   He synneþ no3t, sooþliche, þat so *wynneþ* his foode.
B.20.124   His wepne was al wiles, to *wynnen* and to hiden;
C.Pr.24   And *wonne* þat þis wastors with glotony destrueth.
C. 1.175   For thow 3e ben trewe of 3oure tong[e] and treweliche *wynne*
C. 3.197   Thorw which loueday is loste þat leute myhte *wynne*;
C. 3.248   The leste ladde þat longeth with hym, be þe londe *ywonne*,
C. 3.253   Al þat his men may *wynne*, do ther[mid] here beste.
C. 3.486   That 3eueth 3eftes, taketh 3eme, the victorie a *wynneth*
C. 3.499   Worschipe a *wynneth* þat wol 3eue mede
C. 4.73   And token mede [myd] hem mercy to *wynne*.
C. 4.192   To wage thyn and helpe *wynne* þat thow wilnest aftur
C. 5.126   He bad wastoures [g]o wurche and *wynne* here sustinaunce
C. 6.190   To *wynne* to my wille wymmen with gyle,
C. 6.255   Ne thyn heyres, as y hope, haue ioye of þat thow *wonne*
C. 6.258   'With false wordes and w[ittes] haue y *wonne* my godes
C. 6.310   Al-þat-y-wikkedly-*wan*-sithen-y-witte-hadde-
C. 6.322   Ne neuere wene to *wynne* with craft þat y knowe;
C. 7.234   And al þe wallyng is of wyt for wil ne sholde hit *wynne*;
C. 8.18   Helpeth hym worche wi[3t]liche þat *wynneth* 3oure fode.'
C. 8.63   To pilgrimag[e] as palmeres doen pardon to *wynne*.
C. 8.105   My wyf shal haue of þat y *wan* with treuthe and no more
C. 8.234   Yf thow hast *wonne* auht wikkedliche, wiseliche despene hit:
C. 8.341   Ac y warne 3ow werkmen, *wynneth* whiles 3e mowe
C. 9.252   Ac while a wrouhte in þe world and *wan* his mete with treuthe
C.10.136   And wol[d]e *wynne* here awaye with wyles [3if] he myhte.
C.11.66   Ac þe more a *wynneth* and hath þe world at his wille
C.11.219   And yf we sholde wurche aftur here werkes to *wy[n]nen* vs heuene
C.11.282   That wit ne witnesse *wan* neuere þe maistrie
C.12.6   He shal asoile [the] thus sone how so euere thow *wynne* hit.
C.12.110   And blody bretherne we bycome there of o body *ywonne*,
C.12.227   That chaff[ar]en as chapmen and chide bote they *wynne*
C.12.235   For, how [euere hit] be *ywonne*, bot hit [be] wel despene[d]
C.13.74   That oure lord loketh aftur of vch a lyf þat *wynneth*
C.15.143   Fond [with] wit & word his loue to *wynne*,
C.15.154   Y wolde, and y will hadde, *wynnen* all fraunce
C.16.130   *Wynneth* he nat with w[ih]tus false ne with vnselede mesures
C.16.149   And thogh he chaffare he chargeth no loes may he charite *wynne*:
C.16.276   Ac thyng þat wykkedliche is *wonne* and with fals sleythes
C.17.18   And *wan* with his handes al þat hym nedede.
C.19.236   3ut *wan* ne nat with wrong ne with queynte sleythes;
C.19.244   Sethe he withoute wyles *wan* and wel myhte atymye
C.19.250   [That that wickedliche is *wonne* to wasten hit and make frendes?]
C.20.143   And] that was tynt thorw tre, tre shal hit *wynne*.
C.20.396   So þat [thorw] gyle was gete thorw grace is now *ywonne*
C.21.32   To make lordes of laddes of lond þat he *wynneth*

C.21.230   To *wynne* with treuthe þat the world asketh,
C.21.235   [By] sullyng and buggynge here bileue to *wynne*.
C.21.239   To *wynne* with here lyflode bi lore of his techynge];
C.21.245   And somme to ryde & to rekeuere that vnrihtulliche was *wonne*:
C.21.246   He wissede [h]e[m] *wynne* hit a3eyn thorw whitnesse of handes
C.21.350   Where he *wynne* with riht, with wrong or with vsure.'
C.22.15   He synegeth nat sothlich þat so *wynneth* his fode.
C.22.124   His wepne was al wyles, to *wynnen* and to hyden;

wynneres n *winnere n.* A 1; C 1 wynners
A. 7.148   Fro wastours þat waite *wynneres* to shende.
C.Pr.226   Webbesteres and walkeres and *wynners* with handes,

wynnestere n *n.i.d.* A 1 wynstere; B 1
A. 5.129   My wyf was a *wynstere* & wollene cloþ made,
B. 5.213   My wif was a [*wynnestere*] and wollen cloþ made,

wynnyng ger *winninge ger.(1)* A 3; B 5 wynnyng (3) wynnynge (2); C 14
           wynnyng (1) wynnynge (10) wynnynges (2) wynnyngus (1)
A. 5.33   'Let no *wynnyng* forwanye hem whiles þei ben 3onge'.
A. 5.94   Ac of his *wynnyng* I wepe and weile þe tyme.
A. 8.27   And siþen selle it a3en & saue þe *wynnyng*,
B. 5.35   'Late no *wynnyng* [forwanye hem] while þei be yonge,
B. 5.114   [Ac of his] *wynnyng* I wepe and waille þe tyme.
B. 7.25   And siþenes selle it ayein and saue þe *wynnyng*,
B.19.285   Ne *wynnynge* ne wele of worldliche richesse,
B.19.453   But [it soune], as by sighte, somwhat to *wynnyng*.
C. 5.98   Suche a *wynnynge* hym warth thorw w[y]rdes of grace:
C. 5.137   'Late no *wynnynge* forwanyen hem while thei ben 3onge
C. 6.293   Then haue my fode and my fyndynge of fals menne *wynnyngus*.
C. 6.305   For an hore of here ers *wynnynge* may hardiloker tythe
C. 7.75   But harlotrie and horedom or elles of som *wynnynge*;
C. 9.26   A3en clene Consience for couetyse of *wynnynge*.
C. 9.29   And sethe sullen hit a3eyn and saue þe *wynnyng[e]*,
C. 9.208   Long labour and litte *wynnynge* and at the laste they aspyde
C.11.77   For is no wit worth now but hit of *wynnynge* soune.
C.12.17   To restitute resonably for al vnrihtfole *wynnynge*.
C.16.261   Of vsererus, of hores, of alle euel *wynnynges*,
C.17.36   Toke lyflode of luyther *wynnynges* in all here lyf tyme.
C.21.285   Ne *wynnynge* ne wel[e] o[f] wordliche richesse,
C.21.453   Bote hit sowne, as bi sihte, somwhat to *wynnynge*.

wynse v *wincen v.* C 1
C. 4.22   For hit is þe wone of wil to *wynse* and to kyke

wynstere > wynnestere

wynter n *winter n.* A 8; B 27 wynter (22) wyntre (1) wyntres (4); C 26
           wynter (21) wynteres (1) wyntres (2) wyntur (2)
A. 1.99   And nou3t to fasten a friday in fyue score *wynter*,
A. 3.38   And þei3 falshed hadde folewid þe þis fiftene *wynter*,
A. 3.179   Wendist þat *wynter* wolde han last euere;
A. 5.111   In a torn tabbard of twelue *wynter* age,
A. 5.141   Sheo haþ yholde huxterie elleuene *wynter*.
A. 6.30   I haue ben his folewere al þis fourty *wynter*;
A. 6.101   Happily an hundrit *wynter* er þou eft entre.
A. 8.115   þe foulis in þe firmament, who fynt hem a *wynter*?
B. 1.101   And nau3t to fasten o friday in fyue score *wynter*,
B. 3.39   And [þei3] Fals[hede] hadde yfolwed þee alle þise fift[ene] *wynter*,
B. 3.192   Wendest þat *wynter* wolde han ylasted euere;
B. 5.195   In a [torn] tabard of twelf *wynter* age;
B. 5.225   She haþ holden hukkerye [elleuene *wynter*].
B. 5.415   I haue be preest and person passynge þritty *wynter*,
B. 5.542   I haue ben his folwere al þis [fourty] *wynter*,
B. 5.615   Happily an hundred *wynter* er þow eft entre.
B. 7.133   The foweles in þe [firmament], who fynt hem at *wynter*?
B.11.47   And folwed me fourty *wynter* and a fifte moore,
B.12.3   I haue folwed þee, in feiþ, þise fyue and fourty *wynter*,
B.14.64   It is founden þat fourty *wynter* folk lyuede withouten tulying,
B.14.68   That manye *wyntres* men lyueden and no mete ne tulieden.
B.14.69   Seuene slepe, as seiþ þe book, seuene hundred *wynter*
B.14.113   And wilde wormes in wodes, þoru3 *wyntres* þow hem greuest
B.14.161   And yet is *wynter* for hem worse, for weetshoed þei [gange],
B.14.177   Wo in *wynter* tymes for wantynge of cloþes,
B.14.314   Than he may [soþly] deserue, in somer or in *wynter*;
B.15.288   Foweles hym fedde, fele *wyntres* wiþ alle,
B.17.222   That werchen and waken in *wyntres* ny3tes,
B.17.230   And melteþ hire my3t into mercy, as men may se in *wyntre*
B.17.248   Ac hewe fir at a flynt foure hundred *wynter*;
B.18.133   Siþ þis barn was ybore ben xxxti *wynter* passed,
B.18.284   And siþen I [was] seised seuene [þousand] *wynter*
B.18.296   Thise þritty *wynter*, as I wene, [he wente aboute] and preched.
B.18.299   And þus hath he trolled forþ [lik a tidy man] þise two and þritty
           wynter.
B.20.343   I knew swich oon ones, no3t eighte *wynter* [passed],
C. 3.41   [And] Falshede yfonde the al this fourty *wyntur*,

C. 6.203   In a tore tabard of twelue *wynter* age;
C. 6.233   [He] ha[th] holde hokkerye this eleuene *wynter*.'
C. 7.30   I haue be prest and persoun passynge thritty *wyntur*
C. 7.189   [I]ch haue ybe his foloware al this fourty *wynter*
C. 7.267   Hapliche an hundred *wynter* ar thow eft entre.
C. 9.78   And wo in *wynter* tym[e] and wakynge on nyhtes
C.12.187   A[c] sedes þat ben sowen and mowen soffre *wyntres*
C.12.190   Ne wynde ne wederes as in *wynter* tym[e],
C.12.199   But as an hosebonde hopeth aftur an hard *wynter*,
C.14.3   Y haue folewed the, in fayth, mo then fourty *wynter*
C.15.263   Hit is founde þat fourty *wynter* folke lyuede and tylde nat
C.15.267   That manye *wynter* men lyuede and no mete ne tylede.
C.15.268   Seuene slepen, as saith þe boek, more then syxty *wynter*
C.15.289   And wilde wormes in wodes, thorw *wyntres* thow hem greuest
C.16.14   And ʒut is *wynter* for hem worse for weetshoed þey g[ang]e,
C.16.148   Then he may sothly deserue in Somur or in *wynter*;
C.17.23   Marie Egipciaca eet in thritty *wynter*
C.19.188   That worchen and waken in *wynteres* nyhtes
C.19.196   And melteth myhte into mercy, as we may se a *wynter*
C.19.214   Ac hewe fuyr at a flynt foure hundret *wynter*,
C.20.136   Sethe this barn was ybore ben thritty *wynter* ypassed,
C.20.309   And sethen we haen ben sesed seuene thousand *wynter*
C.20.329   This thritty *wynter*, as y wene, and wente aboute and prechede.
C.20.332   Thus hath he trolled forth lyke a tydy man this two & thritty
       wynter.
C.22.343   Y knewe such oen ones, nat eyhte *wynter* passed,

wiped v *wipen* v. A 2 wypide; B 6 wiped (5) wipeden (1); C 5 wipeden (1) wypede (1) wypeden (2) wypeth (1)

A. 2.182   Wysshen hym & *wypide* him & wounde hym in cloþis,
A. 5.203   Þanne wakide he of his wynkyng & *wypide* his eiʒen;
B. 2.223   Wesshen hym & *wiped* hym & wounden hym in cloutes,
B. 5.361   Thanne waked he of his wynkyng and *wiped* hise eiʒen;
B.13.28   Thei wesshen and *wipeden* and wenten to þe dyner.
B.13.459   Why he ne hadde [w]asshen it or *wiped* it wiþ a brusshe.
B.16.167   And I awaked þerwiþ and *wiped* myne eiʒen
B.16.228   Wessh hir feet and *wiped* hem, and afterward þei eten
C. 2.233   Thei woschen hym and *wypeden* hym and wonden hym in cloutes,
C. 9.251   Wascheth and *wypeth* and with þe furste sitteth.
C.15.31   They woschen and *wypeden* and wenten to þe dyner.
C.15.37   [They] woschen and *wipeden* and wenten to sytten.
C.18.243   Wosch he[re] feet and *wypede* hem and afturward they eten.

wypene > *wepene*

wyr n *wir* n. B 1

B. 2.11   Fetisliche hire fyngres were fretted with gold *wyr*

wirche > *werchen*

wirdes n *werd* n. C 4 wirdes (1) wyrdes (2) wyrdus (1)

C. 3.241   And as his *wyrdus* were ordeyned at þe wille of oure lorde.
C. 5.98   Suche a wynnyng hym warth thorw *w[y]rdes* of grace:
C.12.209   And out of wo into wele ʒoure *wirdes* shal chaunge."
C.14.32   That wit wexeth therof and oþer *w[y]rdes* bothe:

wis adj *wise* adj. &> *wissen* A 13 wys (5) wise (7) wysere (1); B 33 wis (6) wys (3) wise (19) wiser (3) wisest (2); C 37 wis (1) wys (6) wise (2) wyse (25) wiser (1) wisest (1) wysor (1)

A.Pr.48   Wenten forþ in here wey wiþ many *wise* talis,
A. 1.70   Þat suche *wise* wordis of holy writ shewide,
A. 4.55   And warnide wrong þo wiþ suche a *wys* tale:
A. 6.1   Ac þere w[ere] fewe men so *wys* þat þe [wey] þider couþe,
A. 8.169   Þat han þe [welþe of þis] world, & *wise* men ben holden,
A. 9.84   [ʒ]e *wise* suffriþ þe vnwise with ʒow to libbe,
A.10.17   Is a *wys* kniʒt withalle, sire [inwit] he hatte,
A.10.70   Fro folies, & fynde hem til þei ben *wise*.
A.10.71   A[c] iche wiʒt in þis world þat haþ *wys* vndirstonding
A.11.5   'Wel art þou *wys*, wyt,' quaþ she, 'any wisdomis to telle
A.11.8   Wiþ suche *wise* wordis to wisse any foolis!
A.11.272   And was þere neuere in þis world to *wysere* of werkis,
A.12.38   Þan held I vp myn handes to scripture þe *wise*
B.Pr.48   Wenten forþ in hire wey wiþ many *wise* tales,
B.Pr.208   Forþi ech a *wis* wiʒt I warne, wite wel his owene.'
B. 1.72   That swiche *wise* wordes of holy writ shewed,
B. 4.69   And warnede wrong þo with swich a *wis* tale:
B. 5.513   Ac þere was [wye] noon so *wys* þe wey þider kouþe,
B. 7.191   That haue þe welþe of þis world and *wise* men ben holden
B. 8.94   [Ye *wise*] suffreþ þe vnwise wiþ yow to libbe,
B. 9.18   Is a *wis* knyʒt wiþalle, sire Inwit he hatte,
B. 9.81   Than nempnynge of a name and he neuer þe *wiser*.
B.10.5   'Wel artow *wis*, [wit', quod she], 'any wisdomes to telle
B.10.8   'Wiþ swiche *wise* wordes to wissen any sottes!'
B.10.280   That goddes word wercheþ noʒt on [*wis*] ne on lewed
B.10.377   'This is a long lesson', quod I, 'and litel am I þe *wiser*;
B.10.390   Of hir wordes þei wissen vs for *wisest* as in hir tyme,

B.10.403   Forþi *wise* witted men and wel ylettrede clerkes
B.11.256   And alle þe *wise* þat euere were, by auʒt I kan aspye,
B.11.272   *Wiser* þan Salomon was bereþ witnesse and tauʒte
B.11.283   If preestes weren [*wise*] þei wolde no siluer take
B.11.394   The *wise* and þe witty wroot þus in þe bible:
B.12.50   That *wise* wordes wolde shewe and werche þe contrarie:
B.13.292   [Or for his crafty konnynge or of clerkes þe *wisest*,
B.13.434   Ther *wise* men were, witnesseþ goddes wordes,
B.14.18   Dowel shal wasshen it and wryngen it þoruʒ a *wis* confessour:
B.14.167   And yliche witty and *wise*, if þee wel hadde liked.
B.15.548   [Mynne] ye noʒt, *wise* men, how þo men honoured
B.17.262   Forþi beþ war, ye *wise* men þat wiþ þe world deleþ;
B.18.234   That alle þe *wise* of þis world in o wit acor[de]den
B.19.84   Wherfore and why *wise* men þat tyme,
B.19.166   And as alle þise *wise* wyes weren togideres
B.19.244   As Astronomyens þoruʒ Astronomye, and Philosofres *wise*.
B.19.296   And couered hym vnder conseille of Caton þe *wise*:
B.20.33   Wenynge is no wysdom, ne *wys* ymaginacion:
B.20.302   And woundede wel wikkedly many a *wys* techere
C.Pr.49   Wenten forth [i]n here way with many *wyse* tales
C. 1.69   That suche *wyse* wordes of holy writ shewede
C. 3.7   And yf she worche wysely and by *wys* men consayl
C. 4.44   And speke *wyse* wordes a longe while togederes.
C. 5.139   And so wrot the *wyse* to wyssen vs alle:
C. 6.24   Wene y were witty and *wiser* then another;
C. 6.28   To telle eny tale; y trowed me *wysor*
C. 7.94   There *wyse* men were, wittnesseth goddes wordes,
C. 7.158   Ac þer was wye non so *wys* þat þe way thider couthe
C. 8.239   As *wyse* men haen wryten and as witnesseth Genesis
C. 9.51   Beth ywar, ʒe *wis* men and witty of þe lawe,
C. 9.337   That haen þe welthe of this world and *wise* men ben holde
C.10.91   "ʒe wordliche *wyse*, vnwyse þat ʒe soffre,
C.10.144   Is a *wise* knyhte withalle, sire inwit he hatte,
C.10.307   The more he is worthy and worth, of *wyse* and goed ypresed.'
C.11.5   'Wel artow *wyse*,' quod she to wyt, 'suche wysdomes to shewe
C.11.96   And clergi[es] wedded wyf, as *wyse* as hymsulue
C.11.217   Were wonder goed and *wisest* in here tyme
C.11.221   Thenne wrouhte [we] vnwysly for alle ʒoure *wyse* techynge.
C.12.142   And alle þe *wyse* þat euere were, by auhte y can aspye,
C.13.28   Worthiore as by holy writ and *wyse* fylosofres.
C.13.44   Wol no *wys* man be wroth ne his wed take–
C.13.65   ʒe wyte, ʒe *wyse* men, what this is to mene:
C.13.184   'Y haue wonder in my wit, so *wys* as thow art holden,
C.13.202   And so witnesseth *wyse* and wisseth þe frenche:
C.14.193   Wher þey ben in hell or in heuene or Aristotel þe *wyse*.
C.16.20   And yliche witty and *wys* and lyue withoute nede;
C.16.229   "Non plus sapere," saide þe *wyse*, [laste synne of pruyde wexe,]
C.19.228   Forthy beth ywar, ʒe *wyse* men þat with the world deleth,
C.20.243   That alle þe *wyse* of th[is] world in o wit acordede
C.20.354   Beth ywaer, ʒe *wyse* clerkes and ʒe witty of lawe,
C.21.84   [Wherefore & why *wyse* men þat tyme,
C.21.166   And as al thise *wyse* weyes weren togyderes
C.21.244   A[s] astro[nomy]ens thorw astronomye, & philosopheres *wyse*;
C.21.296   And keuered hym vnder consayl of Caton the *wyse*:
C.22.33   Wenyng is no wisdoem ne *wyse* ymaginacioun:
C.22.302   And wounded wel wykkedly many a *wys* techare

wisch- > *wisshen*

wisdom n *wisdom* n. A 15 wisdom (8) wysdom (6) wisdomis (1); B 25 wisdom (18) wysdom (1) wisdomes (2) wisedom (4); C 16 wisdoem (4) wysdoem (2) wisdom (3) wysdom (5) wysdomes (2)

A. 2.98   Werchiþ be *wysdom* & be wyt aftir;
A. 4.24   Ac [o]n wary[n] *wisdom*, and witty his fere
A. 4.49   Wrong was aferd þo & *wisdom* he souʒte
A. 4.53   *Wysdom* wan þo & so dede wyt also
A. 4.60   Wrong þanne on *wisdom* wepi[de] hym to helpe,
A. 4.62   Þanne *wisdom* & wyt wente togidere
A. 4.68   Ac *wisdom* & wyt were aboute faste
A. 4.74   'God wot,' quaþ *wysdom*, 'þat were not þe beste.
A. 4.87   'For he haþ wagid me wel as *wysdom* hym tauʒte
A. 4.141   War[yn] *wisdom* þo, ne [witty] his fere,
A. 7.46   But it be of *wysdom* or of wyt þi werkmen to chaste;
A. 7.198   'Here now,' quaþ hungir, '& holde it for a *wisdom*:
A.10.111   And for *wisdom* is writen & witnessid in chirches:
A.11.5   'Wel art þou wys, wyt,' quaþ she, 'any *wisdomis* to telle
A.11.17   *Wisdom* and wyt now is not worþ a risshe
B. 2.134   Wercheþ by *wisdom* and by wit [after];
B. 4.27   Oon waryn *wisdom* and witty his feere
B. 4.63   Wrong was afered þ[o] and *wisdom* he souʒte
B. 4.67   Tho [wan] *Wisdom* and sire waryn þe witty
B. 4.74   Thanne wowede wrong *wisdom* ful yerne
B. 4.76   [Thanne *Wisdom* and wit] wenten togidres
B. 4.81   Ac *wisdom* and wit were aboute faste

B. 4.87	'God woot', quod *wisdom*, 'þat were noȝt þe beste.
B. 4.100	'For he haþ waged me wel as *wisdom* hym tauȝte
B. 4.154	Waryn *wisdom* wynked vpon Mede
B. 6.51	But if [it be] of *wisdom* or of wit þi werkmen to chaste;
B. 6.212	'Here now', quod hunger, 'and hoold it for a *wisdom*:
B.10.5	'Wel artow wis, [wit', quod she], 'any *wisdomes* to telle
B.10.17	*Wisdom* and wit now is noȝt worþ a [risshe]
B.10.435	Of wit and of *wisedom* wiþ dampned soules wonye.
B.10.456	But wit [ne] *wisedom* wan neuere þe maistrie
B.11.419	The *wisedom* and þe wit of god, he was put fram blisse.
B.12.137	And seiden hir wordes [ne] hir *wisdomes* [w]as but a folye;
B.12.295	And wit and *wisdom*', quod þat wye, 'was som tyme tresor
B.14.209	Of wit and of *wisdom*, þat fer awey is bettre
B.14.310	The seuenþe is welle of *wisedom* and fewe wordes sheweþ
B.15.30	And þat is wit and *wisdom*, þe welle of alle craftes;
B.19.450	And torne hir wit to *wisdom* and to welþe of soule.
B.20.33	Wenynge is no *wysdom*, ne wys ymaginacion:
B.20.133	Muche of þe wit and *wisdom* of westmynstre halle.
C. 2.150	Forthy worcheth by *wisdom* and by witt also,
C. 4.66	Tho was wrong afered and *wisdom* a souhte;
C. 4.72	For *wysdom* and wyt tho wenton togyderes
C. 4.83	'God woot,' quod [*wysdom*], 'þat were nat the beste.
C. 4.96	'For he [hath] waged me wel as *wysdom* hym tauhte
C. 8.222	'Now herkene,' quod hunger, 'and holde hit for a *wysdom*:
C.11.5	'Wel artow *wyse*,' quod she to wyt, 'suche *wysdomes* to shewe
C.11.14	*Wysdom* and wit now is nat worth a carse
C.13.227	The *wisdom* and the wit of god he was pot out of blisse.
C.14.82	And saide here wordes ne here *wysdomes* was but a folye;
C.16.50	Of wit and of *wisdoem* þat fer way is bettere
C.16.144	The seuethe is a welle of *wysdoem* and fewe wordes sheweth
C.16.190	And þat is wit and *wysdoem*, the welle of alle craftes;
C.21.450	And turne here wi[t] to *wisdoem* and to wel[th]e [of] soule.
C.22.33	Wenyng is no *wisdoem* ne *wyse* ymaginacioun:
C.22.133	Moche of þe Wyt and *Wisdoem* of Westmunstre halle.

wise n *wise n.(2)* &> *wis,ooþerwise* A 9 wise (5) wyse (4); B 13; C 16 wyse

A. 2.135	'And let apparaille þise prouisours in palfreis *wise*;
A. 6.4	Aparailid as a paynym in pilgrim[ys] *wyse*.
A. 6.6	In a [weþewindes] *wyse* [ywounden] aboute;
A. 6.51	And þanne ȝoure neiȝebours next in none *wise* apeir[e]
A. 6.92	And ȝif grace graunte þe to gon in [on] þis *wise*,
A. 7.52	'And I shal apparaille me,' quaþ perkyn, 'in pilgrym[ys] *wyse*,
A. 7.289	Ne non halpeny ale in no *wyse* drynke,
A. 9.100	And oþere *wise* & ellis nouȝt but as þei þre assent[e].'
A.10.23	To kepe þise womman þise *wise* men ben chargid,
B. 2.171	'And late apparaille þise prouisours in palfreyes *wise*;
B. 5.516	Apparailled as a paynym in pilgrymes *wise*.
B. 5.518	In a wiþwynde[s] *wise* ywounden aboute.
B. 5.564	And þanne youre neȝebores next in none *wise* apeire
B. 5.605	And if grace graunte þee to go in [in] þis *wise*
B. 6.57	'And I shal apparaille me', quod Perkyn, 'in pilgrymes *wise*
B. 6.305	Ne noon halfpeny ale in none *wise* drynke,
B. 8.110	And ooþer *wise* [and ellis noȝt] but as þei þre assent[e].'
B.12.229	And kynde kenned þe pecok to cauken in swich a [*wise*.
B.13.143	Thyn enemy in alle *wise* eueneforþ wiþ þiselue.
B.17.12	Wheron [was] writen two wordes on þis *wise* yglosed.
B.17.286	Ac þis is þe worste *wise* þat any wight myghte
B.19.142	Killeden hym on cros *wise* at Caluarie on Friday,
C. 5.51	Now with hym, now with here: on this *wyse* y begge
C. 7.161	[A]parayled as a paynyem in pilgrimes *wyse*.
C. 7.163	In a wethewynde *wyse* ywrithe al aboute;
C. 7.211	And thenne ȝoure neyhebores nexst in none *wyse* apayre
C. 7.254	And yf grace graunte the to go in [in] this *wyse*
C. 8.56	'And [y] shal [ap]parayle me,' quod Perkyn, 'in pilgrimes *wyse*
C. 8.327	Ne noon halpeny ale in none *wyse* drynke.
C. 9.33	Amende in som manere *wyse* and ma[y]dones helpe;
C. 9.154	With a bagge at his bak A begyneld *wyse*,
C.10.279	For coueytise of catel in none kyne *wyse*;
C.12.183	[And] oþer sedes also in þe same *wyse*
C.12.207	Angelis in here anger on this *wyse* hem grette;
C.19.13	Whereon was writen two wordes on this *wyse* yglosed:
C.19.151	Vnfolden or folden, a fuste *wyse* or elles,
C.19.267	Ac this is the worste *wyse* þat eny wiht myhte
C.21.142	Culden hym on cros *wyse* at Caluarie on fryday

wisedom > wisdom

wisely adv *wiseli adv.* A 2 wisly; B 5 wisely (4) wisloker (1); C 6 wisely (1) wysely (1) wiseliche (1) wysly (3)

A. 4.33	And wordiden a gret while wel *wisly* togidere.
A.11.268	De[m]de he not wel & *wisly*, as holy [writ] techiþ,
B. 4.46	And wordeden [a gret while wel *wisely*] togideres.
B. 9.183	*Wisely* go wedde and ware [þee] fro synne,

B.10.387	He demed wel and *wisely* as holy writ telleþ;
B.10.434	And þo þat *wisely* wordeden and writen manye bokes
B.13.342	I waitede *wisloker* and þanne was it soilled
C. 3.7	And yf she worche *wysely* and by wys men consayl
C. 8.234	Yf thow hast wonne auht wikkedliche, *wiseliche* despene hit:
C.10.284	*Wysely* go wedde and war þe fro synne;
C.11.213	And demede wel and *wysly*; wymmen bereth wittenesse.
C.15.76	Holy writ byt men be waer and *wysly* hem kepe
C.15.113	And thenne dost thow wel and *wysly*, y dar hit wel avowe.'

wisman n *wiseman n.* C 1

C. 4.27	Ooen wareyn *wisman* and wilyman his felawe

wysor > wis

wispe n *wispe n.* A 1 wysp; B 1; C 1 weps

A. 5.192	And wisshide it hadde be wexid wiþ a *wysp* of firsen.
B. 5.344	And wisshed it hadde ben wexed wiþ a *wispe* of firses.
C. 6.402	And wesched hit hadde [be wexed] with a *weps* of breres.

wissen v *wissen v.* A 19 wis (1) wisse (15) wissen (1) wisside (2); B 27 wisse (12) wissed (4) wissen (9) wisseþ (2); C 22 wisse (7) wissed (1) wissede (4) wissen (5) wyssen (1) wisseth (3) wysseth (1)

A. 1.40	And for þou shuldist be war I *wisse* þe þe beste.'
A. 1.72	What he[o] were witterly þat *wisside* me so faire.
A. 3.17	For we wile *wisse* þe king & þi wey [shape]
A. 6.21	Canst þou *wisse* vs þe wey where þat wy dwelliþ?'
A. 6.42	I [wile] *wisse* ȝow wel riȝt to his place.'
A. 7.150	Warnide wastour & *wisside* hym betere,
A. 8.114	And shewiþ it vs be ensaumple oureselue to *wisse*.
A. 9.6	Was neuere wiȝt as I wen[t]e þat me *wisse* couþe
A. 9.13	'Where þat dowel dwelli[þ], do me to *wisse*'.
A. 9.21	He is oþerwhile elliswhere to *wisse* þe peple.'
A. 9.68	Where dowel dwelliþ, & do me to *wisse*.
A. 9.105	'But wyt can *wisse* þe,' quaþ þouȝt, 'where þo þre dwellen,
A.10.92	Loke þou *wisse* þi wyt & þi werkis aftir;
A.11.8	Wiþ suche wise wordis to *wisse* any foolis!
A.11.109	Shuln *wisse* þe to dowel, I dar wel vndirtake!
A.11.275	And be here werkis & here wordis *wissen* vs to dowel,
A.12.31	Of þat he wolde wite *wis* him no betere;
A.12.40	With þat she wolde me *wisse* wher þe toun were
A.12.46	I shal þe *wisse* [wynlyche] where þat he dwelleþ'.
B. 1.42	And for þow sholdest ben ywar I *wisse* þee þe beste.'
B. 1.74	What she were witterly þat *wissed* me so faire.
B. 3.17	For we wol *wisse* þe kyng and þi wey shape
B. 5.148	I, wraþe, walke wiþ hem and *wisse* hem of my bokes.
B. 5.533	[Kanstow] *wissen* vs þe wey wher þat wye dwelleþ?'
B. 5.555	I [wol] *wisse* yow [wel riȝt] to his place.'
B. 6.165	Warnede wastour and *wissed* hym bettre:
B. 7.132	And sheweþ vs by ensampl[e] vs selue to *wisse*.
B. 8.6	Was neuere wiȝt as I wente þat me *wisse* couþe
B. 8.25	He is ouþerwhile elliswhere to *wisse* þe peple.'
B. 8.77	Where dowel dwelleþ, and do me [to *wisse*].'
B. 8.115	'But wit konne *wisse* þee', quod þoȝt, 'where þo þre dwelle
B.10.8	'Wiþ swiche wise wordes to *wissen* any sottes!'
B.10.91	And whoso litel weldeþ [*wisse*] hym þerafter,
B.10.157	Shullen *wissen* þee to dowel, I dar [wel] vndertake.'
B.10.345	Writen to *wissen* vs to wilne no richesse,
B.10.388	Aristotle and he, who *wissed* men bettre?
B.10.390	Of hir wordes þei *wissen* vs for wisest as in hir tyme,
B.11.383	[Holy writ', quod þat wye, '*wisseþ* men to suffre:
B.11.438	Why ye *wisse* me þus', quod I, 'was for I rebuked Reson.'
B.12.72	For Moyses witnesseþ þat god wroot for to *wisse* þe peple
B.12.273	To *wissen* vs [wyes] þerwiþ þat wiss[h]en to be saued–
B.14.322	That þ[u]s first wroot to *wissen* men what Pouerte was to mene.'
B.15.495	That þei ne wente as crist *wisseþ*, siþen þei wille haue name,
B.19.64	Is to *wissen* vs þerwiþ, þat whan we ben tempted,
B.19.233	And by wit to *wissen* oþere as grace hem wolde teche.
B.19.246	He *wissed* hem wynne it ayein þoruȝ wightnesse of handes
C. 1.40	And *wysseth* þe to ben ywar what wolde þe desseyue.'
C. 1.71	What she were wytterly þat *wissede* me so [faire].
C. 2.202	For to *wisse* hem þe way and with mede abyde.
C. 3.18	For we w[o]l *wisse* the kyng and thy way shape
C. 5.139	And so wrot the wyse to *wyssen* vs alle:
C. 7.178	[Can]st [thow] *wissen* vs [þe w]ay whoderout treuth woneth?'
C. 7.199	Y wol *wissen* ȝow wel ryht to his place.'
C. 8.162	Warnede wastour and *wissede* hym betere:
C.10.6	Was neuere wihte [as y wente] þat me *wisse* couthe
C.10.29	He is otherwhile elleswher to *wisse* the peple.'
C.10.74	'Art thou thouht?' quod y tho; 'thow couthest me *wisse*
C.10.111	'Bote wit wol the *wisse*,' quod thouhte, 'where tho thre dwelleth,
C.11.137	How þat wit and his wyf *wissede* me to hym
C.13.202	And so witnesseth wyse and *wisseth* þe frenche:
C.14.4	And *wissed* the [wel] ofte what dowel was to mene
C.14.195	To *wissen* vs weyes þerwith þat wenen to be saued–

C.15.20   For alle *wisseth* and ȝeueth wit þat walketh oþer crepeth.
C.16.157 That wroet thus to *wisse* men what pouerte was to mene.'
C.17.85   And worcheth nat as ȝe fyndeth ywryte and *wisseth* þe peple.
C.21.64   Is to *wissen* vs þerwith, þat when we ben ytempted
C.21.233 And bi wit to *wissen* oþere as grace hem wolde teche.
C.21.246 He *wissede* [h]e[m] wynne hit aȝeyn thorw whitnesse of handes

wisshen v *wishen v. &> wasshen* A 2 wysshe (1) wisshide (1); B 7
   wisshe (1) wisshed (4) wisshen (2); C 5 wesched (2) weschen (1)
   wisched (1) wischen (1)
A. 5.92   [Þanne] I *wysshe* it were myn [and al þe webbe aftir].
A. 5.192 And *wisshide* it hadde be wexid wiþ a wysp of firsen.
B. 5.112 [Thanne I *wisshe*] it were myn and al þe web after.
B. 5.344 And *wisshed* it hadde ben wexed wiþ a wispe of firses.
B.10.474 And principally hir paternoster; many a persone haþ *wisshed*.
B.12.273 To *wissen* vs [wyes] þerwiþ þat *wiss[h]en* to be saued–
B.13.81   And *wisshed* witterly, wiþ wille ful egre,
B.17.352 Good wille, good word [boþe], *wisshen* and willen
B.20.194 And *wisshed* ful witterly þat I were in heuene.
C. 6.402 And *wesched* hit hadde [be wexed] with a weps of breres.
C.10.268 And wedden here for here welthe and *weschen* on þe morwe
C.15.88 And *wisched* witterly with will ful egre
C.19.332 Goed wil, goed word bothe, *wischen* and wilnen
C.22.194 And *wesched* wel witterly þat y were in heuene.

wisshynges ger *wishinge ger.* B 1; C 1 weschynges
B. 2.91   And in we[n]es and in *wisshynges* and wiþ ydel þouȝtes
C. 2.98   In w[e]des and in *weschynges* and with ydel thouhtes

wissynge ger *wissinge ger.* B 1; C 1 wissyng
B.11.59   By *wissynge* of þis wenche I [dide], hir wordes were so swete,
C.12.11   By *wissyng* of this wenche y dede, here wordes were so swete,

wist(- > witen

wit n *wit n.* A 51 wit (7) wyt (33) wittes (4) wyttes (4) wittis (1) wyttis
   (2); B 113 wit (89) witte (1) wittes (23); C 107 whitus (1) wit (59)
   wyt (18) wytt (5) wytt (3) witte (3) wittes (18)
A.Pr.37 And haue *wyt* at wille to wirche ȝif hem list.
A. 1.15   Boþe wiþ fel & wiþ face, & ȝaf ȝow fyue *wyttes*
A. 1.53   And kynde *wyt* be wardeyn ȝoure welþe to kepe,
A. 1.69   Þanne hadde I wondir in my *wyt* what womman it were
A. 1.129 'Þou dotide daffe,' quaþ heo, 'dulle arn þine *wittes*.
A. 2.93   Wel ȝe *wyte*, wernardis, but ȝif ȝoure *wyt* faile,
A. 2.98   Werchiþ be wysdom & be *wyt* aftir;
A. 2.117 Til mede be þi weddit wyf þoruȝ *wyt* of vs alle,
A. 3.7   And ȝif heo werche be *wyt* & my wil folewe
A. 3.260 [I] consience knowe þis, for kynde [*w*]*it* me tauȝte,
A. 3.275 Ac kynde *wyt* shal come ȝet, & consience togidere,
A. 4.53   Wysdom wan þo & so dede *wyt* also
A. 4.62   Þanne wisdom & *wyt* wente togidere
A. 4.68   Ac wisdom & *wyt* were aboute faste
A. 4.78   *Wyt* accordiþ þerewiþ & seide þe same:
A. 5.228 Al þat I wykkidly wan siþen I *wyt* hadde,
A. 6.27   Clene consience & *wyt* kende me to his place,
A. 6.74   And alle þe wallis ben of *wyt* to holde wil þeroute;
A. 7.46   But it be of wysdom or of *wyt* þi werkmen to chaste;
A. 7.231 Kynde *wyt* wolde þat iche wiȝt wrouȝte
A. 8.55   Ac to bigge watir ne wynd, ne *wyt* is þe þridde,
A. 9.9   Maistris of þe menours, men of gret *wyt*.
A. 9.105 'But *wyt* can wisse þe,' quaþ þouȝt, 'where þo þre dwellen,
A. 9.109 Ac er we ywar were wiþ *wyt* gonne we mete.
A. 9.115 To putte forþ sum purpos [to] prouen hise *wittes*.
A. 9.118 Here is wil wolde wyte ȝif *wit* couþe hym teche.'
A.10.1   'Sire dowel dwelliþ,' quaþ *wyt*, 'nouȝt a day hennes,
A.10.42   Inwit & alle *wyttes* enclosid ben þerinne,
A.10.75   For werche he wel oþer wrong, þe *wyt* is his owene.
A.10.92   Loke þou wisse þi *wyt* & þi werkis aftir;
A.11.1   Þanne hadde *wyt* a wyf þat hatte dame studie,
A.11.3   She was wondirliche wroþ þat *wyt* so tauȝte,
A.11.5   'Wel art þou wys, *wyt*,' quaþ she, 'any wisdomis to telle
A.11.6   To flatereris or to folis þat frentyk ben of *wittis*,'
A.11.17   Wisdom and *wyt* now is not worþ a risshe
A.11.87   And now comiþ a conyon & wolde cacche of my *wittes*
A.11.93   And whanne þat *wyt* was war how his wif tolde
A.11.97   I miȝte gete no g[r]ayn of hise grete *wyttes*,
A.11.123 Þat iche wiȝt be in wille his *wyt* þe to shewen;
A.11.124 So shalt þou come to clergie þat can many *wyttes*.
A.11.159 ȝet arn þere febicchis of Forellis of many manis *wittes*,
A.11.176 Þat I was of *wyttis* hous & wiþ his wyf dame stodie.
A.11.178 And axide how *wyt* ferde & his wif studie,
A.11.277 And for here werkis & here *wyt* wende to pyne,
A.11.278 Þanne wrouȝte I vnwisly wiþ alle þe *wyt* þat I lere.
A.11.293 And ȝet [haue] I forget[e ferþer] of fyue *wyttis* teching
A.12.15   Of þe kynde cardinal *wit*, and cristned in a font,

A.12.41   Kynde [*wit*] hure confessour, hure cosyn was Inne.
A.12.43   And sayde, 'my cosyn kynde *wit* knowen is wel wide,
A.12.53   Ken him to my cosenes hous þat kinde *wit* hyȝth.
A.12.65   [To kyllyn him ȝif I can, þei kynde *wit* helpe].
B.Pr.37 And han *wit* at wille to werken if [hem liste].
B.Pr.114 And þanne cam kynde *wit* and clerkes he made
B.Pr.118 The commune contreued of kynde *wit* craftes,
B.Pr.121 The kyng and þe commune and kynde *wit* þe þridde
B.Pr.156 Miȝte we wiþ any *wit* his wille wiþstonde
B. 1.15   Boþe with fel and with face, and yaf yow fyue *wittes*
B. 1.55   And kynde *wit* be wardeyn youre welþe to kepe
B. 1.71   Thanne hadde I wonder in my *wit* what womman it weere
B. 1.140 'Thow doted daffe!' quod she, 'dulle are þi *wittes*.
B. 2.129 Wel ye witen, wernardes, but if youre *wit* faille,
B. 2.134 Wercheþ by wisdom and by *wit* [after];
B. 2.153 Til Mede be þi wedded wif þoruȝ *wi[t]* of vs alle,
B. 3.7   And if she werche bi *wit* and my wil folewe
B. 3.284 I, Conscience, knowe þis for kynde *wit* me tauȝte,
B. 3.302 That Iewes shul wene in hire *wit*, and wexen glade,
B. 4.76   [Thanne Wisdom and *wit*] wenten togidres
B. 4.81   Ac wisdom and *wit* were aboute faste
B. 4.91   *Wit* acorde[þ] þerwiþ and [witnessede] þe same:
B. 4.158 [Kynde] *wit* acorded þerwiþ and comendede hise wordes,
B. 5.185 That þi wille [ne þi *wit*] to wraþe myȝte turne:
B. 5.456 Al þat I wikkedly wan siþen I *wit* hadde,
B. 5.539 Conscience and kynde *wit* kenned me to his place
B. 5.587 And alle þe walles ben of *wit* to holden wil oute;
B. 6.51   But if [it be] of wisdom or of *wit* þi werkmen to chaste;
B. 6.247 Kynde *wit* wolde þat ech wiȝt wroȝte,
B. 7.53   Ac to bugge water ne wynd ne *wit* ne fir þe ferþe,
B. 8.9   Maistres of þe Menours, men of grete *witte*.
B. 8.53   *Wit* and free wil, to euery wiȝt a porcion,
B. 8.115 'But *wit* konne wisse þee', quod þoȝt, 'where þo þre dwelle
B. 8.119 A[c] er we [war were] wiþ *wit* gonne we mete.
B. 8.125 [To] pute forþ som purpos to preuen hise *wittes*,
B. 8.129 Here is wil wolde wite if *wit* koude [hym teche];
B. 9.1   'SIre Dowel dwelleþ', quod *Wit*, 'noȝt a day hennes
B. 9.44   He moste werche wiþ his word and his *wit* shewe.
B. 9.54   Inwit and alle *wittes* [en]closed ben þerInne.
B.10.1   Thanne hadde *wit* a wif was hote dame Studie.
B.10.3   She was wonderly wroþ þat *wit* [so] tauȝte,
B.10.5   'Wel artow wis, [*wit*, quod she], 'any wisdomes to telle
B.10.6   To flatereres or to fooles þat frenetike ben of *wittes*',
B.10.17   Wisdom and *wit* now is noȝt worþ a [risshe]
B.10.134 And þo þat vseþ þise hauylons [for] to blende mennes *wittes*,
B.10.140 And whan þat *wit* was ywar [how his wif] tolde
B.10.144 I myȝte gete no greyn of his grete *wittes*,
B.10.171 That ech wight be in wille his *wit* þee to shewe.
B.10.172 [So] shaltow come to Clergie þat kan manye [*wittes*].
B.10.216 Yet ar þer fibicches in [forelles] of fele mennes [*wittes*],
B.10.233 That I was of *wittes* hous and wiþ his wif dame Studie.
B.10.235 And askede how *wit* ferde and his wif studie].
B.10.255 For hadde neuere freke fyn *wit* þe feiþ to dispute,
B.10.385 God gaf hym grace of *wit* and alle goodes after
B.10.393 That for hir werkes and *wit* now wonyeþ in pyne,
B.10.401 As Salomon dide and swiche oþere, þat shewed grete *wittes*
B.10.435 Of wit and of wisedom wiþ dampned soules wonye.
B.10.448 [And yet haue I forgete ferþer of fyue *wittes* techyng
B.10.456 But *wit* [ne] wisedom wan neuere þe maistrie
B.11.45 'That *wit* shal torne to wrecchednesse for wil to haue his likyng!'
B.11.323 And þoruȝ þe wondres of þis world wit for to take.
B.11.346 Hadde neuere wye *wit* to werche þe leeste.
B.11.374 'I haue wonder [in my *wit*], þat witty art holden,
B.11.419 The wisedom and þe *wit* of god, he was put fram blisse.
B.12.45 Catel and kynde *wit* was combraunce to hem alle.
B.12.55 [So catel and kynde *wit* acombreþ ful manye;
B.12.64 Clergie and kynde *wit* comeþ of siȝte and techyng
B.12.67 And of quod vidimus comeþ kynde *wit*, of siȝte of diuerse peple.
B.12.69 Knew neuere clerk how it comeþ forþ, ne kynde *wit* þe weyes:
B.12.70 Ac yet is Clergie to comende and kynde *wit* boþe,
B.12.93 For kynde *wit* is of his kyn and neiȝe Cosynes boþe
B.12.108 Come for al his kynde *wit* to cristendom and be saued;
B.12.128 Ac kynde *wit* comeþ of alle kynnes siȝtes,
B.12.132 And helden it an heiȝ science hir *wittes* to knowe;
B.12.169 'That swymme kan noȝt', I seide, 'it semeþ to my *wittes*.'
B.12.224 How euere beest ouþer brid haþ so breme *wittes*.
B.12.225 Clergie ne kynde *wit* ne knew neuere þe cause,
B.12.272 Ac god is so good, I hope þat siþþe he gaf hem *wittes*
B.12.295 And *wit* and wisdom', quod þat wye, 'was som tyme tresor
B.13.154 And al þe *wit* of þe wodnesday of þe nexte wike after;
B.13.168 Nouȝt þoruȝ wicchecraft but þoruȝ *wit*; and þow wilt þiselue
B.13.173 Al þe *wit* of þis world and wiȝt mennes strengþe
B.13.291 Willynge þat men wende his *wit* were þe beste,

B.13.360	And awaited þoruȝ [*wittes* wyes] to bigile;
B.13.362	'The worste withInne was; a greet *wit* I let it.
B.13.365	How I myȝte haue it al my *wit* I caste,
B.14.56	In [ondynge] and in handlynge and in alle þi fyue *wittes*,
B.14.126	Ac god is of [a] wonder wille, by þat kynde *wit* sheweþ,
B.14.209	Of *wit* and of wisdom, þat fer awey is bettre
B.15.3	And so my *wit* weex and wanyed til I a fool weere.
B.15.30	And þat is *wit* and wisdom, þe welle of alle craftes;
B.15.54	Ayein swiche Salomon spekeþ and despiseþ hir *wittes*
B.15.76	And how þat folk in folies [hir fyue *wittes* mysspenden],
B.15.83	If I lye on yow to my lewed *wit*, ledeþ me to brennyng!
B.15.130	Wolde neuere þe *wit* of witty god but wikkede men it hadde,
B.15.370	Astronomyens also aren at hir *wittes* ende;
B.15.400	Into Surrie he souȝte, and þoruȝ hise sotile *wittes*
B.15.409	And þus þoruȝ wiles of his *wit* and a whit Dowue
B.15.553	If knyghthod and kynde *wit* and þe commune [and] conscience
B.16.187	Wardeyn of þat *wit* haþ; was euere wiþouten gynnyng.
B.17.138	And if Conscience carpe þerayein, or kynde *wit* eyþer,
B.18.234	That alle þe wise of þis world in o *wit* acor[de]den
B.19.82	And al þe *wit* of þe world was in þo þre kynges.
B.19.100	And manye wiles and *wit* þat wole ben a ledere.
B.19.118	A faunt[ek]yn ful of *wit*, filius Marie.
B.19.122	He wroȝte þat by no *wit* but þoruȝ word one,
B.19.216	To alle kynne creatures þat [k]an hi[se] fyue *wittes*,
B.19.229	Some [wyes] he yaf *wit* with wordes to shewe,
B.19.233	And by *wit* to wissen oþere as grace hem wolde teche.
B.19.315	'Hareweþ alle þat konneþ kynde *wit* by conseil of þise docto[urs],
B.19.354	Al þe world in a while þoruȝ oure *wit*', quod Pryde.
B.19.360	And þanne kam Kynde *wit* Conscience to teche
B.19.372	Ther nas no cristene creature þat kynde *wit* hadde
B.19.450	And torne hir *wit* to wisdom and to welþe of soule.
B.20.32	Of þat he weneþ wolde falle if his *wit* ne weere;
B.20.133	Muche of þe *wit* and wisdom of westmynstre halle.
B.20.268	Forþi', quod Conscience, 'by crist! kynde *wit* me telleþ
C.Pr.38	And [han] *wytt* at wille to worche yf þei wolde.
C.Pr.141	And thenne cam kynde *wytt* [& clerkis he made
C.Pr.143	Conscience & kynde *wit*] and knyghthed togedres
C.Pr.145	Kynde *wytt* and þe comune contreued alle craftes
C.Pr.148	Thenne kynde *witt* to þe kynge and to þe comune saide:
C.Pr.176	Myghte [we] with eny *wyt* his wille w[i]thsytte
C.1.15	To be fayful to hym [he] ȝaf ȝow fyue *wittes*
C.1.51	And kynde *witte* be wardeyn ȝoure welthe to kepe
C.1.68	Thenne hadde y wonder in my *wit* what woman he were
C.1.139	'Thow dotede daffe!' quod she, 'dulle aren thy *wittes*.
C.2.150	Forthy worcheth by wisdom and by *witt* also,
C.3.212	That al þe *witt* of the world is woxe into Gyle.
C.3.437	[I], Consience, knowe this for kynde *wit* me tauhte,
C.3.455	That iewes shal wene in he[re] *wit*, & wexen so glade,
C.4.23	Lat peytrele [hym] and pole hym with peynted *wittes*.'
C.4.72	For wysdom and *wyt* tho wenton togyderes
C.4.77	Ac wyles and *wyt* were aboute faste
C.4.87	*Witt* acordede therwith and witnessede þe same:
C.4.152	And kynde [*wit*] and Consience corteysliche thonkede
C.5.185	That o *wit* and o wil al ȝoure wardes kepe
C.6.21	Thorw my word and my *witt* here euel werkes to shewe;
C.6.167	That thy wil ne thy *wit* to wr[at]he myhte turne.
C.6.258	'With false wordes and w[*ittes*] haue y ywonne my godes
C.6.261	The worste lay withynne; a greet *wit* y lat hit.
C.6.264	How y myhte haue hit al my *wit* y caste
C.6.310	Al-þat-y-wikkedly-wan-sithen-y-*witte*-hadde:
C.7.184	Consience and kynde *wyt* kenned me to his place
C.7.234	And al þe wallyng is of *wyt* for wil ne sholde hit wynne;
C.8.55	'For to worche by thy *wit* and my wyf bothe.'
C.8.59	His cokeres and his coffes, as kynde *wit* hym tauhte,
C.9.56	Þat is *wit* and watur and wynde and fuyre the ferthe;
C.9.106	Ac hem wanteth *wyt*, men and women bothe,
C.9.116	To ȝeue vch a wyht *wyt*, welthe and his hele
C.10.9	Maystres of þe menore[s], men of gret *witte*.
C.10.51	Ac fre wil and fre *wit* foleweth man euere
C.10.105	And reule alle reumes by here thre *wittes*
C.10.111	'Bote *wit* wol the wisse,' quod thouhte, 'where tho thre dwelleth,
C.10.115	And ar we ywar were with *wit* gan we mete.
C.10.121	And potte forth som purpos to prouen his *wittes*,
C.10.125	Here is oen wolde ywyte yf *wit* couthe teche;
C.10.128	'Sire dowel dwelleth,' quod *wit*, 'nat a day hennes
C.10.152	'Kynde is creatour,' quod *wit*, 'of [alle] kyne thynges,
C.10.171	Inwit and alle *wittes* closed been þerynne:
C.11.1	Thenne hadde *wit* a wyf was hote dame studie
C.11.3	She was wonderly wroth þat *wit* me so tauhte;
C.11.5	'Wel artow wyse,' quod she to *wyt*, 'suche wysdomes to shewe
C.11.14	Wysdom and *wit* now is nat worth a carse
C.11.77	For is no *wit* worth now but hit of wynnynge soune.
C.11.78	Forthy, *wit*,' quod she, 'be waer holy writ to shewe

C.11.81	And when *wit* was ywar what studie menede
C.11.82	I myhte gete no grayn of [his] grete *wittes*
C.11.137	How þat *wit* and his wyf wissede me to hym
C.11.156	For hadde neuere frek fyn *wi[t]* the faith to dispute
C.11.210	God gaf hym grace of *wit* and of goed aftur,
C.11.220	That for here werkes and *wyt* wonyeth now in payne,
C.11.225	Thenne al þe kynde *wyt* þat ȝe can bothe and kunnyng of ȝoure bokes.
C.11.282	That *wit* ne witnesse wan neuere þe maistre
C.12.2	'That *wit* shal turne to wrechednesse for wil hath al his wille!'
C.13.157	Hadde neuere weye *wyt* to worche þe leste.
C.13.169	'Where hadde thise wilde suche *wit* and at what scole?'
C.13.184	'Y haue wonder in my *wit*, so wys as thow art holden,
C.13.227	The wisdom and the *wit* of god he was pot out of blisse.
C.13.237	Of clergie ne of kynde *wyt* counteth he nat a rusche.
C.14.17	Ac catel and kynde *wit* acombreth fol monye;
C.14.30	Ac clergie cometh bote of syhte and kynde *wit* of sterres,
C.14.32	That *wit* wexeth therof and oþer w[y]rdes bothe:
C.14.33	So grace is a gifte of god and kynde *wit* a chaunce
C.14.34	And clergie a connynge of kynde *wittes* techyng.
C.14.36	Then eny connyng of kynde *wit* but clergi hit reule.
C.14.53	Come for al his kynde *wit* thorw cristendoem to be saued,
C.14.109	'He þat can nat swymmen,' y sayde, 'hit semeth to alle *wittes*.'
C.14.157	How creatures han kynde *wit* and how clerkes come to bokes
C.14.163	A cantel of kynde *wyt* here kynde to saue.
C.14.182	Then for eny kyn he come of or for his kynde *wittes*.
C.14.194	Ac god is so gode, y hope þat seth he gaf hem *wittes*
C.15.20	For alle a wisseth and ȝeueth wit þat walketh oþer crepeth.
C.15.74	Ac me wondreth in my *wit* why þat they ne preche
C.15.143	Fond [with] *wit* & word his loue to wynne,
C.15.171	Al th[e] *wit* of this world and wyhte menne strenghe
C.15.255	In [ond]ynge and [in] handlynge [and] in alle thy fyue *wittes*,
C.16.50	Of *wit* and of wisdoem þat fer way is bettere
C.16.190	And þat is *wit* and wysdoem, the welle of alle craftes;
C.16.216	Aȝenes suche salamon speketh and despiseth here *wittes*
C.16.235	And [ho]w that folk [in folies] here fyue *wittes* myspen[en],
C.17.106	Astron[o]myens also aren at here *wittes* ende;
C.17.216	ȝif knyhthoed and kynde *wit* and þe comune and consience
C.18.28	Of o will, of o *wit*; and he[r]with y kepe
C.18.179	In inwit and in alle *wittes* aftur liberum Arbitrium
C.18.189	Of o *wit* and o will, [they] were neuere atwynne
C.19.111	And yf kynde *wit* carpe hereaȝen or eny kyne thouhtes
C.19.248	With wyles and with luyther *whitus* and ȝut wollen nat atymye
C.20.243	That alle þe wyse of th[is] world in o *wit* acordede
C.21.82	And al þe *wit* of the world was in [þo] thre kynges.
C.21.100	And many wyles and *wyt* þat wol be a ledare.
C.21.118	A fauntekyn ful of *wyt*, filius Marie.
C.21.122	He wrouhte þat by no *wyt* bote thorw word one,
C.21.216	To alle kyne creatures þat can his fyue *wittes*,
C.21.229	Som [wyes] he ȝaf *wyt* with wordes to schewe,
C.21.233	And bi *wit* to wissen oþere as grace hem wolde teche.
C.21.315	'Harweth alle þa[t] conneth kynde *wit* bi consail of [this] doctours
C.21.354	Alle the world in a while thorw oure *wit*', quod pruyde.
C.21.360	And thenne cam kynde *wit* Consience to teche
C.21.372	Ther ne was cristene creature that kynde *wit* hadde
C.21.450	And turne here *wi[t]* to wisdoem and to wel[th]e [of] soule.
C.22.32	Of þat he weneth wolde falle yf his *wit* ne were;
C.22.133	Moche of þe *Wyt* and Wisdoem of Westmunstre halle.
C.22.268	For[thy],' quod Consience, 'bi Crist! kynde *wit* me telleth

witen v1 *witen v.(1)* A 48 wiste (7) wisten (1) wistest (1) wite (2) wyte (14) wyten (2) woot (1) wost (2) wot (18); B 110 nyste (1) noot (1) wist (1) wiste (24) wisten (2) wistest (1) wite (28) witen (4) witene (1) witeþ (2) witynge (1) woost (2) woot (42); C 92 neste (1) wete (1) weten (1) wist (2) wiste (16) wyste (1) wisten (3) wite (1) wyte (16) wyten (2) witeth (2) wyteth (3) wytyng (1) woet (33) woot (2) wost (2) wot (5)

A.Pr.12	Þat I was in a wildernesse, wiste I neuere where;
A.Pr.43	In glotonye, god wot, go þei to bedde,
A.2.27	Þere miȝte þou wyte ȝif þou wilt whiche þei ben alle
A.2.57	'Wyten & wytnessen þat wonen vpon erþe,
A.2.86	Þe text[e] tell[iþ] not so, treuþe wot þe soþe;
A.2.93	Wel ȝe wyte, wernardis, but ȝif ȝoure wyt faile,
A.3.50	'Wiste I þat,' quaþ þe womman, 'þere nis wyndowe ne auter
A.3.163	Whanne ȝe wyte wytterly where þe wrong liggeþ;
A.3.167	Wel þou wost, consience, but ȝif þou wilt leiȝe,
A.4.65	'Wiþoute gilt, god wot, gat I þis skaþe?
A.4.67	And wisten wel þat wrong was a shrewe euere.
A.4.74	'God wot,' quaþ wysdom, 'þat were not þe beste.
A.4.92	Wrong wendiþ not so awey er I wyte more.
A.4.122	Shulde neuere wrong in þis world þat I wyte miȝte
A.5.138	A galoun for a grote, god wot no lasse,
A.5.154	'ȝa, glotoun gossib,' quaþ heo, 'god wot, wel hote:
A.5.246	Wel I woot he wep faste watir wiþ his eiȝen,

A. 6.41	And ȝif ȝe wilneþ *wyte* where þat wy dwelliþ	B.10.367	Or delit in wyn and wildefowel and *wite* any in defaute.
A. 6.49	Til ȝe come into consience þat crist *wyte* þe soþe,	B.10.438	In þe hondes of almyȝty god, and he *woot* þe soþe
A. 6.84	Tel hym þis tokne, "treuþe *wot* þe soþe:	B.10.442	And wherby *wiste* men which [is] whit if elle þyng blak were,
A. 6.117	'Wyte god,' quaþ a waffrer, '*wiste* I þat forsoþe,	B.11.101	Þyng þat al þe world *woot*, wherfore sholdestow spare
A. 7.122	Ȝe ben wastours, I *wot* wel, & treuþe wot þe soþe;	B.11.143	For an vncristene creature; clerkes *wite* þe soþe
A. 7.122	Ȝe ben wastours, I wot wel, & treuþe *wot* þe soþe;	B.11.146	Gregorie *wiste* þis wel, and wilned to my soule
A. 7.190	For I *wot* wel, be þou ywent, hy wile werche ille;	B.11.180	Whoso leneþ noȝt he loueþ noȝt, [lord] *woot* þe soþe,
A. 7.196	[Now wolde I] *wite*, ȝif þou wistest, what were þe beste,	B.11.213	For *woot* no man how neiȝ it is to ben ynome fro boþe.
A. 7.196	[Now wolde I] wite, ȝif þou *wistest*, what were þe beste,	B.11.238	So bi hise werkes þei *wisten* þat he was Iesus,
A. 7.241	'I *wot* wel,' quaþ hunger, 'what seknesse hem eileþ;	B.11.409	[To *wite*] what dowel is, [ac wakyng neuere]'.
A. 8.56	Ne wolde neuere holy writ, god *wot* þe soþe.	B.11.434	Thanne *woot* þe dronken [wye] wherfore he is to blame.'
A. 8.61	Ȝe legistris & lawi[er]is, [ȝe] *wyten* ȝif I leiȝe;	B.12.270	And wheiþer he be saaf or noȝt saaf, þe sope *woot* no clergie,
A. 9.4	Ȝif any wiȝt *wiste* where dowel was at Inne;	B.13.25	And þere I [mette] a maister, what man he was I *nyste*,
A. 9.64	'Þat þou *wost* wel,' quaþ he, '& no wiȝt betere.'	B.13.74	Ac I *wiste* neuere freke þat as a frere yede bifore men on englissh
A. 9.65	'*Wot* ich?' quaþ I; 'who art þou?' 'þouȝt,' seide he þanne.	B.13.226	A wafrer, wol ye *wite*, and serue manye lordes,
A. 9.106	Ellis *wot* no man þat now is o lyue.'	B.13.311	Ne wolde he þat men *wiste* of werkes and wordes
A. 9.118	Here is wil wolde *wyte* ȝif wit couþe hym teche.'	B.13.323	Al þat he *wiste* wikked by any wight tellen it,
A.11.30	Or daun[cel]id or drawe forþ; þise disours *wyte* þe soþe.	B.13.325	And þat he *wiste* by wille [to watte tellen it],
A.11.75	Wilneþ neuere to *wyte* why that god wolde	B.13.326	And þat [by] watte [he] *wiste* wille wiste it after,
A.11.80	For alle þat wilneþ to *wyte* þe [whyes] of god almiȝt,	B.13.326	And þat [by] watte [he] wiste wille *wiste* it after,
A.11.82	Þat euere eft wilneþ to *wyte* why [þat] god wolde	B.13.384	Hadde I neuere wille, *woot* god, witterly to biseche
A.11.89	Siþen he wilneþ to *wyte* which þei ben alle.	B.14.8	To agulte god or good man by aught þat I *wiste*,
A.11.175	Þanne myself soþly so sone [as] heo it *wiste*	B.14.83	And þoruȝ feiþ comeþ contricion, conscience *woot* wel,
A.11.194	[Dredles] þis is dobet; [dobest *wot* þe soþe].	B.14.98	'Where wonyeþ Charite?' quod Haukyn; 'I *wiste* neuere in my lyue
A.11.240	Ac cristene men, god *wot*, comiþ not so to heuene,	B.14.106	I *wiste* neuere renk þat riche was, þat whan he rekene sholde,
A.11.259	To *wyte* what is dowel witterly in herte.	B.14.282	Riȝt as contricion is confortable þyng, conscience *woot* wel,
A.12.1	'Crist *wot*,' quod clergie, 'knowe hit ȝif þe lyke,	B.14.332	'I were noȝt worþi, *woot* god', quod haukyn, 'to werien any cloþes,
A.12.10	Ȝif I *wiste* witterly þou woldest don þerafter,	B.15.79	Moore for pompe þan for pure charite; þe peple *woot* þe soþe.
A.12.31	Of þat he wolde *wite* wis him no betere;	B.15.101	A[c] þer þe roote is roten, reson *woot* þe soþe.
A.12.88	'Myȝth I so, god *wot*, ȝoure gates wolde I holden.'	B.15.119	If lewed [ledes] *wiste* what þis latyn meneþ,
A.12.99	Wille þurgh inwit [*wiste*] wel þe soþe,	B.15.146	Ac for goode men, god *woot*, greet doel men maken,
B.Pr.12	That I was in a wildernesse, *wiste* I neuere where.	B.15.263	For wel may euery man *wite*, if god hadde wold hymselue,
B.Pr.43	In glotonye, god *woot*, go þei to bedde,	B.15.362	*Wisten* þo þe walkne what sholde bitide;
B.Pr.166	Men myȝte *witen* wher þei wente and [hire] wey r[oum]e.	B.16.12	Lord!' quod I, 'if any wight *wite* whiderout it groweþ?'
B. 2.45	[There] myȝtow *witen* if þow wilt whiche þei ben alle	B.16.25	'For wyndes, wiltow *wite*', quod he, 'to witen it fro fallyng:
B. 2.75	*Witeþ* and witnesseþ þat wonieþ vpon erþe	B.16.233	He *wiste* my wille bi hym; he wol me it allowe.
B. 2.78	Falsnesse is fayn of hire for he *woot* hire riche,	B.16.258	'I wolde *wite*', quod I þo, 'what is in youre lappe.'
B. 2.122	[The] text telleþ þee noȝt so, Truþe *woot* þe soþe.	B.17.7	And whan it is enseled [þerwiþ] I *woot* wel þe soþe
B. 2.129	Wel ye *witen*, wernardes, but if youre wit faille,	B.18.66	Shal no wight *wite* witterly who shal haue þe maistrie
B. 3.51	'*Wiste* I þat', quod þ[e] womman 'I wolde noȝt spare	B.18.126	'And am wendynge to *wite* what þis wonder meneþ.'
B. 3.74	*Wite* what þow werchest wiþ þi riȝt syde,	B.18.147	It is trufle þat þow tellest; I, truþe, *woot* þe soþe,
B. 3.176	Whan ye *witen* witterly wher þe wrong liggeþ.	B.18.166	For he[o] *woot* moore þan we; he[o] was er we boþe.'
B. 3.180	Wel þow *woost*, [Conscience], but if þow wolt [lie],	B.18.205	For hadde þei *wist* of no wo, wele hadde þei noȝt knowen;
B. 3.332	'I kan no latyn?' quod she, 'clerkes *wite* þe soþe!	B.18.206	For no wight *woot* what wele is þat neuere wo suffrede,
B. 4.37	Thei ne [gy]ueþ noȝt of [good feiþ, *woot* god þe sooþe]:	B.18.209	Sholde *wite* witterly what day is to mene.
B. 4.79	'Wiþouten gilt, god *woot*, gat I þis scaþe.'	B.18.211	*Wite* what wo is, ne were þe deeþ of kynde.
B. 4.87	'God *woot*', quod wisdom, 'þat were noȝt þe beste.	B.18.217	*Woot* no wight, as I wene, what [is ynogh] to mene.
B. 4.105	Wrong wendeþ noȝt so awey [er] I *wite* moore.	B.18.221	To *wite* what wele was, kyndeliche [to] knowe it.
B. 4.139	Sholde neuere wrong in þis world þat I *wite* myȝte	B.18.225	To *wite* what alle wo is [þat woot of] alle ioye.
B. 5.161	For she hadde child in chirietyme; al oure Chapitre it *wiste*.	B.18.225	To wite what alle wo is [þat *woot* of] alle ioye.
B. 5.180	Al þe wikkednesse þat I *woot* by any of oure breþeren,	B.18.228	*Woot* no wight what werre is þer þat pees regneþ.
B. 5.181	I cou[ȝ]e it [vp] in oure Cloistre þat al [þe] Couent *woot* it.'	B.18.308	Wiþ glorie and with gret light; god it is, I *woot* wel.
B. 5.222	A galon for a grote, god *woot* no lesse,	B.19.162	For þat womm[a]n *witeþ* may noȝt wel be counseille.
B. 5.269	And I *wiste* witterly þow were swich as þow tellest.	B.19.358	For witterly, I *woot* wel, we beþ noȝt of strengþe
B. 5.289	And if þow *wite* neuere to [whom] ne [where] to restitue	B.19.370	*Witynge* and wilfully wiþ þe false helden,
B. 5.472	Wel I *woot* he wepte faste water wiþ hise eiȝen,	B.19.371	And for siluer were forswore–sooþly þei *wiste* it.
B. 5.554	And if ye wilneþ *wite* where þat [wye] dwelleþ	B.20.3	I ne *wiste* wher to ete ne at what place,
B. 5.562	Til ye come into Conscience þat crist *wite* þe soþe,	B.20.318	'We han no nede', quod Conscience; 'I *woot* no bettre leche
B. 5.597	Telleþ hym þis tokene: "[truþe *woot*] þe soþe;	C.Pr.100	Al þe world *wot* wel hit myghte nouȝt be trewe
B. 5.632	'Wite god', quod a waf[erer], '*wiste* I þis for soþe	C. 1.122	Euene þe contrarie sitteth Crist, Clerkes *wyteth* þe sothe:
B. 5.642	Thow shalt seye I am þi Suster.' I ne *woot* where þei bicome.	C. 2.82	*Wyten* and witnessen þat wonyen on erthe
B. 6.130	Ye ben wastours, I *woot* wel, and truþe woot þe soþe;	C. 2.85	Falsnesse is fayn of here for he *woot* here ryche;
B. 6.130	Ye ben wastours, I woot wel, and truþe *woot* þe soþe;	C. 2.145	For wel ȝe *wyte*, wernardus, as holy writ telleth,
B. 6.204	For I *woot* wel, be þow went þei wol werche ille;	C. 3.222	When ȝe [*wyten*] witterly [where] þe wrong liggeth.
B. 6.210	Now wolde I *wite*, [if þow wistest], what were þe beste,	C. 3.226	Wel thow *wost*, weye, but yf thow wille gabbe,
B. 6.210	Now wolde I wite, [if þow *wistest*], what were þe beste,	C. 3.286	'Nay,' quod Consience to þe kyng, 'clerkes *witeth* þe sothe,
B. 6.257	'I *woot* wel', quod hunger, 'what siknesse yow eyleþ;	C. 3.297	And *wot* neuere witterly where he lyue so longe
B. 7.70	For if he *wiste* he were noȝt nedy he wolde [it ȝyue]	C. 4.37	They gyue n[ouh]t of good fayth, *woe[t]* god the sothe,
B. 7.78	For *wite* ye neuere who is worþi, ac god woot who haþ nede.	C. 4.75	'Withouten gult, god *wot*, [gat y] this s[c]athe;
B. 7.78	For wite ye neuere who is worþi, ac god *woot* who haþ nede.	C. 4.83	'God *woot*,' quod [wysdom], 'þat were nat the beste.
B. 8.4	If any wiȝt *wiste* wher dowel was at Inne;	C. 4.100	Wrong goth nat so away ar y *wete* more.
B. 8.13	'Where þat dowel dwelleþ, dooþ me to *witene*.'	C. 4.136	Shulde neuere wrong in this worlde þat y *wyte* myhte
B. 8.73	'That þow *woost* wel', quod he, 'and no wiȝt bettre.'	C. 5.1	Thus y awakede, *woet* god, whan y wonede in Cornehull,
B. 8.74	'*Woot* I?' [quod I; 'who art þow]?' 'þouȝt,' seide he þanne.	C. 5.37	Tyl y *wyste* witterly what holy writ menede
B. 8.116	Ellis [n]*oot* [no man] þat now is alyue.'	C. 5.181	'For þe comune is the kynges tresor, Consience *woet* wel.
B. 8.129	Here is wil wolde *wite* if wit koude [hym teche];	C. 6.59	Al [y] wolde þat men *wiste* when it to pruyde souneth,
B. 9.40	Thouȝ he [*wiste* to] write neuer so wel, [and] he hadde [a] penne,	C. 6.70	And þat a *wiste* by wille to watekyn he tolde hit
B. 9.101	[Tynynge] of tyme, truþe *woot* þe soþe,	C. 6.71	And þat he *wiste* by watte tolde hit wille aftur
B.10.122	Wilneþ neuere to *wite* why þat god wolde	C. 6.162	Al þat y *wiste* wykked by eny of oure couent
B.10.127	For alle þat wilneþ to *wite* þe [whyes] of god almyȝty,	C. 6.163	Y cou[ȝ]e hit vp in oure Cloystre þat al þe couent *woet* hit.'
B.10.129	That euere [eft] wilneþ to *wite* why þat god wolde	C. 6.273	Hadde y neuere will, [*woot* god], witterly to byseche
B.10.136	Siþþe he wilneþ to *wite* whiche þei ben [alle].	C. 6.289	Ne take a meles mete of thyn and myn herte hit *wiste*
B.10.232	Than myself sooþly soone so he *wiste*	C. 6.300	Yf he *wiste* thow were such when he resseyued thyn offrynge.

C. 6.303	There shal he *wite* witturly what vsure is to mene		B. 1.31	And al he *witte* it wyn þat wikked dede:
C. 6.326	Wel y *woet* a wepte faste water with his yes		B. 7.60	Ye legistres and lawieres, [if I lye *witeþ* Mathew]:
C. 6.344	And ʒif thow *wyte* neuere to whom ne where to restitue		C. 1.30	And al he *witte* [it] wyn [þat] wikkede dede:
C. 7.198	And hoso wilneth to *wyte* where þat treuthe woneth		C. 6.113	But y hadde weder at my wille y *witte* god þe cause
C. 7.245	Tel hym this tokene: "treuthe *woet* þe sothe;			

witful adj *witful adj.* A 1 wytful; B 1

A. 4.19	And let warroke hym wel wiþ [*wy*]*tful* gerþis.
B. 4.21	And lat warroke hym wel wiþ *wit*[*ful*] gerþes.

wiþ prep *with prep.* &> wiþalle A 214 with (44) wiþ (170); B 572 with (83) wiþ (489); C 532 with (531) wiþ (1)

C. 7.285	'Wyte god,' quod a wafre[re], 'wiste y this for sothe		A.Pr.16	*Wiþ* depe dikes & derke & dredful of siʒt.
C. 8.139	ʒe been wastours, y *woet* wel, and waste and deuouren		A.Pr.22	[Wonne] þat þise wastours *wiþ* glotonye destroiʒeþ.
C. 8.210	For y *woet* wel, be [thow] went, worche þei wol ful ille;		A.Pr.34	And gete gold *wiþ* here gle giltles, I trowe.
C. 8.219	Now wolde y *wyte*, ar thow wendest, what were þe beste;		A.Pr.44	And risen vp *wiþ* ribaudrie as robertis knaues;
C. 8.269	'Y *wot* wel,' quod hungur, 'what sekenesse ʒow ayleth.		A.Pr.48	Wenten forþ in here wey *wiþ* many wise talis,
C. 9.67	Bote ther he *wiste* were wel grete nede		A.Pr.50	Ermytes on an hep, *wiþ* hokide staues,
C. 9.70	*Woet* no man, as y wene, who is worthy to haue		A.Pr.66	Brouʒte forþ a bulle *wiþ* bisshopis selis
C. 9.88	This [y] *woet* witturly, as þe world techeth,		A.Pr.71	He bunchi[de] hem *wiþ* his breuet & bleri[de] here eiʒe[n]
C. 9.128	And alle manere munstrals, me *woet* wel þe sothe,		A.Pr.72	And rauʒte *wiþ* his rageman ryngis & brochis.
C.10.4	Yf eny wiht *wiste* where dowel was at ynne;		A.Pr.103	And driueþ forþ þe longe day *wiþ* dieu saue dame emme;
C.10.22	Fallyng fro ioye, iesu *woet* þe sothe!		A. 1.15	Boþe *wiþ* fel & wiþ face, & ʒaf ʒow fyue wyttes
C.10.71	'That þou [*wost*] w[el],' quod he, 'and no wyht bettere.'		A. 1.15	Boþe wiþ fel & *wiþ* face, & ʒaf ʒow fyue wyttes
C.10.72	'*Woet* y?' quod y; 'who art thow?' 'thouhte,' sayde he thenne.		A. 1.45	Þo þe peple hym aposide *with* a peny in þe temple
C.10.164	God wol nat of hem *wyte* bute lat hem yworthe,		A. 1.65	Iudas he iapide *wiþ* Iewene siluer,
C.10.239	Ac Westm[in]stre lawe, y *woet* wel, worcheth þe contra[r]ye;		A. 1.100	But holde *wiþ* hym & wiþ hire þat aske þe treuþe
C.11.270	By that þat salamon saith hit semeth þat no wyht *woet*		A. 1.100	But holde wiþ hym & *wiþ* hire þat aske þe treuþe
C.11.285	Was Austyn þe oelde þat euere man *wiste*,		A. 1.109	Lucifer *wiþ* legionis leride it in heuene,
C.12.35	Thyng þat al þe world *woet* wherfore sholdest thow spare		A. 1.112	Þanne fil he *wiþ* [his] felawis & fendis bicome;
C.12.78	For an vncristene creature; [clerkes] *woet* þe sothe		A. 1.117	And alle þat werchen *with* wrong wenden þei shuln
C.12.81	Gregori *wiste* this wel and wilned to my soule		A. 1.118	Aftir here deþ day & dwelle *wiþ* þat shrewe
C.12.127	So by [h]is werkes thei *wisten* þat he was iesu		A. 1.141	Lokide on vs *wiþ* loue, & let his sone deiʒe
C.12.161	Crist acordeth efte herwith; clerkes *wyteth* þe sothe,		A. 1.144	But mekly *wiþ* mouþe mercy he besouʒte
C.13.65	ʒe *wyte*, ʒe wyse men, what this is to mene:		A. 1.170	ʒe ben acumbrid *wiþ* coueitise, ʒe [conne] not out crepe;
C.13.82	And other pryue penaunces þe which þe prest *woet* wel		A. 1.177	To counforte þe carful acumbrid *wiþ* synne.
C.13.217	To *wyte* what dowel is Ac wakynge neuere.'		A. 2.9	Ipurfilid *wiþ* pelure, þe pureste [o]n erþe,
C.13.218	And thenne was ther a wyhte, what he was y *neste*.		A. 2.11	Alle here fyue fyngris were frettid *wiþ* rynges
C.13.229	And for thow woldest *wyte* why, resones preue[t]e,		A. 2.13	In red scarlet robid & ribande *wiþ* gold.
C.13.240	And thenne *woet* he wherfore and why he is to blame.'		A. 2.23	Fauel *wiþ* fair speche haþ forgid hem togidere;
C.14.191	And wher he be saef or nat saef þe sothe *woet* no clergie		A. 2.30	ʒif þou wilnest to wone *wiþ* treuþe in his blisse.
C.15.80	Ac y *wiste* neuere freke þat frere is ycald of þe fyue mendynantʒ		A. 2.33	Alle þe riche retenaunce þat regniþ *wiþ* false
C.15.148	And whan he hadde yworded thus *wiste* no man aftur		A. 2.48	To be fastnid *wiþ* fals þe fyn is arerid
C.15.281	[Y *wiste* neuere renke þat ryche was þat whan he rekene sholde]		A. 2.60	*Wiþ* þe Erldom of enuye for euere to laste,
C.16.6	Thenne may men *wyte* what he is worth and what he hath deserued		A. 2.61	*Wiþ* alle þe lordsshipe of leccherie in lengþe & in brede;
C.16.143	As he þat *woet* neuere with wham on nyhtes tyme to mete:		A. 2.62	*Wiþ* þe kingdom of coueitise I croune hem togidere;
C.16.238	More for pompe and pruyde, as þe peple *woet* wel		A. 2.65	*Wiþ* alle þe delites of lust þe deuil for to serue,
C.16.254	Ac þer þe rote is roton, resoun *woet* þe sothe,		A. 2.68	*Wiþ* alle þe purtenaunce of purcatorie into þe pyne of helle;
C.16.342	Ac thorw werkes thow myhte *wyte* wher forth he walketh:		A. 2.71	Þere to wone *wiþ* wrong while god is in heuene.'
C.17.100	*Wisten* w[hi]l[e] and tolde when hit sholde ryne.		A. 2.81	Such weddyng to werche to wraþþe *wiþ* treuþe
C.18.146	And wepte watur with [his] yes; the why *weten* fewe.		A. 2.88	And þou hast fastnid hire *wiþ* fals, fy on þi law[e]!
C.18.180	Y waytede witterly; Ac whoder he wende y ne *wiste*.		A. 2.101	And ʒif þe iustice iugge hire to be ioyned *with* fals,
C.19.9	Were hit þerwith aseled y *woet* wel þe sothe		A. 2.104	And ʒif he fynde ʒow in defaute, & *wiþ* fals holden
C.20.68	Ac shal no wyht *wyte* witturlich ho shal haue þe maistry		A. 2.111	And feffe false wytnesse *wiþ* floreynes ynowe,
C.20.129	'And am wendynge to *wyte* what þis wonder meneth.'		A. 2.118	For we haue mede amaistried *wiþ* oure mery speche
C.20.150	Hit is truyfle þat thow tellest; y, treuthe, *woet* þe sothe,		A. 2.119	Þat he[o] grauntiþ to gon *wiþ* a good wille
C.20.169	For he *woet* more then we; he was ar we bothe.'		A. 2.125	To wende *wiþ* hem to westmynstre to wytnesse þ[is] dede.
C.20.210	For hadde they *wist* of no wo, wele hadde thay nat knowen;		A. 2.174	Ac marchauntis mette *wiþ* hym & made him abide;
C.20.211	For no wiht *woet* what wele is þat neuere wo soffrede		A. 2.183	And senten hym on sundais *wiþ* selis to chirche,
C.20.218	He hadde nat *wist* witterly where deth were sour or swete.		A. 2.186	For to wone *wiþ* hem, watris to loke.
C.20.226	Ne *woet* no wyht, as y wene, what is ynow to mene.		A. 2.187	Spiceris speke *wiþ* h[i]m to aspie here ware,
C.20.230	To *wyte* what wele [was], kyndeliche to knowe [hit].		A. 2.189	Mynstralis & messangeris mette *wiþ* him ones,
C.20.232	To *wyte* what he hath soffred in thre sundry places,		A. 2.191	Freris *wiþ* fair speche fetten hym þennes;
C.20.234	To *wyte* what al wo is þat woet of alle ioye:		A. 2.194	And is welcome whanne he wile & woniþ *wiþ* hem ofte.
C.20.234	To wyte what al wo is þat *woet* of alle ioye:		A. 3.2	*Wiþ* bedelis & baillifs ybrouʒt to þe king.
C.20.237	For *woet* no wiht what werre is þer [þat] pees regneth		A. 3.13	Ientily *wiþ* ioye þe Iustices so[mm]e
C.20.342	With glorie and with [grete] lihte; god hit is ich *woet* wel.		A. 3.22	Rynges *wiþ* rubies & ricchesse manye;
C.20.353	And *wyte*/[th] hem al þe wrechednesse þat wrouhte is on erthe.		A. 3.25	*Wiþ* þat come clerkis to conforten hire þe same,
C.21.162	For þat womman *witeth* [may] nat [wel be] conseyl.		A. 3.92	And brouʒte hire to bo[ure] *wiþ* blisse & wiþ ioye.
C.21.358	For witterly, y *woet* wel, we be nat of strenghe		A. 3.92	And brouʒte hire to bo[ure] wiþ blisse & *wiþ* ioye.
C.21.370	*Wytyng* and wilfully with the false helden		A. 3.136	She is preuy *wiþ* þe pope, prouisours it knowiþ;
C.21.371	And for suluer weren forsswore–soth[ly] thei *wisten* hit.		A. 3.142	Þere she is wel *wiþ* þe king wo is þe reaume,
C.22.3	Y ne *wiste* where to ete ne at what place		A. 3.145	Be Iesu, *wiþ* hire Iuelx ʒoure Iustice she shendiþ,
C.22.318	'We haen no nede,' quod Consience; 'y *woet* no bettere leche		A. 3.159	Þe king grauntide hire grace *wiþ* a good wille.
			A. 3.166	Ne to depraue þi persone *wiþ* a proud herte.
witen v2 *witien v.(1)* A 2 wyte (1) witen (1); B 4 wite (2) witen (2); C 1 wyte			A. 3.171	ʒet I may, as I miʒte, [menske] þe *wiþ* ʒeftis,
A. 6.117	'Wyte god,' quaþ a waffrer, 'wiste I þat forsoþe,		A. 3.184	Þere I lefte *wiþ* my lord his lif for to saue,
A.10.67	But þei *witen* hem fro wauntounesse whiles þei ben ʒon[g]e.		A. 3.198	To alienes, to alle men, to honoure hem *with* ʒeftis.
B.Pr.208	Forþi ech a wis wiʒt I warne, *wite* wel his owene.'		A. 3.202	Þe pope *wiþ* his prelatis presentis vndirfongiþ,
B. 5.632	'*Wite* god', quod a waf[erer], 'wiste I þis for soþe		A. 3.246	Wende þidir *with* þin ost wommen to kille;
B. 7.36	And *witen* yow fro wanhope, if ye wol þus werche,		A. 3.253	But brouʒte *wiþ* hym þe bestis as þe bible [telliþ],
B.16.25	'For wyndes, wiltow *wite*', quod he, 'to *witen* it fro fallyng:		A. 3.271	Ne no ray robe [*wiþ*] riche pelure.
C. 7.285	'Wyte god,' quod a wafre[re], 'wiste y this for sothe		A. 4.11	And counte *wiþ* [þe] consience, so me crist helpe,
			A. 4.19	And let warroke hym wel *wiþ* [wy]tful gerþis.
witenesse > witnesse			A. 4.23	And resoun *wiþ* hym rit & rapiþ hym [swyþe].

witeþ v *witen v.(3)* &> witen A 2 witide (1) wytide (1); B 2 witeþ (1) witte (1); C 2 witte

A. 1.31	And al he *wytide* it wyn þ[at] wykkide dede.
A. 5.205	His wyf [*wit*]*ide* hym þanne of wykkidnesse & synne.

A. 4.30   And rombide forþ *wiþ* resoun riзt to þe king.
A. 4.50   To make his pes *with* his panis & profride hym manye,
A. 4.55   And warnide wrong þo *wiþ* suche a wys tale:
A. 4.63   And tok mede *wiþ* hem mercy to wynne.
A. 4.69   To ouercome þe king *wiþ* catel зif þei miзte.
A. 4.88   I forgyue hym þ[at] gilt *wiþ* a good wille;
A. 4.103   Til childris cherisshing be chastisid *with* зerdis;
A. 4.113   Neiþer grotis ne gold ygraue *wiþ* kynges coyn.
A. 4.115   But it be marchaunt, oþer his man, oþer messang[er] *with* lettres,
A. 4.121   Þat I were king *wiþ* croune to kepe a reaume,
A. 4.126   For nullum malum [þ]e ma[n] met[t]e *with* Inpunitum
A. 4.155   'I am redy,' quaþ resoun, 'to reste *wiþ* зow euere;
A. 5.11   And consience *wiþ* a cros com for to preche.
A. 5.23   How consience *wiþ* a cros cumside to preche.
A. 5.25   And wynne þat he wastide *wiþ* sum maner craft,
A. 5.44   And made wil to wepe watir *wiþ* his eiзen.
A. 5.56   *Wiþ* þat he [shulde] þe satirday, seue зer þeraftir,
A. 5.57   Drinke but *wiþ* þe doke & dyne but ones.
A. 5.58   Enuye *wiþ* heuy herte askide aftir shrift,
A. 5.65   So lokide he *wiþ* lene chekis, lourande foule.
A. 5.68   *Wiþ* werkis [or wiþ] wordis whanne he saiз his tyme.
A. 5.68   *Wiþ* werkis [or *wiþ*] wordis whanne he saiз his tyme.
A. 5.109   He was [betil]browid & babirlippid *wiþ* two bleride eiзen,
A. 5.120   *Wiþ* many maner marchaundise as my maister me hiзte.
A. 5.126   Brochide hem *wiþ* a pakke nedle, & pleit hem togidere;
A. 5.167   Зeue glotoun *wiþ* glad chiere good ale to hansele.
A. 5.184   And grete sire glotoun *wiþ* a galoun ale.
A. 5.192   And wisshide it hadde be wexid *wiþ* a wysp of firsen.
A. 5.196   As whoso leide lynes to lacche *wiþ* [foules].
A. 5.199   Þat *wiþ* al þe wo of þe world his wyf & his wenche
A. 5.231   And *wiþ* þe residue & þe remenaunt, be þe roode of chestre,
A. 5.242   Ne neuere wen[e] to wynne *wiþ* craft þat [I owe],
A. 5.246   Wel I woot he wep faste watir *wiþ* his eiзen.
A. 5.249   And lepe *with* hym ouer lond al his lif tyme,
A. 6.5   He bar a burdoun ybounde *wiþ* a brood list,
A. 6.23   'I sauз neuere palmere *wiþ* pik ne *wiþ* scrippe
A. 6.23   'I sauз neuere palmere *wiþ* pik ne *wiþ* scrippe
A. 6.68   He is fre[þ]id in *wiþ* Floreynes & oþere [fees] manye.
A. 6.76   And boterasid *wiþ* beleue [so] oþer þou [be]st not sauid;
A. 6.78   *Wiþ* no led but [wiþ] loue & louзnesse, as breþeren of o wombe.
A. 6.78   *Wiþ* no led but [*wiþ*] loue & louзnesse, as breþeren of o wombe.
A. 6.80   He may do *wiþ* þe day sterre what hym dere likiþ,
A. 7.6   I wolde wende *wiþ* зow til зe were þere'.
A. 7.18   And зe loueliche ladies *wiþ* зour [longe] fyngris,
A. 7.47   Holde *wiþ* none harlotis ne here nouзt here talis,
A. 7.53   And wende *wiþ* зow þe wey til we fynde treuþe.'
A. 7.61   And make hym mery *wiþ* þe corn whoso it begrucchiþ.
A. 7.67   Deleantur de libro; I shulde not dele *wiþ* hem,
A. 7.76   To penaunce & to pilgrimage wile I passe *wiþ* oþere;
A. 7.88   My wyf shal haue of þat I wan *wiþ* treuþe, & namore,
A. 7.92   And *wiþ* þe residue & þe remenaunt, be þe rode of chestre,
A. 7.108   And holpen [to] ere þe half akir *wiþ* 'hey trolly lolly'.
A. 7.115   And pleynide hem to peris *wiþ* suche pitous wordis:
A. 7.116   'We haue none [lymes] to laboure *wiþ*, lord, ygracid be зe;
A. 7.142   And bad hym go pisse *wiþ* his plouз: 'pilide shrewe!
A. 7.164   N[e] hadde peris [*wiþ*] a pese lof preyede hym beleue,
A. 7.165   And *wiþ* a bene batte he[зe]de [hem] betwene,
A. 7.172   And fla[ppid]e on *wiþ* flailes fro morewe til eue,
A. 7.179   Hungir hem helide *wiþ* an hot[e] cake.
A. 7.182   And preiзede pur charite *wiþ* peris for to dwelle,
A. 7.200   *Wiþ* houndis bred & hors bred holde vp here hertis,
A. 7.201   And [a]baue hem *wiþ* b[e]nes for bollnyng of here wombe.
A. 7.205   *Wiþ* fuyr or *wiþ* false men, fond suche [to] knowen;
A. 7.205   *Wiþ* fuyr or *wiþ* false men, fond suche [to] knowen;
A. 7.206   Counforte hem *wiþ* þi catel for cristis loue of heuene;
A. 7.210   *Wiþ* mete or [*wiþ*] mone let make hem [fare þe betere],
A. 7.210   *Wiþ* mete or [*wiþ*] mone let make hem [fare þe betere],
A. 7.211   [Or *with* werk or with word þe while þou art here].
A. 7.211   [Or with werk or *with* word þe while þou art here].
A. 7.222   Matheu *wiþ* þe manis face [mouþ]iþ þise wordis:
A. 7.232   Oþer *wiþ* teching, oþer telling, or trauaillyng of hondis,
A. 7.235   He þat get his fode here *wiþ* trauaile of his hondis,
A. 7.256   And lerne to laboure *wiþ* lond lest liflode hym faile.
A. 7.284   Þanne was folk fayn, & fedde hunger *wiþ* þe beste;
A. 7.285   *Wiþ* good ale & glotonye h[y] gart hym to slepe.
A. 8.12   *Wiþ* patriarkes in paradis to pleiзe þereaftir.
A. 8.18   Han pardoun *wiþ* þe apostlis whanne þei passe hennis,
A. 8.41   Þat no gile go *wiþ* зow but þe graiþ treuþe.'
A. 8.70   He is fals *wiþ* þe fend & [defraudiþ] þe nedy,
A. 8.73   Þei wedde no womman þat hy *wiþ* delen
A. 8.74   But as wilde bestis *wiþ* wehe, & worþ vp togideris
A. 8.77   And gon & faiten *wiþ* here fauntis for eueremore aftir.
A. 8.83   And wommen *wiþ* childe þat werche ne mowe,

A. 9.31   Þe wynd wolde *wiþ* þe watir þe boot ouerþrowe.
A. 9.81   And *wiþ* mammones money he haþ mad hym frendis,
A. 9.84   [3]e wise suffriþ þe vnwise *with* зow to libbe,
A. 9.85   And *wiþ* glad wil doþ hem good for so god [hiзte].
A. 9.109   Ac er we ywar were *wiþ* wyt gonne we mete.
A.10.4   *Wiþ* wynd & *wiþ* watir wi[tti]liche enioynede.
A.10.4   *Wiþ* wynd & *wiþ* watir wi[tti]liche enioynede.
A.10.9   And wolde wynne hire awey *with* wyles зif he miзte.
A.10.20   Sire werche wel *wiþ* þin hond, [a] wiзt man of strengþe,
A.10.34   And al at his wil was wrouзt *wiþ* a speche,
A.10.39   As muche to mene [as] man *with* his soule,
A.10.40   Þat he wrouзte *wiþ* werkis & *with* wordis boþe.
A.10.40   Þat he wrouзte *wiþ* werkis & *with* wordis boþe.
A.10.58   In зonge fauntes & folis, *wiþ* hem failiþ Inwyt,
A.10.108   Thrift oþer þedom *with* þo is selde yseiзe:
A.10.117   Be paied *wiþ* þe porcioun, pore oþer riche.
A.10.130   Such wer[kis] to werche [þat] he is *wiþ* paied.
A.10.154   For þei mariede hem *wiþ* curside men of caymes kyn.
A.10.156   And alle þat couplide hem *with* þat kyn crist hatide [dedliche].
A.10.161   Þat god was wroþ *wiþ* here werkis & [suche wordis seide]:
A.10.214   And aftir here deþ day·shuln dwelle *with* þe same
A.11.8   *Wiþ* suche wise wordis to wisse any foolis!
A.11.18   But it be cardit *wiþ* coueitise as cloþeris don here wolle:
A.11.50   Þat þus partiþ *wiþ* þe poore a parcel whanne hym nediþ.
A.11.59   To pleise *wiþ* proude men, siþen þe pestilence tyme,
A.11.117   For зif þou coupl[e] þe *with* hym to clergie comist þou neuere;
A.11.133   And bet hem *wiþ* a baleis but зif þei wolde lerne.
A.11.157   Þat þinkeþ werche *wiþ* þo þre þrieue wel late,
A.11.176   Þat I was of wyttis hous & *wiþ* his wyf dame stodie.
A.11.186   *Wiþ* any trewe trauaille toille for here foode,
A.11.188   To breke beggeris bred & bakken hem *with* cloþis,
A.11.193   Sike *with* þe sory, singe *with* þe glade,
A.11.193   Sike with þe sory, singe *with* þe glade,
A.11.217   Þis is þe lif of þis lordis þat lyuen shulde *wiþ* dobet,
A.11.219   'I wende þat kinghed, & kniзthed, & caiseris *wiþ* Erlis
A.11.278   Þanne wrouзte I vnwisly *wiþ* alle þe wyt þat I lere.
A.11.280   Þat hadde lyued al his lyf *wiþ* lesinges & þeft[e],
A.11.284   Þat hadde leyn *with* lucifer manye longe зeris;
A.11.312   Percen *wiþ* a paternoster þe paleis of heuene
A.12.23   "I am not hardy," quod he, "þat I herde *with* erys,
A.12.24   Telle hit *with* tounge to synful wrecches."
A.12.33   But as he seyþ, such I am, when he *with* me carpeþ.'
A.12.40   *With* þat she wolde me wisse wher þe toun were
A.12.44   And his loggyng is *with* lyf þat lord is of erþe,
A.12.45   And зif þou desyre *with* him for to abyde
A.12.48   And þanked hure a þousand syþes *with* þrobbant herte.
A.12.51   'Þou shalt wende *with* wil,' quod she, 'whiles þat him lykyþ,
A.12.56   And wente forþ on my way *with* omnia probate,
A.12.62   'Al hayl,' quod on þo, and I answered, 'welcome, & *with* whom be
          зe?'
A.12.63   'I am dwellyng *with* deth, and hunger I hatte.
A.12.72   Than maunged I *wit[h* him] vp at þe fulle,
A.12.77   *With* þat cam a knaue *with* a confessoures face,
A.12.77   With þat cam a knaue *with* a confessoures face,
A.12.78   [Lene & rewlyche, *with* leggys ful smale].
A.12.81   '*With* deþ I duelle,' quod he, 'dayes and nyзtes,
A.12.91   Þ[ou] tomblest *with* a trepget зif þou my tras folwe,
A.12.95   Þat þi play be plentevous in paradys *with* aungelys.
A.12.96   Þou shalt be lauзth into lyзth *with* loking of an eye
B.Pr.16   *Wiþ* depe diches and derke and dredfulle of siзte.
B.Pr.22   Wonnen þat [þise] wastours *with* glotonye destruyeþ.
B.Pr.34   And geten gold *with* hire glee [gilt]lees, I leeue.
B.Pr.44   And risen [vp] *wiþ* ribaudie [as] Roberdes knaues;
B.Pr.48   Wenten forþ in hire wey *wiþ* many wise tales,
B.Pr.53   Heremytes on an heep *with* hoked staues,
B.Pr.69   Brouзte forþ a bulle *wiþ* Bisshopes seles,
B.Pr.74   He bonched hem *with* his breuet and blered hire eiзen
B.Pr.75   And rauзte *with* his Rageman rynges and broches.
B.Pr.102   How he it lefte *wiþ* loue as oure lord hiзte
B.Pr.146   *Wiþ* þat ran þer a route of Ratons at ones
B.Pr.151   And pleide *wiþ* hem perillousli and possed aboute.
B.Pr.156   Miзte we *wiþ* any wit his wille wiþstonde
B.Pr.190   But fedeþ hym al *wiþ* venyson, defame we hym neuere;
B.Pr.225   And dryueþ forþ þe longe day *with* 'Dieu saue dame Emme'.
B. 1.15   Boþe *with* fel and with face, and yaf yow fyue wittes
B. 1.15   Boþe with fel and *with* face, and yaf yow fyue wittes
B. 1.47   Tho þe poeple hym apposede *wiþ* a peny in þe temple
B. 1.67   Iudas he iaped *wiþ* Iewen siluer
B. 1.102   But holden *wiþ* hym and with here þat [asken þe] truþe,
B. 1.102   But holden wiþ hym and *with* here þat [asken þe] truþe,
B. 1.111   Lucifer *wiþ* legions lerned it in heuene
B. 1.117   Lopen out *wiþ* Lucifer in loþliche forme
B. 1.128   And alle þat werchen *with* wrong wende þei shulle

B. 1.129 After hir deþ day and dwelle *with* þat sherewe.
B. 1.150 And alle hise werkes he wrouȝte *with* loue as hym liste;
B. 1.167 Loked on vs *wiþ* loue and leet his sone dye
B. 1.170 But mekely *wiþ* mouþe mercy [he] bisouȝte
B. 1.196 [Ye] ben acombred *with* coueitise; [ye] konne noȝt [out crepe],
B. 1.203 To conforten þe carefulle acombred *with* synne.
B. 2.9 Purfiled *wiþ* Pelure [þe [pureste on] erþe,
B. 2.11 Fetisliche hire fyngres were fretted *with* gold wyr
B. 2.16 *Wiþ* Ribanes of reed gold and of riche stones.
B. 2.31 And haþ yeuen me mercy to marie *wiþ* myselue,
B. 2.54 That al þe riche retenaunce þat regneþ *with* [fals]
B. 2.64 Were moost pryuee *with* Mede of any men me þouȝte.
B. 2.66 And as a Brocour brouȝte hire to be *wiþ* fals enioyned.
B. 2.70 That Gile *wiþ* hise grete oþes gaf hem togidere',
B. 2.79 And Fauel *wiþ* his fikel speche feffeþ þis chartre
B. 2.85 *Wiþ* þe Chastilet of cheste and chaterynge out of reson,
B. 2.88 In bargaynes and brocages *wiþ* þe Burgh of þefte,
B. 2.89 [*Wiþ*] al þe lordshipe of leccherie in lengþe and in brede,
B. 2.90 As in werkes and in wordes and waityn[g] *wiþ* eiȝes
B. 2.91 And in we[n]es and in wisshynges and *wiþ* ydel þouȝtes
B. 2.100 And þanne wanhope to awaken h[y]m so *wiþ* no wil to amende
B. 2.103 A dwellynge *wiþ* þe deuel and dampned be for euere
B. 2.104 *Wiþ* alle þe [p]urtinaunces of Purgatorie into þe pyne of helle.
B. 2.106 Hire soules to Sathan to suffre *with* hym peynes,
B. 2.107 And *with* hym to wonye [in] wo while god is in heuene.'
B. 2.117 Swic[h] weddyng[e] to werche to wraþe *wiþ* truþe;
B. 2.124 And þow hast fest hire [*wiþ*] Fals; fy on þi lawe!
B. 2.137 And [if þe] Iustic[e] Iugg[e] hire to be Ioyned [*wiþ*] Fals
B. 2.140 And if he fynde yow in defaute, and *with* [fals] holde,
B. 2.147 And feffe fal[s] witness[e] *wiþ* floryns ynowe,
B. 2.154 For we haue Mede amaistried *wiþ* oure murie speche
B. 2.155 That she graunteþ to goon *wiþ* a good wille
B. 2.161 To wenden *wiþ* hem to westmynstre to witnesse þis dede.
B. 2.175 Lat sadle hem *wiþ* siluer oure synne to suffre,
B. 2.215 Ac Marchauntȝ metten *with* hym and made hym abyde
B. 2.224 And senten hym [on Sondayes *wiþ* seles] to chirch[e],
B. 2.227 [For to] wonye *with* hem watres to loke.
B. 2.228 Spycers speken *with* hym to spien hire ware
B. 2.230 A[c] Mynstrales and Messagers mette *with* hym ones
B. 2.232 Freres *wiþ* fair speche fetten hym þennes;
B. 2.235 And is welcome whan he wile and woneþ *with* hem ofte.
B. 3.2 *Wiþ* Bedeles and baillies brouȝt [to] þe kyng.
B. 3.13 Gentilliche *wiþ* ioye þe Iustices somme
B. 3.23 Rynges *wiþ* Rubies and richesses manye,
B. 3.26 *Wiþ* þat comen clerkes to conforten hire þe same
B. 3.74 Wite what þow werchest *wiþ* þi riȝt syde,
B. 3.103 And brouȝte hire to boure *wiþ* blisse and *wiþ* ioye.
B. 3.103 And brouȝte hire to boure *wiþ* blisse and *wiþ* ioye.
B. 3.147 She is pryuee *wiþ* þe pope, prouisours it knoweþ;
B. 3.153 Ther she is wel *wiþ* þe kyng wo is þe Reaume,
B. 3.155 By Iesus! *wiþ* hire Ieweles youre Iustices she shendeþ
B. 3.172 The kyng graunteþ hire grace *wiþ* a good wille.
B. 3.179 Ne [to] depraue þi persone *wiþ* a proud herte.
B. 3.184 Yet I may, as I myȝte, menske þee *wiþ* ȝiftes,
B. 3.197 Ther I lafte *wiþ* my lord his lif for to saue.
B. 3.211 To aliens, to alle men, to honouren hem *with* ȝiftes.
B. 3.215 The Pope [*wiþ* hise] prelates presentȝ vnderfonge[þ],
B. 3.235 Lord, who shal wonye in þi wones *wiþ* þyne holy seintes,
B. 3.239 And han ywroght werkes *wiþ* right and *wiþ* reson,
B. 3.239 And han ywroght werkes *wiþ* right and [*wiþ*] reson,
B. 3.242 And alle þat helpen þe Innocent and holden *with* þe riȝtfulle,
B. 3.266 Weend to Amalec *with* þyn oost & what þow fyndest þere sle it.
B. 3.282 For so is þis world went *wiþ* hem þat han power
B. 3.309 Ech man to pleye *with* a plow, Pykoise or spade,
B. 3.310 Spynne or sprede donge or spille hymself *with* sleuþe.
B. 3.311 Preestes and persons *wiþ* Placebo to hunte
B. 3.352 That þeiȝ we wynne worship and *with* Mede haue victorie,
B. 4.11 And acounte *wiþ* þee, Conscience, so me crist helpe,
B. 4.21 And lat warroke hym wel wit[ful] gerþes.
B. 4.25 And Reson *wiþ* hym ryt, rownynge togideres
B. 4.34 'Ther are wiles in hire wordes, and *with* Mede þei dwelleþ;
B. 4.64 To maken [his] pees *with* hise pens and profred hym manye,
B. 4.69 And warnede wrong þo *with* swich a wis tale:
B. 4.75 To maken [his] pees *wiþ* his pens, handy dandy payed.
B. 4.82 To ouercomen þe kyng *wiþ* catel if þei myȝte.
B. 4.101 I forgyue hym þat gilt *wiþ* a good wille
B. 4.117 And childrene cherissynge be chast[ised] *wiþ* yerdes,
B. 4.130 Neiþer [grotes ne gold ygraue *wiþ* kynges coyn]
B. 4.132 But it be Marchaunt or his man or Messager *wiþ* lettres,
B. 4.138 That I were kyng *with* coroune to kepen a Reaume,
B. 4.143 For Nullum malum þe man mette *wiþ* inpunitum
B. 4.173 And modiliche vpon Mede *wiþ* myȝt þe kyng loked,
B. 4.174 And gan wexe wroþ *with* lawe for Mede almoost hadde shent it,

B. 4.177 Ac Reson shal rekene *wiþ* yow if I regne any while,
B. 4.192 'I am redy', quod Reson, 'to reste *wiþ* yow euere;
B. 5.12 And *wiþ* a cros afore þe kyng comsede þus to techen.
B. 5.25 And wynnen his wastyng *wiþ* som maner crafte.
B. 5.61 And [made] wille to wepe water *wiþ* hise eiȝen.
B. 5.73 *Wiþ* þat he sholde þe Saterday, seuen yer þerafter,
B. 5.74 Drynke but [*wiþ*] þe doke and dyne but ones.
B. 5.75 Enuye *wiþ* heuy herte asked after shrifte,
B. 5.82 So loked he *wiþ* lene chekes, lourynge foule.
B. 5.85 *With* werkes or *wiþ* wordes whan he seyȝe his tyme.
B. 5.85 With werkes or *wiþ* wordes whan he seyȝe his tyme.
B. 5.88 *Wiþ* bakbitynge and bismere and berynge of fals witnesse;
B. 5.135 Now awakeþ Wraþe *wiþ* two white eiȝen,
B. 5.136 And neuelynge *wiþ* þe nose and his nekke hangyng.
B. 5.144 And now persons han parceyued þat freres parte *wiþ* hem
B. 5.148 I, wraþe, walke *wiþ* hem and wisse hem of my bokes.
B. 5.156 Manye Monþes *wiþ* hem, and *wiþ* Monkes boþe.
B. 5.156 Manye Monþes *wiþ* hem, and *wiþ* Monkes boþe.
B. 5.176 Forþi haue I no likyng, [leue me], *wiþ* þo leodes to wonye;
B. 5.190 He was bitelbrowed and baberlipped *wiþ* two blered eiȝen,
B. 5.194 *Wiþ* an hood on his heed, a hat aboue,
B. 5.204 *Wiþ* many manere marchaundise as my maister me hiȝte.
B. 5.210 [P]roche[d] hem *wiþ* a paknedle and playte hem togideres,
B. 5.231 'ȝis, ones I was yherberwed', quod he, '*wiþ* an heep of chapmen;
B. 5.240 To weye pens *wiþ* a peis and pare þe heuyeste
B. 5.246 Eschaunges and cheuysaunces, *wiþ* swich chaffare I dele,
B. 5.248 And *wiþ* lumbardes lettres I ladde gold to Rome
B. 5.264 And þat was wonne *wiþ* wrong *wiþ* wikked men be despended.
B. 5.264 And þat was wonne *wiþ* wrong *wiþ* wikked men be despended.
B. 5.266 I nolde cope vs *wiþ* þi catel ne oure kirk amende
B. 5.271 Til þow make restitucion', [quod Repentaunce], 'and rekene *wiþ* hem alle;
B. 5.281 'Haue mercy in þi mynde, and *wiþ* þi mouþ biseche it—
B. 5.285 For þow hast no good ground to gete þee *wiþ* a wastel
B. 5.286 But if it were *wiþ* þi tonge or ellis *wiþ* þi hondes.
B. 5.286 But if it were *wiþ* þi tonge or ellis *wiþ* þi hondes.
B. 5.287 For þe good þat þow hast geten bigan al *wiþ* falshede,
B. 5.318 Geue Gloton *wiþ* glad chere good ale to hanselle.
B. 5.335 And greten sire Gloton *wiþ* a Galon ale.
B. 5.344 And wisshed it hadde ben wexed *wiþ* a wispe of firses.
B. 5.348 As whoso leiþ lynes to lacche [*wiþ*] foweles.
B. 5.357 *Wiþ* al þe wo of þ[e] world his wif and his wenche
B. 5.365 'As þow *wiþ* wordes & werkes hast wroȝt yuele in þi lyue
B. 5.366 Shryue þee and be shamed þerof and shewe it *with* þi mouþe.'
B. 5.368 That I haue trespased *with* my tonge, I kan noȝt telle how ofte;
B. 5.385 Thanne cam Sleuþe al bislabered *wiþ* two slymy eiȝen.
B. 5.390 He bigan Benedicite *with* a bolk and his brest knokked,
B. 5.401 That I telle *wiþ* my tonge is two myle fro myn herte.
B. 5.403 *Wiþ* ydel tales at þe Ale and ouþerwhile [in] chirche[s];
B. 5.424 Sixe siþes or seuene I forsake it *wiþ* oþes.
B. 5.428 So *wiþ* wikked wil and wraþe my werkmen I paye.
B. 5.432 I am noȝt lured *wiþ* loue but þer ligge auȝt vnder þe þombe.
B. 5.441 'Repente[st]ow noȝt?' quod Repentaunce, & riȝt *wiþ* þat he swowned
B. 5.459 And *wiþ* þe residue and þe remenaunt, bi þe Rode of Chestre,
B. 5.468 Ne neuere wene to wynne *wiþ* craft þat I owe;
B. 5.472 Wel I woot he wepte faste water *wiþ* hise eiȝen,
B. 5.475 And lepe *wiþ* hym ouer lond al his lif tyme,
B. 5.486 And madest þiself *wiþ* þi sone vs synfulle yliche:
B. 5.487 And siþþe *wiþ* þi selue sone in oure s[u]te deidest
B. 5.493 Feddest *wiþ* þi fresshe blood oure forefadres in derknesse:
B. 5.507 And blew it *wiþ* Beati quorum remisse sunt iniquitates,
B. 5.517 He bar a burdoun ybounde *wiþ* a brood liste,
B. 5.535 'I [ne] seiȝ neuere Palmere *wiþ* pyk ne *wiþ* scrippe
B. 5.535 'I [ne] seiȝ neuere Palmere *wiþ* pyk ne *wiþ* scrippe
B. 5.581 He is fryþed In *wiþ* floryns and oþere fees manye;
B. 5.589 Botrased *wiþ* bileef-so-or-þow-beest-noȝt-saued;
B. 5.591 *Wiþ* no leed but *wiþ* loue and lowe[nesse] as breþeren [of o wombe].
B. 5.591 *Wiþ* no leed but *wiþ* loue and lowe[nesse] as breþeren [of o wombe].
B. 5.640 I wol go fecche my box *wiþ* my breuettes & a bulle with bisshopes lettres
B. 5.640 I wol go fecche my box *wiþ* my breuettes & a bulle *with* bisshopes lettres
B. 6.6 I wolde wende *wiþ* yow and þe wey teche.'
B. 6.10 And ye louely ladies *wiþ* youre longe fyngres,
B. 6.47 That he worþ worþier set and *wiþ* moore blisse:
B. 6.52 Hold *wiþ* none harlotes ne here noȝt hir tales,
B. 6.58 And wende *wiþ* yow [þe wey] til we fynde truþe.'
B. 6.75 Deleantur de libro viuencium; I sholde noȝt dele *wiþ* hem,
B. 6.84 To penaunce and to pilgrimage I wol passe *wiþ* oþere;
B. 6.96 My wif shal haue of þat I wan *wiþ* truþe and na moore,

B. 6.100	And *wiþ* þe residue and þe remenaunt, by þe Rode of Lukes!
B. 6.116	And holpen ere þ[e] half acre *wiþ* 'how trolly lolly'.
B. 6.124	'We haue no lymes to laboure *with*; lord, ygraced be [y]e!
B. 6.133	Ye wasten þat men wynnen *wiþ* trauaille and tene.
B. 6.136	But if he be blynd or brokelegged or bolted *wiþ* Irens,
B. 6.147	And catel to [cope] hem *wiþ* þat han Cloistres and chirches.
B. 6.155	And bad hym go pissen *with* his plow3: '[pyuysshe] sherewe!
B. 6.179	Ne hadde Piers *wiþ* a pese loof preyed [hym bileue]
B. 6.181	'[Lat] hem lyue', he seide, 'and lat hem ete *wiþ* hogges,
B. 6.184	And flapten on *wiþ* flailes fro morwe til euen
B. 6.214	*Wiþ* houndes breed and horse breed hoold vp hir hertes,
B. 6.215	[And] aba[u]e hem *wiþ* benes for bollynge of hir womb[e];
B. 6.219	[*Wiþ* fir or wiþ] false men, fonde swiche to knowe.
B. 6.219	[*Wiþ* fir or *wiþ*] false men, fonde swiche to knowe.
B. 6.220	Conforte h[e]m *wiþ* þi catel for cristes loue of heuene.
B. 6.224	*Wiþ* mete or wiþ mone lat make hem fare þe bettre].
B. 6.224	*Wiþ* mete or *wiþ* mone lat make hem fare þe bettre].
B. 6.238	Mathew *wiþ* mannes face mouþe[þ] þise wordes.
B. 6.248	Or [*wiþ* tech]ynge or [tell]ynge or trauaillynge [of hondes],
B. 6.251	The freke þat fedeþ hymself *wiþ* his feiþful labour
B. 6.272	And lerne to laboure *wiþ* lond [lest] liflode [hym faille].
B. 6.295	And profrede Piers þis present to plese *wiþ* hunger.
B. 6.300	Thanne was folk fayn and fedde hunger *wiþ* þe beste;
B. 6.301	*Wiþ* good Ale as Gloton ta3te [þei] garte [hym to] slepe.
B. 7.8	Pardon *wiþ* Piers Plowman truþe haþ ygraunted.
B. 7.12	*Wiþ* Patriarkes and prophetes in paradis to be felawe.
B. 7.16	Arn peres *wiþ* þe Apostles–þ[u]s pardon Piers sheweþ–
B. 7.68	He is fals *wiþ* þe feend and defraudeþ þe nedy,
B. 7.91	[Thei] wedde [no] womman þat [þei] *wiþ* deele
B. 7.92	But as wilde bestes *with* wehee worþen vppe and werchen,
B. 7.95	And goon [and] faiten *with* [hire] fauntes for eueremoore after.
B. 7.101	And wommen *wiþ* childe þat werche ne mowe,
B. 7.141	As diuinour in diuinite, *wiþ* Dixit insipiens to þi teme.'
B. 7.153	And how þe preest inpugned it *wiþ* two propre wordes.
B. 8.35	The wynd wolde *wiþ* þe water þe boot ouerþrowe.
B. 8.90	And *wiþ* Mammonaes moneie he haþ maad hym frendes;
B. 8.94	[Ye wise] suffreþ þe vnwise *wiþ* yow to libbe,
B. 8.95	And *wiþ* glad wille dooþ hem good for so god hoteþ.
B. 8.119	A[c] er we [war were] *wiþ* wit gonne we mete.
B. 9.4	*Wiþ* wynd and *wiþ* water witt[i]ly enioyned.
B. 9.4	*Wiþ* wynd and *wiþ* water witt[i]ly enioyned.
B. 9.9	And wolde wynne hire awey *wiþ* wiles [if] he my3te.
B. 9.11	And [haþ] doo[n] hire *wiþ* sire dowel, duc of þise Marches.
B. 9.21	Sire werch-wel-*wiþ*-þyn-hand, a wi3t man of strengþe,
B. 9.33	[And al at his wil was wrou3t *wiþ* a speche],
B. 9.38	My my3t moot helpe forþ *wiþ* my speche".
B. 9.44	He moste werche *wiþ* his word and his wit shewe.
B. 9.46	*Wiþ* his word and werkmanshipe and *wiþ* lif to laste.
B. 9.46	*Wiþ* his word and werkmanshipe and *wiþ* lif to laste.
B. 9.51	As muche to mene as man *wiþ* a Soule.
B. 9.52	[Th]at he wro3te *wiþ* werk and *wiþ* word boþe;
B. 9.52	[Th]at he wro3te *wiþ* werk and *wiþ* word boþe;
B. 9.93	He is [lugged *wiþ*] Iudas þat 3yueþ a Iaper siluer
B. 9.116	And þus was wedlok ywro3t *wiþ* a mene persone,
B. 9.129	And no3t þi kynde *wiþ* Caymes ycoupled n[e] yspoused".
B. 9.132	Til god wraþed [*wiþ*] hir werkes and swich a word seide,
B. 9.143	And þe foweles þat fleen forþ *wiþ* oþere beestes,
B. 9.181	And þanne gete ye grace of god and good ynou3 to lyue *wiþ*.
B. 9.186	Wreke þee *wiþ* wyuyng if þow wolt ben excused:
B. 9.200	And after hir deeþ day shul dwelle *wiþ* þe same
B.10.8	'*Wiþ* swiche wise wordes to wissen any sottes!'
B.10.18	But it be carded *wiþ* coueitise as cloþeres [don] hir wolle.
B.10.22	Thei lede lordes *wiþ* lesynges and bilieþ truþe.
B.10.39	But þoo þat feynen hem foolis, and *wiþ* faityng libbeþ
B.10.64	That þus parteþ *wiþ* þe pouere a parcell whan hym nedeþ,
B.10.73	To plese *wiþ* proude men syn þe pestilence tyme;
B.10.101	Or in a chambre *wiþ* a chymenee, and leue þe chief halle
B.10.165	For if þow coupl[e] þee [*wiþ*] hym] to clergie comest [þow] neuere;
B.10.181	And bette hem *wiþ* a baleys for þei wolde lerne.
B.10.214	[That] þynkeþ werche *with* þo [þre] þryueþ [wel] late,
B.10.233	That I was of wittes hous and *wiþ* his wif dame Studie.
B.10.239	*Wiþ* alle þe articles of þe feiþ þat falleþ to be knowe.
B.10.326	And Barons *wiþ* Erles beten hem þoru3 Beatus virres techyng.
B.10.346	And preiseden pouerte *with* pacience; þe Apostles bereþ witnesse
B.10.359	That whoso wolde and wilneþ *wiþ* crist to arise,
B.10.409	And his wif *wiþ* hise sones and also hire wyues;
B.10.421	That hadde lyued al his lif *wiþ* lesynges and þefte,
B.10.425	That hadde yleyen *wiþ* lucifer many longe yeres.
B.10.432	And now ben [swiche] as Souereyns *wiþ* Seintes in heuene,
B.10.435	Of wit and of wisedom *wiþ* dampned soules wonye.
B.10.444	Forþi lyue we forþ *wiþ* [liþere] men; I leue fewe ben goode,
B.10.468	Percen *wiþ* a Paternoster þe paleys of heuene

B.11.28	'Man', quod he, 'if I mete *wiþ* þe, by Marie of heuene!
B.11.116	And in a weer gan I wexe, and *wiþ* myself to dispute
B.11.124	By þe blood þat he bou3te vs *wiþ*, and þoru3 bapteme after:
B.11.131	A[c] reson shal rekene *wiþ* hym [and rebuken hym at þe laste,
B.11.132	And conscience acounte *wiþ* hym] and casten hym in arerage,
B.11.136	Mercy for hise mysdedes *wiþ* mouþe [or] *wiþ* herte.'
B.11.136	Mercy for hise mysdedes *wiþ* mouþe [or] *wiþ* herte.'
B.11.169	God wrou3te it and wroot it *wiþ* his [owene] fynger,
B.11.187	And lokeþ on vs in hir liknesse and þat *wiþ* louely chere
B.11.320	Ac muche moore in metynge þus *wiþ* me gan oon dispute,
B.11.330	*Wiþ* fleckede feþeres and of fele colours.
B.11.344	Medled no3t *wiþ* hir makes, [saue man allone].
B.11.400	Al to murþe *wiþ* man þat moste wo þolie,
B.11.420	And ri3t so ferde Reson bi þee; þow *wiþ* rude speche
B.11.440	And I aroos vp ri3t *wiþ* þat and [reuerenced] hym [faire,
B.12.11	*Wiþ* poustees of pestilences, wiþ pouerte and with angres;
B.12.11	*Wiþ* poustees of pestilences, *wiþ* pouerte and with angres;
B.12.11	*Wiþ* poustees of pestilences, *wiþ* pouerte and *with* angres;
B.12.12	And *wiþ* þise bittre baleises god beteþ his deere children:
B.12.14	Alþou3 þow strike me *wiþ* þi staf, *wiþ* stikke or *wiþ* yerde,
B.12.14	Alþou3 þow strike me *wiþ* þi staf, *wiþ* stikke or *wiþ* yerde,
B.12.14	Alþou3 þow strike me *wiþ* þi staf, *wiþ* stikke or *wiþ* yerde,
B.12.16	And þow medlest þee *wiþ* makynges and my3test go seye þi sauter;
B.12.75	*Wiþ* stones men sholde hir strike and stone hire to deþe.
B.12.106	And haþ noon hap *wiþ* his ax his enemy to hitte,
B.12.119	That *wiþ* archa dei [wenten] in [worship and reuerence]
B.12.124	And medle no3t muche *wiþ* hem to meuen any wraþe
B.12.153	Clerkes knewen it wel and comen *wiþ* hir present3
B.12.156	How þow contrariedest clergie *wiþ* crabbede wordes,
B.12.186	Wo was hym marked þat wade moot *wiþ* þe lewed!
B.12.200	As þo þat seten at þe syde table or *wiþ* þe souereynes of þe halle,
B.12.203	He sit neiþer *wiþ* Seint Iohan, Symond ne Iude,
B.12.204	Ne *wiþ* maydenes ne with martires [ne wiþ mylde] wydewes,
B.12.204	Ne *wiþ* maydenes ne *with* martires [ne wiþ mylde] wydewes,
B.12.204	Ne *wiþ* maydenes ne *with* martires [ne *wiþ* mylde] wydewes,
B.12.231	And tau3te hym and Eue to helien hem *wiþ* leues.
B.12.240	And þat [is] þe pecok & þe Pehen [*wiþ* hir proude feþeres
B.12.254	Thou3 he crye to crist þanne *wiþ* kene wil, I leue
B.12.296	To kepe *wiþ* a commune; no catel was holde bettre,
B.12.297	And muche murþe and manhod;' and ri3t *wiþ* þat he vanysshed.
B.13.23	And bad me come to his court, *wiþ* clergie sholde I dyne,
B.13.60	And made hym murþe *wiþ* his mete, ac I mornede euere
B.13.63	Wombe cloutes and wilde brawen and egges yfryed *wiþ* grece.
B.13.78	'Ac þis goddes gloton', quod I, '*wiþ* hise grete chekes
B.13.81	And wisshed witterly, *wiþ* wille ful egre,
B.13.84	'I shal Iangle to þis Iurdan *wiþ* his Iuste wombe
B.13.111	I wolde permute my penaunce *with* youre, for I am in point to dowel.'
B.13.129	Whiche Infinites *wiþ* a feiþ fynden out dobest,
B.13.140	"*Wiþ* wordes and werkes", quod she, "and wil of þyn herte
B.13.143	Thyn enemy in alle wise eueneforþ *wiþ* þiselue.
B.13.145	Boþe *wiþ* wer[k] and with wor[d] fonde his loue to wynne;
B.13.145	Boþe *wiþ* wer[k] and *with* wor[d] fonde his loue to wynne;
B.13.146	And leye on hym þus *with* loue til he lau3e on þe.
B.13.148	Ac for to fare þus *wiþ* þi frend, folie it were;
B.13.151	*Wiþ* half a laumpe lyne in latyn, Ex vi transicionis,,
B.13.156	And herwith am I welcome þer I haue it me.
B.13.159	Misese ne meschief ne man *wiþ* his tonge,
B.13.163	Tene þee any tyme, and þow take it *wiþ* þe:
B.13.181	'For I wol go *wiþ* þis gome, if god wol yeue me grace,
B.13.182	And be Pilgrym *wiþ* pacience til I haue preued moore.'
B.13.206	If Pacience be oure partyng felawe and pryue *with* vs boþe,
B.13.215	Conscience þo *wiþ* Pacience passed, pilgrymes as it were.
B.13.221	Thei mette *wiþ* a Mynstral, as me þo þou3te,
B.13.233	Ne neiþer saille ne [sautrie] ne synge *wiþ* þe gyterne;
B.13.240	Fro Mighelmesse to Mighelmesse I fynde hem *wiþ* wafres.
B.13.242	Faitours and freres and folk *wiþ* brode crounes
B.13.246	Saue a pardon *wiþ* a peis of leed and two polles amyddes.
B.13.254	For siþ he haþ þe power þat Peter hadde he haþ þe pot *wiþ* þe salue:
B.13.266	*Wiþ* [bake] breed fro Stratford; þo gonnen beggeris wepe
B.13.274	Ac it was moled in many places *wiþ* manye sondry plottes,
B.13.278	Ooþerwise þan he haþ *wiþ* herte or si3te shewynge hym;
B.13.280	Forwhy he bosteþ and braggeþ *wiþ* manye bolde oþes,
B.13.288	*Wiþ* Inwit and *wiþ* outwit ymagynen and studie
B.13.288	*Wiþ* Inwit and *wiþ* outwit ymagynen and studie
B.13.320	It was bidropped *wiþ* wraþe and wikkede wille,
B.13.321	*Wiþ* enuye and yuel speche entisynge to fighte,
B.13.328	'Or *wiþ* my3t [of] mouþ or þoru3 m[a]nnes strengþe,
B.13.333	And whan I may no3t haue þe maistrie [*wiþ*] malencolie Itake,
B.13.343	*Wiþ* likynge of lecherie as by lokynge of his ei3e.
B.13.350	Swiche werkes *with* hem were neuere out of seson
B.13.358	[Thoru3] false mesures and met, and *wiþ* fals witnesse;

B.13.374   To seise to me *wiþ* hir sikel þat I sew neuere.
B.13.376   *Wiþ* presentes pryuely, or paide som certeyn;
B.13.393   To marchaunden *wiþ* [my] moneie and maken [here] eschaunges,
B.13.399   [Yet glotoun *wiþ* grete oþes his [garnement] hadde soiled
B.13.400   And foule beflobered it, as *wiþ* fals speche,
B.13.414   Ech day is halyday *with* hym or an heiȝ ferye,
B.13.456   *Wiþ* turpiloquio, a l[a]y of sorwe, and luciferis fiþele.
B.13.459   Why he ne hadde [w]asshen it or wiped it *wiþ* a brusshe.
B.14.6   *Wiþ* þe sope of siknesse þat sekeþ wonder depe,
B.14.7   And [laþered] *wiþ* þe losse of catel [forto me] looþ [were]
B.14.13   That I ne soiled it *wiþ* siȝte or som ydel speche,
B.14.20   And engreynen it *wiþ* good wille and goddes grace to amende þe,
B.14.30   And flour to fede folk *wiþ* as best be for þe soule;
B.14.99   [Wye] þat *wiþ* hym spak, as wide as I haue passed.'
B.14.204   Ac *wiþ* richesse þ[o] Ribaud[es] raþest men bigileþ.
B.14.213   Ther þe poore preesseþ bifore *wiþ* a pak at his rugge:
B.14.225   If wraþe wrastle *wiþ* þe poore he haþ þe worse ende
B.14.295   Wynneþ he noȝt *wiþ* wiȝtes false ne *wiþ* vnseled mesures,
B.14.295   Wynneþ he noȝt *wiþ* wiȝtes false ne wiþ vnseled mesures,
B.14.298   *Wiþ* sobretee fram alle synne and also ȝit moore;
B.14.327   And wepte water *wiþ* hise eighen and weyled þe tyme
B.15.7   As persons in pelure *wiþ* pendauntȝ of siluer;
B.15.18   Is neiþer Peter þe Porter ne Poul *wiþ* [þe] fauchon
B.15.112   That were bisnewed *wiþ* snow and snakes wiþInne,
B.15.115   Ye aren enblaunched *wiþ* bele paroles and wiþ [bele cloþes]
B.15.115   Ye aren enblaunched *wiþ* bele paroles and *wiþ* [bele cloþes]
B.15.124   A baselard or a ballokknyf *wiþ* botons ouergilte,
B.15.127   [He syngeþ seruice bokelees], seiþ it *with* ydel wille.
B.15.129   Ac þing þat wikkedly is wonne, and *wiþ* false sleightes,
B.15.133   [This] þat *wiþ* gile was geten vngraciousliche is [s]pended.
B.15.134   So harlotes and hores arn holpe *wiþ* swiche goodes
B.15.151   'Where sholde men fynde swich a frend *wiþ* so fre an herte?
B.15.169   He is glad *wiþ* alle glade and good til alle wikkede
B.15.181   He kan portreye wel þe Paternoster and peynte it *with* Aues
B.15.189   Pride wiþ al þe appurtenaunces, and pakken hem togideres,
B.15.191   And leggen on longe *wiþ* Laboraui in gemitu meo,
B.15.192   And *wiþ* warm water at hise eiȝen wasshen hem after.
B.15.245   For to wonye *wiþ* hem his wone was som tyme,
B.15.251   For whoso myȝte meete [*wiþ*] hym swiche maneres hym eileþ:
B.15.257   Misdooþ he no man ne *wiþ* his mouþ greueþ.
B.15.291   And wan *wiþ* hise hondes þat his wombe neded.
B.15.300   That ne fil to hir feet and fawned *wiþ* þe tailles;
B.15.339   And wente forþ *wiþ* þat water to woke wiþ Temese.
B.15.339   And wente forþ *wiþ* þat water to woke *wiþ* Temese.
B.15.354   Boþe lettred and lewed beþ alayed now *wiþ* synne
B.15.361   Shipmen and shepherdes þat *wiþ* [shipe] wenten
B.15.389   That sola fides sufficit to saue *wiþ* lewed peple.
B.15.450   As wel þoruȝ hise werkes as *wiþ* hise holy wordes
B.15.454   Wasshen wel *wiþ* water and wiþ taseles cracched,
B.15.454   Wasshen wel *wiþ* water and *wiþ* taseles cracched,
B.15.463   He fedde hem *wiþ* no venyson ne fesauntȝ ybake
B.15.464   But *wiþ* foweles þat fram hym nolde but folwede his whistlyng:
B.15.465   And *wiþ* calues flessh he fedde þe folk þat he louede.
B.15.483   *Wiþ* wederes and wiþ wondres he warneþ vs wiþ a whistlere
B.15.483   Wiþ wederes and *wiþ* wondres he warneþ vs wiþ a whistlere
B.15.483   Wiþ wederes and wiþ wondres he warneþ vs *wiþ* a whistlere
B.15.517   And baptised and bishined *wiþ* þe blode of his herte
B.15.518   Alle þat wilned and wolde *wiþ* Inwit bileue it.
B.15.558   *Wiþ* londes and ledes, lordshipes and rentes,
B.15.573   And feden hem *wiþ* goostly foode and [nedy folk to fynden.
B.15.591   *Wiþ* two fisshes and fyue loues fyue þousand peple,
B.15.594   And vnder stoon deed and stank; *wiþ* stif vois hym callede:
B.15.596   Ac þei seiden and sworen *wiþ* sorcerie he wrouȝte,
B.15.612   [Recorden it and rendren] it *wiþ* remissionem peccatorum
B.16.23   *Wiþ* þre piles was it vnderpight; I parceyued it soone.
B.16.30   Thanne *with* þe firste pil I palle hym doun, potencia de[i patris].
B.16.41   *Wiþ* alle þe wiles þat he kan, and waggeþ þe roote
B.16.48   Ac whan þe fend and þe flessh forþ *wiþ* þe world
B.16.102   To haue yfouȝte *wiþ* þe fend er ful tyme come.
B.16.105   That, þouȝ he were wounded *with* his enemy, to warisshen
               hymselue;
B.16.116   And wepte water *with* hise eiȝen; þer seiȝen it manye.
B.16.120   And seide he wroȝte þoruȝ wichecraft & *with* þe deueles myȝte:
B.16.125   And fed yow *wiþ* two fisshes and wiþ fyue loues,
B.16.125   And fed yow *wiþ* two fisshes and *wiþ* fyue loues,
B.16.128   And knokked on hem *wiþ* a corde, and caste adoun hir stalles
B.16.146   Thanne wente forþ þat wikked man and *wiþ* þe Iewes mette
B.16.147   And tolde hem a tokne to knowe *wiþ* Iesus;
B.16.150   And [þus] was *wiþ* Iudas þo þat Iesus bitrayed:
B.16.172   And þanne mette I *wiþ* a man, a mydlenten sonday,
B.16.223   Wedlok and widwehode *wiþ* virginite ynempned,
B.16.223   So is þe fader forþ *with* þe sone and fre wille of boþe,
B.16.244   And doon hym worship *with* breed and wiþ wyn boþe,

B.16.244   And doon hym worship with breed and *wiþ* wyn boþe,
B.16.272   I wepte for hise wordes; *wiþ* þat sauȝ I anoþer
B.17.3   To rule alle Reames *wiþ*; I bere þe writ [riȝt] here.'
B.17.15   The glose was gloriously writen *wiþ* a gilt penne:
B.17.20   For, þouȝ I seye it myself, I haue saued *with* þis charme
B.17.39   The gome þat gooþ *wiþ* o staf, he semeþ in gretter heele
B.17.40   Than he þat gooþ *wiþ* two staues to sighte of vs alle;
B.17.56   Where a man was wounded and *wiþ* þeues taken.
B.17.63   How he *wiþ* Moyses maundement hadde many men yholpe,
B.17.72   *Wiþ* wyn and oille hise woundes he wasshed,
B.17.72   Wiþ wyn and *with* oille hise woundes he wasshed,
B.17.92   For sighte of þ[e] sorweful [segge] þat robbed was *with* þeues.
B.17.98   And þanne plastred *wiþ* penaunce and passion of þat baby,
B.17.113   That he worþ fettred, þat feloun, faste *wiþ* Cheynes,
B.17.120   Hope shal lede hem forþ *with* loue as his lettre telleþ,
B.17.125   For þe barn was born in Bethleem þat *with* his blood shal saue
B.17.132   O god *wiþ* al my good, and alle gomes after
B.17.137   Thyn euenecristene eueremoore eueneforþ *with* þiselue.
B.17.139   Or Eretikes *wiþ* argumentȝ, þyn hond þow hem shewe.
B.17.141   The fader was first as a fust *wiþ* o fynger foldynge
B.17.143   And profre[d] it forþ as *with* a pawme to what place it sholde.
B.17.152   The fader is [þanne] as a fust *wiþ* fynger to touche–
B.17.160   Thoruȝ foure fyngres and a thombe forþ *with* þe pawme,
B.17.205   God þat he grypeþ *wiþ*, and wolde his grace quenche
B.17.244   For to murþen men [*wiþ*] þat in [m]erke sitten,
B.17.249   But þow haue tow to take it *wiþ*, tonder or broches,
B.17.262   Forþi beþ war, ye wise men þat *wiþ* þe world deleþ;
B.17.278   Sleeþ a man for hise moebles *wiþ* mouþ or with handes.
B.17.278   Sleeþ a man for hise moebles wiþ mouþ or *with* handes.
B.18.27   'Who shal Iuste *wiþ* Iesus', quod I, 'Iewes or Scrybes?'
B.18.36   Thanne cam Pilatus *with* muche peple, sedens pro tribunali,
B.18.51   Nailed hym *with* þre nailes naked on [a] roode:
B.18.67   Er sonday aboute sonne risyng'; and sank *wiþ* þat til erþe.
B.18.78   Ac þer cam forþ a knyȝt *wiþ* a kene spere ygrounde,
B.18.82   To [Iusten wiþ Iesus, þis blynde Iew Longeus]:
B.18.91   Haue on me ruþe, riȝtful Iesu;' and riȝt *wiþ* þat he wepte.
B.18.97   To [bete a body ybounde *wiþ* any briȝt wepene].
B.18.115   Mercy highte þat mayde, a meke þyng *wiþ* alle,
B.18.130   And grace of þe holy goost; weex greet *wiþ* childe;
B.18.143   For Adam and Eue and Abraham *wiþ* oþere
B.18.199   Ayeins Reson. [I], rightwisnesse, recorde þus *wiþ* truþe
B.18.216   For til modicum mete *with* vs, I may it wel auowe,
B.18.230   Thanne was þer a wight *wiþ* two brode eiȝen;
B.18.252   For [Iesus as a] geaunt *wiþ* a gyn [comeþ yonde]
B.18.265   For here comeþ *wiþ* crowne þat kyng is of glorie." '
B.18.282   And dwelle *wiþ* vs deueles; þis þretynge [driȝten] made.
B.18.287   For þow gete hem *wiþ* gile and his Gardyn breke,
B.18.297   I haue assailled hym *with* synne and som tyme yasked
B.18.308   *Wiþ* glorie and with gret light; god it is, I woot wel.
B.18.308   Wiþ glorie and *with* gret light; god it is, I woot wel.
B.18.321   And *wiþ* þat breeþ helle brak with Belialles barres;
B.18.321   And wiþ þat breeþ helle brak *with* Belialles barres;
B.18.334   *Wiþ* gile þow hem gete ageyn alle reson.
B.18.337   Thus ylik a Lusard *wiþ* a lady visage
B.18.371   And þanne shal I come as a kyng, crouned, *wiþ* Aungeles,
B.18.403   Thow shalt abyen it bittre!' and bond hym *wiþ* cheynes.
B.18.425   That men rongen to þe resurexion, and riȝt *wiþ* þat I wakede
B.19.7   And com in *wiþ* a cros bifore þe comune peple,
B.19.14   Is crist *wiþ* his cros, conquerour of cristene.'
B.19.40   And gentil men *wiþ* Iesu, for Iesu[s] was yfulled
B.19.57   And bond [hym] as [he is bounde] *wiþ* bondes of yrene.
B.19.63   Ac þe cause þat he comeþ þus *wiþ* cros of his passion
B.19.73   Reuerenced hym [riȝt] faire *wiþ* richesses of erþe.
B.19.86   That o kyng cam *wiþ* Reson couered vnder sense.
B.19.92   And presented hym *wiþ* pitee apperynge þe Mirre;
B.19.126   And fedde *wiþ* two fisshes and with fyue loues
B.19.126   And fedde wiþ two fisshes and *with* fyue loues
B.19.144   Kepen it fro nyghtcomeris *wiþ* knyghtes yarmed
B.19.153   Verray m[a]n bifore hem alle and forþ *wiþ* hem yede.
B.19.165   Thaddee and ten mo *wiþ* Thomas of Inde.
B.19.171   And feele *wiþ* hise fyngres his flesshliche herte.
B.19.172   Thomas touched it and *wiþ* his tonge seide:
B.19.210   Welcome hym and worshipe hym *wiþ* Veni creator Spiritus.'
B.19.212   And cride *wiþ* Conscience, 'help vs, [crist], of grace!'
B.19.213   [Th]anne bigan grace to go *wiþ* Piers Plowman
B.19.218   And wepne to fighte *wiþ* þat wole neuere faille.
B.19.226   And wepne to fighte *wiþ* whan Antecrist yow assailleþ.'
B.19.227   And gaf ech man a grace to gide *wiþ* hymseluen
B.19.229   Some [wyes] he yaf wit *with* wordes to shewe,
B.19.230   [To wynne *wiþ* truþe þat] þe world askeþ,
B.19.239   To wynne *wiþ* hir liflode bi loore of his techynge;
B.19.247   And fecchen it fro false men *wiþ* Foluyles lawes.
B.19.273   *Wiþ* two [aiþes] þat þei hadde, an oold and a newe:

B.19.279	And lerned men a ladel bugge *wiþ* a long stele
B.19.292	Mighte no [lyere *wiþ* lesynges] ne los of worldly catel
B.19.295	And pleieþ al *wiþ* pacience and Parce michi domine;
B.19.299	*Wiþ* god, and nauȝt agast but of gile one.
B.19.310	*Wiþ* olde lawe and newe lawe þat loue myȝte wexe
B.19.321	And Grace gaf hym þe cros, *wiþ* þe [garland] of þornes,
B.19.326	And watlede it and walled it *wiþ* his[e] peyne[s] and his passion;
B.19.333	As wide as þe world is *wiþ* Piers to tilie truþe
B.19.349	Ne no manere marchaunt þat *wiþ* moneye deleþ
B.19.350	Wheiþer he wynne *wiþ* right, wiþ wrong or wiþ vsure.'
B.19.350	Wheiþer he wynne wiþ right, *wiþ* wrong or wiþ vsure.'
B.19.350	Wheiþer he wynne wiþ right, wiþ wrong or *wiþ* vsure.'
B.19.351	*Wiþ* swiche colours and queyntise comeþ pride yarmed
B.19.352	*Wiþ* þe lord þat layueþ after þe lust of his body,
B.19.359	To goon agayn Pride but Grace weere *wiþ* vs.'
B.19.370	Witynge and wilfully *wiþ* þe false helden,
B.19.397	By Iesu! for al youre Ianglynge, *wiþ* Spiritus Iusticie,
B.19.426	And Piers [þe Plowman] *wiþ* his newe plow and [þe] olde
B.19.463	*Wiþ* Spiritus Intellectus þei [toke] þe reues rolles
B.19.464	And *wiþ* Spiritus fortitudinis fecche it, [wole he, nel he].'
B.19.466	'I am kyng *wiþ* croune þe comune to rule,
B.20.4	And it neghed neiȝ þe noon and *wiþ* me nede I mette
B.20.45	And þe fissh haþ fyn to flete and *wiþ* to reste,
B.20.71	*Wiþ* a lord þat lyueþ after likyng of body,
B.20.74	'I conseille', quod Conscience þo, 'comeþ *wiþ* me, ye fooles,
B.20.89	*Wiþ* deeþ þat is dredful to vndo vs alle!'
B.20.97	Kynde cam after *wiþ* many kene soores
B.20.114	This lecherie leide on *wiþ* [laughynge] chiere
B.20.115	And *wiþ* pryuee speche and peyntede wordes,
B.20.118	Weren feþered *wiþ* fair biheste and many a fals truþe.
B.20.119	*Wiþ* vntidy tales he tened ful ofte
B.20.125	*Wiþ* glosynges and gabbynges he giled þe peple.
B.20.128	To holden *wiþ* Antecrist, hir temporaltees to saue.
B.20.132	And boldeliche bar adoun *wiþ* many a bright Noble
B.20.135	And ouertilte al his truþe *wiþ* 'tak þis vp amendement'.
B.20.149	And prike[d] forþ *wiþ* pride; preiseþ he no vertue,
B.20.168	And wayued awey wanhope and *wiþ* lif he fighteþ.
B.20.174	And dryuen awey deeþ *wiþ* Dyas and drogges.
B.20.176	A Phisicien *wiþ* a furred hood þat he fel in a palsie,
B.20.186	'Sire yuele ytauȝt Elde!' quod I, 'vnhende go *wiþ* þe!
B.20.189	'Ye, leue, lurdeyn?' quod he, and leyde on me *wiþ* Age,
B.20.215	And bisegede [sikerly] *wiþ* seuene grete geauntȝ
B.20.216	That *wiþ* Antecrist helden harde ayein Conscience.
B.20.217	Sleuþe *wiþ* his slynge an hard [s]aut he made.
B.20.218	Proude preestes coome with hym; [passynge an hundred]
B.20.220	Coomen ayein Conscience; *wiþ* Coueitise þei helden.
B.20.225	And shotten ayein *wiþ* shot, many a sheef of oþes,
B.20.237	Lat hem chewe as þei chose and charge hem *with* no cure
B.20.250	*Wiþ* þat ye leue logik and lerneþ for to louye.
B.20.289	And maken hym murie *wiþ* ooþer mennes goodes.
B.20.290	And so it fareþ *with* muche folk þat to freres shryueþ,
B.20.292	A parcel to preye for hem and [pleye] *wiþ* þe remenaunt.
B.20.303	That *wiþ* Conscience acordede and Cardynale vertues.
B.20.326	To curen as a Curatour; and cam *with* hi[s] lettr[e]
B.20.333	Carpe I wolde *wiþ* contricion, and þerfore cam I hider.'
B.20.347	He saluede so oure wommen til some were *wiþ* childe.'
B.20.353	And acorde *wiþ* Conscience and kisse hir eiþer ooþer.'
B.20.374	And comen *wiþ* a kene wille Conscience to assaille.
B.20.378	The frere *wiþ* his phisyk þis folk haþ enchaunted,
C.Pr.24	And wonne þat þis wastors *with* glotony destrueth.
C.Pr.45	And ryseþ *with* rybaudrye, þo robardus knaues;
C.Pr.49	Wenten forth [i]n here way *with* many wyse tales
C.Pr.51	Eremites on an hep *with* hokede staues
C.Pr.67	Brouth forth a bulle *with* bischopis selys
C.Pr.72	A bounchede hem *with* his b[reuet] and blered here yes
C.Pr.73	And raughte *with* his Rageman Rynges and Broches.
C.Pr.87	Ben charged *with* holy chirche charite to tylie,
C.Pr.97	And boxes ben yset forth ybounde *with* yren
C.Pr.130	Hou he it lefte *with* loue as oure lord wolde
C.Pr.133	Thare Crist is in kynedom to close *with* heuene.
C.Pr.147	*With* lele labour to lyue while lif on londe lasteth.
C.Pr.172	And playde *with* somme perilously and potte hem þer hym lykede.
C.Pr.176	Myghte [we] *with* eny wyt his wille w[i]thsytte
C.Pr.226	Webbesteres and walkeres and wynners *with* handes,
C.Pr.229	And dryueth forth [þe longe] da[y] with 'd[ieu] saue dame Emme.'
C.1.67	To combre men *with* coueytise, þat is his kynde and his lore.'
C.1.94	And halden *with* h[y]m and [with] here þat han trewe action
C.1.94	And halden with h[y]m and [*with*] here þat han trewe action
C.1.109	He and oþer *with* hym helden nat with treuthe,
C.1.109	He and oþer with hym helden nat *with* treuthe,
C.1.163	Lokede on vs *with* loue [and] let his sone deye
C.1.166	Bote mekeliche *with* mouth mercy he bysoughte
C.1.191	And ben acombred *with* coueytise: thei can nouȝt [out crepe]
C.1.198	That conforteth alle carefole acombred *with* synne.
C.2.10	She was purfiled [*with*] pelure, non puyrere on erthe,
C.2.16	Here aray *with* here rychesse raueschede my herte;
C.2.66	Were most pryue *with* mede of eny men [me] thoghte.
C.2.68	And [as] a brokor brouhte here to be [*with* fals enioyned].
C.2.92	*With* [þe] chastel of cheste and chaterynge out of resoun;
C.2.94	*With* vsurye and Auaryce and other fals sleythus
C.2.95	In bargaynes and Brocages *with* the borw of thefte,
C.2.96	*With* al þe lordschip of leccherye in lenghe and in Brede,
C.2.98	In w[e]des and in weschynges and *with* ydel thouhtes
C.2.104	*With* spiserye, speke ydelnesse in vayne spe[ch]e and spene
C.2.107	And awake *with* wanhope and no wille to amende,
C.2.110	In lordschip *with* lucifer, as this lettre sheweth,
C.2.111	*With* alle þe [p]urtinaunc[e] of purgatorye and þe peyne of helle.'
C.2.140	And thow hast feffed here *with* fals; fy on suche lawe.
C.2.156	And yf he fynde ȝow in defaute and *with* the fals holde,
C.2.163	And feffe fals witnesse *with* floreynes ynowe,
C.2.170	For we haue mede amaystred [*with*] oure mery [speche]
C.2.171	That he graunteþ to go *with* a goode wille
C.2.177	To wende *with* h[e]m to westminstre [the] weddyng to honoure.
C.2.202	For to wisse hem þe way and *with* mede abyde.
C.2.225	A[c] marchauntes mette *with* hym and made hym abyde
C.2.234	And senten hym on sonendayes *with* seeles to churche.
C.2.237	That lyare sholde wonye *with* hem watres to loke.
C.2.240	Ac mynstrals and mesagers mette *with* lyare ones
C.2.242	Freres [*with*] fayre speche fetten hym thennes,
C.2.245	And is welcome when he cometh and woneth *with* hem ofte.
C.3.2	[*With*] Bedeles and Baylifs ybrouhte byfor þe kyng
C.3.11	Into Boure *with* blisse and by here gan sitte.
C.3.14	Genteliche *with* ioye þe Iustices somme
C.3.24	Rynges *with* rubees and othere riche ȝeftes,
C.3.76	Ywyte what thow delest *with* thi ryhte syde.
C.3.83	*With* that þe pore peple sholde potte in here wombe.
C.3.137	And ay þe lengur y late [the] go þe lasse treuthe is *with* the,
C.3.143	[And marre þe *with* myschef], be seynte mary my lady,
C.3.185	He is priue *with* þe pope, prouysours it knoweth,
C.3.191	Ther she is wel *with* eny kyng wo is þ[e] rewme
C.3.193	By iesu! *with* here ieweles the Iustices she shendeth;
C.3.218	The kyng graunted here grace *with* a goode wille:
C.3.225	Ne to depraue thy persone *with* a pro[u]d herte.
C.3.230	Ȝut y may, as y myhte, menske þe *with* ȝeftes
C.3.248	The leste ladde þat longeth *with* hym, be þe londe ywonne,
C.3.267	To aliens, to alle men, to honoure hem *with* ȝeftes;
C.3.348	As a leel laborer byleueth [*with*] his maister
C.3.356	He acordeth *with* crist in kynde, verbum caro factum est;
C.3.360	And lyue as oure crede vs kenneth *with* crist withouten ende.
C.3.362	Acordeth in alle kyndes *with* his antecedent.
C.3.370	I wolde feffe hym *with* here fayre and [with] here foule taylende.
C.3.370	I wolde feffe hym with here fayre and [*with*] here foule taylende.
C.3.380	Bothe heued and here kyng, haldyng *with* no parteyȝe
C.3.419	Haste þe *with* al thyn oste to þe lond of Amalek
C.3.435	For so is the world went *with* hem þat han power
C.3.462	Vche man to pley *with* a plogh, a pikois oþer a spade,
C.4.11	And acounte *with* the, Consience, so me Crist helpe,
C.4.21	And lat warrokye [hym] w[e]l *with* auys[e]-þe-byfore;
C.4.23	Lat peytrele [hym] and pole hym *with* peynted wittes.'
C.4.25	And resoun *with* hym ry[t], rounynge togederes
C.4.78	To ouercome þe kyng [*with*] catel y[f] they myhte.
C.4.112	And [chyldren] chersyng be chasted *with* ȝerdes
C.4.129	But [it] be marchaunt or his man or messager [*with*] lettres,
C.4.135	That y were kyng *with* c[r]oune to kepe [a] reume,
C.4.140	For nullum malum [þe] man mette *with* inpunitum
C.4.149	In signe þat thei sholde *with* som sotil speche
C.4.163	*With* mede þe mayde out of þe moethalle.
C.4.171	Ac resoun shal rykene *with* ȝow yf y regne eny while
C.4.196	And receyue tho that resoun louede; and riht *with* þat y wakede.
C.5.6	For as y cam by Consience *with* resoun y mette
C.5.8	And lymes to labory *with* and louede wel fare
C.5.23	Y am to wayke to wurcche *with* sykel or with sythe
C.5.23	Y am to wayke to wurcche with sykel or *with* sythe
C.5.45	The lomes þat y labore *with* and lyflode deserue
C.5.51	Now *with* hym, now with here: on this wyse y begge
C.5.51	Now with hym, now *with* here: on this wyse y begge
C.6.1	*With* þat ran repentaunce and rehersede his teme
C.6.2	And made will to wepe water *with* his eyes
C.6.34	Bostyng and braggynge *with* many bolde othes,
C.6.62	Quod repentaunce riht *with* þat; and thenne aroos enuye
C.6.63	Enuye *with* heuy herte asked aftur shrifte
C.6.77	And when y may nat haue þe maystrie [*with*] malecolie ytake,
C.6.103	Thenne awakede wrathe *with* two w[hy]te eyen
C.6.104	And *with* a niuilyng[e] nose, nippynge his lippes
C.6.106	Bothe *with* stoon and with staf and stele vppon myn enemye;
C.6.106	Bothe with stoon and *with* staf and stele vppon myn enemye;

C. 6.109	The harm þat y haue do *with* hand and with tonge.
C. 6.109	The harm þat y haue do with hand and *with* tonge.
C. 6.116	*With* lewed and lered þat leef ben to here
C. 6.124	Til y, wrathe, wexe an hey and walke *with* hem bothe;
C. 6.131	Mony monthes *with* hem and with monkes bothe.
C. 6.131	Mony monthes with hem and *with* monkes bothe.
C. 6.140	And thenne y crye and crache *with* my kene nayles,
C. 6.149	Tyl ayþer clepede oþer "hore!" and o[f] *with* the clothes
C. 6.173	*With* þat y shal,' quod þat shrewe, 'saturdayes for thy loue
C. 6.174	Drynke but *with* þe doke and dyne but ones.
C. 6.184	Such werkes *with* vs were neuere out of sesoun
C. 6.190	To wynne to my wille wymmen *with* gyle,
C. 6.198	He was bitelbrowed and baburlippid *with* two blered eyes
C. 6.202	*With* his hood on his heued and his hat bothe,
C. 6.212	*With* many manere marchandise as my maistre hyhte;
C. 6.218	To brochen hem *with* a batnelde and bande hem togyderes,
C. 6.235	'Þus! ones y was herberwed,' quod he, 'with an heep of chapmen;
C. 6.242	To weye pans *with* a peyse and par[e] þe heuegeste
C. 6.246	And *with* lumbardus lettres le[d]e gold to Rome;
C. 6.252	That chaffared *with* my cheuesaunces cheued selde aftur.'
C. 6.256	For þe pope *with* alle his pentauncers power hem fayleth
C. 6.258	'With false wordes and w[ittes] haue y ywonne my godes
C. 6.259	And *with* Gyle and glosynge ygadered þat y haue,
C. 6.271	To sese to me *with* here sikel þat y sewe neuere.
C. 6.280	To marchaunde *with* my moneye and maken here eschaunges,
C. 6.288	Y ne wolde cope me *with* thy catel ne moar a kyrke mende
C. 6.299	Shal parte *with* the in purgatorye and helpe paye thy dette
C. 6.322	Ne neuere wene to wynne *with* craft þat y knowe;
C. 6.326	Wel y woet a wepte faste water *with* his yes
C. 6.329	[And lepe *wiþ* hym ouer lond al his lif tyme]
C. 6.336	And deyede *with* a drop water; so doth alle synnes
C. 6.341	For thow hast no good, by good fayth, to gete the *with* a wastel
C. 6.342	For the good that thow hast gete bygan al *with* falshede
C. 6.349	What a lered 3ow to lyue *with* and to lette 3ow fram thefte.'
C. 6.369	Dawe þe dikere *with* a dosoyne harlotes
C. 6.375	Geuen glotoun *with* glad chere good ale to hansull.
C. 6.393	And grete syre glotoun *with* a galoun ale.
C. 6.402	And wesched hit hadde [be wexed] *with* a weps of breres.
C. 6.415	*With* alle þe wo of th[e] world his wyf and his wenche
C. 6.426	Of þat y haue trespased *with* tonge, y can nat telle how ofte;
C. 6.434	[On] fastyng dayes bifore noen fedde me *with* ale,
C. 7.1	Thenne cam sleuthe al byslobered *with* two slim[y] yes.
C. 7.6	A bigan benedicite *with* a bolk and his breste knokkede,
C. 7.17	That y telle *with* my tonge is t[wo] myle fro myn herte.
C. 7.19	*With* ydele tales at þe ale and oþerwhile in chirches;
C. 7.33	And holden a knyhtes Court and acounte *with* þe reue
C. 7.37	Sixe sithe oþer seuene y forsake hit *with* othes
C. 7.41	So *with* wikkede will my werkemen y paye.
C. 7.45	Y am nat luyred *with* loue but þer lygge ouht vnder þe t[h]umbe.
C. 7.55	'Repentest th[ow] nat?' quod repentaunce, and ryht *with* þat he swowened
C. 7.104	*With* a lered man to lere the what oure lord suffrede
C. 7.114	There flaterers and foles *with* here foule wordes
C. 7.116	*With* turpiloquio, a lay of sorwe and luciferes fythele,
C. 7.128	And madest thysulue *with* thy sone oure soule & body ilych:
C. 7.133	Feddest tho *with* thy [fresshe] blood oure forfadres in helle:
C. 7.144	And sethen oure sauyour and seydest *with* thy tonge
C. 7.152	And Blewe hit *with* beati quorum remisse sunt iniquitates &
C. 7.153	That alle seyntes for synfol songen *with* dauid:
C. 7.162	He bar a bordoun ybounde *with* a brood liste,
C. 7.180	'I [ne] saw neuere palmere *with* pyk ne with scrip[p]e
C. 7.180	'I [ne] saw neuere palmere with pyk ne *with* scrip[p]e
C. 7.228	Is frithed in *with* floreynes and othere fees monye;
C. 7.236	Ibotrased *with* bileue-so-or-t[hou]-best-not-ysaued;
C. 7.238	*With* no leed but with loue and with lele speche.
C. 7.238	With no leed but *with* loue and with lele speche;
C. 7.238	With no leed but with loue and *with* lele speche;
C. 7.295	To falewe *with* fiue 3o[k]es; 'forthy me bihoueth
C. 7.296	To goo *with* a good wil and graytheliche hem dryue.
C. 8.4	Y wol[de] wende *with* 3ow and þe way teche.'
C. 8.9	And 3e worthily wymmen *with* 3oure longe fyngres,
C. 8.50	Hoold with non harlotes ne here nat here tales
C. 8.57	And wende *with* alle tho þat wolden lyue in treuthe.'
C. 8.77	Del[e]antur de libro viuencium; y sholde nat dele *with* hem
C. 8.86	Lat god yworthe *with* al, as holy wryt techeth:
C. 8.93	To penaunc[e] and [to] pilgrim[age] y wol passe *with* oþere;
C. 8.105	My wyf shal haue of þat y wan *with* treuthe and no more
C. 8.109	And *with* þe res[i]due and þe remenant, by the rode of lukes!
C. 8.123	And holpe erye this half aker *with* 'hey trollilolly.'
C. 8.135	[We haue] none lymes to labory *with*, lord god we thonketh.'
C. 8.143	But yf he be blynde or brokelegged or bolted *with* yren,
C. 8.144	Such poore,' quod [Peres], 'shal parte *with* my godes,
C. 8.151	And bad hym go pisse *with* his plogh, pyuische shrewe.

C. 8.176	Ne hadde [Peres] *with* a pese loof preyede hym b[ile]ue.
C. 8.180	And flapton on *with* f[lay]les fro morwen til euen
C. 8.189	And lame men he lechede *with* longes of bestes.
C. 8.215	'Ther is no fi[al] loue *with* this folk for al here fayre speche
C. 8.224	*With* houndes bred and hors breed hele hem when þei hungren
C. 8.225	And [a]baue hem *with* benes for bollyng of here wombe,
C. 8.229	Conforte hem *with* thy catel, for so comaundeth treuthe;
C. 8.240	Þat sayth, "*with* swynke and with [swetande] face
C. 8.240	Þat sayth, "with swynke and *with* [swetande] face
C. 8.242	And salomon þe sage *with* þe same acordeth:
C. 8.258	Lo! what þe sauter sayth to swynkares *with* handes:
C. 8.272	And sende the of his sauce [t]o sauery *with* thy lyppes
C. 8.284	Part *with* hem of thy payne, of potage or of sowl;
C. 8.293	And lerne to labory *with* lond lest lyflode h[y]m fayle.
C. 8.310	And a cow *with* a calf and a cart m[a]re
C. 8.317	And profrede [Peres] this present to plese *with* hongur.
C. 8.320	*With* craym and with croddes, with cresses and oþere erbes.
C. 8.320	With craym and *with* croddes, with cresses and oþere erbes.
C. 8.320	With craym and with croddes, *with* cresses and oþere erbes.
C. 8.323	And thenne gloton *with* gode ale garte hunger slepe.
C. 8.348	Thre shypes and a schaef *with* [a vii] folwynge
C. 9.8	Pardoun *with* [Peres] þe [Plouhman] perpetuelly he grauntede.
C. 9.12	*With* patriarkes and prophetes in paradis to sitton.
C. 9.21	And deme *with* hem at domesday bothe quyke and dede.
C. 9.31	And wyckede wayes *with* here goed amende
C. 9.58	Alle libbyng laborers þat lyuen *with* here handes
C. 9.73	Charged *with* childrene and chief lordes rente.
C. 9.74	Þat they *with* spynnyng may spare spenen hit [i]n hous huyre,
C. 9.75	Bothe in mylke and in mele to make *with* papelotes
C. 9.76	To aglotye *with* here gurles that greden aftur fode.
C. 9.95	Were a feste *with* suche folk or so fele cockes.
C. 9.98	Ac beggares *with* bagges þe whiche brewhous[es] ben here churches,
C. 9.103	And lymes to labory *with* and lollares lyf vsen
C. 9.111	*With* a good will, witteles, mony wyde contreyes
C. 9.122	And thauh a mete *with* the mayre ameddes þe strete
C. 9.130	For þe lordes loue or þe ladyes þat they *with* longen.
C. 9.135	Welcomen and worschipen and *with* 3oure goed helpen
C. 9.154	*With* a bagge at his bak A begyneld wyse,
C. 9.157	And ouermore to [a]n [ha]tur to hele *with* his bonis
C. 9.168	Ne weddeth none wymmen þat they *with* deleth,
C. 9.171	And goen and fayten *with* here fauntes for eueremore aftur.
C. 9.177	And wymmen *with* childe þat worche ne mowe,
C. 9.187	And pardon *with* the plouhman A pena & a culpa.
C. 9.197	That wonede whilom in wodes *with* beres and lyons.
C. 9.247	Ac aboute myddday at mele tyme y mette *with* hem ofte,
C. 9.251	Wascheth and wypeth and *with* þe furste sitteth.
C. 9.252	Ac while a wrouhte in þe world and wan his mete *with* treuthe
C. 10.18	'Sothly,' saide þe frere, 'a soiourneth *with* vs freres
C. 10.60	And gyue me grace on þis grounde *with* good ende to deye.'
C. 10.94	And halie *with* þe hoked ende [i]lle men to gode
C. 10.95	And *with* the pyk pulte adoun preuaricatores legis.
C. 10.115	And ar we ywar were *with* wit gan we mete.
C. 10.118	Sad of his semblant and *with* a softe speche.
C. 10.131	*With* wynd and with water wittyly enioyned.
C. 10.131	With wynd and *with* water wittyly enioyned.
C. 10.136	And wol[d]e wynne here away *with* wyles [3if] he myhte.
C. 10.138	And hath do here *with* sire dowel, duk of this marches.
C. 10.147	Sire worch-wel-*with*-thyn-hand, a wyht man of strenghe,
C. 10.200	To tulie þe erthe and teche men to louye.
C. 10.231	And þe foules þat fl[e]eth forth *with* oþer bestes,
C. 10.233	That in thi [s]hingled ship shal be *with* þe ysaued."
C. 10.251	Soffre his seed seden *with* Caymus seed his brother.
C. 11.15	Bote hit be cardet *with* coueytise as clotheres kemben here wolle.
C. 11.17	And lette *with* a loueday [lewed] treuthe and bigile
C. 11.39	And gnawen god *with* gorge when here gottes f[u]llen.
C. 11.46	That so parteth *with* þe pore a parsel when hym nedeth.
C. 11.53	To plese *with* proude men senes th[e] pestelenc[e tyme]
C. 11.63	Ne parteth *with* þe pore as puyr charite wolde.
C. 11.89	*With* þat 3e kenne me kyndeliche to knowe what is dowel.'
C. 11.98	So *with* þat clergie can and consail of scripture
C. 11.121	And be[t] hem *with* a baleyse bute yf þei wolde lerne.
C. 11.187	'Man,' quod [he], 'yf y me[t]e *with* the, by marie of heuene.
C. 11.240	And his wyf *with* his sones and his sones wyues;
C. 11.257	That hadde yley *with* lucifer mony longe 3eres.
C. 11.265	Lelly as by his lokes, with a le[tt]re of gyle
C. 11.283	Withoute þe gifte of god w[it]h grace of fortune.
C. 11.294	Persen *with* a paternoster [þe paleys of] heuene
C. 12.51	And in a wer gan y wex and *with* mysulue to despute
C. 12.59	By þ[e] bloed [that] he bouhte vs *with* and bapteme, as he tauhte:
C. 12.66	A[c] reson shal rekene *with* hym and rebuken hym at þe laste
C. 12.67	And consience acounte *with* hym and casten hym in arrerag[e]
C. 12.71	Mercy for his mysdedes *with* mouthe and with herte.'

C.12.71	Mercy for his mysdedes with mouthe and *with* herte.'
C.12.189	Then sedes þat [in somer] sowe ben and mowen nat *with* forstes
C.12.193	In þe feld *with* þe forst and hit frese longe.
C.12.231	Lo! lond ouerleyd *with* marl and with donge,
C.12.231	Lo! lond ouerleyd with marl and *with* donge,
C.13.14	And delyuerede the weye his wyf *with* moche welthe aftur.
C.13.40	Ther þe messager doth no more but *with* his mouth telleth
C.13.47	And þe hayward happe *with* hym for to mete,
C.13.53	The marchaunt *with* his marchauntdyse may nat go so swythe
C.13.54	As þe messager may ne *with* so moche ese.
C.13.56	Ther þe marchaunt l[et] a male *with* many kyne thynges
C.13.58	*With* robbares and reuares þat ryche men despoilen
C.13.70	And haue reuthe and releue *with* his rychesse by his power
C.13.89	And sheweth þe seel and seth by lettre *with* what lord he dwelleth,
C.13.138	*With* flekede fetheres and of fele colours.
C.13.231	Resoun refusede the and wolde nat reste *with* the
C.13.246	And [y] aroes vp riht *with* þat and reuerensed hym fayre
C.14.37	For moyses witnesseth þat god wroet [in stoen *with* his fynger;
C.14.42	To strike *with* stoen or with staf this strompet to dethe."
C.14.42	To strike with stoen or *with* staf this strompet to dethe."
C.14.51	And hath non hap *with* his ax his enemye to hutte,
C.14.67	And medle we nat moche *with* hem to meuen eny wrathe
C.14.97	Clerkes kn[e]we [þe] comet and comen *with* here presentes
C.14.100	How þou contra[r]idest clergie *with* crabbed wordes,
C.14.125	Muchel wo was hym marked þat wade shal *with* þe lewede!
C.14.139	As tho þat sitten at þe syde table or *with* þe souereyns [of þe] halle
C.14.142	A sit noþer *with* seynte Iohan, simond ne Iude,
C.14.143	Ne *with* maydenes ne with martires ne with mylde weddewes,
C.14.143	Ne with maydenes ne *with* martires ne with mylde weddewes,
C.14.143	Ne with maydenes ne with martires ne *with* mylde weddewes,
C.14.172	That is, þe pocok and þe popeiay *with* here proude fetheres
C.15.26	And beden me ryse and rome; *with* reson sholde y dyne.
C.15.27	And y aroos and romede forth and *with* resoun we mette.
C.15.29	And metten *with* a maystre, a man lyk a frere.
C.15.64	And made [hym] mer[þe] *with* [h]is mete Ac y mournede euere
C.15.85	And also a gnedy glotoun *with* two grete chekes,
C.15.88	And wisched witterly *with* will ful egre
C.15.90	Bothe disches and dobelares *with* alle þe deyntees aftur.
C.15.91	'Y schal iangle to þis iurdan *with* his iuyste wombe
C.15.115	In þat 3e parteth nat *with* vs pore, þat 3e passeth dowel
C.15.117	And 3e fare thus *with* 3oure syke freres, ferly me thynketh
C.15.143	Fond [*with*] wit & word his loue to wynne,
C.15.145	Conforte hym *with* thy catel and with thy kynde speche;
C.15.145	Conforte hym with thy catel and *with* thy kynde speche;
C.15.146	And ley on hym thus *with* loue til he lauhe on þe.
C.15.150	And resoun ran aftur and riht *with* hym 3ede;
C.15.158	Meseyse ne meschief ne man *with* his tonge
C.15.161	In þe corner of a car[t]whel *with* a crow croune.
C.15.183	*With* pacience wol y passe parfitnesse to fynde.'
C.15.184	And wenten forth here way; *with* grete wille y folowede.
C.15.190	They mette *with* a mynstral, as me tho thouhte.
C.15.198	As a waf[e]rer *with* wafres, a[nd] welcome godes gestes.
C.15.207	Ne noþer sayle ne sautrien ne syngen *with* þe geterne,
C.15.224	For sethe he hath þe power þat peter hadde he hath þe pott *with* þe salue:
C.15.245	'Hastow,' quod actyf, 'ay such mete *with* the?'
C.16.25	And sende vs contricion [clereliche] to clanse *with* oure soules
C.16.45	Ac *with* rychesse tho rybaudes rathest men bigileth.
C.16.54	There þe pore preseth byfore *with* a pak at his rugge,
C.16.66	Yf wrathe wrastle *with* þe pore he hath þe worse ende
C.16.106	Here fader and alle here frendes and goth forth *with* here paramours:
C.16.130	Wynneth he nat *with* w[ih]tus false ne with vnselede mesures
C.16.130	Wynneth he nat with w[ih]tus false ne *with* vnselede mesures
C.16.134	*With* sobrete fro alle synnes and also 3ut more;
C.16.143	As he þat woet neuere *with* wham on nyhtes tyme to mete:
C.16.169	Is noþer Peter the porter ne poul *with* the fauchen
C.16.177	To do wel or wykke, a will *with* a resoun,
C.16.258	Parte *with* þe pore and pruyde leue
C.16.267	That were bysnewed al *with* snowe and snakes withynne
C.16.270	That ben enblaunched *with* bele paroles and with bele clothes
C.16.270	That ben enblaunched with bele paroles and *with* bele clothes
C.16.276	Ac thyng þat wykkedliche is wonne and *with* fals sleythes
C.16.280	And þat *with* gyle was gete vngraciousliche be yspened.
C.16.302	He is glad *with* alle glade as gurles þat lawhen alle
C.16.323	And purtraye wel þe paternoster and peynten hit *with* Auees.
C.16.332	Pruyde *with* alle [þe] purtinaunces and pakketh hem togyderes
C.16.335	And *with* warm water of his yes woketh h[em] til [t]he[y] white:
C.16.337	'Were y *with* hym by Cr[i]st,' quod y, 'y wolde neuere fro hym
C.16.349	And cheef charite *with* hem and chaste all here lyu[e].
C.16.366	*With* bisshopes a wolde be for beggares sake
C.16.371	As y tolde þe *with* tonge a litel tyme ypassed;
C.17.18	And wan *with* his handes al þat hym nedede.
C.17.31	And faire byfore tho men faunede *with* þe tayles.
C.17.58	*With* þat 3oure bernes and 3oure bloed by goed lawe may clayme!
C.17.74	And to a badde peny *with* a gode printe:
C.17.80	Is alayed *with* leccherye and oþer lustes of synne
C.17.121	That sola fides sufficit to saue *with* lewede peple.
C.17.134	And o god þat al bygan *with* gode herte they honoureth
C.17.146	And ay hopeth eft to be *with* here body at þe laste
C.17.202	To amende and to make, as *with* men of holy churche,
C.17.221	*With* londes and ledes, lordschipes and rentes,
C.17.234	That wyth moneye maynteyneth men [t]o werre vppon cristene
C.17.236	His preyeres *with* his pacience to pees sholde brynge
C.17.238	The pope *with* alle prestes pax vobis sholde make
C.17.268	And baptised and bis[hin]ede *with* þe bloed of his herte
C.17.269	Alle þat wilnede and wolde *with* inwit bileue hit.
C.17.304	Iewes sayde þat hit seye *with* soercerye he wrouhte,
C.17.320	Recorden hit and re[n]d[r]en hit *with* remissionem peccatorum,
C.18.3	Thenne louh liberum Arbitrium and ladde me forth *with* tales
C.18.34	And *with* þe furste planke y palle hym down, potencia dei patris.
C.18.45	And with alle þe wyles þat he can waggeth þe rote
C.18.50	And thenne [f]alle y adoune the pouke *with* the thridde shoriere
C.18.89	For þat is euene *with* angelis and angeles pere.
C.18.120	Filius by þe fadres wille fley *with* spiritus sanctus
C.18.136	To haue yfouthte *with* þe fende Ar fol tyme come.
C.18.146	And wepte watur *with* [his] yes; the why weten fewe.
C.18.149	And some iewes saide *with* sorserie he wrouhte
C.18.153	*With* [two] fisches and [fyue] loues, fyue thousen[d] at ones,
C.18.155	'Vnkynde and vnkunnynge!' quod Crist, and a roep smoet hem
C.18.178	And *with* moche noyse þat nyhte nere frentyk y wakede;
C.18.181	And thenne mette y *with* a man a myddelento[n] sonenday,
C.18.184	'I am *with* fayth,' quod þat freke, 'hit falleth nat me to lye,
C.18.259	As we wilnede and wolde *with* mou[th]e and herte aske.
C.18.261	Worschipe hym *with* wyn and with breed bothe
C.18.261	Worschipe hym with wyn and *with* breed bothe
C.18.272	*With* patriarkes and profetes pleynge togyderes.
C.18.288	[Y] wepte for his wordes; *with* þat saw y [a]nother
C.19.16	The glose was gloriously writen *with* a gult penne:
C.19.21	For, thogh y sey hit mysulue, y haue saued *with* this charme
C.19.62	How he *with* Moyses maundement hadde mony men yholpe
C.19.71	*With* wyn and with oyle his woundes he gan li[th]e,
C.19.71	With wyn and *with* oyle his woundes he gan li[th]e,
C.19.88	And *with* þe bloed of þat barn enbaumed and ybaptised.
C.19.91	And 3ut [b]e plasterud *with* pacience when fondynges [priketh hym]–
C.19.112	Or eretikes *with* argumentis, thien hoend thow hem shewe.
C.19.115	As a fuste wit[h] a fynger yfolde togyderes
C.19.117	And profered hit forth as *with* the paume to what place hit sholde.
C.19.126	The fader is thenne as þe fuste *with* fynger and with paume
C.19.126	The fader is thenne as þe fuste with fynger and *with* paume
C.19.130	A fuste *with* a fynger and a fol paume.
C.19.135	And al þe myhte *with* hym is, was and worth euere.
C.19.147	Bote [be he] greued *with* here grype the holy goost lat falle.
C.19.171	God þ[at] he gripeth [*with*] and wolde his grace quenche
C.19.210	For to murthe men *with* þat in merke sitten,
C.19.215	Bote thow haue tasch to take hit *with*, tender [or] broches,
C.19.228	Forthy beth ywar, 3e wyse men þat *with* the world deleth,
C.19.236	3ut wan he nat *with* wrong ne with queynte sleythes;
C.19.236	3ut wan he nat with wrong ne *with* queynte sleythes;
C.19.243	And dampned a dwelleth *with* þe deuel in helle.
C.19.248	*With* wyles and with luyther whitus and 3ut wollen nat atymye
C.19.248	With wyles and *with* luyther whitus and 3ut wollen nat atymye
C.19.259	Sleth a man for his mebles *with* mouthe or with handes.
C.19.259	Sleth a man for his mebles with mouthe or *with* handes.
C.19.263	Or elles [to] a taper to reuerense *with* the trinite
C.20.26	'Who shal iouste with iesus,' quod y, 'iewes or scrib3?'
C.20.35	Thenne cam Pilatus *with* moche peple, sedens pro tribunali,
C.20.51	[Thei] nayled hym *with* thre nayles naked vpon a rode
C.20.52	And *with* a pole poysen potten vp to his lippes
C.20.69	Ar soneday aboute sonne rysynge'; and sank *with* þat til erthe.
C.20.80	Ac þer cam forth a knyhte *with* a kene spere ygrounde,
C.20.84	[To] iouste *with* iesus, this blynde iewe longies,
C.20.94	Haue [on me reuthe], ri3tful iesu;' and riht *with* þat a wepte.
C.20.100	To bete a body ybounde *with* eny briht wypene.
C.20.118	Mercy hihte þat mayde, a mylde thynge *with* alle,
C.20.133	And grace of the holy gost; wax grete *with* childe,
C.20.146	For Adam and Eue And abraham *with* oþere
C.20.204	A3eynes resoun; y, rihtwysnesse, recorde [þus] *with* treuthe
C.20.225	For til [modicum] mete *with* vs, y may hit wel avowe,
C.20.239	Thenne wa[s] ther a wihte *with* two brode yes;
C.20.261	For iesus as a geaunt *with* a gyn cometh 3ende
C.20.273	For here cometh *with* croune þe kynge of all glorie.'
C.20.282	That Belial, thy beelsyre, beet *with* thy dame
C.20.294	[*With*] crokes and kalketrappes [a]cloye we hem vchone.'
C.20.304	[Sh]olde deye *with* doel and here dwelle euere

C.20.313	For thow gete hem *with* gyle and his gardyn broke,
C.20.318	As two godes, *with* god, bothe goed and ille.
C.20.319	Thus *with* treson and tricherie thow troyledest hem bothe
C.20.330	Y haue ass[a]yled hym *with* synne and som tyme ich askede
C.20.342	*With* glorie and with [grete] lihte; god hit is ich woet wel.
C.20.342	With glorie and with [grete] lihte; god hit is ich woet wel.
C.20.364	And *with* þat breth helle braek with belialles barres;
C.20.364	And with þat breth helle braek *with* belialles barres;
C.20.369	And tho that oure lord louede forth *with* þat liht flowen.
C.20.377	*With* gyle thow hem gete agaynes all resoun.
C.20.413	And thenne shal y come as [a] kynge, croune[d], *with* angeles
C.20.446	Thow shal[t] abuye bittere!' and b[o]nde hym *with* chaynes.
C.20.468	That men rang to þe resureccioun and riht *with* þat y wakede
C.21.7	And cam in *with* a cros bifore þe comune peple
C.21.14	Is Crist *with* his croes, conquerour of Cristene.'
C.21.40	And Ientel men *with* iesu for iesu[s] was yfolled
C.21.57	And bonde [hym] as he is bounde *with* bondes of yre.
C.21.63	Ac the cause that he cometh thus *with* cros [of] his passioun
C.21.73	Reuerensed hym riht fayre *with* richesses of erthe.
C.21.86	That [o] kyng cam *with* reson ykyuered vnder ensense.
C.21.92	And presented hym *with* pyte apperynge bi Mirre
C.21.126	And fedde *with* two fisches and with fyue loues
C.21.126	And fedde with two fisches and *with* fyue loues
C.21.144	Kepen hit fro nyhtecomares *with* knyhtes y[ar]med
C.21.153	Verray man bifore [hem] alle, and forth *with* hem ȝede.
C.21.165	Taddee and ten mo *with* Thomas of ynde.
C.21.171	And fele *with* his fyngeres his flescheliche herte.
C.21.172	Thomas touched hit and and *with* his tonge saide:
C.21.210	Welcome hym and worschipe hym *with* veni creator spiritus.'
C.21.212	And criden *with* Consience, 'helpe vs, [Crist], of grace!'
C.21.213	Thenne bigan grace to go *with* [Peres Plouhman]
C.21.218	And wepne to fihte *with* þat wol neuere fayle.
C.21.226	And wepne to fihte *with* when Auntecrist ȝow assaileth.'
C.21.227	And gaf vch man a grace to gye *with* hymsuluen
C.21.229	Som [wyes] he ȝaf wyt *with* wordes to schewe,
C.21.230	To wynne *with* treuthe þat the world asketh,
C.21.239	To wynne *with* here lyflode bi lore of his techynge];
C.21.247	And fechen hit fro false men *with* foleuiles lawes;
C.21.273	*With* two aythes þat they hadde, an oelde and a newe:
C.21.279	And lered men a ladel bugge *with* a longe stale
C.21.292	Myhte no lyare *with* lesynge[s] ne losse of worldly catel
C.21.295	And ple[ie]þ al *with* pacience and parce michi domine
C.21.299	*With* god and nat agast bote of gyle one.
C.21.310	*With* olde lawe and newe [lawe] that loue myhte wexe
C.21.321	And grace gaf hym þe cros *with* [the garlond] of thornes
C.21.326	And wateled hit and walled hit *with* his paynes and his passio[n]
C.21.333	As wyde as the world is *with* Peres to tulye treuthe
C.21.349	Ne no manere Marchaunt þat *with* moneye deleth
C.21.350	Where he wynne *with* riht, with wrong or with vsure.'
C.21.350	Where he wynne with riht, *with* wrong or with vsure.'
C.21.350	Where he wynne with riht, with wrong or *with* vsure.'
C.21.351	*With* such colours and queyntis[e] cometh pruyde yArmed
C.21.352	*With* the lord þat lyueth aftur the lust of his body,
C.21.359	To goen agayn pruyde bute grace were *with* vs.'
C.21.370	Wytyng and wilfully *with* the false helden
C.21.397	By iesu! for al ȝoure iangelyng, [*with*] spiritus Iusticie
C.21.426	And [Peres the Plowman] *with* his newe [plouh] and [þe] olde
C.21.463	*With* spiritus intellectus they [t]o[k]e þe reues rolles
C.21.464	And *with* spiritus fortitudinis fecche hit, wolle he, null he.'
C.21.466	'Y am kyng *with* croune the comune to reule
C.22.4	And hit neyhed neyh þe noen and *with* nede y mette
C.22.45	And þe fisch hath fyn to flete *with* to reste;
C.22.71	*With* a lord þat lyueth aftur likyng of body
C.22.74	'Y consail,' quod Consi[e]nce tho, 'cometh *with* me, ȝe foles,
C.22.89	*With* deth þat is dredful to vndoen vs alle!'
C.22.97	Kynde cam aftur *with* many k[e]ne sores,
C.22.114	This lecherye leyde [o]n *with* lauhyng chere
C.22.115	And *with* priue speche and paynted wordes
C.22.118	Weren fythered *with* fayre biheste and many a fals treuthe
C.22.119	*With* vntidy tales he tened ful ofte
C.22.125	*With* glosynges and gabbynges he gyled þe peple.
C.22.128	To holde *with* auntecrist, here temperaltee[s] to saue.
C.22.132	And baldeliche baer adoun *with* many a brihte noble
C.22.135	And ouertulde al his treuthe *with* 'taek this [vp] amendement.'
C.22.149	And prike[d] forth *with* pruyde; preyseth he no vertue
C.22.168	And wayued away wanhope *with* lyf he fihteth.
C.22.174	And dryue awey deth *with* dyaes and drogges.
C.22.176	A fisician *with* a forred hoed that he ful in a palesye
C.22.186	'Syre euele yt[a]uȝte Elde,' quod y, 'vnhende go *with* the!
C.22.219	'Ȝe, leue, lordeyne?' quod he, and leide on me *with* age
C.22.215	And biseged s[iker]ly *with* seuene grete geauntes
C.22.216	That *with* auntecrist helden harde aȝeyn Consience.
C.22.217	Sleuthe *with* his slynge a[n] hard sawt he made.

C.22.218	Proute prestes cam *with* hym; passyng an hundred
C.22.220	Comen aȝen Consience; *with* couetyse they helden.
C.22.225	And shoten aȝeyn[e *with*] shotte many a shef of othes
C.22.237	Late hem chewe as thei chose and charge hem *with* no cure.
C.22.250	*With* þat ȝe l[e]ue logyk and lerneth for to louye.
C.22.289	And maken hym murye *with* oþere menne godes.
C.22.290	And so hit fareth *with* moche folke þat to freres shryuen,
C.22.292	A parcel to preye for hem and [pleye] *with* þe remenaunt
C.22.303	That *with* Consience acordede and cardinal vertues.
C.22.326	To curen as a curatour; and kam *with* his lettre
C.22.333	Karpe y wolde *with* Contricioun and þerfore [cam y] heddere.'
C.22.347	He salued so oure wymmen til some were *with* childe.'
C.22.353	And acorde *with* Consience and kusse here ayther oþer.'
C.22.374	And comen *with* a kene wil Consience to assaile.
C.22.378	The frere *with* his fisyk this folk hath enchaunted

wiþalle adv *withal adv.* A 5 withalle (2) wiþal (1) wiþalle (2); B 9 withalle (1) wiþ_al (1) wiþalle (5) wiþ_alle (2); C 4 withalle

A. 5.3	Þanne wakide I of my wynkyng, & wo was *withalle*
A. 7.74	Let god worþe *wiþal* for so his woord techiþ.
A.10.5	Kynde haþ closid þereinne, craftily *withalle*,
A.10.17	Is a wys kniȝt *withalle*, sire [inwit] he hatte,
A.12.50	Hyȝt omnia probate, a pore þing *withalle*;
B.Pr.123	Thanne loked vp a lunatik, a leene þyng *wiþalle*
B. 5.3	Thanne waked I of my wynkyng and wo was *withalle*
B. 6.82	Lat-god-yworþe-*wiþ-al*-for-so-his-word-techeþ.
B. 9.5	Kynde haþ closed þerInne, craftily *wiþalle*,
B. 9.18	Is a wis knyȝt *wiþalle*, sire Inwit he hatte,
B.15.12	Til I seiȝ, as it sorcerie were, a sotil þyng *wiþ alle*.
B.15.288	Foweles hym fedde, fele wyntres *wiþ alle*,
B.16.68	Matrimoyne I may nyme, a moiste fruyt *wiþalle*.
B.16.91	To a maide þat hiȝte Marie, a meke þyng *wiþalle*,
C.10.132	Kynde hath closed therynne, craftily *withalle*,
C.10.144	Is a wise knyhte *withalle*, sire inwit he hatte,
C.17.166	And a cardinal of Court, a gret clerk *withalle*,
C.18.124	To a mayde þat hihte marie, a meke thyng *withalle*,

wiþdrawe v *withdrauen v.* B 5 wiþdrawe (3) wiþdraweþ (1) wiþdrouȝ (1); C 6 withdrawe (3) withdraweth (1) withdrouh (1) withdrow (1)

B. 6.329	Thanne shal deeþ *wiþdrawe* and derþe be Iustice,
B. 9.99	He dooþ best þat *wiþdraweþ* hym by daye and by nyȝte
B.10.82	Ne for drede of þe deeþ *wiþdrawe* noȝt hir pride,
B.18.60	The day for drede *wiþdrouȝ* and derk bicam þe sonne;
B.20.352	And be adrad of deeþ and *wiþdrawe* hym fram pryde
C. 8.350	And thenne shal deth *withdrawe* and derthe be Iustice,
C.11.62	Ne for drede of eny deth *withdraweth* h[e]m fro pruyde
C.17.245	Deuouteliche day and nyhte, *withdrawe* hem fro synne
C.19.64	And dredfully *withdrow* hym and durste go no nerre.
C.20.60	The daye for drede *withdrouh* and derke bicam þe sonne;
C.22.352	And be adrad of deth and *withdrawe* hym fro pruyde

wiþhalt v *withholden v.* A 2 wiþhalt (1) wiþheld (1); B 2 wiþhalt (1) wiþhelden (1); C 3 withhalt (1) withholde (1) wiþhelden (1)

A. 2.190	And *wiþheld* him half [a] ȝer & elleuene dayes.
A. 6.39	He [*wiþ*]halt non hyne his hire þat he ne haþ it at eue.
B. 2.231	And [*wiþ*]helden hym an half yeer and elleuene dayes.
B. 5.552	He *wiþhalt* noon hewe his hire þat he ne haþ it at euen.
C. 2.241	And [*wiþ*]helden hym [a] half ȝere and eleue dayes.
C. 3.307	As by the book þat byt nobody *withholde*
C. 7.196	He *withhalt* non hewe his huyre ouer euen;

wiþinne adv *withinne adv. & prep.* A 1; B 5 withInne (1) wiþInne (4); C 7 withynne

A. 6.34	*Wiþinne* & wiþoute waytide his profit.
B. 5.544	*WiþInne* and wiþouten waited his profit.
B.13.329	Auenge me fele tymes, oþer frete myselue *wiþInne*;
B.13.362	'The worste *withInne* was; a greet wit I let it.
B.15.112	That were bisnewed wiþ snow and snakes *wiþInne*,
B.15.113	Or to a wal þat were whitlymed and were foul *wiþInne*;
C. 6.31	Otherwyse then y haue, *withynne* or withouten
C. 6.74	Venged me vele tymes other vrete myself *withynne*
C. 6.261	The worste lay *withynne*; a greet wit y lat hit.
C. 7.188	*Withynne* and withouten to wayten his profit.
C.12.247	That rote is of robbares, the rychess[e] *withynne*!
C.16.267	That were bysnewed al with snowe and snakes *withynne*
C.16.268	Or to a wal ywhitlymed and were blak *withynne*.

wiþinne prep *withinne adv. & prep.* A 1; B 3; C 2 withynne

A.11.106	He haþ weddit a wif *wiþinne* þise woukes sixe,
B.10.154	He haþ wedded a wif *wiþInne* þise [woukes sixe],
B.17.162	[Halt] al þe wide world *wiþInne* hem þre,
B.18.32	That, for al þat deeþ kan do, *wiþInne* þre daies to walke
C.10.40	That ay is saef and sound þat sitte *withynne* þe borde.
C.20.31	That for al þat deth can do, *withynne* thre dayes to walke

withoute conj *withouten adv. & prep.* C 1
C. 4.176   Quod Consience to þe kyng, '*withoute* þe comune helpe

wiþouten adv *withouten adv. & prep.* A 1 wiþoute; B 4 wiþoute (2)
  wiþouten (2); C 3 withoute (1) withouten (2)
A. 6.34   Wiþinne & *wiþoute* waytide his profit.
B. 5.544   WiþInne and *wiþouten* waited his profit,
B. 5.614   Keyed and cliketted to kepe þee *wiþouten*
B.10.263 But be swich in þi soule as þow semest *wiþoute*.
B.11.260 As on a walnote *wiþoute* is a bitter barke,
C. 6.31   Otherwyse then y haue, withynne or *withouten*
C. 7.188   Withynne and *withouten* to wayten his profit.
C.12.146 As on a walnote *withoute* is a bittere barke

wiþouten prep *withouten adv. & prep.* A 15 wiþoute; B 69 withouten (5)
  wiþoute (13) wiþouten (51); C 81 without (1) withoute (39) withouten
  (40) wiþouten (1)
A. 1.160   Þat feiþ *wiþoute* fait is feblere þan nouȝt,
A. 1.162   Chastite *wiþoute* charite worþ cheynide in helle;
A. 1.168   Such chastite *wiþoute* charite worþ cheynid in helle.
A. 3.78   Or presauntis *wiþoute* panis as pecis of siluer,
A. 3.151   *Wiþoute* presentis or panis he plesiþ [wel] fewe.
A. 3.182   *Wiþoute* pite, pilour, pore men þou robb[ed]est,
A. 3.214   No wiȝt as I wene *wiþoute* mede miȝte libbe.'
A. 4.65   '*Wiþoute* gilt, god wot, gat I þis skaþe.'
A. 8.158   Þe peple *wiþoute* penaunce [to passe to Ioye]?
A. 9.95   And putten hem þere in penaunce *wiþoute* pite or grace,
A.10.57   And ek wantoun & wilde, *wiþoute* any resoun.
A.11.167 And wente wiȝtly my wey *wiþoute* more lettyng,
A.11.261 I was markid *wiþoute* mercy, & myn name entrid
A.11.286 *Wiþoute* penaunce of purcatorie to haue paradis for euere.
A.11.313 *Wiþoute* penaunce at here partyng, into [þe] heiȝe blisse.
B. 1.186   That Feiþ *withouten* feet is [feblere þan nouȝt],
B. 1.188   Chastite *wiþouten* charite worþ cheyned in helle;
B. 1.194   Swich chastite *wiþouten* charite worþ cheyned in helle.
B. 2.30   Oo god *wiþouten* gynnyng, and I his goode douȝter;
B. 3.89   Or presentȝ *wiþouten* pens as pieces of siluer,
B. 3.162   *Wiþouten* presentȝ or pens [he] pleseþ wel fewe.
B. 3.195   *Wiþoute* pite, Pilour, pouere men þow robbedest,
B. 3.227   No wiȝt, as I wene, *wiþouten* Mede may libbe.'
B. 3.243   *Wiþouten* Mede doþ hem good and þe truþe helpeþ,
B. 4.79   '*Wiþouten* gilt, god woot, gat I þis scaþe.'
B. 5.387   I may noȝt stonde ne stoupe ne *wiþoute* stool knele.
B. 7.56   That neuere shul wexe ne wanye *wiþouten* god hymselue.
B. 7.180   [Th]e peple *wiþouten* penaunce to passen [to ioye]?
B. 8.105   And putten hem þer in penaunce *wiþoute* pite or grace],
B. 9.35   And Eue of his ryb bon *wiþouten* any mene.
B.10.225 And wente wightly [my w]ey *wiþoute* moore lettyng,
B.10.357 Ac cristene men *wiþoute* moore maye noȝt come to heuene,
B.10.427 *Wiþouten* penaunce of purgatorie, to perpetuel blisse.
B.10.457 Whan man was at meschief *wiþoute* þe moore grace.
B.11.82   Ac [a] barn *wiþouten* bapteme may noȝt be saued:
B.11.128 *Wiþouten* leue of his lord; no lawe wol it graunte.
B.11.150 *Wiþouten* bede biddyng his boone was vnderfongen
B.11.151 And I saued as ye [may] see, *wiþoute* syngynge of masses,
B.11.171 'Lawe *wiþouten* loue', quod Troianus, 'ley þer a bene!'
B.11.215 Ne vndernyme noȝt foule, for is noon *wiþoute* defaute.
B.12.32   For he dooþ wel, *wiþouten* doute, þat dooþ as lewte techeþ.
B.12.85   For goddes body miȝte noȝt ben of breed *wiþouten* clergie,
B.12.175 And how contricion *wiþoute* confession conforteþ þe soule,
B.12.279 Ne no creature of cristes liknesse *withouten* cristendom worþ
           saued.
B.13.75   Taken it for his teme and telle it *wiþouten* glosyng.
B.13.446 And fiþele þee *wiþoute* flaterynge of good friday þe [geste],
B.14.64   It is founden þat fourty wynter folk lyuede *withouten* tulying,
B.14.70   And lyueden *wiþouten* liflode and at þe laste þei woken.
B.14.130 And greet likynge to lyue *wiþouten* labour of bodye,
B.14.238 *Wiþoute* mournynge amonge, and meschief to bote].
B.14.305 Pouerte myȝte passe *wiþouten* peril of robbyng.
B.14.320 A blessed lif *wiþouten* bisynesse for body and soule:
B.15.13   Oon *wiþouten* tonge and teeþ tolde me whider I sholde
B.15.150 *Wiþouten* fauntelee or folie a fre liberal wille.'
B.15.196 '*Wiþouten* help of Piers Plowman', quod he, 'his persone sestow
           neuere.'
B.15.234 That *wiþouten* wiles ledeþ [wel] hir lyues:
B.15.345 For charite *wiþoute* chalangynge vnchargeþ þe soule,
B.15.461 Rude and vnresonable, rennynge *wiþouten* [keperes].
B.15.473 That loþ ben to louye *wiþouten* lernyng of ensaumples.
B.15.488 *Wiþouten* trauaille þe tiþe deel þat trewe men biswynken?
B.16.72   And swete *wiþouten* swellyng; sour worþ it neuere.'
B.16.99   For to werchen his wille *wiþouten* any synne:
B.16.187 Wardeyn of þat wit haþ; was euere *wiþouten* gynnyng.
B.16.216 As widewe *wiþouten* wedlok was neuere ȝit yseyȝe,
B.16.218 So widewe *withouten* wedlok may noȝt wel stande,

B.16.219 Ne matrimoyne *withouten* Mul[eri]e is noȝt muche to preise:
B.16.240 Lond and lordshipe and lif *wiþouten* ende.
B.17.96   *Wiþouten* þe blood of a barn born of a mayde.
B.17.168 Na moore [may an hand] meue *wiþoute* fyngres.
B.17.195 And þe myddel of myn hand *wiþoute* maleese,
B.17.217 *Wiþouten* leye or light [liþ fir in þe macche]–
B.17.218 So is [þe] holy goost god and grace *wiþoute* mercy
B.17.235 And as wex *wiþouten* moore on a warm glede
B.17.252 So is þe holi goost god and grace *wiþoute* mercy
B.17.273 But þei dwelle þer Diues is dayes *wiþoute* ende.
B.18.12   *Wiþouten* spores oþer spere; spakliche he lokede
B.18.128 A maiden þat highte Marie, and moder *wiþoute* felyng
B.18.131 *Wiþoute* [wommene] wem into þis world broȝte hym.
B.18.227 Shal lere hem what langour is and lisse *wiþoute* ende.
B.18.378 Shul noȝt be dampned to þe deeþ þat [dureþ] *wiþouten* ende:
B.19.76   Mirre and muche gold *wiþoute* merc[ede] askynge
B.19.198 And wikkede to wonye in wo *wiþoute* ende.'
B.20.21   *Wiþouten* conseil of Conscience or Cardynale vertues,
B.20.270 Heuene haþ euene noumbre and helle is *wiþoute* noumbre.
C. 1.182   That fayth *withouten* feet is feblore then nauth
C. 1.184   Chastite *withouten* charite worth c[h]eyned in helle;
C. 2.109   After here deth dwellen day *withouten* ende
C. 2.126   And wilned to be moder amendes mede may [nat] be wedded.
C. 2.131   That god wolde were ydo *withoute* som deseyte.
C. 3.117   Or presentes *without* pans and oþer priue ȝeftes.
C. 3.132   And wilned to be wedded *withouten* his leue,
C. 3.200   *Withoute* presentes oþer pans he pleseth [wel] fewe.
C. 3.206   *Withouten* werre oþer wo oþer wickede lawe
C. 3.360   And lyue as oure crede vs kenneth with crist *withouten* ende.
C. 3.365   And *withoute* ca[s]e to cache [to] and come to bothe nombres,
C. 3.373   *Withouten* coest and care and alle kyn trauayle.
C. 4.75   '*Withouten* gult, god wot, [gat y] this s[c]athe;
C. 4.181   And brynge alle men to bowe *withouten* bittere wounde,
C. 4.182   *Withouten* mercement or manslauht amende alle reumes.'
C. 5.52   *Withoute* bagge or botel but my wombe one.
C. 5.174   Bred *withouten* beggynge to lyue by euere aftur
C. 6.121   *Withoute* licence and leue, and herby lyueth wrathe.
C. 7.3   Y may nat stande ne stoupe ne *withouten* stoel knele.
C. 7.106   And fithele the *withoute* flaterynge of god friday þe [g]este
C. 7.266   Ykeyed and yclyketed to [kepe] the *withouten*,
C. 9.120   *Withoute* bagge and bred as þe book telleth:
C. 9.206   And carteres knaues and Clerkes *withouten* grace,
C. 9.326   To peple *withouten* penaunce to passe into ioye,
C.10.101 And crounede oen to be kyng to kull *withoute* synne
C.10.170 The which is loue and lyf þat last *withouten* ende.
C.10.215 *Withouten* repentaunce of here rechelesnesse a rybaud þei
           engendrede.
C.11.134 Tho wente y my way *withouten* more lettynge
C.11.143 And bycam man of þat maide *withoute* mankynde;
C.11.259 *Withoute* penaunce oþer passioun oþer eny other peyne
C.11.283 *Withoute* þe gifte of god w[it]h grace of fortune.
C.12.63   *Withouten* leue of [his] lord; no lawe wol hit graunte.
C.12.85   *Withouten* bed[e] biddyng his bone vnderfonge
C.12.86   And y saued, as ȝe may se, *withoute* syngynge of masses.
C.12.87   Loue *withoute* lele bileue a[nd] my lawe riht[ful]
C.12.93   For lawe *withouten* leutee, ley þer a bene!
C.13.75   *Withoute* wyles or wronges or wymmen at þe stuyues;
C.14.10   And thenne dost thow wel, *withoute* drede; ho can do bet no force.
C.14.16   That pees be and pacience and pore *withoute* defaute:
C.14.28   So grace *withouten* grace of god and also gode werkes
C.14.115 And how contricion *withoute* confessioun conforteth þe soule,
C.14.201 *Withoute* bapteme, as by here bokes, beth nat ysaued.'
C.15.81   Þat toek this for his teme and tolde hit *withoute* glose.
C.15.155 *Withoute* brutteny[n]ge of buyren or eny bloed shedynge.
C.15.269 [And] lyueden *withouten* lyflode and [at] the laste awakede.
C.16.20   And yliche witty and wys and lyue *withoute* nede;
C.16.32   Thise thre *withoute* doute tholieth alle pouerte
C.16.140 Pouerte myhte passe *withoute* perel of robbynge.
C.16.155 *Withoute* bisinesse bote onelyche for þe soule:
C.16.178 And may nat be *withoute* a body to bere me where hym liketh'.
C.16.367 Ac auaris oþerwhiles halt hym *withoute* þe gate.
C.17.3   And ȝut oþerwhile wroeth *withouten* eny synne.'
C.17.8   *Withoute* borwynge or beggynge bote of god one,
C.17.27   *Withoute* borwynge or beggynge, or þe boek lyeth,
C.17.129 *Withoute* gyle and gabbyng gyue and sulle and lene.
C.17.130 Loue lawe *withoute* leutee? allouable was hit neuere!
C.17.131 God lereth no lyf to l[eu]e *withouten* lele cause.
C.18.99   And swete *withoute* swellynge; sour worth hit neuere'–
C.18.132 For to worchen his wille *withoute* eny synne:
C.18.220 Matrimonye *withoute* moylere is nauht moche to preyse
C.18.223 And man *withoute* a make myhte nat wel of kynde
C.18.224 Multiplie ne moreouer *withoute* a make louye
C.18.225 Ne *withoute* a soware be suche seed; this we seen alle.

C.18.232   Is and ay were [& worþ *wiþouten* ende].
C.18.256   Lond and lordschip ynow and lyf *withouten* ende.
C.19.86   *Withoute* þe bloed of a barn he beth nat ysaued,
C.19.161   And þe myddel of myn hand] *withoute* maleese
C.19.183   *Withouten* leye [or] lihte lith fuyr in þe mache–
C.19.184   So is þe holi gost god and grace *withouten* mercy
C.19.201   And as wex *withouten* more vpo[n] a warm glede
C.19.218   So is þe holy gost god and grace *withouten* mercy
C.19.244   Sethe he *withoute* wyles wan and wel myhte atymye
C.19.254   Bote they dwelle there diues is dayes *withouten* ende.
C.20.10   *Withouten* spores oþer spere; sp[a]keliche he lokede
C.20.131   A mayde þat hoteth Marie, a[nd] moder *withouten* velynge
C.20.134   *Withouten* wommane wem into this world brouhte hym.
C.20.236   Shal lere hem what l[angour] is and lisse *withouten* ende.
C.21.76   Mirre and moche gold *withouten* merc[ede] askynge
C.21.198   And wikked to wonye in wo *withouten* ende.'
C.22.21   *Withouten* consail of Consience or cardinale vertues
C.22.270   [Heuene haeth euene nombre and helle is *withoute* nombre].

withsaet > withsitte

wiþseye v *withseien v.* A 2 wiþsigge; B 1

A. 4.142   Couþe nou3t warpen a word to *wiþsigge* resoun,
A.11.232   'Contra,' quaþ I, 'be crist! þat can I þe *wi[þsigg]e*,
B.10.349   'Contra!' quod I, 'by crist! þat kan I [*wiþseye*],

withsitte v *withsitten v.* C 4 withsaet (1) withsite (1) withsitte (1) withsytte (1)

C.Pr.176   Myghte [we] with eny wyt his wille *w[i]thsytte*
C. 8.202   Þat durste *withsitte* þat [Peres] sayde for fere of syre hunger
C.10.98   Sholde no bisshop be here biddynges to *withsite*.
C.18.249   I *withsaet* nat his heste; y hope and bileue

wiþstonde v *withstonden v.* B 1

B.Pr.156   Mi3te we wiþ any wit his wille *wiþstonde*

wiþwyndes n *withewinde n.* A 1 weþewindes; B 1; C 1 wethewynde

A. 6.6   In a [*weþewindes*] wyse [ywounden] aboute;
B. 5.518   In a *wiþwynde[s]* wise ywounden aboute.
C. 7.163   In a *wethewynde* wyse ywrithe al aboute;

witide > witeþ; wytyng(e > witen

witlees adj *witles adj.* B 1; C 2 witteles

B.13.1   And I awaked þerwiþ, *witlees* nerhande,
C. 9.111   With a good will, *witteles*, mony wyde contreyes
C.15.1   And y awakede þerwith, *witteles* nerhande,

witnesse n *witnesse n.* A 7 witnesse (4) wytnesse (3); B 45 witnesse (44) witnesses (1); C 33 witenesse (1) witnesse (24) witnesses (2) wittenesse (5) wittnesse (1)

A. 2.72   In *witnesse* of whiche þing wrong was þe furste,
A. 2.111   And feffe false *wytnesse* wiþ floreynes ynowe,
A. 6.67   Þanne shalt þou blenche at a b[erw]e, bere no fals *wytnesse*;
A. 8.94   And was writen ri3t þus in *witnesse* of treuþe:
A. 8.135   Ac for þe bible beriþ *wytnesse*
A.11.41   And bringe forþ a ballid resoun, t[a]k[e] bernard to *witnesse*,
A.11.192   Þ[i]s be[þ] dobet; so beriþ *witnesse* þe sauter:
B. 2.38   And how ye shul saue yourself? þe Sauter bereþ *witnesse*:
B. 2.81   To bakbite and to bosten and bere fals *witnesse*,
B. 2.108   In *witnesse* of which þyng wrong was þe furste,
B. 2.147   And feffe fal[s] *witness[e]* wiþ floryns ynowe,
B. 5.88   Wiþ bakbitynge and bismere and berynge of fals *witnesse*;
B. 5.146   And freres fyndeþ hem in defaute, as folk bereþ *witnesse*,
B. 5.580   Thanne shaltow blenche at a Bergh, bere-no-fals-*witnesse*,
B. 7.52   That he ne worþ saaf [sikerly]; þe Sauter bereþ *witnesse*:
B. 7.85   For whoso haþ to buggen hym breed, þe book bereþ *witnesse*,
B. 7.112   And was writen ri3t þus in *witnesse* of truþe:
B. 7.157   Ac for þe book bible bereþ *witnesse*
B. 9.75   And fynde fele *witnesses* among þe foure doctours,
B. 9.76   And þat I lye no3t of þat I lere þee, luc bereþ *witnesse*.
B. 9.120   In erþe [þe] heuene [is]; hymself [was þe] *witnesse*.
B.10.55   And bryngen forþ a balled reson, taken Bernard to *witnesse*,
B.10.89   How þe book bible of hym bereþ *witnesse*:
B.10.252   And Crist cleped hymself so, þe [scripture] bereþ *witnesse*:
B.10.285   The bible bereþ *witnesse* þat al[le] þe [barnes] of Israel
B.10.364   And preiseden pouerte with pacience; þe Apostles bereþ *witnesse*
B.11.87   '3is, by Peter and by Poul!' quod he and took hem boþe to *witnesse*:
B.11.141   '[I] Troianus, a trewe kny3t, [take] *witnesse* at a pope
B.11.157   Was þat Sarsen saued, as Seint Gregorie bereþ *witnesse*.
B.11.227   That saued synful men as Seint Iohan bereþ *witnesse*:
B.11.253   Boþe Marthaes and Maries, as Mathew bereþ *witnesse*.
B.11.269   Than he þat is ri3t riche; Reson bereþ *witnesse*:
B.11.272   Wiser þan Salomon was bereþ *witnesse* and tau3te
B.11.274   And lif moost likynge to god as luc bereþ *witnesse*:
B.12.65   As þe book bereþ *witnesse* to burnes þat kan rede:

B.12.123   Take we hir wordes at worþ, for hir *witnesse* be trewe,
B.12.184   To lere lewed men as luc bereþ *witnesse*:
B.12.261   That was writen, and þei *witnesse* to werche as it wolde.
B.13.94   And þanne shal he testifie of [a] Trinite, and take his felawe to *witnesse*
B.13.135   That no clerk ne kan, as crist bereþ *witnesse*:
B.13.358   [Thoru3] false mesures and met, and wiþ fals *witnesse*;
B.13.440   As he seiþ hymself; seynt Iohan bereþ *witnesse*:
B.14.86   And brynge his soule to blisse, so þat feiþ bere *witnesse*
B.14.180   For how þow confortest alle creatures clerkes bereþ *witnesse*:
B.15.90   Ac of curatours of cristen peple, as clerkes bereþ *witnesse*,
B.15.238   For braulynge and bakbitynge and berynge of fals *witnesse*.
B.15.489   They wol be wrooþ for I write þus, ac to *witnesse* I take
B.17.305   Ac it is but selden ysei3e, þer sooþnesse bereþ *witnesse*,
B.18.132   And þat my tale is trewe I take god to *witnesse*.
B.18.232   'By goddes body', quod þis book, 'I wol bere *witnesse*
B.18.237   And alle þe element3,' quod þe book, 'herof beren *witnesse*.
B.19.446   Ayein þe olde lawe and newe lawe, as Luc [bereþ] *witness[e]*:
C. 2.88   To bacbite and to boste and bere fals *witnesse*,
C. 2.112   In *wittenesse* of [which] thyng wrong was the furste,
C. 2.163   And feffe fals *witnesse* with floreynes ynowe,
C. 6.53   Of werkes þat y wel dede *witnesses* take
C. 7.100   As he sayth hymsulf; seynt Ion bereth *witnesse*:
C. 7.227   Thenne shaltow blenche at a berw, bere-no-fals-*witnesse*,
C. 9.286   And was ywryte ryhte thus in *witnesse* of treuthe:
C. 9.305   Ac for þe boek bible bereth *witnesse*
C.10.212   And þat my sawe is soth þe sauter bereth *witnesse*:
C.11.36   And brynge forth [a] balle[d] reso[n], taken bernard to *witnesse*
C.11.153   [Bisily] bokes; ho beth his *witnesses*?
C.11.213   And demede wel and wysly; wymmen bereth *wittenesse*:
C.11.282   That wit ne *witnesse* wan neuere þe maistre
C.12.76   'I troianes, a trewe knyht, take *witnesse* of a pope
C.12.134   And seynt marie his moder, as Mathew bereth *witnesse*,
C.12.154   Then he þat is rihte ryche; reson bereth *witnesse*:
C.14.66   Take we here wordes at worthe, for here *witteness[e]* b[e] trewe,
C.14.124   To lere lewede men As luk bereth *witnesse*:
C.15.101   And [thenne shal he testifie of] a trinite and take his felowe [t]o *witnesse*
C.15.156   Y take *wittenesse*,' quod [þe wy], 'of holy writ a partye:
C.15.220   As þe boek bereth *witnesse* þat he bere myhte
C.16.291   As poul in his pistul of hym bereth *wittenesse*:
C.16.363   For braulyng and bacbitynge and berynge of fals *witnesse*.
C.18.212   A thre he is þer he is and hereof bereth *witnesse*
C.18.221   As þe bible bereth *witnesse*, A boek of þe olde lawe.
C.19.31   And alle thre bote o god; thus abraham bereth *witenesse*
C.19.240   Clothes of moest cost, as clerkes bereth *witnesse*:
C.19.285   Ac hit is bote selde yseyen, there sothnesse bereth *witnesse*,
C.20.135   And þat my tale [be] trewe y take god to *witnesse*.
C.20.241   'By godes body,' quod this boek, 'y wol [b]ere *witnesse*
C.20.246   And all þe elementis,' quod the boek, 'hereof bereth *witnesse*.
C.20.311   Thenne were he vnwrast of his word þat *witnesse* is of treuthe.'
C.21.446   A3en þe olde lawe and newe lawe, as Luk bereth *witnesse*:

witnesse v *witnessen v.* A 9 wytnesse (2) wytnessen (1) witnesseþ (2) witnessid (1) witnessiþ (2) wytnessiþ (1); B 20 witnesse (4) witnessede (1) witnessen (1) witnesseþ (14); C 33 witnesse (1) witnessede (1) witnessen (1) witnesseth (19) wittenesseth (6) wyttenesse (1) wittnesseth (4)

A. 1.135   For þus [*wytnessiþ*] his woord, werche þou þeraftir,
A. 2.46   Alle to *wytnesse* wel what þe writ wolde,
A. 2.57   'Wyten & *wytnessen* þat wonen vpon erþe,
A. 2.125   To wende wiþ hem to westmynstre to *wytnesse* þ[is] dede.
A.10.94   [And so *witnesseþ* goddis worde and holiwrit boþe]:
A.10.111   And for wisdom is writen & *witnessid* in chirches:
A.11.243   Godis word *witnessiþ* we shuln 3iue & dele
A.11.263   Or ellis [vn]writen for wykkid as *witnessiþ* þe gospel:
A.12.25   And god graunted hit neuere; þe gospel hit *witnesseþ*
B.Pr.195   That *witnesseþ* holy writ, whoso wole it rede:
B. 1.147   [For þus *witnesseþ* his word; werche þow þerafter].
B. 2.75   Witeþ and *witnesseþ* þat wonieþ vpon erþe
B. 2.161   To wenden wiþ hem to westmynstre to *witnesse* þis dede.
B. 3.274   Forbar hym and his beestes boþe as þe bible *witnesseþ*
B. 4.91   Wit acorde[þ] þerwiþ and [*witnessede*] þe same:
B. 4.181   And as moost folk *witnesseþ* wel wrong shal be demed.'
B.10.23   Iob þe gentile in hise gestes *witnesseþ*
B.10.382   Or ellis vnwriten for wikkednesse as holy writ *witnesseþ*
B.11.39   If truþe wol *witnesse* it be wel do Fortune to folwe
B.11.234   *Witnesse* in þe Pask wyke, whan he yede to Emaus;
B.11.398   For al þat he [wrou3t] was wel ydo, as holy writ *witnesseþ*:
B.12.72   For Moyses *witnesseþ* þat god wroot for to wisse þe peple
B.13.306   And of werkes þat he wel dide *witnesse* and siggen,
B.13.434   Ther wise men were, *witnesseþ* goddes wordes,
B.14.46   Lyue þoru3 leel bileue, [as oure lord] *witnesseþ*:
B.14.63   As holy writ *witnesseþ* whan men seye hir graces:

B.16.122   And Sathan youre Saueour; [youre]self now ye *witnessen*.
B.17.253   To alle vnkynde creatures; crist hymself *witnesseþ*:
B.18.242   The water *witnesse[þ]* þat he was god for he wente on it;
C.Pr.208   *Wyttenesse* at holy wryt whoso kan rede:
C. 2.82   *Wyten* and *witnessen* þat wonyen on erthe
C. 2.132   Y, Theo[lo]gie, þe tixt knowe yf trewe doom *wittenesseth*,
C. 3.123   And *wittenesseth* what worth of hem þat wolleth take mede:
C. 3.427   Forbar hym and his beste bestes, as þe byble *witnesseth*,
C. 4.87   Witt acordede therwith and *witnessede* þe same:
C. 5.87   Nec in pane [nec] in pabulo; þe paternoster *wittenesseth*
C. 7.94   There wyse men were, *wittnesseth* goddes wordes,
C. 8.239   As wyse men haen wryten and as *witnesseth* Genesis
C.10.237   Holy writ *witnesseth* þat for no wikkede dede
C.11.21   Iob þe gentele in his g[e]stes *witnesseth*
C.11.216   *Wittenesseth* þat here wordes and here werkes bothe
C.11.232   As holy writ *witnesseth*, goddes word in þe gospel:
C.11.235   *Wittnesseth* godes word þat was neuere vntrewe
C.12.102   And, as þe euaungelie *witnesseth*, when we maken festes
C.12.119   To haue as we haen serued, as holy chirche *witnesseth*:
C.12.123   *Witnesse* in þe paske woke when he ȝede to Emaux:
C.12.155   Holy [writ] *witnesseth* hoso forsaketh
C.13.202   And so *witnesseth* wyse and wisseth þe frenche:
C.14.37   For moyses *witnesseth* þat god wroet [in stoen with his fynger;
C.15.244   Leue thorw lele bileue, As oure lord *wittenesseth*:
C.15.262   As *witnesseth* holy writ when we seggeth oure graces:
C.16.241   Aȝen þe consayl of crist, as holy clergie *witnesseth*:
C.16.242   Lo, what holy writ *wittenesseth* of wikkede techares:
C.16.298   'Charite is a childische thyng, as holy churche *witnesseth*:
C.17.6   Holy writ *witnesseth* þer were suche eremytes,
C.17.37   As *wittnesseth* holy writ what tobie saide
C.17.235   Aȝen þe lore of oure lord as seynt luk *witnesseth*–
C.19.219   To alle vnkynde creatures, as Crist hymsulue *witnesseth*:
C.19.290   That eyþer haue equitee, as holy writ *witnesseth*:
C.20.45   And as wyde as hit euere was; this we *witnesseth* alle.'
C.20.251   The water *witnesseth* þat he was god for a wente on h[it];
C.20.356   *Witnesseth* in his writyng[e] what is lyares mede:

witt > wit; witte > wit,witeþ

witted adj *witted adj.* B 3; C 3 witted (1) wittede (1) ywitted (1)
B.10.403   Forþi wise *witted* men and wel ylettrede clerkes
B.12.107   Na moore kan a kynde *witted* man, but clerkes hym teche,
B.12.158   Than clerkes or kynde *witted* men of cristene peple.
C.11.233   Wel *ywitted* men and wel ylettred clerkes,
C.14.52   No more can a kynde *witted* man, but clerkes hym teche,
C.14.72   Kynde *wittede* men [c]an a clergie by hemsulue;

witteles > witlees; wittenesse(- > witnesse

witterly adv *witterli adv.* A 4 witterly (3) wytterly (1); B 11; C 17
    witterly (11) wytterly (1) witterliche (2) witturly (2) witturlich (1)
A. 1.72   What he[o] were *witterly* þat wisside me so faire.
A. 3.163   Whanne ȝe wyte *wytterly* where þe wrong liggeþ;
A.11.259   To wyte what is dowel *witterly* in herte,
A.12.10   Ȝif I wiste *witterly* þou woldest don þerafter,
B. 1.74   What she were *witterly* þat wissed me so faire.
B. 3.176   Whan ye witen *witterly* wher þe wrong liggeþ.
B. 5.269   And I wiste *witterly* þow were swich as þow tellest.
B.13.81   And wisshed *witterly*, wiþ wille ful egre,
B.13.384   Hadde I neuere wille, woot god, *witterly* to biseche
B.18.66   Shal no wight wite *witterly* who shal haue þe maistrie
B.18.209   Sholde wite *witterly* what day is to meene.
B.18.229   Ne what is *witterly* wele til weylawey hym teche.'
B.19.358   For *witterly*, I woot wel, we beþ noȝt of strengþe
B.20.194   And wisshed ful *witterly* þat I were in heuene.
B.20.271   Forþi I wolde *witterly* þat ye were in þe Registre
C.Pr.11   Wynkyng as hit were, *witterliche* y sigh hit;
C. 1.71   What she were *wytterly* þat wissede me so [faire].
C. 3.222   When ȝe [wyten] *witterly* [where] þe wrong liggeth.
C. 3.297   And not neuere *witterly* where he lyue so longe
C. 5.37   Tyl y wyste *witterly* what holy writ menede
C. 6.273   Hadde y neuere will, [woot god], *witterly* to byseche
C. 6.303   There shal he wite *witturly* what vsure is to mene
C. 9.88   This [y] woet *witturly*, as þe world techeth,
C.15.88   And wisched *witterly* with will ful egre,
C.18.180   Y waytede *witterly*; Ac whoder he wende y ne wiste.
C.20.68   Ac shal no wyht wyte *witturlich* ho shal haue þe maistry
C.20.216   Sholde ywyte *witterly* what day is to mene.
C.20.218   He hadde nat wist *witterly* where deth were sour or swete.
C.20.238   Ne what is *witterliche* wele til welaway hym teche.'
C.21.358   For *witterly*, y woet wel, we be nat of strenghe
C.22.194   And wesched wel *witterly* þat ȝe were in heuene.
C.22.271   Forthy y wolde *witterly* þat ȝe were in [þe] registre

wittes > wit

witty adj *witti adj.* A 3; B 11; C 9 witty (7) wittiore (2)
A. 2.102   Ȝet be war of þe weddyng for *witty* is treuþe.
A. 4.24   Ac [o]n wary[n] wisdom, and *witty* his fere
A. 4.141   War[yn] wisdom þo, ne [*witty*] his fere,
B. 2.138   Yet be war of [þe] weddynge; for *witty* is truþe,
B. 4.27   Oon waryn wisdom and *witty* his feere
B. 4.67   Tho [wan] Wisdom and sire waryn þe *witty*
B.10.395   Ac of fele *witty* in feiþ litel ferly I haue
B.10.437   Ther are *witty* and wel libbynge ac hire werkes ben yhudde
B.11.374   'I haue wonder [in my wit], þat *witty* art holden,
B.11.394   The wise and þe *witty* wroot þus in þe bible:
B.12.143   He spekeþ þere of riche men riȝt noȝt, ne of riȝt *witty*,
B.14.167   And yliche *witty* and wise, if þee wel hadde liked.
B.15.130   Wolde neuere þe wit of *witty* god but wikkede men it hadde,
B.15.357   Wederwise shipmen and *witty* clerkes also
C. 2.154   Ȝut beth ywar of þe weddynge; for *witty* is treuthe.
C. 5.188   Were *wittiore* and worthiore then he þat was his maister.
C. 6.24   Wene y were *witty* and wiser then another;
C. 9.51   Beth ywar, ȝe wis men and *witty* of þe lawe,
C.11.226   For of fele *witty* in faith litel ferly y haue
C.16.20   And yliche *witty* and wys and lyue withoute nede;
C.16.220   The *witt[i]ore* þat eny wihte is, but yf he worche þeraftur,
C.17.95   Wedurwyse shipmen now and oþer *witty* peple
C.20.354   Beth ywaer, ȝe wyse clerkes and ȝe *witty* of lawe,

wittily adv *wittili adv.* A 1 wittiliche; B 1; C 1 wittyly
A.10.4   Wiþ wynd & wiþ watir *wi[tti]liche* enioynede.
B. 9.4   Wiþ wynd and wiþ water *witt[i]ly* enioyned.
C.10.131   With wynd and with water *wittyly* enioyned.

wittyman n *witti adj.* C 1
C. 4.31   [O]n wilyman and *wittyman* and wareyne wrynglawe.

wittiore > witty; wittis > wit; wittnesse(- > witnesse; witturly -liche > witterly; wyue > wif

wyued v *wiven v.* B 1
B. 9.187   Whan ye han *wyued* beþ war and wercheþ in tyme,

wyuen -es > wif

wyuyng ger *wivinge ger.* B 1; C 1 wyfyng
B. 9.186   Wreke þee wiþ *wyuyng* if þow wolt ben excused:
C.10.287   Awrek þe þerwith on *wyfyng*, for godes werk y holde hit:

wo n *wo n.* A 9 wo (7) woo (2); B 31; C 32 wo (31) woo (1)
A. 1.143   And ȝet wolde he hem no *woo* þat wrouȝte him þat pyne
A. 2.82   [And] er þis weddyng be wrouȝt *wo* þe betide!
A. 3.110   Er I wedde such a wif *wo* me betide!
A. 3.142   Þere she is wel wiþ þe king *wo* is þe reaume,
A. 4.71   [Þat wrong for his werkis shulde *woo* þole,
A. 5.3   Þanne wakide I of my wynkyng, & *wo* was wiþalle
A. 5.199   Þat wiþ al þe *wo* of þe world his wyf & his wenche
A.11.69   And alle here seed for here synne þe same *wo* suffride?"
A.11.115   Boþe wele & *wo* ȝif þat þou wile lerne,
B. 1.169   And yet wolde he hem no *wo* þat wrouȝte hym þat peyne,
B. 2.107   And with hym to wonye [in] *wo* while god is in heuene.'
B. 2.118   And er þis weddynge be wroȝt *wo* þee bitide!
B. 3.121   Er I wedde swich a wif *wo* me bitide!
B. 3.153   Ther she is wel wiþ þe kyng *wo* is þe Reaume,
B. 4.84   That wrong for hise werkes sholde *wo* þolie,
B. 5.3   Thanne waked I of my wynkyng and *wo* was withalle
B. 5.357   Wiþ al þe *wo* of þ[e] world his wif and his wenche
B. 9.61   Muche *wo* worþ þat man þat mysruleþ his Inwit,
B.10.163   Boþe-wele-and-*wo* if þat þow wolt lerne,
B.11.4   Tho wepte I for *wo* and wraþe of hir speche
B.11.400   Al to murþe wiþ man þat moste *wo* þolie,
B.11.406   And awaked þerwiþ; *wo* was me þanne
B.12.56   *Wo* is hym þat hem weldeþ but he hem [wel] despende:
B.12.186   *Wo* was hym marked þat wade moot wiþ þe lewed!
B.13.207   Ther nys *wo* in þis world þat we ne sholde amende;
B.13.262   So er my wafres ben ywroȝt muche *wo* I þolye.
B.14.177   *Wo* in wynter tymes for wantynge of cloþes,
B.15.542   And now is werre and *wo*, and whoso why askeþ:
B.18.2   As a recchelees renk þat [reccheþ of no *wo*],
B.18.204   And wo into wele mowe wenden at þe laste.
B.18.205   For hadde þei wist of no *wo*, wele hadde þei noȝt knowen;
B.18.206   For no wight woot what wele is þat neuere *wo* suffrede,
B.18.211   Wite what *wo* is, ne were þe deeþ of kynde.
B.18.225   To wite what alle *wo* is [þat woot of] alle ioye.
B.18.412   Than after werre and *wo* whan loue and pees ben maistres.
B.19.68   And muche *wo* in þis world willen and suffren.
B.19.198   And wikkede to wonye in *wo* wiþouten ende.'
B.19.243   Boþe of wele and of *wo* [and be ware bifore],
B.20.158   Oon þat muche *wo* wroȝte, Sleuþe was his name.
B.20.193   And of þe *wo* þat I was Inne my wif hadde ruþe.

C.Pr.10   Al þe welthe of the world and þe *wo* bothe,
C. 1.165   And ȝut wolde [he] hem no *wo* þat wrouhte hym þat [p]e[y]ne
C. 2.122   And ar this weddyng be wrouhte *wo* to al ȝoure consayle!
C. 3.158   Ar y wedde suche a wyf *wo* me bytyde!
C. 3.191   Ther she is wel with eny kyng *wo* is þ[e] rewme
C. 3.206   Withouten werre oþer *wo* oþer wickede lawe
C. 4.65   How wrong was a wykked man and muche *wo* wrouhte.
C. 4.80   That wrong for his werkes sholde *w[oo]* tholye
C. 6.415   With alle þe *wo* of th[e] world his wyf and his wenche
C. 9.78   And *wo* in wynter tym[e] and wakynge on nyhtes
C. 9.83   The *wo* of this wommen þat wonyeth in cotes
C. 9.84   And of monye oþer men þat moche *wo* soffren,
C. 9.272   And þe wolle worth weye, *wo* is the thenne!
C.10.175   And moche *wo* worth hym þat inwit myspeneth
C.11.105   Bothe-wele-and-*wo* yf þou wilt lerne:
C.11.164   Tho wepte y for *wo* and wrathe of here wordes
C.12.209   And out of *wo* into wele ȝoure wirdes shal chaunge."
C.13.214   And awakede þerwith; *wo* was me thenne
C.14.18   *Wo* is hym þat hem weldeth but he hem wel despene:
C.14.125   Muchel *wo* was hym marked þat wade shal with þe lewede!
C.17.204   And now is werre and *wo* and whoso why asketh:
C.18.174   *Wo* to tho þat thy wyles vysen to þe wo[r]ldes ende:
C.20.209   And *wo* into wele moet wende at þe laste.
C.20.210   For hadde they wist of no *wo*, wele hadde thay nat knowen;
C.20.211   For no wiht woet what wele is þat neuere *wo* soffrede
C.20.220   Ywyte what *wo* is ne were þe deth of kynde.
C.20.234   To wyte what al *wo* is þat woet of alle ioye:
C.21.68   And moche *wo* in this world wilnen and soffren.
C.21.198   And wikked to wonye in *wo* withouten ende.'
C.21.243   Bothe of wele and of *wo* and be ywaer bifore,
C.22.158   Oen þat moche *wo* wrouhte, sleuthe was his name.
C.22.193   And of þe *wo* þat y was ynne my wyf hadde reuthe

wode n *wode n.* A 1; B 6 wode (4) wodes (2); C 8 wode (4) wodes (4)
A. 9.54   [And] as I wente be a *wode*, walkyng myn one,
B. 8.63   And as I wente by a *wode*, walkyng myn one],
B.11.329   Wilde wormes in *wodes*, and wonderful foweles
B.14.113   And wilde wormes in *wodes*, þoruȝ wyntres þow hem greuest
B.16.56   In what *wode* þei woxen and where þat þei growed,
B.17.105   For [an] Outlaw[e is] in þe *wode* and vnder bank lotieþ,
B.17.332   That sholde brynge in bettre *wode* or blowe it til it brende.
C. 9.197   That wonede whilom in *wodes* with beres and lyons.
C. 9.226   That in wilde *wodes* been or in waste places,
C.10.62   By a wi[d]e wildernesse and by a *wode* syde.
C.13.137   Wilde wormes in *wodes* and wondurfol foules
C.15.289   And wilde wormes in *wodes*, thorw wyntres thow hem greuest
C.16.180   Bote as *wode* were afuyre thenne worcheth bothe
C.18.24   And askede [e]fte of hym of what *wode* they were.
C.19.312   That sholde brynge in bettere *wode* or blowen hit til hit brente.

wodewe(s > widewe

wodnesday n *Wednesdai n.* B 1
B.13.154   And al þe wit of þe *wodnesday* of þe nexte wike after;

woen > woon; woet > witen; wok > wake

woke v *woken v. &> wake,wouke* B 1; C 2 woky (1) woketh (1)
B.15.339   And wente forþ wiþ þat water to *woke* wiþ Temese.
C.14.25   And *w[o]ky* thorw gode werkes wikkede hertes.
C.16.335   And with warm water of his yes *woketh* h[em] til [t]he[y] white:

woken > wake; wokes > wouke; woky > woke; wol wolde(- wole > willen

wolf n *wolf n.* A 1 wolues; B 1 wolues; C 5 wolf (2) wolues (3)
A.10.212   But wandriþ [as *wolues*] & wastiþ [ȝif] þei mowe;
B. 9.198   Wandren [as *wolues*] and wasten [if þei] mowe;
C. 9.227   As *wolues* þat wuryeth men, wymmen and childrene
C. 9.260   For many wakere *wolues* ar wr[iþ]en into thy foldes;
C. 9.265   Thy shep ben ner al shabbede; the *wolf* shyt wolle:
C. 9.267   For to go wurye þe *wolf* that the wolle fou[l]leth?
C.16.271   And as lambes they lyen and ly[u]en as *wolues.*

wolkne n *welken n.* B 3 walkne (1) wolkne (2); C 1 welkene
B.15.362   Wisten by þe *walkne* what sholde bitide.
B.17.163   Boþe *wolkne* and þe wynd, water and erþe,
B.18.238   That he was god þat al wroȝte þe *wolkne* first shewed:
C.20.247   That he was god þat al wrouhte the *welkene* furste shewede:

wolle n *wol n. &> willen* A 3; B 2; C 5
A. 7.10   And wyues þat han *woll[e]* werchiþ it faste,
A. 8.17   How þat shabbide shep shu[l] here *wolle* saue,
A.11.18   But it be cardit wiþ coueitise as cloþeris don here *wolle*;
B. 6.13   Wyues and widewes *wolle* and flex spynneþ;
B.10.18   But it be carded wiþ coueitise as cloþeres [don] hir *wolle.*
C. 8.12   Wyue[s] and wyddewes *wolle* an[d] flex spynneth;
C. 9.265   Thy shep ben ner al shabbede; the wolf shyt *wolle:*

C. 9.267   For to go wurye þe wolf that the *wolle* fou[l]leth?
C. 9.272   And þe *wolle* worth weye, wo is the thenne!
C.11.15   Bote hit be cardet with coueytise as clotheres kemben here *wolle.*

wollen adj *wollen adj. &> willen* A 4 wollene; B 5 wollen (4) wollene (1); C 3 wollene (2) wollone (1)
A.Pr.99   *Wollene* websteris and weueris of lynen,
A. 1.18   Of [*woll]ene*, of [lyn]ene, of liflode at nede
A. 5.129   My wyf was a wynstere & *wollene* cloþ made,
A. 8.43   And ȝaf wille for his writyng *wollene* cloþis;
B.Pr.220   *Wollen* webbesters and weueres of lynnen,
B. 1.18   Of *wollene*, of lynnen, of liflode at nede
B. 5.213   My wif was a [wynnestere] and *wollen* cloþ made,
B.11.282   Ne lakkeþ a neuere liflode, lynnen ne *wollen:*
B.11.289   Hem sholde lakke no liflode, neyþer lynnen ne *wollen.*
C. 1.18   And brynge forth ȝoure bilyue, bothe lynnen and *wollene,*
C. 6.221   My wyf was a webbe and *wollone* cloth made,
C.13.103   Hem sholde neuere lacke lyflode, noþer lynnen ne *wollene.*

wolleth > willen

wolleward adj *wolward adj.* B 1; C 1 wollewaerd
B.18.1   *Wolleward* and weetshoed wente I forþ after
C.20.1   *Wollewaerd* and watschoed wente y forth aftur

wollone > wollen; wolt(- > willen

wolueliche adj *wolfli adj.* B 1
B.15.116   Ac youre werkes and wordes þervnder aren ful [*wol]ueliche.*

wolues > wolf

wolueskynnes adj *wolf n.* B 1
B. 6.161   'And fro þise wastours *wolueskynnes* þat makeþ þe world deere,

woman > womman

wombe n *wombe n.* A 10; B 14; C 11
A.Pr.56   Prechinge þe peple for profit of þe *wombe*;
A. 3.73   Of þat þe pore peple shulde putte in here *wombe.*
A. 3.181   And hastide[st] þe homward for hunger of þi *wombe.*
A. 5.70   Walewiþ in my *wombe* & waxiþ as I wene.
A. 5.72   Such wynd in my *wombe* wexiþ er I dyne.
A. 5.210   'Shal neuere fissh on þe Friday defie in my *wombe*
A. 6.78   Wiþ no led but [wiþ] loue & louȝnesse, as breþeren of o *wombe.*
A. 7.160   And wrong hym so be þe *wombe* þat al watride his eiȝen,
A. 7.201   And [a]baue hem wiþ b[e]nes for bollnyng of here *wombe,*
A. 7.240   Of alle þe wyke [hy] werkiþ nouȝt, so here *wombe* akiþ.'
B.Pr.59   Prechynge þe peple for profit of [þe *wombe*];
B. 3.84   [Of] þat þe pouere peple sholde putte in hire *wombe.*
B. 3.194   And [hastedest þee] homward for hunger of þi *wombe.*
B. 5.382   'Shal neuere fyssh on [þe] Fryday defyen in my *wombe*
B. 5.591   Wiþ no leed but wiþ loue and lowe[nesse] as breþeren [of o *wombe*].
B. 6.175   And wrong hym so by þe *wombe* þat [al watrede his eiȝen].
B. 6.215   [And] aba[u]e hem wiþ benes for bollynge of hir *womb[e]*;
B. 6.256   Of al a wike werche noȝt, so oure *wombe* akeþ.'
B. 9.62   And þat ben glotons, glubberes; hir god is hire *wombe:*
B.13.63   *Wombe* cloutes and wilde brawen and egges yfryed wiþ grece.
B.13.84   'I shal Iangle to þis Iurdan wiþ his Iuste *wombe*
B.15.291   And wan wiþ hise hondes þat his *wombe* neded.
B.15.456   [And] so it fareþ by a barn þat born is of *wombe:*
B.16.100   And in þe *wombe* of þat wenche was he fourty woukes
C.Pr.57   Prechyng þe peple for profyt of þe *wombe*;
C. 3.83   With that þe pore peple sholde potte in here *wombe.*
C. 5.52   Withoute bagge or botel but my *wombe* one.
C. 6.439   Shal neuere fysch [o]n þe fryday defyen in my *wombe*
C. 7.239   The barres aren of buxumnesse as bretherne of o *wombe*;
C. 8.172   And wronge hym so by þe *wombe* þat al watrede his yes;
C. 8.225   And [a]baue hem with benes for bollyng of here *wombe*;
C. 8.268   Of al a woke worche nat, so oure *wombe* greueth.'
C. 9.254   Cam no wyn in his *wombe* thorw þe woke longe
C.15.91   'Y schal iangle to þis iurdan with his iuyste *wombe*
C.18.133   And in þe *wombe* of þat wenche was he fourty wokes

womman n *womman n. &> kynnes_womman* A 14 womman (10) wommen (4); B 31 womman (20) wommen (10) wommene (1); C 32 wymmen (11) woman (1) women (3) womman (9) wommane (1) wommen (7)
A. 1.69   Þanne hadde I wondir in my wyt what *womman* it were
A. 2.8   And was war of a *womman* wondirliche cloþide,
A. 2.15   'What is þis *womman*,' quaþ I, 'þus worþily atirid?'
A. 3.50   'Wiste I þat,' quaþ þe *womman*, 'þere nis wyndowe ne auter
A. 3.107   'Wilt þou wedde þis *womman* ȝif I wile assente?
A. 3.246   Wende þidir with þin ost *wommen* to kille;
A. 7.8   'What shulde we *wommen* werche þe while?'
A. 8.73   Þei wedde no *womman* þat hy wiþ delen

A. 8.83	And *wommen* wiþ childe þat werche ne mowe,
A.10.23	To kepe þise *womman* þise wise men ben chargid,
A.10.152	And manye mylions mo of men & of *wommen*
A.10.202	For in [vn]tyme, treweliche, betwyn m[a]n & *womm[a]n*
A.10.208	And [werche] on his wyf & on no *womman* ellis,
A.11.67	Þat he gilide þe *womman* & þe wy aftir,
B. 1.32	Thoruȝ wyn and þoruȝ *wommen* þer was loth acombred,
B. 1.71	Thanne hadde I wonder in my wit what *womman* it weere
B. 2.8	And was war of a *womman* [wonder]liche ycloþed,
B. 2.19	'What is þis *womman*', quod I, 'so worþili atired?'
B. 3.51	'Wiste I þat', quod þ[e] *womman* 'I wolde noȝt spare
B. 3.118	'Woltow wedde þis *womman* if I wole assente?
B. 3.268	Widwes and wyues, *wommen* and children,
B. 5.602	To wayuen vp þe wiket þat þe *womman* shette
B. 5.641	'By crist!' quod a comune *womman*, 'þi compaignie wol I folwe.
B. 6.8	'What sholde we *wommen* werche þe while?'
B. 7.91	[Thei] wedde [no] *womman* þat [þei] wiþ deele
B. 7.101	And *wommen* wiþ childe þat werche ne mowe,
B. 9.189	For in vntyme, trewely, bitwene man and *womman*
B.10.109	That bi[w]iled þe *womman* and þe [wye] after,
B.11.217	Crist to a commune *womman* seide, in [comen] at a feste,
B.11.248	Iesu crist on a Iewes doȝter liȝte, gentil *womman* þouȝ she were,
B.12.74	Of manye swiche I may rede, of men and of *wommen*,
B.12.74	That what *womman* were in auoutrye taken, whe[r] riche or poore,
B.12.76	A *womman*, as [we] fynde[n], was gilty of þat dede,
B.12.80	Than þe *womman* þat þere was, and wenten awey for shame.
B.12.81	[Thus Clergie þere] conforted þe *womman*.
B.12.89	The *womman* þat þe Iewes [iugged] þat Iesus þouȝte to saue:
B.13.447	And a blynd man for a bourdeour, or a bedrede *womman*
B.15.410	Makometh in mysbileue men and *wommen* brouȝte,
B.16.109	And commune *wommen* conuertede and clensed of synne,
B.17.21	Of men and of *wommen* many score þousand.'
B.18.131	Wiþouten [*wommene*] wem into þis world broȝte hym.
B.19.162	For þat *womm[a]n* witeþ may noȝt wel be counseille.
B.19.367	Thanne alle kynne cristene saue comune *wommen*
B.19.433	As brighte as to þe beste man or to þe beste *womman*.
B.20.347	He saluede so oure *wommen* til some were wiþ childe.'
C. 1.31	Thorw wyn and thorw *wom[e]n* there was loot acombred;
C. 1.68	Thenne hadde y wonder in my wit what *woman* he were
C. 2.7	And mony mo of here maners, of men and of *wymmen*.'
C. 2.9	And [was war of] a *womman* wonderly yclothed.
C. 2.149	A myhte kusse the kyng as for his kyn[nes] *womman*.
C. 3.134	And saide, 'vnwittiliche, *womman*, wro[uh]t hastow ofte
C. 3.144	That alle [*women*, wantowen], shal [be] war [by] þe one
C. 3.397	But þat alle maner men, *wymmen* and childrene
C. 3.421	Man, *womman* and wyf, childe, wedewe and bestes,
C. 6.190	To wynne to my wille *wymmen* with gyle,
C. 7.107	And a blynd man for a bordor or a bedredene *womman*
C. 7.206	Ȝe mote go thorw mekenesse, alle men and *wommen*,
C. 8.6	'What sholde we *wommen* wor[c]he þe whiles?'
C. 8.9	And ȝe worthily *wymmen* with ȝoure longe fyngres,
C. 9.83	The wo of this *wommen* þat wonyeth in cotes
C. 9.106	Ac hem wanteth wyt, men and *women* bothe,
C. 9.168	Ne weddeth none *wymmen* þat they with deleth,
C. 9.177	And *wymmen* with childe þat worche ne mowe,
C. 9.227	As wolues þat wuryeth men, *wymmen* and childrene
C.11.85	And when y was war of his wille to þat *womman* gan y louten
C.11.108	Bothe *wymmen* and wyn, wr[a]the, [enuy] and slewthe
C.11.213	And demede wel and wysly; *wymmen* bereth wittenesse:
C.13.75	Withoute wyles or wronges or *wymmen* at þe stuyues;
C.13.189	In *wommen*, in wedes and in wordes bothe
C.17.181	Thus macumeth in misbileue man & *womman* brouhte
C.18.142	And comen *wommen* conuertede and clansed hem of synne
C.19.22	Of men and of *wommen* meny score thousend.'
C.20.134	Withouten *wommane* wem into this world brouhte hym.
C.21.162	For þat *womman* witeth [may] nat [wel be] conseyl.
C.21.367	Thenne alle kyne cristene saue commune *wommen*
C.21.433	As brihte as to þe beste man or to þe beste *womman*.
C.22.347	He salued so oure *wymmen* til some were with childe.'

wonden > wounden

wonder n *wonder n.* A 4 wondir (3) wondris (1); B 16 wonder (12) wondres (4); C 13 wonder (11) wondres (2)

A.Pr.4	Wente wyde in þis world *wondris* to here.
A. 1.69	Þanne hadde I *wondir* in my wyt what womman it were
A. 3.170	Why þou wraþþest þe now *wondir* me þinkiþ.
A. 5.102	Ȝif shrift shulde, it shop[e] a gret *wondir*.'
B.Pr.4	Wente wide in þis world *wondres* to here.
B. 1.71	Thanne hadde I *wonder* in my wit what womman it weere
B. 2.18	I hadde *wonder* what she was and whos wif she were.
B. 3.183	Whi þow wraþþest þee now *wonder* me þynkeþ.
B. 3.304	And haue *wonder* in hire hertes þat men beþ so trewe.
B.11.10	[Siþen] she seide to me, 'here myȝtow se *wondres*

B.11.323	And þoruȝ þe *wondres* of þis world wit for to take.
B.11.347	I hadde *wonder* at whom and wher þe pye
B.11.350	If any Mason made a molde þerto muche *wonder* it were.
B.11.374	'I haue *wonder* [in my wit], þat witty art holden,
B.15.120	And who was myn Auctour, muche *wonder* me þinkeþ
B.15.483	Wiþ wederes and wiþ *wondres* he warneþ vs wiþ a whistlere
B.16.253	I hadde *wonder* of hise wordes and of hise wide cloþes
B.18.122	Eiþer asked ooþer of þis grete *wonder*,
B.18.126	'And am wendynge to wite what þis *wonder* meneþ.'
B.19.119	For bifore his moder Marie made he þat *wonder*
C.Pr.4	Wente forth in þe world *wondres* to here
C. 1.68	Thenne hadde y *wonder* in my wit what woman he were
C. 3.229	Why thow wrathest þe now *wonder* me thynketh!
C.11.169	And senes he saide to me, 'here myhte thow se *wondres*
C.13.158	Y hadde *wonder* at wh[om] and where þe pye
C.13.161	Yf eny mason made a molde þerto moche *wonder* me thynketh.
C.13.184	'Y haue *wonder* in my wit, so wys as thow art holden,
C.16.162	Thenne hadde y *wonder* what he was, þat l[i]berum Arbitrium,
C.18.148	That he was god or godes sone for þat grete *wonder*;
C.18.269	Thenne hadde y *wonder* of his wordes and of [his] wyde clothes
C.20.125	Ayþer asked oþer of this grete *Wonder*,
C.20.129	'And am wendynge to wyte what þis *wonder* meneth.'
C.21.119	For bifore his moder Marie made he þat *wonder*

wonder adj *wonder adj.* B 1
B.14.126	Ac god is of [a] *wonder* wille, by þat kynde wit sheweþ,

wonder adv *wonder adv.* B 3; C 3
B.14.6	Wiþ þe sope of siknesse þat sekeþ *wonder* depe,
B.15.1	AC after my wakynge it was *wonder* longe
B.20.159	Sleuþe wax *wonder* yerne and soone was of age
C.11.217	Were *wonder* goed and wisest in here tyme
C.13.5	Ȝut ret me þat abraham and Iob weren *wonder* ryche
C.22.159	Sleuthe wax *wonder* ȝerne and sone was of age

wonderful adj *wonderful adj.* B 2 wonderful (1) wonderfulle (1); C 2 wonderfol (1) wondurfol (1)
B.11.329	Wilde wormes in wodes, and *wonderful* foweles
B.17.26	'Youre wordes arn *wonderfulle*', quod I, 'which of yow is trewest
C.13.137	Wilde wormes in wodes and *wondurfol* foules
C.19.27	'Ȝoure wordes aren *wonderfol*,' quod y; 'where eny of [hem] be trewe

wonderly adv *wonderli adv.* A 3 wondirliche (1); B 3 wonderly (2) wonderliche (1); C 5 wonderly (3) wonderliche (2)
A. 2.8	And was war of a womman *wondirliche* clo[þ]ide,
A. 6.111	He is *wondirliche* welcome & faire vndirfonge.
A.11.3	She was *wondirliche* wroþ þat wyt so tauȝte,
B. 2.8	And was war of a womman [*wonder*]liche ycloþed,
B. 5.626	He is *wonderly* welcome and faire vnderfongen.
B.10.3	She was *wonderly* wroþ þat wit [so] tauȝte,
C. 2.9	And [was war of] a womman *wonderly* yclothed.
C. 6.308	Thenne was there a walschman was *wonderly* sory,
C. 7.279	Is *wonderliche* welcome and fayre vnderfonge;
C.11.3	She was *wonderly* wroth þat wit me so tauhte;
C.11.165	And in a wynkynge y warth and *wonderliche* me mette

wonderwise adv *wonder adj.* B 1; C 1 wonderwyse
B. 1.124	Whan þise wikkede wenten out *wonderwise* þei fellen,
C. 1.126	*Wonderwyse*, holy wryt telleth, how þei fullen,

wondred v *wondren v.* B 1; C 3 wondred (1) wondrede (1) wondreth (1)
B.19.204	I *wondred* what þat was and waggede Conscience,
C.13.153	Saue man and his make; and þerof me *wondrede*.
C.15.74	Ac me *wondreth* in my wit why þat they ne preche
C.21.204	Y *wondred* what þat was and wagged Consience

wondres > wonder; wondryng > wandre; wondurfol > wonderful

wone n *wone n.* &> *wonye* B 1; C 2
B.15.245	For to wonye wiþ hem his *wone* was som tyme,
C. 4.22	For hit is þe *wone* of wil to wynse and to kyke
C.16.324	And oþerwhile his *wone* is to w[e]nde [o]n pilgrimages

woned > wonye,wont; wonede(n wonen > wonye

wones n *won n.(1)* B 1; C 1
B. 3.235	Lord, who shal wonye in þi *wones* wiþ þyne holy seintes,
C.Pr.18	Woned in tho *wones* and wikkede spiritus.

woneth > wonye; wonid > wont

wonye *wonen v.(1)* A 8 wone (3) wonen (2) woniþ (3); B 19 woneden (2) woneþ (1) wonye (7) wonyen (1) wonieþ (1) wonyeþ (7); C 20 wone (2) woned (1) wonede (3) woneden (2) woneth (4) wonye (2) wonyen (1) wonyeth (5)
A. 1.61	Þereinne *woniþ* a wy þat wrong is yhoten;
A. 2.30	Ȝif þou wilnest to *wone* wiþ treuþe in his blisse,

A. 2.57	'Wyten & wytnessen þat *wonen* vpon erþe,
A. 2.71	Þere to *wone* wiþ wrong while god is in heuene.'
A. 2.186	For to *wone* wiþ hem, watris to loke.
A. 2.194	And is welcome whanne he wile & *woniþ* wiþ hem ofte.
A. 3.12	Þat *woniþ* at westmenstre worsshipeþ hire alle;
A.10.144	Into þis wrecchide world to *wonen* & to libben
B. 1.63	TherInne *wonyeþ* a [wye] þat wrong is yhote;
B. 2.75	Witeþ and witnesseþ þat *wonieþ* vpon erþe
B. 2.107	And with hym to *wonye* [in] wo while god is in heuene.'
B. 2.227	[For to] *wonye* with hem watres to loke.
B. 2.235	And is welcome whan he wile and *woneþ* with hem ofte.
B. 3.12	[That] *wonyeþ* [at] westmynstre worshipeþ hire alle.
B. 3.235	Lord, who shal *wonye* in þi wones wiþ þyne holy seintes,
B. 5.176	Forþi haue I no likyng, [leue me], wiþ þo leodes to *wonye*;
B.10.393	That for hir werkes and wit now *wonyeþ* in pyne,
B.10.435	Of wit and of wisedom wiþ dampned soules *wonye*.
B.13.121	Ther þe lord of lif *wonyeþ*, to leren [hem] what is dowel.
B.14.98	'Where *wonyeþ* Charite?' quod Haukyn; 'I wiste neuere in my lyue
B.15.245	For to *wonye* wiþ hem his wone was som tyme,
B.15.273	*Woneden* in wildernesse among wilde beestes,
B.15.508	And þat is rouþe for riȝtful men þat in þe Reawme *wonyen*,
B.19.36	As wide as þe world is [*wonyeþ* þer noon]
B.19.192	He wente, and *wonyeþ* þere, and wol come at þe laste
B.19.198	And wikkede to *wonye* in wo wiþouten ende.'
B.20.39	And *woneden* [wel elengely] and wolde noȝt be riche.
C.Pr.18	*Woned* in tho wones and wikkede spiritus.
C. 1.59	Therynne *wonyeth* a wyghte þat wrong is [ihote];
C. 2.82	Wyten and witnessen þat *wonyen* on erthe
C. 2.237	That lyare sholde *wonye* with hem watres to loke.
C. 2.245	And is welcome when he cometh and *woneth* with hem ofte.
C. 3.142	Or in a wel wors, *wo[ne* ther as an ancre,
C. 5.1	Thus y awakede, woet god, whan y *wonede* in Cornehull,
C. 7.178	[Can]st [thow] wissen vs [þe w]ay whoderout treuth *woneth*?'
C. 7.198	And hoso wilneth to wyte where þat treuthe *woneth*
C. 9.83	The wo of this wommen þat *wonyeth* in cotes
C. 9.197	That *wonede* whilom in wodes with beres and lyons.
C.11.220	That for here werkes and wyt *wonyeth* now in payne,
C.16.65	And ayther hateth oþer and may nat *wone* togyderes.
C.17.11	Elles foules fedde hem in frythes þer they *wonede*,
C.17.28	And *woneden* in wildernesses amonges wilde bestes.
C.17.259	And þat is reuthe for rihtfole men þat in þ[e] reume *wonyeth*
C.21.36	As wyd[e] as þe worlde is *wonyeth* þer none
C.21.192	He wente and *woneth* there and wol come at þe laste
C.21.198	And wikked to *wonye* in wo withouten ende.'
C.22.39	And *woneden* wel elyngly and wolden nat be riche.

wonne(n > wynnen

wont *ptp wonen v.(1)* A 1 wonid; B 3 woned (1) wont (2); C 4 woned
(3) ywoned (1)

A. 7.152	'I was not *wonid* to werche,' quaþ wastour, 'now wile I not begynne,'
B. 6.167	'I was noȝt *wont* to werche', quod Wastour, 'now wol I noȝt bigynne!'
B.15.182	And ouþerwhile he is *woned* to wenden on pilgrymages
B.20.370	And wake for hise wikked werkes as he was *wont* to doone.
C. 6.143	Amonges wyues and wydewes [y am *woned*] to sitte
C. 8.164	'I was nat *woned* to worche,' quod wastour, 'now wol y nat bygynne!'
C.17.90	As they *ywoned* were; in wham is defaute?
C.22.370	And wake for his wikkede werkes as he was *woned* [to do].

wonte *n wonte n.* C 1

C.15.240	Þe worm and *wonte* vnder erthe and in water fisches,

woo > wo; wook > wake

woon *n won n.(2)* B 1; C 1 woen

B.20.171	[And] gaf hym gold good *woon* þat gladede his herte.
C.22.171	And gaef hym goelde goed *woen* þat gladde h[is] hert[e]

woord(is > word; woost woot > witen; wopen > wepen; worch(- > werchen

word *n word n. &> world* A 38 woord (6) woordis (1) word (7) worde (1)
wordis (23); B 93 word (27) worde (1) wordes (65); C 61 word (15)
worde (1) wordes (45)

A. 1.13	And wolde þat ȝe wrouȝten as his *word* techiþ.
A. 1.41	'A madame mercy,' quaþ I, 'me likiþ wel ȝoure *wordis*.
A. 1.70	Þat suche wise *wordis* of holy writ shewide,
A. 1.89	And ek lyk to oure lord be seint lukis *wordis*.
A. 1.119	Ac þo þat werchen þe *word* þat holy writ techiþ,
A. 1.135	For þus [wytnessiþ] his *woord*, werche þou þeraftir,
A. 1.174	For þise arn þe *wordis* writen in þe Euaungelie:
A. 3.94	To mede þe maide melis þise *wordis*:
A. 4.134	Ac [whanne] resoun among þise renkis reherside þise *wordis*,
A. 4.142	Couþe nouȝt warpen a *word* to wiþsigge resoun,

A. 5.68	Wiþ werkis [or wiþ] *wordis* whanne he saiȝ his tyme.
A. 5.204	Þe ferste *woord* þat he spak was 'where is þe bolle?'
A. 7.35	Curteisliche þ[e] kniȝt [conseyuede] þise *wordis*;
A. 7.51	'For to werche be þi *woord* while my lif duriþ.'
A. 7.65	And robyn þe ribaudour for hise rusty *woordis*.
A. 7.74	Let god worþe wiþal for so his *woord* techeþ.
A. 7.115	And pleynide hem to peris wiþ suche pitous *wordis*:
A. 7.211	[Or with werk or with *word* þe while þou art here].
A. 7.222	Matheu wiþ þe manis face [mouþ]iþ þise *wordis*:
A. 7.259	'Be seint pernel,' quaþ peris, 'þise arn profitable *wordis*,
A. 8.127	And þoruȝ here *wordis* I wok & waitide aboute,
A. 9.48	'I haue no kynde knowyng,' quaþ I, 'to conseyue þi *wordis*,
A. 9.83	And prechiþ þe peple seint poulis *wordis*:
A. 9.116	Þanne bouȝt, in þat tyme, seide þis *wordis*:
A.10.33	For þoruȝ þe *woord* þat he warp wexe forþ bestis,
A.10.40	Þat he wrouȝte wiþ werkis & with *wordis* boþe.
A.10.94	[And so witnesseþ goddis *worde* and holiwrit boþe]:
A.10.95	Ac ȝif þou werchist be godis *word* I warne þe be beste,
A.10.161	Þat god was wroþ wiþ here werkis & [suche *wordis* seide]
A.10.192	Þe fruyt þat þei bringe forþ arn manye foule *wordis*.
A.11.8	Wiþ suche wise *wordis* to wisse any foolis!
A.11.65	And carp[en] aȝens clergie crabbide *wordis*;
A.11.71	And make men to mysbeleue þat musen on here *wordis*.
A.11.150	He kenniþ vs þe contrarie, aȝens catonis *wordis*,
A.11.243	Godis *word* witnessiþ we shuln ȝiue & dele
A.11.269	Boþe in werk & in *woord*, in world in his tyme?
A.11.275	And be here werkis & here *wordis* wissen vs to dowel,
A.12.97	So þat þou werke þe *word* þat holy wryt techeþ,
B.Pr.139	Thanne greued hym a Goliardeis, a gloton of *wordes*,
B.Pr.184	And to þe route of Ratons reherced þise *wordes*:
B. 1.13	And wolde þat ye wrouȝte as his *word* techeþ.
B. 1.43	'[A] madame, mercy', quod I, 'me likeþ wel youre *wordes*.
B. 1.72	That swiche wise *wordes* of holy writ shewed,
B. 1.91	And [ek] ylik to oure lord by Seint Lukes *wordes*.
B. 1.147	[For þus witnesseþ his *word*; werche þow þerafter].
B. 1.200	Fo[r] þise [ben *wordes*] writen in þe [euaungelie]:
B. 2.90	As in werkes and in *wordes* and waityn[g] with eiȝes
B. 3.105	To Mede þe mayde [melleþ] þise *wordes*:
B. 3.342	She sholde haue founden fel[l]e *wordes* folwynge þerafter:
B. 4.34	'Ther are wiles in hire *wordes*, and with Mede þei dwelleþ;
B. 4.158	[Kynde] wit acorded þerwiþ and comendede hise *wordes*,
B. 5.85	With werkes or wiþ *wordes* whan he seyȝe his tyme.
B. 5.86	Ech a *word* þat he warp was of a Neddres tonge;
B. 5.162	Of wikkede *wordes* I, wraþe, hire wortes made
B. 5.362	The firste *word* þat he [spak] was 'where is þe bolle?'
B. 5.365	'As þow wiþ *wordes* & werkes hast wroȝt yuele in þi lyue
B. 5.505	That euere þei wraþed þei in þis world in *word*, þouȝt or dedes.'
B. 6.33	Curteisly þe knyȝt [conseyued] þise *wordes*:
B. 6.56	'For to werche by þi *wor[d]* while my lif dureþ.'
B. 6.73	And Robyn þe Ribaudour for hise rusty *wordes*.
B. 6.82	Lat-god-yworþe-wiþ-al-for-so-his-*word*-techeþ.
B. 6.238	Mathew wiþ mannes face mouþe[þ] þise *wordes*:
B. 6.275	'By Seint [Pernele]', quod Piers, 'þise arn profitable *wordes*!
B. 7.145	And [þoruȝ hir *wordes* I wook] and waited aboute,
B. 7.153	And how þe preest inpugned it wiþ two propre *wordes*.
B. 8.57	'I haue no kynde knowyng', quod I, 'to conceyuen [þi] *wordes*
B. 8.92	And precheþ þe peple Seint Poules *wordes*,
B. 8.127	Thanne þoȝt in þat tyme seide þise *wordes*:
B. 9.32	For þoruȝ þe *word* þat he [warp] woxen forþ beestes,
B. 9.37	As who seiþ, "moore moot herto þan my *word* oone;
B. 9.44	He moste werche wiþ his *word* and his wit shewe.
B. 9.46	Wiþ his *word* and werkmanshipe and wiþ lif to laste.
B. 9.52	[Th]at he wroȝte wiþ werk and wiþ *word* boþe;
B. 9.132	Til god wraþed [wiþ] hir werkes and swich a *word* seide,
B. 9.171	The fruyt þat [þei] brynge forþ arn [manye] foule *wordes*;]
B.10.8	'Wiþ swiche wise *wordes* to wissen any sottes!'
B.10.41	Spitten and spuen and speke foule *wordes*,
B.10.107	And carpen ayein cler[gie] crabbede *wordes*.
B.10.118	And maken men in þire bileue þat muse on hire *wordes*.
B.10.201	He kenneþ vs þe contrarie ayein Catons *wordes*,
B.10.260	Loke þow werche it in werk þat þi *word* sheweþ;
B.10.277	For goddes *word* wolde noȝt be lost, for þat wercheþ euere;
B.10.280	That goddes *word* wercheþ noȝt on [wis] ne on lewed
B.10.294	And drede to wraþe yow in any *word* youre werkmanship to lette,
B.10.390	Of hir *wordes* þei wissen vs for wisest as in hir tyme,
B.10.447	For soþest *word* þat euer god seide was þo he seide Nemo bonus.
B.11.59	By wissynge of þis wenche I [dide], hir *wordes* were so swete,
B.11.176	For Seint Iohan seide it, and soþe arn hise *wordes*:
B.11.226	For some *wordes* I fynde writen, were of Feiþes techyng,
B.11.251	And to oure Saueour self seide þise *wordes*:
B.12.50	That wise *wordes* wolde shewe and werche þe contrarie:
B.12.123	Take we hir *wordes* at worþ, for hir witnesse be trewe,
B.12.137	And seiden hir *wordes* [ne] hir wisdomes [w]as but a folye;

B.12.156 How þow contrariedest clergie wiþ crabbede *wordes*,
B.13.68 Ac o *word* þei ouerhuppen at ech tyme þat þei preche
B.13.88 He shal haue a penaunce in his paunche and puffe at ech a *worde*,
B.13.140 "Wiþ *wordes* and werkes", quod she, "and wil of þyn herte
B.13.145 Boþe wiþ wer[k] and with *wor[d]* fonde his loue to wynne;
B.13.311 Al he wolde þat men wiste of werkes and *wordes*
B.13.340 [For] Goddes *word* [ne grace] gaf me neuere boote,
B.13.417 He wexeþ wroþ, and wol noȝt here but *wordes* of murþe;
B.13.427 Patriarkes and prophetes, prechours of goddes *wordes*,
B.13.434 Ther wise men were, witnesseþ goddes *wordes*,
B.13.454 [There] flateres and fooles þoruȝ hir foule *wordes*
B.14.14 Or þoruȝ werk or þoruȝ *word* or wille of myn herte
B.14.72 Amonges cristene creatures, if cristes *wordes* ben trewe,
B.14.310 The seuenþe is welle of wisedom and fewe *wordes* sheweþ
B.15.116 Ac youre werkes and *wordes* þervnder aren ful [wol]ueliche.
B.15.198 'Clerkes haue no knowyng', quod he, 'but by werkes and *wordes*.
B.15.210 Neiþer þoruȝ *wordes* ne werkes, but þoruȝ wil oone,
B.15.450 As wel þoruȝ hise werkes as wiþ hise holy *wordes*,
B.15.478 And by hire *wordes* and werkes wenen and trowen;
B.16.6 The leues ben lele *wordes*, þe lawe of holy chirche;
B.16.33 That it norisseþ nyce sightes and [anoþer] tyme *wordes*:
B.16.141 Sittynge at þe soper he seide þise *wordes*:
B.16.253 I hadde wonder of hise *wordes* and of hise wide cloþes
B.16.272 I wepte for hise *wordes*; wiþ þat sauȝ I anoþer
B.17.12 Wheron [was] writen two *wordes* on þis wise yglosed.
B.17.26 'Youre *wordes* arn wonderfulle', quod I, 'which of yow is trewest
B.17.352 Good wille, good *word* [boþe], wisshen and willen
B.18.150 Thanne Mercy ful myldely mouþed þise *wordes*,
B.18.283 And [siþen] he þat Sooþnesse is seide þise *wordes*,
B.18.290 And toldest hire a tale, of treson were þe *wordes*;
B.18.389 I [may] do mercy þoruȝ [my] rightwisnesse and alle my *wordes* trewe,
B.19.80 And þere was þat *word* fulfilled þe which þow of speke,
B.19.122 He wroȝte þat by no wit but þoruȝ *word* one,
B.19.229 Some [wyes] he yaf wit with *wordes* to shewe,
B.19.286 Waste *word* of ydelnesse ne wikked speche moeue;
B.19.386 Grace, þoruȝ goddes *word*, [g]af Piers power,
B.20.115 And wiþ pryuee speche and peynted *wordes*,
B.20.144 And armed hym [in] haste [in] harlotes *wordes*,
C.Pr.70 Lewed men leued hym wel and lykede his *wordes*;
C.Pr.201 And to þe route of ratones rehersede thise *wordes*:
C.1.13 And wolde þat ȝe wroghtoun as his *word* techeth.
C.1.41 'A madame, mercy,' [quod I], 'me lyketh wel ȝoure *wordes*.
C.1.69 That suche wyse wordes of holy writ shewede
C.1.87 And also lyk [to] oure lord by saynt Lukes *wordes*.
C.1.195 For this aren *wordes* ywryten in þe ewangelie:
C.2.97 As in werkes and in *wordes* and waytyng[e] of yes,
C.3.494 A sholde iche vyfonde [felle *wordes* folwynge] aftur:
C.4.44 And speke wyse *wordes* a longe while togederes.
C.4.154 And sayden, 'we seyn wel, syre resoun, be thi *wordes*
C.6.21 Thorw my *word* and my witt here euel werkes to shewe;
C.6.65 His clothes were of corsemen[t] and of kene *wordes*.
C.6.84 For god ne goddes *word* ne gras helpe me neuere
C.6.99 Here werkes and here *wordes* where þat y seete.
C.6.177 In *word*, in wedes, in waytynge of eyes.
C.6.258 'With false *wordes* and w[ittes] haue y ywonne my godes
C.6.420 The furste [*word*] þat he spake was '[wh]o halt þe bolle?'
C.7.77 A wexeth wroth and wol not here but *wordes* of murthe;
C.7.87 Patriarkes and prophetes, precheours of goddes *wordes*,
C.7.94 There wyse men were, wittnesseth goddes *wordes*,
C.7.114 There flaterers and foles with here foule *wordes*
C.8.32 Courteisliche the knyhte thenne co[nseyu]ed thise *wordes*:
C.8.75 And Robyn þe rybauder for his rousty *wordes*.
C.9.282 For y can construe vch a *word* and kennen hit the an englische.'
C.9.294 And thorw here *wordes* [y] awoke and waytede aboute
C.9.302 And how þe prest inpugnede hit thorw two propre *wordes*.
C.10.89 And precheth to þe peple seynt paules *wordes*:
C.10.123 Thenne thouht in þat tyme sayde this *wordes*:
C.10.273 The fruyt þat they brynge forth aren many foule *wordes*;
C.11.164 Tho wepte y for wo and wrathe of here *wordes*
C.11.216 Wittenesseth þat here *wordes* and here werkes bothe
C.11.232 As holy writ witnesseth, goddes *word* in þe gospel:
C.11.235 Wittnesseth godes *word* þat was neuere vntrewe:
C.12.11 By wissyng of this wenche y dede, here *wordes* were so swete,
C.12.46 He saide in here sarmon selcouthe *wordes*:
C.12.137 And to oure sauyour sulue saide þis *wordes*:
C.13.189 In wommen, in wedes and in *wordes* bothe
C.14.66 Take we here *wordes* at worthe, for here wittenesse[e] b[e] trewe,
C.14.82 And saide here *wordes* ne here wysdomes was but a folye;
C.14.100 How þou contra[r]idest clergie with crabbed *wordes*,
C.15.95 He shal haue a penaunce in his paunche and poffe at vch a *worde*
C.15.143 Fond [with] wit & *word* his loue to wynne,
C.15.271 Amonges cristene creatures, yf cristes *wordes* be trewe:

C.16.144 The seuethe is a welle of wysdoem and fewe *wordes* sheweth
C.18.37 That hit norischeth nise s[ih]tus and som tyme *wordes*
C.18.269 Thenne hadde y wonder of his *wordes* and of [his] wyde clothes
C.18.288 [Y] wepte for his *wordes*; with þat saw y [a]nother
C.19.13 Whereon was writen two *wordes* on this wyse yglosed:
C.19.27 'Ȝoure *wordes* aren wonderfol,' quod y; 'where eny of [hem] be trewe
C.19.332 Goed wil, goed *word* bothe, wischen and wilnen
C.20.153 Thenne mercy fol myldely mouthed this *wordes*,
C.20.311 Thenne were he vnwrast of his *word* þat witnesse is of treuthe.'
C.20.431 [Y] may do mercy of my rihtwysnesse and alle myn *wordes* trewe
C.21.80 And þer was þat *word* fulfuld þe which þou of speke,
C.21.122 He wrouhte þat by no wyt bote thorw *word* one,
C.21.229 Som [wyes] he ȝaf wyt with *wordes* to schewe,
C.21.286 Wast[e] *word* of ydelnesse ne wikede speche meue:
C.21.386 Grace thorw godes *word* gaf [Peres] power,
C.22.115 And with priue speche and paynted *wordes*
C.22.144 And Armed hym in haste in harlotes *wordes*

worden v *worden v.* A 2 worden (1) wordiden (1); B 3 wordeden (2) wordynge (1); C 3 worden (1) wordyng (1) yworded (1)
A.4.33 And *wordiden* a gret while wel wisly togidere.
A.10.96 Whatso men *worden* of þe wraþþe þe neuere;
B.4.46 And *wordeden* [a gret while wel wisely] togideres.
B.10.434 And þo þat wisely *wordeden* and writen manye bokes
B.17.50 And as we wenten þus in þe wey *wordynge* togideres
C.13.244 Why ȝe *worden* to me thus was for y aresonede Resoun.'
C.15.148 And whan he hadde *yworded* thus wiste no man aftur
C.19.48 And as we wenten in þe way thus *wordyng* of this matere

wordynge ger *OED wording vbl. n. &> worden* C 1
C.8.90 And aftur here warnynge and *wor[d]ynge* worche þou þeraftur:

wordliche > worldly

world n *world n.* A 20; B 51 world (46) worlde (3) worldes (2); C 58 world (48) worlde (8) worldes (2)
A.Pr.4 Wente wyde in þis *world* wondris to here.
A.Pr.19 Worching & wandringe as þe *world* askiþ.
A.1.8 Haue þei worsshipe in þis *world* þei kepe no betere:
A.1.37 Þat is þe wrecchide *world* [wolde] þe betraye.
A.3.6 What man of þis *world* þat hire were leuist;
A.4.122 Shulde neuere wrong in þis *world* þat I wyte miȝte
A.5.199 Þat wiþ al þe wo of þe *world* his wyf & his wenche
A.7.124 Suche wastours in þis *world* his werkmen distroyeþ;
A.7.158 'Awreke me on wasto[urs], 'quaþ peris, 'þat þis *world* [shend]iþ.'
A.8.169 Þat han þe [welþe of þis] *world*, & wise men ben holden
A.9.34 Þe watir is liknid to þe *world* þat waniþ & waxiþ;
A.9.38 Þat þoruȝ þe fend, & þe flessh, & þe false *world*,
A.10.71 A[c] wiȝt in þis *world* þat haþ wys vndirstonding
A.10.89 Wilne þou neuere in þis *world*, [wy], for to do betere,
A.10.133 Þat þoruȝ wedlak þe *world* stant, whoso wile it knowen.
A.10.144 Into þis wrecchide *world* to wonen & to libben
A.11.260 For howso I werche in þis *world*, [wrong] oþer ellis,
A.11.269 Boþe in werk & in woord, in *world* in his tyme?
A.11.272 And was þere neuere in þis *world* to wysere of werkis,
A.11.292 As þise þat wrouȝte wykkidly in *world* whanne þei were.
B.Pr.4 Wente wide in þis *world* wondres to here.
B.Pr.19 Werchynge and wandrynge as þe *world* askeþ.
B.1.8 Haue þei worship in þis *world* þei [kepe] no bettre:
B.1.39 That is þe wrecched *world* wolde þee bitraye.
B.3.6 What man of þis [*world*] þat hire were leuest;
B.3.66 An auenture pride be peynted þere and pomp of þe *world*;
B.3.282 For so is þis *world* went wiþ hem þat han power
B.4.139 Sholde neuere wrong in þis *world* þat I wite myȝte
B.5.282 And al þe wikkednesse in þis *world* þat man myȝte werche or þynke
B.5.357 Wiþ al þe wo of þ[e] *world* his wif and his wenche
B.5.480 God, þat of þi goodnesse [g]onne þe *world* make,
B.5.505 That euere þei wraþed þee in þis *world* in word, þouȝt or dedes.'
B.6.132 Whiche þat were in þis *world* hise werkmen apeired.
B.6.161 'And fro þise wastours woluesskynnes þat makeþ þe *world* deere,
B.6.173 'Awreke me of wastours', quod he, 'þat þis *world* shendeþ.'
B.7.191 That haue þe welþe of þis *world* and wise men ben holden
B.8.38 The water is likned to þe *world* þat wanyeþ and wexeþ;
B.8.42 That þoruȝ þe fend and þe flessh and þe [false] *worlde*
B.9.110 [Dowel in þis *world* is trewe wedded libbynge folk],
B.9.111 For þei mote werche and wynne and þe *world* sustene;
B.10.24 That wikked men he welden þe welþe of þis *worlde*,
B.10.81 And yet þe wrecches of þis *world* is noon ywar by ooþer,
B.10.279 Ac it semeþ now sooþly, to [siȝte of þe *worlde*],
B.10.433 Tho þat wrouȝte wikkedlokest in *world* þo þei were;
B.11.101 Þyng þat al þe *world* woot, wherfore sholdestow spare
B.11.323 And þoruȝ þe wondres of þis *world* wit for to take.
B.13.173 Al þe wit of þis *world* and wiȝt mennes strengþe

B.13.207	Ther nys wo in þis *world* þat we ne sholde amende;
B.14.105	Thouȝ men rede of richesse riȝt to þe *worldes* ende,
B.15.438	Elleuene holy men al þe *world* tornede
B.16.27	The *world* is a wikked wynd to hem þat willen truþe.
B.16.48	Ac whan þe fend and þe flessh forþ wiþ þe *world*
B.16.157	Ac [to] þe [*worldes* ende] þi wikkednesse shal worþe vpon þiselue:
B.17.101	For wente neuere wye in þis *world* þoruȝ þat wildernesse
B.17.162	[Halt] al þe wide *world* wiþInne hem þre,
B.17.262	Forþi beþ war, ye wise men þat wiþ þe *world* deleþ;
B.18.4	Til I weex wery of þe *world* and wilned eft to slepe
B.18.61	The wal waggede and cleef and al þe *world* quaued.
B.18.131	Wiþouten [wommene] wem into þis *world* broȝte hym.
B.18.234	That alle þe wise of þis *world* in o wit acor[de]den
B.18.413	Was neuere werre in þis *world* ne wikkednesse so kene
B.19.36	As wide as þe *world* is [wonyeþ þer noon]
B.19.68	And muche wo in þis *world* willen and suffren.
B.19.82	And al þe wit of þe *world* was in þo þre kynges.
B.19.219	For Antecrist and hise al þe *world* shul greue
B.19.230	[To wynne wiþ truþe þat] þe *world* askeþ,
B.19.333	As wide as þe *world* is wiþ Piers to tilie truþe
B.19.354	Al þe *world* in a while þoruȝ oure wit', quod Pryde.
B.19.427	Emperour of al þe *world*, þat alle men were cristene.
B.20.49	Siþ he þat wroȝte al þe *world* was wilfulliche nedy,
B.20.381	And [wenden] as wide as þe *world* [renneþ]
C.Pr.4	Wente forth in þe *world* wondres to here
C.Pr.10	Al þe welthe of the *world* and þe wo bothe,
C.Pr.21	Worchyng and wondryng as þ[e] *world* ascuth.
C.Pr.100	Al þe *world* wot wel hit myghte nouȝt be trewe
C.Pr.104	That al þe *world* be [þe] wors, as holy writ telleth.
C. 1.8	Ha[u]e thei worschip in this *world* thei wilneth no bettere;
C. 1.37	[That] is þe wrecchede *world* wolde þe bigyle.
C. 3.6	What man of this *world* þat here [were leuest].
C. 3.70	An Auntur pruyde be paynted there and pomp of the *world*,
C. 3.212	That al þe witt of the *world* is woxe into Gyle.
C. 3.435	For so is the *world* went with hem þat han power
C. 4.136	Shulde neuere wrong in this *world* þat y wyte myhte
C. 6.334	For al the wrecchednesse of this *world* and wikkede dedes
C. 6.415	With alle þe wo of th[e] *world* his wyf and his wenche
C. 7.122	God þat of thi goodnesse gonne þe *world* make
C. 8.27	Fro wastores and wikked men þat þis *world* struyen
C. 8.158	'Awreke me of this wastors þat maketh this *world* dere–
C. 8.238	Go to oure bygynnynge tho god the *world* made,
C. 9.88	This [y] woet witturly, as þe *world* techeth,
C. 9.252	Ac while a wrouhte in þe *world* and wan his mete with treuthe
C. 9.337	That haen the welthe of this *world* and wise men ben holde
C.10.44	The water is likned to þe *wor[l]d* þat wanyeth and waxeth;
C.10.48	That thorw the fend and [the] flesch and th[e] freel *worlde*
C.10.199	To wende as wyde as þe *worlde* were
C.10.204	As this wedded men þat this *world* susteyneth,
C.10.245	Ac why þe *world* was adreynt, holy writ telleth,
C.11.61	And ȝut th[e] wrechus of this *world* is noen ywar by oþer
C.11.66	Ac þe more a wynneth and hath þe *world* at his wille
C.11.80	The which is a lykyng and luste, þe loue of þe *world*.'
C.12.35	Thyng þat al þe *world* woet wherfore sholdest thow spare
C.12.157	Or eny welthe in this *world*, his wyf or his childrene,
C.12.171	And al þat þe *world* wolde and my will folowe:
C.12.228	And haen þe *world* at he[re] wille oþerwyse to leuene.
C.15.165	Þer [n]is wyht in this *world* þat wolde the lette
C.15.171	Al th[e] wit of this *world* and wyhte menne strenghe
C.15.280	Thogh men rede of rychesse rihte to þe *worldes* ende
C.18.31	The *world* is a wikkede wynd to hem þat wo[l] treuthe;
C.18.174	Wo to tho þat thy wyles vysen to þe *wo[r]lde* ende:
C.18.213	The werkes þat hymsulue wr[o]uhte and this *world* bothe:
C.18.250	Where y walke in this *worlde* a wol hit me allowe.
C.19.104	Eny wikkedere in þe *worlde* then y were mysulue
C.19.113	For god þat al bygan in bigynnynge of the *worlde*
C.19.228	Forthy beth ywar, ȝe wyse men þat with the *world* deleth;
C.20.4	Til y waxe wery of the *world* and wilnede eefte to slepe
C.20.134	Withouten wommane wem into this *world* brouhte hym.
C.20.214	Yf all þe *world* were whit or swanwhit all thynges?
C.20.243	That alle þe wyse of th[is] *world* in o wit acordede
C.20.456	Was neuere werre in this *world* ne wikkedere enuye
C.21.36	As wyd[e] as þe *worlde* is wonyeth þer none
C.21.68	And moche wo in this *world* wilnen and soffren.
C.21.82	And al þe wit of the *world* was in [þo] thre kynges.
C.21.219	For Auntecrist and hise al the *world* shal greue
C.21.230	To wynne with treuthe þat the *world* asketh,
C.21.333	As wyde as the *world* is with Peres to tulye treuthe
C.21.354	Alle the *world* in a while thorw oure wit,' quod pruyde.
C.21.427	Emperour of al þe *world*, þat all men were cristene.
C.22.49	Sethe [he] þat wrouhte al þe *worlde* was willefolliche nedy
C.22.381	And wenden as wyde as þe *world* re[n]neth

worldly adj *worldli adj.* B 3 worldly (2) worldliche (1); C 5 worldly (3) wordliche (2)

B.19.285	Ne wynnynge ne wele of *worldliche* richesse,
B.19.292	Mighte no [lyere wiþ lesynges] ne los of *worldly* catel
B.20.211	[Weede] ne *worldly* [mete] while þi lif lasteþ.'
C.10.91	"ȝe *wordliche* wyse, vnwyse þat ȝe soffre,
C.12.236	*Worldly* wele y[s] wykked thyng to hem þat hit kepeth.
C.21.285	Ne wynnynge ne wel[e] o[f] *wordliche* richesse,
C.21.292	Myhte no lyare with lesynge[s] ne losse of *worldly* catel
C.22.211	Wede ne *worldly* mete while thy lif lasteth.'

worliche adj *worthli adj.* C 2 worliche (1) worthily (1)

C. 3.369	For hoso wolde to wyue haue my *worliche* douhter
C. 8.9	And ȝe *worthily* wymmen with ȝoure longe fyngres,

worm n *worm n.* A 1; B 5 worm (2) wormes (3); C 4 worm (1) wormes (3)

A.11.66	"Why wolde oure sauiour suffre such a *worm* in his blisse
B.10.108	"Why wolde oure Saueour suffre swich a *worm* in his blisse
B.11.329	Wilde *wormes* in wodes, and wonderful foweles
B.14.41	First þe wilde *worm* vnder weet erþe,
B.14.113	And wilde *wormes* in wodes, þoruȝ wyntres þow hem greuest
B.16.34	And wikkede werkes þerof, *wormes* of synne,
C.13.137	Wilde *wormes* in wodes and wondurfol foules
C.15.240	Þe *worm* and wonte vnder erthe and in water fisches,
C.15.289	And wilde *wormes* in wodes, thorw wyntres thow hem greuest
C.18.38	And manye wikkede werkes, *wormes* of synne,

wors > worse; worschip(- > worship(-

worse adj *werse adj. comp.* A 2 wers; B 8 wers (1) worse (3) worst (1) worste (3); C 11 wors (2) worse (6) worste (3)

A. 1.26	þat þou worþe þe *wers* whanne þou werche shuldist.
A.11.218	And welawey *wers* and I [wo]lde al telle.'
B. 1.26	That þow worþe þe *wers* whan þow werche sholdest.
B. 3.325	And er þis fortune falle fynde men shul þe *worste*
B.10.342	Salomon seiþ also þat siluer is *worst* to louye:
B.13.362	'The *worste* withInne was; a greet wit I let it.
B.14.161	And yet is wynter for hem *worse*, for weetshoed þei [gange],
B.14.225	If wraþe wrastle wiþ þe poore he haþ þe *worse* ende.
B.17.45	And wel awey *worse* ȝit for to loue a sherewe.
B.17.286	Ac þis is þe *worste* wise þat any wight myghte
C.Pr.104	That al þe world be [þe] *wors*, as holy writ telleth.
C. 3.142	Or in a wel *wors*, wo[ne] ther as an ancre,
C. 3.478	Ac ar this fortune falle fynde me shal the *worste*
C. 6.261	The *worste* lay withynne; a greet wit y lat hit.
C. 6.382	And that the bettere thyng, be arbitreres, bote sholde þe *worse*.
C. 6.385	And there were othes an heep for on sholde haue þe *worse*.
C.10.238	That þe sire by hymsulue doth þe sone sholde be þe *worse*.
C.16.14	And ȝut is wynter for hem *worse* for weetshoed þey g[ang]e,
C.16.66	Yf wrathe wrastle with þe pore he hath þe *worse* ende.
C.17.73	Me may now likene lettred men to a loscheborw oþer *worse*
C.19.267	Ac this is the *worste* wyse þat eny wiht myhte

worse adv *werse adv. comp.* A 6 wers; B 8 werse (4) worse (4); C 8 wors (1) worse (6) worste (1)

A. 3.96	Ac *wers* wrouȝtest þou neuere þan þo þou fals toke.
A. 3.162	'Nay lord,' quod þat lady, 'leu[iþ] him þe *wers*
A. 5.95	I deme men þere [hy] don ille, & ȝet I do *wers*;
A. 6.46	For treuþe wolde loue me þe *wers* a long tyme aftir.
A.11.287	Þanne marie þe maudeleyn who miȝte do *wers*?
A.11.288	Or who dede *wers* þanne dauid þat vrie destroyede,
B. 3.107	Ac *worse* wroȝtest [þ]ow neuere þan þo þow Fals toke.
B. 3.175	'Nay lord', quod þat lady, 'leueþ hym þe *werse*
B. 5.115	[I] deme [men þere hij] doon ille, [and yet] I do *werse*;
B. 9.147	And alle for hir [fore]fadres ferden þe *werse*.
B.10.428	Than Marie Maudeleyne [who myȝte do] *werse*?
B.10.429	Or who [dide] *worse* þan Dauid þat vries deeþ conspired,
B.14.227	And if he chide or chatre hym cheueþ þe *worse*,
B.17.328	It dooþ hym *worse* þan his wif or wete to slepe;
C. 3.138	For *wors* wrouhtest [thow] neuere then tho thow fals toke.
C. 3.221	'Nay, lord,' quod þat lady, 'leueth hym þe *worse*
C.10.235	And al for here forfadres ferden þe *worse*.
C.11.73	Get þe loue þerwith thogh thow *worse* fare".
C.11.261	Then marie maudelene who myhte do *worse*?
C.11.269	Tho that *worste* wrouhten while thei here were.
C.16.68	And yf he chyde or chattere hym cheueth þe *worse*
C.19.308	Hit doth hym *worse* then his wyf or wete to slepe;

worship n *worshipe n.* A 1 worsshipe; B 6 worship (4) worshipe (2); C 8 worschip (1) worschipe (7)

A. 1.8	Haue þei *worsshipe* in þis world þei kepe no betere:
B. 1.8	Haue þei *worship* in þis world þei [kepe] no bettre;
B. 3.335	And [muche] *worshipe* ha[þ] þerwiþ as holy writ telleþ:
B. 3.352	That þeiȝ we wynne *worship* and with Mede haue victorie,

B.12.119 That wiþ archa dei [wenten] in [*worship* and reuerence]
B.12.199 [I] hadde mete moore þan ynouȝ, ac noȝt so muche *worshipe*
B.16.244 And doon hym *worship* with breed and wiþ wyn boþe,
C. 1.8 Ha[u]e thei *worschip* in this world thei wilneth no bettere;
C. 3.487 And muche *worschipe* therwith, as holy writ telleth:
C. 3.499 *Worschipe* a wynneth þat wol ȝeue mede
C. 5.75 In confort of the comune and the kynges *worschipe*,
C. 6.142 That alle ladyes me lot[h]eth þat louyet[h] eny *worschipe*.
C.14.138 Ich haue mete more then ynow Ac nat [so] muche *worschipe*
C.18.262 At ones on an auter in *worschipe* of th[e] trinite
C.19.265 A fordoth the lihte þat oure lord loketh to haue *worschipe* of.

worshipe > worship,worshipen

worshipen v *worshipen v.* A 6 worsshipe (3) worsshipeþ (1) worsshipide
(1) yworsshipid (1); B 9 worshipe (4) worshiped (2) worshipen (1)
worshipeþ (1) yworshiped (1); C 9 worschipe (5) worschiped (1)
worschipede (1) worschipen (1) worschipeth (1)

A. 1.16 For to *worsshipe* hym þerewiþ whiles ȝe ben here.
A. 1.46 Ȝif þei [shulde] *worsshipe* þerwiþ cesar þe king.
A. 3.12 Þat woniþ at westmenstre *worsshipeþ* hire alle;
A. 7.93 I wile *worsshipe* þerewiþ treuþe in my lyue,
A.11.85 –Al was as he wolde; lord *yworsshipid* be þou,
A.11.171 And aftirward his wyf I *worsshipide* boþe,
B. 1.16 For to *worshipe* hym þerwiþ while ye ben here.
B. 1.48 [If] þei sholde [*worshipe* þerwiþ Cesar þe kyng].
B. 3.12 [That] wonyeþ [at] westmynstre *worshipeþ* hire alle.
B. 6.101 I wol *worshipe* þerwiþ truþe by my lyue,
B.10.132 Al was as [he] wold[e]–lord, *yworshiped* be þ[ow],
B.10.228 And afterwardes [his] wif [I] *worshiped* boþe,
B.15.484 Where þat his wille is to *worshipen* vs alle,
B.19.210 Welcome hym and *worshipe* hym wiþ Veni creator Spiritus.'
B.19.440 And *worshiped* be he þat wroȝte al, boþe good and wikke,
C.Pr.119 That soffreth men do sacrefyce and *worschipe* maumettes
C. 1.16 For to *worschipe* hym þerwith þe whiles ȝe lyuen here.
C. 3.13 That wendeth to Westmynstre *worschipe*[th] here monye.
C. 8.110 Y wol *worschipe* þerwith treuthe al my lyue
C. 9.135 Welcomen and *worschipen* and with ȝoure goed helpen
C.17.212 How tho corsede cristene catel and richesse *worschipede*;
C.18.261 *Worschipe* hym with wyn and with breed bothe
C.21.210 Welcome hym and *worschipe* hym with veni creator spiritus.'
C.21.440 And *worschiped* be he þat wrouhte all, bothe gode and wicke,

*worsshipe > worship,worshipen; worst > worse,worþe; worste > worse
adj,adv; worstow > worþe*

wortes n *wort n.(1)* A 1 wortis; B 2; C 1
A. 7.292 Deyneþ nouȝt to dyne a day niȝt olde *wortis*.
B. 5.162 Of wikkede wordes I, wraþe, hire *wortes* made
B. 6.308 Deyne[þ] noȝt to dyne a day nyȝt olde *wortes*.
C. 8.330 Deyne[th noght] to dyne a day nyhte olde *wortes*;

worþ n *worth n.(1)* B 3; C 1 worthe
B. 4.170 And yet yeue ye me neuere þe *worþ* of a risshe.'
B.12.123 Take we hir wordes at *worþ*, for hir witnesse be trewe,
B.12.291 And wheiþer it *worþ* [of truþe] or noȝt, [þe] *worþ* [of] bileue is
gret,
C.14.66 Take we here wordes at *worthe*, for here witteness[e] b[e] trewe,

worþ adj *worth adj.* A 4; B 6; C 9 worth (8) worthe (1)
A.Pr.75 Were þe bisshop yblissid & *worþ* boþe hise eris.
A. 5.31 Þat hire hed was *worþ* a mark & his hod not worþ a grote.
A. 5.31 Þat hire hed was worþ a mark & his hod not *worþ* a grote.
A.11.17 Wisdom and wyt now is not *worþ* a risshe.
A.Pr.78 Were þe Bisshop yblessed and *worþ* boþe hise eris
B. 5.31 [That] hire heed was *worþ* [a] marc & his hood noȝt a grote.
B.10.17 Wisdom and wit now is noȝt *worþ* a [risshe]
B.13.381 Moore þan it was *worþ*, and yet wolde I swere
B.14.27 No no Mynstrall ne moore *worþ* amonges pouere and riche
B.14.75 [Ac] mesure is [so] muche *worþ* it may noȝt be to deere.
C.Pr.76 Were þe bischop yblessed and *worth* bothe his eres.
C. 5.133 [That] here hed was *worth* half marc and his hoed nat a grote.
C. 6.244 And more *worth* then the moneye or men þat y lenede.
C. 8.262 That here lyflode be lene and lyte *worth* here clothes.'
C.10.307 The more he is worthy and *worth*, of wyse and goed ypresed.'
C.11.14 Wysdom and wit now is nat *worth* a carse
C.11.77 For is no wit *worth* now but hit of wynnynge soune.
C.13.95 For þe wil is as moche *worthe* of a wrecche beggare
C.16.6 Thenne may men wyte what he is *worth* and what he hath deserued

worþ &> worþe

worþe v *worthen v.* A 16 worst (1) worþ (10) worþe (5); B 42 worstow
(2) worþ (29) worþe (10) worþen (1); C 43 warth (2) worst (1) worth
(34) worthe (2) worthen (3) worþ (1)

A. 1.26 Þat þou *worþe* þe wers whanne þou werche shuldist.
A. 1.162 Chastite wiþoute charite *worþ* cheynide in helle;

A. 1.168 Such chastite wiþoute charite *worþ* cheynid in helle.
A. 2.22 Tomorewe *worþ* þe mariage mad of mede & of fals;
A. 2.26 Tomorewe *worþ* þe mariage ymad as I þe telle;
A. 2.166 Þat holy chirche for hem *worþ* harmid for euere;
A. 3.32 Þat he ne *worþ* ferst auauncid for I am beknowe
A. 5.239 Þi wil w[*orþ*]e vpon me, as I haue wel deserued
A. 6.99 And so *worst* þou dryuen out as dew & þe dore closid,
A. 7.74 Let god *worþe* wiþal for so his woord techiþ.
A. 8.54 Þat he ne *worþ* sauf sykirly, & so seiþ þe sautir.
A. 8.74 But as wilde bestis wiþ wehe, & *worþ* vp togideris
A.11.86 And al *worþ* as þou wilt, whatso we telle–
A.11.88 What is dowel fro dobet; now def mote he *worþe*,
A.11.101 And seide, 'mercy madame, ȝour man shal I *worþe*
A.12.92 And mannes merþe w[*or*]þ no mor þan he deseruyþ here
B.Pr.187 Forþi I counseille al þe commune to late þe cat *worþe*,
B. 1.26 That þow *worþe* þe wers whan þow werche sholdest.
B. 1.188 Chastite wiþouten charite *worþ* cheyned in helle;
B. 1.194 Swich chastite wiþouten charite *worþ* cheyned in helle.
B. 2.40 And now *worþ* þis Mede ymaried [t]o a mansed sherewe,
B. 2.44 Tomorwe *worþ* ymaked þe maydenes bridale;
B. 2.48 And lakke hem noȝt but lat hem *worþe* til leaute be Iustice
B. 2.205 That holy chirche for hem *worþ* harmed for euere.]
B. 3.33 That he ne *worþ* first auaunced, for I am biknowen
B. 3.314 His boost of his benefice *worþ* bynomen hym after.
B. 3.322 Tha[t] *worþ* Trewe-tonge, a tidy man þat tened me neuere.
B. 5.160 And dame Pernele a preestes fyle; Prioresse *worþ* she neuere
B. 5.613 And [so] *worstow* dryuen out as dew & þe dore closed,
B. 6.47 That he *worþ* worþier set and wiþ moore blisse:
B. 6.162 For [þei] wasten and wynnen noȝt and [þo] *worþ* neuere
B. 7.52 That he ne *worþ* saaf [sikerly]; þe Sauter bereþ witnesse:
B. 7.92 But as wilde bestes wiþ wehee *worþen* vppe and werchen,
B. 8.61 And ȝyue yow grace on þis grounde goode men to *worþe*'.
B. 9.61 Muche wo *worþ* þat man þat mysruleþ his Inwit,
B.10.133 And al *worþ* as þow wolt whatso we dispute–
B.10.135 What is dowel fro dobet, [now] deef mote he *worþe*,
B.10.148 And seide, 'mercy, madame; youre man shal I *worþe*
B.10.333 That þis *worþ* sooþ, seke ye þat ofte ouerse þe bible:
B.10.405 Ac I wene it *worþ* of manye as was in Noes tyme
B.10.417 [At domesday þe deluuye *worþ* of deþ and fir at ones;
B.10.419 Wercheþ ye as ye sen ywrite, lest ye *worþe* noȝt þerInne].
B.10.439 Wher fo[r] loue] a man *worþ* allowed þere and hise lele werkes,
B.11.5 And in a wynkynge [*worþ* til I weex] aslepe.
B.11.149 Graunted [me *worþ*] grace [þorȝ his grete wille].
B.12.279 Ne no creature of cristes liknesse withouten cristendom *worþ*
saued.'
B.12.291 And wheiþer it *worþ* [of truþe] or noȝt, [þe] *worþ* [of] bileue is
gret,
B.13.147 And but he bowe for þis betyng blynd mote he *worþe*!"
B.13.406 That into wanhope he [*worþ*] and wende nauȝt to be saued.
B.16.72 And swete wiþouten swellyng; sour *worþ* it neuere.'
B.16.157 Ac [to] þe [worldes ende] þi wikkednesse shal *worþe* vpon þiselue:
B.17.99 He sholde stonde and steppe; ac stalworþe *worþe* he neuere
B.17.113 That he *worþ* fettred, þat feloun, faste wiþ Cheynes,
B.17.199 That whoso synneþ in þe Seint Spirit assoilled *worþ* he neuere,
B.18.101 For be þis derknesse ydo deeþ *worþ* [yvenquisshed];
B.19.344 'And Piers bern *worþ* ybroke; and þei þat ben in vnitee
B.19.406 The chief seed þat Piers sew, ysaued *worstow* neuere.
B.19.430 A[c] wel *worþe* Piers þe plowman þat pursueþ god in doynge,
C. 1.184 Chastite withouten charite *worth* c[h]eyned in helle;
C. 2.43 Tomorwe *worth* mede ymaried to a mansed wrecche,
C. 2.51 Lacke hem nat but lat hem *worthe* til leutte be Iustice
C. 2.78 Leueth hit le[l]ly this *worth* here laste mede
C. 2.251 And holy churche thorw hem *worth* harmed for euere.'
C. 3.36 That he ne *worth* furste vaunsed, for y am byknowe
C. 3.123 And wittenesseth with of hem þat wolleth take mede:
C. 3.475 Þat *worth* trewe-tonge, a tydy man þat tened me neuere.
C. 4.155 That mekenesse *worth* maystre ouer mede at þe laste.'
C. 5.98 Suche a wynnyng hym *warth* thorw w[y]rdes of grace:
C. 6.135 And dame purnele a prestis fyle; Prioresse *worth* he neuere
C. 6.136 For he hadde childe in the chapun co[t]e; he *worth* chalenged at þe
eleccioun."
C. 6.148 And y, wrath, was war and w[o]rthe on hem bothe
C. 7.265 So *worth* thow dryuen out as de[w] and þe dore yclosed,
C. 8.44 He *worth* rather reseyued and reuerentloker s[e]tte:
C. 8.160 For ther *worth* no plente,' quod [Perus], 'and þe plouh lygge.'
C. 9.239 Y drede me, and he dey, hit *worth* for dedly synne
C. 9.272 And þe wolle *worth* weye, wo is the thenne!
C. 9.323 *Worth* fayre vnderfonge byfore god þat tyme
C.10.175 And moche wo *worth* hym þat inwit myspeneth
C.11.22 What shal *worthen* of suche when þei lyf leten:
C.11.86 And saide, 'mercy, madame; ȝoure man shal y *worthen*
C.11.165 And in a wynkynge y *warth* and wonderliche me mette
C.11.236 Ac y wene hit *worth* of monye as was in noes tyme

C.11.249   At domesday a deluuye *worth* of deth and fuyr at ones.
C.12.195   *Worth* allowed of oure lord at here laste ende
C.12.232   Whete þat þeron wexeth *worth* lygge ar hit rype;
C.13.1   Ac wel *worth* pouerte for he may walke vnrobbed
C.14.213   And wher hit *worth* or worth nat, the bileue is gret of treuthe
C.14.213   And wher hit worth or *worth* nat, the bileue is gret of treuthe
C.14.217   For al *worth* as god wol;' and þerwith he vanschede.
C.15.147   And bote he bowe for this betynge blynde mote he *worthen*.'
C.16.329   *Worth* moche meryte to þat man þat hit may soffre.
C.18.99   And swete withoute swellynge; sour *worth* hit neuere'–
C.18.232   Is and ay were [& *worþ* wiþouten ende].
C.19.89   And thouh he stande and steppe riзt strong *worth* he neuere
C.19.135   And al þe myhte with hym is, was and *worth* euere.
C.19.165   That hoso synegeth in þe seynt spirit assoiled *worth* he neuere,
C.20.104   For be this derkenesse ydo deth *worth* yvenkused;
C.20.407   Ac thy drynke *worth* deth and depe helle thy bolle.
C.21.344   'And Peres berne *worth* broke and þei þat ben in vnite
C.21.406   The cheef seed þat [Peres] sewe, ysaued wo[r]st þou neuere.
C.21.430   Ac wel *worth* Peres the plouhman þat pursueth god in doyng[e],

worþi adj *worthi adj.* A 3; B 15 worþi (13) worþier (2); C 16 worthy (12) worthiore (4)

A. 2.87   *Worþi* is þe werkman his mede to haue,
A. 3.216   Mede is *worþi* þe maistrie to haue'.
A.11.195   Sire dobest haþ ben [in office], so is he best *worþi*
B. 3.229   Mede is *worþi*, [me þynkeþ], þe maistrie to haue'.
B. 5.234   Thow haddest be bettre *worþi* ben hanged þerfore.'
B. 6.47   That he worþ *worþier* set and wiþ moore blisse:
B. 7.78   For wite ye neuere who is *worþi*, ac god woot who haþ nede.
B.13.33   This maister was maad sitte as for þe mooste *worþi*,
B.13.255   Ac if myзt of myracle hym faille it is for men ben noзt *worþi*
B.13.453   In a welhope, [for he wrouзte so], amonges *worþi* seyntes],
B.14.90   Ac shrift of mouþ moore *worþi* is if man be y[n]liche contrit,
B.14.138   What he were *worþi* for his werk and what he haþ deserued,
B.14.332   'I were noзt *worþi*, woot god', quod haukyn, 'to werien any cloþes,
B.15.540   Is reuerenced er þe Roode, receyued for [þe] *worþier*
B.16.267   And bettre wed for us [wage] þan we ben alle *worþi*,
B.18.328   For alle synfulle soules, to saue þo þat ben *worþi*.
B.19.24   Is crist moore of myзt and moore *worþi* name
B.19.137   And nempned hym of Naзareth; and no man so *worþi*
C. 3.285   Mede is *worthy*, me thynketh, þe maistrye to haue.'
C. 5.188   Were wittiore and *worthiore* then he þat was his maister.
C. 7.113   In a welhope for a wrouhte so amongus *worthy* seyntes
C. 9.70   Woet no man, as y wene, who is *worthy* to haue
C.10.307   The more he is *worthy* and worth, of wyse and goed ypresed.'
C.11.271   Ho is *worthy* for wele or for wykkede [pyne]:
C.12.192   Aren not so *worthy* as whete ne so wel mowe
C.13.28   *Worthiore* as by holy writ and wyse fylosofres.
C.15.38   The maistre was maed sitte As for þe moste *worthy*;
C.15.225   Ac yf myhte of myracle hym fayle hit is for men beth nat *worthy*
C.17.201   Is reuerenced byfore the rode and resceyued for the *worthiore*
C.18.71   As weddede men and wedewes and riht *worthy* maydones
C.18.87   Wydewhode, more *worthiore* then wedlok, as in heuene;
C.18.283   And bettere wed for vs wagen then we ben alle *worthy*;
C.21.24   Is Crist more of myhte and moore *worth[y]* name
C.21.137   And nempned hym of naзareth; and no man so *worthy*

worþili adv *worthili adv.* A 1 worþily; B 2

A. 2.15   'What is þis womman,' quaþ I, 'þus *worþily* atirid?'
B. 2.19   'What is þis womman', quod I, 'so *worþili* atired?'
B.12.90   Riзt so goddes body, breþeren, but it be *worþili* taken,

wosch- > wasshen

wose n *wose n.(2)* C 1

C.12.229   Riht as wedes waxeth in *wose* and in donge

wost > willen,witen; wot > witen

wouз n *wough n.(1)* A 1; B 1 wowes; C 1 wowes

A. 5.136   Þe beste in my bedchaumbre lay be þe *wouз*.
B. 3.61   *Wowes* do whiten and wyndowes glaзen,
C. 3.65   Bothe wyndowes and *wowes* y wol amende and glase

wouke n *weke n.(3)* A 2 wyke (1) woukes(1); B 7 wike (3) wyke (1) wouke (1) woukes (2); C 4 woke (3) wokes (1)

A. 7.240   Of alle þe *wyke* [hy] werkiþ nouзt, so here wombe akiþ.'
A.11.106   He haþ weddit a wif wiþinne þise *woukes* sixe,
B. 5.92   Than þouз I hadde þis *wouke* ywonne a weye of Essex chese.
B. 6.256   Of al a *wike* werche noзt, so oure wombe akeþ.'
B.10.97   Elenge is þe halle, ech day in þe *wike*,
B.10.154   He haþ wedded a wif wiþInne þise [*woukes* sixe],
B.11.234   Witnesse in þe Pask *wyke*, whan he yede to Emaus;
B.13.154   And al þe wit of þe wodnesday of þe nexte *wike* after;
B.16.100   And in þe wombe of þat wenche was he fourty *woukes*
C. 8.268   Of al a *woke* worche nat, so oure wombe greueth.'

C. 9.254   Cam no wyn in his wombe thorw þe *woke* longe
C.12.123   Witnesse in þe paske *woke* when he зede to Emaux:
C.18.133   And in þe wombe of þat wenche was he fourty *wokes*

wounde n *wound n. &> wounden,wownde* A 1 woundis; B 7 wounde (3) woundes (4); C 6 wounde (3) woundes (3)

A.11.215   Godis flessh, & his fet, & hise fyue *woundis*
B.10.332   Haue a knok of a kyng, and incurable þe *wounde*.
B.14.97   That it neuere eft is sene ne soor, but semeþ a *wounde* yheeled.'
B.17.68   And to þe wye he wente hise *woundes* to biholde,
B.17.72   Wiþ wyn and with oille hise *woundes* he wasshed,
B.17.78   And lo, here siluer', he seide, 'for salue to hise *woundes*.'
B.17.95   Neiþer Feiþ ne fyn hope, so festred be hise *woundes*,
B.18.98   The gree зit haþ he geten for al his grete *wounde*.
C. 4.181   And brynge alle men to bowe withouten bittere *wounde*,
C. 5.177   Shal haue a knok vppon here crounes and incurable þe *wounde*:
C.19.67   And to th[e] wey a wente his *woundes* to byholde
C.19.71   With wyn and with oyle his *woundes* he gan lauen a[li][th]e,
C.19.85   Noþer faith ne fyn hope, so festred aren his *woundes*.
C.20.101   The gre зut hath he geten for al his grete *wound[e]*

wounded(e > wownde

wounden v *winden v.(1)* A 2 wounde (1) ywounden (1); B 2 wounden (1) ywounden (1); C 1 wonden

A. 2.182   Wysshen hym & wypide him & *wounde* hym in cloþis,
A. 6.6   In a [weþewindes] wyse [*ywounden*] aboute;
B. 2.223   Wesshen hym & wiped hym & *wounden* hym in cloutes,
B. 5.518   In a wiþwynde[s] wise *ywounden* aboute.
C. 2.233   Thei woschen hym and wypeden hym and *wonden* hym in cloutes,

woware n *wouere n.* B 1 woweris; C 1

B.11.71   'By my feiþ! frere', quod I, 'ye faren lik þise *woweris*
C.12.19   'By my faith! frere,' quod y, 'зe fare lyke þe *woware*

wowede v *wouen v.* B 1

B. 4.74   Thanne *wowede* wrong wisdom ful yerne

woweris > woware; wowes > wouз

wownde v *wounden v.* B 6 wownde (1) wounded (2) woundede (1) ywounded (2); C 5 wounde (1) wounded (1) ywounded (3)

B.16.105   That, þouз he were *wounded* with his enemy, to warisshen hymselue:
B.17.56   Where a man was *wounded* and wiþ þeues taken.
B.18.88   'Ayein my wille it was, lord, to *wownde* yow so soore.'
B.20.302   And *woundede* wel wikkedly many a wys techere
B.20.305   'Go salue þo þat sike ben and þoruз synne *ywounded*.'
B.20.357   Here is Contricion', quod Conscience, 'my cosyn, *ywounded*.
C.19.82   Were afered and flowe fram þe man *ywounded*.
C.20.90   'Aзeyn my will hit was,' quod he, 'þat y зow *wounde* made.'
C.22.302   And *wounded* wel wykkedly many a wys techare
C.22.305   'Go salue tho þat syke [ben] and thorw synne *ywounded*.'
C.22.357   Here is contricioun,' quod Consience, 'my cosyn, *ywounded*.

woxe(n > wexen

wrake n *wrake n.(1)* C 2

C.17.86   For what thorw werre and *wrake* and wikkede hefdes
C.20.455   Then aftur werre and *wrake* when loue and pees ben maistres.

wrang > wryngen

wranglynge ger *wranglinge ger.* B 1; C 1

B. 4.35   Theras wraþe and *wranglynge* is þer wynne þei siluer,
C. 4.35   For there is wrath and *wranglynge* there wol they abyde;

wrastle v *wrestlen v.* B 1; C 1

B.14.225   If wraþe *wrastle* wiþ þe poore he haþ þe worse ende
C.16.66   Yf wrathe *wrastle* with þe pore he hath þe worse ende

wrath(e > wraþe,wraþen

wraþe n *wrath n.* A 5 wraþþe; B 19; C 18 wrath (5) wrathe (12) wreth (1)

A. 4.56   'Whoso werchiþ be wil *wraþþe* makiþ ofte.
A. 5.66   His body was bolnid for wr[aþþe] þat he bot his lippe[s],
A. 5.79   Betwyn hym & his meyne I haue mad *wraþþe*;
A. 6.95   Ac be war þanne of *wraþþe*, þat wykkide shrewe,
A. 7.109   'Be þe prince of paradis!' quaþ piers þo in *wraþþe*,
B. 4.35   Theras *wraþe* and wranglynge is þer wynne þei siluer,
B. 4.70   'Whoso wercheþ by wille *wraþe* makeþ ofte.
B. 5.83   His body was [b]ollen for *wraþe* þat he boot hise lippes,
B. 5.135   Now awakeþ *Wraþe* wiþ two white eiзen,
B. 5.137   'I am *wraþe*', quod he, 'I was som tyme a frere,
B. 5.148   I, *wraþe*, walke wiþ hem and wisse hem of my bokes.
B. 5.151   Or ellis al riche and ryden; I, *wraþe*, reste neuere
B. 5.162   Of wikkede wordes I, *wraþe*, hire wortes made
B. 5.185   That þi wille [ne þi wit] to *wraþe* myзte turne:

B. 5.400   And if I bidde any bedes, but if it be in *wraþe*,
B. 5.428   So wiþ wikked wil and *wraþe* my werkmen I paye.
B. 5.609   A[c] be war þanne of *Wraþe*, þat wikked sherewe,
B.11.4   Tho wepte I for wo and *wraþe* of hir speche
B.12.124   And medle no3t muche wiþ hem to meuen any *wraþe*
B.13.320   It was bidropped wiþ *wraþe* and wikkede wille,
B.14.53   Shul neuere gyues þee greue ne gret lordes *wraþe*,
B.14.225   If *wraþe* wrastle wiþ þe poore he haþ þe worse ende
B.15.171   Corseþ he no creature ne he kan bere no *wraþe*,
B.19.304   For counteþ he no kynges *wraþe* whan he in Court sitteþ;
C. 4.35   For there is *wrath* and wranglynge there wol they abyde;
C. 6.66   A wroth his f[u]ste vppon *wrath*; hadde [he] wesches at wille
C. 6.103   Thenne awakede *wrathe* with two w[hy]te eyes
C. 6.105   'I am *wr[a]the*,' quod þat weye, 'wol gladliche smyte
C. 6.121   Withoute licence and leue, and herby lyueth *wrathe*.
C. 6.124   Til y, *wrathe*, wexe an hey and walke with hem bothe;
C. 6.126   Or alle riche and ryde, reste shal y nat, *wrathe*,
C. 6.139   And thenne awake y, *wrathe*, and wolde be avenged.
C. 6.148   And y, *wrath*, was war and w[o]rthe on hem bothe
C. 6.167   That thy wil ne thy wit to *wr[at]he* myhte turne.
C. 7.16   And yf y bidde eny bedes, but yf hit be in *wrath*,
C. 7.261   Ac be war thenne of *wrath*, þat wikkede shrewe,
C.11.108   Bothe wymmen and wyn, *wr[a]the*, [enuy] and slewthe
C.11.164   Tho wepte y for wo and *wrathe* of here wordes
C.14.67   And medle we nat moche with hem to meuen eny *wrathe*
C.15.252   Shal neuere gyues the greue ne grete lordes *wrathe*,
C.16.66   Yf *wrathe* wrastle with þe pore he hath þe worse ende
C.21.304   For counteth he no kynges *wreth* when he in Court sitteth;

wraþen v *wratthen v.* A 3 wraþþe (2) wraþþest (1); B 7 wraþe (2) wraþed (2) wraþen (1) wraþeþ (1) wraþeþ (1); C 5 wrath (1) wrathe (1) wrathed (1) wrathest (1) wratheth (1)

A. 2.81   Such weddyng to werche to *wraþþe* wiþ treuþe;
A. 3.170   Why þou *wraþþest* þe now wondir me þinkiþ.
A.10.96   Whatso men worden of þe *wraþþe* þe neuere;
B.Pr.174   And if hym *wraþeþ* be war and his wey shonye.'
B. 2.117   Swic[h] weddyng[e] to werche to *wraþe* wiþ truþe;
B. 3.183   Whi þow *wraþest* þee now wonder me þynkeþ.
B. 5.505   That euere þei *wraþed* þee in þis world in word, þou3t or dedes.'
B. 6.152   [Th]anne gan wastour to *wraþen* hym and wolde haue yfou3te;
B. 9.132   Til god *wraþed* [wiþ] hir werkes and swich a word seide,
B.10.294   And drede to *wraþe* yow in any word youre werkmanship to lette,
C.Pr.191   And yf hym *wratheth* ben war and his way [shonye].'
C. 1.26   Wykked[ly] wroghte and *wrathed* god almyhty.
C. 2.121   Suche a weddyng to wurche þat *wrathe* myhte treuthe;
C. 3.229   Why thow *wrathest* þe now wonder me thynketh!
C. 8.149   Thenne gan wastor to *wrath* hym and wolde haue yfouhte

wraþþe > *wraþe,wraþen*

wrecche n *wrecche n.* A 4 wrecche (1) wrecches (2) wrecchis (1); B 5 wrecche (1) wrecches (4); C 6 wrecche (1) wreche (2) wreches (2) wrechus (1)

A. 2.156   I wolde be wroken of þise *wrecchis* þat werchen so ille,
A. 4.136   Þat he ne held resoun a maister & mede a muche *wrecche*.
A.12.21   Til þo *wrecches* ben in wil here synne to lete."
A.12.24   Telle hit with tounge to synful *wrecches*."
B. 2.195   I wolde be wroken of þo *wrecches* þat wercheþ so ille,
B. 9.122   Wastours and *wrecches* out of wedlok, I trowe,
B.10.81   And yet þe *wrecches* of þis world is noon ywar by ooþer,
B.15.601   And [3it] wenen þo *wrecches* þat he were pseudopropheta
B.19.403   'Caytif!' quod Conscience, 'cursede *wrecche*!
C. 2.43   Tomorwe worth mede ymaried to a mansed *wrecche*,
C. 2.209   Y wolde be awreke [o]n tho *wreches* and on here werkes alle,
C. 8.251   Ac he þat was a *wreche* and wolde nat trauaile
C.10.218   So was Caym conseyued and so ben corsed *wreches*
C.11.61   And 3ut th[e] *wrechus* of this world is noen ywar by oþer,
C.21.403   'Caytyf!' quod Consience, 'corsede *wreche*!

wrecche adj *wrecche adj.* B 1; C 2

B.17.350   For þer nys sik ne sory, ne noon so muche *wrecche*
C.13.95   For þe wil is as moche worthe of a *wrecche* beggare
C.19.330   For þer ne is sike ne sory ne non so moche *wrecche*

wrecched adj *wrecched adj.* A 2 wrecchide; B 2 wrecched (1) wrecchede (1); C 1 wrecchede

A. 1.37   Þat is þe *wrecchide* world [wolde] þe betraye.
A.10.144   Into þis *wrecchide* world to wonen & to libben
B. 1.39   That is þe *wrecched* world wolde þee bitraye.
B.15.142   For a *wrecchede* hous [he held] al his lif tyme,
C. 1.37   [That] is þe *wrecchede* world wolde þe bigyle.

wrecchednesse n *wrecchednesse n.* B 1; C 3 wrecchednesse (1) wrechednesse (2)

B.11.45   'That wit shal torne to *wrecchednesse* for wil to haue his likyng!'
C. 6.334   For al the *wrecchednesse* of this world and wikkede dedes

C.12.2   'That wit shal turne to *wrechednesse* for wil hath al his wille!'
C.20.353   And wyte[th] hem al þe *wrechednesse* þat wrouhte is on erthe.

wrech- > *wrecch-*

wreke v *wreken v.* A 2 wreke (1) wroken (1); B 5 wreke (2) wroke (1) wroken (2); C 2

A. 2.156   I wolde be *wroken* of þise wrecchis þat werchen so ille,
A. 5.67   And wroþliche he wroþ his fest, to *wreke* hym he þou3te,
B. 2.195   I wolde be *wroken* of þo wrecches þat werchen so ille,
B. 5.84   And [wroþliche he wroþ his] fust, to *wreke* hym he þou3te
B. 9.186   *Wreke* þee wiþ wyuyng if þow wolt ben excused:
B.18.390   And þou3 holy writ wole þat I be *wroke* of hem þat diden ille–
B.20.204   'If þow wolt be *wroken* wend into vnitee
B.20.432   For holy writ wol þat y be *wreke* of hem þat wrouhte ille–
C.22.204   'Yf thow wol[t] be *wreke* wende into vnite

wreth > *wraþe*

wrighte n *wrighte n.(1)* B 4 wrighte (1) wrightes (1) wri3te (1) wri3tes (1); C 5 wriht (2) wrihte (1) wryhtes (1) wrihtus (1)

B.10.407   Was neuere *wrighte* saued þat wro3te þeron, ne ooþer werkman ellis,
B.10.410   Of *w[r]ightes* þat it wro3te was noon of hem ysaued.
B.10.418   Forþi I counseille yow clerkes, of holy [kirke] be *wri3tes*,
B.11.349   Ther nys *wri3te*, as I wene, sholde werche hir nes[t] to paye;
C.11.238   Was neuere *wrihte* þat þeron wrouhte ne werkman ysaued
C.11.241   Of *wryhtes* þat hit wrouhte was noen of hem ysaued.
C.11.250   Worcheth, 3e *wrihtus* of holy churche, as holy writ techeth,
C.13.160   Ther is no *wriht*, as y wene, sholde worch here neste to paye;
C.19.138   Sholde n[o] *wri[h]t* worche were they awey.

wryngen v *wringen v.* A 2 wrang (1) wrong (1); B 3 wryngen (1) wrong (2); C 2 wrang (1) wronge (1)

A. 2.198   And ek wep & *wrang* whan heo was atachid.
A. 7.160   And *wrong* hym so be þe wombe þat al watride his ei3en,
B. 2.239   And ek wepte and *wrong* whan she was attached.
B. 6.175   And *wrong* hym so by þe wombe þat [al watrede his ei3en].
B.14.18   Dowel shal wasshen it and *wryngen* it þoru3 a wis confessour:
C. 2.255   And [ek] wepte and *wrang* when she was attached.
C. 8.172   And *wronge* hym so by þe wombe þat al watrede his yes;

wrynglawe n *wringen v.* C 1

C. 4.31   [O]n wilyman and wittyman and wareyne *wrynglawe*.

writ n *writ n.* &> *holy_writ* A 1; B 2; C 1

A. 2.46   Alle to wytnesse wel what þe *writ* wolde,
B.17.3   To rule alle Reames wiþ; I bere þe *writ* [ri3t] here.'
B.17.18   'Whoso wercheþ after þis *writ*, I wol vndertaken,
C.19.19   'And ho[so] worcheth aftur this *writ*, y wol vndertaken,

writen v *writen v.* A 10 write (1) wryte (1) writen (5) wryten (1) wrot (2); B 31 write (9) writen (11) writeþ (1) wroot (9) ywrite (1); C 22 write (1) wryte (3) writen (4) wryten (2) writeth (1) wroet (5) wrot (3) ywryte (2) ywryten (1)

A. 1.174   For þise arn þe wordis *writen* in þe Euaungelie:
A. 3.51   Þat I ne shulde make or mende, & myn name *writen*
A. 3.61   To *writen* in wyndowis of 3oure wel dedis,
A. 7.77   Forþi I wile er I wende do *w[r]yte* my bequest.
A. 8.94   And was *writen* ri3t þus in witnesse of treuþe:
A.10.109   Poule þe apostel in his pistil *wrot* it
A.10.111   And for wisdom is *writen* & witnessid in chirches:
A.11.126   And þat [I] grete wel his wyf for I *wrot* hire þe bible,
A.11.132   Gramer for girles I garte ferst *write*,
A.12.101   And wrou3the þat here is *wryten* and oþer werkes boþe
B. 1.200   Fo[r] þise [ben wordes] *writen* in þe [euaungelie]:
B. 3.65   To *writen* in wyndowes of hir wel dedes,
B. 3.70   To *writen* in wyndowes of youre wel dedes,
B. 5.242   Swiche dedes I dide *write* if he his day breke;
B. 6.85   Forþi I wole er I wende do *write* my biqueste.
B. 7.112   And was *writen* ri3t þus in witnesse of treuþe:
B. 9.40   Thou3 he [wiste to] *write* neuer so wel, [and] he hadde [a] penne,
B.10.174   And þat I grete wel his wif, for I *wroot* hire [þe bible],
B.10.180   Grammer for girles I garte first *write*,
B.10.345   *Writen* to wissen vs to wilne no richesse,
B.10.419   Wercheþ ye as ye sen *ywrite*, lest ye worþe no3t þerInne].
B.10.434   And þo þat wisely wordeden and *writen* manye bokes
B.10.460   Seide þus in a sermon–I seigh it *writen* ones–
B.11.169   God wrou3te it and *wroot* it wiþ his [owene] fynger,
B.11.226   For some wordes I fynde *writen*, were of Feiþes techyng,
B.11.394   The wise and þe witty *wroot* þus in þe bible:
B.12.72   For Moyses witnesseþ þat god *wroot* for to wisse þe peple
B.12.88   [For] þoru3 caractes þat crist *wroot* þe Iewes knewe hemselue
B.12.102   And seint Spirit þe Samplarie, & seide what men sholde *write*.
B.12.261   That was *writen*, and þei witnesse to werche as it wolde.
B.13.71   Holi writ bit men be war–I wol no3t *write* it here

B.13.247   Hadde ich a clerc þat couþe *write* I wolde caste hym a bille
B.14.199   Ellis is al oure labour lost–lo, how men *writeþ*
B.14.322   That þ[u]s first *wroot* to wissen men what Pouerte was to mene.'
B.15.489   They wol be wrooþ for I *write* þus, ac to witnesse I take
B.15.582   And Iewes lyuen in lele lawe; oure lord *wroot* it hymselue
B.17.12   Wheron [was] *writen* two wordes on þis wise yglosed.
B.17.15   The glose was gloriously *writen* wiþ a gilt penne:
B.19.1   Thus I awaked and *wroot* what I hadde ydremed,
B.19.481   And I awakned þerwiþ and *wroot* as me mette.
B.20.259   And if þei wage men to werre þei *write* hem in noumbre;
C. 1.195   For this aren wordes *ywryten* in þe ewangelie:
C. 3.69   To *writen* [i]n wyndowes of eny wel dedes,
C. 5.63   Somme to synge masses or sitten and *wryten*,
C. 5.139   And so *wrot* the wyse to wyssen vs alle:
C. 5.146   Gregory þe grete Clerk gart *wryte* in bokes
C. 8.94   Forthy y wol ar y wende do *wryte* my biqueste.
C. 8.239   As wyse men haen *wryten* and as witnesseth Genesis
C. 9.286   And was *ywryte* ryhte thus in witnesse of treuthe:
C.11.114   And sey y gre[t]e wel his wyf, for y *wrot* here a bible
C.11.120   Gramer for gurles y gart furste *write*
C.14.37   For moyses witnesseth þat god *wroet* [in stoen with his fynger;
C.14.40   And in soend a signe *wroet* and saide to þe iewes,
C.14.47   And seynt spirit þe saumplarie and said what men sholde *wryte*.
C.16.40   Elles is alle oure labour loest–loo how men *writeth*
C.16.157   That *wroet* thus to wisse men what pouerte was to mene.'
C.17.51   Iop þe parfite patriarke this prouerbe *wroet* and tauhte
C.17.85   And worcheth nat as 3e fyndeth *ywryte* and wisseth þe peple.
C.19.13   Whereon was *writen* two wordes on this wyse yglosed:
C.19.16   The glose was gloriously *writen* with a gult penne:
C.21.1   Thus y wakede and *wrot* what y hadde ydremed,
C.21.481   And y [a]wakned þerwith and *wroet* as [me] mette.
C.22.259   And yf thei wage men to werre thei *writen* hem in nombre;

writhen > *wroþ*

writyng ger *writinge ger.* A 2 writyng (1) wrytyng (1); B 3 writyng (1)
     writynge (2); C 3 writyng (1) writynge (1) writynges (1)
A. 3.60   Forþi I lere 3ow lordis, leuiþ such *wrytyng*,
A. 8.43   And 3af wille for his *writyng* wollene cloþis;
B. 3.69   Forþi I lere yow lordes, leueþ swic[h *writynge*],
B.12.82   Holy kirke knoweþ þis þat cristes *writyng* saued;
B.19.462   Counseilleþ me bi hir acounte and my clerkes *writynge*.
C. 3.73   Forthy, l[e]ue lordes, leueth suche *writynges*;
C.20.356   Witnesseth in his *writyng[e]* what is lyares mede:
C.21.462   Conseileth me bi here acounte and my clerkes *writyng*.

wroet > *writen*; *wroeth* > *wroþ*; *wroght- wro3t(-* > *werchen*; *wroke(n* > *wreke*

wrong n *wrong n.(2)* A 18 wrong (17) wrongis (1); B 18 wrong (17)
     wronges (1); C 16 wrong (15) wronges (1)
A. 1.61   Þereinne woniþ a wy þat *wrong* is yhoten;
A. 1.117   And alle þat werchen with *wrong* wenden þei shuln
A. 2.19   And so shulde [heo] not be for *wrong* was hire sire;
A. 2.20   Out of *wrong* heo wex to wroþerhele manye.
A. 2.71   Þere to wone wiþ *wrong* while god is in heuene.'
A. 2.72   In witnesse of whiche þing *wrong* was þe furste,
A. 3.163   Whanne 3e wyte wytterly where þe *wrong* liggeþ;
A. 4.35   How *wrong* a3en his wil hadde his wyf take,
A. 4.49   *Wrong* was aferd þo & wisdom he sou3te
A. 4.54   For þat *wrong* hadde wrou3t so wykkide a dede,
A. 4.55   And warnide *wrong* þo wiþ swich a wys tale:
A. 4.60   *Wrong* þanne on wysdom wepi[de] hym to helpe,
A. 4.67   And wisten wel þat *wrong* was a shrewe euere.
A. 4.71   [Þat *wrong* for his werkis shulde woo þole,
A. 4.84   For I wile wage for *wrong*, he [wile] do so no more.'
A. 4.92   *Wrong* wendiþ not so awey er I wyte more.
A. 4.122   Shulde neuere *wrong* in þis world þat I wyte mi3te
A.11.19   Þat can construe deseites, & conspire *wrongis*,
B. 1.63   TherInne wonyeþ a [wye] þat *wrong* is yhote;
B. 1.128   And alle þat werchen with *wrong* wende þei shulle
B. 2.108   In witnesse of which þyng *wrong* was þe firste,
B. 3.176   Whan ye witen witterly wher þe *wrong* liggeþ.
B. 4.48   How *wrong* ayeins his wille hadde his wif taken,
B. 4.62   That *wrong* was a wikked luft and wro3te muche sorwe.
B. 4.63   *Wrong* was afered þ[o] and wisdom he sou3te
B. 4.68   For þat *wrong* hadde ywro3t so wikked a dede,
B. 4.69   And warnede *wrong* þo with swich a wis tale:

B. 4.74   Thanne wowede *wrong* wisdom ful yerne
B. 4.84   That *wrong* for hise werkes sholde wo þolie,
B. 4.97   For I wol wage for *wrong*, he wol do so na moore.'
B. 4.105   *Wrong* wendeþ no3t so awey [er] I wite moore.
B. 4.139   Sholde neuere *wrong* in þis world þat I wite my3te
B. 4.181   And as moost folk witnesseþ wel *wrong* shal be demed.'
B. 5.264   And þat was wonne wiþ *wrong* wiþ wikked men be despended.
B.10.19   [That] kan con[strue] deceites and conspire *wronges*
B.19.350   Wheiþer he wynne wiþ right, wiþ *wrong* or wiþ vsure.'
C. 1.59   Therynne wonyeth a wyghte þat *wrong* is [ihote];
C. 1.131   Aftur here deth day and dwelle ther *wrong* is;
C. 2.112   In wittenesse of [which] thyng *wrong* was þe furste,
C. 3.222   When 3e [wyten] witterly [where] þe *wrong* liggeth.
C. 4.46   How *wrong* wilfully hadde his wyf forleyn
C. 4.65   How *wrong* was a wykked man and muche wo wrouhte.
C. 4.66   Tho was *wrong* afered and wisdom a souhte:
C. 4.67   On men of lawe *wrong* lokede and largelyche hem profered
C. 4.71   Thorw *wrong* and his werkes there was mede yknowe
C. 4.80   That *wrong* for his werkes sholde w[oo] tholye
C. 4.93   For y wol wage for *wrong*; he wol do so no mare.'
C. 4.100   *Wrong* goth nat so away ar y wete more.
C. 4.136   Shulde neuere *wrong* in this worlde þat y wyte myhte
C.13.75   Withoute wyles or *wronges* or wymmen at þe stuyues;
C.19.236   3ut wan he nat with *wrong* ne with queynte sleythes;
C.21.350   Where he wynne with riht, with *wrong* or with vsure.'

wrong adv *wrong adv. &> wryngen* A 2
A.10.75   For werche he wel oþer *wrong*, þe wyt is his owene.
A.11.260   For howso I werche in þis world, [*wrong*] oþer ellis,

wronge > *wryngen*

wrongly adv *wrongli adv.* C 1
C. 3.92   That bygyleth goode men and greueth hem *wrongly*,

wroot > *writen*; *wrooþ* > *wroþ*; *wrot* > *writen*

wroþ adj *wroth adj.* A 2; B 5 wrooþ (1) wroþ (4); C 7 wroeth (2) wroth
     (4) wrother (1)
A.10.161   Þat god was *wroþ* wiþ here werkis & [suche wordis seide]:
A.11.3   She was wondirliche *wroþ* þat wyt so tau3te,
B. 3.331   Also *wroþ* as þe wynd weex Mede in a while.
B. 4.174   And gan wexe *wroþ* with lawe for Mede almoost hadde shent it,
B.10.3   She was wonderly *wroþ* þat wit [so] tau3te,
B.13.417   He wexeþ *wroþ*, and wol no3t here but wordes of murþe;
B.15.489   They wol be *wrooþ* for I write þus, ac to witnesse I take
C.Pr.117   God was wel þe *wrother* and took þe raþer vengeance.
C. 3.484   As *wroth* as [þe] wynd wax mede þeraftur:
C. 7.77   A wexeth *wroth* and wol not here but wordes of murthe;
C.11.3   She was wonderly *wroth* þat wit me so tauhte;
C.13.44   Wol no wys man be *wroth* ne his wed take–
C.17.3   And 3ut oþerwhile *wroeth* withouten eny synne.'
C.17.4   'Ho is *wroeth* and wolde be awreke, holy writ preueth,' quod he,

wroþ v *writhen v.* A 1; B 2 wriþen (1) wroþ (1); C 4 writhen (1) wriþen
     (1) wroth (1) ywrithe (1)
A. 5.67   And *wroþliche* he *wroþ* his fest, to wreke hym he þou3te,
B. 5.84   And [*wroþliche* he *wroþ* his] fust, to wreke hym he þou3te
B.17.177   Oþerwise þan þe *wriþen* fust or werkmanshipe of fyngres.
C. 6.66   A *wroth* his f[u]ste vppon wrath; hadde [he] wesches at wille
C. 7.163   In a wethewynde wyse *ywrithe* al aboute;
C. 9.260   For many wakere woules ar *wr[iþ]en* into thy foldes;
C.19.142   Oþerwyse then þe *writhen* f[u]ste or werkmanschupe of fyngres.

wroþerhele n *wrotherhele n.* A 1; B 1; C 1
A. 2.20   Out of wrong heo wex to *wroþerhele* manye.
B.14.121   For to *wroþerhele* was he wro3t þat neuere was Ioye shapen.
C.15.297   For to *wroþerhele* was he wrouht þat neuere was ioye yschape.

wroþliche adv *wrothli adv.* A 1; B 1
A. 5.67   And *wroþliche* he wroþ his fest, to wreke hym he þou3te,
B. 5.84   And [*wroþliche* he wroþ his] fust, to wreke hym he þou3te

wrou3t(- wrouht(- wurcche wurche > *werchen*

wurye v *wirien v.* C 2 wurye (1) wuryeth (1)
C. 9.227   As woules þat *wuryeth* men, wymmen and childrene
C. 9.267   For to go *wurye* þe wolf that the wolle fou[l]eth?

X

x > ten; xxxti > þritty

Y

ȝa > ye adv; ȝaf yaf > gyuen; yald > yelden; ȝarde -is > yerde

yarkeþ v *yarken v.* B 1
B. 7.80   For he þat yeueþ yeldeþ and *yarkeþ* hym to reste,

yarn > rennen

yate n *gate n.(1)* A 2 gate (1) ȝate (1); B 16 gate (1) gates (1) yate (6) yates (8); C 21 gate (5) gates (2) ȝate (5) ȝates (9)
A. 6.114   To gete ingang at any *gate* but grace be þe more.'
A.11.45   Ac þe carful may criȝen & carpe at þe *ȝate*,
B.Pr.104   That Cardinals ben called and closynge *yates*
B. 5.594   Of almesdedes are þe hokes þat þe *gates* hangen on.
B. 5.629   To geten ing[o]ng at any *gate* but grace be þe moore.'
B. 9.82   Sholde no cristene creature cryen at þe *yate*
B.10.59   Ac þe carefulle may crie and carpen at þe *yate*
B.11.113   And whan þe peple was plener comen þe porter vnpynned þe *yate*
B.11.164   Yblissed be truþe þat so brak helle *yates*
B.18.262   A spirit spekeþ to helle and biddeþ vnspere þe *yates*:
B.18.319   Dukes of þis dymme place, anoon vndo þise *yates*
B.18.322   For any wye or warde wide opned þe *yates*.
B.19.168   Crist cam In, and al closed boþe dore and *yates*,
B.20.298   And made pees porter to pynne þe *yates*
B.20.301   [Ypocrisie at þe *yate* harde gan fighte]
B.20.329   And cam þere Conscience was and knokked at þe *yate*.
B.20.348   Hende speche heet pees, 'opene þe *yates*.
B.20.376   And [bad] Contricion [come] to kepe þe *yate*.
C.Pr.132   That Cardinales ben cald and closyng *ȝates*
C. 2.135   "God of thy grace heuene *gates* opene,
C. 7.242   The hokes aren Almesdedes þat þe *ȝates* hange on.
C. 7.249   To opene and vndo þe hye *gate* of heuene
C. 7.282   To geten ingang at eny *ȝate* bote grace be þe more.'
C. 8.283   Alle þat gr[eden at] thy *gate* for godes loue aftur fode
C.11.40   Ac þe carfole may crye and quake at þe *ȝate*,
C.12.48   And whan þe peple was plenere ycome þe porter vnpynnede þe *gate*
C.16.367   Ac auaris oþerwhiles halt hym withoute þe *gate*.
C.18.241   Where god [riȝt be my *gate* cam gangynge a thre];
C.20.270   A spirit spekeþ to helle and bit vnspere þe *ȝates*:
C.20.272   'Princ[i]pes of this place, prest vndo this *gates*
C.20.284   Ar we thorw brihtnesse be b[l]ente go barre þe *ȝates*;
C.20.362   Dukes of this demme place, anoen vndoth this *ȝates*
C.20.365   For eny wey or warde wyde open[ed] þe *ȝates*.
C.21.168   Crist cam in, and al closed bothe dore and *ȝates*,
C.22.298   And made pees porter to pynne þe *ȝates*
C.22.301   Ypocrisye at þe *ȝate* harde gan fyhte
C.22.329   And cam þer Consience was and knokked at þe *ȝate*.
C.22.348   Hende speche heet pees, 'opene the *ȝates*.
C.22.376   And baed contricioun come to kepe þe *ȝate*.

ye pron *ye pron.* A 144 ȝe (64) ȝou (1) ȝour (15) ȝoure (22) ȝow (42); B 419 ye (185) youre (110) yow (124); C 358 ȝe (151) ȝou (1) ȝoure (102) ȝow (104)

ȝe A 64
A.Pr.73, A.Pr.97, A.1.13, A.1.16, A.1.51, A.1.127, A.1.150, A.1.151, A.1.152, A.1.152, A.1.153, A.1.155, A.1.157, A.1.169, A.1.170, A.1.170, A.2.91, A.2.92, A.2.93, A.2.167, A.3.62, A.3.63, A.3.75, A.3.163, A.4.2, A.4.89, A.5.17, A.5.36, A.5.39, A.5.40, A.6.17, A.6.41, A.6.47, A.6.48, A.6.49, A.6.50, A.6.54, A.6.56, A.6.112, A.7.6, A.7.18, A.7.110, A.7.112, A.7.116, A.7.119, A.7.121, A.7.122, A.7.125, A.7.129, A.7.302,

A.8.37, A.8.61, A.8.61, A.8.62, A.8.168, A.9.84, A.10.25, A.10.26, A.10.201, A.11.298, A.11.299, A.11.300, A.12.52, A.12.62

ye B 185
B.Pr.76, B.Pr.199, B.Pr.201, B.Pr.201, B.Pr.209, B.Pr.210, B.Pr.218, B.1.13, B.1.16, B.1.53, B.1.138, B.1.176, B.1.177, B.1.178, B.1.178, B.1.179, B.1.181, B.1.183, B.1.195, B.1.196, B.1.196, B.2.38, B.2.127, B.2.128, B.2.129, B.2.206, B.3.53, B.3.55, B.3.71, B.3.72, B.3.86, B.3.176, B.3.344, B.3.344, B.3.345, B.3.346, B.3.348, B.3.348, B.3.351, B.4.2, B.4.102, B.4.170, B.4.178, B.4.187, B.5.17, B.5.42, B.5.44, B.5.47, B.5.52, B.5.53, B.5.56, B.5.56, B.5.529, B.5.554, B.5.560, B.5.561, B.5.562, B.5.563, B.5.567, B.5.569, B.5.627, B.6.10, B.6.11, B.6.118, B.6.120, B.6.124, B.6.127, B.6.129, B.6.130, B.6.133, B.6.135, B.6.139, B.6.143, B.6.258, B.6.321, B.6.327, B.7.36, B.7.60, B.7.78, B.7.84, B.7.84, B.7.190, B.8.14, B.8.94, B.9.180, B.9.181, B.9.187, B.10.88, B.10.113, B.10.275, B.10.276, B.10.276, B.10.289, B.10.290, B.10.296, B.10.333, B.10.378, B.10.379, B.10.394, B.10.419, B.10.419, B.10.419, B.10.451, B.11.71, B.11.73, B.11.74, B.11.83, B.11.151, B.11.154, B.11.158, B.11.290, B.11.290, B.11.291, B.11.435, B.11.438, B.12.34, B.13.106, B.13.107, B.13.107, B.13.109, B.13.115, B.13.183, B.13.226, B.13.307, B.13.315, B.13.421, B.13.441, B.14.144, B.14.144, B.14.145, B.14.277, B.14.304, B.15.22, B.15.40, B.15.71, B.15.80, B.15.82, B.15.84, B.15.103, B.15.115, B.15.128, B.15.128, B.15.315, B.15.317, B.15.317, B.15.322, B.15.336, B.15.336, B.15.340, B.15.340, B.15.341, B.15.341, B.15.462, B.15.548, B.15.551, B.15.554, B.15.555, B.15.564, B.16.53, B.16.121, B.16.122, B.16.135, B.17.9, B.17.262, B.17.266, B.17.266, B.17.267, B.18.102, B.18.104, B.18.104, B.19.15, B.19.23, B.19.252, B.19.319, B.19.320, B.19.383, B.19.470, B.20.74, B.20.244, B.20.248, B.20.250, B.20.253, B.20.269, B.20.271, B.20.322, B.20.365

ȝe C 151
C.Pr.74, C.Pr.96, C.Pr.101, C.Pr.120, C.Pr.217, C.Pr.219, C.Pr.219, C.Pr.220, C.Pr.221, C.Pr.224, C.1.13, C.1.16, C.1.49, C.1.137, C.1.172, C.1.173, C.1.174, C.1.174, C.1.175, C.1.177, C.1.179, C.2.18, C.2.141, C.2.142, C.2.143, C.2.144, C.2.144, C.2.145, C.2.218, C.3.52, C.3.57, C.3.59, C.3.85, C.3.108, C.3.222, C.4.2, C.4.143, C.4.172, C.5.141, C.5.142, C.5.145, C.5.167, C.5.197, C.6.55, C.7.81, C.7.101, C.7.174, C.7.206, C.7.207, C.7.208, C.7.209, C.7.212, C.7.214, C.7.216, C.7.297, C.8.9, C.8.10, C.8.36, C.8.37, C.8.125, C.8.127, C.8.133, C.8.136, C.8.139, C.8.142, C.8.266, C.8.270, C.8.341, C.9.51, C.9.52, C.9.101, C.9.101, C.9.134, C.9.134, C.9.166, C.9.174, C.9.335, C.9.336, C.10.14, C.10.91, C.10.91, C.10.288, C.11.7, C.11.68, C.11.89, C.11.199, C.11.225, C.11.250, C.11.251, C.11.276, C.11.281, C.12.19, C.12.21, C.12.22, C.12.86, C.12.90, C.13.29, C.13.65, C.13.65, C.13.104, C.13.104, C.13.105, C.13.241, C.13.244, C.15.115, C.15.115, C.15.116, C.15.117, C.15.122, C.16.8, C.16.165, C.16.173, C.16.202, C.16.239, C.16.256, C.16.274, C.17.56, C.17.83, C.17.85, C.17.191, C.17.210, C.17.214, C.17.218, C.17.227, C.18.17, C.18.18, C.19.228, C.19.232, C.19.232, C.19.233, C.19.253, C.20.105, C.20.354, C.20.354, C.20.355, C.21.15, C.21.23, C.21.252, C.21.319, C.21.320, C.21.383, C.21.470, C.22.74, C.22.244, C.22.248, C.22.250, C.22.253, C.22.269, C.22.271, C.22.322, C.22.365

ȝour A 15
A.1.54, A.1.150, A.1.169, A.3.52, A.3.102, A.3.218, A.4.156, A.5.38, A.7.18, A.7.118, A.7.119, A.8.38, A.8.166, A.11.101, A.11.102

ȝoure A 22
A.Pr.73, A.1.41, A.1.53, A.1.153, A.2.93, A.2.105, A.3.61, A.3.63, A.3.116, A.3.135, A.3.145, A.5.39, A.6.50, A.6.51, A.6.54, A.6.56, A.7.11, A.7.13, A.7.22, A.7.117, A.8.39, A.12.88

youre B 110
B.Pr.76, B.Pr.201, B.1.43, B.1.55, B.1.56, B.1.176, B.1.179, B.1.195, B.2.129, B.2.141, B.2.174, B.3.52, B.3.60, B.3.60, B.3.63, B.3.70, B.3.72, B.3.72, B.3.113, B.3.127, B.3.146, B.3.155, B.3.231, B.3.345, B.4.155, B.4.175, B.4.180, B.4.184, B.4.186, B.4.193, B.5.46, B.5.47, B.5.52, B.5.564, B.5.567, B.5.569, B.6.10, B.6.14, B.6.20, B.6.125, B.6.126, B.6.127, B.7.35, B.7.37, B.7.88, B.7.188, B.7.200, B.7.200, B.9.136, B.10.112, B.10.119, B.10.148, B.10.150, B.10.282, B.10.283, B.10.294, B.10.295, B.10.296, B.10.323, B.11.76, B.11.193, B.11.194, B.11.194, B.11.293, B.13.109, B.13.111, B.13.114, B.13.136, B.13.425, B.13.442, B.13.448, B.14.141,

B.15.87, B.15.105, B.15.105, B.15.108, B.15.109, B.15.116, B.15.317, B.15.323, B.15.323, B.15.551, B.15.552, B.16.1, B.16.121, B.16.122, B.16.123, B.16.124, B.16.124, B.16.158, B.16.258, B.17.26, B.17.263, B.17.264, B.17.271, B.18.90, B.18.99, B.18.103, B.18.104, B.18.108, B.19.256, B.19.345, B.19.346, B.19.397, B.19.471, B.19.471, B.20.203, B.20.247, B.20.248, B.20.272

ȝoure 102
C.Pr.74, C.Pr.103, C.Pr.124, C.Pr.124, C.Pr.125, C.Pr.125, C.Pr.125, C.Pr.219, C.1.18, C.1.41, C.1.51, C.1.52, C.1.172, C.1.175, C.2.122, C.2.157, C.3.32, C.3.34, C.3.52, C.3.56, C.3.64, C.3.67, C.3.111, C.3.164, C.3.184, C.4.169, C.4.170, C.4.174, C.4.178, C.4.189, C.5.144, C.5.145, C.5.167, C.5.169, C.5.171, C.5.185, C.5.198, C.7.85, C.7.102, C.7.108, C.7.211, C.7.214, C.7.216, C.8.7, C.8.9, C.8.18, C.8.131, C.8.132, C.8.133, C.8.136, C.8.241, C.9.38, C.9.39, C.9.135, C.9.334, C.10.224, C.11.86, C.11.88, C.11.221, C.11.223, C.11.225, C.12.91, C.12.208, C.12.209, C.13.107, C.15.117, C.15.121, C.16.9, C.16.258, C.16.259, C.16.259, C.16.262, C.16.263, C.16.275, C.17.58, C.17.58, C.17.214, C.17.215, C.18.151, C.18.175, C.19.27, C.19.229, C.19.230, C.19.252, C.20.92, C.20.93, C.20.102, C.20.106, C.20.107, C.20.111, C.20.112, C.21.256, C.21.345, C.21.346, C.21.397, C.21.471, C.21.471, C.22.203, C.22.247, C.22.248, C.22.272

ȝow A 42 ȝou (1) ȝow (42)
A.1.2, A.1.14, A.1.15, A.1.17, A.1.19, A.1.52, A.1.54, A.1.169, A.1.171, A.1.175, A.2.103, A.2.104, A.2.121, A.3.60, A.4.1, A.4.155, A.5.36, A.5.41, A.5.42, A.6.42, A.6.55, A.6.83, A.6.88, A.6.113, A.7.6, A.7.53, A.7.110, A.7.111, A.7.117, A.7.119, A.7.126, A.7.156, A.7.302, A.7.307, A.8.37, A.8.41, A.8.165, A.9.20, A.9.50, A.9.84, A.10.199, A.11.180, A.11.300

yow B 124
B.Pr.200, B.1.2, B.1.14, B.1.15, B.1.17, B.1.19, B.1.54, B.1.56, B.1.195, B.1.197, B.1.201, B.2.139, B.2.140, B.2.157, B.2.173, B.3.52, B.3.69, B.3.347, B.4.1, B.4.169, B.4.177, B.4.178, B.4.179, B.4.192, B.5.43, B.5.44, B.5.57, B.5.294, B.5.295, B.5.295, B.5.555, B.5.568, B.5.596, B.5.601, B.5.628, B.6.6, B.6.14, B.6.58, B.6.118, B.6.119, B.6.125, B.6.127, B.6.134, B.6.144, B.6.171, B.6.257, B.6.258, B.6.321, B.6.326, B.7.35, B.7.35, B.7.36, B.7.187, B.8.24, B.8.60, B.8.61, B.8.94, B.9.137, B.9.178, B.10.275, B.10.282, B.10.292, B.10.293, B.10.294, B.10.322, B.10.323, B.10.327, B.10.418, B.10.452, B.11.75, B.11.161, B.11.161, B.11.193, B.11.193, B.11.291, B.11.292, B.11.292, B.11.293, B.13.185, B.13.186, B.13.186, B.13.308, B.13.423, B.13.426, B.13.441, B.14.35, B.14.140, B.14.147, B.14.274, B.15.9, B.15.83, B.15.86, B.15.323, B.15.324, B.15.333, B.15.337, B.15.552, B.15.556, B.15.574, B.16.1, B.16.2, B.16.53, B.16.125, B.16.134, B.16.142, B.17.26, B.17.264, B.17.265, B.18.88, B.18.94, B.18.99, B.19.225, B.19.226, B.19.257, B.19.473, B.19.474, B.20.245, B.20.246, B.20.249, B.20.253, B.20.269, B.20.323, B.20.364, B.20.366

ȝow C 105 ȝou (1) ȝow (104)
C.Pr.9, C.Pr.13, C.Pr.101, C.Pr.118, C.Pr.127, C.1.2, C.1.15, C.1.17, C.1.19, C.1.50, C.1.52, C.1.115, C.1.171, C.1.196, C.2.155, C.2.156, C.3.32, C.3.33, C.3.56, C.4.1, C.4.171, C.4.172, C.4.173, C.5.82, C.5.142, C.5.167, C.5.168, C.5.169, C.5.170, C.5.171, C.5.172, C.5.182, C.5.184, C.5.189, C.6.56, C.6.349, C.6.434, C.6.347, C.7.83, C.7.88, C.7.101, C.7.199, C.7.212, C.7.215, C.7.244, C.7.248, C.7.281, C.7.297, C.8.4, C.8.7, C.8.13, C.8.35, C.8.39, C.8.125, C.8.126, C.8.131, C.8.133, C.8.141, C.8.167, C.8.265, C.8.269, C.8.270, C.8.341, C.8.345, C.9.37, C.9.38, C.9.280, C.9.333, C.9.338, C.10.28, C.10.59, C.10.225, C.10.280, C.11.277, C.13.105, C.13.106, C.13.106, C.13.107, C.15.118, C.15.232, C.16.8, C.17.215, C.17.219, C.18.17, C.18.151, C.18.152, C.18.152, C.19.230, C.19.231, C.20.90, C.20.97, C.20.102, C.20.111, C.21.225, C.21.226, C.21.257, C.21.473, C.21.474, C.22.245, C.22.246, C.22.249, C.22.253, C.22.269, C.22.323, C.22.364, C.22.366

ye adv ye adv. A 6 ȝa (4) ȝe (2); B 16; C 21 ȝe (20) ye (1)
A. 3.101   'Ȝa lord', quaþ þat lady, 'lord forbede ellis;
A. 5.154   'Ȝa, glotoun gossib', quaþ heo, 'god wot, wel hote:
A. 6.43   'Ȝa, leue piers', quaþ þe pilgrimes & profride hym hire.
A. 7.38   'Ȝa, & ȝet a poynt', quaþ perkyn, 'I preye þe more:
A. 7.215   'Ȝe, I hote þe', quaþ hungir, 'oþer ellis þe bible leiȝeþ.
A.10.115   To be blissid for þi beryng, [ȝ/e, b[e]ggere þeiȝ þou were.
B. 3.112   'Ye, lord', quod þat lady, 'lord forbede ellis!
B. 5.251   'Ye, I haue lent lordes loued me neuere after,
B. 5.556   'Ye! leue Piers', quod þise pilgrimes and profred hym huyre.
B. 6.37   'Ye, and yet a point', quod Piers, 'I preye [þee] of moore:
B. 6.231   'Ye I [h]ote þee', quod hunger, 'or ellis þe bible lieþ.
B.10.472   Ye, men knowe clerkes þat han corsed þe tyme
B.11.34   'Ye? recche þee neuere', quod Rechelesnesse, stood forþ in raggede cloþes,
B.11.42   'Ye! farewel, Phippe', quod Faunteltee, and forþ gan me drawe
B.11.140   'Ye? baw for bokes!' quod oon was broken out of helle.
B.14.104   'Ye? quis est ille?' quod Pacience; 'quik, laudabimus eum!
B.15.47   'Ye, sire!' I seide, 'by so no man were greued
B.17.17   [Is] here alle þi lordes lawes?' quod I; 'ye, leue me', he seide.
B.17.25   Ye! and sixti þousand biside forþ þat ben noȝt seyen here.'
B.19.396   'Ye? baw!' quod a Brewere, 'I wol noȝt be ruled,
B.20.189   'Ye, leue, lurdeyn?' quod he, and leyde on me wiþ Age,
B.20.341   'Ye? go þi gate!' quod Pees, 'by god! for al þi phisik,
C. 3.149   'Ȝe, lord', quod that lady, 'lord hit me forbede
C. 5.104   'Ȝe! and contynue', quod Consience, 'and to þe kyrke ywen[d]e.'
C. 6.298   Ȝe! þe prest þat thy tythe t[a]k[eth], trowe y non other,
C. 7.200   'Ȝe! leue Peres', quod thise pilgrimes and profrede Peres mede.
C. 7.292   'Ȝe! villam emi', quod oen, 'and now y moste thedre
C. 8.35   '[Ye], and ȝut a poynt', quod [Peres], 'y praye ȝow of more:

C. 8.237   'Ȝe, y bihote the,' quod hunger, 'or elles þe bible lyeth.
C.11.193   'Ȝe? reche þe neuere,' quod rechelesnesse, stod forth in ragged clothes;
C.11.309   'Ȝe! farewel, fyppe,' quod fauntelete and forth gan me drawe
C.12.75   'Ȝe? bawe for bokes!' quod oen was broken out of helle.
C.13.245   'Ȝe, certes,' quod he, 'þat is soth', and shop hym to walke;
C.15.246   'Ȝe!' quod pacience [paciently], and oute of his poke hente
C.15.279   'Ȝe? quis est ille?' quod pacience; 'quik, lauda[bi]mus eum!
C.16.139   The sixte is a path of pees; ȝe! thorwe þe pase of Aultoun
C.16.209   'Ȝe, sire!' y sayde, 'by so no man were ygreued,
C.18.58   'Ȝe, sertes,' he sayde, 'and sothliche leue hit.
C.18.81   'Ȝe, sire,' y sayde, 'and sethen þer aren but tweyne lyues
C.19.18   'Is here al thy lordes l[aw]es?' quod y; 'ȝe, leef me,' he saide.
C.21.396   'Ȝe? bawe!' quod a breware, 'y wol nat be yruled,
C.22.189   'Ȝe, leue, lordeyne?' quod he, and leide on me with age,
C.22.341   'Ȝe? go thy gate!' quod pees, 'bi god! for al thi fisyk,

ȝedde v yedden v. A 1
A. 1.138   [Þer] þou art m[er]y at mete, ȝif men bidde þe ȝedde.

yede v yeden v. A 9 ȝede (7) ȝeden (1) iotten (1); B 29 yede (21) yeden (6) yedest (1) iotten (1); C 28 ȝede (20) ȝeden (6) ȝedest (2)
A.Pr.40   Bidderis & beggeris faste aboute ȝede
A. 1.71   And h[a]lside hire on þe heiȝe name, er heo þennis ȝede,
A. 2.144   As fo[bb]is & faitours þat on here feet iotten.'
A. 5.202   Þat he slepte satirday & sonneday til sonne ȝede to reste.
A. 7.91   I bar hom þat I borewide er I to bedde ȝede.
A. 8.130   Musyng on þis metelis a myle wey I ȝede;
A. 9.107   Þouȝt & I þus þre dayes we ȝeden,
A.11.273   For alle cunnyng clerkis siþþe crist ȝede on erþe
A.12.60   As I ȝede thurgh ȝouþe, aȝen prime dayes,
B.Pr.40   Bidderes and beggeres faste aboute ȝede
B. 1.73   And [halsede] hire on þe heiȝe name, er she þennes yede,
B. 2.183   As [fobbes] and Faitours þat on hire feet [iotten].'
B. 5.360   That he sleep Saterday and Sonday til sonne yede to reste.
B. 5.496   The þridde day [þer]after þow yedest in oure sute;
B. 6.99   I bar hom þat I borwed er I to bedde yede.
B. 7.148   Musynge on þis metels [a myle] wey ich yede,
B. 8.117   Thoȝt and I þus þre daies we yeden,
B.11.234   Witnesse in þe Pask wyke, whan he yede to Emaus;
B.11.239   Ac by cloþyng þei knewe hym noȝt, [so caitifliche he yede].
B.11.328   And where þat briddes and beestes by hir mak[e þei] yeden,
B.13.74   Ac I wiste neuere freke þat as a frere yede bifore men on englissh
B.13.347   Til eiþeres wille wexeþ kene and to þe werke yeden,
B.13.370   If I yede to þe Plowȝ I pynched so narwe
B.14.61   For þoruȝ his breeþ beestes woxen and abrood yeden:
B.15.304   In likkyng and in lowynge, þer þei on laundes yede].
B.15.535   Fer fro kyth and fro kyn yuele yclopþed yeden,
B.16.151   'Aue, raby', quod þat Ribaud, and riȝt to hym he yede
B.16.170   And yede forþ as an ydiot in contree to aspie
B.17.52   Ridynge ful rapely þe righte wey we yeden,
B.17.102   That he ne was robbed or rifled, rood he þere or yede,
B.18.3   And yede forþ lik a lorel al my lif tyme
B.18.305   For þe body, while it on bones yede, aboute was euere
B.19.4   In myddes of þe masse þo men yede to offryng
B.19.153   Verray m[a]n bifore hem alle and forþ wiþ hem yede.
B.20.2   Heuy chered I yede and elenge in herte.
B.20.136   An[d] to þe Arches in haste he yede anoon after
B.20.183   And Elde after [hym]; and ouer myn heed yede
B.20.185   So harde he ȝede ouer myn heed it wole be sene euere.
C.Pr.41   Bidders and beggers faste aboute ȝede
C. 1.70   And ha[ls]ede here on the hey name or she thennes [ȝede]
C. 4.162   A sysour and a somnour tho softliche forth ȝede
C. 6.181   Til bothe oure wil was oen and to þe werk we ȝeden,
C. 6.267   And yf y ȝede to þe plough y pynched on his half aker
C. 6.418   A sleep saturday and sonenday til sonne ȝede to rcste.
C. 7.53   And ȝede aboute in my ȝouthe and ȝaf me to no thedom
C. 7.136   The thridde day þeraftur thow ȝedest i[n] oure sekte;
C. 8.108   I bar hoem þat y borwed ar y to bedde ȝede.
C. 9.297   Musyng on this meteles A myle way y ȝede.
C.10.113   Thouht and y thus thre dayes we ȝeden,
C.12.123   Witnesse in þe paske woke when he ȝede to Emaux:
C.12.128   Ac by clothyng þei knewe hym nat, so caytifliche he ȝede.
C.13.136   And where þat briddes and bestis by here make þei ȝeden,
C.15.150   And resoun ran aftur and riht with hym ȝede;
C.15.260   [For] thorw his breth bestes wexe and abroed ȝeden:
C.18.168   Fer fro [k]uthe and fro kyn euele yclothed ȝeden,
C.18.168   'Aue raby,' quod th[at] ribaud[e]; and riht til hym [he] ȝede
C.19.50   Rydynge ful raply þe rihte way we ȝeden,
C.20.3   And ȝede forth ylike a lorel al my lyf tyme
C.20.314   Aȝeyne his loue and his leue on his londe ȝedest,
C.20.337   For þe body, whiles hit on bones ȝede, aboute was hit euere
C.21.4   In myddes of þe masse tho men ȝede to offrynge
C.21.153   Verray man bifore [hem] alle, and forth with hem ȝede.

C.22.2   Heuy chered y ȝede and [e]lyng in herte.
C.22.136   And [t]o þe Arches in haste he ȝede anoen aftur
C.22.183   And Elde aftur hym; and ouer myn heued ȝede
C.22.185   So harde he ȝede ouer myn heued hit wol be sene euere.

yeep adj *yepe adj.* B 2; C 2 ȝep
B. 9.185   Whiles þow art yong [and yeep] and þi wepene [yet] kene
B.11.18   And seide, 'þow art yong and yeep and hast yeres ynowe
C.10.286   And whil þou art ȝong an[d] ȝep and thy wepene kene
C.11.177   And saide, 'þou art ȝong and ȝep and hast ȝeres ynowe

ȝeepliche > yepeliche

yeer n *yer n.* A 14 ȝer (7) ȝeris (7); B 21 yeer (4) yer (7) yeres (9) yeris (1); C 21 ȝer (10) ȝere (2) ȝeres (9)
A.Pr.62   Manye ferlis han fallen in a fewe ȝeris.
A. 2.69   Ȝeldinge for þis þing at o ȝeris ende
A. 2.190   And wiþheld him half [a] ȝer & elleuene dayes.
A. 4.73   'He sh[al] not þis seue ȝer se hise feet ones!'
A. 5.56   Wiþ þat he [shulde] þe satirday, seue ȝer þeraftir,
A. 5.122   It hadde be vnsold þis seue ȝer, so me god helpe.
A. 5.222   'Shal no sonneday be þis seue ȝer, but seknesse it make,
A. 7.42   For þou shalt ȝelde it aȝen at one ȝeris ende
A. 7.305   Or fyue ȝer be fulfild such famyn shal arise;
A. 8.20   Marchauntis in þe margyn hadde manye ȝeris,
A. 9.66   'I haue sewide þe seuen ȝer; seiȝe þou me no raþere?'
A.11.227   Helpiþ nouȝt to heuene[ward] at one ȝeris ende,
A.11.284   Þat hadde leyn with lucifer manye longe ȝeris;
A.12.58   Many ferlys me byfel in a fewe ȝeris.
B.Pr.65   Manye ferlies han fallen in a fewe *yeres.*
B.Pr.193   For I herde my sire seyn, seuen *yeer* ypassed,
B. 2.105   Yeldynge for þis þyng at one [*yeres* ende]
B. 2.231   And [wiþ]helden hym an half *yeer* and elleuene dayes.
B. 4.86   '[He shal] noȝt þise seuen *yer* seen his feet ones!'
B. 5.73   Wiþ þat he sholde þe Saterday, seuen *yer* þerafter,
B. 5.121   I myȝte noȝt ete many *yeres* as a man ouȝte
B. 5.206   It hadde ben vnsold þis seuen *yer*, so me god helpe.
B. 5.414   Nouȝt twyes in two *yer*, and þanne [telle I vp gesse].
B. 5.450   'Shal no Sonday be þis seuen *yer*, but siknesse it [make],
B. 6.43   For þow shalt yelde it ayein at one *yeres* [ende]
B. 6.324   Er fyue [*yer*] be fulfilled swich famyn shal aryse.
B. 7.18   Marchauntȝ in þe margyne hadde manye *yeres,*
B. 8.75   'I haue sued þee seuen *yeer*; seye þow me no raþer?'
B.10.339   Helpeþ noȝt to heueneward [at] oone [*y*]*eris* ende,
B.10.425   That hadde ylyen wiþ lucifer many longe *yeres.*
B.11.18   And seide, 'þow art yong and yeep and hast *yeres* ynowe
B.13.3   In manere of a mendynaunt many *yer* after.
B.15.231   Ac it is fern [and fele *yeer* in] Frounceis tyme;
B.15.297   That lyueden þus for oure lordes loue many longe *yeres.*
B.20.287   Yerne of forȝifnesse or lenger *yere* loone.
C.Pr.63   Mony ferlyes han falle in a fewe ȝeres.
C.Pr.206   For y herde my syre sayn, seuene ȝer ypassed,
C. 2.241   And [wiþ]helden hym [a] half ȝere and eleue dayes.
C. 4.82   Ther he sholde nat in seuene ȝer see his feet [ones].
C. 5.35   'When y [ȝut] ȝong was, many ȝer hennes.
C. 6.86   Y myhte nat ete many ȝer as a man ouhte
C. 6.108   Thow y sitte this seuene ȝer, y sholde nat wel telle
C. 6.214   Hit hadde be vnsold this seuene ȝer, so me god helpe.
C. 7.29   Nat twies in ten ȝer and thenne telle y nat þe haluendele.
C. 7.64   'Shal no sonday be this seuene ȝere, but seknesse hit make,
C. 8.344   Ar fewe ȝeres be fulfeld famyne shal aryse.
C. 9.22   Marchauntes in þe margine hadde many ȝeres
C.10.73   'Y haue sued the seuen ȝer; saw thow me no rather?'
C.10.198   Sholde doute no deth ne no dere ȝeres
C.11.177   And saide, 'þou art ȝong and ȝep and hast ȝeres ynowe
C.11.257   That hadde yley with lucifer mony longe ȝeres.
C.15.3   In manere of [a] mendenaunt mony ȝer aftur.
C.16.288   Ich haue yleued in londone monye longe ȝeres
C.16.356   Ac hit is fer and fele ȝer in franceys tyme;
C.17.26   That lyueden thus for oure lordes loue monye longe ȝeres
C.22.287   Ȝerne of forȝeuenesse or lengore ȝeres l[on]e.

ȝef > gyuen,if; ȝefte(s > gifte

yelden v *yelden v.* A 5 ȝelde (3) ȝelden (1) ȝeldinge (1); B 14 ȝilt (1) yald (2) yelde (7) yelden (1) yeldest (1) yeldeþ (1) yeldynge (1); C 12 ȝeld (1) ȝelde (8) ȝelden (1) ȝeldest (1) ȝeldeth (1)
A. 2.69   Ȝeldinge for þis þing at o ȝeris ende
A. 5.227   And ȝet wile I ȝelde aȝen, ȝif I so muchel haue,
A. 7.42   For þou shalt ȝelde it aȝen at one ȝeris ende
A. 7.119   And ȝelde ȝow of ȝour almesse þat ȝe ȝiuen vs here,
A. 8.172   And come [alle] before crist acountes to ȝelden,
B. 2.105   Yeldynge for þis þyng at one [*yeres* ende]
B. 5.288   And as longe as þow lyuest þerwith þow *yeldest* noȝt but borwest;
B. 5.367   'I, Gloton', quod þe [gome], 'gilty me *yelde*

B. 5.455   And yet wole I *yelde* ayein, if I so muche haue,
B. 6.43   For þow shalt *yelde* it ayein at one yeres [ende]
B. 6.127   And *yelde* yow [of] youre Almesse þat ye ȝyue vs here;
B. 7.80   For he þat yeueþ *yeldeþ* and yarkeþ hym to reste,
B. 7.83   To *yelden* hem þat yeueþ hem and yet vsure moore:
B. 7.194   And comen alle [bi]fore crist acountes to *yelde,*
B.12.193   Was for he *yald* hym creaunt to crist & knewliched hym gilty,
B.12.214   A[c] why þat oon þeef on þe cros creaunt hym *yald*
B.15.256   Neiþer he biddeþ ne beggeþ ne borweþ to *yelde.*
B.18.100   ȝilt hym recreaunt re[m]yng, riȝt at Iesus wille.
B.19.391   'How?' quod al þe comune; 'þow conseillest vs to *yelde*
C. 6.309   Hyhte ȝeuan-ȝelde-aȝeyn-yf-y-so-moche-haue-
C. 6.343   And as longe as thow lyuest therwith þou ȝeldest nat bote borwest;
C. 6.425   To the, god, y glotoun, gulty me ȝelde
C. 8.41   For thow shalt ȝelden hit, so may be, or sumdel abuggen hit.
C. 8.133   And ȝelde ȝow of ȝoure Almesse þat ȝe ȝeuen vs here;
C. 9.340   And comen alle bifore Crist acountes to ȝelde,
C.14.132   Was for A ȝeld hym creaunt to crist and his grace askede.
C.14.153   Ac why þat [on] theef vppon þe cros cryant hym ȝelde
C.16.372   For noþer he beggeth ne biddeth ne borweth to ȝelde.
C.17.89   Noþer see ne s[o]nd ne þe seed ȝeldeth
C.20.103   Ȝelde hym [re]creaunt remyng, riht at iesu[s] wille.
C.21.391   'How?' quod alle þe comune; 'thow conseylest vs to ȝelde

ȝeme > yeme,yemen

yeme n *yeme n.* &> *yemen* B 3; C 1 ȝeme
B. 3.334   That ȝyuen ȝiftes, [takeþ *yeme*], þe victorie wynneþ
B.10.200   Ac Theologie techeþ noȝt so, whoso takeþ *yeme;*
B.17.14   This was the tixte, trewely; I took ful good *yeme.*
C. 3.486   That ȝeueth ȝeftes, taketh ȝeme, the victorie a wynneth

ȝemen n *yeman n.* C 1
C. 3.270   Thorw ȝeftes haen ȝemen to ȝerne and to ryde;

yemen v *yemen v.* A 1 ȝeme; B 2 yeme (1) yemen (1); C 1 ȝeme
A.10.72   Is chief souereyn ouer hymself his soule to ȝeme,
B. 8.52   For he yaf þee [to] yeresȝyue to *yeme* wel þiselue
B. 9.205   To ȝyuen and to *yemen* boþe yonge and olde,
C.10.304   To ȝeue and to ȝeme bothe ȝonge and olde,

yemere n *yemer n.* B 1
B.13.170   Yeue þee al þat þei may yeue, as þee for best *yemere;*

ȝende > yonde; ȝent > yond; ȝep > yeep

yepeliche adv *yepeli adv.* B 1; C 1 ȝeepliche
B.15.188   And yerne into youþe and *yepeliche* [seche]
C.16.331   Thenne ȝerneth he into ȝouthe and ȝeepliche he secheth

ȝer(e -es yer(es > yeer

yerde n *yerde n.* A 3 ȝarde (1) ȝardis (1) ȝerdis (1); B 3 yerde (1) yerdes (2); C 2 ȝerde (1) ȝerdes (1)
A. 4.103   Til childris cherisshing be chastisid with ȝerdis;
A. 5.128   Til ten ȝardis oþer twelue tollide out þrittene
A.10.85   Þanne is dobet to ben ywar for betyng of þe ȝarde,
B. 4.117   And childrene cherissynge be chast[ised] wiþ *yerdes,*
B. 5.212   Til ten *yerdes* or twelue tolled out þrittene
B.12.14   Alþouȝ þow strike me wiþ þi staf, wiþ stikke or wiþ *yerde,*
C. 4.112   And [chyldren] chersyng be chasted with ȝerdes
C. 6.220   Til ten ȝerde other twelue tolde out threttene.

yeresȝyue n *yereseve n.* A 2 ȝerisȝiue (1) ȝerisȝiuys (1); B 4 yeresȝeues (1) yeresȝyue (2) yeresyeues (1)
A. 3.89   To haue ȝeftis [or ȝerisȝiuys] in ȝouþe or in elde.
A.11.34   Ȝiue hem to here ȝerisȝiue þe value of a grote.
B. 3.100   Yiftes or *yeresyeues* bycause of hire Offices.
B. 8.52   For he yaf þee [to] *yeresȝyue* to yeme wel þiselue
B.10.48   ȝyue hem to hir *yeresȝyue* þe [value] of a grote.
B.13.184   After *yeresȝeues* or ȝiftes, or *yernen* to rede redels?

ȝerne > yerne,yernen,rennen

yerne adv *yerne adv.* &> *yernen,rennen* A 1 ȝerne; B 6; C 6 ȝerne
A. 7.100   Þerewiþ was perkyn payed, and preisid hem ȝerne.
B. 4.74   Thanne wowede wrong wisdom ful *yerne*
B. 5.423   I foryete it as *yerne*, and if men me it axe
B. 6.108   Therwiþ was Perkyn apayed and preised hem [*yerne*].
B. 6.297   Thanne pouere folk for fere fedden hunger *yerne*
B.20.159   Sleuþe wax wonder *yerne* and soone was of age
B.20.287   *Yerne* of forȝifnesse or lenger yeres loone.
C. 4.53   What wey y wende wel ȝerne he aspyeth
C. 7.36   Y forȝete hit as ȝerne and yf eny man hit aske
C. 8.116   Oþer werkemen þer were þat wrouhten fol ȝerne,
C. 8.319   Pore folk for fere tho fedde honger ȝerne
C.22.159   Sleuthe wax wonder ȝerne and sone was of age
C.22.287   Ȝerne of forȝeuenesse or lengore ȝeres l[on]e.

yernen v *yernen v.* A 1 ȝerne; B 2 yerne (1) yernen (1); C 1 ȝerne
A. 1.33   Mesure is medicine þeiȝ þou muche *ȝerne*.
B. 1.35   Mesure is medicine þouȝ þow muchel *yerne*.
B.13.184   After yeresȝeues or ȝiftes, or *yernen* to rede redels?
C. 1.33   Mesure is medecyne thogh þow muche *ȝerne*;

ȝerneth > rennen

yet adv *yet adv.* A 22 ȝet; B 53 ȝit (12) yet (41); C 75 ȝut
A. 1.127   'Ȝet haue I no kynde knowyng,' quaþ I, '[ȝe mote kenne me bet]
A. 1.143   And ȝet wolde he hem no woo þat wrouȝte him þat pyne,
A. 2.1   Ȝet knelide I on my knes & criȝede hire of grace,
A. 2.102   Ȝet be war of þe weddyng for witty is treuþe.
A. 3.171   Ȝet I may, as I miȝte, [menske] þe wiþ ȝeftis,
A. 3.275   Ac kynde wyt shal come ȝet, & consience togidere,
A. 4.21   And ȝet wile [h]e make many wehe er we come þere.'
A. 4.46   And ȝet he betiþ me þerto & liþ be my maiden.
A. 4.117   And ȝet,' quaþ resoun, 'be þe rode, I shal no reuþe haue
A. 5.95   I deme men þere [hy] don ille, & ȝet I do wers;
A. 5.212   And ȝet haue I hatid hire al my lif tyme.'
A. 5.227   And ȝet wile I ȝelde aȝen, ȝif I so muchel haue,
A. 5.235   And ȝet þe synful shrewe seide to hymselue:
A. 5.247   And knowelechide his [coupe] to crist ȝet eftsones,
A. 7.38   'Ȝa, & ȝet a poynt,' quaþ perkyn, 'I preye þe more:
A. 7.188   'Ac ȝet I preye þe,' quaþ peris, 'er þou passe ferþere:
A. 7.237   'Ȝet I preye þe,' quaþ peris, 'pur charite, ȝif þou kenne
A. 9.29   And ȝet is he sauf & sound, & so hym behouiþ.
A. 9.102   'Ac ȝet sauouriþ me nouȝt þi segging, so me god helpe;
A.11.159   Ȝet arn þere febicchis of Forellis of many manis wittes,
A.11.258   –Ȝet am I neuere þe ner for nouȝt I haue walkid
A.11.293   And ȝet [haue] I forget[e ferþer] of fyue wyttis teching
B.Pr.185   'Thouȝ we [hadde] kille[d] þe cat yet sholde þer come anoþer
B.Pr.211   Yet houed þer an hundred in howues of selk,
B. 1.138   'Yet haue I no kynde knowyng', quod I, 'ye mote kenne me bettre
B. 1.169   And yet wolde he hem no wo þat wrouȝte hym þat peyne,
B. 2.1   YEt [kneled I] on my knees and cried hire of grace,
B. 2.138   Yet be war of [þe] weddynge; for witty is truþe,
B. 3.184   Yet I may, as I myȝte, menske þee wiþ ȝiftes,
B. 3.299   Ac kynde loue shal come ȝit and Conscience togidere
B. 4.59   And yet he beteþ me þerto and lyþ by my mayde.
B. 4.134   And yet', quod Reson, 'by þe Rode! I shal no ruþe haue
B. 4.161   Loue leet of hire liȝt and leaute yet lasse,
B. 4.170   And yet yeue ye me neuere þe worþ of a risshe.'
B. 5.115   [I] deme [men þere hij] doon ille, [and yet] I do werse;
B. 5.384   And yet haue I hated hire al my lif tyme.'
B. 5.399   Ne riȝt sory for my synnes yet, [so þee I], was I neuere.
B. 5.416   Yet kan I neyþer solue ne synge ne seintes lyues rede;
B. 5.455   And yet wole I yelde ayein, if I so muche haue,
B. 5.463   Ac yet þe synfulle sherewe seide to hymselue:
B. 5.473   And knoweliched his [coupe] to crist yet eftsoones,
B. 6.37   'Ye, and yet a point', quod Piers, 'I preye [þee] of moore:
B. 6.253   'Yet I preie [þee]', quod Piers, 'p[u]r charite, and [þow] konne
B. 6.284   And yet I seye, by my soule! I haue no salt bacon
B. 7.83   To yelden hem þat owaþ hem and yet vsure moore:
B. 8.33   Ac yet is he saaf and sound, and so hym bihoueþ,
B. 8.112   'Ac yet sauoreþ me noȝt þi seying, [so me god helpe!
B. 9.130   Yet [seþ], ayein þe sonde of oure Saueour of heuene,
B. 9.185   Whiles þow art yong [and yep] and þi wepene [yet] kene
B.10.81   And yet þe wrecches of þis world is noon ywar by ooþer,
B.10.216   Yet ar þer fibicches in [forelles] of fele mennes [wittes],
B.10.448   [And yet haue I forgete ferþer of fyue wittes techyng
B.11.70   Ac yet I cryde on my Confessour þat [so konnyng heeld hym]:
B.11.351   Ac yet me merueilled moore how many þeere briddes
B.12.70   Ac yet is Clergie to comende and kynde wit boþe,
B.12.276   For lettred men were lewed yet ne were loore of hir bokes.'
B.13.245   Neiþer prouendre ne personage ne of [þe] popes ȝifte,
B.13.381   Moore þan it was worþ, and yet wolde I swere
B.13.399   [Yet glotoun wiþ grete oþes his [garnement] hadde soiled
B.14.161   And yet is wynter for hem worse, for weetshoed þei [gange],
B.14.298   Wiþ sobretee fram alle synne and also ȝit moore;
B.15.349   As in lussheburwes is a luþer alay, and yet lokeþ he lik a sterlyng;
B.15.411   That [lered] þere and [lewed] ȝit leeuen on hise lawes.
B.15.587   And ȝit knewe þei crist þat cristendom tauȝte,
B.15.601   And [ȝit] wenen þo wrecches þat he were pseudopropheta
B.16.3   Ac ȝit I am in a weer what charite is to mene.'
B.16.216   As widewe wiþouten wedlok was neuere ȝit yseiȝe,
B.16.241   To me and to myn issue moore yet he [me] grauntede,
B.17.45   And wel awey worse ȝit for to loue a sherewe.
B.17.216   The blase þerof yblowe out, yet brenneþ þe weke–
B.17.246   Boþe forȝyue and foryete, and ȝit bidde for vs
B.17.285   A[c] yet in mo maneres men offenden þe holy goost;
B.18.44   And ȝit maken it as muche in alle manere poyntes,
B.18.98   The gree ȝit haþ he geten for al his grete wounde,
B.18.367   I fauȝt so me þursteþ ȝit for mannes soule sake;

C.Pr.202   'Thow we hadde ykuld þe Cat ȝut shulde ther come another
C.Pr.222   Ȝut mette me more of mene and of riche,
C. 1.165   And ȝut wolde [he] hem no wo þat wrouhte hym þat [p]e[y]ne
C. 2.154   Ȝut beth ywar of þe weddynge; for witty is treuthe
C. 3.43   And ȝut be thy bedman and brynge adoun Consience
C. 3.77   Ȝut mede the Mayr myldeliche he bysouhte,
C. 3.139   Ȝut y forgyue þis gult; godes forb[o]de eny more
C. 3.210   That no lond ne loueth the and ȝut leeste thyn owene.
C. 3.230   Ȝut y may, as y myhte, menske þe with ȝeftes
C. 3.452   A[c] kynde loue shal come ȝut and Consience togyderes
C. 4.55   Ȝut is he bold for to borw Ac baddelyche he payeth:
C. 4.62   And ȝut he manes[c]heth me and myne and lyth be my mayde.
C. 4.74   Ȝut pees put forth his heued and his panne blody:
C. 4.131   And [ȝut],' quod resoun, 'by þe rode! y shal no reuthe haue
C. 4.156   Loue l[et]te of mede lyhte and leutee ȝut lasse
C. 5.35   'When y [ȝut] ȝong was, many ȝer hennes,
C. 5.94   Ac ȝut y hope, as he þat ofte hath ychaffared
C. 6.36   And ȝut so synguler be mysulue as to syhte of [þe] peple
C. 6.51   Thyng þat neuere was thouhte and ȝut [y] swor [y] seyh hit
C. 6.95   Ȝut am y brokour of bakbytynge to blame menne w[a]re
C. 6.156   Ȝut am y chalenged in oure chapitrehous as y a childe were
C. 6.230   A galon for a grote, and ȝut no grayth mesure
C. 6.292   Ȝut were me leuer, by oure lord, lyue al by wellecresses
C. 6.317   Ac ȝut þ[e] synful shrewe seide to heuene:
C. 6.327   And knolechede [his coupe to Crist] ȝut eftsones,
C. 6.333   [T]rist in his mechel mercy and ȝut þou myhte be saued.
C. 6.441   And ȝut haue y [ha]ted here al my lyf tyme.'
C. 7.31   Ȝut kan y nother solfe ne synge ne a seyntes lyf rede;
C. 8.35   '[Ye], and ȝut a poynt,' quod [Peres], 'y praye ȝow of more:
C. 8.265   Ac ȝut y praye ȝow,' quod [Peres], 'pur charite, syre hungur,
C. 8.279   And ȝut hadde he [hem] nat for y, hungur, culde hym–
C. 8.306   And ȝut y say[e], be my soule! y haue no sal[t] bacoun
C. 9.105   A[nd] ȝut ar ther oþere beggares, in hele as hit semeth
C. 9.132   And ȝut more to suche men me doth ar they passe.
C. 9.134   Ryht so, ȝe ryche, ȝut rather ȝe sholde
C. 9.325   Ȝut hath þe pope power pardoun to graunte
C.10.38   A[c] ȝut is he saef and sound; and so hit fareth by þe rihtfole.
C.10.82   Dobet doth al this Ac ȝut he doth more.
C.10.108   'Ac ȝut sauereth [me nat] thy sawes, so me Crist spede!
C.10.188   Ac thenne dede we alle wel, and wel bet ȝut, to louye
C.10.190   And ȝut were best to ben aboute and brynge hit to hepe
C.11.61   And ȝut th[e] wrechus of this world is noen ywar by oþer
C.12.168   Ȝut conseileth Crist in commen vs all:
C.12.239   And ȝut more hit maketh men mony tymes & ofte
C.13.5   Ȝut ret me þat abraham and Iob weren wonder ryche
C.13.50   And ȝut be ylette, as y leue, for the lawe asketh
C.13.52   And ȝut thow they wende o way as to wynchestre fayre
C.13.61   Ac ȝut myhte þe marchaunt thorw moneye and other ȝeftes
C.13.76   And ȝut more, to maken pees and quyten menne dettes
C.13.162   And ȝut me merueylede more [how] mony [other] briddes
C.14.35   And ȝut is clergie to comende for cristes loue more
C.14.198   For letrede men were lewede ȝut ne were lore of [here bokes].'
C.16.14   And ȝut is wynter for hem worse for weetshoed þey g[ang]e,
C.16.134   With sobrete fro alle synnes and also ȝut more;
C.17.3   And ȝut oþerwhile wroeth withouten eny synne.'
C.17.48   Thenne grace sholde growe ȝut and grene loue wexe
C.17.76   And ȝut is þe printe puyr trewe and parfitliche ygraue.
C.17.133   That lelyche they byleue, and ȝut here lawe diuerseth,
C.17.182   And on his lore thei l[e]uen ȝut, as wel lered as lewed.
C.17.298   And ȝut knewe they crist þat cristendoem tauhte
C.17.307   And ȝut they seyen sothly, and so doen þe sarrasynes,
C.19.91   And ȝut [b]e plasterud with pacience when fondynges [priketh hym]–
C.19.94   And ȝut bote they l[e]ue lelly vpon þat litel baby,
C.19.114   Ferde furste as a f[u]ste, and ȝut is, as y leue,
C.19.182   The blase be yblowen out, ȝut brenneth þe weke–
C.19.212   Bothe forȝeue and forȝete and ȝut bidde for vs
C.19.236   Ȝut wan he nat with wrong ne with queynte sleythes;
C.19.239   Moste lordliche lyue and ȝut [on] his lycame werie
C.19.247   Excuse hem þat ben vnkynde and ȝut here [catel] ywonne
C.19.248   With wyles and with luyther whitus and ȝut wollen nat atymye
C.19.266   And ȝut in mo maneres men [o]ffenden þe holy gost;
C.20.43   And ȝut maken hit as moche in alle manere poyntes,
C.20.101   The gre ȝut hath he geten for al his grete wound[e]
C.20.408   Y fauht so me fursteth ȝut for mannes soule sake:
C.20.435   A[c] ȝut my kynde [in] my kene ire shal constrayne my will–

yeten ptp *yeten v.(1)* B 1; C 1 yȝoten
B. 1.154   Til it hadde of þe erþe [y]eten [hitselue].
C. 1.150   Til hit hadde of erthe yȝoten hitsilue.

ȝeuan n prop *n.i.d.* C 1
C. 6.309   Hyhte ȝeuan-ȝelde-aȝeyn-yf-y-so-moche-haue–

ʒeue(- yeue(- > gyuen; ʒif > gyuen,if; ʒifte(s yiftes > gifte; ʒilt > yelden

ʒis adv *yis adv.* A 2; B 5; C 4 ʒus
A. 5.103 'ʒis, redily,' quaþ repentaunce & redde hym to goode:
A. 6.119 'ʒis,' quaþ peris þe plouʒman & pukide hym to goode:
B. 5.126 'ʒis! redily', quod Repentaunce and radde hym to [goode]:
B. 5.231 'ʒis', ones I was yherberwed', quod he, 'wiþ an heep of chapmen;
B. 5.634 'ʒis!' quod Piers þe Plowman, and poked [hym] to goode,
B.11.87 'ʒis, by Peter and by Poul!' quod he and took hem boþe to witnesse:
B.17.303 'ʒis', seide þe Samaritan, 'so þow myght repente
C. 6.91 'ʒus! redily,' quod repentaunce, 'and thow be ryht sory
C. 6.235 'ʒus! ones y was herberwed,' quod he, 'with an heep of chapmen;
C. 7.287 'ʒus!' quod [Perus] þe [plouhman], and pokede hem alle to gode,
C.19.283 'ʒus,' saide þe samaritaen, 'so thow myhtest repente

ʒit > yet; ʒiue(- > gyuen

ʒokes n *yoke n.* C 1
C. 7.295 To falewe with fiue ʒo[k]es; 'forthy me bihoueth

yolde ptp *yelden v.* B 1
B. 9.166 To yeuen a yong wenche to [a yolde] feble,

yond adj *yond adj.* B 2 yon (1) yond (1); C 3 ʒone (2) ʒent (1)
B.18.145 Leue þow neuere þat yon light hem alofte brynge
B.18.189 Leuestow þat yond light vnlouke myʒte helle
C.15.130 For Peres loue þe palmare ʒent, þat inpugnede ones
C.20.148 Leue [þou] neuere þat ʒone liht hem alofte brynge
C.20.194 Leuest thow þat ʒone lihte vnlouke myhte helle

yonde adv *yond adv.* B 1; C 1 ʒende
B.18.252 For [Iesus as a] geaunt wiþ a gyn [comeþ yonde]
C.20.261 For iesus as a geaunt with a gyn cometh ʒende

ʒone > yond

yong adj *yong adj.* A 5 ʒong (1) ʒonge (4); B 8 yong (4) yonge (4); C 6 ʒong (3) ʒonge (3)
A. 3.201 Þoruʒ ʒeftis han ʒonge men to [ʒerne] & to ride.
A. 5.33 'Let no wynnyng forwanye hem whiles þei ben ʒonge'.
A.10.58 In ʒonge fauntes & folis, wiþ hem failiþ Inwyt,
A.10.67 But þei witen hem fro wauntounesse whiles þei ben ʒon[g]e.
A.10.187 To ʒiuen a ʒong wenche to an old feble,
B. 3.214 [Thoruʒ] ʒiftes han yonge men to [yerne] and to ryde.
B. 5.35 'Late no wynnyng [forwanye hem] while þei be yonge,
B. 9.166 To yeuen a yong wenche to [a yolde] feble,
B. 9.185 Whiles þow art yong [and yeep] and þi wepene [yet] kene
B. 9.205 To ʒyuen and to yemen boþe yonge and olde,
B.11.18 And seide, 'þow art yong and yeep and hast yeres ynowe
B.12.6 And of þi wilde wantownesse [whiles] þow yong were
B.13.110 But cheeste be þer charite sholde be, and yonge children dorste pleyne.
C.Pr.218 Ne were þe Cat of þe Court and ʒonge kitones toward;
C. 5.35 'When y [ʒut] ʒong was, many ʒer hennes,
C. 5.137 'Late no wynnynge forwanyen hem while thei ben ʒonge
C.10.286 And whil þou art ʒong an[d] ʒep and thy wepene kene
C.10.304 To ʒeue and to ʒeme bothe ʒonge and olde,
C.11.177 And saide, 'þou art ʒong and ʒep and hast ʒeres ynowe

ʒorn > rennen; iotten > yede; ʒou(r -e youre > ye; your(e)self > yowself

youþe n *youth n.* A 3 ʒouþe; B 6; C 5 ʒouthe (4) ʒowthe (1)
A. 3.89 To haue ʒeftis [or ʒerisʒiuys] in ʒouþe or in elde.
A. 8.76 Or his bak or his bon þei breken in his ʒouþe,
A.12.60 As I ʒede thurgh ʒouþe, aʒen prime dayes,
B. 1.141 To litel latyn þow lernedest, leode, in þi youþe:
B. 5.238 'Nay, soþly, he seide, 'saue in my youþe.
B. 5.439 I [yarn] aboute in youþe and yaf me nauʒt to lerne,
B. 7.94 Or [his] bak or [his] boon [þei] brekeþ in his youþe
B.11.60 Til I for[yede] youþe and yarn into Elde.
B.15.188 And yerne into youþe and yepeliche [seche]
C. 1.140 To lyte [Latyn þow] lernedest, [leode], in thy ʒowthe:
C. 6.240 'Nay, sothly,' he saide, 'saue in my ʒouthe.
C. 7.53 And ʒede aboute in my ʒouthe and ʒaf me to no thedom
C.12.12 Til y forʒet ʒouthe and ʒorn into elde.
C.16.331 Thenne ʒerneth he into ʒouthe and ʒeepliche he secheth

ʒoue > gyuen; ʒow yow > ye pron

yowself pron *yourself pron.* B 7 youreself (1) yourself (1) yowself (1) yowselue (4); C 4 ʒowsylue (1) ʒowsulue (1) ʒowsuluen (2)
B.Pr.201 For hadde ye rattes youre [raik] ye kouþe noʒt rule yowselue.
B. 2.38 And how ye shul saue yourself? þe Sauter bereþ witnesse:
B. 5.42 'That ye prechen þe peple, preue it yowselue,
B.10.278 [Thouʒ] it auailled noʒt be commune it myʒte auaille yowselue.
B.10.289 Forþi, ye Correctours, claweþ heron and correcteþ first yowselue,
B.16.122 And Sathan youre Saueour; [youre]self now ye witnessen.
B.16.123 For I haue saued yowself and youre sones after,
C.Pr.219 For hadde ʒe ratones ʒoure [reik] ʒe couthe nat reule ʒowsuluen.'
C. 4.187 'Y assente,' sayde resoun, 'by so ʒowsulue yhere
C. 5.141 'That ʒe prechen þe peple, p[ro]ue hit ʒowsylue;
C. 8.14 For profit of the pore and plesaunce of ʒowsuluen.

ʒowthe > youþe; ʒus > ʒis; ʒut > yet

Z

ʒacheus n prop *n.i.d.* B 1
B.13.195 Than ʒacheus for he seide "dimidium bonorum meorum do pauperibus",

LATIN CONCORDANCE

a A 5; B 12; C 11

A. 8.3   And purchac[ide] hym a pardoun *a* pena & a culpa
A. 8.3   And purchac[ide] hym a pardoun a pena & *a* culpa
A. 8.21   But non *a* pena & a culpa þe pope wolde h[e]m graunte,
A. 8.21   But non a pena & *a* culpa þe pope wolde h[e]m graunte,
A. 8.46   Super innocentem munera non accipies; *a* regibus & principibus–
B.Pr.135 Nudum ius *a* te vestiri vult pietate.
B.Pr.141 'Dum rex *a* regere dicatur nomen habere
B. 7.3   And purchaced hym a pardoun *a* pena & a culpa
B. 7.3   And purchaced hym a pardoun a pena & *a* culpa
B. 7.19   Ac noon *A* pena & a culpa þe pope [w]olde hem graunte
B. 7.19   Ac noon A pena & *a* culpa þe pope [w]olde hem graunte
B. 7.44   *A* Regibus & principibus erit merces eorum.
B.13.67   Ter cesus sum & *a* iudeis quinquies quadragenas &c–
B.13.73   Vnusquisque *a* fratre se custodiat quia vt dicitur periculum est in falsis
B.14.46   Quodcumque pecieritis *a* patre in nomine meo &c; Et alibi, Non in solo pane
B.15.55   scrutator est maiestatis opprimitur *a* gloria.
B.16.223 Spiritus procedens *a* patre & filio &c,
C.Pr.156 Nudum ius *a* te vestir[i] vult pietate.
C. 1.122 Dixit dominus domino meo, sede *a* dextris meis.
C. 9.3   And purchasede hym a pardoun *A* pena & A culpa,
C. 9.3   And purchasede hym a pardoun A pena & *A* culpa,
C. 9.23   Ac no [*a*] pena & a culpa treuthe wolde hem graunte
C. 9.23   Ac no [a] pena & *a* culpa treuthe wolde hem graunte
C. 9.187 And pardon with the plouhman *A* pena & a culpa
C. 9.187 And pardon with the plouhman A pena & *a* culpa.
C.13.17   And for a song in his sorwe, "si bona accepimus *a* domino &c,
C.15.244 Quodcumque pecieritis [*a* patre] in nomine meo dab[itur] enim
C.16.217 Sic [qui] scrutator est magestatis opprim[e]tur *a* gloria.

ab B 2; C 2

B.11.255 Maria optimam partem elegit que non [auferetur *ab* ea].
B.12.144 Ibant magi *ab* oriente.
C.12.141 Maria optimam partem elegit que non [auferetur *ab* ea].
C.14.88   Ib[a]nt magi *ab* Oriente &c.

abbas B 1; C 1

B. 5.171 Boþe Prior and Suppriour and oure Pater *Abbas*;
C. 6.153 That is Priour and supriour and oure pater *Abbas*.

ablatum B 1

B. 5.273 Non dimittitur peccatum donec restituatur [*a*]blatum.

abrahe B 1

B.16.242 Quam olim *Abrahe* promisisti & semini eius.

abscondito C 1

C. 5.98   Simile est regnum celorum thesauro *abscondito* in agro;

absit B 1; C 1

*B.15.537 *Absit* nobis gloriari nisi in cruce domini nostri &c.
C.17.198 *Absit* nobis gloriari nisi in cruce domini nostri &c.

absque B 4; C 4

B.14.276 *absque* sollicitudine semita, sapiencie temperatrix, negocium sine
B.14.276 Incerta fortuna, *absque* sollicitudine felicitas.'
B.14.309 Forþi seiþ Seneca Paupertas est *absque* sollicitudine semita.
B.14.320 *Absque* sollicitudine felicitas.
C.16.116 *absque* soli[ci]tudine semita, sapiencie temp[e]ratrix, negocium sine
C.16.116 Incerta fortuna, *absque* solicitudine felicitas.'
C.16.143 Pauper[tas] est *absque* solicitudine semita.
C.16.155 *Absque* solicitudine felicitas.

ac A 1; B 1

A. 8.110 Fuerunt michi lacrime mee panes die *ac* nocte.
B. 7.128 Fuerunt michi lacrime mee panes die *ac* nocte.

accepimus C 1

C.13.17   And for a song in his sorwe, "si bona *accepimus* a domino &c,

accepit C 1

C. 2.42   Et super Innocentem munera non *accepit*.

acceptores B 1; C 1

B.15.88   That seide to hise disciples, "Ne sitis personarum *acceptores*".
C.16.241 Ne sitis *acceptores* personarum.

accionibus B 1; C 1

B.15.39   Anima pro diuersis *accionibus* diuersa nomina sortitur: dum viuificat
C.16.201 Anima pro diuersis [*acc*]ionibus diuersa nomina sortitur: dum

accipere B 1

B. 7.77   Non eligas cui miser[e]aris ne forte pretereas illum qui meretur *accipere*,

accipientium accipiencium B 1; C 1

B. 3.350 Animam autem aufert *accipientium* &c.
C. 3.498 Animam [autem] aufert *Accipiencium*:

accipies A 1; B 1

A. 8.46   Super innocentem munera non *accipies*; a regibus & principibus–
B. 7.42   Super innocentem munera non *accipies*.

accipietis B 1

B.15.428 Petite & *accipietis* &c.

accipis B 3

B.15.343 *accipis* pocius das quam accipis; Si autem non eges & accipis rapis.
B.15.343 accipis pocius das quam *accipis*; Si autem non eges & accipis rapis.
B.15.343 accipis pocius das quam accipis; Si autem non eges & *accipis* rapis.

accipiunt A 1; B 1; C 1

A. 3.85   Ignis deuorabit tabernacula eorum qui libenter *accipiunt* munera.
B. 3.96   Ignis deuorabit tabernacula eorum qui libenter *accipiunt* munera &c.
C. 3.124 Ignis deuorabit tabernacula eorum qui libenter *accipiunt* munera.

actiua B 2; C 5

B.13.224 'I am a Mynstrall', quod þat man, 'my name is *Actiua* vita.
B.14.28   Than Hauky[n] wi[l] þe wafrer, [which is] *Actiua* vita.'
C.15.193 'Ich am a mynstral,' quod this man, 'my name is *actiua* vita,
C.15.272 'What is [properly] parfit pacience?' quod *Actiua* vita.
C.16.117 'Y can nat construe al this,' quod *Actiua* vita.
C.18.80   That [lyf *Actiua*] lettred men in here langage calleth.'
C.18.82   *Actiua* vita & contemplatiua vita,

acutus B 1; C 1

B.13.330 et lingua eorum gladius a[*cutus*].
C. 6.76   & lingua eorum gladius *acutus*.

ad A 5; B 25; C 18

A. 3.221 Qui pecuniam suam [non] dedit *ad* vsuram.
A.10.41   Faciamus hominem *ad* ymaginem nostram.
A.11.245 Dum tempus est operemur bonum *ad* omnes, maxime autem ad
A.11.245 Dum tempus est operemur bonum ad omnes, maxime autem *ad*
A.11.263 Nemo ascendet *ad* celum nisi qui de celo descendit.
B. 3.241 Qui pecuniam suam non dedit *ad* vsuram et munera super innocentem &c,
B. 5.283 Omnis iniquitas quantum *ad* misericordiam dei est quasi sintilla in medio
B. 5.486 Faciamus hominem *ad* ymaginem [et similitudinem] nostram;
B. 5.498 Non veni vocare iustos set peccatores *ad* penitenciam.
B. 7.83   Quare non dedisti pecuniam meam *ad* mensam vt ego veni[ens] cum vsuris ex[egissem illam]?
B. 9.43   Faciamus hominem *ad* imaginem nostram];
B.10.204 Dum tempus [est] operemur bonum *ad* omnes, maxime autem ad domesticos fidei.
B.10.204 Dum tempus [est] operemur bonum ad omnes, maxime autem *ad* domesticos fidei.
B.10.325 And puten [hem] to hir penaunce, *Ad* pristinum statum ire;
B.10.382 Nemo ascendit *ad* celum nisi qui de celo descendit.
B.12.142 Pastores loquebantur *ad* inuicem.
B.13.57   And þanne hadde Pacience a pitaunce, Pro hac orabit *ad* te omnis
B.13.61   Ve vobis qui potentes estis *ad* bibendum vinum.
B.14.131 domine in Ciuitate tua, et *ad* nichilum rediges &c.
B.14.144 De delicijs *ad* delicias difficile est transire.
B.14.180 Conuertimini *ad* me & salui eritis.
B.15.118 totus populus conuertitur *ad* peccandum. Sicut cum videris arborem
B.15.162 [Hic] in enigmate, tunc facie *ad* faciem.
B.17.152 Omnia traham *ad* me ipsum &c–
B.18.111 I drow me in þat derknesse to descendit *ad* inferna
B.18.181 *Ad* vesperum demorabitur fletus & ad matutinum leticia.
B.18.181 Ad vesperum demorabitur fletus & *ad* matutinum leticia.
B.18.244 "Iube me venire *ad* te super aquas."
B.19.479 Omnia tua sunt *ad* defendendum set non ad deprehendendum.'
B.19.479 Omnia tua sunt ad defendendum set non *ad* deprehendendum.'
C. 3.477 Non leuabit gens contra gentem gladium nec excercebuntur vltra *ad* prelium.
C. 5.171 And potte ȝow to ȝoure penaunce, *ad* pristinum statum ire,

C.11.22 Ducunt in bonis dies suos & in fin[e] descendunt *ad* infernum.
C.11.207 Nemo ascendit *ad* celum nisi qui de celo descendit.
C.12.55 /O vos omnes sicientes venite *ad* aquas
C.14.86 Pastores loquebantur *ad* inuicem &c.
C.15.60 And brouhte forth a pytaunce, was pro h[a]c orabit [*ad* te] omnis
C.15.65 Ve vobis qui p[o]tentes estis *ad* bibendum vinum–
C.16.201 dum declina[t] de malo *ad* bonum liberum Arbitrium est;
C.16.273 totus populus conuertitur *ad* peccandum. Sicut cum videri[s]
C.16.296 Hic in enigmate, tunc facie *ad* faciem.
C.19.127 Omnia traham *ad* me ipsum–
C.20.114 Y [d]row [me] in þat derkenesse to descendit *ad* inferna
C.20.184 *Ad* vesperum demorabitur fletus & ad mat[u]tinum leticia.
C.20.184 Ad vesperum demorabitur fletus & *ad* mat[u]tinum leticia.
C.20.253 "Domine, iube me venire *ad* te."
C.21.479 Omnia [tua sunt] *ad* defendendum sed non ad deprehendendum.'
C.21.479 Omnia [tua sunt] ad defendendum sed non *ad* deprehendendum.'

ade B 1; C 1
B. 5.483 O felix culpa, o necessarium peccatum *Ade* &c.
C. 7.125 O felix culpa, [o] necessarium peccatum *Ade*.

adimplere B 1; C 1
B.18.349 Non veni soluere legem set *adimplere*.
C.20.395 Non veni soluere legem set *adimplere*.

adipe B 1; C 1
B.15.318 pabulum commune sufficiat; ex *adipe* prodijt iniquitas tua.
C.17.53 pabulum comune sufficiat; Ex *adipe* prodiit iniquitas tua.

adorant B 1
B.15.81 Confundantur omnes qui *adorant* sculptilia; Et alibi, Vt quid diligitis

adorauit C 1
C.18.241 Tres vidit & vnum *adorauit*.

adquiret B 1; C 1
B. 3.336 Honorem *adquiret* qui dat munera &c.'
C. 3.488 Honorem *adquiret* qui dat munera.'

aduenit B 1; C 2
B.12.286 *Aduenit* ignis diuinus non comburens set illuminans &c.
C.14.208 *A[d]uenit* ignis diuinus non comburens set illuminans &c.
C.15.229 Habundancia panis & vini turpissimum peccatum *aduenit*.

agas B 1; C 1
B.Pr.134 Hoc quod *agas* melius, iustus es, esto pius!
C.Pr.155 Hoc vt *agas* melius, iustus es, esto pius!

agentes B 1; C 1
B.13.426 Consencientes & *agentes* pari pena punientur.
C. 7.86 Consencientes & *agentes* pari pena punientur.

agit A 1
A.10.94 Qui *agit* contra conscientiam &c.

agite B 1; C 1
B.13.49 He sette a sour loof toforn vs and seide '*Agite* penitenciam',
C.15.55 He sette a sour loef and saide, '*Agite* penitenciam',

agnus B 2; C 2
B.16.252 Ecce *agnus* dei &c.'
B.18.324 Songen seint Iohanes song, Ecce *agnus* dei.
C.18.268 Ecce *Agnus* dei.'
C.20.367 Songen seynt Iohann[es songe], ecce *agnus* dei.

agro C 1
C. 5.98 Simile est regnum celorum thesauro abscondito in *agro*;

agunt A 1; B 1
A.11.23 Quare via impiorum p[ros]peratur, [bene] est omnibus qui praue *agunt* & inique?
B.10.25 Quare impij viuunt? bene est omnibus qui preuaricantur & inique *agunt*?

alibi B 9; C 8
B. 5.486 Et *alibi*, Qui manet in caritate in deo manet & deus in eo.
B. 9.67 Amen dico vobis, nescio vos; Et *alibi*, Et dimisi eos secundum desideria
B. 9.94 *alibi*, Perniciosus dispensator est qui res pauperum christi inutiliter
B.12.293 Et *alibi*, si ambulauero in medio vmbre mortis.
B.13.312 Si hominibus placerem christi seruus non essem; Et *alibi*, Nemo potest
B.13.330 labor et dol[or]; Et *alibi*, Filij hominum dentes eorum arma & sagitte
B.14.46 Quodcumque pecieritis a patre in nomine meo &c; Et *alibi*, Non in solo pane
B.14.131 Dormierunt & nichil inuenerunt; [et *alibi*], velud sompn[i]um
B.15.81 Confundantur omnes qui adorant sculptilia; Et *alibi*, Vt quid diligitis

C. 5.60 Dominus pars hereditatis mee &c. Et *alibi*: clemencia non constringit.
C. 9.163 Iunior fui, [et]enim senui; e[t] *alibi*: infirmata est vertus mea paupertate.
C.10.244 Numquam collig[unt] de spinis vuas; Et *Alibi*: Bon[a] Arbor
C.11.23 Et *alibi*: ecce ip[s]i peccatores, habundantes &c.
C.13.224 Philosophus esses si tacuisses; & *alibi*: Locutum me aliquando
C.15.244 vobis. Et *alibi*: Non in solo pane viuit homo &c.'
C.15.306 dormierunt & nichil inuenerunt &c; Et *alibi*: velud sompn[i]um
C.17.40 Videte ne furtum sit: & *alibi*: meli[u]s est mori quam male viuere &c.

alienam B 1; C 1
B.15.530 Nolite mittere falsem in messem *alienam*.
C.17.280 Nolite mittere falcem in messem *alienam* &c.

aliquando C 1
C.13.224 Philosophus esses si tacuisses; & alibi: Locutum me *aliquando*

aliquis B 1
B.12.69 Nescit *aliquis* vnde venit aut quo vadit &c.

alter B 2; C 2
B. 6.221 *Alter* alterius onera portate.
B.11.211 *Alter* alterius onera portate.
C. 8.230 *Alter* alterius onera portate.
C.13.78 *Alter* alterius onera portate.

alteram C 1
C. 4.188 Audiatis *alteram* partem amonges aldremen and comeneres,

alterius B 3; C 3
B. 5.269 Seruus es *alterius* [cum] fercula pinguia queris;
B. 6.221 Alter *alterius* onera portate.
B.11.211 Alter *alterius* onera portate.
C. 6.293 Seruus [es] *alterius* cum fercula pingu[i]a queris;
C. 8.230 Alter *alterius* onera portate.
C.13.78 Alter *alterius* onera portate.

altilia B 1
B.15.464 Ecce *altilia* mea & omnia parata sunt;

altissimo B 2; C 1
B. 1.119 Ponam pedem in aquilone & similis ero *altissimo*.
B.15.51 Ponam pedem meum in aquilone & similis ero *altissimo*.
C. 1.111 Ponam pedem meum in Aquilone & similis ero *altissimo*.'

amare B 1
B.10.342 Nichil iniquius quam *amare* pecuniam;

amaritudine B 1; C 1
B.13.330 Cuius malediccione os plenum est & *amaritudine*; sub lingua eius
C. 6.76 Cuius maledictione os plenum est & *amaritudine*; sub lingua eius

amat B 2; C 2
B.14.60 Si quis *amat* christum mundum non diligit istum.
B.15.39 dum sentit sensus est; dum *amat* Amor est; dum negat vel consentit
C.15.259 Si quis *amat* christum mundum non diligit istum.
C.16.201 dum sentit sensus est; dum *Amat* Amor est; dum declina[t] de malo

ambiciosa B 1; C 1
B.15.157 Non inflatur, non est *ambiciosa*, non querit que sua sunt–
C.16.291 Non inflatur, non est *Ambiciosa*.

ambo B 1
B.10.281 Dum cecus ducit cecum *ambo* in foueam cadunt.

ambula B 1
B.13.254 quod autem habeo tibi do; in nomine domini surge et *amb[ula]*.

ambulabat B 1; C 1
B. 5.494 Populus qui *ambulabat* in tenebris vidit lucem magnam.
C. 7.133 Populus qui *ambulabat* in tenebris vidit lucem magnam &c.

ambulant C 1
C.18.141 Claudi *Ambulant*, leprosi mundantur,

ambulauero A 1; B 2
A. 8.102 & seide 'Si *ambulauero* in medio umbre mortis
B. 7.120 And seide, 'Si *ambulauero* in medio vmbre mortis
B.12.293 Et alibi, si *ambulauero* in medio vmbre mortis.

amen A 6; B 7; C 6
A. 3.64 *Amen* Amen [dico vobis receperunt mercedem suam].
A. 3.64 Amen *Amen* [dico vobis receperunt mercedem suam].
A. 3.233 *Amen* Amen rec[eperu]nt mercedem suam.
A. 3.233 Amen *Amen* rec[eperu]nt mercedem suam.
A. 7.78 In dei nomine *Amen* I make it myseluen:
A.12.117 Þat barn bryng vs to blys þat bled vpon þe rode *amen*.
B. 3.254 *Amen* amen Rec[eperu]nt mercedem suam.
B. 3.254 Amen *amen* Rec[eperu]nt mercedem suam.
B. 5.55 *Amen* dico vobis nescio vos.
B. 6.86 In dei nomine, *amen*. I make it myselue.

B. 9.67   *Amen* dico vobis, nescio vos; Et alibi, Et dimisi eos secundum desideria
B.15.613   Carnis resurreccionem et vitam eternam *amen*.'
B.17.253   *Amen* dico vobis, nescio vos &c.
C. 3.312   *Amen* Amen, Matheu seyth, Mercedem suam rec[e]p[er]unt.
C. 3.312   Amen *Amen*, Matheu seyth, Mercedem suam rec[e]p[er]unt.
C. 8.95   In dei nomine, *Amen*: y make hit mysulue.
C.13.98   *Amen* dico vobis quia hec vidua paupercula &c.
C.17.320   Carnis resurect[i]o[n]em & vitam eternam *amen*.'
C.19.219   *Amen* dico vobis, nescio vos.

amice B 1; C 1
B. 6.47   *Amice*, ascende superius.
C. 8.44   *Amice*, ascende superius.

amicos A 1; B 2; C 3
A. 7.212   Facite vobis *amicos*.'
B. 6.228   Facite vo[bis] *amicos* de mammona iniquitatis.
B.11.191   Cum facitis conuiuia nolite inuitare *amicos*.
C. 8.234   Facite vobis *Amicos* de mammona iniquitatis.'
C.12.103   Cum facitis conuiuia nolite vocare *amicos* &c.
C.19.250   Facite vobis *amicos* de mammona iniquitatis.

amicum C 1
C.17.140   propter mandatum, id est propter legem; & *Amicum* propter Amorem,

amicus A 1; B 1
A.11.147   Qui sim[u]lat verbis, nec corde est fidus *amicus*,
B.10.195   Qui simulat verbis [nec] corde est fidus *amicus*,

amor B 3; C 3
B.15.34   Thanne is lele loue my name, and in latyn *Amor*;
B.15.39   dum sentit sensus est; dum amat *Amor* est; dum negat vel consentit
B.18.408   Post inimicicias [clarior est et *amor*].
C.16.196   Thenne is lele loue my name and in latyn *Amor*;
C.16.201   dum sentit sensus est; dum Amat *Amor* est; dum declina[t] de malo
C.20.451   Post inimicicias Clarior est & *Amor*.

amorem C 1
C.17.140   propter mandatum, id est propter legem; & Amicum propter *Amorem*,

amplius C 1
C. 7.147   omnes iniquitate[s] eius non recordabor *ampli[us]*.

ancilla B 1; C 1
B.16.99   Ecce *ancilla* domini; fiat michi [secundum verbum tuum]'.
C.18.132   Ecce *Ancilla* domini &c.'

anima A 4; B 8; C 9
A.10.7   *Anima* he[o] ha[tte]; to hire [haþ] enuye
A.10.44   Þat is *Anima*, þat oueral in þe body wandriþ,
A.10.47   Inwyt is þe [allie] þat *anima* desiriþ,
A.10.50   For þoruȝ his connyng is kept caro & *anima*
B. 9.7   *Anima* she hatte; [to hir haþ enuye]
B. 9.16   [By his leryng is lad þat lady *Anima*].
B. 9.23   Thise [sixe] ben set to [saue] þis lady *anima*
B. 9.55   For loue of þe lady *anima* þat lif is ynempned.
B. 9.59   What *anima* is leef or looþ; he l[e]t hire at his wille,
B.15.23   'The whiles I quykne þe cors', quod he, 'called am I *anima*;
B.15.39   *Anima* pro diuersis accionibus diuersa nomina sortitur: dum viuificat
C.15.39   dum viuificat corpus *anima* est; dum vult animus est; dum scit mens
C.10.134   *Anima* she hatte; to here hath enuye
C.10.142   And by his leryng is lad þat lady *Anima*.
C.10.149   Thise fyue ben sette for to saue *Anima*
C.10.172   By loue and by leute, þerby lyueth *anima*
C.10.174   Inwit is in þe heued and *anima* in herte
C.12.215   O stulte, ista nocte *anima* tua egredi[e]tur; tezaurisat & ignorat &c.
C.16.183   And whiles y quyke þe cors ycald am y *Anima*;
C.16.201   *Anima* pro diuersis [acc]ionibus diuersa nomina sortitur: dum
C.16.201   dum [v]i[u]ificat corpus *Anima* est; dum vult animus est; [dum scit

animal B 1
B.14.63   Aperis tu manum tuam & imples omne *animal* benediccione.

animalium B 1; C 1
B.15.318   brutorum *animalium* natura te condempnat, quia cum eis pabulum
C.17.53   Brutorum *Animalium* natura te condempnat, quia cum [eis] pabulum

animam B 2; C 2
B. 3.350   *Animam* autem aufert accipientium &c.
B.15.497   Bonus pastor *animam* suam ponit &c.
C. 3.498   *Animam* [autem] aufert Accipiencium:
C.17.193   Bonus Pastor *animam* suam ponit pro ouibus suis &c.

animarum B 1
B.14.286   /And Contricion confort and cura *animarum*;

animo B 1; C 1
B.19.296   Esto forti *animo* cum sis dampnatus inique.
C.21.296   Esto forti *Animo* cum sis dampnatus inique.

animus B 2; C 2
B.15.24   And whan I wilne and wolde *animus* ich hatte;
B.15.39   dum viuificat corpus anima est; dum vult *animus* est; dum scit mens
C.16.184   And when y wilne and wolde *Animus* y hatte;
C.16.201   dum [v]i[u]ificat corpus Anima est; dum vult *animus* est; [dum scit

ante A 1; B 3; C 3
A.11.296   Dum steter[it]is *ante* [reges &] presides nolite cogitare,
B. 4.37   Non est timor dei *ante* oculos eorum &c.
B.10.450   "[D]um steteritis *ante* Reges & presides [nolite cogitare]:
B.15.318   aut mugiet bos cum *ante* plenum presepe steterit? brutorum
C. 4.36   non est timor dei *ante* oculos eorum.
C.11.275   "Dum steteritis *ante* Reges vel presides &c:
C.17.53   aut mugiet bos cum *ante* plenum presepe steterit? Brutorum

antelate C 1
C. 3.344   Quia *antelate* rei recordatiuum est–

aperis B 1; C 2
B.14.63   *Aperis* tu manum tuam & imples omne animal benediccione.
C.15.262   *Aperis* tu manum tuam &c.
C.16.320   Oen *aperis*-tu-manum alle thynges hym fyndeth;

appare B 1
B.10.261   *Appare* quod es vel esto quod appares;

appares B 1
B.10.261   Appare quod es vel esto quod *appares*;

appetitus B 1; C 1
B.15.63   Sciencie *appetitus* hominem inmortalitatis gloria[m] spoliauit.
C.16.225   Sciencie *appetitus* hominem inmortalitatis gloriam spoliauit.

apud B 2; C 2
B.12.138   Sapiencia huius mundi stulticia est *apud* deum.
B.13.39   Edentes & bibentes que *apud* eos sunt.
C.14.83   Sapiencia huius mundi stul[t]icia est *apud* deum.
C.15.44   Edentes & bibentes que *apud* eos sunt &c.

aquas B 1; C 1
B.18.244   "Iube me venire ad te super *aquas*."
C.12.55   /O vos omnes sicientes venite ad *aquas*

aquilone B 2; C 2
B. 1.119   Ponam pedem in *aquilone* & similis ero altissimo.
B.15.51   Ponam pedem meum in *aquilone* & similis ero altissimo.
C. 1.111   Ponam pedem meum in *Aquilone* & similis ero altissimo.'
C.16.213   Ponam pedem meum in *Aquilone* &c.

aquilonis C 1
C. 1.113   Luppen alofte [in lateribus *Aquilonis*]

arbitrium B 4; C 13
B.16.16   And liberum *arbitrium* haþ þe lond [to] ferme,
B.16.46   Ac liberum *arbitrium* letteþ hym som tyme,
B.16.47   est idem qui peccat per liberum *arbitrium* non repugnat.
B.16.50   Thanne liberum *arbitrium* laccheþ þe [þridde] plan[k]e
C.16.158   Thenne hadde Actyf a ledare þat hihte lib[e]rum *arbitrium*;
C.16.162   Thenne hadde y wonder what he was, þat l[i]berum *Arbitrium*,
C.16.165   'Leue liberum *arbitrium*,' quod y, 'of what lond ar ȝe?
C.16.173   'Whareof serue ȝe,' y saide, 'sir liberum *arbitrium*?'
C.16.182   And so is man þat hath his mynde myd liberum *Arbitrium*.
C.16.194   Thenne am y liberum *Arbitrium*, as le[tt]red men telleth;
C.16.201   dum declina[t] de malo ad bonum liberum *Arbitrium* est;
C.18.1   'Leue liberum *Arbitrium*,' quod y, 'y leue, as y hope,
C.18.3   Thenne louh liberum *Arbitrium* and ladde me forth with tales
C.18.104   'Leue liberum *Arbitrium*, lat some lyf hit shake.'
C.18.137   Ac liberum *Arbitrium* lechecraeft hym tauhte
C.18.179   In inwit and in alle wittes aftur liberum *Arbitrium*
C.20.20   'Liberum dei *Arbitrium* for loue hath vndertake

arbor B 1; C 2
B. 2.27   Qualis pater talis filius: Bon[a] *arbor* bonum fructum facit.
C. 2.29   Bona *arbor* bonum fructum facit.
C.10.244   Numquam collig[unt] de spinis vuas; Et Alibi: Bon[a] *Arbor*

arborem B 1; C 1
B.15.118   Sicut cum videris *arborem* pallidam & marcidam intelligis quod
C.16.273   Sicut cum videri[s] *Arborem* pallidam & marcidam intelligis quod

archa arca B 3; C 4
B.10.288   *Archa* dei myshapped and Ely brak his nekke.
B.12.113   *Archa* dei, in þe olde lawe, leuytes it kepten;
B.12.119   That wiþ *archa* dei [wenten] in [worship and reuerence]

C.Pr.108 Thei were discomfited in batayle and losten *Archa* domini
C.Pr.112 Were disconfit in batayle and *Archa* domini lorn
C.11.244 For *Archa* Noe, nymeth hede, ys no more to mene
C.14.58 *Arca* dei in þe olde lawe leuytes hit kepte;

arcana archana A 1; B 1; C 1
A.12.22 Audiui *archan[a* uerba] que non licet homini loqui.
B.18.395 Audiui *archana* verba que non licet homini loqui.
C.20.438 Audiui *arcana* verba que non licet homini loqui.

argentum B 1; C 1
B.13.254 *Argentum* & aurum non est michi; quod autem habeo tibi do; in
nomine
C.15.224 *Argentum* & Aurum non est michi; quod [autem] habeo tibi do &c.

arguam B 1; C 1
B.10.291 Existimasti inique quod ero tui similis; *arguam* te & statuam contra
faciem
C.12.29 Existimasti inique quod ero t[u]i similis; *Arguam* te & statuam

arguas C 1
C.20.435 Domine ne in furore tuo *Arguas* me &c–

argue B 1
B.11.88 Non oderis fratres secrete in corde tuo set publice *argue* illos.

arma B 1; C 1
B.13.330 labor et dol[or]; Et alibi, Filij hominum dentes eorum *arma* &
sagitte
C. 6.76 labor & dolor. Filij hominum dentes eorum *Arma* & sagitte

arrare C 1
C. 8.245 Piger propter frigus noluit *arrare*; mendicabi[t] in yeme & non
dabitur ei”.

ars A 1; B 2; C 2
A.11.148 [Tu quoque fac simile: sic *ars* deluditur arte].
B.10.196 Tu quoque fac simile; sic *ars* deluditur arte.
B.18.162 *Ars* vt artem falleret.'
C.20.165 *Ars* vt Artem falleret.'
C.20.392 *Ars* vt Artem falleret.

arte A 1; B 1
A.11.148 [Tu quoque fac simile: sic ars deluditur *arte*].
B.10.196 Tu quoque fac simile; sic ars deluditur *arte*.

artem B 1; C 2
B.18.162 Ars vt *artem* falleret.'
C.20.165 Ars vt *Artem* falleret.'
C.20.392 Ars vt *Artem* falleret.

ascende B 1; C 1
B. 6.47 Amice, *ascende* superius.
C. 8.44 Amice, *ascende* superius.

ascendet A 1
A.11.263 Nemo *ascendet* ad celum nisi qui de celo descendit.

ascendit B 1; C 1
B.10.382 Nemo *ascendit* ad celum nisi qui de celo descendit.
C.11.207 Nemo *ascendit* ad celum nisi qui de celo descendit.

atque B 1; C 1
B.10.436 [Sunt] iusti *atque* sapientes, & opera eorum in manu dei sunt &c.
C.11.271 Sunt iusti *atque* sapientes & opera eorum in manu dei sunt &c.

attollite B 1; C 1
B.18.262 *Attollite* portas.
C.20.270 *Attollite* portas &c.'

audiatis C 1
C. 4.188 *Audiatis* alteram partem amonges aldremen and comeneres,

audiui A 1; B 1; C 1
A.12.22 *Audiui* archan[a uerba] que non licet homini loqui.
B.18.395 *Audiui* archana verba que non licet homini loqui.
C.20.438 *Audiui* arcana verba que non licet homini loqui.

audiuimus A 1; B 2; C 1
A.11.55 Ecce *audiuimus* eam in effrata, inuenimus eam in campis silue.
B.10.69 Ecce *audiuimus* eam in effrata; inuenimus eam in campis silue.
B.15.490 [Ecce *audiuimus* e[a]m in effrata &c].
C.11.49 Ecce *Audiuimus* eam in Effrata; [inuenimus eam in campis silue].

auferetur B 1; C 1
B.11.255 Maria optimam partem elegit que non [*auferetur* ab ea].
C.12.141 Maria optimam partem elegit que non [*auferetur* ab ea].

aufert B 1; C 1
B. 3.350 Animam autem *aufert* accipientium &c.
C. 3.498 Animam [autem] *aufert* Accipiencium:

aurum B 1; C 1
B.13.254 Argentum & *aurum* non est michi; quod autem habeo tibi do; in
nomine
C.15.224 Argentum & *Aurum* non est michi; quod [autem] habeo tibi do &c.

aut B 2; C 1
B.12.69 Nescit aliquis vnde venit *aut* quo vadit &c.
B.15.318 *aut* mugiet bos cum ante plenum presepe steterit? brutorum
C.17.53 *aut* mugiet bos cum ante plenum presepe steterit? Brutorum

autem A 1; B 9; C 5
A.11.245 Dum tempus est operemur bonum ad omnes, maxime *autem* ad
B. 3.350 Animam *autem* aufert accipientium &c.
B. 9.109 Inquirentes *autem* dominum non minuentur omni bono.
B.10.29 Que perfecisti destruxerunt; iustus *autem* &c.
B.10.89 Si tibi sit copia habundanter tribue; si *autem* exiguum illud
impertiri stude
B.10.204 Dum tempus [est] operemur bonum ad omnes, maxime *autem* ad
domesticos fidei.
B.11.282 Inquirentes *autem* dominum non minuentur omni bono.
B.13.254 Argentum & aurum non est michi; quod *autem* habeo tibi do; in
nomine
B.15.118 Si *autem* corruptum fuerit omnium fides marcida est. Si
B.15.343 accipis pocius das quam accipis; Si *autem* non eges & accipis
rapis.
C. 3.498 Animam [*autem*] aufert Accipiencium:
C.10.202 Inquirentes *autem* dominum [non] minuentur omni bono.
C.11.69 Si tibi sit copia habundanter tribue; Si *Autem* exiguum illud
C.15.224 Argentum & Aurum non est michi; quod [*autem*] habeo tibi do &c.
C.16.273 Si *Autem* corupt[um] fuerit omnium f[i]des marcida est. Si

aue B 2; C 2
B.16.151 '*Aue*, raby', quod þat Ribaud, and ri3t to hym he yede
B.18.50 '*Aue*, raby', quod þat rybaud and þrew reedes at hym.
C.18.168 '*Aue* raby,' quod th[at] ribaud[e]; and riht til hym [he] 3ede
C.20.50 '*Aue*, raby,' quod þat ribaud, and redes shotte vp to his yes.

baculi C 1
C.17.285 In *baculi* forma sit, presul, hec tibi norma;

baculum B 1; C 1
B.10.333 Quomodo cessauit exactor, quieuit tributum? contriuit dominus
baculum
C. 5.177 Contriuit dominus *bac[u]lum* impiorum, virga[m] d[omi]nancium,

baculus A 1; B 1
A.10.87 Virga tua & *baculus* tuus ipsa me consolata sunt.
B.12.13 Virga tua & *baculus* tuus, ipsa me consolata sunt:

baptizatus bapti3atus A 1; B 1; C 2
A.11.234 Qui crediderit et *baptizatus* fuerit saluus erit.'
B.11.124 Qui crediderit & *bapti3atus* fuerit &c.
C.12.59 Qui crediderit & *bapti3atus* fuerit &c.
C.13.87 Qui crediderit & *baptizatus* fuerit &c–

beacius C 1
C.14.16 *Beacius* est dare quam petere.

beati A 1; B 7; C 3
A. 7.234 The sauter seiþ in þe salme of *Beati* omnes:
B. 5.418 Bettre þan in Beatus vir or in *Beati* omnes
B. 5.507 And blew it wiþ *Beati* quorum remisse sunt iniquitates,
B. 6.250 The Sauter seiþ, in þe psalme of *Beati* omnes,
B.12.177 *Beati* quorum remisse sunt iniquitates & quorum tecta sunt &c.
B.13.53 /And he brou3te vs of *Beati* quorum of Beatus virres makyng,
B.14.215 *Beati* pauperes quoniam ipsorum est regnum celorum.
B.19.181 *Beati* qui non viderunt [& crediderunt].
C. 7.152 And Blewe hit with *beati* quorum remisse sunt iniquitates &
C.14.117 *Beati* quorum remisse sunt iniquitates &c.
C.21.181 *Beati* qui non viderunt & crediderunt.”

beatus B 5; C 2
B. 5.418 Bettre þan in *Beatus* vir or in Beati omnes
B.10.326 And Barons wiþ Erles beten hem þoru3 *Beatus* virres techyng;
B.13.53 /And he brou3te vs of Beati quorum of *Beatus* virres makyng,
B.15.60 “*Beatus* est”, seiþ Seint Bernard, “qui scripturas legit
B.15.234 *Beatus* est diues qui &c.
C.16.222 “*Beatus*,” saith seynt Bernard, “qui scripturas legit
C.16.359 *Beatus* est diues sine macula.

bene A 1; B 3; C 1
A.11.23 Quare via impiorum p[ros]peratur, [*bene*] est omnibus qui praue
B.10.25 Quare impij viuunt? *bene* est omnibus qui preuaricantur & inique
agunt
B.12.50 Sunt homines nequam, *bene* de virtute loquentes.
B.13.249 In nomine meo demonia e[j]icient & super egros manus imponent
& *bene*
C.15.221 Super egros manus [in]pone[nt] & *bene* habebunt &c–

benediccione B 1
B.14.63   Aperis tu manum tuam & imples omne animal *benediccione*.

benedicite B 1; C 1
B. 5.390   He bigan *Benedicite* with a bolk and his brest knokked,
C. 7.6   A bigan *benedicite* with a bolk and his breste knokkede,

benedictus B 1; C 1
B.18.17   *Benedictus* qui venit in nomine domini.
C.20.15   *Benedictus* qui venit in nomine domini.

bibendum B 1; C 1
B.13.61   Ve vobis qui potentes estis ad *bibendum* vinum.
C.15.65   Ve vobis qui p[o]tentes estis ad *bibendum* vinum–

bibentes B 1; C 1
B.13.39   Edentes & *bibentes* que apud eos sunt.
C.15.44   Edentes & *bibentes* que apud eos sunt &c.

bisso C 1
C.19.240   Epulabatur splendide & induebatur *bisso* &c.

bona A 1; B 3; C 5
A. 8.95   Et qui *bona* egerunt ibunt in vitam eternam;
B. 2.27   Qualis pater talis filius: *Bon[a]* arbor bonum fructum facit.
B. 7.113   Et qui *bona* egerunt ibunt in vitam eternam;
B.11.398   Et vidit deus cuncta que fecerat & erant valde *bona*.
C. 2.29   *Bona* arbor bonum fructum facit.
C. 9.287   Et qui *bona* egerunt ibunt in vitam eternam;
C.10.244   Numquam collig[unt] de spinis vuas; Et Alibi: *Bon[a]* Arbor
C.12.119   Et qui *bona* egerunt, ibunt &c.
C.13.17   And for a song in his sorwe, "si *bona* accepimus a domino &c,

bonis C 1
C.11.22   Ducunt in *bonis* dies suos & in fin[e] descendunt ad infernum.

bono B 2; C 1
B. 9.109   Inquirentes autem dominum non minuentur omni *bono*.
B.11.282   Inquirentes autem dominum non minuentur omni *bono*.
C.10.202   Inquirentes autem dominum [non] minuentur omni *bono*.

bonorum B 1
B.13.195   Than ʒacheus for he seide "dimidium *bonorum* meorum do
             pauperibus",

bonum A 5; B 11; C 14
A. 4.127   And bad Nullum [*bonum* be] irremuneratum.
A.11.192   Ecce quam *bonum* & quam iocundum habitare Fratres in vnum.
A.11.245   Dum tempus est operemur *bonum* ad omnes, maxime autem ad
A.12.52   Til ʒe come to þe burg[h] quod *bonum* est tenete.
A.12.57   And ere I cam to þe court quod *bonum* est tenete
B. 2.27   Qualis pater talis filius: *Bon[a]* arbor bonum fructum facit.
B. 3.330   For Melius est *bonum* nomen quam diuicie multe.'
B. 3.343   Quod *bonum* est tenete; truþe þat text made.
B. 4.144   And bad Nullum *bonum* be irremuneratum.
B. 9.194   *Bonum* est vt vnusquisque vxorem suam habeat propter
             fornicacionem.
B.10.204   Dum tempus [est] operemur *bonum* ad omnes, maxime autem ad
             domesticos fidei.
B.14.276   'Paupertas,' quod Pacience, 'est odibile *bonum*, Remocio curarum,
B.14.287   Ergo paupertas est odibile *bonum*.
B.15.55   And seiþ, Sicut qui mel comedit multum non est ei *bonum*, Sic qui
B.15.118   Sicut de templo omne *bonum* progreditur, sic de templo omne
B.18.423   Ecce quam *bonum* & quam iocundum &c.
C. 2.29   Bona arbor *bonum* fructum facit.
C. 3.483   [For] melius est *bonum* nomen quam diuicie multe.'
C. 3.495   Quod *bonum* est tenete, a tixst of treuthe [m]akynge.
C. 4.141   And bad nullum *bonum* be irremuneratum.
C.10.244   Numquam collig[unt] de spinis vuas; Et Alibi: Bon[a] Arbor
C.10.293   *Bonum* est [vt] vnusquisque vx[or]em suam habeat propter
             fornicacionem.
C.16.116   'Paupertas,' quod pacience, 'est odibile *bonum*, Remocio curarum,
C.16.122   [Ergo paupertas est odibile *bonum*].
C.16.201   dum declina[t] de malo ad *bonum* liberum Arbitrium est;
C.16.217   And sayth, sicut qui mel comedit multum non est ei *bonum*; Sic
C.16.273   Sicut de templo omne *bonum* progreditur, sic de templo omne
C.20.234   Omnia probate; quod *bonum* est tenete.
C.20.433   As nullum malum inpunitum & nullum *bonum* irremuneratum–
C.20.466   Ecce quam *bonum* & quam iocundum &c.

bonus B 2; C 3
B.10.447   For soþest word þat euer god seide was þo he seide Nemo *bonus*.
B.15.497   *Bonus* pastor animam suam ponit &c.
C.15.135   Nemo *bonus*–
C.17.193   *Bonus* Pastor animam suam ponit pro ouibus suis &c.
C.17.291   *Bonus* pastor &c,

bos B 1; C 1
B.15.318   aut mugiet *bos* cum ante plenum presepe steterit? brutorum
C.17.53   aut mugiet *bos* cum ante plenum presepe steterit? Brutorum

breuis C 1
C.11.295   *Breuis* oratio penetrat celum.

brutorum B 1; C 1
B.15.318   *brutorum* animalium natura te condempnat, quia cum eis pabulum
C.17.53   *Brutorum* Animalium natura te condempnat, quia cum [eis]
             pabulum

cadens C 1
C.12.179   Nisi granum frumenti *cadens* in terram mortuum fuerit &c.

cadit A 1; B 1; C 1
A. 9.16   'Sepcies in die *cadit* iustus.
B. 8.20   'Sepcies in die *cadit* Iustus.
C.10.21   And saide, 'sothly sepcies in die *ca[d]it* iust[u]s,

cadunt B 1
B.10.281   Dum cecus ducit cecum ambo in foueam *cadunt*.

calumpnia B 2; C 2
B.14.276   possessio sine *calumpnia*, donum dei, sanit[atis] mater,
B.14.296   Possessio sine *calumpnia*.
C.16.116   possessio sine *calumpnia*, donum dei, sanitatis mater,
C.16.132   [Possessio sine *calumpnia*].

camelus C 1
C.11.201   Ita possibile est diuiti intrare in regn[um] celorum sicut *camelus*
             &c.

campis A 1; B 1; C 1
A.11.55   Ecce audiuimus eam in effrata, inuenimus eam in *campis* silue.
B.10.69   Ecce audiuimus eam in effrata; inuenimus eam in *campis* silue.
C.11.49   Ecce Audiuimus eam in Effrata; [inuenimus eam in *campis* silue].

canes B 1
B.10.293   *Canes* non valentes latrare,

cantabit B 1
B.14.307   *Cantabit* paupertas coram latrone viato[r],

capias C 1
C. 4.164   A shyreues Clerk cryede, 'a! *capias* mede

captiuam B 1; C 1
B. 5.490   *Captiuam* duxit captiuitatem.
C. 7.130   *Capti[u]am* duxi[t] captiuitatem.

captiuitatem B 1; C 1
B. 5.490   Captiuam duxit *captiuitatem*.
C. 7.130   Capti[u]am duxi[t] *captiuitatem*.

carceratis C 1
C. 4.165   Et saluo custodias set non cum *carcer[a]tis*.'

caristiam B 1
B.14.73   Ac vnkyndenesse *caristiam* makeþ amonges cristen peple,

caritas A 1; B 3; C 7
A. 1.84   I do it on Deus *caritas* to deme þe soþe.
B. 1.86   I do it on Deus *caritas* to deme þe soþe.
B.12.29   Fides, spes, *caritas*, et maior horum &c.
B.13.163   *Caritas* nichil timet.
C. 1.82   I do it [o]n deus *caritas* to deme þe sothe.
C.14.14   Is ycalde *Caritas*, kynde loue an engelysche,
C.15.164   *Caritas* expellit omne[m] timorem.
C.17.5   *Caritas* omnia s[u]ffert.
C.18.14   The whiche is *Caritas* ykald, Cristes oune fode,
C.18.32   Couetyse cometh of þat wynde and *Caritas* hit abiteth
C.18.39   And al forb[i]t *Caritas* rihte to þe bare stalke.

caritate B 2; C 1
B. 5.486   Et alibi, Qui manet in *caritate* in deo manet & deus in eo.
B. 9.65   Qui manet in *caritate* in deo manet &c.
C. 3.403   Qui in *caritate* manet in deo manet et deus in eo.

caritatem C 1
C.17.140   id est propter *caritatem*.

caritatis B 1
B. 2.35   That he shal lese for hire loue a l[i]ppe of *Caritatis*.

carnis B 6; C 6
B.11.13   Concupiscencia *carnis* men called þe elder mayde
B.11.17   Concupiscencia *carnis* colled me aboute þe nekke
B.11.30   And Concupiscencia *carnis* clene þee forsake–
B.11.40   Concupiscencia *carnis* ne Coueitise of eiʒes
B.11.43   Til Concupiscencia *carnis* acorded alle my werkes.
B.15.613   *Carnis* resurreccionem et vitam eternam amen.'
C.11.172   Concupiscencia *carnis* men calde þ[e] eldre maide
C.11.176   Concupiscencia *Carnis* confortede me o[n] this manere
C.11.189   And Concupiscencia *Carnis* clene the forsake–
C.11.307   Concupiscencia *carnis* [ne coueytise-of-yes]
C.11.310   Til Concupiscencia *Carnis* acorded til al my werkes.

C.17.320   *Carnis* resurect[i]o[n]em & vitam eternam amen.'

caro A 2; B 6; C 5
A.10.38   Þat is þe castel þat kynde made, *caro* it hatte,
A.10.50   For þoruȝ his connyng is kept *caro* & anima
B. 5.500   Verbum *caro* factum est & habitauit in nobis.
B. 9.50   [Th]at is þe Castel þat kynde made; *caro* it hatte,
B.17.110   On my Capul þat highte *caro*–of mankynde I took it–
B.18.407   Culpat *caro*, purgat caro, regnat deus dei caro.
B.18.407   Culpat caro, purgat *caro*, regnat deus dei caro.
B.18.407   Culpat caro, purgat caro, regnat deus dei *caro*.
C. 3.356   He acordeth with crist in kynde, verbum *caro* factum est;
C. 7.140   Verbum *caro* factum est.
C.20.450   Culpat *Caro*, purgat Caro, regnat deus dei Caro.
C.20.450   Culpat Caro, purgat *Caro*, regnat deus dei Caro.
C.20.450   Culpat Caro, purgat Caro, regnat deus dei *Caro*.

castigo B 1
B.12.12   Quem diligo *castigo*.

cathedram A 1; B 1; C 2
A.11.223   Super *cathedram* moisi sederunt principes.
B.10.404   Super *cathedra[m]* Moysi &c.
C. 8.86   Super *Cathedram* moysi sede[runt] &c.
C.11.235   Super *cathedra[m]* Moysi &c.

causam B 1
B.11.286   Iudica me deus & discerne *causam* meam.

cauebis B 1
B.10.266   Si culpare velis culpabilis es[se] *cauebis*;

ceciderit B 1
B.16.25   Cum *ceciderit* iustus non collidetur quia dominus supponit ma[num suam];

ceciderunt C 1
C. 5.172   Hij in curribus & [hij] in equis; ipsi obligati sunt & *ceciderunt*.

cecidit B 1
B.18.360   Et *cecidit* in foueam quam fecit.

cecum B 2; C 1
B.10.281   Dum cecus ducit *cecum* ambo in foueam cadunt.
B.12.185   Dum cecus ducit *cecum* &c.
C.14.124   Dum [c]ecus d[u]cit [c]*ecum* &c.

cecus B 2; C 1
B.10.281   Dum *cecus* ducit cecum ambo in foueam cadunt.
B.12.185   Dum *cecus* ducit cecum &c.
C.14.124   Dum [c]*ecus* d[u]cit [c]ecum &c.

cedencium B 1
B.10.333   impiorum, et virgam dominancium *cedencium* plaga insanabili.

celestia B 1; C 1
B.19.80   Omnia *celestia* terrestria flectantur in hoc nomine Iesu;
C.21.80   Omnia *celestia* terrestria flectantur in hoc nomine iesu;

celestibus C 1
C.14.32   Vultus huius seculi sunt subiecti v[u]ltibus *celestibus*.

celi B 1; C 1
B.14.33   Ne soliciti sitis &c; Volucres *celi* deus pascit &c; pacientes vincunt &c.'
C.18.213   *Celi* enarrant gloriam dei &c.

celis B 1; C 2
B. 7.181   Quodcumque ligaueris super terram erit ligatum & in *celis* &c.
C. 9.327   Quodcumque ligaueris super terram erit ligatum & in *celis*.
C.11.153   patrem meum vid[e]t qui in *celis* est &c.

celo A 1; B 1; C 1
A.11.263   Nemo ascendet ad celum nisi qui de *celo* descendit.
B.10.382   Nemo ascendit ad celum nisi qui de *celo* descendit.
C.11.207   Nemo ascendit ad celum nisi qui de *celo* descendit.

celorum A 1; B 3; C 3
A.11.196   Qui facit & docuerit magnus vocabitur in regno *celorum*.
B.13.118   Qui facit & docuerit magnus vocabitur in regno *celorum*.'
B.14.215   Beati pauperes quoniam ipsorum est regnum *celorum*.
B.15.149   'Nisi efficiamini sicut paruuli non intrabitis in regnum *celorum*.
C. 5.98   Simile est regnum *celorum* thesauro abscondito in agro;
C.11.201   Ita possibile est diuiti intrare in regn[um] *celorum* sicut camelus &c.
C.19.232   Non omnis qui dicit domine, domine intrabit in reg[num] *celorum* &c.

celum A 2; B 2; C 3
A.11.263   Nemo ascendet ad *celum* nisi qui de celo descendit.
A.11.305   Ecce ipsi ydiot[e] rapiunt *celum* vbi nos sapientes
B.10.382   Nemo ascendit ad *celum* nisi qui de celo descendit.

B.10.461   "Ecce ipsi ydiot[e] rapiunt *celum* vbi nos sapientes in inferno mergimur".
C.11.207   Nemo ascendit ad *celum* nisi qui de celo descendit.
C.11.287   "Ecce ips[i] idiote rapiunt *celum* vbi nos sapientes in inferno mergimur".
C.11.295   Breuis oratio penetrat *celum*.

cepit B 1; C 1
B.16.115   Ac [er] he made þe maistrie mestus *cepit* esse
C.18.145   Ac ar he made þat miracle mestus *cepit* esse

certare B 1; C 1
B.11.395   De re que te non molestat noli *certare*.
C.13.196   De re que te non molestat noli *certare*.

cesari A 2; B 2; C 2
A. 1.50   "Reddite *cesari*," quaþ god, "þat cesari befall[iþ],
A. 1.50   "Reddite cesari," quaþ god, "þat *cesari* befall[iþ],
B. 1.52   "Reddite *Cesari*", quod god, "þat Cesari bifalleþ,
B. 1.52   "Reddite Cesari", quod god, "þat *Cesari* bifalleþ,
C. 1.48   "Reddite *cesari*," sayde god, "þat cesar[i] byfalleth
C. 1.48   "Reddite cesari," sayde god, "þat *cesar[i]* byfalleth

cesaris B 1
B. 1.51   "*Cesar[i]s*", þei seiden, "we seen wel echone."

cessabit B 2; C 1
B.15.600   Cum sanctus sanctorum veniat *cessabit* vnxio vestra.
B.18.109   Cum veniat sanctus sanctorum *cessabit* vnxio vestra.'
C.20.112   Cum veniat sanctus sanctorum *cessa[bi]t* &c.'

cessauit B 1
B.10.333   Quomodo *cessauit* exactor, quieuit tributum? contriuit dominus baculum

cesus B 1
B.13.67   Ter *cesus* sum & a iudeis quinquies quadragenas &c–

christi cristi B 6; C 3
B.Pr.133   O qui iura regis *christi* specialia regis,
B. 9.94   Proditor est prelatus cum Iuda qui patrimonium *christi* minus distribuit; Et
B. 9.94   alibi, Perniciosus dispensator est qui res pauperum *christi* inutiliter
B.13.312   Si hominibus placerem *christi* seruus non essem; Et alibi, Nemo potest
B.15.388   As clerkes in Corpus *Christi* feeste syngen and reden
B.17.74   And ladde hym so forþ on Lyard to lex *Christi*, a graunge
C.Pr.154   O qui iura regis *christi* specialia regis,
C. 6.60   Si hominibus placerem *christi* seruus non essem; nemo potest duobus
C.17.120   As Clerkes in corpus *cristi* feste syngen and reden

christo B 1
B.10.359   Si cum *christo* sur[r]existis &c,

christos cristos B 1; C 1
B.12.125   Nolite tangere *christos* meos &c.]
C.14.69   Nolite tangere *cristos* meos &c.

christum B 3; C 3
B.14.60   Si quis amat *christum* mundum non diligit istum.
B.15.610   Lere hem litlum and litlum et in Iesum *Christum* filium,
B.19.161   Sic oportet *Christum* pati & intrare &c;
C.15.259   Si quis Amat *christum* mundum non diligit istum.
C.17.318   Lere hem littelum and littelum [et] in iesum *christum* filium
C.21.161   Sic [oportet] *christum* pati & intrare &c;

christus B 3; C 2
B.15.212   But Piers þe Plowman, Petrus id est *christus*.
B.19.152   *Christus* [rex] resurgens, [and it aroos after],
B.19.160   In ech a compaignie þer she cam, *Christus* resurgens.
C.21.152   *Christus* [rex] resurgens, and hit aroos aftur,
C.21.160   In vch a companye þer he cam, *christus* resurgens.

cibus B 1
B.15.578   Inferte omnes [decimas] in orreum meum vt *cibus* in domo mea.

circuit A 1
A.10.108   Qui *circuit* [omne genus in nullo genere est].

ciuiate B 1
B.14.131   velud sompn[i]um surgencium domine in *Ciuitate* tua,

clamat B 1; C 1
B.19.416   The comune *clamat* cotidie, ech a man til ooþer,
C.21.416   The comu[n]e *clamat* cotidie, vch a man to oþer,

clarior B 2; C 2
B.18.408   *Clarior* est solito post maxima nebula phebus;
B.18.408   Post inimicicias [*clarior* est et amor].
C.20.451   *Clarior* est solito [post maxima nebula phebus];
C.20.451   Post inimicicias *Clarior* est & Amor.

claudi C 1
C.18.141 *Claudi* Ambulant, leprosi mundantur,

clausa B 1; C 1
B. 5.603 Per Euam cun[c]tis *clausa* est et per Mariam virginem [iterum]
          patefacta est;
C. 7.250 Per Euam cun[c]tis *clausa* est & per mariam verginem iterum
          patefacta est &c;

clemencia C 1
C. 5.60 Dominus pars hereditatis mee &c. Et alibi: *clemencia* non
         constringit.

cogitaciones B 1; C 1
B.15.200 Et vidit deus *cogitaciones* eorum.
C.16.340 Et vidit deus *cogitaciones* eorum.

cogitare A 1; B 1
A.11.296 Dum steter[it]is ante [reges &] presides nolite *cogitare*,
B.10.450 "[D]um steteritis ante Reges & presides [nolite *cogitare*]:

cognouerunt C 1
C. 4.36 Contricio & infelicitas in viis eorum et viam pacis non
         cognouerunt;

cognoui A 1
A. 8.123 Quoniam literaturam non *cognoui*, þat miȝte be þi teme.'

collidetur B 1
B.16.25 Cum ceciderit iustus non *collidetur* quia dominus supponit
         ma[num suam];

colligunt B 1; C 1
B. 9.155 Numquam *collig[unt]* de spinis vua[s] nec de tribulis ficus.
C.10.244 Numquam *collig[unt]* de spinis vuas; Et Alibi: Bon[a] Arbor

comata B 1; C 1
B.18.239 [The oostes] in heuene token stella *com[a]ta*
C.20.248 Tho þat weren in heuene token stella *comata*

comburens B 1; C 1
B.12.286 Aduenit ignis diuinus non *comburens* set illuminans &c.
C.14.208 A[d]uenit ignis diuinus non *comburens* set illuminans &c.

comedit B 1; C 1
B.15.55 And seiþ, Sicut qui mel *comedit* multum non est ei bonum, Sic qui
C.16.217 And sayth, sicut qui mel *comedit* multum non est ei bonum; Sic

comeditis B 2; C 2
B.13.45 Vos qui peccata hominum *comeditis*, nisi pro eis lacrimas &
         oraciones
B.13.45 eff[u]deritis, ea que in delicijs *comeditis* in tormentis euometis.
C.15.50 Vos qui peccata hominum *comeditis*, nisi pro eis lacrimas &
         orationes
C.15.50 effuderitis, ea que in deliciis *comeditis* in tor[mentis] euo[metis]
         &c.

commodat B 1
B. 5.243 I haue mo Manoirs þoruȝ Rerages þan þoruȝ Miseretur &
          com[m]odat.

commune comune B 1; C 1
B.15.318 pabulum *commune* sufficiat; ex adipe prodijt iniquitas tua.
C.17.53 pabulum *comune* sufficiat; Ex adipe prodiit iniquitas tua.

concepit A 1; B 1; C 1
A.10.150 *Concepit* dolore[m] & peperit iniquitatem.
B. 9.125 *Concepit* dolore[m] & peperit iniquitatem.
C.10.212 *Concepit* dolore[m] & peperit iniquitatem.

conceptus B 1
B.17.151 Qui *conceptus* est de spiritu sancto &c.

concupiscencia B 5; C 5
B.11.13 *Concupiscencia* carnis men called þe elder mayde
B.11.17 *Concupiscencia* carnis colled me aboute þe nekke
B.11.30 And *Concupiscencia* carnis clene þee forsake–
B.11.40 *Concupiscencia* carnis ne Coueitise of eiȝes
B.11.43 Til *Concupiscencia* carnis acorded alle my werkes.
C.11.172 *Concupiscencia* carnis men calde þ[e] eldre maide
C.11.176 *Concupiscencia* Carnis confortede me o[n] this manere
C.11.189 And *Concupiscencia* Carnis clene the forsake–
C.11.307 *Concupiscencia* carnis [ne coueytise-of-yes]
C.11.310 Til *Concupiscencia* Carnis acorded til al my werkes.

concupisces B 1; C 1
B.20.279 Non *concupisces* rem proximi tui.
C.22.279 Non *concupisces* rem proximi tui &c.

condempnat B 1; C 1
B.15.318 brutorum animalium natura te *condempnat*, quia cum eis pabulum
C.17.53 Brutorum Animalium natura te *condempnat*, quia cum [eis]
         pabulum

confessio B 1; C 2
B.14.18 Oris *confessio* &c.
C.16.30 And oris *confessio* cometh of [knowlechyng and] shrifte of mouthe
C.16.31 Cordis contricio, Oris *confessio*, Operis satisfaccio;

confessionem B 1
B.14.92 Per *confessionem* to a preest peccata occiduntur–

confitebor B 1
B.13.55 In a dissh of derne shrifte, Dixi & *confitebor* tibi.

conflabunt B 1; C 1
B. 3.308 *Conflabunt* gladios suos in vomeres &c.
C. 3.461 *Conflabunt* gladios suos in vomeres & lancias [suas] in falces.

confundantur B 1
B.15.81 *Confundantur* omnes qui adorant sculptilia; Et alibi, Vt quid
         diligitis

coniungere C 1
C. 9.213 Non licet uobis legem voluntati, set voluntat[em] *coniungere* legi.

consciencia consiencia B 1; C 1
B.15.39 dum negat vel consentit *consciencia* est; dum spirat spiritus est.'
C.16.201 dum negat vel consentit *consciencia* est; dum sp[i]rat spiritus est.'

conscientiam A 1
A.10.94 Qui agit contra *conscientiam* &c.

consencientes B 1; C 1
B.13.426 *Consencientes* & agentes pari pena punientur.
C. 7.86 *Consencientes* & agentes pari pena punientur.

consentit B 1; C 1
B.15.39 dum negat vel *consentit* consciencia est; dum spirat spiritus est.'
C.16.201 dum negat vel *consentit* consciencia est; dum sp[i]rat spiritus est.'

consideras B 1
B.10.268 Qui[d] *consideras* festucam in oculo fratris tui, trabem in oculo tuo
          &c?

consiencia > consciencia

consolata A 1; B 1
A.10.87 Virga tua & baculus tuus ipsa me *consolata* sunt.
B.12.13 Virga tua & baculus tuus, ipsa me *consolata* sunt:

constituere B 1
B.15.576 In domo mea non est panis neque vestimentum et ideo nolite
          constituere me Regem.

constringit C 1
C. 5.60 Dominus pars hereditatis mee &c. Et alibi: clemencia non
         constringit.

consumit B 1
B. 9.94 qui res pauperum christi inutiliter *consumit*.

consummatum B 1; C 1
B.18.57 '*Consummatum* est', quod crist and comsede for to swoune.
C.20.57 '*Consummatum* est,' quod Crist and comsed for to swoene.

consummatus B 1; C 1
B.18.24 That crist be noȝt [y]knowe here for *consummatus* deus
C.20.23 That Crist be nat yknowe for *consumm[a]tus* deus

contemplatiua C 1
C.18.82 Actiua vita & *contemplatiua* vita,

continens C 1
C.19.114 Mundum pugillo *continens*,

contra A 3; B 5; C 4
A. 9.16 '*Contra*,' quaþ I as a clerk & comside to dispute:
A.10.94 Qui agit *contra* conscientiam &c.
A.11.232 '*Contra*,' quaþ I, 'be crist! þat can I þe wi[þsigg]e,
B. 3.324 Non leuabit gens *contra* gentem gladium &c.
B. 8.20 '*Contra*!' quod I as a clerc and comsed to disputen:
B.10.291 Existimasti inique quod ero tui similis; arguam te & statuam *contra*
          faciem
B.10.349 '*Contra*!' quod I, 'by crist! þat kan I [wiþseye],
B.12.280 '*Contra*!' quod Ymaginatif þoo and comsed to loure,
C. 3.477 Non leuabit gens *contra* gentem gladium nec excercebuntur vltra
          ad prelium.
C.10.20 '*Contra*!' quod y as a Clerk and comsed to despute
C.12.29 Arguam te & statuam *contra* faciem tuam.
C.14.202 '*Contra*!' quod ymagynatif tho and comesed to loure

contricio B 3; C 3
B. 4.36 *Contricio* & infelicitas in viis eorum &c.
B.11.81 Sola *contricio* [delet peccatum]–
B.14.17 Cordis *contricio* &c.
C. 4.36 *Contricio* & infelicitas in viis eorum et viam pacis non
         cognouerunt;

C.16.29 Cordis *contricio* cometh of sor[w]e of herte
C.16.31 Cordis *contricio*, Oris confessio, Operis satisfaccio;

contritum B 2; C 2
B.13.58 Cor *contritum* & humiliatum deus non despicies.
B.15.194 Cor *contritum* & humiliatum deus non despicies.'
C.15.62 And saide, 'cor *contritum* & humiliatum, deus, non despicies.'
C.16.336 Cor *contritum* & humiliatum deus non despicies.

contriuit B 1; C 1
B.10.333 Quomodo cessauit exactor, quieuit tributum? *contriuit* dominus baculum
C. 5.177 *Contriuit* dominus bac[u]lum impiorum, virga[m] d[omi]nancium,

conuersus B 1; C 1
B. 5.506 Thanne hente hope an horn of Deus tu *conuersus* viuificabis [nos]
C. 7.151 Thenne hente [hope] an horn of deus tu *conuersus* viuificabis nos

conuertimini B 1
B.14.180 *Conuertimini* ad me & salui eritis.

conuertitur B 1; C 1
B.15.118 totus populus *conuertitur* ad peccandum. Sicut cum videris arborem
C.16.273 totus populus *conuertitur* ad peccandum. Sicut cum videri[s]

conuiuia B 1; C 1
B.11.191 Cum facitis *conuiuia* nolite inuitare amicos.
C.12.103 Cum facitis *conuiuia* nolite vocare amicos &c.

copia B 1; C 1
B.10.89 Si tibi sit *copia* habundanter tribue; si autem exiguum illud impertiri stude
C.11.69 Si tibi sit *copia* habundanter tribue; Si Autem exiguum illud impertir[i] libenter stude.

cor B 3; C 4
B.13.58 *Cor* contritum & humiliatum deus non despicies.
B.13.398 Vbi thesaurus tuus ibi & *cor* tuum.'
B.15.194 *Cor* contritum & humiliatum deus non despicies.'
C. 6.285 Vbi tezaurus tuus, ibi [&] *cor* tuum.'
C.15.62 And saide, 'cor contritum & humiliatum, deus, non despicies.'
C.16.336 *Cor* contritum & humiliatum deus non despicies.
C.18.4 Til we cam into a contre, *cor* hominis hit heihte,

coram B 1; C 1
B.14.307 /Cantabit paupertas *coram* latrone viato[r],
C.20.420 Tibi soli peccaui & malum *coram* te feci.

corde A 1; B 2; C 1
A.11.147 Qui sim[u]lat verbis, nec *corde* est fidus amicus,
B.10.195 Qui simulat verbis [nec] *corde* est fidus amicus,
B.11.88 Non oderis fratres secrete in *corde* tuo set publice argue illos.
C.12.34 Non oderis fratrem secrete in *corde* &c.

cordis B 1; C 2
B.14.17 *Cordis* contricio &c.
C.16.29 *Cordis* contricio cometh of sor[w]e of herte
C.16.31 *Cordis* contricio, Oris confessio, Operis satisfaccio;

corpus B 2; C 3
B.15.39 dum viuificat *corpus* anima est; dum vult animus est; dum scit mens
B.15.388 As clerkes in *Corpus* Christi feeste syngen and reden
C.10.99 Nolite timere eos qui possunt occidere *corpus* &c.
C.16.201 dum [v]i[u]ificat *corpus* Anima est; dum vult animus est; [dum scit
C.17.120 As Clerkes in *corpus* cristi feste syngen and reden

corruptum coruptum B 1; C 1
B.15.118 Si autem *corruptum* fuerit omnium fides marcida est. Si
C.16.273 Si Autem *corupt[um]* fuerit omnium f[i]des marcida est. Si

cotidianum C 1
C.16.374 Panem nostrum co[tidianum] &c.

cotidie B 1; C 1
B.19.416 The comune clamat *cotidie*, ech a man til ooþer,
C.21.416 The comu[n]e clamat *cotidie*, vch a man to oþer,

creator B 1; C 1
B.19.210 Welcome hym and worshipe hym wiþ Veni *creator* Spiritus.'
C.21.210 Welcome hym and worschipe hym with veni *creator* spiritus.'

creature B 1
B.11.383 Propter deum subiecti estote omni *creature*.

credere C 1
C. 3.357 In case, *credere* in ecclesia, in holy kyrke to bileue;

crediderit A 1; B 1; C 2
A.11.234 Qui *crediderit* et baptizatus fuerit saluus erit.'
B.11.124 Qui *crediderit* & bapti3atus fuerit &c.
C.12.59 Qui *crediderit* & baptizatus fuerit &c.

C.13.87 Qui *crediderit* & baptizatus fuerit &c–

crediderunt B 1; C 1
B.19.181 Beati qui non viderunt [& *crediderunt*]."
C.21.181 Beati qui non viderunt & *crediderunt*."

credite C 1
C.16.342 Operibus *credite*.

credo B 2; C 3
B.10.473 That euere þe[i] couþe [konne on book] moore þan *Credo* in deum patrem,
B.15.608 Konne þe firste clause of oure bileue, *Credo* in deum patrem omnipotentem,
C. 3.481 And saresines for þat syhte shal syng *Credo* in spiritum sanctum
C.16.322 And also a can clergie, *credo* in deum patrem,
C.17.316 Conne þe furste clause of oure bileue, *credo* in deum patrem,

crescant A 1; B 1
A. 8.125 E[j]ice derisores & iurgia cum eis ne *crescant*.'
B. 7.143 E[ji]ce derisores & iurgia cum eis ne *crescant* &c.'

crimina C 1
C.11.18 Qui sapiunt nugas & crim[ina] lege vocantur;

crimine B 1; C 1
B.11.404 Caton acordeþ þerwiþ: Nemo sine *crimine* viuit.'
C.13.212 Caton acordeth therwith: nemo sine *crimine* viuit.'

crist- > christ-

cruce B 1; C 1
B.15.537 Absit nobis gloriari nisi in *cruce* domini nostri &c.
C.17.198 Absit nobis gloriari nisi in *cruce* domini nostri &c.

crucifige B 2; C 2
B.18.39 And al þe court on hym cryde '*crucifige*!' sharpe.
B.18.46 '*Crucifige*!' quod a Cachepol, '[he kan of wicchecraft]!'
C.20.38 And alle þe Court [on hym] cryede '*crucifige*! [sharpe].
C.20.46 '*Crucifige*!' q[uo]d a cachepol, 'he can of wycchecrafte!'

cui B 3; C 1
B. 7.73 *Cui* des videto is Catons techyng,
B. 7.75 Sit elemosina tua in manu tua donec studes *cui* des.
B. 7.77 Non eligas *cui* miser[e]aris ne forte pretereas illum qui meretur accipere,
C. 9.69 Catoun acordeth therwith: *cui* des videto.

cuius B 1; C 1
B.13.330 *Cuius* malediccione os plenum est & amaritudine; sub lingua eius
C. 6.76 *Cuius* maledictione os plenum est & amaritudine; sub lingua eius

culpa A 2; B 4; C 5
A. 8.3 And purchac[ide] hym a pardoun a pena & a *culpa*
A. 8.21 But non a pena & a *culpa* þe pope wolde h[e]m graunte,
B. 5.483 O felix *culpa*, o necessarium peccatum Ade &c.
B. 7.3 And purchaced hym a pardoun a pena & a *culpa*
B. 7.19 Ac noon A pena & a *culpa* þe pope [w]olde hem graunte
B.10.266 Dogma tuum sordet cum te tua *culpa* remordet.
C. 6.64 And cryede 'mea *culpa*', corsynge alle his enemyes;
C. 7.125 O felix *culpa*, o necessarium peccatum Ade.
C. 9.3 And purchasede hym a pardoun A pena & A *culpa*,
C. 9.23 Ac no [a] pena & a *culpa* treuthe wolde hem graunte
C. 9.187 And pardon with the plouhman A pena & a *culpa*.

culpabilis B 1
B.10.266 Si culpare velis *culpabilis* es[se] cauebis;

culpare B 1
B.10.266 Si *culpare* velis culpabilis es[se] cauebis;

culpat B 1; C 1
B.18.407 *Culpat* caro, purgat caro, regnat deus dei caro.
C.20.450 *Culpat* Caro, purgat Caro, regnat deus dei Caro.

cum A 6; B 23; C 15
A. 5.42 Qui *cum* patre & filio; Faire mote 3ow befalle.'
A. 7.68 Et *cum* iustis non scribantur.
A. 8.125 E[j]ice derisores & iurgia *cum* eis ne crescant.'
A.10.98 *Cum* recte viuas ne cures verba malorum,
A.11.193 Gaudere *cum* gaudentibus Et flere cum flentibus,
A.11.193 Gaudere cum gaudentibus Et flere *cum* flentibus,
B. 1.31 Inebri[e]mus eum vino dormiamusque *cum* eo
B. 5.58 Qui *cum* patre & filio; þat faire hem bifalle
B. 5.269 Seruus es alterius [*cum*] fercula pinguia queris;
B. 5.278 *Cum* sancto sanctus eris: construwe me þis on englissh.'
B. 6.76 Quia *cum* iustis non scribantur.
B. 7.83 Quare non dedisti pecuniam meam ad mensam vt ego veni[ens] *cum* vsuris ex[egissem illam]?
B. 7.143 E[ji]ce derisores & iurgia *cum* eis ne crescant &c.'
B. 8.93 Libenter suffertis insipientes *cum* sitis ipsi sapientes:

B. 9.94   Proditor est prelatus *cum* Iuda qui patrimonium christi minus distribuit; Et

B.10.266   Dogma tuum sordet *cum* te tua culpa remordet.

B.10.359   Si *cum* christo sur[r]existis &c,

B.11.191   *Cum* facitis conuiuia nolite inuitare amicos.

B.15.118   Sicut *cum* videris arborem pallidam & marcidam intelligis quod

B.15.118   Ita *cum* videris populum indisciplinatum & irreligiosum, sine dubio

B.15.318   Num[quid], dicit Iob, rugi[e]t onager *cum* herbam habuerit aut

B.15.318   aut mugiet bos *cum* ante plenum presepe steterit? brutorum

B.15.318   brutorum animalium natura te condempnat, quia *cum* eis pabulum

B.15.600   *Cum* sanctus sanctorum veniat cessabit vnxio vestra.

B.16.25   *Cum* ceciderit iustus non colliditur quia dominus supponit ma[num suam];

B.18.109   *Cum* veniat sanctus sanctorum cessabit vnxio vestra.'

B.18.399   Non intres in Iudicium *cum* seruo tuo.

B.19.296   Esto forti animo *cum* sis dampnatus inique.

B.19.422   At Auynoun among Iewes–*Cum* sancto sanctus eris &c–

C. 1.30   Inebriemus eum vino dormiamusque *cum* eo vt seruare possimus

C. 4.165   Et saluo custodias set non *cum* carcer[a]tis.'

C. 5.199   Qui *cum* patre & filio; þat fayre hem byfalle

C. 6.293   Seruus [es] alterius *cum* fercula pingu[i]a queris;

C. 8.78   Quia *cum* iustis non scribantur.

C.12.103   *Cum* facitis conuiuia nolite vocare amicos &c.

C.16.273   Sicut *cum* videri[s] Arborem pallidam & marcidam intelligis quod

C.16.273   Ita *cum* videris populum indissiplinatum & irreligiosum, sine dubio

C.17.53   Nu[mquid], dicit Iop, rugiet onager *cum* habuerit herbam aut

C.17.53   aut mugiet bos *cum* ante plenum presepe steterit? Brutorum

C.17.53   Brutorum Animalium natura te condempnat, quia *cum* [eis] pabulum

C.20.112   *Cum* veniat sanctus sanctorum cessa[bi]t &c.'

C.20.442   Non intres in iudicium *cum* seruo tuo.

C.21.296   Esto forti Animo *cum* sis dampnatus inique.

C.21.422   At Auenon among iewes–*cum* sancto sanctus eris &c–

cuncta B 1

B.11.398   Et vidit deus *cuncta* que fecerat & erant valde bona.

cunctis B 1; C 1

B. 5.603   Per Euam cun[c]tis clausa est et per Mariam virginem [iterum] patefacta est;

C. 7.250   Per Euam cun[c]tis clausa est & per mariam verginem iterum patefacta est &c;

cura B 1

B.14.286   /And Contricion confort and *cura* animarum;

curarum B 2; C 2

B.14.276   'Paupertas,' quod Pacience, 'est odibile bonum, Remocio *curarum*,

B.14.293   Remocio *curarum*.

C.16.116   'Paupertas,' quod pacience, 'est odibile bonum, Remocio *curarum*,

C.16.128   [Remocio *curarum*].

cure B 1; C 1

B.11.251   Domine, non est tibi *cure* quod soror mea reliquit me solam ministrare?

C.12.138   Domine, non est tibi cur[e] quod soror &c?

cures A 2; B 1

A. 8.134   Sompnia ne *cures*.

A.10.98   Cum recte viuas ne *cures* verba malorum,

B. 7.156   To sette sadnesse in Songewarie for sompnia ne *cures*.

curis B 1

B.12.22   Interpone tuis interdum gaudia *curis*.

curribus B 1; C 1

B.10.327   Hij in *curribus* & hij in equis ipsi obligati sunt &c.

C. 5.172   Hij in *curribus* & [hij] in equis; ipsi obligati sunt & ceciderunt.

custodias C 1

C. 4.165   Et saluo *custodias* set non cum carcer[a]tis.'

custodiat B 1

B.13.73   Vnusquisque a fratre se *custodiat* quia vt dicitur periculum est in falsis

dabitur A 1; B 2; C 4

A. 1.175   Date & *dabitur* vobis for I dele ȝow alle.

B. 1.201   "Date & *dabitur* vobis, for I deele yow alle."

B.12.54   Date & *dabitur* vobis.

C. 1.196   "Date & *dabitur* vobis, for y dele ȝow alle."

C. 7.260   Quodcumque pecieritis in nomine meo *dabitur* enim vobis.

C. 8.245   Piger propter frigus noluit arrare; mendicabi[t] in yeme & non *dabitur* ei".

C.15.244   Quodcumque pecieritis [a patre] in nomine meo dab[itur] enim

dabo C 1

C.15.271   *Dabo* tibi secundum peticionem tuam.

dampnatus B 1; C 1

B.19.296   Esto forti animo cum sis *dampnatus* inique.

C.21.296   Esto forti Animo cum sis *dampnatus* inique.

dampno B 2; C 2

B.14.276   negocium sine *dampno*, Incerta fortuna, absque sollicitudine

B.14.315   Negocium sine *dampno*.

C.16.116   negocium sine *dampno*, Incerta fortuna, absque solicitudine

C.16.149   Negocium sine *dampno*.

dans B 1

B.12.293   For Deus dicitur quasi *dans* [eternam vitam] suis, hoc est fidelibus;

dare B 2; C 2

B.15.343   Quia sacrilegium est res pauperum non pauperibus *dare*. Item, peccatoribus

B.15.343   *dare* est demonibus immolare. Item, monache, si indiges &

C. 7.118   *Dare* histrionibus &c.

C.14.16   Beacius est *dare* quam petere.

das B 1

B.15.343   accipis pocius *das* quam accipis; Si autem non eges & accipis rapis.

dat B 1; C 1

B. 3.336   Honorem adquiret qui *dat* munera &c.'

C. 3.488   Honorem adquiret qui *dat* munera.'

date A 1; B 2; C 1

A. 1.175   *Date* & dabitur vobis for I dele ȝow alle.

B. 1.201   "*Date* & dabitur vobis, for I deele yow alle."

B.12.54   *Date* & dabitur vobis.

C. 1.196   "*Date* & dabitur vobis, for y dele ȝow alle."

de A 2; B 18; C 15

A. 7.67   Deleantur *de* libro; I shulde not dele wiþ hem,

A.11.263   Nemo ascendet ad celum nisi qui *de* celo descendit.

B.Pr.137   Si ius nudatur nudo *de* iure metatur;

B.Pr.138   Si seritur pietas *de* pietate metas.'

B. 1.31   Vt seruare possimus *de* patre nostro semen.

B. 6.75   Deleantur *de* libro viuencium; I sholde noȝt dele wiþ hem,

B. 6.228   Facite vo[bis] amicos *de* mammona iniquitatis.

B. 9.155   Numquam collig[unt] *de* spinis vua[s] nec de tribulis ficus.

B. 9.155   Numquam collig[unt] de spinis vua[s] nec *de* tribulis ficus.

B.10.270   E[j]ice primo trabem [*de*] oculo tuo &c–

B.10.382   Nemo ascendit ad celum nisi qui *de* celo descendit.

B.11.395   *De* re que te non molestat noli certare.

B.12.50   Sunt homines nequam, bene *de* virtute loquentes.

B.12.207   *De* peccato propiciato noli esse sine metu.

B.14.46   viuit homo set in omni verbo quod procedit *de* ore dei.'

B.14.144   *De* delicijs ad delicias difficile est transire.

B.15.118   Sicut *de* templo omne bonum progreditur, sic de templo omne

B.15.118   sic *de* templo omne malum procedit. Si sacerdocium integrum fuerit

B.15.552   Deposuit potentes *de* sede &c.

B.17.151   Qui conceptus est *de* spiritu sancto &c.

C.Pr.158   [Si ius nudatur nudo *de* iure metatur];

C.Pr.159   Si seritur pietas *de* pietate metas.'

C. 1.30   vt seruare possimus *de* patre nostro semen.

C. 5.86   Non *de* solo,' y sayde, 'for sothe viuit homo,

C. 8.77   Del[e]antur *de* libro viuencium; y sholde nat dele with hem

C. 8.234   Facite vobis Amicos *de* mammona iniquitatis.'

C.10.244   Numquam collig[unt] *de* spinis vuas; Et Alibi: Bon[a] Arbor

C.11.207   Nemo ascendit ad celum nisi qui *de* celo descendit.

C.13.196   *De* re que te non molestat noli certare.

C.14.146   *De* peccato propiciato noli esse sine metu.

C.16.201   dum declina[t] *de* malo ad bonum liberum Arbitrium est;

C.16.273   Sicut *de* templo omne bonum progreditur, sic de templo omne

C.16.273   sic *de* templo omne malum procedit. Si sacerdocium integrum fuerit

C.17.215   Deposuit potentes *de* sede &c.

C.19.250   Facite vobis amicos *de* mammona iniquitatis.

dealbabor C 1

C.16.335   Lauabis me & super niuem *dealbabor*.

debes B 4; C 4

B.19.187   To Piers pardon þe Plowman redde quod *debes*.

B.19.259   And Registrer to receyue redde quod *debes*.

B.19.390   To Piers pardon þe Plowman redde quod *debes*.'

B.20.308   And þat Piers [pardon] were ypayed, redde quod *debes*.

C.21.187   To Peres pardoun þe plouhman Redde quod *debes*.

C.21.259   And Registrer to reseyuen Redde quod *debes*.

C.21.390   To [Peres] pardon þe [plouhman] Redde quod debe[s].'

C.22.308   And þat Peres pardon were ypayd, redde quod *debes*.

debet B 1; C 1

B.19.193   And rewarde hym right wel þat reddit quod *debet*,

C.21.193 And rewarde hym riht wel that redd[it] quod *debet*,

debita B 1; C 1
B.19.394 Et dimitte nobis *debita* nostra &c,
C.21.394 Et dimitte nobis *debita* nostra &c,

decem B 1; C 1
B.19.135 The burdes þo songe, Saul interfecit mille et dauid *decem* milia.
C.21.135 The buyrdes tho songe, Saul interfecit mille & dauid *decem* milia.

decimas B 2; C 1
B.15.556 Per primicias & *decimas* &c.
B.15.578 Inferte omnes [*decimas*] in orreum meum vt cibus in domo mea.
C.17.219 Per pr[i]micias & *decimas* &c.

declinat C 1
C.16.201 dum *declina[t]* de malo ad bonum liberum Arbitrium est;

dedisti B 1
B. 7.83 Quare non *dedisti* pecuniam meam ad mensam vt ego veni[ens]
    cum vsuris ex[egissem illam]?

dedit A 1; B 2
A. 3.221 Qui pecuniam suam [non] *dedit* ad vsuram.
B. 3.241 Qui pecuniam suam non *dedit* ad vsuram et munera super
    innocentem &c,
B.15.327 Dispersit, *dedit* pauperibus?

defendendum B 1; C 1
B.19.479 Omnia tua sunt ad *defendendum* set non ad deprehendendum.'
C.21.479 Omnia [tua sunt] ad *defendendum* sed non ad deprehendendum.'

dei A 2; B 18; C 23
A. 1.51 Et que sunt *dei* deo oþer ellis ȝe don ille."
A. 7.78 In *dei* nomine Amen I make it myseluen:
B. 1.53 Et que sunt *dei* deo or ellis ye don ille."
B. 4.37 Non est timor *dei* ante oculos eorum &c.
B. 5.283 Omnis iniquitas quantum ad misericordiam *dei* est quasi sintilla in
    medio
B. 6.86 In *dei* nomine, amen. I make it myselue.
B. 7.46 Than pro *dei* pietate [pleden at þe barre].
B.10.288 Archa *dei* myshapped and Ely brak his nekke.
B.10.436 [Sunt] iusti atque sapientes, & opera eorum in manu *dei* sunt &c.
B.12.113 Archa *dei*, in þe olde lawe, leuytes it kepten;
B.12.119 That wiþ archa *dei* [wenten] in [worship and reuerence]
B.14.46 viuit homo set in omni verbo quod procedit de ore *dei*.'
B.14.276 possessio sine calumpnia, donum *dei*, sanit[atis] mater,
B.14.30 Donum *dei*.
B.16.30 Thanne with þe firste pil I palle hym doun, potencia *de[i* patris].
B.16.36 Thanne sette I to þe secounde pil, sapiencia *dei* patris,
B.16.252 Ecce agnus *dei* &c.'
B.18.68 Vere filius *dei* erat iste.
B.18.324 Songen seint Iohanes song, Ecce agnus *dei*.
B.18.407 Culpat caro, purgat caro, regnat deus *dei* caro.
C. 1.49 Et que sunt *dei* deo or [elles] ȝe don ylle."
C. 2.31 The fader þat me forth brouhte filius *dei* he hoteth,
C. 4.36 non est timor *dei* ante oculos eorum.
C. 5.88 Fiat voluntas *dei* fynt vs alle thynges.'
C. 6.338 Omnis iniquitas quoad misericordiam *dei* est quasi sintilla in
    medio maris.
C. 8.95 In *dei* nomine, Amen: y make hit mysulue.
C.11.271 Sunt iusti atque sapientes & opera eorum in manu *dei* sunt &c.
C.14.58 Arca *dei* in þe olde lawe leuytes hit kepte;
C.16.116 posessio sine calumpnia, donum *dei*, sanitatis mater,
C.16.136 Donum *dei*.
C.18.7 That hihte ymago *dei*, graciousliche hit growede.
C.18.34 And with þe furste planke y palle hym down, potencia *dei* patris.
C.18.40 Thenne sette y þe seconde planke, sapiencia *dei* patris,
C.18.117 Thenne moued hym moed [in] magestate *dei*
C.18.118 That libera voluntas *dei* lauhte þe myddel Shoriare
C.18.213 Celi enarrant gloriam *dei* &c.'
C.18.268 Ecce Agnus *dei*.'
C.19.73 And ladde hym forth to lauacrum lex *dei*, a grang[e]
C.19.140 Dextere *dei* tu digitus.
C.20.20 'Liberum *dei* Arbitrium for loue hath vndertake
C.20.70 Vere filius *dei* erat iste;
C.20.367 Songen seynt Iohann[es songe], ecce agnus *dei*.
C.20.450 Culpat Caro, purgat Caro, regnat deus *dei* Caro.

deinceps B 1; C 1
B.Pr.132 'Sum Rex, sum princeps; neutrum fortasse *deinceps*.
C.Pr.153 'Sum Rex, sum Princeps; neutrum fortasse *deinceps*.

deitate B 1; C 1
B.18.26 For no dynt shal hym dere as in *deitate* patris.'
C.20.25 For no d[yn]t shal hym dere as in *deitate* patris.'

deleantur A 1; B 1; C 1
A. 7.67 *Deleantur* de libro; I shulde not dele wiþ hem,

B. 6.75 *Deleantur* de libro viuencium; I sholde noȝt dele wiþ hem,
C. 8.77 *Del[e]antur* de libro viuencium; y sholde nat dele with hem

delet B 1
B.11.81 Sola contricio [*delet* peccatum]–

delicias B 1
B.14.144 De delicijs ad *delicias* difficile est transire.

delicijs deliciis B 2; C 1
B.13.45 eff[u]deritis, ea que in *delicijs* comeditis in tormentis euometis.
B.14.144 De *delicijs* ad delicias difficile est transire.
C.15.50 effuderitis, ea que in *deliciis* comeditis in tor[mentis] euo[metis]
    &c.

delictis B 1
B.11.58 Pena pecuniaria non sufficit pro spiritualibus *delictis*.

deluditur A 1; B 1
A.11.148 [Tu quoque fac simile: sic ars *deluditur* arte].
B.10.196 Tu quoque fac simile; sic ars *deluditur* arte.

demonia B 1
B.13.249 In nomine meo *demonia* e[j]icient & super egros manus imponent
    & bene

demonibus B 1
B.15.343 dare est *demonibus* immolare. Item, monache, si indiges &

demonium B 1; C 1
B.16.120 *Demonium* habe[s] &c.
C.18.150 *Demonium* habes.

demorabitur B 1; C 1
B.18.181 Ad vesperum *demorabitur* fletus & ad matutinum leticia.
C.20.184 Ad vesperum *demorabitur* fletus & ad mat[u]tinum leticia.

denarium B 1
B.10.343 Dilige *denarium* set parce dilige formam.

dente B 1; C 1
B.18.339 Dentem pro *dente* & oculum pro oculo.
C.20.385 Dentem p[ro] *dente* & oculum pro oculo.

dentem B 1; C 1
B.18.339 *Dentem* pro dente & oculum pro oculo.
C.20.385 *Dentem* p[ro] dente & oculum pro oculo.

dentes B 1; C 1
B.13.330 labor et dol[or]; Et alibi, Filij hominum *dentes* eorum arma &
    sagitte
C. 6.76 labor & dolor. Filij hominum *dentes* eorum Arma & sagitte

deo A 1; B 9; C 6
A. 1.51 Et que sunt dei *deo* oþer ellis ȝe don ille."
B. 1.53 Et que sunt dei *deo* or ellis ye don ille."
B. 5.486 Et alibi, Qui manet in caritate in *deo* manet & deus in eo.
B. 7.77 Quia incertum est pro quo *deo* magis placeas.
B. 9.65 Qui manet in caritate in *deo* manet &c.
B.11.287 Spera in *deo* spekeþ of preestes þat haue no spendyng siluer,
B.11.311 Psallite *deo* nostro; psallite quoniam rex terre deus Israel; psallite
B.12.150 And songe a song of solas, Gloria in excelsis *deo*.
B.15.180 And if he soupeþ eteþ but a sop of Spera in *deo*.
B.19.74 Gloria in excelsis *deo* &c.
C. 1.49 Et que sunt dei *deo* or [elles] ȝe don ylle."
C. 3.403 Qui in caritate manet in *deo* manet et deus in eo.
C.13.101 For spera in *deo* speketh of prestis þat han no spendynge suluer
C.13.123 Psallite *deo* nostro, psallite; quoniam Rex [terre] deus, psallite
    sapienter.
C.14.94 And song a song of solace, Gloria in excelcis *deo*.
C.21.74 Gloria in excelsis *deo*.

deposuit B 1; C 1
B.15.552 *Deposuit* potentes de sede &c.
C.17.215 *Deposuit* potentes de sede &c.

deprehendendum B 1; C 1
B.19.479 Omnia tua sunt ad defendendum set non ad *deprehendendum*.'
C.21.479 Omnia [tua sunt] ad defendendum sed non ad *deprehendendum*.'

derelictum B 1
B. 7.89 Iunior fui etenim senui, & non vidi iustum *derelictum* ne[c] semen
    eius

dereliquisti B 1
B.16.214 Deus meus, Deus meus, vt quid *dereliquisti* me?

derisores A 1; B 1
A. 8.125 E[j]ice *derisores* & iurgia cum eis ne crescant.'
B. 7.143 E[ji]ce *derisores* & iurgia cum eis ne crescant &c.'

des B 3; C 2
B. 7.73 Cui *des* videto is Catons techyng,
B. 7.75 Sit elemosina tua in manu tua donec studes cui *des*.

B. 9.186   Dum sis vir fortis ne *des* tua robora scortis;
C. 9.69   Catoun acordeth therwith: cui *des* videto.
C.10.287   Dum sis vir fortis ne *des* tua robora scortis;

descendit A 1; B 2; C 2
A.11.263   Nemo ascendet ad celum nisi qui de celo *descendit.*
B.10.382   Nemo ascendet ad celum nisi qui de celo *descendit.*
B.18.111   I drow me in þat derknesse to *descendit* ad inferna
C.11.207   Nemo ascendet ad celum nisi qui de celo *descendit.*
C.20.114   Y [d]row [me] in þat derkenesse to *descendit* ad inferna

descendunt C 1
C.11.22   Ducunt in bonis dies suos & in fin[e] *descendunt* ad infernum.

desideria B 1; C 1
B. 9.67   Amen dico vobis, nescio vos; Et alibi, Et dimisi eos secundum
           desideria
C.10.165   Et dimisi eos secundum *desideria* eorum.

despicies B 2; C 2
B.13.58   Cor contritum & humiliatum deus non *despicies.*
B.15.194   Cor contritum & humiliatum deus non *despicies.*'
C.15.62   And saide, 'cor contritum & humiliatum, deus, non *despicies.*'
C.16.336   Cor contritum & humiliatum deus non *despicies.*

destruxerunt B 1; C 1
B.10.29   Que perfecisti *destruxerunt*; iustus autem &c.
C.11.25   Que perfecisti *destruxerunt* &c.

deum A 1; B 8; C 9
A.11.242   Dilige *deum* &c, Et proximum tuum sicut teipsum.
B.10.473   That euere þe[i] kouþe [konne on book] moore þan Credo in *deum*
           patrem,
B.11.383   Propter *deum* subiecti estote omni creature.
B.12.138   Sapiencia huius mundi stulticia est apud *deum.*
B.13.127   But Dilige *deum* and Domine quis habitabit;
B.15.584   Dilige *deum* & proximum is parfit Iewen lawe;
B.15.608   Konne þe firste clause of oure bileue, Credo in *deum* patrem
           omnipotentem,
B.17.13   Dilige *deum* & proximum tuum,
B.18.422   Truþe trumpede þo and song Te *deum* laudamus,
C.14.83   Sapiencia huius mundi stul[t]icia est apud *deum.*
C.15.134   Bote dilige *deum* & p[roximu]m [and] domine quis habitabit
C.15.140   That disce, doce, dilige *deum* and thyn enemy,
C.16.322   And also a can clergie, credo in *deum* patrem,
C.17.140   Dilige *deum* propter deum, id est propter veritatem; & inimicum
           tuum
C.17.140   Dilige deum propter *deum*, id est propter veritatem; & inimicum
           tuum
C.17.316   Conne þe furste clause of oure bileue, credo in *deum* patrem,
C.19.14   Dilige *deum* & proximum [tuum].
C.20.465   Treuth trompede tho and song te *deum* laudamus

deus A 1; B 26; C 17
A. 1.84   I do it on *Deus* caritas to deme þe soþe.
B. 1.86   I do it on *Deus* caritas to deme þe soþe.
B. 5.277   In Miserere mei *deus*, wher I mene truþe:
B. 5.486   Et alibi, Qui manet in caritate in deo manet & *deus* in eo.
B. 5.506   Thanne hente hope an horn of *Deus* tu conuersus viuificabis [nos]
B. 5.509   quemadmodum multiplicasti misericordiam tuam, *deus*'.
B. 9.62   Quorum *deus* venter est.
B.10.45   Than Munde þe Millere of Multa fecit *deus.*
B.10.246   *Deus* pater, deus filius, deus spiritus sanctus:
B.10.246   Deus pater, *deus* filius, deus spiritus sanctus:
B.10.246   Deus pater, deus filius, *deus* spiritus sanctus:
B.11.38   'And *Deus* disponit', quod he; 'lat god doon his wille.
B.11.286   Iudica me *deus* & discerne causam meam.
B.11.311   Psallite deo nostro; psallite quoniam rex terre *deus* Israel; psallite
B.11.398   Et vidit *deus* cuncta que fecerat & erant valde bona.
B.12.293   For *Deus* dicitur quasi dans [eternam vitam] suis, hoc est fidelibus;
B.13.54   And þanne a mees of ooþer mete of Miserere mei *deus*,
B.13.58   Cor contritum & humiliatum *deus* non despicies.
B.14.33   Ne soliciti sitis &c; Volucres celi *deus* pascit &c; pacientes vincunt
           &c.'
B.15.194   Cor contritum & humiliatum *deus* non despicies.'
B.15.200   Et vidit *deus* cogitaciones eorum.
B.16.214   *Deus* meus, Deus meus, vt quid dereliquisti me?
B.16.214   Deus meus, *Deus* meus, vt quid dereliquisti me?
B.18.24   That crist be noȝt [y]knowe here for consummatus *deus*
B.18.407   Culpat caro, purgat caro, regnat *deus* dei caro.
B.19.172   "[Dominus] meus & [*deus*] meus.
B.20.33   Homo proponit & *deus* disponit;
C. 1.82   I do it [o]n *deus* caritas to deme þe sothe.
C. 3.340   Retribuere dignare domine *deus* &c.'
C. 3.402   *Deus* homo–
C. 3.403   Qui in caritate manet in deo manet et *deus* in eo.
C. 3.406   Of thre trewe termisonus, trinitas vnus *deus*:

C. 7.151   Thenne hente [hope] an horn of *deus* tu conuersus viuificabis nos
C. 7.154   multiplicasti misericordiam [tu]am, *deus*.'
C.11.304   'Et *deus* disponit,' quod he; 'la[t] god do his wille.
C.13.123   Psallite deo nostro, psallite; quoniam Rex [terre] *deus*, psallite
           sapienter.
C.15.62   And saide, 'cor contritum & humiliatum, *deus*, non despicies.'
C.16.336   Cor contritum & humiliatum *deus* non despicies.
C.16.340   Et vidit *deus* cogitaciones eorum.
C.18.190   And, sondry to se vpon, solus *deus* he hoteth.'
C.20.23   That Crist be nat yknowe for consumm[a]tus *deus*
C.20.450   Culpat Caro, purgat Caro, regnat *deus* dei Caro.
C.21.172   "Dominus meus & *deus* meus.
C.22.33   Homo proponit [&] *deus* dispo[n]it;

deuorabit A 1; B 1; C 1
A. 3.85   Ignis *deuorabit* tabernacula eorum qui libenter accipiunt munera.
B. 3.96   Ignis *deuorabit* tabernacula eorum qui libenter accipiunt munera
           &c.
C. 3.124   Ignis *deuorabit* tabernacula eorum qui libenter accipiunt munera.

dextera dextra A 2; B 2; C 1
A. 3.54   And seiþ Nesciat sinist[ra] quid faciat *dexter[a]*.
A. 3.228   In quorum manibus iniquitates sunt; *dextera* eorum repleta est
           muneribus.
B. 3.72   Nesciat sinistra quid faciat *dextra*:
B. 3.249   In quorum manibus iniquitates sunt; *dextra* eorum repleta est
           muneribus.
C. 3.74   Nesciat [sinistra] quid faciat [*dextera*]:

dextere C 1
C.19.140   *Dextere* dei tu digitus.

dextris C 1
C. 1.122   Dixit dominus domino meo, sede a *dextris* meis.

dicatur B 1
B.Pr.141   'Dum rex a regere *dicatur* nomen habere

dicis B 1
B.16.145   It was hymself sooþly and seide 'tu *dicis*'.

dicit B 2; C 2
B.15.318   Num[quid], *dicit* Iob, rugi[e]t onager cum herbam habuerit aut
B.17.266   Non omnis qui *dicit* domine, domine, intrabit &c.
C.17.53   Nu[mquid], *dicit* Iop, rugiet onager cum habuerit herbam aut
C.19.232   Non omnis qui *dicit* domine, domine intrabit in reg[num] celorum
           &c.

dicitur B 2
B.12.293   For Deus *dicitur* quasi dans [eternam vitam] suis, hoc est fidelibus;
B.13.73   Vnusquisque a fratre se custodiat quia vt *dicitur* periculum est in
           falsis

dico A 1; B 3; C 2
A. 3.64   Amen Amen [*dico* vobis receperunt mercedem suam].
B. 5.55   Amen *dico* vobis nescio vos.
B. 9.67   Amen *dico* vobis, nescio vos; Et alibi, Et dimisi eos secundum
           desideria
B.17.253   Amen *dico* vobis, nescio vos &c.
C.13.98   Amen *dico* vobis quia hec vidua paupercula &c.
C.19.219   Amen *dico* vobis, nescio vos.

dicunt C 1
C. 8.90   Omnia que *dicunt* facite & seruate.

die A 2; B 3; C 4
A. 8.110   Fuerunt michi lacrime mee panes *die* ac nocte.
A. 9.16   'Sepcies in *die* cadit iustus.
B. 7.128   Fuerunt michi lacrime mee panes *die* ac nocte.
B. 8.20   'Sepcies in *die* cadit Iustus.
B.12.281   And seide, 'Saluabitur vix Iustus in *die* Iudicij;
C.10.21   And saide, 'sothly sepcies in *die* ca[d]it iust[u]s,
C.14.203   And saide, 'Vix saluabitur iustus in *die* iudicij;
C.15.22   That iustus bifore iesu in *die* iudicij non saluabitur bote vix helpe;
C.15.118   [Bu]t dowel endite ȝow in *die* iudicij.'

dies C 1
C.11.22   Ducunt in bonis *dies* suos & in fin[e] descendunt ad infernum.

difficile B 1
B.14.144   De delicijs ad delicias *difficile* est transire.

digitus C 1
C.19.140   Dextere dei tu *digitus*.

dignare C 1
C. 3.340   Retribuere *dignare* domine deus &c.'

dignus A 1; B 1
A. 2.86   *Dignus* est operarius mercede [sua].
B. 2.123   For *Dignus* est operarius his hire to haue,

dilexisti B 1; C 1
B. 5.277   Ecce enim veritatem *dilexisti* &c.
C. 6.302   On Ecce enim veritatem *dilexisti*.

dilige A 1; B 7; C 4
A.11.242   *Dilige* deum &c, Et proximum tuum sicut teipsum.
B.10.343   *Dilige* denarium set parce dilige formam.
B.10.343   Dilige denarium set parce *dilige* formam.
B.13.127   But *Dilige* deum and Domine quis habitabit;
B.13.137   Disce', quod he, 'doce, *dilige* inimicos.
B.13.138   Disce and dowel, doce and dobet, *dilige* and dobest:
B.15.584   *Dilige* deum & proximum is parfit Iewen lawe;
B.17.13   *Dilige* deum & proximum tuum,
C.15.134   Bote *dilige* deum & p[roximu]m [and] domine quis habitabit
C.15.140   That disce, doce, *dilige* deum and thyn enemy,
C.17.140   *Dilige* deum propter deum, id est propter veritatem; & inimicum
          tuum
C.19.14   *Dilige* deum & proximum [tuum].

diligit B 2; C 2
B.11.176   Qui non *diligit* manet in morte.
B.14.60   Si quis amat christum mundum non *diligit* istum.
C.12.99   Qui non *diligit* manet in morte.
C.15.259   Si quis Amat christum mundum non *diligit* istum.

diligitis B 1
B.15.81   Confundantur omnes qui adorant sculptilia; Et alibi, Vt quid
          diligitis

diligo B 1
B.12.12   Quem *diligo* castigo.

dimidium B 1
B.13.195   Than ȝacheus for he seide "*dimidium* bonorum meorum do
          pauperibus",

dimisi B 1; C 1
B. 9.67   Amen dico vobis, nescio vos; Et alibi, Et *dimisi* eos secundum
          desideria
C.10.165   Et *dimisi* eos secundum desideria eorum.

dimitte B 1; C 1
B.19.394   Et *dimitte* nobis debita nostra &c,
C.21.394   Et *dimitte* nobis debita nostra &c,

dimittitur B 2; C 2
B. 5.273   Non *dimittitur* peccatum donec restituatur [a]blatum.
B.17.310   Numquam *dimittitur* peccatum &c.
C. 6.257   Numquam *dimittitur* peccatum &c.'
C.19.290   Nunquam *dimittitur* peccatum &c.

disce B 2; C 1
B.13.137   *Disce*', quod he, 'doce, dilige inimicos.
B.13.138   *Disce* and dowel, doce and dobet, dilige and dobest:
C.15.140   That *disce*, doce, dilige deum and thyn enemy,

discerne B 1
B.11.286   Iudica me deus & *discerne* causam meam.

dispensator B 1
B. 9.94   alibi, Perniciosus *dispensator* est qui res pauperum christi inutiliter

dispergentur C 1
C. 9.262   *Dispergentur* oues, þe dogge dar nat berke.

dispersit B 1
B.15.327   *Dispersit*, dedit pauperibus?

disponit B 2; C 2
B.11.38   'And Deus *disponit*', quod he; 'lat god doon his wille.
B.20.33   Homo proponit & deus *disponit*;
C.11.304   'Et deus *disponit*,' quod he; 'la[t] god do his wille.
C.22.33   Homo proponit [&] deus *dispo[n]it*;

distribuit B 1
B. 9.94   Proditor est prelatus cum Iuda qui patrimonium christi minus
          distribuit; Et

diu B 1; C 1
B.13.50   And siþþe he [drouȝ] vs drynke, *Di[u]* perseuerans,
C.15.56   And sethe he drow vs drynke, *di[u]* p[er]seuerans,

diuersa B 1; C 1
B.15.39   Anima pro *diuersis* accionibus diuersa nomina sortitur: dum
          viuificat
C.16.201   Anima pro *diuersis* [acc]ionibus diuersa nomina sortitur: dum

diuersis B 1; C 1
B.15.39   Anima pro *diuersis* accionibus diuersa nomina sortitur: dum
          viuificat
C.16.201   Anima pro *diuersis* [acc]ionibus diuersa nomina sortitur: dum

diuersorio B 1
B.12.147   Set non erat ei locus in *diuersorio*, et pauper non habet
          diuersorium.

diuersorium B 1
B.12.147   Set non erat ei locus in diuersorio, et pauper non habet
          diuersorium.

diues B 3; C 2
B. 7.87   Satis *diues* est qui non indiget pane.
B.11.269   Pauper ego ludo dum tu *diues* meditaris.
B.15.234   Beatus est *diues* qui &c.
C.12.154   Pauper ego ludo dum tu *diues* m[e]ditaris.
C.16.359   Beatus est *diues* sine macula.

diuicias B 2
B.10.26   Ecce ipsi peccatores! habundantes in seculo obtinuerunt *diuicias*.
B.11.271   *Diuicias* nec paupertates &c,

diuicie B 1; C 1
B. 3.330   For Melius est bonum nomen quam *diuicie* multe.'
C. 3.483   [For] melius est bonum nomen quam *diuicie* multe.'

diuidatur C 1
C.11.213   Nec michi nec tibi, set *diuidatur*.

diuinus B 1; C 1
B.12.286   Aduenit ignis *diuinus* non comburens set illuminans &c.
C.14.208   A[d]uenit ignis *diuinus* non comburens set illuminans &c.

diuisiones B 1; C 1
B.19.228   *Diuisiones* graciarum sunt &c.
C.21.228   *Diuisiones* graciarum sunt.

diuiti B 1; C 1
B.14.212   Ita inpossibile *diuiti* &c,
C.11.201   Ita possibile est *diuiti* intrare in regn[um] celorum sicut camelus
          &c.

dixi B 1
B.13.55   In a dissh of derne shrifte, *Dixi* & confitebor tibi.

dixit A 1; B 3; C 3
A.10.34   *Dixit* & facta sunt &c,
B. 7.141   As diuinour in diuinite, wiþ *Dixit* inspiens to þi teme.'
B. 9.33   *Dixit* & facta sunt,
B.14.61   *Dixit* & facta sunt &c;
C. 1.122   *Dixit* dominus domino meo, sede a dextris meis.
C.14.165   *Dixit* & facta sunt.
C.15.260   *Dixit* & facta [s]unt;

do B 2; C 1
B.13.195   Than ȝacheus for he seide "dimidium bonorum meorum *do*
          pauperibus",
B.13.254   Argentum & aurum non est michi; quod autem habeo tibi *do*; in
          nomine
C.15.224   Argentum & Aurum non est michi; quod [autem] habeo tibi *do* &c.

doce B 2; C 1
B.13.137   Disce', quod he, '*doce*, dilige inimicos.
B.13.138   Disce and dowel, *doce* and dobet, dilige and dobest:
C.15.140   That disce, *doce*, dilige deum and thyn enemy,

docuerit A 1; B 1; C 1
A.11.196   Qui facit & *docuerit* magnus vocabitur in regno celorum.
B.13.118   Qui facit & *docuerit* magnus vocabitur in regno celorum.'
C.15.126   Qui facit & *docuerit* magnus vocabitur.'

dogma B 1
B.10.266   *Dogma* tuum sordet cum te tua culpa remordet.

dolor B 1; C 1
B.13.330   labor et *dol[or]*; Et alibi, Filij hominum dentes eorum arma &
          sagitte
C. 6.76   labor & *dolor*. Filij hominum dentes eorum Arma & sagitte

dolorem A 1; B 1; C 1
A.10.150   Concepit *dolore[m]* & peperit iniquitatem.
B. 9.125   Concepit *dolore[m]* & peperit iniquitatem.
C.10.212   Concepit *dolore[m]* & peperit iniquitatem.

domesticos A 1; B 1
A.11.245   ad omnes, maxime autem ad *domesticos* fidei.
B.10.204   Dum tempus [est] operemur bonum ad omnes, maxime autem ad
          domesticos fidei.

dominancium B 1; C 1
B.10.333   impiorum, et virgam *dominancium* cedencium plaga insanabili.
C. 5.177   Contriuit dominus bac[u]lum impiorum, virga[m] *d[omi]nancium*,

domine B 11; C 9
B. 2.39   *Domine* quis habitabit in tabernaculo tuo &c.
B. 3.234   *Domine*, quis habitabit in tabernaculo tuo?

B. 7.52   *Domine*, quis habitabit in tabernaculo tuo.
B.10.416   Homines & iumenta saluabis, *domine* &c.
B.11.251   *Domine*, non est tibi cure quod soror mea reliquit me solam ministrare?
B.13.127   But Dilige deum and *Domine* quis habitabit;
B.14.131   velud sompn[i]um surgencium *domine* in Ciuitate tua,
B.15.490   Boþe Mathew and Marc and Memento *domine* dauid:
B.17.266   Non omnis qui dicit *domine*, domine, intrabit &c.
B.17.266   Non omnis qui dicit *domine*, domine, intrabit &c.
B.19.295   And pleieþ al wiþ pacience and Parce michi *domine*;
C. 2.40   *Domine* quis habitabit in tabernaculo tuo &c.
C. 3.340   Retribuere dignare *domine* deus &c.'
C.12.138   *Domine*, non est tibi cur[e] quod soror &c?
C.15.134   Bote dilige deum & p[roximu]m [and] *domine* quis habitabit
C.19.232   Non omnis qui dicit *domine*, domine intrabit in reg[num] celorum &c.
C.19.232   Non omnis qui dicit domine, *domine* intrabit in reg[num] celorum &c.
C.20.253   "*Domine*, iube me venire ad te."
C.20.435   *Domine* ne in furore tuo Arguas me &c–
C.21.295   And ple[ieþ] al with pacience and parce michi *domine*

domini A 1; B 6; C 5
A.10.81   Inicium sapiencie timor *domini*.
B. 9.96   Inicium sapiencie timor *domini*.
B.13.254   quod autem habeo tibi do; in nomine *domini* surge et amb[ula].
B.14.190   Pateat &c: Per passionem *domini*,
B.15.537   Absit nobis gloriari nisi in cruce *domini* nostri &c.
B.16.99   Ecce ancilla *domini*; fiat michi [secundum verbum tuum]'.
B.18.17   Benedictus qui venit in nomine *domini*.
C.Pr.108   Thei were discomfited in batayle and losten Archa *domini*
C.Pr.112   Were disconfit in batayle and Archa *domini* lorn
C.17.198   Absit nobis gloriari nisi in cruce *domini* nostri &c.
C.18.132   Ecce Ancilla *domini* &c.'
C.20.15   Benedictus qui venit in nomine *domini*.

dominis B 1; C 1
B.13.312   Et alibi, Nemo potest duobus *dominis* seruire.
C. 6.60   nemo potest duobus *dominis* seruire.'

domino C 2
C. 1.122   Dixit dominus *domino* meo, sede a dextris meis.
C.13.17   And for a song in his sorwe, "si bona accepimus a *domino* &c,

dominum B 2; C 1
B. 9.109   Inquirentes autem *dominum* non minuentur omni bono.
B.11.282   Inquirentes autem *dominum* non minuentur omni bono.
C.10.202   Inquirentes autem *dominum* [non] minuentur omni bono.

dominus B 6; C 5
B.10.333   Quomodo cessauit exactor, quieuit tributum? contriuit *dominus* baculum
B.10.336   'Thanne is dowel and dobet', quod I, '*dominus* and knyȝthode?'
B.12.189   *Dominus* pars hereditatis mee is a murye verset
B.16.25   Cum ceciderit iustus non collidetur quia *dominus* supponit ma[num suam];
B.18.318   *Dominus* virtutum.
B.19.172   "[*Dominus*] meus & [deus] meus.
C. 1.122   Dixit *dominus* domino meo, sede a dextris meis.
C. 5.60   *Dominus* pars hereditatis mee &c. Et alibi: clemencia non constringit.
C. 5.177   Contriuit *dominus* bac[u]lum impiorum, virga[m] d[omi]nancium,
C.14.128   *Dominus* pars hereditatis [mee] is A merye verset
C.21.172   "*Dominus* meus & deus meus.

domo B 2
B.15.576   In *domo* mea non est panis neque vestimentum et ideo nolite constituere me Regem.
B.15.578   Inferte omnes [decimas] in orreum meum vt cibus in *domo* mea.

domos B 1; C 1
B.20.340   'Certes', seide his felawe, 'sire Penetrans *domos*.'
C.22.340   'Certes,' saide his felawe, 'sire penetrans *domos*.'

domum C 1
C. 9.125   Et egenos vagos[que] induc in *domum* tuam,

domus B 3; C 1
B.13.432   Non habitabit in medio *domus* mee qui facit superbiam & qui loquitur iniqua.
B.16.135   *Domus* mea domus oracionis vacabitur.'
B.16.135   Domus mea *domus* oracionis vacabitur.'
C. 7.92   Non habitabit in medio *domus* mee qui facit superbiam [&] qui

donec B 2
B. 5.273   Non dimittitur peccatum *donec* restituatur [a]blatum.
B. 7.75   Sit elemosina tua in manu tua *donec* studes cui des.

donum B 2; C 2
B.14.276   possessio sine calumpnia, *donum* dei, sanit[atis] mater,
B.14.300   *Donum* dei.
C.16.116   posessio sine calumpnia, *donum* dei, sanitatis mater,
C.16.136   *Donum* dei.

dormiam B 2; C 1
B.15.254   In pace in idipsum *dormiam* &c.
B.18.187   And þat þis dede shal dure *dormiam* & requiescam.'
C.20.192   And that this dede shal duyre, *dormiam* & requiescam.'

dormiamusque B 1; C 1
B. 1.31   Inebri[e]mus eum vino *dormiamusque* cum eo
C. 1.30   Inebriemus eum vino *dormiamusque* cum eo vt seruare possimus

dormierunt B 1; C 1
B.14.131   *Dormierunt* & nichil inuenerunt; [et alibi], velud sompn[i]um
C.15.306   *dormierunt* & nichil inuenerunt &c; Et alibi: velud sompn[i]um

dormit C 1
C. 9.258   Certes, hoso durste sygge hit, Simon quasi *dormit*;

dos B 2; C 2
B.15.552   Shal þei demen *dos* ecclesie, and [depose yow for youre pride]:
B.15.560   "*Dos* ecclesie þis day haþ ydronke venym
C.17.215   Shal dampne *dos* ecclesie and depose ȝow for ȝoure pruyde:
C.17.223   "*Dos* ecclesie this day hath ydronke venym

dragmam C 1
C. 5.98   Mulier qu[e] inuenit d[ra]gmam.

dubio B 1; C 1
B.15.118   sine *dubio* sacerdocium eius non est sanum.
C.16.273   sine *dubio* sacerdocium eius non est sanum.

ducit B 2; C 1
B.10.281   Dum cecus *ducit* cecum ambo in foueam cadunt.
B.12.185   Dum cecus *ducit* cecum &c.
C.14.124   Dum [c]ecus d[u]cit [c]ecum &c.

ducunt C 1
C.11.22   *Ducunt* in bonis dies suos & in fin[e] descendunt ad infernum.

dum A 2; B 16; C 14
A.11.245   *Dum* tempus est operemur bonum ad omnes, maxime autem ad
A.11.296   *Dum* steter[it]is ante [reges &] presides nolite cogitare,
B.Pr.141   '*Dum* rex a regere dicatur nomen habere
B. 9.186   *Dum* sis vir fortis ne des tua robora scortis;
B.10.204   *Dum* tempus [est] operemur bonum ad omnes, maxime autem ad domesticos fidei.
B.10.281   *Dum* cecus ducit cecum ambo in foueam cadunt.
B.10.450   "[D]um steteritis ante Reges & presides [nolite cogitare]:
B.11.269   Pauper ego ludo *dum* tu diues meditaris.
B.12.185   *Dum* cecus ducit cecum &c.
B.15.39   *dum* viuificat corpus anima est; dum vult animus est; dum scit mens
B.15.39   dum viuificat corpus anima est; *dum* vult animus est; dum scit mens
B.15.39   *dum* scit mens est; dum recolit memoria est; dum iudicat racio est;
B.15.39   dum scit mens est; *dum* recolit memoria est; dum iudicat racio est;
B.15.39   dum scit mens est; dum recolit memoria est; *dum* iudicat racio est;
B.15.39   *dum* sentit sensus est; dum amat Amor est; dum negat vel consentit
B.15.39   dum sentit sensus est; *dum* amat Amor est; dum negat vel consentit
B.15.39   *dum* negat vel consentit consciencia est; dum spirat spiritus est.'
B.15.39   dum negat vel consentit consciencia est; *dum* spirat spiritus est.'
C.10.287   *Dum* sis vir fortis ne des tua robora scortis;
C.11.275   "*Dum* steteritis ante Reges vel presides &c:
C.12.154   Pauper ego ludo *dum* tu diues m[e]ditaris.
C.14.124   *Dum* [c]ecus d[u]cit [c]ecum &c.
C.16.201   *dum* [v]i[u]ificat corpus Anima est; dum vult animus est; [dum scit
C.16.201   dum [v]i[u]ificat corpus Anima est; *dum* vult animus est; [dum scit
C.16.201   [*dum* scit mens est]; dum recolit memoria est; dum iudicat racio est;
C.16.201   [dum scit mens est]; *dum* recolit memoria est; dum iudicat racio est;
C.16.201   [dum scit mens est]; dum recolit memoria est; *dum* iudicat racio est;
C.16.201   *dum* sentit sensus est; dum Amat Amor est; dum declina[t] de malo
C.16.201   dum sentit sensus est; *dum* Amat Amor est; dum declina[t] de malo
C.16.201   dum sentit sensus est; dum Amat Amor est; *dum* declina[t] de malo ad bonum liberum Arbitrium est; dum negat
C.16.201   dum declina[t] de malo ad bonum liberum Arbitrium est; *dum* negat
C.16.201   *dum* negat vel consentit consciencia est; dum sp[i]rat spiritus est.'
C.16.201   dum negat vel consentit consciencia est; *dum* sp[i]rat spiritus est.'

duobus B 2; C 2
B.13.312   Et alibi, Nemo potest *duobus* dominis seruire.
B.17.16   In hijs *duobus* mandatis tota lex pendet & prophet[e].
C. 6.60   Si hominibus placerem christi seruus non essem; nemo potest *duobus*

C.19.17   In hijs *duobus* [mandatis tota lex pendet & prophete].

duxi B 3; C 3
B. 1.141   Heu michi quia sterilem *duxi* vitam Iuuenilem.
B. 5.440   Heu michi quia sterilem vitam *duxi* Iuuenilem.'
B.14.3   Vxorem *duxi* & ideo non possum venire–
C. 1.140   Heu michi quod ste[r]ilem *duxi* vitam iuuenilem.
C. 7.54   Heu michi quod ster[i]lem *duxi* vitam iuuenilem.'
C. 7.304   Vxorem *duxi* & ideo non possum venire.'

duxit B 1; C 1
B. 5.490   Captiuam *duxit* captiuitatem.
C. 7.130   Capti[u]am *duxi[t]* captiuitatem.

ea B 2; C 2
B.11.255 Maria optimam partem elegit que non [auferetur ab *ea*].
B.13.45   eff[u]deritis, *ea* que in delicijs comeditis in tormentis euometis.
C.12.141 Maria optimam partem elegit que non [auferetur ab *ea*].
C.15.50   *ea* que in deliciis comeditis in tor[mentis] euo[metis] &c.

eadem A 1; B 2; C 3
A.10.112 In *eadem* vocacione qua vocati estis state.
B. 1.178 *Eadem* mensura qua mensi fueritis remecietur vobis.
B.11.228 *Eadem* mensura qua mensi fueritis remecietur vobis.
C. 1.174 *Eadem* mensura qua mensi fueritis Remetietur vobis.
C. 5.43   In *eadem* vocacione qu[a] vocati estis [&c]
C.11.232 *Eadem* mensura &c.

eam A 2; B 3; C 2
A.11.55   Ecce audiuimus *eam* in effrata, inuenimus eam in campis silue.
A.11.55   Ecce audiuimus eam in effrata, inuenimus *eam* in campis silue.
B.10.69   Ecce audiuimus *eam* in effrata; inuenimus eam in campis silue.
B.10.69   Ecce audiuimus eam in effrata; inuenimus *eam* in campis silue.
B.15.490 [Ecce audiuimus e[a]m in effrata &c]
C.11.49   Ecce Audiuimus *eam* in Effrata; [inuenimus eam in campis silue].
C.11.49   Ecce Audiuimus eam in Effrata; [inuenimus *eam* in campis silue].

ecce A 3; B 10; C 8
A.11.55   *Ecce* audiuimus eam in effrata, inuenimus eam in campis silue.
A.11.192 *Ecce* quam bonum & quam iocundum habitare Fratres in vnum.
A.11.305 *Ecce* ipsi ydiot[e] rapiunt celum vbi nos sapientes
B. 5.277 *Ecce* enim veritatem dilexisti &c.
B.10.26   *Ecce* ipsi peccatores! habundantes in seculo obtinuerunt diuicias.
B.10.69   *Ecce* audiuimus eam in effrata; inuenimus eam in campis silue.
B.10.461 "*Ecce* ipsi ydiot[e] rapiunt celum vbi nos sapientes in inferno mergimur".
B.15.464 *Ecce* altilia mea & omnia parata sunt;
B.15.490 [*Ecce* audiuimus e[a]m in effrata &c].
B.16.99   *Ecce* ancilla domini; fiat michi [secundum verbum tuum]'.
B.16.252 *Ecce* agnus dei &c.'
B.18.324 Songen seint Iohanes song, *Ecce* agnus dei.
B.18.423 *Ecce* quam bonum & quam iocundum &c.
C. 6.302 On *Ecce* enim veritatem dilexisti.
C.11.23   Et alibi: ecce ip[s]i peccatores, habundantes &c.
C.11.49   *Ecce* Audiuimus eam in Effrata; [inuenimus eam in campis silue].
C.11.287 "*Ecce* ips[i] idiote rapiunt celum vbi nos sapientes in inferno mergimur".
C.18.132 *Ecce* Ancilla domini &c.'
C.18.268 *Ecce* Agnus dei.'
C.20.367 Songen seynt Iohann[es songe], *ecce* agnus dei.
C.20.466 *Ecce* quam bonum & quam iocundum &c.

ecclesia B 1; C 2
B.15.118 Si sacerdocium integrum fuerit tota floret *ecclesia*; Si autem
C. 3.357 In case, credere in *ecclesia*, in holy kyrke to bileue;
C.16.273 Si sacerdocium integrum fuerit tota floret *ecclesia*; Si Autem

ecclesie B 2; C 2
B.15.552 Shal þei demen dos *ecclesie*, and [depose yow for youre pride]:
B.15.560 "Dos *ecclesie* þis day haþ ydronke venym
C.17.215 Shal dampne dos *ecclesie* and depose ȝow for ȝoure pruyde:
C.17.223 "Dos *ecclesie* this day hath ydronke venym

edentes B 1; C 1
B.13.39   *Edentes* & bibentes que apud eos sunt.
C.15.44   *Edentes* & bibentes que apud eos sunt &c.

efficiamini B 1; C 1
B.15.149 'Nisi *efficiamini* sicut paruuli non intrabitis in regnum celorum.
C.16.298 Nisi *efficiamini* sicut paruuli &c,

effrata A 1; B 2; C 1
A.11.55   Ecce audiuimus eam in *effrata*, inuenimus eam in campis silue.
B.10.69   Ecce audiuimus eam in *effrata*; inuenimus eam in campis silue.
B.15.490 [Ecce audiuimus e[a]m in *effrata* &c].
C.11.49   Ecce Audiuimus eam in *Effrata*; [inuenimus eam in campis silue].

effuderitis B 1; C 1
B.13.45   *eff[u]deritis*, ea que in delicijs comeditis in tormentis euometis.

C.15.50   *effuderitis*, ea que in deliciis comeditis in tor[mentis] euo[metis] &c.

egenos C 1
C. 9.125 Et *egenos* vagos[que] induc in domum tuam,

egerunt A 1; B 1; C 2
A. 8.95   Et qui bona *egerunt* ibunt in vitam eternam;
B. 7.113 Et qui bona *egerunt* ibunt in vitam eternam;
C. 9.287 Et qui bona *egerunt* ibunt in vitam eternam;
C.12.119 Et qui bona *egerunt*, ibunt &c.

eges B 1
B.15.343 accipis pocius das quam accipis; Si autem non *eges* & accipis rapis.

egipciaca C 1
C.17.23 Marie *Egipciaca* eet in thritty wynter

ego A 1; B 6; C 3
A.11.255 For Michi vindictam et *ego* retribuam.
B. 6.226 Michi vindictam & *ego* retribuam.
B. 7.83   Quare non dedisti pecuniam meam ad mensam vt *ego* veni[ens] cum vsuris ex[egissem illam]?
B.10.209 Michi vindictam & *ego* retribuam.
B.10.252 [*Ego* in patre et pater in me est, et qui videt me videt et patrem meum]
B.10.374 [For michi vindictam et *ego* retribuam]:
B.11.269 Pauper *ego* ludo dum tu diues meditaris.
C. 7.128 *Ego* in patre & pater in me [est] et qui me videt videt [&] patrem meum &c;
C.11.153 *Ego* in patre & pater in me est; Et qui me vid[e]t, patrem meum
C.12.154 Pauper *ego* ludo dum tu diues m[e]ditaris.

egredietur C 1
C.12.215 O stulte, ista nocte anima tua *egredi[e]tur*; tezaurisat & ignorat &c.

egros B 1; C 1
B.13.249 In nomine meo demonia e[j]icient & super *egros* manus imponent & bene
C.15.221 Super *egros* manus [in]pone[nt] & bene habebunt &c–

ei B 2; C 2
B.12.147 Set non erat *ei* locus in diuersorio, et pauper non habet diuersorium.
B.15.55   And seiþ, Sicut qui mel comedit multum non est *ei* bonum, Sic qui
C. 8.245 Piger propter frigus noluit arrare; mendicabi[t] in yeme & non dabitur *ei*".
C.16.217 And sayth, sicut qui mel comedit multum non est *ei* bonum; Sic

eiicietur B 1
B.18.315 Nunc princeps huius mundi e[i]icietur foras.'

eis A 1; B 5; C 3
A. 8.125 E[j]ice derisores & iurgia cum *eis* ne crescant.'
B. 7.60   Quodcumque vultis vt faciant vobis homines facite *eis*.
B. 7.143 E[ji]ce derisores & iurgia cum *eis* ne crescant &c.'
B.13.45   Vos qui peccata hominum comeditis, nisi pro *eis* lacrimas & oraciones
B.15.318 brutorum animalium natura te condempnat, quia cum *eis* pabulum
B.20.256 Qui numerat multitudinem stellarum et omnibus *eis* [nomina vocat].
C.15.50   Vos qui peccata hominum comeditis, nisi pro *eis* lacrimas & orationes
C.16.309 Quodcumque vultis vt faciant vobis homines, facite *eis*.
C.17.53   Brutorum Animalium natura te condempnat, quia cum [*eis*] pabulum

eius B 10; C 8
B. 5.281 [Misericordia *eius* super omnia opera eius &c]–
B. 5.281 [Misericordia eius super omnia opera *eius* &c]–
B. 7.89   Iunior fui etenim senui, & non vidi iustum derelictum ne[c] semen *eius*
B.11.139 Misericordia *eius* super omnia opera eius.'
B.11.139 Misericordia eius super omnia opera *eius*.'
B.13.330 Cuius malediccione os plenum est & amaritudine; sub lingua *eius*
B.15.118 sine dubio sacerdocium *eius* non est sanum.
B.16.242 Quam olim Abrahe promisisti & semini *eius*.
B.17.318 Misericordia *eius* super omnia opera eius–
B.17.318 Misericordia eius super omnia opera *eius*–
C. 6.76   Cuius maledictione os plenum est & amaritudine; sub lingua *eius*
C. 7.147 Quandocumque ingemuerit peccator omnes iniquitate[s] *eius* non
C.12.74   Misericordia *eius* super omnia opera [eius].'
C.12.74   Misericordia eius super omnia opera [*eius*].'
C.16.273 sine dubio sacerdocium *eius* non est sanum.
C.17.66   Iusticia *eius* manet in eternum.
C.19.298 Misericordia *eius* super omnia opera eius.
C.19.298 Misericordia eius super omnia opera *eius*.

ejice A 1; B 2
A. 8.125   E[j]ice derisores & iurgia cum eis ne crescant.'
B. 7.143   E[ji]ce derisores & iurgia cum eis ne crescant &c.'
B.10.270   E[j]ice primo trabem [de] oculo tuo &c–

ejicient B 1
B.13.249   In nomine meo demonia e[j]icient & super egros manus imponent
                & bene

elegit B 1; C 1
B.11.255   Maria optimam partem elegit que non [auferetur ab ea].
C.12.141   Maria optimam partem elegit que non [auferetur ab ea].

elemosina B 1
B. 7.75   Sit elemosina tua in manu tua donec studes cui des.

eligas B 1
B. 7.77   Non eligas cui miser[e]aris ne forte pretereas illum qui meretur
                accipere,

emi C 1
C. 7.292   'Ʒe! villam emi,' quod oen, 'and now y moste thedre

enarrant C 1
C.18.213   Celi enarrant gloriam dei &c.

enigmate B 1; C 1
B.15.162   [Hic] in enigmate, tunc facie ad faciem.
C.16.296   Hic in enigmate, tunc facie ad faciem.

enim B 2; C 4
B. 5.277   Ecce enim veritatem dilexisti &c.
B.14.213   Opera enim illorum sequ[u]ntur illos,
C. 6.302   On Ecce enim veritatem dilexisti.
C. 7.260   Quodcumque pecieritis in nomine meo dabitur enim vobis.
C.15.244   Quodcumque pecieritis [a patre] in nomine meo dab[itur] enim
C.16.54   Opera [enim ill]orum sequ[u]ntur illos,

eo B 2; C 2
B. 1.31   Inebri[e]mus eum vino dormiamusque cum eo
B. 5.486   Et alibi, Qui manet in caritate in deo manet & deus in eo.
C. 1.30   Inebriemus eum vino dormiamusque cum eo vt seruare possimus
C. 3.403   Qui in caritate manet in deo manet et deus in eo.

eorum A 2; B 10; C 8
A. 3.85   Ignis deuorabit tabernacula eorum qui libenter accipiunt munera.
A. 3.228   In quorum manibus iniquitates sunt; dextera eorum repleta est
                muneribus.
B. 3.96   Ignis deuorabit tabernacula eorum qui libenter accipiunt munera
                &c.
B. 3.249   In quorum manibus iniquitates sunt; dextra eorum repleta est
                muneribus.
B. 4.36   Contricio & infelicitas in viis eorum &c.
B. 4.37   Non est timor dei ante oculos eorum &c.
B. 7.44   A Regibus & principibus erit merces eorum.
B. 9.67   Et dimisi eos secundum desideria eorum.
B.10.436   [Sunt] iusti atque sapientes, & opera eorum in manu dei sunt &c.
B.13.330   labor et dol[or]; Et alibi, Filij hominum dentes eorum arma &
                sagitte
B.13.330   et lingua eorum gladius a[cutus].
B.15.200   Et vidit deus cogitaciones eorum.
C. 3.124   Ignis deuorabit tabernacula eorum qui libenter accipiunt munera.
C. 4.36   Contricio & infelicitas in viis eorum et viam pacis non
                cognouerunt;
C. 4.36   non est timor dei ante oculos eorum.
C. 6.76   labor & dolor. Filij hominum dentes eorum Arma & sagitte
C. 6.76   & lingua eorum gladius acutus.
C.10.165   Et dimisi eos secundum desideria eorum.
C.11.271   Sunt iusti atque sapientes & opera eorum in manu dei sunt &c.
C.16.340   Et vidit deus cogitaciones eorum.

eos B 2; C 3
B. 9.67   Amen dico vobis, nescio vos; Et alibi, Et dimisi eos secundum
                desideria
B.13.39   Edentes & bibentes que apud eos sunt.
C.10.99   Nolite timere eos qui possunt occidere corpus &c.
C.10.165   Et dimisi eos secundum desideria eorum.
C.15.44   Edentes & bibentes que apud eos sunt &c.

episcopos B 1
B.11.317   Non excusat episcopos nec ydiotes preestes'.

episcopus B 1; C 1
B.15.43   And oþere names an heep, Episcopus and Pastor.'
C.16.205   And oþere names an heep, Episcopus and pastor.'

epulabatur C 1
C.19.240   Epulabatur splendide & induebatur bisso &c.

equis B 1; C 1
B.10.327   Hij in curribus & hij in equis ipsi obligati sunt &c.

C. 5.172   Hij in curribus & [hij] in equis; ipsi obligati sunt & ceciderunt.

erant B 1
B.11.398   Et vidit deus cuncta que fecerat & erant valde bona.

erat B 2; C 1
B.12.147   Set non erat ei locus in diuersorio, et pauper non habet
                diuersorium.
B.18.68   Vere filius dei erat iste.
C.20.70   Vere filius dei erat iste;

ergo A 1; B 8; C 7
A. 9.20   Ergo he nis not alwey at hom among Ʒow Freris;
B. 8.24   Ergo he nys noʒt alwey [at hoom] amonges yow freres;
B.12.282   Ergo saluabitur', quod he and seide na moore latyn.
B.14.62   Ergo þoruʒ his breeþ [boþe] men and beestes lyuen,
B.14.88   Ergo contricion, feiþ and conscience is kyndeliche dowel,
B.14.287   Ergo paupertas est odibile bonum.
B.14.292   /Ergo pouerte and poore men parfournen þe comaundement
B.18.340   Ergo soule shal soule quyte and synne to synne wende,
B.19.19   Ergo is no name to þe name of Iesus,
C.10.28   Ergo he [n]is nat alwey at hom amonges Ʒow freres;
C.14.204   Ergo saluabitur,' quod he and saide no more latyn.
C.15.261   Ergo thorw his breth bestes lyueth, bothe men and fisches,
C.16.122   [Ergo paupertas est odibile bonum.]
C.16.127   Ergo pouerte and pore men parforme þe comandement
C.20.388   Ergo soule shal soule quyte and synne to synne wende
C.21.19   Ergo is no name to þe name of iesus

eris B 3; C 2
B. 5.269   Pane tuo pocius vescere: liber eris.
B. 5.278   Cum sancto sanctus eris: construwe me þis on englissh.'
B.19.422   At Auynoun among Iewes–Cum sancto sanctus eris &c–
C. 6.293   Pane tuo pocius vescere: liber eris.
C.21.422   At Auenon among iewes–cum sancto sanctus eris &c–

erit A 1; B 2; C 1
A.11.234   Qui crediderit et baptizatus fuerit saluus erit.'
B. 7.44   A Regibus & principibus erit merces eorum.
B. 7.181   Quodcumque ligaueris super terram erit ligatum & in celis &c.
C. 9.327   Quodcumque ligaueris super terram erit ligatum & in celis.

eritis B 1
B.14.180   Conuertimini ad me & salui eritis.

ero B 6; C 3
B. 1.119   Ponam pedem in aquilone & similis ero altissimo.
B.10.291   Existimasti inique quod ero tui similis; arguam te & statuam contra
                faciem
B.11.95   Existimasti inique quod ero tui similis &c.
B.15.51   Ponam pedem meum in aquilone & similis ero altissimo.
B.17.114   [O mors ero mors tua &c].
B.18.35   O mors ero mors tua.'
C. 1.111   Ponam pedem meum in Aquilone & similis ero altissimo.'
C.12.29   Existimasti inique quod ero t[u]i similis; Arguam te & statuam
C.20.34   O mors [ero] mors tua.'

es A 1; B 4; C 2
A. 8.103   Non timebo mala quoniam tu mecum es.
B.Pr.134   Hoc quod agas melius, iustus es, esto pius!
B. 5.269   Seruus es alterius [cum] fercula pinguia queris;
B. 7.121   Non timebo mala quoniam tu mecum es.
B.10.261   Appare quod es vel esto quod appares;
C.Pr.155   Hoc vt agas melius, iustus es, esto pius!
C. 6.293   Seruus [es] alterius cum fercula pingu[i]a queris;

esse B 4; C 3
B.10.266   Si culpare velis culpabilis es[se] cauebis;
B.11.274   Si vis perfectus esse vade & vende [&c].
B.12.207   De peccato propiciato noli esse sine metu.
B.16.115   Ac [er] he made þe maistrie mestus cepit esse
C.12.167   Si vis perfectus esse vade & vende &c.
C.14.146   De peccato propiciato noli esse sine metu.
C.18.145   Ac ar he made þat miracle mestus cepit esse

essem B 1; C 1
B.13.312   Si hominibus placerem christi seruus non essem; Et alibi, Nemo
                potest
C. 6.60   Si hominibus placerem christi seruus non essem; nemo potest
                duobus

esses B 1; C 1
B.11.416   Philosophus esses si tacuisses.
C.13.224   Philosophus esses si tacuisses; & alibi: Locutum me aliquando

est A 10; B 70; C 61
A. 2.86   Dignus est operarius mercede [sua].
A. 3.228   In quorum manibus iniquitates sunt; dextera eorum repleta est
                muneribus.
A.10.108   Qui circuit [omne genus in nullo genere est].

A.11.23 [bene] *est* omnibus qui praue agunt & inique?
A.11.147 Qui sim[u]lat verbis, nec corde *est* fidus amicus,
A.11.154 Necesse *est* vt veniant scandala.
A.11.245 Dum tempus *est* operemur bonum ad omnes, maxime autem ad
A.12.28 "Quid *est* ueritas?" quod he; "verilyche tel vs."
A.12.52 Til ȝe come to þe burg[h] quod bonum *est* tenete.
A.12.57 And ere I cam to þe court quod bonum *est* tenete
B.Pr.196 Ve terre vbi puer Rex *est* &c.
B. 1.187 Fides sine operibus mortua *est* &c.
B. 2.123 For Dignus *est* operarius his hire to haue,
B. 3.249 In quorum manibus iniquitates sunt; dextra eorum repleta *est* muneribus.
B. 3.330 For Melius *est* bonum nomen quam diuicie multe.'
B. 3.343 Quod bonum *est* tenete; truþe þat text made.
B. 4.37 Non *est* timor dei ante oculos eorum &c.
B. 5.283 Omnis iniquitas quantum ad misericordiam dei *est* quasi sintilla in medio
B. 5.412 Come I to Ite missa *est* I holde me yserued.
B. 5.500 Verbum caro factum *est* & habitauit in nobis.
B. 5.603 Per Euam cun[c]tis clausa *est* et per Mariam virginem [iterum] patefacta est;
B. 5.603 Per Euam cun[c]tis clausa est et per Mariam virginem [iterum] patefacta *est*;
B. 7.77 Quia incertum *est* pro quo deo magis placeas.
B. 7.87 Satis diues *est* qui non indiget pane.
B. 9.62 Quorum deus venter *est*.
B. 9.94 Proditor *est* prelatus cum Iuda qui patrimonium christi minus distribuit; Et
B. 9.94 alibi, Perniciosus dispensator *est* qui res pauperum christi inutiliter
B. 9.100 Qui offendit in vno in omnibus *est* reus.
B. 9.186 Scribitur in portis, meretrix *est* ianua mortis.
B. 9.194 Bonum *est* vt vnusquisque vxorem suam habeat propter fornicacionem.
B.10.25 Quare impij viuunt? bene *est* omnibus qui preuaricantur & inique agunt?
B.10.195 Qui simulat verbis [nec] corde *est* fidus amicus,
B.10.204 Dum tempus [*est*] operemur bonum ad omnes, maxime autem ad domesticos fidei.
B.10.252 [Ego in patre et pater in me *est*, et qui videt me videt et patrem meum]
B.11.204 Qui facit peccatum seruus *est* peccati.
B.11.231 Melius *est* scrutari scelera nostra quam naturas rerum.
B.11.251 Domine, non *est* tibi cure quod soror mea reliquit me solam ministrare?
B.11.309 Qui offendit in vno in omnibus *est* reus.
B.12.138 Sapiencia huius mundi stulticia *est* apud deum.
B.12.293 For Deus dicitur quasi dans [eternam vitam] suis, hoc *est* fidelibus;
B.13.70 Periculum *est* in falsis fratribus.'
B.13.73 Vnusquisque a fratre se custodiat quia vt dicitur periculum *est* in falsis
B.13.254 Argentum & aurum non *est* michi; quod autem habeo tibi do; in nomine
B.13.330 Cuius maledICcione os plenum *est* & amaritudine; sub lingua eius
B.14.104 'Ye? quis *est* ille?' quod Pacience; 'quik, laudabimus eum!
B.14.144 De delicijs ad delicias difficile *est* transire.
B.14.215 Beati pauperes quoniam ipsorum *est* regnum celorum.
B.14.276 'Paupertas,' quod Pacience, '*est* odibile bonum, Remocio curarum,
B.14.287 Ergo paupertas *est* odibile bonum.
B.14.309 Forþi seiþ Seneca Paupertas *est* absque sollicitudine semita.
B.15.39 dum viuificat corpus anima *est*; dum vult animus est; dum scit mens
B.15.39 dum viuificat corpus anima est; dum vult animus *est*; dum scit mens
B.15.39 dum scit mens *est*; dum recolit memoria est; dum iudicat racio est;
B.15.39 dum scit mens est; dum recolit memoria *est*; dum iudicat racio est;
B.15.39 dum scit mens est; dum recolit memoria est; dum iudicat racio *est*;
B.15.39 dum sentit sensus *est*; dum amat Amor est; dum negat vel consentit
B.15.39 dum sentit sensus est; dum amat Amor *est*; dum negat vel consentit
B.15.39 dum negat vel consentit consciencia *est*; dum spirat spiritus est.'
B.15.39 dum negat vel consentit consciencia est; dum spirat spiritus *est*.'
B.15.55 And seiþ, Sicut qui mel comedit multum non *est* ei bonum, Sic qui
B.15.55 scrutator *est* maiestatis opprimitur a gloria.
B.15.60 "Beatus *est*", seiþ Seint Bernard, "qui scripturas legit
B.15.118 Si autem corruptum fuerit omnium fides marcida *est*. Si
B.15.118 sine dubio sacerdocium eius non *est* sanum.
B.15.157 Non inflatur, non *est* ambiciosa, non querit que sua sunt—
B.15.212 But Piers þe Plowman, Petrus id *est* christus.
B.15.234 Beatus *est* diues qui &c.
B.15.343 Quia sacrilegium *est* res pauperum non pauperibus dare. Item, peccatorum
B.15.343 dare *est* demonibus immolare. Item, monache, si indiges &
B.15.576 In domo mea non *est* panis neque vestimentum et ideo nolite constituere me Regem.

B.16.47 *est* idem qui peccat per liberum arbitrium non repugnat.
B.16.110 Non *est* sanis opus medicus set in[firmis].
B.16.157 Necesse *est* vt veniant scandala; ve homini illi per quem scandalum venit.
B.17.151 Qui conceptus *est* de spiritu sancto &c.
B.18.57 'Consummatum *est*', quod crist and comsede for to swoune.
B.18.149 Quia in Inferno nulla *est* redempcio.'
B.18.316 'Quis *est* iste?'
B.18.408 Clarior *est* solito post maxima nebula phebus;
B.18.408 Post inimicicias [clarior *est* et amor].
B.19.273 Id *est* vetus testamentum & nouum.
C.Pr.209 Ve terre vbi puer *est* Rex.
C. 1.143 Melius *est* mori quam male viuere.
C. 1.183 Fides sine operibus mortua *est*.
C. 3.344 Quia antelate rei recordatiuum *est*—
C. 3.356 He acordeth with crist in kynde, verbum caro factum *est*;
C. 3.483 [For] melius *est* bonum nomen quam diuicie multe.'
C. 3.495 Quod bonum *est* tenete, a tixst of treuthe [m]akynge.
C. 4.36 non *est* timor dei ante oculos eorum.
C. 5.98 Simile *est* regnum celorum thesauro abscondito in agro;
C. 6.76 Cuius maledictione os plenum *est* & amaritudine; sub lingua eius
C. 6.290 Melius *est* mori quam male viuere.
C. 6.338 Omnis iniquitas quoad misericordiam dei *est* quasi sintilla in medio maris.
C. 7.128 Ego in patre & pater in me [*est*] et qui me videt videt [&] patrem meum &c;
C. 7.140 Verbum caro factum *est*.
C. 7.250 Per Euam cun[c]tis clausa *est* & per mariam verginem iterum patefacta est &c;
C. 7.250 Per Euam cun[c]tis clausa est & per mariam verginem iterum patefacta *est* &c;
C. 9.163 Iunior fui, [et]enim senui; e[t] alibi: infirmata *est* vertus mea paupertate.
C.10.287 Scribitur in portis, meretrix *est* ianua mortis.
C.10.293 Bonum *est* [vt] vnusquisque vx[or]em suam habeat propter fornicacionem.
C.11.153 Ego in patre & pater in me *est*; Et qui me vid[e]t, patrem meum
C.11.153 patrem meum vid[e]t qui in celis *est* &c.
C.11.201 Ita possibile *est* diuiti intrare in regn[um] celorum sicut camelus &c.
C.12.112 Qui facit peccatum seruus *est* peccati.
C.12.138 Domine, non *est* tibi cur[e] quod soror &c?
C.13.122 Qui offendit in vno in om[n]ibus *est* reus.
C.14.16 Beacius *est* dare quam petere.
C.14.42 Quis vestrum sine peccato *est*.
C.14.83 Sapiencia huius mundi stul[t]icia *est* apud deum.
C.15.75 Periculum *est* in falsis fratribus.'
C.15.224 Argentum & Aurum non *est* michi; quod [autem] habeo tibi do &c.
C.15.279 'ȝe? quis *est* ille?' quod pacience; 'quik, lauda[bi]mus eum!
C.16.116 'Paupertas,' quod pacience, '*est* odibile bonum, Remocio curarum,
C.16.122 [Ergo paupertas *est* odibile bonum].
C.16.143 Pauper[tas] *est* absque solicitudine semita.
C.16.201 dum [v]i[u]ificat corpus Anima *est*; dum vult animus est; [dum scit
C.16.201 dum [v]i[u]ificat corpus Anima est; dum vult animus *est*; [dum scit
C.16.201 [dum scit mens *est*]; dum recolit memoria est; dum iudicat racio est;
C.16.201 [dum scit mens est]; dum recolit memoria *est*; dum iudicat racio est;
C.16.201 [dum scit mens est]; dum recolit memoria est; dum iudicat racio *est*;
C.16.201 dum sentit sensus *est*; dum Amat Amor est; dum declina[t] de malo
C.16.201 dum sentit sensus est; dum Amat Amor *est*; dum declina[t] de malo
C.16.201 dum declina[t] de malo ad bonum liberum Arbitrium *est*; dum negat
C.16.201 dum negat vel consentit consciencia *est*; dum sp[i]rat spiritus est.'
C.16.201 dum negat vel consentit consciencia est; dum sp[i]rat spiritus *est*.'
C.16.217 And sayth, sicut qui mel comedit multum non *est* ei bonum; Sic
C.16.217 [qui] scrutator *est* magestatis opprim[e]tur a gloria.
C.16.273 Si Autem corupt[um] fuerit omnium f[i]des marcida *est*. Si
C.16.273 sine dubio sacerdocium eius non *est* sanum.
C.16.291 Non inflatur, non *est* Ambiciosa.
C.16.359 Beatus *est* diues sine macula.
C.17.40 Videte ne furtum sit: & alibi: meli[u]s *est* mori quam male viuere &c.
C.17.140 Dilige deum propter deum, id *est* propter veritatem; & inimicum tuum
C.17.140 propter mandatum, id *est* propter legem; & Amicum propter Amorem,
C.17.140 id *est* propter caritatem.
C.19.125 Natus *est* ex maria virgine.
C.20.57 'Consummatum *est*,' quod Crist and comsed for to swoene.
C.20.152 Quia in inferno nulla *est* redempcio.'
C.20.234 Omnia probate; quod bonum *est* tenete.

C.20.451   Clarior *est* solito [post maxima nebula phebus];
C.20.451   Post inimicicias Clarior *est* & Amor.
C.21.273   Id *est* vetus testamentum & nouum.

estis   A 1; B 2; C 2
A.10.112   In eadem vocacione qua vocati *estis* state.
B.13.61   Ve vobis qui potentes *estis* ad bibendum vinum.
B.15.429   Vos *estis* sal terre &c.
C. 5.43   In eadem vocacione qu[a] vocati *estis* [&c]
C.15.65   Ve vobis qui p[o]tentes *estis* ad bibendum vinum–

esto   B 4; C 3
B.Pr.134   Hoc quod agas melius, iustus es, *esto* pius!
B. 5.186   *Esto* sobrius!' he seide and assoiled me after,
B.10.261   Appare quod es vel *esto* quod appares;
B.19.296   *Esto* forti animo cum sis dampnatus inique.
C.Pr.155   Hoc vt agas melius, iustus es, *esto* pius!
C. 6.168   *Esto* sobrius!' he saide, and assoiled hym aftur
C.21.296   *Esto* forti Animo cum sis dampnatus inique.

estote   B 1
B.11.383   Propter deum subiecti *estote* omni creature.

esurienti   B 1; C 1
B.10.85   Frange *esurienti* panem tuum &c.
C.11.65   Frange *esurienti* panem tuum.

et   &   A 21; B 130; C 120
A. 1.51   *Et* que sunt dei deo oþer ellis ȝe don ille."
A. 1.175   Date & dabitur vobis for I dele ȝow alle.
A. 5.42   Qui cum patre & filio; Faire mote ȝow befalle.'
A. 7.68   *Et* cum iustis non scribantur.
A. 8.3   And purchac[ide] hym a pardoun a pena & a culpa
A. 8.21   But non a pena & a culpa þe pope wolde h[e]m graunte,
A. 8.46   Super innocentem munera non accipies; a regibus & principibus–
A. 8.95   *Et* qui bona egerunt ibunt in vitam eternam;
A. 8.125   E[j]ice derisores & iurgia cum eis ne crescant.'
A.10.34   Dixit & facta sunt &c,
A.10.87   Virga tua & baculus tuus ipsa me consolata sunt.
A.10.150   Concepit dolore[m] & peperit iniquitatem.
A.11.23   [bene] est omnibus qui praue agunt & inique?
A.11.192   Ecce quam bonum & quam iocundum habitare Fratres in vnum.
A.11.193   Gaudere cum gaudentibus *Et* flere cum flentibus,
A.11.196   Qui facit & docuerit magnus vocabitur in regno celorum.
A.11.234   Qui crediderit *et* baptizatus fuerit saluus erit.'
A.11.242   Dilige deum &c, *Et* proximum tuum sicut teipsum.
A.11.255   For Michi vindictam *et* ego retribuam.
A.11.296   Dum steter[it]is ante [reges &] presides nolite cogitare,
A.12.19   Vidi preuarica[nt]es & tabescebam.
B. 1.53   *Et* que sunt dei deo or ellis ye don ille."
B. 1.119   Ponam pedem in aquilone & similis ero altissimo.
B. 1.201   "Date & dabitur vobis, for I deele yow alle."
B. 2.74   'Sciant presentes & futuri &c.
B. 3.237   Qui ingreditur sine macula & operatur Iusticiam.
B. 3.241   Qui pecuniam suam non dedit ad vsuram *et* munera super innocentem &c,
B. 4.36   Contricio & infelicitas in viis eorum &c.
B. 5.58   Qui cum patre & filio; þat faire hem bifalle
B. 5.243   I haue mo Manoirs þoruȝ Rerages þan þoruȝ Miseretur & com[m]odat.
B. 5.486   Faciamus hominem ad ymaginem [*et* similitudinem] nostram;
B. 5.486   *Et* alibi, Qui manet in caritate in deo manet & deus in eo.
B. 5.486   Et alibi, Qui manet in caritate in deo manet & deus in eo.
B. 5.500   Verbum caro factum est & habitauit in nobis.
B. 5.509   'Homines & iumenta saluabis quemadmodum multiplicasti misericordiam
B. 5.567   Honora patrem & matrem &c;
B. 5.603   Per Euam cun[c]tis clausa *est* & per Mariam virginem [iterum] patefacta est;
B. 6.226   Michi vindictam & ego retribuam.
B. 7.3   And purchaced hym a pardoun a pena & a culpa
B. 7.19   Ac noon A pena & a culpa þe pope [w]olde hem graunte
B. 7.44   A Regibus & principibus erit merces eorum.
B. 7.89   Iunior fui etenim senui, & non vidi iustum derelictum ne[c] semen eius
B. 7.113   *Et* qui bona egerunt ibunt in vitam eternam;
B. 7.143   E[ji]ce derisores & iurgia cum eis ne crescant &c.'
B. 7.181   Quodcumque ligaueris super terram erit ligatum & in celis &c.
B. 9.33   Dixit & facta sunt,
B. 9.67   Amen dico vobis, nescio vos; *Et* alibi, Et dimisi eos secundum desideria
B. 9.67   Amen dico vobis, nescio vos; Et alibi, *Et* dimisi eos secundum desideria
B. 9.94   Proditor est prelatus cum Iuda qui patrimonium christi minus distribuit; *Et*
B. 9.125   Concepit dolore[m] & peperit iniquitatem.

B. 9.149   Filius non portabit iniquitatem patris *et* pater non portabit iniquitatem filij.
B. 9.164   "I am via & veritas", seiþ crist, "I may auaunce alle."
B.10.25   Quare impij viuunt? bene est omnibus qui preuaricantur & inique agunt?
B.10.209   Michi vindictam & ego retribuam.
B.10.252   [Ego in patre *et* pater in me est, et qui videt me videt et patrem meum]
B.10.252   [Ego in patre et pater in me est, *et* qui videt me videt et patrem meum]
B.10.252   [Ego in patre et pater in me est, et qui videt me videt *et* patrem meum]
B.10.291   Existimasti inique quod ero tui similis; arguam te & statuam contra faciem
B.10.327   Hij in curribus & hij in equis ipsi obligati sunt &c.
B.10.333   impiorum, *et* virgam dominancium cedencium plaga insanabili.
B.10.374   [For michi vindictam *et* ego retribuam]:
B.10.416   Homines & iumenta saluabis, domine &c.
B.10.436   [Sunt] iusti atque sapientes, & opera eorum in manu dei sunt &c.
B.10.450   "[D]um steteritis ante Reges & presides [nolite cogitare]:
B.11.3   And seide 'Multi multa sciunt *et* seipsos nesciunt'.
B.11.124   Qui crediderit & baptiȝatus fuerit &c.
B.11.274   Si vis perfectus esse vade & vende [&c.]
B.11.286   Iudica me deus & discerne causam meam.
B.11.398   *Et* vidit deus cuncta que fecerat & erant valde bona.
B.11.398   Et vidit deus cuncta que fecerat & erant valde bona.
B.12.13   Virga tua & baculus tuus, ipsa me consolata sunt:
B.12.29   Fides, spes, caritas, & maior horum &c.
B.12.54   Date & dabitur vobis.
B.12.56   Scient[es] *et* non facient[es] varijs flagellis vapulab[un]t.
B.12.89   Nolite iudicare & non iudicabimini.
B.12.147   Set non erat ei locus in diuersorio, *et* pauper non habet diuersorium.
B.12.177   Beati quorum remisse sunt iniquitates & quorum tecta sunt &c.
B.12.293   *Et* alibi, si ambulauero in medio vmbre mortis.
B.13.39   Edentes & bibentes que apud eos sunt.
B.13.45   Vos qui peccata hominum comeditis, nisi pro eis lacrimas & oraciones
B.13.54   *Et* quorum tecta sunt peccata
B.13.55   In a dissh of derne shrifte, Dixi & confitebor tibi.
B.13.58   Cor contritum & humiliatum deus non despicies.
B.13.67   In fame & frigore and flappes of scourges;
B.13.67   Ter cesus sum & a iudeis quinquies quadragenas &c–
B.13.118   Qui facit & docuerit magnus vocabitur in regno celorum.'
B.13.249   In nomine meo demonia e[j]icient & super egros manus imponent & bene
B.13.249   In nomine meo demonia e[j]icient & super egros manus imponent & bene
B.13.254   Argentum & aurum non est michi; quod autem habeo tibi do; in nomine
B.13.254   quod autem habeo tibi do; in nomine domini surge *et* amb[ula].
B.13.312   Si hominibus placerem christi seruus non essem; *Et* alibi, Nemo potest
B.13.330   Cuius malediccione os plenum est & amaritudine; sub lingua eius
B.13.330   labor *et* dol[or]; Et alibi, Filij hominum dentes eorum arma & sagitte
B.13.330   labor et dol[or]; *Et* alibi, Filij hominum dentes eorum arma & sagitte
B.13.330   labor et dol[or]; Et alibi, Filij hominum dentes eorum arma & sagitte
B.13.330   *et* lingua eorum gladius a[cutus].
B.13.398   Vbi thesaurus tuus ibi & cor tuum.'
B.13.426   Consencientes & agentes pari pena punientur.
B.13.432   Non habitabit in medio domus mee qui facit superbiam & qui loquitur iniqua.
B.14.3   Vxorem duxi & ideo non possum venire–
B.14.46   Quodcumque pecieritis a patre in nomine meo &c; *Et* alibi, Non in solo pane
B.14.61   Dixit & facta sunt &c;
B.14.63   Aperis tu manum tuam & imples omne animal benediccione.
B.14.77   Ociositas & habundancia panis peccatum turpissimum nutriuit;
B.14.94   As Dauid seiþ in þe Sauter: *et* quorum tecta sunt peccata.
B.14.131   Dormierunt & nichil inuenerunt; [et alibi], velud sompn[i]um
B.14.131   Dormierunt & nichil inuenerunt; [*et* alibi], velud sompn[i]um
B.14.131   domine in Ciuitate tua, *et* ad nichilum rediges &c.
B.14.180   Conuertimini ad me & salui eritis.
B.15.51   Ponam pedem meum in aquilone & similis ero altissimo.
B.15.61   *Et* verba vertit in opera fulliche to his power."
B.15.81   Confundantur omnes qui adorant sculptilia; *Et* alibi, Vt quid diligitis
B.15.81   Vt quid diligitis vanitatem & queritis mendacium?
B.15.118   Sicut cum videris arborem pallidam & marcidam intelligis quod

B.15.118 Ita cum videris populum indisciplinatum & irreligiosum, sine dubio
B.15.194 Cor contritum & humiliatum deus non despicies.'
B.15.200 *Et* vidit deus cogitaciones eorum.
B.15.343 accipis pocius das quam accipis; Si autem non eges & accipis rapis.
B.15.343 dare est demonibus immolare. Item, monache, si indiges &
B.15.428 Petite & accipietis &c.
B.15.431 *Et* si sal euanuerit in quo salietur?
B.15.464 Ecce altilia mea & omnia parata sunt;
B.15.491 Ite in vniuersum mundum, & predicate &c?
B.15.503 Querite & inuenietis &c.
B.15.556 Per primicias & decimas &c.
B.15.576 In domo mea non est panis neque vestimentum *et* ideo nolite constituere me Regem.
B.15.584 Dilige deum & proximum is parfit Iewen lawe;
B.15.610 Lere hem litlum and litlum *et* in Iesum Christum filium,
B.15.611 Til þei kouþe speke and spelle *et* in Spiritum sanctum,
B.15.613 Carnis resurreccionem *et* vitam eternam amen.'
B.16.223 Spiritus procedens a patre & filio &c,
B.16.242 Quam olim Abrahe promisisti & semini eius.
B.17.13 Dilige deum & proximum tuum,
B.17.16 In hijs duobus mandatis tota lex pendet & prophet[e].
B.18.181 Ad vesperum demorabitur fletus & ad matutinum leticia.
B.18.187 And þat þis dede shal dure dormiam & requiescam.'
B.18.339 Dentem pro dente & oculum pro oculo.
B.18.360 *Et* cecidit in foueam quam fecit.
B.18.408 Post inimicicias [clarior est *et* amor].
B.18.421 Misericordia & veritas obuiauerunt sibi; Iusticia & pax osculate su[nt]
B.18.421 Misericordia & veritas obuiauerunt sibi; Iusticia & pax osculate su[nt]
B.18.423 Ecce quam bonum & quam iocundum &c.
B.19.135 The burdes þo songe, Saul interfecit mille *et* dauid decem milia.
B.19.161 Sic oportet Christum pati & intrare &c;
B.19.172 "[Dominus] meus & [deus] meus.
B.19.181 Beati qui non viderunt [& crediderunt]."
B.19.273 Id est vetus testamentum & nouum.
B.19.394 *Et* dimitte nobis debita nostra &c,
B.19.431 Qui pluit super Iustos & iniustos at ones
B.20.33 Homo proponit & deus disponit;
B.20.256 Qui numerat multitudinem stellarum *et* omnibus eis [nomina vocat]
C. 1.49 *Et* que sunt dei deo or [elles] ȝe don ylle."
C. 1.111 Ponam pedem meum in Aquilone & similis ero altissimo.'
C. 1.196 "Date & dabitur vobis, for y dele ȝow alle."
C. 2.42 *Et* super Innocentem munera non accepit.
C. 2.81 Sciant presentes & futuri &c.
C. 3.403 Qui in caritate manet in deo manet *et* deus in eo.
C. 3.405 As hic & hec homo askyng an adiectyf
C. 3.406 Nominatiuo, pater & filius & spiritus sanctus.
C. 3.406 Nominatiuo, pater & filius & spiritus sanctus.
C. 3.461 Conflabunt gladios suos in vomeres & lancias [suas] in falces.
C. 4.36 Contricio & infelicitas in viis eorum *et* viam pacis non cognouerunt;
C. 4.36 Contricio & infelicitas in viis eorum *et* viam pacis non cognouerunt;
C. 4.165 *Et* saluo custodias set non cum carcer[a]tis.'
C. 5.60 Dominus pars hereditatis mee &c. *Et* alibi: clemencia non constringit.
C. 5.172 Hij in curribus & [hij] in equis; ipsi obligati sunt & ceciderunt.
C. 5.172 Hij in curribus & [hij] in equis; ipsi obligati sunt & ceciderunt.
C. 5.199 Qui cum patre & filio; þat fayre hem byfalle
C. 6.76 Cuius maledictione os plenum est & amaritudine; sub lingua eius
C. 6.76 labor & dolor. Filij hominum dentes eorum Arma & sagitte
C. 6.76 labor & dolor. Filij hominum dentes eorum Arma & sagitte
C. 6.76 & lingua eorum gladius acutus.
C. 6.285 Vbi tezaurus tuus, ibi [&] cor tuum.'
C. 7.86 Consencientes & agentes pari pena punientur.
C. 7.92 Non habitabit in medio domus mee qui facit superbiam [&] qui
C. 7.128 Ego in patre & pater in me [est] *et* qui me videt videt [&] patrem meum &c;
C. 7.128 Ego in patre & pater in me [est] *et* qui me videt videt [&] patrem meum &c;
C. 7.128 Ego in patre & pater in me [est] et qui me videt videt [&] patrem meum &c;
C. 7.152 beati quorum remisse sunt iniquitates & quorum tecta sunt peccata,
C. 7.154 'Homines & iumenta saluabis; qu[e]madmodum multiplicasti
C. 7.216 Honora patrem & matrem &c.
C. 7.250 Per Euam cun[c]tis clausa est & per mariam verginem iterum patefacta est &c;
C. 7.304 Vxorem duxi & ideo non possum venire.'
C. 8.90 Omnia que dicunt facite & seruate.

C. 8.241 In [labore & sudore] vultus tui vesceris pane tuo".
C. 8.245 Piger propter frigus noluit arrare; mendicabi[t] in yeme & non dabitur ei".
C. 9.3 And purchasede hym a pardoun A pena & A culpa,
C. 9.23 Ac no [a] pena & a culpa treuthe wolde hem graunte
C. 9.120 [Q]uando misi vos sine pane & pera &c.
C. 9.125 *Et* egenos vagos[que] induc in domum tuam,
C. 9.163 Iunior fui, [et]enim senui; e[t] alibi: infirmata est vertus mea paupertate.
C. 9.187 And pardon with the plouhman A pena & a culpa.
C. 9.287 *Et* qui bona egerunt ibunt in vitam eternam;
C. 9.327 Quodcumque ligaueris super terram erit ligatum & in celis.
C.10.165 *Et* dimisi eos secundum desideria eorum.
C.10.212 Concepit dolore[m] & peperit iniquitatem.
C.10.244 Numquam collig[unt] de spinis vuas; Et Alibi: Bon[a] Arbor
C.10.255 For y am via & veritas and may avauncen alle."
C.11.18 Qui sapiunt nugas & crim[ina] lege vocantur;
C.11.22 Ducunt in bonis dies suos & in fin[e] descendunt ad infernum.
C.11.23 *Et* alibi: ecce ip[s]i peccatores, habundantes &c.
C.11.23 Ibunt in progenie patrum suorum & vsque in eternum non videbunt lumen;
C.11.153 Ego in patre & pater in me est; Et qui me vid[e]t, patrem meum
C.11.153 Ego in patre & pater in me est; *Et* qui me vid[e]t, patrem meum
C.11.163 And saide, 'multi multa sciunt & seipsos nessiunt.'
C.11.248 Homines & iumenta saluabis &c.
C.11.271 Sunt iusti atque sapientes & opera eorum in manu dei sunt &c.
C.11.304 '*Et* deus disponit,' quod he; 'la[t] god do his wille.
C.12.29 Existimasti inique quod ero t[u]i similis; Arguam te & statuam
C.12.59 Qui crediderit & baptizatus fuerit &c.
C.12.119 *Et* qui bona egerunt, ibunt &c.
C.12.160 Quicumque reli[querit] patrem & matrem &c.
C.12.167 Si vis perfectus esse vade & vende &c.
C.12.215 O stulte, ista nocte anima tua egredi[e]tur; tezaurisat & ignorat &c.
C.13.87 Qui crediderit & baptizatus fuerit &c–
C.13.224 Philosophus esses si tacuisses; & alibi: Locutum me aliquando
C.14.18 Scient[es] & non facient[es] varijs flagellis vapulab[unt].
C.14.152 *Et* reddet vnicu[i]que iuxta opera sua.
C.14.165 Dixit & facta sunt.
C.15.44 Edentes & bibentes que apud eos sunt &c.
C.15.50 Vos qui peccata hominum comeditis, nisi pro eis lacrimas & orationes
C.15.62 And saide, 'cor contritum & humiliatum, deus, non despicies.'
C.15.73 In fame [*et*] frygore &c.
C.15.116 *Et* visitauit & fecit redempcionem &c.
C.15.116 Et visitauit & fecit redempcionem &c.
C.15.126 Qui facit & docuerit magnus vocabitur.'
C.15.134 Bote dilige deum & p[roximu]m [and] domine quis habitabit
C.15.221 Super egros manus [in]pone[nt] & bene habebunt &c–
C.15.224 Argentum & Aurum non est michi; quod [autem] habeo tibi do &c.
C.15.229 Habundancia panis & vini turpissimum peccatum aduenit.
C.15.244 vobis. *Et* alibi: Non in solo pane viuit homo &c.'
C.15.260 Dixit & facta [s]unt.
C.15.306 dormierunt & nichil inuenerunt &c; Et alibi: velud sompn[i]um
C.15.306 dormierunt & nichil inuenerunt &c; *Et* alibi: velud sompn[i]um
C.16.223 *Et* verba vertit in opera emforth his power."
C.16.273 Sicut cum videri[s] Arborem pallidam & marcidam intelligis quod
C.16.273 Ita cum videris populum indissiplinatum & irreligiosum, sine dubio
C.16.335 Lauabis me & super niuem dealbabor.
C.16.336 Cor contritum & humiliatum deus non despicies.
C.16.340 *Et* vidit deus cogitaciones eorum.
C.17.40 Videte ne furtum sit: & alibi: meli[u]s est mori quam male viuere &c.
C.17.59 Honora patrem & matrem &c–
C.17.140 Dilige deum propter deum, id est propter veritatem; & inimicum tuum
C.17.140 propter mandatum, id est propter legem; & Amicum propter Amorem,
C.17.219 Per pr[i]micias & decimas &c.
C.17.318 Lere hem littelum and littelum [*et*] in iesum christum filium
C.17.319 Til they couthe speke and spele *et* in spiritum sanctum,
C.17.320 Carnis resurect[i]o[n]em & vitam eternam amen.'
C.18.82 Actiua vita & contemplatiua vita,
C.18.241 Tres vidit & vnum adorauit.
C.18.264 Fiet vnum ouile & vnus pastor.
C.19.14 Dilige deum & proximum [tuum].
C.19.17 In hijs duobus [mandatis tota lex pendet & prophete].
C.19.240 Epulabatur splendide & induebatur bisso &c.
C.20.184 Ad vesperum demorabitur fletus & ad mat[u]tinum leticia.
C.20.192 And that this dede shal duyre, dormiam & requiescam.'
C.20.385 Dentem p[ro] dente & oculum pro oculo.
C.20.420 Tibi soli peccaui & malum coram te feci.
C.20.433 As nullum malum inpunitum & nullum bonum irremuneratum–

C.20.451 Post inimicicias Clarior est & Amor.
C.20.464 Misericordia & veritas obuiauerunt sibi; Iusticia & pax osculate sunt.
C.20.464 Misericordia & veritas obuiauerunt sibi; Iusticia & pax osculate sunt.
C.20.466 Ecce quam bonum & quam iocundum &c.
C.21.135 The buyrdes tho songe, Saul interfecit mille & dauid decem milia.
C.21.161 Sic [oportet] christum pati & intrare &c;
C.21.172 "Dominus meus & deus meus.
C.21.181 Beati qui non viderunt & crediderunt."
C.21.273 Id est vetus testamentum & nouum.
C.21.394 *Et* dimitte nobis debita nostra &c,
C.21.431 Qui pluit super iustos & iniustos at ones
C.22.33 Homo proponit [&] deus dispo[n]it;

&c   A 8; B 93; C 98

A. 7.234 Labores manuum tuarum quia manducabis &c.
A. 8.159 Quodcumque ligaueris super terram &c.
A. 9.83 Libenter suffert[is] &c.
A.10.34 Dixit & facta sunt &c,
A.10.90 For intencio indicat hominem &c.
A.10.94 Qui agit contra conscientiam &c.
A.10.120 Qui se humiliat exaltabitur &c.
A.11.242 Dilige deum &c, Et proximum tuum sicut teipsum.
B.Pr.196 Ve terre vbi puer Rex est &c.
B. 1.187 Fides sine operibus mortua est &c.
B. 2.39 Domine quis habitabit in tabernaculo tuo &c.
B. 2.74 'Sciant presentes & futuri &c.
B. 3.96 Ignis deuorabit tabernacula eorum qui libenter accipiunt munera &c.
B. 3.241 Qui pecuniam suam non dedit ad vsuram et munera super innocentem &c,
B. 3.308 Conflabunt gladios suos in vomeres &c.
B. 3.324 Non leuabit gens contra gentem gladium &c.
B. 3.328 And Sar3ynes for þat si3te shul synge Gloria in excelsis &c,
B. 3.336 Honorem adquiret qui dat munera &c.'
B. 3.350 Animam autem aufert accipientium &c.
B. 4.36 Contricio & infelicitas in viis eorum &c.
B. 4.37 Non est timor dei ante oculos eorum &c.
B. 5.277 Ecce enim veritatem dilexisti &c.
B. 5.281 [Misericordia eius super omnia opera eius &c]–
B. 5.483 O felix culpa, o necessarium peccatum Ade &c.
B. 5.567 Honora patrem & matrem &c;
B. 6.252 Labores manuum tuarum &c.'
B. 7.143 E[ji]ce derisores & iurgia cum eis ne crescant &c.'
B. 7.181 Quodcumque ligaueris super terram erit ligatum & in celis &c.
B. 9.65 Qui manet in caritate in deo manet &c.
B.10.29 Que perfecisti destruxerunt; iustus autem &c.
B.10.85 Frange esurienti panem tuum &c.
B.10.114 Filius non portabit iniquitatem patris &c.
B.10.116 Vnusquisque portabit onus suum &c.
B.10.268 Qui[d] consideras festucam in oculo fratris tui, trabem in oculo tuo &c?
B.10.270 E[j]ice primo trabem [de] oculo tuo &c–
B.10.327 Hij in curribus & hij in equis ipsi obligati sunt &c.
B.10.359 Si cum christo sur[r]existis &c.
B.10.404 Super cathedra[m] Moysi &c.
B.10.416 Homines & iumenta saluabis, domine &c.
B.10.436 [Sunt] iusti atque sapientes, & opera eorum in manu dei sunt &c.
B.11.95 Existimasti inique quod ero tui similis &c.
B.11.120 O vos omnes sicientes venite &c,
B.11.124 Qui crediderit & bapti3atus fuerit &c.
B.11.271 Diuicias nec paupertates &c,
B.11.274 Si vis perfectus esse vade & vende [&c].
B.12.9 Si non in prima vigilia nec in secunda &c.
B.12.29 Fides, spes, caritas, et maior horum &c.
B.12.57 Sapiencia inflat &c];
B.12.69 Nescit aliquis vnde venit aut quo vadit &c.
B.12.125 Nolite tangere christos meos &c.]
B.12.177 Beati quorum remisse sunt iniquitates & quorum tecta sunt &c.
B.12.185 Dum cecus ducit cecum &c.
B.12.286 Aduenit ignis diuinus non comburens set illuminans &c.
B.13.67 Ter cesus sum & a iudeis quinquies quadragenas &c–
B.13.135 Pacientes vincunt &c.'
B.13.423 Ve vobis qui ridetis &c–
B.14.14 Cordis contricio &c.
B.14.18 Oris confessio &c.
B.14.33 Ne soliciti sitis &c; Volucres celi deus pascit &c; pacientes vincunt &c.'
B.14.33 Ne soliciti sitis &c; Volucres celi deus pascit &c; pacientes vincunt &c.'
B.14.33 Ne soliciti sitis &c; Volucres celi deus pascit &c; pacientes vincunt &c.'

B.14.46 Quodcumque pecieritis a patre in nomine meo &c; Et alibi, Non in solo pane
B.14.61 Dixit & facta sunt &c;
B.14.131 domine in Ciuitate tua, et ad nichilum rediges &c.
B.14.190 Pateat &c: Per passionem domini,
B.14.212 Ita inpossibile diuiti &c,
B.15.219 Nolite fieri sicut ypocrite tristes &c.
B.15.234 Beatus est diues qui &c.
B.15.254 In pace in idipsum dormiam &c.
B.15.428 Petite & accipietis &c.
B.15.429 Vos estis sal terre &c.
B.15.490 [Ecce audiuimus e[a]m in effrata &c].
B.15.491 Ite in vniuersum mundum & predicate &c?
B.15.497 Bonus pastor animam suam ponit &c.
B.15.500 Ite vos in vineam meam &c.
B.15.503 Querite & inuenietis &c.
B.15.537 Absit nobis gloriari nisi in cruce domini nostri &c.
B.15.552 Deposuit potentes de sede &c.
B.15.556 Per primicias & decimas &c.
B.16.47 Videatis qui peccat in spiritum sanctum numquam remittetur &c; Hoc
B.16.120 Demonium habe[s] &c.
B.16.223 Spiritus procedens a patre & filio &c,
B.16.252 Ecce agnus dei &c.'
B.17.114 [O mors ero mors tua &c].
B.17.151 Qui conceptus est de spiritu sancto &c.
B.17.152 Omnia traham ad me ipsum &c–
B.17.170 Tu fabricator omnium &c.
B.17.200 Qui peccat in spiritu[m] sanct[um] &c,
B.17.253 Amen dico vobis, nescio vos &c.
B.17.261 Si linguis hominum loquar &c.
B.17.266 Non omnis qui dicit domine, domine, intrabit &c.
B.17.310 Numquam dimittitur peccatum &c.
B.18.378 Tibi soli peccaui &c.
B.18.390 Nullum malum impunitum &c–
B.18.423 Ecce quam bonum & quam iocundum &c.
B.19.74 Gloria in excelsis deo &c.
B.19.161 Sic oportet Christum pati & intrare &c;
B.19.228 Diuisiones graciarum sunt &c.
B.19.394 Et dimitte nobis debita nostra &c,
B.19.422 At Auynoun among Iewes–Cum sancto sanctus eris &c–
B.19.446 Non occides: michi vindictam &c.
C. 2.27 [Qu]alis pater talis fili[us] &c.
C. 2.40 Domine quis habitabit in tabernaculo tuo &c.
C. 2.81 Sciant presentes & futuri &c.
C. 3.308 Non morabit[ur] opus mersenarii &c.
C. 3.340 Retribuere dignare domine deus &c.'
C. 5.43 In eadem vocacione qu[a] vocati estis [&c]
C. 5.60 Dominus pars hereditatis mee &c. Et alibi: clemencia non constringit.
C. 6.257 Numquam dimittitur peccatum &c.'
C. 7.83 Ve vobis qui ridetis &c–
C. 7.92 qui facit superbiam [&] qui loquitur iniqua &c.
C. 7.118 Dare histrionibus &c.
C. 7.128 Ego in patre & pater in me [est] et qui me videt videt [&] patrem meum &c;
C. 7.133 Populus qui ambulabat in tenebris vidit lucem magnam &c.
C. 7.138 Non veni vocare iustos set peccatores &c.
C. 7.216 Honora patrem & matrem &c.
C. 7.250 Per Euam cun[c]tis clausa est & per mariam verginem iterum patefacta est &c;
C. 8.86 Super Cathedram moysi sede[runt] &c.
C. 8.260 Labores manuum tuarum quia manducabis &c".
C. 9.120 [Q]uando misi vos sine pane & pera &c.
C. 9.265 Sub molli pastore &c.
C.10.90 Libenter suffertis in[s]ipientes &c;
C.10.99 Nolite timere eos qui possunt occidere corpus &c.
C.10.236 Filius non portabit iniquitatem patris &c.
C.11.23 Et alibi: ecce ip[s]i peccatores, habundantes &c.
C.11.25 Que perfecisti destruxerunt &c.
C.11.153 patrem meum vid[e]t qui in celis est &c.
C.11.157 Fides non habet meritum vbi humana racio &c.
C.11.201 Ita possibile est diuiti intrare in regn[um] celorum sicut camelus &c.
C.11.232 Eadem mensura &c.
C.11.235 Super cathedra[m] Moysi &c.
C.11.248 Homines & iumenta saluabis &c.
C.11.271 Sunt iusti atque sapientes & opera eorum in manu dei sunt &c.
C.11.275 "Dum steteritis ante Reges vel presides &c:
C.12.10 Pena peccuniaria non sufficit &c.
C.12.34 Non oderis fratrem secrete in corde &c.
C.12.59 Qui crediderit & baptizatus fuerit &c.
C.12.103 Cum facitis conuiuia nolite vocare amicos &c.

C.12.119 Et qui bona egerunt, ibunt &c.
C.12.138 Domine, non est tibi cur[e] quod soror &c?
C.12.160 Quicumque reli[querit] patrem & matrem &c.
C.12.167 Si vis perfectus esse vade & vende &c.
C.12.171 Nisi renunciaueritis omnia que po[s]sid[etis] &c."
C.12.179 Nisi granum frumenti cadens in terram mortuum fuerit &c.
C.12.215 O stulte, ista nocte anima tua egredi[e]tur; tezaurisat & ignorat &c.
C.13.4 Tanquam nichil habentes &c.
C.13.17 And for a song in his sorwe, "si bona accepimus a domino &c,
C.13.87 Qui crediderit & baptizatus fuerit &c.
C.13.98 Amen dico vobis quia hec vidua paupercula &c.
C.14.69 Nolite tangere cristos meos &c.
C.14.86 Pastores loquebantur ad inuicem &c.
C.14.88 Ib[a]nt magi ab Oriente &c.
C.14.117 Beati quorum remisse sunt iniquitates &c.
C.14.124 Dum [c]ecus d[u]cit [c]ecum &c.
C.14.134 Nolo mortem peccatoris &c.
C.14.155 Quare placuit? qui[a] voluit &c.
C.14.208 A[d]uenit ignis diuinus non comburens set illuminans &c.
C.14.214 Quia super pauca fuisti fidelis &c.
C.15.44 Edentes & bibentes que apud eos sunt &c.
C.15.50 effuderitis, ea que in deliciis comeditis in tor[mentis] euo[metis] &c.
C.15.73 In fame [et] frygore &c.
C.15.116 Et visitauit & fecit redempcionem &c.
C.15.156 Pacientes vincunt &c.
C.15.221 Super egros manus [in]pone[nt] & bene habebunt &c–
C.15.224 Argentum & Aurum non est michi; quod [autem] habeo tibi do &c.
C.15.244 vobis. Et alibi: Non in solo pane viuit homo &c.'
C.15.262 Aperis tu manum tuam &c.
C.15.306 dormierunt & nichil inuenerunt &c; Et alibi: velud sompn[i]um
C.15.306 velud sompn[i]um surgencium &c.
C.16.213 Ponam pedem meum in Aquilone &c.
C.16.298 Nisi efficiamini sicut paruuli &c,
C.16.374 Panem nostrum co[tidianum] &c.
C.17.40 Videte ne furtum sit: & alibi: meli[u]s est mori quam male viuere &c.
C.17.59 Honora patrem & matrem &c–
C.17.193 Bonus Pastor animam suam ponit pro ouibus suis &c.
C.17.198 Absit nobis gloriari nisi in cruce domini nostri &c.
C.17.215 Deposuit potentes de sede &c.
C.17.219 Per pr[i]micias & decimas &c.
C.17.235 Mihi vindictam &c–
C.17.280 Nolite mittere falcem in messem alienam &c.
C.17.291 Bonus pastor &c,
C.18.132 Ecce Ancilla domini &c.'
C.18.213 Celi enarrant gloriam dei &c.
C.19.166 Qui peccat in spiritu[m] sanct[um] &c,
C.19.227 Si linguis hominum loqu[a]r &c.
C.19.232 Non omnis qui dicit domine, domine intrabit in reg[num] celorum &c.
C.19.240 Epulabatur splendide & induebatur bisso &c.
C.19.290 Nunquam dimittitur peccatum &c.
C.20.112 Cum veniat sanctus sanctorum cessa[bi]t &c.'
C.20.259 Non visurum se mortem &c.
C.20.270 Attollite portas &c.'
C.20.435 Domine ne in furore tuo Arguas me &c–
C.20.466 Ecce quam bonum & quam iocundum &c.
C.21.161 Sic [oportet] christum pati & intrare &c;
C.21.394 Et dimitte nobis debita nostra &c,
C.21.422 At Auenon among iewes–cum sancto sanctus eris &c–
C.21.446 Non occides: Michi vindictam &c.
C.22.256 Qui numerat multitudinem stellarum &c.
C.22.279 Non concupisces rem proximi tui &c.

etenim B 1; C 1
B. 7.89 Iunior fui etenim senui, & non vidi iustum derelictum ne[c] semen eius
C. 9.163 Iunior fui, [et]enim senui; e[t] alibi: infirmata est vertus mea paupertate.

eternam A 1; B 3; C 2
A. 8.95 Et qui bona egerunt ibunt in vitam eternam;
B. 7.113 Et qui bona egerunt ibunt in vitam eternam;
B.12.293 For Deus dicitur quasi dans [eternam vitam] suis, hoc est fidelibus;
B.15.613 Carnis resurreccionem et vitam eternam amen.'
C. 9.287 Et qui bona egerunt ibunt in vitam eternam;
C.17.320 Carnis resurect[i]o[n]em & vitam eternam amen.'

eternum A 1; B 1; C 3
A. 8.96 Qui vero mala in ignem eternum.
B. 7.114 Qui vero mala in ignem eternum.
C. 9.288 Qui vero mala in ignem etern[u]m.
C.11.23 Ibunt in progenie patrum suorum & vsque in eternum non videbunt lumen;

C.17.66 Iusticia eius manet in eternum.

eum B 2; C 2
B. 1.31 Inebri[e]mus eum vino dormiamusque cum eo
B.14.104 'Ye? quis est ille?' quod Pacience; 'quik, laudabimus eum!
C. 1.30 Inebriemus eum vino dormiamusque cum eo vt seruare possimus
C.15.279 'ʒe? quis est ille?' quod pacience; 'quik, lauda[bi]mus eum!

euam B 1; C 1
B. 5.603 Per Euam cun[c]tis clausa est et per Mariam virginem [iterum] patefacta est;
C. 7.250 Per Euam cun[c]tis clausa est & per mariam verginem iterum patefacta est &c;

euanuerit B 1
B.15.431 Et si sal euanuerit in quo salietur?

euometis B 1; C 1
B.13.45 eff[u]deritis, ea que in delicijs comeditis in tormentis euometis.
C.15.50 effuderitis, ea que in deliciis comeditis in tor[mentis] euo[metis] &c.

ex B 2; C 2
B.13.151 Wiþ half a laumpe lyne in latyn, Ex vi transicionis,
B.15.318 pabulum commune sufficiat; ex adipe prodijt iniquitas tua.
C.17.53 pabulum comune sufficiat; Ex adipe prodiit iniquitas tua.
C.19.125 Natus est ex maria virgine.

exactor B 1
B.10.333 Quomodo cessauit exactor, quieuit tributum? contriuit dominus baculum

exaltabitur A 1
A.10.120 Qui se humiliat exaltabitur &c.

excelcis C 1
C.14.94 And song a song of solace, Gloria in excelcis deo.

excelsis B 3; C 1
B. 3.328 And Sarʒynes for þat siʒte shul synge Gloria in excelsis &c,
B.12.150 And songe a song of solas, Gloria in excelsis deo.
B.19.74 Gloria in excelsis deo &c.
C.21.74 Gloria in excelsis deo.

excercebuntur C 1
C. 3.477 Non leuabit gens contra gentem gladium nec excercebuntur vltra ad prelium.

excusat B 1; C 1
B.11.317 Non excusat episcopos nec ydiotes preestes'.
C.13.128 For ignorancia non excusat as ych haue herd in bokes.'

exegissem B 1
B. 7.83 vt ego veni[ens] cum vsuris ex[egissem] illam]?

exiguum B 1; C 1
B.10.89 Si tibi sit copia habundanter tribue; si autem exiguum illud impertiri stude
C.11.69 Si tibi sit copia habundanter tribue; Si Autem exiguum illud impertir[i] libenter stude.

existimasti B 2; C 1
B.10.291 Existimasti inique quod ero tui similis; arguam te & statuam contra faciem
B.11.95 Existimasti inique quod ero tui similis &c.
C.12.29 Existimasti inique quod ero t[u]i similis; Arguam te & statuam

expellit C 1
C.15.164 Caritas expellit omne[m] timorem.

experimentum B 1
B.10.256 Fides non habet meritum vbi humana racio prebet experimentum.

extremis A 1; B 1
A.11.235 'Þat is in extremis,' quaþ scripture, 'as sarisines & Iewis
B.10.352 'That is in extremis', quod Scripture, '[as] Sarʒens & Iewes

fabricator B 1; C 1
B.17.170 Tu fabricator omnium &c.
C.19.134 Tu fabricator omnium–

fac A 1; B 1
A.11.148 [Tu quoque fac simile: sic ars deluditur arte].
B.10.196 Tu quoque fac simile; sic ars deluditur arte.

faciamus A 1; B 3
A.10.41 Faciamus hominem ad ymaginem nostram.
B. 5.486 Faciamus hominem ad ymaginem [et similitudinem] nostram;
B. 9.36 For he was synguler hymself and seide faciamus
B. 9.43 Faciamus hominem ad imaginem nostram];

faciant B 1; C 1
B. 7.60 Quodcumque vultis vt faciant vobis homines facite eis.
C.16.309 Quodcumque vultis vt faciant vobis homines, facite eis.

faciat A 1; B 1; C 1
A. 3.54 And seiþ Nesciat sinist[ra] quid *faciat* dexter[a].
B. 3.72 Nesciat sinistra quid *faciat* dextra:
C. 3.74 Nesciat [sinistra] quid *faciat* [dextera]:

facie B 1; C 1
B.15.162 [Hic] in enigmate, tunc *facie* ad faciem.
C.16.296 Hic in enigmate, tunc *facie* ad faciem.

faciem B 2; C 2
B.10.291 Existimasti inique quod ero tui similis; arguam te & statuam contra *faciem*
B.15.162 [Hic] in enigmate, tunc facie ad *faciem*.
C.12.29 Arguam te & statuam contra *faciem* tuam.
C.16.296 Hic in enigmate, tunc facie ad *faciem*.

facientes B 1; C 1
B.12.56 Scient[es] et non *facient[es]* varijs flagellis vapulab[un]t.
C.14.18 Scient[es] & non *facient[es]* varijs flagellis vapulab[unt].

facit A 1; B 4; C 5
A.11.196 Qui *facit* & docuerit magnus vocabitur in regno celorum.
B. 2.27 Qualis pater talis filius: Bon[a] arbor bonum fructum *facit*.
B.11.204 Qui *facit* peccatum seruus est peccati.
B.13.118 Qui *facit* & docuerit magnus vocabitur in regno celorum.'
B.13.432 Non habitabit in medio domus mee qui *facit* superbiam & qui loquitur iniqua.
C. 2.29 Bona arbor bonum fructum *facit*.
C. 7.92 Non habitabit in medio domus mee qui *facit* superbiam [&] qui
C.10.244 Bon[a] Arbor bonum fructum *facit*.
C.12.112 Qui *facit* peccatum seruus est peccati.
C.15.126 Qui *facit* & docuerit magnus vocabitur.'

facite A 1; B 2; C 4
A. 7.212 *Facite* vobis amicos.'
B. 6.228 *Facite* vo[bis] amicos de mammona iniquitatis.
B. 7.60 Quodcumque vultis vt faciant vobis homines *facite* eis.
C. 8.90 Omnia que dicunt *facite* & seruate.
C. 8.234 *Facite* vobis Amicos de mammona iniquitatis.'
C.16.309 Quodcumque vultis vt faciant vobis homines, *facite* eis.
C.19.250 *Facite* vobis amicos de mammona iniquitatis.

facitis B 1; C 1
B.11.191 Cum *facitis* conuiuia nolite inuitare amicos.
C.12.103 Cum *facitis* conuiuia nolite vocare amicos &c.

facta A 1; B 2; C 2
A.10.34 Dixit & *facta* sunt &c,
B. 9.33 Dixit & *facta* sunt,
B.14.61 Dixit & *facta* sunt &c;
C.14.165 Dixit & *facta* sunt.
C.15.260 Dixit & *facta* [s]unt;

factum B 1; C 2
B. 5.500 Verbum caro *factum* est & habitauit in nobis.
C. 3.356 He acordeth with crist in kynde, verbum caro *factum* est;
C. 7.140 Verbum caro *factum* est.

falcem C 1
C.17.280 Nolite mittere *falcem* in messem alienam &c.

falces C 1
C. 3.461 Conflabunt gladios suos in vomeres & lancias [suas] in *falces*.

falleret B 1; C 2
B.18.162 Ars vt artem *falleret*.'
C.20.165 Ars vt artem *falleret*.'
C.20.392 Ars vt Artem *falleret*.

falsem B 1
B.15.530 Nolite mittere *falsem* in messem alienam.

falsis B 2; C 1
B.13.70 Periculum est in *falsis* fratribus.'
B.13.73 Vnusquisque a fratre se custodiat quia vt dicitur periculum est in *falsis*
C.15.75 Periculum est in *falsis* fratribus.'

fame B 1; C 1
B.13.67 In *fame* & frigore and flappes of scourges:
C.15.73 In *fame* [et] frygore &c.

fautores B 1
B.15.215 Fy on faitours and in *fautores* suos!

fecerat B 1
B.11.398 Et vidit deus cuncta que *fecerat* & erant valde bona.

feci C 1
C.20.420 Tibi soli peccaui & malum coram te *feci*.

fecisse A 1; B 1; C 1
A.10.162 Penitet me *fecisse* hominem.
B. 9.133 Penitet me *fecisse* hominem.
C.10.222 Penitet me *fecisse* hominem;

fecit B 2; C 1
B.10.45 Than Munde þe Millere of Multa *fecit* deus.
B.18.360 Et cecidit in foueam quam *fecit*.
C.15.116 Et visitauit & *fecit* redempcionem &c.

felicitas B 2; C 2
B.14.276 Incerta fortuna, absque sollicitudine *felicitas*.'
B.14.320 Absque sollicitudine *felicitas*.
C.16.116 Incerta fortuna, absque solicitudine *felicitas*.'
C.16.155 Absque solicitudine *felicitas*.

felix B 1; C 1
B. 5.483 O *felix* culpa, o necessarium peccatum Ade &c.
C. 7.125 O *felix* culpa, [o] necessarium peccatum Ade.

fer C 1
C.17.285 *Fer*, trahe, punge gregem, seruando per omnia legem–

fercula B 1; C 1
B. 5.269 Seruus es alterius [cum] *fercula* pinguia queris;
C. 6.293 Seruus [es] alterius cum *fercula* pingu[i]a queris;

ferre B 1; C 1
B. 6.315 Paupertatis onus pacienter *ferre* memento;
C. 8.336 Paupertatis onus pacienter *ferre* memento.

festucam B 1
B.10.268 Qui[d] consideras *festucam* in oculo fratris tui, trabem in oculo tuo &c?

fiat B 3; C 3
B.14.50 And þanne was it *fiat* voluntas tua [sholde fynde vs alle].
B.15.179 *Fiat* voluntas tua fynt hym eueremoore,
B.16.99 Ecce ancilla domini; *fiat* michi [secundum verbum tuum]'.
C. 5.88 *Fiat* voluntas dei fynt vs alle thynges.'
C.15.249 And thenne was hit *fiat* voluntas tua þat sholde fynde vs alle.
C.16.321 *Fiat*-voluntas-tua festeth hym vch a daye.

ficus B 1
B. 9.155 Numquam collig[unt] de spinis vua[s] nec de tribulis *ficus*.

fidei A 1; B 1
A.11.245 ad omnes, maxime autem ad domesticos *fidei*.
B.10.204 Dum tempus [est] operemur bonum ad omnes, maxime autem ad domesticos *fidei*.

fidelibus B 1
B.12.293 For Deus dicitur quasi dans [eternam vitam] suis, hoc est *fidelibus*;

fidelis C 1
C.14.214 Quia super pauca fuisti *fidelis* &c.

fides B 6; C 4
B. 1.187 *Fides* sine operibus mortua est &c.
B.10.256 *Fides* non habet meritum vbi humana racio prebet experimentum.
B.11.218 That *Fides* sua sholde sauen hire and saluen hire of synnes.
B.12.29 *Fides*, spes, caritas, et maior horum &c.
B.15.118 Si autem corruptum fuerit omnium *fides* marcida est. Si
B.15.389 That sola *fides* sufficit to saue wiþ lewed peple.
C. 1.183 *Fides* sine operibus mortua est.
C.11.157 *Fides* non habet meritum vbi humana racio &c.
C.16.273 Si Autem corupt[um] fuerit omnium f[i]des marcida est. Si
C.17.121 That sola *fides* sufficit to saue with lewede peple.

fidus A 1; B 1
A.11.147 Qui sim[u]lat verbis, nec corde est *fidus* amicus,
B.10.195 Qui simulat verbis [nec] corde est *fidus* amicus,

fieret C 1
C.18.164 Ne forte tumultus *fieret* in populo–

fieri B 1; C 1
B.15.219 Nolite *fieri* sicut ypocrite tristes &c.
C.16.344 Nolite [*fieri* sicut ypocrite tristes].

fiet C 2
C. 9.127 Si quis videtur sapiens, *fiet* stultus vt sit sapiens.
C.18.264 *Fiet* vnum ouile & vnus pastor.

fili B 3; C 3
B.18.15 Thanne was feiþ in a fenestre and cryde 'a! *fili* dauid!'
B.19.133 For þe dedes þat he dide, *Fili* dauid, Iesus.
B.19.136 Forþi þe contree þer Iesu cam called hym *fili* dauid,
C.20.13 Thenne was faith in a fenestre and criede 'a! *fil[i]* dauid!'
C.21.133 For þe dedes þat he dede, *fili* dauid, iesus.
C.21.136 Forthy þe contre þer iesu cam calde hym *fili* dauid

filij B 2; C 1
B. 9.149 Filius non portabit iniquitatem patris et pater non portabit iniquitatem *filij*.

B.13.330   labor et dol[or]; Et alibi, *Filij* hominum dentes eorum arma &
         sagitte
C. 6.76   labor & dolor. *Filij* hominum dentes eorum Arma & sagitte

filio A 1; B 2; C 1
A. 5.42   Qui cum patre & *filio*; Faire mote ȝow befalle.'
B. 5.58   Qui cum patre & *filio*; þat faire hem bifalle
B.16.223   Spiritus procedens a patre & *filio* &c,
C. 5.199   Qui cum patre & *filio*; þat fayre hem byfalle

filium B 2; C 2
B. 5.39   Qui parcit virge odit *filium*:
B.15.610   Lere hem litlum and litlum et in Iesum Christum *filium*,
C. 5.139   Qui parcit virge odit *filium*.'
C.17.318   Lere hem littelum and littelum [et] in iesum christum *filium*

filius B 9; C 9
B. 2.27   Qualis pater talis *filius*: Bon[a] arbor bonum fructum facit.
B. 9.149   *Filius* non portabit iniquitatem patris et pater non portabit
         iniquitatem filij.
B.10.114   *Filius* non portabit iniquitatem patris &c.
B.10.246   Deus pater, deus *filius*, deus spiritus sanctus:
B.16.88   *Filius* by þe fader wille and frenesse of spiritus sancti
B.16.186   The secounde of þa[t] sire is Sothfastnesse *filius*,
B.17.229   And þanne flawmeþ he as fir on fader and on *filius*
B.18.68   Vere *filius* dei erat iste.
B.19.118   A faunt[ek]yn ful of wit, *filius* Marie.
C. 2.27   [Qu]alis pater talis *fili[us]* &c.
C. 2.31   The fader þat me forth brouhte *filius* dei he hoteth,
C. 3.406   Nominatiuo, pater & *filius* & spiritus sanctus.
C.10.236   *Filius* non portabit iniquitatem patris &c.
C.18.120   *Filius* by þe fadres wille fley with spiritus sanctus
C.18.193   And þe seconde is a sone of þe sire, *filius*;
C.19.195   And thenne flaumeth he as fuyr on fader and on *filius*
C.20.70   Vere *filius* dei erat iste.
C.21.118   A fauntekyn ful of wyt, *filius* Marie.

fine C 1
C.11.22   Ducunt in bonis dies suos & in *fin[e]* descendunt ad infernum.

flagellis B 1; C 1
B.12.56   Scient[es] et non facient[es] varijs *flagellis* vapulab[un]t.
C.14.18   Scient[es] & non facient[es] varijs *flagellis* vapulab[unt].

flectantur B 1; C 1
B.19.80   Omnia celestia terrestria *flectantur* in hoc nomine Iesu;
C.21.80   Omnia celestia terrestria *flectantur* in hoc nomine iesu;

flentibus A 1
A.11.193   Gaudere cum gaudentibus Et flere cum *flentibus*,

flere A 1
A.11.193   Gaudere cum gaudentibus Et *flere* cum flentibus,

fletus B 1; C 1
B.18.181   Ad vesperum demorabitur *fletus* & ad matutinum leticia.
C.20.184   Ad vesperum demorabitur *fletus* & ad mat[u]tinum leticia.

floret B 1; C 1
B.15.118   Si sacerdocium integrum fuerit tota *floret* ecclesia; Si autem
C.16.273   Si sacerdocium integrum fuerit tota *floret* ecclesia; Si Autem

foras B 2; C 1
B.15.594   Laȝare veni *foras*;
B.18.315   Nunc princeps huius mundi e[i]icietur *foras*.'
C.11.18   Qui recte sapiunt lex iubet ire *foras*.

forma C 1
C.17.285   In baculi *forma* sit, presul, hec tibi norma;

formam B 1
B.10.343   Dilige denarium set parce dilige *formam*.

fornicacionem B 1; C 1
B. 9.194   Bonum est vt vnusquisque vxorem suam habeat propter
         fornicacionem.
C.10.293   Bonum est [vt] vnusquisque vx[or]em suam habeat propter
         fornicacionem.

fornicatores B 1; C 1
B. 2.181   And fecchen [oure] vitailles at *Fornicatores*.
C. 2.194   And fecchen oure vitailes a[t] *fornicatores*,

fortasse B 1; C 1
B.Pr.132   'Sum Rex, sum princeps; neutrum *fortasse* deinceps.
C.Pr.153   'Sum Rex, sum Princeps; neutrum *fortasse* deinceps.

forte B 1; C 1
B. 7.77   Non eligas cui miser[e]aris ne *forte* pretereas illum qui meretur
         accipere,
C.18.164   Ne *forte* tumultus fieret in populo–

forti B 1; C 1
B.19.296   Esto *forti* animo cum sis dampnatus inique.
C.21.296   Esto *forti* Animo cum sis dampnatus inique.

fortis B 1; C 1
B. 9.186   Dum sis vir *fortis* ne des tua robora scortis;
C.10.287   Dum sis vir *fortis* ne des tua robora scortis;

fortitudinis B 4; C 4
B.19.289   The þridde seed þat Piers sew was Spiritus *fortitudinis*,
B.19.464   And wiþ Spiritus *fortitudinis* fecche it, [wole he, nel he].'
B.20.24   Ne[iþer] Spiritus Iusticie ne Spiritus *fortitudinis*.
B.20.25   For Spiritus *fortitudinis* forfeteþ [wel] ofte;
C.21.289   The thridde seed that [Peres] sewe was spiritus *fortitudinis*
C.21.464   And with spiritus *fortitudinis* fecche hit, wolle he, null he.'
C.22.24   Noythe[r] spiritus iusticie ne spiritus *fortitudinis*.
C.22.25   For spiritus *fortitudinis* forfeteth wel ofte;

fortuna B 1; C 1
B.14.276   negocium sine dampno, Incerta *fortuna*, absque sollicitudine
C.16.116   negocium sine dampno, Incerta *fortuna*, absque solicitudine

foueam B 2
B.10.281   Dum cecus ducit cecum ambo in *foueam* cadunt.
B.18.360   Et cecidit in *foueam* quam fecit.

frange C 1; B 1
B.10.85   *Frange* esurienti panem tuum &c.
C.11.65   *Frange* esurienti panem tuum.

fratre B 1
B.13.73   Vnusquisque a *fratre* se custodiat quia vt dicitur periculum est in
         falsis

fratrem B 1; C 1
B.11.195   Non oderis *fratrem*.
C.12.34   Non oderis *fratrem* secrete in corde &c.

fratres A 1; B 1
A.11.192   Ecce quam bonum & quam iocundum habitare *Fratres* in vnum.
B.11.88   Non oderis *fratres* secrete in corde tuo set publice argue illos.

fratribus B 2; C 1
B.13.70   Periculum est in falsis *fratribus*.'
B.13.73   quia vt dicitur periculum est in falsis *fratribus*.
C.15.75   Periculum est in falsis *fratribus*.'

fratris B 1
B.10.268   Qui[d] consideras festucam in oculo *fratris* tui, trabem in oculo tuo
         &c?

frigore frygore B 1; C 1
B.13.67   In fame & *frigore* and flappes of scourges:
C.15.73   In fame [et] *frygore* &c.

frigus A 1; B 1; C 1
A. 7.220   Piger propter *frigus* no feld wolde tilie;
B. 6.236   Piger [propter *frigus*] no feeld [w]olde tilie;
C. 8.245   Piger propter *frigus* noluit arrare; mendicabi[t] in yeme & non
         dabitur ei".

fructum B 1; C 2
B. 2.27   Qualis pater talis filius: Bon[a] arbor bonum *fructum* facit.
C. 2.29   Bona arbor bonum *fructum* facit.
C.10.244   Bon[a] Arbor bonum *fructum* facit.

frumenti C 1
C.12.179   Nisi granum *frumenti* cadens in terram mortuum fuerit &c.

fuerit A 1; B 5; C 6
A.11.234   Qui crediderit et baptizatus *fuerit* saluus erit.'
B.11.82   Nisi quis renatus *fuerit*.
B.11.124   Qui crediderit & baptiȝatus *fuerit* &c.
B.15.118   Si sacerdocium integrum *fuerit* tota floret ecclesia; Si autem
B.15.118   Si autem corruptum *fuerit* omnium fides marcida est. Si
B.15.118   Si sacerdocium *fuerit* in peccatis totus populus conuertitur ad
C.12.59   Qui crediderit & baptizatus *fuerit* &c.
C.12.179   Nisi granum frumenti cadens in terram mortuum *fuerit* &c.
C.13.87   Qui crediderit & baptizatus *fuerit* &c–
C.16.273   Si sacerdocium integrum *fuerit* tota floret ecclesia; Si Autem
C.16.273   Si Autem corupt[um] *fuerit* omnium f[i]des marcida est. Si
C.16.273   Si sacerdocium *fuerit* in peccatis totus populus conuertitur ad

fueritis B 2; C 1
B. 1.178   Eadem mensura qua mensi *fueritis* remecietur vobis.
B.11.228   Eadem mensura qua mensi *fueritis* remecietur vobis.
C. 1.174   Eadem mensura qua mensi *fueritis* Remetietur vobis.

fuerunt A 1; B 1
A. 8.110   *Fuerunt* michi lacrime mee panes die ac nocte.
B. 7.128   *Fuerunt* michi lacrime mee panes die ac nocte.

fui B 1; C 1

B. 7.89 Iunior *fui* etenim senui, & non vidi iustum derelictum ne[c] semen
eius

C. 9.163 Iunior *fui*, [et]enim senui; e[t] alibi: infirmata est vertus mea
paupertate.

fuisti C 1

C.14.214 Quia super pauca *fuisti* fidelis &c.

furore C 1

C.20.435 Domine ne in *furore* tuo Arguas me &c–

furtum C 1

C.17.40 Videte ne *furtum* sit: & alibi: meli[u]s est mori quam male viuere
&c.

futuri B 1; C 1

B. 2.74 'Sciant presentes & *futuri* &c.

C. 2.81 Sciant presentes & *futuri* &c.

gaudentibus A 1

A.11.193 Gaudere cum *gaudentibus* Et flere cum flentibus,

gaudere A 1

A.11.193 *Gaudere* cum gaudentibus Et flere cum flentibus,

gaudia B 1

B.12.22 Interpone tuis interdum *gaudia* curis.

gaudium C 1

C.12.207 "Tristicia vestra vertetur in *gaudium*:

gemitu B 1; C 1

B.15.191 And leggen on longe wiþ Laboraui in *gemitu* meo,

C.16.333 And laueth hem in þe lauendrie, labora[ui] in *gemitu* meo,

genere B 1; A 1

A.10.108 Qui circuit [omne genus in nullo *genere* est].

B.14.181 Thus in *genere* of gentries Iesu crist seide

geniti B 1; C 1

B.11.203 As quasi modo *geniti* gentil men echone,

C.12.111 As quasi modo *geniti* gentel men vchone,

gens B 1; C 1

B. 3.324 Non leuabit *gens* contra gentem gladium &c.

C. 3.477 Non leuabit *gens* contra gentem gladium nec excercebuntur vltra
ad prelium.

gentem B 1; C 1

B. 3.324 Non leuabit gens contra *gentem* gladium &c.

C. 3.477 Non leuabit gens contra *gentem* gladium nec excercebuntur vltra
ad prelium.

genus A 1

A.10.108 Qui circuit [omne *genus* in nullo genere est].

gladios B 1; C 1

B. 3.308 Conflabunt *gladios* suos in vomeres &c.

C. 3.461 Conflabunt *gladios* suos in vomeres & lancias [suas] in falces.

gladium B 1; C 1

B. 3.324 Non leuabit gens contra gentem *gladium* &c.

C. 3.477 Non leuabit gens contra gentem *gladium* nec excercebuntur vltra
ad prelium.

gladius B 1; C 1

B.13.330 et lingua eorum *gladius* a[cutus].

C. 6.76 & lingua eorum *gladius* acutus.

gloria B 5; C 4

B. 3.328 And Sarȝynes for þat siȝte shul synge *Gloria* in excelsis &c,

B.12.150 And songe a song of solas, *Gloria* in excelsis deo.

B.15.55 scrutator est maiestatis opprimitur a *gloria*.

B.18.7 Of gerlis and of *Gloria* laus gretly me dremed,

B.19.74 *Gloria* in excelsis deo &c.

C.14.94 And song a song of solace, *Gloria* in excelcis deo.

C.16.217 Sic [qui] scrutator est magestatis opprim[e]tur a *gloria*.

C.20.6 Of gurles and of *gloria* laus greetliche me dremede

C.21.74 *Gloria* in excelsis deo.

gloriam B 1; C 2

B.15.63 Sciencie appetitus hominem inmortalitatis *gloria[m]* spoliauit.

C.16.225 Sciencie appetitus hominem inmortalitatis *gloriam* spoliauit.

C.18.213 Celi enarrant *gloriam* dei &c.

gloriari B 1; C 1

B.15.537 Absit nobis *gloriari* nisi in cruce domini nostri &c.

C.17.198 Absit nobis *gloriari* nisi in cruce domini nostri &c.

glorie B 1

B.18.317 'Rex *glorie*,

gracia B 1

B.15.268 Pacientes Vincunt verbi *gracia*, and [verred] ensamples manye.

graciarum B 1; C 1

B.19.228 Diuisiones *graciarum* sunt &c.

C.21.228 Diuisiones *graciarum* sunt.

grana B 1; C 1

B.Pr.136 Qualia vis metere, talia *grana* sere.

C.Pr.157 Qualia vis metere, talia *grana* sere.

granum C 1

C.12.179 Nisi *granum* frumenti cadens in terram mortuum fuerit &c.

gregem C 1

C.17.285 Fer, trahe, punge *gregem*, seruando per omnia legem–

habeat B 2; C 1

B. 9.194 Bonum est vt vnusquisque vxorem suam *habeat* propter
fornicacionem.

B.15.343 Porro non indiget monachus si *habeat* quod nature sufficit.

C.10.293 Bonum est [vt] vnusquisque vx[or]em suam *habeat* propter
fornicacionem.

habebunt B 1; C 1

B.13.249 & super egros manus imponent & bene *habebunt*.

C.15.221 Super egros manus [in]pone[nt] & bene *habebunt* &c–

habentes C 1

C.13.4 Tanquam nichil *habentes* &c.

habeo B 1; C 1

B.13.254 Argentum & aurum non est michi; quod autem *habeo* tibi do; in
nomine

C.15.224 Argentum & Aurum non est michi; quod [autem] *habeo* tibi do &c.

habere B 1

B.Pr.141 'Dum rex a regere dicatur nomen *habere*

habes B 1; C 1

B.16.120 Demonium *habe[s]* &c.

C.18.150 Demonium *habes*.

habet B 4; C 3

B.Pr.142 Nomen *habet* sine re nisi studet iura tenere.'

B.10.256 Fides non *habet* meritum vbi humana racio prebet experimentum.

B.12.147 Set non erat ei locus in diuersorio, et pauper non *habet*
diuersorium.

B.15.118 intelligis quod vicium *habet* in radice, Ita cum videris populum

C.11.157 Fides non *habet* meritum vbi humana racio &c.

C.13.44 Necessitas non *habet* legem–

C.16.273 intelligis quod vicium *habet* in radice, Ita cum videris populum

habitabit B 5; C 3

B. 2.39 Domine quis *habitabit* in tabernaculo tuo &c.

B. 3.234 Domine, quis *habitabit* in tabernaculo tuo?

B. 7.52 Domine, quis *habitabit* in tabernaculo tuo.

B.13.127 But Dilige deum and Domine quis *habitabit*;

B.13.432 Non *habitabit* in medio domus mee qui facit superbiam & qui
loquitur iniqua.

C. 2.40 Domine quis *habitabit* in tabernaculo tuo &c.

C. 7.92 Non *habitabit* in medio domus mee qui facit superbiam [&] qui

C.15.134 Bote dilige deum & p[roximu]m [and] domine quis *habitabit*

habitare A 1

A.11.192 Ecce quam bonum & quam iocundum *habitare* Fratres in vnum.

habitauit B 1

B. 5.500 Verbum caro factum est & *habitauit* in nobis.

habuerit B 1; C 1

B.15.318 Num[quid], dicit Iob, rugi[e]t onager cum herbam *habuerit* aut

C.17.53 Nu[mquid], dicit Iop, rugiet onager cum *habuerit* herbam aut

habundancia B 1; C 1

B.14.77 Ociositas & *habundancia* panis peccatum turpissimum nutriuit;

C.15.229 *Habundancia* panis & vini turpissimum peccatum aduenit.

habundanter B 1; C 1

B.10.89 Si tibi sit copia *habundanter* tribue; si autem exiguum illud
impertiri stude

C.11.69 Si tibi sit copia *habundanter* tribue; Si Autem exiguum illud
impertir[i] libenter stude.

habundantes B 1; C 1

B.10.26 Ecce ipsi peccatores! *habundantes* in seculo obtinuerunt diuicias.

C.11.23 Et alibi: ecce ip[s]i peccatores, *habundantes* &c.

hac B 1; C 1

B.13.57 And þanne hadde Pacience a pitaunce, Pro *hac* orabit ad te omnis;

C 1

C.15.60 And brouhte forth a pytaunce, was pro h[a]c orabit [ad te] omnis

hec C 3

C. 3.405 As hic & *hec* homo askyng an adiectyf

C.13.98 Amen dico vobis quia *hec* vidua paupercula &c.

C.17.285 In baculi forma sit, presul, *hec* tibi norma;

herbam B 1; C 1
B.15.318 Num[quid], dicit Iob, rugi[e]t onager cum *herbam* habuerit aut
C.17.53 Nu[mquid], dicit Iop, rugiet onager cum habuerit *herbam* aut

hereditatis B 1; C 2
B.12.189 Dominus pars *hereditatis* mee is a murye verset
C. 5.60 Dominus pars *hereditatis* mee &c. Et alibi: clemencia non constringit.
C.14.128 Dominus pars *hereditatis* [mee] is A merye verset;

heremita B 1; C 1
B.15.286 Poul primus *heremita* hadde parroked hymselue
C.17.13 Paul primus *heremita* hadde yparrokede hymsulue

heu B 2; C 2
B. 1.141 *Heu* michi quia sterilem duxi vitam Iuuenilem.
B. 5.440 *Heu* michi quia sterilem vitam duxi Iuuenilem.'
C. 1.140 *Heu* michi quod ste[r]ilem duxi vitam iuuenilem.
C. 7.54 *Heu* michi quod ster[i]lem duxi vitam iuuenilem.'

hic B 1; C 2
B.15.162 [*Hic*] in enigmate, tunc facie ad faciem.
C. 3.405 As *hic* & hec homo askyng an adiectyf
C.16.296 *Hic* in enigmate, tunc facie ad faciem.

hij B 2; C 2
B.10.327 *Hij* in curribus & hij in equis ipsi obligati sunt &c.
B.10.327 Hij in curribus & *hij* in equis ipsi obligati sunt &c.
C. 5.172 *Hij* in curribus & [hij] in equis; ipsi obligati sunt & ceciderunt.
C. 5.172 Hij in curribus & [*hij*] in equis; ipsi obligati sunt & ceciderunt.

hijs B 1; C 1
B.17.16 In *hijs* duobus mandatis tota lex pendet & prophet[e].
C.19.17 In *hijs* duobus [mandatis tota lex pendet & prophete].

histrionibus C 1
C. 7.118 Dare *histrionibus* &c.

hoc B 4; C 2
B.Pr.134 *Hoc* quod agas melius, iustus es, esto pius!
B.12.293 For Deus dicitur quasi dans [eternam vitam] suis, *hoc* est fidelibus;
B.16.47 Videatis qui peccat in spiritum sanctum numquam remittetur &c; *Hoc*
B.19.80 Omnia celestia terrestria flectantur in *hoc* nomine Iesu;
C.Pr.155 *Hoc* vt agas melius, iustus es, esto pius!
C.21.80 Omnia celestia terrestria flectantur in *hoc* nomine iesu;

hominem A 3; B 4; C 2
A.10.41 Faciamus *hominem* ad ymaginem nostram.
A.10.90 For intencio indicat *hominem* &c.
A.10.162 Penitet me fecisse *hominem*.
B. 5.486 Faciamus *hominem* ad ymaginem [et similitudinem] nostram;
B. 9.43 Faciamus *hominem* ad imaginem nostram];
B. 9.133 Penitet me fecisse *hominem*.
B.15.63 Sciencie appetitus *hominem* inmortalitatis gloria[m] spoliauit.
C.10.222 Penitet me fecisse *hominem*;
C.16.225 Sciencie appetitus *hominem* inmortalitatis gloriam spoliauit.

homines B 4; C 3
B. 5.509 'Homines & iumenta saluabis quemadmodum multiplicasti misericordiam
B. 7.60 Quodcumque vultis vt faciant vobis *homines* facite eis.
B.10.416 *Homines* & iumenta saluabis, domine &c.
B.12.50 Sunt *homines* nequam, bene de virtute loquentes.
C. 7.154 '*Homines* & iumenta saluabis; qu[e]madmodum multiplicasti
C.11.248 *Homines* & iumenta saluabis &c.
C.16.309 Quodcumque vultis vt faciant vobis *homines*, facite eis.

homini A 1; B 2; C 2
A.12.22 Audiui archan[a uerba] que non licet *homini* loqui.
B.16.157 Necesse est vt veniant scandala; ve *homini* illi per quem scandalum venit.
B.18.395 Audiui archana verba que non licet *homini* loqui.
C.18.174 Ve *homini* illi per quem scand[a]lum venit.
C.20.438 Audiui arcana verba que non licet *homini* loqui.

hominibus B 1; C 1
B.13.312 Si *hominibus* placerem christi seruus non essem; Et alibi, Nemo potest
C. 6.60 Si *hominibus* placerem christi seruus non essem; nemo potest duobus

hominis C 1
C.18.4 Til we cam into a contre, cor *hominis* hit heihte,

hominum B 3; C 3
B.13.45 Vos qui peccata *hominum* comeditis, nisi pro eis lacrimas & oraciones

B.13.330 labor et dol[or]; Et alibi, Filij *hominum* dentes eorum arma & sagitte
B.17.261 Si linguis *hominum* loquar &c.
C. 6.76 labor & dolor. Filij *hominum* dentes eorum Arma & sagitte
C.15.50 Vos qui peccata *hominum* comeditis, nisi pro eis lacrimas & orationes
C.19.227 Si linguis *hominum* loqu[a]r &c.

homo B 4; C 7
B.11.37 '*Homo* proponit', quod a poete, and Plato he hiȝte,
B.14.46 viuit *homo* set in omni verbo quod procedit de ore dei.'
B.16.219 Maledictus *homo* qui non reliquit semen in Israel.
B.20.33 *Homo* proponit & deus disponit;
C. 3.402 Deus *homo*–
C. 3.405 As hic & hec *homo* askyng an adiectyf
C. 5.86 Non de solo, y sayde, 'for sothe viuit *homo*,
C.11.303 '*Homo* pr[o]ponit,' quod a poete tho, and plato he hihte,
C.15.244 vobis. Et alibi: Non in solo pane viuit *homo* &c.'
C.18.222 Maledictus *homo* qui non reliquit semen in Israel.
C.22.33 *Homo* proponit [&] deus dispo[n]it;

honora B 1; C 2
B. 5.567 *Honora* patrem & matrem &c;
C. 7.216 *Honora* patrem & matrem &c.
C.17.59 *Honora* patrem & matrem &c–

honorem B 1; C 1
B. 3.336 *Honorem* adquiret qui dat munera &c.'
C. 3.488 *Honorem* adquiret qui dat munera.'

horum B 1
B.12.29 Fides, spes, caritas, et maior *horum* &c.

huius A 2; B 3; C 4
A.10.8 A proud prikere of Fraunce, Princeps *huius* mundi,
A.10.62 Thanne haþ þe pouk power, sire princeps *huius* mundi,
B. 9.8 A proud prikere of Fraunce, Princeps *huius* mundi,
B.12.138 Sapiencia *huius* mundi stulticia est apud deum.
B.18.315 Nunc princeps *huius* mundi e[i]icietur foras.'
C.10.135 A proued prikeare of fraunce, princeps *huius* mundi,
C.14.32 Vultus *huius* seculi sunt subiecti v[u]ltibus celestibus.
C.14.83 Sapiencia *huius* mundi stul[t]icia est apud deum.
C.20.349 Nunc princeps *huius* mundi.'

humana B 2; C 2
B.10.256 Fides non habet meritum vbi *humana* racio prebet experimentum.
B.18.23 In his helm and in his haubergeon, *humana* natura;
C.11.157 Fides non habet meritum vbi *humana* racio &c.
C.20.22 In his helm and in his haberion, *humana* natura;

humiliat A 1
A.10.120 Qui se *humiliat* exaltabitur &c.

humiliatum B 2; C 2
B.13.58 Cor contritum & *humiliatum* deus non despicies.
B.15.194 Cor contritum & *humiliatum* deus non despicies.'
C.15.62 And saide, 'cor contritum & *humiliatum*, deus, non despicies.'
C.16.336 Cor contritum & *humiliatum* deus non despicies.

ianua B 1; C 1
B. 9.186 Scribitur in portis, meretrix est *ianua* mortis.
C.10.287 Scribitur in portis, meretrix est *ianua* mortis.

ibant B 1; C 1
B.12.144 *Ibant* magi ab oriente.
C.14.88 *Ib[a]nt* magi ab Oriente &c.

ibi C 1; B 1
B.13.398 Vbi thesaurus tuus *ibi* & cor tuum.'
C. 6.285 Vbi tezaurus tuus, *ibi* [&] cor tuum.'

ibunt A 1; B 1; C 3
A. 8.95 Et qui bona egerunt *ibunt* in vitam eternam;
B. 7.113 Et qui bona egerunt *ibunt* in vitam eternam;
C. 9.287 Et qui bona egerunt *ibunt* in vitam eternam;
C.11.23 *Ibunt* in progenie patrum suorum & vsque in eternum non videbunt lumen;
C.12.119 Et qui bona egerunt, *ibunt* &c.

id B 2; C 4
B.15.212 But Piers þe Plowman, Petrus *id* est christus.
B.19.273 *Id* est vetus testamentum & nouum.
C.17.140 Dilige deum propter deum, *id* est propter veritatem; & inimicum tuum
C.17.140 propter mandatum, *id* est propter legem; & Amicum propter Amorem,
C.17.140 *id* est propter caritatem.
C.21.273 *Id* est vetus testamentum & nouum.

idem B 1
B.16.47 est *idem* qui peccat per liberum arbitrium non repugnat.

ideo B 2; C 1

B.14.3 Vxorem duxi & *ideo* non possum venire–

B.15.576 In domo mea non est panis neque vestimentum et *ideo* nolite
constituere me Regem.

C. 7.304 Vxorem duxi & *ideo* non possum venire.'

ydiote idiote A 1; B 1; C 1

A.11.305 Ecce ipsi *ydiot[e]* rapiunt celum vbi nos sapientes

B.10.461 "Ecce ipsi *ydiot[e]* rapiunt celum vbi nos sapientes in inferno
mergimur".

C.11.287 "Ecce ips[i] *idiote* rapiunt celum vbi nos sapientes in inferno
mergimur".

idipsum B 2; C 1

B.15.254 In pace in *idipsum* dormiam &c.

B.18.186 Lo! here þe patente', quod Pees, 'In pace in *idipsum*,

C.20.191 Loo! here þe patente,' quod pees, 'In pace in *idipsum*,

yeme C 1

C. 8.245 Piger propter frigus noluit arrare; mendicabi[t] in *yeme* & non
dabitur ei".

iesu B 1; C 1

B.19.80 Omnia celestia terrestria flectantur in hoc nomine *Iesu*;

C.21.80 Omnia celestia terrestria flectantur in hoc nomine *iesu*;

iesum B 1; C 1

B.15.610 Lere hem litlum and litlum et in *Iesum* Christum filium,

C.17.318 Lere hem littelum and littelum [et] in *iesum* christum filium

iesus B 1; C 1

B.19.133 For þe dedes þat he dide, Fili dauid, *Iesus*.

C.21.133 For þe dedes þat he dede, fili dauid, *iesus*.

ignem A 1; B 1; C 1

A. 8.96 Qui vero mala in *ignem* eternum.

B. 7.114 Qui vero mala in *ignem* eternum.

C. 9.288 Qui vero mala in *ignem* etern[u]m.

ignis A 1; B 2; C 2

A. 3.85 *Ignis* deuorabit tabernacula eorum qui libenter accipiunt munera.

B. 3.96 *Ignis* deuorabit tabernacula eorum qui libenter accipiunt munera
&c.

B.12.286 Aduenit *ignis* diuinus non comburens set illuminans &c.

C. 3.124 *Ignis* deuorabit tabernacula eorum qui libenter accipiunt munera.

C.14.208 A[d]uenit *ignis* diuinus non comburens set illuminans &c.

ignorancia B 1; C 1

B.11.316 For hir eiþer is endited, and that [of] '*Ignorancia*

C.13.128 For *ignorancia* non excusat as ych haue herd in bokes.'

ignorat C 1

C.12.215 O stulte, ista nocte anima tua egredi[e]tur; tezaurisat & *ignorat* &c.

illam B 1

B. 7.83 vt ego veni[ens] cum vsuris ex[egissem *illam*]?

ille B 1; C 1

B.14.104 'Ye? quis est *ille*?' quod Pacience; 'quik, laudabimus eum!

C.15.279 'ʒe? quis est *ille*?' quod pacience; 'quik, lauda[bi]mus eum!

illi B 1; C 1

B.16.157 Necesse est vt veniant scandala; ve homini *illi* per quem scandalum
venit.

C.18.174 Ve homini *illi* per quem scand[a]lum venit.

illorum B 1; C 1

B.14.213 Opera enim *illorum* sequ[u]ntur illos,

C.16.54 Opera [enim *ill]orum* sequ[u]ntur illos,

illos B 2; C 1

B.11.88 Non oderis fratres secrete in corde tuo set publice argue *illos*.

B.14.213 Opera enim illorum sequ[u]ntur *illos*,

C.16.54 Opera [enim ill]orum sequ[u]ntur *illos*,

illud B 1; C 1

B.10.89 Si tibi sit copia habundanter tribue; si autem exiguum *illud*
impertiri stude

C.11.69 Si Autem exiguum *illud* impertir[i] libenter stude.

illum B 1

B. 7.77 Non eligas cui miser[e]aris ne forte preterea *illum* qui meretur
accipere,

illuminans B 1; C 1

B.12.286 Aduenit ignis diuinus non comburens set *illuminans* &c.

C.14.208 A[d]uenit ignis diuinus non comburens set *illuminans* &c.

ymaginem imaginem A 1; B 2

A.10.41 Faciamus hominem ad *ymaginem* nostram.

B. 5.486 Faciamus hominem ad *ymaginem* [et similitudinem] nostram;

B. 9.43 Faciamus hominem ad *imaginem* nostram];

ymago C 1

C.18.7 That hihte *ymago* dei, graciousliche hit growede.

immolare B 1

B.15.343 dare est demonibus *immolare*. Item, monache, si indiges &

impertiri B 1; C 1

B.10.89 Si tibi sit copia habundanter tribue; si autem exiguum illud
impertiri stude

C.11.69 Si Autem exiguum illud *impertir[i]* libenter stude.

impij B 1

B.10.25 Quare *impij* viuunt? bene est omnibus qui preuaricantur & inique
agunt?

impiorum A 1; B 1; C 1

A.11.23 Quare via *impiorum* p[ros]peratur, [bene] est omnibus qui praue

B.10.333 *impiorum*, et virgam dominancium cedencium plaga insanabili.

C. 5.177 Contriuit dominus bac[u]lum *impiorum*, virga[m] d[omi]nancium,

imples B 1

B.14.63 Aperis tu manum tuam & *imples* omne animal benediccione.

imponent B 1

B.13.249 In nomine meo demonia e[j]icient & super egros manus *imponent*
& bene

impunitum B 1

B.18.390 Nullum malum *impunitum* &c–

in A 15; B 109; C 97

A. 3.228 *In* quorum manibus iniquitates sunt; dextera eorum repleta est
muneribus.

A. 7.78 *In* dei nomine Amen I make it myseluen:

A. 7.217 *In* sudore & swynke þou shalt þi mete tilen

A. 8.95 Et qui bona egerunt ibunt *in* vitam eternam;

A. 8.96 Qui vero mala *in* ignem eternum.

A. 8.102 & seide 'Si ambulauero *in* medio umbre mortis

A. 9.16 'Sepcies *in* die cadit iustus.

A.10.108 Qui circuit [omne genus in nullo genere est].

A.10.112 *In* eadem vocacione qua vocati estis state.

A.11.55 Ecce audiuimus eam *in* effrata, inuenimus eam in campis silue.

A.11.55 Ecce audiuimus eam in effrata, inuenimus eam *in* campis silue.

A.11.192 Ecce quam bonum & quam iocundum habitare Fratres *in* vnum.

A.11.196 Qui facit & docuerit magnus vocabitur *in* regno celorum.

A.11.235 'Þat is *in* extremis,' quaþ scripture, 'as sarisines & Iewis

A.11.305 vbi nos sapientes *in* infernum mergemur.

B. 1.119 Ponam pedem *in* aquilone & similis ero altissimo.

B. 2.39 Domine quis habitabit *in* tabernaculo tuo &c.

B. 3.234 Domine, quis habitabit *in* tabernaculo tuo?

B. 3.249 *In* quorum manibus iniquitates sunt; dextra eorum repleta est
muneribus.

B. 3.308 Conflabunt gladios suos *in* vomeres &c.

B. 3.328 And Sarʒynes for þat siʒte shul synge Gloria *in* excelsis &c,

B. 4.36 Contricio & infelicitas *in* viis eorum &c.

B. 5.283 Omnis iniquitas quantum ad misericordiam dei est quasi sintilla *in*
medio

B. 5.486 Et alibi, Qui manet *in* caritate in deo manet & deus in eo.

B. 5.486 Et alibi, Qui manet in caritate *in* deo manet & deus in eo.

B. 5.486 Et alibi, Qui manet in caritate in deo manet & deus *in* eo.

B. 5.493 Populus qui ambulabat *in* tenebris vidit lucem magnam.

B. 5.500 Verbum caro factum est & habitauit *in* nobis.

B. 6.86 *In* dei nomine, amen. I make it myselue.

B. 6.233 *In* sudore and swynk þow shalt þi mete tilie

B. 7.52 Domine, quis habitabit *in* tabernaculo tuo.

B. 7.75 Sit elemosina tua *in* manu tua donec studes cui des.

B. 7.113 Et qui bona egerunt ibunt *in* vitam eternam;

B. 7.114 Qui vero mala *in* ignem eternum.

B. 7.120 And seide, 'Si ambulauero *in* medio vmbre mortis

B. 7.181 Quodcumque ligaueris super terram erit ligatum & *in* celis &c.

B. 8.20 'Sepcies *in* die cadit Iustus.

B. 9.65 Qui manet *in* caritate in deo manet &c.

B. 9.65 Qui manet in caritate *in* deo manet &c.

B. 9.100 Qui offendit *in* vno in omnibus est reus.

B. 9.100 Qui offendit in vno *in* omnibus est reus.

B. 9.186 Scribitur *in* portis, meretrix est ianua mortis.

B.10.26 Ecce ipsi peccatores! habundantes *in* seculo obtinuerunt diuicias.

B.10.69 Ecce audiuimus eam *in* effrata; inuenimus eam in campis silue.

B.10.69 Ecce audiuimus eam in effrata; inuenimus eam *in* campis silue.

B.10.252 [Ego *in* patre et pater in me est, et qui videt me videt et patrem
meum]

B.10.252 [Ego in patre et pater *in* me est, et qui videt me videt et patrem
meum]

B.10.268 Qui[d] consideras festucam *in* oculo fratris tui, trabem in oculo tuo
&c?

B.10.268 Qui[d] consideras festucam in oculo fratris tui, trabem *in* oculo tuo
&c?

B.10.281 Dum cecus ducit cecum ambo *in* foueam cadunt.
B.10.327 Hij *in* curribus & hij in equis ipsi obligati sunt &c.
B.10.327 Hij in curribus & hij *in* equis ipsi obligati sunt &c.
B.10.352 'That is *in* extremis', quod Scripture, '[as] Sarȝens & Iewes
B.10.436 [Sunt] iusti atque sapientes, & opera eorum *in* manu dei sunt &c.
B.10.461 "Ecce ipsi ydiot[e] rapiunt celum vbi nos sapientes *in* inferno
             mergimur"'.
B.10.473 That euere þe[i] kouþe [konne on book] moore þan Credo *in* deum
             patrem,
B.10.481 Ite vos *in* vineam meam.'
B.11.88   Non oderis fratres secrete *in* corde tuo set publice argue illos.
B.11.176 Qui non diligit manet *in* morte.
B.11.287 Spera *in* deo spekeþ of preestes þat haue no spendyng siluer,
B.11.309 Qui offendit *in* vno in omnibus est reus.
B.11.309 Qui offendit in vno *in* omnibus est reus.
B.12.9   Si non *in* prima vigilia nec in secunda &c.
B.12.9   Si non in prima vigilia nec *in* secunda &c.
B.12.147 Set non erat ei locus *in* diuersorio, et pauper non habet
             diuersorium.
B.12.150 And songe a song of solas, Gloria *in* excelsis deo.
B.12.281 And seide, 'Saluabitur vix Iustus *in* die Iudicij;
B.12.293 Et alibi, si ambulauero *in* medio vmbre mortis.
B.13.45   eff[u]deritis, ea que *in* delicijs comeditis in tormentis euometis.
B.13.45   eff[u]deritis, ea que in delicijs comeditis *in* tormentis euometis.
B.13.57   Pro hac orabit ad te omnis sanctus *in* tempore oportuno;
B.13.67   *In* fame & frigore and flappes of scourges:
B.13.70   Periculum est *in* falsis fratribus.'
B.13.73   Vnusquisque a fratre se custodiat quia vt dicitur periculum est *in*
             falsis
B.13.118 Qui facit & docuerit magnus vocabitur *in* regno celorum.'
B.13.249 *In* nomine meo demonia e[j]icient & super egros manus imponent
             & bene
B.13.254 Argentum & aurum non est michi; quod autem habeo tibi do; *in*
             nomine
B.13.432 Non habitabit *in* medio domus mee qui facit superbiam & qui
             loquitur iniqua.
B.14.46   Quodcumque pecieritis a patre *in* nomine meo &c; Et alibi, Non in
             solo pane
B.14.46   Quodcumque pecieritis a patre in nomine meo &c; Et alibi, Non *in*
             solo pane
B.14.46   viuit homo set *in* omni verbo quod procedit de ore dei.'
B.14.131 velud sompn[i]um surgencium domine *in* Ciuitate tua,
B.14.181 Thus *in* genere of gentries Iesu crist seide
B.15.51   Ponam pedem meum *in* aquilone & similis ero altissimo.'
B.15.61   Et verba vertit *in* opera fulliche to his power."
B.15.118 Si sacerdocium fuerit *in* peccatis totus populus conuertitur ad
B.15.118 intelligis quod vicium habet *in* radice, Ita cum videris populum
B.15.149 'Nisi efficiamini sicut paruuli non intrabitis *in* regnum celorum.
B.15.162 [Hic] *in* enigmate, tunc facie ad faciem.
B.15.180 And if he soupeþ eteþ but a sop of Spera *in* deo.
B.15.191 And leggen on longe wiþ Laboraui *in* gemitu meo,
B.15.215 Fy on faitours and *in* fautores suos!
B.15.254 *In* pace in idipsum dormiam &c.
B.15.254 In pace *in* idipsum dormiam &c.
B.15.431 Et si sal euanuerit *in* quo salietur?
B.15.490 [Ecce audiuimus e[a]m *in* effrata &c].
B.15.491 Ite *in* vniuersum mundum & predicate &c?
B.15.500 Ite vos *in* vineam meam &c.
B.15.530 Nolite mittere falsem *in* messem alienam.
B.15.537 Absit nobis gloriari nisi *in* cruce domini nostri &c.
B.15.576 *In* domo mea non est panis neque vestimentum et ideo nolite
             constituere me Regem.
B.15.578 Inferte omnes [decimas] *in* orreum meum vt cibus in domo mea.
B.15.578 Inferte omnes [decimas] in orreum meum vt cibus *in* domo mea.
B.15.608 Konne þe firste clause of oure bileue, Credo *in* deum patrem
             omnipotentem,
B.15.610 Lere hem litlum and litlum et *in* Iesum Christum filium,
B.15.611 Til þei kouþe speke and spelle et *in* Spiritum sanctum,
B.16.47   Videatis qui peccat *in* spiritum sanctum numquam remittetur &c;
             Hoc
B.16.84   And made of holy men his hoord *In* limbo Inferni,
B.16.219 Maledictus homo qui non reliquit semen *in* Israel.
B.17.16   *In* hijs duobus mandatis tota lex pendet & prophet[e].
B.17.111 He was vnhardy, þat harlot, and hidde hym *in* Inferno.
B.17.200 Qui peccat *in* spiritu[m] sanct[um] &c,
B.17.201 For he prikeþ god as *in* þe pawme þat peccat in spiritu[m]
             sanct[um].
B.17.341 Virtus *in* infirmitate perficitur.
B.18.17   Benedictus qui venit *in* nomine domini.
B.18.26   For no dynt shal hym dere as *in* deitate patris.'
B.18.149 Quia *in* Inferno nulla est redempcio.'
B.18.186 Lo! here þe patente', quod Pees, '*In* pace in idipsum.
B.18.186 Lo! here þe patente', quod Pees, 'In pace *in* idipsum,

B.18.323 Patriarkes and prophetes, populus *in* tenebris,
B.18.360 Et cecidit *in* foueam quam fecit.
B.18.399 Non intres *in* Iudicium cum seruo tuo.
B.19.74   Gloria *in* excelsis deo &c.
B.19.80   Omnia celestia terrestria flectantur *in* hoc nomine Iesu;
C. 1.111 Ponam pedem meum *in* Aquilone & similis ero altissimo.'
C. 1.113 Luppen alofte [*in* lateribus Aquilonis]
C. 2.40   Domine quis habitabit *in* tabernaculo tuo &c.
C. 3.118 *In* quorum manibus iniquitates sunt:
C. 3.357 In case, credere *in* ecclesia, in holy kyrke to bileue;
C. 3.403 Qui *in* caritate manet in deo manet et deus in eo.
C. 3.403 Qui in caritate manet *in* deo manet et deus in eo.
C. 3.403 Qui in caritate manet in deo manet et deus *in* eo.
C. 3.461 Conflabunt gladios suos *in* vomeres & lancias [suas] in falces.
C. 3.461 Conflabunt gladios suos in vomeres & lancias [suas] *in* falces.
C. 3.481 And saresines for þat syhte shal syng Credo *in* spiritum sanctum
C. 4.36   Contricio & infelicitas *in* viis eorum et viam pacis non
             cognouerunt;
C. 5.43   *In* eadem vocacione qu[a] vocati estis [&c]
C. 5.87   Nec *in* pane [nec] in pabulo; the paternoster wittenesseth
C. 5.87   Nec in pane [nec] *in* pabulo; the paternoster wittenesseth
C. 5.98   Simile est regnum celorum thesauro abscondito *in* agro;
C. 5.172 Hij *in* curribus & [hij] in equis; ipsi obligati sunt & ceciderunt.
C. 5.172 Hij in curribus & [hij] *in* equis; ipsi obligati sunt & ceciderunt.
C. 6.338 Omnis iniquitas quoad misericordiam dei est quasi sintilla *in*
             medio maris.
C. 7.92   Non habitabit *in* medio domus mee qui facit superbiam [&] qui
C. 7.128 Ego *in* patre & pater in me [est] et qui me videt videt [&] patrem
             meum &c;
C. 7.128 Ego in patre & pater *in* me [est] et qui me videt videt [&] patrem
             meum &c;
C. 7.133 Populus qui ambulabat *in* tenebris vidit lucem magnam &c.
C. 7.260 Quodcumque pecieritis *in* nomine meo dabitur enim vobis.
C. 8.95   *In* dei nomine, Amen: y make hit mysulue.
C. 8.241 *In* [labore & sudore] vultus tui vesceris pane tuo".
C. 8.245 Piger propter frigus noluit arrare; mendicabi[t] *in* yeme & non
             dabitur ei".
C. 9.125 Et egenos vagos[que] induc *in* domum tuam,
C. 9.287 Et qui bona egerunt ibunt *in* vitam eternam;
C. 9.288 Qui vero mala *in* ignem etern[u]m.
C. 9.327 Quodcumque ligaueris super terram erit ligatum & *in* celis.
C.10.21   And saide, 'sothly sepcies *in* die ca[d]it iust[u]s,
C.10.287 Scribitur *in* portis, meretrix est ianua mortis.
C.11.22   Ducunt *in* bonis dies suos & in fin[e] descendunt ad infernum.
C.11.22   Ducunt in bonis dies suos & *in* fin[e] descendunt ad infernum.
C.11.23   Ibunt *in* progenie patrum suorum & vsque in eternum non videbunt
             lumen;
C.11.23   Ibunt in progenie patrum suorum & vsque *in* eternum non videbunt
             lumen;
C.11.49   Ecce Audiuimus eam *in* Effrata; [inuenimus eam in campis silue].
C.11.49   Ecce Audiuimus eam in Effrata; [inuenimus eam *in* campis silue].
C.11.153 Ego *in* patre & pater in me est; Et qui me vid[e]t, patrem meum
C.11.153 Ego in patre & pater *in* me est; Et qui me vid[e]t, patrem meum
C.11.153 vid[e]t qui *in* celis est &c.
C.11.201 Ita possibile est diuiti intrare *in* regn[um] celorum sicut camelus
             &c.
C.11.271 Sunt iusti atque sapientes & opera eorum *in* manu dei sunt &c.
C.11.287 "Ecce ips[i] idiote rapiunt celum vbi nos sapientes *in* inferno
             mergimur".
C.12.34   Non oderis fratrem secrete *in* corde &c.
C.12.99   Qui non diligit manet *in* morte.
C.12.179 Nisi granum frumenti cadens *in* terram mortuum fuerit &c.
C.12.207 "Tristicia vestra vertetur *in* gaudium:
C.13.101 For spera *in* deo speketh of prestis þat han no spendynge suluer
C.13.122 Qui offendit *in* vno in om[n]ibus est reus.
C.13.122 Qui offendit in vno *in* om[n]ibus est reus.
C.14.94   And song a song of solace, Gloria *in* excelcis deo.
C.14.203 And saide, 'Vix saluabitur iustus *in* die iudicij;
C.15.22   That iustus bifore iesu *in* die iudicij non saluabitur bote vix helpe;
C.15.50   effuderitis, ea que *in* deliciis comeditis in tor[mentis] euo[metis]
             &c.
C.15.50   effuderitis, ea que in deliciis comeditis *in* tor[mentis] euo[metis]
             &c.
C.15.60   pro h[a]c orabit [ad te] omnis sanctus *in* tempore oportuno.
C.15.73   *In* fame [et] frygore &c.
C.15.75   Periculum est *in* falsis fratribus.'
C.15.118 [Bu]t dowel endite ȝow *in* die iudicij.'
C.15.244 Quodcumque pecieritis [a patre] *in* nomine meo dab[itur] enim
C.15.244 vobis. Et alibi: Non *in* solo pane viuit homo &c.'
C.16.213 Ponam pedem meum *in* Aquilone &c.
C.16.223 Et verba vertit *in* opera emforth his power."
C.16.273 Si sacerdocium fuerit *in* peccatis totus populus conuertitur ad
C.16.273 intelligis quod vicium habet *in* radice, Ita cum videris populum

C.16.296 Hic *in* enigmate, tunc facie ad faciem.
C.16.322 And also a can clergie, credo *in* deum patrem,
C.16.333 And laueth hem *in* þe lauendrie, labora[ui] *in* gemitu meo,
C.17.66 Iusticia eius manet *in* eternum.
C.17.191 Ite *in* vniuersum mundum, sethe ȝe wilne þe name
C.17.198 Absit nobis gloriari nisi *in* cruce domini nostri &c.
C.17.280 Nolite mittere falcem *in* messem alienam &c.
C.17.285 *In* baculi forma sit, presul, hec tibi norma:
C.17.316 Conne þe furste clause of oure bileue, credo *in* deum patrem,
C.17.318 Lere hem littelum and littelum [et] *in* iesum christum filium
C.17.319 Til they couthe speke and spele et *in* spiritum sanctum,
C.18.115 And made of holy men his hoerd *in* limbo inferni
C.18.117 Thenne moued hym moed [*in*] magestate dei
C.18.164 Ne forte tumultus fieret *in* populo–
C.18.222 Maledictus homo qui non reliquit semen *in* Israel.
C.19.17 *In* hijs duobus [mandatis tota lex pendet & prophete].
C.19.166 Qui peccat *in* spiritu[m] sanct[um] &c,
C.19.167 For he priketh god as in [the] paume that peccat *in* spiritum sanctum.
C.19.232 Non omnis qui dicit domine, domine intrabit *in* reg[num] celorum &c.
C.19.321 Virtus *in* infirmitate perficitur.
C.20.15 Benedictus qui venit *in* nomine domini.
C.20.25 For no d[yn]t shal hym dere as *in* deitate patris.'
C.20.152 Quia *in* inferno nulla est redempcio.'
C.20.191 Loo! here þe patente,' quod pees, '*In* pace in idipsum,
C.20.191 Loo! here þe patente,' quod pees, 'In pace *in* idipsum,
C.20.366 Patriarkes and profetes, populus *in* tenebris,
C.20.435 Domine ne *in* furore tuo Arguas me &c–
C.20.442 Non intres *in* iudicium cum seruo tuo.
C.21.74 Gloria *in* excelsis deo.
C.21.80 Omnia celestia terrestria flectantur *in* hoc nomine iesu;

incerta B 1; C 1
B.14.276 negocium sine dampno, *Incerta* fortuna, absque sollicitudine
C.16.116 negocium sine dampno, *Incerta* fortuna, absque solicitudine

incertum B 1
B. 7.77 Quia *incertum* est pro quo deo magis placeas.

indicat A 1
A.10.90 For intencio *indicat* hominem &c.

indiges B 1
B.15.343 dare est demonibus immolare. Item, monache, si *indiges* &

indiget B 2
B. 7.87 Satis diues est qui non *indiget* pane.
B.15.343 Porro non *indiget* monachus si habeat quod nature sufficit.

indisciplinatum indissiplinatum B 1; C 1
B.15.118 Ita cum videris populum *indisciplinatum* & irreligiosum, sine dubio
C.16.273 Ita cum videris populum *indissiplinatum* & irreligiosum, sine dubio

induc C 1
C. 9.125 Et egenos vagos[que] *induc* in domum tuam,

induebatur C 1
C.19.240 Epulabatur splendide & *induebatur* bisso &c.

inebriemus B 1; C 1
B. 1.31 *Inebri[e]mus* eum vino dormiamusque cum eo
C. 1.30 *Inebriemus* eum vino dormiamusque cum eo vt seruare possimus

infelices C 1
C. 3.190 Sunt *infelices* quia matres sunt meretrices.

infelicitas B 1; C 1
B. 4.36 Contricio & *infelicitas* in viis eorum &c.
C. 4.36 Contricio & *infelicitas* in viis eorum et viam pacis non cognouerunt;

inferna B 1; C 1
B.18.111 I drow me in þat derkenesse to descendit ad *inferna*
C.20.114 Y [d]row [me] in þat derkenesse to descendit ad *inferna*

inferni B 1; C 1
B.16.84 And made of holy men his hoord In limbo *Inferni*,
C.18.115 And made of holy men his hoerd in limbo *inferni*

inferno B 3; C 2
B.10.461 "Ecce ipsi ydiot[e] rapiunt celum vbi nos sapientes in *inferno* mergimur".
B.17.111 He was vnhardy, þat harlot, and hidde hym in *Inferno*.
B.18.149 Quia in *Inferno* nulla est redempcio.'
C.11.287 "Ecce ips[i] idiote rapiunt celum vbi nos sapientes in *inferno* mergimur".
C.20.152 Quia in *inferno* nulla est redempcio.'

infernum A 1; C 1
A.11.305 vbi nos sapientes in *infernum* mergemur.
C.11.22 Ducunt in bonis dies suos & in fin[e] descendunt ad *infernum*.

inferte B 1
B.15.578 *Inferte* omnes [decimas] in orreum meum vt cibus in domo mea.

infirmata C 1
C. 9.163 Iunior fui, [et]enim senui; e[t] alibi: *infirmata* est vertus mea paupertate.

infirmis B 1
B.16.110 Non est sanis opus medicus set *in[firmis]*.

infirmitate B 1; C 1
B.17.341 Virtus in *infirmitate* perficitur.
C.19.321 Virtus in *infirmitate* perficitur.

inflat B 1
B.12.57 Sapiencia *inflat* &c];

inflatur B 1; C 1
B.15.157 Non *inflatur*, non est ambiciosa, non querit que sua sunt–
C.16.291 Non *inflatur*, non est Ambiciosa.

ingemuerit C 1
C. 7.147 Quandocumque *ingemuerit* peccator omnes iniquitate[s] eius non

ingrati B 1
B.14.169 Of þe good þat þow hem gyuest *ingrati* ben manye;

ingratus B 1; C 1
B.17.257 And Indulgences ynowe, and be *ingratus* to þi kynde,
C.19.223 And indulgences ynowe and be *ingrat[u]s* to thy kynde,

ingreditur B 1
B. 3.237 Qui *ingreditur* sine macula & operatur Iusticiam.

inicium A 1; B 1
A.10.81 *Inicium* sapiencie timor domini.
B. 9.96 *Inicium* sapiencie timor domini.

inimicicias B 1; C 1
B.18.408 Post *inimicicias* [clarior est et amor].
C.20.451 Post *inimicicias* Clarior est & Amor.

inimicos B 1
B.13.137 Disce', quod he, 'doce, dilige *inimicos*.

inimicum C 1
C.17.140 Dilige deum propter deum, id est propter veritatem; & *inimicum* tuum

iniqua B 1; C 1
B.13.432 Non habitabit in medio domus mee qui facit superbiam & qui loquitur *iniqua*.
C. 7.92 qui facit superbiam [&] qui loquitur *iniqua* &c.

inique A 1; B 4; C 2
A.11.23 [bene] est omnibus qui praue agunt & *inique*?
B.10.25 Quare impij viuunt? bene est omnibus qui preuaricantur & *inique* agunt?
B.10.291 Existimasti *inique* quod ero tui similis; arguam te & statuam contra faciem
B.11.95 Existimasti *inique* quod ero tui similis &c.
B.19.296 Esto forti animo cum sis dampnatus *inique*.
C.12.29 Existimasti *inique* quod ero t[u]i similis; Arguam te & statuam
C.21.296 Esto forti Animo cum sis dampnatus *inique*.

iniquitas B 2; C 2
B. 5.283 Omnis *iniquitas* quantum ad misericordiam dei est quasi sintilla in medio
B.15.318 pabulum commune sufficiat; ex adipe prodijt *iniquitas* tua.
C. 6.338 Omnis *iniquitas* quoad misericordiam dei est quasi sintilla in medio maris.
C.17.53 pabulum comune sufficiat; Ex adipe prodiit *iniquitas* tua.

iniquitatem A 1; B 4; C 3
A.10.150 Concepit dolore[m] & peperit *iniquitatem*.
B. 9.125 Concepit dolore[m] & peperit *iniquitatem*.
B. 9.149 Filius non portabit *iniquitatem* patris et pater non portabit iniquitatem filij.
B. 9.149 Filius non portabit iniquitatem patris et pater non portabit *iniquitatem* filij.
B.10.114 Filius non portabit *iniquitatem* patris &c.
C.10.212 Concepit dolore[m] & peperit *iniquitatem*.
C.10.236 Filius non portabit *iniquitatem* patris &c.
C.20.356 Odisti omnes qui operantur *iniquitatem*;

iniquitates A 1; B 3; C 4
A. 3.228 In quorum manibus *iniquitates* sunt; dextera eorum repleta est muneribus.

B. 3.249 In quorum manibus *iniquitates* sunt; dextra eorum repleta est muneribus.
B. 5.507 And blew it wiþ Beati quorum remisse sunt *iniquitates*,
B.12.177 Beati quorum remisse sunt *iniquitates* & quorum tecta sunt &c.
C. 3.118 In quorum manibus *iniquitates* sunt:
C. 7.147 Quandocumque ingemuerit peccator omnes *iniquitate[s]* eius non
C. 7.152 And Blewe hit with beati quorum remisse sunt *iniquitates* &
C.14.117 Beati quorum remisse sunt *iniquitates* &c.

iniquitatis B 1; C 2
B. 6.228 Facite vo[bis] amicos de mammona *iniquitatis*.
C. 8.234 Facite vobis Amicos de mammona *iniquitatis*.'
C.19.250 Facite vobis amicos de mammona *iniquitatis*.

iniquius B 1
B.10.342 Nichil *iniquius* quam amare pecuniam;

iniustos B 1; C 1
B.19.431 Qui pluit super Iustos & *iniustos* at ones
C.21.431 Qui pluit super iustos & *iniustos* at ones

inmortalitatis B 1; C 1
B.15.63 Sciencie appetitus hominem *inmortalitatis* gloria[m] spoliauit.
C.16.225 Sciencie appetitus hominem *inmortalitatis* gloriam spoliauit.

innocentem A 1; B 2; C 1
A. 8.46 Super *innocentem* munera non accipies; a regibus & principibus–
B. 3.241 Qui pecuniam suam non dedit ad vsuram et munera super *innocentem* &c,
B. 7.42 Super *innocentem* munera non accipies.
C. 2.42 Et super *Innocentem* munera non accepit.

inponent C 1
C.15.221 Super egros manus [*in*]*pone[nt]* & bene habebunt &c–

inpossibile B 2
B.11.281 Nichil *inpossibile* volenti,
B.14.212 Ita *inpossibile* diuiti &c,

inpunitum A 1; B 1; C 2
A. 4.126 For nullum malum [þ]e ma[n] met[t]e with *Inpunitum*
B. 4.143 For Nullum malum þe man mette wiþ *inpunitum*
C. 4.140 For nullum malum [þe] man mette with *inpunitum*
C.20.433 As nullum malum *inpunitum* & nullum bonum irremuneratum–

inquirentes B 2; C 1
B. 9.109 *Inquirentes* autem dominum non minuentur omni bono.
B.11.282 *Inquirentes* autem dominum non minuentur omni bono.
C.10.202 *Inquirentes* autem dominum [non] minuentur omni bono.

insanabili B 1; C 1
B.10.333 impiorum, et virgam dominancium cedencium plaga *insanabili*.
C. 5.177 bac[u]lum impiorum, virga[m] d[omi]nancium, plaga *insanabili*.

insipiens B 1
B. 7.141 As diuinour in diuinite, wiþ Dixit *insipiens* to þi teme.'

insipientes B 1; C 1
B. 8.93 Libenter suffertis *insipientes* cum sitis ipsi sapientes:
C.10.90 Libenter suffertis *in[s]ipientes* &c;

integrum B 1; C 1
B.15.118 Si sacerdocium *integrum* fuerit tota floret ecclesia; Si autem
C.16.273 Si sacerdocium *integrum* fuerit tota floret ecclesia; Si Autem

intellectus B 1; C 1
B.19.463 Wiþ Spiritus *Intellectus* þei [toke] þe reues rolles
C.21.463 With spiritus *intellectus* they [t]o[k]e þe reues rolles

intelligis B 1; C 1
B.15.118 *intelligis* quod vicium habet in radice, Ita cum videris populum
C.16.273 *intelligis* quod vicium habet in radice, Ita cum videris populum

intencio A 1
A.10.90 For *intencio* indicat hominem &c.

interdum B 1
B.12.22 Interpone tuis *interdum* gaudia curis.

interfecit B 1; C 1
B.19.135 The burdes þo songe, Saul *interfecit* mille et dauid decem milia.
C.21.135 The buyrdes tho songe, Saul *interfecit* mille & dauid decem milia.

interpone B 1
B.12.22 *Interpone* tuis interdum gaudia curis.

intrabit B 1; C 1
B.17.266 Non omnis qui dicit domine, domine, *intrabit* &c.
C.19.232 Non omnis qui dicit domine, domine *intrabit* in reg[num] celorum &c.

intrabitis B 1
B.15.149 'Nisi efficiamini sicut paruuli non *intrabitis* in regnum celorum.

intrare B 1; C 2
B.19.161 Sic oportet Christum pati & *intrare* &c;
C.11.201 Ita possibile est diuiti *intrare* in regn[um] celorum sicut camelus &c.
C.21.161 Sic [oportet] christum pati & *intrare* &c;

intres B 1; C 1
B.18.399 Non *intres* in Iudicium cum seruo tuo.
C.20.442 Non *intres* in iudicium cum seruo tuo.

inutiliter B 1
B. 9.94 alibi, Perniciosus dispensator est qui res pauperum christi *inutiliter*

inuenerunt B 1; C 1
B.14.131 Dormierunt & nichil *inuenerunt*; [et alibi], velud sompn[i]um
C.15.306 dormierunt & nichil *inuenerunt* &c; Et alibi: velud sompn[i]um

inuenietis B 1
B.15.503 Querite & *inuenietis* &c.

inuenimus A 1; B 1; C 1
A.11.55 Ecce audiuimus eam in effrata, *inuenimus* eam in campis silue.
B.10.69 Ecce audiuimus eam in effrata; *inuenimus* eam in campis silue.
C.11.49 Ecce Audiuimus eam in Effrata; [*inuenimus* eam in campis silue].

inuenit C 1
C. 5.98 Mulier qu[e] *inuenit* d[ra]gmam.

inuicem B 1; C 1
B.12.142 Pastores loquebantur ad *inuicem*.
C.14.86 Pastores loquebantur ad *inuicem* &c.

inuitare B 1
B.11.191 Cum facitis conuiuia nolite *inuitare* amicos.

iob iop B 1; C 1
B.15.318 Num[quid], dicit *Iob*, rugi[e]t onager cum herbam habuerit aut
C.17.53 Nu[mquid], dicit *Iop*, rugiet onager cum habuerit herbam aut

iocundum A 1; B 1; C 1
A.11.192 Ecce quam bonum & quam *iocundum* habitare Fratres in vnum.
B.18.423 Ecce quam bonum & quam *iocundum* &c.
C.20.466 Ecce quam bonum & quam *iocundum* &c.

ypocrite B 1; C 1
B.15.219 Nolite fieri sicut *ypocrite* tristes &c.
C.16.344 Nolite [fieri sicut *ypocrite* tristes].

ipsa A 1; B 1
A.10.87 Virga tua & baculus tuus *ipsa* me consolata sunt.
B.12.13 Virga tua & baculus tuus, *ipsa* me consolata sunt:

ipsi A 1; B 4; C 3
A.11.305 Ecce *ipsi* ydiot[e] rapiunt celum vbi nos sapientes
B. 8.93 Libenter suffertis insipientes cum sitis *ipsi* sapientes:
B.10.26 Ecce *ipsi* peccatores! habundantes in seculo obtinuerunt diuicias.
B.10.327 Hij in curribus & hij in equis *ipsi* obligati sunt &c.
B.10.461 "Ecce *ipsi* ydiot[e] rapiunt celum vbi nos sapientes in inferno mergimur".
C. 5.172 Hij in curribus & [hij] in equis; *ipsi* obligati sunt & ceciderunt.
C.11.23 Et alibi: ecce ip[s]i peccatores, habundantes &c.
C.11.287 "Ecce ips[i] idiote rapiunt celum vbi nos sapientes in inferno mergimur".

ipsorum B 1
B.14.215 Beati pauperes quoniam *ipsorum* est regnum celorum.

ipsum B 1; C 1
B.17.152 Omnia traham ad me *ipsum* &c–
C.19.127 Omnia traham ad me *ipsum*–

ire B 1; C 2
B.10.325 And puten [hem] to hir penaunce, Ad pristinum statum *ire*;
C. 5.171 And potte ȝow to ȝoure penaunce, ad pristinum statum *ire*,
C.11.18 Qui recte sapiunt lex iubet *ire* foras.

irreligiosum B 1; C 1
B.15.118 Ita cum videris populum indisciplinatum & *irreligiosum*, sine dubio
C.16.273 Ita cum videris populum indissiplinatum & *irreligiosum*, sine dubio

irremuneratum A 1; B 1; C 2
A. 4.127 And bad Nullum [bonum be] *irremuneratum*.
B. 4.144 And bad Nullum bonum be *irremuneratum*.
C. 4.141 And bad nullum bonum be *irremuneratum*.
C.20.433 As nullum malum inpunitum & nullum bonum *irremuneratum*–

israel B 2; C 1
B.11.311 Psallite deo nostro; psallite quoniam rex terre deus *Israel*; psallite
B.16.219 Maledictus homo qui non reliquit semen in *Israel*.
C.18.222 Maledictus homo qui non reliquit semen in *Israel*.

ista C 1
C.12.215   O stulte, *ista* nocte anima tua egredi[e]tur; tezaurisat & ignorat &c.

iste B 2; C 1
B.18.68   Vere filius dei erat *iste*.
B.18.316   'Quis est *iste*?
C.20.70   Vere filius dei erat *iste*;

istum B 1; C 1
B.14.60   Si quis amat christum mundum non diligit *istum*.
C.15.259   Si quis Amat christum mundum non diligit *istum*.

ita B 2; C 2
B.14.212   *Ita* inpossibile diuiti &c,
B.15.118   *Ita* cum videris populum indisciplinatum & irreligiosum, sine dubio
C.11.201   *Ita* possibile est diuiti intrare in regn[um] celorum sicut camelus &c.
C.16.273   *Ita* cum videris populum indissiplinatum & irreligiosum, sine dubio

ite B 4; C 1
B. 5.412   Come I to *Ite* missa est I holde me yserued.
B.10.481   *Ite* vos in vineam meam.'
B.15.491   *Ite* in vniuersum mundum & predicate &c?
B.15.500   *Ite* vos in vineam meam &c.
C.17.191   *Ite* in vniuersum mundum, sethe 3e wilne þe name

item B 2
B.15.343   Quia sacrilegium est res pauperum non pauperibus dare. *Item*, peccatoribus
B.15.343   dare est demonibus immolare. *Item*, monache, si indiges &

iterum B 1; C 1
B. 5.603   Per Euam cun[c]tis clausa est et per Mariam virginem [*iterum*] patefacta est;
C. 7.250   Per Euam cun[c]tis clausa est & per mariam verginem *iterum* patefacta est &c;

iube B 1; C 1
B.18.244   "*Iube* me venire ad te super aquas."
C.20.253   "Domine, *iube* me venire ad te."

iubet C 1
C.11.18   Qui recte sapiunt lex *iubet* ire foras.

iuda B 1
B. 9.94   Proditor est prelatus cum *Iuda* qui patrimonium christi minus distribuit; Et

iudeis B 1
B.13.67   Ter cesus sum & a *iudeis* quinquies quadragenas &c–

iudica B 1
B.11.286   *Iudica* me deus & discerne causam meam.

iudicabimini B 1
B.12.89   Nolite iudicare & non *iudicabimini*.

iudicare B 3; C 2
B.11.90   Nolite *iudicare* quemquam.'
B.12.89   Nolite *iudicare* & non iudicabimini.
B.14.293   Nolite *iudicare* quemquam.'
C.12.31   Nolite *iudicare* quemquam.'
C.16.128   Nolite *iudicare* quemquam:

iudicat B 1; C 1
B.15.39   dum scit mens est; dum recolit memoria est; dum *iudicat* racio est;
C.16.201   [dum scit mens est]; dum recolit memoria est; dum *iudicat* racio est;

iudicij B 1; C 3
B.12.281   And seide, 'Saluabitur vix Iustus in die *Iudicij*;
C.14.203   And saide, 'Vix saluabitur iustus in die *iudicij*;
C.15.22   That iustus bifore iesu in die *iudicij* non saluabitur bote vix helpe;
C.15.118   [Bu]t dowel endite 3ow in die *iudicij*.'

iudicium B 1; C 1
B.18.399   Non intres in *Iudicium* cum seruo tuo.
C.20.442   Non intres in *iudicium* cum seruo tuo.

iumenta B 2; C 2
B. 5.509   'Homines & *iumenta* saluabis quemadmodum multiplicasti misericordiam
B.10.416   Homines & *iumenta* saluabis, domine &c.
C. 7.154   'Homines & *iumenta* saluabis; qu[e]madmodum multiplicasti
C.11.248   Homines & *iumenta* saluabis &c.

iunior B 1; C 1
B. 7.89   *Iunior* fui etenim senui, & non vidi iustum derelictum ne[c] semen eius
C. 9.163   *Iunior* fui, [et]enim senui; e[t] alibi: infirmata est vertus mea paupertate.

iura B 2; C 1
B.Pr.133   O qui *iura* regis christi specialia regis,
B.Pr.142   Nomen habet sine re nisi studet *iura* tenere.'
C.Pr.154   O qui *iura* regis christi specialia regis,

iure B 1; C 1
B.Pr.137   Si ius nudatur nudo de *iure* metatur;
C.Pr.158   [Si ius nudatur nudo de *iure* metatur];

iurgia A 1; B 1
A. 8.125   E[j]ice derisores & *iurgia* cum eis ne crescant.'
B. 7.143   E[ji]ce derisores & *iurgia* cum eis ne crescant &c.'

ius B 2; C 2
B.Pr.135   Nudum *ius* a te vestiri vult pietate.
B.Pr.137   Si *ius* nudatur nudo de iure metatur;
C.Pr.156   Nudum *ius* a te vestir[i] vult pietate.
C.Pr.158   [Si *ius* nudatur nudo de iure metatur];

iusti B 1; C 1
B.10.436   [Sunt] *iusti* atque sapientes, & opera eorum in manu dei sunt &c.
C.11.271   Sunt *iusti* atque sapientes & opera eorum in manu dei sunt &c.

iusticia B 1; C 2
B.18.421   Misericordia & veritas obuiauerunt sibi; *Iusticia* & pax osculate su[nt]
C.17.66   *Iusticia* eius manet in eternum.
C.20.464   Misericordia & veritas obuiauerunt sibi; *Iusticia* & pax osculate sunt.

iusticiam B 1
B. 3.237   Qui ingreditur sine macula & operatur *Iusticiam*.

iusticie B 9; C 9
B.19.297   The ferþe seed þat Piers sew was Spiritus *Iusticie*,
B.19.301   [Shal] nou3t ben espied [þoru3] Spiritus *Iusticie*.
B.19.302   Spiritus *Iusticie* spareþ no3t to spille [þe] gilty,
B.19.397   By Iesu! for al youre Ianglynge, wiþ Spiritus *Iusticie*,
B.19.402   Of Spiritus *Iusticie* þow spekest muche on ydel.'
B.19.405   But þow lyue by loore of Spiritus *Iusticie*,
B.19.474   Of Spiritus *Iusticie* for I Iugge yow alle.
B.20.24   Ne[iþer] Spiritus *Iusticie* ne Spiritus fortitudinis.
B.20.29   And Spiritus *Iusticie* shal Iuggen, wole he, nel he,
C.21.297   The ferthe seed that [Peres] sewe was spiritus *Iusticie*
C.21.301   [Shal] nat be aspyed thorw spiritus *iusticie*.
C.21.302   Spiritus *iusticie* spareth nat to spille [the] gulty
C.21.397   By iesu! for al 3oure iangelyng, [with] spiritus *Iusticie*
C.21.402   Of spiritus *Iusticie* thow spekest moche an ydel.'
C.21.405   Bote thow lyue bi lore of spiritus *Iusticie*,
C.21.474   Of spiritus *iusticie* for y iuge 3ow alle.
C.22.24   Noythe[r] spiritus *iusticie* ne spiritus fortitudinis.
C.22.29   And spiritus *iusticie* shal iugen, wol he, nel he,

iustis A 1; B 1; C 1
A. 7.68   Et cum *iustis* non scribantur.
B. 6.76   Quia cum *iustis* non scribantur.
C. 8.78   Quia cum *iustis* non scribantur.

iustorum B 1; C 1
B.17.293   Vindica sanguinem *iustorum*."
C.19.274   Vindic[a] sanguinem *iustorum*."

iustos B 2; C 2
B. 5.498   Non veni vocare *iustos* set peccatores ad penitenciam.
B.19.431   Qui pluit super *Iustos* & iniustos at ones
C. 7.138   Non veni vocare *iustos* set peccatores &c.
C.21.431   Qui pluit super *iustos* & iniustos at ones

iustum B 1
B. 7.89   Iunior fui etenim senui, & non vidi *iustum* derelictum ne[c] semen eius

iustus A 1; B 6; C 4
A. 9.16   'Sepcies in die cadit *iustus*.
B.Pr.134   Hoc quod agas melius, *iustus* es, esto pius!
B. 8.20   'Sepcies in die cadit *Iustus*.
B.10.29   Que perfecisti destruxerunt; *iustus* autem &c.
B.12.281   And seide, 'Saluabitur vix *Iustus* in die Iudicij;
B.13.19   And siþen how ymaginatif seide 'vix saluabitur [*iustus*]',
B.16.25   Cum ceciderit *iustus* non collidetur quia dominus supponit má[num suam];
C.Pr.155   Hoc vt agas melius, *iustus* es, esto pius!
C.10.21   And saide, 'sothly sepcies in die ca[d]it *iust[u]s*,
C.14.203   And saide, 'Vix saluabitur *iustus* in die iudicij;
C.15.22   That *iustus* bifore iesu in die iudicij non saluabitur bote vix helpe;

iuuenilem B 2; C 2
B. 1.141   Heu michi quia sterilem duxi vitam *Iuuenilem*.
B. 5.440   Heu michi quia sterilem vitam duxi *Iuuenilem*.'
C. 1.140   Heu michi quod ste[r]ilem duxi vitam *iuuenilem*.

C. 7.54   Heu michi quod ster[i]lem duxi vitam *iuuenilem*.'

iuxta B 1; C 2
B.12.213   Qui[a] reddit vnicuique *iuxta* opera sua.
C. 5.32   Reddet vnicuique *iuxta* opera sua–
C.14.152   Et reddet vnicu[i]que *iuxta* opera sua.

labor B 1; C 1
B.13.330   *labor* et dol[or]; Et alibi, Filij hominum dentes eorum arma &
                sagitte
C. 6.76   *labor* & dolor. Filij hominum dentes eorum Arma & sagitte

laboraui B 1; C 1
B.15.191   And leggen on longe wiþ *Laboraui* in gemitu meo,
C.16.333   And laueth hem in þe lauendrie, *labora[ui]* in gemitu meo,

labore C 1
C. 8.241   In [*labore* & sudore] vultus tui vesceris pane tuo".

labores A 1; B 1; C 1
A. 7.234   *Labores* manuum tuarum quia manducabis &c.
B. 6.252   *Labores* manuum tuarum &c.'
C. 8.260   *Labores* manuum tuarum quia manducabis &c".

lacrimas B 1; C 1
B.13.45   Vos qui peccata hominum comeditis, nisi pro eis *lacrimas* &
                oraciones
C.15.50   Vos qui peccata hominum comeditis, nisi pro eis *lacrimas* &
                orationes

lacrime A 1; B 1
A. 8.110   Fuerunt michi *lacrime* mee panes die ac nocte.
B. 7.128   Fuerunt michi *lacrime* mee panes die ac nocte.

lancias C 1
C. 3.461   Conflabunt gladios suos in vomeres & *lancias* [suas] in falces.

lateribus C 1
C. 1.113   Luppen alofte [in *lateribus* Aquilonis]

latrare B 1
B.10.293   Canes non valentes *latrare*,

latro A 1; B 1; C 1
A. 5.250   For he hadde lei3e be *latro* luciferis [aunte].
B. 5.476   For he hadde leyen by *Latro*, luciferis Aunte.
C. 6.330   For he hadde lay3e by *latro*, luciferes aunte.

latrone B 1
B.14.307   /Cantabit paupertas coram *latrone* viato[r],

lauda B 1; C 1
B.11.106   Parum *lauda*; vitupera parcius.'
C.12.40   Pa[r]um *lauda*; vit[u]pera parcius.'

laudabimus B 1; C 1
B.14.104   'Ye? quis est ille?' quod Pacience; 'quik, *laudabimus* eum!
C.15.279   '3e? quis est ille?' quod pacience; 'quik, *lauda[bi]mus* eum!

laudamus B 1; C 1
B.18.422   Truþe trumpede þo and song Te deum *laudamus*,
C.20.465   Treuth trompede tho and song te deum *laudamus*

laus B 1; C 1
B.18.7   Of gerlis and of Gloria *laus* gretly me dremed,
C.20.6   Of gurles and of gloria *laus* greetliche me dremede

lauabis C 1
C.16.335   *Lauabis* me & super niuem dealbabor.

lauacrum C 1
C.19.73   And ladde hym forth to *lauacrum* lex dei, a grang[e]

la3are B 1
B.15.594   *La3are* veni foras;

lege C 1
C.11.18   Qui sapiunt nugas & crim[ina] *lege* vocantur;

legem B 1; C 5
B.18.349   Non veni soluere *legem* set adimplere.
C. 9.213   Non licet uobis *legem* voluntati, set voluntat[em] coniungere legi.
C.13.44   Necessitas non habet *legem*–
C.17.140   propter mandatum, id est propter *legem*; & Amicum propter
                Amorem,
C.17.285   Fer, trahe, punge gregem, seruando per omnia *legem*–
C.20.395   Non veni soluere *legem* set adimplere.

legenda B 3
B.11.161   The *legend[a]* sanctorum yow lereþ more largere þan I yow telle.
B.11.220   Of logyk [ne] of lawe in *legenda* sanctorum
B.15.269   [Lo]! in *legenda* sanctorum, þe lif of holy Seintes,

legi C 1
C. 9.213   Non licet uobis legem voluntati, set voluntat[em] coniungere *legi*.

legis B 1; C 1
B.Pr.145   'Precepta Regis sunt nobis vincula *legis*'.
C.10.95   And with the pyk pulte adoun preuaricatores *legis*.

legit B 1; C 1
B.15.60   "Beatus est", seiþ Seint Bernard, "qui scripturas *legit*
C.16.222   "Beatus," saith seynt Bernard, "qui scripturas *legit*

leprosi C 1
C.18.141   Claudi Ambulant, *leprosi* mundantur,

leticia B 1; C 1
B.18.181   Ad vesperum demorabitur fletus & ad matutinum *leticia*.
C.20.184   Ad vesperum demorabitur fletus & ad mat[u]tinum *leticia*.

leuabit B 1; C 1
B. 3.324   Non *leuabit* gens contra gentem gladium &c.
C. 3.477   Non *leuabit* gens contra gentem gladium nec excercebuntur vltra
                ad prelium.

leuitici leuyticy B 1; C 2
B.15.556   And lyuen as *Leuitici* as oure lord [yow] techeþ:
C. 5.55   For by þe lawe of *leuyticy* þat oure lord ordeynede,
C.17.219   And lyuen as *leuitici*, as oure lord 3ow techeth:

lex B 2; C 3
B.17.16   In hijs duobus mandatis tota *lex* pendet & prophet[e].
B.17.74   And ladde hym so forþ on Lyard to *lex* Christi, a graunge
C.11.18   Qui recte sapiunt *lex* iubet ire foras.
C.19.17   In hijs duobus [mandatis tota *lex* pendet & prophete].
C.19.73   And ladde hym forth to lauacrum *lex* dei, a grang[e]

libenter A 2; B 3; C 3
A. 3.85   Ignis deuorabit tabernacula eorum qui *libenter* accipiunt munera.
A. 9.83   *Libenter* suffert[is] &c.
B. 3.96   Ignis deuorabit tabernacula eorum qui *libenter* accipiunt munera
                &c.
B. 8.93   *Libenter* suffertis insipientes cum sitis ipsi sapientes:
B.10.89   si autem exiguum illud impertiri stude *libenter*.
C. 3.124   Ignis deuorabit tabernacula eorum qui *libenter* accipiunt munera.
C.10.90   *Libenter* suffertis in[s]ipientes &c;
C.11.69   Si Autem exiguum illud impertir[i] *libenter* stude.

liber B 1; C 1
B. 5.269   Pane tuo pocius vescere: *liber* eris.
C. 6.293   Pane tuo pocius vescere: *liber* eris.

libera C 1
C.18.118   That *libera* voluntas dei lauhte þe myddel Shoriare

liberum B 4; C 13
B.16.16   And *liberum* arbitrium haþ þe lond [to] ferme,
B.16.46   Ac *liberum* arbitrium letteþ hym som tyme,
B.16.47   est idem qui peccat per *liberum* arbitrium non repugnat.
B.16.50   Thanne *liberum* arbitrium laccheþ þe [þridde] plan[k]e
C.16.158   Thenne hadde Actyf a ledare þat hihte *lib[e]rum* arbitrium;
C.16.162   Thenne hadde y wonder what he was, þat *l[i]berum* Arbitrium,
C.16.165   'Leue *liberum* arbitrium,' quod y, 'of what lond ar 3e?
C.16.173   'Whareof serue 3e,' y saide, 'sir *liberum* arbitrium?'
C.16.182   And so is man þat hath his mynde myd *liberum* Arbitrium.
C.16.194   Thenne am y *liberum* Arbitrium, as le[tt]red men telleth;
C.16.201   dum declina[t] de malo ad bonum *liberum* Arbitrium est;
C.18.1   'Leue *liberum* Arbitrium,' quod y, 'y leue, as y hope,
C.18.3   Thenne louh *liberum* Arbitrium and ladde me forth with tales
C.18.104   'Leue *liberum* Arbitrium, lat some lyf hit shake.'
C.18.137   Ac *liberum* Arbitrium lechecraeft hym tauhte
C.18.179   In inwit and in alle wittes aftur *liberum* Arbitrium
C.20.20   '*Liberum* dei Arbitrium for loue hath vndertake

libro A 1; B 1; C 1
A. 7.67   Deleantur de *libro*; I shulde not dele wiþ hem,
B. 6.75   Deleantur de *libro* viuencium; I sholde no3t dele wiþ hem,
C. 8.77   Del[e]antur de *libro* viuencium; y sholde nat dele with hem

licet A 1; B 1; C 2
A.12.22   Audiui archan[a uerba] que non *licet* homini loqui.
B.18.395   Audiui archana verba que non *licet* homini loqui.
C. 9.213   Non *licet* uobis legem voluntati, set voluntat[em] coniungere legi.
C.20.438   Audiui arcana verba que non *licet* homini loqui.

licitum B 1
B.11.96   It is *licitum* for lewed men to [legge] þe soþe

ligatum B 1; C 1
B. 7.181   Quodcumque ligaueris super terram erit *ligatum* & in celis &c.
C. 9.327   Quodcumque ligaueris super terram erit *ligatum* & in celis.

ligaueris A 1; B 1; C 1
A. 8.159   Quodcumque *ligaueris* super terram &c.
B. 7.181   Quodcumque *ligaueris* super terram erit ligatum & in celis &c.
C. 9.327   Quodcumque *ligaueris* super terram erit ligatum & in celis.

limbo B 1; C 1
B.16.84   And made of holy men his hoord In *limbo* Inferni,
C.18.115   And made of holy men his hoerd in *limbo* inferni

lingua B 2; C 2
B.13.330 Cuius malediccione os plenum est & amaritudine; sub *lingua* eius
B.13.330 et *lingua* eorum gladius a[cutus].
C. 6.76   Cuius maledictione os plenum est & amaritudine; sub *lingua* eius
C. 6.76   & *lingua* eorum gladius acutus.

linguis B 1; C 1
B.17.261 Si *linguis* hominum loquar &c.
C.19.227 Si *linguis* hominum loqu[a]r &c.

literaturam A 1
A. 8.123 Quoniam *literaturam* non cognoui, þat miȝte be þi teme.'

locus B 1
B.12.147 Set non erat ei *locus* in diuersorio, et pauper non habet
            diuersorium.

locutum C 1
C.13.224 Philosophus esses si tacuisses; & alibi: *Locutum* me aliquando

loquar B 1; C 1
B.17.261 Si linguis hominum *loquar* &c.
C.19.227 Si linguis hominum *loqu[a]r* &c.

loquebantur B 1; C 1
B.12.142 Pastores *loquebantur* ad inuicem.
C.14.86   Pastores *loquebantur* ad inuicem &c.

loquentes B 1
B.12.50   Sunt homines nequam, bene de virtute *loquentes*.

loqui A 1; B 1; C 1
A.12.22   Audiui archan[a uerba] que non licet homini *loqui*.
B.18.395 Audiui archana verba que non licet homini *loqui*.
C.20.438 Audiui arcana verba que non licet homini *loqui*.

loquimur B 1
B.12.65   Quod scimus *loquimur*, quod vidimus testamur.

loquitur A 1; B 2; C 2
A.Pr.39   Qui *loquitur* turpiloquium [is] luciferis hyne.
B.Pr.39   Qui *loquitur* turpiloquium is luciferes hyne.
B.13.432 Non habitabit in medio domus mee qui facit superbiam & qui
            loquitur iniqua.
C.Pr.40   Qui turpiloquium *loquitur* [is] luciferes knaue.
C. 7.92   qui facit superbiam [&] qui *loquitur* iniqua &c.

loquuntur C 1
C.20.356 Perdes omnes qui *loqu[u]ntur* mendacium.

lucem B 1; C 1
B. 5.493 Populus qui ambulabat in tenebris vidit *lucem* magnam.
C. 7.133 Populus qui ambulabat in tenebris vidit *lucem* magnam &c.

ludo B 1; C 1
B.11.269 Pauper ego *ludo* dum tu diues meditaris.
C.12.154 Pauper ego *ludo* dum tu diues m[e]ditaris.

lumen C 1
C.11.23   Ibunt in progenie patrum suorum & vsque in eternum non videbunt
            lumen;

macula B 1; C 1
B. 3.237 Qui ingreditur sine *macula* & operatur Iusticiam.
C.16.359 Beatus est diues sine *macula*.

magestate C 1
C.18.117 Thenne moued hym moed [in] *magestate* dei

magestatis C 1
C.16.217 Sic [qui] scrutator est *magestatis* opprim[e]tur a gloria.

magi B 1; C 1
B.12.144 Ibant *magi* ab oriente.
C.14.88   Ib[a]nt *magi* ab Oriente &c.

magis B 1
B. 7.77   Quia incertum est pro quo deo *magis* placeas.

magnam B 1; C 1
B. 5.493 Populus qui ambulabat in tenebris vidit lucem *magnam*.
C. 7.133 Populus qui ambulabat in tenebris vidit lucem *magnam* &c.

magnus A 1; B 1; C 1
A.11.196 Qui facit & docuerit *magnus* vocabitur in regno celorum.
B.13.118 Qui facit & docuerit *magnus* vocabitur in regno celorum.'
C.15.126 Qui facit & docuerit *magnus* vocabitur.'

maiestatis B 1
B.15.55   scrutator est *maiestatis* opprimitur a gloria.

maior B 1
B.12.29   Fides, spes, caritas, et *maior* horum &c.

mala A 2; B 2; C 2
A. 8.96   Qui vero *mala* in ignem eternum.
A. 8.103 Non timebo *mala* quoniam tu mecum es.
B. 7.114 Qui vero *mala* in ignem eternum.
B. 7.121 Non timebo *mala* quoniam tu mecum es.
C. 9.288 Qui vero *mala* in ignem etern[u]m.
C.13.18   Derworthe and dere god, do we so *mala*",

male C 3
C. 1.143 Melius est mori quam *male* viuere.
C. 6.290 Melius est mori quam *male* viuere.
C.17.40   Videte ne furtum sit: & alibi: meli[u]s est mori quam *male* viuere
            &c.

malediccione maledictione B 1; C 1
B.13.330 Cuius *malediccione* os plenum est & amaritudine; sub lingua eius
C. 6.76   Cuius *maledictione* os plenum est & amaritudine; sub lingua eius

maledictus B 1; C 1
B.16.219 *Maledictus* homo qui non reliquit semen in Israel.
C.18.222 *Maledictus* homo qui non reliquit semen in Israel.

malo C 2
C. 5.58   Non reddas malum pro *malo*.
C.16.201 dum declina[t] de *malo* ad bonum liberum Arbitrium est;

malorum A 1
A.10.98   Cum recte viuas ne cures verba *malorum*,

malum A 1; B 3; C 5
A. 4.126 For nullum *malum* [þ]e ma[n] met[t]e with Inpunitum
B. 4.143 For Nullum *malum* þe man mette wiþ inpunitum
B.15.118 sic de templo omne *malum* procedit. Si sacerdocium integrum
            fuerit
B.18.390 Nullum *malum* impunitum &c–
C. 4.140 For nullum *malum* [þe] man mette with inpunitum
C. 5.58   Non reddas *malum* pro malo.
C.16.273 sic de templo omne *malum* procedit. Si sacerdocium integrum
            fuerit
C.20.420 Tibi soli peccaui & *malum* coram te feci.
C.20.433 As nullum *malum* inpunitum & nullum bonum irremuneratum–

mammona B 1; C 2
B. 6.228 Facite vo[bis] amicos de *mammona* iniquitatis.
C. 8.234 Facite vobis Amicos de *mammona* iniquitatis.'
C.19.250 Facite vobis amicos de *mammona* iniquitatis.

mandatis B 1; C 1
B.17.16   In hijs duobus *mandatis* tota lex pendet & prophet[e].
C.19.17   In hijs duobus [*mandatis* tota lex pendet & prophete].

mandatum C 1
C.17.140 propter *mandatum*, id est propter legem; & Amicum propter
            Amorem,

manducabis A 1; C 1
A. 7.234 Labores manuum tuarum quia *manducabis* &c.
C. 8.260 Labores manuum tuarum quia *manducabis* &c".

manet B 5; C 4
B. 5.486 Et alibi, Qui *manet* in caritate in deo manet & deus in eo.
B. 5.486 Et alibi, Qui manet in caritate in deo *manet* & deus in eo.
B. 9.65   Qui *manet* in caritate in deo manet &c.
B. 9.65   Qui manet in caritate in deo *manet* &c.
B.11.176 Qui non diligit *manet* in morte.
C. 3.403 Qui in caritate *manet* in deo manet et deus in eo.
C. 3.403 Qui in caritate manet in deo *manet* et deus in eo.
C.12.99   Qui non diligit *manet* in morte.
C.17.66   Iusticia eius *manet* in eternum.

manibus A 1; B 1; C 3
A. 3.228 In quorum *manibus* iniquitates sunt; dextera eorum repleta est
            muneribus.
B. 3.249 In quorum *manibus* iniquitates sunt; dextra eorum repleta est
            muneribus.
C. 3.118 In quorum *manibus* iniquitates sunt:
C. 3.300 That pre *manibus* is paied or his pay asketh.
C. 9.45   But they pre *manibus* were payed for pledynge at þe barre;

manu B 2; C 1
B. 7.75   Sit elemosina tua in *manu* tua donec studes cui des.
B.10.436 [Sunt] iusti atque sapientes, & opera eorum in *manu* dei sunt &c.
C.11.271 Sunt iusti atque sapientes & opera eorum in *manu* dei sunt &c.

manum B 2; C 2
B.14.63   Aperis tu *manum* tuam & imples omne animal benediccione.
B.16.25   Cum ceciderit iustus non colliditur quia dominus supponit ma[*num*
            suam];

C.15.262   Aperis tu *manum* tuam &c.
C.16.320   Oen aperis-tu-*manum* alle thynges hym fyndeth;

manus B 1; C 1
B.13.249   In nomine meo demonia e[j]icient & super egros *manus* imponent & bene
C.15.221   Super egros *manus* [in]pone[nt] & bene habebunt &c–

manuum A 1; B 1; C 1
A. 7.234   Labores *manuum* tuarum quia manducabis &c.
B. 6.252   Labores *manuum* tuarum &c.'
C. 8.260   Labores *manuum* tuarum quia manducabis &c".

marcida B 1; C 1
B.15.118   Si autem corruptum fuerit omnium fides *marcida* est. Si
C.16.273   Si Autem corupt[um] fuerit omnium f[i]des *marcida* est. Si

marcidam B 1; C 1
B.15.118   Sicut cum videris arborem pallidam & *marcidam* intelligis quod
C.16.273   Sicut cum videri[s] Arborem pallidam & *marcidam* intelligis quod

maria B 1; C 2
B.11.255   *Maria* optimam partem elegit que non [auferetur ab ea].
C.12.141   *Maria* optimam partem elegit que non [auferetur ab ea].
C.19.125   Natus est ex *maria* virgine.

mariam B 1; C 1
B. 5.603   Per Euam cun[c]tis clausa est et per *Mariam* virginem [iterum] patefacta est;
C. 7.250   Per Euam cun[c]tis clausa est & per *mariam* verginem iterum patefacta est &c;

marie B 1; C 1
B.19.118   A faunt[ek]yn ful of wit, filius *Marie*.
C.21.118   A fauntekyn ful of wyt, filius *Marie*.

maris B 1; C 1
B. 5.283   quasi sintilla in medio *m[aris]*.
C. 6.338   Omnis iniquitas quoad misericordiam dei est quasi sintilla in medio *maris*.

mater B 2; C 2
B.14.276   possessio sine calumpnia, donum dei, sanit[atis] *mater*,
B.14.303   Sani[tatis] *mater*.
C.16.116   posessio sine calumpnia, donum dei, sanitatis *mater*,
C.16.138   Sanitatis *mater*.

matrem B 1; C 3
B. 5.567   Honora patrem & *matrem* &c;
C. 7.216   Honora patrem & *matrem* &c.
C.12.160   Quicumque reli[querit] patrem & *matrem* &c.
C.17.59   Honora patrem & *matrem* &c–

matres C 1
C. 3.190   Sunt infelices quia *matres* sunt meretrices.

matutinum B 1; C 1
B.18.181   Ad vesperum demorabitur fletus & ad *matutinum* leticia.
C.20.184   Ad vesperum demorabitur fletus & ad *mat[u]tinum* leticia.

maxima B 1; C 1
B.18.408   Clarior est solito post *maxima* nebula phebus;
C.20.451   Clarior est solito [post *maxima* nebula phebus];

maxime A 1; B 1
A.11.245   Dum tempus est operemur bonum ad omnes, *maxime* autem ad
B.10.204   Dum tempus [est] operemur bonum ad omnes, *maxime* autem ad domesticos fidei.

me A 2; B 12; C 11
A.10.87   Virga tua & baculus tuus ipsa *me* consolata sunt.
A.10.162   Penitet *me* fecisse hominem.
B. 9.133   Penitet *me* fecisse hominem.
B.10.252   [Ego in patre et pater in *me* est, et qui videt me videt et patrem meum]
B.10.252   [Ego in patre et pater in me est, et qui videt *me* videt et patrem meum]
B.11.251   Domine, non est tibi cure quod soror mea reliquit *me* solam ministrare?
B.11.286   Iudica *me* deus & discerne causam meam.
B.12.13   Virga tua & baculus tuus, ipsa *me* consolata sunt:
B.13.440   Qui vos spernit *me* spernit.
B.14.180   Conuertimini ad *me* & salui eritis.
B.15.576   neque vestimentum et ideo nolite constituere *me* Regem.
B.16.214   Deus meus, Deus meus, vt quid dereliquisti *me*?
B.17.152   Omnia traham ad *me* ipsum &c–
B.18.244   "Iube *me* venire ad te super aquas."
C. 7.100   Qui vos spernit *me* spernit.
C. 7.128   Ego in patre & pater in *me* [est] et qui me videt videt [&] patrem meum &c;

C. 7.128   Ego in patre & pater in me [est] et qui *me* videt videt [&] patrem meum &c;
C.10.222   Penitet *me* fecisse hominem;
C.11.153   Ego in patre & pater in *me* est; Et qui me vid[e]t, patrem meum
C.11.153   Ego in patre & pater in me est; Et qui me vid[e]t, patrem meum
C.13.224   Philosophus esses si tacuisses; & alibi: Locutum *me* aliquando
C.16.335   Lauabis *me* & super niuem dealbabor.
C.19.127   Omnia traham ad *me* ipsum–
C.20.253   "Domine, iube *me* venire ad te."
C.20.435   Domine ne in furore tuo Arguas *me* &c–

mea B 5; C 2
B.11.251   Domine, non est tibi cure quod soror *mea* reliquit me solam ministrare?
B.15.464   Ecce altilia *mea* & omnia parata sunt;
B.15.576   In domo *mea* non est panis neque vestimentum et ideo nolite constituere me Regem.
B.15.578   Inferte omnes [decimas] in orreum meum vt cibus in domo *mea*.
B.16.135   Domus *mea* domus oracionis vacabitur.'
C. 6.64   And cryede '*mea* culpa', corsynge alle his enemyes;
C. 9.163   Iunior fui, [et]enim senui; e[t] alibi: infirmata est vertus *mea* paupertate.

meam B 4
B. 7.83   Quare non dedisti pecuniam *meam* ad mensam vt ego veni[ens] cum vsuris ex[egissem illam]?
B.10.481   Ite vos in vineam *meam*.'
B.11.286   Iudica me deus & discerne causam *meam*.
B.15.500   Ite vos in vineam *meam* &c.

mecaberis A 1; B 1
A.11.254   Ne *mecaberis*, ne sle nouȝt, is þe kynde englissh;
B.10.372   But if I sende þee som tokene", and seiþ Non *mecaberis*,

mecum A 1; B 1
A. 8.103   Non timebo mala quoniam tu *mecum* es.
B. 7.121   Non timebo mala quoniam tu *mecum* es.

medicus B 1
B.16.110   Non est sanis opus *medicus* set in[firmis].

medio A 1; B 4; C 2
A. 8.102   & seide 'Si ambulauero in *medio* umbre mortis
B. 5.283   Omnis iniquitas quantum ad misericordiam dei est quasi sintilla in *medio*
B. 7.120   And seide, 'Si ambulauero in *medio* vmbre mortis
B.12.293   Et alibi, si ambulauero in *medio* vmbre mortis.
B.13.432   Non habitabit in *medio* domus mee qui facit superbiam & qui loquitur iniqua.
C. 6.338   Omnis iniquitas quoad misericordiam dei est quasi sintilla in *medio* maris.
C. 7.92   Non habitabit in *medio* domus mee qui facit superbiam [&] qui

meditaris B 1; C 1
B.11.269   Pauper ego ludo dum tu diues *meditaris*.
C.12.154   Pauper ego ludo dum tu diues *m[e]ditaris*.

mee A 1; B 3; C 3
A. 8.110   Fuerunt michi lacrime *mee* panes die ac nocte.
B. 7.128   Fuerunt michi lacrime *mee* panes die ac nocte.
B.12.189   Dominus pars hereditatis *mee* is a murye verset
B.13.432   Non habitabit in medio domus *mee* qui facit superbiam & qui loquitur iniqua.
C. 5.60   Dominus pars hereditatis *mee* &c. Et alibi: clemencia non constringit.
C. 7.92   Non habitabit in medio domus *mee* qui facit superbiam [&] qui
C.14.128   Dominus pars hereditatis [*mee*] is A merye verset;

mei B 2
B. 5.277   In Miserere *mei* deus, wher I mene truþe:
B.13.54   And þanne a mees of ooþer mete of Miserere *mei* deus,

meis C 1
C. 1.122   Dixit dominus domino meo, sede a dextris *meis*.

mel B 1; C 1
B.15.55   And seiþ, Sicut qui *mel* comedit multum non est ei bonum, Sic qui
C.16.217   And sayth, sicut qui *mel* comedit multum non est ei bonum; Sic

melius B 3; C 5
B.Pr.134   Hoc quod agas *melius*, iustus es, esto pius!
B. 3.330   For *Melius* est bonum nomen quam diuicie multe.'
B.11.231   *Melius* est scrutari scelera nostra quam naturas rerum.
C.Pr.155   Hoc vt agas *melius*, iustus es, esto pius!
C. 1.143   *Melius* est mori quam male viuere.
C. 3.483   [For] *melius* est bonum nomen quam diuicie multe.'
C. 6.290   *Melius* est mori quam male viuere.
C.17.40   Videte ne furtum sit: & alibi: *meli[u]s* est mori quam male viuere &c.

memento B 2; C 1 *cf. M.E.*
B. 6.315   Paupertatis onus pacienter ferre *memento*;
B.15.490 Boþe Mathew and Marc and *Memento* domine dauid:
C. 8.336   Paupertatis onus pacienter ferre *memento*.

memoria B 3; C 3
B.15.26   And whan I make mone to god *memoria* is my name;
B.15.39   dum scit mens est; dum recolit *memoria* est; dum iudicat racio est;
B.20.366 And make [of] yow [*memoria*] in masse and in matyns
C.16.186 And when y make mone to god *Memoria* y hatte;
2C.16.201 [dum scit mens est]; dum recolit *memoria* est; dum iudicat racio est;
C.22.366 And make [of] ȝow [*memoria*] in masse and in matynes

mendacium B 1; C 1
B.15.81   Et alibi, Vt quid diligitis vanitatem & queritis *mendacium*?
C.20.356 Perdes omnes qui loqu[u]ntur *mendacium*.

mendicabit C 1
C. 8.245   Piger propter frigus noluit arrare; *mendicabi[t]* in yeme & non dabitur ei".

mens B 2; C 2
B.15.25   And for þat I kan [and] knowe called am I *mens*;
B.15.39   dum scit *mens* est; dum recolit memoria est; dum iudicat racio est;
C.16.185 And [for] þat y can and knowe ycald am y [*mens*];
C.16.201 [dum scit *mens* est]; dum recolit memoria est; dum iudicat racio est;

mensam B 1
B. 7.83   Quare non dedisti pecuniam meam ad *mensam* vt ego veni[ens] cum vsuris ex[egissem illam]?

mensi B 2; C 1
B. 1.178   Eadem mensura qua *mensi* fueritis remecietur vobis.
B.11.228 Eadem mensura qua *mensi* fueritis remecietur vobis.
C. 1.174   Eadem mensura qua *mensi* fueritis Remetietur vobis.

mensura B 2; C 2
B. 1.178   Eadem *mensura* qua mensi fueritis remecietur vobis.
B.11.228 Eadem *mensura* qua mensi fueritis remecietur vobis.
C. 1.174   Eadem *mensura* qua mensi fueritis Remetietur vobis.
C.11.232 Eadem *mensura* &c.

meo B 3; C 4
B.13.249 In nomine *meo* demonia e[j]icient & super egros manus imponent & bene
B.14.46   Quodcumque pecieritis a patre in nomine *meo* &c; Et alibi, Non in solo pane
B.15.191 And leggen on longe wiþ Laboraui in gemitu *meo*,
C. 1.122   Dixit dominus domino *meo*, sede a dextris meis.
C. 7.260   Quodcumque pecieritis in nomine *meo* dabitur enim vobis.
C.15.244 Quodcumque pecieritis [a patre] in nomine *meo* dab[itur] enim
C.16.333 And laueth hem in þe lauendrie, labora[ui] in gemitu *meo*,

meorum B 1
B.13.195 Than ȝacheus for he seide "dimidium bonorum *meorum* do pauperibus",

meos B 1; C 1
B.12.125 Nolite tangere christos *meos* &c.]
C.14.69   Nolite tangere cristos *meos* &c.

mercede A 1
A. 2.86   Dignus est operarius *mercede* [sua].

mercedem A 2; B 1; C 1
A. 3.64   Amen Amen [dico vobis receperunt *mercedem* suam].
A. 3.233   Amen Amen rec[eperu]nt *mercedem* suam.
B. 3.254   Amen amen Rec[eperu]nt *mercedem* suam.
C. 3.312   Amen Amen, Matheu seyth, *Mercedem* suam rec[e]p[er]unt.

merces B 1
B. 7.44   A Regibus & principibus erit *merces* eorum.

meretrices C 1
C. 3.190   Sunt infelices quia matres sunt *meretrices*.

meretrix B 1; C 1
B. 9.186   Scribitur in portis, *meretrix* est ianua mortis.
C.10.287 Scribitur in portis, *meretrix* est ianua mortis.

meretur B 1
B. 7.77   Non eligas cui miser[e]aris ne forte pretereas illum qui *meretur* accipere,

mergemur A 1
A.11.305 vbi nos sapientes in infernum *mergemur*.

mergimur B 1; C 1
B.10.461 "Ecce ipsi ydiot[e] rapiunt celum vbi nos sapientes in inferno *mergimur*".

C.11.287 "Ecce ips[i] idiote rapiunt celum vbi nos sapientes in inferno *mergimur*".

meritum B 1; C 1
B.10.256 Fides non habet *meritum* vbi humana racio prebet experimentum.
C.11.157 Fides non habet *meritum* vbi humana racio &c.

mersenarii C 1
C. 3.308   Non morabit[ur] opus *mersenarii* &c.

messem B 1; C 1
B.15.530 Nolite mittere falsem in *messem* alienam.
C.17.280 Nolite mittere falcem in *messem* alienam &c.

mestus B 1; C 1
B.16.115 Ac [er] he made þe maistrie *mestus* cepit esse
C.18.145 Ac ar he made þat miracle *mestus* cepit esse

metas B 1; C 1
B.Pr.138   Si seritur pietas de pietate *metas*.'
C.Pr.159   Si seritur pietas de pietate *metas*.'

metatur B 1; C 1
B.Pr.137   Si ius nudatur nudo de iure *metatur*;
C.Pr.158   [Si ius nudatur nudo de iure *metatur*];

metere B 1; C 1
B.Pr.136   Qualia vis *metere*, talia grana sere.
C.Pr.157   Qualia vis *metere*, talia grana sere.

metropolitanus B 2; C 2
B.15.42   Presul and Pontifex and *Metropolitanus*,
B.15.516 And bicam man of a maide and *metropolitanus*,
C.16.204 Presul and Pontifex and *metropol[it]anus*
C.17.267 And bicam man of a mayde and *metropol[it]anus*

metu B 1; C 1
B.12.207 De peccato propiciato noli esse sine *metu*.
C.14.146 De peccato propiciato noli esse sine *metu*.

meum B 3; C 4
B.10.252 [Ego in patre et pater in me est, et qui videt me videt et patrem *meum*]
B.15.51   Ponam pedem *meum* in aquilone & similis ero altissimo.
B.15.578 Inferte omnes [decimas] in orreum *meum* vt cibus in domo mea.
C. 1.111   Ponam pedem *meum* in Aquilone & similis ero altissimo.'
C. 7.128   Ego in patre & pater in me [est] et qui me videt videt [&] patrem *meum* &c;
C.11.153 Ego in patre & pater in me est; Et qui me vid[e]t, patrem *meum*
C.16.213 Ponam pedem *meum* in Aquilone &c.

meus B 4; C 2
B.16.214 Deus *meus*, Deus meus, vt quid dereliquisti me?
B.16.214 Deus meus, Deus *meus*, vt quid dereliquisti me?
B.19.172 "[Dominus] *meus* & [deus] meus.
B.19.172 "[Dominus] meus & [deus] *meus*.
C.21.172 "Dominus *meus* & deus meus.
C.21.172 "Dominus meus & deus *meus*.

michi mihi A 2; B 10; C 7
A. 8.110   Fuerunt *michi* lacrime mee panes die ac nocte.
A.11.255 For *Michi* vindictam et ego retribuam.
B. 1.141   Heu *michi* quia sterilem duxi vitam Iuuenilem.
B. 5.440   Heu *michi* quia sterilem vitam duxi Iuuenilem.'
B. 6.226   *Michi* vindictam & ego retribuam.
B. 7.128   Fuerunt *michi* lacrime mee panes die ac nocte.
B.10.209 *Michi* vindictam & ego retribuam.
B.10.374 [For *michi* vindictam et ego retribuam]:
B.13.254 Argentum & aurum non est *michi*; quod autem habeo tibi do; in nomine
B.16.99   Ecce ancilla domini; fiat *michi* [secundum verbum tuum]'.
B.19.295 And pleieþ al wiþ pacience and Parce *michi* domine;
B.19.446 Non occides: *michi* vindictam &c.
C. 1.140   Heu *michi* quod ste[r]ilem duxi vitam iuuenilem.
C. 7.54   Heu *michi* quod ster[i]lem duxi vitam iuuenilem.'
C.11.213 Nec *michi* nec tibi, set diuidatur.
C.15.224 Argentum & Aurum non est *michi*; quod [autem] habeo tibi do &c.
C.17.235 *Mihi* vindictam &c–
C.21.295 And ple[ieþ] al with pacience and parce *michi* domine
C.21.446 Non occides: *Michi* vindictam &c.

milia B 1; C 1
B.19.135 The burdes þo songe, Saul interfecit mille et dauid decem *milia*.
C.21.135 The buyrdes tho songe, Saul interfecit mille & dauid decem *milia*.

mille B 1; C 1
B.19.135 The burdes þo songe, Saul interfecit *mille* et dauid decem milia.
C.21.135 The buyrdes tho songe, Saul interfecit *mille* & dauid decem milia.

ministrare B 1
B.11.251 Domine, non est tibi cure quod soror mea reliquit me solam
ministrare?

minuentur B 2; C 1
B. 9.109 Inquirentes autem dominum non *minuentur* omni bono.
B.11.282 Inquirentes autem dominum non *minuentur* omni bono.
C.10.202 Inquirentes autem dominum [non] *minuentur* omni bono.

minus B 1
B. 9.94 Proditor est prelatus cum Iuda qui patrimonium christi *minus*
distribuit; Et

miserearis B 1
B. 7.77 Non eligas cui *miser[e]aris* ne forte pretereas illum qui meretur
accipere.

miserere B 2
B. 5.277 In *Miserere* mei deus, wher I mene truþe:
B.13.54 And þanne a mees of ooþer mete of *Miserere* mei deus,

miseretur B 1
B. 5.243 I haue mo Manoirs þoruȝ Rerages þan þoruȝ *Miseretur* &
com[m]odat.

misericordia B 4; C 3
B. 5.281 [*Misericordia* eius super omnia opera eius &c]–
B.11.139 *Misericordia* eius super omnia opera eius.'
B.17.318 *Misericordia* eius super omnia opera eius–
B.18.421 *Misericordia* & veritas obuiauerunt sibi; Iusticia & pax osculate
su[nt]
C.12.74 *Misericordia* eius super omnia opera [eius].'
C.19.298 *Misericordia* eius super omnia opera eius.
C.20.464 *Misericordia* & veritas obuiauerunt sibi; Iusticia & pax osculate
sunt.

misericordiam B 2; C 2
B. 5.283 Omnis iniquitas quantum ad *misericordiam* dei est quasi sintilla in
medio
B. 5.509 'Homines & iumenta saluabis quemadmodum multiplicasti
misericordiam
C. 6.338 Omnis iniquitas quoad *misericordiam* dei est quasi sintilla in
medio maris.
C. 7.154 'Homines & iumenta saluabis; qu[e]madmodum multiplicasti

misi C 1
C. 9.120 [Q]uando *misi* vos sine pane & pera &c.

missa B 1
B. 5.412 Come I to Ite *missa* est I holde me yserued.

mittere A 1; B 2; C 2
A.11.9 And seide, 'Nolite *mittere*, Man, margerie perlis
B.10.9 And seide, 'noli[te] *mittere*, man, margery perles
B.15.530 Nolite *mittere* falsem in messem alienam.
C.11.7 And sayde, 'nolite *mittere*, ȝe men, Margerie perles
C.17.280 Nolite *mittere* falcem in messem alienam &c.

modicum B 1; C 1
B.18.216 For til *modicum* mete with vs, I may it wel auowe,
C.20.225 For til [*modicum*] mete with vs, y may hit wel avowe,

modo B 1; C 1
B.11.203 As quasi *modo* geniti gentil men echone,
C.12.111 As quasi *modo* geniti gentel men vchone,

moisi moysi A 1; B 1; C 2
A.11.223 Supe cathedram *moisi* sederunt principes.
B.10.404 Super cathedra[m] *Moysi* &c.
C. 8.86 Super Cathedram *moysi* sede[runt] &c.
C.11.235 Super cathedra[m] *Moysi* &c.

molestat B 1; C 1
B.11.395 De re que te non *molestat* noli certare.
C.13.196 De re que te non *molestat* noli certare.

molli C 1
C. 9.265 Sub *molli* pastore &c.

monache B 1
B.15.343 dare est demonibus immolare. Item, *monache*, si indiges &

monachus B 1
B.15.343 Porro non indiget *monachus* si habeat quod nature sufficit.

morabitur C 1
C. 3.308 Non *morabit[ur]* opus mersenarii &c.

mori C 3
C. 1.143 Melius est *mori* quam male viuere.
C. 6.290 Melius est *mori* quam male viuere.
C.17.40 Videte ne furtum sit: & alibi: meli[u]s est *mori* quam male viuere
&c.

mors B 4; C 2
B.17.114 [O *mors* ero mors tua &c].
B.17.114 [O *mors* ero mors tua &c].
B.18.35 O *mors* ero mors tua.'
B.18.35 O mors ero *mors* tua.'
C.20.34 O *mors* [ero] mors tua.'
C.20.34 O mors [ero] *mors* tua.'

morte B 1; C 1
B.11.176 Qui non diligit manet in *morte*.
C.12.99 Qui non diligit manet in *morte*.

mortem B 1; C 3
B.13.44 In a morter, Post *mortem*, of many bitter peyne
C.14.134 Nolo *mortem* peccatoris &c.
C.15.49 In a morter, post *mortem*, of many bittere peynes
C.20.259 Non visurum se *mortem* &c.

mortis A 1; B 3; C 1
A. 8.102 & seide 'Si ambulauero in medio umbre *mortis*
B. 7.120 And seide, 'Si ambulauero in medio vmbre *mortis*
B. 9.186 Scribitur in portis, meretrix est ianua *mortis*.
B.12.293 Et alibi, si ambulauero in medio vmbre *mortis*.
C.10.287 Scribitur in portis, meretrix est ianua *mortis*.

mortua B 1; C 1
B. 1.187 Fides sine operibus *mortua* est &c.
C. 1.183 Fides sine operibus *mortua* est.

mortuorum B 1; C 1
B.18.370 That I drynke riȝt ripe Must, Resureccio *mortuorum*.
C.20.412 And [y] drynke riht rype m[o]st, resureccio *mortuorum*.

mortuum C 1
C.12.179 Nisi granum frumenti cadens in terram *mortuum* fuerit &c.

mugiet B 1; C 1
B.15.318 aut *mugiet* bos cum ante plenum presepe steterit? brutorum
C.17.53 aut *mugiet* bos cum ante plenum presepe steterit? Brutorum

mulier C 1
C. 5.98 *Mulier* qu[e] inuenit d[ra]gmam.

multa B 2; C 1
B.10.45 Than Munde þe Millere of *Multa* fecit deus.
B.11.3 And seide 'Multi *multa* sciunt et seipsos nesciunt'.
C.11.163 And saide, 'multi *multa* sciunt & seipsos nessiunt.'

multe B 1; C 1
B. 3.330 For Melius est bonum nomen quam diuicie *multe*.'
C. 3.483 [For] melius est bonum nomen quam diuicie *multe*.'

multi B 2; C 2
B.11.3 And seide '*Multi* multa sciunt et seipsos nesciunt'.
B.11.112 '*Multi* to a mangerie and to þe mete were sompned,
C.11.163 And saide, '*multi* multa sciunt & seipsos nessiunt.'
C.12.47 '*Multi* to a mangerye and to þe mete were sompned

multiplicasti B 1; C 1
B. 5.509 'Homines & iumenta saluabis quemadmodum *multiplicasti*
misericordiam
C. 7.154 'Homines & iumenta saluabis; qu[e]madmodum *multiplicasti*
misericordiam

multitudinem B 1; C 1
B.20.256 Qui numerat *multitudinem* stellarum et omnibus eis [nomina
vocat].
C.22.256 Qui numerat *multitudinem* stellarum &c.

multum B 1; C 1
B.15.55 And seiþ, Sicut qui mel comedit *multum* non est ei bonum, Sic qui
C.16.217 And sayth, sicut qui mel comedit *multum* non est ei bonum; Sic

mundantur C 1
C.18.141 Claudi Ambulant, leprosi *mundantur*,

mundi A 2; B 3; C 3
A.10.8 A proud prikere of Fraunce, Princeps huius *mundi*,
A.10.62 Thanne haþ þe pouk power, sire princeps huius *mundi*,
B. 9.8 A proud prikere of Fraunce, Princeps huius *mundi*,
B.12.138 Sapiencia huius *mundi* stulticia est apud deum.
B.18.315 Nunc princeps huius *mundi* e[i]icietur foras.'
C.10.135 A proued prikeare of fraunce, princeps huius *mundi*,
C.14.83 Sapiencia huius *mundi* stul[t]icia est apud deum.
C.20.349 Nunc princeps huius *mundi*.'

mundum B 2; C 3
B.14.60 Si quis amat christum *mundum* non diligit istum.
B.15.491 Ite in vniuersum *mundum* & predicate &c?
C.15.259 Si quis Amat christum *mundum* non diligit istum.
C.17.191 Ite in vniuersum *mundum*, sethe ȝe wilne þe name
C.19.114 *Mundum* pugillo continens,

munera A 2; B 4; C 3
A. 3.85   Ignis deuorabit tabernacula eorum qui libenter accipiunt *munera*.
A. 8.46   Super innocentem *munera* non accipies; a regibus & principibus–
B. 3.96   Ignis deuorabit tabernacula eorum qui libenter accipiunt *munera* &c.
B. 3.241   Qui pecuniam suam non dedit ad vsuram et *munera* super innocentem &c,
B. 3.336   Honorem adquiret qui dat *munera* &c.'
B. 7.42   Super innocentem *munera* non accipies.
C. 2.42   Et super Innocentem *munera* non accepit.
C. 3.124   Ignis deuorabit tabernacula eorum qui libenter accipiunt *munera*.
C. 3.488   Honorem adquiret qui dat *munera*.'

muneribus A 1; B 1
A. 3.228   In quorum manibus iniquitates sunt; dextera eorum repleta est *muneribus*.
B. 3.249   In quorum manibus iniquitates sunt; dextra eorum repleta est *muneribus*.

natura B 2; C 2
B.15.318   brutorum animalium *natura* te condempnat, quia cum eis pabulum
B.18.23   In his helm and in his haubergeon, humana *natura*;
C.17.53   Brutorum Animalium *natura* te condempnat, quia cum [eis] pabulum
C.20.22   In his helm and in his haberion, humana *natura*;

naturas B 1
B.11.231   Melius est scrutari scelera nostra quam *naturas* rerum.

nature B 1
B.15.343   Porro non indiget monachus si habeat quod *nature* sufficit.

natus C 1
C.19.125   *Natus* est ex maria virgine.

ne A 4; B 7; C 5
A. 8.113   *Ne* soliciti sitis he seiþ in his gospel,
A. 8.125   E[j]ice derisores & iurgia cum eis *ne* crescant.'
A. 8.134   Sompnia *ne* cures.
A.10.98   Cum recte viuas *ne* cures verba malorum,
B. 7.77   Non eligas cui miser[e]aris *ne* forte pretereas illum qui meretur accipere,
B. 7.131   *Ne* soliciti sitis he seiþ in þe gospel,
B. 7.143   E[ji]ce derisores & iurgia cum eis *ne* crescant &c.'
B. 7.156   To sette sadnesse in Songewarie for sompnia *ne* cures.
B. 9.186   Dum sis vir fortis *ne* des tua robora scortis,
B.14.33   *Ne* soliciti sitis &c; Volucres celi deus pascit &c; pacientes vincunt &c.'
B.15.88   That seide to hise disciples, "*Ne* sitis personarum acceptores".
C.10.287   Dum sis vir fortis *ne* des tua robora scortis;
C.16.241   *Ne* sitis acceptores personarum.
C.17.40   Videte *ne* furtum sit: & alibi: meli[u]s est mori quam male viuere &c.
C.18.164   *Ne* forte tumultus fieret in populo–
C.20.435   Domine *ne* in furore tuo Arguas me &c–

nebula B 1; C 1
B.18.408   Clarior est solito post maxima *nebula* phebus;
C.20.451   Clarior est solito [post maxima *nebula* phebus];

nec A 1; B 6; C 5
A.11.147   Qui sim[u]lat verbis, *nec* corde est fidus amicus,
B. 7.89   Iunior fui etenim senui, & non vidi iustum derelictum *ne[c]* semen eius
B. 9.155   Numquam collig[unt] de spinis vua[s] *nec* de tribulis ficus.
B.10.195   Qui simulat verbis [*nec*] corde est fidus amicus,
B.11.271   Diuicias *nec* paupertates &c,
B.11.317   Non excusat episcopos *nec* ydiotes preestes'.
B.12.9   Si non in prima vigilia *nec* in secunda &c.
C. 3.477   Non leuabit gens contra gentem gladium *nec* excercebuntur vltra ad prelium.
C. 5.87   *Nec* in pane [*nec*] in pabulo; the paternoster wittenesseth
C. 5.87   Nec in pane [*nec*] in pabulo; the paternoster wittenesseth
C.11.213   *Nec* michi nec tibi, set diuidatur.
C.11.213   Nec michi *nec* tibi, set diuidatur.

necessarium B 1; C 1
B. 5.483   O felix culpa, o *necessarium* peccatum Ade &c.
C. 7.125   O felix culpa, [o] *necessarium* peccatum Ade.

necesse A 1; B 1
A.11.154   *Necesse* est vt veniant scandala.
B.16.157   *Necesse* est vt veniant scandala; ve homini illi per quem scandalum venit.

necessitas C 1
C.13.44   *Necessitas* non habet legem–

negat B 1; C 1
B.15.39   dum *negat* vel consentit consciencia est; dum spirat spiritus est.'

C.16.201   dum *negat* vel consentit consciencia est; dum sp[i]rat spiritus est.'

negocium B 2; C 2
B.14.276   *negocium* sine dampno, Incerta fortuna, absque sollicitudine
B.14.315   *Negocium* sine dampno.
C.16.116   *negocium* sine dampno, Incerta fortuna, absque solicitudine
C.16.149   *Negocium* sine dampno.

nemini C 1
C. 9.123   *Nemini* salutauerit[is] per viam.

nemo A 1; B 4; C 4
A.11.263   *Nemo* ascendet ad celum nisi qui de celo descendit.
B.10.382   *Nemo* ascendit ad celum nisi qui de celo descendit.
B.10.447   For soþest word þat euer god seide was þo he seide *Nemo* bonus.
B.11.404   Caton acordeþ þerwiþ: *Nemo* sine crimine viuit.'
B.13.312   Si hominibus placerem christi seruus non essem; Et alibi, *Nemo* potest
C. 6.60   Si hominibus placerem christi seruus non essem; *nemo* potest duobus
C.11.207   *Nemo* ascendit ad celum nisi qui de celo descendit.
C.13.212   Caton acordeth therwith: *nemo* sine crimine viuit.'
C.15.135   *Nemo* bonus–

nequam A 1; B 2
A. 7.223   Seruus *nequam* had a nam, & for he nolde it vsen,
B. 6.239   Seruus *nequam* hadde a Mnam and for he [n]olde [it vse]
B.12.50   Sunt homines *nequam*, bene de virtute loquentes.

neque B 1
B.15.576   In domo mea non est panis *neque* vestimentum et ideo nolite constituere me Regem.

nesciat A 1; B 1; C 1
A. 3.54   And seiþ *Nesciat* sinist[ra] quid faciat dexter[a].
B. 3.72   *Nesciat* sinistra quid faciat dextra:
C. 3.74   *Nesciat* [sinistra] quid faciat [dextera]:

nescio B 3; C 1
B. 5.55   Amen dico vobis *nescio* vos.
B. 9.67   Amen dico vobis, *nescio* vos; Et alibi, Et dimisi eos secundum desideria
B.17.253   Amen dico vobis, *nescio* vos &c.
C.19.219   Amen dico vobis, *nescio* vos.

nescit B 1
B.12.69   *Nescit* aliquis vnde venit aut quo vadit &c.

nesciunt nessiunt B 1; C 1
B.11.3   And seide 'Multi multa sciunt et seipsos *nesciunt*'.
C.11.163   And saide, 'multi multa sciunt & seipsos *nessiunt*.'

neutrum B 1; C 1
B.Pr.132   'Sum Rex, sum princeps; *neutrum* fortasse deinceps.
C.Pr.153   'Sum Rex, sum Princeps; *neutrum* fortasse deinceps.

nichil B 4; C 2
B.10.342   *Nichil* iniquius quam amare pecuniam;
B.11.281   *Nichil* inpossibile volenti.
B.13.163   Caritas *nichil* timet.
B.14.131   Dormierunt & *nichil* inuenerunt; [et alibi], velud sompn[i]um
C.13.4   Tanquam *nichil* habentes &c.
C.15.306   dormierunt & *nichil* inuenerunt &c; Et alibi: velud sompn[i]um

nichilum B 1
B.14.131   domine in Ciuitate tua, et ad *nichilum* rediges &c.

nisi A 1; B 6; C 6
A.11.263   Nemo ascendet ad celum *nisi* qui de celo descendit.
B.Pr.142   Nomen habet sine re *nisi* studet iura tenere.'
B.10.382   Nemo ascendit ad celum *nisi* qui de celo descendit.
B.11.82   *Nisi* quis renatus fuerit.
B.13.45   Vos qui peccata hominum comeditis, *nisi* pro eis lacrimas & oraciones
B.15.149   '*Nisi* efficiamini sicut paruuli non intrabitis in regnum celorum.
B.15.537   Absit nobis gloriari *nisi* in cruce domini nostri &c.
C.11.207   Nemo ascendit ad celum *nisi* qui de celo descendit.
C.12.171   *Nisi* renunciaueritis omnia que po[s]sid[etis] &c."
C.12.179   *Nisi* granum frumenti cadens in terram mortuum fuerit &c.
C.15.50   Vos qui peccata hominum comeditis, *nisi* pro eis lacrimas & orationes
C.16.298   *Nisi* efficiamini sicut paruuli &c,
C.17.198   Absit nobis gloriari *nisi* in cruce domini nostri &c.

niuem C 1
C.16.335   Lauabis me & super *niuem* dealbabor.

nobis B 4; C 2
B.Pr.145   'Precepta Regis sunt *nobis* vincula legis'.
B. 5.500   Verbum caro factum est & habitauit in *nobis*.
B.15.537   Absit *nobis* gloriari nisi in cruce domini nostri &c.

B.19.394 Et dimitte *nobis* debita nostra &c,
C.17.198 Absit *nobis* gloriari nisi in cruce domini nostri &c.
C.21.394 Et dimitte *nobis* debita nostra &c,

nocte A 1; B 1; C 1
A. 8.110 Fuerunt michi lacrime mee panes die ac *nocte*.
B. 7.128 Fuerunt michi lacrime mee panes die ac *nocte*.
C.12.215 O stulte, ista *nocte* anima tua egredi[e]tur; tezaurisat & ignorat &c.

noe C 1
C.11.244 For Archa *Noe*, nymeth hede, ys no more to mene

noli B 2; C 2
B.11.395 De re que te non molestat *noli* certare.
B.12.207 De peccato propiciato *noli* esse sine metu.
C.13.196 De re que te non molestat *noli* certare.
C.14.146 De peccato propiciato *noli* esse sine metu.

nolite A 2; B 10; C 8
A.11.9 And seide, '*Nolite* mittere, Man, margerie perlis
A.11.296 Dum steter[it]is ante [reges &] presides *nolite* cogitare,
B.10.9 And seide, '*noli[te]* mittere, man, margery perles
B.10.450 "[D]um steteritis ante Reges & presides [*nolite* cogitare]:
B.11.90 *Nolite* iudicare quemquam.'
B.11.191 Cum facitis conuiuia inuitare amicos.
B.12.89 *Nolite* iudicare & non iudicabimini.
B.12.125 *Nolite* tangere christos meos &c.]
B.14.293 *Nolite* iudicare quemquam:
B.15.219 *Nolite* fieri sicut ypocrite tristes &c.
B.15.530 *Nolite* mittere falsem in messem alienam.
B.15.576 In domo mea non est panis neque vestimentum et ideo *nolite*
constituere me Regem.
C.10.99 *Nolite* timere eos qui possunt occidere corpus &c.
C.11.7 And sayde, '*nolite* mittere, ȝe men, Margerie perles
C.12.31 *Nolite* iudicare quemquam.'
C.12.103 Cum facitis conuiuia *nolite* vocare amicos &c.
C.14.69 *Nolite* tangere cristos meos &c.
C.16.128 *Nolite* iudicare quemquam:
C.16.344 *Nolite* [fieri sicut ypocrite tristes].
C.17.280 *Nolite* mittere falcem in messem alienam &c.

nolo C 1
C.14.134 *Nolo* mortem peccatoris &c.

noluit C 1
C. 8.245 Piger propter frigus *noluit* arrare; mendicabi[t] in yeme & non
dabitur ei".

nomen B 3; C 1
B.Pr.141 'Dum rex a regere dicatur *nomen* habere
B.Pr.142 *Nomen* habet sine re nisi studet iura tenere.'
B. 3.330 For Melius est bonum *nomen* quam diuicie multe.'
C. 3.483 [For] melius est bonum *nomen* quam diuicie multe.'

nomina B 2; C 1
B.15.39 Anima pro diuersis accionibus diuersa *nomina* sortitur: dum
viuificat
B.20.256 Qui numerat multitudinem stellarum et omnibus eis [*nomina*
vocat].
C.16.201 Anima pro diuersis [acc]ionibus diuersa *nomina* sortitur: dum

nominatiuo C 1
C. 3.406 *Nominatiuo*, pater & filius & spiritus sanctus.

nomine A 1; B 6; C 5
A. 7.78 In dei *nomine* Amen I make it myseluen:
B. 6.86 In dei *nomine*, amen. I make it myselue.
B.13.249 In *nomine* meo demonia e[j]icient & super egros manus imponent
& bene
B.13.254 Argentum & aurum non est michi; quod autem habeo tibi do; in
nomine
B.14.46 Quodcumque pecieritis a patre in *nomine* meo &c; Et alibi, Non in
solo pane
B.18.17 Benedictus qui venit in *nomine* domini.
B.19.80 Omnia celestia terrestria flectantur in hoc *nomine* Iesu;
C. 7.260 Quodcumque pecieritis in *nomine* meo dabitur enim vobis.
C. 8.95 In dei *nomine*, Amen; y make hit mysulue.
C.15.244 Quodcumque pecieritis [a patre] in *nomine* meo dab[itur] enim
C.20.15 Benedictus qui venit in *nomine* domini.
C.21.80 Omnia celestia terrestria flectantur in hoc *nomine* iesu;

non A 7; B 66; C 52
A. 3.221 Qui pecuniam suam [*non*] dedit ad vsuram.
A. 7.68 Et cum iustis *non* scribantur.
A. 8.46 Super innocentem munera *non* accipies; a regibus & principibus–
A. 8.103 *Non* timebo mala quoniam tu mecum es.
A. 8.123 Quoniam literaturam *non* cognoui, þat miȝte be þi teme.'
A.11.74 *Non* plus sapere quam oportet.
A.12.22 Audiui archan[a uerba] que *non* licet homini loqui.

B. 3.241 Qui pecuniam suam *non* dedit ad vsuram et munera super
innocentem &c,
B. 3.324 *Non* leuabit gens contra gentem gladium &c.
B. 4.37 *Non* est timor dei ante oculos eorum &c.
B. 5.273 *Non* dimittitur peccatum donec restituatur [a]blatum.
B. 5.498 *Non* veni vocare iustos set peccatores ad penitenciam.
B. 6.76 Quia cum iustis *non* scribantur.
B. 7.42 Super innocentem munera *non* accipies.
B. 7.77 *Non* eligas cui miser[e]aris ne forte pretereas illum qui meretur
accipere,
B. 7.83 Quare *non* dedisti pecuniam meam ad mensam vt ego veni[ens]
cum vsuris ex[egissem illam]?
B. 7.87 Satis diues est qui *non* indiget pane.
B. 7.89 Iunior fui etenim senui, & *non* vidi iustum derelictum ne[c] semen
eius
B. 7.121 *Non* timebo mala quoniam tu mecum es.
B. 9.109 Inquirentes autem dominum *non* minuentur omni bono.
B. 9.149 Filius *non* portabit iniquitatem patris et pater non portabit
iniquitatem filij.
B. 9.149 Filius non portabit iniquitatem patris et pater *non* portabit
iniquitatem filij.
B.10.114 Filius *non* portabit iniquitatem patris &c.
B.10.121 *Non* plus sapere quam oportet.
B.10.256 Fides *non* habet meritum vbi humana racio prebet experimentum.
B.10.293 Canes *non* valentes latrare,
B.10.372 But if I sende þee som tokene", and seiþ *Non* mecaberis,
B.11.58 Pena pecuniaria *non* sufficit pro spiritualibus delictis.
B.11.88 *Non* oderis fratres secrete in corde tuo set publice argue illos.
B.11.93 *Non* oderis fratrem.
B.11.176 Qui *non* diligit manet in morte.
B.11.251 Domine, *non* est tibi cure quod soror mea reliquit me solam
ministrare?
B.11.255 Maria optimam partem elegit que *non* [auferetur ab ea].
B.11.282 Inquirentes autem dominum *non* minuentur omni bono.
B.11.317 *Non* excusat episcopos nec ydiotes preestes'.
B.11.395 De re que te *non* molestat noli certare.
B.12.9 Si *non* in prima vigilia nec in secunda &c.
B.12.56 Scient[es] et *non* facient[es] varijs flagellis vapulab[un]t.
B.12.89 Nolite iudicare & *non* iudicabimini.
B.12.147 Set *non* erat ei locus in diuersorio, et pauper non habet
diuersorium.
B.12.147 Set non erat ei locus in diuersorio, et pauper *non* habet
diuersorium.
B.12.286 Aduenit ignis diuinus *non* comburens set illuminans &c.
B.13.58 Cor contritum & humiliatum deus *non* despicies.
B.13.254 Argentum & aurum *non* est michi; quod autem habeo tibi do; in
nomine
B.13.312 Si hominibus placerem christi seruus *non* essem; Et alibi, Nemo
potest
B.13.432 *Non* habitabit in medio domus mee qui facit superbiam & qui
loquitur iniqua.
B.14.3 Vxorem duxi & ideo *non* possum venire–
B.14.46 Quodcumque pecieritis a patre in nomine meo &c; Et alibi, *Non* in
solo pane
B.14.60 Si quis amat christum mundum *non* diligit istum.
B.15.55 And seiþ, Sicut qui mel comedit multum *non* est ei bonum, Sic qui
B.15.69 That is *Non* plus sapere quam oportet sapere.
B.15.118 sine dubio sacerdocium eius *non* est sanum.
B.15.149 'Nisi efficiamini sicut paruuli *non* intrabitis in regnum celorum.
B.15.157 *Non* inflatur, non est ambiciosa, non querit que sua sunt–
B.15.157 Non inflatur, *non* est ambiciosa, non querit que sua sunt–
B.15.157 Non inflatur, non est ambiciosa, *non* querit que sua sunt–
B.15.194 Cor contritum & humiliatum deus *non* despicies.'
B.15.343 Quia sacrilegium est res pauperum *non* pauperibus dare. Item,
peccatorum
B.15.343 accipis pocius das quam accipis; Si autem *non* eges & accipis
rapis.
B.15.343 Porro *non* indiget monachus si habeat quod nature sufficit.
B.15.576 In domo mea *non* est panis neque vestimentum et ideo nolite
constituere me Regem.
B.16.25 Cum ceciderit iustus *non* collidetur quia dominus supponit ma[num
suam];
B.16.47 est idem qui peccat per liberum arbitrium *non* repugnat.
B.16.110 *Non* est sanis opus medicus set in[firmis].
B.16.219 Maledictus homo qui *non* reliquit semen in Israel.
B.17.266 *Non* omnis qui dicit domine, domine, intrabit &c.
B.18.349 *Non* veni soluere legem set adimplere.
B.18.395 Audiui archana verba que *non* licet homini loqui.
B.18.399 *Non* intres in Iudicium cum seruo tuo.
B.19.181 Beati qui *non* viderunt [& crediderunt]."
B.19.446 *Non* occides: michi vindictam &c.
B.19.479 Omnia tua sunt ad defendendum set *non* ad deprehendendum.'
B.20.279 *Non* concupisces rem proximi tui.

C. 2.42   Et super Innocentem munera *non* accepit.
C. 3.308   *Non* morabit[ur] opus mersenarii &c.
C. 3.477   *Non* leuabit gens contra gentem gladium nec excercebuntur vltra ad prelium.
C. 4.36   Contricio & infelicitas in viis eorum et viam pacis *non* cognouerunt;
C. 4.36   *non* est timor dei ante oculos eorum.
C. 4.165   Et saluo custodias set *non* cum carcer[a]tis.'
C. 5.58   *Non* reddas malum pro malo.
C. 5.60   Dominus pars hereditatis mee &c. Et alibi: clemencia *non* constringit.
C. 5.86   *Non* de solo,' y sayde, 'for sothe viuit homo,
C. 6.60   Si hominibus placerem christi seruus *non* essem; nemo potest duobus
C. 7.92   *Non* habitabit in medio domus mee qui facit superbiam [&] qui
C. 7.138   *Non* veni vocare iustos set peccatores &c.
C. 7.147   Quandocumque ingemuerit peccator omnes iniquitate[s] eius *non*
C. 7.304   Vxorem duxi & ideo *non* possum venire.'
C. 8.78   Quia cum iustis *non* scribantur.
C. 8.245   Piger propter frigus noluit arrare; mendicabi[t] in yeme & *non* dabitur ei".
C. 9.213   *Non* licet uobis legem voluntati, set voluntat[em] coniungere legi.
C.10.202   Inquirentes autem dominum [*non*] minuentur omni bono.
C.10.236   Filius *non* portabit iniquitatem patris &c.
C.11.23   Ibunt in progenie patrum suorum & vsque in eternum *non* videbunt lumen;
C.11.157   Fides *non* habet meritum vbi humana racio &c.
C.12.10   Pena peccuniaria *non* sufficit &c.
C.12.34   *Non* oderis fratrem secrete in corde &c.
C.12.99   Qui *non* diligit manet in morte.
C.12.138   Domine, *non* est tibi cur[e] quod soror &c?
C.12.141   Maria optimam partem elegit que *non* [auferetur ab ea].
C.13.44   Necessitas *non* habet legem–
C.13.128   For ignorancia *non* excusat as ych haue herd in bokes.'
C.13.196   De re que te *non* molestat noli certare.
C.14.18   Scient[es] & *non* facient[es] varijs flagellis vapulab[unt].
C.14.208   A[d]uenit ignis diuinus *non* comburens set illuminans &c.
C.15.22   That iustus bifore iesu in die iudicij *non* saluabitur bote vix helpe;
C.15.62   And saide, 'cor contritum & humiliatum, deus, *non* despicies.'
C.15.224   Argentum & Aurum *non* est michi; quod [autem] habeo tibi do &c.
C.15.244   vobis. Et alibi: *Non* in solo pane viuit homo &c.'
C.15.259   Si quis Amat christum mundum *non* diligit istum.
C.16.217   And sayth, sicut qui mel comedit multum *non* est ei bonum; Sic
C.16.229   "*Non* plus sapere," saide þe wyse, [laste synne of pruyde wexe,]
C.16.273   sine dubio sacerdocium eius *non* est sanum.
C.16.291   Cor contritum & humiliatum deus *non* despicies.
C.16.291   Non inflatur, *non* est Ambiciosa.
C.16.291   *Non* inflatur, non est Ambiciosa.
C.18.222   Maledictus homo qui *non* reliquit semen in Israel.
C.19.232   *Non* omnis qui dicit domine, domine intrabit in reg[num] celorum &c.
C.20.259   *Non* visurum se mortem &c.
C.20.395   *Non* veni soluere legem set adimplere.
C.20.438   Audiui arcana verba que *non* licet homini loqui.
C.20.442   *Non* intres in iudicium cum seruo tuo.
C.21.181   Beati qui *non* viderunt & crediderunt."
C.21.446   *Non* occides: Michi vindictam &c.
C.21.479   Omnia [tua sunt] ad defendendum sed *non* ad deprehendendum.'
C.22.279   *Non* concupisces rem proximi tui &c.

norma C 1
C.17.285   In baculi forma sit, presul, hec tibi *norma*;

nos A 1; B 2; C 2
A.11.305   Ecce ipsi ydiot[e] rapiunt celum vbi *nos* sapientes
B. 5.506   Thanne hente hope an horn of Deus tu conuersus viuificabis [*nos*]
B.10.461   "Ecce ipsi ydiot[e] rapiunt celum vbi *nos* sapientes in inferno mergimur".
C. 7.151   Thenne hente [hope] an horn of deus tu conuersus viuificabis *nos*
C.11.287   "Ecce ips[i] idiote rapiunt celum vbi *nos* sapientes in inferno mergimur".

nostra B 2; C 1
B.11.231   Melius est scrutari scelera *nostra* quam naturas rerum.
B.19.394   Et dimitte nobis debita *nostra* &c.
C.21.394   Et dimitte nobis debita *nostra* &c,

nostram A 1; B 2
A.10.41   Faciamus hominem ad ymaginem *nostram*.
B. 5.486   Faciamus hominem ad ymaginem [et similitudinem] *nostram*;
B. 9.43   Faciamus hominem ad imaginem *nostram*];

nostri B 1; C 1
B.15.537   Absit nobis gloriari nisi in cruce domini *nostri* &c.
C.17.198   Absit nobis gloriari nisi in cruce domini *nostri* &c.

nostro B 2; C 2
B. 1.31   Vt seruare possimus de patre *nostro* semen.
B.11.311   Psallite deo *nostro*; psallite quoniam rex terre deus Israel; psallite
C. 1.30   vt seruare possimus de patre *nostro* semen.
C.13.123   Psallite deo *nostro*, psallite; quoniam Rex [terre] deus, psallite sapienter.

nostrum C 1
C.16.374   Panem *nostrum* co[tidianum] &c.

nouum B 1; C 1
B.19.273   Id est vetus testamentum & *nouum*.
C.21.273   Id est vetus testamentum & *nouum*.

nudatur B 1; C 1
B.Pr.137   Si ius *nudatur* nudo de iure metatur;
C.Pr.158   [Si ius *nudatur* nudo de iure metatur];

nudo B 1; C 1
B.Pr.137   Si ius nudatur *nudo* de iure metatur;
C.Pr.158   [Si ius nudatur *nudo* de iure metatur];

nudum B 1; C 1
B.Pr.135   *Nudum* ius a te vestiri vult pietate.
C.Pr.156   *Nudum* ius a te vestir[i] vult pietate.

nugas C 1
C.11.18   Qui sapiunt *nugas* & crim[ina] lege vocantur;

nulla B 1; C 1
B.18.149   Quia in Inferno *nulla* est redempcio.'
C.20.152   Quia in inferno *nulla* est redempcio.'

nullo A 1
A.10.108   Qui circuit [omne genus in *nullo* genere est].

nullum A 2; B 3; C 4
A. 4.126   For *nullum* malum [þ]e ma[n] met[t]e with Inpunitum
A. 4.127   And bad *Nullum* [bonum be] irremuneratum.
B. 4.143   For *Nullum* malum þe man mette wiþ inpunitum
B. 4.144   And bad *Nullum* bonum be irremuneratum.
B.18.390   *Nullum* malum inpunitum &c–
C. 4.140   For *nullum* malum [þe] man mette with inpunitum
C. 4.141   And bad *nullum* bonum be irremuneratum.
C.20.433   As *nullum* malum inpunitum & nullum bonum irremuneratum–
C.20.433   As nullum malum inpunitum & *nullum* bonum irremuneratum–

numerat B 1; C 1
B.20.256   Qui *numerat* multitudinem stellarum et omnibus eis [nomina vocat].
C.22.256   Qui *numerat* multitudinem stellarum &c.

numquam B 3; C 2
B. 9.155   *Numquam* collig[unt] de spinis vua[s] nec de tribulis ficus.
B.16.47   Videatis qui peccat in spiritum sanctum *numquam* remittetur &c; Hoc
B.17.310   *Numquam* dimittitur peccatum &c.
C. 6.257   *Numquam* dimittitur peccatum &c.'
C.10.244   *Numquam* collig[unt] de spinis vuas; Et Alibi: Bon[a] Arbor

numquid B 1; C 1
B.15.318   *Num[quid]*, dicit Iob, rugi[e]t onager cum herbam habuerit aut
C.17.53   *Nu[mquid]*, dicit Iop, rugiet onager cum habuerit herbam aut

nunc B 1; C 1
B.18.315   *Nunc* princeps huius mundi e[i]icietur foras.'
C.20.349   *Nunc* princeps huius mundi.'

nunquam C 2
C.13.224   Locutum me aliquando penituit, tacuisse *nunquam*.
C.19.290   *Nunquam* dimittitur peccatum &c.

nutriuit B 1
B.14.77   Ociositas & habundancia panis peccatum turpissimum *nutriuit*;

o B 6; C 6
B.Pr.133   *O* qui iura regis christi specialia regis,
B. 5.483   *O* felix culpa, o necessarium peccatum Ade &c.
B. 5.483   O felix culpa, *o* necessarium peccatum Ade &c.
B.11.120   *O* vos omnes sicientes venite &c,
B.17.114   [*O* mors ero mors tua].
B.18.35   *O* mors ero mors tua.'
C.Pr.154   *O* qui iura regis christi specialia regis,
C. 7.125   O felix culpa, [o] necessarium peccatum Ade.
C. 7.125   O felix culpa, [*o*] necessarium peccatum Ade.
C.12.55   /*O* vos omnes sicientes venite ad aquas
C.12.215   *O* stulte, ista nocte anima tua egredi[e]tur; tezaurisat & ignorat &c.
C.20.34   *O* mors [ero] mors tua.'

obligati B 1; C 1
B.10.327   Hij in curribus & hij in equis ipsi *obligati* sunt &c.
C. 5.172   Hij in curribus & [hij] in equis; ipsi *obligati* sunt & ceciderunt.

obtinuerunt B 1
B.10.26   Ecce ipsi peccatores! habundantes in seculo *obtinuerunt* diuicias.

obuiauerunt B 1; C 1
B.18.421   Misericordia & veritas *obuiauerunt* sibi; Iusticia & pax osculate
su[nt]
C.20.464   Misericordia & veritas *obuiauerunt* sibi; Iusticia & pax osculate
sunt.

occidere C 1
C.10.99   Nolite timere eos qui possunt *occidere* corpus &c.

occides B 1; C 1
B.19.446   Non *occides*: michi vindictam &c.
C.21.446   Non *occides*: Michi vindictam &c.

occiduntur B 1
B.14.92   Per confessionem to a preest peccata *occiduntur*–

ociositas B 1
B.14.77   *Ociositas* & habundancia panis peccatum turpissimum nutriuit;

oculo B 4; C 1
B.10.268   Qui[d] consideras festucam in *oculo* fratris tui, trabem in oculo tuo
&c?
B.10.268   Qui[d] consideras festucam in oculo fratris tui, trabem in *oculo* tuo
&c?
B.10.270   E[j]ice primo trabem [de] *oculo* tuo &c–
B.18.339   Dentem pro dente & oculum pro *oculo*.
C.20.385   Dentem p[ro] dente & oculum pro *oculo*.

oculos B 1; C 1
B. 4.37   Non est timor dei ante *oculos* eorum &c.
C. 4.36   non est timor dei ante *oculos* eorum.

oculum B 1; C 1
B.18.339   Dentem pro dente & *oculum* pro oculo.
C.20.385   Dentem p[ro] dente & *oculum* pro oculo.

oderis B 2; C 1
B.11.88   Non *oderis* fratres secrete in corde tuo set publice argue illos.
B.11.93   Non *oderis* fratrem.
C.12.34   Non *oderis* fratrem secrete in corde &c.

odibile B 2; C 2
B.14.276   'Paupertas,' quod Pacience, 'est *odibile* bonum, Remocio curarum,
B.14.287   Ergo paupertas est *odibile* bonum.
C.16.116   'Paupertas,' quod pacience, 'est *odibile* bonum, Remocio curarum,
C.16.122   [Ergo paupertas est *odibile* bonum].

odisti C 1
C.20.356   *Odisti* omnes qui operantur iniquitatem;

odit B 1; C 1
B. 5.39   Qui parcit virge *odit* filium:
C. 5.139   Qui parcit virge *odit* filium.'

offendit B 2; C 1
B. 9.100   Qui *offendit* in vno in omnibus est reus.
B.11.309   Qui *offendit* in vno in omnibus est reus.
C.13.122   Qui *offendit* in vno in om[n]ibus est reus.

olim B 1
B.16.242   Quam *olim* Abrahe promisisti & semini eius.

omne A 1; B 3; C 2
A.10.108   Qui circuit [*omne* genus in nullo genere est].
B.14.63   Aperis tu manum tuam & imples *omne* animal benediccione.
B.15.118   Sicut de templo *omne* bonum progreditur, sic de templo omne
B.15.118   sic de templo *omne* malum procedit. Si sacerdocium integrum
fuerit
C.16.273   Sicut de templo *omne* bonum progreditur, sic de templo omne
C.16.273   sic de templo *omne* malum procedit. Si sacerdocium integrum
fuerit

omnem C 1
C.15.164   Caritas expellit *omne[m]* timorem.

omnes A 2; B 6; C 4
A. 7.234   The sauter seiþ in þe salme of Beati *omnes*:
A.11.245   Dum tempus est operemur bonum ad *omnes*, maxime autem ad
B. 5.418   Bettre þan in Beatus vir or in Beati *omnes*
B. 6.250   The Sauter seiþ, in þe psalme of Beati *omnes*,
B.10.204   Dum tempus [est] operemur bonum ad *omnes*, maxime autem ad
domesticos fidei.
B.11.120   O vos *omnes* sicientes venite &c,
B.15.81   Confundantur *omnes* qui adorant sculptilia; Et alibi, Vt quid
diligitis
B.15.578   Inferte *omnes* [decimas] in orreum meum vt cibus in domo mea.
C. 7.147   Quandocumque ingemuerit peccator *omnes* iniquitate[s] eius non
C.12.55   /O vos *omnes* sicientes venite ad aquas
C.20.356   Odisti *omnes* qui operantur iniquitatem;

C.20.356   Perdes *omnes* qui loqu[u]ntur mendacium.

omni B 4; C 1
B. 9.109   Inquirentes autem dominum non minuentur *omni* bono.
B.11.282   Inquirentes autem dominum non minuentur *omni* bono.
B.11.383   Propter deum subiecti estote *omni* creature.
B.14.46   viuit homo set in *omni* verbo quod procedit de ore dei.'
C.10.202   Inquirentes autem dominum [non] minuentur *omni* bono.

omnia A 2; B 8; C 11
A.12.50   Hy3t *omnia* probate, a pore þing withalle;
A.12.56   And wente forþ on my way with *omnia* probate,
B. 3.339   Was *omnia* probate, and þat plesed hire herte
B. 5.281   [Misericordia eius super *omnia* opera eius &c]–
B.11.139   Misericordia eius super *omnia* opera eius.'
B.15.464   Ecce altilia mea & *omnia* parata sunt;
B.17.152   *Omnia* traham ad me ipsum &c–
B.17.318   Misericordia eius super *omnia* opera eius–
B.19.80   *Omnia* celestia terrestria flectantur in hoc nomine Iesu;
B.19.479   *Omnia* tua sunt ad defendendum set non ad deprehendendum.'
C. 3.491   Was *omnia* probate; þat plesede here herte.
C. 8.90   *Omnia* que dicunt facite & seruate.
C.12.74   Misericordia eius super *omnia* opera [eius].'
C.12.171   Nisi renunciaueritis *omnia* que po[s]sid[etis] &c.''
C.17.5   Caritas s[u]ffert.
C.17.285   Fer, trahe, punge gregem, seruando per *omnia* legem–
C.19.127   *Omnia* traham ad me ipsum–
C.19.298   Misericordia eius super *omnia* opera eius.
C.20.234   *Omnia* probate; quod bonum est tenete.
C.21.80   *Omnia* celestia terrestria flectantur in hoc nomine iesu;
C.21.479   *Omnia* [tua sunt] ad defendendum sed non ad deprehendendum.'

omnibus A 1; B 4; C 1
A.11.23   Quare via impiorum p[ros]peratur, [bene] est *omnibus* qui praue
B. 9.100   Qui offendit in vno in *omnibus* est reus.
B.10.25   Quare impij viuunt? bene est *omnibus* qui preuaricantur & inique
agunt.
B.11.309   Qui offendit in vno in *omnibus* est reus.
B.20.256   Qui numerat multitudinem stellarum et *omnibus* eis [nomina
vocat].
C.13.122   Qui offendit in vno in *om[n]ibus* est reus.

omnipotentem B 1
B.15.608   Konne þe firste clause of oure bileue, Credo in deum patrem
omnipotentem,

omnis B 3; C 3
B. 5.283   *Omnis* iniquitas quantum ad misericordiam dei est quasi sintilla in
medio
B.13.57   And þanne hadde Pacience a pitaunce, Pro hac orabit ad te *omnis*
B.17.266   Non *omnis* qui dicit domine, domine, intrabit &c.
C. 6.338   *Omnis* iniquitas quoad misericordiam dei est quasi sintilla in medio
maris.
C.15.60   And brouhte forth a pytaunce, was pro h[a]c orabit [ad te] *omnis*
C.19.232   Non *omnis* qui dicit domine, domine intrabit in reg[num] celorum
&c.

omnium B 2; C 2
B.15.118   Si autem corruptum fuerit *omnium* fides marcida est. Si
B.17.170   Tu fabricator *omnium* &c.
C.16.273   Si Autem corupt[um] fuerit *omnium* f[i]des marcida est. Si
C.19.134   Tu fabricator *omnium*–

onager B 1; C 1
B.15.318   Num[quid], dicit Iob, rugi[e]t *onager* cum herbam habuerit aut
C.17.53   Nu[mquid], dicit Iop, rugiet *onager* cum habuerit herbam aut

onera B 2; C 2
B. 6.221   Alter alterius *onera* portate.
B.11.211   Alter alterius *onera* portate.
C. 8.230   Alter alterius *onera* portate.
C.13.78   Alter alterius *onera* portate.

onus B 2; C 1
B. 6.315   Paupertatis *onus* pacienter ferre memento;
B.10.116   Vnusquisque portabit *onus* suum &c.''
C. 8.336   Paupertatis *onus* pacienter ferre memento.

opera B 7; C 7
B. 5.281   [Misericordia eius super omnia *opera* eius &c]–
B.10.436   [Sunt] iusti atque sapientes, & *opera* eorum in manu dei sunt &c.
B.11.139   Misericordia eius super omnia *opera* eius.'
B.12.213   Qui[a] reddit vnicuique iuxta *opera* sua.
B.14.213   *Opera* enim illorum sequ[u]ntur illos,
B.15.61   Et verba vertit in *opera* fulliche to his power.''
B.17.318   Misericordia eius super omnia *opera* eius–
C. 5.32   Reddet vnicuique iuxta *opera* sua–
C.11.271   Sunt iusti atque sapientes & *opera* eorum in manu dei sunt &c.
C.12.74   Misericordia eius super omnia *opera* [eius].'

C.14.152　Et reddet vnicu[i]que iuxta *opera* sua.
C.16.54　*Opera* [enim ill]orum sequ[u]ntur illos,
C.16.223　Et verba vertit in *opera* emforth his power."
C.19.298　Misericordia eius super omnia *opera* eius.

operarius A 1; B 1
A. 2.86　Dignus est *operarius* mercede [sua].
B. 2.123　For Dignus est *operarius* his hire to haue,

operatur B 1
B. 3.237　Qui ingreditur sine macula & *operatur* Iusticiam.

operantur C 1
C.20.356　Odisti omnes qui *operantur* iniquitatem;

operemur A 1; B 1
A.11.245　Dum tempus est *operemur* bonum ad omnes, maxime autem ad
B.10.204　Dum tempus [est] *operemur* bonum ad omnes, maxime autem ad
　　　　　domesticos fidei.

operibus B 1; C 2
B. 1.187　Fides sine *operibus* mortua est &c.
C. 1.183　Fides sine *operibus* mortua est.
C.16.342　*Operibus* credite.

operis C 2
C.16.31　And [*operis* satisfaccio] for soules paieth and alle synnes quyteth.
C.16.31　Cordis contricio, Oris confessio, *Operis* satisfaccio:

oportet A 1; B 3; C 2
A.11.74　Non plus sapere quam *oportet*.
B.10.121　Non plus sapere quam *oportet*.
B.15.69　That is Non plus sapere quam *oportet* sapere.
B.19.161　Sic *oportet* Christum pati & intrare &c;
C.16.230　"Quam *oportet* sapere."
C.21.161　Sic [*oportet*] christum pati & intrare &c;

oportuno B 1; C 1
B.13.57　Pro hac orabit ad te omnis sanctus in tempore *oportuno*;
C.15.60　pro h[a]c orabit [ad te] omnis sanctus in tempore *oportuno*.

opprimetur opprimitur B 1; C 1
B.15.55　scrutator est maiestatis *opprimitur* a gloria.
C.16.217　Sic [qui] scrutator est magestatis *opprim[e]tur* a gloria.

optimam B 1; C 1
B.11.255　Maria *optimam* partem elegit que non [auferetur ab ea].
C.12.141　Maria *optimam* partem elegit que non [auferetur ab ea].

opus B 1; C 1
B.16.110　Non est sanis *opus* medicus set in[firmis].
C. 3.308　Non morabit[ur] *opus* mersenarii &c.

orabit B 1; C 1
B.13.57　And þanne hadde Pacience a pitaunce, Pro hac *orabit* ad te omnis
C.15.60　And brouhte forth a pytaunce, was pro h[a]c *orabit* [ad te] omnis

oratio C 1
C.11.295　Breuis *oratio* penetrat celum.

oraciones orationes B 1; C 1
B.13.45　Vos qui peccata hominum comeditis, nisi pro eis lacrimas &
　　　　　oraciones
C.15.50　Vos qui peccata hominum comeditis, nisi pro eis lacrimas &
　　　　　orationes

oracionis B 1
B.16.135　Domus mea domus *oracionis* vacabitur.'

ore B 1
B.14.46　viuit homo set in omni verbo quod procedit de *ore* dei.'

oriente B 1; C 1
B.12.144　Ibant magi ab *oriente*.
C.14.88　Ib[a]nt magi ab *Oriente* &c.

oris B 1; C 2
B.14.18　*Oris* confessio &c.
C.16.30　And *oris* confessio cometh of [knowlechyng and] shrifte of mouthe
C.16.31　Cordis contricio, *Oris* confessio, Operis satisfaccio:

orreum B 1
B.15.578　Inferte omnes [decimas] in *orreum* meum vt cibus in domo mea.

os B 1; C 1
B.13.330　Cuius malediccione *os* plenum est & amaritudine; sub lingua eius
C. 6.76　Cuius maledictione *os* plenum est & amaritudine; sub lingua eius

osculate B 1; C 1
B.18.421　Misericordia & veritas obuiauerunt sibi; Iusticia & pax *osculate*
　　　　　su[nt]
C.20.464　Misericordia & veritas obuiauerunt sibi; Iusticia & pax *osculate*
　　　　　sunt.

oues C 1
C. 9.262　Dispergentur *oues*, þe dogge dar nat berke.

ouibus C 1
C.17.193　Bonus Pastor animam suam ponit pro *ouibus* suis &c.

ouile C 1
C.18.264　Fiet vnum *ouile* & vnus pastor.

pabulo C 1
C. 5.87　Nec in pane [nec] in *pabulo*; the paternoster wittenesseth

pabulum B 1; C 1
B.15.318　*pabulum* commune sufficiat; ex adipe prodijt iniquitas tua.
C.17.53　*pabulum* comune sufficiat; Ex adipe prodiit iniquitas tua.

pace B 2; C 1
B.15.254　In *pace* in idipsum dormiam &c.
B.18.186　Lo! here þe patente', quod Pees, 'In *pace* in idipsum,
C.20.191　Loo! here þe patente,' quod pees, 'In *pace* in idipsum,

pacienter B 1; C 1
B. 6.315　Paupertatis onus *pacienter* ferre memento;
C. 8.336　Paupertatis onus *pacienter* ferre memento.

pacientes B 6; C 3
B.13.135　*Pacientes* vincunt &c.'
B.13.171　*Pacientes* vincunt].'
B.14.33　Ne soliciti sitis &c; Volucres celi deus pascit &c; *pacientes* vincunt
　　　　　&c.'
B.14.54　Prison ne peyne, for *pacientes* vincunt.
B.15.268　*Pacientes* Vincunt verbi gracia, and [verred] ensamples manye.
B.15.598　*Pacientes* vincunt.
C.15.137　Quod Peres the ploghman, '*Pacientes* vinc[u]nt.
C.15.156　*Pacientes* vincunt &c.
C.15.253　Prisoun ne payne, for [*pacientes*] vincunt.

pacis C 1
C. 4.36　Contricio & infelicitas in viis eorum et viam *pacis* non
　　　　　cognouerunt;

pallidam B 1; C 1
B.15.118　Sicut cum videris arborem *pallidam* & marcidam intelligis quod
C.16.273　Sicut cum videri[s] Arborem *pallidam* & marcidam intelligis quod

palmarum B 1
B.18.6　Reste me þere and rutte faste til Ramis *palmarum*.

pane B 3; C 5
B. 5.269　*Pane* tuo pocius vescere: liber eris.
B. 7.87　Satis diues est qui non indiget *pane*.
B.14.46　Quodcumque pecieritis a patre in nomine meo &c; Et alibi, Non in
　　　　　solo *pane*
C. 5.87　Nec in *pane* [nec] in pabulo; the paternoster wittenesseth
C. 6.293　*Pane* tuo pocius vescere: liber eris.
C. 8.241　In [labore & sudore] vultus tui vesceris *pane* tuo".
C. 9.120　[Q]uando misi vos sine *pane* & pera &c.
C.15.244　vobis. Et alibi: Non in solo *pane* viuit homo &c.'

panem B 2; C 2
B. 7.89　& non vidi iustum derelictum ne[c] semen eius [querens *panem*].
B.10.85　Frange esurienti *panem* tuum &c.
C.11.65　Frange esurienti *panem* tuum.
C.16.374　*Panem* nostrum co[tidianum] &c.

panes A 1; B 1
A. 8.110　Fuerunt michi lacrime mee *panes* die ac nocte.
B. 7.128　Fuerunt michi lacrime mee *panes* die ac nocte.

panis B 2; C 1
B.14.77　Ociositas & habundancia *panis* peccatum turpissimum nutriuit;
B.15.576　In domo mea non est *panis* neque vestimentum et ideo nolite
　　　　　constituere me Regem.
C.15.229　Habundancia *panis* & vini turpissimum peccatum aduenit.

paraclitus B 2; C 2
B.19.201　Oon Spiritus *paraclitus* to Piers and to hise felawes.
B.19.206　Spiritus *paraclitus* ouerspradde hem alle.
C.21.201　Oen spiritus *paraclitus* to Peres and to his felawes.
C.21.206　Spiritus *paraclitus* ouerspradde hem alle.

parata B 1
B.15.464　Ecce altilia mea & omnia *parata* sunt;

parce B 3; C 1
B.10.343　Dilige denarium set *parce* dilige formam.
B.18.392　In my prisone Purgatorie til *parce* it hote.
B.19.295　And pleieþ al wiþ pacience and *Parce* michi domine;
C.21.295　And ple[ieþ] al with pacience and *parce* michi domine

parcit B 1; C 1
B. 5.39　Qui *parcit* virge odit filium:
C. 5.139　Qui *parcit* virge odit filium.'

parcius B 1; C 1
B.11.106   Parum lauda; vitupera *parcius*.'
C.12.40   Pa[r]um lauda; vit[u]pera *parcius*.'

pari B 1; C 1
B.13.426   Consencientes & agentes *pari* pena punientur.
C. 7.86   Consencientes & agentes *pari* pena punientur.

pars B 1; C 2
B.12.189   Dominus *pars* hereditatis mee is a murye verset
C. 5.60   Dominus *pars* hereditatis mee &c. Et alibi: clemencia non
           constringit.
C.14.128   Dominus *pars* hereditatis [mee] is A merye verset;

partem B 1; C 2
B.11.255   Maria optimam *partem* elegit que non [auferetur ab ea].
C. 4.188   Audiatis alteram *partem* amonges aldremen and comeneres,
C.12.141   Maria optimam *partem* elegit que non [auferetur ab ea].

parum B 1; C 1
B.11.106   *Parum* lauda; vitupera parcius.'
C.12.40   *Pa[r]um* lauda; vit[u]pera parcius.'

paruuli B 1; C 1
B.15.149   'Nisi efficiamini sicut *paruuli* non intrabitis in regnum celorum.
C.16.298   Nisi efficiamini sicut *paruuli* &c,

pascit B 1
B.14.33   Ne soliciti sitis &c; Volucres celi deus *pascit* &c; pacientes vincunt
           &c.'

passionem B 1
B.14.190   Pateat &c: Per *passionem* domini,

pastor B 2; C 4
B.15.43   And oþere names an heep, Episcopus and *Pastor*.'
B.15.497   Bonus *pastor* animam suam ponit &c.
C.16.205   And oþere names an heep, Episcopus and *pastor*.'
C.17.193   Bonus *Pastor* animam suam ponit pro ouibus suis &c.
C.17.291   Bonus *pastor* &c,
C.18.264   Fiet vnum ouile & vnus *pastor*.

pastore C 1
C. 9.265   Sub molli *pastore* &c.

pastores B 1; C 1
B.12.142   *Pastores* loquebantur ad inuicem.
C.14.86   *Pastores* loquebantur ad inuicem &c.

pateat B 1
B.14.190   *Pateat* &c: Per passionem domini,

patefacta B 1; C 1
B. 5.603   Per Euam cun[c]tis clausa est et per Mariam virginem [iterum]
           patefacta est;
C. 7.250   Per Euam cun[c]tis clausa est & per mariam verginem iterum
           patefacta est &c;

pater B 6; C 6
B. 2.27   Qualis *pater* talis filius: Bon[a] arbor bonum fructum facit.
B. 5.171   Boþe Priour and Suppriour and oure *Pater* Abbas;
B. 9.149   Filius non portabit iniquitatem patris et *pater* non portabit
           iniquitatem filij.
B.10.246   Deus *pater*, deus filius, deus spiritus sanctus:
B.10.252   [Ego in patre et *pater* in me est, et qui videt me videt et patrem
           meum]
B.16.185   *Pater* is his propre name, a persone by hymselue.
C. 2.27   [Qu]alis *pater* talis fili[us] &c.
C. 3.406   Nominatiuo, *pater* & filius & spiritus sanctus.
C. 6.153   That is Priour and supriour and oure *pater* Abbas.
C. 7.128   Ego in patre & *pater* in me [est] et qui me videt videt [&] patrem
           meum &c;
C.11.153   Ego in patre & *pater* in me est; Et qui me vid[e]t, patrem meum
C.18.192   'That is soth,' saide he thenne, 'the syre hatte *pater*

pati B 2; C 1
B.10.445   For quant oportet vient en place il nyad que *pati*.
B.19.161   Sic oportet Christum *pati* & intrare &c;
C.21.161   Sic [oportet] christum *pati* & intrare &c;

patre A 1; B 5; C 5
A. 5.42   Qui cum *patre* & filio; Faire mote ȝow befalle.'
B. 1.31   Vt seruare possimus de *patre* nostro semen.
B. 5.58   Qui cum *patre* & filio; þat faire hem bifalle
B.10.252   [Ego in *patre* et pater in me est, et qui videt me videt et patrem
           meum]
B.14.46   Quodcumque pecieritis a *patre* in nomine meo &c; Et alibi, Non in
           solo pane
B.16.223   Spiritus procedens a *patre* & filio &c,
C. 1.30   vt seruare possimus de *patre* nostro semen.
C. 5.199   Qui cum *patre* & filio; þat fayre hem byfalle

C. 7.128   Ego in *patre* & pater in me [est] et qui me videt videt [&] patrem
           meum &c;
C.11.153   Ego in *patre* & pater in me est; Et qui me vid[e]t, patrem meum
C.15.244   Quodcumque pecieritis [a *patre*] in nomine meo dab[itur] enim

patrem B 4; C 7
B. 5.567   Honora *patrem* & matrem &c;
B.10.252   [Ego in patre et pater in me est, et qui videt me videt et *patrem*
           meum]
B.10.473   That euere þe[i] kouþe [konne on book] moore þan Credo in deum
           patrem,
B.15.608   Konne þe firste clause of oure bileue, Credo in deum *patrem*
           omnipotentem,
C. 7.128   Ego in patre & pater in me [est] et qui me videt videt [&] *patrem*
           meum &c;
C. 7.216   Honora *patrem* & matrem &c.
C.11.153   Ego in patre & pater in me est; Et qui me vid[e]t, *patrem* meum
C.12.160   Quicumque reli[querit] *patrem* & matrem &c.
C.16.322   And also a can clergie, credo in deum *patrem*,
C.17.59   Honora *patrem* & matrem &c–
C.17.316   Conne þe furste clause of oure bileue, credo in deum *patrem*,

patrimonium B 1
B. 9.94   Proditor est prelatus cum Iuda qui *patrimonium* christi minus
           distribuit; Et

patris B 5; C 4
B. 9.149   Filius non portabit iniquitatem *patris* et pater non portabit
           iniquitatem filij.
B.10.114   Filius non portabit iniquitatem *patris* &c.
B.16.30   Thanne with þe firste pil I palle hym doun, potencia de[i *patris*].
B.16.36   Thanne sette I to þe secounde pil, sapiencia dei *patris*,
B.18.26   For no dynt shal hym dere as in deitate *patris*.'
C.10.236   Filius non portabit iniquitatem *patris* &c.
C.18.34   And with þe furste planke y palle hym down, potencia dei *patris*.
C.18.40   Thenne sette y þe seconde planke, sapiencia dei *patris*,
C.20.25   For no d[yn]t shal hym dere as in deitate *patris*.'

patrum C 1
C.11.23   Ibunt in progenie *patrum* suorum & vsque in eternum non videbunt
           lumen;

pauca C 1
C.14.214   Quia super *pauca* fuisti fidelis &c.

pauci B 1; C 1
B.11.114   And plukked in *Pauci* pryueliche and leet þe remenaunt go rome.'
C.12.49   And plihte in *pauci* preueiliche and lette þe remenaunt go rome.'

pauper B 2; C 1
B.11.269   *Pauper* ego ludo dum tu diues meditaris.
B.12.147   Set non erat ei locus in diuersorio, et *pauper* non habet
           diuersorium.
C.12.154   *Pauper* ego ludo dum tu diues m[e]ditaris.

paupercula C 1
C.13.98   Amen dico vobis quia hec vidua *paupercula* &c.

pauperes B 1
B.14.215   Beati *pauperes* quoniam ipsorum est regnum celorum.

pauperibus B 3
B.13.195   Than ȝacheus for he seide "dimidium bonorum meorum do
           pauperibus",
B.15.327   Dispersit, dedit *pauperibus*?
B.15.343   Quia sacrilegium est res pauperum non *pauperibus* dare. Item,
           peccatoribus

paupertas B 4; C 3
B.14.276   '*Paupertas*,' quod Pacience, 'est odibile bonum, Remocio curarum,
B.14.287   Ergo *paupertas* est odibile bonum.
B.14.307   /Cantabit *paupertas* coram latrone viato[r],
B.14.309   Forþi seiþ Seneca *Paupertas* est absque sollicitudine semita.
C.16.116   '*Paupertas*,' quod pacience, 'est odibile bonum, Remocio curarum,
C.16.122   [Ergo *paupertas* est odibile bonum].
C.16.143   *Pauper[tas]* est absque solicitudine semita.

paupertate C 1
C. 9.163   Iunior fui, [et]enim senui; e[t] alibi: infirmata est vertus mea
           paupertate.

paupertates B 1
B.11.271   Diuicias nec *paupertates* &c,

paupertatis B 1; C 1
B. 6.315   *Paupertatis* onus pacienter ferre memento;
C. 8.336   *Paupertatis* onus pacienter ferre memento.

pauperum B 2
B. 9.94   alibi, Perniciosus dispensator est qui res *pauperum* christi inutiliter

B.15.343   Quia sacrilegium est res *pauperum* non pauperibus dare. Item, peccatoribus

pax B 2; C 3

B.18.421   Misericordia & veritas obuiauerunt sibi; Iusticia & *pax* osculate su[nt]

B.19.169   To Peter and to [h]ise Apostles and seide *pax* vobis;

C.17.238   The pope with alle prestes *pax* vobis sholde make

C.20.464   Misericordia & veritas obuiauerunt sibi; Iusticia & *pax* osculate sunt.

C.21.169   To peter and to his apostlis and saide *pax* vobis;

peccandum B 1; C 1

B.15.118   totus populus conuertitur ad *peccandum*. Sicut cum videris arborem

C.16.273   totus populus conuertitur ad *peccandum*. Sicut cum videri[s]

peccat B 4; C 2

B.16.47   Videatis qui *peccat* in spiritum sanctum numquam remittetur &c; Hoc

B.16.47   est idem qui *peccat* per liberum arbitrium non repugnat.

B.17.200   Qui *peccat* in spiritu[m] sanct[um] &c,

B.17.201   For he prikeþ god as in þe pawme þat *peccat* in spiritu[m] sanct[um].

C.19.166   Qui *peccat* in spiritu[m] sanct[um] &c,

C.19.167   For he priketh god as in [the] paume that *peccat* in spiritum sanctum.

peccata B 4; C 2

B.13.45   Vos qui *peccata* hominum comeditis, nisi pro eis lacrimas & oraciones

B.13.54   Et quorum tecta sunt *peccata*

B.14.92   Per confessionem to a preest *peccata* occiduntur–

B.14.94   As Dauid seiþ in þe Sauter: et quorum tecta sunt *peccata*.

C. 7.152   quorum tecta sunt *peccata*,

C.15.50   Vos qui *peccata* hominum comeditis, nisi pro eis lacrimas & orationes

peccati B 1; C 1

B.11.204   Qui facit peccatum seruus est *peccati*.

C.12.112   Qui facit peccatum seruus est *peccati*.

peccatis B 1; C 1

B.15.118   Si sacerdocium fuerit in *peccatis* totus populus conuertitur ad

C.16.273   Si sacerdocium fuerit in *peccatis* totus populus conuertitur ad

peccato B 1; C 2

B.12.207   De *peccato* propiciato noli esse sine metu.

C.14.42   Quis vestrum sine *peccato* est.

C.14.146   De *peccato* propiciato noli esse sine metu.

peccator C 1

C. 7.147   Quandocumque ingemuerit *peccator* omnes iniquitate[s] eius non

peccatores B 2; C 2

B. 5.498   Non veni vocare iustos set *peccatores* ad penitenciam.

B.10.26   Ecce ipsi *peccatores*! habundantes in seculo obtinuerunt diuicias.

C. 7.138   Non veni vocare iustos set *peccatores* ad penitenciam.

C.11.23   Et alibi: ecce ip[s]i *peccatores*, habundantes &c.

peccatoribus B 1

B.15.343   Quia sacrilegium est res pauperum non pauperibus dare. Item, *peccatoribus*

peccatoris C 1

C.14.134   Nolo mortem *peccatoris* &c.

peccatorum B 1; C 1

B.15.612   [Recorden it and rendren] it wiþ remissionem *peccatorum*

C.17.320   Recorden hit and re[n]d[r]en hit with remissionem *peccatorum*,

peccatum B 6; C 5

B. 5.273   Non dimittitur *peccatum* donec restituatur [a]blatum.

B. 5.483   O felix culpa, o necessarium *peccatum* Ade &c.

B.11.81   Sola contricio [delet *peccatum*]–

B.11.204   Qui facit *peccatum* seruus est peccati.

B.14.77   Ociositas & habundancia panis *peccatum* turpissimum nutriuit;

B.17.310   Numquam dimittitur *peccatum* &c.

C. 6.257   Numquam dimittitur *peccatum* &c.'

C. 7.125   O felix culpa, [o] necessarium *peccatum* Ade.

C.12.112   Qui facit *peccatum* seruus est peccati.

C.15.229   Habundancia panis & vini turpissimum *peccatum* aduenit.

C.19.290   Nunquam dimittitur *peccatum* &c.

peccaui B 1; C 1

B.18.378   Tibi soli *peccaui* &c.

C.20.420   Tibi soli *peccaui* & malum coram te feci.

peccuniaria C 1

C.12.10   Pena *peccuniaria* non sufficit &c.

peccuniosus C 1

C.12.10   And preeye for the pol by pol yf thow be *peccuniosus*.'

pecieritis B 1; C 2

B.14.46   Quodcumque *pecieritis* a patre in nomine meo &c; Et alibi, Non in solo pane

C. 7.260   Quodcumque *pecieritis* in nomine meo dabitur enim vobis.

C.15.244   Quodcumque *pecieritis* [a patre] in nomine meo dab[itur] enim

pecuniam A 1; B 3

A. 3.221   Qui *pecuniam* suam [non] dedit ad vsuram.

B. 3.241   Qui *pecuniam* suam non dedit ad vsuram et munera super innocentem &c,

B. 7.83   Quare non dedisti *pecuniam* meam ad mensam vt ego veni[ens] cum vsuris ex[egissem illam]?

B.10.342   Nichil iniquius quam amare *pecuniam*;

pecuniaria B 1

B.11.58   Pena *pecuniaria* non sufficit pro spiritualibus delictis.

pecuniosus B 1

B.11.58   And preien for þee pol by pol if þow be *pecuniosus*.'

pedem B 2; C 2

B. 1.119   Ponam *pedem* in aquilone & similis ero altissimo.

B.15.51   Ponam *pedem* meum in aquilone & similis ero altissimo.

C. 1.111   Ponam *pedem* meum in Aquilone & similis ero altissimo.'

C.16.213   Ponam *pedem* meum in Aquilone &c.

pena A 2; B 4; C 5

A. 8.3   And purchac[ide] hym a pardoun a *pena* & a culpa

A. 8.21   But non a *pena* & a culpa þe pope wolde h[e]m graunte,

B. 7.3   And purchaced hym a pardoun a *pena* & a culpa

B. 7.19   Ac noon A *pena* & a culpa þe pope [w]olde hem graunte

B.11.58   *Pena* pecuniaria non sufficit pro spiritualibus delictis.

B.13.426   Consencientes & agentes pari *pena* punientur.

C. 7.86   Consencientes & agentes pari *pena* punientur.

C. 9.3   And purchasede hym a pardoun A *pena* & a culpa,

C. 9.23   Ac no [a] *pena* & a culpa treuthe wolde hem graunte

C. 9.187   And pardon with the plouhman A *pena* & a culpa.

C.12.10   *Pena* peccuniaria non sufficit &c.

pendet B 1; C 1

B.17.16   In hijs duobus mandatis tota lex *pendet* & prophet[e].

C.19.17   In hijs duobus [mandatis tota lex *pendet* & prophete].

penetrans B 1; C 1

B.20.340   'Certes', seide his felawe, 'sire *Penetrans* domos.'

C.22.340   'Certes,' saide his felawe, 'sire *penetrans* domos.'

penetrat C 1

C.11.295   Breuis oratio *penetrat* celum.

penitencia A 1; B 1; C 1

A. 5.248   Þat *penitencia* his pik he shulde pulsshe newe

B. 5.474   That *penitencia* his pik he sholde polshe newe

C. 6.328   That [*penitencia*] is pykstaff a wolde polesche newe

penitenciam B 2; C 1

B. 5.498   Non veni vocare iustos set peccatores ad *penitenciam*.

B.13.49   He sette a sour loof toforn vs and seide 'Agite *penitenciam*',

C.15.55   He sette a sour loef and saide, 'Agite *penitenciam*',

penitet A 1; B 1; C 1

A.10.162   *Penitet* me fecisse hominem.

B. 9.133   *Penitet* me fecisse hominem.

C.10.222   *Penitet* me fecisse hominem;

penituit C 1

C.13.224   Locutum me aliquando *penituit*, tacuisse nunquam.

peperit A 1; B 1; C 1

A.10.150   Concepit dolore[m] & *peperit* iniquitatem.

B. 9.125   Concepit dolore[m] & *peperit* iniquitatem.

C.10.212   Concepit dolore[m] & *peperit* iniquitatem.

per B 8; C 7

B. 5.603   *Per* Euam cun[c]tis clausa est et per Mariam virginem [iterum] patefacta est;

B. 5.603   Per Euam cun[c]tis clausa est et *per* Mariam virginem [iterum] patefacta est;

B.14.92   *Per* confessionem to a preest peccata occiduntur–

B.14.190   Pateat &c: *Per* passionem domini,

B.15.556   *Per* primicias & decimas &c.

B.16.47   est idem qui peccat *per* liberum arbitrium non repugnat.

B.16.157   Necesse est vt veniant scandala; ve homini illi *per* quem scandalum venit.

B.18.421   Pees, and pees h[i]re, *per* secula seculorum:

C. 7.250   *Per* Euam cun[c]tis clausa est & per mariam verginem iterum patefacta est &c;

C. 7.250 Per Euam cun[c]tis clausa est & *per* mariam verginem iterum
       patefacta est &c;
C. 9.123 Nemini salutauerit[is] *per* viam.
C.17.219 *Per* pr[i]micias & decimas &c.
C.17.285 Fer, trahe, punge gregem, seruando *per* omnia legem–
C.18.174 Ve homini illi *per* quem scand[a]lum venit.
C.20.464 Pees, and pees here, *per* secula seculorum:

pera C 1
C. 9.120 [Q]uando misi vos sine pane & *pera* &c.

perdes C 1
C.20.356 *Perdes* omnes qui loqu[u]ntur mendacium.

perfecisti B 1; C 1
B.10.29 Que *perfecisti* destruxerunt; iustus autem &c.
C.11.25 Que *perfecisti* destruxerunt &c.

perfectus B 1; C 1
B.11.274 Si vis *perfectus* esse vade & vende [&c].
C.12.167 Si vis *perfectus* esse vade & vende &c.

perficitur B 1; C 1
B.17.341 Virtus in infirmitate *perficitur*.
C.19.321 Virtus in infirmitate *perficitur*.

periculum B 2; C 1
B.13.70 *Periculum* est in falsis fratribus.'
B.13.73 Vnusquisque a fratre se custodiat quia vt dicitur *periculum* est in
       falsis
C.15.75 *Periculum* est in falsis fratribus.'

perniciosus B 1
B. 9.94 alibi, *Perniciosus* dispensator est qui res pauperum christi inutiliter

perseuerans B 1; C 1
B.13.50 And siþþe he [drouȝ] vs drynke, Di[u] *perseuerans*,]
C.15.56 And sethe he drow vs drynke, di[u] *p[er]seuerans*,

personarum B 1; C 1
B.15.88 That seide to hise disciples, "Ne sitis *personarum* acceptores".]
C.16.241 Ne sitis acceptores *personarum*.

petere C 1
C.14.16 Beacius est dare quam *petere*.

peticionem C 1
C.15.271 Dabo tibi secundum *peticionem* tuam.

petite B 2
B.15.428 *Petite* & accipietis &c.]

petrus B 1
B.15.212 But Piers þe Plowman, *Petrus* id est christus.]

phebus B 1; C 1
B.18.408 Clarior est solito post maxima nebula *phebus*;]
C.20.451 Clarior est solito [post maxima nebula *phebus*];

philosophus B 1; C 1
B.11.416 *Philosophus* esses si tacuisses.]
C.13.224 *Philosophus* esses si tacuisses; & alibi: Locutum me aliquando

pietas B 1; C 1
B.Pr.138 Si seritur *pietas* de pietate metas.']
C.Pr.159 Si seritur *pietas* de pietate metas.'

pietate B 3; C 2
B.Pr.135 Nudum ius a te vestiri vult *pietate*.
B.Pr.138 Si seritur pietas de *pietate* metas.'
B. 7.46 Than pro dei *pietate* [pleden at þe barre].]
C.Pr.156 Nudum ius a te vestir[i] vult *pietate*.
C.Pr.159 Si seritur pietas de *pietate* metas.'

piger A 1; B 1; C 1
A. 7.220 *Piger* propter frigus no feld wolde tilie;
B. 6.236 *Piger* [propter frigus] no feeld [w]olde tilie;]
C. 8.245 *Piger* propter frigus noluit arrare; mendicabi[t] in yeme & non
       dabitur ei".

pinguia B 1; C 1
B. 5.269 Seruus es alterius [cum] fercula *pinguia* queris;]
C. 6.293 Seruus [es] alterius cum fercula *pingu[i]a* queris;

pius B 1; C 1
B.Pr.134 Hoc quod agas melius, iustus es, esto *pius*!]
C.Pr.155 Hoc vt agas melius, iustus es, esto *pius*!

placeas B 1
B. 7.77 Quia incertum est pro quo deo magis *placeas*.]

placerem B 1; C 1
B.13.312 Si hominibus *placerem* christi seruus non essem; Et alibi, Nemo
       potest

C. 6.60 Si hominibus *placerem* christi seruus non essem; nemo potest
       duobuss

placuit B 1; C 1
B.12.216 Quare *placuit*? quia voluit.
C.14.155 Quare *placuit*? qui[a] voluit &c.

plaga B 1; C 1
B.10.333 baculum impiorum, et virgam dominancium cedencium *plaga*
       insanabili.
C. 5.177 bac[u]lum impiorum, virga[m] d[omi]nancium, *plaga* insanabili.

plenitudo B 1; C 2
B.16.93 Til *plenitudo* temporis [tyme] comen were
B.18.126 Til *plenitudo* temporis tyme ycome were
C.18.138 Til *plenitudo* temporis [h]y tyme aprochede,

plenum B 2; C 2
B.13.330 Cuius malediccione os *plenum* est & amaritudine; sub lingua eius
B.15.318 aut mugiet bos cum ante *plenum* presepe steterit? brutorum
C. 6.76 Cuius maledictione os *plenum* est & amaritudine; sub lingua eius
C.17.53 aut mugiet bos cum ante *plenum* presepe steterit? Brutorum

pluit B 1; C 1
B.19.431 Qui *pluit* super Iustos & iniustos at ones
C.21.431 Qui *pluit* super iustos & iniustos at ones

plus A 1; B 2; C 1
A.11.74 Non *plus* sapere quam oportet.
B.10.121 Non *plus* sapere quam oportet.
B.15.69 That is Non *plus* sapere quam oportet sapere.
C.16.229 "Non *plus* sapere," saide þe wyse, [laste synne of pruyde wexe,]

pocius B 2; C 1
B. 5.269 Pane tuo *pocius* vescere: liber eris.
B.15.343 accipis *pocius* das quam accipis; Si autem non eges & accipis
       rapis.
C. 6.293 Pane tuo *pocius* vescere: liber eris.

ponam B 2; C 2
B. 1.119 *Ponam* pedem in aquilone & similis ero altissimo.
B.15.51 *Ponam* pedem meum in aquilone & similis ero altissimo.
C. 1.111 *Ponam* pedem meum in Aquilone & similis ero altissimo.'
C.16.213 *Ponam* pedem meum in Aquilone &c.

ponit B 1; C 1
B.15.497 Bonus pastor animam suam *ponit* &c.
C.17.193 Bonus Pastor animam suam *ponit* pro ouibus suis &c.

pontifex B 1; C 1
B.15.42 Presul and *Pontifex* and Metropolitanus,
C.16.204 Presul and *Pontifex* and metropol[it]anus

populo C 1
C.18.164 Ne forte tumultus fieret in *populo*–

populum B 1; C 1
B.15.118 Ita cum videris *populum* indisciplinatum & irreligiosum, sine
       dubio
C.16.273 Ita cum videris *populum* indissiplinatum & irreligiosum, sine dubio

populus B 3; C 3
B. 5.493 *Populus* qui ambulabat in tenebris vidit lucem magnam.
B.15.118 totus *populus* conuertitur ad peccandum. Sicut cum videris
       arborem
B.18.323 Patriarkes and prophetes, *populus* in tenebris,
C. 7.133 *Populus* qui ambulabat in tenebris vidit lucem magnam &c.
C.16.273 totus *populus* conuertitur ad peccandum. Sicut cum videri[s]
C.20.366 Patriarkes and profetes, *populus* in tenebris,

porro B 1
B.15.343 *Porro* non indiget monachus si habeat quod nature sufficit.

portabit B 4; C 1
B. 9.149 Filius non *portabit* iniquitatem patris et pater non portabit
       iniquitatem filij.
B. 9.149 Filius non portabit iniquitatem patris et pater non *portabit*
       iniquitatem filij.
B.10.114 Filius non *portabit* iniquitatem patris &c.
B.10.116 Vnusquisque *portabit* onus suum &c."
C.10.236 Filius non *portabit* iniquitatem patris &c.

portas B 1; C 1
B.18.262 Attollite *portas*.
C.20.270 Attollite *portas* &c.'

portate B 2; C 2
B. 6.221 Alter alterius onera *portate*.
B.11.211 Alter alterius onera *portate*.
C. 8.230 Alter alterius onera *portate*.
C.13.78 Alter alterius onera *portate*.

portis B 1; C 1
B. 9.186 Scribitur in *portis*, meretrix est ianua mortis.
C.10.287 Scribitur in *portis*, meretrix est ianua mortis.

possessio posesio B 2; C 2
B.14.276 *possessio* sine calumpnia, donum dei, sanit[atis] mater,
B.14.296 *Possessio* sine calumpnia.
C.16.116 *possessio* sine calumpnia, donum dei, sanitatis mater,
C.16.132 [*Possessio* sine calumpnia].

possibile C 1
C.11.201 Ita *possibile* est diuiti intrare in regn[um] celorum sicut camelus &c.

possidetis C 1
C.12.171 Nisi renunciaueritis omnia que *po[s]sid[etis]* &c."

possimus B 1; C 1
B. 1.31 Vt seruare *possimus* de patre nostro semen.
C. 1.30 vt seruare *possimus* de patre nostro semen.

possum B 1; C 1
B.14.3 Vxorem duxi & ideo non *possum* venire–
C. 7.304 Vxorem duxi & ideo non *possum* venire.'

possunt C 1
C.10.99 Nolite timere eos qui *possunt* occidere corpus &c.

post B 3; C 3
B.13.44 In a morter, *Post* mortem, of many bitter peyne
B.18.408 Clarior est solito *post* maxima nebula phebus;
B.18.408 *Post* inimicicias [clarior est et amor].
C.15.49 In a morter, *post* mortem, of many bittere peynes
C.20.451 Clarior est solito [*post* maxima nebula phebus];
C.20.451 *Post* inimicicias Clarior est & Amor.

potencia B 1; C 1
B.16.30 Thanne with þe firste pil I palle hym doun, *potencia* de[i patris].
C.18.34 And with þe furste planke y palle hym down, *potencia* dei patris.

potentes B 2; C 2
B.13.61 Ve vobis qui *potentes* estis ad bibendum vinum.
B.15.552 Deposuit *potentes* de sede &c.
C.15.65 Ve vobis qui *p[o]tentes* estis ad bibendum vinum–
C.17.215 Deposuit *potentes* de sede &c.

potest B 1; C 1
B.13.312 Si hominibus placerem christi seruus non essem; Et alibi, Nemo *potest*
C. 6.60 Si hominibus placerem christi seruus non essem; nemo *potest* duobus

praue A 1
A.11.23 Quare via impiorum p[ros]peratur, [bene] est omnibus qui *praue*

pre C 2
C. 3.300 That *pre* manibus is paied or his pay asketh.
C. 9.45 But they *pre* manibus were payed for pledynge at þe barre;

prebet B 1
B.10.256 Fides non habet meritum vbi humana racio *prebet* experimentum.

precepta B 1
B.Pr.145 '*Precepta* Regis sunt nobis vincula legis'.

predicate B 1
B.15.491 Ite in vniuersum mundum & *predicate* &c?

prelatus B 1
B. 9.94 Proditor est *prelatus* cum Iuda qui patrimonium christi minus distribuit; Et

prelium C 1
C. 3.477 Non leuabit gens contra gentem gladium nec excercebuntur vltra ad *prelium*.

presentes B 1; C 1
B. 2.74 'Sciant *presentes* & futuri &c.
C. 2.81 Sciant *presentes* & futuri &c.

presepe B 1; C 1
B.15.318 aut mugiet bos cum ante plenum *presepe* steterit? brutorum
C.17.53 aut mugiet bos cum ante plenum *presepe* steterit? Brutorum

presides A 1; B 1; C 1
A.11.296 Dum steter[it]is ante [reges &] *presides* nolite cogitare,
B.10.450 "[D]um steteritis ante Reges & *presides* [nolite cogitare]:
C.11.275 "Dum steteritis ante Reges vel *presides* &c:

presul B 1; C 2
B.15.42 *Presul* and Pontifex and Metropolitanus,
C.16.204 *Presul* and Pontifex and metropol[it]anus,
C.17.285 In baculi forma sit, *presul*, hec tibi norma;

pretereas B 1
B. 7.77 Non eligas cui miser[e]aris ne forte *pretereas* illum qui meretur accipere,

preuaricantes A 1
A.12.19 Vidi *preuarica[nt]es* & tabescebam.

preuaricantur B 1
B.10.25 Quare impij viuunt? bene est omnibus qui *preuaricantur* & inique agunt?

preuaricatores C 1
C.10.95 And with the pyk pulte adoun *preuaricatores* legis.

prima B 1
B.12.9 Si non in *prima* vigilia nec in secunda &c.

primicias B 1; C 1
B.15.556 Per *primicias* & decimas &c.
C.17.219 Per *pr[i]micias* & decimas &c.

primo B 1
B.10.270 E[j]ice *primo* trabem [de] oculo tuo &c–

primus B 1; C 1
B.15.286 Poul *primus* heremita hadde parroked hymselue
C.17.13 Paul *primus* heremita hadde yparrokede hymsulue

princeps A 2; B 3; C 3
A.10.8 A proud prikere of Fraunce, *Princeps* huius mundi,
A.10.62 Thanne haþ þe pouk power, sire *princeps* huius mundi,
B.Pr.132 'Sum Rex, sum *princeps*; neutrum fortasse deinceps.
B. 9.8 A proud prikere of Fraunce, *Princeps* huius mundi,
B.18.315 Nunc *princeps* huius mundi e[i]icietur foras.'
C.Pr.153 'Sum Rex, sum *Princeps*; neutrum fortasse deinceps.
C.10.135 A proued prikeare of fraunce, *princeps* huius mundi,
C.20.349 Nunc *princeps* huius mundi.'

principes A 1; C 1
A.11.223 Super cathedram moisi sederunt *principes*.
C.20.272 '*Princ[i]pes* of this place, prest vndo this gates

principibus A 1; B 1
A. 8.46 Super innocentem munera non accipies; a regibus & *principibus*–
B. 7.44 A Regibus & *principibus* erit merces eorum.

pristinum B 1; C 1
B.10.325 And puten [hem] to hir penaunce, Ad *pristinum* statum ire;
C. 5.171 And potte 3ow to 3oure penaunce, ad *pristinum* statum ire,

pro B 9; C 8
B. 7.46 Than *pro* dei pietate [pleden at þe barre].
B. 7.77 Quia incertum est *pro* quo deo magis placeas.
B.11.58 Pena pecuniaria non sufficit *pro* spiritualibus delictis.
B.13.45 Vos qui peccata hominum comeditis, nisi *pro* eis lacrimas & oraciones
B.13.57 And þanne hadde Pacience a pitaunce, *Pro* hac orabit ad te omnis
B.15.39 Anima *pro* diuersis accionibus diuersa nomina sortitur: dum viuificat
B.18.36 Thanne cam Pilatus with muche peple, sedens *pro* tribunali,
B.18.339 Dentem *pro* dente & oculum pro oculo.
B.18.339 Dentem pro dente & oculum *pro* oculo.
C. 5.58 Non reddas malum *pro* malo.
C.15.50 Vos qui peccata hominum comeditis, nisi *pro* eis lacrimas & orationes
C.15.60 And brouhte forth a pytaunce, was *pro* h[a]c orabit [ad te] omnis
C.16.201 Anima *pro* diuersis [acc]ionibus diuersa nomina sortitur: dum
C.17.193 Bonus Pastor animam suam ponit *pro* ouibus suis &c.
C.20.35 Thenne cam Pilatus with moche peple, sedens *pro* tribunali,
C.20.385 Dentem *p[ro]* dente & oculum pro oculo.
C.20.385 Dentem p[ro] dente & oculum *pro* oculo.

probate A 2; B 1; C 2
A.12.50 Hy3t omnia *probate*, a pore þing withalle;
A.12.56 And wente forþ on my way with omnia *probate*,
B. 3.339 Was omnia *probate*, and þat plesed hire herte
C. 3.491 Was omnia *probate*; þat plesede here herte.
C.20.234 Omnia *probate*; quod bonum est tenete.

procedens B 1
B.16.223 Spiritus *procedens* a patre & filio &c,

procedit B 2; C 1
B.14.46 viuit homo set in omni verbo quod *procedit* de ore dei.'
B.15.118 sic de templo omne malum *procedit*. Si sacerdocium integrum fuerit
C.16.273 sic de templo omne malum *procedit*. Si sacerdocium integrum fuerit

prodijt prodiit B 1; C 1
B.15.318 pabulum commune sufficiat; ex adipe *prodijt* iniquitas tua.
C.17.53 pabulum commune sufficiat; Ex adipe *prodiit* iniquitas tua.

proditor B 1
B. 9.94   *Proditor* est prelatus cum Iuda qui patrimonium christi minus
           distribuit; Et

progenie C 1
C.11.23   Ibunt in *progenie* patrum suorum & vsque in eternum non videbunt
           lumen;

progreditur B 1; C 1
B.15.118   Sicut de templo omne bonum *progreditur*, sic de templo omne
C.16.273   Sicut de templo omne bonum *progreditur*, sic de templo omne

promisisti B 1
B.16.242   Quam olim Abrahe *promisisti* & semini eius.

prophete B 1; C 1
B.17.16   In hijs duobus mandatis tota lex pendet & *prophet[e]*.
C.19.17   In hijs duobus [mandatis tota lex pendet & *prophete*].

propiciato B 1; C 1
B.12.207   De peccato *propiciato* noli esse sine metu.
C.14.146   De peccato *propiciato* noli esse sine metu.

proponit B 2; C 2
B.11.37   'Homo *proponit*', quod a poete, and Plato he hiȝte,
B.20.33   Homo *proponit* & deus disponit;
C.11.303   'Homo *pr[o]ponit*,' quod a poete tho, and plato he hihte,
C.22.33   Homo *proponit* [&] deus dispo[n]it;

propter A 1; B 3; C 8
A. 7.220   Piger *propter* frigus no feld wolde tilie;
B. 6.236   Piger [*propter* frigus] no feeld [w]olde tilie;
B. 9.194   Bonum est vt vnusquisque vxorem suam habeat *propter*
           fornicacionem.
B.11.383   *Propter* deum subiecti estote omni creature.
C. 8.245   Piger *propter* frigus noluit arrare; mendicabi[t] in yeme & non
           dabitur ei".
C.10.293   Bonum est [vt] vnusquisque vx[or]em suam habeat *propter*
           fornicacionem.
C.17.140   Dilige deum *propter* deum, id est propter veritatem; & inimicum
           tuum
C.17.140   Dilige deum propter deum, id est *propter* veritatem; & inimicum
           tuum
C.17.140   *propter* mandatum, id est propter legem; & Amicum propter
           Amorem,
C.17.140   propter mandatum, id est *propter* legem; & Amicum propter
           Amorem,
C.17.140   propter mandatum, id est propter legem; & Amicum *propter*
           Amorem,
C.17.140   id est *propter* caritatem.

prosperatur A 1
A.11.23   Quare via impiorum *p[ros]peratur*, [bene] est omnibus qui praue

proximi B 1; C 1
B.20.279   Non concupisces rem *proximi* tui.
C.22.279   Non concupisces rem *proximi* tui &c.

proximum A 1; B 2; C 2
A.11.242   Dilige deum &c, Et *proximum* tuum sicut teipsum.
B.15.584   Dilige deum & *proximum* is parfit Iewen lawe;
B.17.13   Dilige deum & *proximum* tuum,
C.15.134   Bote dilige deum & *p[roximu]m* [and] domine quis habitabit
C.19.14   Dilige deum & *proximum* [tuum].

prudencie B 3; C 3
B.19.276   Spiritus *prudencie* þe firste seed highte,
B.19.455   For Spiritus *prudencie* among þe peple is gyle,
B.20.31   And Spiritus *prudencie* in many a point shal faille
C.21.276   Spiritus *prudencie* the furste seed hihte,
C.21.455   For spiritus *prudencie* among þe peple is gyle
C.22.31   And spiritus *Prudencie* in many a poynt shal faile

psallite B 3; C 3
B.11.311   *Psallite* deo nostro; psallite quoniam rex terre deus Israel; psallite
B.11.311   Psallite deo nostro; *psallite* quoniam rex terre deus Israel; psallite
B.11.311   Psallite deo nostro; psallite quoniam rex terre deus Israel; *psallite*
C.13.123   *Psallite* deo nostro, psallite; quoniam Rex [terre] deus, psallite
           sapienter.
C.13.123   Psallite deo nostro, *psallite*; quoniam Rex [terre] deus, psallite
           sapienter.
C.13.123   Psallite deo nostro, psallite; quoniam Rex [terre] deus, *psallite*
           sapienter.

pseudopropheta seudopropheta B 1; C 1
B.15.601   And [ȝit] wenen þo wrecches þat he were *pseudopropheta*
C.17.309   And a sofistre of soercerie and *seudopropheta*

publice B 1
B.11.88   Non oderis fratres secrete in corde tuo set *publice* argue illos.

puer B 1; C 1
B.Pr.196   Ve terre vbi *puer* Rex est &c.
C.Pr.209   Ve terre vbi *puer* est Rex.

pugillo C 1
C.19.114   Mundum *pugillo* continens,

punge C 1
C.17.285   Fer, trahe, *punge* gregem, seruando per omnia legem–

punientur B 1; C 1
B.13.426   Consencientes & agentes pari pena *punientur*.
C. 7.86   Consencientes & agentes pari pena *punientur*.

purgat B 1; C 1
B.18.407   Culpat caro, *purgat* caro, regnat deus dei caro.
C.20.450   Culpat Caro, *purgat* Caro, regnat deus dei Caro.

qua A 1; B 2; C 2
A.10.112   In eadem vocacione *qua* vocati estis state.
B. 1.178   Eadem mensura *qua* mensi fueritis remecietur vobis.
B.11.228   Eadem mensura *qua* mensi fueritis remecietur vobis.
C. 1.174   Eadem mensura *qua* mensi fueritis Remetietur vobis.
C. 5.43   In eadem vocacione *qu[a]* vocati estis [&c]

quadragenas B 1
B.13.67   Ter cesus sum & a iudeis quinquies *quadragenas* &c–

quadriduanus quatriduanus B 1; C 2
B.16.114   *Quatriduanus* quelt quyk dide hym walke.
C.17.303   *Quadriduanus* coeld quyk dede hym walke.
C.18.144   *Quadriduanus* coeld, quyk dede hym rome.

qualia B 1; C 1
B.Pr.136   *Qualia* vis metere, talia grana sere.
C.Pr.157   *Qualia* vis metere, talia grana sere.

qualis B 1; C 1
B. 2.27   *Qualis* pater talis filius: Bon[a] arbor bonum fructum facit.
C. 2.27   [*Qu]alis* pater talis fili[us] &c.

quam A 3; B 10; C 8
A.11.74   Non plus sapere *quam* oportet.
A.11.192   Ecce *quam* bonum & quam iocundum habitare Fratres in vnum.
A.11.192   Ecce quam bonum & *quam* iocundum habitare Fratres in vnum.
B. 3.330   For Melius est bonum nomen *quam* diuicie multe.'
B.10.121   Non plus sapere *quam* oportet.
B.10.342   Nichil iniquius *quam* amare pecuniam;
B.11.231   Melius est scrutari scelera nostra *quam* naturas rerum.
B.15.69   That is Non plus sapere *quam* oportet sapere.
B.15.343   accipis pocius das *quam* accipis; Si autem non eges & accipis
           rapis.
B.16.242   *Quam* olim Abrahe promisisti & semini eius.
B.18.360   Et cecidit in foueam *quam* fecit.
B.18.423   Ecce *quam* bonum & quam iocundum &c.
B.18.423   Ecce quam bonum & *quam* iocundum &c.
C. 1.143   Melius est mori *quam* male viuere.
C. 3.483   [For] melius est bonum nomen *quam* diuicie multe.'
C. 6.290   Melius est mori *quam* male viuere.
C.14.16   Beacius est dare *quam* petere.
C.16.230   "*Quam* oportet sapere."
C.17.40   Videte ne furtum sit: & alibi: meli[u]s est mori *quam* male viuere
           &c.
C.20.466   Ecce *quam* bonum & quam iocundum &c.
C.20.466   Ecce quam bonum & *quam* iocundum &c.

quando C 1
C. 9.120   [*Q]uando* misi vos sine pane & pera &c.

quandocumque C 1
C. 7.147   *Quandocumque* ingemuerit peccator omnes iniquitate[s] eius non

quantum B 1
B. 5.283   Omnis iniquitas *quantum* ad misericordiam dei est quasi sintilla in
           medio

quare A 1; B 3; C 1
A.11.23   *Quare* via impiorum p[ros]peratur, [bene] est omnibus qui praue
B. 7.83   *Quare* non dedisti pecuniam meam ad mensam vt ego veni[ens]
           cum vsuris ex[egissem illam]?
B.10.25   *Quare* impij viuunt? bene est omnibus qui preuaricantur & inique
           agunt?
B.12.216   *Quare* placuit? quia voluit.
C.14.155   *Quare* placuit? qui[a] voluit &c.

quasi B 3; C 3
B. 5.283   Omnis iniquitas quantum ad misericordiam dei est *quasi* sintilla in
           medio
B.11.203   As *quasi* modo geniti gentil men echone,
B.12.293   For Deus dicitur *quasi* dans [eternam vitam] suis, hoc est fidelibus;

C. 6.338   Omnis iniquitas quoad misericordiam dei est *quasi* sintilla in medio maris.
C. 9.258   Certes, hoso durste sygge hit, Simon *quasi* dormit;
C.12.111   As *quasi* modo geniti gentel men vchone,

quatriduanus > *quadriduanus*

que A 2; B 9; C 10
A. 1.51   Et *que* sunt dei deo oþer ellis ȝe don ille."
A.12.22   Audiui archan[a uerba] *que* non licet homini loqui.
B. 1.53   Et *que* sunt dei deo or ellis ye don ille."
B.10.29   *Que* perfecisti destruxerunt; iustus autem &c.
B.11.255   Maria optimam partem elegit *que* non [auferetur ab ea].
B.11.395   De re *que* te non molestat noli certare.
B.11.398   Et vidit deus cuncta *que* fecerat & erant valde bona.
B.13.39   Edentes & bibentes *que* apud eos sunt.
B.13.45   eff[u]deritis, ea *que* in delicijs comeditis in tormentis euometis.
B.15.157   Non inflatur, non est ambiciosa, non querit *que* sua sunt–
B.18.395   Audiui archana verba *que* non licet homini loqui.
C. 1.49   Et *que* sunt dei deo or [elles] ȝe don ylle."
C. 5.98   Mulier *qu[e]* inuenit d[ra]gmam.
C. 8.90   Omnia *que* dicunt facite & seruate.
C.11.25   *Que* perfecisti destruxerunt &c.
C.12.141   Maria optimam partem elegit *que* non [auferetur ab ea].
C.12.171   Nisi renunciaueritis omnia *que* po[s]sid[etis] &c."
C.13.196   De re *que* te non molestat noli certare.
C.15.44   Edentes & bibentes *que* apud eos sunt &c.
C.15.50   effuderitis, ea *que* in deliciis comeditis in tor[mentis] euo[metis] &c.
C.20.438   Audiui arcana verba *que* non licet homini loqui.

quem B 2; C 1
B.12.12   *Quem* diligo castigo.
B.16.157   Necesse est vt veniant scandala; ve homini illi per *quem* scandalum venit.
C.18.174   Ve homini illi per *quem* scand[a]lum venit.

quemadmodum B 1; C 1
B. 5.509   'Homines & iumenta saluabis *quemadmodum* multiplicasti misericordiam
C. 7.154   'Homines & iumenta saluabis; *qu[e]madmodum* multiplicasti misericordiam

quemquam B 2; C 2
B.11.90   Nolite iudicare *quemquam*.'
B.14.293   Nolite iudicare *quemquam*:
C.12.31   Nolite iudicare *quemquam*.'
C.16.128   Nolite iudicare *quemquam*:

querens B 1
B. 7.89   & non vidi iustum derelictum ne[c] semen eius [*querens* panem].

queris B 1; C 1
B. 5.269   Seruus es alterius [cum] fercula pinguia *queris*;
C. 6.293   Seruus [es] alterius cum fercula pingu[i]a *queris*;

querit B 1
B.15.157   Non inflatur, non est ambiciosa, non *querit* que sua sunt–

querite B 1
B.15.503   *Querite* & inuenietis &c.

queritis B 1
B.15.81   Et alibi, Vt quid diligitis vanitatem & *queritis* mendacium?

qui A 14; B 48; C 42
A.Pr.39   *Qui* loquitur turpiloquium [is] luciferis hyne.
A. 3.85   Ignis deuorabit tabernacula eorum *qui* libenter accipiunt munera.
A. 3.221   *Qui* pecuniam suam [non] dedit ad vsuram.
A. 5.42   *Qui* cum patre & filio; Faire mote ȝow befalle.'
A. 8.95   Et *qui* bona egerunt ibunt in vitam eternam;
A. 8.96   *Qui* vero mala in ignem eternum.
A.10.94   *Qui* agit contra conscientiam &c.
A.10.108   *Qui* circuit [omne genus in nullo genere est].
A.10.120   *Qui* se humiliat exaltabitur &c.
A.11.23   Quare via impiorum p[ros]peratur, [bene] est omnibus *qui* praue
A.11.147   *Qui* sim[u]lat verbis, nec corde est fidus amicus,
A.11.196   *Qui* facit & docuerit magnus vocabitur in regno celorum.
A.11.234   *Qui* crediderit et baptizatus fuerit saluus erit.'
A.11.263   Nemo ascendet ad celum nisi *qui* de celo descendit.
B.Pr.39   *Qui* loquitur turpiloquium is luciferes hyne.
B.Pr.133   O *qui* iura regis christi specialia regis,
B. 3.96   Ignis deuorabit tabernacula eorum *qui* libenter accipiunt munera &c.
B. 3.237   *Qui* ingreditur sine macula & operatur Iusticiam.
B. 3.241   *Qui* pecuniam suam non dedit ad vsuram et munera super innocentem &c,
B. 3.336   Honorem adquiret *qui* dat munera &c.'
B. 5.39   *Qui* parcit virge odit filium:

B. 5.58   *Qui* cum patre & filio; þat faire hem bifalle
B. 5.486   Et alibi, *Qui* manet in caritate in deo manet & deus in eo.
B. 5.493   Populus *qui* ambulabat in tenebris vidit lucem magnam.
B. 7.77   Non eligas cui miser[e]aris ne forte pretereas illum *qui* meretur accipere,
B. 7.87   Satis diues est *qui* non indiget pane.
B. 7.113   Et *qui* bona egerunt ibunt in vitam eternam;
B. 7.114   *Qui* vero mala in ignem eternum.
B. 9.65   *Qui* manet in caritate in deo manet &c.
B. 9.94   Proditor est prelatus cum Iuda *qui* patrimonium christi minus distribuit;
B. 9.94   alibi, Perniciosus dispensator est *qui* res pauperum christi inutiliter
B. 9.100   *Qui* offendit in vno in omnibus est reus.
B.10.25   Quare impij viuunt? bene est omnibus *qui* preuaricantur & inique agunt?
B.10.195   *Qui* simulat verbis [nec] corde est fidus amicus,
B.10.252   [Ego in patre et pater in me est, et *qui* videt me videt et patrem meum]
B.10.382   Nemo ascendit ad celum nisi *qui* de celo descendit.
B.11.124   *Qui* crediderit & baptiȝatus fuerit &c.
B.11.176   *Qui* non diligit manet in morte.
B.11.204   *Qui* facit peccatum seruus est peccati.
B.11.309   *Qui* offendit in vno in omnibus est reus.
B.13.45   Vos *qui* peccata hominum comeditis, nisi pro eis lacrimas & oraciones
B.13.61   Ve vobis *qui* potentes estis ad bibendum vinum.
B.13.118   *Qui* facit & docuerit magnus vocabitur in regno celorum.'
B.13.423   Ve vobis *qui* ridetis &c–
B.13.432   Non habitabit in medio domus mee *qui* facit superbiam & qui loquitur iniqua.
B.13.432   Non habitabit in medio domus mee qui facit superbiam & *qui* loquitur iniqua.
B.13.440   *Qui* vos spernit me spernit.
B.15.55   And seiþ, Sicut *qui* mel comedit multum non est ei bonum, Sic qui
B.15.55   And seiþ, Sicut qui mel comedit multum non est ei bonum, Sic *qui*
B.15.60   "Beatus est", seiþ Seint Bernard, "*qui* scripturas legit
B.15.81   Confundantur omnes *qui* adorant sculptilia; Et alibi, Vt quid diligitis
B.15.234   Beatus est diues *qui* &c.
B.16.47   Videatis *qui* peccat in spiritum sanctum numquam remittetur &c; Hoc
B.16.47   est idem *qui* peccat per liberum arbitrium non repugnat.
B.16.219   Maledictus homo *qui* non reliquit semen in Israel.
B.17.151   *Qui* conceptus est de spiritu sancto &c.
B.17.200   *Qui* peccat in spiritu[m] sanct[um] &c,
B.17.266   Non omnis *qui* dicit domine, domine, intrabit &c.
B.18.17   Benedictus *qui* venit in nomine domini.
B.19.181   Beati *qui* non viderunt [& crediderunt]."
B.19.431   *Qui* pluit super Iustos & iniustos at ones
B.20.256   *Qui* numerat multitudinem stellarum et omnibus eis [nomina vocat].
C.Pr.40   *Qui* turpiloquium loquitur [is] luciferes knaue.
C.Pr.154   O *qui* iura regis christi specialia regis,
C. 3.124   Ignis deuorabit tabernacula eorum *qui* libenter accipiunt munera.
C. 3.403   *Qui* in caritate manet in deo manet et deus in eo.
C. 3.488   Honorem adquiret *qui* dat munera.'
C. 5.139   *Qui* parcit virge odit filium.'
C. 5.199   *Qui* cum patre & filio; þat fayre hem byfalle
C. 7.83   Ve vobis *qui* ridetis &c–
C. 7.92   Non habitabit in medio domus mee *qui* facit superbiam [&] qui
C. 7.92   Non habitabit in medio domus mee qui facit superbiam [&] *qui*
C. 7.100   *Qui* vos spernit me spernit.
C. 7.128   Ego in patre & pater in me [est] et *qui* me videt videt [&] patrem meum &c;
C. 7.133   Populus *qui* ambulabat in tenebris vidit lucem magnam &c.
C. 9.287   Et *qui* bona egerunt ibunt in vitam eternam;
C. 9.288   *Qui* vero mala in ignem etern[u]m.
C.10.99   Nolite timere eos *qui* possunt occidere corpus &c.
C.11.18   *Qui* sapiunt nugas & crim[ina] lege vocantur;
C.11.18   *Qui* recte sapiunt lex iubet ire foras.
C.11.153   Ego in patre & pater in me est; Et *qui* me vid[e]t, patrem meum
C.11.153   patrem meum vid[e]t *qui* in celis est &c.
C.11.207   Nemo ascenderit ad celum nisi *qui* de celo descendit.
C.12.59   *Qui* crediderit & baptizatus fuerit &c.
C.12.99   *Qui* non diligit manet in morte.
C.12.112   *Qui* facit peccatum seruus est peccati.
C.12.119   Et *qui* bona egerunt, ibunt &c.
C.13.87   *Qui* crediderit & baptizatus fuerit &c–
C.13.122   *Qui* offendit in vno in om[n]ibus est reus.
C.15.50   Vos *qui* peccata hominum comeditis, nisi pro eis lacrimas & oraciones
C.15.65   Ve vobis *qui* p[o]tentes estis ad bibendum vinum–
C.15.126   *Qui* facit & docuerit magnus vocabitur.'

C.16.217 And sayth, sicut *qui* mel comedit multum non est ei bonum; Sic
C.16.217 [*qui*] scrutator est magestatis opprim[e]tur a gloria.
C.16.222 "Beatus," saith seynt Bernard, "*qui* scripturas legit
C.18.222 Maledictus homo *qui* non reliquit semen in Israel.
C.19.166 *Qui* peccat in spiritu[m] sanct[um] &c,
C.19.232 Non omnis *qui* dicit domine, domine intrabit in reg[num] celorum &c.
C.20.15 Benedictus *qui* venit in nomine domini.
C.20.356 Odisti omnes *qui* operantur iniquitatem;
C.20.356 Perdes omnes *qui* loqu[u]ntur mendacium.
C.21.181 Beati *qui* non viderunt & crediderunt."
C.21.431 *Qui* pluit super iustos & iniustos at ones
C.22.256 *Qui* numerat multitudinem stellarum &c.

quia A 1; B 11; C 9
A. 7.234 Labores manuum tuarum *quia* manducabis &c.
B. 1.141 Heu michi *quia* sterilem duxi Iuuenilem.
B. 5.440 Heu michi *quia* sterilem vitam duxi Iuuenilem.'
B. 6.76 *Quia* cum iustis non scribantur.
B. 7.77 *Quia* incertum est pro quo deo magis placeas.
B.12.213 *Qui[a]* reddit vnicuique iuxta opera sua.
B.12.216 Quare placuit? *quia* voluit.
B.13.73 Vnusquisque a fratre se custodiat *quia* vt dicitur periculum est in falsis
B.15.318 brutorum animalium natura te condempnat, *quia* cum eis pabulum
B.15.343 *Quia* sacrilegium est res pauperum non pauperibus dare. Item, peccatoribus
B.16.25 Cum ceciderit iustus non collidetur *quia* dominus supponit ma[num suam];
B.18.149 *Quia* in Inferno nulla est redempcio.'
C. 3.190 Sunt infelices *quia* matres sunt meretrices.
C. 3.344 *Quia* antelate rei recordatiuum est–
C. 8.78 *Quia* cum iustis non scribantur.
C. 8.260 Labores manuum tuarum *quia* manducabis &c".
C.13.98 Amen dico vobis *quia* hec vidua paupercula &c.
C.14.155 Quare placuit? *qui[a]* voluit &c.
C.14.214 *Quia* super pauca fuisti fidelis &c.
C.17.53 Brutorum Animalium natura te condempnat, *quia* cum [eis] pabulum
C.20.152 *Quia* in inferno nulla est redempcio.'

quicumque C 1
C.12.160 *Quicumque* reli[querit] patrem & matrem &c.

quid A 2; B 4; C 1
A. 3.54 And seiþ Nesciat sinist[ra] *quid* faciat dexter[a].
A.12.28 "*Quid* est ueritas?" quod he; "verilyche tel vs."
B. 3.72 Nesciat sinistra *quid* faciat dextra:
B.10.268 *Qui[d]* consideras festucam in oculo fratris tui, trabem in oculo tuo &c?
B.15.81 Confundantur omnes qui adorant sculptilia; Et alibi, Vt *quid* diligitis
B.16.214 Deus meus, Deus meus, vt *quid* dereliquisti me?
C. 3.74 Nesciat [sinistra] *quid* faciat [dextera]:

quieuit B 1
B.10.333 Quomodo cessauit exactor, *quieuit* tributum? contriuit dominus baculum

quinquies B 1
B.13.67 Ter cesus sum & a iudeis *quinquies* quadragenas &c–

quis B 8; C 6
B. 2.39 Domine *quis* habitabit in tabernaculo tuo &c.
B. 3.234 Domine, *quis* habitabit in tabernaculo tuo?
B. 7.52 Domine, *quis* habitabit in tabernaculo tuo.
B.11.82 Nisi *quis* renatus fuerit.
B.13.127 But Dilige deum and Domine *quis* habitabit;
B.14.60 Si *quis* amat christum mundum non diligit istum.
B.14.104 'Ye? *quis* est ille?' quod Pacience; 'quik, laudabimus eum!
B.18.316 '*Quis* est iste?'
C. 2.40 Domine *quis* habitabit in tabernaculo tuo &c.
C. 9.127 Si *quis* videtur sapiens, fiet stultus vt sit sapiens.
C.14.42 *Quis* vestrum sine peccato est.
C.15.134 Bote dilige deum & p[roximu]m [and] domine *quis* habitabit
C.15.259 Si *quis* Amat christum mundum non diligit istum.
C.15.279 'ʒe? *quis* est ille?' quod pacience; 'quik, lauda[bi]mus eum!

quoad C 1
C. 6.338 Omnis iniquitas *quoad* misericordiam dei est quasi sintilla in medio maris.

quo B 3
B. 7.77 Quia incertum est pro *quo* deo magis placeas.
B.12.69 Nescit aliquis vnde venit aut *quo* vadit &c.
B.15.431 Et si sal euanuerit in *quo* salietur?

quod A 2; B 20; C 13
A.12.52 Til ʒe come to þe burg[h] *quod* bonum est tenete.
A.12.57 And ere I cam to þe court *quod* bonum est tenete.
B.Pr.134 Hoc *quod* agas melius, iustus es, esto pius!
B. 3.343 *Quod* bonum est tenete; truþe þat text made.
B.10.261 Appare *quod* es vel esto quod appares;
B.10.261 Appare quod es vel esto *quod* appares;
B.10.291 Existimasti inique *quod* ero tui similis; arguam te & statuam contra faciem
B.11.95 Existimasti inique *quod* ero tui similis &c.
B.11.251 Domine, non est tibi cure *quod* soror mea reliquit me solam ministrare?
B.12.65 *Quod* scimus loquimur, quod vidimus testamur.
B.12.65 Quod scimus loquimur, *quod* vidimus testamur.
B.12.66 Of *quod* scimus comeþ Clergie, [a] konnynge of heuene,
B.12.67 And of *quod* vidimus comeþ kynde wit, of siʒte of diuerse peple.
B.13.254 Argentum & aurum non est michi; *quod* autem habeo tibi do; in nomine
B.14.46 viuit homo set in omni verbo *quod* procedit de ore dei.'
B.15.118 intelligis *quod* vicium habet in radice, Ita cum videris populum
B.15.343 Porro non indiget monachus si habeat *quod* nature sufficit.
B.19.187 To Piers pardon þe Plowman redde *quod* debes.
B.19.193 And rewarde hym wel þat reddit *quod* debet,
B.19.259 And Registrer to receyue redde *quod* debes.
B.19.390 To Piers pardon þe Plowman redde *quod* debes.'
B.20.308 And þat Piers [pardon] were ypayed, redde *quod* debes.
C. 1.140 Heu michi *quod* ste[r]ilem duxi vitam iuuenilem.
C. 3.495 *Quod* bonum est tenete, a tixst of treuthe [m]akynge.
C. 7.54 Heu michi *quod* ster[i]lem duxi vitam iuuenilem.'
C.12.29 Existimasti inique *quod* ero t[u]i similis; Arguam te & statuam
C.12.138 Domine, non est tibi cur[e] *quod* soror &c?
C.15.224 Argentum & Aurum non est michi; *quod* [autem] habeo tibi do &c.
C.16.273 intelligis *quod* vicium habet in radice, Ita cum videris populum
C.20.234 Omnia probate; *quod* bonum est tenete.
C.21.187 To Peres pardoun þe plouhman Redde *quod* debes.
C.21.193 And rewarde hym riht wel þat redd[it] *quod* debet,
C.21.259 And Registrer to reseyuen Redde *quod* debes.
C.21.390 To [Peres] pardon þe [plouhman] Redde *quod* debe[s].'
C.22.308 And þat Peres pardon were ypayd, redde *quod* debes.

quodcumque A 1; B 3; C 4
A. 8.159 *Quodcumque* ligaueris super terram &c.
B. 7.60 *Quodcumque* vultis vt faciant vobis homines facite eis.
B. 7.181 *Quodcumque* ligaueris super terram erit ligatum & in celis &c.
B.14.46 *Quodcumque* pecieritis a patre in nomine meo &c; Et alibi, Non in solo pane
C. 7.260 *Quodcumque* pecieritis in nomine meo dabitur enim vobis.
C. 9.327 *Quodcumque* ligaueris super terram erit ligatum & in celis.
C.15.244 *Quodcumque* pecieritis [a patre] in nomine meo dab[itur] enim
C.16.309 *Quodcumque* vultis vt faciant vobis homines, facite eis.

quomodo B 1
B.10.333 *Quomodo* cessauit exactor, quieuit tributum? contriuit dominus baculum

quoniam A 2; B 3; C 1
A. 8.103 Non timebo mala *quoniam* tu mecum es.
A. 8.123 *Quoniam* literaturam non cognoui, þat miʒte be þi teme.'
B. 7.121 Non timebo mala *quoniam* tu mecum es.
B.11.311 Psallite deo nostro; psallite *quoniam* rex terre deus Israel; psallite
B.14.215 Beati pauperes *quoniam* ipsorum est regnum celorum.
C.13.123 Psallite deo nostro, psallite; *quoniam* Rex [terre] deus, psallite sapienter.

quoque A 1; B 1
A.11.148 [Tu *quoque* fac simile: sic ars deluditur arte].
B.10.196 Tu *quoque* fac simile: sic ars deluditur arte.

quorum A 1; B 8; C 4
A. 3.228 In *quorum* manibus iniquitates sunt; dextera eorum repleta est muneribus.
B. 3.249 In *quorum* manibus iniquitates sunt; dextra eorum repleta est muneribus.
B. 5.507 And blew it wiþ Beati *quorum* remisse sunt iniquitates,
B. 9.62 *Quorum* deus venter est.
B.12.177 Beati *quorum* remisse sunt iniquitates & quorum tecta sunt &c.
B.12.177 Beati quorum remisse sunt iniquitates & *quorum* tecta sunt &c.
B.13.53 /And he brouʒte vs of Beati *quorum* of Beatus virres makyng,
B.13.54 Et *quorum* tecta sunt peccata
B.14.94 As Dauid seiþ in þe Sauter: et *quorum* tecta sunt peccata.
C. 3.118 In *quorum* manibus iniquitates sunt:
C. 7.152 *quorum* tecta sunt peccata,
C. 7.152 *quorum* tecta sunt peccata,
C.14.117 Beati *quorum* remisse sunt iniquitates &c.

raby B 2; C 2
B.16.151 'Aue, *raby*', quod þat Ribaud, and riȝt to hym he yede
B.18.50 'Aue, *raby*', quod þat rybaud and þrew reedes at hym.
C.18.168 'Aue *raby*,' quod th[at] ribaud[e]; and riht til hym [he] ȝede
C.20.50 'Aue, *raby*,' quod þat ribaud, and redes shotte vp to his yes.

racio B 3; C 3
B.10.256 Fides non habet meritum vbi humana *racio* prebet experimentum.
B.15.28 Thanne is *Racio* my riȝte name, reson on englissh;
B.15.39 dum scit mens est; dum recolit memoria est; dum iudicat *racio* est;
C.11.157 Fides non habet meritum vbi humana *racio* &c.
C.16.188 Thenne ys *racio* my rihte name, reson an englische;
C.16.201 [dum scit mens est]; dum recolit memoria est; dum iudicat *racio* est;

racionem C 1
C. 9.273 Redde *racionem* villicacionis or in arrerage fall!

radice B 1; C 1
B.15.118 intelligis quod vicium habet in *radice*, Ita cum videris populum
C.16.273 intelligis quod vicium habet in *radice*, Ita cum videris populum

ramis B 1
B.18.6 Reste me þere and rutte faste til *Ramis* palmarum.

rapis B 1
B.15.343 accipis pocius das quam accipis; Si autem non eges & accipis *rapis*.

rapiunt A 1; B 1; C 1
A.11.305 Ecce ipsi ydiot[e] *rapiunt* celum vbi nos sapientes
B.10.461 "Ecce ipsi ydiot[e] *rapiunt* celum vbi nos sapientes in inferno mergimur".
C.11.287 "Ecce ips[i] idiote *rapiunt* celum vbi nos sapientes in inferno mergimur".

re B 2; C 1
B.Pr.142 Nomen habet sine *re* nisi studet iura tenere.'
B.11.395 De *re* que te non molestat noli certare.
C.13.196 De *re* que te non molestat noli certare.

receperunt A 2; B 1; C 1
A. 3.64 Amen Amen [dico vobis *receperunt* mercedem suam].
A. 3.233 Amen Amen *rec[eperu]nt* mercedem suam.
B. 3.254 Amen amen *Rec[eperu]nt* mercedem suam.
C. 3.312 Amen Amen, Matheu seyth, Mercedem suam *rec[e]p[er]unt*.

recolit B 1; C 1
B.15.39 dum scit mens est; dum *recolit* memoria est; dum iudicat racio est;
C.16.201 [dum scit mens est]; dum *recolit* memoria est; dum iudicat racio est;

recordabor C 1
C. 7.147 omnes iniquitate[s] eius non *recordabor* ampli[us].

recordare B 1
B. 4.120 And Religiouse Romeris *Recordare* in hir cloistres

recordatiuum C 1
C. 3.344 Quia antelate rei *recordatiuum* est–

recte A 1; C 1
A.10.98 Cum *recte* viuas ne cures verba malorum,
C.11.18 Qui *recte* sapiunt lex iubet ire foras.

rectores C 1
C. 2.187 Wol Ryde vppon *Rectores* and ryche men deuoutours,

reddas C 1
C. 5.58 Non *reddas* malum pro malo.

redde B 4; C 5
B.19.187 To Piers pardon þe Plowman *redde* quod debes.
B.19.259 And Registrer to receyue *redde* quod debes.
B.19.390 To Piers pardon þe Plowman *redde* quod debes.'
B.20.308 And þat Piers [pardon] were ypayed, *redde* quod debes.
C. 9.273 *Redde* racionem villicacionis or in arrerage fall!
C.21.187 To Peres pardoun þe plouhman *Redde* quod debes.
C.21.259 And Registrer to reseyuen *Redde* quod debes.
C.21.390 To [Peres] pardon þe [plouhman] *Redde* quod debe[s].
C.22.308 And þat Peres pardon were ypayd, *redde* quod debes.

reddere A 1; B 1; C 1
A. 5.241 So rewe on þis robert þat *red[dere]* ne hauiþ,
B. 5.467 So rewe on þis Robbere þat *Reddere* ne haue
C. 6.321 So rewe on Robert þat *reddere* ne haue

reddet C 2
C. 5.32 *Reddet* vnicuique iuxta opera sua–
C.14.152 Et *reddet* vnicu[i]que iuxta opera sua.

reddit B 2; C 1
B.12.213 Qui[a] *reddit* vnicuique iuxta opera sua.

B.19.193 And rewarde hym right wel þat *reddit* quod debet,
C.21.193 And rewarde hym riht wel that *redd[it]* quod debet,

reddite A 2; B 2; C 2
A. 1.50 "*Reddite* cesari," quaþ god, "þat cesari befall[iþ],
A. 5.233 Robert þe robbour on *reddite* lokide,
B. 1.52 "*Reddite* Cesari", quod god, "þat Cesari bifalleþ,
B. 5.461 Roberd þe Robbere on *Reddite* loked,
C. 1.48 "*Reddite* cesari," sayde god, "þat cesar[i] byfalleth
C. 6.315 Robert the ruyflare on *reddite* lokede

redempcio B 1; C 1
B.18.149 Quia in Inferno nulla est *redempcio*.'
C.20.152 Quia in inferno nulla est *redempcio*.'

redempcionem C 1
C.15.116 Et visitauit & fecit *redempcionem* &c.

redemptor B 1; C 1
B.11.207 And after his resurexcion *Redemptor* was his name,
C.12.115 And aftur his resureccoun *redemptor* was his name

rediges B 1
B.14.131 domine in Ciuitate tua, et ad nichilum *rediges* &c.

regem B 1
B.15.576 neque vestimentum et ideo nolite constituere me *Regem*.

regere B 1
B.Pr.141 'Dum rex a *regere* dicatur nomen habere

reges A 1; B 1; C 1
A.11.296 Dum steter[it]is ante [*reges* &] presides nolite cogitare,
B.10.450 "[D]um steteritis ante *Reges* & presides [nolite cogitare]:
C.11.275 "Dum steteritis ante *Reges* vel presides &c:

regibus A 1; B 1
A. 8.46 Super innocentem munera non accipies; a *regibus* & principibus–
B. 7.44 A *Regibus* & principibus erit merces eorum.

regis B 3; C 2
B.Pr.133 O qui iura *regis* christi specialia regis,
B.Pr.133 O qui iura regis christi specialia *regis*,
B.Pr.145 'Precepta *Regis* sunt nobis vincula legis'.
C.Pr.154 O qui iura *regis* christi specialia regis,
C.Pr.154 O qui iura regis christi specialia *regis*,

regnat B 1; C 1
B.18.407 Culpat caro, purgat caro, *regnat* deus dei caro.
C.20.450 Culpat Caro, purgat Caro, *regnat* deus dei Caro.

regno A 1; B 1
A.11.196 Qui facit & docuerit magnus vocabitur in *regno* celorum.
B.13.118 Qui facit & docuerit magnus vocabitur in *regno* celorum.'

regnum B 2; C 3
B.14.215 Beati pauperes quoniam ipsorum est *regnum* celorum.
B.15.149 'Nisi efficiamini sicut paruuli non intrabitis in *regnum* celorum.
C. 5.98 Simile est *regnum* celorum thesauro abscondito in agro;
C.11.201 Ita possibile est diuiti intrare in *regn[um]* celorum sicut camelus &c.
C.19.232 Non omnis qui dicit domine, domine intrabit in *reg[num]* celorum &c.

regum A 1; B 1; C 2
A. 3.238 Ac reddist þou neuere *Regum*, þou recreiȝede mede,
B. 3.259 Ac reddestow neuere *Regum*, þow recrayed Mede,
C. 3.407 Ac hoso rat of *regum* rede me may of mede,
C. 3.413 As me ret in *regum* [of þe reuthe] of kynges,

rei C 1
C. 3.344 Quia antelate *rei* recordatiuum est–

reliquerit C 1
C.12.160 Quicumque *reli[querit]* patrem & matrem &c.

reliquit B 2; C 1
B.11.251 Domine, non est tibi cure quod soror mea *reliquit* me solam ministrare?
B.16.219 Maledictus homo qui non *reliquit* semen in Israel.
C.18.222 Maledictus homo qui non *reliquit* semen in Israel.

rem B 1; C 1
B.20.279 Non concupisces *rem* proximi tui.
C.22.279 Non concupisces *rem* proximi tui &c.

remecietur B 2
B. 1.178 Eadem mensura qua mensi fueritis *remecietur* vobis.
B.11.228 Eadem mensura qua mensi fueritis *remecietur* vobis.

remetietur C 1
C. 1.174 Eadem mensura qua mensi fueritis *Remetietur* vobis.

remisse B 2; C 2
B. 5.507   And blew it wiþ Beati quorum *remisse* sunt iniquitates,
B.12.177   Beati quorum *remisse* sunt iniquitates & quorum tecta sunt &c.
C. 7.152   And Blewe hit with beati quorum *remisse* sunt iniquitates &
C.14.117   Beati quorum *remisse* sunt iniquitates &c.

remissionem B 1; C 1
B.15.612   [Recorden it and rendren] it wiþ *remissionem* peccatorum
C.17.320   Recorden hit and re[n]d[r]en hit with *remissionem* peccatorum,

remittetur B 1
B.16.47   Videatis qui peccat in spiritum sanctum numquam *remittetur* &c;
           Hoc

remocio B 2; C 2
B.14.276   'Paupertas,' quod Pacience, 'est odibile bonum, *Remocio* curarum,
B.14.293   *Remocio* curarum.
C.16.116   'Paupertas,' quod pacience, 'est odibile bonum, *Remocio* curarum,
C.16.128   [*Remocio* curarum].

remordet B 1
B.10.266   Dogma tuum sordet cum te tua culpa *remordet*.

renatus B 1
B.11.82   Nisi quis *renatus* fuerit.

renunciaueritis C 1
C.12.171   Nisi *renunciaueritis* omnia que po[s]sid[etis] &c."

repleta A 1; B 1
A. 3.228   In quorum manibus iniquitates sunt; dextera eorum *repleta* est
           muneribus.
B. 3.249   In quorum manibus iniquitates sunt; dextra eorum *repleta* est
           muneribus.

repugnat B 1
B.16.47   est idem qui peccat per liberum arbitrium non *repugnat*.

requiescam B 1; C 1
B.18.187   And þat þis dede shal dure dormiam & *requiescam*.'
C.20.192   And that this dede shal duyre, dormiam & *requiescam*.'

rerum B 1
B.11.231   Melius est scrutari scelera nostra quam naturas *rerum*.

res B 2
B. 9.94   alibi, Perniciosus dispensator est qui *res* pauperum christi inutiliter
B.15.343   Quia sacrilegium est *res* pauperum non pauperibus dare. Item,
           peccatoribus

restituatur B 1
B. 5.273   Non dimittitur peccatum donec *restituatur* [a]blatum.

restitucione C 1
C. 6.257   To assoyle the of th[y] synne sine *restitucion[e]*:

resureccio B 1; C 1
B.18.370   That I drynke riȝt ripe Must, *Resureccio* mortuorum.
C.20.412   And [y] drynke riht rype m[o]st, *resureccio* mortuorum.

resurgens B 2; C 2
B.19.152   Christus [rex] *resurgens*, [and it aroos after],
B.19.160   In ech a compaignie þer she cam, Christus *resurgens*.
C.21.152   Christus [rex] *resurgens*, and hit aroos aftur,
C.21.160   In vch a companye þer he cam, christus *resurgens*.

resurreccionem resurectionem B 1; C 1
B.15.613   Carnis *resurreccionem* et vitam eternam amen.'
C.17.320   Carnis *resurect[i]o[n]em* & vitam eternam amen.'

retribuam A 1; B 3
A.11.255   For Michi vindictam et ego *retribuam*.
B. 6.226   Michi vindictam & ego *retribuam*.
B.10.209   Michi vindictam & ego *retribuam*.
B.10.374   [For michi vindictam et ego *retribuam*]:

retribuere C 1
C. 3.340   *Retribuere* dignare domine deus &c.'

reus B 2; C 1
B. 9.100   Qui offendit in vno in omnibus est *reus*.
B.11.309   Qui offendit in vno in omnibus est *reus*.
C.13.122   Qui offendit in vno in om[n]ibus est *reus*.

rex B 6; C 4
B.Pr.132   'Sum *Rex*, sum princeps; neutrum fortasse deinceps.
B.Pr.141   'Dum *rex* a regere dicatur nomen habere
B.Pr.196   Ve terre vbi puer *Rex* est &c.
B.11.311   Psallite deo nostro; psallite quoniam *rex* terre deus Israel; psallite
B.18.317   '*Rex* glorie,
B.19.152   Christus [*rex*] resurgens, [and it aroos after],
C.Pr.153   'Sum *Rex*, sum Princeps; neutrum fortasse deinceps.
C.Pr.209   Ve terre vbi puer *Rex*.

C.13.123   Psallite deo nostro, psallite; quoniam *Rex* [terre] deus, psallite
           sapienter.
C.21.152   Christus [*rex*] resurgens, and hit aroos aftur,

ridetis B 1; C 1
B.13.423   Ve vobis qui *ridetis* &c–
C. 7.83   Ve vobis qui *ridetis* &c–

robora B 1; C 1
B. 9.186   Dum sis vir fortis ne des tua *robora* scortis;
C.10.287   Dum sis vir fortis ne des tua *robora* scortis;

rugiet B 1; C 1
B.15.318   Num[quid], dicit Iob, *rugi[e]t* onager cum herbam habuerit aut
C.17.53   Nu[mquid], dicit Iop, *rugiet* onager cum habuerit herbam aut

sacerdocium B 3; C 3
B.15.118   Si *sacerdocium* integrum fuerit tota floret ecclesia; Si autem
B.15.118   Si *sacerdocium* fuerit in peccatis totus populus conuertitur ad
B.15.118   sine dubio *sacerdocium* eius non est sanum.
C.16.273   Si *sacerdocium* integrum fuerit tota floret ecclesia; Si Autem
C.16.273   Si *sacerdocium* fuerit in peccatis totus populus conuertitur ad
C.16.273   sine dubio *sacerdocium* eius non est sanum.

sacrilegium B 1
B.15.343   Quia *sacrilegium* est res pauperum non pauperibus dare. Item,
           peccatoribus

sagitte B 1; C 1
B.13.330   labor et dol[or]; Et alibi, Filij hominum dentes eorum arma &
           sagitte
C. 6.76   labor & dolor. Filij hominum dentes eorum Arma & *sagitte*

sal B 2
B.15.429   Vos estis *sal* terre &c.
B.15.431   Et si *sal* euanuerit in quo salietur?

salietur B 1
B.15.431   Et si sal euanuerit in quo *salietur*?

salutaueritis C 1
C. 9.123   Nemini *salutauerit[is]* per viam.

saluabis B 2; C 2
B. 5.509   'Homines & iumenta *saluabis* quemadmodum multiplicasti
           misericordiam
B.10.416   Homines & iumenta *saluabis*, domine &c.
C. 7.154   'Homines & iumenta *saluabis*; qu[e]madmodum multiplicasti
C.11.248   Homines & iumenta *saluabis* &c.

saluabitur B 3; C 3
B.12.281   And seide, '*Saluabitur* vix Iustus in die Iudicij;
B.12.282   Ergo *saluabitur*', quod he and seide na moore latyn.
B.13.19   And siþen how ymaginatif seide 'vix *saluabitur* [iustus]',
C.14.203   And saide, 'Vix *saluabitur* iustus in die iudicij;
C.14.204   Ergo *saluabitur*,' quod he and saide no more latyn.
C.15.22   That iustus bifore iesu in die iudicij non *saluabitur* bote vix helpe;

salui B 1
B.14.180   Conuertimini ad me & *salui* eritis.

saluo C 1
C. 4.165   Et *saluo* custodias set non cum carcer[a]tis.'

saluus A 1
A.11.234   Qui crediderit et baptizatus fuerit *saluus* erit.'

sancti B 1
B.16.88   Filius by þe fader wille and frenesse of spiritus *sancti*

sancto B 3; C 1
B. 5.278   Cum *sancto* sanctus eris: construwe me þis on englissh.'
B.17.151   Qui conceptus est de spiritu *sancto* &c.
B.19.422   At Auynoun among Iewes–Cum *sancto* sanctus eris &c–
C.21.422   At Auenon among iewes–cum *sancto* sanctus eris &c–

sanctorum B 5; C 2
B.11.161   The legend[a] *sanctorum* yow lereþ more largere þan I yow telle.
B.11.220   Of logyk [ne] of lawe in legenda *sanctorum*
B.15.269   [Lo]! in legenda *sanctorum*, þe lif of holy Seintes,
B.15.600   Cum sanctus *sanctorum* veniat cessabit vnxio vestra.
B.18.109   Cum veniat sanctus *sanctorum* cessabit vnxio vestra.'
C.17.157   Louyeth nat þat lord aryht as by þe legende *sanctorum*
C.20.112   Cum veniat sanctus *sanctorum* cessa[bi]t &c.'

sanctum B 4; C 4
B.15.611   Til þei kouþe speke and spelle et in Spiritum *sanctum*,
B.16.47   Videatis qui peccat in spiritum *sanctum* numquam remittetur &c;
           Hoc
B.17.200   Qui peccat in spiritu[m] *sanct[um]* &c,
B.17.201   For he prikeþ god as in þe pawme þat peccat in spiritu[m]
           sanct[um].
C. 3.481   And saresines for þat syhte shal syng Credo in spiritum *sanctum*

C.17.319 Til they couthe speke and spele et in spiritum *sanctum*,
C.19.166 Qui peccat in spiritu[m] *sanct[um]* &c,
C.19.167 For he priketh god as in [the] paume that peccat in spiritum
          sanctum.

sanctus B 8; C 7
B. 5.278 Cum sancto *sanctus* eris: construwe me þis on englissh.'
B.10.246 Deus pater, deus filius, deus spiritus *sanctus:*
B.13.57   Pro hac orabit ad te omnis *sanctus* in tempore oportuno;
B.15.600 Cum *sanctus* sanctorum veniat cessabit vnxio vestra.
B.16.90   And þanne spak spiritus *sanctus* in Gabrielis mouþe
B.17.212 So dooþ þe Sire and þe sone and also spiritus *sanctus*
B.18.109 Cum veniat *sanctus* sanctorum cessabit vnxio vestra.'
B.19.422 At Auynoun among Iewes–Cum sancto *sanctus* eris &c–
C. 3.406 Nominatiuo, pater & filius & spiritus *sanctus.*
C.15.60   pro h[a]c orabit [ad te] omnis *sanctus* in tempore oportuno.
C.18.51   The whiche is spiritus *sanctus* and sothfaste bileue
C.18.120 Filius by þe fadres wille fley with spiritus *sanctus*
C.18.123 And thenne spak spiritus *sanctus* in gabrieles mouthe
C.20.112 Cum veniat *sanctus* sanctorum cessa[bi]t &c.'
C.21.422 At Auenon among iewes–cum sancto *sanctus* eris &c–

sanguinem B 1; C 1
B.17.293 Vindica *sanguinem* iustorum."
C.19.274 Vindic[a] *sanguinem* iustorum."

sanis B 1
B.16.110 Non est *sanis* opus medicus set in[firmis].

sanitatis B 2; C 2
B.14.276 possessio sine calumpnia, donum dei, *sanit[atis]* mater,
B.14.303 *Sani[tatis]* mater.
C.16.116 posessio sine calumpnia, donum dei, *sanitatis* mater,
C.16.138 *Sanitatis* mater.

sanum B 1; C 1
B.15.118 sine dubio sacerdocium eius non est *sanum.*
C.16.273 sine dubio sacerdocium eius non est *sanum.*

sapere A 1; B 3; C 2
A.11.74   Non plus *sapere* quam oportet.
B.10.121 Non plus *sapere* quam oportet.
B.15.69   That is Non plus *sapere* quam oportet sapere.
B.15.69   That is Non plus sapere quam oportet *sapere.*
C.16.229 "Non plus *sapere*," saide þe wyse, [laste synne of pruyde wexe,]
C.16.230 "Quam oportet *sapere.*"

sapiencia B 3; C 2
B.12.57   *Sapiencia* inflat &c];
B.12.138 *Sapiencia* huius mundi stulticia est apud deum.
B.16.36   Thanne sette I to þe secounde pil, *sapiencia* dei patris,
C.14.83   *Sapiencia* huius mundi stul[t]icia est apud deum.
C.18.40   Thenne sette y þe seconde planke, *sapiencia* dei patris,

sapiencie A 1; B 3; C 2
A.10.81   Inicium *sapiencie* timor domini.
B. 9.96   Inicium *sapiencie* timor domini.
B.14.276 absque sollicitudine semita, *sapiencie* temperatrix, negocium sine
B.14.312 *Sapiencie* temperatrix.
C.16.116 absque soli[ci]tudine semita, *sapiencie* temp[e]ratrix, negocium
          sine
C.16.146 [*Sapiencie* temperatrix].

sapiens C 2
C. 9.127 Si quis videtur *sapiens*, fiet stultus vt sit sapiens.
C. 9.127 Si quis videtur sapiens, fiet stultus vt sit *sapiens.*

sapienter B 2; C 2
B.11.311 psallite quoniam rex terre deus Israel; psallite *sapien[ter].*
B.11.313 That crouneþ swiche goddes kny3tes, þat konneþ no3t *sapienter*
C.13.123 Psallite deo nostro, psallite; quoniam Rex [terre] deus, psallite
          sapienter.
C.13.125 That crouneth suche goddes knyhtes that conne [nat] *sapienter*

sapientes A 1; B 3; C 2
A.11.305 Ecce ipsi ydiot[e] rapiunt celum vbi nos *sapientes*
B. 8.93   Libenter suffertis insipientes cum sitis ipsi *sapientes:*
B.10.436 [Sunt] iusti atque *sapientes*, & opera eorum in manu dei sunt &c.
B.10.461 "Ecce ipsi ydiot[e] rapiunt celum vbi nos *sapientes* in inferno
          mergimur".
C.11.271 Sunt iusti atque *sapientes* & opera eorum in manu dei sunt &c.
C.11.287 "Ecce ips[i] idiote rapiunt celum vbi nos *sapientes* in inferno
          mergimur".

sapiunt C 2
C.11.18   Qui *sapiunt* nugas & crim[ina] lege vocantur;
C.11.18   Qui recte *sapiunt* lex iubet ire foras.

satis B 1
B. 7.87   *Satis* diues est qui non indiget pane.

satisfaccio B 1; C 2
B.14.21   *Satisfaccio.*
C.16.31   And [operis *satisfaccio*] for soules paieth and alle synnes quyteth.
C.16.31   Cordis contricio, Oris confessio, Operis *satisfaccio:*

scandala A 1; B 1
A.11.154 Necesse est vt veniant *scandala.*
B.16.157 Necesse est vt veniant *scandala*; ve homini illi per quem
          scandalum venit.

scandalum B 1; C 1
B.16.157 Necesse est vt veniant scandala; ve homini illi per quem
          scandalum venit.
C.18.174 Ve homini illi per quem *scand[a]lum* venit.

scelera B 1
B.11.231 Melius est scrutari *scelera* nostra quam naturas rerum.

sciant B 1; C 1
B. 2.74   '*Sciant* presentes & futuri &c.
C. 2.81   *Sciant* presentes & futuri &c.

sciencie B 1; C 1
B.15.63   *Sciencie* appetitus hominem inmortalitatis gloria[m] spoliauit.
C.16.225 *Sciencie* appetitus hominem inmortalitatis gloriam spoliauit.

scientes B 1; C 1
B.12.56   *Scient[es]* et non facient[es] varijs flagellis vapulab[un]t.
C.14.18   *Scient[es]* & non facient[es] varijs flagellis vapulab[unt].

scimus B 2
B.12.65   Quod *scimus* loquimur, quod vidimus testamur.
B.12.66   Of quod *scimus* comeþ Clergie, [a] konnynge of heuene,

scit B 1; C 1
B.15.39   dum *scit* mens est; dum recolit memoria est; dum iudicat racio est;
C.16.201 [dum *scit* mens est]; dum recolit memoria est; dum iudicat racio
          est;

sciunt B 1; C 1
B.11.3   And seide 'Multi multa *sciunt* et seipsos nesciunt'.
C.11.163 And saide, 'multi multa *sciunt* & seipsos nessiunt.'

scortis B 1; C 1
B. 9.186 Dum sis vir fortis ne des tua robora *scortis*;
C.10.287 Dum sis vir fortis ne des tua robora *scortis*;

scribantur A 1; B 1; C 1
A. 7.68   Et cum iustis non *scribantur.*
B. 6.76   Quia cum iustis non *scribantur.*
C. 8.78   Quia cum iustis non *scribantur.*

scribitur B 1; C 1
B. 9.186 *Scribitur* in portis, meretrix est ianua mortis.
C.10.287 *Scribitur* in portis, meretrix est ianua mortis.

scripturas B 2; C 2
B.15.60   "Beatus est", seiþ Seint Bernard, "qui *scripturas* legit
B.18.112 And þere I sau3 sooþly, secundum *scripturas*,
C.16.222 "Beatus," saith seynt Bernard, "qui *scripturas* legit
C.20.115 And there y seyh sothly, secundum *scripturas*,

scrutari B 1
B.11.231 Melius est *scrutari* scelera nostra quam naturas rerum.

scrutator B 1; C 1
B.15.55   *scrutator* est maiestatis opprimitur a gloria.
C.16.217 Sic [qui] *scrutator* est magestatis opprim[e]tur a gloria.

sculptilia B 1
B.15.81   Confundantur omnes qui adorant *sculptilia*; Et alibi, Vt quid
          diligitis

se A 1; B 1; C 1
A.10.120 Qui *se* humiliat exaltabitur &c.
B.13.73   Vnusquisque a fratre *se* custodiat quia vt dicitur periculum est in
          falsis
C.20.259 Non visurum *se* mortem &c.

secrete B 1; C 1
B.11.88   Non oderis fratres *secrete* in corde tuo set publice argue illos.
C.12.34   Non oderis fratrem *secrete* in corde &c.

secula B 1; C 1
B.18.421 Pees, and pees h[i]re, per *secula* seculorum:
C.20.464 Pees, and pees here, per *secula* seculorum:

seculi C 1
C.14.32   Vultus huius *seculi* sunt subiecti v[u]ltibus celestibus.

seculo B 1
B.10.26   Ecce ipsi peccatores! habundantes in *seculo* obtinuerunt diuicias.

seculorum B 1; C 1
B.18.421 Pees, and pees h[i]re, per secula *seculorum*:
C.20.464 Pees, and pees here, per secula *seculorum*:

secunda B 1
B.12.9 Si non in prima vigilia nec in *secunda* &c.

secundum B 3; C 3
B. 9.67 Amen dico vobis, nescio vos; Et alibi, Et dimisi eos *secundum*
          desideria
B.16.99 Ecce ancilla domini; fiat michi [*secundum* verbum tuum]'.
B.18.112 And þere I sauȝ sooþly, *secundum* scripturas,
C.10.165 Et dimisi eos *secundum* desideria eorum.
C.15.271 Dabo tibi *secundum* peticionem tuam.
C.20.115 And there y seyh sothly, *secundum* scripturas,

sed set B 9; C 7
B. 5.498 Non veni vocare iustos *set* peccatores ad penitenciam.
B.10.343 Dilige denarium *set* parce dilige formam.
B.11.88 Non oderis fratres secrete in corde tuo *set* publice argue illos.
B.12.147 *Set* non erat ei locus in diuersorio, et pauper non habet
          diuersorium.
B.12.286 Aduenit ignis diuinus non comburens *set* illuminans &c.
B.14.46 viuit homo *set* in omni verbo quod procedit de ore dei.'
B.16.110 Non est sanis opus medicus *set* in[firmis].
B.18.349 Non veni soluere legem *set* adimplere.
B.19.479 Omnia tua sunt ad defendendum *set* non ad deprehendendum.'
C. 4.165 Et saluo custodias *set* non cum carcer[a]tis.'
C. 7.138 Non veni vocare iustos *set* peccatores &c.
C. 9.213 Non licet uobis legem voluntati, *set* voluntat[em] coniungere legi.
C.11.213 Nec michi nec tibi, *set* diuidatur.
C.14.208 A[d]uenit ignis diuinus non comburens *set* illuminans &c.
C.20.395 Non veni soluere legem *set* adimplere.
C.21.479 Omnia [tua sunt] ad defendendum *sed* non ad deprehendendum.'

sede B 1; C 2
B.15.552 Deposuit potentes de *sede* &c.
C. 1.122 Dixit dominus domino meo, *sede* a dextris meis.
C.17.215 Deposuit potentes de *sede* &c.

sedens B 1; C 1
B.18.36 Thanne cam Pilatus with muche peple, *sedens* pro tribunali,
C.20.35 Thenne cam Pilatus with moche peple, *sedens* pro tribunali,

sederunt A 1; C 1
A.11.223 Super cathedram moisi *sederunt* principes.
C. 8.86 Super Cathedram moysi *sede[runt]* &c.

seipsos B 1; C 1
B.11.3 And seide 'Multi multa sciunt et *seipsos* nesciunt'.
C.11.163 And saide, 'multi multa sciunt & *seipsos* nessiunt.'

semen B 3; C 2
B. 1.31 Vt seruare possimus de patre nostro *semen*.
B. 7.89 Iunior fui etenim senui, & non vidi iustum derelictum ne[c] *semen*
          eius
B.16.219 Maledictus homo qui non reliquit *semen* in Israel.
C. 1.30 vt seruare possimus de patre nostro *semen*.
C.18.222 Maledictus homo qui non reliquit *semen* in Israel.

semini B 1
B.16.242 Quam olim Abrahe promisisti & *semini* eius.

semita B 2; C 2
B.14.276 absque sollicitudine *semita*, sapiencie temperatrix, negocium sine
B.14.309 Forþi seiþ Seneca Paupertas est absque sollicitudine *semita*.
C.16.116 absque soli[ci]tudine *semita*, sapiencie temp[e]ratrix, negocium
         sine
C.16.143 Pauper[tas] est absque solicitudine *semita*.

sensus B 2; C 2
B.15.29 And whan I feele þat folk telleþ my firste name is *sensus*,
B.15.39 dum sentit *sensus* est; dum amat Amor est; dum negat vel consentit
C.16.189 And when y fele þat folke telleth my furste name is *sensus*
C.16.201 dum sentit *sensus* est; dum Amat Amor est; dum declina[t] de malo

sentit B 1; C 1
B.15.39 dum *sentit* sensus est; dum amat Amor est; dum negat vel consentit
C.16.201 dum *sentit* sensus est; dum Amat Amor est; dum declina[t] de malo

senui B 1; C 1
B. 7.89 Iunior fui etenim *senui*, & non vidi iustum derelictum ne[c] semen
         eius
C. 9.163 Iunior fui, [et]enim *senui*; e[t] alibi: infirmata est vertus mea
         paupertate.

sepcies A 1; B 1; C 1
A. 9.16 '*Sepcies* in die cadit iustus.
B. 8.20 '*Sepcies* in die cadit Iustus.
C.10.21 And saide, 'sothly *sepcies* in die ca[d]it iust[u]s,

sequuntur B 1; C 1
B.14.213 Opera enim illorum *sequ[u]ntur* illos,
C.16.54 Opera [enim ill]orum *sequ[u]ntur* illos,

sere B 1; C 1
B.Pr.136 Qualia vis metere, talia grana *sere*.
C.Pr.157 Qualia vis metere, talia grana *sere*.

seritur B 1; C 1
B.Pr.138 Si *seritur* pietas de pietate metas.'
C.Pr.159 Si *seritur* pietas de pietate metas.'

seruando C 1
C.17.285 Fer, trahe, punge gregem, *seruando* per omnia legem–

seruare B 1; C 1
B. 1.31 Vt *seruare* possimus de patre nostro semen.
C. 1.30 Inebriemus eum vino dormiamusque cum eo vt *seruare* possimus

seruate C 1
C. 8.90 Omnia que dicunt facite & *seruate*.

seruire B 1; C 1
B.13.312 Et alibi, Nemo potest duobus dominis *seruire*.
C. 6.60 nemo potest duobus dominis *seruire*.'

seruo B 1; C 1
B.18.399 Non intres in Iudicium cum *seruo* tuo.
C.20.442 Non intres in iudicium cum *seruo* tuo.

seruus A 1; B 4; C 3
A. 7.223 *Seruus* nequam had a nam, & for he nolde it vsen.
B. 5.269 *Seruus* es alterius [cum] fercula pinguia queris;
B. 6.239 *Seruus* nequam hadde a Mnam and for he [n]olde [it vse]
B.11.204 Qui facit peccatum *seruus* est peccati.
B.13.312 Si hominibus placerem christi *seruus* non essem; Et alibi, Nemo
         potest
C. 6.60 Si hominibus placerem christi *seruus* non essem; nemo potest
         duobus
C. 6.293 *Seruus* [es] alterius cum fercula pingu[i]a queris;
C.12.112 Qui facit peccatum *seruus* est peccati.

set > sed

seudopropheta > pseudopropheta

si A 1; B 21; C 15
A. 8.102 & seide '*Si* ambulauero in medio umbre mortis
B.Pr.137 *Si* ius nudatur nudo de iure metatur;
B.Pr.138 *Si* seritur pietas de pietate metas.'
B. 7.120 And seide, '*Si* ambulauero in medio vmbre mortis
B.10.89 *Si* tibi sit copia habundanter tribue; si autem exiguum illud
         impertiri stude
B.10.89 Si tibi sit copia habundanter tribue; *si* autem exiguum illud
         impertiri stude
B.10.266 *Si* culpare velis culpabilis es[se] cauebis;
B.10.359 *Si* cum christo sur[r]existis &c,
B.11.274 *Si* vis perfectus esse vade & vende [&c].
B.11.416 Philosophus esses *si* tacuisses.
B.12.9 *Si* non in prima vigilia nec in secunda &c.
B.12.293 Et alibi, *si* ambulauero in medio vmbre mortis.
B.13.312 *Si* hominibus placerem christi seruus non essem; Et alibi, Nemo
         potest
B.14.60 *Si* quis amat christum mundum non diligit istum.
B.15.118 *Si* sacerdocium integrum fuerit tota floret ecclesia; Si autem
B.15.118 *Si* autem corruptum fuerit omnium fides marcida est. Si
B.15.118 *Si* sacerdocium fuerit in peccatis totus populus conuertitur ad
B.15.343 dare est demonibus immolare. Item, monache, *si* indiges &
B.15.343 accipis pocius das quam accipis; *Si* autem non eges & accipis rapis.
B.15.343 Porro non indiget monachus *si* habeat quod nature sufficit.
B.15.431 Et *si* sal euanuerit in quo salietur?
B.17.261 *Si* linguis hominum loquar &c.
C.Pr.158 [*Si* ius nudatur nudo de iure metatur];
C.Pr.159 *Si* seritur pietas de pietate metas.'
C. 3.329 So god gyueth no [grace] þat "*si*" [ne] is the glose
C. 6.60 *Si* hominibus placerem christi seruus non essem; nemo potest
         duobus
C. 9.127 *Si* quis videtur sapiens, fiet stultus vt sit sapiens.
C.11.69 *Si* tibi sit copia habundanter tribue; Si Autem exiguum illud
C.11.69 Si tibi sit copia habundanter tribue; *Si* Autem exiguum illud
C.12.167 *Si* vis perfectus esse vade & vende &c.
C.13.17 And for a song in his sorwe, "*si* bona accepimus a domino &c,
C.13.224 Philosophus esses *si* tacuisses; & alibi: Locutum me aliquando
C.15.259 *Si* quis Amat christum mundum non diligit istum.
C.16.273 *Si* sacerdocium integrum fuerit tota floret ecclesia; Si Autem
C.16.273 *Si* Autem corupt[um] fuerit omnium f[i]des marcida est. Si
C.16.273 *Si* sacerdocium fuerit in peccatis totus populus conuertitur ad
C.19.227 *Si* linguis hominum loqu[a]r &c.

sibi B 1; C 1
B.18.421 Misericordia & veritas obuiauerunt *sibi*; Iusticia & pax osculate
              su[nt]
C.20.464 Misericordia & veritas obuiauerunt *sibi*; Iusticia & pax osculate
              sunt.

sic A 1; B 4; C 3
A.11.148 [Tu quoque fac simile: *sic* ars deluditur arte].
B.10.196 Tu quoque fac simile; *sic* ars deluditur arte.
B.15.55   And seiþ, Sicut qui mel comedit multum non est ei bonum, *Sic* qui
B.15.118 *sic* de templo omne malum procedit. Si sacerdocium integrum
              fuerit
B.19.161 *Sic* oportet Christum pati & intrare &c;
C.16.217 *Sic* [qui] scrutator est magestatis opprim[e]tur a gloria.
C.16.273 *sic* de templo omne malum procedit. Si sacerdocium integrum
              fuerit
C.21.161 *Sic* [oportet] christum pati & intrare &c;

sicientes B 1; C 1
B.11.120 O vos omnes *sicientes* venite &c,
C.12.55   /O vos omnes *sicientes* venite ad aquas

sicio C 1
C.20.408 *S[i]cio.*

sicut A 1; B 5; C 6
A.11.242 Dilige deum &c, Et proximum tuum *sicut* teipsum.
B.15.55   And seiþ, *Sicut* qui mel comedit multum non est ei bonum, Sic qui
B.15.118 *Sicut* de templo omne bonum progreditur, sic de templo omne
B.15.118 *Sicut* cum videris arborem pallidam & marcidam intelligis quod
B.15.149 'Nisi efficiamini *sicut* paruuli non intrabitis in regnum celorum.
B.15.219 Nolite fieri *sicut* ypocrite tristes &c.
C.11.201 Ita possibile est diuiti intrare in regn[um] celorum *sicut* camelus
              &c.
C.16.217 And sayth, *sicut* qui mel comedit multum non est ei bonum; Sic
C.16.273 *Sicut* de templo omne bonum progreditur, sic de templo omne
C.16.273 *Sicut* cum videri[s] Arborem pallidam & marcidam intelligis quod
C.16.298 Nisi efficiamini *sicut* paruuli &c,
C.16.344 Nolite [fieri *sicut* ypocrite tristes].

silue A 1; B 1; C 1
A.11.55   Ecce audiuimus eam in effrata, inuenimus eam in campis *silue*.
B.10.69   Ecce audiuimus eam in effrata; inuenimus eam in campis *silue*.
C.11.49   Ecce Audiuimus eam in Effrata; [inuenimus eam in campis *silue*].

simile A 1; B 1; C 1
A.11.148 [Tu quoque fac *simile*: sic ars deluditur arte].
B.10.196 Tu quoque fac *simile*; sic ars deluditur arte.
C. 5.98   *Simile* est regnum celorum thesauro abscondito in agro;

similis B 4; C 2
B. 1.119 Ponam pedem in aquilone & *similis* ero altissimo.
B.10.291 Existimasti inique quod ero tui *similis*; arguam te & statuam contra
              faciem
B.11.95   Existimasti inique quod ero tui *similis* &c.
B.15.51   Ponam pedem meum in aquilone & *similis* ero altissimo.
C. 1.111 Ponam pedem meum in Aquilone & *similis* ero altissimo.'
C.12.29   Existimasti inique quod ero t[u]i *similis*; Arguam te & statuam

similitudinem B 1
B. 5.486 Faciamus hominem ad ymaginem [et *similitudinem*] nostram;

simulat A 1; B 1
A.11.147 Qui sim[u]lat verbis, nec corde est fidus amicus,
B.10.195 Qui *simulat* verbis [nec] corde est fidus amicus,

sine B 10; C 12
B.Pr.142 Nomen habet *sine* re nisi studet iura tenere.'
B. 1.187 Fides *sine* operibus mortua est &c.
B. 3.237 Qui ingreditur *sine* macula & operatur Iusticiam.
B.11.404 Caton acordeþ þerwiþ: Nemo *sine* crimine viuit.'
B.12.207 De peccato propiciato noli esse *sine* metu.
B.14.276 possessio *sine* calumpnia, donum dei, sanit[atis] mater,
B.14.276 negocium *sine* dampno, Incerta fortuna, absque sollicitudine
B.14.296 Possessio *sine* calumpnia.
B.14.315 Negocium *sine* dampno.
B.15.118 *sine* dubio sacerdocium eius non est sanum.
C. 1.183 Fides *sine* operibus mortua est.
C. 6.257 To assoyle the of th[y] synne *sine* restitucion[e]:
C. 9.120 [Q]uando misi vos *sine* pane & pera &c.
C.13.212 Caton acordeth therwith: nemo *sine* crimine viuit.'
C.14.42   Quis vestrum *sine* peccato est.
C.14.146 De peccato propiciato noli esse *sine* metu.
C.16.116 posessio *sine* calumpnia, donum dei, sanitatis mater,
C.16.116 negocium *sine* dampno, Incerta fortuna, absque solicitudine
C.16.132 [Possessio *sine* calumpnia].
C.16.149 Negocium *sine* dampno.
C.16.273 *sine* dubio sacerdocium eius non est sanum.

C.16.359 Beatus est diues *sine* macula.

sinistra A 1; B 1; C 1
A. 3.54   And seiþ Nesciat *sinist[ra]* quid faciat dexter[a].
B. 3.72   Nesciat *sinistra* quid faciat dextra:
C. 3.74   Nesciat [*sinistra*] quid faciat [dextera]:

sintilla B 1; C 1
B. 5.283 Omnis iniquitas quantum ad misericordiam dei est quasi *sintilla* in
              medio
C. 6.338 Omnis iniquitas quoad misericordiam dei est quasi *sintilla* in
              medio maris.

sis B 2; C 2
B. 9.186 Dum *sis* vir fortis ne des tua robora scortis;
B.19.296 Esto forti animo cum *sis* dampnatus inique.
C.10.287 Dum *sis* vir fortis ne des tua robora scortis;
C.21.296 Esto forti Animo cum *sis* dampnatus inique.

sit B 2; C 4
B. 7.75   *Sit* elemosina tua in manu tua donec studes cui des.
B.10.89   Si tibi *sit* copia habundanter tribue; si autem exiguum illud
              impertiri stude
C. 9.127 Si quis videtur sapiens, fiet stultus vt *sit* sapiens.
C.11.69   Si tibi *sit* copia habundanter tribue; Si Autem exiguum illud
C.17.40   Videte ne furtum *sit*: & alibi: meli[u]s est mori quam male viuere
              &c.
C.17.285 In baculi forma *sit*, presul, hec tibi norma;

sitis A 1; B 4; C 1
A. 8.113 Ne soliciti *sitis* he seiþ in his gospel,
B. 7.131 Ne soliciti *sitis* he seiþ in þe gospel,
B. 8.93   Libenter suffertis insipientes cum *sitis* ipsi sapientes:
B.14.33   Ne soliciti *sitis* &c; Volucres celi deus pascit &c; pacientes vincunt
              &c.'
B.15.88   That seide to hise disciples, "Ne *sitis* personarum acceptores".
C.16.241 Ne *sitis* acceptores personarum.

sobrius B 1; C 1
B. 5.186 Esto *sobrius*!' he seide and assoiled me after,
C. 6.168 Esto *sobrius*!' he saide, and assoiled hym aftur

sola B 2; C 1
B.11.81   *Sola* contricio [delet peccatum]–
B.15.389 That *sola* fides sufficit to saue wiþ lewed peple.
C.17.121 That *sola* fides sufficit to saue with lewede peple.

solam B 1
B.11.251 Domine, non est tibi cure quod soror mea reliquit me *solam*
              ministrare?

soli B 1; C 2
B.18.378 Tibi *soli* peccaui &c.
C.20.316 Ve *soli*!–
C.20.420 Tibi *soli* peccaui & malum coram te feci.

soliciti A 1; B 2
A. 8.113 Ne *soliciti* sitis he seiþ in his gospel,
B. 7.131 Ne *soliciti* sitis he seiþ in þe gospel,
B.14.33   Ne *soliciti* sitis &c; Volucres celi deus pascit &c; pacientes vincunt
              &c.'

solito B 1; C 1
B.18.408 Clarior est *solito* post maxima nebula phebus;
C.20.451 Clarior est *solito* [post maxima nebula phebus];

sollicitudine solicitudine B 4; C 4
B.14.276 absque *sollicitudine* semita, sapiencie temperatrix, negocium sine
B.14.276 Incerta fortuna, absque *sollicitudine* felicitas.'
B.14.309 Forþi seiþ Seneca Paupertas est absque *sollicitudine* semita.
B.14.320 Absque *sollicitudine* felicitas.
C.16.116 absque *soli[ci]tudine* semita, sapiencie temp[e]ratrix, negocium
              sine
C.16.116 Incerta fortuna, absque *solicitudine* felicitas.'
C.16.143 Pauper[tas] est absque *solicitudine* semita.
C.16.155 Absque *solicitudine* felicitas.

solo B 1; C 2
B.14.46   Quodcumque pecieritis a patre in nomine meo &c; Et alibi, Non in
              solo pane
C. 5.86   Non de *solo*,' y sayde, 'for sothe viuit homo,
C.15.244 vobis. Et alibi: Non in *solo* pane viuit homo &c.'

solus C 1
C.18.190 And, sondry to se vpon, *solus* deus he hoteth.'

soluere B 1; C 1
B.18.349 Non veni *soluere* legem set adimplere.
C.20.395 Non veni *soluere* legem set adimplere.

sompnia A 1; B 1
A. 8.134 *Sompnia* ne cures.

B. 7.156   To sette sadnesse in Songewarie for *sompnia* ne cures.

sompnium B 1; C 1
B.14.131   velud *sompn[i]um* surgencium domine in Ciuitate tua,
C.15.306   velud *sompn[i]um* surgencium &c.

sordet B 1
B.10.266   Dogma tuum *sordet* cum te tua culpa remordet.

soror B 1; C 1
B.11.251   Domine, non est tibi cure quod *soror* mea reliquit me solam
           ministrare?
C.12.138   Domine, non est tibi cur[e] quod *soror* &c?

sortitur B 1; C 1
B.15.39   Anima pro diuersis accionibus diuersa nomina *sortitur*: dum
          viuificat
C.16.201   Anima pro diuersis [acc]ionibus diuersa nomina *sortitur*: dum

specialia B 1; C 1
B.Pr.133   O qui iura regis christi *specialia* regis,
C.Pr.154   O qui iura regis christi *specialia* regis,

spera B 2; C 1
B.11.287   *Spera* in deo spekeþ of preestes þat haue no spendyng siluer,
B.15.180   And if he soupeþ eteþ but a sop of *Spera* in deo.
C.13.101   For *spera* in deo speketh of prestis þat han no spendynge suluer

spernit B 2; C 2
B.13.440   Qui vos *spernit* me spernit.
B.13.440   Qui vos spernit me *spernit*.
C. 7.100   Qui vos *spernit* me spernit.
C. 7.100   Qui vos spernit me *spernit*.

spes B 7; C 6
B.12.29   Fides, *spes*, caritas, et maior horum &c.
B.17.1   'I am *Spes*, [a spie', quod he], 'and spire after a Knyght
B.17.35   And now com[s]eþ *Spes* and spekeþ, þat [haþ] aspied þe lawe,
B.17.48   Go þi gate!' quod I to *Spes*, 'so me god helpe,
B.17.84   And *Spes* spakliche hym spedde, spede if he my3te,
B.17.91   How þat feiþ flei3 awey and *Spes* his felawe boþe
B.17.103   Saue feiþ and [myselue and] *Spes* [his felawe],
C.19.1   'I am *spes*, a spie,' quod he, 'and spere aftur a kny3te
C.19.36   And now cometh this *sp[es* and speketh] that hath aspyed þe lawe,
C.19.46   Go thy gate!' quod y to *spes*; 'so me god helpe,
C.19.53   Bothe abraham and *sp[e]s* and he mette at ones
C.19.80   Bothe fayth and his felawe *spes* folewede faste aftur
C.19.97   As faith and his felawe *spes* enfourmede me bothe,

spinis B 1; C 1
B. 9.155   Numquam collig[unt] de *spinis* vua[s] nec de tribulis ficus.
C.10.244   Numquam collig[unt] de *spinis* vuas; Et Alibi: Bon[a] Arbor

spirat B 2; C 2
B.12.63   Spiritus vbi vult *spirat*.
B.15.39   dum negat vel consentit consciencia est; dum *spirat* spiritus est.'
C.14.27   Spiritus vbi vult *spirat*.
C.16.201   dum negat vel consentit consiencia est; dum *sp[i]rat* spiritus est.'

spiritu B 1
B.17.151   Qui conceptus est de *spiritu* sancto &c.

spiritualibus B 1
B.11.58   Pena pecuniaria non sufficit pro *spiritualibus* delictis.

spiritum B 4; C 4
B.15.611   Til þei kouþe speke and spelle et in *Spiritum* sanctum,
B.16.47   Videatis qui peccat in *spiritum* sanctum numquam remittetur &c;
          Hoc
B.17.200   Qui peccat in *spiritu[m]* sanct[um] &c,
B.17.201   For he prikeþ god as in þe pawme þat peccat in *spiritu[m]*
          sanct[um].
C. 3.481   And saresines for þat syhte shal syng Credo in *spiritum* sanctum
C.17.319   Til they couthe speke and spele et in *spiritum* sanctum,
C.19.166   Qui peccat in *spiritu[m]* sanct[um] &c,
C.19.167   For he priketh god as in [the] paume that peccat in *spiritum*
          sanctum.

spiritus B 32; C 32
B.10.246   Deus pater, deus filius, deus *spiritus* sanctus:
B.12.63   *Spiritus* vbi vult spirat.
B.15.36   Thanne am I spirit spechelees; *Spiritus* þanne ich hatte.
B.15.39   dum negat vel consentit consciencia est; dum spirat *spiritus* est.'
B.16.88   Filius by þe fader wille and frenesse of *spiritus* sancti
B.16.90   And þanne spak *spiritus* sanctus in Gabrielis mouþe
B.16.223   *Spiritus* procedens a patre & filio &c,
B.17.212   So dooþ þe Sire and þe sone and also *spiritus* sanctus
B.19.201   Oon *Spiritus* paraclitus to Piers and to hise felawes.
B.19.206   *Spiritus* paraclitus ouerspradde hem alle.
B.19.210   Welcome hym and worshipe hym wiþ Veni creator *Spiritus*,'
B.19.276   *Spiritus* prudencie þe firste seed highte,

B.19.281   The seconde seed highte *Spiritus* temperancie.
B.19.289   The þridde seed þat Piers sew was *Spiritus* fortitudinis,
B.19.297   The ferþe seed þat Piers sew was *Spiritus* Iusticie,
B.19.301   [Shal] nou3t ben espied [þoru3] *Spiritus* Iusticie.
B.19.302   *Spiritus* Iusticie spareþ no3t to spille [þe] gilty,
B.19.397   By Iesu! for al youre langlynge, wiþ *Spiritus* Iusticie,
B.19.402   Of *Spiritus* Iusticie þow spekest muche on ydel.'
B.19.405   But þow lyue by loore of *Spiritus* Iusticie,
B.19.455   For *Spiritus* prudencie among þe peple is gyle,
B.19.463   Wiþ *Spiritus* Intellectus þei [toke] þe reues rolles
B.19.464   And wiþ *Spiritus* fortitudinis fecche it, [wole he, nel he].'
B.19.474   Of *Spiritus* Iusticie for I Iugge yow alle.
B.20.8   [Was] by techynge and by tellynge of *Spiritus* temperancie,
B.20.22   So þat he sewe and saue *Spiritus* temperancie.
B.20.23   For is no vertue bi fer to *Spiritus* temperancie,
B.20.24   Ne[iþer] *Spiritus* Iusticie ne Spiritus fortitudinis.
B.20.24   Ne[iþer] Spiritus Iusticie ne *Spiritus* fortitudinis.
B.20.25   For *Spiritus* fortitudinis forfeteþ [wel] ofte;
B.20.29   And *Spiritus* Iusticie shal Iuggen, wole he, nel he,
B.20.31   And *Spiritus* prudencie in many a point shal faille
C.Pr.18   Woned in tho wones and wikkede *spiritus*.
C. 3.406   Nominatiuo, pater & filius & *spiritus* sanctus.
C.14.27   *Spiritus* vbi vult spirat.
C.16.198   Thenne am [y] spirit spechelees; *spiritus* then y hote.
C.16.201   dum negat vel consentit consiencia est; dum sp[i]rat *spiritus* est.'
C.18.51   The whiche is *spiritus* sanctus and sothfaste bileue
C.18.120   Filius by þe fadres wille fley with *spiritus* sanctus
C.18.123   And thenne spak *spiritus* sanctus in gabrieles mouthe
C.21.201   Oen *spiritus* paraclitus to Peres and to his felawes.
C.21.206   *Spiritus* paraclitus ouerspradde hem alle.
C.21.210   Welcome hym and worschipe hym with veni creator *spiritus*.'
C.21.276   *Spiritus* prudencie the furste seed hihte
C.21.281   The seconde se[d]e hihte *Spiritus* temperancie.
C.21.289   The thridde seed that [Peres] sewe was *spiritus* fortitudinis
C.21.297   The ferthe seed that [Peres] sewe was *spiritus* Iusticie
C.21.301   [Shal] nat be aspyed thorw *spiritus* iusticie.
C.21.302   *Spiritus* iusticie spareth nat to spille [the] gulty
C.21.397   By iesu! for al 3oure iangelyng, [with] *spiritus* Iusticie
C.21.402   Of *spiritus* Iusticie thow spekest moche an ydel.'
C.21.405   Bote thow lyue bi lore of *spiritus* Iusticie,
C.21.455   For *spiritus* prudencie among þe peple is gyle
C.21.463   With *spiritus* intellectus they [t]o[k]e þe reues rolles
C.21.464   And with *spiritus* fortitudinis fecche hit, wolle he, null he.'
C.21.474   Of *spiritus* iusticie for y iuge 3ow alle.
C.22.8   Was bi techyng and by tellyng of *spiritus* temperancie
C.22.22   So þat he sewe and saue *spiritus* temperancie.
C.22.23   [For is no vertue by fer to *spiritus* temperancie],
C.22.24   Noythe[r] *spiritus* iusticie ne spiritus fortitudinis.
C.22.24   Noythe[r] spiritus iusticie ne *spiritus* fortitudinis.
C.22.25   For *spiritus* fortitudinis forfeteth wel ofte;
C.22.29   And *spiritus* iusticie shal iugen, wol he, nel he,
C.22.31   And *spiritus* Prudencie in many a poynt shal faile

splendide C 1
C.19.240   Epulabatur *splendide* & induebatur bisso &c.

spoliauit B 1; C 1
B.15.63   Sciencie appetitus hominem inmortalitatis gloria[m] *spoliauit*.
C.16.225   Sciencie appetitus hominem inmortalitatis gloriam *spoliauit*.

state A 1
A.10.112   In eadem vocacione qua vocati estis *state*.

statuam B 1; C 1
B.10.291   Existimasti inique quod ero tui similis; arguam te & *statuam* contra
          faciem
C.12.29   Existimasti inique quod ero t[u]i similis; Arguam te & *statuam*

statum B 1; C 1
B.10.325   And puten [hem] to hir penaunce, Ad pristinum *statum* ire;
C. 5.171   And potte 3ow to 3oure penaunce,ad pristinum *statum* ire,

stella B 1; C 1
B.18.239   [The oostes] in heuene token *stella* com[a]ta
C.20.248   Tho þat weren in heuene token *stella* comata

stellarum B 1; C 1
B.20.256   Qui numerat multitudinem *stellarum* et omnibus eis [nomina
          vocat].
C.22.256   Qui numerat multitudinem *stellarum* &c.

sterilem B 2; C 2
B. 1.141   Heu michi quia *sterilem* duxi vitam Iuuenilem.
B. 5.440   Heu michi quia *sterilem* vitam duxi Iuuenilem.'
C. 1.140   Heu michi quod *ste[r]ilem* duxi vitam iuuenilem.
C. 7.54   Heu michi quod *ster[i]lem* duxi vitam iuuenilem.'

steterit B 1; C 1
B.15.318   aut mugiet bos cum ante plenum presepe *steterit*? brutorum
C.17.53   aut mugiet bos cum ante plenum presepe *steterit*? Brutorum

steteritis A 1; B 1; C 1
A.11.296   Dum *steter[it]is* ante [reges &] presides nolite cogitare,
B.10.450   "[D]um *steteritis* ante Reges & presides [nolite cogitare]:
C.11.275   "Dum *steteritis* ante Reges vel presides &c:

stude B 1; C 1
B.10.89   Si tibi sit copia habundanter tribue; si autem exiguum illud
           impertiri *stude*
C.11.69   Si Autem exiguum illud impertir[i] libenter *stude*.

studes B 1
B. 7.75   Sit elemosina tua in manu tua donec *studes* cui des.

studet B 1
B.Pr.142   Nomen habet sine re nisi *studet* iura tenere.'

stulte C 1
C.12.215   O *stulte*, ista nocte anima tua egredi[e]tur; tezaurisat & ignorat &c.

stulticia B 1; C 1
B.12.138   Sapiencia huius mundi *stulticia* est apud deum.
C.14.83   Sapiencia huius mundi *stul[t]icia* est apud deum.

stultus C 1
C. 9.127   Si quis videtur sapiens, fiet *stultus* vt sit sapiens.

sua A 1; B 3; C 2
A. 2.86   Dignus est operarius mercede [*sua*].
B.11.218   That Fides *sua* sholde sauen hire and saluen hire of synnes.
B.12.213   Qui[a] reddit vnicuique iuxta opera *sua*.
B.15.157   Non inflatur, non est ambiciosa, non querit que *sua* sunt–
C. 5.32   Reddet vnicuique iuxta opera *sua*–
C.14.152   Et reddet vnicu[i]que iuxta opera *sua*.

suam A 3; B 5; C 3
A. 3.64   Amen Amen [dico vobis receperunt mercedem *suam*].
A. 3.221   Qui pecuniam *suam* [non] dedit ad vsuram.
A. 3.233   Amen Amen rec[eperu]nt mercedem *suam*.
B. 3.241   Qui pecuniam *suam* non dedit ad vsuram et munera super
           innocentem &c,
B. 9.194   Bonum est vt vnusquisque vxorem *suam* habeat propter
           fornicacionem.
B.15.497   Bonus pastor animam *suam* ponit &c.
B.16.25   Cum ceciderit iustus non colliditur quia dominus supponit ma[num
           suam];
C. 3.312   Amen Amen, Matheu seyth, Mercedem *suam* rec[e]p[er]unt.
C.10.293   Bonum est [vt] vnusquisque vx[or]em *suam* habeat propter
           fornicacionem.
C.17.193   Bonus Pastor animam *suam* ponit pro ouibus suis &c.

suas C 1
C. 3.461   Conflabunt gladios suos in vomeres & lancias [*suas*] in falces.

sub B 1; C 2
B.13.330   Cuius malediccione os plenum est & amaritudine; *sub* lingua eius
C. 6.76   Cuius maledictione os plenum est & amaritudine; *sub* lingua eius
C. 9.265   *Sub* molli pastore &c.

subiecti B 1; C 1
B.11.383   Propter deum *subiecti* estote omni creature.
C.14.32   Vultus huius seculi sunt *subiecti* v[u]ltibus celestibus.

sudore A 1; B 1; C 1
A. 7.217   In *sudore* & swynke þou shalt þi mete tilen
B. 6.233   In *sudore* and swynk þow shalt þi mete tilie
C. 8.241   In [labore & *sudore*] vultus tui vesceris pane tuo".

suffert C 1
C.17.5   Caritas omnia *s[u]ffert*.

suffertis A 1; B 1; C 1
A. 9.83   Libenter *suffert[is]* &c.
B. 8.93   Libenter *suffertis* insipientes cum sitis ipsi sapientes:
C.10.90   Libenter *suffertis* in[s]ipientes &c;

sufficiat B 1; C 1
B.15.318   pabulum commune *sufficiat*; ex adipe prodijt iniquitas tua.
C.17.53   pabulum commune *sufficiat*; Ex adipe prodiit iniquitas tua.

sufficit B 3; C 2
B.11.58   Pena pecuniaria non *sufficit* pro spiritualibus delictis.
B.15.343   Porro non indiget monachus si habeat quod nature *sufficit*.
B.15.389   That sola fides *sufficit* to saue wiþ lewed peple.
C.12.10   Pena peccuniaria non *sufficit* &c.
C.17.121   That sola fides *sufficit* to saue with lewede peple.

suis B 1; C 1
B.12.293   For Deus dicitur quasi dans [eternam vitam] *suis*, hoc est fidelibus;

C.17.193   Bonus Pastor animam suam ponit pro ouibus *suis* &c.

sum B 3; C 2
B.Pr.132   '*Sum* Rex, sum princeps; neutrum fortasse deinceps.
B.Pr.132   'Sum Rex, *sum* princeps; neutrum fortasse deinceps.
B.13.67   Ter cesus *sum* & a iudeis quinquies quadragenas &c–
C.Pr.153   '*Sum* Rex, sum Princeps; neutrum fortasse deinceps.
C.Pr.153   'Sum Rex, *sum* Princeps; neutrum fortasse deinceps.

sunt A 4; B 21; C 17
A. 1.51   Et que *sunt* dei deo oþer ellis ȝe don ille."
A. 3.228   In quorum manibus iniquitates *sunt*; dextera eorum repleta est
           muneribus.
A.10.34   Dixit & facta *sunt* &c,
A.10.87   Virga tua & baculus tuus ipsa me consolata *sunt*.
B.Pr.145   'Precepta Regis *sunt* nobis vincula legis'.
B. 1.53   Et que *sunt* dei deo or ellis ye don ille."
B. 3.249   In quorum manibus iniquitates *sunt*; dextra eorum repleta est
           muneribus.
B. 5.507   And blew it wiþ Beati quorum remisse *sunt* iniquitates,
B. 9.33   Dixit & facta *sunt*,
B.10.327   Hij in curribus & hij in equis ipsi obligati *sunt* &c.
B.10.436   [*Sunt*] iusti atque sapientes, & opera eorum in manu dei sunt &c.
B.10.436   [Sunt] iusti atque sapientes, & opera eorum in manu dei *sunt* &c.
B.12.13   Virga tua & baculus tuus, ipsa me consolata *sunt*:
B.12.50   *Sunt* homines nequam, bene de virtute loquentes.
B.12.177   Beati quorum remisse *sunt* iniquitates & quorum tecta sunt &c.
B.12.177   Beati quorum remisse sunt iniquitates & quorum tecta *sunt* &c.
B.13.39   Edentes & bibentes que apud eos *sunt*.
B.13.54   Et quorum tecta *sunt* peccata
B.14.61   Dixit & facta *sunt* &c;
B.14.94   As Dauid seiþ in þe Sauter: et quorum tecta *sunt* peccata.
B.15.157   Non inflatur, non est ambiciosa, non querit que sua *sunt*–
B.18.421   Misericordia & veritas obuiauerunt sibi; Iusticia & pax osculate
           su[nt]
B.19.228   Diuisiones graciarum *sunt* &c.
B.19.479   Omnia tua *sunt* ad defendendum set non ad deprehendendum.'
C. 1.49   Et que *sunt* dei deo or [elles] ȝe don ylle."
C. 3.118   In quorum manibus iniquitates *sunt*:
C. 3.190   *Sunt* infelices quia matres sunt meretrices.
C. 3.190   Sunt infelices quia matres *sunt* meretrices.
C. 5.172   Hij in curribus & [hij] in equis; ipsi obligati *sunt* & ceciderunt.
C. 7.152   And Blewe hit with beati quorum remisse *sunt* iniquitates &
C. 7.152   quorum tecta *sunt* peccata,
C.11.271   *Sunt* iusti atque sapientes & opera eorum in manu dei sunt &c.
C.11.271   Sunt iusti atque sapientes & opera eorum in manu dei *sunt* &c.
C.14.32   Vultus huius seculi *sunt* subiecti v[u]ltibus celestibus.
C.14.117   Beati quorum remisse *sunt* iniquitates &c.
C.14.165   Dixit & facta *sunt*.
C.15.44   Edentes & bibentes que apud eos *sunt* &c.
C.15.260   Dixit & facta [*s]unt*;
C.20.464   Misericordia & veritas obuiauerunt sibi; Iusticia & pax osculate
           sunt.
C.21.228   Diuisiones graciarum *sunt*.
C.21.479   Omnia [tua *sunt*] ad defendendum sed non ad deprehendendum.'

suorum C 1
C.11.23   Ibunt in progenie patrum *suorum* & vsque in eternum non videbunt
           lumen;

suos B 2; C 2
B. 3.308   Conflabunt gladios *suos* in vomeres &c.
B.15.215   Fy on faitours and in fautores *suos*!
C. 3.461   Conflabunt gladios *suos* in vomeres & lancias [suas] in falces.
C.11.22   Ducunt in bonis dies *suos* & in fin[e] descendunt ad infernum.

super A 3; B 10; C 10
A. 8.46   *Super* innocentem munera non accipies; a regibus & principibus–
A. 8.159   Quodcumque ligaueris *super* terram &c.
A.11.223   *Super* cathedram moisi sederunt principes.
B. 3.241   Qui pecuniam suam non dedit ad vsuram et munera *super*
           innocentem &c,
B. 5.281   [Misericordia eius *super* omnia opera eius &c]–
B. 7.42   *Super* innocentem munera non accipies.
B. 7.181   Quodcumque ligaueris *super* terram erit ligatum & in celis &c.
B.10.404   *Super* cathedra[m] Moysi &c.
B.11.139   Misericordia eius *super* omnia opera eius.'
B.13.249   In nomine meo demonia e[j]icient & *super* egros manus imponent
           & bene
B.17.318   Misericordia eius *super* omnia opera eius–
B.18.244   "Iube me venire ad te *super* aquas."
B.19.431   Qui pluit *super* Iustos & iniustos at ones
C. 2.42   Et *super* Innocentem munera non accepit.
C. 8.86   *Super* Cathedram moysi sede[runt] &c.
C. 9.327   Quodcumque ligaueris *super* terram erit ligatum & in celis.

C.11.235 *Super* cathedra[m] Moysi &c.
C.12.74 Misericordia eius *super* omnia opera [eius].'
C.14.214 Quia *super* pauca fuisti fidelis &c.
C.15.221 *Super* egros manus [in]pone[nt] & bene habebunt &c–
C.16.335 Lauabis me & *super* niuem dealbabor.
C.19.298 Misericordia eius *super* omnia opera eius.
C.21.431 Qui pluit *super* iustos & iniustos at ones

superbiam B 1; C 1
B.13.432 Non habitabit in medio domus mee qui facit *superbiam* & qui loquitur iniqua.
C. 7.92 Non habitabit in medio domus mee qui facit *superbiam* [&] qui

superius B 1; C 1
B. 6.47 Amice, ascende *superius.*
C. 8.44 Amice, ascende *superius.*

supponit B 1
B.16.25 Cum ceciderit iustus non collidetur quia dominus *supponit* ma[num suam];

surge B 1
B.13.254 quod autem habeo tibi do; in nomine domini *surge* et amb[ula].

surgencium B 1; C 1
B.14.131 velud sompn[i]um *surgencium* domine in Ciuitate tua,
C.15.306 velud sompn[i]um *surgencium* &c.

surrexistis B 1
B.10.359 Si cum christo *sur[r]existis* &c,

suum B 1
B.10.116 Vnusquisque portabit onus *suum* &c."

tabernacula A 1; B 1; C 1
A. 3.85 Ignis deuorabit *tabernacula* eorum qui libenter accipiunt munera.
B. 3.96 Ignis deuorabit *tabernacula* eorum qui libenter accipiunt munera &c.
C. 3.124 Ignis deuorabit *tabernacula* eorum qui libenter accipiunt munera.

tabernaculo B 3; C 1
B. 2.39 Domine quis habitabit in *tabernaculo* tuo &c.
B. 3.234 Domine, quis habitabit in *tabernaculo* tuo?
B. 7.52 Domine, quis habitabit in *tabernaculo* tuo.
C. 2.40 Domine quis habitabit in *tabernaculo* tuo &c.

tabescebam A 1
A.12.19 Vidi preuarica[nt]es & *tabescebam.*

tacuisse C 1
C.13.224 Locutum me aliquando penituit, *tacuisse* nunquam.

tacuisses B 1; C 1
B.11.416 Philosophus esses si *tacuisses.*
C.13.224 Philosophus esses si *tacuisses*; & alibi: Locutum me aliquando

talia B 1; C 1
B.Pr.136 Qualia vis metere, *talia* grana sere.
C.Pr.157 Qualia vis metere, *talia* grana sere.

talis B 1; C 1
B. 2.27 Qualis pater *talis* filius: Bon[a] arbor bonum fructum facit.
C. 2.27 [Qu]alis pater *talis* fili[us] &c.

tangere B 1; C 1
B.12.125 Nolite *tangere* christos meos &c.]
C.14.69 Nolite *tangere* cristos meos &c.

tanquam C 1
C.13.4 *Tanquam* nichil habentes &c.

te B 8; C 8
B.Pr.135 Nudum ius a *te* vestiri vult pietate.
B.10.266 Dogma tuum sordet cum *te* tua culpa remordet.
B.10.291 Existimasti inique quod ero tui similis; arguam *te* & statuam contra faciem
B.11.395 De re que *te* non molestat noli certare.
B.13.57 And þanne hadde Pacience a pitaunce, Pro hac orabit ad *te* omnis
B.15.318 brutorum animalium natura *te* condempnat, quia cum eis pabulum
B.18.244 "Iube me venire ad *te* super aquas."
B.18.422 Truþe trumpede þo and song *Te* deum laudamus,
C.Pr.156 Nudum ius a *te* vestir[i] vult pietate.
C.12.29 Existimasti inique quod ero t[u]i similis; Arguam *te* & statuam
C.13.196 De re que *te* non molestat noli certare.
C.15.60 And brouhte forth a pytaunce, was pro h[a]c orabit [ad *te*] omnis
C.17.53 Brutorum Animalium natura *te* condempnat, quia cum [eis] pabulum
C.20.253 "Domine, iube me venire ad *te.*"
C.20.420 Tibi soli peccaui & malum coram *te* feci.
C.20.465 Treuth trompede tho and song *te* deum laudamus

tecta B 3; C 1
B.12.177 Beati quorum remisse sunt iniquitates & quorum *tecta* sunt &c.

B.13.54 Et quorum *tecta* sunt peccata
B.14.94 As Dauid seiþ in þe Sauter: et quorum *tecta* sunt peccata.
C. 7.152 quorum *tecta* sunt peccata,

teipsum A 1
A.11.242 Dilige deum &c, Et proximum tuum sicut *teipsum.*

temperancie B 4; C 4
B.19.281 The seconde seed highte Spiritus *temperancie.*
B.20.8 [Was] by techynge and by tellynge of Spiritus *temperancie,*
B.20.22 So þat he sewe and saue Spiritus *temperancie.*
B.20.23 For is no vertue bi fer to Spiritus *temperancie.*
C.21.281 The seconde se[d]e hihte Spiritus *temperancie.*
C.22.8 Was bi techyng and by tellyng of spiritus *temperancie*
C.22.22 So þat he sewe and saue spiritus *temperancie.*
C.22.23 [For is no vertue by fer to spiritus *temperancie*],

temperatrix B 2; C 2
B.14.276 absque sollicitudine semita, sapiencie *temperatrix*, negocium sine
B.14.312 Sapiencie *temperatrix.*
C.16.116 absque soli[ci]tudine semita, sapiencie *temp[e]ratrix*, negocium sine
C.16.146 [Sapiencie *temperatrix*].

templo B 2; C 2
B.15.118 Sicut de *templo* omne bonum progreditur, sic de templo omne
B.15.118 sic de *templo* omne malum procedit. Si sacerdocium integrum fuerit
C.16.273 Sicut de *templo* omne bonum progreditur, sic de templo omne
C.16.273 sic de *templo* omne malum procedit. Si sacerdocium integrum fuerit

tempore B 1; C 1
B.13.57 Pro hac orabit ad te omnis sanctus in *tempore* oportuno;
C.15.60 pro h[a]c orabit [ad te] omnis sanctus in *tempore* oportuno.

temporis B 1; C 2
B.16.93 Til plenitudo *temporis* [tyme] comen were
C.18.126 Til plenitudo *temporis* tyme ycome were
C.18.138 Til plenitudo *temporis* [h]y tyme aprochede,

tempus A 1; B 1
A.11.245 Dum *tempus* est operemur bonum ad omnes, maxime autem ad
B.10.204 Dum *tempus* [est] operemur bonum ad omnes, maxime autem ad domesticos fidei.

tenebris B 2; C 2
B. 5.493 Populus qui ambulabat in *tenebris* vidit lucem magnam.
B.18.323 Patriarkes and prophetes, populus in *tenebris,*
C. 7.133 Populus qui ambulabat in *tenebris* vidit lucem magnam &c.
C.20.366 Patriarkes and profetes, populus in *tenebris,*

tenere B 1
B.Pr.142 Nomen habet sine re nisi studet iura *tenere.*'

tenete A 2; B 1; C 2
A.12.52 Til ȝe come to þe burg[h] quod bonum est *tenete.*
A.12.57 And ere I cam to þe court quod bonum est *tenete*
B. 3.343 Quod bonum est *tenete*; truþe þat text made.
C. 3.495 Quod bonum est *tenete*, a tixst of treuthe [m]akynge.
C.20.234 Omnia probate; quod bonum est *tenete.*

ter B 1
B.13.67 *Ter* cesus sum & a iudeis quinquies quadragenas &c–

terram A 1; B 1; C 2
A. 8.159 Quodcumque ligaueris super *terram* &c.
B. 7.181 Quodcumque ligaueris super *terram* erit ligatum & in celis &c.
C. 9.327 Quodcumque ligaueris super *terram* erit ligatum & in celis.
C.12.179 Nisi granum frumenti cadens in *terram* mortuum fuerit &c.

terre B 3; C 2
B.Pr.196 Ve *terre* vbi puer Rex est &c.
B.11.311 Psallite deo nostro; psallite quoniam rex *terre* deus Israel; psallite
B.15.429 Vos estis sal *terre* &c.
C.Pr.209 Ve *terre* vbi puer est Rex.
C.13.123 Psallite deo nostro, psallite; quoniam Rex [*terre*] deus, psallite sapienter.

terrestria B 1; C 1
B.19.80 Omnia celestia *terrestria* flectantur in hoc nomine Iesu;
C.21.80 Omnia celestia *terrestria* flectantur in hoc nomine iesu;

testamentum B 1; C 1
B.19.273 Id est vetus *testamentum* & nouum.
C.21.273 Id est vetus *testamentum* & nouum.

testamur B 1
B.12.65 Quod scimus loquimur, quod vidimus *testamur.*

tezaurisat C 1
C.12.215 O stulte, ista nocte anima tua egredi[e]tur; *tezaurisat* & ignorat &c.

tezaurus C 1
C. 6.285   Vbi *tezaurus* tuus, ibi [&] cor tuum.'

thesauro C 1
C. 5.98   Simile est regnum celorum *thesauro* abscondito in agro;

thesaurus B 1
B.13.398   Vbi *thesaurus* tuus ibi & cor tuum.'

tibi B 5; C 7
B.10.89   Si *tibi* sit copia habundanter tribue; si autem exiguum illud impertiri stude
B.11.251   Domine, non est *tibi* cure quod soror mea reliquit me solam ministrare?
B.13.55   In a dissh of derne shrifte, Dixi & confitebor *tibi*.
B.13.254   Argentum & aurum non est michi; quod autem habeo *tibi* do; in nomine
B.18.378   *Tibi* soli peccaui &c.
C.11.69   Si *tibi* sit copia habundanter tribue; Si Autem exiguum illud
C.11.213   Nec michi nec *tibi*, set diuidatur.
C.12.138   Domine, non est *tibi* cur[e] quod soror &c?
C.15.224   Argentum & Aurum non est michi; quod [autem] habeo *tibi* do &c.
C.15.271   Dabo *tibi* secundum peticionem tuam.
C.17.285   In baculi forma sit, presul, hec *tibi* norma;
C.20.420   *Tibi* soli peccaui & malum coram te feci.

timebo A 1; B 1
A. 8.103   Non *timebo* mala quoniam tu mecum es.
B. 7.121   Non *timebo* mala quoniam tu mecum es.

timere C 1
C.10.99   Nolite *timere* eos qui possunt occidere corpus &c.

timet B 1
B.13.163   Caritas nichil *timet*.

timor A 1; B 2; C 1
A.10.81   Inicium sapiencie *timor* domini.
B. 4.37   Non est *timor* dei ante oculos eorum &c.
B. 9.96   Inicium sapiencie *timor* domini.
C. 4.36   non est *timor* dei ante oculos eorum.

timorem C 1
C.15.164   Caritas expellit omne[m] *timorem*.

tolle B 2; C 2
B.18.47   '*Tolle*, tolle!' quod anoþer, and took of kene þornes
B.18.47   'Tolle, *tolle*!' quod anoþer, and took of kene þornes
C.20.47   '*Tolle*, tolle!' quod another, and toek of kene thornes
C.20.47   'Tolle, *tolle*!' quod another, and toek of kene thornes

tormentis B 1; C 1
B.13.45   eff[u]deritis, ea que in delicijs comeditis in *tormentis* euometis.
C.15.50   effuderitis, ea que in deliciis comeditis in *tor[mentis]* euo[metis] &c.

tota B 2; C 2
B.15.118   Si sacerdocium integrum fuerit *tota* floret ecclesia; Si autem
B.17.16   In hijs duobus mandatis *tota* lex pendet & prophet[e].
C.16.273   Si sacerdocium integrum fuerit *tota* floret ecclesia; Si Autem
C.19.17   In hijs duobus [mandatis *tota* lex pendet & prophete].

totus B 1; C 1
B.15.118   *totus* populus conuertitur ad peccandum. Sicut cum videris arborem
C.16.273   *totus* populus conuertitur ad peccandum. Sicut cum videri[s]

trabem B 2
B.10.268   Qui[d] consideras festucam in oculo fratris tui, *trabem* in oculo tuo &c?
B.10.270   E[j]ice primo *trabem* [de] oculo tuo &c–

traham B 1; C 1
B.17.152   Omnia *traham* ad me ipsum &c–
C.19.127   Omnia *traham* ad me ipsum–

trahe C 1
C.17.285   Fer, *trahe*, punge gregem, seruando per omnia legem–

transgressores B 1; C 1
B. 1.96   And taken *transgressores* and tyen hem faste
C. 1.92   And take *transgressores* and teyen hem faste

transicionis B 1
B.13.151   Wiþ half a laumpe lyne in latyn, Ex vi *transicionis*,

transire B 1
B.14.144   De delicijs ad delicias difficile est *transire*.

tres C 1
C.18.241   *Tres* vidit & vnum adorauit.

tribue B 1; C 1
B.10.89   Si tibi sit copia habundanter *tribue*; si autem exiguum illud impertiri stude
C.11.69   Si tibi sit copia habundanter *tribue*; Si Autem exiguum illud

tribulis B 1
B. 9.155   Numquam collig[unt] de spinis vua[s] nec de *tribulis* ficus.

tribunali B 1; C 1
B.18.36   Thanne cam Pilatus with muche peple, sedens pro *tribunali*,
C.20.35   Thenne cam Pilatus with moche peple, sedens pro *tribunali*,

tributum B 1
B.10.333   Quomodo cessauit exactor, quieuit *tributum*? contriuit dominus baculum

trinitas C 1
C. 3.406   Of thre trewe termisonus, *trinitas* vnus deus:

tristes B 1; C 1
B.15.219   Nolite fieri sicut ypocrite *tristes* &c.
C.16.344   Nolite [fieri sicut ypocrite *tristes*].

tristicia C 1
C.12.207   "*Tristicia* vestra vertetur in gaudium:

tu A 2; B 7; C 6
A. 8.103   Non timebo mala quoniam *tu* mecum es.
A.11.148   [*Tu* quoque fac simile: sic ars deluditur arte].
B. 5.506   Thanne hente hope an horn of Deus *tu* conuersus viuificabis [nos]
B. 7.121   Non timebo mala quoniam *tu* mecum es.
B.10.196   *Tu* quoque fac simile; sic ars deluditur arte.
B.11.269   Pauper ego ludo dum *tu* diues meditaris.
B.14.63   Aperis *tu* manum tuam & imples omne animal benediccione.
B.16.145   It was hymself sooþly and seide '*tu* dicis'.
B.17.170   *Tu* fabricator omnium &c.
C. 7.151   Thenne hente [hope] an horn of deus *tu* conuersus viuificabis nos
C.12.154   Pauper ego ludo dum *tu* diues m[e]ditaris.
C.15.262   Aperis *tu* manum tuam &c.
C.16.320   Oen aperis-*tu*-manum alle thynges hym fyndeth;
C.19.134   *Tu* fabricator omnium–
C.19.140   Dextere dei *tu* digitus.

tua A 1; B 12; C 7
A.10.87   Virga *tua* & baculus tuus ipsa me consolata sunt.
B. 7.75   Sit elemosina *tua* in manu tua donec studes cui des.
B. 7.75   Sit elemosina tua in manu *tua* donec studes cui des.
B. 9.186   Dum sis vir fortis ne des *tua* robora scortis;
B.10.266   Dogma tuum sordet cum te *tua* culpa remordet.
B.12.13   Virga *tua* & baculus tuus, ipsa me consolata sunt:
B.14.50   And þanne was it fiat voluntas *tua* [sholde fynde vs alle].
B.14.131   velud sompn[i]um surgencium domine in Ciuitate *tua*,
B.15.179   Fiat voluntas *tua* fynt hym eueremoore.
B.15.318   pabulum commune sufficiat; ex adipe prodijt iniquitas *tua*.
B.17.114   [O mors ero mors *tua* &c].
B.18.35   O mors ero mors *tua*.'
B.19.479   Omnia *tua* sunt ad defendendum set non ad deprehendendum.'
C.10.287   Dum sis vir fortis ne des *tua* robora scortis;
C.12.215   O stulte, ista nocte anima *tua* egredi[e]tur; tezaurisat & ignorat &c.
C.15.249   And thenne was hit fiat voluntas *tua* þat sholde fynde vs alle.
C.16.321   Fiat-voluntas-*tua* festeth hym vch a daye.
C.17.53   pabulum commune sufficiat; Ex adipe prodiit iniquitas *tua*.
C.20.34   O mors [ero] mors *tua*.'
C.21.479   Omnia [*tua* sunt] ad defendendum sed non ad deprehendendum.'

tuam B 3; C 5
B. 5.509   quemadmodum multiplicasti misericordiam *tuam*, deus'.
B.10.291   arguam te & statuam contra faciem *tuam*.
B.14.63   Aperis tu manum *tuam* & imples omne animal benediccione.
C. 7.154   multiplicasti misericordiam [*tu]am*, deus.'
C. 9.125   Et egenos vagos[que] induc in domum *tuam*,
C.12.29   Arguam te & statuam contra faciem *tuam*.
C.15.262   Aperis tu manum *tuam* &c.
C.15.271   Dabo tibi secundum peticionem *tuam*.

tuarum A 1; B 1; C 1
A. 7.234   Labores manuum *tuarum* quia manducabis &c.
B. 6.252   Labores manuum *tuarum* &c.'
C. 8.260   Labores manuum *tuarum* quia manducabis &c".

tui B 4; C 3
B.10.268   Qui[d] consideras festucam in oculo fratris *tui*, trabem in oculo tuo &c?
B.10.291   Existimasti inique quod ero *tui* similis; arguam te & statuam contra faciem
B.11.95   Existimasti inique quod ero *tui* similis &c.
B.20.279   Non concupisces rem proximi *tui*.
C. 8.241   In [labore & sudore] vultus *tui* vesceris pane tuo".
C.12.29   Existimasti inique quod ero t[u]i similis; Arguam te & statuam

C.22.279 Non concupisces rem proximi *tui* &c.

tuis B 1

B.12.22 Interpone *tuis* interdum gaudia curis.

tumultus C 1

C.18.164 Ne forte *tumultus* fieret in populo–

tunc B 1; C 1

B.15.162 [Hic] in enigmate, *tunc* facie ad faciem.
C.16.296 Hic in enigmate, *tunc* facie ad faciem.

tuo B 8; C 5

B. 2.39 Domine quis habitabit in tabernaculo *tuo* &c.
B. 3.234 Domine, quis habitabit in tabernaculo *tuo*?
B. 5.269 Pane *tuo* pocius vescere: liber eris.
B. 7.52 Domine, quis habitabit in tabernaculo *tuo*.
B.10.268 Qui[d] consideras festucam in oculo fratris tui, trabem in oculo *tuo* &c?
B.10.270 E[j]ice primo trabem [de] oculo *tuo* &c–
B.11.88 Non oderis fratres secrete in corde *tuo* set publice argue illos.
B.18.399 Non intres in Iudicium cum seruo *tuo*.
C. 2.40 Domine quis habitabit in tabernaculo *tuo* &c.
C. 6.293 Pane *tuo* pocius vescere: liber eris.
C. 8.241 In [labore & sudore] vultus tui vesceris pane *tuo*".
C.20.435 Domine ne in furore *tuo* Arguas me &c–
C.20.442 Non intres in iudicium cum seruo *tuo*.

turpiloquio B 1; C 1

B.13.456 Wiþ *turpiloquio*, a l[a]y of sorwe, and luciferis fiþele.
C. 7.116 With *turpiloquio*, a lay of sorwe and luciferes fythele,

turpiloquium A 1; B 1; C 1

A.Pr.39 Qui loquitur *turpiloquium* [is] luciferis hyne.
B.Pr.39 Qui loquitur *turpiloquium* is luciferes hyne.
C.Pr.40 Qui *turpiloquium* loquitur [is] luciferes knaue.

turpissimum B 1; C 1

B.14.77 Ociositas & habundancia panis peccatum *turpissimum* nutriuit;
C.15.229 Habundancia panis & vini *turpissimum* peccatum aduenit.

tuum A 1; B 5; C 4

A.11.242 Dilige deum &c, Et proximum *tuum* sicut teipsum.
B.10.85 Frange esurienti panem *tuum* &c.
B.10.266 Dogma *tuum* sordet cum te tua culpa remordet.
B.13.398 Vbi thesaurus tuus ibi & cor *tuum*.'
B.16.99 Ecce ancilla domini; fiat michi [secundum verbum *tuum*]'.
B.17.13 Dilige deum & proximum *tuum*,
C. 6.285 Vbi tezaurus tuus, ibi [&] cor *tuum*.'
C.11.65 Frange esurienti panem *tuum*.
C.17.140 Dilige deum propter deum, id est propter veritatem; & inimicum *tuum*
C.19.14 Dilige deum & proximum [*tuum*].

tuus A 1; B 2; C 1

A.10.87 Virga tua & baculus *tuus* ipsa me consolata sunt.
B.12.13 Virga tua & baculus *tuus*, ipsa me consolata sunt:
B.13.398 Vbi thesaurus *tuus* ibi & cor tuum.'
C. 6.285 Vbi tezaurus *tuus*, ibi [&] cor tuum.'

vbi A 1; B 5; C 5

A.11.305 Ecce ipsi ydiot[e] rapiunt celum *vbi* nos sapientes
B.Pr.196 Ve terre *vbi* puer Rex est &c.
B.10.256 Fides non habet meritum *vbi* humana racio prebet experimentum.
B.10.461 "Ecce ipsi ydiot[e] rapiunt celum *vbi* nos sapientes in inferno mergimur".
B.12.63 Spiritus *vbi* vult spirat.
B.13.398 *Vbi* thesaurus tuus ibi & cor tuum.'
C.Pr.209 Ve terre *vbi* puer est Rex.
C. 6.285 *Vbi* tezaurus tuus, ibi [&] cor tuum.'
C.11.157 Fides non habet meritum *vbi* humana racio &c.
C.11.287 "Ecce ips[i] idiote rapiunt celum *vbi* nos sapientes in inferno mergimur".
C.14.27 Spiritus *vbi* vult spirat.

vltra C 1

C. 3.477 Non leuabit gens contra gentem gladium nec excercebuntur *vltra* ad prelium.

umbre vmbre A 1; B 2

A. 8.102 & seide 'Si ambulauero in medio *umbre* mortis
B. 7.120 And seide, 'Si ambulauero in medio *vmbre* mortis
B.12.293 Et alibi, si ambulauero in medio *vmbre* mortis.

vnde B 1

B.12.69 Nescit aliquis *vnde* venit aut quo vadit &c.

vnicuique B 1; C 2

B.12.213 Qui[a] reddit *vnicuique* iuxta opera sua.
C. 5.32 Reddet *vnicuique* iuxta opera sua–
C.14.152 Et reddet *vnicu[i]que* iuxta opera sua.

vniuersum B 1; C 1

B.15.491 Ite in *vniuersum* mundum & predicate &c?
C.17.191 Ite in *vniuersum* mundum, sethe ʒe wilne þe name

vno B 2; C 1

B. 9.100 Qui offendit in *vno* in omnibus est reus.
B.11.309 Qui offendit in *vno* in omnibus est reus.
C.13.122 Qui offendit in *vno* in om[n]ibus est reus.

vnum A 1; C 2

A.11.192 Ecce quam bonum & quam iocundum habitare Fratres in *vnum*.
C.18.241 Tres vidit & *vnum* adorauit.
C.18.264 Fiet *vnum* ouile & vnus pastor.

vnus C 2

C. 3.406 Of thre trewe termisonus, trinitas *vnus* deus:
C.18.264 Fiet vnum ouile & *vnus* pastor.

vnusquisque B 3; C 1

B. 9.194 Bonum est vt *vnusquisque* vxorem suam habeat propter fornicacionem.
B.10.116 *Vnusquisque* portabit onus suum &c."
B.13.73 *Vnusquisque* a fratre se custodiat quia vt dicitur periculum est in falsis
C.10.293 Bonum est [vt] *vnusquisque* vx[or]em suam habeat propter fornicacionem.

vnxio B 2

B.15.600 Cum sanctus sanctorum veniat cessabit *vnxio* vestra.
B.18.109 Cum veniat sanctus sanctorum cessabit *vnxio* vestra.'

vsque C 1

C.11.23 Ibunt in progenie patrum suorum & *vsque* in eternum non videbunt lumen;

vsuram A 1; B 1

A. 3.221 Qui pecuniam suam [non] dedit ad *vsuram*.
B. 3.241 Qui pecuniam suam non dedit ad *vsuram* et munera super innocentem &c,

vsuris B 1

B. 7.83 Quare non dedisti pecuniam meam ad mensam vt ego veni[ens] cum *vsuris* ex[egissem illam]?

vt A 1; B 10; C 7

A.11.154 Necesse est *vt* veniant scandala.
B. 1.31 *Vt* seruare possimus de patre nostro semen.
B. 7.60 Quodcumque vultis *vt* faciant vobis homines facite eis.
B. 7.83 Quare non dedisti pecuniam meam ad mensam *vt* ego veni[ens] cum vsuris ex[egissem illam]?
B. 9.194 Bonum est *vt* vnusquisque vxorem suam habeat propter fornicacionem.
B.13.73 Vnusquisque a fratre se custodiat quia *vt* dicitur periculum est in falsis
B.15.81 Confundantur omnes qui adorant sculptilia; Et alibi, *Vt* quid diligitis
B.15.578 Inferte omnes [decimas] in orreum meum *vt* cibus in domo mea.
B.16.157 Necesse est *vt* veniant scandala; ve homini illi per quem scandalum venit.
B.16.214 Deus meus, Deus meus, *vt* quid dereliquisti me?
B.18.162 Ars *vt* artem falleret.'
C.Pr.155 Hoc *vt* agas melius, iustus es, esto pius!
C. 1.30 Inebriemus eum vino dormiamusque cum eo *vt* seruare possimus
C. 9.127 Si quis videtur sapiens, fiet stultus *vt* sit sapiens.
C.10.293 Bonum est [*vt*] vnusquisque vx[or]em suam habeat propter fornicacionem.
C.16.309 Quodcumque vultis *vt* faciant vobis homines, facite eis.
C.20.165 Ars *vt* Artem falleret.'
C.20.392 Ars *vt* Artem falleret.

vuas B 1; C 1

B. 9.155 Numquam collig[unt] de spinis *vua[s]* nec de tribulis ficus.
C.10.244 Numquam collig[unt] de spinis *vuas*; Et Alibi: Bon[a] Arbor

vxorem B 2; C 2

B. 9.194 Bonum est vt vnusquisque *vxorem* suam habeat propter fornicacionem.
B.14.3 *Vxorem* duxi & ideo non possum venire–
C. 7.304 *Vxorem* duxi & ideo non possum venire.'
C.10.293 Bonum est [vt] vnusquisque *vx[or]em* suam habeat propter fornicacionem.

vacabitur B 1

B.16.135 Domus mea domus oracionis *vacabitur*.'

vade B 1; C 1

B.11.274 Si vis perfectus esse *vade* & vende [&c].
C.12.167 Si vis perfectus esse *vade* & vende &c.

vadit B 1

B.12.69 Nescit aliquis vnde venit aut quo *vadit* &c.

vagosque C 1
C. 9.125 Et egenos *vagos[que]* induc in domum tuam,

valde B 1
B.11.398 Et vidit deus cuncta que fecerat & erant *valde* bona.

valentes B 1
B.10.293 Canes non *valentes* latrare,

vanitatem B 1
B.15.81 Et alibi, Vt quid diligitis *vanitatem* & queritis mendacium?

vapulabunt B 1; C 1
B.12.56 Scient[es] et non facient[es] varijs flagellis *vapulab[un]*t.
C.14.18 Scient[es] & non facient[es] varijs flagellis *vapulab[unt]*.

varijs B 1; C 1
B.12.56 Scient[es] et non facient[es] *varijs* flagellis vapulab[un]t.
C.14.18 Scient[es] & non facient[es] *varijs* flagellis vapulab[unt].

ve B 4; C 5
B.Pr.196 *Ve* terre vbi puer Rex est &c.
B.13.61 *Ve* vobis qui potentes estis ad bibendum vinum.
B.13.423 *Ve* vobis qui ridetis &c–
B.16.157 Necesse est vt veniant scandala; *ve* homini illi per quem scandalum venit.
C.Pr.209 *Ve* terre vbi puer est Rex.
C. 7.83 *Ve* vobis qui ridetis &c–
C.15.65 *Ve* vobis qui p[o]tentes estis ad bibendum vinum–
C.18.174 *Ve* homini illi per quem scand[a]lum venit.
C.20.316 *Ve* soli!–

vel B 2; C 2
B.10.261 Appare quod es *vel* esto quod appares;
B.15.39 dum negat *vel* consentit consciencia est; dum spirat spiritus est.'
C.11.275 "Dum steteritis ante Reges *vel* presides &c:
C.16.201 dum negat *vel* consentit consiencia est; dum sp[i]rat spiritus est.'

velis B 1
B.10.266 Si culpare *velis* culpabilis es[se] cauebis;

velud B 1; C 1
B.14.131 *velud* sompn[i]um surgencium domine in Ciuitate tua,
C.15.306 *velud* sompn[i]um surgencium &c.

vende B 1; C 1
B.11.274 Si vis perfectus esse vade & *vende* [&c].
C.12.167 Si vis perfectus esse vade & *vende* &c.

veni B 4; C 3
B. 5.498 Non *veni* vocare iustos set peccatores ad penitenciam.
B.15.594 Laȝare *veni* foras,
B.18.349 Non *veni* soluere legem set adimplere.
B.19.210 Welcome hym and worshipe hym wiþ *Veni* creator Spiritus.'
C. 7.138 Non *veni* vocare iustos set peccatores &c.
C.20.395 Non *veni* soluere legem set adimplere.
C.21.210 Welcome hym and worschipe hym with *veni* creator spiritus.'

veniant A 1; B 1
A.11.154 Necesse est vt *veniant* scandala.
B.16.157 Necesse est vt *veniant* scandala; ve homini illi per quem scandalum venit.

veniat B 2; C 1
B.15.600 Cum sanctus sanctorum *veniat* cessabit vnxio vestra.
B.18.109 Cum *veniat* sanctus sanctorum cessabit vnxio vestra.'
C.20.112 Cum *veniat* sanctus sanctorum cessa[bi]t &c.'

veniens B 1
B. 7.83 Quare non dedisti pecuniam meam ad mensam vt ego *veni[ens]* cum vsuris ex[egissem illam]?

venire B 2; C 2
B.14.3 Vxorem duxi & ideo non possum *venire*–
B.18.244 "Iube me *venire* ad te super aquas."
C. 7.304 Vxorem duxi & ideo non possum *venire*.'
C.20.253 "Domine, iube me *venire* ad te."

venit B 3; C 2
B.12.69 Nescit aliquis vnde *venit* aut quo vadit &c.
B.16.157 Necesse est vt veniant scandala; ve homini illi per quem scandalum *venit*.
B.18.17 Benedictus qui *venit* in nomine domini.
C.18.174 Ve homini illi per quem scand[a]lum *venit*.
C.20.15 Benedictus qui *venit* in nomine domini.

venite B 1; C 1
B.11.120 O vos omnes sicientes *venite* &c,
C.12.55 /O vos omnes sicientes *venite* ad aquas

venter B 1
B. 9.62 Quorum deus *venter* est.

uerba verba A 2; B 2; C 2
A.10.98 Cum recte viuas ne cures *verba* malorum,
A.12.22 Audiui archan[a *uerba*] que non licet homini loqui.
B.15.61 Et *verba* vertit in opera fulliche to his power."
B.18.395 Audiui archana *verba* que non licet homini loqui.
C.16.223 Et *verba* vertit in opera emforth his power."
C.20.438 Audiui arcana *verba* que non licet homini loqui.

verbi B 1
B.15.268 Pacientes Vincunt *verbi* gracia, and [verred] ensamples manye.

verbis A 1; B 1
A.11.147 Qui sim[u]lat *verbis*, nec corde est fidus amicus,
B.10.195 Qui simulat *verbis* [nec] corde est fidus amicus,

verbo B 1
B.14.46 viuit homo set in omni *verbo* quod procedit de ore dei.'

verbum B 2; C 2
B. 5.500 *Verbum* caro factum est & habitauit in nobis.
B.16.99 Ecce ancilla domini; fiat michi [secundum *verbum* tuum]'.
C. 3.356 He acordeth with crist in kynde, *verbum* caro factum est;
C. 7.140 *Verbum* caro factum est.

vere B 1; C 1
B.18.68 *Vere* filius dei erat iste.
C.20.70 *Vere* filius dei erat iste;

verginem > virginem

ueritas veritas A 1; B 2; C 2
A.12.28 "Quid est *ueritas*?" quod he; "verilyche tel vs."
B. 9.164 "I am via & *veritas*", seiþ crist, "I may auaunce alle."
B.18.421 Misericordia & *veritas* obuiauerunt sibi; Iusticia & pax osculate su[nt]
C.10.255 For y am via & *veritas* and may avauncen alle."
C.20.464 Misericordia & *veritas* obuiauerunt sibi; Iusticia & pax osculate sunt.

veritatem B 1; C 2
B. 5.277 Ecce enim *veritatem* dilexisti &c.
C. 6.302 On Ecce enim *veritatem* dilexisti.
C.17.140 Dilige deum propter deum, id est propter *veritatem*; & inimicum tuum

vero A 1; B 1; C 1
A. 8.96 Qui *vero* mala in ignem eternum.
B. 7.114 Qui *vero* mala in ignem eternum.
C. 9.288 Qui *vero* mala in ignem etern[u]m.

vertetur C 1
C.12.207 "Tristicia vestra *vertetur* in gaudium:

vertit B 1; C 1
B.15.61 Et verba *vertit* in opera fulliche to his power."
C.16.223 Et verba *vertit* in opera emforth his power."

vertus > virtus

vescere B 1; C 1
B. 5.269 Pane tuo pocius *vescere*: liber eris.
C. 6.293 Pane tuo pocius *vescere*: liber eris.

vesceris C 1
C. 8.241 In [labore & sudore] vultus tui *vesceris* pane tuo".

vesperum B 1; C 1
B.18.181 Ad *vesperum* demorabitur fletus & ad matutinum leticia.
C.20.184 Ad *vesperum* demorabitur fletus & ad mat[u]tinum leticia.

vestimentum B 1
B.15.576 In domo mea non est panis neque *vestimentum* et ideo nolite constituere me Regem.

vestiri B 1; C 1
B.Pr.135 Nudum ius a te *vestiri* vult pietate.
C.Pr.156 Nudum ius a te *vestir[i]* vult pietate.

vestra B 2; C 1
B.15.600 Cum sanctus sanctorum veniat cessabit vnxio *vestra*.
B.18.109 Cum veniat sanctus sanctorum cessabit vnxio *vestra*.'
C.12.207 "Tristicia *vestra* vertetur in gaudium:

vestrum C 1
C.14.42 Quis *vestrum* sine peccato est.

vetus B 1; C 1
B.19.273 Id est *vetus* testamentum & nouum.
C.21.273 Id est *vetus* testamentum & nouum.

vi B 1
B.13.151 Wiþ half a laumpe lyne in latyn, Ex *vi* transicionis,

via A 1; B 1; C 1
A.11.23 Quare *via* impiorum p[ros]peratur, [bene] est omnibus qui praue

B. 9.164   "I am *via* & veritas", seiþ crist, "I may auaunce alle."
C.10.255   For y am *via* & veritas and may avauncen alle."

viam C 2
C. 4.36   Contricio & infelicitas in viis eorum et *viam* pacis non
             cognouerunt;
C. 9.123   Nemini salutauerit[is] per *viam*.

viator B 1
B.14.307   /Cantabit paupertas coram latrone *viato[r]*,

vicium B 1; C 1
B.15.118   intelligis quod *vicium* habet in radice, Ita cum videris populum
C.16.273   intelligis quod *vicium* habet in radice, Ita cum videris populum

videatis B 1
B.16.47   *Videatis* qui peccat in spiritum sanctum numquam remittetur &c;
             Hoc

videbunt C 1
C.11.23   Ibunt in progenie patrum suorum & vsque in eternum non *videbunt*
             lumen;

videris B 2; C 2
B.15.118   Sicut cum *videris* arborem pallidam & marcidam intelligis quod
B.15.118   Ita cum *videris* populum indisciplinatum & irreligiosum, sine
             dubio
C.16.273   Sicut cum *videri[s]* Arborem pallidam & marcidam intelligis quod
C.16.273   Ita cum *videris* populum indissiplinatum & irreligiosum, sine
             dubio

viderunt B 1; C 1
B.19.181   Beati qui non *viderunt* [& crediderunt]."
C.21.181   Beati qui non *viderunt* & crediderunt."

videt B 2; C 4
B.10.252   [Ego in patre et pater in me est, et qui *videt* me videt et patrem
             meum]
B.10.252   [Ego in patre et pater in me est, et qui videt me *videt* et patrem
             meum]
C. 7.128   Ego in patre & pater in me [est] et qui me *videt* videt [&] patrem
             meum &c;
C. 7.128   Ego in patre & pater in me [est] et qui me videt *videt* [&] patrem
             meum &c;
C.11.153   Ego in patre & pater in me est; Et qui me *vid[e]t*, patrem meum
C.11.153   *vid[e]t* qui in celis est &c.

videte C 1
C.17.40   *Videte* ne furtum sit: & alibi: meli[u]s est mori quam male viuere
             &c.

videto B 1; C 1
B. 7.73   Cui des *videto* is Catons techyng,
C. 9.69   Catoun acordeth therwith: cui des *videto*.

videtur C 1
C. 9.127   Si quis *videtur* sapiens, fiet stultus vt sit sapiens.

vidi A 1; B 1
A.12.19   *Vidi* preuarica[nt]es & tabescebam.
B. 7.89   Iunior fui etenim senui, & non *vidi* iustum derelictum ne[c] semen
             eius

vidimus B 2
B.12.65   Quod scimus loquimur, quod *vidimus* testamur.
B.12.67   And of quod *vidimus* comeþ kynde wit, of siȝte of diuerse peple.

vidit B 3; C 3
B. 5.493   Populus qui ambulabat in tenebris *vidit* lucem magnam.
B.11.398   Et *vidit* deus cuncta que fecerat & erant valde bona.
B.15.200   Et *vidit* deus cogitaciones eorum.
C. 7.133   Populus qui ambulabat in tenebris *vidit* lucem magnam &c.
C.16.340   Et *vidit* deus cogitaciones eorum.
C.18.241   Tres *vidit* & vnum adorauit.

vidua C 1
C.13.98   Amen dico vobis quia hec *vidua* paupercula &c.

vigilare C 1
C. 9.259   *Vigilare* were fayrere for thow haste a greet charge.

vigilate A 1; B 1; C 1
A. 5.214   Til *Vigilate* [þe veil] fet watir [at] his eiȝen,
B. 5.442   Til *vigilate* þe veille fette water at hise eiȝen
C. 7.56   Til *vigilate* the veile fette water at his eyus

vigilia B 1
B.12.9   Si non in prima *vigilia* nec in secunda &c.

viis B 1; C 1
B. 4.36   Contricio & infelicitas in *viis* eorum &c.
C. 4.36   Contricio & infelicitas in *viis* eorum et viam pacis non
             cognouerunt;

villam C 1
C. 7.292   'ȝe! *villam* emi,' quod oen, 'and now y moste thedre

villicacionis C 1
C. 9.273   Redde racionem *villicacionis* or in arrerage fall!

vincula B 1
B.Pr.145   'Precepta Regis sunt nobis *vincula* legis'.

vincunt B 6; C 3
B.13.135   Pacientes *vincunt* &c.'
B.13.171   Pacientes *vincunt*].'
B.14.33   Ne soliciti sitis &c; Volucres celi deus pascit &c; pacientes *vincunt*
             &c.'
B.14.54   Prison ne peyne, for pacientes *vincunt*.
B.15.268   Pacientes *Vincunt* verbi gracia, and [verred] ensamples manye.
B.15.598   Pacientes *vincunt*.
C.15.137   Quod Peres the ploghman, 'Pacientes *vinc[u]nt*.
C.15.156   Pacientes *vincunt* &c.
C.15.253   Prisoun ne payne, for [pacientes] *vincunt*.

vindica B 1; C 1
B.17.293   *Vindica* sanguinem iustorum."
C.19.274   *Vindic[a]* sanguinem iustorum."

vindictam A 1; B 4; C 2
A.11.255   For Michi *vindictam* et ego retribuam.
B. 6.226   Michi *vindictam* & ego retribuam.
B.10.209   Michi *vindictam* & ego retribuam.
B.10.374   [For michi *vindictam* et ego retribuam]:
B.19.446   Non occides: michi *vindictam* &c.
C.17.235   Mihi *vindictam* &c–
C.21.446   Non occides: Michi *vindictam* &c.

vineam B 2
B.10.481   Ite vos in *vineam* meam.'
B.15.500   Ite vos in *vineam* meam &c.

vini C 1
C.15.229   Habundancia panis & *vini* turpissimum peccatum aduenit.

vino B 1; C 1
B. 1.31   Inebri[e]mus eum *vino* dormiamusque cum eo
C. 1.30   Inebriemus eum *vino* dormiamusque cum eo vt seruare possimus

vinum B 1; C 1
B.13.61   Ve vobis qui potentes estis ad bibendum *vinum*.
C.15.65   Ve vobis qui p[o]tentes estis ad bibendum *vinum*–

vir B 2; C 1 *cf. ME virres*
B. 5.418   Bettre þan in Beatus *vir* or in Beati omnes
B. 9.186   Dum sis *vir* fortis ne des tua robora scortis;
C.10.287   Dum sis *vir* fortis ne des tua robora scortis;

virga A 1; B 1
A.10.87   *Virga* tua & baculus tuus ipsa me consolata sunt.
B.12.13   *Virga* tua & baculus tuus, ipsa me consolata sunt:

virgam B 1; C 1
B.10.333   impiorum, et *virgam* dominancium cedencium plaga insanabili.
C. 5.177   Contriuit dominus bac[u]lum impiorum, *virga[m]* d[omi]nancium,

virge B 1; C 1
B. 5.39   Qui parcit *virge* odit filium:
C. 5.139   Qui parcit *virge* odit filium.'

virgine C 1
C.19.125   Natus est ex maria *virgine*.

virginem verginem B 1; C 1
B. 5.603   Per Euam cun[c]tis clausa est et per Mariam *virginem* [iterum]
             patefacta est;
C. 7.250   Per Euam cun[c]tis clausa est & per mariam *verginem* iterum
             patefacta est &c;

virtus vertus B 1; C 2
B.17.341   *Virtus* in infirmitate perficitur.
C. 9.163   Iunior fui, [et]enim senui; e[t] alibi: infirmata est *vertus* mea
             paupertate.
C.19.321   *Virtus* in infirmitate perficitur.

virtute B 1
B.12.50   Sunt homines nequam, bene de *virtute* loquentes.

virtutum B 1
B.18.318   Dominus *virtutum*.

vis B 2; C 2
B.Pr.136   Qualia *vis* metere, talia grana sere.
B.11.274   Si *vis* perfectus esse vade & vende [&c].
C.Pr.157   Qualia *vis* metere, talia grana sere.
C.12.167   Si *vis* perfectus esse vade & vende &c.

visitauit C 1
C.15.116   Et *visitauit* & fecit redempcionem &c.

visurum C 1
C.20.259   Non *visurum* se mortem &c.

vita B 2; C 5
B.13.224   'I am a Mynstrall', quod þat man, 'my name is Actiua *vita*.
B.14.28   Than Hauky[n] wi[l] þe wafrer, [which is] Actiua *vita*.'
C.15.193   'Ich am a mynstral,' quod this man, 'my name is actiua *vita*,
C.15.272   'What is [properly] parfit pacience?' quod Actiua *vita*.
C.16.117   'Y can nat construe al this,' quod Actiua *vita*.
C.18.82   Actiua *vita* & contemplatiua vita,
C.18.82   Actiua vita & contemplatiua *vita*,

vitam A 1; B 5; C 4
A. 8.95   Et qui bona egerunt ibunt in *vitam* eternam;
B. 1.141   Heu michi quia sterilem duxi *vitam* Iuuenilem.
B. 5.440   Heu michi quia sterilem *vitam* duxi Iuuenilem.'
B. 7.113   Et qui bona egerunt ibunt in *vitam* eternam;
B.12.293   For Deus dicitur quasi dans [eternam *vitam*] suis, hoc est fidelibus;
B.15.613   Carnis resurreccionem et *vitam* eternam amen.'
C. 1.140   Heu michi quod ste[r]ilem duxi *vitam* iuuenilem.
C. 7.54   Heu michi quod ster[i]lem duxi *vitam* iuuenilem.'
C. 9.287   Et qui bona egerunt ibunt in *vitam* eternam;
C.17.320   Carnis resurect[i]o[n]em & *vitam* eternam amen.'

vitupera B 1; C 1
B.11.106   Parum lauda; *vitupera* parcius.'
C.12.40   Pa[r]um lauda; *vit[u]pera* parcius.'

viuas A 1
A.10.98   Cum recte *viuas* ne cures verba malorum,

viuencium B 1; C 1
B. 6.75   Deleantur de libro *viuencium*; I sholde noȝt dele wiþ hem,
C. 8.77   Del[e]antur de libro *viuencium*; y sholde nat dele with hem

viuere C 3
C. 1.143   Melius est mori quam male *viuere*.
C. 6.290   Melius est mori quam male *viuere*.
C.17.40   Videte ne furtum sit: & alibi: meli[u]s est mori quam male *viuere* &c.

viuificabis B 1; C 1
B. 5.506   Thanne hente hope an horn of Deus tu conuersus *viuificabis* [nos]
C. 7.151   Thenne hente [hope] an horn of deus tu conuersus *viuificabis* nos

viuificat B 1; C 1
C.16.201   dum *[v]i[u]ificat* corpus Anima est; dum vult animus est; [dum scit
B.15.39   dum *viuificat* corpus anima est; dum vult animus est; dum scit mens

viuit B 2; C 3
B.11.404   Caton acordeþ þerwiþ: Nemo sine crimine *viuit*.'
B.14.46   *viuit* homo set in omni verbo quod procedit de ore dei.'
C. 5.86   Non de solo,' y sayde, 'for sothe *viuit* homo,
C.13.212   Caton acordeth therwith: nemo sine crimine *viuit*.'
C.15.244   vobis. Et alibi: Non in solo pane *viuit* homo &c.'

viuunt B 1
B.10.25   Quare impij *viuunt*? bene est omnibus qui preuaricantur & inique agunt?

vix B 2; C 2
B.12.281   And seide, 'Saluabitur *vix* Iustus in die Iudicij;
B.13.19   And siþen how ymaginatif seide '*vix* saluabitur [iustus]',
C.14.203   And saide, '*Vix* saluabitur iustus in die iudicij;
C.15.22   That iustus bifore iesu in die iudicij non saluabitur bote *vix* helpe;

uobis vobis A 3; B 12; C 14
A. 1.175   Date & dabitur *vobis* for I dele ȝow alle.
A. 3.64   Amen Amen [dico *vobis* receperunt mercedem suam].
A. 7.212   Facite *vobis* amicos.'
B. 1.178   Eadem mensura qua mensi fueritis remecietur *vobis*.
B. 1.201   "Date & dabitur *vobis*, for I deele yow alle."
B. 5.55   Amen dico *vobis* nescio vos.
B. 6.228   Facite *vo[bis]* amicos de mammona iniquitatis.
B. 7.60   Quodcumque vultis vt faciant *vobis* homines facite eis.
B. 9.67   Amen dico *vobis*, nescio vos; Et alibi, Et dimisi eos secundum desideria
B.11.228   Eadem mensura qua mensi fueritis remecietur *vobis*.
B.12.54   Date & dabitur *vobis*.
B.13.61   Ve *vobis* qui potentes estis ad bibendum vinum.
B.13.423   Ve *vobis* qui ridetis &c–
B.17.253   Amen dico *vobis*, nescio vos &c.
B.19.169   To Peter and to [h]ise Apostles and seide pax *vobis*;
C. 1.174   Eadem mensura qua mensi fueritis Remetietur *vobis*.
C. 1.196   "Date & dabitur *vobis*, for y dele ȝow alle."
C. 7.83   Ve *vobis* qui ridetis &c–

C. 7.260   Quodcumque pecieritis in nomine meo dabitur enim *vobis*.
C. 8.234   Facite *vobis* Amicos de mammona iniquitatis.'
C. 9.213   Non licet *uobis* legem voluntati, set voluntat[em] coniungere legi.
C.13.98   Amen dico *vobis* quia hec vidua paupercula &c.
C.15.65   Ve *vobis* qui p[o]tentes estis ad bibendum vinum–
C.15.244   *vobis*. Et alibi: Non in solo pane viuit homo &c.'
C.16.309   Quodcumque vultis vt faciant *vobis* homines, facite eis.
C.17.238   The pope with alle prestes pax *vobis* sholde make
C.19.219   Amen dico *vobis*, nescio vos.
C.19.250   Facite *vobis* amicos de mammona iniquitatis.
C.21.169   To peter and to his apostlis and saide pax *vobis*;

vocabitur A 1; B 1; C 1
A.11.196   Qui facit & docuerit magnus *vocabitur* in regno celorum.
B.13.118   Qui facit & docuerit magnus *vocabitur* in regno celorum.'
C.15.126   Qui facit & docuerit magnus *vocabitur*.'

vocacione A 1; C 1
A.10.112   In eadem *vocacione* qua vocati estis state.
C. 5.43   In eadem *vocacione* qu[a] vocati estis [&c]

vocantur C 1
C.11.18   Qui sapiunt nugas & crim[ina] lege *vocantur*;

vocare B 1; C 2
B. 5.498   Non veni *vocare* iustos set peccatores ad penitenciam.
C. 7.138   Non veni *vocare* iustos set peccatores &c.
C.12.103   Cum facitis conuiuia nolite *vocare* amicos &c.

vocat B 1
B.20.256   Qui numerat multitudinem stellarum et omnibus eis [nomina *vocat*].

vocati A 1; C 1
A.10.112   In eadem vocacione qua *vocati* estis state.
C. 5.43   In eadem vocacione qu[a] *vocati* estis [&c]

volenti B 1
B.11.281   Nichil inpossibile *volenti*,

volucres B 1
B.14.33   Ne soliciti sitis &c; *Volucres* celi deus pascit &c; pacientes vincunt &c.'

voluit B 1; C 1
B.12.216   Quare placuit? quia *voluit*.
C.14.155   Quare placuit? qui[a] *voluit* &c.

voluntas B 2; C 4
B.14.50   And þanne was it fiat *voluntas* tua [sholde fynde vs alle].
B.15.179   Fiat *voluntas* tua fynt hym eueremoore,
C. 5.88   Fiat *voluntas* dei fynt vs alle thynges.'
C.15.249   And thenne was hit fiat *voluntas* tua þat sholde fynde vs alle.
C.16.321   Fiat-*voluntas*-tua festeth hym vch a daye.
C.18.118   That libera *voluntas* dei lauhte þe myddel Shoriare

voluntatem C 1
C. 9.213   Non licet uobis legem voluntati, set *voluntat[em]* coniungere legi.

voluntati C 1
C. 9.213   Non licet uobis legem *voluntati*, set voluntat[em] coniungere legi.

vomeres B 1; C 1
B. 3.308   Conflabunt gladios suos in *vomeres* &c.
C. 3.461   Conflabunt gladios suos in *vomeres* & lancias [suas] in falces.

vos B 9; C 5
B. 5.55   Amen dico vobis nescio *vos*.
B. 9.67   Amen dico vobis, nescio *vos*; Et alibi, Et dimisi eos secundum desideria
B.10.481   Ite *vos* in vineam meam.'
B.11.120   O *vos* omnes sicientes venite &c,
B.13.45   *Vos* qui peccata hominum comeditis, nisi pro eis lacrimas & oraciones
B.13.440   Qui *vos* spernit me spernit.
B.15.429   *Vos* estis sal terre &c.
B.15.500   Ite *vos* in vineam meam &c.
B.17.253   Amen dico vobis, nescio *vos* &c.
C. 7.100   Qui *vos* spernit me spernit.
C. 9.120   [Q]uando misi *vos* sine pane & pera &c.
C.12.55   /O *vos* omnes sicientes venite ad aquas
C.15.50   *Vos* qui peccata hominum comeditis, nisi pro eis lacrimas & orationes
C.19.219   Amen dico vobis, nescio *vos*.

vult B 3; C 3
B.Pr.135   Nudum ius a te vestiri *vult* pietate.
B.12.63   Spiritus vbi *vult* spirat.
B.15.39   dum viuificat corpus anima est; dum *vult* animus est; dum scit mens
C.Pr.156   Nudum ius a te vestir[i] *vult* pietate.

C.14.27   Spiritus vbi *vult* spirat.
C.16.201 dum [v]i[u]ificat corpus Anima est; dum *vult* animus est; [dum scit

vultibus C 1
C.14.32   Vultus huius seculi sunt subiecti *v[u]ltibus* celestibus.

vultis B 1; C 1
B. 7.60   Quodcumque *vultis* vt faciant vobis homines facite eis.
C.16.309 Quodcumque *vultis* vt faciant vobis homines, facite eis.

vultus C 2
C. 8.241   In [labore & sudore] *vultus* tui vesceris pane tuo".
C.14.32   *Vultus* huius seculi sunt subiecti v[u]ltibus celestibus.

a B 1; C 1
B.11.386 Bien dire et bien suffrir fait lui suffra[ble] *a* bien venir.
C.13.204 Ben dire & ben suffrer fait lui suffrable *a* bien venir.

beau A 1; B 1; C 1
A. 8.145 '*Beau* fitʒ,' quaþ his fadir, 'for defaute we shuln,
B. 7.168 '*Beau* fitʒ', quod his fader, 'for defaute we shullen,
C. 9.312 '*Beau* fitʒ', quod the fadur, 'for defaute we shal,

bele B 2; C 2
B.11.385 [B]*ele* vertue est suffrance; mal dire est pet[ite] vengeance.
B.15.115 Ye aren enblaunched wiþ *bele* paroles and wiþ [bele cloþes]
C.13.203 *Bele* vertue est suffrance, mal dire est petit vengeance.
C.16.270 That ben enblaunched with *bele* paroles and with bele clothes

ben bien B 3; C 3
B.11.386 *Bien* dire et bien suffrir fait lui suffra[ble] a bien venir.
B.11.386 Bien dire et *bien* suffrir fait lui suffra[ble] a bien venir.
B.11.386 Bien dire et bien suffrir fait lui suffra[ble] a *bien* venir.
C.13.204 *Ben* dire & ben suffrer fait lui suffrable a bien venir.
C.13.204 Ben dire & *ben* suffrer fait lui suffrable a bien venir.
C.13.204 Ben dire & ben suffrer fait lui suffrable a *bien* venir.

charite A 3; B 3; C 4
A. 7.182 And preiʒede pur *charite* wiþ peris for to dwelle,
A. 7.237 'ʒet I preye þe,' quaþ peris, 'pur *charite*, ʒif þou kenne
A. 9.11 And preiʒede hem, pur *charite*, er þei passide ferþere,
B. 6.253 'Yet I preie [þee]', quod Piers, 'p[u]r *charite*, and [þow] konne
B. 8.11 And preide hem, p[u]r *charite*, er þei passed ferþer
B.13.30 And preyde mete 'p[u]r *charite*, for a pouere heremyte'.
C. 8.169 'Y preye the,' quod [Perus] tho, 'pur *charite*, sire hunger,
C. 8.265 Ac ʒut y praye ʒow,' quod [Peres], 'pur *charite*, syre hungur,
C.10.11 And preyde hem, pur *charite*, ar they passede forthere
C.15.32 [Pacience as a pore thyng cam] and preeyede mete pur *charite*;

chaud chaut A 2; B 2; C 2
A. 7.295 And *chaud*, & pluys chaud, for chillyng of h[ere] mawe.
A. 7.295 And chaud, & pluys *chaud*, for chillyng of h[ere] mawe.
B. 6.311 And þat *chaud* and plus chaud for chillynge of hir mawe.
B. 6.311 And þat chaud and plus *chaud* for chillynge of hir mawe.
C. 8.333 And þat *chaut* and pluchaut for chillyng of h[ere] mawe.
C. 8.333 And þat chaut and plu*chaut* for chillyng of h[ere] mawe.

dame A 1; B 1; C 1
A.Pr.103 And driueþ forþ þe longe day wiþ dieu saue *dame* emme;
B.Pr.225 And dryueþ forþ þe longe day with 'Dieu saue *dame* Emme'.
C.Pr.229 And dryueth forth [þe longe] da[y] with 'd[ieu] saue *dame* Emme.'

dieu A 1; B 1; C 1
A.Pr.103 And driueþ forþ þe longe day wiþ *dieu* saue dame emme;
B.Pr.225 And dryueþ forþ þe longe day with '*Dieu* saue dame Emme'.
C.Pr.229 And dryueth forth [þe longe] da[y] with '*d[ieu]* saue dame Emme.'

dire B 2; C 2
B.11.385 [B]ele vertue est suffrance; mal *dire* est pet[ite] vengeance.
B.11.386 Bien *dire* et bien suffrir fait lui suffra[ble] a bien venir.
C.13.203 Bele vertue est suffrance, mal *dire* est petit vengeance.
C.13.204 Ben *dire* & ben suffrer fait lui suffrable a bien venir.

douce B 1; C 1
B.14.123 And diues in deyntees lyuede and in *douce* vie;
C.15.299 And dyues in deyntees lyuede and [in] *douce* vie

emme A 1; B 1; C 1
A.Pr.103 And driueþ forþ þe longe day wiþ dieu saue dame *emme*;
B.Pr.225 And dryueþ forþ þe longe day with 'Dieu saue dame *Emme*'.
C.Pr.229 And dryueth forth [þe longe] da[y] with 'd[ieu] saue dame *Emme*.'

en B 1
B.10.445 For quant oportet vient *en* place il nyad que pati.

est B 2; C 2
B.11.385 [B]ele vertue *est* suffrance; mal dire est pet[ite] vengeance.
B.11.385 [B]ele vertue est suffrance; mal dire *est* pet[ite] vengeance.
C.13.203 Bele vertue *est* suffrance, mal dire est petit vengeance.
C.13.203 Bele vertue est suffrance, mal dire *est* petit vengeance.

et & B 1; C 1
B.11.386 Bien dire *et* bien suffrir fait lui suffra[ble] a bien venir.
C.13.204 Ben dire *&* ben suffrer fait lui suffrable a bien venir.

fait B 1; C 1
B.11.386 Bien dire et bien suffrir *fait* lui suffra[ble] a bien venir.
C.13.204 Ben dire & ben suffrer *fait* lui suffrable a bien venir.

fitʒ A 1; B 1; C 1
A. 8.145 'Beau *fitʒ*,' quaþ his fadir, 'for defaute we shuln,
B. 7.168 'Beau *fitʒ*', quod his fader, 'for defaute we shullen,
C. 9.312 'Beau *fitʒ*', quod the fadur, 'for defaute we shal,

il B 1
B.10.445 For quant oportet vient en place *il* nyad que pati.

lui B 1; C 1
B.11.386 Bien dire et bien suffrir fait *lui* suffra[ble] a bien venir.
C.13.204 Ben dire & ben suffrer fait *lui* suffrable a bien venir.

mal B 1; C 1
B.11.385 [B]ele vertue est suffrance; *mal* dire est pet[ite] vengeance.
C.13.203 Bele vertue est suffrance, *mal* dire est petit vengeance.

nyad B 1
B.10.445 For quant oportet vient en place il *nyad* que pati.

oportet B 1
B.10.445 For quant *oportet* vient en place il nyad que pati.

paroles B 1; C 1
B.15.115 Ye aren enblaunched wiþ bele *paroles* and wiþ [bele cloþes]
C.16.270 That ben enblaunched with bele *paroles* and with bele clothes

petit petite B 2; C 1
B.11.385 [B]ele vertue est suffrance; mal dire est *pet[ite]* vengeance.
C.13.203 Bele vertue est suffrance, mal dire est *petit* vengeance.

place B 1
B.10.445 For quant oportet vient en *place* il nyad que pati.

plus pluys plu A 1; B 1; C 1
A. 7.295 And chaud, & *pluys* chaud, for chillyng of h[ere] mawe.
B. 6.311 And þat chaud and *plus* chaud for chillynge of hir mawe.
C. 8.333 And þat chaut and *plu*chaut for chillyng of h[ere] mawe.

pur A 3; B 3; C 4
A. 7.182 And preiʒede *pur* charite wiþ peris for to dwelle,
A. 7.237 'ʒet I preye þe,' quaþ peris, '*pur* charite, ʒif þou kenne
A. 9.11 And preiʒede hem, *pur* charite, er þei passide ferþere,
B. 6.253 'Yet I preie [þee]', quod Piers, '*p[u]r* charite, and [þow] konne
B. 8.11 And preide hem, *p[u]r* charite, er þei passed ferþer
B.13.30 And preyde mete '*p[u]r* charite, for a pouere heremyte'.
C. 8.169 'Y preye the,' quod [Perus] tho, '*pur* charite, sire hunger,
C. 8.265 Ac ʒut y praye ʒow,' quod [Peres], '*pur* charite, syre hungur,
C.10.11 And preyde hem, *pur* charite, ar they passede forthere
C.15.32 [Pacience as a pore thyng cam] and preeyede mete *pur* charite;

quant B 1
B.10.445 For *quant* oportet vient en place il nyad que pati.

que B 1
B.10.445 For quant oportet vient en place il nyad *que* pati.

saue A 1; B 1; C 1
A.Pr.103 And driueþ forþ þe longe day wiþ dieu *saue* dame emme;
B.Pr.225 And dryueþ forþ þe longe day with 'Dieu *saue* dame Emme'.
C.Pr.229 And dryueth forth [þe longe] da[y] with 'd[ieu] *saue* dame Emme.'

signiure A 1
A. 2.66 In al þe *signiure* of slouþe I se[se] hem togidere;

suffrable B 1; C 1
B.11.386 Bien dire et bien suffrir fait lui *suffra[ble]* a bien venir.
C.13.204 Ben dire & ben suffrer fait lui *suffrable* a bien venir.

suffrance B 1; C 1
B.11.385 [B]ele vertue est *suffrance*; mal dire est pet[ite] vengeance.
C.13.203 Bele vertue est *suffrance*, mal dire est petit vengeance.

suffrer suffrir B 1; C 1
B.11.386 Bien dire et bien *suffrir* fait lui suffra[ble] a bien venir.
C.13.204 Ben dire & ben *suffrer* fait lui suffrable a bien venir.

vengeance B 1; C 1
B.11.385 [B]ele vertue est suffrance; mal dire est pet[ite] *vengeance*.
C.13.203 Bele vertue est suffrance, mal dire est petit *vengeance*.

venir B 1; C 1
B.11.386 Bien dire et bien suffrir fait lui suffra[ble] a bien *venir*.
C.13.204 Ben dire & ben suffrer fait lui suffrable a bien *venir*.

vertue B 1; C 1
B.11.385 [B]ele *vertue* est suffrance; mal dire est pet[ite] vengeance.
C.13.203 Bele *vertue* est suffrance, mal dire est petit vengeance.

vie B 1; C 1
B.14.123 And diues in deyntees lyuede and in douce *vie*;
C.15.299 And dyues in deyntees lyuede and [in] douce *vie*

vient B 1
B.10.445 For quant oportet *vient* en place il nyad que pati.

APPENDICES

LIST OF HOMOGRAPHS

This lists all spellings which will be found under two or more headwords. It includes forms spelled identically; thus lyking | lykyng are not treated here as homographs, nor are the | þe. If a spelling is identical to the headword, only the part of speech tag follows the form (e.g., aboute: adv, prep).

a: art indef, exclam, letter, num, prep, he pron, heo pron
abite: v, habite n
aboute: adv, prep
abouten: aboute adv, prep
aboue: adv, prep
afore: adv, prep
after: adv, prep, conj
aftir: after adv, prep, conj
aftur: after adv, prep, conj
agayne: ayein adv, prep
ageyn: ayein adv, prep
ayr: eyr n, heir n
al: adj, adv, oueral adv, wiþalle adv
ale: n, penyale n
alisaundre: n1_prop, n2_prop
alle: adj, adv, wiþalle adv
alowed: allowe v, aloud adv
als: also adv, as conj
an: a art, num, prep, on prep
angre: n, v
any: adj, pron
anoþer: pron, adj
answere: n, v
ar: ben v, er prep, er conj
aray: array n, v
armure: n, cote_armure n
ars: art n, ers n
art: n, ben v
as: conj, theras conj
assente: assent n, assenten v
auȝt: pron, adv
auȝte: n, owe v
auht: auȝt adv, auȝt pron
aȝeyne: ayein adv, prep
aȝen: ayein adv, prep
ayein: adv, prep

B

baer: bare adj, beren v2
bake: ptp, bak n
bakkes: n, bak n
bale: adj, n
bar: bare adj, beren v2
barre: n, v
be: ben v; by prep
bede: n, bidden v
beest: n, ben v
before: bifore adv, prep
begge: v, buggen v
beggeris: beggere n, buggere n
beggeth: begge v, buggen v
behynde: bihynde adv, prep
beleue: bileue n, bileuen v1, bileuen v2
bere: n, v1, beren v2
bern: n, brennen v, burn n
berne: bern n, brennen v
bernes: barn n, bern n
best > adj, adv, ben v
beste > best adj, best adv, beest n
bet: adv, beten v2
beten: v2, bete v1
betere: bettre adj, bettre adv

bette: n prop, bet adv, beten v2
bettere: bettre adj, bettre adv
bettre: adj, adv
betwene: bitwene adv, bitwene prep
by: prep, by_so conj
bi: by prep, by_so conj
biddynge: bidden v, biddyng ger
bide: bidden v, biden v
byfore: bifore adv, bifore prep
bigge: adj, buggen v
bygge: bigge adj, buggen v
bihynde: adv, prep
byhynde: bihynde adv, bihynde prep
bileeue: bileue n, bileuen v2
bileue: n, bilyue n, bileuen v1, bileuen v2
byleue: bileuen v2, bileue n
bileuen: v1, v2
byleueth: bileuen v1, bileuen v2
biside: adv, prep
bite: byte n, biten v
bitter: n, adj
bittere: bitter adj, bittre adv
bittre: adv, bitter adj
bitwene: adv, prep
bytwene: bitwene adv, bitwene prep
blase: n, blasen v
blasen: n, v
blew: adj, blowe v
blissen: v, blesse v
bond: n, bynden v
bonde: n, bynden v
boot: n, biten v
borw: borgh n, borwe v, burgh n
borwe: v, borgh n
borwes: borgh n, burgh n
bowe: n, bowen v
bowen v
bowen > bown adj
bowes: bouȝ n, bowe n
brake: n, v, breke v
brede: n, v1
breed: n, bredcorn n
bren: n, brennen v
brennyng: ger, brennen v
brent: ptp, brennen v
broke: breke v, brook n
but: conj, prep, iohan_but n prop

C

caytif: n, adj
can: konne v, gynneþ v
cardinal: cardynal n, cardinale adj
cardinales: cardynal n, cardinale adj
cardynales: cardynal n, cardinale adj
cardinals: cardynal n, cardinale adj
care: n, v
certein: n, adj
certeyn: certein n, certein adj
certeyne: certein n, certein adj
chaffare: n, v

champion: n, adj
charge: n, v
chaste: adj, adv, v
chaumbre: chambre n, bedchambre n
cherche: chirche n, holy_chirche n
chield: ptp, child n
chirche: n, holy_chirche n
cockes: n, cokkeslane n
cold: n, adj
colde: cold n, cold adj
coles: n2, cole n1
comen: v, commune adj
comyng: comen v, comynge ger
commune: n, adj
comune: commune n, commune adj
conforte: confort n, conforten v
connynge: konnyng adj, konnyng ger
consail: counseil n, counseillen v
consayl: counseil n, counseillen v
consayle: counseil n, counseillen v
conseile: counseil n, counseillen v
conseyle: counseil n, counseillen v
conseille: counseil n, counseillen v
contrarie: n, v
cope: n, v, coupe n
corn: n, bredcorn n
cors: n, cours n
cost: n1, n2
coste: n, costed v
cote: n1, n2, cote_armure n
connynge: konnyng adj, konnyng ger
couden: kidde v, konne v
counseille: counseil n, counseillen v
counte: v, countee n
couple: n, coupleþ v
couþe: kidde v, konne v
cristen: adj, v
cristene: cristen adj, cristen v
croune: v, crowne n
cure: n, curen v

D

day: n, holy_day n
daies: day n, holy_day n
dayes: day n, holy_day n
dar: v1, darstow v2
dawe: n, v
ded: adj, ptp, doon v
dede: n, ded adj, doon v
dedly: adj, adv
deel: n, dele v
deere: adj, adv, deren v
dees: n, deys n
degre: n, decree n
demme: dym adj, dymme adv
depe: adj, deep adj
dere: deere adj, deere adv, deren v
derke: n, derk adj
derne: adj, adv
dymme: adv, dym adj
diuerse: adj, adv
do: doon v, dowel n
done: n, doon v
dore: n, dorenail n
doun: adv, vp_so_doun

doute: n, douten v
down: doun adv, vp_so_doun adv
dred: drede n, drede v
drede: n, v
drye: n, adj
drynk: drynke n, drynken v
drynke: n, drynken v
dwellyng: dwellen v, dwellynge ger

E

ech: adj, echone pron
eiȝe: n1, n2
elles: ellis adj, ellis adv
ellis: adj, adv
ende: n, v
englisch: englissh n, englissh adj
englissh: n, adj
eny: any pron, any adj
entre: entree n, entreþ v
er: adv, prep, conj
ere: n, er conj, erien v
eten: v, eten v
etynge: ger, eten v
eue: n prop, euen n
euel: yuel n, yuel adj, yuele adv
euele: yuel n, yuel adj, yuele adv
euene: adj, euen n, euene adv
eueneforþ: adv, prep
euil: yuel n, yuel adj

F

fayn: adj, fayne adv
fair: adj, faire adv
fayr: fair adj, faire adv
faire: adv, fair adj
fayre: fair adj, faire adv, feire n, fayre n
fairer: fair adj, faire adv
fallyng: ger, falle v
fals: n, adj
false: fals n, fals adj
fare: n, v
faste: adj, adv, fasten v
fastyng: ger, fasten v
fatte: n, fat adj
feere: n, fere n
feeris: n, feere n
feeste: feste n, festen v
feet: n, foot n
fel: n, adj, falle v
felde: feld n, felle v
fele: adj, feele v
felle: v, falle v, fel adj, fille v
fende: fend n, fenden v
fer: adj, adv, fere n
fere: n, v, feere n
ferme: n, adv, ferm adj
ferthynge: ferþyng n, ferþyng n
fest: festne v, fust n
fet: fette v, foot n
fille: n, v, falle v
fyn: n1, n2, adj
first: adj, adv
firste: first adj, first adv
fisyk: phisik n, phisike v

849

fiþele: n, fiþelen v
flaterynge: ger, flatere v
fle: flee v1, fleen v2
flee: v1, fleen v2
fleen: v2, flee v1
fleeth: flee v1, fleen v2
fleeþ: flee v1, fleen v2
fley: flee v1, fleen v2
flour: n1, n2
fol: fool n, ful adj, ful adv
fold: n1, n2
folde: v, fold n2
foles: n, fool n
folis: foles n, fool n
fond: fonde v, founded v, fynden v
fonde: v, fynden v
for: prep, conj, for_to adv&particle,
    forto conj
forbode: n, forbedeþ v
fore: n, for prep
forth: forþ n, forþ adv
forþ: n, adv
foul: adj, fowel n
foule: adv, foul adj, fowel n
foulest: foul adj, foule adv
founded: v, fonde v
fourme: forme n, formen v
frenche: adj, frenssh n
ful: adj, adv, falle v, potte_ful
fulle: n, fille v
fullen: v, falle v
fullyng: ger1, ger2
furst: first adj, first adv
furste: first adj, first adv, þurst n

G

gate: n, yate n
gates: gate n, yate n
gentil: adj, gentile n
gentile: n, gentil adj
geste: n, gest n
gestes: gest n, geste n
gide: n, v
gyle: v, gile n, gyles n prop
gyles: n, gile n
gilt: n, ptp
glade: glad adj, gladen v
glosynge: gloseþ v, glosyng ger
gode: good n, good adj
godes: god n, good n
godis: god n, good n
goed: good n, good adj
goest: goost n, holy_goost n
goynge: go v, goyng ger
gold: n, adj
golde: gold n, gold adj
gome: n1, n2
good: n, adj, adv
goode: good n, good adj
goost: n, holy_goost n
gost: goost n, holy_goost n
gray: adj, grey n
graue: n, v
greete: v, gret adj
grete: greete v, gret adj, greten v
gretter: adv, gret adj
grettere: gret adj, gretter adv
grettore: gret adj, gretter adv
grype: n, gripeþ v
grys: n1, n2
grounde: ptp, ground n
gult: gilt n, gilt ptp

H

hayl: n1, n2
half: n, adj
haly: holy adj, holy_day n
halle: hallen, moot_halle n
hangynge: ger, hangen v
harde: adv, hard adj
hardere: hard adj, harde adv
hardier: adv, hardy adj
harpe: n, harpen v
haste: n, hasteþ v, hauen v
hatte: hat n, hote v
he: pron, heo pron
hed: hede n, heed n
heed: n, hede n
heele: n, helen v
hey: hei3 adv, hei3 adj,
    how_trolly_lolly
heye: hei3 adv, hei3 adj
heighe: hei3 adv, hei3 adj
hei3: adv, adj
hei3e: hei3 adv, hei3 adj
helde: v, holden v
hele: n, heele n, helen v, helien v
help: n, helpen v
helpe: help n, helpen v
her: heo pron, here adv, hij pron
herberwe: n, v
herde: n, heren v
here: adv, heo pron, heren v, hij pron,
    hire n
herte: n, hurte v
hete: n, hote v
heuy: adj, adv
hewe: n, v, hugh n prop
hewes: n, hewe n
hy: hei3 adj, hij pron
hye: v, hei3 adv, hei3 adj
hir: heo pron, hij pron
hire: n, heo pron, hij pron
his: he pron, it pron
hise: he pron, it pron
hit: it pron, hitte v
hode: hood n, robyn_hood n prop
hoem: hoom n, hoom adv
hoet: hoot adj, hote v
holde: adj, holden v
holdyng: ger, holden v
hole: n, hool adj
holy: adj, holy_day n, holy_chirche n,
    holy_goost n, holy_writ n,
    pope_holy adj
hom: hoom n, hoom adv
home: hoom n, hoom adv
honeste: n, adj
hood: n, robyn_hood n prop
hoom: n, adv
hope: n, v
hore: n, hoor adj
hote: v, hoot adj, otes n
how: adv, conj, how_trolly_lolly

I

ycalled: adj, callen v
ydel: n, adj
yherd: heren v, herie v
yknowe: v, knowen v
ylet: leten v, lette v
yleued: leued ptp, lyuen v
yliche: ylik adj, ylike adv
ylike: ylik adj, ylik adj
ylyke: ylike adv, ille n

ille: n, adj, adv
ylle: ille n, ille adv
in: adv, prep
inne: n, adv, prep
ynne: inne n, inne adv, inne prep
ynogh: ynou3 n, ynou3 adj
yno3: ynou3 n, ynou3 adj
YNOU3:, YNOU3 N
ynow: ynou3 adj, ire n
yre: ire n, yren n
is: ben v, he pron
ysaye: n prop, seen v
ysey: yse v, seen v
yseye: yse v, seen v
yuel: n, adj
yuele: adv, yuel n
ywonne: v, wynnen v

J

ianglyng: ger, iangle v
iape: n, v
ioyned: v1, v2
iuge: iugge n, iuggen v
iugge: n, iuggen v
iuste: adj, iusten v

K

kenne: kyn n, kennen v
kep: kepe n, kepen v
kepe: n, kepen v
keuered: couere v, keuere v
kynde: n, adj
kyne: cow n, kyn n
kynnes: kyn n, kynnes_womman n
kirk: chirche n, holy_chirche n
kirke: chirche n, holy_chirche n
kyrke: chirche n, holy_chirche n
kitte: kutte v, kytte n prop
knelyng: ger, knelen v
knowyng: ger, knowen v
knowynge: knowen v, knowyng ger
konnyng: adj, ger
konnynge: konnyng adj, konnyng ger
kouþe: kidde v, konne v

L

laboure: labour n, labouren v
ladde: leden v, ligge v
layes: n, lay n
layk: n, laike v
layn: v, ligge v
lakkynge: lakke v, lakkyng ger
large: n, adj
lasse: n, adj, adv
laste: adj, v, lest conj
lat: leden v, leten v
late: adv, leten v
laughynge: lau3en v, laughyng ger
leche: n, lechen n
lede: leden v, leode n
leef: n1, n2, adj, adv, leue v1, leuen v
leeste: adv, leest adj
leeue: leef adj, leue n, leue v1
lef: leef n1, leef adj, leef adv, leue v1
lege: leggen v2, lige adj
legge: v1, leggen v2
ley: leggen v2, ligge v
leye: n, adj, leggen v2, ligge v
leyen: legge v, ligge v
leiþ: leggen v2, lyen v
lei3e: ligge v, lyen v
lene: adj, lenen v2
lened: v1, lenen v2

lenede: lened v1, lenen v2
lenger: long adj, longe adv
lengere: long adj, longe adv
lenghe: lengþe n, lengþe v
lengore: long adj, longe adv
lengþe: n, v
lengur: long adj, longe adv
lente: lenen v2, lenten n
lere: leere n, leren v
lese: v1, lesen v2
lesynge: n, ger
lesse: lasse n, lasse adj, lasse adv
lest: conj, leest adj, list v
let: leden v, leten v, lette v
lette: v, leten v
lettynge: ger2, lettyng ger1
leue: n, v1, v2, leef n1, leef adj, leef
    adv, leuen v, lyuen v
leued: ptp, leue v1
leuen: v, leue v1, lyuen v
leuere: leef adj, leef adv
leuest: leef adj, leef adv, leue v1,
    leuen v
leueth: leue v1, leuen v, lyuen v
leueþ: leue v1, leuen v
leuiþ: leue v1, leuen v
lich: liche n, lik prep
liche: n, lik prep
lye: leye n, lyen v
lyen: v, ligge v
lyeth: ligge v, lyen v
lif: n, lif_tyme n
lyft: left adj, lifte n
lifte: n, liften v
lygge: adj, ligge v
li3t: adj, adv, light n
li3te: li3t adv, li3teþ v
liht: li3t adj, light n
lihte: li3t adv, li3teþ v, light n
lyhte: li3t adv, li3teþ v
lik: adj, prep
lyk: lik adj, lik prep
like: adv, lik prep, likeþ v
lyke: lik adj, lik prep, like adv, likeþ v
lykyng: likyng ger1, likynge adj
likynge: adj, ger2, prp, likyng ger1
liste: list n, list v
litel: adj, adv
lytel: litel adj, litel adv
liþ: ligge v, lyen v
lyth: n, lyen v, ligge v
liþed: liþeþ v, liþen v
lythed: liþeþ v, liþen v
lyue: leuen v, lif n, lyuen v
lyues: adj, lif n
lyuyng: ger, lyuen v
lyuynge: leuynges ger, lyuen v,
    lyuyng ger
li3en: ligge v, lyen v
lok: n, loken v
lokes: n, lok n
lokynge: ger, loken v
long: adj, longe adv
longe: n, adv, v1, long adj
looue: v, loue v2
lordliche: adv, lordlich adj
lore: lesen v2, loore n
los: loos n, losse n
lost: lesen v2, lust n
loth: looþ adj, lot n prop
loþe: v, looþ adj
loude: adv, loud adj

loue (loue): see loue (love)
louȝ: lauȝen v, lowe adj
louh: lauȝen v, lowe adj, lowe adv
louhe: lauȝen v, lowe adj
lourynge: ger, loure v
loue: (loue) n, lowe v; (love) n1, n2,
    v1, v2, looue n
loued: loue v1, loue v2
louede: loue v1, loue v2
loueliche: adv, louely adj
loues: loof n, loue n1
loueth: loue v1, loue v2
loueþ: loue v1, loue v2
louid: loue v1, loue v2
louye: loue v1, loue v2
louyen: loue v1, loue v2
low: lauȝen v, lowe adj, lyen v
lowe: adj, adv, v, lyen v
lowed: loue v2, lowe v
luft: left adj, liften v
lukes: n prop, luc n prop
lust: n, list v
luste: list v, lust n

M

macche: n, v
may: n1, n2, v
mayne: mayn n, meynee n
maynprise: n, v
maistre: maister n, maistrie n
make: n, maken v
male: n, adj
males: n, male n
maner: n, manoir n
manere: maner n, manoir n
maneres: maner n, manoir n
marc: n, n prop, mark n
mare: n, moore adv
marie: n prop, marien v
marye: marie n prop, marien v
mark: n, marc n, marc n prop
maugre: maugree n, maugree prep
maugree: n, prep
meene: mene n, mene adj1, mene v
mees: n, mous n
meete: mete v1, mete vb2
meke: adj, meken v
mele: n, v, meel n
mene: n, adj1, adj2, v, meynee n
menede: mene v, mened v
menyng: ger, mene v
menynge: mene v, menyng ger
mery: murye adv, murye adj
merye: murye adv, murye adj
merk: adj, mark n
messe: masse n, massepens n
mesure: n, v
met: n, mete vb2, meten v
mete: n, v1, v2, meten v
meteles: meteleos adj, metels n
meten: v, mete v1, mete vb2
metyng: ger, meten v
mette: n, met n, mete v1, mete v2,
    meten v
myddel: n, adj
myght: may v, myȝt n
myghte: may v, myȝt n
myȝt: n, may v
miȝt: may v, myȝt n
miȝte: may v, myȝt n
myȝte: may v, myȝt n
myhte: may v, myȝt n

mynne: adj, v
mysdede: n, mysdo v
myseise: n, adj
mo: n, adv, adv
moche: muche n, muche adv,
    muche adj
moest: moost adv, moost adj
moet: moot n, moot v
moiste: adj, v
molde: n1, n2
mone: n, moneie n, moone n
moneye: many adj, moneie n
mony: many adj, moneie n
moore: n, adj, adv, neueremoore adv
moost: adv, adj
mooste: moost adv, moost adj
moot: n, v, moot_halle n
more: n, moore n, moore adv,
    moore adj
mores: moores n, more n
mornyng: moorne n, morwenyng n,
    mournynge ger
morter: n1, n2
most: moost adv, moost adj, moot v,
    must n
moste: moost adv, moost adj, moot v
mot: moot n, moot v
mote: n, v, moot n, moot v
mournynge: ger, moorne n
mouþe: mouþ n, mouþen v
mowen: v, may v
muche: n, adj, adv
muchel: muche n, muche adv,
    muche adj
murye: adj, adv
murthe: murþe n, murþen v
murþe: n, murþen v

N

nat: noȝt n, noȝt adv
nauȝt: noȝt n, noȝt adv, noȝt n
nauht: noȝt n, noȝt adv
nauhte: adj, noȝt n
nauhte: noȝt n, noȝt adv
ne: adv, conj
nede: n, adv, nedy adj
nedes: adv, nede n
nedle: n, paknedle n
neer: adv, prep
neiȝ: adj, adv, prep
neyh: neiȝ adv, neiȝ prep
neiþer: pron, adv, conj
neyther: neiþer pron, neiþer adv,
    neiþer conj
ner: adj, neer adv, neer prep
nere: neer adv, neuere adv, ben v
neste: nest n, witen v1
neuere: adv, neueremoore adv
newe: adj, adv
next: adj, adv, prep
no: adj, adv, body n
noen: noon n, noon pron, noon adj
noȝt: n, pron, adv
noyther: neiþer adv, neiþer conj
nombre: v, noumbre n
non: noon n, noon pron, noon adj
none: noon pron, noon adj
nones: n1, n2
noon: n, pron, adj
north: n, adj
nother: neiþer adv, neiþer conj

noþer: neiþer pron, neiþer adv,
    neiþer conj
nouȝt: noȝt n, noȝt n, noȝt adv
nouht: noȝt n, noȝt adv
now: n, adv
noye: noy n, noyen v

O

o: on prep, oon num, oon pron
oen: oon num, oon pron
of: adv, prep, out_of prep
ofte: adj, adv
on: adv, prep, oon num, oon pron
one: oon num, oon pron, oone adv,
    echone pron
only: oonly adj, oonliche adv
oon: num, pron
oonly: adj, oonliche adv
ooþer: pron, adj, oþer conj,
    ooþerwise adv
or: correl adv, conj, er conj
oþer: conj, ooþer pron, ooþer adj,
    ouþerwhile adv
other: ooþer pron, ooþer adj, oþer
    conj, ouþerwhile adv
othere: ooþer pron, ooþer adj, oþere
    adv, oþer conj
oþere: adv, ooþer pron, ooþer adj,
    ooþer adv, oþergates adv
ouȝt: auȝt adv, auȝt pron
out: adv, out_of prep
oute: adj, out adv, out_of prep
ouþer: oþer conj, ooþer pron,
    ouþerwhile adv
ouer: adv, prep, oueral adv
ouerlonge: adj, adv
owen: owe v, owene adj

P

pay: paien v, paye n
paie: paien v, paye n
paye: n, paien v
payne: payn n, peyne n
palays: paleis n1, paleys n2
paleis: n1, paleys n2
pans: peny n, massepens n
part: n, parteþ v
partyng: ger, parteþ v
peeren: v1, v2
peny: n, penyale n
penis: peny n, massepens n
pere: peere n, peeris n
peres: peere n, piers n prop
persone: n2, person n1
persones: person n1, persone n2
persons: person n1, persone n2
pes: pees n, pese n
pye: n, pies n
pies: n, pye n
plastre: n, v
plaunte: n, ptp
plener: adv, adj
plihte: v, pliȝte v
plogh: plouȝ n, plouȝ v
plouȝ: n, v
pole: poole n, pulle v
pope: n, pope_holy adj
pors: v, purs n
pot: n, putten v
potte: potte_ful, putten v
praye: n, preien v
prechyng: ger, prechen v
prechynge: prechen v, prechyng ger

preyede: prayed ptp, preien v
present: n, adj
prest: adj, adv, preest n, preest n
printe: n, preynte v
pris: n, adj
prouendre: n1, n2
prouendres: n3, prouendre n2
puyr: pure adv, pure adj
puyre: pure adv, pure adj
pulte: pulle v, pult v
pure: adv, adj
put: n, putten v

Q

queynte: adj, quenche v
quyk: adj, quik adv
quik: adv, quyk adj
quyke: quyk adj, quykne v

R

rape: n, rapiþ v
reche: recche v, rechen v
recheth: recche v, rechen v
red: reden v, reed adj, reed n
rede: reden v, reed adj, reed n
reed: n, adj, reden v
reyne: reyn n, reyneþ v
rekne: adj, rekene v
religious: n, religiouse adj
religiouse: adj, religious n
rest: reste n, resten v
reste: n, resten v
reule: n, rule n, rulen v
reumes: reaume n, rewmes n
reue: n, v
reuerence: n, reuerencen v
rewe: n, v
rewele: rule n, rulen v
riche: n, adj
right: riȝt n, riȝt adv, riȝt adj
righte: riȝt adv, riȝt adj
riȝt: n, adj, adv
riȝte: riȝt adj, riȝt n
riht: riȝt adv, riȝt n
rihte: riȝt n, riȝt adj, riȝt adv
ryhte: riȝt n, riȝt adj, riȝt adv
ryne: v, ryn n prop
ripe: adj, ripen v
rype: ripe adj, ripen v
robyn: n, robyn_hood n prop
rome: n prop, v
roten: adj, v1, v2
roteth: roten v1, roten v2
rule: n, rulen v

S

sadde: v, sad adj
sadder: adv, sad adj
saddere: sad adj, sadder adv
saef: fouchensaf v, saaf adj
say: seen v, siggen v
saynt: seint adj, seint n
salt: n, saluen v
sauf: adv, saaf adj
saue: n, prep, sauen v
scorne: v, scorn n
se: see n, seen v
see: n, seen v
segge: n, siggen v
sey: seen v, siggen v
seye: seen v, siggen v
seyen: v, seen v, siggen v
seyn: seen v, siggen v

seint: n, adj
seynt: seint n, seint adj
seynte: seint n, seint adj
seiȝe: seen v, siggen v
seke: seken v, sik adj
selk: silk n, silk adj
selle: n, v
selles: n, selle n
semed: v, semest v
semede: semed v, semest v
senes: siþen adv, siþen prep
sennes: synne n, siþen adv, siþen
    prep, siþen conj
serued: v1, seruen v2
sese: cessen v, seise v
seth: seþ n prop, seen v, siþen adv,
    siþen conj
sethe: siþen adv, siþen prep,
    siþen conj
sethen: siþen adv, siþen conj
sewe: sowe v1, sowe v2, suwen v
sewiþ: sowe v2, suwen v
shap: n, shape v
shape: v, shap n
sharpe: adv, sharp adj
shewynge: shewen v, shewyng ger
shon: shyne v, shoon n
shotte: sheteth v, shot n
shrewed: adj, v
siȝte: siȝt n, sighed v
sike: v, sik adj
syke: sik adj, sike v
siker: adv, adj
sikir: siker adv, siker adj
silk: n, adj
syn: siþen prep, siþen conj
synne: n, synnen v
synnes: synne n, synnen v
syse: n, n prop
siþ: siþen prep, siþen conj
sithe: siþen conj, siþes n
sythe: siþe n, siþen conj, siþes n
siþen: adv, prep, conj
siþþe: siþen adv, siþen prep,
    siþen conj
skolde: n, scolde v
sleep: n, slepe v
slepe: v, sleep n
slepyng: ger, slepe v
slepynge: slepe v, slepyng ger
slow: adj, sleen v
slowe: sleen v, slow adj
smerte: adv, smerteþ v
so: adv, by_so conj, vp_so_doun adv,
    whatso pron
soeth: sooþ adj, sooþ n
softe: adv, adj
solace: n, solacen v
som: pron, adj
some: som pron, som adj
somme: n, adv, som pron
somwhat: pron, adv
sone: n, soone adv
song: n, syngen v
songe: song n, syngen v
sooþ: n, adj
sore: n, soore adv
soth: sooþ n, sooþ adj
soþ: sooþ n, sooþ adj
soþe: sooþ n, sooþ adj
sotile: v, sotil adj
soule: n1, n2

soure: adv, sour adj
souereyn: adj, n
sowe: n, v1, v2
spele: v, spelle v
spere: n, spire v
spire: n, v
stable: adj, v
stale: stele n1, stele v
stede: n1, n2
stele: n1, n2, v
stere: v, steere n
stif: adj, adv
stille: adj, adv
stodie: studie n, studie v
strenghe: n, v
strengþe: n, strengþeþ v
studie: n, v
such: swich pron, swich adj
suche: swich pron, swich adj
sum: som pron, som adj
summe: som pron, som adj
swete: adj, v
swetter: adv, swete adj
swich: pron, adj
swiche: swich pron, swich adj
swynke: v, swynk n
swowe: n, v

T

tale: n, taletelleris n
teeme: teme n1, teme n2
tellynge: ger1, ger2
tem: teme n1, teme n2
teme: n1, n2
tene: n, v, ten num
þan: conj, thanne adv1
than: þan conj, thanne adv1
þanne: adv2, þan conj, thanne adv1
þat: pron rel, pron dem, adj dem, conj
that: þat pron rel, þat pron dem, þat
    adj dem, þat conj
þe: def art, thee v, þow pron
the: þe def art, þow pron
þee: thee v, þow pron
þei: pron, þeiȝ conj
then: þan conj, thanne adv1
thenne: þan conj, thanne adv1,
    þanne adv2
þer: adv, conj, þei pron, theras conj
ther: þei pron, þer adv, þer conj,
    theras conj
þere: þer adv, þer conj
there: þer adv, þer conj, theras conj
these: þis pron dem, þis adj dem
þynke: v1, þynkeþ v2
þynkeþ: v2, þynke v1
þinkeþ: þynke v1, þynkeþ v2
þis: pron dem, adj dem
this: þis pron dem, þis adj dem
þise: þis pron dem, þis adj dem
thise: þis pron dem, þis adj dem
thyse: þis pron dem, þis adj dem
þo: pron dem, adj dem, adv, conj
tho: þo pron dem, þo adj dem, þo adv,
    þo conj
þoȝte: þynke v1, þynkeþ v2
þoo: þo pron dem, þo adv
þouȝt: n, þynke v1
þouȝte: þynke v1, þynkeþ v2
thouhte: þynke v1, þynkeþ v2, þouȝt n
thow: þouȝ conj, þow pron
þrowe: n, v

til: prep, conj
tyme: n, lif_tyme n
tiþe: n, num
tythe: v, tiþe sb
to: adv1, adv2, prtcl, prep, two num,
    for_to adv&prtcl, forto conj
toke: v, taken v
tolde: tellen v, tolled v
toward: adj, prep
trauaile: trauaille n, trauaille v
trauayle: trauaille n, trauaille v
trauaille: n, v
trewe: n, adj
trist: trust n, truste v
truste: v, trust n

U

vnlouely: adv, vnlouelich adj
vp: adv, prep, vp_so_doun adv
vpon: adv, prep
vppon: vpon adv, vpon prep

W

waer: war adj, ware v
waiten: v1, v2
wakynge: ger, wake v
walled: v, wellede v
war: adj, ware v
warde: n, v
ware: n, v, war adj
wareyne: n, waryn n prop
waste: adj, wasten v
webbe: n, web n
wedde: wed n, wedden v
wedes: weed n, weede n
weet: n, adj
wey: n, wye n
weye: wey n, wye n
weyes: wey n, wye n
weiȝe: wey n, weye v
wel: adj, adv, dowwel
wende: wenden v, wene v
wente: wenden v, wene v
wepyng: ger, wepen v
wer: ben v, weer n
werchynge: ger, werchen v
were: v, ben v
werke: werchen v, werk n
werre: n, v
wers: worse adj, worse adv
wete: weet n, weet adj, witen v1
weue: v, wayuen v
wex: n, wexen v
wexe: wex n, wexen v
weye: n, v
what: adj, adv, exclam, pron,
    whatso pron
wheder: whider adv, wheiþer conj
wheiþer: pron, conj
when: adv, whan conj
wher: wheiþer conj, where conj
where: adv, conj, wheiþer pron,
    wheiþer conj
wheþer: wheiþer pron, wheiþer conj
why: n, adv
which: pron, adj
whiche: which pron, which adj
whil: while n, while conj
while: n, adv, conj, ouþerwhile adv
whiles: adv, conj
white: whit adj, whiten v
wy: n prop, wye n
wyddore: wid adj, wide adv

wide: adv, wid adj
wyde: wid adj, wide adv
wiȝt: adj, wight n
wyht: wight n, wiȝt adj
wyhte: wight n, wiȝt adj
wyke: weke n, wouke n
wil: wille n, wille n prop, willen v
will: wille n, wille n prop
wille: n, n prop, willen v
wynde: v, wynd n
wynkyng: ger, wynke v
wis: adj, wissen v
wise: n, wis adj, ooþerwise adv
wyse: wise n, wis adj
wite: witen v1, witen v2
wyte: witen v1, witen v2
witen: v1, v2
witeþ: v, witen v1
wiþ: prep, wiþalle adv
wiþinne: adv, prep
withynne: wiþinne adv, wiþinne prep
withoute: conj, wiþouten adv,
    wiþouten prep
wiþoute: wiþouten adv, wiþouten
    prep
withouten: wiþouten adv,
    wiþouten prep
wiþouten: adv, prep
witnesse: n, v
wytnesse: witnesse n, witnesse v
witte: wit n, witeþ v
woke: v, wake v, wouke n
wolle: n, willen v
wollen: adj, willen v
womman: n, kynnes_womman n
wonder: n, adj, adv
wone: n, wonye
woned: wonye, wont ptp
wordynge: ger, worden v
wors: worse adj, worse adv
worschipe: worship n, worshipen v
worse: adj, adv
worshipe: worship n, worshipen v
worsshipe: worship n, worshipen v
worst: worse adj, worþe v
worste: worse adj, worse adv
worth: worþ adj, worþe v
worþ: n, adj, worþe v
worthe: worþ n, worþ adj, worþe v
wost: willen v, witen v1
wounde: n, wounden v, wownde v
wrath: wraþe n, wraþen v
wrathe: wraþe n, wraþen v
wraþe: n, wraþen v
wraþþe: wraþe n, wraþen v
wrecche: n, adj
writ: n, holy_writ n
wrong: n, adv, wryngen v
wroth: wroþ adj, wroþ v
wroþ: adj, v

Y

ye: pron, adv
ȝe: ye pron, ye adv
ȝef: gyuen v, if conj
yeme: n, yemen v
ȝeme: yeme n, yemen v
ȝerne: yerne adv, yernen v, rennen v
yerne: adv, yernen v
ȝif: gyuen v, if conj

LIST OF FORMS SEPARATED OR COMBINED IN ANALYSIS

The following, written as a single word in the copy text, have been analyzed as two separate words.

attese (1) > at prep, ese n
bycause (1) > by prep, cause n
dowel (3) > doon v, wel adv
farewel (2) > fare v, wel adv
fastyngdayes (1) > fastyng ger, day n
fastyngdays (2) > fastyng ger, day n
fenelsed (1) > fenel n, seed n

foreuere (1) > for prep, euere adv
fremen (1) > fre adj, man n
nobody (1) > no adj, body n
ouersour (1) > ouer adv, sour adj
namore (2) > no adj, moore n, moore adv
roteyetyme (1) > rotey adj, tyme n
welawey (1) > wel adv, awey adv

The following, written as two (or three) separate forms in the copy text, have been analyzed as a single word. Headwords composed of forms written separately are joined with an underscore, as in by_so.

bed chaumbre > bedchambre n
by_so conj
bi so > by_so conj
breed corn > bredcorn n
cockes lane > cokkeslane n
cote_armure n
dore nayl > dorenail n
do wel > dowel n
ech one > echone pron
for_to adv&prtcl
fouchen saef > fouchensaf v
handy_dandy n
haly daies > holy_day n
haly dayes > holy_day n
hey trolly lolly > how_trolly_lolly exclam
hey trollilolly > how_trolly_lolly exclam
holy_chirche n
holi cherches > holy_chirche n
holy cherche > holy_chirche n
holi chirch > holy_chirche n
holy chirche > holy_chirche n
holy chirches > holy_chirche n
holi church > holy_chirche n
holy church > holy_chirche n
holi churche > holy_chirche n
holy churche > holy_chirche n
holy kerke > holy_chirche n
holy kirk > holy_chirche n
holi kirke > holy_chirche n
holy kirke > holy_chirche n
holy_day n
holi goest > holy_goost n
holy goest > holy_goost n
holy_goost n
holi goost > holy_goost n
holi gost > holy_goost n
holy gost > holy_goost n

holy goste > holy_goost n
holy_writ n
holi writ > holy_writ n
holy wryt > holy_writ n
how_trolly_lolly exclam
iohan_but n prop
iohannes_crisostomus n prop
kynnes_womman n
lif_tyme n
lyf tyme > lif_tyme n
mas pans > massepens n
mesonis deux > mesondieux n
messe penis > massepens n
moot_halle n
neuere moore > neueremoore adv
pakke nedle > paknedle n
peny ale > penyale n
pere_ionettes n
pope_holy adj
potte_ful n
robyn hode > robyn_hood n prop
robyn_hood n prop
som_tyme adv
some tyme > som_tyme adv
some tymes > sometymes adv
sum tyme > som_tyme adv
sume tyme > som_tyme adv
summe tyme > som_tyme adv
tale telleris > taletelleris n
ther as > theras conj
þer as > theras conj
there as > theras conj
vp_so_doun adv
vp so down > vp_so_doun adv
what so > whatso pron
wiþ al > wiþalle adv
wiþ alle > wiþalle adv

WORDS UNIQUE TO A, B, C OR AC

The following distinguishes the vocabulary found only in one version or in A and C but not B.

Words Unique to A

aaron n prop
allie n
arerid ptp
asshamidest v
axesse n
bakken v
banisshit ptp
begynnere n
begon ptp
belouȝ v
beloure v
bidowe n
bode n
bodyward adv
bollnyng ger
brayn n
braynwood adj
brokesshankid adj
browes n
cateles adj
chapellis n
cheuisshen v
childhod n
clerioun n
clyf n
clom n
comaundour n
conyon n
copiede v
cotidian n
courrour n
cowes n
dauncelid ptp
declynede v
delites n
derling n
destreris n
deuyn n
dignites n
dredles adv
drinkeres n
faste adj
fyn n2
foretolde v
forgid ptp
fornicatouris n
foundours n
gronyng ger
growel n
hayl n2
harpe n
hauer n
helde v
hendeþ v
heryng ger
hobelide v
hogge n prop
ygulpid ptp
ile n
iohan_but n prop
loggyng ger
may n2
marbil n
mydmorewe adj
mylionis n

mynchons n
mysbeleue v
mosseþ v
next adv
nones n
outtake prep
pauyloun n
pencioun n
pilewhey n
pitous adj
play n
plete v
pluralites n
poperiþ v
present adj
presumptuowsly adv
ray adj
rekne adj
rewlyche adj
ribande ptp
richard n prop
rouȝ adj
routen v
sauf adv
semble n
sengle adj
setis n
seweris n
skornfully adv
spedelich adj
spedily adv
spousid v
stable adj
stodyenge ger
swage v
swowe n
tentis n
tercian n
thrift n
þrobbant prp
tide n
toille v
tokkeris n
tomblest v
tras n
trepget n
trespassours n
vnche n
vnpossible adj
verilyche adv
verious n
vynegre n
walewiþ v
wepyng ger
when adv
wynlyche adv
wrong adv
ȝedde v

Words Unique to B

abyngdoun n prop
ablyndeþ v
acouped ptp
acquitaunce n
adayes adv
affrayned v

afore adv
afore prep
ago ptp
aiels n
alay n
aliche adv
alisaundre n1 prop
allone adj
alouȝ adv
amercy v
amyddes adv
amonge adv
anoþer adj
appele v
appultree n
appurtenaunces n
aprill n
argueres n
articles n
asondry adj
aspare v
assay n
assaut n
assembled ptp
assemblee n
atones adv
attre n
auynet n
auoutrye n
baddenesse n
ballokknyf n
banyer n
baptiȝynge ger
barm n
baþed ptp
beem n
beflobered v
benyson n
bidropped ptp
biggyng prp
bile n
bymeneþ v2
bymolen v
biquasshed v
birewe v
bisherewed v
bisperede v
bistowe v
biswatte ptp
biwiled v
biyete n
blameworþy adj
blasen n
blosmede v
blowyng ger
bodily adj
bokelees adj
bollen ptp
bosard n
bostere n
botons n
breden v2
bredyng ger
breide v
brennyng ger
brent ptp
breþyng ger

brewecheste adj
brusshe n
buylden v
buyldynge ger
burel adj
buryinge ger
burioneþ v
cakebreed n
caractes n
castynge ger
catecumelynges n
caue n
cene n
chastilet n
chaumbrere n
chichestre n prop
chief n
chymenee n
chirietyme n
chiteryng ger
clausemele adv
cleef v
colomy adj
compasynge ger
confortable adj
confortatif adj
confortour n
congie n
conynges n
coniured v
contrit adj
corde n
correctours n
costned v
crauynge ger
cristnyng gen
cruwel adj
dampnacion n
decourreþ v
decretals n
deel n
derkliche adv
derne adv
desiryng ger
deuoutrye n
diamaundes n
disalowed ptp
dolful adj
done n
dongehill n
double adj
driȝte n
dropped v
ely n prop
emme n prop
emperesse n
encreesse v
engreynen v
enseled ptp
entente n
entisyng ger
entremetten v
enuenymes n
enuenymeþ v
erchebisshopes n
eschetes n
esy adj

esily adv
espied ptp
essex n prop
eueneforþ adv
ewages n
executours n
expounen v
faderlese adj
faityng ger
fautes n
feeris n
feynte adj
ferme n
fermerye n
fern adj
fernyeres n
fesaunt₃ n
festynge ger
festu n
fetisliche adv
fight n
fightyng ger
filþe n
fiþelere n
flappes n
flobre v
floured v
forgrynt v
forster n
forwalked ptp
forwhy conj
forwit n
frenche adj
frenesse n
frounces n
fulled ptp
fulliche adv
fullyng ger2
gape v
gardyner n
garlekhiþe n prop
ga₃ophilacium n
geffrey n prop
generacion n
gesene adj
gesse v
gybbe n prop
gide v
glubberes n
godchildren n
godfader n
godmoder n
goere n
goliardeis n
goostly adj
graffen v
gramariens n
grape n
grece n
greetnesse n
grekes n prop
greuaunces n
hardie v
harpour n
haterynge ger
haukyn n prop
hauylons n
heeþ n
helyng ger
herafterward adv
heron adv
hethynesse n

homliche adv
hostele v
hostrie n
ydiot n
ydiotes adj
yfruyted ptp
yhabited ptp
impe v
infamis adj
infinites n
inparfitly adv
intestate adj
intil prep
ypocras n prop
ysherewed v
yspoused ptp
yteynted ptp
kaylewey n
kalender n
kennyng ger
keruynge ger
kynnesmen n
lakkes n
largere adv
laþered ptp
laweful adj
leef n2
legge v1
leopard n
lernyng ger
liberal adj
lieutenaunt n
lyinge ger
likynge ger2
likkyng ger
listres n
lyth n
londleperis n
loseþ v
lotieþ v
louedreem n
lowynge ger
lusard n
madde adj
makere n
manlich adj
meditacion n
mees n
menged v
menyson n
merciful adj
mercymonye n
mesure v
mete₃yueres n
myldenesse n
minute n
mys n
myscheued v
mysruleþ v
myx n
moled ptp
moles n
morsel n
mote n
moþeeten adj
mute adj
narwe adv
neddres n
nempnynge ger
nor conj
northfolk n prop
ofgon v

ofrau₃te v
ofte adj
orientals n
outcomen ptp
outlawe n
outwit n
ouergilte ptp
ouermaistreþ v
ouertaken v
o₃ias n prop
paast n
parchemyn n
parlour n
pedlere n
peel n
peeren v1
peeris n
pendaunt₃ n
personage n
pharisees n
pil n1
plaunte ptp
pledours n
plener adj
plot n
plurel adj
po n
porthors n
possed v
possessioners n
postes n
poustee n
praye n
praktisour n
pried v
principally adv
pryuees n
proched v
prophecie n
prouendre n1
purueie v
quartron n
quaued v
queed n
quelt ptp
quiete n
rattes n
raunsoun n
raued v
raxed v
rebukynge ger
reconforted v
redels n
redyng ger
renable adj
renaboute n
rerages n
ribanes n
riche n
riflynge ger
ri₃twise adj
ryuer n
rochemador n prop
rogged v
rolle v
rosamounde n prop
sadde v
sadnesse n
salt n
saphires n
saufte n
saulee n

scape v
scoffyng ger
scornyng ger
scourges n
semblaunce n
serpent n
seyen v
shaft n
shamedest v
shappere n
sherte n
shilden v
shynes n
shipe n
shordych n prop
skynnes n
sliken v
sobbed v
sobreliche adv
soiled v
sonnen v
soor adj
sop n
sope n
sothfastnesse n
soude n
spekes n
spelonkes n
sperhauk n
spien v
spiritual adj
spitten v
spottes n
spuen v
stable v
stalworþe adj
stank v
stekie v
sterne adv
stone v
stories n
stratford n prop
surgenrie n
swymmere n
swymmyng ger
tacches n
talke v
tarse n
taseles n
tastes n
termes n
thefliche adv
þerf adj
þesternesse n
thilke pron
þresshe v
þretynge ger
þreve n
þursday n
tynynge ger
tiþe num
tonne n
torende ptp
tow n
trailynge ger
trauaillours n
tunycle n
vnchargeþ v
vncoupled ptp
vnderpight ptp
vndignely adv
vndoynge ger

vnglade adj
vngodly adv
vnmaken v
vnmesurable adj
vnresonable adj
vnrosted ptp
vnsauory adj
vnsesonable adj
vntempred ptp
unþende adj
vntiled ptp1
vsage n
venial adj
verred v
vers n
viker n
vile adj
virgile n prop
virres n
visage n
viseden v
visitynge ger
voideþ v
waast n
wakynge ger
walis n prop
wantynge ger
wareyne n
warisshen v
wastyng ger
wenes n
weue v
weuyng ger
weye n
whatsoeuere pron
whistlen v
whistlere n
whistlyng ger
wildefowel n
wynde v
wyr n
wiþstonde v
wyued v
wodnesday n
wolueliche adj
wolueskynnes adj
wonder adj
wowede v
yarkeþ v
yemere n
yolde ptp
ȝacheus n prop

Words Unique to C

abeggeth adv
abel n prop
abostede v
abrede adv
abribeth adv
absoloun n prop
acloye v
acordaunce n
acountable adj
action n
aday adv
adiectyf n
ado n
aferes n
afuyre adj
aglotye v
aysches n
aknowe ptp
aldremen n

alenghe adv
alyhte v
allouable adj
almesfull adj
alose v
amorwe adv
angryliche adv
anhengede
antecedent n
apartye adv
apeel n
arbitreres n
aredy adj
aryht adv
arseny n prop
arwed ptp
aspele v
atake ptp
atyer n
atymye v
atwene adv
atwynne adv
auȝte n
auer n
awurchynge adv
aȝeynward adv
bande v
bannebury n prop
barnhoed n
barre v
batnelde n
becauȝte v
beden v
beggynge ger
begyneld n
beyre num
bendeth v
berye n
berke v
berkeres n
bygat v
byglosedest v
byhofte n
bysemede v
byteche v
bythenke v
bytrauayle v
bytulye v
blanket n
blete v
blew adj
bloweth v2
boylaunt prp
bollares n
bonchef n
bonde n
borwynge
bote v
brake n
brake v
brasene adj
breuhwyf n
brewhouses n
brihtnesse n
brumstoen
bruttene v
bruttenynge ger
cammaca n
cantel n
capede v
cappe n
car n

carse n
carte v
carteres n
cartwhel n
chayere n
chaste adv
chaunceller n
cheke v
cher adj
chetes n
chield ptp
chine n
claymes n
clees n
clemynge prp
clergyse n
clerkysh adj
cliauntes n
clymat n
cockes n
coked ptp
cokeres n2
coltyng n prop
comet n
compas n
confounde v
connesaunce n
consenteth v
constrayne v
contumax adj
conturrollor n
corf n prop
cornehull n prop
corner n
corsement n
corsynge ger
coterelles n
countresegge v
couerour n
cradel n
crocer n
crokes n
crommes n
cronicles n
cropward n
crow n
daubynge ger
daunsynge ger
decretistre n
dedeynus adj
delicat adj
deluynge ger
demynge ger
denyede v
dentiefliche adv
derfly adv
dernely adv
desauowe v
descendeth v
desert n
despeyre v
despoilen v
deuouren v
deuouteliche adv
deuoutours n
dirige n
discomfited ptp
discrete adj
dispit n
diuerse adv
diuerseth v
dompynges n

donghep n
dronkenesse n
drop n
drosenes n
druie adv
ducchesse n
ducherie n
ebrew n
eg n
enchesoun n
encountre prep
endaunted v
enhanced ptp
ennedy n prop
enquestes n
ensense n
enspireth v
enterely adv
episteles n
erbes n
errant adj
erren v
espirit n
fayre n
falaes adj
falewe v
fallas n
fenkel n
ferlyede v
festedayes n
fial adj
fyge n
figuratyfly adv
fiscuth v
flees n
flonke n
foldes n
folowynge ger
force n
fore n
foreynes n
foreteth n
forgo v
forleyn ptp
forthermore adv
fouchensaf v
gabbe v
garlekmonger n
gyles n prop
gyse n
gnedy adj
gobet n
gome n2
gonnes n
graffe n
gredyre n
greut n
grype n
hacches n
hakeneys n
halie v
halsyng ger
haluendele n
hangeman n
hangynge ger
hastite n
heggen v
helynge ger
herby adv
herde n
hereaboute adv
herkene v

herodes n prop
hertely adv
holdyng ger
hostiele n
hundredfold n
ydolatrie n
yesyhte n
yfranchised ptp
yknowe v
ille adj
imade v
indepartable adj
indirect adj
infirmite n
inhabiten v
insolibles adj
yreuestede ptp
yrynged ptp
yse v
ythryueth v
ywende v
ywyte v
ywonne v
iolyf adj
ionettes n
kalketrappes n
kembe v
kerne v
kyke v
kyndly adj
kynnes_womman n
laboryng ger
lachdraweres n
layes n
layn v
later adj
lauhfollyche adv
launseth v
laurence n prop
lechyng ger
legityme adj
leiaunce n
leye adj
leksed n
lentesedes n
letyse n prop
lettynge ger2
lycour n
lygge adj
likynge prp
lykyngliche adv
lynsed n
lyther adv
lithereth v
lokes n
lomes n
lompe n
longe n
longede v2
longes n
lordliche adv
lossum adj
lotus n
louable adj
loue n
loupe n
loueknotte n
louer n
madden v
mayntenour n
mangnel n
manschipes n

manslauht n
marl n
marre v
maumettes n
me pron indef
megre adj
mere n
mersyen v
mylked ptp
mynne adj
myntewhile n
myres n
myshap n
mysliked v
mysturnynge ger
mytrede ptp
mywen v
moreouer adv
morreyne n
mortel adj
moskeles n
mowen v
mullestones n
nacion n
nauhte adj
neyhele v
nese n
nippynge prp
nythynge n
north adj
northerne adj
obediencer n
ofwalked ptp
orysones n
ouh exclam
outryderes n
ouerdoen v
ouerleyd ptp
ouermore adv
ouerplente n
ouersopped v
ouerturnynge ger
ouerward adv
palpable adj
paniter n
papelotes n
parail n
paramours n
parfay exclam
pauper n
peccunie n
peytrele v
penyles adj
pensel n
pere_ionettes n
perpetuelly adv
persecucoun n
pyement n
pykares n
pikeporses n
pykstaff n
pynnes n
plesaunce n
plihte v
plommes n
poyntest v
pomade n
popeiay n
porfirie n prop
pors v
portours n
potte_ful n

predestinaet ptp
prescit adj
prest adv
preuete n
primer n
printe n
printede v
profiteþ v
prouendreth v
prouerbe n
pues n
pult v
pursward adv
putour n
putrie n
queene n
quoer n
ragamoffyn n
rage n
rayme v
ransake v
raueners n
raxlede v
recetteth v
reclused ptp
rect adj
relacion n
relatif n
rele v
remembraunce n
repaest n
rescetour n
retribucoun n
reule n
reueled ptp
reuers n
rewe n
rybbe v
richeliche adv
ryhtfulnesse n
rypereue n
robynge ger
roep n
ronde n
roste v
roued v
rowe v1
ruyflare n
safly adv
sambure n
samrede adj
saue n
saueriore adj
scale n
schalkes n
sciense n
seden v
seemely adj
seyntwarie n
selles n
seluerles adj
semeliche adv
senatours n
seneschalles n
serued v1
sharpeliche adv
shille adv
shyt v
shoriare n
shrewed adj
shrewed v
shryuars n

shuyuen v
sykeren v
simile n
syse n
syse n prop
skalones n
skilfole adj
sleyliche adv
sloo n
sofistre n
solempneliche adv
solitarie adj
sopares n
sotiltees n
souche v
soule n2
soware n
spele v
spendour n
spiek n
spyer n
spilletyme n
spynnyng ger
spiserye n
spitteden v
spouse n
squier n1
squire n2
stake n
stalke n
stele n2
steryng ger
sterte v
styfliche adv
styhlede v
stikede v
style n
straunge adj
strenede v
strenghe n
strenghe v
strikares n
strompet n
supersedias n
suspectioun n
sustantyf n
swanwhit adj
swettenesse n
tanners n
tarre n
tasch n
termisonus n
thankes n
thekynge ger
þertyl adv
thewes n
threschynge ger
thusgates adv
thwytinge ger
tythe v
togrynt v
tol n
tolle v
tolomeus n prop
tombe n
toquasched v
toreueth v
toroef v
tortle n
tothdraweres n
touore adj
toward adj

transuerseth v
treys n
tribulacions n
tripe n
troyledest v
tulius n prop
vnbokelede v
vnconnyngliche adv
vncorteysliche adv
vncrounede ptp
vndernymynge ger
vndershored ptp
vngraue ptp
vnknowe ptp
vnlawefulliche adv
vnlele adj
vnlikyng prp
vnlofsum adj
unnit adj
vnredy adj
vnrihtfole adj
vnrobbed ptp
vnsemely adj
vnsittyng prp
vnstable adj
vnstedefast adj
vnwrast adj
vpon adv
vayne adj
vaynglorie n
vantyng ger
variable adj
vaunsed ptp
vowe v
vowes n
wayke adj
wakere adj
walet n
walkeres n
wallyng ger
walschman n
wanne adj
warde v
warnynge ger
webbe n
wellecresses n
wentes n
werynesse n
werre v
wesches n
wetheres n
while adv
whiles adv
wilyman n
willed adj
wynse v
wirdes n
wisman n
withoute conj
withsitte v
wittyman n
wonte n
wordynge ger
worliche adj
wose n
wrake n
wrynglawe n
wrongly adv
wurye v
ȝemen n
ȝeuan n prop
ȝokes n

Words in AC but not in B

bane n
batte n
brere n
brochen n
busily adv
charge n
clymbe v
combre v
constellacioun n
croce n
hosebonde n
leperis n
mende v
mendis n
myssyng ger
obedient adj
part n
piche v
queynte adj
roten v2
shabbide adj
þedom n
þeroute adv
þropis n
vnderstondyng ger
wantoun
wynneres n

LIST OF PROPER NOUNS

In this list, proper nouns which appear in the Latin or French are italicized.

aaron	elyes	iurdan	samuel
abel	emaus	kytte	sathan
abyngdoun	emme	*laȝare*	saturne
abraham	*emme*	laurence	saul
abrahe	engelond	letyse	scribes
absoloun	ennedy	londoun	seneca
ade	essex	longeus	seþ
agag	*euam*	lot	shordych
albertes	eue	luc	symme
amalec	felice	lucifer	symond
ambrose	fynes	lukes	synay
andrew	flaundres	lumbardes	syse
antony	foluyles	macabeus	sodome
aristotle	fraunce	mahoun	sortes
arseny	fraunceis	makometh	southwerk
astroth	gabrielis	malkyn	spayne
aultoun	galilee	maluerne	stowue
austyn	galis	marc	stratford
auereys	garlekhiþe	margrete	surrie
auynoun	gascoigne	*maria*	thaddee
bannebury	geffrey	marie	themese
beneyt	gybbe	martha	thomas
bernard	gyles	mathew	tybourne
bethleem	godefray	maudeleyne	tymme
beton	gregorie	michel	tobye
bette	grekes	moyses	tolomeus
bokynghamshire	griffyn	*moisi*	tomme
bromholm	haukyn	morales	troianus
brugges	heyne	munde	tulius
caym	herodes	nabugodonosor	vrie
cayphas	hertford	naȝareth	virgile
caleis	heruy	neptalym	walis
calote	hikke	nynyue	walsyngham
caluarie	hogge	noe	waryn
caton	hugh	normandie	watte
caunterbury	*iesu(-*	northfolk	westmynstre
cesar	ynde	offyn	wy
cesari(s	*iob*	oseye	wille
cesse	ypocras	oȝias	wynchestre
chepe	irlonde	pampilon	ȝeuan
chestre	ysaak	paulynes	ȝacheus
chichestre	ysaye	perkyn	
christus	ysodorus	pernele	
clarice	*israel*	peter	
clement	israel	*petrus*	
cleophas	*iuda*	piers	
coltyng	iacob	pilat	
corf	iakke	plato	
cornehull	iames	porfirie	
costantyn	ierico	poul	
crist	ierom	prucelond	
damaske	ierusalem	randolf	
daniel	iesus	reynald	
dauid	iew	richard	
dawe	iob	ryn	
denote	iohan	roberd	
dysmas	iohan_but	robyn	
diues	iohane	robyn_hood	
dominyk	iohannes_crisostomus	rochel	
douere	ionette	rochemador	
dunmowe	iosaphat	romaynes	
edmond	ioseph	rome	
edward	iosue	rosamounde	
egidie	iuda	rutland	
egipciaca	iudas	salomon	
egipte	iude	samaritan	
ely	iudith	sampson	

This lists in descending order the highest frequency headwords in Langland's Middle English vocabulary, each with its absolute and relative frequency (in parentheses); included are words which occur at least eight times (relative frequency of 0.005 or greater).

and conj 10,620 (6.719)
þe def art 5,024 (3.178)
he pron 5,012 (3.171)
ben v 4,619 (2.922)
i pron 4,403 (2.786)
of prep 3,366 (2.130)
to prtcl 2,492 (1.577)
þat pron rel 2,421 (1.532)
a art 2,378 (1.504)
in prep 2,262 (1.431)
hij pron 2,032 (1.286)
þow pron 1,704 (1.078)
hauen v 1,570 (0.993)
to prep 1,529 (0.967)
as conj 1,477 (0.934)
it pron 1,445 (0.914)
al adj 1,407 (0.890)
for prep 1,401 (0.886)
wiþ prep 1,318 (0.834)
man n 1,298 (0.821)
shal v 1,133 (0.717)
for conj 1,077 (0.681)
þat conj 1,028 (0.650)
we pron 937 (0.593)
ye pron 921 (0.583)
by prep 853 (0.540)
noȝt adv 815 (0.516)
so adv 797 (0.504)
þei pron 777 (0.492)
ne conj 763 (0.483)
willen v 739 (0.468)
quod v 709 (0.449)
on prep 693 (0.438)
þis adj dem 691 (0.437)
or conj 685 (0.433)
no adj 684 (0.433)
god n 678 (0.429)
siggen v 676 (0.428)
ac conj 654 (0.414)
may v 652 (0.412)
but conj 633 (0.400)
at prep 569 (0.360)
maken v 559 (0.354)
doon v 539 (0.341)
if conj 528 (0.334)
heo pron 520 (0.329)
comen v 515 (0.326)
thanne adv1 497 (0.314)
lord n 444 (0.281)
þat adj dem 430 (0.272)
boþe num 414 (0.262)
wel adv 411 (0.260)
neuere adv 386 (0.244)
kyng n 383 (0.242)
many adj 367 (0.232)
conscience n 348 (0.220)
þoruȝ prep 342 (0.216)
þer adv 330 (0.209)
seen v 328 (0.208)
crist n prop 322 (0.204)
konne v 321 (0.203)
whan conj 317 (0.201)
tellen v 311 (0.197)
lif n 310 (0.196)

lawe n 305 (0.193)
lyuen v 300 (0.190)
taken v 290 (0.183)
truþe n 287 (0.182)
knowen v 286 (0.181)
loue n1 283 (0.179)
mede n 282 (0.178)
þan conj 276 (0.175)
wit n 271 (0.171)
piers n prop 266 (0.168)
werchen v 257 (0.163)
gyuen v 256 (0.162)
grace n 252 (0.159)
witen v1 250 (0.158)
til conj 247 (0.156)
wille n 247 (0.156)
þus adv 245 (0.155)
reson n 243 (0.154)
tyme n 240 (0.152)
what pron 239 (0.151)
soule n1 232 (0.147)
loue v1 228 (0.144)
þat pron dem 226 (0.143)
after adv 226 (0.143)
any adj 224 (0.142)
swich adj 224 (0.142)
techen v 222 (0.140)
peple n 217 (0.137)
holden v 215 (0.136)
pouere adj 214 (0.135)
helpen v 210 (0.133)
day n 209 (0.132)
fro prep 209 (0.132)
good adj 208 (0.132)
clerk n 207 (0.131)
synne n 205 (0.130)
forþ adv 200 (0.127)
riȝt adv 200 (0.127)
how conj 199 (0.126)
ne adv 197 (0.125)
now adv 196 (0.124)
kynde n 195 (0.123)
mercy n 195 (0.123)
riche adj 195 (0.123)
þer conj 194 (0.123)
go v 194 (0.123)
heuene n 194 (0.123)
leten v 192 (0.121)
word n 192 (0.121)
ooþer pron 189 (0.120)
hote v 188 (0.119)
loken v 188 (0.119)
euere adv 185 (0.117)
beren v2 183 (0.116)
wenden v 183 (0.116)
for_to adv&prtcl 178 (0.113)
hymself pron 178 (0.113)
sauen v 178 (0.113)
after prep 176 (0.111)
fynden v 176 (0.111)
þo adv 171 (0.108)
leue v1 169 (0.107)
suffren v 169 (0.107)
holy_chirche n 167 (0.106)

dowel n 165 (0.104)
wiþouten prep 165 (0.104)
þouȝ conj 164 (0.104)
bidden v 163 (0.103)
she pron 162 (0.102)
brynge v 161 (0.102)
gret adj 159 (0.101)
þis pron dem 158 (0.100)
folk n 158 (0.100)
here adv 157 (0.099)
er conj 156 (0.099)
among prep 151 (0.096)
deeþ n 150 (0.095)
maner n 150 (0.095)
yet adv 150 (0.095)
frere n 148 (0.094)
kepen v 148 (0.094)
lewed adj 146 (0.092)
heren v 143 (0.090)
oon num 142 (0.090)
good n 140 (0.089)
herte n 139 (0.088)
togideres adv 137 (0.087)
som pron 134 (0.085)
erþe n 132 (0.084)
þyng n 130 (0.082)
deye v 130 (0.082)
knyȝt n 130 (0.082)
asken v 129 (0.082)
kyn n 129 (0.082)
preest n 129 (0.082)
whoso pron 129 (0.082)
world n 129 (0.082)
ech adj 128 (0.081)
ayein prep 125 (0.079)
clergie n 125 (0.079)
sire n 125 (0.079)
trewe adj 125 (0.079)
cristen adj 123 (0.078)
werk n 123 (0.078)
iesus n prop 122 (0.077)
leren v 122 (0.077)
lond n 122 (0.077)
shewen v 122 (0.077)
speche n 122 (0.077)
book n 121 (0.077)
wif n 121 (0.077)
amenden v 119 (0.075)
callen v 117 (0.074)
folwen v 117 (0.074)
wynnen v 117 (0.074)
falle v 116 (0.073)
moore adv 116 (0.073)
name n 116 (0.073)
noon adj 116 (0.073)
ligge v 115 (0.073)
kynde adj 114 (0.072)
no adv 114 (0.072)
ful adv 113 (0.071)
feiþ n 112 (0.071)
sitten v 112 (0.071)
likeþ v 111 (0.070)
moore n 110 (0.070)
sende v 110 (0.070)

ooþer adj 109 (0.069)
siþen adv 109 (0.069)
forþi adv 108 (0.068)
out_of prep 108 (0.068)
pees n 108 (0.068)
sone n 108 (0.068)
þre num 106 (0.067)
coueitise n 105 (0.066)
mete n 105 (0.066)
penaunce n 105 (0.066)
helle n 104 (0.066)
reden v 104 (0.066)
seint adj 104 (0.066)
who pron 104 (0.066)
into prep 103 (0.065)
oþer conj 103 (0.065)
ofte adv 103 (0.065)
pacience n 101 (0.064)
worþe v 101 (0.064)
iew n prop 100 (0.063)
counseil n 99 (0.063)
fals adj 98 (0.062)
maister n 98 (0.062)
preien v 98 (0.062)
two num 98 (0.062)
mayde n 97 (0.061)
putten v 96 (0.061)
cryen v 95 (0.060)
plowman n 95 (0.060)
wey n 95 (0.060)
beest n 94 (0.059)
lady n 94 (0.059)
heiȝ adj 93 (0.059)
muche adj 93 (0.059)
nede n 92 (0.058)
sooþ n 92 (0.058)
vpon prep 92 (0.058)
also adv 91 (0.058)
pride n 91 (0.058)
what adj 91 (0.058)
prechen v 90 (0.057)
where conj 90 (0.057)
al adv 89 (0.056)
neiþer conj 89 (0.056)
þynkeþ v2 87 (0.055)
commune n 87 (0.055)
aboute adv 86 (0.054)
beggere n 86 (0.054)
moot v 86 (0.054)
pouerte n 86 (0.054)
hunger n 85 (0.054)
seruen v2 85 (0.054)
witnesse n 85 (0.054)
body n 84 (0.053)
hand n 84 (0.053)
myȝt n 84 (0.053)
myself pron 84 (0.053)
noon pron 84 (0.053)
bifore prep 83 (0.053)
ende n 83 (0.053)
fader n 83 (0.053)
lesen v2 83 (0.053)
longe adv 83 (0.053)
siluer n 83 (0.053)

tonge n 83 (0.053)
wis adj 83 (0.053)
fair adj 82 (0.052)
bileue n 81 (0.051)
charite n 81 (0.051)
gynneþ v 81 (0.051)
vp adv 81 (0.051)
wikked adj 81 (0.051)
eten v 80 (0.051)
faste adv 79 (0.050)
lyen v 79 (0.050)
vnder prep 79 (0.050)
graunte v 78 (0.049)
pardon n 78 (0.049)
som_tyme adv 78 (0.049)
þerwiþ adv 77 (0.049)
best adj 77 (0.049)
child n 77 (0.049)
long adj 77 (0.049)
which pron 77 (0.049)
womman n 77 (0.049)
eiȝe n1 75 (0.047)
faillen v 75 (0.047)
passen v 75 (0.047)
seuen num 75 (0.047)
water n 75 (0.047)
dede n 74 (0.047)
place n 74 (0.047)
sette v 74 (0.047)
siȝt n 74 (0.047)
bisshop n 73 (0.046)
gile n 73 (0.046)
lele adj 73 (0.046)
pope n 73·(0.046)
seken v 73 (0.046)
semest v 73 (0.046)
stonden v 73 (0.046)
bileuen v2 72 (0.046)
lenen v2 72 (0.046)
lerne v 72 (0.046)
wexen v 72 (0.046)
wo n 72 (0.046)
creature n 71 (0.045)
ioye n 71 (0.045)
leden v 71 (0.045)
sorwe n 71 (0.045)
a prep 70 (0.044)
speken v 70 (0.044)
tale n 70 (0.044)
bettre adv 69 (0.044)
blisse n 69 (0.044)
dobet n 69 (0.044)
kennen v 69 (0.044)
liflode n 69 (0.044)
catel n 68 (0.043)
craft n 68 (0.043)
drynken v 68 (0.043)
wissen v 68 (0.043)
leuen v 67 (0.042)
ones adv 67 (0.042)
preuen v 67 (0.042)
siþen conj 67 (0.042)
syngen v 67 (0.042)
bettre adj 66 (0.042)
power n 66 (0.042)
yede v 66 (0.042)
coueiten v 65 (0.041)
lettre n 65 (0.041)
out adv 65 (0.041)
paien v 65 (0.041)
raþe adv 65 (0.041)
soone adv 65 (0.041)

gifte n 64 (0.040)
sooþly adv 64 (0.040)
while conj 64 (0.040)
breke v 63 (0.040)
conforten v 63 (0.040)
court n 63 (0.040)
dar v1 63 (0.040)
fend n 63 (0.040)
writen v 63 (0.040)
first adv 62 (0.039)
lette v 62 (0.039)
mete v2 62 (0.039)
oon pron 62 (0.039)
richesse n 62 (0.039)
som adj 62 (0.039)
witnesse v 62 (0.039)
awey adv 61 (0.039)
holy_writ n 61 (0.039)
lakke v 61 (0.039)
wynter n 61 (0.039)
counseillen v 60 (0.038)
dwellen v 60 (0.038)
fare v 60 (0.038)
laste adj 60 (0.038)
sonne n 60 (0.038)
swich pron 60 (0.038)
þo adj dem 59 (0.037)
dobest n 59 (0.037)
first adj 59 (0.037)
light n 59 (0.037)
lucifer n prop 59 (0.037)
wedden v 59 (0.037)
geten v 58 (0.037)
heed n 58 (0.037)
leaute n 58 (0.037)
þerinne adv 57 (0.036)
þiself pron 57 (0.036)
adam n 57 (0.036)
blood n 57 (0.036)
frend n 57 (0.036)
gold n 57 (0.036)
mene v 57 (0.036)
turne v 57 (0.036)
þo pron dem 56 (0.035)
blesse v 56 (0.035)
deuel n 56 (0.035)
drawe v 56 (0.035)
faire adv 56 (0.035)
flessh n 56 (0.035)
ouer prep 56 (0.035)
reaume n 56 (0.035)
ruþe n 56 (0.035)
til prep 56 (0.035)
vertue n 56 (0.035)
wisdom n 56 (0.035)
yeer n 56 (0.035)
breed n 55 (0.035)
buggen v 55 (0.035)
ellis adv 55 (0.035)
greuen v 55 (0.035)
lelly adv 55 (0.035)
mouþ n 55 (0.035)
pure adj 55 (0.035)
riden v 55 (0.035)
wight n 55 (0.035)
cros n 54 (0.034)
knelen v 54 (0.034)
leef adj 54 (0.034)
leggen v2 54 (0.034)
slepe v 54 (0.034)
carpen v 53 (0.034)
fals n 53 (0.034)

tresor n 53 (0.034)
ale n 52 (0.033)
leue n 52 (0.033)
moost adv 52 (0.033)
owene adj 52 (0.033)
wilne v 52 (0.033)
wrong n 52 (0.033)
arise v 51 (0.032)
cloþ n 51 (0.032)
lo exclam 51 (0.032)
marie n prop 51 (0.032)
meschief n 51 (0.032)
moore adj 51 (0.032)
old adj 51 (0.032)
þynke v1 50 (0.032)
chirche n 50 (0.032)
moneie n 50 (0.032)
prophete n 50 (0.032)
roode n 50 (0.032)
sauter n 50 (0.032)
bisechen v 49 (0.031)
commune adj 49 (0.031)
fecchen v 49 (0.031)
fiȝte v 49 (0.031)
hangen v 49 (0.031)
hennes adv 49 (0.031)
hous n 49 (0.031)
litel adj 49 (0.031)
why adv 49 (0.031)
fruyt n 48 (0.030)
fynger n 48 (0.030)
seed n 48 (0.030)
wepen v 48 (0.030)
beten v2 47 (0.030)
noȝt pron 47 (0.030)
same adj 47 (0.030)
seint n 47 (0.030)
suwen v 47 (0.030)
wonye 47 (0.030)
bigynnen v 46 (0.029)
curseþ v 46 (0.029)
defaute n 46 (0.029)
drede v 46 (0.029)
feden v 46 (0.029)
foode n 46 (0.029)
lauȝen v 46 (0.029)
preiere n 46 (0.029)
bifore adv 45 (0.028)
demen v 45 (0.028)
hope v 45 (0.028)
in adv 45 (0.028)
masse n 45 (0.028)
poul n prop 45 (0.028)
rennen v 45 (0.028)
wene v 45 (0.028)
wheiþer conj 45 (0.028)
cacchen v 44 (0.028)
dauid n prop 44 (0.028)
enuye n 44 (0.028)
foul adj 44 (0.028)
peny n 44 (0.028)
selle v 44 (0.028)
wastour n 44 (0.028)
wye n 44 (0.028)
aboute prep 43 (0.027)
casten v 43 (0.027)
clene adj 43 (0.027)
ellis adj 43 (0.027)
fowel n 43 (0.027)
lowe adj 43 (0.027)
rulen v 43 (0.027)
saue prep 43 (0.027)

sleuþe n 43 (0.027)
trinite n 43 (0.027)
ye adv 43 (0.027)
barn n 42 (0.027)
blynd adj 42 (0.027)
dome n 42 (0.027)
elde n 42 (0.027)
holy_goost n 42 (0.027)
lecherie n 42 (0.027)
likyng ger1 42 (0.027)
parfit adj 42 (0.027)
peyne n 42 (0.027)
symonye n 42 (0.027)
synnen v 42 (0.027)
wraþe n 42 (0.027)
þeiȝ conj 41 (0.026)
þo conj 41 (0.026)
aungel n 41 (0.026)
comseþ v 41 (0.026)
contree n 41 (0.026)
doctour n 41 (0.026)
fyue num 41 (0.026)
holy adj 41 (0.026)
liere n 41 (0.026)
walken v 41 (0.026)
a num 40 (0.025)
assoillen v 40 (0.025)
destruye v 40 (0.025)
drynke n 40 (0.025)
eue n prop 40 (0.025)
hemself pron 40 (0.025)
lordshipe n 40 (0.025)
nyȝt n 40 (0.025)
preisen v 40 (0.025)
shape v 40 (0.025)
sowe v1 40 (0.025)
bold adj 39 (0.025)
contricion n 39 (0.025)
drede n 39 (0.025)
fir n 39 (0.025)
ful adj 39 (0.025)
lepen v 39 (0.025)
moost adj 39 (0.025)
muche adv 39 (0.025)
pilgrym n 39 (0.025)
riȝt n 39 (0.025)
trewely adv 39 (0.025)
yate n 39 (0.025)
þerafter adv 38 (0.024)
þerof adv 38 (0.024)
acorden v 38 (0.024)
adoun adv 38 (0.024)
blame v 38 (0.024)
broþer n 38 (0.024)
dele v 38 (0.024)
eiþer pron 38 (0.024)
fer adv 38 (0.024)
help n 38 (0.024)
killen v 38 (0.024)
murþe n 38 (0.024)
murye adj 38 (0.024)
wise n 38 (0.024)
almyȝty adj 37 (0.023)
ensample n 37 (0.023)
forsaken v 37 (0.023)
gome n1 37 (0.023)
hatien v 37 (0.023)
iustice n 37 (0.023)
plouȝ 37 (0.023)
shryuen v 37 (0.023)
sweren v 37 (0.023)
vnkynde adj 37 (0.023)

anoon adv 36 (0.023)
apostle n 36 (0.023)
bicome v 36 (0.023)
bynden v 36 (0.023)
ek adv&conj 36 (0.023)
heremyte n 36 (0.023)
lacchen v 36 (0.023)
laste v 36 (0.023)
loore n 36 (0.023)
nedy adj 36 (0.023)
nempne v 36 (0.023)
peter n prop 36 (0.023)
repentaunce n 36 (0.023)
selde adv 36 (0.023)
sherewe n 36 (0.023)
trowe v 36 (0.023)
þef n 35 (0.022)
fauel n 35 (0.022)
fortune n 35 (0.022)
gloton n 35 (0.022)
hope n 35 (0.022)
leode n 35 (0.022)
lettred adj 35 (0.022)
litel adv 35 (0.022)
louely adj 35 (0.022)
mynstral n 35 (0.022)
nymen v 35 (0.022)
plese v 35 (0.022)
soore adv 35 (0.022)
synful adj 35 (0.022)
tilien v 35 (0.022)
wombe n 35 (0.022)
bifalle v 34 (0.022)
gospel n 34 (0.022)
mankynde n 34 (0.022)
nedeþ v 34 (0.022)
persone n2 34 (0.022)
pite n 34 (0.022)
sake n 34 (0.022)
worþi adj 34 (0.022)
wynd n 34 (0.022)
anoþer pron 33 (0.021)
bigile v 33 (0.021)
cloþen v 33 (0.021)
cristendom n 33 (0.021)
crowne n 33 (0.021)
ded adj 33 (0.021)
defende v 33 (0.021)
fette v 33 (0.021)
fleen v2 33 (0.021)
fool n 33 (0.021)
friday n 33 (0.021)
growe v 33 (0.021)
heele n 33 (0.021)
honouren v 33 (0.021)
liȝtly adv 33 (0.021)
looþ adj 33 (0.021)
molde n1 33 (0.021)
riȝtful adj 33 (0.021)
sooþ adj 33 (0.021)
vnitee n 33 (0.021)
wonder n 33 (0.021)
but prep 32 (0.020)
curteisly adv 32 (0.020)
deserue v 32 (0.020)
echone pron 32 (0.020)
foure num 32 (0.020)
knaue n 32 (0.020)
konnyng ger 32 (0.020)
laborer n 32 (0.020)
moder n 32 (0.020)
muche n 32 (0.020)

oone adv 32 (0.020)
patriark n 32 (0.020)
peril n 32 (0.020)
person n1 32 (0.020)
prelat n 32 (0.020)
rome n prop 32 (0.020)
scripture n 32 (0.020)
swete adj 32 (0.020)
ten num 32 (0.020)
vsen v 32 (0.020)
witterly adv 32 (0.020)
þerto adv 31 (0.020)
þouȝt n 31 (0.020)
abide v 31 (0.020)
assenten v 31 (0.020)
awaken v 31 (0.020)
bible n 31 (0.020)
cleymen v 31 (0.020)
cyuylle n 31 (0.020)
felawe n 31 (0.020)
fewe adj 31 (0.020)
foot n 31 (0.020)
inwit n 31 (0.020)
iohan n prop 31 (0.020)
latyn n 31 (0.020)
lesynge ger 31 (0.020)
lif_tyme n 31 (0.020)
maistrie n 31 (0.020)
purgatorie n 31 (0.020)
sarsen n 31 (0.020)
tree n 31 (0.020)
yelden v 31 (0.020)
yuele adv 31 (0.020)
borwe v 30 (0.019)
caym n prop 30 (0.019)
chiden v 30 (0.019)
comaunde v 30 (0.019)
deere adj 30 (0.019)
eft adv 30 (0.019)
fere n 30 (0.019)
fre adj 30 (0.019)
gilt n 30 (0.019)
ground n 30 (0.019)
labouren v 30 (0.019)
lik prep 30 (0.019)
owe v 30 (0.019)
prince n 30 (0.019)
reuerencen v 30 (0.019)
signe n 30 (0.019)
suster n 30 (0.019)
warne v 30 (0.019)
ynouȝ adj 30 (0.019)
bitwene prep 29 (0.018)
enemy n 29 (0.018)
erien v 29 (0.018)
fissh n 29 (0.018)
hire n 29 (0.018)
labour n 29 (0.018)
leef n1 29 (0.018)
list v 29 (0.018)
present n 29 (0.018)
profit n 29 (0.018)
profrest v 29 (0.018)
proud adj 29 (0.018)
resten v 29 (0.018)
salomon n prop 29 (0.018)
seruaunt n 29 (0.018)
sory adj 29 (0.018)
techyng ger 29 (0.018)
which adj 29 (0.018)
while n 29 (0.018)
begge v 28 (0.018)

brid n 28 (0.018)
dedly adj 28 (0.018)
hard adj 28 (0.018)
hundred num 28 (0.018)
leest adj 28 (0.018)
meuen v 28 (0.018)
monk n 28 (0.018)
nay adv 28 (0.018)
regne v 28 (0.018)
religion n 28 (0.018)
science n 28 (0.018)
sleen v 28 (0.018)
syde n 28 (0.018)
war adj 28 (0.018)
wyn n 28 (0.018)
yuel n 28 (0.018)
þerfor adv 27 (0.017)
aspie v 27 (0.017)
ay adv 27 (0.017)
boote n 27 (0.017)
chief adj 27 (0.017)
dame n 27 (0.017)
eueremoore adv 27 (0.017)
holynesse n 27 (0.017)
luþer adj 27 (0.017)
mysdede n 27 (0.017)
reherce v 27 (0.017)
risen v 27 (0.017)
shrift n 27 (0.017)
spende v 27 (0.017)
sprynge v 27 (0.017)
þridde num 26 (0.016)
biddyng ger 26 (0.016)
cardinale adj 26 (0.016)
dette n 26 (0.016)
dyne v 26 (0.016)
kyndely adv 26 (0.016)
marchaunt n 26 (0.016)
noumbre n 26 (0.016)
pryue adj 26 (0.016)
repente v 26 (0.016)
swynke v 26 (0.016)
werkman n 26 (0.016)
whiles conj 26 (0.016)
widewe n 26 (0.016)
þousand num 25 (0.016)
best adj 25 (0.016)
care n 25 (0.016)
counte v 25 (0.016)
dampneþ v 25 (0.016)
doun adv 25 (0.016)
dryuen v 25 (0.016)
ese n 25 (0.016)
falsnesse n 25 (0.016)
fordoon v 25 (0.016)
fust n 25 (0.016)
likne v 25 (0.016)
lyuyng ger 25 (0.016)
mayntene v 25 (0.016)
mo n 25 (0.016)
mylde adj 25 (0.016)
newe adj 25 (0.016)
parissh n 25 (0.016)
pawme n 25 (0.016)
recche v 25 (0.016)
reste n 25 (0.016)
siknesse n 25 (0.016)
somer n 25 (0.016)
tene v 25 (0.016)
to adv2 25 (0.016)
wasshen v 25 (0.016)
wele n 25 (0.016)

þeron adv 24 (0.015)
abien v 24 (0.015)
afere v 24 (0.015)
bulle n 24 (0.015)
caton n prop 24 (0.015)
cause n 24 (0.015)
dure v 24 (0.015)
er prep 24 (0.015)
fele adj 24 (0.015)
feste n 24 (0.015)
kene adj 24 (0.015)
knowyng ger 24 (0.015)
lenten n 24 (0.015)
likame n 24 (0.015)
loue v2 24 (0.015)
mynde n 24 (0.015)
ordre n 24 (0.015)
passion n 24 (0.015)
rule n 24 (0.015)
shenden v 24 (0.015)
siþes n 24 (0.015)
sik adj 24 (0.015)
spille v 24 (0.015)
vengeaunce n 24 (0.015)
wake v 24 (0.015)
worshipen v 24 (0.015)
appose v 23 (0.015)
brennen v 23 (0.015)
construe v 23 (0.015)
corn n 23 (0.015)
curatour n 23 (0.015)
ere n 23 (0.015)
forȝyue v 23 (0.015)
foule adv 23 (0.015)
glad adj 23 (0.015)
goodnesse n 23 (0.015)
half adj 23 (0.015)
hente v 23 (0.015)
lemman n 23 (0.015)
marien v 23 (0.015)
messager n 23 (0.015)
meten v 23 (0.015)
namely adv 23 (0.015)
oþes n 23 (0.015)
ouþerwhile adv 23 (0.015)
rightwisnesse n 23 (0.015)
roote n 23 (0.015)
seel n 23 (0.015)
text n 23 (0.015)
wilde adj 23 (0.015)
witty adj 23 (0.015)
abraham n prop 22 (0.014)
auȝt pron 22 (0.014)
ayein adv 22 (0.014)
brode adj 22 (0.014)
cheke n 22 (0.014)
chese v 22 (0.014)
close v 22 (0.014)
craue v 22 (0.014)
croune v 22 (0.014)
curteisie n 22 (0.014)
dore n 22 (0.014)
douȝter n 22 (0.014)
euen n 22 (0.014)
faitour n 22 (0.014)
glotonye n 22 (0.014)
half n 22 (0.014)
hede n 22 (0.014)
heir n 22 (0.014)
herof adv 22 (0.014)
iuggen v 22 (0.014)
kissen v 22 (0.014)

late adv 22 (0.014)
leche n 22 (0.014)
lest conj 22 (0.014)
mair n 22 (0.014)
mesure n 22 (0.014)
paternoster n 22 (0.014)
perkyn n prop 22 (0.014)
quyte v 22 (0.014)
spirit n 22 (0.014)
vnderfonge v 22 (0.014)
worse adv 22 (0.014)
wynnyng ger 22 (0.014)
þole v 21 (0.013)
allas exclam 21 (0.013)
apeire v 21 (0.013)
bihote v 21 (0.013)
certes adv 21 (0.013)
deuyne v 21 (0.013)
fayn adj 21 (0.013)
flood n 21 (0.013)
fulfille v 21 (0.013)
hardy adj 21 (0.013)
harlot n 21 (0.013)
heep n 21 (0.013)
hei3 adv 21 (0.013)
ille n 21 (0.013)
lasse adv 21 (0.013)
makometh n prop 21 (0.013)
me pron indef 21 (0.013)
meke adj 21 (0.013)
mene adj1 21 (0.013)
ne3ebore n 21 (0.013)
nouþe adv 21 (0.013)
on adv 21 (0.013)
pestilence n 21 (0.013)
pleyne v 21 (0.013)
point n 21 (0.013)
prison n 21 (0.013)
renk n 21 (0.013)
ri3t adj 21 (0.013)
scole n 21 (0.013)
segge n 21 (0.013)
spare v 21 (0.013)
vnkyndenesse n 21 (0.013)
wanhope n 21 (0.013)
whete n 21 (0.013)
worse adj 21 (0.013)
careful adj 20 (0.013)
cherl n 20 (0.013)
confessour n 20 (0.013)
conquerour n 20 (0.013)
despise v 20 (0.013)
englissh n 20 (0.013)
feble adj 20 (0.013)
feld n 20 (0.013)
freke n 20 (0.013)
greyn n 20 (0.013)
hood n 20 (0.013)
lasse adj 20 (0.013)
lesson n 20 (0.013)
londoun n prop 20 (0.013)
loure v 20 (0.013)
lowe adv 20 (0.013)
matere n 20 (0.013)
mathew n prop 20 (0.013)
parfournen v 20 (0.013)
pleye v 20 (0.013)
rente n 20 (0.013)
rome v 20 (0.013)
saaf adj 20 (0.013)
saul n prop 20 (0.013)
shame n 20 (0.013)

sondry adj 20 (0.013)
werre n 20 (0.013)
wide adv 20 (0.013)
appul n 19 (0.012)
austyn n prop 19 (0.012)
bagge n 19 (0.012)
bak n 19 (0.012)
bed n 19 (0.012)
bene n 19 (0.012)
blowe v1 19 (0.012)
buxom adj 19 (0.012)
caas n 19 (0.012)
castel n 19 (0.012)
colour n 19 (0.012)
depe adv 19 (0.012)
fastyng ger 19 (0.012)
ferly n 19 (0.012)
flee v1 19 (0.012)
fonde v 19 (0.012)
greten v 19 (0.012)
harde adv 19 (0.012)
issue n 19 (0.012)
iudas n prop 19 (0.012)
luc n prop 19 (0.012)
madame n 19 (0.012)
make n 19 (0.012)
marchaundise n 19 (0.012)
matyns n 19 (0.012)
parteþ v 19 (0.012)
sisour n 19 (0.012)
skile n 19 (0.012)
studie n 19 (0.012)
welþe n 19 (0.012)
wikkedly adv 19 (0.012)
worþ adj 19 (0.012)
yong adj 19 (0.012)
þennes adv 18 (0.011)
aboue prep 18 (0.011)
allowe v 18 (0.011)
biholde v 18 (0.011)
boot n 18 (0.011)
by_so conj 18 (0.011)
conceyuen v 18 (0.011)
euene adv 18 (0.011)
hulle n 18 (0.011)
inparfit adj 18 (0.011)
knees n 18 (0.011)
liknesse n 18 (0.011)
mawe n 18 (0.011)
mekely adv 18 (0.011)
mene n 18 (0.011)
morwe n 18 (0.011)
moyses n prop 18 (0.011)
paradis n 18 (0.011)
peynten v 18 (0.011)
phisik n 18 (0.011)
pursueþ v 18 (0.011)
religious n 18 (0.011)
robbe v 18 (0.011)
sapience n 18 (0.011)
sathan n prop 18 (0.011)
sleighte n 18 (0.011)
sonday n 18 (0.011)
teme n2 18 (0.011)
tokene n 18 (0.011)
waiten v1 18 (0.011)
wenche n 18 (0.011)
wiþalle adv 18 (0.011)
wille n prop 18 (0.011)
wrecche n 18 (0.011)
yuel adj 18 (0.011)
actif adj 17 (0.011)

bale n 17 (0.011)
cart n 17 (0.011)
cat n 17 (0.011)
confort n 17 (0.011)
crepe v 17 (0.011)
desire v 17 (0.011)
erl n 17 (0.011)
euery adj 17 (0.011)
flaterere n 17 (0.011)
folie n 17 (0.011)
foryete v 17 (0.011)
haukyn n prop 17 (0.011)
hitte v 17 (0.011)
hoom adv 17 (0.011)
iames n prop 17 (0.011)
kyngdom n 17 (0.011)
left adj 17 (0.011)
lik adj 17 (0.011)
loof n 17 (0.011)
lyme n 17 (0.011)
maugree prep 17 (0.011)
mekenesse n 17 (0.011)
metels n 17 (0.011)
moorne n 17 (0.011)
noble n 17 (0.011)
parauenture adv 17 (0.011)
parceyue v 17 (0.011)
payn n 17 (0.011)
prechours n 17 (0.011)
pryueliche adv 17 (0.011)
receyue v 17 (0.011)
rekene v 17 (0.011)
sad adj 17 (0.011)
salue n 17 (0.011)
saueour n 17 (0.011)
see n 17 (0.011)
spede v 17 (0.011)
tail n 17 (0.011)
trauaille v 17 (0.011)
wed n 17 (0.011)
welcome adj 17 (0.011)
wiles n 17 (0.011)
ywar adj 17 (0.011)
almesse n 16 (0.010)
armes n2 16 (0.010)
baroun n 16 (0.010)
bitokneþ v 16 (0.010)
borgh n 16 (0.010)
chere n 16 (0.010)
cloke n 16 (0.010)
disputen v 16 (0.010)
excuse v 16 (0.010)
feele v 16 (0.010)
fourty num 16 (0.010)
gare v 16 (0.010)
grene adj 16 (0.010)
haste n 16 (0.010)
iusten v 16 (0.010)
lappe n 16 (0.010)
large adj 16 (0.010)
leef adv 16 (0.010)
louten v 16 (0.010)
lust n 16 (0.010)
meynee n 16 (0.010)
myle n 16 (0.010)
notarie n 16 (0.010)
ouercomen v 16 (0.010)
pernele n prop 16 (0.010)
prikeþ v 16 (0.010)
raton n 16 (0.010)
rechen v 16 (0.010)
reue n 16 (0.010)

rewarden v 16 (0.010)
seruice n 16 (0.010)
sib adj 16 (0.010)
somonour n 16 (0.010)
stok n 16 (0.010)
touchen v 16 (0.010)
auarice n 15 (0.009)
bacon n 15 (0.009)
bet adv 15 (0.009)
bihynde adv 15 (0.009)
bilongeþ v 15 (0.009)
blody adj 15 (0.009)
boldely adv 15 (0.009)
boy n 15 (0.009)
bymeene v1 15 (0.009)
cardynal n 15 (0.009)
chaffare n 15 (0.009)
chaste v 15 (0.009)
cold n 15 (0.009)
constable n 15 (0.009)
couenaunt n 15 (0.009)
elleuene num 15 (0.009)
enioigne v 15 (0.009)
euencristen n 15 (0.009)
gladen v 15 (0.009)
grote n 15 (0.009)
hallen 15 (0.009)
harlotrie n 15 (0.009)
heruest n 15 (0.009)
heste n 15 (0.009)
hiden v 15 (0.009)
holy_day n 15 (0.009)
hoot adj 15 (0.009)
hound n 15 (0.009)
ille adv 15 (0.009)
ledere n 15 (0.009)
lettrure n 15 (0.009)
lorel n 15 (0.009)
matrimoyne n 15 (0.009)
ooþerwise adv 15 (0.009)
pacient adj 15 (0.009)
partie n 15 (0.009)
perpetuel adj 15 (0.009)
pli3te v 15 (0.009)
purchace v 15 (0.009)
pyne n 15 (0.009)
route n 15 (0.009)
sermon n 15 (0.009)
softely adv 15 (0.009)
solace n 15 (0.009)
strengþe n 15 (0.009)
trauaille n 15 (0.009)
tweyne num 15 (0.009)
tyne v 15 (0.009)
wage v 15 (0.009)
wandre v 15 (0.009)
welcome v 15 (0.009)
wepene n 15 (0.009)
wherfore adv 15 (0.009)
wode n 15 (0.009)
worship n 15 (0.009)
wraþen v 15 (0.009)
ylike adv 15 (0.009)
þider adv 14 (0.009)
acombre v 14 (0.009)
antecrist n 14 (0.009)
any pron 14 (0.009)
apparaille v 14 (0.009)
assaille v 14 (0.009)
auenture n 14 (0.009)
bake ptp 14 (0.009)
banne v 14 (0.009)

bataille n 14 (0.009)	compaignye n 13 (0.008)	hikke n prop 12 (0.008)	gilour n 11 (0.007)
biknowen v 14 (0.009)	contrarie v 13 (0.008)	indulgence n 12 (0.008)	girles n 11 (0.007)
biten v 14 (0.009)	couent n 13 (0.008)	iob n prop 12 (0.008)	goos n 11 (0.007)
caluarie n prop 14 (0.009)	couere v 13 (0.008)	kepe n 12 (0.008)	happe v 11 (0.007)
caytif n 14 (0.009)	coupleþ v 13 (0.008)	laȝar n 12 (0.008)	harm n 11 (0.007)
cessen v 14 (0.009)	croft n 13 (0.008)	lene adj 12 (0.008)	hendely adv 11 (0.007)
chapman n 14 (0.009)	deluen v 13 (0.008)	lippes n 12 (0.008)	hostiler n 11 (0.007)
charge v 14 (0.009)	deying ger 13 (0.008)	lynnen n 12 (0.008)	konnyng adj 11 (0.007)
cloistre n 14 (0.009)	feloun n 13 (0.008)	makyng ger 12 (0.008)	lolleþ v 11 (0.007)
confession n 14 (0.009)	floryns n 13 (0.008)	manhede n 12 (0.008)	loueday n 11 (0.007)
consistorie n 14 (0.009)	forȝifnesse n 13 (0.008)	meble n 12 (0.008)	lowenesse n 11 (0.007)
contrarie n 14 (0.009)	frayned v 13 (0.008)	meken v 12 (0.008)	medicyne n 11 (0.007)
cope v 14 (0.009)	goost n 13 (0.008)	membre n 12 (0.008)	medle v 11 (0.007)
coppe n 14 (0.009)	gregorie n prop 13 (0.008)	mete v1 12 (0.008)	menyng ger 11 (0.007)
derknesse n 14 (0.009)	gut n 13 (0.008)	moone n 12 (0.008)	mirour n 11 (0.007)
donge n 14 (0.009)	hete n 13 (0.008)	muse v 12 (0.008)	mo adj 11 (0.007)
face n 14 (0.009)	hewe n 13 (0.008)	myddel n 12 (0.008)	myracle n 11 (0.007)
feere n 14 (0.009)	hoor adj 13 (0.008)	ordeyne v 12 (0.008)	neiþer adv 11 (0.007)
forbedeþ v 14 (0.009)	inne prep 13 (0.008)	ouer adv 12 (0.008)	noon n 11 (0.007)
gaderen v 14 (0.009)	knyȝthod n 13 (0.008)	palmere n 12 (0.008)	oonliche adv 11 (0.007)
gate n 14 (0.009)	lengþe n 13 (0.008)	punysshen v 12 (0.008)	palfrey n 11 (0.007)
gentil adj 14 (0.009)	lomb n 13 (0.008)	rapiþ v 12 (0.008)	paye n 11 (0.007)
gloseþ v 14 (0.009)	longe v1 13 (0.008)	rauysshed v 12 (0.008)	pece n 11 (0.007)
helen v 14 (0.009)	lyne n 13 (0.008)	reed adj 12 (0.008)	plentee n 11 (0.007)
hende adj 14 (0.009)	mendynaunt n 13 (0.008)	releue v 12 (0.008)	porter n 11 (0.007)
heuy adj 14 (0.009)	meschaunce n 13 (0.008)	ripe adj 12 (0.008)	possession n 11 (0.007)
hoom n 14 (0.009)	noyen v 13 (0.008)	robbere n 12 (0.008)	profitable adj 11 (0.007)
iangle v 14 (0.009)	of adv 13 (0.008)	rose n 12 (0.008)	psalme n 11 (0.007)
lasse n 14 (0.009)	pecok n 13 (0.008)	sawe n 12 (0.008)	pure adv 11 (0.007)
logyk n 14 (0.009)	pese n 13 (0.008)	secounde num 12 (0.008)	recorden v 11 (0.007)
lollare n 14 (0.009)	pouke n 13 (0.008)	ship n 12 (0.008)	restitucion n 11 (0.007)
mo adv 14 (0.009)	refuse v 13 (0.008)	somdel adv 12 (0.008)	ribaud n 11 (0.007)
myldely adv 14 (0.009)	remenaunt n 13 (0.008)	sooþness n 12 (0.008)	sage n 11 (0.007)
naked adj 14 (0.009)	samaritan n prop 13 (0.008)	souereyn n 12 (0.008)	sauacion n 11 (0.007)
pardoner n 14 (0.009)	score adj 13 (0.008)	teme n1 12 (0.008)	selkouþ adj 11 (0.007)
parfitly adv 14 (0.009)	self adj 13 (0.008)	tene n 12 (0.008)	sherreue n 11 (0.007)
pilgrymage n 14 (0.009)	sergeaunt n 13 (0.008)	theologie n 12 (0.008)	smyte v 11 (0.007)
poete n 14 (0.009)	souereyn adj 13 (0.008)	treson n 12 (0.008)	styward n 11 (0.007)
prentice n 14 (0.009)	sterre n 13 (0.008)	vnderstonden v 12 (0.008)	swiþe adv 11 (0.007)
quyk adj 14 (0.009)	westmynstre n prop 13 (0.008)	vp prep 12 (0.008)	tiþe n 11 (0.007)
rebuken v 14 (0.009)	weye v 13 (0.008)	weddynge ger 12 (0.008)	vndertaken v 11 (0.007)
riȝtfully adv 14 (0.009)	wiþinne adv 13 (0.008)	wedlok n 12 (0.008)	vndo v 11 (0.007)
samuel n prop 14 (0.009)	wiped v 13 (0.008)	wel adj 12 (0.008)	vnlouken 11 (0.007)
secte n 14 (0.009)	wisely adv 13 (0.008)	welden v 12 (0.008)	ware n 11 (0.007)
siker adj 14 (0.009)	wouke n 13 (0.008)	wightly adv 12 (0.008)	warm adj 11 (0.007)
sixe num 14 (0.009)	yerne adv 13 (0.008)	wollen adj 12 (0.008)	weder n 11 (0.007)
solacen v 14 (0.009)	acounte n 12 (0.008)	ydel n 12 (0.008)	wiþdrawe v 11 (0.007)
sour adj 14 (0.009)	amendes n 12 (0.008)	ypocrisie n 12 (0.008)	wikkednesse n 11 (0.007)
staf n 14 (0.009)	arme n1 12 (0.008)	yren n 12 (0.008)	wonderly adv 11 (0.007)
thomas n prop 14 (0.009)	awreke v 12 (0.008)	ȝis adv 11 (0.007)	wownde v 11 (0.007)
vsurie n 14 (0.009)	belle n 12 (0.008)	answere v 11 (0.007)	ylik adj 11 (0.007)
wisshen v 14 (0.009)	bethleem n prop 12 (0.008)	aside adv 11 (0.007)	yowself pron 11 (0.007)
wounde n 14 (0.009)	bilyue n 12 (0.008)	aslepe adv 11 (0.007)	þanne adv2 10 (0.006)
wroþ adj 14 (0.009)	bitwene adv 12 (0.008)	bapteme n 11 (0.007)	þonken v 10 (0.006)
youþe n 14 (0.009)	blasen v 12 (0.008)	bedrede adj 11 (0.007)	þorn n 10 (0.006)
acounten v 13 (0.008)	brest n 12 (0.008)	bern n 11 (0.007)	þritty num 10 (0.006)
acre n 13 (0.008)	briȝt adj 12 (0.008)	bidderis n 11 (0.007)	a exclam 10 (0.006)
afterward adv 13 (0.008)	burgeises n 12 (0.008)	bihoueþ v 11 (0.007)	afyngred ptp 10 (0.006)
amyd prep 13 (0.008)	chambre n 12 (0.008)	bitraye v 11 (0.007)	age n 10 (0.006)
angre n 13 (0.008)	cope n 12 (0.008)	bitter adj 11 (0.007)	ancre n 10 (0.006)
assayen v 13 (0.008)	daniel n prop 12 (0.008)	confessen v 11 (0.007)	arerage n 10 (0.006)
barre n 13 (0.008)	defyen v2 12 (0.008)	congeien v 11 (0.007)	aristotle n prop 10 (0.006)
bastard n 13 (0.008)	deren v 12 (0.008)	contenaunce n 11 (0.007)	armed v 10 (0.006)
beryng ger 13 (0.008)	derk adj 12 (0.008)	contreue v 11 (0.007)	auaunce v 10 (0.006)
bitide v 13 (0.008)	domesday n 12 (0.008)	cosyn n 11 (0.007)	baptist n 10 (0.006)
borde n 13 (0.008)	er adv 12 (0.008)	cote n2 11 (0.007)	bede n 10 (0.006)
bowen v 13 (0.008)	feffeþ v 12 (0.008)	curteis adj 11 (0.007)	biheste n 10 (0.006)
burn n 13 (0.008)	fikel adj 12 (0.008)	deep adj 11 (0.007)	blede v 10 (0.006)
chartre n 13 (0.008)	formest adv 12 (0.008)	deere adv 11 (0.007)	bolle n 10 (0.006)
clepe v 13 (0.008)	forsoþe adv 12 (0.008)	entreþ v 11 (0.007)	bon n 10 (0.006)
cloþyng ger 13 (0.008)	greden v 12 (0.008)	falshede n 11 (0.007)	bosten v 10 (0.006)
cofre n 13 (0.008)	heraud n 12 (0.008)	formen v 11 (0.007)	bour n 10 (0.006)

brewere n 10 (0.006)
capul n 10 (0.006)
care v 10 (0.006)
certein adj 10 (0.006)
certein n 10 (0.006)
chalange v 10 (0.006)
chewe v 10 (0.006)
clause n 10 (0.006)
clement n prop 10 (0.006)
clennesse n 10 (0.006)
cote n1 10 (0.006)
crafty adj 10 (0.006)
dale n 10 (0.006)
deceyue v 10 (0.006)
doute n 10 (0.006)
dykere n 10 (0.006)
ende v 10 (0.006)
feire n 10 (0.006)
folde v 10 (0.006)
founded v 10 (0.006)
fullyng ger1 10 (0.006)
godhede n 10 (0.006)
gripeþ v 10 (0.006)
hals n 10 (0.006)
helþe n 10 (0.006)
hireself pron 10 (0.006)
hore n 10 (0.006)
how adv 10 (0.006)
hungry adj 10 (0.006)
hyne n 10 (0.006)
ierusalem n prop 10 (0.006)
keye n 10 (0.006)
knoweliched v 10 (0.006)
li3t adj 10 (0.006)
li3t adv 10 (0.006)
lige adj 10 (0.006)
maluerne n prop 10 (0.006)
maudeleyne n prop 10 (0.006)
more n 10 (0.006)
myd prep 10 (0.006)
myddes n 10 (0.006)
mysdo v 10 (0.006)
nekke n 10 (0.006)
newe adv 10 (0.006)
no3t n 10 (0.006)
noe n prop 10 (0.006)
offreth v 10 (0.006)
paciently adv 10 (0.006)
parcel n 10 (0.006)
peere n 10 (0.006)
pelure n 10 (0.006)
pik n 10 (0.006)
pilat n prop 10 (0.006)
plaunte n 10 (0.006)
pleden v 10 (0.006)
precious n 10 (0.006)
prouysour n 10 (0.006)
quenche v 10 (0.006)
reyn n 10 (0.006)
risshe n 10 (0.006)
saterday n 10 (0.006)
scaþe n 10 (0.006)
siþen prep 10 (0.006)
stille adv 10 (0.006)
stuwes n 10 (0.006)
surgien n 10 (0.006)
swete v 10 (0.006)
towne n 10 (0.006)
truste v 10 (0.006)
vncristen adj 10 (0.006)
vnfolde v 10 (0.006)
vyce n 10 (0.006)

wal n 10 (0.006)
wasten v 10 (0.006)
watte n prop 10 (0.006)
wherof adv 10 (0.006)
whit adj 10 (0.006)
wid adj 10 (0.006)
wolle n 10 (0.006)
worm n 10 (0.006)
wyndow n 10 (0.006)
ydelnesse n 10 (0.006)
þrowe v 9 (0.006)
acurseþ v 9 (0.006)
alþou3 conj 9 (0.006)
amaistrye v 9 (0.006)
appere v 9 (0.006)
attachen v 9 (0.006)
bapti3e v 9 (0.006)
bare adj 9 (0.006)
benche n 9 (0.006)
bisy adj 9 (0.006)
bittre adv 9 (0.006)
bocher n 9 (0.006)
bondeman n 9 (0.006)
brewestere n 9 (0.006)
burye v 9 (0.006)
buxomnesse n 9 (0.006)
careyne n 9 (0.006)
chaffare v 9 (0.006)
cheste n2 9 (0.006)
cheue v 9 (0.006)
cite n 9 (0.006)
comende v 9 (0.006)
cook n 9 (0.006)
cours n 9 (0.006)
cow n 9 (0.006)
cure n 9 (0.006)
deuoir n 9 (0.006)
doel n 9 (0.006)
douhty adj 9 (0.006)
dredful adj 9 (0.006)
dro3te n 9 (0.006)
duc n 9 (0.006)
elliswhere adv 9 (0.006)
engendreþ v 9 (0.006)
eyr n 9 (0.006)
fasten v 9 (0.006)
faunt n 9 (0.006)
feþere n 9 (0.006)
felawship n 9 (0.006)
fer adj 9 (0.006)
fettren v 9 (0.006)
flatere v 9 (0.006)
flour n1 9 (0.006)
fonge v 9 (0.006)
foo n 9 (0.006)
fraunce n prop 9 (0.006)
fressh adj 9 (0.006)
galon n 9 (0.006)
gentile n 9 (0.006)
gilty adj 9 (0.006)
glose n 9 (0.006)
gras n 9 (0.006)
graue v 9 (0.006)
gruccheþ v 9 (0.006)
grys n1 9 (0.006)
hailsed v 9 (0.006)
harewen v 9 (0.006)
hastily adv 9 (0.006)
haunteþ v 9 (0.006)
hider adv 9 (0.006)
hoost n 9 (0.006)
ianglyng ger 9 (0.006)

iape v 9 (0.006)
impugnen v 9 (0.006)
kaiser n 9 (0.006)
knokked v 9 (0.006)
lened v1 9 (0.006)
lenge v 9 (0.006)
likerous adj 9 (0.006)
losse n 9 (0.006)
loude adv 9 (0.006)
meel n 9 (0.006)
merciable adj 9 (0.006)
muliere adj 9 (0.006)
murþere n 9 (0.006)
mynstralcie n 9 (0.006)
nayles n 9 (0.006)
nedeful adj 9 (0.006)
nose n 9 (0.006)
opene v 9 (0.006)
peynen v 9 (0.006)
plato n prop 9 (0.006)
pound n 9 (0.006)
prechyng ger 9 (0.006)
prest adj 9 (0.006)
propre adj 9 (0.006)
purs n 9 (0.006)
rechelesnesse n 9 (0.006)
redily adv 9 (0.006)
resurexion n 9 (0.006)
reue v 9 (0.006)
roberd n prop 9 (0.006)
rynges n 9 (0.006)
shef n 9 (0.006)
softe adv 9 (0.006)
sompne v 9 (0.006)
song n 9 (0.006)
sorcerie n 9 (0.006)
sotil adj 9 (0.006)
sotile v 9 (0.006)
sprede v 9 (0.006)
stille adj 9 (0.006)
stoon n 9 (0.006)
studie v 9 (0.006)
swymmen v 9 (0.006)
table n 9 (0.006)
techere n 9 (0.006)
temple n 9 (0.006)
triennals n 9 (0.006)
troianus n prop 9 (0.006)
twelf num 9 (0.006)
venym n 9 (0.006)
where adv 9 (0.006)
wreke v 9 (0.006)
wrighte n 9 (0.006)
ydel adj 9 (0.006)
ymaginatif adj 9 (0.006)
þurst n 8 (0.005)
abstinence n 8 (0.005)
aloft adv 8 (0.005)
apparaill n 8 (0.005)
art n 8 (0.005)
auaille v 8 (0.005)
auarous adj 8 (0.005)
aunte n 8 (0.005)
auowe v1 8 (0.005)
auter n 8 (0.005)
awayte v 8 (0.005)
baude n 8 (0.005)
bayard n 8 (0.005)
bedel n 8 (0.005)
bette n prop 8 (0.005)
bihynde prep 8 (0.005)
boost n 8 (0.005)

cairen v 8 (0.005)
calf n 8 (0.005)
chastite n 8 (0.005)
chaunge v 8 (0.005)
cogheþ v 8 (0.005)
coluere n 8 (0.005)
commissarie n 8 (0.005)
cors n 8 (0.005)
coueitous adj 8 (0.005)
coupe n 8 (0.005)
debat n 8 (0.005)
degre n 8 (0.005)
despende v 8 (0.005)
deuyse v 8 (0.005)
doynge ger 8 (0.005)
dremeþ v 8 (0.005)
dych n 8 (0.005)
engelond n prop 8 (0.005)
euensong n 8 (0.005)
faytest v 8 (0.005)
felle v 8 (0.005)
feuere n 8 (0.005)
forme n 8 (0.005)
gadelyng n 8 (0.005)
glede n 8 (0.005)
gleman n 8 (0.005)
glorie n 8 (0.005)
graiþ adj 8 (0.005)
hap n 8 (0.005)
harme v 8 (0.005)
hat n 8 (0.005)
heþen n 8 (0.005)
heritage n 8 (0.005)
hoked ptp 8 (0.005)
holly adv 8 (0.005)
hors n 8 (0.005)
howue n 8 (0.005)
hunte v 8 (0.005)
hurte v 8 (0.005)
ioseph n prop 8 (0.005)
kepere n 8 (0.005)
kiþ n 8 (0.005)
kidde v 8 (0.005)
kutte v 8 (0.005)
launde n 8 (0.005)
lechecraft n 8 (0.005)
leg n 8 (0.005)
lippe n 8 (0.005)
manoir n 8 (0.005)
marc n prop 8 (0.005)
mariage n 8 (0.005)
merite n 8 (0.005)
messie n 8 (0.005)
monþe n 8 (0.005)
mote v 8 (0.005)
mouþen v 8 (0.005)
mous n 8 (0.005)
neer adv 8 (0.005)
neghen v 8 (0.005)
neueremoore adv 8 (0.005)
peire n 8 (0.005)
pitously adv 8 (0.005)
poke n 8 (0.005)
potage n 8 (0.005)
preesthod n 8 (0.005)
pulle v 8 (0.005)
pureliche adv 8 (0.005)
quake v 8 (0.005)
rendren v 8 (0.005)
robe n 8 (0.005)
rouneþ v 8 (0.005)
saluen v 8 (0.005)

scorne v 8 (0.005)
seþ n prop 8 (0.005)
seson n 8 (0.005)
shire n 8 (0.005)
short adj 8 (0.005)
sikerly adv 8 (0.005)
sobretee n 8 (0.005)
somwhat pron 8 (0.005)
sooþfast adj 8 (0.005)
souereynly adv 8 (0.005)
soupen v 8 (0.005)
spynnen v 8 (0.005)
stede n1 8 (0.005)
stele v 8 (0.005)
sterneliche adv 8 (0.005)
sterue v 8 (0.005)
strike v 8 (0.005)
swoune v 8 (0.005)
taillours n 8 (0.005)
tidy adj 8 (0.005)
title n 8 (0.005)
torche n 8 (0.005)
tour n 8 (0.005)
tried ptp 8 (0.005)
vitailles n 8 (0.005)
waggeþ v 8 (0.005)
weed n 8 (0.005)
weke n 8 (0.005)
welle n 8 (0.005)
were v 8 (0.005)
wex n 8 (0.005)
what adv 8 (0.005)
whennes adv 8 (0.005)
wiþouten adv 8 (0.005)
wikke adj 8 (0.005)
wildernesse n 8 (0.005)
wont ptp 8 (0.005)
worden v 8 (0.005)
worldly adj 8 (0.005)
writyng ger 8 (0.005)
yerde n 8 (0.005)

RANKED LIST OF HIGH-FREQUENCY SPELLINGS

This lists in descending order the highest frequency spellings in Langland's Middle English vocabulary, each with its absolute and relative frequency (in parentheses); included are forms which occur at least eight times (relative frequency of 0.005 or greater).

and 9,836 (6.223)
þe 4,336 (2.743)
to 4,052 (2.564)
of 3,379 (2.138)
þat 3,205 (2.028)
for 2,474 (1.565)
a 2,406 (1.522)
in 2,307 (1.460)
he 1,945 (1.231)
his 1,636 (1.035)
i 1,605 (1.015)
is 1,571 (0.994)
as 1,476 (0.934)
hym 1,162 (0.735)
be 1,103 (0.698)
hem 1,102 (0.697)
y 1,036 (0.655)
the 977 (0.618)
ne 960 (0.607)
alle 908 (0.574)
here 905 (0.573)
that 900 (0.569)
me 878 (0.555)
it 849 (0.537)
so 797 (0.504)
& 784 (0.496)
no 769 (0.487)
men 734 (0.464)
my 734 (0.464)
on 724 (0.458)
was 722 (0.457)
or 696 (0.440)
wiþ 660 (0.418)
with 658 (0.416)
ac 654 (0.414)
by 629 (0.398)
haue 626 (0.396)
quod 613 (0.388)
hit 593 (0.375)
shal 565 (0.357)
at 564 (0.357)
god 560 (0.354)
but 523 (0.331)
al 522 (0.330)
were 492 (0.311)
man 455 (0.288)
þei 449 (0.284)
wel 423 (0.268)
þis 383 (0.242)
hadde 383 (0.242)
ben 382 (0.242)
neuere 363 (0.230)
oure 352 (0.223)
loue 348 (0.220)
nat 345 (0.218)
what 344 (0.218)
noȝt 335 (0.212)
wolde 335 (0.212)
hire 315 (0.199)
sholde 313 (0.198)
kynde 307 (0.194)
hir 306 (0.194)
may 303 (0.192)

til 297 (0.188)
this 296 (0.187)
we 295 (0.187)
lord 288 (0.182)
vs 288 (0.182)
thow 281 (0.178)
mede 278 (0.176)
þi 277 (0.175)
crist 266 (0.168)
lawe 264 (0.167)
if 261 (0.165)
þow 257 (0.163)
grace 248 (0.157)
ȝe 237 (0.150)
seide 224 (0.142)
boþe 223 (0.141)
leue 219 (0.139)
an 218 (0.138)
they 218 (0.138)
do 216 (0.137)
peple 215 (0.136)
kyng 214 (0.135)
þanne 207 (0.131)
how 206 (0.130)
ye 202 (0.128)
þou 200 (0.127)
made 198 (0.125)
now 198 (0.125)
come 195 (0.123)
tyme 195 (0.123)
mercy 194 (0.123)
heuene 193 (0.122)
after 192 (0.121)
soule 192 (0.121)
thenne 192 (0.121)
out_of 95 (0.060)
bothe 186 (0.118)
wille 185 (0.117)
wol 184 (0.116)
many 183 (0.116)
haþ 182 (0.115)
þer 180 (0.114)
consience 180 (0.114)
euere 180 (0.114)
yf 175 (0.111)
make 174 (0.110)
tho 173 (0.109)
helpe 172 (0.109)
þoruȝ 168 (0.106)
þee 166 (0.105)
good 166 (0.105)
hise 166 (0.105)
þere 162 (0.102)
synne 162 (0.102)
she 161 (0.102)
thy 161 (0.102)
dowel 160 (0.101)
oþer 160 (0.101)
more 156 (0.099)
whan 155 (0.098)
wit 155 (0.098)
conscience 151 (0.096)
aftur 148 (0.094)
þo 146 (0.092)

ȝow 146 (0.092)
bote 146 (0.092)
fro 144 (0.091)
ful 144 (0.091)
lif 144 (0.091)
thorw 144 (0.091)
go 141 (0.089)
thus 141 (0.089)
cam 139 (0.088)
folk 139 (0.088)
myhte 139 (0.088)
resoun 138 (0.087)
clerkes 135 (0.085)
day 134 (0.085)
lordes 133 (0.084)
se 132 (0.084)
saue 131 (0.083)
herte 130 (0.082)
lyf 130 (0.082)
lyue 130 (0.082)
riche 128 (0.081)
moore 125 (0.079)
trewe 125 (0.079)
ȝoure 124 (0.078)
aboute 124 (0.078)
any 124 (0.078)
yow 124 (0.078)
þise 123 (0.078)
manye 123 (0.078)
piers 123 (0.078)
som_tyme 61 (0.039)
speche 122 (0.077)
knowe 121 (0.077)
thanne 121 (0.077)
pore 120 (0.076)
am 119 (0.075)
clergie 118 (0.075)
er 118 (0.075)
holy_chirche 59 (0.037)
cristene 117 (0.074)
treuthe 117 (0.074)
forþ 114 (0.072)
saide 114 (0.072)
world 114 (0.072)
eny 113 (0.071)
fals 113 (0.071)
hath 113 (0.071)
han 112 (0.071)
dede 111 (0.070)
longe 111 (0.070)
mete 111 (0.070)
myn 111 (0.070)
holy_writ 55 (0.035)
when 110 (0.070)
wordes 110 (0.070)
youre 110 (0.070)
suche 108 (0.068)
peres 107 (0.068)
sone 107 (0.068)
telle 106 (0.067)
then 106 (0.067)
oþere 105 (0.066)
þus 104 (0.066)
ther 104 (0.066)

bileue 103 (0.065)
into 103 (0.065)
myȝte 103 (0.065)
pees 103 (0.065)
helle 102 (0.065)
pacience 101 (0.064)
riȝt 101 (0.064)
manere 100 (0.063)
reson 100 (0.063)
þan 99 (0.063)
amende 99 (0.063)
grete 98 (0.062)
nede 97 (0.061)
ofte 97 (0.061)
truþe 97 (0.061)
where 97 (0.061)
kepe 96 (0.061)
lewed 96 (0.061)
muche 96 (0.061)
name 96 (0.061)
quaþ 95 (0.060)
two 95 (0.060)
penaunce 94 (0.059)
sire 94 (0.059)
loke 93 (0.059)
o 93 (0.059)
ȝif 92 (0.058)
take 90 (0.057)
can 89 (0.056)
forth 89 (0.056)
thei 89 (0.056)
ende 88 (0.056)
vp 88 (0.056)
while 87 (0.055)
faste 85 (0.054)
pouerte 84 (0.053)
noon 83 (0.053)
fynde 82 (0.052)
whoso 82 (0.052)
charite 81 (0.051)
laste 81 (0.051)
bifore 80 (0.051)
holde 80 (0.051)
nouȝt 80 (0.051)
ar 79 (0.050)
body 79 (0.050)
comune 79 (0.050)
iewes 79 (0.050)
there 79 (0.050)
werkes 79 (0.050)
holy_churche 39 (0.025)
kynges 78 (0.049)
also 77 (0.049)
beste 77 (0.049)
witnesse 77 (0.049)
bi 76 (0.048)
rede 76 (0.048)
vnder 76 (0.048)
ȝut 75 (0.047)
erþe 75 (0.047)
freres 75 (0.047)
hope 75 (0.047)
lat 75 (0.047)
mene 75 (0.047)

goddes 74 (0.047)
kan 74 (0.047)
wende 73 (0.046)
litel 72 (0.046)
tolde 71 (0.045)
blisse 70 (0.044)
iesus 70 (0.044)
lond 70 (0.044)
sayde 70 (0.044)
among 69 (0.044)
dobet 69 (0.044)
wente 69 (0.044)
wo 69 (0.044)
catel 68 (0.043)
ioye 68 (0.043)
louye 68 (0.043)
mette 68 (0.043)
ouer 68 (0.043)
seiþ 68 (0.043)
drynke 67 (0.042)
ooþer 67 (0.042)
riht 67 (0.042)
tonge 67 (0.042)
aftir 66 (0.042)
gan 66 (0.042)
hymself 66 (0.042)
vpon 66 (0.042)
werche 66 (0.042)
amonges 65 (0.041)
not 65 (0.041)
power 65 (0.041)
such 65 (0.041)
bad 64 (0.040)
feiþ 64 (0.040)
frere 64 (0.040)
lady 64 (0.040)
ones 64 (0.040)
somme 64 (0.040)
wil 64 (0.040)
som 63 (0.040)
forþi 62 (0.039)
ryche 62 (0.039)
thre 62 (0.039)
all 61 (0.039)
hunger 61 (0.039)
bettre 60 (0.038)
fader 60 (0.038)
out 60 (0.038)
pouere 60 (0.038)
arn 59 (0.037)
dobest 59 (0.037)
lele 59 (0.037)
swiche 59 (0.037)
aren 58 (0.037)
coueitise 58 (0.037)
ech 58 (0.037)
ellis 58 (0.037)
goode 58 (0.037)
king 58 (0.037)
pope 58 (0.037)
shalt 58 (0.037)
sonne 58 (0.037)
which 58 (0.037)
court 57 (0.036)
deeþ 57 (0.036)
erthe 57 (0.036)
shul 57 (0.036)
sorwe 57 (0.036)
wole 57 (0.036)
deth 56 (0.035)
oon 56 (0.035)
seint 56 (0.035)

sente 56 (0.035)
sette 56 (0.035)
dayes 55 (0.035)
drede 55 (0.035)
brynge 54 (0.034)
hymsulue 54 (0.034)
mannes 54 (0.034)
wiþouten 54 (0.034)
wrong 54 (0.034)
faire 53 (0.034)
foule 53 (0.034)
non 53 (0.034)
none 53 (0.034)
saued 53 (0.034)
siluer 53 (0.034)
synnes 53 (0.034)
treuþe 53 (0.034)
who 53 (0.034)
worþ 53 (0.034)
adam 52 (0.033)
iesu 52 (0.033)
than 52 (0.033)
bere 51 (0.032)
cristes 51 (0.032)
heo 51 (0.032)
herde 51 (0.032)
siþen 51 (0.032)
suffre 51 (0.032)
wyf 51 (0.032)
wynter 51 (0.032)
wyt 51 (0.032)
þouȝ 50 (0.032)
ale 50 (0.032)
deye 50 (0.032)
gold 50 (0.032)
lene 50 (0.032)
place 50 (0.032)
swich 50 (0.032)
bokes 49 (0.031)
dide 49 (0.031)
goed 49 (0.031)
marie 49 (0.031)
moche 49 (0.031)
neiþer 49 (0.031)
reste 49 (0.031)
seuene 49 (0.031)
word 49 (0.031)
wynne 49 (0.031)
falle 48 (0.030)
furste 48 (0.030)
lette 48 (0.030)
mo 48 (0.030)
sauter 48 (0.030)
shewe 48 (0.030)
awey 47 (0.030)
euc 47 (0.030)
godes 47 (0.030)
hoso 47 (0.030)
mowe 47 (0.030)
same 47 (0.030)
shulde 47 (0.030)
wey 47 (0.030)
wiste 47 (0.030)
withouten 47 (0.030)
creature 46 (0.029)
doon 46 (0.029)
holy_kirke 23 (0.015)
lasse 46 (0.029)
maner 46 (0.029)
wise 46 (0.029)
art 45 (0.028)
fayre 45 (0.028)

half 45 (0.028)
lede 45 (0.028)
lered 45 (0.028)
lucifer 45 (0.028)
tymes 45 (0.028)
vertues 45 (0.028)
whiche 45 (0.028)
wittes 45 (0.028)
woot 45 (0.028)
wyse 45 (0.028)
craft 44 (0.028)
defaute 44 (0.028)
forthy 44 (0.028)
gaf 44 (0.028)
kyne 44 (0.028)
maken 44 (0.028)
olde 44 (0.028)
pardon 44 (0.028)
thogh 44 (0.028)
þre 43 (0.027)
clene 43 (0.027)
enuye 43 (0.027)
gode 43 (0.027)
haen 43 (0.027)
hennes 43 (0.027)
holden 43 (0.027)
plowman 43 (0.027)
tauȝte 43 (0.027)
teche 43 (0.027)
vch 43 (0.027)
why 43 (0.027)
clerk 42 (0.027)
dauid 42 (0.027)
elde 42 (0.027)
fruyt 42 (0.027)
gyle 42 (0.027)
lowe 42 (0.027)
worth 42 (0.027)
betere 41 (0.026)
liflode 41 (0.026)
lyuen 41 (0.026)
rome 41 (0.026)
soþe 41 (0.026)
taken 41 (0.026)
telleth 41 (0.026)
togideres 41 (0.026)
whanne 41 (0.026)
withoute 41 (0.026)
yet 41 (0.026)
children 40 (0.025)
doth 40 (0.025)
fyue 40 (0.025)
him 40 (0.025)
holy_goost 20 (0.013)
hote 40 (0.025)
hymselue 40 (0.025)
lo 40 (0.025)
meschief 40 (0.025)
mony 40 (0.025)
sethe 40 (0.025)
some 40 (0.025)
wile 40 (0.025)
are 39 (0.025)
counseil 39 (0.025)
cros 39 (0.025)
elles 39 (0.025)
gyue 39 (0.025)
lerne 39 (0.025)
moste 39 (0.025)
other 39 (0.025)
pride 39 (0.025)
trinite 39 (0.025)

womman 39 (0.025)
called 38 (0.024)
com 38 (0.024)
holy 38 (0.024)
kyn 38 (0.024)
lere 38 (0.024)
prest 38 (0.024)
pruyde 38 (0.024)
putte 38 (0.024)
sey 38 (0.024)
seye 38 (0.024)
seynt 38 (0.024)
thise 38 (0.024)
water 38 (0.024)
wif 38 (0.024)
FALSE 38 (0.024)
cometh 37 (0.023)
commune 37 (0.023)
fram 37 (0.023)
kenne 37 (0.023)
mayde 37 (0.023)
myself 37 (0.023)
owene 37 (0.023)
telleþ 37 (0.023)
vnkynde 37 (0.023)
dar 36 (0.023)
hatte 36 (0.023)
hele 36 (0.023)
plouhman 36 (0.023)
repentaunce 36 (0.023)
selde 36 (0.023)
soules 36 (0.023)
took 36 (0.023)
þyng 35 (0.022)
beestes 35 (0.022)
bereþ 35 (0.022)
book 35 (0.022)
comen 35 (0.022)
dooþ 35 (0.022)
ek 35 (0.022)
fauel 35 (0.022)
first 35 (0.022)
fortune 35 (0.022)
graunte 35 (0.022)
hast 35 (0.022)
lawes 35 (0.022)
makeþ 35 (0.022)
masse 35 (0.022)
newe 35 (0.022)
seiȝ 35 (0.022)
soffre 35 (0.022)
tauhte 35 (0.022)
thyng 35 (0.022)
wombe 35 (0.022)
þeiȝ 34 (0.022)
þerwiþ 34 (0.022)
ayein 34 (0.022)
beth 34 (0.022)
byfore 34 (0.022)
dere 34 (0.022)
lettre 34 (0.022)
lewede 34 (0.022)
miȝte 34 (0.022)
mote 34 (0.022)
oen 34 (0.022)
one 34 (0.022)
pardoun 34 (0.022)
richesse 34 (0.022)
sake 34 (0.022)
see 34 (0.022)
symonye 34 (0.022)
wisse 34 (0.022)

þerof 33 (0.021)
comeþ 33 (0.021)
flessh 33 (0.021)
gete 33 (0.021)
late 33 (0.021)
likeþ 33 (0.021)
lyuede 33 (0.021)
mankynde 33 (0.021)
nedy 33 (0.021)
rode 33 (0.021)
seed 33 (0.021)
tales 33 (0.021)
way 33 (0.021)
wite 33 (0.021)
woet 33 (0.021)
best 32 (0.020)
bestes 32 (0.020)
breed 32 (0.020)
ete 32 (0.020)
foure 32 (0.020)
gospel 32 (0.020)
hand 32 (0.020)
hous 32 (0.020)
knewe 32 (0.020)
lay 32 (0.020)
leef 32 (0.020)
lye 32 (0.020)
lyuynge 32 (0.020)
most 32 (0.020)
poore 32 (0.020)
pure 32 (0.020)
tale 32 (0.020)
wikkede 32 (0.020)
wyte 32 (0.020)
bereth 31 (0.020)
bettere 31 (0.020)
deuel 31 (0.020)
don 31 (0.020)
fend 31 (0.020)
fewe 31 (0.020)
greue 31 (0.020)
ille 31 (0.020)
latyn 31 (0.020)
maister 31 (0.020)
maistres 31 (0.020)
maketh 31 (0.020)
moost 31 (0.020)
noþer 31 (0.020)
parfit 31 (0.020)
scripture 31 (0.020)
swete 31 (0.020)
techeþ 31 (0.020)
techeth 31 (0.020)
wiþoute 31 (0.020)
þou3te 30 (0.019)
bible 30 (0.019)
bidde 30 (0.019)
blood 30 (0.019)
by_so 15 (0.009)
contricion 30 (0.019)
gile 30 (0.019)
gret 30 (0.019)
hei3e 30 (0.019)
hy 30 (0.019)
ich 30 (0.019)
lif_tyme 15 (0.009)
moder 30 (0.019)
my3t 30 (0.019)
peris 30 (0.019)
serue 30 (0.019)
togyderes 30 (0.019)
turne 30 (0.019)

wher 30 (0.019)
wonder 30 (0.019)
þerto 29 (0.018)
a3en 29 (0.018)
adoun 29 (0.018)
blynde 29 (0.018)
care 29 (0.018)
doctour 29 (0.018)
drawe 29 (0.018)
ei3en 29 (0.018)
fecche 29 (0.018)
fele 29 (0.018)
fer 29 (0.018)
ho 29 (0.018)
let 29 (0.018)
na 29 (0.018)
preche 29 (0.018)
preestes 29 (0.018)
siþþe 29 (0.018)
sory 29 (0.018)
ten 29 (0.018)
tresor 29 (0.018)
wisdom 29 (0.018)
beþ 28 (0.018)
dedly 28 (0.018)
frendes 28 (0.018)
from 28 (0.018)
hi3te 28 (0.018)
lettres 28 (0.018)
lyf_tyme 14 (0.009)
lyflode 28 (0.018)
molde 28 (0.018)
nay 28 (0.018)
peter 28 (0.018)
prelates 28 (0.018)
right 28 (0.018)
sende 28 (0.018)
sothly 28 (0.018)
togidere 28 (0.018)
vppon 28 (0.018)
wedde 28 (0.018)
þerwith 27 (0.017)
þyn 27 (0.017)
3ede 27 (0.017)
ay 27 (0.017)
barn 27 (0.017)
bete 27 (0.017)
couthe 27 (0.017)
fayth 27 (0.017)
fere 27 (0.017)
iustice 27 (0.017)
mennes 27 (0.017)
pite 27 (0.017)
preest 27 (0.017)
reule 27 (0.017)
seke 27 (0.017)
sitte 27 (0.017)
sones 27 (0.017)
sooþ 27 (0.017)
trowe 27 (0.017)
war 27 (0.017)
whiles 27 (0.017)
wrouhte 27 (0.017)
wyn 27 (0.017)
þerinne 26 (0.016)
armes 26 (0.016)
dame 26 (0.016)
eten 26 (0.016)
gome 26 (0.016)
her 26 (0.016)
hihte 26 (0.016)
kepen 26 (0.016)

knoweth 26 (0.016)
labour 26 (0.016)
lelly 26 (0.016)
lik 26 (0.016)
lore 26 (0.016)
mone 26 (0.016)
mysulue 26 (0.016)
oute_of 13 (0.008)
persones 26 (0.016)
plese 26 (0.016)
speke 26 (0.016)
summe 26 (0.016)
thyn 26 (0.016)
wikked 26 (0.016)
worche 26 (0.016)
bar 25 (0.016)
beggeris 25 (0.016)
caste 25 (0.016)
coueytise 25 (0.016)
creatures 25 (0.016)
ese 25 (0.016)
falsnesse 25 (0.016)
fode 25 (0.016)
fre 25 (0.016)
inwit 25 (0.016)
knowen 25 (0.016)
konne 25 (0.016)
kouþe 25 (0.016)
lese 25 (0.016)
long 25 (0.016)
louede 25 (0.016)
passe 25 (0.016)
patriarkes 25 (0.016)
poul 25 (0.016)
preye 25 (0.016)
profit 25 (0.016)
reuthe 25 (0.016)
taketh 25 (0.016)
wele 25 (0.016)
wene 25 (0.016)
witterly 25 (0.016)
anoþer 24 (0.015)
beggares 24 (0.015)
briddes 24 (0.015)
brou3te 24 (0.015)
cause 24 (0.015)
crye 24 (0.015)
dwelle 24 (0.015)
fare 24 (0.015)
felawe 24 (0.015)
handes 24 (0.015)
hard 24 (0.015)
holi_churche 12 (0.008)
kene 24 (0.015)
loked 24 (0.015)
lyueth 24 (0.015)
myne 24 (0.015)
prestes 24 (0.015)
ryde 24 (0.015)
sothe 24 (0.015)
sum_tyme 12 (0.008)
swynke 24 (0.015)
will 24 (0.015)
þerfore 23 (0.015)
aske 23 (0.015)
bloed 23 (0.015)
bred 23 (0.015)
euene 23 (0.015)
fair 23 (0.015)
fayn 23 (0.015)
lete 23 (0.015)
light 23 (0.015)

lost 23 (0.015)
meke 23 (0.015)
mouþ 23 (0.015)
mynde 23 (0.015)
places 23 (0.015)
prophetes 23 (0.015)
raþer 23 (0.015)
science 23 (0.015)
seruen 23 (0.015)
sleuþe 23 (0.015)
teme 23 (0.015)
tene 23 (0.015)
welcome 23 (0.015)
wexe 23 (0.015)
wordis 23 (0.015)
wot 23 (0.015)
þiselue 22 (0.014)
þynkeþ 22 (0.014)
3af 22 (0.014)
3et 22 (0.014)
aboue 22 (0.014)
bitwene 22 (0.014)
conforte 22 (0.014)
dedes 22 (0.014)
fuyr 22 (0.014)
knoweþ 22 (0.014)
kynge 22 (0.014)
leten 22 (0.014)
lettred 22 (0.014)
londe 22 (0.014)
maistrie 22 (0.014)
monkes 22 (0.014)
mylde 22 (0.014)
paternoster 22 (0.014)
perkyn 22 (0.014)
peyne 22 (0.014)
ruþe 22 (0.014)
segge 22 (0.014)
shuln 22 (0.014)
slepe 22 (0.014)
spirit 22 (0.014)
syre 22 (0.014)
takeþ 22 (0.014)
thouhte 22 (0.014)
toek 22 (0.014)
werk 22 (0.014)
weye 22 (0.014)
wilde 22 (0.014)
wrou3te 22 (0.014)
wyues 22 (0.014)
þeron 21 (0.013)
3eue 21 (0.013)
assente 21 (0.013)
bisshopes 21 (0.013)
blame 21 (0.013)
breke 21 (0.013)
brouhte 21 (0.013)
chief 21 (0.013)
cristendom 21 (0.013)
depe 21 (0.013)
euele 21 (0.013)
firste 21 (0.013)
foode 21 (0.013)
fyngres 21 (0.013)
greet 21 (0.013)
knyhte 21 (0.013)
lokede 21 (0.013)
loueth 21 (0.013)
monye 21 (0.013)
noen 21 (0.013)
rihte 21 (0.013)
rule 21 (0.013)

scole 21 (0.013)
selle 21 (0.013)
semeth 21 (0.013)
siȝte 21 (0.013)
sitten 21 (0.013)
thoruȝ 21 (0.013)
vnkyndenesse 21 (0.013)
wanhope 21 (0.013)
werre 21 (0.013)
whete 21 (0.013)
wiȝt 21 (0.013)
witty 21 (0.013)
wommen 21 (0.013)
wraþe 21 (0.013)
wynd 21 (0.013)
yede 21 (0.013)
ysaued 21 (0.013)
abraham 20 (0.013)
allas 20 (0.013)
begge 20 (0.013)
bisshop 20 (0.013)
boek 20 (0.013)
cacche 20 (0.013)
caym 20 (0.013)
conne 20 (0.013)
conquerour 20 (0.013)
corn 20 (0.013)
fol 20 (0.013)
gate 20 (0.013)
goodnesse 20 (0.013)
grounde 20 (0.013)
hede 20 (0.013)
heed 20 (0.013)
holi_chirche 10 (0.006)
holy_kyrke 10 (0.006)
holynesse 20 (0.013)
knyȝt 20 (0.013)
kynne 20 (0.013)
large 20 (0.013)
loueþ 20 (0.013)
maide 20 (0.013)
neuer 20 (0.013)
prechen 20 (0.013)
rather 20 (0.013)
seintes 20 (0.013)
shame 20 (0.013)
soone 20 (0.013)
sore 20 (0.013)
sowe 20 (0.013)
spak 20 (0.013)
stande 20 (0.013)
studie 20 (0.013)
thynges 20 (0.013)
toke 20 (0.013)
wedded 20 (0.013)
wenten 20 (0.013)
writen 20 (0.013)
wye 20 (0.013)
yes 20 (0.013)
bale 19 (0.012)
blessed 19 (0.012)
carpe 19 (0.012)
croune 19 (0.012)
deme 19 (0.012)
destruye 19 (0.012)
doþ 19 (0.012)
dome 19 (0.012)
dore 19 (0.012)
dyne 19 (0.012)
eft 19 (0.012)
faith 19 (0.012)
help 19 (0.012)

hente 19 (0.012)
heued 19 (0.012)
issue 19 (0.012)
knyhtes 19 (0.012)
kynnes 19 (0.012)
ladies 19 (0.012)
lente 19 (0.012)
lest 19 (0.012)
lesynges 19 (0.012)
leuere 19 (0.012)
leueth 19 (0.012)
madame 19 (0.012)
mysdedes 19 (0.012)
names 19 (0.012)
potte 19 (0.012)
purgatorie 19 (0.012)
rychesse 19 (0.012)
salue 19 (0.012)
seyntes 19 (0.012)
stille 19 (0.012)
thynketh 19 (0.012)
trewely 19 (0.012)
vnite 19 (0.012)
wastour 19 (0.012)
wepte 19 (0.012)
werkis 19 (0.012)
wilneþ 19 (0.012)
witnesseth 19 (0.012)
worse 19 (0.012)
ydel 19 (0.012)
yuel 19 (0.012)
þerafter 18 (0.011)
þey 18 (0.011)
asken 18 (0.011)
bet 18 (0.011)
bigan 18 (0.011)
castel 18 (0.011)
clerkis 18 (0.011)
defende 18 (0.011)
deyede 18 (0.011)
eet 18 (0.011)
fende 18 (0.011)
fette 18 (0.011)
fond 18 (0.011)
glotonye 18 (0.011)
hardy 18 (0.011)
haste 18 (0.011)
herof 18 (0.011)
hey 18 (0.011)
highte 18 (0.011)
honoure 18 (0.011)
iohan 18 (0.011)
iudas 18 (0.011)
lakke 18 (0.011)
mesure 18 (0.011)
preue 18 (0.011)
proud 18 (0.011)
saith 18 (0.011)
seyh 18 (0.011)
solace 18 (0.011)
sondry 18 (0.011)
synge 18 (0.011)
thouȝ 18 (0.011)
ȝer 17 (0.011)
amenden 17 (0.011)
anoon 17 (0.011)
arise 17 (0.011)
asketh 17 (0.011)
austyn 17 (0.011)
ayeins 17 (0.011)
bestis 17 (0.011)
bulle 17 (0.011)

calde 17 (0.011)
chaffare 17 (0.011)
construe 17 (0.011)
cryede 17 (0.011)
dele 17 (0.011)
dette 17 (0.011)
ere 17 (0.011)
euery 17 (0.011)
faille 17 (0.011)
fedde 17 (0.011)
folke 17 (0.011)
geten 17 (0.011)
goodes 17 (0.011)
harde 17 (0.011)
hundred 17 (0.011)
knaues 17 (0.011)
knowyng 17 (0.011)
lerned 17 (0.011)
liketh 17 (0.011)
lordis 17 (0.011)
menne 17 (0.011)
moneye 17 (0.011)
peril 17 (0.011)
persone 17 (0.011)
prestis 17 (0.011)
put 17 (0.011)
reue 17 (0.011)
roode 17 (0.011)
sapience 17 (0.011)
sayth 17 (0.011)
sewe 17 (0.011)
spille 17 (0.011)
suluer 17 (0.011)
togederes 17 (0.011)
wastours 17 (0.011)
wolle 17 (0.011)
þin 16 (0.010)
þing 16 (0.010)
þridde 16 (0.010)
ȝyue 16 (0.010)
askeþ 16 (0.010)
bak 16 (0.010)
beleue 16 (0.010)
chekes 16 (0.010)
clothes 16 (0.010)
contrarie 16 (0.010)
cote 16 (0.010)
couetyse 16 (0.010)
craftes 16 (0.010)
deere 16 (0.010)
doun 16 (0.010)
feld 16 (0.010)
folwe 16 (0.010)
foul 16 (0.010)
fourty 16 (0.010)
friday 16 (0.010)
glotoun 16 (0.010)
grene 16 (0.010)
haukyn 16 (0.010)
heiȝ 16 (0.010)
helden 16 (0.010)
holy_gost 8 (0.005)
knele 16 (0.010)
lefte 16 (0.010)
lemman 16 (0.010)
lepe 16 (0.010)
lihte 16 (0.010)
likynge 16 (0.010)
lust 16 (0.010)
maad 16 (0.010)
matere 16 (0.010)
mawe 16 (0.010)

messager 16 (0.010)
murþe 16 (0.010)
nolde 16 (0.010)
nombre 16 (0.010)
peny 16 (0.010)
puyr 16 (0.010)
ryht 16 (0.010)
salomon 16 (0.010)
seth 16 (0.010)
shaltow 16 (0.010)
sheweþ 16 (0.010)
shryue 16 (0.010)
soth 16 (0.010)
stonde 16 (0.010)
syde 16 (0.010)
tellen 16 (0.010)
vengeaunce 16 (0.010)
wan 16 (0.010)
witnesseþ 16 (0.010)
worþi 16 (0.010)
wroȝte 16 (0.010)
yuele 16 (0.010)
þiself 15 (0.009)
ȝour 15 (0.009)
aȝeyn 15 (0.009)
aryse 15 (0.009)
asked 15 (0.009)
blody 15 (0.009)
bold 15 (0.009)
breþeren 15 (0.009)
cardinale 15 (0.009)
certes 15 (0.009)
chirche 15 (0.009)
cloke 15 (0.009)
confort 15 (0.009)
conseil 15 (0.009)
counseille 15 (0.009)
curatours 15 (0.009)
deþ 15 (0.009)
eiþer 15 (0.009)
ensaumple 15 (0.009)
fel 15 (0.009)
ferly 15 (0.009)
freke 15 (0.009)
fust 15 (0.009)
fynden 15 (0.009)
gloton 15 (0.009)
heye 15 (0.009)
knaue 15 (0.009)
knew 15 (0.009)
leaute 15 (0.009)
lecherye 15 (0.009)
leet 15 (0.009)
legge 15 (0.009)
liþ 15 (0.009)
liknesse 15 (0.009)
londes 15 (0.009)
lordshipe 15 (0.009)
louely 15 (0.009)
louen 15 (0.009)
lyues 15 (0.009)
myselue 15 (0.009)
nempned 15 (0.009)
ordre 15 (0.009)
othere 15 (0.009)
ouþer 15 (0.009)
paye 15 (0.009)
payn 15 (0.009)
pilgrymes 15 (0.009)
prechours 15 (0.009)
prince 15 (0.009)
pyne 15 (0.009)

religioun 15 (0.009)
rentes 15 (0.009)
route 15 (0.009)
semeþ 15 (0.009)
seuen 15 (0.009)
sheweth 15 (0.009)
shrewe 15 (0.009)
signe 15 (0.009)
songen 15 (0.009)
sooþly 15 (0.009)
soore 15 (0.009)
techiþ 15 (0.009)
tresour 15 (0.009)
walke 15 (0.009)
ware 15 (0.009)
weere 15 (0.009)
werkmen 15 (0.009)
wheiþer 15 (0.009)
wight 15 (0.009)
wissen 15 (0.009)
worþe 15 (0.009)
ywar 15 (0.009)
ȝeftes 14 (0.009)
abyde 14 (0.009)
acorde 14 (0.009)
almyhty 14 (0.009)
apostles 14 (0.009)
bagge 14 (0.009)
bedde 14 (0.009)
biddyng 14 (0.009)
bihynde 14 (0.009)
bolde 14 (0.009)
chaste 14 (0.009)
cloþes 14 (0.009)
consayl 14 (0.009)
couþe 14 (0.009)
deueles 14 (0.009)
doute 14 (0.009)
echone 14 (0.009)
englissh 14 (0.009)
face 14 (0.009)
fastyng 14 (0.009)
feet 14 (0.009)
fir 14 (0.009)
fle 14 (0.009)
flood 14 (0.009)
folowe 14 (0.009)
founde 14 (0.009)
foweles 14 (0.009)
gilt 14 (0.009)
graunted 14 (0.009)
hadden 14 (0.009)
harlotes 14 (0.009)
hemselue 14 (0.009)
hende 14 (0.009)
hete 14 (0.009)
hood 14 (0.009)
iche 14 (0.009)
inne 14 (0.009)
knyȝtes 14 (0.009)
ladde 14 (0.009)
lappe 14 (0.009)
leche 14 (0.009)
lecherie 14 (0.009)
lef 14 (0.009)
leute 14 (0.009)
likyng 14 (0.009)
maistre 14 (0.009)
miȝt 14 (0.009)
moot 14 (0.009)
mowen 14 (0.009)
muchel 14 (0.009)

murye 14 (0.009)
myle 14 (0.009)
nameliche 14 (0.009)
pacient 14 (0.009)
passion 14 (0.009)
payne 14 (0.009)
perpetuel 14 (0.009)
pilgrimes 14 (0.009)
quyte 14 (0.009)
reaume 14 (0.009)
sat 14 (0.009)
saul 14 (0.009)
sent 14 (0.009)
sethen 14 (0.009)
sleuthe 14 (0.009)
somer 14 (0.009)
spede 14 (0.009)
strengþe 14 (0.009)
techynge 14 (0.009)
thomas 14 (0.009)
trauaille 14 (0.009)
tree 14 (0.009)
vnitee 14 (0.009)
warne 14 (0.009)
werchen 14 (0.009)
whom 14 (0.009)
wide 14 (0.009)
wys 14 (0.009)
yblessed 14 (0.009)
ynowe 14 (0.009)
þerynne 13 (0.008)
þousand 13 (0.008)
þynges 13 (0.008)
ȝiftes 13 (0.008)
afered 13 (0.008)
almesse 13 (0.008)
askede 13 (0.008)
auȝt 13 (0.008)
benes 13 (0.008)
blynd 13 (0.008)
boote 13 (0.008)
bouȝte 13 (0.008)
byleue 13 (0.008)
chere 13 (0.008)
cherles 13 (0.008)
cryde 13 (0.008)
ded 13 (0.008)
dorste 13 (0.008)
durste 13 (0.008)
eueremore 13 (0.008)
fendes 13 (0.008)
frend 13 (0.008)
fynt 13 (0.008)
heep 13 (0.008)
heuy 13 (0.008)
hitte 13 (0.008)
hungir 13 (0.008)
knees 13 (0.008)
knowest 13 (0.008)
knyghtes 13 (0.008)
kyndely 13 (0.008)
leeste 13 (0.008)
lereth 13 (0.008)
lettrure 13 (0.008)
liȝt 13 (0.008)
ligge 13 (0.008)
liht 13 (0.008)
liked 13 (0.008)
loore 13 (0.008)
lordschipe 13 (0.008)
lyare 13 (0.008)
makiþ 13 (0.008)

maydenes 13 (0.008)
mekenesse 13 (0.008)
myddel 13 (0.008)
nere 13 (0.008)
nyme 13 (0.008)
oþes 13 (0.008)
paume 13 (0.008)
popes 13 (0.008)
preide 13 (0.008)
preuen 13 (0.008)
preyede 13 (0.008)
prophete 13 (0.008)
religion 13 (0.008)
reume 13 (0.008)
samuel 13 (0.008)
score 13 (0.008)
semede 13 (0.008)
sherewe 13 (0.008)
shewed 13 (0.008)
sholden 13 (0.008)
siþ 13 (0.008)
signes 13 (0.008)
siknesse 13 (0.008)
softe 13 (0.008)
song 13 (0.008)
suster 13 (0.008)
swere 13 (0.008)
togideris 13 (0.008)
watir 13 (0.008)
wenche 13 (0.008)
wepe 13 (0.008)
wherfore 13 (0.008)
wilt 13 (0.008)
wrathe 13 (0.008)
þereinne 12 (0.008)
þouȝt 12 (0.008)
ȝit 12 (0.008)
artow 12 (0.008)
barnes 12 (0.008)
been 12 (0.008)
before 12 (0.008)
beggeres 12 (0.008)
brode 12 (0.008)
broke 12 (0.008)
bute 12 (0.008)
caluarie 12 (0.008)
carpen 12 (0.008)
cat 12 (0.008)
chide 12 (0.008)
comsed 12 (0.008)
confessour 12 (0.008)
couenaunt 12 (0.008)
couent 12 (0.008)
cristendoem 12 (0.008)
curteisie 12 (0.008)
cyuyle 12 (0.008)
deþe 12 (0.008)
doen 12 (0.008)
ermytes 12 (0.008)
euen 12 (0.008)
feble 12 (0.008)
folwede 12 (0.008)
forsake 12 (0.008)
fynger 12 (0.008)
glad 12 (0.008)
goth 12 (0.008)
grette 12 (0.008)
gyueth 12 (0.008)
halle 12 (0.008)
heele 12 (0.008)
hemsulue 12 (0.008)
holy_goest 6 (0.004)

hom 12 (0.008)
inparfit 12 (0.008)
konnynge 12 (0.008)
laborers 12 (0.008)
leste 12 (0.008)
leues 12 (0.008)
lokeþ 12 (0.008)
looþ 12 (0.008)
loth 12 (0.008)
lyke 12 (0.008)
lyueþ 12 (0.008)
marchaunt 12 (0.008)
mathew 12 (0.008)
mouthe 12 (0.008)
moyses 12 (0.008)
myghte 12 (0.008)
nauht 12 (0.008)
paradis 12 (0.008)
pawme 12 (0.008)
persons 12 (0.008)
praye 12 (0.008)
pryde 12 (0.008)
puyre 12 (0.008)
rape 12 (0.008)
religious 12 (0.008)
remenaunt 12 (0.008)
rose 12 (0.008)
ryhte 12 (0.008)
sauȝ 12 (0.008)
saueour 12 (0.008)
say 12 (0.008)
siþes 12 (0.008)
sighte 12 (0.008)
sike 12 (0.008)
sixe 12 (0.008)
soffrede 12 (0.008)
synfulle 12 (0.008)
techyng 12 (0.008)
thi 12 (0.008)
thouh 12 (0.008)
tunge 12 (0.008)
wed 12 (0.008)
weren 12 (0.008)
whenne 12 (0.008)
worschipe 12 (0.008)
worthy 12 (0.008)
wyde 12 (0.008)
wynnynge 12 (0.008)
wysdom 12 (0.008)
þy 11 (0.007)
ȝelde 11 (0.007)
ȝerne 11 (0.007)
ȝeueth 11 (0.007)
aȝens 11 (0.007)
abide 11 (0.007)
actif 11 (0.007)
almyȝty 11 (0.007)
amongus 11 (0.007)
aslepe 11 (0.007)
aungeles 11 (0.007)
awake 11 (0.007)
beggare 11 (0.007)
beggere 11 (0.007)
berynge 11 (0.007)
bette 11 (0.007)
biseche 11 (0.007)
boot 11 (0.007)
buxum 11 (0.007)
chapmen 11 (0.007)
childrene 11 (0.007)
cold 11 (0.007)
concience 11 (0.007)

conforted 11 (0.007)	reuerenced 11 (0.007)	gyueþ 10 (0.006)	treweliche 10 (0.006)
consail 11 (0.007)	rightwisnesse 11 (0.007)	hanged 10 (0.006)	trouþe 10 (0.006)
contree 11 (0.007)	sathan 11 (0.007)	harlotrie 10 (0.006)	tyne 10 (0.006)
coueite 11 (0.007)	seiʒe 11 (0.007)	harm 10 (0.006)	watre 10 (0.006)
croft 11 (0.007)	seten 11 (0.007)	helpen 10 (0.006)	welthe 10 (0.006)
daies 11 (0.007)	seyn 11 (0.007)	heraud 10 (0.006)	wercheþ 10 (0.006)
dampned 11 (0.007)	shrift 11 (0.007)	hold 10 (0.006)	wollen 10 (0.006)
deserue 11 (0.007)	sib 11 (0.007)	iames 10 (0.006)	wy 10 (0.006)
deserued 11 (0.007)	slepynge 11 (0.007)	iustices 10 (0.006)	wyles 10 (0.006)
doctours 11 (0.007)	somur 11 (0.007)	knelede 10 (0.006)	yeue 10 (0.006)
donge 11 (0.007)	suffrede 11 (0.007)	knelynge 10 (0.006)	yliche 10 (0.006)
doom 11 (0.007)	synful 11 (0.007)	kniʒt 10 (0.006)	ymaked 10 (0.006)
enemyes 11 (0.007)	tel 11 (0.007)	kniʒtes 10 (0.006)	þeraftur 9 (0.006)
eueremoore 11 (0.007)	thysulue 11 (0.007)	kyndeliche 10 (0.006)	ʒates 9 (0.006)
faile 11 (0.007)	tweyne 11 (0.007)	laʒar 10 (0.006)	ʒeftis 9 (0.006)
faitours 11 (0.007)	wedes 11 (0.007)	ledes 10 (0.006)	ʒeres 9 (0.006)
falleth 11 (0.007)	wenden 11 (0.007)	leeue 10 (0.006)	ʒyueþ 9 (0.006)
fareþ 11 (0.007)	wolt 11 (0.007)	lenger 10 (0.006)	amydde 9 (0.006)
fayle 11 (0.007)	wonne 11 (0.007)	lippes 10 (0.006)	anoen 9 (0.006)
fede 11 (0.007)	worlde 11 (0.007)	lokide 10 (0.006)	anon 9 (0.006)
ferþer 11 (0.007)	write 11 (0.007)	louʒ 10 (0.006)	appul 9 (0.006)
feste 11 (0.007)	wymmen 11 (0.007)	loude 10 (0.006)	assoile 9 (0.006)
fikel 11 (0.007)	wynneþ 11 (0.007)	loued 10 (0.006)	assoiled 9 (0.006)
foules 11 (0.007)	wynnen 11 (0.007)	lycame 10 (0.006)	aungel 9 (0.006)
frende 11 (0.007)	yaf 11 (0.007)	lygge 10 (0.006)	banne 9 (0.006)
fryday 11 (0.007)	ybounde 11 (0.007)	lyued 10 (0.006)	bastard 9 (0.006)
fulfille 11 (0.007)	yknowe 11 (0.007)	maiden 10 (0.006)	bicam 9 (0.006)
fyndeth 11 (0.007)	þennes 10 (0.006)	maistris 10 (0.006)	bifel 9 (0.006)
fyngeres 11 (0.007)	þeues 10 (0.006)	maluerne 10 (0.006)	bigiled 9 (0.006)
glade 11 (0.007)	age 10 (0.006)	matynes 10 (0.006)	bisshopis 9 (0.006)
godis 11 (0.007)	als 10 (0.006)	moet 10 (0.006)	bit 9 (0.006)
ground 11 (0.007)	amendes 10 (0.006)	mooste 10 (0.006)	born 9 (0.006)
halde 11 (0.007)	another 10 (0.006)	morwe 10 (0.006)	borwe 9 (0.006)
hange 11 (0.007)	apostel 10 (0.006)	munstrals 10 (0.006)	bouhte 9 (0.006)
hed 11 (0.007)	aspie 10 (0.006)	neiʒ 10 (0.006)	broken 9 (0.006)
helpeþ 11 (0.007)	auarice 10 (0.006)	noumbre 10 (0.006)	brood 9 (0.006)
huyre 11 (0.007)	baer 10 (0.006)	oþerwhile 10 (0.006)	bynde 9 (0.006)
ichone 11 (0.007)	barre 10 (0.006)	pardoner 10 (0.006)	casten 9 (0.006)
kepeth 11 (0.007)	beden 10 (0.006)	passed 10 (0.006)	cheste 9 (0.006)
laboure 11 (0.007)	belle 10 (0.006)	passioun 10 (0.006)	cloth 9 (0.006)
lacche 11 (0.007)	biddeþ 10 (0.006)	pelure 10 (0.006)	colours 9 (0.006)
lacke 11 (0.007)	bidden 10 (0.006)	plouh 10 (0.006)	comaunde 9 (0.006)
ladyes 11 (0.007)	bigile 10 (0.006)	possession 10 (0.006)	comaundede 9 (0.006)
land 11 (0.007)	boke 10 (0.006)	pouke 10 (0.006)	consayle 9 (0.006)
left 11 (0.007)	bolle 10 (0.006)	precheþ 10 (0.006)	cosyn 9 (0.006)
lesson 11 (0.007)	bringe 10 (0.006)	pryue 10 (0.006)	counteth 9 (0.006)
leued 11 (0.007)	cald 10 (0.006)	putten 10 (0.006)	cursed 9 (0.006)
leuest 11 (0.007)	cart 10 (0.006)	rekene 10 (0.006)	dale 9 (0.006)
libbe 11 (0.007)	cast 10 (0.006)	renkes 10 (0.006)	daniel 9 (0.006)
likned 11 (0.007)	caton 10 (0.006)	reumes 10 (0.006)	deuil 9 (0.006)
loo 11 (0.007)	chartre 10 (0.006)	roote 10 (0.006)	dispute 9 (0.006)
luste 11 (0.007)	childe 10 (0.006)	salamon 10 (0.006)	done 9 (0.006)
lyketh 11 (0.007)	clause 10 (0.006)	sarʒens 10 (0.006)	down 9 (0.006)
lymes 11 (0.007)	comunes 10 (0.006)	seel 10 (0.006)	drow 9 (0.006)
lytel 11 (0.007)	connynge 10 (0.006)	semed 10 (0.006)	dryue 9 (0.006)
mad 11 (0.007)	constable 10 (0.006)	seruauntʒ 10 (0.006)	dwelleþ 9 (0.006)
merye 11 (0.007)	coueiteþ 10 (0.006)	seue 10 (0.006)	eche 9 (0.006)
moneie 11 (0.007)	crafty 10 (0.006)	seyde 10 (0.006)	ensample 9 (0.006)
naked 11 (0.007)	criede 10 (0.006)	seynte 10 (0.006)	feche 9 (0.006)
nauʒt 11 (0.007)	cure 10 (0.006)	shewen 10 (0.006)	felle 9 (0.006)
nedeth 11 (0.007)	curteisliche 10 (0.006)	ship 10 (0.006)	feloun 9 (0.006)
noble 11 (0.007)	curteisly 10 (0.006)	sour 10 (0.006)	ferme 9 (0.006)
nother 11 (0.007)	demen 10 (0.006)	spare 10 (0.006)	fissh 9 (0.006)
nouthe 11 (0.007)	domesday 10 (0.006)	stokkes 10 (0.006)	foles 9 (0.006)
nyhte 11 (0.007)	efte 10 (0.006)	suffren 10 (0.006)	folwen 9 (0.006)
plouʒ 11 (0.007)	euel 10 (0.006)	sulle 10 (0.006)	forbede 9 (0.006)
preieres 11 (0.007)	fadir 10 (0.006)	synneþ 10 (0.006)	fordo 9 (0.006)
present 11 (0.007)	fareth 10 (0.006)	tail 10 (0.006)	forgyue 9 (0.006)
profitable 11 (0.007)	flesch 10 (0.006)	techen 10 (0.006)	forsoke 9 (0.006)
reche 11 (0.007)	folweþ 10 (0.006)	text 10 (0.006)	fraunce 9 (0.006)
releue 11 (0.007)	fooles 10 (0.006)	theologie 10 (0.006)	freris 9 (0.006)
repente 11 (0.007)	gees 10 (0.006)	thridde 10 (0.006)	fuste 9 (0.006)

glose 9 (0.006)
godhede 9 (0.006)
golde 9 (0.006)
gomes 9 (0.006)
growe 9 (0.006)
gyuen 9 (0.006)
halt 9 (0.006)
happe 9 (0.006)
hastow 9 (0.006)
heires 9 (0.006)
hemself 9 (0.006)
hertes 9 (0.006)
heruest 9 (0.006)
hilles 9 (0.006)
hole 9 (0.006)
hore 9 (0.006)
hostiler 9 (0.006)
houses 9 (0.006)
hungry 9 (0.006)
hungur 9 (0.006)
hye 9 (0.006)
hymseluen 9 (0.006)
iangle 9 (0.006)
ierusalem 9 (0.006)
iob 9 (0.006)
iugge 9 (0.006)
kam 9 (0.006)
knowynge 9 (0.006)
knyght 9 (0.006)
labory 9 (0.006)
lakkeþ 9 (0.006)
lasteth 9 (0.006)
leautee 9 (0.006)
leccherie 9 (0.006)
leelly 9 (0.006)
lengþe 9 (0.006)
leueþ 9 (0.006)
likede 9 (0.006)
list 9 (0.006)
logyk 9 (0.006)
loketh 9 (0.006)
lokynge 9 (0.006)
lollares 9 (0.006)
lyk 9 (0.006)
makometh 9 (0.006)
marchaundise 9 (0.006)
maried 9 (0.006)
maugree 9 (0.006)
maynprise 9 (0.006)
menynge 9 (0.006)
merciable 9 (0.006)
meschaunce 9 (0.006)
metels 9 (0.006)
metes 9 (0.006)
meue 9 (0.006)
mouþe 9 (0.006)
mouth 9 (0.006)
myldeliche 9 (0.006)
nedeþ 9 (0.006)
nedes 9 (0.006)
nose 9 (0.006)
notaries 9 (0.006)
ouercome 9 (0.006)
ouhte 9 (0.006)
oute 9 (0.006)
paie 9 (0.006)
parauntur 9 (0.006)
parceyued 9 (0.006)
payed 9 (0.006)
perel 9 (0.006)
pestilence 9 (0.006)
plato 9 (0.006)

preched 9 (0.006)
preie 9 (0.006)
preyeres 9 (0.006)
princes 9 (0.006)
profrede 9 (0.006)
propre 9 (0.006)
refuse 9 (0.006)
reherce 9 (0.006)
riȝte 9 (0.006)
rihtwisnesse 9 (0.006)
rype 9 (0.006)
saaf 9 (0.006)
sage 9 (0.006)
seconde 9 (0.006)
sennes 9 (0.006)
serued 9 (0.006)
seruice 9 (0.006)
seyen 9 (0.006)
shrifte 9 (0.006)
siȝt 9 (0.006)
sihte 9 (0.006)
soffren 9 (0.006)
souȝte 9 (0.006)
spene 9 (0.006)
stede 9 (0.006)
sterres 9 (0.006)
surgien 9 (0.006)
syhte 9 (0.006)
syngen 9 (0.006)
takiþ 9 (0.006)
temple 9 (0.006)
tened 9 (0.006)
theues 9 (0.006)
tre 9 (0.006)
vertue 9 (0.006)
vncristene 9 (0.006)
wage 9 (0.006)
warm 9 (0.006)
watte 9 (0.006)
wedlok 9 (0.006)
weex 9 (0.006)
wern 9 (0.006)
wers 9 (0.006)
westmynstre 9 (0.006)
wex 9 (0.006)
wherof 9 (0.006)
wiþinne 9 (0.006)
withynne 9 (0.006)
wode 9 (0.006)
woldest 9 (0.006)
wonye 9 (0.006)
wroot 9 (0.006)
wyht 9 (0.006)
wykkide 9 (0.006)
wynneth 9 (0.006)
ybore 9 (0.006)
ydelnesse 9 (0.006)
yeres 9 (0.006)
yerne 9 (0.006)
yholde 9 (0.006)
ynne 9 (0.006)
ynow 9 (0.006)
ywonne 9 (0.006)
þider 8 (0.005)
þoo 8 (0.005)
þynke 8 (0.005)
acounte 8 (0.005)
acountes 8 (0.005)
angeles 8 (0.005)
answere 8 (0.005)
apeire 8 (0.005)

aspye 8 (0.005)
assoille 8 (0.005)
aunte 8 (0.005)
awakede 8 (0.005)
away 8 (0.005)
awreke 8 (0.005)
bacoun 8 (0.005)
bake 8 (0.005)
bisouȝte 8 (0.005)
blowe 8 (0.005)
bowe 8 (0.005)
broþer 8 (0.005)
bryngen 8 (0.005)
calle 8 (0.005)
canst 8 (0.005)
carte 8 (0.005)
case 8 (0.005)
catoun 8 (0.005)
chastite 8 (0.005)
child 8 (0.005)
chosen 8 (0.005)
chyde 8 (0.005)
clement 8 (0.005)
clennesse 8 (0.005)
colde 8 (0.005)
colour 8 (0.005)
connyng 8 (0.005)
contrees 8 (0.005)
contricioun 8 (0.005)
corsed 8 (0.005)
cortesye 8 (0.005)
coueyte 8 (0.005)
cours 8 (0.005)
crepe 8 (0.005)
crowne 8 (0.005)
deiȝe 8 (0.005)
deide 8 (0.005)
derke 8 (0.005)
derknesse 8 (0.005)
derne 8 (0.005)
dethe 8 (0.005)
dettes 8 (0.005)
diuerse 8 (0.005)
doone 8 (0.005)
dredful 8 (0.005)
dronke 8 (0.005)
erles 8 (0.005)
falshede 8 (0.005)
faren 8 (0.005)
ferst 8 (0.005)
festes 8 (0.005)
floreynes 8 (0.005)
fonde 8 (0.005)
fonge 8 (0.005)
forsoþe 8 (0.005)
fyhte 8 (0.005)
fyn 8 (0.005)
garte 8 (0.005)
giftes 8 (0.005)
glorie 8 (0.005)
gon 8 (0.005)
gras 8 (0.005)
grayn 8 (0.005)
gretter 8 (0.005)
greyn 8 (0.005)
grote 8 (0.005)
groweþ 8 (0.005)
had 8 (0.005)
hals 8 (0.005)
held 8 (0.005)
helpeth 8 (0.005)
hewe 8 (0.005)

hoem 8 (0.005)
holpen 8 (0.005)
holy_wryt 4 (0.003)
hondes 8 (0.005)
hoten 8 (0.005)
hulles 8 (0.005)
hyne 8 (0.005)
iew 8 (0.005)
iewene 8 (0.005)
indulgences 8 (0.005)
kenneþ 8 (0.005)
kepeþ 8 (0.005)
kille 8 (0.005)
knyht 8 (0.005)
koude 8 (0.005)
lauȝte 8 (0.005)
leden 8 (0.005)
leiȝe 8 (0.005)
leide 8 (0.005)
lened 8 (0.005)
lenten 8 (0.005)
leode 8 (0.005)
lesse 8 (0.005)
leutee 8 (0.005)
lewid 8 (0.005)
leye 8 (0.005)
libbeþ 8 (0.005)
like 8 (0.005)
liste 8 (0.005)
loken 8 (0.005)
loues 8 (0.005)
louyeth 8 (0.005)
lyeth 8 (0.005)
lykyng 8 (0.005)
lykynge 8 (0.005)
macometh 8 (0.005)
madest 8 (0.005)
maneres 8 (0.005)
manhede 8 (0.005)
marc 8 (0.005)
masses 8 (0.005)
maugre 8 (0.005)
mayntene 8 (0.005)
mebles 8 (0.005)
meene 8 (0.005)
mekeliche 8 (0.005)
messie 8 (0.005)
meteles 8 (0.005)
mot 8 (0.005)
myddes 8 (0.005)
myght 8 (0.005)
nauhte 8 (0.005)
nekke 8 (0.005)
nelle 8 (0.005)
ner 8 (0.005)
next 8 (0.005)
nobles 8 (0.005)
nouþe 8 (0.005)
othes 8 (0.005)
ouþer_while 4 (0.003)
oune 8 (0.005)
paied 8 (0.005)
pans 8 (0.005)
parsche 8 (0.005)
parte 8 (0.005)
passeth 8 (0.005)
pens 8 (0.005)
pestilences 8 (0.005)
peynted 8 (0.005)
plouȝman 8 (0.005)
point 8 (0.005)
porter 8 (0.005)

pound 8 (0.005)
poynt 8 (0.005)
preise 8 (0.005)
presentes 8 (0.005)
pris 8 (0.005)
proude 8 (0.005)
quyk 8 (0.005)
radde 8 (0.005)
ran 8 (0.005)
rechelesnesse 8 (0.005)
redily 8 (0.005)
regne 8 (0.005)
renk 8 (0.005)
restitucion 8 (0.005)
rewarde 8 (0.005)
rewe 8 (0.005)
riȝtful 8 (0.005)
rise 8 (0.005)
rote 8 (0.005)
rynges 8 (0.005)
sad 8 (0.005)
saef 8 (0.005)
secte 8 (0.005)
seen 8 (0.005)
seiden 8 (0.005)
seluer 8 (0.005)
set 8 (0.005)
sholdest 8 (0.005)
shoop 8 (0.005)
sle 8 (0.005)
slepyng 8 (0.005)
soffreth 8 (0.005)
songe 8 (0.005)
sorewe 8 (0.005)
souereyn 8 (0.005)
sowen 8 (0.005)
spende 8 (0.005)
sprynge 8 (0.005)
suffreþ 8 (0.005)
sum 8 (0.005)
syke 8 (0.005)
synegeth 8 (0.005)
table 8 (0.005)
therwith 8 (0.005)
thousend 8 (0.005)
tok 8 (0.005)
tokene 8 (0.005)
torche 8 (0.005)
tour 8 (0.005)
twelue 8 (0.005)
vices 8 (0.005)
welþe 8 (0.005)
welle 8 (0.005)
wepne 8 (0.005)
wis 8 (0.005)
wone 8 (0.005)
worcheth 8 (0.005)
wounde 8 (0.005)
wroþ 8 (0.005)
wroȝt 8 (0.005)
wrouȝt 8 (0.005)
wynde 8 (0.005)
yates 8 (0.005)
ydo 8 (0.005)
yserued 8 (0.005)